Recognition for
Superior Academic Achievement

Spring 2005
Eighth Edition

Volume 1

National Honor Roll, LLC

Students are listed alphabetically within the state where they live.
Students in this volume live in:

Connecticut, Delaware, District of Columbia, Indiana, Kentucky, Maine, Maryland, Massachusetts, New Hampshire, New Jersey, New York, North Carolina, Ohio, Pennsylvania, Rhode Island, Tennessee, Vermont, Virginia, West Virginia

Copyright © 2005 by National Honor Roll, LLC

All rights reserved. No part of this book may be reproduced or copied in any form or by any means, including but not limited to, electronic, mechanical, photographical, photocopying or information storage and retrieval systems without the express written consent of the publisher.

is a registered trademark owned by National Honor Roll, LLC.

Digital Imagery ©copyright 2001 PhotoDisc, Inc.
Digital Imagery © copyright 2001 image100Ltd. Images reproduced by license from image100 Ltd. All rights reserved.

National Honor Roll, LLC
777 Sunrise Highway
Lynbrook, New York 11563
www.nationalhonorroll.org

All rights reserved.
Printed in U.S.A.

Vol. I	1-932-654-26-7
Vol. II	1-932-654-27-5
Vol. III	1-932-654-28-3

National Honor Roll Staff

Publisher and Editor	Lynn Romeo
Associate Publisher	Monica Stumacher
Art Director	AnneLouise Burns/Blue Sky Design
Production Director	Stephani Simoes Hoyle
Customer Service	Thea Pettaway
	Jane Fitzpatrick
	Wendy Haynes
	Dawn Failla
	Aimee Saunier
	Allison O'Day
	Kim Malone
Office Support	Chris A. Betty
	Nora Hinojosa
	Laura Klein
	Maria Masson
	Angela Pinson
	Altagracia R. Prince
Student Intern	Marin Kaplansky
Contributors	Dr. William D. Abbott
	Kenneth Barone
	Robert Guy Dilts, Ph.D.
	Eugene Eli Dubois, Ed.D.
	Dr. Victor E. Gatto
	Marin Kaplansky
	Julie Ntem
Proofreaders	Louise Asperas
	Bill Given
	Tom Guadagno
	Beth Levine
	Kelly Spampinato

Student Nominations Standards Committee

Lynn Romeo	Publisher National Honor Roll
Dr. William D. Abbott, Ed.D.	Former President Ricker College Houlton, ME
Steffany Bane	Author, Educational Consultant New York, NY
Kenneth C. Barone	President College Bound Selection Service Medfield, MA
Dr. Bryan E. Carlson	Former President Mt. Ida College Newton, MA
Robert Guy Dilts, Ph.D.	Facilitator, Gifted Studies-Retired Schenley High School Pittsburgh, PA
Dr. Eugene Eli Du Bois, Ed.D.	Academic Dean, Retired Urban College of Boston Boston, MA
Scott G. Failla	Lecturer Barnard College/Columbia University New York, NY
Dr. Victor E. Gatto	Achieve Telecom Network Peabody, MA
Dr. Joseph A. Greenburg	Regional Director of Admissions The George Washington University Washington D.C.
Dr. John C. Norman	Dean of Student Affairs Northwestern Connecticut Community College Winsted, CT
Nancy Williams	President AIB College of Business Des Moines, IA
Margo Ewing Bane Woodacre	Author, Educational Consultant Former State Senator Margo Ewing Bane Services Wilmington, DE

Organizations

Allied Member of AASA
American Library Association
American School Counselors Association
Association of Educational Publishers
BPA
DECA
FBLA-PBL
FFA
HOSA
Junior Achievement
Key Club International
LeadAmerica
National American Miss
Quill and Scroll Society

Contents

4	Our Mission
5	Publisher's Page
6	Benefits
7	NHR Supports Education
8	NHR Student Stats
9	Award For Academic Achievement Winners
13	Scholarship Winners From Associated Organizations
14	Why College?
15	What Kinds of Jobs Are Available To College Grads?
16	What Courses Should I Take To Prepare For College?
17	Preparing For College
21	Understanding The Financial Aid Process
23	The International Baccalaureate Diploma Program
24	The Importance of Interning
25	The College Credit & College Unit
26	Your (IQ) Intelligence Quotient
27	In A World of Lifelong Learning
28	Doors Open From Both Sides
30	The Education Consumer – Transition To A New Attitude
31	What To Take To The Dorm
32	Abbreviations

Our Mission

The National Honor Roll program was developed to give high school and middle school students who have attained outstanding academic success the recognition they deserve, and to provide customized services as they apply to college.

At National Honor Roll, we firmly believe that the future is in the hands of our children, and that young people who are applauded for their accomplishments will achieve even more.

Encouraging and assisting these students benefits everyone. Short-term, the students and their families are rewarded for their efforts and are assisted as they move on in their academic careers. Long-term, the impact these future leaders have on society will be good for everyone.

Publisher's Page

One of the benefits of being inducted into National Honor Roll is that you become eligible to compete for a $1000 National Honor Roll Award for Academic Achievement.

We awarded 100 of these scholarships to inductees from the 2003/2004 school year.

Applicants were required to write a 100-word paragraph explaining what their long-term educational goals were, why they wanted to achieve them, and how they expected to benefit once they did. Our scholarship screening committee narrowed the applications down to 200 based on these essays; then grade point average, activities, and teacher references were factored in to determine the final 100 winners.

We asked inductees to write this essay so we could identify which of them had the maturity and the focus to succeed in life. We at National Honor Roll are great believers in goal setting. In general, people who have identified long-term goals which they are willing to work for are far more likely to achieve than people who go through life without setting goals.

Goal setting is a formal process for personal planning. A game plan, a road map for life, setting short-term and long-term goals is important in helping people achieve their objectives. Setting goals, and writing them down, helps a person focus their energies and monitor their success as they go along.

There isn't enough space here to go into the "how-to's" of goal setting. You can get plenty of information about that on the internet (Google, alone, has over 1,500,000 English language page references on the subject!), at your public library, or in your local book stores.

I know I achieve a lot more when I have compiled for myself a list of long-term and short-term goals than when I take each day as it comes with no plan in mind. If you haven't already begun to set life goals for yourself, there is no time like the present.

You can see the 2003/2004 scholarship recipients on pages 9 through 13 of this volume. Congratulations to them and their families!

Will you be able to qualify for a National Honor Roll Award For Academic Achievement this year? Do you have a plan?

All the best,

Lynn Romeo

Lynn Romeo
Publisher

"There are risks and costs to a program of action. But they are far less than the long-range risks and costs of comfortable inaction."
John F. Kennedy

Benefits

Being a National Honor Roll Student is not only an honor, but offers qualified students some exciting benefits!

NATIONAL HONOR ROLL AWARD FOR ACADEMIC ACHIEVEMENT

Since our inception, National Honor Roll has awarded $115,000 in scholarship monies. For the 2004/2005 school year, National Honor Roll has set aside $25,000 to be shared among 25 of its qualifying inductees. Students who are in grades 9 through 12 during the 2004/2005 school year, have been inducted into the National Honor Roll, are legal residents of the United States or its possessions, and have completed the scholarship application in its entirety can compete for one of these National Honor Roll Awards For Academic Achievement.

THE COLLEGE ADMISSIONS NOTIFICATION SERVICE

Every high school student published in the National Honor Roll is eligible to take advantage of the College Admissions Notification Service. Depending on timing, this could be a student's first introduction to the Admissions Officers at the schools he/she designates.

Once it has been determined that a student is qualified for acceptance into the National Honor Roll, we send out a letter of acceptance. Along with this letter, we include a list of colleges in the United States. The student can select as many schools for us to notify of his/her acceptance as he/she wishes. (There is a nominal processing fee for this service.) We then write to the Office of Admissions at each school the student has chosen announcing that the student has been inducted into the National Honor Roll and is interested in learning more about their school. The letter also contains a copy of the student's printed biography. This is an excellent way to let schools know about this prestigious award.

We notify any college or university a student wants. If a school is not listed in the CANS brochure, the student can give us the full name of the school (no initials, nicknames, or abbreviations) and its mailing address. We will be pleased to send the CANS notification to them.

THE NEWSPAPER NOTIFICATION SERVICE

National Honor Roll's Newspaper Notification Service is another way we publicize a student's induction. Only students whose biographies have been published receive this benefit.

Approximately six to eight weeks after the Commemorative Editions are released, we send a press release to daily and weekly newspapers across the United States announcing the publication of the National Honor Roll Commemorative Edition. We provide each paper with electronic access to a list of all student inductees in their areas. (The list includes students living in zip codes within a 50-mile radius of each daily paper's home office and a 20-mile radius of each weekly paper's home office.) The editors can access the list of students, or view individual student's profiles. The papers are advised that inductees have attained a level of academic achievement shared by a very small percentage of all U.S. students.

GOVERNOR AND U.S. SENATOR NOTIFICATION

Approximately six to eight weeks after the Commemorative Editions are released, we send a copy of the book to each state governor and all U.S. senators, along with a CD listing the name and address of each student who was inducted in their state (for use in the event they wish to send a letter of congratulations).

FREE BOOK PROGRAM

Each year, National Honor Roll sends a free copy of the Commemorative Edition to selected high school libraries across the country.

Being a National Honor Roll Student is not only an honor, but offers qualified students some exciting benefits!

NHR Supports Education

This year, in our ongoing crusade to encourage academic achievement, National Honor Roll has entered into relationships with several organizations and youth groups whose missions are to promote excellence in education. We are proud to announce our association with the following . . .

Professional Organziations

Allied member of AMERICAN ASSOCIATION OF SCHOOL ADMINISTRATORS (AASA). The mission of the American Association of School Administrators is to support and develop effective school leaders who are dedicated to the highest quality public education for all children.

AMERICAN LIBRARY ASSOCIATION (ALA). The mission of the American Library Association is to provide leadership for the development, promotion, and improvement of library and information services and the profession of librarianship in order to enhance learning and ensure access to information for all.

THE ASSOCIATION OF EDUCATIONAL PUBLISHERS (AEP) is a professional organization supporting the growth of educational publishing and its positive impact on learning and teaching. AEP's vision is of a thriving educational publishing industry that provides quality materials for every educator and student.

ASCA's mission is to represent professional school counselors and to promote professionalism and ethical practices.

Student Organizations and Youth Groups

BUSINESS PROFESSIONAL OF AMERICA (BPA). The mission of Business Professionals of America is to contribute to the preparation of a world-class workforce through the advancement of leadership, citizenship, academic, and technological skills.

DECA Inc. The mission of DECA is to enhance the co-curricular education of students with interests in marketing, management, and entrepreneurship. DECA helps students develop skills and competence for marketing careers, build self-esteem, experience leadership, and practice community service. DECA is committed to the advocacy of marketing education and the growth of business and education partnerships.

FBLA-PBL. The FBLA-PBL mission is to bring business and education together in a positive working relationship through innovative leadership and career development programs.

THE NATIONAL FFA ORGANIZATION. FFA makes a positive difference in the lives of students by developing their potential for premier leadership, personal growth and career success through agricultural education.

HOSA. Health Occupations Students of America (HOSA) is a national student organization endorsed by the U.S. Department of Education and the Health Occupations Education Division of ACTE. HOSA's two-fold mission is to promote career opportunities in the health care industry and to enhance the delivery of quality health care to all people. HOSA's goal is to encourage all health occupations instructors and students to join and be actively involved in the HOE-HOSA Partnership.

JUNIOR ACHIEVEMENT is passionate people inspiring kids to learn the economics of life through free enterprise education. JA enables caring business professionals to share their experience with students to show them what it takes to be successful. After all, kids are our future.

KEY CLUB INTERNATIONAL is an international student-led organization which provides its members with opportunities to provide service, build character and develop leadership.

LEADAMERICA's mission is to transform the next generation of young leaders by inspiring, educating, and instilling in them ethical and principled leadership values, attitudes, and skills through sponsorship of the academic-based leadership conferences, the Congressional Student Leadership Conference (high school) and the National Junior Leaders Conference (middle school). LeadAmerica conferences are approved programs on the 2004/2005 National Association of Secondary School Principals' National Advisory List of Student Contests and Activities and the only organization endorsed by the American Mock Trial Association.

NATIONAL AMERICAN MISS. As the nation's leading pageant system for teens, National American Miss provides a high-energy competition environment to encourage and reward excellence in academics, athletics, and community service. With concert-level effects, laser lights, and a hip-hop beat, the event recognizes the individual and group accomplishments of outstanding young women across the country.

QUILL AND SCROLL SOCIETY is an international honorary society for high school journalists founded on April 10, 1926. The mission of Quill and Scroll Society is to champion and improve the future of scholastic journalism and to recognize and reward student journalists for their outstanding work in the various forms of media that exist in their school communities.

National Honor Roll Students...

AWARDS 92.3% of National Honor Roll Students Have Received Academic and Community Honors

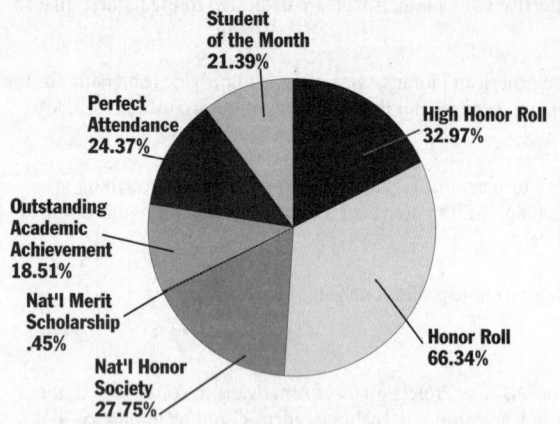

- Student of the Month 21.39%
- Perfect Attendance 24.37%
- Outstanding Academic Achievement 18.51%
- Nat'l Merit Scholarship .45%
- Nat'l Honor Society 27.75%
- Honor Roll 66.34%
- High Honor Roll 32.97%

- 25.29% ARE EMPLOYED (PART TIME/VACATION)
- 25% PARTICIPATE IN SCHOOL GOVERNMENT
- 15.99% WORK ON THEIR SCHOOL PUBLICATIONS
- 61.61% VOLUNTEER IN THEIR COMMUNITY

GENDER –
Male Students 33%
Female Students 67%

CLASS
Seniors (Class of 2005)	18%
Juniors (Class of 2006)	31%
Sophomores (Class of 2007)	26%
Freshmen (Class of 2008)	22%
Middle School (Class of 2009)	3%

Tomorrow's leaders facing today's challenges

88% Participate in Activities and Clubs

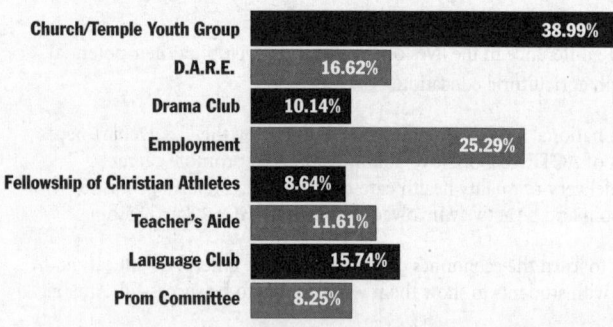

- Church/Temple Youth Group 38.99%
- D.A.R.E. 16.62%
- Drama Club 10.14%
- Employment 25.29%
- Fellowship of Christian Athletes 8.64%
- Teacher's Aide 11.61%
- Language Club 15.74%
- Prom Committee 8.25%

GRADES:
A+, A, A- 64.6%
B+, B 35.4%

PERFORMING ARTS
55% Are Involved In the Performing Arts

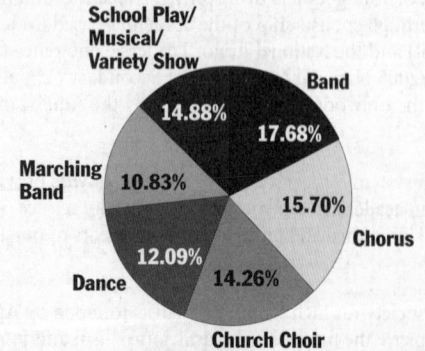

- School Play/Musical/Variety Show 14.88%
- Band 17.68%
- Marching Band 10.83%
- Chorus 15.70%
- Church Choir 14.26%
- Dance 12.09%

61% Participate in Sports

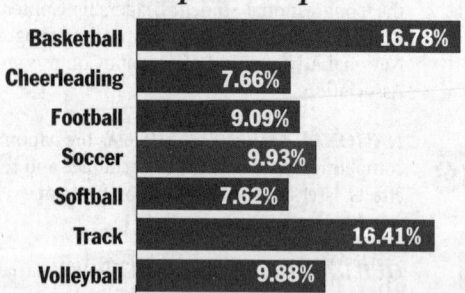

- Basketball 16.78%
- Cheerleading 7.66%
- Football 9.09%
- Soccer 9.93%
- Softball 7.62%
- Track 16.41%
- Volleyball 9.88%

Note: Because students can receive multiple honors or participate in multiple programs or activities, percentages will not add up to 100%.

AWARD FOR ACADEMIC ACHIEVEMENT

2003/2004 SCHOLARSHIP WINNERS

Out of almost 13,000 applicants, 100 students were chosen to receive the 2003/2004 National Honor Roll Award For Academic Achievement. Winners were selected based on an essay they wrote concerning what their after high school education goals were, why they wanted to achieve these goals, and how achieving the goals will benefit them. Grade point average and a reference written by a teacher or other youth leader were other factors used to select the final winners. The awards are sent directly to each student's college after they send us instructions concerning when and where to send their award.

Congratulations on a job well done!

Zijian An
River Edge, NJ
River Dell Senior HS
Class of 2004

Cody Bailey
Clemson, SC
Daniel HS
Class of 2004

Ann Bakeman
Langley, WA
So Whidbey HS
Class of 2004

Jason D Baker
King Of Prussia, PA
Archbishop John Carroll HS
Class of 2004

Brooke Barneck
Bountiful, UT
Bountiful HS
Class of 2004

Laurel Bennett
Redding, CA
Foothill HS
Class of 2004

Avery Justin Brown
Goose Creek, SC
Stratford HS
Class of 2004

Josh Brox
Peoria, AZ
Sunrise Mountain HS
Class of 2004

Kirsti A Burr
Corona, CA
Centennial HS
Class of 2004

Julie Byrom
Smithville, TX
Smithville HS
Class of 2004

Sara E Carter
Lexington, KY
Lafayette HS
Class of 2004

Andrew Thomas Cramer
Struthers, OH
Struthers HS
Class of 2004

Melissa Erin Crosby
Germantown, TN
Houston HS
Class of 2004

Gregory Scott Davison
St Clairsville, OH
St Clairsville HS
Class of 2004

Travis M Dowden
Medford, WI
Medford Area Sr HS
Class of 2004

Jarrett S Dziuk
San Antonio, TX
Canyon HS
Class of 2004

Noah Robert Ellingson
Maddock, ND
Maddock Public School
Class of 2004

Lacey Anne Ferro
Jonesville, MI
Jonesville HS
Class of 2004

Mark Fox
Grand Terrace, CA
Calvary Chapel School
Class of 2004

Valerie L Haenny
Highland, IN
Highland HS
Class of 2004

Jason Coit Harkey
Iron Station, NC
East Lincoln HS
Class of 2004

Sarah Henry
Fremont, CA
Irvington HS
Class of 2004

Lauren Hering
Edison, NJ
John P Stevens HS
Class of 2004

Katrina Joy Heyrana
Fairfax Station, VA
Hayfield Secondary School
Class of 2004

Jessica Jeanty
Fredericksburg, VA
Massaponax HS
Class of 2004

Megan Karl
Henderson, NV
Foothill HS
Class of 2004

Leah Katz
Chesapeake, VA
Western Branch HS
Class of 2004

Jason Kixmiller
Indianapolis, IN
Perry Meridian HS
Class of 2004

Heather Marie Lorigan
Jamestown, PA
Jamestown Jr/Sr HS
Class of 2004

Jason Bradley McCoy
San Angelo, TX
Lake View HS
Class of 2004

Kara Elizabeth Orr
Huntsville, AL
Sparkman HS
Class of 2004

Michael J. Phillips
New Knoxville, OH
New Knoxville Local HS
Class of 2004

Tara Price
Wichita, KS
Northeast Magnet
Class of 2004

Kathryn S Roberts
Marathon, FL
Marathon Jr/Sr HS
Class of 2004

Taanisha Rodgers
Elmont, NY
Elmont Memorial HS
Class of 2004

Kailyn Rogers
Midland, TX
Robert E Lee HS
Class of 2004

Justin Ross
Marietta, GA
North Cobb Christian School
Class of 2004

Dianna Rowe
Mobile, AL
Alabama School Of
Mathematics & Science
Class of 2004

Amby Schniers
San Angelo, TX
Wall HS
Class of 2004

Honor Schwartz
McDonough, NY
Cincinnatus Central School
Class of 2004

Jenessa Sprague
Miami, FL
Gulliver Prep School
Class of 2004

Eric Michael Sterling
Grand Blanc, MI
Grand Blanc HS
Class of 2004

Rachel M Taylor
Lakeland, FL
Harrison Arts Center
Class of 2004

Stephanie Westberry
Indianapolis, IN
Southport HS
Class of 2004

Caroline Westman
Akron, OH
Our Lady of the Elms HS
Class of 2004

Stefanie Noelle Whitmore
Kissimmee, FL
Gateway HS IB Program
Class of 2004

Homer Wiland
Canfield, OH
Canfield HS
Class of 2004

Timothy Allomong
Vermilion, OH
Firelands HS
Class of 2004

Nicholas Basso
Canonsburg, PA
Canon-McMillan
Class of 2005

Timothy Daniel Berkland
Sibley, IA
Sibley-Ocheyedan HS
Class of 2005

Joshua Burr
Glenpool, OK
Glenpool HS
Class of 2005

Katelyn Donohue
Clifton Park, NY
Shenendehowa HS
Class of 2005

Casandra Farlow
Basin, WY
Riverside HS
Class of 2005

Maurilio Garcia
Humble, TX
Humble HS
Class of 2005

Kathleen Goodwin
Mansfield, TX
Mansfield HS
Class of 2005

Adam Greenberg
Glen Head, NY
North Shore HS
Class of 2005

Emily Hovermale
Chambersburg, PA
St Maria Goretti HS
Class of 2005

John Johnson
Cleveland, TX
Caney Creek HS
Class of 2005

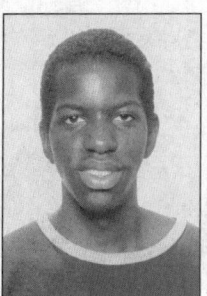
Eru Kyeyune-Nyombi Jr
Loma Linda, CA
Redlands HS
Class of 2005

Si-Cheng Liu
Millburn, NJ
Millburn HS
Class of 2005

William Joseph Michael III
Columbia, AL
Abbeville Christian Academy
Class of 2005

Sara Mosher
Wichita, KS
Goddard HS
Class of 2005

Sara New
Cape Coral, FL
Mariner HS
Class of 2005

Tara Elizabeth Payne
Pelham, TN
Grundy City HS
Class of 2005

Leila Perkins
San Jose, CA
Lynbrook HS
Class of 2005

Sarah Rivard
Williston, FL
Williston HS
Class of 2005

Megan Schafer
Canadian, TX
Canadian HS
Class of 2005

Stuart Schutta
Pitcher, NY
Cincinnatus Christian Academy
Class of 2005

Stephanie Shaheen
Rochester, NY
Our Lady Of Mercy HS
Class of 2005

Stephanie Skeens
Portsmouth, OH
Sciotoville Community School
Class of 2005

Adrienne Smith
Severn, MD
Meade Sr HS
Class of 2005

Torie Steitler
Texarkana, TX
Texas HS
Class of 2005

Lia Ronay Walker
Merryhill, NC
Bertie HS
Class of 2005

Phillip Wright
Britton, MI
Britton-Macon HS
Class of 2005

Jessica Lynn Hall
Richmond, VA
Mills E Godwin HS
Class of 2006

Meghan Hanrahan
Danville, IL
Schlarman HS
Class of 2006

Michelle Henry
Glen Mills, PA
Penncrest HS
Class of 2006

Amanda Jones
Houston, TX
Memorial HS
Class of 2006

Demian Kendall
St Michaels, MD
Easton HS
Class of 2006

Ashley Kennedy
Waunakee, WI
Waunakee HS
Class of 2006

Jennifer Lackey
Lenore, WV
Tug Valley HS
Class of 2006

Elizabeth Laferriere
Manchester, NH
Central HS
Class of 2006

Patrick J Melton
Phoenix, AZ
Tolleson Union HS
Class of 2006

H Maurice Mills Jr
New York, NY
Christ the King Regional HS
Class of 2006

Andrea Peterson
San Diego, CA
Westview HS
Class of 2006

Charles Franklin Preslar
Polkton, NC
Anson Sr HS
Class of 2006

Melissa Satibanez
Miami, FL
South Miami Sr HS
Class of 2006

Zachary T Simpson
Lancaster, KY
Garrard County HS
Class of 2006

Aydria Jeanne Smith
Carrollton, GA
Carroll Central HS
Class of 2006

Lindsay Wagner
Gaithersburg, MD
Damascus HS
Class of 2006

Jessica Hughes Willis
Selma, AL
John T Morgan Academy
Class of 2006

Megan Bollish
Wellfleet, NE
Maywood Public School
Class of 2007

Kevin Brent
Lancaster, PA
Penn Manor HS
Class of 2007

Julia Chung
Dinuba, CA
Dinuba HS
Class of 2007

Michael Frongello
Raleigh, NC
Middle Creek HS
Class of 2007

Charlie Arsena Grigoryon
Anaheim Hills, CA
Canyon HS
Class of 2007

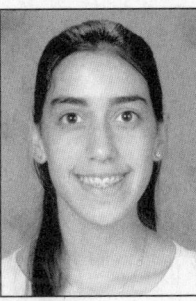
Wendy Pino
Miami, FL
Miami Coral Park Sr HS
Class of 2007

Ryan Prunty
Freeport, PA
Freeport Senior HS
Class of 2007

Michael Morgan Ulmer
N Augusta, SC
North Augusta HS
Class of 2007

Ana Maria Vascan
Land O'Lakes, WI
Northland Pines HS
Class of 2007

National Honor Roll supports the scholarship initiatives of several organizations and youth groups. During the 2003/2004 school year, students received National Honor Roll-sponsored scholarships from the following organizations:

HOSA:
Sarah Lee Sexton, Dover, TN

NATIONAL AMERICAN MISS:
Joi Mar, Shelby Twp, MI
Meaghan Jamison, Springfield, MO
Megan Marler, Oakdale, LA

NATIONAL FFA:
Joseph Moroni, Oran, MO

QUILL AND SCROLL SOCIETY:
Dennis Shane Mitchell, Phoenix, AZ

National Honor Roll also contributed to the general scholarship funds of:

LEADAMERICA
NEW GROUND

WHY College?

Why should you think seriously about college now?
Because college can be the key to the kind of life you want!

By "College", we mean:
- Public and private four-year colleges and universities
- Two-year community colleges or junior colleges
- Business schools
- Proprietary schools, and
- Vocational Technical schools

A college education can take you out of a minimum-wage job and into good-paying work you enjoy. It gives you choices. Compared with folks who don't continue their education beyond high school, people who go to college:

- Develop lifelong learning skills, and

- Get a good start in life. College trains you to express your thoughts clearly, make informed decisions, and use technology – useful skills on and off the job and for life.

- Have a wider range of job possibilities and options. More and more jobs require education beyond high school. With a college education, you will have more jobs from which to choose.

- Earn more money. A person who goes to college usually earns more than a person who doesn't. On average, over a lifetime, someone who spends two years in college earns $250,000 more than someone who doesn't – a quarter of a million dollars more over a lifetime.

- Are in a better position to help their families and communities.

Even if you're not sure what your future holds, prepare as if you'll be going to college. What you learn will help you get the very most from life.

U.S. Department of Education, Office of Postsecondary Education, "Think College? Me? Now? A Handbook for Students in Middle School and Junior High School, Think College Early", Washington D.C.

What kinds of jobs are available to college graduates?

One of the best things about getting a college education is that you have more jobs to choose from. Certificates and degrees earned by graduates of two- and four-year colleges or universities lead to different kinds of professional opportunities. As you explore possible careers, find out what kind of education is needed for them. Many professions require graduate degrees beyond the traditional four-year degree, such as a medical degree or a law degree.

You might change your mind several times about the type of job you want to have. Changing your mind is not a problem – but not planning ahead is.

Following is a partial listing of different occupations and the educational background generally required or recommended for each. Some people who go on to acquire jobs in the four-year college column obtain a graduate degree or some graduate education, but many of these jobs can be filled by people who do not have more than a four-year college education. For more information on the educational requirements of specific jobs, contact a guidance counselor or check the latest copy of the Occupational Outlook Handbook, published by the U.S. Department of Labor, in your library.

Examples of Jobs in Which a College Education May Be Recommended or Required

Two-Year College (Associate's Degree)	Four-Year College (Bachelor's Degree)	More than four years of college (Various Graduate Degrees Required)
Administrative Assistant	Accountant	Architect
Automotive Mechanic	Computer Systems Analyst	Biologist
Cardiovascular Technician	Dietitian	Chiropractor
Commercial Artist	Editor	Dentist
Computer Technician	Engineer	Diplomat
Dental Hygienist	FBI Agent	Doctor
Drafter	Investment Banker	Economist
Engineering Technician	Journalist	Geologist
Funeral Director	Medical Illustrator	Lawyer
Graphic Designer	Pharmacist	Librarian
Heating, Air-Conditioning, and Refrigeration Technician (HVAC)	Public Relations Specialist	Management Consultant
	Recreational Therapist	Paleontologist
Hotel or Restaurant Manager	Research Assistant	Priest
Medical Laboratory Technician	Social Worker	Psychologist
Medical Record Technician	Teacher	Public Policy Analyst
Insurance Agent	Writer	Rabbi
Registered Nurse		Scientist
Surgical Technologist		Sociologist
Surveyor		University Professor
Visual Artist		Veterinarian
Water and Wastewater Treatment Plant Operator		Zoologist

U.S. Department of Education, Office of Postsecondary Education, "Think College? Me? Now? A Handbook for Students in Middle School and Junior High School, Think College Early", Washington D.C.
U.S. Department of Education, Office of the Under Secretary, Preparing Your Child for College, Washington D.C., 2000

What Courses Should I Take to Prepare for College?

To prepare for college, you must obtain a solid and broad academic education. This means taking challenging courses in academic subjects and maintaining good grades throughout high school.

It is recommended that students begin planning their high school course schedule in the seventh or eighth grade. Research indicates that the earlier you start preparing, the more likely it will be that you will go on to college.

Although academic requirements differ among colleges, the admissions requirements listed below are typical for four-year colleges. The specific classes listed here are examples of the types of courses students can take.

- **Mathematics (3 to 4 years)**
  Types of classes:
  Algebra I; Geometry; Algebra II; Trigonometry; Precalculus; Calculus.

  Mathematical and scientific concepts learned in these classes are used in many disciplines outside these courses.

- **English (4 years)**
  Types of classes:
  Composition; English; Literature; American Literature; World Literature.

  These courses improve writing skills, reading comprehension, and vocabulary.

- **Laboratory Science (2 to 4 years)**
  Types of classes:
  Biology; Earth Science; Chemistry; Physics.

- **History or Geography (2 to 3 years)**
  Types of classes:
  Geography; U.S. History; U.S. Government; World History; World Cultures; Civics.

  These courses help you understand the world around you and make you a more informed citizen.

- **Foreign Language (2 to 4 years)**
  Language skills show you can learn basics and you're preparing to work in the global economy.

Many high schools offer advanced placement (AP) courses and exams. AP courses are college-level courses given in high school in approximately 16 different subjects. They help students prepare for college-level work while still in high school. If you score a 3 or higher on an AP exam, you can often receive advanced placement in college or credit for a college course (which can provide you with significant cost savings!) Check with the college of your choice to determine their policies regarding AP credit.

If you are interested in pursuing a technical program in a community, junior, or technical college, it is recommended that you take all of the core courses listed here in math, science, English, history, and geography, and supplement some of the electives in the chart with vocational or technical courses in your field of interest. You can speak with an administrator, dean of a technical program or professor from a community, junior, or technical college to learn which high school courses are best to take to prepare for a particular technical program.

Remember, the earlier you start preparing for your post-high school education, the more likely your chances will be of fulfilling your goals.

- **Arts Courses (1 year)**
  Types of classes:
  Art; Dance; Drama; Music.
  Arts courses broaden your understanding and appreciation of the world and develop your skills to see differences, figure out patterns, and examine how you make decisions.

- **Computer Science (as much as you can take)**
  Computer technology can help you find more information and do schoolwork better and faster. Also, more and more college courses and jobs require a knowledge of computers.

- **Other Challenging Courses (1 to 3 years)**
  Types of classes:
  Economics; Psychology; Statistics; Astronomy; Research Projects and Independent Projects; Oral and Written Communication.

U.S. Department of Education, Office of Postsecondary Education, "Think College? Me? Now? A Handbook for Students in Middle School and Junior High School, Think College Early", Washington D.C.; U.S. Department of Education, Office of the Under Secretary, Preparing Your Child for College, Washington D.C., 2000

Preparing for College

Getting into the college of your choice doesn't just happen. If you plan to continue your education beyond high school graduation, you must begin laying the groundwork for your post-secondary future the day you begin high school.

The following checklist highlights some of the most important things you must do to ultimately receive that coveted letter of acceptance.

9TH GRADE

- Enroll in your school's college-prep program.
- Take challenging classes in English, mathematics, science, history, geography, a foreign language, government, civics, economics, and the arts.
- Concentrate on getting good grades. Grades earned in ninth grade will be included in the high school transcript you will have to send to every college you apply to.
- Get to know your career counselor or guidance counselor, and other college resources available in your school.
- Talk to adults in a variety of professions to determine what they like and dislike about their jobs and what kind of education is needed for each kind of job.
- Get involved in some extracurricular activities you enjoy and can stay with throughout high school.
- Start researching colleges. You can find information in your guidance counselor's office, on the web, and in your public library.
- Continue to save for college.

10TH GRADE

- Continue in your school's college-prep program. Take challenging courses in English, mathematics, science, history, geography, a foreign language, government, civics, economics, and the arts. Look into the possibility of taking Advanced Placement (AP) and post-secondary enrollment options.
- Concentrate on getting good grades. You want to achieve the highest GPA and class rank possible.
- Continue to talk to adults in a variety of professions to determine what they like and dislike about their jobs, and what kind of education is needed for each kind of job.
- Stay involved in the school- or community-based extracurricular (before or after school) activities you started with in ninth grade and find others that interest you and enable you to explore career interests.
- Meet with your career counselor or guidance counselor to discuss colleges and their requirements.
- Start thinking about the kind of college you would like to go to.
- Write to colleges and ask them for information about their academic requirements for admission.
- Practice taking the PSAT/NMSQT.
- Take the Preliminary Scholastic Assessment Test/National Merit Scholarship Qualifying Test (PSAT/NMSQT). You must register early. If you have difficulty paying the registration fee, see your guidance counselor about getting a fee waiver.

- Find out about the American College Testing program's PLAN (pre-ACT) assessment program, which helps determine your study habits, academic progress, and interests. It is also a way to prepare yourself for the ACT Assessment which you may take in the Eleventh Grade.

- Read as many books as you can. Obtain a comprehensive reading list from your English teacher, your public library, or in one of the college and career planning books which can be found in most book stores.

- Work on your writing skills. Learn how to focus your thoughts and express them clearly using proper grammar and correct spelling.

- Take advantage of opportunities to visit colleges and talk to students.

- Consider taking SAT II Subject Tests in the subjects you took this year while the information is still fresh in your mind. You can take these tests in May and June.

- Continue to save for college.

11TH GRADE

- Continue in your school's college-prep program. Take challenging classes in English, mathematics, science, history, geography, a foreign language, government, civics, economics, and the arts.

- Prepare a list of features you want in a college.

- Meet with your career counselor or guidance counselor to discuss the courses you have already taken and those you still must take. Also review colleges in which you are interested and their requirements.

- Check your class rank.

- If you haven't already done so, sign up for - and take - the PSAT/NMSQT. This is the qualifying test for the National Merit Scholarships, the National Scholarship Service, the Fund for Negro Students, and the National Hispanic Scholar Recognition Program.

- Continue to be involved with school- or community-based extracurricular activities. Work your way into a leadership role in these activities.

- Develop a list of schools. Write them requesting information and an application for admission. Be sure to ask about special admissions requirements, financial aid, deadlines, and which standardized tests (SAT I, ACT, or SAT II) they require.

- Talk to college representatives at college fairs.

- Visit colleges and talk to the students there.

- Decide which colleges interest you most.

- Think about which people you can ask for recommendations - teachers, counselors, employers, etc.

- Prepare for the standardized tests you will have to take (SAT I, SAT II, ACT).

- Investigate the availability of financial aid from federal, state, local, and private sources. Call the Student Aid Hotline at the U.S. Department of Education (1-800-4FED-AID) for a student guide to Federal financial aid. Talk to your guidance counselor for more information.

- Look into the availability of scholarships provided by organizations such as corporations, labor unions, professional associations, religious organizations, and credit unions.

- If applicable, go to the library and look for directories of scholarships for women, minorities, and disabled students.

- If you want to participate in Division I or Division II sports in college, start the certification process. Check with your Guidance Counselor to make sure you are taking the core curriculum required by NCAA.

- If you are interested in applying to one of the military academies, speak with your counselor about beginning the application process.

- Learn about AmeriCorps by calling 1-800-942-2677 or TDD 1-800-833-3722. Or go to www.americorps.org.

- Register for and take the Scholastic Assessment Test (SAT), the ACT, SAT Subject Tests, or any other exams required for admission to colleges you might want to attend. If you have difficulty paying the registration fees, see your guidance counselor about getting fee waivers.

- Continue to save for college.

- In the Spring, meet with your Counselor to review Senior-year course selection and graduation requirements.

- Discuss your ACT/SAT I assessment scores with your counselor. Register to retake these tests if you are unhappy with your original scores.
- Request applications from schools you are interested in and practice filling them out. Start working on your college essays and have a teacher critique them.
- In May, take SAT IIs for courses you have just finished, as well as any Advanced Placement (AP) exams.

12TH GRADE

- Continue with your college prep course load. Take challenging classes in English, mathematics, science, history, geography, a foreign language, government, civics, economics, the arts, and advanced technologies.
- Meet with your counselor early in the year to discuss your plans. Make sure you have taken all of the courses necessary for graduation.
- Continue to participate in and take a leadership role in your extracurricular activities.
- Write to the colleges you are interested in to request information and applications for admission. Be sure to ask about financial aid, admissions requirements, and deadlines.
- Complete all necessary financial aid forms. Make sure that you fill out at least one form that can be used for Federal aid.
- If you are male, you must register for Selective Service on your eighteenth birthday. You will not be eligible for federal and state financial aid if you don't.
- Complete the Free Application for Federal Student Aid (FAFSA) and, if necessary, the Financial Aid Profile (FAP) and submit after January 1. Be sure you receive a FAFSA acknowledgement after you have submitted this application.
- Finalize your list of potential schools.
- If possible, visit the colleges that most interest you.
- Register for, and take, any standardized tests you plan to re-take (Scholastic Assessment Test (SAT), American College Test (ACT), SAT Subject Tests), or any other exams required for admission to the colleges to which you are applying. If you have difficulty paying any registration fee, see your guidance counselor about getting a fee waiver. Be sure to request that your scores be sent to the schools of your choice.
- If you are applying Early Decision or Early Action, remember that this process begins in September. BE VERY SURE TO PAY CLOSE ATTENTION TO DEADLINES.

- Prepare your applications carefully. Follow the instructions, work on your essay and have it reviewed by two teachers. PAY CLOSE ATTENTION TO DEADLINES! Make copies of every application you send. Be sure to ask your counselor and teachers at least two weeks before your application deadlines to submit all necessary documents to your colleges (your transcript, letters of recommendation, etc.). Follow up with each college to confirm that your application and all supporting documents have been received.

- Finish your applications, college visits, college interviews.

- Mail or send electronically all remaining applications and financial aid forms before winter break.

- Register for CSS Profile, if necessary.

- Confirm that your first semester transcripts were sent to all colleges to which you applied.

- If you receive Early Decision admission, you must accept in January and withdraw applications from all other institutions to which you may have applied.

- You will receive acceptance notices from colleges between March 1 and April 1.

- In April, consider all of your choices. Be sure to accept a college by May 1, send in the non-refundable deposit, and decline the others.

- Complete follow-up paperwork for the college of your choice.

- Take your final AP exams. They can save you time and money once you are in college.

Understanding the Financial Aid Process

By Julie Ntem

What…???
It Costs Money to Learn to Make Money!???

College is the beginning of the path that will carry you through life. To continue on life's path of success, you are going to have to pass over dollar sign obstacles littering the trail throughout your years of schooling. Once your college years are behind you, the dollar signs will seem to dissolve from the ground and they will begin falling from the sky ready for you to catch. Financial aid has the power to ensure that your path is not blocked by dollar sign barriers. You just need to do your part and you will fly over the obstacles!

It's never too early to start planning for college. In fact, it can save you money if you do plan early! By getting information on your preferred colleges early, you will know about deadlines that must be met. Deadlines can be crucial to qualifying for certain aid programs. You should check with the financial aid office at your school(s) of interest regarding their deadlines. Oftentimes, schools have an institutional deadline, so it's important to inquire into each school you are interested in.

What Does it Mean??

Let's start by getting familiar with common financial aid terms:

- *Scholarships and Grants* – This is gift assistance that does not need to be repaid. Amounts may be based on merit and/or need.

- *Loans* – This money must be paid back to the lender over time. Loans may be interest free or interest bearing while the student is attending the institution.

- *Work study* – This is aid that may provide part-time jobs on campus or in the community for students who qualify.

- *Dependency Status* – The Free Application for Federal Student Aid (FAFSA) will determine whether you are considered dependent or independent. If you're considered dependent, you must report your parents' income and assets as well as your own on the FAFSA. If you're independent, you'll report only your own income and assets (and those of your spouse if married).

- *Expected Family Contribution (EFC)* – The EFC is a measure of your family's financial strength and is used to determine your eligibility for student aid.

- *Need Analysis* – The official evaluation that determines how much a family must contribute to the cost of the college.

- *Financial Need* – Need is based on the following equation:

   Cost of Attendance
   - Expected Family Contribution (EFC)
   = Financial Need

The internet can offer endless information on college decisions and financial aid. Be aware of your source; you should never pay for scholarship searches or application processing.

HELPFUL WEB SITES TO VISIT:
www.studentaid.ed.gov
http://mapping-your-future.org/
www.studentaid.ed.gov/completefafsa
www.fafsa.ed.gov
www.pin.ed.gov
www.allscholar.com

What do I do Now??

You should not rule out any college due to financial obligation until you can clearly see the bottom line. You get to the bottom line by applying for financial aid and factoring in your financial aid awards from each institution.

In order to qualify for financial aid programs, students must complete a FAFSA form. The FAFSA application can be obtained from your high school guidance office, college financial aid office, or you can access it on the Web at http://www.fafsa.ed.gov. Everyone is encouraged to apply for financial aid, even if you think you may not be eligible. There may be other options for federal assistance such as low-interest loan programs.

FAFSA forms are available in December and should be submitted as soon after January 1 as possible. Remember, deadlines vary from state to state and each college has its own aid deadlines you must be aware of. Apply as early as you can to avoid missing out on any aid you may be eligible to receive!

You will need a Personal Identification Number (PIN) number to complete the FAFSA online. You can register for a PIN number online at www.pin.ed.gov. The PIN number assigned to you will serve as your electronic signature and you may have to use it for other purposes while you are in school. A parent of a dependent student will also need a PIN to sign the FAFSA.

After your FAFSA has been received by the processing center, you will receive a Student Aid Report (SAR). The SAR confirms the information reported on your FAFSA and will contain your Expected Family Contribution (EFC). Your EFC will remain the same for each college, but the amount of your award will be different at each college.

Whether you applied electronically or on paper, the processing center will send your financial data electronically to the school(s) you listed on the FAFSA. The college(s) you are interested in attending may collect other necessary documentation from you in order to determine the amount of aid available to you. It is important to respond to any requests in a timely manner. Once your aid has been determined, a Financial Award Notice will be sent to you by the college(s).

You must complete the financial aid process every academic year. After your first year completing a full FAFSA, the process becomes simpler as a Renewal FAFSA will be available to you the following year. You'll be required to update information that has changed from the prior year and fill in a few new answers.

As you begin your path of success with college, always put your educational goals first and then weigh the financial factors. Be sure to examine your Award Notice carefully. Determine the source of your aid. How much gift assistance are you receiving? How much loan debt will need to be incurred during the first year? What will be your out-of-pocket expenses?

Decisions you make now will determine the quality of your future journey down life's path. Your path is just beginning and financial aid can help you get off to a running start!

**Julie Ntem is a graduate of AIB College of Business and Graceland University with degrees in Business Administration. She is currently a Financial Aid Advisor/Loan Specialist at AIB College of Business.
Special thanks to Connie Jensen, Director of Financial Aid at AIB for her advice and input.**

The International Baccalaureate Diploma Program: a personal view

Robert Guy Dilts

My involvement with the International Baccalaureate Diploma Program, hereafter referred to as "IB program", spanned 16 years (1985 - 2001) as a teacher of the IB Mathematical Studies course and an advisor to gifted students at Schenley who were pursuing the IB Diploma or taking IB courses. The IB Diploma program is the crown jewel of a 12-year international studies magnet program of the Pittsburgh Public Schools. The IB courses serve as alternatives to AP and advanced courses restricted to students designated as gifted according to Pennsylvania Department of Education regulations.

The IB Diploma Program was created in 1968, designed to serve a population of highly motivated high school age students who for various reasons transferred among schools mostly throughout Europe but also in and to other areas of the world. It provided one curriculum so students were able to easily adapt their studies wherever their families relocated. Schools in North America began offering the program to accommodate these same students. Today there are IB schools in nearly every nation.

What is the program? The IB Diploma Program has syllabi in six academic areas plus three significant features which must be completed by all candidates. The six academic areas are: 1) the individual's own language incorporating one's cultural and literary heritage; 2) a second language, used in various contexts and expressed both orally and in writing; 3) individuals and society – those studies involving primarily the social sciences; 4) the experimental sciences; 5) mathematics and computer science; and 6) the arts. Syllabi have been developed at standard and higher levels, allowing for individual differences in talents across the board. At least three (at most four) subjects must be taken at the higher level, the others at the standard level, the latter being comparable to advanced academic high school offerings, higher level first year college level. These studies are completed during the 11th and 12th grades. Standard level examinations and portfolios may be completed in 11th grade; higher level in 12th grade since they involve a two-year syllabus.

You mentioned "additional significant features" of the program. What are they? The IB program is comprehensive, all-inclusive. The first additional feature is a course called "Theory of Knowledge". This experience challenges students to investigate the bases of knowledge across academic disciplines, developing awareness of biases that affect the communication of knowledge and developing analytical and evaluative skills. At Schenley, experts from various academic fields met with students, made somewhat easier because we were located within a mile of four colleges and research universities. We encouraged students to take this seminar even if they weren't IB candidates.

The second feature is "creativity, action, and service", which focuses on each candidate sharing their talents and time in such activities as theatre, sports, or working in community agencies. The focus is on personal development. Each student has to document their involvement.

The third feature is "an extended essay of 4,000 words". Each candidate is required to produce an essay investigating a topic related to a master list of 60 general subject areas, the purpose being to develop independent research and writing skills required in higher education.

Why pursue an IB Diploma? First, depending upon where you might want to go to college, successfully completing the diploma could save you a year of college. I had a student one year who applied to a university in Holland. She was informed that since she went to an American high school, she would have to complete a preparatory year at the university before being officially admitted. She indicated that she was completing the IB program and was admitted immediately. Many others were admitted as sophomores at their various schools.

But foremost, the rigor and academic demands prepare anyone to move from a high school environment to a collegiate environment - much more capable of being an independent, self-motivated learner, and therefore a successful college student. We've heard this expressed year after year by graduates who return to talk with students and faculty. And the best reason I ever heard was "This was the most challenging and demanding experience of my life and I succeeded."

You can learn more about the IB program at http://www.ibo.org

■ Robert Guy Dilts, Ph.D.
Retired Facilitator of
Gifted Studies, Schenley
High School Teacher Center,
Pittsburgh, Pennsylvania

The Importance of Interning

Ever since I was a little girl I have been amazed by commercials, billboards, and magazine advertisements. The colors, characters, and text all seemed to draw me in, my attention never drifting from what I was looking at. As I grew older, I began to wonder how these advertisements drew me in, made me want their product or take an interest in the person or company the marketers were promoting. When I entered high school, I took a class called "Principles of Marketing" to fill up my schedule. What I thought would be an extra class became the love of my life. Marketing became what I ate, drank, and breathed. After learning about how consumers buy products due to marketing strategy, my eyes began to spot every type of promotion and its target audience. Everything was clear in my head, it made sense to me, and marketing was my world.

After taking "College Marketing" and "Advertising", my love of and interest in the field grew. For my senior experience, in which each high school Advanced Placement student volunteers at an organization of their choice, I am interning at National Honor Roll.

Internships are a great way to learn about the working world. While it may not be possible to find an internship in your desired field, working in any business situation can be a rewarding experience. During my internship, I have learned skills needed for any type of business, including how to properly file, how to achieve high standards, how to use computer programs, and how to set up presentation folders. I have even been involved in data entry. Since the publication revolves around students, I have had the opportunity to conduct several forms of research. National Honor Roll works with many student organizations and I have done research on organizations that National Honor Roll could develop relationships with in the future. I was also able to compare student profile statistics from year to year.

Interning is a way to learn about a field you're interested in and to see if you actually want to pursue that type of career. Working in an office is much different than many people perceive it to be, and it can change or reinforce your career aspirations. Interning is the best way to make yourself familiar with the working world, no matter where you have the chance to work. Some experiences can be bad and some can be good, but in the end what you learn most from interning is where you might want to go in the future.

■ **Marin Kaplansky,**
High School Senior,
Hewlett High School,
Intern, National Honor Roll

The College Credit & College Unit

By Eugene Eli Dubois, Ed.D.

Introduction

Higher Education has historically been measured by a credit system. This has sometimes been referred to as the Carnegie System. This is the result of the attempt by Andrew Carnegie and the Carnegie Foundation to quantify a system for institutions of higher education to qualify professors and their survivors for his retirement program. Due to economic changes, this original program failed. However, it evolved into the very successful TIAA-CREF (Teachers Annuity Association and College Retirement Education Fund).

Most high school students are familiar with the high school GPA (Grade Point Average) system, particularly athletes, who must qualify for sports participation.

Not as many people understand what the college credit system means.

The Higher Education Experience

What is the credit system? Students must complete a certain number of credits over a period of time to earn their degrees. A number of credits is assigned to each course, based on how many hours of coursework (time spent in the classroom or what the professor requires for completion of independent study) is required to complete it. As a student completes his/her course load, the number of credits per successfully completed class is added to his/her credit "bank" until he/she has accumulated the requisite number of credits for graduation.

In the United States there is no uniform system of higher education, except for, perhaps, Certificates, Associate Degrees, Bachelors, Masters, and Doctorates. Therefore, the system of course credit varies between institutions. (There are several undergraduate institutions where grading systems do not adhere to the more common Carnegie unit of in-class instruction found at most colleges and universities.)

Some institutions prefer the semester system, others the quarter system. With adult learners, there are a variety of "open" systems. This is particularly true in non-traditional institutions. These are usually those colleges where open enrollment and student-centered learning is a major focus.

The non-traditional institution is usually, although not always, for the adult student.

Continuing education is increasingly becoming popular not only in colleges and universities, but also in corporations and business and professional organizations.

In these latter situations, the C.E.U. (Continuing Education Unit) may be awarded. These are not college credits, however they may be applied toward continued certification in a particular field or profession.

Although it is necessary to quantify a student's progress through the required course load for his/her degree, the fact is that the student is in a course of higher education to obtain an education. Francis C. Rosecrance has stated the role of the college experience most succinctly: "The academic is not designed to make students "serve time" nor to give them degrees. Someone has quite properly said that education does not come by degrees. The purpose of the program is to produce a cultivated person, one who has knowledge and appreciation of great literature, art, music and science, who has some knowledge of how to live with others and some insight into world affairs. Certainly he should have an understanding of the democratic way of life and of democratic values as well as to achieve and sustain them. A good college program should enable graduates to do difficult things well and should make them eternally curious about life - its opportunities, challenges and meanings. Perhaps Lessing, the great German critic and dramatist, summed it all up in the statement, "The end of all education is to make men see things that are big as big and things that are small as small." [2]

■ Eugene Eli Dubois, Ed.D.
Academic Dean, Retired
The Urban College of Boston, MA

---

1. See: Brubacher, John S. and Rudy, Willis Higher Education in Transition. An American History 1636-1956. New York: Harper and Brothers, 1958.
2. Rosecrance, Francis C. The American College and Its Teachers. New York: The MacMillan Company, 1962 p.104

Your (IQ) Intelligence Quotient

Dr. William D Abbott, Ed.D.

"IQ", or Intellegence Quotient, is a term you often hear. Common wisdom says that having a high IQ means you are smart and having a low IQ means you aren't. But what, exactly, is an IQ, how is it measured, and how important is it in terms of determining how successful you will be?

The Intelligence Quotient Defined

The intelligence quotient is the way mental abilities are scored on an intelligence test, resulting in a number that places a person above or below the score considered average, . . . most often 100.[1]

Intelligence, in educational practice, is usually defined by measuring many functions which include: cognitive skills; numerical and verbal reasoning; comprehension and memory; and the ability to learn new information, solve problems, and grasp concepts. It is important to note, however, that these areas do not comprise all types of human ability and functioning.[1]

How IQ Testing Came To Be

The IQ came of age when Robert M. Yerks, a member of Harvard University's faculty, convinced the US Army to use tests developed by American psychometrics in 1917 to test Army personnel. This was a start. It generated a lot of data, but compared to modern testing was lacking.[2]

Are you the brightest bulb on the tree?

For many years people noted that some were "smart", and others "dumb." Ways were sought to predict the enabled from less skilled people, as well as to find reasons for this occurrence. Some theories suggested causative factors included:

- Brain Size
- Size of Head
- Race
- Sex
- Class

They were wrong. None of the above affects how intelligent you are.

Your IQ Does Not Guarantee Automatic Success or Failure In Life

What does this mean to you, a college bound student? In the estimation of the writer, the fact that you are a member of the National Honor Roll confirms that you are blessed with a higher than average IQ. However, having a robust IQ is not a guarantee of success in college. Many other factors come into play which may include:

- The quality of your education
- Your desire to succeed
- Emotional support from family and friends
- Your study habits
- Taking, and paying attention to, accurate class notes (Keep good records and review them).

Summary

It's what you do – not a high IQ – that counts. Don't blow your stepping stone to success. Avoid the "party life". Have fun in school, but don't forget that the main reason you are there is to get a solid education. All the brains in the world won't help you if you don't apply yourself.

Years ago, a teacher of mine wrote on the chalkboard (I do not know the source):

"On the plains of hesitation, bleach the bones of countless millions, who at the dawn of victory, sat down to rest, and resting died."

Don't rest – excel!

[1] McCullough, Virginia E. "Testing and Your Child," Penguin Books USA, Inc N.Y. N.Y. 10014, 1992

[2] Gould, Stephen Jay. "The Mismeasure of Man," W. Norton & Company, N.Y., N.Y., 1981

(Note: You can test your I.Q. on the Internet in the privacy of your own home. Search "intelligence quotient" and you will find tests that you can take online.)

■ Dr. William D. Abbott, Ed.D.
**Former President,
Ricker College,
Houlton, ME**

In A World of Lifelong Learning...

Ken Barone

You Must Learn... How To Learn!

Many young people believe that after high school, college and perhaps two years of graduate school, the "learning" part of an individual's life is completed and it is time to start the "doing" or "working" part of life. Over the past 25 years that notion has become less and less true; and over the next 10 years it will become completely incorrect. If you Google on the phrase "Lifelong Learning" today, you will find 3,580,000 hits.

Why will you need to make learning a lifelong pursuit? In our rapidly developing world, careers, businesses, whole fields of knowledge and technology have arisen that our parents and grandparents could not imagine. Twenty-five years ago there weren't any Massage Therapists or Digital Animation Developers. Fields of expertise quickly arise or become obsolete and businesses eliminate jobs as more efficient processes are developed. Small appliance repairmen are disappearing as we find it cheaper to replace toasters and computer printers than to fix them.

The experts all agree that a lifelong commitment to learning new skills and information will be critical to our future career success and personal satisfaction. Already in many career fields, lifelong learning is a requirement. Certified Home Inspectors, Licensed Electricians, Public Accountants, Social Workers, Licensed Massage Therapists and Nurses must all complete continuing education requirements throughout their careers in order to maintain their credentials.

How should the knowledge that you will need to continue your education throughout your life affect the decisions you make as you evaluate colleges and majors? You may be thinking that it is important to pick a career path, find a college that has a major with a good reputation in that field and take as many employment skill courses as possible in order to get a good job after college. However, with the way our world shifts so rapidly, those skills may not be important in 10 to 15 years. There are courses offered in colleges that will enhance your ability to learn. These courses teach you to form intelligent questions, to conduct appropriate research, to extract relevant information, to draw conclusions, to communicate and implement a plan. Those are the skills that are essential to all learning, regardless of the subject. The courses that teach these skills are found in the Liberal Arts, in Literature, Logic, Psychology, Sociology and basic Sciences. Colleges have long recognized the importance of these courses as a base for all learning. Most colleges require every student to complete a "core" of some of these courses regardless of a student's specific "career" major.

Students often find it difficult to be motivated for an 8:00 A.M. Literature class when they really want to be an Accountant or a Graphic Designer, but it's important to realize that a Designer must use language effectively to understand the client's aspirations before achieving them in color and shape. The Designer will also have to continually research and master new techniques, new computer software, and perhaps, business, accounting and management skills as they decide to open their own practice.

Experienced professionals will tell you that all of your courses will provide important contributions to your ability to adapt and succeed. They also agree that the Liberal Arts courses provide a critical foundation on which to build a lifetime of experience and learning. The ability to learn provides flexibility. Flexibility results in choice. Having choices enables you to control your future in the manner which will be the most fulfilling.

■ **Ken Barone**
Former Head of Admissions, Enrollment, and Financial Aid
Mt. Ida College
Newton, MA

Doors Open...

Excerpts from co-authors Margo Woodacre and Steffany Bane's book, **Doors Open From Both Sides**, an Off to College guide that takes you from the senior year of high school through the senior year of college.

These excerpts outline parent's and student's responses and reactions to the senior year in high school (Chapter 1) and jump to when the child first arrives at college (Chapter 3).

"We chose to symbolize the many transitions we went through with a door. There are always two sides to a door."

...Margo Woodacre and Steffany Bane

Chapter #1 "The Revolving Door"

Entering high school senior year is like moving through a revolving door: attention needs to be focused on making a good exit. The senior year calls for careful planning for that exit - whether it be to college or to a job. It is a year of activities that focus on the child's future. If the goal is college, much of the school year revolves around choosing and getting into a college.

It is also a year for parents facing an imminent empty nest to reflect upon the past and think about their future. Just as high school seniors remind themselves, "This is the last game, the last test, the last dance, the last play", the parents begin to realize that they, too, will be involved in a series of "lasts". Questions suddenly enter one's mind, "What's next?" "How can I handle this?"

> When one door closes, another opens, but we often look so long and regretfully upon the closed door that we do not see the one that has opened for us.
>
> -Alexander Graham Bell

Mom

The first "College Night" at the high school was overwhelming to us when we learned about the decisions to be made concerning final SAT schedules, applications, essays and college interviews. As a somewhat congenital worrier, I felt the pressure to get those chores accomplished. I became torn between my good intention to hand over responsibility to my child and my worry-based impatience to jump in and help her get it done!

Senior year was filled with many emotions and culminated with graduation. For many parents and their children, graduation was an emotional experience. For months, we were wrapped up in the excitement leading up to the actual event and suddenly, there we were, sitting at our final high school event!

Steff

The whole idea of going off to college was exciting: new places, new faces, choice of major and a class schedule I could select on my own, so much freedom! My friends and I would meet during our breaks at school and chat about how we were ready to graduate. By mid-year, our familiar robot-like schedules were becoming a bit boring but we still felt comfortable and safe.

Kids react in different ways to their last year in high school. Some feel emotional ties to their school and some are ecstatic at the prospect of leaving. However, along with most of my friends, I was starting to feel a bit melancholy about the approaching "end."

From Both Sides

Chapter #3 "Doors Apart"

Two separate doors now exist: the one at home and the one on campus. For parents, the challenge is to adjust to a more stable, yet quiet, homefront. For the young adult, the challenge is to adjust to a more dynamic and unaccustomed habitat. For both parents and child, the changes in their environments can produce a variety of emotions.

Mom

Our house seemed abnormally quiet. The phone didn't ring as much. The familiar sounds of chatter were gone, as were the whispers, the music, and the laughter from my daughter's upstairs room. Any reminders of her that remained - a book bag, sneakers, her key ring, the yearbook - all helped bring a heavy feeling to my stomach and tears to my eyes. I actually changed my traffic pattern around the house so that I would not have to walk by her room.

The real emptiness I felt in my life hit me when I went grocery shopping for the first time after Steffany had left home. Suddenly I was shopping only for my husband and myself. I felt sad as I walked to the aisle of Steff's favorite cereals and sadder as I passed her favorite snacks. There was now no need to add these to my cart so I passed by quickly, but I couldn't hold back my tears. I felt as empty as my cart looked.

Steff

College was nothing like I had ever expected. Adjustment to life without my parents nearby was easier than I thought. At times, however, when I felt alone, I felt a little scared. I knew all of us freshman had our own adjustments to make. Some of my new friends described feelings similar to mine. I could see the same look in their eyes that I had: the "I'm not sure how to feel" look. It was comforting to find that my feelings were quite normal.

The Orientation Days were great! Interactive games threw us together and proved to be a good way of getting to meet each other… After the orientation period, the start of classes was a rude awakening. I think some of us had almost forgotten why we were at school! ("You mean this isn't just one big party?")

Doors Open From Both Sides is a ten chapter book, starting with the senior year in high school and running through the senior year in college.

www.frombothsides.com

Reprinted with permission.

The Education Consumer

Dr. Victor E. Gatto

A large majority of entering college freshmen must learn a new set of education consumer behaviors to achieve the greatest value from their college experience.

Old Attitude – "Brown-nosing"

Example as often described to the Dean: "I don't like to talk to my professors. I had no respect for kids in my high school who were always brown-nosing the teachers."

Transition to a New Attitude…

"Pay the money; call the tune."

K-12 Education is teacher-directed. Teachers teach, and students learn. College Education is student-directed. Students must take responsibility for their own learning experience. Professors are only one source of knowledge.

What matters is what you learn.

Be open to learning from a rich variety of resources:

- *Students who share classes with you.* Your analysis of the classwork together will help make meaning from the new chaos of college work.

- *Roommates and Dormmates.* The spin of information – current news, college issues, fierce debates - will provide the foundation for your best learning.

- *Professors and Advisors.* They are the most expensive educational resource at your college – you pay for them; you should use them. You must transition from Professor-directed: "The way it's supposed to be" to… Student-directed: "The way it is for me!"

- *Internet and other resources.* Everything you need to know is available in two clicks or up a few library steps.

Your Mission:

Make sense for yourself – What do you want to learn – What do you need to learn? Don't consider yourself a brown-nose – consider all the sources of knowledge as a myriad of colored balloons that lift you to understanding.

Summary:

If you read this section first, you are on your way to making the transition to the attitudes of a successful education consumer. In high school your teachers provided the initiative for your education; now in college you will direct your own learning. Use many resources to develop your learning path, including the professors and advisors whose salaries comprise greater than 50% of your college's fiscal commitment to support your learning. Find effective strategies and shortcuts to learn what you want and need to learn.

■ Dr. Victor E. Gatto,
Achieve Telecom Network,
Peabody, MA

what 2 take 2 the DORM!

FIRST DAY AT COLLEGE! AT LAST YOU'VE ARRIVED!

You get to your room...

You find it's just like all the others on the floor.

You have a bed, a desk, a desk chair, a dresser, a closet. And, maybe, a new roommate. THAT'S IT!

Now it's up to you to make it a home.

Thank goodness you had this checklist, so you have the basics!...

STUDYING
- Computer and Printer
- Dictionary
- Thesaurus
- Strunk & White's The Elements of Style
- Bulletin Board/1 Desk Lamp/1 Floor Lamp
- 1 Desk Organizer Set
- Pens/Pencils/Pads/Highlighters/Scotch Tape/Stapler and Staples/Post-it Notes/Scissors/Hole Punch/Paper Clips
- Sticky Arrows To Mark Place On Pages
- 1 Backpack
- 1 Beanbag Base Lap Desk

KITCHEN/FOOD PREPARATION
- Flatware
- Glassware
- Dishes
- Mug
- Kitchen Utensils
- Frying Pan
- Saucepan
- 1 Dorm-Size Microwave
- 1 Dorm-Size Refrigerator
- 1 Blender
- 1 Coffee Machine
- 1 Electric Teakettle
- 1 Brita® Pitcher and Filter

LAUNDRY/CLEAN-UP
- Detergent
- 1 Iron
- 1 Portable Ironing Board
- 2 Laundry Bags
- 1 Drying Rack
- 1 Hand Vacuum
- Quarters

MISCELLANEOUS
- 1 Calendar/Organizer
- 1 Calculator
- 1 Tool Kit/Multipurpose Tool With Screwdriver, Measuring Tape, and Pliers
- 1 Sewing Kit
- 1 First Aid Kit
- 1 Alarm Clock
- 1 Personal CD Player
- 1 Portable TV
- 1 MP3 Player
- 1 Cell Phone with Voicemail
- 2 Extension Cords
- 1 Surge Protector
- 1 Pocket Calculator
- 1 Flashlight
- Wall Hooks
- Batteries
- Handi Wipes
- Plastic Bags
- 1 Backrest
- 1 Fan
- Lightbulbs
- Waste Basket
- Museum Putty and/or Adhesive Tape That Won't Damage Walls
- Disposable Cameras

BEDDING
- 2 Sheet Sets Flat, Fitted, & Pillowcases (Check with your college to determine whether you'll need extra long sheets.)
- 1 Comforter
- 1 Comforter Cover
- 2 Blankets
- 2 Pillows
- 4 Pillow Protectors
- 1 Mattress Pad

BATHROOM
- 3 Sets of Towels
- 1 Tote for Carrying Personal Items
- 1 Blow Drier
- 1 Robe and Slippers
- Flip-Flops
- Personal Hygiene Supplies
- Bath Rug
- Tub Mat

STORAGE/ORGANIZERS
- 2 Under-the-Bed Storage Containers
- Storage Cubes
- Bed Elevators
- Shoe Rack
- Organizing Unit
- Over-the-Door Grid System
- 1 CD/DVD Storage
- 1 Folding Bookcase

(This is a general list. Some schools provide more items for their students' use than others. So please be sure to check with your school to ask what items will be provided for you in your room, which appliances you should bring, and what you should not bring.)

Abbreviations

4H 4-H
4H Awd 4-H Award
Acpl Chr A Cappella Choir
Adv Cncl Advisory Council
All Am Sch All-American Scholar
AL Aux Boys/Girls American Legion Auxiliary Boys/Girls State
Amnsty Intl Amnesty International Volunteer
Aqrium Clb Aquarium Club
Arch Archery
Bdmtn Badminton
Bnd Band
Bsball Baseball
Bskball Basketball
Biology Clb Biology Club
BPA Business Professionals of America
CARE C.A.R.E.
C Captain
Chrldg Cheerleading
Chr Chorus
Ch Chr Church Choir
Chrch Yth Grp Church Youth Group
Ctznshp Aw Citizenship Award
Civil Air Pat Civil Air Patrol
Cl Off Class Officer
CR Class Representative
Clr Grd Color Guard
Comm Volntr Community Volunteer
Cmptr Clb Computer Club
Cr Ctry Cross Country
Cr Ct Ski Cross Country Skiing
Cyclg Cycling
Dnce Dance
DAR Daughters of the American Revolution
Dbte Team Debate Team
Dvng Diving
Drma Clb Drama Club
Drl Tm Drill Team
Drm Mjr Drum Major(ette)
Duke TS Duke Talent Search
E Editor
Emplmnt Employment (part-time, vacation)
FCA Fellowship of Christian Athletes
Fncg Fencing
Fld Hky Field Hockey
Flg Crps Flag Corps
Ftball Football

F Lan Hn Soc Foreign Language Honor Society
Fr Freshman
Fr of Library Friends of the Library
FBLA Future Business Leaders of America
FCCLA Family, Career and Community Leaders of America
Fut Prb Slvr Future Problem Solvers
FTA Future Teachers of America
GAA Girls Athletic Association
Gov Hnr Prg Governor's Honor Program
Gmnstcs Gymnastics
Hab For Humty Volntr Habitat For Humanity Volunteer
Hi Hnr Roll High Honor Roll
Hnr Roll Honor Roll
Hsbk Rdg Horseback Riding
Hosp Aide Hospital Aide (Candy Striper)
HO'Br Yth Ldrshp Hugh O'Brian Youth Leadership
Ice Hky Ice Hockey
Ice Sktg Ice Skating
Jzz Bnd Jazz Band
Jr Junior
Jr Ach Junior Achievement
Jr Cls League Junior Classical League
Jr Eng Tech Junior Engineering Technical Society Award
Jr Mshl Junior Marshal
Jr Rot Junior Rotarian
JSA Junior Statesmen of America
JV Junior Varsity
Kwnis Aw Kiwanis Award
Lcrsse Lacrosse
L Letter Winner
Lttrmn Clb Letterman Club
Lib Aide Library Aide
Lit Mag Literary Magazine
Mch Bnd Marching Band
Mar Art Martial Arts
Mas Aw Masonic Lodge Award
Mth Clb/Tm Math Club/Team
Mod UN Model U.N.
MVP Most Valuable Player
MuAlphaTh MuAlphaTheta
Mus Clb Music Club
Ntl Beta Clb National Beta Club
Ntl FFA National FFA
NtlFrnscLg National Forensic League

Nat Hon Sy National Honor Society
Nat Ldrshp Svc National Leadership Service Award
Nat Mrt Fin National Merit Finalist
Nat Mrt LOC National Merit Letter Of Commendation
Nat Mrt Sch Recip National Merit Scholarship Recipient
Nat Mrt Semif National Merit Semifinalist
Nat Sci Aw National Science Award
Nat Stu Ath Day Aw National Student Athlete Day Award
NYLC National Young Leaders Conference
Sch Ppr Newspaper
Off Aide Office Aide
Orch Orchestra
Outdrs Clb Outdoors Club
Otst Ac Ach Awd Outstanding Academic Achievement Award
Peer Tut/Med Peer Tutoring/Mediator
P to P St Amb Prg People to People Student Ambassador Program
Pep Bnd Pep Band
Pep Squd Pep Squad/Club
Perf Att Perfect Attendance
P Photographer
Photog Photography
PPSqd Pom Pom Squad
PP Ftbl Powder Puff Football
P President
Pres Ac Ftns Aw Presidential Academic Fitness Award
Pres Sch Presidential Scholar
Prom Com Prom Committee
Red Cr Aide Red Cross Aide/Volunteer
R Reporter
R Representative
Rlr Hky Roller Hockey
Rqtball Racquetball
Salutrn Salutatorian
Schol Bwl Scholastic Bowl
SP/M/VS School Play/Musical/Variety Show
Sci Clb Science Club
Sci Fairs Science Fairs
Sci/Math Olympn Science/Math Olympians
Scr Kpr Score Keeper
S Secretary

Sr Senior
Svce Clb Service Club
Skt Tgt Sh Skeet/Target Shooting
Sccr Soccer
Sftball Softball
So Sophomore
Spec Olymp Vol Special Olympics Volunteer
Spch Team Speech Team
Stg Cre State Crew
St Schl State Scholar
Stu Cncl Student Council
St of Mnth Student of the Month
St Optmst of Yr Student Optimist of the Year
SADD Students Against Drunk Driving
Swmg Swimming
Swg Chr Swing Chorus
Tchrs Aide Teacher's Aide
Tech Clb Technology Club
Tmpl Yth Grp Temple Youth Group
T Treasurer
USAA U.S. Achievement Society/Academy
US Army Sch Ath Aw U.S. Army Scholar Athlete Award
USMC Stu Ath Aw U.S. Marine Corps Student Athlete Award
UW Svce Awd United Way Service to Community Award
Valdctrian Valedictorian
Vsy Clb Varsity Club
V Varsity
Vsity Clb Varsity Club
V Vice President
Voc Ind Clb Am Vocational Industrial Club of America
Vllyball Volleyball
Wt Lftg Weight Lifting
WWAAHSS Who's Who Among American HS Students
Wdwrkg Clb Woodworking
Wrstlg Wrestling
Yrbk Yearbook
Yth Ldrshp Prog Youth Leadership Program

SAMPLE BIOGRAPHICAL SKETCH
This sample illustrates the format of the biographical listings. Students are identified by name, home city and state, school, and class year. To protect inductees' privacy, home addresses and personal information are not published.

1. Name
2. Home City and State
3. High School
4. Year in School
5. Achievements
6. Future Plans, including colleges to which student plans to apply

(1)RANDALL, STEVEN: (2)Massapequa, NY; (3)Massapequa High School; (4)JR; (5) Hnr Roll;Tchrs Aide; Tmpl Yth Grp; Bnd; Mch Bnd; Bsball; Bskball; Cr Ctry; Sccr; Tennis(V); Sch Ppr, R; Teacher Helper at Religious School; Piano For 7 Years; (6) Elementary School Teacher Harvard University, Yale.

Although National Honor Roll has endeavored to correctly enter all personal information in each listing, it does not guarantee the accuracy of the content of any information contained herein. Accordingly, National Honor Roll expressly disclaims any liability that may occur as a result of any listing, typographical error and/or any error in printing contained herein or as a result of any reliance on such information.

STUDENT BIOGRAPHIES
Connecticut

ABBAZIA, DANIELLE; STAMFORD, CT; STAMFORD HS; (SO); Hnr Roll; Comm Volntr; Tennis (V); Camp Counselor; Foreign Language; U of Virginia; U of Connecticut

ABDUL-MALAK, TANYA; STAMFORD, CT; STAMFORD HS; (SO); Ctznshp Aw; Hi Hnr Roll; Hnr Roll; St of Mnth; Latin Clb; Dnce; Mch Bnd; Ice Sktg; Advanced Ballet Dancer

ABE, SESHIA; FAIRFIELD, CT; FAIRFIELD WARDE HS; (SO); Hi Hnr Roll; Hnr Roll; USAA; WWAHSS; Comm Volntr; Red Cr Aide; Key Club; Orch; The Greater Bridgeport Youth Orchestras (Symphony Orchestra); Violin; MIT; Columbia U

ABERCROMBIE III, RICHARD K; RIDGEFIELD, CT; IMMACULATE HS; (SO); Hnr Roll; WWAHSS; Comm Volntr; Dbte Team; Ftball (J); Lcrsse (V); Business

ACOSTA, MIGUEL A; HARTFORD, CT; A I PRINCE TECH; (JR); Ctznshp Aw; Hi Hnr Roll; Hnr Roll; Nat Hon Sy; Otst Ac Ach Awd; Perf Att; St of Mnth; Comm Volntr; Chrch Yth Grp; Emplmnt; Mth Clb/Tm; SINA Scholar of the Month; RYA Student of the Cycle and Year; Bachelor's Degree- Business Management; Entrepreneur; Central Connecticut State College; Bridgeport U

ALBINO, NICOLE R; CHESHIRE, CT; CHOATE ROSEMARY HALL; (JR); Fut Prb Slvr; Gov Hnr Prg; Hi Hnr Roll; Nat Hon Sy; Pres Ac Ftns Aw; Pres Sch; WWAHSS; Yth Ldrshp Prog; Comm Volntr; Chrch Yth Grp; DARE; Mth Clb/Tm; Swmg (V); Chosen for Science Research Program; Chosen for National Youth Forum in Medicine; Pre-Med to Medical School / Pediatrician; Dartmouth College

ALCORTA, ANDREW S; GLASTONBURY, CT; GLASTONBURY HS; (SO); F Lan Hn Soc; Hi Hnr Roll; Sci Fairs; St of Mnth; WWAHSS; DARE; Drma Clb; Outdrs Clb; Russian Clb; Chr; SP/M/VS; Sccr (J); Vllyball (J); Stu Cncl (R); Vice President of Ski Club; CT Association of Schools Scholar Leader Award; Performing in Theatre; Government; Yale U; Georgetown U

ALDRICH, KATHRYN; BOLTON, CT; BOLTON HS; (JR); Hnr Roll; Comm Volntr; Hosp Aide; Peer Tut/Med; Chrch Yth Grp; DARE; Off Aide; Scouts; Medusa National Latin Exam-Bronze Medal; Outstanding Effort in English; Elementary Education; Criminal Justice; Manchester Community College CT; University of Connecticut Storrs

ALESSI, SARA N; FAIRFIELD, CT; FAIRFIELD WARDE HS; (JR); F Lan Hn Soc; Hi Hnr Roll; Nat Hon Sy; WWAHSS; Key Club; Dnce; Orch; Lit Mag; Pequot House Council Secretary, Vice-President; Key Club Can Tab Drive Chairperson, Recording Secretary; English

ALEXANDER, ASHLEY T; ANSONIA, CT; BRIDGE AC; (JR); Nat Hon Sy; Peer Tut/Med; Chrch Yth Grp; Emplmnt; Dnce; Psychology; New York U; Wheelock College

ALIBERTI, SAMANTHA; MILFORD, CT; FORAN HS; (FR); Hnr Roll; Peer Tut/Med; Key Club; Ntl FFA; Sccr

ALICEA, FRANCISCO; MERIDEN, CT; ORVILLE H PLATT HS; (FR); Hi Hnr Roll; Hnr Roll; Otst Ac Ach Awd; St of Mnth; Comm Volntr; Peer Tut/Med; Chess; Chrch Yth Grp; DARE; Dbte Team; Drma Clb; Mus Clb; Chr; Ch Chr; SP/M/VS; Stu Cncl (R); Theatre; Vocalist

ALICKOLLI, XHENSILIA; WATERBURY, CT; CROSBY HS; (SO); Hi Hnr Roll; Hnr Roll; WWAHSS; Comm Volntr; HO'Br Yth Ldrshp; Mock Trial; Lawyer; Nursing; Fairfield U; Trinity College

ALMEIDA, LAURA B; CHESHIRE, CT; CHESHIRE HS; Hi Hnr Roll; Hnr Roll; Yth Ldrshp Prog; Comm Volntr; Hab For Humty Volntr; Spec Olymp Vol; Emplmnt; Dnce; SP/M/VS; Chrldg (V L); Relay for Life; Big Brothers / Big Sisters; Teaching; Nursing; U of Connecticut; Southern CT State U

ALSTON-SMITH, CHANISE; BLOOMFIELD, CT; NORTHWEST CATHOLIC HS; (JR); Hi Hnr Roll; Hnr Roll; Nat Hon Sy; Perf Att; Sci Fairs; Yth Ldrshp Prog; Comm Volntr; Peer Tut/Med; Emplmnt; NYLC; Bnd; Jzz Bnd; Pep Bnd; SP/M/VS; Cr Ctry (J); Lcrsse (J); Track (V); Rotary Youth Leadership Conference; Pre-Medicine; Tufts U; Boston U

ANDERSON, KELLY; BETHLEHEM, CT; NONNEWAUG HS; (FR); Hi Hnr Roll; Otst Ac Ach Awd; Pres Ac Ftns Aw; St of Mnth; Comm Volntr; Peer Tut/Med; Lib Aide; NYLC; Scouts; Flg Crps; Sccr (J L); Cl Off (R); Teach Sunday School for Church; Woodbury Middle School Spirit Award; Middle School Math Teacher; Guidance Counselor/Social Worker; U of Connecticut

ANDERSON, KIMBERLY; BRIDGEPORT, CT; CENTRAL HS; (SO); Nat Hon Sy; Comm Volntr; Chrldg (V); Business; Southern Connecticut State U; Western Connecticut State U

ANDERSON, MEGAN M; NEW MILFORD, CT; HENRY ABBOTT REG TECH HS; (SO); Hnr Roll; Off Aide; Sch Ppr (R, P); Yrbk (R, P); Culinary Arts; Culinary Institute of America; Johnson & Wales U

ANDREASEN, MELISSA; NEW FAIRFIELD, CT; NEW FAIRFIELD HS; (SR); Ctznshp Aw; F Lan Hn Soc; Hnr Roll; WWAHSS; Comm Volntr; DARE; DECA; Emplmnt; FBLA; Chrldg (J); Fld Hky (VJCL); Sftball (J); Track (J); Sportsmanship Award - Cheerleading; All Patriot Player-Field Hockey; Interior Design; Business; Sage College of Albany - Attending Fall 2005

ANDREOZZI JR, SCOTT G; NEW FAIRFIELD, CT; NEW FAIRFIELD HS; (FR); Hi Hnr Roll; Pres Ac Ftns Aw; FBLA; Bsball (J); Ftball (J); Cl Off (P); Jaycee Basketball; Business; Entrepreneurship; Rutgers U-The State U of New Jersey; U of Rhode Island, Princeton U

ANGLIN, ROMAN A; DANBURY, CT; DANBURY HS; (FR); Hi Hnr Roll; Hnr Roll; Otst Ac Ach Awd; Perf Att; Peer Tut/Med; Emplmnt; Mus Clb; Bnd; Jzz Bnd; Orch; Bsball; Bskball; Rlr Hky; Vllyball; Outstanding Jazz Instrumentalist; Attorney-Real Estate; Professional Musician; U of Connecticut; U of Florida

ARPIE, JOANNA; MILFORD, CT; JOSEPH A FORAN HS; (SO); Hi Hnr Roll; St of Mnth; Comm Volntr; Hosp Aide; Red Cr Aide; Emplmnt; Key Club; Photog; Spanish Clb; Dnce; Sccr (VJ); Sftball (J); Volunteer At a Vacation Bible School; Part of Interact Club; Journalism; Photography; Northeastern; NYU

ASZKLAR, MELISSA A; MERIDEN, CT; ORVILLE H PLATT HS; (JR); Hnr Roll; Otst Ac Ach Awd; St of Mnth; Comm Volntr; Red Cr Aide; Drma Clb; Mus Clb; Acpl Chr; Chr; SP/M/VS; Yrbk (P); Student of the Month; Project Excel; Vocal Performing; Criminal Psychology; Berklee College of Music; U Conn

ATKINS, GEORGIA; HARTFORD, CT; WEAVER HS; (FR); Hi Hnr Roll; Sci Fairs; Adv Cncl (P); Medicine; Yale U

AUGUST, JOSHUA T; DERBY, CT; DERBY HS; (JR); F Lan Hn Soc; Hi Hnr Roll; Nat Hon Sy; Nat Mrt Fin; WWAHSS; Yth Ldrshp Prog; Comm Volntr; Hosp Aide; HO'Br Yth Ldrshp; Spch Team; Vsity Clb; Spanish Clb; Fncg (V); Sccr (V C); Cl Off (P, V); Stu Cncl (R)

AVILA, CARLOS D; WATERBURY, CT; W F KAYNOR REG VOC TECH SCH; (SO); Hnr Roll; Nat Hon Sy; St of Mnth; WWAHSS; Wdwrkg Clb; Bsball; Bskball; Swmg; Engineer/Master Carpentry; Navy Seals; Virginia Technical

AWAN, ADNAN; HAMDEN, CT; NOTRE DAME HS; (JR); Hnr Roll; St of Mnth; Yth Ldrshp Prog; Comm Volntr; Peer Tut/Med; Drma Clb; SADD; French Clb; National Junior Honor Society of Secondary School; Latin Honor Society; Medicine; Bio/Medical; Johns Hopkins U; George Washington U

AWODELE, OLUSEGUN; BRIDGEPORT, CT; WARREN HARDING HS; (SR); Hnr Roll; Chrch Yth Grp; Ch Chr; Mar Art; 1st Place in Medical Math At HOSA (State); Honor Roll in Senior Year; Pharmacy (Pharm.D)-6 year Program; Research Scientist; U of Connecticut

BAEZ, JENNIFER; HARTFORD, CT; A I PRINCE TECH; (FR); Ctznshp Aw; Hi Hnr Roll; Hnr Roll; Perf Att; Sci Fairs; St of Mnth; Was in Stock Market in Elementary; Culinary Artist / Chef; Caterer; U Conn

BAEZ, JISANNI; NEW LONDON, CT; ELLA T GRASSO RVT SCH; (JR); Hi Hnr Roll; Hnr Roll; Pres Sch; St of Mnth; WWAHSS; Comm Volntr; Emplmnt; Off Aide; Prom Com; Voc Ind Clb Am; Cl Off (S); Stu Cncl (S); Sch Ppr (R); Yrbk (E); Skills USA VICA President; Major in Nursing; Minor in Business; College of New Rochelle; American International College

BAILEY JR, EVERTON; BRIDGEPORT, CT; CENTRAL HS; (JR); Ctznshp Aw; Hnr Roll; DARE; Emplmnt; Track (V); Sch Ppr (E); Member of the African-American Club; Farmer Member of the Junior Police; Journalism; St John's U; American U

BALINT, DAN; CHESHIRE, CT; CHESHIRE HS; (JR); Hi Hnr Roll; Hnr Roll; MVP; Comm Volntr; Chess; Scouts; Acpl Chr; Chr; SP/M/VS; Swg Chr; Cr Ctry (J); Mar Art; Skiing (J); Vllyball; Sch Ppr (R); All Eastern Honor Choir; Tri-M Music Honor Society; Music Education; U of Connecticut; St Michael's College

BALKARAN, JENNIFER; NEW HAVEN, CT; WILBUR CROSS HS; (JR); Hnr Roll; Sci Fairs; WWAHSS; Comm Volntr; Emplmnt; Tennis (V); Adv Cncl (R); Cl Off (R); Stu Cncl (R); Nursing; Social Work; UConn; Quinnpiac

BANTEN, CHRISTOPHER C; FAIRFIELD, CT; FAIRFIELD LUDLOWE HS; (SO); DAR; Hnr Roll; St of Mnth; Chrch Yth Grp; DARE; Key Club; P to P St Amb Prg; Bskball (V)

BARNES, NATHAN D; ORANGE, CT; CHRISTIAN HERITAGE SCH; (SO); Hi Hnr Roll; Hnr Roll; Sci Fairs; Chrch Yth Grp; Bnd; Jzz Bnd; SP/M/VS; Stg Cre; Bsball (V); Cyclg; Wrstlg; Engineering; Rensselaer Polytechnic Institute

BARONE, STEPHANIE; CHESHIRE, CT; CHESHIRE HS; (JR); Hi Hnr Roll; Hnr Roll; St of Mnth; Hab For Humty Volntr; Chrch Yth Grp; Emplmnt; P to P St Amb Prg; SADD; Sftball (VJ); Co-Chairman of B2 Day; Accounting; Business Management; Bryant U; Sacred Heart U

BARR, LINDSAY; OLD LYME, CT; LYME-OLD LYME HS; (JR); 4H Awd; Hi Hnr Roll; Hnr Roll; Nat Hon Sy; Otst Ac Ach Awd; WWAHSS; Comm Volntr; Hab For Humty Volntr; 4-H; Chrch Yth Grp; Emplmnt; Key Club; Sci Clb; Scouts; Chr; Fncg (V L); CR (R); Lit Mag; Yrbk (R, P); Marine Scholar - U Conn; Marine Biology Major

BARRIGA, DIANA Y; EAST HARTFORD, CT; EAST HARTFORD HS; (JR); Hnr Roll; Yth Ldrshp Prog; Comm Volntr; Peer Tut/Med; Chrch Yth Grp; Mus Clb; Chr; Ch Chr; Dnce; Swg Chr; Vllyball (J); Student-Guide (For New Students); Manager (For Volleyball Also); Architecture; Interior Decorating; U of Connecticut; Central Connecticut State U

BARRY, JENNIFER K; ENFIELD, CT; ENFIELD HS; (SR); F Lan Hn Soc; Hi Hnr Roll; Hnr Roll; Nat Hon Sy; Comm Volntr; Drma Clb; Emplmnt; Scouts; Bnd; SP/M/VS; Ice Sktg (C); Sch Ppr (E); Will Be Attending-U of Connecticut

BARTELL, ZACHARY; HAMDEN, CT; THE SOUND SCH; (JR); Hi Hnr Roll; Nat Hon Sy; WWAHSS; Yth Ldrshp Prog; Ntl FFA; NYLC; Tmpl Yth Grp; Mar Art; Rowing Team

BASHER, KRISTINA; STRATFORD, CT; BUNNELL HS; (MS); All Am Sch; Ctznshp Aw; Hi Hnr Roll; Otst Ac Ach Awd; Pres Ac Ftns Aw; Pres Sch; Comm Volntr; Hosp Aide; Spec Olymp Vol; Chrch Yth Grp; DARE; Drma Clb; Mus Clb; Pep Squd; P to P St Amb Prg; Chr; Chrldg (J); Yrbk (E); Law Degree; Doctorate; Yale U; U of Conn

BATISTA, ADRIELA E; TERRYVILLE, CT; TERRYVILLE HS; (FR); Reporter/Publishing; Communications; Columbia U; U of Massachusetts

BAUCICAUT, HARRY; STAMFORD, CT; STAMFORD HS; (SO); Hnr Roll; DARE; Emplmnt; Jr Ach

BAYLIS, ALLISON; WEST HAVEN, CT; WEST HAVEN HS; (SR); Hi Hnr Roll; Nat Hon Sy; Nat Sci Aw; Otst Ac Ach Awd; Pres Sch; St of Mnth; WWAHSS; Comm Volntr; DECA; Emplmnt; Bnd; Drm Mjr; Mch Bnd; Ice Hky (V C); Lcrsse (J); Sftball (J); Stu Cncl (R); CR (R); Sch Ppr (R); Bayer Academic Achievement; Rotary Speech Contest; Dentistry; Biology; U of Connecticut

BEAL, ADAM; NORWALK, CT; NORWALK HS; (SO); Hi Hnr Roll; Yth Ldrshp Prog; Comm Volntr; Key Club; NYLC; P to P St Amb Prg; Tmpl Yth Grp; Sccr (VJC); Tennis (V); People to People Sports Ambassador World Friendship Games-England/Armsterdam; NJLC-Defense and Diplomacy; Stanford U; Tufts U

BEAN, KATELYN; WINDSOR LOCKS, CT; WINDSOR LOCKS HS; (SO); Hi Hnr Roll; Hnr Roll; Otst Ac Ach Awd; Comm Volntr; FBLA; Sccr (J); Track (V); North Central Connecticut Conference Scholar Athlete Award 2003 and 2004; Business; Obstetrician; U of Connecticut; Boston College

BEATTY, BRETT; SHELTON, CT; CHRISTIAN HERITAGE SCH; (JR); Hi Hnr Roll; Hnr Roll; MVP; Nat Hon Sy; WWAHSS; Yth Ldrshp Prog; Chrch Yth Grp; Acpl Chr; Bnd; Chr; Ch Chr; Sccr (V C); Elementary Education; Youth Ministry; Gordon College

BECK, ERIC S; NORWALK, CT; NORWALK HS; (SO); Ctznshp Aw; Hi Hnr Roll; Pres Ac Ftns Aw; Pres Sch; DARE; Scouts; Wdwrkg Clb

BEHRENT, SHAUN; COLCHESTER, CT; BARON AC; (SR); Hnr Roll; Emplmnt; Photog; French Clb; Cl Off (V); Sch Ppr (R, P); Yrbk (P); Hartford Courant Journalism Contest Photography 1st Place; Photo Journalism; Eastern Connecticut State U

BELAGORUDSKY, JULIA; ORANGE, CT; AMITY HS; (JR); Ctznshp Aw; F Lan Hn Soc; Hi Hnr Roll; WWAHSS; Emplmnt; Dnce; Yrbk (E)

BELIVEAU, JACQUELINE; NORTH GRANBY, CT; NORTHWEST CATHOLIC HS; (SO); Hi Hnr Roll; WWAHSS; Comm Volntr; Peer Tut/Med; Sccr (V L); Track (V L); Business; Law

BEMBER, BIANCA L; BRIDGEPORT, CT; BULLARD-HAVENS TECH SCH; (FR); Ctznshp Aw; Hnr Roll; Otst Ac Ach Awd; Perf Att; St of Mnth; Chrch Yth Grp; DARE; Drma Clb; Off Aide; Bnd; Ch Chr; Dnce; Drl Tm; National American Miss Pageant; Model / Actress; Lawyer; U of Connecticut - Department of Dramatic Arts; Yale Law School

Bean, Katelyn
Windsor Locks HS
Windsor Locks, CT

Baucicaut, Harry
Stamford HS
Stamford, CT

Bember, Bianca L
Bullard-Havens Tech Sch
Bridgeport, CT

Basher, Kristina
Bunnell HS
Stratford, CT

Andreozzi Jr, Scott G
New Fairfield HS
New Fairfield, CT

Alston-Smith, Chanise
Northwest Catholic HS
Bloomfield, CT

Alicea, Francisco
Orville H Platt HS
Meriden, CT

Acosta, Miguel A
A I Prince Tech
Hartford, CT

Abbazia, Danielle
Stamford HS
Stamford, CT

Abe, Seshia
Fairfield Warde HS
Fairfield, CT

Almeida, Laura B
Cheshire HS
Cheshire, CT

Anderson, Kelly
Nonnewaug HS
Bethlehem, CT

Banten, Christopher C
Fairfield Ludlowe HS
Fairfield, CT

Barone, Stephanie
Cheshire HS
Cheshire, CT

BENBOW, TIPHANI; BRIDGEPORT, CT; CHRISTIAN HERITAGE SCH; (SO); Chrch Yth Grp; Bnd; Mch Bnd; SP/M/VS; Bskball (V); Scr Kpr (VJ); Sccr (V); Sftball (V); Most Improved Player - Varsity Soccer; Most Valuable Player - AYSO; Architecture; Culinary Arts; Rensselaer Polytechnic Institute; Otis College

BENTO, OLIVIA; FAIRFIELD, CT; FAIRFIELD LUDLOWE JHS; (FR); Hi Hnr Roll; Hnr Roll; Nat Hon Sy; Pres Sch; St of Mnth; WWAHSS; Peer Tut/Med; DARE; Key Club; Dnce; Lawyer; Pediatrician; Brown U; U of California in L.A

BERKY, BRITTANY J; MADISON, CT; DANIEL HAND HS; (SR); Hnr Roll; Pres Ac Ftns Aw; WWAHSS; Comm Volntr; Chrch Yth Grp; Drma Clb; Emplmnt; Wdwrkg Clb; Chr; Chrldg (V); Sccr (J); Culinary Arts; Food Service; Southern New Hampshire U

BEST, CHRISTOPHER M; BRIDGEPORT, CT; BASSICK HS; (SO); Hnr Roll; Emplmnt; Success Program Graduate; Graphic Design & Animation; Morehouse College; Central CT State

BETANCOURT, SHANIA K; NEW BRITAIN, CT; E C GOODWIN REG VOC TECH SCH; (SO); Hi Hnr Roll; Hnr Roll; Bskball (J); Sftball (J); Vllyball (J); Hairdressing; Automotive; State U

BETKOSKI, KOURTNEY; BEACON FALLS, CT; WOODLAND REG HS; (MS); Hi Hnr Roll; Hnr Roll; Nat Hon Sy; Perf Att; Sci Fairs; Comm Volntr; Peer Tut/Med; Red Cr Aide; DARE; Dbte Team; Drma Clb; Emplmnt; Mus Clb; Outdrs Clb; Pep Squd; Photog; Chr; Ch Chr; SP/M/VS; Stg Cre; Bskball; Mar Art; Sccr; Sftball; Swmg; Tennis; Vllyball; Stu Cncl (R); High Honors; Business; U of Connecticut; Fairfield U

BIGLEY, SARA M; STRATFORD, CT; STRATFORD HS; (JR); F Lan Hn Soc; Hi Hnr Roll; Hnr Roll; Nat Hon Sy; Perf Att; Yth Ldrshp Prog; Hosp Aide; Drma Clb; Emplmnt; Quill & Scroll; Sci Clb; French Clb; SP/M/VS; Stg Cre; Cr Ctry (V CL); Lit Mag (E); Treasurer of the Earth Club; Youth As Resources Award of Stratford, CT; Organic Sciences; Theater; New York U; Fairfield U

BINNS, SHAWN; WATERBURY, CT; CROSBY HS; (JR); Hi Hnr Roll; Hnr Roll; Perf Att; WWAHSS; SP/M/VS; Cr Ctry (J); Track (J); Sch Ppr (E); Psychology; Drama

BIRCH, KRISTIN; SOUTH WINDSOR, CT; SOUTH WINDSOR HS; (JR); Hi Hnr Roll; Hnr Roll; Nat Hon Sy; Otst Ac Ach Awd; Comm Volntr; Chrch Yth Grp; Emplmnt; Dnce; Physical Therapy; Psychology; Boston U; U of Connecticut

BIRCH, MICHELLE A; NEW HAVEN, CT; JAMES HILLHOUSE HS; (FR); Ctznshp Aw; Hi Hnr Roll; Hnr Roll; Perf Att; St of Mnth; Peer Tut/Med; Chrch Yth Grp; Emplmnt; Spanish Clb; Ch Chr; Clr Grd; Drl Tm; Chrldg (J); Tennis (J); Stu Cncl (R); CR (R); Trophies in Piano; Lawyer; Doctor; Florida State, Spelman, Yale; Howard U, Harvard

BLAIS, KELLY E; SUFFIELD, CT; SUFFIELD HS; (SR); Hi Hnr Roll; Hnr Roll; Nat Hon Sy; Pres Ac Ftns Aw; St of Mnth; Comm Volntr; Chrch Yth Grp; Drma Clb; Emplmnt; Mus Clb; Prom Com; Vsity Clb; Chr; Ch Chr; Dnce; SP/M/VS; Sftball (V C); Yrbk (R, P); NCCC-Vocal; All American Dance; Secondary Education; American History; Central Connecticut State U; Westfield State College

BOCCAROSSA, STEPHEN C; ORANGE, CT; LIVING WORD CHRISTIAN AC; (SO); Hi Hnr Roll; Chess; Chrch Yth Grp; Emplmnt; Bskball (V L); Cl Off (S); National Anthology of Young Poets; Global Expeditions Mission Trip to Mexico; Business Administration & Economics; Northeastern U; U of Connecticut

BOGAN, DANA L; MILFORD, CT; JOSEPH A. FORAN HS; (JR); Hnr Roll; St of Mnth; WWAHSS; Hosp Aide; Key Club; Sccr (V L); Track (V CL); Cl Off (V); Stu Cncl (V); Pre-Medicine; Boston College; Tufts U

BOHORQUEZ, SOAD V; NEW HAVEN, CT; HS IN THE CMTY; (JR); Sci/Math Olympn; St of Mnth; Comm Volntr; Chrch Yth Grp; Drma Clb; Mth Clb/Tm; Chr; Sccr (V); Excellence in Mathematics and Science Award (Fairfield U); Health Professions Recruitment and Exposure Program At Yale.; Pre-Medicine; Finance; Yale U; Fairfield U

BONILLA, HARBIN; STAMFORD, CT; AC OF INFORMATION TECH; (JR); Hnr Roll; Comm Volntr; DARE; Ftball; Architecture; Norwalk Community College; U of Bridgeport

BOTERO, GABRIEL; GREENWICH, CT; GREENWICH HS; (SR); Hi Hnr Roll; Hnr Roll; Nat Mrt LOC; Yth Ldrshp Prog; Comm Volntr; Emplmnt; Mod UN; SADD; Tech Clb; Mar Art; Wrstlg (J); National Student Leadership Conference; Vice-President of School's Hispanic Club (Vision); Pre-Law; History or Business; U of Connecticut (Accepted); St. John's U (Accepted)

BOUCHARD, KATELIN; PLAINVILLE, CT; PLAINVILLE HS; (SO); Gov Hnr Prg; Hnr Roll; Nat Hon Sy; Pres Ac Ftns Aw; Pres Sch; St of Mnth; WWAHSS; Chrch Yth Grp; DARE; Drma Clb; Jr Ach; Scouts; Chr; SP/M/VS; Swg Chr; Chrldg (V); Gmnstcs (V); All-Star Cheerleader (Sr.) (V); GPA-4.71205; Nurse; Teacher-Biology/Science; St. Joseph's College; UConn

BRADLEY, ALEXANDRA; BETHEL, CT; IMMACULATE HS; (SO); F Lan Hn Soc; Hi Hnr Roll; WWAHSS; Comm Volntr; Chrch Yth Grp; Dbte Team; Emplmnt; Chr; Ch Chr; Dnce; Lit Mag (E); The President's Volunteer Service Award; World Language Department Outstanding Achievement Award; English Education; French; Dartmouth College; State U of New York, U At Albany

BRIGHT, QUINTON; HAMDEN, CT; HAMDEN HS; (JR); St of Mnth; WWAHSS; Comm Volntr; Peer Tut/Med; HO'Br Yth Ldrshp; Prom Com; Mch Bnd; Ftball (J); Track (V); Cl Off (P); Stu Cncl (R); Vice President of the Black and Hispanic Student Union; Vice President of Jack & Jill of America Inc.; Johnson C. Smith U. Charlotte, North Carolina

BRION, CHRISTINE C; COLCHESTER, CT; BACON AC; (JR); Hi Hnr Roll; Hnr Roll; Nat Hon Sy; Comm Volntr; DARE; FBLA; Off Aide; Scouts; Vsity Clb; Bnd; Ch Chr; Tennis (V); Vllyball (V); Communications; Wheaton College; Northeastern U

BROOKINS, VALAYSHIA T; BRIDGEPORT, CT; CENTRAL HS; (FR); Ctznshp Aw; Hi Hnr Roll; Hnr Roll; Jr Rot; Nat Hon Sy; Otst Ac Ach Awd; Salutrn; St Schl; St of Mnth; Peer Tut/Med; ArtClub; Chess; Chrch Yth Grp; DARE; Jr Ach; Mus Clb; Scouts; Chr; Ch Chr; Sccr (V); Fashion; Psychology; NY Fashion Institute; Florida State U

BROUGH, CARYN H; FAIRFIELD, CT; FAIRFIELD WARDE HS; (SO); Hi Hnr Roll; Pres Sch; Sci Fairs; WWAHSS; Yth Ldrshp Prog; Comm Volntr; Peer Tut/Med; Chrch Yth Grp; Key Club; P to P St Amb Prg; Vsity Clb; Fncg (V CL); Adv Cncl (R); CR (R); Yrbk (E); Student Ambassador to Australia; U of Notre Dame; Duke U

BROWN, KIMBERLY N; STAMFORD, CT; WESTHILL HS; (SR); Hnr Roll; Nat Mrt LOC; WWAHSS; Comm Volntr; Peer Tut/Med; ArtClub; Emplmnt; Bnd; Flg Crps; Mch Bnd; Stg Cre; Winter Guard Captain; Explorer Post 135-Secretary; Art; Temple U; Drexel U

BROWN, NICOLE A; WINDSOR LOCKS, CT; WINDSOR LOCKS HS; (JR); Comm Volntr; Emplmnt; FBLA; Photog; Dnce; Yrbk (E); FBLA (Future Business Leader of America); Accounting; Nursing; U of Connecticut; U of Hartford

BRUNO, COLLEEN; RIDGEFIELD, CT; IMMACULATE HS; (JR); Hnr Roll; St of Mnth; Comm Volntr; Hosp Aide; Chrch Yth Grp; DARE; Emplmnt; Scouts; Chr; SP/M/VS; Fld Hky (V); Stu Cncl (R); CR (R); Nominated for Student of the Month; Girl Scout Silver Award; Nursing; College of Mount St Vincent; Catholic U of America

BRUNSON, JESSE; MIDDLETOWN, CT; VINAL TECH; (SO); Hi Hnr Roll; Hnr Roll; New England Technical Institute

BUCKLEY, AMANDA M; GLASTONBURY, CT; GLASTONBURY HS; Duke TS; F Lan Hn Soc; Hi Hnr Roll; Nat Hon Sy; Sci Fairs; WWAHSS; Comm Volntr; Hab For Humty Volntr; Chrch Yth Grp; Key Club; Spanish Clb; Mch Bnd; Yrbk (E); Thoracic Surgery; U of Connecticut (Honors Program)

BUCKLIN, ALEX; GREENWICH, CT; GREENWICH HS; (SO); F Lan Hn Soc; Hi Hnr Roll; Pres Ac Ftns Aw; Pres Sch; WWAHSS; Comm Volntr; Chrch Yth Grp; Lttrmn Clb; Photog; Bskball (J); PP Ftbl; Sccr (V, L); Track (V, L); CR; Leading Scorer for the Varsity Girl's Soccer Team During the Fall '04 Season - Sophomore Year; Business / Finance; Law; Harvard University; Columbia University

BUERGER, MEGAN M; OLD LYME, CT; LYME-OLD LYME HS; (JR); Hi Hnr Roll; Hnr Roll; Nat Hon Sy; Otst Ac Ach Awd; Peer Tut/Med; Mus Clb; Photog; Prom Com; Svce Clb; Vsity Clb; Bnd; Jzz Bnd; Lcrsse (V L); Tennis (J); Stu Cncl (R); Lit Mag (R); Sch Ppr (E, R, P); Yrbk (E, R, P); 11 Years of Piano Study; Studied English Literature - Cambridge U; Print Journalism; Foreign Policy; Columbia U; U of Virginia

BUI, JEFFREY T; SOUTH WINDSOR, CT; SOUTH WINDSOR HS; (JR); Fut Prb Slvr; Hi Hnr Roll; Nat Hon Sy; Pres Sch; Yth Ldrshp Prog; Comm Volntr; Chess; Mth Clb/Tm; Mus Clb; Vsity Clb; French Clb; Chr; Orch; Track (J); Vllyball (V); Wrstlg (J); Adv Cncl (R); Pianist (10 Yrs); Medical; Yale, Tuft, Princeton, U Conn

BURCHARD, KAYLA M; MIDDLETOWN, CT; VINAL TECH; (SO); Hi Hnr Roll; Hnr Roll; Otst Ac Ach Awd; St of Mnth; Spec Olymp Vol; Chrch Yth Grp; FCA; Voc Ind Clb Am; Sftball (V L); Vllyball (V L); Cl Off (S); Yrbk (E)

BURNEY, CATRENNA L; NEW HAVEN, CT; HILL REG CAREER HS; (JR); Hi Hnr Roll; Hnr Roll; MVP; Otst Ac Ach Awd; Perf Att; WWAHSS; Yth Ldrshp Prog; Comm Volntr; Peer Tut/Med; Emplmnt; Prom Com; Vsity Clb; Ftball (V); Wrstlg (V); Youth Rights Media, Youth Organizer; Yale New Haven Hospital Day Care Volunteer; Pre-Med; Obstetrician/Gynecologist; Spelman College; Johnson C Smith U

BURPEE, DANA A; LEDYARD, CT; NORTH STONINGTON CHRISTIAN AC; (FR); Ctznshp Aw; Hnr Roll; Nat Ldrshp Svc; Nat Sci Aw; Sci Fairs; St Optmst of Yr; Peer Tut/Med; Chess; Chrch Yth Grp; DARE; Drma Clb; Mus Clb; Photog; Sci Clb; Scouts; Ch Chr; SP/M/VS; Bskball (C); Cl Off (T); Stu Cncl (V); Yrbk (P); Drama Award; Sharon Moon Award; PhD; URI

BURROWS, MADISON; ESSEX, CT; VALLEY REG HS; (SO); Hnr Roll; St of Mnth; Comm Volntr; Aqrium Clb; DARE; FBLA; Mod UN; Chr; Dnce; Tennis (J); National Junior Leadership Conference/Lead America; National Outdoor Leadership School; Marine Biology; U of California Los Angeles; Northeastern

BURRUANO, TATIANA; FAIRFIELD, CT; FAIRFIELD LUDLOWE HS; MS; All Am Sch; Ctznshp Aw; Hi Hnr Roll; Hnr Roll; Otst Ac Ach Awd; Perf Att; St of Mnth; Yth Ldrshp Prog; Comm Volntr; DARE; Drma Clb; Emplmnt; Key Club; Pep Squd; Bnd; Chr; SP/M/VS; Chrldg (C); Sftball; Lead America; Nominee for Superintendent's Award; Pediatrician (Pediatrics); Psychology; Michigan U; Yale

BUTKIEWICZ, ADAM; NEW BRITAIN, CT; E C GOODWIN TECH; (JR); Hi Hnr Roll; Hnr Roll; Nat Hon Sy; Otst Ac Ach Awd; Perf Att; St of Mnth; Hosp Aide

CABRERA, KAYLA; HARTFORD, CT; PRINCE TECH; (FR); Hnr Roll; Nat Sci Aw; Otst Ac Ach Awd; Perf Att; Sci Fairs; St of Mnth; Capital Community College; Trinity College

CADORET, KAITLYN; ORANGE, CT; AMITY SR HS; (SR); Hnr Roll; Perf Att; Yth Ldrshp Prog; Comm Volntr; Hosp Aide; Chrch Yth Grp; Drma Clb; Emplmnt; Mus Clb; Scouts; Chr; Clr Grd; SP/M/VS; Chrldg (J); Yrbk (E, P); Girl Scout Silver Award; Music Teacher Education; Central Connecticut State U

CAMACHO, SAMANTHA E; STRATFORD, CT; FRANK SCOTT BUNNELL HS; (SR); Hnr Roll; WWAHSS; Comm Volntr; Emplmnt; Who's Who of America; Community Service; Master's in Social Work; Sacred Heart U; Southern Connecticut State

CAMACHO, TOMAS; BRIDGEPORT, CT; (JR); Nat Hon Sy; Chess; Chrch Yth Grp; DARE; Mth Clb/Tm; Duke U; Maryland U

CAMPBELL, ASHLEY; NEW CANAAN, CT; NEW CANAAN HS; (FR); Hnr Roll; Comm Volntr; Chrch Yth Grp; Photog; Chr; Dnce; SP/M/VS; Chrldg (V L); 2nd Runner Up Miss Jr Teen Connecticut & Most Promising Model; Senior Varsity All Star Cheer Leading Squad At Local Gym; Business Mayor; Fashion Design; U of North Carolina; Boston College

CANTARANO, NOELLE; STRATFORD, CT; BURNETT HS; (SR); Hnr Roll; Otst Ac Ach Awd; Hosp Aide; Peer Tut/Med; Emplmnt; Mod UN; PP Ftbl; Swmg (V); Stu Cncl (R); CR (R); Yrbk (E); Volunteer - St Vincent's Medical Center; Model UN; Journalism; Business; U of Massachusetts Amherst

CAPISTRAN, MAGALI; BRIDGEPORT, CT; WARREN HARDING HS; (SO); Hnr Roll; Perf Att; St of Mnth; Comm Volntr; I Do Community Service; (Cosmetology) College Majors/Professional Degrees; (Law) College Major/Professional Degrees That Interest Me; Iona College

CARDINAL, ANGELA L; TAFTVILLE, CT; ST BERNARD; (SR); Hi Hnr Roll; Nat Hon Sy; Otst Ac Ach Awd; WWAHSS; Yth Ldrshp Prog; Comm Volntr; Peer Tut/Med; Chrch Yth Grp; Drma Clb; Emplmnt; HO'Br Yth Ldrshp; Ch Chr; Orch; SP/M/VS; Fncg (V CL); Stu Cncl (R); CR (R); History; Scandinavian Studies; Saint Michael's College; Gustavus Adolphus College

CARLSON, ELIZABETH; ENFIELD, CT; ENFIELD HS; (SR); Hi Hnr Roll; Hnr Roll; WWAHSS; Chrch Yth Grp; DECA; Emplmnt; Prom Com; DECA-Reporter; Finance; Western New England College

CARRINGTON, JUSTIN D; PROSPECT, CT; W F KAYNOR REG VOC TECH SCH; (JR); Ctznshp Aw; Hi Hnr Roll; Hnr Roll; Nat Hon Sy; St of Mnth; Peer Tut/Med; Emplmnt; Stu Cncl (R); CR (R); SR Modified Race Car Pit Crew Member @16; Teacher's Association Award, Citizenship Award; NASCAR Engineering Degree; Universal Technical Institute

CARS, MARIANA; GROTON, CT; FITCH SR HS; (SR); Jr Cls League; Sci Clb; SADD; Tchrs Aide; Tennis (J); Hotel Management; Accepted-Three Rivers Community College

CARTIER, ADAM; ELLINGTON, CT; ELLINGTON HS; (JR); Hi Hnr Roll; Hnr Roll; Nat Hon Sy; Perf Att; Pres Ac Ftns Aw; WWAHSS; Yth Ldrshp Prog; Peer Tut/Med; Drma Clb; FBLA; HO'Br Yth Ldrshp; Bnd; Mch Bnd; Pep Bnd; SP/M/VS; Track (J); Stu Cncl (R); Junior Ice Hockey-Non School Sponsored; Aerospace Engineering; United States Naval Academy

CASSELL, SHAUN; ENFIELD, CT; ENFIELD HS; (SO); Hnr Roll; Perf Att; Sci Fairs; WWAHSS; Comm Volntr; Peer Tut/Med; ArtClub; Sci Clb; Stu Cncl (R); Architectural Engineer; Mathematics; Massachusetts Institute of Technology; Northeastern U

CASSIDY, KATELYN; STONINGTON, CT; ST BERNARD HS; (JR); Hnr Roll; MVP; Perf Att; St of Mnth; Comm Volntr; Orch; Sftball (CVL); Norwich Bulletin / All-Area Sports Teams; Eastern Connecticut All-Star Team; Nursing; Teaching

Carrington, Justin D
W F Kaynor Reg Voc Tech Sch
Prospect, CT

Burrows, Madison
Valley Reg HS
Essex, CT

Burchard, Kayla M
Vinal Tech
Middletown, CT

Brough, Caryn H
Fairfield Warde HS
Fairfield, CT

Bohorquez, Soad V
HS In The Cmty
New Haven, CT

Berky, Brittany J
Daniel Hand HS
Madison, CT

Boccarossa, Stephen C
Living Word Christian AC
Orange, CT

Buerger, Megan M
Lyme-Old Lyme HS
Old Lyme, CT

Burney, Catrenna L
Hill Reg Career HS
New Haven, CT

Burruano, Tatiana
Fairfield Ludlowe HS
Fairfield, CT

Cabrera, Kayla
Prince Tech
Hartford, CT

CASTILLO, BERNARDA B; EAST HAVEN, CT; AC OF OUR LADY OF MERCY; (JR); F Lan Hn Soc; Hnr Roll; Nat Hon Sy; WWAHSS; Spanish Clb; LH Cares (Minority Club That Promotes Awareness); Volunteer Work Helping Kids with Homework; Accounting; Finance; New York U; Johns Hopkins

CHAMBERS, JEFFREY; KILLINGWORTH, CT; HADDAM-KILLINGWORTH HS; (JR); Hi Hnr Roll; Drma Clb; SADD; Bnd; Mch Bnd; Stg Cre; Member of Spanish Honor Society; Pre-Medicine; Biology

CHANNER, MELVIN; HARTFORD, CT; WEAVER HS; (SO); Hnr Roll; Comm Volntr; BPA; Bskball (J); CR (S); I Would Like to Be Selected to a Division I College; Capital U; Providence Rhode Island

CHAO, EILEEN Y; ORANGE, CT; AMITY SR HS; (SO); Hi Hnr Roll; Hnr Roll; Comm Volntr; Hosp Aide; Peer Tut/Med; Chess; Emplmnt; Mus Clb; SADD; Asian Clb; Acpl Chr; Chr; Stu Cncl (R); CR (R); Leadership Award For Choir; Temporarily Helped At Children's Show in China - CCTV; Public Relations / Telecommunications; Journalism / Communications; U of Michigan Ann Arbor; New York U

CHAU, CARMEN; EAST HARTFORD, CT; EAST HARTFORD HS; (JR); Hi Hnr Roll; Hnr Roll; Otst Ac Ach Awd; Sci/Math Olympn; St of Mnth; WWAHSS; Spec Olymp Vol; Emplmnt; FBLA; Ntl FFA; P to P St Amb Prg; Svce Clb; Tennis (J); Track (J); Vllyball (J); Special Olympics-Unified Track; Unified Soccer & Basketball; Journalism; Broadcasting-News Reporter; U of Connecticut; Quinnipiac U

CHEUNG, LISA; WINGFORD, CT; MARK T SHEEHAN HS; (MS); Perf Att; St of Mnth; Comm Volntr; Peer Tut/Med; Chess; DARE; Drma Clb; Mus Clb; Chr; Clr Grd; SP/M/VS; Stg Cre; Stu Cncl (R); Sch Ppr (R, P); Yrbk (P); President's Award for Educational Excellence; Physical Education Award; Bachelor's Degree; Doctors of Veterinary Medicine; Cornell U; Boston U

CHIN, SHAUNETTE; BRIDGEPORT, CT; CENTRAL HS; (JR); Hnr Roll; Nat Hon Sy; Chr; National History Day Award; Gear Up Award; Accounting; U of Connecticut; Quinnipiac U

CHMIELEWSKI, ELIZABETH; NEWINGTON, CT; NEWINGTON HS; (SR); F Lan Hn Soc; Hi Hnr Roll; Nat Hon Sy; Comm Volntr; Emplmnt; Key Club; Mod UN; Scouts; Latin Clb; Stu Cncl (R); St. Joseph's Book Award; Outstanding Junior Award for History; Social Studies; Secondary Education; Providence College; Assumption College

CHOI, KWANG-IL; KENT, CT; THE MARLWOOD SCH; (SR); Hi Hnr Roll; Yth Ldrshp Prog; Comm Volntr; Hosp Aide; Peer Tut/Med; NYLC; SP/M/VS; Bskball (J); Lcrsse (V); Sccr (VJ); Management; Engineering; Case Western Reserve U (OH); Pennsylvania State U-U Park

CHOMCHEON, MELINDA; LEDYARD, CT; ELLA T GRASSO SOUTHEASTERN VOC HS; (JR); Hnr Roll; Comm Volntr; Peer Tut/Med; ArtClub; Emplmnt; Photog; Prom Com; Dnce; Vllyball (VJ); Stu Cncl (R); CR (R); Started the School Dance Team; Was in VICA-Skills USA; I Enjoy Writing (Creative Writing); Designing & Managing; New York U; Elmira College

CHRISTIAN, VICTORIA R; SUFFIELD, CT; SUFFIELD HS; (SR); 4H Awd; Hi Hnr Roll; Hnr Roll; Jr Rot; Nat Hon Sy; Otst Ac Ach Awd; Comm Volntr; Red Cr Aide; 4-H; Chrch Yth Grp; Drma Clb; Emplmnt; Mus Clb; Ntl FFA; Photog; Scouts; Acpl Chr; Chr; SP/M/VS; Cr Ctry (V L); Sccr (J); Track (V L); Community Theatre; FFA Officer Team; Agriculture Education; Horticulture; Cornell U; SUNY Cobleskill

CLARK, LOGAN; GRANBY, CT; (JR); Hi Hnr Roll; Hnr Roll; MVP; Nat Hon Sy; Nat Mrt LOC; WWAHSS; Yth Ldrshp Prog; Drma Clb; HO'Br Yth Ldrshp; Cr Ctry (L); Lcrsse (C); Cl Off (P); Political Science; Economics; Queens U; Mc Gill U

CLARK, SUZANNAH J; MERIDEN, CT; ORVILLE H PLATT HS; (JR); Hnr Roll; MVP; ArtClub; DARE; Emplmnt; FBLA; Latin Clb; Dnce; Sccr (V); CR (R); Yrbk (E); National Art Awards; Latin Club Tribune; Business Management; Fashion Merchandising; U of Mass; U of Rhode Island

COELHO, DAVID; SEYMOUR, CT; SEYMOUR HS; Hnr Roll; Sccr (J); Mechanical Engineering; Computer Science; U of Connecticut; Central Connecticut U

COLE, PIA S; DANBURY, CT; DANBURY HS; (FR); Hnr Roll; Dnce; Architecture; Fashion Design; Florida International U; New York U

COLE, RYAN J; MILFORD, CT; FORAN HS; (SR); Hnr Roll; Perf Att; Comm Volntr; Red Cr Aide; Spec Olymp Vol; Emplmnt; Key Club; P to P St Amb Prg; Scouts; Tchrs Aide; Bskball (J); Golf (V CL); Sccr (VJCL); Medal Excellence in Business; Key Club; Business Management; U of Rhode Island

COLLIN-DESCHAINE, OLIVIA; BRISTOL, CT; E C GOODWIN REG VOC TECH SCH; (SO); Hi Hnr Roll; Otst Ac Ach Awd; ArtClub; Sftball; Art Achievement Award; Pediatrician; Dentist

COLON, ERICA; BRIDGEPORT, CT; BULLARD-HAVENS VOC TECH SCH; (SO); Hnr Roll; Perf Att; St of Mnth; DARE; Business; Administrative; St Vincent Medical; Sacred Heart

COLON, JUDIAN; NEW HAVEN, CT; HS IN THE CMTY; (JR); 4H Awd; Hi Hnr Roll; Otst Ac Ach Awd; Perf Att; St of Mnth; Yth Ldrshp Prog; Comm Volntr; Peer Tut/Med; 4-H; Cmptr Clb; Emplmnt; Tchrs Aide; Stu Cncl (R); Sch Ppr (R); Speak Spanish & English; Criminal Justice; Pre-Law to Law; U of New Haven; Quinniplac U

COMBELIC, ALEXA A; MERIDEN, CT; ORVILLE H PLATT HS; (JR); Hi Hnr Roll; Nat Hon Sy; Pres Ac Ftns Aw; Pres Sch; Comm Volntr; Emplmnt; Key Club; Prom Com; Bnd; Jzz Bnd; Mch Bnd; Orch; Tennis (VJ L); Track (J L); Stu Cncl (R); Governor, New England District of Key Club International (2005-2006); Business Management & Finance; Political Science; Georgetown U; Duke U

COOK, JOSHUA R; BRIDGEPORT, CT; BASSICK BUSINESS MAGNET; (SO); Ctznshp Aw; Hi Hnr Roll; Hnr Roll; Nat Hon Sy; Otst Ac Ach Awd; Chrch Yth Grp; Ch Chr; Stu Cncl (R); Accountant; Business Management / Music Major; New York U; U of Rochester

COOPER, MARK; HARTFORD, CT; SPORTS SCIENCES AC; (SO); Hnr Roll; Comm Volntr; Emplmnt; Bskball (J); Sccr (V)

COPE, AISHAN; STAMFORD, CT; STAMFORD HS; (JR); Hnr Roll; Comm Volntr; Peer Tut/Med; DARE; Emplmnt; Lib Aide; Scouts; Dnce; Cr Ctry (V); Track (V); I Have Been a Mediator for 5 Years; Elementary Teacher; Guidance Counselor; Bridgeport U; U Conn

CORBETT, MEGAN; DANBURY, CT; DANBURY HS; (SO); Hi Hnr Roll; Sci Fairs; Yth Ldrshp Prog; Comm Volntr; Chrch Yth Grp; Emplmnt; Key Club; Chr; Fld Hky (V L); Golf (V L); Nominated For: Hugh O'Brian Youth; Leadership, National Young Leaders Corp, People to People Student Ambassador Program; Sports Management; Physical Therapy; Duke U; Springfield College

CORREA, JUAN D; NORWALK, CT; BRIEN MC MAHON HS; (SO); Emplmnt; Sccr; Architectural Design; Engineering; Norwalk Community College

CORTINA, DANIELLE S; NORTH STONINGTON, CT; ELLA GRASSO SE VOC TECH SCH; (SO); Hi Hnr Roll

COSTA, PAMELA C; BRIDGEPORT, CT; BULLARD-HAVENS VOC TECH SCH; (SO); Hnr Roll; Otst Ac Ach Awd; Ch Chr; CR (R); Architectural Drafting

COSTANZO, MARC E; SEYMOUR, CT; SEYMOUR HS; (JR); Ctznshp Aw; Hi Hnr Roll; Hnr Roll; Otst Ac Ach Awd; Pres Ac Ftns Aw; Comm Volntr; DARE; Drma Clb; Mus Clb; Spanish Clb; Acpl Chr; Chr; Jzz Bnd; SP/M/VS; Qualified and Participated in CMEA; Communications; Psychology; Southern Connecticut State U; U of Connecticut

CROPSEY, ELIZABETH S; WETHERSFIELD, CT; WETHERSFIELD HS; (JR); Hi Hnr Roll; Hnr Roll; Nat Hon Sy; Yth Ldrshp Prog; Comm Volntr; Spec Olymp Vol; ArtClub; DARE; Mod UN; Sci Clb; Black Belt in Tae Kwon Do; Sergeant in Wethersfield Police Explorers; Biology; Criminal Justice; Norwich U; State U of New York Maritime

CULLEN, LEIGHANN; MILFORD, CT; FORAN HS; (SO); Hi Hnr Roll; Hnr Roll; WWAHSS; Comm Volntr; Peer Tut/Med; Key Club; Tchrs Aide; Latin Clb; Scr Kpr (J); Key Club Latin Club; Mentoring; Psychology; Forensic Psychology; U of Connecticut; Fairfield U

CUTLER, CHELSEA M; DAYVILLE, CT; KILLINGLY HS; (JR); 4H Awd; Hnr Roll; WWAHSS; Comm Volntr; 4-H; Emplmnt; Bnd; Chr; Jzz Bnd; Mch Bnd; Tennis (V); Great Garage Band; Music Teacher; U of Southern Maine

DA CRUZ, CAROLINE; NORWALK, CT; BRIEN MC MAHON HS; (JR); Hi Hnr Roll; Sci Fairs; Peer Tut/Med; 1st Place Science Fair - 2 Years, 2nd Place NHD (County); 2 Years of African American Culture Club, Capt Master; 2 Yrs Associate's Degree in Nursing; Bachelor's / Master's Degree; College of New Rochelle; Norwalk Community College

D'ADEMO, DANIEL; MILFORD, CT; FORAN HS; (FR); Hnr Roll; WWAHSS; Comm Volntr; Key Club; SP/M/VS; Cl Off (V); CR (R); Co-Founder of Respect Group At Foran; Active Member/Secretary of Milford Youth Commission; U of Connecticut

DAILEY, CHASSIDY S; HARTFORD, CT; SPORTS SCIENCES AC; (SR); Hnr Roll; Perf Att; WWAHSS; Yth Ldrshp Prog; Peer Tut/Med; Chrch Yth Grp; Emplmnt; Jr Ach; Pep Squd; Chr; Ch Chr; Dnce; Drl Tm; Chrldg (V); Sccr (V); Track (V); Stu Cncl (T); Culinary Arts; Johnson and Wales

DAKIN, JENNIFER; DANBURY, CT; BROADVIEW MS; (MS); Hi Hnr Roll; St of Mnth; Yth Ldrshp Prog; Comm Volntr; Chrch Yth Grp; Lib Aide; Scouts; Svce Clb; Chr; Dnce; SP/M/VS; Fld Hky (J); Stu Cncl (R); Various Christian Achievement Awards; National American Miss Academic Achievement; Political Science; Law; U of Michigan; Yale U

DAMALAS, GREG; DANBURY, CT; DANBURY HS; (JR); Hi Hnr Roll; WWAHSS; Comm Volntr; DECA; Bskball (V L); Sccr (V CL); Volunteer Town Rec Sports Leagues; Business; Management; Villanova U of Connecticut; Boston College

DAMICI, LINDSAY A; DANBURY, CT; DANBURY HS; (JR); Hnr Roll; Yth Ldrshp Prog; Comm Volntr; Peer Tut/Med; Chrch Yth Grp; DARE; DECA; Emplmnt; Prom Com; Sftball (V); Vllyball (V C); Cl Off (V); DECA State Competition Winner; Business / Marketing

DAMJANOVIC, LUCAS J; STRATFORD, CT; FRANK S BONNELL HS; (JR); Hnr Roll; Comm Volntr; Chrch Yth Grp; Drma Clb; Photog; SP/M/VS; Ftball (J); Track (J); Sch Ppr (R, P); Outstanding Achievement in Spanish II; Outstanding Achievement in Theatre Arts; Pre-Medical; Investments/Security; UConn (U of Conn); Boston U

DANIEL, ANDREW; NORWALK, CT; TRINITY CATHOLIC HS; (SO); Perf Att; Yth Ldrshp Prog; Comm Volntr; Peer Tut/Med; Chess; Chrch Yth Grp; Drma Clb; NYLC; Tchrs Aide; Vsity Clb; Bnd; Jzz Bnd; Mch Bnd; SP/M/VS; Bskball (J); Mar Art; Sccr (J); Wt Lftg (J); Tae Kwon Do Black White (High); Law

DA SILVA, ARIANE; WEST HAVEN, CT; HILL REG CAREER HS; (FR); Hi Hnr Roll; Hnr Roll; Nat Hon Sy; St of Mnth; Chrch Yth Grp; DARE; Ch Chr; Physical Therapy; Occupational Therapy; Yale U

D'AVANZO, OLIVIA; NEW FAIRFIELD, CT; NEW FAIRFIELD HS; (SO); Ctznshp Aw; Hi Hnr Roll; Hnr Roll; MVP; Otst Ac Ach Awd; Pres Ac Ftns Aw; St of Mnth; Comm Volntr; Peer Tut/Med; DARE; FBLA; Off Aide; Bskball (J); Hsbk Rdg (J); Vllyball (V); Future Teachers Award; Psychology; Journalism; UConn U of Connecticut; Florida State U

DAVIS-KOS, STEPHEN; WESTON, CT; WESTON HS; (JR); F Lan Hn Soc; Hi Hnr Roll; Nat Hon Sy; Nat Mrt Semif; Hosp Aide; Lib Aide; NYLC; Jzz Bnd; Sch Ppr (E, R); Registered MRT (Medical Response Technician); Westport Youth Film Festival Board Member; Pre-Medicine; French; Amherst College; U of Chicago

DAY, TIMOTHY J; WESTPORT, CT; STAPLES HS; (JR); Hnr Roll; WWAHSS; Jr Cls League; Bnd; Orch; Sccr (V); Track (V); National Latin Historical Honor Society; Attorney; Georgetown U; Johns Hopkins U

DEBIASE, AMANDA L; STRATFORD, CT; STRATFORD HS; (SO); Hi Hnr Roll; Hnr Roll; St of Mnth; Hosp Aide; Chrch Yth Grp; Photog; SADD; Stu Cncl (R); CR (R); Forensic Science; Psychology; Cedar Crest College; U of New Haven

DEEB, JESSICA; TRUMBULL, CT; TRUMBULL HS; (SO); Hi Hnr Roll; Hnr Roll; St of Mnth; Peer Tut/Med; Spec Olymp Vol; Emplmnt; Spanish Clb; Chrldg (V); Lcrsse (J); Cl Off (T); Stu Cncl (R); Major in Math

DEGENNARO, ELLEN; FAIRFIELD, CT; FAIRFIELD WARDE HS; (FR); Hi Hnr Roll; Hnr Roll; Perf Att; Pres Sch; Sci/Math Olympn; St of Mnth; WWAHSS; Comm Volntr; Hab For Humty Volntr; Spec Olymp Vol; Chrch Yth Grp; Key Club; Mth Clb/Tm; Svce Clb; Chr; Orch; SP/M/VS; Sccr (J); Tennis (J); Cl Off (R); Stu Cncl (R)

DE LA CRUZ, JESSICA; GLASTONBURY, CT; GLASTONBURY HS; (SO); Ctznshp Aw; Hnr Roll; Perf Att; Comm Volntr; Key Club; Chr; Drl Tm; Team Work Medals, CIT Awards (Counselor in Training) Most Dedicated, Coach's Award; Blue Ribbon Award, MVP, Most Improved; Psychiatrist (Work with Mentally Retarded Kids); Law; U Conn; Trinity College

DELACRUZ, ROSSY E; NEW BRITAIN, CT; NEW BRITAIN HS; (FR); Otst Ac Ach Awd; Perf Att; Comm Volntr; Mus Clb; Spanish Clb; Dnce; Actress; Nurse; UConn; Capitol College

DE LEON, NATHANIEL; HAMDEN, CT; HAMDEN HS; (SO); F Lan Hn Soc; Hnr Roll; Mth Clb/Tm; Mus Clb; NYLC; Stg Cre; Human Relations Club Officer; National Junior Leaders Conference; Forensic Psychology; Criminal Law; Yale U; U of Connecticut

DEL FRANCO, AMARA; FAIRFIELD, CT; LUDLOWE HS; (SO); Hnr Roll; Comm Volntr; Hab For Humty Volntr; Peer Tut/Med; Key Club; Italian Clb; Sociology; Criminal Law; U of Connecticut; Quinnipiac U

DELGADO, KRISTINA M; BRIDGEPORT, CT; KOLBE CATHEDRAL HS; (SO); F Lan Hn Soc; Hnr Roll; Comm Volntr; Hosp Aide; DARE; Off Aide; P to P St Amb Prg; Ch Chr; SP/M/VS; Chrldg (V); Medical; Yale U; Fairfield U

DELISLE, AMANDA; TOLLAND, CT; TOLLAND HS; (SR); Hnr Roll; Dnce; Stg Cre; Line Dance Intermediate Teen World Champion; Zoology; Theatre-Design & Tech; U of Central Florida; U of New Hampshire

DE LUCA, EMILY; FAIRFIELD, CT; FAIRFIELD LUDLOWE HS; (SO); Hnr Roll; Otst Ac Ach Awd; Pres Ac Ftns Aw; Comm Volntr; Chrch Yth Grp; Skiing (V); Sccr (J); Tennis (V); Biology; Law; Holy Cross; Colgate

DEOCAMPO, KRISTINE; SEYMOUR, CT; SEYMOUR HS; (JR); Hnr Roll; Comm Volntr; Hosp Aide; FBLA; Tennis (V); Pharmacy; Architecture; U of Houston; U of Texas

DEVALDA, EBONY L; NORWALK, CT; NORWALK HS; (JR); Hnr Roll; Sci Fairs; Dnce; Drl Tm; SP/M/VS; Stg Cre

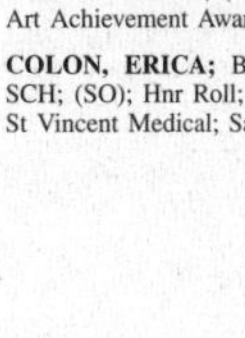
De Leon, Nathaniel
Hamden HS
Hamden, CT

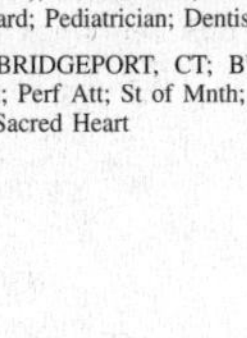
Damici, Lindsay A
Danbury HS
Danbury, CT

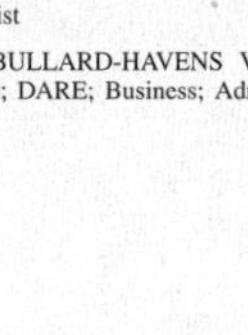
Cortina, Danielle S
Ella Grasso SE Voc Tech Sch
North Stonington, CT

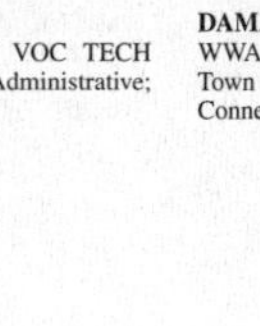
Cooper, Mark
Sports Sciences AC
Hartford, CT

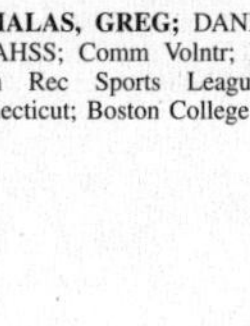
Combelic, Alexa A
Orville H Platt HS
Meriden, CT

National
Honor Roll
Spring 2005

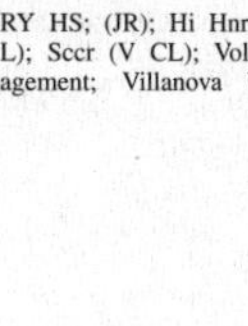
Channer, Melvin
Weaver HS
Hartford, CT

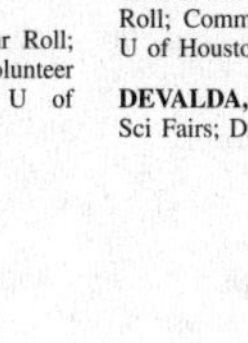
Correa, Juan D
Brien Mc Mahon HS
Norwalk, CT

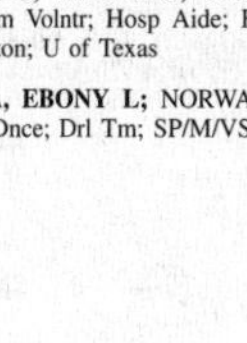
Da Cruz, Caroline
Brien Mc Mahon HS
Norwalk, CT

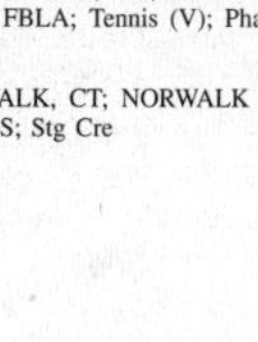
Daniel, Andrew
Trinity Catholic HS
Norwalk, CT

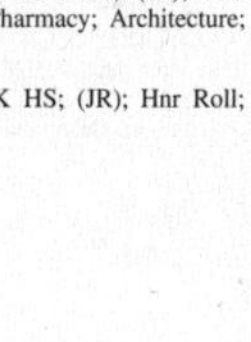
Debiase, Amanda L
Stratford HS
Stratford, CT

DE VORE, LAUREN; FAIRFIELD, CT; FAIRFIELD LUDLOWE HS; (FR); Ctznshp Aw; Hi Hnr Roll; Otst Ac Ach Awd; Perf Att; Pres Ac Ftns Aw; Pres Sch; Comm Volntr; Hab For Humty Volntr; Chrch Yth Grp; Emplmnt; Key Club; Scouts; Chr; Gmnstcs (J); Light the Night-Spin Odyssey for Cancer-Breast; Fold Family Missions, Cancer Walk; Teacher; Azusa Pacific College

DE VORE, RYAN; FAIRFIELD, CT; FAIRFIELD LUDLOWE HS; (SO); Ctznshp Aw; Hi Hnr Roll; Perf Att; Pres Ac Ftns Aw; Comm Volntr; Hab For Humty Volntr; Chrch Yth Grp; Emplmnt; Key Club; Outdrs Clb; Scouts; Bnd; Mch Bnd; Bsball (J); Scr Kpr (J); Sccr (J); Track (J); Light the Night Walk Spin Odyssey for Cancer; Fold Family Missions-Breast Cancer Walk; Architecture; Engineering; U of CA State of Long Beach; USC, Fullerton

DIAS, JESSICA N; BRIDGEPORT, CT; BULLARD-HAVENS VOC TECH SCH; (JR); Hnr Roll; Architect

DIAZ, DESIREE; NEW BRITAIN, CT; EC GOODWIN TECH HS; (FR); Drma Clb; SP/M/VS; Fashion Designer; Parsons School of Design

DILLON, TATIANA; BRIDGEPORT, CT; CHRISTIAN HERITAGE SCH; (JR); Comm Volntr; ArtClub; DARE; Photgz; Spanish Clb; Bskball (J); National Art Award / Membership; Economics; Photography; NYU; Cornell U

DI MAURO, JENNIFER; WEST HARTFORD, CT; WESTMINSTER SCH; (JR); Hi Hnr Roll; Otst Ac Ach Awd; Comm Volntr; Drma Clb; Emplmnt; Dnce; SP/M/VS; Fld Hky (J); Scr Kpr (J); Lit Mag (E, R); Sch Ppr (R); Student Organization for the Needy; Johns Hopkins Talent Search; English / Journalism/Creative Writing; Psychology; Vassar; Hamilton

DI MEOLA, BETSY; TOLLAND, CT; TOLLAND HS; (JR); Hi Hnr Roll; Hnr Roll; Nat Hon Sy; Comm Volntr; Hosp Aide; Peer Tut/Med; Prom Com; Dnce; Sccr (V); Track (V C); Scholar Athlete (Grades 9, 10, 11); Irish Step Dancing-2nd Place New England; Physical Therapy; Pre-Med; Salve Regina U; Fairfield U

DOLAN, JACQUELINE; WETHERSFIELD, CT; WETHERSFIELD HS; (JR); Ctznshp Aw; F Lan Hn Soc; Hi Hnr Roll; MVP; Nat Hon Sy; Sci/Math Olympn; WWAHSS; Comm Volntr; Hab For Humty Volntr; Key Club; Mth Clb/Tm; Vsity Clb; Swmg (V CL); Track (V); Yrbk (R); All-State Athlete-Swimming; Business; U of Notre Dame

DOMINGUEZ, JESSICA; STAMFORD, CT; STAMFORD HS; (SO); Ctznshp Aw; Hnr Roll; Comm Volntr; Emplmnt; Art Club; Multicultural Student Union (MSU); Marine Biology; Art

DONOVAN, KAILEE; CHESHIRE, CT; CHESHIRE HS; (JR); St of Mnth; Comm Volntr; Peer Tut/Med; Chrch Yth Grp; Drma Clb; Chr; Dnce; SP/M/VS; Stg Cre; Fundraisers-Relay for Life / Food Drive; Elementary Education; Performing Arts; Cornell U; Ithaca College

DRAYTON, LACHELLE; NEW LONDON, CT; ELLA GRASSO SE VOC TECH SCH; (JR); Hi Hnr Roll; Hnr Roll; Perf Att; Yth Ldrshp Prog; Comm Volntr; DARE; Wdwrkg Clb; Bskball (VJ L); Track (V); Cabinetry Work; Business College

DUBLIN, SHEMIKA; HARTFORD, CT; WEAVER HS; (FR); Hnr Roll; Otst Ac Ach Awd; Perf Att; St of Mnth; WWAHSS; Comm Volntr; Chrch Yth Grp; I Volunteer At St Francis Hospital, I Work on the Maternity Floor; Pediatrician

DUBUC, DAVID L; WESTBROOK, CT; WESTBROOK HS; (JR); F Lan Hn Soc; Gov Hnr Prg; Hi Hnr Roll; Pres Sch; St of Mnth; WWAHSS; Comm Volntr; Chrch Yth Grp; Drma Clb; Emplmnt; SP/M/VS; Skiing; Lit Mag (E); Sch Ppr (R); Film Critic Club-Organizer; Multicultural Club; Film; Rochester Institute of Technology; Temple U

DUNLEVY, KIMBERLY; MILFORD, CT; JOSEPH A FORAN HS; (SR); All Am Sch; Hnr Roll; Comm Volntr; DARE; Drma Clb; Jr Ach; Photgz; Scouts; Stg Cre; Sch Ppr (E); Yrbk (P); Girl Scout Silver Award; Art Contest Awards; Marketing; Health Care Management; U of Connecticut

EAGAM, VIKRAM; STAMFORD, CT; STAMFORD HS; (SO); Hnr Roll; Kwnis Aw; Otst Ac Ach Awd; Comm Volntr; Hosp Aide; Chess; FBLA; Jr Ach; Mth Clb/Tm; Connecticut Pre-Engineering Program; Doctorate; MGA

ECKENRODE, KAELYN F; NEWTOWN, CT; NEWTOWN HS; (SR); F Lan Hn Soc; Hi Hnr Roll; Hnr Roll; Nat Hon Sy; Otst Ac Ach Awd; Pres Sch; USAA; Peer Tut/Med; Emplmnt; NYLC; Bnd; Mch Bnd; Mar Art; Lit Mag; Sch Ppr (E); Yrbk (E); Michael's Jewelers Award Recipient; Ranked 14th Out of 368 Students; Broadcast Journalism for Television; Political Science; U of Southern California; American U

EDWARDS, YINKA; WINDSOR, CT; WINDSOR HS; (SO); DAR; Hi Hnr Roll; Hnr Roll; Otst Ac Ach Awd; WWAHSS; Yth Ldrshp Prog; Peer Tut/Med; Chrch Yth Grp; HO'Br Yth Ldrshp; Photgz; Prom Com; Track (V); Vllyball (J); Stu Cncl (R); Yrbk (E, P); Superintendent's Award of Excellence; Black Teachers of Windsor (BTOW Awards); Pre-Medicine; Social Psychology; Yale U; U of Pennsylvania

ELLIS, COLLEEN; FAIRFIELD, CT; FAIRFIELD LUDLOWE HS; (FR); Hi Hnr Roll; Otst Ac Ach Awd; Key Club; Chr; SP/M/VS; Make a Wish Club; Fairfield County Children's Choir; Communications/Marketing; TV Production; Quinnipiac U; Caldwell College

EL-MASSRI, NANCEE A; SEYMOUR, CT; SEYMOUR HS; (JR); Hi Hnr Roll; Hnr Roll; Drma Clb; Chr; Stg Cre; Studio Technician / Stage Engineering; Website Designing; Five Towns College

EMMANOUIL, RHODA E; SEYMOUR, CT; SEYMOUR HS; (SR); Hi Hnr Roll; Hnr Roll; Nat Hon Sy; WWAHSS; Comm Volntr; Chrch Yth Grp; Emplmnt; FBLA; Swmg (V CL); Tennis (V CL); Joseph J Gesek Certificate of Excellence; CT Colt Poetry Recitation Contest; Bachelor's Degree / Biology; Master's Degree / Secondary Education; Quinnipiac U

EMOND JR, RAYMOND; NORWALK, CT; J M WRIGHT REG VOC TECH SCH; (FR); Hnr Roll; Nat Hon Sy; Sci Fairs; Bsball (V); Ftball (V); Athletic Warrior of the Year Award.; Electrician; Florida State

ERIKSEN, KATRINE; FAIRFIELD, CT; FAIRFIELD LUDLOWE HS; (SO); F Lan Hn Soc; Hi Hnr Roll; Hnr Roll; Perf Att; Pres Ac Ftns Aw; Pres Sch; Comm Volntr; Peer Tut/Med; Key Club; Orch; Psychology; Columbia U; New York U

ESPINOZA, CLAUDIA; HARTFORD, CT; BULKELEY HS; (JR); Hi Hnr Roll; Nat Hon Sy; Sci Fairs; St of Mnth; WWAHSS; Yth Ldrshp Prog; Comm Volntr; Peer Tut/Med; HO'Br Yth Ldrshp; NYLC; "Take the Lead" - Mt Holyoke College; Mass Mutual Academic Achiever; Biochemistry; Mathematics; Massachusetts Institute of Technology; Harvard U

ESTRELLA, HECTOR F; NORWALK, CT; J M WRIGHT REG VOC TECH SCH; (SR); Hnr Roll; Perf Att; St of Mnth; Sccr; Computer Programmer; Website Designer; Gibbs College

ESTREMERA, MARITZA; BRIDGEPORT, CT; BULLARD-HAVENS RVTS; (JR); Hi Hnr Roll; Hnr Roll; Nat Hon Sy; DARE; Emplmnt

FAY, JACQUELINE; FAIRFIELD, CT; FAIRFIELD LUDLOWE HS; (JR); Hi Hnr Roll; Hnr Roll; Prom Com; Cl Off (S); Varsity Sailing Team (2 Years); Sportsmanship Award; Major: Political Science; Law Degree; U of Delaware; St Mary's U of Maryland

FEDORKO, STEPHEN J; ORANGE, CT; AMITY REG HS; (JR); Ctznshp Aw; F Lan Hn Soc; Hi Hnr Roll; Hnr Roll; Nat Hon Sy; WWAHSS; Yth Ldrshp Prog; Comm Volntr; Hab For Humty Volntr; Svce Clb; Bsball (J); CT Assoc of Public School Superintendent Cert & Excellence Award; Accounting; Economics; Bachelor's Degree; Wesleyan U

FELT, AMBER L; NEW LONDON, CT; ELLA GRASSO SE VOC TECH SCH; (FR); Ctznshp Aw; Hnr Roll; Otst Ac Ach Awd; Sci Fairs; St of Mnth; Comm Volntr; DARE; Scouts; SADD; Wdwrkg Clb; Bnd; Chr; Sftball (V); President's Award; Young Educator Society; Medical School; Hairdressing; U of Connecticut; Mitchell College

FERMIN, PERLA; DANBURY, CT; DANBURY HS; (SR); Hi Hnr Roll; WWAHSS; Comm Volntr; Chrch Yth Grp; Emplmnt; Tennis (V)

FERREIRA, JOSE; FAIRFIELD, CT; FAIRFIELD WARDE HS; (SR); Hnr Roll; Otst Ac Ach Awd; St of Mnth; WWAHSS; Comm Volntr; Key Club; Ftball (J); Vllyball (J); Wrstlg (VJ L); Political Science; Biology; U of Vermont; U of Miami

FERREIRA, SAMARA C; DANBURY, CT; DANBURY HS; (JR); Hi Hnr Roll; Hnr Roll; WWAHSS; Comm Volntr; Chrch Yth Grp; DECA; Emplmnt; Pep Squd; Dnce; Tennis (J); Perry Award Winner; Captain of Step Squad; Registered Nurse; Social Worker; U of Connecticut; Temple U

FESHEE, KEITHAN; MERIDEN, CT; PLATT HS; (SO); Hi Hnr Roll; Hnr Roll; Otst Ac Ach Awd; St of Mnth; Consistent Honor Rolls; Game Designer; Animator; Yale U; Harvard U

FIELDS, SHAYNE L; EAST HARTFORD, CT; EAST HARTFORD HS; (JR); Ctznshp Aw; Hnr Roll; Nat Hon Sy; Nat Ldrshp Svc; WWAHSS; Yth Ldrshp Prog; Hab For Humty Volntr; Hosp Aide; Chrch Yth Grp; Emplmnt; Scouts; Ch Chr; Clr Grd; Drl Tm; Drm Mjr; Bskball (J); National Student Leadership Conference Honoree; Who's Who Among American High School Students; Corporate Lawyer; Morehouse College; U Conn

FILDES, CLARISSA; STRATFORD, CT; STRATFORD HS; (JR); Hi Hnr Roll; Otst Ac Ach Awd; St of Mnth; WWAHSS; Comm Volntr; Mth Clb/Tm; Sci Clb; Excellence in Chemistry Award; Excellence in Spanish III Award; Secondary Education in Mathematics; Sacred Heart U

FILIPOWICH, NINA; FAIRFIELD, CT; FAIRFIELD LUDLOWE HS; (FR); Ctznshp Aw; Hi Hnr Roll; Pres Sch; Nat Hon Sy; St Schl; St of Mnth; WWAHSS; Comm Volntr; DARE; Drma Clb; Key Club; Acpl Chr; Bnd; Chr; Dnce; Yrbk (P); Dance Team; Art Shows

FITZGERALD, COLBY; HAMDEN, CT; LYMAN HALL HS; (SR); Hi Hnr Roll; Nat Hon Sy; Otst Ac Ach Awd; St of Mnth; Comm Volntr; Emplmnt; Ntl FFA; Spanish Clb; PP Ftbl (V L); Sftball (V CL); Nursery Landscape CDE Number 1 in State; Secondary Education / English; Southern Connecticut State U

FITZGERALD, JOCLYN A; MADISON, CT; DANIEL HAND HS; (SR); Hi Hnr Roll; Hnr Roll; Pres Ac Ftns Aw; Chrldg (V); Self Defense Award; LEAP Project Award; Childcare Programs; Nurse; Southern Connecticut State U; Gateway

FITZGERALD, LINDSAY; MADISON, CT; (SR); Hi Hnr Roll; Hnr Roll; WWAHSS; Chrldg (V); Self-Defense Award; L.E.A.P. Award; Early Childhood Education; Nurse; Southern Connecticut U; UConn

FLANAGAN, KELLINA R; WINDSOR LOCKS, CT; WINDSOR LOCKS HS; (SO); Hi Hnr Roll; Hnr Roll; St of Mnth; Comm Volntr; Peer Tut/Med; DARE; Mus Clb; Scouts; Chr; Dnce; SP/M/VS; Stg Cre; Chrldg (V); Graphic Arts; Biology; Central Connecticut State U; Regis College

FLORES, REINA; NEW BRITAIN, CT; E C GOODWIN REG VOC TECH SCH; (JR); Hi Hnr Roll; Hnr Roll; Otst Ac Ach Awd; Perf Att; St of Mnth; Emplmnt; Lib Aide; Prom Com; Lcrsse (J); Sftball (J); Swmg (J); Cl Off (S); Stu Cncl (R); CR (P, S); Yrbk (E); Take Culinary As a Trade; Teacher; Midwife; CCSU; Tunxis Community College

FLOREZ, CHRISTIAN; NORWALK, CT; AC OF INFORMATION TECH; (FR); Hnr Roll; Perf Att; St of Mnth; Jzz Bnd; West Rocks HS Scholars' Circle; President's Education Awards Program; Piano Performance; Musical Composition; The Juilliard School; The Curtis Institute of Music

FLUKER, DONYEA F; GROTON, CT; ELLA GRASSO SE VOC TECH SCH; (FR); Hnr Roll; Nat Hon Sy; DARE; Mus Clb; Bnd; Chr; Ch Chr; Dnce; Bskball (J); Cr Ctry (J); Sftball (J); Track (J); Vllyball (J); Electronics and Engineering; Neuro Science; U of Connecticut; Georgia Technical College

FLYNN, MICHAEL D; WEST HAVEN, CT; NOTRE DAME HS; (SR); F Lan Hn Soc; Hi Hnr Roll; Nat Hon Sy; Otst Ac Ach Awd; St of Mnth; WWAHSS; Comm Volntr; Peer Tut/Med; Chrch Yth Grp; Emplmnt; Vsity Clb; Bsball (VJCL); Ftball (VJ L); Rotary Club Youth Leadership Award; Providence College Book Award; Business Management; Finance; Boston College; Wesleyan U

FOLEY, BRENDON T; VERNON ROCKVILLE, CT; ROCKVILLE HS; (JR); Hi Hnr Roll; Hnr Roll; Nat Hon Sy; Otst Ac Ach Awd; Comm Volntr; Peer Tut/Med; Red Cr Aide; Chrch Yth Grp; Drma Clb; Emplmnt; Drm Mjr; Jzz Bnd; Mch Bnd; SP/M/VS; Ftball (J); Wrstlg (J); Yrbk (E); National Honor Society Vice President; Stage Manager/Technical Director; Education; Architecture; U of Connecticut; U of Maryland

FONG, VALENE; HARTFORD, CT; SPORTS SCIENCES AC; (SO); Hi Hnr Roll; Hnr Roll; Vllyball (J); Jumpstart Academy; Nursing; Psychology; Howard State U; U of Connecticut

FOSTER, CRAIG; FAIRFIELD, CT; FAIRFIELD LUDLOWE HS; (JR); Hnr Roll; Comm Volntr; Peer Tut/Med; Spec Olymp Vol; Drma Clb; Key Club; Prom Com; Acpl Chr; Chr; SP/M/VS; Ftball (V L); Lcrsse (V L); Wrstlg (V CL); Football Scholar Athlete; All Conference Honorable Mention Wrestling; Psychology; U of Delaware; U of Charleston

FOULK, ZACHARY J; FAIRFIELD, CT; FAIRFIELD LUDLOWE HS; (FR); Hi Hnr Roll; Hnr Roll; Nat Hon Sy; Otst Ac Ach Awd; Key Club; Tchrs Aide; Tmpl Yth Grp; Bnd; Mch Bnd; Tennis (J); Track (V); Stu Cncl (R); Attends "The Community High School for Judaic Studies-Merkaz"

FOURNIER, AIMEE; EAST HARTFORD, CT; EAST HARTFORD HS; (SO); Hnr Roll; Pres Ac Ftns Aw; St of Mnth; Comm Volntr; Spec Olymp Vol; Bnd; Clr Grd; Dnce; Mch Bnd; Chrldg (V); Cr Ctry (V); Physical Therapy; Simmons College

FREDRIKSSON, ALAN; TORRINGTON, CT; TORRINGTON HS; Hi Hnr Roll; Hnr Roll; MVP; Pres Ac Ftns Aw; WWAHSS; Comm Volntr; Emplmnt; Vsity Clb; Bsball (V L); Bskball (J); Ftball (VJ); Torrington Collegiate Baseball Inc; Academic Award; Eckerd College; Lynchburg College

FREEMAN, DEMICHE O; EAST HARTFORD, CT; EAST HARTFORD HS; (FR); Hi Hnr Roll; Hnr Roll; St of Mnth; Scouts; Bskball; Cr Ctry; Ftball; Sccr; Track; Wt Lftg; Computer Technology; Computer Engineer; Duke; U Conn

FRIEDMAN, MAXWELL; NEW MILFORD, CT; NEW MILFORD HS; (JR); Ctznshp Aw; Hi Hnr Roll; Hnr Roll; St of Mnth; WWAHSS; Comm Volntr; Dbte Team; Drma Clb; Emplmnt; Quiz Bowl; Svce Clb; Stu Cncl (R); CR; Political Science; Journalism; George Washington U; American U

FRIEDMAN, NIZAN; CHESHIRE, CT; CHESHIRE HS; Hi Hnr Roll; Nat Hon Sy; Nat Sci Aw; Pres Ac Ftns Aw; Pres Sch; Comm Volntr; Red Cr Aide; Emplmnt; Key Club; Ntl Beta Clb; Tmpl Yth Grp; Vllyball

GAGLIANO, JODI; FAIRFIELD, CT; FAIRFIELD WARDE HS; (JR); Hi Hnr Roll; Hnr Roll; Nat Hon Sy; Pres Sch; Comm Volntr; Peer Tut/Med; Emplmnt; Key Club; Prom Com; Chrldg (V CL); Vllyball (J); Cl Off (S); Psychology; U of Connecticut

GALLACHER, RYAN J; WESTBROOK, CT; WESTBROOK HS; (SO); Hi Hnr Roll; Hnr Roll; Otst Ac Ach Awd; WWAHSS; Bskball; Cyclg; Golf; Skiing; Sccr; Track; BMX Bicycling State Champ; Chemistry; Mathematics

GARAY, JOSIAN; BRIDGEPORT, CT; BULLARD-HAVENS VOC TECH SCH; (SO); Hnr Roll; CR (R); Master Mechanic; UTI

GARCIA, RAQUEL; NEW HAVEN, CT; WILBUR CROSS HS; (JR); WWAHSS; Drma Clb; P to P St Amb Prg; SP/M/VS; I Really Want to Major in Theatre or Music Mainly Acting; New York U; Southern Connecticut State U

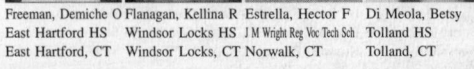

GARCZYNSKI, MAGDALENA; BRISTOL, CT; MISS PORTER'S SCH; (JR); Hi Hnr Roll; Hnr Roll; Nat Hon Sy; Nat Mrt Fin; Comm Volntr; Peer Tut/Med; ArtClub; Chrch Yth Grp; Photog; Scouts; Polish Clb; Chr; Orch; SP/M/VS; Stg Cre; Tennis (VJC); Stu Cncl (R); Yrbk (E); International Business Management; International Politics; Boston U; American U

GARZI, CAITLIN; NEW MILFORD, CT; CANTERBURY SCH; (JR); Hnr Roll; WWAHSS; Comm Volntr; Dbte Team; Emplmnt; Mod UN; Scouts; Fld Hky (V); Ice Hky (J); Lcrsse (J); Adv Cncl (R); Sch Ppr (R); Silver Award; Psychology; Sociology

GASCINSKI, HEATHER N; THOMASTON, CT; THOMASTON HS; (JR); All Am Sch; Hi Hnr Roll; MVP; Nat Hon Sy; Nat Mrt LOC; Otst Ac Ach Awd; Perf Att; USAA; WWAHSS; Comm Volntr; Peer Tut/Med; Emplmnt; Prom Com; Bskball (V CL); Cr Ctry (V CL); Fld Hky (V L); Sftball (V CL); CR (R); Yrbk (R); Marine Biologist

GASKINS, AIDELLE; HAMDEN, CT; JAMES HILLHOUSE HS; (JR); Hnr Roll; Perf Att; Sci Fairs; Drma Clb; HO'Br Yth Ldrshp; Mth Clb/Tm; Dnce; Cr Ctry (J); Stu Cncl (T); To be a chef and become successful.; Cordon Blu in Georgia.

GENTILE, NICOLE; HAMDEN, CT; HAMDEN HS; (JR); F Lan Hn Soc; Hi Hnr Roll; Hnr Roll; Nat Hon Sy; St of Mnth; WWAHSS; DECA; Emplmnt; Italian Clb; Bnd; Stg Cre; National DECA Competitor, Anaheim, CA; DECA Vice President Community Service, Hamden Chamber of Commerce Business Student of the Year; Play Writing/Screen Writing

GERSON, KELLY A; MADISON, CT; DANIEL HAND HS; (JR); Hi Hnr Roll; Hnr Roll; Pres Sch; Comm Volntr; Emplmnt; HO'Br Yth Ldrshp; Prom Com; French Clb; Chr; Bskball (V L); Cr Ctry (J); Lcrsse (J); PP Ftbl (V); Adv Cncl (R); Cl Off (R); Stu Cncl (R); Sch Ppr (R); World Affairs Seminar; Democratic Internship Recipient Under Sen Liberman; Political Science; International Relations; Georgetown U; Penn U

GIAMBRONE, DANIELLE; GREENWICH, CT; GREENWICH HS; (SO); Hnr Roll; Nat Hon Sy; Otst Ac Ach Awd; Perf Att; Yth Ldrshp Prog; Comm Volntr; Hosp Aide; Red Cr Aide; ArtClub; Emplmnt; Svce Clb; Chr; Dnce; SP/M/VS; Yrbk (E); Marketing; Interior Design; Boston College; Fairfield U

GILBERT, JOSEPH J; WEST GRANBY, CT; GRANBY MEMORIAL HS; (JR); Hi Hnr Roll; Hnr Roll; Perf Att; St of Mnth; Comm Volntr; Cmptr Clb; Mth Clb/Tm; Bnd; Jzz Bnd; Mch Bnd; Skiing

GIVEN, ASHBY; REDDING, CT; JOEL BARLOW HS; (JR); Hi Hnr Roll; Hnr Roll; Nat Hon Sy; Peer Tut/Med; Emplmnt; Hsbk Rdg (V); Cadet Major of Barn New Canaan Mounted Troop; Organized Fundraiser for St Jude Children's Research Hospital; International Business; Babson College; Boston U

GLASS, CHRISTOPHER; OLD GREENWICH, CT; GREENWICH HS; (JR); Duke TS; Hi Hnr Roll; Otst Ac Ach Awd; WWAHSS; Hab For Humty Volntr; Red Cr Aide; AL Aux Boys; Svce Clb; Orch; Cr Ctry (V C); Track (V); Biological Anthropology; Primatology; Pomona College; Wesleyan U

GLAUDE, NADEGE; BRIDGEPORT, CT; BULLARD-HAVENS HS; (JR); Hi Hnr Roll; Hnr Roll; Nat Hon Sy; Was a Nominee for National Honor Society; Major in Business; To Have My Own Clothing Business; U of Connecticut; Eastern Conn State U

GLIDDEN JR, ROBERT D; EAST HAMPTON, CT; EAST HAMPTON HS; (SR); Hi Hnr Roll; Hnr Roll; Bsball (J); Bskball (J); Mechanical Engineering; New England Technical Institute; New Hampshire Technical Institute

GOETZ, MARISSA; SIMSBURY, CT; SIMSBURY HS; (JR); Hi Hnr Roll; Hnr Roll; Comm Volntr; Emplmnt; FBLA; Tmpl Yth Grp; Cr Ctry (J); Track (J); Interact - Community Help Group; U Conn; Connecticut College

GOKARN, RISHI; SIMSBURY, CT; SIMSBURY HS; (JR); Ctznshp Aw; Hi Hnr Roll; Hnr Roll; Nat Hon Sy; Yth Ldrshp Prog; Comm Volntr; Hosp Aide; DARE; FBLA; Mod UN; Tmpl Yth Grp; Bdmtn (V); Tennis (V); Sch Ppr (E); Business Management; Finance; U of North Carolina Chapel Hill; New York U

GOLDBACH, STEPHANIE M; WALLINGFORD, CT; MARK T SHEEHAN HS; (JR); Hi Hnr Roll; Hnr Roll; Comm Volntr; Hosp Aide; ArtClub; DARE; Emplmnt; Scouts; Spanish Clb; Dnce; Fld Hky (J); PP Ftbl (V); Yrbk (E); BMX Girls Bike Racing; Dance Club / Choreographer; Pediatric RN / Master's Degree; Southern Connecticut State U; Quinnipiac U

GOMES, LATANYA M L; BRIDGEPORT, CT; CTRL MAGNET / AQUA HS; (SO); 4H Awd; Ctznshp Aw; Hi Hnr Roll; Hnr Roll; Nat Hon Sy; Otst Ac Ach Awd; Perf Att; St of Mnth; Comm Volntr; DARE; Svce Clb; Ch Chr; Track (J); Psychology; Computer Science; Yale U; U Conn

GONZALEZ, OSCAR; WEST HAVEN, CT; WEST HAVEN HS; (SO)

GORDON, DWAYNE; HARTFORD, CT; AI PRINCE TECH; (FR); Hnr Roll; Plumbing & Heating; Business Management; U of Connecticut; U of Hartford

GORDON, KELLIE; TRUMBULL, CT; TRUMBULL HS; (SR); Hnr Roll; Perf Att; St of Mnth; CARE; Jr Ach; Key Club; Spanish Clb; SP/M/VS; Stg Cre; Sccr (J); Track (V); Business; Nursing; U of Connecticut; Quinnipiac U

GOULD, AMY; REDDING, CT; (JR); Comm Volntr; 4-H; ArtClub; Chrch Yth Grp; Photog; SADD; SP/M/VS; Bskball (J); Cr Ctry (V L); Sccr (J); Track (V L); National Charity League; Large Animal Vet; U of Connecticut Storrs; U of Massachusetts Amherst

GRACE, KAREEM; BRIDGEPORT, CT; BULLARD-HAVENS VOC TECH SCH; (SO); Hi Hnr Roll; Hnr Roll; Perf Att; St of Mnth; Comm Volntr; U of Connecticut

GRANGER, BRIGITTE; TRUMBULL, CT; TRUMBULL HS; (JR); Hi Hnr Roll; Nat Hon Sy; WWAHSS; Comm Volntr; Drma Clb; Emplmnt; Key Club; SADD; French Clb; Chr; SP/M/VS; Cr Ctry (V); Tennis (J); Track (V); Sch Ppr (E, R); Internship At Boardroom Inc. Publishing Company; Competitive Ski Road Races; Doctorate in Biomedicine; Master's in Journalism; Columbia U; U of Virginia

GRANT, MEGAN; FAIRFIELD, CT; FAIRFIELD LUDLOWE HS; (JR); F Lan Hn Soc; Hi Hnr Roll; Hnr Roll; Nat Hon Sy; Key Club; Bnd; SP/M/VS; Ice Hky (V); American Field Society (Member); Pre-Medicine; Journalism; Lehigh U; Syracuse U

GRAY, RASHELL; BRIDGEPORT, CT; BULLARD HAVENS TECH HS; (JR); Hi Hnr Roll; Hnr Roll; Pres Sch; Sci Fairs; Comm Volntr; DARE; Mth Clb/Tm; Prom Com; Drl Tm; Adv Cncl (R); CR (R); Yrbk (E, P); Medical/Forensic; Law; Georgia Tech; A & T of North Carolina

GREEN, ALLI; STAMFORD, CT; STAMFORD HS; (SO); Yth Ldrshp Prog; Comm Volntr; Hab For Humty Volntr; Tmpl Yth Grp; Latin Clb; Fld Hky (J); Lcrsse (J); Chapter Vice President for BBYO; Brown U; Emory U

GREEN, NATALIE; MILFORD, CT; JOSEPH A FORAN HS; (SO); Hnr Roll; Comm Volntr; Chrch Yth Grp; Best Budding Club; Honor Roll Since 6th Grade; Interior Design; Journalism; Yale; Cornel U

GRIFFIN, JENNIFER; CHESHIRE, CT; CHESHIRE HS; (SO); Hi Hnr Roll; Hnr Roll; Comm Volntr; Emplmnt; Sch Ppr (E, P); B- 1 Day Committee / Band Co-President; Interior Designer; Communications; Philadelphia U; American U

GRILLO, GINA; HAMDEN, CT; (SR); Hnr Roll; P to P St Amb Prg; Gmnstcs (V); Business Management; New Mexico State U

GRISSLER, MEGHAN; NEW CANAAN, CT; ST LUKE'S SCH; (SR); Hi Hnr Roll; Nat Hon Sy; Salutrn; WWAHSS; Comm Volntr; Hosp Aide; Dnce; Brown Book Award; Top Scholar Junior Year; Double Major History & Business; Law School; Washington U in St Louis

GROSSMAN, REBECCA; SOUTHPORT, CT; FAIRFIELD LUDLOWE HS; (FR); Hi Hnr Roll; Hnr Roll; Sci Fairs; Peer Tut/Med; Emplmnt; Key Club; Tmpl Yth Grp; Fld Hky; Adv Cncl (R); Stu Cncl (R); CR (R); Hebrew High School; Summer Camp State Science Fair; International Law; American Law; George Washington U; Brandeis U

GUERRERA, ASHLEY A; IVORYTON, CT; MERCY HS; (FR); Hi Hnr Roll; St of Mnth; WWAHSS; Comm Volntr; Dnce; Sccr; National Junior Leadership Conference; Forensics; Ivy League Hopeful

GUERTIN, JULIA; BETHEL, CT; IMMACULATE HS; (JR); Hnr Roll; Yth Ldrshp Prog; Comm Volntr; Chrch Yth Grp; Drma Clb; Mus Clb; NYLC; Pep Squd; P to P St Amb Prg; Prom Com; Chr; Ch Chr; SP/M/VS; Chrldg (V L); Piano (6 Years); Spiritual Life; Music Therapy; Duquesne U; Berklee College

GUZMAN, GRACIELA; NEW LONDON, CT; NEW LONDON HS; (JR); Hnr Roll; Emplmnt; Key Club; Hotel Mgmt.; Merchandise; U of CT; Connecticut College

GUZMAN, IVELISSE; WATERBURY, CT; CROSBY HS; (JR); Hnr Roll; USAA; WWAHSS; Comm Volntr; Key Club; Cr Ctry (J); Ace Program; Accounting; Barnard College; Iona College

HAGEL, KRISTEN; FAIRFIELD, CT; FAIRFIELD LUDLOWE HS; (SO); Hi Hnr Roll; MVP; Pres Sch; St of Mnth; Comm Volntr; Hab For Humty Volntr; Chrch Yth Grp; DARE; Emplmnt; Photog; Vsity Clb; Bskball (V L); Lcrsse (V L); Sccr (V L); Yrbk (P); Honorable Mention for Soccer As Varsity Goalie; Math Award; Architecture/Design; Biology

HAILE-MARIAM, HANA; FAIRFIELD, CT; FAIRFIELD LUDLOWE HS; (SO); Hi Hnr Roll; Hnr Roll; Perf Att; Pres Sch; Comm Volntr; Chrch Yth Grp; Emplmnt; Key Club; Mod UN; Chr; Dnce; Vice President of Key Club 2005-2006; Annual Volunteer At Vacation Bible School; Law; Psychology; Boston U; New York U

HALKOVIC, JACLYN; MILFORD, CT; JOSEPH A FORAN HS; (SR); Hnr Roll; St of Mnth; WWAHSS; Emplmnt; Dnce; Sch Ppr (R, P); Math & English Awards; Homecoming Princess; Human Services; Nursing; Gateway Community College; Southern Connecticut State U

HALL, MAEGAN; TORRINGTON, CT; OLIVER WOLCOTT VOC TECH SCH; (FR); Hi Hnr Roll; Hnr Roll; Bnd; I Want to Be an Architect.; I Would Major in Architecture.; Lehigh U-Located in Pennsylvania

HALL, SONCHERAY S; EAST HARTFORD, CT; EAST HARTFORD HS; (SO); Hi Hnr Roll; Hnr Roll; Otst Ac Ach Awd; Sci/Math Olympn; Peer Tut/Med; Scouts; Tchrs Aide; Chr; Sftball (JC); Track (J); Wt Lftg; Cl Off (S); Stu Cncl (R); Multicultural Club; Business; Law; Spelman, Harvard; U Conn

HALPERT, DAN; FAIRFIELD, CT; FAIRFIELD WARDE HS; (FR); Hi Hnr Roll; Hnr Roll; WWAHSS; Emplmnt; Key Club; Tmpl Yth Grp; Bnd; Jzz Bnd; Lcrsse (J); Stu Cncl (R); Sch Ppr (R); Officer in Key Club; Community Hebrew High School

HALPERT, SARAH R; FAIRFIELD, CT; FAIRFIELD WARDE HS; (SR); F Lan Hn Soc; Hi Hnr Roll; Nat Hon Sy; WWAHSS; Comm Volntr; Hosp Aide; Emplmnt; Key Club; MuAlphaTh; Photog; Tmpl Yth Grp; Fld Hky (VJ); Lcrsse (J); Track (J); Stu Cncl (R); Sch Ppr (P); Community Hebrew High School, Tutor to Learning Disabled Students, Colby College Book Prize; Architecture; Tufts U

HANSON, MICHAEL E; NEW HAVEN, CT; CONNECTICUT STATE SCHOLARS AC; (FR); Hi Hnr Roll; Hnr Roll; Peer Tut/Med; Cmptr Clb; Dbte Team; Adv Cncl (R); Stu Cncl (R); CR (V); Lawyer; Computer Programmer; Southern CT; U Conn

HARDY, SOLOMON; WATERFORD, CT; NEW LONDON HS; (SO); 4H Awd; Ctznshp Aw; Hi Hnr Roll; Hnr Roll; Otst Ac Ach Awd; Perf Att; Sci Fairs; St of Mnth; Yth Ldrshp Prog; Peer Tut/Med; 4-H; Cmptr Clb; DARE; Emplmnt; Lib Aide; Photog; ROTC; Tech Clb; Bnd; Clr Grd; Drl Tm; Mch Bnd; Adv Cncl (R); Stu Cncl (T); CR (R); Channel 21 Student Program Manager; Communications (TV, Radio)

HARINARAYAN, NEHAH; SOUTH WINDSOR, CT; SOUTH WINDSOR HS; MS; Hnr Roll; Otst Ac Ach Awd; CARE; DARE; Scouts; SP/M/VS; Stg Cre; Bskball; Tennis; Vllyball; Spelling Bee; Doctor; Scientist; Duke; Yale, Johns Hopkins

HARRIS, BRIAN S; EAST HARTFORD, CT; EAST HARTFORD HS; (SO); Hi Hnr Roll; Hnr Roll; Chrch Yth Grp; Bnd; Ch Chr; Mch Bnd; Stg Cre; Bsball (VJ); Sccr (VJ); Track (J); 3 State Championship Ice Hockey Teams; Major League Baseball; Architecture; A1 Baseball Schools; U of Connecticut

HARRIS, KEVIN M; NAUGATUCK, CT; NAUGATUCK HS; (SO); Hi Hnr Roll; Hnr Roll; Pres Ac Ftns Aw; Comm Volntr; Sccr (J L); Accounting; Criminal Justice; U of Connecticut; Argosy U

HARRY, LAUREN; MERIDEN, CT; ORVILLE H PLATT HS; (FR); Ctznshp Aw; Hi Hnr Roll; Hnr Roll; Otst Ac Ach Awd; Perf Att; St of Mnth; Comm Volntr; Dbte Team; Bskball; Debate Club President; Student Senate; Corporate Attorney; New York U

HART JR, ADRAIN G; NEW HAVEN, CT; CT SCHOLARS AC; (FR); Hi Hnr Roll; Hnr Roll; DARE; Chr; Dnce; Drl Tm; MALES; To Become Choreographer; To Become Magazine Editor; New York U; Princeton U

HASTINGS, BRIDGET A; COLCHESTER, CT; MERCY HS; (JR); Hi Hnr Roll; Hnr Roll; Yth Ldrshp Prog; Comm Volntr; Hosp Aide; Emplmnt; Cr Ctry (V C); Track (V); Pharmacy; Physical Therapy; U of Connecticut; U of Rhode Island

HEADY, NICOLE; WATERTOWN, CT; W F KAYNOR REG VOC TECH SCH; (SO); Hi Hnr Roll; Hnr Roll; Comm Volntr; Chrch Yth Grp; Drma Clb; Emplmnt; Quiz Bowl; SP/M/VS; Creative Writing; Drama; New York U; Pratt Institute

HEALY, RACHEL; WINDSOR LOCKS, CT; WINDSOR LOCKS HS; (FR); Hnr Roll; Nat Hon Sy; Otst Ac Ach Awd; WWAHSS; Bskball (J); Sccr (VJ L); Track (VJ)

HEFFERON, LAUREN; LITCHFIELD, CT; CHASE COLLEGIATE SCH; (JR); F Lan Hn Soc; Hi Hnr Roll; Nat Mrt LOC; Mod UN; Spanish Clb; Bnd; Chr; Dnce; Jzz Bnd; Cr Ctry (V C); Swmg (V); Rensselaer Medal Winner - 2005; CT Statewide Prose Winner of IMPAC - CSU Young Writers Contest - 2003; International Relations; Spanish

HEITZ, CAT; FAIRFIELD, CT; FAIRFIELD LUDLOWE HS; (SO); F Lan Hn Soc; Hi Hnr Roll; Hnr Roll; Hab For Humty Volntr; Chrch Yth Grp; Key Club; Mus Clb; Scouts; Tchrs Aide; Vsity Clb; Chr; Ch Chr; Cr Ctry (V); Track (V); Secondary Education; Physical Education; New York U; Fordham U

HENDRIE, RACHEL; TRUMBULL, CT; CHRISTIAN HERITAGE SCH; (JR); Hi Hnr Roll; Hnr Roll; MVP; Nat Hon Sy; Sci Fairs; Hab For Humty Volntr; Chrch Yth Grp; Emplmnt; Bnd; SP/M/VS; Stg Cre; Bskball (VJ); Sccr (V C); Tennis (VJ); Connecticut State Cup Soccer Champs - '03; Medical Field / Health Care

HEWITT, LAUREN; FAIRFIELD, CT; FAIRFIELD WARDE HS; (FR); Hi Hnr Roll; Hnr Roll; Otst Ac Ach Awd; Pres Ac Ftns Aw; St of Mnth; Comm Volntr; DARE; Key Club; Sign Clb; Chr; Dnce; SP/M/VS; Cr Ctry; Gmnstcs; Track; Nurse; Coaching/Teaching; Coastal Carolina; U of South Carolina

Heitz, Cat
Fairfield Ludlowe HS
Fairfield, CT

Hardy, Solomon
New London HS
Waterford, CT

Hagel, Kristen
Fairfield Ludlowe HS
Fairfield, CT

Guerrera, Ashley A
Mercy HS
Ivoryton, CT

Goldbach, Stephanie M
Mark T Sheehan HS
Wallingford, CT

Gordon, Kellie
Trumbull HS
Trumbull, CT

Hanson, Michael E
Connecticut State Scholars AC
New Haven, CT

Hart Jr, Adrain G
CT Scholars AC
New Haven, CT

Hendrie, Rachel
Christian Heritage Sch
Trumbull, CT

HILL, TOMANISHA N; HARTFORD, CT; SPORTS SCIENCES AC; (SR); Hi Hnr Roll; Hnr Roll; Nat Hon Sy; Perf Att; WWAHSS; Comm Volntr; Peer Tut/Med; Cmptr Clb; Dnce; Drl Tm; Chrldg (VJ); Track (VJ); Yrbk; Psychology; Child Psychologist; U of Connecticut; Eastern Connecticut State U

HO, TRUONG K; BRIDGEPORT, CT; HARDING HS; (JR); Hnr Roll; Nat Hon Sy; Perf Att; Comm Volntr; Peer Tut/Med; Emplmnt; Sci Clb; Mar Art (J); Wt Lftg (J); King of Harding in Barnum Festival; Medical; Doctor's Degree; Harvard U; Yale U

HODGE, CELESTINA D; NEW LONDON, CT; NEW LONDON HS; (JR); Hi Hnr Roll; Nat Hon Sy; Pres Sch; Sci Fairs; WWAHSS; Comm Volntr; ArtClub; FTA; JSA; Key Club; P to P St Amb Prg; SADD; Bnd; SP/M/VS; Swmg (V); Cl Off (S); Lit Mag; Sch Ppr; NAACP; On a Math/Science Scholarship for 2 Summers; Creative Writing/Journalism; Forensic Science & Fashion Design; Connecticut College; Boston College

HOERLE, R EVAN; NEW HARTFORD, CT; OLIVER WOLCOTT VOC TECH SCH; (SO); Hnr Roll; Comm Volntr; Chrch Yth Grp; Drma Clb; Scouts; Voc Ind Clb Am; Sccr (VJ); Skills USA

HOLMES-LAU, NATALIA; STAMFORD, CT; STAMFORD HS; (SO); Hnr Roll; WWAHSS; Comm Volntr; Hosp Aide; Chrch Yth Grp; Off Aide; Chr; Ch Chr; Bdmtn (J); Biology; Pre-Med; Princeton U; Yale U

HOPKINS, LINA M; STRATFORD, CT; BUNNELL HS; (SR); Comm Volntr; Hab For Humty Volntr; Chrch Yth Grp; Teacher; Housatonic Community College; U of Bridgeport

HOPKINS, SHAYNA; DANBURY, CT; DANBURY HS; (JR); Ctznshp Aw; Hi Hnr Roll; Otst Ac Ach Awd; Comm Volntr; Chrldg (J); Graphic Arts; Nursing; West Conn

HUBBARD, JESSE L; WESTPORT, CT; STAPLES HS; (FR); Hnr Roll; Yth Ldrshp Prog; Dbte Team; Bnd; Jzz Bnd; Orch; Pep Bnd; Martial Arts; Writing; Politics

HURLEY, OUVEANNA H; ENFIELD, CT; ENFIELD HS; (SR); Hi Hnr Roll; Hnr Roll; Pres Sch; Comm Volntr; Chrch Yth Grp; Emplmnt; Lib Aide; Ch Chr; Excellence in Chemistry; Excellence in Visual Art Skills; Liberal Studies; Editor/Writer; Bay Path College

HURST-FARRELL, KAITLIN; OXFORD, CT; SEYMOUR HS; (JR); Hnr Roll; Nat Hon Sy; Pres Ac Ftns Aw; Yth Ldrshp Prog; Comm Volntr; Peer Tut/Med; Spec Olymp Vol; Chrch Yth Grp; Emplmnt; Prom Com; Scouts; Spanish Clb; Cr Ctry (V L); Track (V CL); Wt Lftg (V); Yrbk (E); Athletic Excellence Award; Pre-Med; Mary Washington U; Marist College

HURWITZ, AMY M; SOUTH GLASTONBURY, CT; LOOMIS CHAFFEE SCH; (SR); Hi Hnr Roll; Sci Fairs; WWAHSS; Spec Olymp Vol; Chess; Cmptr Clb; Mth Clb/Tm; Mus Clb; Svce Clb; Dnce; Orch; Track (V CL); Vllyball (V L); Sch Ppr (R); Scottish Highland Dance-Nationally Ranked; Cum Laude; Biochemistry; Biological Sciences; Johns Hopkins U; U of Southern California

IFERT-MILLER, KATHERINE; RIDGEFIELD, CT; RIDGEFIELD HS; (SR); Hnr Roll; Nat Hon Sy; Ceramics; SUNY New Paltz

ILLESCAS, ANJALI; DANBURY, CT; IMMACULATE HS; (JR); Hi Hnr Roll; Hnr Roll; Otst Ac Ach Awd; Comm Volntr; Chrch Yth Grp; Emplmnt; Criminal Justice; Teacher; Fordham U; Columbia U

JACKSON, KENTRELL A; BRIDGEPORT, CT; J M WRIGHT TECH HS; (SO); Hi Hnr Roll; Hnr Roll; Chrch Yth Grp; Voc Ind Clb Am; Track (J); Bowling; To Be an Architect; To Own My Own Plumbing & Heating Company; U of Connecticut; Yale U

JAMILKOWSKI, JACLYN A; NORTH HAVEN, CT; NORTH HAVEN HS; (JR); Hnr Roll; Comm Volntr; Hosp Aide; Red Cr Aide; Drma Clb; Emplmnt; Mus Clb; SADD; Chr; Ch Chr; Dnce; SP/M/VS; Gmnstcs; PP Ftbl; Vllyball; Adv Cncl; Usher At 2005 Graduation; Biology/Chemistry; Pre-Med; D'youville College New York; Boston U

JARRETT JR, DAVID D; HARTFORD, CT; WEAVER HS; (JR); Hnr Roll; Kwnis Aw; Otst Ac Ach Awd; WWAHSS; Yth Ldrshp Prog; Comm Volntr; Peer Tut/Med; Chess; Chrch Yth Grp; Cmptr Clb; Drma Clb; Key Club; Mth Clb/Tm; Mus Clb; Vsity Clb; Ch Chr; Dnce; SP/M/VS; Stg Cre; Sccr (V); Tennis (V); Wt Lftg (J); Sch Ppr (R, P); Dragon Boat; Rowing; Pre-Law; Criminology; Harvard U; Yale U

JAWADEKAR, EMILY N; EAST LYME, CT; EAST LYME HS; (JR); F Lan Hn Soc; Hnr Roll; Nat Hon Sy; Comm Volntr; Spec Olymp Vol; ArtClub; Key Club; Spanish Clb; Dnce; Tennis (J); Spanish Honor Society; CIT Japanese Exchange Host/Volunteer; Speech Pathology; Psychology; Connecticut College; U of Connecticut

JECROIS, ANNE M; STAMFORD, CT; STAMFORD HS; (JR); Hnr Roll; Nat Hon Sy; Otst Ac Ach Awd; Comm Volntr; Chrch Yth Grp; Emplmnt; Clb; Ch Chr; Lit Mag (E, R); Degree in Medical Field; Major in Fashion

JEWETT, LAUREN; S GLASTONBURY, CT; GLASTONBURY HS; (SO); Hi Hnr Roll; St of Mnth; WWAHSS; Comm Volntr; Hab For Humty Volntr; Peer Tut/Med; Chrch Yth Grp; DARE; Emplmnt; Key Club; Vsity Clb; Spanish Clb; Chr; Crew-Varsity and Letter Winner; Marine Biology; Secondary Education

JIMINIAN, ELIZABETH; HARTFORD, CT; BULKELEY HS; (JR); Dnce; Hartford College for Women / Comp Acad; Criminal Justice; Psychology; Central CT State U; Saint Joseph's College Maine

JOHNSON, CHANTEL; WATERBURY, CT; W F KAYNOR REG VOC TECH SCH; (JR); Hnr Roll; WWAHSS; Comm Volntr; Drl Tm; Yrbk; Nursing; Dental Hygiene; Gibbs College

JOHNSON, JESSICA L; BLOOMFIELD, CT; BLOOMFIELD HS; (JR); F Lan Hn Soc; Hi Hnr Roll; Hnr Roll; Comm Volntr; Red Cr Aide; Emplmnt; Prom Com; Scouts; Tennis (J); Team Spirit Award; Child Development; Temple U; U of Maryland

JOHNSON, KEVIN; RIDGEFIELD, CT; RIDGEFIELD HS; (JR); Hnr Roll; WWAHSS; Comm Volntr; DECA; Emplmnt; Scouts; Bsball (J); Sccr (V L); Vllyball (J); Boy Scouts of America - Eagle Scout; DECA Competition - 4th Place Business Administration; Marketing; Economics; Bucknell U; U of Richmond

JONES, TIM; HARTFORD, CT; WEAVER HS; (JR); Hnr Roll; St of Mnth; Comm Volntr; Chrch Yth Grp; Ftball (J); Major in Finance; Major in Business; Yale U; Fisk, Harvard

JOSITAS, GRETCHEN E; TRUMBULL, CT; TRUMBULL HS; (JR); Ctznshp Aw; Hi Hnr Roll; Hnr Roll; Pres Ac Ftns Aw; Sci Fairs; WWAHSS; Comm Volntr; Emplmnt; Spanish Clb; Chr; Sccr (J); Track (V); Health Award; Early Elementary Teacher; Southern Connecticut State U; Central Connecticut State U

JOUKHADAR, JENNIFER; FAIRFIELD, CT; FAIRFIELD LUDLOWE HS; (JR); F Lan Hn Soc; Hi Hnr Roll; Nat Hon Sy; USAA; Comm Volntr; Peer Tut/Med; Drma Clb; Emplmnt; Key Club; MuAlphaTh; Mus Clb; Spanish Clb; Acpl Chr; Chr; Ch Chr; SP/M/VS; Lit Mag (E, R); Local Nominee for Nat'l Council of Teachers of English Award; Received COLT Spanish Language Award-9th Grade; Genetic Engineer; Singer; Massachusetts Institute of Technology; Brown U

JOWERS, KIMBERLY; NEW HAVEN, CT; JAMES HILLHOUSE HS; Hi Hnr Roll; Hnr Roll; Nat Hon Sy; Otst Ac Ach Awd; St of Mnth; Chrch Yth Grp; Ch Chr; Dnce; Chrldg (V); Principal's Award; Secretary of State Award; A Masters Degree in Psychology; A Bachelors Degree in Psycho-Biology; North Carolina Agricultural & Technical College, U of CT

JURGENS, CHRISTOPHER; SEYMOUR, CT; SEYMOUR HS; (JR); Hnr Roll; Nat Hon Sy; Perf Att; Sci Fairs; Red Cr Aide; Sccr (J); Architecture; Carpenter; Roger Williams U; Salve Regina U

KAPPLAN, DAVID A; UNION, CT; KEYSTONE NATIONAL HS; (SR); Hi Hnr Roll; Comm Volntr; Emplmnt; Ntl FFA; Bnd; Mch Bnd; Dvng; Mar Art; Wt Lftg; Star Greenhand (FFA Award); BS Nursing; Masters in Anesthesia; U of Connecticut

KAPUSTINSKI, JACOB; MERIDEN, CT; ORVILLE H PLATT HS; (SO); Hnr Roll; Otst Ac Ach Awd; WWAHSS; Chess; Chrch Yth Grp; Emplmnt; Key Club; Skt Tgt Sh (V); Rifle Team Sportsmanship Award; O.H. Platt HS Academic Achievement Award; Computers, Game Design; Business

KARAR, SARA K; ENFIELD, CT; ENFIELD HS; (FR); Hi Hnr Roll; Sci Fairs; St of Mnth; Chr; Medicine (PhD); Pediatric Dentistry (PhD); Harvard U; Yale U

KASPAREK, DARIA; MILFORD, CT; FORAN HS; (FR); Hi Hnr Roll; St of Mnth; Key Club; Dnce; Spelling Bee Winner 5th & 6th Grade; Lorraine Nicefaro Scholarship-5th Grade; Broadcasting; Performing Arts; New York U; Columbia U

KATEVATIS, CONSTANTINOS; STRATFORD, CT; FRANK SCOTT BUNNELL HS; (JR); Hi Hnr Roll; Pres Ac Ftns Aw; Sci Fairs; St of Mnth; Comm Volntr; Chrch Yth Grp; Emplmnt; Mth Clb/Tm; Mod UN; Sci Clb; Dnce; Ftbll (J L); Track (J); CR (R); EMT-B Certification; Winner School Physics Competition 2003 & 2004; Biomedical Engineering; Medicine; Harvard U; Yale U

KAUSHIK, ANSHIKA; FAIRFIELD, CT; FAIRFIELD LUDLOWE HS; (FR); DAR; F Lan Hn Soc; Hi Hnr Roll; Pres Sch; Comm Volntr; Peer Tut/Med; Dbte Team; Key Club; Mth Clb/Tm; Orch; Badminton State Champion; Doctor

KEEGAN, CHRISTINE; ORANGE, CT; CHRISTIAN HERITAGE SCH; (SO); Ctznshp Aw; Hi Hnr Roll; MVP; Nat Hon Sy; Perf Att; 4-H; Chrch Yth Grp; DARE; Drma Clb; Prom Com; Chr; Ch Chr; SP/M/VS; Stg Cre; Bskball (V); Sccr (V); Sftball (V); Vllyball (V); Cl Off (P); CR (R); Yrbk (P); Basketball Sportsmanship Award; Education; Music, Medicine (Nurse Practitioner)

KEENE, DENISE; DANBURY, CT; DANBURY HS; (FR); Hi Hnr Roll; Hnr Roll; Otst Ac Ach Awd; Off Aide; Prom Com; Chrldg (J); Tumbling; Psychology; Elementary Education; Western Connecticut State U; Bridgeport U

KELLEY, ALESHA L; STRATFORD, CT; BUNNELL HS; (JR); Ctznshp Aw; Fut Prb Slvr; Hnr Roll; MVP; Perf Att; Yth Ldrshp Prog; Comm Volntr; Peer Tut/Med; Chrch Yth Grp; DARE; Emplmnt; FTA; Dnce; Dvng (V); Swmg (V); Track (J); CR (R); Natural Helpers; Medical Field; U of Connecticut

KELLY, COLLEEN P B; FAIRFIELD, CT; FAIRFIELD WARDE HS; (SR); Hi Hnr Roll; Nat Hon Sy; Pres Sch; WWAHSS; Comm Volntr; Peer Tut/Med; Chrch Yth Grp; Emplmnt; Key Club; MuAlphaTh; Bnd; Mch Bnd; Pep Bnd; Dvng (V CL); Golf (V CL); Spanish Honor Society; Spanish COLT Award for Excellence; Commerce & Finance At Villanova U; Accounting; Villanova U (Accepted); Boston College (Accepted)

KERSCHNER, BRYAN S; NORWALK, CT; BRIEN MC MAHON HS; (SR); Hi Hnr Roll; Hnr Roll; Sci Fairs; Chr; Ftball (V L); Lcrsse (J); Marine Biology; Oceanography; Eckerd College; Colgate U

KHAN, SADAF; BRIDGEPORT, CT; BASSICK HS; (SO); Hnr Roll; Perf Att; Sci Fairs; Key Club; Advanced Placement Classes; Business Magnet; Pharmacist; U of Miami; U of Connecticut

KIESEWETTER, ELAINE; MADISON, CT; DANIEL HAND HS; (JR); Hnr Roll; Comm Volntr; Outdrs Clb; Scouts; Member of Cardinal Figure Skating Team (4yr) 6 Yrs Figure Skating; Exercise Science; Athletic Training; U of Delaware; New England College

KIGHT, RENEE L; WATERBURY, CT; W F KAYNOR REG VOC TECH SCH; (JR); Hi Hnr Roll; Hnr Roll; St of Mnth; Comm Volntr; Dnce; Stu Cncl (R); Sociology; Radiologic Technology; UConn; Naugatuck Valley

KIMBALL, JOSH; WASHINGTON DEPOT, CT; SHEPAUG VALLEY HS; (SR); Hi Hnr Roll; Hnr Roll; MVP; Nat Ldrshp Svc; Pres Ac Ftns Aw; WWAHSS; Comm Volntr; Hosp Aide; Emplmnt; Outdrs Clb; P to P St Amb Prg; Vsity Clb; Cr Ctry (C); Swmg (C); Tennis (C); All-Star All-State in Swimming & Tennis; 4 School / 1 National YMCA Records; Pre-Med Studies; Environmental Science; Bowdoin College

KINDL, ROB; TRUMBULL, CT; TRUMBULL HS; (JR); Hi Hnr Roll; Hnr Roll; Nat Hon Sy; Comm Volntr; Dbte Team; Key Club; Mus Clb; Spanish Clb; Acpl Chr; Chr; Vllyball (VJ); Western Region Music Festival; Relay for Life Volunteer; U of Connecticut; U of Miami (OH)

KING, CARLY; GAYLORDSVILLE, CT; NEW MILFORD HS; (SO); Hi Hnr Roll; Hnr Roll; Pres Ac Ftns Aw; St of Mnth; Emplmnt; Mth Clb/Tm; P to P St Amb Prg; Prom Com; Orch; Lcrsse (J); Swmg (V); Cl Off (T); Business; Finance

KING, MICHELLE M; MIDDLEBURY, CT; POMPERAUG REG HS; (JR); Hi Hnr Roll; Emplmnt; Arabic Clb; Orch; Language; Music

KINGSLEY, CAITLIN W; BRANFORD, CT; BRANFORD HS; (SR); Hi Hnr Roll; Nat Hon Sy; Otst Ac Ach Awd; WWAHSS; Amnsty Intl; Comm Volntr; Peer Tut/Med; Emplmnt; Chrldg (V CL); PP Ftbl; Yrbk (E); English; Lehigh U

KINSCHERF, MEREDITH; MADISON, CT; DANIEL HAND HS; (JR); Hnr Roll; Lcrsse (J); PP Ftbl; Sccr (J)

KLAUBER, KIMBERLY; THOMASTON, CT; THOMASTON HS; (JR); Hi Hnr Roll; Nat Hon Sy; WWAHSS; Comm Volntr; Drma Clb; Spanish Clb; SP/M/VS; Sccr (V L); Yrbk; Captain of Relay for Life for Cancer Society; EMT State of CT/National Jr. Ski Patrol; Physical Therapy; Teaching; Quinnipiac U; St Michael's

KLEIN, TRISTEN; FAIRFIELD, CT; FAIRFIELD WARDE HS; (SO); Hnr Roll; Yth Ldrshp Prog; Comm Volntr; Peer Tut/Med; Key Club; P to P St Amb Prg; Spanish Clb; Sftball (J); Vllyball (J); Foreign Affairs

KNOX, CLINTON; NEW HAVEN, CT; CT STATE SCHOLARS AC; (FR); Hnr Roll; U of Connecticut; Yale U

KNUFF, CAROLINE; FAIRFIELD, CT; FAIRFIELD LUDLOWE HS; (FR); Kwnis Aw; WWAHSS; Peer Tut/Med; Chrch Yth Grp; Key Club; SP/M/VS; Stu Cncl (R); CR (R); Key Club; Boston College

KOCH, JESSICA L; FAIRFIELD, CT; FAIRFIELD WARDE HS; (SR); F Lan Hn Soc; Hi Hnr Roll; Nat Hon Sy; WWAHSS; Comm Volntr; Peer Tut/Med; Chrch Yth Grp; Emplmnt; Key Club; MuAlphaTh; Committee Co-Chair Person for Relay for Life; Co-Chair Person for Walk for Cyclic Vomiting Syndrome; Occupational Therapy; Quinnipiac U

KOCIUBINSKI, LISA; WETHERSFIELD, CT; WETHERSFIELD HS; (SR); F Lan Hn Soc; Hi Hnr Roll; Hnr Roll; WWAHSS; Yth Ldrshp Prog; Comm Volntr; Spec Olymp Vol; Mus Clb; French Clb; Bnd; Dnce; Jzz Bnd; Mch Bnd; Northern Region Music Festival; Section Leader (Band); Biology; Music Therapy; Loyola U New Orleans

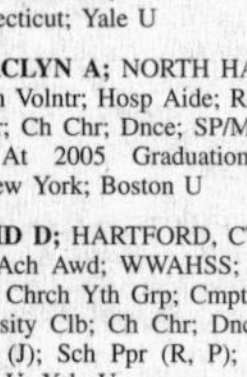
Keene, Denise
Danbury HS
Danbury, CT

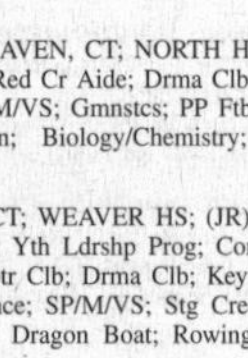
Kapplan, David A
Keystone National HS
Union, CT

Jecrois, Anne M
Stamford HS
Stamford, CT

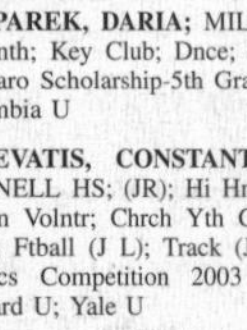
Jawadekar, Emily N
East Lyme HS
East Lyme, CT

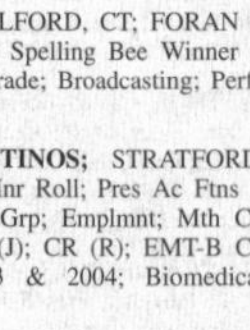
Hodge, Celestina D
New London HS
New London, CT

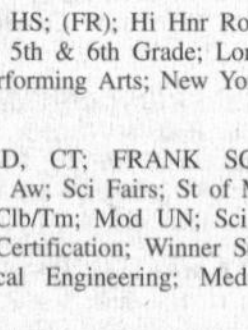
Holmes-Lau, Natalia
Stamford HS
Stamford, CT

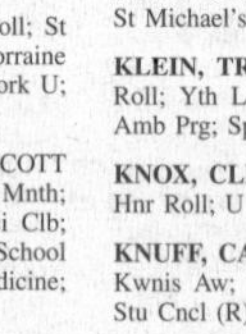
Jones, Tim
Weaver HS
Hartford, CT

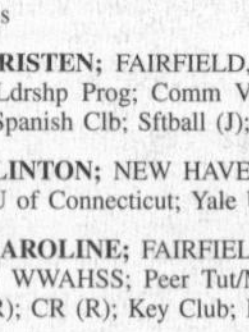
Karar, Sara K
Enfield HS
Enfield, CT

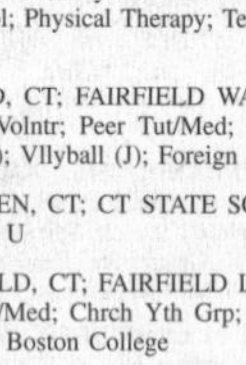
Klauber, Kimberly
Thomaston HS
Thomaston, CT

KONOPKA, IVETTE; SHELTON, CT; SHELTON HS; (JR); Hi Hnr Roll; Nat Hon Sy; WWAHSS; Comm Volntr; Hab For Humty Volntr; Spec Olymp Vol; DECA; FBLA; Off Aide; P to P St Amb Prg; Spch Team; Vsity Clb; Spanish Clb; Bskball (VJ L); Sccr (J); Tennis (VJCL); Sch Ppr (E)

KOVEL, CHRISTOPHER S; COS COB, CT; GREENWICH HS; (SR); Hnr Roll; Comm Volntr; Red Cr Aide; Chrch Yth Grp; Key Club; Scouts; Vsity Clb; Ftball (V L); Senior Babe Ruth; Basketball- GYBA; Liberal Arts & Sciences; Arizona State U - Accepted

KUPIDURA, JARED L; EAST HARTFORD, CT; EAST HARTFORD HS; (SO); Hnr Roll; Emplmnt; Bsball (J); Golf (J); Wrstlg (J)

KWONG, EMILY; SOUTHPORT, CT; FAIRFIELD LUDLOWE HS; (FR); Hi Hnr Roll; Hnr Roll; St Schl; St of Mnth; Yth Ldrshp Prog; Comm Volntr; Peer Tut/Med; Red Cr Aide; Chr; Orch; SP/M/VS; Fld Hky; CR (T); CT Scholar Leader Award; Student Representative Speaker At 8th Grade Graduation; English; Columbia U; Yale U

LA COMBE, BRIANNE M; WATERBURY, CT; CROSBY HS; (FR); Hi Hnr Roll; Hnr Roll; WWAHSS; Comm Volntr; Key Club; Latin Clb; ACE-Academic Choose for Excellence-College Prep Classes (Highest); Business Major; Law Major; Yale U; U of Connecticut

LACRETE, NATHALIE; TRUMBULL, CT; TRUMBULL HS; (JR); Hnr Roll; Comm Volntr; Peer Tut/Med; Chrch Yth Grp; Pep Squd; Chr; Drl Tm; Toped Varsity Boys Basketball; I Was a Letter Winner; U of Bridgeport; Southern

LAGACE, ANDREW D; NEW LONDON, CT; ELLA GRASSO SE VOC TECH SCH; (SR); Hi Hnr Roll; Hnr Roll; Sci Fairs; Comm Volntr; DARE; Emplmnt; 2 Years Police Explorer New London; 1 Year Volunteer Fire Fighter; Electrical Engineering; Business Management; U Conn

LAGONICK-WEITZEL, CHELSEA; MARLBOROUGH, CT; RHAM HS; (SR); 4H Awd; Hnr Roll; WWAHSS; Yth Ldrshp Prog; Comm Volntr; Red Cr Aide; 4-H; Drma Clb; Emplmnt; Mus Clb; Chr; SP/M/VS; Cl Off (S); Stu Cncl (R); Connecticut Quarter Horse Youth Association President; 4-H VP; Equine Studies; Minor in Music; Kirkwood Community College; U Conn

LAM, CHING; STAMFORD, CT; STAMFORD HS; (SO); Emplmnt; Track; Student Recognition Award; Psychology; Computer; U Conn

LAM, SUSAN; WALLINGFORD, CT; LYMAN HALL HS; (SO); Hi Hnr Roll; Nat Hon Sy; WWAHSS; Comm Volntr; Key Club; Financial Analysis; Business Management; Tulane U

LAPONTE, MATTHEW; FAIRFIELD, CT; FAIRFIELD LUDLOWE HS; (FR); Hi Hnr Roll; WWAHSS; Comm Volntr; Dbte Team; Key Club; NtlFrnscLg; Orch; Fairfield County Strings Festival Honors Orchestra; Greater Bridgeport Youth Orchestra; Law

LARSON, KAITLYN L; BURLINGTON, CT; LEWIS S. MILLS HS; (SR); Hi Hnr Roll; Hnr Roll; Nat Hon Sy; St of Mnth; Comm Volntr; ArtClub; Drma Clb; Emplmnt; FBLA; Mod UN; Mus Clb; Photog; Prom Com; Chr; SP/M/VS; Stg Cre; Yrbk; Scholastic Art & Writing Award 2005-Silver Key-Visual Arts Sculpture, 2005 Distinguished Finalist; Prudential Spirit of Community Award-Senior Citizen Program; Business Administration-Honors; Southern New Hampshire U

LARSON, NATALIE; NEW CANAAN, CT; NEW CANAAN HS; (JR); Hnr Roll; Yth Ldrshp Prog; Comm Volntr; Chrch Yth Grp; Emplmnt; Key Club; Svce Clb; Ch Chr; SP/M/VS; Cr Ctry (V); Golf (V); Lcrsse (J); National Charity League; Speech Pathologist; Brigham Young U; Utah State

LARTEY, REINA; BRIDGEPORT, CT; CENTRAL HS; (FR); Sci Fairs; Comm Volntr; Chrch Yth Grp; Stock Market Game Award; National Junior Honor Society; Pediatrics / Master's Degree; Medicine; Cornell U; Quinnipiac U

LAVALLEE, KAITLYN; MIDDLEBURY, CT; POMPERAUG REG HS; (FR); Hi Hnr Roll; Hnr Roll; Otst Ac Ach Awd; Chrch Yth Grp; DARE; Scouts; Chr; Ch Chr; Dnce; Piano / Grade 8 - Highest Academic Avg Award Pre-Algebra Class / Valuable Contributions to Chorus Award / Art Service Award; Master's Degree / Teaching; Master's Degree / Fashion Design; Pepperdine U; Livingstone College

LAVERY, WHITNEY; MILFORD, CT; J.A. FORAN HS; (SR); Sftball (J); Vice President of Best Buddies; Plan to Major in Education; Southern CT State U

LA VISTA, ALLISON C; FAIRFIELD, CT; FAIRFIELD LUDLOWE HS; (FR); Hi Hnr Roll; Comm Volntr; Chrch Yth Grp; Key Club; Mus Clb; Chr; Ch Chr; Mch Bnd; SP/M/VS; Swmg (V); Track; CR; Headmaster's List; Psychology; Music; Redlands College; U Conn

LAWRENCE, CATHERINE; FAIRFIELD, CT; FAIRFIELD LUDLOWE HS; (JR); Hi Hnr Roll; Nat Hon Sy; Comm Volntr; Key Club; Bnd; Swmg (V); Chemistry; Psychology; Middlebury; Dickinson

LAZUK, KATIE; COLCHESTER, CT; BACON AC; (SO); Hi Hnr Roll; Drma Clb; Mod UN; Quill & Scroll; Fncg (V); Sch Ppr (R); Journalism; Communications

LEE, RONA; WOODBURY, CT; WESTOVER SCH; (JR); Hi Hnr Roll; Hnr Roll; MVP; Otst Ac Ach Awd; Comm Volntr; Hosp Aide; Red Cr Aide; ArtClub; Photog; Dnce; SP/M/VS; Sccr (L); Tennis (J); Sch Ppr (R); Yrbk (R); Head of Asian Cultural Club; Win 25th Annual College Photo Contest; Dentist; Photographer; Tufts U; Wesleyan U

LEE, SAMUEL; GLASTONBURY, CT; GLASTONBURY HS (GHS); (SO); Hi Hnr Roll; Hnr Roll; Perf Att; Comm Volntr; Chrch Yth Grp; Key Club; Mth Clb/Tm; French Clb; Track (J); 1st Degree (Don) Black Belt in Tae-Kwon-Do; 3rd Place on a Korean Essay; Pharmacy (Pharmacist); Mechanical Engineering; (UConn) U of Connecticut; (UCLA) U of California, Los Angeles

LEITERMANN, SAMUEL L; HAMDEN, CT; SOUND SCH; (SO); Hi Hnr Roll; Yth Ldrshp Prog; Comm Volntr; Peer Tut/Med; Spec Olymp Vol; Chrch Yth Grp; Dbte Team; Mth Clb/Tm; Ntl FFA; P to P St Amb Prg; Scouts; Adv Cncl (R); Stu Cncl (R); CR (R); Sailing Team, Debate Member, Life Scout, People to People Ambassador; Marine Science; Environmental Engineering; Yale; RIT

LENOIR, DANIELLE; CHESHIRE, CT; CHESHIRE HS; (SO); Hnr Roll; MVP; St of Mnth; DARE; Emplmnt; German Clb; Clr Grd; Dnce; Flg Crps; Mch Bnd; World Champion Winter Guard; Book Club; History Teacher; Photography; Roger Williams U; U of Amherst MA

LEVITZ, SCOTT; ORANGE, CT; AMITY SR HS; (JR); F Lan Hn Soc; Peer Tut/Med; Emplmnt; Tmpl Yth Grp; Bnd; Jzz Bnd; Mch Bnd; SP/M/VS; Peer Tutor; Badminton Association of CT; Dentistry

LEWIS, JOANAIR; HARTFORD, CT; SPORTS SCIENCES AC; (SO); Hnr Roll; Emplmnt; Dental Hygienist; Pharmacist; U Conn; Trinity College

LEWIS II, VICTOR J; BRIDGEPORT, CT; BULLARD-HAVENS RVTS; (JR); 4H Awd; Hnr Roll; Perf Att; Sci Fairs; St of Mnth; Peer Tut/Med; Chrch Yth Grp; Ch Chr; Ftball (J); Law; Computer Sciences; U of Hartford

LI, JERRY; FAIRFIELD, CT; FAIRFIELD WARDE HS; (FR); Hi Hnr Roll; Otst Ac Ach Awd; Pres Sch; St of Mnth; Comm Volntr; FBLA; Key Club; Orch; Vice President of Key Club; High School Chamber Orchestra; Law; Business; Yale; Stanford

LIDDY, CAROLINE; MILFORD, CT; FORAN HS; (FR); Comm Volntr; Hosp Aide; Key Club; Swmg (V); Track (J); Cl Off (S); Pre-Med; Washington U (St. Louis)

LIPOVETSKY, BORIS; NEW CANAAN, CT; NEW CANAAN HS; (SO); Hnr Roll; Hab For Humty Volntr; Tmpl Yth Grp; Dnce; SP/M/VS; Bsball (J); Ftball (J); Lcrsse (J); Track (J)

LOJKO, PAWEL; SEYMOUR, CT; SEYMOUR HS; (JR); Nat Sci Aw; Sci Fairs; Sci/Math Olympn; St of Mnth; Comm Volntr; Polish Clb; Acpl Chr; Cr Ctry (V); Gmnstcs (V); Sccr (C); Sch Ppr (R); Architecture; Engineering

LOULOUDIS, YANNI; FAIRFIELD, CT; FAIRFIELD LUDLOWE HS; (FR); Hi Hnr Roll; Hnr Roll; Pres Sch; St Schl; Comm Volntr; Peer Tut/Med; Chrch Yth Grp; DARE; Key Club; Bnd; Chr; Jzz Bnd; Lcrsse (J); CR (R); Certificate of Greek Knowledge from Greek Consulate of New York

LUNA, JOSE; WATERBURY, CT; W F KAYNOR REG VOC TECH SCH; (SO); Hnr Roll; St of Mnth; Comm Volntr; Chrch Yth Grp; Mth Clb/Tm; Quiz Bowl; Voc Ind Clb Am; Spanish Clb; SP/M/VS; Stg Cre; Tennis (J); Yrbk; Elected Parliamentarian-Skills USA; Nominated to Run Class Secretary; Police Officer; FBI Agent; Oberlin; Yale New Haven

LUPACCHINO, MICHAEL R; EAST HARTFORD, CT; EAST HARTFORD HS; (JR); Hi Hnr Roll; Hnr Roll; Nat Hon Sy; Pres Sch; St of Mnth; WWAHSS; Drma Clb; Emplmnt; Acpl Chr; Chr; Dnce; SP/M/VS; Dance Team Choreographer; Nat History Day Finalist; Communications/ Advertising; Theater/Dance; Boston U; Emerson College

LYNCH, MARK; PAWCATUCK, CT; ELLA GRASSO SE VOC TECH SCH; (SR); Hi Hnr Roll; Nat Hon Sy; Comm Volntr; Chrch Yth Grp; Emplmnt; Bsball (V); Bskball (V); Environmental Engineering; Nuclear Engineering; Three Rivers Community College

MAC FARLANE, ASHLEY; EAST HARTFORD, CT; EAST HARTFORD HS; (JR); Hnr Roll; St of Mnth; Chrldg (V); Business Management; Finance; U of Connecticut; U of California in Los Angeles

MACHIDA, NATALIE L; FAIRFIELD, CT; FAIRFIELD WARDE HS; (SR); F Lan Hn Soc; Hi Hnr Roll; Nat Hon Sy; St of Mnth; WWAHSS; Comm Volntr; Peer Tut/Med; Chrch Yth Grp; Emplmnt; Key Club; MuAlphaTh; Orch; Sch Ppr (E, R); Rotary Club Student Achievement Recognition Day; Loyola Marymount U

MACKEY, LAURA; OLD LYME, CT; LYME-OLD LYME; (SO); Hi Hnr Roll; Perf Att; Comm Volntr; Key Club; Prom Com; Chr; Cr Ctry (J); Tennis (V); Track (V)

MACURA, HEATHER; STRATFORD, CT; (SR); Comm Volntr; Clr Grd; Dnce; Mch Bnd; PPSqd (V); Southern Conn. State U; Western Conn State U

MAHDER, MEGHAN E; FAIRFIELD, CT; FAIRFIELD LUDLOWE HS; (FR); Hi Hnr Roll; Comm Volntr; Key Club; Svce Clb; Orch; Bskball (V L); Sccr (J); Track (V); CR (R); Youth American Cancer Society; Relay for Life

MAHENDRAN, RADHAKRISHNAN R; TRUMBULL, CT; TRUMBULL HS; (JR); Hi Hnr Roll; Nat Mrt LOC; WWAHSS; Comm Volntr; Hosp Aide; Peer Tut/Med; Chess; Cmptr Clb; Dbte Team; Key Club; SP/M/VS; Stg Cre; Sccr (J); Swmg (J); Stu Cncl (S, R); Sch Ppr (E); Yrbk (E); Student Achievement in English; Finance; Business Management; New York U; U of Michigan Ann Arbor

MAJEWSKA, ARLETA A; NEW BRITAIN, CT; NEW BRITAIN HS; (SR); Hnr Roll; Nat Hon Sy; Comm Volntr; ArtClub; Outdrs Clb; Sci Clb; SADD; Polish Clb; Alternatives to Violence and Creating Positive Role Model Award; Renaissance Award; Dentistry; U of Connecticut

MALINOWSKI, CAITLIN A; SOUTH WINDSOR, CT; SOUTH WINDSOR HS; (JR); Hi Hnr Roll; Hnr Roll; Nat Hon Sy; Comm Volntr; Peer Tut/Med; Emplmnt; Bnd; Dnce; Mch Bnd; Stu Cncl (R)

MANCUSO, MARCELLO; TRUMBULL, CT; TRUMBULL HS; (JR); Hnr Roll; St of Mnth; Peer Tut/Med; SADD; Italian Clb; Choir During Freshman Year; Spanish/Italian Tutor; Foreign Language Teacher; Business Major; Boston U; U of Manitoba

MANNING, JODI N; BRIDGEPORT, CT; CHRISTIAN HERITAGE SCH; (JR); Hi Hnr Roll; Hnr Roll; Sci Fairs; Yth Ldrshp Prog; Comm Volntr; Key Club; NYLC; Tchrs Aide; Dnce; Track (V); Sch Ppr (R); Captain of the Netball Team; Prefect; History; Pre-Law; New York U; Fordham U

MANSFIELD, LISA; BRIDGEPORT, CT; CENTRAL HS; (FR); Hnr Roll; Perf Att; Yth Ldrshp Prog; Pharmacist; Bachelor's Degree; U of Miami; U of South Florida

MANUEL, MANDY; FAIRFIELD, CT; FAIRFIELD WARDE HS; (JR); Ctznshp Aw; Hi Hnr Roll; Hnr Roll; Nat Hon Sy; WWAHSS; Comm Volntr; Spec Olymp Vol; Chrch Yth Grp; Key Club; P to P St Amb Prg; Svce Clb; Track (J); Vllyball (V); Stu Cncl (R); National Society of High School Scholars; Psychology; English-Creative Writing; Indiana U-Bloomington; U of Massachusetts-Amherst

MANZUETA, ANDREINA; WATERBURY, CT; LINCOLN HS; (SO); Hi Hnr Roll; Hnr Roll; Lttrmn Clb; Lib Aide; Quill & Scroll; Quiz Bowl; Bnd; Culinary Arts; Accounting; Yale U; NYU-New York U

MAPP, KAILYN N; BLOOMFIELD, CT; SPORTS SCIENCES AC; (SO); Hi Hnr Roll; Perf Att; DECA; Track; Business Management; Forensic Science; U of Southern California; Spelman

MARCEL, NEDJINE; BRIDGEPORT, CT; HARDING HS; (SR); Hi Hnr Roll; Hnr Roll; Nat Hon Sy; Nat Mrt Fin; Otst Ac Ach Awd; Perf Att; WWAHSS; Yth Ldrshp Prog; Comm Volntr; Photog; SP/M/VS; Second Honor Bowl Year 2004-2005; Outstanding Achievement 2003-2004; Nursing Pediatrician; Early Childhood Education/Writing; U of Bridgeport

MARINI, CATHERINE; TRUMBULL, CT; TRUMBULL HS; (JR); Hi Hnr Roll; Hnr Roll; Nat Hon Sy; Otst Ac Ach Awd; Pres Ac Ftns Aw; St of Mnth; Comm Volntr; Peer Tut/Med; Emplmnt; Key Club; Prom Com; SADD; French Clb; Lcrsse (V); Track; Vllyball (J); Mathematics; Business; Villanova; Boston College

MARQUES, VALERIE; BETHEL, CT; BETHEL HS; (JR); All Am Sch; F Lan Hn Soc; Hi Hnr Roll; Hnr Roll; Nat Ldrshp Svc; Nat Sci Aw; Otst Ac Ach Awd; Dnce; Track (J); AFS; National World Language Honor Society; Dancing; Acting

MARTIN, AMANDA; BRISTOL, CT; BRISTOL CTRL HS; (JR); Hnr Roll; FBLA; Clb; Sccr (J); Sftball (J); Stu Cncl (R); Massage Therapist / Minor in Accounting; Central Connecticut State University; University of New Haven

MARTIN, AMBER M; BRISTOL, CT; BRISTOL CTRL HS; (JR); Hnr Roll; Otst Ac Ach Awd; Perf Att; St of Mnth; Yth Ldrshp Prog; Comm Volntr; Chrch Yth Grp; DARE; Emplmnt; Mus Clb; Quiz Bowl; Scouts; Tchrs Aide; Chr; Ch Chr; Sccr (J); Bristol Police Explorer Program; United Way Youth Board; Criminal Justice; Forensics; Bay Path College; Long Island U

MARTINEZ, MELISSA; LEBANON, CT; LYMAN MEMORIAL HS; (SR); Ctznshp Aw; Hnr Roll; Nat Ldrshp Svc; Otst Ac Ach Awd; Pres Ac Ftns Aw; Comm Volntr; Hosp Aide; Red Cr Aide; Chrch Yth Grp; Outdrs Clb; Photog; Prom Com; Scouts; French Clb; Member of Girl Scouts of America; Architecture; Civil Engineer; Wentworth Institute of Technology

MARTONE, JESSICA J; NORWALK, CT; CHRISTIAN HERITAGE SCH; (JR); Hi Hnr Roll; Hnr Roll; Nat Hon Sy; Sci Fairs; Yth Ldrshp Prog; Spec Olymp Vol; Chrch Yth Grp; DARE; Emplmnt; Tchrs Aide; Acpl Chr; Chr; SP/M/VS; Stg Cre; Bskball (J); Cl Off (S, T); Ancient Near East History / Medieval Europe

MAURO, DANA; WETHERSFIELD, CT; WETHERSFIELD HS; (JR); Hi Hnr Roll; Hnr Roll; WWAHSS; Comm Volntr; Emplmnt; Lttrmn Clb; Vsity Clb; Chr; Bskball (V L); Vsy Clb (V); Stu Cncl (R); All-State Basketball Player; Business

Martin, Amber M
Bristol Ctrl HS
Bristol, CT

Lupacchino, Michael R
East Hartford HS
East Hartford, CT

Lazuk, Katie
Bacon AC
Colchester, CT

Larson, Kaitlyn L
Lewis S. Mills HS
Burlington, CT

Kovel, Christopher S
Greenwich HS
Cos Cob, CT

National
Honor Roll
Spring 2005

Konopka, Ivette
Shelton HS
Shelton, CT

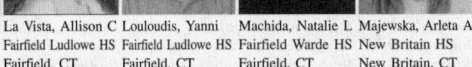

La Vista, Allison C
Fairfield Ludlowe HS
Fairfield, CT

Louloudis, Yanni
Fairfield Ludlowe HS
Fairfield, CT

Machida, Natalie L
Fairfield Warde HS
Fairfield, CT

Majewska, Arleta A
New Britain HS
New Britain, CT

MAYNARD, DAREEM E; TORRINGTON, CT; OLIVER WOLCOTT VOC TECH SCH; (FR); Hnr Roll; Perf Att; DARE; Bnd; Chr; Jzz Bnd; Mch Bnd; Chrldg (J); Vllyball (J); Diversity Club; Human Relations Club; Plumbing, Heating and Cooling; Graphic Communications; (UConn) U of Connecticut; New England Technical Institute

MAYS, RYAN; HARTFORD, CT; WEAVER HS; (FR); Hi Hnr Roll; Hnr Roll; MVP; Perf Att; Sci Fairs; WWAHSS; Hab For Humty Volntr; Chrch Yth Grp; DARE; Bskball (V); Landscaping; Doctor's Degrees; Mississippi State; Georgetown U

MC ARDLE, BRIAN P; SOUTHPORT, CT; FAIRFIELD LUDLOWE HS; (SO); Ctznshp Aw; Hi Hnr Roll; Hnr Roll; St of Mnth; Comm Volntr; Key Club; Vsity Clb; Bnd; Sccr (V L); Track (J); Member of Stratton Mountain Snowboard Team; United States Soccer Federation Referee

MC CRAE, CANDICE; STRATFORD, CT; BUNNELL HS; (SR); Hi Hnr Roll; Hnr Roll; Chrch Yth Grp; Dnce; Accounting Major; Bachelor's Degree; Central Connecticut State; Eastern Connecticut State

MC CUE, ALYSSA; OLD LYME, CT; LYME-OLD LYME HS; (SR); Hi Hnr Roll; Hnr Roll; St of Mnth; WWAHSS; FBLA; Jr Cls League; Key Club; Bnd; AFS - American Field Service; Academic Letter; Food & Beverage Management; Johnson & Wales U

MC CUE, MICKI A; NEW FAIRFIELD, CT; NEW FAIRFIELD HS; (SO); Hnr Roll; Comm Volntr; Fld Hky (J); Leo's Club

MC DOWELL, AMBER; NEW HAVEN, CT; JAMES HILLHOUSE HS; (FR); Hnr Roll; Peer Tut/Med; Chrch Yth Grp; Drl Tm; Chrldg; Journalism; Newscaster; Law

MC FADDEN, TYRRELL D; MERIDEN, CT; ORVILLE H PLATT HS; (JR); Hnr Roll; Comm Volntr; Hosp Aide; DECA; Ch Chr; Dnce; Cl Off (V); Keystone Club; RN (Registered Nurse)

MC GOLDRICK, PAUL; STRATFORD, CT; BUNNELL HS; (JR); Bnd; Junior B Level Ice Hockey; New England Regional Ice Hockey Championship; Political Science; Psychology; U of Michigan; Saint Lawrence U

MC GUIRE, PATRICK; SOUTHPORT, CT; (SO); Hnr Roll; Hab For Humty Volntr; Chrch Yth Grp; Emplmnt; Key Club; Golf (VJ); Business; Pre-Med; Villanova U; Boston College

MC LELLAN, LEA; COLCHESTER, CT; BACON AC; (SO); Hi Hnr Roll; Otst Ac Ach Awd; HO'Br Yth Ldrshp; Quill & Scroll; Sccr (J); Tennis (V); Sch Ppr (E); English/Writing; New York U; Sarah Lawrence U

MC LELLAN, MARIZA; BRISTOL, CT; OLIVER WOLCOTT VOC TECH SCH; (SO); Hi Hnr Roll; Hnr Roll; Nat Hon Sy; Otst Ac Ach Awd; St of Mnth; Hosp Aide; ArtClub; Chess; DARE; Sci Clb; Student of the Month Grade 7; Pursue a Career As a Physician's Assistant; Registered Nurse; U of Connecticut

MELCHIONNO, SCOTT; STRATFORD, CT; STRATFORD HS; (JR); Hi Hnr Roll; Nat Hon Sy; St of Mnth; Comm Volntr; Mod UN; P to P St Amb Prg; French Clb; Sccr (V); Track (V); Debbie Diaz Award; Mechanical Engineering; Computer Sciences; Boston College

MELLINGER, MOLLY S; FAIRFIELD, CT; FAIRFIELD WARDE HS; (SR); Hi Hnr Roll; Nat Hon Sy; Nat Mrt LOC; Chrch Yth Grp; Emplmnt; Key Club; Lit Mag (E); Winner of 1st Prize, Wallace Stevens Poetry Contest; Relay for Life Team Captain/Committee Member; English; Pediatric Psychology; Santa Clara U

MELNIKOV, ILYA; STAMFORD, CT; AC OF INFORMATION TECH; (JR); Hnr Roll; Salutrn; Sci Fairs; St of Mnth; Comm Volntr; Key Club; Bsball (L); Mar Art (J); Boston U; Massachusetts Institute of Tech

MENDELBAUM, ANDREW; FAIRFIELD, CT; FAIRFIELD WARDE HS; (JR); Hnr Roll; Yth Ldrshp Prog; Comm Volntr; Key Club; Mus Clb; Svce Clb; Tech Clb; Tmpl Yth Grp; Bnd; Mch Bnd; Pep Bnd; Sccr (J); Honor Roll; Computer Science; Computer Engineering; Rensselaer Polytechnic Institute; Rochester Institute of Technology

MENDEZ, NICHOLAS; BRIDGEPORT, CT; J.M. WRIGHT TECH HS; (SO); Hi Hnr Roll; Hnr Roll; Nat Ldrshp Svc; Red Cr Aide; Bskball (VJ); Ftball (VJ); Track (V); Adv Cncl (T); Stu Cncl (V); Get My Master's in My Trade; Play College Football; Florida Tech; Florida State

MENEZES, ROHINI; NEW CANAAN, CT; GREENWICH AC; (JR); Hnr Roll; Yth Ldrshp Prog; Photog; Bskball (J); Tennis (J); Adv Cncl (R); Sch Ppr (R)

MENSAH, MERCY; BRIDGEPORT, CT; CENTRAL HS; (JR); Hnr Roll; Sci Fairs; St of Mnth; Chrch Yth Grp; Svce Clb; Bskball (J); Track (J); Vllyball (V); Future Nurses Club; African-American Club; Registered Nurse; Lawyer / Criminal Justice; Central Connecticut State U; Southern Connecticut State U

MERCALDI, JESSICA; TRUMBULL, CT; TRUMBULL HS; (SO); Hnr Roll; WWAHSS; Comm Volntr; DECA; Key Club; Dentistry; UConn; Rhode Island

MEYERS, BENJAMIN; VERNON ROCKVILLE, CT; WESTMINSTER SCH; (JR); Hnr Roll; MVP; Nat Hon Sy; Perf Att; Pres Ac Ftns Aw; Yth Ldrshp Prog; Comm Volntr; BPA; Chrch Yth Grp; Cmptr Clb; DARE; Lttrmn Clb; Scouts; Vsity Clb; Wdwrkg Clb; Bsball (VL); Bskball (VL); Ftball (VL); Cl Off (V); Stu Cncl (V); Most Valuable Player Basketball; Business; Sales

MIKO, REBECCA E; SEYMOUR, CT; SEYMOUR HS; (JR); Hi Hnr Roll; Hnr Roll; Nat Hon Sy; Dnce; Physical Therapist; U of Connecticut; Quinnipiac U

MILES, ZACHARY; FAIRFIELD, CT; FAIRFIELD WARDE HS; (FR); Hi Hnr Roll; Hnr Roll; Nat Hon Sy; Otst Ac Ach Awd; St of Mnth; Key Club; Cr Ctry (J); Tennis (V); Track (J); President's Education Awards Program: Outstanding Academic Excellence; Headmaster's List; Business/Finance; Computer Science

MILLER, KEILAH; BRIDGEPORT, CT; KOLBE CATHEDRAL HS; (MS); Hnr Roll; Perf Att; Chrch Yth Grp; Sccr; Won Several Medals and Trophies for Soccer; Team Won the Danbury State Soccer Tournament - 2002; Professional Soccer; Pediatrician; Yale U

MILLS, ASHLEY N; BLOOMFIELD, CT; BLOOMFIELD HS; (JR); Hi Hnr Roll; Hnr Roll; Nat Hon Sy; WWAHSS; Comm Volntr; Ntl FFA; Nursing; U of Connecticut; Quinnipiac U

MIRANDA, MAGADALENA; HARTFORD, CT; SPORTS SCIENCES AC; (SO); Hi Hnr Roll; Hnr Roll; St of Mnth; DECA; Drma Clb; Chrldg (V); Track (J); Sch Ppr (R); Received a Leadership Award; Cosmetic Surgery (Doctoral Degree); Psychology (Master's); Princeton U; Oxford U

MITRIK, KRISTEN M; WOLCOTT, CT; W F KAYNOR REG VOC TECH SCH; (JR); Hnr Roll; Nat Hon Sy; Comm Volntr; Chess; Emplmnt; Fr of Library; Prom Com; Scouts; Chrldg (V); Girl Scouts Silver Award; Captain, USA All Star Cheer; Early Childhood Education; Teaching K-8, Special Education; Naugatuck Valley Community College; U of Connecticut

MOKRITSKI, HEATHER S; MERIDEN, CT; ORVILLE H PLATT HS; (JR); Hi Hnr Roll; Hnr Roll; Comm Volntr; Scouts; Sign Clb; Bnd; Mch Bnd; Vllyball (VJ); Science-Chemistry

MONAHAN, SIOBHAN K; SOUTHPORT, CT; FAIRFIELD LUDLOWE HS; (SO); Hi Hnr Roll; Hnr Roll; Otst Ac Ach Awd; Pres Sch; St Schl; St of Mnth; Yth Ldrshp Prog; Comm Volntr; Peer Tut/Med; DARE; Emplmnt; Key Club; Pep Squd; Svce Clb; Fld Hky (V); Boys/Girls Club-Keystone Club; Helps Homeless Shelter

MONROE, BRITNEY; MERIDEN, CT; AC WILCOX TECH; (JR); Hnr Roll; Perf Att; Comm Volntr; ArtClub; DARE; Dbte Team; Drma Clb; Emplmnt; Mus Clb; Prom Com; Scouts; Chrldg (V); Dnce; SP/M/VS; Bskball (VJ); Tennis (J); Vllyball (J); Cl Off (S); CR (R); Hotel & Hospitality; Johnson & Wales

MONTAQUE, STACIA; WATERBURY, CT; W F KAYNOR REG VOC TECH SCH; (JR); Ctznshp Aw; Hi Hnr Roll; Hnr Roll; St of Mnth; ArtClub; Chrch Yth Grp; Prom Com; Scouts; Ch Chr; Dnce; Stu Cncl (R); Student of the Month in Jan.; Social Worker; Fashion Design; U of Bridgeport; Southern U.

MONTEALEGRE, HARLYN; HARTFORD, CT; (JR); Perf Att; St of Mnth; Comm Volntr; ArtClub; Emplmnt; Scouts; Dnce; SP/M/VS; Ftball (V); Architect Degree; Savannah

MORALES, NICOLE F; STRATFORD, CT; PLATT RVTS; (SR); Hnr Roll; Peer Tut/Med; Voc Ind Clb Am; SP/M/VS; Stu Cncl (R); Social Work; Iona College

MORENO, CRISTIANA; WATERBURY, CT; CROSBY; (JR); Hnr Roll; Perf Att; Red Cr Aide; ROTC; Clr Grd; Drl Tm

MORGILLO, TERI; NIANTIC, CT; ELLA GRASSO SE VOC TECH SCH; (SR); Hi Hnr Roll; Hnr Roll; Otst Ac Ach Awd; Perf Att; Comm Volntr; Peer Tut/Med; Emplmnt; Prom Com; Cl Off (S); Business Management; Environmental/Marine Biology; Three Rivers Community College; U Conn Avery Point

MOY, TIFFANY; DANBURY, CT; DANBURY HS; (JR); Hi Hnr Roll; Sci Fairs; Comm Volntr; Peer Tut/Med; Chrch Yth Grp; FBLA; Key Club; Mth Clb/Tm; Orch; Tennis (V); Track (J); Vllyball (V); USAA National English Merit Award Winner; Washington U in St Louis; Wheaton College (IL)

MUJCINOVIC, ZEHRUDIN; HARTFORD, CT; BULKELEY HS; (JR); Hi Hnr Roll; Hnr Roll; Nat Hon Sy; St of Mnth; WWAHSS; Yth Ldrshp Prog; Comm Volntr; Hab For Humty Volntr; Red Cr Aide; Cmptr Clb; Emplmnt; Sccr (V); Track (J); Computer Science; Engineering; Trinity College; U of Connecticut

MUNIZ, ERICA L; BRIDGEPORT, CT; BULLARD-HAVENS RVTS; (JR); Ctznshp Aw; Hi Hnr Roll; Hnr Roll; Otst Ac Ach Awd; Perf Att; Chrch Yth Grp; DARE; Fashion Designer; Photography

MURCIER, AMANDA R; WINDSOR LOCKS, CT; WINDSOR LOCKS HS; (SO); Hnr Roll; MVP; Otst Ac Ach Awd; WWAHSS; Emplmnt; Tchrs Aide; Chrldg (V); Cl Off (R); Stu Cncl (V); CR (T); 9th Grade-Honors for 4 Straight Semesters; Education; Central Connecticut State U

MURPHY, MEGHAN; BETHLEHEM, CT; NONNEWAUG HS; (SR); Hi Hnr Roll; Nat Hon Sy; Pres Ac Ftns Aw; Pres Sch; Peer Tut/Med; Chrch Yth Grp; Fld Hky (V C); Yrbk (R); Capt. Scholar; Nursing; U of New Hampshire

MURRELL, LESHAWNA; NEW HAVEN, CT; JAMES HILLHOUSE HS; (FR); Nat Hon Sy; Comm Volntr; Schol Bwl; Chr; Medical Field; PhD; Yale U; U of California Los Angeles

NAPIER-RUZEK, ALEXANDRA; NEWTOWN, CT; NEWTON HS; (MS); Hi Hnr Roll; Hnr Roll; Comm Volntr; Chrch Yth Grp; DARE; Drma Clb; Scouts; SP/M/VS; Teaching Acting to Younger Children; Actress

NAPOLI, LAUREN; MILFORD, CT; JOSEPH A FORAN HS; (JR); Hnr Roll; WWAHSS; Comm Volntr; Spec Olymp Vol; Key Club; Prom Com; Spanish Clb; Child/Adolescent Psychology; Spanish (Minor); U of Connecticut

NARDOZZI, NICOLE; TRUMBULL, CT; TRUMBULL HS; (SO); Hi Hnr Roll; Hnr Roll; Otst Ac Ach Awd; Pres Sch; St of Mnth; Yth Ldrshp Prog; Comm Volntr; Peer Tut/Med; DARE; Lib Aide; Orch; Stg Cre; Cr Ctry (J); Fld Hky (J L); Sftball (J); Track (J); Yrbk (E); Field Hockey Team Manager; Program of Excellence; Psychology; Teaching; Brown U; Boston U

NASON, SHANNON; EAST HAVEN, CT; EAST HAVEN HS; (SR); Marine Biology; Roger Williams U; U of New England

NIGRO, STEPHANIE A; FAIRFIELD, CT; FAIRFIELD WARDE HS; (SO); Hnr Roll; Comm Volntr; Chrch Yth Grp; Key Club; Spanish Clb; Acpl Chr; Chr; Lcrsse; Sccr (J); English, Writing; Cultural Arts; New York U; Boston U

NOAKE, ROBERT; SIMSBURY, CT; SIMSBURY HS; (JR); Hi Hnr Roll; Nat Hon Sy; Cmptr Clb; Sci Clb; Student Pilot; Embry-Riddle Aeronautical U Prescott; Worcester Polytechnic Institute

NORFLEET, SHAYLA; WATERBURY, CT; W F KAYNOR REG VOC TECH SCH; (JR); Hi Hnr Roll; Hnr Roll; WWAHSS; Prom Com; Bskball (VJ); Hair Competition Participation Certificate; Business Management; Cosmetology

NOWELL, JUSTIN; SOUTHPORT, CT; FAIRFIELD LUDLOWE HS; (SO); Ctznshp Aw; Hi Hnr Roll; Hnr Roll; Otst Ac Ach Awd; Perf Att; Pres Ac Ftns Aw; St of Mnth; WWAHSS; Chrch Yth Grp; DARE; P to P St Amb Prg; Tchrs Aide; Spanish Clb; Bnd; Stg Cre; Bskball (V L); AAU Basketball; Business Management; Law; Yale U; Princeton U

NUZZACI, BRITTANY L; STRATFORD, CT; BUNNELL HS; (JR); Hi Hnr Roll; Hnr Roll; Otst Ac Ach Awd; Yth Ldrshp Prog; Chrch Yth Grp; Dbte Team; Emplmnt; Mod UN; Yrbk (P); Working 2 Jobs; Yale Co-Op Program - German; Law; Political Science

NYAMAIA, TAMBU; NORWALK, CT; BRIEN MC MAHON HS; (SO); Hnr Roll; Perf Att; Peer Tut/Med; Chrch Yth Grp; Acpl Chr; Chr; Ch Chr; Music; Psychology; Barnard College; Adelphi U

O'BRIEN, ROBERT J; WEST HARTFORD, CT; NORTHWEST CATHOLIC HS; (SO); Hi Hnr Roll; Hnr Roll; Comm Volntr; Chess; Drma Clb; French Clb; Bnd; Chr; Jzz Bnd; Pep Bnd; Jazz Choir; Music; History

O CONNELL, ASHLEY L; BEACON FALLS, CT; WOODLAND REG; (SR); Hi Hnr Roll; Hnr Roll; Nat Mrt Sch Recip; St of Mnth; Comm Volntr; Peer Tut/Med; Drma Clb; Photog; SP/M/VS; Stg Cre; Swmg (V); Yrbk; Human Relations Organization-President; GSA; Secondary Education; Performing Arts; Southern Connecticut State U

O'CONNELL, CHARLOTTE C; FAIRFIELD, CT; FAIRFIELD WARDE HS; (SO); Ctznshp Aw; Hi Hnr Roll; Sci Fairs; St of Mnth; WWAHSS; Comm Volntr; Peer Tut/Med; ArtClub; DARE; Key Club; Spanish Clb; Ice Hky (J); Church Group; Pre Medical; Biochemistry; Mc Gill U; Georgetown U

OJEDA, PAULA; GREENWICH, CT; (JR); Hi Hnr Roll; Hnr Roll; WWAHSS; Comm Volntr; Chrldg (V C); Accounting; Actuarial Science; U of North Carolina; Villanova

OLSEN-ECKER, BRITT H; OLD GREENWICH, CT; GREENWICH HS; (SR); Hi Hnr Roll; Hnr Roll; Nat Hon Sy; Drma Clb; Mus Clb; Acpl Chr; Chr; SP/M/VS; Leadership in Theatrical Arts; Voice Performance; Musical Theater; Will Be Attending the Peabody Conservatory of Music, Part of Johns Hopkins U

OLSON, ALAN; DERBY, CT; CHRISTIAN HERITAGE SCH; (JR); Hi Hnr Roll; Nat Hon Sy; Sci Fairs; Sci/Math Olympn; Clb; Bskball (J); Sccr (VJC); Tennis (V); Cl Off (V); History Club President; Physician's Assistant; Quinnipiac College; Wake Forest U

OSPINA, JUAN D; GREENWICH, CT; GREENWICH HS; (JR); Hi Hnr Roll; Yth Ldrshp Prog; Comm Volntr; Hosp Aide; Peer Tut/Med; Cmptr Clb; Vsity Clb; Ftball (J); Wrstlg (V L); Lit Mag (R); England Tour for Every Team; French Study Abroad Program; Business/Finance; Modeling/Actor; Columbia U; Lynn U

OTERO, MATTHEW; STAMFORD, CT; STAMFORD AC; (SO); Hnr Roll; MVP; Nat Hon Sy; Nat Stu Ath Day Aw; Otst Ac Ach Awd; St of Mnth; Comm Volntr; Chess; Cmptr Clb; DARE; Drma Clb; SP/M/VS; Ftball (C); Wrstlg (V); Robotics; Business, Stocks, Bonds; Veterinarian; Penn State; Yale

Ospina, Juan D — Greenwich HS — Greenwich, CT
O'Brien, Robert J — Northwest Catholic HS — West Hartford, CT
Nowell, Justin — Fairfield Ludlowe HS — Southport, CT
Noake, Robert — Simsbury HS — Simsbury, CT
Nuzzaci, Brittany L — Bunnell HS — Stratford, CT
Olson, Alan — Christian Heritage Sch — Derby, CT
Otero, Matthew — Stamford AC — Stamford, CT

Monahan, Siobhan K — Fairfield Ludlowe HS — Southport, CT
Meyers, Benjamin — Westminster Sch — Vernon Rockville, CT
Mendez, Nicholas — J.M. Wright Tech HS — Bridgeport, CT
Mc Goldrick, Paul — Bunnell HS — Stratford, CT
Mc Dowell, Amber — James Hillhouse HS — New Haven, CT 
Maynard, Dareem E — Oliver Wolcott Voc Tech Sch — Torrington, CT
Melchionno, Scott — Stratford HS — Stratford, CT 
Mensah, Mercy — Central HS — Bridgeport, CT 
Mitrik, Kristen M — W F Kaynor Reg Voc Tech Sch — Wolcott, CT
Mokritski, Heather S — Orville H Platt HS — Meriden, CT

PADULA, DANIELLE E; SOUTHBURY, CT; POMPERAUG REG HS; (FR); Hi Hnr Roll; Otst Ac Ach Awd; Comm Volntr; Drma Clb; Mus Clb; Bnd; Chr; Jzz Bnd; Mch Bnd; Ice Hky (V C); Ice Sktg (C); Sftball (J); Best Drama Student Award; Ice Hockey with Select Regional Team

PAGAN, YESENIA; HARTFORD, CT; SPORTS SCIENCES AC; (SO); Hi Hnr Roll; Hnr Roll; Sci Fairs; Comm Volntr; Writing Award; Social Work, Clinical; Clinical Psychology; Boston U; Syracuse U

PAGE, FORREST W; EAST HAVEN, CT; HS IN THE CMTY; (JR); Hi Hnr Roll; Hnr Roll; Sch Ppr (E, R); Co-President of Gay/Straight Alliance; Historian/History Teacher; Psychologist; U of Auburn; Rhode Island U

PAGE, MARTY; MILFORD, CT; JOSEPH A FORAN HS; (FR); Hi Hnr Roll; WWAHSS; Hosp Aide; Chrch Yth Grp; Key Club; Scouts; Swmg (V L); Track (V); Swam in SCCS and Placed Second in Heat.; Medicine; Biology; Penn State U; U of Virginia

PALADINO, LAUREN; MILFORD, CT; JOSEPH FORAN HS; (SR); F Lan Hn Soc; Hnr Roll; Nat Hon Sy; WWAHSS; Peer Tut/Med; Red Cr Aide; Spec Olymp Vol; Key Club; Spanish Clb; Bskball (V L); Vllyball (V L); Scholar Athlete Award (Tap-Off Club); Elementary Education; Syracuse U

PALELLA, ANASTASIA; NEW PRESTON, CT; SHEPAUG VALLEY HS; (SR); Hnr Roll; St of Mnth; Comm Volntr; ArtClub; DARE; Emplmnt; Photog; Prom Com; Scouts; Mar Art; Skiing (J); Sccr (J); Yrbk (P); Community Service - Over 46 Hours; 43 Commitment Credits in High School; Photography; Photography / Teacher; Wesleyan U; Cazenovia College

PALMER, MARY; BETHEL, CT; BETHEL HS; (JR); Hi Hnr Roll; Comm Volntr; Red Cr Aide; DECA; Prom Com; PP Ftbl (C); Sftball (J); Adv Cncl (R); Yrbk (E); VP BHS DECA Chapter; Marketing; Business Management; U of Connecticut; U of Rhode Island

PALTER, ARIEL; WEST HARTFORD, CT; HALL HS; (JR); F Lan Hn Soc; Hi Hnr Roll; Comm Volntr; Spec Olymp Vol; Emplmnt; Tmpl Yth Grp; Bnd; Jzz Bnd; Mch Bnd; Pep Bnd; Swmg (V); Track (V); Sch Ppr (E, P); Photo Editor of School Newspaper; USY (United Synagogue Youth); Doctor; Children/Child Development; Skidmore College; Brandeis U

PARE, JONATHAN; MADISON, CT; DANIEL HAND HS; (JR); Hnr Roll; ArtClub; Chrch Yth Grp; Drma Clb; Mus Clb; Acpl Chr; Chr; SP/M/VS; Waes Hael Honorary Performance for Music Educ(only High School Chosen); Dramatic Arts

PARE JR, GEORGE; EAST HARTFORD, CT; EAST HARTFORD HS; (SR); Hi Hnr Roll; Hnr Roll; Spec Olymp Vol; Emplmnt; Bskball (J); Student of the Week; Recognition of Commitment for Olympics; Entrepreneurship; Business Management; Central Connecticut State U; Southern Connecticut State U

PAREKH, DIVYA D; NORWICH, CT; NORWICH FREE AC; (JR); Hi Hnr Roll; Hnr Roll; St of Mnth; Hosp Aide; Sci Clb; Asian Clb; Bdmtn (J); Pathologist; Radiologist; First Two Year in Community College; U Conn

PARISI, AMANDA; WALLINGFORD, CT; (FR); Hi Hnr Roll; Hnr Roll; Pres Ac Ftns Aw; Sci Fairs; Sch Ppr; Comm Volntr; Chrch Yth Grp; DARE; Pep Squd; Bnd; Dnce; Mch Bnd; Ftball (J); Tennis (J); CR (R); Summer Diving; Math Education; Phys. Ed.; U of Connecticut

PARSONS, TULISSA S; CHESHIRE, CT; CHESHIRE HS; (SO); Hnr Roll; Pres Ac Ftns Aw; Sci Fairs; Sch Ppr; Comm Volntr; WWAHSS; Yth Ldrshp Prog; Chrch Yth Grp; DARE; Emplmnt; Scouts; Stg Cre; Sch Ppr (E); Art; YMCA Leader's Club; Art; Marketing; Berklee College of Music; Drexel U

PASCAL, BRENDON; BRIDGEPORT, CT; BULLARD-HAVENS VOC TECH SCH; (JR); Hi Hnr Roll; Hnr Roll; WWAHSS; Peer Tut/Med; DARE; Mus Clb; Bnd; Dnce; SP/M/VS; Bskball (J); Ftball (V); Sccr (V); Track (V); CR (R); Psychology; Engineering; Princeton U; Lynchburg College

PASCALE, DAN; MERIDEN, CT; ORVILLE H PLATT HS; (FR); DAR; Hnr Roll; Nat Sci Aw; Otst Ac Ach Awd; Perf Att; Pres Ac Ftns Aw; Sci/Math Olympn; Comm Volntr; DARE; Key Club; Scouts; Bsball (J); Ftball (V L); Wt Lftg (J); CR (S); Project Excel; D.A.R.E. Essay Winner; Sports Management; Communications; U Of Notre Dame; U of Southern California

PATEL, KHUSHBU; DANBURY, CT; DANBURY HS; (FR); Hi Hnr Roll; Hnr Roll; Nat Hon Sy; Nat Ldrshp Svc; Nat Hon Sy; St of Mnth; Yth Ldrshp Prog; Comm Volntr; Red Cr Aide; ArtClub; Chrch Yth Grp; DARE; Dbte Team; Drma Clb; Key Club; Photog; Sci Clb; Dnce; SP/M/VS; Bharatanatyam (Dance); Physical Therapy; Photography; Yale; Harvard

PATEL, KINAL; MILFORD, CT; JOSEPH A. FORAN HS; (FR); Hi Hnr Roll; WWAHSS; Comm Volntr; Spec Olymp Vol; Key Club; Scouts; Bskball; Track; Vllyball; Cl Off (T)

PATELLA, GREGORY; BROOKFIELD, CT; (JR); Hi Hnr Roll; Pres Sch; WWAHSS; Comm Volntr; Peer Tut/Med; DECA; Bsball (V); Ftball (V CL); PP Ftbl (C); Treasurer of DECA Program; Engineering; US Coast Guard Academy; U of Rhode Island

PATERNOSTER, MELISSA; WATERBURY, CT; CROSBY HS; (SO); Hnr Roll; Comm Volntr; Key Club; Skt Tgt Sh (J); Mock Trial; Law; Psychology; Quinnipiac U; Connecticut College

PATRICK, CHRISTY; MILFORD, CT; JOSEPH A FORAN HS; (FR); Hnr Roll; Perf Att; WWAHSS; Comm Volntr; Peer Tut/Med; Chrch Yth Grp; Key Club; Pharmacy; Psychology

PAULEKAS, AMY; GLASTONBURY, CT; GLASTONBURY HS; (SO); Hi Hnr Roll; WWAHSS; Yth Ldrshp Prog; Peer Tut/Med; Chrch Yth Grp; Emplmnt; Key Club; Latin Clb; Orch; Fld Hky (J); Lcrsse (J); Track (J); Who's Who American High School Students; Math; Architecture; Colby College; College of William & Mary

PENROD, CASEY; EAST HAVEN, CT; EAST HAVEN HS; (SR); Nat Hon Sy; Otst Ac Ach Awd; Comm Volntr; Peer Tut/Med; Emplmnt; Scouts; Vsity Clb; Sccr (VJCL); Track; Vsy Clb; Animal Science; English; Fordham U; Pennsylvania State U

PEREIRA, ARIADNI M; BRIDGEPORT, CT; BASSICK HS; (SO); Hi Hnr Roll; Hnr Roll; Sci Fairs; St of Mnth; Comm Volntr; Peer Tut/Med; ArtClub; Chrch Yth Grp; DARE; Emplmnt; Key Club; Ch Chr; Dnce; SP/M/VS; Scr Kpr (V); Sftball (VJ L); Vllyball (VJCL); Cl Off (R); Stu Cncl (S, R); Sch Ppr (R, P); Yrbk (R, P); Asian Club; Poetry.Com; GSA Member; Pediatric Cardiologist / Neurologist; Poet; Johns Hopkins U; Yale U

PERKINS, ERIC; BRIDGEPORT, CT; HARDING HS; (SO); Hnr Roll; Nat Hon Sy; Nat Sci Aw; Nat Stu Ath Day Aw; Perf Att; St of Mnth; CARE; Comm Volntr; Red Cr Aide; Bnd; Drm Mjr; Jzz Bnd; Pep Bnd; Bskball; Cr Ctry; Cyclg; Ftball; Scr Kpr; Swmg; Wt Lftg; Wrstlg; Boston College Business, Sport; Boston College

PERSAUD, RICHARD; HARTFORD, CT; BULKELEY HS; (JR); Perf Att; Sci Fairs; Hosp Aide; Chrch Yth Grp; Cr Ctry; Nursing; New York U; U

PESKETT, ALEXANDRA; WEST HARTFORD, CT; CONARD HS; (JR); F Lan Hn Soc; Hi Hnr Roll; Hnr Roll; Comm Volntr; Chrch Yth Grp; Stg Cre; Computer Science; Graphic Design; Rochester Institute of Technology; U of Connecticut

PETONITO, CRISTINA; EAST HAVEN, CT; SACRED HEART AC; (JR); Hnr Roll; Perf Att; ArtClub; Emplmnt; Key Club; Scouts; Latin Clb; Orch; Swmg (V L); Track (V); Chemistry Award; Perfect Attendance Award; Pre-Dentistry; Biology

PETROSKY, KATHERINE M; MERIDEN, CT; ORVILLE H PLATT HS; (FR); Hnr Roll; Perf Att; St of Mnth; DARE; Scouts; SP/M/VS; Yrbk (P); St. Stanislaus School Sister Magdalene Award for 3 Yr. Old Pre-K Through 8th Grade; Project Excel Award for Outstanding Contributions to Platt HS; Work with Animals; Culinary Arts

PHAM, JESSICA; BETHEL, CT; BETHEL HS; (FR); Hi Hnr Roll; Hnr Roll; Comm Volntr; Doctor / Pediatrician; Medical Field; U of Connecticut

PHAM, NHUT; HARTFORD, CT; HARTFORD HS; (SO); Ctznshp Aw; Fut Prb Slvr; Hnr Roll; Nat Hon Sy; Nat Sci Aw; Otst Ac Ach Awd; Perf Att; Sci Fairs; St of Mnth; Peer Tut/Med; ArtClub; Chess; Photog; Sci Clb; Tech Clb; Spanish Clb; SP/M/VS; First Place City Science Fair; Attended Space Camp, Due to Essay Writing; Video Game Development; Acting; Stanford U; Westwood College

PHILLIPS, CAMERON; FAIRFIELD, CT; CHRISTIAN HERITAGE SCH; (SO); Hnr Roll; MVP; Comm Volntr; Chrch Yth Grp; Chr; Ch Chr; Dnce; SP/M/VS; Cr Ctry (V); Swmg (V); Tennis (V); Piano Trio; Architecture; Music; Oberlin U

PHUNG, SHIRLEY; WATERFORD, CT; WATERFORD HS; (SR); Hi Hnr Roll; Hnr Roll; Drma Clb; Emplmnt; Stg Cre; Multicultural Club; Learning Through Service Committee; Childhood Education; U of Rhode Island, Salve Regina U; U of Connecticut, Wagner College

PIAO, FENGYAN; EAST HARTFORD, CT; EAST HARTFORD HS; (JR); Hi Hnr Roll; Perf Att; St of Mnth; Chrch Yth Grp; Emplmnt; Mth Clb/Tm; Off Aide; Chr; SP/M/VS; Computer Graphics; Business Advertising; U of Connecticut; Union College, NY

PIERRE-NOISETTE, LEAH; BRIDGEPORT, CT; HARDING HS; (JR); Hi Hnr Roll; Hnr Roll; Nat Mrt LOC; Otst Ac Ach Awd; Perf Att; Sci Fairs; Comm Volntr; Chrch Yth Grp; Ch Chr; Science; Math; Yale U; U of Connecticut

PILIERO, JOANNA; FAIRFIELD, CT; FAIRFIELD LUDLOWE HS; (FR); Hi Hnr Roll; WWAHSS; Comm Volntr; Chrch Yth Grp; Key Club; Svce Clb; Sccr (J)

PONTURO, GRACE; REDDING, CT; JOEL BARLOW HS; (JR); Hi Hnr Roll; Nat Hon Sy; St of Mnth; Comm Volntr; Peer Tut/Med; Chrch Yth Grp; Hsbk Rdg; Honorable Mention: Women's History Month Essay Contest; Honorable Mention-Statewide Reflections Contest (Musical Composition); Business Marketing; Psychology; Villanova U; Boston College

PRECIADO, ALMA S; WEST HAVEN, CT; WEST HAVEN HS; (FR); Otst Ac Ach Awd; Emplmnt; Pep Squd; Chr; Ob/Gyn; Nurse; UConn U of Connecticut; Southern Connecticut U

PRINGLE, LATRESE; NEW HAVEN, CT; HILL REG CAREER HS; (JR); Hnr Roll; Comm Volntr; Peer Tut/Med; Career Against Tobacco; Nurse Practitioner; Southern

PROPIESCUS, CRYSTAL; COVENTRY, CT; COVENTRY HS; (JR); Hnr Roll; Nat Hon Sy; WWAHSS; Bnd; Mch Bnd; Optometry; Nursing; U of Connecticut; Robert Morris

PRZYBYSZ, BRANDAN A; OLD LYME, CT; LYME-OLD LYME HS; (SO); Hi Hnr Roll; Otst Ac Ach Awd; Yth Ldrshp Prog; Comm Volntr; Emplmnt; NYLC; Off Aide; Bskball (VJC); Golf (V); Volunteer Work-Basketball & Baseball Coach; Accounting; U of NC Chapel Hill; Vanderbilt U

PUGLISE, PATRICIA; GROTON, CT; FITCH SR HS; (JR); Hnr Roll; Comm Volntr; DARE; Hotel Management; Child Care; Lehigh Valley College; Johnson and Wales U

PURDY, SARA; FAIRFIELD, CT; FAIRFIELD WARDE HS; (SO); Hi Hnr Roll; Hnr Roll; Nat Hon Sy; WWAHSS; Comm Volntr; Emplmnt; Key Club; CR (R); Fashion Magazine Editor; Magazine Layout Designer; New York U; Fashion Institute of Technology

PURPLE, KATHERINE E; AVON, CT; NORTHWEST CATHOLIC HS; (SO); Hi Hnr Roll; Comm Volntr; Chrch Yth Grp; Dnce; Lit Mag (E); Sch Ppr (R); Johns Hopkins Talent Search; Honors Biology, Honors World History & Honors Spanish II Awards, President's Award for Educational Excellence; Creative Writing; Education; Providence College; Villanova U

PUSSER, BRITTANY; GREENWICH, CT; GREENWICH HS; (SR); Hi Hnr Roll; Hnr Roll; Chrch Yth Grp; Drma Clb; Emplmnt; Mus Clb; Chr; Ch Chr; SP/M/VS; Music Education; Manhattanville College; U of Connecticut

QUEIROZ JR, ALBERTO S; DANBURY, CT; NEW HOPE CHRISTIAN AC; (FR); Hi Hnr Roll; Hnr Roll; Otst Ac Ach Awd; Pres Ac Ftns Aw; Sci Fairs; Chrch Yth Grp; DARE; Outdrs Clb; Bskball (J); Track (V); Child Psychology; Law

QUINN, ONIKA; HARTFORD, CT; WEAVER HS; (SR); Gov Hnr Prg; Hi Hnr Roll; Hnr Roll; Nat Hon Sy; Perf Att; St of Mnth; WWAHSS; Hosp Aide; Peer Tut/Med; Chrch Yth Grp; Emplmnt; Ch Chr; Tennis (V); President of National Honor Society; Received Governor's Achievement Award; Biology; Columbia U; New York U

RACZKOWSKI, JASON A; NAUGATUCK, CT; W F KAYNOR REG VOC TECH SCH; (SO); Hnr Roll; Hnr Roll; Comm Volntr; Chrch Yth Grp; DARE; Emplmnt; Church Volunteer-Holy Savior Church; Altar Server for 7 Years; Automotive Technology; Daytona Beach Community College; Embry Riddle Aeronautical College

RAISSI, ALI; STAMFORD, CT; WEST HILL HS; (JR); Hnr Roll; Sci Fairs; Hosp Aide; Lib Aide; Bskball; Skiing; Sccr; Sch Ppr; Civil Engineering-Master Degree; Mathematics Computer Sciences; NYU

RAMADAN, IMAN; NEW HAVEN, CT; HS IN THE CMTY; (JR); Hnr Roll; Nat Hon Sy; Perf Att; Wdwrkg Clb; Computer Science; Photography; New Haven U; U of Connecticut

RAPHAEL, ADAM E; WESTPORT, CT; STAPLES HS; (JR); Hi Hnr Roll; Nat Sci Aw; Pres Ac Ftns Aw; Yth Ldrshp Prog; Comm Volntr; Dbte Team; Key Club; Bnd; Pep Bnd; Golf (V); Sccr (J); Track (J); Sch Ppr (N); National Student Leadership Conference; United Way Youth Initiatives Board, Jake Carter Board; History; Political Science

RARDIN, JESSICA; SANDY HOOK, CT; CHRISTIAN HERITAGE SCH; (JR); Hi Hnr Roll; Hnr Roll; Nat Hon Sy; Sci Fairs; Comm Volntr; Chrch Yth Grp; Drma Clb; Tchrs Aide; Chr; Stg Cre; Yrbk (E, R, P); Church Leadership Team; Church Media Team; Computer Science; Georgia Tech; Clemson U

RAYMOND, SEAN M; PLAINVILLE, CT; BRISTOL TECH ED CTR; (JR); Hnr Roll; St of Mnth; Comm Volntr; Civil Air Pat; DECA; FBLA; Stu Cncl; Work Study Apprenticeship Program; HVAC; HVAC S-2 License; Own Business By Age 25; New England Technical Institute

REDGATE, MOLLY E; TRUMBULL, CT; ST JOSEPH'S HS; (SO); Ctznshp Aw; Hnr Roll; Nat Ldrshp Svc; Nat Mrt Sch Recip; Yth Ldrshp Prog; Comm Volntr; Peer Tut/Med; Drma Clb; Emplmnt; Mus Clb; Spanish Clb; Chr; SP/M/VS; Swg Chr; Lcrsse (J); Stu Cncl; CR; National Young Leaders Conference 7/30- 8/9 Washington DC; Medicine; Law Enforcement

RENCURREL, KRISTY L; BROAD BROOK, CT; EAST WINDSOR HS; (FR); Ctznshp Aw; Hnr Roll; Otst Ac Ach Awd; Perf Att; DARE; French Clb; Chr; SP/M/VS; Stu Cncl (R); Yrbk (R); Caring Award; Responsibility / Citizenship; Literature Arts; History; New York U; U of California

REYES, GABRIELLE; HAMDEN, CT; HAMDEN HS; (SO); Hi Hnr Roll; Hnr Roll; Nat Hon Sy; Otst Ac Ach Awd; Perf Att; Pres Sch; St of Mnth; WWAHSS; Hosp Aide; Chrch Yth Grp; Italian Clb; Chrldg (L); Sccr (L); Vllyball (L); US Navy Sea Cadets; Italian Honor Society; Pre-Med; US History; Yale; Southern Connecticut State U

RIBEIRO, BIANCA A; OXFORD, CT; SEYMOUR HS; (MS); Ctznshp Aw; F Lan Hn Soc; Hnr Roll; Nat Stu Ath Day Aw; Otst Ac Ach Awd; St of Mnth; ArtClub; DARE; Wdwrkg Clb; Clr Grd; Dnce; Most Consistent Effort; Most Improved; Psychology; Acting/Modeling; U Conn, U of CO; Fashion Institute of Technology

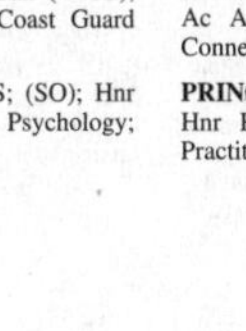

Redgate, Molly E
St Joseph's HS
Trumbull, CT

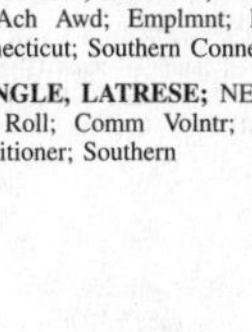

Raissi, Ali
West Hill HS
Stamford, CT

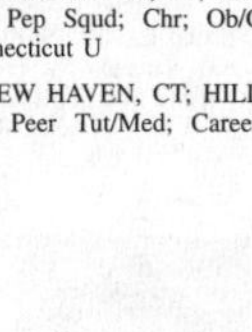

Palella, Anastasia
Shepaug Valley HS
New Preston, CT

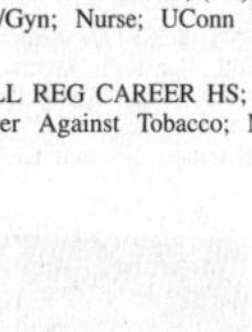

Raczkowski, Jason A
W F Kaynor Reg Voc Tech Sch
Naugatuck, CT

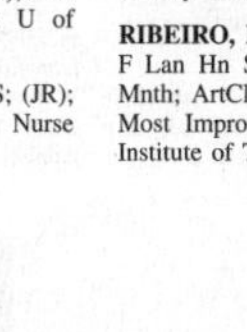

Rencurrel, Kristy L
East Windsor HS
Broad Brook, CT

RICHEME, DANIEL; DANBURY, CT; DANBURY HS; (FR); Hnr Roll; DARE; Scouts; Mch Bnd; Track (J); Science; West Point Military Academy; Yale U

RIVERA, RANGY; FARMINGTON, CT; BRISTOL TECH ED CTR; (JR); Hnr Roll; Comm Volntr; Emplmnt; Wrstlg (V); Automotive Design; Custom Hot Rod; Universal Technical Institute

RIZZARDI, ALEXA J; MILFORD, CT; ST JOSEPH; (MS); Ctznshp Aw; DAR; Hnr Roll; Nat Hon Sy; Perf Att; Sci/Math Olympn; Peer Tut/Med; Chrch Yth Grp; DARE; FTA; Pep Squd; Prom Com; Scouts; Italian Clb; SP/M/VS; Stg Cre; Bskball (J); Lcrsse (J); Sftball (J); Vllyball (J); Stu Cncl (S); Yrbk (P); Snowboarding; Physical Education Award; Teaching; Special Education; Central Connecticut State U; Clemson U

RODRIGUEZ, ERIKA; BRIDGEPORT, CT; BULLARD-HAVENS VOC TECH SCH; (SO); Hi Hnr Roll; Hnr Roll; Perf Att; St of Mnth; DARE; Stu Cncl (R); CR (P); CNC-I; Blueprint Reading; Housatonic Community College; Gateway Community College

RODRIGUEZ, SACHA LEE; BRIDGEPORT, CT; J.M. WRIGHT TECH HS; (SR); Ctznshp Aw; Hi Hnr Roll; Salutrn; St of Mnth; Hab For Humty Volntr; SP/M/VS; Yrbk (E); Pediatrician; U of Arizona; U of Connecticut

RODRIGUEZ SANTIAGO, MARIA C; NEW HAVEN, CT; HS IN THE CMTY; (JR); Hi Hnr Roll; Hnr Roll; Otst Ac Ach Awd; Mth Clb/Tm; Photog; Chr; Sccr

ROGERS, SHANELE H; EAST HARTFORD, CT; EAST HARTFORD HS; (SO); Hi Hnr Roll; Hnr Roll; Otst Ac Ach Awd; Sci Fairs; St of Mnth; Yth Ldrshp Prog; Comm Volntr; ArtClub; Chrch Yth Grp; DARE; Emplmnt; Mus Clb; Tchrs Aide; Bnd; Dnce; Drl Tm; Cr Ctry (J); Track (J); Stu Cncl (T); Nursing; Doctor; U of Georgia; U of Florida

ROLLINS, MEGAN; MILFORD, CT; FORAN HS; (JR); All Am Sch; Hi Hnr Roll; Hnr Roll; Spec Olymp Vol; Chrch Yth Grp; Key Club; Tennis (J); Fairfield U; Roger Williams College

ROSA JR, ANTHONY C P; HARTFORD, CT; SPORTS SCIENCES AC; (SO); Hi Hnr Roll; Nat Hon Sy; High Honors Every Semester; Physician; Computer Technology; Syracuse; U of Florida

ROSE, LESLIE K; FAIRFIELD, CT; FAIRFIELD LUDLOWE HS; Hi Hnr Roll; USAA; WWAHSS; Comm Volntr; Key Club; Dnce; Hsbk Rdg; Skiing; Various Art Awards & Shows; Member of Mensa; Art & Computer Art

ROSEMOND, TIONA; WINDSOR, CT; ALBERT PRINCE TECH; (FR); Hi Hnr Roll; Hnr Roll; Otst Ac Ach Awd; St of Mnth; Chrch Yth Grp; Drma Clb; Key Club; Dnce; Drl Tm; CR (P); Windsor Cheerleading Team - Outside School; Drill Team; Accounting; Law School - Tort or Contracts; U of Hartford; U of Virginia

ROSEN, JUSTIN M; MILFORD, CT; JOSEPH A FORAN HS; (SR); Hnr Roll; WWAHSS; Red Cr Aide; Spec Olymp Vol; Key Club; Swmg (V CL); Cl Off (V); Stu Cncl (V); CR (V); Sch Ppr (R, P); Inter for Speaker of House of Representative (State A); Connecticut Board of Education Leadership Awards; Lawyer; Lobbyist; U of Connecticut; Drexel U

ROSS, MICHAEL F; WILTON, CT; WILTON HS; (JR); Hi Hnr Roll; Hnr Roll; Hab For Humty Volntr; Emplmnt; Key Club; Swmg (L); Stu Cncl (R); Varsity Crew; Columbia U; Fordham U

ROUSSEAU, JON P; UNIONVILLE, CT; BRISTOL TECH ED CTR; (JR); Hi Hnr Roll; Otst Ac Ach Awd; St of Mnth; Emplmnt; Electrical - E2 Master Level

RUBINO, JOEL M; SOUTHBURY, CT; POMPERAUG REG HS; (FR); Hi Hnr Roll; Pres Sch; St Schl; Comm Volntr; Mth Clb/Tm; Golf (J); Ice Hky (V); Sccr (V)

RUDD, ROBIN; BRIDGEPORT, CT; CTRL MAGNET HS; (FR); Hi Hnr Roll; Hnr Roll; Nat Hon Sy; Otst Ac Ach Awd; Chr; SP/M/VS; Bowling Team - J; Superintendent Award-Academic Prowess; Foreign Language / Spanish; Music; Howard U; Fordham U

RUIZ, FRANCIS; WEST HAVEN, CT; WEST HAVEN HS; (SO); Hnr Roll; St of Mnth; Chrch Yth Grp; Ch Chr; Medicine; Dentist; Harvard; Cornell

RUSCHMEYER, ELYSSE; S GLASTONBURY, CT; GLASTONBURY HS; (JR); Hi Hnr Roll; Hnr Roll; Nat Hon Sy; Comm Volntr; Chrch Yth Grp; Emplmnt; Russian Clb; Hsbk Rdg; Numerous Equestrian Awards; Piano Student; Business; Law; Lehigh U; Fairfield U

RUSSELL, ANNE S; FAIRFIELD, CT; FAIRFIELD LUDLOWE HS; (JR); Hi Hnr Roll; Hnr Roll; Nat Hon Sy; St of Mnth; Comm Volntr; Peer Tut/Med; Spec Olymp Vol; Emplmnt; Key Club; Photog; Vsity Clb; Sccr (V L); Tennis (V CL); Track (V CL); Coaches' Award for Track; Student of the Marking Period; Business; Boston College; Villanova

RUSSELL, MISHIKA A; HARTFORD, CT; (FR); Ctznshp Aw; F Lan Hn Soc; Hnr Roll; MVP; Otst Ac Ach Awd; Perf Att; St of Mnth; Yth Ldrshp Prog; Outdrs Clb; Dnce; Drl Tm; Track (V); Virgina U; Moore House U

RYAN, KRISTIN; CHESHIRE, CT; CHESHIRE HS; (JR); F Lan Hn Soc; Hi Hnr Roll; St of Mnth; WWAHSS; Comm Volntr; Red Cr Aide; Chrch Yth Grp; Emplmnt; SADD; Swmg (V CL); Yrbk; Co-Captain - Relay for Life; Facilitator- St Bridget Church; Economics; Business; Boston College; Wake Forest U

SAARI, ASHLEY; STRATFORD, CT; BUNNELL HS; (JR); Hnr Roll; Chrch Yth Grp; DARE; Emplmnt; Vsity Clb; Track (V); Helping to Feed Homeless; Psychology; Flagler College

SABIN, TARA; FAIRFIELD, CT; FAIRFIELD LUDLOWE HS; (FR); Hi Hnr Roll; Hnr Roll; Otst Ac Ach Awd; Pres Ac Ftns Aw; Comm Volntr; Hab For Humty Volntr; Key Club; Wdwrkg Clb; Chr; SP/M/VS; Fld Hky (J); Tennis (J); Yrbk (P); Architect; Business; U of North Carolina; U of Miami

SAMPSON, DANA; EASTON, CT; JOEL BARLOW HS; (JR); Hi Hnr Roll; Hnr Roll; MVP; Nat Hon Sy; WWAHSS; Comm Volntr; Sccr (V); Track (V); National Charity League Member; Curriculum Development Task Force-H.S.; Elementary Education; Muhlenberg College; Holy Cross

SANCHEZ, TAINA; HARTFORD, CT; AI PRINCE TECH; (FR); Hnr Roll; Peer Tut/Med; Chess; Bskball (J); Tennis (J); Child Care; Law / Lawyer; U Conn; Trinity College

SANDELIN, EBONY; WATERBURY, CT; W F KAYNOR REG VOC TECH SCH; (JR); Hi Hnr Roll; Hnr Roll; WWAHSS; Comm Volntr; Peer Tut/Med; ArtClub; Pep Squd; Prom Com; Voc Ind Clb Am; Chr; Dnce; SP/M/VS; Pep Squad Leader (Captain); Dance Choreographer Captain; Fashion Majors; Dance Choreography Majors

SANDERS, NATALI N; NEW HAVEN, CT; WILBUR L CROSS HS; (FR); Nat Hon Sy; St Schl; Comm Volntr; Drma Clb; Adv Cncl (S); Sch Ppr (E); Criminal Law; Pediatrics; U of New York; Florida State U

SANDREY, JILLIAN L; MADISON, CT; DANIEL HAND HS; (JR); Hnr Roll; Nat Hon Sy; Pres Ac Ftns Aw; Comm Volntr; ArtClub; DARE; Mus Clb; Photog; SADD; French Clb; Dnce; Cl Off (R); Stu Cncl (R); CR (R); Lit Mag (R); Art Awards; Art Work Nominations; Art Major; Literature Major

SANGUINO, OTTO; EAST HARTFORD, CT; EAST HARTFORD HS; (JR); Hnr Roll; St of Mnth; Chrch Yth Grp; Bnd; Dnce; Drl Tm; Mch Bnd; Bdmtn (J); Dvng (J); Mar Art (J); Sccr (J); Swmg (J); Tennis (J); Vllyball (J); Medicine; Technology in Computers; Manchester Community College; U of Connecticut

SANTHOSH, SARIGA; GLASTONBURY, CT; GLASTONBURY HS; (JR); Hi Hnr Roll; Hnr Roll; WWAHSS; Hosp Aide; Dbte Team; Emplmnt; Dnce; French Concours Award-Placed 9th in CT; Latin National Award-Bronze Medal; Finance; Chemist

SANTIAGO, LORIMAR; NEW BRITAIN, CT; E C GOODWIN REG VOC TECH SCH; (SO); Hi Hnr Roll; Hnr Roll; WWAHSS; Chrch Yth Grp; Drma Clb; SP/M/VS; Vllyball (J); CR (R); I'm At the Top of My Hairdressing Class; Psychiatry

SANTIAGO, MAURICIO A; STAMFORD, CT; AC OF INFORMATION TECH; (SO); Hi Hnr Roll; Hnr Roll; Otst Ac Ach Awd; Perf Att; St of Mnth; Lawyer; History Major; Yale; Harvard

SANTORO, DANA; AVON, CT; AVON HS; (FR); Hnr Roll; Nat Stu Ath Day Aw; St of Mnth; CARE; Comm Volntr; Peer Tut/Med; DARE; Emplmnt; Lib Aide; Photog; Scouts; Tchrs Aide; Lcrsse (J); Vllyball (J); Cl Off (J); Yrbk (P); Made the Northern Stars Lacrosse League; Journalism-Magazine Editor; Boston College; U of North Carolina At Chapel Hill

SAVOPOULOS, ABRAM; NORWALK, CT; NORWALK HS; (JR); F Lan Hn Soc; Hi Hnr Roll; Perf Att; Comm Volntr; Cmptr Clb; DARE; Greek Clb; Sccr (VJ); Wrstlg (VJ); Six Year Graduation Diploma in Greek; Greek Archdiocese New York Regents Exam Honors; Computer Installation/Repair, Telecommunications; Computer Science, Computer Engineering; Sacred Heart U, U of Connecticut; Fairfield U, Quinnipiac U

SAWYER, DIREES D; NEW HAVEN, CT; CONNECTICUT STATE SCHOLARS AC; (FR); Hnr Roll; St of Mnth; DARE; A & T College NC

SCANLON, TREVOR R; FAIRFIELD, CT; (JR); St of Mnth; WWAHSS; Yth Ldrshp Prog; Drma Clb; SADD; Tchrs Aide; SP/M/VS; Sch Ppr (R); Film Producer/Director/Writer; NYU-Tisch Film School

SCHELLENS, TORREY W; ESSEX, CT; VALLEY REG HS; (JR); Hi Hnr Roll; Peer Tut/Med; Scouts; Chr; SP/M/VS; Tennis (VJ); Cl Off (T); Madrigal Choir; Early Childhood Education; Psychology; UConn (U of Connecticut); U of Vermont

SCHENA, JOSEPH; FAIRFIELD, CT; FAIRFIELD WARDE HS; (SR); Hi Hnr Roll; Hnr Roll; Kwnis Aw; Nat Hon Sy; Pres Sch; Sci/Math Olympn; WWAHSS; Comm Volntr; Key Club; Mth Clb/Tm; MuAlphaTh; NYLC; Svce Clb; Vsity Clb; Golf (VJCL); Keystone Club Member; Business Administration; Accounting; Wake Forest U

SCHER, HADLEY; WEST REDDING, CT; WILTON HS; (JR); Hnr Roll; Otst Ac Ach Awd; WWAHSS; Aqrium Clb; Emplmnt; Key Club; Outdrs Clb; Sci Clb; Dnce; The Wilton Conservation Land Trust Award (05); Veterinary Science & Medicine; Zoology & Husbandry; Quinnipiac U-CT; Mount Ida College-Mass.

SCHLEIFER, HAILEY; FAIRFIELD, CT; FAIRFIELD LUDLOWE HS; (JR); Hnr Roll; Chrch Yth Grp; Chrldg (V L); Psychologist; Southern Methodist U; Clemson U

SCHMIDT, KYLE; HEBRON, CT; RHAM HS; (SR); Hi Hnr Roll; Hnr Roll; MVP; Nat Hon Sy; US Army Sch Ath Aw; WWAHSS; Comm Volntr; Peer Tut/Med; DECA; Emplmnt; Sccr (V CL); All-Conference Soccer Player; Major in Economics; U of Connecticut

SCHNEIDER, BENJAMIN A; TRUMBULL, CT; TRUMBULL HS; (JR); Pres Ac Ftns Aw; St of Mnth; Key Club; Outdrs Clb; Bnd; SP/M/VS; Lcrsse (VJ); Assistant Coach-Trumbull Youth Lacrosse; Marketing; Advertising/Graphic Design; Syracuse U; Marist College

SCOTT, EBONY J; NEW HAVEN, CT; CT SCHOLARS AC; (FR); Hi Hnr Roll; Hnr Roll; Nat Hon Sy; Otst Ac Ach Awd; Perf Att; St of Mnth; Peer Tut/Med; Chrch Yth Grp; Ch Chr; Adv Cncl (R); Cl Off (R); CR (R); Vice-Pres of the National Junior Honor Society; Peer Mediator; Business; Entrepreneurship; U of Connecticut; Howard U

SEBASTIAN, SAMANATHA; FAIRFIELD, CT; FAIRFIELD LUDLOWE HS; (SO); Hi Hnr Roll; WWAHSS; Key Club; Lcrsse (JC); Sccr; Track; Journalism; Broadcast Television; U of California Los Angeles; Columbia U

SELVACHANDRAN, ADARSHA; MILFORD, CT; JONATHAN LAW HS; (FR); Hi Hnr Roll; Nat Hon Sy; Otst Ac Ach Awd; St of Mnth; Hosp Aide; Peer Tut/Med; Bnd; Jzz Bnd; Mch Bnd; First Degree Black Belt in Shaolin Kempo; Diversity Club Member; Chemistry; Biology; New York U; U of California

SHAPIRO, HANNAH; TRUMBULL, CT; TRUMBULL HS; (JR); Ctznshp Aw; Hi Hnr Roll; Nat Hon Sy; Pres Ac Ftns Aw; WWAHSS; Comm Volntr; ArtClub; Chrch Yth Grp; Key Club; French Clb; Bnd; Jzz Bnd; Mch Bnd; Orch; Lcrsse (V); Sch Ppr (R); Clarinet Section Leader-Marching Band; Biology; Medicine; Stanford U; Columbia U

SHARMA, MONICA; EAST HARTFORD, CT; CONNECTICUT INT BACCALAUREATE AC; (JR); Hnr Roll; Comm Volntr; Hab For Humty Volntr; Hosp Aide; Dbte Team; Mod UN; Yrbk (E); Business / Business Management; Finance; Boston U; New York U

SHARON, A J; ENFIELD, CT; ENRICO FERMI HS; (JR); Comm Volntr; Spec Olymp Vol; DECA; Emplmnt; Scouts; 2nd Place Food Marketing Series At The State Leadership Conference 2005; Culinary Arts Major; Own a Restaurant; Johnson & Wales U; Connecticut Culinary Institute

SHAYER, JUSTIN; GALES FERRY, CT; ELLA GRASSO SE VOC TECH SCH; (FR); Hnr Roll; Comm Volntr; DARE; Fr of Library; Outdrs Clb; Scouts; Culinary; Johnson & Wales

SHEEHAN, JOHN; MADISON, CT; DANIEL HAND HS; (JR); Hnr Roll; Nat Hon Sy; Comm Volntr; DARE; Outdrs Clb; Ftball (V); Track (V); Safe Rider P/T Video Store Mgr; Interact Club; Film; Communications; U of California Los Angeles; U of Southern California

SHEEHAN, RACHEL L; GROTON, CT; ELLA GRASSO SE VOC TECH SCH; (JR); Hi Hnr Roll; Hnr Roll; Nat Hon Sy; Otst Ac Ach Awd; Peer Tut/Med; ArtClub; DARE; Chr; Ch Chr; Bskball (V C); Sccr (V C); Sch Ppr (R); National Honor Society-Vice President; Peer Mediation-Student Coordinator; Culinary Arts-Chef; Culinary Institute of America; Johnson & Wales U

SHETH, HETAL; GREENWICH, CT; GREENWICH HS; (JR); F Lan Hn Soc; Hi Hnr Roll; Nat Hon Sy; St of Mnth; Yth Ldrshp Prog; Comm Volntr; Hab For Humty Volntr; Hosp Aide; Svce Clb; Dnce; SP/M/VS; Yrbk (E); 3 Years of Bharatanatyam (Indian Classical Dance); Reading and Writing Gujarati; Medicine

SHETTY, PRIYANKA; MIDDLEBURY, CT; POMPERAUG REG HS; (FR); Mch Bnd; Tennis (V); Vllyball (J); Science-Biology / Medicine; Yale U; Brown U

SIDELINGER, AMANDA E; TORRINGTON, CT; OLIVER WOLCOTT VOC TECH SCH; (SO); Hi Hnr Roll; Hnr Roll; Otst Ac Ach Awd; Comm Volntr; Law Degree; New York U; U of Connecticut

SIMMONS, JENA' L; BRIDGEPORT, CT; BASSICK HS; (JR); Hnr Roll; DARE; Jr Ach; Ntl FFA; Chr; Ch Chr; Bskball (J); Cr Ctry (VJ); Nursing Degree / Health; Pre-Med; Duke U; Russell Sage College

SIMMS, NICOLE E; DARIEN, CT; DARIEN HS; (SR); Hi Hnr Roll; Hnr Roll; Nat Hon Sy; Pres Sch; WWAHSS; Yth Ldrshp Prog; Comm Volntr; Spec Olymp Vol; Emplmnt; Off Aide; Svce Clb; Fld Hky (VJCL); Lcrsse (J L); Track (VJ L); President-Teen Center; Student Life Committee; International Relations; Vanderbilt; NYU

SIMS, ANDREW M; FAIRFIELD, CT; FAIRFIELD WARDE HS; (SO); Hi Hnr Roll; Otst Ac Ach Awd; St of Mnth; Comm Volntr; Emplmnt; Key Club; Prom Com; Scouts; Tmpl Yth Grp; Chr; Class of 2001-Club/National Junior Honor Society; Soccer Referee; Architecture; Law/Sports Representation; U of Pennsylvania; George Washington U

SLATTERY, MATTHEW P; MILFORD, CT; JOSEPH A FORAN HS; (JR); Track (J); Certa Program; Key Club; Business/Accounting; U of CT; Bryant U.

SLAVINSKI, KATE; MERIDEN, CT; OH PLATT HS; (JR); Hi Hnr Roll; Nat Hon Sy; WWAHSS; Comm Volntr; Peer Tut/Med; Drma Clb; Key Club; Spanish Clb; Bnd; Jzz Bnd; Mch Bnd; SP/M/VS

SLIVA, JAMES; MONROE, CT; ST JOSEPH HS; (JR); WWAHSS; Comm Volntr; Chess; Sccr (V L); Vllyball (V CL); Business Administration; Accounting; Sacred Heart U; Rivier College

SMALDONE, COLLEEN; FAIRFIELD, CT; FAIRFIELD WARDE HS; (JR); Hi Hnr Roll; Hnr Roll; Nat Hon Sy; Spec Olymp Vol; Chrch Yth Grp; Key Club; P to P St Amb Prg; Bulletin Editor (Key Club); Communications/ Journalism; Albright College; Loyola College of Maryland

SMITH, ALANA K; NEW HAVEN, CT; WILBUR CROSS HS; (SR); Hnr Roll; Nat Hon Sy; Comm Volntr; Peer Tut/Med; Emplmnt; Bnd; Dnce; Jzz Bnd; SP/M/VS; Swmg (V); Tennis (V); Sch Ppr (R); Volunteering At the YMCA; Driving School; Pharmacy; U of Connecticut; Massachusetts College of Pharmacy & Health Services

SMITH, ARIELLE A; MILFORD, CT; JA FORAN HS; (FR); Hnr Roll; WWAHSS; Comm Volntr; Spec Olymp Vol; Chrch Yth Grp; Emplmnt; Key Club; Off Aide; Tchrs Aide; Bnd; Dnce; Mch Bnd; Orch; Yrbk (E); Mentor to 3rd Grade Student; Dance Teacher (Assistant); Medicine; Pediatrician; U of Connecticut; New York U

SMITH, HILARY; OLD GREENWICH, CT; GREENWICH HS; (JR); F Lan Hn Soc; Hi Hnr Roll; Comm Volntr; Photog; Prom Com; Fld Hky (J); Tennis (J); CR (R); Yrbk (E); Crew-Junior Varsity; Volunteered 200 Hours At YMCA; Liberal Arts; Amherst College; U of Virginia

SMITH, JOSHUA; NEW HAVEN, CT; JAMES HILLHOUSE HS; (JR); F Lan Hn Soc; Hnr Roll; Nat Hon Sy; Perf Att; WWAHSS; Comm Volntr; Chrch Yth Grp; Emplmnt; Tchrs Aide; Bnd; Ch Chr; Drl Tm; Mch Bnd; Mathematics Award Trig ++; Science Award-Chemistry 2nd Place

SMITH, VERONICA A; WINDSOR LOCKS, CT; WINDSOR LOCKS HS; (JR); Hi Hnr Roll; Nat Hon Sy; Otst Ac Ach Awd; WWAHSS; Yth Ldrshp Prog; Comm Volntr; Peer Tut/Med; Chrch Yth Grp; DARE; Emplmnt; FBLA; Prom Com; SADD; Tchrs Aide; Sftball (J); National Honor Society Member; Peer Facilitator; Architecture; Business; Roger Williams U; Yale U

SNIETKA, BENJAMIN; HEBRON, CT; RHAM HS; (SO); Hi Hnr Roll; Hnr Roll; Otst Ac Ach Awd; St of Mnth; WWAHSS; Chrch Yth Grp; DECA; Mth Clb/Tm; Golf (V); Business; Duke U; U Penn

SNOEK, LAURA; BROOKFIELD, CT; CHRISTIAN HERITAGE SCH; (SO); Hnr Roll; Perf Att; ArtClub; Art Show Awards / Studies / Plays; Math Competition / Piano & Violin; Neurologist; Animal Trainer

SO, KRISTINE; BROOKFIELD, CT; BROOKFIELD HS; (JR); F Lan Hn Soc; Hi Hnr Roll; Pres Sch; WWAHSS; Comm Volntr; Hab For Humty Volntr; Emplmnt; Scouts; Svce Clb; The National Society of High School Scholars; Pre-Med; Engineering; Columbia U

SOARES, JAY; PLYMOUTH, CT; OLIVER WOLCOTT VOC TECH SCH; (SO); Comm Volntr; DARE; Emplmnt; Mus Clb; Scouts; Bnd; SP/M/VS; Chrldg (V); Varsity Softball Manager

SOARES, JORDAN R; PLYMOUTH, CT; OLIVER WOLCOTT VOC TECH SCH; (SR); Hi Hnr Roll; MVP; Nat Hon Sy; Comm Volntr; Spec Olymp Vol; ArtClub; Drma Clb; P to P St Amb Prg; Prom Com; Sftball (V CL); Vllyball (V CL); Cl Off (P); National Honor Society-Vice Pres.; CIAC Most Scholar Athlete 2005; M.D.; Orthopedic Surgery; U of Rochester; UConn-U of CT

SOKOLSKI, CASEY; FAIRFIELD, CT; FAIRFIELD LUDLOWE HS; (FR); Hi Hnr Roll; Hnr Roll; Comm Volntr; Key Club; History; Astronomy; Columbia U; Boston U

SOLOMON, MATTHEW R; AVON, CT; AVON OLD FARMS SCH; (FR); Hnr Roll; Perf Att; Comm Volntr; Cmptr Clb; SADD; Tech Clb; Chr; Bskball (J L); Sccr (J L); Yrbk; Computer Information Systems; Management; Bentley College; Babson College

SONICK, BECKY; FAIRFIELD, CT; FAIRFIELD WARDE HS; (JR); F Lan Hn Soc; Hi Hnr Roll; Nat Hon Sy; Pres Ac Ftns Aw; St of Mnth; WWAHSS; Key Club; Dnce; Stu Cncl (R); Freshman Advisor; Key Club Co-President; Pre-Med; Dance; Goucher College, Skidmore College; Connecticut College, Union College

SORBO, RACHEL; EAST HAVEN, CT; WILBUR CROSS HS; (JR); F Lan Hn Soc; Hnr Roll; Nat Hon Sy; Otst Ac Ach Awd; Comm Volntr; Emplmnt; Jr Ach; Adv Cncl (R); Cl Off (R); Stu Cncl (S); CR (R); Yrbk (R); Psychology; Pre-Medical; Emory U; Spelman U

STANEK, PATRICK; SEYMOUR, CT; SEYMOUR HS; (JR); Ctznshp Aw; Hi Hnr Roll; Hnr Roll; Comm Volntr; FBLA; Spanish Clb; Skiing; Sccr (VJ); Stu Cncl (R); History; Criminal Justice; Siena College; Merrimack College

STEBBINS, HAYDEN B; FAIRFIELD, CT; FAIRFIELD LUDLOWE HS; (FR); Hi Hnr Roll; Comm Volntr; DARE; Key Club

STERN, BRADLEY; MILFORD, CT; JOSEPH A FORAN HS; (JR); Hnr Roll; Nat Hon Sy; WWAHSS; Comm Volntr; Key Club; Spanish Clb; Stu Cncl (R); Black Belt in Karate; International Relations

STEVENS, PATRICIA; FAIRFIELD, CT; FAIRFIELD LUDLOWE HS; (JR); Hnr Roll; WWAHSS; Comm Volntr; Chrch Yth Grp; Emplmnt; Key Club; Photog; Vsity Clb; Italian Clb; Orch; Ice Hky (VJ L); Ice Sktg; Yrbk; Art Education (Elementary)

SUBRAMANYAM, SHRUTHI; SOUTH GLASTONBURY, CT; GLASTONBURY HS; (SO); F Lan Hn Soc; Hi Hnr Roll; Comm Volntr; Hosp Aide; Key Club; Mod UN; Latin Clb; Orch; West Hartford Symphony Orchestra-2 years Complete; Teen Advisory Board At Welles Turner Library-5 yrs Complete; Biology; World History; Wesleyan U; Trinity College

SULLIVAN, RYAN K; COLCHESTER, CT; BACON AC; (SO); Hi Hnr Roll; Hnr Roll; Quill & Scroll; Sch Ppr (E); Journalism; Criminal Justice

SUNDERHAUF, ALLYSHA; MERIDEN, CT; ORVILLE H PLATT HS; (FR); Hnr Roll; Perf Att; Comm Volntr; DARE; Scouts; Outstanding Achievement in Art; Major in Medical (Pediatric Nurse)

SUNDERLAND, EDEN; GROTON, CT; FITCH MS; Hi Hnr Roll; Hnr Roll; Sci Fairs; St of Mnth; Comm Volntr; Chrch Yth Grp; DARE; Drma Clb; Chrldg; Business Management; Architecture; U of Maryland; U of Virginia

SUSSMANE, ALEXA; WESTPORT, CT; STAPLES HS; (FR); Hi Hnr Roll; Comm Volntr; Spec Olymp Vol; Earth Club, Amnesty International Radio DJ; Marine Biology; Northeastern U

SUSSMANE, NICOLE; WESTPORT, CT; STAPLES HS; (FR); Hi Hnr Roll; Sci Fairs; Amnsty Intl; Comm Volntr; Spec Olymp Vol; Earth Club, Amnesty International; Northeastern U

SWANSON III, DAVID R; WESTPORT, CT; CHRISTIAN HERITAGE SCH; (JR); Hi Hnr Roll; Nat Hon Sy; Sci Fairs; Yth Ldrshp Prog; Comm Volntr; Hab For Humty Volntr; Peer Tut/Med; Chrch Yth Grp; Emplmnt; Bnd; Jzz Bnd; Mch Bnd; SP/M/VS; Bskball (V); Cl Off (S); Private Instruction at the Jim Royle Drum Studio; Junior Leader in Boy's Brigade Program at Church; Law; Law Enforcement; Wheaton College; Yale U

SYPHER, BRITTNEY; DEEP RIVER, CT; VALLEY REG HS; (MS); Hi Hnr Roll; St of Mnth; Comm Volntr; Photog; Prom Com; Chr; Dnce; PPSqd (V); Track (J); Business Administration; Photography; Business Administration; Photography; U Conn; Eastern Connecticut State

SZYMASZEK, JULIE F; MERIDEN, CT; ORVILLE PLATT HS; (FR); DAR; Hi Hnr Roll; Hnr Roll; Comm Volntr; Key Club; French Clb; Bnd; Mch Bnd; Biology; Film Production; Massachusetts Institute of Technology; Emerson College

TAKACS, CHRISTOPHER T; FAIRFIELD, CT; FAIRFIELD LUDLOWE HS; (JR); Hnr Roll; Comm Volntr; Emplmnt; Prom Com; Bnd; Mch Bnd; Pep Bnd; Lcrsse (V); Coach Basketball for Middle Schoolers At Boys Club; Physical Therapy; Business; Fairfield U

TARASCIO, LINDSAY; WINDSOR LOCKS, CT; WINDSOR LOCKS HS; (JR); Hi Hnr Roll; Hnr Roll; Perf Att; Comm Volntr; Peer Tut/Med; Emplmnt; Chr; CR (R); Major in Secondary Education; Math; Central Connecticut State U; Eastern Connecticut State U

TAYLOR, JOSHUA; BRIDGEPORT, CT; BASSICK HS; (JR); Photog; Ch Chr; Photography; Arts; Music Production; Syracuse U; U of Connecticut

THOMAS, JADE; BRIDGEPORT, CT; BULLARD-HAVENS VOC TECH SCH; (SO); Hnr Roll; DARE; Wdwrkg Clb; Bnd; Cr Ctry (J); Track (J); Doctor; U of Connecticut; Georgia Tech

THOMAS, JESSIE; BLOOMFIELD, CT; AI PRINCE TECH; (FR); 4H Awd; Pres Ac Ftns Aw; St of Mnth; Yth Ldrshp Prog; Comm Volntr; Peer Tut/Med; Spec Olymp Vol; Chess; Cmptr Clb; Tech Clb; Bsball; Track; Computer Technology; Culinary Arts

THOMAS, SEAN; TERRYVILLE, CT; TERRYVILLE HS; (FR); Hi Hnr Roll; Hnr Roll; St of Mnth; Comm Volntr; Chr; Football-Pop Warner 2nd Runner Up League Championship; Certificate Appreciation-Am Legion; Juris Doctorate; Criminal Justice; Yale U; U of Connecticut

THOMPSON, CASSANDRA; COLCHESTER, CT; BACON AC; (SO); Hi Hnr Roll; Hnr Roll; St of Mnth; Comm Volntr; Chrch Yth Grp; DARE; Emplmnt; Mod UN; Prom Com; Chr; Ch Chr; Stg Cre; Sftball (JC); Vllyball (V); Public Relations-Choir Council; Athletic Trainer; English Teacher; North Park U; Northwestern U

THORPE, ANDREW; NEW HAVEN, CT; CONNECTICUT STATE SCHOLARS AC; (FR); Hnr Roll; Peer Tut/Med; Clr Grd; Ftball (J); CR (R); Auto Mechanics Technician; Southern Connecticut State U

THOTTAM, MICHAEL A; FAIRFIELD, CT; FAIRFIELD LUDLOWE HS; (FR); Hi Hnr Roll; Pres Sch; WWAHSS; Comm Volntr; Hab For Humty Volntr; Peer Tut/Med; Key Club; Chr; SP/M/VS; Sch Ppr (R)

TOBIN III, DONALD; BRIDGEPORT, CT; CENTRAL HS; (JR); Hi Hnr Roll; Hnr Roll; DECA; Pep Squd; Pep Bnd; Bsball (J); Graphic Designs; Entertainment Business; U of Connecticut; Miami U

TOLOSA, CYNTHIA E; BLOOMFIELD, CT; METROPOLITAN LEARNING CTR; (JR); Hi Hnr Roll; Pres Ac Ftns Aw; Drma Clb; Emplmnt; Mod UN; French Clb; Chr; SP/M/VS; Swg Chr; Member of Students for Social Justice; Architecture; Interior Design; Columbia U; New York U

TORRE, STEPHEN D; WESTPORT, CT; STAPLES HS; (JR); Hi Hnr Roll; Hnr Roll; Bnd; Pep Bnd; Bsball (V); NSMA USAA National Science Merit Award; Study Medicine; Colgate U; U of Connecticut

TORRES, YADIRA; NORWALK, CT; BRIEN MC MAHON HS; (JR); Hnr Roll; Web Page Designer; Pace U; U of South Florida

TOSCANO, ELISE; AVON, CT; AVON HS; (JR); Hi Hnr Roll; Nat Hon Sy; WWAHSS; Comm Volntr; AL Aux Girls; Emplmnt; Acpl Chr; Chr; SP/M/VS; Sccr (J); Sch Ppr (R); Participation In All-State Music Festival 2004 and 2005; Music; Mathematics; Vassar College; Colgate U

TRAPP, JAMES; FAIRFIELD, CT; FAIRFIELD WARDE HS; (JR); Hi Hnr Roll; Comm Volntr; Key Club; Bskball (VJ L); Cr Ctry (J); Tennis (J); American College of Musicians; French Hospitality Club; Business; Mathematics

TRAPP, JESSICA; FAIRFIELD, CT; FAIRFIELD WARDE HS; (FR); Hnr Roll; Comm Volntr; Key Club; Lcrsse (J); Sccr (J); Track (V L); American College of Musicians; Red Cross, School Store

TRERICE, ROBERT P; WATERBURY, CT; W F KAYNOR REG VOC TECH SCH; (SO); Hi Hnr Roll; Hnr Roll; Perf Att; St of Mnth; Voc Ind Clb Am; Officer-VICA Club-(Vocational Industrial Club of Amer); Engineering; Architecture; U of Connecticut

TRINIDAD, BRIAN R; VERNON ROCKVILLE, CT; ROCKVILLE HS; (SR)

TUCKER, KWAME H; HAMDEN, CT; HAMDEN HS; (FR); Hi Hnr Roll; Comm Volntr; Peer Tut/Med; DARE; Drma Clb; Lib Aide; Stg Cre

TYRA, KAMILA; PLANTSVILLE, CT; SOUTHINGTON HS; (JR); Hnr Roll; Otst Ac Ach Awd; St of Mnth; Comm Volntr; Emplmnt; Dnce; Family, Career and Community Leaders of America-Club; International Business; Pre-Medicine; U of Connecticut

UNG, RICKY; PAWCATUCK, CT; STONINGTON HS; (JR); Hnr Roll; St of Mnth; DARE; Cr Ctry (J); Chemical Engineering; Architectural Engineering; Fordham U; Virginia Commonwealth U

VALDEZ, VINSON M; WATERBURY, CT; W F KAYNOR; (JR); Hi Hnr Roll; Hnr Roll; MVP; Perf Att; St of Mnth; WWAHSS; Emplmnt; Mus Clb; Bnd; Bsball (V); Bskball (VJ); Mechanical Engineering; Law; U of Miami; U of Connecticut

VATSAL, EISHA; MILFORD, CT; JOSEPH A FORAN HS; (FR); Hnr Roll; Hosp Aide; Peer Tut/Med; Red Cr Aide; Drma Clb; Key Club; Latin Clb; Bnd; Mch Bnd; Pep Bnd; Swmg; Medicine; Surgeon; Yale U

VELEZ, GRISEL A; NEW HAVEN, CT; (FR); Home Maker and Companion; Pediatrician; Yale U

VETTER, BEN; NORWALK, CT; NORWALK HS; (FR); Hnr Roll; Otst Ac Ach Awd; Perf Att; Sci Fairs; Sci/Math Olympn; St of Mnth; Comm Volntr; Chrch Yth Grp; Emplmnt; Mus Clb; NYLC; Bnd; Jzz Bnd; Mch Bnd; SP/M/VS; Swmg (V); Music; Criminal Justice; Bowdoin College; Berklee School of Music

VIDA, ROBERT; BROOKFIELD, CT; IMMACULATE HS; (SO); Hi Hnr Roll; Hab For Humty Volntr; Chrch Yth Grp; Chemistry; Environmental Sciences; Massachusetts Institute of Technology

VIGNERON, KELLY; FAIRFIELD, CT; FAIRFIELD LUDLOWE HS; (JR); Hi Hnr Roll; Hnr Roll; Nat Mrt Fin; Yth Ldrshp Prog; Comm Volntr; Key Club; Svce Clb; Vsity Clb; Fld Hky (J); Lcrsse (V L); Yrbk (E); Nominated for National Honor Society; Business Major; James Madison U; U of Delaware

VINDIGNI, ALYSSA; STAMFORD, CT; STAMFORD HS; (SO); Hi Hnr Roll; Hnr Roll; MVP; Otst Ac Ach Awd; Perf Att; Pres Sch; St of Mnth; Yth Ldrshp Prog; Comm Volntr; Peer Tut/Med; Red Cr Aide; ArtClub; Chrch Yth Grp; DARE; Drma Clb; Scouts; Tchrs Aide; Tech Clb; Latin Clb; Bnd; Chr; SP/M/VS; Stg Cre; Cr Ctry (V); 2nd Place History Day County Competition; Scholarship with Sons of Italy; Vet; Psychology; Boston College; Princeton

VITELLO, MICHAEL T; CHESHIRE, CT; CHESHIRE HS; (JR); Hi Hnr Roll; Hnr Roll; WWAHSS; Yth Ldrshp Prog; Peer Tut/Med; Red Cr Aide; Chrch Yth Grp; Emplmnt; Ftball (V L); Track (V CL); National Society of High School Scholars; Military Career; United States Naval Academy; United States Air Force Academy

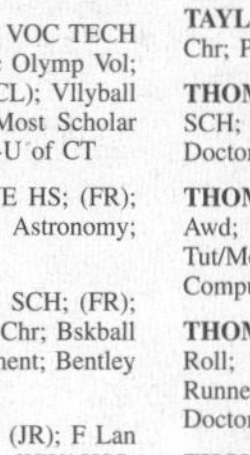

Thorpe, Andrew
Connecticut State Scholars AC
New Haven, CT

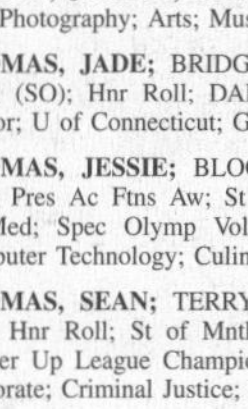

Thomas, Sean
Terryville HS
Terryville, CT

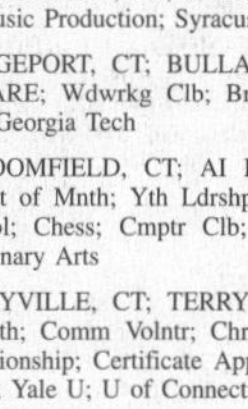

Soares, Jordan R
Oliver Wolcott Voc Tech Sch
Plymouth, CT

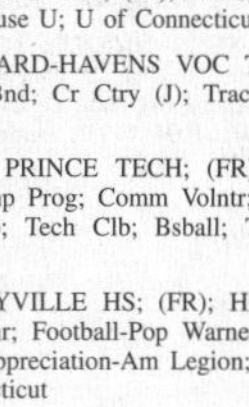

Taylor, Joshua
Bassick HS
Bridgeport, CT

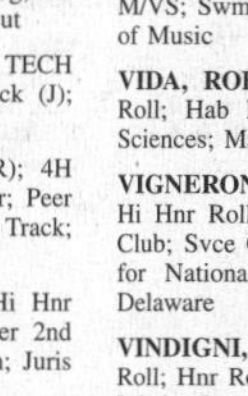

Tyra, Kamila
Southington HS
Plantsville, CT

VITHAYATHIL, PAUL J; BETHANY, CT; AMITY HS; (JR); F Lan Hn Soc; Hnr Roll; Peer Tut/Med; Dbte Team; JSA; Bnd; Jzz Bnd; Mch Bnd; Pep Bnd; Tennis (V CL); Sch Ppr (R); New England Open Doubles Tennis Champion; All State, All Housatonic Doubles Team; Biochemist; Biologist; Washington U Saint Louis; UC San Diego

VLACICH, AMY L; STRATFORD, CT; FRANK SCOTT BUNNELL HS; (JR); Hnr Roll; Otst Ac Ach Awd; Comm Volntr; Drma Clb; Emplmnt; Photog; SP/M/VS; Secretary of Bunnell S.T.A.G.E. (Drama Club); Anchor on the Bulldog Bulletin (School News Show), Ski/Snowboard Club; Drama/Theater; Education; Skidmore College; Emerson College

VO, ANHDAO; NEWINGTON, CT; CHESHIRE AC; (SR); Hnr Roll; WWAHSS; Yth Ldrshp Prog; Comm Volntr; Hab For Humty Volntr; Peer Tut/Med; Chrch Yth Grp; Emplmnt; Key Club; Prom Com; Tmpl Yth Grp; Tennis (JC); Vllyball (VJC); Yrbk (E, P); National Youth Leadership on Law; Robert R Brown Scholarship; Pre-Pharmacy; Pharmacy; Whittier College; Coastal Carolina U

VOONASIS, ELENA M; FAIRFIELD, CT; FAIRFIELD LUDLOWE HS; (FR); Ctznshp Aw; Hi Hnr Roll; Otst Ac Ach Awd; WWAHSS; Comm Volntr; Chrch Yth Grp; Dbte Team; Key Club; Debate Team

WALKER, ANTHONY; DERBY, CT; DERBY HS; (SO); Chrch Yth Grp; DARE; Emplmnt; Wdwrkg Clb; Spanish Clb; I Work At Derby Day Care After School; Psychology; New Haven U; Western State U

WALLACE, ALISHA M; WATERBURY, CT; W F KAYNOR REG VOC TECH SCH; (JR); Hi Hnr Roll; Hnr Roll; Nat Hon Sy; Comm Volntr; DARE; Drma Clb; Mus Clb; Scouts; Yrbk (R); Honor Roll; Fashion Design; Fashion Institute of Technology; St. John

WALSH, ALLYSON S; BETHEL, CT; BETHEL HS; (JR); DAR; Hi Hnr Roll; Nat Hon Sy; Sci Fairs; USMC Stu Ath Aw; WWAHSS; Yth Ldrshp Prog; Hosp Aide; Peer Tut/Med; Emplmnt; ROTC; Drl Tm; Fld Hky (V L); Track (J)

WANG, JASON; AVON, CT; AVON HS; (JR); Hi Hnr Roll; Hnr Roll; Amnsty Intl; Comm Volntr; Emplmnt; Orch; Cr Ctry (L); Sccr (J); Track (L); US Naval Sea Cadets Corp.; Music Festival Solo & Ensemble "2" Rating; Engineering / Automotive, Aeronautical, Architectural; Pre-Med; College of William & Mary; McGill U

WARGO, HEATHER; MONROE, CT; MASUK HS; (JR); Hi Hnr Roll; ArtClub; Journalism; Psychology; Salem State College; Ithaca College

WARZYSKI, AMANDA L; ENFIELD, CT; ENFIELD HS; (SR); Hi Hnr Roll; Nat Ldrshp Svc; Pres Ac Ftns Aw; Sci Fairs; WWAHSS; Yth Ldrshp Prog; Comm Volntr; Red Cr Aide; DARE; DECA; FBLA; Prom Com; Scouts; Dnce; Chrldg (J); Gmnstcs (V); Sccr (J); Vllyball (J); Cl Off (R); Most Spirited Award; Class Individual; Merchandising Product Development; Fashion Design; Fashion Institute of Design and Merchandising

WASHINGTON, SHANTA; BRIDGEPORT, CT; BULLARD-HAVENS VOC TECH SCH; (JR); Hnr Roll; Nat Hon Sy; WWAHSS; Comm Volntr; Chrch Yth Grp; Prom Com; Scouts; Track; Vllyball (VJ); Stu Cncl (P); CR (R); Business; Doctor; Spelman College; Harvard College

WATTS, SHANAY; NEW HAVEN, CT; CO-OP HS; (SR); Hnr Roll; WWAHSS; Comm Volntr; Prom Com; SP/M/VS; Bskball (VJ L); Track (VJ L); Vllyball (J L); CR (S); Marketing; Accounting; U of Connecticut

WEBEL, KAITLIN; REDDING, CT; JOEL BARLOW HS; (JR); Hi Hnr Roll; Nat Hon Sy; Otst Ac Ach Awd; Comm Volntr; Emplmnt; Svce Clb; Fld Hky (C); Yrbk (R); National Charity League; EMT Trainee; Nursing; Villanova U; Fairfield U

WEINER, ELIZABETH; EAST LYME, CT; EAST LYME HS; (JR); Hi Hnr Roll; Comm Volntr; Jzz Bnd; Mch Bnd; Orch; SP/M/VS; History; Psychology; Skidmore College; Wheaton College

WESCOTT, TYLER L; HARWINTON, CT; OLIVER WOLCOTT VOC TECH SCH; (FR); Hnr Roll; Pres Ac Ftns Aw; Sci Fairs; St of Mnth; Chess; Cmptr Clb; DARE; Emplmnt; Scouts; French Clb; Sccr (J); Vllyball (J); NRA Certificate; CPR Certificate; Culinary Arts; Culinary Institute of America

WEST, MALLORY; NEW BRITAIN, CT; MISS PORTERS SCH; (JR); Hi Hnr Roll; WWAHSS; Comm Volntr; Peer Tut/Med; Mth Clb/Tm; Fld Hky (V C); Swmg (V C); Tennis (V); Lit Mag (R)

WEZENSKI, NICOLE; KILLINGWORTH, CT; HADDAM-KILLINGWORTH HS; (FR); Hnr Roll; Comm Volntr; Pep Squd; Scouts; Bnd; Dnce; Chrldg (J); Nursing; UConn; Boston College

WHEELER, ALYSSA; OLD LYME, CT; LYME-OLD LYME HS; (JR); Hi Hnr Roll; Hnr Roll; Nat Hon Sy; Otst Ac Ach Awd; St of Mnth; WWAHSS; Comm Volntr; Emplmnt; Key Club; Mus Clb; Prom Com; Acpl Chr; Bnd; Chr; Dnce; Mar Art (V CL); Cl Off (V); Martial Arts (Outside School) Rank of Black Belt; Neuroscience / Biology; Brown U; New York U

WHITE, MICHELLE; NEW HAVEN, CT; JAMES HILLHOUSE HS; (FR); Ctznshp Aw; Hi Hnr Roll; MVP; Otst Ac Ach Awd; Perf Att; Sci Fairs; St of Mnth; Valdctrian; Comm Volntr; Peer Tut/Med; Spec Olymp Vol; Cmptr Clb; Emplmnt; Fr of Library; FBLA; Lib Aide; Off Aide; P to P St Amb Prg; Tchrs Aide; Stg Cre; Bskball (V); Track (J); Vllyball (J); Stu Cncl (R); CR (R); Yrbk (P)

WHITE, STEPHANIE; BRIDGEPORT, CT; WARREN HARDING HS; (SO); Hnr Roll; Perf Att; Sci Fairs; St of Mnth; Red Cr Aide; Chrch Yth Grp; DARE; Scouts; Chr; Dnce; Cl Off (R); Stu Cncl (T); Forensic Pathology; Criminal Justice; New York U; Adelphi U

WHITMORE, BRITTANY; BETHEL, CT; CANTERBURY SCH; (JR); Hi Hnr Roll; Yth Ldrshp Prog; Comm Volntr; Peer Tut/Med; Biology Clb; Chrch Yth Grp; Emplmnt; Key Club; Bskball (V L); Fld Hky (V L); Sftball (V CL); Sch Ppr (R); Ditullio Merit Scholarship; Montana Leadership Program; English; Communications; Boston College; Brown U

WIELGOSZ, KRISTYN; MERIDEN, CT; OH PLATT HS; Hi Hnr Roll; Hnr Roll; Nat Hon Sy; St of Mnth; Key Club; Bskball (J); Tennis (V); Wt Lftg; Adv Cncl (V); U of Connecticut; U of Rhode Island

WILLIAMS, KEYMANIE; HARTFORD, CT; (FR); Perf Att; Comm Volntr; Ftball (V); Masonry; Masters Degree's; U of Hartford

WILSON, DARYL; NEW HAVEN, CT; ELI WHITNEY TECH HS; (SO); Hnr Roll; Voc Ind Clb Am; Computer Science; Electronics; South Central Community College; New England Technical College

WILSON, NICK; SEYMOUR, CT; SEYMOUR HS; (JR); Hnr Roll; Comm Volntr; AL Aux Boys; Outdrs Clb; Vsity Clb; Spanish Clb; Bsball (V); Wt Lftg (V); International Business; Central Connecticut State U; Ithaca College

WOODWARD, AYATO; HARTFORD, CT; WEAVER HS; (FR); Hnr Roll; Otst Ac Ach Awd; WWAHSS; Peer Tut/Med; Chrch Yth Grp; Drma Clb; Mth Clb/Tm; Chr; Actor-Masters Degree; Lawyer-Masters Degree; Boston College; Morehouse College

WUHRER, MALLORY; MILFORD, CT; JONATHAN LAW HS; (FR); Hnr Roll; Pres Ac Ftns Aw; Yth Ldrshp Prog; Comm Volntr; Chrch Yth Grp; DARE; Key Club; NYLC; P to P St Amb Prg; Latin Clb; Cr Ctry (J); Sftball (J); Yrbk (P); Superintendent's Award; Nominated for "Homecoming Princess"; Marketing; Business; Teacher; Art; U-Conn; Duke

WYSKIEL, HEATHER M; MERIDEN, CT; PLATT HS; (JR); Hi Hnr Roll; Nat Hon Sy; Nat Mrt Semif; St of Mnth; Comm Volntr; Chrch Yth Grp; Drma Clb; Key Club; Outdrs Clb; Prom Com; French Clb; Ch Chr; SP/M/VS; Tennis (V); Vllyball (V CL); Stu Cncl (R); Platt Key Club President; District Convention Chair for New England District of Key Clubs; Elementary Education; Deaf Studies; Boston U; Pennsylvania State U

XAMA, AJANA; WATERBURY, CT; KENNEDY HS; (JR); F Lan Hn Soc; Hi Hnr Roll; Hnr Roll; WWAHSS; Peer Tut/Med; Key Club; Italian Clb; Tennis (J); Biochemistry; Architecture; U of Connecticut

YORANIDIS, NICOLE; STAMFORD, CT; STAMFORD HS; (SO); Hi Hnr Roll; Hnr Roll; MVP; Otst Ac Ach Awd; Perf Att; Comm Volntr; DARE; Jr Ach; Scouts; Chr; Sccr (V L); Track (V); All-FCIAC Honorable Mention 2003 & 2004; 2004 MVP; Business and Management; Finances; Villanova U; Brown U

YOSHIKAMI, ROBIN K; STAMFORD, CT; WESTHILL HS; (JR); Hnr Roll; Comm Volntr; Red Cr Aide; Chess; Cmptr Clb; Tech Clb; Bnd; Wrstlg (V); Stu Cncl (R); CR (R); Sch Ppr (R); AIT Winner of Talent Show/Rock Band; Vice President of Paintball Club; Military Officer Career; Historian; Liberal Arts; Virginia Military Institute; U of Connecticut

YOUNG, ALEX; FAIRFIELD, CT; FAIRFIELD WARDE HS; (FR); Hi Hnr Roll; Pres Sch; St of Mnth; FBLA; Key Club; Bsball; Law Degree; Math Major; Duke; Princeton

YOUNG, SHANIVA C; NEW HAVEN, CT; ELI WHITNEY TECH HS; (SO); Hnr Roll; Nat Stu Ath Day Aw; Perf Att; St of Mnth; Ch Chr; Dnce; Bachelor's Degree in Science; Temple U; Southern Connecticut State U

YOUNG, TODDCHELLE J; NEW HAVEN, CT; JAMES HILLHOUSE HS; (FR); Hi Hnr Roll; Hnr Roll; Nat Hon Sy; Otst Ac Ach Awd; Sci Fairs; St of Mnth; Valdctrian; Yth Ldrshp Prog; Comm Volntr; Chrch Yth Grp; Mth Clb/Tm; Schol Bwl; Scouts; Chr; Ch Chr; Bskball (J); Cl Off (P); Stu Cncl (R); Yrbk (P); Medical; PhD; Yale U; Duke U

YUN, HYEONG-SEON T; WILLIMANTIC, CT; MANSFIELD MS; MS; Comm Volntr; Mth Clb/Tm; Bnd; Mch Bnd; Pep Bnd; Bsball (J); Sccr (J); History Day; Math Counts; Medical Doctor; Biology; Harvard U; Princeton U

ZAPPI, CHRISTOPHER; WESTPORT, CT; STAPLES HS; (JR); All Am Sch; Hi Hnr Roll; Nat Hon Sy; Otst Ac Ach Awd; USAA; WWAHSS; Comm Volntr; Emplmnt; Mus Clb; Bnd; Jzz Bnd; Orch; SP/M/VS; Swmg (V L); Track (J); Stu Cncl (R); Sch Ppr (R); USAA National Science Merit Award; AAPT 2005 Outstanding Physics Student of the Year; Science; Business

ZAWACKI, MITCH; PLAINVILLE, CT; E C GOODWIN REG VOC TECH SCH; (JR); Hi Hnr Roll; Hnr Roll; Mus Clb; Bnd; Stu Cncl (R); CR (R); Play Guitar/6 String Bags; Go to Tunxis for College Credits; HVAC; Building Automation, Rock Star; STCC; UAI

ZAYAS, JOHANNAH; BRIDGEPORT, CT; HARDING HS; Hnr Roll; Comm Volntr; Volunteer Work At Bridgeport Hospital; Worked At Science Fair; Oral Hygienist; Dentist; Southern St U; Sacred Heart U

ZEMBKO, KAYLEE; BERLIN, CT; BERLIN HS; (JR); Hnr Roll; PP Ftbl; Belong to "Upbeat" Organization

ZIGLAR, JEREMY; WINDSOR, CT; METROPOLITAN LEARNING CTR; (SR); Hnr Roll; St of Mnth; Comm Volntr; Mus Clb; Jzz Bnd; Sch Ppr (E); Student Exchange to Poland; Participated in First Ever Iraqi Teleconference; International Business; Music; Pace U

ZRELAK, GORDON; SEYMOUR, CT; SEYMOUR HS; (SR); Hnr Roll; Nat Hon Sy; USMC Stu Ath Aw; WWAHSS; Peer Tut/Med; Chrch Yth Grp; Scouts; Cr Ctry (V CL); Track (V); RPI Medal Award Winner; CAS CIAC Scholar Athlete Award; Biochemistry

ZUBRILINA, VERONICA; OAKDALE, CT; MONTVILLE HS; (SO); Hi Hnr Roll; Nat Hon Sy; Nat Sci Aw; Otst Ac Ach Awd; Perf Att; Sci Fairs; Sci/Math Olympn; WWAHSS; Yth Ldrshp Prog; Comm Volntr; Peer Tut/Med; Biology Clb; Chrch Yth Grp; Emplmnt; Mus Clb; Sci Clb; German Clb; Chr; Dnce; Royal Swedish Family Water Contest Award; Distinguished Participant of Country Civics Contest; Psychology; Biology; Connecticut College; Central Connecticut State U

ZUCHELLI, DAN; STAMFORD, CT; STAMFORD HS; (SO); Hnr Roll; WWAHSS; Hosp Aide; Dbte Team; Latin Clb; Cr Ctry (V); Lcrsse (C); Cl Off (T); Pre-Med; Harvard; Yale

Ziglar, Jeremy — Metropolitan Learning Ctr — Windsor, CT
Yun, Hyeong-Seon T — Mansfield MS — Willimantic, CT
Whitmore, Brittany — Canterbury Sch — Bethel, CT
Wezenski, Nicole — Haddam-Killingworth HS — Killingworth, CT
Vithayathil, Paul J — Amity HS — Bethany, CT
Wescott, Tyler L — Oliver Wolcott Voc Tech Sch — Harwinton, CT
Woodward, Ayato — Weaver HS — Hartford, CT
Zayas, Johannah — Harding HS — Bridgeport, CT
Zubrilina, Veronica — Montville HS — Oakdale, CT

Delaware

ABBOTT, VERONICA D; NEWARK, DE; CAB CALLOWAY SCH OF ARTS; (SO); Hi Hnr Roll; Hnr Roll; Nat Hon Sy; Pres Ac Ftns Aw; St of Mnth; Drma Clb; Off Aide; Tchrs Aide; Chr; Dnce; SP/M/VS; CR (R); Member - Ballet Elite of Delaware Ballet Co; Soloist - Elite; Physical Therapy; Dance; Rutgers U; U of Delaware

ADEYANJU, ELIZABETH; NEW CASTLE, DE; WILLIAM PENN HS; (JR); Hnr Roll; St of Mnth; WWAHSS; BPA; Stu Cncl (R); Yrbk (E); Nursing-R.N.; Montclair State U; Temple U

AHMED, SARISH S; NEWARK, DE; ALEXIS I DUPONT HS; (SR); Ctznshp Aw; Hi Hnr Roll; Hnr Roll; Nat Hon Sy; Otst Ac Ach Awd; Sci/Math Olympn; Valdctrian; WWAHSS; Yth Ldrshp Prog; Comm Volntr; Peer Tut/Med; Chrch Yth Grp; HO'Br Yth Ldrshp; Key Club; Mth Clb/Tm; Prom Com; Sci Clb; Chr; Cl Off (P, V, S); Stu Cncl (R); AAUW Award for Excellence in Science & Math; Governor's School of Excellence; Pediatrician / Doctor; Biology; U of Delaware

AKHIMIEN, SARAH-JOY; BEAR, DE; CHRISTIANA HS; (FR); Hi Hnr Roll; WWAHSS; Comm Volntr; Chrch Yth Grp; Cmptr Clb; DARE; P to P St Amb Prg; Spanish Clb; Orch; Swmg (J); Vllyball (J); Vice President of School Volunteer Club; Biology Major; Medical Doctor / Surgeon; Princeton U; New York U

ALLEN, KEVIN L; NEWARK, DE; PAUL HODGSON VOC TECH HS; (SO); Hnr Roll; St of Mnth; Chrch Yth Grp; Culinary Arts; Food Catering; U of Delaware; Johnson & Wales U

ALPHIN, MATTHEW J; NEWARK, DE; ST MARK'S HS; (SR); Hi Hnr Roll; Hnr Roll; Sci/Math Olympn; WWAHSS; Hab For Humty Volntr; Drma Clb; Key Club; Invited to National Youth Leadership Conference; Mechanical Engineering; Psychology; U of Delaware, Newark

ANTALIK, CINDY M; NEWARK, DE; CHRISTIANA HS; (JR); F Lan Hn Soc; Hi Hnr Roll; Nat Hon Sy; Perf Att; St of Mnth; Comm Volntr; Hab For Humty Volntr; Chrch Yth Grp; Drma Clb; Emplmnt; Mus Clb; Off Aide; Prom Com; Tchrs Aide; Chr; Dnce; SP/M/VS; Cl Off (V); Stu Cncl (R); CR (R); Yrbk (E); Psychology; Education; U of Delaware; Yale U

ASHABI, MOHAMMAD; NEWARK, DE; CHRISTIAN HS; (SO); Otst Ac Ach Awd; Perf Att; Computer Programming / Bachelor's Degree; U of Delaware

AUCK, KARA; BEAR, DE; MIDDLETOWN HS; (JR); Hi Hnr Roll; Hnr Roll; Comm Volntr; Emplmnt; Prom Com; Tchrs Aide; Chr; SP/M/VS; Chrldg (V L); Won 1st Prize on School Related Events; Putting Myself Out There and Giving 100%; Own My Own Business As a Wedding Planner; Hotel and Restaurant Management; U of Delaware

AVILES, CHELSEA B; GREENWOOD, DE; WOODBRIDGE SR HS; (FR); Hi Hnr Roll; Hnr Roll; Pres Sch; St of Mnth; DARE; Ntl FFA; Scouts; Sftball (VJ); U of Miami; U of Delaware

AYALASOMAYAJULA, SUDHEE; NEWARK, DE; CHRISTIANA HS; (JR); Hnr Roll; Nat Hon Sy; Perf Att; WWAHSS; DECA; Tchrs Aide; Sccr (J); Stu Cncl (V); Computer Science; Computer Programming; U of Delaware; New York Institute of Technology

BAKER, JILL; SEAFORD, DE; NORTH DORCHESTER HS; (JR); Hi Hnr Roll; MVP; Nat Hon Sy; St of Mnth; WWAHSS; Emplmnt; Key Club; Prom Com; Bnd; Chr; Mch Bnd; Sccr (V); Cl Off (T); Elementary Education

BAKER, MELISSA; GREENWOOD, DE; WOODBRIDGE SR HS; (FR); Hi Hnr Roll; Otst Ac Ach Awd; Perf Att; St of Mnth; 4-H; Chrch Yth Grp; Photog; ROTC; Bnd; Hsbk Rdg (V); Sccr (V); Marine Corps Junior Reserve Officers Training Corps (MCJROTC); Criminal Justice; U of Delaware; U of Maryland

BARINEAU, MARK; HOCKESSIN, DE; CHARTER SCH OF WILMINGTON; (JR); Hi Hnr Roll; Jr Eng Tech; Nat Hon Sy; Nat Mrt LOC; Sci Fairs; Sci/Math Olympn; WWAHSS; Yth Ldrshp Prog; Comm Volntr; AL Aux Boys; Emplmnt; Key Club; Mth Clb/Tm; Quiz Bowl; Schol Bwl; Sci Clb; Bskball (J); Sccr (V); Track (V); CR (R); Lit Mag (R); Science Olympiad National Medalist; First Robotics Competition; Mechanical Engineer

BARLOW WARREN, WILLIS; FELTON, DE; LAKE FOREST HS; (FR); Hnr Roll; Chrch Yth Grp; DARE; Bskball (J); Ftball (J); Track (V); Doctor, MD; Boston College; Syracuse College

BAZZOLI, TYLER C; NEWARK, DE; ST MARK'S HS; (JR); Hi Hnr Roll; Perf Att; Sci/Math Olympn; WWAHSS; Yth Ldrshp Prog; Hab For Humty Volntr; Peer Tut/Med; Chrch Yth Grp; Emplmnt; Key Club; Mth Clb/Tm; Off Aide; Tchrs Aide; Bsball (VJ); Lit Mag (E); Sch Ppr (R); Reporter for the News Journal "Crossroads"; Member of the Peer Counseling Club; Medicine; Engineering; Columbia School of General Studies; Duke

BECHARD, MICHAEL; NEWARK, DE; CAB CALLOWAY SCH OF ARTS; (SO); Hi Hnr Roll; Hnr Roll; Perf Att; Sci/Math Olympn; WWAHSS; Mth Clb/Tm; Photog; Lcrsse (V); Cab Calloway Spirit Award; Biomedical Engineering; Columbia U; U of Delaware

BENNETT, JESSICA L; NEWARK, DE; HOWARD HS OF TECH; (SR); Hnr Roll; Chrch Yth Grp; Emplmnt; Voc Ind Clb Am; Ms. Engine Tech; Best Vision Statement; Certified Nursing Assistant; Registered Nurse; Delaware Technical Community College; Wilmington College

BINDER MACLEOD, RINA; NEWARK, DE; CHARTER SCH OF WILMINGTON; (SO); Hi Hnr Roll; WWAHSS; Comm Volntr; Chrch Yth Grp; Emplmnt; Key Club; Scouts; Svce Clb; Bnd; Lcrsse (V); Swmg (V); Girl Scouts - Outward Bound in Costa Rica; Peaceworks Volunteer in Belize; Communications; Economics; Wellesley College; University of Delaware

BINETTI, JON; WILMINGTON, DE; WILMINGTON FRIENDS SCH; (SO); Comm Volntr; Emplmnt; Chr; Bsball (V); Bskball (J); Sccr (V); Sch Ppr (R); All Conference Soccer; Distinguished School Award; Engineering; U of Virginia; Bucknell

BISSON, TRACY; BRIDGEVILLE, DE; WOODBRIDGE SR HS; (JR); Hi Hnr Roll; Hnr Roll; Nat Hon Sy; BPA; Drma Clb; Bnd; Chr; Clr Grd; SP/M/VS; Color Guard Captain; Tri-M music Honor Society; Music Education; Music Theatre; Catholic U of America

BLANCO, MELANIE C; MIDDLETOWN, DE; MIDDLETOWN HS; (JR); Ctznshp Aw; Hi Hnr Roll; Hnr Roll; Pres Ac Ftns Aw; St of Mnth; Comm Volntr; Hosp Aide; Peer Tut/Med; Chrch Yth Grp; Drma Clb; Lib Aide; Mus Clb; Prom Com; SADD; Tchrs Aide; Bnd; Chr; Mch Bnd; SP/M/VS; Cr Ctry (V L); Track (V L); CR (R); Indoor Track; Tri-M Music Honor Society; Nursing / RN; Nursing / Pediatrics; West Virginia U; U of Delaware

BODINE, TIFFANY L; CLAYTON, DE; POLYTECH HS; (SO); Hnr Roll; St of Mnth; Comm Volntr; Emplmnt; Community Service for Disabled Children / Read to Day Care Children; Community Service at Opera House; Massage Therapist; Chiropractor; Del Tech

BOLESLAWSKI, MELISSA; NEWARK, DE; HODGSON VO-TECH HS; (JR); Hi Hnr Roll; Hnr Roll; St of Mnth; All-Star Cheerleading Team; Servsafe Certified; Nutritionist; Personal Trainer; U of Delaware; Del Tech

BOLTON, PERRY; NEWARK, DE; CHRISTIANA HS; (JR); Hi Hnr Roll; Hnr Roll; Nat Hon Sy; Pres Sch; WWAHSS; Comm Volntr; Track (V L); Yrbk (R); Business Administration; Finance; New York U; U of Delaware

BONSALL, AMBER L; NEWARK, DE; ST MARK'S HS; (SR); Hnr Roll; Nat Hon Sy; Chess; Key Club; Stg Cre; Fld Hky; Yrbk (R); National Honor Society; Psychology; U of Delaware, Newark

BOSTON, ISATU; NEWARK, DE; HODGSON VO-TECH HS; (FR); Hnr Roll; Perf Att; Off Aide; Michael C. Ferguson Scholarship; Architecture; Business Management; New York U; Yale U

BOYD, TERESA; WILMINGTON, DE; MC KEAN HS; (JR); Hnr Roll; Chr; Bskball (L); Basketball Manager; Upward Bound Math / Science; Elementary Education; Early Childhood Education; Delaware State U; Wilmington College

BRADLEY, ARIEL R; LEWES, DE; CAPE HENLOPEN HS; (FR); Hnr Roll; Sci Fairs; WWAHSS; Comm Volntr; ArtClub; Chess; Key Club; 1st Place in Science Fair; President's Education Award; Zoology; Veterinary Medicine; U of Pennsylvania

BRALEY, HOPE; WILMINGTON, DE; CONCORDVILLE PREP SCH; (FR); Hi Hnr Roll; Hnr Roll; Perf Att; Comm Volntr; Chrch Yth Grp; Lib Aide; Tchrs Aide; Ch Chr; Dnce; SP/M/VS; Adv Cncl (R); Cl Off (R); Stu Cncl (R); CR (R); Yrbk (E, P); Physical Therapy / Doctorate; Child Development; U of Sciences of Philadelphia; U of Delaware

BRALEY, JOHN B; WILMINGTON, DE; CONCORDVILLE PREP SCH; (SO); Hi Hnr Roll; Hnr Roll; Sci Fairs; Comm Volntr; Chrch Yth Grp; Lib Aide; Quiz Bowl; SP/M/VS; Stg Cre; Bskball (J); Adv Cncl (P); Stu Cncl (P); CR (P); Sch Ppr (E); Yrbk (E); President's Award for Educational Excellence; Architectural Engineering; Drexel U

BURNS, LAUREN; NEWARK, DE; ST MARK'S HS; (SR); Ctznshp Aw; Hnr Roll; Perf Att; Pres Ac Ftns Aw; St of Mnth; Comm Volntr; Hab For Humty Volntr; Drma Clb; Emplmnt; Key Club; Photog; SP/M/VS; Vllyball (J L); Early Education; U of Delaware

CAMARA, BRITNI E; BEAR, DE; MIDDLETOWN HS; (FR); Hnr Roll; Perf Att; Comm Volntr; Chrch Yth Grp; Lib Aide; Off Aide; Tchrs Aide; Chrldg (V); Vllyball (C); CR; Lit Mag; Yrbk (P); Most Improved Student in Science - 8th Grade; Character, Attitude, Vision and Success Award - Jan 2005; High School Education / Teaching; Web Design; U of Delaware; Pennsylvania State U

CANADY, CHRISSY; NEWARK, DE; CHRISTIANA HS; (FR); Ctznshp Aw; Hi Hnr Roll; Hnr Roll; Nat Hon Sy; Comm Volntr; Chrch Yth Grp; ROTC; Scouts; German Clb; Drl Tm; NSI Drill Team Commander / JROTC Class; Excel 8th Grade / Shakespeare Course / Study Buddy - Leader; Philosophy / Psychology; World Religions; U of Delaware

CANNAVO, TANNER D; HOUSTON, DE; LAKE FOREST HS; (FR); Hi Hnr Roll; Hnr Roll; Emplmnt; Bsball (J); Ftball (V L); Wrstlg (V L)

CARINO, AMBER N; FREDERICA, DE; LAKE FOREST HS; (JR); Hi Hnr Roll; Hnr Roll; Nat Hon Sy; Comm Volntr; Chrch Yth Grp; Emplmnt; Scouts; Tchrs Aide; Medical; Computer Programming; Delaware Technical; Wesley College

CARNCROSS, CHAD; WILMINGTON, DE; CONCORD HS; (JR); Hi Hnr Roll; Perf Att; WWAHSS; Comm Volntr; Tennis (J); Leader Corps; Pre-Law; Psychology; U of Delaware; Villanova U

CARTER, SHYMERE D; SMYRNA, DE; SMYRNA HS; (JR); Hnr Roll; Chr; Dnce; Business Major; Medical Major; Delaware State U; Morgan State U

CARVAJAL, ELDER; GREENWOOD, DE; WOODBRIDGE SR HS; (FR); Hnr Roll; St of Mnth; Comm Volntr; Chrch Yth Grp; Ntl FFA; Swg Chr; Sccr (V); CR (S, T); Yrbk (R); Student of the Month; Nation Physical Fitness Award; Bachelor's Degrees; Master's Degree; Delaware State U

CHARLOT, KATHLEEN; DOVER, DE; DOVER HS; (SO); Hnr Roll; Nat Hon Sy; Spanish Clb; Vllyball (J); Dover High History Club; Delaware State U FAME Program; Broadcast Journalism; Psychology; Florida State U; Temple U

CHAU, ALEX; WILMINGTON, DE; BRANDYWINE HS; (FR); Hi Hnr Roll; Perf Att; St of Mnth; Mth Clb/Tm; Tech Clb; Bnd; Jzz Bnd; Crew - JV; Mock Trial Team / All-State Band; Brown U; Harvard U

CHINMAYA, NIKHIL; WILMINGTON, DE; BRANDYWINE HS; (SO); Hnr Roll; Perf Att; Yth Ldrshp Prog; Amnsty Intl; Comm Volntr; Hosp Aide; Chess; Emplmnt; Mth Clb/Tm; NYLC; SP/M/VS; Stg Cre; Swmg (J); Tennis (V); Founder of Badminton Club; Medicine; Bioengineering; Johns Hopkins U; Vanderbilt U

CLARK, HANNAH R; MILLSBORO, DE; INDIAN RIVER HS; (SO); Hi Hnr Roll; Mth Clb/Tm; Bnd; Dnce; Mch Bnd; Orch; Odyssey of the Mind-3 years, State Champs 2004; Competitive Dance Troupe; Education; Fashion, Fashion Merchandising; Florida State U; U of Delaware

CLOUTIER, KAYLA N; NEWARK, DE; GLASGOW HS; (SO); F Lan Hn Soc; Hi Hnr Roll; Hnr Roll; MVP; Perf Att; Chrch Yth Grp; Bskball (J); Fld Hky (V L); Sccr (V L); Swmg (V L); Cl Off (S); MVP for Field Hockey; Coach's Award for Field Hockey; Engineer; Teacher/Lawyer; U of Delaware

COLES, CAROLYN; WILMINGTON, DE; CONCORD HS; (JR); Ctznshp Aw; Fut Prb Slvr; Hnr Roll; Nat Ldrshp Svc; Perf Att; Sci Fairs; Sci/Math Olympn; Yth Ldrshp Prog; Comm Volntr; Peer Tut/Med; Chrch Yth Grp; Emplmnt; Lib Aide; Off Aide; Pep Squd; Prom Com; Scouts; Tchrs Aide; Chr; Dnce; Drl Tm; PPSqd (V C); Scr Kpr (V); Sftball (J); Stu Cncl (R); CR (R); Yrbk (E); FAME - Forum to Advance Minorities in Engineering; Xinos - The National Sorority of Phi Delta Kapp; Mechanical Engineer / Foreign Language; Psychology; Georgia Institute of Technology; Morgan State U

COLLISON, CHELSEA; BRIDGEVILLE, DE; WOODBRIDGE SR HS; (FR); Duke TS; Hi Hnr Roll; MVP; Perf Att; USAA; WWAHSS; Comm Volntr; Key Club; Lib Aide; Vsity Clb; Spanish Clb; Bnd; Mch Bnd; Fld Hky (V); Sccr (V); Track (V C); Cl Off (P); Honorable Mention All Conference-Soccer; Space Camp-NASA; Architecture; Engineering

Camara, Britni E
Middletown HS
Bear, DE

Binetti, Jon
Wilmington Friends Sch
Wilmington, DE

Blanco, Melanie C
Middletown HS
Middletown, DE

CONNELLY, ERIN M; WILMINGTON, DE; ST MARK'S HS; (JR); Hnr Roll; Otst Ac Ach Awd; WWAHSS; Comm Volntr; Chrch Yth Grp; Emplmnt; Key Club; Svce Clb; Bskball (L); Sftball (L); Track (V L); Who's Who Among American High School Students; Achievement Award in Spanish; Criminal Justice; U of Hartford; Boston U

COTTINGHAM, STEPHANIE M; WILMINGTON, DE; CAB CALLOWAY SCH OF ARTS; (SO); Hnr Roll; Perf Att; St of Mnth; ArtClub; DARE; Drma Clb; Bnd; Chr; Ch Chr; Dnce; Bskball; Stu Cncl (S); Sch Ppr (R); Communications; U of Delaware; Morgan State U

COUGHLAN, BRENDAN; WILMINGTON, DE; CAB CALLOWAY SCH OF ARTS; (SO); Hi Hnr Roll; Hnr Roll; Perf Att; Sci/Math Olympn; Comm Volntr; DARE; Mth Clb/Tm; Sci Clb; Chr; Dnce; SP/M/VS; Swmg (V); Cl Off (P, T); Law; History; Harvard U; Boston U

COVERT, MEGAN; WILMINGTON, DE; CONCORD HS; (JR); F Lan Hn Soc; Hi Hnr Roll; Hnr Roll; Nat Mrt LOC; Perf Att; Comm Volntr; BPA; Emplmnt; Prom Com; Sci Clb; French Clb; Chrldg (V L); Fld Hky (V L); Sftball (V L); Cl Off (R); French National Honors Society Secretary; Business Professionals of America Secretary; Physical Therapy Major; Master's Degree; West Chester U; College of William and Mary

COX, REBECCA; BEAR, DE; MIDDLETOWN HS; (SR); 4H Awd; All Am Sch; Hi Hnr Roll; Hnr Roll; Nat Hon Sy; Comm Volntr; 4-H; Emplmnt; Ntl FFA; Tchrs Aide; Track; Vllyball (J); CR (R); Travel Club; Psychology; Physical Therapy; U of Delaware

CRAWFORD, AMANDA; NEWARK, DE; ST MARKS HS; (FR); Hi Hnr Roll; Pres Sch; Salutrn; DARE; Drma Clb; Key Club; Ntl Beta Clb; Svce Clb; SP/M/VS; Graduate of John Robert Powers Finishing School; Enrolled in Trinity College of Music Program, Through Towson U; Horseback Riding

CROPPER, TARA L; NEW CASTLE, DE; CAB CALLOWAY SCH OF ARTS; (SO); Hi Hnr Roll; Hnr Roll; WWAHSS; Chrch Yth Grp; NYLC; Ch Chr; Stg Cre; Hsbk Rdg; Author / Fiction Writer

CROSBY, JESSICA L; NEWARK, DE; ST MARK'S HS; (FR); Hnr Roll; WWAHSS; Comm Volntr; Key Club; Sftball (J); Nursing; U of Delaware

CRUMP, ASHLEY S; DOVER, DE; DOVER HS; (SR); Gov Hnr Prg; Hi Hnr Roll; Nat Hon Sy; Nat Mrt Fin; Nat Sci Aw; Comm Volntr; HO'Br Yth Ldrshp; Jr Ach; Off Aide; Prom Com; Dnce; Adv Cncl (R); National Achievement Finalist; AP Scholar; Pre-Medicine; Biology; U of Pennsylvania; Howard U

CRUMP, DEBORAH; FREDERICA, DE; LAKE FOREST HS; (FR); Hnr Roll; Peer Tut/Med; Mth Clb/Tm

CURRIE, AMANDA; LINCOLN, DE; MILFORD HS; (JR); Hi Hnr Roll; Nat Hon Sy; Comm Volntr; Key Club; Prom Com; French Clb; Bnd; Mch Bnd; Stg Cre; Fld Hky (VJ); Sccr (J); Track (VJ L); Odyssey of the Mind-A Problem Solving Competition; Lead America 2005; Bio-Chemistry-BS, PhD; U of Delaware; Elon U

DALECKI, MARISSA; WILMINGTON, DE; CAB CALLOWAY SCH OF ARTS; (SO); Hi Hnr Roll; Hnr Roll; Nat Ldrshp Svc; Otst Ac Ach Awd; Perf Att; Yth Ldrshp Prog; Comm Volntr; Hab For Humty Volntr; Peer Tut/Med; Jr Ach; Photog; French Clb; SP/M/VS; Stg Cre; Chrldg (L); Track (L); Academic Honors in All Honor Classes; Volunteer at Library Every Summer; Black & White Photography; Photography; College of the Atlantic; U of Delaware

DANIELS, RENICIA; LINCOLN, DE; CAPE HENLOPEN HS; (JR); Hnr Roll; WWAHSS; Comm Volntr; Hab For Humty Volntr; Chrch Yth Grp; DARE; Drma Clb; Emplmnt; FCCLA; FTA; Key Club; Prom Com; Ch Chr; Dnce; SP/M/VS; Bskball (J); Chrldg (J); Cl Off (V); Stu Cncl (P, V); Started a New Club for Cape; Lawyer / Domestic Violence; Doctorate; Clark Atlanta U; Savannah College

DAVIS, SHANICE; NEWARK, DE; CHRISTIANA HS; (JR); Hnr Roll; Comm Volntr; Emplmnt; Off Aide; Ch Chr; Dnce; Nursing; Performing Arts; Baltimore Community College

DEAN, CARLY; WILMINGTON, DE; CONCORD HS; (JR); Hnr Roll; Perf Att; Sci Fairs; Comm Volntr; BPA; Chrch Yth Grp; DARE; Emplmnt; Photog; Chrldg (J); Dvng (J); Fld Hky (V); Sccr (J); CR (R); Lit Mag (E); Leader Corp; Business Professionals-Senator; Communications; Journalism; U of Delaware; Villanova U

DEL COLLO, ALEXANDRA M; HOCKESSIN, DE; ST MARK'S HS; (SO); Hi Hnr Roll; Hnr Roll; MVP; Perf Att; Comm Volntr; DARE; Key Club; Chr; Sftball (J); Swmg (J); National Junior Honor Society; Medical Degree; Business Degree; Virginia Tech; Penn State

DICKERSON, KIRSTEN C; DOVER, DE; DOVER HS; (SR); Hnr Roll; Comm Volntr; Spec Olymp Vol; DECA; Emplmnt; Lib Aide; ROTC; Spanish Clb; Clr Grd; Drl Tm; Vllyball (V L); ROTC - Varsity Letter / Community Service Officer; Athletic Scholar Award; Nursing / Pediatrician; Norfolk State U

DIXON, BROOKE; MIDDLETOWN, DE; MIDDLETOWN HS; (SO); Ctznshp Aw; Hi Hnr Roll; Hnr Roll; Emplmnt; Medicine/Medical; Journalism; U of Delaware; Temple U

DOMBROSKI, JUSTINE; WILMINGTON, DE; ST MARK'S HS; (FR); Hnr Roll; Sci/Math Olympn; Comm Volntr; Chrch Yth Grp; Key Club; Mth Clb/Tm; Track (V); Stu Cncl (R); Sch Ppr (R); Private Piano Lessons Since Jan 1998; Psychology; Business Person; U of Delaware; St Joe's College

DORMAN, MYTIA T; BRIDGEVILLE, DE; WOODBRIDGE SR HS; (JR); Hnr Roll; Spec Olymp Vol; ArtClub; DARE; Bnd; Clr Grd; Drl Tm; Flg Crps; Bskball (V); Physician; College Professor of Science; Hampton U; Delaware State U

DOWNES, MARQUES R; NEW CASTLE, DE; ST ELIZABETH HS; (JR); Hnr Roll; Perf Att; WWAHSS; Hab For Humty Volntr; Chrch Yth Grp; Engineering; U of Delaware; Drexel U

EUM, SO Y; WILMINGTON, DE; ST MARK'S HS; (JR); Hi Hnr Roll; Hnr Roll; WWAHSS; Comm Volntr; Red Cr Aide; Chrch Yth Grp; Key Club; Mth Clb/Tm; Mod UN; Tennis (VJ); CR; Competed & Participated in Red Cross's Youth Disaster Preparedness; Dentistry; Business

FORAKER, JACQUELINE; FELTON, DE; LAKE FOREST HS; (SO); Hi Hnr Roll; Hnr Roll; Veterinary; Animal Classes; U of Delaware, Dover

FOX, STEPHANIE; WILMINGTON, DE; ST MARK'S HS; (FR); Hnr Roll; Nat Hon Sy; Perf Att; St of Mnth; Chrch Yth Grp; Emplmnt; Key Club; Chr; Student of the Month; National Junior Honor Society; Scientist; Teacher; The U of Delaware

GAFFIGAN, HEATHER M; MIDDLETOWN, DE; HODGSON VO-TECH HS; (SR); Hi Hnr Roll; Nat Hon Sy; St of Mnth; WWAHSS; BPA; Sch Ppr (R); Yrbk (E); Placed 1st Twice & 2nd Twice in Business Professionals of America Competition; Bio Informatics; Biological Sciences; U of Delaware

GALBREATH, COREY; REHOBOTH BEACH, DE; CAPE HENLOPEN HS; (FR); Hnr Roll; Kwnis Aw; Sci Fairs; St of Mnth; WWAHSS; Comm Volntr; Hab For Humty Volntr; Spec Olymp Vol; Key Club; P to P St Amb Prg; Chr; Ch Chr; Dnce; Fld Hky (J); Sftball (J); Yrbk (E); Miss Teen Delaware Pageant; Forensic Science; Elementary Teacher; U of Delaware; Cedar Crest College

GANGLOFF JR, JOHN J; NEWARK, DE; ST MARK'S HS; (SR); Hi Hnr Roll; Hnr Roll; Nat Hon Sy; Sci/Math Olympn; WWAHSS; Yth Ldrshp Prog; Comm Volntr; Hab For Humty Volntr; Peer Tut/Med; Emplmnt; Key Club; Svce Clb; Mar Art; Roman Catholic Eucharistic Minister; Law Club Member; Mechanical Engineering / Biomedical; Medical Doctor; U of Delaware

GIMBUS, JAMIE; MIDDLETOWN, DE; MIDDLETOWN HS; (JR); Hi Hnr Roll; Nat Hon Sy; Otst Ac Ach Awd; Ntl FFA; Tchrs Aide; French Clb; Lcrsse (V); Swmg (V); JD National Gymnastics Champion; Avid Horseback Rider; Penn State; Pittsburgh

GINN, LAUREN; MIDDLETOWN, DE; MIDDLETOWN HS; (SR); Ctznshp Aw; F Lan Hn Soc; Hi Hnr Roll; Hnr Roll; Perf Att; St of Mnth; Emplmnt; Tchrs Aide; Bnd; Chr; Mch Bnd; SP/M/VS; Fld Hky (J); Track (J); Business Major; U of Delaware; U of North Carolina Wilmington

GOLDSBOROUGH, RASHAD T.; NEWARK, DE; CAB CALLOWAY SCH OF ARTS; (SO); Hnr Roll; Nat Ldrshp Svc; Otst Ac Ach Awd; St of Mnth; WWAHSS; Yth Ldrshp Prog; Comm Volntr; NYLC; P to P St Amb Prg; Bskball (J); Ftball (J); Track (V); Wt Lftg (J); Film Club; Multi-Cultural Club; Film; Entertainment Law; Harvard U; NYU

GORDY, CHRISTINE E; SEAFORD, DE; SEAFORD SR HS; (SO); Gov Hnr Prg; Hi Hnr Roll; Otst Ac Ach Awd; Pres Ac Ftns Aw; WWAHSS; Yth Ldrshp Prog; Comm Volntr; 4-H; Chrch Yth Grp; Drma Clb; Emplmnt; Off Aide; Prom Com; Tchrs Aide; Spanish Clb; Bnd; Jzz Bnd; Pep Bnd; SP/M/VS; Arch (J); Fld Hky (V); Sftball (V); Cl Off (V); Stu Cncl; Yrbk (R, P); United Nations Pilgrimage for Youth; Spanish Club Treasurer; Chemical Engineering; Anesthesiology; U of Delaware; York College

GOSCH, BRITTANY; BRIDGEVILLE, DE; WOODBRIDGE HS; (FR); Hi Hnr Roll; Hnr Roll; Nat Hon Sy; St of Mnth; Chrch Yth Grp; Drma Clb; Key Club; Lttrmn Clb; Spanish Clb; Chr; Ch Chr; Dnce; SP/M/VS; Fld Hky (VJ L); Performing Arts (Singing, Dance, Drama); Journalism; Lee U

HAMMONS, ALEXANDREA N; LEWES, DE; CAPE HENLOPEN HS; (SO); Hnr Roll; St of Mnth; Comm Volntr; Chrch Yth Grp; HO'Br Yth Ldrshp; Key Club; Mth Clb/Tm; Bnd; Mch Bnd; Chrldg (V L); Sccr (J); CR (R); Geometry Student of the Year; Four 5's on DSTP; Pre-Med; Pennsylvania State U; Johns Hopkins U

HANNUM, ALISON; HOCKESSIN, DE; CHARTER SCH OF WILMINGTON; (FR); Hi Hnr Roll; Otst Ac Ach Awd; Pres Sch; Sci Fairs; St of Mnth; Chrch Yth Grp; Emplmnt; Bskball (V L); Scr Kpr (V); Vllyball (J L); Stu Cncl (R); Received First Degree Black Belt in Kempo Karate 12/04; Business; Sports Medicine / Physical Therapy; U of Delaware; UNC Chapel Hill

HARDING, SHEILA; HARRINGTON, DE; LAKE FOREST HS; (JR); Hi Hnr Roll; Hnr Roll; Nat Hon Sy; Perf Att; Comm Volntr; Peer Tut/Med; Chrch Yth Grp; Emplmnt; Pep Squd; Photog; Prom Com; Ch Chr; Chrldg (V L); Sftball (V L); Cl Off (S); Yrbk; Cheerleading State Champs 02 & 05; Elementary Education Teacher; Psychologist; Salisbury State U; U of Georgia Athens

HARRIS, COURTNEY A; FELTON, DE; LAKE FOREST HS; (JR); Hi Hnr Roll; Nat Hon Sy; Otst Ac Ach Awd; Pres Ac Ftns Aw; Yth Ldrshp Prog; Comm Volntr; Peer Tut/Med; BPA; Chrch Yth Grp; DARE; Drma Clb; Emplmnt; FCCLA; Off Aide; Bnd; Ch Chr; Cr Ctry (V); Track (V); Stu Cncl (R); CR (R); National Honor Society Member; BPA State Conference 1st Place-Presentation Mang.; Business Administration; Law; Wake Forest (U); Howard U

HAWKINS, SALAH; WILMINGTON, DE; MC KEAN HS; (JR); All Am Sch; Hnr Roll; MVP; St Schl; WWAHSS; Bnd; Bskball (VJ); Ftball (V C); Track (V); All-Conference Football Player; All-Conference Scholar; Lawyer / Doctor; Master's / Doctorate Degree; U of Miami; West Virginia U

HICKMAN, WENDY; HARRINGTON, DE; LAKE FOREST HS; (FR); Hi Hnr Roll; BPA; Chrch Yth Grp; HO'Br Yth Ldrshp; Fld Hky (J); U of Delaware; New York U

HILLMAN, AUSTIN R; HARRINGTON, DE; LAKE FOREST HS; (FR); Hnr Roll; St of Mnth; Chrch Yth Grp

HOLLAND, TARA L; LEWES, DE; DELMARVA CHRISTIAN SCH; (FR); Duke TS; Hnr Roll; Pres Sch; St of Mnth; ArtClub; Chrch Yth Grp; DARE; Drma Clb; Emplmnt; Mth Clb/Tm; Scouts; SADD; SP/M/VS; Stg Cre; Bskball; Gmnstcs; Hsbk Rdg; Sccr (V); Sftball; Volunteering At Church, W/ Ushering & Nursery; Learning Spanish & Teaching Myself Guitar; Psychology; Teaching; U of Delaware; Eastern U

HOLLINGSWORTH, MATT; LEWES, DE; CAPE HENLOPEN; (SR); Key Club

HOPKINS, TIMOTHY J; FELTON, DE; LAKE FOREST HS; (FR); All Am Sch; Hi Hnr Roll; Nat Ldrshp Svc; Nat Sci Aw; Sci/Math Olympn; USAA; WWAHSS; Comm Volntr; Chrch Yth Grp; Emplmnt; Spanish Clb; Bsball (J); Sccr (V L); DIAA Scholar Athlete Award - Soccer

HOUSTON, CHRISTINE; LEWES, DE; CAPE HENLOPEN HS; (FR); Hnr Roll; Pres Ac Ftns Aw; Sci/Math Olympn; St of Mnth; WWAHSS; ArtClub; Key Club; Dnce; Chrldg (V); Stu Cncl (R); Psychology; Veterinarian Science; U of Delaware

HUGHES, JUSTIN; WILMINGTON, DE; CHARTER SCH OF WILMINGTON; (SR); Hi Hnr Roll; Hnr Roll; Nat Hon Sy; Perf Att; Sci Fairs; Sci/Math Olympn; Comm Volntr; Peer Tut/Med; Chrch Yth Grp; DARE; Emplmnt; Key Club; Spanish Clb; Bskball (J); Cr Ctry (VJ); DSTP-High Math Score Achievement; Freshman Basketball-Highest GPA; Pharmacy Doctorate Program; U of the Sciences in Philadelphia

HUGHES, LAUREN; FELTON, DE; POLYTECH HS; (SO); Hi Hnr Roll; Hnr Roll; MVP; Perf Att; Emplmnt; Scouts; Voc Ind Clb Am; Bnd; Chr; Ch Chr; Mch Bnd; Fld Hky (J); Sccr (V L); CR (R); Yrbk (R); Recreational Basketball; Physical Therapy; Delaware Technical Community; U of Delaware

HULL, JALESA; DELMAR, DE; DELMAR HS; (SO); Ctznshp Aw; Hi Hnr Roll; Hnr Roll; WWAHSS; Comm Volntr; Chrch Yth Grp; Emplmnt; Key Club; Tchrs Aide; Chr; Ch Chr; Chrldg (VJC); Cr Ctry (V L); CR (R); Classic Upward Bound; African American Club

INSKEEP, JESSICA S; NEW CASTLE, DE; WILLIAM PENN HS; (FR); Hi Hnr Roll; Hnr Roll; Otst Ac Ach Awd; St of Mnth; Comm Volntr; Chrch Yth Grp; Yrbk (R); Elementary Education; U of Delaware; New York U

IYER, SRUTI; HOCKESSIN, DE; WILMINGTON CHARTER; (FR); Hnr Roll; Perf Att; St of Mnth; Mod UN; Tmpl Yth Grp; Acpl Chr; Chr; Stg Cre; Fld Hky (J); Fergusson Scholarship for DSTP Maths; Medical School; U of Delaware; Penn State

Hopkins, Timothy J
Lake Forest HS
Felton, DE

Harding, Sheila
Lake Forest HS
Harrington, DE

Inskeep, Jessica S
William Penn HS
New Castle, DE

Goldsborough, Rashad T.
Cab Calloway Sch Of Arts
Newark, DE

Fox, Stephanie
St Mark's HS
Wilmington, DE

Del Collo, Alexandra M
St Mark's HS
Hockessin, DE

Cropper, Tara L
Cab Calloway Sch Of Arts
New Castle, DE

Cox, Rebecca
Middletown HS
Bear, DE

National
Honor Roll
Spring 2005

Cottingham, Stephanie M
Cab Calloway Sch Of Arts
Wilmington, DE

Dalecki, Marissa
Cab Calloway Sch Of Arts
Wilmington, DE

Dickerson, Kirsten C
Dover HS
Dover, DE

Gaffigan, Heather M
Hodgson Vo-Tech HS
Middletown, DE

Gangloff Jr, John J
St Mark's HS
Newark, DE

JONES, JESSICA L; CLAYMONT, DE; CAB CALLOWAY SCH OF ARTS; (SO); Hnr Roll; Otst Ac Ach Awd; Perf Att; Sci/Math Olympn; WWAHSS; Comm Volntr; Chrch Yth Grp; French Clb; Orch; Fncg; National Jr Honor Society; National Society of High School Students; Medical Sciences; Psychology

JONES JR, ENOCH; BEAR, DE; GLASGOW HS; (JR); Hnr Roll; Perf Att; Chrch Yth Grp; Bskbll (J); Ftball (V); Track (V); Computer Technology; Business Administration; U of Delaware; Morgan State U

KAMARA, FATMATA; NEWARK, DE; GLASGOW HS; (JR); Hnr Roll; Nat Mrt LOC; Nat Mrt Sch Recip; WWAHSS; Sccr (J); Nursing; Computer Science; U of Delaware; Delaware State U

KAYE, BRIAN; SMYRNA, DE; SMYRNA HS; (JR); Hi Hnr Roll; Otst Ac Ach Awd; Sci/Math Olympn; Emplmnt; FTA; Lttrmn Clb; Sccr (V CL); Sports Medicine; Audition; East Carolina U; U of North Carolina

KELANI, KAFAYAT; NEW CASTLE, DE; WILLIAM PENN HS; (JR); F Lan Hn Soc; Hi Hnr Roll; Nat Hon Sy; St of Mnth; WWAHSS; Comm Volntr; BPA; Tchrs Aide; French Clb; Dnce; Scr Kpr (VJ); Presidential Service Award; Management; Accounting; U of Maryland College Park; Morgan State U

KELLAM, MAYA L; NEWARK, DE; GLASGOW HS; (JR); Hnr Roll; WWAHSS; Dbte Team; Drma Clb; Emplmnt; Clr Grd; Mch Bnd; SP/M/VS; Stg Cre; Stu Cncl (R); Neonatology / Nursing; U of Delaware; Delaware State U

KELLER, LISA; MIDDLETOWN, DE; MIDDLETOWN HS; (SO); Ctznshp Aw; Hi Hnr Roll; Hnr Roll; Lib Aide; Tchrs Aide; CR (R); FCCLA Member; Advertising; U of Delaware; Boston U

KENNEDY, TIFFANY M; NEWARK, DE; PAUL HODGSON VOC TECH HS; (SO); Ctznshp Aw; Hi Hnr Roll; Hnr Roll; Otst Ac Ach Awd; Pres Sch; BPA; Dnce; Fld Hky (J); Sccr (J); Business Degree; A Degree in Computers; Widener College; U of Delaware

KNOX, ERIKA; GREENWOOD, DE; WOODBRIDGE HS; (SO); Hnr Roll; Kwnis Aw; Comm Volntr; FTA; Jr Ach; Key Club; Vsity Clb; Spanish Clb; Bnd; Fld Hky (V L); Sftball (V L); Track (V L); Athletic Training; Gym Teacher; U of Delaware

KOSER, LINDSAY; MILTON, DE; CAPE HENLOPEN HS; (SO); Duke TS; F Lan Hn Soc; Hnr Roll; Comm Volntr; Hab For Humty Volntr; Hosp Aide; AL Aux Girls; Chrch Yth Grp; DARE; Emplmnt; FCCLA; Key Club; Kwanza Clb; Lib Aide; Flg Crps; Nurse; Dentist; U of Boston; U of Delaware

KOTHARI, KINNERI; WILMINGTON, DE; CHARTER SCH OF WILMINGTON; (SR); F Lan Hn Soc; Hnr Roll; Nat Hon Sy; Hosp Aide; Peer Tut/Med; Emplmnt; SADD; Spanish Clb; Dnce; Track (J); Democrat Club; Business and Management; Communications; U of Delaware

KRAMER, MARISSA N; MILFORD, DE; MILFORD HS; (SR); Hi Hnr Roll; Hnr Roll; Nat Hon Sy; St of Mnth; WWAHSS; Comm Volntr; Peer Tut/Med; DECA; FTA; Key Club; Quill & Scroll; Lit Mag (E); Future Educators of America-Treasurer; Graduate with Full Honors; Join a Fortune 500 Company; Goldey-Beacom College; Western Michigan U

KROUSE, TASHAUNA L; REHOBOTH BCH, DE; CAPE HENLOPEN HS; (FR); St of Mnth; Comm Volntr; Emplmnt; Key Club; ROTC; Clr Grd; Drl Tm; Yrbk (P); Pennsylvania State U; U of North Carolina Wilmington

LAPANNE, ALEXANDRA; WILMINGTON, DE; CONCORD HS; (JR); Ctznshp Aw; Hnr Roll; Sci Fairs; St of Mnth; Yth Ldrshp Prog; Comm Volntr; Emplmnt; Ntl FFA; Prom Com; Tchrs Aide; Bnd; Scr Kpr (V); Yrbk (E); Biology; U of Delaware

LEEDS, STEPHEN D; NEWARK, DE; ST MARK'S HS; (JR); Hnr Roll; Comm Volntr; Key Club; Tennis (VJ); Math Award; U of Delaware; U of Maryland

LESLIE, JOANNA; MILFORD, DE; MILFORD HS; (JR); Hnr Roll; Nat Hon Sy; Otst Ac Ach Awd; WWAHSS; Key Club; Law; U of Delaware; Salisbury U

LINGO, ROBERT J; MILTON, DE; CAPE HENLOPEN HS; (FR); Hi Hnr Roll; Otst Ac Ach Awd; St of Mnth; WWAHSS; Key Club; Bnd; Jzz Bnd; Mch Bnd; Lcrsse (J); Voice of Democracy Contest-2nd Place; U of Delaware

LONERGAN JR, KEVIN P; MILFORD, DE; MILFORD SR HS; (SR); Hi Hnr Roll; MVP; Nat Hon Sy; WWAHSS; Comm Volntr; Chrch Yth Grp; Emplmnt; Key Club; Scouts; Tchrs Aide; French Clb; Chr; Ch Chr; SP/M/VS; Swg Chr; Swmg (V CL); Track (V L); Academic All Conference; Who's Who Among HS Students - Sports Edition; Clinical Child Psychologist; Washington College Chestertown MD

LOPEZ, KIMBERLY; NEW CASTLE, DE; WILLIAM PENN HS; (FR); Hnr Roll; Perf Att; St of Mnth; Comm Volntr; Stu Cncl (R); Law; Medicine; Johns Hopkins; U of Pennsylvania

LOTT, EDWARD L; DOVER, DE; CAESAR RODNEY HS; (SO); Hnr Roll; Perf Att; Comm Volntr; Chrch Yth Grp; DARE; Ftball (J); Volunteer- US Army Hospitals; Finance and Economics Major; Georgia Southern U

LOUNSBURY, ANNA; WILMINGTON, DE; CHARTER SCH OF WILMINGTON; (FR); 4H Awd; Hnr Roll; Sci Fairs; Comm Volntr; 4-H; Chrch Yth Grp; Drma Clb; Italian Clb; Chr; Ch Chr; SP/M/VS; Stg Cre; Bskball; Teacher; Magazine Editor; U of Delaware; Virginia Tech

MACASEVICH, KYLE T; WILMINGTON, DE; CHARTER SCH OF WILMINGTON; (JR); Hi Hnr Roll; Hnr Roll; Otst Ac Ach Awd; Sci/Math Olympn; WWAHSS; Comm Volntr; Chess; Chrch Yth Grp; Key Club; Mth Clb/Tm; Mus Clb; Scouts; Tech Clb; Yrbk (P); Presidents Education Awards Program; Michael C Ferguson Scholarship; Engineering; Villanova U; Drexel U

MACK, BRYAN; REHOBOTH BEACH, DE; CAPE HENLOPEN HS; (FR); Ctznshp Aw; Hi Hnr Roll; Hnr Roll; MVP; Nat Hon Sy; Otst Ac Ach Awd; Perf Att; Sci Fairs; Sci/Math Olympn; St of Mnth; Comm Volntr; Spec Olymp Vol; Chrch Yth Grp; DARE; Drma Clb; Emplmnt; Key Club; Mus Clb; P to P St Amb Prg; Sci Clb; Stg Cre; Bsball (J); Bskball (J); Sccr (J); Cl Off (T); Stu Cncl (R); CR (R); Journalism; Teacher; Virginia Tech; U of Delaware

MAKDAD, JESSICA A; HARRINGTON, DE; LAKE FOREST HS; (JR); Hnr Roll; Otst Ac Ach Awd; St of Mnth; DARE; Emplmnt; Fld Hky; Sftball

MAO, QIUSHI; BEAR, DE; CHARTER SCH OF WILMINGTON; (SR); F Lan Hn Soc; Hi Hnr Roll; Jr Eng Tech; Nat Hon Sy; Nat Mrt LOC; WWAHSS; Comm Volntr; Mth Clb/Tm; Mus Clb; French Clb; Orch; Cr Ctry (V); Track (V); 2nd in State American Chemical Society Contest; Score of 122 on AMC-12; Engineering; Computer Science; MIT; California Institute of Technology

MARTE, LADY; WILMINGTON, DE; NEWARK HS; (MS); Hnr Roll; Who's Who Poetry Award; Master's Degree in Photography; Associate's Degree in Photography; Brooks Institute of Photography; Citrus College

MASTEN JR, STEPHEN T; MILFORD, DE; MILFORD HS; (SR); Ctznshp Aw; Hi Hnr Roll; Hnr Roll; Kwnis Aw; Nat Hon Sy; WWAHSS; Comm Volntr; Hosp Aide; Red Cr Aide; Emplmnt; Pep Squd; Prom Com; Scouts; Tchrs Aide; Vsity Clb; Bsball (V L); Sccr (V L); Swmg (V CL); Vsy Clb (V L); Wt Lftg; Wrstlg (J); Adv Cncl (R); Cl Off (V); Stu Cncl (R); Lit Mag; Eagle Scout; Wendy's High School Heisman Award; Physical Therapy; Chiropractics; Salisbury U; U of Delaware

MATTSON, NICOLE; NEWARK, DE; CHRISTIANA HS; (SO); Hnr Roll; MVP; Perf Att; Scouts; Vllyball (J); Registered Nurse; Practical Nurse; Wilmington College; U of Delaware

MC AULIFFE, ERIN; HOCKESSIN, DE; ST MARK'S HS; (JR); Hnr Roll; MVP; Nat Hon Sy; Sci/Math Olympn; WWAHSS; Comm Volntr; Peer Tut/Med; Key Club; Mth Clb/Tm; Rlr Hky (V); Ice Hockey-Phil Little Flyers-8 years; Rugby; Engineering; Rensselaer Polytechnic Institute; Union College

MC COOL, KELSEY L; GEORGETOWN, DE; SUSSEX TECH HS; (JR); Hi Hnr Roll; Hnr Roll; Comm Volntr; Bnd; Chr; SP/M/VS; Stg Cre; Bsball; Sftball (J); Cl Off (S); Stu Cncl; CR (V); Yrbk (E); Interior Design; Textile Design

MC DOWELL, ASHLEY; CAMDEN WYO, DE; POLYTECH HS; (SO); Hi Hnr Roll; Comm Volntr; Chrch Yth Grp; Drma Clb; Quiz Bowl; Voc Ind Clb Am; Bnd; Chr; Ch Chr; SP/M/VS; Sccr (L); Tennis (J); All-State Band - 2 Times / County Band - 4 Times / All-State Chorus - 2 Times; Engineering; James Madison U; Virginia Tech

MC GEE, CHA'TEEDRA; GREENWOOD, DE; WOODBRIDGE SR HS; (FR); Hi Hnr Roll; Hnr Roll; St of Mnth; WWAHSS; Red Cr Aide; Drma Clb; FBLA; Clr Grd; SP/M/VS; Stg Cre; Mar Art; USAA National Honor Student Award; Psychology; Japanese; Pennsylvania State U Park; New York U

MC KEE, EMILY; MILFORD, DE; MILFORD SR HS; (FR); Hi Hnr Roll; St of Mnth; Comm Volntr; Key Club; Sftball (V L); Interior Design; Psychiatrist; UCLA; Florida State

MC LEAN, THOMAS J; WILMINGTON, DE; TALLEY MS; (MS); Ctznshp Aw; Hnr Roll; Perf Att; St of Mnth; Drma Clb; Bnd; Orch; SP/M/VS; Sccr (V); Wrstlg (V); Yrbk (P); FAME-Forum to Advance Minor in Engineering; Acting, Movie or Performing Arts; Veterinary Science; U of California Los Angeles; Notre Dame

MC MILLEN, MATT; NEWARK, DE; CHRISTIANA HS; (JR); Hi Hnr Roll; Nat Hon Sy; WWAHSS; Pre-Law; Political Science / Government; U of Delaware

MERIDA, CYNTHIA; NEWARK, DE; HODGSON VO-TECH HS; (SR); All Am Sch; Hi Hnr Roll; Hnr Roll; Nat Hon Sy; St of Mnth; WWAHSS; Comm Volntr; Sftball (J); Stu Cncl (S); Nursing; Physician; U of DE

METHVIN, LAURA J; NEWARK, DE; CHARTER SCH OF WILMINGTON; (SR); F Lan Hn Soc; Hi Hnr Roll; Nat Hon Sy; Perf Att; WWAHSS; Yth Ldrshp Prog; Comm Volntr; Prom Com; Svce Clb; Vsity Clb; Bskball (V CL); Sccr (V L); Football Team Letter-Manager; Medicine; Drew U; U of Delaware

METHVIN, THOMAS W; NEWARK, DE; CHARTER SCH OF WILMINGTON; (SR); Hi Hnr Roll; MVP; Nat Hon Sy; Sci Fairs; Comm Volntr; Peer Tut/Med; Emplmnt; Jr Ach; Scouts; Svce Clb; Vsity Clb; Bskball (V L); Ftball (V CL); Track (V L); First Team All State Football Player; Princeton U; U of Delaware

MILLER, JAZMYN; WILMINGTON, DE; JOHN DICKINSON HS; (SO); Hi Hnr Roll; Hnr Roll; Perf Att; St of Mnth; Peer Tut/Med; Chrch Yth Grp; DARE; Drma Clb; Emplmnt; Chr; SP/M/VS; Track; Concession Stand; Japanese; Literacy

MILLER, JOSH; SEAFORD, DE; SEAFORD SR HS; (FR); Hi Hnr Roll; Hnr Roll; MVP; Nat Hon Sy; Otst Ac Ach Awd; Comm Volntr; Peer Tut/Med; Emplmnt; FBLA; Key Club; Spanish Clb; SP/M/VS; Bsball (J); Sccr (VJ); Tennis (J); Cl Off (R); Stu Cncl (R); CR (R); Community Service with Key Club; Business; Music; U of North Carolina Wilmington; Old Dominion U

MILLER, KRISTEN; FELTON, DE; LAKE FOREST HS; (JR); Hi Hnr Roll; Hnr Roll; Comm Volntr; Dbte Team; Drma Clb; Spch Team; SP/M/VS; Vllyball (V); Social Psychology; U of Delaware; Wesley College

MINTZER, KRISTEN; LEWES, DE; CAPE HENLOPEN HS; (FR); Hi Hnr Roll; Sci Fairs; St of Mnth; WWAHSS; Comm Volntr; ArtClub; Emplmnt; Key Club; Ntl FFA; P to P St Amb Prg; Sccr (J); Ranked #2 in Class Out of 363 Students; Marine Biology; U of Delaware; Florida Atlantic U

MITCHELL, RHONDA F; NEWARK, DE; PINE FORGE AC; (SR); Ctznshp Aw; Hi Hnr Roll; Hnr Roll; Nat Hon Sy; WWAHSS; Comm Volntr; Off Aide; P to P St Amb Prg; Biology; Oakwood College

MOLESKI, JEANNETTE; WILMINGTON, DE; CONCORD HS; (JR); Hi Hnr Roll; Otst Ac Ach Awd; Drma Clb; FTA; Mus Clb; Svce Clb; Bnd; Clr Grd; SP/M/VS; Stg Cre; Business Management; Dramatic Arts / Theater; Millersville U; Westchester U

MONTALVO, YESENIA; WILMINGTON, DE; GLASGOW HS; (JR); 4H Awd; Perf Att; St of Mnth; Comm Volntr; 4-H; Drma Clb; Bnd; Bskball (L); Sftball; Tennis; Track; Vllyball; Girl Scout; SP/M/VS; Ntl FFA; Scouts; Tchrs Aide; Spanish Clb; Ch Chr; Sftball; Tennis; Track; Vllyball; Girl Scout (Fashion, and Working with Toddlers); Become a Model or Become a Lawyer; U of Delaware

MOTT, CORTNEY M; CLAYTON, DE; SMYRNA HS; (FR); Hnr Roll; Spanish Clb; Chr; Dnce; Chrldg (C); Yrbk (P); All-Star Cheerleading - Competitive Only; Medical; Cheerleading or Languages; Delaware Technical Community College; U of Delaware

MULLETT, MIKE; GREENWOOD, DE; WOODBRIDGE HS; (SO); Ctznshp Aw; Hnr Roll; Perf Att; Yth Ldrshp Prog; Emplmnt; HO'Br Yth Ldrshp; Key Club; Ntl FFA; Vsity Clb; Voc Ind Clb Am; Ftball (V L); Wt Lftg (V); CR (T); Construction Technology; Construction Technical School

MUNOZ, ELZY; CLAYMONT, DE; CONCORD HS; (JR); Hi Hnr Roll; Hnr Roll; Nat Mrt Sch Recip; Perf Att; Sci Fairs; WWAHSS; Yth Ldrshp Prog; Comm Volntr; BPA; Drma Clb; Mus Clb; P to P St Amb Prg; Sci Clb; Acpl Chr; Chr; SP/M/VS; Chrldg (J); Science National Honor Society; Law; International Business / Relations; Georgetown U; College of Notre Dame Maryland

MURRAY, MEGAN; BEAR, DE; ST MARK'S HS; (SO); Hi Hnr Roll; Comm Volntr; Peer Tut/Med; Scouts; Svce Clb; Bnd; Swmg (V); Stu Cncl (R); Silver Award in Girl Scouts; National Junior Leaders Conference; Elementary Education; U of Delaware; U of Pittsburgh

NARVELL, AMANDA; BEAR, DE; CHRISTIANA HS; (SO); Hnr Roll; Nat Hon Sy; Comm Volntr; Dnce; Sch Ppr (R); Competition Dance Team; Gold or Higher Awards; English; Journalism; New York City U; U of Florida

NELSON, STEVEN; NEWARK, DE; HOWARD HS; (JR); Hnr Roll; Sci Fairs; St of Mnth; Comm Volntr; Chrch Yth Grp; Emplmnt; Tchrs Aide; SP/M/VS; Stg Cre; Bsball (J); Sccr (VJCL); Stu Cncl (R); Church Teen Group Volunteer; Electrical

Mott, Cortney M — Smyrna HS — Clayton, DE
Mattson, Nicole — Christiana HS — Newark, DE
Kellam, Maya L — Glasgow HS — Newark, DE
National Honor Roll Spring 2005
Kelani, Kafayat — William Penn HS — New Castle, DE
Miller, Kristen — Lake Forest HS — Felton, DE
Nelson, Steven — Howard HS — Newark, DE

NYHUS, MEGAN C; MIDDLETOWN, DE; MIDDLETOWN HS; (JR); WWAHSS; Comm Volntr; Emplmnt; Lib Aide; Off Aide; Tchrs Aide; Education; Psychology; Millersville U; Shippensburg U

O'KANE, ERICA N; WILMINGTON, DE; ST MARK'S HS; (JR); Hi Hnr Roll; WWAHSS; Yth Ldrshp Prog; Comm Volntr; Hab For Humty Volntr; Hosp Aide; Emplmnt; HO'Br Yth Ldrshp; Jr Ach; Key Club; NYLC; P to P St Amb Prg; Photog; Stg Cre; Fld Hky; Skiing; Cl Off (P); Stu Cncl; CR; Yrbk (E, P); Guitar Player; Medical Doctor Specializing in Neonatology; U of Pennsylvania; Pennsylvania State College

ORSINI, ANGIE; HOCKESSIN, DE; ST ELIZABETH'S HS; (SO); Hnr Roll; WWAHSS; DARE; Drma Clb; Pep Squd; Chrldg (V); Yrbk (R); Psychology; Photography; U of California in Los Angeles; Temple U

PALMER, NATASHA; NEW CASTLE, DE; HODGSON VO-TECH; (SR); Hi Hnr Roll; Hnr Roll; St of Mnth; Yth Ldrshp Prog; Spec Olymp Vol; ArtClub; Emplmnt; Fr of Library; Scouts; Lit Mag (E); Won Scholarships for College; PhD in Interior Design; Art Institute of Atlanta

PARKER, LARYSSA; HOCKESSIN, DE; ALEXIS I DUPONT HS; (JR); Hi Hnr Roll; Hnr Roll; St of Mnth; Comm Volntr; Peer Tut/Med; Emplmnt; Key Club; Off Aide; Compete in Horseback Riding Shows; Camp Counselor; Computer Science; Graphic Design; Champlain College; U of Delaware

PARSONS, HEATHER J; SMYRNA, DE; SMYRNA HS; (SR); Gov Hnr Prg; Hi Hnr Roll; Hnr Roll; Jr Mshl; Nat Hon Sy; Otst Ac Ach Awd; St Schl; Valdctrian; WWAHSS; Yth Ldrshp Prog; Comm Volntr; Peer Tut/Med; BPA; Chrch Yth Grp; Drma Clb; FTA; Jr Ach; Tchrs Aide; SP/M/VS; Stg Cre; Stu Cncl (R); Elementary Education; Bible; Columbia International U; Bible College

PATEL, CHIRAYU; NEWARK, DE; CARAVEL AC; (JR); Hi Hnr Roll; Hnr Roll; Otst Ac Ach Awd; Perf Att; Sci Fairs; Sci/Math Olympn; Yth Ldrshp Prog; Comm Volntr; Hosp Aide; Peer Tut/Med; Emplmnt; Sci Clb; Vsity Clb; Ftball (V); Wt Lftg (V); MD / Professional Degree in Medicine; Pre-Med; Rutgers; Penn State U

PATTERSON, STEPHANIE; NEWARK, DE; ST MARK'S HS; (SR); Hnr Roll; Comm Volntr; Key Club; SP/M/VS; Lit Mag; The President's Volunteer Service Award; Child Psychology; U of Delaware

PAUCIULO, ALEXANDRA; WILMINGTON, DE; ST. MARKS; (FR); Hi Hnr Roll; Hnr Roll; Key Club; Svce Clb

PERRY, VANESSA M; WILMINGTON, DE; WILLIAM PENN HS; (JR); Hnr Roll; Perf Att; Yth Ldrshp Prog; Comm Volntr; BPA; Drma Clb; Scouts; SP/M/VS; Vllyball (J); Presidential Community Service Award; Architectural Design; Interior Design; Northeastern U; Drexel U

PHILLIPS, KIMBERLY M; FELTON, DE; LAKE FOREST HS; (FR); Ctznshp Aw; Hi Hnr Roll; Perf Att; Pres Ac Ftns Aw; St of Mnth; Yth Ldrshp Prog; Comm Volntr; DARE; FCCLA; HO'Br Yth Ldrshp; Field Hockey Manager; Journalism; Optometry; U of Delaware; Princeton U

PIERRE, CINDY; SEAFORD, DE; SEAFORD HS; (JR); Hi Hnr Roll; Hnr Roll; WWAHSS; Comm Volntr; 4-H; Emplmnt; Key Club; ROTC; Scouts; Tchrs Aide; Bnd; Clr Grd; Drl Tm; Mch Bnd; Bskball (J); Sccr (V L); Track (V); Cl Off (P); CR (R); Girl State; Pharmaceuticals; Business Administration; Howard U; Georgetown U

PIZZADILI, ANTONIA; FELTON, DE; LAKE FOREST HS; (SR); Hi Hnr Roll; Hnr Roll; Nat Hon Sy; Comm Volntr; Peer Tut/Med; Chrch Yth Grp; Emplmnt; Ntl FFA; NYLC; Tchrs Aide; Fld Hky (V); Tennis; Cl Off (P); Stu Cncl (P); Student Internship with Dept of Ed, Delaware; Medical; Political; U of Maryland; James Madison U

PRITCHETT, SARAH; BRIDGEVILLE, DE; WOODBRIDGE HS; (SR); F Lan Hn Soc; Hi Hnr Roll; Nat Hon Sy; Perf Att; Pres Ac Ftns Aw; St of Mnth; WWAHSS; Hosp Aide; Emplmnt; Key Club; Off Aide; Prom Com; Svce Clb; Vsity Clb; French Clb; Fld Hky (V CL); Sccr (V CL); Cl Off (S); Yrbk (E, R); Psychology; Salisbury U

RIFENBURG, JUSTIN; NEW CASTLE, DE; PAUL HODGSON VOC TECH HS; (SO); Hnr Roll; Perf Att; DARE; Lib Aide; Mus Clb; Off Aide; Bnd; Jzz Bnd; Plumber; Lawyer; Harvard U

ROBINSON, JULIA; FELTON, DE; LAKE FOREST HS; (SO); Hi Hnr Roll; WWAHSS; Comm Volntr; Hab For Humty Volntr; Hosp Aide; Chrch Yth Grp; Clr Grd; Swmg (V); Vllyball (J); Stu Cncl (R); Scuba Diving Certified; Odyssey of the Mind State Champion; Veterinary Medicine; U of Delaware; U of Miami

RODGERS, SAMANTHA; BEAR, DE; GLASGOW HS; (JR); Hi Hnr Roll; Hnr Roll; Nat Hon Sy; Perf Att; WWAHSS; Drma Clb; Acpl Chr; Bnd; Chr; Jzz Bnd; Tennis (VJ); National Member of Guild for Piano Playing / Member of Delaware's All-State Women's Choir - 9th in the State of Sopranos II; Music Education / Voice Major; Music Therapy; West Chester U; U of Delaware

ROGERS, DAJUNA; SMYRNA, DE; SMYRNA HS; (FR); Hnr Roll; Sci Fairs; St of Mnth; Yth Ldrshp Prog; Comm Volntr; DECA; Tchrs Aide; Chr; Bskball (J); Cl Off (R); CR (R); Class Officer / Historian; Pharmacy; Law; Spelman College; Clark Atlanta U

RUST, ASHLEY N; BRIDGEVILLE, DE; WOODBRIDGE SR HS; (FR); Hnr Roll; WWAHSS; Chrch Yth Grp; Drma Clb; Mus Clb; Spanish Clb; Bnd; Mch Bnd; SP/M/VS; Stg Cre; Hampton Master's Commission

SACHER, LAUREN N; MIDDLETOWN, DE; MIDDLETOWN HS; (FR); Ctznshp Aw; Hi Hnr Roll; Perf Att; Pres Sch; Comm Volntr; Off Aide; Chr; Clr Grd; SP/M/VS; Lcrsse (J); Cl Off (V); Stu Cncl; CR; Yrbk (P); DSTP 5 Award; Medical Field; Interior Design; Yale U; New York U

SAMUELS, DANIELLE; NEWARK, DE; GLASGOW HS; (JR); Hnr Roll; Nat Hon Sy; WWAHSS; Off Aide; Tchrs Aide; Chrldg (J); Who's Who Among High School Students; National Honor Society; Computer Science; Pre-Law; U of Delaware; Cecil Community College

SANDELIER, MICHAEL R; WILMINGTON, DE; HOWARD HS OF TECH; (FR); Ctznshp Aw; Hi Hnr Roll; Hnr Roll; MVP; Nat Hon Sy; Otst Ac Ach Awd; Perf Att; St of Mnth; Peer Tut/Med; Chess; Chrch Yth Grp; DARE; Dbte Team; SP/M/VS; Stg Cre; Bsball (V C); Bskball (V CL); Ftball (J); All Star in Baseball 5 Years; 100 Point Club in Basketball All City Team Foul Shooting Champ; Computer Networking Engineer with Finance/Business Degree; U of Delaware; Delaware Technical Community College

SAVIDGE, TIFFANY S; TOWNSEND, DE; MIDDLETOWN HS; (JR); Hnr Roll; Perf Att; Comm Volntr; Chrch Yth Grp; Emplmnt; Ntl FFA; Nursing; Medicine; Delaware Tech; Penn State

SCALISE, JOSEPH M; MIDDLETOWN, DE; MIDDLETOWN HS; (FR); Ctznshp Aw; Hnr Roll; Sci/Math Olympn; St of Mnth; Lib Aide; Mth Clb/Tm; Off Aide; Tchrs Aide; Stu Cncl (R); Major in Meteorology; Penn State U; U of Delaware

SCARBOROUGH, NICOLE; NEWARK, DE; ST MARK'S HS; (FR); Hi Hnr Roll; Comm Volntr; Key Club; Mth Clb/Tm; Bnd; Chr; Jzz Bnd; Mch Bnd; Mock Trial; Biology; Genetics; U of North Carolina; U of Delaware

SCHAFFER, KRISTEN; FRANKFORD, DE; SUSSEX CTRL HS; (SO); Hi Hnr Roll; Nat Hon Sy; St of Mnth; WWAHSS; Comm Volntr; Peer Tut/Med; Lib Aide; Mth Clb/Tm; Bnd; Mch Bnd; Stu Cncl (R); CR (R); Band Lieutenant; Bowling Participant; Elementary Education; Psychology; College of William and Mary; Salisbury State

SCHILL, STEPHAN; MIDDLETOWN, DE; CHARTER SCH OF WILMINGTON; (SR); Hi Hnr Roll; Hnr Roll; Emplmnt; Tchrs Aide; Sccr (V C); High School Soccer - 2nd Team All-State; U of North Carolina Chapel Hill

SCHROCK, JENNA L; GREENWOOD, DE; WOODBRIDGE SR HS; (FR); Hi Hnr Roll; Hnr Roll; Otst Ac Ach Awd; Perf Att; St of Mnth; USAA; WWAHSS; Comm Volntr; Drma Clb; Emplmnt; Key Club; Vsity Clb; Chr; SP/M/VS; Stg Cre; Bskball (V L); Chrldg (V CL); Sftball (V L); Vsy Clb (V); Cl Off (V); Gatorade Rookie of the Year Award (Basketball)

SCHWANDER, ANDREA; NEWARK, DE; ST MARK'S HS; (JR); Hi Hnr Roll; WWAHSS; Comm Volntr; Drma Clb; FTA; Key Club; Mus Clb; Bnd; Mch Bnd; SP/M/VS; Stg Cre; Lit Mag; Elementary Education; Special Education; Syracuse U; New York U

SESSOMS, BRITTANY N; WILMINGTON, DE; CAB CALLOWAY SCH OF ARTS; (FR); Hnr Roll; Otst Ac Ach Awd; Chrch Yth Grp; DARE; Mus Clb; SADD; Bnd; Chr; Ch Chr; Dnce; Playing with Bill Cosbys Jazz Band / 2-Time Apollo Live CD Recorded That Was Played with Many National Stars; Church Head Musician / Produced Own CD; Music Director; Producer; Juilliard / Coppin State; U of the Arts

SETHI, SAMIR; NEWARK, DE; ST MARK'S HS; (SO); Hi Hnr Roll; Hnr Roll; Comm Volntr; Hosp Aide; Key Club; Mth Clb/Tm; Mod UN; Quiz Bowl; Sci Clb; Scouts; Tennis; Black Belt in Kenpo Karate; Medicine; Biology; U of Delaware

SHEEHAN JR, ROBERT P; HOCKESSIN, DE; ST. MARK'S HS; (SO); Hi Hnr Roll; Nat Sci Aw; Otst Ac Ach Awd; Sci/Math Olympn; St Schl; WWAHSS; Key Club; Mth Clb/Tm; Schol Bwl; Sci Clb; CYM Basketball Team; Naamans Baseball Team

SIERER, KIRSTIN; HOCKESSIN, DE; CAB CALLOWAY SCH OF ARTS; (JR); Hi Hnr Roll; Hnr Roll; Perf Att; WWAHSS; Comm Volntr; Scouts; Dnce; Attended Virginia School of Arts; Attended Joffrey Ballet School; Business / Economics; U of Delaware

SILVA, ERIN; CLAYTON, DE; SMYRNA HS; (FR); Hnr Roll; Otst Ac Ach Awd; St of Mnth; ArtClub; Drma Clb; Jr Ach; Pep Squd; Scouts; Bnd; Chr; Clr Grd; Dnce; Chrldg (J); Sccr (V); Tennis (J); Track (J); Philadelphia Art Institution

SMALL, NAKITA; SELBYVILLE, DE; INDIAN RIVER HS; (JR); Comm Volntr; Hosp Aide; Chr; Hotel Management; Certified Nurses Assistant; Delaware State U; Salisbury U

SMITH, HEATHER L; SEAFORD, DE; LAUREL SR HS; (JR); F Lan Hn Soc; Hi Hnr Roll; Hnr Roll; Otst Ac Ach Awd; Perf Att; Sci Fairs; Comm Volntr; Peer Tut/Med; Photog; Spanish Clb; Chr; Sch Ppr (R); Yrbk (P); Upward Bound-Community Service Award; Spanish Translator; Salisbury U; Delaware Technical Community College

SMOOT, AMBER R; BRIDGEVILLE, DE; WOODBRIDGE SR HS; (FR); Hi Hnr Roll; Hnr Roll; St of Mnth; BPA; DARE; ROTC; Spanish Clb; Chr; Sftball (J L); Nurse Practitioner; Delaware State U

SOTO, JESUS R M; SELBYVILLE, DE; INDIAN RIVER HS; (SR); Hnr Roll; Chrch Yth Grp; DARE; Tchrs Aide; (AAS) Associate in Applied Science; Delaware Tech & Community College

SPIVEY, CATLYN; NEWARK, DE; ST MARK'S HS; (JR); Hnr Roll; Yth Ldrshp Prog; Peer Tut/Med; Key Club; Chr; Blue/Gold Buddies; Key Club; Pre-Veterinary; Radford College; Virginia Tech

TARNOCK, SARAH; WILMINGTON, DE; ST MARK'S HS; (SO); Hi Hnr Roll; Valdctrian; WWAHSS; Key Club; Mth Clb/Tm; Scouts; Bnd; Vllyball (J); Principal Scholarship to St Mark's for Full Tuition, Winner Of 2005 Colonial Names Essay Contest; Received a Scholarship to Attend Washington Workshops Congressional Seminar in June; Pre-Law

TAYLOR, VALERIE; HOCKESSIN, DE; ST MARK'S HS; (JR); Hnr Roll; Nat Hon Sy; WWAHSS; Comm Volntr; Hosp Aide; Chrch Yth Grp; Key Club; Scouts; Bnd; Chr; Mch Bnd; SP/M/VS; Work Camp; Nursing/Medicine; Animals & Sciences; U of Delaware; York College of Pennsylvania

TEETER, KRYSTAL; LAUREL, DE; LAUREL SR HS; (SO); Hnr Roll; Otst Ac Ach Awd; Peer Tut/Med; Spec Olymp Vol; BPA; DARE; Drma Clb; Chr; SP/M/VS; Bachelor Degree in Science & Law; Science & Law and Society; Delaware U; New Mexico U

THIBEAU, KELLY; LAUREL, DE; LAUREL SR HS; (FR); Hi Hnr Roll; Hnr Roll; Comm Volntr; Peer Tut/Med; Chrch Yth Grp; Bnd; Ch Chr; Dnce; Mch Bnd; Bskball (J); Chrldg (V); Fld Hky (J); Sccr (V); Stu Cncl (R); CR (R); Student Government Association; Volunteer At the Boys and Girls Club; Lawyer/Paralegal; Dance; U of Maryland Eastern Shore; U of Miami

THOMAS, ANGELA M; GEORGETOWN, DE; MILFORD SR HS; (JR); Hi Hnr Roll; Hnr Roll; Comm Volntr; Emplmnt; Key Club; Ntl FFA; Chr; Clr Grd; Flg Crps; Mch Bnd; Chrldg (VJ); Sccr (J); Nursing; Fashion Design; U of Delaware

THOMAS, ANNIE; WILMINGTON, DE; ST MARK'S HS; (SO); WWAHSS; Comm Volntr; Emplmnt; Key Club; Mod UN; Scouts; Tennis (V); CR (R); Key Club Class Representative; Girl Scout Silver Award; Film/ Cinema Arts; Business; New York U; Pace U

THOMPKINS, COURTNEY L; BEAR, DE; CHRISTIANA HS; (FR); Hnr Roll; Otst Ac Ach Awd; Chrch Yth Grp; Emplmnt; Scouts; Drl Tm; Bskball (J); Math Award; Licensed Nurse; Basketball Player; Temple U; U of Delaware

TOMLIN, CHARIS R; SELBYVILLE, DE; SUSSEX TECH HS; (JR); Hnr Roll; Nat Hon Sy; Pres Sch; WWAHSS; Comm Volntr; Hosp Aide; Chrch Yth Grp; Emplmnt; Key Club; Prom Com; Bnd; Ch Chr; Mch Bnd; Bskball (V L); Sftball (J); All County Band Participant-Trumpet; Nursing; Hampton U; North Carolina A & T U

TURNER, ASHLEY; LINCOLN, DE; MILLFORD SR HS; (JR); Hnr Roll; WWAHSS; Bnd; Chr; Mch Bnd; SP/M/VS; Chrldg (V)

TUTINI, ADRIANNA G; NEWARK, DE; CHRISTIANA HS; (SO); Ctznshp Aw; Hnr Roll; Nat Hon Sy; Otst Ac Ach Awd; Comm Volntr; Tchrs Aide; Bskball (J); Sftball (V L); Swmg (V L); Vllyball (V L); Culinary Arts; English and Literature Major; U of Delaware; Culinary Arts Institute of Philadelphia

VANDER LEE, DAVID J; DOVER, DE; LAKE FOREST HS; (SR); Hnr Roll; WWAHSS; Hosp Aide; Drma Clb; FCCLA; Tchrs Aide; SP/M/VS; Wrstlg (V); Social Studies Education; Delaware State U

Sierer, Kirstin
Cab Calloway Sch Of Arts
Hockessin, DE

Sandelier, Michael R
Howard HS Of Tech
Wilmington, DE

Parker, Laryssa
Alexis I Dupont HS
Hockessin, DE

Rogers, Dajuna
Smyrna HS
Smyrna, DE

Smoot, Amber R
Woodbridge SR HS
Bridgeville, DE

VAN REES, ASHLEY; MILTON, DE; CAPE HENLOPEN HS; (JR); Mth Clb/Tm; Mus Clb; ROTC; Fld Hky (J); Lcrsse (V L); CR (R); Business Professionals of America; Honor Society; Business; Fashion; U of Delaware; U of Virginia

VAN SANT, HANNAH R; GREENWOOD, DE; WOODBRIDGE SR HS; (FR); Hi Hnr Roll; Hnr Roll; St of Mnth; Peer Tut/Med; Chrch Yth Grp; FCA; Wdwrkg Clb; Ch Chr; Youth Leader At Church; Missionary; Anderson U, Ind; Bible Baptist Institute, Pensacola

WAGNER, MELISSA R; GREENWOOD, DE; WOODBRIDGE SR HS; (FR); 4H Awd; Hi Hnr Roll; Hnr Roll; St of Mnth; Comm Volntr; 4-H; Chrch Yth Grp; DARE; Drma Clb; Emplmnt; Key Club; Spanish Clb; SP/M/VS; Stg Cre; Fld Hky (J); National PTA Reflections Contest; Runner-Up in School Spelling Bee; Stock-Broker; Financial Advisor; New York U; Lynchburg College

WALLACE, BENJAMIN L; HOCKESSIN, DE; THE CHARTER SCH OF WILMINGTON; (FR); Hi Hnr Roll; Hnr Roll; Otst Ac Ach Awd; Pres Ac Ftns Aw; Sci/Math Olympn; Comm Volntr; Hosp Aide; Spec Olymp Vol; ArtClub; Mth Clb/Tm; Mod UN; Quiz Bowl; Spch Team; Chr; Bsball (JC); Bskball (JC); Ftball (J); Stu Cncl (V)

WALLS, JORDAN; HARRINGTON, DE; LAKE FOREST HS; (SO); Hnr Roll; Perf Att; St of Mnth; Scouts; Tech Clb; U of Delaware; Drexel U

WALTON, LOVESHA A; NEW CASTLE, DE; WILLIAM PENN HS; (SO); Hnr Roll; Otst Ac Ach Awd; Perf Att; St of Mnth; Comm Volntr; Chrch Yth Grp; DARE; Dbte Team; Drma Clb; ROTC; Scouts; Tchrs Aide; Dnce; Yrbk (E, R, P); Entered Poetry Contest; 2 Poems Publish in Anthology Book; English Writing/Writing; Fashion & Design; North Carolina Central U; Delaware State U

WAWERU, BRIAN; MIDDLETOWN, DE; MIDDLETOWN HS; (FR); Hnr Roll; ArtClub; Sci Clb; Bskball (J); Sccr (J); Aeronautical Engineering; Chemistry; Massachusetts Institute of Technology; Harvard U

WHARTON, KYLE J; WILMINGTON, DE; THE CHARTER SCH OF WILMINGTON; (FR); Sci Fairs; Latin Clb; Bsball (J); National Latin Exam - Silver Medal; Master's Degree in Business Administration; U of Delaware; U of Pennsylvania - Wharton School of Business

WHITE, CASSIE; HOCKESSIN, DE; ST MARK'S HS; (SO); Hnr Roll; MVP; Pres Ac Ftns Aw; St of Mnth; Hab For Humty Volntr; Chrch Yth Grp; Emplmnt; Key Club; Cr Ctry (V); Lcrsse (J); Swmg (V); CR (R); Home Room Rep; Key Club Member; Physical Therapist; U of Delaware; U of South Florida

WILD, KRISTEN; NEWARK, DE; ST MARK'S HS; (SO); Hnr Roll; Nat Ldrshp Svc; WWAHSS; Key Club; Dnce; SP/M/VS; Karate Outside of School; Psychology; Graphic Design

WILLEY, CHAD T; GREENWOOD, DE; WOODBRIDGE HS; (JR); Hnr Roll; Otst Ac Ach Awd; St of Mnth; WWAHSS; Comm Volntr; Emplmnt; Key Club; Vsity Clb; Wdwrkg Clb; Spanish Clb; Ftball (VJCL); Wt Lftg (V); Doctor of Medicine; Pharmacist; U of Delaware; U of South Carolina

WILLEY, ERIC; GREENWOOD, DE; WOODBRIDGE SR HS; (FR); Hi Hnr Roll; St of Mnth; USAA; WWAHSS; Yth Ldrshp Prog; BPA; Drma Clb; HO'Br Yth Ldrshp; Lib Aide; Mus Clb; Bnd; Mch Bnd; SP/M/VS; Stg Cre; Mar Art

WILLIAMS, LISA; MILTON, DE; CAPE HENLOPEN HS; (SR); Hnr Roll; MVP; Nat Hon Sy; Pres Ac Ftns Aw; WWAHSS; Comm Volntr; Key Club; Ntl FFA; Prom Com; Tchrs Aide; Bskball (V CL); Fld Hky (V L); Sftball (V CL); Stu Cncl (R); First Team All State Field Hockey and Softball Player; Physical Education; Elementary Education; Drexel U

WILLIAMSON, NICOLE M; MIDDLETOWN, DE; PAUL HODGSON VOC TECH HS; (SO); Hnr Roll; Comm Volntr; Vsity Clb; Chrldg (V); Sftball (V); Yrbk (E); Nursing; Math Teacher; U of North Carolina

WINN, RACHQUEL T; WILMINGTON, DE; MT PLEASANT SR; (SR); Hi Hnr Roll; Hnr Roll; Perf Att; WWAHSS; Comm Volntr; Peer Tut/Med; BPA; DARE; Drma Clb; Emplmnt; Mth Clb/Tm; Pep Squd; Tchrs Aide; Dnce; SP/M/VS; Chrldg (V C); Cl Off (T); Stu Cncl (R); Yrbk (R); Pre-Law / Entertainment Lawyer; Fashion Merchandising / Designer; Morgan State U; Princeton U

WYNDER, DONAEYA; NEWARK, DE; CHRISTIANA HS; (SO); Hnr Roll; Comm Volntr; Off Aide; Tchrs Aide; Chr; Sccr (J); Stu Cncl (S); Yrbk (E); Physical Therapist; Fashion Designers; Hampton U; Clark U

YU, LAWRENCE; WILMINGTON, DE; ST MARK'S HS; (SO); Hi Hnr Roll; Hnr Roll; Comm Volntr; Chrch Yth Grp; Key Club; Cr Ctry (J); Tennis (J); I Play Drums for My Church; Business; Music; UD; U Penn

District of Columbia

ALLOTEY, EUGENE; WASHINGTON, DC; (SR); Hnr Roll; Otst Ac Ach Awd; Comm Volntr; Cmptr Clb; Clr Grd; Drl Tm; Sccr (V); Tennis (V); CR (R); Yrbk (P); Chemistry; Howard U; St. Mary's College of Maryland

BAILEY, JAEL A; WASHINGTON, DC; FRIENDSHIP-EDISON COLLEGIATE AC; (SR); Hnr Roll; Comm Volntr; ArtClub; Prom Com; Tech Clb; Graphic Design; Biology; Hampton U; North Carolina Agricultural and Technical State U

BARLOW JR, AUDWIN T; WASHINGTON, DC; ENTERPRISE PCS; (FR); Ctznshp Aw; Hnr Roll; Otst Ac Ach Awd; Perf Att; Peer Tut/Med; Chess; DARE; Dbte Team; Mus Clb; ROTC; Scouts; Bnd; Chr; Drm Mjr; Bsball (V); Bskball (V); Ftball (V); Wt Lftg (V); Wrstlg (J); Cl Off (S); CR (R); Sch Ppr (P); Computer Engineer; Bachelor's Degree; Virginia Tech, U of North Carolina; U of Georgia

BARNETT, RAYMOND; WASHINGTON, DC; HOWARD D WOODSON SR HS; (FR); Ctznshp Aw; Hnr Roll; Otst Ac Ach Awd; Perf Att; Sci Fairs; ROTC; Sci Clb; CR (R); Sch Ppr (P); Computer Programming; Howard; Maryland

BELL, CHRISTOPHER R; WASHINGTON, DC; NEW ENTERPRISE & DVLMNT SCH; (JR); Hnr Roll; Perf Att; Comm Volntr; Youth Opportunity Summit (Police Dept 7.D); The Inaugural Soul of the City Program; Business Management; Criminal Law; American U; George Washington U

BELLETE, DAGMAWI; WASHINGTON, DC; FRIENDSHIP EDISON COLLEGIATE AC; (SO); Hnr Roll; ArtClub; Chrch Yth Grp; Sccr (C); Wt Lftg (L); Intro to Computer; Reading; Technology and Engineering; Pharmacology; Harvard; ITT Tech

BRANNON, LEONA; WASHINGTON, DC; BANNEKER SR HS; (SO); Ctznshp Aw; Hnr Roll; MVP; Comm Volntr; Cmptr Clb; Emplmnt; Sftball (V); CR (R); Psychology; Medical Degree; George Washington U; Pennsylvania State U

CAMPBELL, ASHLEY M; WASHINGTON, DC; NEW ENTERPRISE & DVLMNT SCH; (JR); Ctznshp Aw; Comm Volntr; Peer Tut/Med; Prom Com; Marine Science (Biology); Spanish Interpreter; Meredith College; Newman College

CARNEY, CYNTHIA V; WASHINGTON, DC; CALVIN COOLIDGE HS; (FR); Hnr Roll; Perf Att; Sci Fairs; ROTC; Tchrs Aide; Bnd; Mch Bnd; SP/M/VS; Stg Cre; Psychology; Sociology; Delaware State U; North Carolina A & T State U

CHERRY, NAJA T; WASHINGTON, DC; FRIENDSHIP-EDISON COLLEGIATE AC; (SR); Hi Hnr Roll; Hnr Roll; Nat Hon Sy; St of Mnth; WWAHSS; Peer Tut/Med; Emplmnt; Chr; Orch; Chrldg (J); Track (V); Journalism; Communications; Winston-Salem-NC; U of North Carolina At Chapel Hill

COOLEY, SAMUEL; WASHINGTON, DC; COOLIDGE SR HS; (FR); Business Management; Computer Technician; Virginia Tech; Atlanta Georgia, Miami U

CORBIN, ALEXIS M; WASHINGTON, DC; DUNBAR SR HS; (SR); Hnr Roll; Perf Att; Sci Fairs; Comm Volntr; Peer Tut/Med; Chrch Yth Grp; Lib Aide; Prom Com; Dnce; SP/M/VS; PPSqd (J); Stu Cncl (V); Criminal Justice; Accountant; Trinity U; UDC

CRUZ, SIERRA; WASHINGTON, DC; CARDOZO SHS; (SR); DARE; Emplmnt; ROTC; Criminal Justice; Business; Morgan State U

DESHIELDS, DANIELLE; WASHINGTON, DC; COOLIDGE SR HS; (FR); DARE; Tchrs Aide; Chrldg (V)

DUONG, NGOC B; WASHINGTON, DC; BANNEKER SR HS; (SO); Hnr Roll; Comm Volntr; Sccr (V); Silver Medal - National Latin Exam - 9th Grade; Nurse; George Washington U; Georgetown U

ELLIOTT, PATRICK D; WASHINGTON, DC; COOLIDGE SR HS; (FR); Hnr Roll; Play in the NFL; Graphics Design; Miami U; Ohio State

FORREST, CALVIN M; WASHINGTON, DC; CARDOZO SHS; (SO); Ctznshp Aw; Hi Hnr Roll; Hnr Roll; Otst Ac Ach Awd; Perf Att; Comm Volntr; Spec Olymp Vol; Chrch Yth Grp; Emplmnt; Quiz Bowl; ROTC; Schol Bwl; Tchrs Aide; Bnd; Clr Grd; Drl Tm; Mch Bnd; Bskball (J); Ftball (V); Best Men Program / Howard U Upward Bound; SEDARHOC - Outstanding Scholarship Citizenship Service; Culinary Arts; Doctor / Plastic Surgery; Orlando & Chicago Culinary Academy; Johns Hopkins U

GILMORE, LAKIA; WASHINGTON, DC; FRIENDSHIP EDISON COLLEGIATE AC; (JR); Hnr Roll; Pres Sch; Comm Volntr; DARE; Emplmnt; Wdwrkg Clb; Clb; Dnce; Drl Tm; Drm Mjr; SP/M/VS; PPSqd; Lit Mag (R); Step Team 2003-2004-2005; Higher Achievement Program 2001; To Attend Business School; Morgan State U

GOINS, SHARNITA P; WASHINGTON, DC; FRIENDSHIP EDISON COLLEGIATE AC; (SO); Ctznshp Aw; Hnr Roll; Perf Att; Sci Fairs; Comm Volntr; Chrch Yth Grp; Emplmnt; Ch Chr; Dnce; Pre-Med; Howard U; U of Maryland Eastern Shore

GOMEZ, ANGIE; WASHINGTON, DC; (JR); Hnr Roll; Otst Ac Ach Awd; Perf Att; Pres Sch; St of Mnth; Yth Ldrshp Prog; Comm Volntr; Hosp Aide; Red Cr Aide; P to P St Amb Prg; Photog; ROTC; Ch Chr; Clr Grd; Dnce; SP/M/VS; Swmg; Vllyball; Stu Cncl (V); Yrbk (P); President's Education Awards Program; National Society of High School Scholars; Pre-Med; Science Major; United States Naval Academy; Georgetown U

GONZALEZ, JENNY N; WASHINGTON, DC; BANNEKER SR HS; (SO); Hnr Roll; Perf Att; Comm Volntr; Emplmnt; Off Aide; Sccr (V); CR (V); Pediatrician; Veterinarian; George Washington U; Howard U

GORHAM III, NORMAN C; WASHINGTON, DC; HYDE LEADERSHIP P.C.S; (JR); Comm Volntr; DARE; Emplmnt; Scouts; SP/M/VS; Stg Cre; Golf (V); Sch Ppr (E); Internship Program; Culinary Program; Culinary School; History Major; Johnson and Wales; Columbia

GRAHAM, MONIQUE L; WASHINGTON, DC; WOODROW WILSON SHS; (JR); Ctznshp Aw; Hi Hnr Roll; Hnr Roll; Nat Hon Sy; Comm Volntr; Peer Tut/Med; Chrch Yth Grp; Drma Clb; Emplmnt; Tchrs Aide; Dnce; Mch Bnd; SP/M/VS; Adv Cncl (R); Stu Cncl (S); Lit Mag (R); Congressional Black Caucus Spouses Essay Winner; Mass Communications; Theater; Clark Atlanta U; Temple U

GRAYTON, RANELLE S; WASHINGTON, DC; BANNEKER SR HS; (FR); Hnr Roll; Sci Fairs; Comm Volntr; Chrch Yth Grp; Ch Chr; Dnce; SP/M/VS; Journalism; Spanish; Syracuse U; George Washington U

GREEN, MARCUS; WASHINGTON, DC; SCH WITHOUT WALLS SHS; (JR); Hnr Roll; WWAHSS; Yth Ldrshp Prog; Amnsty Intl; Comm Volntr; Peer Tut/Med; Emplmnt; Chr; Cl Off (S, R); Yrbk (P); Youth of the Year 2002 & 2004 - Boys and Girls Club of Greater Washington - Hopkins Branch; Friends of Tyler School Board of Directors Student Representative; Education; Finance; Georgia State U; North Carolina A & T U

HATTON, DIONA M; WASHINGTON, DC; BANNEKER SR HS; (SO); Hi Hnr Roll; Nat Hon Sy; Sci Fairs; WWAHSS; Comm Volntr; Ntl Beta Clb; Sci Clb; Bnd; Dnce; SP/M/VS; Chrldg (V C); Golf (J); Skiing (J); CR (R); Medicine; Law; Yale U; Xavier U New Orleans

HAYES, JAMAAL; WASHINGTON, DC; SCH FINDERS LEARNING FACILITY; (SR); Ctznshp Aw; Hi Hnr Roll; Nat Mrt Semif; Otst Ac Ach Awd; Perf Att; St of Mnth; St Optmst of Yr; WWAHSS; Peer Tut/Med; Chess; Mus Clb; P to P St Amb Prg; Spch Team; Chr; SP/M/VS; Stg Cre; Adv Cncl (P); Stu Cncl (R); Psychology; Theology; New York U; Morgan State U

ISMAEL, QUADIR; WASHINGTON, DC; SPINGARN STAY HS; (SR); Hnr Roll; Kwnis Aw; Nat Hon Sy; WWAHSS; Comm Volntr; Peer Tut/Med; Red Cr Aide; Key Club; Key Club; Non Profit Organization ("Break The Cycle"); Business; Pharmacology; Delaware State

JACKSON, ARZELLA; WASHINGTON, DC; FRIENDSHIP-EDISON COLLEGIATE AC; (JR); Hi Hnr Roll; Hnr Roll; Otst Ac Ach Awd; Sci/Math Olympn; Chrch Yth Grp; Emplmnt; Lib Aide; Mth Clb/Tm; Off Aide; Photog; Tchrs Aide; Vsity Clb; Drm Mjr; Flg Crps; Mch Bnd; Chrldg (V); Step Team; Executive Manager; Child Development; George Washington U; Howard U

JACKSON, SARAH; WASHINGTON, DC; BANNEKER SR HS; (FR); Ctznshp Aw; Hi Hnr Roll; Hnr Roll; Comm Volntr; German Clb; Adv Cncl (S); Cl Off (S); CR (S); Music Medal Award; Master's Degree; Fashion Institute of New York; New York U

JEFFERSON, SHAMIA M; WASHINGTON, DC; FRIENDSHIP-EDISON COLLEGIATE AC; (JR); Hnr Roll; Sci Fairs; St of Mnth; WWAHSS; Yth Ldrshp Prog; Comm Volntr; Peer Tut/Med; Chrch Yth Grp; Tchrs Aide; Latin Clb; Dnce; Yrbk (P); Pharmacy; Nursing; Johnson C. Smith U; Howard U

JIMENEZ, ALISHA; WASHINGTON, DC; INTEGRATED DESIGN ELECTRONICS AC (PUB CHARTER SCH); (FR); Hi Hnr Roll; Hnr Roll; Sci/Math Olympn; Comm Volntr; Emplmnt; ROTC; Sci Clb; Scouts; Wdwrkg Clb; Lit Mag (P); JROTC Drill Team; JROTC Academic Challenge; Law; Engineering; Air Force Academy; Navy Academy

KELLY, CRYSTAL I; WASHINGTON, DC; CARDOZO SHS; (FR); Ctznshp Aw; Otst Ac Ach Awd; Perf Att; Sci/Math Olympn; St of Mnth; CARE; Comm Volntr; Hosp Aide; ArtClub; Drma Clb; Emplmnt; Mod UN; Off Aide; Outdrs Clb; Pep Squd; Prom Com; Clr Grd; Dnce; Drm Mjr; SP/M/VS; Chrldg (J); Gmnstcs (J); Hsbk Rdg (J); PPSqd (V); Scr Kpr (J); Swmg (J); Track (J); Cl Off (S); CR (V); Swimming; Nurse; Secretary; Howard U; Virginia State U

KIM, TRINH; WASHINGTON, DC; BANNEKER SR HS; (SO); Hnr Roll; Perf Att; St of Mnth; Valdctrian; Comm Volntr; ArtClub; Cmptr Clb; Drma Clb; Sci Clb; SP/M/VS; Stg Cre; Bskball (J); Adv Cncl (T); Computer Engineer; Astronomer; UC Berkeley; Pennsylvania State U

KINGSBURY, KRYSTINA B; WASHINGTON, DC; BALLOU STAY SR HS; (SR); Ctznshp Aw; Jr Mshl; Perf Att; Comm Volntr; DARE; P to P St Amb Prg; ROTC; SADD; Ch Chr; Oratorical Contest Raby & Jenning; Project Y Com Program; Business & Computer; Drama; NC A & Technical Greensboro; Howard U

KIRKSEY, ERIC C; WASHINGTON, DC; HOWARD D WOODSON SR HS; (FR); Ctznshp Aw; Hi Hnr Roll; Hnr Roll; Perf Att; ROTC; Drl Tm; Mch Bnd; Ftball (J); Virginia Technology; The U of Okla.

LEWIS, DOMINIC; WASHINGTON, DC; NEW ENTERPRISE & DVLMNT SCH; (JR); Hnr Roll; Nat Hon Sy; St of Mnth; Emplmnt; Bskball (V); Most Improved Student; Business Management; Accounting; Grambling State U; Virginia Tech

LEWIS, TIARA N; WASHINGTON, DC; FRIENDSHIP-EDISON COLLEGIATE AC; (JR); Hnr Roll; St of Mnth; Ch Chr; Dnce; Mch Bnd; SP/M/VS; CR; Johnson C Smith U; Howard U

LIEBERMAN, HANNAH; WASHINGTON, DC; CHARLES E SMITH JEWISH DAY SCH; (JR); F Lan Hn Soc; Hnr Roll; MVP; Comm Volntr; Peer Tut/Med; JSA; Bskball (JC); Sccr (VJ); Sftball (V C); Cl Off (V); Stu Cncl (R); President of Junior Statesmen Chapter; Lions Trophy Winner; Political Science; Biology; U of Michigan Ann Arbor; U of Wisconsin Madison

LIGHTFOOT, LAQUAN T; WASHINGTON, DC; BANNEKER SR HS; (SO); Hi Hnr Roll; Hnr Roll; Sci Fairs; WWAHSS; Peer Tut/Med; Mth Clb/Tm; Sci Clb; Ch Chr; Drl Tm; Track (V); Stu Cncl (P); CR (R); Lawyer; History; Fordham U; George Washington U

LINGHAM, KRISTEN M; WASHINGTON, DC; BANNEKER SR HS; (JR); Ctznshp Aw; Hnr Roll; Sci Fairs; Comm Volntr; DARE; Jr Ach; Ntl Beta Clb; Ch Chr; Dnce; Pep Bnd; Sftball (J); CR (P); Theater; Fashion

LLOYD, DAVINA T; WASHINGTON, DC; CALVIN COOLIDGE HS; (JR); Ctznshp Aw; Hnr Roll; Nat Sci Aw; Otst Ac Ach Awd; Perf Att; Sci Fairs; Yth Ldrshp Prog; Comm Volntr; DARE; FBLA; Jr Ach; Outdrs Clb; ROTC; Tchrs Aide; Bnd; Chr; Clr Grd; Dnce; Bskball (V); Chrldg (V); Skiing (J); Swmg (V); College Tour 2004 Youth Leader; United Way 2004 Teenage Appreciation; Business Management; Case Management; North Carolina A & T U; Morgan State U

MARIN, CARLA; WASHINGTON, DC; ST JOHN'S COLLEGE HS; (JR); Hi Hnr Roll; Hnr Roll; Nat Hon Sy; Comm Volntr; Peer Tut/Med; ArtClub; Svce Clb; French Clb; Dnce; Multicultural Student Alliance; Diversity Workshops, Gold Star Finalist From National Honor Society; Dentist; Orthodontist; Maryland U; Georgetown U

MARTINEZ, KRALIA L; WASHINGTON, DC; IDEA PUBLIC CHARTER SCH; (SR); Comm Volntr; Peer Tut/Med; Drma Clb; Emplmnt; Off Aide; Prom Com; ROTC; Tchrs Aide; Drl Tm; Vllyball; Cl Off (P); Yrbk (P); High Diploma Obtained in 4 Years Due to Set-Backs.; Auto CAB Trained (Computer Engineering); Business Economics (Major); PhD in Business Law/ Criminal Law; Morgan State U; Georgetown U

MATTHEWS, KAMILLAH; WASHINGTON, DC; BANNEKER SR HS; (FR); Hnr Roll; Sci Fairs; Comm Volntr; Drma Clb; Emplmnt; Ntl Beta Clb; Tchrs Aide; Chr; Dnce; SP/M/VS; Bachelor's Degree in Science; Juris Doctorate of Laws; Stanford U; Howard U

MC DONALD, ASHLEY D; WASHINGTON, DC; IDEA PUBLIC CHARTER SCH; (JR); Hnr Roll; ROTC; Tchrs Aide; Mch Bnd; Yrbk (P); Psychology; U of Maryland; Norfolk State

MC NAIR JR, DAVID E; WASHINGTON, DC; PINE FORGE AC; (FR); Hnr Roll; Emplmnt; Architecture; Engineering; U of Connecticut; Duke U

MILLER, BREA M; WASHINGTON, DC; HYDE LEADERSHIP P.C.S; (FR); Hi Hnr Roll; Hnr Roll; St of Mnth; ArtClub; Dbte Team; Mus Clb; P to P St Amb Prg; Svce Clb; SP/M/VS; Sccr (V); Track (V); Stu Cncl (S); Community Service At BC.; Majoring in Acting; Major in the Medical Field

MORRISON IV, CURTIS; WASHINGTON, DC; HOWARD D WOODSON SR HS; (SO); Hnr Roll; Peer Tut/Med; ArtClub; Bnd; Ch Chr; Mch Bnd; Band Award; Business/Management Degree; Bowie State U/George Mason U; Georgetown U

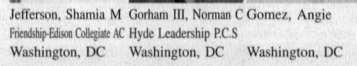

Jefferson, Shamia M
Friendship-Edison Collegiate AC
Washington, DC

Gorham III, Norman C
Hyde Leadership P.C.S
Washington, DC

Gomez, Angie
Washington, DC

Bellete, Dagmawi
Friendship Edison Collegiate AC
Washington, DC

Gilmore, Lakia
Friendship Edison Collegiate AC
Washington, DC

Jackson, Arzella
Friendship-Edison Collegiate AC
Washington, DC

Marin, Carla
St John's College HS
Washington, DC

NATIONAL HONOR ROLL SPRING 2005 — District of Columbia — WOODWARD / 51

NANAY, ILONA; WASHINGTON, DC; WASHINGTON INTERNATIONAL HS; (SO); Hi Hnr Roll; Hnr Roll; Otst Ac Ach Awd; Hab For Humty Volntr; Peer Tut/Med; Stg Cre; Sch Ppr (R, P); Created Documentary on Youth in Senegal; Model UN & Model OAS; Speak 3 Languages; Film Maker; Screen Writer; New York U; U of Toronto

NEELEY, MILAN N; WASHINGTON, DC; CHARLES HERBERT FLOWERS HS; (SO); Ctznshp Aw; Hnr Roll; Nat Hon Sy; Perf Att; Comm Volntr; Peer Tut/Med; Vsity Clb; Swmg (V); SAT High Performer Among 7th & 8th Graders; Zoology; Foreign Language; U of California Berkeley; Brown U

NIBBLINS, VALERIE; WASHINGTON, DC; NEW ENTERPRISE & DVLMNT SCH; (JR); Ctznshp Aw; Hnr Roll; Perf Att; Yth Ldrshp Prog; Teacher; Business; Morgan State U; Howard U

NICHOLSON, MARK J; WASHINGTON, DC; (MS) Ctznshp Aw; Gov Hnr Prg; Hnr Roll; Nat Hon Sy; Perf Att; Pres Sch; Sci Fairs; St of Mnth; Valdctrian; Yth Ldrshp Prog; Peer Tut/Med; Red Cr Aide; Spec Olymp Vol; Aqrium Clb; ArtClub; Chess; Cmptr Clb; Jr Ach; Mus Clb; Outdrs Clb; Wdwrkg Clb; Bnd; Dnce; Mch Bnd; Stg Cre; Bskball; Dvng; Ftball; Gmnstcs; Mar Art; Skiing; Sccr; Swmg; Cl Off; Policeman; Lifeguard; Businessman; Scientist

OLAWOYIN, OLATUNDUN; WASHINGTON, DC; HIGH POINT HS; (JR); Hnr Roll; WWAHSS; Off Aide; Medicine; Doctorate (Medical); Howard U, Washington, DC; U of Maryland, College Park

PETERSON, MICHELLE; WASHINGTON, DC; DUKE ELLINGTON SCH FOR THE ARTS; (FR); Comm Volntr; Acpl Chr; Chr; Performer (Music/ Vocal); UC Berkeley-U of California

PETERSON, THOMEISHA; WASHINGTON, DC; ARCHBISHOP CARROLL HS; (JR); Hnr Roll; Nat Hon Sy; Peer Tut/Med; Red Cr Aide; Emplmnt; FBLA; Off Aide; SP/M/VS; Member of FBLA - Future Business Leaders of America; Fashion Club / Leadership 101; Business / Finance Real Estate; Communications / Criminal Justice; Howard U; Florida A & M

PINKNEY, JOHN; WASHINGTON, DC; BALLOU STAY SR HS; (SR); WWAHSS; Comm Volntr; Hosp Aide; Peer Tut/Med; Chrch Yth Grp; Emplmnt; Photog; Ch Chr; Higher Achievement Program Ambassador; MBA; Clark Atlanta U; Howard U

ROBERTSON, NAKEEA; WASHINGTON, DC; WASHINGTON MATH SCI AND TECH PUBLIC CHARTER HS; Yth Ldrshp Prog; Emplmnt; Mod UN; ROTC; Bnd; Own My Own Day Care Center; Create a Clothing Line; Trinity U; Southeastern U

ROBINSON, STACIA T; WASHINGTON, DC; BANNEKER SR HS; (FR); Ctznshp Aw; Hnr Roll; Perf Att; Comm Volntr; Pep Squd; Dnce; Yrbk (E); Member of Banneker's Junior Sorority; English; Psychology; Spelman College; Stanford U

ROBINSON, TIFFANY S; WASHINGTON, DC; BENJAMIN BANNEKER AC HS; (JR); F Lan Hn Soc; Hnr Roll; Nat Hon Sy; Otst Ac Ach Awd; Sci Fairs; WWAHSS; Yth Ldrshp Prog; Amnsty Intl; Comm Volntr; ArtClub; Emplmnt; NYLC; Pep Squd; Photog; Prom Com; Tech Clb; Spanish Clb; Pep Bnd; Swmg; Adv Cncl (T); Cl Off (T); Stu Cncl (R); Community Service Award -YWCA; Top 10 Miss DC Teen USA Pageant 2005; Business; Political Science; U of Michigan; Duke U

SCOTT, KARIMA; WASHINGTON, DC; FRIENDSHIP-EDISON COLLEGIATE AC; (SO); Ctznshp Aw; Hnr Roll; Otst Ac Ach Awd; Perf Att; Salutrn; St of Mnth; Peer Tut/Med; Chess; Photog; Tchrs Aide; Chr; Dnce; Stu Cncl (R); Yrbk (E); 10 Who Are 10 Scholarship Competition; Award of Merit: Essay Contest; Paralegal; Newscasting/Television; U of District of Columbia; Howard U

SHERMAN, IVORY; WASHINGTON, DC; BANNEKER SR HS; (FR); Ctznshp Aw; Hnr Roll; Otst Ac Ach Awd; Perf Att; Sci Fairs; Comm Volntr; Spec Olymp Vol; ArtClub; DARE; Drma Clb; Lib Aide; Mod UN; Mus Clb; Photog; Vsity Clb; SP/M/VS; Cr Ctry (V); Track (C); National Junior Honor Society; Excellence in Acting; Communications; Biology; Hampton U; George Washington U

SPENCER, JOSHUA; WASHINGTON, DC; (FR); Hnr Roll; Perf Att; Sci Fairs; Chrch Yth Grp; DARE; Georgetown U

STALEY, JAKIA M; WASHINGTON, DC; HOWARD D WOODSON SR HS; (SR); Hi Hnr Roll; Hnr Roll; Nat Hon Sy; Otst Ac Ach Awd; Sci Fairs; Yth Ldrshp Prog; Comm Volntr; Peer Tut/Med; Prom Com; Vsity Clb; Bskball (V L); Sftball (V); Vllyball (V); College Major: Accounting; Interest: Accounting, Fashion Design and Sports; Winston-Salem State U; Virginia State U

TAYLOR, ABDUL; WASHINGTON, DC; NEW ENTERPRISE & DEVELOPMENT SCH; (FR); Ctznshp Aw; Hnr Roll; MVP; Otst Ac Ach Awd; Comm Volntr; Mus Clb; Vsity Clb; Bskball (V); Ftball (V); Captain (Football, Basketball, Baseball); Engineering Master's; Education-Master's; Florida State U; U of Miami

THOMPKINS, ERNEST; WASHINGTON, DC; (SO); Hnr Roll; Perf Att; Comm Volntr

WALKER, COURTNEY D; WASHINGTON, DC; MM WASHINGTON CAREER SR HS; (SO); Hnr Roll; WWAHSS; Comm Volntr; Chrch Yth Grp; Ch Chr; Clr Grd; Drm Mjr; Mch Bnd; Chrldg (J); Pediatrician / Medical; Broadcasting; Hampton U; George Washington Med U

WARE, ANTOINETTE R; WASHINGTON, DC; ARCHBISHOP CARROLL HS; (JR); Hnr Roll; WWAHSS; Comm Volntr; Lib Aide; Off Aide; Scouts; Track (V); Stu Cncl (R); CR (R); Sociology; Criminal Science; Clark Atlanta U; Benedict College

WARWICK, RYAN; WASHINGTON, DC; ARCHBISHOP CARROLL HS; (JR); Hnr Roll; Otst Ac Ach Awd; Pres Sch; WWAHSS; Comm Volntr; Peer Tut/Med; Dbte Team; Emplmnt; SP/M/VS; Stg Cre; Chrldg (V); Vllyball (J); CR (R); Secondary Education; Sociology; Howard U; Temple U

WELCH, LATOYA T; WASHINGTON, DC; EASTERN HS; (JR); Ctznshp Aw; Hnr Roll; Otst Ac Ach Awd; St of Mnth; Comm Volntr; Peer Tut/Med; Chess; Chrch Yth Grp; Emplmnt; Pep Squd; Scouts; Clb; Chr; Ch Chr; Dnce; SP/M/VS; Chrldg (C); Stu Cncl (V); Participation in Howard U Upward Bound Program; Outstanding Student of Wheatley Elem School; Chemical Engineering; Master's Degree in Engineering and Mathematics; Rutgers U in New Jersey; Pennsylvania State

WELLS, NASHELLE; WASHINGTON, DC; MC KINLEY TECH; (SO); Hnr Roll; Otst Ac Ach Awd; Sci Fairs; Comm Volntr; DARE; Emplmnt; ROTC; Bnd; Chr; Dnce; Chrldg (V); Scr Kpr (J); Track (V); Vllyball (V); Best Friend / Diamond Girl Organization; March of Dimes Volunteer; Child Psychology / Social Worker; Real Estate Agent; Hampton U Virginia; University of Miami

WHITE, CHRISTINA; WASHINGTON, DC; (MS); Hnr Roll; Nat Mrt Fin; Nat Sci Aw; Sci Fairs; St of Mnth; Comm Volntr; Fr of Library; Mth Clb/Tm; Mus Clb; Off Aide; Outdrs Clb; Sci Clb; Svce Clb; Tchrs Aide; Bnd; Dnce; Mch Bnd; SP/M/VS; Bsball; Chrldg; Ftball; GAA; Mar Art; Skiing; Sccr; Tennis; Cl Off (P)

WILLIAMS, TA'LIESHA; WASHINGTON, DC; SPINGARN STAY HS; (SR); Ctznshp Aw; Hi Hnr Sy; Hnr Roll; Nat Hon Sy; Otst Ac Ach Awd; Perf Att; Sci Fairs; CARE; Comm Volntr; ArtClub; DARE; Drma Clb; Jr Ach; Mth Clb/Tm; Off Aide; Quiz Bowl; Tchrs Aide; Ch Chr; Dnce; Drl Tm; SP/ M/VS; Bskball (J); Chrldg (J); PPSqd (J); Skiing (V); Sftball (J); Tennis (V); Vllyball (J); Cl Off (T); CR (T); Yrbk (P); Kickball; Teacher/Childhood Care; Nurse/Nurse's Aide; Virginia State U Norfolk State; Delaware State U DC

WILLIFORD, BIANCA; WASHINGTON, DC; NEW ENTERPRISE & DVLMNT SCH; (FR); Ctznshp Aw; Hnr Roll; Otst Ac Ach Awd; Sci Fairs; Comm Volntr; Bell Choir; Art; Georgetown U; American U

WOODWARD, DOMINIQUE A; WASHINGTON, DC; ARCHBISHOP CARROLL HS; (JR); Hnr Roll; Comm Volntr; Red Cr Aide; ArtClub; Chrch Yth Grp; Dbte Team; Ch Chr; SP/M/VS; Vllyball (J); Debate Team; Athletic Trainer For Sports At Carroll; Culinary Arts; Forensics Science Research; Clark Atlanta; Xavier College New Orleans

Welch, Latoya T — Eastern HS — Washington, DC

Sherman, Ivory — Banneker SR HS — Washington, DC

Peterson, Michelle — Duke Ellington Sch For The Arts — Washington, DC

Olawoyin, Olatundun — High Point HS — Washington, DC

National Honor Roll Spring 2005

Nibblins, Valerie — New Enterprise & Dvlmnt Sch — Washington, DC

Robinson, Stacia T — Banneker SR HS — Washington, DC

Walker, Courtney D — Mm Washington Career SR HS — Washington, DC

Williams, Ta'Liesha — Spingarn Stay HS — Washington, DC

Indiana

ABRAHAM, PAULOS M; INDIANAPOLIS, IN; ARLINGTON HS; Technology; Pharmacy; Purdue U; Indiana U

ACAMOVIC, DANIJELA; SCHERERVILLE, IN; LAKE CTRL HS; (JR); Hi Hnr Roll; Hnr Roll; Nat Hon Sy; St of Mnth; WWAHSS; Peer Tut/Med; Emplmnt; Photog; Quill & Scroll; Yrbk (P); Super Fan; Law (Family); IU Bloomington (Indiana U); Michigan State

ACKERMAN, ASHLYN M; JASPER, IN; JASPER HS; (SO); Hi Hnr Roll; Hnr Roll; Sci Fairs; WWAHSS; 4-H; Chrch Yth Grp; Drma Clb; Emplmnt; Key Club; Scouts; Acpl Chr; Bnd; Chr; Mch Bnd; National Society of High School Scholars; Architecture; Spanish, Music; Ball State U

ADAIR, EMILY; SPENCER, IN; OWEN VALLEY HS; (SO); Ctznshp Aw; Hi Hnr Roll; Hnr Roll; Nat Hon Sy; Otst Ac Ach Awd; WWAHSS; Yth Ldrshp Prog; Comm Volntr; Emplmnt; Lib Aide; Chr; Sccr; Sftball; Top 10% of My Class; American Legion Award; Doctor/Physician; English Major; IU Uhalaha U; Case Western U

ADAMS, JACLYN; JASPER, IN; JASPER HS; (SO); Perf Att; WWAHSS; Comm Volntr; Hosp Aide; Spec Olymp Vol; ArtClub; Chrch Yth Grp; Emplmnt; FCA; Key Club; Scouts; SADD; Tchrs Aide; Sccr (V); Sftball (V); Key Club, Spanish Club, Art Club; Varsity Letter Club, FCA; Cosmetology; Massage Therapy; Edutech-Clearwater, Florida; Louisiana State U

ADAMS, JESSICA; GRANGER, IN; PENN HS; (FR); Hi Hnr Roll; Pres Ac Ftns Aw; Comm Volntr; 4-H; Chrch Yth Grp; Drma Clb; Chr; Ch Chr; SP/M/VS; Stg Cre; Hsbk Rdg; Equine Studies; Murray State U

ADAMS, MEGAN E; PORTLAND, IN; JAY CTY HS; (FR); Hi Hnr Roll; Otst Ac Ach Awd; Comm Volntr; FCA; Fr of Library; Key Club; Spanish Clb; Swg Chr; Chrldg (J); Gmnstcs (J); Tennis (J); 2003 Member of East Jay Academic Bowl Team; 2002 County & District Speech Winner-Optimist Contest

ADAMS, SEAN A; PORTLAND, IN; JAY CTY HS; (JR); Hi Hnr Roll; Nat Hon Sy; Otst Ac Ach Awd; Comm Volntr; FCA; Fr of Library; Key Club; Spanish Clb; Swg Chr; Scr Kpr (V); Sccr (V L); Fall 2004 Academic All State Soccer Team; 2004 Stay in Bounds Ambassador Program

ADAMS, TRACEY; RICHMOND, IN; RICHMOND HS; (SO); Hnr Roll; Nat Hon Sy; Chrch Yth Grp; German Clb; Chr; Dnce; Accounting; International Business Foundation

ADKINS, CHRISTINA D; GEORGETOWN, IN; LANESVILLE HS; (SO); Hnr Roll; Perf Att; Pres Ac Ftns Aw; St of Mnth; Chrch Yth Grp; DARE; FCA; ROTC; French Clb; Chr; Bskball (VJ); Sftball (V); Vllyball (J); CR (S, T); ROTC Outstanding Cadet; Young Artisans; Astronomical Engineering; Space Science; Purdue U

AHEE, ADRIENNE; FORT WAYNE, IN; HOMESTEAD HS; (SR); Hi Hnr Roll; Hnr Roll; Otst Ac Ach Awd; Pres Ac Ftns Aw; St of Mnth; WWAHSS; Comm Volntr; Peer Tut/Med; Emplmnt; Key Club; Mth Clb/Tm; Off Aide; Photog; Tchrs Aide; Vsity Clb; French Clb; Bnd; Dnce; SP/M/VS; Bskball; Ice Sktg; Tennis (J); Vsy Clb (V); 2004 Ameridance Varsity Dance Soloist National; 2004 In-State Figure Skating - Runner-up Champion; Biology Major; Medical School; U of Wisconsin-Madison

AHMED, HENA; CARMEL, IN; STONE BRIDGE HS; (FR); Hi Hnr Roll; Key Club; Off Aide; Scr Kpr (J)

ALBERTS, TIFFANY C; ELKHART, IN; ELKHART CTRL HS; (SO); Hnr Roll; Kwnis Aw; Sci Fairs; St of Mnth; Comm Volntr; Hab For Humty Volntr; Peer Tut/Med; DARE; Emplmnt; Key Club; Scouts; Orch; I Teach Sunday School At My Church; Active in Clubs At My Church; Archaeology; History

ALCORN, JAY T; BAINBRIDGE, IN; NORTH PUTNAM HS; (SR); 4H Awd; Hi Hnr Roll; Nat Hon Sy; Otst Ac Ach Awd; St of Mnth; WWAHSS; Yth Ldrshp Prog; 4-H; Emplmnt; Key Club; Ntl FFA; Bsball (V L); Cl Off (R); TSLA; Livestock Judging-Top Individual; Agriculture Economics; Agriculture Science; Purdue U

ALEXANDER, KELYN A; ANDERSON, IN; HIGHLAND HS; (FR); Hnr Roll; Chrch Yth Grp; Drma Clb; Ch Chr; Stg Cre; Sccr (V); Sftball (J)

ALI, MAIDUM F; INDIANAPOLIS, IN; PIKE HS; (JR); ROTC; Wdwrkg Clb; Rugby Team - Varsity; Rugby Club; Business Management; Hotel Management; Indiana U; IUPUI

ALLEN, CHRISTINE E; ELKHART, IN; ELKHART CTRL HS; (JR); 4H Awd; Hi Hnr Roll; Nat Hon Sy; Otst Ac Ach Awd; St of Mnth; WWAHSS; Comm Volntr; 4-H; Chrch Yth Grp; DARE; Drma Clb; Emplmnt; Key Club; Photog; Spch Team; Orch; Stg Cre; PP Ftbl (V); Swmg (J); Track (J); Top Ten of Students in Junior Class; #8 Out of 400 Students; Obstetric Nursing; Indiana U Purdue U; Indianapolis

ALLEN, DEREK; ELBERFELD, IN; WALDO J WOOD MEMORIAL HS; (FR); Bsball (V); Bskball (J); Architecture; Indiana U

ALLEN, JESSICA; COVINGTON, IN; COVINGTON CHRISTIAN SCH; (JR); 4H Awd; Hnr Roll; Pres Ac Ftns Aw; Sci Fairs; 4-H; Chrch Yth Grp; Emplmnt; Off Aide; Tchrs Aide; SP/M/VS; Bskball (JC); Vllyball (J); Cl Off (S); Stu Cncl (T); Yrbk (E); Early Education

ALLENSWORTH, BRITTANY S; INDIANAPOLIS, IN; ARLINGTON HS; (FR); Ctznshp Aw; Hi Hnr Roll; Hnr Roll; Otst Ac Ach Awd; Perf Att; Sci Fairs; St of Mnth; Peer Tut/Med; Jr Ach; Lib Aide; Off Aide; Tchrs Aide; Stu Cncl (R); Selected For Science Bound; Honors Student - Top Of Class; Criminal Justice; Forensic Science; Purdue U; Georgia Tech U

ALLISON, KAYLA N; LOGANSPORT, IN; LEWIS CASS HS; (JR); Hnr Roll; Otst Ac Ach Awd; Pres Ac Ftns Aw; Peer Tut/Med; Chrch Yth Grp; Emplmnt; FCA; Key Club; Lttrmn Clb; SADD; Tchrs Aide; SP/M/VS; Bskball (V); Golf (V); Vllyball (J); Telecommunications; Sports Management; Ball State U; Purdue U

ALLMAN, KYLA R; COLUMBUS, IN; COLUMBUS EAST HS; (SO); Chrch Yth Grp; Quill & Scroll; Ch Chr; Sch Ppr (E); Most Improved Student-Into Health 6 Years; Law-Lawyer; Bible-Pastoral Ministry; Pensacola Christian College; Christian Bible College (CBC)

ANDERSON, CARLY; CARMEL, IN; CARMEL HS; (JR); F Lan Hn Soc; Hi Hnr Roll; Nat Hon Sy; WWAHSS; Peer Tut/Med; AL Aux Girls; DECA; Emplmnt; Mod UN; Prom Com; Quill & Scroll; Cr Ctry (V CL); Sccr (J); Cl Off (V); Sch Ppr (E); Top 10 at Nationals for DECA; Mental Attitude Award for Carmel Cross Country; Public Relations; Business; Indiana U; Boston U

ANDERSON, GINA; CLOVERDALE, IN; CLOVERDALE HS; (SR); 4H Awd; Nat Hon Sy; Perf Att; St of Mnth; 4-H; Ntl FFA; Prom Com; SADD; Spanish Clb; Golf (V L); PP Ftbl; Track (V L); Stu Cncl; VP of FFA; Horticulture Production and Marketing; Purdue U

ANDREWS, DEREK J; BROWNSBURG, IN; BROWNSBURG HS; (SO); F Lan Hn Soc; Hi Hnr Roll; Nat Hon Sy; WWAHSS; Yth Ldrshp Prog; Comm Volntr; Peer Tut/Med; FCA; Jr Cls League; Key Club; NYLC; Outdrs Clb; Schol Bwl; Latin Clb; Bnd; Mch Bnd; Pep Bnd; Spell Bowl; Medicine; Indiana U; Purdue U

ANDREWS, ELLIOT; SOUTH BEND, IN; RILEY HS; (FR); Hnr Roll; Sci Fairs; Sci/Math Olympn; Chrch Yth Grp; Ch Chr; Track (J); Law; Notre Dame U; U of Chicago

ANG, NOEL; TERRE HAUTE, IN; TERRE HAUTE SOUTH VIGO HS; (SO); Hi Hnr Roll; Perf Att; Hab For Humty Volntr; Latin Clb; Track (J); Designed T-Shirts Asian American Club; Architecture

ANSPACH, LANDON M; ELKHART, IN; ELKHART CTRL HS; (JR); Bnd; Jzz Bnd; Mch Bnd; Orch; Bsball (VJ); Cr Ctry (V L)

APPLE, ELIZABETH D; KNOX, IN; KNOX HS; (SO); Hnr Roll; Yth Ldrshp Prog; Spec Olymp Vol; 4-H; DARE; Lib Aide; Sci Clb; Tchrs Aide; Vsity Clb; Hsbk Rdg; PP Ftbl (V); Sftball (V); Stu Cncl (R); Sch Ppr (R); Veterinarian Science Degree; Purdue North Central

AQUIRRE, MONICA; INDIANAPOLIS, IN; BEN DAVIS HS; (SO); Ctznshp Aw; Hi Hnr Roll; Otst Ac Ach Awd; WWAHSS; Presidents Education Awards Program; Secondary Education; Butler U; Saint Mary's of the Woods

ARBUCKLE, ALEXANDRIA N; SAINT PAUL, IN; NORTH DECATUR JR/SR HS; (SO); Hnr Roll; Nat Hon Sy; WWAHSS; Comm Volntr; Peer Tut/Med; Chrch Yth Grp; Key Club; Pep Squd; Clb; Bnd; Chr; Dnce; Mch Bnd; PPSqd (V C); CR (P); Big Brothers/Big Sisters Volunteer; Page to the Indiana State House; Political Science; Pre-Law; Harvard U; George Washington U

ARCHER, ASHLYN; GREENCASTLE, IN; GREENCASTLE HS; (FR); 4H Awd; Hi Hnr Roll; Comm Volntr; 4-H; Fr of Library; Key Club; Lib Aide; Scouts; Bnd; Chr; Pep Bnd; SP/M/VS; Stu Cncl (R); Latin Clb; Key Club, Student Council; Journalism; English Major; DePauw U; Purdue U

ARMAO, TYLER W; INDIANAPOLIS, IN; LUTHERAN HS OF INDIANAPOLIS; (JR); F Lan Hn Soc; Hi Hnr Roll; Nat Hon Sy; Otst Ac Ach Awd; Sci/Math Olympn; USAA; WWAHSS; Comm Volntr; Hab For Humty Volntr; Peer Tut/Med; Chrch Yth Grp; Drma Clb; Jr Ach; Schol Bwl; Chr; SP/M/VS; Ice Hky (J L); Vllyball (VJCL); Stu Cncl (S); CR (R); Yrbk (E, R, P); Journalism - Print / Mass Media; Advertising; Ball State U; Syracuse U

ARNDT, KAITLIN M; LEBANON, IN; WESTERN BOONE JR/SR HS; (JR); Hnr Roll; Nat Hon Sy; Nat Mrt Fin; Nat Mrt Semif; WWAHSS; Yth Ldrshp Prog; Comm Volntr; Peer Tut/Med; Emplmnt; Key Club; Off Aide; Prom Com; Quiz Bowl; Scouts; Tchrs Aide; Foreign Clb; Attended National Youth Leadership Program on Medicine; Attending IU Honors Program in Mexico, 2005; Medicine; Physical Therapy; Purdue U; DePaul U

ARNOLD, AYMBER M; WEST BADEN SPRINGS, IN; PAOLI HS; (FR); Hi Hnr Roll; Hnr Roll; Otst Ac Ach Awd; Sci Fairs; Peer Tut/Med; Off Aide; SADD; Tchrs Aide; Wdwrkg Clb; Spanish Clb; Bnd; Chr; Clr Grd; Mch Bnd; Tutored Peers/Talked Out Problems With Peers; I Also Help Take Care of My Severely Autistic Brother; Anything in Medical Field; Indiana U

ARNOLD, RACHELLE; WOODBURN, IN; BISHOP LUERS HS; (SR); Hi Hnr Roll; Hnr Roll; Jr Rot; Nat Hon Sy; Nat Sci Aw; Perf Att; WWAHSS; Peer Tut/Med; NtlFrnscLg; Spch Team; SADD; Chr; Dnce; SP/M/VS; Swg Chr; Lit Mag (R); Peer Ministry; Mass Server; Chemistry; Forensic Chemist; U of Indianapolis

ARROWOOD, LORI R; SCOTTSBURG, IN; SCOTTSBURG HS; (SR); Hi Hnr Roll; MVP; Nat Hon Sy; Otst Ac Ach Awd; Pres Sch; USAA; Red Cr Aide; Emplmnt; Photog; Quill & Scroll; Sftball (V L); Sch Ppr (E); National Honor Society; Indiana U Southeast

ASHBY, CARRISSA B; HIGHLAND, IN; HIGHLAND HS; (JR); Hnr Roll; Pres Sch; Chrch Yth Grp; Emplmnt; Key Club; Pep Squd; Tchrs Aide; Chr; Orch; Chrldg (V C); Scr Kpr (V L); Key Club; 1st Place At ISSMA for Orchestra; Pediatrician; I Would Like to Open Up My Own Pediatric Clinic.; Indiana U of Bloomington; Indiana U, Purdue U

ATKINSON, ASHLEY; KOKOMO, IN; KOKOMO HS; (JR); Hnr Roll; Jr Rot; Perf Att; Pres Ac Ftns Aw; St of Mnth; Comm Volntr; Hab For Humty Volntr; Drma Clb; Emplmnt; FCA; Prom Com; Quill & Scroll; Sci Clb; Vsity Clb; Spanish Clb; Sccr (V L); Swmg (J); Vsy Clb (V); Stu Cncl (R); Yrbk (R); Turn-Around Award; Elementary Education; U of Southern Indiana; Indiana U

AUER, ALYSSA B D; COLUMBIA CITY, IN; COLUMBIA CITY HS; (SR); Nat Hon Sy; WWAHSS; Comm Volntr; Peer Tut/Med; Ntl FFA; SADD; Bnd; Jzz Bnd; Mch Bnd; Pep Bnd; Adv Cncl; Junior Miss; Veterinarian of Large & Small Animals; Purdue U

AVERY, TAKENDRIA; INDIANAPOLIS, IN; BROAD RIPPLE HS; (FR); Hnr Roll; WWAHSS; Key Club; Ch Chr; Orch; Key Club Member; Music Major; Juilliard; Kentucky State

AYALA, ANA C; INDIANAPOLIS, IN; NORTHWEST HS; (FR); Ctznshp Aw; Hnr Roll; St of Mnth; Chr; Lawyer

BABBS, KELLAN W; SPENCER, IN; OWEN VALLEY CMTY HS; (SO); Hi Hnr Roll; Hnr Roll; Perf Att; Sci Fairs; Sci/Math Olympn; WWAHSS; Comm Volntr; Jr Cls League; Lttrmn Clb; Golf (V L); Scr Kpr; Stu Cncl (R); Announcer-Football & Basketball; Who's Who Member; Anesthesiologist; Chemical Engineer; Massachusetts Institute of Technology; Indiana U

BAIEL, JOSHUA J; WHEATFIELD, IN; KANKAKEE VALLEY HS; (SO); Hi Hnr Roll; Nat Hon Sy; Perf Att; Sci/Math Olympn; St of Mnth; Drma Clb; Emplmnt; Jr Ach; Mth Clb/Tm; Schol Bwl; Foreign Clb; Chr; SP/M/VS; Cl Off (T); Stu Cncl (R); All-State Chorus/1st in State Vocal; 1st in Regional Piano Competition; Mathematics; Paleontology; U of Evansville; Harvard U

BAILEY, ALEISHA K; EDINBURGH, IN; EDINBURGH HS; (FR); Hnr Roll; WWAHSS; 4-H; Chrch Yth Grp; French Clb; Chr; Dnce; Tennis (V); Cl Off (V); FCCLA; 4-H Junior Leaders; Pediatric Nursing

BAKER, CHARLIE W; SPENCER, IN; OWEN VALLEY CMTY HS; (FR); Hnr Roll; Perf Att; Science Major; Chemist Major; Indiana State U; Hanover College

BAKER, JULIE; HIGHLAND, IN; HIGHLAND HS; (SO); F Lan Hn Soc; Hi Hnr Roll; Hnr Roll; Nat Hon Sy; Comm Volntr; Emplmnt; Key Club; Track (V); National Art Honor Society; Business; Chemistry; Indiana U; Northwestern U

BALLARD, CHRISTOPHER A; SOUTH BEND, IN; RILEY HS; (FR); Hi Hnr Roll; Hnr Roll; Kwnis Aw; Perf Att; Pres Sch; Sci/Math Olympn; St of Mnth; Comm Volntr; Peer Tut/Med; Chrch Yth Grp; Ch Chr; Orch; Bsball (J); Ftball (J); Swmg (J); Stu Cncl (V); CR; Yrbk (P); Friends, Inc Organization; Purdue U; US Naval Academy

BALTIERRA, ROBERTO; INDIANAPOLIS, IN; NORTHWEST HS; (SO); Hnr Roll; Perf Att; Computers; IUPUI; Franklin College

BANKSON, PATRICE; CHURUBUSCO, IN; CHURUBUSCO HS; (JR); Hi Hnr Roll; Nat Hon Sy; Otst Ac Ach Awd; WWAHSS; Yth Ldrshp Prog; Comm Volntr; FCA; Key Club; Lttrmn Clb; SADD; Bskball (J); Sftball (V L); Vllyball (V L); CR (R); Yrbk; Advisor on Gifted and Talented Board; Student Tutor; Law; St Mary's at Notre Dame; Indiana U

BARGER, JOHN; INDIANAPOLIS, IN; BEN DAVIS HS; (JR); Hnr Roll; Writing; Physics; Indiana U Purdue U Indianapolis; Purdue

Bailey, Aleisha K
Edinburgh HS
Edinburgh, IN

Arnold, Aymber M
Paoli HS
West Baden Springs, IN

Ahee, Adrienne
Homestead HS
Fort Wayne, IN

Acamovic, Danijela
Lake Ctrl HS
Schererville, IN

National
Honor Roll
Spring 2005

Abraham, Paulos M
Arlington HS
Indianapolis, IN

Andrews, Derek J
Brownsburg HS
Brownsburg, IN

Arrowood, Lori R
Scottsburg HS
Scottsburg, IN

Ballard, Christopher A
Riley HS
South Bend, IN

BARKER, ALLISON P; NOBLESVILLE, IN; NOBLESVILLE HS; (SO); Hnr Roll; Key Club; P to P St Amb Prg; Spanish Clb; Stu Cncl (R); Ballet Medical Explorer Program; Doctorate; Indiana U-Bloomington; Northeastern-Boston

BARKER, CORY; HARTFORD CITY, IN; (JR); Hnr Roll; Nat Hon Sy; WWAHSS; BPA; Key Club; Sci Clb; Spanish Clb; Bskball (J); Journalism; Psychology; Michigan State U; UCLA

BARKER, WHITTNEY M; COLUMBUS, IN; COLUMBUS EAST HS; (JR); Hnr Roll; Nat Hon Sy; Pres Sch; St of Mnth; Yth Ldrshp Prog; Comm Volntr; Red Cr Aide; Emplmnt; Key Club; Prom Com; Quill & Scroll; Spanish Clb; Bskball (J); Golf (V L); Swmg (V L); Tennis (V L); Vllyball (J); Cl Off; Stu Cncl; CR; Yrbk (R); Youth Salute; Television Crew; Purdue U; Indiana U

BARLETT, AMANDA L; ROCKPORT, IN; SOUTH SPENCER HS; (SO); Ctznshp Aw; Hi Hnr Roll; Pres Sch; WWAHSS; Tennis (J); Fish and Game Club.; Forensic Scientist (C.S.I); Prosecuting Attorney; Tulane U; U of North Carolina

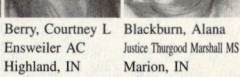

BARLOW, JONATHAN E; INDIANAPOLIS, IN; BROAD RIPPLE HS; (SO); Hi Hnr Roll; Kwnis Aw; Nat Hon Sy; Otst Ac Ach Awd; Perf Att; Pres Sch; Sci Fairs; Yth Ldrshp Prog; Comm Volntr; Peer Tut/Med; ArtClub; Cmptr Clb; Emplmnt; Key Club; Mth Clb/Tm; Quiz Bowl; Schol Bwl; Stu Cncl (P); Youth Mentor At Young Audiences of Indiana; YARCI Board Member; Engineering; Robotics; Harvard U; NYU

BARNETT, JASMINE M; MARION, IN; MARION HS; (SO); Hnr Roll; Yth Ldrshp Prog; Comm Volntr; Peer Tut/Med; Chrch Yth Grp; Lib Aide; Bnd; Ch Chr; Dnce; Mch Bnd; Track (J); Black History Club; Criminal Justice; Central State U; Ball State U

BARNETT, NATASHA; BRAZIL, IN; NORTHVIEW HS; (SR); Hnr Roll; Jr Eng Tech; WWAHSS; BPA; Emplmnt; Key Club; Off Aide; Pep Squd; SADD; Tech Clb; Vsity Clb; Ch Chr; Dnce; SP/M/VS; Bskball (J); Chrldg (V C); Sccr (V); Track (V C); Vllyball (J); Cl Off (V/S); Stu Cncl (R); Super Mileage Team Captain; Technology Club President; Architectural Engineering; Wentworth Institute of Technology

BARNICKLE, CRAIG; LANESVILLE, IN; LANESVILLE CMTY SCH; (JR); Hnr Roll; Sci Fairs; Sci/Math Olympn; St of Mnth; WWAHSS; Comm Volntr; Chrch Yth Grp; DARE; Ntl FFA; Tchrs Aide; Bskball (V); Indiana Science Olympiad State Finalist; Professional Commercial Pilot; Indiana State U; Embry Riddle Aeronautical U

BARR, TRAMAINE F; SOUTH BEND, IN; CLAY HS; (SR); Ctznshp Aw; Hi Hnr Roll; Hnr Roll; Otst Ac Ach Awd; Perf Att; St of Mnth; DARE; ROTC; Voc Ind Clb Am; Ch Chr; Drm Mjr; Camera Operator; Movie Producer; Ivy Tech

BARTLETT, JOSH; DEPUTY, IN; SOUTHWESTERN MS/SR HS; (JR); Hnr Roll; Emplmnt; Bsball (V); Wrstlg (V CL); Ball State; Vincennes U

BATES, SHANE; EVANSVILLE, IN; CENTRAL HS; (SO); Ctznshp Aw; Hi Hnr Roll; Perf Att; Emplmnt; Bsball (V); Bskball (V); Ftball (V); U of Evansville; U Notre Dame

BAUER, AMOS; TERRE HAUTE, IN; TERRE HAUTE SOUTH VIGO HS; (JR); Hi Hnr Roll; Quiz Bowl; Tech Clb; Indiana State U; Ivy Tech

BAUM, ANDREW J; EVANSVILLE, IN; (FR); Hnr Roll; Pres Sch; Comm Volntr; Hab For Humty Volntr; Peer Tut/Med; ArtClub; FCA; SADD; German Clb; Ice Hky (V); Teacher; Communications; U of Nebraska

BAUM, ASHLEY N; EVANSVILLE, IN; F J REITZ HS; (SR); F Lan Hn Soc; Hi Hnr Roll; MVP; Nat Hon Sy; Otst Ac Ach Awd; Pres Ac Ftns Aw; WWAHSS; Yth Ldrshp Prog; Comm Volntr; Hab For Humty Volntr; Peer Tut/Med; BPA; Chrch Yth Grp; DARE; DECA; Emplmnt; FCA; Schol Bwl; Svce Clb; Vllyball (V CL); Academic All City, 1st Team All State, 1st Team All City; Who's Who Among HS Athletes; Marketing/Business; Teaching; Kentucky Wesleyan College

BAWEL, HEATHER; JASPER, IN; JASPER HS; (SO); Hnr Roll; St of Mnth; Peer Tut/Med; 4-H; Chrch Yth Grp; DARE; Emplmnt; Key Club; Prom Com; SADD; Spanish Clb; Stu Cncl (R); Advertising; Indiana U; Western Kentucky

BAXTER, ERIÇA N; MARION, IN; JUSTICE THURGOOD MARSHALL MS; MS; Hi Hnr Roll; Perf Att; Chrch Yth Grp; Jr Ach; Lib Aide; Mth Clb/Tm; Bnd; Jzz Bnd; Mch Bnd; Yrbk (E); Mayor's Math Award; President's Award for Educational Excellence; Computers; Science

BAYON, AMIE D; INDIANAPOLIS, IN; LAWRENCE CTRL HS; (FR); Hi Hnr Roll; Hnr Roll; Perf Att; Pres Ac Ftns Aw; St of Mnth; Chrch Yth Grp; Key Club; Spch Team; Ch Chr; Orch; Tennis (J); Adv Cncl (V); National Forensic League, Degree of Merit; First Place Division 3 ISSMA; Major in Finance; Stock Broker; Indiana U (Bloomington)

BAYS, JENNIFER L; ARCADIA, IN; HAMILTON HEIGHTS HS; (JR); Hi Hnr Roll; Hnr Roll; Nat Hon Sy; Comm Volntr; 4-H; FCA; NYLC; Prom Com; Sci Clb; Scouts; Spanish Clb; Cr Ctry (J L); Track (V L); Stu Cncl (R); CR (R); Volunteer EMT; Community Emergency Response Team Member; Pre-Medicine; Medicine; Cornell U; Hanover College

BAZYK, KYLE C; SOUTH BEND, IN; ADAMS HS; (SO); Ctznshp Aw; Hi Hnr Roll; Otst Ac Ach Awd; Perf Att; St of Mnth; Bnd; Jzz Bnd; Mch Bnd; Pep Bnd; Tae Kwon Do Awards and Trophies - Out of School; Mechanical Engineer; Architect; Purdue U; Ball State

BEABOUT, LEANDRA N; ELKHART, IN; CONCORD HS; (SR); Hi Hnr Roll; Hnr Roll; Nat Hon Sy; Nat Mrt LOC; WWAHSS; Comm Volntr; Chrch Yth Grp; Emplmnt; Key Club; Photog; Schol Bwl; Creative Writing; English; Taylor U

BEAM, KAYLEE R; PERU, IN; PERU HS; (FR); Hnr Roll; Nat Hon Sy; Emplmnt; Writer; Lawyer; Purdue; Ohio State

BEAM, MICHAEL; INDIANAPOLIS, IN; BEN DAVIS HS; (JR); F Lan Hn Soc; Hnr Roll; Perf Att; Quill & Scroll; Spch Team; Bnd; Sch Ppr (E, R); Harvey Award-Division 3-1st Place-Newspaper Division Sports Writing; 2004 Quill and Scroll's National Award Gold Key-Feature Story; Journalism; History

BEARDSLEY, CARL; CARMEL, IN; CARMEL HS; (SR); Hnr Roll; Nat Hon Sy; St of Mnth; Chrch Yth Grp; DECA; Cr Ctry (V L); Track (J L); Academic Honors; Scholar Athlete & Class Award; Economics; Spanish; DePauw U

BEAULIEU, ANDREA; FORT WAYNE, IN; NORTH SIDE HS; (JR); Hi Hnr Roll; Hnr Roll; Nat Hon Sy; Comm Volntr; Peer Tut/Med; Photog; Quill & Scroll; Quiz Bowl; Spch Team; Stu Cncl (R); Yrbk (R, P); Outstanding Photojournalism Award; Graphic Design; Photographer; U of Saint Francis; Webster U

BECKER, SCOTT; WINAMAC, IN; WEST CTRL SR HS; (FR); 4H Awd; Hnr Roll; 4-H; Ftball; GAA (J); Golf (J)

BECKMAN, ALI; JASPER, IN; JASPER HS; (JR); Hnr Roll; Kwnis Aw; Nat Hon Sy; WWAHSS; Comm Volntr; Hosp Aide; Peer Tut/Med; FCA; Key Club; Off Aide; Prom Com; SADD; Bnd; Mch Bnd; Pep Bnd; Swmg (J); Track (V); Majoring in Nursing; Majoring in Occupational Therapy; Indiana U; Indiana State U

BECKMAN, LACY; JASPER, IN; JASPER HS; (FR); Hnr Roll; WWAHSS; Comm Volntr; Chrch Yth Grp; Key Club; Spanish Clb; Chrldg (V); Gmnstcs; Sftball; (Cheerleading) 2004-05 NCA National Champions; 4-H champs, Regional Champs, NCA All-American, Top Team; Interior Design; Indiana U; U of Southern Indiana

BECKMAN, ROSS; JASPER, IN; JASPER HS; (FR); WWAHSS; DARE; Key Club; SADD; Spanish Clb; Bnd; Mch Bnd; Pep Bnd; Tennis (J); December Student of the Month; Instrumental Music; Visual Arts

BELANGER, KENDRA; SUNMAN, IN; SOUTH DEARBORN HS; (JR); Gov Hnr Prg; Hi Hnr Roll; Otst Ac Ach Awd; Pres Ac Ftns Aw; St of Mnth; WWAHSS; Bnd; Mch Bnd; Pep Bnd; Stg Cre; Chemistry; Engineering; Purdue U; U of Southern Indiana

BENDER, AMANDA E; ELKHART, IN; ELKHART CTRL; (FR); Hi Hnr Roll; Hnr Roll; MVP; Nat Hon Sy; Otst Ac Ach Awd; St of Mnth; Comm Volntr; Chrch Yth Grp; Emplmnt; FCA; Key Club; Bnd; Mch Bnd; Pep Bnd; PP Ftbl; 10 Yrs of Dance Outside of School; About 5 Yrs of Softball Outside of School; Zoologist; Veterinarian; Olivet Nazarene U; Pensacola Christian College

BENDER, EMILY; POSEYVILLE, IN; NORTH POSEY HS; (SR); 4H Awd; Hnr Roll; Perf Att; 4-H; Ntl FFA; Off Aide; Pep Squd; German Clb; Dnce; Bskball (J); Cr Ctry (V); Sccr (V); Vllyball (J); Ball State U

BENNETT, ETHAN; PETERSBURG, IN; PIKE CTRL HS; (FR); Hnr Roll; SADD; Bnd; Mch Bnd; SP/M/VS; Swg Chr; Golf (V); Medical Field

BERCOT, ROSS; FORT WAYNE, IN; NORTHROP HS; (FR); Hi Hnr Roll; Chess; Jr Ach; Mth Clb/Tm; Schol Bwl; Sci Clb; Spch Team; Jzz Bnd; Mch Bnd; Orch; SP/M/VS; Butler U; Ball State U

BERMUDEZ, ADRIAN; BLUFFTON, IN; BLUFFTON HS; (JR); Hnr Roll; Comm Volntr; Chrch Yth Grp; DARE; Emplmnt; Off Aide; Prom Com; SADD; Swg Chr; Bskball (J); Ftball (V); Golf (J); Criminal Justice; Design; Ball State; IPFW

BERO, ZACK; CROWN POINT, IN; LAKE CTRL HS; (SR); Hnr Roll; FCA; Lttrmn Clb; Off Aide; Bskball (V L); Track (V L); Business Marketing; Indiana U

BERRY, COURTNEY L; HIGHLAND, IN; ENSWEILER AC; (SO); Hnr Roll; Otst Ac Ach Awd; Perf Att; Pres Sch; Sci Fairs; Sci/Math Olympn; St of Mnth; Comm Volntr; ArtClub; DARE; Drma Clb; Mus Clb; Photog; Quiz Bowl; Sci Clb; Scouts; Acpl Chr; Chr; SP/M/VS; Stg Cre; Art (Visual) Awards; Poetry Awards; Fashion Design; Cosmetic Surgery; International Academy of Design and Technology; U of Arizona, Purdue Calumet

BERRYMAN, TABATHA; ANDERSON, IN; HIGHLAND HS; (FR); Hi Hnr Roll; Hnr Roll; Chrch Yth Grp; Bnd; Clr Grd; Mch Bnd; Sftball (J); Marine Biology; Lawyer; Ball State U; Harvard U

BESS, KELSEY E; RUSHVILLE, IN; RUSHVILLE CONSOLIDATED HS; (SO); 4H Awd; Hnr Roll; Peer Tut/Med; 4-H; Chrch Yth Grp; Emplmnt; FCA; Key Club; Photog; Scouts; SADD; Chr; Golf (V L); Tennis (V L); Adv Cncl (R); Yrbk (R, P); Dental Hygiene; Doctor; Butler; Hanover

BIDDLE II, RICHARD J; GRABILL, IN; WOODLAN JR/SR HS; (MS); Hi Hnr Roll; Pres Sch; St of Mnth; Comm Volntr; Peer Tut/Med; Chess; Chrch Yth Grp; Bnd; Stu Cncl; Peer Mediation Team; EF Tours-Student Explorer; Law; Photography; Ball State; Purdue U

BIEHL, DARA; URBANA, IN; NORTHFIELD JR-SR HS; (SO); 4H Awd; Hi Hnr Roll; Otst Ac Ach Awd; 4-H; Chrch Yth Grp; Bnd; Pep Bnd; Tennis (J L); Vllyball (J L); Academic Super Bowl; Top Sophomore

BIGNELL, LACHELLE J; WEST TERRE HAUTE, IN; WEST VIGO HS; (SO); Hi Hnr Roll; Hnr Roll; Sci Fairs; Comm Volntr; Spec Olymp Vol; DARE; Clb; SP/M/VS; Bskball (V); Sccr (J); Vllyball (V); Veterinary; Basket Ball Player; Perdue; ISU

BIKOS, ATHINA I; MICHIGAN CITY, IN; MICHIGAN CITY HS; (FR); Hi Hnr Roll; Hnr Roll; Nat Hon Sy; Otst Ac Ach Awd; St of Mnth; Peer Tut/Med; Photog; Presidential Education Awards Program; Computer Programmer; Indiana U; Ball State U

BISHOP, AMY; NEW ALBANY, IN; NEW ALBANY HS; (FR); Hi Hnr Roll; Hnr Roll; Otst Ac Ach Awd; Perf Att; Pres Sch; FCA; Photog; German Clb; Dnce; PPSqd (V C); Sch Ppr (E, P); Journalism; Broadcasting; Indiana U; U of Louisville

BLACKBURN, ALANA; MARION, IN; JUSTICE THURGOOD MARSHALL MS; MS; Hnr Roll; DARE; Bnd; Chrldg (V); Gmnstcs (J); Ball State U, Indiana U; Purdue U, Taylor U

BLACKBURN, BRITTANY; HARTFORD CITY, IN; BLACKFORD HS; (JR); 4H Awd; Hnr Roll; Nat Hon Sy; Otst Ac Ach Awd; Pres Ac Ftns Aw; 4-H; Key Club; Pep Squd; Prom Com; SADD; Spanish Clb; Bnd; Chr; Dnce; Chrldg (VJ L); Gmnstcs (VJ L); Track (V L); Vllyball (VJ L); Cl Off (S); UCA All-Star - 2 Yrs; All-State Choir - 4 Yrs; Elementary Teaching; Ball State U; Indiana U

BLAIR, ALYSSA; BOONVILLE, IN; BOONVILLE HS; (SO); 4H Awd; Hnr Roll; Perf Att; St of Mnth; WWAHSS; Peer Tut/Med; 4-H; Chrch Yth Grp; Emplmnt; Key Club; Lttrmn Clb; Dnce; Tennis (J); Interior Designing; Auburn U

BLAIR, KELLY; OSGOOD, IN; (SO); Hnr Roll; Nat Hon Sy; ArtClub; Chrch Yth Grp; Drma Clb; Emplmnt; Spanish Clb; SP/M/VS; Private Flute Lessons; Spell Bowl, Academic Bowl; Computer Science; School of Advertising Art; Indiana U

BLAKE, LARRY; INDIANAPOLIS, IN; ARLINGTON HS; (SR); Hnr Roll; Otst Ac Ach Awd; Perf Att; WWAHSS; Comm Volntr; Tennis (V); Wrstlg (V); Voice Representative; Multi-Cultural Youth Congress Member; Christian Ministry; Psychology; Kentucky Wesleyan College

BLOOM, CHRIS; CONNERSVILLE, IN; CONNERSVILLE HS; (JR); Hi Hnr Roll; MVP; Perf Att; WWAHSS; Chrch Yth Grp; FCA; Key Club; Vsity Clb; Spanish Clb; Bskball (V); Tennis (V); Vsy Clb (V); Cl Off (R); Stu Cncl (R); Radiation Therapist

BLUHM, CHRISTY A; DECATUR, IN; ADAMS CTRL HS; (SR); 4H Awd; Hi Hnr Roll; Hnr Roll; Nat Hon Sy; Otst Ac Ach Awd; Perf Att; WWAHSS; Comm Volntr; Hosp Aide; Peer Tut/Med; 4-H; ArtClub; Chrch Yth Grp; DARE; Emplmnt; Mth Clb/Tm; Ntl FFA; Off Aide; Chrldg (J); Hsbk Rdg (J); PP Ftbl (J); Nursing; Indiana State U

BLUMENSTOCK, KACI; ELKHART, IN; ELKHART CTRL HS; (FR); 4H Awd; Hi Hnr Roll; Otst Ac Ach Awd; Pres Sch; Sci Fairs; WWAHSS; Comm Volntr; Chrch Yth Grp; DARE; Key Club; Quiz Bowl; Tchrs Aide; Orch; SP/M/VS; Celebration of Excellence; Academic Super Bowl; Chemistry; Engineering; Indiana U; Stanford

BLUNK, DAVID; FLOYDS KNOBS, IN; FLOYD CTRL HS; (SO); Hnr Roll; Sci Fairs; St of Mnth; WWAHSS; Chrch Yth Grp; SADD; Latin Clb; Bsball; Bskball; Pharmacy; U of Kentucky; Butler U

BODKIN, JOE; WILKINSON, IN; GREENFIELD CTRL HS; (FR); 4H Awd; Hnr Roll; Perf Att; Sci Fairs; Yth Ldrshp Prog; Comm Volntr; 4-H; Chrch Yth Grp; Tchrs Aide; Spanish Clb; Chr; Ftball (J); Swmg (V); Cl Off (V); Stu Cncl (R); Biomedical Engineering; Doctor; Purdue U; Indiana Medical School

BOER, JESSICA L; VALPARAISO, IN; PORTAGE HS; (SR); Hnr Roll; Yth Ldrshp Prog; Comm Volntr; Chrch Yth Grp; Emplmnt; Spch Team; Bnd; Jzz Bnd; Orch; SP/M/VS; Sftball; Freshman of the Year Award; Indiana All-State Honor Band - 11th & 12th Grade; Music Education; U of Evansville

Blunk, David
Floyd Ctrl HS
Floyds Knobs, IN

Bermudez, Adrian
Bluffton HS
Bluffton, IN

Beam, Kaylee R
Peru HS
Peru, IN

Barnickle, Craig
Lanesville Cmty Sch
Lanesville, IN

Barnett, Jasmine M
Marion HS
Marion, IN

Barker, Allison P
Noblesville HS
Noblesville, IN

Barlett, Amanda L
South Spencer HS
Rockport, IN

Bazyk, Kyle C
Adams HS
South Bend, IN

Beckman, Ali
Jasper HS
Jasper, IN

Berry, Courtney L
Ensweiler AC
Highland, IN

Blackburn, Alana
Justice Thurgood Marshall MS
Marion, IN

BOGGESS, STEPHANIE; NINEVEH, IN; BROWN CTY HS; (FR); 4H Awd; Hi Hnr Roll; Hnr Roll; Perf Att; Pres Ac Ftns Aw; Pres Sch; Comm Volntr; 4-H; Chrch Yth Grp; Scouts; Tchrs Aide; Spanish Clb; Stg Cre; Chrldg; Stu Cncl (S); Medical Study; Marine Biology; Indiana U

BOLLENBACHER, JOSHUA P; DECATUR, IN; BLUFFTON HS; (SO); 4H Awd; Hnr Roll; Peer Tut/Med; 4-H; Tchrs Aide; Swmg (V)

BONA, ANNA; SCHERERVILLE, IN; LAKE CTRL HS; (FR); Hi Hnr Roll; Nat Hon Sy; St of Mnth; Peer Tut/Med; Spec Olymp Vol; ArtClub; Lttrmn Clb; Clr Grd; Cr Ctry (V L); Swmg (V L); Track (V L); Stu Cncl (V); All American Swimmer 200 Fr Relay & 400 Fr Relay; 3rd At State (Swimming) 200 Fr & 400 Fr Relays; Pre-Medical; Pre-Veterinary; Indiana U; Purdue U

BONCZEK, WESTON; MEDARYVILLE, IN; WEST CTRL SR HS; (FR); Perf Att; BPA; Chrch Yth Grp; Scouts; SADD; Bnd; Chr; Pep Bnd; SP/M/VS; Yrbk (R, P); Psychiatry; Psychology

BONICK, MATT; VALPARAISO, IN; VALPARAISO HS; (JR); Cmptr Clb; DARE; Key Club; Scouts; Computer Technology; Architectural Technology (Art); Purdue U (Lafayette); Ivy Tech Community College

BONTRAGER, MORIAH R; GRABILL, IN; WOODLAN JR/SR HS; (MS); Hnr Roll; Perf Att; Chrch Yth Grp; Bnd; Bskball; Vllyball

BOOCHER, AMANDA; SOUTH BEND, IN; RILEY HS; (FR); Hi Hnr Roll; Hnr Roll; MVP; Otst Ac Ach Awd; Perf Att; St of Mnth; DARE; French Clb; Bskball (J); Sccr (J); Sftball (J); Track (L); Psychology; Teaching; Purdue; Ball State

BOOKER, URSULA; INDIANAPOLIS, IN; EMMERICH MANUAL HS; (FR); Hnr Roll; Comm Volntr; Hosp Aide; Chrch Yth Grp; Key Club; Ntl FFA; Spch Team; Ch Chr; Cr Ctry (V); Sftball (V); Track (V); Yrbk (P)

BORDERS, JORDAN; RUSHVILLE, IN; RUSHVILLE CONSOLIDATED HS; (FR); Hnr Roll; WWAHSS; FCA; Key Club; SADD; French Clb; Chr; Varsity Scholars; Business; Teaching; Ball State U; Anderson U

BOSSI, RACHEL A; INDIANAPOLIS, IN; LAWRENCE CTRL HS; (JR); Peer Tut/Med; Key Club; Chr; SP/M/VS; Swg Chr; Cr Ctry (V L); Sccr (V L); Secretary for Key Club; National Honor Society; Music; Butler U

BOURDAGE, ALEXA S; CARMEL, IN; CARMEL HS; (SO); Hi Hnr Roll; Sci Fairs; Comm Volntr; Peer Tut/Med; Chrch Yth Grp; Tchrs Aide; Chr; Clr Grd; Dnce; Flg Crps; 2002 Silver Medal Jr Pairs World Baton Twirling Fed - World Championship; 2003 / 2004 6th Place Jr Woman World Baton Twirling Fed - World Championship; Medicine; Business; Purdue U; New York U

BOWERMAN, LAURA; MILFORD, IN; WAWASEE HS; (SR); 4H Awd; Hi Hnr Roll; Nat Hon Sy; WWAHSS; Yth Ldrshp Prog; Comm Volntr; Peer Tut/Med; 4-H; Chrch Yth Grp; Drma Clb; Emplmnt; FCA; FTA; Key Club; Acpl Chr; Dnce; Orch; SP/M/VS; Gmnstcs (V L); Chemistry Education; Physical Therapy; Purdue U West Lafayette

BOWERS, VALERIE; DUNKIRK, IN; JAY CTY HS; (FR); 4H Awd; Ctznshp Aw; Hnr Roll; Perf Att; St of Mnth; WWAHSS; 4-H; Chrch Yth Grp; DARE; Drma Clb; Key Club; Quiz Bowl; Jzz Bnd; Mch Bnd; SP/M/VS; Stg Cre; Music; Dramatic Arts; Ohio State U; Miami U of Oxford, Ohio

BOWKER, JANE; VALPARAISO, IN; VALPARAISO HS; (JR); Hi Hnr Roll; Hnr Roll; WWAHSS; Yth Ldrshp Prog; Comm Volntr; Peer Tut/Med; Spec Olymp Vol; AL Aux Girls; Chrch Yth Grp; Emplmnt; Key Club; Lib Aide; Tchrs Aide; French Clb; Bnd; Jzz Bnd; Mch Bnd; Orch; Pep Bnd; CASS mentor to middle school children; Butler U; U of Dayton

BOWMAN, LEEANNA R; CROTHERSVILLE, IN; SEYMOUR CHRISTIAN AC; (SO); Hnr Roll; Nat Hon Sy; Chrch Yth Grp; DARE; Ntl Beta Clb; Chr; Ch Chr; SP/M/VS; Vllyball (V); Nursing; Design; U of Louisville; New York U

BOWMAN, WILLIAM; LAFAYETTE, IN; JEFFERSON HS; (SR); Hi Hnr Roll; Nat Hon Sy; WWAHSS; AL Aux Boys; Chrch Yth Grp; Emplmnt; Ftball (V CL); Sch Ppr (E); Congressional Student Leadership Conference; Business; History; Purdue U

BRADFORD, ALANA M; SULLIVAN, IN; SULLIVAN HS; (SR); Hi Hnr Roll; MVP; Nat Hon Sy; Otst Ac Ach Awd; Pres Ac Ftns Aw; Pres Sch; St of Mnth; WWAHSS; Comm Volntr; Peer Tut/Med; 4-H; BPA; Drma Clb; Key Club; Ntl Beta Clb; Ntl FFA; Spanish Clb; Chr; SP/M/VS; Stg Cre; Bskball (V); Track (V); Vllyball (J); Cl Off (R); Stu Cncl (R); Who's Who (Academic & Athletic); Business Administration; Marketing; Indiana State U

BRADY, MALLORI N; MENTONE, IN; TIPPECANOE VALLEY HS; (SO); Hi Hnr Roll; Bskball; Sftball; Veterinarian

BRAMES, ELIZABETH C; WOODBURN, IN; WOODLAN JR SR HS; (FR); Perf Att; Pres Sch; Sci Fairs; St of Mnth; Peer Tut/Med; Scouts; Clr Grd; SP/M/VS; Stu Cncl (R); Elementary Education; U of Saint Francis; Indiana U Purdue U

BRANHAM, ALEXANDRA E M; LANESVILLE, IN; LANESVILLE JR/SR HS; (SO); Hnr Roll; St of Mnth; USAA; WWAHSS; Off Aide; Quiz Bowl; Tchrs Aide; Spanish Clb; Sftball (V); Cl Off (S); Stu Cncl (R); Renaissance Steering Committee Member; Psychology; Medicine; Indiana U Southeast; Notre Dame U

BRATTAIN, DERICK; NEW HAVEN, IN; NEW HAVEN HS; (SR); Hnr Roll; Nat Hon Sy; Perf Att; St of Mnth; Photog; Bsball (VJ); Sch Ppr (E, R, P); Yrbk (E, P); 1st Place Superior for Photo Essay At Ball State; 1st Place Excellence for Sports Photo At Ball State; Photography; Journalism; Ball State U

BRAUN, RANDALL; WINCHESTER, IN; UNION CITY CMTY HS; (SO); 4H Awd; Hnr Roll; Perf Att; Pres Ac Ftns Aw; 4-H; Lttrmn Clb; Ntl FFA; Bsball (VJ L); Bskball (J); Sccr (V L); Agriculture; Mechanics; Northwestern of Ohio

BRAWNER, BRANDON; HANOVER, IN; SOUTHWESTERN MIDDLE/SR HS; (JR); 4H Awd; MVP; St of Mnth; WWAHSS; Comm Volntr; 4-H; P to P St Amb Prg; Wrstlg (V CL); Congressional Student Leadership Conference; Physical Education; Sports Marketing; U of Purdue; Franklin College

BRECKLER, JOSEPH R; AVILLA, IN; BISHOP DWENGER HS; (JR); 4H Awd; Ctznshp Aw; Hnr Roll; MVP; Nat Hon Sy; Perf Att; Sci Fairs; Comm Volntr; 4-H; Emplmnt; Jr Ach; Bsball (J); Chemical Engineering; Civil Engineering; U of Notre Dame; Purdue U

BREMER, LUKE D; MONROEVILLE, IN; WOODLAN JR/SR HS; (SO); Hi Hnr Roll; Perf Att; St of Mnth; Chrch Yth Grp; Bskball (V L); Ftball (V L); Most Improved Player (Basketball); Education; Coaching Sports; Purdue

BREMMER, JESS; COLUMBUS, IN; COLUMBUS NORTH HS; (JR); Hnr Roll; WWAHSS; Yth Ldrshp Prog; Emplmnt; Key Club; Pep Squd; Dnce; Dance-Varsity and Letter Winner; Physical Therapy; Sports Medicine; U of Evansville; U of Indianapolis

BRESCHER, HALEY; VELPEN, IN; JASPER HS; (JR); 4H Awd; Ctznshp Aw; Hi Hnr Roll; Hnr Roll; WWAHSS; Yth Ldrshp Prog; Comm Volntr; 4-H; Chrch Yth Grp; Emplmnt; FCA; Key Club; Prom Com; Vsity Clb; French Clb; Cr Ctry (V); Track (J); Vsy Clb (V); Wrstlg (V L); Cl Off (P, V); Stu Cncl (R); CR (R); Lit Mag (R); Mat Club, a Wrestling Bester Club; Outstanding Sophomore Student Council Rep; Real Estate; Activities Director/ Coordinator

BRICKENS, LINDSAY; GREENSBURG, IN; NORTH DECATUR JR/SR HS; (SO); Nat Hon Sy; Chrch Yth Grp; Drma Clb; Emplmnt; FCA; Key Club; Mth Clb/Tm; Svce Clb; SADD; Bnd; Chr; Mch Bnd; SP/M/VS; Cr Ctry (V); Sftball (J); CR (R); Jr Optimist Vice President; SADD Vice President; Physician; Health Sciences

BRIDGEGROOM, AMANDA R; GARY, IN; CALUMET HS; (SO); Nat Hon Sy; Perf Att; ArtClub; Mth Clb/Tm; Schol Bwl; Sch Ppr (E, R); Culinary Arts; Nursing; Indiana U; Purdue U-Calumet

BRIDGES, EVAN; LANESVILLE, IN; LANESVILLE HS; (JR); Hi Hnr Roll; Hnr Roll; Perf Att; St of Mnth; WWAHSS; Comm Volntr; Chrch Yth Grp; FCA; Ntl FFA; French Clb; Bnd; Pep Bnd; Bskball (V L); Cr Ctry (V L); Track (V L); FCA, FFA President, Renaissance Club; French Club, FFA Awards, Sports Awards; Secondary Education; Athletic Director; Louisville U; Indiana U Southeast

BRISTLE, CODY; FREMONT, IN; FREMONT HS; (SO); Hi Hnr Roll; Hnr Roll; Emplmnt; Scouts; Wdwrkg Clb; Bsball (J); Industry Award; Criminal Justice; Law Enforcement

BRITTEN, JOSH; HUNTINGTON, IN; HUNTINGTON NORTH HS; (SR); Hnr Roll; Nat Hon Sy; Perf Att; St of Mnth; Peer Tut/Med; Chrch Yth Grp; Drma Clb; Chr; Ch Chr; SP/M/VS; Swg Chr; Community Theatre-"Best Newcomer"; Who's Who Among American High School Students; Business Management/International Studies; Entrepreneurship; Indiana U-Purdue U/ Indianapolis

BRITTON, KENDRA; SOLSBERRY, IN; EASTERN GREENE HS; (JR); 4H Awd; Hi Hnr Roll; Hnr Roll; Nat Hon Sy; Perf Att; WWAHSS; Peer Tut/ Med; 4-H; AL Aux Girls; Ntl FFA; Bnd; Mch Bnd; Pep Bnd; Nursing; Vet; Vincennes U; U of Indianapolis

BROCK, ABIGAIL; LAWRENCEBURG, IN; LAWRENCEBURG HS; (SO); Ctznshp Aw; Hnr Roll; Perf Att; Emplmnt; Tchrs Aide; Acpl Chr; Chr; CCHA (Heritage Reenactment, Pioneer); Young Voices of Southeastern Indiana; Psychology; Business

BROGAN, ASHLEY N; NEW ROSS, IN; SOUTHMONT HS; (SO); Hnr Roll; Perf Att; WWAHSS; Comm Volntr; Emplmnt; Key Club; Ntl FFA; Greenhand Officer of the Year; Greenhand Degree in FFA; Nursing; U of Evansville; Purdue U

BROGDON, HILLARY; CROWN POINT, IN; CROWN POINT HS; (JR); Hnr Roll; WWAHSS; Emplmnt; Spanish Clb; Chr; Stg Cre; Apparel Merchandising; Business; Indiana U in Bloomington; The Art Institute of Chicago

BROOKS, MARGARET; NOBLESVILLE, IN; NOBLESVILLE HS; (FR); Hnr Roll; Comm Volntr; Scouts; Chr; Culinary School; Journalism

BROONER, LESLEY A; JASPER, IN; JASPER HS; (SO); Hnr Roll; WWAHSS; Key Club; SADD; Spanish Clb; Bnd; Mch Bnd; Pep Bnd; Sch Ppr (R); Yrbk (R)

BROWN, ASHLEY; EVANSVILLE, IN; CENTRAL HS; (SO); Ctznshp Aw; Hnr Roll; Otst Ac Ach Awd; Perf Att; Hosp Aide; DARE; Pep Squd; Photog; Spanish Clb; Chr; Clr Grd; Dnce; Flg Crps; Honor Roll; Law - Business / Personal; Ob/Gyn; U of Southern Indiana; Indiana State U

BROWN, HEATHER B; HARTFORD CITY, IN; BLACKFORD HS; (JR); Hnr Roll; Pres Sch; Chrch Yth Grp; Drma Clb; Lib Aide; Bnd; Orch; Pep Bnd; SP/M/VS; Surgical Degree; PhD / MD; Indiana Wesleyan U; Indiana U

BROWN, KEITH; CONNERSVILLE, IN; UNION CTY HS; (SR); Ctznshp Aw; DAR; Hnr Roll; USAA; Comm Volntr; Peer Tut/Med; Prom Com; Tchrs Aide; Ftball (V L); Track (V); Network Administration; Computer Programming; Ivy Tech State College

BROWN, LAURA; INDIANAPOLIS, IN; CARDINAL RITTER HS; (SO); Ctznshp Aw; Hi Hnr Roll; Otst Ac Ach Awd; Pres Sch; St of Mnth; WWAHSS; Chrch Yth Grp; Dnce; PP Ftbl; Sch Ppr; Yrbk; Ambassadors for Children; News Editor; Journalism; History Major; Indiana U; Loyola U Chicago

BROWN, MEGAN; VALPARAISO, IN; VALPARAISO HS; (JR); Hi Hnr Roll; Hnr Roll; Nat Hon Sy; Perf Att; Pres Ac Ftns Aw; Comm Volntr; Peer Tut/Med; Spec Olymp Vol; Drma Clb; Key Club; Off Aide; Tchrs Aide; Spanish Clb; Chr; Dnce; Hope Club (Vice President) Tutoring; Journalism; Law Degree; U of Notre Dame; DePauw U

BROWN, TERA; LIBERTY, IN; UNION CTY HS; (SO); Hnr Roll; Hosp Aide; Peer Tut/Med; Emplmnt; Pep Squd; Prom Com; SADD; Spanish Clb; Chrldg (J); PP Ftbl; Vllyball (VJCL); Family Community Career Leaders of America; Peer Helper, Freshman Court; Communications; Marketing/ Advertising; Ball State U, Ohio Wesleyan; Xavier

BROWNELL, JENNIFER; COLUMBUS, IN; COLUMBUS EAST HS; (JR); F Lan Hn Soc; Hi Hnr Roll; Hnr Roll; Nat Hon Sy; Pres Ac Ftns Aw; WWAHSS; Yth Ldrshp Prog; Comm Volntr; Hosp Aide; Spec Olymp Vol; Chrch Yth Grp; NYLC; Quill & Scroll; Quiz Bowl; French Clb; Cr Ctry (J); Track (J); CR (R); Sch Ppr (E, R); Journalism; Law; U of Notre Dame; Northwestern U

BROWNELL, STEVEN; SOUTH BEND, IN; ADAMS HS; (SO); 4H Awd; Hi Hnr Roll; Hnr Roll; Perf Att; Sci Fairs; Comm Volntr; 4-H; Golf (V); Business; Engineering; U of Notre Dame

BROWNLEE, JEREMY L; FRANKLIN, IN; FRANKLIN CMTY HS; (SR); Ctznshp Aw; Hi Hnr Roll; Nat Hon Sy; Nat Mrt Sch Recip; Valdctrian; Comm Volntr; Peer Tut/Med; Chrch Yth Grp; Emplmnt; FCA; Key Club; Tchrs Aide; Bnd; Pep Bnd; SP/M/VS; Cr Ctry (V L); Track (V); Stu Cncl (R); Indiana U Summer Honors Program & Foreign Language; Have a Nice Day Club; Linguistics; Religious Studies; U of Oklahoma

BRUNNER, MITCHELL; LANESVILLE, IN; LANESVILLE JR/SR HS; (SO); Hnr Roll; Sci Fairs; Sci/Math Olympn; Chrch Yth Grp; Emplmnt; Photog; Spanish Clb; Acpl Chr; SP/M/VS; Degree in Engineering; Purdue; U of Southern Indiana

BRYANT, ALLYSON R; BOONVILLE, IN; BOONVILLE HS; (JR); Hnr Roll; Nat Hon Sy; WWAHSS; Emplmnt; FCA; Key Club; Prom Com; Sftball (VJ); Yrbk (R); Mentor to Freshman Class; Indiana U Southeast; Butler U

BUENING, JONATHAN; COLUMBUS, IN; COLUMBUS NORTH HS; (SO); Hnr Roll; Sci/Math Olympn; Drma Clb; Key Club; Outdrs Clb; Schol Bwl; Sci Clb; SP/M/VS; Stg Cre; English Team Captain; Physical Sciences; Bio Technology; Purdue U; U of Chicago

BUILTA, COLE A; ANDERSON, IN; ANDERSON HS; (FR); Ctznshp Aw; DAR; Hi Hnr Roll; Jr Rot; Pres Ac Ftns Aw; Comm Volntr; Hosp Aide; Chess; Fr of Library; Schol Bwl; Chr; Knowledge Master Open

BULINGTON, SHELLEY D; LAFAYETTE, IN; MC CUTCHEON HS; (SO); Gov Hnr Prg; Hnr Roll; 4-H; Chrch Yth Grp; Jr Ach; Tchrs Aide; Chr; Vllyball (J); Pediatric Nurse; Elementary Teacher; St Joe's College; Purdue U

BULLOCK, JESSICA L; PORTLAND, IN; JAY CTY HS; (FR); Hi Hnr Roll; Otst Ac Ach Awd; 4-H; DARE; Drma Clb; Pep Squd; Scouts; French Clb; Stg Cre; Stu Cncl (R); Registered Nurse; Pediatrician; U of Notre Dame; U of Saint Francis

BUNTON, JOEY; AMBIA, IN; BENTON CTRL HS; (SR); Hnr Roll; Nat Hon Sy; St of Mnth; WWAHSS; Chrch Yth Grp; Emplmnt; Bsball (V L); Ftball (V L); Athletic Training Major; Purdue U

BURGDORF, ALLISON R; HOPE, IN; HAUSER HS; (JR); Hi Hnr Roll; Hnr Roll; MVP; Otst Ac Ach Awd; WWAHSS; Hosp Aide; Peer Tut/Med; Chrch Yth Grp; Emplmnt; FCA; Key Club; Chr; SP/M/VS; Bskball (J); Track (V L); Vllyball (J); Yrbk (R); Pre-Med; Secondary Education; Franklin College; Anderson U

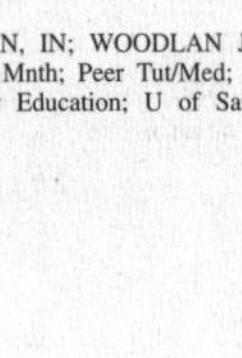
Brown, Keith
Union Cty HS
Connersville, IN

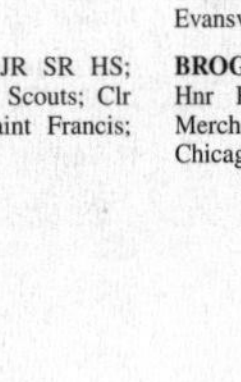
Brattain, Derick
New Haven HS
New Haven, IN

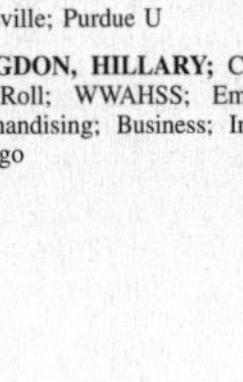
Branham, Alexandra E M
Lanesville JR/SR HS
Lanesville, IN

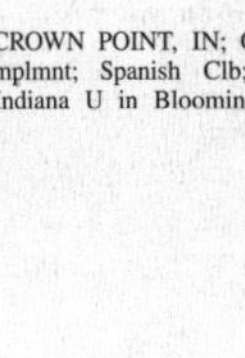
Bossi, Rachel A
Lawrence Ctrl HS
Indianapolis, IN

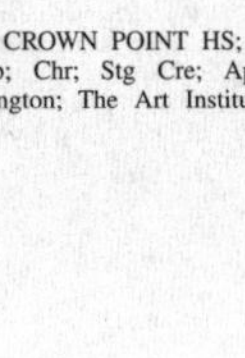
Bourdage, Alexa S
Carmel HS
Carmel, IN

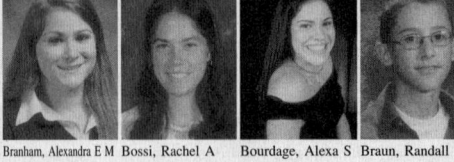

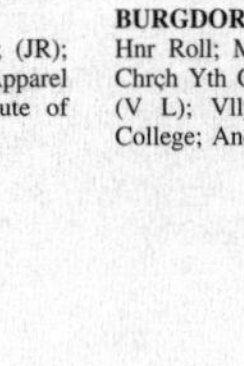
Braun, Randall
Union City Cmty HS
Winchester, IN

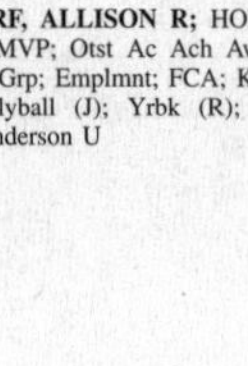
Builta, Cole A
Anderson HS
Anderson, IN

BURGESS, MICHAEL; CONNERSVILLE, IN; CONNERSVILLE HS; (JR); F Lan Hn Soc; Hi Hnr Roll; Hnr Roll; Otst Ac Ach Awd; Pres Sch; St of Mnth; WWAHSS; Comm Volntr; Peer Tut/Med; ArtClub; Chess; Dbte Team; Fr of Library; FBLA; Jr Ach; Key Club; Mth Clb/Tm; Stg Cre; Golf (J); Adv Cncl; Cl Off (P); Stu Cncl; CR (R); Lit Mag; Founder of CHS Chess Club; All Academic Teams; Mathematics; Computer Science; Purdue U; Rose-Hulman Institute

BURNS, ANDREA C; MACY, IN; NORTH MIAMI HS; (SR); Hnr Roll; Nat Hon Sy; Nat Stu Ath Day Aw; WWAHSS; Comm Volntr; Peer Tut/Med; Chrch Yth Grp; Ntl FFA; Prom Com; SADD; Bskball (V C); Cr Ctry (V); PP Ftbl (V); Sccr (V); Track (V C); Cl Off (S); Stu Cncl (R); Professional Writing; Taylor U - Ft Wayne

BURNS, ANDREA R; ANDERSON, IN; HIGHLAND HS; (FR); Hnr Roll; St of Mnth; DARE

BURNS, KERRY L; MEDARYVILLE, IN; WEST CTRL SR HS; (FR); Hi Hnr Roll; Hnr Roll; Perf Att; Comm Volntr; Red Cr Aide; Chrch Yth Grp; Mth Clb/Tm; Scouts; Bnd; Chr; Flg Crps; SP/M/VS; Golf (VJ); Track (V); Sun Shine Society; Student Correlation of Positive Energy; Lawyer; Forensic Science; Indiana U School of Law (Indianapolis); Harvard Law

BURRIS, AUDRIANA; INDIANAPOLIS, IN; LAWRENCE NORTH; Ctznshp Aw; Hnr Roll; Perf Att; WWAHSS; Chrch Yth Grp; Tchrs Aide; Drl Tm; Stu Cncl (R); Dentistry; IUPUI; Tennessee State

BURRIS, TY O; EDINBURGH, IN; EDINBURGH HS; (JR); Hnr Roll; St of Mnth; ArtClub; Bskball (L); Track (L); Major-Graphic Design; Marian College; Full Sail

BURTON, CRYSTAL; INDIANAPOLIS, IN; EMMERICH MANUAL HS; (SO); WWAHSS; Red Cr Aide; Flg Crps; Bskball (J); Private Detective; Cosmetology, Nurse; Alabama; Bloomington U

BURTON, JULIANNE; INDIANAPOLIS, IN; AVON HS; (SO); Hi Hnr Roll; Hnr Roll; St of Mnth; Comm Volntr; Drma Clb; Quill & Scroll; Vsity Clb; Wdwrkg Clb; French Clb; SP/M/VS; Sch Ppr (R); Indianapolis Zoo Naturalist; Forensic Psychology; Journalism / Writing; San Jose U; U of Evansville

BURZYNSKI, CHRISTOPHER; SOUTH BEND, IN; RILEY HS; (FR); Hnr Roll; Chrch Yth Grp; Bnd; Jzz Bnd; Mch Bnd; Pep Bnd; Track (V); Stu Cncl (S); Meteorology; Real Estate; Purdue U; Notre Dame U

BUSCH, KOLTER P; MONTICELLO, IN; TWIN LAKES HS; (SR); Hi Hnr Roll; Nat Hon Sy; Otst Ac Ach Awd; Pres Ac Ftns Aw; Pres Sch; WWAHSS; Comm Volntr; Peer Tut/Med; Chrch Yth Grp; Drma Clb; Emplmnt; Jr Ach; Lttrmn Clb; Pep Squd; Quill & Scroll; Quiz Bowl; Acpl Chr; Chr; SP/M/VS; Bsball (J); Bskball (J); Skiing; Tennis (V CL); Cl Off (P); Stu Cncl; Sch Ppr (E, R); Scholar Athlete; Business, Computer Graphics, Communications; Purdue U (Enrolled)

BUSH, DALE W; SPENCER, IN; OWEN VALLEY CMTY HS; (JR); Hnr Roll; Perf Att; WWAHSS; Red Cr Aide; Chrch Yth Grp; Emplmnt; FCA; Tchrs Aide; Fld Hky (L); Ftball (VJCL); Track (V L); Major in Fire Science/ Safety Technology; Homeland Security; Purdue U; Eastern Kentucky U

BUSH, KATY; SHERIDAN, IN; SHERIDAN HS; (JR); Hnr Roll; Nat Hon Sy; St of Mnth; Comm Volntr; ArtClub; Chrch Yth Grp; Drma Clb; FCA; Off Aide; Quiz Bowl; Stg Cre; PP Ftbl (V); Sccr (VJCL); Bible / Biblical Studies; Missionary; Anderson U

BUSH, VICTORIA N; GARY, IN; LEW WALLACE HS; (JR); Hnr Roll; Chrch Yth Grp; Vllyball (J); Chicago U; IUN

BUSZ, JESSICA L; PORTLAND, IN; JAY CTY HS; (SO); Hnr Roll; WWAHSS; Peer Tut/Med; Emplmnt; Photog; Chr; Dnce; National American Miss Pageant State Finalist; National Society for High School Scholars; Interior Designer; Cosmetology; Ball State U; Indiana U

BUTCHER, JESSICA; WASHINGTON, IN; WASHINGTON HS; (JR); Hnr Roll; Chrch Yth Grp; Emplmnt; Ntl Beta Clb; Prom Com; Tchrs Aide; Sftball (J); CR (R); Beta Treasurer; USI Education; USI

BUTLER, SAMANTHA A; SEYMOUR, IN; SEYMOUR HS; (JR); Hi Hnr Roll; Nat Hon Sy; St of Mnth; WWAHSS; Comm Volntr; 4-H; AL Aux Girls; Key Club; Mus Clb; Bnd; Drm Mjr; Mch Bnd; Pep Bnd; Music Education; Elementary Education; Butler U; Indiana U

BUTTS, RACHEL; FORT WAYNE, IN; HOMESTEAD HS; (FR); Hnr Roll; Pres Ac Ftns Aw; Chrch Yth Grp; Stu Cncl (R); Lit Mag (R); Sophomore (2005-2006) Class Vice President; Psychology; Journalism; U of Notre Dame; Butler U

BUUCK, BRANDON; HOAGLAND, IN; HERITAGE JR/SR HS; (SO); Hnr Roll; St of Mnth; Emplmnt; Business; Health Care; Purdue U; Ball State U

BUUCK, JORDAN; HOAGLAND, IN; HERITAGE JR/SR HS; (FR); Hi Hnr Roll; Comm Volntr; Ftball (J); Wrstlg (V); BS in Biology; Medical Degree; Indiana U; Purdue U

BUXTON, JESSIE; BOONVILLE, IN; BOONVILLE HS; (FR); 4H Awd; Hnr Roll; Nat Hon Sy; WWAHSS; 4-H; Key Club; Bskball (JC); Golf (J); Radiology Major; Stock Broking Major; Murray U; Kentucky Wesleyan

BYERS, MATTHEW; SOUTH BEND, IN; ADAMS HS; (SO); Ctznshp Aw; DAR; Hnr Roll; Emplmnt; Scouts; Cr Ctry (J); Track (J); Eagle Scout Award; Junior Leadership Training Conference; Political Science; Business

BYRD-FORD, SALITA M; INDIANAPOLIS, IN; BROAD RIPPLE HS; (FR); Chrch Yth Grp; Emplmnt; ROTC; Doctor / Surgeon; Ohio State; Georgia State

BYRUM, DALENE; LAFAYETTE, IN; MC CUTCHEON HS; (JR); Ctznshp Aw; Hnr Roll; Comm Volntr; Chrch Yth Grp; Tchrs Aide; Early Childhood Education; Accountant; Franklin College; U of North Carolina Pembroke

CAI, YI; CARMEL, IN; CARMEL SR HS; (SO); Hi Hnr Roll; WWAHSS; Comm Volntr; Key Club; French Clb; Chr; CR (S); Chinese School Student - Sundays; Top 25 in Freshman Year - Out of 986; Pre-Med; Psychology; Northwestern U; Johns Hopkins U

CALDEMEYER, BRENT; STENDAL, IN; PIKE CTRL HS; (SO); Hi Hnr Roll; Hnr Roll; Perf Att; St of Mnth; Scouts; Bnd; Mch Bnd; Bsball (J); Bskball (VJ); Midwest Talent Search; Order of Arrow, Life Scout Rank; Engineering; Purdue U; U of Evansville

CALDWELL, ALYSIA; DELPHI, IN; DELPHI CMTY HS; (JR); Hi Hnr Roll; Hnr Roll; DARE; Emplmnt; Pep Squd; Prom Com; Tchrs Aide; Vsity Clb; French Clb; Chrldg (V L); Tennis (J); Vsy Clb (V); Vllyball (J); Academic Decathlon; Physical Therapy; Pre-Med; Indianapolis U; Indiana U

CALDWELL, CARRIE; ADVANCE, IN; WESTERN BOONE JR/SR HS; (SO); 4H Awd; Hnr Roll; WWAHSS; Peer Tut/Med; 4-H; Chrch Yth Grp; FCA; Key Club; Quiz Bowl; Foreign Clb; Chr; Dnce; SP/M/VS; Sftball (J); Tennis (J); Vllyball (J); Stu Cncl (R); Nursing; Social Science; Ball State U; DePauw U

CALVIN, ZARAH; CARMEL, IN; CARMEL SR HS; (SO); Hi Hnr Roll; Hnr Roll; Nat Stu Ath Day Aw; Comm Volntr; Chrch Yth Grp; Pep Squd; Tchrs Aide; Chr; Clr Grd; Mch Bnd; Chrldg (J); All-Star Leading Co-Ed Squad; Carmel Marching Band / Color Guard; Education; Medical Field; Indiana U; Purdue U

CAMPBELL, JENNY M; TIPTON, IN; CLINTON CTRL HS; (SR); Ctznshp Aw; DAR; Hnr Roll; Nat Hon Sy; WWAHSS; Comm Volntr; Chrch Yth Grp; Ntl FFA; Tchrs Aide; Foreign Clb; Yrbk (E); Hoosier Girls State Delegate; Crop and Soil Science Major; Purdue U

CAMPOS, CHELSEA; GOSHEN, IN; GOSHEN HS; (SO); Hi Hnr Roll; Hnr Roll; Otst Ac Ach Awd; Perf Att; Comm Volntr; Chrch Yth Grp; DARE; Emplmnt; Chr; Ch Chr; Quality Engineering; Pharmacist; Purdue U; Indiana U

CANTRELL, ARTHUR; INDIANAPOLIS, IN; BROAD RIPPLE HS; (SO); DARE; Ftball; Track; Wt Lftg; Wrstlg; Purdue U; Indiana U

CARLSGAARD, JESSLYN C; BARGERSVILLE, IN; CTR GROVE HS; (SO); F Lan Hn Soc; Hi Hnr Roll; Otst Ac Ach Awd; Sci Fairs; St of Mnth; Comm Volntr; Chrch Yth Grp; Key Club; Spanish Clb; Key Club Secretary; Spanish; Mathematics; Indiana Wesleyan U; Washington U in St Louis

CARNES, JEREMY M; EDINBURGH, IN; EDINBURGH HS; (FR); Ctznshp Aw; Hi Hnr Roll; Hnr Roll; Otst Ac Ach Awd; Comm Volntr; Peer Tut/Med; Chrch Yth Grp; Emplmnt; French Clb; Bnd; Ch Chr; Pep Bnd; Golf (V); Stu Cncl (R); Journalism/Writing; English/Literature; Indiana U; Stanford U

CARPENTER, AMANDA; GALVESTON, IN; LEWIS CASS JR SR HS; (SO); Hnr Roll; WWAHSS; Chrch Yth Grp; DARE; SADD; Chr; Ch Chr; SP/M/VS; Psychologist; Spanish Major or Minor; Indiana U; Purdue U

CARRASCO, ASHLEY; MUNSTER, IN; LAS VEGAS HS; (JR); Hi Hnr Roll; Hnr Roll; Nat Hon Sy; St of Mnth; WWAHSS; Hosp Aide; Peer Tut/Med; Emplmnt; FTA; Key Club; Tchrs Aide; Chr; Track (J); Stu Cncl (R); Sch Ppr (E); Yrbk (E); Student of the Month-Science; Teacher (Math); Advertising; U of Miami; U of Texas-Austin

CARROLL, MEGAN; DEMOTTE, IN; KANKAKEE VALLEY HS; (SO); Hi Hnr Roll; Hnr Roll; MVP; Otst Ac Ach Awd; Pres Ac Ftns Aw; Peer Tut/Med; Chrch Yth Grp; Drma Clb; FCA; Mus Clb; Quiz Bowl; Sci Clb; Tchrs Aide; Foreign Clb; Bnd; Chr; Dnce; Jzz Bnd; Cl Off (T); Stu Cncl (T); Lit Mag (R); Submission of Poems to the School Newspaper; Journalism; Creative Writing; Davenport U; Indiana U

CARTER, DANIELLE; FORT WAYNE, IN; WAYNE HS; (SO); Ctznshp Aw; Hnr Roll; Emplmnt; Photog; Youth Group; Pre-Law; Business Management; Florida State; Miami U

CARTER, KRISTA; LAPORTE, IN; (FR); Hnr Roll; Peer Tut/Med; Chr; Sccr (J); Tennis (J); Elementary Teacher; Medical (RN); Ball State U; Purdue U

CARTER, MARQUESE S; MARION, IN; JUSTICE THURGOOD MARSHALL MS; MS; Hi Hnr Roll; Hnr Roll; Perf Att; Chrch Yth Grp; DARE; Mth Clb/Tm; Quiz Bowl; Bnd; Chr; Ch Chr; Yrbk (E); Marriage Psychology; Southern Adventist U; Purdue U

CASE, SAMANTHA D; DEPUTY, IN; MADISON CONSOLIDATED HS; Hnr Roll; Nat Hon Sy; WWAHSS; DARE; Ntl FFA; P.R.I.D.E Club; Vet; Health Careers; Purdue College; St. Mary's

CASTANEDA, ELAINE R; HOBART, IN; HOBART HS; (JR); Hnr Roll; St of Mnth; Yth Ldrshp Prog; Comm Volntr; Emplmnt; Key Club; Spanish Clb; Clr Grd; Dnce; Cr Ctry (V L); Tennis (V); Vice President of Hobart Key Club; International Marketing; Foreign Language; Indiana U of Bloomington; U of Evansville

CAUGHELL, BRITTANY; VALPARAISO, IN; MORGAN TOWNSHIP HS; (SO); Hnr Roll; Otst Ac Ach Awd; Perf Att; St of Mnth; Comm Volntr; ArtClub; Chrch Yth Grp; DARE; Mus Clb; Off Aide; Pep Squd; Tchrs Aide; German Clb; Competition Cheerleading; Horizon Gymnastics; Psychology; Philosophy; U of Portland; Indiana U

CECIL, EMILY; LAWRENCEBURG, IN; LAWRENCEBURG HS; (JR); Hi Hnr Roll; Nat Hon Sy; Nat Stu Ath Day Aw; Otst Ac Ach Awd; Perf Att; Comm Volntr; Chrch Yth Grp; Emplmnt; Key Club; Prom Com; French Clb; Sccr (V L); Track (V L); Academic Medallion Winner (3X); Chemical Engineering; U of Cincinnati; Ohio State

CECIL, KRISTEN; MARTINSVILLE, IN; EMINENCE HS; (SR); Hnr Roll; Nat Sci Aw; WWAHSS; Chrch Yth Grp; Ntl FFA; Prom Com; SADD; Bskball (V CL); Sftball (V L); Vllyball (V CL); Cl Off (T); Stu Cncl (T); Pediatrician; Veterinary; Indiana U Purdue U Indianapolis; Indiana U

CHADD, HANNAH; FORT WAYNE, IN; R NELSON SNIDER; (SO); Hnr Roll; WWAHSS; Emplmnt; Sccr (J); Accounting; Physical Therapy; Indiana Purdue Fort Wayne

CHAGNON, ALYSSA; SULLIVAN, IN; SULLIVAN HS; (FR); 4H Awd; Hi Hnr Roll; Yth Ldrshp Prog; 4-H; Chrch Yth Grp; FCA; Key Club; Ntl Beta Clb; Quiz Bowl; French Clb; Track (V); Vllyball (V); Lawyer

CHALFIN, CHELSEA; FISHERS, IN; HAMILTON SOUTHEASTERN HS; (FR); Hnr Roll; Comm Volntr; Key Club; High School Guidance Counselor-Psychology/Ed; Indiana U

CHAMBERLAIN, DAVID; SOUTH BEND, IN; WASHINGTON HS; (SO); Hnr Roll; Chrch Yth Grp; ROTC; Wrstlg (V L); Stu Cncl (R)

CHAMEM, FERDAWS; INDIANAPOLIS, IN; NORTHWEST HS; (SO); Ctznshp Aw; Hi Hnr Roll; Hnr Roll; Nat Hon Sy; Nat Sci Aw; Perf Att; St of Mnth; WWAHSS; Mth Clb/Tm; Sci Clb; Bskball (VJ); Golf (V); Tennis (VJ); Vllyball (VJ); Stu Cncl (V); Academic Team; Math Club; Pediatrician; IUPUI; Purdue U

CHANDLER, BREANNA P; ROCKPORT, IN; SOUTH SPENCER HS; (SO); Ctznshp Aw; Hnr Roll; Pres Ac Ftns Aw; WWAHSS; Yth Ldrshp Prog; HO'Br Yth Ldrshp; Key Club; Ntl FFA; Outdrs Clb; Pep Squd; SADD; Chrldg (V L); Who's Who; HOBY Leadership; Interior Design; Pharmaceutical Sales; Ivy Tech; USI

CHANDLER, KATIE; LAWRENCEBURG, IN; LAWRENCEBURG HS; (FR); Ctznshp Aw; Hnr Roll; Kwnis Aw; Perf Att; Comm Volntr; Key Club; Quiz Bowl; Chr; Golf (J); Professional Chef; New York U

CHEEK, LACI; KENNARD, IN; KNIGHTSTOWN HS; (SO); Hi Hnr Roll; Perf Att; Sci Fairs; St of Mnth; WWAHSS; Peer Tut/Med; Chrch Yth Grp; Lttrmn Clb; Off Aide; Tchrs Aide; French Clb; Chrldg (V); Optometrist; Pharmacist; Butler

CHERRY II, BRIAN; BEECH GROVE, IN; BEECH GROVE HS; (FR); Hnr Roll; Hosp Aide; Quill & Scroll; Schol Bwl; SADD; French Clb; Bnd; Pep Bnd; Stu Cncl (R); Yrbk (R, P); Veterinarian; Lawyer; Purdue U; Indiana U

CHEVIRON, COURTNEY L; NEW HAVEN, IN; NEW HAVEN HS; (SO); Hnr Roll; Kwnis Aw; Perf Att; Pres Ac Ftns Aw; WWAHSS; Chrch Yth Grp; Key Club; Spanish Clb; Chr; Dnce; Chrldg (J); Vllyball (J); Stu Cncl (R); Yrbk (R)

CHILTON, ALESHA C; HANOVER, IN; SOUTHWESTERN MIDDLE/SR HS; (JR); Hi Hnr Roll; Hnr Roll; Nat Hon Sy; Sci Fairs; WWAHSS; Comm Volntr; ArtClub; Chrch Yth Grp; Emplmnt; FCA; Lttrmn Clb; Prom Com; GAA; Sftball (V L); Track (J); Vllyball (J); Mission Trips; Spell Bowl; General Practitioner; Communications; Hanover College; Franklin College

CHINN, LEA; LAWRENCEBURG, IN; LAWRENCEBURG HS; (JR); Hnr Roll; Nat Hon Sy; Comm Volntr; Chrch Yth Grp; Emplmnt; Key Club; Prom Com; Spanish Clb; Chr; Track (J); Education, Math Teacher; Chemical Engineer; Ball State U; Indiana U

CHOGA, TATENDA V; FRANKLIN, IN; FRANKLIN CMTY HS; (SO); Fut Prb Slvr; Hnr Roll; Perf Att; St of Mnth; Yth Ldrshp Prog; Chrch Yth Grp; DARE; Quill & Scroll; Sch Ppr (R); English and Fine Arts Academic Teams; Spell Bowl; Physical Therapy; Massage Therapy

Cecil, Emily
Lawrenceburg HS
Lawrenceburg, IN

Campos, Chelsea
Goshen HS
Goshen, IN

Calvin, Zarah
Carmel SR HS
Carmel, IN

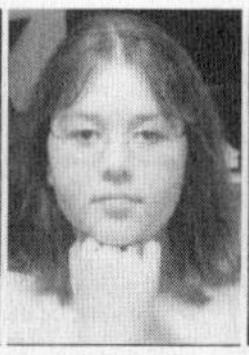

Burns, Kerry L
West Ctrl SR HS
Medaryville, IN

Caldwell, Alysia
Delphi Cmty HS
Delphi, IN

Carter, Danielle
Wayne HS
Fort Wayne, IN

Chamem, Ferdaws
Northwest HS
Indianapolis, IN

CHRISTIAN, DESIREE; LAKE STATION, IN; RIVER FOREST SR HS; (FR); Perf Att; Comm Volntr; Chrch Yth Grp; Emplmnt; Bnd; Architecture; Valparaiso U; Indiana U

CHTCHEDRINA, ALEXANDRA; INDIANAPOLIS, IN; NORTH CTRL HS; (JR); Hi Hnr Roll; Hnr Roll; Nat Hon Sy; Otst Ac Ach Awd; St of Mnth; WWAHSS; Yth Ldrshp Prog; Comm Volntr; Peer Tut/Med; Dbte Team; Drma Clb; NtlFrnscLg; Svce Clb; Spch Team; GERMANY Clb; Dnce; SP/M/VS; Stu Cncl (R); Sch Ppr (R); Class Rank 17/700; 2 Academic Letters; Law; Economics Political; Boston College; Tufts U

CHU, BINGBING; MUNCIE, IN; MUNCIE CTRL HS; (SR); Hi Hnr Roll; Hnr Roll; Jr Mshl; Jr Rot; Kwnis Aw; Nat Hon Sy; Otst Ac Ach Awd; Pres Ac Ftns Aw; Pres Sch; St of Mnth; Comm Volntr; Peer Tut/Med; BPA; Drma Clb; Emplmnt; FBLA; Key Club; MuAlphaTh; Mus Clb; Prom Com; Chr; Dnce; SP/M/VS; Swg Chr; Cl Off (R); Stu Cncl (R); Sch Ppr (R); Yrbk (E); President of National Honor Society; VP - Key Club; Accounting; Ball State U

CISNEY, JOSH; BERNE, IN; SOUTH ADAMS JR/SR HS; (SO); Hi Hnr Roll; Sci Fairs; WWAHSS; Comm Volntr; Chrch Yth Grp; Jr Ach; Ntl FFA; Ftball (J); PP Ftbl (JCL); Track (V)

CLANTON, CATHERINE; THORNTOWN, IN; WESTERN BOONE JR/SR HS; (SO); Hnr Roll; WWAHSS; Key Club; Quiz Bowl; Tchrs Aide; Sftball (J); Vllyball (J); Stu Cncl (R); Pediatrics; Indiana U

CLARK, ASHLEY M; GARY, IN; WEST SIDE HS; (SO); Hi Hnr Roll; Nat Hon Sy; Otst Ac Ach Awd; USAA; WWAHSS; Comm Volntr; Chrch Yth Grp; Emplmnt; P to P St Amb Prg; Ch Chr; Sftball (V); Business/Marketing; Computers; Howard U; North Carolina A & T

CLARK, CHARLES R; SOUTH BEND, IN; JAMES WHITCOMB RILEY HS; (SO); Hi Hnr Roll; 4-H; Mth Clb/Tm; Latin Clb; Cr Ctry (J); State Runner Up in Storm the Castle: Science Olympiad; PhD in Chemistry or Biology; Doctorate in Pharmacy; Notre Dame; Butler

CLARK, EMILY M; SOUTH BEND, IN; MARIAN HS; (SO); WWAHSS; Tennis (J)

CLARK, ERICA; CHESTERFIELD, IN; HIGHLAND SR HS; (JR); WWAHSS; Chrch Yth Grp; DARE; Chr; Clr Grd; Mch Bnd; PP Ftbl (V); Sftball (J); Culinary Arts; Sullivan U; Purdue U

CLARK, KANDI D; KOKOMO, IN; KOKOMO HS; (JR); Hnr Roll; Nat Hon Sy; Sci Fairs; Comm Volntr; Peer Tut/Med; 4-H; Chrch Yth Grp; DARE; FBLA; NYLC; Off Aide; Quill & Scroll; Tchrs Aide; Ch Chr; Dnce; SP/M/VS; PP Ftbl (J); Yrbk (E); Mayor's Youth Advisory Board; Diversity Group; Health Inspector; Fashion Design; Ohio State U; Ball State U

CLARK, MATTHEW R; INDIANAPOLIS, IN; (JR); Hnr Roll; WWAHSS; Comm Volntr; Peer Tut/Med; Prom Com; Vsity Clb; Bskball (VJ); Tennis (V CL); Cl Off (P); Stu Cncl; Miami of Ohio; Indiana U

CLAUSMAN, MACKENZIE; VINCENNES, IN; VINCENNES LINCOLN HS; (SR); 4H Awd; Nat Hon Sy; WWAHSS; Yth Ldrshp Prog; Comm Volntr; 4-H; Chrch Yth Grp; DARE; Emplmnt; Foreign Clb; Bnd; Clr Grd; Flg Crps; Tennis (V CL); Stu Cncl (R); Yrbk (R, P); Major in Chemistry; Pre-Veterinary Medicine; Franklin College

CLEM, KELLY; CYNTHIANA, IN; NORTH POSEY HS; (JR); 4H Awd; Hi Hnr Roll; Nat Hon Sy; Comm Volntr; 4-H; Mth Clb/Tm; Off Aide; Prom Com; Spanish Clb; Chr; Cr Ctry (V CL); Sftball (V CL); Cl Off (T); Stu Cncl (V); Mentor to Junior High Students Through the Peers Project; Athlete of the Week; Elementary Education; U of Southern Indiana

CLEMENTS, ALISON M; PETERSBURG, IN; PIKE CTRL HS; (FR); 4H Awd; All Am Sch; Hnr Roll; Perf Att; St of Mnth; Comm Volntr; Hab For Humty Volntr; Peer Tut/Med; 4-H; Chrch Yth Grp; DARE; Drma Clb; Jr Ach; Mus Clb; Scouts; SADD; Bnd; Mch Bnd; SP/M/VS; Swg Chr; Sccr (V); Tennis (V); Stu Cncl (R); Marine Biologist; Indiana U (IU)

CLENDENEN, STEPHANIE M; BOGGSTOWN, IN; SOUTHWESTERN HS; (FR); Hnr Roll; St of Mnth; Peer Tut/Med; Ntl FFA; Prom Com; Quiz Bowl; SADD; Wdwrkg Clb; German Clb; Sch Ppr (R); 21st Century Scholar Pledge; Honor Roll All My Life; Master's Degree; Bachelor's Degree; Purdue U; Manchester

CLERC, CHRIS; COLUMBUS, IN; COLUMBUS NORTH HS; (JR); Hnr Roll; Nat Hon Sy; Nat Mrt LOC; WWAHSS; Comm Volntr; Red Cr Aide; FCA; Mth Clb/Tm; Sci Clb; Bnd; Jzz Bnd; Mch Bnd; Orch; Biology/ Pre-Med; Tuba Studies / Music Major; Columbia U; Wabash U

CLINGLER, JACOB; INDIANAPOLIS, IN; PIKE HS; (FR); Hi Hnr Roll; Hnr Roll; Ftball (V); Wt Lftg (J); Architect; Computer Programming; Ohio State U; Michigan U

COFFING, CAMERON; NEW PARIS, IN; FAIRFIELD JR/SR HS; (JR); Hi Hnr Roll; MVP; Nat Hon Sy; St of Mnth; WWAHSS; Comm Volntr; Emplmnt; Key Club; Tchrs Aide; Ftball (V CL); Track (V CL); Pharmacy; Butler U; Purdue U

COHEN, CARLY; BATESVILLE, IN; BATESVILLE HS; (JR); Bnd; Mch Bnd; Pep Bnd; SP/M/VS; Bsball (J); Bskball (J); Skiing; Tennis (J); Track (V); Stu Cncl (R); Key Club; Drama Club; Indiana U; Purdue U

COHERNOUR, COLTEN A; LAFAYETTE, IN; MC CUTCHEON HS; (SO); Hnr Roll; Perf Att; Comm Volntr; Chrch Yth Grp; Emplmnt; FCA; Scouts; Tchrs Aide; Ftball (J); Wt Lftg (V); Wrstlg (J); Young Life; Engineering; Purdue U; Indiana U

COLBY, AMIE J; HOBART, IN; HOBART HS; (FR); Hi Hnr Roll; Hnr Roll; St of Mnth; WWAHSS; Student Council (Different from Yours Listed); Student Handbook Committee

COLE, TANYA G; SHELBYVILLE, IN; (JR); Hnr Roll; ArtClub; Sccr (V); Art Club; Dental Hygiene; Degree in Law; Purdue U; Indiana Wesleyan U

COLEMAN, DANIELLE L; EAST CHICAGO, IN; EAST CHICAGO CTRL HS; (SO); Hnr Roll; Nat Hon Sy; SP/M/VS; Vllyball (J); Law Degree and Business Degree; Indiana College

COLEY, MARIAH E; JASPER, IN; JASPER HS; (SR); Hi Hnr Roll; Nat Hon Sy; Nat Mrt Fin; Nat Mrt Semif; Otst Ac Ach Awd; St of Mnth; Valdctrian; WWAHSS; Comm Volntr; Hosp Aide; Peer Tut/Med; DARE; Drma Clb; Key Club; Quiz Bowl; Svce Clb; Spch Team; SADD; French Clb; Chr; Dnce; SP/M/VS; Stg Cre; All Star; Foreign Language Outstanding Student; Theatre; Astro Physics; Indiana U

COLLINS, BRIGID; COLUMBUS, IN; (SO); Hnr Roll; WWAHSS; Key Club; Chr; Stg Cre; Astrophysics; Indiana U

COLLINS, CHRISTINE; NEWBURGH, IN; CASTLE HS; (SO); Hi Hnr Roll; Nat Hon Sy; Otst Ac Ach Awd; St of Mnth; WWAHSS; Comm Volntr; Peer Tut/Med; Key Club; Quill & Scroll; German Clb; Bnd; Mch Bnd; Stu Cncl (R); Yrbk (E); Vice President of Key Club; Member of Quill & Scroll Society; Vanderbilt; Miami of Ohio

COLLINS, RENESHA; FORT WAYNE, IN; NORTHSIDE HS; (MS); Hnr Roll; Chr; Ch Chr; Dnce; Swg Chr; PPSqd (V C); National School Choral Award; Music; Ball State U; Northwestern U

COMBEST, KATRINA L; NORTH VERNON, IN; JENNINGS CTY HS; (SO); St of Mnth; WWAHSS; Drawing (Art); Acting

CONLEY, AMBER N; EVANSVILLE, IN; CENTRAL HS; (JR); Ctznshp Aw; Hnr Roll; ArtClub; ROTC; Clr Grd; Drl Tm; Flg Crps; Received the Sons of the American Revolution Award; Color Guard Commander / Medals / Honors; Art; Pilot; Norwich U; US Naval Academy

CONLEY, KARA; MUNCIE, IN; YORKTOWN HS; (SO); Ctznshp Aw; Hnr Roll; Perf Att; WWAHSS; Comm Volntr; Chrch Yth Grp; Key Club; Ch Chr; Oncology; Medical Field; Indiana U Medical School

CONLEY, LAUREN E; WANATAH, IN; SOUTH CTRL HS; (SO); Hi Hnr Roll; Nat Hon Sy; Perf Att; WWAHSS; Yth Ldrshp Prog; Peer Tut/Med; Drma Clb; Key Club; Lttrmn Clb; Chr; SP/M/VS; Swg Chr; Chrldg (J); Track (V L); Science: Chemistry/Medicine; Communications; Purdue U; Notre Dame

CONLEY, NIKKI; ANDERSON, IN; HIGHLAND HS; (FR); Duke TS; Nat Hon Sy; Comm Volntr; Chrch Yth Grp; Emplmnt; Ntl Beta Clb; Scouts; Stu Cncl (V); C Team Basketball; Psychology; Law Enforcement; Ball State U; U of Tennessee

CONNER, DONALD W; AUSTIN, IN; AUSTIN HS; (SO); Hnr Roll; Nat Hon Sy; Comm Volntr; Emplmnt; Lttrmn Clb; Off Aide; Vsity Clb; Bskball (V); Tennis (V); USI; Ivy Tech

CONOVER, AMANDA; PENDLETON, IN; PENDLETON HEIGHTS HS; (FR); 4H Awd; Hnr Roll; St of Mnth; 4-H; Chrch Yth Grp; Emplmnt; Outdrs Clb; Photog; Spanish Clb; Ch Chr; Stg Cre; Cr Ctry (J); Track (J); Markleville Princess 2002; Photography; Design; UCLA; U of Miami

COOK, JUSTIN; FORT WAYNE, IN; NEW HAVEN HS; (FR); Hnr Roll; Chrch Yth Grp; Ftball (J); Engineering; Indiana-Purdue Fort Wayne; Purdue U

COOL, KEVIN; MOORELAND, IN; BLUE RIVER VALLEY JR/SR HS; (SR); 4H Awd; Ctznshp Aw; Hnr Roll; Nat Hon Sy; Otst Ac Ach Awd; Perf Att; Comm Volntr; 4-H; Chrch Yth Grp; Emplmnt; Ntl FFA; Tchrs Aide; Spanish Clb; Cr Ctry (V L); Golf (VJ L); Track (V L); Wrstlg (V L); Governor of Model Legislator; Agribusiness Management; Agriculture Systems Management; Purdue U

COOPER, KAILEE; ELWOOD, IN; ELWOOD HS; (SO); Ctznshp Aw; DAR; F Lan Hn Soc; Hi Hnr Roll; MVP; Otst Ac Ach Awd; Perf Att; Sci Fairs; St of Mnth; Yth Ldrshp Prog; Peer Tut/Med; Chrch Yth Grp; DARE; Drma Clb; Emplmnt; Jr Cls League; Mus Clb; Photog; Latin Clb; Bnd; Jzz Bnd; Mch Bnd; SP/M/VS; Cr Ctry (V); Track (V L); Yrbk (E, P); 2003/2004 Latin Club Officer (Senator); 2005/2006 Panther Band Drum Major; Computer Science; Cryptography; DePauw U; Rose-Hulman Technical College

COSTAKIS, ALEXANDER J; VALPARAISO, IN; VALPARAISO HS; (JR); F Lan Hn Soc; Hi Hnr Roll; Nat Hon Sy; Yth Ldrshp Prog; Comm Volntr; AL Aux Boys; Emplmnt; Key Club; Spanish Clb; Orch; SP/M/VS; Cr Ctry (V); Track (J); Winner of 2005 Sociedad Honoraria Hispanic Travel Award to Spain; 2005 Hoosier Boys State Delegate; International Studies; Journalism; Boston U; Indiana U

COTTERMAN, TREVOR H; MONTICELLO, IN; FRONTIER HS; (SO); 4H Awd; Hnr Roll; WWAHSS; Comm Volntr; Peer Tut/Med; 4-H; FCA; Quiz Bowl; Schol Bwl; Bskball (J); Cr Ctry (V L); Stu Cncl (R); CR (R); 7 Year Member of 4-H Program; Shooting Sports President; Law; Secondary Education; Indiana U; Syracuse U

COUNCIL, AMANDA; INDIANAPOLIS, IN; ARLINGTON HS; (FR); Ctznshp Aw; Hnr Roll; St of Mnth; Peer Tut/Med; Chrch Yth Grp; Emplmnt; Dnce; Bskball (J); Cr Ctry (V L); Track (V); Cross Country Mental Attitude Award; Computer Technology / Engineering; Psychology; U of Tennessee Knoxville; Purdue U

COX, HEATHER; KOKOMO, IN; KOKOMO HS; (SO); FCA; Photog; Quill & Scroll; Spanish Clb; Yrbk (P); Elementary Education; Indiana U of Kokomo; Ball State U

COX, JORDAN; FOWLER, IN; BENTON CTRL HS; (SR); 4-H; Emplmnt; Ntl FFA; NYLC

COX, KAYLA; SEYMOUR, IN; SEYMOUR HS; (FR); Hi Hnr Roll; Perf Att; Pres Ac Ftns Aw; Sci/Math Olympn; St of Mnth; WWAHSS; Comm Volntr; Peer Tut/Med; Key Club; Lib Aide; Mth Clb/Tm; Off Aide; Schol Bwl; Tchrs Aide; Spanish Clb; Bskball (J); Track (V); Microbiology; Medical Technology / Science; Duke U School of Medicine; Purdue U

COX, RACHEAL N; ODON, IN; NORTH DAVIESS JR/SR HS; (JR); Hnr Roll; WWAHSS; ArtClub; Ntl Beta Clb; Tchrs Aide; Tennis (L); Psychology

CRAIG, DEANNA; CHURUBUSCO, IN; CHURUBUSCO HS; (SR); 4H Awd; DAR; Hi Hnr Roll; Nat Hon Sy; Perf Att; Salutrn; WWAHSS; Comm Volntr; Peer Tut/Med; Spec Olymp Vol; 4-H; Chrch Yth Grp; Drma Clb; FCCLA; FTA; Jr Ach; Key Club; SADD; Chr; Ch Chr; Elementary Education; Special Education; Indiana Wesleyan U

CRANE, RACHEL N; LIBERTY, IN; UNION CTY HS; (SO); 4H Awd; Hi Hnr Roll; Otst Ac Ach Awd; Yth Ldrshp Prog; Comm Volntr; Peer Tut/Med; 4-H; Chrch Yth Grp; Drma Clb; Emplmnt; FCA; Fr of Library; Tchrs Aide; Spanish Clb; SP/M/VS; Stg Cre; PP Ftbl; Sftball (J); Adv Cncl; Volunteered At Summer Children's Program; Scholar Athlete-Softball 04' Season; Music Business/Entertainment Business; Law; New York U; U of California Los Angeles

CRANEY, BRITTANY F; PETERSBURG, IN; PIKE CTRL HS; (SO); Hnr Roll; Chrch Yth Grp; SADD; German Clb; Bskball (V C); Cr Ctry (V); Track (V); Cl Off (V)

CRANEY, WHITNEY; PETERSBURG, IN; PIKE CTRL HS; (SO); Hnr Roll; MVP; Pres Ac Ftns Aw; Comm Volntr; Chrch Yth Grp; Vsity Clb; German Clb; Bskball (V L); Cr Ctry (V L); Track (V L); Stu Cncl; Pre-School Teacher; Athletic Trainer; ISU; IU

CRAWFORD, CHANDLER; INDIANAPOLIS, IN; PIKE HS; (SR); Hnr Roll; Orch; Section Leader; Lettered in Symphony Orchestra; Psychology; Social Work; Indiana U, Purdue U Indianapolis (IN)

CREAGER, NICHOLAS M; WOODBURN, IN; WOODLAN JR/SR HS; (SR); Hi Hnr Roll; Hnr Roll; Jr Rot; MVP; Nat Hon Sy; Perf Att; St of Mnth; Comm Volntr; Peer Tut/Med; Red Cr Aide; Chrch Yth Grp; FCA; Jr Ach; Prom Com; Svce Clb; Tchrs Aide; Wdwrkg Clb; Bsball (V CL); Ftball (V L); Wrstlg (V CL); Cl Off (P); Stu Cncl (V); State Qualifier in Wrestling; Evan Bayh Service Leader; Civil Engineering; Construction Engineering and Management; Tri-State U; Purdue U

CREEL, LEAH; POLAND, IN; OWEN VALLEY HS; (MS); Hnr Roll; Otst Ac Ach Awd; St of Mnth; 4-H; P to P St Amb Prg; Clr Grd; Sccr; Stu Cncl (R); CR (R); Midwest Academic Talent Search; Gifted and Talented Program; Medical; Journalism

CRESS, MEGAN; NOBLESVILLE, IN; ROY C KETCHAM HS; (SR); Hi Hnr Roll; Hnr Roll; Otst Ac Ach Awd; Perf Att; St of Mnth; Comm Volntr; Chrch Yth Grp; DARE; Emplmnt; Key Club; Off Aide; Pep Squd; Photog; Spanish Clb; Chrldg (J L); Cr Ctry (V); Track (V L); Wrestling Manager/ Trainer; Donate Blood; Elementary Education; Ball State U

CRIM, ELIZABETH M; WARSAW, IN; WARSAW CMTY HS; (JR); Hnr Roll; St of Mnth; Yth Ldrshp Prog; Comm Volntr; Chrch Yth Grp; FCA; Mus Clb; Off Aide; SADD; Latin Clb; Bnd; Clr Grd; Mch Bnd; Pep Bnd; Sch Ppr (R, P); Yrbk (P); Athletic Trainer; Indiana Wesleyan U; Ohio State U

CRISWELL, COURTNEY; PITTSBORO, IN; TRI-WEST HS; (SO); Hnr Roll; Chrch Yth Grp; FCA; Sftball (J); Vllyball (J); Stu Cncl (R); Psychology; Elementary Education; Indiana U; Purdue U

Coleman, Danielle L
East Chicago Ctrl HS
East Chicago, IN

Coffing, Cameron
Fairfield JR/SR HS
New Paris, IN

Clark, Erica
Highland SR HS
Chesterfield, IN

Clark, Kandi D
Kokomo HS
Kokomo, IN

Cox, Kayla
Seymour HS
Seymour, IN

CROSS, HEATHER R; GREENWOOD, IN; CTR GROVE HS; (FR); Hi Hnr Roll; Hnr Roll; Pres Sch; Comm Volntr; Chrch Yth Grp; Spanish Clb; Chr; SP/M/VS; Ice Sktg; Swmg; Bronze Award for Girl Scouts; Pre-Med; Pharmacy; U of Florida; Purdue U

CROSS, MEGHAN J; KNIGHTSTOWN, IN; KNIGHTSTOWN HS; (SO); Hi Hnr Roll; Hnr Roll; Otst Ac Ach Awd; St of Mnth; Ntl FFA; Spanish Clb; Sftball (V L); Vllyball (JC); Chemistry Major; Biology Major; Purdue U; Franklin Community College

CROUCH, JAMISON P; MARTINSVILLE, IN; MARTINSVILLE HS; (FR); Hi Hnr Roll; Hnr Roll; Pres Ac Ftns Aw; Chrch Yth Grp; Emplmnt; Bnd; Bskball; Golf; Sports Management; U of Indianapolis; Evangel U

CROWE, KELSEY R; BLUFFTON, IN; BLUFFTON HS; (FR); Hi Hnr Roll; Otst Ac Ach Awd; Emplmnt; Scouts; Swmg (V L); Computer Animation; Swim Coach; Purdue U; Notre Dame

CROYLE, JORDAN W; RIDGEVILLE, IN; MONROE CTRL HS; (SR); Hnr Roll; MVP; Comm Volntr; Drma Clb; Emplmnt; Off Aide; Tchrs Aide; Stg Cre; Bskball (JC); Sccr (V CL); Track (V CL); School Record Holder - Track- 300M Hurdles; Athletic Training; Anderson U

CRUZ, SOCORRO; CROWN POINT, IN; BLOOM HS; (SR); Hi Hnr Roll; Hnr Roll; Perf Att; WWAHSS; Key Club; Off Aide; Quill & Scroll; Tchrs Aide; Vllyball (V); CR (R); Yrbk (E, R, P); Pre-Med; Purdue U

CRUZ, YESSICA; JASPER, IN; JASPER HS; (SR); Perf Att; Comm Volntr; Peer Tut/Med; DARE; Key Club; SADD; Spanish Clb; Business Administration; Real Estate; Vincennes Jasper; U of Evansville

CUDWORTH, CASSIE J; BROWNSBURG, IN; BROWNSBURG HS; (SO); Hnr Roll; Pres Sch; WWAHSS; DARE; FCA; Jr Cls League; Key Club; Spch Team; Bnd; Jzz Bnd; Mch Bnd; Pep Bnd; Journalism; Band / Music; Butler U; Ball State U

CUEVAS, SILVIA; HAMMOND, IN; BISHOP NOLL INST; (MS); Hi Hnr Roll; Hnr Roll; MVP; Otst Ac Ach Awd; Pres Sch; Salutrn; Sci Fairs; Sci/Math Olympn; Valdctrian; Comm Volntr; Peer Tut/Med; Chrch Yth Grp; DARE; Emplmnt; Jr Ach; Svce Clb; Spch Team; Spanish Clb; Ch Chr; Dnce; Bskball (C); Sccr (V); Sftball (J); Stu Cncl; CR; Civil Engineer; U of Notre Dame; Valparaiso U

CULLISON, TOMMY; INDIANAPOLIS, IN; EMMERICH MANUAL HS; (SO); Hnr Roll; Comm Volntr; Emplmnt; A Member of Lilly Boys & Girls Club for 8 Years; Automotive; Lincoln Tech

CUMBERWORTH, STEVEN R; RUSHVILLE, IN; RUSHVILLE HS; (JR); Hi Hnr Roll; Nat Hon Sy; Nat Mrt LOC; Otst Ac Ach Awd; WWAHSS; Yth Ldrshp Prog; Chess; Chrch Yth Grp; FCA; Key Club; Mth Clb/Tm; Pep Squd; Prom Com; French Clb; Acpl Chr; Chr; Cr Ctry (V L); Track (V CL); Adv Cncl (R); Stu Cncl (R); CR (R); Nuclear Engineering; Aerospace Engineering; Massachusetts Institute of Technology; U of Notre Dame

CUMMINGS II, JAMES; BLOOMINGTON, IN; BLOOMINGTON HS NORTH; (SR); WWAHSS; Society for Creative Anachronism; Gay / Straight Alliance; Computer Science; Art; Indiana U

CUNNINGHAM, CADIS J; INDIANAPOLIS, IN; WARREN CTRL HS; (JR); Hi Hnr Roll; Hnr Roll; Nat Hon Sy; Perf Att; NYLC; Quill & Scroll; Bskball (VJ); Tennis (V CL); Wt Lftg (C); Adv Cncl (R); Cl Off (R); Stu Cncl (R); Sch Ppr (R); Yrbk (E, R); Selected from My School Participate Circle City Classic; Journalism; Athletic Training; Ball State U; Howard U

CUNNINGHAM, CYNTHIA; WESTVILLE, IN; WESTVILLE HS; (JR); Hnr Roll; Perf Att; Sftball (V L); Yrbk (E, P); Education; Business Management; Purdue North Central

CURRY, ASHLEY N; NEW ALBANY, IN; NEW ALBANY HS; (MS); Hnr Roll; Nat Hon Sy; Otst Ac Ach Awd; St of Mnth; Comm Volntr; DARE; Dnce; Bskball (V); Swmg (L); Vllyball (V); Competing in Pageants Since 14 Mos. Old; Donated (12 Inches) of Hair to Locks of Love, Collected Money for Disabled Children; Child Therapist for Abused' Children

CURTIS, SHEA W; SANDBORN, IN; NORTH KNOX HS; (SR); Hnr Roll; Nat Hon Sy; Pres Ac Ftns Aw; WWAHSS; Comm Volntr; Peer Tut/Med; DARE; FCA; NYLC; Off Aide; Prom Com; Sci Clb; SADD; Dnce; Bskball (J); Sftball (V L); Vllyball (V CL); Adv Cncl (R); Cl Off (P); Stu Cncl (S); UDA All-Star (Dance); Record Holder in Softball & Volleyball; Pre-Med; Dermatology; U of Southern Indiana; Indiana U/Purdue U

CUSKADEN, JORDAN; GREENSBURG, IN; GREENSBURG CMTY HS; (SR); MVP; Nat Hon Sy; WWAHSS; Yth Ldrshp Prog; BPA; FCA; French Clb; Bnd; Mch Bnd; Pep Bnd; Stg Cre; Bskball (J); Sccr (V CL); Swmg (V CL); Tennis (J); Stu Cncl (R); Yrbk (R, P); Lilly Scholarship Runner-Up Recipient; Swimming MVP; Radiography; Indiana U

CUTRERA, MAUREEN C; BLOOMINGTON, IN; BLOOMINGTON HS NORTH; (SR); Hi Hnr Roll; MVP; Nat Hon Sy; Pres Sch; Sci/Math Olympn; Yth Ldrshp Prog; Comm Volntr; Hab For Humty Volntr; Hosp Aide; Chrch Yth Grp; Emplmnt; Prom Com; Sci Clb; Bnd; Orch; Pep Bnd; Bskball (J); Sccr (V CL); Cl Off (V); Stu Cncl (R); Yrbk (P); Nursing; Pre-Med; St Louis U; Xavier U

CYB, KAREN; CARMEL, IN; CARMEL HS; (JR); Hi Hnr Roll; Nat Hon Sy; DECA; Emplmnt; Key Club; Spanish Clb; Tennis (J); Departmental Award for Spanish II; National DECA Participant; Marketing; International Business; U of Florida; Indiana U

CYRILL, NICOLLE; JASPER, IN; JASPER HS; (SO); Hi Hnr Roll; Hnr Roll; Otst Ac Ach Awd; Sci Fairs; WWAHSS; Yth Ldrshp Prog; Comm Volntr; Hosp Aide; Peer Tut/Med; Chess; DARE; Jr Ach; Key Club; Quiz Bowl; Schol Bwl; Svce Clb; SADD; Bnd; Pep Bnd; Golf (JV); Track (V); Pharmacy; Sales / Marketing; Arizona State University; Purdue University

CZARKOWSKI, BRIAN; CARMEL, IN; CARMEL HS; (JR); Hi Hnr Roll; Nat Hon Sy; Yth Ldrshp Prog; Peer Tut/Med; DARE; DECA; Emplmnt; Spanish Clb; Bskball (J); Golf (J); Track; CR (T); Sch Ppr (R); DECA; Indiana U-Kelly School of Business; Accounting, Finance, Marketing; Indiana U

DAILEY, MICHELLE A; FORT WAYNE, IN; (SO); Pre-Medicine

DANFORTH, DINAH; COLUMBUS, IN; COLUMBUS NORTH HS; (JR); DAR; Hi Hnr Roll; Nat Hon Sy; Nat Mrt LOC; WWAHSS; Yth Ldrshp Prog; Comm Volntr; Chrch Yth Grp; FCA; Key Club; Mth Clb/Tm; French Clb; Chr; Choir Officer; French Club Officer; Psychology; Math; Washington U; Washington and Lee U

DANNER, AMANDA L; NEW HAVEN, IN; NEW HAVEN HS; (SR); Hnr Roll; Nat Hon Sy; St of Mnth; WWAHSS; Peer Tut/Med; FCA; Quill & Scroll; Spanish Clb; Acpl Chr; Bskball; PP Ftbl; Track (J); Vllyball (J); Cl Off (S); Stu Cncl (R); Yrbk (E, R); Elementary Education Teacher; Ball State U

DATES, CATHERINE; INDIANAPOLIS, IN; EMMERICH MANUAL HS; (FR); Hnr Roll; Perf Att; Drl Tm; SP/M/VS; Stg Cre; A Teacher; A Lawyer; IUPUI, Georgia Tech Spelman Collage; Indiana U, Morris Brown College

DATZEK, KRISTA N; GREENFIELD, IN; NEW PALESTINE HS; (JR); Comm Volntr; DARE; PP Ftbl; Track (V L); Wt Lftg; SAVE Program; Business Degree; Communications Degree; Indiana U; Ball State U

DAVENPORT III, ROBERT M; INDIANAPOLIS, IN; BROAD RIPPLE HS; (JR); Hi Hnr Roll; Hnr Roll; MVP; Comm Volntr; Peer Tut/Med; Track (V); Wrstlg (V); Red Belt in Karate; Business; Engineering; Indiana U

DAVIS, ADRIENE F; AVON, IN; AVON HS; (SO); Hi Hnr Roll; Hnr Roll; Nat Hon Sy; Perf Att; Chrch Yth Grp; DARE; SADD; Chr; Ftbll (J); Sccr (J); Wt Lftg (J); National Junior Honor Society; Business and Management; Broadcast Journalism; U of Florida; U of Georgia

DAVIS, ALICIA N; INDIANAPOLIS, IN; BROAD RIPPLE HS; (SO); Hnr Roll; Nat Hon Sy; Yth Ldrshp Prog; Comm Volntr; Key Club; Lttrmn Clb; Scouts; Sch Ppr; Key Club Vice President; Rugby Player; Major in Fashion Photography; Minor in Fashion Design; International Academy of Design & Tech; Parsons School of Design

DAVIS, ANGELA M; INDIANAPOLIS, IN; (SR); Hnr Roll; WWAHSS; Yth Ldrshp Prog; Hab For Humty Volntr; Chrch Yth Grp; Emplmnt; Key Club; Mus Clb; Orch; Yrbk (E); Key Clubber of the Month (Sept.); French Major/ Business; U of Evansville

DAVIS, ANTHONY; KOKOMO, IN; KOKOMO HS; (SO); Hnr Roll; Perf Att; Chrch Yth Grp; Photog; Quill & Scroll; Ftball (V); Yrbk (P); Adult/ Youth 3rd Place Bowling; Adult/Youth High Series Handicap; Purdue U; Indiana U

DAVIS, BRANDON A; WESTPORT, IN; SOUTH DECATUR JR/SR HS; (SO); Chr; Ch Chr; SP/M/VS; Stg Cre; Teacher's Asst.-Algebra; Who's Who Among High School Students; Stage Production/Acting; Johnson Bible College; Ball State U

DAVIS, CAMERON A; AVON, IN; AVON HS; (FR); Hi Hnr Roll; Hnr Roll; Perf Att; Sci Fairs; Comm Volntr; Hosp Aide; Sccr (J); Medicine; Engineering

DAVIS, KACIE L; CARMEL, IN; CARMEL HS; (JR); Hnr Roll; Nat Hon Sy; WWAHSS; Comm Volntr; Chrch Yth Grp; Emplmnt; Key Club; Photog; Quill & Scroll; Sccr; Track; Yrbk; Indiana Professional Photographers Guild; International Studies / Spanish; Miami of Ohio Oxford College; Indiana U

DAVIS, KENDRA M; INDIANAPOLIS, IN; BEN DAVIS HS; (SO); Hnr Roll; Perf Att; Comm Volntr; Chrch Yth Grp; Emplmnt; Clb; Bskball (J L); Wayne Success Team; Judge / Law; Tennessee State; Ball State U

DAVIS, KERI J; HARTSVILLE, IN; HAUSER JR/SR HS; (SO); Hnr Roll; Perf Att; St of Mnth; WWAHSS; FCA; Key Club; SADD; Spanish Clb; Chr; Dnce; PPSqd (V L); Tennis (V L); Vllyball (J); Stu Cncl (R); Psychology-Master's; Human Resources-Master's in Business Minor; DePauw U; Ball State U

DAVIS, LOGAN M; CHURUBUSCO, IN; CHURUBUSCO HS; (JR); Hi Hnr Roll; Hnr Roll; Nat Hon Sy; WWAHSS; Comm Volntr; Red Cr Aide; Spec Olymp Vol; Chrch Yth Grp; FCA; Key Club; Lttrmn Clb; Schol Bwl; SADD; Tchrs Aide; Spanish Clb; Bnd; Mch Bnd; Pep Bnd; SP/M/VS; Cr Ctry (V L); Golf (J); Advertising; Indiana U; Ball State U

DAVIS, MARK; GREENCASTLE, IN; GREENCASTLE HS; (JR); Hi Hnr Roll; Hnr Roll; Nat Hon Sy; Pres Ac Ftns Aw; Comm Volntr; Chess; Chrch Yth Grp; Cmptr Clb; Emplmnt; Key Club; Mth Clb/Tm; Schol Bwl; Scouts; Bnd; Chr; Pep Bnd; SP/M/VS; Golf (V L); Sccr (J); Cl Off (V)

DAVIS, RACHEL E; BEDFORD, IN; STONE CITY CHRISTIAN AC; (SO); Ctznshp Aw; Hnr Roll; St of Mnth; Chrch Yth Grp; Mus Clb; Chr; Ch Chr; Orch; Vllyball; Placed 1st in Piano Competition in a 4 State Region; Nurse; Music Career; Hobe Sound Bible College; God's Bible School & College

DAVIS, SCOTT L; PENDLETON, IN; PENDLETON HEIGHTS HS; (SR); Bsball; Communication; Business; Indiana U Bloomington

DAVIS, SYDNI; SOUTH BEND, IN; (SO); Hi Hnr Roll; Hnr Roll; Perf Att; Comm Volntr; Bskball (V L); Stu Cncl (R); Law; Veterinarian; Tennessee State U; USC U Southern Cal.

DAY, DANIEL; INDIANAPOLIS, IN; LAWRENCE NORTH HS; (JR); Hi Hnr Roll; Hnr Roll; Key Club; Spch Team; Orch; SP/M/VS; Earlham College; Indiana U

DEAL, BRITTANY N; EDINBURGH, IN; EDINBURGH HS; (FR); 4H Awd; Ctznshp Aw; Hnr Roll; Perf Att; Sci Fairs; Comm Volntr; 4-H; French Clb; Bnd; Drm Mjr; Mch Bnd; Pep Bnd; Tennis (J); Best Section-Woodwind Band; Solo & Ensemble 1st, 2nd, 2nd; Psychology; Psychiatry; Indiana U; Purdue

DEAN, MATT; SCOTTSBURG, IN; AUSTIN HS; (JR); F Lan Hn Soc; Hi Hnr Roll; Hnr Roll; Nat Hon Sy; Pres Sch; WWAHSS; Comm Volntr; Peer Tut/Med; Chrch Yth Grp; Emplmnt; Lib Aide; Pep Squd; Sci Clb; French Clb; Bnd; Pep Bnd; Golf (V); Hoosier Boy's State; Sons of Liberty; Pre-Med; Medical Schooling; U of L; Evansville

DEAN, RACHEL J; VALPARAISO, IN; WHEELER HS; (JR); Hi Hnr Roll; Nat Hon Sy; Chrch Yth Grp; FCA; Key Club; Quiz Bowl; Tchrs Aide; Chr; Bskball (V CL); PP Ftbl (V); Vllyball (V CL); History Academic Team; Natural Helpers Program; Athletic Training; Physical Therapy; Indiana Wesleyan U; Anderson U

DEATON, BLAKE O; WARSAW, IN; WARSAW CMTY HS; (JR); Hnr Roll; Perf Att; Emplmnt; Ntl FFA; Off Aide; Ftball (VJ L); Track (J); Wrstlg (V L)

DE BOY, LAUREN E; FRANKLIN, IN; FRANKLIN CMTY HS; (SR); Hi Hnr Roll; Nat Hon Sy; Comm Volntr; Hosp Aide; Peer Tut/Med; Chrch Yth Grp; FCA; Key Club; Off Aide; Prom Com; Chr; PP Ftbl (V); Swmg (V L); Tennis (V L); Vllyball (J); Stu Cncl; VFW Essay Prize Winner; AmeriCorps; Nursing

DEEK, CHRISTINE; VALPARAISO, IN; WHEELER HS; (FR); Hi Hnr Roll; WWAHSS; Chrch Yth Grp; Key Club; Schol Bwl; Ch Chr; Bskball (J); Golf (V L); Stu Cncl (R)

DEEK, SYLVIA; VALPARAISO, IN; WHEELER HS; (JR); Hi Hnr Roll; Nat Hon Sy; Otst Ac Ach Awd; WWAHSS; Chrch Yth Grp; Key Club; Prom Com; Schol Bwl; Bskball (J); Golf (V); Cl Off (T); Stu Cncl (V)

DEGROFF KIRCHGRABER, MICHAEL A; SPENCER, IN; OWEN VALLEY CMTY HS; (FR); Hnr Roll; Bnd; Jzz Bnd; Mch Bnd; Pep Bnd; USNAA-USAA National Band Award 2005; Earlham College, Richmond Indiana

DEHRING, KATHY; VALPARAISO, IN; VALPARAISO HS; (JR); Hnr Roll; Nat Hon Sy; Perf Att; WWAHSS; Comm Volntr; Drma Clb; Emplmnt; Key Club; Mus Clb; Tchrs Aide; Bnd; Jzz Bnd; Orch; SP/M/VS; Intramural Water Polo; Music Therapy; Music Education; Michigan State U (East Lansing); Indiana U (Bloomington)

DEITERING, NICK; WOODBURN, IN; WOODLAN JR/SR HS; (MS); Bsball (J); Bskball; Ftbll (J); Mental Attitude Award in 8th Basketball; Teacher; Chiropractor; Indiana U; Notre Dame U

DEMAREE, BEN; OSGOOD, IN; (SO); Hnr Roll; Bskball (VJ); Track (V); Philosophy, History; Foreign Language; Hanover College; IUPUI

DEMOND, CHELSEA; HOBART, IN; RIVER FOREST SR HS; (FR); Hi Hnr Roll; Hnr Roll; Otst Ac Ach Awd; Perf Att; St of Mnth; Peer Tut/Med; Chrch Yth Grp; Drma Clb; Emplmnt; Mus Clb; Chr; Ch Chr; SP/M/VS; Scr Kpr (J); Stu Cncl (P, V); All-State Honor Choir; Circle of the State with Song; Choral Director; English Majors; U of Notre Dame; Indiana U

DEMOS, LYNN; ANDERSON, IN; HIGHLAND HS; (SO); Hnr Roll; Jr Rot; WWAHSS; Comm Volntr; Drma Clb; Off Aide; Quill & Scroll; Svce Clb; Swg Chr; Cl Off (V); Yrbk (R)

DE PYPER, ADAM J; ROCHESTER, IN; CASTON HS; (SR); Hnr Roll; MVP; St of Mnth; WWAHSS; Comm Volntr; Peer Tut/Med; AL Aux Boys; Chrch Yth Grp; FCA; Key Club; Sci Clb; Bnd; Golf (J); Sccr (V CL); Stu Cncl; Yrbk (R); Boys State Candidate; Computer Engineering; Tri-State U

Cutrera, Maureen C
Bloomington HS North
Bloomington, IN

Cullison, Tommy
Emmerich Manual HS
Indianapolis, IN

Croyle, Jordan W
Monroe Ctrl HS
Ridgeville, IN

National
Honor Roll
Spring 2005

Cross, Heather R
Center Grove HS
Greenwood, IN

Curry, Ashley N
New Albany HS
New Albany, IN

Davis, Adriene F
Avon HS
Avon, IN

DERBY, JACK; NEW HAVEN, IN; NEW HAVEN HS; (SO); DAR; St of Mnth; Comm Volntr; Chrch Yth Grp; Drma Clb; NtlFrnscLg; Quiz Bowl; Schol Bwl; Spch Team; Acpl Chr; SP/M/VS; Cr Ctry (V L); Track (J); Most Improved Runner (Cross Country 2004); Best Newcomer-Male (Drama Club 2004); Doctor of Optometry (OD); Bachelor of Arts; Indiana U-Bloomington; Taylor U-Upland

DE SANTO, ISAAC; FORT WAYNE, IN; HOMESTEAD; (SO); Hnr Roll; Chess

DEUTSCH, NICHOLAS E; EVANSVILLE, IN; F J REITZ HS; (SR); 4H Awd; Hi Hnr Roll; Hnr Roll; Kwnis Aw; Nat Hon Sy; WWAHSS; Comm Volntr; Hab For Humty Volntr; 4-H; Chrch Yth Grp; Key Club; Ntl FFA; Scouts; Bnd; Jzz Bnd; Mch Bnd; Pep Bnd; Reitz Chapter FFA-President 2 Yrs; National Honor Society, Academic Honors Diploma; Mechanical Engineering; Agricultural Engineering; Purdue U

DEVALK, DANIELLE N; NORTH WEBSTER, IN; WAWASEE HS; (FR); Hnr Roll; Kwnis Aw; Otst Ac Ach Awd; St of Mnth; Comm Volntr; Hab For Humty Volntr; Chrch Yth Grp; Emplmnt; Key Club; Off Aide; Tchrs Aide; PP Ftbl (J); Sccr (V); Track (J); Yrbk (E, R, P); Presidential Award Educational Achievement; Child Psychologist

DEVER, JOSEPH; GREENVILLE, IN; FLOYD CTRL HS; (SO); Hnr Roll; St of Mnth; WWAHSS; Comm Volntr; Peer Tut/Med; Off Aide; Tchrs Aide; Spanish Clb; Reading Club

DEVRIES, ASHTON; DEMOTTE, IN; KANKAKEE VALLEY HS; (JR); Hi Hnr Roll; Nat Hon Sy; Otst Ac Ach Awd; St of Mnth; WWAHSS; Yth Ldrshp Prog; Peer Tut/Med; Chrch Yth Grp; Drma Clb; Prom Com; Schol Bwl; Svce Clb; Foreign Clb; Chr; Ch Chr; SP/M/VS; Stg Cre; PP Ftbl (V); Indiana All-State Choir; Academic Decathlon; Music Business; Jazz Studies; Belmont U; Elmhurst College

DIAZ, M J; ELIZABETHTOWN, IN; COLUMBUS EAST HS; (SO); Hnr Roll; Kwnis Aw; St of Mnth; Comm Volntr; Hosp Aide; DARE; Kindness and Justice Challenge; Registered Nurse; Ball State; Indiana U

DIEHL, KATHRYN E; MERRILLVILLE, IN; MERRILLVILLE HS; (SR); All Am Sch; Hi Hnr Roll; Jr Eng Tech; Nat Hon Sy; Nat Ldrshp Svc; Valdctrian; Yth Ldrshp Prog; Emplmnt; NYLC; Bnd; Ch Chr; Mch Bnd; Pep Bnd; Adv Cncl (R); Cl Off (T, R); Stu Cncl (P, V, R); Indiana U Honors Program in Foreign Language; Student Government President; Pharmacy; Purdue U West Lafayette

DIESER, KIMBERLY C; CARMEL, IN; CARMEL HS; (SR); All Am Sch; Hi Hnr Roll; Jr Eng Tech; MVP; Nat Hon Sy; Otst Ac Ach Awd; CARE; Biology Clb; Chrch Yth Grp; Cmptr Clb; DARE; Drma Clb; Fr of Library; Mth Clb/Tm; Sci Clb; Bskball (J); Sccr (V); Electronic Engineer; Purdue U W. Lafayette IN

DIKO, EMILY; ELWOOD, IN; ELWOOD HS; (JR); Nat Hon Sy; Sci Fairs; ArtClub; Chrch Yth Grp; Emplmnt; Prom Com; Latin Clb; Tennis (J); Cl Off (S); UC Berkeley

DILLARD, ASHLEY R; SEYMOUR, IN; SEYMOUR HS; (SO); Hi Hnr Roll; Nat Hon Sy; St of Mnth; USAA; WWAHSS; Comm Volntr; Key Club; Off Aide; Spanish Clb; Dnce; Chrldg (VJ L); All-Star Cheerleading; One Step Above-Dance Team; Business

DINKELMAN, JENN; VALPARAISO, IN; VALPARAISO HS; (SO); Hnr Roll; Peer Tut/Med; Emplmnt; Key Club; Tchrs Aide; Bnd; Track (V); Vllyball (J); Key Club Class Representative; Veterinary; Culinary; Purdue U; Ball State U

DISHER, ERICA N; INDIANAPOLIS, IN; SOUTHPORT HS; (SR); Hnr Roll; Nat Hon Sy; Comm Volntr; Emplmnt; Prom Com; Clr Grd; Orch; SHAPE President; PEER Mentor; Doctor of Pharmacy; Spanish Minor; Purdue U

DIXON, JALENA E; HOBART, IN; HOBART HS; (SR); Ctznshp Aw; Hnr Roll; St of Mnth; Comm Volntr; Chrch Yth Grp; Key Club; Off Aide; Tchrs Aide; Spanish Clb; Ch Chr; Swmg (V L); Stu Cncl (R); Sch Ppr (E, R); Yrbk (E, R); Miss Swimmer of the Year (2004-2005); Management/Finance; Biology; Ball State U; Purdue U Calumet

DOCTOR, RACHEL; HUNTINGTON, IN; HUNTINGTON NORTH HS; (SR); 4H Awd; Hi Hnr Roll; Hnr Roll; Nat Hon Sy; St of Mnth; USAA; WWAHSS; Comm Volntr; 4-H; AL Aux Girls; Emplmnt; Jr Ach; Ntl FFA; Off Aide; Photog; French Clb; Bnd; PP Ftbl (V); Track (V); Sunshine Society; Agricultural Communications; Purdue U

DONALDSON, KARISA; PERU, IN; NORTH MIAMI HS; (SR); DAR; Hnr Roll; MVP; Nat Hon Sy; St Schl; Valdctrian; WWAHSS; Ntl FFA; German Clb; Bskball (V L); Sftball (V CL); Vllyball (V CL); Taken Private Piano Lessons 10 Yrs; Biology/Pre-Med; Optometry; Huntington U

DONOVAN, NICK; UNION CITY, IN; UNION CITY CMTY HS; (SO); Video Game Design; Forensics

DORGAY, BETH; LANESVILLE, IN; LANESVILLE JR/SR HS; (JR); Hi Hnr Roll; Nat Hon Sy; WWAHSS; Chrch Yth Grp; FCA; Prom Com; Scouts; SADD; Tchrs Aide; French Clb; Bnd; Sftball (V); Vllyball (V)

DORGAY, JOSEPH; LANESVILLE, IN; LANESVILLE JR/SR HS; (JR); Hnr Roll; WWAHSS; Scouts; Bnd; Tennis (V)

DOUBMAN, KYLIE S; KENNARD, IN; KNIGHTSTOWN HS; (SO); Hi Hnr Roll; Sci Fairs; St of Mnth; USAA; WWAHSS; Chrch Yth Grp; Off Aide; Chrldg (VJ L); Stu Cncl; Pre-Optometry; Pre-Med; Indiana Wesleyan; U of Notre Dame

DOUCET, KELLY A; FT WAYNE, IN; R NELSON SNIDER HS; (SR); Ctznshp Aw; WWAHSS; Comm Volntr; Peer Tut/Med; Chrch Yth Grp; Off Aide; Prom Com; Tchrs Aide; Spanish Clb; Ch Chr; Tennis (V); National Urban League Scholars Society; Attorney / Pre-Law Major; Spanish / Psychology; Tennessee State U; Ball State U

DOWNS, CRAIG; ELKHART, IN; CONCORD HS; (JR); Hi Hnr Roll; Nat Hon Sy; Otst Ac Ach Awd; WWAHSS; Comm Volntr; Peer Tut/Med; Chrch Yth Grp; Emplmnt; FCA; Key Club; Off Aide; Chr; Bsball (V L); Bskball (JC); Ftball (V L); Stu Cncl (P); Medical Field; Business; Indiana; U of Notre Dame

DOWNTON, JASMINE; FORT WAYNE, IN; WAYNE HS; (JR); Hi Hnr Roll; Hnr Roll; Nat Hon Sy; Nat Mrt LOC; WWAHSS; Speech Pathologist, Doctoral Degree; Pediatrician; Indiana Purdue Fort Wayne; Ivy Tech

DOZIER, KHIRY A; SOUTH BEND, IN; WASHINGTON HS; (FR); Fld Hky (J); Ftball (J); Wt Lftg (V); CR (R); Sports Psychology; Sports Broadcasting; Purdue U; U of Michigan

DRUBA, JUSTIN A; HANOVER, IN; SOUTHWESTERN MIDDLE SR HS; (JR); Hi Hnr Roll; Nat Hon Sy; Otst Ac Ach Awd; Perf Att; WWAHSS; Yth Ldrshp Prog; Comm Volntr; Prom Com; Bskball (J); Cr Ctry (V L); Track (V L); Cl Off (V); Stu Cncl (R); National Honor Society; Engineering; Rose Hulman Institute of Technology; Purdue U

DUBOIS, JONATHON; ELKHART, IN; JIMTOWN HS; (FR); Ctznshp Aw; Hnr Roll; Chrch Yth Grp; FCA; French Clb; Chr; Bsball (J); Bskball (J); Tennis (J); Teaching; Medicine; Northwestern U; Bethel College

DUNAWAY, BRENT R; GRANGER, IN; PENN HS; (JR); Hi Hnr Roll; Nat Hon Sy; Yth Ldrshp Prog; Comm Volntr; Chrch Yth Grp; DARE; Emplmnt; Bskball (V L); Student Athlete of the Week / Academic Letter; Big Brother / Big Sister Program / Northern Indiana Conference Award for Basketball - Honorable Mention; Medical Doctor / Sports Medicine; Dentist; Purdue U West Lafayette; Michigan U Ann Arbor

DUNHAM, SARAH; ANDERSON, IN; HIGHLAND HS; (FR); Hnr Roll; Nat Hon Sy; Comm Volntr; Chrch Yth Grp; Chrldg (V L); Orthodontistry; Indiana U; U of Louisville, Kentucky

DUNIGAN, LINDSEY; GARY, IN; THE ENSWEILER AC; (JR); Comm Volntr; Drma Clb; SP/M/VS; Chrldg (V); Assistant Cheerleading Coach At Lake Ridge Middle School; Business Management; Dance; Purdue U Calumet

DUNKERLY, CALEB A; LINTON, IN; LINTON-STOCKTON; (SO); Comm Volntr; Lttrmn Clb; Spanish Clb; Bnd; Mch Bnd; Bskball (VJ); Golf (V L); Tennis (V L)

DUNNINGTON, DAVID; YORKTOWN, IN; YORKTOWN HS; (JR); Hnr Roll; Earn a philosophy doctorate in Computer Analysis; Become a professor in my field; Massachusetts Institute of Technology; California Institute of Technology

DUNSIL, PAEGAN D; BATESVILLE, IN; JAC-CEN-DEL JR/SR HS; (SO); Hnr Roll; Chrch Yth Grp; Drma Clb; Emplmnt; FCA; Schol Bwl; SADD; German Clb; Bnd; Mch Bnd; Pep Bnd; Chrldg; Vllyball (J); Yrbk; Sunshine Society; Pre-Medicine; Chemistry; Indiana State U; Indiana U

DUNSMORE, LACEY; MUNCIE, IN; MUNCIE CTRL HS; (SR); Hnr Roll; Nat Hon Sy; Comm Volntr; Chrch Yth Grp; Jr Cls League; Key Club; Chr; Cl Off (V); Nursing; Ball State U

DUPIN, JENNY; SALEM, IN; WEST WASHINGTON JR/SR HS; (SR); Comm Volntr; ArtClub; Pep Squd; Prom Com; Sci Clb; Pep Bnd; Chrldg (V C); PP Ftbl; Outstanding Community Leaders; Business. Law; IUS; U of Louisville

DUPONT, EMILY; JASPER, IN; JASPER HS; (SO); Hnr Roll; Emplmnt; FCA; Key Club; Vsity Clb; German Clb; Swmg (V); Pharmacy; Teacher; Indiana U, Purdue U At Indianapolis; Purdue U

DURAN, TINA M; MUNSTER, IN; BISHOP NOLL INST; (SR); Hnr Roll; WWAHSS; Comm Volntr; Emplmnt; Mth Clb/Tm; P to P St Amb Prg; Prom Com; Schol Bwl; Sci Clb; Svce Clb; Bskball; Chrldg (J); Tennis (VJ); Vllyball; Cl Off (T); CR (R); Business Marketing & Advertising; Master's Degree / Finance; Hawaii Pacific U; Northern Illinois

DYKES, JOHN; ANDERSON, IN; (SR); 4H Awd; Hnr Roll; WWAHSS; Comm Volntr; 4-H; Chrch Yth Grp; Scouts; Tchrs Aide; Latin Clb; Cr Ctry; English Literature; Purdue U

EARLS, NICK A; BEDFORD, IN; MITCHELL HS; (SO); 4H Awd; Hi Hnr Roll; Nat Hon Sy; Otst Ac Ach Awd; Pres Ac Ftns Aw; St of Mnth; USAA; WWAHSS; Yth Ldrshp Prog; Comm Volntr; Peer Tut/Med; 4-H; Chrch Yth Grp; Scouts; SADD; Spanish Clb; Cr Ctry (V L); Track (V L); Wrstlg (V L); Optometry; Indiana U; Butler U

EARNEST, MEGAN E; RUSHVILLE, IN; RUSHVILLE CONSOLIDATED HS; (SR); 4H Awd; WWAHSS; Comm Volntr; 4-H; Chrch Yth Grp; Emplmnt; Key Club; Pep Squd; SADD; Spanish Clb; Bnd; Mch Bnd; Orch; Pep Bnd; Swmg (V CL); 2005 Indiana Horatio Alger Scholar; Pediatric Endocrinology; U of Southern Indiana

EAST, KEISHA D; WESTPORT, IN; SOUTH DECATUR JR/SR HS; (SR); WWAHSS; Comm Volntr; Chrch Yth Grp; Emplmnt; Mus Clb; Off Aide; Pep Squd; Photog; Bnd; Pep Bnd; PPSqd (J); PP Ftbl (V); Sch Ppr (E, R, P); Yrbk (E, R, P); Twenty-First Century Scholars; National Junior Honor Society; Photography; Interior Design; Ivy Tech

EATON, TAYLOR C; VINCENNES, IN; LINCOLN HS; Hi Hnr Roll; MVP; Nat Hon Sy; Perf Att; WWAHSS; Comm Volntr; Chrch Yth Grp; Off Aide; Prom Com; Foreign Clb; SP/M/VS; Cr Ctry (V L); Swmg (V L); Track (V L); Stu Cncl (R); Yrbk (R, P); American Legion Award-Cross Country; Biology; Sports Medicine; U of Evansville; Anderson U

EBER, LEAH; COLUMBIA CITY, IN; COLUMBIA CITY HS; (SO); 4H Awd; Hi Hnr Roll; Hnr Roll; MVP; Otst Ac Ach Awd; Yth Ldrshp Prog; Comm Volntr; 4-H; Chrch Yth Grp; Emplmnt; FCA; Key Club; Photog; SADD; SP/M/VS; Track (V); Vllyball (V C); 2nd in State in Long Jump Track; 1st Team All-Conference in Volleyball; Interior Design; Fashion Design; U of Illinois; Wheaton U (Norton Mass)

EBERLEIN, MARCUS; TERRE HAUTE, IN; SOUTH VIGO HS; (JR); Hi Hnr Roll; Hnr Roll; Hab For Humty Volntr; Emplmnt; ROTC; Scouts; Tchrs Aide; WREASTLING Clb; Wt Lftg (L); Wrstlg (L); Building Trades-Helped Built a House; Wrestling; Building Trades; Indiana State U; Michigan (Allendale)

EBY, KATIE M; ELKHART, IN; CONCORD HS; (SR); Ctznshp Aw; Hi Hnr Roll; Hnr Roll; Kwnis Aw; Otst Ac Ach Awd; Perf Att; Pres Ac Ftns Aw; Pres Sch; St of Mnth; Yth Ldrshp Prog; Comm Volntr; Chrch Yth Grp; FCA; Key Club; Mus Clb; Chr; Ch Chr; SP/M/VS; Bskball (J); Lcrsse (V C); Sccr (J); Track (V L); Honorable Mention in the Scholastic Art Award for Computer Art; Advertising / Graphic Design; Interior Design; Clark State College; The Illinois Institute of Art Chicago

ECENBARGER, EMILY; FORT WAYNE, IN; NORTH SIDE HS; (JR); Hi Hnr Roll; Hnr Roll; Kwnis Aw; Nat Hon Sy; Comm Volntr; Golf (V); Tennis (V); Yrbk (R); Indiana U

ECKER, DUSTIN L; RICHMOND, IN; CTRVILLE HS; (SR); Ctznshp Aw; Hnr Roll; MVP; Nat Hon Sy; Pres Ac Ftns Aw; Comm Volntr; Chrch Yth Grp; DARE; Emplmnt; FCA; Key Club; Lttrmn Clb; Off Aide; Prom Com; Bnd; Jzz Bnd; SP/M/VS; Bskball (J); Tennis (V CL); Track (V L); Vsy Clb; Wt Lftg; Adv Cncl (S); Cl Off (S); Stu Cncl (R); CR (R); Yrbk (R, P); National Honor Society / Young Life Leader; Physical Trainer; Huntington U

ECKERLE, CASSIE; JASPER, IN; JASPER HS; (JR); Hnr Roll; Nat Hon Sy; Perf Att; WWAHSS; Comm Volntr; FCA; Key Club; Prom Com; SADD; Spanish Clb; Chrldg (J); Stu Cncl (R); Sch Ppr (R); Yrbk (R); Elementary Education; Indiana U-Bloomington; Indiana State U

ECKERLE, JUSTIN S; JASPER, IN; JASPER HS; (SR); Hnr Roll; Nat Hon Sy; Otst Ac Ach Awd; WWAHSS; Comm Volntr; AL Aux Boys; Chrch Yth Grp; DARE; Key Club; SADD; Voc Ind Clb Am; Stg Cre; Bsball (J); Bskball (J); Tennis (V L); Motorcycle Mechanic; Motorcycle Mechanics Institute

EDISON, TIFFANY M; ANDERSON, IN; HIGHLAND HS; (SO); Hnr Roll; Chr; Swg Chr; Psychology; Pre-Law; Ball State U; Anderson U

EDMUNDSON, AMBER; PORTLAND, IN; JAY CTY HS; (FR); Hnr Roll; Perf Att; Spanish Clb; Bskball (J); Sftball (J); Indiana U

EDWARDS, SABRINA L; PALMYRA, IN; FLOYD CTRL HS; (FR); Sci Fairs; Comm Volntr; FCA; Schol Bwl; Tchrs Aide; Chr; Clr Grd; Skiing; Track (V); CR (R); Academic Super Bowl Russian History; Community Service; Doctoral Degree; Law Degree; U of Florida; Bloomington

EDWARDSON, STEPHEN; NEWBURGH, IN; CASTLE HS; (SR); Hi Hnr Roll; Nat Hon Sy; St of Mnth; Yth Ldrshp Prog; Comm Volntr; Hab For Humty Volntr; Peer Tut/Med; Chrch Yth Grp; DARE; Emplmnt; FCA; Photog; Quill & Scroll; Svce Clb; SADD; SP/M/VS; Yrbk (R, P); Vice President of Teen Power; United Way Volunteer of the Year; Medicine; Biology; U of Southern Indiana

EFFINGER, LAURA R; BOONVILLE, IN; BOONVILLE HS; (JR); Hnr Roll; Nat Hon Sy; WWAHSS; Hosp Aide; Spec Olymp Vol; Emplmnt; FCA; Key Club; Vsity Clb; Bskball (V); Golf (V); Engineer; Physician; U of Michigan; U of Indiana

EGGINK, ALFONS G; ELKHART, IN; ELKHART MEMORIAL HS; (SR); Hi Hnr Roll; Hnr Roll; Emplmnt; Ftball (VJ); Elkhart Memorial Dollars for Scholars Phon-A-Thon; Close-Up US History Trip to Washington, DC; Accounting; Economics; Indiana U Bloomington

Edison, Tiffany M
Highland HS
Anderson, IN

Earls, Nick A
Mitchell HS
Bedford, IN

Dunsil, Paegan D
Jac-Cen-Del JR/SR HS
Batesville, IN

Dieser, Kimberly C
Carmel HS
Carmel, IN

Dixon, Jalena E
Hobart HS
Hobart, IN

Eberlein, Marcus
South Vigo HS
Terre Haute, IN

Edmundson, Amber
Jay Cty HS
Portland, IN

EHRGOTT, TAYLOR; ANDERSON, IN; ANDERSON HS; (FR); Hnr Roll; Nat Hon Sy; Perf Att; Chrch Yth Grp; DARE; Chrldg (V); Swmg (V); Tennis (J); Medical; U of Tennessee; U of Florida

EICHLER, JASON; OSSIAN, IN; NORWELL HS; (SO); Hi Hnr Roll; 4-H; Bsball (J); Ftball (V); Wells County Rotary Club Award; Business Management; Purdue U; Manchester College

ELDER, WILLIAM C; NOBLESVILLE, IN; HAMILTON SOUTHEASTERN HS; (JR); F Lan Hn Soc; Hi Hnr Roll; Pres Ac Ftns Aw; St of Mnth; Comm Volntr; Peer Tut/Med; Spec Olymp Vol; Emplmnt; Vsity Clb; Latin Clb; Ftball (J); Vllyball (J); Wt Lftg (V); Rugby; Leadership Award Winner; Aeronautical Engineering; US History Major; Purdue U; Embry Riddle Aeronautical U

ELDRIDGE, KELSIE; ELKHART, IN; CONCORD HS; (JR); Hi Hnr Roll; Kwnis Aw; MVP; Nat Hon Sy; WWAHSS; Peer Tut/Med; Emplmnt; FCA; Key Club; Off Aide; Prom Com; SADD; Tchrs Aide; Bskball (V CL); Sftball (V CL); Vllyball (V CL); Stu Cncl (R); Nominated Who's Who Soph Jr Yrs, Softball-All Conference/Channel 46 Athlete March; Softball-All District/ Kiwanis Athlete of Year Nom; Occupational Therapy; Speech & Language/ Education; Indian U; Purdue U, Anderson U, Oakland U-MI, Grand Valley State U MI; Butler U, U of Indianapolis, Bethel College, De Pauw U, Valparaiso U

ELLIS, KATY; BRISTOL, IN; ELKHART CTRL HS; (SO); Hi Hnr Roll; Hnr Roll; WWAHSS; Chrch Yth Grp; Emplmnt; Key Club; Mod UN; Ch Chr; Jzz Bnd; Orch; Swmg (V L); Music Education Major; Chemistry Education Major; Indiana U Bloomington

ELPERS, ASHLEY R; EVANSVILLE, IN; CENTRAL HS; (JR); 4H Awd; Ctznshp Aw; Hi Hnr Roll; Nat Hon Sy; Pres Ac Ftns Aw; Sci/Math Olympn; St of Mnth; Yth Ldrshp Prog; Comm Volntr; 4-H; BPA; DECA; P to P St Amb Prg; Prom Com; French Clb; Dnce; PPSqd (V CL); Adv Cncl (R); Yrbk (R); Numerous Awards for 4-H; Food Science / Dietitian; Purdue U; Ball State U

ELSHABAZZ, KHADIJAH; INDIANAPOLIS, IN; ARSENAL TECH HS; (SR); Hi Hnr Roll; Nat Hon Sy; Perf Att; WWAHSS; Key Club; Mch Bnd; Pep Bnd; SP/M/VS; Tennis; CR (R); Sch Ppr; Yrbk; Upward Bound; HOSA; Biology / Pre-Med; Indiana U Bloomington

EMERSON, HALEY; ELKHART, IN; CONCORD HS; (JR); Hi Hnr Roll; Nat Hon Sy; WWAHSS; Comm Volntr; Chrch Yth Grp; FCA; Key Club; Lttrmn Clb; Pep Squd; Bskball (V CL); Sccr (V L); Sftball (V L); Cl Off (V); Stu Cncl; National Key Club; Physical Therapy; Architecture

EMERY, KURT; GALVESTON, IN; LEWIS CASS JR/SR HS; (SO); Ftball (VJ)

ENGLAND, ERICA; EDINBURGH, IN; EDINBURGH HS; (JR); Hnr Roll; Nat Hon Sy; Perf Att; WWAHSS; Comm Volntr; Peer Tut/Med; Chrch Yth Grp; Emplmnt; Prom Com; SADD; Vsity Clb; Spanish Clb; Bskball (V); Track (V); Vllyball (V); Yrbk (P); CTA's in Hand Washing, Meal Planning, Lesson Planning, Most Improved Chemistry; Social Work; Early Childhood Educational; Sullivan U

ENGLERT, AMBER M; HUNTINGBURG, IN; SOUTHRIDGE HS; (FR); 4H Awd; Hi Hnr Roll; Hnr Roll; 4-H; BPA; Ntl FFA; Outdrs Clb; SADD; Acpl Chr; Yrbk (R); Architecture; Purdue U

ESCALANTE, MARITSA; MERRILLVILLE, IN; HOBART HS; (SO); All Am Sch; F Lan Hn Soc; Hnr Roll; Spec Olymp Vol; Chrch Yth Grp; Bnd; Ch Chr; Clr Grd; Dnce; Cr Ctry (V); Swmg (V); Track (V); Calumet Strutter (Runners Club); Lawyer; Criminal Justice; Indiana U

ESTEP, BRADLEY; MUNCIE, IN; MUNCIE CTRL HS; (SR); Ctznshp Aw; Hi Hnr Roll; Hnr Roll; Nat Hon Sy; Otst Ac Ach Awd; Perf Att; St of Mnth; WWAHSS; Comm Volntr; Hab For Humty Volntr; Chrch Yth Grp; Key Club; Chr; Ch Chr; Secondary Education; English Education; IVU Tech State College; Ball State U

ESTER, BRITNE; LAKE STATION, IN; RIVER FOREST SR HS; (FR); Hi Hnr Roll; MVP; Nat Hon Sy; St of Mnth; DARE; Chrldg (V); Education

EVANCHO, CATHY; INDIANAPOLIS, IN; PERRY MERIDIAN HS; (JR); Hi Hnr Roll; Hnr Roll; Nat Hon Sy; Otst Ac Ach Awd; Perf Att; Comm Volntr; Peer Tut/Med; Spec Olymp Vol; Emplmnt; Key Club; Mth Clb/Tm; NYLC; Pep Squd; Prom Com; Bskball (J); Cr Ctry (J); Track (J); Pediatrics; U of Miami; Clemson U

EVANS, KEVIN; FRANKFORT, IN; FRANKFORT HS; (FR); Comm Volntr; Chrch Yth Grp; Scouts; Chr; Music Producer; Singer; Norwich U

EVANS, RAVENE D; INDIANAPOLIS, IN; NORTHWEST HS; (SO); Hnr Roll; Perf Att; St of Mnth; Comm Volntr; Red Cr Aide; Chrch Yth Grp; Chr; Tennis (J); Vllyball (J); Fashion & Design; Pediatrician; Texas Southern U; Butler U

EWING, KYLAH E; COLUMBIA CITY, IN; COLUMBIA CITY HS; (FR); Hi Hnr Roll; Chrch Yth Grp; Photog; Chrldg (J); Gmnstcs

EYKHOLT, JACKIE; FORT WAYNE, IN; ANTHIS CAREER CTR/ ELMHURST; (JR); Iupui

FAILAUGA, TEUILA M; HONOLULU, IN; RADFORD HS; (SR); Hnr Roll; Perf Att; Comm Volntr; Peer Tut/Med; Chrch Yth Grp; Emplmnt; Off Aide; ROTC; SADD; Tchrs Aide; Ch Chr; Clr Grd; Sccr (V L); CR (R); Lit Mag (R, P); Sch Ppr (R, P); Cosmetology; Honolulu Community College; U of Hawaii

FARMER, ALLISON; EVANSVILLE, IN; CENTRAL HS; (SO); Ctznshp Aw; Hnr Roll; Nat Hon Sy; Perf Att; Chrch Yth Grp; DARE; Drma Clb; Emplmnt; Pep Squd; Photog; Scouts; German Clb; Clr Grd; Dnce; Flg Crps; SP/M/VS; PPSqd (V); Stu Cncl; Sch Ppr (R, P); Yrbk (R, P); Journalism; Photography; U of Kentucky; Indiana U

FARRIS, HANNAH M; SEYMOUR, IN; SEYMOUR CHRISTIAN AC; (SO); Hi Hnr Roll; Hnr Roll; MVP; Nat Hon Sy; Perf Att; St of Mnth; Comm Volntr; Chrch Yth Grp; DARE; Drma Clb; Emplmnt; Ntl Beta Clb; Pep Squd; Prom Com; Tchrs Aide; Ch Chr; SP/M/VS; Vllyball (VJ L); Stu Cncl (T); Lit Mag (R); Yrbk (P); Ensemble Group; Medical; Law; Indiana U

FAULKENBURG, AUDREY G; DE PAUW, IN; AMERICAN SCH; (JR); Hnr Roll; Nat Hon Sy; Perf Att; WWAHSS; Comm Volntr; Peer Tut/Med; Ntl FFA; World Qualifier in Barrel Racing; State Champion Barrel Racer; Equine Business Management; U of Louisville

FAULKNER, NATALIE; CARMEL, IN; CARMEL HS; (SO); Hnr Roll; WWAHSS; Comm Volntr; Chrch Yth Grp; DARE; DECA; Chr; Dnce; Stg Cre

FEATHERSTON, BRIANA; EDINBURGH, IN; SOUTHWESTERN HS; (JR); Hnr Roll; Nat Hon Sy; WWAHSS; Drma Clb; SP/M/VS; Track (V); Journalism; Education; Ball State U; Purdue U

FEDERICI, LAUREN M; GREENFIELD, IN; GREENFIELD-CTRL HS; (SO); 4H Awd; Hi Hnr Roll; Nat Hon Sy; Perf Att; Salutrn; Sci Fairs; St of Mnth; Comm Volntr; 4-H; Chrch Yth Grp; Drma Clb; FCA; Key Club; Bnd; Chr; Ch Chr; Clr Grd; Cl Off (V); Sch Ppr (R); Medicine; History; John Carroll U; Butler U

FEGETT, CATHERINE; INDIANAPOLIS, IN; PERRY MERIDIAN HS; (FR); Ctznshp Aw; F Lan Hn Soc; Hnr Roll; WWAHSS; Peer Tut/Med; Chrch Yth Grp; Drma Clb; Emplmnt; FCA; Key Club; NtlFrnscLg; Spch Team; Spanish Clb; Bnd; Mch Bnd; Pep Bnd; SP/M/VS; Cr Ctry (J); Track (J); Bass Drum Section Leader; Robotics & Marion County Cadette Officer; Music; Ministry; Baylor; Ball State

FEILEN, DEBORAH; RUSSELLVILLE, IN; NORTH PUTNAM HS; (SR); Hnr Roll; Nat Hon Sy; WWAHSS; Comm Volntr; Emplmnt; Key Club; Mth Clb/Tm; Sci Clb; SADD; Spanish Clb; Bskball (V); Sccr (V); Sftball (V); Stu Cncl (P); Dean's Scholarship from Manchester; Athletic Training Major; Pre-Med; Manchester College

FELTER, MARIANNE E; INDIANAPOLIS, IN; CARDINAL RITTER HS; (SO); Hnr Roll; Comm Volntr; Peer Tut/Med; Tchrs Aide; Spanish Clb; Vllyball; Promise to Keep; School Ambassador; Pediatric Nursing; Butler U; Marian College

FELTON, KAYLA R; HUNTINGTON, IN; HUNTINGTON NORTH HS; (FR); Hi Hnr Roll; Nat Hon Sy; Pres Ac Ftns Aw; Comm Volntr; 4-H; Chrch Yth Grp; Sftball (V L); Vllyball (J); Adv Cncl; Served As Page for State Representative; Physical Therapy; Indiana U

FERGUSON, LAURA K; EVANSVILLE, IN; CENTRAL HS; (SO); Ctznshp Aw; Hi Hnr Roll; Kwnis Aw; Otst Ac Ach Awd; Sci Fairs; St of Mnth; Comm Volntr; Peer Tut/Med; Spec Olymp Vol; Chrch Yth Grp; Pep Squd; Schol Bwl; Scouts; Svce Clb; Spanish Clb; Bnd; Mch Bnd; Pep Bnd; Stu Cncl (R)

FIELDS, SHATALYA; INDIANAPOLIS, IN; BROAD RIPPLE HS; (SO); Hi Hnr Roll; Key Club; Chrldg (JC); CR (P); Criminal Justice; Music; Indiana U

FINKE, BENJAMIN; HOPE, IN; HAUSER HS; (SR); Ctznshp Aw; DAR; Hnr Roll; Nat Hon Sy; Nat Mrt Semif; Otst Ac Ach Awd; Valdctrian; WWAHSS; Yth Ldrshp Prog; Comm Volntr; AL Aux Boys; Chrch Yth Grp; FCA; Off Aide; Schol Bwl; German Clb; Cr Ctry (L); Track (L); Cl Off (S); Stu Cncl (V); Yrbk (R, P); Valparaiso U; Washington and Lee U

FINLEY, CALEB R; FARMERSBURG, IN; NORTH CTRL HS; (FR); Comm Volntr; Chrch Yth Grp; Emplmnt; Chr; SP/M/VS; Tennis (V); Track (V); Gold in Choir; Airplane Mechanic; Air Force; Purdue U

FINN, KELSEY M; INDIANAPOLIS, IN; LAWRENCE CTRL HS; (FR); Hnr Roll; Key Club

FIREOVED, JOHN W; ELKHART, IN; ELKHART CTRL HS; (SO); Hi Hnr Roll; Otst Ac Ach Awd; Sci/Math Olympn; USAA; WWAHSS; Yth Ldrshp Prog; Chess; Emplmnt; Key Club; Mod UN; Sci Clb; Svce Clb; Ftball (J); Track (J); Wrstlg (V L); Stu Cncl (R); Engineer; Naval Academy

FISCHER, ELIZABETH; FORT WAYNE, IN; SOUTHSIDE HS; (JR); Hnr Roll; Comm Volntr; Chrch Yth Grp; FCA; Off Aide; Tech Clb; Spanish Clb; Cr Ctry (V); Tennis (J); Track (V); Law Enforcement Explorer; Criminal Justice; Psychology; Indiana U, Purdue U; Fort Wayne

FISHBURN, MICHELLE A; DENVER, IN; NORTH MIAMI HS; (SR); 4H Awd; Ctznshp Aw; Hnr Roll; Nat Hon Sy; Comm Volntr; 4-H; Chrch Yth Grp; Jr Ach; Ntl FFA; Vsity Clb; Bskball (V L); Vllyball (V CL); Accounting; Manchester College

FISHER, ALLYSE M; TOPEKA, IN; WESTVIEW HS; (SR); 4H Awd; Hnr Roll; Pres Ac Ftns Aw; St of Mnth; Peer Tut/Med; 4-H; Photog; Prom Com; Scouts; Tchrs Aide; German Clb; Bskball (V CL); Vllyball (V CL); Yrbk (P); IHSAA Sportsmanship Committee; Athletic Training; Physical Education; Indiana U-Purdue U Indianapolis

FISHER, JAMES; LANESVILLE, IN; LANESVILLE HS; (SO); Hi Hnr Roll; Hnr Roll; Pres Ac Ftns Aw; St of Mnth; WWAHSS; Chrch Yth Grp; FCA; Photog; Bnd; Pep Bnd; Bskball (J); Photojournalism; Dentistry; Indiana U Southeast

FITZPATRICK, KRISTIN; CARMEL, IN; HERITAGE CHRISTIAN SCH; (SO); Hi Hnr Roll; Sci Fairs; Chrch Yth Grp; German Clb; Chr; Sftball (V L); Swmg (V L); Civics Student of the Year; Select Vocal Ensemble; Dietetics; Religion; Princeton U; Harvard U

FITZPATRICK, MEGAN; EDINBURGH, IN; EDINBURGH HS; (JR); Hnr Roll; Nat Hon Sy; St of Mnth; WWAHSS; Comm Volntr; Chrch Yth Grp; Emplmnt; Prom Com; Spanish Clb; Bnd; Mch Bnd; Pep Bnd; SP/M/VS; Bskball; Chrldg (J); Cr Ctry (V L); Track (V L); Cl Off (T); Stu Cncl (T); Nursing; Zoology; Marian College; St Joseph's U

FLATER, VICTORIA; SULLIVAN, IN; SULLIVAN HS; (SR); Hnr Roll; Nat Hon Sy; WWAHSS; Comm Volntr; Chrch Yth Grp; Emplmnt; Key Club; Ntl Beta Clb; Medicine; Business; Ivy Tech State College

FLECK, JOSHUA; HUNTINGBURG, IN; SOUTHRIDGE HS; (FR); Ctznshp Aw; Hnr Roll; Perf Att; Comm Volntr; BPA; Spanish Clb; Zoology; World History; Indiana State; Purdue U

FLEDDERMAN, TARYN K; BATESVILLE, IN; ADENBURG AC; (SR); Ctznshp Aw; Hnr Roll; Nat Hon Sy; WWAHSS; Peer Tut/Med; Chrch Yth Grp; Drma Clb; Emplmnt; Prom Com; SADD; SP/M/VS; Chrldg (J L); Sftball (V CL); Vllyball (VJCL); Stu Cncl (R); Athletic Training; Purdue U

FLEENER, RACHEL L; SPRINGVILLE, IN; STONE CITY CHRISTIAN AC; (FR); Ctznshp Aw; Hi Hnr Roll; Hnr Roll; Otst Ac Ach Awd; St of Mnth; Ch Chr; SP/M/VS; Bskball; Sftball; Vllyball; Play in Chime Choir (Won Regional 1st Competition); CPA; God's Bible College

FLEMING, RACHEL L; EVANSVILLE, IN; CENTRAL HS; (JR); 4H Awd; Ctznshp Aw; Hi Hnr Roll; Perf Att; Comm Volntr; Hab For Humty Volntr; Spec Olymp Vol; 4-H; Chrch Yth Grp; Prom Com; Svce Clb; German Clb; Ch Chr; Dnce; PPSqd (V L); United Methodist Conference Board of Youth Ministries - Evansville Representative; Forensic Psychology; U of Southern Indiana; Purdue U

FLINT, SAMANTHA; INDIANAPOLIS, IN; AVON HS; (FR); Ctznshp Aw; Hi Hnr Roll; Hnr Roll; Drma Clb; FCA; Photog; German Clb; Chr; Stg Cre; PP Ftbl (J); Sch Ppr (P); Yrbk (P); Psychology; North Carolina U; Texas U

FLOTOW, CODY; FORT WAYNE, IN; SOUTH SIDE HS; (SO); Hnr Roll; Perf Att; Comm Volntr; Chrch Yth Grp; Emplmnt; Bskball (J); Ftball (VJ); Wt Lftg (J); Perfect Attendance; Sports Medicine; Computer Programming; Indiana U; U of Michigan

FLYNN, COLT R; CARLISLE, IN; SULLIVAN HS; (JR); 4H Awd; Mas Aw; Nat Hon Sy; Nat Sci Aw; Otst Ac Ach Awd; Pres Ac Ftns Aw; Sci Fairs; Sci/Math Olympn; WWAHSS; Yth Ldrshp Prog; Comm Volntr; Hosp Aide; Peer Tut/Med; 4-H; Aqrium Clb; Chrch Yth Grp; Cmptr Clb; Drma Clb; Lib Aide; Mth Clb/Tm; Sci Clb; Chr; SP/M/VS; Who's Who Award; In Science Olympiad We Won State!; Electrical Engineer; Computer Engineer; Rose Hulman Institute of Technology; Purdue U

FOELLINGER, KURT; FORT WAYNE, IN; NORTHROP HS; (SO); Hi Hnr Roll; Otst Ac Ach Awd; Scouts; Ftball (J); Cl Off (R); Stu Cncl (R); Pharmacy; Physical Therapy

FOLAND, KARA; FORT WAYNE, IN; NORTHROP HS; (SO); Ctznshp Aw; Hnr Roll; Otst Ac Ach Awd; Comm Volntr; Chrch Yth Grp; Emplmnt; Jr Ach; Key Club; I Am a Member of Key Club.; Education; Medical; Indiana Wesleyan U; Anderson U

FORD, DONTE L; INDIANAPOLIS, IN; BEN DAVIS HS; (SO); Hnr Roll; Perf Att; St of Mnth; Comm Volntr; Chrch Yth Grp; Emplmnt; Bnd; Mch Bnd; Big Plans Club; Ob/Gyn Medical Doctor; IUPUI Medical U

FORST, ALLIE; NOBLESVILLE, IN; NOBLESVILLE HS; (JR); WWAHSS; Comm Volntr; Hab For Humty Volntr; 4-H; Chrch Yth Grp; Emplmnt; Key Club; Tchrs Aide; SP/M/VS; Nursing; Veterinary Medicine; Purdue U; U of Redlands

FORSYTHE, BEN; LEBANON, IN; LEBANON HS; (JR); 4H Awd; Ctznshp Aw; Hnr Roll; St of Mnth; WWAHSS; Comm Volntr; Chrch Yth Grp; Emplmnt; FCA; Key Club; Ntl FFA; Tchrs Aide; Ch Chr; Bsball (J); Audio Technology; Business; Belmont U; Indiana U

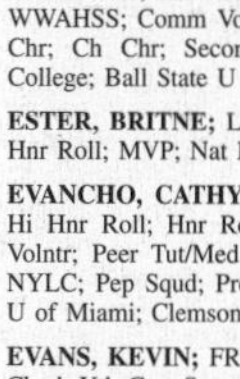
Ford, Donte L
Ben Davis HS
Indianapolis, IN

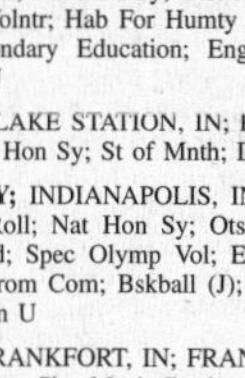
Faulkner, Natalie
Carmel HS
Carmel, IN

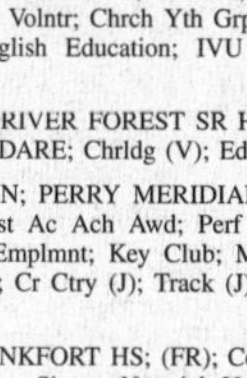
Evans, Ravene D
Northwest HS
Indianapolis, IN

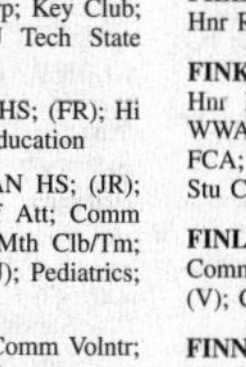
Escalante, Maritsa
Hobart HS
Merrillville, IN

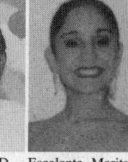

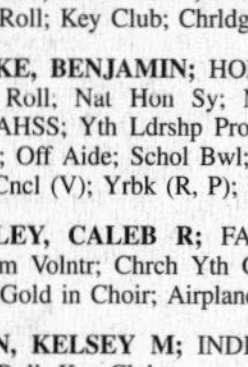
Emerson, Haley
Concord HS
Elkhart, IN

National
Honor Roll
Spring 2005

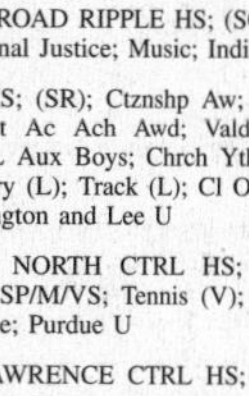
Eldridge, Kelsie
Concord HS
Elkhart, IN

Evancho, Cathy
Perry Meridian HS
Indianapolis, IN

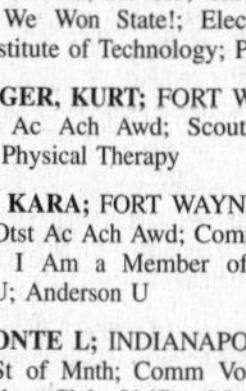
Faulkenburg, Audrey G
American Sch
De Pauw, IN

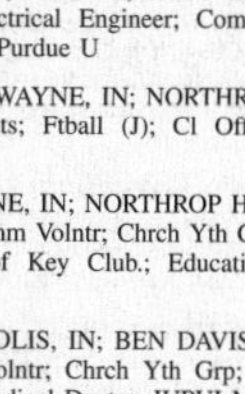
Fleck, Joshua
Southridge HS
Huntingburg, IN

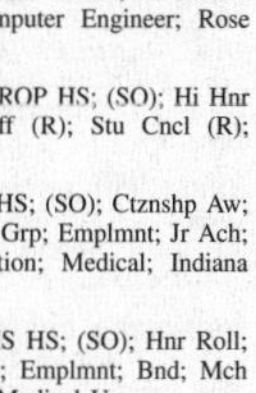
Flint, Samantha
Avon HS
Indianapolis, IN

FOSTER, BARBARA A; HOBART, IN; WHEELER HS; (SO); 4H Awd; Hnr Roll; Perf Att; WWAHSS; 4-H; Emplmnt; Key Club; Chrldg (V L); PP Ftbl (V); Sccr (V L); Track (V L); Physical/Occupational/Recreational Therapist; Forensic Investigator; Purdue U; Missouri State

FOSTER, KYLE; MARKLEVILLE, IN; PENDLETON HEIGHTS HS; (SR); 4H Awd; Hi Hnr Roll; Hnr Roll; Sci Fairs; St of Mnth; Comm Volntr; 4-H; Chrch Yth Grp; Emplmnt; Lib Aide; Off Aide; Wt Lftg; 4-H-President of Pendleton Livestock; FFA; Fire Science/EMT; Vincennes U

FOWLER, ASHLEY; COLUMBUS, IN; COLUMBUS NORTH HS; (JR); Hnr Roll; Comm Volntr; Peer Tut/Med; BPA; DECA; Emplmnt; Key Club; Tchrs Aide; Volunteer Work in Community; Senior Project Board; Communications; Public Relations; Franklin College; High Point U

FOWLER, KAREESHA L; INDIANAPOLIS, IN; ARLINGTON HS; (JR); Ctznshp Aw; Hi Hnr Roll; Hnr Roll; Nat Sci Aw; Otst Ac Ach Awd; Peer Tut/Med; Emplmnt; FTA; Key Club; Ch Chr; Tennis (V L); Vllyball (V L); Magnet Student of the Year; Mental Attitude Award for Volleyball & Tennis; Analysis; Engineering; U of Tennessee; IUPUI

FOX, DANIEL G; TERRE HAUTE, IN; TERRE HAUTE SOUTH VIGO HS; (JR); Hi Hnr Roll; Jr Eng Tech; Nat Hon Sy; Perf Att; Sci Fairs; Sci/Math Olympn; WWAHSS; Comm Volntr; Hab For Humty Volntr; Chess; Chrch Yth Grp; DECA; Emplmnt; Mth Clb/Tm; Schol Bwl; Bnd; Tennis (J); Wrstlg (J L); Stu Cncl (V); Deca-1st in State, National Competitor; Knowledge Master's-1st State; Jets-1st State; Marketing; Entrepreneurship; Indiana U; Harvard U

FOX, EMILY; NEW PARIS, IN; FAIRFIELD JR/SR HS; (JR); Hi Hnr Roll; Nat Hon Sy; Otst Ac Ach Awd; St of Mnth; WWAHSS; Spec Olymp Vol; Chrch Yth Grp; Emplmnt; Key Club; Off Aide; Chr; SP/M/VS; Swg Chr; PP Ftbl (V); Vllyball (VJ); Sch Ppr (R); Best Attitude Award-Show Choir; Mental Attitude-Volleyball

FOXWORTHY, ANDREA; INDIANAPOLIS, IN; SPEEDWAY SR HS; (FR); Hi Hnr Roll; Perf Att; FCA; Sccr (J); Swmg (V L); Cl Off (T); Top 10; Medical Degree; Indiana U

FRADY, SPENCER; HOPE, IN; HAUSER JR/SR HS; (FR); 4H Awd; Hi Hnr Roll; 4-H; Emplmnt; German Clb; Bnd; Jzz Bnd; Mch Bnd; Pep Bnd; Bsball (J); Bskball (J); Tennis (J)

FRANCIS, LINDSAY R; WARSAW, IN; WARSAW CMTY HS; (JR); Ctznshp Aw; Hi Hnr Roll; Peer Tut/Med; Chrch Yth Grp; DARE; Scouts; Bskball (L); Track (L); Vllyball (L); Elementary Education; Ball State U

FRANK, ALLISON; CROWN POINT, IN; (JR); Hnr Roll; Nat Hon Sy; Otst Ac Ach Awd; Pres Ac Ftns Aw; Hab For Humty Volntr; Chrch Yth Grp; Key Club; SADD; Japanese Clb; Bskball (J); Tennis (V); Forensic Science; Psychology; Indiana U; Boston U

FRANKLIN, ASHLEY D; INDIANAPOLIS, IN; ARSENAL TECH HS; (SO); Ctznshp Aw; Hnr Roll; St of Mnth; Hosp Aide; ROTC; Drl Tm; ROTC; Nursing; Doctor; Indiana U

FRANZ, KATY; FORT WAYNE, IN; NORTHROP HS; (SO); Hnr Roll; Perf Att; Chr; Pediatrician; Elementary School Teacher; Indiana U; Ball State U

FRAZIER, DEREK; INDIANAPOLIS, IN; DECATUR CTRL HS; (SR); Hi Hnr Roll; Hnr Roll; Perf Att; WWAHSS; Emplmnt; Photog; Software Designer; Computer Technician; Purdue U; Rose-Hulman Institute of Technology

FRAZIER, KENDALL; GREENFIELD, IN; GREENFIELD CTRL HS; (FR); Ctznshp Aw; F Lan Hn Soc; Hi Hnr Roll; MVP; Nat Ldrshp Svc; Comm Volntr; Aqrium Clb; Chrch Yth Grp; Emplmnt; FCA; Key Club; Off Aide; Schol Bwl; Tchrs Aide; Bskball (J); Sccr (V L); Track (V L); Adv Cncl (R); Stu Cncl (V); Olympic Torch Bearer; Key Club; Dentistry; Indiana U; Wake Forest U

FREEL, PHILLIP M; HARTFORD CITY, IN; BLACKFORD HS; (FR); 4H Awd; Kwnis Aw; Otst Ac Ach Awd; WWAHSS; 4-H; Chrch Yth Grp; FCA; Key Club; Swg Chr; Bskball; Cr Ctry (V); Track (V); Cl Off (P); Freshman Basketball Team; Pre-Med; Neurosurgeon; Indiana U; Ball State U

FREEMYER, REBEKAH P; MARION, IN; LAKEVIEW HS; (SO); Hi Hnr Roll; Nat Hon Sy; Otst Ac Ach Awd; USAA; WWAHSS; Chrch Yth Grp; Bnd; Pep Bnd; Sftball (V); Vllyball (V); Volleyball Conference Champions; Elementary Ed; Languages

FRIDDLE, HOLLY C; LEESBURG, IN; WAWASEE HS; (FR); Ctznshp Aw; Hi Hnr Roll; Hnr Roll; Comm Volntr; Emplmnt; Key Club; Orch; Track (J); Managing Volleyball; Business; Home Town College

FRITZ, ERIC M; CARMEL, IN; CARMEL HS; (JR); Hi Hnr Roll; Hnr Roll; Nat Hon Sy; Peer Tut/Med; Emplmnt; NtlFrnscLg; Quill & Scroll; Svce Clb; Spch Team; Participated on School Radio Station; Play Intramural Sports; Agricultural Sciences; Biological Sciences; Hanover College; Purdue U

FROST, CHRIS; MONTICELLO, IN; (SO); Hi Hnr Roll; Nat Hon Sy; Otst Ac Ach Awd; St of Mnth; Comm Volntr; Spec Olymp Vol; Chrch Yth Grp; Emplmnt; Spanish Clb; Stg Cre; Ftball (V); Track (V); Wt Lftg (V); Elementary/Pre-School Teacher; Business Management; Ball State U; Purdue U

FRY, LEAH; NEW PARIS, IN; FAIRFIELD HS; (JR); Hnr Roll; 4-H; Key Club; Bnd; Clr Grd; Mch Bnd; Pep Bnd; Key Club; Sunshine Club; Interior Design; Social Worker; Indiana U; Purdue U

FRY, TARA; LYNN, IN; RANDOLPH SOUTHERN JR/SR HS; (MS); Hnr Roll; Perf Att; Sci Fairs; St of Mnth; Chrldg; Sftball; Vllyball; Pediatrician; Obstetrician; Indiana U; Purdue U

FUHS, SARAH E; JASPER, IN; JASPER HS; (SO); Hi Hnr Roll; Hnr Roll; Sci Fairs; Comm Volntr; Hosp Aide; Chrch Yth Grp; Emplmnt; Key Club; SADD; Spanish Clb; Bnd; Mch Bnd; Pep Bnd; Bskball (J); Cr Ctry (V); Sftball (J); Medicine; Physical Therapy; St Louis U; Purdue U

FURRY, ERIC S; GREENWOOD, IN; CTR GROVE HS; (JR); Hi Hnr Roll; Nat Hon Sy; WWAHSS; FCA; Key Club; Bskball (V); Golf (V); Spanish National Honors Society; Architecture; Landscape Architecture; Ball State U; U of Notre Dame

GAMEON, JORDAN O O; DALE, IN; SOUTHRIDGE HS; (FR); Hi Hnr Roll; Hnr Roll; St of Mnth; Comm Volntr; Emplmnt; Jr Ach; Outdrs Clb; Pep Squd; Quiz Bowl; Schol Bwl; SADD; Bnd; Chr; SP/M/VS; Ftball (J); Varsity High School Bowling Team; Member of Indiana All State Honor Choir; Engineering; Architecture; Purdue U; Indiana U

GARCIA, ELISE M; GRIFFITH, IN; GRIFFITH SR HS; (SO); Nat Hon Sy; Otst Ac Ach Awd; Perf Att; Valdctrian; WWAHSS; Yth Ldrshp Prog; DARE; Emplmnt; Scouts; Bskball (JC); Sftball (V L); Vllyball (V L); Cl Off (P); Best Mental Attitude Basketball 2 Years; Who's Who Academics and Sports; Pre-Med; Indiana U Bloomington; U of Michigan Notre Dame U

GARG, DEEPIKA; GREENWOOD, IN; GREENWOOD CMTY HS; (JR); WWAHSS; Comm Volntr; Quill & Scroll; Spanish Clb; Tennis (J L); Yrbk (R); Medicine / Dentistry; Pharmacy; Indiana U; Stanford U

GARLAND, CASSY; JASPER, IN; JASPER HS; (FR); Indiana U; ISU

GARLAND, STACIE; LEXINGTON, IN; SOUTHWESTERN MIDDLE/SR HS; (JR); 4H Awd; Hnr Roll; Nat Hon Sy; Nat Sci Aw; 4-H; FCA; FCCLA; Prom Com; Tchrs Aide; Spanish Clb; Sftball (L); Vllyball (L); Cl Off (S); Stu Cncl (V); CR (T); Yrbk (P); History Major; Ball State U; Franklin College

GARRISON, WHITNEY N; INDIANAPOLIS, IN; PIKE HS; (JR); Hnr Roll; Nat Hon Sy; St of Mnth; WWAHSS; Comm Volntr; MuAlphaTh; Off Aide; Sci Clb; Tchrs Aide; Peers Project Mentor; Volunteer At Day Care; Pre-Med; Psychology; Xavier U of Louisiana; Alabama A & M U

GARSIDE, REBECCA F; VALPARAISO, IN; WHEELER HS; (SR); Hi Hnr Roll; Nat Hon Sy; Otst Ac Ach Awd; WWAHSS; Yth Ldrshp Prog; Comm Volntr; Peer Tut/Med; Chrch Yth Grp; Drma Clb; Key Club; Mod UN; Tchrs Aide; French Clb; Chr; SP/M/VS; Mar Art; Stu Cncl (R); Yrbk; Pre-Med; U of Chicago

GASTON, DESIRE; INDIANAPOLIS, IN; PIKE HS; (MS); All Am Sch; Ctznshp Aw; Hi Hnr Roll; Nat Hon Sy; Otst Ac Ach Awd; St of Mnth; Comm Volntr; Chrch Yth Grp; Drma Clb; Emplmnt; Ch Chr; Dnce; SP/M/VS; Bskball (C); Stu Cncl (V); National Junior Honor Society Member; Queen of Spring Court; Law Degree; Business; Indiana U Purdue U Indps; Ball State U, Harvard Law School

GAUTHIER, DANIELLE; FORT WAYNE, IN; HOMESTEAD HS; (SO); Hi Hnr Roll; MVP; Otst Ac Ach Awd; Pres Ac Ftns Aw; St of Mnth; Comm Volntr; French Clb; SP/M/VS; Vllyball (V L); Black Belt in Tae Kwon Do; Club Volleyball; Physician; CIA; Dartmouth College; Duke U

GAY, SPENCER P; FREMONT, IN; FREMONT HS; (SO); Hnr Roll; Perf Att; Comm Volntr; Photog; Golf (J); Skiing; Tennis (J); Stu Cncl (R)

GAZA, MEGAN; INDIANAPOLIS, IN; CARMEL HS; (JR); F Lan Hn Soc; Hi Hnr Roll; Nat Hon Sy; Nat Mrt LOC; Otst Ac Ach Awd; WWAHSS; Comm Volntr; Chrch Yth Grp; Quill & Scroll; Bnd; Sch Ppr (E); Accounting; Ball State U; Calvin College

GENG, DAVID M; AKRON, IN; TIPPECANOE VALLEY HS; (FR); 4H Awd; Hi Hnr Roll; Hnr Roll; Otst Ac Ach Awd; Perf Att; Comm Volntr; Red Cr Aide; 4-H; AL Aux Boys; Chess; Chrch Yth Grp; FCA; Sci Clb; Ftball (J); Golf (J); CR (R); Tippecanoe Valley Science Achievement Award; Master's of Geology; Paleontology; Purdue U; Bowling Green U

GENTRY, STEVEN C; ANDERSON, IN; ANDERSON HS; (JR); Hnr Roll; Perf Att; School Spelling Champ; Sports Journalism; Ivy Tech

GEORGIEFSKI, TIANA; SAINT JOHN, IN; LAKE CTRL HS; (JR); Hi Hnr Roll; Emplmnt; Off Aide; Bskball (V); Business; Sports Medicine; U of Florida; U of Indiana

GIBBS, JONATHAN M; FORT WAYNE, IN; NORTHROP HS; (SO); Hi Hnr Roll; Chess; Chrch Yth Grp; Mth Clb/Tm; Ch Chr; President-Explorer Scouts Post 2829; Engineering; Computer Programming; Ball State U; Purdue U

GIBSON, ANDREW J; LEBANON, IN; LEBANON HS; (JR); Hnr Roll; WWAHSS; Chrch Yth Grp; Emplmnt; FCA; Key Club; Lttrmn Clb; Prom Com; Ftball (V L); Wt Lftg (V); Optometry; Indiana U; Purdue U

GIBSON, CHRISTY; CHURUBUSCO, IN; CHURUBUSCO HS; (JR); 4H Awd; Hi Hnr Roll; MVP; Nat Hon Sy; 4-H; Chrch Yth Grp; Key Club; SADD; Spanish Clb; Ch Chr; Bskball (V L); Sftball (V L); Vllyball (J); Pharmaceutical Sales; Chiropractor; Indiana Wesleyan U; U of Kentucky

GIBSON, VICKI; NINEVEH, IN; BROWN CTY HS; (FR); Hnr Roll; Emplmnt; Stg Cre; Stu Cncl (R); Peers Project - 6th Grade; Marine Biology; Theatre; Franklin College; Purdue U

GIESE, ANTON; FORT WAYNE, IN; HOMESTEAD HS; Hnr Roll; Chess; Chrch Yth Grp; Foreign Language; Game Design; ITT Technical Institute; U Of Notre Dame

GILBERT, LACEY; MARION, IN; JUSTICE THURGOOD MARSHALL MS; MS; Hi Hnr Roll; Hnr Roll; Otst Ac Ach Awd; Perf Att; Chrch Yth Grp; DARE; Jr Ach; Chr; Yrbk (E, P); Softball; Fashion Design; Choir Teacher; NYU; Ball State

GILLENWATER, LAUREN; NEW ALBANY, IN; OUR LADY OF PROVIDENCE HS; (FR); Hi Hnr Roll; Hnr Roll; Nat Hon Sy; Pres Sch; Sci Fairs; St of Mnth; USAA; WWAHSS; Drma Clb; Mth Clb/Tm; Dnce; SP/M/VS; PPSqd (V); Sccr (V); Indiana U

GILLESPIE, KURTESS R; MICHIGAN CITY, IN; MICHIGAN CITY HS; (FR); Hnr Roll; Otst Ac Ach Awd; St of Mnth; Comm Volntr; Chrch Yth Grp; Ch Chr; Steering Committee; Law; Computer Technology; Ball State U; Indiana U

GILPIN, CAPRICE; COLUMBUS, IN; COLUMBUS NORTH HS; (JR); Hi Hnr Roll; Nat Hon Sy; Sci/Math Olympn; USAA; WWAHSS; Comm Volntr; Hosp Aide; Peer Tut/Med; ArtClub; BPA; Drma Clb; Emplmnt; Key Club; Mth Clb/Tm; Quiz Bowl; Sci Clb; Orch; Stg Cre; Sccr (J); International Business; Notre Dame U; Northwestern U

GINGERICH, SUSANNAH M R; VALPARAISO, IN; VALPARAISO HS; (SO); Hi Hnr Roll; Hnr Roll; Sci Fairs; WWAHSS; Comm Volntr; Peer Tut/Med; Chrch Yth Grp; Drma Clb; Emplmnt; Key Club; Mus Clb; Acpl Chr; Chr; Ch Chr; SP/M/VS; Sch Ppr (R); Co-Host of F.M. Radio Show (Weekly); Soccer (Independent League); Psychology; Music; U of California-San Diego; Indiana U

GIPSON, ERIKA; ROLLING PR, IN; NEW PRAIRIE HS; (FR); Hnr Roll; Perf Att; St of Mnth; Chrch Yth Grp; DARE; Scouts; Scr Kpr (VJ L); Track (J); Vllyball (J); Wrestling Manager 1/2 Letter; Geography Bee Finalist; Physical Therapy; IUPUI; Purdue U

GIPSON, JESSICA L; ROLLING PR, IN; NEW PRAIRIE HS; (FR); Hnr Roll; Perf Att; St of Mnth; Chrch Yth Grp; DARE; Scouts; Physical Therapist; Physical Therapist in Sports Medicine; Indiana U of South Bend

GLASCOCK, TRAVIS H; SULLIVAN, IN; SULLIVAN HS; (SO); 4H Awd; Hnr Roll; Sci Fairs; Sci/Math Olympn; Comm Volntr; 4-H; Chess; Chrch Yth Grp; FCA; Key Club; Ntl Beta Clb; Sci Clb; Sccr (VJ L); FIFA Soccer Referee; Architecture Engineer

GLASGOW, SAMANTHA; UNION MILLS, IN; SOUTH CTRL HS; (FR); Hi Hnr Roll; 4-H; Member of 4-H Horse and Pony Club

GLESSNER, JESSICA D; SHELBYVILLE, IN; SHELBYVILLE HS; (JR); Hnr Roll; WWAHSS; Comm Volntr; Chr; Volunteer at Brickyard 400; Volunteer at Indy 500; Accounting; Business; Ivy Tech State College

GLIDEWELL, CODY R; CLARKSVILLE, IN; CLARKSVILLE HS; (SO); Hnr Roll; Comm Volntr; Lib Aide; Off Aide; Bnd; Pep Bnd; Sch Ppr (P); Yrbk (P); Outstanding Effort Band 2001-2004; Optimist Club's Youth Appreciation & Achievement 2002

GODBEY, KATHERINE; VALPARAISO, IN; VALPARAISO HS; (JR); Hi Hnr Roll; Nat Hon Sy; Sci Fairs; WWAHSS; Comm Volntr; Peer Tut/Med; Red Cr Aide; Chrch Yth Grp; Emplmnt; Key Club; Photog; Prom Com; Tchrs Aide; Clr Grd; Dnce; Flg Crps; SP/M/VS; PPSqd (V CL); Scr Kpr; Track (V CL); Stu Cncl (R); CR (R); Pharmacy; Interior Design; Butler U

GOEBEL, JONATHAN M; MT VERNON, IN; MT VERNON HS; (SR); 4H Awd; Hi Hnr Roll; Hnr Roll; Nat Hon Sy; Perf Att; Comm Volntr; 4-H; Chrch Yth Grp; Emplmnt; FCA; Lttrmn Clb; SADD; Tchrs Aide; Vsity Clb; Ftball (VJ L); Wt Lftg; Pre-Med; Pre-Law; U of Indianapolis; Indiana U Bloomington

GOEDDE, JAMIE; CARMEL, IN; CARMEL SR HS; (SO); F Lan Hn Soc; Hi Hnr Roll; Nat Hon Sy; Otst Ac Ach Awd; Perf Att; Yth Ldrshp Prog; Comm Volntr; Peer Tut/Med; Chrch Yth Grp; Emplmnt; Photog; French Clb; Chr; Ch Chr; Placed Nationally on National French Exam; Have Had Writings Published; Writer / Lyricist; Translator / French; Purdue U

Geng, David M
Tippecanoe Valley HS
Akron, IN

Franklin, Ashley D
Arsenal Tech HS
Indianapolis, IN

Foxworthy, Andrea
Speedway SR HS
Indianapolis, IN

Frank, Allison
Crown Point, IN

Glidewell, Cody R
Clarksville HS
Clarksville, IN

GOLDSCHMIDT, JILL; LAWRENCEBURG, IN; LAWRENCEBURG HS; (JR); DAR; Hi Hnr Roll; Nat Hon Sy; Otst Ac Ach Awd; Perf Att; Pres Ac Ftns Aw; WWAHSS; Comm Volntr; Peer Tut/Med; Emplmnt; Key Club; Prom Com; Vsity Clb; French Clb; Bnd; Jzz Bnd; Mch Bnd; Sccr (V L); Sftball (V L); Track (J); Cl Off (P, V); Stu Cncl; World Piano Competition & Other Piano Competitions; Piano Competition Awards; Purdue U; Indiana U

GOMEZ, ALYS; ELKHART, IN; ELKHART CTRL; (FR); Hi Hnr Roll; Hnr Roll; Key Club; Clr Grd; Mch Bnd; Chrldg; Plastic Surgeon; Indiana Purdue At Fort Wayne

GONZALES, CRISTAL L; OAKLAND CITY, IN; WALDO J WOOD MEMORIAL HS; (FR); Ctznshp Aw; Hnr Roll; Kwnis Aw; Perf Att; Pres Ac Ftns Aw; Sci Fairs; WWAHSS; Comm Volntr; Chrch Yth Grp; DARE; Jr Ach; Tchrs Aide; Bskball (J); Track (J); Vllyball (J); Indiana U, Purdue U

GONZALEZ, JOANNA; WALTON, IN; LEWIS CASS HS; (SO); ArtClub; Key Club; SADD; Track (V); Registered Nurse; IUK; Saint Josephs College

GONZALEZ, PAUL A; ELKHART, IN; CONCORD HS; (JR); Hi Hnr Roll; Nat Hon Sy; Chrch Yth Grp; Emplmnt; FCA; Key Club; Chr; Swg Chr; Bsball (J); Tennis (J); Stu Cncl (R); Criminal Psychology; Indiana Wesleyan U

GONZALEZ, RENEE; VALPARAISO, IN; CHESTERTON HS; (SR); Hi Hnr Roll; Nat Hon Sy; Otst Ac Ach Awd; Perf Att; WWAHSS; Yth Ldrshp Prog; Comm Volntr; Emplmnt; Tchrs Aide; Spanish Clb; Chr; Dnce; SP/M/VS; National Honor Society - Treasurer; Nursing; Saint Mary's College

GONZALEZ CARRASCO, MANUEL A; INDIANAPOLIS, IN; BEN DAVIS HS; (JR); Ctznshp Aw; Hnr Roll; Nat Hon Sy; Otst Ac Ach Awd; Perf Att; St Schl; St of Mnth; Comm Volntr; Peer Tut/Med; Chrch Yth Grp; Emplmnt; Mus Clb; Quill & Scroll; Spanish Clb; Chr; Ch Chr; SP/M/VS; Stu Cncl (R); Sch Ppr (E); 2 Times - Invited to the National Young Leaders Conference; Invited to the Presidential Classroom Program; Journalism / Communications; Business; Indiana U; Butler U

GOOTEE, PHILLIP; JASPER, IN; JASPER HS; (JR); Hnr Roll; WWAHSS; Peer Tut/Med; Drma Clb; Key Club; Mus Clb; Prom Com; Spch Team; SADD; French Clb; Bnd; Chr; Ch Chr; Mch Bnd; Yrbk; Teaching; Music; Indiana State; Butler

GORDON, GRANT; SOUTH BEND, IN; CLAY HS; (SO); 4H Awd; Hi Hnr Roll; 4-H; Chrch Yth Grp; Vsity Clb; Orch; Cr Ctry (V L); Track (J); Wrstlg (J); MD; Indiana U

GORTAT, HEATHER; HIGHLAND, IN; HIGHLAND HS; (JR); F Lan Hn Soc; Hi Hnr Roll; Nat Hon Sy; Otst Ac Ach Awd; Perf Att; Sci/Math Olympn; Peer Tut/Med; DARE; Emplmnt; Jr Ach; Key Club; Quiz Bowl; Scouts; Tchrs Aide; German Clb; Tennis J and Exhibition; Psychology; Physical Therapy; Purdue U West Lafayette; Purdue U Calumet

GOSHERT, SARAH; WARSAW, IN; WARSAW CMTY HS; (JR); Hi Hnr Roll; Hnr Roll; Perf Att; Pres Ac Ftns Aw; Comm Volntr; Peer Tut/Med; Schol Bwl; Scouts; Tchrs Aide; Latin Clb; Sftball (JCL); Optimist Student of the Week; Secretary for FCCLA (Family Career & Community Leaders of America); Elementary Education; Communications; U of Michigan; U of Arizona

GOULD, DAVID C; LEBANON, IN; LEBANON HS; (JR); Hnr Roll; Kwnis Aw; Nat Hon Sy; WWAHSS; Comm Volntr; Key Club; Ftball (V); Track (V); Stu Cncl (R); Law; Political Science; Indiana U; Ball State U

GRAMELSPACHER, MARIA; JASPER, IN; JASPER HS; (FR); Hi Hnr Roll; MVP; Comm Volntr; Peer Tut/Med; 4-H; Chrch Yth Grp; FCA; Key Club; Off Aide; Scouts; SADD; Cr Ctry (V L); Swmg (V L); Track (V L); Stu Cncl (R)

GRANSON, ABIGAIL B; KOKOMO, IN; TAYLOR HS; (JR); Hi Hnr Roll; Peer Tut/Med; Emplmnt; Off Aide; Prom Com; Clr Grd; Flg Crps; Mch Bnd; Sch Ppr (R); Yrbk (R); Veterans History Project for the Page At the State House/Library of Congress; Business Management; Business Administration-Sales; Indiana U; Purdue U

GRAVES, JOSHUA R; MARTINSVILLE, IN; MARTINSVILLE HS; (JR); Hnr Roll; WWAHSS; Emplmnt; Ftball (V L); Wrstlg (V L); All A's in English and History in 2002; Construction Engineer; Heavy Equipment Operator; Purdue U; IUPUI

GRAVES, KEICHUN L; INDIANAPOLIS, IN; LAWRENCE CTRL HS; (SR); Hnr Roll; MVP; WWAHSS; Comm Volntr; Peer Tut/Med; Red Cr Aide; Emplmnt; Key Club; P to P St Amb Prg; Vsity Clb; Chr; Orch; Chrldg (V L); Cr Ctry (V CL); Scr Kpr (L); Track (V CL); Psychology PhD; Clark Atlanta U

GRAY, EMILY; HUNTINGBURG, IN; SOUTHRIDGE HS; (FR); Hi Hnr Roll; St of Mnth; 4-H; BPA; Chrch Yth Grp; Pep Squd; Quiz Bowl; SADD; Spanish Clb; Chr; Ch Chr; Mch Bnd; SP/M/VS; Tennis (V); Cl Off (P); Play Piano, Flute, Violin, & Guitar, Bible Study Club; All-State Choir, Participated in BPA State Competition; Oncologist; Music; Vanderbilt U; Centre College

GRAY, KIESHA; ELKHART, IN; ELKHART CTRL HS; (JR); Hi Hnr Roll; Nat Hon Sy; Otst Ac Ach Awd; Comm Volntr; Spec Olymp Vol; 4-H; Emplmnt; Key Club; Off Aide; Photog; Prom Com; SADD; Vsity Clb; Bnd; Mch Bnd; Pep Bnd; Bskball (V CL); Sccr (VJ); Track (V L); Wt Lftg (J); Pre-Med Then Med School To Be An Oncologist; Michigan State U

GREEN, VAN; HANOVER, IN; SOUTHWESTERN MIDDLE SR HS; (JR); Hnr Roll; MVP; Nat Hon Sy; Perf Att; Pres Ac Ftns Aw; St of Mnth; WWAHSS; Comm Volntr; Peer Tut/Med; Emplmnt; FCA; Mod UN; Schol Bwl; Vsity Clb; Spanish Clb; Dnce; Sccr (V CL); Track (V); Cl Off (P); CR (P); School Record Holder in Soccer; 1st in Class Ranking; Pre-Medicine; Psychology; U of Indianapolis; U of Evansville

GREENE, KAILA M; INDIANAPOLIS, IN; BEN DAVIS HS; (SO); Ctznshp Aw; Hnr Roll; Perf Att; St of Mnth; WWAHSS; Emplmnt; Dnce; Drl Tm; Track (J); Dentistry; Georgia Medical Center

GREESON, TAYLOR M; INDIANAPOLIS, IN; BEN DAVIS HS; MS; Ctznshp Aw; Hnr Roll; Bskball; Sftball; Vllyball; Wt Lftg; Radiologist; Registered Nurse; Purdue U; IUPUI

GREGORY, DILLION; OAKLAND CITY, IN; WALDO J WOOD MEMORIAL HS; (FR); Hi Hnr Roll; Hnr Roll; Comm Volntr; Bskball (J); Golf (V); Tennis (V); I'm in CLAY; Law School-Lawyer; Teacher/Coach; Ball State U; U of Southern Indiana

GREGORY, LAURA E; WESTVILLE, IN; WESTVILLE HS; (JR); Hi Hnr Roll; Hnr Roll; MVP; Nat Hon Sy; WWAHSS; Comm Volntr; Peer Tut/Med; AL Aux Girls; Emplmnt; Mus Clb; Off Aide; Prom Com; Svce Clb; Bnd; Chr; Pep Bnd; Bskball (V L); Chrldg (V L); Sftball (V L); Vllyball (V L); Stu Cncl (R); Yrbk (P); Radiology; Purdue U

GREINER, GARRETT; CARMEL, IN; CARMEL HS; (JR); Ctznshp Aw; F Lan Hn Soc; Hnr Roll; Nat Hon Sy; WWAHSS; Yth Ldrshp Prog; Amnsty Intl; Comm Volntr; Peer Tut/Med; Chrch Yth Grp; Emplmnt; Key Club; Lttrmn Clb; Mod UN; Quill & Scroll; Spch Team; Spanish Clb; Ch Chr; SP/M/VS; Stg Cre; Bskball (J); Lcrsse (V); Swmg (V L); Adv Cncl (R); Stu Cncl (R); Radio Broadcaster on School Station; Exchange Student to Costa Rica - 2005; Engineering; International Relations; Princeton U; Duke U

GRIMM, LUCY; INDIANAPOLIS, IN; BROWNSBURG HS; (SO); Hi Hnr Roll; Otst Ac Ach Awd; Yth Ldrshp Prog; Comm Volntr; Emplmnt; Key Club; Quiz Bowl; Spanish Clb; Swmg (V L); Law; U of Notre Dame; Butler U

GRISSOM, SAMANTHA; JASONVILLE, IN; SHAKAMAK HS; (SR); Hnr Roll; MVP; Nat Hon Sy; Perf Att; Peer Tut/Med; Chrch Yth Grp; Emplmnt; Prom Com; Tchrs Aide; Bskball (V CL); Vllyball (V L); Cl Off (S); Yrbk (R, P); Nursing; Indiana State U

GROFF, HILLARY; CROWN POINT, IN; CROWN POINT HS; (SO); F Lan Hn Soc; Hnr Roll; Pres Ac Ftns Aw; WWAHSS; Jr Cls League; Key Club; SADD; Vsity Clb; Latin Clb; Bnd; Gmnstcs (V L); PP Ftbl; Vsy Clb (V); Wt Lftg; Pediatrician; Physical Therapist

GRUBBS, BRANDON J; CARTHAGE, IN; KNIGHTSTOWN HS; (SO); 4H Awd; Hnr Roll; MVP; Otst Ac Ach Awd; St of Mnth; Comm Volntr; Peer Tut/Med; 4-H; ArtClub; Lttrmn Clb; Photog; Scouts; SADD; Vsity Clb; Spanish Clb; Ftball (V CL); Track (V L); Wt Lftg; Wrstlg (V L); Cl Off (V); CR (V); Architecture; Business; Purdue; Ball State

GRUBER, NICOLAS S; MOROCCO, IN; NORTH NEWTON JR/SR HS; (SR); Hi Hnr Roll; Hnr Roll; Nat Hon Sy; Otst Ac Ach Awd; Pres Ac Ftns Aw; Sci/Math Olympn; St of Mnth; Comm Volntr; Peer Tut/Med; Chrch Yth Grp; Emplmnt; Mth Clb/Tm; Ntl FFA; Prom Com; Sci Clb; Spanish Clb; Bsball (V CL); Bskball (J); Sccr (V C); FFA President; National Honor Society President; Civil Engineering; Biological Engineering; Purdue U

GRUELL, RYAN T; RUSHVILLE, IN; RUSHVILLE CONSOLIDATED HS; (JR); 4H Awd; Hnr Roll; Nat Hon Sy; Perf Att; 4-H; Chrch Yth Grp; FCA; Key Club; Pep Squd; Prom Com; Quiz Bowl; Scouts; Acpl Chr; Bnd; Chr; Drm Mjr; Swmg (L); Chamber of Commerce Junior Leadership Award; Engineering; Purdue U; Tri-State U

GUDORF, AMBER; JASPER, IN; JASPER HS; (JR); Hnr Roll; Nat Hon Sy; Perf Att; Pres Ac Ftns Aw; WWAHSS; Yth Ldrshp Prog; Comm Volntr; Hab For Humty Volntr; Peer Tut/Med; Chrch Yth Grp; Emplmnt; Key Club; Prom Com; SADD; Tchrs Aide; Spanish Clb; Bskball (V); Stu Cncl (R)

GUINTO, JOSEPH M; RICHLAND, IN; SOUTH SPENCER HS; (SO); Hi Hnr Roll; Pres Ac Ftns Aw; St of Mnth; WWAHSS; Comm Volntr; Spec Olymp Vol; DARE; Key Club; Ntl Beta Clb; Bsball (V); Bskball (V); Ftball (V); Wt Lftg (V); Weight Lifting (Above) Not Competitive; Medical; Sports Medicine; U of Evansville

GUNSELMAN, JESSE R; HOLLAND, IN; SOUTHRIDGE HS; (JR); Hi Hnr Roll; Hnr Roll; Perf Att; Comm Volntr; Peer Tut/Med; Chrch Yth Grp; Drma Clb; Mus Clb; Outdrs Clb; Pep Squd; Prom Com; SADD; Bnd; Chr; Mch Bnd; Orch; Bskball (V); Scr Kpr (V); CR (T); Violin for 10 Years; Voice for 2 Years; Education; Music; Indiana U; U of Evansville

GURIDY, TIFFANY; RICHMOND, IN; RICHMOND HS; (JR); Hnr Roll; Nat Hon Sy; Comm Volntr; Hosp Aide; Peer Tut/Med; BPA; Emplmnt; Jr Ach; Key Club; Clb; Sccr (J); Tennis (J); Sch Ppr; Pharmacy; Social Worker; Florida International U; New York U

HAAFF, ERIN; HATFIELD, IN; SOUTH SPENCER HS; (JR); Otst Ac Ach Awd; Perf Att; Pres Ac Ftns Aw; St of Mnth; WWAHSS; Emplmnt; HO'Br Yth Ldrshp; Key Club; Ntl Beta Clb; Pep Squd; Bskball (V L); Cr Ctry (V L); Track (V L); Dermatology; U of Cincinnati; Indiana U

HACKLER, CALANDRA R; VALPARAISO, IN; VALPARAISO HS; (SO); Hi Hnr Roll; Perf Att; WWAHSS; Comm Volntr; Key Club; Svce Clb; SADD; German Clb; Psychology; Valparaiso U; Purdue U

HAFNER, KEISHA; FORT WAYNE, IN; HERITAGE JR/SR HS; (SO); Hnr Roll; Chrch Yth Grp; DARE; Mus Clb; Chr; SP/M/VS; Swg Chr; Bachelor's Degree; Pediatric Nursing; Saint Francis; Indiana/Purdue U Fort Wayne

HAGAN, LELAH; GRANDVIEW, IN; SOUTH SPENCER HS; (JR); Ctznshp Aw; Hnr Roll; Perf Att; St of Mnth; HO'Br Yth Ldrshp; Key Club; Ntl Beta Clb; Pep Squd; Bskball (V L); Cr Ctry (V L); Track (V L); Physical Therapy Major; Indiana U Purdue U Indianapolis (IUPUI); U of Evansville

HAGEMAN, HOLLY A; HAMMOND, IN; MORTON SR HS; (FR); Hi Hnr Roll; Hnr Roll; Pres Sch; St of Mnth; Comm Volntr; Hosp Aide; ArtClub; Chrch Yth Grp; DARE; Emplmnt; P to P St Amb Prg; Sci Clb; Scouts; French Clb; Bnd; Ch Chr; Mch Bnd; Stu Cncl (P); American Legion Award; President's Award; Medical Degree; Engineering Degree; Notre Dame U; Yale U

HAGLER, ANDREW; GEORGETOWN, IN; FLOYD CTRL HS; (SO); Hnr Roll; St of Mnth; Yth Ldrshp Prog; Comm Volntr; Chrch Yth Grp; Emplmnt; FCA; Orch; Ftball (J); Track (V); Leader of 1st Grade Small Group At Church; Attended Congressional Student Leadership Conference; Aviation; Business (Stock Market); Naval Academy; U Of Notre Dame

HAINES, RYAN; FORT WAYNE, IN; HOMESTEAD HS; (FR); Ctznshp Aw; Hnr Roll; Pres Ac Ftns Aw; Sci Fairs; St of Mnth; Chrch Yth Grp; Key Club; Mus Clb; Bnd; Jzz Bnd; Mch Bnd; Pep Bnd; Golf (J); Architecture; Engineering; Duke U; US Naval Academy

HALE, DUSTIN; FORT WAYNE, IN; NORTHROP HS; (SO); Hi Hnr Roll; Hnr Roll; Perf Att; WWAHSS; Red Belt in Tae Kwon Do; Engineering; Indiana Telephone Telegraph Technology

HALEY, ELIZABETH; HIGHLAND, IN; HIGHLAND HS; (SO); DARE; Key Club; Off Aide; SADD; Vsity Clb; Japanese Clb; Sftball (V L); Vllyball (J); Teaching; Nebraska; U of Florida

HALL, COTY; HOWE, IN; PRAIRIE HEIGHTS SR HS; (FR); Ctznshp Aw; Hnr Roll; Nat Hon Sy; Perf Att; DARE; Bsball; Bskball (J); Ftball (J); Track; Track- 1st Place Shot Put; Indiana U

HALL, KYLE; MUNCIE, IN; MUNCIE CTRL HS; (SO), F Lan Hn Soc; Hi Hnr Roll; Hnr Roll; MVP; Sci Fairs; Comm Volntr; Peer Tut/Med; Emplmnt; Key Club; P to P St Amb Prg; French Clb; Tennis (V L); Secretary of Key Club; Engineering; Chemistry; Hobart & William Smith Colleges; U of Michigan

HALLER, EMILY; SOUTH BEND, IN; JOHN ADAMS HS; (JR); Hnr Roll; Nat Hon Sy; Comm Volntr; Hab For Humty Volntr; Emplmnt; Quill & Scroll; Schol Bwl; Dnce; PPSqd (V); Adv Cncl (R); Stu Cncl (P); Yrbk (E, P); Club: (PSI) Postponing Sexual Involvement; Club: Junior Civitan; Nutritionist; Business; Indiana U; San Diego State

HALLFORD, ASHLEY; HARTFORD CITY, IN; BLACKFORD HS; (SO); Hnr Roll; WWAHSS; Comm Volntr; ArtClub; Emplmnt; Key Club; Off Aide; Chr; Ch Chr; Swg Chr; Bskball (VJ); Sccr (V); Track (V); Vllyball (L); Cl Off (V); Stu Cncl (R); Most Outstanding Freshman Girl Award; Outstanding Health/P.E. Student; Pre Medicine; Indiana U; Goshen College

HALTER, KEITH L; VINCENNES, IN; LINCOLN HS; (SR); Ctznshp Aw; Hi Hnr Roll; Nat Hon Sy; Perf Att; WWAHSS; Chrch Yth Grp

HAM, LOREN; FLOYDS KNOBS, IN; FLOYD CTRL; (JR); Hnr Roll; St of Mnth; WWAHSS; DECA; Jr Ach; Spanish Clb; Bskball (J); National Technical Honor Society; Floyd Central Christian Ministries; Pharmacy; Law; Purdue U-Main Campus; U of Louisville

HAMERSLEY, MEGAN S; DANVILLE, IN; AVON HS; (FR); 4H Awd; Hi Hnr Roll; WWAHSS; Comm Volntr; 4-H; Chrch Yth Grp; Drma Clb; Mus Clb; Scouts; Bnd; Mch Bnd; SP/M/VS; Stg Cre

HAMILTON, JORDAN R; PETERSBURG, IN; PIKE CTRL HS; (SO); Hi Hnr Roll; Hnr Roll; Perf Att; Chrch Yth Grp; DARE; FCA; Pep Squd; Scouts; SADD; Chr; Bsball (L); Chrldg (V L); Cl Off (R); Advertising; U of Kentucky

HAMILTON, NICOLAS; TERRE HAUTE, IN; TERRE HAUTE SOUTH VIGO HS; (SR); Duke TS; Hi Hnr Roll; Nat Hon Sy; WWAHSS; Mth Clb/Tm; MuAlphaTh; Sci Clb; Swmg (V CL); Admission to Rose Hulman Institute Technology; Recipient of Full Tuition Airforce ROTC Scholarship; Electrical Engineering; Computer Science; Rose-Hulman Institute of Technology

Hagler, Andrew
Floyd Ctrl HS
Georgetown, IN

Green, Van
Southwestern Middle SR HS
Hanover, IN

Granson, Abigail B
Taylor HS
Kokomo, IN

National
Honor Roll
Spring 2005

Goshert, Sarah
Warsaw Cmty HS
Warsaw, IN

Hageman, Holly A
Morton SR HS
Hammond, IN

Hall, Coty
Prairie Heights SR HS
Howe, IN

HAMILTON II, RONALD E.; INDIANAPOLIS, IN; EMMERICH MANUAL HS; (JR); Ctznshp Aw; Hi Hnr Roll; Hnr Roll; Perf Att; Valdctrian; Chess; Emplmnt; French Clb; Graphic Design Technology; IUPUI; Purdue

HAMMER, ALLISON; WINSLOW, IN; PIKE CTRL HS; (SO); Hnr Roll; Comm Volntr; SADD; Tchrs Aide; German Clb; Bnd; Chr; Ch Chr; Mch Bnd; Yrbk (R, P); Who's Who Among Babe Ruth Youth League Softball; Assistant in SADD; Optometry; Culinary; Vincennes U; U of Evansville

HAMMOND, JORDAN; SPENCER, IN; OWEN VALLEY CMTY HS; (JR); Hnr Roll; Perf Att; WWAHSS; Comm Volntr; Lttrmn Clb; Bskball (V C); Sftball (V L); Vllyball (V CL); All-Conference in Volleyball; Engineering; Hotel Management; Purdue U; Rose-Hulman Institute of Tech

HANCOCK, CHRISTINA N; VALPARAISO, IN; PORTAGE HS; (SR); Hnr Roll; Comm Volntr; ROTC; Bnd; Drl Tm; Orch; Cl Off (V); CR (R); MCJROTC - Cadet 1st Lt Class Commander; Associate's Degree / Bachelor's Degree; Art School

HANCOCK, ELIZABETH; GRIFFITH, IN; GRIFFITH SR HS; (SO); Hnr Roll; Chrch Yth Grp; Schol Bwl; Chr; Swg Chr; Tennis (J); Interior Decorating; Purdue U, Lafayette College

HANEY, ALICIA; LAWRENCEBURG, IN; LAWRENCEBURG HS; (SO); Nat Hon Sy; Nat Stu Ath Day Aw; Perf Att; Pres Ac Ftns Aw; Pres Sch; WWAHSS; Key Club; Lttrmn Clb; Clb; Bskball (V L); Sccr (V L); Sftball (V L); Awarded 2 Academic Medallions; Inducted Into My High School National Honor Society; Athletic Trainer; Physical Therapist

HANEY, HEATHER K; VINCENNES, IN; VINCENNES LINCOLN HS; Ctznshp Aw; Hnr Roll; Perf Att; WWAHSS; Peer Tut/Med; DARE; Lib Aide; Off Aide; Prom Com; Tchrs Aide; Bnd; Mch Bnd; Chrldg (J); Who's Who Amer. High School; Airline Industry; Vincennes U; Airline Academy

HANN, RYAN W; LEESBURG, IN; WARSAW CMTY HS; (JR); Ctznshp Aw; Hi Hnr Roll; Hnr Roll; Comm Volntr; Svce Clb; Octagon; Teaching; Law; Purdue U; Indiana U (Bloomington)

HANNA, COURTNEY; ANGOLA, IN; PRAIRIE HEIGHTS SR HS; (FR); Ctznshp Aw; Hnr Roll; Nat Hon Sy; Perf Att; Comm Volntr; Pep Squd; Scouts; German Clb; Chr; Chrldg (J); Gmnstcs (J); PPSqd (J); Track (J); Yrbk (E, P); Cheerleading; Dental Hygienist; Optometrist; Vincennes U; IPFW Fort Wayne

HANNAN, GREER E; MISHAWAKA, IN; TRINITY SCH AT GREENLAWN; (SR); Nat Mrt Fin; Otst Ac Ach Awd; Comm Volntr; Chrch Yth Grp; Emplmnt; Chr; SP/M/VS; Lit Mag; Translated John's Gospel from Latin to English on My Own; Translated Harry Potter and the Sorcerer's Movie from German to English; Joint Major in Philosophy and Theology; Minor in Irish Studies; U of Notre Dame

HANSFORD, BRITTANY N; EDINBURGH, IN; SOUTHWESTERN HS; (SO); Comm Volntr; Chrch Yth Grp; Ntl FFA; Pep Squd; Scouts; SADD; Dnce; Golf (V); Tennis (J); Cl Off (T); Yrbk (E, R, P); United States Achievement Academy for International Foreign Language Award; Design; Business/Management; Cincinnati Bible College; Anderson

HANSON, CHRISTINE M; MERRILLVILLE, IN; MERRILLVILLE HS; (SR); Hi Hnr Roll; Hnr Roll; Nat Mrt LOC; Pres Sch; WWAHSS; Red Cr Aide; Emplmnt; Tchrs Aide; Orch; BS / Nursing; Master's Degree / Physician's Assistant; Indiana U Northwest; Midwestern U Chicago

HARDEN, AUDREY; FISHERS, IN; HAMILTON SOUTHEASTERN HS; (JR); F Lan Hn Soc; Hi Hnr Roll; Hnr Roll; Nat Mrt LOC; St of Mnth; WWAHSS; Drma Clb; Emplmnt; Spch Team; French Clb; SP/M/VS; Stg Cre; Mechanical Engineering; Purdue U

HARDESTY, AMANDA; GOSHEN, IN; FAIRFIELD JR/SR HS; (JR); Ctznshp Aw; Hnr Roll; WWAHSS; Emplmnt; Key Club; SADD; Bnd; Chr; SP/M/VS; Swg Chr; Social Work; Indiana U

HARDWICK, BRITNEY; INDIANAPOLIS, IN; GEORGE WASHINGTON CMTY SCH; (SO); Chrldg (J); Drama / Theater; Photography; College for Creative Studies; Indiana U Purdue U Indianapolis

HARMAN, BRADY; BRISTOL, IN; ELKHART CTRL HS; (SO); Hi Hnr Roll; Sci/Math Olympn; WWAHSS; Key Club; Mod UN; Bnd; Jzz Bnd; Mch Bnd; Pep Bnd; Cl Off (T); Stu Cncl (R); Medicine; Chemistry; Washington & Lee U; Indiana U

HARMON, AZUREA; GARY, IN; GARY CAREER CTR; (JR); Ctznshp Aw; Hnr Roll; Nat Ldrshp Svc; Nat Sci Aw; Otst Ac Ach Awd; Perf Att; Sci Fairs; St of Mnth; USAA; Yth Ldrshp Prog; CARE; Hosp Aide; Spec Olymp Vol; Chrch Yth Grp; Drma Clb; Mod UN; Mus Clb; Off Aide; Prom Com; ROTC; SADD; Dnce; Drl Tm; Flg Crps; Stg Cre; Chrldg (J); Cl Off (S); Pediatrician; Nursing; Indiana U

HARMON, GEORGE; COLUMBUS, IN; COLUMBUS EAST; (SR); Hnr Roll; St of Mnth; Comm Volntr; Chrch Yth Grp; Cl Off (P); Architectural Drawing; Social Worker; Ball State; Indiana U

HARMON, KAITLIN; BEECH GROVE, IN; BEECH GROVE HS; (SO); Hnr Roll; Pres Ac Ftns Aw; Emplmnt; Quill & Scroll; Spanish Clb; Sftball (JC); Vllyball (J); Yrbk (R, P); Teaching License; Degree in History; Ball State U; Evansville U

HARRIS, ALYSIA; NEW CARLISLE, IN; NEW PRAIRIE HS; (FR); Hnr Roll; WWAHSS; Emplmnt; Bnd; Mch Bnd; Pep Bnd; Journalism; Elementary Teaching; Indiana U; Ball State U

HARRIS, JESSICA; INDIANAPOLIS, IN; BEN DAVIS HS; (SO); Hi Hnr Roll; Hnr Roll; Comm Volntr; Spanish Clb; Education; Business; Indiana U; Purdue U

HARRIS, KEVIN; CARMEL, IN; CARMEL HS; (SO); Hi Hnr Roll; MVP; Nat Ldrshp Svc; Perf Att; Pres Sch; WWAHSS; Comm Volntr; Peer Tut/Med; DARE; Emplmnt; Wdwrkg Clb; Bsball (J); Ftball (J); Gold Key Award for Art; Nominated for Scholar Athlete; Computers; Science

HARRIS, RACHEL S; INDIANAPOLIS, IN; BROAD RIPPLE HS; (SO); Hi Hnr Roll; Hnr Roll; WWAHSS; Comm Volntr; Chrch Yth Grp; Key Club; ROTC; National Society of High School Scholars; Biology; Dentistry; Jackson State U; Fisk U

HARRIS, ZACHARY; NEW PALESTINE, IN; NEW PALESTINE HS; (SR); Hnr Roll; Emplmnt; Jr Ach; Bnd; Jzz Bnd; Mch Bnd; Pep Bnd; Sch Ppr (R, P); National Honor Roll; Visual Communications/Graphic Design; Music (Minor); IUPUI Indiana U Purdue U of Indianapolis

HARSHMAN, LATICIA; ALBION, IN; CHURUBUSCO HS; (JR); Hi Hnr Roll; Nat Hon Sy; WWAHSS; Spec Olymp Vol; Chrch Yth Grp; Key Club; SADD; Tchrs Aide; Bnd; Ch Chr; SP/M/VS; Swg Chr; Stu Cncl (R); Pediatrics; Olivet Nazarene U

HARSIN, RACHEL; HANOVER, IN; SOUTHWESTERN MIDDLE SR HS; (JR); Hi Hnr Roll; Nat Hon Sy; St of Mnth; Valdctrian; Yth Ldrshp Prog; Comm Volntr; Chrch Yth Grp; Mod UN; NtlFrnscLg; Off Aide; Prom Com; Schol Bwl; Spch Team; French Clb; Chr; Bskball; President of French Club; Spanish Club; International Business; Foreign Languages, General; Washington U in St Louis; The George Washington U

HART, SAMANTHA; FT WAYNE, IN; CONCORDIA LUTHERAN HS; (SO); Hi Hnr Roll; Hnr Roll; Comm Volntr; Peer Tut/Med; Chrch Yth Grp; P to P St Amb Prg; Photog; Spch Team; Cl Off (T); International Relations; Political Science & Government; Carleton College; Johns Hopkins U

HARTER, KAYLA; OAKVILLE, IN; COWAN HS; (JR); Hnr Roll; Nat Hon Sy; Comm Volntr; ArtClub; Emplmnt; Prom Com; Vllyball (J); Nursing; Ivy Tech State College

HARTLEY, AMY E; PETERSBURG, IN; PIKE CTRL HS; (FR); Hnr Roll; DARE; Fr of Library; SADD; German Clb; Chr; SP/M/VS; Cr Ctry (V L); Sftball (J); Stu Cncl; Cross Country-Mental Attitude 9th & 8th; Lawyer; Federal Bureau of Investigation (FBI); Indiana U

HARVEY, KATHRYN B; LAWRENCEBURG, IN; LAWRENCEBURG HS; (SR); Hi Hnr Roll; Nat Hon Sy; Nat Stu Ath Day Aw; Otst Ac Ach Awd; Perf Att; Salutrn; WWAHSS; Peer Tut/Med; Emplmnt; Key Club; French Clb; Bnd; Mch Bnd; Pep Bnd; Sftball (V CL); Academic Team Conference Champs; TD; MBA; U of Chicago

HASS, GRETA; FRANKLIN, IN; FRANKLIN CMTY HS; (JR); F Lan Hn Soc; Nat Hon Sy; Perf Att; Pres Ac Ftns Aw; Peer Tut/Med; Chrch Yth Grp; Emplmnt; FCA; Pep Squd; Photog; Prom Com; Quill & Scroll; Svce Clb; PP Ftbl (V); Swmg (V L); Sch Ppr (E, R, P); Yrbk (R, P); Career in Journalism; Indiana U Bloomington

HATCH, ELIZABETH K; CARMEL, IN; CARMEL HS; (SR); Otst Ac Ach Awd; WWAHSS; Comm Volntr; DARE; Drma Clb; Emplmnt; Mus Clb; Chr; SP/M/VS; Swg Chr; 2003 National Age Group Synchronized Swimming Trip; ISSMA Division I Solo Vocal Award Champion; Vocal Performance Major; Aspire to Be a Country Music Recording Artist; Clemson U; Mercer U

HATCH, KAYTE; CRAWFORDSVILLE, IN; SOUTHMONT HS; (JR); Hi Hnr Roll; Hnr Roll; MVP; Nat Hon Sy; WWAHSS; Chrch Yth Grp; DARE; Emplmnt; Key Club; Prom Com; German Clb; PP Ftbl (V C); Sccr (V L); Swmg (V CL); Cl Off (S); Key Club; German Club-Vice President; Physical Therapy; Athletic Training; Indiana U Purdue U Indianapolis; U of Western Michigan

HAWA, KRISTINE; MICHIGAN CITY, IN; MICHIGAN CITY HS; (FR); Hnr Roll; WWAHSS; French Clb; Tennis (J); Medicine; Indiana U Bloomington; Purdue U West Lafayette

HAWKINS, LINDSAY; FRENCH LICK, IN; INDIANA AC; (SO); Hi Hnr Roll; Hnr Roll; Otst Ac Ach Awd; WWAHSS; Comm Volntr; Drma Clb; Key Club; Lib Aide; Pep Squd; SADD; Track (V); Cl Off (P); Sch Ppr (R); Orange County Youth Council; Talent Board; English; Computer Science

HAY, MELANIE; ROCKPORT, IN; SOUTH SPENCER HS; (FR); 4H Awd; Hi Hnr Roll; St of Mnth; WWAHSS; 4-H; FCA; Key Club; Pep Squd; SADD; Bnd; Sftball (VJ); Vllyball (J)

HAYDEN, MICHEAL A; OAKLAND CITY, IN; WALDO J WOOD MEMORIAL HS; (FR); Hnr Roll; Otst Ac Ach Awd; Perf Att; Chrch Yth Grp; Bskball; Ftball (V); Track (V); Bachelors Degree; Masters Degree; U of Tennessee; U of Kentucky

HAYS, STEVEN; ROCKPORT, IN; SOUTH SPENCER HS; (SR); Nat Hon Sy; Otst Ac Ach Awd; St of Mnth; Valdctrian; Red Cr Aide; Emplmnt; Key Club; Ntl Beta Clb; Tennis (V CL); Track (V CL); Wrstlg (V CL); Cl Off (S); IMSTEA Super Mileage State Champions; Wrestling Academic All-State 1st Team; Software Engineering; Rose-Hulman Institute of Technology

HECK, CASEY L; LEBANON, IN; LEBANON HS; (JR); Hi Hnr Roll; Nat Hon Sy; Otst Ac Ach Awd; Perf Att; Pres Ac Ftns Aw; Pres Sch; St of Mnth; WWAHSS; Yth Ldrshp Prog; Peer Tut/Med; Chrch Yth Grp; Emplmnt; FCA; Key Club; Pep Squd; Prom Com; Svce Clb; Tchrs Aide; Chrldg (V CL); Track (V L); Cl Off (P); Stu Cncl; CR; Outstanding Sophomore Girl Award; Highest GPA for Her Sport; Major; Bachelors Degree; DePauw U; Franklin College

HEHMAN, JOSHUA; COLUMBUS, IN; COLUMBUS NORTH HS; (JR); Hnr Roll; Comm Volntr; Emplmnt; Quill & Scroll; Lit Mag (E, P); Sch Ppr (E); Engineering; Software Application; Purdue U

HEIN, DOMINIQUE; SOUTH BEND, IN; WASHINGTON HS; (SO); Hi Hnr Roll; Nat Stu Ath Day Aw; Otst Ac Ach Awd; St of Mnth; WWAHSS; Emplmnt; P to P St Amb Prg; Quiz Bowl; Vllyball (J); Purdue U; Hanover

HELTON, MAEGGAN; SULLIVAN, IN; SULLIVAN HS; (SR); Hnr Roll; Nat Hon Sy; Comm Volntr; Peer Tut/Med; Drma Clb; Emplmnt; Key Club; Ntl Beta Clb; SP/M/VS; Sftball (V); Yrbk (E); National Honor Society; Beta Club; Elementary Education; Purdue U

HEMMEGER, TATUM M; KOKOMO, IN; KOKOMO HS; (SR); Hnr Roll; Nat Hon Sy; WWAHSS; Chrch Yth Grp; Lttrmn Clb; Quill & Scroll; Vsity Clb; German Clb; Bskball (J); Sccr (V L); Track (V L); NCC All-Academic Award - Soccer; Chiropractor; Optometry; Indiana U Bloomington

HENDERSON, ALEX; INDIANAPOLIS, IN; BEN DAVIS HS; (SO); Ctznshp Aw; Hi Hnr Roll; Hnr Roll; Nat Hon Sy; Otst Ac Ach Awd; Perf Att; Mus Clb; Bnd; Mch Bnd; Pep Bnd; Motorcycle Mechanics; Custom Paint

HENGEN JR, JOHN; SOUTH BEND, IN; ST JOSEPH HS; (JR); Hnr Roll; Comm Volntr; ArtClub; Chrch Yth Grp; Emplmnt; Scouts; Spanish Clb; Skiing (J); Swmg (V L); Business; Science

HENKLE, SHAUNA; INDIANAPOLIS, IN; PERRY MERIDIAN HS; (JR); Hnr Roll; Comm Volntr; Spec Olymp Vol; Emplmnt; Key Club; Pep Squd; Tchrs Aide; Bskball (J); Cr Ctry (J); Track (V L); CR (R); Sch Ppr (E, R, P); President of Best Buddies; Communications-Journalism; Advertising; U of Kentucky; Northwestern U

HENLEY, KIMBERLY; CRAWFORDSVILLE, IN; SOUTHMONT HS; (JR); Hnr Roll; Nat Hon Sy; St of Mnth; WWAHSS; Comm Volntr; 4-H; Chrch Yth Grp; DARE; FCA; Key Club; Prom Com; Ch Chr; Swg Chr; PP Ftbl; Cl Off (R); Stu Cncl; Purdue U

HENNEY, JENN; GRIFFITH, IN; GRIFFITH HS; (SO); Hnr Roll; Perf Att; WWAHSS; Emplmnt; Computer Information Systems; Website Design; Purdue U Calumet; Indiana Institute of Technology

HENNIGAN, THOMAS; INDIANAPOLIS, IN; (JR); Perf Att; ROTC; Scouts; Bsball (J); Ftball (V L); Wt Lftg (V); Wrstlg (J L); CR (V); Race Kenyon Midgets; Mechanical Engineer; Purdue U; Michigan U

HENRICH, JAMES; WEST LAFAYETTE, IN; HARRISON HS; (SR); Hi Hnr Roll; Hnr Roll; Pres Sch; Sci Fairs; Comm Volntr; Hab For Humty Volntr; P to P St Amb Prg; Spch Team; SADD; Bsball (J); Ftball; Sccr (J); Stu Cncl (R); Architecture; Marketing; Florida Atlantic U

HENRY, KYLE S; JAMESTOWN, IN; WESTERN BOONE JR/SR HS; (JR); 4H Awd; Hnr Roll; Perf Att; Comm Volntr; Hab For Humty Volntr; 4-H; Chrch Yth Grp; Emplmnt; Key Club; Ntl FFA; Tchrs Aide; Bskball (J); Ftball (V); Ag/Landscaping; Auto/Diesel Mechanic; Purdue U; WyoTech

HERROLD, BRANDON J; KEWANNA, IN; CASTON ED CTR; (SR); 4H Awd; Hnr Roll; MVP; WWAHSS; 4-H; ArtClub; Emplmnt; FCA; Key Club; Lttrmn Clb; Ntl FFA; Tchrs Aide; Bskball (V L); Ftball (V L); Golf (V L); Stu Cncl (R); All State Football-1st Team; All Logan Land MVP - Football & Basketball; University of St Francis

HERROLD, KAYLYN; KEWANNA, IN; CASTON HS; (SO); 4H Awd; Hi Hnr Roll; Perf Att; 4-H; Drma Clb; FCA; FCCLA; Key Club; Sci Clb; Bnd; Chr; Mch Bnd; Pep Bnd; Bskball (V); Sftball (V); Vllyball (V); Dietetics; Food Science; Purdue U; Ball State U

HERSKEDAL, REBEKAH S; CLOVERDALE, IN; CLOVERDALE HS; (SR); Hi Hnr Roll; Hnr Roll; Nat Hon Sy; Perf Att; St of Mnth; 4-H; AL Aux Girls; Chrch Yth Grp; Emplmnt; FCA; Ntl FFA; Prom Com; Tchrs Aide; Bnd; Ch Chr; Pep Bnd; SP/M/VS; Golf (V L); Cl Off (S); Rosewater Book Club; Cloverdale Ambassador; Large Animal Veterinarian; Purdue U

HERVEY, JANEE; MICHIGAN CITY, IN; MARQUETTE; (JR); Ctznshp Aw; Hnr Roll; Pres Sch; St of Mnth; Emplmnt; Dnce; Bskball (V L)

Hayden, Micheal A
Waldo J Wood Memorial HS
Oakland City, IN

Harsin, Rachel
Southwestern Middle SR HS
Hanover, IN

Hanson, Christine M
Merrillville HS
Merrillville, IN

National
Honor Roll
Spring 2005

Hamilton II, Ronald E.
Emmerich Manual HS
Indianapolis, IN

Harter, Kayla
Cowan HS
Oakville, IN

Hays, Steven
South Spencer HS
Rockport, IN

HESS, BRITTANI; DECATUR, IN; BELLMONT HS; (SO); 4H Awd; Hnr Roll; Comm Volntr; 4-H; DARE; Emplmnt; Scouts; French Clb; Bnd; Dnce; Mch Bnd; Chrldg; Sccr (J); Sftball; Swmg (V); Tennis (J); Fashion and Interior Design; Modeling; Orlando FL International Academy of Design & Tech; Art Institute of New York City

HESS, GWENDOLYN; GRANGER, IN; PENN HS; (JR); Hi Hnr Roll; WWAHSS; Comm Volntr; Drma Clb; Emplmnt; Off Aide; Chr; SP/M/VS; Swg Chr; Induction to National Thespian Society; Secondary Education; Biology; Ball State U

HESSER, ANNA D; GOSHEN, IN; NORTHRIDGE HS; (SR); 4H Awd; Hi Hnr Roll; Nat Hon Sy; Nat Mrt Fin; Pres Sch; Salutrn; 4-H; Emplmnt; Photog; Schol Bwl; Sci Clb; Stu Cncl (R); Academic Letter Winner; Scholastic of Awards / Honorable Mentions; Linguistics; Italian; Indiana U

HESSIG, MICHAEL A; VALLONIA, IN; SALEM HS; (SR); Hnr Roll; Nat Hon Sy; Otst Ac Ach Awd; Perf Att; Pres Ac Ftns Aw; St of Mnth; WWAHSS; ArtClub; Chrch Yth Grp; DARE; Emplmnt; Jr Ach; Scouts; SADD; Sccr (VJ); Track (VJ); Wt Lftg (VJ); Legal Attorney; Computer Technology; Berea College

HEVIA, HANNAH; BLOOMINGTON, IN; BLOOMINGTON HS NORTH; (JR); Sci Fairs; WWAHSS; Key Club; Ntl FFA; Florida State Science Fair Runner Up in Botany; Top 5 State FFA Parliamentary Procedure Competition; Business Administration; Marketing; Indiana U; Ivy Tech College

HICKS, BRITTANY E; INDIANAPOLIS, IN; BROAD RIPPLE HS; (FR); Hnr Roll; Otst Ac Ach Awd; Perf Att; Peer Tut/Med; Chrch Yth Grp; Drma Clb; Bskball (VJ); Sftball; Track; Philosophy; WNBA Pro Basketball Player; Indiana U Purdue U; Ivy Tech State College

HIGDON, AMANDA; ROCKPORT, IN; SOUTH SPENCER HS; (SO); 4H Awd; Ctznshp Aw; Hi Hnr Roll; Perf Att; St of Mnth; WWAHSS; Yth Ldrshp Prog; Comm Volntr; 4-H; Chrch Yth Grp; DARE; FCA; HO'Br Yth Ldrshp; Key Club; Pep Squd; SADD; Ch Chr; Chrldg (V); Tennis (J); Elementary Education; Psychology; Indiana U; Western Kentucky U

HIGGINS, BETHANY; MADISON, IN; MADISON CONSOLIDATED HS; (JR); F Lan Hn Soc; Hi Hnr Roll; Hnr Roll; Nat Hon Sy; Comm Volntr; Peer Tut/Med; Chrch Yth Grp; Svce Clb; French Clb; Ch Chr; Adv Cncl; Stu Cncl; National Honor Society; Church Camp Counselor; Elementary Education (Kindergarten); Franklin College; Anderson U

HIGGINS III, HARVIST; INDIANAPOLIS, IN; ARLINGTON HS; (FR); Hnr Roll; Tech Clb; Master's Degree; Purdue

HIGHSMITH, JENNIFER N; VALPARAISO, IN; MERRILLVILLE HS; (SR); Hi Hnr Roll; Hnr Roll; WWAHSS; Hosp Aide; Peer Tut/Med; DARE; Emplmnt; Off Aide; Quill & Scroll; Tchrs Aide; Chr; Dnce; PPSqd (V); Scr Kpr (V); Sftball (J); Sch Ppr (R); Yrbk (E); Academic Honors Diploma; Veterinary Medicine; Purdue U North Central

HILGEMAN, SEAN M; OTWELL, IN; PIKE CTRL HS; (SR); Hnr Roll; Perf Att; WWAHSS; Cr Ctry (V); Track (J); Multi-Media; Associate's & Bachelor's; ITT Technical Institute

HILL, HEATHER R; SEYMOUR, IN; SEYMOUR HS; (SR); Ctznshp Aw; Hi Hnr Roll; Hnr Roll; Nat Hon Sy; Otst Ac Ach Awd; St of Mnth; USAA; WWAHSS; Comm Volntr; Peer Tut/Med; ArtClub; Emplmnt; Key Club; Lttrmn Clb; Off Aide; Tchrs Aide; SP/M/VS; Stg Cre; Published Author; Paint Murals at Local Nursing Home; Teaching Degree / High School Art; Art Design / Advertising; Committed to Indiana U, Purdue U of Columbus; Indiana U

HILL, KATHERINE L A; OTWELL, IN; PIKE CTRL HS; (FR); Hi Hnr Roll; Otst Ac Ach Awd; Pres Ac Ftns Aw; St of Mnth; WWAHSS; Comm Volntr; 4-H; Chrch Yth Grp; DARE; Jr Ach; Tchrs Aide; Bskball (J); Tennis (J); Top 10 in Class; Indiana Farm Bureau County Essay Winner; Guidance Counselor; Elementary School Teacher; Oakland City U

HILL, TYLER B; CARMEL, IN; CARMEL HS; (SO); Hnr Roll; Hab For Humty Volntr; Chrch Yth Grp; Emplmnt; Cr Ctry (J); Track (J); Medicine; Law; Anderson U; Taylor U

HIMSEL, ANDREA M; JASPER, IN; JASPER HS; (FR); Hnr Roll; Yth Ldrshp Prog; Comm Volntr; Chrch Yth Grp; Drma Clb; Key Club; SADD; French Clb; Bnd; Chr; Ch Chr; Mch Bnd; Music

HINTON, JODI; MARTINSVILLE, IN; (JR); Hnr Roll; WWAHSS; Wdwrkg Clb; Chr; Wt Lftg (J); PCI-Nursing; ITT Tech-Cars; PCI; ITT Tech

HIVELY, LINDSEY M; CHURUBUSCO, IN; CHURUBUSCO HS; (JR); Hi Hnr Roll; Nat Hon Sy; Pres Sch; Yth Ldrshp Prog; ArtClub; Emplmnt; FBLA; Key Club; Prom Com; SADD; French Clb; Chrldg (V CL); Track (V L); Stu Cncl (P, V); Yrbk (P); SADD; Future Business Leaders of America; Entrepreneurship; Art and Design; U of Notre Dame; Indiana U

HOCHGESANG, BETH; JASPER, IN; JASPER HS; (FR); Bnd; Mch Bnd; Pep Bnd; Track (J); Stu Cncl (R); 4-H-7 Yrs; U of Evansville

HODGES, CHERELL; INDIANAPOLIS, IN; ARLINGTON HS; (JR); Hi Hnr Roll; Hnr Roll; Nat Hon Sy; Nat Mrt LOC; Otst Ac Ach Awd; Perf Att; Sci Fairs; St of Mnth; WWAHSS; Yth Ldrshp Prog; Peer Tut/Med; Chrch Yth Grp; DARE; Emplmnt; ESC, Basketball Manager; Psychology / Nursing; Engineering; Indiana U

HOEING, ALLISON; RUSHVILLE, IN; RUSHVILLE CONSOLIDATED HS; (FR); 4H Awd; Hi Hnr Roll; Hnr Roll; Perf Att; 4-H; Chrch Yth Grp; Key Club; Pep Squd; Chr; Chrldg (J); Sccr (J); Medical; Indiana U

HOEING, KEITH; RUSHVILLE, IN; RCHS; (SO); 4H Awd; Hnr Roll; WWAHSS; Comm Volntr; 4-H; Emplmnt; FCA; Key Club; Ntl FFA; SADD; Spanish Clb; Acpl Chr; Cr Ctry (V L); Track (V L); Stu Cncl (R); CR (R); FFA Treasurer; Key Club Secretary; Something Agriculture Related; Conservational Officer; Purdue U

HOEPPNER, MARC D; WOODBURN, IN; WOODLAN JR/SR HS; (SR); Hi Hnr Roll; Jr Rot; MVP; Nat Hon Sy; Perf Att; St of Mnth; Comm Volntr; Peer Tut/Med; Chrch Yth Grp; FCA; Prom Com; Tchrs Aide; Bsball (V CL); Bskball (VJCL); Ftball (V CL); Cl Off (V, S); Stu Cncl (R); Richard Lugar's Leadership Symposium; IHSAA; Medical Doctor; Orthopedic Surgeon; DePauw U; Wabash Coll, IU-Bloomington

HOFFMAN, ELIZABETH; VALPARAISO, IN; VALPARAISO HS; (JR); Hnr Roll; Kwnis Aw; Comm Volntr; Hab For Humty Volntr; Spec Olymp Vol; Key Club; Off Aide; Prom Com; Tchrs Aide; Tennis (J); Distinguished Club Treasurer-Key Club; Indiana State Board Member-Key Club; Marine Biology; Environmental Science; U of Hawaii, Hilo; U of North Carolina

HOFFMAN, SARAH; INDIANAPOLIS, IN; BROAD RIPPLE HS; (SR); Hi Hnr Roll; Hnr Roll; Nat Hon Sy; WWAHSS; Comm Volntr; Chrch Yth Grp; Dbte Team; Drma Clb; Emplmnt; FCA; Key Club; Mod UN; Chr; Stg Cre; Cr Ctry (V L); Sftball (J); Pre-Med; Indiana U

HOFFNER, AARON J; SULLIVAN, IN; SULLIVAN HS; (SR); Drma Clb; Emplmnt; Chr; SP/M/VS; Bskball (V CL); Ftball (V CL); Track (V CL); Waiter At a Restaurant; Flying Planes and Helicopters; Vincennes U; USI

HOGUE, NICHOLAS; ANDERSON, IN; HIGHLAND HS; (FR); St of Mnth; Peer Tut/Med; DARE; Photog; Scouts; Pilot; Purdue U; Indiana State U

HOKE, SAMANTHA K; LIBERTY, IN; UNION CTY HS; (JR); 4H Awd; Perf Att; Comm Volntr; 4-H; ArtClub; Chrch Yth Grp; Emplmnt; FCA; Spanish Clb; Drl Tm; Vllyball (J); Stu Cncl (S); Yrbk (E, R, P); Science Academic Team; Award for Excellence in Biology; Wildlife Biologist; Veterinary Medicine; Purdue U; Indiana U East

HOLDEN, JENNIFER L; FRANKLIN, IN; WHITELAND CMTY HS; (SO); Hi Hnr Roll; Hnr Roll; Perf Att; Comm Volntr; DARE; Ntl FFA; Tchrs Aide; Published Poet; Veterinary Medicine; Zoology; Purdue U; Texas A & M U

HOLDER, RACHEL M; EVANSVILLE, IN; CENTRAL HS; (SO); Hi Hnr Roll; Hnr Roll; Pres Sch; Hab For Humty Volntr; ArtClub; HO'Br Yth Ldrshp; Pep Squd; Sci Clb; German Clb; Cl Off (S); Stu Cncl (R); Star Power; Law Explorers; Political Science; Law

HOLDERMAN, BRANDON; MISHAWAKA, IN; CHARLESTON HS; (SR); 4H Awd; Hi Hnr Roll; Hnr Roll; Nat Hon Sy; Perf Att; St of Mnth; WWAHSS; Comm Volntr; DARE; P to P St Amb Prg; Cyclg; Scr Kpr; Swmg; Cl Off; Culinary Arts; IUSB; Purdue U

HOLLAND, FELICIA R; AUSTIN, IN; AUSTIN HS; (SO); DAR; Nat Hon Sy; Perf Att; Comm Volntr; Peer Tut/Med; Chrch Yth Grp; Drma Clb; Emplmnt; Off Aide; Sci Clb; French Clb; SP/M/VS; Bskball; Tennis; Vllyball; Cl Off (P); Stu Cncl (T); CR (P); 4.0 GPA; Member of the Future Leaders of Austin; News Media; Telecommunications; Ball State U; New York U

HOLLON, LESLEY; MUNCIE, IN; YORKTOWN HS; (JR); Hnr Roll; Nat Hon Sy; Otst Ac Ach Awd; WWAHSS; Comm Volntr; Peer Tut/Med; FBLA; Key Club; Sci Clb; Spanish Clb; Cr Ctry (V); Tennis (V); Track (V); English

HOLMES, JOSHUA L; ELKHART, IN; ELKHART CTRL HS; (JR); Hi Hnr Roll; Hnr Roll; Perf Att; Yth Ldrshp Prog; Comm Volntr; Key Club; Mus Clb; Tchrs Aide; Bnd; Jzz Bnd; Mch Bnd; Orch; Cr Ctry (V L); Cyclg; Swmg (J); Track (J); Glassmen Drama Bugle Corp; HS Grant Winner; Master's Computer Integrated Manufacturing Tech at Purdue U; Purdue U; Arizona U

HOLTSCLAW, AMBER D; INDIANAPOLIS, IN; BROAD RIPPLE HS; (FR); Hnr Roll; USAA

HOMBURG, REEGAN; TWELVE MILE, IN; CASTON JR/SR HS; (FR); Hi Hnr Roll; Hnr Roll; Key Club; Spanish Clb; Bskball (J); Golf (V); Stu Cncl (R); Accounting; Hotel Management; Purdue U; Indiana U

HOPF, EMILY; HUNTINGBURG, IN; JASPER HS; (JR); 4H Awd; Hnr Roll; Nat Hon Sy; WWAHSS; Comm Volntr; 4-H; Emplmnt; FCA; Key Club; Lttrmn Clb; Off Aide; Prom Com; Vsity Clb; Sccr (V); Stu Cncl (R); Physical Therapy; Nursing; U of Indianapolis; U of Evansville

HOPF, HEATHER; JASPER, IN; JASPER HS; (FR); Gov Hnr Prg; Hi Hnr Roll; Pres Ac Ftns Aw; Sci Fairs; WWAHSS; Hosp Aide; ArtClub; Key Club; SADD; Spanish Clb; Orch; Swmg (V); Vllyball (J); Stu Cncl (R)

HOPF, RACHEL K; JASPER, IN; JASPER HS; (FR); Hnr Roll; Comm Volntr; Emplmnt; Key Club; Scouts; Track (J L); Marketing; Accounting & Business; U of Southern Indiana; Indiana State U

HOPF, RYAN; HUNTINGBURG, IN; JASPER HS; (JR); 4H Awd; Hnr Roll; Otst Ac Ach Awd; Perf Att; WWAHSS; Comm Volntr; AL Aux Boys; Chrch Yth Grp; Emplmnt; FCA; Key Club; Lttrmn Clb; SADD; Spanish Clb; Bsball (J); Bskball (J); Sccr (V L); Vsy Clb (V); Vllyball (V); Wt Lftg (V); Academic All-State-Soccer; Football Home-Coming Court.; Surveying; Engineering; U of Southern Indiana; Indiana U

HOPKINS, LACY; COLUMBUS, IN; JEFFERSON EDUCATION CTR; (JR); Hnr Roll; Nat Hon Sy; St of Mnth; WWAHSS; Comm Volntr; DARE; Emplmnt; Svce Clb; Chr; Orch; Sccr; Honor Roll; Student of the Month; Early Childhood Development; Interior Design; U of Indiana; Indiana U, Purdue U, Columbus

HORD, ANNA; MADISON, IN; SOUTHWESTERN MIDDLE SR HS; (JR); 4H Awd; Hnr Roll; Peer Tut/Med; 4-H; Emplmnt; Pep Squd; Dnce; Chrldg (VJCL); Current Job; Nursing; Physical Therapy; Ball State U; U Southern Indiana

HORMANN, KRISTIN L; HOAGLAND, IN; HERITAGE JR/SR HS; (FR); Hi Hnr Roll; Perf Att; Comm Volntr; Chr; SP/M/VS; Stg Cre; Medical Field; Indiana U; Georgetown U

HORTON, ALLISON; CORYDON, IN; LANESVILLE HS; (JR); Hi Hnr Roll; Hnr Roll; MVP; Nat Hon Sy; Bskball (V L); Cr Ctry (V); Sftball (V CL); Cl Off (S); Stu Cncl (R); CR (S); Yrbk (E, R, P); Ranked 1st; Renaissance Steering Committee; Secondary Education; Chemistry; U of Louisville; U of Southern Indiana

HORTON, KAYLISSA; CARLISLE, IN; SULLIVAN HS; (SO); 4H Awd; DAR; Hi Hnr Roll; Hnr Roll; Kwnis Aw; Nat Hon Sy; Otst Ac Ach Awd; Perf Att; Pres Ac Ftns Aw; WWAHSS; Comm Volntr; Hosp Aide; 4-H; Emplmnt; Key Club; Ntl Beta Clb; Ntl FFA; Chr; Ch Chr; Track (V L); 4-H; FFA; Agribusiness; Physical Therapy; Purdue U; Vincennes U

HOSKINS, BETTY; MARYSVILLE, IN; NEW WASHINGTON HS; (FR); Drma Clb; SP/M/VS; Academic Team; Drama Club; Accounting

HOSTETLER, HALEY; PLYMOUTH, IN; HIGAS HS; (FR); Hnr Roll; Nursing; U of Miami; Indiana U

HOUGHTELIN, BRIDGET; BLOOMINGTON, IN; BLOOMING HS NORTH; (JR); Ctznshp Aw; Hnr Roll; Nat Hon Sy; Pres Sch; Comm Volntr; Chrch Yth Grp; Vllyball (J); Indiana U

HOUSIER, BRIDGET E; BEDFORD, IN; BEDFORD NORTH LAWRENCE HS; MS; Ctznshp Aw; Hi Hnr Roll; Kwnis Aw; Otst Ac Ach Awd; Pres Sch; Sci Fairs; Comm Volntr; Peer Tut/Med; Chrch Yth Grp; DARE; Scouts; Orch; Vllyball; Stu Cncl (R); AWANA Timothy Award; Polly Holtsclaw Memorial Mental Attitude Award-Volleyball; Medical Doctor; Michigan State U; Indiana U

HUCK, SARAH M; INDIANAPOLIS, IN; PERRY MERIDIAN HS; (JR); Hi Hnr Roll; Kwnis Aw; Nat Hon Sy; Sci Fairs; St of Mnth; Comm Volntr; Key Club; Mus Clb; Svce Clb; Tchrs Aide; SP/M/VS; Swg Chr; Tennis (V); Stu Cncl (V, S); Sch Ppr (R); Secretary of Key Club; District 1st Place for Key Club Newsletters; Nursing; Anderson U; U of Indianapolis

HUDI, KORTNEY; CROWN POINT, IN; CROWN POINT HS; (JR); Hi Hnr Roll; Hnr Roll; Nat Hon Sy; Comm Volntr; 4-H; Spanish Clb; Chr; Hsbk Rdg; Ice Sktg; Stu Cncl (R); Equine Veterinarian; Purdue Calumet; Purdue Lafayette

HUDSON, DAREN L; GREENSBURG, IN; SOUTH DECATUR JR/SR HS; (SR); Ctznshp Aw; DAR; Hi Hnr Roll; Kwnis Aw; Nat Hon Sy; St Schl; St of Mnth; WWAHSS; Comm Volntr; 4-H; Emplmnt; Mth Clb/Tm; Ntl FFA; Prom Com; Quiz Bowl; Bsball; Ftball; Cl Off (P); Stu Cncl (V); Aerospace Engineering; Purdue U

HUFFER, KENDALL A; LAFAYETTE, IN; LAFAYETTE JEFFERSON HS; (SR); 4H Awd; Ctznshp Aw; Hi Hnr Roll; Jr Rot; Nat Hon Sy; Otst Ac Ach Awd; Perf Att; Sci Fairs; St Optmst of Yr; WWAHSS; 4-H; Emplmnt; Mus Clb; Bnd; Drm Mjr; Mch Bnd; American Fisheries Soc. Hutton Biology Program; Biomedical Engineering; Purdue U

HUFFMAN, BRANDAL L; ALEXANDRIA, IN; JOHN H HINDS CAREER CTR; (SR); Ctznshp Aw; Hnr Roll; Nat Hon Sy; Otst Ac Ach Awd; Perf Att; Lib Aide; Photog; Wdwrkg Clb; Manager Basketball Team; Manager Baseball Team

HUGGLER, LAURA; MUNCIE, IN; BURRIS LABORATORY SCH; (SR); 4H Awd; Kwnis Aw; Nat Stu Ath Day Aw; Otst Ac Ach Awd; St Schl; Hab For Humty Volntr; 4-H; Emplmnt; Key Club; Prom Com; Orch; Sccr (V L); Tennis (V L); Vllyball (J); Cl Off (V, T); Stu Cncl (R); Sch Ppr (R); Lilly Endowment Finalist; Landscape Architecture; Apparel Design; Purdue U West Lafayette

HUGHBANKS, DANIELLE; CARBON, IN; NORTHVIEW HS; (SR); Hnr Roll; Perf Att; WWAHSS; Emplmnt; Key Club; Pep Squd; Tchrs Aide; French Clb; Radiologist Technician; Ivy Tech State College; Indiana State U

Huffer, Kendall A
Lafayette Jefferson HS
Lafayette, IN

Hess, Brittani
Bellmont HS
Decatur, IN

Holder, Rachel M
Central HS
Evansville, IN

HUMAN, NICKI; MICHIGAN CITY, IN; MICHIGAN CITY HS; (FR); Ctznshp Aw; Hnr Roll; Otst Ac Ach Awd; Comm Volntr; Drma Clb; Chr; SP/M/VS; Perform in Community Plays; A-H Diploma; Purdue North Central

HUNTZINGER, AUDI; ANDERSON, IN; ANDERSON HS; (FR); Hnr Roll; Otst Ac Ach Awd; WWAHSS; Chrch Yth Grp; Chr; Ch Chr; SP/M/VS; Church Volleyball Team; Church Membership; English Major / Literature; Business Major; Purdue U; IUPUI

HUNTZINGER, NICHOLE; ANDERSON, IN; ANDERSON HS; (SO); Ctznshp Aw; Hnr Roll; Jr Rot; Nat Hon Sy; Chrch Yth Grp; Tchrs Aide; Piano Lessons / Recitals; Art Shows / Awards; Art Major; Dental Hygiene; Indiana U; Anderson U

HURT, TAYLOR; HOPE, IN; HAUSER JR/SR HS; (FR); Ctznshp Aw; DAR; Hi Hnr Roll; Pres Sch; Key Club; Schol Bwl; Svce Clb; German Clb; Track (V); Cl Off (P); Stu Cncl (R); Educator; Doctor; U Of Notre Dame

HUSTON, CHRIS B; CARLISLE, IN; SULLIVAN HS; (SO); 4H Awd; Hnr Roll; Perf Att; Sci Fairs; Sci/Math Olympn; Comm Volntr; 4-H; Chrch Yth Grp; Emplmnt; Key Club; Ntl Beta Clb; Schol Bwl; Sccr (V); Track (V); Cl Off (R); Stu Cncl (R); Most Improved Player-Soccer; Spell Bowl, French Club, Relay for Life

HUTCHISON, ASHLEY N; COLUMBUS, IN; JEFFERSON EDUCATION CTR; (SO); Hi Hnr Roll; Hnr Roll; Perf Att; Comm Volntr; Peer Tut/Med; Chrch Yth Grp; DARE; Drma Clb; Emplmnt; Mus Clb; Photog; Prom Com; Bnd; Ch Chr; Clr Grd; Dnce; Golf (C); Hsbk Rdg (C); Ice Sktg (L); PPSqd (C); Stu Cncl (S); Sch Ppr (E); Scholarship to Great Lakes; Music Camp; Psychology/Sociology; Music/Culinary Arts; Indiana U; Purdue

HYLAND, GARY; MARION, IN; MARION HS; (JR); Hi Hnr Roll; Hnr Roll; Perf Att; WWAHSS; Photog; Chr; Bowling League- 3 Yrs of High School; Join the Air Force / Flying & Engineering; Military College

IANNOPOLLO, EMILY C; LAWRENCEBURG, IN; LAWRENCEBURG HS; (SO); Hi Hnr Roll; Nat Hon Sy; WWAHSS; Comm Volntr; Emplmnt; Key Club; French Clb; English Academic Team

IGO, ALESIA; AKRON, IN; TIPPECANOE VALLEY HS; (SR); Hi Hnr Roll; Hnr Roll; Nat Hon Sy; Pres Sch; WWAHSS; Comm Volntr; Peer Tut/Med; Drma Clb; Emplmnt; Lib Aide; Tchrs Aide; Spanish Clb; Bnd; Dnce; Pep Bnd; SP/M/VS; Sftball (J); Wrstlg (L); Get Doctoral for Veterinarian; Purdue U

ILES, LAURA; PLAINFIELD, IN; PLAINFIELD HS; (FR); Hnr Roll; Comm Volntr; Chrch Yth Grp; FCA; Key Club; Chr; Cr Ctry (V L); Track (V L); Nursing; Indiana U; Butler U

IRVIN, AUDRA O; MEROM, IN; SULLIVAN HS; (SR); Hi Hnr Roll; Nat Hon Sy; St of Mnth; Valdctrian; WWAHSS; Comm Volntr; Peer Tut/Med; AL Aux Girls; Chrch Yth Grp; Emplmnt; Key Club; Ntl Beta Clb; Pep Squd; Quiz Bowl; Schol Bwl; Bnd; Pep Bnd; SP/M/VS; Swg Chr; Chrldg (JC); Track (VJ); Yrbk (E); Beta Club Oratory Winner 1st Place State Level; National Level-Beta Oratory Winner 2nd Place; English Major; Indiana U

ISENBARGER, DANA; SARATOGA, IN; WINCHESTER CMTY HS; (SR); Hnr Roll; Nat Hon Sy; WWAHSS; Yth Ldrshp Prog; Peer Tut/Med; Ntl FFA; Prom Com; Tchrs Aide; Cl Off (S); Football Manager-Freshman Year; Elementary Education; Indiana U East

JACKSON, SHANE; EVANSVILLE, IN; CENTRAL HS; (JR); Ctznshp Aw; Hnr Roll; WWAHSS; Red Cr Aide; Quiz Bowl; French Clb; Sch Ppr (R); Academic Super Bowl-2nd Place in Area Meet; Creative Writing; Journalism; U of Evansville; Hanover U

JACKSON, SHAVONNE M; ELKHART, IN; CONCORD HS; (JR); Perf Att; Yth Ldrshp Prog; Comm Volntr; Chrch Yth Grp; DARE; Key Club; Mus Clb; Outdrs Clb; Photog; Prom Com; Chr; Lcrsse (VJ); Social Worker; Own My Own Business

JACKSON, STEFANNE; SOUTH BEND, IN; RILEY HS; (FR); Hi Hnr Roll; Otst Ac Ach Awd; Pres Ac Ftns Aw; Chrch Yth Grp; Quiz Bowl; Nursing; Political Science; Ball State U; U of Notre Dame

JAMES, ASHLEIGH N; LOGANSPORT, IN; LOGANSPORT HS; (JR); Ctznshp Aw; Hi Hnr Roll; Otst Ac Ach Awd; Perf Att; Pres Sch; Sci Fairs; Peer Tut/Med; Spec Olymp Vol; Drma Clb; Emplmnt; Jr Ach; Pep Squd; Svce Clb; SADD; Tchrs Aide; Bnd; Tennis (J); Century Career Center Honor Society; Elementary Education; Ball State U; Purdue U

JAMES, MELISSA S; GRIFFITH, IN; GRIFFITH HS; (SO); Hi Hnr Roll; Comm Volntr; Emplmnt; Tchrs Aide; Nutritionist; Photographer; U of Arizona

JAWORSKI, KAYLA N; MISHAWAKA, IN; PENN HS; (JR); F Lan Hn Soc; Hi Hnr Roll; WWAHSS; Hab For Humty Volntr; Peer Tut/Med; Emplmnt; Ntl FFA; Bnd; Clr Grd; Dnce; Mch Bnd; Varsity Winterguard: 2004 State Champs; Interact Club; Graphic Design; Advertising; Purdue U; Indiana U

JEFFRIES, KRISTYN; ROCKPORT, IN; SOUTH SPENCER HS; (FR); 4H Awd; Hi Hnr Roll; St of Mnth; WWAHSS; Yth Ldrshp Prog; 4-H; Chrch Yth Grp; FCA; Key Club; Ch Chr; Bskball (J); Golf (J); Track (V L); Cl Off (T); Key Club Officer; Leadership Spencer County Graduate

JENKINS, CORTEZ; SOUTH BEND, IN; WASHINGTON HS; (JR); Hi Hnr Roll; Hnr Roll; St of Mnth; WWAHSS; Honor Roll; Certificate of Honor; Computers; Business; Purdue; U of Evansville

JENNINGS, AUSTIN; NOBLESVILLE, IN; NOBLESVILLE HS; (FR); WWAHSS; Comm Volntr; Sccr (V); Health Sciences; Indiana U

JENSEN, KATRINA M; HIGHLAND, IN; HIGHLAND HS; (SR); WWAHSS; Comm Volntr; Cmptr Clb; Emplmnt; Key Club; Off Aide; Tchrs Aide; French Clb; Dnce; Stg Cre; Yrbk (R); Pre-Dentistry; Indiana U Bloomington

JETER, ASHLEY; GARY, IN; CALUMET HS; (FR); Hnr Roll; Nat Hon Sy; Otst Ac Ach Awd; Perf Att; Comm Volntr; Peer Tut/Med; ArtClub; Jr Ach; Off Aide; Pep Squd; French Clb; Dnce; Cr Ctry; Tennis; Vllyball; Pediatrician; Physical Therapist; Howard U; Columbia U

JOHNSON, ANDRE'; INDIANAPOLIS, IN; ARLINGTON HS; (SO); Hnr Roll; Perf Att; Pres Sch; Business; Texas Southern; Florida A & M

JOHNSON, BOBBI M; GENEVA, IN; SOUTH ADAMS JR/SR HS; (SR); Hnr Roll; Yth Ldrshp Prog; Chrch Yth Grp; Emplmnt; Jr Ach; Ntl FFA; Tchrs Aide; Ch Chr; PP Ftbl (VJ); Sftball (J); FFA Member; FFA Officer; Cosmetology; Rudae's School of Cosmetology

JOHNSON, BRITTANY; CORYDON, IN; LANESVILLE HS; (JR); Hi Hnr Roll; Hnr Roll; MVP; Nat Hon Sy; WWAHSS; Peer Tut/Med; Emplmnt; Prom Com; French Clb; Bskball (V); Sftball (V L); Vllyball (V); All Conference Team-Softball; Social Work; Criminal Justice; U of Southern Indiana; U of Indianapolis

JOHNSON, EMANUEL; INDIANAPOLIS, IN; NORTHWEST HS; (SO); Hnr Roll; Comm Volntr; Chrch Yth Grp; FCA; Mth Clb/Tm; Bskball (C); Math Major; Degree in Computer Engineering; Ball State U; Purdue U

JOHNSON, HEATHER N; COLUMBIA CITY, IN; COLUMBIA CITY HS; (FR); Hi Hnr Roll; Dvng (J); Swmg (J); Architecture; Interior Design; Ball State U; Purdue U

JOHNSON, JENNIE; HAMMOND, IN; MORTON HS; (JR); Hnr Roll; Comm Volntr; Drma Clb; Key Club; Prom Com; Spch Team; Wdwrkg Clb; Chr; Dnce; SP/M/VS; Chrldg (V); PPSqd (V CL); PP Ftbl; Cl Off (V); Arts and Entertainment Club Pres; 13 Years of Private Dance Instruction; Business Management; Performing Arts; Ball State U; Purdue U

JOHNSON, JENNIFER; BRISTOL, IN; ELKHART CTRL HS; (SO); Hi Hnr Roll; Nat Hon Sy; Otst Ac Ach Awd; Sci Fairs; Sci/Math Olympn; St of Mnth; USAA; WWAHSS; Comm Volntr; Peer Tut/Med; 4-H; Chrch Yth Grp; Emplmnt; Key Club; Quiz Bowl; Scouts; Bnd; Ch Chr; Mch Bnd; Pep Bnd; Cr Ctry (L); Sftball; Track (L); Sch Ppr (E); US Dept of Health and Human Services-Participation Awards for the National Health and Nutrition Exams; Elementary Education with Spanish; Secondary Education, Algebra and Spanish; Ball State U; St Mary's College, Hanover College

JOHNSON, JILL E; JASPER, IN; JASPER HS; (JR); Hnr Roll; Nat Hon Sy; WWAHSS; Comm Volntr; Key Club; SADD; Bnd; Mch Bnd; Pep Bnd; Swmg (V); Speech Language Pathology; U of Kentucky; U of Louisville

JOHNSON, KRESTINA; VALPARAISO, IN; VALPARAISO HS; (JR); Ctznshp Aw; F Lan Hn Soc; Hi Hnr Roll; Nat Hon Sy; Perf Att; Pres Ac Ftns Aw; Comm Volntr; Hosp Aide; Peer Tut/Med; Chrch Yth Grp; Cmptr Clb; Emplmnt; Fr of Library; Key Club; Lib Aide; Prom Com; SADD; PP Ftbl; Friend of the Dunes; Cass-Mentor Program; Pre-Med; Psychology; Valparaiso U; Notre Dame

JOHNSON, KRISTEN; GALVESTON, IN; LEWIS CASS HS; (SO); Hnr Roll; WWAHSS; Chrch Yth Grp; Emplmnt; FCA; Key Club; SADD; Ch Chr; SP/M/VS; Swg Chr; Chrldg (J); Tennis (J); Sch Ppr; Indiana Leadership Seminar Winner; Cosmetology; Music Major

JOHNSON, PETER S; WEST BADEN SPRINGS, IN; (FR); 4H Awd; Hnr Roll; Sci Fairs; Comm Volntr; Peer Tut/Med; Spec Olymp Vol; 4-H; Tchrs Aide; Church Activities; 4-H, Academic Teams, FFA; Graphic Design; History; Purdue U; Indiana U

JOHNSON, SHALONDA; INDIANAPOLIS, IN; PIKE HS; (JR); Pres Sch; WWAHSS; Yth Ldrshp Prog; Comm Volntr; Chrch Yth Grp; Off Aide; Ch Chr; PP Ftbl; Cl Off (R); Stu Cncl (S, T); CR (R); Sch Ppr (R); Yrbk (E, R, P); Congressional Student Leadership Conference; Business Administration; Finance; Purdue U; Indiana State U

JOHNSON, TRACIE; POSEYVILLE, IN; NORTH POSEY HS; (SR); Hnr Roll; Nat Hon Sy; St of Mnth; Emplmnt; Prom Com; Spanish Clb; Bnd; Drm Mjr; Mch Bnd; Pep Bnd; Bskball (J); Track (J); National Honor Society-Secretary; Nursing; U of Southern Indiana; Indiana State U

JOHNSON JR, RONNIE G; FREMONT, IN; FREMONT HS; (SO); Hnr Roll; ArtClub; Chess; Outdrs Clb; Wdwrkg Clb; Ftball (J); Wt Lftg (J); Numerous Most Improved Awards; Math Achievement Award; Engineer; Automotive Design; (Wyotech) Wyoming Technical; Ohio Technical College

JOINTER, LATIA D; INDIANAPOLIS, IN; EMMERICH MANUAL HS; (JR); 4H Awd; Hi Hnr Roll; WWAHSS; Comm Volntr; 4-H; Chrch Yth Grp; Scouts; French Clb; Bskball (V L); Golf (V L); Sftball (V L); Vllyball (V); Medical; Pharmacy; Indiana U; Purdue U

JONES, AMY; PETERSBURG, IN; PIKE CTRL HS; (SO); Hi Hnr Roll; Hnr Roll; Pres Ac Ftns Aw; St of Mnth; Chrch Yth Grp; DARE; FCA; SADD; Tchrs Aide; Ch Chr; SP/M/VS; Swg Chr; Bskball; Track; Vllyball; Wt Lftg; Adv Cncl (R); Cl Off (P); Stu Cncl (R); CR (P); Secretary of FCA & S; Student Government; Speech Therapist; Indiana U; Southern Indiana U

JONES, GABRIELLE; ANDERSON, IN; HIGHLAND HS; (FR); Hnr Roll; Nat Hon Sy; Pres Ac Ftns Aw; WWAHSS; Comm Volntr; Chrch Yth Grp; DARE; Emplmnt; Pep Squd; SADD; Chrldg (J L); Track (V); National Cheerleader Assoc. Winner (JV); Vet. Med; Purdue U

JONES, JACINTA; SOUTH BEND, IN; ADAMS HS; (MS); Chrch Yth Grp; Ch Chr; Dnce; Bskball; Law Office; Law Office

JONES, JESSICA L; STENDAL, IN; PIKE CTRL HS; (SO); Hi Hnr Roll; MVP; WWAHSS; Peer Tut/Med; Chrch Yth Grp; Chrldg (V L); Cr Ctry; Teacher; Lawyer; U of Evansville; U of Southern Indiana

JONES, JORDAN P; MADISON, IN; SHAWE MEM JR/SR HS; (SO); Hi Hnr Roll; Nat Hon Sy; Otst Ac Ach Awd; Pres Ac Ftns Aw; Yth Ldrshp Prog; Peer Tut/Med; Mth Clb/Tm; Pep Squd; Scouts; Spanish Clb; Bnd; Pep Bnd; Swg Chr; Chrldg (V); Gmnstcs; Swmg (J); Tennis; Cl Off (P); Mayor's Youth Council; Bowl for Kid's Sake; Business/Accounting; Elementary Education; U of Kentucky; U of Tennessee

JONES, KRISTI; MARION, IN; THE KING'S AC; (JR); Hnr Roll; Sci/Math Olympn; Comm Volntr; Peer Tut/Med; Chrch Yth Grp; Off Aide; Tchrs Aide; Chr; SP/M/VS; Elementary Education; Missions; Indiana Wesleyan U

JONES, KYLE D; RICHLAND, IN; SOUTH SPENCER HS; (JR); Ctznshp Aw; Hi Hnr Roll; Nat Hon Sy; St of Mnth; WWAHSS; Comm Volntr; Chrch Yth Grp; Drma Clb; Emplmnt; FCA; Key Club; Ntl Beta Clb; Prom Com; SP/M/VS; Stg Cre; Golf; Tennis; Cl Off (V); CR (R); Youth Leadership Board Spencer Cty; Orthodontist; Indiana U-Purdue U Indianapolis

JONES, MEAGAN; RICHLAND, IN; SOUTH SPENCER HS; (SO); 4H Awd; Ctznshp Aw; Hnr Roll; Otst Ac Ach Awd; Perf Att; Pres Ac Ftns Aw; Sci Fairs; St of Mnth; WWAHSS; Yth Ldrshp Prog; 4-H; Chrch Yth Grp; DARE; HO'Br Yth Ldrshp; Key Club; Ntl Beta Clb; Yrbk (P); Photographer; Graphic Design; U of Evansville; Indiana U

JONES, NATHAN D; RICHLAND, IN; SOUTH SPENCER HS; (FR); Hi Hnr Roll; Hnr Roll; Perf Att; Pres Ac Ftns Aw; St of Mnth; Comm Volntr; Drma Clb; Emplmnt; FCA; Key Club; SP/M/VS; Stg Cre; Golf; Medical

JONES, SEAN P O; INDIANAPOLIS, IN; BISHOP CHATARD HS; (SR); Hi Hnr Roll; Hnr Roll; Comm Volntr; Mod UN; Ftball (V L); Wrstlg (V CL); Doc Kennedy Award; Purdue U

JONES, TALISSE; INDIANAPOLIS, IN; PERRY MERIDIAN HS; (JR); Chrch Yth Grp; Key Club; Ch Chr; Nursing; Maternity Nurse; North Carolina State; Fayetteville Technical

JONES, TARA L A; HIGHLAND, IN; HIGHLAND HS; (SO); F Lan Hn Soc; Hnr Roll; Nat Hon Sy; WWAHSS; Comm Volntr; ArtClub; Emplmnt; Key Club; Prom Com; Spanish Clb; Track (J); Cl Off (V, S); Member of T.A. T.U.; Participated in 9th Grade Basketball; Journalism; Art; Notre Dame (The U of Notre Dame); Ball State U

JORDAN, ALEXIA; MICHIGAN CITY, IN; MICHIGAN CITY HS; (FR); Hnr Roll; Perf Att; Sci Fairs; St of Mnth; Scouts; Bnd; Ch Chr; SP/M/VS; Chrldg (J); Stu Cncl (P, S); Law; Music; Indiana U; New York U

JORDAN, BRITTANY; INDIANAPOLIS, IN; ARLINGTON HS; (JR); Hi Hnr Roll; Hnr Roll; Otst Ac Ach Awd; Sci Fairs; WWAHSS; Emplmnt; Drl Tm; Chrldg (V); Cr Ctry (V); Scr Kpr (J); Tennis (V); Cl Off (S, T); Psychology; Criminal Justice; Howard U; Tennessee State U

JORDAN, TIM; SOUTH BEND, IN; JOHN ADAM HS; (SR); WWAHSS; Hab For Humty Volntr; Quill & Scroll; SADD; Sccr (V); Wrstlg (V C); Yrbk (E); Medicine; Indiana U

JOYCE, LE SHA; GARY, IN; THEODORE ROOSEVELT HS; (JR); Ctznshp Aw; Fut Prb Slvr; Hnr Roll; Otst Ac Ach Awd; Perf Att; Sci Fairs; Comm Volntr; Peer Tut/Med; Chrch Yth Grp; Drma Clb; Emplmnt; Tchrs Aide; Spanish Clb; Ch Chr; Dnce; Cl Off (V); Stu Cncl (V); Elementary Education; Fashion Design; Langston U; U of Iowa

KAMINSKY, LAUREN; MUNCIE, IN; BURN'S LABORATORY SCH; (JR); MVP; Nat Stu Ath Day Aw; Otst Ac Ach Awd; WWAHSS; Comm Volntr; Chrch Yth Grp; FCA; Key Club; Prom Com; Svce Clb; Chr; Track (V L); Vllyball (V CL); Stu Cncl (P, T); Sch Ppr (R, P); All State-Volleyball; Business; Xavier U

KANTENWEIN, DAVID J; WARSAW, IN; WARSAW CMTY HS; (JR); Ctznshp Aw; Hi Hnr Roll; St of Mnth; Chrch Yth Grp; Emplmnt; Mth Clb/Tm; Optimist Club-Student of the Week; Math Education; Architecture; Grace College & Theological Seminary

Johnson, Heather N
Columbia City HS
Columbia City, IN

Jeter, Ashley
Calumet HS
Gary, IN

Isenbarger, Dana
Winchester Cmty HS
Saratoga, IN

National
Honor Roll
Spring 2005

Hyland, Gary
Marion HS
Marion, IN

Johnson, Emanuel
Northwest HS
Indianapolis, IN

Johnson Jr, Ronnie G
Fremont HS
Fremont, IN

KASINJA, PRUDENCE D.; GRANGER, IN; PENN HS; (SR); Track; 1 JV Track Certificate (Junior Year); Accounting/Business; Nursing; Saint Joseph's College; Southwestern Michigan College

KAUFFMAN, LEANDER M; COLUMBIA CITY, IN; COLUMBIA CITY HS; (FR); DAR; Comm Volntr; Chrch Yth Grp; Drma Clb; Mus Clb; P to P St Amb Prg; Spch Team; Bnd; Ch Chr; Mch Bnd; Pep Bnd; Major in Elementary Education; Music; Ball State U; Purdue U

KAYS, KRISTEN A; CARMEL, IN; CARMEL HS; (FR); Hnr Roll; Perf Att; Chrch Yth Grp; Chr; Cr Ctry (J L); Track (J); Veterinary Medicine; Pharmacy; Purdue U; St Louis College of Pharmacy

KAZMIERCZAK, JILLIAN R; BATTLE GROUND, IN; HARRISON HS; (SO); Hi Hnr Roll; St of Mnth; DARE; Emplmnt; Scouts; Clr Grd; SP/M/VS; Stg Cre; Did Band and Basketball Team in Middle School; Purdue U

KEARBY, BRANDON L; FRENCH LICK, IN; SPRINGS VALLEY HS; (JR); Hnr Roll; WWAHSS; Stu Cncl (P); History Award; Computer Tech; Automobile Restoration & Repair; Vincennes U; Lincoln Tech

KELICH, JESSICA C; BRISTOL, IN; ELKHART CTRL HS; (JR); 4H Awd; Hnr Roll; Kwnis Aw; Comm Volntr; 4-H; Chrch Yth Grp; Key Club; Swmg (V L); Bristol Homecoming Queen 2004; Registered Nurse; Specializing in Obstetrics; Indiana U Purdue U of Indy; Indiana U of South Bend

KELLAMS, JULIANN; FRANKLIN, IN; (JR); Ctznshp Aw; Hi Hnr Roll; Hnr Roll; Nat Hon Sy; Otst Ac Ach Awd; Perf Att; WWAHSS; Yth Ldrshp Prog; Comm Volntr; AL Aux Girls; Chrch Yth Grp; FCCLA; Mus Clb; P to P St Amb Prg; Scouts; Bnd; Jzz Bnd; Mch Bnd; Pep Bnd; Tennis (J); Stu Cncl (R); FCCLA District President, VP; Figure Skating; Elementary Education; Franklin College

KELLEHER, RYAN W; CARMEL, IN; CARMEL HS; (FR); Hnr Roll; Otst Ac Ach Awd; Sci/Math Olympn; Sci Clb; Scouts; Bnd; Jzz Bnd; Mch Bnd; Pep Bnd; Full Orchestra; Volunteer for Alzheimer's Association; Doctorate / Medical Degree; Indiana U; Purdue

KELLER, ANDY; BROWNSBURG, IN; BROWNSBURG HS; (JR); Hi Hnr Roll; Hnr Roll; Nat Hon Sy; Nat Mrt Semif; Otst Ac Ach Awd; Perf Att; Comm Volntr; DECA; Emplmnt; FCA; Off Aide; Quiz Bowl; Schol Bwl; Scouts; Tchrs Aide; Bskball (J); Ftball (V L); Track (V CL); Wt Lftg (V); Stu Cncl (R); 2 Time State Champion Hammer Throw/Weight Throw; Basketball Broadcaster; Business; Law; U of Southern California; Harvard College

KELLER, JESSICA A; MANILLA, IN; RUSHVILLE CONSOLIDATED HS; (SR); Hi Hnr Roll; Hnr Roll; MVP; Nat Hon Sy; WWAHSS; Comm Volntr; Hab For Humty Volntr; 4-H; Chrch Yth Grp; Drma Clb; FCA; Key Club; Mus Clb; Pep Squd; Spanish Clb; Acpl Chr; Chr; SP/M/VS; Dvng (V L); Sccr (V CL); Sftball (J); Swmg (V CL); Tennis (J); Track (V L); Adv Cncl (R); Stu Cncl (R); Rush County Republican Party Top 20 Senior Award; Indiana U

KELLEY, MADISON P; ROCKPORT, IN; SOUTH SPENCER HS; (SO); 4H Awd; Hi Hnr Roll; Hnr Roll; Perf Att; Pres Sch; St of Mnth; WWAHSS; Yth Ldrshp Prog; 4-H; Chrch Yth Grp; DARE; Emplmnt; FCA; Key Club; Ntl Beta Clb; Pep Squd; Chr; Dnce; Chrldg (V L); Tennis (V L); Cl Off (T); Stu Cncl (R); Fashion Merchandising / Design; Travel Management; Purdue U

KELLEY, SCOTT; NEW HAVEN, IN; NEW HAVEN HS; (JR); All Am Sch; Hnr Roll; Nat Hon Sy; Otst Ac Ach Awd; Perf Att; Pres Sch; St of Mnth; WWAHSS; Peer Tut/Med; Chrch Yth Grp; DARE; Dbte Team; Drma Clb; Emplmnt; Jr Ach; Mus Clb; NtlFrnscLg; Acpl Chr; Chr; SP/M/VS; Ftball (V); Track (J); Vsy Clb (L); Cl Off (R); Stu Cncl (R); President-Speech & Debate Team; School News (Channel 4); Pre-Medicine-Plastic Surgeon (Graduate); Acting & Directing; Indiana U; Ball State U

KELLY, ELIZABETH; ANDERSON, IN; HIGHLAND HS; (SO); Hnr Roll; WWAHSS; Yth Ldrshp Prog; Hosp Aide; Peer Tut/Med; Chrch Yth Grp; Off Aide; Vsity Clb; Bdmtn (V); Scr Kpr (V); Swmg (V L); Wt Lftg (V); Nursing; Marian College

KELSER, SAMANTHA; KOKOMO, IN; TAYLOR HS; (JR); Hnr Roll; Pres Ac Ftns Aw; ArtClub; Scouts; Chr; Swg Chr; Kids to College; Dance; Music; Indiana U; Huntington College

KEMKER, LIZ; JASPER, IN; JASPER HS; (FR); Sci Fairs; Comm Volntr; 4-H; Emplmnt; Key Club; SADD; Spanish Clb; Bnd; Pep Bnd; Hsbk Rdg; Track

KENDALL, AMY; SHIRLEY, IN; KNIGHTSTOWN HS; (SO); Hi Hnr Roll; Otst Ac Ach Awd; St of Mnth; WWAHSS; ArtClub; Drma Clb; Spch Team; French Clb; Jzz Bnd; SP/M/VS; Tennis (V); Academic Bowl-Eng, Science, S.S. Teams; Freshman Mentor; Literature; Psychology; Indiana U; Butler U

KENDALL, MICHAEL A; JASONVILLE, IN; SHAKAMAK HS; (JR); Hnr Roll; Nat Hon Sy; Perf Att; St of Mnth; WWAHSS; Peer Tut/Med; Chess; Emplmnt; Chr; SP/M/VS; Golf; Aviation Mechanic; Criminal Justice; Ivy Tech; Rose-Hulman IT

KENNEDY, NICHOLAS; CARMEL, IN; CARMEL HS; (JR); F Lan Hn Soc; Hi Hnr Roll; Hnr Roll; MVP; Nat Hon Sy; Perf Att; WWAHSS; Chrch Yth Grp; Emplmnt; Photog; Quill & Scroll; Scouts; Vsity Clb; Bnd; Orch; Lcrsse (V L); CR (R); Sch Ppr (E); Eagle Scout; First Team All-State Lacrosse; U of North Carolina At Chapel Hill; Miami (Ok) U

KERCHEVAL, SAMUEL; BLOOMINGTON, IN; BLOOMINGTON SOUTH HS; (JR); Hnr Roll; Nat Hon Sy; Yth Ldrshp Prog; Emplmnt; Stg Cre; Cyclg (V); Tennis (V L); Panther Activity Council

KERCHNER, KATIE B; MISHAWAKA, IN; MISHAWAKA HS; (SR); Hnr Roll; WWAHSS; Comm Volntr; DECA; Emplmnt; Chr; Stg Cre; Vllyball (J); U of Southern Indiana

KEY, JESSICA; CAMBY, IN; MOORESVILLE HS; (JR); Ctznshp Aw; Duke TS; Hi Hnr Roll; MVP; Otst Ac Ach Awd; Perf Att; Sci Fairs; St of Mnth; WWAHSS; Yth Ldrshp Prog; Comm Volntr; Hab For Humty Volntr; Red Cr Aide; Chrch Yth Grp; FCA; Mus Clb; Outdrs Clb; Prom Com; Spch Team; Tchrs Aide; Spanish Clb; Chr; Ch Chr; Dnce; Drl Tm; Hsbk Rdg; PP Ftbl; Sftball (J); Helping the Homeless; Helping Children with No Parents; Medicine Degree; Spanish and Law; Indiana U; Loyola U Chicago

KEYS, ASHLEY L; WINSLOW, IN; PIKE CTRL HS; (SR); Hnr Roll; Peer Tut/Med; Emplmnt; Prom Com; Tchrs Aide; Swmg (V L); Childhood Education; Vincennes U

KILNER, NICOLE; ENGLISH, IN; PERRY CTRL JR/SR HS; (JR); Perf Att; WWAHSS; 4-H; Emplmnt; Mus Clb; German Clb; Bnd; Drm Mjr; Jzz Bnd; Mch Bnd; Yrbk

KIMBLER, DUSTIN C; EDINBURGH, IN; EDINBURGH HS; (FR); Hi Hnr Roll; Otst Ac Ach Awd; Chess; Emplmnt; Scouts; Wdwrkg Clb; Outstanding Science Student Award; Outstanding History Student Award; Video Game Designer; Psychologist; ITT Technical Institute; Ball State U

KINCAID, AMBER N; AVON, IN; INDIANA AC; (SO); F Lan Hn Soc; Hi Hnr Roll; Hnr Roll; Nat Hon Sy; Otst Ac Ach Awd; Pres Sch; Comm Volntr; Hab For Humty Volntr; Hosp Aide; BPA; Chrch Yth Grp; Emplmnt; FCA; Key Club; Quill & Scroll; Stu Cncl (R); Sch Ppr (R); French Club Treasurer; Quill and Scroll Member; Pre-Law; Business Management; Pepperdine U; Duke

KINDER, LAURA; WINSLOW, IN; PIKE CTRL HS; (SO); Hi Hnr Roll; Hnr Roll; Perf Att; Emplmnt; SADD; German Clb; Bnd; Track (V L); Accounting; Pharmaceuticals; Indiana U; U of Evansville

KINDIG, WHITNEY; MISHAWAKA, IN; (JR); Hi Hnr Roll; Hnr Roll; Nat Hon Sy; WWAHSS; Comm Volntr; 4-H; DECA; Prom Com; SP/M/VS; Sftball (V L); Vllyball (V L); Wrstlg (V L); Accounting; Business Management; Manchester College; Ball State U

KING, AMANDA; COLUMBIA CITY, IN; COLUMBIA CITY HS; (FR); Hi Hnr Roll; Hnr Roll; Scouts; Bnd; Clr Grd; Mch Bnd; Pep Bnd; Accounting; Marine Biology; Indiana U; Miami U

KING, KACY J; LEBANON, IN; LEBANON HS; (JR); Hi Hnr Roll; Hnr Roll; Nat Hon Sy; Otst Ac Ach Awd; Pres Sch; WWAHSS; Comm Volntr; Hab For Humty Volntr; Chrch Yth Grp; Emplmnt; Key Club; Prom Com; Acpl Chr; Chr; Swg Chr; Chrldg (V L); Sftball (J); Cl Off (P, R); Stu Cncl (R); Sch Ppr (E, R); Physical Therapy; Indiana U; U of Evansville

KING, LYNLEY; FORT WAYNE, IN; SOUTHSIDE HS; (JR); Hnr Roll; WWAHSS; Peer Tut/Med; Photog; Tennis (J); Vllyball (V); Peers Educating Peers Program; Corporate Lawyer, Major in English; FBI Agent; U of Miami (In Miami, FL)

KING, MARIAH L; WINSLOW, IN; PIKE CTRL HS; (FR); Hi Hnr Roll; Chrch Yth Grp; DARE; Jr Ach; SADD; Ch Chr; SP/M/VS; Swg Chr; Chrldg (V L); Cl Off (V); Stu Cncl (R); Teacher; Oakland City U

KING, SARAH; COLUMBUS, IN; COLUMBUS NORTH HS; (JR); Hnr Roll; Yth Ldrshp Prog; Emplmnt; FCA; Quill & Scroll; Tchrs Aide; Track (V L); Vllyball (V L); Stu Cncl (R); Lit Mag (E); Sch Ppr (R); Member of CNHS Student Assembly; Sports Marketing; Business Management; Northwestern U; Miami of Ohio

KINSER, STEPHANIE; WILLIAMS, IN; MITCHELL HS; (SO); Ctznshp Aw; Hnr Roll; Perf Att; St of Mnth; Comm Volntr; Peer Tut/Med; SADD; Chr; Varsity Singers; Cosmetology; Vincennes U

KIRBY, SPENCER; MUNCIE, IN; YORKTOWN HS; (SR); Hnr Roll; WWAHSS; CARE; Comm Volntr; Chrch Yth Grp; DECA; Drma Clb; Emplmnt; Key Club; Off Aide; Tchrs Aide; Ch Chr; SP/M/VS; Stg Cre; Golf (J); Stu Cncl (R); CR (R); Aviation, Commercial Pilot or Flight Instruction; Medical, Physical Therapist; Ball State U; Purdue U

KIRTLEY, CHELSIE; ALEXANDRIA, IN; ALEXANDRIA-MONROE HS; (SO); 4H Awd; Ctznshp Aw; Hnr Roll; CARE; Comm Volntr; Peer Tut/Med; 4-H; Drma Clb; Emplmnt; Spanish Clb; Chr; SP/M/VS; Stg Cre; Bskball; Chrldg; Stu Cncl; TATU Club - Teens Against Tobacco Use; 4-H - 9 Yrs; Art; Animals; Ball State; Butler

KISER, JOSHUA J; HIGHLAND, IN; HIGHLAND HS; (SO); All Am Sch; Hnr Roll; Pres Ac Ftns Aw; Pres Sch; USAA; Comm Volntr; DARE; Emplmnt; Key Club; Spanish Clb; Bskball (J); Sccr (J); Track (V L); Architecture; Ball State U

KISER, MATTHEW S; HIGHLAND, IN; HIGHLAND HS; (FR); Hnr Roll; Pres Ac Ftns Aw; Pres Sch; Sci Fairs; Comm Volntr; DARE; Emplmnt; Key Club; Bskball (J); Sccr (J); Track (J); Business Lawyer; Valparaiso U; Wabash College

KITTO, ELIZABETH; FORT WAYNE, IN; HOMESTEAD HS; (SO); Hi Hnr Roll; Key Club; Tchrs Aide; Bnd; Mch Bnd; Pep Bnd; Psychology; Writing Arts; Duke U; New York U

KIVETT, KIM; INDIANAPOLIS, IN; PERRY MERIDIAN HS; (JR); Ctznshp Aw; Hnr Roll; Otst Ac Ach Awd; Perf Att; Pres Ac Ftns Aw; St of Mnth; Comm Volntr; Peer Tut/Med; DARE; Emplmnt; Key Club; Bskball (J); Chrldg (J); Medical; Criminal Justice; Indiana U; Indiana U and Purdue U

KLEHFOTH, ELIZABETH; ELKHART, IN; ELKHART CTRL HS; (SO); Hi Hnr Roll; Hnr Roll; Otst Ac Ach Awd; WWAHSS; Comm Volntr; Peer Tut/Med; Chrch Yth Grp; Drma Clb; Emplmnt; Key Club; Schol Bwl; Bnd; Mch Bnd; Pep Bnd; SP/M/VS; Cr Ctry (J); Creative Writing

KLEM, HEATHER L; JASPER, IN; JASPER HS; (JR); Hnr Roll; Perf Att; WWAHSS; Comm Volntr; Hosp Aide; Peer Tut/Med; Chrch Yth Grp; Emplmnt; Key Club; Prom Com; Scouts; SADD; Spanish Clb; Bnd; Clr Grd; Mch Bnd; Pep Bnd; Nursing Home Volunteer; Respiratory Therapist; Dental Hygienist; U of Southern Indiana

KLUESENER, EMILY; AVON, IN; AVON HS; (FR); Hnr Roll; Emplmnt; German Clb; Bnd; Jzz Bnd; Mch Bnd; Pep Bnd

KNIES, KATHERINE; JASPER, IN; JASPER HS; (FR); 4H Awd; Hi Hnr Roll; Pres Sch; Key Club; SADD; German Clb; Active in Key Club, SADD, German Club Also Play the Piano & Am a Former Girl Scout; Elementary Special Education; Occupational Therapy; U of Evansville; U of Southern Indiana

KOEHLER, LINDSAY M; VALPARAISO, IN; WHEELER HS; (JR); Hnr Roll; MVP; Nat Hon Sy; Key Club; French Clb; Dnce; SP/M/VS; PPSqd (V CL); Stu Cncl (R); Secretary of Key Club; Business Major; Valparaiso U; Hope U

KOEHNE, KIMBERLY R; GREENSBURG, IN; OLDENBURG AC; (SR); Hnr Roll; MVP; Nat Hon Sy; WWAHSS; Yth Ldrshp Prog; Peer Tut/Med; 4-H; Emplmnt; Mth Clb/Tm; Bskball (J); Vllyball (JC); Business; Accounting; Purdue U

KOEPKE, KAYLEE; AVON, IN; AVON HS; (SO); Ctznshp Aw; Hi Hnr Roll; Hnr Roll; Perf Att; Peer Tut/Med; Chrch Yth Grp; Key Club; Quill & Scroll; Ch Chr; Sch Ppr (R, P); Mission Work; Journalism; Psychology; Purdue U; U of Notre Dame

KONOPINSKI, TY; MIDDLEBURY, IN; NORTHRIDGE HS; (SR); Hi Hnr Roll; Nat Hon Sy; Perf Att; Peer Tut/Med; Chrch Yth Grp; DARE; Drma Clb; Emplmnt; SP/M/VS; CR (R); Sch Ppr (R); A Lead Role in Musical Sophomore Year; Secondary Education; Business Management; Indiana Wesleyan U

KOSCIELNY II, MICHAEL J; ELKHART, IN; CONCORD HS; (JR); Hi Hnr Roll; Nat Hon Sy; Otst Ac Ach Awd; Perf Att; Sci Fairs; Sci/Math Olympn; Yth Ldrshp Prog; Spec Olymp Vol; Chess; Chrch Yth Grp; Emplmnt; Key Club; Mth Clb/Tm; Quill & Scroll; Sci Clb; Scouts; Bnd; Mch Bnd; Pep Bnd; Cr Ctry (V); Track (V); Stu Cncl (R); Lit Mag (R); Sch Ppr (E); Eagle Scout; Secondary Teaching; Creative Writing; Butler U; Saint Joseph's College

KRAMER, DEREK; ANDERSON, IN; ANDERSON HS; (SO); Ctznshp Aw; Hi Hnr Roll; Hnr Roll; Nat Hon Sy; Comm Volntr; Spec Olymp Vol; Chrch Yth Grp; Bible Quiz Team

KRAMER, EMILY A; JAMESTOWN, IN; WESTERN BOONE JR/SR HS; (SO); 4H Awd; Hi Hnr Roll; Hnr Roll; Otst Ac Ach Awd; Pres Ac Ftns Aw; Comm Volntr; Chrch Yth Grp; Emplmnt; FCA; Key Club; Ntl FFA; Quiz Bowl; Scouts; Chr; SP/M/VS; Sccr; Sftball (V); Social Work; Spanish; Taylor; Indiana U

KRAMPE, RACHEL; EVANSVILLE, IN; CENTRAL HS; (SO); Hi Hnr Roll; St of Mnth; Yth Ldrshp Prog; Comm Volntr; Hab For Humty Volntr; Hosp Aide; ArtClub; Chrch Yth Grp; Emplmnt; Pep Squd; Chr; Swmg (V); Track (V); Stu Cncl (R); CR (R); Teen Advisory Council; Ohio Northern U; Indiana U

KRANZMAN, JUSTIN; WARSAW, IN; WARSAW CMTY HS; (JR); Hi Hnr Roll; Hnr Roll; Otst Ac Ach Awd; Sci/Math Olympn; Yth Ldrshp Prog; Comm Volntr; Peer Tut/Med; Red Cr Aide; AL Aux Boys; Chrch Yth Grp; Emplmnt; Mth Clb/Tm; Quiz Bowl; Schol Bwl; Sci Clb; Scouts; Track (J); Academic Social Studies Super Bowl Captain; Cardiology; Neurology; Cornell U; Harvard U

Kiser, Joshua J
Highland HS
Highland, IN

Kilner, Nicole
Perry Ctrl JR/SR HS
English, IN

Kemker, Liz
Jasper HS
Jasper, IN

Keller, Andy
Brownsburg HS
Brownsburg, IN

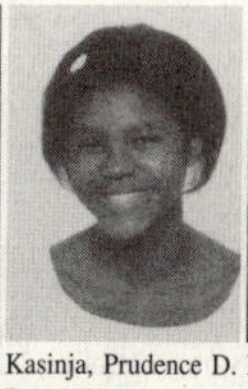
Kasinja, Prudence D.
Penn HS
Granger, IN

Kelleher, Ryan W
Carmel HS
Carmel, IN

Kendall, Michael A
Shakamak HS
Jasonville, IN

Kinser, Stephanie
Mitchell HS
Williams, IN

Kiser, Matthew S
Highland HS
Highland, IN

KREILEIN, STEPHANIE; JASPER, IN; (FR); Hnr Roll; Comm Volntr; Chrch Yth Grp; Key Club; SADD; Tchrs Aide; Spanish Clb; Tennis (J); Cross Country-Student Manager; Nursing

KREPS, KAITLIN; COLUMBUS, IN; COLUMBUS NORTH HS; (SO); Ctznshp Aw; Hnr Roll; Perf Att; WWAHSS; Comm Volntr; 4-H; Chrch Yth Grp; FCA; Key Club; Sftball (J); First Christian Church Basketball League; Fall and Summer League Softball; Indiana U; Ball State U

KRILL, BRETT A; ANGOLA, IN; FREMONT HS; (SO); Hnr Roll; Criminal Justice; Accounting; U of Pennsylvania; U Of Notre Dame

KRISTY, MELISSA; HIGHLAND, IN; HIGHLAND HS; (JR); F Lan Hn Soc; Hi Hnr Roll; MVP; Nat Hon Sy; Otst Ac Ach Awd; WWAHSS; Chrch Yth Grp; Key Club; Off Aide; Tchrs Aide; Spanish Clb; Mar Art; Tennis (V L); Vllyball (V L); Stu Cncl (R); National Society of High School Scholars; National Art Honor Society; Medicine; Indiana U

KRUGER, TERRA R; AKRON, IN; TIPPECANOE VALLEY HS; (SO); Ctznshp Aw; Hnr Roll; Peer Tut/Med; DARE; Scouts; Mar Art (J); Spanish Degree in College; Nursing Degree in College; Ivy Tech; Indiana U

KUEBLER, EMILY A; JASPER, IN; JASPER HS; (FR); Hnr Roll; Perf Att; Pres Ac Ftns Aw; Comm Volntr; Chrch Yth Grp; Key Club; Spanish Clb; Bnd; Mch Bnd; Pep Bnd; College; USI

KUHN, AMY E; EVANSVILLE, IN; EVANSVILLE CTRL HS; (SR); Ctznshp Aw; Hi Hnr Roll; Kwnis Aw; Nat Hon Sy; Perf Att; WWAHSS; Comm Volntr; Hab For Humty Volntr; Hosp Aide; 4-H; Chrch Yth Grp; DECA; Drma Clb; Emplmnt; German Clb; Bnd; Mch Bnd; Orch; Pep Bnd; Yrbk (E); Psychology; U of Louisville

KUHN, LUCYANNE; EVANSVILLE, IN; SIGNATURE SCH; (FR); 4H Awd; Ctznshp Aw; Hi Hnr Roll; Comm Volntr; 4-H; Chrch Yth Grp; Key Club; NtlFrnscLg; Spch Team; German Clb; CR (R); Journalism; History; Winston-Salem U; Florida State U

KUMAR, SAJEL; INDIANAPOLIS, IN; COVENANT CHRISTIAN HS; (JR); Hnr Roll; Perf Att; Drma Clb; Emplmnt; Spch Team; Chr; Ch Chr; SP/M/VS; Stg Cre; Lcrsse (V); Basketball Manager for V & J; Concert Choir; Pre-Medicine; Pediatric Surgery; Washington U in St Louis; Indiana U in Bloomington,

KUNTZ, PATRICIA A; INDIANAPOLIS, IN; BROAD RIPPLE HS; (JR); Hnr Roll; WWAHSS; Comm Volntr; Chrch Yth Grp; Key Club; Dnce; Key Club; Para Legal; Vincennes U

KUPER, TODD W; JASPER, IN; JASPER HS; (JR); Hnr Roll; MVP; Nat Hon Sy; Pres Ac Ftns Aw; Sci Fairs; WWAHSS; Yth Ldrshp Prog; Peer Tut/Med; Emplmnt; FCA; Key Club; SADD; Golf (V L); Tennis (J); Cl Off (P); Stu Cncl (S); Business Management; Purdue U; Indiana U

KURIC, KATIE; EVANSVILLE, IN; MEMORIAL HS; (SO); Hi Hnr Roll; WWAHSS; Key Club; Sccr (VJ L); Swmg (V L); Stu Cncl (R); Business; Psychology; Notre Dame U

KURIC, KYLE; EVANSVILLE, IN; MEMORIAL HS; (FR); Hnr Roll; Key Club; Bsball (J); Bskball (V L); Duke U; Indiana

KUROSKY, ERICKA; WARSAW, IN; WARSAW CMTY HS; (JR); Hi Hnr Roll; Hnr Roll; Nat Hon Sy; Nat Mrt LOC; Peer Tut/Med; Emplmnt; Prom Com; SADD; Vsity Clb; Cr Ctry (V L); Sftball (V CL); Track (V); Vllyball (J); Cl Off (S); Softball, All-Conference; Psychology; Medical (Osteopathy); Indiana U

KURUPPU, DULANJI; PLAINFIELD, IN; PLAINFIELD HS; (JR); Hi Hnr Roll; Nat Hon Sy; Otst Ac Ach Awd; Perf Att; St of Mnth; St Optmst of Yr; Yth Ldrshp Prog; Comm Volntr; Hosp Aide; Peer Tut/Med; Emplmnt; Key Club; P to P St Amb Prg; Svce Clb; Tchrs Aide; Spanish Clb; Cl Off (T); Secretary of Key Club; Plainfield Optimist Youth of the Year (2003); Biology; Biochemistry; Case Western Reserve U; Indiana U

KVRGIC, ZORAN; GRIFFITH, IN; GRIFFITH SR HS; (SO); Hi Hnr Roll; Nat Hon Sy; St Schl; St of Mnth; Comm Volntr; Mth Clb/Tm; Vsity Clb; Sccr (V); Track (V); CR (R); State Winner of Americanism Test; Team MVP Soccer; Medicine; Science; I.U. Bloomington; Purdue U, Calumet, Valparaiso U

LADIG, DANIEL A; NEW HAVEN, IN; NEW HAVEN HS; (SR); Hi Hnr Roll; Hnr Roll; Kwnis Aw; WWAHSS; Chrch Yth Grp; FCA; Quill & Scroll; Ftball (V L); Track (V CL); Wrstlg (V CL); Adv Cncl (R); Sch Ppr (E); Business Major; Ball State U

LAIN, JULIANN; SHELBYVILLE, IN; SOUTHWESTERN HS; (FR); Hi Hnr Roll; Perf Att; Pep Squd; Bnd; Pep Bnd; Tennis (V); BS Nursing; IUPUI (Indiana U) Purdue U Indianapolis; Vincennes U

LA JEUNESSE, ELIZABETH; VALPARAISO, IN; VALPARAISO HS; (SO); Hnr Roll; Otst Ac Ach Awd; Comm Volntr; Chrch Yth Grp; Key Club; Sch Ppr (R); Drama Class Performances; Intramural Water Polo; Journalism Major; Education Major; Marquette U

LAMARCHE, BRITTANY; JASPER, IN; JASPER HS; (FR); Hi Hnr Roll; Hnr Roll; Perf Att; WWAHSS; Comm Volntr; Key Club; SADD; French Clb; Bnd; Chr; Ch Chr; Mch Bnd; All-State Choir

LAMBERT, SARAH; BROWNSBURG, IN; BROWNSBURG HS; (SO); 4H Awd; Hi Hnr Roll; Hnr Roll; WWAHSS; 4-H; Chrch Yth Grp; FCA; Key Club; Bnd; Mch Bnd; Pep Bnd

LAMBERTH, GLEN; GALVESTON, IN; LEWIS CASS JR/SR HS; (SO); Ctznshp Aw; Hnr Roll; Sci/Math Olympn; St of Mnth

LA MOTHE, COLLIN; INDIANAPOLIS, IN; CATHEDRAL HS; (FR); Hi Hnr Roll; Comm Volntr; Chrch Yth Grp; Drma Clb; Jr Ach; Scouts; Spch Team; SP/M/VS; Life Scout; Journalism; Theater; U of Notre Dame; Stanford U

LAMPERT, MEGAN; HUNTINGBURG, IN; FOREST PARK HS; (SO); Hnr Roll; Perf Att; WWAHSS; Comm Volntr; Chrch Yth Grp; Emplmnt; Key Club; Pep Squd; Chr; Sftball (J); Clinical Psychology; Educational Counseling; Indiana U; U of Evansville

LANCASTER, EMILEE; COLUMBUS, IN; COLUMBUS NORTH HS; (JR); Hnr Roll; Nat Hon Sy; Comm Volntr; Hab For Humty Volntr; Drma Clb; Emplmnt; Key Club; Quill & Scroll; Cr Ctry (J); Track (J); Sch Ppr (E); PhD; MD; Indiana U; Purdue U

LANCE, KELSEY R; OAKLAND CITY, IN; WALDO J WOOD MEMORIAL HS; (FR); All Am Sch; Hnr Roll; Nat Ldrshp Svc; USAA; Jr Ach; Sftball (J); Yrbk (P); Pediatrician; Medical Technology; U of Southern Indiana; U of Kentucky

LAND, CHELSEA; ANDERSON, IN; HIGHLAND HS; (FR); Hi Hnr Roll; Hnr Roll; Otst Ac Ach Awd; Comm Volntr; DARE; Bskball (C); National Junior Honors Society; Child Protective Attorney; Physical Therapy; Purdue U; Butler U

LAND, SARAH; GREENCASTLE, IN; GREENCASTLE HS; (FR); Hnr Roll; Yth Ldrshp Prog; Peer Tut/Med; Spanish Clb; Chr; SP/M/VS; Chrldg (J L); Dvng (V L); Hsbk Rdg; Sftball (J L); Vllyball (J L); Wt Lftg

LAND, WHITNEY; JASPER, IN; JASPER HS; (SO); Sccr (J); Tennis (J); Stu Cncl (R)

LANE, STEVEN M; HOPE, IN; HAUSER HS; (JR); 4H Awd; Hnr Roll; WWAHSS; 4-H; Chr; SP/M/VS

LARGE, KELSEY; LEBANON, IN; LEBANON HS; (FR); Ctznshp Aw; Hi Hnr Roll; Otst Ac Ach Awd; Perf Att; St of Mnth; Comm Volntr; DARE; Scouts; Chr; SP/M/VS; Bskball; Hsbk Rdg; PP Ftbl; President's Award for Educational Excellence; Law; PhD; Harvard Law School; Indiana U

LARSON, CHRISTY; CARMEL, IN; CARMEL HS; (SO); Hnr Roll; Pres Ac Ftns Aw; Chrch Yth Grp; Pep Squd; Chr; Dnce; PPSqd (V); Dance Team; Psychology; Communications; Indiana U; Ball State U

LASHER, SARAH; ROCKPORT, IN; SOUTH SPENCER HS; (FR); 4H Awd; Hi Hnr Roll; Hnr Roll; Perf Att; 4-H; Chrch Yth Grp; Key Club; Ntl FFA; Bskball; Sccr

LATHREM, AMANDA; INDIANAPOLIS, IN; BEN DAVIS HS; (SO); 4H Awd; Hnr Roll; WWAHSS; Peer Tut/Med; 4-H; Photog; Scouts; Chr; Stg Cre; Handicapable Camp; Football Manager; Teaching; Conseling

LA VIGNE, STEPHANIE; INDIANAPOLIS, IN; PERRY MERIDIAN HS; (FR); Hnr Roll; St of Mnth; Comm Volntr; Chrch Yth Grp; FCA; Key Club; Chr; Tennis (J); Track (J); Cl Off (S, T); Stu Cncl; CR (S, T); Criminal Justice; Business; Indiana U; Butler U

LAWRENCE, ERIN; PORTLAND, IN; JAY CTY HS; (SR); 4H Awd; Hnr Roll; Nat Hon Sy; Red Cr Aide; 4-H; Chrch Yth Grp; Ntl FFA; Bnd; Mch Bnd; FFA Officer, Jr. Fair Board, Portland Chamber Student Board; FFA Hoosier Farmer Recipient; Agriculture Education; Purdue U

LAWSON, BRITTANY; SOUTH BEND, IN; ADAMS HS; (SO); Hi Hnr Roll; Hnr Roll; Otst Ac Ach Awd; Perf Att; Sci Fairs; St of Mnth; Comm Volntr; Peer Tut/Med; Chrch Yth Grp; Bnd; Jzz Bnd; Mch Bnd; Pep Bnd; Dvng (V); Sftball (J); Swmg (V); Tennis (J); CR (R); South Bend Honor Band - 4 Years; ISSMA Solo and Ensemble - 6 Years; Radiology; US Air Force

LAWTON, MELODY; WINONA LAKE, IN; WARSAW CMTY HS; (JR); Ctznshp Aw; Fut Prb Slvr; Hi Hnr Roll; Hnr Roll; MVP; Otst Ac Ach Awd; Pres Sch; St of Mnth; Peer Tut/Med; BPA; Chrch Yth Grp; DARE; Emplmnt; FCA; FBLA; Jr Ach; Mth Clb/Tm; SP/M/VS; Cr Ctry (J L); Track (V L); BPA-District Champion, State Qualifier; SADD-Representative; Pre-Med; Secondary Education; Purdue U; Anderson U

LAY, BRANDON; MONROEVILLE, IN; HERITAGE JR/SR HS; (FR); Hi Hnr Roll; Hnr Roll; Otst Ac Ach Awd; Perf Att; Comm Volntr; Chess; DARE; Emplmnt; Jr Ach; Chr; Wrstlg (V L); Teaching; Chemistry; Ball State U; Indiana U

LAYTON, ASHLEY; SOUTH BEND, IN; CLAY HS; (SR); All Am Sch; Hnr Roll; WWAHSS; Emplmnt; Mus Clb; Bnd; Mch Bnd; Sftball (J); Swmg (V L); Sch Ppr (R)

LEBRYK, JENNIFER N; SCHERERVILLE, IN; LAKE CTRL; (SR); Hi Hnr Roll; Nat Hon Sy; WWAHSS; Comm Volntr; Lttrmn Clb; Dnce; PPSqd (V CL)

LECHNER, CHAD; JASPER, IN; SOUTHRIDGE HS; (JR); Hnr Roll; Scouts; Ftball (J); Wt Lftg (V); School Sports Were At Jasper High School; Auto Technician; Diesel Technician; WyoTech; Lincoln Tech

LEE, HEATHER; OAKLAND CITY, IN; WALDO J WOOD MEMORIAL HS; (FR); 4H Awd; Hi Hnr Roll; Hnr Roll; Sci Fairs; 4-H; Chrch Yth Grp; Tennis (V); Vllyball (J); Sch Ppr (R); Yrbk (E); Volunteer-Assist W/ Hypnotherapy At Lazy G Ranch; Volunteer-(GCAS) Gibson Co Animal Services; Dolphin Trainer, Biology, Marine Biology

LEFFLER, MEGAN; LANESVILLE, IN; LANESVILLE JR/SR HS; (SO); 4H Awd; Hnr Roll; St of Mnth; Comm Volntr; 4-H; Chrch Yth Grp; FCA; Pep Squd; ROTC; Scouts; Tchrs Aide; French Clb; Chr; Bskball (J); Chrldg (J); Tennis (V); Vllyball (J); Silver 3 Years in Solo Ensemble Singing; Music Ministry; Evangel U; Central Bible College

LEHMAN, NATHAN D; MONROE, IN; ADAMS CTRL HS; (SR); 4H Awd; Ctznshp Aw; Hnr Roll; Nat Hon Sy; St of Mnth; Comm Volntr; Peer Tut/Med; 4-H; Chess; Chrch Yth Grp; Emplmnt; Jr Ach; Ntl FFA; Quiz Bowl; Voc Ind Clb Am; Ch Chr; Bskball (V CL); Adv Cncl (R); Stu Cncl (R); Section Star In Indiana FFA; National Honor Society; Agribusiness Marketing & Technology Management; U of Northwestern Ohio

LEICHTER, LANDON; SPENCER, IN; OWEN VALLEY CMTY HS; (FR); Hnr Roll; Perf Att; Comm Volntr; 4-H; Chrch Yth Grp; Emplmnt; Scouts; Ch Chr; Bskball; Sccr (V L); Track (V L); Eagle Scout; Elementary Education; Indiana U; Ball State

LEITHAUSER, EMILY; CARMEL, IN; CARMEL HS; (JR); F Lan Hn Soc; Hi Hnr Roll; Nat Hon Sy; Otst Ac Ach Awd; WWAHSS; Comm Volntr; Chrch Yth Grp; Drma Clb; Quill & Scroll; SP/M/VS; CR (R); Yrbk (E); Samford U; Elon U

LEMAN, NATASHA Y; LADOGA, IN; SOUTHMONT HS; (JR); Hi Hnr Roll; Hnr Roll; Nat Hon Sy; WWAHSS; Comm Volntr; Chrch Yth Grp; DARE; Emplmnt; Key Club; Lib Aide; Prom Com; German Clb; Chr; Swg Chr; Cr Ctry (VJ L); PP Ftbl (V); Track (V); Music Performance; Music Business Management; DePaul U; Saint Joseph's College

LENTS, HOLLY M; BROWNSBURG, IN; BROWNSBURG HS; (SO); Hnr Roll; Nat Ldrshp Svc; Otst Ac Ach Awd; Perf Att; St of Mnth; WWAHSS; Yth Ldrshp Prog; Comm Volntr; Peer Tut/Med; Chrch Yth Grp; DARE; FCA; Jr Cls League; Key Club; Spch Team; Chr; Tennis (J); Stu Cncl (R); Secretary of Choir / Treasurer; Nursing; U Southern Indiana; Indiana U

LESSING, ERIN M; FORT WAYNE, IN; HOMESTEAD HS; (FR); F Lan Hn Soc; Hi Hnr Roll; Hnr Roll; Hosp Aide; Emplmnt; Jr Cls League; Sccr (V L); Tennis (J); Recognized As a Hoosier Champion Because of Contribution to Women's Sports; Become a Doctor; Become a Pilot; Indiana U; Purdue U

LEUNG, STEPHEN; CORYDON, IN; PORTLAND CHRISTIAN SCH; (JR); Hnr Roll; Otst Ac Ach Awd; Sci Fairs; Sci/Math Olympn; Acpl Chr; Bnd; Chr; Ch Chr; Music; Indiana U Bloomington; U of Louisville

LEVI, CORENA N; MUNCIE, IN; MUNCIE CTRL HS; (JR); Hi Hnr Roll; Hnr Roll; Nat Hon Sy; Otst Ac Ach Awd; Comm Volntr; Peer Tut/Med; 4-H; Chrch Yth Grp; DARE; DECA; Emplmnt; Key Club; Mth Clb/Tm; MuAlphaTh; Ch Chr; SP/M/VS; Cl Off (V); 21st Century Scholar; The Presidential Award; Nursing; Spanish; Purdue; Indiana U

LEWIS, KAYLM; WEST TERRE HAUTE, IN; WEST VIGO HS; (SO); Hi Hnr Roll; Hnr Roll; Nat Hon Sy; WWAHSS; Comm Volntr; Ftball (V L); Track (V L); Wrstlg (L); Education; Indiana State U

LEWIS, MICHELLE; INDIANAPOLIS, IN; PIKE HS; (JR); Ctznshp Aw; F Lan Hn Soc; Hi Hnr Roll; Nat Hon Sy; Pres Sch; St of Mnth; WWAHSS; Comm Volntr; Peer Tut/Med; Spec Olymp Vol; BPA; Chrch Yth Grp; Emplmnt; Key Club; MuAlphaTh; Tchrs Aide; Orch; Key Club President; Academic Super Bowl; Pharmacy

LEWIS-MANNING, GINAI M; INDIANAPOLIS, IN; BROAD RIPPLE HS; (JR); Hi Hnr Roll; Hnr Roll; Nat Hon Sy; WWAHSS; Yth Ldrshp Prog; Comm Volntr; Chrch Yth Grp; Key Club; Lttrmn Clb; Prom Com; Chr; Ch Chr; Dnce; SP/M/VS; Sftball (V L); Cl Off (T); Stu Cncl (R); National Youth Leadership Forum on Law; Indianapolis Professional Youth Leadership Award; Political Science; Entertainment Lawyer; Winston-Salem State U (NC); Case Western Reserve (Oh)

LIBBERT, KEITH M; EVANSVILLE, IN; NORTH POSEY HS; (JR); Hi Hnr Roll; Otst Ac Ach Awd; Perf Att; Ftball (VJ); Engineering; CAD; Ivy Tech Evansville

LIETZ, ASHLEY; HIGHLAND, IN; HIGHLAND HS; (FR); Hnr Roll; Key Club; Track (J)

LIGHT, ASTARA C; BLOOMINGTON, IN; HOMESCHOOL; (SR); Comm Volntr; Emplmnt; Dnce; SP/M/VS; Wt Lftg; Philosophy and Religion; Architecture; Indiana U Bloomington; Ball State U

Lechner, Chad
Southridge HS
Jasper, IN

Land, Whitney
Jasper HS
Jasper, IN

Lance, Kelsey R
Waldo J Wood Memorial HS
Oakland City, IN

Kuruppu, Dulanji
Plainfield HS
Plainfield, IN

Kvrgic, Zoran
Griffith SR HS
Griffith, IN

Lane, Steven M
Hauser HS
Hope, IN

Leman, Natasha Y
Southmont HS
Ladoga, IN

LIM, JEONGKI; INDIANAPOLIS, IN; COVENANT CHRISTIAN HS; (JR); Nat Hon Sy; Peer Tut/Med; Chess; Mth Clb/Tm; MuAlphaTh; NtlFrnscLg; Sci Clb; Spch Team; Tchrs Aide; Tennis (J); Track (J); Stu Cncl (R); Sch Ppr (R); National Day of Prayer Oratorical Contest 2nd Place; Communication; Journalism; Northwestern U; Columbia U (College)

LINDEMAN, SAMANTHA; JASPER, IN; JASPER HS; (SO); Hnr Roll; WWAHSS; Peer Tut/Med; Emplmnt; Key Club; SADD; Spanish Clb; Bowling Team; National Society of High School Scholars; Elementary Education; Nursing; Indiana U-Purdue U-Indy; Indiana State U

LINNEMEIER, AMANDA; FORT WAYNE, IN; HERITAGE JR/SR HS; (FR); Hnr Roll; Perf Att; Medical Degree

LISTON, CASEY; HIGHLAND, IN; HIGHLAND HS; (FR); Hi Hnr Roll; Sci Fairs; Sci/Math Olympn; Comm Volntr; ArtClub; Key Club; Scouts; Clr Grd

LITTELL, OLIVIA; JAMESTOWN, IN; WESTERN BOONE JR/SR HS; (JR); Nat Hon Sy; WWAHSS; Comm Volntr; Emplmnt; Key Club; Foreign Clb; Student Assistant; Baseball statistician; Dental; Business Administration; Indiana U; Indiana U Purdue U Indianapolis

LLOYD, AMANDA M; INDIANAPOLIS, IN; BEN DAVIS HS; (SR); Hi Hnr Roll; Hnr Roll; WWAHSS; Chrch Yth Grp; Bnd; Chr; Mch Bnd; Academic Giant; Nursing; Special Education; Purdue U

LOCH, KATIE; FORT WAYNE, IN; NORTHROP HS; (SO); Ctznshp Aw; Hi Hnr Roll; Otst Ac Ach Awd; Comm Volntr; Emplmnt; Spch Team; Bnd; Dnce; PPSqd (J); Sccr (V L); Swmg (V L); Yrbk (R); Community Softball; Medicine

LOCKWOOD, ASHLEY; SYRACUSE, IN; FAIRFIELD HS; (JR); Hi Hnr Roll; Nat Hon Sy; WWAHSS; Peer Tut/Med; Spec Olymp Vol; 4-H; Chrch Yth Grp; Emplmnt; Key Club; Prom Com; Tchrs Aide; Tennis (V); Vllyball (V); Stu Cncl (T); National Honor Society; National Honor Society of Scholars; Medical Imaging; Radiology; Indiana U, Purdue U At Indianapolis; Ball State

LOECHEL, HALEY; MOORESVILLE, IN; MOORESVILLE HS; (MS); Hi Hnr Roll; Hnr Roll; Nat Hon Sy; Otst Ac Ach Awd; Chrch Yth Grp; Mus Clb; Orch; Sftball (L); Tennis (L); Law; History; Harvard

LOMPKIN, ELIZABETH; GALVESTON, IN; LEWIS CASS JR/SR HS; (JR); Hi Hnr Roll; Nat Hon Sy; Salutrn; USAA; WWAHSS; Comm Volntr; Peer Tut/Med; Chrch Yth Grp; Key Club; Scouts; SADD; Bnd; Drm Mjr; Mch Bnd; Pep Bnd; Golf (V); Swmg (V); Tennis (V); Sch Ppr (E); Church Music; Youth Ministry; Indiana Wesleyan U; Anderson U

LONG, CODY; ROCHESTER, IN; TIPPECANOE VALLEY HS; (FR); Hnr Roll; Otst Ac Ach Awd; Pres Ac Ftns Aw; St of Mnth; Comm Volntr; 4-H; DARE; Emplmnt; Lib Aide; Ftball (VJC); Stu Cncl (R); Teacher; Business; Purdue; IU

LONG, NICHOLAS; HOPE, IN; HAUSER JR/SR HS; (FR); Bsball (V L); Bskball (J); Tennis (V L); Cl Off (P); IHSAA 04-05 Baseball State Runner-Up; Sports Med/Sports Management; Architecture Design

LONGHI, EMILY K; VALPARAISO, IN; VALPARAISO HS; (FR); Hi Hnr Roll; Kwnis Aw; Nat Hon Sy; Pres Ac Ftns Aw; Comm Volntr; Peer Tut/Med; Chrch Yth Grp; Key Club; Bnd

LONGSTAFF, ALEXA M; EVANSVILLE, IN; MEMORIAL HS; (SR); Hnr Roll; Nat Hon Sy; Comm Volntr; Key Club; PP Ftbl (V); Sccr (J); Pre-Pharmacy; U of Kentucky; U of Mississippi

LOPEZ, ALEXIA J; SHERIDAN, IN; SHERIDAN HS; (JR); Hnr Roll; Hosp Aide; DARE; Emplmnt; Prom Com; Quiz Bowl; Clb; Chrldg (J); PP Ftbl (J); Track (J); Cl Off (T); Stu Cncl (P); Medical School; Surgeon; St John's U; U of Southern California

LOPEZ, LINDA; GARY, IN; CALUMET HS; (SO); Hnr Roll; Nat Hon Sy; WWAHSS; Chrch Yth Grp; DARE; Dnce; PP Ftbl; Tennis; PUSH, Pace and Guitar lessons; Dance Team; Art; Cosmetology

LOUGH, MICHAELA R; THORNTOWN, IN; WESTERN BOONE HS; (SO); Hi Hnr Roll; WWAHSS; Comm Volntr; Chrch Yth Grp; Emplmnt; Key Club; Quiz Bowl; Chrldg (V); Tennis (J); Cl Off (V); Winner of Biology Award; 2005 Sophomore Top Ten; Pharmacy; Purdue; Ball State

LOUVIERE, TYLER; GRIFFITH, IN; GRIFFITH HS; (SO); Hnr Roll; Perf Att; Pres Sch; Sci Fairs; Emplmnt; Scouts; Chr; SP/M/VS; Bsball (J); Sch Ppr (R); I Took the American Legion Flag and Government Test; Biology or US History Major; I Want to Teach in Biology or US History; Butler U; Louisiana State U

LOVALL, ELIZABETH; CRAWFORDSVILLE, IN; SOUTHMONT JR/SR HS; (FR); Hi Hnr Roll; Hnr Roll; 4-H; NYLC; Bnd; Mch Bnd; Pep Bnd; Family Doctor; MD Degree; Indiana U; Indiana U Purdue U Indianapolis

LOWS, MELISSA A; OSGOOD, IN; JAC-CEN-DEL HS; (SO); Bnd; Chr; Flg Crps; Pep Bnd; Yrbk; Medical Billing

LOYDA, KERSTIN; CARMEL, IN; CARMEL HS; (SR); F Lan Hn Soc; Hnr Roll; Nat Hon Sy; Comm Volntr; Chrch Yth Grp; Emplmnt; German Clb; Sccr; President-German Club; Medical Field; Purdue U

LUCAS, ALISHA; ST JOHN, IN; MERRILLVILLE HS; (SR); Hi Hnr Roll; Hnr Roll; Nat Hon Sy; WWAHSS; Peer Tut/Med; Red Cr Aide; DARE; Emplmnt; Key Club; French Clb; Chr; Chrldg; Bowling Team - 4 Yrs Captain; Pre-Med Pathology; Bio Medical Engineering Technology; Loyola U Chicago; DeVry U Chicago

LUCAS, JANNETTE; POLAND, IN; OWEN VALLEY CMTY HS; (JR); Hnr Roll; Nat Hon Sy; Perf Att; WWAHSS; Chrch Yth Grp; Emplmnt; FCA; Lttrmn Clb; Prom Com; ROTC; SADD; Spanish Clb; Bskball (J); Sftball (V L); Vllyball (VJCL); Chemical Engineering; Aerospace Engineering; Rose Hulman Inst of Tech, Terre Haute, IN; Purdue U, West Lafayette, IN

LUCAS, RACHEL; WALTON, IN; LEWIS CASS JR/SR HS; (JR); Hi Hnr Roll; Hnr Roll; Nat Hon Sy; Pres Ac Ftns Aw; St of Mnth; WWAHSS; Red Cr Aide; Spec Olymp Vol; Drma Clb; Emplmnt; Key Club; Lttrmn Clb; Off Aide; SADD; SP/M/VS; Stg Cre; Bskball (V); Cr Ctry (V); PP Ftbl (V); Track (V); Vllyball (J); Cl Off (S); Stu Cncl (P); Sch Ppr (E); SADD President; Key Club Secretary/Treasurer; Forensic Psychology; Web Design; Brevard Community College; Purdue U

LUEBCKE, SARAH P; CROWN POINT, IN; CROWN POINT HS; (SO); 4H Awd; Hnr Roll; Perf Att; Comm Volntr; Hosp Aide; Peer Tut/Med; 4-H; Chrch Yth Grp; DARE; FCA; Key Club; Pep Squd; Quiz Bowl; SADD; Bnd; Chr; Ch Chr; Pep Bnd; Stu Cncl (T); Sch Ppr (R); The Jon Milstead Reading Award; Spell Bowl Achievement; 4 Year Nursing Program; Radiology; Valparaiso U; Indiana U Concordia Riverford

LUEKEN, JOSHUA P; SAINT ANTHONY, IN; FOREST PARK HS; (SO); Ctznshp Aw; DAR; Gov Hnr Prg; Hi Hnr Roll; Hnr Roll; Otst Ac Ach Awd; Perf Att; Sci Fairs; WWAHSS; Peer Tut/Med; Chrch Yth Grp; Key Club; Quiz Bowl; Schol Bwl; Scouts; SP/M/VS; Stu Cncl (V); Marine Biology; U of Evansville, IN

LUNG, ALYSSA S; ELKHART, IN; CONCORD HS; (SO); Hi Hnr Roll; Perf Att; Scouts; Clr Grd; Dnce; Orch

LUTHER, CARISSA M; NORTH LIBERTY, IN; JOHN GLENN HS; (JR); 4H Awd; Hnr Roll; Perf Att; Yth Ldrshp Prog; Peer Tut/Med; 4-H; AL Aux Girls; Chrch Yth Grp; DARE; Mus Clb; Scouts; SADD; Spanish Clb; Bnd; Clr Grd; Mch Bnd; Pep Bnd; Chrldg (J); Tennis (J); 4-H Horse & Pony; Elementary Education; U of Southern Indiana; Bethel College

LYLES, NAOMI; GRIFFITH, IN; GRIFFITH SR HS; (SO); Hnr Roll; Hab For Humty Volntr; Chrch Yth Grp; DECA; FCA; Mus Clb; Chr; Ch Chr; Dnce; Bskball (L); Tennis (J); DECA; Candidate for Northern Indiana Pageant 05; Acting; Law; Georgia State U; Harvard School of Law

LYTTLE, AMBER M; FORT WAYNE, IN; HERITAGE JR/SR HS; (SR); Hi Hnr Roll; Hnr Roll; Nat Hon Sy; Perf Att; Comm Volntr; Peer Tut/Med; Sch Ppr (R); Yrbk (E); Over 127 Hrs. of Community Service; Sterling Sentinel Award Nominee; Business Administration-Finance; Ivy Tech; Indiana-Purdue Fort Wayne

MABE, SYLVIA L; GRANGER, IN; ADAMS HS; (SO); Hnr Roll; St of Mnth; Drma Clb; Photog; Bnd; SP/M/VS; Chrldg (J); Sftball (J); Drama; Business; Medical; Indiana U; Michigan State

MACEDO, DAISY; SOUTH BEND, IN; JOHN ADAMS HS; (SO); Hnr Roll; Perf Att; USAA; Clb; Law; IUSB

MACK, KIMBERLY M; MEMPHIS, IN; HENRYVILLE HS; (JR); Peer Tut/Med; Emplmnt; FCA; Off Aide; Prom Com; Chrldg (V); Elementary Education; Indian U Southeast

MADZONGUE, RUFARO; INDIANAPOLIS, IN; DECATUR CTRL H.S.; (JR); Hnr Roll; WWAHSS; Key Club; Prom Com; CR (R)

MAHAN, LAURA N; PRINCETON, IN; WALDO J WOOD MEMORIAL HS; (FR); Ctznshp Aw; Hi Hnr Roll; St of Mnth; Comm Volntr; Chrch Yth Grp; Tennis (V); Vllyball (V); Cl Off (S, T)

MALATINKA, RACHEL; HAMMOND, IN; MORTON HS; (SO); Hi Hnr Roll; Hnr Roll; Perf Att; St of Mnth; Yth Ldrshp Prog; Comm Volntr; Dbte Team; Dnce; PPSqd (V); Dentist; Pharmacist; Indiana State U; Arizona State U

MALLABER, BLAINE; NOBLESVILLE, IN; NOBLESVILLE HS; (FR); Hnr Roll; WWAHSS; Comm Volntr; Peer Tut/Med; Become a Helicopter Pilot in the Military; Purdue U

MANGOLD, CODY L; EVANSVILLE, IN; F J REITZ; (SR); Emplmnt; Quill & Scroll; Ftball (C); Sch Ppr (E, R, P); Journalism; History; U of Southern Indiana

MANLEY, PAIGE; SOUTH BEND, IN; RILEY HS; (FR); Hi Hnr Roll; Hnr Roll; Comm Volntr; Chrch Yth Grp; Sccr (V); Track (V); Teacher; Indiana U; Notre Dame U

MANN, JUSTIN; MEROM, IN; SULLIVAN HS; (FR); Hnr Roll; Sci/Math Olympn; Chrch Yth Grp; Ntl Beta Clb; Ntl FFA; Chr; Engineering; Purdue

MANNERING, CLAYTON; WALTON, IN; LEWIS CASS JR/SR HS; (JR); Ctznshp Aw; Hi Hnr Roll; Hnr Roll; MVP; Nat Hon Sy; Otst Ac Ach Awd; Pres Ac Ftns Aw; St of Mnth; WWAHSS; Comm Volntr; AL Aux Boys; Drma Clb; Emplmnt; FCA; Lttrmn Clb; Prom Com; SP/M/VS; Swg Chr; Bsball (J L); Ftball (V); Track (V L); Wrstlg (V CL); Cl Off (P); Stu Cncl (P); Sch Ppr (R); Yrbk (R); Conference Champion in Wrestling; Sectional Champion in Wrestling; Journalism; Political Science; DePaul U; Wabash College

MANNING, PATRICK; ANDERSON, IN; HIGHLAND HS; (SO); Hnr Roll; Pres Sch; Comm Volntr; ArtClub; Chrch Yth Grp; Drma Clb; SP/M/VS; Swmg (V); Yrbk (R); Literature & Writing; Journalism; Florida; Texas

MANSMANN, ERIN; CARMEL, IN; CARMEL HS; (JR); Hi Hnr Roll; Nat Hon Sy; Comm Volntr; Emplmnt; Quill & Scroll; Bnd; Sch Ppr (R); Yrbk (R); Rugby Team (V) (L); Psychology; Purdue U

MARKER, BETHANN R; LIBERTY, IN; UNION CTY HS; (JR); 4H Awd; Hnr Roll; Nat Hon Sy; St of Mnth; Comm Volntr; 4-H; Emplmnt; Ntl FFA; Tchrs Aide; Bskball (J); United States Senate Page; Indiana State Senate Page; Political Science; Government; U of Baltimore; U of Maryland

MARSCHAND, BETSY; GALVESTON, IN; LEWIS CASS JR/SR HS; (SR); Hi Hnr Roll; Nat Hon Sy; St of Mnth; Yth Ldrshp Prog; Comm Volntr; Peer Tut/Med; Red Cr Aide; AL Aux Girls; Chrch Yth Grp; Emplmnt; FCA; Key Club; Lttrmn Clb; SADD; Vsity Clb; Chrldg (V CL); PP Ftbl; Tennis (V L); Vllyball (V CL); Wt Lftg; Cl Off (V); Stu Cncl (R); United Youth of the United Way Secretary; Science; Business; U of Notre Dame; Boise-Hulman Institute of Technology

MARSHALL, ERICA R; INDIANAPOLIS, IN; PIKE HS; (FR); Hnr Roll; Kwnis Aw; WWAHSS; Yth Ldrshp Prog; Comm Volntr; Spec Olymp Vol; BPA; Dbte Team; Key Club; P to P St Amb Prg; Spch Team; Orch; PP Ftbl (V); Ran for Student Council Secretary; In United Council of Negro Women; Law (Juris Doctorate); Political Science; Valparaiso U; Fisk U

MARTIN, ANGELICIA C; LAFAYETTE, IN; (SO); Ctznshp Aw; Hnr Roll; Perf Att; Sci Fairs; St of Mnth; Comm Volntr; Peer Tut/Med; FTA; Ch Chr; Dnce; Chrldg (J); Sch Ppr (R); Creative Writing; Dance; Michigan State U; American Musical and Drama Academy

MARTIN, DAVID; COLUMBUS, IN; COLUMBUS NORTH HS; (SO); 4H Awd; Hi Hnr Roll; St of Mnth; WWAHSS; Comm Volntr; 4-H; Chrch Yth Grp; DARE; Key Club; Off Aide; Scouts; Ch Chr; Swg Chr; Cr Ctry (J L); Swmg (V L); Pre-Med; Pharmacy; Michigan State U; Arizona State U

MARTIN, LATRISHA; INDIANAPOLIS, IN; ARLINGTON HS; (MS); Hi Hnr Roll; Hnr Roll; Sci Fairs; Chrch Yth Grp; Bnd; Mch Bnd; Pep Bnd; Bskball (J L); 04-Healthy Living Award / '04 Science Bound; 05-Top Offensive Player; Computer Technology; WNBA Owner; Tennessee State; Ball State U

MARTIN, LEAH; CHANDLER, IN; BOONVILLE HS; (JR); 4H Awd; Hi Hnr Roll; Nat Hon Sy; WWAHSS; Hosp Aide; 4-H; AL Aux Girls; Chrch Yth Grp; Emplmnt; Key Club; Ntl FFA; Sftball (J); Vllyball (L); Stu Cncl (R); Dental Hygienist; Industrial Safety; U of Southern Indiana; U of Illinois

MARTIN, MEGAN M; PORTAGE, IN; PORTAGE HS; (SR); Ctznshp Aw; F Lan Hn Soc; Hnr Roll; Perf Att; St of Mnth; Comm Volntr; Prom Com; SADD; Tchrs Aide; French Clb; Orch; Arrowhead Ambassador; Academic Letter Orchestra Letter; Elementary Education; French; Purdue U North Central

MARTIN, REBECCA; ALEXANDRIA, IN; ALEXANDRIA-MONROE HS; (SO); Hnr Roll; Perf Att; DARE; Emplmnt; NYLC; Scouts; Spanish Clb; Chr; Dnce; SP/M/VS; Move to NYC, Do Broadway

MARTIN, SHARIESE L; INDIANAPOLIS, IN; H L HARSHMAN (MS); Hi Hnr Roll; Hnr Roll; Nat Hon Sy; Chrch Yth Grp; Drma Clb; Sci Clb; Tchrs Aide; Ch Chr; Flg Crps; SP/M/VS; Bskball; Cr Ctry; Track; People to People; Grad School; Harvard Law School; Ball State U

MARTINEZ, SARAH; INDIANAPOLIS, IN; BEN DAVIS HS; (SO); Hi Hnr Roll; Hnr Roll; Comm Volntr; Chrch Yth Grp; Mth Clb/Tm; Scouts; Chr; Sccr (J); Tennis (J); Stu Cncl (R); Nursing; Pediatrician; Ivy Tech; Indiana U Purdue U Indianapolis

MARTLAGE, EMELIE; GREENWOOD, IN; RONCALLI HS; (SR); Hnr Roll; WWAHSS; Comm Volntr; Spec Olymp Vol; Svce Clb; Spanish Clb; Chr; Stg Cre; CR (P); Evan Bayn Service Leaders Summit; Honor Roll; Occupational Therapy; Speech Pathology; Ball State U

MASSENGALE, HALEY; WILKINSON, IN; EASTERN HANCOCK HS; (SO); Nat Hon Sy; Otst Ac Ach Awd; Perf Att; DARE; Drma Clb; Acpl Chr; SP/M/VS; Chrldg (J); Sftball (J); Swmg (J); Vllyball (J); In Softball-Most Improved; Perfect Attendance; Nursing (RN) Dental Assistant; Ball State, IUPUI, U of Southern Indiana; Indiana U; Purdue U

MASSIE, MEGAN A; GREENSBURG, IN; NORTH DECATUR JR/SR HS; (SR); Perf Att; WWAHSS; Peer Tut/Med; 4-H; Emplmnt; Key Club; Lib Aide; Ntl FFA; SADD; Bnd; Clr Grd; Mch Bnd; Pep Bnd; Sftball (J); 4-H Horse Color Guard; Pre-Vet; U of Findlay

Martin, Shariese L
H L Harshman (MS)
Indianapolis, IN

Martin, Latrisha
Arlington HS
Indianapolis, IN

Lovall, Elizabeth
Southmont JR/SR HS
Crawfordsville, IN

Mangold, Cody L
F J Reitz
Evansville, IN

Massengale, Haley
Eastern Hancock HS
Wilkinson, IN

MASTERS, MICHAEL T; INDIANAPOLIS, IN; NEW BEGINNINGS HS; (SO); Hnr Roll; Sci Fairs; Peer Tut/Med; Chess; Bnd; Ftball (V); Stu Cncl (P); Automotive Mechanics; Automotive Management; Ivy Tech State College; U of Indiana

MATTINGLY, BRITNI; GARY, IN; CALUMET HS; (SO); Ctznshp Aw; Hnr Roll; MVP; Otst Ac Ach Awd; Perf Att; Sci Fairs; St of Mnth; WWAHSS; Comm Volntr; DARE; Lib Aide; Pep Squd; Scouts; Tchrs Aide; Vsity Clb; Bsball (V); Chrldg (J); Scr Kpr (V); Vllyball (J); Nursing; IU; Purdue

MAX, KAITLYN; ELKHART, IN; ELKHART CTRL HS; (FR); Hi Hnr Roll; Key Club; Bnd; Mch Bnd; Pep Bnd; Cl Off (S); Nursing Career

MAY, DANIEL; ELKHART, IN; CONCORD HS; (JR); Hi Hnr Roll; WWAHSS; Comm Volntr; Key Club; Off Aide; Quill & Scroll; Chr; SP/M/VS; Ftball (V); Lcrsse (V L); Stu Cncl (R); Sch Ppr (R); History Professor; Butler U; U of Notre Dame

MAY, MICHELLE K; LOGANSPORT, IN; LEWIS CASS JR/SR HS; (SR); Hnr Roll; WWAHSS; ArtClub; Chrch Yth Grp; Emplmnt; Key Club; Photog; Spanish Clb; Chr; Ch Chr; Cr Ctry (VJ); Track (V); Wt Lftg; Yrbk (P); I Am Involved in SADD; To Obtain a Career As a Graphic Designer; International Business College Fort Wayne, IN

MC ADAMS, MEGAN; MARION, IN; LAKEVIEW CHRISTIAN HS; (SO); 4H Awd; Hi Hnr Roll; Perf Att; Yth Ldrshp Prog; Comm Volntr; Peer Tut/Med; 4-H; Chrch Yth Grp; Emplmnt; Pep Squd; Bnd; Pep Bnd; Stu Cncl (R); Yrbk (P); 4-H Achievement Awards; Art Education; Indiana Wesleyan U; Huntington College

MC AVOY, JESSICA; HIGHLAND, IN; HIGHLAND HS; (SO); F Lan Hn Soc; Hnr Roll; Nat Hon Sy; Emplmnt; Key Club; Prom Com; Dnce; Scr Kpr (J); Track (J); Sports Marketing; Early Child Development; Indiana U Bloomington; Purdue U

MC BRIDE, MEGAN; NEW HAVEN, IN; NEW HAVEN HS; (FR); Ctznshp Aw; Hi Hnr Roll; Hnr Roll; Kwnis Aw; Perf Att; St of Mnth; Hosp Aide; DARE; Sftball (V); Vllyball (J); Honor Roll; Orthopedic Surgeon

MC CABE, JORDAN C; LAFAYETTE, IN; CTRL CATHOLIC HS; (FR); 4H Awd; Hnr Roll; Comm Volntr; 4-H; Chrldg (V L); Lafayette Ballet Co; Violin 4-H; Marine Biology; Medical Field; Indiana U; California State U

MC CALLISTER, KATIE E; ARLINGTON, IN; RUSHVILLE CONSOLIDATED HS; (SO); 4H Awd; Hnr Roll; Comm Volntr; Peer Tut/Med; 4-H; Chrch Yth Grp; Emplmnt; Key Club; Off Aide; Pep Squd; Scouts; Spch Team; Chr; Cheer Block; Jr Leaders; Nursing; Ball State U; Indiana State U

MC CAULEY, PHILIP S; INDIANAPOLIS, IN; LAWRENCE CTRL HS; (JR); Hi Hnr Roll; Hnr Roll; Nat Hon Sy; Perf Att; Comm Volntr; Peer Tut/Med; Chrch Yth Grp; Emplmnt; FCA; Key Club; Quill & Scroll; Spanish Clb; Track (J); Sch Ppr (R); Yrbk (E); Center for Leadership Development (Alumni); Students for the Betterment of Society; Architecture; International Affairs; U of Virginia; Washington U of St Louis

MC CLEERY, AMY; EDINBURGH, IN; EDINBURGH HS; (FR); Lawyer; Cosmetologist; Indiana Business; IUPUI

MC CLURE, KARA; SHELBURN, IN; NORTH CTRL HS; (SO); Hi Hnr Roll; Hnr Roll; MVP; Chess; Lib Aide; Mus Clb; Chr; SP/M/VS; Golf (V); Sftball (VJ); Music; ISU; Chicago U

MC COIN, KURTIS E; INDIANAPOLIS, IN; ARLINGTON HS; (JR); Ctznshp Aw; Hnr Roll; MVP; Sci Fairs; CARE; Emplmnt; Mus Clb; Bsball (V CL); Ftball (V L); Wt Lftg (V); Honor Roll Entire Year; World History Award; Aviation; Media; North Carolina State U; Purdue U

MC COLLUM, SHAWNA; LAGRANGE, IN; PRAIRIE HEIGHTS SR HS; (FR); Chrch Yth Grp; Pep Squd; Chrldg (J); Art; Business

MC CORD, ELENA; HIGHLAND, IN; HIGHLAND HS; (SO); F Lan Hn Soc; Hi Hnr Roll; Hnr Roll; Nat Hon Sy; Otst Ac Ach Awd; Comm Volntr; Chrch Yth Grp; Emplmnt; Key Club; Prom Com; French Clb; Chr; Dnce; PPSqd (V L); Track (V L); Stu Cncl (R); CR (R); Teach Sunday School, Vacation Bible School; Key Club Class Chase (Sec); Physical Therapy; Teaching; Purdue U, W Lafayette; Indiana U, Bloomington

MC CORMICK, KRISSY; WASHINGTON, IN; WASHINGTON HS; (JR); Hi Hnr Roll; Hnr Roll; WWAHSS; Hab For Humty Volntr; Drma Clb; Mus Clb; SADD; Acpl Chr; Chr; Clr Grd; Mch Bnd; Psychology; Musical Theatre; Indiana State U; Ball State U

MC CORY, CHELSEY; SEYMOUR, IN; SEYMOUR HS; (JR); Hi Hnr Roll; MVP; Nat Hon Sy; Yth Ldrshp Prog; Comm Volntr; Hab For Humty Volntr; Chrch Yth Grp; Emplmnt; Lttrmn Clb; Lib Aide; Quill & Scroll; Tchrs Aide; Vsity Clb; Latin Clb; PP Ftbl (V); Track (V L); Vsy Clb (V); Vllyball (V L); Yrbk (E); Chemistry Major; Law; Vanderbilt U

MC CRORY, AMY; HOPE, IN; HAUSER JR/SR HS; (SO); 4H Awd; Hnr Roll; 4-H; Chrch Yth Grp; FCA; Key Club; SADD; Tchrs Aide; German Clb; Track (V L); Ob Nurse; Physical Therapist; IUPUC; Evansville U

MC CULLOUGH, ANDREA; HOAGLAND, IN; HERITAGE JR/SR HS; (FR); Hnr Roll; Perf Att; Comm Volntr; Bnd; Mch Bnd; Pep Bnd; Winterguard Two Years; Medical/Health Services; Education

MC CULLOUGH, ANN; FT WAYNE, IN; HOMESTEAD HS; (SR); Hi Hnr Roll; Hnr Roll; Nat Hon Sy; WWAHSS; Yth Ldrshp Prog; Comm Volntr; Chrch Yth Grp; DECA; Emplmnt; Jr Ach; Prom Com; SP/M/VS; Chrldg (V L); Sftball (V CL); Adv Cncl (S); Stu Cncl (S); Student Leader in Campus Life; Dance Marathon Winner; Pre-Physician's Assistant; Pre-Med; Butler - Will Attend in August

MC CULLOUGH, MAURA-ANN V; SHERIDAN, IN; SHERIDAN HS; (JR); 4H Awd; Yth Ldrshp Prog; Peer Tut/Med; 4-H; Lib Aide; Vsity Clb; Bskball (V L); Track (V CL); Yrbk (R, P); Vet; Physician; Purdue; IU

MC CULLOUGH, SARAH; MONROEVILLE, IN; HERITAGE JR/SR HS; (SO); Hi Hnr Roll; Hnr Roll; Perf Att; Comm Volntr; DARE; FCA; Jr Ach; Off Aide; Sftball (V L); Genetics; Biological Sciences; Purdue U; Indiana U

MC DOWELL, MORGAN M; INDIANAPOLIS, IN; PIKE HS; (JR); Hi Hnr Roll; Hnr Roll; St of Mnth; Peer Tut/Med; Emplmnt; Key Club; Off Aide; Tchrs Aide; Now Certified As a C.N.A.; Law/Political Science; Radiology; Kentucky State U; U of Southern Indiana

MC GEE, RAQUAEL C; MUNCIE, IN; MUNCIE CTRL HS; (FR); Ctznshp Aw; Hnr Roll; WWAHSS; Comm Volntr; Peer Tut/Med; Key Club; Spanish Clb; Chr; Ch Chr; SP/M/VS; CR (R); VP - Key Club; Public Relations; Jackson State U

MC GHEHEY, MATTHEW L; CROWN POINT, IN; BOONE GROVE HS; (JR); 4H Awd; F Lan Hn Soc; Hnr Roll; 4-H; Chrch Yth Grp; DARE; Mus Clb; Spanish Clb; Bnd; Jzz Bnd; Mch Bnd; Orch; Bsball (J); Swmg (J); 8 Year Member - 4-H; Soccer Referee; Chemistry / Pharmaceutical; Computer Science; Purdue U; Butler U

MC GILL, CODY A; BOONVILLE, IN; WARRICK CHRISTIAN HS; (FR); Hi Hnr Roll; Perf Att; WWAHSS; Chrch Yth Grp; SP/M/VS; Bsball (J); Teachers Award, Perfect Attendance; Highest GPA; U of Evansville; Indiana State U

MCGRAW, ADRIAN; FISHERS, IN; INTERNATIONAL HS; (JR); Comm Volntr; Emplmnt; Mod UN; Acpl Chr; Bskball (V CL); Tennis (V); Stu Cncl (P, T); Yrbk (E, R, P)

MC GREW, BREEANNA; FRANCISCO, IN; WALDO J WOOD MEMORIAL HS; (FR); Ctznshp Aw; Hnr Roll; St of Mnth; Peer Tut/Med; 4-H; Chrch Yth Grp; DARE; Emplmnt; Jr Ach; Pep Squd; Scouts; Tchrs Aide; Stg Cre; Chrldg (JC); Golf (V); Stu Cncl; Nursing; Teaching; Indiana U; Indiana State U

MC INTYRE, DANIELLE; INDIANAPOLIS, IN; THE RENAISSANCE SCH; (SO); Chrch Yth Grp; Indiana U; Indiana State

MC KINNEY, ALYSSA; WINSLOW, IN; PIKE CTRL HS; (FR); Hnr Roll; Otst Ac Ach Awd; Perf Att; Chrch Yth Grp; Bnd; Mch Bnd; Pep Bnd; SP/M/VS; Track (J)

MC KINNEY, ASHLEY M; SAINT MARY OF THE WOODS, IN; WEST VIGO HS; (JR); Hi Hnr Roll; Hnr Roll; Chrch Yth Grp; RN; Forensic Scientist; Ivy Tech; Indiana State U

MC KINNEY, ELIZABETH; SEYMOUR, IN; SEYMOUR HS; (SO); Hi Hnr Roll; Nat Hon Sy; USAA; Chrch Yth Grp; Drma Clb; Emplmnt; Key Club; Tchrs Aide; Spanish Clb; Bnd; Ch Chr; Jzz Bnd; Mch Bnd; Tri-M Music Honor Society; Medical Doctor / Medical Missionary; Missionary; Indiana U; Indiana Bible College

MC KNIGHT, KELLI A; MITCHELL, IN; MITCHELL HS; (SO); Hnr Roll; Perf Att; 4-H; Drma Clb; SADD; Spanish Clb; SP/M/VS; Hsbk Rdg (V); High School Education; Northeastern Oklahoma U; Murray State U

MC LAUGHLIN, LAUREN; LAWRENCEBURG, IN; LAWRENCEBURG HS; (FR); Hi Hnr Roll; Key Club; Bskball (J); Sccr (V); Track (V)

MC MILLAN, KELLY; VALPARAISO, IN; VALPARAISO HS; (FR); Orch; SP/M/VS; Medicine; Neonatologist; Valparaiso U; Purdue

MC MULLEN, KELSEY M; LAWRENCEBURG, IN; LAWRENCEBURG HS; (JR); Hi Hnr Roll; Kwnis Aw; Nat Hon Sy; Perf Att; WWAHSS; Yth Ldrshp Prog; Comm Volntr; Hab For Humty Volntr; Chrch Yth Grp; Emplmnt; FCA; Key Club; Prom Com; Svce Clb; SP/M/VS; Stg Cre; Sccr (J); Tennis (V L); Cl Off (V, S, T); Stu Cncl (P, S); President-Secretary of Key Club; Attended Richard Lugar Future World Leaders Symposium; Political Science; International Relations; Cincinnati Christian U; Wheaton U

MC NEAL, SHANICE; INDIANAPOLIS, IN; (JR); Hnr Roll; Nat Hon Sy; DECA; Emplmnt; Candidate for National Honors Society; To Be a Pediatrician; Indiana State U; IUPUI

MEADOWS, ALAINA J; HANOVER, IN; SOUTHWESTERN MIDDLE SR HS; (FR); Hi Hnr Roll; Hnr Roll; Comm Volntr; Hab For Humty Volntr; Peer Tut/Med; 4-H; Chrch Yth Grp; Drma Clb; FCA; Pep Squd; Scouts; SADD; Spanish Clb; Clr Grd; Flg Crps; Mch Bnd; SP/M/VS; Sftball (V); Cl Off (T); Stu Cncl (R); CR (R); Jefferson County Pride; Pediatrician; Early Education; U of North Carolina; Saint Mary of the Woods

MEDLOCK, LESLIE M; JASONVILLE, IN; SHAKAMAK HS; (SR); Nat Hon Sy; WWAHSS; Peer Tut/Med; BPA; Emplmnt; FCCLA; Quill & Scroll; Foreign Clb; Chr; Bskball (L); Cr Ctry; Stu Cncl (R); Sch Ppr (R, P); Radiography; Ivy Tech State College

MEHRINGER, BROGAN; JASPER, IN; JASPER HS; (SO); DAR; Hi Hnr Roll; Perf Att; Hosp Aide; Peer Tut/Med; FCA; Key Club; Lttrmn Clb; SADD; Vsity Clb; Spanish Clb; Sccr (V L); Track (V L); Stu Cncl (R); Student Council-Outstanding Class Rep.; Texas U; Indiana U

MEINECKE, KAYLAN M; CARMEL, IN; CARMEL SR HS; (SO); Hi Hnr Roll; Hnr Roll; Otst Ac Ach Awd; Perf Att; Sci Fairs; St of Mnth; Yth Ldrshp Prog; Comm Volntr; Chrch Yth Grp; DARE; Emplmnt; Lib Aide; Chr; Ch Chr; SP/M/VS; Stu Cncl (R); CR (R); Michigan State U Kid's College; Tennis - High School All-Stars; Secondary Teaching; Astronomical Science; Michigan State U; Purdue U

MELLINGER, MELISSA; CARMEL, IN; CARMEL SR HS; (SO); Hi Hnr Roll; Hnr Roll; Pres Ac Ftns Aw; Comm Volntr; DARE; Drma Clb; Scouts; Chr; Dnce; SP/M/VS; Stg Cre; Chrldg (J); Track (J); Stu Cncl (R); Sch Ppr (R); Honor Bar Thespian; Musical Theatre; Education; U of Michigan; Indiana U

MENDENHALL, SARAH; TIPTON, IN; TIPTON HS; (SO); 4H Awd; Hi Hnr Roll; Hnr Roll; Otst Ac Ach Awd; Pres Ac Ftns Aw; Yth Ldrshp Prog; Comm Volntr; Peer Tut/Med; 4-H; Chrch Yth Grp; DARE; Emplmnt; Key Club; Photog; Scouts; SADD; SP/M/VS; Swg Chr; Swmg (V); SADD Officer (Vice President); Key Club Officer (Bulletin Board Editor); Meteorology; Graphic Design; Purdue U; Ball State U

MERIDA, MECAYLA; BLOOMINGTON, IN; BLOOMINGTON HS; (SR); Ctznshp Aw; Hnr Roll; Perf Att; St of Mnth; Comm Volntr; DARE; Volunteer at Bloomington Hospital Cytology Department and Offered Full Time Job; Surgical Technology; Ivy Tech, Bloomington; Surgical Technology Program at Hospital, Bloomington, IN

MERRITT, DAVID B; EVANSVILLE, IN; F J REITZ HS; (SR); Hnr Roll; Comm Volntr; 4-H; BPA; Cmptr Clb; DECA; Emplmnt; FCA; Photog; Quill & Scroll; Ftball (VJ); Sch Ppr (P); Yrbk (R, P); DECA State Qualifier; Web Developer Entrepreneur; U of Southern Indiana

MERWIN, LINDSAY; EVANSVILLE, IN; CENTRAL HS; (JR); Hi Hnr Roll; Nat Hon Sy; St of Mnth; WWAHSS; Chrch Yth Grp; Drma Clb; Emplmnt; Mus Clb; Prom Com; Spch Team; Spanish Clb; Chr; SP/M/VS; Tennis (J); Cl Off (R); Stu Cncl (R); English Literature; Communications / Media Journalism; Vanderbilt U; Northwestern U

MESSERSMITH, BRACHLA R; MARION, IN; OAK HILL HS; (JR); 4H Awd; Ctznshp Aw; F Lan Hn Soc; Hi Hnr Roll; Hnr Roll; Nat Hon Sy; St of Mnth; Comm Volntr; Peer Tut/Med; 4-H; Dbte Team; FCA; NtlFrnscLg; Pep Squd; Prom Com; Quiz Bowl; Tchrs Aide; Chr; Dnce; Chrldg (V CL); PP Ftbl (L); Vsy Clb (L); Stu Cncl (R); The National Society of High School Scholars; Optometry; Corporate Law; Boston U/Miami U (Miami Florida); Florida State U/Indiana U

MESSICK, CADE P; JASPER, IN; JASPER HS; (JR); 4H Awd; Hi Hnr Roll; Pres Ac Ftns Aw; WWAHSS; Yth Ldrshp Prog; Comm Volntr; Peer Tut/Med; 4-H; AL Aux Boys; Chrch Yth Grp; DARE; Emplmnt; Key Club; SADD; Bnd; Mch Bnd; Pep Bnd; 4-H junior Leaders; Engineering; Purdue U

MESSICK, CODY P; JASPER, IN; JASPER HS; (FR); Hi Hnr Roll; WWAHSS; Comm Volntr; 4-H; Emplmnt; Key Club; SADD; Bnd; Mch Bnd; Pep Bnd; Computer Graphics Design.; Journalism; Purdue U; Rose Hulman

MESSMER, ALISON; JASPER, IN; JASPER HS; (JR); Hnr Roll; WWAHSS; Comm Volntr; Hosp Aide; Peer Tut/Med; Chrch Yth Grp; FCA; Key Club; Pep Squd; Prom Com; SADD; Spanish Clb; Bnd; Ch Chr; Clr Grd; Mch Bnd; JHS Color Guard Director's Award; Psychology; Indiana U

METTERT, CARRIE; FORT WAYNE, IN; NORTHROP HS; (JR); Ctznshp Aw; Hi Hnr Roll; Nat Hon Sy; Otst Ac Ach Awd; Perf Att; WWAHSS; Comm Volntr; Emplmnt; Svce Clb; Bnd; Chr; Clr Grd; Dnce; National Honor Society; Color Guard Captain; Nursing; Medicine; Indiana U, Purdue U-Indianapolis; Purdue U-West Lafayette, IN

MEYER, ALEXANDRA; FERDINAND, IN; FOREST PARK HS; (JR); Hnr Roll; Nat Hon Sy; WWAHSS; Comm Volntr; Peer Tut/Med; 4-H; AL Aux Girls; Emplmnt; Key Club; Ntl Beta Clb; Pep Squd; Prom Com; SADD; Chr; Clr Grd; Dnce; SP/M/VS; Chrldg (J); Sccr (J); Track (V); Sch Ppr (R); Yrbk (P); State Champion-Dance; Journalism-Advertising; Indiana U; U of Southern Indiana

Merritt, David B
F J Reitz HS
Evansville, IN

Mellinger, Melissa
Carmel SR HS
Carmel, IN

May, Michelle K
Lewis Cass JR/SR HS
Logansport, IN

Mc Cory, Chelsey
Seymour HS
Seymour, IN

Messersmith, Brachla R
Oak Hill HS
Marion, IN

MEYER, BECKY; GREENWOOD, IN; CTR GROVE HS; (SO); Hnr Roll; St of Mnth; WWAHSS; Comm Volntr; Hab For Humty Volntr; Hosp Aide; Chrch Yth Grp; FCA; Key Club; Prom Com; Tchrs Aide; Spanish Clb; Chr; Nursing; Indiana Wesleyan U; Anderson U

MEYER, SCOTT E; JASPER, IN; JASPER HS; (SO); Hnr Roll; WWAHSS; Peer Tut/Med; Emplmnt; Key Club; Spanish Clb; Bnd; Jzz Bnd; Mch Bnd; Pep Bnd; Football Homecoming Court; Peer Mentor/Outstanding Bandsman; Finance; Accounting; Indiana U; U of Evansville

MEYER, TESSA L; VALPARAISO, IN; VALPARAISO HS; (FR); Hi Hnr Roll; Hnr Roll; Kwnis Aw; Nat Hon Sy; Perf Att; Yth Ldrshp Prog; Comm Volntr; Spec Olymp Vol; Chrch Yth Grp; Key Club; Prom Com; Svce Clb; Bnd; Church Acolyte; Leader of Local K-Kids Club; Education; Pediatrics

MICHAEL, MEGAN; ANDERSON, IN; HIGHLAND HS; (FR); Hnr Roll; Comm Volntr; Chrch Yth Grp; Emplmnt; Chr; Wrestling Manager; Psychology; Ball State; Indiana U Bloomington

MICHEL, STEPHANIE L; NEWBURGH, IN; REITZ MEMORIAL HS; (JR); Hnr Roll; WWAHSS; Spec Olymp Vol; Chrch Yth Grp; Emplmnt; Key Club; Pep Squd; P to P St Amb Prg; Spanish Clb; Chr; SP/M/VS; Stg Cre; Sch Ppr (R); Modern Music Masters Society - Tri-M; Chaplain of "Co Ed 4" - YMCA Club; Hotel Management; Business Management; Western Kentucky U

MIKA, KATELYN M; VALPARAISO, IN; VALPARAISO HS; (FR); Hnr Roll; Nat Hon Sy; Perf Att; Sci/Math Olympn; WWAHSS; Peer Tut/Med; ArtClub; Chrch Yth Grp; DARE; Drma Clb; Fr of Library; Key Club; Sci Clb; Scouts; Bnd; Mch Bnd; National Science Olympiad Finalist 2003/2004; Certified Open Water Scuba Diver; Genetic Engineer; Marine Biologist; Indiana U

MILAM, GREGORY C; LEBANON, IN; LEBANON HS; (JR); Hnr Roll; Perf Att; Pres Sch; Comm Volntr; Key Club; Lttrmn Clb; Prom Com; Tchrs Aide; Bskball (V); Golf (V); Tennis (V); Spanish Award; Key Club Secretary; Attorney; Business

MILES, LA'TASHA; EAST CHICAGO, IN; EAST CHICAGO CTRL HS; (JR); Hnr Roll; Peer Tut/Med; Mus Clb; Chr; Track

MILLER, AMBER N; POSEYVILLE, IN; NORTH POSEY HS; (JR); Hi Hnr Roll; Hnr Roll; Peer Tut/Med; Spanish Clb; School Committee Sophomore Year; Nursing, Criminal Law; Indiana State U; U of Southern Indiana

MILLER, ASHLEY M; INDIANAPOLIS, IN; LAWRENCE CTRL HS; (SO); Hnr Roll; St of Mnth; WWAHSS; Key Club; Chr; SP/M/VS; Swmg (V); Running the Indianapolis Mini Marathon; Teaching; Nursing; Ball State U; Indiana U

MILLER, BRIAN; OTWELL, IN; PIKE CTRL HS; (FR); 4-H; Wrstlg (J); Architecture; Art; Oakland City U; Purdue U

MILLER, CASEY; ELWOOD, IN; ELWOOD HS; (JR); Hi Hnr Roll; MVP; Nat Hon Sy; Latin Clb; Chrldg (JC); PP Ftbl (V C); Sftball (V CL); Swmg (V L); Vllyball (V CL); Stu Cncl (R); Yrbk (E); English; Law; Indiana U-Bloomington; Purdue U

MILLER, DAVID L; KIMMELL, IN; WEST NOBLE HS; (SR); Eagle Scout; Automotive Technician; Lincoln Technical Institute

MILLER, D LUKE; ELKHART, IN; JIMTOWN HS; (SR); Bnd; Ch Chr; Jzz Bnd; Pep Bnd; Ftball (V C); National Honor Society Member; Postponing Sexual Involvement Leader; Communications / Business Administration; Broadcasting; Bethel College

MILLER, DUSTIN; ANGOLA, IN; PRAIRIE HEIGHTS SR HS; (JR); Ctznshp Aw; F Lan Hn Soc; Hnr Roll; Wrstlg (V); Army National Guard; Economics; Electronic and Information Technology Systems; United States Military Academy; Lincoln Tech

MILLER, JACKIE; HARTFORD CITY, IN; BLACKFORD HS; (FR); Hnr Roll; USAA; Comm Volntr; Drma Clb; Sci Clb; Spanish Clb; SP/M/VS; Golf (J); Registered Nurse; Ball State U

MILLER, JACOB; AVON, IN; AVON HS; (SO); Hi Hnr Roll; Hnr Roll; Nat Hon Sy; Otst Ac Ach Awd; WWAHSS; Chrch Yth Grp; Emplmnt; FCA; Key Club; Golf (V L); Sccr (J); Architecture; Engineering; Purdue; Ball State

MILLER, KATHERINE; EVANSVILLE, IN; SIGNATURE SCH; (SO); All Am Sch; Nat Hon Sy; Comm Volntr; ArtClub; NtlFrnscLg; Spch Team; Stu Cncl; National Qualifier in Speech; PTSA Reflection State Qualifier - Art; Museum Curator / Art History; English / Writing; Indiana U; Chicago Art Institute

MILLER, LEAH; JASPER, IN; JASPER HS; (FR); 4H Awd; Hi Hnr Roll; Perf Att; 4-H; FCA; Key Club; Spanish Clb; Chr; Bskball (J); Hsbk Rdg; Sftball (VJ); Medicine

MILLER, NICK; JASPER, IN;; Hnr Roll; Perf Att; WWAHSS; Emplmnt; Jr Ach; Junior Achievement; Key Club-Perfect Attendance-2 Yrs.

MILLER, TIMOTHY; HAMMOND, IN; MORTON SR HS; (FR); Engineering; Computer Programming; Purdue U; Indiana U

MILLIGAN, JOHN; ANDERSON, IN; HIGHLAND HS; (FR); All Am Sch; Hnr Roll; Track (J); Pharmaceuticals; Doctor; U Of Notre Dame; Purdue U

MILLS, ABBY; MUNCIE, IN; SHENANDOAH HS; (JR); F Lan Hn Soc; Hi Hnr Roll; Nat Hon Sy; WWAHSS; Comm Volntr; Chrch Yth Grp; Drma Clb; Emplmnt; Prom Com; Bnd; Mch Bnd; Pep Bnd; SP/M/VS; Stu Cncl (V); Middletown Lions Club Fair Queen of 2005; Nominated Twice for "You Make a Difference"; Business Major; English Literature; Ball State U

MILLS, STEPHEN R; EVANSVILLE, IN; CENTRAL HS; (SO); Ctznshp Aw; Hnr Roll; Chess; Chrch Yth Grp; Mus Clb; Bnd; Mch Bnd; Orch; Pep Bnd; All-City Honors Band; All-City Honors Orchestra; Business; Finance; U of Kentucky; Samford U

MINOR, FRANK; INDIANAPOLIS, IN; ARLINGTON HS; (SO); Hnr Roll; Comm Volntr; Chrch Yth Grp; Lib Aide

MINTON, KATHERINE; CARMEL, IN; CARMEL HS; (JR); Ctznshp Aw; F Lan Hn Soc; Hi Hnr Roll; Nat Hon Sy; Otst Ac Ach Awd; Comm Volntr; Peer Tut/Med; Chrch Yth Grp; Emplmnt; Key Club; Photog; Prom Com; Quill & Scroll; Lcrsse (V); Cl Off (V); CR (R); Yrbk (P); National Honor Society - President; International Business; Marketing / Advertising; Indiana U; Southern Methodist U TX

MITCHELL, AMANDA L; LEBANON, IN; WESTERN BOONE JR/SR HS; (JR); 4H Awd; F Lan Hn Soc; Hnr Roll; Otst Ac Ach Awd; Perf Att; WWAHSS; Comm Volntr; Hab For Humty Volntr; 4-H; Chrch Yth Grp; FCA; Key Club; Prom Com; Tchrs Aide; Ch Chr; SP/M/VS; Stu Cncl (R); Sunshine Society, Campus Life; Business; Art; Purdue U; Indiana U

MOED, MEGHAN; CARMEL, IN; CARMEL HS; (JR); F Lan Hn Soc; Hi Hnr Roll; Nat Hon Sy; Chrch Yth Grp; DECA; Emplmnt; Key Club; Quill & Scroll; German Clb; Chrldg (VJ); Yrbk (E); Scholar Athlete Award; Quill and Scroll Award; Business Management; Law Degree; Butler U; Syracuse U

MOELLER, COREY; FORT WAYNE, IN; NORTHSIDE HS; (MS); Hnr Roll; Orch; Ftball (V); Music; Computer Technology; Indiana U-Bloomington; Saint Francis

MOELLER, ERIC; NEW HAVEN, IN; NEW HAVEN HS; (SO); Hi Hnr Roll; Hnr Roll; Kwnis Aw; MVP; Perf Att; St of Mnth; WWAHSS; Chess; Drma Clb; Vsity Clb; Chr; SP/M/VS; Stg Cre; Cr Ctry (V L); Sccr (V L); Track (J); Softball Manager; Architecture; Aviation Mechanics; Purdue U

MOLLAUN, CHELSIE; LAWRENCEBURG, IN; LAWRENCEBURG HS; (FR); Ctznshp Aw; F Lan Hn Soc; Hi Hnr Roll; Otst Ac Ach Awd; Perf Att; Pres Ac Ftns Aw; Comm Volntr; Key Club; Lttrmn Clb; Quiz Bowl; Vsity Clb; Swg Chr; Bskball (V L); Chrldg; Track (V L); Vllyball (J); Journalism/ Broadcasting; Physical Therapy; Indiana U

MONCADA, ELISHA; VALPARAISO, IN; VALPARAISO HS; (FR); Comm Volntr; Key Club; Doctor; Lawyer; Northwestern; DePaul

MONESMITH, CAITLIN; JASPER, IN; JASPER HS; (FR); 4H Awd; DAR; Hi Hnr Roll; Otst Ac Ach Awd; Sci Fairs; WWAHSS; Comm Volntr; 4-H; Chrch Yth Grp; Key Club; Schol Bwl; Spch Team; SADD; Spanish Clb; Bnd; Chr; Ch Chr; Jzz Bnd; Science/Pre-Med; Education; Northwestern U; Indiana U

MONK, KAYLA M; SULLIVAN, IN; SULLIVAN HS; (SO); 4H Awd; Hnr Roll; Nat Hon Sy; Pres Ac Ftns Aw; Sci Fairs; St of Mnth; WWAHSS; Comm Volntr; Peer Tut/Med; 4-H; HO'Br Yth Ldrshp; Ntl Beta Clb; Ntl FFA; Chr; 1st Runner Up 4-8 Fair Queen; Indiana Leadership Rep.; Culinary Arts; Sullivan U

MONROE, CHELSI; MADISON, IN; SOUTHWESTERN MIDDLE/SR HS; (FR); Hnr Roll; St of Mnth; Comm Volntr; Pep Squd; Dnce

MONTGOMERY, BRANDON A; MAUCKPORT, IN; CORYDON CTRL HS; (FR); Competes in Special Olympics; Would Like to Work in Construction

MONTRASTELLE, LAUREN E; EVANSVILLE, IN; REITZ MEMORIAL HS; (JR); Chrch Yth Grp; Key Club; Prom Com; Cr Ctry (V); Sccr (V); Track (V); Stu Cncl; CR; IUPUI; Western Kentucky U

MOORE, ASHLEY M; SCOTTSBURG, IN; SCOTTSBURG HS; (JR); Hnr Roll; Emplmnt; Photog; Quill & Scroll; Sch Ppr (E); Bachelors of Elementary Education; Indiana U Southeast; U of Florida

MOORE, BRITTANI L; HAMMOND, IN; MORTON SR HS; (FR); Hi Hnr Roll; Hnr Roll; Flg Crps; SP/M/VS; Pediatrician; Physical Therapist; DePaul U; Morehouse College

MOORE, HANNA L; BRAZIL, IN; CLAY CITY JR/SR HS; (FR); Hi Hnr Roll; MVP; Nat Stu Ath Day Aw; Pres Ac Ftns Aw; Pres Sch; Yth Ldrshp Prog; BPA; Chrch Yth Grp; FCA; Lib Aide; Pep Squd; SADD; Vsity Clb; Dnce; Chrldg (J); GAA (V); Track (V L); Vsy Clb (V); Vllyball (V L); Cl Off (P); 8th Gr. Outstanding Math, Science Student; Medical Degree (Surgeon); Chemical Engineering; Rose Hulman; Indiana U/Purdue U

MOORE, JAMIE L; WHEATFIELD, IN; KANKAKEE VALLEY HS; (FR); Hi Hnr Roll; Otst Ac Ach Awd; Pres Sch; Sci Fairs; St of Mnth; Comm Volntr; Chrch Yth Grp; Jr Ach; Schol Bwl; Svce Clb; Foreign Clb; Chr; Ch Chr; Track (L); Vllyball (J); Lit Mag (R); National Junior Honor Society; Most Improved and Sportsmanship Awards; Medical Technology (Pediatrician); Nutritional Science (Nutritionist); Purdue U; Valparaiso U

MOORE, JAY E; HAMMOND, IN; MORTON HS; (SO); Hnr Roll; St of Mnth; Comm Volntr; Peer Tut/Med; Chrch Yth Grp; DARE; Emplmnt; Key Club; Mus Clb; Pep Squd; Photog; Prom Com; Acpl Chr; Bnd; Chr; Dnce; Sch Ppr (E, R, P); Marched in Chicago State Street Parade; Cosmetology; Music; Ball State U; Indiana State U

MOORE, KARI N; OSGOOD, IN; SOUTH RIPLEY JR/SR HS; (JR); Hnr Roll; Chrch Yth Grp; Emplmnt; FCA; Lib Aide; Pep Squd; Prom Com; Spanish Clb; Bnd; Flg Crps; Mch Bnd; Pep Bnd; Varsity Volleyball Manager; Media Broadcast Through School (CNN-SR); Nursing Ob/Gyn; Public Relations; Indiana U; U of North Carolina

MOORE, LEAERIN; WEST TERRE HAUTE, IN; WEST VIGO HS; (FR); Hnr Roll; MVP; Pres Ac Ftns Aw; Chrch Yth Grp; P to P St Amb Prg; Bskball (J); Sccr (V); Track (V); Travel Soccers 4 Years; People to People Sports Ambassador 2000; Teaching; Urban Planning; Texas A & M U; Ball State U

MORALES, AMANDA K; PORTAGE, IN; PORTAGE HS; (SR); Hi Hnr Roll; Hnr Roll; Nat Hon Sy; St of Mnth; Comm Volntr; Peer Tut/Med; Chrch Yth Grp; Drma Clb; Emplmnt; Lttrmn Clb; Mus Clb; Off Aide; Pep Squd; Prom Com; Chr; Dnce; SP/M/VS; Stg Cre; PPSqd (V L); Adv Cncl (R); Cl Off (R); Stu Cncl (R); CR (R); Yrbk (R); Academic Letters - Jr & Sr Year; Academic Hall of Fame / Junior Miss Winner; English; Political Science; Butler U; IU Bloomington

MORALES, ANDREA M; LAFAYETTE, IN; MC CUTCHEON HS; (SO); Hi Hnr Roll; Hnr Roll; Nat Hon Sy; Sci/Math Olympn; Peer Tut/Med; Chrch Yth Grp; Emplmnt; Sci Clb; Spanish Clb; Chr; Ch Chr; Vllyball (J); Sch Ppr (R); Top Scholar; Academic Award for Outstanding Scholastic Endeavors; Doctor / MD; Indiana U; Princeton U

MORALES, JENNIFER; HIGHLAND, IN; HIGHLAND HS; (SR); F Lan Hn Soc; Hi Hnr Roll; Nat Hon Sy; Otst Ac Ach Awd; Pres Sch; WWAHSS; Comm Volntr; Peer Tut/Med; Chrch Yth Grp; Emplmnt; Key Club; Tchrs Aide; Spanish Clb; Stu Cncl (R); Yrbk (E); National Honor Society Secretary; Spanish Club Secretary; Education; Psychology

MORGAN, JESSICA; PORTLAND, IN; JAY CTY HS; (SO); Hi Hnr Roll; Hnr Roll; Nat Hon Sy; WWAHSS; Hab For Humty Volntr; Chrch Yth Grp; FCA; PP Ftbl (J); Sccr (J); Sftball (J); Stu Cncl (V); Psychology; PhD; Purdue U; Duke U

MORGAN, KATY L; LAWRENCEBURG, IN; LAWRENCEBURG HS; (SR); Ctznshp Aw; Hnr Roll; Nat Hon Sy; WWAHSS; Comm Volntr; AL Aux Girls; Drma Clb; Emplmnt; Key Club; Prom Com; French Clb; SP/M/VS; Chrldg (VJCL); Stu Cncl (P); Academic Medallion; Jack Anderson Academic Award; International Business Management; Saint Mary's College; Purdue U

MORGAN, MALLIE; MARION, IN; MISSISSINEWA HS; (JR); Hi Hnr Roll; Hnr Roll; Nat Hon Sy; WWAHSS; Comm Volntr; Emplmnt; FCA; PP Ftbl; Sftball (J); Cl Off (V); Nursing; Indiana Wesleyan U

MORNINGSTAR, JULIE; ELKHART, IN; ELKHART CTRL HS; (SO); Hi Hnr Roll; WWAHSS; Comm Volntr; Chrch Yth Grp; Key Club; Svce Clb; Chr; Swg Chr; Sccr (V L); Tennis (VJ L); Stu Cncl (R); Physical Therapy; Indiana U Purdue U Indianapolis

MORRIS, KHRISTOPHER; INDIANAPOLIS, IN; BROAD RIPPLE HS; (JR); WWAHSS; Bnd; Mch Bnd; Associate's Degree / Law Enforcement; Vincennes U

MORRIS, LUCAS; LAKEVILLE, IN; JOHN GLENN HS; (JR); Hnr Roll; MVP; Nat Hon Sy; Pres Sch; WWAHSS; Ftball (V); Wrstlg (V C); Wrestling State Qualifier in 2005; ISWA State Champion 2003; Conservation Officer; Medicine; Purdue U; U of Indianapolis

MOSER, CLARK A; ELWOOD, IN; ELWOOD HS; (SO); 4H Awd; Hi Hnr Roll; MVP; Sci Fairs; St of Mnth; Comm Volntr; Peer Tut/Med; 4-H; Chrch Yth Grp; Emplmnt; Mth Clb/Tm; Latin Clb; Ch Chr; SP/M/VS; Cr Ctry (V); Swmg (V); Track (V); Medicine; Computer; Indiana U

MOTT, CAITLIN; FT WAYNE, IN; CONCORDIA LUTHERAN HS; (SO); Hnr Roll; Perf Att; Chrch Yth Grp; Mus Clb; Pep Squd; Chr; Chrldg (L); Gmnstcs (L); Marine Biology; Forensics

MULDOON, KERRI; EDINBURGH, IN; SOUTHWESTERN HS; (JR); Hnr Roll; Otst Ac Ach Awd; Perf Att; Emplmnt; Pep Squd; Tchrs Aide; German Clb; Clr Grd; Dnce; Drl Tm; Chrldg (J L); PPSqd (V C); Stu Cncl (R); Plan on Working on Senior Video This Year; German Club; Elementary Education; Dance; Franklin College; Indiana U, Purdue U Indianapolis

MULL, MACIE; NORTH VERNON, IN; JENNINGS CTY HS; (FR); Hi Hnr Roll; Hnr Roll; WWAHSS; Key Club; SADD; Bnd; Mch Bnd; Pep Bnd; Cr Ctry; Scr Kpr (J); Track (V); Vllyball (JCL); Lawyer; Indiana U; Harvard U

Moore, Hanna L
Clay City JR/SR HS
Brazil, IN

Meyer, Becky
Center Grove HS
Greenwood, IN

Minor, Frank
Arlington HS
Indianapolis, IN

MUNDY, ERIC M; JASPER, IN; JASPER HS; (FR); Hi Hnr Roll; Perf Att; WWAHSS; Comm Volntr; 4-H; Emplmnt; Key Club; Scouts; Eagle Scout; 4-H; Engineering

MUNDY, JESSICA; ROACHDALE, IN; NORTH PUTNAM HS; (SO); Hnr Roll; WWAHSS; Spec Olymp Vol; Key Club; SADD; Chr; SP/M/VS; Stg Cre; Choir Award; Nursing for RN or Pediatrics; Purdue U; IUPUI

MUNFORD, KATHLEEN; CRAWFORDSVILLE, IN; SOUTHMONT HS; (JR); Hi Hnr Roll; Nat Hon Sy; WWAHSS; Comm Volntr; Peer Tut/Med; AL Aux Girls; Drma Clb; Key Club; Lttrmn Clb; Mus Clb; Prom Com; Schol Bwl; Spanish Clb; Bnd; Mch Bnd; Pep Bnd; SP/M/VS; Stu Cncl (R); Pride (Drug-Free Program); Psychology; Drama; Earlham College; Denison U

MURPHY, BRANDI; INDIANAPOLIS, IN; LAWRENCE CTRL HS; (JR); Hnr Roll; Comm Volntr; Key Club; Ch Chr; Helping Hands; Black History Committee; Social Worker; RN; International Business College; Atlanta Clarks U

MURPHY, TRISTAN; HAMMOND, IN; MORTON HS; (JR); Hnr Roll; Dbte Team; Key Club; Spch Team; Cr Ctry (V L); Swmg (V L); Sch Ppr (R); Political Science

MURRAY, AMANDA; LOGANSPORT, IN; PIONEER JR/SR HS; (FR); Hnr Roll; Otst Ac Ach Awd; St of Mnth; Yth Ldrshp Prog; Comm Volntr; Mus Clb; Pep Squd; Spanish Clb; Chr; SP/M/VS; Swg Chr; Chrldg (J); Nursing; Doctor of Medicine; Indiana U; Purdue U

MURRAY, NICHOLAS; LOGANSPORT, IN; LOGANSPORT HS; (FR); Hnr Roll; Perf Att; Spec Olymp Vol; 4-H; Dbte Team; NtlFrnscLg; Spch Team; German Clb; Bsball (J); Tennis (J); Business

MUSKAT, LAUREN; INDIANAPOLIS, IN; BISHOP CHATARD HS; (JR); Hi Hnr Roll; Nat Hon Sy; WWAHSS; Comm Volntr; Chrch Yth Grp; Fr of Library; Key Club; Vsity Clb; SP/M/VS; Stg Cre; Lcrsse (VJCL); Sccr (VJ L); Sch Ppr; Pro-Life Club; Thespian Society; Communications; Law; Indiana U Bloomington; Harvard U

MUSSELMAN, HOLLY; HARTFORD CITY, IN; BLACKFORD HS; (FR); Hnr Roll; Otst Ac Ach Awd; Perf Att; WWAHSS; Key Club; Bskball (V); Ftball (L); Golf (V); Track (V); Radiology; Nursing; Indiana U; Duke U

MYERS, LAURA; WHEATFIELD, IN; KANKAKEE VALLEY HS; (FR); 4H Awd; Hnr Roll; WWAHSS; 4-H; DARE; Jr Ach; Photog; SADD; Chr; Track (J); Vllyball (J); Journalism TV/Radio; U of Indianapolis; Ohio Northern U

MYERS, NILA; KOKOMO, IN; KOKOMO HS; (SR); Perf Att; Chrch Yth Grp; Quill & Scroll; Stg Cre; Member of Diversity Group; Member of Drama Club (Backstage); I Want to Be a Veterinarian Technician

MYERS, SARAH D; GREENFIELD, IN; GREENFIELD CTRL HS; (FR); Hi Hnr Roll; Chrch Yth Grp; Key Club; Bnd; Mch Bnd; Pep Bnd; Artistic Achievement Award

MYNETT, JESSIE R; MUNCIE, IN; MUNCIE CTRL HS; (SO); Ctznshp Aw; Hnr Roll; WWAHSS; Comm Volntr; Chrch Yth Grp; Emplmnt; Key Club; Spanish Clb; Chr; Golf (J); Sftball (J); Cl Off (R); Stu Cncl (R); 22nd in Sophomore Class; Elementary Education; Public Relations; Ball State U, Indiana U

NAGEL, PATRICK O; FORT WAYNE, IN; HOMESTEAD HS; (SO); Hnr Roll; Ftball (J); Track (J); Wrstlg (J); At Homestead High School Wrestling Club Work with Young Wrestlers; Medicine/General Practitioner/Dr.; Purdue U; Indiana U, U Of Notre Dame

NAGLE, SADIE S; VALPARAISO, IN; WHEELER HS; (SO); Hnr Roll; Comm Volntr; Spec Olymp Vol; Key Club; Tchrs Aide; Sccr (V L); Tennis (J); Clear Lake Ski Team; Family Law; Business; Xavier U-Cincinnati, Oh.; Michigan State U

NAGY, ERIN M; EVANSVILLE, IN; CENTRAL HS; (SO); Ctznshp Aw; Hnr Roll; Otst Ac Ach Awd; WWAHSS; Comm Volntr; Spanish Clb; Chrldg (V); Stu Cncl (R); All-American Cheerleader; Accounting; Business; Indiana U

NARSINGHANI, MICHAEL; COLUMBUS, IN; COLUMBUS NORTH HS; (JR); Hnr Roll; MVP; Perf Att; Yth Ldrshp Prog; Comm Volntr; Hosp Aide; Key Club; French Clb; Ice Hky (J); New York U; Boston U

NASH, KELLY; INDIANAPOLIS, IN; LAWRENCE CTRL HS; (SO); Hi Hnr Roll; Hnr Roll; Perf Att; Comm Volntr; Chrch Yth Grp; Photog; Quill & Scroll; Dnce; Chrldg (VJ L); Sftball (V L); Sch Ppr (E, R); Vice President-Freshman Mentor Council; Psychology; Journalism; U of Notre Dame; Xavier U

NAULT, BENJAMIN; WARSAW, IN; WHITKO HS; (JR); Hi Hnr Roll; Nat Hon Sy; WWAHSS; Comm Volntr; Peer Tut/Med; Drma Clb; Emplmnt; Sci Clb; Bnd; Drm Mjr; Jzz Bnd; Mch Bnd; Adv Cncl (R); Stu Cncl (P, T, R); Discover Card Tribute Winner; Chemistry; Chemical Engineering; Purdue U; Tri State U

NAYROCKER, ALAN; WARSAW, IN; WARSAW CMTY HS; (JR); Ctznshp Aw; Hi Hnr Roll; Otst Ac Ach Awd; Perf Att; Chrch Yth Grp; Jr Ach; Mth Clb/Tm; Schol Bwl; Spanish Clb; Chr; Tennis (J); Award for Citizenship Perfect Attendance and GPA Above 12 on a 12 Point Scale; Political Science; Law

NDAYISENGA, CHRISTELLE; SOUTH BEND, IN; JOHN ADAMS HS; (FR); Nat Hon Sy; USAA; Chr; Ch Chr; Dnce; Drl Tm; Chrldg (L); PPSqd (L); Track (J); MD; Doctor; Notre Dame

NEAL, CLARISSA A; ENGLISH, IN; CRAWFORD CTY JR/SR HS; (SO); 4H Awd; Hnr Roll; Nat Hon Sy; Nat Sci Aw; Perf Att; Sci Fairs; CARE; Comm Volntr; Peer Tut/Med; 4-H; Chrch Yth Grp; Emplmnt; Off Aide; Sci Clb; Tchrs Aide; Track (V); Poetry/Arts; Child Care Worker; Ivy Tech; Vincennes U Jasper Campus

NEELY, DARREN K; INDIANAPOLIS, IN; BROAD RIPPLE HS; (FR); Ctznshp Aw; Hnr Roll; MVP; Bskball (J); Track (J)

NEIL, JENNIFER; MC CORDSVILLE, IN; MT VERNON HS; (SR); Hi Hnr Roll; Hnr Roll; Perf Att; WWAHSS; Comm Volntr; Dbte Team; Drma Clb; Chr; Elementary Education; Criminology; Ball State U

NELSON, KALI R; MISHAWAKA, IN; PENN HS; (JR); F Lan Hn Soc; Hi Hnr Roll; WWAHSS; Peer Tut/Med; Prom Com; Cr Ctry (V CL); Track (V L); Dietetics; Purdue U

NELSON, NATASHA; JASPER, IN; JASPER HS; (FR); Hi Hnr Roll; MVP; St of Mnth; WWAHSS; Comm Volntr; Chrch Yth Grp; Emplmnt; FCA; Key Club; SADD; Chrldg (V L); Dvng (V L); Track (V L); Stu Cncl; Diving-Mental Attitude Award/Most Valuable Diver; Cheerleading-NCA Small Varsity National Champion; Medical School/Pediatrician; U of Kentucky; Purdue U

NEPOMUCENO, JOSEPH KARL T; JASPER, IN; JASPER HS; (FR); DARE; Key Club; SADD; French Clb; Sccr (J); Medicine; Engineering; Purdue U; Indiana U

NEUENSCHWANDER, KYLA R; BERNE, IN; SOUTH ADAMS JR/SR HS; (SR); Hi Hnr Roll; Hnr Roll; Chrch Yth Grp; Emplmnt; Off Aide; Tchrs Aide; Tennis (J); Vllyball (J); Accounting; Business Management; International Business College

NEWBAUER, ABBY R; KNOX, IN; KNOX HS; (JR); Hi Hnr Roll; Hnr Roll; Nat Hon Sy; Perf Att; Prom Com; Bnd; Mch Bnd; Pep Bnd; Veterinary Medicine; Pharmacy; Purdue U; Indiana U

NEWMAN, LAURA; NOBLESVILLE, IN; NOBLESVILLE HS; (SR); Fut Prb Slvr; Hi Hnr Roll; Hnr Roll; Nat Hon Sy; Nat Mrt LOC; Sci Fairs; WWAHSS; Comm Volntr; Peer Tut/Med; AL Aux Girls; Chrch Yth Grp; Quiz Bowl; Schol Bwl; Orch; Teams Test; Rugby; Biology; Medical License; Indiana U Bloomington

NEWPORT, JESSICA L; SPENCER, IN; OWEN VALLEY HS; (SO); Hnr Roll; Comm Volntr; Hosp Aide; Lib Aide; SADD; Dnce; 4th Place in Dance Nationals; RN Registered Nurse; MD Medical Doctor; V.U. Vincennes; Ivy Tech

NEWTON, CHRISTOPHER; ECKERTY, IN; CRAWFORD CTY JR/SR HS; (FR); 4H Awd; Hnr Roll; Perf Att; Pres Ac Ftns Aw; Sci Fairs; 4-H; FCA; Mth Clb/Tm; Pep Squd; Tchrs Aide; Bsball (V); Bskball (J); Cr Ctry (V); Dentist; Arizona; Duke

NG'ANDWE, MUKA; SOUTH BEND, IN; ADAMS HS; (JR); French Clb; Sccr (J); Medicine; Accounting; Butler U; Washington U

NGUYEN, VIET; WARSAW, IN; WARSAW CMTY HS; (JR); Hi Hnr Roll; Perf Att; Comm Volntr; HO'Br Yth Ldrshp; Mth Clb/Tm; Spanish Clb; Spanish Club Officer and Treasurer; Octagon Club Class Rep. and Officer; Pre-Medicine; U of Notre Dame; Indiana U (Bloomington)

NIEUWLANDT, LAUREN; SPENCERVILLE, IN; WOODLAN JR/SR HS; MS; 4H Awd; Hnr Roll; Perf Att; St of Mnth; Peer Tut/Med; 4-H; Chrch Yth Grp; Ch Chr; Swg Chr; Bskball; Vllyball; Stu Cncl (S); 4-H Horseback Riding-State Qualifier; NEIVA Elite Volleyball Club; Nursing; Dental Hygiene; IPFW; Notre Dame

NIKSCH, GREGORY; CROWN POINT, IN; MERRILLVILLE HS; (SR); Hi Hnr Roll; Nat Hon Sy; Comm Volntr; Scouts; French Clb; Bnd; Mch Bnd; Tennis (J); Eagle Scout; Mechanical Engineer; Purdue U

NIX, KRISTA; EVANSVILLE, IN; F J REITZ HS; (SO); Ctznshp Aw; Hi Hnr Roll; USAA; WWAHSS; BPA; Chrch Yth Grp; Spanish Clb; Dnce; PP Ftbl (J); Stu Cncl (R); CR (R); Yrbk (R); National Level BPA; Who's Who Among American Scholars; Indiana U; Butler U

NOBLE, ALLISON; MUNCIE, IN; MUNCIE CTRL HS; (JR); Hi Hnr Roll; Jr Mshl; Nat Hon Sy; Otst Ac Ach Awd; Yth Ldrshp Prog; Comm Volntr; Hab For Humty Volntr; Peer Tut/Med; Chrch Yth Grp; Emplmnt; Key Club; MuAlphaTh; Prom Com; Quill & Scroll; Tchrs Aide; German Clb; Bnd; Sccr (V); Swmg (V); Tennis (J); Stu Cncl (T); Yrbk (E); Secondary Education; Brigham Young U; Utah State U

NOBLE, CRYSTALYN; FORT WAYNE, IN; NEW HAVEN HS; (FR); Hi Hnr Roll; Hnr Roll; DARE; Bnd; Jzz Bnd; Mch Bnd; Pep Bnd; Cr Ctry; Track; Doctorates in Physical Science; Arizona State U

NORTH, EMILY K S; ROME CITY, IN; EAST NOBLE HS; (JR); 4H Awd; Hi Hnr Roll; Nat Hon Sy; Comm Volntr; 4-H; AL Aux Girls; Chrch Yth Grp; Emplmnt; Key Club; Prom Com; Quill & Scroll; German Clb; Bnd; Drm Mjr; Mch Bnd; Orch; Cl Off (S); Three Rivers Honor Band; Regional All Honors Band; Plant Genetics; Purdue U; Indiana U

NUNLEY, JOANNA; PLAINFIELD, IN; PLAINFIELD HS; (JR); Ctznshp Aw; Hi Hnr Roll; Nat Hon Sy; St of Mnth; WWAHSS; Key Club; Spanish Clb; Bnd; Chr; SP/M/VS; PP Ftbl; Plainfield Ambassador; Vice President of Key Club; Law; Music Performance; Princeton U; Georgetown U

O'BRYAN, EMILY R; NEWBURGH, IN; REITZ MEMORIAL HS; (JR); Hi Hnr Roll; Nat Hon Sy; WWAHSS; Hab For Humty Volntr; Chrch Yth Grp; Key Club; Prom Com; Spanish Clb; PP Ftbl; Sftball (V L); Swmg (J); Yrbk (E, R, P); Academic All-City; President of Teens in Drug Education Club - TIDE; Business Administration; Accounting

OCHS, TRAVIS K; MILAN, IN; MILAN HS; (SO); Hi Hnr Roll; Hnr Roll; DARE; Bskball (J); Golf (J); Math; Engineering; Indiana State; Duke U

O'DELL, SHANNON; PENNVILLE, IN; JAY CTY HS; (SR); Ctznshp Aw; Hnr Roll; Nat Hon Sy; Otst Ac Ach Awd; St of Mnth; USAA; Chrch Yth Grp; Emplmnt; FCA; Spanish Clb; Bnd; Ch Chr; Mch Bnd; Bskball (J); Track (V L); Vllyball (V L); Actuarial Science; Accounting; Defiance College

OEDING, LACEY K; JASPER, IN; (FR); MVP; Perf Att; WWAHSS; ArtClub; Chrch Yth Grp; Emplmnt; Key Club; Scouts; SADD; Spanish Clb; Cr Ctry (V L); Swmg (V L); Track (V L); Architecture

OFFETT, CANDYCE; INDIANAPOLIS, IN; ARLINGTON HS; (JR); Hnr Roll; Nat Hon Sy; Comm Volntr; Peer Tut/Med; Chrch Yth Grp; Key Club; Lttrmn Clb; Scouts; Ch Chr; Bskball (J); Vllyball (J); Manager Of Basketball & Volleyball; Sports Management; U of Miami; Florida State U

OGDEN, HEATHER; CTRVILLE, IN; CTRVILLE HS; (JR); 4-H; Drma Clb; Key Club; Scouts; Chr; SP/M/VS; Stg Cre; Member of Voice; Member of Green Club; Art Teacher; Designer; Ball State U; Indiana U

OGDEN, KAITLYN; INDIANAPOLIS, IN; NORTH CTRL HS; (SO); Hnr Roll; Comm Volntr; Scouts; Latin Clb; Ftball (V L); Wrstlg (V L); Rugby; Japanese; Zoology; Sports Medicine; Ohio State-Columbus; Purdue U-Lafayette

OGLE, JORDAN; INDIANAPOLIS, IN; BROAD RIPPLE HS; (JR); Hnr Roll; WWAHSS; Peer Tut/Med; Key Club; Sch Ppr (R); Corporate Law; Fashion Marketing; Florida State; Texas Southern U

OKERSON, JOHN P; INDIANAPOLIS, IN; SCECINA MEMORIAL HS; (FR); Hi Hnr Roll; Chrch Yth Grp; Bskball; Ftball (J); Golf (J); Scholar Athlete; William Bevan Scholar Athlete Award

OLINGER, MICHAEL A; HUNTINGBURG, IN; SOUTHRIDGE HS; (FR); Hi Hnr Roll; Hnr Roll; Perf Att; St of Mnth; BPA; Outdrs Clb; Quiz Bowl; SADD; Spanish Clb; Acpl Chr; Chr; Bsball (J); Bskball; Tennis (V L); PAC Tennis 1 Doubles Runner Up; Dentist; Indiana U

OLIVER, QUENTIN; INDIANAPOLIS, IN; ARLINGTON HS; (SO); Perf Att; St Schl; Comm Volntr; Peer Tut/Med; Chrch Yth Grp; DARE; Emplmnt; Tech Clb; Ch Chr; Chef; Ball State; IUPUI

OLSON, JUSTIN R; WESTFIELD, IN; THE SUMMIT AC; (JR); Ctznshp Aw; Hnr Roll; Yth Ldrshp Prog; Comm Volntr; Chrch Yth Grp; Emplmnt; Acpl Chr; Chr; Orch; SP/M/VS; Bskball (V); Stu Cncl (P); CYO Music Contest: Outstanding Performer; Political Science; Law; Grove City College; Wheaton College

O'MARA, ERIC J; SEYMOUR, IN; SEYMOUR HS; (FR); WWAHSS; Key Club; Off Aide; Bskball (J); Ftball (J); Track (V); Stu Cncl (V); St Ambrose Youth Group Member; Engineering; Business; Purdue; Indiana U

ORBIK, JOSEPH; ANDERSON, IN; ANDERSON HS; (SO); Hi Hnr Roll; Hnr Roll; Perf Att; Pres Ac Ftns Aw; Comm Volntr; Bsball (J); Ftball (V L); Sportsmanship Phillips Award Football; History Teacher; Architect; Ball State U; Notre Dame U

O'RILEY, KATHLEEN; GREENWOOD, IN; GREENWOOD HS; (JR); Hnr Roll; WWAHSS; Peer Tut/Med; Chrch Yth Grp; Drma Clb; Emplmnt; FCA; Quill & Scroll; French Clb; Dnce; Stg Cre; Yrbk (E); Fashion Merchandising; Business; Indiana U; Savannah Art College

ORR, STACI; DALEVILLE, IN; BURRIS LABORATORY SCH; (SO); Ctznshp Aw; Hnr Roll; WWAHSS; Comm Volntr; Hosp Aide; Drma Clb; Jr Cls League; Key Club; Prom Com; SADD; Latin Clb; Bnd; Dnce; Pep Bnd; SP/M/VS; Bskball (L); Cl Off (S); Pride; Pre-Med; Medical School; Ball State University

OSBORN, REBEKAH; WEST BADEN SPRINGS, IN; HOMESCHOOLED; (FR); Comm Volntr; Peer Tut/Med; Chrch Yth Grp; Ch Chr; Piano 4yrs; Indiana DNR 6 Youth Badges; Biologist; Veterinarian; Indiana Wesleyan; Michigan State

O'Dell, Shannon
Jay Cty HS
Pennville, IN

Nix, Krista
F J Reitz HS
Evansville, IN

Neely, Darren K
Broad Ripple HS
Indianapolis, IN

Neal, Clarissa A
Crawford Cty JR/SR HS
English, IN

Mynett, Jessie R
Muncie Ctrl HS
Muncie, IN

Nagy, Erin M
Central HS
Evansville, IN

Nelson, Kali R
Penn HS
Mishawaka, IN

Ochs, Travis K
Milan HS
Milan, IN

Offett, Candyce
Arlington HS
Indianapolis, IN

OSBORNE, ROBERT; DALEVILLE, IN; DALEVILLE JR/SR HS; (JR); MVP; Nat Hon Sy; WWAHSS; Schol Bwl; Cr Ctry (J L); Track (V L); Wrstlg (V CL); Stu Cncl (T)

OTTE, ELIZABETH; CROTHERSVILLE, IN; CROTHERSVILLE JR/SR HS; (SR); 4H Awd; DAR; Hi Hnr Roll; MVP; Nat Hon Sy; St Schl; Valdctrian; WWAHSS; Comm Volntr; Peer Tut/Med; 4-H; Chrch Yth Grp; DARE; Emplmnt; Mod UN; Ntl FFA; Schol Bwl; SADD; Pep Bnd; Bskball (V CL); Cr Ctry (V CL); Track (CL); Vllyball (V L); Cl Off (P); Stu Cncl (V); Yrbk (R, P); John R Wooden Award; FFA National Agri-Science Fair; Medical Physician; Hanover College

OWENS, ERICA L; EVANSVILLE, IN; CENTRAL HS; (JR); Hnr Roll; Perf Att; WWAHSS; Yth Ldrshp Prog; Hab For Humty Volntr; Bnd; Mch Bnd; Actuarial Science; Mathematics; Purdue U

PACK, AMBER; INDIANAPOLIS, IN; BEN DAVIS HS; (JR); Hnr Roll; Perf Att; Comm Volntr; Peer Tut/Med; Chrch Yth Grp; FCA; Key Club; Prom Com; Quill & Scroll; Tchrs Aide; Spanish Clb; Stu Cncl (V); Yrbk (E); Special Education Teacher; Ball State U; Indiana U

PAINTER, MICHELLE; HUNTINGBURG, IN; SOUTHRIDGE HS; (FR); Hnr Roll; Otst Ac Ach Awd; Perf Att; Hab For Humty Volntr; BPA; DARE; Emplmnt; Jr Ach; Pep Squd; Schol Bwl; SADD; Bnd; Chr; Mch Bnd; Pep Bnd; Chrldg (J); Went Through Modeling School; Pediatric Surgeon; Pediatrician; Indiana U; Ball State U

PANOJA, SAMMY; ELKHART, IN; ELKHART CTRL HS; (SO); Hi Hnr Roll; St of Mnth; USAA; WWAHSS; Yth Ldrshp Prog; Key Club; Photog; Bnd; Mch Bnd; Pep Bnd; SP/M/VS; Key Club; Society for a Better Earth; Writer; Photography; Notre Dame; Ball State

PARKS, MEGAN E K; SHELBYVILLE, IN; BLUE RIVER CAREER CTR; (FR); Hnr Roll; Comm Volntr; Chrch Yth Grp; Mus Clb; P to P St Amb Prg; Bowling Team; Culinary Arts; Astronomy

PARRISH, SHURE-NACHELLE; NORTH MANCHESTER, IN; MANCHESTER; (SO); Hnr Roll; Perf Att; Pres Sch; Hab For Humty Volntr; ArtClub; Tchrs Aide; Acpl Chr; Chr; Ch Chr; Swmg (VJ); Track (VJ); Cl Off (S); 2003-2004 Manchester High School / JV Girls Swimming - Most Improved; Creative Writing; English; U of Notre Dame; DePauw U

PARSONS, AIMEE E; LANESVILLE, IN; LANESVILLE JR/SR HS; (SO); Hnr Roll; St of Mnth; WWAHSS; Peer Tut/Med; FCA; Bskball (J); Sftball (V); Pharmacy; Pre-Veterinary Medicine; Purdue U; U of Southern Indiana

PARSONS, TOMMY; JASPER, IN; JASPER HS; (JR); Hnr Roll; WWAHSS; Comm Volntr; ArtClub; DARE; Jr Ach; Key Club; Mus Clb; Photog; Scouts; Lit Mag (R); Sch Ppr (R); Yrbk (R); Major in Radio Broadcasting, Major in Music Guitar; U of Vincennes; Vincennes U Jasper Campus

PARTON, JENNA A; EDINBURGH, IN; EDINBURGH HS; (FR); Hi Hnr Roll; Hnr Roll; Perf Att; Pres Sch; Comm Volntr; DARE; Mus Clb; Pep Squd; SADD; French Clb; Chr; Dnce; Chrldg (V); Wt Lftg (J); Sang At Basketball Games; Sang for the Mayor of Columbus; Degree in Nursing, Culinary Arts; Purdue U; Indiana U

PATEL, DIMPLE; EVANSVILLE, IN; REITZ MEMORIAL HS; (SO); Hi Hnr Roll; Otst Ac Ach Awd; Perf Att; Pres Sch; Comm Volntr; Hosp Aide; Emplmnt; Key Club; SP/M/VS; Stg Cre; Service Award; Superior Performance in Mathematics Award; Veterinarian Medicine; Indiana U; Purdue U

PATEL, NEEL; FT WAYNE, IN; HOMESTEAD HS; (SR); Hi Hnr Roll; Nat Hon Sy; Otst Ac Ach Awd; Sci Fairs; Comm Volntr; Hosp Aide; Chrch Yth Grp; DECA; Emplmnt; Key Club; NtlFrnscLg; P to P St Amb Prg; Prom Com; Tennis (J); Stu Cncl (P); AP Scholar; Cognitive Science; Pre-Med; Indiana University

PATEL, RITEN; COLUMBIA CITY, IN; COLUMBIA CITY HS; (FR); Hi Hnr Roll; Otst Ac Ach Awd; Perf Att; Key Club; Schol Bwl; Track (J); Architect; Engineer; U of Chicago; Northwestern U

PATRON, RICARDO; COLUMBUS, IN; COLUMBUS NORTH HS; (JR); Hnr Roll; Nat Mrt LOC; Yth Ldrshp Prog; Comm Volntr; BPA; Chrch Yth Grp; Emplmnt; Key Club; Quill & Scroll; SP/M/VS; Track (J); Yrbk (E); National Hispanic Youth Recognition Program; Accounting; Business Administration; Indiana U

PATTERSON III, JAMES; SOUTH BEND, IN; CLAY HS; (FR); Bskball (J); On a Basketball Scouting Website; Biology; Social Studies; U of Maryland; U of North Carolina

PATTON, NINA L; CAMPBELLSBURG, IN; WEST WASHINGTON JR/SR HS; (JR); DAR; Hnr Roll; Nat Hon Sy; Sci/Math Olympn; WWAHSS; ArtClub; Ntl FFA; Tchrs Aide; Spanish Clb; Bnd; Jzz Bnd; Mch Bnd; Pep Bnd; FFA State Soil Judging Team; Academic Team State Fine Arts Squad; Music Education; Soil Scientist; Hanover College; Indiana U Bloomington

PATTON, SARA; JASPER, IN; JASPER HS; (FR); 4H Awd; Hnr Roll; Pres Ac Ftns Aw; WWAHSS; Comm Volntr; Hosp Aide; Peer Tut/Med; 4-H; Chrch Yth Grp; Key Club; Svce Clb; SADD; Spanish Clb; Bnd; Mch Bnd; Pep Bnd; Outstanding Freshman in Band; Outstanding Freshman in Junior Optimist; Elementary Music Education; Occupational Therapist; U of Evansville; Indiana State U

PAYNE, AMELIA; HOPE, IN; HAUSER JR/SR HS; (JR); Hnr Roll; Yth Ldrshp Prog; ArtClub; Key Club; Ntl FFA; SADD; Spanish Clb; SP/M/VS; Sftball (V L); Yrbk (R); Basketball Statistician; Anthropology; English; Eastern Kentucky U; Purdue U

PAYNE, KERI; WESTVILLE, IN; WESTVILLE HS; (SO); Hi Hnr Roll; Hnr Roll; Perf Att; Comm Volntr; Svce Clb; Chr; Dnce; SP/M/VS; PPSqd (J); Black Hawk Award; USAA National Honor Student Award; Law Degree; Dance; Ball State U; Duke U

PAYNE II, VERNARD J; DANA, IN; SOUTH VERMILLION HS; (SO); Hi Hnr Roll; Hnr Roll; Otst Ac Ach Awd; Pres Ac Ftns Aw; Sci/Math Olympn; St of Mnth; Comm Volntr; Peer Tut/Med; Red Cr Aide; Chess; Chrch Yth Grp; DARE; Emplmnt; Bnd; Mch Bnd; Pep Bnd; SP/M/VS; Track (V); Adv Cncl (R); CR (R); Sch Ppr (E); Work-Oriented Person (Workaholic); Amateur Pool Player; Education-Teacher-Science/Math; Marines; Indiana State U; Taylor U-Upland

PAYNE JR, RODNEY W; FORT BRANCH, IN; WALDO J WOOD MEMORIAL HS; (FR); Hi Hnr Roll; Yth Ldrshp Prog; Chrch Yth Grp; DARE; Pep Squd; SADD; Vsity Clb; Spanish Clb; Stg Cre; Sccr (V); Track (C); MD Cardiovascular Surgeon; MD Family Practice; Harvard Medical School; U of Kentucky

PEAKS, CORTNIE J; FORT WAYNE, IN; NEW HAVEN HS; (SO); Hnr Roll; MVP; Perf Att; Pres Ac Ftns Aw; St of Mnth; Comm Volntr; Key Club; Acpl Chr; Chrldg (J); Tennis (J); Vllyball (J); Yrbk (R); Medical; Master's; Ball State U; Indiana U

PEARMAN, KELSEY R; ROCKVILLE, IN; ROCKVILLE HS; (JR); 4H Awd; Hnr Roll; Nat Hon Sy; Yth Ldrshp Prog; Comm Volntr; 4-H; Drma Clb; Svce Clb; SADD; Chr; Sftball (V); Cl Off (S); Stu Cncl (R); Indiana Youth Advisory - Board Member; Pre-Med

PEARSON, ANNA N; KIRKLIN, IN; CLINTON CTRL HS; (SR); 4H Awd; Hnr Roll; Nat Hon Sy; WWAHSS; Yth Ldrshp Prog; Comm Volntr; 4-H; Chrch Yth Grp; Emplmnt; Prom Com; Sci Clb; Foreign Clb; Bnd; Mch Bnd; Pep Bnd; Swmg (V CL); Track (V L); Cl Off (S); 4-H Fair Queen 2004; Biology; Purdue U; Arizona State U

PEARSON, KAYLA; CHURUBUSCO, IN; CHURUBUSCO HS; (JR); Hi Hnr Roll; Nat Hon Sy; WWAHSS; Peer Tut/Med; Key Club; SADD; Tchrs Aide; Bskball (J); Physical Therapy; Sports Medicine; Indiana U Purdue U Fort Wayne

PEARSON, MEGAN; BAINBRIDGE, IN; NORTH PUTNAM HS; (SR); 4H Awd; Hi Hnr Roll; Kwnis Aw; MVP; Nat Hon Sy; Otst Ac Ach Awd; Perf Att; Comm Volntr; 4-H; Chrch Yth Grp; Key Club; Ntl FFA; Prom Com; Vsity Clb; Spanish Clb; Bskball (V L); Golf (V CL); Sftball (V CL); Vllyball (V L); Cl Off (V); Stu Cncl (R); Business Marketing; Spanish; U of Indianapolis

PEART, JENNIFER N; GREENCASTLE, IN; GREENCASTLE HS; (FR); Hnr Roll; Perf Att; Sci Fairs; WWAHSS; ArtClub; Chrch Yth Grp; Key Club; French Clb; Clr Grd; Dnce; Track (V); Art; Journalism; DePauw U; Webster U

PEDIGO, ZACHARY L; FRENCH LICK, IN; PAOLI JR/SR HS; (SR); Hi Hnr Roll; Otst Ac Ach Awd; Sci Fairs; Comm Volntr; Red Cr Aide; Lttrmn Clb; Off Aide; Prom Com; SADD; Vsity Clb; Bskball (V CL); Ftball (V CL); Tennis (J); Track (V CL); Wt Lftg; All-Conference Track Team; Pre-Law; Political Science; Franklin College

PELFREY, JOSH; HOWE, IN; HOWE MILITARY SCH; (SO); All Am Sch; Ctznshp Aw; Hnr Roll; MVP; Otst Ac Ach Awd; USAA; WWAHSS; Yth Ldrshp Prog; Comm Volntr; Red Cr Aide; Emplmnt; Svce Clb; Vsity Clb; Clr Grd; Drl Tm; Bsball (V); Bskball (V); Sccr (V); Cl Off (P); CR (R); All Conference Baseball; Defensive MVP Soccer; Engineering/Mechanical; Purdue; North Carolina

PELLAR, JOSEPH W; SCHERERVILLE, IN; ANDREAN HS; (SR); F Lan Hn Soc; Hnr Roll; Nat Hon Sy; WWAHSS; Emplmnt; German Clb; Bsball (J); Bskball (V L); Cr Ctry (J); Sccr (J); Cl Off (S, T); University Scholarship; Presidential Youth Leadership Conference; Public Policy; International Studies; U of Denver

PENELTON, ERICA; INDIANAPOLIS, IN; EMMERICH MANUAL HS; (SO); Hi Hnr Roll; Perf Att; JSA; Dnce; Tennis (J); State Finalist for Miss Indiana-American Co-ed Pageants; Microbiology; U of Notre Dame; Georgetown U

PENN, JAMEKA; MUNSTER, IN; MUNSTER HS; (JR); Hi Hnr Roll; Hnr Roll; St of Mnth; Emplmnt; ROTC; Dnce; Chrldg (J); Adv Cncl; English Achievement; Therapist; Sociology; IUPUI; Butler U

PENNINGTON, SARA; CORYDON, IN; NORTH HARRISON HS; 4H Awd; Ctznshp Aw; DAR; Hnr Roll; Sci/Math Olympn; St of Mnth; Chrch Yth Grp; FTA; Tchrs Aide; Bnd; Clr Grd; Pep Bnd; Yrbk (E, P); YMCA Soccer; NAMISS State Finalist; Fashion & Design; Optometry; Purdue U; IUS

PENROD, BROOKE E; MILLERSBURG, IN; FAIRFIELD JR/SR HS; (SO); 4H Awd; Ctznshp Aw; Hnr Roll; Otst Ac Ach Awd; WWAHSS; 4-H; Emplmnt; Key Club; Ntl FFA; Chr; Ch Chr; SP/M/VS; Wrstlg (V); Major in Nursing

PERIGO, REIDE; EVANSVILLE, IN; CENTRAL HS; (SO); Ctznshp Aw; Hi Hnr Roll; Hnr Roll; St of Mnth; Hab For Humty Volntr; Chrch Yth Grp; Sccr (J); Architecture; Computer Engineering; Ball State U; Indiana U

PERKINS, JORDAN A; HOPE, IN; HAUSER HS; (JR); Ctznshp Aw; Hi Hnr Roll; Hnr Roll; Nat Hon Sy; Nat Ldrshp Svc; Otst Ac Ach Awd; Perf Att; Pres Ac Ftns Aw; St of Mnth; Yth Ldrshp Prog; AL Aux Boys; Chrch Yth Grp; Emplmnt; Tchrs Aide; Vsity Clb; Bsball (VJ L); Bskball (VJCL); Tennis (VJ L); Secondary Education; Law; Tennessee (Knoxville); Kentucky (Lexington)

PETERS, ELIZABETH M; FORT WAYNE, IN; HOMESTEAD HS; (FR); Hi Hnr Roll; Hnr Roll; Otst Ac Ach Awd; Sci Fairs; St of Mnth; Comm Volntr; Chrch Yth Grp; Scouts; Bnd; Ch Chr; Dnce; SP/M/VS; Horseback Riding At a Local Barn; Teaching; Animal Behavior/Training Horses/Dogs; Indiana U; Purdue U

PETERSOHN, ADAM; BLOOMINGTON, IN; BLOOMINGTON HS SOUTH; (JR); Hi Hnr Roll; Hnr Roll; MVP; Nat Hon Sy; WWAHSS; Prom Com; Cr Ctry (V L); Track (V L); National Honor Society, 3-Yrs 40+; National Society of HS scholars, Leaders of Tomorrow; Biomedical Engineering; Doctor of Orthopedics; Purdue U; Washington U, St Louis

PHILLIPS, AMANDA R; ROSEDALE, IN; RIVERTON PARKE JR/SR HS; (SO); Comm Volntr; Chrch Yth Grp; FCA; Pep Squd; SADD; Bnd; Chr; SP/M/VS; Teaching; Neonatal Nurse; Indiana State U; Saint Mary's of the Woods

PHILLIPS, JENNIFER; NAPPANEE, IN; BREMEN SR HS; (SO); Hi Hnr Roll; Hnr Roll; Nat Hon Sy; Otst Ac Ach Awd; Perf Att; Sci Fairs; St Schl; St of Mnth; St Optmst of Yr; Comm Volntr; Peer Tut/Med; Chrch Yth Grp; Cmptr Clb; DARE; Emplmnt; Fr of Library; Mus Clb; NYLC; Off Aide; Acpl Chr; Chr; Ch Chr; Dnce; Golf (V); Gmnstcs (V); Scr Kpr (J); Vllyball (V); Teaching High School Lit/Creative Writing; Author; Elmira College; Ancilla College

PHILLIPS, JESSICA; GRIFFITH, IN; GRIFFITH SR HS; (SO); Hnr Roll; Pep Squd; Tmpl Yth Grp; Chr; Dnce; PPSqd (V L); Vsy Clb (V); Ballet, Senior Corps Company Member for Indiana Youth Ballet; Ballet/Dance; IU; The Juilliard School

PHILLIPS, KATRINA; FRANKLIN, IN; FRANKLIN CMTY HS; (JR); Hnr Roll; MVP; Nat Hon Sy; Otst Ac Ach Awd; WWAHSS; Comm Volntr; AL Aux Girls; Chrch Yth Grp; Emplmnt; FCA; Key Club; Off Aide; Prom Com; Tchrs Aide; Bskball (J); Sccr (V L); Tennis (V CL); FCTV; Mentor's Advisory Council; Medical; U of Evansville; Indiana U

PHILLIPS, REBEKAH J; GENTRYVILLE, IN; HERITAGE HILLS HS; (SR); 4H Awd; Hnr Roll; Perf Att; WWAHSS; Comm Volntr; Hab For Humty Volntr; 4-H; Chrch Yth Grp; Ntl FFA; Off Aide; Tchrs Aide; FFA Chapter Vice President 2004-2005; 4-H Club Treasurer 2001-2005; Associate's Degree in Photography; Ivy Tech State College

PHILLIPS, SARA; WEST TERRE HAUTE, IN; WEST VIGO HS; (SO); Otst Ac Ach Awd; St of Mnth; WWAHSS; Emplmnt; Key Club; Cl Off (P); Stu Cncl (R); Number One in Class; Business Management; Indiana State U; Indiana U

PIERCE, BRETT J; HIGHLAND, IN; HIGHLAND HS; (SO); F Lan Hn Soc; Hi Hnr Roll; Nat Hon Sy; Perf Att; Sci/Math Olympn; WWAHSS; Comm Volntr; Key Club; Off Aide; German Clb; Tennis (J); Track (J L); Science Olympiad Gold Medalist; Engineering; Computer Science; Purdue U; Notre Dame

PIERCE, DANIEL J; ADVANCE, IN; WESTERN BOONE JR/SR HS; (SO); Hi Hnr Roll; Hnr Roll; WWAHSS; Peer Tut/Med; Emplmnt; FCA; Key Club; Bsball (J); Bskball (J); Ftball (V L); Oncology Radiologist; Indiana U-Bloomington

PIKE, JONATHAN; RUSHVILLE, IN; RUSHVILLE CONSOLIDATED HS; (SO); 4H Awd; Ctznshp Aw; Hi Hnr Roll; Hnr Roll; Perf Att; Salutrn; Sci Fairs; Sci/Math Olympn; WWAHSS; Comm Volntr; Hab For Humty Volntr; 4-H; Chrch Yth Grp; FCA; Key Club; Lttrmn Clb; Mth Clb/Tm; Quiz Bowl; Schol Bwl; Bnd; Orch; Pep Bnd; SP/M/VS; Tennis (V L); Track (V L); Adv Cncl (R); Cl Off (S); Stu Cncl (S); CR (R); Yrbk (E); Named to Indiana SADD Student Leadership Council - SLC; Named to Indiana State Fair School - ISFYLC / 4-H; PhD / Chemistry; MD / Neurology; U of Notre Dame; Butler U

Pearman, Kelsey R
Rockville HS
Rockville, IN

Patterson III, James
Clay HS
South Bend, IN

Patel, Dimple
Reitz Memorial HS
Evansville, IN

Parsons, Tommy
Jasper HS
Jasper, IN

National
Honor Roll
Spring 2005

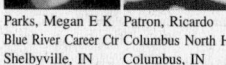

Parks, Megan E K
Blue River Career Ctr
Shelbyville, IN

Patron, Ricardo
Columbus North HS
Columbus, IN

Payne II, Vernard J
South Vermillion HS
Dana, IN

Phillips, Katrina
Franklin Cmty HS
Franklin, IN

PITMAN, DANIELLE; HOPE, IN; HAUSER JR/SR HS; (JR); Hnr Roll; Otst Ac Ach Awd; WWAHSS; Yth Ldrshp Prog; Peer Tut/Med; Prom Com; SADD; Tchrs Aide; Spanish Clb; Chrldg (V L); Cr Ctry (V L); Track (V); Level 9 Junior Olympic Gymnast; Best All Around Varsity Cheerleader; U of Kentucky; Indiana U

PLUTA, MICHELLE E; BLOOMINGTON, IN; BLOOMINGTON HS SOUTH; (JR); 4H Awd; Hnr Roll; Nat Hon Sy; Otst Ac Ach Awd; Pres Sch; St of Mnth; Yth Ldrshp Prog; Comm Volntr; Chrch Yth Grp; DARE; Drma Clb; Fr of Library; Photog; Tchrs Aide; Ch Chr; Dnce; SP/M/VS; Stg Cre; Mar Art (C); Track (J); Volunteered at Bloomington Playwrights Project; Received a $1000 Scholarship for Volunteering; Theatre Arts; Forensic Science; Indiana U; U of Evansville

POBANZ, TESSA; CTRVILLE, IN; CTRVILLE HS; (JR); F Lan Hn Soc; Hi Hnr Roll; Hnr Roll; Nat Hon Sy; St of Mnth; Yth Ldrshp Prog; Comm Volntr; Spec Olymp Vol; ArtClub; Chess; Drma Clb; Key Club; Mth Clb/Tm; Quiz Bowl; Spch Team; SADD; Clb; Bnd; Chr; Mch Bnd; SP/M/VS; Golf (V, J); Sftball (V, L); Tennis (V, L); Cl Off (T); CR (R); MaintainedHigh Grades and Standards, While Attending 10 different Schools.; Traveled the World. Experienced, and Learned About, Other Cultures, Foreign to My Own.; Architecture; Cornell U, Ithaca, New York; Cooper Union, New York, New York

POLEN, ASHLEY D; PETERSBURG, IN; PIKE CTRL HS; (FR); All Am Sch; Hi Hnr Roll; St of Mnth; Comm Volntr; 4-H; DARE; FCA; Jr Ach; SADD; German Clb; Chr; Clr Grd; Dnce; SP/M/VS; Chrldg (J L); Gmnstcs (J); PPSqd (V); Tennis (J); Wt Lftg (J); Stu Cncl (R); Dance Team; All Star Scholar; Law Degree; Performing Arts; NYU-New York U; U of Evansville IN

PONDS, TIEISHA S; MARION, IN; JUSTICE THURGOOD MARSHALL MS; MS; Hi Hnr Roll; Hnr Roll; Chrch Yth Grp; DARE; Chr; Ch Chr; Law; Medicine; Indiana Wesleyan U; Indiana Business College

PONTZIUS, JESSICA E; ORLAND, IN; PRAIRIE HEIGHTS SR HS; (SR); Ctznshp Aw; Hnr Roll; WWAHSS; Forensic Science; Tri-State U

POPE, TONISHA; MOORESVILLE, IN; MOORESVILLE HS; (JR); Hnr Roll; MVP; Sci Fairs; St of Mnth; WWAHSS; Yth Ldrshp Prog; Comm Volntr; Aqrium Clb; DARE; Emplmnt; Mus Clb; Off Aide; Tchrs Aide; Vsity Clb; Chr; Dnce; Stg Cre; Cr Ctry (J); PP Ftbl (J); Sftball (J); Swmg (V); Special Education Teacher; Personal Trainer; Indiana State; Purdue

PORTER, ANDREW W; WASHINGTON, IN; WASHINGTON HS; (JR); Hnr Roll; St of Mnth; Comm Volntr; Chrch Yth Grp; NYLC; ROTC; Schol Bwl; Tchrs Aide; Clr Grd; Drl Tm; Scr Kpr (J); NJROTC XO Jr & Sr Letter in Rifle, Drill, Color Guard; Junior War College CLSC & Leadership Academy NJROTC; Naval Career; History

POSEY, MEGAN L; COMMISKEY, IN; JENNINGS CTY HS; (SO); 4H Awd; Ctznshp Aw; Hi Hnr Roll; Otst Ac Ach Awd; Perf Att; Sci Fairs; St of Mnth; Yth Ldrshp Prog; Comm Volntr; 4-H; Chrch Yth Grp; Key Club; Quiz Bowl; Svce Clb; German Clb; Orch; Jennings County Youth Leadership; State Science Honor Program (2003); Pharmacy; Chemistry; Purdue U; Butler U

POST, THERESA; NEW HAVEN, IN; WOODLAN JR/SR HS; (MS); Ctznshp Aw; Hi Hnr Roll; Hnr Roll; Perf Att; St of Mnth; Peer Tut/Med; ArtClub; DARE; Mth Clb/Tm; Ntl FFA; Track; Accounting/Business; Math; Indiana Purdue Fort Wayne; Ivy Tech

POTTER, KATIE; NEW HAVEN, IN; WOODLAN JR/SR HS; (SO); 4H Awd; Hi Hnr Roll; Kwnis Aw; Perf Att; St of Mnth; Comm Volntr; Spec Olymp Vol; 4-H; Chrch Yth Grp; Schol Bwl; Svce Clb; Mch Bnd; Pep Bnd; Chrldg (V); Stu Cncl; Academic Super Bowl Team; Principals Award; Engineering; Accounting; Purdue U

POWELL, JERIKA R; SULLIVAN, IN; SULLIVAN HS; (JR); F Lan Hn Soc; Perf Att; Emplmnt; Ntl Beta Clb; Chrldg (V CL); Gmnstcs (V L); Nursing; Vincennes U

POWERS, KATHRYN; COLUMBUS, IN; COLUMBUS NORTH HS; (SR); Hi Hnr Roll; St of Mnth; Comm Volntr; DARE; Emplmnt; Mth Clb/Tm; Bnd; Mch Bnd; Pep Bnd; Sftball (VJC); Biology; Forensic Science; Chaminade U; Alaska Pacific U

POWLEN, BRYAN; KEWANNA, IN; CASTON HS; (JR); 4H Awd; Hnr Roll; Perf Att; 4-H; ArtClub; FCA; Key Club; Sci Clb; SADD; Spanish Clb; Ftball (V CL); Track (V CL); Wt Lftg (V L); Wrstlg (V CL); State Qualifier in Shot-put, Track 2005; Chemical Engineering; Georgia Tech; Florida

POWLEN, LUCAS; KEWANNA, IN; CASTON HS; (JR); Hi Hnr Roll; Nat Hon Sy; WWAHSS; 4-H; FCA; Ntl FFA; Bskball (VJ L); Ftball (VJ L); 4-H; FFA; Agriculture; Purdue U; Vincennes U

POWLESS, MATT; NEWBURGH, IN; REITZ MEMORIAL HS; (SO); Hi Hnr Roll; Perf Att; St of Mnth; DARE; Key Club; Ftball (J); Wrstlg (V); Stu Cncl (R); Team Indiana-Wrestling; Key Club; Secondary Education; Psychology; U of Notre Dame; Purdue U

PRENTOSKI, KLIME; CROWN POINT, IN; CROWN POINT HS; (SO); Hnr Roll; Honor Roll; Business; Purdue U

PREVO, AMANDA; FRANKLIN, IN; FRANKLIN CMTY HS; (MS); Hi Hnr Roll; Hnr Roll; Otst Ac Ach Awd; St of Mnth; Peer Tut/Med; Chrch Yth Grp; Bnd; Student Voice; Project Peace Award; Performing Arts; Legal System; Juilliard School; Harvard Law School

PROCTOR, CORY; GREENCASTLE, IN; NORTH PUTNAM HS; (SR); Hi Hnr Roll; Hnr Roll; Nat Hon Sy; Perf Att; WWAHSS; Comm Volntr; Chess; Key Club; Off Aide; SADD; Spanish Clb; Bsball (V); Engineering; Purdue U; Rose-Hulman

PURCELL, BRANDI; GARY, IN; CALUMET HS; (SO); Hnr Roll; Nat Hon Sy; Perf Att; WWAHSS; Dnce; PP Ftbl (V); Sccr; Sch Ppr (R); Wrestling State - Girl; Doctor / Medical; Purdue Calumet; Indiana U

PURKHISER, MARIAH; SALEM, IN; SALEM HS; (SR); 4H Awd; Ctznshp Aw; Hnr Roll; Nat Hon Sy; WWAHSS; Yth Ldrshp Prog; Comm Volntr; 4-H; Emplmnt; Ntl FFA; Pep Squd; Sci Clb; SADD; Tchrs Aide; French Clb; FFA President; 4-H Junior Leader President; Nursing; Nurse Practitioner; Indiana U Southeast

PYNERT, BRIAN A; SOUTH BEND, IN; JOHN ADAMS HS; (SR); Hnr Roll; WWAHSS; Comm Volntr; Photog; SP/M/VS; Lit Mag (E); Been Published; Become Best Teacher I Can Be; IUSB (Indiana U of South Bend)

QUANDT, CHAD; SOUTH BEND, IN; JOHN ADAMS HS; (JR); Hnr Roll; Nat Hon Sy; Yth Ldrshp Prog; Amnsty Intl; Comm Volntr; Peer Tut/Med; Chrch Yth Grp; Drma Clb; Emplmnt; Prom Com; Quill & Scroll; SP/M/VS; Swg Chr; Ftball (V C); Cl Off (P); Sch Ppr (E); Scholar Athlete; Football-1st Team-All Conference NIC; Business; Psychology; Indiana U; Purdue U

QUINONES, MARISELA; SOUTH BEND, IN; RILEY HS; (FR); Dnce; Vllyball (L); Stu Cncl (R); Medical Field; Performing Arts / Actress; U of Notre Dame; Indiana U

RACE, CAITLIN; GRIFFITH, IN; GRIFFITH SR HS; (SO); Hi Hnr Roll; Nat Hon Sy; Otst Ac Ach Awd; St of Mnth; Chrch Yth Grp; Drma Clb; Emplmnt; Schol Bwl; International Clb; Chr; Stg Cre; ACES Member; Public Library Volunteer; Entomology; Botany

RAHM, BRYAN; COVINGTON, IN; COVINGTON CHRISTIAN SCH; (JR); Hi Hnr Roll; Hnr Roll; Nat Hon Sy; Perf Att; Pres Sch; USAA; WWAHSS; Chrch Yth Grp; Emplmnt; Lib Aide; Spch Team; Stu Cncl (P); Yrbk (R); Math Award; Aeronautical Engineering; Meteorology; Purdue U; U of Illinois

RAJECKI, ERIKA; GREENWOOD, IN; RONCALLI HS; (JR); Hi Hnr Roll; MVP; Nat Hon Sy; WWAHSS; Comm Volntr; Peer Tut/Med; Spanish Clb; Bnd; Pep Bnd; Chrldg (V L); Gmnstcs (V L); All-American Cheerleader; French Club Member; Near Eastern Languages / Cultures; Arabic; Syracuse U; Indiana U

RAMER, TIFFANIE; FORT WAYNE, IN; NORTHSIDE HS; (SO); Ctznshp Aw; Hnr Roll; Comm Volntr; ArtClub; Chrch Yth Grp; DARE; Jr Ach; Bnd; Jzz Bnd; Mch Bnd; Pep Bnd; Cosmetology; Child Care; Indiana U Purdue U Fort Wayne

RAMIREZ, HEATHER; INDIANAPOLIS, IN; LAWRENCE NORTH; (JR); Hnr Roll; MVP; Perf Att; Peer Tut/Med; Chrch Yth Grp; Scouts; Spanish Clb; Ch Chr; Dnce; Swmg; Wt Lftg; National American Miss Hispanic Women's Fashion Show; Education / Elementary School Teacher; Fashion Designer; Indiana U; Ball State U

RAMSEY, TIFFANY; NORTH VERNON, IN; SEYMOUR CHRISTIAN AC; (SO); Hi Hnr Roll; Hnr Roll; Nat Hon Sy; St of Mnth; WWAHSS; Comm Volntr; Chess; Chrch Yth Grp; Drma Clb; Tchrs Aide; Chr; Ch Chr; SP/M/VS; Vllyball (V); President's Education Awards Program / 1st Century Scholars; Egyptologist; Pediatrician; Brown U; U of California

RASCHE, LOGAN R; JASPER, IN; JASPER HS; (FR); 4H Awd; Hnr Roll; Perf Att; 4-H; Key Club; Spanish Clb; Bsball; Wrstlg (J); Math Teacher

RATCLIFF, DARIUS L; HAMMOND, IN; HAMMOND HS; (FR); Ctznshp Aw; Hnr Roll; Perf Att; St of Mnth; Chrch Yth Grp; DARE; Emplmnt; Mth Clb/Tm; Mus Clb; Spch Team; Track (J); Wt Lftg (J); Bachelor's Degree; Master's Degree; Columbia College; Illinois Institute of Art

RATCLIFF, SABRINA L; INDIANAPOLIS, IN; INDIANAPOLIS METROPOLITAN CAREER AC; (SO); Hi Hnr Roll; Hnr Roll; Otst Ac Ach Awd; Perf Att; Comm Volntr; Peer Tut/Med; Chrch Yth Grp; P to P St Amb Prg; Prom Com; Ch Chr; Drl Tm; Adv Cncl (R); Cl Off (R); Stu Cncl (S); CR (R); Sch Ppr (R); Peer Educators for Planned Parenthood; Teen Court for Reach for Youth; Political Science; Social Work; Tennessee State U; Howard U

RAVENSCROFT, JUSTINA E; BOURBON, IN; TRITON JR/SR HS; (SR); Hnr Roll; Nat Hon Sy; Pres Ac Ftns Aw; WWAHSS; Peer Tut/Med; Emplmnt; Prom Com; Sci Clb; Spanish Clb; Cr Ctry (V); Tennis (V C); Stu Cncl; Physical Therapy Assistant; Exercise Science; U of Indianapolis; U of Evansville

RAY, LACEY; SEYMOUR, IN; SEYMOUR CHRISTIAN AC; (SO); Hi Hnr Roll; Hnr Roll; MVP; Nat Hon Sy; Otst Ac Ach Awd; Perf Att; St of Mnth; Yth Ldrshp Prog; Comm Volntr; Chrch Yth Grp; Drma Clb; Ntl Beta Clb; Tchrs Aide; Chr; Ch Chr; SP/M/VS; Stg Cre; Vllyball (VJC); Sportsmanship Award; President's Education Award; OB Nurse; Pediatrician; IUPUI; U of Cincinnati

RAYL, ADDIE L; KEMPTON, IN; TRI-CENTRAL HS; (JR); 4H Awd; Hi Hnr Roll; MVP; Nat Hon Sy; WWAHSS; Comm Volntr; Peer Tut/Med; 4-H; HO'Br Yth Ldrshp; Lib Aide; Prom Com; SADD; Spanish Clb; Chrldg (V L); Cr Ctry (V L); PP Ftbl; Track (V L); Stu Cncl (R); Veterinary Medicine; Nutrition; Purdue U

RAYNOR, ADAM; VALPARAISO, IN; VALPARAISO HS; (SO); Hi Hnr Roll; Hnr Roll; Sci Fairs; Chrch Yth Grp; DARE; Bsball; Bskball; Wt Lftg; Babe Ruth Baseball; Intramural Basketball; Meteorology; Astronomy; Purdue U; Michigan U At Ann Arbor

RECTOR, TRACEY; INDIANAPOLIS, IN; SCECINA MEMORIAL HS; (SR); Hnr Roll; WWAHSS; Peer Tut/Med; Emplmnt; Spanish Clb; Promise to Keep Peer Mentor - 2 Yrs; Journalism; Indiana U Purdue U Indianapolis

REDDING, DEASHA L; ANDERSON, IN; ANDERSON HS; (SO); Ctznshp Aw; F Lan Hn Soc; Hnr Roll; Nat Hon Sy; Perf Att; St of Mnth; Yth Ldrshp Prog; Comm Volntr; Peer Tut/Med; Chrch Yth Grp; DARE; Tchrs Aide; Spanish Clb; Chr; Ch Chr; Bskball; PP Ftbl (V); Sftball; 5 "A" Sophomore Exec; Physical Therapy; Dental Specialist; Indiana U; Indiana State U

REDMAN, ASHLEY N; BROWNSBURG, IN; BROWNSBURG HS; (SO); Hi Hnr Roll; Hnr Roll; Otst Ac Ach Awd; Perf Att; St of Mnth; FCA; Key Club; Sci Clb; German Clb; Chr; Ch Chr; Biology; Teacher; DePaul U; Purdue U

REECER, COURTNEY E; GOLDSMITH, IN; TIPTON HS; (SO); Hnr Roll; St of Mnth; Emplmnt; Key Club; Pep Squd; Photog; SADD; Spanish Clb; Vllyball (J); Vice President-Key Club; Member of Student Council, Voice & TYMAD; Journalism-Personal Relations; Photography; Ball State U; Purdue U

REED, ANDREW B; ANDERSON, IN; CALVARY AC; (JR); Ctznshp Aw; Hnr Roll; MVP; Nat Hon Sy; Sci Fairs; Comm Volntr; Hosp Aide; Chrch Yth Grp; Emplmnt; Ntl Beta Clb; Scouts; Spch Team; Tchrs Aide; Wdwrkg Clb; Ch Chr; Clr Grd; Bskball (V); Stu Cncl (T, R); Eagle Scout; Ball State U

REED, ERIK; FORT BRANCH, IN; WALDO J WOOD MEMORIAL HS; (FR); Hnr Roll; Bsball (J); Army Ranger

REESE, TAYLOR J; HUNTINGBURG, IN; SOUTHRIDGE HS; (FR); Gov Hnr Prg; Hi Hnr Roll; Nat Hon Sy; Otst Ac Ach Awd; Pres Ac Ftns Aw; St of Mnth; DARE; Lttrmn Clb; Mth Clb/Tm; Quiz Bowl; Vsity Clb; Bskball; Ftball; Golf; Cl Off (R); Stu Cncl (R); CR (R); 4.0 GPA; #1 Rank in Class; Engineering; Mathematics; Rose Hulman; U of Evansville

REEVES, RANDY; GREENFIELD, IN; EASTERN HANCOCK HS; (SR); F Lan Hn Soc; Hi Hnr Roll; Hnr Roll; MVP; Nat Hon Sy; Otst Ac Ach Awd; Perf Att; St of Mnth; WWAHSS; Yth Ldrshp Prog; Comm Volntr; Peer Tut/Med; Chrch Yth Grp; DARE; Lib Aide; Mth Clb/Tm; Off Aide; Sci Clb; Scouts; Tchrs Aide; Bskball (J); Ftball (V CL); Track (V L); Stu Cncl (R); Bruce Russell Award; Bachelor's Degree; Radiation Therapy; Indiana U Purdue U

REISING, LEAH M; POSEYVILLE, IN; NORTH POSEY HS; (JR); Hi Hnr Roll; Hnr Roll; Pres Ac Ftns Aw; Comm Volntr; 4-H; BPA; Chrch Yth Grp; Emplmnt; FBLA; Prom Com; German Clb; Bskball (J); Tennis (V L); Vllyball (J); Cl Off (P); Stu Cncl (P); President Class of 2006; Student Council President; Marketing; Communication; U of Evansville; Murray State U

RENNER, KYAIRA N; LAWRENCEBURG, IN; LAWRENCEBURG HS; (JR); Hnr Roll; Nat Hon Sy; WWAHSS; Yth Ldrshp Prog; Comm Volntr; Emplmnt; Key Club; NYLC; Prom Com; Spanish Clb; Chr; Swg Chr; Sccr (JC); Track (V L); PhD in Pharmacy; U of Cincinnati; Butler U

REUST, MEGAN; HUNTINGTON, IN; HUNTINGTON NORTH HS; (JR); Hnr Roll; Otst Ac Ach Awd; Perf Att; Sci Fairs; Peer Tut/Med; Drma Clb; Mus Clb; Vsity Clb; Clr Grd; Flg Crps; Mch Bnd; On the HNHS Varsity Bowling Team; On News Show At Huntington North; TV Broadcasting-Bachelors; Huntington College; U of Indianapolis

RHOADES, BRITTANY; DECATUR, IN; BELLMONT HS; (SR); Hi Hnr Roll; Hnr Roll; Nat Hon Sy; WWAHSS; Comm Volntr; Peer Tut/Med; AL Aux Girls; Emplmnt; SADD; Tchrs Aide; Spanish Clb; Bskball (J); PP Ftbl (V); Vllyball (V L); Occupational Therapy; Psychology; U of Indianapolis

RHOADES, DEENA; BUTLER, IN; EASTSIDE JR/SR HS; (SO); Hnr Roll; St of Mnth; Amnsty Intl; Chess; DARE; Emplmnt; Spch Team; Tchrs Aide; Bnd; Chr; Mch Bnd; Cr Ctry (L); Track (J); Amnesty International; Art; Music; Holy Cross College

RICH, ELIZABETH; CLOVERDALE, IN; CLOVERDALE HS; (SO); Hi Hnr Roll; Hnr Roll; WWAHSS; Chrch Yth Grp; Lib Aide; French Clb; Bnd; Clr Grd; Dnce; Pep Bnd; Golf (V CL); Sch Ppr (R); Cumulative Honors; Student Ambassadors; Astronomy; Astrophysics; U of Hawaii Hilo; Indiana U Bloomington

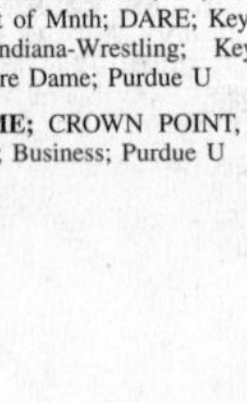
Reeves, Randy
Eastern Hancock HS
Greenfield, IN

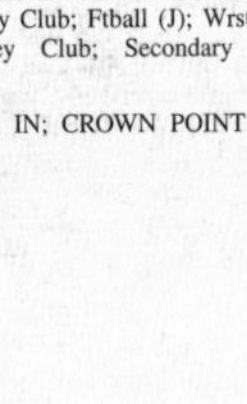
Rayl, Addie L
Tri-Central HS
Kempton, IN

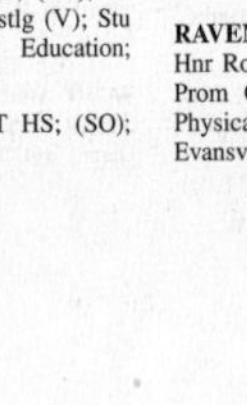
Ramer, Tiffanie
Northside HS
Fort Wayne, IN

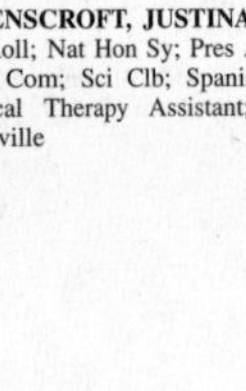
Polen, Ashley D
Pike Ctrl HS
Petersburg, IN

National
Honor Roll
Spring 2005

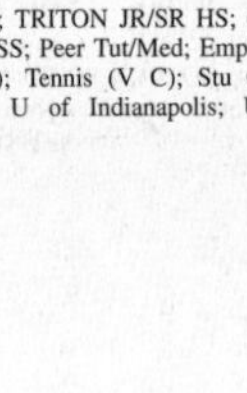
Pluta, Michelle E
Bloomington HS South
Bloomington, IN

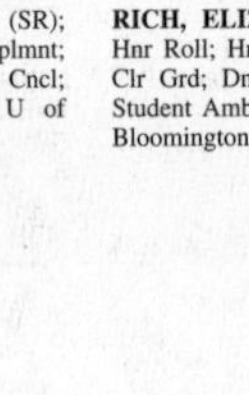
Ratcliff, Darius L
Hammond HS
Hammond, IN

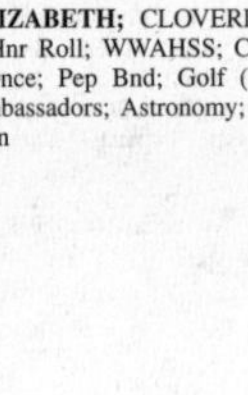
Redding, Deasha L
Anderson HS
Anderson, IN

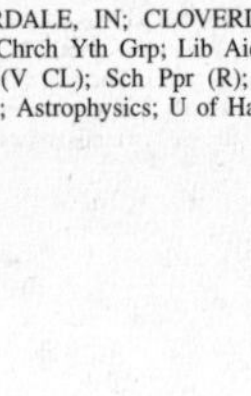
Rhoades, Deena
Eastside JR/SR HS
Butler, IN

RICHARDS, TRACI L; MONTICELLO, IN; TWIN LAKES HS; (SR); Ctznshp Aw; Hi Hnr Roll; Hnr Roll; Nat Hon Sy; Pres Sch; St of Mnth; Peer Tut/Med; Drma Clb; Jr Ach; Quill & Scroll; Tchrs Aide; Chr; SP/M/VS; Stu Cncl (R); Sch Ppr (E); Elementary Education; Indiana U - Accepted

RICHARDSON, ASHLEY; LAKE STATION, IN; RIVER FOREST SR HS; (FR); Hi Hnr Roll; DARE; Tchrs Aide; Sftball (L); Vllyball (J); Sch Ppr (E); Physical Therapy; Indiana U Purdue U Indy

RICHARDSON, HEATHER N; LEBANON, IN; WESTERN BOONE; (JR); DAR; Hnr Roll; Nat Hon Sy; Perf Att; Sci Fairs; 4-H; Chrch Yth Grp; Emplmnt; FCA; Key Club; Pep Squd; Tchrs Aide; Foreign Clb; Bnd; Mch Bnd; Pep Bnd; Golf (V); Scr Kpr (V); Sftball (V C); Swmg (L); Vllyball (J).

RICHARDSON, KERRI; LEBANON, IN; WESTERN BOONE JR/SR HS; (SO); 4H Awd; Hnr Roll; Otst Ac Ach Awd; USAA; WWAHSS; Comm Volntr; 4-H; ArtClub; Chrch Yth Grp; Key Club; Golf (V L); Swmg (V L); Yrbk (E, R, P); National Art Honor Society (NAHS); Top Ten in Class; Journalism; Northwestern U; Butler U

RICHARDSON, KIMBERLY L; AVON, IN; AVON HS; (SO); Ctznshp Aw; F Lan Hn Soc; Hi Hnr Roll; Hnr Roll; Nat Hon Sy; Perf Att; St of Mnth; Comm Volntr; Chrch Yth Grp; Emplmnt; Pep Squd; Tchrs Aide; Vsity Clb; Bnd; Dnce; Drl Tm; Stu Cncl (S); Psychology; Ball State U; Purdue U

RICHMOND, ASHLEY; HIGHLAND, IN; HIGHLAND HS; (FR); Hi Hnr Roll; Hnr Roll; Comm Volntr; Key Club; Track (J); Stu Cncl (R); Relay for Life; Library Volunteer; Accounting; Engineering; West Point Academy; Indiana U

RICKE, LAUREN; HUNTINGTON, IN; CANTERBURY SCH; (SR); Hi Hnr Roll; Hnr Roll; WWAHSS; Chrch Yth Grp; Emplmnt; Key Club; Lib Aide; Prom Com; SP/M/VS; Chrldg (V); Sftball (V); Cl Off (V); Lit Mag (R); Sch Ppr (R); Japanese; International Affairs; Mt Holyoke College

RICKETT, AMANDA; SPENCER, IN; OWEN VALLEY CMTY HS; (FR); Hnr Roll; Perf Att; St of Mnth; WWAHSS; Bskball (J); Track (V L); Yrbk (R); VFW-Won 2nd Place in District for Patriot Pen Writing Contest; MATS-Midwest Talent Search Participant

RIDENOUR, MADYSON L; PITTSBORO, IN; TRI-WEST HS; (SO); Hnr Roll; Pres Ac Ftns Aw; 4-H; DARE; Emplmnt; Off Aide; Chrldg (V); Member of the 2004 State Fair; Small Varsity Squad That Received 1st Place; Business; Spanish; Indiana U; Ball State U

RIGGS, BRITNEY; MILTON, IN; LINCOLN SR HS; (SO); All Am Sch; Hi Hnr Roll; MVP; USAA; WWAHSS; Peer Tut/Med; P to P St Amb Prg; Schol Bwl; French Clb; Gmnstcs (V L); Track (V L); Yrbk (R, P); Athletic Scholar; MVP - 2 Yrs - Gymnastics; Writing a Book; St Mary of the Woods; U of Notre Dame

RILEY, BREANNA; AURORA, IN; SOUTH DEARBORN HS; (JR); Hnr Roll; Nat Hon Sy; Otst Ac Ach Awd; St of Mnth; WWAHSS; Comm Volntr; Peer Tut/Med; Emplmnt; SADD; Tchrs Aide; Spanish Clb; Vllyball (JC); Elementary Teacher; Physical Therapists; Northern Kentucky; Evansville

RINCKEL, DANIEL T; BLOOMINGTON, IN; BLOOMINGTON HS NORTH; (SR); Hi Hnr Roll; Nat Hon Sy; Comm Volntr; Peer Tut/Med; Emplmnt; Outdrs Clb; Scouts; Tchrs Aide; Bnd; Jzz Bnd; Mch Bnd; Swmg (V CL); Eagle Scout; Mental Attitude Award - Swimming; Mechanical Engineering; Rose-Hulman Institute of Technology

RINKENBERGER, JEFFREY J; VALPARAISO, IN; VALPARAISO HS; (FR); Hnr Roll; Sci/Math Olympn; Key Club; Sci Clb; Science Olympiad Team Member; Engineering; Indiana

RISHER, TIFFIANY R; WABASH, IN; NORTHFIELD JR/SR HS; (SO); Pres Ac Ftns Aw; Yth Ldrshp Prog; 4-H; Drm Mjr; Chrldg (V); Sftball (J); Baton Coach-Saint Bernard Summer Program; Member of United States Twirling Association; Nursing; Aviation; Purdue U; U Of Notre Dame

RITTER, LINDSAY; EVANSVILLE, IN; CENTRAL HS; (JR); Hi Hnr Roll; DECA; Emplmnt; Pep Squd; Sci Clb; Special Needs Volunteer; Pediatrics; Physical / Occupational Therapy; Indiana U; Purdue U

RITTER, NIKI; PLAINFIELD, IN; PLAINFIELD HS; (JR); Hi Hnr Roll; MVP; Nat Hon Sy; Perf Att; WWAHSS; Comm Volntr; Spec Olymp Vol; Chrch Yth Grp; Key Club; French Clb; Sccr (V L); Key Club President; Octagon Club; Biology; Psychology; Franklin College; Purdue U

RITZ, CARSON D; BROOKVILLE, IN; FRANKLIN CTY HS; (SR); Hi Hnr Roll; Jr Mshl; Nat Hon Sy; Valdctrian; WWAHSS; Yth Ldrshp Prog; Comm Volntr; ArtClub; Chrch Yth Grp; Emplmnt; Lib Aide; Mus Clb; Prom Com; Tchrs Aide; Spanish Clb; SP/M/VS; Bsball (VJ L); Bskball (JC); Tennis (VJ L); Adv Cncl (R); Stu Cncl (S, R); Accomplished Piano Player (Lessons for 12 Years); Academic All State Tennis; Audio Production; Sound Engineer; Webster U; Belmont U

ROBARGE, MARK; GREENTOWN, IN; EASTERN (HOWARD) HS; (SR); Hi Hnr Roll; MVP; Nat Hon Sy; Valdctrian; Peer Tut/Med; Chrch Yth Grp; Quiz Bowl; Tchrs Aide; Chr; Swmg (V CL); Tennis (V CL); Track (J); Science Fair Judge; Biochemistry; Veterinarian

ROBERTSON, BRADLEY S; HOPE, IN; HAUSER JR/SR HS; (SO); Hi Hnr Roll; Hnr Roll; WWAHSS; Comm Volntr; Chrch Yth Grp; DARE; Emplmnt; FCA; Key Club; Tchrs Aide; Spanish Clb; Sccr (V L); Stu Cncl (R); Lit Mag; Computer Science; Web Design; Butler U; Northern Kentucky U

ROBERTSON, BRITTANY; FRANKFORT, IN; FRANKFORT SR HS; (FR); Ctznshp Aw; Hi Hnr Roll; St of Mnth; Chrch Yth Grp; Chr; SP/M/VS; Swg Chr; Tennis (J); Vllyball (J); Music; Education; Indiana Wesleyan U; Butler U

ROBERTSON, JEREMY D; JASONVILLE, IN; SHAKAMAK HS; (SO); Hnr Roll; Drma Clb; Mus Clb; Chr; SP/M/VS; Swg Chr; Computer Systems Management; Computer Programming; U of Southern Indiana; Purdue U

ROBINSON, CHANAE R; MERRILLVILLE, IN; MERRILLVILLE HS; (MS); Ctznshp Aw; Gov Hnr Prg; Hi Hnr Roll; Hnr Roll; St of Mnth; Comm Volntr; Chrch Yth Grp; Chr; Ch Chr; Dnce; Drl Tm; Chrldg (C); Gmnstcs; PPSqd; Tennis; Stu Cncl (V, R); American Legion Award; Principal's Award; Pediatrician; Doctor's Degree; IU Bloomington; Michigan State U

ROBINSON, COREY; GENEVA, IN; SOUTH ADAMS JR/SR HS; (SR); Hnr Roll; Perf Att; DARE; Emplmnt; Lib Aide; Off Aide; Tchrs Aide; Medical Assistant; International Business College (Fort Wayne)

ROBINSON, KIMBERLY; ANDERSON, IN; HIGHLAND HS; (FR); Hnr Roll; Chrch Yth Grp; Ch Chr; Tennis (J); Medical Degree; Dentistry; Indiana U; Ball State U

ROBINSON, RICHELL; EVANSVILLE, IN; CENTRAL HS; (JR); Ctznshp Aw; Hi Hnr Roll; Hnr Roll; Perf Att; Sci Fairs; Sci/Math Olympn; CARE; Comm Volntr; Chrch Yth Grp; DARE; Voc Ind Clb Am; Spanish Clb; Dnce; Vllyball (J); Stu Cncl (R); Business; Computer Applications; U of Indianapolis; Ball State U

ROBINSON, STEVE; WARSAW, IN; WARSAW CMTY HS; (JR); Ctznshp Aw; Hi Hnr Roll; Hnr Roll; Cr Ctry (V L); Track (V L); Freshmen Mentor; Octagon Club

ROBISON, MARK D; BROWNSTOWN, IN; INDIANA AC; (SR); Nat Mrt Fin; WWAHSS; Chrch Yth Grp; Emplmnt; Key Club; German Clb; CR (R); Students Standing Against Genocide; History; Ball State U (Attending This Fall)

ROBLING, DANIELLE; JASPER, IN; JASPER HS; (FR); WWAHSS; Key Club; SADD; Spanish Clb; Bnd; Dnce; Mch Bnd; Pep Bnd; Bat Girl; Dance Lessons 12 Years; Therapy; Indiana U

RODRIGUEZ, OPHY; INDIANAPOLIS, IN; NORTHWEST HS; (JR); Hnr Roll; Dnce; Art; Modeling; I U Indianapolis; IUPUI

RODRIGUEZ, RAFAEL; FORT WAYNE, IN; NEW HAVEN HS; (FR); Sccr (VJ L); Student of the Month Careers Class; Law Enforcement (Police Officer)

ROGALA, BRYAN; CARMEL, IN; CARMEL HS; (SO); Duke TS; Hi Hnr Roll; Hnr Roll; Sch Ppr (R); Started on the Rugby Team as a Freshman & Sophomore; On Radio Staff - WHJE; Journalism; Telecommunications; Ohio State U; Syracuse U

ROGERS, ASHLEY B; TIPTON, IN; TIPTON HS; (JR); Hi Hnr Roll; Hnr Roll; Emplmnt; Key Club; Prom Com; Chrldg (J); Stu Cncl (R); 3.75 GPA Award (2 Years); Nursing; Midwifery; Indiana U of Kokomo; Indiana U/ Purdue U of Indy

ROGERS, TANYA M; TIPTON, IN; TIPTON HS; (JR); Hnr Roll; WWAHSS; Emplmnt; Chr; Dental Assistant; Nursing; Ivy Tech State College; International Business College

ROLAND, NATASHA R; WASHINGTON, IN; WASHINGTON HS; (SO); Hi Hnr Roll; Hnr Roll; Peer Tut/Med; DARE; Jr Ach; Yrbk (P); Job, Baby Sitting; Church Activities; Master's Degree; Medical Careers; U of Evansville; Purdue U

ROLLINS, JONATHAN M; VALPARAISO, IN; WHEELER HS; (JR); Hnr Roll; Key Club; Scouts; Mar Art; Rqtball; Black Belt; Business; Accounting; Indiana U; Purdue U

ROMERO, ATALYA; FRANKFORT, IN; FRANKFORT SR HS; (FR); WWAHSS; Chr; Ch Chr; In Honors English; Marine Biologist; Cosmetic Surgeon; Purdue U; U of Miami

ROMESBURG, ERIC; GRIFFITH, IN; GRIFFITH HS; (SR); Hnr Roll; St of Mnth; WWAHSS; Ftball (J); Doctorate in Pharmacy / Pharmacist; Purdue U Calumet; Purdue U West Lafayette

ROOS, MORGAN; JASPER, IN; JASPER HS; (SO); Hnr Roll; Nat Stu Ath Day Aw; Otst Ac Ach Awd; Perf Att; Pres Ac Ftns Aw; WWAHSS; Key Club; SADD; Spanish Clb; Clr Grd; Nursing Degrees; Butler; Purdue

ROSENBAUM, JON M A; LAUREL, IN; FRANKLIN CTY HS; (SR); Hi Hnr Roll; Hnr Roll; Nat Hon Sy; St Schl; St of Mnth; WWAHSS; Yth Ldrshp Prog; Comm Volntr; Peer Tut/Med; ArtClub; Drma Clb; Emplmnt; Key Club; NYLC; Spanish Clb; SP/M/VS; Cl Off (V); USGA Certified Gymnastics Instructor; Senatorial & Congressional Nominee to Naval & A.F. Acad., Academic Hall of Fame-FCHS; Serve As an Officer in U.S. Air Force or Navy; Work At NASA As an Engineering Physicist; US Naval (Or) Air Force Academy; Embry Riddle Aeronautical U

ROSS, NICOLE; MICHIGAN CITY, IN; MICHIGAN CITY HS; (FR); Hnr Roll; Chess; Bnd; Sftball (J); Criminal Justice; Pre-Med; Indiana U; Purdue U

ROSS, RICKI L; BEDFORD, IN; STONE CITY CHRISTIAN AC; (FR); Hnr Roll; St of Mnth; Hosp Aide; Chrch Yth Grp; Emplmnt; Chr; Ch Chr; Stu Cncl (R); Yrbk (E); Pre-Med; Gods Bible School & College; Indiana State U

ROUSH, KENNETH R; SOUTH BEND, IN; ANDREW JACKSON HS; (MS); 4H Awd; Hi Hnr Roll; MVP; 4-H; Orch; Cr Ctry; Ftball; Track; Stu Cncl; Concert Master of Orchestra

ROUSSEAU, EMMANUELLE A; MUNCIE, IN; YORKTOWN HS; (SO); Hnr Roll; Sci Fairs; WWAHSS; Hab For Humty Volntr; Peer Tut/Med; Chrch Yth Grp; Dbte Team; Emplmnt; FBLA; Key Club; Off Aide; Quiz Bowl; Sci Clb; Sccr (V); Tennis (V); Stu Cncl (R); Sch Ppr (R); Pre-Law; Notre Dame U

RUBLE, ANN M; ARLINGTON, IN; RUSHVILLE CONSOLIDATED HS; (SR); 4H Awd; Ctznshp Aw; Hi Hnr Roll; Hnr Roll; Nat Hon Sy; Otst Ac Ach Awd; Perf Att; WWAHSS; Comm Volntr; Peer Tut/Med; 4-H; Chrch Yth Grp; Key Club; Quiz Bowl; Svce Clb; SADD; Spanish Clb; Acpl Chr; Bnd; Chr; Ch Chr; Stu Cncl; Art Department Award; Outstanding Musicians Workmanship Award; Music Major in Instrumental Music Education; Indiana State U Terre Haute

RUCH, JENNA R; MILFORD, IN; WAWASEE HS; (JR); 4H Awd; Hnr Roll; WWAHSS; Comm Volntr; 4-H; Chrch Yth Grp; Cmptr Clb; Drma Clb; FCA; Key Club; Off Aide; Ch Chr; Golf (VJ); Vllyball (J); Hoosier Girls State; Dietetics; Health Care; Purdue U; North Manchester

RUEBEL, KYLE; HIGHLAND, IN; HIGHLAND HS; (JR); Hnr Roll; WWAHSS; Yth Ldrshp Prog; Chrch Yth Grp; DARE; Key Club; Mus Clb; Off Aide; SADD; Chr; Bsball (V L); Swmg (J L); Tennis (J L); Stu Cncl (R); Sch Ppr (R); Bowling Team Varsity Lettered/Perfect First Vocal Solo State; T. R.E.N.D. Group-Mentor Group; Pediatrics; Engineering; South Suburban College; St. Joseph's College (Rennselaer)

RUPPEL, RYAN; PETERSBURG, IN; PIKE CTRL HS; (FR); All Am Sch; Hnr Roll; USAA; Emplmnt; Outdrs Clb; Midwest Talent Search; Academic Team; Bachelor's Degree; Master's Degree; ITT Technical Institutes; Purdue U

RUSH, LAUREN; SHELBYVILLE, IN; SOUTHWESTERN HS; (FR); Hnr Roll; USAA; Comm Volntr; 4-H; Chrch Yth Grp; DARE; Ntl FFA; Pep Squd; Tchrs Aide; Dnce; Chrldg (V); Most Spirited Award-9th Grade-Varsity; Athletic Honor Roll; Math; Teaching; Franklin College; Indiana U

RYAN, PATRICK C; COLUMBUS, IN; COLUMBUS NORTH HS; (JR); Hnr Roll; Nat Hon Sy; St of Mnth; WWAHSS; Peer Tut/Med; BPA; Chrch Yth Grp; Key Club; NYLC; Off Aide; Cr Ctry (J L); Track (V L); Voice Anti-Tobacco Group; Freedom's Answer Leadership Team; Military Officer; History; United States Military Academy; U of Notre Dame

SAEED, SIDRA A; PLAINFIELD, IN; PLAINFIELD HS; (SO); Hi Hnr Roll; Perf Att; St Optmst of Yr; Comm Volntr; Key Club; French Clb; Track (J); Stu Cncl (R); Pre-Med; Pharmacy; Indiana U Purdue U Indianapolis; Butler U

SANDERS, ELIJAH L; MT VERNON, IN; MT VERNON HS; (JR); Hnr Roll; Nat Hon Sy; Comm Volntr; Biology Clb; Chrch Yth Grp; DARE; DECA; FCA; Vsity Clb; German Clb; Cr Ctry (V L); Sccr (J); Swmg (V L); Track (V); Yrbk (P); Cross Country - Semi-State Champs; Swimming - Sectional Champ; School Administration; Business Management; SIU Carbondale; Home College

SANDERS, KIMBERLY; FORT WAYNE, IN; HOMESTEAD HS; (SO); Hi Hnr Roll; Sci/Math Olympn; WWAHSS; Comm Volntr; Chrch Yth Grp; Jr Ach; Key Club; Orch; Swmg (J); Track (J); Pharmacy; Biomedical Engineering; Purdue U

SANDS, JENNIFER; SYRACUSE, IN; WAWASEE HS; (SR); 4H Awd; Hi Hnr Roll; Hnr Roll; Nat Hon Sy; Otst Ac Ach Awd; WWAHSS; Comm Volntr; Peer Tut/Med; 4-H; BPA; Chrch Yth Grp; Drma Clb; Emplmnt; Key Club; Prom Com; Ch Chr; Orch; SP/M/VS; Stg Cre; Chrldg; Dvng (V CL); Xavier U, Cincinnati, OH

SANTO, CORBIN T; PITTSBORO, IN; TRI-WEST HS; (SO); Hi Hnr Roll; Perf Att; St of Mnth; Emplmnt; NtlFrnscLg; French Clb; Scr Kpr (L); Track (L); Stu Cncl (R); Freshman Mentoring Program; Biology; Economics; U of Notre Dame; Northwestern U

SARBER, MELLISA; SOUTH BEND, IN; JOHN ADAMS HS; (JR); Hnr Roll; Emplmnt; Photog; Scholastics Art Award; Dentistry; Mortuary Science

Ruble, Ann M
Rushville Consolidated HS
Arlington, IN

Rosenbaum, Jon M A
Franklin Cty HS
Laurel, IN

Robinson, Richell
Central HS
Evansville, IN

Rinkenberger, Jeffrey J
Valparaiso HS
Valparaiso, IN

National
Honor Roll
Spring 2005

Riggs, Britney
Lincoln SR HS
Milton, IN

Rogers, Tanya M
Tipton HS
Tipton, IN

Ross, Ricki L
Stone City Christian AC
Bedford, IN

Ruppel, Ryan
Pike Ctrl HS
Petersburg, IN

SATTERFIELD, JORDAN; WINSLOW, IN; PIKE CTRL HS; (SO); 4H Awd; Emplmnt; German Clb; Bachelor's; Hanover U

SAYA, PETER; FORT WAYNE, IN; HOMESTEAD HS; (FR); Ctznshp Aw; Hi Hnr Roll; St of Mnth; Travel Hockey Player; Communications; Career in Medicine; Syracuse U; Michigan State U

SCHAEFER, HEATHER; LANESVILLE, IN; LANESVILLE JR/SR HS; (JR); Hi Hnr Roll; Nat Hon Sy; WWAHSS; Peer Tut/Med; Chrch Yth Grp; FCA; Photog; Prom Com; Quiz Bowl; Scouts; SADD; French Clb; Bskball (V); Cr Ctry (V); Youth Philanthropy Council Member; Girl Scout Silver Award; Biology/Chemistry-Pre-Medicine; Business; Indiana U (Bloomington); U of Chicago

SCHAEFER, KYLE J; EVANSVILLE, IN; CENTRAL HS; (SO); Hi Hnr Roll; Pres Sch; Bskball (J); Engineering; Business; U of Evansville; U of Notre Dame

SCHAFER II, BRENDAN; CROWN POINT, IN; MERRILLVILLE HS; (SR); Hi Hnr Roll; Nat Hon Sy; Nat Mrt LOC; Otst Ac Ach Awd; Pres Sch; USAA; WWAHSS; Emplmnt; Quill & Scroll; Bsball (V L); Adv Cncl (R); Stu Cncl (R); Sch Ppr (R); Yrbk (E); Accounting; Sports Broadcasting; Indiana U Bloomington

SCHIEBER, EMILY; GOSHEN, IN; NORTHRIDGE HS; (SR); Hi Hnr Roll; Hnr Roll; Nat Hon Sy; Perf Att; WWAHSS; 4-H; Chrch Yth Grp; Emplmnt; Scouts; Chr; Girl Scout Silver Award; Elementary Education; Manchester College

SCHLUND, NATHAN; NEW HAVEN, IN; NEW HAVEN HS; (FR); Bsball (J); Ftball (V); Wrstlg (VL)

SCHLUTTENHOFER, CRAIG M; THORNTOWN, IN; WESTERN BOONE JR/SR HS; (SR); 4H Awd; Hi Hnr Roll; Hnr Roll; Nat Hon Sy; Comm Volntr; Hab For Humty Volntr; 4-H; ArtClub; Chrch Yth Grp; Emplmnt; Ntl FFA; Scouts; Tchrs Aide; Adv Cncl (R); National Art Honor Society (Member); National Jr. Horticulture Society (Member); Horticulture Science; Purdue U

SCHMELZ, JAMES; GEORGETOWN, IN; LANESVILLE HS; (SO); Hnr Roll; St of Mnth; Peer Tut/Med; Computer Networking; U of Southern U

SCHMELZ, JESSICA; GEORGETOWN, IN; (JR); Hnr Roll; Nat Hon Sy; St of Mnth; WWAHSS; Yth Ldrshp Prog; Comm Volntr; Chrch Yth Grp; FCA; FCCLA; Prom Com; Quiz Bowl; SADD; Tchrs Aide; French Clb; Bnd; Chr; Bskball (V); Tennis (V); Vllyball (V); Cl Off (V); Stu Cncl (R); CR (R); Indiana Leadership Seminar; Camp Wyman Attendee; Medical Field; Purdue U; Indiana U Bloomington

SCHMIDT, JESSICA L; MICHIGAN CITY, IN; MICHIGAN CITY HS; (FR); Hnr Roll; Comm Volntr; Chrch Yth Grp; Prom Com; Tchrs Aide; French Clb; Vllyball (JC); Cl Off (V); Stu Cncl (R); CR (R); Athletic Training Asst.; Sports Medicine; UCLA; U of Illinois

SCHMITT, AMY; JASPER, IN; JASPER HS; (FR); Hnr Roll; Pres Ac Ftns Aw; Key Club; SADD; Spanish Clb; Sftball (J); Vllyball (VJ); Teaching

SCHMITT, LARYSSA J; LYNNVILLE, IN; TECUMSEH HS; (FR); Hnr Roll; Ntl Beta Clb; Tchrs Aide; Dnce; Mch Bnd; Pep Bnd; SP/M/VS; Sftball (J); Vllyball (J); Cl Off (V), Dance Team Varsity; Teacher; Architect; Indiana U

SCHNAUS, ALYSSA; JASPER, IN; JASPER HS; (FR); Hnr Roll; Perf Att; Key Club; Mus Clb; Scouts; SADD; Spanish Clb; Bnd; Mch Bnd; Pep Bnd; Swmg (V); Pediatrics; Surgery; Indiana U; U of Tennessee

SCHNEIDER, ANTHONY; HENRYVILLE, IN; HENRYVILLE JR/SR HS; (SO); Hnr Roll; Chrch Yth Grp; Lib Aide; Golf (J); P.A.C.E. Award; Marine Biologist; Florida State U; U of Florida

SCHNELL, ISAIAH; STENDAL, IN; PIKE CTRL HS; (FR); 4H Awd; Comm Volntr; 4-H; Chrch Yth Grp; Emplmnt; Marketing; Business Management; Indiana U

SCHNITZ, CASSANDRA S; AKRON, IN; TIPPECANOE VALLEY HS; (JR); Ctznshp Aw; Hnr Roll; Perf Att; Pres Ac Ftns Aw; Mus Clb; Bnd; Mch Bnd; Pep Bnd; Kick Boxing; Registered Nurse; Dentist; Ivy Tech State College; Manchester College

SCHOENHERR, JONAS P; PORTLAND, IN; JAY CTY HS; (SR); Hi Hnr Roll; Nat Hon Sy; WWAHSS; Chrch Yth Grp; Emplmnt; Key Club; Bnd; Sccr (V)

SCHOENLE, JODY R; NEW HAVEN, IN; NEW HAVEN HS; (FR); Hi Hnr Roll; Otst Ac Ach Awd; Perf Att; Sci Fairs; St of Mnth; Chrch Yth Grp; DARE; Drma Clb; Jr Ach; Key Club; Scouts; SADD; Acpl Chr; Chr; Ch Chr; SP/M/VS; Vllyball (J); Adv Cncl (R); Stu Cncl (S); Non Public School Association Distinguished Student Award; Girl Scout Silver Award; Nursing; Social Work with Children; Indiana Purdue U of Fort Wayne; Saint Francis U

SCHOETTLE, JEANETTE; GREENBORO, IN; PERRY MERIDIAN HS; (JR); Hi Hnr Roll; Nat Hon Sy; Comm Volntr; Peer Tut/Med; Chrch Yth Grp; Key Club; Off Aide; Pep Squd; Spanish Clb; Cr Ctry (V L); Sftball (V L); Best Buddies Club; Spanish Club; Indiana U; Purdue U

SCHOETTMER, SARA L; GREENSBURG, IN; NORTH DECATUR JR/SR HS; (SR); Ctznshp Aw; DAR; Hnr Roll; Nat Hon Sy; Otst Ac Ach Awd; USAA; WWAHSS; Comm Volntr; Emplmnt; FTA; Key Club; Lib Aide; Svce Clb; SADD; Tchrs Aide; Clb; Chr; Clr Grd; Adv Cncl (R); Cl Off (S); Homecoming Court-Princess; Radiology; Indiana U-Purdue U-Indianapolis

SCHOLL, AMANDA; ANDERSON, IN; HIGHLAND HS; (SO); Hnr Roll; Sci Fairs; WWAHSS; Comm Volntr; Chrch Yth Grp; Volunteer At the Second Harvest Food Bank; Red Belt in Tae Kwon Do (Martial Arts); Special Education; Forensics; Indiana U; Ball State U

SCHROEDER, BRITTANY; JASPER, IN; JASPER HS; (SO); Perf Att; WWAHSS; Comm Volntr; Peer Tut/Med; Key Club; Spanish Clb; Pediatric Nurse; Beautician; Indiana State U; Purdue U

SCHROEDER, PAIGE R; JASPER, IN; JASPER HS; (FR); Hi Hnr Roll; Pres Ac Ftns Aw; Sci Fairs; Chrch Yth Grp; Emplmnt; FCA; Key Club; SADD; Vsity Clb; Spanish Clb; Chrldg (V); Golf (V); Cl Off (T); Stu Cncl (R); Sch Ppr (R, P); Yrbk (R, P); Double Major in Business; Major in Designing; Indiana U

SCHUCK, HEIDI A; ROCKPORT, IN; SOUTH SPENCER HS; (FR); Hnr Roll; Key Club; SADD; Bnd; Pep Bnd; Bskball (L); Sccr (L); Track (L); Nursing; U of Southern Indiana; Vincennes U

SCHULTZ, ERIC R; FORT WAYNE, IN; HOMESTEAD HS; (SO); Hi Hnr Roll; Perf Att; WWAHSS; Bnd; Jzz Bnd; Mch Bnd; Orch; IPFW Honor Band; Fort Wayne Youth Symphony

SCHULZ, SYDNEY M; SEYMOUR, IN; SEYMOUR HS; (SO); F Lan Hn Soc; Hi Hnr Roll; Nat Hon Sy; Otst Ac Ach Awd; WWAHSS; Yth Ldrshp Prog; Comm Volntr; Peer Tut/Med; Chrch Yth Grp; DARE; Emplmnt; Lttrmn Clb; Off Aide; Photog; Prom Com; Tchrs Aide; Bskball (V); Tennis (J); Vllyball (V); Stu Cncl (R); Sch Ppr (E); Medicine; Notre Dame

SCHUM, AMANDA; JASPER, IN; JASPER HS; (SO); Hnr Roll; Pres Ac Ftns Aw; Sci Fairs; Yth Ldrshp Prog; Comm Volntr; Peer Tut/Med; ArtClub; Chrch Yth Grp; Emplmnt; Key Club; Scouts; SADD; Spanish Clb; Bskball (J); Sftball (VJ); Vllyball (J); Medical; U of Southern Indiana

SCHUMACHER, KELLY N; SANTA CLAUS, IN; HERITAGE HILLS HS; (JR); Hnr Roll; WWAHSS; DARE; Scouts; Tchrs Aide; Tennis (J); Natural Helpers; Twenty-First Century Scholar; Psychology; Sociology; Marion College

SCHWANHOLT, JOSHUA; MILAN, IN; MILAN HS; (SO); Hnr Roll; Nat Hon Sy; Perf Att; Sci Fairs; St of Mnth; Bnd; Bskball (VJ L); Ftball (VJ L); Track (V L); Cl Off (V); Basketball 110% Award; Track-Rookie of the Year Award

SCOLLEY, KESHA D; FRANKFORT, IN; FRANKFORT SR HS; (FR); Hnr Roll; Chr; I Am Having a Poem Published in an Anthology; Interior Decorator/Design; Indiana State U; Purdue U

SCOTT, CARRIE N; SPENCER, IN; OWEN VALLEY CMTY HS; (FR); Peer Tut/Med; 4-H; Chrch Yth Grp; Ntl FFA; Volunteer for Kids Volleyball; Was in Helping Hands for 2 Yrs; Pediatrician-Masters; Doctor-Masters; Indiana U; Ivy Tech State College

SCOTT, JONATHAN; OAKLAND CITY, IN; WALDO J WOOD MEMORIAL HS; (FR); Hi Hnr Roll; Chrch Yth Grp; Emplmnt, Stg Cre; Bsball (J); Bskball (J); Cl Off (V); Religious Education; Business Management; Oakland City U; Trevecca U

SCOTT, KAYLA; PERU, IN; PERU HS; (FR); Perf Att; Fashion Designer; Stylist; Purdue U; Indiana

SCOTT, LAURA; OSCEOLA, IN; PENN HS; (SR); F Lan Hn Soc; Hnr Roll; St of Mnth; Comm Volntr; Chrch Yth Grp; Orch; Lcrsse (C); Law; Purdue U; Indiana U Law School

SCULLY, ASHLEIGH A; FREMONT, IN; ANGOLA HS; (JR); F Lan Hn Soc; Hi Hnr Roll; Hnr Roll; Nat Hon Sy; Otst Ac Ach Awd; Perf Att; Comm Volntr; Peer Tut/Med; Chess; Chrch Yth Grp; Emplmnt; Photog; Prom Com; Tchrs Aide; Spanish Clb; Bskball (V L); Vllyball (V L); Kids League Softball; Secondary Education; Indiana U

SEALS, CRISTA K; EVANSVILLE, IN; MT VERNON HS; (JR); Hab For Humty Volntr; Tchrs Aide; Sophomore English Teachers Assistant; Radio Broadcasting; TV Personality; U of Southern Indiana; U of Kentucky

SEAY, ANDREW R; EVANSVILLE, IN; REITZ MEMORIAL HS; (FR); Hi Hnr Roll; WWAHSS; Comm Volntr; Chrch Yth Grp; Dbte Team; Key Club; Spch Team; Bnd; Jzz Bnd; Mch Bnd; Stg Cre; Swmg (V L); Medicine; Engineering; Indiana U

SEBERGER, AMANDA B; CEDAR LAKE, IN; CROWN POINT HS; (SO); Hnr Roll; Emplmnt; Scouts; Bnd; Jzz Bnd; Mch Bnd; Pep Bnd; Received Superior Rating At ISSMA Solo Competitions; Purdue U; Ball State U

SEE, WHITNEY; GALVESTON, IN; LEWIS CASS JR/SR HS; (SO); Hnr Roll; MVP; Bnd; Jzz Bnd; Mch Bnd; Pep Bnd; Cr Ctry (V); Swmg (J); Track (V); Learning to Fly a Airplane; Commercial Pilot; Ball State; Purdue

SEGER, BUCK A; WINSLOW, IN; PIKE CTRL HS; (SR); WWAHSS; Emplmnt; Ftball (V CL); Wrstlg (V CL); Conservation Officer; Vincennes U

SEGER, JOHN P; HUNTINGBURG, IN; SOUTHRIDGE HS; (SO); 4H Awd; Hnr Roll; Comm Volntr; 4-H; Chrch Yth Grp; Emplmnt; Ntl FFA; Bsball (VJ L); Ftball (VJ L); FFA Awards; History; Indiana State U

SEGERT, BRADLEY R; PETERSBURG, IN; (SO); 4H Awd; Hnr Roll; Sci/Math Olympn; USAA; 4-H; Chrch Yth Grp; Mth Clb/Tm; Pep Squd; Quiz Bowl; Schol Bwl; German Clb; Bnd; Mch Bnd; Pep Bnd; German Club; Physical Therapy; U of Evansville

SEIBEL, DAVID; GREENFIELD, IN; MT VERNON HS; (SO); Hi Hnr Roll; Hnr Roll; MVP; Peer Tut/Med; Chrch Yth Grp; Ntl FFA; Bsball (L); Bskball (J); Ftball (V); Wt Lftg (J); All - A Honor Roll; Accounting Degree; Indiana U; Tulane U

SEIBERT, ANTHONY W; NEW HARMONY, IN; NORTH POSEY HS; (FR); Hi Hnr Roll; Hnr Roll; Otst Ac Ach Awd; Peer Tut/Med; Chrch Yth Grp; Emplmnt; Ntl FFA; Scouts; Spch Team; German Clb; Ftball (V); Indiana Top 8 FFA Parliamentary Procedure Team; Agricultural Engineer; Purdue U; Lincoln Tech

SEILER, COURTNEY; BOONVILLE, IN; BOONVILLE; (JR); Hnr Roll; Nat Hon Sy; WWAHSS; FCA; Key Club; Prom Com; Sftball (V); Cl Off (R); Yrbk (R); Civil Engineering; U of Evansville; Purdue U

SELJAN, ERIC; HIGHLAND, IN; HIGHLAND HS; (JR); Hnr Roll; Key Club; Golf (V L); Architecture; Design; Vincennes U; Ball State U

SENECHAL, DANIEL A; CORYDON, IN; LANESVILLE HS; (SO); Hnr Roll; St of Mnth; USAA; WWAHSS; French Clb; Bnd

SERGESKETTER, KAYLA; JASPER, IN; JASPER HS; (SO); Hi Hnr Roll; MVP; WWAHSS; Peer Tut/Med; Chrch Yth Grp; FCA; Key Club; SADD; Tchrs Aide; Vsity Clb; Spanish Clb; Cr Ctry (V L); Swmg (V L); Track (V L); 5 Time High School All American Swimmer

SERMERSHEIM, NATHANIEL; MOORESVILLE, IN; (SO); Hnr Roll; Nat Hon Sy; WWAHSS; Chrch Yth Grp; Scouts; Bnd; Jzz Bnd; Mch Bnd; Pep Bnd; Ftball (V); Wt Lftg (L); Medical; Physician; Ball State U; U of Southern Indiana

SERWACKI, MEGAN; HIGHLAND, IN; HIGHLAND HS; (JR); F Lan Hn Soc; Hi Hnr Roll; Hnr Roll; Nat Hon Sy; Otst Ac Ach Awd; Sci/Math Olympn; WWAHSS; Yth Ldrshp Prog; Comm Volntr; Peer Tut/Med; Key Club; Lttrmn Clb; NYLC; Sci Clb; Spanish Clb; Bnd; Mch Bnd; Pep Bnd; Sftball (J); Stu Cncl (R); President's Award for Academic Excellence; 2 State Science Olympiad Medals; Sciences; Purdue U

SHADDAY, JORDAN; WALTON, IN; LEWIS CASS HS; (SO); Hi Hnr Roll; Nat Hon Sy; Pres Ac Ftns Aw; St of Mnth; WWAHSS; Yth Ldrshp Prog; FBLA; Key Club; Lttrmn Clb; Bsball (J L); Cr Ctry (V L); Engineering; Purdue

SHAFER, STEPHINE; MARION, IN; MARION HS; (JR); Hnr Roll; Nat Stu Ath Day Aw; WWAHSS; Comm Volntr; Off Aide; Pep Squd; Bskball (V L); Sccr (V L); Sftball (V L); Sports Medicine; Physical Therapy; Indiana U Bloomington; Purdue U

SHAFFER, JOHN; HARLAN, IN; WOODLAN JR/SR HS; (JR); Hi Hnr Roll; Hnr Roll; MVP; Nat Hon Sy; St of Mnth; Peer Tut/Med; Chrch Yth Grp; Bsball (J); Bskball; Ftball (V L); Track (V CL); Wt Lftg; National Honor Society; Academic Super Bowl; Physical Therapy; Business; Indiana U (Bloomington); Ball State U

SHAFFNER, WHITNEY; JEFFERSONVILLE, IN; JEFFERSONVILLE HS; (JR); St of Mnth; Comm Volntr; Emplmnt; ROTC; Clr Grd; Drl Tm; (RN) Registered Nurse; Associate of Science in Culinary Arts; U of Kentucky; U of Louisville

SHAMMAS, NATALIA N; EDINBURGH, IN; SOUTHWESTERN HS; (SO); Hi Hnr Roll; MVP; Nat Hon Sy; Nat Sci Aw; Otst Ac Ach Awd; Sci Fairs; WWAHSS; Yth Ldrshp Prog; Comm Volntr; Peer Tut/Med; ArtClub; Chrch Yth Grp; DARE; Pep Squd; SADD; Tchrs Aide; German Clb; Ch Chr; Dnce; Tennis (V); Vllyball (V); Stu Cncl (T); CR (T); SADD, Student Govt.; Pharmacy; U of Southern California; Butler U

SHAN, NANCY; CARMEL, IN; CARMEL HS; (SR); F Lan Hn Soc; Nat Hon Sy; Nat Mrt Fin; WWAHSS; Yth Ldrshp Prog; Comm Volntr; Peer Tut/Med; Chrch Yth Grp; Emplmnt; Tchrs Aide; Orch; 2nd Place-Indiana Music Teachers' Association's State Auditions for Piano - 2002; Physician; U of Pennsylvania; Rice U

SHANK, MELISSA; SHIRLEY, IN; KNIGHTSTOWN HS; (FR); 4H Awd; Ctznshp Aw; Nat Hon Sy; Otst Ac Ach Awd; St of Mnth; DARE; Bnd; Pep Bnd; SP/M/VS; Stg Cre; Track (L); Vsy Clb; Yrbk (P)

SHANNON, IAN A; DUNKIRK, IN; JAY CTY HS; (JR); All Am Sch; Hnr Roll; Nat Hon Sy; WWAHSS; Drma Clb; Jr Cls League; Key Club; Latin Clb; Bnd; Chr; Drm Mjr; Jzz Bnd; Cr Ctry (J); Track (VJ); Cl Off (V); United Way King; Music Director; Studio Engineer (Music); Ball State U

Seberger, Amanda B
Crown Point HS
Cedar Lake, IN

Scott, Kayla
Peru HS
Peru, IN

Schumacher, Kelly N
Heritage Hills HS
Santa Claus, IN

National
Honor Roll
Spring 2005

Schultz, Eric R
Homestead HS
Fort Wayne, IN

Seals, Crista K
Mt Vernon HS
Evansville, IN

Shaffer, John
Woodlan JR/SR HS
Harlan, IN

SHARKEY, MOLLY; SOUTH BEND, IN; JOHN ADAMS HS; (JR); Hnr Roll; Nat Hon Sy; St of Mnth; Comm Volntr; Scouts; Clr Grd; Mch Bnd; Orch; SP/M/VS; Math Professor

SHARP, JOSH; HARTFORD CITY, IN; BLACKFORD HS; (FR); 4H Awd; Hnr Roll; Perf Att; Pres Ac Ftns Aw; St of Mnth; WWAHSS; 4-H; Key Club; Wdwrkg Clb; Bskball (L); Ftball (L); Track (J); Sports Medicine; Sports Administration; Indiana U; Michigan U

SHATTO, AIMEE; FRANKLIN, IN; FRANKLIN CMTY HS; (SO); FCA; Key Club; Photog; Quill & Scroll; Cr Ctry (J); Track (J); Sch Ppr (P); Yrbk (P); Photo Journalist

SHEPARD, ANDREAS; VALPARAISO, IN; VALPARAISO HS; (SO); Hnr Roll; Sci/Math Olympn; Dbte Team; Key Club; Scouts; Bnd; Orch; Indiana All-State Band 2004; All-State Orchestra 2005

SHEPARD, MEGAN; CTRVILLE, IN; CTRVILLE HS; (SO); Ctznshp Aw; Hnr Roll; MVP; Otst Ac Ach Awd; Perf Att; Pres Sch; Sci Fairs; St of Mnth; Yth Ldrshp Prog; Comm Volntr; Peer Tut/Med; Spec Olymp Vol; Chrch Yth Grp; DARE; FCA; Key Club; Off Aide; Prom Com; SADD; Tchrs Aide; Stg Cre; Bskball (J); Sftball (J); Tennis (J); Vllyball (J); Executive Council; Neurology; Social Fields; Butler U; Indiana U

SHEPHERD, CATHERINE; HOAGLAND, IN; HERITAGE JR/SR HS; (FR); Hi Hnr Roll; WWAHSS; Stu Cncl (R); Business

SHEPHERD, NATHAN; WARSAW, IN; TIPPECANOE VALLEY HS; (SO); Hnr Roll; Perf Att; Chess; Schol Bwl; Sci Clb; National Junior Honor Society; Kick Boxing Club; Explosives Engineer; Purdue U

SHEPHERD, NIKKI; COLUMBUS, IN; COLUMBUS NORTH HS; (JR); Hnr Roll; Nat Hon Sy; Nat Mrt LOC; St of Mnth; WWAHSS; Yth Ldrshp Prog; Comm Volntr; Hosp Aide; Chrch Yth Grp; Drma Clb; Emplmnt; Key Club; Mth Clb/Tm; Quill & Scroll; Svce Clb; Clb; SP/M/VS; Stg Cre; Sch Ppr (E); 4-H Fair Queen's Court (Second Runner-Up); Bartholomew County Top Teen 2004; International Law; Psychology; College of William and Mary, Williamsburg, Virginia; Amherst College, Amherst, Massachusetts

SHERLOCK, STEPHANIE; INDIANAPOLIS, IN; WARREN CTRL HS; (SO); Ctznshp Aw; F Lan Hn Soc; Gov Hnr Prg; Hi Hnr Roll; Hnr Roll; Otst Ac Ach Awd; Chr; Track (L); Yrbk (R); Sophomore Council; Archaeology; Psychology; Indiana U; IUPUI

SHERMAN, RODRIQUEZ; INDIANAPOLIS, IN; BEN DAVIS HS; (JR); Hi Hnr Roll; Hnr Roll; Nat Hon Sy; Chrch Yth Grp; FCA; Key Club; Bskball (V); Wt Lftg (V); Sports Management; Broadcasting

SHERRILL, FAITH; FORT WAYNE, IN; NORTHROP HS; (JR); Hi Hnr Roll; Nat Hon Sy; Perf Att; Comm Volntr; Chrch Yth Grp; FTA; Bskball (V CL); Track (V CL); Vllyball (V CL); Stu Cncl (R); National Honors Society Member; Athletic Council Member; Elementary Education; Administration in Schools; Coastal Carolina U; Ball State U

SHIFLET, BRITTANY R; KOKOMO, IN; KOKOMO HS; (JR); Hnr Roll; Nat Hon Sy; Perf Att; Pres Ac Ftns Aw; Chrch Yth Grp; Emplmnt; FCA; Pep Squd; Quill & Scroll; Scouts; Tchrs Aide; Vsity Clb; Sftball (V L); Sch Ppr (R); Yrbk (R); Dental Field; Elementary Education; Indiana U At Kokomo; Indiana U Bloomington

SHLAKMAN, STEVE; GRANGER, IN; MARIAN HS; (SO); Hnr Roll; Comm Volntr; Hosp Aide; Emplmnt; Quiz Bowl; German Clb; SP/M/VS; Stg Cre; Cl Off; Stu Cncl (R); Medical; Bio med Engineering; Notre Dame; U of Chicago

SHORT, MATTHEW; LYNN, IN; RANDOLPH SOUTHERN JR/SR HS; (MS); 4H Awd; Hnr Roll; Perf Att; Comm Volntr; 4-H; Chrch Yth Grp; Bsball; Bskball; Cr Ctry; Track; Cl Off (V); Sportsmanship Award-Baseball; Business Major; Computer Science; Purdue U; Franklin College

SHORT, RYAN; MUNCIE, IN; YORKTOWN HS; (SO); Ctznshp Aw; Hi Hnr Roll; Hnr Roll; WWAHSS; Yth Ldrshp Prog; Comm Volntr; Chrch Yth Grp; Emplmnt; FCA; Key Club; Svce Clb; Ch Chr; Jzz Bnd; Pep Bnd; Sccr (J); Tennis (VJ); Cl Off (S); Stu Cncl (R); CR (R); Most Improved Tennis Player; Landscape Architecture, Elementary Education; Business Management; Ball State U; Purdue U

SHORTER, RACHEL L; CARLISLE, IN; (FR); Hnr Roll; Stu Cncl; Indiana U; Indiana State U

SHREFFLER, NICHOLAS A; HIGHLAND, IN; HIGHLAND HS; (JR); Hnr Roll; WWAHSS; Comm Volntr; Emplmnt; Key Club; Off Aide; Prom Com; Chr; Tennis (J L); Cl Off (P); Stu Cncl (V); Yrbk (R); Key Club Lieutenant Governor; IUPUI

SHREVE, MASON; REDKEY, IN; JAY CTY HS; (SO); Hnr Roll; German Clb; Sccr (V L); Track (V L); German Club President; Communications; U of Toledo; U of Southern California

SHULER, MORGAN; FORT WAYNE, IN; HERITAGE JR/SR HS; (FR); Hi Hnr Roll; Perf Att; Jr Ach; Bskball (J); Vllyball; 4 Year College Degree; Business Management; Indiana U; Saint Francis

SHUTE, TOSHEENA; INDIANAPOLIS, IN; INDIANAPOLIS CHRISTIAN SCH; (SR); Ctznshp Aw; Hnr Roll; MVP; Comm Volntr; Off Aide; Tchrs Aide; Bskball (V C); Sftball (V); Vllyball (V C); Major in Sport and Medicine in Training; IUPUI; U of Tennessee

SIDEBOTTOM, CHRISTOPHER C R; HOBART, IN; THE INDIANA AC; (SO); Hi Hnr Roll; Otst Ac Ach Awd; Perf Att; Pres Ac Ftns Aw; Pres Sch; Sci/Math Olympn; St of Mnth; WWAHSS; Drma Clb; Mth Clb/Tm; Quiz Bowl; Scouts; SP/M/VS; Stg Cre; Sccr (VJ); Biochemist; Chemist; Harvard; Yale

SIDNEY, TERRENCE; PERU, IN; PERU HS; (FR); Bskball (J); Ftball (V); Track (J); NBA Player; Architect; Indiana U; Michigan State

SIGGERS, AMBERA; INDIANAPOLIS, IN; ARLINGTON HS; (JR); Nat Hon Sy; Tennis (V); President of National Honor Society; Volunteer At Indianapolis Zoo; Medicine; Butler U; IUPUI

SILLS, HANNAH C; EVANSVILLE, IN; REITZ MEMORIAL HS; (FR); Hnr Roll; Perf Att; WWAHSS; Comm Volntr; Chrch Yth Grp; Key Club; Spanish Clb; Stg Cre; Sccr (J); Track (V); Physical Therapist

SILVEY, JESSICA; INDIANAPOLIS, IN; LAWRENCE NORTH HS; (JR); Hnr Roll; Yth Ldrshp Prog; Comm Volntr; Peer Tut/Med; Chrch Yth Grp; DARE; Emplmnt; Mus Clb; Pep Squd; Photog; Quill & Scroll; Scouts; Chr; Swg Chr; Chrldg (J); Yrbk (P); Photography; Purdue U (West Lafayette); Indiana U (Bloomington)

SIMLER, ASHLEY R; CORYDON, IN; MAPLE LANESVILLE JR/SR HS; (SO); Hnr Roll; Nat Hon Sy; Otst Ac Ach Awd; St of Mnth; USAA; WWAHSS; SADD; Tchrs Aide; Sftball (V); Cl Off (V); Stu Cncl (R)

SIMMONS, ALEX; LANESVILLE, IN; (JR); Hnr Roll; Nat Hon Sy; Perf Att; St of Mnth; WWAHSS; Comm Volntr; Red Cr Aide; Chrch Yth Grp; FCA; Ntl FFA; Pep Squd; Prom Com; SADD; French Clb; Chr; Sftball (J); Architecture; Engineering; U of Kentucky; U of Evansville

SIMMONS, BETH; TAYLORSVILLE, IN; COLUMBUS NORTH HS; (JR); Hi Hnr Roll; Hnr Roll; Nat Hon Sy; St of Mnth; WWAHSS; Yth Ldrshp Prog; Comm Volntr; Chrch Yth Grp; Drma Clb; Emplmnt; FCA; Key Club; Mus Clb; Quill & Scroll; Chr; Ch Chr; SP/M/VS; Stg Cre; Yrbk (E); Sunday School Teacher; Producer of School Plays; Broadcasting; Communications; Ball State U; Butler U

SIMPSON, ALYSSA M; ROACHDALE, IN; NORTH PUTNAM HS; (SO); Hi Hnr Roll; Nat Hon Sy; Otst Ac Ach Awd; Perf Att; Comm Volntr; Peer Tut/Med; Chrch Yth Grp; Key Club; Pep Squd; Spch Team; Golf (V); Sftball (V); Stu Cncl (R); Sch Ppr (R); Teen Student Leadership Academy (TSLH); Medical; Pediatrics; DePauw U; Purdue U

SIMPSON, JOANNA L; LADOGA, IN; SOUTHMONT HS; (JR); 4H Awd; Ctznshp Aw; Hnr Roll; St of Mnth; WWAHSS; 4-H; Chrch Yth Grp; DARE; Emplmnt; Key Club; Ntl FFA; Photog; Prom Com; Swg Chr; Pre School Education; Medical Assistant; Ivy Tech of Lafayette or Crawfordsville; St Mary's of the Woods

SIMS, BRYAN; CHURUBUSCO, IN; CHURUBUSCO HS; (SO); Hi Hnr Roll; Emplmnt; Bsball (V L); Bskball (J); Ftball (V L); Bowling 300 Game at Age 15; Top Male Freshman; Landscaping; Construction; Ball State; Tri-State

SIMS, DUSTIN; ODON, IN; NORTH DAVIESS JR/SR HS; (JR); Hnr Roll; Peer Tut/Med; Chrch Yth Grp; DARE; Ntl Beta Clb; Prom Com; French Clb; Bskball (L); Golf (L); Yrbk (R, P); Boys Varsity Basketball 2004-2005 Most Recognized; Beta Club Member; Accounting; Business Management; Oakland City; USI

SIMS, LAURA C; COLUMBUS, IN; COLUMBUS NORTH HS; (SR); 4H Awd; Hi Hnr Roll; Hnr Roll; Nat Hon Sy; WWAHSS; Comm Volntr; 4-H; Emplmnt; Key Club; Vllyball (VJ); Yrbk (E, P); Freshman Volleyball Coach; Football Manager; Ball State U

SIMS, ROBERT; HANOVER, IN; SOUTHWESTERN MIDDLE SR HS; (JR); Hnr Roll; Otst Ac Ach Awd; Yth Ldrshp Prog; Comm Volntr; Drma Clb; Emplmnt; P to P St Amb Prg; Bsball (V L); Tennis (V L); Nominated for Presidential Classroom and Presidential Symposium on Law; Invited to Attend Congressional Student Leadership Conference, Alternate to Hoosiers Boys' State; Criminal Justice; Law Enforcement; Eastern Kentucky U, Richmond; U of Southern Indiana, Evansville

SINDERS, ANTHONY J; HANOVER, IN; SOUTHWESTERN MIDDLE SR HS; (JR); 4H Awd; Hnr Roll; Nat Hon Sy; Perf Att; Comm Volntr; Peer Tut/Med; 4-H; Drma Clb; FCA; Prom Com; Bsball (V CL); Bskball (VJ L); Cr Ctry (V L); Cl Off (T); Stu Cncl (R); Honorable Mention All State in Cross Country; Degree in Sports Marketing/Management; Major in Business Administration; Xavier U; Indiana (Bloomington) U

SINGH, ALINA; INDIANAPOLIS, IN; PIKE HS; (SR); Ctznshp Aw; F Lan Hn Soc; Hi Hnr Roll; Nat Hon Sy; Otst Ac Ach Awd; Perf Att; WWAHSS; Comm Volntr; Peer Tut/Med; Spec Olymp Vol; DARE; Emplmnt; Key Club; MuAlphaTh; Sci Clb; Tmpl Yth Grp; Spanish Clb; Ch Chr; Orch; SP/M/VS; Stu Cncl (R); Placed 1st in Punjabi Class (Language of Origin); Placed 1st in Indian Dance Competition; Pharmacy; Indiana U Purdue U Indianapolis; Butler U

SINGLETON, BRADY; VINCENNES, IN; LINCOLN HS; (SR); Hnr Roll; Nat Hon Sy; Perf Att; Emplmnt; Ftball (V); Golf (J); Wrstlg (V C); Yrbk (E); Competition Government Cast Captain; National Honor Society; Psychology; Political Science; Indiana U; Purdue U

SINGLETON, JOSEPH P; WADESVILLE, IN; NORTH POSEY HS; (JR); Hi Hnr Roll; Hnr Roll; Comm Volntr; Hab For Humty Volntr; Peer Tut/Med; AL Aux Boys; Chrch Yth Grp; Dbte Team; Lib Aide; NtlFrnscLg; NYLC; Prom Com; Schol Bwl; Bnd; Chr; Ch Chr; Drm Mjr; Stu Cncl (R); Hoosiers Boy State; Spanish Club Treasurer & Thespian Society; Marketing; Accounting & Architect; U of Southern Indiana; Purdue U & Ball State U.

SINK, ALISHA M; ANDERSON, IN; HIGHLAND HS; (FR); Hi Hnr Roll; Nat Hon Sy; Perf Att; Pres Ac Ftns Aw; Chrch Yth Grp; Tchrs Aide; Chr; Swmg (V)

SITTLER, JAKE; COLUMBIA CITY, IN; COLUMBIA CITY HS; (FR); Hnr Roll; Chrch Yth Grp; FCA; Bskball (J)

SLATTERY, CHELSEA; FORT WAYNE, IN; WOODLAN JR/SR HS; (SO); Hi Hnr Roll; Hnr Roll; Perf Att; St of Mnth; Bnd; Mch Bnd; SP/M/VS; Swg Chr; Music; Engineering; Ball State U; Indiana U

SLOAN, NAOMI; FORT WAYNE, IN; HOMESTEAD HS; (SO); Hi Hnr Roll; Hnr Roll; Perf Att; WWAHSS; Comm Volntr; Chrch Yth Grp; Key Club; Quiz Bowl; Spch Team; Psychology; Wheaton College

SMITH, AMANDA; NEW ROSS, IN; SOUTHMONT SR HS; (FR); Ctznshp Aw; Hnr Roll; Emplmnt; Key Club; SADD; PP Ftbl; Sftball (J); Vllyball; Yrbk (P); Columnist; Butler U

SMITH, ASHANTI; INDIANAPOLIS, IN; BROAD RIPPLE HS; (JR); Kwnis Aw; Comm Volntr; Key Club; Decathlon; Clothing Designing; Nursing; Ball State; U of Indianapolis

SMITH, AUSTIN D; LAFAYETTE, IN; MC CUTCHEON HS; (SO); Hi Hnr Roll; Hnr Roll; MVP; Pres Ac Ftns Aw; Yth Ldrshp Prog; Chrch Yth Grp; Photog; Wdwrkg Clb; Nominated for the National Young Leaders Conference; AMC 10 Math Test; Computer Graphics; Movie Production; Purdue U; Ivy Tech

SMITH, BRANDON W; EDINBURGH, IN; SOUTHWESTERN HS; (SO); Hnr Roll; Perf Att; Sci Fairs; WWAHSS; Tchrs Aide; Computer Science; Computer Programming; Brown College; Purdue U

SMITH, BRIAN D; EATON, IN; BLACKFORD HS; (JR); 4H Awd; Hnr Roll; Nat Hon Sy; Nat Ldrshp Svc; WWAHSS; Comm Volntr; Peer Tut/Med; 4-H; ArtClub; Emplmnt; Key Club; Off Aide; Svce Clb; Bnd; Track (V); Stu Cncl (R); Landscape Architecture; Business Management; Indiana U; Purdue U

SMITH, CHRISTOPHER R; NEEDHAM, IN; SOUTHWESTERN; (SO); WWAHSS; Peer Tut/Med; Chrch Yth Grp; Ntl FFA; Off Aide; Tchrs Aide; Ch Chr; Bsball (V); Bskball (L)

SMITH, ERIN D; LANESVILLE, IN; LANESVILLE CMTY SCH; (JR); Hnr Roll; Nat Hon Sy; Perf Att; WWAHSS; Peer Tut/Med; Chrch Yth Grp; Ntl FFA; Pep Squd; Prom Com; Track (V); Reporter in Lanesville FFA; Dairy Foods Competition; Special Education Teacher; Radiologist; Indiana U Southeast; U Southern Indiana

SMITH, EZEKIEL J; CAMBY, IN; COVENANT CHRISTIAN SCH; (SR); Hnr Roll; Comm Volntr; Chrch Yth Grp; Photog; Ch Chr; Sch Ppr (E, R, P); Creative Writing; Education; Butler U; U of Indianapolis

SMITH, HANNAH M; ENGLISH, IN; CRAWFORD CTY JR/SR HS; (FR); Hnr Roll; Comm Volntr; Tchrs Aide; Tutor Younger Students; Education; Criminal Justice; Indiana State; I U Southeast

SMITH, JAYME L; MITCHELL, IN; MITCHELL HS; (JR); Hnr Roll; Nat Hon Sy; WWAHSS; ArtClub; Chrch Yth Grp; Emplmnt; Key Club; Spanish Clb; Chrldg (VJ); Sftball (VJ L); Track (V); Vllyball (VJ L); Radiation Therapy / Oncology; Psychiatric Medicine / Psychiatry; Indiana U Purdue U Indianapolis; Butler U

SMITH, KARA; ROCKPORT, IN; SOUTH SPENCER HS; (FR); Ctznshp Aw; Hnr Roll; Key Club; Pep Squd; SADD; Bskball (J); Vllyball (J); Stu Cncl (R); Athletic Training; Physical Therapy; U of Evansville

SMITH, KARRI L; SOUTH BEND, IN; RILEY HS; (FR); Hnr Roll; Yth Ldrshp Prog; Chrch Yth Grp; Schol Bwl; Bowling; GAP INC; Psychology

SMITH, KYLE A; MILLTOWN, IN; CRAWFORD CTY JR/SR HS; (JR); Hnr Roll; Otst Ac Ach Awd; WWAHSS; Comm Volntr; Peer Tut/Med; 4-H; Chrch Yth Grp; Emplmnt; Pep Squd; Tchrs Aide; Arch (V); Skt Tgt Sh (V); Track (V); Electrical Engineering; Mechanical Engineering; Rose Hulman Institute of Technology; Louisville Speeds

SMITH, LAMONICA Y; MUNCIE, IN; MUNCIE CTRL HS; (JR); Hi Hnr Roll; Hnr Roll; Nat Hon Sy; Comm Volntr; Peer Tut/Med; Chrch Yth Grp; DECA; Key Club; Mth Clb/Tm; MuAlphaTh; Off Aide; SADD; Radiology Technologist; Spanish; Ball State U

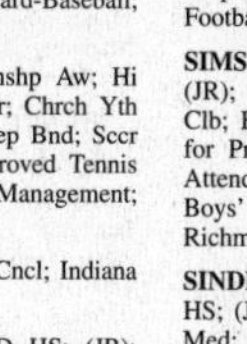
Shreffler, Nicholas A
Highland HS
Highland, IN

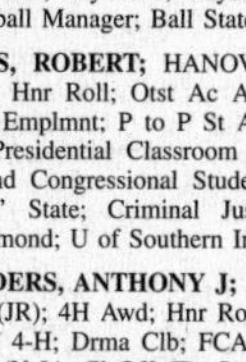
Shiflet, Brittany R
Kokomo HS
Kokomo, IN

National
Honor Roll
Spring 2005

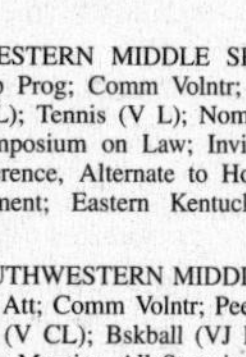
Shepherd, Nathan
Tippecanoe Valley HS
Warsaw, IN

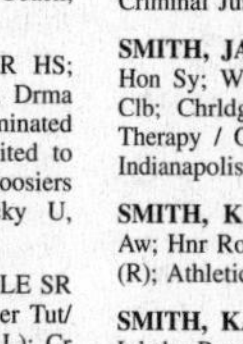
Singleton, Joseph P
North Posey HS
Wadesville, IN

76 / SMITH — Indiana — NATIONAL HONOR ROLL SPRING 2005

SMITH, LINDSAY; SYRACUSE, IN; WAWASEE HS; (SO); Hnr Roll; Comm Vlntr; Chrch Yth Grp; Key Club; Tchrs Aide; Ch Chr; Orch; Vice President of Key Club 2 Years; Senators Page; Athletic Training; Youth Ministry

SMITH, MICHAEL J; ANDERSON, IN; ANDERSON HS; (FR); Ctznshp Aw; Hnr Roll; MVP; Nat Hon Sy; Perf Att; Pres Ac Ftns Aw; Comm Vlntr; Hab For Humty Vlntr; Peer Tut/Med; DARE; Mth Clb/Tm; Pep Squd; SADD; Latin Clb; Ftball; Wt Lftg; Wrstlg; Honor Society

SMITH, RACHELL; INDIANAPOLIS, IN; ARLINGTON HS; (SO)

SMITH, STACI J; BREMEN, IN; BREMEN HS; (SO); Hnr Roll; Perf Att; Chrch Yth Grp; FCA; Off Aide; Chr; Ch Chr; Scr Kpr

SMITH, TIMISHA J; GARY, IN; WESTSIDE HS; (MS); Ctznshp Aw; Hnr Roll; Comm Vlntr; Chess; Svce Clb; Chr; Miss Photogenic Northern Indiana 2003; Live Theatre Performance - Drama; Writer; Obstetrician; U of Pennsylvania; Bradley U

SMITH, WHITNEY; FLOYDS KNOBS, IN; (FR); Hi Hnr Roll; St of Mnth; Comm Vlntr; French Clb; Sccr (V L); Interior Designing; Indiana U of Bloomington

SMITH-VANCE, TORIN R; INDIANAPOLIS, IN; ARLINGTON HS; (FR); Indianapolis Public School Pre-Algebra - 2nd Place Winner

SMOKER, JACOB A; WANATAH, IN; SOUTH CTRL HS; (JR); 4H Awd; Hi Hnr Roll; Nat Hon Sy; Perf Att; St of Mnth; WWAHSS; Yth Ldrshp Prog; 4-H; Chrch Yth Grp; DARE; Drma Clb; Emplmnt; Key Club; Lttrmn Clb; Mus Clb; Bnd; Mch Bnd; Pep Bnd; SP/M/VS; Cl Off (S); Who's Who Among American HS Students; Ag-Horticulture; Engineering

SMYTHE, RYAN; NEWBURGH, IN; (FR); WWAHSS; Comm Vlntr; Spec Olymp Vol; Drma Clb; French Clb; Sccr (J); Track (V); Medical Degree; Business Degree; Indiana U; Duke U

SNETHEN, ARIELL N; LAFAYETTE, IN; MC CUTCHEON HS; (SO); Hi Hnr Roll; Hnr Roll; Nat Hon Sy; Otst Ac Ach Awd; St of Mnth; Yth Ldrshp Prog; Peer Tut/Med; 4-H; Drma Clb; Jr Ach; Scouts; Tchrs Aide; Spanish Clb; Tennis (V); Spanish Club; Pharmacy; Radiology Technician; Purdue U

SNODGRASS, AMBER N; INDIANAPOLIS, IN; AVON HS; (JR); 4H Awd; Hnr Roll; Comm Vlntr; 4-H; ArtClub; Chrch Yth Grp; DARE; Drma Clb; Emplmnt; FCA; FCCLA; Bnd; Chr; Drm Mjr; Jzz Bnd; Bskball (V); Chrldg (V); Mar Art (V); Vllyball (V); Psychology; Forensic Science; Purdue U; Indiana U

SNOW, STEPHANIE; HOBART, IN; RIVER FOREST SR HS; (FR); Hi Hnr Roll; Hnr Roll; Nat Hon Sy; Perf Att; DARE; Chr; Perdue

SNYDER, DAVID; EVANSVILLE, IN; NORTH POSEY HS; (JR); Ctznshp Aw; Hnr Roll; Perf Att; Chrch Yth Grp; DARE; Schol Bwl; Scouts; Spanish Clb; Bnd; Mch Bnd; Pep Bnd; Bskball (VJC); Track (VL); Yrbk; Graphic Arts; Elementary Education; Purdue U; U of Evansville

SNYDER, ROSE M; NOBLESVILLE, IN; SNYDER HOME SCH; (SR); 4H Awd; Hnr Roll; St of Mnth; WWAHSS; Yth Ldrshp Prog; Comm Vlntr; 4-H; DARE; Emplmnt; FCA; Ntl FFA; Hsbk Rdg (V); Mar Art (V); Skt Tgt Sh (V); Multiple World & National Horseback Riding Champions; State Tae Kwon Do Champion; Teaching Degree in History; Business Degree; Transylvania U; Otterbein College

SOKOLSKI, MELISSA S; KOKOMO, IN; KOKOMO HS; (JR); Hi Hnr Roll; Hnr Roll; Yth Ldrshp Prog; Comm Vlntr; Chrch Yth Grp; Dbte Team; NtlFrnscLg; Quill & Scroll; Schol Bwl; Sci Clb; Spch Team; German Clb; Stu Cncl (R); CR (P); Sch Ppr (E, R); English Team; Fine Arts Team; Journalism; Creative Writing; New York U; Columbia U

SOLANO, ASHLEY; MICHIGAN CITY, IN; MICHIGAN CITY HS; (FR); Ctznshp Aw; Hnr Roll; Chrch Yth Grp; Drma Clb; Mus Clb; Chr; SP/M/VS; Stg Cre; Psychologist; Lawyer; Indiana U; Ball State U

SOLIDAY, CHAD E; COLUMBUS, IN; COLUMBUS NORTH HS; (SR); Hnr Roll; Nat Hon Sy; Perf Att; Pres Ac Ftns Aw; St of Mnth; Comm Vlntr; Peer Tut/Med; Quill & Scroll; Sch Ppr (E, R); Mayor's Art Award - Christmas Card Design; Student of the Year Nominee; Informatics; Indiana U Purdue U Columbus

SOMMER, ASHLEY; MONROEVILLE, IN; HERITAGE JR/SR HS; (FR); Hi Hnr Roll; Perf Att; WWAHSS; SP/M/VS; Chrldg (J); Stu Cncl (S); Health Service-Surgeon; Health Service-Pediatrician

SORBER, BECKY; RUSHVILLE, IN; RUSHVILLE CONSOLIDATED HS; (SO); 4H Awd; Hi Hnr Roll; Otst Ac Ach Awd; WWAHSS; Comm Vlntr; 4-H; Chrch Yth Grp; Key Club; Mth Clb/Tm; Spanish Clb; Acpl Chr; Bnd; Chr; Ch Chr; Sccr (V L); Track (V L); Cl Off (S); Stu Cncl (R)

SORG, SARAH E; CHURUBUSCO, IN; CHURUBUSCO HS; (SO); Hi Hnr Roll; Kwnis Aw; Perf Att; WWAHSS; DARE; Key Club; SP/M/VS; Swg Chr; Cr Ctry (V); Mar Art (V); Track (V)

SPARKS, MATTHEW A; BOONVILLE, IN; BOONVILLE HS; (MS); Hnr Roll; Nat Stu Ath Day Aw; Comm Vlntr; Aqrium Clb; ArtClub; Chrch Yth Grp; Outdrs Clb; SADD; Tchrs Aide; Wdwrkg Clb; Ch Chr; Arch; Bskball; Ftball; Swmg; Track; Special Olympic - Swimming & Track; Basketball; Mechanical Work; Architect; ITT Technical Institute; Purdue U Cooperative Service

SPEGELE, BRIAN; FORTVILLE, IN; HAMILTON SOUTHEASTERN HS; (JR); Hnr Roll; Nat Hon Sy; St of Mnth; Yth Ldrshp Prog; Peer Tut/Med; Chrch Yth Grp; Emplmnt; Key Club; Quill & Scroll; Spanish Clb; Bnd; Swmg (J); Sch Ppr (E); Participated on High School Rugby Team; Holds Various Leadership Positions Within Church; International Studies; Journalism; Northeastern U; Mc Gill U

SPEITH, STACEY; MONROEVILLE, IN; HERITAGE JR/SR HS; (FR); Hnr Roll; Become a High School Teacher; Counseling; Indiana U, Purdue U, Fort Wayne; Ball State U

SPENGLER, ELLIOT; MUNCIE, IN; BURRIS LABORATORY SCH; (SO); Hi Hnr Roll; Comm Vlntr; Chrch Yth Grp; Key Club; Prom Com; French Clb; Bnd; Jzz Bnd; Pep Bnd; Bsball (V L); Bskball (V L); Sccr (V L); Cl Off (V); Stu Cncl (V); Psychology; Sports Trainer

SPIERING, LISA A; COVINGTON, IN; COVINGTON CHRISTIAN SCH; (SO); Hi Hnr Roll; Pres Sch; Chrch Yth Grp; Emplmnt; Chr; Ch Chr; SP/M/VS; Bskball (V); Chrldg (V); Vllyball (C); Cl Off (V); Yrbk (E, P); Elementary Education; Nursing; Indiana U

SPINOLA, SUZANNE; INDIANAPOLIS, IN; PIKE HS; (JR); Hi Hnr Roll; Nat Hon Sy; WWAHSS; Hosp Aide; Key Club; MuAlphaTh; Dnce; Orch; Tennis (V); I Am in the Top 25 of 700.; I Am in Pre-Med Club.; Pediatric Oncology; Indiana U; Northwestern U

SPRADLEY, AMBER; INDIANAPOLIS, IN; ARLINGTON HS; (FR); Hnr Roll; St of Mnth; Mth Clb/Tm; Bnd; Bskball (J); Aerospace Engineer; Purdue U

SPRADLEY, KATIE; BOONVILLE, IN; BOONVILLE HS; (SO); Hnr Roll; WWAHSS; Key Club; Cr Ctry (V L); Tennis (J); Stu Cncl (R); Interior Design; Veterinarian; Ivy Tech State College; U of Southern Indiana

SPRECHER, CORTNEY; INDIANAPOLIS, IN; GEORGE WASHINGTON CMTY HS; (JR); Hnr Roll; Nat Hon Sy; Otst Ac Ach Awd; St of Mnth; Comm Vlntr; Peer Tut/Med; DARE; Emplmnt; Prom Com; ROTC; Vsity Clb; Bskball (V); Sftball (V); Vllyball (V); Wt Lftg (V); Neo-Natal Nursing; Indianapolis Purdue U; Indianapolis U

SPRINGER, JOEL; BUTLER, IN; EASTSIDE JR/SR HS; (SO); Hnr Roll; St of Mnth; Off Aide; Tchrs Aide; French Clb; High School Math Teacher; Graphic Designer; Butler U; Ball State U

SPRINGHETTI, BRYAN; NEWBURGH, IN; REITZ MEMORIAL HS; (SO); Pres Ac Ftns Aw; Chrch Yth Grp; Key Club; SADD; Bskball (J); Ftball (J); Wt Lftg (J); Stu Cncl (R); CR (R); Go to College for 4 Years Then Med School; Wabash U

SPRINKLE, KELLEY; PLAINVILLE, IN; NORTH DAVIESS JR/SR HS; (JR); Hnr Roll; Perf Att; Pres Ac Ftns Aw; Chrch Yth Grp; Ntl Beta Clb; Prom Com; Sci Clb; Bskball (VJC); Cl Off (R); Stu Cncl (R); CR (R); Journalism; Physical Therapy; Ball State U

SPURGEON, ASHLEY; GOSPORT, IN; (JR); Hnr Roll; Perf Att; Pres Ac Ftns Aw; Comm Vlntr; Emplmnt; Prom Com; Spanish Clb; Bnd; Mch Bnd; Pep Bnd; Pediatrics; Ob/Gyn; Nursing; Purdue U

SPURLOCK, CHARLES; SUNMAN, IN; (SO); Oceanography

STACK, BRANDON; HOBART, IN; RIVER FOREST SR HS; (FR); Hi Hnr Roll; DARE; Bskball (J); Tennis (J); Degree in Architecture; U of Notre Dame; Ball State

STAHL, KATELYN M; TIPTON, IN; TIPTON HS; (FR); 4H Awd; Ctznshp Aw; Hnr Roll; Pres Ac Ftns & Emplmnt; Comm Vlntr; 4-H; Chrch Yth Grp; DARE; Emplmnt; Key Club; Pep Squd; Photog; Sci Clb; Chrldg (J L); PP Ftbl (J); Swmg (V); Track (V L); Stu Cncl (R); CR (R); Top 25 in National American Miss-Indiana; Medical Field; Architecture / Interior Designs; Ball State; Indiana U

STANLEY, JENNIFER A; FORT WAYNE, IN; HOMESTEAD HS; (SR); Hi Hnr Roll; MVP; Nat Hon Sy; Otst Ac Ach Awd; Emplmnt; Sccr (VJ); Medical School; Medical Research; Washington U in St Louis; Purdue U

STANTON, SARAH V; LIBERTY, IN; UNION CTY HS; (SO); 4H Awd; Gov Hnr Prg; MVP; Perf Att; Pres Ac Ftns Aw; 4-H; FCA; Ch Chr; Hsbk Rdg (V); PP Ftbl (V); Vllyball (V L); President of Hoofbeats 4-H club; Physical Therapist; Chiropractor

STARK, AMY L; LANESVILLE, IN; LANESVILLE HS; (JR); Hi Hnr Roll; Hnr Roll; Nat Hon Sy; St of Mnth; WWAHSS; Yth Ldrshp Prog; Comm Vlntr; Peer Tut/Med; Emplmnt; FCA; FCCLA; HO'Br Yth Ldrshp; Off Aide; Pep Squd; Prom Com; Scouts; Dnce; Chrldg (V L); Scr Kpr (V); Stu Cncl (R); CR (R); HOBY World Representative; Journalism; Indiana U

STARKEY, JEFFREY; ROLLING PR, IN; NEW PRAIRIE HS; (FR); Hnr Roll; Perf Att; Comm Vlntr; Chrch Yth Grp; Sccr (J); Volunteer Church Work; Teaching; Arts; Butler U; Ivy Tech

STAWICKI, MICHELLE; COLUMBUS, IN; COLUMBUS NORTH HS; (JR); Hi Hnr Roll; Nat Hon Sy; WWAHSS; Yth Ldrshp Prog; Comm Vlntr; Chrch Yth Grp; Dbte Team; Drma Clb; Emplmnt; FCA; Key Club; Off Aide; Outdrs Clb; SP/M/VS; Stg Cre; Cr Ctry (L); Track (J); Vllyball (J); Adv Cncl (R); Cl Off (P); Stu Cncl (V); CR (R); Lit Mag (E); Sch Ppr (E); Turning Point Dance Marathon - Chair; Graphic Design; Visual Communications; U of Dayton; Xavier U

STEDMAN, MANDEE L; INDIANAPOLIS, IN; BEN DAVIS HS; (JR); Comm Vlntr; Chr; Sch Ppr; Interior Design; Fashion Design

STEFFE, KACEE; WARSAW, IN; WARSAW CMTY HS; (SR); 4H Awd; Ctznshp Aw; Hnr Roll; Otst Ac Ach Awd; WWAHSS; Yth Ldrshp Prog; Peer Tut/Med; 4-H; Emplmnt; Jr Ach; Ntl FFA; Quiz Bowl; Tchrs Aide; National FFA Champions-Horse Judging; Major in Pre-Veterinary Medicine; Minor in Animal Science; Purdue U

STEINBARGER, MICHELLE R; EDINBURGH, IN; SOUTHWESTERN HS; (FR); 4H Awd; Gov Hnr Prg; Hnr Roll; Nat Hon Sy; USAA; WWAHSS; Comm Vlntr; 4-H; Chrch Yth Grp; Emplmnt; Ntl FFA; SADD; German Clb; Bnd; Mch Bnd; Pep Bnd; Bskball (V); Track (V); Vllyball (V); Cl Off (P); Stu Cncl (V); Agriculture; Nursing; Purdue U

STEINKE, SARAH; BROWNSBURG, IN; BROWNSBURG HS; (SR); F Lan Hn Soc; Hnr Roll; MVP; Nat Hon Sy; St of Mnth; WWAHSS; Hab For Humty Vlntr; Chrch Yth Grp; DECA; FCA; Jr Cls League; Key Club; Off Aide; Stg Cre; Stu Cncl (R); CR (R); Academic Letter; DECA National Qualifier; Nursing / Master's Degree; Doctor; Indiana U

STELZEL, ZACH; DANVILLE, IN; TRI-WEST HS; (SO); 4H Awd; Ctznshp Aw; Hnr Roll; Nat Stu Ath Day Aw; Pres Ac Ftns Aw; Sci Fairs; St of Mnth; 4-H; Chess; DARE; Scouts; Bsball (J); Ftball (V); Wrstlg (V L); National Society of High School Scholars; Neurosurgeon; Surgeon / Specialty

STENFTENAGEL, LOGAN B; JASPER, IN; JASPER HS; (FR); Hnr Roll; Otst Ac Ach Awd; Pres Ac Ftns Aw; Pres Sch; WWAHSS; Comm Vlntr; ArtClub; Drma Clb; Key Club; Mus Clb; Svce Clb; French Clb; SP/M/VS; Chrldg; Dvng (V); Gmnstcs; Track (VJ); Stu Cncl (R); Lit Mag; Cheerleading-Club; Region Qual. Gymnastics-Optional 5th All Around; Theater/Dance Performance; U of Southern California

STETLER, MARIA; BEDFORD, IN; STONE CITY CHRISTIAN AC; (SO); Ctznshp Aw; Hnr Roll; Perf Att; St of Mnth; Chrch Yth Grp; Emplmnt; Photog; Tchrs Aide; Chr; Ch Chr; Orch; SP/M/VS; Stu Cncl (R); Yrbk (E); Education; Business; Gods Bible School & College; Hobe Sound Bible College

STEUP, ROXANNE; FORT WAYNE, IN; WAYNE HS; (SR); Ctznshp Aw; Hnr Roll; CAN; Nurse; International Business College

STEVENS, LAURA; CARMEL, IN; CARMEL HS; (JR); Hnr Roll; Nat Hon Sy; Comm Vlntr; DECA; Drma Clb; Emplmnt; Business, Marketing; Fitness and Nutrition; Indiana U; Purdue U

STEVENS, MARY E; JASONVILLE, IN; SHAKAMAK HS; (SR); 4H Awd; Ctznshp Aw; Hi Hnr Roll; Nat Hon Sy; Salutrn; WWAHSS; Comm Vlntr; Peer Tut/Med; 4-H; AL Aux Girls; Chrch Yth Grp; Ntl FFA; Quill & Scroll; Schol Bwl; Chr; Swg Chr; Vllyball (J); Sch Ppr (E, R, P); Choir President; Elementary / Special Education

STEWART, ALYSSA D; WALTON, IN; LEWIS CASS HS; (SO); Hi Hnr Roll; Hnr Roll; Nat Hon Sy; Perf Att; WWAHSS; Comm Vlntr; Spec Olymp Vol; 4-H; Chrch Yth Grp; Emplmnt; FCA; FBLA; Key Club; SADD; Mch Bnd; Pep Bnd; PP Ftbl; Sftball (V L); Vllyball (V L); Sch Ppr (R); Marching Band State Champions 2003; Mathematics-Medical Field; Indiana Wesleyan U; Bethel College

STEWART, HOLLIE; UNION CITY, IN; UNION CITY CMTY HS; (SO); Hnr Roll; Spanish Clb; Sccr (V); Ball State U; Indiana State U

STIDHAM, AMANDA L; NEW HAVEN, IN; NEW HAVEN HS; (JR); Hi Hnr Roll; Hnr Roll; Perf Att; St of Mnth; WWAHSS; Chrch Yth Grp; Dbte Team; Drma Clb; Jr Cls League; Mus Clb; Schol Bwl; Svce Clb; Spch Team; Chr; Dnce; SP/M/VS; Swg Chr; PP Ftbl (V); Stu Cncl (R); Mayor's Youth Advisory Council; Vocal Jazz, National Society of High School Scholars; Dentistry; Music

STIEN, DAVONNA; LAWRENCEBURG, IN; LAWRENCEBURG HS; (MS); Ctznshp Aw; Gov Hnr Prg; Hnr Roll; Nat Mrt Fin; Perf Att; Pres Ac Ftns Aw; Comm Vlntr; Hab For Humty Vlntr; ArtClub; Chrch Yth Grp; DARE; Lib Aide; Pep Squd; Photog; Bnd; Dnce; Drl Tm; Flg Crps; Swmg; Sch Ppr (E, R); Crime Scene Investigation; Law; Purdue U; All State U

STIFFLER, DANIEL; MICHIGAN CITY, IN; MICHIGAN CITY HS; (FR); Hnr Roll; Perf Att; Peer Tut/Med; ROTC; Drl Tm; Bsball (J); Chrldg (V L); Cr Ctry (V L); Presidential Physical Fitness Award; Major in Personal Training; Professional Degree in Physical Fitness; Ball State U; Valparaiso U

Stidham, Amanda L — New Haven HS — New Haven, IN
Stanton, Sarah V — Union Cty HS — Liberty, IN
Soliday, Chad E — Columbus North HS — Columbus, IN
National Honor Roll Spring 2005
Smoker, Jacob A — South Ctrl HS — Wanatah, IN
Stedman, Mandee L — Ben Davis HS — Indianapolis, IN
Stiffler, Daniel — Michigan City HS — Michigan City, IN

STILGER, KAYLA N; CORYDON, IN; LANESVILLE HS; (JR); Hnr Roll; Nat Hon Sy; WWAHSS; Hab For Humty Volntr; 4-H; Chrch Yth Grp; Emplmnt; FCA; Scouts; Bskball (J); Cr Ctry (V); Tennis (V); Vllyball (J)

STILLABOWER, ASHLEY L; EDINBURGH, IN; EDINBURGH HS; (SO); Hi Hnr Roll; Nat Hon Sy; WWAHSS; Yth Ldrshp Prog; Comm Volntr; Chrch Yth Grp; Emplmnt; Mth Clb/Tm; P to P St Amb Prg; SADD; Bskball (V L); Scr Kpr (V L); Track (V L); Vllyball (V L); Sch Ppr (E); Pediatrician-Medical Field; Indiana U

STILLERMAN, AARON M; INDIANAPOLIS, IN; WARREN CTRL HS; (FR); Hi Hnr Roll; Hnr Roll; Sci Fairs; WWAHSS; Bnd; SP/M/VS; Ice Hky (J); Criminal Law; Music; Indiana U

STIPP, KEVIN; BEDFORD, IN; (SO); Peer Tut/Med; DARE; Lttrmn Clb; Photog; SADD; Bskball (L); Ftball (V); Track (V); Yrbk (P); Trainer, Athletic; Training; Indiana U

STOCKBERGER, DANIEL; LAFAYETTE, IN; (SO); Hnr Roll; Emplmnt; P to P St Amb Prg; Bnd; Pep Bnd; SP/M/VS; Cr Ctry (V CL); Track (V L); Indiana U

STOKES, CHRISTOPHER R; SOUTH BEND, IN; RILEY HS; (SO); Ctznshp Aw; Fut Prb Slvr; Hi Hnr Roll; Otst Ac Ach Awd; Perf Att; Pres Sch; Sci Fairs; Sci/Math Olympn; Yth Ldrshp Prog; Comm Volntr; Peer Tut/Med; DARE; Emplmnt; Bnd; Bskball (J L); Cr Ctry (J); Golf (J L); Notre Dame-Engineering Program

STOKES, FAYE C; MICHIGAN CITY, IN; MARQUETTE HS; (JR); Hi Hnr Roll; Hnr Roll; Nat Hon Sy; Sci/Math Olympn; Comm Volntr; AL Aux Girls; Chrch Yth Grp; Emplmnt; NYLC; Schol Bwl; Dnce; Jzz Bnd; SP/M/VS; PPSqd; Sccr; Track; Cl Off (S); Edward Paine Scholastic Achievement Award English; 2 Years President of Ski Club

STOLL, KATHERINE M; LAPORTE, IN; MICHIGAN CITY HS; (FR); Ctznshp Aw; Hi Hnr Roll; Hnr Roll; Perf Att; Scouts; French Clb; Bnd; Sccr (V); Track (V)

STONE, HEIDI; ELKHART, IN; ELKHART CTRL HS; (SO); Hi Hnr Roll; Hnr Roll; WWAHSS; Comm Volntr; Chrch Yth Grp; Emplmnt; Key Club; Photog; PP Ftbl (V); Sccr (V L); Sftball (J L); Swmg (V L); Homecoming Court-2004; Health/Physical Education PE-2 Female of the Year; Indiana U

STOOPS, JAY B; ELKHART, IN; ELKHART CTRL HS; (JR); Hi Hnr Roll; Comm Volntr; Key Club; Chr; Swg Chr; Bsball (V); Tennis (V); V President/ President-Key Club; Business Degree

STORY, CECELIA R; MICHIGAN CITY, IN; MICHIGAN CITY HS; (FR); Hnr Roll; MVP; Pres Ac Ftns Aw; Chess; DARE; Bskball (V); Sccr (J); Sftball (J); To Become a Cardiovascular Surgeon; U of Tennessee

STOUDER, ELIZABETH; CARMEL, IN; CARMEL HS; (SO); Hi Hnr Roll; Comm Volntr; Chrch Yth Grp; Ch Chr; Orch; Received Letter in Athletic Training; Business; Education; U of Notre Dame; Indiana U

STRANGE, COURTNEY; LAGRO, IN; NORTHFIELD JR/SR HS; (SO); Hnr Roll; Chrch Yth Grp; FCA; Spch Team; Bnd; Pep Bnd; SP/M/VS; Psychology; Counseling; Anderson U

STRAZZABASCO, NICOLE; HIGHLAND, IN; HIGHLAND HS; (JR); Hnr Roll; Nat Hon Sy; WWAHSS; Key Club; Dvng (V L); Sftball (J); Medical Degree; Vet Degree; Purdue; Indiana U

STRINGER, ANDREA; SEYMOUR, IN; SEYMOUR HS; (JR); Hi Hnr Roll; Nat Hon Sy; St of Mnth; WWAHSS; Chrch Yth Grp; Key Club; Bnd; Ch Chr; Mch Bnd; Indiana Federation of Music Clubs - Superior & Excellent Ratings; ISSHA -District - Gold/ State - Silver; Elementary Education; Indiana U Purdue U; Indiana U Southeast

STUCKEY, JARRED V; WASHINGTON, IN; WASHINGTON HS; (JR); Hnr Roll; Comm Volntr; DECA; Tchrs Aide; Bskball (J); Ftball (V CL); Track (V L); All Area Football Team 2004; Athletic Training; Engineering; Purdue U; Indiana U

STUERZENBERGER, ELLEN; MONROEVILLE, IN; NEW HAVEN HS; (SO); Hnr Roll; WWAHSS; Comm Volntr; Peer Tut/Med; Chrch Yth Grp; Emplmnt; Chr; Swg Chr; Bskball (V); Cr Ctry (V); Track (V); Vllyball (V); Pre-Physical Therapy; Purdue

STUGLIK, MICHAEL; CARMEL, IN; CARMEL HS; (JR); Hnr Roll; Chrch Yth Grp; Emplmnt; Chr; Sccr (J L); Computer Technology; U of Southern Indiana

STULL, JOSHUA L; BROWNSBURG, IN; BROWNSBURG HS; (JR); Hnr Roll; Nat Hon Sy; Comm Volntr; Peer Tut/Med; Chrch Yth Grp; DECA; Emplmnt; FCA; Mus Clb; Chr; Bsball (V); Bskball (V); Ftball (VJ L); Wt Lftg (V); Stu Cncl (R); 1st in Indiana State DECA Competition; Representative in 1st IHSAA Student Leadership Conference; MBA; U of Southern California; U of Notre Dame

STUNSON, MICHAEL; NEWBURGH, IN; SIGNATURE SCH; (FR); Hnr Roll; Perf Att; Sci Fairs; Comm Volntr; Emplmnt; Key Club; Spch Team; Orch; Bskball; Key Club President - 2006; Key Club Treasurer - 2005; Communications / Sports Analyst; Indiana State U

SUAREZ, NICKI; FORT WAYNE, IN; NORTHSIDE HS; (SO); Hnr Roll; Scouts; Orch; Bowling; Veterinary

SUDROFF, JENNIFER L; HOBART, IN; HOBART HS; (JR); F Lan Hn Soc; Hi Hnr Roll; St of Mnth; Chrch Yth Grp; Mus Clb; Tchrs Aide; Spanish Clb; Bnd; Drm Mjr; Jzz Bnd; Mch Bnd; IMEA Honor Band; All-District Honor Band; Music Education; Indiana State U; Vandercook College of Music

SUITORS, LAUREN; NEW PARIS, IN; FAIRFIELD HS; (JR); Hi Hnr Roll; Hnr Roll; Nat Hon Sy; Peer Tut/Med; 4-H; Chrch Yth Grp; Emplmnt; Key Club; Prom Com; Chr; SP/M/VS; Tennis (J); Cl Off (S); Stu Cncl (S); Speech Pathology; Interior Design; Indiana U; Indian Purdue U India

SULLIVAN, KEN; PORTAGE, IN; PORTAGE HS; (JR); Ctznshp Aw; Hnr Roll; Otst Ac Ach Awd; WWAHSS; Chess; Emplmnt; Photog; ROTC; Scouts; Tech Clb; Order of the Arrow - Scouts; Engineering; Veterinarian; Purdue North Central; Indiana U

SUMMERFIELD, JACOB; NORTH VERNON, IN; JENNINGS CTY HS; (FR); Hnr Roll; Otst Ac Ach Awd; St of Mnth; Key Club; Wt Lftg; Veterinarian; Pharmacist; Indiana U

SUMMITT, RYAN; DANVILLE, IN; TRI-WEST HS; (SO); Hnr Roll; St of Mnth; Yth Ldrshp Prog; Chrch Yth Grp; FCA; Bsball (VJ)

SUTTON, SARAH; PETERSBURG, IN; PIKE CTRL HS; (FR); Hi Hnr Roll; Hnr Roll; Perf Att; Pres Sch; St of Mnth; Comm Volntr; Chrch Yth Grp; DARE; FCA; Jr Ach; SADD; German Clb; Bnd; Dnce; Mch Bnd; Stu Cncl (R)

SWAGER, ELIZABETH; FREMONT, IN; FREMONT HS; (JR); All Am Sch; Ctznshp Aw; Hi Hnr Roll; Hnr Roll; Nat Hon Sy; Perf Att; St of Mnth; Comm Volntr; DARE; Off Aide; Prom Com; Scouts; Tchrs Aide; Chrldg (VJ L); Track (V L); Cl Off (V, T); Stu Cncl (R); All-Star Cheerleader; All-American Cheerleader Nominee; Purdue U

SWARTS, PHILLIP F; WARSAW, IN; WARSAW CMTY HS; (JR); Hi Hnr Roll; Nat Hon Sy; Otst Ac Ach Awd; Pres Sch; ArtClub; Drma Clb; Fr of Library; Lib Aide; Mth Clb/Tm; P to P St Amb Prg; SP/M/VS; Stg Cre; Sch Ppr (E, R, P); Yrbk (R, P); People to People Student Ambassador to Antarctica; Journalism

SYVERSON, KRISTINA; INDIANAPOLIS, IN; BEN DAVIS HS; (SR); Hnr Roll; Nat Hon Sy; Peer Tut/Med; Sci Clb; Spanish Clb; Chrldg (V CL); National Spanish Honor Society; Nursing; Marion College; U of Indianapolis

TAFLINGER, LESLIE M; SHERIDAN, IN; SHERIDAN HS; (JR); Hi Hnr Roll; Hnr Roll; Nat Hon Sy; Perf Att; Comm Volntr; Spec Olymp Vol; ArtClub; Chrch Yth Grp; DARE; Drma Clb; Mus Clb; Pep Squd; Schol Bwl; Foreign Clb; Bnd; Chr; Ch Chr; Mch Bnd; Presiding Officer of Job's Daughters; Medical Degree, Specialist in Children; Degree in Special Education; Butler U; Indiana U

TARR, KYLE; SHOALS, IN; SHOALS JR/SR HS; (SR); Hi Hnr Roll; WWAHSS; Comm Volntr; Peer Tut/Med; Chrch Yth Grp; Emplmnt; Ntl Beta Clb; Off Aide; Tchrs Aide; Spanish Clb; Bsball (V); Bskball (V); Film Club; Senior Video; Occupational Therapy / MS; U of Southern Indiana

TAYLOR, JUSTIN; SPENCER, IN; OWEN VALLEY CMTY HS; (SO); Hi Hnr Roll; Hnr Roll; Mas Aw; MVP; Otst Ac Ach Awd; Perf Att; Pres Ac Ftns Aw; Emplmnt; Lttrmn Clb; Spanish Clb; Bsball (J); Bskball (J); Sccr (V L); Insight; Bachelor Engineering; Kansas U; U of Southern California

TAYLOR, KAITLYN; FISHERS, IN; HAMILTON SOUTHEASTERN HS; (SO); F Lan Hn Soc; Hi Hnr Roll; Nat Hon Sy; Otst Ac Ach Awd; St of Mnth; WWAHSS; Comm Volntr; Peer Tut/Med; Chrch Yth Grp; Key Club; Mth Clb/Tm; P to P St Amb Prg; Vsity Clb; French Clb; Vsy Clb; Vllyball (V L); French Club Secretary; National American Miss State Finalist; French Major; Orthopedic Surgeon; Washington U (St. Louis); Dartmouth

TAYLOR, KAYLA; CARMEL, IN; WESTFIELD HS; (MS); Hi Hnr Roll; Hnr Roll; Comm Volntr; Peer Tut/Med; DARE; Off Aide; Clr Grd; Mch Bnd; SP/M/VS; Bachelor's Degree; Interior Design; Purdue U

TAYLOR, TANEQUA A; MERRILLVILLE, IN; GARY CAREER CTR; (JR); Hi Hnr Roll; Hnr Roll; Chrch Yth Grp; Emplmnt; Chr; Ch Chr; SP/M/VS; Most Employable; Business Management; Indiana U Purdue U Indianapolis; U of Southern Mississippi

TEDDER, BRANDI; HARTSVILLE, IN; HAUSER JR-SR HS; (FR); Ctznshp Aw; DAR; Hnr Roll; Perf Att; Sci Fairs; Comm Volntr; Chrch Yth Grp; DARE; Key Club; Spanish Clb; Vllyball (J)

TEETERS, BARTON W; LYNN, IN; RANDOLPH SOUTHERN JR/SR HS; (SO); 4H Awd; Ctznshp Aw; Hi Hnr Roll; Hnr Roll; Otst Ac Ach Awd; Pres Sch; Sci Fairs; St of Mnth; WWAHSS; Yth Ldrshp Prog; Comm Volntr; 4-H; Chrch Yth Grp; DARE; Drma Clb; Lttrmn Clb; Ntl FFA; Photog; Quiz Bowl; Bskball (J); Golf (V L); Hsbk Rdg; Scr Kpr; Tennis (VJ); Cl Off (P); Stu Cncl; 4 -Time State Runner-Up Destination Imagination; Top Dairy Award-Randolph County Farmers Achievement; Political Science; Law; Duke U; Georgetown U

TERRY, LINDSAY; MUNCIE, IN; MUNCIE CTRL HS; (SR); Hnr Roll; Jr Mshl; Kwnis Aw; Nat Hon Sy; Pres Sch; Valdctrian; WWAHSS; Peer Tut/Med; DARE; Emplmnt; Key Club; Svce Clb; Tchrs Aide; Bnd; Sftball (J); Swmg (V L); Stu Cncl (P, V, S, R); Secondary Education Math; Ball State U

THOMAS, CHAD A; LAKE STATION, IN; RIVER FOREST SR HS; (FR); Ctznshp Aw; Gov Hnr Prg; Hi Hnr Roll; Hnr Roll; Otst Ac Ach Awd; St Schl; DARE; SADD; Indiana District Spell Bowl Winners; Architectural Engineer; Pyrotechnics; Purdue U Lafayette; Indiana U Bloomington

THOMAS, DARIUS; EVANSVILLE, IN; REITZ MEMORIAL HS; (SO); Ctznshp Aw; Hnr Roll; MVP; St of Mnth; Spec Olymp Vol; Chrch Yth Grp; Lttrmn Clb; Vsity Clb; Ch Chr; Bskball (V); Cr Ctry (V); Track (V); Future National Runner Up in Basketball; State Track Meet As Freshman; Gym Teacher; Basketball Coach; USI

THOMAS, JOHNATHON; CORYDON, IN; LANESVILLE JR/SR; (JR); Hnr Roll; Otst Ac Ach Awd; Perf Att; St of Mnth; WWAHSS; Comm Volntr; Peer Tut/Med; Chrch Yth Grp; FCA; ROTC; Bnd; French Major; Theology; World Harvest Bible College

THOMPSON, ERICA L; CTRVILLE, IN; CTRVILLE SR HS; (SO); Ctznshp Aw; Hnr Roll; Otst Ac Ach Awd; Pres Sch; St of Mnth; Emplmnt; Lttrmn Clb; Vsity Clb; Golf (V L); Sftball (J); Vsy Clb (L); Girl's Bowling Team All-Conference Champs; December Student of the Month - French; Elementary Education; Nursing; Ball State U; Indiana U

THOMPSON, JACOB; CRAWFORDSVILLE, IN; SOUTHMONT HS; (JR); 4H Awd; Hi Hnr Roll; Nat Hon Sy; WWAHSS; 4-H; Chrch Yth Grp; Emplmnt; FCA; German Clb; Bsball (V); Tennis (V); Cl Off (T); Pharmacy; Purdue

THOMPSON, MEGAN E; NEWBURGH, IN; REITZ MEMORIAL HS; (FR); Hi Hnr Roll; Otst Ac Ach Awd; Perf Att; Pres Sch; Sci Fairs; WWAHSS; Peer Tut/Med; Chrch Yth Grp; Key Club; Pep Squd; Scouts; Spch Team; Sccr (J); Certified Lifeguard, Horseback Riding; Music - Guitar / Piano / Flute; Veterinary Science; Purdue U

THOMPSON, SKYLAR; HOPE, IN; HAUSER HS; (JR); Hi Hnr Roll; Hnr Roll; Nat Hon Sy; Yth Ldrshp Prog; Comm Volntr; Emplmnt; Pep Squd; Spanish Clb; Dnce; Cr Ctry (V); Psychology; Purdue U; Indiana U

THORNBURG, TARA; RUSSELLVILLE, IN; NORTH PUTNAM HS; (JR); 4H Awd; Hi Hnr Roll; Nat Hon Sy; Otst Ac Ach Awd; WWAHSS; Yth Ldrshp Prog; Comm Volntr; Peer Tut/Med; 4-H; Chrch Yth Grp; Key Club; Prom Com; Bskball (V); Sftball (V); Track (V); Vllyball (V C); Cl Off (P); Stu Cncl (R); Pre-Medicine; Pediatrician; Veterinarian; Indiana U; Purdue U

THORPE, CHRISTINA; INDIANAPOLIS, IN; ARSENAL TECH HS; (SR); Hnr Roll; Otst Ac Ach Awd; Perf Att; Yth Ldrshp Prog; Peer Tut/Med; BPA; Drma Clb; Emplmnt; FBLA; ROTC; Bskball; Chrldg; Ftball; Track; PASS Program; Dental Hygienist; Indiana University of Bloomington; Indiana U Indianapolis

THRUSH, MICHAEL J; GARRETT, IN; GARRETT HS; (SR); 4H Awd; Ctznshp Aw; Hi Hnr Roll; Nat Hon Sy; Otst Ac Ach Awd; Perf Att; Pres Ac Ftns Aw; Pres Sch; USMC Stu Ath Aw; WWAHSS; Comm Volntr; Peer Tut/Med; 4-H; Chrch Yth Grp; DARE; Emplmnt; Ntl FFA; Off Aide; Prom Com; SADD; Bskball (J); Cr Ctry (V CL); Track (V CL); Cl Off (V); Stu Cncl (R); Building Construction Management; Purdue U

THURMAN, EMILY; HARTFORD CITY, IN; BLACKFORD HS; (JR); 4H Awd; Hnr Roll; Nat Hon Sy; WWAHSS; Comm Volntr; Hab For Humty Volntr; 4-H; Chrch Yth Grp; Emplmnt; FCA; Key Club; Lttrmn Clb; Prom Com; Spanish Clb; Acpl Chr; Chr; Ch Chr; Bskball (VJ); Track (VJ L); Vllyball (VJ L); Elected to Go Hoosier Girls State - 4-H; Award for Hard Work & Leadership; Physical Therapy; Vet. Technician; Manchester College; U of Indianapolis

TIMMONS, ERIC; VALPARAISO, IN; WHEELER HS; (JR); Hi Hnr Roll; Nat Hon Sy; Otst Ac Ach Awd; Sci/Math Olympn; WWAHSS; 4-H; Drma Clb; Emplmnt; Key Club; Mth Clb/Tm; Schol Bwl; Scouts; Tech Clb; Bnd; Mch Bnd; Stg Cre; Captain of US First Robotics Team; Engineering

TIMMONS, JORDAN I A; KIRKLIN, IN; CLINTON CTRL HS; (SO); 4H Awd; All Am Sch; Ctznshp Aw; Hnr Roll; Pres Ac Ftns Aw; WWAHSS; Comm Volntr; 4-H; Chrch Yth Grp; Emplmnt; FCA; Pep Squd; 4-H Champion & Officer; Mechanical Engineering; Purdue U

TITOVA, MAYA; INDIANAPOLIS, IN; PIKE HS; (JR); Hi Hnr Roll; Hnr Roll; Nat Hon Sy; WWAHSS; Spec Olymp Vol; Key Club; Mod UN; MuAlphaTh; Off Aide; Quiz Bowl; Schol Bwl; Orch; SP/M/VS; Concert Orchestra Leadership Award; Best Soloist Award

TITZER, SARAH; BOONVILLE, IN; BOONVILLE HS; (SO); 4H Awd; Hnr Roll; WWAHSS; Hosp Aide; Peer Tut/Med; 4-H; Chrch Yth Grp; Emplmnt; FCA; Jr Cls League; Key Club; Lttrmn Clb; Sccr (V); Stu Cncl; Yrbk; Elementary Education; Secondary Education; U of Evansville; U of Southern Indiana

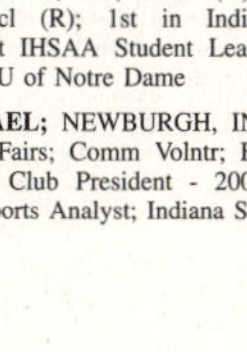
Thompson, Jacob
Southmont HS
Crawfordsville, IN

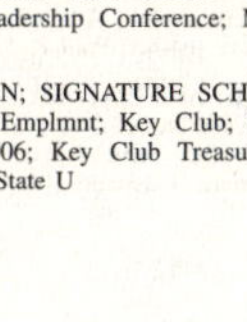
Teeters, Barton W
Randolph Southern JR/SR HS
Lynn, IN

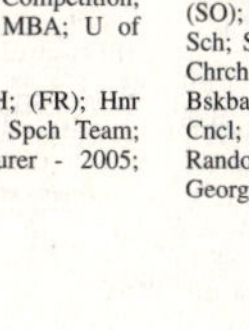
Swager, Elizabeth
Fremont HS
Fremont, IN

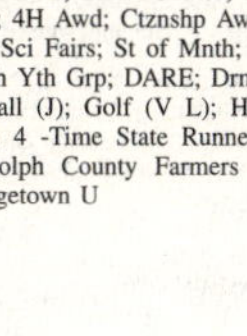
Stull, Joshua L
Brownsburg HS
Brownsburg, IN

National
Honor Roll
Spring 2005

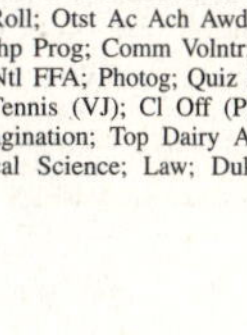
Stouder, Elizabeth
Carmel HS
Carmel, IN

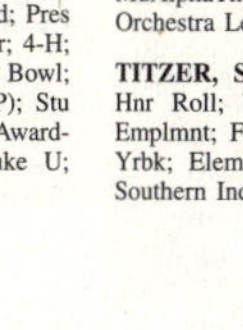
Taylor, Kaitlyn
Hamilton Southeastern HS
Fishers, IN

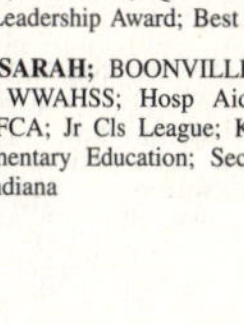
Thomas, Darius
Reitz Memorial HS
Evansville, IN

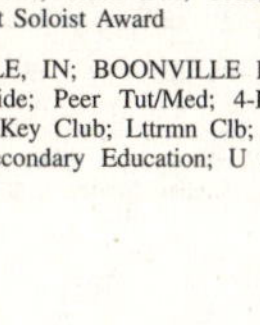
Timmons, Eric
Wheeler HS
Valparaiso, IN

TODD, TRACY E; PETERSBURG, IN; PIKE CTRL HS; (SR); All Am Sch; F Lan Hn Soc; Hnr Roll; Nat Hon Sy; Otst Ac Ach Awd; Pres Ac Ftns Aw; St of Mnth; ArtClub; Cmptr Clb; Emplmnt; Spanish Clb; Bnd; Chr; Mch Bnd; Stu Cncl (R); Art Show Achievement & Awards; 2001-2002 Jasper Marching Band Finalist; Computer Graphic & Design; Commercial Art & Multimedia; Vincennes U; Indiana State U

TOMPKINS, JIM B; SHIRLEY, IN; KNIGHTSTOWN HS; (SO); Hnr Roll; St of Mnth; USAA; Comm Volntr; Chrch Yth Grp; Emplmnt; Spanish Clb; Ftball (J); Wrstlg (V); Stu Cncl (R); CR (R); Officer in the Marines; Degree in Psychology; Purdue U; United States Naval Academy

TOOMBS, CASEY; ELKHART, IN; JIMTOWN HS; (FR); 4H Awd; Hi Hnr Roll; WWAHSS; 4-H; FCA; Pep Squd; Chrldg (V); Track (V L); Vllyball (VJ L); Elementary Education

TOSCHLOG, KIMBERLY; RICHMOND, IN; CTRVILLE SR HS; (SR); 4H Awd; Ctznshp Aw; Hnr Roll; Nat Hon Sy; Perf Att; 4-H; Chrch Yth Grp; Jr Ach; Key Club; Tchrs Aide; Vsity Clb; Bnd; Chr; Pep Bnd; Bskball (V L); Agricultural Finance; Purdue U

TOWNSEND, JOSH; INDIANAPOLIS, IN; WARREN CTRL HS; (SR); Hi Hnr Roll; Hnr Roll; WWAHSS; Orch; Culinary Arts; Computer Applications; Ivy Tech; Purdue U

TREXLER, CIERA; ELKHART, IN; JIMTOWN HS; Hi Hnr Roll; Hnr Roll; Otst Ac Ach Awd; St of Mnth; Comm Volntr; Peer Tut/Med; 4-H; ArtClub; Chrch Yth Grp; Kwanza Clb; Mth Clb/Tm; Mus Clb; Schol Bwl; Scouts; Chr; Vllyball (L); National American Miss State Finalist; Young Achievers of America; Business Degree; Interior Design; Indiana U; Ball State

TRIMM, CHARLENE M; MARION, IN; MC CULLOCH MS; (MS); Hi Hnr Roll; Orch; Mayor's Math Champion - 3 Years; Excel Classes; Doctor; Lawyer; Ball State; Purdue U

TRIPP, TROY D; NEW HAVEN, IN; NEW HAVEN HS; (SO); Hnr Roll; St of Mnth; Chrch Yth Grp; DARE; Emplmnt; Jr Ach; Chr; Ftball (J); Wrstlg (J); Scorekeeper for the Middle School Wrestling Team; Helped with the Handicapped; X-Ray Technician; Fireman; U of Arizona; Purdue U/West Point

TROUTMAN, KATHRYN A; NORTH VERNON, IN; SOUTH DECATUR JR/SR HS; (SO); Hnr Roll; Kwnis Aw; Pres Sch; WWAHSS; Comm Volntr; Peer Tut/Med; Chrch Yth Grp; Drma Clb; Key Club; Quiz Bowl; Scouts; SADD; Bnd; Chr; Ch Chr; Jzz Bnd; PP Ftbl (J); Scr Kpr (V); Track (V); Stu Cncl (R); National Jr. Honor Society; Music Education; Drama; Indiana State U; Butler U

TROWBRIDGE, BECKY; VERSAILLES, IN; SOUTH RIPLEY HS; (JR); Hi Hnr Roll; Hnr Roll; WWAHSS; Comm Volntr; Chrch Yth Grp; Emplmnt; FCA; Mth Clb/Tm; Prom Com; Quill & Scroll; Vsity Clb; Spanish Clb; SP/M/VS; Track (V); Sch Ppr (E); Local Voice of Democracy Contest Finalist; Top Ten Ranking in Class; English; Biology; Purdue U-West Lafayette; Xavier U (Cincinnati)

TROXEL, KELSEY L; GRIFFITH, IN; GRIFFITH SR HS; (SO); Hnr Roll; Otst Ac Ach Awd; St of Mnth; Comm Volntr; DARE; Pep Squd; Chrldg (V); Neuroscience/Neurologist; F.B.I./Secret Service; U of Los Angeles; New York U

TRZCINSKI, ERIN M; CROWN POINT, IN; LAKE CTRL HS; (SO); Hi Hnr Roll; Hnr Roll; Perf Att; Peer Tut/Med; DARE; Emplmnt; Photog; Quill & Scroll; Yrbk (E, R, P); Journalism; Broadcasting; Ball State U; Purdue U

TURKETTE, STEPHANIA; FORT WAYNE, IN; HOMESTEAD HS; (SO); Hi Hnr Roll; WWAHSS; Comm Volntr; Hosp Aide; Emplmnt; Key Club; Bnd; Mch Bnd; Pep Bnd; Anesthesiology; Cornell U; Indiana U

TURNER, DEREK E; FLAT ROCK, IN; SOUTHWESTERN HS; (FR); Ctznshp Aw; Hi Hnr Roll; Nat Hon Sy; Otst Ac Ach Awd; Pres Ac Ftns Aw; Sci Fairs; WWAHSS; Chrch Yth Grp; Schol Bwl; Scouts; SADD; Bnd; Mch Bnd; Pep Bnd; Sccr (V L); Track (V L); Freshman Basketball; Law; Indiana U

UBELHOR, LAUREN; JASPER, IN; JASPER HS; (SO); Comm Volntr; Chrch Yth Grp; Emplmnt; Key Club; SADD; Spanish Clb; Education; Occupational Therapy; Indiana U; Indiana State U

UEBELHOR, JONATHAN; JASPER, IN; JASPER HS; (SO); Hnr Roll; Perf Att; WWAHSS; Key Club; Scouts; Spanish Clb; Ftball (J); Golf (V)

UMBARGER, ASHLEY; HAMMOND, IN; MORTON HS; (JR); Hnr Roll; Peer Tut/Med; Emplmnt; Key Club; Chr; Fashion Merchandising; Elementary Education; Ball State U; U of Southern Indiana

UMPHRESS, KAYLA S; BEDFORD, IN; BEDFORD NORTH LAWRENCE HS; (SR); Hnr Roll; Nat Hon Sy; USAA; WWAHSS; Comm Volntr; Chrch Yth Grp; Drma Clb; Emplmnt; Ntl Beta Clb; Photog; Spanish Clb; Orch; SP/M/VS; Active in Youth Group; Archangel Russia Mission Team 2001; Psychology; Religious Studies; Indiana U Bloomington

UNGER, ADAIR; CARLISLE, IN; SULLIVAN HS; (SR); 4H Awd; F Lan Hn Soc; Hi Hnr Roll; Nat Hon Sy; Pres Ac Ftns Aw; USAA; WWAHSS; Peer Tut/Med; 4-H; Chrch Yth Grp; Ntl Beta Clb; Ntl FFA; Bskball (V L); Track (V CL); Vllyball (V CL); All-State Academic Honorable Mention-Volleyball; WIC All-Conference-2 Yrs-Volleyball; Ag Business; Ag Communications; Vincennes U

UNGER, BRANDON M; SOUTH BEND, IN; WASHINGTON HS; (JR); Hnr Roll; Nat Hon Sy; Perf Att; DARE; Emplmnt; Wdwrkg Clb; Bsball (V); Ftball (V); Wt Lftg (V); Accountant; Criminal Justice; Florida; Florida State

URQUIZA, WENDY; HIGHLAND, IN; HIGHLAND HS; (SO); Otst Ac Ach Awd; Accounting; Business Administration; DeVry U; Robert Morris College

UTLEY, NICHOLAS; INDIANAPOLIS, IN; IPS CAREER & TECH CTR; (SO); Hnr Roll; Otst Ac Ach Awd; Perf Att; Chrch Yth Grp; JROTC Promotion to Sergeant; Perfect Attendance; Rose Hulman; Purdue

VALENZUELA, JOEL; ELKHART, IN; CONCORD HS; (JR); Hnr Roll; Perf Att; WWAHSS; Comm Volntr; Emplmnt; Key Club; Off Aide; Photog; Spanish Clb; Ftball; Stu Cncl (R); Employee of the Month At Work for the Month of January; Landscape Architecture; Photography; Texas A & M U; Ball State U

VANDENBARK, LEEANN; INDIANAPOLIS, IN; PERRY MERIDIAN HS; (SO); Hnr Roll; Perf Att; Chrch Yth Grp; Key Club; Scouts; Bnd; Mch Bnd; Pep Bnd; SP/M/VS; Swmg (J); Girl Scouts; Middle or High School Band Director; Professional Flutist/Piccolo Player; Indiana U; Brigham Young U Utah

VANDER WIER, MICHAEL A; INDIANAPOLIS, IN; SUBURBAN BAPTIST SCH; (JR); Ctznshp Aw; Hi Hnr Roll; Nat Hon Sy; Nat Mrt LOC; Perf Att; WWAHSS; Comm Volntr; Peer Tut/Med; Chrch Yth Grp; Emplmnt; Lttrmn Clb; Chr; SP/M/VS; Bsball (V); Bskball (V L); Sccr (V L); Cl Off (P); LUGAR Symposium for Tomorrow's Leaders; Medicine; Indiana U

VANDIVER, STEPHANIE; HIGHLAND, IN; HIGHLAND HS; (SR); Ctznshp Aw; Gov Hnr Prg; Hnr Roll; Kwnis Aw; MVP; WWAHSS; Yth Ldrshp Prog; Comm Volntr; Hab For Humty Volntr; AL Aux Girls; Emplmnt; Key Club; Off Aide; Pep Squd; Prom Com; Tchrs Aide; Vsity Clb; Chr; Dnce; SP/M/VS; PPSqd (JCL); Sftball (V L); Track (J L); Vllyball (JC); Wt Lftg (J); Cl Off (P); Stu Cncl (R); CR (P); Yrbk (R); Key Club District Board Member; Broadcasting (TV); Purdue U

VANKIRK, JERI; HUDSON, IN; PRAIRIE HEIGHTS SR HS; (JR); F Lan Hn Soc; Hnr Roll; WWAHSS; Bskball (J); Cr Ctry (V); Track (V); Elementary Education; Physical Therapy; Indiana U; Indiana U-Purdue U

VANNARSDALL, HALEY D; AUSTIN, IN; SCOTTSBURG HS; (FR); 4H Awd; Hnr Roll; Perf Att; WWAHSS; 4-H; Chrch Yth Grp; Photog; Chrldg (J); Tennis (J); Outside of School - Gymnastics & Dance

VAN NOTE, RACHEL R; RICHMOND, IN; CTRVILLE SR HS; (SR); Hnr Roll; Chrch Yth Grp; Drma Clb; Key Club; Lib Aide; SADD; Tchrs Aide; Chr; SP/M/VS; Swg Chr; Musical Fine Arts; Musical Theatre; Vincennes U; Ball State U

VAN NOY, ANDREA; INDIANAPOLIS, IN; PERRY MERIDIAN HS; (JR); Hnr Roll; Kwnis Aw; Comm Volntr; Peer Tut/Med; Emplmnt; Key Club; Bnd; Pep Bnd; Dental Hygienist; Indiana U (Bloomington); Indiana U Purdue U Indianapolis

VAN ORDEN, D J; HOWE, IN; HOWE MILITARY SCH; (FR); Ctznshp Aw; Hnr Roll; Nat Ldrshp Svc; Otst Ac Ach Awd; USAA; WWAHSS; Yth Ldrshp Prog; Comm Volntr; Chrch Yth Grp; Vsity Clb; Chr; Bsball (V); Bskball (J); Sccr (V); CR (R); Best Effort Basketball; Rookie of the Year-Baseball; Law; Notre Dame

VANTWOUD, MICHELLE R; MONTICELLO, IN; TWIN LAKES HS; (SR); F Lan Hn Soc; Hnr Roll; Nat Hon Sy; St of Mnth; WWAHSS; Peer Tut/Med; 4-H; Chrch Yth Grp; Emplmnt; Jr Ach; Prom Com; Quill & Scroll; SADD; Spanish Clb; Bnd; Mch Bnd; SP/M/VS; Stg Cre; Cr Ctry (V L); Track (V L); Cl Off (P); Stu Cncl (V); CR (R); Yrbk (E); Lilly Endowment Recipient; Outstanding Junior Achievement Economics Student of the Year; Certified Public Accountant; Indiana U Bloomington

VARGSON, KRISTI; NEW PARIS, IN; FAIRFIELD JR/SR HS; (SO); Hnr Roll; WWAHSS; Chrch Yth Grp; Key Club; Chr; Medical

VAUGHAN, CARLA G; INDIANAPOLIS, IN; LAWRENCE NORTH HS; (SR); Hi Hnr Roll; Nat Hon Sy; Otst Ac Ach Awd; Perf Att; Comm Volntr; Hosp Aide; Key Club; NYLC; Photog; Dnce; PP Ftbl; Sftball (J); Academic and Athletic Letter-Dance; Tri-Hi-Y and Peers Program; Nursing; Purdue U

VAUGHN, AMANDA; BLOOMINGTON, IN; BLOOMINGTON HS NORTH; (JR); Hnr Roll; Yth Ldrshp Prog; Hab For Humty Volntr; Peer Tut/Med; Emplmnt; Lib Aide; ROTC; German Clb; Bnd; Mch Bnd; NJROTC Awards; Young Poets Contest Award; Education-High School English; Special Needs Education; Indiana U

VEACH, JUSTIN; FORT WAYNE, IN; NORTHROP HS; (SR); Ctznshp Aw; Hnr Roll; Kwnis Aw; St of Mnth; DARE; Emplmnt; Tchrs Aide; Voc Ind Clb Am; Welding; Fabricating; Ivy Tech State College; Indiana Institute of Technology

VEENSTRA, ALICE; GOSHEN, IN; FAIRFIELD JR/SR HS; (SO); Hnr Roll; Otst Ac Ach Awd; ArtClub; Key Club; CR (S); Bowling (Varsity); National Art Honor Society; Math Teaching; Animal Anatomy; Nebraska U; Oxford U

VELDMAN, STEPHEN; GRANGER, IN; JOHN ADAMS HS; (JR); Hi Hnr Roll; Nat Hon Sy; WWAHSS; Amnsty Intl; Comm Volntr; Hab For Humty Volntr; Chrch Yth Grp; Drma Clb; Emplmnt; Quiz Bowl; SP/M/VS; Fncg; Mock Trial-Team Finished 1st in State and Is Going to Nationals in May 2005; Business; Pre-Law; Notre Dame; Northwestern

VENARD, NATHAN; WASHINGTON, IN; WASHINGTON HS; (JR); 4H Awd; Hnr Roll; Nat Mrt Fin; Perf Att; Pres Ac Ftns Aw; 4-H; AL Aux Boys; ArtClub; DARE; Drma Clb; Emplmnt; Mus Clb; Sci Clb; Acpl Chr; Chr; Ch Chr; SP/M/VS; Cr Ctry (V L); Track (V L); Modern Music Masters-Tri-M; Musical Theatre; Music Education (Chorus); Ball State U; U of Southern Indiana

VEZINA, RACHAEL; INDIANAPOLIS, IN; LAWRENCE CTRL HS; 4H Awd; Hnr Roll; Perf Att; St of Mnth; Key Club; Swmg (V); 4-H Photography-Grand Champion; Occupational Therapy; Pediatric Nurse; Indiana U; U of Indiana

VIA, NICOLE C; HUDSON, IN; PRAIRIE HEIGHTS SR HS; (FR); Hnr Roll; Comm Volntr; Peer Tut/Med; Outdrs Clb; Spanish Clb; Chr; Sftball (J); 1st Place in Singing Solo Competition; Anesthesiology; Veterinary; Weill Cornell Medical College; U of Iowa

VINCENT, ASHLEY A; KOKOMO, IN; KOKOMO HS; (SO); Hi Hnr Roll; Hnr Roll; Nat Hon Sy; Perf Att; Sci Fairs; WWAHSS; ArtClub; Chrch Yth Grp; Emplmnt; FBLA; Quill & Scroll; Spanish Clb; Stu Cncl (R); Yrbk (E); Academic Honors; National Youth Leadership on Medicine Nominee; Chemical Engineering; Cytology; Rose-Hulman Technology Institute; Purdue U

VINCENT, COLTON R; ELKHART, IN; JIMTOWN HS; (FR); 4H Awd; Hnr Roll; Pres Ac Ftns Aw; Sci Fairs; St of Mnth; 4-H; Chrch Yth Grp; Drma Clb; Emplmnt; FCA; Mus Clb; P to P St Amb Prg; Photog; Dnce; SP/M/VS; Swg Chr; Bskball (J); Ftball (VJ); Track (V); Marine Biology

VINSON, AMANDA L; KENDALLVILLE, IN; EAST NOBLE HS; (FR); Hnr Roll; WWAHSS; Key Club; Chr; Sch Ppr (R); Show Choir; Vocalist; Journalist

VITS, CALEB J; CARMEL, IN; CARMEL HS; (SR); F Lan Hn Soc; Hi Hnr Roll; Hnr Roll; Nat Hon Sy; Pres Ac Ftns Aw; St of Mnth; WWAHSS; Yth Ldrshp Prog; Comm Volntr; Peer Tut/Med; Chrch Yth Grp; Dbte Team; Drma Clb; FCA; Mus Clb; NtlFrnscLg; NYLC; Pep Squd; Bnd; Chr; Ch Chr; Jzz Bnd; Cl Off (T); CR (R); Representative to National Forum on Law; International Baccalaureate Degree Committee; Pre-Law; Entertainment Law; Grove City College

VOEGEL, ASHLI; POSEYVILLE, IN; NORTH POSEY HS; (JR); Hnr Roll; 4-H; Quill & Scroll; Tchrs Aide; German Clb; Clr Grd; Stu Cncl (V); Yrbk (R, P); Spell Bowl; President of German Club; Nursing; Psychology; U of Southern Indiana; Purdue U

VOEGERL, HEATHER; HUNTINGBURG, IN; FOREST PARK JR/SR HS; (SO); 4H Awd; Hnr Roll; Nat Hon Sy; WWAHSS; Comm Volntr; 4-H; Emplmnt; FCCLA; Key Club; SADD; Chr; Bskball (L); Tennis (J); National Honors Society; Secretary for FCCLA; Business; U of Southern Indiana

VOGLER, LAURA J; PORTLAND, IN; JAY CTY HS; (FR); Hnr Roll; Otst Ac Ach Awd; Comm Volntr; Chrch Yth Grp; Drma Clb; Key Club; German Clb; Acpl Chr; Bnd; Dnce; Mch Bnd; I Won the Optimist Speech Contest At District Level; Music; Theater; Taylor U; Anderson U

VOIGT, JAMIE A; FORT WAYNE, IN; SOUTH SIDE HS; (SO); Hnr Roll; Otst Ac Ach Awd; Chrch Yth Grp; FCA; Tennis (J); Stu Cncl (V); Ft Wayne Medical Education; History Club; Physician; Business; Indiana U; U of Dayton

VOLTZ, TIM; WESTFIELD, IN; COLONIAL CHRISTIAN SCH; (SR); Ctznshp Aw; Hi Hnr Roll; Salutrn; WWAHSS; Chrch Yth Grp; Tchrs Aide; Chr; SP/M/VS; Bskball (V CL); Sccr (V L); Cl Off (V); CR (R); 2004 Athlete of the Year; Bible Bachelor of Arts; Cedarville U

VOLZ, ALICIA L; OSGOOD, IN; JAC-CEN-DEL HS; (SO); Hnr Roll; Nat Hon Sy; Comm Volntr; ArtClub; Bnd; Mch Bnd; Pep Bnd; SP/M/VS; Track (J); Pharmacy; Teacher; Purdue U; Butler U

VONGSKUL, MALISA; SEYMOUR, IN; SEYMOUR HS; (JR); Hi Hnr Roll; Hnr Roll; Nat Hon Sy; Comm Volntr; Peer Tut/Med; Emplmnt; Key Club; Quill & Scroll; Spanish Clb; Sccr (VJ L); Sch Ppr (E); Communications; International Relations

Vargson, Kristi
Fairfield JR/SR HS
New Paris, IN

Troxel, Kelsey L
Griffith SR HS
Griffith, IN

Trexler, Ciera
Jimtown HS
Elkhart, IN

Tripp, Troy D
New Haven HS
New Haven, IN

Volz, Alicia L
Jac-Cen-Del HS
Osgood, IN

WADE, SARAH K; EVANSVILLE, IN; NORTH POSEY HS; (JR); Hnr Roll; Spanish Clb; I Am a Counter Salesperson At a Local Bakery.; Culinary Arts; Business; The Illinois Institute of Art-Chicago; Sullivan U

WAGNER, MOLLY R; HARTFORD CITY, IN; BLACKFORD HS; (FR); Nat Hon Sy; Key Club; Ball State U

WAGNER JR, JAMES B; HUNTINGBURG, IN; SOUTHRIDGE HS; (SO); 4H Awd; Hnr Roll; St of Mnth; Comm Volntr; 4-H; Emplmnt; Outdrs Clb; Ftball (J L); 4-H; FFA; Landscape Management; Electrician; Purdue; IV Tech

WAINSCOTT, SETH; NORTH VERNON, IN; JENNINGS CTY HS; (SO); Hnr Roll; Pres Ac Ftns Aw; St of Mnth; Comm Volntr; Peer Tut/Med; Drma Clb; Off Aide; Cr Ctry (V); Ftball (J); Wrstlg (V); Bachelors/Masters in Elementary Education; Ball State U; Indiana U

WAITE, DUSTYN B; FT WAYNE, IN; R NELSON SNIDER HS; (SR); Hi Hnr Roll; Pharmacist; Purdue U

WALASCHMIDT, ELISE; SOUTH BEND, IN; RILEY HS; (FR); 4H Awd; Hi Hnr Roll; Hnr Roll; Perf Att; Sci Fairs; Comm Volntr; 4-H; ArtClub; Drma Clb; Swmg (J); TREES; History; Education; Holy Cross College; Indiana U South Bend

WALDRON, NICOLE; TERRE HAUTE, IN; NORTH VIGO HS; (SO); Hi Hnr Roll; Amnsty Intl; ArtClub; Emplmnt; Prom Com; Stg Cre; Yrbk; Artwork Displayed At Swope Art Gallery, Terre Haute, IN; Fine Arts, Graphic Arts, Marketing

WALKER, CASSIE; LAFAYETTE, IN; MC CUTCHEON HS; (JR); 4H Awd; 4-H; French Clb; Elementary Education; Early Childhood Education; Ivy Tech State College; Purdue U

WALKER, KRISTINA; COLUMBUS, IN; COLUMBUS NORTH HS; (FR); Hnr Roll; WWAHSS; Comm Volntr; Hosp Aide; Chrch Yth Grp; DARE; Drma Clb; Key Club; Medical Doctor; Indiana University; Duke University

WALL, SARAH E; COLUMBUS, IN; COLUMBUS EAST HS; (SO); Ch Chr; Dnce; Chrldg (V L); Yrbk (P); Stanford U; Yale U

WALLACE, ALEXANDRA M; INDIANAPOLIS, IN; BEN DAVIS HS; (SO); Hnr Roll; Nat Hon Sy; Yth Ldrshp Prog; Comm Volntr; DARE; NYLC; P to P St Amb Prg; Prom Com; Tchrs Aide; Chr; Chrldg (J L); Scr Kpr (L); Sftball (J L); Tennis (J L); Cl Off (S); Stu Cncl (R); CR (S); National Junior Honor Society Member; Student Council Cabinet Member; Architecture; Medicine; Indiana U; Duke U

WALSDORF, AMANDA N; HOBART, IN; RIVER FOREST SR HS; (FR); Hnr Roll; MVP; Emplmnt; Bnd; Clr Grd; Mch Bnd; Pep Bnd; Bskball (J); Sftball (J); Track (J); Vllyball (J); Outstanding Academic Achievement French I; Forensic Science; Medical; Valparaiso U

WALSH, HOLLY R; VALPARAISO, IN; VALPARAISO HS; (JR); Hnr Roll; Nat Hon Sy; Comm Volntr; Peer Tut/Med; Spec Olymp Vol; Emplmnt; Key Club; Kwanza Clb; Tchrs Aide; PP Ftbl (J); Track (J); Treasurer of Hope Club; Mentor for Children; Optometry; Nursing; Purdue (West Lafayette); Indiana U

WALTER, ALYSSA; VALPARAISO, IN; VALPARAISO HS; (FR); Hnr Roll; Kwnis Aw; Yth Ldrshp Prog; Comm Volntr; Spec Olymp Vol; Chrch Yth Grp; Key Club; Tchrs Aide; Bnd; Starting a K-Kids Club; Nursing; Education; Indiana U; Ball State U

WALTERS, AMANDA; CROWN POINT, IN; CROWN POINT HS; (SO); Hi Hnr Roll; Kwnis Aw; Otst Ac Ach Awd; Pres Sch; St Optmst of Yr; WWAHSS; Jr Cls League; Quill & Scroll; Vsity Clb; Latin Clb; Track (V L); Vsy Clb (V); Vllyball (J); Stu Cncl (R); Sch Ppr (E); USAA International Foreign Lang Award; Communications; Biology (Genetics); Notre Dame; Columbia U

WALTERS, JESSICA L; OTTERBEIN, IN; BENTON CTRL HS; (JR); 4H Awd; St of Mnth; 4-H; Chess; Chrch Yth Grp; Dbte Team; Drma Clb; Emplmnt; FCA; Lib Aide; Clr Grd; SP/M/VS; Stg Cre; PP Ftbl (V); Legal Secretary; Early Childhood Education; Ball State U; Purdue U

WALTERS, LAURA M; PETERSBURG, IN; PIKE CTRL HS; (JR); All Am Sch; Hi Hnr Roll; Hnr Roll; Nat Hon Sy; WWAHSS; Comm Volntr; Peer Tut/Med; Prom Com; SADD; Spanish Clb; Chr; SP/M/VS; Stu Cncl (R); Yrbk (E); Engineering; Computer Technology; U of Southern Indiana; Purdue U

WALTON, VANESSA; PAOLI, IN; PAOLI HS; (SR); Hi Hnr Roll; Nat Hon Sy; WWAHSS; Comm Volntr; Peer Tut/Med; BPA; Chrch Yth Grp; Emplmnt; Ntl FFA; Tchrs Aide; Spanish Clb; Agriculture Education; Purdue U

WALULU, LILLIAN; WEST LAFAYETTE, IN; HARRISON HS; (JR); Hnr Roll; Perf Att; Nursing; Pharmacy; Texas Tech U; New York U

WANNINGER, TARYN; JASPER, IN; JASPER HS; (FR); Hnr Roll; Pres Ac Ftns Aw; WWAHSS; FCA; Key Club; Spanish Clb; Chrldg (V); Dvng (V); Swmg (V)

WANTZ, BRADLEY; NEW CASTLE, IN; THE INDIANA AC; (SR); 4H Awd; Hnr Roll; WWAHSS; Peer Tut/Med; 4-H; Chrch Yth Grp; Drma Clb; Emplmnt; Prom Com; Spanish Clb; Chr; Ch Chr; Mch Bnd; SP/M/VS; Swmg (V L); Tennis (J); Stu Cncl; All-State Choir; El Premio Del Oro (Spanish Excellence); Musical Theatre; Spanish; New York U; Indiana U

WAQAR, HIRA; FLOYDS KNOBS, IN; FLOYD CTRL HS; (FR); Hnr Roll; Comm Volntr; Latin Clb

WARD, STARR A; ELKHART, IN;; Hnr Roll; Sci Fairs; ArtClub; Chrch Yth Grp; DARE; Mus Clb; Acpl Chr; Ch Chr; SP/M/VS; Bsball (L); Bskball (L); Chrldg (L); Sccr (L); Sftball (L); Track (L); Sch Ppr (E); Won a Poetry Contest.; Invited to Miss Pre-Teen Pageant; Veterinarian; Artist; IU; Notre Dame

WARE, JACOB; INDIANAPOLIS, IN; EMMERICH MANUAL HS; (FR); Ctznshp Aw; Hnr Roll; WWAHSS; Chrch Yth Grp; Ntl FFA; Reporter for Agriculture Class; Botanist; Artist; Purdue

WARE, KERRI L; INDIANAPOLIS, IN; PERRY MERIDIAN HS; (JR); Hnr Roll; Otst Ac Ach Awd; St of Mnth; Comm Volntr; Peer Tut/Med; ArtClub; Key Club; Acpl Chr; Chr; Stg Cre; Swg Chr; Stu Cncl (R); Blue Crew (School Spirit Club); Psychology; Counseling; Indiana/Purdue U; Indiana U

WARREN, KELSEY V; MARION, IN; EASTBROOK HS; (JR); Ctznshp Aw; Hi Hnr Roll; Hnr Roll; MVP; Nat Hon Sy; Nat Mrt Semif; Otst Ac Ach Awd; WWAHSS; Yth Ldrshp Prog; Comm Volntr; ArtClub; Chrch Yth Grp; Emplmnt; FCA; Photog; Tchrs Aide; Chr; Cr Ctry (V L); Track (V L); Cl Off (P); Stu Cncl (S); Sch Ppr (E, R); Completed a Marathon (26.2 miles) in 2005; English Education; Journalism; Taylor U-Upland Campus; Wheaton College

WEAVER, BRANDI; REYNOLDS, IN; FRONTIER HS; (SO); 4H Awd; Comm Volntr; 4-H; Ntl FFA; Spanish Clb; Chr; Vllyball; 4-H (Officer); Accountant; Business Management; St. Joseph College; Purdue U

WEAVER, ROSE; BRYANT, IN; JAY CTY HS; (SO); DAR; Hnr Roll; Pres Ac Ftns Aw; Sci Fairs; Peer Tut/Med; Chrch Yth Grp; FCA; Key Club; Spanish Clb; Chr; Swg Chr; Cr Ctry (V L); Track (V L); Broke 3200 Meter Relay Record Freshman Year in Track; Psychology; Medical; Indiana U; Ball State U

WEBB, DAVID; FORT WAYNE, IN; HERITAGE JR/SR HS; (SO); Ctznshp Aw; Hi Hnr Roll; Hnr Roll; Nat Hon Sy; Pres Ac Ftns Aw; Pres Sch; St of Mnth; Peer Tut/Med; Ch Chr; Bskball (J); Ftball (J); Track (V); National Urban League Inductee; Medical Degree; U of Michigan; U of North Carolina

WEBB, LYLE J; RENSSELAER, IN; RENSSELAER CTRL HS; (SR); Hi Hnr Roll; Hnr Roll; Nat Hon Sy; WWAHSS; Emplmnt; Jr Ach; SADD; Spanish Clb; Bnd; Mch Bnd; Pep Bnd; Cl Off (V); Stu Cncl (R); Architecture; Ball State U

WEDDLE, MELISSA; SPENCER, IN; OWEN VALLEY HS; (SO); 4H Awd; Hi Hnr Roll; Perf Att; WWAHSS; 4-H; Emplmnt; Scouts; Bnd; Mch Bnd; Stu Cncl (R); CR (R); Biomedical Engineering; Photography; Case Western Reserve U; Rose Hulman Institute for Technology

WEEMS, PATRICIA; ROACHDALE, IN; NORTH PUTNAM HS; (SO); Hnr Roll; Perf Att; St of Mnth; Peer Tut/Med; Chrch Yth Grp; DARE; Emplmnt; Key Club; Off Aide; Pep Squd; Scouts; Spanish Clb; Acpl Chr; Chr; Ch Chr; Scr Kpr; Vllyball (J); Best English Student Award (Sophomore); Neo Natal; Pediatrician; Indiana U; Saint Mary of the Woods

WEHNER, BRANDON; MADISON, IN; MADISON CONSOLIDATED; (SR); 4H Awd; Ctznshp Aw; DAR; Peer Tut/Med; 4-H; Chrch Yth Grp; DARE; Emplmnt; Key Club; Ntl FFA; Wdwrkg Clb; Spanish Clb; Bnd; Mch Bnd; Pep Bnd; FFA; Electrical Engineering Technology; Purdue U; Indiana U Southeast

WELCH, BREYAUNA; ANDERSON, IN; HIGHLAND HS; (SO); Hi Hnr Roll; Hnr Roll; Otst Ac Ach Awd; WWAHSS; Comm Volntr; Emplmnt; Bskball (J); Dr. Martin Luther King Jr. Award; Nursing; Bachelor's Degree

WELCH, MATTHEW L; CARMEL, IN; CARMEL HS; (JR); F Lan Hn Soc; Hi Hnr Roll; Nat Hon Sy; Perf Att; WWAHSS; Comm Volntr; Chrch Yth Grp; Mus Clb; Quill & Scroll; Bnd; Jzz Bnd; Mch Bnd; Pep Bnd; Sch Ppr (E)

WENDLING, LAUREN; ROACHDALE, IN; NORTH PUTNAM HS; (SR); Hi Hnr Roll; Nat Hon Sy; Otst Ac Ach Awd; Valdctrian; WWAHSS; Comm Volntr; Hab For Humty Volntr; Peer Tut/Med; AL Aux Girls; Chrch Yth Grp; Key Club; Prom Com; SADD; Spanish Clb; Bskball (V CL); Golf (V L); Track (V L); Vllyball (V L); Cl Off (T); Stu Cncl (R); CR (R); Sch Ppr (R); 2004 Evan Bayh Student Volunteer; 2005 LHSAA "What's Your Choice" Poster Role Model; English Education; Non-For-Profit Work; DePauw U; Earlham College

WENNING, THOMAS C; GREENSBURG, IN; JAC-CEN-DEL HS; (SO); Hnr Roll; Nat Hon Sy; Otst Ac Ach Awd; Perf Att; Chrch Yth Grp; Emplmnt; Ntl FFA; Tchrs Aide; Bskball (J); Architecture; Agricultural Engineering; Purdue; Ohio State U

WERNER, HOLLY; JASPER, IN; JASPER HS; (SO); Hi Hnr Roll; WWAHSS; FCA; Key Club; Spanish Clb; Bskball (JC); Vllyball (J); Stu Cncl (R); Lawyer; Teaching; Ball State U; Indiana U

WERNER, TRAVIS; JASPER, IN; JASPER HS; (FR); Hnr Roll; Perf Att; WWAHSS; Emplmnt; FCA; Key Club; Spanish Clb; Sccr (J)

WESLEY, KEVIN; CHESTERTON, IN; CHESTERTON HS; (SO); Ctznshp Aw; Hnr Roll; Perf Att; Yth Ldrshp Prog; Comm Volntr; Hab For Humty Volntr; Red Cr Aide; Chrch Yth Grp; Quill & Scroll; Scouts; Svce Clb; German Clb; Ch Chr; Stg Cre; Firehooper for Sakima Lodge in the Order of the Arrow; DJ for WDSO - FM in Chesterton HS; Marine Biology; Alaska Pacific U; Indiana U South Bend

WEST, KLARISSA R; ANDERSON, IN; ANDERSON HS; (FR); Hi Hnr Roll; Hnr Roll; Otst Ac Ach Awd; Perf Att; St Schl; St of Mnth; Comm Volntr; Hosp Aide; Chrch Yth Grp; DARE; Mus Clb; Chr; Swg Chr; Students Undercover; RN; Teacher; IUPUI; Purdue U

WESTERN, DAVID B; COLUMBIA CITY, IN; COLUMBIA CITY HS; (FR); 4H Awd; Hnr Roll; Sci/Math Olympn; Comm Volntr; Peer Tut/Med; 4-H; Chrch Yth Grp; Emplmnt; FCA; Quiz Bowl; Bsball (J); Ftball (J); Stu Cncl (R); CR (R); 7 Year 4-H Member; Won Showmanship Several Times; Mechanical Engineering; Purdue U

WETLER, KATIE; CROWN POINT, IN; CROWN POINT HS; (SO); Hnr Roll; Kwnis Aw; Sci Fairs; WWAHSS; Chrch Yth Grp; DARE; P to P St Amb Prg; Quill & Scroll; Tchrs Aide; Spanish Clb; Stg Cre; Sch Ppr (E); Yrbk (E); Quill & Scroll Member; History; International Studies; Georgetown U; Loyola U

WHEATLEY, KRISTIN; ELIZABETHTOWN, IN; COLUMBUS NORTH HS; (JR); Hnr Roll; MVP; FCA; Key Club; Off Aide; Swmg (V L); Track (J); Key Club Treasurer; Donner Swim Club - Top 10 Athlete in Indiana; Health Careers; Nursing

WHEELER, ADAM J; ECKERTY, IN; CRAWFORD CTY JR/SR HS; (JR); Nat Hon Sy; Perf Att; WWAHSS; Pep Squd; Tchrs Aide; Golf (J); Guitar Club President; Intramural Sports; Music Education; Business Administration; Oakland City U; U of Evansville

WHETSTONE, BROGUEN; BRYANT, IN; JAY CTY HS; (SO); 4H Awd; Hi Hnr Roll; Nat Hon Sy; WWAHSS; 4-H; Drma Clb; Jr Cls League; Schol Bwl; Chr; Flg Crps; SP/M/VS; Stg Cre; Stu Cncl (R); business; fashion design

WHITE, AMBER D; INDIANAPOLIS, IN; ARLINGTON HS; (SO); Otst Ac Ach Awd; Peer Tut/Med; Chrch Yth Grp; Mus Clb; ROTC; Chr; Ch Chr; Drl Tm; Track (V); Cl Off (R); Bachelor's / Master's Degree; Florida A & M; Alabama A & M

WHITE, GARY L; LAWRENCEBURG, IN; EAST CTRL HS; (SR); Nat Hon Sy; National Honor Society; General Studies; Computer Graphic & Design; Vincennes U

WHITE, KENDAL L; SWITZ CITY, IN; WHITE RIVER VALLEY HS; (JR); 4H Awd; Hnr Roll; Nat Hon Sy; Yth Ldrshp Prog; Comm Volntr; 4-H; ArtClub; Chrch Yth Grp; Drma Clb; Prom Com; Svce Clb; Spanish Clb; Bnd; Chr; Ch Chr; Mch Bnd; Tennis (J L); Homecoming-Freshman Representative; Nursing-Associate Degree; Purdue U; Vincennes U

WHITE, NATALIE; COLUMBUS, IN; COLUMBUS EAST; (SO); Hnr Roll; MVP; Perf Att; Pres Sch; Comm Volntr; Spec Olymp Vol; Mth Clb/Tm; Quiz Bowl; Sccr (V L); Track (V L); Stu Cncl (R); CR (R); Sch Ppr (R); Journalism

WHITEMAN, HANNAH; MUNCIE, IN; DELTA HS; (SO); Hi Hnr Roll; Nat Hon Sy; Perf Att; WWAHSS; Comm Volntr; Prom Com; Tchrs Aide; Spanish Clb; Chrldg (V); Tennis (J); Yrbk (R, P); Advertising; Public Relations; DePauw U; Butler U

WHITFIELD, AMANDA; CARTHAGE, IN; KNIGHTSTOWN HS; (SO); Ctznshp Aw; Hi Hnr Roll; Otst Ac Ach Awd; St of Mnth; ArtClub; Drma Clb; Emplmnt; Off Aide; Voc Ind Clb Am; French Clb; SP/M/VS; Bskball (J); PP Ftbl; Aries Youth Council; Top Ten in My Class; Practicing Medicine; Ph.D.; Indiana State U; Indiana U Purdue U

WHITLOW, RACHELE F; OSCEOLA, IN; PENN HS; (SR); Prom Com; Bnd; Jzz Bnd; Mch Bnd; Pep Bnd; Tap Dance; History Major; Ministry Major; Indiana U Bloomington

WIAND, ANDREW; SOUTH BEND, IN; ANDREW JACKSON; (SO); All Am Sch; Fut Prb Slvr; Hi Hnr Roll; Mth Clb/Tm; Mus Clb; Vsity Clb; Latin Clb; Orch; Bsball (V); Ftball (V); Swmg (J); Fischoff National Competition; All-Conference Football-Baseball; Architecture; Engineering; U of Notre Dame; Stanford U

WILBER, MORGAN M; RICHMOND, IN; RICHMOND HS; (SO); 4H Awd; Hi Hnr Roll; Nat Hon Sy; Otst Ac Ach Awd; Comm Volntr; 4-H; Pep Squd; Clr Grd; Dnce; Drl Tm; Bskball (J); Hsbk Rdg (V); Tennis (J); Pre-Med; Radiologist; Earlham College; U of Kentucky Medical School

WILHITE, KEELY D; FRANCISCO, IN; WALDO J WOOD MEMORIAL HS; (FR); 4H Awd; Hi Hnr Roll; USAA; WWAHSS; 4-H; Emplmnt; Bskball (V); Ftball; Sftball (V); Football-Manager; 4-H; Oakland City U

White, Gary L
East Ctrl HS
Lawrenceburg, IN

West, Klarissa R
Anderson HS
Anderson, IN

Welch, Breyauna
Highland HS
Anderson, IN

Ware, Kerri L
Perry Meridian HS
Indianapolis, IN

National
Honor Roll
Spring 2005

Waqar, Hira
Floyd Ctrl HS
Floyds Knobs, IN

Wesley, Kevin
Chesterton HS
Chesterton, IN

Wheeler, Adam J
Crawford Cty JR/SR HS
Eckerty, IN

Wilhite, Keely D
Waldo J Wood Memorial HS
Francisco, IN

WILKERSON, BRITTANY; INDIANAPOLIS, IN; LAWRENCE CTRL HS; (JR); Hi Hnr Roll; Hnr Roll; Nat Hon Sy; WWAHSS; Comm Volntr; Key Club; Quill & Scroll; Spanish Clb; Tennis; CR (P); Sch Ppr (E); Congressional Youth Caucus; Indiana U Honors Program; Law; Business; Purdue; U of Michigan

WILKINSON, TRENT; FORT WAYNE, IN; NORTHROP HS; (JR); Hnr Roll; Comm Volntr; Chrch Yth Grp; Golf (J); Law; Indiana U; Butler U

WILL, COURTNEY; FORT WAYNE, IN; HOMESTEAD HS; (SO); Psychology; Business; Indiana U

WILL, KYLE; FORT WAYNE, IN; HOMESTEAD; (JR); Hi Hnr Roll; Hnr Roll; DECA; Bsball (J)

WILLIAMS, AMANDA T; GARY, IN; WEST SIDE HS; (SO); Ctznshp Aw; Hnr Roll; WWAHSS; Ch Chr; Business Management; Interior Decorating; Purdue Calumet; Ball State U

WILLIAMS, CASANDRA; FORT WAYNE, IN; SOUTH SIDE HS; (SO); Hi Hnr Roll; Otst Ac Ach Awd; Pres Ac Ftns Aw; Sci Fairs; St of Mnth; WWAHSS; Comm Volntr; Peer Tut/Med; ArtClub; Emplmnt; FTA; Key Club; Spanish Clb; SP/M/VS; Chrldg (V L); Cl Off (V); Stu Cncl (P); African American Club; Alpha Omega Club; Psychology; Biomedical Engineering; Notre Dame U; Xavier U

WILLIAMS, DARCI L; ELKHART, IN; JIMTOWN HS; (FR); Ctznshp Aw; Hnr Roll; Comm Volntr; Scouts; Bnd; Jzz Bnd; Pep Bnd; SP/M/VS; Interior Designing; Business; Bethel College

WILLIAMS, GUY L; INDIANAPOLIS, IN; BEN DAVIS HS; (SO); Ctznshp Aw; Hnr Roll; Perf Att; Yth Ldrshp Prog; BPA; NYLC; Bnd; Jzz Bnd; Mch Bnd; Louie Armstrong Jazz Award; Architecture / Exterior Design; Engineer; Purdue; Florida St

WILLIAMS, HANNAH; PORTLAND, IN; JAY CTY HS; (JR); Hnr Roll; Nat Hon Sy; FCA; Chrldg (V L); Gmnstcs (V L); PP Ftbl (V); Education; Ball State U; Huntington College

WILLIAMS, KHADESHIA; MICHIGAN CITY, IN; MICHIGAN CITY HS; (FR); Hi Hnr Roll; Hnr Roll; Perf Att; Spec Olymp Vol; Chrch Yth Grp; Mus Clb; Chr; Dnce; Education; Food Science; Purdue U; Indiana U

WILLIAMS, MAHOGANY; INDIANAPOLIS, IN; ARLINGTON HS; (FR); Hi Hnr Roll; Hnr Roll; Kwnis Aw; Perf Att; Peer Tut/Med; Sci Clb; Bskball (VJ L); Cr Ctry (J L); African American History Challenge; Computer Technology; Sports Doctor; U of Tennessee; Ball State U

WILLIAMS, MALLORY; STENDAL, IN; PIKE CTRL HS; (SO); Hi Hnr Roll; Nat Ldrshp Svc; Perf Att; Yth Ldrshp Prog; Comm Volntr; Peer Tut/Med; Chrch Yth Grp; Emplmnt; Mth Clb/Tm; Sci Clb; Spanish Clb; Ch Chr; Clr Grd; Flg Crps; Swmg (V L); National English Merit Award; Medical Degree; U of Evansville; Indiana State U

WILLIAMS, SCOTT T; EVANSVILLE, IN; CENTRAL HS; (JR); Ctznshp Aw; Hnr Roll; WWAHSS; Emplmnt; Bsball (VJ); Bskball (J)

WILLIAMSON, BRITTANY; GREENCASTLE, IN; NORTH PUTNAM HS; (SR); Hi Hnr Roll; Hnr Roll; Nat Hon Sy; Otst Ac Ach Awd; WWAHSS; Yth Ldrshp Prog; Comm Volntr; Chrch Yth Grp; Emplmnt; Key Club; Ntl FFA; Prom Com; SADD; Chrldg (J); Golf (V L); Scr Kpr (V L); CR (R); Yrbk (R, P); Communications; Psychology; DePauw U

WILLIS, PAUL E; EVANSVILLE, IN; CTRL; (JR); Hnr Roll; Electric; Cable Guy; U of Evansville; Ivy Tech State College

WILLOUGHBY, BRITTNEY; EVANSVILLE, IN; CENTRAL HS; (JR); Ctznshp Aw; Hnr Roll; Otst Ac Ach Awd; USAA; Comm Volntr; Chrch Yth Grp; Chr; Veterinarian; Business; Purdue U; U of Southern Indiana

WILLS, LINDSAY; YODER, IN; WAYNE HS; (SR); Ctznshp Aw; Hnr Roll; Nat Hon Sy; Otst Ac Ach Awd; WWAHSS; Emplmnt; SP/M/VS; Chrldg (V); Track (J); Elementary Education; Radiologist Technician; Indiana Purdue U of Fort Wayne; Indiana Purdue U of Indianapolis

WILSON, DIANA M; BEECH GROVE, IN; BEECH GROVE HS; (JR); Hnr Roll; Nat Hon Sy; WWAHSS; Chrch Yth Grp; Emplmnt; FCA; Quill & Scroll; Tennis (V CL); Vllyball (JC); Stu Cncl (R); Sch Ppr (R); Speech Therapy; History; Indiana U; Butler U

WILSON, JULIE M; SOUTH BEND, IN; ADAMS HS; (SO); F Lan Hn Soc; Hnr Roll; Nat Hon Sy; Nat Sci Aw; Nat Stu Ath Day Aw; Otst Ac Ach Awd; Perf Att; Sci Fairs; St of Mnth; Comm Volntr; Peer Tut/Med; Red Cr Aide; 4-H; Chrch Yth Grp; DARE; Emplmnt; Mus Clb; Outdrs Clb; P to P St Amb Prg; Photog; Chr; Ch Chr; Orch; SP/M/VS; Gmnstcs (V); Hsbk Rdg (C); Track (VJ); Lit Mag (E); Japanese National Honor Society; Honor Roll; Cardiology or Radiology; IUPUI of Indianapolis; Ball State U

WILSON, MICHAEL A; PETERSBURG, IN; PIKE CTRL HS; (JR); Hnr Roll; Perf Att; Emplmnt; Lib Aide; Voc Ind Clb Am; First Place in School Art; Master's Degree in Architectural Engineering; To Own My Own Engineering Firm; Vincennes U; Evansville U

WILTRAKIS, SUSAN M; SAINT JOHN, IN; HOMESCHOOL; (SO); Otst Ac Ach Awd; Comm Volntr; Jzz Bnd; SP/M/VS; Performed on National Television, Chicago Jazz Festival; Member of Screen Actors Guild, Academic Talent Search Award; Career in Medicine; Northwestern; Loyola Chicago

WINDLAN, KATHRYN E; ANDERSON, IN; HIGHLAND HS; (FR); Ctznshp Aw; Hi Hnr Roll; Hnr Roll; Pres Ac Ftns Aw; Comm Volntr; Chrch Yth Grp; Lib Aide; Vsity Clb; Golf (V); Swmg (V)

WINGATE, ALICIA R; CHESTERTON, IN; CHESTERTON HS; (JR); 4H Awd; Hi Hnr Roll; St of Mnth; Comm Volntr; 4-H; Chrch Yth Grp; Spanish Clb; Bnd; Orch; Indiana State Music Award; Medicine; Indiana U; Ball State U

WININGER, CRYSTAL N; WASHINGTON, IN; WASHINGTON HS; (JR); Hi Hnr Roll; USAA; Comm Volntr; Peer Tut/Med; Chrch Yth Grp; Ntl Beta Clb; ROTC; Chr; Ch Chr; Drl Tm; SP/M/VS; NJROTC; Beta Club; Neonatal Nurse; Psychology/Social Work; U of Southern Indiana; Vincennes U

WINK, SCOTT R M; COLUMBIA CITY, IN; COLUMBIA CITY HS; (SO); Ctznshp Aw; Hi Hnr Roll; Nat Hon Sy; Otst Ac Ach Awd; WWAHSS; Comm Volntr; Peer Tut/Med; DARE; FTA; Key Club; Lib Aide; Ntl FFA; P to P St Amb Prg; Quiz Bowl; Schol Bwl; SP/M/VS; Adv Cncl; Cl Off (T); Stu Cncl; CR (P); Key Club President; Class Rank #1 of 279; Pediatrician; Biochemistry; U of Notre Dame; Harvard U

WINTER, ASHLEY; BLOOMINGTON, IN; EDGEWOOD HS; (FR); Hnr Roll; Junior Church Helper; Science & Math & Spanish; Purdue U

WINTERS, MEAGAN R; WALTON, IN; LEWIS CASS HS; (SR); Hi Hnr Roll; Nat Hon Sy; Pres Ac Ftns Aw; WWAHSS; Peer Tut/Med; FCA; Key Club; Prom Com; SADD; Chrldg (V CL); Golf (V CL); Sftball (V CL); Stu Cncl (P); Sch Ppr (E); Pre-Law; Communication/Political Science; Butler U

WIRTS, DEVIN B; WASHINGTON, IN; WASHINGTON HS; (JR); Hi Hnr Roll; Hnr Roll; St of Mnth; WWAHSS; Hab For Humty Volntr; Peer Tut/Med; BPA; Chrch Yth Grp; Drma Clb; Emplmnt; Key Club; Mus Clb; Ntl Beta Clb; Pep Squd; Ch Chr; SP/M/VS; Stg Cre; Swg Chr; Tennis (J); Stu Cncl (R); CR (R); Madrigal Dinner Singer & Actor; Talent Show Host; Acting; Commercial/Television Broadcasting; Indiana U; U of Southern Indiana

WITHERS, BRYANT K; MILAN, IN; MILAN HS; (SO); Perf Att; SADD; Vsity Clb; Bskball (VJ); Ftball (VJ); Track (V); Wt Lftg (V); MVP Award Basketball - 2004

WITTE, ALLISON; VALPARAISO, IN; VALPARAISO HS; (JR); Hi Hnr Roll; Nat Hon Sy; Otst Ac Ach Awd; Perf Att; Comm Volntr; Chrch Yth Grp; Emplmnt; Key Club; Ch Chr; Tennis (J); Education; Foreign Language; Ball State U; Indiana U

WITTMER, CHELSEA J; ODON, IN; NORTH DAVIESS JR/SR HS; (JR); Hnr Roll; Sci Fairs; WWAHSS; Chrch Yth Grp; Ntl Beta Clb; Pep Squd; Sci Clb; Dnce; Chrldg (V L); Sftball (V L); Beta Club; Science Club; Medical Field; Radiology; Indiana State U; U of Southern Indiana

WOLCOTT, JENNIFER L; MARION, IN; MARION HS; (SR); Hi Hnr Roll; WWAHSS; Peer Tut/Med; Chrch Yth Grp; Drma Clb; FCA; Dnce; SP/M/VS; Swg Chr; Dance Captain of Innovations Show Choir; To Star on Broadway; Taylor U

WOLSIFFER, EMILY J; NEW PALESTINE, IN; TRITON CTRL HS; (JR); 4H Awd; Hnr Roll; Kwnis Aw; Nat Hon Sy; Otst Ac Ach Awd; Comm Volntr; 4-H; Emplmnt; Pep Squd; Prom Com; SADD; Tchrs Aide; Chrldg (V L); Tennis (V L); Cl Off (P, V); Stu Cncl (P, V); Zoology; Ball State U

WOLTER, MADDIE; GRANGER, IN; PENN HS; (MS); Hi Hnr Roll; Pep Squd; Bnd; Chrldg (J); Track (J); Daughters of American Revolution Nominee; Medical School

WOOD, JASON; COLUMBUS, IN; COL NORTH HS; (SO); Hnr Roll; WWAHSS; Chess; Key Club; Mth Clb/Tm; Voc Ind Clb Am; Bnd; Mch Bnd; Engineer; Vincennes U; Purdue U

WOODARD, MONICA; KOKOMO, IN; TAYLOR HS; (SO); All Am Sch; Hi Hnr Roll; Nat Hon Sy; Peer Tut/Med; Chrch Yth Grp; FCA; FBLA; Prom Com; Spanish Clb; Ch Chr; Sccr (V L); Track (V L); Stu Cncl (R); Pre-Med; Degree in Medicine; IUPUI; Northwestern U

WOODS, ASHLEE R M; INDIANAPOLIS, IN; EMMERICH MANUAL HS; (FR); Hi Hnr Roll; Hnr Roll; Nat Mrt Sch Recip; Nat Sci Aw; Perf Att; Sci Fairs; Sci/Math Olympn; ArtClub; Fr of Library; Sci Clb; Spanish Clb; Won in Children's Museum Twice (Art); Won 5th Place in Science Fair of 2004; Crime Investigation (Master/Dr); Biology, Chemistry, Math (Master/Dr); Indiana U; St Francis CSI

WOODWORTH, KYLE P; NEW CARLISLE, IN; JOHN ADAMS HS; (JR); Hi Hnr Roll; St of Mnth; Comm Volntr; Chrch Yth Grp; DARE; Emplmnt; Mus Clb; Sci Clb; Svce Clb; Spanish Clb; Bnd; Ch Chr; Mch Bnd; Sccr (V); Principal's Award; Biology; Hope College; Notre Dame U

WOOLSEY, JESSICA; BOONVILLE, IN; BOONVILLE HS; (SO); 4H Awd; Hnr Roll; WWAHSS; Spec Olymp Vol; 4-H; Jr Cls League; Key Club; Bskball (J L); Golf (V L); Stu Cncl (R); 4-H Fine Arts State Fair Entry; Art Education

WORKMAN, WHITNEY; MAYS, IN; RUSHVILLE CONSOLIDATED HS; (SO); Hnr Roll; Otst Ac Ach Awd; Sci Fairs; St of Mnth; WWAHSS; 4-H; Chrch Yth Grp; Emplmnt; FCA; Key Club; Scouts; SADD; French Clb; Major in Education or Astronomy; Graduate from Ball State U; Ball State U; Butler U

WRIGHT, SHEMEKA; MERRILLVILLE, IN; MERRILLVILLE HS; (JR); Hi Hnr Roll; Hnr Roll; Nat Mrt LOC; Perf Att; WWAHSS; Peer Tut/Med; Jr Ach; Off Aide; SADD; French Clb; Future Community Leaders of America; Business; Fashion; Indiana U Purdue U; Indianapolis Indiana U Bloomington

WU, LANCE; GRANGER, IN; PENN HS; (FR); Pres Ac Ftns Aw; Dbte Team; Orch; SP/M/VS; Cr Ctry (L); Track (J); Mechanical Engineering; Aerospace Engineering; Purdue U; U of Michigan

WUELFING, AURELIA; WHITESTOWN, IN; LEBANON HS; (SO); 4H Awd; Hnr Roll; 4-H; Emplmnt; Scouts; Sftball (j/v); Mathalete; Medical Field; Indiana U

WYATT, KIRK L; COLUMBIA CITY, IN; COLUMBIA CITY HS; (FR); Hnr Roll; WWAHSS; Chrch Yth Grp; Emplmnt; Chr; Ch Chr; SP/M/VS; Cl Off (S); CR; Poetry.Com Award; Mary Hallowell / Tri Kappa Honor Award; Dentistry; Mathematics; Indiana U; Indiana U Purdue U Fort Wayne

YACK, RACHEL M; RENSSELAER, IN; KANKAKEE VALLEY HS; (SR); Hnr Roll; Chrch Yth Grp; Emplmnt; Photog; Quill & Scroll; Yrbk (R, P); Business Management; History; Purdue U Calumet

YANKAUSKAS, MICHAEL; HEBRON, IN; HEBRON HS; (SR); Hnr Roll; Emplmnt; FCA; Off Aide; Tchrs Aide; Spanish Clb; Bnd; Mch Bnd; Pep Bnd; Bsball (VJC); Bskball (VJ); Cr Ctry (J); Track (V); Cl Off (T); Bowling; Engineering; Purdue West Lafayette, IN

YATES, DAVID; HANOVER, IN; SOUTHWESTERN MIDDLE SR HS; (FR); Hnr Roll; Nat Hon Sy; ArtClub; Chrch Yth Grp; Build & Program Computers; Work On & Fix Cars; To Be a Pastor; Oral Roberts U

YEZBICK, TYLER J; EVANSVILLE, IN; SIGNATURE SCH; (SO); Ctznshp Aw; Hnr Roll; St of Mnth; Comm Volntr; Chess; DARE; Spch Team; Golf (V); Tennis (V); Stock Market Simulation

YORK, STEPHANIE; ELKHART, IN; JIMTOWN HS; (FR); Hi Hnr Roll; Perf Att; WWAHSS; Comm Volntr; FCA; Mth Clb/Tm; Bnd; Jzz Bnd; Pep Bnd; SP/M/VS; Tennis (V L); Vllyball (J); Cl Off (S)

YOUNG, LAUREN A; INDIANAPOLIS, IN; PERRY MERIDIAN HS; (FR); Ctznshp Aw; Hi Hnr Roll; Otst Ac Ach Awd; Chrch Yth Grp; FCA; Pep Squd; SADD; Chr; SP/M/VS; Swg Chr; Vllyball (C); Cl Off (V); Ambassador Corps

YOUNG, MELISSA; WHITING, IN; WHITING HS; (SR); Hnr Roll; Off Aide; Spanish Clb; Participated in Spanish Club; Nursing; Teaching; Purdue U Calumet; Indiana U Northwest

YOUNG, NICHOLE; HUNTINGBURG, IN; SOUTHRIDGE HS; (FR); 4H Awd; Hnr Roll; 4-H; BPA; Outdrs Clb; SADD; Spanish Clb; Hsbk Rdg

YOUNGGREEN, RYAN L; HANNA, IN; SOUTH CTRL HS; (FR); 4H Awd; Hnr Roll; 4-H; Bsball (J); Ftball (J); Agriculture-Animals; Construction Management; Purdue U; Indiana U, Vincennes U

ZEHR, ALICIA; ENGLISH, IN; CRAWFORD CTY JR/SR HS; (FR); Hi Hnr Roll; WWAHSS; ArtClub; Chrch Yth Grp; Tchrs Aide; Dnce; Golf (V); Sftball (V); Ski Club; Dance Team; Pharmacy; Dentistry

ZIENTA, JORDIN E; FREMONT, IN; FREMONT HS; (SO); Hnr Roll; WWAHSS; Chrch Yth Grp; DARE; FTA; Off Aide; Tchrs Aide; Bnd; Track (V L); Vllyball (V); Yrbk (E, P); Massage Therapy; Purdue U; Ohio State U

ZOOK, JADA; GREENFIELD, IN; GREENFIELD-CTRL HS; (FR); Hnr Roll; WWAHSS; Key Club; Svce Clb; French Clb; Chr; Swg Chr; Sister City Program (Sent Me to Japan for Exchange); Archaeology; Graphic Design; Michigan State U; Missouri State U

Wright, Shemeka
Merrillville HS
Merrillville, IN

Wininger, Crystal N
Washington HS
Washington, IN

Willoughby, Brittney
Central HS
Evansville, IN

Williams, Mallory
Pike Ctrl HS
Stendal, IN

Williams, Hannah
Jay Cty HS
Portland, IN

National
Honor Roll
Spring 2005

Williams, Amanda T
West Side HS
Gary, IN

Willis, Paul E
Central
Evansville, IN

Wiltrakis, Susan M
Homeschool
Saint John, IN

Wirts, Devin B
Washington HS
Washington, IN

Wood, Jason
Col North HS
Columbus, IN

Kentucky

ABERNATHY, WHITNEY; HOPKINSVILLE, KY; HOPKINSVILLE HS; (FR); Ctznshp Aw; Duke TS; Hi Hnr Roll; Hnr Roll; Otst Ac Ach Awd; Yth Ldrshp Prog; Chrch Yth Grp; Chr; Ch Chr; Bskball (VJ); Law; General History; Duke U; Texas Southern U

ADAMS, BRITTANY; NEWPORT, KY; NEWPORT HS; (SO); Duke TS; Hi Hnr Roll; Nat Hon Sy; WWAHSS; Hosp Aide; Drma Clb; Key Club; SP/M/VS; Mar Art (V); Microbiology; U of Kentucky

ADAMS, JENNIFER B; WOOTON, KY; LESLIE CTY HS; (SO); Ctznshp Aw; Hnr Roll; Perf Att; Sci Fairs; Comm Volntr; Drma Clb; FBLA; Prom Com; Scouts; Dnce; SP/M/VS; Stg Cre; Bskball (V); Sftball (V); The Show Most Go on Award (Drama Club); Academic English Award; Major in History; Degree in Teaching; Eastern Kentucky U; Alice Lloyd

ADAMS, KIMBERLY; BARDSTOWN, KY; NELSON CTY HS; (SO); Hnr Roll; Nat Hon Sy; WWAHSS; Comm Volntr; Hosp Aide; FCA; Key Club; Ntl FFA; National Honors Society; Nursing; U of Kentucky; U of Louisville

ADAMS, MEGAN A; GERMANTOWN, KY; MASON CTY HS; (SO); Ctznshp Aw; Gov Hnr Prg; Hi Hnr Roll; Hnr Roll; WWAHSS; Comm Volntr; Chrch Yth Grp; Mod UN; Ntl Beta Clb; Pep Squd; Svce Clb; Chr; Dnce; Orch; Top 10 USA - Gymnastics Finalist; Professional Ballet Dancer; New York U; U of California

ADAMS, RYAN; DRY RIDGE, KY; GRANT CO HS; (SO); Chrch Yth Grp; Ftball (VJ L)

ADCOCK, BRANDON S; FRANKFORT, KY; FRANKLIN CTY HS; (FR); Ctznshp Aw; Hi Hnr Roll; Nat Ldrshp Svc; Perf Att; USAA; WWAHSS; Comm Volntr; Chrch Yth Grp; DARE; FCA; Key Club; Bnd; Mch Bnd; Pep Bnd; Sftball (CL); Key Club Award, Most Points for a Freshman; Medical Field; Centre College

AGNEW, KELLSEY A; FREDONIA, KY; CALDWELL CTY HS; (SO); 4H Awd; Hi Hnr Roll; Nat Hon Sy; St of Mnth; 4-H; Emplmnt; FCA; FBLA; Sccr (V); Yrbk (R, P); Medicine; U of Michigan; U of Kentucky

AKER, JENNIFER; MIDDLESBORO, KY; MIDDLESBORO HS; (FR); Hnr Roll; Perf Att; ROTC; ROTC; Veterinary Assistant; Physician's Assistant; U of Kentucky

AKERS, BRANDON K; BARDSTOWN, KY; NELSON CTY HS; (SO); All Am Sch; Duke TS; Hi Hnr Roll; Nat Hon Sy; Otst Ac Ach Awd; St of Mnth; USAA; WWAHSS; Comm Volntr; Key Club; Schol Bwl; Bnd; Mch Bnd; SP/M/VS; Mar Art; Sophomore of the Year; Young Leaders Program; Major in Biochemistry/Molecular; Biology-Graduate or Medical School; Yale U, Harvard U, Brown U, Boston, Cornell U, Tulane U, Northwestern U, Centre College

ALLEN, JACLYN D; LA CTR, KY; BALLARD MEMORIAL HS; (SR); 4H Awd; Hi Hnr Roll; Nat Sci Aw; Perf Att; Pres Sch; Valdctrian; WWAHSS; Peer Tut/Med; 4-H; Chrch Yth Grp; FCCLA; FTA; Lib Aide; Ntl Beta Clb; Quill & Scroll; Spanish Clb; Bnd; Mch Bnd; Pep Bnd; Sch Ppr (R, P); Yrbk (E); Presidential Classroom Scholar; FTA - President; Spanish; Kentucky Wesleyan College

ALLEN, JAMIE; LEXINGTON, KY; HENRY CLAY SR HS; (FR); WWAHSS; ROTC; JROTC Assistant S-5; JROTC Color Guard & Drill Team; Law Enforcement; Eastern Kentucky U

ALLEN, KELLY; LOUISVILLE, KY; SACRED HEART AC; (SO); Duke TS; Hi Hnr Roll; Sci Fairs; Sci/Math Olympn; WWAHSS; Comm Volntr; Chrch Yth Grp; Emplmnt; Outdrs Clb; Sci Clb; Spch Team; Cr Ctry (J); Fld Hky (J); PP Ftbl; Track (V L); Stu Cncl (R); Law; Eartham College

ALLENDER, BRANDON; LATONIA, KY; SCOTT HS; (SO); Hnr Roll; Perf Att; St of Mnth; Chrch Yth Grp; DARE; Emplmnt; Sccr (VJ L); National Junior Honor Society; U of Kentucky

AMBROISE, DARLYN; LOUISVILLE, KY; (MS); Hnr Roll; Chrch Yth Grp; Mod UN; Spanish Clb; Chr; Dnce; Orch; Step Team; Music Artist; Princeton

AMBURGEY, MICHAEL; MT STERLING, KY; MONTGOMERY CTY HS; Hi Hnr Roll; Ntl FFA; Tmpl Yth Grp; Hunting; Demolition Derby Driver; Welder; Auto Mechanic; Rowan Tech College

AMMON, HEATHER D; LONDON, KY; NORTH LAUREL HS; (SO); St of Mnth; Comm Volntr; DARE; Drma Clb; FCA; ROTC; SADD

AMORES, KRISTY A; LOUISVILLE, KY; FERN CREEK TRADITIONAL HS; (FR); Hi Hnr Roll; WWAHSS; Comm Volntr; Hosp Aide; DECA; Pep Squd; Spanish Clb; Pharmacology; Medical Doctor; U of Louisville; Baylor College of Medicine-Houston, TX

ANDERSON, COREY; BURKESVILLE, KY; CUMBERLAND CTY HS; (JR); Hnr Roll; WWAHSS; DARE; FCA; FBLA; Jr Ach; Ntl Beta Clb; Ntl FFA; Bskball (VJ); FFA Officer-Reporter; Engineering; Land Surveying; Western Kentucky U; Lindsey Wilson College

ANDERSON, MATT; LOUISVILLE, KY; SENECA HS; (SR); Hi Hnr Roll; Nat Hon Sy; Perf Att; USAA; WWAHSS; Peer Tut/Med; Red Cr Aide; Key Club; Mth Clb/Tm; Ntl Beta Clb; Tchrs Aide; Sccr (J); Participated in Imagining the Future of Learning; Computer Engineering; Electrical Engineering; U of Louisville

ANDERSON, REBECCA; LOUISVILLE, KY; SENECA HS; (SO); Hi Hnr Roll; Nat Hon Sy; WWAHSS; Comm Volntr; Key Club; Ntl Beta Clb; Chr; Outstanding Zoo Volunteer Award; Biology; U of Louisville

ANDERSON RICE, SEAN C; SCOTTSVILLE, KY; ALLEN CTY HS; (SO); All Am Sch; Duke TS; Hnr Roll; USAA; WWAHSS; Chrch Yth Grp; FCA; Ntl Beta Clb; Scouts; Bnd; Ch Chr; Jzz Bnd; Mch Bnd; Western KY U Honors Band; All-District Band; Mathematics; Science; Michigan State U; U of Michigan

ANDRECHT, MELISSA; PADUCAH, KY; REIDLAND HS; (SO); Ctznshp Aw; Fut Prb Slvr; Nat Hon Sy; Sci Fairs; WWAHSS; Hosp Aide; Peer Tut/Med; FCA; Key Club; Kwanza Clb; Bnd; Chr; Mch Bnd; Pep Bnd; Lawyer; Family Consumer; U of Michigan; U of Kentucky

ANTLE, ERIKA; JAMESTOWN, KY; ADAIR CTY HS; (SO); Chrch Yth Grp; Voc Ind Clb Am; Chr; HOSA; Obstetrics/Gynecology; Pediatrics; Western Kentucky U; U of Kentucky

ARANT, CODY L; BARLOW, KY; BALLARD MEMORIAL HS; (JR); Duke TS; Hnr Roll; Nat Hon Sy; WWAHSS; Comm Volntr; Chrch Yth Grp; Emplmnt; Schol Bwl; USSF Soccer Referee; Journalism; West Kentucky U; U of Kentucky

ARMSTRONG, NICOLE M A; BERRY, KY; HARRISON CTY HS; (FR); Ctznshp Aw; Hnr Roll; Otst Ac Ach Awd; Comm Volntr; Chrch Yth Grp; FCA; Lib Aide; Chr; Cr Ctry (V L); FCA; Medicine-Human; Medicine-Vet; U of Dayton; U of Xavier

ARNETT, RACHEL; WALTON, KY; LARRY A RYLE HS; (SO); Hnr Roll; Bskball (V); Cr Ctry (J); Track (J); USAA National Mathematics Award Nominee; Juris Doctor; Psychology; U of Virginia; Vanderbilt U

ARTIS, LINDSEY M; PADUCAH, KY; HEATH HS; (SO); Hnr Roll; Drma Clb; Bnd; Mch Bnd; 3 Years of Marching Band; Inductee in Duke Talent Search in 7th Grade; Culinary Arts; Meteorology; Murray State U; Chicago Culinary Arts School

ARTRIP, KRISTIN; FRANKFORT, KY; FRANKLIN CTY HS; (JR); Hi Hnr Roll; Hnr Roll; Nat Hon Sy; Nat Ldrshp Svc; Nat Mrt LOC; Nat Mrt Sch Recip; Otst Ac Ach Awd; St of Mnth; USAA; WWAHSS; Chrch Yth Grp; DARE; Drma Clb; Emplmnt; Key Club; Scouts; Chr; SP/M/VS; Sch Ppr (R); Lifeguard CPR; Fashion-Interior Design; Education; Eastern Kentucky; U of Kentucky

ASHLEY, TASHA L; BEE SPRING, KY; EDMONSON CTY HS; (FR); Perf Att; Chr; Bskball; Veterinary; U of Kentucky

ATHA, ERIN; FRANKFORT, KY; FRANKLIN CTY HS; (JR); Hnr Roll; WWAHSS; Comm Volntr; Chrch Yth Grp; FCA; Key Club; Mod UN; Ntl Beta Clb; Pep Squd; SADD; Chr; Dnce; PP Ftbl (J); Tennis (J); Cl Off (S); Stu Cncl (R); CR (R); Pre-Physical Therapy

AUSTIN, BRITTANY E; MADISONVILLE, KY; MADISONVILLE NORTH HOPKINS HS; (JR); Hnr Roll; Nat Hon Sy; Nat Stu Ath Day Aw; WWAHSS; Comm Volntr; Spec Olymp Vol; FCA; Key Club; Ntl Beta Clb; Prom Com; Dnce; Sftball; Academic All-State Award; Psychology; Psychiatrist; U of Kentucky; Western Kentucky U

AUSTIN, WHITNEY; FRANKFORT, KY; FRANKLIN CTY HS; (FR); Hi Hnr Roll; Hnr Roll; Nat Hon Sy; Sci Fairs; Comm Volntr; Peer Tut/Med; Chrch Yth Grp; DARE; Key Club; Bnd; Drm Mjr; Mch Bnd; Pep Bnd; PP Ftbl (J); Sccr (J); Kuna; Y-Club; Pediatrician; Registered Nurse; Midway College; LCC

BAILEY, CLARICE N; RINEYVILLE, KY; NORTH HARDIN HS; (JR); Hnr Roll; Nat Hon Sy; Yth Ldrshp Prog; Chrch Yth Grp; Emplmnt; FBLA; FCCLA; Jr Ach; French Clb; Vllyball (VJCL); National Honor Society; National Youth Salute; Business Management; MBA; Tulane U; Howard U

BAIRD, COURTNEY; BENTON, KY; MARSHALL CTY HS; (JR); Perf Att; Red Cr Aide; FBLA; Pep Squd; All American Scholar in 7th Grade; Volunteer for Harvey Brewers Fire Department; Criminology / Major; Forensics; Murray State U; West Kentucky Community Technical College

BAKER, BLAKE; FRANKFORT, KY; WESTERN HILLS HS; (JR); Hnr Roll; Ntl Beta Clb; Bsball; Golf; Yrbk

BAKER, ERIN; GEORGETOWN, KY; SCOTT CTY HS; (SO); 4H Awd; Hi Hnr Roll; MVP; St of Mnth; USAA; WWAHSS; Comm Volntr; 4-H; FCCLA; Key Club; Scouts; Bnd; Mch Bnd; Pep Bnd; Swmg (V L); Tennis (V L); National Make It Yourself with Wool Finalist; Girl Scout Silver Award; Interior Design; U of Kentucky; Kansas State U

BAKER, JESSICA L; SCALF, KY; KNOX CTRL HS; (JR); Hnr Roll; Otst Ac Ach Awd; Perf Att; Sci Fairs; St of Mnth; Comm Volntr; FBLA; Pep Squd; Business Administration; Psychology; Eastern Kentucky U; Union College

BAKER, LUKE R; LEWISPORT, KY; HANCOCK CTY HS; (SO); Duke TS; Fut Prb Slvr; Hi Hnr Roll; Otst Ac Ach Awd; Perf Att; St of Mnth; Comm Volntr; FBLA; Ntl Beta Clb; Bnd; Mch Bnd; Pep Bnd; Stu Cncl (R); CR (R); Conservation Essay Winner; Medical Doctor; Medical Examiner; Duke U; Columbia U

BALDWIN, JOSEPH C; LIVERMORE, KY; MC LEAN CTY HS; (SO); Ctznshp Aw; Hnr Roll; Nat Hon Sy; Otst Ac Ach Awd; Perf Att; Pres Ac Ftns Aw; Sci Fairs; St of Mnth; USAA; WWAHSS; Comm Volntr; Peer Tut/Med; Spec Olymp Vol; 4-H; ArtClub; Chrch Yth Grp; DARE; Emplmnt; Lttrmn Clb; Ntl FFA; Pep Squd; Bnd; Ch Chr; Mch Bnd; Pep Bnd; Ftball (J L); Tennis (V L); Eagle Scout Preparation; Veterinary Science; U of Kentucky

BALL, KIMBERLY A; PARKERS LAKE, KY; MC CREARY CTRL HS; (SO); Hnr Roll; Comm Volntr; Outdrs Clb; ROTC; Clr Grd; Drl Tm; Chrldg (V); Ftball; Vet; U of Kentucky

BALL, RYAN K; LOUISVILLE, KY; SOUTHERN HS MAGNET; (JR); Hnr Roll; WWAHSS; Comm Volntr; Chrch Yth Grp; DARE; Key Club; ROTC; Clr Grd; Cr Ctry (J); Track (J); Wt Lftg (J); Wrstlg (J); Criminal Justice; Western KY U; U of L-U of Louisville

BALLARD, BRYON J; GLASGOW, KY; BARREN CTY HS; (SO); Hnr Roll; Perf Att; Sci Fairs; St of Mnth; WWAHSS; Comm Volntr; Chrch Yth Grp; DARE; Drma Clb; Emplmnt; FBLA; FTA; Key Club; Foreign Clb; Ch Chr; SP/M/VS; Bskball (J); Sccr (J); Swmg (J); Track (J); Vsy Clb (J); Vllyball (J); Yrbk (P); Key Club / Foreign Language Club; Elementary School Teacher; Meteorologist / Storm Chaser; U of Kentucky; U of Nebraska

BALLARD, CASSANDRA; OWENSBORO, KY; DAVIESS CTY HS; (FR); All Am Sch; Duke TS; Hi Hnr Roll; Hnr Roll; MVP; Otst Ac Ach Awd; Pres Sch; St Schl; St of Mnth; WWAHSS; Comm Volntr; Peer Tut/Med; Chrch Yth Grp; DARE; Emplmnt; FCA; Mth Clb/Tm; Pep Squd; SADD; Spanish Clb; Vllyball (C); Best Server Award (For Volleyball); Veterinary (Large Animal); Pediatrician; Duke; Auburn

BANEY, TRAVIS; MAGNOLIA, KY; (SR); Hnr Roll; Nat Hon Sy; Nat Stu Ath Day Aw; WWAHSS; Yth Ldrshp Prog; Chrch Yth Grp; FBLA; Ntl FFA; Ftball; Wrstlg; Stu Cncl (T); Agriculture; U of KY

BARBEE, AMBER; LOUISVILLE, KY; FAIRDALE HS; (SR); Hnr Roll; Nat Hon Sy; WWAHSS; Red Cr Aide; Mth Clb/Tm; Ntl Beta Clb; Prom Com; Voc Ind Clb Am; French Clb; Dnce; PP Ftbl; Governor Scholar Program; Pre-Med; U of Louisville

BARKER, CAITLIN M; FRANKFORT, KY; FRANKLIN CTY HS; (SO); All Am Sch; Duke TS; Gov Hnr Prg; Hnr Roll; Nat Ldrshp Svc; Pres Sch; WWAHSS; Peer Tut/Med; Key Club; Ntl Beta Clb; Cr Ctry (V L); PP Ftbl (V); Sccr (V L); Track (V L); Cl Off (S)

BARLOW, BENJAMIN R; LIBERTY, KY; CASEY CTY HS; (SR); Hnr Roll; Perf Att; St of Mnth; Comm Volntr; 4-H; Chrch Yth Grp; DARE; FCA; Ntl FFA; Pep Squd; Prom Com; Voc Ind Clb Am; Bskball (V C); Scr Kpr; Industrial Maintenance / Electrical; Central KY Technical College

BARR, JOSEPH M; VERSAILLES, KY; WOODFORD CTY HS; (FR); Hnr Roll; MVP; Pres Ac Ftns Aw; Golf (V L); Business; Sports Management; U of Tennessee; U of Kentucky

BARRETT, ANDREW R; VERSAILLES, KY; WOODFORD CTY HS; (JR); Ctznshp Aw; Duke TS; Hi Hnr Roll; Hnr Roll; Nat Hon Sy; Emplmnt; Ntl Beta Clb; Tech Clb; Kentucky National Guard; U of Kentucky; Eastern Kentucky U

BARRIE II, FLORIAN A; BARDSTOWN, KY; NELSON CTY SR HS; (SO); 4H Awd; All Am Sch; Nat Mrt Fin; Nat Mrt Sch Recip; WWAHSS; Key Club; Ntl Beta Clb; Ntl FFA; Off Aide; Scouts; Bskball (J); Forensic Engineering; U of Kentucky

BARTLETT, MAGAN A; MACEO, KY; DAVIESS CTY HS; (SR); Hnr Roll; Perf Att; Comm Volntr; Hab For Humty Volntr; Emplmnt; FCA; FBLA; Ntl Beta Clb; Pep Squd; Photog; SADD; Tchrs Aide; Chr; Ch Chr; Sch Ppr (R); Yrbk (R); 1st Runner Up Miss Teen Daviess Cty; Coached Junior Cheer Squads; Communication Disorders; Western Kentucky U; U of Kentucky

Ballard, Bryon J
Barren Cty HS
Glasgow, KY

Allender, Brandon
Scott HS
Latonia, KY

National
Honor Roll
Spring 2005

Adcock, Brandon S
Franklin Cty HS
Frankfort, KY

Barker, Caitlin M
Franklin Cty HS
Frankfort, KY

BARTOLO, PATRICIA; MAYFIELD, KY; GRAVES CTY HS; (JR); Hnr Roll; Nat Mrt LOC; Perf Att; St of Mnth; Comm Volntr; Track (J); Nurse; Paduca Community College; Murray State U

BARTSCH, RACHEL; ERLANGER, KY; BOONE CTY HS; (FR); Ctznshp Aw; Duke TS; Hi Hnr Roll; Pres Sch; Comm Volntr; Chrch Yth Grp; Drma Clb; FCA; Spanish Clb; Bnd; Dnce; Sch Ppr (R); Psychology; Pediatrician

BATES, PATRICIA; LEXINGTON, KY; PAUL LAURENCE DUNBAR HS; (JR); Hi Hnr Roll; Hnr Roll; Sci Fairs; St of Mnth; Yth Ldrshp Prog; Comm Volntr; Hab For Humty Volntr; DARE; Tchrs Aide; Ch Chr; Chrldg (J); Talent Search; Black Achievers; Biology; UK, Alabama State; Tenn State

BAUER, ZACK; FRANKFORT, KY; FRANKLIN CTY HS; (SO); Duke TS; Hnr Roll; Otst Ac Ach Awd; WWAHSS; Chrch Yth Grp; Outdrs Clb; Vsity Clb; Sccr (V); Track (V); Wrstlg (V); Aerospace Engineering; US Air Force Academy; Embry-Riddle Aeronautical U

BAYS, BETHANY; TYNER, KY; JACKSON CTY HS; (FR); 4H Awd; Hnr Roll; St of Mnth; WWAHSS; 4-H; Chrch Yth Grp; DARE; FCA; Ntl FFA; Spanish Clb; SP/M/VS; Bskball (V); Veterinarian; U of Kentucky

BEAM, CANDACE; BARDSTOWN, KY; NELSON CTY HS; (FR); Hi Hnr Roll; Hnr Roll; MVP; WWAHSS; Comm Volntr; Chrch Yth Grp; Key Club; Pep Squd; Sccr (V); Pharmacy; U of Kentucky

BEAM, LAURA; LEXINGTON, KY; SCAPA/LAFAYETTE HS; (JR); Hi Hnr Roll; Hnr Roll; Nat Hon Sy; WWAHSS; Yth Ldrshp Prog; Comm Volntr; Hosp Aide; Chrch Yth Grp; Drma Clb; Emplmnt; FCA; Key Club; MuAlphaTh; Ntl Beta Clb; Prom Com; Acpl Chr; Chr; SP/M/VS; Sccr (V L); Stu Cncl (R); CR (R); Sch Ppr (R); Attended GSA (Governor School for the Arts); Vocal Performing; Musical Theatre; Belmont U; Florida State U

BEARD, JACOB R; ELIZABETHTOWN, KY; CTRL HARDIN HS; (FR); Wt Lftg; Architecture / Engineering; Biology; U of Kentucky; Vanderbilt U

BEAVER, SAMANTHA; WILLIAMSTOWN, KY; WILLIAMSTOWN JR/SR HS; (JR); Hi Hnr Roll; Hnr Roll; Nat Hon Sy; Peer Tut/Med; DARE; Lib Aide; Ntl Beta Clb; Yrbk (R, P); Pediatric Nursing; Northern Kentucky U; Beckfield College

BECKER, STARR; DAYTON, KY; DAYTON HS; (JR); Hi Hnr Roll; Hnr Roll; Nat Hon Sy; Perf Att; WWAHSS; Comm Volntr; Bnd; Mch Bnd; Pep Bnd; Sftball (J); Tennis (V); Vllyball (VJ); Cl Off (T); Bowling; Veterinarian; Eastern Kentucky U

BELL, BRANDON Q; LOUISVILLE, KY; BUECHEL METROPOLITAN HS; (SO); Hnr Roll; Nat Ldrshp Svc; Yth Ldrshp Prog; Comm Volntr; Emplmnt; SP/M/VS; Bskball (J); Mar Art (V); Youth Resident & Leadership Facilitation Training; YPY Young Powerful Youth Award; Web Master; Music; U of Louisville; U of Kentucky

BELL, KRISTEN K; BURLINGTON, KY; CONNER HS; (FR); Ctznshp Aw; Hi Hnr Roll; Hnr Roll; St of Mnth; DARE; Scouts; Lawyer; Chef; Thomas More College; N KY U

BELLAMY, JOSHUA P; WHITESVILLE, KY; TRINITY HS; (JR); Hnr Roll; Nat Hon Sy; WWAHSS; Yth Ldrshp Prog; Comm Volntr; Peer Tut/Med; Chrch Yth Grp; Emplmnt; FBLA; HO'Br Yth Ldrshp; Prom Com; SADD; Bskball (V); Cl Off (V, S, T); Hugh O'Brian Youth Leadership (HOBY); Gillette Company Economics for Leaders; Political Science; Sports Broadcasting; U of Kentucky; Gonzaga U

BENNETT, MARIE; TOMPKINSVILLE, KY; MONROE CTY HS; (SO); Duke TS; Hnr Roll; Comm Volntr; FCA; FBLA; Pep Squd; Bskball (VJ); Sftball (V); Tennis (J); Vllyball (V); Yrbk (E); Nursing; Physical Therapist; Western; UK

BENOIST, MICHAEL B; FLORENCE, KY; BOONE CTY HS; (FR); Hi Hnr Roll; Hnr Roll; Perf Att; Peer Tut/Med; Drma Clb; FBLA; Bnd; Ftball (J L); Forensics; U of Miami; Northern Kentucky U

BENTLEY, WHITLEY; JACKHORN, KY; FLEMING NEON HS; (SO); Ctznshp Aw; Hi Hnr Roll; Hnr Roll; Valdctrian; Comm Volntr; Peer Tut/Med; Ntl Beta Clb; Sftball (V); Sch Ppr (R); Anesthesiologist; CRNA (Certified Registered Nurse of Anesthetics); Southeast Community College

BEVILLE, WILLIAM H; HOPKINSVILLE, KY; HOPKINSVILLE HS; (SO); Hi Hnr Roll; Hnr Roll; MVP; Nat Hon Sy; Perf Att; Emplmnt; Tchrs Aide; Vsity Clb; Ftball (VJ L); Wt Lftg (VJ); Engineering; Law; U of Kentucky; U of Missouri

BIANCHI DI CARCANO, ALEJANDRO; WALTON, KY; LARRY A RYLE HS; (FR); Hnr Roll; 4-H; Chess; Chrch Yth Grp; DARE; Tech Clb; Track (V); On World Competition '04; Architecture; NYU

BILLINGSLEY, BRITTANY; GLASGOW, KY; BARREN CTY HS; (SO); Hnr Roll; Pres Ac Ftns Aw; WWAHSS; 4-H; Chrch Yth Grp; Key Club; Ntl Beta Clb; Pep Squd; Sccr (VJ L); Track (V); U of Kentucky

BINGHAM, BRANDON R; WALKER, KY; KNOX CTRL; (SR)

BIRD, JESSICA E M; HOPKINSVILLE, KY; HOPKINSVILLE HS; (FR); Gov Hnr Prg; Hi Hnr Roll; Hnr Roll; Chrch Yth Grp; Ntl Beta Clb; Chr; Vllyball (J); Jr. Beta; Jr. Optimist; Registered Nurse; Math Major; Yale U; Columbia U

BISIG, TARA; SHELBYVILLE, KY; SHELBY CTY HS; (FR); Duke TS; Peer Tut/Med; Pep Squd; Chr; Poem Award; Counseling Degree; U of Kentucky; U of Florida

BITTER, SHAUN; FT MITCHELL, KY; SCOTT HS; (SO); Hnr Roll; Pres Ac Ftns Aw; St of Mnth; Bsball (VJ); Bskball (J); College Baseball; Louisville; U of Kentucky

BLACK, RANDI; VERSAILLES, KY; WOODFORD CTY HS; (SR); All Am Sch; Duke TS; Hnr Roll; Nat Hon Sy; WWAHSS; Comm Volntr; Ntl Beta Clb; Dnce; Cr Ctry (V L); Track (V L); CR (R); Veterinary; U of Kentucky (Undergraduate Work); Auburn U (Graduate Doctorial)

BLACKWOOD, JESSICA L; CORBIN, KY; LYNN CAMP HS; (MS); Duke TS; Hi Hnr Roll; Otst Ac Ach Awd; Sci Fairs; Yth Ldrshp Prog; Peer Tut/Med; FCA; Prom Com; Bskball (V); Track (V); Yrbk (E, P); Honor Club 4.0; Law; Teaching; U of Kentucky; U of the Cumberlands

BLAIR, ADRIENNE V; REGINA, KY; EAST RIDGE HS; (JR); Hi Hnr Roll; Hnr Roll; Otst Ac Ach Awd; Pres Sch; St of Mnth; WWAHSS; Comm Volntr; 4-H; Biology Clb; Emplmnt; Ntl Beta Clb; Pep Squd; French Clb; Cl Off (V); Biology; Math-Algebra; Pikeville College; U of Kentucky

BLAIR, JACOB; LOUISVILLE, KY; LOUISVILLE MALE HS; (JR); F Lan Hn Soc; Hnr Roll; WWAHSS; Comm Volntr; ArtClub; Cmptr Clb; Quill & Scroll; ROTC; Spanish Clb; Chr; Ch Chr; SP/M/VS; Skt Tgt Sh (J); Sch Ppr (E); Journalism; Western Kentucky U

BLAKE, KACI; ALLENSVILLE, KY; TODD CTY CTRL HS; (SO); Hnr Roll; St of Mnth; WWAHSS; Spanish Clb; Bskball (VJ); I Played Both JV and Varsity Basketball During 2004-2005

BLAKLEY, LAJOLLA M; WILLIAMSBURG, KY; WHITLEY CTY HS; (FR); 4H Awd; Hnr Roll; Perf Att; Sci Fairs; St of Mnth; Comm Volntr; Peer Tut/Med; Spec Olymp Vol; 4-H; Chrch Yth Grp; Ch Chr; Dnce; SP/M/VS; Stg Cre; Radiology; Berea College; Lindsay Wilson College

BLANKENSHIP, WHITNEY H; RACCOON, KY; PIKE CTY CTRL HS; (SO); 4H Awd; Hi Hnr Roll; Hnr Roll; Nat Hon Sy; Perf Att; WWAHSS; Ntl Beta Clb; Sci Clb; Spanish Clb; Chr; Golf (V); Awarded for Foreign Language Achievement Academy; Interior Design; Cosmetology; Pikeville College; Transylvania U

BLEVINS, ASHLEY; MOUNT STERLING, KY; MONTGOMERY CTY HS; (FR); Ctznshp Aw; Hi Hnr Roll; Kwnis Aw; Otst Ac Ach Awd; Perf Att; Sci Fairs; 4-H; Chrch Yth Grp; Ch Chr; Junior Beta; Youth Group Council Member; Masters in Primary Education; Zoology; U of Kentucky; Morehead State U

BLEVINS, CANDACE; WELLINGTON, KY; MENIFEE CTY HS; (SO); 4H Awd; Hnr Roll; MVP; Nat Mrt LOC; Otst Ac Ach Awd; Sci Fairs; St of Mnth; US Army Sch Ath Aw; WWAHSS; Yth Ldrshp Prog; CARE; Peer Tut/Med; Red Cr Aide; ArtClub; Chrch Yth Grp; Drma Clb; Lttrmn Clb, Ntl FFA; Photog; SADD; German Clb; Bnd; Ch Chr; Clr Grd; Drl Tm; Bskball (V); Mar Art (V); Sccr (V); Sftball (V); Swmg (V); Tennis (V); Vllyball (V); Wt Lftg (V); Yrbk (P); Photographer; Morehead State U; College in Kentucky

BLOOM, SARAH; LOUISVILLE, KY; WALDEN SCH; (SO); Duke TS; Otst Ac Ach Awd; Perf Att; WWAHSS; Comm Volntr; Key Club; Mth Clb/Tm; Ntl Beta Clb; Tmpl Yth Grp; Spanish Clb; Tennis (Outside School); Black Belt in Karate (Outside School); Environment

BLUE, EMILY M; MADISONVILLE, KY; MADISONVILLE NORTH HOPKINS HS; (JR); Hnr Roll; WWAHSS; Chrch Yth Grp; Key Club; Ntl Beta Clb; Bnd; Mch Bnd; Pep Bnd; Outstanding Freshmen Bandsmen; All-State / All-District Band; Spanish; Criminal / Child Development Psychology; Georgetown College; Murray State U

BOARD, EMILY K M; BARDSTOWN, KY; NELSON CTY HS; (FR); Ctznshp Aw; DAR; Hi Hnr Roll; Hnr Roll; Pres Sch; USAA; WWAHSS; Chess; Key Club; P to P St Amb Prg; Bnd; Pep Bnd; Sch Ppr (R); People to People Student Ambassador Twice; Culinary Arts; Creative Writing; U of Kentucky; Western Kentucky U

BODELL, CHARLES A; BANDANA, KY; BALLARD MEMORIAL HS; (SR); 4H Awd; Hi Hnr Roll; Hnr Roll; Otst Ac Ach Awd; USAA; WWAHSS; Yth Ldrshp Prog; Comm Volntr; Peer Tut/Med; 4-H; Chrch Yth Grp; DARE; Emplmnt; FCA; Ntl FFA; Bsball (V L); Cr Ctry (V); Ftball (VJ); CR (R); State FFA Degree; Mechanical Engineer; West Kentucky Community and Technical College; U of KY School of Engineering

BOGGS, AUDRA; MILLSTONE, KY; FLEMING NEON HS; (SR); Duke TS; F Lan Hn Soc; Hnr Roll; Nat Hon Sy; WWAHSS; FBLA; Ntl Beta Clb; Pep Squd; Prom Com; Bskball (V CL); Vllyball (V CL); Stu Cncl (S); Sch Ppr; Yrbk; Psychology; Pikeville College

BOGGS, JOSH; CORBIN, KY; SOUTH LAUREL HS; Duke TS; Hnr Roll; Perf Att; 4-H; Chrch Yth Grp; DARE; Drma Clb; FCA; Scouts; Chr; Ch Chr; SP/M/VS; Arts and Humanities Bowl; Academic Achievement Award; Forensic Science Technician; Computer Technician; Eastern Kentucky U; U of Tennessee

BOHANNON, ZACH; WEST PADUCAH, KY; HEATH HS; (JR); Duke TS; Hnr Roll; Nat Sci Aw; Chrch Yth Grp; Bsball (V L); Ftball (C); Academic 3 Years; Pre-Medicine; Sports Medicine

BOLAND, VICTORIA K; CORBIN, KY; SOUTH LAUREL HS; (FR); Hi Hnr Roll; Nat Hon Sy; Yth Ldrshp Prog; Peer Tut/Med; Chrch Yth Grp; Emplmnt; Ntl Beta Clb; Quiz Bowl; Ch Chr; Won a Writing Award in 8th Grade; U of Kentucky

BOLEN, SARAH J; LANGLEY, KY; ALLEN CTRL HS; (FR); Hnr Roll; Nat Hon Sy; Otst Ac Ach Awd; St of Mnth; USAA; WWAHSS; Comm Volntr; Peer Tut/Med; Emplmnt; Mth Clb/Tm; Ntl Beta Clb; ROTC; Chrldg (V); Gymnastics Outside of School; Nursing; Social Workers

BONDY, JESSICA L; VINE GROVE, KY; NORTH HARDIN HS; (JR); Hnr Roll; Nat Hon Sy; Otst Ac Ach Awd; Pres Ac Ftns Aw; St of Mnth; WWAHSS; Yth Ldrshp Prog; Comm Volntr; Red Cr Aide; DARE; Pep Squd; Sci Clb; SADD; French Clb; Stu Cncl (R); CR (R); Team Captain-City League Softball-District Champions; Highest on Honors Test-Social Science Issues, French, Geometry; Dentistry; College History Professor; Washington U in St. Louis; Western Kentucky U

BOONE, JUSTIN M; PRINCETON, KY; CALDWELL CTY HS; (SR); All Am Sch; Duke TS; F Lan Hn Soc; Hi Hnr Roll; Nat Hon Sy; Nat Mrt LOC; Perf Att; St Schl; USAA; Valdctrian; Comm Volntr; 4-H; Chrch Yth Grp; FCCLA; HO'Br Yth Ldrshp; Key Club; Ntl FFA; Off Aide; Spanish Clb; Bsball (V); Bskball (J); Kentucky Colonel / Governor's Scholar; Business; Economics; U of Kentucky

BOOTH, LISA M; LOUISVILLE, KY; BULLITT CTY AREA TECH CTR; (JR); All Am Sch; Hnr Roll; Nat Hon Sy; WWAHSS; Yth Ldrshp Prog; Hosp Aide; DARE; FCA; Off Aide; Sci Clb; Ch Chr; Yrbk (E, R, P); Medical Nursing Assistant; Licensed Practical Nurse; Registered Nurse; U of Louisville; Jefferson Community College

BORDERS, JESSICA M; BARDSTOWN, KY; NELSON CTY HS; (JR); DAR; Gov Hnr Prg; Nat Hon Sy; USAA; WWAHSS; Comm Volntr; Peer Tut/Med; DARE; Emplmnt; Key Club; Ntl Beta Clb; Ntl FFA; Chr; Bskball; Vllyball (J); Stu Cncl; Elementary Education; Spaulding U; U of Louisville

BOSTIC, MALORI; CRESTWOOD, KY; OLDHAM CTY HS; (JR); Hnr Roll; Nat Hon Sy; WWAHSS; Comm Volntr; Chrch Yth Grp; Emplmnt; FCA; Ntl Beta Clb; Radio Broadcasting; Education; Union U; Georgetown College

BOSWELL, ALEXANDRIA M; EDMONTON, KY; METCALFE CTY HS; (FR); 4H Awd; DAR; Hnr Roll; USAA; Comm Volntr; Peer Tut/Med; 4-H; Ntl Beta Clb; Sftball (J); Vllyball (J); Kentucky Junior Historical Society; Doctorate; Western KY U

BOWEN, DAVID; MT WASHINGTON, KY; BULLITT EAST HS; (FR); Hnr Roll; Sci Fairs; Comm Volntr; FCA; Off Aide; Pep Squd; Scouts; Tchrs Aide; Bnd; Stg Cre; Cr Ctry (VJCL); Track; CR (R); Life Scout; Diesel Mechanic; Lima Technical College; Nashville Auto Diesel College

BOWLING, BRANDEN; ASHLAND, KY; BOYD CTY CTRL; (SR); Perf Att; FCA; ROTC; Clr Grd; Drl Tm

BOWLING, SARAH; GREENUP, KY; GREENUP CTY HS; (JR); Hnr Roll; Perf Att; WWAHSS; 4-H; FBLA; FCCLA; Tech Clb; Business Management; Shawnee State U

BOWMAN, STEPHANIE L; BEATTYVILLE, KY; LEE CTY HS; (SO); 4H Awd; Ctznshp Aw; Hnr Roll; Otst Ac Ach Awd; St of Mnth; Comm Volntr; Chrch Yth Grp; DARE; Emplmnt; FCA; FTA; Ntl FFA; Scouts; Ch Chr; SP/M/VS; Vice President of Future Educators; Education; Medicine; Eastern Kentucky U; Alice Lloyd

BOYD, CHRISTOPHER; LOUISVILLE, KY; FAIRDALE HS; (FR); Hi Hnr Roll; Hnr Roll; Comm Volntr; Chrch Yth Grp; Bskball (J); Ftball (VJ); Attended Manual HS Art Classes & Picture Was Picked to Be Put on Display; Degree in Architecture; Master's Degree in Architecture; Miami U; Kentucky U

BRADBURY, MARCUS; ELIZABETHTOWN, KY; CTRL HARDIN HS; (SR); Hi Hnr Roll; MVP; Nat Hon Sy; Pres Ac Ftns Aw; St of Mnth; WWAHSS; Yth Ldrshp Prog; Chrch Yth Grp; Ntl Beta Clb; Ntl FFA; Wrstlg (C); Pre-Vet; Secondary Education; Cumberland College

BRADY, TAMANTHA D; ADAIRVILLE, KY; LOGAN CTY HS; (JR); Ctznshp Aw; Hnr Roll; Nat Sci Aw; Otst Ac Ach Awd; Perf Att; Pres Sch; Sci Fairs; St Schl; ArtClub; Chrch Yth Grp; Mus Clb; Ntl FFA; Outdrs Clb; Quiz Bowl; ROTC; SADD; Chr; Ch Chr; Clr Grd; SP/M/VS; Hsbk Rdg; Skt Tgt Sh; Wt Lftg; PE 1 & 2; Child Care; Doctor; Army National Guard; Western U KY

BRANN, ALEXANDER; BURLINGTON, KY; CONNER; (FR); Hnr Roll; Ftball

Boland, Victoria K
South Laurel HS
Corbin, KY

Bell, Kristen K
Conner HS
Burlington, KY

Beam, Candace
Nelson Cty HS
Bardstown, KY

National
Honor Roll
Spring 2005

Bates, Patricia
Paul Laurence Dunbar HS
Lexington, KY

Bianchi Di Carcano, Alejandro
Larry A Ryle HS
Walton, KY

Bowman, Stephanie L
Lee Cty HS
Beattyville, KY

NATIONAL HONOR ROLL SPRING 2005 — Kentucky

BRASHEARS, JORDAN; CADIZ, KY; TRIGG CTY HS; (FR); 4H Awd; Hnr Roll; Perf Att; 4-H; DARE; Key Club; Ch Chr; Dnce; Drm Mjr; Pep Bnd; Arch; Bskball; Cyclg; Ftball; Mar Art; Rlr Hky; Sccr; Wt Lftg; Basket Ball; Murray State U

BRATCHER, NATALIE R; COXS CREEK, KY; NELSON CTY HS; (SO); Hi Hnr Roll; Nat Hon Sy; WWAHSS; Comm Volntr; Chrch Yth Grp; DARE; Key Club; Pep Squd; Chr; Ch Chr; PP Ftbl (J); Sccr (V); Stu Cncl (R); Yrbk (P); Communications; Law; U of Louisville

BRELT, SAMANTHA; LOUISVILLE, KY; FERN CREEK TRADITIONAL HS; (FR); Hnr Roll; Comm Volntr; Jr Ach; Chrldg (V); Communications; Western; U of L

BREWER, HEATHER; LEXINGTON, KY; EASTSIDE CTR FOR APPLIED TECH HS; (JR); SP/M/VS; Chrldg (VJ L); Cl Off (P); CR (P); National Technical Honor Society Member; German; Ophthalmology; U of Los Angeles California; U of Santa Barbara California

BRIDGES, A J; CADIZ, KY; TRIGG CTY HS; (FR); Hi Hnr Roll; MVP; WWAHSS; 4-H; Chrch Yth Grp; Emplmnt; Key Club; Ntl Beta Club; Pep Squd; Tchrs Aide; Ch Chr; Cr Ctry (V); Sccr (VJ L); Odyssey of Mind (6 Yrs) Academic Team National Winner; (6 Yrs), Governors Minority Cup Participant; U of Kentucky; Duke U

BRIERLEY, JESSICA; JONESVILLE, KY; GRANT CTY HS; (SO); Hnr Roll; Otst Ac Ach Awd; WWAHSS; Comm Volntr; Peer Tut/Med; Chrch Yth Grp; Yrbk (R, P); Highest Algebra 2 Rank in Entire 9th; Psychology; Accountant; Morehead; EKU

BRIGGS, ATHENA M; UNION, KY; LARRY A RYLE HS; (SO); Hi Hnr Roll; Hnr Roll; Sci Fairs; Emplmnt; Bskball; Track (J); Vllyball (L); Selected for Young Authors; Lawyer; Marine Biologist; U of Southern California; Illinois State U

BRILEY, CARRIE; AUGUSTA, KY; AUGUSTA HS; (JR); Hnr Roll; St of Mnth; WWAHSS; Emplmnt; Prom Com; Sftball (V); Cl Off (V); Sch Ppr (R); Yrbk (R, P); Small Business Management; Finances; Northern Kentucky U; Lexington Community College

BRIM, ASHLEY; COVINGTON, KY; HOLMES HS; (SR); Hnr Roll; FBLA; Bachelor's Degree in Surgical Nursing; The Christ Hospital School of Nursing

BROCK, BRANDON B; MOREHEAD, KY; ROWAN CTY SR HS; (FR); Ctznshp Aw; Hi Hnr Roll; Nat Hon Sy; Pres Ac Ftns Aw; Perf Att; Sci/Math Olympn; WWAHSS; Comm Volntr; 4-H; Chrch Yth Grp; Cmptr Club; FCA; Mth Clb/Tm; Spanish Clb; Golf (V); All A's Kindergarten-8th Gr / Nomination to People Student Ambassador Program /Congressional Student Leadership Conference; Distinguished Scholar in Math / Social Studies & Practical Living; Medicine; U of Kentucky; Morehead State U

BROCK, DANIEL G; LONDON, KY; CORNERSTONE CHRISTIAN SCH; (SR); Ctznshp Aw; Hnr Roll; Pres Ac Ftns Aw; Emplmnt; Ntl Beta Club; Sch Ppr (R); Forestry; Computer Graphics; Eastern Kentucky U; Spencerian College

BROMAGEN, ASHLEY; CARLISLE, KY; NICHOLAS CTY HS; (FR); Nat Hon Sy; WWAHSS; FCA; Ntl FFA; Pep Squd; Sftball (VJ L); Vllyball (V L); Cl Off (V); Stu Cncl (R); CR; Lit Mag (R); Sch Ppr (R); Sports Medicine; Journalism; U of Kentucky; Eastern Kentucky U

BROWN, CHELSEA; HOPKINSVILLE, KY; HOPKINSVILLE HS; (FR); Hnr Roll; Pres Sch; WWAHSS; Lttrmn Clb; Chrldg (V L); Stu Cncl (R); Who's Who Among American High School Athletes; Master's Degree; CRNA (Certified Registered Nurse Anesthetist); U of Kentucky; U of Louisville

BROWN, CORISHA; COLUMBIA, KY; ADAIR CO HS; (FR); Hnr Roll; Otst Ac Ach Awd; Perf Att; St of Mnth; Yth Ldrshp Prog; Comm Volntr; Peer Tut/Med; DARE; FCA; FBLA; Pep Squd; Bnd; Clr Grd; Mch Bnd; Orch; Competed In FBLA Regionals; English; Pre-Law; U of Louisville; Harvard U

BROWN, DANIELLE N; ALEXANDRIA, KY; CAMPBELL CTY HS; (FR); Ctznshp Aw; Hnr Roll; Otst Ac Ach Awd; Pres Sch; St of Mnth; Ntl FFA; Scouts; Spanish Clb; Chr; Stu Cncl (T); CR (S); Law; U of Louisville; Northern Kentucky U

BROWN, KEEVA M; LOUISVILLE, KY; DUPONT MANUAL HS; (SR); Ctznshp Aw; Duke TS; Comm Volntr; Peer Tut/Med; Red Cr Aide; Chrch Yth Grp; Emplmnt; Key Club; Off Aide; Pep Squd; Photog; Prom Com; Tchrs Aide; Chr; SP/M/VS; Chrldg (V); PP Ftbl (V); Principal's Forum, Parker Scholarship-U of Kentucky; Porter Scholarship-U of Louisville; Attain Law Degree; U of Louisville; U of Kentucky

BROWN, LYDIA; BLOOMFIELD, KY; NELSON CTY HS; (JR); All Am Sch; Hnr Roll; Jr Mshl; MVP; Nat Hon Sy; Nat Ldrshp Svc; St of Mnth; USAA; WWAHSS; Yth Ldrshp Prog; Comm Volntr; Peer Tut/Med; Key Club; Ntl FFA; Pep Squd; Chr; Vsy Clb (V C); National Honor Society President; Business Management; Political Science; Saint Catharine College; U of Kentucky

BROWN, SAMANTHA; VINE GROVE, KY; NORTH HARDIN HS; (JR); Hnr Roll; Hab For Humty Volntr; FBLA; Pep Squd; Clr Grd; Mch Bnd; Finance & Economics; Market Research; NYU-New York U

BROWN, SARAH; LEXINGTON, KY; LEXINGTON CHRISTIAN AC; (JR); All Am Sch; Hi Hnr Roll; Hnr Roll; Nat Hon Sy; Pres Ac Ftns Aw; USAA; WWAHSS; Yth Ldrshp Prog; Comm Volntr; Hosp Aide; Peer Tut/Med; Chrch Yth Grp; Drma Clb; Ntl Beta Club; NYLC; Prom Com; Svce Clb; Tchrs Aide; Bnd; Chr; Ch Chr; Clr Grd; Sccr (V L); Yrbk (E, P); Pre-Law/Forensics/Pre-Med; Spanish; Asbury College; William & Mary

BRUNO, JUSTIN; BARDSTOWN, KY; NELSON CTY HS; (JR); All Am Sch; Duke TS; Hi Hnr Roll; Nat Hon Sy; St of Mnth; WWAHSS; Yth Ldrshp Prog; Comm Volntr; Chrch Yth Grp; Cmptr Club; Dbte Team; Emplmnt; FCA; Key Club; NYLC; Scouts; Bsball (J); Golf (J); Life Scout (Boy Scouts); Duke U; Miami (OH) U

BRYANT, CHRISTOPHER; LA CTR, KY; BALLARD MEMORIAL HS; (FR); Hi Hnr Roll; Hnr Roll; Perf Att; WWAHSS; Chess; Spanish Clb; Bnd; Mch Bnd; Pep Bnd; Chemical Engineering; Civil Engineering

BRYANT, CRYSTAL A; COLUMBIA, KY; ADAIR CO HS; (FR); Ctznshp Aw; Hnr Roll; Salutrn; Comm Volntr; Peer Tut/Med; 4-H; DARE; FCA; Pep Squd; Chrldg (V); GAA (V); Gmnstcs (V); Pediatrician; Earn A Cheerleading Scholarship; U of Kentucky; Lindsey Willison College

BUCKNER, SARA E; CAMPBELLSVILLE, KY; TAYLOR CTY HS; (SR); Duke TS; Hi Hnr Roll; Nat Hon Sy; WWAHSS; Comm Volntr; Chrch Yth Grp; Emplmnt; FCA; Chr; Bskball (J); Sccr (V CL); Who's Who Among American HS Students-4 Yrs; Beta Club Treasurer; Pharmacy; U of Kentucky

BULLOCK, MORGAN; FRANKFORT, KY; FRANKLIN CTY HS; (SO); Ctznshp Aw; Duke TS; Hnr Roll; Comm Volntr; Chrch Yth Grp; FCA; Key Club; Mod UN; Ntl Beta Club; Bnd; Mch Bnd; Pep Bnd; Bskball (VJ); PP Ftbl (V); Sftball (VJ L); Cl Off (T); Teen Court; Social Sciences; Engineering; Georgetown College

BUMPHUS, CLARISSA; PADUCAH, KY; PADUCAH TILGHMAN HS; (FR); WWAHSS; Comm Volntr; Chrch Yth Grp; ROTC; Ch Chr; Dnce; Pediatrician; Nurse; Kentucky State U; Alabama State U

BURBA, TYLER T; BARDSTOWN, KY; NELSON CO HS; (FR); Hi Hnr Roll; Perf Att; Comm Volntr; Chess; Chrch Yth Grp; Key Club

BURCHETT, APRIL; BARDWELL, KY; CLINTON CTY AREA TECH CTR; (SR); Comm Volntr; FCA; Chr; X-Ray Technician; Tennessee Technological U; Lindsey Wilson College

BURDINE, DEXTER; RADCLIFF, KY; NORTH HARDIN HS; (JR); Hnr Roll; Perf Att; Comm Volntr; DARE; Emplmnt; Ftball (VJ); Track (V); Business Management; U North Carolina Chapel Hill; North Carolina State

BURGIE, BRANDON K; HARDIN, KY; EASTWOOD CHRISTIAN AC; (JR); Duke TS; Hi Hnr Roll; Hnr Roll; Chrch Yth Grp; DARE; Emplmnt; FCA; Vsity Clb; Ch Chr; SP/M/VS; Bskball (V L); Sch Ppr (E); Murray State U; Golden State Baptist College

BURGIN, AMANDA; BARDSTOWN, KY; NELSON CTY HS; (FR); Hnr Roll; WWAHSS; ArtClub; Key Club; Distinguished on CATS Testing; U of Kentucky, Eastern KY U; U of Louisville

BURK, JENNIFER N; WHITLEY CITY, KY; MC CREARY CTRL HS; (SR); Hnr Roll; WWAHSS; Comm Volntr; Chrch Yth Grp; Key Club; Mth Clb/Tm; Cl Off (S); Stu Cncl (S); Yrbk; National Society of High School Scholars; Education; Mathematics; U of the Cumberlands

BURKE, BAILEY; MEALLY, KY; DAVID SCH; (JR); 4H Awd; Hnr Roll; St of Mnth; WWAHSS; Comm Volntr; 4-H; Ntl FFA; Pep Squd; Photog; Prom Com; Wdwrkg Clb; Chrldg (V); Gmnstcs; Sftball (V); Sch Ppr (P); Yrbk (P); Spirit Club; To Become a Nurse; Mayo; Eastern Kentucky U

BURKE, TONY; PIKEVILLE, KY; PIKE CTY CTRL; (JR); Comm Volntr; 4-H; ROTC; Chr

BURKEEN, KANDICE; CADIZ, KY; TRIGG CTY HS; (FR); Hnr Roll; Comm Volntr; Key Club; Pep Squd; Bsball (J); Bskball (J); Who's Who; Proficient on Portfolio; Ob/Gyn; Vanderbilt U; U of Louisville

BURKHARDT, ANDREW E; NICHOLASVILLE, KY; TRINITY CHRISTIAN AC; (SO); Yth Ldrshp Prog; Comm Volntr; Peer Tut/Med; Chrch Yth Grp; Ntl Beta Club; Chr; SP/M/VS; Sccr (V C); Stu Cncl (R); CR; Out of Country Missions; In State Missions (Construction); Physical Therapist; History/International Studies; U of Kentucky

BURNETT, ELIZABETH A; ELIZABETHTOWN, KY; JOHN HARDIN HS; (JR); Hnr Roll; Comm Volntr; Drma Clb; Scouts; Bnd; Mch Bnd; Silver Award Through Girl Scouts; Foreign Language Medal-Second Place Listening; Veterinary Medicine; Child Psychology; Western Kentucky U; Kentucky Wesleyan

BURRIS, JUSTIN R; COLUMBIA, KY; ADAIR CTY HS; (JR); Nat Hon Sy; Perf Att; WWAHSS; Peer Tut/Med; FCA; Ntl Beta Clb; Pep Squd; Bsball (V); Sccr (V); Cl Off (T); Stu Cncl (V); 2004 Rogers Scholar; Pharmacy; Anesthesiology; U of Kentucky; Lindsey Wilson College

BURROUGHS, SLOAN; HOPKINSVILLE, KY; HOPKINSVILLE HS; (FR); Hi Hnr Roll; Hnr Roll; Perf Att; Drma Clb; Spch Team; Chr; Accelerator Reader Award; Education/Master's; Doctoral; Western Kentucky U; U of Kentucky

BURTON, ASHLEY; FRANKFORT, KY; (SO); Hnr Roll; 4-H; Chrch Yth Grp; Cmptr Clb; FCA; Ntl FFA; Tmpl Yth Grp; Dnce

BURTON, BRANDON; PARTRIDGE, KY; CUMBERLAND HS; (JR); Hnr Roll; Sci Fairs; Chrch Yth Grp; Ntl Beta Club; Bsball (VJ); Law Enforcement; Southeast Kentucky Community & Technical College

BUSH, KATIE; JACKSON, KY; BREATHITT CO AREA TECH CTR; (FR); Mechanics; Nursing

BUTLER, ALIZABETH; MURRAY, KY; CALLOWAY CTY HS; (FR); Duke TS; Ntl Beta Clb; Pep Squd; Track; U of Kentucky

BUTLER, CODY E; LAWRENCEBURG, KY; ANDERSON CTY HS; (FR); Hi Hnr Roll; Hnr Roll; Peer Tut/Med; Chrch Yth Grp; FCA; Acpl Chr; Chr; Ch Chr; In FCCLA, ALICC, FCA; Science / ER Doctor; Sports Medicine / Trainer; Vanderbilt U; U of Kentucky

BUTLER, DEBRA; CALVERT CITY, KY; MARSHALL CTY HS; (SO); Emplmnt; Bnd; Mch Bnd; Prom Committee; Peer Intervention; Radiology Diploma; West Kentucky Community and Technical College

BUTLER, RACHEL; WESTVIEW, KY; BRECKINRIDGE CTY HS; (SR); Hnr Roll; WWAHSS; Comm Volntr; Hosp Aide; FBLA; Jr Ach; SADD; Tchrs Aide; Voc Ind Clb Am; Bnd; Chr; Clr Grd; Mch Bnd; Owensboro Community College; Elizabethtown Community College

BYERLEY, HOLLY; KEVIL, KY; BALLARD MEMORIAL HS; (JR); Duke TS; Hnr Roll; WWAHSS; Peer Tut/Med; Chrch Yth Grp; FCCLA; Clr Grd; Regional President of FCCLA; Dentistry; Music; Georgetown; Indiana Tech

CALDWELL, LAURA; GEORGETOWN, KY; SCOTT CTY HS; (JR); Hnr Roll; Yth Ldrshp Prog; Peer Tut/Med; DARE; DECA; FCA; Key Club; Pep Squd; Dnce; DECA Chapter VP of Fundraising; Won State Advertising Event in DECA 2004; Advertising; International Business Management; U of Kentucky; U of Louisville

CALLAHAN, CASEY; LOUISVILLE, KY; ASSUMPTION HS; (SO); Hi Hnr Roll; Outdrs Clb; Pep Squd; Cr Ctry (V L); Hsbk Rdg (V); Track (J L); Most Improved Runner for Cross Country; Journalism; Public Relations; U of Louisville

CALLAHAN, JENNIFER; LOUISVILLE, KY; BALLARD MEMORIAL HS; (SO); Hi Hnr Roll; Sci Fairs; Comm Volntr; Emplmnt; Ntl Beta Clb; Spanish Clb; Veterinarian; Elementary School Teacher; U of Kentucky; Purdue

CAMPBELL, COURTNEY; EKRON, KY; MEADE CTY HS; (FR); 4H Awd; Hi Hnr Roll; Hnr Roll; Nat Sci Aw; Otst Ac Ach Awd; St of Mnth; Comm Volntr; 4-H; Chess; Chrch Yth Grp; DARE; DECA; FCA; Ntl FFA; Outdrs Clb; Chr; Arch (L); Hsbk Rdg (V); Vllyball (V); NASP - Archery Scholarship; World Champion Barrel Racer; Nursing; Ob/Gyn; Murray State U; U of Kentucky

CAMPBELL, DANIELLE; HINDMAN, KY; KNOTT CTY CTRL HS; (JR); All Am Sch; Gov Hnr Prg; Hi Hnr Roll; Hnr Roll; Sci Fairs; USAA; WWAHSS; Yth Ldrshp Prog; Peer Tut/Med; Chrch Yth Grp; Cmptr Clb; DARE; Emplmnt; Prom Com; SADD; Voc Ind Clb Am; Cl Off (S); CR (T); Engineering/Drafting

CAMPBELL, DOROTHY; HEBRON, KY; CONNER HS; (MS); Ctznshp Aw; Duke TS; Hnr Roll; St of Mnth; DARE; Outdrs Clb; Chr; Law; Northern Kentucky U; U of Cincinnati

CAMPBELL, MEGAN E; PRINCETON, KY; CALDWELL CTY HS; (JR); Hnr Roll; Comm Volntr; Chess; Chrch Yth Grp; FCA; Key Club; Pep Squd; Prom Com; Spanish Clb; Cl Off (T); Hotel Management; Business; Western Kentucky U; U of Kentucky

CAMPBELL, VERONICA L; RADCLIFF, KY; NORTH HARDIN HS; (JR); Hnr Roll; Nat Hon Sy; Nat Ldrshp Svc; Nat Mrt Fin; WWAHSS; Yth Ldrshp Prog; Comm Volntr; Peer Tut/Med; Chrch Yth Grp; Emplmnt; Pep Squd; Spanish Clb; Bnd; Mch Bnd; Pep Bnd; Secretary of Youth in Charge; Physician's Assistant; U of Kentucky

CAMPLIN, LAURA; MADISONVILLE, KY; MADISONVILLE NORTH HOPKINS HS; (JR); Hi Hnr Roll; MVP; Otst Ac Ach Awd; WWAHSS; Peer Tut/Med; Spec Olymp Vol; Chrch Yth Grp; FCA; FBLA; Key Club; Ntl Beta Clb; Pep Squd; Prom Com; Tchrs Aide; Chrldg (V CL); Gmnstcs (V); CR (R); All District Cheer Team; Criminal Forensics; Western KY U

CAO, ANGELA; LOUISVILLE, KY; DUPONT MANUAL HS; (SO); Fut Prb Slvr; Hi Hnr Roll; Perf Att; Yth Ldrshp Prog; Comm Volntr; Hab For Humty Volntr; Chrch Yth Grp; FBLA; Ntl Beta Clb; Spanish Clb; Chr; SP/M/VS; Sccr (J L); CR (P); Cell Biology and Neuroscience; Chemistry; U of Notre Dame; Centre College

CAPPS, JOSHUA I; GILBERTSVILLE, KY; MARSHALL CTY HS; (JR); Duke TS; Gov Hnr Prg; Hnr Roll; Nat Hon Sy; Sci/Math Olympn; WWAHSS; Hab For Humty Volntr; Peer Tut/Med; Chess; Emplmnt; Ntl Beta Clb; Pep Squd; Prom Com; Sci Clb; Sccr (VJCL); Cl Off (S); Stu Cncl (R); College; Environmental Attorney; Transylvania; Vanderbilt

CARPENTER, ASHLEY R; LOUISVILLE, KY; FERN CREEK TRADITIONAL HS; (FR); Hnr Roll; Hab For Humty Volntr; DECA; Chr; Forensic Science; Doctoral Degree; U of Louisville

CARR, ADAIR L; FOSTER, KY; BRACKEN CTY HS; (JR); Hnr Roll; Perf Att; WWAHSS; Chrch Yth Grp; DARE; Bnd; Drm Mjr; Mch Bnd; Pep Bnd; Track (J); Yrbk; Band Officer Sec/Treas; English; Graphic Design

CARRICO, HEATHER M; PADUCAH, KY; LONE OAK HS; (SO); Duke TS; Hnr Roll; Perf Att; Comm Volntr; Ntl Beta Clb; Clr Grd; Teaching; Veterinary Medicine; Murray State U; Auburn U

CARRICO, KENNY; LOUISVILLE, KY; ST FRANCIS DE SALES HS; (JR); Hnr Roll; Nat Hon Sy; Perf Att; St of Mnth; Key Club; Ftball (VJ L); Wrstlg (VJ L); Yrbk (R); Computer Engineering; Accounting; U of Louisville; Purdue U

CARRINGTON, TINA; MAYSLICK, KY; DEMING HS; (SR); Emplmnt; FCCLA; Tchrs Aide; Massage Therapist; Maysville Community College; Morehead Community College

CARROLL, MARY; PIKEVILLE, KY; PIKE CTY CTRL HS; (FR); 4H Awd; Hnr Roll; FBLA; Sign Clb; Cosmetologist; Pediatrician; Moorhead State

CARROLL, SARAH; FAIRDALE, KY; FAIRDALE HS; (FR); Hnr Roll; Peer Tut/Med; Chrch Yth Grp; Veterinarian; EMT Therapist; U of Louisville; Georgia Tech

CARTER, HEATHER; SCOTTSVILLE, KY; ALLEN CTY HS; (SO); All Am Sch; Hi Hnr Roll; Hnr Roll; WWAHSS; Comm Volntr; Chrch Yth Grp; DARE; FCCLA; FTA; Jr Ach; Ntl Beta Clb; Co-Ed Y; Perfect Attendance Award; Dentistry; Western Kentucky U

CARTER, JESSICA; ADAIRVILLE, KY; LOGAN HS; (JR); Hnr Roll; DECA; ROTC; Tchrs Aide; Spanish Clb; Chr; Clr Grd; Drl Tm; Business Management; Nursing; Western Kentucky U

CARTER, KRISTIN; COLUMBIA, KY; ADAIR CTY HS; (SO); Hi Hnr Roll; Hnr Roll; WWAHSS; Ntl Beta Clb; Psychology; Law; Vanderbilt U; Wittenberg U

CARTER, LAUREN; SCOTTSVILLE, KY; ALLEN CTY HS; (JR); Hi Hnr Roll; Hab For Humty Volntr; Chrch Yth Grp; FCA; Ntl Beta Clb; Bnd; Ch Chr; Pep Bnd; SP/M/VS; Tennis (V); Vllyball (J); Cl Off (V); Medicine; Vanderbilt U; Belmont U

CARTER, MARY; HAZARD, KY; HAZARD HS; (JR); Hi Hnr Roll; MVP; Nat Hon Sy; Sci Fairs; Comm Volntr; Peer Tut/Med; Chr; SP/M/VS; Chrldg (V); Cl Off (V); Communications; Western KY U; Charleston U

CARTER, RACHEL; LOUISVILLE, KY; LOUISVILLE MALE HS; (FR); Ctznshp Aw; Hnr Roll; St of Mnth; Comm Volntr; Dnce; Orch; Kentucky Music Educators Association - Distinguished Award 2004 / 2005; Dentistry / Orthodontics; Pediatrics / Veterinary Medicine; U of Louisville; U of Kentucky

CARTER, SHERRY; VANCEBURG, KY; LEWIS CTY HS; (FR); Adv Cncl (S); Cl Off (T); Stu Cncl (S); JROTC; RN Nurse; Morehead State

CARTER, WILLIAM C; ADOLPHUS, KY; ALLEN CTY HS; (FR); All Am Sch; Ctznshp Aw; Duke TS; Nat Ldrshp Svc; Nat Sci Aw; Sci/Math Olympn; St of Mnth; WWAHSS; Chrch Yth Grp; Cmptr Clb; FBLA; Ntl Beta Clb; Bnd; Mch Bnd; Pep Bnd; Stu Cncl (T); Science Olympiad; Academic Team; Forensic Biology Major; Forensic Anthropology Major; Guilford College Greensboro, NC; U of Tennessee Knoxville

CARTER JR, TERRY D; LOUISVILLE, KY; CHRISTIAN AC OF LOUISVILLE; (SR); Hnr Roll; Nat Hon Sy; Comm Volntr; Chrch Yth Grp; Emplmnt; Jr Ach; Ntl Beta Clb; Vsity Clb; Ftball (V L); Academic All-State Honorable Mention in Football; Finance; Accounting; U of Kentucky

CASE, KARA J; LOUISVILLE, KY; VALLEY HS; (SR); Hnr Roll; Perf Att; Emplmnt; Lib Aide; Photog; ROTC; Orch; Stu Cncl (R); I'm an Officer in Valley's NJROTC; Completing My Portfolio Successfully; Major in Broadcasting Electronics; Minor in Music; Eastern Kentucky U

CASON, JALISA R; OWENSBORO, KY; OWENSBORO HS; (SO); Hnr Roll; Otst Ac Ach Awd; Perf Att; St of Mnth; Chrch Yth Grp; DARE; Quiz Bowl; SADD; Ch Chr; President of Champions Against Drugs; Nurse Midwife; Pediatric Nurse; Western Kentucky U; Kentucky Wesleyan College

CASTELLON, RUTH; CARROLLTON, KY; CHRISTIAN AC OF CARROLTON; (FR); Hnr Roll; WWAHSS; Chess; Spanish Clb; Chr; SP/M/VS; Pediatrician; Pre-Med

CATLETT, ASHLEY N; LAWRENCEBURG, KY; ANDERSON CTY HS; (FR); Hnr Roll; Perf Att; Peer Tut/Med; Chrch Yth Grp; Drma Clb; FCCLA; Chr; Ch Chr; SP/M/VS; Bachelor's Degree In Forensic Science; Psychology; Eastern Kentucky U; Hanover College

CATLETT, WILLIAM R; FRANKFORT, KY; FRANKLIN CTY HS; (SO); Hnr Roll; Otst Ac Ach Awd; Pres Sch; St of Mnth; WWAHSS; Comm Volntr; Chrch Yth Grp; Scouts; Bnd; Mch Bnd; Pep Bnd; Eagle Scout Rank

CAUDILL, VIRGINIA; LEBURN, KY; KNOTT CTY CTRL HS; (JR); All Am Sch; WWAHSS; ArtClub; Drma Clb; Lib Aide; Chr; Ch Chr; Tennis; Yrbk (E); Teacher; Liberty U

CAULEY, KARI M; GRAND RIVERS, KY; LIVINGSTON CTRL HS; (SR); WWAHSS; Mth Clb/Tm; Bnd; Clr Grd; Mch Bnd; Pep Bnd; Attend College; Military; West Kentucky Community & Technical College

CAUSEY, BEN; DRY RIDGE, KY; GRANT CTY HS; (FR); Duke TS; Perf Att; Comm Volntr; Chrch Yth Grp; Video Game Designer; Engineer; Northern Kentucky U; Eastern Kentucky U

CAVANAUGH, AMANDA G; LA CTR, KY; BALLARD MEMORIAL HS; (SO); Hnr Roll; Nat Hon Sy; Otst Ac Ach Awd; St of Mnth; WWAHSS; ArtClub; Spanish Clb; Bnd; Mch Bnd; Pep Bnd; SP/M/VS; Honor Band; Music; Medicine; Murray State U; U of Kentucky

CAVINS, JOSIE; FALMOUTH, KY; PENDLETON CTY HS; (FR); Hnr Roll; Perf Att; St of Mnth; USAA; Cmptr Clb; DARE; Scouts; Chr; Become a Nurse; Northern Kentucky U

CHAMBERLAIN, JAMES; MADISONVILLE, KY; MADISONVILLE NORTH HOPKINS HS; (SR); Ctznshp Aw; Fut Prb Slvr; Hi Hnr Roll; WWAHSS; Chrch Yth Grp; DECA; Emplmnt; FCA; Quiz Bowl; Tech Clb; Chr; Sch Ppr (R); Academic Team Member; President of Strategy Gaming Club; Political Science; Law; Murray State U

CHAMPION, BECKY; NEON, KY; FLEMING NEON HS; (SR); Hi Hnr Roll; Nat Hon Sy; Otst Ac Ach Awd; USAA; WWAHSS; Comm Volntr; Peer Tut/Med; Chrch Yth Grp; Emplmnt; Lttrmn Clb; Ntl Beta Clb; Off Aide; Pep Squd; Prom Com; Tchrs Aide; Ch Chr; Chrldg (V); Track (V); Sch Ppr (E); Yrbk (E); Dentistry; Doctor; Morehead State U

CHANDLER, JOSHUA; BULAN, KY; PERRY CTY CTRL HS; (SO); Nat Stu Ath Day Aw; Bskball; Art; Physical Education Teacher; Auto Body; Hazard Tech College; Eastern

CHANEY, KAYLA; PIKEVILLE, KY; PIKE CTRL HS; Nat Hon Sy; Spanish Clb; Chr; Dnce; Bskball (VJC); PP Ftbl (V); Nursing Classes, Spanish Club; National Honor Society, HOSA; Registered Nurse; Pikeville College; Prestonburg Community College

CHANEY, KELLI; STEARNS, KY; MC CREARY CTRL HS; (JR); Duke TS; Hi Hnr Roll; Hnr Roll; Nat Hon Sy; WWAHSS; Chrch Yth Grp; Emplmnt; FCA; Mth Clb/Tm; Ntl Beta Clb; Prom Com; SADD; Vllyball (V); Champions Against Drugs (President); National Society of High School Scholars; Criminal Psychology; Veterinary Medicine; U of Kentucky; Centre College

CHAPE, ASHLEIGH; WILLIAMSBURG, KY; WHITLEY CTY MS; Hi Hnr Roll; 4-H; Chrch Yth Grp; DARE; Drma Clb; Chr; Ch Chr; Performing Arts; Medical; U of Kentucky; UCLA

CHAPPELL, ROBIN; CAMPBELLSVILLE, KY; TAYLOR CTY HS; (JR); WWAHSS; Yth Ldrshp Prog; Comm Volntr; 4-H; FCA; Ntl FFA; SADD; Taylor County Jr. Fair Board; Relay for Life; High School English Teacher; Elementary Education; Campbellsville U

CHARLES, ANGELA; EDDYVILLE, KY; LYON CTY HS; (JR); Hnr Roll; Perf Att; St of Mnth; Ntl FFA; Pep Squd; Prom Com; Chr; CR (R); Sch Ppr (R); Psychology; Murray State U; Western U

CHARLTON, ANNE; VERSAILLES, KY; WOODFORD CTY HS; (FR); Duke TS; Fut Prb Slvr; Hnr Roll; Ntl Beta Clb; SADD; Stg Cre; Bskball (J); Academic Team-5 years; Pharmacy; Journalism; Purdue U; Miami U

CHENAULT, BETH; WOODBURN, KY; FRANKLIN-SIMPSON HS; (JR); Hnr Roll; WWAHSS; Comm Volntr; Emplmnt; Ntl Beta Clb; Ntl FFA; Bnd; Pep Bnd; FFA Officers and Committee Chairman; Agriculture Education; US History; Murray State U; Western Kentucky U

CHENAULT, HEATHER N; ALVATON, KY; BOWLING GREEN CHRISTIAN AC; MS; Duke TS; Hnr Roll; USAA; Dnce; Vllyball (J); Fashion Design; Culinary Arts

CHENAULT, MATTHEW; WOODBURN, KY; FRANKLIN-SIMPSON HS; (JR); Hi Hnr Roll; Hnr Roll; Perf Att; WWAHSS; Chrch Yth Grp; Ntl Beta Clb; Voc Ind Clb Am; Bnd; Mch Bnd; Pep Bnd; Stu Cncl; Yrbk; Aeronautical Engineering

CHILTON, CAITLIN M; CRESTWOOD, KY; SOUTH OLDHAM HS; (JR); Duke TS; F Lan Hn Soc; Hnr Roll; MVP; Otst Ac Ach Awd; Perf Att; Pres Ac Ftns Aw; WWAHSS; Hab For Humty Volntr; Chrch Yth Grp; FCA; Ntl Beta Clb; Photog; Prom Com; Quill & Scroll; SADD; Vsity Clb; Sftball (V CL); Adv Cncl (R); Stu Cncl (R); CR (R); Yrbk (E, R, P); English (Journalism); Political Science; Georgetown College; Transylvania U

CHINN JR, RONNIE L; VANCEBURG, KY; LEWIS CTY HS; (SR); Hi Hnr Roll; Otst Ac Ach Awd; Perf Att; WWAHSS; ArtClub; DARE; ROTC; Tchrs Aide; Outstanding Achievement on CATS Testing; Information Technology; Electrical Energies; Morehead State U

CHIPLEY, SHAWNA N; SPRINGFIELD, KY; MOREHEAD YOUTH DEVELOPMENT CTR ALT SCH; (JR); Hi Hnr Roll; Otst Ac Ach Awd; Comm Volntr; Chrch Yth Grp; Bskball; Office Technology; Computers; St Catherine; Centre College

CHOI, TIM; PROSPECT, KY; DUPONT MANUAL HS; (SO); Hnr Roll; Sci/Math Olympn; Yth Ldrshp Prog; Comm Volntr; FBLA; Mth Clb/Tm; Mus Clb; Ntl Beta Clb; Sci Clb; Orch; Tennis (J); Adv Cncl (R); Pre-Med; Economics; Harvard College; Stanford

CHOWPHURY, SUDIPA; LEXINGTON, KY; TATES CREEK HS; (SO); Duke TS; F Lan Hn Soc; Hi Hnr Roll; Hnr Roll; Nat Hon Sy; Otst Ac Ach Awd; Perf Att; Sci Fairs; Comm Volntr; Hosp Aide; Peer Tut/Med; Chess; Drma Clb; Fr of Library; Lib Aide; Ntl Beta Clb; P to P St Amb Prg; French Clb; Dnce; Bdmtn (J); Track (J); Stu Cncl (R); Selected for Honors Program At School; Internal Medicine; Pharmacy; Duke U; U of Kentucky

CHRISTY, ASHLEY G; GARRISON, KY; LEWIS CTY HS; (SR); Hnr Roll; St of Mnth; DARE; FBLA; Off Aide; Tchrs Aide; Chr; Sch Ppr (P); Radiology; Occupational Therapist; Morehead State U; U of Kentucky

CINNAMON, MEREDITH L; SALVISA, KY; MERCER CTY HS; (FR); Hnr Roll; Chrch Yth Grp; FCA; Ntl FFA; Bskball (VJ L); Sftball (VJ L); Church Youth Group

CIRESI, ERICA; LOUISVILLE, KY; J GRAHAM BROWN SCH; (FR); Hnr Roll; Comm Volntr; French Clb; Bnd; Bskball (V); Vllyball (V); CR (S); Sports Medicine; U of Kentucky; U of Louisville

CLARK, BROOKLYN; NORTONVILLE, KY; HOPKINS CTY CTRL HS; (SO); Hnr Roll; Perf Att; FCA; Ntl Beta Clb; Ntl FFA; Pep Squd; Bskball (VJ L); Cr Ctry (V L); Tennis (V L); Medicine; Law; U of Tennessee; U of Kentucky

CLARK, KAYLA; NEW HAVEN, KY; NELSON CTY HS; (FR); Hnr Roll; Perf Att; Sci Fairs; WWAHSS; Comm Volntr; DARE; Drma Clb; Key Club; Key Club International; National Honor Roll; Actress; Pediatrician/Teacher; Western Kentucky; UK (U of Kentucky)

CLARK, SAMUEL J; LOUISVILLE, KY; SOUTHERN HS; (JR); Fut Prb Slvr; Perf Att; Emplmnt; FBLA; ROTC; Scouts; Tchrs Aide; Marine Corps; Starting Own Business; Jefferson Community College; U of Louisville

CLAYTON, AUTUMN; CRITTENDEN, KY; GRANT CTY HS; (JR); Hnr Roll; Comm Volntr; 4-H; Pep Squd; Rewards for Ag Sales and Marketing/ Relationship Also Wildlife Management; Major in Zoology; Doctorate Degree; U of Kentucky; Georgetown U

CLEAR, JEANNIE; RACCOON, KY; PIKE CTY CTRL HS; (SO); 4H Awd; Hnr Roll; 4-H; DARE; FBLA; Lib Aide; Criminal Law; Veterinarian; U of Louisville; Moorehead State

CLEGG, PAUL R; GEORGETOWN, KY; LEXINGTON CHRN AC HS; (SO); Ctznshp Aw; Hnr Roll; Sci Fairs; Chrch Yth Grp; Emplmnt; Ntl Beta Clb; Engineering; Computer Science/Business

CLEMONS, ALISHA; CAMPTON, KY; WOLFE CTY HS; (FR); Hnr Roll; Otst Ac Ach Awd; Perf Att; St of Mnth; Drma Clb; Ntl Beta Clb; Ntl FFA; Chrldg (J); Gmnstcs (J); Pediatric Nurse; Doctor; Morehead State U; UK

COATS, TOSHA; GLASGOW, KY; GLASGOW HS; (JR); Hnr Roll; Nat Hon Sy; WWAHSS; Comm Volntr; Peer Tut/Med; Red Cr Aide; Emplmnt; FCCLA; Ntl Beta Clb; Spanish Clb; Bnd; Clr Grd; Dnce; Mch Bnd; Elementary Education; Interior Design; Western Kentucky U; Campbellsville U

COLE, AMANDA; KEVIL, KY; HEATH HS; (JR); 4H Awd; Hnr Roll; Otst Ac Ach Awd; 4-H; Chrch Yth Grp; Emplmnt; Ntl FFA; FFA for 3 Years; Highest Grade in Gym Freshman Year; Registered Nurse; Doctor; U of Tennessee; Shawnee Community College

COLE, KAYLA A; PIPPA PASSES, KY; KNOTT CTY AREA TECH CTR; (JR); Ctznshp Aw; Hnr Roll; Nat Hon Sy; Perf Att; Sci Fairs; WWAHSS; Comm Volntr; FBLA; Pep Squd; Prom Com; Law Enforcement; Social Work; Eastern Kentucky U; Hazard Community College

COLEMAN, BRITTANY; KIMPER, KY; PIKE CTY CTRL HS; (FR); Hnr Roll; Otst Ac Ach Awd; Comm Volntr; 4-H; Chrch Yth Grp; FBLA; Bskball (V); Homecoming Queen/Representative; Law Major; Biology Major; Princeton U; Sullivan U

COLEMAN, CAROLINE; LEXINGTON, KY; PAUL LAURENCE DUNBAR HS; (SR); Hi Hnr Roll; Hnr Roll; WWAHSS; DARE; Emplmnt; FCA; Tchrs Aide; U of Kentucky

COLEY, WILLIAM; KEVIL, KY; HEATH HS; (FR); Duke TS; Hi Hnr Roll; Hnr Roll; Nat Hon Sy; Sci Fairs; Hab For Humty Volntr; Chrch Yth Grp; DARE; Bnd; Computer Technology; X-Ray Technician; Murray State U

Chinn Jr, Ronnie L
Lewis Cty HS
Vanceburg, KY

Carter, William C
Allen Cty HS
Adolphus, KY

Carter, Jessica
Logan HS
Adairville, KY

Carrington, Tina
Deming HS
Mayslick, KY

Carpenter, Ashley R
Fern Creek Traditional HS
Louisville, KY

Carrico, Heather M
Lone Oak HS
Paducah, KY

Carter, Sherry
Lewis Cty HS
Vanceburg, KY

Cavins, Josie
Pendleton Cty HS
Falmouth, KY

Clemons, Alisha
Wolfe Cty HS
Campton, KY

COLGAN, RACHEL M; FLEMINGSBURG, KY; FLEMING CTY HS; (SO); Ctznshp Aw; Hi Hnr Roll; Hnr Roll; St of Mnth; WWAHSS; Comm Volntr; Peer Tut/Med; Chrch Yth Grp; FCA; Ntl Beta Clb; Bnd; Mch Bnd; Pep Bnd; PP Ftbl (V); Vllyball (J); Cl Off (T); Member of Champions Against Drugs; Sports Medicine/Athletic Training; U of Kentucky; Duke U

COLLEY, MATTHEW H; FARMINGTON, KY; GRAVES CO HS; (JR); Hnr Roll; WWAHSS; Chrch Yth Grp; DARE; FCA; Bskball (V); Ftball (V)

COLLIE, JAMA L N; JEREMIAH, KY; LETCHER CTY CTRL HS; (FR); Hnr Roll; Otst Ac Ach Awd; Comm Volntr; Academic Achievement Award; Satisfactory Attendance; X-Ray Technician; Attend Morehead State U; Howard Community College; Morehead State U

COLLINS, ANDREA; PIKEVILLE, KY; PIKE CTY CTRL HS; (SO); Hnr Roll; Perf Att; WWAHSS; 4-H; Chr; Vllyball (VJ); Lawyer; Physical Therapist

COLLINS, BRITTANY A; PRESTONSBURG, KY; PRESTONSBURG HS; (FR); 4H Awd; Hnr Roll; MVP; Perf Att; Pres Ac Ftns Aw; Yth Ldrshp Prog; Peer Tut/Med; 4-H; Chrch Yth Grp; FCA; FBLA; Bskball (VJ); Sftball (VJ); Vllyball (VJ); Talented and Gifted Program; Top 10 in Graduating 8th Grade Class; Physical Therapist; U of Kentucky; Transylvania U

COLLINS, DUSTIN B; LEBURN, KY; KNOTT CTY AREA TECH CTR; (JR); Hnr Roll; Perf Att; WWAHSS; Cmptr Clb; FBLA; Voc Ind Clb Am; Computer Repair; Law Enforcement; Hazard Community College

COLLINS, JORDEN; PINE TOP, KY; KNOTT CTY AREA TECH CTR; (SO); Gov Hnr Prg; Hnr Roll; Nat Hon Sy; Sci Fairs; WWAHSS; Yth Ldrshp Prog; Chrch Yth Grp; DARE; FCA; Chr; Ftball; Wt Lftg; Cl Off (V); Motor Cycle Repair; Morehead State

COLLINS, KAYLA B; PIKEVILLE, KY; PIKE CTY CTRL HS; (FR); 4H Awd; Ctznshp Aw; Hnr Roll; Perf Att; Chrch Yth Grp; FBLA; Bachelors Degree; Degree in Nursing; Prestonburg Community College

COLLINS, KIMBERLY; PADUCAH, KY; REIDLAND HS; (SR); Hnr Roll; Perf Att; Chrch Yth Grp; DECA; Emplmnt; FCCLA; Key Club; Scouts; Acpl Chr; Bnd; Clr Grd; Mch Bnd; Culinary Skills Test; DECA Officer; Teaching; Business Marketing; West Kentucky Community Tech College; Murray State U

COLLINS, SARA; AUGUSTA, KY; AUGUSTA HS; (SO); Hi Hnr Roll; St of Mnth; USAA; WWAHSS; Comm Volntr; Peer Tut/Med; Chrch Yth Grp; Drma Clb; Emplmnt; FCCLA; Ntl Beta Clb; Pep Squd; Pep Bnd; SP/M/VS; Bskball (V); Sftball (V); Tennis (V); Vllyball (J); Cl Off (V); Sch Ppr (R); Psychology; Law; Nebraska Wesleyan U; U of Nebraska Lincoln

COLLINS, TYLER; E BERNSTADT, KY; SOUTH LAUREL HS; (FR); Hnr Roll; Comm Volntr; Chrch Yth Grp; FCA; Spanish Clb; Sccr; Pre Medicine; U of Kentucky; U of Louisville

COMBS, ASHLEY L; LOUISVILLE, KY; LOUISVILLE MALE HS; (SO); Hnr Roll; Perf Att; ArtClub; Chrch Yth Grp; Emplmnt; FCA; Jr Ach; Ch Chr; Orch; Fld Hky (V L); Saddleseat Horse Riding; Art; Photo Journalism; Asbury College; Western Kentucky U

COMBS, BRETT; ALLEN, KY; CADET LEADERSHIP & ED ALT PROGRAM; (JR); 4H Awd; Hi Hnr Roll; Hnr Roll; MVP; Nat Hon Sy; Perf Att; St of Mnth; Comm Volntr; Peer Tut/Med; 4-H; DARE; Lib Aide; Off Aide; ROTC; Tchrs Aide; Vsity Clb; Wdwrkg Clb; Clr Grd; Drl Tm; Bsball (V); Bskball (V); Ftball (C); Golf (V); Sftball (V); Track (V); Wt Lftg (C); Wrstlg (V); Adv Cncl (R); Cl Off (R); Stu Cncl (R); Sch Ppr (R); Pharmacy; Morehead State U; U of Kentucky

COMPTON, COURTNEY S; SOMERSET, KY; SOUTHWESTERN HS; (FR); Hi Hnr Roll; Hnr Roll; Perf Att; Yth Ldrshp Prog; Comm Volntr; Chrch Yth Grp; DECA; FCA; Bnd; Ch Chr; SP/M/VS; Chrldg (J); Golf (V); Swmg (J); Vllyball (J); Yrbk (E, R, P); Bible Drill Competitions; Major in Business; Master's Degree; UK; Ohio State

CONATSER, JESSICA; DANVILLE, KY; BOYLE CTY HS; (SR); Hnr Roll; Emplmnt; State Finalist in National American Miss Pageant; $500 Sullivan U Scholarship; Travel / Tourism & Event Management; Sullivan U Lexington KY

CONDER, JONATHAN B; GRAVEL SWITCH, KY; BOYLE CTY HS; (SR); Hnr Roll; Nat Hon Sy; Otst Ac Ach Awd; USAA; WWAHSS; Comm Volntr; Ntl Beta Clb; Ntl FFA; Youth Salute Junior Yr; President of FFA; Veterinary; U of Kentucky

CONN, AMANDA L; PRESTONSBURG, KY; PRESTONSBURG HS; (FR); Comm Volntr; Volunteer - Local Shop with a Cop Program; Pikeville College; Marshall U

CONNER, CYNTHIA; ALBANY, KY; CLINTON CTY HS; (JR); 4H Awd; Hnr Roll; Otst Ac Ach Awd; Perf Att; Comm Volntr; 4-H; FCA; FTA; Mus Clb; Pep Squd; Chr; Pep Bnd; Cl Off (V); Education Talent Search - ETS; Degree in Education; Degree in Music; Eastern Kentucky U; Transylvania U

COOK, ANTHONY A; LAWRENCEBURG, KY; HARRODSBURG AREA TECH CTR; (JR); Hi Hnr Roll; Hnr Roll; Comm Volntr; 4-H; Chrch Yth Grp; DARE; Emplmnt; Ntl FFA; Tchrs Aide; Voc Ind Clb Am; Chr; Hsbk Rdg (V); Wt Lftg (V); Diesel Mechanic or Tech; Nashville Auto Diesel College; Lincoln Tech

COOK, STACY; SOMERSET, KY; SOUTHWESTERN HS; (SO); Comm Volntr; ROTC; Nursing; Somerset Community College

COOK, TIMOTHY; BOONS CAMP, KY; JOHNSON CTRL HS; (FR); Wdwrkg Clb; Computer Design; Game Design; Mayo Technical; U of Kentucky

COOLEY, ERICA; SHEPHERDSVILLE, KY; BULLITT CTRL HS; (MS); 4H Awd; Ctznshp Aw; Fut Prb Slvr; Hnr Roll; MVP; Otst Ac Ach Awd; Pres Sch; Sci Fairs; St of Mnth; Yth Ldrshp Prog; Comm Volntr; Peer Tut/Med; Red Cr Aide; DARE; Dbte Team; Drma Clb; FCA; FBLA; Lib Aide; Photog; Tchrs Aide; Mch Bnd; Pep Bnd; SP/M/VS; Stg Cre; Chrldg; Hsbk Rdg; Sftball; Track; Stu Cncl (S); CR (R); Sch Ppr (R); Yrbk (P); Bachelor's in Psychology; Bachelor's in Business; Louisville U; Moorhead U

COOMER, LINDSY R; BEATTYVILLE, KY; LEE CTY HS; (SO); Ctznshp Aw; Hnr Roll; Otst Ac Ach Awd; Perf Att; 4-H; DARE; FTA; Mus Clb; Ntl Beta Clb; Photog; Scouts; Track (V); Stu Cncl (R); CR (R); Gifted and Talented for 6 Year; Psychology; Nursing; Eastern Kentucky U

COONS, ALANA B; VINE GROVE, KY; NORTH HARDIN HS; (JR); Hnr Roll; Nat Hon Sy; Perf Att; WWAHSS; German Clb; Sccr (V L); German Club Historian; Social Work; Psychology; Morehead State U; U of Louisville

COOPER, MARIA L; JAMESTOWN, KY; RUSSELL CTY HS; (FR); Hnr Roll; Comm Volntr; ROTC; Drl Tm; General Education; Psychology; U of Kentucky; Campbellsville U

COOPER, SARAH E; AUGUSTA, KY; AUGUSTA HS; (JR); Hnr Roll; Nat Hon Sy; Nat Mrt Sch Recip; WWAHSS; Peer Tut/Med; Emplmnt; FCCLA; Pep Squd; Prom Com; Tchrs Aide; Vsity Clb; Bnd; Mch Bnd; Pep Bnd; Chrldg (V); Sftball (V); Tennis (V); Stu Cncl (S); CR (S); Sch Ppr (R); Nurse; Pediatrician; U of Bellarmine; Thomas Moore College

COOTS, LACEY N; VICCO, KY; PERRY CTY CTRL HS; (SO); Hnr Roll; ArtClub; Ntl Beta Clb; Patriot Pen Award; Art Major (Visual Art); Journalist; EKU; Art Institute

COPELAND, BREANNA N; EDDYVILLE, KY; LYON CTY HS; (JR); Hnr Roll; Perf Att; Sci Fairs; WWAHSS; 4-H; ArtClub; Chrch Yth Grp; DARE; Emplmnt; FCA; FBLA; Ntl Beta Clb; Chrldg (V); Sccr (V); Cl Off (S); Stu Cncl (S); Sch Ppr (R); Mississippi State U; Western Kentucky

COPLEY, MICHELLE; DUNNVILLE, KY; RUSSELL CTY HS; (FR); Hi Hnr Roll; MVP; Perf Att; St of Mnth; Hab For Humty Volntr; FBLA; SP/M/VS; Bskball (VJ L); Track (V); Vllyball (V L); Cl Off (S); Stu Cncl (R); Education; Business; Campbellsville U; Lindsey Wilson College

COPPOLA, BRITTANY; LOUISVILLE, KY; SACRED HEART AC; (SO); Duke TS; Hi Hnr Roll; Hnr Roll; Comm Volntr; Hab For Humty Volntr; Peer Tut/Med; ArtClub; Chrch Yth Grp; FCA; Jr Ach; Ntl Beta Clb; Scouts; SADD; Spanish Clb; Acpl Chr; Cr Ctry (J); Fld Hky (L); PP Ftbl (V); Swmg (J); Track (J); Plays the Piano; Was a Gymnast for 9 Yrs; Journalism; Languages

CORBETT, MATTHEW; JENKINS, KY; JENKINS HS; (FR); Bnd; Pep Bnd; Bsball (V); Bskball (J); Cr Ctry (V); Golf (V); Track (V); Work At Church Camp; Fire Science; Paramedic; Eastern Kentucky U

CORBIN, JOSHUA; CYNTHIANA, KY; HARRISON CTY HS; (SO); Hnr Roll; WWAHSS; Foreign Clb; Ftball (V); Forensic Science; Sports Medicine; U of Kentucky; Western Kentucky U

CORBIN, MARILYN; LA GRANGE, KY; OLDHAM CTY HS; (JR); Fut Prb Slvr; Hnr Roll; Perf Att; WWAHSS; DARE; Drma Clb; Emplmnt; Jr Ach; Ntl Beta Clb; Prom Com; Tchrs Aide; Chr; Dnce; SP/M/VS; PPSqd (V); Cl Off (T); All-State Choir; Governor's School for the Arts; Reconstructive Surgeon; Vocal Performance; Stanford U; Boston U

CORDERO, FRANCHESKA M; RADCLIFF, KY; NORTH HARDIN HS; (JR); Pep Squd; Track (J); Vllyball (V); Medical Examiner; Forensic Investigator; New York U; U of Puerto Rico

CORDIAL, STEPHANIE N; ASHLAND, KY; PAUL G BLAZER HS; (FR); Hnr Roll; Drma Clb; Scouts; Sftball (J); Theatre Arts; Major in English; Major in Drama; U of Kentucky; U of Louisville

CORNETT, BRITTANY; GORDON, KY; CUMBERLAND HS; (JR); Hnr Roll; Perf Att; Off Aide; Prom Com

CORNETT, JEFFREY B; LEBURN, KY; KNOTT CO CTRL HS; (FR); Fut Prb Slvr; Hnr Roll; Ntl FFA

CORUM, CHANCE M; LEWISBURG, KY; LOGAN CTY HS; (SO); Hi Hnr Roll; Hnr Roll; Perf Att; St of Mnth; USAA; WWAHSS; Comm Volntr; Red Cr Aide; Chrch Yth Grp; FCA; Ntl Beta Clb; Ntl FFA; FFA Seed Contest - 10th in State; FFA Officer & Land Judging Team 4th in Form; Western Kentucky U; U of Kentucky

COSTELLO, MICHAEL W; SCOTTSVILLE, KY; ALLEN CTY HS; (SO); 4H Awd; Hnr Roll; St of Mnth; Comm Volntr; Red Cr Aide; 4-H; Chrch Yth Grp; DARE; Scouts; Ch Chr; Eagle Scout with Boy Scouts of America; United States Army; Architect; Western Kentucky U; U of Kentucky

COSTIGAN, BEN; FRANKFORT, KY; FRANKLIN CTY HS; (FR); Hi Hnr Roll; WWAHSS; Chrch Yth Grp; FCA; Key Club; Bnd; Mch Bnd; Pep Bnd; Sccr (VJ)

COSTIGAN, MOLLY; FRANKFORT, KY; FRANKLIN CTY HS; (JR); Nat Hon Sy; WWAHSS; Yth Ldrshp Prog; Comm Volntr; Chrch Yth Grp; FCA; Key Club; Ntl Beta Clb; Bnd; Mch Bnd; Pep Bnd; SP/M/VS; Key Club Vice-President

COTHERN, AMANDA; BOSTON, KY; NELSON CTY HS; (SR); All Am Sch; Hnr Roll; Nat Hon Sy; St of Mnth; USAA; WWAHSS; Chrch Yth Grp; Ntl FFA; Sftball (J); Stu Cncl (R); Chemistry; College of Pharmacy; U of Kentucky; U of K College of Pharmacy

COUCH, ASHLEY L; WILLIAMSBURG, KY; WHITLEY CTY HS; (JR); Hnr Roll; WWAHSS; Yth Ldrshp Prog; Chrch Yth Grp; Prom Com; Ch Chr; Track (J); I Am Miss Junior of WCHS '04'-'05'; Physical Therapist; X-Ray Technician; Summerset U

COUCH, MARY; COLUMBIA, KY; ADAIR CO HS; (FR); 4H Awd; Ctznshp Aw; F Lan Hn Soc; Hi Hnr Roll; Hnr Roll; Nat Stu Ath Day Aw; Otst Ac Ach Awd; Salutrn; St of Mnth; WWAHSS; Comm Volntr; Peer Tut/Med; Red Cr Aide; 4-H; Chrch Yth Grp; Cmptr Clb; DARE; Drma Clb; Ntl Beta Clb; Pep Squd; Prom Com; Ch Chr; SP/M/VS; Stu Cncl (S); Criminal Law; Master's of Public Administration; Harvard U; Yale U

COURSEY, CASEY L; LEWISBURG, KY; LOGAN CTY HS; (FR); 4H Awd; Ctznshp Aw; Fut Prb Slvr; Hi Hnr Roll; Hnr Roll; Nat Mrt Sch Recip; Otst Ac Ach Awd; Perf Att; St of Mnth; WWAHSS; Comm Volntr; Peer Tut/Med; 4-H; Chrch Yth Grp; DECA; Drma Clb; Emplmnt; FTA; Ntl FFA; Outdrs Clb; Ch Chr; SP/M/VS; Adv Cncl (R); Cl Off (V); CR (P); Sch Ppr (R); Yrbk (E, P); Teen Court / Lawyer; Logan County Lamb/Goat Clubs; Advertisement; Business / Real Estate; Western Kentucky U

COWDEN, COURTNEY; LEXINGTON, KY; LEXINGTON CATHOLIC HS; (SO); Duke TS; F Lan Hn Soc; Hi Hnr Roll; WWAHSS; Comm Volntr; Hosp Aide; DARE; Key Club; Ntl Beta Clb; Photog; SADD; Spanish Clb; Swmg (V L); Tennis (V L); Spanish Honors Society; Beta Club; Business; Medicine; U of Virginia; U of North Carolina

COWLES, CHELSAE R; SMITHS GROVE, KY; EDMONSON CTY HS; (FR); Hnr Roll; Perf Att; Yth Ldrshp Prog; Comm Volntr; Chrch Yth Grp; DARE; Drma Clb; Ntl Beta Clb; Ch Chr; SP/M/VS; Vllyball (J); Dentistry; Pharmacist; Western Kentucky U; U of Louisville

COX, JORDAN T; MT WASHINGTON, KY; BULLITT EAST HS; (FR); Hnr Roll; Perf Att; St of Mnth; Comm Volntr; DARE; Scouts; Computer Technology; Engineering; U of Louisville; Michigan Institute of Technology

COX, KENDALL T; TURNERS STATION, KY; HENRY CTY HS; (FR); Hnr Roll; FCA; Lib Aide; Ntl FFA; Bsball (V); Mechanical Engineer

COY, AMANDA M; CYNTHIANA, KY; HARRISON CTY HS; (SR); Hnr Roll; ArtClub; Veterinarian; Eastern Kentucky U; Maysville College

COY, JOSEPH R; HODGENVILLE, KY; LARUE CTY HS; (JR); Hnr Roll; Nat Hon Sy; Ntl FFA; Tech Clb; Cl Off (P, R); E-Town Technical College; E-Town Community College; E-Town Technical College; E-Town Community College

COZORT, RYAN; PADUCAH, KY; HEATH HS; (MS); DAR; Duke TS; Hnr Roll; St of Mnth; Chrch Yth Grp; Ntl Beta Clb; Bnd; Mch Bnd; 1st Place At West Kentucky History Day; Bachelor of Science in Aeronautical Science; Embry-Riddle Aeronautical U

CRAWFORD, NATALIE; TOMPKINSVILLE, KY; MONROE CTY HS; (FR); 4H Awd; Duke TS; Hi Hnr Roll; 4-H; Emplmnt; FCCLA; Ntl Beta Clb; Ntl FFA; Pep Squd; Tech Clb; Bnd; Clr Grd; Drm Mjr; Mch Bnd; Sftball; CR (S, R); KY Coal Coalition Scholarship; Medical; UK Lexington; UC Louisville

CRAWFORD, RANDALL J; LEXINGTON, KY; BRYAN STATION HS; (SO); Hnr Roll; Nat Hon Sy; DARE; Emplmnt; SADD; Wdwrkg Clb; Ftball (V L); Architecture; U of Kentucky; Auburn U

CRESS, AMANDA; ERMINE, KY; FLEMING NEON HS; (SR); Hnr Roll; Otst Ac Ach Awd; Perf Att; Comm Volntr; Photog; Prom Com; Tech Clb; Sch Ppr (R, P); Yrbk (R, P); Vice President of HOSA Organization; Registered Nurse; Physical Therapist; Southeast Community College (Whitesburg)

CRIDER, KELLYE J; MARION, KY; CRITTENDEN CTY HS; (JR); Ctznshp Aw; Hnr Roll; St of Mnth; WWAHSS; Chrch Yth Grp; Emplmnt; FCA; FTA; Ntl Beta Clb; SADD; Vllyball (V L); Career in Education; Murray State U; Western Kentucky U

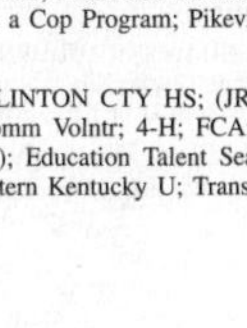
Cozort, Ryan
Heath HS
Paducah, KY

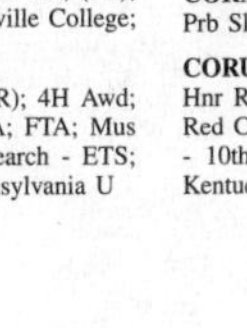
Costello, Michael W
Allen Cty HS
Scottsville, KY

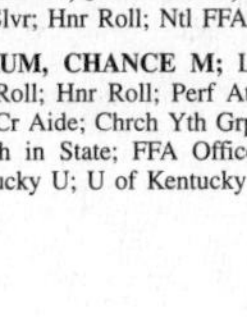
Cook, Timothy
Johnson Ctrl HS
Boons Camp, KY

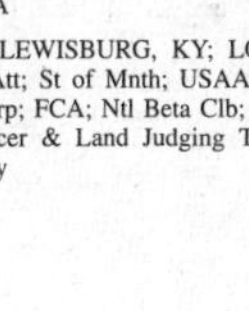
Combs, Ashley L
Louisville Male HS
Louisville, KY

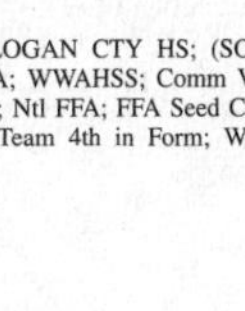
Conn, Amanda L
Prestonsburg HS
Prestonsburg, KY

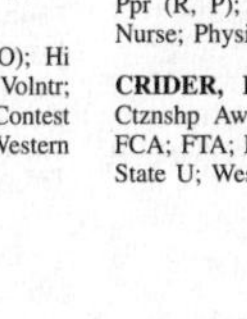
Cowden, Courtney
Lexington Catholic HS
Lexington, KY

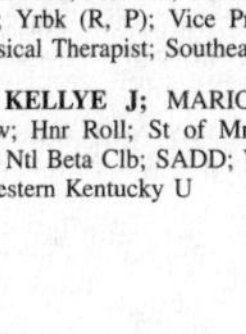
Crawford, Randall J
Bryan Station HS
Lexington, KY

CRIPE, ELIZABETH M; LOUISVILLE, KY; ASSUMPTION HS; (JR); Hnr Roll; Perf Att; WWAHSS; Comm Volntr; Hab For Humty Volntr; Hosp Aide; Emplmnt; FCA; Ntl Beta Clb; Pep Squd; Svce Clb; Fld Hky (J); Crew Team (JV and Varsity); Psychology; Nursing; Western Kentucky U; Bellarmine Mine U

CROFFORD, CALYN; ALLENSVILLE, KY; LOGAN CTY HS; (FR); Hi Hnr Roll; Otst Ac Ach Awd; Pres Ac Ftns Aw; St of Mnth; DARE; FCA; FBLA; Ntl Beta Clb; Ntl FFA; Pep Squd; Tchrs Aide; Flg Crps; Bskball (V); Tennis (V L); Vllyball (V); Aerospace Engineering; Virginia Tech U; U of Kansas

CROLEY, CHRISTOPHER S; GEORGETOWN, KY; SCOTT CTY HS; (JR); Duke TS; Hi Hnr Roll; Nat Hon Sy; Otst Ac Ach Awd; St of Mnth; WWAHSS; Yth Ldrshp Prog; Comm Volntr; Hab For Humty Volntr; Chrch Yth Grp; FCA; Key Club; Ntl Beta Clb; Pep Squd; Sci Clb; Svce Clb; French Clb; Bnd; Cl Off (T); Stu Cncl (T, R); National Honor Society - VP; Central KY - Council on Youth Leadership Award; U of Kentucky; Transylvania U

CROPPER, BRIAN; VANCEBURG, KY; LEWIS CTY HS; (SO); Perf Att; Sci Fairs; DARE; Ntl FFA; Welding; Carpenter; Rowan Technical

CROUCH, DAVID M; MURRAY, KY; CALLOWAY CTY HS; (SR); Ctznshp Aw; Hnr Roll; WWAHSS; Chrch Yth Grp; FCA; Lib Aide; Ntl Beta Clb; Ntl FFA; Pep Squd; Prom Com; Tchrs Aide; Bskball (V); FFA President; Star Farmer Award; Agriculture; Murray State U

CROWDER, VICTORIA; LOUISVILLE, KY; DUPONT MANUAL HS; (JR); Hnr Roll; Comm Volntr; Chrch Yth Grp; Emplmnt; FCA; Photog; Prom Com; Tchrs Aide; Latin Clb; Political Science; History; U of Kentucky; Centre College

CRUTCHFIELD, JESSICA; FRANKFORT, KY; FRANKLIN CTY HS; (JR); Hnr Roll; WWAHSS; Chrch Yth Grp; DECA; Who's Who; Accounting; Business Management; U of Kentucky; U of Louisville

CULVER, CASEY; BARDSTOWN, KY; NELSON CTY HS; (SR); Duke TS; Hi Hnr Roll; Nat Sci Aw; Otst Ac Ach Awd; USAA; WWAHSS; Emplmnt; Ntl FFA; Pep Squd; PP Ftbl (VJ); Nursing; Business; U of Kentucky; Lexington Community College

CULVER, SAMANTHA; BARDSTOWN, KY; NELSON CTY HS; (FR); Duke TS; Hnr Roll; WWAHSS; Comm Volntr; ArtClub; Drma Clb; Key Club; SP/M/VS; PP Ftbl (J); Sccr (V); Marine Biology; U of North Carolina

CUNDIFF, WESTLEY; HAZARD, KY; PERRY CTY CTRL HS; (FR); Hnr Roll; Otst Ac Ach Awd; DARE; Drma Clb; SP/M/VS; Stg Cre; Bsball (J); Fncg; Art Awards; Game Designing; History/Acting; AI Art Institutes of America

CUNNINGHAM, RYAN D; FT MITCHELL, KY; SCOTT HS; (SR); Hnr Roll; Pres Ac Ftns Aw; St of Mnth; WWAHSS; CARE; ArtClub; DARE; Emplmnt; SADD; Cr Ctry (V); Dvng (V); Swmg (V); Track (V); Stu Cncl (R); Music; Northern KY U

CURTIS, DUSTIN R; OWENTON, KY; OWEN CTY HS; (SO); Ctznshp Aw; Hnr Roll; St of Mnth; DARE; Ftball (V); Wt Lftg (V); Equine Veterinarian; U of Kentucky; Northern Kentucky U

CURTIS, KRISTIN; CYNTHIANA, KY; HARRISON CTY HS; (FR); 4H Awd; Hnr Roll; Perf Att; Sci Fairs; 4-H; Vllyball (J)

CURTIS, MARGARET; LOUISVILLE, KY; SACRED HEART AC; (SO); Duke TS; Hnr Roll; WWAHSS; Peer Tut/Med; Mod UN; Pep Squd; Bskball (J); Fld Hky (J); Cl Off (S, T); CR (R); Peer Leaders; Student Council Executive Board; Business; Miami U; U of Kentucky

DAILEY, REBEKAH; LEXINGTON, KY; HENRY CLAY HS; (FR); Duke TS; Hi Hnr Roll; Otst Ac Ach Awd; Pres Ac Ftns Aw; Pres Sch; WWAHSS; Comm Volntr; Peer Tut/Med; Mth Clb/Tm; Ntl Beta Clb; Ch Chr; Cl Off (T); Stu Cncl (P); Early Childhood Association; Lewis M Thompson Award; Pre-Med; Pre-Law; U of Kentucky; U of Louisville

DANIEL, BRITTANY; WINCHESTER, KY; GEORGE ROGERS CLARK HS; (FR); Hi Hnr Roll; Perf Att; Comm Volntr; 4-H; Chrch Yth Grp; FCA; FBLA; Ntl Beta Clb; Pep Squd; SADD; Ch Chr; Chrldg (L); Gmnstcs; PP Ftbl; Stu Cncl (R); Presidential Award; Nursing; U of Louisville

DARBY, MASON A; RUSSELL, KY; RUSSELL HS; (SO); Hnr Roll; WWAHSS; Chrch Yth Grp; FCA; Key Club; French Clb; Golf (V); Beta Club Member; Key Club Member - Treasurer; Communications Degree; Sports Broadcasting; Eastern Kentucky U; U of Kentucky

DAUGHERTY, SASHA; ELKHORN CITY, KY; EAST RIDGE HS; (JR); Hnr Roll; WWAHSS; Ntl Beta Clb; HOSA; Radiology Technician; Marketing; Pikeville College

DAVENPORT, AMY P; WALTON, KY; LARRY A RYLE HS; (FR); Duke TS; Hnr Roll; Nat Sci Aw; Sccr (J); (Section A) USAA National Mathematics Award; Veterinary School

DAVENPORT, MAGGIE; MANITOU, KY; MADISONVILLE NORTH HOPKINS HS; (JR); Hnr Roll; MVP; WWAHSS; Hab For Humty Volntr; Spec Olymp Vol; Chrch Yth Grp; FCA; FBLA; Key Club; Ntl Beta Clb; Cr Ctry (V L); Sccr (V CL); Swmg (V L); Track (V L); Pre-Law / Criminal Justice; Pharmacy; U of Kentucky

DAVENPORT, MOLLY; MANITOU, KY; MADISONVILLE NORTH HOPKINS HS; (JR); Fut Prb Slvr; Hi Hnr Roll; Jr Mshl; MVP; Nat Mrt LOC; WWAHSS; Spec Olymp Vol; Chrch Yth Grp; FCA; Key Club; Ntl Beta Clb; Spanish Clb; Sccr (V CL); Sftball (V L); Swmg (V L); Track (V L); Governor's Scholar; National Merit Scholar Consideration

DAVIDSON, STEPHANIE; LOUISVILLE, KY; FAIRDALE HS; (SO); Hi Hnr Roll; Hnr Roll; Amnsty Intl; Comm Volntr; Peer Tut/Med; ArtClub; Emplmnt; Fr of Library; Mth Clb/Tm; Stg Cre; All Honors Classes; Business Owner; Architecture; Brown U; Boston U

DAVIS, BRADLEY S; HOPKINSVILLE, KY; CHRISTIAN CTY HS; (FR); Hnr Roll; Perf Att; Sci Fairs; Chrch Yth Grp; Cmptr Clb; DARE; Chr; Computer Repair; Murray State U

DAVIS, CLAYTON B; PILGRIM, KY; MARTIN CTY AREA TECH CTR; (JR); Hnr Roll; Nat Hon Sy; WWAHSS; Comm Volntr; Peer Tut/Med; Red Cr Aide; FCA; FBLA; Ntl Beta Clb; Tennis (V C); President of Health Occupations Students of America; President of National Technical Vocational Honor Society; Doctor-Orthopedic Surgeon; Nurse-Registered Nurse; Alice Lloyd College; Berea College

DAVIS, DAMIEYAUNTA; LA GRANGE, KY; OLDHAM CTY HS; (FR); Hnr Roll; Perf Att; Comm Volntr; Chrch Yth Grp; Dbte Team; Emplmnt; Bskball (J); Ftball (J); Track (J); Wt Lftg (J); Volunteer for Salvation Army; Science, Basketball; Accountant, Track

DAVIS, GABRIEL P; LOUISVILLE, KY; BRECKINRIDGE METROPOLITAN HS; (JR); Hnr Roll; St of Mnth; Tchrs Aide; Working on Cars

DAVIS, JENNIFER A; SOUTH SHORE, KY; GREENUP CTY HS; (SO); Chrch Yth Grp; Pep Squd; Counseling and Guidance; Medical Radiologic Technology; U of Kentucky; Lexington Community College

DAVIS, JOHNNA K; GRAYSON, KY; EAST CARTER HS; (MS); Hnr Roll; MVP; Pres Ac Ftns Aw; Sci Fairs; St of Mnth; Peer Tut/Med; Chrch Yth Grp; DARE; Emplmnt; Ntl Beta Clb; P to P St Amb Prg; SADD; Dnce; SP/M/VS; Bskball (J); GAA (J); Stu Cncl (P); Beta Club (Must Be on Honor Roll); W.VA AAU Third Place-Basketball; Sexual Abuse Counselor; Psychologist; U of Kentucky; Michigan U

DAVIS, MORGAN; MAYSVILLE, KY; MASON CTY HS; (SO); Hi Hnr Roll; Nat Hon Sy; Pres Sch; Sci Fairs; WWAHSS; Chrch Yth Grp; FCA; Ntl Beta Clb; Chr; SP/M/VS; Elementary Education; Physical Therapy; Northern Kentucky University; University of Kentucky

DAVIS, RICHARD; FORT KNOX, KY; FORT KNOX HS; (SR); Hnr Roll; Nat Hon Sy; Pres Sch; WWAHSS; Yth Ldrshp Prog; Comm Volntr; Hab For Humty Volntr; Ftball (VJCL); Track (V L); Wt Lftg (V CL); Information Studies; Business Administration; Syracuse U; Carthage College

DAVIS, WHITNEY; HANSON, KY; MADISONVILLE NORTH HOPKINS HS; (SO); Fut Prb Slvr; Hnr Roll; WWAHSS; Spec Olymp Vol; Chrch Yth Grp; Key Club; Bnd; Mch Bnd; Pep Bnd; Pre-Med; Elementary Education; U of Kentucky; Campbellsville U

DAVIS-ROBERTS, SHELLENA; BEAVER DAM, KY; OHIO CTY HS; (SR); Hnr Roll; Nat Hon Sy; Perf Att; Comm Volntr; Peer Tut/Med; Chrch Yth Grp; FCA; Mus Clb; Ntl Beta Clb; P to P St Amb Prg; Tchrs Aide; French Clb; Chr; Academic Team; Beta Club VP; English-Journalism; Vocal Music; Lindsey Wilson College

DAWS, KENDRA M; SOMERSET, KY; SOUTHWESTERN HS; (JR); Hnr Roll; WWAHSS; Peer Tut/Med; Chrch Yth Grp; FCA; Ch Chr; Sccr (V); Criminal Justice; Real Estate/Social Worker; Eastern Kentucky U; Cumberland College

DEAN, BLAKE; LEXINGTON, KY; BRYAN STATION HS; (SO); Hnr Roll; Comm Volntr; Stg Cre; Bsball (VJ L); Carried Part Time Job, While Playing Sports and Doing Well in School; Architecture; Engineering; U of Kentucky; Purdue U

DE BERNARDI, NATHAN; SYMSONIA, KY; GRAVES CTY HS; (JR); Hi Hnr Roll; MVP; Otst Ac Ach Awd; St of Mnth; WWAHSS; AL Aux Boys; Chrch Yth Grp; FCA; Ntl Beta Clb; Pep Squd; Bsball (V L); Optometry; Pharmacy; Belmont U; U of Louisville

DELANEY, ANDREW L; BARDSTOWN, KY; NELSON CTY SR HS; (FR); All Am Sch; Duke TS; Hi Hnr Roll; Perf Att; USAA; WWAHSS; Chrch Yth Grp; FCA; Key Club; SADD; Ftball (V L); Cl Off (P); Pharmacy; UK U of KY; Western KY U

DE NARDI, JAMIE; LOUISVILLE, KY; FERN CREEK HS; (JR); Hi Hnr Roll; Red Cr Aide; DECA; Emplmnt; Jr Ach; Ntl Beta Clb; Tchrs Aide; Major in Business or Marketing; Major in Accounting; U of Louisville; U of Kentucky

DENNER, MARIE; CLAY, KY; WEBSTER CTY HS; (SO); Hnr Roll; Otst Ac Ach Awd; Emplmnt; Ntl FFA; SP/M/VS; Educational Talent Search Member; Animal/Veterinary Sciences Major; Cosmetology; Murry State U; U of Kentucky

DENNIS, SHAYNA M; HUDSON, KY; BETHEL CHRISTIAN AC; (JR); Hnr Roll; WWAHSS; 4-H; Chrch Yth Grp; Chr; Ch Chr; SP/M/VS; Bskball (V); Sch Ppr (E); Yrbk (E, P); Cosmetology; Elementary Education; Elizabethtown Community College; U of Kentucky

DENNISON, MAEGHAN; FAIRDALE, KY; ATHERTON HS; (FR); Hnr Roll; Pres Sch; Bnd; Mch Bnd; Pep Bnd; Indiana U Bloomington

DENTON, KATIE; HENDERSON, KY; HENDERSON CTY HS; (FR); Hnr Roll; Perf Att; Comm Volntr; Peer Tut/Med; 4-H; Ntl FFA; Bnd; Parliamentary Procedure Speaking Contest 9th Grade Regional Winner; Veterinarian; Western Kentucky U; Auburn U

DERRINGER, MICHAEL; RICHMOND, KY; MODEL LABORATORY SCH; (JR); Hi Hnr Roll; WWAHSS; FCA; Key Club; Pep Squd; Tchrs Aide; Bsball (VJCL); Bskball (VJCL); All Region Baseball 2004; All District Baseball 2004; BRU

DICK, KELLY; MURRAY, KY; MURRAY HS; (JR); Hnr Roll; Nat Hon Sy; WWAHSS; Comm Volntr; Key Club; Ntl Beta Clb; Pep Squd; Prom Com; Quill & Scroll; Tchrs Aide; French Clb; Chrldg (VJCL); Golf (V L); Sftball (V L); Cl Off (T); Stu Cncl (R); CR (R); Sch Ppr (E); Yrbk (E); Sports Medicine/Physical Therapy; Photography; Murray State U; U of Kentucky

DICKENS, JOSEPH; FT MITCHELL, KY; CALVARY CHRISTIAN SCH; (FR); All Am Sch; Hi Hnr Roll; Nat Hon Sy; USAA; WWAHSS; Comm Volntr; Chrch Yth Grp; Mth Clb/Tm; Svce Clb; Bnd; Pep Bnd; Cl Off (R); Cedarville U

DITTO, DAVID T; LEXINGTON, KY; LEXINGTON CHRN AC HS; (SO); Hi Hnr Roll; Chrch Yth Grp; Ntl Beta Clb; Cr Ctry; Track; The Citadel; U of Kentucky

DIXON, DUSTIN; BURLINGTON, KY; (SO); Hnr Roll; WWAHSS; Hab For Humty Volntr; Computer Programmer; Northern KY U

DIXON, EBONY; LOUISVILLE, KY; ATHERTON HS; (JR); Gov Hnr Prg; Hnr Roll; Nat Hon Sy; WWAHSS; Peer Tut/Med; Off Aide; Prom Com; Tchrs Aide; Chr; Cl Off (V); CR (V); U of K; Kentucky State

DIXON, JARED L; COVINGTON, KY; SCOTT HS; (SO); Duke TS; Hnr Roll; MVP; Nat Hon Sy; Pres Ac Ftns Aw; Pres Sch; St of Mnth; Yth Ldrshp Prog; DARE; Bskball (VJ L); Ftball (JC); Track; Offered a Spot in National Honor Society; Offered a Spot on Northern KY Area Planning Commission; Major in Business; Doctor-Pediatrician; Duke U; U of Kentucky

DONAHUE, RYAN; BARDSTOWN, KY; NELSON CTY HS; (SO); Hnr Roll; WWAHSS; Chrch Yth Grp; Key Club; Ch Chr; Computer Hardware Engineer; Computer Programmer; Elizabethtown Community College; U of Kentucky

DONALDSON, WHITNEY; MT STERLING, KY; MONTGOMERY CTY HS; (FR); Hnr Roll; 4-H; Chrch Yth Grp; Drma Clb; Mod UN; Ntl Beta Clb; Ntl FFA; Scouts; Chr; Orch; SP/M/VS; Agriculture Law; Government; U of Kentucky

DONG, DAN L; EDMONTON, KY; METCALFE CO HS; (FR); Bskball (J)

DONOHUE, JAMES; VINE GROVE, KY; MEADE CTY HS; (SO); Hi Hnr Roll; Perf Att; USAA; DARE; Pep Squd; Ftball (VJ L); Automotive; Math; U of Louisville; U of Kentucky

DORRIS, CLAIRE; MADISONVILLE, KY; MADISONVILLE NORTH HOPKINS HS; (SO); Duke TS; Nat Hon Sy; WWAHSS; Key Club; Ntl Beta Clb; Swmg (V L); Coaches Choice 2003-2004 Swim Team; Girl Scout Silver Award; Law

DORTCH, CARRIE L; PADUCAH, KY; HEATH HS; (JR); Hnr Roll; Otst Ac Ach Awd; Emplmnt; FBLA; Ntl Beta Clb; Off Aide; Prom Com; Tchrs Aide; Chr; SP/M/VS; Chrldg (V); Pediatrician; Orthodontist; U of Kentucky; Eastern Kentucky U

DOTY, HUDSON; WILMORE, KY; WEST JESSAMINE HS; (FR); Hnr Roll; Chess; Chrch Yth Grp; Emplmnt; Mar Art; Veterinarian; U of Kentucky; Purdue U

DOWNEY, CHRISTOPHER R; CRESTWOOD, KY; OLDHAM CTY HS; (FR); Hnr Roll; Nat Hon Sy; Drma Clb; Chr; SP/M/VS; KYA, Acting in Plays/Musicals; Theatre; Journalism; UL; UK

DOWNEY, SHANNA; AUBURN, KY; LOGAN CTY HS; (FR); Hnr Roll; Salutrn; Comm Volntr; Chrch Yth Grp; FBLA; Ntl Beta Clb; Ch Chr; SP/M/VS; Journalism; U of Kentucky; Vanderbilt U

DOYLE, RYAN; KIMPER, KY; PIKE CTY CTRL HS; (FR); WWAHSS; Comm Volntr; Wdwrkg Clb; Architect; Eastern College; Pikeville College

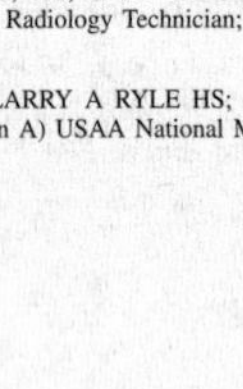
Denton, Katie
Henderson Cty HS
Henderson, KY

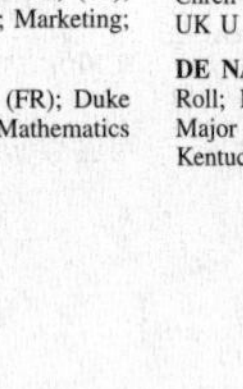
Davis, Johnna K
East Carter HS
Grayson, KY

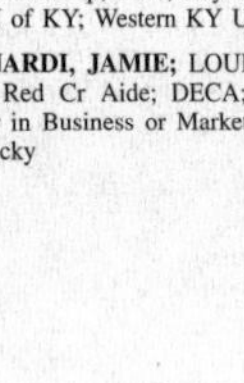
Davis, Clayton B
Martin Cty Area Tech Ctr
Pilgrim, KY

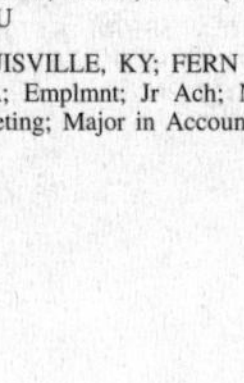
Crofford, Calyn
Logan Cty HS
Allensville, KY

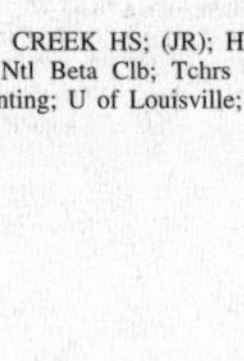
Curtis, Margaret
Sacred Heart AC
Louisville, KY

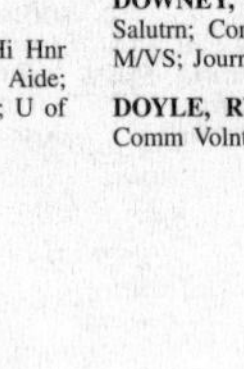
De Nardi, Jamie
Fern Creek HS
Louisville, KY

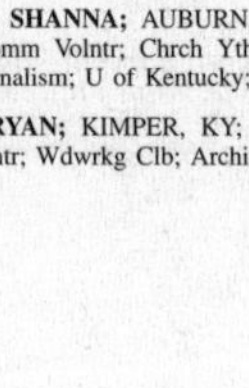
Dixon, Jared L
Scott HS
Covington, KY

DRAKE, DANIEL S; BARDSTOWN, KY; NELSON CTY HS; (FR); Duke TS; Hnr Roll; WWAHSS; Red Cr Aide; Key Club; Pep Squd; Bskball (J); Stu Cncl (R); American Red Cross Youth Volunteer; Medicine; Georgetown College; U of Kentucky

DUNAWAY, JASON D; WILLIAMSTOWN, KY; WILLIAMSTOWN HS; (SR); Hi Hnr Roll; Nat Hon Sy; Nat Ldrshp Svc; St of Mnth; WWAHSS; Comm Volntr; Peer Tut/Med; Chrch Yth Grp; DARE; Emplmnt; FCA; FBLA; Pep Squd; Prom Com; Scouts; Bnd; Mch Bnd; Orch; Pep Bnd; Bsball (V); Wt Lftg (V); Adv Cncl (R); Cl Off (V); Stu Cncl (S); CR (V); Marching Band State Champion; Music; Criminal Justice; Morehead

DUNCAN, CRISTIN T; RUSSELL SPRINGS, KY; (FR); Hnr Roll; Chrch Yth Grp; Speech Pathology; Beautician; U of Kentucky; Somerset Beauty School

DUNCAN, DENICE; VERSAILLES, KY; LEXINGTON CHRN AC HS; (SO); Ch Chr; Missions-Missionary; Usbury College Wilmore, KY; Other Christian College

DUNCAN, JARED L; GRAND RIVERS, KY; LIVINGSTON CTRL HS; (SR); Hi Hnr Roll; Otst Ac Ach Awd; Pres Ac Ftns Aw; Sci Fairs; WWAHSS; Yth Ldrshp Prog; Comm Volntr; Chrch Yth Grp; Emplmnt; FCA; Ntl Beta Clb; Ntl FFA; Prom Com; Scr Kpr (VJ); Cl Off (T); Stu Cncl (R); Telecommunications Systems Management; Murray State U

DUNCAN, JORDAN T; STEARNS, KY; MC CREARY CTRL HS; (SO); Comm Volntr; Chess; Mus Clb; Bnd; Jzz Bnd; Mch Bnd; Pep Bnd; Track; Wrstlg; Distinguished at Ensemble; All Fest; Science; Technology; Berea College; Cumberland College

DUNN, RUSSELL C; OWENTON, KY; OWEN CTY HS; (SO); Ftball (V); Play Drums; Computer Technician; Northern KY U; KY State U

DUNNING, MARTY; PADUCAH, KY; BALLARD MEMORIAL HS; (SO); Hnr Roll; WWAHSS; Comm Volntr; Chrch Yth Grp; Emplmnt; FCA; FBLA; Spanish Clb; Bnd; Ch Chr; Mch Bnd; Pep Bnd; Cr Ctry (V L); Track (V L); FBLA Reporter (Rep KY at FBLA Nationals in FBLA Principles & Procedures 2005); FCA Officer; Education-High School-Science/Math/Music or Spanish; Murray State U; Campbellsville U

DURR, CAROLINE; NICHOLASVILLE, KY; LEXINGTON CHRN AC HS; (SO); Hosp Aide; Pep Squd; PP Ftbl (V); Nursing; Chef

DURRETT, BRITTANY; CAMPBELLSBURG, KY; HENRY CTY HS; (JR); St of Mnth; Chrch Yth Grp; FCA; Tchrs Aide; Cl Off (S); Stu Cncl (R); Business Management; Music; U of Louisville

DUSZYNSKI, EVAN J; CYNTHIANA, KY; HARRISON CTY HS; (SO); Hi Hnr Roll; St of Mnth; WWAHSS; Yth Ldrshp Prog; Peer Tut/Med; Red Cr Aide; Biology Clb; Bskball (VJ L); Ftball (V); Sccr (V L); NEED Project-National Winner; Class of Kentucky Award; Computers; Dentistry; U of Kentucky; Wake Forest U

DUVALL, SEAIRRA B; ALBANY, KY; CLINTON CTY HS; (FR); 4H Awd; Hnr Roll; Otst Ac Ach Awd; Comm Volntr; 4-H; Chrch Yth Grp; DARE; FBLA; Mus Clb; Chr; Registered Nurse; Physical Therapist; Lindsey Wilson College; Somerset Community College

DUVALL II, DALLAS; SWEEDEN, KY; EDMONSON CTY HS; (SO); All Am Sch; Hi Hnr Roll; Nat Hon Sy; Yth Ldrshp Prog; Drma Clb; MuAlphaTh; Ntl Beta Clb; Prom Com; Tech Clb; SP/M/VS; Stg Cre; Skt Tgt Sh; Sch Ppr (E); Yrbk (E); Law; Medicine; U of Kentucky; Western Kentucky U

DYER, WESLEY A; GAMALIEL, KY; MONROE CTY HS; (JR); Ctznshp Aw; Duke TS; Hnr Roll; Perf Att; DARE; Ntl Beta Clb; Pep Squd; Tech Clb; Clb; Cl Off (S, T, R); Beta Top Scholar; Most Likely to Succeed & Most Dependable of Class; Veterinary; Pre-Med; Western Kentucky; Auburn U

EARL, KARA; LEXINGTON, KY; LEXINGTON CHRN AC HS; (SO); Hnr Roll; WWAHSS; Comm Volntr; Svce Clb; Bskball (J); PP Ftbl (V); Sftball (VJ L); Veterinarian; Art/English; U of Kentucky

EASLEY JR, DALE R; LOUISVILLE, KY; JEFFERSONTOWN HS; (JR); Hnr Roll; MVP; Perf Att; Pres Ac Ftns Aw; Pres Sch; Comm Volntr; Emplmnt; Pep Squd; Tchrs Aide; Bskball (V CL); Track (V); Who's Who Sports Edition; Computer Engineering; UNC; Purdue

EASTERLING, ANDREW J; MOUNT STERLING, KY; (JR); Ctznshp Aw; Hi Hnr Roll; Hnr Roll; Perf Att; St of Mnth; Yth Ldrshp Prog; Comm Volntr; Hab For Humty Volntr; Peer Tut/Med; Chrch Yth Grp; Emplmnt; Key Club; Tech Clb; Ftball (J); Wt Lftg (J); Adv Cncl (R); CR (R); Engineering: Electrical; Mechanical; Georgia Tech

ECKARD, CHRISTINA D; LOUISA, KY; SHELDON CLARK HS; (FR); Nursing; Veterinarian; Ohio State U; Kentucky State U

EDMONDS, MEGAN; PIKEVILLE, KY; PIKE CTY CTRL HS; (FR); 4H Awd; Hi Hnr Roll; Otst Ac Ach Awd; USAA; Comm Volntr; 4-H; Chrch Yth Grp; FBLA; Ntl Beta Clb; Pep Squd; Prom Com; Tech Clb; Ch Chr; Vllyball (J); Pikeville College Upward-Bound; Pikeville College; U of Kentucky

EDWARDS, AARON D; HENDERSON, KY; HENDERSON CTY HS; (FR); Duke TS; Hi Hnr Roll; Sci/Math Olympn; Chrch Yth Grp; Prom Com; Ch Chr; Swmg (V L); Stu Cncl; Regional Swimming Champion 2005; Law; Politics; U of Kentucky; Auburn U

EICHBERGER, JESSI A; LOUISVILLE, KY; WALDEN SCH; (JR); Gov Hnr Prg; Hi Hnr Roll; Nat Hon Sy; Nat Sci Aw; Pres Ac Ftns Aw; USAA; WWAHSS; Comm Volntr; ArtClub; Drma Clb; Key Club; Mod UN; Ntl Beta Clb; Spanish Clb; Stg Cre; Bskball (V); Sccr (V); Cl Off (V); Sch Ppr (R); Honorable Mention for Prudential Spirit of Community Award; Placed 1st in State for Construction Model At Foreign Language Festival; Fine Arts; Theater Technology; Bellarmine U; Savannah School of Art and Design

ELDER, JORDAN; BARDSTOWN, KY; NELSON CTY HS; (FR); Hi Hnr Roll; Hnr Roll; WWAHSS; Comm Volntr; Hab For Humty Volntr; Red Cr Aide; 4-H; Chrch Yth Grp; Emplmnt; Kwanza Clb; Chr; Dnce; Drl Tm; PPSqd (V); Nelson County Dance Team; Job At Fit Kids Sports Center; Forensic Scientist; Fashion Designer; Auburn U; Yale

ELDRIDGE, MARGARET; WHITESBURG, KY; FLEMING NEON HS; (SR); Gov Hnr Prg; Hi Hnr Roll; Hnr Roll; Pres Sch; St of Mnth; Valdctrian; WWAHSS; Comm Volntr; Peer Tut/Med; Photog; Prom Com; Tchrs Aide; Tech Clb; Sch Ppr (R, P); Yrbk (R, P); Most Outstanding Sophomore; Rank 1 of Senior Class of 59; Business/Accounting; Southeast Community College; Hazard Community College

ELLIOTT, ROBBIE M; LEXINGTON, KY; LAFAYETTE HS; (SO); Hnr Roll; Perf Att; Sci Fairs; Comm Volntr; Lib Aide; Mus Clb; P to P St Amb Prg; Bnd; Jzz Bnd; Mch Bnd; Orch; KY All-State Band; Architecture; Music

ELLIS, TABITHA L; LAWRENCEBURG, KY; ANDERSON CTY HS; (FR); Duke TS; Hnr Roll; Perf Att; Comm Volntr; AL Aux Girls; DARE; Lib Aide; Off Aide; Dnce; Gifted and Talented; Choreographer; Pediatrician; U of Louisville; Central Michigan U

ELMORE, JAMES L; BURKESVILLE, KY; CLINTON CTY AREA TECH CTR; (SO); Drl Tm; Bsball (VJ); Bskball (J); Tennis (J); Track; Have Been in Jr Guard 5 Years; Assistant Staff Leader; Probably Military First

ELROD, JON L; FOSTER, KY; (JR); Ctznshp Aw; Hi Hnr Roll; Nat Hon Sy; Otst Ac Ach Awd; Perf Att; St of Mnth; USAA; WWAHSS; Chrch Yth Grp; FBLA; Off Aide; Tchrs Aide; Bskball (V L); Sccr (V L); Stu Cncl (T)

EMBRY, CHRISTINA; LEITCHFIELD, KY; BETHEL CHRISTIAN AC; (FR); Hi Hnr Roll; Hnr Roll; Chrch Yth Grp; Drma Clb; Pep Squd; Ch Chr; Bskball (V); Vllyball (V); Pre-Med; Forensics; Western Kentucky U; Elizabethtown Community College

EMBRY, TRENTON; MORGANTOWN, KY; (SR); Comm Volntr; Bsball (J); Sccr (VJCL); NJROTC Commanding Officer; NJROTC Rifle Team Commander; Pre-Law; Law; U of Kentucky; Western Kentucky U

ENGLAND, JAKE; HEBRON, KY; CONNER HS; (FR); Ctznshp Aw; Duke TS; Hnr Roll; Otst Ac Ach Awd; Pres Sch; Sci/Math Olympn; WWAHSS; Comm Volntr; Hosp Aide; Red Cr Aide; Chrch Yth Grp; DARE; Dbte Team; Drma Clb; Emplmnt; FTA; Lib Aide; NtlFrnscLg; Chr; SP/M/VS; Sccr (J L); Adv Cncl (T); Duke Tip Program; Presidential Service Award; Doctor; Lawyer; Duke U; Transylvania U

ENGLAND, LAURA; AUGUSTA, KY; AUGUSTA HS; (SO); Hnr Roll; Nat Hon Sy; Otst Ac Ach Awd; USAA; DARE; Cl Off (R); CR (R)

ENGLAND, OLIVIA M; FALLS OF ROUGH, KY; GRAYSON CTY HS; (SO); Hnr Roll; Otst Ac Ach Awd; WWAHSS; Comm Volntr; Chrch Yth Grp; DECA; Pep Squd; Certified Firefighter; DECA / HOSA Secretary '05-'06; Career Firefighter; Marketing Director / Crusade for Children; U of Kentucky; Eastern Kentucky U

ENGLE, KATHRYN; RICHMOND, KY; MODEL LABORATORY SCH; (SO); Duke TS; Hi Hnr Roll; Spec Olymp Vol; Chrch Yth Grp; FCA; Key Club; Sci Clb; Bnd; Bskball (V L); Sccr (V L); Sftball (V L); Numerous Awards- Science, English, Arts & Humanities - Honors

ERICKSON, JENNIFER; BARDSTOWN, KY; NELSON CTY HS; (SO); Hnr Roll; WWAHSS; 4-H; Chrch Yth Grp; DARE; Drma Clb; Key Club; Ntl Beta Clb; Dnce; Medical Field-Radiology; U of Kentucky; U of Louisville

ERIKSEN, MAXWELL H; ELIZABETHTOWN, KY; JOHN HARDIN HS; (SR); Duke TS; Fut Prb Slvr; Comm Volntr; Chess; Tech Clb; Races Professionally with the SCCA-For Mazda's Car Races; Chiropractic; Western Kentucky U; Palmer College of Chiropractic

ERNSPERGER, COLIN; OWENTON, KY; OWEN CTY HS; (FR); Hnr Roll; DARE; Emplmnt; Bsball (J); Ftball (J); Wt Lftg (J); Marine Biology; Oceanology; Florida State U; Miami Community College

EVANS, AMANDA; INEZ, KY; SHELDON CLARK HS; (SO); Nat Hon Sy; Nat Ldrshp Svc; WWAHSS; Lib Aide; Ntl Beta Clb; Pharmacist; Doctor; U of Kentucky; Marshall U

EWINGS, JESSICA D; CTRL CITY, KY; MUHLENBERG NORTH HS; (JR); Hnr Roll; WWAHSS; Comm Volntr; Drma Clb; Pep Squd; Tchrs Aide; HOSA Treasurer; Biology Major; Medicine; Kentucky Western U; U of Louisville

FAESY, SHANA; FRANKFORT, KY; FRANKLIN CTY HS; (SO); Hnr Roll; WWAHSS; ArtClub; Key Club; Mod UN; Ntl Beta Clb; Scouts; Voc Ind Clb Am; Stg Cre; Golf (V L); Tennis (J); Cl Off (R); Sch Ppr (E); Girl Scout Silver Award; Teaching; Graphic Design; Savannah College of Art and Design; Centre College

FARLEY, BRAD; SCOTTSVILLE, KY; ALLEN CTY HS; (FR); Ntl FFA; Member of FFA; Farming; Automotive; Western Kentucky U

FARLEY, ELIZABETH; FRANKLIN, KY; FRANKLIN SIMPSON HS; (JR); 4H Awd; Hi Hnr Roll; Hnr Roll; Otst Ac Ach Awd; Perf Att; Comm Volntr; 4-H; ArtClub; Chrch Yth Grp; Emplmnt; Ntl Beta Clb; Ntl FFA; Photog; Veterinary Medicine

FARRIS, AARIKA J; LAWRENCEBURG, KY; ANDERSON CTY HS; (JR); Hnr Roll; WWAHSS; Comm Volntr; 4-H; Cmptr Clb; Emplmnt; FCCLA; Ntl Beta Clb; Svce Clb; Tech Clb; Chrldg (J); Sch Ppr (R); Academic Team; Young Engineers Program; Civil Engineering; Architecture; Reed College; U of Kentucky

FASSOLD, SHANE; DAWSON SPRINGS, KY; HOPKINS CTY CTRL HS; (SO); Hnr Roll; Comm Volntr; ROTC; Clr Grd; Drl Tm; Electronics; ITT Technical Institute

FAUGHT, DUSTY; PERRYVILLE, KY; BOYLE CTY HS; (JR); Comm Volntr; Ntl FFA; Wild Life Management; Law Enforcement; EKU

FEIST, PETER; BURLINGTON, KY; CONNER SR HS; (FR); Hi Hnr Roll; Otst Ac Ach Awd; Perf Att; St of Mnth; Cr Ctry (J L); Track (VJ L)

FELTON, CALLY A; CADIZ, KY; TRIGG CTY HS; (SO); Hnr Roll; Perf Att; WWAHSS; Chrch Yth Grp; Emplmnt; Ntl Beta Clb; Ntl FFA; Vllyball (J); State Champion FFA Parliamentary Procedure Team; Agriculture Education; Forensic Science; Murray State U

FEOLE, IAN; SHELBYVILLE, KY; CORNERSTONE CHRISTIAN AC; (JR); Gov Hnr Prg; Hnr Roll; USAA; WWAHSS; Chess; Chrch Yth Grp; Key Club; Outdrs Clb; Tchrs Aide; Ch Chr; Stg Cre; Bskball (J); Golf (J); Sccr (V L); Wt Lftg; Yrbk (P); President's Education Award; Black Belt Tae Kwon Do; Engineering; Business; U of Louisville; Clemson

FIELDS, ASHTON; HAZARD, KY; HAZARD HS; (SO); Hnr Roll; Comm Volntr; Chrch Yth Grp; Bnd; Chr; Ch Chr; Clr Grd; Medical-Surgeon; Law; U of Kentucky; U of Southern Maine

FIELDS, CHARLES S; CUMBERLAND, KY; CUMBERLAND HS; (JR); Ctznshp Aw; Hnr Roll; Yth Ldrshp Prog; Chrch Yth Grp; Emplmnt; FBLA; Ntl Beta Clb; Prom Com; ROTC; Scouts; Ch Chr; Clr Grd; Attained the Rank of Eagle Scout 2004; Commissioned a Kentucky Colonel 2005; Mechanical Engineer; Civil Engineer; Southeast Community College; U of Kentucky

FILBACK III, JESSE T; WESTVIEW, KY; BETHEL CHRISTIAN AC; (SO); Ctznshp Aw; Fut Prb Slvr; Hnr Roll; MVP; Otst Ac Ach Awd; Perf Att; St of Mnth; WWAHSS; Comm Volntr; Hab For Humty Volntr; Spec Olymp Vol; Chrch Yth Grp; Cmptr Clb; Dbte Team; Emplmnt; FCA; Spanish Clb; Chr; Ch Chr; Bsball (V L); Bskball (VJ L); Scr Kpr (VJ); Sccr (V L); Vllyball (V); Sch Ppr (R); Teaching; Lawyer / Law School; Western Kentucky U

FINN, AMANDA; GLASGOW, KY; BARREN CTY HS; (SO); Hnr Roll; Biology Clb

FITCH, EMMA; CATLETTSBURG, KY; BOYD CTY HS; (FR); Hnr Roll; Perf Att; Chrch Yth Grp; Jr Ach; Outdrs Clb; Pep Squd; Dance; Modeling; Barbizon; Juilliard

FITZPATRICK, JENNIFER; HOPKINSVILLE, KY; HOPKINSVILLE HS; (SO); WWAHSS; Chrch Yth Grp; Sci Clb; Veterinarian

FLAKE, ALAYNA J; HAWESVILLE, KY; HANCOCK CTY HS; (SO); 4H Awd; Hnr Roll; St of Mnth; 4-H; Ntl FFA; Pep Squd; Tchrs Aide; Chrldg (V L); Hsbk Rdg (V); Vllyball (V); Veterinary Tech; Murray U; Midway College

FLANNERY, ALLISON; LOUISVILLE, KY; SACRED HEART AC; (SO); All Am Sch; Duke TS; Hi Hnr Roll; Hnr Roll; Otst Ac Ach Awd; Perf Att; Pres Ac Ftns Aw; WWAHSS; Yth Ldrshp Prog; Comm Volntr; Hosp Aide; Peer Tut/Med; Chrch Yth Grp; DARE; Drma Clb; Emplmnt; Jr Ach; Pep Squd; Photog; Scouts; Chr; SP/M/VS; Vllyball (J); Freshman Christian Leadership Award; Freshman & JV Volleyball Defense Award; Psychology; Medicine / Pediatrics; U of Kentucky; Xavier U

FLEMING, BRITANEY; LOUISVILLE, KY; FERN CREEK TRADITIONAL HS; (FR); Duke TS; Hnr Roll; Perf Att; Yth Ldrshp Prog; Comm Volntr; Drma Clb; Emplmnt; FCA; Orch; Cr Ctry (J); Track (J); Spanish Club; Real Estate; Business; U of Louisville

FLEMING, JON M H; ERMINE, KY; JENKINS HS; (FR); Duke TS; Hnr Roll; St of Mnth; Vsity Clb; Ftball (V); Vsy Clb (V); Wt Lftg (V); Duke Map Program; Pikeville College; U of Virginia

FLENER, GABRIELLE A E; COLUMBIA, KY; ADAIR CTY HS; (FR); Chrch Yth Grp; FBLA; Gifted and Talented Program; Family Practice Doctor; U of Louisville; U of Kentucky

Fields, Charles S
Cumberland HS
Cumberland, KY

Ernsperger, Colin
Owen Cty HS
Owenton, KY

Eriksen, Maxwell H
John Hardin HS
Elizabethtown, KY

Earl, Kara
Lexington Chrn AC HS
Lexington, KY

Eichberger, Jessi A
Walden Sch
Louisville, KY

Fields, Ashton
Hazard HS
Hazard, KY

Fleming, Jon M H
Jenkins HS
Ermine, KY

FLETCHER JR, RAY L; AVAWAM, KY; PERRY CTY CTRL HS; (JR); Hnr Roll; Otst Ac Ach Awd; Sci Fairs; Chrch Yth Grp; DARE; Ftball (V); Sccr (V); Member of F.C. Kentucky Select Soccer Team; Member of London White Sharks Soccer Team; I Want to Play Soccer.; Pharmacy; U of Kentucky

FLORA, SARAH E; LEXINGTON, KY; BRYAN STATION HS; (SO); Duke TS; Hnr Roll; Pres Ac Ftns Aw; St of Mnth; 4-H; Chrch Yth Grp; DARE; Emplmnt; Chr; Ch Chr; Clr Grd; Flg Crps; Forensic Science; Medicine; Asbury College; Eastern Kentucky U

FLOYD, KAYLA; RUSSELL SPGS, KY; RUSSELL CTY HS; (SO); Ctznshp Aw; Hi Hnr Roll; Hnr Roll; Otst Ac Ach Awd; Perf Att; Comm Volntr; 4-H; Chrch Yth Grp; DARE; Lib Aide; Ntl FFA; ROTC; Tech Clb; Voc Ind Clb Am; Ch Chr; Library Service Award; Outstanding Technology Award; Technology Education; U of Kentucky

FOGLE, SYDNEY; LOUISVILLE, KY; LOUISVILLE MALE HS; (FR); Comm Volntr; Chrch Yth Grp; DARE; Orch; SP/M/VS; Medical Doctor; Music / Fine Arts; Bellermine University; University of Louisville

FOLEN, BRITTNEY N; WOOLLUM, KY; KNOX CTRL HS; (SR); Gov Hnr Prg; Hi Hnr Roll; Hnr Roll; Nat Hon Sy; St of Mnth; WWAHSS; Chrch Yth Grp; DARE; Drma Clb; Pep Squd; Spanish Clb; SP/M/VS; Stg Cre; Cr Ctry (V L); PP Ftbl (V); Sftball (J L); Yrbk (R); Drama- 3 Yrs; Pep Club - 2 Yrs; Veterinary / DVM; Purdue U; U of North Carolina

FOLEY, REBECCA; KNIFLEY, KY; ADAIR CTY HS; (FR); 4H Awd; Hnr Roll; Nat Hon Sy; 4-H; Ntl FFA; Bskball (J); Sftball (J); Landscape Design - Master's; U of Kentucky; U of Louisville

FOLLOWELL, STEVEN L; BRADFORDSVILLE, KY; MARION CTY HS; (SR); Hnr Roll; Perf Att; St of Mnth; WWAHSS; FTA; ROTC

FOLTZ, KELLEY; BURLINGTON, KY; CONNER HS; (JR); F Lan Hn Soc; Hnr Roll; Jr Mshl; MVP; Nat Hon Sy; Perf Att; Pres Ac Ftns Aw; St of Mnth; Yth Ldrshp Prog; Comm Volntr; Peer Tut/Med; Spec Olymp Vol; Chrch Yth Grp; FCA; Prom Com; Spanish Clb; Golf (V); Sftball (V); Cl Off (T); Education; Counseling; Eastern Kentucky U; Cincinnati Bible College

FOSTER, CHRISTINA; LOUISVILLE, KY; LOUISVILLE MALE HS; (FR); Hi Hnr Roll; Hnr Roll; Junior Beta Club; Calligraphy Club; Psychology

FOSTER, EMILY; SHELBYVILLE, KY; SHELBY CTY HS; (JR); Ctznshp Aw; Hnr Roll; Yth Ldrshp Prog; Comm Volntr; Spec Olymp Vol; ArtClub; Chrch Yth Grp; Drma Clb; FCA; NYLC; Photog; Prom Com; Bnd; Ch Chr; SP/M/VS; Stg Cre; PP Ftbl (V); Tennis; Cl Off (T); CR (T); Yrbk (E, P); Southern Seminary Piano Conference - Superior and Excellent Ratings; Miss Congeniality in 2005 / Shelby Fair Queen Pageant; Sports Photojournalism; Youth Ministries; Southwest Baptist University in Bolivar Missouri; Western Kentucky U

FOSTER, SIERRA N; MURRAY, KY; MURRAY HS; (FR); Hi Hnr Roll; Hnr Roll; Pres Sch; USAA; Comm Volntr; Chrch Yth Grp; Civil Air Pat; Drma Clb; Pep Squd; French Clb; Ch Chr; Yrbk (P); Major in Medicine; Master's Degree; Spelman College; Murray State U

FRANKE, REBECCA E; FRANKFORT, KY; FRANKLIN CTY HS; (SO); Ctznshp Aw; Duke TS; Hi Hnr Roll; WWAHSS; Comm Volntr, Chrch Yth Grp; FCA, Key Club; Ntl Beta Clb; Svce Clb; Acpl Chr; Chr; SP/M/VS; Sccr (J); Tennis (J); Y-Club - Co-President; Key Club Secretary; U of Kentucky

FRANKLIN, PAIGE; PADUCAH, KY; LONE OAK HS; (JR); Comm Volntr; Chrch Yth Grp; DARE; Emplmnt; FBLA; Quill & Scroll; Tchrs Aide; Vsity Clb; Chrldg; Tennis; Vsy Clb; Yrbk (E); PSI Teen Leader; Elementary Education

FRENCH, ASHLEY; DOVER, KY; MASON CTY HS; (SO); Ctznshp Aw; Hi Hnr Roll; Hnr Roll; Nat Hon Sy; Sci Fairs; St of Mnth; WWAHSS; Comm Volntr; Peer Tut/Med; Red Cr Aide; Dbte Team; Drma Clb; FCA; JSA; Ntl Beta Clb; Off Aide; Pep Squd; Prom Com; Bnd; Chr; Ch Chr; SP/M/VS; Chrldg (V L); Gmnstcs (V); PPSqd (V L); Stu Cncl (R); CR (R); Sch Ppr (R); Yrbk (R); Obstetrics; Forensic Science; Xavier U; Bellarmine U

FRENCH, BRANDON H; HAWESVILLE, KY; HANCOCK CTY HS; (SO); Hnr Roll; MVP; Pres Ac Ftns Aw; Yth Ldrshp Prog; 4-H; Chrch Yth Grp; DARE; FCA; Lttrmn Clb; Vsity Clb; Ch Chr; Bskball (J); Cr Ctry (V L); Track (V L); Middle School Cross Country Records; Math Award-Algebra I; Social Studies; Law; U of Kentucky; Campbellsville U

FRENCH, CRYSTAL D; SCOTTSVILLE, KY; ALLEN CTY HS; (FR); Duke TS; Hi Hnr Roll; Nat Hon Sy; Perf Att; Sci Fairs; Sci/Math Olympn; Comm Volntr; Chrch Yth Grp; FCCLA; Chinese Clb; Ch Chr; Dnce; FCCLA Member (Previously FHA); Community Service Volunteer; Health Sciences; Biology; Western Kentucky U; Eastern Kentucky U

FRY, MATT; BELLEVUE, KY; C E MC CORMICK AREA TECH CTR BELLEVUE HS; (JR); Hnr Roll; St of Mnth; Chess; Bsball (VJ L); Ftball (VJ L); Paint Ball Player; Military

FRYE, MELISSA; LOUISVILLE, KY; PLEASURE RIDGE PARK HS; (SO); Hnr Roll; St of Mnth; 4-H

FUGATE, KAYLA; FRANKLIN, KY; FRANKLIN-SIMPSON HS; (JR); Ctznshp Aw; Gov Hnr Prg; Hnr Roll; Nat Hon Sy; Sci Fairs; St Schl; WWAHSS; Comm Volntr; Peer Tut/Med; Chrch Yth Grp; Emplmnt; FBLA; Lib Aide; Ntl Beta Clb; Ntl FFA; Off Aide; Prom Com; Dnce; Chrldg (J); Cl Off (P); Stu Cncl (P); Sch Ppr (R); President of Gifted and Talented; Psychology; Journalism; Georgetown College; Western Kentucky U

FULKERSON, TARA N; BARDSTOWN, KY; NELSON CTY HS; (FR); Hnr Roll; WWAHSS; Hosp Aide; Key Club; Highest Average in Social Studies; Distinguished on CATS Test; Law; Medicine; U of Louisville; U of Kentucky

FULLER, LUKE; FT MITCHELL, KY; HOLY CROSS HS; (SO); DAR; Duke TS; Hnr Roll; Perf Att; St of Mnth; Comm Volntr; Sccr (J); Track (V); Stu Cncl (R); Accelerated Geometry Award; Thomas More College; U of Kentucky

FULMER, JESSICA N; BROOKSVILLE, KY; BRACKEN CTY HS; (JR); 4H Awd; Hnr Roll; MVP; Perf Att; WWAHSS; Comm Volntr; Peer Tut/Med; Red Cr Aide; 4-H; Chrch Yth Grp; FCA; FBLA; FCCLA; Ntl FFA; Prom Com; Tchrs Aide; Ch Chr; SP/M/VS; Chrldg (J); Hsbk Rdg (J); Scr Kpr (VJ); Tennis (V); Track (C); Vllyball (V L); Adv Cncl (T); Stu Cncl (P); Sch Ppr (R); Medicinal Researcher; Biological Scientist; Morehead State U; U of Kentucky

FURCHES, GINNY A; HAZEL, KY; CALLOWAY CTY HS; (SO); Duke TS; Hnr Roll; Nat Hon Sy; St of Mnth; USAA; FCA; Ntl Beta Clb; Pep Squd; Foreign Clb; Chrldg; Competitive Cheerleader; Journalism / Communications / Spanish; Political Science

FURNISH, NICOLE; BARDSTOWN, KY; NELSON CTY HS; (SO); 4H Awd; All Am Sch; Hnr Roll; WWAHSS; Peer Tut/Med; 4-H; Drma Clb; Key Club; Bnd; Mch Bnd; Pep Bnd; SP/M/VS; Cr Ctry (V); Track (V); English; History; Eastern Kentucky U

FURROW, MORGAN R; FRANKLIN, KY; ALLEN CTY HS; (FR); All Am Sch; Ctznshp Aw; Duke TS; Hi Hnr Roll; Nat Sci Aw; Sci Fairs; Sci/Math Olympn; WWAHSS; Yth Ldrshp Prog; Comm Volntr; Peer Tut/Med; FCA; Ntl Beta Clb; P to P St Amb Prg; Clr Grd; Pep Bnd; Bskball (J); Yrbk (E, P); HOSA; Modeling; Pharmacy School; Television Journalism; U of Georgia; U of Southern California

FUTRELL, ERIC; LOUISVILLE, KY; TRINITY HS; (SR); Duke TS; F Lan Hn Soc; Hi Hnr Roll; Hnr Roll; WWAHSS; Comm Volntr; Peer Tut/Med; Red Cr Aide; FCA; Spanish Clb; Bskball (J L); Golf (V CL); CR (R); Political Science; Law; Florida State U

GABBARD, BETHANY; BEREA, KY; BEREA CMTY HS; (JR); Hnr Roll; MVP; Otst Ac Ach Awd; Comm Volntr; Dbte Team; Drma Clb; FTA; Key Club; Ntl Beta Clb; Tchrs Aide; Bnd; SP/M/VS; Sccr (VJ L); Tennis (V CL); Stu Cncl (R); Sch Ppr (E, R); President of Future Educators of America; Member of Mock Trial Team; Anthropology; Marketing; College of William and Mary; Centre College

GAGLIARDI, ANTHONY; MT WASHINGTON, KY; BULLITT EAST; (SO); Hnr Roll; Perf Att; DARE; FBLA; Outdrs Clb

GAINES, ANN M; LAWRENCEBURG, KY; HARRODSBURG AREA TECH CTR; (JR); St of Mnth; WWAHSS; Emplmnt; FCCLA; Voc Ind Clb Am; E-Town Comm. Coll.-Diesel Technician; Elizabethtown Community College; Central Kentucky Technical College

GALAVIZ GONZALEZ, MAGDA Y; MAYFIELD, KY; MAYFIELD HS; (FR); Perf Att; Peer Tut/Med; DARE; Lib Aide; P to P St Amb Prg; SADD; Tchrs Aide; Sccr (V); Teacher; Nurse

GALLAGHER, LEVI; DOVER, KY; AUGUSTA INDEPENDENT SCH; (JR); Hnr Roll; MVP; Perf Att; Comm Volntr; Drma Clb; Emplmnt; FCCLA; Pep Squd; Prom Com; Scouts; SADD; Bskball (VJC); Cl Off (R); Xavier U; Northern Kentucky U

GAMEZ, MADISON; LOUISVILLE, KY; MANUAL HS; (SO); 4H Awd; Fut Prb Slvr; Hi Hnr Roll; MVP; Nat Stu Ath Day Aw; Pres Ac Ftns Aw; Sci Fairs; Yth Ldrshp Prog; 4-H; Chrch Yth Grp; DARE; Emplmnt; FCA; Jr Ach; Mus Clb; Ntl Beta Clb; Chr; Ch Chr; Bskball (J); Dvng (V); Fld Hky (JC); Skiing (V); Swmg (V); Stu Cncl (R); Marine Biologist; Arizona State U; Florida State U

GANDY, MEGAN; MAGNOLIA, KY; HART CTY HS; (SO); Hi Hnr Roll; Hnr Roll; MVP; Otst Ac Ach Awd; Sci Fairs; Sci/Math Olympn; St of Mnth; WWAHSS; Yth Ldrshp Prog; Comm Volntr; Chrch Yth Grp; Drma Clb; Emplmnt; JSA; Mth Clb/Tm; Svce Clb; Korean Clb; Bnd; Jzz Bnd; Mch Bnd; SP/M/VS; Chrldg (V); Cl Off (S); Stu Cncl (S); Business; Politics; Princeton U; Brigham Young U

GARRETT, ALEXIS; LOUISVILLE, KY; DUPONT MANUAL HS; (JR); Hnr Roll; WWAHSS; Chrch Yth Grp; Emplmnt; Ch Chr; Ob/Gyn; U North Carolina-Chapel Hill; Ohio State U

GARRETT, DEBORAH A; BELTON, KY; MUHLENBERG SOUTH HS; (SR); Hnr Roll; Perf Att; Peer Tut/Med; DECA; Emplmnt; FBLA; Ntl Beta Clb; Tchrs Aide; Senior Beta; Medical Field; Eastern Kentucky U; U of Louisville

GARRETT, HANNAH M; CARLISLE, KY; NICHOLAS CTY HS; (FR); Hnr Roll; Nat Hon Sy; Perf Att; USAA; WWAHSS; 4-H; Chrch Yth Grp; Drma Clb; FCA; Pep Squd; SP/M/VS; Chrldg (V L); Gmnstcs; Who's Who Among High School Students; USAA; Athletic Trainer; Labor and Delivery Nurse; Eastern Kentucky U; Morehead State U

GARRUTO, CHRISTINA M; LOUISVILLE, KY; DUPONT MANUAL HS; (JR); F Lan Hn Soc; Hi Hnr Roll; Nat Hon Sy; Perf Att; WWAHSS; Comm Volntr; Peer Tut/Med; Emplmnt; Key Club; Mod UN; Ntl Beta Clb; Stu Cncl; Executive Council (Dupont Manual); Communications; Tulane; George Washington U in St Louis

GAYHART, ALEXANDER; KITE, KY; KNOTT CTY CTRL HS; (SO); Hnr Roll; ArtClub; DARE; Ntl Beta Clb; Spch Team; Film Director; U of Kentucky

GE, CHONGTANG; LOUISVILLE, KY; SOUTHERN HS; (JR); Gov Hnr Prg; Hi Hnr Roll; Hnr Roll; Nat Hon Sy; Otst Ac Ach Awd; Perf Att; St Schl; WWAHSS; Comm Volntr; Peer Tut/Med; Emplmnt; FCA; Key Club; Lib Aide; Mth Clb/Tm; Ntl Beta Clb; Off Aide; Quiz Bowl; Chr; SP/M/VS; Tennis (V); Club Officers; Governor's Scholar; Lawyer; International Relations; U of Kentucky; Georgetown U

GEDDES, JANELLE; LEXINGTON, KY; P L DUNBAR HS; (FR); 4H Awd; Duke TS; F Lan Hn Soc; Hi Hnr Roll; Hnr Roll; Pres Ac Ftns Aw; Pres Sch; Sci Fairs; Sci/Math Olympn; WWAHSS; Comm Volntr; 4-H; DARE; Jr Ach; Mth Clb/Tm; Mod UN; Ntl Beta Clb; NtlFrnscLg; Spch Team; Orch; Sccr (J); Tennis (J); Doctor of Philosophy (Ph.D); Juris Doctor (J.D.); Stanford; Princeton

GETZ, MICHAEL A; LOUISVILLE, KY; LOUISVILLE MALE HS; (FR); Bnd; Bsball (J); Ice Hky (V); Production; Sound Engineering; Denver U; Miami U Ohio

GIBSON, BREA M; RAVEN, KY; KNOTT CTY AREA TECH CTR; (SO); 4H Awd; Hnr Roll; Nat Hon Sy; Sci Fairs; WWAHSS; Comm Volntr; Peer Tut/Med; ArtClub; DARE; Lttrmn Clb; Ntl Beta Clb; Tech Clb; Vllyball (VJ); Major in Fine Arts; Master/Bachelors Degree in Art; Morehead State U; Corcoran College of Art & Design

GIBSON, COURTNEY; GLENDALE, KY; CTRL HARDIN HS; (SO); 4H Awd; Duke TS; Fut Prb Slvr; Hi Hnr Roll; Pres Ac Ftns Aw; FBLA; Ntl Beta Clb; Pep Squd; Vsity Clb; Vsy Clb (V); Academic Team; Psychology; Medical; U of Kentucky; Bellarmine U

GIBSON, JOSH; OWENTON, KY; (SO); Hnr Roll; MVP; Perf Att; Outdrs Clb; Bsball (J)

GIBSON, LESLIE R; MANCHESTER, KY; CLAY CTY HS; (FR); Ctznshp Aw; Duke TS; Fut Prb Slvr; Hi Hnr Roll; Otst Ac Ach Awd; Perf Att; St of Mnth; Peer Tut/Med; Mth Clb/Tm; Pep Squd; SP/M/VS; Bskball; Tennis (V); U.S. Achievement Academy National Award Winner; Distinguished Scholar; PHD / in the Medical Field; U of Kentucky; Alice Lloyd College

GILDERBLOOM, MAX; LOUISVILLE, KY; ATHERTON HS; (SO); Hi Hnr Roll; Hnr Roll; St of Mnth; Peer Tut/Med; Mth Clb/Tm; Private Kung Fu / Martial Arts Lessons; Tibetan Buddhist / Tibetan Language Class; Psychology; Medicine; UC Berkeley; Stanford U

GILES, CHRISTINA; VERSAILLES, KY; WOODFORD CTY HS; (SO); Hi Hnr Roll; Comm Volntr; Key Club; Pep Squd; Dnce; Sccr (V L); CR (R); Medical Science Medal Academic All-State in Soccer; Freshman Homecoming Attendant/Soph. Court; Physician, Pre-Med; Clinical Research-Biology; Vanderbilt U; Transylvania U

GILREATH, JORDAN; MARSHES SIDING, KY; MC CREARY CTRL HS; (JR); Hnr Roll; Pres Sch; Sci Fairs; St of Mnth; DARE; Outdrs Clb; ROTC; Scouts; SADD; Received the Highest Possible Grades on My CATS Test; Teaching At High School Level; Medicine; U of Kentucky; U of Tennessee

GIST, DERRICK; LOUISVILLE, KY; FERNCREEK TRADITIONAL HS; (FR); Ctznshp Aw; Perf Att; Sci Fairs; Chrch Yth Grp; Basketball W/J-Town Optimist; Basketball W/Derrick Anderson's Camp; Computer Engineer; Veterinarian; U of Louisville; U of Kentucky

GIVIDEN, JONATHAN E; DRY RIDGE, KY; GRANT CTY HS; (SR); Gov Hnr Prg; Nat Hon Sy; Perf Att; Valdctrian; WWAHSS; Comm Volntr; ArtClub; Chrch Yth Grp; Cmptr Clb; Art Awards; Computer Engineering; U of Louisville

GLASS, MICHELE L; HOPKINSVILLE, KY; HOPKINSVILLE HS; (FR); Hnr Roll; Otst Ac Ach Awd; Chrch Yth Grp; Emplmnt; Lib Aide; Ntl Beta Clb; Pep Squd; Chr; Cr Ctry (V); Sftball (V); Anesthetist; Radiologist; U of Kentucky; Murray State U

GLASS, TOMMY R; OWENTON, KY; OWEN CO. HS; (JR); Hnr Roll; WWAHSS

GLASSCOCK, KELLI; LEBANON, KY; MARION CTY HS; (JR); 4H Awd; Hi Hnr Roll; Hnr Roll; Otst Ac Ach Awd; Perf Att; St of Mnth; Yth Ldrshp Prog; Comm Volntr; 4-H; Emplmnt; Key Club; Ntl Beta Clb; Pep Squd; Prom Com; Tchrs Aide; Spanish Clb; SP/M/VS; Adv Cncl (R); Cl Off (R); Stu Cncl (R); CR (R); Ranked 1 in Class 9th & 10th; Business

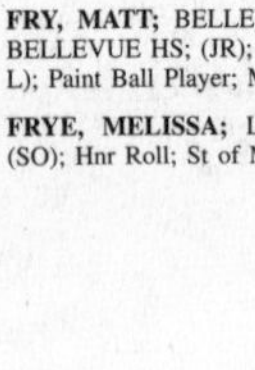
Gist, Derrick
Ferncreek Traditional HS
Louisville, KY

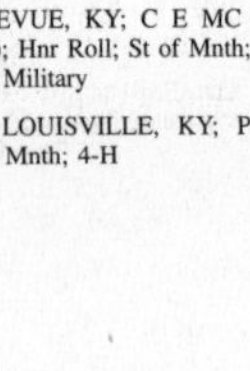
Gayhart, Alexander
Knott Cty Ctrl HS
Kite, KY

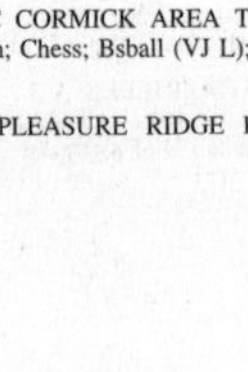
Garrett, Deborah A
Muhlenberg South HS
Belton, KY

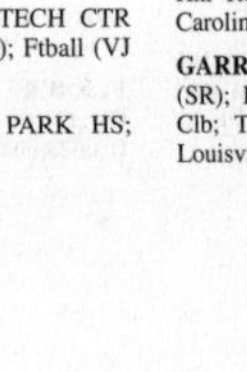
Foster, Sierra N
Murray HS
Murray, KY

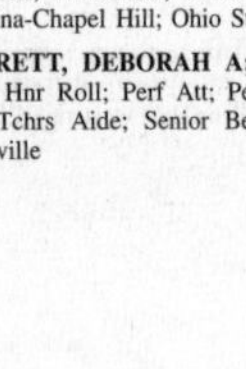
Foster, Christina
Louisville Male HS
Louisville, KY

National
Honor Roll
Spring 2005

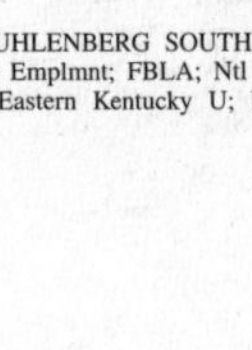
Flora, Sarah E
Bryan Station HS
Lexington, KY

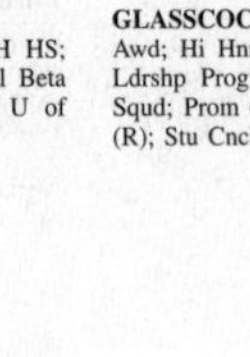
Furrow, Morgan R
Allen Cty HS
Franklin, KY

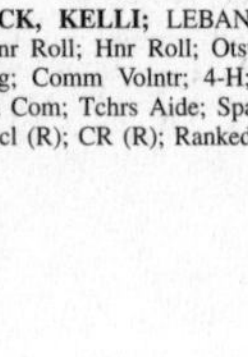
Garruto, Christina M
Dupont Manual HS
Louisville, KY

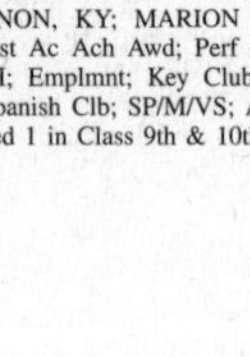
Gibson, Brea M
Knott Cty Area Tech Ctr
Raven, KY

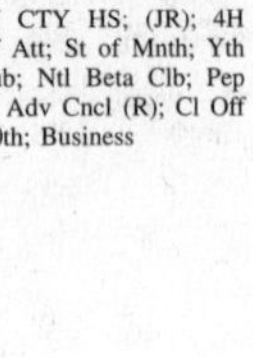
Giles, Christina
Woodford Cty HS
Versailles, KY

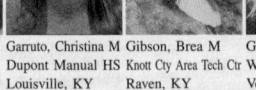

GODBEY, NATALIE; LIBERTY, KY; CASEY CTY HS; (JR); Hi Hnr Roll; Nat Ldrshp Svc; Nat Sci Aw; Otst Ac Ach Awd; Perf Att; Sci Fairs; Sci/Math Olympn; St Schl; Yth Ldrshp Prog; Comm Volntr; Peer Tut/Med; Chrch Yth Grp; FCA; FTA; Ntl Beta Clb; Pep Squd; Prom Com; Sci Clb; Stg Cre; Bskball (V); Sftball (V); Wt Lftg (V); Adv Cncl; Cl Off; Stu Cncl; CR; Yrbk; Rogers Scholars; Postponing Sexual Involvement; Orthopedic Surgeon; Dietician; Western Kentucky U; U of Kentucky

GOETZ, CHRISTOPHER W; BURLINGTON, KY; LARRY A RYLE HS; (SR); Hnr Roll; WWAHSS; Chrch Yth Grp; FBLA; Voc Ind Clb Am; Ch Chr; Ftball (J); 5th Place At National Comp. for VICA; 1st Place At State Comp. for VICA

GOODE, ERIN L; SPRINGFIELD, KY; WASHINGTON CTY HS; (SO); 4H Awd; Hnr Roll; Yth Ldrshp Prog; Comm Volntr; 4-H; Chrch Yth Grp; DARE; DECA; Pep Squd; Prom Com; Tmpl Yth Grp; Vsity Clb; Chrldg (V); Public Relations; Lexington Community College; St Catherine College

GOODMAN, SARAH; HICKMAN, KY; FULTON CTY HS; (FR); Duke TS; Hnr Roll; Comm Volntr; 4-H; Chrch Yth Grp; FCA; FBLA; Ntl Beta Clb; Schol Bwl; Sci Clb; Bskball (V); Cl Off (P); AAU Girls Basketball; Play Piano

GOODRICH, CRYSTAL L; OWENTON, KY; OWEN CTY HS; (FR); Sci Fairs; St of Mnth; Peer Tut/Med; 4-H; DARE; Drma Clb; Ntl FFA; Outdrs Clb; SADD; Bnd; Chr; Clr Grd; Cr Ctry; Yrbk; Forensic Science/Nursing

GOODWIN, KAYLA E; VANCEBURG, KY; LEWIS CTY HS; (JR); WWAHSS; ROTC; Tchrs Aide; Bnd; Clr Grd; Drl Tm; Mch Bnd; PP Ftbl (J); Doctor (MD); Shawnee State U; Morehead State U

GORD, DOUG; LOUISVILLE, KY; TRINITY HS; (SR); Hnr Roll; Emplmnt; Photog; Ice Hky (V C); Sch Ppr (R, P); Yrbk (R, P); Journalism; Economics; U of Kentucky

GORDON, LINDSEY C; RICHMOND, KY; MODEL HS; (SO); Emplmnt; Key Club; Pep Squd; Chr; Chrldg (V); U of Kentucky

GORDON, SHAMICA; NEWPORT, KY; NEWPORT HS; (SO); Ctznshp Aw; Hnr Roll; Otst Ac Ach Awd; St of Mnth; Hosp Aide; DARE; Drma Clb; FBLA; Key Club; Drl Tm; Cr Ctry (J); Sftball (VJ); CR (R); Upward Bound; S.O.S. Club; Corp. Lawyer; Tennessee State U; U of Cincinnati

GOSNEY, SARAH R; BUTLER, KY; PENDLETON CTY HS; (FR); Hnr Roll; Perf Att; WWAHSS; Yth Ldrshp Prog; Hosp Aide; FBLA; Svce Clb; Chr; Vllyball; Stu Cncl (R); Volleyball Club-Team Traveling; Nursing; Northern KY U; Thomas More

GOSSETT, FELICIA M; WILMORE, KY; WEST JESSAMINE HS; (FR); 4H Awd; Hnr Roll; Otst Ac Ach Awd; WWAHSS; Dnce; Chrldg (V); Lawyer or Cosmetologist

GOWENS, ASHLEY; LEXINGTON, KY; LAFAYETTE HS; (SR); Hnr Roll; Nat Hon Sy; Otst Ac Ach Awd; Pres Ac Ftns Aw; Emplmnt; Acpl Chr; Chr; Orch; PP Ftbl (V); Sccr (V L); National Honor Society; Physical Therapy; Sports Medicine; Transylvania U

GRABOVA, KRISTINA; LOUISVILLE, KY; LOUISVILLE MALE HS; (FR); Comm Volntr; Chrch Yth Grp; Emplmnt; Mus Clb; Pep Squd; Bnd; Clr Grd; Flg Crps; Mch Bnd; Gmnstcs (V); Lcrsse (J); Sccr (J); Cancer Research; Architect; Murray State U; UK

GRALHEER, LORA E; LEXINGTON, KY; LEXINGTON CHRN AC HS; (SO); Ctznshp Aw; Duke TS; Hi Hnr Roll; MVP; USAA; FCA; Ntl Beta Clb; Bskball (VJ L); PP Ftbl (V); Sccr (V L); ODP State Team Beta Club; Kentucky Youth Assembly

GRAVES, AMBER D; WINCHESTER, KY; GEORGE ROGERS CLARK HS; (JR); 4H Awd; Hi Hnr Roll; Hnr Roll; Otst Ac Ach Awd; St of Mnth; WWAHSS; Comm Volntr; Peer Tut/Med; 4-H; Chrch Yth Grp; Emplmnt; Off Aide; Scouts; Tchrs Aide; Bnd; Ch Chr; Mch Bnd; Yrbk (R); Peer Club; Youth Group Secretary; Real Estate Management; Teaching (All Levels); U of Kentucky; Eastern Kentucky U

GRAY, ANN A M; PARK CITY, KY; BARREN CTY HS; (SO); F Lan Hn Soc; Hi Hnr Roll; Otst Ac Ach Awd; DARE; FBLA; Key Club; Ntl Beta Clb; Pep Squd; P to P St Amb Prg; National Beta Club, Spanish Honor Society; Pep Club, Key Club, Beta Service Award; Child Psychiatry; Forensic Science / Pathology; U of Kentucky

GRAY, BRITTANY J; LAWRENCEBURG, KY; ANDERSON CTY HS; (FR); Hnr Roll; Nat Hon Sy; Perf Att; St of Mnth; WWAHSS; Chrch Yth Grp; FCA; FCCLA; Scouts; French Clb; Chr; Swmg; Forensic Scientist; Police Officer; U of Kentucky; U of Florida

GREENWELL, ASHLEY; BARDSTOWN, KY; NELSON CTY; (SR); 4H Awd; All Am Sch; St of Mnth; WWAHSS; 4-H; Emplmnt; Ntl FFA; Quiz Bowl; Bskball; Hsbk Rdg; Skt Tgt Sh; FFA Green Hand Degree; FFA Chapter Degree; Education; Equine; St Catherine's

GREER, KELSIE; FARMINGTON, KY; CALLOWAY CO HS; (FR); 4H Awd; 4-H; Sccr (J)

GREER, LINDSEY; FRANKLIN, KY; FRANKLIN-SIMPSON HS; (JR); Hi Hnr Roll; WWAHSS; Comm Volntr; ArtClub; Chrch Yth Grp; Emplmnt; FBLA; Ntl Beta Clb; Art & Design; Photography

GREER, TRAVIS R; VERSAILLES, KY; WOODFORD CTY HS; (FR); Hi Hnr Roll; Hnr Roll; Perf Att; Pres Ac Ftns Aw; Pres Sch; Sci Fairs; USAA; CARE; Comm Volntr; Peer Tut/Med; Chess; DARE; Emplmnt; Sci Clb; Scouts; SADD; Tchrs Aide; Wdwrkg Clb; Bnd; Ftball (VJ L); Wt Lftg (VJ); Wrstlg (VJ); Sch Ppr (R); Surgeon; Cardiovascular; U of Kentucky; Duke U

GREGORY, JENNIFER; AUBURN, KY; LOGAN CTY HS; (SO); Perf Att; ArtClub; Photog; Welding; Photography

GREGORY, WILLIAM; RUSSELLVILLE, KY; LOGAN CTY HS; (FR); Ntl FFA; Ftball (V); Lawyer; Engineer; Murray State U

GRESCHEL, SHAWN M; LOUISVILLE, KY; ST XAVIER HS; (SR); Hi Hnr Roll; Hnr Roll; MVP; Nat Stu Ath Day Aw; Comm Volntr; Peer Tut/Med; Biology Clb; Emplmnt; Swmg (V L); USS Swimming - Captain 2 Yrs; BS in Biology / BA in English; Medical Doctorate; Transylvania U; U of Louisville

GRIDER, LESLI J; LIBERTY, KY; CASEY CTY HS; (SR); Hnr Roll; Nat Hon Sy; WWAHSS; Comm Volntr; Chrch Yth Grp; FCA; FBLA; Ntl Beta Clb; Ntl FFA; Off Aide; Pep Squd; Prom Com; Sftball (V C); Physical Therapist; Accounting; Eastern Kentucky U; Campbellsville U

GRIDER, SETH E; SCIENCE HILL, KY; PULASKI CTY HS; (FR); Hnr Roll; Perf Att; Chess; Ntl Beta Clb; Bnd; Mch Bnd; Pep Bnd

GRISE, TEIA; RUSSELLVILLE, KY; LOGAN CTY HS; (SO); Hnr Roll; Perf Att; Pres Ac Ftns Aw; St of Mnth; Yth Ldrshp Prog; Comm Volntr; Peer Tut/Med; Red Cr Aide; Chrch Yth Grp; Emplmnt; ROTC; Scouts; Tchrs Aide; Ch Chr; Clr Grd; CR (P); Venturing Crew (BSA), Silver Award (Girl Scouts); Rifle Team (ROTC), National Physical Fitness Award; Medical Degree; Business Degree; Western Kentucky U; U of Louisville, NKU

GRISE III, THOMAS M; LOUISVILLE, KY; ATHERTON HS; (FR); Duke TS; Hi Hnr Roll; Nat Hon Sy; Otst Ac Ach Awd; Comm Volntr; Chrch Yth Grp; Emplmnt; Scouts; Ftball (VJ L); Boy Scouts-Eagle Candidate; Engineering

GROSS, ANNA; LATONIA, KY; SCOTT HS; (JR); Hnr Roll; MVP; Perf Att; Pres Sch; Chrch Yth Grp; Emplmnt; Prom Com; French Clb; Chrldg (V L); Sftball (VJCL); Vllyball (J L); Cl Off (P); Stu Cncl (R); CR (R); Dean's List; Chemistry Degree; Pre-Med; Morehead State U; U of Kentucky

GROSS, JERRI A; JACKSON, KY; JACKSON CITY SCH; (SR); Hnr Roll; Nat Hon Sy; Otst Ac Ach Awd; WWAHSS; Peer Tut/Med; HO'Br Yth Ldrshp; Pep Squd; Clr Grd; Chrldg (V); Sftball (V); Cl Off (P); Forensic Science; Education "Math"; Morehead State U; Hazard Community Technical College

GROSS, THOMAS D; CUMBERLAND, KY; CUMBERLAND HS; (JR); Hi Hnr Roll; Hnr Roll; Nat Ldrshp Svc; US Army Sch Ath Aw; Peer Tut/Med; DARE; Emplmnt; Pep Squd; Prom Com; ROTC; Voc Ind Clb Am; Bsball (J); National Beta Club; ROTC; General Physician; Accounting; Penn State U; Franklin & Marshall

GROVE, MACKENZIE; CORBIN, KY; CORBIN HS; (JR); Duke TS; Hi Hnr Roll; WWAHSS; Peer Tut/Med; ArtClub; FTA; Mod UN; Ntl Beta Clb; Pep Squd; Adv Cncl (R); Member of CHS YMCA Club; Elementary Education

GROVES, JUSTINE M; COLUMBIA, KY; ADAIR CTY HS; (SO); Ctznshp Aw; Hnr Roll; Chrch Yth Grp; FBLA; Chr; Dnce; Bskball (J); Track (V); Sch Ppr (R); Criminal Justice; Forensic Pathologist; U of Louisville; ITT Technical Institute

GROVES, MATT; AUGUSTA, KY; AUGUSTA HS; (SO); All Am Sch; Ctznshp Aw; Hi Hnr Roll; Hnr Roll; Nat Hon Sy; Nat Ldrshp Svc; St of Mnth; USAA; WWAHSS; Yth Ldrshp Prog; Chrch Yth Grp; Drma Clb; FCCLA; Ntl Beta Clb; Pep Squd; Ch Chr; Pep Bnd; Bsball (V); Bskball (V); Tennis (V); Sch Ppr (E); Negligence Attorney; Photography; Northern Kentucky U; Sullivan U

GRUBB, AARON; GIRDLER, KY; BARBOURVILLE HS; (JR); All Am Sch; Hnr Roll; Nat Hon Sy; WWAHSS; Bskball; Golf; Bachelor's in Chemistry / Math / Medical Field; Teaching; Union College; U of Kentucky

GRUBB, COURTNEY; MANCHESTER, KY; CLAY CTY HS; (FR); Fut Prb Slvr; Nat Mrt Fin; Otst Ac Ach Awd; St of Mnth; Comm Volntr; Chrch Yth Grp; DARE; FBLA; Lib Aide; Pep Squd; Tchrs Aide; Dnce; Pep Bnd; Cl Off (V); Lawyer; U California of Los Angeles; Charlotte At North Carolina

GRUBB, KASEY; LOUISVILLE, KY; PLEASURE RIDGE PARK HS; (SO); Ctznshp Aw; Hnr Roll; St of Mnth; 4-H; DARE; Jr Ach; Tchrs Aide; Interior Designer; Dermatologist; U of Kentucky; Sullivan U

GRUBER, KELLY D; BURLINGTON, KY; CONNER HS; (SO); Duke TS; Hi Hnr Roll; Hnr Roll; Nat Hon Sy; Perf Att; Sci Fairs; WWAHSS; Chrch Yth Grp; Emplmnt; Chr; Cr Ctry (V); Scr Kpr (V); Sftball (V); Track (V); Cougarette - Wrestling Support Team; National Honors Society; Psychology; Teaching; U of Kentucky

GUELTZOW, LAURA C; LOUISVILLE, KY; ASSUMPTION HS; (SR); Duke TS; Hi Hnr Roll; Hnr Roll; Nat Hon Sy; WWAHSS; Comm Volntr; Hosp Aide; Peer Tut/Med; Chrch Yth Grp; Mod UN; MuAlphaTh; Ntl Beta Clb; Prom Com; Scouts; Svce Clb; French Clb; Bskball (VJ L); Cl Off (R); Rowing

GUERRA, HILDALICIA; LOUISVILLE, KY; SENECA HS; (JR); Hnr Roll; Otst Ac Ach Awd; Perf Att; WWAHSS; Peer Tut/Med; Red Cr Aide; Emplmnt; FCA; Key Club; Lttrmn Clb; Ntl Beta Clb; Prom Com; SADD; French Clb; Bsball; Fld Hky (JC); PP Ftbl; Wrstlg; Played in Orchestra; Taking 3 College Classes This Year; Medicine; Sciences; U of Louisville; U of Kentucky

GUESS, GARRETT R; EDDYVILLE, KY; LYON CTY HS; (JR); Hnr Roll; Nat Hon Sy; USAA; WWAHSS; Ntl Beta Clb; Pep Squd; Jzz Bnd; Mch Bnd; Pep Bnd; SP/M/VS; CR; Tri-M Honor Society; State STLP Conference Associate; Murray State U; U of Louisville

GUFFEY, BRITTANY S; ALBANY, KY; CLINTON CTY HS; (SO); Ctznshp Aw; Hnr Roll; Comm Volntr; Chrch Yth Grp; FCA; FBLA; Chr; Ch Chr; SP/M/VS; Cl Off (P); Stu Cncl (P); Psychology; Poetry; Western Kentucky U; Transylvania U

GUY, JASMINE; BUTLER, KY; PENDLETON CTY HS; (JR); Ctznshp Aw; Gov Hnr Prg; Hi Hnr Roll; Hnr Roll; MVP; Otst Ac Ach Awd; Perf Att; Chrch Yth Grp; DECA; Emplmnt; FTA; Lttrmn Clb; Photog; Chrldg (V L); Gmnstcs (VJ); Sftball (VJ L); Vllyball (VJ L); Principal's Award; Best-Defensive Player; History; Art; Northern Kentucky U

HABERMEHL, KIM; DOVER, KY; AUGUSTA HS; (JR); Hnr Roll; MVP; Perf Att; St of Mnth; WWAHSS; Peer Tut/Med; DARE; FCCLA; Ntl Beta Clb; Pep Squd; Prom Com; Vsity Clb; Bnd; Pep Bnd; Bskball (V C); Tennis (V); Cl Off (T); Sch Ppr (R); All Region Team; Class 'A' Tournament Team; Education; Morehead State; U of KY

HADLEY, MEGAN; COLUMBIA, KY; ADAIR CTY HS; (SO); Hi Hnr Roll; Hnr Roll; WWAHSS; Peer Tut/Med; 4-H; ArtClub; Chrch Yth Grp; DARE; Scouts; Ch Chr; Psychology; CSI; Duke U

HAFER, JUSTIN D; TOLLESBORO, KY; LEWIS CTY HS; (JR); Hnr Roll; ROTC; Sci Clb; Tchrs Aide; Clr Grd; Drl Tm; JROTC; Computer Science; Military; Morehead State U; U of Kentucky

HAGAN, ALEX H; BARDSTOWN, KY; NELSON CTY HS; (JR); 4H Awd; Gov Hnr Prg; Hnr Roll; Nat Hon Sy; USAA; WWAHSS; 4-H; Chrch Yth Grp; Key Club; Ntl FFA; Sccr (V); Track (J); Stu Cncl; Business; U of Kentucky

HAGAN, CHRISTINE; WHITESVILLE, KY; TRINITY HS; (JR); Hnr Roll; Pres Ac Ftns Aw; Comm Volntr; Hosp Aide; Peer Tut/Med; Chrch Yth Grp; DARE; Emplmnt; Lib Aide; Sci Clb; Scouts; Bnd; Ch Chr; Stg Cre; Vllyball (J); Yrbk (E)

HAGAN, GEORGE H; BARDSTOWN, KY; NELSON CTY HS; (FR); 4H Awd; Hnr Roll; St of Mnth; WWAHSS; 4-H; Chrch Yth Grp; Key Club; Ntl FFA; Sccr (J); Stu Cncl; Business; U of Kentucky

HAGAN, JOSHUA T; TOMPKINSVILLE, KY; MONROE CTY HS; (SO); Hi Hnr Roll; Hnr Roll; Sci Fairs; Ntl FFA; Pep Squd; Kentucky Tech School Standards; Western Kentucky U; U of Louisville

HALEY, CHRIS; MANITOU, KY; HOPKINS CTY CTRL HS; (SO); Hnr Roll; MVP; Otst Ac Ach Awd; Perf Att; Spec Olymp Vol; 4-H; Chrch Yth Grp; DARE; DECA; Ntl FFA; Pep Squd; Tchrs Aide; Ch Chr; Bskball (VJ); Communications; Technology; U of Louisville; U of North Carolina

HALEY, SARAH; BENTON, KY; MARSHALL CTY HS; (SO); Duke TS; Hnr Roll; Perf Att; Sci Fairs; Comm Volntr; Hab For Humty Volntr; Chrch Yth Grp; DARE; Emplmnt; FBLA; FCCLA; Mod UN; Ntl Beta Clb; Pep Squd; Cr Ctry (VJ L); Sccr (V CL); Track (VJ L); Cl Off (V); (Soccer) Assistant Coach for Handicapped Children Called Tops; Treasurer Church Youth Group; Pharmacy; Child Psychology; Murray State U; U of Kentucky

HALL, ANGELA; FRANKFORT, KY; CORNERSTONE; (SR); Hi Hnr Roll; Hnr Roll; MVP; Otst Ac Ach Awd; Valdctrian; WWAHSS; Chrch Yth Grp; Key Club; Off Aide; Ch Chr; Bskball (VJCL); Sccr (V CL); Stu Cncl (S); CR (R); Yrbk (P); Miss Basketball for KCAA; Medicine; Lee U; U of Kentucky

HALL, COLLEEN; LOUISVILLE, KY; ATHERTON HS; (JR); Hi Hnr Roll; Hnr Roll; Perf Att; Comm Volntr; Hab For Humty Volntr; 4-H; Chrch Yth Grp; DARE; Emplmnt; FCA; FBLA; Ntl Beta Clb; Scouts; Ch Chr; Orch; Fld Hky (J L); Interior Design; Business Management; U of Kentucky; Western Kentucky U

HALL, DONNIE J; NEON, KY; FLEMING NEON HS; (SO); Ctznshp Aw; Gov Hnr Prg; Hi Hnr Roll; Otst Ac Ach Awd; Perf Att; Valdctrian; Cmptr Clb; Pep Squd; Bnd; Mch Bnd; Pep Bnd; Bskball (VJ); Marched in Band At Inaugural Parade; Devote Time to Ministries in Church; Become a Neurologist; Law; U of Kentucky; U of Cincinnati

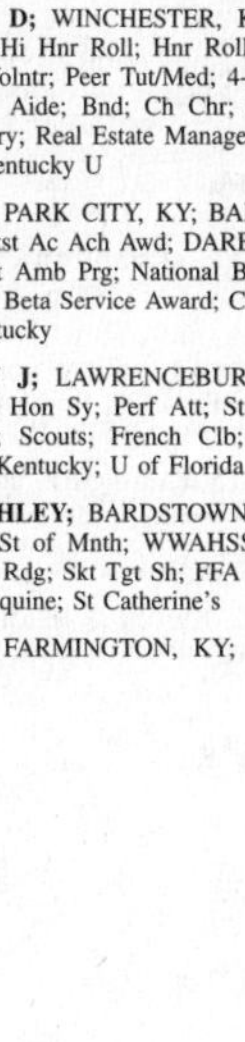
Guess, Garrett R
Lyon Cty HS
Eddyville, KY

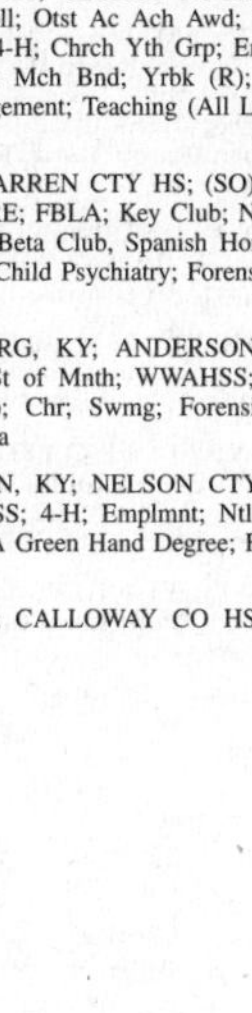
Gross, Anna
Scott HS
Latonia, KY

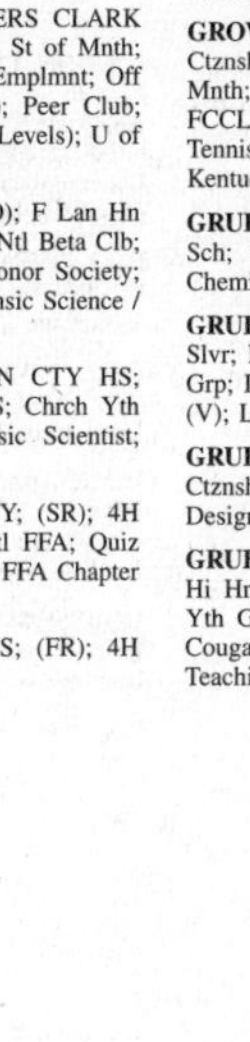
Greer, Travis R
Woodford Cty HS
Versailles, KY

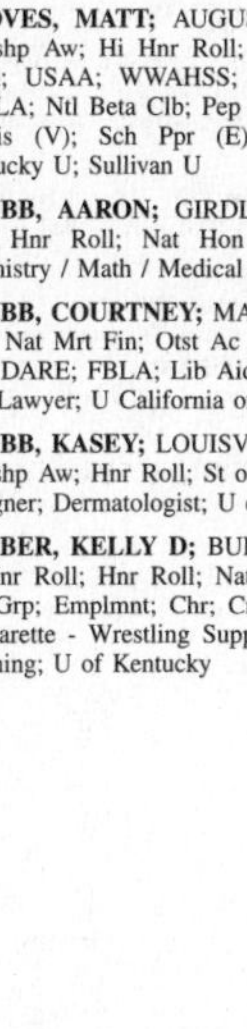
Greenwell, Ashley
Nelson Cty
Bardstown, KY

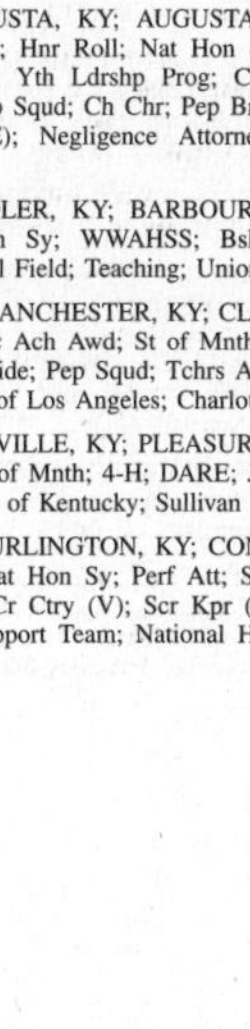
Goodrich, Crystal L
Owen Cty HS
Owenton, KY

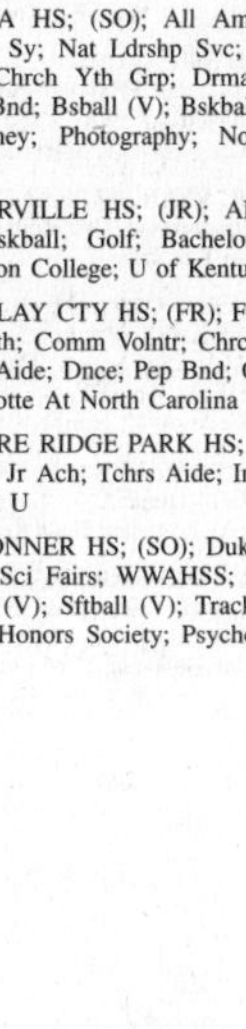
Goodwin, Kayla E
Lewis Cty HS
Vanceburg, KY

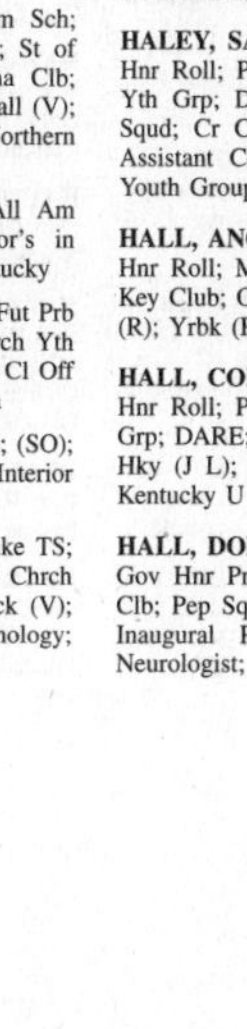
Greschel, Shawn M
St Xavier HS
Louisville, KY

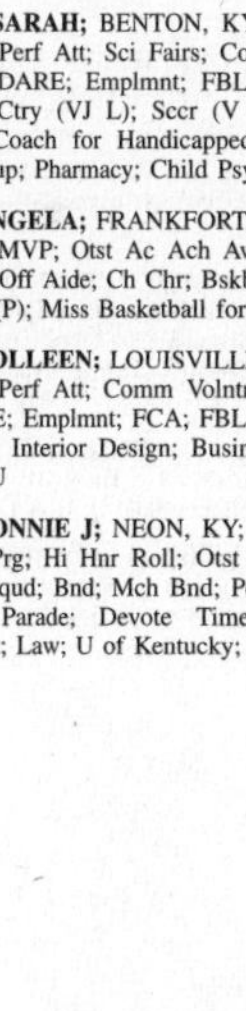
Grubb, Kasey
Pleasure Ridge Park HS
Louisville, KY

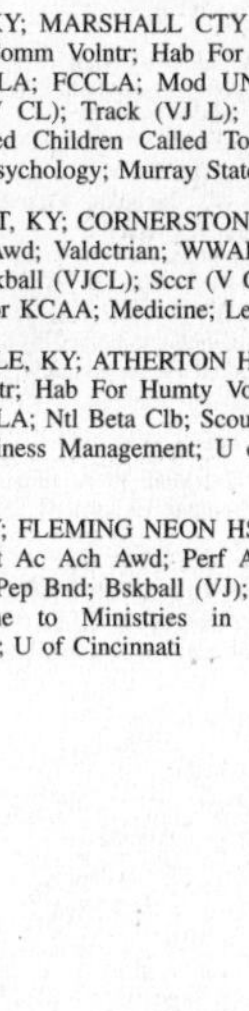
Guy, Jasmine
Pendleton Cty HS
Butler, KY

HALL, KRISTY; NEON, KY; FLEMING NEON HS; (SR); Gov Hnr Prg; Hi Hnr Roll; Hnr Roll; Nat Hon Sy; Perf Att; Pres Sch; Valdctrian; WWAHSS; Comm Volntr; Peer Tut/Med; Chrch Yth Grp; Emplmnt; Photog; Prom Com; Tchrs Aide; Sch Ppr (R, P); Yrbk (R, P); Usher for 2004 Graduation; Highest GPA in English III; Registered Nurse; Physical Therapy; Southeast Community College; Hazard Community College

HALL, TIARRA L S; LEBANON, KY; MARION CTY HS; (SO); 4H Awd; Duke TS; Hnr Roll; Nat Hon Sy; WWAHSS; Yth Ldrshp Prog; Hab For Humty Volntr; Peer Tut/Med; 4-H; DARE; Drma Clb; Ntl Beta Clb; Pep Squd; Scouts; Chr; Dnce; Chrldg (V); Track (V); Intern with Local Channel 6 Television; Co-Captain of Step Team; Performing Arts; Literature; Spelman College; Swarthmore College

HAMILTON, SARAH M; LOUISVILLE, KY; SOUTHERN HS; (FR); 4H Awd; Hnr Roll; Perf Att; St of Mnth; CARE; 4-H; Chrch Yth Grp; DARE; Drma Clb; Emplmnt; FCA; Ntl Beta Clb; P to P St Amb Prg; Chr; Orch; Sccr (V); Cl Off (P); Rifle Team (Varsity); Venture Crew; Culinary Arts; Law; Yale U; U of U of L

HAMPTON, MADISON; NICHOLASVILLE, KY; BLUEGRASS BAPTIST SCH; (JR); Hnr Roll; MVP; DARE; Emplmnt; Pep Squd; Quiz Bowl; Bskball (V C); Vllyball (V); Cl Off (P); Sch Ppr (P); Sports Management; Marketing

HANCOCK, BRACEY D; OAK GROVE, KY; HOPKINSVILLE HS; (FR); Hnr Roll; Perf Att; FCA; Lttrmn Clb; Mus Clb (Pre: CR); Chr; Sftball (VJ L); Psychology; Criminal Law (F.B.I.); U of Kentucky; Eastern Kentucky

HANDLEY, CANDICE L; HODGENVILLE, KY; LARUE CTY HS; (SO); Comm Volntr; Ntl FFA; PP Ftbl; Healthcare Professional; Western Kentucky U

HANEY, JENA B; HICKMAN, KY; FULTON CTY HS; (FR); Hnr Roll; 4-H; Chrch Yth Grp; Emplmnt; Bnd; Ch Chr; Mch Bnd; Chrldg (V); Acting; Interior Design; New York U; Murray State U

HANKS, CALLIE; VERSAILLES, KY; ANDERSON CTY HS; (JR); F Lan Hn Soc; Gov Hnr Prg; Hi Hnr Roll; Nat Hon Sy; St of Mnth; Yth Ldrshp Prog; Comm Volntr; Peer Tut/Med; Chrch Yth Grp; Drma Clb; FCA; FCCLA; Ntl Beta Clb; Prom Com; SADD; French Clb; Acpl Chr; Chr; Mch Bnd; SP/M/VS; Cl Off (P); Stu Cncl (R); Sch Ppr (R); Theatre; Psychology; U of Kentucky

HANKS, RACHEL M; CLOVERPORT, KY; FREDERICK FRAIZE HS; (JR); Hi Hnr Roll; Hnr Roll; Otst Ac Ach Awd; Comm Volntr; Emplmnt; Prom Com; Mar Art (J); Cl Off (V); Stu Cncl (R); Yrbk (R, P); Participating in Dual Credit College Programs; Homecoming Princess; Psychology; Journalism; Georgetown College; U of Kentucky

HARBIN, TAYLOR W; PADUCAH, KY; CMTY CHRISTIAN AC; (SO); Hnr Roll; Nat Hon Sy; Nat Ldrshp Svc; Sci Fairs; WWAHSS; Comm Volntr; Svce Clb; Chaplain of Leo Club; Computers / Graphic Design; Creative Writing; Florida College; Western Kentucky U

HARBISON, WINSTON B; EDMONTON, KY; METCALFE CO; (FR); Hi Hnr Roll; Perf Att; St of Mnth; 4-H; Chrch Yth Grp; DARE; FCA; FTA; Ntl Beta Clb; Ntl FFA; Pep Squd; Bsball (V); Bskball (V); Ftball (V); Wt Lftg (V)

HARDIN, BEE JAY; ROUNDHILL, KY; EDMONSON CTY HS; (FR); Hnr Roll; Ntl Beta Clb; Bnd; Mch Bnd; Took a Advanced Math Course; Kindergarten Teacher; Social Worker; U of Louisville; Western Kentucky U

HARDYMON, JEREMY; AUGUSTA, KY; AUGUSTA HS; (SO); Hnr Roll; Perf Att; St of Mnth; WWAHSS; Comm Volntr; DARE; FCCLA; Pep Squd; Bsball (V); Bskball (VJC); Cl Off (T); Elementary Education; Georgetown College; Thomas Moore College

HARGROVE, JENNY; LOUISVILLE, KY; DOSS HS MAG CAREER AC; (JR); Comm Volntr; Chrch Yth Grp; Ch Chr; Dnce; Stu Cncl (R)

HARP, RACHEL; WILLIAMSBURG, KY; WHITLEY CTY HS; (FR); Hnr Roll; Nat Stu Ath Day Aw; WWAHSS; Chrch Yth Grp; FCA; Ntl Beta Clb; Pep Squd; Chr; Sftball (J); Bachelors Degree/Biology; Masters/Biology; U of the Cumberlands; Eastern Kentucky U

HARPER, AMANDA E; LOUISVILLE, KY; SENECA HS; (SO); Hnr Roll; Nat Hon Sy; Sci Fairs; Yth Ldrshp Prog; Comm Volntr; Peer Tut/Med; FCA; Key Club; Ntl Beta Clb; Scouts; Tech Clb; Spanish Clb; Tennis (J); Adv Cncl (R); Stu Cncl (R); National Honors Society; Teen Court; Pre-Med; Biology; U of Kentucky; Purdue U

HARPER, DURAND L; LOUISVILLE, KY; WESTERN HS; (SO); Hnr Roll; WWAHSS; Peer Tut/Med; FCA; Ftball (V CL); Track (J); Wt Lftg (V C); Wrstlg (V CL); Computer Technology; Atlanta State U; U of Louisville

HARPER, MELISSA; SCOTTSVILLE, KY; ALLEN CTY HS; (JR); Hnr Roll; WWAHSS; Comm Volntr; Peer Tut/Med; Red Cr Aide; 4-H; Chrch Yth Grp; DARE; Emplmnt; FCCLA; FTA; Ntl FFA; SADD; CR (V); Elem Education; Home Ec Extension; Murray State U; Western Kentucky U

HARPER, SUNNY; EDDYVILLE, KY; LYON CTY HS; (JR); Hi Hnr Roll; Nat Hon Sy; WWAHSS; ArtClub; Chrch Yth Grp; FCA; FCCLA; Ntl Beta Clb; Ntl FFA; Pep Squd; Prom Com; Chrldg (C); Scr Kpr (V); Cl Off (V); Yrbk (P); FCCLA Regional Vice President; FFA Chapter Treasurer; Anesthesiology; Agriculture Education; Murray State U; U of Kentucky

HARRIS, DAVID K; AUBURN, KY; LOGAN CTY HS; (FR); Hnr Roll; Perf Att; Comm Volntr; DARE; Scouts; Bnd; Jzz Bnd; Mch Bnd; Pep Bnd; Cyclg (J); Dvng (J); Swmg (J); Lawyer; Western KY

HARRIS, KATIE; BEREA, KY; BEREA CMTY HS; (JR); Hi Hnr Roll; Hnr Roll; Nat Hon Sy; Otst Ac Ach Awd; WWAHSS; Yth Ldrshp Prog; Comm Volntr; Emplmnt; FBLA; FCCLA; Key Club; Ntl Beta Clb; NYLC; Outdrs Clb; Flg Crps; Bskball (V); Cl Off (V); Yrbk (P); Business; Berea College; U of Kentucky

HARSHBARGER, LOGAN; BURLINGTON, KY; CONNER HS; (FR); Hnr Roll; St of Mnth; WWAHSS; Yth Ldrshp Prog; Comm Volntr; Chrch Yth Grp; FCA; FBLA; Pep Squd; U of Kentucky

HARVEY, DENISE; ERLANGER, KY; DIXIE HEIGHTS HS; (JR); Hnr Roll; WWAHSS; Peer Tut/Med; Chrch Yth Grp; Emplmnt; Tchrs Aide; Chrldg (V); Sccr (J); Sftball (V); Yrbk; Wrestling State Girl; Business; Nursing; Northern Kentucky U

HASH, MEGAN R; CAMPBELLSVLLE, KY; TAYLOR CTY HS; (SO); Hi Hnr Roll; WWAHSS; Comm Volntr; Peer Tut/Med; FCA; Key Club; Pep Squd; Sci Clb; SADD; Chr; Sftball (VJ); Vllyball (VJCL); Member of Who's Who Among American High School Students; Business; Physical Therapy; Campbellsville U; U of Kentucky

HATFIELD, HALEY G; CANADA, KY; BELFRY HS; (MS); 4H Awd; Hnr Roll; Chrch Yth Grp; DARE; FTA; Chr; Ch Chr; Orch; Music / Piano

HATFIELD, JARED; NEWPORT, KY; NEWPORT HS; (JR); Hi Hnr Roll; Nat Hon Sy; Otst Ac Ach Awd; Sci Fairs; St Schl; WWAHSS; Comm Volntr; Emplmnt; FBLA; Key Club; Photog; Prom Com; Track (V L); Stu Cncl (R); Sch Ppr (R, P); Yrbk (P); FBLA Region & State Conf. Runner-Up; Kentucky Governor's Scholar Program; Computer Science

HATFIELD, JUSTINA; CARLISLE, KY; NICHOLAS CTY HS; (FR); Hnr Roll; Perf Att; FCA; Scouts; SP/M/VS; Vllyball (J); Yrbk (P); Teaching; U of Kentucky

HATFIELD RAWDON, EMILY A; GEORGETOWN, KY; SCOTT CTY HS; (JR); Duke TS; Hnr Roll; WWAHSS; Comm Volntr; Chess; Chrch Yth Grp; Dbte Team; Drma Clb; Key Club; Mod UN; Mus Clb; Ntl Beta Clb; Chr; SP/M/VS; Stg Cre; Sccr (J L); Track (V L); Stu Cncl; Sch Ppr (R); Yrbk (E, R, P); Academic Team; Theatre; Law; Dartmouth College; Williams College

HAWES, KYLE; PADUCAH, KY; LONE OAK HS; (SR); All Am Sch; Hnr Roll; Yth Ldrshp Prog; Chrch Yth Grp; Emplmnt; FCA; Key Club; Ntl Beta Clb; Tchrs Aide; Bnd; Ch Chr; Mch Bnd; Pep Bnd; Marching Band Section Leader; Electrical Engineer; Computer Science; U of Kentucky; Murray State U

HAWKINS, REESE H; PRINCETON, KY; CALDWELL CTY HS; (SR); Gov Hnr Prg; Hi Hnr Roll; Hnr Roll; Nat Hon Sy; Nat Mrt Fin; Nat Mrt LOC; Otst Ac Ach Awd; WWAHSS; Comm Volntr; Peer Tut/Med; Chrch Yth Grp; FCA; Pep Squd; Tech Clb; Ch Chr; SP/M/VS; Bskball (J); Ftball (J); Scr Kpr (J); Wt Lftg (V); Praise & Worship Band at Church; After School Tutor at Church; Computer Technology; Journalism; Murray State U

HAWKINS, SARAH M; LOUISVILLE, KY; LOUISVILLE COLLEGIATE SCH; (JR); Duke TS; Nat Hon Sy; WWAHSS; NYLC; P to P St Amb Prg; Chr; Dnce; Lit Mag (E); Kentucky All-State Chorus; Pre-Med

HAY, JESSICA; UPTON, KY; HART CTY HS; (JR); Hi Hnr Roll; Hnr Roll; WWAHSS; Ntl FFA; Key Club; Prom Com; Foreign Clb; Ch Chr; Blue and Gold Award in FFA; Land Judging Team; History; Music; Elizabethtown Community College; Western Kentucky College

HAYES, RYAN; ALEXANDRIA, KY; CAMPBELL CTY HS; (FR); All Am Sch; Ctznshp Aw; Hnr Roll; Perf Att; St of Mnth; USAA; Published Author; Northern Kentucky U

HAZZARD, CARA M; BUCKNER, KY; OLDHAM CTY HS; (JR); Hnr Roll; WWAHSS; Yth Ldrshp Prog; Comm Volntr; Chrch Yth Grp; Drma Clb; FCA; Mus Clb; Scouts; Chr; Ch Chr; SP/M/VS; Stg Cre; PP Ftbl; Part of Church Leadership Team; Work with Missions Team; Vocal Music; Theatre; Ohio Wesleyan U; Northern Kentucky U

HEAD, SAMANTHA J; LA GRANGE, KY; NORTH OLDHAM HS; (FR); Hnr Roll; Drma Clb; Emplmnt; Photog; Scouts; SADD; Chr; SP/M/VS; Equine Veterinarian; Animal Behavior; Auburn U

HEARN, DERRICK L; LOUISVILLE, KY; DOSS HS MAG CAREER AC; (SO); Comm Volntr; Hosp Aide; BPA; Emplmnt; Spanish Clb; Ch Chr; Cl Off (V); Elementary School Tutor; Children's Hospital Volunteer; Technology; Education/Business; U of Louisville; Tennessee State U

HEATH, CATHERINE; WESTVIEW, KY; BETHEL CHRISTIAN AC; (SO); Hnr Roll; Perf Att; Chrch Yth Grp; Emplmnt; Pep Squd; Tchrs Aide; Ch Chr; Bskball (J); Sch Ppr (R); Yrbk (R); Business; Marine Biologist; Campbellsville U; U of Kentucky

HEATON, ANDREA; LOUISVILLE, KY; ATHERTON HS; (SO); Hi Hnr Roll; Otst Ac Ach Awd; Perf Att; Pres Ac Ftns Aw; Pres Sch; Sci Fairs; St of Mnth; Peer Tut/Med; DARE; Emplmnt; Chrldg (V); Cl Off (P); Beta Club Award; Education; Business; Winthrop U; Franklin College

HELTON, KRISTEN; SHARPSBURG, KY; BATH CTY HS; (JR); Hnr Roll; Perf Att; Emplmnt; Ntl Beta Clb; Ntl FFA; Spanish Clb; Outstanding Scholarship in US History; Certificate of Achievement in Floriculture; Nursing RN; Medical Field; U of Kentucky; Morehead U

HENDERSON, KRISTI; FRANKLIN, KY; FRANKLIN-SIMPSON HS; (JR); WWAHSS; AL Aux Girls; Chrch Yth Grp; DECA; FBLA; Ntl Beta Clb; Ntl FFA; Prom Com; Spch Team; Dnce; SP/M/VS; Chrldg (V L); Cl Off (V); Stu Cncl (R); Fashion Design; Apparel Marketing

HENRY, D J; MADISONVILLE, KY; MADISONVILLE NORTH HOPKINS HS; (FR); Hi Hnr Roll; Key Club; Scouts; Bnd; Mch Bnd; Orch; Pep Bnd; All District Band (2 Years); Quad State Band; Music Major

HENRYHAND, BRIANNA L; ELIZABETHTOWN, KY; ELIZABETHTOWN HS; (JR); Hi Hnr Roll; Perf Att; WWAHSS; Hab For Humty Volntr; Chrch Yth Grp; FBLA; Ntl Beta Clb; Svce Clb; Spanish Clb; Ch Chr; Clr Grd; Track (V); Cl Off (T); CR (T); American Private Enterprise Systems Seminar Regional and State Delegate; Color Guard Member of the Year 2003; Marketing/Business Administration; Marketing Manager; U of Maryland College Park; Morgan State U

HENSLEY, HELEN M; SIMPSONVILLE, KY; WALDEN HS; (SO); Hi Hnr Roll; Kwnis Aw; Nat Sci Aw; Otst Ac Ach Awd; Pres Sch; WWAHSS; Comm Volntr; Peer Tut/Med; ArtClub; Key Club; Mth Clb/Tm; Mod UN; Ntl Beta Clb; Svce Clb; Tchrs Aide; Spanish Clb; SP/M/VS; Cl Off (P); Stu Cncl (R); Attend Walden Theatre (9 Yrs); Member of Swim Team (11 Yrs); Theatre; Psychology; Juilliard; Cal Arts

HENSON, MITCHEL T; BOWLING GREEN, KY; GREENWOOD HS; (FR); Ctznshp Aw; Duke TS; Hnr Roll; WWAHSS; Chrch Yth Grp; FCA; Stu Cncl; Business Management; U of Kentucky

HERALD, ASHLY; BOWLING GREEN, KY; WARREN EAST HS; (SR); 4H Awd; Ctznshp Aw; Perf Att; Peer Tut/Med; 4-H; DARE; Jr Ach; Lib Aide; Pep Squd; SADD; Tchrs Aide; Chr; Ch Chr; Chrldg; Computer Technology; Doctorial Degree; WKU; Bowling Green Technical College

HERALD, DEANNA; COVINGTON, KY; HOLMES HS; (SO); Ctznshp Aw; F Lan Hn Soc; Hnr Roll; Comm Volntr; Peer Tut/Med; DARE; Tchrs Aide; Chr; SP/M/VS; Bsball (V); Sftball; Social Work; Human Child Development; NKU; UC

HERRINGTON, ROBERT S; ADOLPHUS, KY; ALLEN CTY HS; (SO); Hnr Roll, WWAHSS; DARE; Cr Ctry (L); Wt Lftg

HESCH II, JAMES E; NEWPORT, KY; NEWPORT HS; (SO); Ctznshp Aw; Hi Hnr Roll; MVP; Perf Att; Sci Fairs; Emplmnt; Bsball (V L); Bskball (V L); Ftball (V L)

HESTAND, LOLITA; TOMPKINSVILLE, KY; MONROE CTY HS; (SO); Hnr Roll; ArtClub; Ntl FFA; Wdwrkg Clb; Astronomy; U of Kentucky

HICKS, RAYLENE; NEW HAVEN, KY; NELSON CTY HS; (SO); Hnr Roll; WWAHSS; Key Club; Pep Squd; Sccr (J); Medical Field; Pediatrician; St. Catherine's; U of Kentucky

HIGDON, LINDSAY; LOUISVILLE, KY; LOUISVILLE MALE HS; (SR); F Lan Hn Soc; Gov Hnr Prg; Hi Hnr Roll; Nat Hon Sy; Otst Ac Ach Awd; Perf Att; Salutrn; WWAHSS; Comm Volntr; Peer Tut/Med; Red Cr Aide; DARE; Off Aide; Photog; French Clb; Dnce; Sch Ppr; Governors Scholar (Kentucky); Commonwealth Diploma Dance Team VCL; Psychology; U of Louisville; Cumberland College

HILL, ERIN E; JAMESTOWN, KY; RUSSELL CTY HS; (FR); 4H Awd; Fut Prb Slvr; Hi Hnr Roll; 4-H; Chrch Yth Grp; Ntl FFA; Track (VJ); Agriculture Law; U of Louisville

HILL, MARKEETA E; MAMMOTH CAVE, KY; EDMONSON CTY HS; (FR); Hi Hnr Roll; Comm Volntr; Drma Clb; Emplmnt; FBLA; Pep Squd; Many Math Awards; Psychiatry; Radiology; Western K U; U of Louisville

HIMES, AARON C; WINCHESTER, KY; GEORGE ROGERS CLARK HS; (FR); Hnr Roll; Perf Att; Sci Fairs; Chrch Yth Grp; DARE; Ntl FFA; SADD; Bskball (J); Ftball (V); Wt Lftg (V); FFA; Law Enforcement; Professional Football Player; E.K.U. Eastern KY U; Marshall U-Any Division

HOBBS, MATT; FT MITCHELL, KY; DIXIE HEIGHTS HS; (SO); Hnr Roll; WWAHSS; Cmptr Clb; Computer Programming; Psychology; DigiPen Institute of Tech

HOBDY, AMANDA; LEXINGTON, KY; BRYAN STATION HS; (SO); Hi Hnr Roll; Hnr Roll; WWAHSS; Chrch Yth Grp; Drma Clb; Ntl Beta Clb; Spch Team; French Clb; SP/M/VS; Stg Cre; Tennis (J); Cl Off (P); Sch Ppr (E); Journalism; Psychology; U of Kentucky

HODGE, SARAH E; PADUCAH, KY; REIDLAND HS; (SR); Hnr Roll; Nat Hon Sy; Nat Mrt Fin; Otst Ac Ach Awd; WWAHSS; Comm Volntr; Chrch Yth Grp; DECA; FCA; FCCLA; Key Club; Pep Squd; Prom Com; Scouts; Bnd; Ch Chr; Clr Grd; Tennis (V); Adv Cncl; Cl Off (T); Stu Cncl (V); CR (R); Yrbk (R, P); Secondary Education; Western Kentucky U

HOFFMAN, DEVIN; ALEXANDRIA, KY; CAMPBELL CTY HS; (FR); Hi Hnr Roll; Hnr Roll; Perf Att; Nursing; Business; U of Louisville; U of Kentucky

HOGAN, BRETTE; FRANKFORT, KY; FRANKLIN CTY HS; (SO); 4H Awd; Duke TS; Hi Hnr Roll; Hnr Roll; WWAHSS; Chrch Yth Grp; FCA; Key Club; Ntl Beta Clb; Svce Clb; PP Ftbl (V); Sftball (J); Swmg (V L); High School Teacher; Accounting; Centre College

HOGGE, RICHARD M; RUSSELLVILLE, KY; LOGAN CTY HS; (FR); Ctznshp Aw; PC Repair Hardware / Software; Bowling Green Tech; ITT Tech

HOLCOMB, KELSEY M; LONDON, KY; SOUTH LAUREL HS; (JR); Hnr Roll; Spec Olymp Vol; DARE; Emplmnt; FCA; Chrldg (J); Track (J); Yrbk (R, P); Early Elementary Education; Eastern Kentucky U; Somerset Community College

HOLDEN, PATRICIA; PROSPECT, KY; BALLARD HS; (SR); Hnr Roll; Nat Hon Sy; Otst Ac Ach Awd; Sci Fairs; WWAHSS; Comm Volntr; Hab For Humty Volntr; Drma Clb; FCA; Ntl Beta Clb; Sci Clb; Tchrs Aide; Spanish Clb; Dnce; Drl Tm; Stg Cre; PPSqd (V); Lit Mag (E, R); Pre-Dentistry Major; Business; Ohio U; Ball State U

HOLLAN, CHASITY; CAMPTON, KY; WOLFE CO HS; (JR); Hnr Roll; WWAHSS; ArtClub; Tech Clb

HOLLAN, JESSICA L; JACKSON, KY; BREATHITT HS; (SO); Hnr Roll; Otst Ac Ach Awd; WWAHSS; 4-H; DARE; RN / Registered Nurse; Teacher; Eastern U of Kentucky; Lees College

HOLLOMAN, KENDRA; LEXINGTON, KY; BRYAN STATION HS; (SO); Ctznshp Aw; Hi Hnr Roll; MVP; St of Mnth; Emplmnt; Bnd; Track (V); Business / Marketing; Cosmetology; U of Louisville; Clark Atlanta U

HOLMES, AMANDA D; CORYDON, KY; HENDERSON CTY HS; (FR); Hnr Roll; Perf Att; Pres Ac Ftns Aw; Comm Volntr; Chrch Yth Grp; ROTC; Clr Grd; Drl Tm; Track (J); Lawyer; Interior Design; Howard Law School; Yale U

HOLMES, COLLIN; LOUISVILLE, KY; FERN CREEK TRADITIONAL HS; (FR); Gov Hnr Prg; Hnr Roll; St of Mnth; WWAHSS; DARE; Wrstlg (J); U of Louisville; U of Kentucky

HOLT, ASHLEY S; BLOOMFIELD, KY; NELSON CTY HS; (FR); All Am Sch; Hnr Roll; WWAHSS; Chrch Yth Grp; FCA; Key Club; Dnce; Sch Ppr (R); FCA; Communications//Phot.; Advertising; WKU (Western Kentucky U); UK (U of Kentucky)

HOLT, BRITTANY; BROWNSVILLE, KY; EDMONSON CTY HS; (FR); Hnr Roll; Emplmnt; Ntl FFA; Photog; Education(Agriculture); Physician; Morehead State U; Western Kentucky U

HOLT, MATTHEW D; LAWRENCEBURG, KY; ANDERSON CTY HS; (SR); Duke TS; Hi Hnr Roll; Hnr Roll; Nat Hon Sy; St of Mnth; WWAHSS; DARE; Emplmnt; FCA; Ntl Beta Clb; Ntl FFA; Off Aide; Tchrs Aide; Bsball (VJCL); Bskball (VJ); Sch Ppr (E); Equine Business / Management; Business

HOOK, KRYSTAL; CLAY, KY; WEBSTER CTY HS; (SO); Hnr Roll; Peer Tut/Med; Ntl FFA; Educational Talent Search (CTS); Zoology Major; Murry State U; BelRea Inst

HOOPER, STARR; LOUISVILLE, KY; MARY RYAN AC; (SO); Hi Hnr Roll; Hnr Roll; Perf Att; Bnd; SP/M/VS; Stg Cre; Sch Ppr (E, R); Art; Harvard U; Yale U

HOPKINS, KAREN; RICHMOND, KY; MODEL LABORATORY SCH; (JR); Hnr Roll; WWAHSS; Yth Ldrshp Prog; Comm Volntr; Drma Clb; Emplmnt; Key Club; Pep Squd; Prom Com; Dnce; SP/M/VS; Stg Cre; PPSqd (V); Swmg (V); Cl Off (R); Sch Ppr (E); Youth Salute; Theatre Major; Film Production; Northern Kentucky; Western Kentucky

HOPPES, BRIQUELLE; PEWEE VALLEY, KY; WALDEN SCH; (FR); Hnr Roll; WWAHSS; Key Club; Sch Ppr (R); Newspaper Secretary; Pediatrics; Psychiatrics; U of Louisville

HORD, CHRISTOPHER S; TOLLESBORO, KY; FLEMING CTY HS; (SR); Ctznshp Aw; Duke TS; Hnr Roll; St of Mnth; Chrch Yth Grp; Ftball (V); Cl Off (T); Optometry; Dentistry; Morehead State U

HOUK, ELEAH M; SCOTTSVILLE, KY; ALLEN CTY HS; (SR); Hnr Roll; Nat Hon Sy; Comm Volntr; Peer Tut/Med; ArtClub; FCCLA; SADD; Ch Chr; Sch Ppr (E); FCCLA Club; Community Service; Massage Therapy; Teaching; Natural Health Institute

HOWARD, EMILY J; JACKSON, KY; BREATHITT HS; (SO); Gov Hnr Prg; Hnr Roll; Perf Att; Peer Tut/Med; Chrldg (V); Psychology; Pharmacy; Eastern Kentucky U; Morehead State U

HOWARD, JACOB; WILLIAMSBURG, KY; WILLIAMSBURG SCH; (MS); Spec Olymp Vol; 4-H; Ntl Beta Clb; Bnd; Mch Bnd; Pep Bnd; SP/M/VS; Architecture; Lawyer; Cumberland College

HOWARD, SHANNON N; LEXINGTON, KY; THE AMERICAN SCH; (FR); Emplmnt; Orch; Interior Design; Lawyer; U of Kentucky

HOWELL, ALEX J; LOUISVILLE, KY; LOUISVILLE MALE HS; (SO); Hnr Roll; St of Mnth; Comm Volntr; FCA; French Clb; Ftball (VJ L); Engineering; Math; Western KY U; Murray State U

HOWELL, JESSICA D; KNOB LICK, KY; METCALFE CTY HS; (SO); Hi Hnr Roll; Hnr Roll; Otst Ac Ach Awd; WWAHSS; Ntl Beta Clb; Pep Squd; Tech Clb; Fashion; Western Kentucky U; Campbellsville U

HUBBARD, LINDSEY R; EDMONTON, KY; METCALFE CTY HS; (FR); 4H Awd; Fut Prb Slvr; Hi Hnr Roll; Hnr Roll; Nat Hon Sy; Sci Fairs; USAA; WWAHSS; Peer Tut/Med; 4-H; Chrch Yth Grp; Cmptr Clb; DARE; FCA; Ntl Beta Clb; Pep Squd; Quiz Bowl; Ch Chr; Vllyball (J); Stu Cncl (R); US Achievement Academy / English & Leadership; Creative Communication "03" Young Poets Award; Computer Information / Undergraduate; Juris Doctor of Law / Graduate; U of Louisville; U of Kentucky

HUBBARD, MATTHEW; EDMONTON, KY; METCALFE CTY HS; (FR); Hnr Roll; Perf Att; St of Mnth; Chrch Yth Grp; Ntl FFA; Quiz Bowl; Aviation; Boston College; Stanford U

HUGHES, AMY; MARTIN, KY; DAVID SCH; (JR); Perf Att; Comm Volntr; Emplmnt; Prom Com; Wdwrkg Clb; Yrbk (R); Bachelor Degree in Office Assistance; Secretarial; Mayo Technical; Prestonsburg Community

HUGHES, ASHLEY N; FLORENCE, KY; BOONE CTY HS; (FR); Comm Volntr; Hab For Humty Volntr; ArtClub; Chrch Yth Grp; DARE; Dnce; Chrldg; Freshman Representative For Citi Best; Helping Hands; Social Work; Architect; U of Cincinnati; U of Kentucky

HUGHEY, SAMANTHA; CRESTWOOD, KY; OLDHAM CTY HS; (SR); Hi Hnr Roll; Nat Hon Sy; WWAHSS; Comm Volntr; Red Cr Aide; Emplmnt; Ntl Beta Clb; Photog; Tchrs Aide; Sccr (JC); Adv Cncl; Sch Ppr (E, P); Yrbk (P); Certificate of Merit in Photography from Columbia; Photojournalism; Western KY U

HULKER, JACOB; FRANKFORT, KY; WESTERN HILLS HS; (SR); Hnr Roll; Nat Hon Sy; WWAHSS; 4-H; Ntl Beta Clb; Ntl FFA; Quiz Bowl; Tech Clb; SP/M/VS; U of Kentucky

HULTMAN, MITCHELL; PADUCAH, KY; LONE OAK HS; (SR); Bnd; Ch Chr; Mch Bnd; Pep Bnd; 2005 Humanitarian Award; MSU Honor Award / John Robinson Award; Murray State U

HUNDLEY, DERRICK N; JUNCTION CITY, KY; BOYLE CTY HS; (SR); All Am Sch; Hnr Roll; Nat Ldrshp Svc; Perf Att; USAA; WWAHSS; Emplmnt; Voc Ind Clb Am; Electrical Engineering; U of Kentucky

HUNT, KEITH; ADOLPHUS, KY; ALLEN CTY HS; (SO); Hnr Roll; WWAHSS; Comm Volntr; Bnd; Jzz Bnd; Mch Bnd; Pep Bnd; Mar Art (V); Radiologist; Vandy; Wku

HUNT, NATOSHA M; BROWNSVILLE, KY; EDMONSON CTY HS; (FR); Hnr Roll; FCA; Pep Squd; Bskball (VJ L); Social Sciences

HUNTER, MOLLY J; GREENUP, KY; GREENUP CTY HS; (FR); Duke TS; Fut Prb Slvr; WWAHSS; Red Cr Aide; Chrch Yth Grp; Quiz Bowl; Golf (J); Adv Cncl (R); CR (R); Piano Student; Duke U; Georgetown College

HUNTSMAN, CYBILE D; SCOTTSVILLE, KY; ALLEN CTY HS; (JR); Gov Hnr Prg; Hnr Roll; WWAHSS; DARE; Jr Ach; Golf; Honor Roll / Invited to Governor Scholars; Radiologist; Western Kentucky U; Bowling Green Tech

HUNTSMAN, STEPHANIE; PRINCETON, KY; CALDWELL CTY HS; (SR); All Am Sch; DAR; F Lan Hn Soc; Gov Hnr Prg; Hi Hnr Roll; Nat Hon Sy; Valdctrian; WWAHSS; Chrch Yth Grp; DARE; Emplmnt; FCA; HO'Br Yth Ldrshp; Key Club; Tchrs Aide; Chr; Ch Chr; Dnce; Pep Bnd; Sccr (VJC); Swmg (J); Stu Cncl; CR; Yrbk (R, P); National Honor Society - Reporter; Outstanding Senior of Class; Math Major; U of Kentucky

HUTCHISON, SHAWNA L; STANTON, KY; POWELL CTY HS; (FR); Hnr Roll; Comm Volntr; Chrch Yth Grp; FCA; Bskball (VJ); Sftball (J); Nursing; Physical Therapy; Morehead State U; U of Kentucky

HUYNH, QUETRANG; LOUISVILLE, KY; BUTLER TRADITIONAL HS; (JR); Hnr Roll; WWAHSS; Comm Volntr; Peer Tut/Med; Ntl Beta Clb; Accounting; U of Louisville

IMHOFF, DANIELLE M; PADUCAH, KY; REIDLAND HS; (JR); Duke TS; F Lan Hn Soc; Hnr Roll; WWAHSS; Peer Tut/Med; Biology Clb; DARE; Key Club; Lib Aide; Ntl Beta Clb; Pep Squd; Scouts; Tchrs Aide; Mar Art (V)

IRVIN, REBECA J; JAMESTOWN, KY; RUSSELL CTY HS; (SO); Hnr Roll; Otst Ac Ach Awd; Perf Att; WWAHSS; Comm Volntr; Chrch Yth Grp; Emplmnt; Dnce; Sccr (J); Tennis (V); Sch Ppr (R); Football Management; Homecoming Queen; Psychology; Journalism; U of Kentucky; Harvard U

ISAAC JR, DWIGHT; PINE TOP, KY; KNOTT CTY CTRL HS; (FR); Hnr Roll; Nat Hon Sy; WWAHSS; 4-H; DARE; FCA; Scouts; Bskball (J); Ftball (JC); Engineering

ISON, SARA; MT STERLING, KY; MONTGOMERY CTY HS; (FR); 4H Awd; Hnr Roll; Nat Ldrshp Svc; Otst Ac Ach Awd; Sci Fairs; Yth Ldrshp Prog; Comm Volntr; Hab For Humty Volntr; Spec Olymp Vol; 4-H; Chrch Yth Grp; Drma Clb; FCA; Mth Clb/Tm; Ntl FFA; Pep Squd; Bnd; Chr; Dnce; Chrldg (V); Sccr (J); Track (J); Vllyball (J); Yrbk (E, P); FFA - Member-Public Speaking / Lambs; 4-H-Reporter; Marine Biology / Trainer; Education; Georgetown College; U of Kentucky

IVEY, LINSEY; HICKORY, KY; GRAVES CTY HS; (JR); Hi Hnr Roll; Hnr Roll; Nat Mrt LOC; WWAHSS; Comm Volntr; Peer Tut/Med; Chrch Yth Grp; Lib Aide; Ntl Beta Clb; Tchrs Aide; Chrldg (J); PP Ftbl (V); Sonographer; West Kentucky Community & Technical College; Murray State U

JACKSON, AMBER; CRITTENDEN, KY; GRANT CTY HS; (SR); All Am Sch; Hnr Roll; WWAHSS; Comm Volntr; Chrch Yth Grp; FCA; Ntl FFA; Sftball (VJ); Nursing; Thomas More College

JACKSON, ANDREW; GEORGETOWN, KY; EASTSIDE CTR FOR APPLIED TECH; (SR); Hnr Roll; Nat Hon Sy; Perf Att; Become a NASCAR Mechanic; NASCAR Technical Institute

JACKSON, CORNELIA; LEXINGTON, KY; BRYAN STATION HS; (SR); Hnr Roll; Comm Volntr; Chrch Yth Grp; DARE; Lib Aide; Prom Com; Svce Clb; Tchrs Aide; Chr; Ch Chr; Pre-Med; Pre-Pharmacy; University of Louisville; University of Kentucky

JACKSON, JAMES A; PHILPOT, KY; TRINITY HS; (SR); Hi Hnr Roll; Hnr Roll; Who's Who Among American High School Students; Agriculture; Owensboro Community & Technical College

JACKSON, TRENTON; HENDERSON, KY; HENDERSON CTY HS; (SR); Ctznshp Aw; Hnr Roll; Nat Hon Sy; Ntl FFA; Voc Ind Clb Am; Western Kentucky U

JEFFREY, ERICA S; FREDONIA, KY; CALDWELL CTY HS; (JR); Nat Hon Sy; WWAHSS; Chrch Yth Grp; Emplmnt; FCA; FCCLA; President 2005-2006 of FCCLA; Vice President of Public Relations Region 2; Clinical Psychologist; Paducah Community College; U of Kentucky

JELLISON, LAUREN N; HOPKINSVILLE, KY; CHRISTIAN CTY HS; (JR); Hi Hnr Roll; Hnr Roll; Nat Hon Sy; Otst Ac Ach Awd; Sci Fairs; WWAHSS; Yth Ldrshp Prog; Comm Volntr; Emplmnt; Key Club; Ntl Beta Clb; Photog; Dnce; Chrldg (V L); Cl Off (P); CR (P); Dance - Varsity Captain; Key Club - Vice President; Law; Psychology; U of Kentucky; Murray State U

JENKINS, ALEX; CADIZ, KY; TRIGG CTY HS; (FR); 4H Awd; Hi Hnr Roll; Nat Hon Sy; Otst Ac Ach Awd; USAA; WWAHSS; Yth Ldrshp Prog; Comm Volntr; Peer Tut/Med; 4-H; Chrch Yth Grp; DARE; Key Club; Ntl Beta Clb; NYLC; Pep Squd; Quiz Bowl; Bnd; Pep Bnd; Bskball (V); Ftball (V); Scr Kpr (V); Track (J); Stu Cncl (R); CR (R); Odyssey of the Mind; Keys Club International; Pediatrician; Medical Doctor; U of Kentucky; Murray State U

JENKINS, JACOB; PRINCETON, KY; CALDWELL CTY HS; (FR); Hnr Roll; Chrch Yth Grp; FCA; Bskball (J); Ftball (J); Criminal Justice; U of North Carolina; U of Kentucky

JENKINS, JOY; LOUISVILLE, KY; J.M. ATHERTON HS; (JR); Hnr Roll; Nat Hon Sy; Comm Volntr; Tchrs Aide; Pharmacy; Secondary Education; U of Louisville; Bellarmine U

JENKINS, KYLE; SALYERSVILLE, KY; MAGOFFIN CTY HS; (JR); Hi Hnr Roll; Nat Hon Sy; Otst Ac Ach Awd; Sci Fairs; WWAHSS; Comm Volntr; Chrch Yth Grp; Dbte Team; Drma Clb; FCA; FCCLA; Key Club; MuAlphaTh; Pep Squd; Ch Chr; SP/M/VS; Tennis (V); Cl Off (P); FCCLA Star Events Winner; Creative Writing; U of Kentucky

JEWELL, MARY B; CANMER, KY; HART CTY HS; (JR); Duke TS; Hi Hnr Roll; Otst Ac Ach Awd; Perf Att; Sci Fairs; St of Mnth; WWAHSS; Yth Ldrshp Prog; Comm Volntr; Peer Tut/Med; FCA; Ntl Beta Clb; Pep Squd; Prom Com; Sci Clb; Svce Clb; Spanish Clb; Bskball (VJC); Track (V); Vllyball (VJC); Cl Off (S, T); Stu Cncl (R); 1st Place Winner in the KASA Statewide Writing Contest; Competed in the 2004 Governor's Cup State Finals for Written Composition; Physical Therapy; Sports Medicine/Athletic Training; Campbellsville U; Western Kentucky U

JOHNSON, AMANDA K; ULYSSES, KY; SHELDON CLARK HS; (SR); Ctznshp Aw; Hi Hnr Roll; Nat Hon Sy; Otst Ac Ach Awd; Perf Att; WWAHSS; Comm Volntr; Peer Tut/Med; Ntl Beta Clb; Bskball (V CL); Sftball (V CL); Commonwealth Scholar; WYMT- TV Scholar; Radiological Technologist; Morehead State U

Jenkins, Kyle
Magoffin Cty HS
Salyersville, KY

Jenkins, Jacob
Caldwell Cty HS
Princeton, KY

Hundley, Derrick N
Boyle Cty HS
Junction City, KY

Hulker, Jacob
Western Hills HS
Frankfort, KY

National
Honor Roll
Spring 2005

Hughes, Amy
David Sch
Martin, KY

Huntsman, Cybile D
Allen Cty HS
Scottsville, KY

Jenkins, Joy
J.M. Atherton HS
Louisville, KY

Jewell, Mary B
Hart Cty HS
Canmer, KY

JOHNSON, ANDREA; FRANKFORT, KY; (SR); Nat Hon Sy; Pres Sch; WWAHSS; DECA; Key Club; Ntl Beta Clb; Bskball (J); Accounting; Nursing; Eastern Kentucky U

JOHNSON, BRAD; MADISONVILLE, KY; MADISONVILLE NORTH HOPKINS HS; (JR); Duke TS; Hi Hnr Roll; Nat Hon Sy; Otst Ac Ach Awd; Perf Att; Comm Volntr; Spec Olymp Vol; AL Aux Boys; Chrch Yth Grp; Emplmnt; FCA; FBLA; Key Club; Ntl Beta Clb; Cr Ctry (V); Wt Lftg (V L); Yrbk (R, P); Selected to Commonwealth Honors Academy - 2005; Selected to American Legion Boys State - 2005; Political Science; Criminal Justice / Pre-Law; Kentucky Wesleyan College; Murray State U

JOHNSON, CAMRI M; RUSSELL SPRINGS, KY; RUSSELL CTY HS; (SO); Peer Tut/Med; Emplmnt; Chrldg (V); Tennis (V); Pharmaceutical Representative; U of Louisville; Western Kentucky U

JOHNSON, DULCE C; VERSAILLES, KY; WOODFORD CTY HS; (FR); 4H Awd; Duke TS; Hi Hnr Roll; 4-H; Quiz Bowl; Schol Bwl; Wdwrkg Clb; Spanish Clb; Hsbk Rdg; CR; Academic Team; Horse and Pony Club 4-H; Marine Biology; Oceanography; United States Naval Academy; West Point Military Academy

JOHNSON, ELIZABETH; ADAIRVILLE, KY; LOGAN CTY HS; (FR); Hnr Roll; Otst Ac Ach Awd; Perf Att; Sci Fairs; Valdctrian; Comm Volntr; Chrch Yth Grp; DECA; FCA; FCCLA; Ntl Beta Clb; Ch Chr; Golf (V); Vllyball (J); Communications; Broadcasting/Journalism; Eastern Kentucky U; U of Kentucky

JOHNSON, HOPE; WINGO, KY; GRAVES CTY HS; (JR); Duke TS; Hi Hnr Roll; Nat Hon Sy; Nat Sci Aw; Otst Ac Ach Awd; Perf Att; St of Mnth; WWAHSS; Comm Volntr; Chrch Yth Grp; FCA; Lib Aide; Ntl Beta Clb; Pep Squd; Photog; Prom Com; Svce Clb; Ch Chr; SP/M/VS; Chrldg (V L); Yrbk (P); School Talent Show 1st in Solo & Duet Best in Show; Agape' Club; Elementary Education; Murray State U

JOHNSON, LISA M; LATONIA, KY; J D PATTON AREA TECH CTR; (SR); Hnr Roll; Yth Ldrshp Prog; FCCLA; Voc Ind Clb Am; Family Career and Community Leaders of America / HOSA; Respiratory Therapist / Associate's Degree; Cincinnati State Community & Tech; Northern Kentucky U

JOHNSON, SARAH; LOUISVILLE, KY; DOSS HS MAG CAREER AC; (JR); Ctznshp Aw; Hnr Roll; Peer Tut/Med; Chrch Yth Grp; Golf (J); PP Ftbl (J); Tennis (V CL); Vllyball (V L); Stu Cncl (R); Congressional Student Leadership Conference; Master's in Health and Physical Education; U of Louisville; U of Kentucky

JOHNSON, SHAWN D; TOMAHAWK, KY; MARTIN CTY AREA TECH CTR; (JR); Hnr Roll; Nat Hon Sy; Perf Att; Sci/Math Olympn; USAA; WWAHSS; Comm Volntr; Hosp Aide; Red Cr Aide; Chrch Yth Grp; FCA; SADD; Voc Ind Clb Am; Ch Chr; Bsball (V); Bskball (V); Golf (V); Health Sciences; Sports Medicine; Spencerian U; Morehead State

JOHNSON, SIERRA L; FORT KNOX, KY; FORT KNOX HS; (SR); Hi Hnr Roll; Hnr Roll; Otst Ac Ach Awd; Salutrn; St of Mnth; Valdctrian; WWAHSS; Red Cr Aide; AL Aux Girls; Emplmnt; Tchrs Aide; Dnce; Bskball (J); Track (VJCL); Vllyball (VJCL); Cl Off (P); Stu Cncl (R); Yrbk (R); National Society of High School Scholars; 2nd Runner Up Hardin County Junior Miss 2005; Bachelor's Degree in Nursing; Florida State U

JOHNSON, WILLIAM; HEBRON, KY; (SO); Hnr Roll; Nat Hon Sy; St of Mnth; Drma Clb; Mus Clb; Ntl FFA; Pep Squd; Bnd; Jzz Bnd; Mch Bnd; Pep Bnd; Chrldg (V); Ftball; Wt Lftg; Music Degree; Culinary Degree; Morehead State U; Texas A & M U

JOHNSTON, MATTHEW; MADISONVILLE, KY; MADISONVILLE NORTH HOPKINS HS; (SR); Ctznshp Aw; Duke TS; Hnr Roll; Sci Fairs; WWAHSS; Spec Olymp Vol; Chrch Yth Grp; DARE; FBLA; Key Club; Ntl Beta Clb; Medicine

JOHNSTON, MEGAN; LEXINGTON, KY; (JR); Hnr Roll; WWAHSS; Comm Volntr; Chrch Yth Grp; French Clb; SP/M/VS; Chrldg (V); Tennis (J)

JONES, ALEXANDRA; HENDERSON, KY; CTY HS; (MS); Hnr Roll; Perf Att; St of Mnth; Comm Volntr; Chrch Yth Grp; DARE; Emplmnt; Ch Chr; Drama; Journalism; Juilliard; U of Kentucky

JONES, AUSTIN; MADISONVILLE, KY; MADISONVILLE NORTH HOPKINS HS; (JR); Duke TS; Gov Hnr Prg; Jr Mshl; WWAHSS; Key Club; Ntl Beta Clb; Quiz Bowl; Scouts; Eagle Scout; Biomedical Engineering; Washington U; Vanderbilt U

JONES, CASSIE M; MT STERLING, KY; MONTGOMERY CTY HS; (SO); Hnr Roll; WWAHSS; Hosp Aide; Dnce; Accounting Major; Dentistry; Morehead State U; U of Kentucky

JONES, DE ANDRA; RADCLIFF, KY; NORTH HARDIN HS; (SO); Ctznshp Aw; F Lan Hn Soc; Hi Hnr Roll; Hnr Roll; Otst Ac Ach Awd; Perf Att; St of Mnth; Peer Tut/Med; Chrch Yth Grp; DARE; Emplmnt; FBLA; Jr Ach; Off Aide; Tchrs Aide; Wdwrkg Clb; Ch Chr; Dnce; Stu Cncl (R); CR (R); Academic Team; Emergency/Trauma Surgeon; U of Kentucky; U of Alabama At Birmingham

JONES, JASON R; MURRAY, KY; CALLOWAY CTY HS; (FR); Ctznshp Aw; Hnr Roll; MVP; Otst Ac Ach Awd; Sci Fairs; Comm Volntr; Peer Tut/Med; ArtClub; Chess; Chrch Yth Grp; Drma Clb; Off Aide; SADD; Tchrs Aide; Tech Clb; Bnd; Ch Chr; Jzz Bnd; SP/M/VS; Adv Cncl (R); Most Likely to Succeed Science Award; Park League Baseball; Neurology; Anesthesiology; Baylor College of Medicine; Vanderbilt U School of Medicine

JONES, JENNIFER D; FRANKLIN, KY; FRANKLIN-SIMPSON HS; (JR); 4H Awd; Ctznshp Aw; Hnr Roll; Comm Volntr; 4-H; Chrch Yth Grp; FCA; Ntl Beta Clb; Ntl FFA; Photog; Scouts; Tchrs Aide; Sftball (J); 4-H Citizenship Award; 4-H Maude Mequiar Award; Animal Science; Veterinary Medicine; Western Kentucky U; Auburn State U

JONES, NICOLETTE J; HOPKINSVILLE, KY; CHRISTIAN CTY HS; (FR); Ctznshp Aw; Hnr Roll; Perf Att; Sci Fairs; St of Mnth; Peer Tut/Med; Chrch Yth Grp; DARE; ROTC; Renaissance Card; Performing Arts; Spelman; T.S.U

JONES, VALERIE; SOMERSET, KY; SOMERSET HS; (SO); ArtClub; Chrch Yth Grp; DARE; FCA; Sftball; FCA; Lawyer, Government; Forensic Scientist; EKU

JUSTICE, KRISTI N; SHELBIANA, KY; SHELBY VALLEY HS; (SR); All Am Sch; Hi Hnr Roll; Nat Ldrshp Svc; Nat Mrt LOC; Perf Att; USAA; WWAHSS; 4-H; Emplmnt; FTA; Ntl Beta Clb; German Clb; Sch Ppr (R, P); Kentucky Administrative Support Skill Standards Certificate of Recognition; Early Childhood Education; Sullivan U Lexington; Eastern Kentucky U

KAELIN, JOSHUA; LOUISVILLE, KY; PLEASURE RIDGE PARK HS; (JR); Hnr Roll; WWAHSS; Engineering; Jefferson Community College; University of Louisville

KAESER, JASMIN; LOUISVILLE, KY; WALDEN SCH; (SO); Duke TS; Hi Hnr Roll; Nat Hon Sy; WWAHSS; Comm Volntr; Drma Clb; Key Club; Ntl Beta Clb; Scouts; Spanish Clb; SP/M/VS; Vllyball (V); Forensic Science; Psychology; Carnegie Mellon; Eastern Kentucky U

KAIMA, JOEL S; VANCLEVE, KY; MT CARMEL SCH; (JR); Gov Hnr Prg; Hnr Roll; Otst Ac Ach Awd; Perf Att; Pres Sch; Salutrn; St of Mnth; St Optmst of Yr; WWAHSS; Amnsty Intl; Comm Volntr; Red Cr Aide; BPA; Emplmnt; FCA; Mus Clb; SADD; Chr; Ch Chr; Bsball (V); Ftball (V); Skt Tgt Sh (V); Sftball (V); Finance & Business Management; Computer Science; Pensacola Christian College; Virginia Tech

KAPUR, ABHINAV; PROSPECT, KY; DUPONT MANUAL HS; (SR); Duke TS; F Lan Hn Soc; MVP; Nat Hon Sy; Nat Mrt Fin; Sci Fairs; Sci/Math Olympn; WWAHSS; Yth Ldrshp Prog; Hosp Aide; Lttrmn Clb; Lib Aide; Mth Clb/Tm; Ntl Beta Clb; Cr Ctry (L); Physician; Biomedical Engineer; Duke U; Johns Hopkins U

KEARNS, TARA M; LEXINGTON, KY; LEXINGTON CHRN AC HS; (SO); Hi Hnr Roll; Hnr Roll; Otst Ac Ach Awd; Yth Ldrshp Prog; Comm Volntr; Spec Olymp Vol; Chrch Yth Grp; FCA; NYLC; Pep Squd; Svce Clb; Chrldg (V L); Gmnstcs (V L); PP Ftbl (V); Medicine; Florida State U; U of Kentucky

KEEL, BRANDI; WHITESBURG, KY; FLEMING NEON HS; (SR); Hnr Roll; Otst Ac Ach Awd; Perf Att; WWAHSS; Comm Volntr; Peer Tut/Med; Emplmnt; FCCLA; Lttrmn Clb; Photog; Prom Com; Vllyball (V C); Sch Ppr (R, P); Yrbk (R, P); Biology; Sociology; Alice Lloyd College; Eastern Kentucky U

KEENE, KRISTIN; RACCOON, KY; IKE CTY CTRL HS; (FR); 4H Awd; Ctznshp Aw; Hnr Roll; Nat Hon Sy; Otst Ac Ach Awd; Sci Fairs; Comm Volntr; 4-H; DARE; Bskball (J); PP Ftbl (V); Sftball (VJ); Vllyball (VJ); Mathematics Teachers; PE Teacher; Pikeville College; UNC

KEETON, SAMANTHA H; CAMPTON, KY; WOLFE CTY HS; (SR); Gov Hnr Prg; Hi Hnr Roll; Hnr Roll; Nat Hon Sy; St of Mnth; WWAHSS; Comm Volntr; Chrch Yth Grp; FCCLA; Ntl Beta Clb; Ntl FFA; Prom Com; Tchrs Aide; Yrbk (E); Elementary Education; Kentucky Christian U

KEITH, HEATHER-ANN; OWENTON, KY; OWEN CTY HS; (MS); Duke TS; Hnr Roll; St of Mnth; Comm Volntr; Peer Tut/Med; 4-H; Chrch Yth Grp; Key Clb; Pep Squd; Bnd; Clr Grd; Dnce; Pep Bnd; Chrldg (L); PPSqd (L); CR (R); Northern Kentucky U; Kentucky State

KEITH, NATHANIEL; BEREA, KY; BEREA CMTY HS; (FR); St of Mnth; 4-H; Chrch Yth Grp; Emplmnt; FCA; Key Club; Bnd; Skt Tgt Sh (V); Swmg (V L); CR; Eastern Kentucky U

KELLY, CLAIRE; CTRL CITY, KY; MUHLENBERG NORTH HS; (SO); Hnr Roll; Perf Att; WWAHSS; Hab For Humty Volntr; 4-H; ArtClub; Chrch Yth Grp; DARE; FBLA; Tchrs Aide; Sccr (V); Swmg (V L); Architect; Western Kentucky U

KELSCH, V ROSS; AUGUSTA, KY; AUGUSTA HS; (JR); Ctznshp Aw; Fut Prb Slvr; Hnr Roll; Nat Hon Sy; Nat Ldrshp Svc; St of Mnth; WWAHSS; Comm Volntr; Cmptr Clb; FBLA; FCCLA; Off Aide; Prom Com; Tech Clb; Ch Chr; Adv Cncl (S); Cl Off (P, V, T); Sch Ppr (E); Yrbk (E); Church Musician; Computer Aide; U of Kentucky; Northern Kentucky U

KENNEDY, RACHEAL; RUSSELLVILLE, KY; (SR); Hnr Roll; Hab For Humty Volntr; Red Cr Aide; Emplmnt; SADD; Ch Chr

KENNEY, NATALIE R; LOUISVILLE, KY; HOLY ANGELS AC; (FR); Hi Hnr Roll; WWAHSS; Comm Volntr; SP/M/VS; Vllyball (J); Piano; Tennis; Nurse; Pharmacist; Bellarmine U; U of Louisville

KEOWN, DANIEL; HAWESVILLE, KY; HANCOCK CTY HS; (SO); Duke TS; Fut Prb Slvr; Hi Hnr Roll; Pres Ac Ftns Aw; Ntl Beta Clb; Scouts; Tchrs Aide; Bsball (VJ L); Bskball (VJ); Who's Who Among Youth League Baseball 2003; Forensic Science; U of Kentucky

KEPPLE, ASHLEY M; LOUISVILLE, KY; ATHERTON HS; (SO); Duke TS; Gov Hnr Prg; Hi Hnr Roll; Pres Sch; St of Mnth; WWAHSS; Comm Volntr; Red Cr Aide; Dbte Team; Drma Clb; Emplmnt; FCA; FBLA; JSA; Ntl Beta Clb; Photog; Sccr (V L); Yrbk (P); FBLA Local Chapter Parliamentarian; Varsity Soccer Rookie of the Year; Psychology; Public Relations; New York U; U of Louisville

KERLEY, JOHN; NEWPORT, KY; NEWPORT HS; (SR); Duke TS; Hi Hnr Roll; Nat Hon Sy; Otst Ac Ach Awd; Perf Att; Comm Volntr; Peer Tut/Med; Aqrium Clb; Cmptr Clb; Emplmnt; Key Club; Pep Squd; P to P St Amb Prg; Prom Com; Tech Clb; Bnd; Mch Bnd; Pep Bnd; Cl Off (T); Stu Cncl (P); CR (T); Sch Ppr (R); Varsity Scholar; Biology; Transylvania U

KIDWELL, BRITTANY; BLOOMFIELD, KY; NELSON CTY HS; (JR); Hi Hnr Roll; Nat Hon Sy; St of Mnth; USAA; WWAHSS; Comm Volntr; Key Club; Dnce; Cr Ctry (V); Stu Cncl (R)

KILCOYNE, BRANDON; HICKORY, KY; GRAVES CTY HS; (JR); Hi Hnr Roll; Hnr Roll; Perf Att; St of Mnth; WWAHSS; Comm Volntr; Hosp Aide; Peer Tut/Med; FCA; FBLA; Lttrmn Clb; Ntl FFA; Off Aide; Pep Squd; SADD; Vsity Clb; Bskball (V); Dental; Business Management; Murray State U; U of Louisville

KILLEBREW, JESSICA D; CADIZ, KY; TRIGG CTY HS; (FR); Hi Hnr Roll; Hnr Roll; WWAHSS; Key Club; Pep Squd; Chrldg; College After High School; Major in Communications; Rice; UCLA, or UK

KILLINGBECK, SARAH R; CLARKSON, KY; GRAYSON CTY HS; (SO); All Am Sch; Duke TS; Hi Hnr Roll; Perf Att; Comm Volntr; Chrch Yth Grp; DARE; Ntl Beta Clb; Scouts; Bnd; Ch Chr; Mch Bnd; Pep Bnd; Tennis (V L); Stu Cncl (R); All District Band; Junior Beta President; U of Louisville

KING, JOCELYN M; HOPKINSVILLE, KY; HOPKINSVILLE HS; (FR); Hnr Roll; Red Cr Aide; Chrch Yth Grp; ROTC; Chr; Ch Chr; Bskball (J); Sftball (J); Vllyball (J); Best Server Award for Volleyball; Published on Poetry.Com; I Want to Become a Successful Woman; I Want to Become a Psychologist.; U of Kentucky; U of Louisville

KING, STEVEN D; HUSTONVILLE, KY; LINCOLN CTY; (JR); Hnr Roll; Perf Att; St of Mnth; FCA; Ntl Beta Clb; Outdrs Clb; Pep Squd; Missed Only 1/2 day of School Since High School; Education Talent Search; Pre Medical; Math; U of Kentucky; Somerset Community College

KINNAMAN, KEVIN; LOUISVILLE, KY; BETH HAVEN CHRISTIAN SCH; (JR); Hnr Roll; Bskball (VJ); U of Louisville; U of Kentucky

KINNEY, NICOLE; GEORGETOWN, KY; SCOTT CTY HS; (JR); Duke TS; Hi Hnr Roll; Nat Hon Sy; WWAHSS; Comm Volntr; DECA; Emplmnt; FCA; FBLA; Key Club; Ntl Beta Clb; Pep Squd; Prom Com; Sccr (V L); Stu Cncl (R); DECA Officer; Defensive Player of the Year in Soccer; Advertising; Marketing; U of Kentucky

KIPER, KELSEY H; LOUISVILLE, KY; SACRED HEART AC; (SO); Hnr Roll; Pres Ac Ftns Aw; WWAHSS; Yth Ldrshp Prog; Peer Tut/Med; Chrch Yth Grp; Jr Ach; Pep Squd; German Clb; Chr; Bskball (C); Fld Hky (J); PP Ftbl; Track (V L); Stu Cncl (R); CR (R); Best Sprinter - Track; Business Marketing; Business Advertising; U of Virginia; U of North Carolina

KIRBY, BROOKE; CLAY CITY, KY; POWELL CTY HS; (JR); Hnr Roll; Otst Ac Ach Awd; Perf Att; Comm Volntr; Peer Tut/Med; Chrch Yth Grp; DARE; FBLA; Chr; Radiology/Nuclear Medicine; Lexington Community College; Somerset Community College

KIRKLAND, ELYSE; LEXINGTON, KY; BRYAN STATION HS; (JR); Hnr Roll; WWAHSS; Comm Volntr; FBLA; Spch Team; Orch; PP Ftbl (J); Stu Cncl (R); CR (R); FCCLA; Pharmacy; Doctor; U of Kentucky; U of Louisville

KIRKWOOD, DEMETRICE; HOPKINSVILLE, KY; HOPKINSVILLE HS; (JR); Hi Hnr Roll; Hnr Roll; Perf Att; Ntl Beta Clb; Vsity Clb; Chr; Track (VJCL); Physical Therapist; Psychologist; U of Louisville; U of Kentucky

KLOCKE, JEFFERSON T; GEORGETOWN, KY; SCOTT CTY HS; (SO); Duke TS; Hi Hnr Roll; Nat Hon Sy; Otst Ac Ach Awd; Perf Att; Pres Sch; WWAHSS; Comm Volntr; Chrch Yth Grp; DARE; FCA; Jr Ach; Key Club; P to P St Amb Prg; Scouts; French Clb; Bnd; Jzz Bnd; Mch Bnd; Orch; Adv Cncl (R); Boy Scouts; Capital City Community Band; Medical; Music; Ohio State U; U of Michigan

Keene, Kristin
Ike Cty Ctrl HS
Raccoon, KY

Jones, De Andra
North Hardin HS
Radcliff, KY

National
Honor Roll
Spring 2005

Johnson, Hope
Graves Cty HS
Wingo, KY

Kilcoyne, Brandon
Graves Cty HS
Hickory, KY

KNEZEVICH, KYLE; RICHMOND, KY; MODEL LABORATORY SCH; (JR); Hnr Roll; MVP; Nat Hon Sy; WWAHSS; Key Club; Pep Squd; Prom Com; Swmg (V C); Cl Off (T); Sch Ppr (R); Yrbk (R, P); Swim Team MVP & 110% for 2005; Aviation Administration; Florida Institute of Technology

KNIGHT, LYNSEY; RUSSELL SPRINGS, KY; RUSSELL CTY HS; (JR); Hnr Roll; WWAHSS; Accounting; Somerset Community College KY

KOHL, AMANDA L; MAYFIELD, KY; GRAVES CTY HS; (JR); Hnr Roll; Nat Hon Sy; Perf Att; 4-H; Drma Clb; NtlFrnscLg; Pep Squd; Dnce; Drl Tm; SP/M/VS; PPSqd (V L); Scr Kpr; Drama/Dance; Musical; Broadcasting/ Production; Psychology; Murray State U; Western Kentucky U

KOLLMANN, JACOB; BURLINGTON, KY; CONNER HS; (SO); Hnr Roll; Nat Hon Sy; St of Mnth; WWAHSS; Chrch Yth Grp; FCA; FBLA; Ftball (VJ L); Track (V L); Wt Lftg (V L); Who's Who- 2 Years; Lawyer; Judge; Indiana U; Notre Dame U

KOONAPAREDDY, JESSICA R; ONEIDA, KY; ONEIDA BAPTIST INST; (JR); F Lan Hn Soc; Gov Hnr Prg; Hi Hnr Roll; Hnr Roll; Nat Sci Aw; Otst Ac Ach Awd; Perf Att; Sci Fairs; St of Mnth; Yth Ldrshp Prog; Comm Volntr; Peer Tut/Med; Red Cr Aide; Biology Clb; Chrch Yth Grp; Drma Clb; Lib Aide; Mus Clb; Off Aide; Schol Bwl; Sci Clb; Chr; Ch Chr; SP/M/VS; Stg Cre; Bdmtn; Bskball; Golf; Rlr Hky; Sccr; Sftball; Tennis; Track; Cl Off (S); Stu Cncl (V); CR (S); Lit Mag (R); Yrbk (R); National Junior Honor Society; Medicine; Nursing; Mysore Medical College (India); Transey U

KOONTZ, JONATHON; STANTON, KY; POWELL CTY HS; (FR); 4H Awd; Perf Att; 4-H; Chrch Yth Grp; Ntl FFA; Ftball (VJ); Wt Lftg (V); Marine Biologist; Forest Ranger; Eastern KY U; South Carolina U

KYLOR, SHELLEY; RADCLIFF, KY; NORTH HARDIN HS; (SR); Hnr Roll; Nat Hon Sy; St of Mnth; WWAHSS; Hab For Humty Volntr; FCA; Pep Squd; Prom Com; Scouts; Chrldg (V); Adv Cncl (R); Stu Cncl (R); U of Kentucky

LADD, ALYSIA F; HOPKINSVILLE, KY; HOPKINSVILLE HS; (FR); Hnr Roll; Sci Fairs; St of Mnth; Comm Volntr; Chrch Yth Grp; Pep Squd; Ch Chr; Upward Bound; James White Scholars Program; Pediatrician; Accountant; U of Louisville; U of Virginia

LADD, JON; MAYFIELD, KY; GRAVES CTY HS; (SR); Hnr Roll; MVP; Otst Ac Ach Awd; WWAHSS; Yth Ldrshp Prog; Comm Volntr; Chrch Yth Grp; Ftball (V L); Track (V L); KY CATS Test Achievement Award Winner X2; KY House of Rep. Science Academic Ex., Who's Who Sports Ed.; Business & Sports Mktg./Mark Shelton Leadership Award; Murray State U; U of Kentucky

LAFFERTY, ALAN W; SHELBYVILLE, KY; SHELBY CTY HS; (JR); Ctznshp Aw; Hnr Roll; Nat Hon Sy; Otst Ac Ach Awd; USAA; WWAHSS; Chrch Yth Grp; FCA; Jr Ach; Ntl Beta Clb; Bnd; Pep Bnd; Academic Team; Meteorologist; Atmospheric Science; Western Kentucky U

LAIR, COURTNEY; LOUISVILLE, KY; SOUTHERN HS; (SO); Hnr Roll; Otst Ac Ach Awd; St of Mnth; WWAHSS; DECA; FBLA; Key Club; Swmg; Vllyball; Veterinarian; Radiologist; U of R; U of L

LAMB, CHERYL R; PRINCETON, KY; CALDWELL CTY HS; (SR); Hnr Roll; WWAHSS; FCCLA; Key Club; Up for Peer Education; Region 2 Up for Membership; Nursing or History; Hopkinsville Community College; Murray State U

LAMOND, LIANA; SCOTTSVILLE, KY; ALLEN CTY HS; (SO); All Am Sch; Hi Hnr Roll; Hnr Roll; Nat Ldrshp Svc; Otst Ac Ach Awd; Pres Sch; USAA; WWAHSS; Peer Tut/Med; Spec Olymp Vol; FCCLA; FTA; JSA; Ntl Beta Clb; Bnd; Mch Bnd; Pep Bnd; Cr Ctry (J); Track (V); Vllyball (J); VP of Public Relations - FCCLA-FHA; Presidential Classroom; Supreme Court Justice; Lawyer; Vanderbilt U; Indiana U

LANEY, AMANDA; ASHLAND, KY; PAUL G BLAZER HS; (FR); Sci Fairs; DARE; Tmpl Yth Grp; Lawyer; Sales Executive; New York U; California State U

LANIER, ANDREW C; WEST PADUCAH, KY; HEATH HS; (JR); Hnr Roll; Otst Ac Ach Awd; Comm Volntr; Chrch Yth Grp; Emplmnt; FBLA; Tchrs Aide; Participated in KY Mock Trial; Received a GPA Award in Social Studies; Major in Criminal Law; Minor in Psychology; U of Kentucky; U of Louisville

LAPHAM, GARRETT C; GLASGOW, KY; BARREN CTY HS; (SR); Hnr Roll; Perf Att; Sci Fairs; Chess; Chrch Yth Grp; Bnd; Mch Bnd; Pep Bnd; Civil Engineering; Western KY U

LARISON, ANGELA L; JEFFERSONVILLE, KY; MONTGOMERY CTY HS; (SO); Hi Hnr Roll; WWAHSS; Key Club; Ntl Beta Clb; Ntl FFA; Who's Who Poetry; Animal Science / Veterinarian; Eastern Kentucky U; U of Kentucky

LASCH, MISTY N; LOUISVILLE, KY; DUPONT MANUAL HS; (SR); Hnr Roll; Perf Att; WWAHSS; Comm Volntr; Spec Olymp Vol; Chrch Yth Grp; Drma Clb; Emplmnt; FCA; Mus Clb; Scouts; Chr; Ch Chr; SP/M/VS; Chrldg (V); PP Ftbl (V); Perfect Attendance 15 Yrs; FCA Athlete of the Year 03-04; Communications-Broadcast Journalism; Vocal Music Performance; Lindsey Wilson College

LASSELL, DANIEL; CRESTWOOD, KY; HOLY ANGELS AC; (SO); 4H Awd; Hnr Roll; WWAHSS; Comm Volntr; 4-H; Chrch Yth Grp; Emplmnt; Scouts; Bskball (J); 4-H President; State Fair Merit Award in Art; Veterinary; Writing

LAWSON, HEATHER; JEFFERSONVILLE, KY; MONTGOMERY CTY HS; (FR); Ctznshp Aw; Hi Hnr Roll; Hnr Roll; Otst Ac Ach Awd; Perf Att; St of Mnth; WWAHSS; Key Club; School Bank Officer; Part of Junior Beta Club; Dental Hygienist; Pediatrician; Morehead State U; U of Kentucky

LAY, STACY; LOUISVILLE, KY; DOSS HS MAG CAREER AC; (JR); Hnr Roll; Peer Tut/Med; Bsball (VJ); Sccr (V L); Sftball (J); Teacher for the ECE, Major In Education; Jefferson County

LAYNE, JORDAN E; NICHOLASVILLE, KY; LEXINGTON CHRN AC HS; (SO); Hi Hnr Roll; USAA; Chrch Yth Grp; Ntl Beta Clb; Svce Clb; Chr; Golf (V L); Academic All-State 2003, 2004; 9th Individual (KYKHSAA Golf Tournament 2004); Accounting; Business-Finance/Golf Management; U of Kentucky; U of Tennessee

LEAVELL, JOE; HOPKINSVILLE, KY; HOPKINSVILLE HS; (SO); Ctznshp Aw; Duke TS; Hnr Roll; MVP; Perf Att; Sci Fairs; Peer Tut/Med; Chrch Yth Grp; DARE; FCA; FBLA; Vsity Clb; Ch Chr; Bskball (VJ); Ftball (VJ); Track (V); Stu Cncl (R); Sports Medicine / Physical Therapy; Business Management; University of Louisville; Western Kentucky University

LEE, CALVIN; LEXINGTON, KY; PAUL LAWRENCE DUNBAR HS; (SO); Duke TS; Hi Hnr Roll; Hnr Roll; Otst Ac Ach Awd; Peer Tut/Med; DARE; Ntl Beta Clb; Orch; Tennis (V); First Place Bach Piano Competition Lexington; Federated Music Club; Engineering; Medicine

LEE, CHELSEA M; LEXINGTON, KY; LEXINGTON CHRN AC HS; (SO); Hnr Roll; Chrch Yth Grp; Chr; Fncg (V); PP Ftbl (J); Vllyball (V)

LEE, HEATHER; LANCASTER, KY; GARRARD CTY HS; (SR); Hnr Roll; Nat Hon Sy; Otst Ac Ach Awd; USAA; WWAHSS; Comm Volntr; Emplmnt; FCCLA; Vsity Clb; Chrldg (V); PP Ftbl (J); Cl Off (T); Yrbk (R, P); CNA License; HOSA Club; Medical Field; Lexington Community College; Midway College

LEE, JASON R; PROSPECT, KY; ST XAVIER HS; (SR); Hnr Roll; WWAHSS; Comm Volntr; Drma Clb; Emplmnt; Mus Clb; Scouts; Bnd; SP/ M/VS; Stu Cncl (R); CR (R); Music: Guild-2001-2004; Eagle Scout 2003; Engineering; Purdue U

LEE, MICHELLE D; MT WASHINGTON, KY; MT WASHINGTON MS; Hnr Roll; Perf Att; St of Mnth; DARE; Lib Aide; Chrldg; Computer Tech; U of Louisville

LEECH, KAYLA; PRINCETON, KY; CALDWELL CTY HS; (FR); Hnr Roll; St of Mnth; FCA; Pep Squd; Chrldg; Gmnstcs; Dietician; Sex Therapist; U of Louisville

LESTER, WHITNEY; MADISONVILLE, KY; MADISONVILLE NORTH HOPKINS HS; (JR); Duke TS; Gov Hnr Prg; Hi Hnr Roll; Hnr Roll; Jr Mshl; Nat Hon Sy; Perf Att; WWAHSS; Comm Volntr; Chrch Yth Grp; Emplmnt; FCA; FBLA; Key Club; Ntl Beta Clb; Prom Com; Sccr (VJ L); Cl Off (S); FCA - Junior Representative; Church Mission Trip; Transylvania U; Center College

LE VAUGHN, MEGHAN; MADISONVILLE, KY; HOPKINS CTY CTRL HS; (SO); Hnr Roll; Perf Att; St of Mnth; ArtClub; Pep Squd; Photog; Prom Com; Sccr; Yrbk (P); A Manager of the Soccer Team; Cartoonist of Anime At Toronto, Canada; Architect; The Art Institute of Toronto

LEWIS, BRENDA L; ALLEN, KY; ALLEN CTRL HS; (JR); Hnr Roll; Perf Att; WWAHSS; Chrch Yth Grp; DARE; FCA; Prom Com; ROTC; Chr; Clr Grd; Drl Tm; Mch Bnd; Chrldg (J); Track (V); Cl Off (S); Chemical Specialist; Eastern Kentucky U; U of Kentucky

LEWIS, DUSTIN; CYNTHIANA, KY; HARRISON CTY HS; (SO); Hnr Roll; Chrch Yth Grp; Bsball (VJ); Sccr (VJ); Sports Management; U of Kentucky; Western Kentucky

LEWIS, HILLARY N; CORBIN, KY; WHITLEY CTY HS; (FR); Hi Hnr Roll; Otst Ac Ach Awd; Sci/Math Olympn; Yth Ldrshp Prog; Comm Volntr; ArtClub; Chrch Yth Grp; FCA; Ntl Beta Clb; Pep Squd; SADD; Spanish Clb; Chrldg (V); Top Math Student of the Year; Outstanding Art Student of the Year; Anesthesiology; Pharmacy; U of Kentucky; U of Louisville

LEWIS, SARAH E; VANCEBURG, KY; LEWIS CTY HS; (SO); Duke TS; WWAHSS; Chrch Yth Grp; Ch Chr; Degree in Radiology or Teaching Degree; U of Kentucky; Northern Kentucky U

LILLPOP, CANDACE; BOWLING GREEN, KY; EDMONSON CTY HS; (FR); All Am Sch; Hnr Roll; DARE; Drma Clb; Mus Clb; Bnd; Jzz Bnd; Mch Bnd; Pep Bnd; Tri M Honor Society; Drama; Librarian; Band Teacher; Western Kentucky U; Murray State U

LIMPACH JR, STEPHEN J; ASHLAND, KY; PAUL G BLAZER HS; (FR); 4H Awd; Duke TS; Hnr Roll; MVP; Sci Fairs; Yth Ldrshp Prog; Comm Volntr; Peer Tut/Med; 4-H; ArtClub; Chrch Yth Grp; DARE; Emplmnt; FCA; Jr Ach; Key Club; SP/M/VS; Bsball; Bskball (J); Golf (V L); Wt Lftg (V); Art Awards; Kiwanis Bowl Court; 4 Yr. Degree; U of KY; U of Louisville KY

LINK, MATTHEW; OWINGSVILLE, KY; BATH CTY HS; (JR); Hnr Roll; Ntl FFA; Teaching; Criminal Justice; Morehead State U; Eastern Kentucky U

LITTLE, FAITH; MELVIN, KY; SOUTH FLOYD HS; (FR); Hi Hnr Roll; Otst Ac Ach Awd; Perf Att; St of Mnth; USAA; WWAHSS; Peer Tut/Med; 4-H; DARE; FCA; French Clb; Bskball (V); Track (V); Stu Cncl (R); People to People Leadership; Conservation Essay Winner

LITTLE, NOLAN; LOUISVILLE, KY; FERN CREEK TRADITIONAL HS; (SR); F Lan Hn Soc; Hi Hnr Roll; Hnr Roll; Nat Hon Sy; Otst Ac Ach Awd; St of Mnth; WWAHSS; Comm Volntr; Chess; Chrch Yth Grp; Emplmnt; P to P St Amb Prg; Photog; French Clb; Golf (V); Mar Art (V); Tennis (V); Lit Mag; Distinguished Scholar Award; Medicine-Doctor; Communications; U of Louisville; Western Kentucky U

LITTRELL, ADAM; UNION, KY; COVINGTON LATIN HS; (JR); Duke TS; Hi Hnr Roll; St of Mnth; Comm Volntr; Spch Team; Golf (V); Medicine

LOCH, SAMBATH; BARDSTOWN, KY; NELSON CTY HS; (SO); Ctznshp Aw; Hnr Roll; Perf Att; Comm Volntr; Key Club; Cr Ctry (VJ); Tennis (V); Track (V); Computer Programmer; Computer Engineer; U of Louisville; U of Kentucky

LOCKHART, SARAH; SOMERSET, KY; PULASKI CO HS; (SO); Hi Hnr Roll; Otst Ac Ach Awd; WWAHSS; Yth Ldrshp Prog; 4-H; DECA; FCA; Mod UN; Ntl Beta Clb; Pep Squd; Prom Com; Vsity Clb; Chrldg (V); Cl Off (T); Stu Cncl (T); CR (T)

LOCKWOOD, JENKA M; DRY RIDGE, KY; GRANT CTY HS; (SO); 4H Awd; Hnr Roll; Otst Ac Ach Awd; St of Mnth; WWAHSS; 4-H; Chrch Yth Grp; Emplmnt; Ntl FFA; Stu Cncl (R); The National Society of High School; Overall Distinguished on CATS/Scholars; Veterinary Medicine; Ag Education-(High School); Murray State U; Auburn U

LOGSDON, GLENNIS A; HARDYVILLE, KY; HART CTY HS; (SO); 4H Awd; Hi Hnr Roll; Hnr Roll; St of Mnth; WWAHSS; Comm Volntr; 4-H; Chrch Yth Grp; Pep Squd; Bnd; Jzz Bnd; Mch Bnd; Pep Bnd; Academic Team-State Finals; Lifesmarts Team; Anesthesiologist; Physical Therapist; U of Florida; U of Kentucky

LOGSDON, KAYLA R; OLMSTEAD, KY; LOGAN CTY HS; (FR); Hnr Roll; St of Mnth; Chrch Yth Grp; FCA; FBLA; Ntl FFA; Pep Squd; Clr Grd; Health Science; Agriculture; Western Kentucky; Columbia

LONG, KAYLA; LOUISVILLE, KY; LOUISVILLE MALE HS; (JR); Hnr Roll; Biology Clb; Emplmnt; Softball - Lyndon (Not In School); Nursing; Elementary Education; U of Louisville

LOPEZ, AMANDA; HUSTONVILLE, KY; LINCOLN CTY HS; (JR); Duke TS; Hnr Roll; Nat Hon Sy; Otst Ac Ach Awd; Pres Ac Ftns Aw; Emplmnt; Ntl Beta Clb; Chr; Tennis (V); Physical Therapy; U of Kentucky

LOUSIGNONT, COLIN; LEXINGTON, KY; PAUL LAURENCE DUNBAR HS; (FR); Comm Volntr; Chrch Yth Grp; Ftball (J); Culinary Arts; Marine Biology; U of Kentucky; U of Miami

LOWE, JACOB T; WILLIAMSBURG, KY; WHITLEY CTY HS; (FR); Hnr Roll; Comm Volntr; Chrch Yth Grp; Ch Chr; Ftball (J); Wt Lftg (V); Football 8th Colonel Team; Education; Computer Science; U of Kentucky, Cumberland College; Morehead State U

LOWE, KAYLA D; PIKEVILLE, KY; PIKE CTY CTRL HS; (FR); 4H Awd; Hnr Roll; Perf Att; Sci Fairs; USAA; WWAHSS; Comm Volntr; 4-H; Chrch Yth Grp; DARE; Ntl Beta Clb; Sci Clb; Vsity Clb; Ch Chr; Bskball (V); Sftball (V); Vsy Clb (V); Vllyball (V); Booth Scholar Recipient, Double Promoted; Who's Who Among High School Students; Trauma Surgeon or Physician; Astronomical Engineer or Archeology; U of Tennessee; UNC At Chapel Hill

LOWE, SHANNON R; FLEMINGSBURG, KY; FLEMING CTY HS; (SO); Hnr Roll; Emplmnt; FCCLA; Ntl FFA; PP Ftbl; Vllyball; Pharmacy; X-Ray Technician; U of Kentucky; Morehead State U

LYNCH, NATIA; HOPKINSVILLE, KY; CHRISTIAN CTY HS; (SO); Perf Att; FCCLA; Ch Chr; Track (V); Pediatrician Assistant (Nurse); Louisville

MACK, KANETHA; SHELBYVILLE, KY; SHELBY CTY HS; (FR); Fut Prb Slvr; Hnr Roll; Yth Ldrshp Prog; Comm Volntr; Peer Tut/Med; Chrch Yth Grp; Jr Ach; Pep Squd; Ch Chr; Dnce; Stg Cre; Track (J); Stu Cncl (S); Black Achievers; Tennessee State U; Murray State U

Le Vaughn, Meghan
Hopkins Cty Ctrl HS
Madisonville, KY

MADDEN, LAURA; LA GRANGE, KY; OLDHAM CTY HS; (FR); Hnr Roll; Otst Ac Ach Awd; Comm Volntr; Hosp Aide; Chrch Yth Grp; Drma Clb; FCA; Chr; SP/M/VS; Theatre (Acting); Communications (Media); Georgetown College; Butler U

MAGUIRE, KIERNAN; LOUISVILLE, KY; ST FRANCIS DE SALES HS; (JR); Hnr Roll; Nat Hon Sy; WWAHSS; Emplmnt; Key Club; Bsball (V); Sccr (V); Wrstlg (V); Key Club President

MAHNKEN-HOULE, KIERRA K; VINE GROVE, KY; NORTH HARDIN HS; (JR); Hnr Roll; Bnd; Pep Bnd; Sftball (J); Swmg (V); Animal Care; Doctor; Elizabethtown Community College; U of Louisville

MAJOR, EMILY A; CAMPBELLSVILLE, KY; CAMPBELLSVILLE HS; (SO); St of Mnth; Peer Tut/Med; 4-H; Chrch Yth Grp; DARE; FBLA; Off Aide; Pep Squd; Tchrs Aide; Bnd; Ch Chr; Clr Grd; Dnce; Law School; Criminal Justice; Eastern KY U

MALOY, MATTHEW; LEXINGTON, KY; LEXINGTON CHRN AC HS; (SO); Gov Hnr Prg; Hnr Roll; Comm Volntr; Chrch Yth Grp; Ntl Beta Clb; Sccr (VJ); Business; Insurance; Harvard Business School; Western Kentucky U

MANN, JAMI E; CALHOUN, KY; MC LEAN CTY HS; (SR); Chrldg (V L); Track (V L); Cl Off (V); Stu Cncl (R); CR (V); Kentucky Governor's Scholar; Western Kentucky U; U of Kentucky

MANNING, KELLY; WILLIAMSBURG, KY; WHITLEY CTY HS; (FR); Hi Hnr Roll; Hnr Roll; Comm Volntr; Drma Clb; FCA; Writer; Video Game Developer; Bard College; Virginia Polytechnic Institute and State U

MANZULLO, CHARLES; GEORGETOWN, KY; SCOTT CTY HS; (SO); 4H Awd; Hi Hnr Roll; Hnr Roll; Nat Hon Sy; Perf Att; Sci Fairs; Comm Volntr; 4-H; Chess; DARE; Ntl Beta Clb; Scouts; German Clb; Bnd; Mch Bnd; Orch; Pep Bnd; Hsbk Rdg; Mar Art (L); Sccr; IT Professional; Kentucky Community and Technical College

MARKER, AMANDA; LONDON, KY; NORTH LAUREL HS; (SO); Hnr Roll; Nat Hon Sy; Chrch Yth Grp; DARE; Chr; Pediatric Nurse Practitioner; Nurse; Bellarmine U; Berea College

MARLETT, LINDSEY; MT WASHINGTON, KY; BULLITT EAST HS; (FR); Hi Hnr Roll; Hnr Roll; WWAHSS; Comm Volntr; Chrch Yth Grp; DARE; FCA; FBLA; Lib Aide; Tchrs Aide; Bskball (J); PP Ftbl (J); Scr Kpr; Sccr (VJ); Tennis (V); Wt Lftg; U of Louisville; U of Kentucky

MARSH, KAYLA; CYNTHIANA, KY; HARRISON CTY HS; (SO); F Lan Hn Soc; Hnr Roll; Perf Att; WWAHSS; Chrch Yth Grp; Ntl FFA; Sftball (V); Forensic Pathology; Crime Lab Analyst; Eastern Kentucky U; U of Kentucky

MARSHALL, MEGAN D; COXS CREEK, KY; NELSON CTY HS; (FR); Hnr Roll; Perf Att; Comm Volntr; Chess; Chrch Yth Grp; DARE; Key Club; CR (S); Sch Ppr (R); Yrbk (R, P); Nursing; Business & Law; U of Louisville; U of Kentucky

MARSH-CUNNINGHAM, TREVOR; CYNTHIANA, KY; HARRISON CTY HS; (FR); Hnr Roll; Otst Ac Ach Awd; Perf Att; WWAHSS; 4-H; Chrch Yth Grp; Ntl FFA; Harrison County High School Academic Excellence Pin; Academic Excellence in Science; Truck Driver; Carpenter; Maysville Community College; U of Kentucky

MARTIN, AMBER N; MAYSVILLE, KY; MASON CTY; (JR); Ntl FFA

MARTIN, REENA; FRANKFORT, KY; WESTERN HILLS; (MS); Duke TS; Hnr Roll; St of Mnth; Comm Volntr; Peer Tut/Med; ArtClub; Chrch Yth Grp; Drma Clb; Tchrs Aide; Bnd; SP/M/VS; Sch Ppr (R); Yrbk (E); Psychology / Bachelor's Degree; Master's Degree in Anesthesiology; Stanford U; U of Louisville

MARTIN, SARAH M; COLUMBIA, KY; ADAIR CO HS; (FR); Hnr Roll; Chrch Yth Grp; Orch; Chrldg (V); CANAM National Cheerleading Competition

MARTIN, SHIRLEY; HINDMAN, KY; KNOTT CTY CTRL HS; (FR); Hnr Roll; Comm Volntr; Chrch Yth Grp; DARE; FCA; Ch Chr; Dnce; Chrldg; Gmnstcs; Vllyball (J); Physical Therapy; Teaching

MASON, SHAMON; LOUISVILLE, KY; LOUISVILLE MALE HS; (FR); Hnr Roll; Otst Ac Ach Awd; Perf Att; Comm Volntr; Ntl Beta Clb; Pep Squd; ROTC; Dnce; Yrbk (E, P); The Whitney M Young Scholars Program; Entrepreneur; Morehouse College; University of Louisville

MASSEY, JILL A; PADUCAH, KY; LONE OAK HS; (SR); Hnr Roll; MVP; Lttrmn Clb; Mth Clb/Tm; Quill & Scroll; Sftball (V C); CR (R); Sch Ppr; Yrbk; Nurse Practioner; Physician's Assistant; U of Kentucky

MATHENA, STEPHANIE; HEBRON, KY; CONNER HS; (FR); Duke TS; Hnr Roll; St of Mnth; Stu Cncl; Journalism; Directing

MATHIS, AISSA A; LOUISVILLE, KY; SOUTHERN HS; (SO); Ctznshp Aw; Hnr Roll; St of Mnth; Comm Volntr; Dbte Team; Drma Clb; Off Aide; ROTC; Bnd; Ch Chr; Outstanding Citizenship Award; Obstetrician; U of Louisville

MATTA, LAURA; LOUISVILLE, KY; FERN CREEK TRADITIONAL HS; (FR); Hnr Roll; Nat Hon Sy; Perf Att; WWAHSS; Comm Volntr; Peer Tut/Med; DECA; FCA; Ntl Beta Clb; Tchrs Aide; Ch Chr; Orch; Poetry Awards; Social Worker

MATTINGLY, ALLISON E; BARDSTOWN, KY; NELSON CTY HS; (SO); 4H Awd; Hnr Roll; Pres Ac Ftns Aw; Sci/Math Olympn; WWAHSS; Key Club; Pep Squd; Dnce; Physical Therapy; Nursing; U of Kentucky

MATTINGLY, KAYLA N; COXS CREEK, KY; NELSON CTY HS; (FR); Hnr Roll; Nat Hon Sy; WWAHSS; Comm Volntr; Chrch Yth Grp; FCA; Key Club; Active in Church; FCCLA; Pediatric Nurse; U of Louisville

MATTINGLY, KELSEY; BARDSTOWN, KY; NELSON CTY HS; (SO); Hnr Roll; Nat Hon Sy; Comm Volntr; Key Club; Early Childhood Education; U of Kentucky; Western U

MATTINGLY, MICHAEL T; MAYSVILLE, KY; MASON CTY HS; (SO); Hnr Roll; Nat Hon Sy; St of Mnth; Comm Volntr; ArtClub; Cmptr Clb; Emplmnt; Ntl Beta Clb; Scouts; Bsball (VJ); J.V. Baseball Coach's Award 2004-2005; Major in Environmental Science; Minor in Forestry; Eastern Kentucky U; U of Tennessee

MAULDEN, PAM; MAGNOLIA, KY; HART CTY HS; (JR); Layout & Editor of Art Club Magazine; Nursing, Interior Design; Pre-Medicine, Cosmetology; Lindsey Wilson College

MAXEDON, ASHLEY R; FOSTER, KY; PENDLETON CTY HS; (SR); WWAHSS; Chrch Yth Grp; Mus Clb; Tchrs Aide; Foreign Clb; Chr; Ch Chr; SP/M/VS; Yrbk (P); Member of Senior Council; President of Foreign Language Club; Accounting; Northern Kentucky U

MAY, RICK; ASHLAND, KY; PAUL G BLAZER HS; (FR); Duke TS; Hnr Roll; Nat Hon Sy; Pres Sch; Comm Volntr; Chrch Yth Grp; Off Aide; Tech Clb; Ftball (J); Wt Lftg (V); Stu Cncl (R); CR (R); Martial Arts (Aikido); Church Gospel Singer Volunteer, Church Charity Event Volunteer; Professional/Specialist in Reconstructive Plastic Surgery; Professional/Specialist in Elective Cosmetic Surgery; U of Kentucky; U of Louisville

MAYS, HEATHER E; WILLIAMSBURG, KY; WILLIAMSBURG HS; (SO); WWAHSS; Chr; Williamsburg Lady Jacket Basketball Manager; Only Person to Get a 100 on Every Word of Day 3rd Nine Weeks; Writer; English; U of Connecticut; U of Tennessee

MC ANINCH, CASSIE; CYNTHIANA, KY; HARRISON CTY HS; (SO); Hnr Roll; Perf Att; Comm Volntr; ArtClub; FBLA; Foreign Clb; Ch Chr; Art

MC CAIN, BIANCA; BROWNSVILLE, KY; EDMONSON CTY HS; (FR); All Am Sch; ArtClub; Pep Squd; Vllyball (J); Cl Off (T); Law; Photography; U of Kentucky; U of Louisville

MC CARTY, KRISTI; PADUCAH, KY; REIDLAND HS; (JR); Spanish Clb

MC CLURE, COURTNEY; FRANKFORT, KY; FRANKLIN CTY HS; (FR); Hnr Roll; WWAHSS; Chrch Yth Grp; Emplmnt; FCA; Bnd; Jzz Bnd; Mch Bnd; Stg Cre; Golf (J); Tennis; MBA in Business; Minor in Interior Design; U of Kentucky; Hillsdale College

MC CUBBINS, HEATHER; BARDSTOWN, KY; (FR); Key Club; Ntl FFA; Registered Nurse

MC CUMBERS, JORDAN; WILLIAMSBURG, KY; WHITLEY CTY HS; (FR); Hnr Roll; MVP; WWAHSS; Comm Volntr; Pep Squd; P to P St Amb Prg; Bsball (V); Bskball (V); Ftball (V); Cl Off (R); Veterinarian; Teacher; U of Kentucky; Duke U

MC CUTCHEN, LAUREN; WEST PADUCAH, KY; CMTY CHRISTIAN AC; (SO); Duke TS; Hnr Roll; Pres Ac Ftns Aw; Sci Fairs; Comm Volntr; Chrch Yth Grp; FCA; Pep Squd; Svce Clb; Bnd; Chrldg (V L); Gmnstcs (V); Track (V); Young Republican's Club; Cheers Elite - Competitive Cheerleading; Pharmacy; Psychology; U of Kentucky; Murray State U

MC DANIEL, JAMES; RICHMOND, KY; MADISON CTRL HS; (SO); Nat Hon Sy; Perf Att; Comm Volntr; Bsball (J); Astrology; Geology; Eastern Kentucky U; The U of Kentucky

MC DONALD, BRITTANY N; VANCEBURG, KY; LEWIS CTY HS; (FR); Hnr Roll; Perf Att; Sci Fairs; Comm Volntr; FCA; ROTC; Teaching; Military Service; Morehead State U; Duke U

MC DOWELL, KIM; BUFFALO, KY; LAWRENCE CTY HS; (JR); Hnr Roll; Nat Hon Sy; Emplmnt; FCA; FBLA; Pep Squd; Prom Com; Bskball (V L); PP Ftbl (L); Sftball (V); Vllyball (V); Cl Off (R); Stu Cncl (R); CR (R); Yrbk (R); Community Volunteer Service; Elementary Education; Nursing; U of Kentucky; Eastern Kentucky U

MC ELROY, JAYSON; FRANKLIN, KY; FRANKLIN-SIMPSON HS; (SO); WWAHSS; NtlFrnscLg; Spch Team; Chr; Bsball (L); Zoology; Transylvania U, Brown U; Bellarmine U

MC FARLAND, MELISSA R; ASHLAND, KY; PAUL G BLAZER HS; (FR); Hi Hnr Roll; WWAHSS; Drma Clb; Orch; Stg Cre; Management; Dance; Transylvania State U; U of Louisville

MC GILL, ZACHARY R; BOAZ, KY; LONE OAK HS; (JR); Duke TS; WWAHSS; Comm Volntr; Biology Clb; Chess; Chrch Yth Grp; Emplmnt; FCA; Scouts; Bnd; Chr; Mch Bnd; Sccr (VJ L); Eagle Scout; U of Kentucky

MC GUFFIN, ASHLEY; LOUISVILLE, KY; DOSS HS MAG CAREER AC; (JR); Ctznshp Aw; Hnr Roll; Nat Hon Sy; ArtClub; DARE; Emplmnt; Lib Aide; Off Aide; Spanish Clb; Had a Job Since I Was 14; Interior Design; Architecture; Louisville Technical Institute; U of Kentucky

MC HONE, MYSHELL; LEXINGTON, KY; PAUL LAURENCE DUNBAR HS; (FR); Hi Hnr Roll; Hnr Roll; Comm Volntr; Hosp Aide; 4-H; Ntl Beta Clb; Off Aide; Tech Clb; Bnd; Jzz Bnd; Mch Bnd; Teacher; Berea College; University of Kentucky

MC INNIS, CHRISTINA G; COVINGTON, KY; HOLMES HS; (SR); Gov Hnr Prg; Hnr Roll; St of Mnth; WWAHSS; Comm Volntr; Voc Ind Clb Am; Orch; Chemical Engineer; Medical Examiner; U of Kentucky; Oregon State U

MC INTOSH, TIA; LA GRANGE, KY; OLDHAM CTY HS; (FR); Chr; Sftball (J); Vllyball (J); Pageants, Won Princess 2000 OC; Lawyer; Nursing; U of Kentucky; U of Louisville

MC KEIGHEN, JUSTIN; STEARNS, KY; MC CREARY CTRL HS; (JR); Hnr Roll; Nat Hon Sy; St of Mnth; ArtClub; Bnd; Wt Lftg (J); Wrstlg (J); Art; Drama; Ball State U; U of Louisville

MC KENZIE, LINDSEY; WILMORE, KY; WEST JESSAMINE HS; (MS); 4H Awd; Ctznshp Aw; Duke TS; Hnr Roll; USAA; Chrch Yth Grp; FCA; Off Aide; Chr; Vllyball (J); Childhood & Adolescent Psychology; Elementary Teaching; Asbury Theological Seminary; U of Kentucky

MC KINLEY, BRANDON M; HOPKINSVILLE, KY; HOPKINSVILLE HS; (FR); Hnr Roll; Otst Ac Ach Awd; Chrch Yth Grp; ROTC; Bnd; Mch Bnd; Pep Bnd; Attorney; U of Kentucky

MC KINNEY, ELIOT; WINGO, KY; NORTHSIDE BAPTIST CHRISTIAN SCH; (SO); Yth Ldrshp Prog; Emplmnt; HO'Br Yth Ldrshp; Bnd; Wt Lftg; Music-Teaching; Murray State U; Transylvania U

MC NEIL, MICHAEL; PADUCAH, KY; LONE OAK HS; (SO); Hnr Roll; WWAHSS; Comm Volntr; Chrch Yth Grp; FCA; Ntl Beta Clb; Scouts; Ch Chr; Track (V); Completing Eagle Scout; Named Outstanding Student- '04-'05; Military Intelligence; Christian Missionary; West Point; U of Kentucky

MC QUEEN, GLORIA; LATONIA, KY; HOLMES HS; (JR); Hnr Roll; Nat Hon Sy; Sci Fairs; Comm Volntr; DARE; Off Aide; Tchrs Aide; Chr; Dnce; Orch; Accounting; Pediatrician; Georgetown College; Thomas More College

MC SORLEY, SARA R; LEXINGTON, KY; LEXINGTON CHRN AC HS; (SO); Ctznshp Aw; Hi Hnr Roll; Hnr Roll; Nat Hon Sy; WWAHSS; Comm Volntr; Ntl Beta Clb; Photog; Sftball (V L); Softball Dedication Award; Softball Sportsmanship Award; U of Kentucky

MEANS III, GLENN L; MT STERLING, KY; MONTGOMERY CTY HS; (SO); All Am Sch; Hi Hnr Roll; USAA; WWAHSS; Comm Volntr; Peer Tut/Med; 4-H; Chrch Yth Grp; Emplmnt; Key Club; Ntl Beta Clb; Orch; SP/M/VS; Stu Cncl (T); SERVE and Tri - M; YAB; Medical Field; U of Kentucky; Morehead State U

MEEKS, BETHANY J; LEXINGTON, KY; THOMPSON EDUCATION DIRECT; (FR); Hnr Roll; Comm Volntr; Chrch Yth Grp; Hsbk Rdg (J); Artist; Marine Biology

MEFFORD, LANDON S; FRANKFORT, KY; FRANKLIN CTY HS; (FR); Duke TS; Hi Hnr Roll; Pres Ac Ftns Aw; Pres Sch; WWAHSS; Comm Volntr; Chrch Yth Grp; Emplmnt; FCA; Key Club; Bsball (J L); Veterinarian; U of KY/Auburn; Duke U or Miami U

MEHL, JULIAN; FAIRFIELD, KY; NELSON CTY HS; (SO); DAR; Hi Hnr Roll; Nat Hon Sy; WWAHSS; Yth Ldrshp Prog; Comm Volntr; Chrch Yth Grp; Emplmnt; Key Club; Vsity Clb; Mar Art (J); Sccr (V); Tennis (V); Stu Cncl (R)

MELANCON, SAMANTHA; BARDSTOWN, KY; NELSON CTY HS; (SO); 4H Awd; Hnr Roll; WWAHSS; Comm Volntr; 4-H; Chrch Yth Grp; Key Club; Pep Squd; Ftball (V); PP Ftbl (J); Scr Kpr (V); Stu Cncl (R); CR (R); I'm Football Manager for V, J. I Don't Play.; Teaching (Education); Personal Trainer; U of Kentucky; Eastern Kentucky

MELIKANT, DAWN M; AUBURN, KY; LOGAN CTY HS; (SR); Hnr Roll; St of Mnth; Peer Tut/Med; ArtClub; Chrch Yth Grp; FCA; FBLA; FCCLA; Ntl Beta Clb; Pep Squd; Tchrs Aide; Ch Chr; SP/M/VS; Stg Cre; Sch Ppr (R); Yrbk (E); Zoology; Wildlife Conservation; Murray State U; Western Kentucky U

MEREDITH, AUSTIN; BROWNSVILLE, KY; EDMONSON CTY HS; (FR); 4H Awd; 4-H; DARE; Ntl FFA; Bnd; Ftball (V L); Skt Tgt Sh; Wt Lftg; Electro Mechanical Engineer; Western Kentucky U; U of Kentucky

MEREDITH, WESTLEY; MUNFORDVILLE, KY; HART CTY HS; (SO); Hnr Roll; FCA; Pep Squd; Academic Team (JV); PhD in Law; Master's in Business; U of Kentucky; U of Louisville

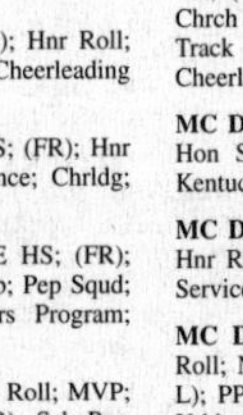

Means III, Glenn L
Montgomery Cty HS
Mt Sterling, KY

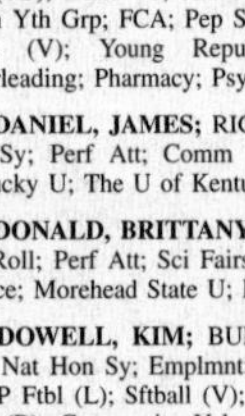

Mc Cumbers, Jordan
Whitley Cty HS
Williamsburg, KY

National
Honor Roll
Spring 2005

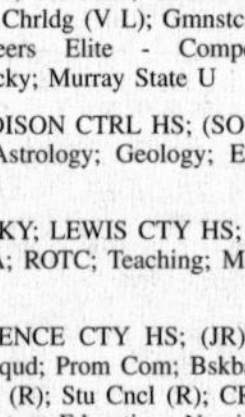

Mathis, Aissa A
Southern HS
Louisville, KY

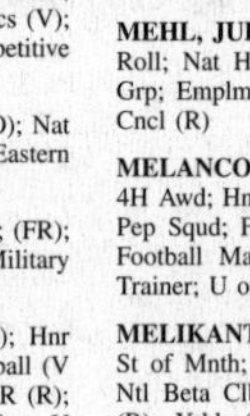

Meredith, Austin
Edmonson Cty HS
Brownsville, KY

MERSON, JESSICA A; ALBANY, KY; CLINTON CTY HS; (SR) Ctznshp Aw; Hnr Roll; Nat Ldrshp Svc; Otst Ac Ach Awd; St of Mnth; US Army Sch Ath Aw; WWAHSS; Comm Volntr; Peer Tut/Med; 4-H; Emplmnt; FCA; ROTC; Scouts; Tchrs Aide; Voc Ind Clb Am; Bnd; Chr; Clr Grd; Drl Tm; Sch Ppr (R); Numerous JROTC Awards; Criminal Justice; Forensic Science; Eastern Kentucky U

METZGER, KRISTA L; VERSAILLES, KY; WOODFORD CTY HS; (SR); Hnr Roll; WWAHSS; Yth Ldrshp Prog; Comm Volntr; Hab For Humty Volntr; Chrch Yth Grp; Ntl Beta Clb; Off Aide; SADD; Tchrs Aide; Ch Chr; CR (J); President of Church Youth Group; Interior Designer; Interior Decorator; U of Kentucky; Eastern Kentucky U

MICALLEF, STEPHANIE A; LEXINGTON, KY; PAUL LAURENCE DUNBAR HS; (SR); Hi Hnr Roll; WWAHSS; Chrch Yth Grp; DARE; Tchrs Aide; Clr Grd; Orch; Sch Ppr (R, P); Winter Guard; Secondary Education; Western Kentucky U

MIDDLETON, ZACH; STANFORD, KY; LINCOLN CTY HS; (JR); Hnr Roll; Jr Eng Tech; Peer Tut/Med; FCA; Outdrs Clb; Criminal Justice; Eastern Kentucky U; U of Kentucky

MIDKIFF, BRANDI; WEST LIBERTY, KY; MORGAN CTY AREA TECH CTR; (SO); Hnr Roll; Perf Att; Comm Volntr; FCA; Ntl Beta Clb; Ntl FFA; Tech Clb; Dnce; Vice President Juniorettes; Education Major; 4-Year Degree / Bachelor's; U of Kentucky; Morehead State U

MILES, BRITTANY K; ALMO, KY; MURRAY HS; (SR); Hnr Roll; Nat Hon Sy; St of Mnth; WWAHSS; Chrch Yth Grp; Emplmnt; FBLA; Key Club; Pep Squad; Prom Com; Quill & Scroll; Tchrs Aide; Ch Chr; Sccr (V CL); Yrbk; Voted Best Dressed of Sr. Class Was on the Miss Murray High Court, Prom Ct & Football Homecoming Queen Ct; Communication Disorders; Murray State U

MILES, MEGAN R; WILLIAMSTOWN, KY; GRANT CTY HS; (SO); Duke TS; Hnr Roll; MVP; WWAHSS; Comm Volntr; Chrch Yth Grp; Sccr (V); Sftball (V L); Most Athletic Award (Softball) (2004); Steals Leader (Softball 2004); Accounting; Medical Administration; Eastern Kentucky U; Northern Kentucky U

MILLER, ALLYSON; MURRAY, KY; CALLOWAY CTY HS; (FR); Ctznshp Aw; Fut Prb Slvr; Hnr Roll; Chrch Yth Grp; Dbte Team; Drma Clb; Emplmnt; FTA; NtlFrmscLg; Spch Team; Ch Chr; SP/M/VS; Cl Off (R); CR (R); Child Psychology; Pediatrics; U of Kentucky; Brigham Young U

MILLER, ERIC; MAYFIELD, KY; GRAVES CTY HS; (JR); Hnr Roll; Nat Hon Sy; Perf Att; Yth Ldrshp Prog; Ntl FFA; Pre-Med; Pre-Pharm; West Kentucky Community and Technical College; Murray State U

MILLER, KAYLA R; ASHLAND, KY; BOYD CTY HS; (SO); Ctznshp Aw; Hi Hnr Roll; Otst Ac Ach Awd; Yth Ldrshp Prog; Comm Volntr; FCA; Ntl Beta Clb; Chr; CR (R); VP of BCHS FCCLA; Law; Pediatric Medicine; Marshall U; U of Kentucky

MILLER, KORY; BOSTON, KY; NELSON CTY HS; (SR); Ctznshp Aw; St of Mnth; WWAHSS; 4-H; Chess; Key Club; Voc Ind Clb Am; Wdwrkg Clb; Sccr (J); Stu Cncl; Kentucky State Engineering Scholarship; 1st State Cabinet Making 2005, 2nd Place 2004; Engineering; Morehead State

MILLER, KRYSTOL; BOSTON, KY; NELSON CTY HS; (SO); Ctznshp Aw; Hnr Roll; MVP; St of Mnth; WWAHSS; Yth Ldrshp Prog; Comm Volntr; 4-H; Key Club; Ntl Beta Clb; PP Ftbl (J); Sccr (VJCL); Stu Cncl (R); Young Leaders; Key Club Vice-President; Pediatrician; Medical Field; U of Kentucky; Western U

MILLER, LAURA; JAMESTOWN, KY; RUSSELL CTY HS; (SO); Hnr Roll; FCA; Somerset Community College; Campbellsville U

MILLER, TESSA P; ASHLAND, KY; BOYD CTY HS; (FR); Hnr Roll; WWAHSS; Chrch Yth Grp; P to P St Amb Prg; Chr; Ch Chr; Clr Grd; Labor and Delivery Nurse; Pediatrics Nurse; U of Kentucky; Berea College

MILLER, TIFFANY; COXS CREEK, KY; NELSON CTY HS; (FR); All Am Sch; Duke TS; Hi Hnr Roll; MVP; Sci Fairs; WWAHSS; Key Club; Ntl FFA; Pep Squd; Bskball (VJ L); Sccr (V L); Track (V L); Stu Cncl; U of Kentucky; U of Louisville

MILLS, ASHLEY; WINCHESTER, KY; GEORGE ROGERS CLARK HS; (FR); 4H Awd; Ctznshp Aw; DAR; Hnr Roll; Pres Sch; 4-H; DARE; FCCLA; Chr; Teaching; Business; Eastern Kentucky U

MILLS, COURTNEY R; LOUISVILLE, KY; FERN CREEK TRADITIONAL HS; (FR); 4H Awd; Hnr Roll; Perf Att; 4-H; Drma Clb; Jr Ach; Ntl Beta Clb; Spanish Clb; Sch Ppr (R); Law; Design; U of Louisville; U of Kentucky

MILLS, SARA J; CORBIN, KY; AMERICAN SCH/HOME SCH; (FR); Ctznshp Aw; Hi Hnr Roll; Hnr Roll; Comm Volntr; Peer Tut/Med; Ntl Beta Clb; Spanish Clb; Dental Hygienist; U of Kentucky

MINKS, TIFFANY; NEW CASTLE, KY; HENRY CTY HS; (FR); Hnr Roll; Perf Att; 4-H; Chr; PP Ftbl; Sftball; Pediatrician; Registered Nurse; U of Louisville; Sullivan U

MINTON, SAVANNAH N; WOODBINE, KY; CORBIN HS; (SO); Hnr Roll; Perf Att; Sci Fairs; Peer Tut/Med; 4-H; Lib Aide; Mus Clb; Off Aide; Pep Squd; Scouts; Svce Clb; SADD; Acpl Chr; Chr; Dnce; English; Teaching; Nurse; Eastern Kentucky U; Richmond U

MIRACLE, MARY E; CALVIN, KY; MEDICAL LAKE HS; (SO); Hnr Roll; Perf Att; St of Mnth; Chrch Yth Grp; Pep Squd; Chrldg (J)

MITCHELL, MARQUETA; HICKMAN, KY; FULTON CTY HS; (SO); CARE; Comm Volntr; Hosp Aide; DARE; Mth Clb/Tm; Chr; Clr Grd; Cl Off (S); Nursing; Day Care; West Kentucky Technical College; Murray State U

MITCHELL, SHADEA D; PADUCAH, KY; LONE OAK HS; (SR); 4H Awd; Gov Hnr Prg; Hi Hnr Roll; Hnr Roll; Pres Ac Ftns Aw; WWAHSS; Yth Ldrshp Prog; 4-H; Chrch Yth Grp; Drma Clb; Emplmnt; FCA; Ntl Beta Clb; Prom Com; Quill & Scroll; Chr; Ch Chr; SP/M/VS; Cr Ctry (J); Golf (J); Sccr (V); Sftball (J); Track (V); Cl Off (R); Yrbk (E); Governor's School for the Arts (Creative Writing); English; U of Louisville

MIZE, ASHLEY; MT VERNON, KY; ROCKCASTLE CTY HS; (SR); Duke TS; Nat Hon Sy; WWAHSS; FCA; Bskball (V); Occupational Therapy; Eastern Kentucky U

MOFFATT, LADREKUS D; HICKMAN, KY; FULTON CTY HS; (FR); Hi Hnr Roll; Hnr Roll; Otst Ac Ach Awd; Chr; Bskball (J); Ftball (VJ); Track (V); Wt Lftg (J); Most Improved Player Track; Defensive Back Award Football; Pro Football Player; Science; Murray State U

MOK, NANCY; LOUISVILLE, KY; ATHERTON HS; (FR); Hnr Roll; Otst Ac Ach Awd; Perf Att; Comm Volntr; Chess; Photog; Japanese Clb; Orch; Track; Vllyball; Table Tennis / Ping-Pong Club; Music / Performing Arts; U of Louisville

MOK, SUNNY G; LEXINGTON, KY; SAYRE HS; (JR); Perf Att; Comm Volntr; Red Cr Aide; French Clb; Swmg (V); Tennis (V); Architecture; Design; North Carolina State U; U of Kentucky

MONTGOMERY, LISA; MIDWAY, KY; WOODFORD CTY HS; (JR); Hnr Roll; Nat Hon Sy; Comm Volntr; Hosp Aide; Chrch Yth Grp; Emplmnt; FCA; FTA; Ntl Beta Clb; Prom Com; Bnd; Mch Bnd; Pep Bnd; Elementary Ed; Special Ed; Asbury College; Western U

MONTS, TOBY J; ALMO, KY; CALLOWAY CTY HS; (JR); Gov Hnr Prg; Hnr Roll; Nat Hon Sy; WWAHSS; Comm Volntr; Lawyer; Business

MOODY, AUSTIN K; OWENSBORO, KY; DAVIESS CTY HS; (JR); Duke TS; Chrch Yth Grp; Vllyball; Plays Guitar; Business; Florida State

MOORE IV, JOHN R; ALMO, KY; MURRAY HS; (SR); Swmg (V); Reef Environmental Education Foundation - Appointee and Participant Scuba Marine Bio Survey; English Studies / Writing / History, Video-Production, Science; Video-Production / Science; Murray State U

MORAN, BRITTANY; MELBER, KY; GRAVES CTY HS; (SR); Hnr Roll; WWAHSS; Comm Volntr; Hosp Aide; 4-H; ArtClub; DARE; Emplmnt; FCCLA; Pep Squd; Biology (Pre-Med)-To Become Ob/Gyn; Spanish; U of Louisville; Murray State U

MORENO, LESLIE; MOUNT STERLING, KY; MONTGOMERY; (MS); Ctznshp Aw; Chrch Yth Grp; Chr; Dnce; Drl Tm; Chrldg (V); Cr Ctry (V); Cyclg (V); Sccr; Swmg

MORGAN, BRYAN; MAYFIELD, KY; GRAVES CTY HS; (JR); Hnr Roll; Nat Hon Sy; Nat Mrt Fin; Otst Ac Ach Awd; Comm Volntr; Chrch Yth Grp; FCA; FBLA; Pep Squd; Prom Com; Chr; Ch Chr; SP/M/VS; TV Dept of School-News Show, Etc; Commonwealth Honors Academy; Computer Science/Software Programming; Murray State U; U of Kentucky

MORGAN, JESSICA; LAWRENCEBURG, KY; ANDERSON HS; (FR); Hnr Roll; Perf Att; St of Mnth; Chrch Yth Grp; DARE; French Clb; Chr; SP/M/VS; Chrldg (V); Sftball (J); Doctor In A Hospital; Psychiatrist / MD; U of Texas; U of Kentucky

MORGAN, KAREN L; FRANKFORT, KY; WESTERN HILLS HS; (SR); F Lan Hn Soc; Gov Hnr Prg; Nat Hon Sy; USAA; WWAHSS; Comm Volntr; 4-H; Drma Clb; Ntl Beta Clb; Ntl FFA; Scouts; Bnd; Flg Crps; Mch Bnd; Pep Bnd; State Adv. Board KY Jr Historians; Animal Science; U of Kentucky

MORGAN, SIERRA; BURKESVILLE, KY; CUMBERLAND CTY HS; (FR); Hi Hnr Roll; Hnr Roll; USAA; Comm Volntr; Chrch Yth Grp; 4-H; FBLA; FCCLA; Jr Ach; Ntl Beta Clb; Mar Art (J); 8th Grade Diploma; FCCLA Vice President of Membership; Psychology; Journalism & Photography; Oxford U; U of California in Los Angeles

MORROW, JULIE A; COXS CREEK, KY; NELSON CTY HS; (FR); Duke TS; Hi Hnr Roll; Hnr Roll; WWAHSS; Key Club; Ntl FFA; Stu Cncl; Barrel Racing (Equestrian Sport); HOSA Club; Crime Scene Investigation; Forensic Nursing; Eastern Kentucky U; U of Kentucky

MOSELEY, MARCUS; CALHOUN, KY; MC LEAN CTY HS; (JR); All Am Sch; Hnr Roll; Nat Hon Sy; Chrch Yth Grp; DARE; Emplmnt; FBLA; Lttrmn Clb; Ntl Beta Clb; Bskball; Tennis (V L); Track (V L); U of Kentucky; Western Kentucky U

MOSES, BRITTANY; CORBIN, KY; WHITLEY CTY HS; (FR); Ctznshp Aw; Hi Hnr Roll; Hnr Roll; Perf Att; Sci/Math Olympn; WWAHSS; Comm Volntr; Hosp Aide; Chrch Yth Grp; FCA; Mth Clb/Tm; Ntl Beta Clb; Pep Squd; Chr; Ch Chr; Track (J); Cl Off; CR (P); Yrbk (E); Pharmacy; Law; U of Kentucky; Eastern Kentucky U

MOSLEY, TAYLOR E; MARTIN, KY; ALLEN CTRL HS; (JR); 4H Awd; Hi Hnr Roll; Hnr Roll; MVP; Nat Hon Sy; Perf Att; US Army Sch Ath Aw; WWAHSS; Comm Volntr; Peer Tut/Med; 4-H; ArtClub; FTA; Ntl Beta Clb; Pep Squd; Prom Com; ROTC; Latin Clb; Chr; Dnce; Drl Tm; SP/M/VS; Bskball (V L); Cr Ctry (V CL); Sccr (L); Sftball (V); Tennis (V L); Track (V CL); Vllyball (V L); Yrbk (R, P); RHSAA - State Track Champion; Region 1st Place Track 100 Dash; Secondary Education; High School Sports Coach; Pikeville; Alice Lloyd

MOTHERAL, AMY; MAYFIELD, KY; GRAVES CTY HS; (JR); Gov Hnr Prg; Hi Hnr Roll; Otst Ac Ach Awd; St of Mnth; WWAHSS; Yth Ldrshp Prog; Comm Volntr; Peer Tut/Med; Chrch Yth Grp; FCA; Ntl Beta Clb; Off Aide; Pep Squd; Sci Clb; Tchrs Aide; Golf (V); PP Ftbl (V); Tennis (V); Cl Off (V); Stu Cncl (S, T); Home Published Author "Heroes Among Us"; Christian Leadership Institution; Pharmacy; Communications/Journalism

MOTLEY, CHRISTOPHER; SCOTTSVILLE, KY; ALLEN CTY HS; (SO); Hnr Roll; Chrch Yth Grp; Bnd; Mch Bnd; Marching Band for Two Years; Literary Club; Philosophy / Theology; Political Science; U of Kentucky; Oxford U

MOUGHLER, MEGHAN; LEXINGTON, KY; TATES CREEK HS; (JR); Duke TS; Gov Hnr Prg; Hi Hnr Roll; Nat Hon Sy; WWAHSS; Comm Volntr; Peer Tut/Med; Chrch Yth Grp; DARE; DECA; FCA; Ntl Beta Clb; Off Aide; Prom Com; Tchrs Aide; PP Ftbl (V); Cl Off (P, V); Middle Childhood Education; Education; Furman U; Centre College

MOUNTZ, LAUREN; LOUISVILLE, KY; WALDEN HS; (FR); Ctznshp Aw; Hnr Roll; Kwnis Aw; Pres Sch; Comm Volntr; Drma Clb; Key Club; Pep Squd; Scouts; Svce Clb; Dnce; SP/M/VS; Stg Cre; Chrldg (V); Cr Ctry (V); Sccr (V); Track (V); Vllyball; Cl Off (V); CR (P); Sch Ppr (V); President of Builders Club; Got Most Improved & Spirited in Volleyball; Be a Teacher; Be a Relief Worker; Centre; Murray State

MOWRY, JESSICA; RADCLIFF, KY; JOHN HARDIN HS; (SR); F Lan Hn Soc; Hnr Roll; Comm Volntr; Foreign Language Festival Scholar; Bachelor of Science in Equine Therapy; Western Kentucky; Midway College

MOYER, LAUREN; LA GRANGE, KY; SOUTH OLDHAM HS; (SO); F Lan Hn Soc; Fut Prb Slvr; Hnr Roll; Perf Att; Sci Fairs; Yth Ldrshp Prog; Comm Volntr; Peer Tut/Med; Red Cr Aide; Chess; DARE Dbte Team; FCA; FBLA; Jr Ach; Ntl Beta Clb; Pep Squd; Dnce; SP/M/VS; Stg Cre; Gmnstcs (J); Adv Cncl (R); Stu Cncl (R); Captain of JV Dance Team; Architecture; Education; Auburn U; U of Georgia

MULLETT, JAMIE; LOUISVILLE, KY; PRESENTATION AC; (FR); Hi Hnr Roll; Hnr Roll; St of Mnth; Comm Volntr; Peer Tut/Med; 4-H; Chrch Yth Grp; Mod UN; Chr; Fld Hky (V); Track (V); Stu Cncl (V); Law Degree; Saint Louis U; Notre Dame

MULLINS, CATRINA; BUTLER, KY; PENDLETON CTY HS; (SR); Hnr Roll; ArtClub; Chrch Yth Grp; FCA; Prom Com; Foreign Clb; Chr; Dnce; SP/M/VS; Sftball (V); Computers; Psychology; Brown Mackie College; Gateway

MULLINS, NATHANIEL K; BEREA, KY; ROCKCASTLE CTY HS; (FR); Hnr Roll; Comm Volntr; Chrch Yth Grp; FCA; Church Band- Acoustic Guitar / Lead Rhythm; Youth Fellowship Group at Church; Automotive Technician; Master Automotive Mechanic; Somerset Community College; Berea College

MUNDY, CHRISTOPHER; OWENSBORO, KY; OWENSBORO SR HS; (JR); Hnr Roll; WWAHSS; Comm Volntr; ArtClub; Chess; Tchrs Aide; Tech Clb; Chr; Sccr (V L); Track (J); Bachelor of Arts; Game Art Design; The Institute of Arts; Millikin U

MURPHY, COURTNEY; BEREA, KY; MADISON SOUTHERN HS; (SO); Hi Hnr Roll; Hnr Roll; Nat Hon Sy; Otst Ac Ach Awd; WWAHSS; Yth Ldrshp Prog; Hab For Humty Volntr; Peer Tut/Med; Chrch Yth Grp; DECA; FCA; FBLA; Ntl Beta Clb; Pep Squd; Spanish Clb; Bnd; Ch Chr; Chrldg (V L); Major:Pre-Law; Minor: Criminal Justice; U of Florida

MURPHY, SHAWN R; LAWRENCEBURG, KY; ANDERSON CTY HS; (FR); Hi Hnr Roll; Hnr Roll; Bnd; Ftball (J); Wt Lftg (VJ); Western Kentucky U; U of Kentucky

MYERS, MADISON; GLASGOW, KY; GLASGOW HS; (SO); DECA; Pep Squd; Spanish Clb; Golf (V); Law; Business; New York U; U of Kentucky

NALL, DEANNA L; ASHLAND, KY; PAUL G BLAZER HS; (FR); Hnr Roll; Comm Volntr; Peer Tut/Med; Key Club; P to P St Amb Prg; French Clb; Orch; Track (V); Medical Field; Science Field

NANCE, LAURA B; HANSON, KY; MADISONVILLE NORTH HOPKINS HS; (SO); Hi Hnr Roll; MVP; Otst Ac Ach Awd; WWAHSS; Spec Olymp Vol; Chrch Yth Grp; FCA; FBLA; Key Club; Ntl Beta Clb; Bskball (V L); Sccr (V L); Cl Off (S); Yrbk (R); Law; Physical Therapy; Western Kentucky U; U of Louisville

Morrow, Julie A
Nelson Cty HS
Coxs Creek, KY

Miller, Allyson
Calloway Cty HS
Murray, KY

Miles, Brittany K
Murray HS
Almo, KY

Micallef, Stephanie A
Paul Laurence Dunbar HS
Lexington, KY

Midkiff, Brandi
Morgan Cty Area Tech Ctr
West Liberty, KY

Miracle, Mary E
Medical Lake HS
Calvin, KY

Mowry, Jessica
John Hardin HS
Radcliff, KY

NAPIER, JOSHUA; IRVINE, KY; ESTILL CTY HS; (FR); Hnr Roll; St of Mnth; Peer Tut/Med; Chrch Yth Grp; DARE; FCA; FBLA; Bsball (VJ); Bskball (VJ); Golf (J); Architecture; Electrical Engineering; U of Kentucky; Eastern Kentucky U

NAVE, TIFFANIE M; LANCASTER, KY; GARRARD CTY HS; (JR); 4H Awd; All Am Sch; Ctznshp Aw; Hnr Roll; Nat Ldrshp Svc; Sci Fairs; USAA; WWAHSS; Comm Volntr; Hosp Aide; Red Cr Aide; 4-H; Chrch Yth Grp; DARE; FCCLA; Jr Ach; Lib Aide; Ntl Beta Clb; Chrldg (V); Sec. of FCCLA for 2 Plus Years; Sec. of HOSA for 1 Year; I Want to Major in Pediatrics.; Nursing; U of Louisville; Eastern Kentucky U

NEBEN, BRITTANY L; BRANDENBURG, KY; MEADE CTY HS; (SO); Hnr Roll; WWAHSS; Comm Volntr; Peer Tut/Med; Mod UN; Svce Clb; Swmg (V L); Cl Off (P, V); Sch Ppr; RUNA Outstanding Ambassador; Kentucky Youth Assembly; Broadcasting Journalism; U of Kentucky

NEUMANN, MEGAN; LOUISVILLE, KY; SACRED HEART AC; (JR); Hi Hnr Roll; Nat Hon Sy; Otst Ac Ach Awd; WWAHSS; Comm Volntr; Peer Tut/Med; SP/M/VS; Founder of Scrapbook Club; Ophelia Mentor; Dentistry; Advertising; U of Illinois; Xavier

NEWMAN, TIMOTHY; MT WASHINGTON, KY; BULLITT EAST HS; (FR); Chrch Yth Grp; Ftball (V); Computers; ITT Tech

NEYHART, BRIAN; LOUISVILLE, KY; DUPONT MANUAL MAGNET HS; (JR); Hi Hnr Roll; Hnr Roll; Nat Hon Sy; Perf Att; Pres Sch; Comm Volntr; Peer Tut/Med; Chrch Yth Grp; Emplmnt; FCA; Ntl Beta Clb; Bnd; Ch Chr; Jzz Bnd; Nominated for 2006 Kentucky Ambassadors of Music; 2004 Servant of the Year at Kentucky Christian U; Music Education; Secondary Education; Kentucky Christian U; U of Louisville

NICELY, MARY B; MC KEE, KY; JACKSON CTY HS; (FR); Hnr Roll; Ntl FFA; Who's Who Among American High School Student; Any Educational Major; Any Child Care Major; Eastern Kentucky U; U of Kentucky

NICKERSON, AMANDA N; GERMANTOWN, KY; MASON CTY HS; (SR); Hi Hnr Roll; Hnr Roll; Sci Fairs; Yth Ldrshp Prog; Peer Tut/Med; DARE; Off Aide; Quiz Bowl; Voc Ind Clb Am; Sch Ppr (E); Yrbk (E, P); Massage Therapist; Hair Stylist; Maysville Community College; Massage College

NIX, ASHLEY N; LOUISVILLE, KY; LOUISVILLE MALE HS; (SO); 4H Awd; Ctznshp Aw; F Lan Hn Soc; Hnr Roll; MVP; Comm Volntr; Peer Tut/Med; 4-H; Chrch Yth Grp; Emplmnt; FCA; Spanish Clb; Soccer in Middle School / Then Had to Get Job for Family; Pediatrician; Lawyer; U of Louisville; U of Kentucky

NOLAN, CORY; STANTON, KY; POWELL CTY HS; (FR); Nat Hon Sy; Ntl FFA; Bachelor's Degree; Eastern Kentucky U

NOLAN, MICHELLE L; SCOTTSVILLE, KY; (SO); DAR; Hnr Roll; Otst Ac Ach Awd; Perf Att; Yth Ldrshp Prog; Peer Tut/Med; Red Cr Aide; Spec Olymp Vol; Chrch Yth Grp; Emplmnt; FCA; Ntl FFA; ROTC; Clr Grd; Drl Tm; Hsbk Rdg (L); FCCLA Certificate of Appreciation; Veterinarian; Western Kentucky U

NORTON, JOHN P; LOUISVILLE, KY; HOLY ANGELS AC; (MS); Hnr Roll; WWAHSS; Comm Volntr; Hosp Aide; Emplmnt; Photog; Scouts; Bskball (J); Ftball (L); Cum Laude National Latin Exam; Journalism; History; U of Kentucky; Franciscan U of Steubenville

O'BRYAN, PATRICK J; COXS CREEK, KY; NELSON CTY HS; (SO); All Am Sch; Hi Hnr Roll; Hnr Roll; Nat Hon Sy; Otst Ac Ach Awd; WWAHSS; Comm Volntr; Chess; Key Club; Voc Ind Clb Am; Tennis (J); Architectural Engineering Degree; Civil Engineering Degree; U of Kentucky; Lexington Community College

OEHLER, HEATHER M; NEWPORT, KY; NEWPORT HS; (SO); Hnr Roll; WWAHSS; Comm Volntr; Peer Tut/Med; Chrch Yth Grp; DECA; Key Club; Bnd; Dnce; Mch Bnd; Pep Bnd; Most Dedicated Dancer of the Year; Sophomore Class Princess; Education; Social Worker; Western Kentucky U; U of Kentucky

OLDHAM JR, WILLIAM; WINCHESTER, KY; GEORGE ROGERS CLARK HS; (SO); Fut Prb Slvr; Hnr Roll; MVP; Pres Ac Ftns Aw; Yth Ldrshp Prog; BPA; Chrch Yth Grp; FBLA; Ftball (V C); Wt Lftg (V L); Sports Management; Law; U of Georgia; U of Tennessee

OLIVER, ASHLEY D; CARLISLE, KY; NICHOLAS CTY HS; (FR); Gov Hnr Prg; Sci Fairs; Drma Clb; FCCLA; FTA; SP/M/VS; Sccr (L); Yrbk (E); Member of FCCLA; Member of the Drama Club; Social Worker; Registered Nurse; Morehead State U; Kentucky U

OLIVER, RAINER; UNION, KY; LARRY A RYLE HS; (SO); Hi Hnr Roll; Hnr Roll; Perf Att; Emplmnt; FCA; FBLA; Lttrmn Clb; Bsball (J L); Ftball (J L); Medical

OLIVER III, R V; MURRAY, KY; MURRAY HS; (SO); Hnr Roll; Perf Att; Chrch Yth Grp; Ch Chr; Bskball (VJ); Scr Kpr (VJ); Interior Design; Cal State U; Murray State U

OLSON, JEANETTE; LOUISVILLE, KY; HOLY ANGELS AC; (FR); Hnr Roll; MVP; Perf Att; Comm Volntr; Drma Clb; Lib Aide; Mth Clb/Tm; Prom Com; Ch Chr; Bskball (J); Vllyball (J); Yrbk (R); I Served As an Altar Girl for Mass; Law Enforcement (Detective); Nursing; U of Louisville; Bellarmine U/Jefferson Community College

O'NEAL, RACHEL; ROBARDS, KY; HENDERSON CTY HS; (FR); Hi Hnr Roll; Hnr Roll; Perf Att; St of Mnth; Peer Tut/Med; Chrch Yth Grp; Bnd; Chr; Ch Chr; Dnce; Chrldg (J); Gmnstcs (J); Cl Off; Stu Cncl (P); CR; Involved in Summer Work Program @ Niagara Elem. School; Elementary School Teacher; Child Psychologist; Henderson Community College & Then to U of Southern Indiana (USI)

ORR, KASI M; BUTLER, KY; PENDLETON CTY HS; (SR); Ctznshp Aw; Hi Hnr Roll; Hnr Roll; Perf Att; St of Mnth; WWAHSS; Comm Volntr; ArtClub; Chrch Yth Grp; Drma Clb; Emplmnt; FCA; Scouts; Tchrs Aide; Chr; Dnce; SP/M/VS; Stg Cre; Sccr (VJCL); Track (L); Stu Cncl (R); Theatre; Education; Morehead State

ORR, SHARRY; FLORENCE, KY; BOONE CTY HS; (SR); Hi Hnr Roll; Nat Stu Ath Day Aw; Otst Ac Ach Awd; Perf Att; St of Mnth; WWAHSS; Comm Volntr; Spec Olymp Vol; Chrch Yth Grp; FCA; FBLA; Off Aide; Pep Squd; Quiz Bowl; Chr; Dnce; Chrldg (V); Accounting; Northern Kentucky U

OSBORNE, ALLISON; ASHLAND, KY; PAUL G BLAZER HS; (FR); Duke TS; Hnr Roll; Perf Att; Comm Volntr; 4-H; Chrch Yth Grp; FCA; Pep Squd; Bskball; Sftball; Physical Education Teacher/Athletic Coach; Preschool Teacher; University of Tennessee; University of Kentucky

OSBORNE, JAMES; LOUISVILLE, KY; LIBERTY HS; (SO); St of Mnth; ArtClub; Drma Clb; ROTC; Tchrs Aide; Bnd; Cr Ctry

OSBORNE, TIFFANY; HARDINSBURG, KY; BRECKINRIDGE CTY HS; (SO); Duke TS; Hnr Roll; WWAHSS; Pep Squd; SADD; Spanish Clb; Chr; Murray State U; Western Kentucky U

OTTIS, SARAH E; STAMPING GRD, KY; SCOTT CTY HS; (JR); Hnr Roll; Nat Ldrshp Svc; Otst Ac Ach Awd; St of Mnth; WWAHSS; Comm Volntr; Mus Clb; Ntl Beta Clb; Ntl FFA; ROTC; Chr; Clr Grd; Drl Tm; Sccr (V L); Sftball (VJ L); JROTC Drill Team /JROTC Color Guard; Beta Club / Rocket Club; Georgetown College; U of Kentucky

OVERTON, WHITNEY B; GREENVILLE, KY; MUHLENBERG NORTH HS; (SO); 4H Awd; Hnr Roll; WWAHSS; Peer Tut/Med; DARE; FBLA; Clr Grd; Sch Ppr (R); Yrbk (P); FBLA Historian; Big Brothers / Big Sisters; Psychologist; Doctor; U of Kentucky; U of Louisville

OWINGS, JUSTIN; LOUISVILLE, KY; TRINITY HS; (SR); Hi Hnr Roll; MVP; Nat Hon Sy; Otst Ac Ach Awd; WWAHSS; Hab For Humty Volntr; Spec Olymp Vol; Emplmnt; FCA; Mus Clb; Ntl Beta Clb; Photog; Svce Clb; Bskball; Lcrsse; Sch Ppr (R, P); Yrbk (R, P); 2nd Place in City Wide Photo Contest; All Tournament Lacrosse Team, All Zone Player; Music Business (Production/Engineering); Psychology; Belmont U; Middle Tennessee State U

PACE, AUDREY; BENTON, KY; CHRISTIAN FELLOWSHIP SCH; (SO); Hi Hnr Roll; USAA; Comm Volntr; Chrch Yth Grp; DECA; Drma Clb; Emplmnt; Spanish Clb; Vllyball (VJ L); Cl Off (T); Forensic Scientist; Criminal Lawyer; U of Kentucky; Murray State U

PACE, BARCLEY; LEXINGTON, KY; LEXINGTON CATHOLIC HS; (FR); Hi Hnr Roll; Otst Ac Ach Awd; WWAHSS; Comm Volntr; Chrch Yth Grp; Drma Clb; Emplmnt; Lib Aide; Pep Squd; SP/M/VS; Ice Sktg; U of Kentucky

PACK, BRANDON; BRANDENBURG, KY; MEADE CTY HS; (FR); Hnr Roll; Automotive Design; Criminal Investigation

PACK, KELSEY J; MAYFIELD, KY; NORTHSIDE BAPTIST CHRISTIAN; (SO); All Am Sch; Hi Hnr Roll; Hnr Roll; Nat Ldrshp Svc; Nat Mrt Sch Recip; Perf Att; USAA; WWAHSS; DARE; Ntl Beta Clb; Pep Squd

PAPILA, MELIS; PADUCAH, KY; LONE OAK HS; (JR); Comm Volntr; Drma Clb; Prom Com; Chr; SP/M/VS; Bskball (J); Ice Hky; Sftball; Wt Lftg; Lawyer; U of San Francisco; San Francisco Conservatory of Music

PARISH, LAURA A; LEXINGTON, KY; LEXINGTON CHRN AC HS; (SO); Hi Hnr Roll; Hnr Roll; Chrch Yth Grp; Ntl Beta Clb; Svce Clb; Ch Chr; Vllyball (VJ); Member of National Society of HS Scholars; Business; Broadcast Journalsm; U of Texas Austin, TX; U of Kentucky Lexington, KY

PARMAN, CATHERINE L; LOUISVILLE, KY; JM ATHERTON HS; (SR); Hi Hnr Roll; Hnr Roll; St of Mnth; Emplmnt; Tchrs Aide; Jzz Bnd; SP/M/VS; Stg Cre; Track; Helped Start Amateur Kickball League; Member of a Band That Plays Frequently; Fashion Design; Creative Writing; U of Cincinnati

PARSONS, PAMELLA; PENROD, KY; SOUTH HS; (SR); Hnr Roll; Peer Tut/Med; Cr Ctry (J); ROTC for 2 Years; Psychology; Art Therapy; U of Kentucky; Brescia U

PATE, WES; LEWISPORT, KY; HANCOCK CTY HS; (FR); Hnr Roll; Yth Ldrshp Prog; Chrch Yth Grp; Tech Clb; Bskball (J); Stu Cncl (R); Gifted/Talented Leadership; Sports Medicine; U of Kentucky; Western Kentucky U

PATEL, NICK; WINCHESTER, KY; GEORGE ROGERS CLARK HS; (FR); F Lan Hn Soc; Hi Hnr Roll; Perf Att; St of Mnth; WWAHSS; CARE; ArtClub; Emplmnt; Jr Ach; Mth Clb/Tm; Sci Clb; Spch Team; Tmpl Yth Grp; Wdwrkg Clb; Honor Roll (In India); Pharmacy-Exploratory Medicine; Harvard U; Oxford U

PATIL, MEENAKSHI R; ASHLAND, KY; PAUL G BLAZER HS; (FR); Comm Volntr; Biology Clb; Key Club; Spanish Clb; Dnce; Swmg (V); Economics Major

PATRICK, AMANDA K; LEXINGTON, KY; P L DUNBAR HS; (SR); Hi Hnr Roll; WWAHSS; Comm Volntr; Chrch Yth Grp; Emplmnt; Vsity Clb; Dnce; Vsy Clb (V C); Kentucky Family Services Skills Standards Test; Dental Hygienist; Orthodontist; Lexington Community College

PATTON, MACKENZIE; HENDERSON, KY; HENDERSON CTY HS; (SO); Duke TS; Hnr Roll; WWAHSS; DARE; Dnce; Sccr (V, L); Yrbk (R, P); Member of Dance Company - Children's Center for Dance Education; Physical Therapy; Photography; U of Kentucky; Notre Dame

PAWSAT, BRAD T; MAYSVILLE, KY; MASON CO HS; (SO); Hnr Roll; St of Mnth; WWAHSS; Chrch Yth Grp; FCA; Chr; Orch; SP/M/VS; Bskball (VJ L); Golf (V L)

PAYNE, BRITTANY N; MT VERNON, KY; ROCKCASTLE CTY HS; (FR); Ctznshp Aw; Duke TS; Perf Att; Sci Fairs; Yth Ldrshp Prog; Comm Volntr; Chrch Yth Grp; FCA; Key Club; NYLC; Pep Squd; Quiz Bowl; Bnd; Chr; Ch Chr; Dnce; Scored Distinguished on all CAT Tests; 1st Place in English Grammar Olympics; Psychology / Drama/Acting / Journalism / Politics; Yale U; U of Southern Florida

PAYNE, ERIC; NEWPORT, KY; NEWPORT HS; (FR); Mus Clb; Bnd; Drm Mjr; Mch Bnd; Pep Bnd; Bsball (V); Auto Mechanic; Book Writer; Northern Kentucky U

PAYNE, JONATHAN M; FLATWOODS, KY; RUSSELL HS; (JR); Hi Hnr Roll; Kwnis Aw; Nat Hon Sy; Perf Att; St of Mnth; WWAHSS; Comm Volntr; Peer Tut/Med; 4-H; Key Club; Latin Clb; Bnd; Jzz Bnd; Mch Bnd; Pep Bnd; CR (R); All-State Band - Best Tuba Player in Kentucky; The Kentucky Center - Governor's School for the Arts; Music Education; Professor of Tuba; Morehead State U; U of Kentucky

PAYTON, JESSICA R; ELK HORN, KY; CASEY CTY HS; (SO); 4H Awd; Perf Att; Comm Volntr; 4-H; Chrch Yth Grp; Emplmnt; Bnd; Mch Bnd; Sch Ppr (R); Pediatrician

PAYTON, LAUREN A; FRANKFORT, KY; WESTERN HILLS HS; (JR); Hnr Roll; WWAHSS; BPA; FBLA; Ntl Beta Clb; Pep Squd; Prom Com; Vsity Clb; SP/M/VS; Chrldg (V); PP Ftbl (V); Vsy Clb (V); Major in Literature and Minor in Speech; U of Kentucky

PEARCE, MANDALYNNE G; LEXINGTON, KY; BRYAN STATION HS; (FR); Ctznshp Aw; Hnr Roll; Otst Ac Ach Awd; Perf Att; Pres Ac Ftns Aw; Sci Fairs; St of Mnth; Peer Tut/Med; Chrch Yth Grp; DARE; Key Club; Ntl Beta Clb; Bskball (V); Chrldg (V); Pharmacist; Kentucky; Murray State

PEAVLER, SARA; DANVILLE, KY; DANVILLE HS; (SR); Hnr Roll; Yth Ldrshp Prog; Comm Volntr; 4-H; FCA; Ntl Beta Clb; Off Aide; Clr Grd; Dnce; Cr Ctry (V CL); PP Ftbl, Track (V CL), Stu Cncl (R), Sch Ppr (E, R), Yrbk (E, R); Architecture; U of Kentucky

PEAVLEY, ERIK M; BARBOURVILLE, KY; KNOX CTRL HS; (FR); Hnr Roll; Otst Ac Ach Awd; St of Mnth; Gifted & Talented-Student of MD; Academic Team-Honor Roll

PECK, WHITNEY; SCOTTSVILLE, KY; ALLEN CTY HS; (SO); Nat Hon Sy; WWAHSS; Peer Tut/Med; FTA; Clr Grd; Mch Bnd; Pep Bnd; Axis Winter Guard; Forensic Science; Elementary Education; Vanderbilt U; Transylvania U

PEE, LESLIE R; RINEYVILLE, KY; NORTH HARDIN HS; (SR); Hnr Roll; WWAHSS; Yth Ldrshp Prog; Chrch Yth Grp; Pep Squd; Prom Com; Chr; Chrldg (V); Gmnstcs; Adv Cncl (R); Spanish Club (Vice President); National Youth Leadership Forum on Medicine; Pediatrician; Fashion Design; U of Kentucky; Washington U in St. Louis

PEEK, WHITNEY N; WINCHESTER, KY; GEORGE ROGERS CLARK HS; (FR); Hnr Roll; Sci Fairs; St of Mnth; Comm Volntr; Chrch Yth Grp; FBLA; Off Aide; Ch Chr; Adv Cncl (R); Clogging; FBLA (At School); Real Estate; Marketing; Eastern Kentucky U; U of Tennessee

PEGRAM, JASON; PADUCAH, KY; HEATH HS; (JR); Duke TS; Gov Hnr Prg; Hnr Roll; Nat Hon Sy; Perf Att; WWAHSS; Prom Com; Bnd; Jzz Bnd; Mch Bnd; CR (S); Sch Ppr; Governor's Scholar 2005; U of Kentucky

PEKRUL, KATELIN P; LEXINGTON, KY; PARIS INDEPENDENT HS; (FR); 4H Awd; Hnr Roll; Comm Volntr; 4-H; FBLA; Scouts; Tennis (J); Academic Team; Berea College

PENCE, JEREMY M; WORTHVILLE, KY; CARROLL CTY HS; (SR); Hnr Roll; MVP; St of Mnth; WWAHSS; Drma Clb; Ntl FFA; Off Aide; Bsball (VJ); Sccr (V); Yrbk; Who's Who Among American HS Athletes

Payne, Brittany N
Rockcastle Cty HS
Mt Vernon, KY

Pack, Kelsey J
Northside Baptist Christian
Mayfield, KY

O'Neal, Rachel
Henderson Cty HS
Robards, KY

Oehler, Heather M
Newport HS
Newport, KY

Newman, Timothy
Bullitt East HS
Mt Washington, KY

Nix, Ashley N
Louisville Male HS
Louisville, KY

Overton, Whitney B
Muhlenberg North HS
Greenville, KY

Patil, Meenakshi R
Paul G Blazer HS
Ashland, KY

Peavler, Sara
Danville HS
Danville, KY

PENDLETON, KATLIN B; HOPKINSVILLE, KY; CHRISTIAN CTY HS; (SO); Ctznshp Aw; Hi Hnr Roll; Nat Hon Sy; Yth Ldrshp Prog; Comm Volntr; Chrch Yth Grp; FBLA; Ntl Beta Clb; Ch Chr; Chrldg (V); Angel's Cheer Stars Cheerleading; Sub-Deb 1; Engineering; U of Kentucky

PENNINGTON, STEVEN R; VERSAILLES, KY; WOODFORD CTY HS; (FR); Duke TS; Hnr Roll; 4-H; DARE; Scouts; Wdwrkg Clb; Arch; Ftball (V); Wt Lftg (V); Wrstlg (J); Psychology; Military History Major; Florida State U; U of Nebraska

PEREZ LEON, ROCIO; LOUISVILLE, KY; (FR); Hi Hnr Roll; Hnr Roll; ArtClub; Chrch Yth Grp; CR; I Recorded Many Commercials in Mexico; I Was in the Volleyball Team in Mexico; Business; Languages; Sullivan

PERKINS, AMBER; ALEXANDRIA, KY; CAMPBELL CTY HS; (FR); Hi Hnr Roll; Hnr Roll; Pres Ac Ftns Aw; Chrch Yth Grp; Pep Squd; Chr; Ch Chr; Bskball (J); Sftball (J); Stu Cncl; Dentistry; Lawyer

PERRY, JESSICA D; LA GRANGE, KY; OLDHAM CTY HS; (SR); Hnr Roll; Pres Ac Ftns Aw; WWAHSS; Comm Volntr; Peer Tut/Med; Chrch Yth Grp; Emplmnt; Mth Clb/Tm; Ntl Beta Clb; Ntl FFA; French Clb; Engineering; U of Louisville Speed School of Engineering

PERRY, KELLY; PRESTONSBURG, KY; PRESTONSBURG HS; (FR); St of Mnth; Comm Volntr; Chrch Yth Grp; Chr; Counselor; U of Kentucky; Morehead U

PESTERFIELD, JOSHUA; BOWLING GREEN, KY; WARREN CTRL HS; (SO); Duke TS; Fut Prb Slvr; Hnr Roll; Sci Fairs; Sci/Math Olympn; Comm Volntr; Spec Olymp Vol; FCA; Ntl Beta Clb; Bnd; Pep Bnd; Duke TIP (Talent Identification Program); English Literature; Sociology/Theology

PETERS, PAUL; FRENCHBURG, KY; MENIFEE CTY HS; (JR); Duke TS; Hi Hnr Roll; Nat Hon Sy; Otst Ac Ach Awd; Perf Att; Valdctrian; Comm Volntr; Emplmnt; Lttrmn Clb; Ntl Beta Clb; Ntl FFA; Prom Com; Tchrs Aide; Vsity Clb; Bskball (V); Sccr (V); Cl Off (R); CR (R); Prom Prince; Robinson Scholar; Major in Engineering; Minor in Sports Medicine; U of Kentucky

PETERSON, CHRISTOPHER A; RADCLIFF, KY; NORTH HARDIN HS; (JR); Hnr Roll; Nat Hon Sy; Comm Volntr; Quiz Bowl; ROTC; German Clb; Ftball (J); Skt Tgt Sh (V); MS in Genetic Engineering; PhD in Biology; U of Kentucky; South Dakota School of Mines and Technology

PETITT, MARY B; SHARPSBURG, KY; BATH CTY HS; (JR); All Am Sch; Hi Hnr Roll; Nat Hon Sy; Otst Ac Ach Awd; Sci/Math Olympn; WWAHSS; Comm Volntr; Peer Tut/Med; Chrch Yth Grp; FCA; Ntl Beta Clb; Off Aide; Prom Com; Tech Clb; Adv Cncl (R); Cl Off (P, S); Sch Ppr (R); Drug and Tobacco Advisory Board; Doctor; Morehead State U; U of Kentucky

PETRI, IVICA; LOUISVILLE, KY; SENECA HS; (JR); Comm Volntr; Ntl FFA; Sccr (V); Record Own Music; Computer Engineering; ITT Tech; U of L

PHELPS, JAMES C; FRENCHBURG, KY; MENIFEE CTY HS; (JR); Hi Hnr Roll; MVP; Salutrn; FCA; Ntl Beta Clb; Ntl FFA; Pep Squd; Prom Com; SADD; Spanish Clb; Bsball (V); Bskball; Golf (V); CR (R); Distinguished on CATS Test; Transylvania U; U of Louisville

PHILLIPS, CARRIE; HICKMAN, KY; FULTON CTY HS; (FR); Hnr Roll; Chrch Yth Grp; Sci Clb; Clr Grd; Criminal Justice; Paralegal; Murray State U

PHILLIPS, JOSH; COLUMBIA, KY; ADAIR CO HS; (FR); Hnr Roll; Perf Att; Comm Volntr; ArtClub; Bsball (J)

PHILLIPS, KAYLA; PADUCAH, KY; HEATH HS; (JR); Peer Tut/Med; FBLA; FCCLA; Ntl FFA; Early Childhood Education; Murray State U; U of California

PHILLIPS, TAMARA; BENTON, KY; CHRISTIAN FELLOWSHIP SCH; (FR); F Lan Hn Soc; Hnr Roll; Chrch Yth Grp; Drma Clb; Ntl Beta Clb; Spanish Clb; Chr; Dnce; Bskball (V L); Sftball (J); CR (V); Governors Cup Champion; Homecoming Representative; Princeton U; New York U

PHILOT, MEGAN; DRY RIDGE, KY; GRANT CTY HS; (FR); Hnr Roll; Chrch Yth Grp; FCA; Ch Chr; Bskball (J); Vllyball (J); Sports Medicine; Athletic Training; Georgetown College; Eastern Kentucky U

PHIPPS, KARA M; FRANKFORT, KY; FRANKLIN CTY; (JR); PP Ftbl; Sccr (V); CR; Sch Ppr (R); Engineering; U of Kentucky; Western Kentucky

PIERROT, DEAN A; LOUISVILLE, KY; SENECA HS; (FR); MVP; Comm Volntr; Chrch Yth Grp; DARE; Bskball (VJ); Going to the NBA / Drawing / Cartoonist; U of Louisville

PIERSON, JEREMY; BOONEVILLE, KY; OWSLEY CTY HS; (FR); 4H Awd; Hnr Roll; Perf Att; Comm Volntr; 4-H; Chess; Bnd; Bsball (VJ); Bskball (VJ); Wt Lftg (VJ); 4-H Demonstration Award; Education-Math

PINKERTON, KATE; GEORGETOWN, KY; SCOTT CTY HS; (JR); 4H Awd; F Lan Hn Soc; Fut Prb Slvr; Hi Hnr Roll; Otst Ac Ach Awd; Sci Fairs; Yth Ldrshp Prog; Comm Volntr; Peer Tut/Med; Spec Olymp Vol; Chrch Yth Grp; DARE; Key Club; Mod UN; French Clb; Bnd; Dnce; Drm Mjr; Mch Bnd; Swmg (V L); Yrbk (P); All State Band - Bassoon; State Swim Team - Scott County; International Business; Georgetown College KY; Harvard U

PITMAN, SABRINA N; NANCY, KY; SOUTHWESTERN HS; (SR); Hnr Roll; FCCLA; Bnd; Computer Science; Music; Transylvania U

PITTMAN, SHANICE; PADUCAH, KY; PADUCAH TILGHMAN HS; (SO); Hnr Roll; Chrch Yth Grp; Chrldg (V); Gmnstcs; NAACP Youth of the Year; Social Worker; Kentucky State U; Spelman College

PITTMAN III, DAVEY; LEBANON, KY; MARION CTY HS; (JR); Hnr Roll; St of Mnth; Ntl Beta Clb; Wt Lftg; Welding; Universal Technical Institute

PLUMLEY, SHAYNA; GRAVEL SWITCH, KY; BOYLE CTY HS; (SO); Hnr Roll; Sci Fairs; Comm Volntr; Ntl FFA; Greenhand Degree in FFA; 2nd Place County Conservation Essay; Law; Social Worker; Eastern Kentucky; Morehead U

PODAPATI, PALLAVI; LEXINGTON, KY; SAYRE SCH; (MS); Ctznshp Aw; Duke TS; F Lan Hn Soc; Gov Hnr Prg; Otst Ac Ach Awd; Perf Att; Hosp Aide; ArtClub; Chess; DARE; Spanish Clb; Chr; SP/M/VS; Sccr (J); Received School English Award; Received School Science Award; Premedicine; Harvard, Boston, Massachusetts; Vanderbilt, Nashville, Tennessee

POER, LINDSAY M; DRY RIDGE, KY; (SR); Hnr Roll; Nat Hon Sy; WWAHSS; Comm Volntr; Peer Tut/Med; Emplmnt; FCCLA; Mus Clb; Pep Squd; Bnd; Chr; Drm Mjr; Mch Bnd; Chrldg (VJCL); Gmnstcs (V); PPSqd (VJ); Cl Off (T); Medical; U of Kentucky

POLLEY, NICHOLE; LATONIA, KY; HOLMES HS; (SO); Ctznshp Aw; Hnr Roll; Nat Hon Sy; Otst Ac Ach Awd; Comm Volntr; Pep Squd; Bnd; Pep Bnd; Northern Kentucky U

POND, STEVEN; BARDSTOWN, KY; NELSON CTY HS; (SR); 4H Awd; Hnr Roll; St of Mnth; WWAHSS; 4-H; Emplmnt; Key Club; Ntl FFA; State Champion-Youth Hunter Education Challenge; Law Enforcement & Criminal Justice; Wildlife Management; Eastern Kentucky U

PORTER, BRITTANY; RICHMOND, KY; MODEL LAB HS; (SO); All Am Sch; Duke TS; Hnr Roll; MVP; WWAHSS; Comm Volntr; Chrch Yth Grp; Emplmnt; FCA; Key Club; Pep Squd; Chrldg (VJ); Swmg (V); Adv Cncl (R); Sch Ppr; Yrbk

PORTER, JENNIFER A; FRANKFORT, KY; FRANKLIN CTY HS; (JR); Hnr Roll; WWAHSS; Comm Volntr; Emplmnt; Key Club; Mod UN; Pep Squd; SADD; Chr; SP/M/VS; PP Ftbl (V); Sftball (V); Track (V); Stu Cncl (R); CR (R); Passed Kentucky Allied Health Skills Standard Test; Pre-Med; A Degree in Business; U of Louisville; Kentucky State U

PORTER, ROBERT; ASHLAND, KY; PAUL G BLAZER HS; (FR); 4H Awd; Hnr Roll; Perf Att; Yth Ldrshp Prog; Chrch Yth Grp; Tchrs Aide; Ftball; Sccr; Tennis; Louisville, U of Louisville; Kentucky, U of Kentucky

POTEET, KRISTAN N; BOWLING GREEN, KY; WARREN EAST HS; (SR); Hi Hnr Roll; Otst Ac Ach Awd; USAA; WWAHSS; Chrch Yth Grp; Dbte Team; FCA; Ntl Beta Clb; NtlFrnscLg; Spch Team; Tchrs Aide; French Clb; Acpl Chr; Chr; Ch Chr; SP/M/VS; Top Degree in Sword Bearer Bible Club; 4th in Class of 150; Missionary to France; French Language; Heartland Baptist Bible College; Western Kentucky U

POTTS, CAMERON; LA GRANGE, KY; OLDHAM CTY HS; (JR); Duke TS; Hnr Roll; Perf Att; Pres Ac Ftns Aw; St of Mnth; WWAHSS; Chrch Yth Grp; Emplmnt; FCA; Bskball (VJCL); Yrbk (R, P); Communications-Public Relations; Theology; Eastern Kentucky U; Campbellsville U

POWELL, CAMERON; LOUISVILLE, KY; FAIRDALE HS; (FR); Hnr Roll; Nat Hon Sy; Perf Att; Architecture; Marine Biology; UR; UL

POWELL, CRYSTAL; MOREHEAD, KY; ROWAN CTY SR HS; (JR); Hnr Roll; St of Mnth; Yth Ldrshp Prog; Comm Volntr; Peer Tut/Med; 4-H; AL Aux Girls; ArtClub; Chrch Yth Grp; DARE; Drma Clb; FCA; Fr of Library; Chr; Ch Chr; Clr Grd; Drl Tm; Bskball (J); Nominated Commander for Honor Guard; Music Voice; Morehead College; Florida State

POWELL, VICTORIA; FLATWOODS, KY; RUSSELL HS; (FR); Hnr Roll; Nat Hon Sy; St of Mnth; Comm Volntr; Chrch Yth Grp; FCA; Ntl Beta Clb; French Clb; Tennis (V); CR (S); Orthodontia / Cosmetic Dentistry; Plastic Surgery; U of Kentucky; Ohio State U

POWELL, WES; HENDERSON, KY; HENDERSON CTY HS; (SR); Hnr Roll; Chrch Yth Grp; DARE; Ntl FFA; Off Aide; Quiz Bowl; 2nd Vice-President of the FFA; Full Time Employment

PRESTON, HEATHER; HARRODSBURG, KY; MERCER CTY HS; (SO); Hnr Roll; Nat Hon Sy; Otst Ac Ach Awd; St of Mnth; Comm Volntr; DARE; FCA; Ntl FFA; Tchrs Aide; TATU - Teens Against Tobacco Use; Technical School; Computers; Eastern Kentucky U Technical School

PRESTON, MATTHEW; LEXINGTON, KY; LEXINGTON CHRN AC HS; (SO); Duke TS; Hi Hnr Roll; Chrch Yth Grp; Ntl Beta Clb; Svce Clb; Track (V); Computer Sciences; U of Kentucky

PRICE, JENNY F; EDMONTON, KY; METCALFE CTY HS; (FR); 4H Awd; Hi Hnr Roll; Hnr Roll; Nat Hon Sy; Otst Ac Ach Awd; Sci Fairs; Comm Volntr; 4-H; ArtClub; Chrch Yth Grp; DARE; FCA; FTA; Mus Clb; Ntl Beta Clb; Bnd; Ch Chr; Dnce; SP/M/VS; Dance Team / MCMS, MCHS; Dance; Counselor; Western Kentucky U

PRICE, SHAWN; LOUISVILLE, KY; SACRED HEART AC; (SO); Duke TS; Hnr Roll; Comm Volntr; Emplmnt; Mth Clb/Tm; Chr; Track (V); Achieved "B" in United States Pony Club; 25 Hours of Service in 2005-Spring; Psychiatry; Medicine; Vanderbilt; UVA

PRIEST, CARRIE L; WEBSTER, KY; BRECKINRIDGE CTY HS; (MS); Hnr Roll; Perf Att; Yth Ldrshp Prog; Comm Volntr; Chrch Yth Grp; Ntl Beta Clb; Ch Chr; Vllyball (V); Playing the Piano; Murray State U; Accountant; Murray State U; U of Louisville

PRUITT, DAMESHA; MULDRAUGH, KY; MEADE CTY HS; (FR); FBLA; Major Business; Minor Dance; Morehouse and Howard U

PRUITT, SHONDA; MULDRAUGH, KY; MEADE CTY HS; (FR); Hnr Roll; WWAHSS; Spec Olymp Vol; Chrch Yth Grp; DARE; DECA; Special Olympics Bowling; Special Olympics Cheerleader; Nursing; Dancing; Western Kentucky; U of Hawaii

PUERTO, AMY; SOMERSET, KY; SOUTHWESTERN HS; (SO); 4H Awd; Hi Hnr Roll; Hnr Roll; Otst Ac Ach Awd; Perf Att; WWAHSS; Yth Ldrshp Prog; Comm Volntr; Chrch Yth Grp; DECA; Lttrmn Clb; Outdrs Clb; Spanish Clb; SP/M/VS; Stg Cre; Tennis (V C); Adv Cncl (R); Stu Cncl (T); Reporter and Newsletter Editor of the Conservation/Rap for Club; Varsity Academic Team Member; Broadcast Journalism/Communications; World Government/ Politics & Law; Kentucky Wesleyan College; Southern Adventist U

PUFFER, MEGAN; LOUISVILLE, KY; SENECA HS; (SR); Hnr Roll; Nat Hon Sy; WWAHSS; Red Cr Aide; Chrch Yth Grp; Key Club; Tchrs Aide; Spanish Clb; Bnd; Flg Crps; Pep Bnd; Stg Cre; PP Ftbl (V); Business; Elementary Education; U of Louisville

PYKE, JESSICA N; UNION, KY; LARRY A RYLE HS; (SO); Ctznshp Aw; Duke TS; F Lan Hn Soc; Hnr Roll; FCA; French Clb; Ch Chr; Tumbling; Radio Technologists; Cosmetologists; Northern Kentucky U

PYLAND, JESSICA; EUBANK, KY; PULASKI CTY HS; (JR); Hnr Roll; Comm Volntr; ArtClub; Chrch Yth Grp; FCA; SADD; Cr Ctry (V); Sccr (V); Second Team All-County - Soccer; Law Enforcement; Military; Eastern Kentucky U; Somerset Community College

PYLES, CODY; MONTICELLO, KY; WAYNE CTY HS; (SO); Fut Prb Slvr; Gov Hnr Prg; Hi Hnr Roll; Nat Hon Sy; Nat Stu Ath Day Aw; Otst Ac Ach Awd; Sci/Math Olympn; WWAHSS; Ftball (V); Wt Lftg (V)

QUINN, ERIC; PARK HILLS, KY; COVINGTON CATHOLIC HS; (SR); Hi Hnr Roll; Hnr Roll; MVP; Pres Ac Ftns Aw; Comm Volntr; Jr Ach; Quill & Scroll; Bnd; Bsball (V); Sch Ppr (R); Yrbk (E, P); Business Award; Accounting; Law; U of Kentucky

RAINEY, DAVID; LOUISVILLE, KY; DOSS; (JR); Perf Att; Lib Aide; Off Aide; SADD; Stg Cre; Scr Kpr (V); Sccr (V)

RANNEY, SAMUEL; LOUISVILLE, KY; PLEASURE RIDGE PARK HS; (SO); Hnr Roll; Nat Hon Sy; Perf Att; Comm Volntr; Hosp Aide; Red Cr Aide; Chrch Yth Grp; HO'Br Yth Ldrshp; SADD; Tennis (V); In the Red Cross; Students Against Drunk Drivers; Biology; Health Field; U of Louisville; Murray State U

RAPIER, KATIE; BARDSTOWN, KY; NELSON CTY HS; (FR); Fut Prb Slvr; Hi Hnr Roll; Otst Ac Ach Awd; Pres Sch; St of Mnth; WWAHSS; Key Club; Stg Cre; Sftball (VJ L); Vllyball (J); Stu Cncl (R)

RAY, ALICIA; LOUISVILLE, KY; SOUTHERN HS; (FR); Hnr Roll; Key Club; Sccr (V L); Business; Wildlife Biologist; U of Kentucky; Eastern Kentucky

RAY, BRITTANY; CLAY, KY; WEBSTER CTY HS; (JR); Hi Hnr Roll; MVP; Nat Hon Sy; Otst Ac Ach Awd; Perf Att; St of Mnth; WWAHSS; Chrch Yth Grp; DARE; Ntl Beta Clb; Prom Com; Bskball (V L); Sccr (V CL); Sftball (V L); Cl Off (V); Stu Cncl (V); CR (V); Health Science; Radiology

RAY, HILLARY N; PIKEVILLE, KY; PIKE CTRL HS; (FR); Hi Hnr Roll; WWAHSS; Chrch Yth Grp; Sftball (J); Orthodontist; Ohio State U

RAY, STEPHANIE R; MIDDLESBORO, KY; MIDDLESBORO HS; (SO); Hnr Roll; FCCLA; Pharmacist; Psychiatrist; U of Kentucky; Eastern Kentucky U

REDMAN, MARK J; LAWRENCEBURG, KY; ANDERSON CTY HS; (FR); Hnr Roll; St of Mnth; Chess; Chrch Yth Grp; Civil Air Pat

REECE, HEATHER N; FRANKLIN, KY; FRANKLIN SIMPSON HS; (SO); All Am Sch; Ctznshp Aw; Hi Hnr Roll; Hnr Roll; Nat Hon Sy; Nat Mrt LOC; Nat Sci Aw; Otst Ac Ach Awd; Sci Fairs; St of Mnth; CARE; Peer Tut/Med; BPA; DECA; FTA; Tchrs Aide; Bnd; Clr Grd; Wt Lftg (V); 5 Yrs Straight Highest In Nation on SATs; Teacher; Western KY U

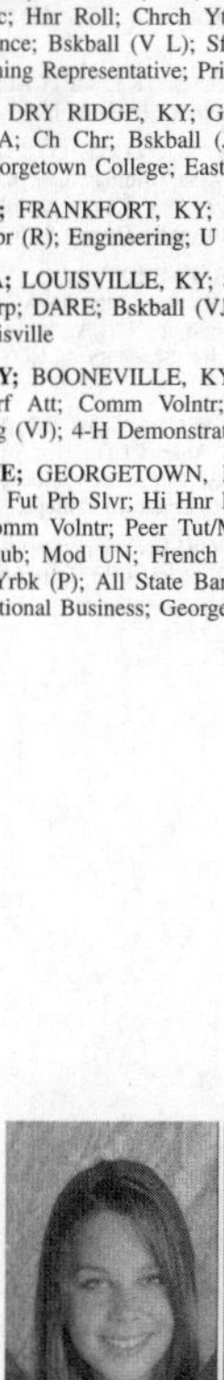
Powell, Victoria
Russell HS
Flatwoods, KY

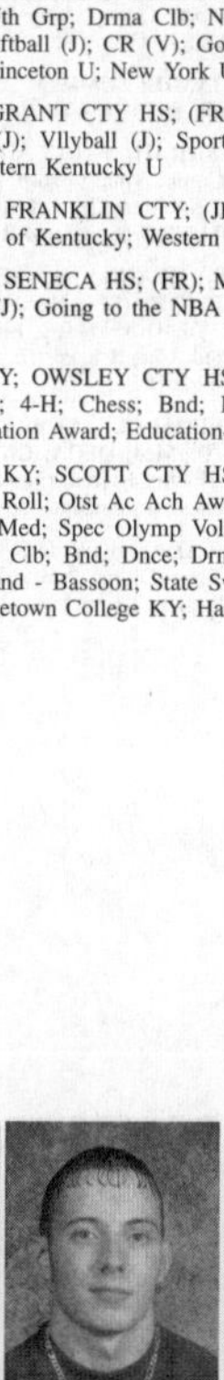
Pittman III, Davey
Marion Cty HS
Lebanon, KY

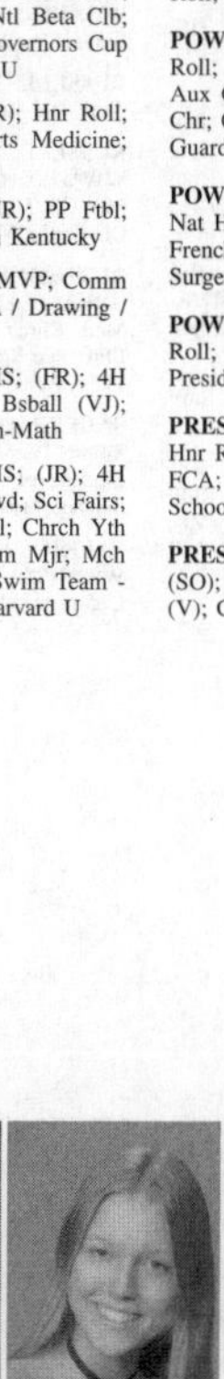
Perry, Jessica D
Oldham Cty HS
La Grange, KY

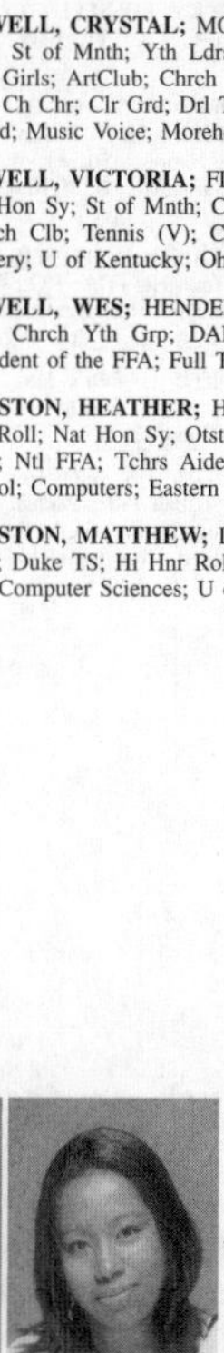
Perez Leon, Rocio
Louisville, KY

National
Honor Roll
Spring 2005

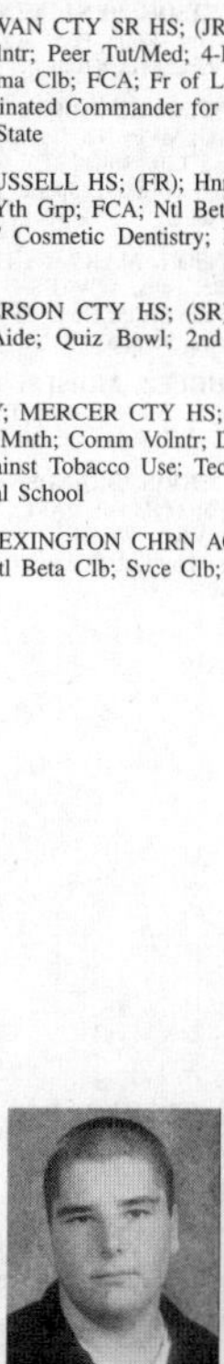
Pennington, Steven R
Woodford Cty HS
Versailles, KY

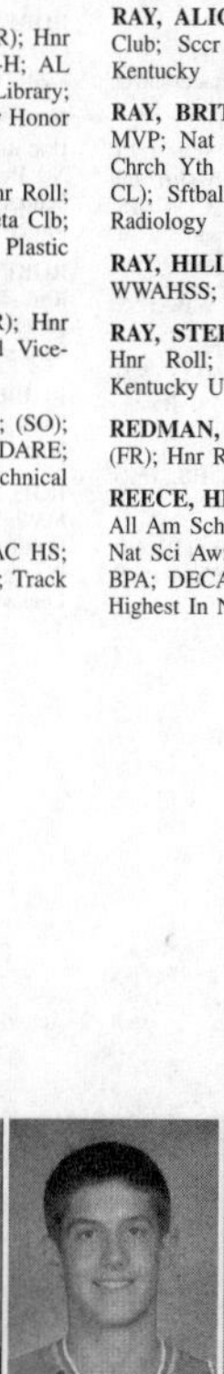
Pierson, Jeremy
Owsley Cty HS
Booneville, KY

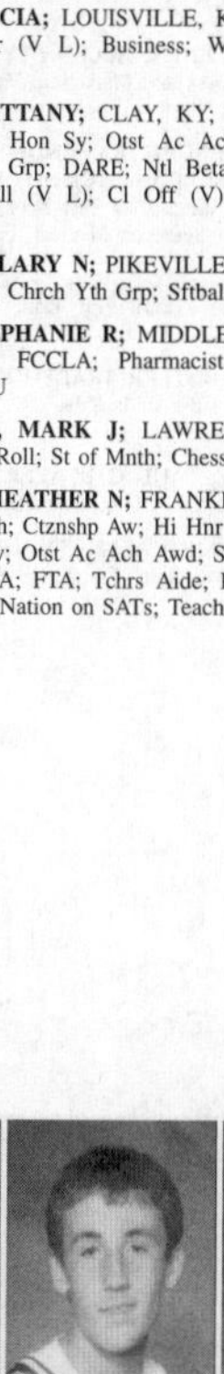
Porter, Robert
Paul G Blazer HS
Ashland, KY

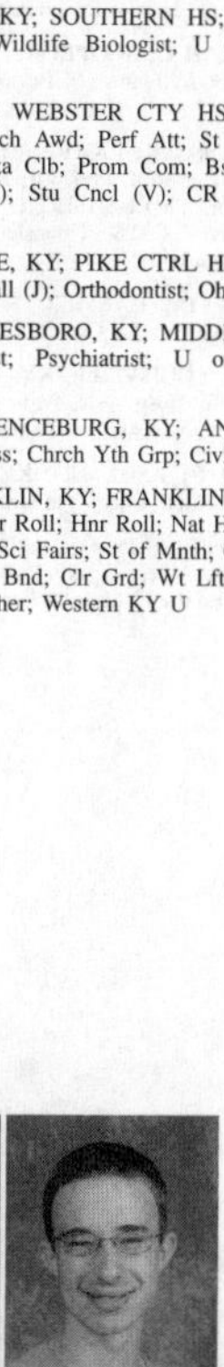
Redman, Mark J
Anderson Cty HS
Lawrenceburg, KY

REED, GERALD; HOPKINSVILLE, KY; CHRISTIAN CTY HS; (JR); Ctznshp Aw; Hnr Roll; Perf Att; WWAHSS; Business; U of Louisville; U of Kentucky

REEVES, DYNASTY N; LOUISVILLE, KY; WAGGENER HS; (FR); Hnr Roll; Sci Clb; Dnce; 11-04 Wrote Music Review in Courier Journal and Featured Teen; 8-04 Named "Totally Awesome Teen" in Local Magazine; Accounting; Nursing; U of Miami; New York U

REEVES, MARI C; BOWLING GREEN, KY; GREENWOOD HS; (MS); Duke TS; Hi Hnr Roll; Otst Ac Ach Awd; Perf Att; Pres Sch; Sci/Math Olympn; Yth Ldrshp Prog; Comm Volntr; Chrch Yth Grp; FCA; Ntl Beta Clb; NYLC; Pep Squd; P to P St Amb Prg; Scouts; Ch Chr; Chrldg (V); Cl Off (S); Congressional Youth Leadership Forum; Pediatrician; Foreign Mission Work; College of William and Mary

REMY, AMANDA K; LANCASTER, KY; LEXINGTON CHRN AC HS; (SO); Hnr Roll; Perf Att; Peer Tut/Med; Svce Clb; Sccr (V); Marketing; Nursing; Oklahoma U; Eastern Kentucky U

RENFROW, WENSDI L; CTRL CITY, KY; MUHLENBERG NORTH HS; (JR); St of Mnth; Red Cr Aide; 4-H; Chrch Yth Grp; DARE; Emplmnt; Ntl Beta Clb; Off Aide; Photog; Tchrs Aide; CR (R); Yrbk (R, P); HOSA; Nursing / RN; Pediatrician; Madisonville Co College; Western

RENO, CHARITY R; NORTONVILLE, KY; HOPKINS CTY CTRL HS; (SR); Hi Hnr Roll; Nat Hon Sy; St of Mnth; Valdctrian; WWAHSS; Comm Volntr; Hab For Humty Volntr; Chrch Yth Grp; DARE; DECA; FCA; Key Club; Mth Clb/Tm; Ntl Beta Clb; Pep Squd; Pharmacy; U of Kentucky

REVEL, PATRICIA M; RICHMOND, KY; MADISON CTRL HS; (JR); Hi Hnr Roll; Hnr Roll; Nat Hon Sy; Perf Att; Yth Ldrshp Prog; Comm Volntr; Hab For Humty Volntr; 4-H; Chrch Yth Grp; DECA; Emplmnt; FCA; Prom Com; Spanish Clb; Dnce; Cl Off (T); Central Kentucky Youth Salute; Varsity Dance Team; PhD in Radiology; Major in Fashion Merchandising; U of Kentucky; Morehead State U

REXING, BRITTANY L; CADIZ, KY; TRIGG CTY HS; (FR); Hi Hnr Roll; Pres Ac Ftns Aw; WWAHSS; 4-H; Chrch Yth Grp; FBLA; Key Club; Scouts; SADD; Ch Chr; Bskball (VJ); Track (V); Basketball 2005 Best Team Mate Award; Neonatology; Murray State; U of Tennessee

REXROAT, ANDREW B; RUSSELL SPRINGS, KY; RUSSELL CTY HS; (SO); All Am Sch; Hi Hnr Roll; Otst Ac Ach Awd; 4-H; FCA; Bnd; Ch Chr; Bsball (J); Bskball (J); Plays Bass Guitar in Christian Rock Band; Industrial Arts; Computer Design

REYNOLDS, COURTNEY; MAGNOLIA, KY; LARUE CTY HS; (JR); Duke TS; Hnr Roll; Nat Hon Sy; WWAHSS; Yth Ldrshp Prog; Comm Volntr; Chrch Yth Grp; FCA; FCCLA; Spch Team; Tennis (V L); Vsy Clb (V L); Lincoln Trail Youth Salute; National Honor Society; Medicine (Pediatrics); Church Music; U of Louisville; Campbellsville U

REYNOLDS, EMILY R; OWINGSVILLE, KY; ST MARGARET'S SCH; (JR); Fut Prb Slvr; Hi Hnr Roll; Otst Ac Ach Awd; Pres Sch; Yth Ldrshp Prog; Comm Volntr; Hab For Humty Volntr; Peer Tut/Med; Ntl Beta Clb; Ntl FFA; NYLC; Off Aide; Photog; Sftball (J); Swmg (J); Converse College Award; EPA Intern; MD; Mt Holyoke College; Smith College

RHEA, NICK; FRANKLIN, KY; FRANKLIN-SIMPSON HS; (SO); WWAHSS; Ntl Beta Clb; Ntl FFA; Voc Ind Clb Am; FFA Chapter Degree; Agricultural Engineer; Agricultural Scientist; U of Kentucky; Western Kentucky U

RHINERSON, MEGAN R; OWENSBORO, KY; OWENSBORO HS; (JR); Gov Hnr Prg; Hnr Roll; Perf Att; Sci Fairs; St of Mnth; Emplmnt; Scouts; Chrldg (V); Cosmetology; Interior Decorating

RICHARDS, REBEKAH C; SCOTTSVILLE, KY; ALLEN CTY HS; (SO); Hi Hnr Roll; DECA; FCA; Tennis (J); Business and Marketing; Vanderbilt U; U of Tennessee

RICHARDSON, ALYSSA K; LAWRENCEBURG, KY; ANDERSON CTY HS; (FR); Duke TS; Hnr Roll; Perf Att; St of Mnth; Chrch Yth Grp; Lib Aide; French Clb; Chr; Ch Chr; Dnce; Distinguished Test Scores - CATS; Proficient Test Scores - CATS; Forensic Science; Medical Field; U of Kentucky; Eastern Kentucky U

RICHARDSON, OLIVIA; CANMER, KY; (SO); Hnr Roll; WWAHSS; Chrch Yth Grp; Ntl Beta Clb; Ch Chr

RIGSBY, AMANDA; LOUISVILLE, KY; BUTLER TRADITIONAL; (FR); Ctznshp Aw; Hnr Roll; Hosp Aide; Mus Clb; Bnd; Yrbk (R, P); Band - Marching / Concert; Photographer; U of Louisville

RIGSBY, JINIFERD G; ASHLAND, KY; PAUL G BLAZER HS; (FR); Comm Volntr; Peer Tut/Med; Chrch Yth Grp; Law; U of Kentucky

RIGSBY, MAKESHA; EDMONTON, KY; METCALFE CTY HS; (FR); Hnr Roll; DARE; Ntl FFA; Pep Squd; Pediatrician; Computer Engineering; Western Kentucky U; Lindsey Wilson College

RILEY, BARBARA M; WEST PADUCAH, KY; HEATH HS; (JR); Duke TS; Hnr Roll; WWAHSS; Emplmnt; Bnd; Clr Grd; I Was Elected President of Environmental Club.; Received Junior Class Directors Award 2004-2005; Pre-Med; Surgery; U of Kentucky; Vanderbilt U

RILEY, DONIA K; CORYDON, KY; WEBSTER CTY HS; (JR); Ctznshp Aw; Hi Hnr Roll; Otst Ac Ach Awd; WWAHSS; Yth Ldrshp Prog; Comm Volntr; Peer Tut/Med; Chrch Yth Grp; Emplmnt; FBLA; Ntl Beta Clb; Off Aide; Mock Trial Team; Art/Design; Religion

RILEY, KELLY; NICHOLASVILLE, KY; ST MARY HS; (SR); MVP; Comm Volntr; Swmg (V); Volunteer At Annual Church Picnic; Named Most Improved Swimmer Twice; Major in Political Science; Minor in International Studies; Accepted to the U of Evansville

RILEY, KYNDAL; LEXINGTON, KY; HOMESCHOOLED; (MS); Hnr Roll; Chrch Yth Grp; Ch Chr; 2 Gold Cups in Piano from Nat'l Federation of Music; Honor Roll At Abeka Academy; International Missionary; Teaching English As a Second Language; Liberty U; Bethany College of Missions

RILEY, MATT; GLASGOW, KY; BARREN CTY HS; (FR); Duke TS; Hi Hnr Roll; Hnr Roll; Otst Ac Ach Awd; Pres Ac Ftns Aw; Pres Sch; St of Mnth; USAA; WWAHSS; Yth Ldrshp Prog; Comm Volntr; Peer Tut/Med; DARE; Emplmnt; FCA; Key Club; Ntl Beta Clb; Pep Squd; Foreign Clb; Bsball (V); Bskball (V); 2002-2003 National Jr. Beta President; 2003 John W Harris Leadership Award Winner; Major Pre-Med / Minor Spanish; Orthopedic Surgeon; U of Alabama; Centre College

RINEBOLD, BRANDON; HAGERHILL, KY; JOHNSON CTRL HS; (SR); WWAHSS; Chess; Emplmnt; Quiz Bowl; 2001 Governor's Cup State Champion (Science); Network Administration; Computer Repair; Big Sandy Technical College; Spencerian

RISNER, KARA J; HINDMAN, KY; KNOTT CTY CTRL HS; (FR); Hi Hnr Roll; Comm Volntr; Chrch Yth Grp; SP/M/VS; Vllyball (J); Computer Technology; X-Ray Technician; U of Kentucky; Eastern State

RIZENBERGS, CHRISTOPHER R; JAMESTOWN, KY; RUSSELL CTY HS; (JR); Hnr Roll; St of Mnth; Comm Volntr; Chrch Yth Grp; FCA; FBLA; Voc Ind Clb Am; Bskball; Ftball; Sccr; Swmg; Wt Lftg; Cl Off (S);'CR (S); Business; Christian Ministry; Western Kentucky U; Lindsay Wilson College

ROACH, ALEXANDREA R; PADUCAH, KY; PADUCAH TILGHMAN HS; (SO); Hnr Roll; Perf Att; Sci Fairs; Hab For Humty Volntr; DARE; Pep Squd; Chr; Bskball (J); NAACP; NIA Dancers; Major in Nursing; Major in Nursing; U of L (U of Louisville); U of St Louis

ROBBINS, LYNSEY; WAYNESBURG, KY; LINCOLN CTY HS; (SO); Ctznshp Aw; Hi Hnr Roll; Otst Ac Ach Awd; Sci Fairs; St of Mnth; Comm Volntr; Hab For Humty Volntr; Chrch Yth Grp; DARE; Emplmnt; FCA; Ntl Beta Clb; Ntl FFA; Outdrs Clb; Pep Squd; Chr; Dnce; SP/M/VS; Bskball (J); PP Ftbl (V); Scr Kpr (V); Tennis (V); Vllyball (V); Cl Off (S); 2005 Rogers Scholar; Full Scholarship to Lindsey Wilson College; Pre-Med / Doctor; Dentist; Georgetown College; U of Kentucky

ROBERTS, SHYMONE E; LOUISVILLE, KY; LOUISVILLE MALE HS; (JR); Hnr Roll; Perf Att; WWAHSS; Yth Ldrshp Prog; Comm Volntr; Hosp Aide; ArtClub; DARE; Drma Clb; Emplmnt; FCA; FBLA; FTA; Jr Ach; Bnd; Dnce; Chrldg (V); Track (V); Dietary Aide at Nursing Home; Pediatrician; Fashion Designer; Tennessee State U; Savannah College of Art and Design

ROBERTS, STACEY L; LANCASTER, KY; GARRARD CTY HS; (MS); 4H Awd; Fut Prb Slvr; Gov Hnr Prg; Hnr Roll; Nat Hon Sy; Otst Ac Ach Awd; Sci Fairs; USAA; Peer Tut/Med; 4-H; Chrch Yth Grp; DARE; Mus Clb; Chr; Ch Chr; Clr Grd; Dnce; Sccr (J); Presidential Award; US History Major; Pre-Law Major; Harvard Law School

ROBERTSON, BENJAMIN R; RUSSELL SPGS, KY; RUSSELL CTY HS; (SO); Hnr Roll; Perf Att; WWAHSS; Ntl FFA; Ch Chr; Sccr (VJ); Agriculture; U of Kentucky; Western Kentucky U

ROBINSON, KIMBERLY N; PILGRIM, KY; SHELDON CLARK HS; (JR); Hnr Roll; MVP; Nat Hon Sy; Perf Att; Peer Tut/Med; 4-H; FCA; Key Club; Ntl Beta Clb; Sftball (C); Vllyball (V); FCCLA; National Society of High School Scholars; Pediatric Physical Therapist; Journalism; U of Kentucky; Morehead U

ROBINSON, MARY K; LOUISVILLE, KY; ATHERTON HS; (FR); Hnr Roll; Sci Fairs; WWAHSS; Comm Volntr; Peer Tut/Med; FCA; FTA; Tchrs Aide; French Clb; Orch; SP/M/VS; Cl Off (P); Teaching; Real Estate; Eastern U; Central Florida

RODRIGUEZ, MOISES; RADCLIFF, KY; NORTH HARDIN HS; (SO); Duke TS; Nat Sci Aw; Tech Clb; State Champion in TSA for 2 Years; Electronic Engineering; Art Certification; Duke U; Columbia U

ROE, CHRIS; BRANDENBURG, KY; MEADE CTY HS; (FR); Hnr Roll; MVP; St of Mnth; DARE; FCA; FBLA; SADD; Bsball (VJ); Bskball (VJ); Ftball (VJC); Wt Lftg; Yrbk; Who's Who Among Youth League Baseball Players; Physical Education Teacher; Athletic Trainer; U of Kentucky; U of Louisville

ROE, CLARISSA; VANCEBURG, KY; LEWIS CTY HS; (FR); Hi Hnr Roll; Sci Fairs; St of Mnth; ROTC; Yrbk (P); 4th in Social Studies-Academic Team; 4th Place in Knockout Drill-ROTC; Teaching/Therapy, Physical; Drama/Theatre; Shawnee State U; Morehead State U

ROGERS, JENNIFER S; LOUISVILLE, KY; BULLITT CTY AREA TECH CTR; (SR); Hnr Roll; Pres Ac Ftns Aw; Comm Volntr; FCA; Pep Squd; Dnce; SP/M/VS; Track (C); CR (R); HOSA; MNA / Medical Nurse Aide - Student; Bachelor's Degree / Medical Field; RN / Pediatrician; U of Louisville; Jefferson Community College

ROGERS, SAMANTHA; CAMPBELLSVLLE, KY; (SO); Hnr Roll; WWAHSS; Emplmnt; FBLA; E-Town Community College

ROOF, STETSON; LEITCHFIELD, KY; GRAYSON CTY HS; (JR); Hnr Roll; Perf Att; Emplmnt; Bnd; Drm Mjr; Jzz Bnd; Mch Bnd; Music; Engineering; Murray State U; U of Kentucky

ROSENBLUM, NATHANIEL; PROSPECT, KY; DUPONT MANUAL HS; (JR); Hnr Roll; Kwnis Aw; Nat Hon Sy; Otst Ac Ach Awd; WWAHSS; Comm Volntr; Hosp Aide; Peer Tut/Med; Key Club; Tchrs Aide; Tmpl Yth Grp; Cr Ctry (J L); Started a Fellowship of Jewish Athletes; Nominated for Hometown Hero; Emergency Room Doctor (MD); Bates; Brandeis

ROSS JR, JOHNNY R; LOUISVILLE, KY; BRECKINRIDGE METROPOLITAN HS; (SR); Ctznshp Aw; Hnr Roll; Nat Stu Ath Day Aw; Otst Ac Ach Awd; WWAHSS; Comm Volntr; Chrch Yth Grp; Emplmnt; Jr Ach; Mus Clb; Outdrs Clb; SADD; Voc Ind Clb Am; Wdwrkg Clb; Acpl Chr; Bnd; Chr; SP/M/VS; Bskball (V); Cyclg (V); Dvng (V); Swmg (V); Track (V); Vsy Clb (V); Wrstlg (V); Stu Cncl (R); CR (R); Safe Sex Among Teens; Writing; Engineering; U of Louisville; Jefferson Community College

ROUTION, JENNIFER; CAMPBELLSVILLE, KY; CAMPBELLSVILLE HS; (JR); 4H Awd; Hnr Roll; Comm Volntr; 4-H; Chrch Yth Grp; DARE; Ntl Beta Clb; Dnce; FCCLA Historian; FCCLA Nationals; Medical Field; Pediatrics; Campbellsville U; U of Kentucky (UK)

ROWE, KOCIA; TOMAHAWK, KY; MARTIN CTY AREA TECH CTR; (JR); Hi Hnr Roll; Hnr Roll; Nat Hon Sy; WWAHSS; Peer Tut/Med; Physical Therapy; Marshall U; U of Kentucky

ROWLAND, MEGHAN B; WICKLIFFE, KY; BALLARD MEMORIAL HS; (JR); DARE; FCA; Sci Clb; Spanish Clb; Bnd; Mch Bnd; Pep Bnd; Stg Cre; Dentist; Music Major; Murray State U; Campbellsville U

ROWLAND, SARA R; WICKLIFFE, KY; BALLARD MEMORIAL HS; (JR); ArtClub; FCA; Sci Clb; Spanish Clb; Bnd; Mch Bnd; Pep Bnd; SP/M/VS; Art; Music; Murray State U; Bellarmine U

ROY, HILLARY; NANCY, KY; SOUTHWESTERN PULASKI CTY HS; (FR); Ctznshp Aw; Sci Fairs; Sci/Math Olympn; Comm Volntr; Chrch Yth Grp; Emplmnt; FCA; Ntl FFA; ROTC; Ch Chr; Drl Tm; Paramedic; Firefighter; EKU; Somerset Community College

RUNYON, JAMES W; PIKEVILLE, KY; PIKE CTY CTRL HS; (SO); Hi Hnr Roll; ArtClub; Sci Clb; 1st Place 9-12 (Art) Cedar Coal Fair; Veterinarian; Engineering; Morehead State U; Pikeville College

RUSHING, SAMUEL E; CLINTON, KY; HICKMAN CTY HS; (JR); Hnr Roll; DARE; FCA; FBLA; Mth Clb/Tm; Ntl Beta Clb; Off Aide; Prom Com; Sci Clb; Bsball (V L); Bskball (V CL); Golf (V L); Murray State U; Eastern Kentucky U

RUSSELL, BRITTANY; HOPKINSVILLE, KY; HOPKINSVILLE HS; (FR); Hnr Roll; Key Club; Sccr; U of Kentucky, Western Kentucky U; Murray State U

RUSSELL, COURTNEY; FOUNTAIN RUN, KY; MONROE CTY HS; (SO); WWAHSS; Spec Olymp Vol; Bnd; Mch Bnd; Medicine; Science; U of Louisville; Western U

RUSSELL, JAMIE; SUMMER SHADE, KY; METCALFE CO HS; (FR); 4H Awd; Hnr Roll; Perf Att; 4-H; Ntl Beta Clb; Quiz Bowl; Chr

RUSSELL, SARAH; PADUCAH, KY; LONE OAK HS; (SR); Hnr Roll; WWAHSS; Comm Volntr; Hosp Aide; Biology Clb; Chrch Yth Grp; FCA; Mth Clb/Tm; Ntl Beta Clb; Off Aide; Prom Com; Spanish Clb; Chr; Ch Chr; Clr Grd; SP/M/VS; International Business; Murray State U

RUTLEDGE, DEANNA J; SHEPHERDSVILLE, KY; BULLITT CTY AREA TECH CTR; (SR); Hnr Roll; Perf Att; WWAHSS; CARE; Peer Tut/Med; Chrch Yth Grp; DARE; Emplmnt; FBLA; Jr Ach; Ntl Beta Clb; Ntl FFA; Pep Squd; Chr; Sch Ppr (E, R); Secretary of HOSA; Nursing / Medical Field; Bellarmine U

SADLER, DREW; GLASGOW, KY; GLASGOW HS; (SR); Hnr Roll; Comm Volntr; Peer Tut/Med; DECA; Off Aide; Cl Off (P); Stu Cncl (S, T); Rotary Student of Month; Barren County Community Council Member; Political Science; Business Administration; Georgetown College; Western Kentucky U

SALKIC, SUADA; BOWLING GREEN, KY; GREENWOOD HS; (FR); WWAHSS; Spec Olymp Vol; Ntl Beta Clb; International Clb; Dentistry; Optometry; Western Kentucky U; U of Kentucky

Roberts, Shymone E
Louisville Male HS
Louisville, KY

Reynolds, Emily R
St Margaret's Sch
Owingsville, KY

Revel, Patricia M
Madison Ctrl HS
Richmond, KY

National
Honor Roll
Spring 2005

Reeves, Dynasty N
Waggener HS
Louisville, KY

Riley, Kyndal
Homeschooled
Lexington, KY

Robinson, Kimberly N
Sheldon Clark HS
Pilgrim, KY

SALLEE, LOGAN M; WINCHESTER, KY; GEORGE ROGERS CLARK HS; (JR); 4H Awd; Duke TS; Gov Hnr Prg; Hi Hnr Roll; Nat Hon Sy; Otst Ac Ach Awd; WWAHSS; Yth Ldrshp Prog; Comm Volntr; Peer Tut/Med; Spec Olymp Vol; Emplmnt; Outdrs Clb; Wdwrkg Clb; French Clb; Bskball; Tennis (V); Adv Cncl (R); National Honor Society Member; Outstanding Conservation Award (Ducks Unlimited); Civil Engineering; Architectural Engineering; U of Kentucky; Georgetown College

SAMMONS, REBECCA; COVINGTON, KY; HOLMES HS; (JR); Hi Hnr Roll; Nat Hon Sy; Perf Att; WWAHSS; Yth Ldrshp Prog; Peer Tut/Med; Prom Com; Quill & Scroll; Schol Bwl; Tech Clb; Stg Cre; Cl Off (P); Stu Cncl (V); Sch Ppr (E); CAS for IB Diploma; Psychology; Teaching; Georgetown College; Thomas More College

SAMPLES, JULIE; HICKORY, KY; GRAVES CTY HS; (JR); Duke TS; Hnr Roll; WWAHSS; Comm Volntr; Chrch Yth Grp; DARE; Emplmnt; FCA; Pep Squd; Chrldg (V L); Yrbk (E, R, P); KAPOS State Champions-2005-Cheerleading; 4th in the Nation-NHSCC-UCA-Cheerleading, State Championships in Media 2005; Broadcasting; Western Kentucky U

SANCHEZ, JORGE; VERSAILLES, KY; WOODFORD CTY HS; (FR); Ctznshp Aw; Hnr Roll; Otst Ac Ach Awd; St of Mnth; DARE; Wdwrkg Clb; Sccr (J); Computer Engineer; Pro Soccer Player; U of North Carolina; U of Kentucky

SANDERS, AUMBREA S; RADCLIFF, KY; NORTH HARDIN HS; (SR); Hnr Roll; Nat Hon Sy; WWAHSS; Hab For Humty Volntr; FCA; Prom Com; Bnd; Ch Chr; Pep Bnd; Chrldg (V); Treasury At Church for the Youth; Biology; Forensic Science; Eastern Kentucky U

SANDERS, KYLE; EMINENCE, KY; HENRY CTY HS; (SR); 4H Awd; Hi Hnr Roll; Nat Hon Sy; Otst Ac Ach Awd; Perf Att; St of Mnth; WWAHSS; Yth Ldrshp Prog; Comm Volntr; Peer Tut/Med; 4-H; FBLA; Ntl Beta Clb; Vsity Clb; German Clb; Chrldg; Cr Ctry (V); Track (V); Cl Off (P); Stu Cncl (P); CR; Nationally Renowned Public Speaker; Producer of School News Broadcast; Broadcast Journalism; Communications; Western Kentucky U

SANDLIN, COURTNEY R; LOUISVILLE, KY; FAIRDALE HS; (JR); DARE; PP Ftbl (V); Bowling Team; U of Louisville

SANDOVAL, JHONATAN J; COVINGTON, KY; HOLMES HS; (SO); St of Mnth; Comm Volntr; DARE; Ftball (J); Sccr (V); Architecture; U of Kentucky

SANDOVAL, MELISSA J; GEORGETOWN, KY; SCOTT CTY HS; (JR); Hi Hnr Roll; Comm Volntr; Peer Tut/Med; Chrch Yth Grp; FCA; Key Club; Ntl Beta Clb; Pep Squd; Spch Team; Bnd; Mch Bnd; Pep Bnd; Chrldg (V); Track (V); National Cheerleaders Association - All-American Cheerleader; Forensics; Mathematics; U of Central Florida; Eastern Kentucky U

SANTIAGO, NATALIE; LOUISVILLE, KY; ASSUMPTION HS; (FR); Fut Prb Slvr; Gov Hnr Prg; Hnr Roll; Comm Volntr; FBLA; Pep Squd; Photog; Quiz Bowl; Tennis (V); CR (R); Photography Club - Secretary; CPA; Business

SAPP, KHRYSTEN G; MAYSVILLE, KY; MASON CTY HS; (SO); Ctznshp Aw; Duke TS; Hnr Roll; MVP; Nat Hon Sy; Peer Tut/Med; Chrch Yth Grp; DARE; Emplmnt; FCA; Ntl Beta Clb; SADD; Chr; Orch; SP/M/VS; Chrldg (V); Gmnstcs (V); Cl Off (R); CR (P); Elementary Education; Counseling / Social Work; Northern KY U; Morehead State

SARGENT, EMILY F; PINE KNOT, KY; MC CREARY CTRL HS; (SO); HOSA; HOSA - Treasurer; Registered Nurse; Eastern Kentucky U

SATTERFIELD, LAUREN A; HOPKINSVILLE, KY; HOPKINSVILLE HS; (FR); Duke TS; Hi Hnr Roll; Hnr Roll; Chrch Yth Grp; Key Club; Lttrmn Clb; Pep Squd; Scouts; Vsity Clb; Chr; Dnce; Sccr (V L); Tennis (V L); Stu Cncl (R); Principal's List; Business and Marketing; Fashion Marketing; New York U; Florida State U

SAUNDERS, JONATHON; GEORGETOWN, KY; SC HS; (SO); Hnr Roll; Perf Att; Pres Ac Ftns Aw; Sci Fairs; WWAHSS; Chrch Yth Grp; DECA; Key Club; Mus Clb; Ntl Beta Clb; Pep Squd; Scouts; Chr; CR (P)

SCHACKOW, VERONICA; RUSSELL SPRINGS, KY; RUSSELL CTY HS; (JR); WWAHSS; Scouts; Bnd; Mch Bnd; Pep Bnd; Forensics; Sociology; Eastern Kentucky U; Campbellsville U

SCHANIE, GRANT; LOUISVILLE, KY; PORTLAND CHRISTIAN; (SO); Hnr Roll; USAA; Comm Volntr; Chrch Yth Grp; Chr

SCHEIB, CHRISTIANA L; NICHOLASVILLE, KY; IDYLLWILD ARTS AC; (JR); Duke TS; F Lan Hn Soc; Hi Hnr Roll; Otst Ac Ach Awd; WWAHSS; Comm Volntr; Drma Clb; Ntl Beta Clb; Photog; Spch Team; French Clb; Bnd; Chr; Dnce; Jzz Bnd; Adv Cncl (R); Beta Club; Senior Prefect / Top 10 Scholar; Film & Television Production; Screenwriting; UCLA; U of Southern California

SCHEITLIN, JANET L; RADCLIFF, KY; NORTH HARDIN HS; (JR); Fut Prb Slvr; Hi Hnr Roll; Hnr Roll; Nat Hon Sy; Perf Att; WWAHSS; Hab For Humty Volntr; Peer Tut/Med; Red Cr Aide; ArtClub; Emplmnt; Off Aide; P to P St Amb Prg; Prom Com; Scouts; French Clb; Ch Chr; Stg Cre; Stu Cncl (R); CR (R); Art Club President; Girl Scout Silver Award; Pre-Med; Chemistry Major; Cumberland College

SCHEUMANN, BECKY; LEXINGTON, KY; TATES CREEK HS; (JR); MVP; WWAHSS; Yth Ldrshp Prog; Hosp Aide; Peer Tut/Med; Chrch Yth Grp; DARE; DECA; Emplmnt; FCA; Off Aide; Prom Com; Tchrs Aide; PP Ftbl (V); Tennis (C); Adv Cncl (S, R); Cl Off (S); Stu Cncl (R); CR (S); Accounting; U of Kentucky

SCHMIDT JR, PAUL H; INEZ, KY; SHELDON CLARK HS; (SR); Hi Hnr Roll; WWAHSS; Comm Volntr; Peer Tut/Med; Chrch Yth Grp; Emplmnt; FCA; Pep Squd; Prom Com; Tchrs Aide; Ftball (VJC); Wt Lftg (VJC); Wrstlg (J); Cl Off (T); Stu Cncl (T); History; Cumberland College; Morehead U

SCHMITT, BETHANY G; BURLINGTON, KY; CONNER HS; (SO); 4H Awd; Hnr Roll; Nat Hon Sy; Nat Stu Ath Day Aw; Otst Ac Ach Awd; Comm Volntr; 4-H; Chrch Yth Grp; Emplmnt; FCA; FBLA; Tennis (V L); Vllyball (VJCL); Vice President of FCA / Fellowship of Christian Athletes; Straight A's Award; Medical Field / Nurse Practitioner; Law School / Patent Lawyer; Eastern Kentucky U; U of Kentucky

SCHOENBACHLER, DAVID W; LOUISVILLE, KY; PLEASURE RIDGE PARK HS; (FR); Hnr Roll; Otst Ac Ach Awd; Perf Att; Comm Volntr; Emplmnt; Ftball; Track; Jr. Beta Club; Computer Tech; U of L-U of Louisville; UCLA

SCHWARTZ, PAUL J; LOUISVILLE, KY; ATHERTON HS; (JR); Duke TS; Hnr Roll; ArtClub; Photog; Scouts; Bnd; Stg Cre; English; History

SCHWEINHART, ALISHIA; BARDSTOWN, KY; NELSON CTY HS; (SO); Hnr Roll; Pres Ac Ftns Aw; Sci Fairs; Comm Volntr; Hosp Aide; Peer Tut/Med; DARE; Key Club; Bnd; Clr Grd; Mch Bnd; Pep Bnd; Yrbk (P); Soccer, Played for 2 Years; Medical Subjects-(First Aid, CPR); Pediatric Oncology; Pediatrician; U of Louisville; Baylor U

SCOTT, CANDACE; LOUISVILLE, KY; DOSS HIGH MAG CAREER AC; (JR); Hnr Roll; Nat Hon Sy; Vllyball; Yrbk (P); FCCLA; Psychology; Forensic Science; U of Louisville; Western U

SCOTT, DEREK; MADISONVILLE, KY; MADISONVILLE NORTH HOPKINS HS; (JR); Duke TS; Hnr Roll; WWAHSS; Comm Volntr; Hab For Humty Volntr; Spec Olymp Vol; FCA; FBLA; Key Club; Ntl Beta Clb; Bskball (V L); Academic All-State First Team; Business-Management; Transylvania U

SCOTT, WINFRED; LOUISA, KY; LELY HS; (FR); Comm Volntr; Chrch Yth Grp; Emplmnt; FBLA; Clr Grd; Mch Bnd; Solo for 1st Gov Jennings (National Anthem); Taps Solo for Changing of the Watch on Marco Island, FL; Vet

SCRIVNER, KELLY; RICHMOND, KY;; Duke TS; Hnr Roll; 4-H; DARE; Scouts; Bskball (L); Chrldg (L); Sftball (L); Yrbk (P); Wildlife Management; Education; Duke U; Eastern Kentucky U

SCRUGGS, MYRAH; BEATTYVILLE, KY; LEE CTY HS; (JR); 4H Awd; Hnr Roll; MVP; Nat Hon Sy; Otst Ac Ach Awd; St of Mnth; WWAHSS; 4-H; FBLA; Ntl Beta Clb; Ntl FFA; NYLC; Photog; Prom Com; Schol Bwl; Clr Grd; Cr Ctry (V); Tennis (V); Track (V C); Kentucky River Region FFA Vice President; BA Animal Science; PhD Veterinary Medicine; U of Kentucky; U of Australia

SEAL, CARLA R; WILLIAMSTOWN, KY; WILLIAMSTOWN IND; (JR); Chrch Yth Grp; DARE; Emplmnt; Ntl FFA; Psychology; Registered Nurse; Georgetown U; U of Kentucky

SEARS, ERICKA P; CORBIN, KY; CORNERSTONE CHRISTIAN SCH; (SO); Hnr Roll; Chrch Yth Grp; FCA; Ntl Beta Clb; Sch Ppr (E, R, P); Beta Club; Oncology; U of Kentucky; U of Tennessee

SEBASTION, LAUREN; AUGUSTA, KY; AUGUSTA HS; (SO); Ctznshp Aw; Hnr Roll; St of Mnth; Chrch Yth Grp; Pep Squd; Bnd; Pep Bnd; Bskball (VJ); Sftball (V); Psychologist; Choreographer; U of Kentucky; New York State U

SECOR, JAMES R; MOREHEAD, KY; ROWAN CTY HS; (JR); French Clb; Sccr (V); Tennis (V); French Oral Proficiency Festival Winner, Level 3; 2nd Place, Local Art Show

SEGURA, ALEXANDRIA K; LOUISVILLE, KY; LOUISVILLE MALE HS; (SO); Hnr Roll; DARE; FCA; FBLA; Pep Squd; Photog; Scouts; Swmg (J); Nursing; Law School; U of Louisville; U of Kentucky

SEIBERT, RENEE A; NEWPORT, KY; NEWPORT HS; (JR); Hnr Roll; Nat Hon Sy; DECA; Emplmnt; FBLA; Key Club; Prom Com; Scouts; Bnd; Clr Grd; Flg Crps; Mch Bnd; Cl Off (S); Sch Ppr (E); Yrbk (E); Business Accounting; Secondary Education; Western Kentucky U

SEITZ, ASHLEIGH; NICHOLASVILLE, KY; EAST JESSAMINE HS; (SO); Hi Hnr Roll; Hnr Roll; Civil Air Pat; Ntl Beta Clb; Scouts; Tchrs Aide; Ch Chr; Dnce; Medical Degree; Cedarville; Georgetown

SENN, KAYLA R; FRANKFORT, KY; FRANKLIN CTY HS; (SO); Hnr Roll; Nat Hon Sy; Pres Sch; WWAHSS; Emplmnt; Ntl Beta Clb; Pep Squd; Bnd; Mch Bnd; Pep Bnd; PP Ftbl (J); Swmg (J); Vllyball (J); Who's Who Among High School Students; Honor Roll; Accountant; Business/ Management; U of Kentucky; Sullivan College

SETTLES, KELLY; VERSAILLES, KY; WOODFORD CTY; (SR); Hnr Roll; WWAHSS; Peer Tut/Med; Tchrs Aide; French Clb; French Award; Business Management; Sullivan U

SEXTON, BRITTANY; NEWPORT, KY; (FR); Ctznshp Aw; Duke TS; Hnr Roll; Sci Fairs; Peer Tut/Med; I Volunteer At the Salvation Army After School Program; I Want to Go Into Child Care

SEXTON, RICKY; NEON, KY; FLEMING NEON HS; (SR); Hnr Roll; MVP; WWAHSS; Comm Volntr; Pep Squd; Tech Clb; Bsball (V CL); Bskball (V CL); Sch Ppr (E); Yrbk (P); Computer Science; Electrical; Pikeville College; Hazard Community College

SHABAN, DANIA; LOUISVILLE, KY; SENECA HS; (FR); Hnr Roll; Otst Ac Ach Awd; St of Mnth; FTA; Business / Marketing; Running Own Business; U of Louisville

SHACKLETTE, BRADLEY; LOUISVILLE, KY; ATHERTON HS; (SO); St of Mnth; WWAHSS; Chess; Golf (V L); Engineering

SHACKLETTE, JOSHUA; LOUISVILLE, KY; LOUISVILLE MALE HS; (SO); Hnr Roll; Nat Hon Sy; Comm Volntr; FBLA; French Clb; Communications; Veterinary Medicine; U of Louisville; Eastern Kentucky U

SHAFFERY, ANGIE; BARDSTOWN, KY; NELSON CTY HS; (SO); Hnr Roll; Nat Hon Sy; WWAHSS; 4-H; DARE; Emplmnt; Key Club; Prom Com; SADD; 4-H Teen Volunteer; NCH National Honor Society; Pharmacy; Physical Therapy; U of Kentucky

SHAH, REECHA S; MADISONVILLE, KY; MADISONVILLE NORTH HOPKINS HS; (SO); Ctznshp Aw; Hi Hnr Roll; Nat Hon Sy; WWAHSS; Yth Ldrshp Prog; Comm Volntr; Hosp Aide; Spec Olymp Vol; DARE; FBLA; Key Club; Ntl Beta Clb; Dnce; SP/M/VS; Cr Ctry (V L); Tennis (V L); Cl Off (S); Stu Cncl (R); Pre-Med; U of Louisville; Vanderbilt U

SHAHIN, RAWAN; COLUMBIA, KY; ADAIR CTY HS; (FR); All Am Sch; Hi Hnr Roll; Hnr Roll; Kwnis Aw; Otst Ac Ach Awd; Sci Fairs; WWAHSS; Yth Ldrshp Prog; 4-H; Pep Squd; Bskball; Cr Ctry; Sftball; Stu Cncl (R); Math Award; Accelerated Reader Award; Obstetrician; Chemistry; Duke U; Michigan State

SHARER, CODY M; UNION, KY; LARRY A RYLE HS; (SO); Ctznshp Aw; F Lan Hn Soc; Hi Hnr Roll; Hnr Roll; Otst Ac Ach Awd; St of Mnth; WWAHSS; Comm Volntr; Cmptr Clb; DARE; FBLA; P to P St Amb Prg; Hispanic Clb; Bsball (J); Ftball (J); Pre-Medical; Architecture/Engineering

SHATHER, BRETT; PADUCAH, KY; LONE OAK HS; (SR); Hnr Roll; Sci/ Math Olympn; WWAHSS; Mus Clb; Sci Clb; Scouts; Bnd; Mch Bnd; Pep Bnd; SP/M/VS; Track (VJ); Eagle Scout; Secondary Education / Biology; Conservation Biology; Murray State U

SHAUGHNESSY, PADDY; LOUISVILLE, KY; SACRED HEART AC; (SR); Hi Hnr Roll; Hnr Roll; Nat Hon Sy; Yth Ldrshp Prog; Comm Volntr; DARE; Jr Ach; Mod UN; Photog; Svce Clb; SADD; Ch Chr; Cr Ctry (V L); Sftball (J L); Track (V L); Marine Science; Psychologist; Coastal Carolina U

SHAW, ANDREA; LOUISVILLE, KY; ASSUMPTION HS; (SO); Hnr Roll; WWAHSS; Comm Volntr; Drma Clb; Mch Bnd; Pep Bnd; Stg Cre; Ice Hky (V); 10 Year Award Received from Deaf Youth Sports Festival; Outstanding Camper-Lions Camp Lacasanda; Education-History; Theatrics; U of Connecticut; U of Louisville

SHELLEY, HALEIGH R; WINCHESTER, KY; GEORGE ROGERS CLARK HS; (FR); 4H Awd; MVP; Perf Att; Pres Ac Ftns Aw; Sci Fairs; Comm Volntr; 4-H; Chrch Yth Grp; DARE; FCA; Ntl Beta Clb; Pep Squd; Chr; Ch Chr; Sccr (VJC); Track; All Tournament Team Rachel Sutherland Memorial; Best Defense Award; Dentistry; Occupational Therapy; UK; Transylvania U

SHEPARD, LINDSEY R; JAMESTOWN, KY; RUSSELL CTY HS; (SO); WWAHSS; Voc Ind Clb Am; Lindsey Wilson College

SHEPPARD, SHEA; GEORGETOWN, KY; SCOTT CTY HS; (JR); Duke TS; Hnr Roll; Nat Hon Sy; Perf Att; Pres Sch; WWAHSS; Comm Volntr; Peer Tut/Med; Key Club; Ntl Beta Clb; Sci Clb; Tech Clb; Bnd; Mch Bnd; Pep Bnd; Leader of Build Team in Robotics Club; On Teen Advisory Board at Local Library; Political Science; US Government; Miami U; U of Kentucky

SHERRELL, COURTNEY; MADISONVILLE, KY; MADISONVILLE NORTH HOPKINS HS; (SR); Gov Hnr Prg; Hnr Roll; Perf Att; St of Mnth; WWAHSS; Comm Volntr; Spec Olymp Vol; Chrch Yth Grp; DARE; FCA; Key Club; Ntl Beta Clb; Off Aide; Prom Com; Yrbk; Registered Nurse; Nurse; Madisonville Community College; Western Kentucky U

SHIPE, TYLER; UNION, KY; LARRY A RYLE HS; (SO); F Lan Hn Soc; Hi Hnr Roll; Hnr Roll; Otst Ac Ach Awd; Comm Volntr; Chrch Yth Grp; DARE; FCA; FBLA; Jr Ach; Tech Clb; SP/M/VS; Cr Ctry (V); Track (V); Stu Cncl (R); Business; Law

SHIRLEY, MATTHEW W; COLUMBIA, KY; ADAIR CO HS; (FR); 4H Awd; Hi Hnr Roll; Hnr Roll; Perf Att; Pres Sch; Bnd; Mch Bnd; Pep Bnd; District Honors Band; Teaching; Western KY U

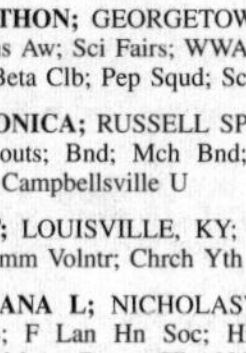
Shaban, Dania
Seneca HS
Louisville, KY

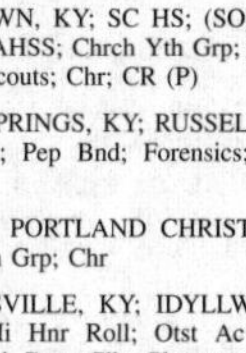
Schweinhart, Alishia
Nelson Cty HS
Bardstown, KY

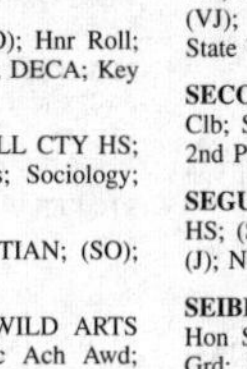
Schmitt, Bethany G
Conner HS
Burlington, KY

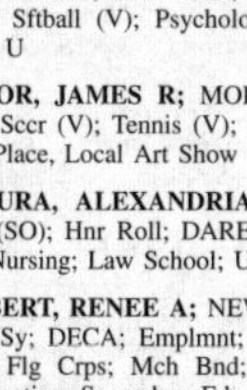
Scheitlin, Janet L
North Hardin HS
Radcliff, KY

National
Honor Roll
Spring 2005

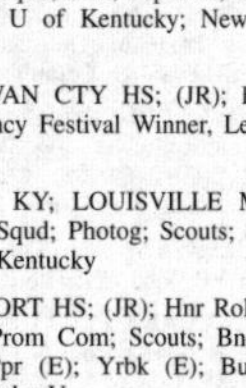
Sanders, Aumbrea S
North Hardin HS
Radcliff, KY

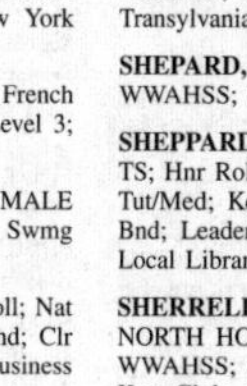
Schwartz, Paul J
Atherton HS
Louisville, KY

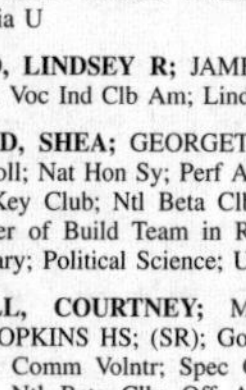
Sexton, Brittany
Newport, KY

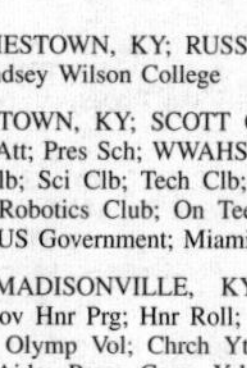
Shepard, Lindsey R
Russell Cty HS
Jamestown, KY

SHIRLEY, TIMOTHY P; SUMMERSVILLE, KY; GREEN CTY HS; (SR); All Am Sch; Hnr Roll; Nat Hon Sy; WWAHSS; Yth Ldrshp Prog; Comm Volntr; Chrch Yth Grp; Emplmnt; FBLA; Ntl Beta Clb; Spanish Clb; Ch Chr; Cl Off (P); Yrbk (R, P); Academic Team/Governor's Cup; Evangelism; Architecture; Engineering; U of Kentucky; Western Kentucky U

SHOEMAKER, TERESA J; HENDERSON, KY; REITZ MEMORIAL HS; (FR); Sccr (J); Track (V); Most Improved - Soccer; Key Club Officer; Math Major; PhD; Vanderbilt U; Georgia Tech

SHOUSE, JOSEPH D; BARDSTOWN, KY; NELSON CTY HS; (FR); All Am Sch; Ctznshp Aw; DAR; Hi Hnr Roll; Hnr Roll; WWAHSS; Key Club; Ntl Beta Clb; Bsball (JC); Bskball (J); Captain of Freshman Baseball Team; Computer Engineer; Basketball Coach

SHRYOCK, CHARLES T; LAWRENCEBURG, KY; ANDERSON HS; (SO); St of Mnth; Emplmnt; Ntl FFA; Hsbk Rdg (J); Secretary of FFA; Welding; Blocksmith; Anderson Technical School; Mt. Elden Blocksmithing School

SIEWINSKI, FRANNIE; FLORENCE, KY; BOONE CTY HS; (MS); Straight "A" Science Certificate; Health Care Administration; Health Care Field; Gateway Technical College; Northern Kentucky U

SIMMONS, ELISABETH; MIDDLESBORO, KY; MIDDLESBORO HS; (SO); Hnr Roll; Yth Ldrshp Prog; Comm Volntr; Peer Tut/Med; Chrch Yth Grp; Emplmnt; Pep Squd; Prom Com; Ch Chr; Adv Cncl (R); Junior Beta Club; Vice President- London District Association Youth; Dentistry; Orthodonist; U of Louisville; U of Kentucky

SIMS, AMANDA; SHELBYVILLE, KY; (SR); Hnr Roll; USAA; WWAHSS; Chrch Yth Grp; Key Club; Stg Cre; Yrbk (E); Asbury College

SINGER, TYLER H; VERSAILLES, KY; WOODFORD CTY HS; (FR); Hnr Roll; Ftball (J); Wt Lftg (J); Architect; Civil Engineering; U of Kentucky; Eastern Kentucky U

SKAGGS, G MICAH; LOUISVILLE, KY; JEFFERSONTOWN HIGH MAGNET SCH; Hnr Roll; Chrch Yth Grp; Bsball (V L); Article Published in "Muse"-School Sponsored Literature Book

SKEES, ALEXANDRA; JEFFERSONVILLE, KY; MONTGOMERY CTY HS; (SO); Duke TS; Hnr Roll; WWAHSS; Comm Volntr; 4-H; ArtClub; Chrch Yth Grp; JSA; Key Club; Ntl Beta Clb; Svce Clb; Mock Trial; President of Key Club; Art; Political Science; College of Charleston; Duke U

SKIPWORTH, ASHLEY L; LEWISBURG, KY; LOGAN CTY HS; (FR); Hnr Roll; Nat Hon Sy; Comm Volntr; FBLA; Elected Fundraiser Committee Chair of FBLA; Business; Law; Western Kentucky U; Murray State U

SLONE, JORDAN B; TOPMOST, KY; KNOTT CTY AREA TECH CTR; (SO); Hnr Roll; WWAHSS; Chrch Yth Grp; FCA; Bnd; Mch Bnd; Pep Bnd; Physical Therapy Assistant; Computer Tech; Hazard Community College

SLONE, SONYA; BEREA, KY; (SO); 4H Awd; Hnr Roll; Sci Fairs; St of Mnth; Comm Volntr; Hosp Aide; 4-H; ArtClub; BPA; Chrch Yth Grp; DARE; FCA; FBLA; Lib Aide; Ch Chr; Dnce; Bskball; Gmnstcs; PP Ftbl; Sftball; Vllyball; Stu Cncl (S); Yrbk (P); Volunteer Work; Nurse; Doctor; EKD; UK

SLONE, STEPHANIE R; MC DOWELL, KY; DAVID SCH; (SR); Sci Fairs; WWAHSS; Comm Volntr; Pep Squd; Yrbk (E); Radiologist/Radiology; Morehead State U; Big Sandy Cmty & Tech College

SMALLS II, CARL; RADCLIFF, KY; NORTH HARDIN HS; (JR); Hnr Roll; St of Mnth; Red Cr Aide; DARE; Emplmnt; FCA; SADD; Bnd; Jzz Bnd; Ftball (V); Mar Art (L); Sftball (L); Christian Band State Winner; Business Management; U of Louisville

SMILEY, BRITTANY D; PADUCAH, KY; REIDLAND HS; (SR); Otst Ac Ach Awd; WWAHSS; Comm Volntr; DECA; FCA; FCCLA; Key Club; Pep Squd; Bnd; Clr Grd; Pep Bnd; Bskball (V); Track (V); Winter Guard; Pre-Vet; Murray State U

SMITH, ASHLEY D; BULAN, KY; KNOTT CTY CTRL HS; (SO); 4H Awd; Fut Prb Slvr; Gov Hnr Prg; Hnr Roll; Nat Ldrshp Svc; Sci Fairs; 4-H; Chrch Yth Grp; DARE; Drma Clb; Ntl FFA; Scouts; Wdwrkg Clb; SP/M/VS; Skt Tgt Sh (V); 4-H; FFA-Sentinel; Agriculture; Medical; U of Kentucky; Eastern KY U

SMITH, DEREK; HEBRON, KY; CONNER HS; (SO); Hnr Roll; Perf Att; Yth Ldrshp Prog; Comm Volntr; Chrch Yth Grp; Emplmnt; Mus Clb; Bnd; Jzz Bnd; Mch Bnd; Pep Bnd; Section Leader / Marching Band; Music Teacher; Architect; U of Louisville; U of Kentucky

SMITH, DONNA M; WILLIAMSBURG, KY; WHITLEY CTY HS; (FR); Hnr Roll; Comm Volntr; 4-H; Chrch Yth Grp; DARE; SP/M/VS; Lawyer; Psychologist; Sullivan U; Eastern Kentucky U

SMITH, GREGORY; LOUISVILLE, KY; DOSS HS MAG CAREER AC; (JR); Hnr Roll; Nat Hon Sy; WWAHSS; Tennis (J); Track (V); PhD in Doctor; U of South Alabama; U of Louisville

SMITH, JESSICA L; FLORENCE, KY; LARRY A RYLE HS; (SO); WWAHSS; FBLA; Chr; FCCLA and National Society of High School Scholars; Tri-M music Honor Society; Communications; Music (Vocal); Northern Kentucky U; U of Kentucky

SMITH, LINDSAY; ALBANY, KY; CLINTON CTY HS; (SO); Perf Att; Chrch Yth Grp; FCA; Chr; Vllyball (J); Cl Off (V); LPN; Teaching; Lindsey Wilson College; Somerset Community College

SMITH, MACON; FRANKFORT, KY; WESTERN HILLS HS; (JR); Hnr Roll; WWAHSS; Bsball (V); Member of HOSA; Physical Therapy; U of Kentucky; Georgetown U

SMITH, MEGAN; FRANKLIN, KY; FRANKLIN-SIMPSON HS; (JR); Hnr Roll; Nat Hon Sy; St of Mnth; WWAHSS; Emplmnt; Ntl Beta Clb; Prom Com; Tchrs Aide; Stu Cncl (R); Secretary of Teenage Republican Club; Gifted & Talented Program; Business Management; Accounting; Western Kentucky U; U of Kentucky

SMITH, SAMANTHA; RUSSELL SPRINGS, KY; RUSSELL CTY HS; (FR); 4H Awd; Hi Hnr Roll; Nat Hon Sy; Perf Att; Peer Tut/Med; 4-H; Chrch Yth Grp; DARE; Ntl Beta Clb; SADD; Ch Chr; Tennis (J); Pediatrician; U of Kentucky

SMITH, SEAN; LOUISVILLE, KY; (SO); Hnr Roll; Nat Hon Sy; Bskball (J); Ftball (J); Wt Lftg (J); U of Kentucky

SMITH, TERESA N; RUSSELL SPGS, KY; RUSSELL CTY HS; (JR); Hnr Roll; ArtClub; ROTC; Ch Chr

SNIDER, AARON R; ANNVILLE, KY; JACKSON CTY HS; (FR); Hi Hnr Roll; Nat Hon Sy; Chrch Yth Grp; Cmptr Clb; DARE; FCA; Spanish Clb; Computer Programmer; Berea College; EKU

SOLOMON, AMBER; CALVERT CITY, KY; CHRISTIAN FELLOWSHIP SCH; (SO); F Lan Hn Soc; Hi Hnr Roll; Hnr Roll; Otst Ac Ach Awd; Sci Fairs; USAA; Yth Ldrshp Prog; Comm Volntr; Hab For Humty Volntr; Chrch Yth Grp; Emplmnt; Ntl Beta Clb; Pep Squd; Spanish Clb; Bskball (V L); Vllyball (V C); Stu Cncl (T); KHSAA- Academic All-State; Child Psychology

SOLOMON, ASHLEY; CALVERT CITY, KY; CHRISTIAN FELLOWSHIP SCH; (JR); Duke TS; F Lan Hn Soc; Hi Hnr Roll; Hnr Roll; Nat Hon Sy; Otst Ac Ach Awd; Sci Fairs; Sci/Math Olympn; USAA; Yth Ldrshp Prog; Comm Volntr; Hab For Humty Volntr; Chrch Yth Grp; Emplmnt; Mth Clb/Tm; Ntl Beta Clb; Pep Squd; Spanish Clb; Ch Chr; Bskball (V CL); Vllyball (V CL); Stu Cncl; KHSAA - Academic All-State; ORUEF National Honor Society; Cedarville U

SPARKMAN, SAMANTHA; GORDON, KY; CUMBERLAND HS; (JR); WWAHSS; Ntl Beta Clb; Off Aide; ROTC; Sftball (J); Vllyball (V); Child Psychologist; Berea; Alice Lloyd

SPARKS, NIKKI; RUSH, KY; BOYD CTY HS; (SO); Hi Hnr Roll; St Schl; Peer Tut/Med; Chrch Yth Grp; Fr of Library; Outdrs Clb; Chr; Ch Chr; Drl Tm; Sftball

SPARKS, RICKY D; SOUTH PORTSMOUTH, KY; LEWIS CTY HS; (SR); Nat Hon Sy; WWAHSS; ArtClub; Tchrs Aide; Voc Ind Clb Am; Drafting; Ashland Technical College

SPAW, BRANDI N; STANFORD, KY; LINCOLN CTY HS; (JR); Hnr Roll; Perf Att; WWAHSS; Comm Volntr; Chrch Yth Grp; Physical Therapy; Psychologist; Eastern Kentucky U; U of Kentucky

SPEARS, LANDRY; BURKESVILLE, KY; CUMBERLAND CO HS; (FR); Hnr Roll; Comm Volntr; Chrch Yth Grp; Emplmnt; FCA; FBLA; Ntl Beta Clb; Ntl FFA; Vsity Clb; Golf (V); Tennis (V)

SPENCER, NATASIA; LOUISVILLE, KY; LOUISVILLE MALE HS; (FR); Hnr Roll; Otst Ac Ach Awd; WWAHSS; Pep Squd; The Whitney M Young Scholars Program; The Quick Recall Team; Pediatric Medicine; Fashion Design; Harvard U; Columbia U

SPILLMAN, DUSTY; CLINTON, KY; FULTON CTY HS; (JR); All Am Sch; Hnr Roll; Nat Hon Sy; WWAHSS; Ntl Beta Clb; Ntl FFA; Sci Clb; French Clb; Cl Off (T); CR; Yrbk (P); Mortuary Science; Agriculture; Mid America College of Funeral Science; Murray State U

SPURR, RYAN; LOUISVILLE, KY; LOUISVILLE MALE HS; (SO); Hnr Roll; MVP; Mod UN; Photog; Sccr (V)

STACY, CLARA P; CAMPTON, KY; WOLFE CTY HS; (JR); Gov Hnr Prg; Hi Hnr Roll; Hnr Roll; Nat Ldrshp Svc; Sci Fairs; Sci/Math Olympn; USAA; WWAHSS; Comm Volntr; DARE; Ntl Beta Clb; Ntl FFA; Prom Com; Sftball (J); Cl Off (S); Zoologist; National Guards; Morehead State U; Eastern Kentucky U

STANFIELD, JOSEPH; MT STERLING, KY; MONTGOMERY CTY HS; (FR); Hnr Roll; MVP; Otst Ac Ach Awd; Perf Att; ArtClub; Ntl FFA; Ftball (C); Wt Lftg (VJ); Football; Computers; U of Eastern Kentucky; U of Louisville

STANFIELD, SARAH; ADOLPHUS, KY; ALLEN CTY HS; (FR); 4H Awd; All Am Sch; Hnr Roll; USAA; Bskball (J); Renaissance; Teacher / Coach; Accountant; Western Kentucky U; U of Tennessee

STANLEY, ALLISON L; HARDY, KY; BELFRY HS; (JR); Hi Hnr Roll; Nat Hon Sy; USAA; WWAHSS; Yth Ldrshp Prog; Comm Volntr; Peer Tut/Med; 4-H; MuAlphaTh; Pep Squd; Quill & Scroll; SADD; German Clb; Yrbk (E); Academic Team; PCVL Leader of the Month; Graphic Design; Business; Pikeville College; Eastern Kentucky U

STANLEY, CLAY; LOUISVILLE, KY; LOUISVILLE MALE HS; (FR); Duke TS; Hi Hnr Roll; Otst Ac Ach Awd; Perf Att; Comm Volntr; Chrch Yth Grp; Sccr (J)

STAUSS, SARAH M; LOUISVILLE, KY; HOLY ANGELS AC; (SO); Hnr Roll; WWAHSS; Drma Clb; Dnce; SP/M/VS; Vllyball (V); Law; Centre College; Loyola U

STEELE, JACQUELINE; LOUISVILLE, KY; SOUTHERN HS; (FR); St of Mnth; WWAHSS; FBLA; Key Club; Ch Chr; Scr Kpr (J); Track (V); Wt Lftg (J); Chef; Sullivan U

STEINFELD, SAMANTHA; HOPKINSVILLE, KY; HOPKINSVILLE HS; (FR); Duke TS; Hnr Roll; Comm Volntr; Chrch Yth Grp; Dnce; Tennis (J); Fashion Design Marketing; Forensic Science

STEPHENS, FALISHA; LOUISVILLE, KY; FERN CREEK TRADITIONAL HS; (FR); Duke TS; Hnr Roll; Otst Ac Ach Awd; Pres Sch; WWAHSS; Comm Volntr; Peer Tut/Med; Drma Clb; FCA; Ntl Beta Clb; Sci Clb; Tchrs Aide; French Clb; Chr; SP/M/VS; Tennis (J); CR (V); Environmental Club; STARS Club; DMD; Math and Science; Harvard U; Duke U

STEPHENS, MILES L; UNION, KY; LARRY A RYLE HS; (SO); Chrch Yth Grp; FBLA; Bsball (J); Golf (J); Skiing; Hispanic Honors Society; Guitar Club; Aerospace Engineering; Mechanical Engineering; Embry-Riddle U; Massachusetts Institute of Technology

STERRY, TAYLOR L; LEXINGTON, KY; PAUL LAURENCE DUNBAR HS; MS; 4H Awd; Duke TS; Fut Prb Slvr; Hi Hnr Roll; Hnr Roll; Otst Ac Ach Awd; Pres Sch; Yth Ldrshp Prog; Comm Volntr; Peer Tut/Med; ArtClub; DARE; Emplmnt; SP/M/VS; Chrldg (V CL); Equine Veterinarian; Auburn U; Ohio State U

STEVENS, RANDAL; STRUNK, KY; MC CREARY CTRL HS; (SO); Duke TS; Ftball (VJ); Wt Lftg (V); Wrstlg (V); Cumberland College; Berea College

STEVENSON II, JAMES T; HOPKINSVILLE, KY; HOPKINSVILLE HS; (JR); Gov Hnr Prg; Hnr Roll; MVP; Nat Hon Sy; Otst Ac Ach Awd; Perf Att; Pres Ac Ftns Aw; Pres Sch; St of Mnth; WWAHSS; Comm Volntr; Peer Tut/Med; Chrch Yth Grp; FCA; Lttrmn Clb; Ntl Beta Clb; NYLC; Scouts; Vsity Clb; Chr; Golf (V CL); President's Educational Award; RAGE - Gifted Student Association of KY; Business; Finance; U of Kentucky; Georgetown College Kentucky

STEWART, AMANDA C; SMITHS GROVE, KY; EDMONSON CO HS; (FR); Hi Hnr Roll; Perf Att; Comm Volntr; FBLA; Ntl Beta Clb; Pep Squd; SADD; Bskball (VJ L); Stu Cncl (P)

STEWART, CANDICE; LOUISVILLE, KY; FAIRDALE HS; (JR); Hnr Roll; Otst Ac Ach Awd; Perf Att; Chrch Yth Grp; DARE; FCA; Prom Com; Scouts; Bskball (J); Becoming a Police Officer; Criminal Justice; Western Kentucky U; U of Louisville

STILES, ALEXANDRA; ST HELENS, KY; KEYSTONE NATIONAL HS; (JR); Hi Hnr Roll; Peer Tut/Med; DARE; Emplmnt; Photog; Tchrs Aide; Play Various Musical Instruments - Home Schooled / Can't Join Band; Journalism Club; Public Relations; Film; U of Kentucky; Ball State

STITH, ABBY; BARDSTOWN, KY; NELSON CTY HS; (SO); All Am Sch; Hnr Roll; WWAHSS; Comm Volntr; 4-H; Chrch Yth Grp; DARE; Key Club; Sftball (J); Vllyball (J); Labor & Delivery Nurse; U of Louisville; Western Kentucky

STOCKTON, JENNIFER A; ALBANY, KY; CLINTON CTY HS; (JR); 4H Awd; Hnr Roll; Perf Att; Hosp Aide; 4-H; Chrch Yth Grp; FCCLA; Chr; Gymnastics / Choir / Softball; Kindergarten Teacher; Western KY U College; Somerset Community College

STOKES, REBECCA E; KEVIL, KY; HEATH HS; (SR); Hi Hnr Roll; Hnr Roll; WWAHSS; 4-H; ArtClub; Chess; Emplmnt; Spanish Clb; Bnd; Mch Bnd; Pep Bnd; History & English Major; Wish to Teach High School; Murray State U

STOUT, JARED E; LOUISVILLE, KY; FERN CREEK TRADITIONAL HS; (FR); FCA; Bsball (VJ); Ftball (J); Captain 8th Grade Quick Recall Team District Champions-Quick Recall 2004; Sports Profession; U of Kentucky; U of Louisville

STRAIN, JACKIE; LOUISVILLE, KY; SENECA HS; (SR); Hi Hnr Roll; MVP; Nat Stu Ath Day Aw; WWAHSS; Red Cr Aide; Key Club; Ntl Beta Clb; Sccr (VJ L); Pharmacy; U of Kentucky

STRANEY, AUDREY N; VINE GROVE, KY; MEADE CTY HS; (SR); 4H Awd; Hnr Roll; Nat Hon Sy; Perf Att; St of Mnth; WWAHSS; Comm Volntr; 4-H; Chrch Yth Grp; Emplmnt; FCA; Ntl FFA; VP of FFA Chapter; Agriculture; Elizabethtown Community College; Western Kentucky U

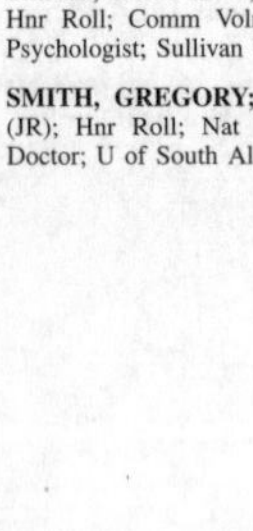
Stokes, Rebecca E
Heath HS
Kevil, KY

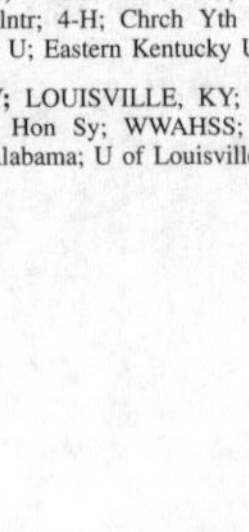
Smith, Macon
Western Hills HS
Frankfort, KY

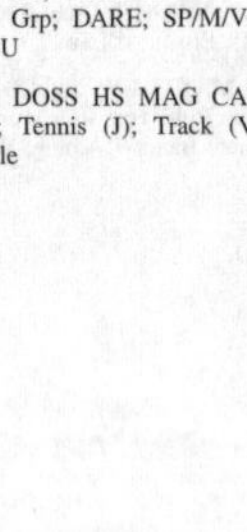
Smalls II, Carl
North Hardin HS
Radcliff, KY

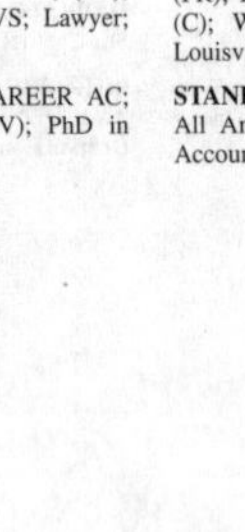
Singer, Tyler H
Woodford Cty HS
Versailles, KY

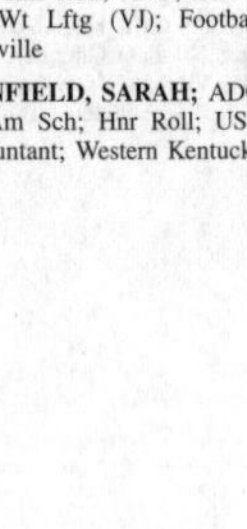
Simmons, Elisabeth
Middlesboro HS
Middlesboro, KY

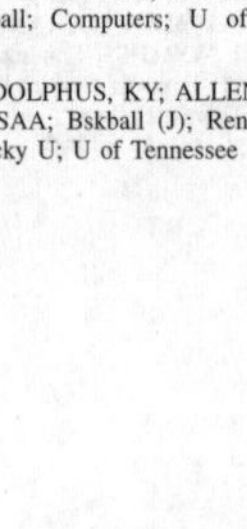
Shouse, Joseph D
Nelson Cty HS
Bardstown, KY

Siewinski, Frannie
Boone Cty HS
Florence, KY

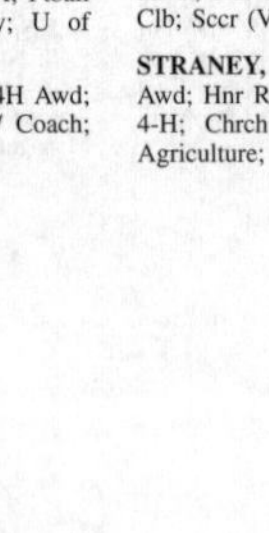
Skipworth, Ashley L
Logan Cty HS
Lewisburg, KY

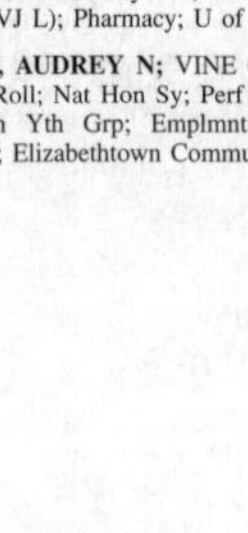
Smith, Derek
Conner HS
Hebron, KY

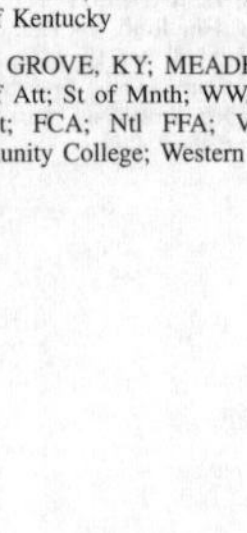
Sparks, Ricky D
Lewis Cty HS
South Portsmouth, KY

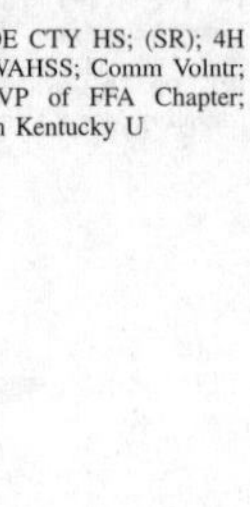
Stanfield, Sarah
Allen Cty HS
Adolphus, KY

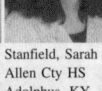

STRATTON, ELIZABETH A; FRANKFORT, KY; WESTERN HILLS HS; (JR); All Am Sch; Hnr Roll; Otst Ac Ach Awd; Comm Volntr; Emplmnt; Bnd; Music Business; NYU New York U; Berklee College of Music

STRICKLAND, WILLIAM F; KEVIL, KY; BALLARD MEMORIAL HS; (JR); Duke TS; Otst Ac Ach Awd; Comm Volntr; Chrch Yth Grp; Emplmnt; SP/M/VS; Ftball (J); Member of Christian Bands; Sound Technician; Mid Tennessee State

STROM, CLAIRE; LEXINGTON, KY; HENRY CLAY HS; (SO); Duke TS; Hnr Roll; Otst Ac Ach Awd; USAA; Peer Tut/Med; ArtClub; Fr of Library; Chr; SP/M/VS; National Junior Leaders' Conference (9th Grade); Social Activism Award (9th Grade); Business; Medicine; Smith College; Centre College

STURDIVANT, RACHEL E; WALTON, KY; LARRY A RYLE HS; (FR); Chrch Yth Grp; FBLA; Tennis (J); Communications; Business Administration; U of Tennessee; U of Kentucky

SUBLETT, TERRELL; ELIZABETHTOWN, KY; ELIZABETHTOWN HS; (SO); Hnr Roll; Perf Att; Sci Fairs; St of Mnth; Chrch Yth Grp; Mus Clb; Tech Clb; Wdwrkg Clb; Ch Chr; SP/M/VS; Ftball (V); Track (V); Wt Lftg (J); CR (S); Most Improved; Proficient in Science & Language Arts; Computer Technology; Music Theory; Western Kentucky; U of Louisville

SUBRAMANIAN, ANIRUDH; LOUISVILLE, KY; DUPONT MANUAL HS; (SO); Duke TS; Hi Hnr Roll; Otst Ac Ach Awd; Perf Att; Pres Ac Ftns Aw; Pres Sch; Comm Volntr; Hosp Aide; Peer Tut/Med; Chess; Dbte Team; Key Club; Ntl Beta Clb; Spch Team; Tmpl Yth Grp; Orch; Lcrsse (J); Mar Art (V); Member of Indiana State Youth Orchestra; Indiana State Chess Champion; Medicine; Music

SULLIVAN, CASEY; LOUISVILLE, KY; VALLEY TRADITIONAL HS; (JR); Hi Hnr Roll; Nat Hon Sy; Otst Ac Ach Awd; Perf Att; WWAHSS; Comm Volntr; Peer Tut/Med; Emplmnt; FBLA; Ntl Beta Clb; Pep Squd; Prom Com; Bnd; Pep Bnd; SP/M/VS; Chrldg (V); Cl Off (T); Nursing-RN; U of Louisville; Sullivan U

SULLIVAN, CHELSEA D; SCOTTSVILLE, KY; ALLEN CTY HS; (JR); Hnr Roll; Nat Mrt Sch Recip; WWAHSS; Chrch Yth Grp; Emplmnt; FCA; FBLA; FTA; Ntl Beta Clb; Pep Squd; Ch Chr; Clr Grd; Mch Bnd; Pep Bnd; Tennis (V L); Teaching; Business Degree; Oakland City U

SUTTON, TERRI N; HINDMAN, KY; KNOTT CTY CTRL HS; (SR); Hnr Roll; Nat Hon Sy; Ntl FFA; Sign Clb; Bnd; Vocational Agriculture Educator; Veterinary Tech; Hazard Community College; Morehead

SWAIM, HUNTER H; NICHOLASVILLE, KY; LEXINGTON CHRN AC HS; (SO); 4H Awd; Hnr Roll; Otst Ac Ach Awd; Sci Fairs; USAA; WWAHSS; Yth Ldrshp Prog; Comm Volntr; 4-H; Chrch Yth Grp; Emplmnt; FCA; Ntl FFA; Cr Ctry (VJ); Ftball (J); Track (V); Wt Lftg (V); Stu Cncl (V); CR; U of Tennessee; U of the South-Sewanee

SWEENEY, MICHAEL; MAYSLICK, KY; MASON CTY HS; (SO); Duke TS; Hnr Roll; WWAHSS; Chess; Ntl Beta Clb; Bnd; Mch Bnd; Pep Bnd; Computer Science Major; Rose-Hulman Institute of Technology; Xavier U

SYDNOR, TIANDREA; LOUISVILLE, KY; LOUISVILLE MALE HS; (SO); St of Mnth; Chrch Yth Grp; ROTC; Latin Clb; Ch Chr; Cr Ctry (VJ); Track (VJCL); Tennessee State U; U of Kentucky

SYKES, KELSEY; MURRAY, KY; MURRAY HS; (JR); Hnr Roll; Nat Hon Sy; Hosp Aide; Chrch Yth Grp; DARE; Emplmnt; FBLA; Ntl Beta Clb; Pep Squd; Prom Com; Quill & Scroll; Dnce; SP/M/VS; Stg Cre; PP Ftbl; Stu Cncl (R); Sch Ppr (R); Leadership Tomorrow Graduate; International Society of Poets-Editors Choice Award; Journalism, Business, Marketing; Public Relations, Sociology; Murray State U; Lipscomb U

SYMPSON, JENNA; BARDSTOWN, KY; NELSON CTY HS; (SR); All Am Sch; Hi Hnr Roll; Hnr Roll; Nat Hon Sy; St of Mnth; St Optmst of Yr; USAA; WWAHSS; Yth Ldrshp Prog; Comm Volntr; BPA; Chrch Yth Grp; Emplmnt; FCA; FBLA; Key Club; Off Aide; Pep Squd; Sccr (VJCL); Stu Cncl (R); Key Club President; Young Leader's Institute; Accounting; Bellarmine U

TALCOTT, MEGAN; ALVATON, KY; GREENWOOD HS; (SR); 4H Awd; Hnr Roll; Nat Hon Sy; Perf Att; WWAHSS; 4-H; FCCLA; Ntl Beta Clb; Bnd; Mch Bnd; Pep Bnd; Beta Club; National Honor Society; Auburn U; DePauw U

TARDY, LACEY; ASHLAND, KY; RUSSELL HS; (JR); F Lan Hn Soc; Nat Hon Sy; St of Mnth; Yth Ldrshp Prog; Comm Volntr; Red Cr Aide; ArtClub; Chrch Yth Grp; Emplmnt; FCA; Key Club; Ntl Beta Clb; Photog; Prom Com; Chrldg (L); Track (V); CR; Tri State Leadership Board; U of Kentucky; Georgetown College

TAYLOR, JENNIFER M; CLAY CITY, KY; POWELL CTY HS; (FR); Scouts; Cheerleading 2003-2004; Cross Country 2003-2004

TAYLOR, JOE; LEXINGTON, KY; TATES CREEK SR HS; (JR); Hnr Roll; WWAHSS; Yth Ldrshp Prog; Comm Volntr; DECA; Bskball (J L); Sch Ppr (R); Regional DECA Champion 2004; Runner-Up DECA State 2004; Bloodstock Agent-Business Mgmt; U of Kentucky; Eastern Kentucky U

TAYLOR, JOHN-TERRENCE B; GAMALIEL, KY; MONROE CTY HS; (FR); Duke TS; Hnr Roll; MVP; Sci Fairs; Peer Tut/Med; DARE; Ntl Beta Clb; Pep Squd; Voc Ind Clb Am; Bsball (VJ); Ftball (VJ); Wt Lftg (VJ); Athletic Trainer; U of Louisville; U of Kentucky

TAYLOR, KELLY E; HAZEL, KY; CALLOWAY CTY HS; (SR); All Am Sch; Duke TS; F Lan Hn Soc; Hnr Roll; Kwnis Aw; Otst Ac Ach Awd; St of Mnth; USAA; Valdctrian; Yth Ldrshp Prog; Comm Volntr; Emplmnt; FCA; Ntl Beta Clb; Ntl FFA; Pep Squd; Prom Com; Sci Clb; Tchrs Aide; Bskball (V CL); Tennis (V CL); Stu Cncl (R); CR (R); Member of National Science Honors Society; Pre-Pharmacy Major; U of Mississippi

TAYLOR, NICK; GEORGETOWN, KY; SCOTT CTY HS; (SO); Duke TS; Hi Hnr Roll; Hnr Roll; Otst Ac Ach Awd; Perf Att; WWAHSS; DECA; FCA; Key Club; Mus Clb; Pep Squd; Stu Cncl; Music; Business; Transylvania U; Centre U

TEAL, ALYSSA K; WITTENSVILLE, KY; JOHNSON CTRL HS; (SO); 4H Awd; Hnr Roll; Otst Ac Ach Awd; Perf Att; St of Mnth; Comm Volntr; 4-H; Chrch Yth Grp; DARE; Drma Clb; FCA; Pep Squd; Scouts; Ch Chr; SP/M/VS; Cr Ctry (V); Track (V); Cl Off (R); Pediatrician; Ob/Gyn; Ohio State U; U of Kentucky

TEMPLIN, SAMANTHA M; MT STERLING, KY; MONTGOMERY CTY HS; (FR); 4H Awd; Hnr Roll; Perf Att; Sci Fairs; Chrch Yth Grp; Ntl Beta Clb; Ch Chr; Dnce; Pediatrician; Wedding Planner; Transylvania U; Morehead State U

TERPIN, BRIANNA C; MT STERLING, KY; MONTGOMERY CTY HS; (JR); Ctznshp Aw; Hi Hnr Roll; Hnr Roll; Nat Hon Sy; Otst Ac Ach Awd; Perf Att; Sci Fairs; WWAHSS; Yth Ldrshp Prog; Peer Tut/Med; Chrch Yth Grp; Key Club; Acpl Chr; Chr; Ch Chr; SP/M/VS; Psychology; Pediatrics; Anderson U; Asbury College

TERRY, JOSH; COLUMBIA, KY; ADAIR CTY HS; (SO); Comm Volntr; ArtClub; Bnd; Mch Bnd; Orch; Pep Bnd; Physical Therapist; University of Kentucky; University of Louisville

THOMAS, FELICIA J Y; VANCEBURG, KY; LEWIS CTY HS; (SO); Hnr Roll; Perf Att; Sci Fairs; WWAHSS; 4-H; Chrch Yth Grp; DARE; FBLA; Scouts; Tchrs Aide; Chr; Ch Chr; CR (P); Yrbk (E); All Years of Elementary Cheer Captain; Fashion Designing

THOMAS, HEATHER A; HENDERSON, KY; HENDERSON CTY HS; MS; Hnr Roll; St of Mnth; Comm Volntr; Chrch Yth Grp; Chr; Dnce; Dance Team (School); Dentist; Nurse; U of Kentucky

THOMASON, ASHLEY; MADISONVILLE, KY; MADISONVILLE NORTH HOPKINS HS; (SR); Hnr Roll; Yth Ldrshp Prog; Hab For Humty Volntr; Spec Olymp Vol; Chrch Yth Grp; DECA; FBLA; Key Club; Off Aide; Outdrs Clb; Prom Com; Tchrs Aide; DECA - President 2004-2005; Elementary Education; Western Kentucky U

THOMPSON, BRITTANY; CAMPBELLSVILLE, KY; TAYLOR CTY HS; (SO); Fut Prb Slvr; Hnr Roll; WWAHSS; Comm Volntr; DECA; Emplmnt; Quiz Bowl; DECA Chapter Secretary; DECA Region III Reporter; Philosophy; Journalism; Tulane U; New York U

THOMPSON, ERIC; BARDSTOWN, KY; NELSON CTY HS; (FR); Hnr Roll; MVP; WWAHSS; Comm Volntr; DARE; Key Club; Ntl Beta Clb; Pep Squd; Bsball (V); Bskball (J); Cl Off (V); Freshman "Pitcher of the Year"; Designing Stadiums; Medical Field; U of KY

THOMPSON, LINDSAY; FRANKFORT, KY; FRANKIN CTY HS; (JR); F Lan Hn Soc; Fut Prb Slvr; Hi Hnr Roll; Otst Ac Ach Awd; St Schl; WWAHSS; Comm Volntr; Peer Tut/Med; Chrch Yth Grp; Drma Clb; Emplmnt; FCA; Key Club; Ntl Beta Clb; Prom Com; SADD; Bnd; Drm Mjr; Mch Bnd; Pep Bnd; Golf (L); PP Ftbl; Tennis; Adv Cncl (R); Cl Off (R); Stu Cncl (R); CR; Key Club Secretary; Computer Animation; Eastern Kentucky U; Western Kentucky U

THOMPSON, MATTHEW G; SALT LICK, KY; BATH CTY HS; (JR); Ctznshp Aw; Gov Hnr Prg; St of Mnth; WWAHSS; Comm Volntr; Peer Tut/Med; Chrch Yth Grp; FCA; Ntl Beta Clb; Spanish Clb; Y-Club Treasurer; Medical Field; Engineering; U of Kentucky

THOMPSON, MEGAN; VINE GROVE, KY; NORTH HARDIN HS; (JR); DAR; Hnr Roll; WWAHSS; ROTC; Bnd; Drl Tm; National Youth Leadership Forum; Future World Leaders Forum; Chemical Engineering; Military Science; West Point; Naval Academy

THORNE, ASHLEY; MT STERLING, KY; MONTGOMERY CTY HS; (FR); Hi Hnr Roll; Chrch Yth Grp; Ntl Beta Clb; Chr; Dnce; Yrbk (R); Photography

THORNSBEARY, MARLENA; LEBURN, KY; KNOTT CTY CTRL HS; (FR); Peer Tut/Med; Spec Olymp Vol; ArtClub; Meteorologist; Broadcasting News; Western Kentucky U; Eastern Kentucky U

THORNSBERRY, BRIAN; MT WASHINGTON, KY; BULLITT EAST HS; (SO); Hi Hnr Roll; Otst Ac Ach Awd; Pres Ac Ftns Aw; Sci Fairs; WWAHSS; Comm Volntr; Chrch Yth Grp; FCA; Spanish Clb; Bsball (J); Ftball (V L); PP Ftbl; Wt Lftg; Stu Cncl (R); Sophomore Homecoming Representative - Football Season; Math / PE Distinguished Student Award; Aeronautical Engineering; Juris Doctorate; United States Air Force Academy; United States Naval Academy

TIGUE, SHANNON N; PINEVILLE, KY; PINEVILLE HS; (MS); Hi Hnr Roll; Hnr Roll; Nat Hon Sy; Perf Att; Peer Tut/Med; Ntl Beta Clb; Psychology; Veterinarian Medicine; U of Kentucky; Lincoln Memorial U

TILFORD, CLINT; WEST PADUCAH, KY; HEATH HS; (JR); Hi Hnr Roll; Pres Sch; WWAHSS; Comm Volntr; Chrch Yth Grp; Ntl FFA; Prom Com; Bsball (V L); Bskball (V L); Ftball (V L); U of Kentucky; U of Louisville

TOBIN, KRISTIN; BRANDENBURG, KY; MEADE CTY HS; (SR); Gov Hnr Prg; Hi Hnr Roll; Nat Hon Sy; St of Mnth; St Optmst of Yr; WWAHSS; Comm Volntr; Peer Tut/Med; Chrch Yth Grp; FCA; Mus Clb; SADD; French Clb; Chr; Ch Chr; Chrldg (J L); Swmg (J L); CR (T); Governor's Scholar Program; Child Studies; Vanderbilt U

TODD, ARIC; LOUISVILLE, KY; (SO); Ctznshp Aw; Hnr Roll; Nat Hon Sy; Otst Ac Ach Awd; Perf Att; Cmptr Clb; Mus Clb; Scouts; Tech Clb; Bnd; Jzz Bnd; Mch Bnd; Pep Bnd; Beta Club; National Honor Society; Cryptology; Programming

TODD, MARIE; NICHOLASVILLE, KY; EAST JESSAMINE HS; (JR); Hnr Roll; Otst Ac Ach Awd; WWAHSS; Peer Tut/Med; Drma Clb; Spch Team; Tchrs Aide; Spanish Clb; SP/M/VS; Stg Cre; History; Education; U of Kentucky

TRACEY, CHRISTOPHER; CORBIN, KY; WHITLEY CTY HS; (FR); Hnr Roll; Nat Hon Sy; Perf Att; Pres Sch; Sci Fairs; USAA; WWAHSS; Peer Tut/Med; Mth Clb/Tm; Ntl Beta Clb; Spanish Clb; Mch Bnd; Pep Bnd; Computer Programming & Design

TRACY, SETH A; EDDYVILLE, KY; LYON CTY HS; (JR); Hnr Roll; MVP; Perf Att; WWAHSS; ArtClub; Emplmnt; FCA; Pep Squd; Prom Com; Sccr (V L); Engineering; Computer Science; Murray State U; Western Kentucky U

TRAVELSTEAD, JESSICA; LOUISVILLE, KY; JEFFERSON CTY HS; (SR); Ctznshp Aw; Hnr Roll; WWAHSS; DARE; FCA; Ntl Beta Clb; P to P St Amb Prg; Scouts; Chr; Ch Chr; Law; Political Science; U of Louisville; Bellarmine College

TRIMBLE, KATHRYN; WINCHESTER, KY; MARS HILL AC; (JR); 4H Awd; Duke TS; F Lan Hn Soc; Hnr Roll; Comm Volntr; Peer Tut/Med; 4-H; Chrch Yth Grp; Emplmnt; Off Aide; Tchrs Aide; French Clb; Dnce; Stg Cre; Treasurer of the Lexington Baker Senior Company Club; 4-H Volunteer Leader; Pre-Med; Biology; Vanderbilt U; U of Louisville

TRIMBLE, TAMMY; ASHLAND, KY; BOYD CTY HS; (SO); Duke TS; Comm Volntr; Peer Tut/Med; FBLA; Adv Cncl (P); FCCLA Representative; Lawyer Juvenile / Family Court; U of Kentucky; Morehead State

TRIPLETT, HOPE; LOUISVILLE, KY; BUTLER HS; (JR); Hnr Roll; Comm Volntr; Chr; Animal Rights Advocate; PETA; Veterinarian; U of Kentucky; U of Louisville

TROBAUGH, TASHA; LONDON, KY; SOUTH LAUREL HS; (MS); 4H Awd; Ctznshp Aw; Gov Hnr Prg; Hnr Roll; Kwnis Aw; Perf Att; St of Mnth; Hab For Humty Volntr; 4-H; Chrch Yth Grp; DARE; FCA; Kwanza Clb; Scouts; Dnce; Gmnstcs (J); U of Kentucky

TRULOCK, KATRINA A; MAMMOTH CAVE, KY; EDMONSON CTY HS; (FR); Hnr Roll; FCCLA; Clr Grd; An Art Degree or Veterinarian Degree

TUCK, SIERRA P; SPRINGFIELD, KY; WASHINGTON CTY HS; (FR); Duke TS; Fut Prb Slvr; Hnr Roll; 4-H; Chrch Yth Grp; Drma Clb; FCA; Scouts; Spanish Clb; Bnd; Jzz Bnd; Mch Bnd; Orch; Tennis (V); Cl Off (R); Stu Cncl (R); CR (R); Centre College; Campbellsville U

TUCKER, BRITTANY N; LEITCHFIELD, KY; BETHEL CHRISTIAN AC; (FR); Hnr Roll; Chrch Yth Grp; Drma Clb; Chr; Bskball (VJCL); Christian Character Award; Automotive Technician; Western Kentucky U

TUCKER, GARRETT; HOPKINSVILLE, KY; HOPKINSVILLE HS; (SO); Pep Squd; Bnd; Clr Grd; Mch Bnd; Pep Bnd; Band Contest State; Computer Design; Work on Computers; Western Kentucky U; Murray State U

TURNER, TREY; RUSSELLVILLE, KY; LOGAN CO HS; (SO); 4H Awd; Hnr Roll; St of Mnth; WWAHSS; 4-H; FCA; Ntl Beta Clb; Ntl FFA; Bskball (VJ L); Tennis (V L)

UNDERWOOD, LINDSEY; WICKLIFFE, KY; BALLARD MEMORIAL HS; (JR); Gov Hnr Prg; Hnr Roll; Nat Hon Sy; WWAHSS; Yth Ldrshp Prog; Peer Tut/Med; Chrch Yth Grp; FCA; FBLA; Ntl Beta Clb; Prom Com; Ch Chr; Chrldg (V); Cl Off (V); West Kentucky Community and Technical College

Thornsbeary, Marlena
Knott Cty Ctrl HS
Leburn, KY

Thomas, Heather A
Henderson Cty HS
Henderson, KY

Sykes, Kelsey
Murray HS
Murray, KY

Teal, Alyssa K
Johnson Ctrl HS
Wittensville, KY

Triplett, Hope
Butler HS
Louisville, KY

UTZ, CANDICE; BUTLER, KY; PENDLETON CTY HS; (JR); Perf Att; WWAHSS; Chrch Yth Grp; DECA; Ch Chr; Sftball (V); Vllyball (V); Marine Biology; Psychology; Hawaii Pacific U; Coastal Carolina

VALLEJO, REYMOND; PADUCAH, KY; PADUCAH TILGHMAN HS; (SO); Ctznshp Aw; Hi Hnr Roll; Hnr Roll; Nat Sci Aw; Perf Att; Pres Ac Ftns Aw; Pres Sch; Sci Fairs; St of Mnth; Yth Ldrshp Prog; Comm Volntr; Peer Tut/Med; 4-H; Biology Clb; Chrch Yth Grp; DARE; Drma Clb; Emplmnt; Ntl FFA; Off Aide; Acpl Chr; Ch Chr; Bsball (V); Bskball (J); Cr Ctry (V); Sccr (V); Wrstlg (V); Yrbk (E)

VAN BIBBER, EDEN; SOUTH SHORE, KY; GREENUP CTY HS; (JR); Gov Hnr Prg; Hnr Roll; Nat Sci Aw; WWAHSS; Chrch Yth Grp; Ntl Beta Clb; Photog; Chr; Homecoming Junior Candidate; Journalism; Psychology; Eastern U of Kentucky; Transylvania U

VANCE, DONNA M; ASHLAND, KY; BOYD CTY HS; (FR); Otst Ac Ach Awd; Perf Att; Chr; Forensic Science; Nurse Practitioner; Morehead State U; Brea State College

VAN CLEVE, JAMES; CALHOUN, KY; MC LEAN CTY HS; (SO); Hnr Roll; USAA; WWAHSS; Chrch Yth Grp; FCA; Ntl Beta Clb; Sci Clb; Spanish Clb; Tennis; Forensics; Eastern Kentucky U

VAN CLEVE, MICHAEL; CALHOUN, KY; MC LEAN CTY HS; (FR); Hnr Roll; WWAHSS; Peer Tut/Med; Chrch Yth Grp; Lttrmn Clb; Lib Aide; Quill & Scroll; Quiz Bowl; Bskball; Skiing; Business; U of Kentucky; Western Kentucky U

VANDERMOSTEN III, GUY; BURLINGTON, KY; CONNER HS; (SO); Hnr Roll; MVP; Nat Hon Sy; Perf Att; St of Mnth; Emplmnt; Cr Ctry (V CL); Sccr (J); Track (V CL); Sports Medicine; Physical Therapist; U Kentucky; U Louisville

VAN METER, JESSICA M; CECILIA, KY; CTRL HARDIN HS; (FR); Ctznshp Aw; Hnr Roll; Perf Att; Chrch Yth Grp; Chr; Master's Degree in Teaching; New York U; Yale

VAN METER, SHAUNA B; LEITCHFIELD, KY; GRAYSON CTY HS; (SR); Hnr Roll; Peer Tut/Med; Prom Com; Chr; Medical Office Assistant; Elizabethtown Community College

VANOVER, SARAH L; WILLIAMSBURG, KY; WHITLEY CTY HS; (FR); 4H Awd; Ctznshp Aw; Hnr Roll; Perf Att; Sci Fairs; 4-H; Chrch Yth Grp; Mus Clb; ROTC; Scouts; Chr; Poem Published In: a Celebration of Young Poets; Achievement Award/Reading; Nurse; Counselor; Berea College; U of Kentucky

VANSEAH, JEREMY; BOWLING GREEN, KY; WARREN EAST HS; (FR); Hnr Roll; SADD; Bskball (J); Ftball (J)

VAUGHN, AMBER; LA GRANGE, KY; OLDHAM CTY HS; (JR); Comm Volntr; FCCLA (Family, Community & Career Leaders of America); Interior Design; U of Kentucky; Northern Kentucky U

VAUGHN, ROCHELLE L; LAWRENCEBURG, KY; ANDERSON CTY HS; (SR); F Lan Hn Soc; Hnr Roll; St of Mnth; WWAHSS; Comm Volntr; Peer Tut/Med; Chrch Yth Grp; Emplmnt; FCCLA; Ntl Beta Clb; Pep Squd; Prom Com; Acpl Chr; Chr; Ch Chr; Tennis (J); Stu Cncl (R); Peers Assisting with Student Success, Mentor to Freshman Students; Psychology; Communications; U of Kentucky; Lexington Community College KY

VAUGHN, TAYLOR; LA GRANGE, KY; OLDHAM CTY HS; (FR); Hi Hnr Roll; Hnr Roll; Nat Hon Sy; Otst Ac Ach Awd; Peer Tut/Med; Pep Squd; Chrldg (VJ); Cl Off (R); OCMS Colonel Pin Recipient; 2 Star Oldham Co. Middle School Recipient; I Am Interested in Broadcast Journalism.; The Real Estate Business; Georgetown College (Kentucky); U of Kentucky

VICARS, HEATHER R; ALEXANDRIA, KY; CAMPBELL CTY HS; (FR); 4H Awd; Ctznshp Aw; Hi Hnr Roll; Hnr Roll; Otst Ac Ach Awd; St of Mnth; 4-H; DARE; Drma Clb; Chr; Chrldg (J); Adv Cncl (R); Explore More Classes at Thomas More; Dreamfest Classes at NKU / Completed Modeling; Photographer; Social Worker; U of North Carolina; U of Kentucky

VICKERS V, JOHN R; SACRAMENTO, KY; MC LEAN CTY HS; (FR); 4H Awd; DAR; Duke TS; WWAHSS; Yth Ldrshp Prog; Chrch Yth Grp; DARE; Emplmnt; FBLA; Ntl FFA; Ch Chr; Bsball (VJ); District FFA Creed Contest Winner & Quiz Bowl Winner; Regional FFA Creed Contest Winner; Engineering Field & Agriculture; Law / History; Western Kentucky U

VIEHLAND, KAILEE; PRINCETON, KY; CALDWELL CTY HS; (SO); Hnr Roll; Nat Hon Sy; USAA; WWAHSS; Peer Tut/Med; Chrch Yth Grp; FCA; FBLA; Key Club; Ntl Beta Clb; Ntl FFA; Pep Squd; Vsity Clb; Chrldg (V); Gmnstcs; Cl Off (P); Stu Cncl (V); CR; Yrbk; Journalism; Law; U of Kentucky; Western Kentucky U

VINCENT, ALEX T; LOUISVILLE, KY; JEFFERSONTOWN HS; (JR); Hnr Roll; Nat Hon Sy; Otst Ac Ach Awd; WWAHSS; 4-H; Chess; Chrch Yth Grp; Cmptr Clb; DARE; Drma Clb; Emplmnt; FCA; Orch; SP/M/VS; Stg Cre; Cr Ctry (J); U of Louisville

VINCENT, CHRISTOPHER M; LEWISBURG, KY; LOGAN CTY HS; (FR); Duke TS; Hnr Roll; Mar Art; Purple Belt Tae Kwon Do - Martial Arts; Academic Team; Information Technology; MIT; U Florida

WAFFORD, KIMBERLY; NICHOLASVILLE, KY; WEST JESSAMINE HS; (FR); Hnr Roll; Chrch Yth Grp; Ch Chr; Business; Lexington Community College; Eastern Kentucky U

WAFFORD JR, DANIEL; LEXINGTON, KY; EASTSIDE CTR FOR APPLIED TECH; (SO); Hnr Roll; Chrch Yth Grp; ROTC; Scouts; Wdwrkg Clb; Ch Chr; Orch; Bsball (V); Golf (V C); Wrstlg (V C); Member of Skills USA; Law Degree; Baseball; U of Kentucky; Eastern Kentucky

WAINSCOTT, LOGAN S; FRANKFORT, KY; FRANKLIN CTY HS; (FR); Duke TS; Gov Hnr Prg; Hi Hnr Roll; Nat Hon Sy; USAA; WWAHSS; Comm Volntr; Peer Tut/Med; Emplmnt; Key Club; Mod UN; Dnce; Stg Cre; Dance Team; Presidential Honor Roll; Centre College; Transylvania U

WALDEN, SARA; RUSH, KY; BOYD CTY HS; (FR); Ctznshp Aw; Duke TS; Hnr Roll; Perf Att; Chrch Yth Grp; Mod UN; Sci Clb

WALKER, KATIE; LOUISVILLE, KY; BALLARD MEMORIAL HS; (SO); Hi Hnr Roll; Hnr Roll; Sci Fairs; Comm Volntr; Emplmnt; Mod UN; Ntl Beta Clb; Quiz Bowl; Sci Clb; Latin Clb; SP/M/VS; Stu Cncl (S); Anchor for School News Show - WBHS; Volunteer-Juvenile Diabetes Research Foundation; Liberal Arts

WALKER, MINDY S; BARLOW, KY; BALLARD MEMORIAL HS; (SO); Hi Hnr Roll; Hnr Roll; WWAHSS; Chrch Yth Grp; Emplmnt; FCA; Pep Squd; Spanish Clb; Bnd; Clr Grd; Dnce; Flg Crps; Medical Field

WALKER, RAVEN B; GLASGOW, KY; BARREN CTY HS; (SO); Hi Hnr Roll; Hnr Roll; Perf Att; Sci Fairs; St of Mnth; WWAHSS; Comm Volntr; DARE; FBLA; Pep Squd; SADD; Spanish Clb; Lawyer; Paralegal; Western Kentucky U; Lindsey Wilson College

WALLACE, ANDREA; BOSTON, KY; NELSON CTY HS; (JR); Hnr Roll; Comm Volntr; FBLA; Key Club; Ntl FFA; Pep Squd; Vllyball (J); Key Club Secretary; Master's in Business Administration; Western Kentucky; U of Louisville

WALLACE, BLYTHE L; ROBARDS, KY; HENDERSON CTY HS; (FR); Hnr Roll; Hab For Humty Volntr; Chrch Yth Grp; DARE; Cr Ctry (V L); Track (V L); Health Science; Zoologist; Western Kentucky U

WALLACE, JESSICA S; PADUCAH, KY; REIDLAND HS; (JR); Duke TS; Sci Fairs; WWAHSS; Comm Volntr; Hab For Humty Volntr; ArtClub; Chrch Yth Grp; DECA; FCA; Key Club; Pep Squd; Sci Clb; Tchrs Aide; Chr; Clr Grd; Scr Kpr (VJ); Sccr (V); Vllyball (V); Second Place DECA State; DECA Region I President; Athletic Training; Sports Medicine; Western Kentucky U; U of Kentucky

WALLACE, KRISTINA K; HOPKINSVILLE, KY; HOPKINSVILLE HS; (FR); Duke TS; Hnr Roll; Sci Fairs; Chrch Yth Grp; Lib Aide; Ntl Beta Clb; Acpl Chr; Chr; Ch Chr; Sftball (J); Vllyball (J); Sch Ppr (R); Kentucky New Era Teen Focus Group; Club: First Priority; Anthropology; Journalism

WALLS, APRIL; LOUISVILLE, KY; FERN CREEK TRADITIONAL HS; (FR); Hi Hnr Roll; Hnr Roll; Perf Att; WWAHSS; Chrch Yth Grp; FCA; FTA; Pep Squd; Chr

WALLS, ERIN; LOUISVILLE, KY; FERN CREEK TRADITIONAL HS; (FR); Hnr Roll; Perf Att; WWAHSS; Chrch Yth Grp; FCA; Pep Squd; Chr

WARD, ANGELINA C; LOUISVILLE, KY; LOUISVILLE MALE HS; (JR); Hnr Roll; Comm Volntr; Hosp Aide; Peer Tut/Med; FCA; FBLA; Pep Squd; French Clb; Involved in Red Cross; Pediatrics; Elementary Education; U of Kentucky; U of Louisville

WARD, TYLER; KIMPER, KY; PIKE CTY CTRL HS; (SO); All Am Sch; Hnr Roll; Nat Hon Sy; USAA; WWAHSS; Emplmnt; Ntl Beta Clb; Criminology; Morehead State U; Eastern Kentucky U

WARFORD, JORDAN; VINE GROVE, KY; MEADE CTY HS; (FR); Duke TS; Hi Hnr Roll; WWAHSS; Chrch Yth Grp; DARE; FCA; Chr; Cl Off (T); Duke Tip Award Winner; Member of Youth in Charge; Veterinary License; Masters Degree; Western Kentucky U; U of Kentucky

WARNOCK, ASHLEY N; OIL SPRINGS, KY; JOHNSON CTRL HS; (JR); 4-H; Chrch Yth Grp; Drma Clb; FCA; Mus Clb; Pep Squd; Prom Com; SADD; Acpl Chr; Chr; Ch Chr; SP/M/VS; Anesthesia/Anestheologist; Moorehead State U; Florida State U

WARRIX, HOLLY L; PIKEVILLE, KY; PIKE CTRL HS; (SR); 4H Awd; Hnr Roll; WWAHSS; 4-H; ArtClub; DARE; Chr; Yrbk (P); Member and VP of FCCLA; Art Education; Art; EKU; Pikeville College

WASH, AMBER M; FRANKFORT, KY; FRANKLIN CTY HS; (JR); Hnr Roll; Pres Sch; WWAHSS; Yth Ldrshp Prog; Comm Volntr; Red Cr Aide; DARE; DECA; Emplmnt; Key Club; Ntl Beta Clb; Quill & Scroll; SADD; Dnce; PPSqd (V L); Stu Cncl (R); CR (R); Sch Ppr (R, P); Captain of Dance Team; Leadership Award on Dance Team; Business Management; Cosmetology; Western Kentucky U; Eastern Kentucky U

WASHBURN, JASON A; CHAPLIN, KY; NELSON CTY HS; (JR); WWAHSS; Key Club; Biology-Human; Chemistry; Transylvania U; U of Kentucky

WATKINS, BRITTANY; CARLISLE, KY; NICHOLAS CTY HS; (FR); Hnr Roll; Nat Hon Sy; Perf Att; WWAHSS; Scouts; National Junior Honor Society; Pediatric Nursing; Master's Degree; Eastern Kentucky U; Michigan State U

WEAVER, LAUREN M; DRY RIDGE, KY; GRANT CTY HS; (SO); Fut Prb Slvr; Hi Hnr Roll; Otst Ac Ach Awd; St of Mnth; Key Club; Orch; Sccr (J); Stu Cncl (P); Tutoring; Young Professionals Organization; Liberal Arts; U of Kentucky; Morehead State

WEAVER, MEREDITH L; SCOTTSVILLE, KY; ALLEN CTY HS; (SR); All Am Sch; Hnr Roll; Nat Hon Sy; Nat Mrt Semif; Perf Att; USAA; Valdctrian; WWAHSS; Comm Volntr; Chrch Yth Grp; FCA; Ntl Beta Clb; Bnd; Ch Chr; Mch Bnd; Pep Bnd; Host Treas.; Occupational Therapy; Music Therapy; U of Louisville

WEAVER, WHITNEY N; DAWSON SPRINGS, KY; DAWSON SPRINGS HS; (FR); Hnr Roll; WWAHSS; DARE; Ntl Beta Clb; Scouts; Sccr (J); Nurse; Teacher; Madisonville Community College; Murray State U

WEBB, BRANDI; PLEASUREVILLE, KY; HENRY CTY HS; (SR); Hnr Roll; Perf Att; Drma Clb; Emplmnt; Mus Clb; Pep Squd; Prom Com; ROTC; Sci Clb; SADD; Chr; Dnce; SP/M/VS; Stg Cre; A Member of U of Louisville Ohio; Flight Commander in JROTC; Performing Arts; Theater; Eastern Kentucky U

WEBB, JESSICA; CARLISLE, KY; NICHOLAS CTY HS; (JR); All Am Sch; Hi Hnr Roll; Hnr Roll; Pres Ac Ftns Aw; USAA; WWAHSS; Comm Volntr; Peer Tut/Med; Chrch Yth Grp; DARE; Drma Clb; Emplmnt; FTA; Lib Aide; Mod UN; Off Aide; SP/M/VS; Chrldg (V L); Tennis (V L); Cl Off (V); Stu Cncl (P); Yrbk (E, R, P); Y-Club-President; Communications; U of Kentucky; Northern Kentucky U

WEBB, LAURA M; PERRYVILLE, KY; BOYLE CTY HS; (SR); Ctznshp Aw; Hnr Roll; Perf Att; St of Mnth; Comm Volntr; Ntl FFA; Bnd; Orch; Pep Bnd; Vice President of FFA 2004/2005; Reporter of FFA 2003/2004; Biology / Pre-Vet; Campbellsville U

WEBER, CHRISTOPHER; BELLEVUE, KY; BELLEVUE HS; (FR); Hi Hnr Roll; Hnr Roll; MVP; Perf Att; Pres Ac Ftns Aw; St of Mnth; Aqrium Clb; Chess; Chrch Yth Grp; Cmptr Clb; DARE; Emplmnt; Mth Clb/Tm; Stg Cre; Bsball (J L); Bskball (J L); Cr Ctry (J L); Golf (J); Track (J L); Wt Lftg (J); Stu Cncl (R); Science; Athletics; Duke U; Northern KY U Louisville

WEDDING, JUSTIN A; HENDERSON, KY; REITZ MEMORIAL HS; (JR); Duke TS; Hi Hnr Roll; Nat Hon Sy; WWAHSS; Hab For Humty Volntr; Chrch Yth Grp; Key Club; Vsity Clb; Spanish Clb; Sccr (J); Wrstlg (V); Dentistry; Pre-Med; U of Kentucky; U of Louisville

WEDEL, JACQUELINE; RICHMOND, KY; MODEL LABORATORY SCH; (JR); All Am Sch; Hi Hnr Roll; Nat Hon Sy; Otst Ac Ach Awd; Pres Ac Ftns Aw; St Schl; USAA; WWAHSS; Comm Volntr; Spec Olymp Vol; Emplmnt; Key Club; Mth Clb/Tm; Prom Com; Sci Clb; Sccr (V); Tennis (V); Track (V); Cl Off (P, V); Lit Mag; Governor's Scholar 2005

WELLS, HIMELLA; RICHMOND, KY; MODEL LABORATORY SCH; (JR); 4H Awd; All Am Sch; Duke TS; Hi Hnr Roll; Nat Hon Sy; Nat Ldrshp Svc; Nat Mrt LOC; Otst Ac Ach Awd; USAA; WWAHSS; Comm Volntr; Hosp Aide; Drma Clb; FCA; Key Club; NYLC; P to P St Amb Prg; Sci Clb; Scouts; SADD; Bnd; Mch Bnd; Pep Bnd; SP/M/VS; Arch (V); Cl Off (R); Stu Cncl (V, R); Sch Ppr (E); Yrbk (R); Health and Wellness Award; Youth Salute; Political Science / Law; Journalism; Florida State; Yale U

WELLS, KARA B; CARLISLE, KY; NICHOLAS CTY HS; (JR); All Am Sch; Ctznshp Aw; DAR; Hi Hnr Roll; Nat Mrt LOC; Perf Att; Pres Sch; St of Mnth; USAA; WWAHSS; Comm Volntr; Chrch Yth Grp; FTA; Off Aide; Pep Squd; Prom Com; Ch Chr; Chrldg (V); Gmnstcs (V); Tennis (V); Cl Off (T); Stu Cncl (R); Lit Mag; Piano; Y-Club; Biology; Photography; U of Kentucky; Transylvania U

WELLS, STEPHEN T; WACO, KY; MODEL LABORATORY SCH; (SR); All Am Sch; Hi Hnr Roll; Hnr Roll; Otst Ac Ach Awd; WWAHSS; Comm Volntr; Key Club; Prom Com; Bdmtn (J); Cyclg; Sccr (J); Track (V); Civil Engineer; Math Teacher; Eastern Kentucky U; U of Kentucky

WENTLING, CHARLES; LOUISVILLE, KY; BUTLER TRADITIONAL HS; Hi Hnr Roll; Hnr Roll; Perf Att; Yth Ldrshp Prog; Chess; DARE; Engineering; Law School; U of Louisville

WESLEY, EMILY; RUSSELL SPRINGS, KY; RUSSELL CTY HS; (FR); 4H Awd; Hnr Roll; Perf Att; St of Mnth; Yth Ldrshp Prog; Comm Volntr; Chrch Yth Grp; Ch Chr; Chrldg (J); Gmnstcs (J); Pharmacist; Western; Somerset Community College

WEST, ASHLEY L; FRANKLIN, KY; ALLEN CTY HS; (FR); All Am Sch; Hnr Roll; Perf Att; Chrch Yth Grp; Ntl Beta Clb; Tchrs Aide; Beta; Perfect Attendance; Teaching; Hair Stylist; Indiana U; Western Kentucky U

WESTMORELAND, CRYSTAL R; SUMMER SHADE, KY; METCALFE CTY HS; (FR); Pep Squd; Business; Teacher's Aide; U of Kentucky; Western Kentucky

Wallace, Andrea
Nelson Cty HS
Boston, KY

Wafford Jr, Daniel
Eastside Ctr For Applied Tech
Lexington, KY

Vicars, Heather R
Campbell Cty HS
Alexandria, KY

Vickers V, John R
Mc Lean Cty HS
Sacramento, KY

Wells, Himella
Model Laboratory Sch
Richmond, KY

WHALEN, SHEENA M; COVINGTON, KY; HOLMES HS; (SO); Hnr Roll; Sccr (VJ); A-B Honor Roll; Outstanding All-Star; Dance; Interior Designer

WHEATLEY, BROOKE; BARDSTOWN, KY; NELSON CTY HS; (SO); 4H Awd; Hnr Roll; Nat Hon Sy; Sci Fairs; WWAHSS; Yth Ldrshp Prog; Comm Volntr; Peer Tut/Med; 4-H; Chrch Yth Grp; DARE; FCA; Key Club; Ntl FFA; Pep Squd; Chr; Bskball; Sccr (VJ); FFA

WHEATLEY, MATTHEW P; PROSPECT, KY; SOUTH OLDHAM HS; (SR); Hnr Roll; MVP; Nat Hon Sy; Perf Att; St of Mnth; ArtClub; Drma Clb; FCA; Prom Com; Quill & Scroll; LATIN GERM Clb; Adv Cncl (R); Yrbk (E, R, P); Most Artistic Senior Superlative; 2004-2005 KHSSA First Place Editorial Cartoon, Newspaper AA; BFA in Filmmaking; North Carolina School of the Arts Filmmaking

WHITAKER, NICK; CROMONA, KY; FLEMING NEON HS; (SR); Gov Hnr Prg; Hnr Roll; Nat Hon Sy; Otst Ac Ach Awd; WWAHSS; Comm Volntr; Chess; Lttrmn Clb; Bsball (V CL); Golf (V CL); Sch Ppr (E, P); Yrbk (E, R); Computer Science & Engineering; U of Louisville

WHITAKER, SHANE; WEST LIBERTY, KY; MORGAN CTY AREA TECH CTR HS; (SO); Hi Hnr Roll; Hnr Roll; Ntl FFA; Bskball (V); Ftball (J); Eastern Kentucky U; U of Kentucky

WHITAKER, TRESTON; COLD SPRING, KY; CAMPBELL CTY HS; (SO); Ctznshp Aw; Duke TS; Fut Prb Slvr; Hi Hnr Roll; Hnr Roll; Nat Hon Sy; Nat Ldrshp Svc; Otst Ac Ach Awd; Sci Fairs; Sci/Math Olympn; Peer Tut/Med; BPA; Chrch Yth Grp; Emplmnt; FBLA; Mth Clb/Tm; Sci Clb; Scouts; Tech Clb; Skiing (V); Sccr (J); Track (J); Robotics Team Area-1st Place Award; Working on Boy Scout Eagle Project; Business; Law; U of Kentucky

WHITE, BRYAN C; MT WASHINGTON, KY; BULLITT EAST HS; (FR); Hnr Roll; Chrch Yth Grp; DARE; Scouts; Tech Clb; Bnd; Skt Tgt Sh (J); Eagle Scout; Computer Science; U of Kentucky; U of Louisville

WHITE, KIRSTEN E; MADISONVILLE, KY; MADISONVILLE NORTH HOPKINS HS; (JR); Hnr Roll; St Schl; USAA; WWAHSS; Spec Olymp Vol; Chrch Yth Grp; FCA; FBLA; Key Club; Lttrmn Clb; Ntl Beta Clb; Bskball (V L); Vllyball (V L); Chrysalis Board of Directors

WHITE, PEARL M; PADUCAH, KY; LIGHTHOUSE CHRISTIAN AC; (SO); Hnr Roll; Sci Fairs; St of Mnth; WWAHSS; Yth Ldrshp Prog; Comm Volntr; Peer Tut/Med; Chrch Yth Grp; DARE; Fr of Library; FBLA; Photog; Prom Com; Scouts; SADD; Ch Chr; Dnce; SP/M/VS; Bskball (J); Sccr (J); Track (J); Adv Cncl (V); Stu Cncl (V); CR (V); Yrbk (P); Psychology; Law Enforcement; Boston U; Kentucky U

WHITEHEAD, MISTY; BURKESVILLE, KY; CUMBERLAND CTY HS; (SO); 4H Awd; MVP; Sci Fairs; St of Mnth; Peer Tut/Med; Red Cr Aide; 4-H; Chrch Yth Grp; DARE; FCA; Ntl FFA; Scouts; Ch Chr; Fld Hky (V); Cl Off (V); Yrbk (P); Physical Therapist; Veterinarian; U of Kentucky

WHITT, JOSHUA D; CALHOUN, KY; MC LEAN CTY HS; (FR); FCA; Sci Clb; SP/M/VS; Bskball (VJ L); Track (V L)

WHITTINGTON, AMANDA; LEXINGTON, KY; LAFAYETTE HS; (SR); Hi Hnr Roll; Hnr Roll; Sci Fairs; Comm Volntr; 4-H; ArtClub; Chrch Yth Grp; DARE; Emplmnt; Ntl FFA; Tchrs Aide; Dnce; Certification in Hort. from Skills Standard; Plant Biology; Zoology; U of Kentucky; Florida Southern College

WIGGINS, BRAD; SEBREE, KY; WEBSTER CTY HS; (JR); WWAHSS; Peer Tut/Med; Ntl FFA; Pep Squd; Tech Clb; Ftball (V L); Wt Lftg (V CL); 2002 KY State Power Lifting Trophy Winner; Physical Therapy; Sports Medicine; Murray State U; Western KY U

WILDER, STACY; LOUISVILLE, KY; BETH HAVEN CHRISTIAN SCH; (JR); All Am Sch; Hnr Roll; Nat Hon Sy; Nat Ldrshp Svc; USAA; WWAHSS; Hosp Aide; Peer Tut/Med; Chrch Yth Grp; Drma Clb; Ch Chr; SP/M/VS; Vllyball (VJ); Cl Off (P, S); MD / Anesthesiology; U of Kentucky

WILEY, KAYLA; WALTON, KY; LARRY A RYLE HS; (SO); Hnr Roll; Comm Volntr; FCA; FBLA; Tchrs Aide; Chrldg (JC); Gmnstcs (J); Five Star Cheerleading; Dentist; NKU

WILFONG, RYNE; DAYTON, KY; NEWPORT HS; (FR); Comm Volntr; Emplmnt; Bsball (VJ); Bskball (J); Ftball (VJ); PE/Health Teacher, Coaching; Business Owner; Georgetown U KY

WILLIAMS, AUTUMN; SHEPHERDSVILLE, KY; NORTH BULLITT HS; (JR); All Am Sch; Gov Hnr Prg; Hi Hnr Roll; Nat Hon Sy; Otst Ac Ach Awd; Pres Sch; WWAHSS; Yth Ldrshp Prog; Comm Volntr; Peer Tut/Med; Chrch Yth Grp; DARE; Emplmnt; FCA; FBLA; Ntl Beta Clb; Sci Clb; SADD; Bnd; Chr; Ch Chr; Stg Cre; Bskball (J L); Sftball (J); Track (J); Vllyball (V CL); Mission Trip At Church (Mexico); Teach Special Needs At Church; Medical Field; Cosmetology; U of Louisville; Jefferson Community College

WILLIAMS, BRANDI R; LOUISVILLE, KY; CENTRAL HS; (SO); Hnr Roll; Perf Att; St of Mnth; Comm Volntr; 4-H; Drma Clb; Jr Ach; Ntl Beta Clb; Dnce; Stu Cncl (S); Step Team; JROTC; Dance; Business; Tennessee State U; North Carolina U

WILLIAMS, HEATHER; CYNTHIANA, KY; HARRISON CTY HS; (SO); Hi Hnr Roll; Perf Att; Comm Volntr; Sftball (V); Wrstlg (V)

WILLIAMS, KRISTOPHER; LOUISVILLE, KY; LOUISVILLE MALE HS; (FR); Hnr Roll; Perf Att; Hosp Aide; Spanish Clb; Pep Bnd; Usher at Church; Black Achievers; Pre-Dentistry; U of Kentucky; Tennessee State U

WILLIAMS, SARA N; LOUISVILLE, KY; FERN CREEK TRADITIONAL HS; (FR); Ctznshp Aw; Hi Hnr Roll; Hnr Roll; Sci Fairs; Yth Ldrshp Prog; Ntl Beta Clb; Advanced Program; Beta Club; Interior Designer; Business Administration; U of Kentucky; Western Kentucky U

WILLIAMS, SHELIA; LOUISVILLE, KY; SENECA HS; (JR); Hnr Roll; Nat Hon Sy; Otst Ac Ach Awd; WWAHSS; Comm Volntr; Key Club; SP/M/VS; Student of the Year Award 2001-2002; In the Liberal Arts Magnet Program; Medical Field; U of Louisville

WILLIAMSON, CARRIE A; LEXINGTON, KY; BRYAN STATION HS; (FR); Duke TS; Hi Hnr Roll; Hnr Roll; Bnd; Ch Chr; Mch Bnd; Pep Bnd; Track (V); Stu Cncl (R); Sch Ppr (E); Journalism; Law; Howard U

WILLIAMSON, MICHAEL P; RUSSELLVILLE, KY; LOGAN CTY HS; (FR); Hnr Roll; St of Mnth; Quiz Bowl; SP/M/VS; Plays Classical Violin; Poetry Slam (1st Place); Film; Political Science; Juilliard School of Arts; Harvard U

WILLINGER, KRISTEN; LOUISVILLE, KY; MERCY AC; (SO); Duke TS; Hnr Roll; Nat Hon Sy; St of Mnth; USAA; WWAHSS; Comm Volntr; 4-H; Chrch Yth Grp; Jr Ach; SADD; Bskball (J); Vllyball (J); CR (R); Who's Who Among High School Students; Pathways to Leadership Gold Medal Award; Business; Interior Design; Bellarmine U; U of Kentucky

WILLOUGHBY, REBECCA C; MT STERLING, KY; MONTGOMERY CTY HS; (JR); Hi Hnr Roll; Hnr Roll; WWAHSS; Comm Volntr; AL Aux Girls; Chrch Yth Grp; Key Club; Svce Clb; Chr; Varsity Letter for Girls Basketball Managing; Most Outstanding Geometry Student - 2003-2004; Elementary Education; Photography; Campbellsville U; Asbury College

WILSON, ETHAN J; RUSSELLVILLE, KY; LOGAN CTY HS; (FR); Ctznshp Aw; Duke TS; Hnr Roll; Otst Ac Ach Awd; Comm Volntr; Chrch Yth Grp; Jr Ach; Ntl Beta Clb; P to P St Amb Prg; Scouts; Bnd; Jzz Bnd; Mch Bnd; Pep Bnd; Wadoryu - Orange Belt; Flying; Air Force

WILSON, JOHN M; HICKMAN, KY; FULTON CTY HS; (FR); Duke TS; Hi Hnr Roll; Hnr Roll; Comm Volntr; FBLA; Ntl Beta Clb; Sci Clb; Bnd; Jzz Bnd; Mch Bnd; Pep Bnd; Cl Off (V); KY Governor's Cup Science 9th Place in State, 2004-District Winner 2005; M.D., Genetics, Biological Sciences

WILSON, KELLY; VERSAILLES, KY; (JR); Hi Hnr Roll; Nat Hon Sy; Pres Ac Ftns Aw; WWAHSS; Comm Volntr; Peer Tut/Med; Chrch Yth Grp; Key Club; Ntl Beta Clb; SADD; Spanish Clb; Sccr (V L); Tennis (VJ); Track (V L); Stu Cncl (R); CR (R); Pre-Med; Physical Therapy; Transylvania U; Centre College

WILSON, KEVIN A; ASHLAND, KY; BOYD CTY HS; (FR); Hnr Roll; Nat Hon Sy; Wdwrkg Clb; Ftball (J); Track (V); Wt Lftg (V); Academic Achievement Awards '04-'05; Academic Achievement Awards '05-'06; Law Enforcement; Physical Education Teacher; Morehead State U; U of Kentucky

WILSON, MARCKIA R; LEXINGTON, KY; LEXINGTON CHRN AC HS; (SO); Hi Hnr Roll; Pres Sch; St Schl; WWAHSS; Comm Volntr; 4-H; Chrch Yth Grp; FCA; Ntl Beta Clb; Tchrs Aide; Bskball (VJ L); Cl Off (S, T); CR (S, T); YMCA Black Achievers; Secondary/Post Secondary English; Secondary/Post-Secondary Counselor; Wake Forest U; U of Southern California

WILSON, TIFFANY M; STEARNS, KY; MC CREARY CTRL HS; (JR); Gov Hnr Prg; Otst Ac Ach Awd; Hab For Humty Volntr; Ntl Beta Clb; Ntl FFA; ROTC; Bskball (J); Chrldg (J); Auto Mechanics; Agriculture - FFA; Nursing; Lindsey Wilson College; Carson Newman College

WILSON, VICTORIA C; LIVERMORE, KY; MC LEAN CTY HS; (FR); Hnr Roll; WWAHSS; 4-H; Chrch Yth Grp; Drma Clb; Ntl FFA; Tennis (V); Forensic Pathology; U of Louisville

WILSON, VICTORIA R; SALYERSVILLE, KY; MAGOFFIN CTY HS; (FR); 4H Awd; Ctznshp Aw; Hnr Roll; Kwnis Aw; Mas Aw; Nat Hon Sy; Nat Ldrshp Svc; Otst Ac Ach Awd; Sci Fairs; USAA; Comm Volntr; Peer Tut/Med; 4-H; Chrch Yth Grp; Drma Clb; Photog; Svce Clb; SADD; Tech Clb; Bnd; Ch Chr; Mch Bnd; Pep Bnd; Rainbow for Girls State Miss Service; Pharmacy; 4-H Agent; Alice Lloyd College; Eastern Kentucky U

WIMBERLY, KATE; RICHMOND, KY; MODEL LABORATORY SCH; (SO); Duke TS; Fut Prb Slvr; Hnr Roll; USAA; WWAHSS; Comm Volntr; FCA; Photog; Sci Clb; Cr Ctry (V); Swmg (V); Class of Kentucky; Medicine; Education; Centre College; Transylvania U

WIMSATT, ASHLEY R; FAIRDALE, KY; FAIRDALE HS; (SO); Hnr Roll; Comm Volntr; Chrch Yth Grp; Chr; PP Ftbl (J); JCPS All County Music Festival; Pharmacist; Prosecuting Attorney; U of Kentucky; Campbellsville U

WINDSOR, HOLLY A; MAYFIELD, KY; GRAVES CTY HS; (JR); Hi Hnr Roll; Hnr Roll; Nat Hon Sy; Off Aide; Pep Squd; Tchrs Aide; Pre-Law; U of Southern Florida; U of Kentucky

WINSTEAD, CORIE; MADISONVILLE, KY; MADISONVILLE NORTH HOPKINS HS; (SR); Hnr Roll; WWAHSS; Yth Ldrshp Prog; Spec Olymp Vol; Chrch Yth Grp; FCA; Key Club; Ntl Beta Clb; Off Aide; P to P St Amb Prg; Prom Com; Dnce; PPSqd (V C); Cl Off (P); Stu Cncl (S); Yrbk (P); Dance Team- UDA All-Star - 2 Years; Future U of Kentucky Dancer; Elementary Education / Minor in Dance; Special-Ed / Fashion Merchandising; U of Kentucky

WINTERS, BRANDON; HICKMAN, KY; FULTON CTY HS; (FR); Hi Hnr Roll; Hnr Roll; MVP; Nat Hon Sy; Perf Att; Sci Fairs; Comm Volntr; Chess; Chrch Yth Grp; DARE; Mus Clb; Ntl FFA; Scouts; Chr; Ch Chr; Dnce; SP/M/VS; Bsball (V); Bskball (V); Ftball (J); Track (V); Stu Cncl (R); Wrote and Produced Song for School; All Star Softball Team/Honor Roll; Business Management Master's; Computer Specialist; U of KY; Duke U

WITT, VICTORIA M; IRVINE, KY; ESTILL CTY HS; (SR); Ctznshp Aw; Hi Hnr Roll; Perf Att; Salutrn; WWAHSS; Yth Ldrshp Prog; Comm Volntr; Peer Tut/Med; Chrch Yth Grp; Emplmnt; FBLA; HO'Br Yth Ldrshp; Ntl Beta Clb; Off Aide; Pep Squd; Prom Com; Chr; Ch Chr; SP/M/VS; PP Ftbl (V); Sftball (V); Cl Off (V); Stu Cncl (R); Pharmacy; Psychology; Georgetown College

WOLFE, KRIS; BEECHMONT, KY; MUHLENBERG SOUTH HS; (SO); Ntl FFA; Off Aide; Bsball (VJ)

WOOD, HERMAN; LIVERMORE, KY; MC LEAN CTY HS; (FR); Hnr Roll; St of Mnth; Auto Body Technician

WOODS, ASHLEY; NEWPORT, KY; NEWPORT HS; (JR); Ctznshp Aw; Duke TS; Hnr Roll; Otst Ac Ach Awd; St of Mnth; WWAHSS; Emplmnt; Jr Ach; Key Club; Lib Aide; Off Aide; Pep Squd; Prom Com; Tchrs Aide; Chr; Dnce; Chrldg (J); PP Ftbl (C); A Pediatric Oncologist; Ob/Gyn; U of Kentucky; Northern Kentucky U

WOODS, DEANNA; PADUCAH, KY; REIDLAND HS; (JR); WWAHSS; Chrch Yth Grp; Emplmnt; FCA; FBLA; Key Club; Sci Clb; Spanish Clb; Kindergarten Teacher; Beautician; West Kentucky Community Technical College; Brooks College

WOODSON, CLINTON C; GEORGETOWN, KY; SCOTT CTY HS; (SO); Duke TS; Hi Hnr Roll; Hnr Roll; Otst Ac Ach Awd; Pres Sch; Comm Volntr; Chrch Yth Grp; FCA; Scouts; Eagle Scout Rank; Computer Engineering

WOOSLEY, MINDY; SADIEVILLE, KY;; Chrldg (V L); Dvng (V L); Sftball (V L); Beta Club; All District Softball Player; Teacher; Kentucky Wesleyan College; Campbellsville College

WOOTON, JOSHUA E; JAMESTOWN, KY; RUSSELL CTY HS; (SO); Hnr Roll; Perf Att; 4-H; Chrch Yth Grp; DARE; Emplmnt; Scouts; Software Designer; Computer Technologist; I.T.T. Technology School

WORLEY, JEREMY; MARSHES SIDING, KY; MC CREARY CTRL HS; (SO); All Am Sch; Hnr Roll; Comm Volntr; Mth Clb/Tm; Degree in Pharmacy; U of Kentucky

WRIGHT, AMBER; LOUISVILLE, KY; HOLY CROSS HS; (JR); Hi Hnr Roll; Hnr Roll; MVP; Nat Hon Sy; Otst Ac Ach Awd; WWAHSS; Hosp Aide; Emplmnt; Outdrs Clb; Vsity Clb; French Clb; Bskball (V C); PP Ftbl (J); Sccr (V); Sftball (V); KHSAA-2004 Basketball, 2003 Soccer; Honor Awards-2003, Humanities, Theology, Health; Degree in Nursing; Jefferson Community College-Downtown; U of Louisville

WRIGHT, CRYSTAL D; CALHOUN, KY; MC LEAN CTY HS; (SO); 4H Awd; All Am Sch; Hnr Roll; Nat Hon Sy; Otst Ac Ach Awd; WWAHSS; Comm Volntr; 4-H; Chrch Yth Grp; FBLA; Ch Chr; Hsbk Rdg; 4-H variety Act Winner; Lawyer; Western Kentucky U; Southeastern College

WRIGHT, HEATHER L; CLAY CITY, KY; POWELL CTY HS; (SR); Hnr Roll; Chrch Yth Grp; Chr; Chrldg (J); Accounting; Lexington Community College

WRIGHT, JANCEE; RUSSELL SPRINGS, KY; RUSSELL CTY HS; (FR); Duke TS; Fut Prb Slvr; Hnr Roll; Nat Sci Aw; Chrch Yth Grp; FCA; Ch Chr; Sftball (J); Academic Team; Pharmacy; Medicine; U of Kentucky; U of Louisville

WRIGHT, RYAN H; FRANKFORT, KY; FRANKLIN CTY HS; (JR); Duke TS; Hi Hnr Roll; WWAHSS; Yth Ldrshp Prog; Drma Clb; Emplmnt; Ntl Beta Clb; SP/M/VS; Vice President State Beta Club; Chemical Engineering; Mechanical Engineering; U of Kentucky; Purdue U

WRIGHT II, DONALD L; DORTON, KY; SHELBY VALLEY HS; (SR); Hi Hnr Roll; Hnr Roll; Nat Hon Sy; WWAHSS; Pharmacy; Pikeville College

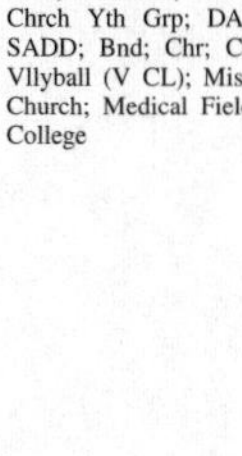
Woosley, Mindy
Sadieville, KY

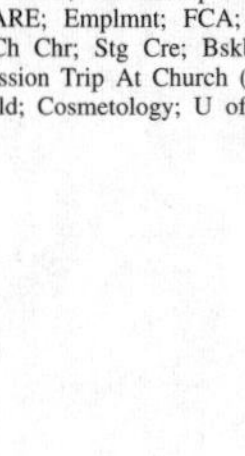
Wilson, Kevin A
Boyd Cty HS
Ashland, KY

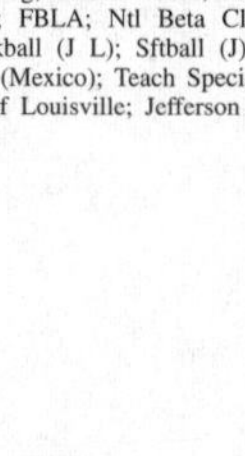
Williamson, Michael P
Logan Cty HS
Russellville, KY

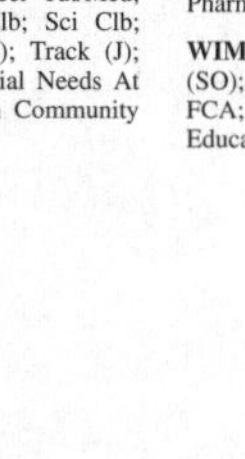
Wilder, Stacy
Beth Haven Christian Sch
Louisville, KY

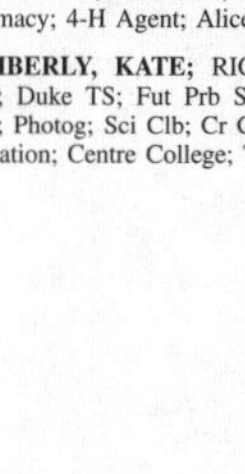
Whitt, Joshua D
Mc Lean Cty HS
Calhoun, KY

National
Honor Roll
Spring 2005

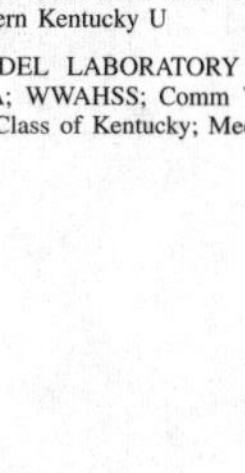
Wheatley, Brooke
Nelson Cty HS
Bardstown, KY

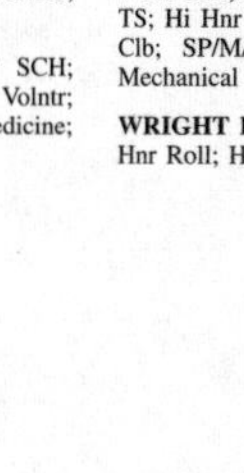
Williams, Kristopher
Louisville Male HS
Louisville, KY

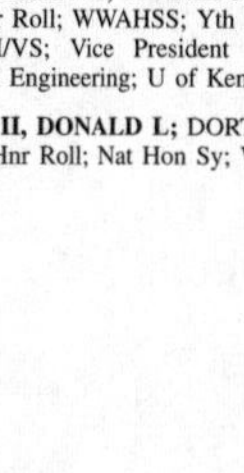
Willoughby, Rebecca C
Montgomery Cty HS
Mt Sterling, KY

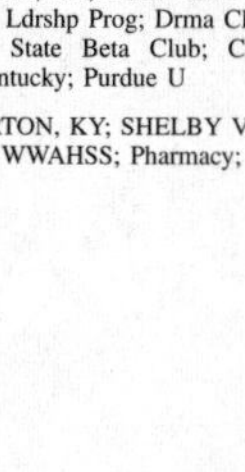
Wilson, Tiffany M
Mc Creary Ctrl HS
Stearns, KY

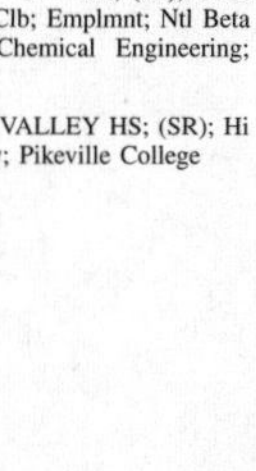
Wimsatt, Ashley R
Fairdale HS
Fairdale, KY

WYATT, AMBER; CROMONA, KY; FLEMING NEON HS; (SR); Fut Prb Slvr; Hi Hnr Roll; Hnr Roll; Nat Hon Sy; WWAHSS; Comm Volntr; Peer Tut/Med; Chrch Yth Grp; Emplmnt; FTA; Lttrmn Clb; NYLC; Prom Com; Tchrs Aide; Vllyball (V); CR (R); Sch Ppr (R, P); Yrbk (R, P); Physical Therapy; Forensic Science; Southeast Community College; Howard Community College

WYATT, APRIL DAWN; HAZEL, KY; CALLOWAY CTY HS; (FR); Hnr Roll; 4-H; DARE; Chef; Counselor; Murray State U

YAGER, SARAH; KEVIL, KY; BALLARD MEMORIAL HS; (SR); WWAHSS; Comm Volntr; Emplmnt; Sci Clb; Tchrs Aide; Marketing; Western Kentucky U; U of Southern Indiana

YATES, ANNE K; LEXINGTON, KY; LEXINGTON CHRN AC HS; (SO); Duke TS; Hi Hnr Roll; MVP; Otst Ac Ach Awd; Comm Volntr; Chrch Yth Grp; Emplmnt; Svce Clb; Bskball (V L); PP Ftbl (V); Sftball (V L); Young Life Club; Education; Media; U of Kentucky; Campbellsville U

YOKLEY, SARA B; SMITHS GROVE, KY; EDMONSON CTY HS; (FR); Gov Hnr Prg; Hi Hnr Roll; Hnr Roll; DARE; FBLA; Ntl Beta Clb; Clb; Bskball (V); Vllyball (V); Governor Scholar; Elementary Education; Social Work; Western Kentucky U; Lindsay-Wilson College

YONTS, AARON; NEON, KY; FLEMING NEON HS; Hi Hnr Roll; Hnr Roll; Nat Hon Sy; WWAHSS; Comm Volntr; ArtClub; NYLC; P to P St Amb Prg; Tech Clb; German Clb; Stu Cncl (T); Sch Ppr (R)

YORK, BAILLIE; SCOTTSVILLE, KY; ALLEN CTY HS; (FR); 4H Awd; All Am Sch; Duke TS; Hnr Roll; Sci/Math Olympn; Comm Volntr; Peer Tut/Med; FCA; Ntl Beta Clb; Bnd; Sftball (J); Pre-Med; U of Kentucky; U of Louisville

YOUNG, AMBER L; EDMONTON, KY; METCALFE CTY HS; (FR); Ctznshp Aw; Fut Prb Slvr; Hnr Roll; Nat Hon Sy; Otst Ac Ach Awd; Perf Att; St of Mnth; Peer Tut/Med; 4-H; Chrch Yth Grp; DARE; FCA; Ntl Beta Clb; Ntl FFA; Pep Squd; Bskball (VJ L); Track (VJ L); Cl Off (S); Yrbk; Academic Team; Criminal Investigation; Education; Lindsey Wilson College; Campbellsville U

YOUNG, CANDACE; CAMPBELLSVLLE, KY; TAYLOR CTY HS; (SO); 4H Awd; Hnr Roll; Perf Att; Comm Volntr; 4-H; Chrch Yth Grp; DARE; FCA; Ntl Beta Clb; Pep Squd; Sci Clb; Chr; Ch Chr; Cr Ctry (V L); Track (V L); Never Missed Any School Days; Dentistry; Teaching; U of Kentucky

YOUNG, KAYLA A; ASHLAND, KY; BOYD CTY HS; (JR); 4H Awd; Hi Hnr Roll; Otst Ac Ach Awd; Sci/Math Olympn; Peer Tut/Med; Biology Clb; Mod UN; Ntl Beta Clb; Prom Com; Sci Clb; German Clb; SP/M/VS; Stu Cncl (R); Sch Ppr (E, R); Yrbk (E); Varsity Academic Team; Mock Trial Team; Bio Chemistry; Ecology; Reed College; U of Glasgow Scotland

YOUNG, R TYLER; LEXINGTON, KY; LEXINGTON CHRN AC HS; (SO); All Am Sch; Ctznshp Aw; Hi Hnr Roll; Nat Hon Sy; USAA; Ntl Beta Clb; Off Aide; Svce Clb; Cl Off (R); Joseph Service Award; Presidential Education Award; Economics; Finance; Centre College, Transylvania; U of Kentucky U

YOUNG, VALERIE; CALIFORNIA, KY; CAMPBELL CTY HS; (JR); Ctznshp Aw; Duke TS; Hi Hnr Roll; Hnr Roll; Nat Hon Sy; Nat Mrt Semif; WWAHSS; Yth Ldrshp Prog; Comm Volntr; Chrch Yth Grp; Drma Clb; Emplmnt; FCA; Lib Aide; Ntl Beta Clb; NYLC; Quill & Scroll; Bnd; Chr; Ch Chr; Clr Grd; National Youth Leadership for Law; Law Internship; Law; Georgetown College

ZAITSU, RISA; UNION, KY; LARRY A RYLE HS; (SO); Hnr Roll; ArtClub; Bnd; Arch

ZAPLO, KAROLIN; WHITLEY CITY, KY; MC CREARY CTRL HS; (SR); St of Mnth; ArtClub; Bnd; Mch Bnd; Orch; Pep Bnd; Track (J); Vllyball (J); History; Political Science

Young, R Tyler
Lexington Chrn AC HS
Lexington, KY

Maine

ADAMS, MICHAEL; FRANKFORT, ME; SEARSPORT DISTRICT HS; (SR); DAR; Hi Hnr Roll; Nat Hon Sy; WWAHSS; Comm Volntr; Emplmnt; Bnd; Mch Bnd; Pep Bnd; Bsball (C); Bskball (C); Golf (C); CR (R); Aviation / Air Traffic Management; Civil Engineering; Daniel Webster College; Northeastern U

AHERN, SARAH; ELLSWORTH, ME; ELLSWORTH HS; (SO); 4H Awd; Hi Hnr Roll; Comm Volntr; Spec Olymp Vol; 4-H; Chrch Yth Grp; Mth Clb/Tm; Golf (J); Swmg (V); Biology; Dalhousie U; Case Western Reserve

ALBEE, JESSICA L; ELLSWORTH, ME; ELLSWORTH HS; (JR); Hi Hnr Roll; Comm Volntr; Peer Tut/Med; ArtClub; DARE; Emplmnt; Key Club; Civil Rights Team Pres; Big Brothers Big Sisters; BFA; Art Education; Maine College of Art; Wheelock

ALBERT, JACOB R; AUGUSTA, ME; ST DOMINIC REG HS; (SR); Ctznshp Aw; Hi Hnr Roll; Nat Hon Sy; Valdctrian; WWAHSS; Yth Ldrshp Prog; Drma Clb; Emplmnt; Key Club; Mth Clb/Tm; Bnd; SP/M/VS; Bsball (V L); Bskball (V L); Stu Cncl (R); Sch Ppr (E); Harvard Book Award; Princeton Book Award; English; New York U

ALLEN, ASHLEY; ROBBINSTON, ME; CALAIS HS; (SO); Hnr Roll; MVP; Sci Fairs; Comm Volntr; Peer Tut/Med; ArtClub; Chrch Yth Grp; Emplmnt; Bskball (V); Sccr (V); Sftball (V); Big Brother / Big Sister; Recreational Basketball Coach; Business; Management; Bowdoin College; Bates College

AMELINA, ALINA; ORONO, ME; APOSTOLIC CHRISTIAN AC; (SO); F Lan Hn Soc; Nat Hon Sy; WWAHSS; Comm Volntr; Peer Tut/Med; Fr of Library; Key Club; Lib Aide; Chr; Member of National Geographic; Knowledge of 2 Foreign Languages; Anthropology Major; Art History Degree; College of Saint Rose; Art Institute of Portland

ANDREWS, EMILY; HOLDEN, ME; JOHN BAPST MEM. HS; (SO); Gov Hnr Prg; Hnr Roll; Kwnis Aw; Nat Hon Sy; Perf Att; Pres Ac Ftns Aw; Sci Fairs; Comm Volntr; Red Cr Aide; Dbte Team; Key Club; Outdrs Clb; Bnd; Mch Bnd; Orch; Bskball (J); Golf (V L); Key Club; Outing Club; Medical Field; Military (Air Force); New York U; West Point

ARTINYAN, SARA; PORTLAND, ME; PORTLAND HS; (SR); Hi Hnr Roll; Comm Volntr; FBLA; Off Aide; Photog; Environmental Club; Students for World Awareness; Nursing; U of Southern Maine

ASRIYAN, YUNA; PORTLAND, ME; CHEVERUS HS; (SR); Hnr Roll; Nat Hon Sy; WWAHSS; Peer Tut/Med; ArtClub; Key Club; Pep Squd; P to P St Amb Prg; Photog; Prom Com; Bskball (V CL); Sccr (V L); Sftball (J); Track (V); Stu Cncl (T); Yrbk (E, P); Publicity Committee; Dentistry; Doctor; Saint Anselm College; Tufts U

BARNES, AMY M; EASTON, ME; EASTON AREA HS; (JR); Hnr Roll; Nat Hon Sy; St of Mnth; WWAHSS; Spec Olymp Vol; AL Aux Girls; Chrch Yth Grp; Drma Clb; Emplmnt; Key Club; Ntl FFA; Vsity Clb; Bnd; Chr; SP/M/VS; Bskball (V); Chrldg (V); Vsy Clb (V); Stu Cncl (R); CR (R); Yrbk (E); NHS; Jazz Chorus Jr Exhibition; Elementary School Teacher; U of Maine Presque Isle

BEACH JR, JOHN R; STRATTON, ME; MT ABRAM HS; (FR); Pep Squd; Bnd; SP/M/VS; Chrldg (V); Steel Drums-All Stars; Theatre; Paranormal Investigator; Foriegn Affairs Worker; U of Farmington

BEAULIEU, MICHELLE; FALMOUTH, ME; FALMOUTH HS; (JR); Hnr Roll; WWAHSS; Key Club; Bskball (J); Cr Ctry (J); Cr Ct Ski (V); Tennis (J); Adventure Leadership; Northeastern U

BEAVERS, DAVID A; OAKLAND, ME; MESSALONSKEE HS; (SR); Hi Hnr Roll; Nat Hon Sy; Drma Clb; Emplmnt; Mth Clb/Tm; Bnd; Jzz Bnd; Mch Bnd; Pep Bnd; Aerospace Engineering; Mechanical Engineering; Worcester Polytechnic Institute; Massachusetts Institute of Technology

BECK, BRIONNE; ROCKPORT, ME; CAMDEN HILLS REG HS; (JR); Hnr Roll; Yth Ldrshp Prog; Amnsty Intl; Comm Volntr; Red Cr Aide; Emplmnt; Prom Com; Dnce; SP/M/VS; Stg Cre; Nominated for Global Young Leaders Conference; Nominated for Who's Who Among American High School Students; Journalism; Business Management; American U, Washington, DC; Mercer U, Macon, GA

BERNIER, CHASTITY L; EAGLE LAKE, ME; FORT KENT CMTY HS; (SO); Hnr Roll; Comm Volntr; Spec Olymp Vol; Chrch Yth Grp; Key Club; Dnce; Cr Ctry (V L); PPSqd (V); Track (V); Wrstlg (L); Architecture

BLAIS, ADAM P; AUBURN, ME; ST DOMINIC REG HS; (SO); Hi Hnr Roll; Hnr Roll; Perf Att; Sci Fairs; Valdctrian; Comm Volntr; Hosp Aide; Drma Clb; Key Club; SP/M/VS; Stg Cre; Twin Cities Swim Team; Piano for 9 Years/Community Little Theatre; Theatre Management; Business Management; Boston U

BOUCHER, ASHLEY; FORT KENT, ME; FORT KENT CMTY HS; (SO); F Lan Hn Soc; Hnr Roll; Pres Sch; Emplmnt; Karate Soon Black Belt; Law Degree; Nursing Degree; Tulane U; Drexel U

BOUYEA, NICOLE L; LEWISTON, ME; LEWISTON HS; (SO); Ctznshp Aw; Hi Hnr Roll; Hnr Roll; DARE; Emplmnt; Scouts; Dnce; Doctor MD Heart Surgeon; Plastic Surgeon; U of Maine; U of Tennessee

BRIGHTMAN, CHETARA S M; LEBANON, ME; NOBLE HS; (JR); Hnr Roll; Nat Hon Sy; Otst Ac Ach Awd; Comm Volntr; Emplmnt; NYLC; Photog; Tchrs Aide; Chr; Dnce; Lit Mag (R, P); Journalist; Actress; New York U; U of Colorado At Boulder

BROOKS, KATHRYN; STANDISH, ME; BONNY EAGLE HS; (SR); All Am Sch; F Lan Hn Soc; Hi Hnr Roll; Hnr Roll; Kwnis Aw; Nat Hon Sy; Nat Mrt LOC; Pres Sch; WWAHSS; Yth Ldrshp Prog; Comm Volntr; Hab For Humty Volntr; Emplmnt; Key Club; Foreign Clb; Bnd; Sccr (J L); Sftball (J L); Teens Who Care Award Nomination; Biochemistry; Medicine-Pediatrics; Boston U Attending Fall 2005

BROOKS, SHAUNA; ROBBINSTON, ME; CALAIS HS; (SR); Hnr Roll; Perf Att; DARE; Emplmnt; Voc Ind Clb Am; Clr Grd; Adv Cncl (R); Skills USA Member; Washington County Community College; Johnson & Wales U

BROWN, SONYA M; PORTLAND, ME; PORTLAND HS; (JR); Hnr Roll; St of Mnth; Yth Ldrshp Prog; Hab For Humty Volntr; DARE; Emplmnt; Graduate of Portland Arts Technology High School Two Year Program; Early Childhood Occupation; Office Management; Southern Maine Community College

BROWN, TASHA; POLAND, ME; B WHITTIER MS/POLAND REG HS; (MS); Hi Hnr Roll; Hnr Roll; Nat Hon Sy; Nat Stu Ath Day Aw; Pres Ac Ftns Aw; Comm Volntr; Hab For Humty Volntr; Chrch Yth Grp; Emplmnt; Off Aide; Prom Com; Scouts; Bnd; Jzz Bnd; SP/M/VS; Chrldg (V); Gmnstcs (J); Hsbk Rdg (V); Mar Art (J); Skiing (J); Sccr (V); Sftball (V C); Sch Ppr (E); Yrbk (E); Vet; Doctor or Navy

BUCK, BRADLEY; STILLWATER, ME; OLD TOWN HS; (SO); Hi Hnr Roll; Hnr Roll; Kwnis Aw; Otst Ac Ach Awd; WWAHSS; Comm Volntr; Key Club; ROTC; Sci Clb; Scouts; Chr; Track (V); Completed an Outdoor Achievement Course; Animal Rehabilitation; Marine Biology/Zoology; U of Maine, Orono

BURKE, ELIZA; PORTLAND, ME; PORTLAND HS; (SR); Hnr Roll; WWAHSS; Comm Volntr; Emplmnt; Quill & Scroll; Vsity Clb; Fld Hky (V); Psychology; Zoology; Florida Gulf Coast U

CABALLERO, MIA; OLD TOWN, ME; OLD TOWN HS; (SO); Hi Hnr Roll; Otst Ac Ach Awd; Biology Clb; Key Club; Bnd; Mch Bnd; Orch; Pep Bnd; Mar Art (J); Sccr (V); Sftball (J); Tennis (V); Vllyball (V); Cardiologist/ Surgical

CARDAMONE, ANDREW; HOLLIS CTR, ME; BONNY EAGLE HS; (SO); Ctznshp Aw; Hi Hnr Roll; Kwnis Aw; Nat Hon Sy; Otst Ac Ach Awd; Perf Att; WWAHSS; Comm Volntr; Drma Clb; Emplmnt; Key Club; Lib Aide; Mus Clb; Prom Com; Svce Clb; Tchrs Aide; Acpl Chr; Chr; SP/M/VS; Stg Cre; Cl Off (T); CR (T); Member of Natural Helpers-Peer Listening Group; Winner of Science and English Awards in 2004; Secondary Education-College Teaching; Theatre; U of Maine Orono; UCLA

CARTER, EVA; EASTPORT, ME; CALAIS HS; (SO); Ctznshp Aw; Hi Hnr Roll; Hnr Roll; Comm Volntr; 4-H; ArtClub; Principal's Award; Nursing; Pharmacist; Washington County Community College; U of Maine St Machias

CAWOOD, CHRISTINA; HOLLIS CTR, ME; BONNY EAGLE HS; (SO); Key Club; Key Club Treasurer

CHILELLI, DAVID R; MILFORD, ME; OLDTOWN HS; (SR); Ctznshp Aw; Hi Hnr Roll; Jr Eng Tech; MVP; Nat Hon Sy; St of Mnth; Valdctrian; WWAHSS; Chrch Yth Grp; Emplmnt; Mth Clb/Tm; Bnd; Jzz Bnd; Mch Bnd; Pep Bnd; Bsball (V CL); Bskball (J); Sccr (V CL); Swmg (V CL); Bausch & Lomb Science Award; Most Promising Scholar; Sports Management; U of Massachusetts At Amherst

CHOOLANI, MEGHA P; PORTLAND, ME; DEERING HS; (JR); Ctznshp Aw; Hi Hnr Roll; Kwnis Aw; Nat Hon Sy; St of Mnth; Comm Volntr; Peer Tut/Med; Key Club; SADD; Spanish Clb; Track (J); Stu Cncl (R); Key Club Member - 4 Yrs / President - 2 Yrs; Natural Helper; Business Management / Advertising; Fashion Merchandising; Boston U; Johnson & Wales U

CLEMENS, CODY W; POLAND, ME; B WHITTIER MS/POLAND REG HS; MS; Gov Hnr Prg; Hnr Roll; Emplmnt; Wdwrkg Clb; Golf (J); Stu Cncl (R); Automotive Technician; Hot Rod U; U Technical Institute

CLIFFORD, TIMOTHY; AUGUSTA, ME; CONY HS; (JR); Hi Hnr Roll; Hnr Roll; Perf Att; Chess; Emplmnt; French Clb; Lit Mag (R); Sch Ppr (E); Yale Book Award; English; Philosophy; Boston U; Syracuse U

CONLEY, BRANDON L; OXFORD, ME; OHC HS; (FR); Ctznshp Aw; Hi Hnr Roll; Hnr Roll; Perf Att; Comm Volntr; ArtClub; Cmptr Clb; Drma Clb; Key Club; SP/M/VS; Lawyer; Actor/Drama Major; Harvard U; California State

COOKSON, TAWNY; CORINNA, ME; NOKOMIS REG HS; (SO); Hi Hnr Roll; Hnr Roll; Otst Ac Ach Awd; Sci Fairs; St of Mnth; WWAHSS; Mth Clb/Tm; Bskball (JC); Sch Ppr (R); Writing; Radiology

COOPER, ERIC; WINDHAM, ME; WINDHAM HS; (JR); 4H Awd; Hnr Roll; WWAHSS; Comm Volntr; 4-H; DARE; Emplmnt; Sccr (J); AIJCA-Bronze & Silver Achievement Awards; NRA/Jr Olympic Target Shooting; Aviation; Embry-Riddle Aeronautical U

COUTURE, THERESE M; AUGUSTA, ME; HOMESCHOOLED; (SO); WWAHSS; Chrch Yth Grp; Lib Aide; Member of Dead Theologians Society; Play Piano and Violin; Russian Studies; Chemistry; Franciscan U of Steubenville; Christendom College

CROSBY, AMBER; LITCHFIELD, ME; OAK HILL HS; (JR); Hnr Roll; 4-H; Chr; Tennis (J); Nursing; Central Maine Community College; U of Southern Maine

DANSE, WHITNEY; LISBON, ME; ST DOMINIC REG HS; (JR); Hi Hnr Roll; Hnr Roll; Nat Hon Sy; Perf Att; Pres Sch; WWAHSS; Peer Tut/Med; ArtClub; Drma Clb; Emplmnt; Key Club; SP/M/VS; Stg Cre; Chrldg (V CL); Fld Hky (J); Vllyball (V); Stu Cncl (R); National Honor Society-Treasurer; Humane Society Volunteer; Engineering; Advertising/Marketing; Northeastern U; Boston U

DEBURRA, DEZARAY; POLAND, ME; B WHITTIER MS/POLAND REG HS; MS; DARE; Scouts; Wdwrkg Clb; Bnd; Bskball (V); Fld Hky (VJ); Sftball (V); Primatology; Zoology

DEMERS, KEVIN; WINN, ME; LEE AC; (SO); Hi Hnr Roll; WWAHSS; ArtClub; Emplmnt; Mth Clb/Tm; Cl Off (V); Civil Rights Team; Margaret Dingley Award; Computer Engineering; U of Maine Orono; MIT

DEPREY, JESSICA; BANGOR, ME; HERMAN HS; (SR); Hnr Roll; Nat Hon Sy; WWAHSS; Comm Volntr; Peer Tut/Med; Spec Olymp Vol; Emplmnt; Key Club; Tchrs Aide; Chr; Bskball (J); Fld Hky (V CL); Track (V L); Cl Off (S); Stu Cncl (R); CR (S); Sch Ppr (E); Business Preparation Award; Elementary Education; Husson College; Thomas College

DODGE, LAURA; ROCKLAND, ME; ROCKLAND DISTRICT HS; (SO); Hi Hnr Roll; Hnr Roll; WWAHSS; Key Club; Key Club; English; Art; Brown U; Northeastern U

DONAHUE, JAMES G B; GARDINER, ME; ST DOMINIC REG HS; (JR); DAR; Hi Hnr Roll; Hnr Roll; Nat Hon Sy; Nat Mrt LOC; WWAHSS; Comm Volntr; Peer Tut/Med; Drma Clb; Emplmnt; Key Club; Lib Aide; Mth Clb/Tm; Mus Clb; NYLC; Bnd; Ch Chr; Jzz Bnd; Stg Cre; Bskball (V L); Sccr (J); Cl Off (T); Member of Rock Band; Psychology; Brandeis U; Bates College

DOUCETTE, CASEY R; SOUTH PORTLAND, ME; SOUTH PORTLAND HS; (SR); DAR; F Lan Hn Soc; Nat Hon Sy; WWAHSS; Comm Volntr; Drma Clb; Key Club; Spanish Clb; Bnd; Clr Grd; Flg Crps; SP/M/VS; Fld Hky (V); Cl Off (S); CR (R); Wellesley College Book Award; Biology; Marine Biology; Dartmouth College; U of Connecticut

DOUIN, D JOSHUA; HOLLIS CTR, ME; BONNY EAGLE HS; (JR); F Lan Hn Soc; Hi Hnr Roll; Nat Hon Sy; Pres Sch; WWAHSS; Comm Volntr; Emplmnt; Key Club; Prom Com; Bnd; Jzz Bnd; Pep Bnd; Bskball (J); Sccr (V); Tennis (V); Cl Off (T); Stu Cncl; Engineering; Medicine; Boston College; Northwestern U

DUFOUR, TAMMY L; MADISON, ME; MADISON AREA HS; (SR); Hnr Roll; Nat Hon Sy; Perf Att; Sci Fairs; St of Mnth; WWAHSS; Red Cr Aide; Photog; Prom Com; Bnd; Stg Cre; Track (J); Cl Off (V); Senior Mentor and Biology Tutor; Animal Science Major; Biology; U of Maine

DUMONT, IAN P; AUGUSTA, ME; LONG HS; (SR); Hi Hnr Roll; MVP; Nat Hon Sy; Otst Ac Ach Awd; Valdctrian; WWAHSS; Yth Ldrshp Prog; Comm Volntr; Peer Tut/Med; AL Aux Boys; Emplmnt; HO'Br Yth Ldrshp; Key Club; Mth Clb/Tm; Outdrs Clb; Sci Clb; Svce Clb; Chr; SP/M/VS; Bskball (V C); Sccr (V C); Track (V C); Adv Cncl (R); Pre-Med; Middlebury College; Harvard College

DUVAL, BRIDGET C; MINOT, ME; ST DOMINIC REG HS; (JR); Hnr Roll; Nat Hon Sy; Otst Ac Ach Awd; WWAHSS; Comm Volntr; Hosp Aide; Peer Tut/Med; Drma Clb; Emplmnt; Key Club; SP/M/VS; Sccr (J); Yrbk (E); Participation in Local, State, and National Beauty Pageants Talent Competition Winner.; Music-Concentration in Vocal Performance/Opera; Musical Theater; Boston U; Northeastern U

Brown, Sonya M
Portland HS
Portland, ME

Amelina, Alina
Apostolic Christian AC
Orono, ME

National
Honor Roll
Spring 2005

Adams, Michael
Searsport District HS
Frankfort, ME

Crosby, Amber
Oak Hill HS
Litchfield, ME

DYER, HEATHER M; ALBION, ME; LAWRENCE HS; (SR); 4H Awd; Hi Hnr Roll; Pres Ac Ftns Aw; Hosp Aide; 4-H; DARE; Drma Clb; Emplmnt; Scouts; SP/M/VS; Ftball (J); Medical School; Harvard; Yale

DYLESKI, KAITLYN J; ORRINGTON, ME; JOHN BAPST MEMORIAL; (JR); Hnr Roll; Perf Att; Pres Ac Ftns Aw; Pres Sch; WWAHSS; Emplmnt; Key Club; Scouts; Acpl Chr; Chr; SP/M/VS; Bskball (J); Fld Hky (JC); Sftball (JC); Swmg (L)

EASTMAN, SHAWNA; LIMINGTON, ME; BONNY EAGLE HS; (JR); F Lan Hn Soc; Hi Hnr Roll; Kwnis Aw; Nat Hon Sy; Pres Sch; St of Mnth; WWAHSS; Comm Volntr; Emplmnt; Key Club; Prom Com; Sccr (V L); Track (V L); U of New Hampshire; U of Maine Orono

ELLIS, SARAH; FARMINGTON, ME; MT BLUE HS; (JR); Hi Hnr Roll; WWAHSS; Comm Volntr; Emplmnt; FBLA; Bskball (JCL); Vice President and Secretary for JMG; Volunteer for Community; Business Management

EMBREY, EVAN; BUXTON, ME; BONNY EAGLE HS; (JR); Hnr Roll; Kwnis Aw; MVP; Nat Hon Sy; WWAHSS; Comm Volntr; Hab For Humty Volntr; AL Aux Boys; Emplmnt; Key Club; Prom Com; Svce Clb; Cr Ctry (V CL); Track (V L)

EMERSON, ANDREW W; YORK, ME; ST THOMAS AQUINAS; (JR); F Lan Hn Soc; Hi Hnr Roll; Nat Hon Sy; Perf Att; Sci Fairs; WWAHSS; Yth Ldrshp Prog; Comm Volntr; Drma Clb; Emplmnt; Scouts; Acpl Chr; Chr; SP/M/VS; Eagle Scout / All-State Choir; Music Dept Award / All-State Jazz Choir / American Legion Award; Worcester Polytechnic Institute; Villanova U

EVERETT, JESSICA; FALMOUTH, ME; FALMOUTH HS; (JR); Hi Hnr Roll; Otst Ac Ach Awd; WWAHSS; Comm Volntr; Chrch Yth Grp; Key Club; Mth Clb/Tm; Chr; Dnce; Mar Art; Skiing; Pre-Med; Spanish; Princeton, Stanford, Brown

FEENEY, ASHLEY; PORTLAND, ME; PORTLAND HS; (SO); Hi Hnr Roll; Hnr Roll; Otst Ac Ach Awd; St of Mnth; Yth Ldrshp Prog; Drma Clb; Off Aide; SADD; Bskball (V L); Sccr (V L); Sftball (V L); Cl Off (V, S); Stu Cncl (R); Sports Medicine; Sports Business; West Virginia U; Holy Cross College

FERRY, AMY; PLYMOUTH, ME; NOKOMIS REG HS; (SO); Hi Hnr Roll; Hnr Roll; Scouts; Bnd; Mch Bnd; Pep Bnd; Fld Hky (VJ L); Registered Nursing; U of Maine; Husson College

FIKES, KATIE; BANGOR, ME; JOHN BAPST MEM. HS; (JR); Hnr Roll; Red Cr Aide; Spec Olymp Vol; Chrch Yth Grp; Drma Clb; Key Club; Mus Clb; Photog; Bnd; Ch Chr; Stg Cre; Swmg (V L); Hope to Own My Own Restaurant; Culinary Institute of America; Johnson and Wales

FILIMONOW, ASHLEY M; NEW SWEDEN, ME; CARIBOU HS; (JR); Hnr Roll; Emplmnt; Key Club; Sftball (V); Marine Biology; Maine Maritime U; Regis College

FOSTER, KAYLA M; WINDHAM, ME; WINDHAM HS; (JR); Hnr Roll; Peer Tut/Med; Lib Aide; Fld Hky (J); Hsbk Rdg (J); Tennis (VJ); Track (V); Elementary Education; U of Maine

FREDERICK, TAMLYN M; DOVER FOXCROFT, ME; FOXCROFT AC; (SR); Ctznshp Aw; Hi Hnr Roll; Hnr Roll; MVP; Nat Hon Sy; Sci Fairs; Sci/Math Olympn; WWAHSS; Yth Ldrshp Prog; Comm Volntr; Peer Tut/Med; AL Aux Girls; Chrch Yth Grp; Drma Clb; Key Club; Latin Clb; Chr; Ch Chr; SP/M/VS; Cr Ctry (V L); Fld Hky (V L); Swmg (V CL); Tennis (V L); Track (V L); Cl Off (T); Stu Cncl (R); Maine Youth Leadership Seminar; Maine Event Field Hockey; Chemistry; Physics; Bowdoin College

GAGLIARDO, KELLY; NEWPORT, ME; NOKOMIS REG HS; (JR); Hi Hnr Roll; Hnr Roll; Otst Ac Ach Awd; Pres Sch; DARE; Emplmnt; Bnd; Mch Bnd; Pep Bnd; Zoology; Veterinary Medicine; U of Maine

GALLICK, KATHRIN O; AUBURN, ME; ST DOMINIC REG HS; (SO); Hi Hnr Roll; Hnr Roll; Nat Hon Sy; Pres Ac Ftns Aw; WWAHSS; Comm Volntr; Peer Tut/Med; Emplmnt; Key Club; Prom Com; Vsity Clb; Ice Hky (V); Sccr (V); Stu Cncl (S); Student Senate, Secretary; Board of Directors-Key Club; Medicine/Biology Sciences; U of Virginia; U California Los Angeles

GEYER, SHEA; HARPSWELL, ME; MT ARARAT HS; (FR); Hi Hnr Roll; Hnr Roll; Pep Squd; Bnd; WWAHSS; Art Piece Selected for District Art Show; Environmental Studies; French; Yale U; Brown U

GIRARD, DESIREE; BIDDEFORD, ME; BIDDEFORD HS; (SO); Hi Hnr Roll; Hnr Roll; St of Mnth; Bnd; Jzz Bnd; Mch Bnd; Orch; All-State Music Festival; Portland Youth Symphony Orchestra & Wind Ensemble; Physical Therapy; Music Performance; Slippery Rock U; Ithaca College

GIROUARD, DANIELLE; EAST POLAND, ME; POLAND REG HS; (MS); Hnr Roll; Comm Volntr; DARE; Chr; Bskball (J); Fld Hky (J); Sftball (J); Stu Cncl (R); Criminology Degree; Crime Scene Investigator / Career; Northeastern U; U of Southern Maine

GROSS, BRITTNY E; WARREN, ME; MORNINGSTAR AC; (FR); Hi Hnr Roll; Hnr Roll; Perf Att; St of Mnth; Comm Volntr; Peer Tut/Med; Red Cr Aide; Chrch Yth Grp; Emplmnt; Lib Aide; Mth Clb/Tm; Tchrs Aide; Ch Chr; Ice Sktg; MSSM Summer Camp / Maine School for Science & Math - 4 Yrs; Care Wear Crochet Volunteer; Media Studies; Child Development; Middlebury College VT; U of Maine

GUHAD, MOHAMED; PORTLAND, ME; PORTLAND HS; (SO); Hnr Roll; SP/M/VS; Computer Technology; Nurse

GUTEK, SASHA L; PORTLAND, ME; PORTLAND HS; (SO); Ctznshp Aw; Hnr Roll; WWAHSS; Comm Volntr; DARE; Emplmnt; P to P St Amb Prg; Tchrs Aide; Chr; Stg Cre; Chrldg (V); Tennis (V); Chemistry With Forensic Investigation; Biotechnology; U of Surrey - Guilford; U of Keele - UK

HAASS, JANEKA; SURRY, ME; ELLSWORTH HS; (SO); Ctznshp Aw; Gov Hnr Prg; Hi Hnr Roll; WWAHSS; Comm Volntr; Key Club; Sftball (C); Cl Off (S); Accountant-CPA; Husson College; Thomas College

HACKETT, BRIAN E; BANGOR, ME; (SR); Bsball (V L); Bskball (V); Ftball (V L); CR (R); Who's Who Sports; Pharmacy; U of Maine

HADDIX, KELSEY; HOLDEN, ME; JOHN BAPST MEM. HS; (SR); Hnr Roll; Sci Fairs; Comm Volntr; Hab For Humty Volntr; Chrch Yth Grp; DARE; Key Club; Outdrs Clb; Bnd; Ch Chr; SP/M/VS; Stg Cre; Bmtn; Bskball; Cr Ctry (J); Hsbk Rdg (V); Mar Art; Swmg (V); Vllyball; Yrbk; Nursing; Husson College; U of New Brunswick

HAEUSER, EMILY; SOUTH PORTLAND, ME; SOUTH PORTLAND HS; (JR); Hi Hnr Roll; Nat Hon Sy; Nat Mrt LOC; Nat Mrt Semif; Yth Ldrshp Prog; Comm Volntr; DARE; Jzz Bnd; Bskball (V); Cr Ctry (V); Sccr (J); Lit Mag (E); Rotary Youth Leadership Awards Participant; Brown U; Princeton U

HALE, SHANNA E; AUBURN, ME; ST DOMINIC REG HS; (JR); Hi Hnr Roll; Hnr Roll; WWAHSS; Comm Volntr; ArtClub; Emplmnt; Key Club; Photog; Svce Clb; Dnce; Lit Mag (E, P); Yrbk (E, R, P); Dance-Out of School; Photography Class Scholarship; Art-Photography-Graphic Design; Psychology; Maine College of Art

HAMANN, MICHELLE S; AUBURN, ME; ST DOMINIC REG HS; (SR); Hi Hnr Roll; Hnr Roll; Perf Att; WWAHSS; Comm Volntr; Key Club; Mus Clb; French Clb; Chrldg (V); Sccr (V); Biology / Criminal Science; Elmira College

HAMANN, PAUL A; AUBURN, ME; ST DOMINIC REG HS; (FR); Perf Att; WWAHSS; Comm Volntr; Chrch Yth Grp; Emplmnt; Key Club; Ice Hky (J); Lcrsse (J); Sccr (J); Adv Cncl (R); Key Club; Mortician (Human Science); Elmira College

HANIFI, DAVID; FALMOUTH, ME; FALMOUTH HS; (JR); Hnr Roll; Comm Volntr; Key Club; Mth Clb/Tm; SP/M/VS; Swmg (V); Blue Belt in Karate; Community Services Volunteer; BS in the Field of Math/Science; MS in the Field of Math/Science; Bowdoin; Stanford

HARDING, CHRISTOPHER A; LEVANT, ME; HERMON HS; (SR); Hi Hnr Roll; Hnr Roll; MVP; Otst Ac Ach Awd; Perf Att; Sci Fairs; St of Mnth; Valdctrian; Comm Volntr; AL Aux Boys; Emplmnt; Key Club; Prom Com; Vsity Clb; Bskball (VJCL); Sccr (VJCL); Tennis (V CL); Track (V L); Stu Cncl (R); CR (R); Big East Conference Scholar Athlete-Basketball; All-Conference Honorable Mention-Soccer; Master's in Business Management; U of Maine At Orono; Bentley College

HARRIS, ADRENNA L; PORTLAND, ME; PORTLAND HS; (SO); Hnr Roll; Otst Ac Ach Awd; St of Mnth; Comm Volntr; DECA; Key Club; Off Aide; Tchrs Aide; Chr; Bskball; Part of - Teen Leadership Connection / TLC; Business; Cosmetology; New York U; UCLA

HERSOM, MICHAEL A; AUGUSTA, ME; LAWRENCE HS; (SO); Hi Hnr Roll; Bsball (V); Ftball (V); Ice Hky (V L); Major in Education; Sports Medicine; U of Maine At Orono; Bates College

HERSOM, THOMAS L; AUGUSTA, ME; LAWRENCE HS; (SO); Hi Hnr Roll; Hnr Roll; Bsball (V); Ftball (V L); Ice Hky (V L); Education; Coaching; U of Maine-Orono; Springfield College

HILLS, MELISSA; HERMON, ME; HERMON HS; (SR); Hi Hnr Roll; Nat Hon Sy; St of Mnth; Comm Volntr; Peer Tut/Med; Emplmnt; Key Club; Spanish Clb; Bnd; Bskball (V); Fld Hky (V); Sftball (V); Tennis (V); Cl Off (P); Stu Cncl (R); School Committee Student Representative; Biochemistry; Accepted-U of Maine Orono-Attending

HINKLEY, WILLIAM; CHARLESTON, ME; BANGOR CHRISTIAN; (JR); Hi Hnr Roll; St Optmst of Yr; Valdctrian; Comm Volntr; 4-H; Chr; Ch Chr; SP/M/VS; Bskball (V L); Bskball (J); Dvng (V); Sccr (V L); Wrstlg (V L); Cl Off (P); Stu Cncl (R); Scholar Athlete; Accepted USMA - Summer Leader Seminar; Military History; Geography; US Military Academy; US Naval Academy

HOPKINS, KYLIE; HOLDEN, ME; JOHN BAPST MEM. HS; (SO); Ctznshp Aw; Hi Hnr Roll; Hnr Roll; Kwnis Aw; MVP; Otst Ac Ach Awd; Perf Att; Pres Sch; Sci Fairs; WWAHSS; Key Club; Bskball (J); Sccr (VJ L); Sftball; Swmg (V L); Track (V); Sch Ppr (R); Highest Average Award in 6 of My 7 Classes My Freshman Year; Scholastic Excellence for All A's All Year; Nursing; Colby-Sawyer College; U of Maine/Farmington

HOPKINS, SKYLAR; OLD TOWN, ME; OLD TOWN HS; (SO); Ctznshp Aw; Hi Hnr Roll; St of Mnth; Pep Squd; Bnd; Jzz Bnd; Mch Bnd; Pep Bnd; All-State Band; International Affairs; Psychology; Georgetown - Affairs

HUBBARD, GABRIELLE; POLAND, ME; B WHITTIER MS/POLAND REG HS; MS; Ctznshp Aw; Hnr Roll; Otst Ac Ach Awd; St of Mnth; DARE; Drma Clb; Dnce; SP/M/VS; Chrldg (J); Sftball (J); Selected the HOW Student of the Year - 2005; Registered Nurse; Bates College

HULBERT, CAITLIN M; HEBRON, ME; HEBRON AC; (SR); Hi Hnr Roll; Hnr Roll; WWAHSS; Yth Ldrshp Prog; Comm Volntr; Peer Tut/Med; Red Cr Aide; Chrch Yth Grp; Emplmnt; NYLC; Prom Com; SP/M/VS; Stg Cre; Scr Kpr (VJ); Sccr (J); Tennis (VJ L); Track (V); CR (T); Presidential Youth Leadership Conference Participant; Foreign Affairs; International Relations; Catholic U of America

JACOBSON, NICOLE L; FALMOUTH, ME; FALMOUTH HS; (FR); Hi Hnr Roll; Comm Volntr; Key Club; Chr; Dnce

JANOSIK, ZACHARY; WINDHAM, ME; WINDHAM HS; (JR); F Lan Hn Soc; Hi Hnr Roll; Nat Hon Sy; WWAHSS; Comm Volntr; Spec Olymp Vol; Chrch Yth Grp; Emplmnt; Sccr (V); Tennis (V); Maine Metro FC, Captain (Premier Soccer Club); SMAA All Star Award Honorable Mention 2004; Mathematics; Computer Engineering; U of Maine At Orono; Worcester Polytechnical Institute

JARO, BRIANNA; SOUTH PORTLAND, ME; SOUTH PORTLAND HS; (SO); Ctznshp Aw; Hnr Roll; Nat Hon Sy; Comm Volntr; DARE; Key Club; Outdrs Clb; P to P St Amb Prg; Prom Com; Spanish Clb; Bskball (JV); Sccr (JV); Tennis (V); Cl Off (P); 2nd Place Ribbon for Youth Federal Duck Stamp Contest 2005; Portland-Shinagawa Cultural Youth Exchange 2003; Next Generation Most Improved Student Award 2004; Entrepreneur; Marketing; Boston College; Columbia U

JEFFRIES, ASHLEY M; WINTHROP, ME; WINTHROP SR HS; (SR); Hi Hnr Roll; Hnr Roll; Otst Ac Ach Awd; Perf Att; Comm Volntr; Peer Tut/Med; Red Cr Aide; Drma Clb; Emplmnt; Latin Clb; SP/M/VS; Psychology-Clinical; Theater; Keene State College; Plymouth State U

JENSEN, KYLE P; EAST DIXFIELD, ME; FOSTER REG APPLIED TECH CTR; (SR); 4H Awd; Hi Hnr Roll; Hnr Roll; Otst Ac Ach Awd; USAA; Comm Volntr; Peer Tut/Med; 4-H; Track (V); Member of East Dixfield Fire Dept.; Keep Me Warm Program; Mechanical Engineering Technology; The U of Maine; Southern Maine Community College

JENSEN, ZACHARY R; LEWISTON, ME; LEWISTON HS; (SO); Hnr Roll; WWAHSS; Comm Volntr; Chess; P to P St Amb Prg; Tchrs Aide; Sccr (J); History

JOHNDRO, AMY; ORRINGTON, ME; JBM HS; (SO); Hnr Roll; WWAHSS; Comm Volntr; Key Club; Outdrs Clb; Bnd; Chr; Pep Bnd; Veterinarian; Forensic Scientist; U of North Carolina; Cedar Crest

JOHNSTON, COREY; CALAIS, ME; CALAIS HS; (SO); Bsball (V); Bskball (J); Sccr (V CL); Business; Wildlife Management; U of Maine Orono; Husson College

JOHNSTON, HEATHER; LINCOLN, ME; MATTANAWCOOK AC; (SO); Ctznshp Aw; Hnr Roll Prg; Hi Hnr Roll; Nat Hon Sy; DARE; St of Mnth; Valdctrian; Comm Volntr; Peer Tut/Med; Chess; Drma Clb; Mth Clb/Tm; Mus Clb; Photog; Scouts; French Clb; Bnd; Ch Chr; Jzz Bnd; Bskball (J); Ftball (J); Track (V L); Yrbk (E, P); Civil Rights Team; Destination Imagination; Business /Law / Political Science; Music / Theatre / Creative Writing; Goucher College; Stanford U

JONES, MOLLY; VEAZIE, ME; JOHN BAPST MEM. HS; (SO); Hi Hnr Roll; Otst Ac Ach Awd; Perf Att; Sci Fairs; Comm Volntr; Emplmnt; Jr Cls League; Key Club; Mth Clb/Tm; Sccr (V L); Swmg (V L); Track (V L); Stu Cncl (V); Aeronautical Engineering; Astrophysics; Cornell U; Notre Dame

JUSKEWITCH, ELLEN W; HOLDEN, ME; JOHN BAPST MEM. HS; (SR); Ctznshp Aw; Hnr Roll; MVP; Pres Ac Ftns Aw; WWAHSS; Spec Olymp Vol; Emplmnt; Key Club; Mus Clb; Outdrs Clb; Pep Squd; Photog; Prom Com; Vsity Clb; Bnd; Jzz Bnd; Pep Bnd; SP/M/VS; Bskball (JC); Scr Kpr (J); Sccr (V CL); Tennis (V CL); Vsy Clb (V CL); Stu Cncl (R); CR (R); Yrbk (E, R); Politics; Attorney; Ithaca

KALEY, LINDSEY; MANCHESTER, ME; MARANACOOK CMTY HS; (SR); Gov Hnr Prg; Hi Hnr Roll; Nat Mrt Fin; Pres Sch; Salutrn; WWAHSS; Yth Ldrshp Prog; Comm Volntr; Peer Tut/Med; Dbte Team; Drma Clb; NtlFrnscLg; Photog; Prom Com; Tchrs Aide; Tmpl Yth Grp; Acpl Chr; Chr; SP/M/VS; Stu Cncl (V); CR (R); Lit Mag (P); Participant in the National Forensic League National Debate Tournament; Toyota Community Regional Scholar; International Relations and Affairs; Diplomacy; Columbia U

Hanifi, David
Falmouth HS
Falmouth, ME

Haass, Janeka
Ellsworth HS
Surry, ME

National Honor Roll Spring 2005

Feeney, Ashley
Portland HS
Portland, ME

Johnston, Heather
Mattanawcook AC
Lincoln, ME

KANE, SAMANTHA M; PORTLAND, ME; DEERING HS; (JR); Hi Hnr Roll; Nat Hon Sy; Otst Ac Ach Awd; Yth Ldrshp Prog; Comm Volntr; Clb; Fld Hky (V L); Lcrsse (V CL); Scr Kpr (L); Wrstlg (V L); John Casa Gold Award for Lacrosse

KARANTZA, ALEXANDER; WINDHAM, ME; WINDHAM HS; (JR); Hnr Roll; Mas Aw; Otst Ac Ach Awd; Sci/Math Olympn; Peer Tut/Med; Spec Olymp Vol; Chrch Yth Grp; Cmptr Clb; Emplmnt; Acpl Chr; Chr; Ch Chr; Orch; Computer Programming; Full Sail-Real World Education

KENAHAN, CASEY; WINDHAM, ME; WINDHAM HS; (JR); Hnr Roll; MVP; Emplmnt; Fld Hky (JC); Lcrsse (J); Skiing (V CL); Castleton State College; U of Vermont

KENNEY, RYAN; BRADLEY, ME; OLD TOWN HS; (JR); Hi Hnr Roll; Hnr Roll; Chrch Yth Grp; DARE; Emplmnt; Key Club; Scouts; Bskball (J); Sccr (V L); Track (L); Junior Bowling Champion 1999; Father/Son Bowling Champions 2000; Marine Biology; U of Maine Orono

KILGOUR, MICHELLE L; SOUTH BERWICK, ME; MARSHWOOD HS; (JR); Hi Hnr Roll; Hnr Roll; Comm Volntr; Peer Tut/Med; HO'Br Yth Ldrshp; Scouts; Tchrs Aide; Fld Hky (JC); Stu Cncl (P); Psychology; Business Associates; Elmira College

KING, JENNA; OLD TOWN, ME; OLD TOWN HS; (FR); Hi Hnr Roll; MVP; Red Cr Aide; Key Club; SADD; Vsity Clb; Bskball (V L); Fld Hky (V L); Track (V L); Cl Off (P); Stu Cncl (R); Yrbk (E)

KINNEY, NATHAN; PHILLIPS, ME; MT ABRAM HS; (FR); Ctznshp Aw; Hi Hnr Roll; Hnr Roll; Tennis (VJ); Cl Off (P); Stu Cncl (R); Prudential Spirit of Community Award; Accountant; Lawyer

KRASSIKOFF, MELISSA; ORONO, ME; ORONO HS; (JR); Hi Hnr Roll; Hnr Roll; Nat Hon Sy; Otst Ac Ach Awd; Comm Volntr; Spec Olymp Vol; Cmptr Clb; Drma Clb; Key Club; Clb; Chr; Dnce; SP/M/VS; CR (R); Lit Mag; Yrbk (E); Diversity Team; Film Club; Cinematography; Psychology; Columbia U, New York, New York; Ithaca College, Ithaca, New York

LABBE, CRYSTAL; EAST BALDWIN, ME; SACOPEE VALLEY HS; (SR); Hi Hnr Roll; Hnr Roll; Otst Ac Ach Awd; Perf Att; WWAHSS; Jr Cls League; Mth Clb/Tm; Fld Hky (V); Math Team- 11th & 12th Grade; Dental Hygiene; U of Maine Augusta

LEVESQUE, ROSS A; EAST ORLAND, ME; JOHN BAPST MEM. HS; (JR); Hi Hnr Roll; Nat Hon Sy; Valdctrian; WWAHSS; Key Club; Bnd; Bsball (V); Bskball (J); Skiing (J); Stu Cncl (R); Doctor; Boston College; U of Maine Orono

LIBBY, PAIGE M; POLAND, ME; B WHITTIER MS/POLAND REG HS; (MS); Hi Hnr Roll; Hnr Roll; Nat Hon Sy; Otst Ac Ach Awd; Sci Fairs; Sci/Math Olympn; St of Mnth; Comm Volntr; ArtClub; DARE; Chr; Dnce; 2003 Fly Cheering Senior Champions; Art / Animation; Graphics Art Designing; California State U

LIN, ILKA; HAMPDEN, ME; JOHN BAPST MEM. HS; (SO); Hi Hnr Roll; Hnr Roll; Nat Stu Ath Day Aw; Pres Ac Ftns Aw; Sci Fairs; Comm Volntr; ArtClub; Key Club; Mth Clb/Tm; Scouts; Chr; Dnce; SP/M/VS; Dvng (V L); Track (J); Bangor Area Children's Choir; Cty Talent Search; Architecture; Cornell U; Massachusetts Institute of Technology

LOFTON, JESSIE; LAMOINE, ME; ELLSWORTH HS; (SO); Hi Hnr Roll; Hnr Roll; Otst Ac Ach Awd; Comm Volntr; ArtClub; Chrch Yth Grp; Key Club; Bskball; Mar Art; Sftball; Academic Excellence Award 2004 Foreign Language; Academic Excellence Award 2004 Intro to Tech; Zoology; Early Childhood Development; U of Maine; Pensacola Christian College

LOW, MATTHEW; FAIRFIELD, ME; LAWRENCE HS; (SO); Hi Hnr Roll; Perf Att; St of Mnth; Yth Ldrshp Prog; Emplmnt; Mth Clb/Tm; Bsball (J); Bskball (J); Sccr (V L); CR (R); Aeronautical Engineering; Chemical Engineering; Massachusetts Institute of Technology; Boston U

MARSTON, BRITTNEY L; FAIRFIELD, ME; LAWRENCE HS; (FR); Hi Hnr Roll; Hnr Roll; DARE; Mus Clb; Bnd; Chr; Dnce; Chrldg (V); Sftball (J); Snowmobile Racing/Speed Run; 6 Years of Dance; Interior Designer; Race Car Driver.; U of Maine At Orono; U of Maine in Farmington

MARTIN-HUNT, ARIEL; BUXTON, ME; BONNY EAGLE HS; (SO); Hi Hnr Roll; Hnr Roll; Nat Hon Sy; Otst Ac Ach Awd; WWAHSS; Comm Volntr; Hosp Aide; Peer Tut/Med; Key Club; Off Aide; Svce Clb; Bnd; Dnce; Piano; Medical Explorers; Medical Field

MATTHEWS, KYLE; OWLS HEAD, ME; ROCKLAND DIST HS; (SO); Hnr Roll; Comm Volntr; Spec Olymp Vol; Key Club; Scouts; Ice Hky; Sccr (J); Tennis (V); PE Teacher

MC CLARIE, MARIE N; WATERVILLE, ME; WINSLOW HS; (SR); Hnr Roll; WWAHSS; Comm Volntr; Chrch Yth Grp; Vsity Clb; SP/M/VS; Bskball (V C); Sccr (V); Tennis (V); Yrbk (R); Homecoming Queen 2004; U of Southern Maine

MC GRATH, JOSHUA; BOWDOIN, ME; MT ARARAT HS; (FR); Hi Hnr Roll; Hnr Roll; Hab For Humty Volntr; ArtClub; Chrch Yth Grp; Bnd; Jzz Bnd; Mch Bnd; Pep Bnd; Cr Ctry (J); Sch Ppr (R); Artwork Chosen for State Art Show; Spectrum - Gifted and Talented Program; Software Programmer; Illustrator; Bowdoin College; U of Maine

MC MASTER, CHELSEA; LISBON, ME; LISBON HS; (SR); Hi Hnr Roll; Jr Mshl; Nat Hon Sy; Otst Ac Ach Awd; Perf Att; Pres Sch; St of Mnth; Valdctrian; WWAHSS; Comm Volntr; Spec Olymp Vol; AL Aux Girls; Drma Clb; Emplmnt; Prom Com; Svce Clb; SP/M/VS; Cl Off (P); Yrbk (E); US Senate Page; International Affairs; George Washington U

MILLAY, SENAIT M; SURRY, ME; ELLSWORTH HS; (SO); Hnr Roll; WWAHSS; Comm Volntr; Chrch Yth Grp; Key Club; American Foreign Students Club; Key Club; Nursing; U of Maine-Augusta; U of Maine-Fort Kent

MORRILL, ELLYSEA J; BANGOR, ME; HERMON HS; (SR); Red Cr Aide; Chrch Yth Grp; Emplmnt; Key Club; Scouts; Spanish Clb; Bnd; Dnce; Chrldg (J); Fld Hky (J); Track (V); Yrbk (E); Teaching; Medical Field

MOWER, EMILY; SAINT ALBANS, ME; NOKOMIS REG HS; (SO); Hi Hnr Roll; Pres Sch; WWAHSS; Bnd; Jzz Bnd; Mch Bnd; Chrldg (V); Track (V); Engineering; Medical Field

MULLINS, JULIE; BANGOR, ME; BANGOR AREA HS; (JR); Hnr Roll; Nat Hon Sy; Peer Tut/Med; DARE; Mus Clb; ROTC; French Clb; Bnd; Chr; Drl Tm; Jzz Bnd; Zoology; Animal Science / Medicine; SUNY Oswego; North Carolina State U

MURRY, NOELLE B; FALMOUTH, ME; FALMOUTH HS; (SO); Pres Sch; Comm Volntr; Chrch Yth Grp; Key Club; Mth Clb/Tm; Sccr (JC); Sftball (J); Track (J); Yrbk (E); Youth Ref of the Year; Pre-Med/Biology; Arizona State U; U of Michigan

MURRY JR, CHRISTOPHER B; FALMOUTH, ME; FALMOUTH HS; (JR); Hnr Roll; Amnsty Intl; Comm Volntr; Emplmnt; Prom Com; Track (V L); Cl Off (V); CR (R); Sch Ppr (R); Yrbk (R); Captain of the Mock Trial Team; Student Representative to the School Board; Political Science; History; George Washington U; Catholic U of America

NELSON, NICK; SHAWMUT, ME; LAWRENCE; (FR); Civil Air Pat; Mth Clb/Tm; Bsball; Bskball; Ftball

NEWMAN, BRANDON; SOUTH CHINA, ME; ERSKINE AC; (SO); Hi Hnr Roll; MVP; Nat Hon Sy; Otst Ac Ach Awd; Perf Att; Valdctrian; WWAHSS; Comm Volntr; Peer Tut/Med; Red Cr Aide; Drma Clb; Mth Clb/Tm; Ntl Beta Clb; NYLC; Outdrs Clb; Bsball (J); Hsbk Rdg (V); Swmg (V L); Tennis (V); Cl Off (P); Stu Cncl (V); Engineering

NICKERSON, RYAN D; HOULTON, ME; REGION 2 SCH-APPLIED TECH; (SR); Hi Hnr Roll; Hnr Roll; WWAHSS; Emplmnt; Black Belt 1st Degree; Who's Who - 3 Times; Computer Science; U of Maine Orono; Northeastern U

O'NEAL, MATTHEW; MT VERNON, ME; MARANACOOK HS; (SR); Hnr Roll; Comm Volntr; Mus Clb; Outdrs Clb; Tchrs Aide; Bnd; Jzz Bnd; SP/M/VS; Cyclg (V); 2nd Place in State Championship - Cycling; Wildlife; Wildlife Biology; Unity College

OUELLET, MITCHELL; FORT KENT, ME; FORT KENT CMTY HS; (SR); All Am Sch; Ctznshp Aw; Hi Hnr Roll; Hnr Roll; MVP; Nat Hon Sy; Otst Ac Ach Awd; WWAHSS; Yth Ldrshp Prog; Comm Volntr; Peer Tut/Med; Spec Olymp Vol; Chrch Yth Grp; Emplmnt; HO'Br Yth Ldrshp; Key Club; Lttrmn Clb; Prom Com; Quiz Bowl; SADD; Bnd; Pep Bnd; Bskball (V CL); Sccr (V L); Tennis (V CL); Vllyball (V CL)

OUELLETTE, JUSTIN; POLAND, ME; ST DOMINIC REG HS; (JR); Hnr Roll; Kwnis Aw; Perf Att; WWAHSS; Comm Volntr; Hosp Aide; ArtClub; Drma Clb; Emplmnt; Key Club; Mth Clb/Tm; Vsity Clb; SP/M/VS; Stg Cre; Bsball (V L); Bskball (V L); Scr Kpr (VJ L); Sccr (J); Vsy Clb (V L); Volunteer of the Year-2001; 9th, 10th Grade Effort/Achievement; Marketing; Advertising

PAQUET, JORDAN E; LEWISTON, ME; ST DOMINIC REG HS; (SO); Hnr Roll; WWAHSS; Comm Volntr; Emplmnt; Key Club; Dnce; Sccr; Stu Cncl (R); CR (R); Soup Kitchen Volunteer; Dentistry; Nutritionist/Personal Counselor

PERKINS, SARA E; MILLINOCKET, ME; STEARNS HS; (SR); Hi Hnr Roll; Nat Hon Sy; WWAHSS; Peer Tut/Med; AL Aux Girls; Chrch Yth Grp; Emplmnt; Mth Clb/Tm; Off Aide; Prom Com; SADD; Dnce; Chrldg (V C); Tennis (V); Cl Off (P); Stu Cncl (R); Yrbk; State Silver Medal in Health Math; State Bronze Medal in Pharmacology Knowledge; Pharmacy 6 Year Program; U Rhode Island

PERRY, LINDSEY; OXFORD, ME; OXFORD HILLS TECH SCH; (JR); Chrldg (VJ); Lcrsse (V); DECA State Officer - Treasurer; Lawyer; Marietta; Western New England College

PERUFFO, NICK; FARMINGTON, ME; MT BLUE HS; (SO); Hnr Roll; Bnd; Chr; Bskball (J); Golf (J); Cl Off (P); Stu Cncl (R); Coach Kids Basketball During the Summer; Knowledge Master Captain; History; Politics; Boston College; New York U

PETERSON, KENNY; CALAIS, ME; CALAIS HS; (FR); Chrch Yth Grp; Member of the Church of Jesus Christ of Latter Day Saints; Read Book of Mormon At Age 3; Psychology / Counselor; Accounting

PRIOR, KIMBERLY A; CUSHING, ME; GEORGES VALLEY HS; (SR); Hi Hnr Roll; Nat Hon Sy; Sci Fairs; St of Mnth; Valdctrian; WWAHSS; Chrch Yth Grp; Emplmnt; Bnd; Chr; Dnce; Pep Bnd; National Honor Society President; All-State and District Honor Bands; Pre-Med Psychology; Gordon College

RALLIS, NEVIN; WINDHAM, ME; WINDHAM HS; (SR); Hi Hnr Roll; Hnr Roll; Perf Att; Sci/Math Olympn; St of Mnth; Emplmnt; Latin Clb; Bnd; Jzz Bnd; Mch Bnd; Pep Bnd; Bsball (J); Skiing (V C); Track (V L); Scholar Athlete Awards; Most Improve Award-Track; Mechanical Engineer; Cornell U; U of Vermont, U of Maine Orono

RAMSEY, DIANN; OXFORD, ME; OXFORD HILLS TECH CTR; (SO); Hnr Roll; DECA; Bskball (J); Fld Hky (V); Sftball (V); KVAC Rookie Team (Field Hockey); Majoring in Psychology; U of New England

RAYDER, BROOKE E; FALMOUTH, ME; NORTH YARMOUTH AC; (SO); Hi Hnr Roll; Nat Hon Sy; Otst Ac Ach Awd; Yth Ldrshp Prog; Comm Volntr; Hab For Humty Volntr; Chrch Yth Grp; Key Club; Bnd; Pep Bnd; Bskball (V L); Sccr (V L); Stu Cncl (R); Sch Ppr (R); Yrbk (R)

RAYMOND, BRIANA; AUGUSTA, ME; CONY HS; (SR); Hnr Roll; MVP; Pres Ac Ftns Aw; Sci Fairs; St of Mnth; Comm Volntr; Peer Tut/Med; DARE; Emplmnt; Key Club; Photog; Spanish Clb; Stg Cre; Ice Hky (V); Cl Off (S); Yrbk (P); Volunteer at Food Kitchen; Volunteer Work for Community; Business Major; Georgia State U; Long Island U Brooklyn Campus

REYNOLDS, CYLE J; KINGFIELD, ME; MT ABRAM HS; (FR); Mth Clb/Tm; Tennis (V); Computer Programming; DigiPen

RIBEIRO, PATRICIA C; FALMOUTH, ME; FALMOUTH HS; (SR); Hnr Roll; Nat Hon Sy; Otst Ac Ach Awd; Comm Volntr; Chrch Yth Grp; Emplmnt; Key Club; Prom Com; Spanish Clb; Dnce; Tennis (J); Yrbk (R, P); Secretary of Civil Rights Team; Psychology Degree; Communications Degree; Gordon College

RICHARDSON, KAYLIN E; EDDINGTON, ME; BANGOR HS; (JR); Hnr Roll; Nat Hon Sy; Otst Ac Ach Awd; Perf Att; Yth Ldrshp Prog; Comm Volntr; Peer Tut/Med; ArtClub; DARE; Dbte Team; Drma Clb; Emplmnt; Key Club; Mth Clb/Tm; P to P St Amb Prg; Stg Cre; Tennis (V); Sch Ppr (E, R); Student Ambassador; Film & Theatre; Photography; Emerson; Boston U

RINDLAUB, NATHANIEL C; PEAKS ISLAND, ME; PORTLAND HS; (SO); ArtClub; Lcrsse (J); Film Club; Film Maker; Car Design

ROBINSON, BRIAN; POLAND, ME; ST DOMINIC REG HS; (SR); Hnr Roll; Nat Hon Sy; WWAHSS; Red Cr Aide; Key Club; Scouts; Sccr (J); Cl Off (P); CR (R); Saint Joseph College Book Award; Key Club 110+ Hours Community Service; Business; Political Science / Law; Bryant U

ROBINSON, RACHAEL; NORWAY, ME; OXFORD HILLS COMP HS; (JR); Hi Hnr Roll; Hnr Roll; Comm Volntr; Peer Tut/Med; Emplmnt; French Clb; Bnd; Mch Bnd; Pep Bnd; Fashion Show 2004 & 2005; Going Abroad to France in April 2005; Pilot; Lawyer; Air Force Academy

ROY, JONATHAN; BANGOR, ME; HARMON HS; (SO); Hnr Roll; MVP; St of Mnth; WWAHSS; Comm Volntr; Hab For Humty Volntr; Key Club; P to P St Amb Prg; Bsball (J); Bskball (J); Golf (V L); Cl Off (S, T); Athletic Director; Coach; U of Maine Presque Isle

ROY, KEVIN R; PHIPPSBURG, ME; MORSE HS; (SR); Hi Hnr Roll; Hnr Roll; MVP; Nat Hon Sy; Otst Ac Ach Awd; Pres Ac Ftns Aw; Comm Volntr; Chrch Yth Grp; DARE; Emplmnt; Jr Ach; Scouts; Wdwrkg Clb; Bskball (V L); Cr Ctry (V CL); Track (V CL); John Cakouros Award; Letter of Achievement from Maine's Gov King; Engineering; U of New Hampshire; U of Connecticut

RUNES, CORRI E; SUMNER, ME; OXFORD HILLS HS; (SR); Hnr Roll; St of Mnth; WWAHSS; Comm Volntr; Peer Tut/Med; DECA; Emplmnt; Prom Com; Scouts; Bskball; Sccr; Sftball; Business Mgmt-Major in Marketing; U of Denver

RUPARD, STACEY L; LEWISTON, ME; LEWISTON HS; (SO); F Lan Hn Soc; Hnr Roll; St of Mnth; Comm Volntr; Peer Tut/Med; DARE; Lib Aide; Off Aide; Scouts; Latin Clb; Dnce; Bskball (V); Wt Lftg (V); Big Brothers Big Sisters; Nursing; Law Enforcement; Northeastern U; Bentley College

RYDER, BRITTANY D; DEXTER, ME; DEXTER CHRISTIAN AC; (JR); Hi Hnr Roll; Chrch Yth Grp; Ch Chr; Christian Character Award; Animation; Psychology; Southwest Baptist U; Geneva College

Nickerson, Ryan D
Region 2 Sch-Applied Tech
Houlton, ME

Murry, Noelle B
Falmouth HS
Falmouth, ME

Mc Clarie, Marie N
Winslow HS
Waterville, ME

National
Honor Roll
Spring 2005

Marston, Brittney L
Lawrence HS
Fairfield, ME

Murry Jr, Christopher B
Falmouth HS
Falmouth, ME

Paquet, Jordan E
St Dominic Reg HS
Lewiston, ME

SANSOM, SAMANTHA; ROCKLAND, ME; ROCKLAND DISTRICT HS; (JR); Hi Hnr Roll; Hnr Roll; Comm Volntr; ArtClub; Emplmnt; Key Club; Prom Com; Svce Clb; Tchrs Aide; Chr; Stu Cncl (R); Sch Ppr; Yrbk; Key Club President 2 Years; Secondary Education; Social Work; U of Southern Maine; Western New England College

SAUCIER, ERIN; LEWISTON, ME; ST DOMINIC REG HS; (SO); Hnr Roll; Otst Ac Ach Awd; Pres Ac Ftns Aw; WWAHSS; Comm Volntr; Emplmnt; Key Club; Mth Clb/Tm; French Clb; Sccr (J); Tennis (V L); Key Club International; Cosmetic Dentistry; Journalism; Florida State

SCALORA, FRANK; CARIBOU, ME; CARIBOU HS; (SR); Hi Hnr Roll; Nat Hon Sy; DECA; Ntl FFA; Sch Ppr (E); Business Administration; Northern Maine Community College

SEAVEY, KATHERINE E; WINDHAM, ME; CHEVERUS HS; (SO); Hnr Roll; WWAHSS; Emplmnt; Key Club; Hsbk Rdg; Stu Cncl (R); Central Maine Team Penning Champion; Key Club; Veterinary Medicine; Tufts College; Saint Josephs College

SHEPARD, LINDSAY; DEER ISLE, ME; DEER ISLE STONINGTON HS; (SO); Hi Hnr Roll; Hnr Roll; Comm Volntr; Scouts; Wdwrkg Clb; Dnce; Chrldg (V); Sccr (V); Cl Off (V); Stu Cncl (R)

SHOLES, JEFFREY A; BELFAST, ME; ROCKLAND DIST HS; (SR); Hnr Roll; Automotive Technology / Diesel Engine; Advanced Technological Institute

SIMONSEN, KIMBERLY; BUXTON, ME; BONNY EAGLE HS; (JR); F Lan Hn Soc; Hi Hnr Roll; Nat Hon Sy; Sci Fairs; WWAHSS; Yth Ldrshp Prog; Comm Volntr; ArtClub; Chrch Yth Grp; Emplmnt; Key Club; NYLC; Prom Com; Scouts; Latin Clb; SP/M/VS; Stg Cre; Swmg (V CL); Tennis (V L); National History State & National Winner 9-11; Occupational Therapy; Utica College Quinnipiac College; Ithaca College

SKINNER, MAKALA; ORLAND, ME; ELLSWORTH HS; (JR); Hi Hnr Roll; Hnr Roll; WWAHSS; Comm Volntr; Drma Clb; Emplmnt; Key Club; French Clb; Chr; SP/M/VS; Chrldg (J); Track (J); Sch Ppr (R); Second Degree Black Belt (Not Through My School); President of Key Club; Major in English; Minor in the Performing Arts; Harvard U; Princeton U

SKOLD, RACQUEL; FREEPORT, ME; FREEPORT HS; (SR); Hi Hnr Roll; Nat Hon Sy; Pres Sch; Sci/Math Olympn; WWAHSS; Comm Volntr; Peer Tut/Med; Red Cr Aide; Chrch Yth Grp; Drma Clb; Emplmnt; Mth Clb/Tm; Mus Clb; Prom Com; Sci Clb; Svce Clb; Bnd; Chr; SP/M/VS; Bskball (VJ); Sccr (VJC); Tennis (J); Sch Ppr (R); Biomedical Engineering; Medical School-Doctor; U of Pennsylvania

SOMERS, SARAH J; HOLDEN, ME; BREWER HS; (JR); Ctznshp Aw; Hi Hnr Roll; Hnr Roll; Perf Att; WWAHSS; Peer Tut/Med; Drma Clb; Emplmnt; Key Club; Mus Clb; Bnd; Chr; Jzz Bnd; Mch Bnd; Cl Off (S); Key Club; U of Maine

STEANNS, ERIN R; ALFRED, ME; CATHERINE MC AULEY HS; (JR); Hnr Roll; Kwnis Aw; Comm Volntr; Key Club; Vsity Clb; French Clb; Fld Hky (V); Lcrsse (V); Vsy Clb (V); Stu Cncl (R); Key Club President 2005-2006; Doctor; Architect; U of Notre Dame; Miami U

STEVENSON, MAXWELL; LEWISTON, ME; LEWISTON HS; (SO); Hnr Roll; Sci Fairs; Comm Volntr; Civil Air Pat; DARE; Emplmnt; Cr Ctry (J); Track (J); Wt Lftg (J); I Have a Radio Show At Bates; Business Stratagies; Investment Banking; Princeton U; Brandeis U

STILES, EMILY E; OAKFIELD, ME; SOUTHERN AROOSTOOK HS; (JR); Ctznshp Aw; Hi Hnr Roll; Hnr Roll; Jr Mshl; Jr Rot; Nat Hon Sy; Otst Ac Ach Awd; Sci Fairs; St of Mnth; Yth Ldrshp Prog; Comm Volntr; Hab For Humty Volntr; Peer Tut/Med; Chrch Yth Grp; Drma Clb; Emplmnt; Jr Ach; Prom Com; Scouts; Svce Clb; Tchrs Aide; Ch Chr; SP/M/VS; Stg Cre; Bskball (V); Cr Ct Ski (V); Hsbk Rdg (V CL); Skiing (V); Sccr (J); Sftball (V); Adv Cncl (V); Cl Off (S); Stu Cncl (S); CR (P); Sch Ppr (E); Yrbk (E, P); Student of the Quarter; Member of Youth in Government; Pre-Law Major; Law School; U of Vermont; Pennsylvania State

STILLMAN, CHELSEA M; PORTLAND, ME; PORTLAND HS; (JR); Hi Hnr Roll; Hnr Roll; Nat Hon Sy; WWAHSS; Comm Volntr; Hosp Aide; Peer Tut/Med; Key Club; Tchrs Aide; Vsity Clb; Skiing; Swmg (V L); Pre-Med; Psychiatry; Washington U St Louis; Yale U

ST PIERRE, EMILY; LEWISTON, ME; ST DOMINIC REG HS; (FR); Hnr Roll; St Optmst of Yr; Key Club; Mth Clb/Tm; Ice Hky (V); Sccr (V); Tennis (V); Teaching; Pediatrics; Boston College; U of Maine (Orono)

ST PIERRE, KATIE; LEWISTON, ME; ST DOMINIC REG HS; (JR); Hi Hnr Roll; Nat Hon Sy; WWAHSS; Comm Volntr; Peer Tut/Med; Chrch Yth Grp; Dbte Team; Drma Clb; Key Club; Mth Clb/Tm; NYLC; Scouts; Ch Chr; SP/M/VS; Stg Cre; Chrldg (V L); Sch Ppr (E); Yrbk (E, P); Vice President Key Club; President Drama Society; Law; Medicine; Yale, Dartmouth; Wellesley

STUART, ASHLEY M; LEWISTON, ME; LEWISTON HS; (SO); Hnr Roll; Sci Fairs; ArtClub; Key Club; Chrldg; Fld Hky (V); Gmnstcs; Hsbk Rdg; Track; Vllyball; Participated in Beauty Pageant; Best of Fair in Science Fair (2004); Psychology, Veterinary; Art(S)/Modeling; U of Maine Orono; Maine College of Art (Portland)

TAREILA, COLIN; BROOKLIN, ME; GEORGE STEVENS AC; (SR); Hi Hnr Roll; Hnr Roll; Chess; Mth Clb/Tm; Skiing (V); Sccr (V); Tennis (V); 2004 State Tennis Class C Champions; Engineering; Lafayette College

TEKO, TCHOTCHO S; LEWISTON, ME; LEWISTON HS; (SO); F Lan Hn Soc; Hnr Roll; Perf Att; Comm Volntr; Chrch Yth Grp; DARE; Photog; Dnce; Bskball (J); Track; Civil Rights Team; I'm an Ambassador of Seeds of Peace; Lawyer; Forensic Science

THIBODEAU, ASHLEY C; MILFORD, ME; OLD TOWN HS; (SR); Hi Hnr Roll; Prom Com; Bnd; Jzz Bnd; Mch Bnd; Pep Bnd; Veterinary Medicine; Nursing; U of Maine At Orono

THORNTON, KELLY; SCARBOROUGH, ME; SCARBOROUGH HS; (SR); Hnr Roll; Perf Att; WWAHSS; Comm Volntr; Chrch Yth Grp; Chrldg (V CL); Fld Hky (J); Yrbk (R); Gymnastics - Not with School; Dance; Physical Therapy; U of New England

TOOMEY, SHEILA R; HOLDEN, ME; JOHN BAPST MEMORIAL HS; (FR); Ctznshp Aw; Hi Hnr Roll; Hnr Roll; Otst Ac Ach Awd; Pres Ac Ftns Aw; Pres Sch; Sci Fairs; WWAHSS; Comm Volntr; Chrch Yth Grp; Key Club; Bnd; Ch Chr; SP/M/VS; Stg Cre; Chrldg (V L); Gmnstcs; PP Ftbl; Sccr; Sftball (J)

TRANT, MARQUISE; PORTLAND, ME; PORTLAND HS; (JR); Hnr Roll; Comm Volntr; Drma Clb; Ftball (V); Physical Education & Athletic Training; Business; Palm Beach Atlantic; South Florida U

VISLOSKY, KYLE; CARIBOU, ME; CARIBOU HS; (JR); Hnr Roll; U of Maine Presque Isle; Northern Maine Community College

WATSON, MEGAN L; BANGOR, ME; HERMON HS; (SR); Hi Hnr Roll; Nat Hon Sy; Otst Ac Ach Awd; St of Mnth; WWAHSS; Peer Tut/Med; Emplmnt; HO'Br Yth Ldrshp; Key Club; Tchrs Aide; Vsity Clb; Bskball (V); Sccr (V CL); Track (J); Cl Off (P); Stu Cncl (P, S, R); CR (R); Secondary Education; Coaching; U of Maine At Fort Kent; U of Maine At Presque Isle

WENTWORTH, SHARISSE; WEST KENNEBUNK, ME; KENNEBUNK HS; (JR); Hnr Roll; Comm Volntr; DARE; Emplmnt; Chr; Lit Mag; President's Education Awards Program; Nursing; U of New England

WHEELER, BETHANY; PHILLIPS, ME; MT ABRAM HS; (FR); Hi Hnr Roll; Hnr Roll; Perf Att; Prom Com; Bskball (V C); Sccr (VJ); Sftball (V C); Cl Off (T); American Legion Certificate of School Award; American Legion's School Award for Citizenship; Athletic Trainer; Travel Agent

WILLIAMS, CHELSEA; BOWDOIN, ME; MT ARARAT HS; (FR); Hi Hnr Roll; Sci Fairs

WILLIAMS, CINDY; BRUNSWICK, ME; MAINE REGION 10 VOC SCH; (SR); Hi Hnr Roll; Hnr Roll; Perf Att; Comm Volntr; Voc Ind Clb Am; Chr; Skills-USA; Girl Scouts; Own My Own Restaurant; Culinary Arts; Southern Maine Community College

WOOD, LYNDSAY; ORRINGTON, ME; BREWER HS; (SR); Hi Hnr Roll; Hnr Roll; WWAHSS; Peer Tut/Med; Emplmnt; Yrbk (E, R, P); Yearbook Editor; METS - Maine Talent Search; Art Education; Photography; U of Maine Orono; Colby-Sawyer College

YORK, DANIEL R; PALMYRA, ME; NOKOMIS REG HS; (SR); Hi Hnr Roll; Hnr Roll; Nat Hon Sy; Otst Ac Ach Awd; St of Mnth; Comm Volntr; Peer Tut/Med; Chrch Yth Grp; Emplmnt; Mth Clb/Tm; Mus Clb; Vsity Clb; Bnd; Jzz Bnd; Mch Bnd; Pep Bnd; Bsball (V); Sccr (V); Track (V L); Stu Cncl (V); Berklee Jazz Festival Judges Choice Award for Guitar; Jazz Performance (Guitar); U of North Texas

Toomey, Sheila R — John Bapst Memorial HS — Holden, ME
Sansom, Samantha — Rockland District HS — Rockland, ME
Skinner, Makala — Ellsworth HS — Orland, ME

Maryland

ACOSTA, ZARETH; GERMANTOWN, MD; WATKINS MILL HS; (SR); Hnr Roll; Perf Att; St of Mnth; Peer Tut/Med; ArtClub; Off Aide; Sci Clb; Officer of Interactive Club; Most Artistic Senior Yearbook Superlative; Interior Design; Graphic Design; Montgomery College

ACREE, NINA R; CAPITOL HEIGHTS, MD; CHARLES HERBERT FLOWERS HS; (JR); Hi Hnr Roll; Hnr Roll; Comm Volntr; Prom Com; Tech Clb; CR (R); UMCP-Spanish Conference; Science and Technology; Chemical Engineer; Protection Engineer; U of Maryland

ADAMS, AMY; CATONSVILLE, MD; MT DE SALES AC; (JR); Hnr Roll; Nat Hon Sy; Pres Sch; Comm Volntr; Chrch Yth Grp; Emplmnt; Vsity Clb; Sccr (J); Track (V L); Veterinary Medicine; Biology Major; Muskingum College

ADAMS, ASHLEY M; HAVRE DE GRACE, MD; ABERDEEN HS; (SO); Hnr Roll; Comm Volntr; Chrch Yth Grp; Pep Squd; Prom Com; Dnce; Chrldg (V L); Lcrsse (J); PPSqd (V); Cl Off (R); Stu Cncl (R); CR (R); Dance; Florida State; Salisbury State

ADAMS-BROWN, RYAN L; UPPER MARLBORO, MD; OXON HILL HS; (FR); Hnr Roll; Perf Att; Acpl Chr; Chr; Performs with the Washington Performing Arts Society Children of the Gospel Choir Since '98; To Become a Forensic Scientist; George Washington U

ADEKUNBI, SHEWA; BOWIE, MD; BOWIE HS; (JR); Hnr Roll; Nat Mrt LOC; WWAHSS; Comm Volntr; Peer Tut/Med; Chrch Yth Grp; DARE; Dbte Team; Emplmnt; FBLA; Pep Squd; Prom Com; Ch Chr; Dnce; Track (J); Step Team; Ladies with Class Assn.; Dentistry; Pre-Medicine; U of Maryland; Penn State U

ADENIRAN, ADEBOLA V; SALISBURY, MD; PARKSIDE HS; (SO); Hi Hnr Roll; Hnr Roll; Nat Hon Sy; Pres Sch; St of Mnth; Mth Clb/Tm; Scouts; Spanish Clb; Bnd; Dnce; Jzz Bnd; Mch Bnd; Sftball (J); Tennis (V L); Track (V L); Cl Off (V); Silver Award-Girl Scouts; Biomedical Engineering; Chemical Engineering; Carnegie Mellon U; Columbia U

ADEWOLE, OLAMIDE; CATONSVILLE, MD; CATONSVILLE HS; (JR); Hi Hnr Roll; Hnr Roll; MVP; Otst Ac Ach Awd; Perf Att; St of Mnth; Peer Tut/Med; Red Cr Aide; ArtClub; Dbte Team; FBLA; Lib Aide; SADD; French Clb; Chr; SP/M/VS; Sccr (J L); Yrbk (R); School Representative for French Poetry Contest; Made Principal's List Twice; Science; Pre-Med; U of Maryland College Park; Villa Julie College

ADKINS, MEGAN E; FREDERICK, MD; WALKERSVILLE HS; (JR); Hnr Roll; Comm Volntr; ArtClub; FTA; Mus Clb; Chr; Sch Ppr (R); Music Education; Computer Technology; U of Maryland; Mc Daniel College

ADNANI, JESSICA; OWINGS MILLS, MD; ROLAND PARK CTRY SCH; (SO); Comm Volntr; Hab For Humty Volntr; Peer Tut/Med; Mod UN; Prom Com; SADD; Tech Clb; Stg Cre; Sftball (V); Animal Rights Coalition President; Member of Mock Trial & Model UN; Law; Politics; U California Los Angeles; U California Irvine

AFRICA, BROOKE E; CORRIGANVILLE, MD; BEALL HS; (JR); Hi Hnr Roll; Hnr Roll; Nat Stu Ath Day Aw; Otst Ac Ach Awd; Perf Att; Sci Fairs; St of Mnth; WWAHSS; Comm Volntr; Chrch Yth Grp; DARE; Emplmnt; Prom Com; Vsity Clb; French Clb; Ch Chr; SP/M/VS; GAA (VJ); PP Ftbl (V); Sccr (VJCL); Sftball (J); Track (V); Vsy Clb (V); Sch Ppr (R); Employee of the Month; Minds in Motion Athlete Award; Lawyer; Psychologist; Maryland State U; North Carolina State U

AGBOKE, FADEKE; UPPER MARLBORO, MD; CHARLES HERBERT FLOWERS HS; (JR); Hi Hnr Roll; Hnr Roll; Nat Hon Sy; Otst Ac Ach Awd; Perf Att; Pres Sch; Sci Fairs; St of Mnth; Yth Ldrshp Prog; Comm Volntr; BPA; FBLA; Mus Clb; NYLC; Outdrs Clb; Quiz Bowl; Chr; Science and Technology Program; Academy of Finance; Pre-Med; Biology; Johns Hopkins U; Penn State U

AGUSTIN, REA MAE S; WALDORF, MD; OXON HS; (JR); Hnr Roll; Nat Hon Sy; Otst Ac Ach Awd; Perf Att; Sci Fairs; WWAHSS; ROTC; Cadet of the Quarter; Chief-Of-Staff of AFJROTC MD-11 Wing; Psychology; Criminology; Longwood U; State U of New York (Cortland)

AKANDE, IDIYATU; GAITHERSBURG, MD; (JR); Chr; Ch Chr; Track (J); CR (R); Lit Mag (R); Founder & President of a Club Called Women; Law / Nursing; Psychology; Princeton U; Brown U

AKINRINMADE, ADELANKE; FORT WASHINGTON, MD; OXON HILL HS; (JR); Ctznshp Aw; Fut Prb Slvr; Hi Hnr Roll; Hnr Roll; Nat Hon Sy; Perf Att; Sci Fairs; Comm Volntr; Peer Tut/Med; Biology Clb; Chrch Yth Grp; DARE; NYLC; Off Aide; Prom Com; Sci Clb; Tchrs Aide; Chr; Ch Chr; Cl Off (S); CR (R); Student of Month; Pre-Medicine; Biology; Pennsylvania State U; U of MD-Baltimore County

AKPORJI, YVONNE; WALDORF, MD; ST MARY'S RYKEN HS; (SO); F Lan Hn Soc; Hi Hnr Roll; Hnr Roll; Nat Ldrshp Svc; Nat Sci Aw; Otst Ac Ach Awd; Perf Att; CARE; Comm Volntr; Peer Tut/Med; ArtClub; Biology Clb; Cmptr Clb; Key Club; Mth Clb/Tm; Mus Clb; Sci Clb; French Clb; Bnd; Jzz Bnd; Orch; Sftball (J); Adv Cncl (R); President's Honor List; Principal's Honor List; Medical Doctor; Pediatrician (Children's Doctor); Harvard College; Yale U

ALABI, SAYODE; ELKRIDGE, MD; LONG REACH HS; (SO); Hnr Roll; Nat Mrt LOC; Otst Ac Ach Awd; Perf Att; Comm Volntr; Telecommunication Engineering; Stanford U; Syracuse U

ALBANDOZ, COLETTE; BROOKLYN, MD; (JR); Hi Hnr Roll; Hnr Roll; MVP; Perf Att; St of Mnth; Yth Ldrshp Prog; Chrch Yth Grp; Outdrs Clb; Use to Play Basketball in Jr High School; Nursing Doctor; 4-Year Degree; Easternshore College

ALBOWICZ, JOSHUA R; JOPPA, MD; JOPPATOWNE HS; (FR); Hnr Roll; Perf Att; Bsball (J); Ftball (J); Wrstlg (J); Perfect Attendance; Sports; Physics; Colorado U; Maryland U

ALLEN, AMY E; HUNTINGTOWN, MD; NORTHERN HS; (SR); Hi Hnr Roll; Hnr Roll; Nat Hon Sy; Nat Sci Aw; Otst Ac Ach Awd; Pres Sch; Sci Fairs; St Schl; WWAHSS; Yth Ldrshp Prog; Comm Volntr; Chrch Yth Grp; Emplmnt; Key Club; Mus Clb; Quill & Scroll; Svce Clb; Bnd; Chr; Ch Chr; Jzz Bnd; CR (R); Sch Ppr (R, P); Key Club President & Secretary; Tri-County Honor Band, All-County Honor Band/Chorus; Communications (Major); Political Science (Minor); Salisbury U

ALLEN, LAUREN; FORT WASHINGTON, MD; FRIENDLY HS; (SO); Hnr Roll; Nat Hon Sy; Perf Att; WWAHSS; Comm Volntr; Peer Tut/Med; Chrch Yth Grp; FTA; NYLC; ROTC; Scouts; Chr; Dnce; Sftball; Sch Ppr (R, P); Top 25 Achiever, Class of 2007; Education/English/Business; Hampton U; Spelman College

ALLEN, RONDINE; WINDSORMILL, MD; MILFORD MILL AC; (SO); Hnr Roll; Nat Hon Sy; Spec Olymp Vol; ROTC; Clr Grd; Sftball (J); MESA-Math Engineering Science Achievement; National Sojourner's Award; Nursing; Psychology; Johns Hopkins U; U Maryland Eastern Shore

ALLEN, SASHA M C; UPPER MARLBORO, MD; CHARLES HERBERT FLOWERS HS; (JR); Ctznshp Aw; Hnr Roll; Nat Hon Sy; Sci Fairs; St of Mnth; Yth Ldrshp Prog; Comm Volntr; Hosp Aide; Peer Tut/Med; Mus Clb; Bnd; Jzz Bnd; Mch Bnd; Pep Bnd; Neonatologist; Biology; U of Maryland Baltimore County; George Washington U

ALLES, JENELL; WESTMINSTER, MD; SOUTH CARROLL HS; (JR); Hnr Roll; WWAHSS; Yth Ldrshp Prog; Comm Volntr; Peer Tut/Med; Spec Olymp Vol; Emplmnt; Key Club; NYLC; Prom Com; Tchrs Aide; Chr; SP/M/VS; Fld Hky (J); PP Ftbl (J); Stu Cncl (R); CR (R); Communications, Social Services; Villa Julie; Frostburg

ALO, SAMUEL; BALTIMORE, MD; BALTIMORE CITY COLLEGE HS; (FR); Ctznshp Aw; Hnr Roll; Perf Att; Chrch Yth Grp; Mod UN; Bnd; Ch Chr; Mch Bnd; Pep Bnd; Law Attorney / Defense; Civil Engineer; Harvard U; Howard U

ALSHEIKHLY, MELODY; POTOMAC, MD; CHURCHILL HS; (MS); Hnr Roll; Comm Volntr; Peer Tut/Med; ArtClub; Drma Clb; Jr Cls League; Tchrs Aide; Tech Clb; French Clb; Chr; SP/M/VS; Bskball (L); Ice Sktg (L); Sccr (L); Swmg (L); Selective Performing Arts Academy; Selective Math/Science/Technology Academy; Film Directing/Producing; Columbia U; Stanford U

ALT, JESSICA A; WESTERNPORT, MD; WESTMAR HS; (FR); Hnr Roll; Sci Fairs; Comm Volntr; Peer Tut/Med; Dbte Team; JSA; Clr Grd; Drl Tm; SHOP (Students Helping Other People); Lawyer; Frostburg State U

ALUCULESEI, SIMONA; HAGERSTOWN, MD; NORTH HAGERSTOWN HS; (SR); Ctznshp Aw; Gov Hnr Prg; Hnr Roll; Perf Att; WWAHSS; Comm Volntr; Emplmnt; Key Club; Cl Off (R); CR (R); National Honor Club; Architectural Engineering; U of Maryland-College Park; Hagerstown Community College

AMELANG, MEGAN A; PARKVILLE, MD; LOCH RAVEN HS; (SO); Hnr Roll; Nat Hon Sy; Drma Clb; SADD; Physician; Forensic Science

AMELGA, MAKEDA; BOWIE, MD; BOWIE HS; (SO); All Am Sch; Hnr Roll; Pres Sch; Track (J); Vllyball (J); Business; History; U of Maryland College Park; Boston U

AMES, LACY R; WESTMINSTER, MD; WESTMINSTER HS; (JR); Hi Hnr Roll; Hnr Roll; Otst Ac Ach Awd; Pres Sch; WWAHSS; Peer Tut/Med; Emplmnt; Lib Aide; P to P St Amb Prg; Scouts; Law; Psychology; Villa Julie; Washington College

ANDERSON, JASMINE M; WINDSOR MILL, MD; PINE FORGE AC; (SO); Ctznshp Aw; Hi Hnr Roll; Hnr Roll; Nat Hon Sy; Otst Ac Ach Awd; Sci Fairs; St of Mnth; Valdctrian; WWAHSS; Comm Volntr; Peer Tut/Med; Chrch Yth Grp; Emplmnt; Off Aide; Quiz Bowl; Tchrs Aide; Chr; Ch Chr; SP/M/VS; Cl Off (T); Stu Cncl (R); Sign Language Choir; Graphic Engineering; Oakwood College

ANDERSON, MICHELLE K; WHITE PLAINS, MD; MAURICE J MC DONOUGH HS; (JR); Ctznshp Aw; Hi Hnr Roll; Hnr Roll; MVP; St of Mnth; WWAHSS; Comm Volntr; Chrch Yth Grp; DARE; Emplmnt; Off Aide; Outdrs Clb; Vsity Clb; Chr; SP/M/VS; Sccr (V CL); Track (V L); Wt Lftg (V); MVP in Soccer & Track; Physical and Wellness; Physical Therapist; Penn State; U of Virginia

ANDERSON III, PHILIP L; CRISFIELD, MD; CRISFIELD CHRISTIAN AC; (JR); Hnr Roll; Comm Volntr; Chrch Yth Grp; Emplmnt; SP/M/VS; Stg Cre; Bsball; Hsbk Rdg; Sccr; Psychology; High School Counselor; A & M Florida U; U of Florida

ANDERSSON, MATILDA; ANNAPOLIS, MD; BROADNECK HS; (JR); Hnr Roll; Nat Hon Sy; Comm Volntr; Peer Tut/Med; Fld Hky (V); Lcrsse (V); Pre-Med; Stanford; Middlebury

ANDREWS, LAURA; WALDORF, MD; MC DONOUGH HS; (SR); Drma Clb; Emplmnt; SP/M/VS; Stg Cre; Thespian; Associate Degree in Mortuary Science; College of Southern Maryland; Catonsville College

APUGO, SANDY C; UPPER MARLBORO, MD; FREDERICK DOUGLASS HS; (JR); Hi Hnr Roll; Nat Hon Sy; Otst Ac Ach Awd; WWAHSS; Comm Volntr; Hosp Aide; Red Cr Aide; FBLA; Tchrs Aide; Cr Ctry (V); Track (V); Secretary of Nat'l. Honor Society; Pre-Medicine (Chemistry/Biology); Accounting; Georgetown U; Columbia U

ARMITAGE, TRACEY; WESTMINSTER, MD; SOUTH CARROLL HS; (SO); Hi Hnr Roll; Nat Hon Sy; USAA; WWAHSS; 4-H; Key Club; Fld Hky; Sftball (J); Tennis (J); Track; Sch Ppr (R, P); Member of NHS, Key Club; Participate in 4-H; Communications/Journalism

ARRINGTON, DEKEBRA; HYATTSVILLE, MD; NORTHWESTERN HS; (SO); Ctznshp Aw; Hnr Roll; Sci Fairs; WWAHSS; Yth Ldrshp Prog; Comm Volntr; Peer Tut/Med; 4-H; NYLC; Scouts; Chrldg (J); Vllyball (J); Nurse Anesthetist; Johns Hopkins U; Carnegie Mellon U

ASHKIN, GRIFFIN; ROCKVILLE, MD; GEORGETOWN PREP HS; (JR); F Lan Hn Soc; Hi Hnr Roll; Nat Hon Sy; Pres Ac Ftns Aw; Yth Ldrshp Prog; Comm Volntr; Chess; Chrch Yth Grp; Emplmnt; Mth Clb/Tm; Mus Clb; Scouts; Bnd; SP/M/VS; Ftball (J); Golf (J); Swmg (C); Business; Engineering; Georgetown U; Notre Dame

ASSANAH, SAMANTHA; WINDSOR MILL, MD; BALTIMORE POLY TECH INST 403; (SO); Hnr Roll; Nat Hon Sy; Perf Att; WWAHSS; Comm Volntr; Mus Clb; Bnd; SP/M/VS; Meritorious Scholar 4 Times; Feed the Homeless During Holidays; Pediatrician; Medicine; Johns Hopkins U; Howard U

ATANGA, ROSALINE A; COLLEGE PARK, MD; HIGH POINT HS; (SO); Hnr Roll; MVP; Nat Hon Sy; Perf Att; Sci Fairs; St of Mnth; Comm Volntr; Hosp Aide; ArtClub; Chrch Yth Grp; Drma Clb; Kwanza Clb; Lib Aide; Mus Clb; Off Aide; Sci Clb; Bnd; Ch Chr; Mch Bnd; Chrldg (V); Gmnstcs (J); Lit Mag (R); Nursing; Pharmacist; Prince George's Community College

ATCHERSON, HEATHER; ANNAPOLIS, MD; BROADNECK HS; (SO); Hnr Roll; Nat Hon Sy; Otst Ac Ach Awd; Perf Att; Pres Ac Ftns Aw; WWAHSS; Chrch Yth Grp; Key Club; Scouts; Gmnstcs (V L); All-Star Cheerleading; Modeling & Pageants; Orthopedic Surgeon; Stanford U

ATHANASIOU, NIKOLAS; BALTIMORE, MD; ARCHBISHOP CURLEY HS; (SO); Lcrsse (J); Sccr (V); Speaks 2nd Language - Greek; International Business; Towson U; U of MD Baltimore Country

AUSHERMAN, JACOB R K; LAUREL, MD; ST VINCENT PALLOTTI HS; (FR); Hi Hnr Roll; Hnr Roll; Comm Volntr; Scouts; Lcrsse (J); Sccr (J); Swmg (V); Master's Degree; U of Maryland, College Park

AUSTIN, ALLYSON A; WOODSBORO, MD; WALKERSVILLE HS; (SO); Hi Hnr Roll; Comm Volntr; Emplmnt; Japanese Clb; Vllyball (V); Hood College; U of MD

AUSTIN, DOMINIQUE A; BOWIE, MD; CHARLES HERBERT FLOWERS HS; (SO); Nat Hon Sy; Chrch Yth Grp; Dnce; GAA (J); Track (V); CR; Environmental Scientists; Athletic Coach; Howard U; U of Maryland

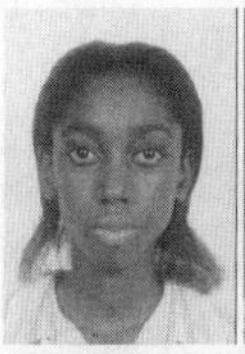
Austin, Dominique A
Charles Herbert Flowers HS
Bowie, MD

Anderson III, Philip L
Crisfield Christian AC
Crisfield, MD

Allen, Rondine
Milford Mill AC
Windsormill, MD

Akande, Idiyatu
Gaithersburg, MD

Adkins, Megan E
Walkersville HS
Frederick, MD

National
Honor Roll
Spring 2005

Adams-Brown, Ryan L
Oxon Hill HS
Upper Marlboro, MD

Allen, Lauren
Friendly HS
Fort Washington, MD

Allen, Sasha M C
Charles Herbert Flowers HS
Upper Marlboro, MD

Ashkin, Griffin
Georgetown Prep HS
Rockville, MD

Atcherson, Heather
Broadneck HS
Annapolis, MD

AWAD, AEKEAM; GWYNN OAK, MD; RANDALLSTOWN HS; (JR); Hnr Roll; Nat Hon Sy; Nat Sci Aw; Otst Ac Ach Awd; Perf Att; Sci Fairs; WWAHSS; Yth Ldrshp Prog; Comm Volntr; Peer Tut/Med; Emplmnt; SADD; Spanish Clb; Ch Chr; SP/M/VS; Stu Cncl (R); Member of National Honor Society; Member of Student Government Assn; Computer Science; Computer Engineering; U of Virginia; U of Maryland College Park

AWANI, OLAYINKA R; BALTIMORE, MD; PATAPSCO HS; (SO); Hnr Roll; Perf Att; Peer Tut/Med; Chr; Ch Chr; Pediatrician; Musician; Johns Hopkins U; U of Maryland.

AYENSU, KEVIN K; SILVER SPRING, MD; WHEATON HS; (FR); Hnr Roll; Perf Att; Tchrs Aide; Ch Chr; Ftball (J); Vllyball (J); Stu Cncl (R); Sch Ppr (R); BROTHERS; Medical Doctor; Dermatologist; U of Maryland, College Park; Howard U

AZAM, AYESHA S; GERMANTOWN, MD; POOLESVILLE HS; (JR); Hi Hnr Roll; Hnr Roll; Comm Volntr; Hosp Aide; ArtClub; Fr of Library; Outdrs Clb; Svce Clb; Spanish Clb; Stg Cre; Lit Mag (R); Child Development; Pediatrician / MD; U of Missouri Kansas City; George Washington U

BAE, CRYSTAL; LUTHERVILLE TIMONIUM, MD; DULANEY HS; (SO); Hnr Roll; Nat Hon Sy; Perf Att; WWAHSS; Comm Volntr; Peer Tut/Med; FTA; Jr Cls League; Key Club; Bnd; Dnce; Mar Art; Certamen (Latin "It's Academic"), Lancers Club; Dulanians (School Touring Club)

BAIG, KASIM; BURTONSVILLE, MD; ST VINCENT PALLOTTI HS; (FR); Hnr Roll; Ftball (J); Medicine; Law; Georgetown; Johns Hopkins

BAKER, FRANCIS J; CLINTON, MD; CROOM VOC SCH; (JR); Chrch Yth Grp; Basketball; Architecture

BALAGUER, AMY; BEL AIR, MD; BEL AIR HS; (JR); Hi Hnr Roll; Hnr Roll; Nat Hon Sy; Pres Ac Ftns Aw; St of Mnth; WWAHSS; Emplmnt; Vsity Clb; Bnd; Mch Bnd; Lcrsse (VJ L); Sccr (VJ L); Swmg (V CL); Stu Cncl (R); CR (R); St Joseph's U; Loyola College of Maryland

BALINT, EMMA; HAGERSTOWN, MD; NORTH HAGERSTOWN HS; (FR); All Am Sch; Ctznshp Aw; Hi Hnr Roll; Otst Ac Ach Awd; Pres Ac Ftns Aw; WWAHSS; Comm Volntr; Chrch Yth Grp; Emplmnt; Key Club; Pep Squd; Dnce; Chrldg (JC); GAA (J); Lcrsse (V); Skiing (V); Swmg (V); Stu Cncl (R); CR (R); Key Club, Student Govt; Lawyer; Politics; Cornell; Bucknell

BALL, SHANICKA C; TEMPLE HILLS, MD; FRIENDLY HS; (JR); Ctznshp Aw; Hnr Roll; Otst Ac Ach Awd; St of Mnth; Comm Volntr; Peer Tut/Med; Chrch Yth Grp; DARE; Scouts; Ch Chr; Sftball (J); I Take Honors Courses.; I Am A Part of the Student Leadership Committee.; I Would Like to Major in Medicine.; I Would Like to Major in Business Administration.; George Washington U; Spelman College

BALLEW, KATHLEEN; ROCKY RIDGE, MD; CATOCTIN HS; (SR); Hnr Roll; Nat Hon Sy; Comm Volntr; Chrch Yth Grp; Emplmnt; Prom Com; Svce Clb; Tchrs Aide; Fld Hky (VJ L); Maryland Distinguished Scholar - Honorable Mention; Frederick News Post 2nd Team Field Hockey All-Stars; Elementary Education; Shippensburg U

BALSAMO, JUSTIN C; WESTMINSTER, MD; WINTERS MILL HS; (SO); Ctznshp Aw; Hi Hnr Roll; Nat Hon Sy; WWAHSS; Yth Ldrshp Prog; Comm Volntr; Key Club; Chr; Dnce; SP/M/VS; Yrbk (E, R); Doctor; Dancer; New York U; Towson U

BANADDA, ANDREW; GAITHERSBURG, MD; THE BULLIS SCH; (JR); Sccr; Track; Wrstlg; Cl Off (R); Academic Achievement Faculty Selected 2003; 2004 All Interstate Athletic Conference Jr.; Sports Medicine; Duke U; U of Maryland

BANSAL, ROBIN; LAUREL, MD; LAUREL HS; (JR); Hnr Roll; Perf Att; WWAHSS; Comm Volntr; Cmptr Clb; Sccr (J); Computer Engineering; Finance; U of Maryland College Park; U of Maryland Baltimore County

BAPTISTE, RIMMEL; RIVERDALE, MD; SUITLAND HS; (FR); Ctznshp Aw; Hnr Roll; Otst Ac Ach Awd; Comm Volntr; Acpl Chr; Chr; Ch Chr; Music; Psychology; Juilliard School (NYC); Yale

BARBEE, CARLIKA L; UPPER MARLBORO, MD; KETTERING MS; Ctznshp Aw; Hnr Roll; Comm Volntr; Chrch Yth Grp; Off Aide; Ch Chr; Dnce; Entrepreneur-Sewing (Pillows & Blankets By Carlika); Volunteer-Wash. Ctr for Life Aging; Dance; Hair Stylist of Fashion Design; U of MD-Baltimore County; Towson U

BARBIERRI, CHRISTEN A; POCOMOKE CITY, MD; POCOMOKE HS; (SO); Hnr Roll; Otst Ac Ach Awd; WWAHSS; Comm Volntr; Chrch Yth Grp; Key Club; Tchrs Aide; Bnd; Mch Bnd; Fld Hky (VJCL); Sftball (J); All County Band; Band Officer; Sports Medicine; Doctor / Pediatrician; James Madison U; U of Maryland College Park

BARLOW, MATT; NOTTINGHAM, MD; CALVERT HALL HS; (SR); F Lan Hn Soc; Hnr Roll; Nat Hon Sy; Nat Mrt LOC; St Schl; Comm Volntr; Peer Tut/Med; Emplmnt; Track (J); Rugby- Letter for Sophomore & JV Years; NHS-Letter Winner / History Club; Plastic Surgeon; Oncologist; U of Maryland College Park; Gettysburg College

BARNES, KAYMARIE; GWYNN OAK, MD; THE NEW MARK OF EXCELLENCE SCH; (SO); Hnr Roll; Nat Hon Sy; Otst Ac Ach Awd; St of Mnth; Peer Tut/Med; Chrch Yth Grp; FBLA; P to P St Amb Prg; CR (P); Psychology; Business; Columbia U; Johns Hopkins U

BARNES, LATRICE; GWYNN OAK, MD; WOODLAWN HS; (FR); Hnr Roll; Nat Hon Sy; Mch Bnd; Police Officer; Doctor; Morgan State U; U of Maryland

BARRETT, AMANDA; BALTIMORE, MD; THE CATHOLIC HS OF BALTIMORE; (JR); Hnr Roll; MVP; Nat Hon Sy; WWAHSS; Comm Volntr; Bskball (V); GAA (V C); Sccr (V); Sftball (V); Sports Medicine; Physical Therapy; Towson U; Radford U

BASELEY, BRETT; THURMONT, MD; CATOCTIN HS; (FR); Hi Hnr Roll; Comm Volntr; Vsity Clb; Sccr (V); Track (V); Physics

BATES, JOHN; MECHANICSVILLE, MD; CHOPTICAN HS; (JR); Hi Hnr Roll; Nat Hon Sy; Perf Att; St of Mnth; WWAHSS; Comm Volntr; Outdrs Clb; Teen Court; Mechanical Engineering; Electrical Engineering; Louisiana State U; U of Maryland

BATTLE, MARIAH; RIVERDALE, MD; (MS); Hnr Roll; Comm Volntr; Ch Chr; Chrldg (V); Miss Maryland Pre-Teen Queen-2004-2005; Pageants & Modeling; Pediatric Doctor; Clark Atlanta U; Spelman College

BATTON, BRIGETTE; DUNDALK, MD; PATAPSCO CTR FOR THE ARTS; (SO); Perf Att; Comm Volntr; Chrch Yth Grp; Chrldg (J); Business; Cosmetology; Dundalk Community College

BAUER, SKYLAR; MOUNT AIRY, MD; SOUTH CARROLL HS; (SO); Hi Hnr Roll; Hnr Roll; Nat Hon Sy; Perf Att; WWAHSS; Comm Volntr; Drma Clb; Key Club; Tchrs Aide; Stg Cre; Bskball (JC); Sccr (VJ L); Organized "Walking for Water" Fundraiser At My School; Received Minds in Motion Award; Johns Hopkins U; York College

BAXI, JAY; SILVER SPRING, MD; SPRINGBROOK HS; (FR); Hnr Roll; Otst Ac Ach Awd; Comm Volntr; Peer Tut/Med; Chess; Cmptr Clb; DARE; Off Aide; Tchrs Aide; Tech Clb; German Clb; Bdmtn (L); Well Over Community Service Hours (60) - 284 Hours; Computer Engineer; Business Management; U of Maryland-College Park; U of Maryland-Baltimore College

BAYLISS, JENNIFER; WESTMINSTER, MD; SOUTH CARROLL HS; (SO); Hi Hnr Roll; Nat Hon Sy; WWAHSS; Comm Volntr; Drma Clb; Key Club; Chr; SP/M/VS; Volunteering with Children; Helping At Middle School; Medical School; Physician/Pediatrician

BAZEMORE, ALONZO; BALTIMORE, MD; PATTERSON HS; (JR); Ctznshp Aw; Hi Hnr Roll; Hnr Roll; St of Mnth; Comm Volntr; Emplmnt; Ftball (V); Lcrsse; I Attend Towson Gear Up Program For Over a Year.; I Am a Member of a Weightlifting Club-Bally's.; Engineering; Football; Maryland State U; Towson U

BEALL, DANIELA; COLUMBIA, MD; WILDE LAKE HS; (SO); Hi Hnr Roll; Nat Hon Sy; Perf Att; St of Mnth; Amnsty Intl; Comm Volntr; Peer Tut/Med; Chrch Yth Grp; Mth Clb/Tm; P to P St Amb Prg; Svce Clb; French Clb; Stu Cncl (R); Landscape Architecture; U of Maryland-College Park; Morgan State U

BEAN, MANTI D; GWYNN OAK, MD; WOODLAWN HS; (JR); Hnr Roll; Comm Volntr; Peer Tut/Med; Cmptr Clb; FCA; Lib Aide; Mod UN; Tchrs Aide; Lcrsse (V); Sccr (V); Howard U Participant in IASEP; All Star Attorney in MD Mock Trial; Political Science; Constitutional Law; Howard U; American U

BEARDSLEY, NICKI; UNION BRIDGE, MD; FRANCIS SCOTT KEY HS; (SO); Hi Hnr Roll; Hnr Roll; Otst Ac Ach Awd; Perf Att; Pres Sch; Comm Volntr; Spec Olymp Vol; Chrch Yth Grp; DARE; FCA; Chr; Lcrsse (JC); Sccr (JC); Wt Lftg; Adv Cncl (R); Over 500 Community Service Hrs.; Interior Design; Business-Major; Nazareth College; St. John Fisher College

BEASLEY, VICTORIA; COLUMBIA, MD; LONG BEACH HS; (SR); Hnr Roll; Nat Hon Sy; Perf Att; WWAHSS; Red Cr Aide; Spec Olymp Vol; NtlFrnscLg; NYLC; Off Aide; Tchrs Aide; Bskball (V CL); Skiing (C); Sccr (J); CR (T); Bat Ball; Robot Challenge; Engineering; Pharmacist; U of Maryland

BEATTIE, LINDSAY; HAGERSTOWN, MD; SOUTH HAGERSTOWN HS; (JR); Hi Hnr Roll; Nat Hon Sy; Prom Com; Bnd; Drm Mjr; Jzz Bnd; Mch Bnd; Cr Ctry (V L); Sftball (VJ); Stu Cncl (T); Physician's Assistant; Music; Georgia Washington U

BEATTY, AMANDA; BOWIE, MD; BOWIE HS; (MS); Hnr Roll; P to P St Amb Prg; Scouts; Bnd; Dnce; PPSqd (V); Outstanding Merit Student; Business Major; Culinary Arts Degree

BEAVER, MELANIE; BELTSVILLE, MD; HIGH POINT HS; (JR); Hi Hnr Roll; St of Mnth; WWAHSS; Comm Volntr; Emplmnt; Off Aide; Hsbk Rdg; Sch Ppr (R); Physics Club: Poetry Club; National Youth Rights Association (NYRA); Pre-Veterinarian/Veterinary Medicine; Environmental Sciences; Sweet Briar College; College Park-U of MD

BEHNKE-HANSON, HELEN; BALDWIN, MD; (SO); Hnr Roll; Nat Hon Sy; Comm Volntr; Drma Clb; Stg Cre; Track (J); Lit Mag (R); Sch Ppr (E); School Improvement Team; Journalism; Columbia U; Yale U

BELL, CRYSTAL; MONTGOMERY VILLAGE, MD; WATKINS MILL HS; (JR); Hnr Roll; Perf Att; ArtClub; Drma Clb; Scouts; Spch Team; Chr; SP/M/VS; Stg Cre; Adv Cncl (V); Congressional Recognition in Art By Congressman Wynn; Speech Team 2nd in State Duet; U of Maryland

BELL, EMILY; GAITHERSBURG, MD; NORTHWEST HS; (SR); Hnr Roll; MVP; Nat Hon Sy; Comm Volntr; Chrch Yth Grp; Prom Com; Quill & Scroll; Svce Clb; Tchrs Aide; Cr Ctry (V CL); Track (V CL); Yrbk (E, R); MVP - Indoor Track 2004-2005; Business; Fordham U

BENDU, THOMLINA A; BOWIE, MD; BOWIE HS; (SO); Hnr Roll; Sci Fairs; St of Mnth; Comm Volntr; Peer Tut/Med; Chrch Yth Grp; DARE; Fr of Library; Lib Aide; Mod UN; Scouts; Tchrs Aide; Bnd; Dnce; Lit Mag (R)

BENNETT, MARIA E; PRINCESS ANNE, MD; WASHINGTON HS; (SR); Nat Hon Sy; Otst Ac Ach Awd; St of Mnth; WWAHSS; Emplmnt; Key Club; Prom Com; Bnd; Mch Bnd; Chrldg (JC); Sftball (J); Stu Cncl; Students Helping Other People (Shop) Club; Biology-Pre-Professional; Education; Wor-Wic Community College; Salisbury U

BERGAMY, RYAN; DUNDALK, MD; DUNDALK HS; (SO); Hnr Roll; Nat Mrt LOC; Perf Att; Comm Volntr; P to P St Amb Prg; ROTC; Scouts; Chr; Forensic; U of MD; Towson State

BERGERIS, ANDREW S; SILVER SPRING, MD; PAINT BRANCH HS; Hi Hnr Roll; Hnr Roll; Nat Hon Sy; WWAHSS; Chrch Yth Grp; FCA; Tchrs Aide; Bsball (VJCL); Bskball (J); Ftball (VJCL); Wt Lftg (V); Sportsmanship Award-Football & Baseball; Aerospace/Aeronautical Engineering; Air Force Academy; Embry Riddle U

BERNEY, SARA; ROCKVILLE, MD; RICHARD MONTGOMERY HS; (JR); Hnr Roll; Nat Hon Sy; Comm Volntr; Emplmnt; Pep Squd; Tchrs Aide; Chr; Dnce; Drl Tm; Mar Art (C); PPSqd (C); Dance Awards; Shooting Star Award; International Development; Columbia U; Vanderbilt U

BERRIOS, TATIANA; HYATTSVILLE, MD; HIGH POINT HS; (FR); Comm Volntr

BERRY JR, RODELL; OWINGS, MD; NORTHERN HS; (SR); Ctznshp Aw; Hnr Roll; WWAHSS; Chrch Yth Grp; Emplmnt; FBLA; Chr; Ch Chr; Ftball (V L); Track (L); Wrstlg (V L); First Team All-County-Football; Major in Finance; Salisbury-Accepted; Pennsylvania State U-Accepted

BIELEWICZ, ANNA; GREAT MILLS, MD; ST MARY'S RYKEN HS; (SO); Hi Hnr Roll; Chrch Yth Grp; Key Club; Bnd; Ch Chr; Bskball (VJCL); Sccr (VJ L); Class of '05 Booster Club Representative; Weather Club; Meteorology; Physical Training; Virginia Tech U; Miami U (Oxford, OH)

BINDRA, SUMRITA; SILVER SPRING, MD; J H BLAKE HS; (SO); Hnr Roll; Otst Ac Ach Awd; Perf Att; St of Mnth; Yth Ldrshp Prog; Comm Volntr; Hab For Humty Volntr; ArtClub; Emplmnt; Off Aide; Svce Clb; Spch Team; Tchrs Aide; Tmpl Yth Grp; Dnce; SP/M/VS; Stg Cre; President & Founder of International Club, Elected Blood Drive Chair; Business Major; MBA; U of Maryland; American U

BINION, BERNARD; CLINTON, MD; SURRATTSVILLE HS; (SO); Hnr Roll; MVP; Chess; Chrch Yth Grp; Fr of Library; ROTC; Bnd; Ch Chr; Mch Bnd; Pep Bnd; Bskball (J); Automotive Engineering

BISHOP, ASHLEY C; POCOMOKE CITY, MD; POCOMOKE HS; (FR); Hi Hnr Roll; Hnr Roll; Perf Att; Chrch Yth Grp; Emplmnt; FCA; Scouts; Bskball (V); Sftball; Vllyball (V); CPA / Accountant; U of Maryland College Park; U Conn

BITANGO, KATHERINE; ODENTON, MD; ARUNDEL SR HS; (SO); Hnr Roll; Track (J); Business Management; Child Care; Salisbury U; Towson U

BLAMBLE, CLARISSA P; OAKLAND, MD; SOUTHERN GARRETT HS; (FR); Hnr Roll; Comm Volntr; Chrch Yth Grp; Bnd; Sccr (J); Sftball (J); Law; West Virginia U; U of Maryland

BLASZKIEWICZ, KAREN; FREDERICK, MD; GOVERNOR THOMAS JOHNSON HS; (SR); Hi Hnr Roll; Nat Hon Sy; WWAHSS; Comm Volntr; Peer Tut/Med; Scouts; Tchrs Aide; German Clb; Mch Bnd; Lit Mag (E); Sociology; History; Roanoke College

BLOCKINGER, AMBER; BROOKLYN, MD; DIGITAL HARBOR HS 416; (JR); Hnr Roll; Jr Ach; Off Aide; Tchrs Aide; CR (R); Class Award (Outstanding Student); Business Management; Lawyer; U of Baltimore; U of Maryland Baltimore Cty

BLOOD, AMANDA; ROSEDALE, MD; OVERLEA HS; (SO); Hnr Roll; Nat Hon Sy; Otst Ac Ach Awd; Pres Sch; Sci Fairs; St of Mnth; St Optmst of Yr; Comm Volntr; Peer Tut/Med; ArtClub; Chess; Drma Clb; Emplmnt; Mus Clb; Acpl Chr; Chr; SP/M/VS; Stg Cre; CR (R); Drama Club; Law; North Point U; Richmond U

Bindra, Sumrita
J H Blake HS
Silver Spring, MD

Bergamy, Ryan
Dundalk HS
Dundalk, MD

Barbee, Carlika L
Kettering MS
Upper Marlboro, MD

Ball, Shanicka C
Friendly HS
Temple Hills, MD

National
Honor Roll
Spring 2005

Ayensu, Kevin K
Wheaton HS
Silver Spring, MD

Barlow, Matt
Calvert Hall HS
Nottingham, MD

Berry Jr, Rodell
Northern HS
Owings, MD

Blaszkiewicz, Karen
Governor Thomas Johnson HS
Frederick, MD

BLUBAUGH, KEISHA; LONACONING, MD; WESTMAR HS; (FR); Hnr Roll; Sci Fairs; Peer Tut/Med; Chrch Yth Grp; DARE; FTA; Lib Aide; Ch Chr; Hsbk Rdg (J); Sccr (J); CR (R); Veterinary; U of Georgia; U of Maryland

BOBBITT, DEVIN G; CLINTON, MD; SURRATTSVILLE HS; (SR); Hnr Roll; Perf Att; WWAHSS; Comm Volntr; Hab For Humty Volntr; Chess; Cmptr Clb; Emplmnt; ROTC; Tchrs Aide; Bskball (J); Ftball (J); CR (R); Yrbk (R); Management Information Systems; Computer Science; North Carolina A & T State U; Florida A & M U

BOBBITT, MATTHEW; SMITHSBURG, MD; SMITHSBURG HS; (SO); Freshman Stars

BOGGS, COREY D; ELKRIDGE, MD; LONG BEACH HS; Hi Hnr Roll; Otst Ac Ach Awd; Perf Att; St of Mnth; WWAHSS; Yth Ldrshp Prog; Comm Volntr; Peer Tut/Med; Red Cr Aide; DARE; NYLC; Prom Com; Scouts; Acpl Chr; Chr; Ch Chr; Bskball (J); Track (VJ); Adv Cncl (T); Stu Cncl (P); CR (R); National Congressional Leader Award; Medicine; Nursing; U of North Carolina Greensboro; U of Maryland School of Nursing

BOLDEN, CALEB A; GLENN DALE, MD; ST VINCENT PALLOTTI HS; (FR); Hnr Roll; Scouts; Bnd; Ftball (J)

BOLLING, DEVIN; GWYNN OAK, MD; WOODLAWN HS; (JR); Nat Hon Sy; Chrch Yth Grp; ROTC; Scouts; Chr; Seaman Rank in JROTC; Carpentry; Architectural Design; DeVry; Norwich

BONSER, ROBERT J; OAKLAND, MD; SOUTHERN GARRETT HS; (SR); All Am Sch; Hi Hnr Roll; Hnr Roll; MVP; Nat Hon Sy; Otst Ac Ach Awd; Perf Att; St of Mnth; WWAHSS; Chess; Chrch Yth Grp; Drma Clb; Emplmnt; Lib Aide; Tchrs Aide; Chr; Ch Chr; SP/M/VS; Gmnstcs (V); Sccr; Track; Yrbk (P); MVP-Boy's Varsity Soccer; German II Student of the Year; Research Scientist; Environmental Science; Frostburg State U

BOONE, ASHLEE A; SEVERN, MD; ARUNDEL HS; (JR); Hnr Roll; MVP; WWAHSS; Yth Ldrshp Prog; Comm Volntr; Peer Tut/Med; Emplmnt; P to P St Amb Prg; Bskball (V CL); Sccr (J); CR (R); English; Sports Medicine; Howard U; Morgan State U

BOONE, EDWARD; CAPITOL HEIGHTS, MD; SUITLAND HS; (JR); Hnr Roll; Otst Ac Ach Awd; Comm Volntr; Certified as an Apprentice Plumber; Computer Engineering; Electrical / Electronic Engineering; Bowie State U; Duke U

BOROWIAK, SHANE J; EDGEWOOD, MD; EDGEWOOD HS; (SR); Hi Hnr Roll; Hnr Roll; WWAHSS; Scouts; Ftball (VJCL); Lcrsse (VJCL); 2 X Who's Who Among America High Sch Students; National Football Foundation & College Hall of Fame Scholar Athlete, NSHSS; Sciences; Medical; Towson U

BOUDREAU, TRYSHA; CROFTON, MD; ANNE ARUNDEL HS; (FR); Hnr Roll; Comm Volntr; Hab For Humty Volntr; Peer Tut/Med; DARE; FBLA; Key Club; Dnce; SP/M/VS; CR (P); Interact Club; Environmentalist / Biologist; Dancer; Florida State U; Harvard U

BOURJOLLY, WIDELYNE; HYATTSVILLE, MD; BLADENSBURG HS; (JR); Hnr Roll; Comm Volntr; Hab For Humty Volntr; Spec Olymp Vol; Chrch Yth Grp; DARE; Drma Clb; Ch Chr; CR (R); Yrbk (P); Volunteer for Parks & Recreation; Doctor; Business; Howard U College Park; Simmons College

BOWE, BREONNA; DUNDALK, MD; DUNDALK HS; (SO); Hi Hnr Roll; Perf Att; Drma Clb; Lit Mag (E); Step Squad (Stepper of Week); Anime Club; Drama & Dance; Biology; New York U; Towson U

BOWLES, ANGELA; SAINT LEONARD, MD; CALVERT HS; (FR); Hnr Roll; St of Mnth; Criminal Justice / Law Enforcement; Cosmetology; Howard U; New York U

BOWMAN, ANDRIA; BALTIMORE, MD; PATAPSCO HS; (SO); Hi Hnr Roll; Otst Ac Ach Awd; Perf Att; Chrch Yth Grp; FTA; Chr; Dnce; Chrldg (J); Gmnstcs (V); Lcrsse (J); Forensic Science; English Literature; Berkeley; U of Maryland

BOWMAN, KAMI; DUNDALK, MD; KENWOOD HS; (JR); Hnr Roll; Nat Hon Sy; Perf Att; WWAHSS; Mod UN; Tchrs Aide; Spanish Clb; Chr; Manager of JV and Varsity Football; A Part of a Tutoring Program; Become a Registered Nurse; Villa Julie; Johns Hopkins U

BOYD, MARNAY; BALTIMORE, MD; MEDIC ARTS AC; (FR); Hnr Roll; Perf Att; St of Mnth; Comm Volntr; ArtClub; Cmptr Clb; Fr of Library; Mth Clb/Tm; Outdrs Clb; Chrldg (J); Scr Kpr (J); Sftball (J); Vllyball (J); Own A Business; Yale U

BRANCH, SHAWNIECE; HAGERSTOWN, MD; NORTH HS; (JR); Ctznshp Aw; Hnr Roll; Otst Ac Ach Awd; Perf Att; Comm Volntr; Hab For Humty Volntr; Emplmnt; Dnce; Bskball (J); Sch Ppr (R); Yrbk (P); Psychology (D); Sociology (D); U of Maryland College Park; Morgan State U

BRAND, ALINA C E; SYKESVILLE, MD; CENTURY HS; (SO); DAR; Hnr Roll; Comm Volntr; Chrch Yth Grp; Emplmnt; Mus Clb; Spanish Clb; Bnd; Chr; Dnce; Orch; Arch (J); PPSqd (J); Primary Education-Teacher / English; College of Charleston; Carroll Community College, Maryland

BRANSON, TIFFANY; ABERDEEN, MD; ABERDEEN HS; (JR); Hnr Roll; Nat Hon Sy; WWAHSS; Pep Squd; Prom Com; Dnce; Chrldg (V L); Track (V L); CR (R); Dance Team Placed in Top 3 At Nat'ls; Psychology; Law; U of Georgia; U of Maryland

BRASHEARS, JESSICA; FT WASHINGTON, MD; CROSSLAND HS; (SO); Hnr Roll; Otst Ac Ach Awd; Perf Att; Sci Fairs; Peer Tut/Med; Chrch Yth Grp; Drma Clb; Fr of Library; Scouts; Tchrs Aide; Chr; Dnce; Mch Bnd; SP/M/VS; Graduating from Modeling School; NA Miss Pageant; CSI / Master's Degree; Dance; New York U; Atlanta U

BREWER, NIKKIA R; FORT WASHINGTON, MD; FRIENDLY HS; (SO); Hnr Roll; Comm Volntr; Chrch Yth Grp; Emplmnt; Pep Squd; ROTC; Scouts; Chrldg (JC); Child Psychology; Clinical Psychology; Howard U; Spelman College

BRIDGEFORTH, RANDALL K; OWINGS MILLS, MD; PIKESVILLE HS; (SO); Hnr Roll; Nat Hon Sy; Perf Att; WWAHSS; Peer Tut/Med; ArtClub; FBLA; Ftball (J); Yrbk (P); Architect; Computer Technician; New York U; UCLA

BRIGHT, JUSTIN C; BALTIMORE, MD; WESTERN SCH OF TECH; (FR); Hnr Roll; Nat Hon Sy; Perf Att; Comm Volntr; Peer Tut/Med; Ftball (J); Wt Lftg (J); Certificate of Honor; Citizenship Award; Business Administration; Dentistry; Howard U; Florida State

BRISCOE, TIERRA; TEMPLE HILLS, MD; GWYNN PARK HS; (FR); Ctznshp Aw; Hi Hnr Roll; Hnr Roll; St of Mnth; Comm Volntr; Drma Clb; Pep Squd; Scouts; Chrldg (V); Cr Ctry (V); Track (V); Cl Off (V); National Junior Honor Society; Delta Academy; Forensic Scientist; Criminologist, Cosmetologist; North Carolina State U; Christopher Newport U

BRITTINGHAM, LAFFEON I; POCOMOKE CITY, MD; POCOMOKE HS; (JR); Hnr Roll; St of Mnth; Chrch Yth Grp; Computer Programmer; Georgetown U; U of MD Eastern Shore

BRITTINGHAM JR, TROY S; WESTOVER, MD; CRISFIELD HS; (JR); Hi Hnr Roll; Hnr Roll; WWAHSS; Comm Volntr; Chrch Yth Grp; Key Club; Photog; Prom Com; Tchrs Aide; Bnd; Chr; Ch Chr; Pep Bnd; Yrbk (E, P); Key Club; Shop; Accounting, Business Management; Real Estate; Clark Atlanta U; U of Maryland College Park

BRIZUELA, TONY; BOWIE, MD; BOWIE HS; (SO); Hi Hnr Roll; Hnr Roll; Nat Hon Sy; Pres Sch; Sci Fairs; Comm Volntr; Peer Tut/Med; Chrch Yth Grp; DARE; Dbte Team; Mod UN; Tech Clb; Orch; CR (R); Church Tech - Pep Choir; Spanish Tutor; Genetic Engineering; Computer Software & Hardware; Massachusetts Institute of Technology; Maryland U

BROCIOUS, DANA; ANNAPOLIS, MD; BROADNECK HS; (JR); Hnr Roll; Nat Hon Sy; Comm Volntr; Peer Tut/Med; DARE; Emplmnt; Key Club; Photog; Scouts; Sailing Team Captain; Graphic Design; Photography / Photo Journalism; NYU; Charleston

BROCK, ANTHONIQUE; DISTRICT HEIGHTS, MD; LARGO SR HS; (JR); Ctznshp Aw; Hnr Roll; Comm Volntr; Emplmnt; ROTC; Tchrs Aide; Stu Cncl (R); Yrbk (E, R, P); Big Sister Program; Business/Finance; Temple U

BROCKINGTON, BRANDON; WINDSOR MILL, MD; WOODLAWN HS; (SO); Hi Hnr Roll; Hnr Roll; Otst Ac Ach Awd; Sci Fairs; St of Mnth; Peer Tut/Med; Cmptr Clb; Bsball (J); Ftball (J); Wrstlg (J); Cooking/Chef; Art; Maryland; Florida State

BRODE, FELICIA M; LONACONING, MD; WESTMAR HS; (FR); Hnr Roll; St of Mnth; WWAHSS; 4-H; Emplmnt; Registered Nurse; Penn State; U of Maryland

BRODSKY, RONNIE; ROCKVILLE, MD; WALTER JOHNSON HS; (JR); F Lan Hn Soc; Hnr Roll; Nat Hon Sy; Nat Mrt LOC; Sci Fairs; St Schl; Comm Volntr; Mod UN; Scouts; Tchrs Aide; Bnd; Chr; Dnce; CR (R); Lit Mag (E); 2004 AP Scholar; Earned Over 530 Student Service Learning Hours (Will Receive Certificate of Merit); President of French Honor Society; Fluent in Hebrew, Russian & English, & Semi-Fluent in French; International Relations; French Studies (Language and Literature); Psychology; U of Pennsylvania; U of Maryland, College Park

BROMWELL, ZACHARY; HAMPSTEAD, MD; LOYOLA BLAKEFIELD HS; (SR); Hi Hnr Roll; Nat Hon Sy; Perf Att; Pres Sch; Yth Ldrshp Prog; Comm Volntr; Hab For Humty Volntr; Peer Tut/Med; Emplmnt; NYLC; Scouts; SADD; Vsity Clb; Spanish Clb; Bsball (VJ L); Ftball (J); Track (VJ L); Adv Cncl (R); CR (R); Yrbk (R, P); Kairos; Business / Accounting-CPA; Loyola College

BROOKS, JANEE; UPPER MARLBORO, MD; CHARLES HERBERT FLOWERS HS; (SO); Hnr Roll; Otst Ac Ach Awd; Perf Att; Mus Clb; ROTC; Drl Tm; Track (J); Barbizon Modeling School; Nursing; Culinary Arts; U of Maryland; U of Florida

BROOKS, KANDICE C; BALTIMORE, MD; NEW ERA AC; (FR); Hi Hnr Roll; Otst Ac Ach Awd; Yth Ldrshp Prog; Comm Volntr; Chrch Yth Grp; Dbte Team; Drma Clb; Ch Chr; SP/M/VS; Stg Cre; Bskball (V); Sccr (J); CR (P); Most Reader; Most Improved Player; Teacher; Bowie State; U Maryland

BROOKS, LARRY; GWYNN OAK, MD; WOODLAWN HS; (SO); Hnr Roll; Sci/Math Olympn; Chess; Bsball (J); Wrstlg (J); Engineering; Miami

BROWN, BRANDON M; ANNAPOLIS, MD; ANNAPOLIS HS; (JR); Hnr Roll; MVP; Nat Mrt Fin; Otst Ac Ach Awd; Pres Ac Ftns Aw; Sci Fairs; WWAHSS; Comm Volntr; Peer Tut/Med; Emplmnt; Mus Clb; Photog; Bskball (J); Golf (V); Lcrsse (J); Computers; Sciences; U of North Carolina; Elon U

BROWN, ERICK J; JOPPA, MD; JOPPATOWNE HS; (SR); Hi Hnr Roll; Hnr Roll; MVP; Nat Hon Sy; Comm Volntr; Peer Tut/Med; Emplmnt; P to P St Amb Prg; Quiz Bowl; Sci Clb; Scouts; Bnd; Mch Bnd; Lcrsse (J); PP Ftbl (V); Tennis (V L); Wrstlg (V CL); Its Academic Team; Chemathon Team; Chemical/Bio Molecular Engineering; Tulane U

BROWN, JAMES R; BOWIE, MD; BOWIE HS; (FR); Ctznshp Aw; Hnr Roll; St of Mnth; Comm Volntr; Chrch Yth Grp; Off Aide; Ch Chr; Bskball (J); Intern-Congressman Albert Wynn's Office; Accounting; Sports Management; U of North Carolina; U of Maryland

BROWN, JASMINE C; ROCKVILLE, MD; WHEATON HS; (JR); Ctznshp Aw; Otst Ac Ach Awd; Comm Volntr; Key Club; Chr; Ch Chr; Dnce; SP/M/VS; Bdmtn; Chrldg; Gmnstcs; Lcrsse; Mar Art; PPSqd; Tennis; Vllyball; Key Club; Performing Arts; Chef; U of Maryland; George Town U

BROWN, KAISHA C; LAUREL, MD; LAUREL HS; (JR); Hnr Roll; WWAHSS; Comm Volntr; Chr; Sftball (J); Leaders of Promise; Piano; Accounting; Math; Spelman; Hampton U

BROWN, KIMBERLEY; BEL AIR, MD; FALLSTON HS; (SR); WWAHSS; Peer Tut/Med; Mod UN; Off Aide; Spanish Clb; Chrldg (V); Tennis (V); Vllyball (V); Cl Off (V); National Youth Leadership Forum on Medicine 2001; Communications; English; Northeastern U, Boston; U of Maryland-College Park

BROWN, KIMBERLY B; ANNAPOLIS, MD; BROADNECK HS; (SO); Hi Hnr Roll; Hnr Roll; Nat Hon Sy; Otst Ac Ach Awd; Perf Att; Pres Sch; Comm Volntr; Emplmnt; Key Club; Lib Aide; Outdrs Clb; Photog; Foreign Clb; Chr; Dnce; Carson Scholarship for 3 Years; National Piano Playing Auditions; Photographer; Graduate Degree; Princeton U; U of Virginia

BROWN, MATTHEW D; WALDORF, MD; GONZAGA COLLEGE HS; (SO); Hi Hnr Roll; Hnr Roll; Nat Hon Sy; Valdctrian; WWAHSS; Peer Tut/Med; Chess; Chrch Yth Grp; Ch Chr; US National English Merit Award; English, Law School; Engineering; Georgetown U, Harvard U; Duke U, Columbia U

BROWN, PORSHA; DISTRICT HEIGHTS, MD; ELEANOR ROOSEVELT; (FR); Hnr Roll; Hosp Aide; Spec Olymp Vol; Chr; SP/M/VS

BROWN, SHANAH; BALTIMORE, MD; DIGITAL HARBOR HS 416; (JR); Hnr Roll; Perf Att; St of Mnth; Photog; Scouts; Dnce; Nursing; Teacher; U of Maryland Eastern Shore; BCCC

BROWNE, HOLLY; ESSEX, MD; BALTIMORE LUTHERAN HS; (JR); Hi Hnr Roll; Nat Hon Sy; Nat Mrt LOC; Otst Ac Ach Awd; Perf Att; Pres Sch; Hosp Aide; Chrch Yth Grp; Drma Clb; HO'Br Yth Ldrshp; Bnd; Chr; Ch Chr; Dnce; Bskball (J); Vllyball (JC); Cl Off (P); CR (R); Kodak Young Leader's Award; High Performance Award on National Latin Exam; Pre-Med; Loyola College Maryland; Villa Julie College

BROWN JR, VON; WALDORF, MD; GRACE BRETHREN CHRISTIAN SCH; (JR); Hi Hnr Roll; Hnr Roll; MVP; Valdctrian; Comm Volntr; Chrch Yth Grp; Prom Com; Stg Cre; Bsball (V); Bskball (VJ); Cl Off (P); Criminal Justice; Pre-Law; Stanford U; U of California-Los Angeles

BROWNLEE, ERICKA D; UPPER MARLBORO, MD; BOWIE HS; (JR); Ctznshp Aw; Hi Hnr Roll; Hnr Roll; WWAHSS; Comm Volntr; Chrch Yth Grp; Emplmnt; Mod UN; Chr; Ch Chr; Track (V); Cl Off (V); Homecoming Court Princess 2004-2005; 1st Place Essay Contest-Kappa Alpha Psi Fraternity; Business Admin/Marketing; Law

BRUNO, EMILY; BOWIE, MD; BOWIE HS; (JR); Hnr Roll; Sci Fairs; St of Mnth; WWAHSS; Peer Tut/Med; Emplmnt; Tchrs Aide; Foreign Languages; International Affairs; U of Connecticut; SUNY Binghamton

BRYANT, AISHA; FORT WASHINGTON, MD; FRIENDLY HS; (JR); Hnr Roll; Otst Ac Ach Awd; Sci Fairs; WWAHSS; Peer Tut/Med; Prom Com; ROTC; Gmnstcs; Sftball (V); CR (R); Step Team Member; National Technical Honor Society Member; Computer Science; Computer Information Systems; U of Maryland College Park; Spelman College

BRYANT, BLAIRE; UPPER MARLBORO, MD; CHARLES HERBERT FLOWERS HS; (JR); Hnr Roll; Sci Fairs; WWAHSS; Comm Volntr; Chrch Yth Grp; Emplmnt; Ch Chr; Dnce; Science and Technology Program; PhD; Pre-Med

BRYANT, BRITTANY; SILVER SPRING, MD; WHEATON HS; (FR); Ctznshp Aw; Hnr Roll; Otst Ac Ach Awd; Comm Volntr; Chrch Yth Grp; Scouts; Chr; Ch Chr; Chrldg (J); Argyle Eagle Award; African American Academic of Achievement; Engineering/Education; Fashion Designer; Spelman College; Clark Atlanta U

Brown Jr, Von
Grace Brethren Christian Sch
Waldorf, MD

Brown, Kaisha C
Laurel HS
Laurel, MD

Bryant, Brittany
Wheaton HS
Silver Spring, MD

Brown, James R
Bowie HS
Bowie, MD

Brooks, Janee
Charles Herbert Flowers HS
Upper Marlboro, MD

Briscoe, Tierra
Gwynn Park HS
Temple Hills, MD

Brashears, Jessica
Crossland HS
Ft Washington, MD

Brand, Alina C E
Century HS
Sykesville, MD

Borowiak, Shane J
Edgewood HS
Edgewood, MD

Boudreau, Trysha
Anne Arundel HS
Crofton, MD

Brewer, Nikkia R
Friendly HS
Fort Washington, MD

Brock, Anthonique
Largo SR HS
District Heights, MD

Brooks, Larry
Woodlawn HS
Gwynn Oak, MD

Brown, Erick J
Joppatowne HS
Joppa, MD

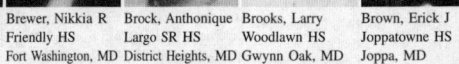

BRYANT, MARCUS; UPPER MARLBORO, MD; OXON HILL HS; (FR); Ctznshp Aw; Hnr Roll; Nat Hon Sy; Perf Att; St of Mnth; Chrch Yth Grp; Lib Aide; Prom Com; ROTC; Scouts; Bskball (J); National Junior Honor Society; AFJROTC Cadet of the Year; Criminal Justice; Automobile Mechanics; U of North Carolina-Chapel Hill; Howard U

BUCHHOLZ JR, WILLIAM R; PRINCESS ANNE, MD; WASHINGTON HS; (SR); Gov Hnr Prg; Nat Hon Sy; Nat Mrt LOC; St of Mnth; Ftball (V CL); Wt Lftg (V); Computer Repair; Computer Programming; Wor-Wic Community College; Salisbury U

BUCK, KELLY; SALISBURY, MD; JAMES M BENNETT HS; (SO); DAR; F Lan Hn Soc; Hnr Roll; Nat Hon Sy; Otst Ac Ach Awd; Perf Att; St of Mnth; Hab For Humty Volntr; Chrch Yth Grp; Emplmnt; Mth Clb/Tm; MuAlphaTh; Scouts; Spanish Clb; Bnd; Dnce; SP/M/VS; Lcrsse (V L); Sccr (J); Cl Off (T); Stu Cncl (S); CR (R); Rock N' Roll Revival; Pre-Med; Architecture; U of Texas Austin; Rice U

BUCK, RYAN J; SALISBURY, MD; JAMES M BENNETT HS; (SO); Hnr Roll; Nat Hon Sy; St of Mnth; Emplmnt; Mth Clb/Tm; MuAlphaTh; Bnd; Chr; Bsball (J); Golf (V); Certified Scuba Diver; Red Cross Certified Lifeguard; Science/Medicine; Law

BUDZENSKI, DANIEL; CALIFORNIA, MD; ST MARY'S RYKEN HS; (JR); Hi Hnr Roll; Nat Hon Sy; WWAHSS; FBLA; Jr Cls League; Key Club; Jzz Bnd; Tennis (J); Track (J L); Wrstlg (V L); Aeronautical/Aerospace Engineering

BUKOWSKI, ANNIE; ANNAPOLIS, MD; ANNAPOLIS HS; (FR); Hi Hnr Roll; Hnr Roll; Perf Att; Pres Ac Ftns Aw; Pres Sch; St of Mnth; Comm Volntr; Peer Tut/Med; Emplmnt; Mth Clb/Tm; ROTC; Svce Clb; Bnd; Drl Tm; Flg Crps; Mch Bnd; Swmg (V); Track (J); Vllyball (J); Cl Off (T); Member of a Crew / Rowing Team; Intelligence Field

BULLARD, BRIAN L; MECHANICSVLLE, MD; CHOPTICAN HS; (FR); Hnr Roll; Otst Ac Ach Awd; Computer Programming; ITT Tech

BUNCH, AMBER; WALKERSVILLE, MD; WALKERSVILLE HS; (FR); Ctznshp Aw; Hnr Roll; Emplmnt; Photog; Scouts; Chr; Play GVAA Soccer from Ages 9-18; Psychology; Journalism; U of Maryland; Penn State

BURCH, CORINNE J; DISTRICT HEIGHTS, MD; KETTERING MS; (MS); Ctznshp Aw; Hi Hnr Roll; Hnr Roll; Otst Ac Ach Awd; Sci Fairs; Peer Tut/Med; Drma Clb; CR (P); National Junior Honor Society; Veterinary Medicine; Animation; St. Joseph's Catholic U; New York U

BURNS, JENNA M; SMITHSBURG, MD; SMITHSBURG HS; (SO); Ctznshp Aw; Hi Hnr Roll; Hnr Roll; Perf Att; WWAHSS; Comm Volntr; Chrch Yth Grp; Latin Clb; Bnd; Mch Bnd; Bskball (J); Sccr (V); Track (V); Frostburg U; York College Pennsylvania

BURTON, NATASHIA; DISTRICT HEIGHTS, MD; LARGO HS; (FR); Hnr Roll; Otst Ac Ach Awd; ROTC; Chr; Dnce; Singer / Actress; Poet; Bowie State U; Morgan State U

BUSHROD, BRANDON; GWYNN OAK, MD; CARDINAL GIBBONS HS; (JR); Nat Hon Sy; Perf Att; Comm Volntr; Emplmnt; Bsball (V); Bskball (V); Ftball (V); Wt Lftg (V); Stu Cncl; Perfect Attendance; Computer Programmer; Seton Hall U; Capital College

BUSKIRK, DAVID, FROSTBURG, MD; BEALL HS; (SR); Hnr Roll; WWAHSS; Comm Volntr; Emplmnt; FTA; Tchrs Aide; SP/M/VS; Tennis (J); Cl Off (T); Winning Treasurer All Four Years/Girl's Basketball Manager; The Lead of Julius Caesar; Elementary Education; Frostburg State U

BUSLER, CHELSEA D; DUNKIRK, MD; NORTHERN HS; (FR); Hi Hnr Roll; Hnr Roll; Comm Volntr; Chrch Yth Grp; Bnd; Ch Chr; Dnce; Chrldg (J); Forensic Science; Psychiatry; U of Pittsburgh; Loyola U

BUTLER, DAVID B; HYATTSVILLE, MD; DUVAL HS; (SO); Ctznshp Aw; Hi Hnr Roll; Hnr Roll; MVP; Otst Ac Ach Awd; Perf Att; Yth Ldrshp Prog; Peer Tut/Med; DARE; Drma Clb; Vsity Clb; SP/M/VS; Bskball (V); Ftball (V); Sports Medicine; Business; Florida State U; U of Miami

BUTLER, LAUREN A; POCOMOKE CITY, MD; POCOMOKE HS; (SO); Hi Hnr Roll; St of Mnth; WWAHSS; Chrch Yth Grp; Bnd; Mch Bnd; Fld Hky (V L); Sftball (J); Physical Therapy / Sports Medicine

BYRD, MEGAN; JARRETTSVILLE, MD; NORTH HARFORD HS; (SR); Hi Hnr Roll; Hnr Roll; Otst Ac Ach Awd; Perf Att; St of Mnth; ArtClub; Chrch Yth Grp; Drma Clb; Prom Com; Tchrs Aide; Lcrsse (JC); PP Ftbl (V); Sccr (J); Track (V); Adv Cncl (R); Cl Off (R); Sch Ppr (E); Varsity Bowling; School Play; Broadcast Journalism; Mass Communications; Salisbury U

BYRON, ANTONIA; BALTIMORE, MD; PATTERSON HS; (JR); Perf Att; Peer Tut/Med; Dbte Team; Mus Clb; Scouts; Chr; Dnce; Traveling Nurse; York College; Morgan State U

CALANDRELLE, TONI; HAGERSTOWN, MD; NORTH HAGERSTOWN HS; (JR); Hi Hnr Roll; Hnr Roll; Nat Hon Sy; WWAHSS; Comm Volntr; Peer Tut/Med; Red Cr Aide; Chrch Yth Grp; DARE; Mus Clb; Prom Com; Acpl Chr; Chr; SP/M/VS; Chrldg (VJ L); Stu Cncl (R); Journalism; Communications

CALHOUN, MARISSA; UPPER MARLBORO, MD; SUITLAND HS; (SO); Ctznshp Aw; Hi Hnr Roll; Hnr Roll; Nat Hon Sy; Nat Ldrshp Svc; Otst Ac Ach Awd; Pres Ac Ftns Aw; Pres Sch; Yth Ldrshp Prog; Comm Volntr; Peer Tut/Med; DARE; Emplmnt; Scouts; SADD; SP/M/VS; Stg Cre; Bskball; Ftball; Track; Wrstlg; Adv Cncl (P); Cl Off (S); Stu Cncl (R); CR (P); Started a Modeling Team That Raised Scholarship Money for Student; MBA / Master's Degree in Business; MFA - Film / Television Production; Florida State U; U of Southern California

CALLAHAN, BRANDON; BOWIE, MD; BOWIE HS; (FR); Hnr Roll; Otst Ac Ach Awd; Sci Fairs; Comm Volntr; Chess; Chrch Yth Grp; Lib Aide; Bnd; Chr; SP/M/VS; 1st Degree Black Belt - 2005; Electronic Technology; U of Maryland

CANEDY, RONALD M; SILVER SPRING, MD; PAINT BRANCH HS; (JR); WWAHSS; Comm Volntr; Chrch Yth Grp; Emplmnt; Photog; Scouts; Chr; Ch Chr; Jzz Bnd; Swg Chr; Wt Lftg (J); Music; Engineering; Hampton U; North Carolina A & T U

CANIGLIA, CHRISTOPHER J; WALDORF, MD; THOMAS STONE HS; (SR); All Am Sch; Ctznshp Aw; Hi Hnr Roll; Nat Hon Sy; Nat Mrt LOC; Otst Ac Ach Awd; Sci Fairs; St Schl; Valdctrian; WWAHSS; Comm Volntr; Key Club; NYLC; Tchrs Aide; Bnd; Hsbk Rdg (V C); Sccr (JC); Tennis (V C); Adv Cncl (R); Stu Cncl (R); Yrbk (R); Student Member Charles County Board of Ed; Student Member Maryland State Board of Ed; Pre-Veterinary & Equine Studies; Veterinary Science; Bridgewater College

CANNON, BRANDY R; PRINCESS ANNE, MD; WASHINGTON HS; (SR); Hi Hnr Roll; Nat Hon Sy; Otst Ac Ach Awd; St Schl; WWAHSS; Comm Volntr; Chrch Yth Grp; FBLA; Key Club; Prom Com; Bnd; Jzz Bnd; Mch Bnd; Pep Bnd; Sftball (VJCL); Cl Off (R); Stu Cncl (V); Yrbk (R); Envirothon Team; First Chair Clarinet; Pre-Law; Music; Villa Julie College

CANNON, MEGAN L; WALDORF, MD; MC DONOUGH HS; (SO); Ctznshp Aw; Hi Hnr Roll; Hnr Roll; Otst Ac Ach Awd; Perf Att; Sci Fairs; Chrldg (VJCL); CR (R); Most Spirited Award - Cheerleading; Academic Letter - 9th Grade 2004; Nursing Major; Teaching / Working with Children; U North Carolina; U of Maryland

CAOUETTE, COLLEEN; CALIFORNIA, MD; ST MARY'S RYKEN HS; (JR); Hi Hnr Roll; Hnr Roll; MVP; Comm Volntr; Hosp Aide; Key Club; Lttrmn Clb; Sci Clb; Bnd; Bskball (VJ L); Sccr (VJCL); Track (V L); Letter of Appreciation from US Navy for Community Service; Environmental Science; Environmental Studies; Warren Wilson College; Brevard College

CARDER, MADISON S; WESTERNPORT, MD; WESTMAR HS; (FR); Ctznshp Aw; Hnr Roll; St of Mnth; Dbte Team; Art-Awards; Orthopedic Surgeon

CARKHUFF, ASHTON; MECHANICSVILLE, MD; ST MARY'S RYKEN HS; (JR); Hnr Roll; Pres Ac Ftns Aw; Comm Volntr; FBLA; P to P St Amb Prg; French Clb; Sftball (J); Sailing Team - V; Rowing Crew - J; International Diplomacy; Foreign Affairs; Schiller International U

CARNIE, ANDREA V; BETHESDA, MD; WALT WHITMAN; (SO); Hnr Roll; Emplmnt; Bnd; Mch Bnd; Sccr (VJ); Vllyball (JC); 1st Chair Award (Flute); Straight "A" Report; Biology; Chemistry; Georgetown U; Amherst College

CARR, JAMES B; UPPER MARLBORO, MD; ST MARY'S RYKEN HS; (JR); Hnr Roll; MVP; Nat Hon Sy; Comm Volntr; FBLA; Cr Ctry (V CL); Track (V L); Scholastic Achievement (Algebra 2 & Old Testament); Future Award (FBLA); Biology; JLD; U of Maryland (Baltimore Campus); Drexel U

CARTER, ASHLEY L; CLINTON, MD; OXON HILL HS; (FR); Hnr Roll; Sci Fairs; Chrch Yth Grp; Center for Talented Youth Program; Hall of Fame At Stephen Decatur Middle School; Dentistry; Pediatrics; Howard U; North Carolina A & T.

CARTER, DARREN; BELTSVILLE, MD; HIGH POINT HS; (JR); Hnr Roll; MVP; Perf Att; Ftball (VJCL); Track (V C); Sports/Business Management; Aeronautical Engineering; Morgan State U

CARTER, KIA; BUSHWOOD, MD; CHOPTICAN HS; (JR); Hnr Roll; St of Mnth; Spec Olymp Vol; FBLA; ROTC; Chr; SP/M/VS; Fashion Merchandising; Fashion Design; U of Maryland Eastern Shore; Radford U

CARTER, LAUREN E; JOPPA, MD; JOPPATOWNE HS; (FR); Hi Hnr Roll; Hnr Roll; WWAHSS; Red Cr Aide; Spch Team; Orch; SP/M/VS; Lcrsse (J); Sccr (J); Cl Off (P); Stu Cncl (R); Leo Club Member; Best All-Around Award - JV Lacrosse; Writer; English Major

CARTER, MECHALE T; HYATTSVILLE, MD; ELEANOR ROOSEVELT HS; (JR); All Am Sch; Hnr Roll; Nat Hon Sy; Peer Tut/Med; Chrch Yth Grp; Emplmnt; Tchrs Aide; Ch Chr; Bskball (J); PP Ftbl (V C); Scr Kpr (VJ); CR (R); Yrbk (E, R, P); Human Resources Management; Business Management; UNC Chapel Hill; U of Maryland College Park

CASTRENCE, FIDEL; WALDORF, MD; WESTLAKE HS; (FR); Bskball; Fine Arts

CATLETTE, MICHAEL; GLEN BURNIE, MD; GLEN BURNIE SR HS; (SO); Ctznshp Aw; Hi Hnr Roll; Hnr Roll; Otst Ac Ach Awd; Perf Att; St of Mnth; Yth Ldrshp Prog; CARE; Comm Volntr; Red Cr Aide; Chess; Chrch Yth Grp; DARE; Drma Clb; Fr of Library; Mus Clb; Outdrs Clb; SADD; Acpl Chr; Bnd; Chr; Ch Chr; Lcrsse (J); Track (J); CR (R); Music Major; Business and Administration; Howard U; Morgan State U

CAUDLE, ERICKA M; LEXINGTON PK, MD; GREAT MILLS HS; (SR); Hi Hnr Roll; Nat Hon Sy; Otst Ac Ach Awd; Chrch Yth Grp; Emplmnt; FTA; Tchrs Aide; Yrbk (E); Young Life; Wyldlife; Special Education; Early Childhood Education; Towson U

CAZARES, GABRIEL; BOWIE, MD; BOWIE HS; (SO); Hi Hnr Roll; Hnr Roll; MVP; Nat Hon Sy; Nat Ldrshp Svc; Yth Ldrshp Prog; Comm Volntr; Hosp Aide; Emplmnt; Ftball (V); Anthropology; Psychology; U of Maryland College Park; Arizona State U

CERDA, GERARDO; HAGERSTOWN, MD; SOUTH HAGERSTOWN HS; (JR); Hi Hnr Roll; Hnr Roll; Perf Att; Comm Volntr; FCA; Prom Com; Scouts; Spanish Clb; Bskball (V); Member of FCA; Teacher; Sports Broadcaster

CHASE, ASHLEY T; LAUREL, MD; ST VINCENT PALLOTTI HS; (MS); Ctznshp Aw; Hnr Roll; Otst Ac Ach Awd; Pres Sch; St of Mnth; Comm Volntr; Peer Tut/Med; Chrch Yth Grp; Mth Clb/Tm; Vsity Clb; Chr; Ch Chr; Dnce; Chrldg; GAA; Gmnstcs; Mar Art; Sccr; Stu Cncl (V); Yrbk (R); State Finalist Miss MD Junior / Teen Program; US National Martial Arts Team; Medical Field; Law; Spelman College; Howard U

CHAU, TERENCE; CLARKSVILLE, MD; ATHOLTON HS; (FR); Hnr Roll; Perf Att; Sci/Math Olympn; St of Mnth; Chess; DARE; Tech Clb; Psychologist; Computer Science; U of Maryland; Johns Hopkins U

CHEN, JENNIFER; ROCKVILLE, MD; ROCKVILLE HS; (JR); Hnr Roll; Sci Fairs; Yth Ldrshp Prog; Comm Volntr; Emplmnt; Prom Com; Quill & Scroll; Vsity Clb; Vllyball (VJ); Adv Cncl (T); Cl Off (P, S, T); Stu Cncl (R); CR (R); Sch Ppr (E); Communications / Graphic Design; Marketing; Carnegie Mellon U; U of Maryland College Park

CHENG, VANESSA; PARKVILLE, MD; PERRY HALL HS; (SO); Hnr Roll; Perf Att; Sci Fairs; St of Mnth; Comm Volntr; ArtClub; Biology Clb; Cmptr Clb; DARE; Orch; Tennis (V); Track (V); Sch Ppr (E); Columbia U

CHERRY, KHIAL D; BOWIE, MD; BOWIE HS; (FR); Hnr Roll; Chrch Yth Grp; Law; Psychology; U of Maryland; Towson State U

CHESLEY, TIA D; BALTIMORE, MD; BALTIMORE POLY TECH INST 403; (SO); Ctznshp Aw; Hi Hnr Roll; Jr Mshl; Nat Mrt LOC; Otst Ac Ach Awd; Valdctrian; Yth Ldrshp Prog; Comm Volntr; Peer Tut/Med; Chrch Yth Grp; Drma Clb; Quiz Bowl; Clb; Dnce; SP/M/VS; Gmnstcs (J); Math Award; Science Award; Medical Major / Pediatrics; Howard U; U MD College Park

CHESNICK, KELLY; BOWIE, MD; ARCHBISHOP SPALDING; (JR); Hi Hnr Roll; Hnr Roll; Nat Hon Sy; Perf Att; Yth Ldrshp Prog; Comm Volntr; Peer Tut/Med; Emplmnt; CR

CHI, ANDREW; ELLICOTT CITY, MD; WILDE LAKE HS; (JR); Duke TS; Hnr Roll; Perf Att; St of Mnth; Comm Volntr; Peer Tut/Med; Chrch Yth Grp; Emplmnt; FCA; Key Club; Ch Chr; Orch; Emergency Medical Tech; Pre-Medicine; Pre-Law; Baylor U

CHIALASTRI, VALERIE; BELTSVILLE, MD; HIGH POINT HS; (SR); Hnr Roll; Sci Fairs; Peer Tut/Med; Drma Clb; Emplmnt; Tchrs Aide; SP/M/VS; Cr Ctry (J); Sftball (J); Kennedy Center Singer; County Choir; Drama; U of Maryland, College Park; Salisbury U

CHILCOAT, MOLLY; COLUMBIA, MD; OAKLAND MILLS HS; (JR); Hnr Roll; Nat Hon Sy; Sci Fairs; St of Mnth; Yth Ldrshp Prog; Dnce; Fld Hky (J); Sftball (V L); Vllyball (V L); Academic Letter, National Honor Society; Physical Therapy

CHILDRESS, CRYSTAL M; OXON HILL, MD; ARCHBISHOP CARROLL HS; (JR); Hnr Roll; Otst Ac Ach Awd; WWAHSS; Comm Volntr; Peer Tut/Med; FBLA; Chr; SP/M/VS; Bskball (J); Vllyball (VJ); Rising To Glory; Master's Degree; Law Degree; Brown U; Spelman College

CHIN, ALEX; BOWIE, MD; BOWIE HS; (FR); Hnr Roll; Otst Ac Ach Awd; Sccr (J); Engineering; Maryland State U

CHO, MARISSA C; HAGERSTOWN, MD; NORTH HAGERSTOWN HS; (SR); Hnr Roll; Nat Hon Sy; Perf Att; Pres Ac Ftns Aw; Sci Fairs; WWAHSS; Comm Volntr; Peer Tut/Med; ArtClub; Chrch Yth Grp; Emplmnt; Key Club; Lttrmn Clb; Prom Com; Vsity Clb; Chr; Clr Grd; SP/M/VS; Tennis (V CL); Vllyball (J); Stu Cncl (R); CR (R); Senior Night Committee; Published Poet

CHONG, JESSICA; ROCKVILLE, MD; ROCKVILLE HS; (JR); Hnr Roll; Sci Fairs; Peer Tut/Med; Red Cr Aide; Chrch Yth Grp; Emplmnt; Jr Ach; Prom Com; Quill & Scroll; Vsity Clb; Bnd; Dnce; Mch Bnd; Lcrsse (V L); Tennis (V L); Adv Cncl (R); Stu Cncl (S); Sch Ppr (E, R); Spirit and Rededication Committee; Chief of Staff Student Council; Business Communications; Journalism or Law; U of Maryland College Park; U of Maryland Baltimore County

Chesley, Tia D
Baltimore Poly Tech Inst 403
Baltimore, MD

Cannon, Megan L
Mc Donough HS
Waldorf, MD

Calhoun, Marissa
Suitland HS
Upper Marlboro, MD

Bushrod, Brandon
Cardinal Gibbons HS
Gwynn Oak, MD

Busler, Chelsea D
Northern HS
Dunkirk, MD

Carter, Mechale T
Eleanor Roosevelt HS
Hyattsville, MD

Chi, Andrew
Wilde Lake HS
Ellicott City, MD

CHONG, KEZIAH; GAITHERSBURG, MD; WOOTTON HS; (JR); Hnr Roll; Perf Att; WWAHSS; Comm Volntr; Key Club; Business/Economics; Psychology

CHOU, DANIEL; ROCKVILLE, MD; ROCKVILLE HS; (SR); Hnr Roll; MVP; Nat Hon Sy; Nat Mrt LOC; Pres Sch; St of Mnth; WWAHSS; Comm Volntr; Peer Tut/Med; Chrch Yth Grp; Quill & Scroll; Ch Chr; Orch; Track (V); Vllyball (V CL); Sch Ppr (E); Maryland High School Journalist of the Year; City of Rockville Martin Luther King Youth Award; Print Journalism; U of Southern California

CHURCHEY, DESIRAE M; SHARPSBURG, MD; FAITH CHRISTIAN AC; (FR); Sci Fairs; Yrbk (E)

CLARK, ELISIA M; UPPER MARLBORO, MD; CHARLES HERBERT FLOWERS HS; (FR); All Am Sch; Hnr Roll; Nat Hon Sy; Otst Ac Ach Awd; Perf Att; Pres Sch; Comm Volntr; Chrch Yth Grp; Emplmnt; Scouts; Chr; Dnce; Chrldg (JC); Stu Cncl; Swimming / Dance; Psychology; Medicine; Spelman College; Hampton U

CLAYE, EMMA J; BELTSVILLE, MD; ELEANOR ROOSEVELT HS; (SO); Ctznshp Aw; Hnr Roll; Comm Volntr; Peer Tut/Med; Chr; Dnce; Accepted in Science/Technology Program At Roosevelt; Black Saga Champion (Former); Child Psychologist; Performing Arts (Dance/Drama); Marymount Manhattan College; York College

CLEVELAND, RASHAD D; UPPER MARLBORO, MD; CHARLES HERBERT FLOWERS HS; (FR); Ctznshp Aw; Hnr Roll; Otst Ac Ach Awd; Perf Att; Pres Sch; Comm Volntr; Chrch Yth Grp; Ch Chr; Ftball (J); President's Academic Award; CEO of Kings & Queens Mentoring / Enrichment Program; Computer Engineering / Software; Computer Programmer / Hardware; Michigan Institute of Technology; U of Maryland

COCHRAN, CORTNEY E; WESTMINSTER, MD; WINTERS MILL HS; (SO); Hi Hnr Roll; Hnr Roll; Kwnis Aw; Nat Hon Sy; Otst Ac Ach Awd; Perf Att; St of Mnth; WWAHSS; Comm Volntr; Peer Tut/Med; Chrch Yth Grp; Emplmnt; FCA; Key Club; Chr; Ch Chr; Lcrsse (J); Scr Kpr (J); Gospel Choir; English Teacher; Special Education Teacher; Mc Daniel College; Maryland U

COE, BRITTANY; GERMANTOWN, MD; NORTHWEST HS; (JR); Hi Hnr Roll; Hnr Roll; Emplmnt; Scouts; Tchrs Aide; Cr Ctry (VJ); Yrbk (P); I Plan to Be a Homicide Detective; I Will Major in Criminal Justice; RIT; Albany U

COFFEE, SHENEIR; BALTIMORE, MD; BALTIMORE POLY TECH INST 403; (JR); Ctznshp Aw; Hi Hnr Roll; Hnr Roll; Nat Mrt LOC; Otst Ac Ach Awd; Perf Att; Comm Volntr; Peer Tut/Med; Emplmnt; Lib Aide; Mth Clb/Tm; NYLC; Off Aide; Tchrs Aide; Ch Chr; Dnce; Mch Bnd; PP Ftbl (J); Cl Off (R); CR (R); Pre-Med; Nursing; Johns Hopkins U; U of Maryland

COLEMAN, BRYAN; FORT WASHINGTON, MD; FRIENDLY HS; (SO); F Lan Hn Soc; Hi Hnr Roll; Hnr Roll; Nat Hon Sy; Otst Ac Ach Awd; St of Mnth; Yth Ldrshp Prog; Comm Volntr; Peer Tut/Med; HO'Br Yth Ldrshp; French Clb; Drl Tm; Ftball (J); Wt Lftg (V); CR (R); Principal's Award; National Academy Achievement Award; Lawyer Studies; Medical Field; Morehouse College; U Pennsylvania

COLEMAN, TREASURE C; RANDALLSTOWN, MD; RANDALLSTOWN HS; (JR); F Lan Hn Soc; Hnr Roll; Sci Fairs; Chrch Yth Grp; Emplmnt; Chr; Track (J); Doctor; Forensic Science; U of Maryland Baltimore County; Drexel U

COLLADO, STEPHANIE; MOUNT RAINIER, MD; ARCHBISHOP CARROLL HS; (JR); Hnr Roll; Comm Volntr; Peer Tut/Med; Emplmnt; Photog; SP/M/VS; Lcrsse (J); Scr Kpr (V); Sccr (J); Wt Lftg (J); Have My Own Fashion Magazine; St John's U; New York U

COLLETON, AYNE-KA; SILVER SPRING, MD; JOHN F KENNEDY HS; (JR); Ctznshp Aw; Hnr Roll; St of Mnth; WWAHSS; Comm Volntr; Peer Tut/Med; Chrch Yth Grp; Off Aide; Outdrs Clb; ROTC; Tchrs Aide; Clr Grd; Drl Tm; Bskball (J); Sccr (J); Sftball (V C); Psychology; Northwestern U; Washington U of St Louis

COLLIFLOWER, BRITTNEY M; CHESAPEAKE BEACH, MD; NORTHERN HS; MS; Hnr Roll; MVP; Emplmnt; Mus Clb; Off Aide; Chr; Chrldg; Sftball; Academic Excellence Award for Both Math & Science 2004-2005; All County Honor Chorus Member & Tri-County Honor Chorus Mentor; Trauma Physician; Medical Forensics; U of Maryland

COLLINS, JESSICA; CLINTON, MD; BISHOP MC NAMARA HS; (FR); Hi Hnr Roll; Sci Fairs; Red Cr Aide; Scouts; Dnce; Swmg (V L); CR; Girl Scout Leadership Award; Silver Award; Business; Fashion Design

COLLINS, PORSCHE; SILVER SPRING, MD; ARCHBISHOP CARROLL HS; (JR); MVP; WWAHSS; Yth Ldrshp Prog; Comm Volntr; Peer Tut/Med; ArtClub; DARE; Emplmnt; Prom Com; SP/M/VS; Stg Cre; Bskball (JC); Sccr (V); Cl Off (V); Sch Ppr (R); Journalism; Business; U of Georgia; Tuskegee U

COLLINS, TANISHA; DISTRICT HEIGHTS, MD; SUITLAND HS; (JR); Hnr Roll; MVP; Otst Ac Ach Awd; St of Mnth; Yth Ldrshp Prog; Comm Volntr; DARE; Emplmnt; Fr of Library; Mod UN; NYLC; Tchrs Aide; Chr; Dnce; SP/M/VS; CR (R); Yrbk (P); Dance/BASU; Model/PASC; Business; Child Development; Carnegie Mellon U; Morgan U

COMBS, RORY B; SEVERNA PARK, MD; SEVERNA PARK HS; (SR); Hnr Roll; Perf Att; WWAHSS; Chrch Yth Grp; Emplmnt; Key Club; Scouts; Key Club; Boy Scouts; Pre-Med; Anne Arundel Community College

COMPTON, KRYSTLE C; CLINTON, MD; SURRATTSVILLE HS; (SO); Hnr Roll; Otst Ac Ach Awd; Sci Fairs; St of Mnth; Comm Volntr; ROTC; Bnd; Mch Bnd; Bskball (J); Sftball (V L); Vllyball (V); Most Motivated Cadet/Outstanding Cadet (AFJROTC); Architecture; Graphic Arts; U of Maryland; U of South Florida

CONAWAY, KENNETH N; BALTIMORE, MD; LOYOLA-BLAKEFIELD HS; (JR); Hnr Roll; Comm Volntr; Emplmnt; Civil Engineering; Computer Engineering; Drexel, Morgan State U; Georgia Tech

CONCEPCION, MARIA M L S; OXON HILL, MD; OXON HILL HS; MS; Ctznshp Aw; Hnr Roll; Sci Fairs; Sci Clb; Bnd; Orch; Stu Cncl (R); Master's Degree; To Be Successful

CONNELL, GAELAN; SILVER SPRING, MD; BALTIMORE ACTORS THEATER CONS; (SO); Hnr Roll; MVP; Sci Fairs; St of Mnth; Comm Volntr; Hab For Humty Volntr; Chess; Drma Clb; Emplmnt; Mus Clb; Spch Team; Acpl Chr; Chr; Dnce; SP/M/VS; Fncg; Skiing (J); Sccr (J); Adv Cncl (R); CR (R); Three Major Movies; Eleven City and Community Theater; Acting; Film Making; McGill U; U S California

CONNOR, KAT; PARKVILLE, MD; PATAPSCO HS; (SO); Hnr Roll; Emplmnt; Chr; Dnce; Orch; SP/M/VS; Job; Actress; Lawyer; The Juilliard School; Virginia Commonwealth

CONTEH, HAJA M; LAUREL, MD; LAUREL HS; (FR); Ctznshp Aw; Hnr Roll; Otst Ac Ach Awd; Perf Att; Sci Fairs; St of Mnth; Comm Volntr; Drma Clb; ROTC; Spanish Clb; SP/M/VS; Stg Cre; Stu Cncl (R); Lit Mag (E, R); Most Improved; Engineer; Lawyer; Georgetown U; U of Maryland

CONTEH, ISATU; FT WASHINGTON, MD; FRIENDLY HS; (SO); Hnr Roll; Otst Ac Ach Awd; Perf Att; Pres Sch; Sci Fairs; St of Mnth; Comm Volntr; Skiing (JC); Yrbk (P); Top 25 Achiever in Class of 2007; Chemistry; Georgetown U; George Mason U

CONWELL, SIMONE E; BALTIMORE, MD; TOWSON HS; (JR); F Lan Hn Soc; Hnr Roll; Peer Tut/Med; Emplmnt; Key Club; Orch; Sch Ppr (R); National French Honor Society; Doctor of Medicine; U of Maryland; U of Virginia

COOKE, PAUL J; GLEN BURNIE, MD; NORTH CTY SR HS; (SO); Hnr Roll; Otst Ac Ach Awd; Perf Att; St of Mnth; Comm Volntr; Emplmnt; P to P St Amb Prg; Sccr (V); President's Education Award; Scholar Athlete Award; Engineering; Mechanical & Information Technologies; U of Maryland; U of Virginia

COOLS, LIANA; HYATTSVILLE, MD; NORTHWESTERN HS; (SO); Hnr Roll; Yth Ldrshp Prog; Spec Olymp Vol; FBLA; Best Buddies, Mock Trial, Youth Inc., Youth Leadership Program; Pre-Law (Prosecutor); Psychology; Duke U; Yale U

COOPER, BRITNE' I; BURTONSVILLE, MD; PAINT BRANCH HS; (JR); Duke TS; Hnr Roll; Jr Eng Tech; Otst Ac Ach Awd; Perf Att; Sci Fairs; St of Mnth; St Optmst of Yr; WWAHSS; Yth Ldrshp Prog; Comm Volntr; Hosp Aide; Peer Tut/Med; Chrch Yth Grp; DARE; Emplmnt; FCA; Key Club; Off Aide; SADD; Tchrs Aide; Ch Chr; Lit Mag (R); Environmental Club Vice President; Cosmetology Student At Thomas Edison High School of Technology; Major-Business Management; Salon Owning Cosmetologist; Morgan State U; U of Maryland Eastern Shore

COOPER, BRITTANIE; FORT WASHINGTON, MD; FRIENDLY HS; (SO); Ctznshp Aw; Hi Hnr Roll; Hnr Roll; Perf Att; Pres Sch; Sci Fairs; Comm Volntr; Peer Tut/Med; Emplmnt; FTA; Jr Ach; ROTC; Clr Grd; Track (V); Student of the Quarter; National Junior Honor Society; Mathematics (Education); Accounting; Pepperdine U; UCLA

COOPER, JUDITH E; CAPITOL HEIGHTS, MD; HOWARD UNIVERSITY HS; (JR); Hnr Roll; Sci/Math Olympn; St of Mnth; St Optmst of Yr; Hosp Aide; Spec Olymp Vol; Fr of Library; Sci Clb; Major in Master Physical Therapy

COPE, SAMANTHA; BOWIE, MD; BOWIE HS; (FR); Hi Hnr Roll; Perf Att; Chrch Yth Grp; Ch Chr; Stu Cncl (R); Bowling League - Most Improved; Guitar - Going Into Advanced / Piano; Creative Writing; Education; Columbia U; Brigham Young U

COPPLE, MATT; SILVER SPRING, MD; PAINT BRANCH HS; (SO); Hi Hnr Roll; Hnr Roll; MVP; Sci Fairs; 4-H; Sccr (J); Business; Economics; U of North Carolina at Chapel Hill

CORNELL, CHARLES; OWINGS, MD; NORTHERN HS; (JR); Hnr Roll; Yth Ldrshp Prog; FBLA; President of Chapter Future Business Leaders; Vice President of Academy of Finance; Medical; U of Maryland; U of Miami

CORNELL, JOANNA; GAITHERSBURG, MD; THOMAS S WOOTTON HS; (FR); Hnr Roll; Otst Ac Ach Awd; Perf Att; Sci Fairs; Yth Ldrshp Prog; Comm Volntr; Peer Tut/Med; ArtClub; Dbte Team; Mth Clb/Tm; Mod UN; NtlFrnscLg; P to P St Amb Prg; Svce Clb; Spch Team; Orch; Stu Cncl (R); Sch Ppr (R); Superintendent's Award - SSL; Gottlieb Memorial Competition; Business; Law; Yale U; Harvard U

COSBY, TANEA; WINDSOR MILL, MD; MILFORD MILL AC; (SO); Bnd; 100 Hrs of Community Student Service; 3.3 GPA, Volunteer at Men's Shelter; Accounting; Psychology; Towson State U; Morgan State U

COSSENTINO, CHARLES; PASADENA, MD; MT ST JOSEPH; (SR); Hnr Roll; Villa Julie College; Capital College

COSTA, DANIELLE; BEL ALTON, MD; ST MARY'S RYKEN HS; (SO); Ctznshp Aw; Sci Fairs; DARE; Key Club; Scouts; Tchrs Aide; Latin Clb; Bnd; Fld Hky (J); Sch Ppr (R); Communications; Journalism

COSTANZA, AMANDA; BEL AIR, MD; C MILTON WRIGHT HS; (JR); Hnr Roll; Pres Sch; Peer Tut/Med; Chr; Stu Cncl; Peer Helper; Master Tutor Special Education; Psychology; Sociology; Coastal Carolina; U of Vermont

COUNTEE, MELANIE; LARGO, MD; KETTERING MS; (MS); Hi Hnr Roll; Hnr Roll; Nat Hon Sy; Sci Fairs; Comm Volntr; Drma Clb; P to P St Amb Prg; CR (P); Good Morning Kettering; Pre-Medicine; Spelman College; Howard U

COWARD, DARREN T; BOWIE, MD; BOWIE HS; (JR); Hnr Roll; Perf Att; WWAHSS; Mod UN; Bskball (JC); Ftball (J); President-Gentleman's Club; Business Administration; Law; Morehouse College; UNC Chapel Hill

CRAIG, MARISSA M; BOWIE, MD; BOWIE HS; (JR); Hnr Roll; Nat Hon Sy; Poetry.Com Award; Japanese Translator; Creative Writing; Maryland U; Gettysburg College

CRAMER, MAEGAN; FREDERICK, MD; CATOCTIN HS; (FR); Hnr Roll; Comm Volntr; Spec Olymp Vol; Chrch Yth Grp; Ch Chr; Dnce; Worked at Craft Shows; Dance Teacher; Teaching; Special Education; Frederick Community College; Hood College

CRAMER, MALLORY L; ANNAPOLIS, MD; BROADNECK HS; Hnr Roll; Perf Att; Comm Volntr; Chrch Yth Grp; Key Club; P to P St Amb Prg; Bnd; Chr; Ch Chr; Dnce; Swmg; Pilot; Bachelor of Arts; Towson State U; U of Maryland

CRAWFORD, BRANDI; SUITLAND, MD; SUITLAND HS; (JR); Hnr Roll; Perf Att; Comm Volntr; Peer Tut/Med; Chrch Yth Grp; Tchrs Aide; Spanish Clb; Ch Chr; Dnce; PPSqd (V); CR (R); Social Work; Psychology; Delaware U; Howard U

CRENSON, LEAH; TOWSON, MD; TOWSON HS; (FR); Hnr Roll; WWAHSS; Comm Volntr; Key Club; Mus Clb; P to P St Amb Prg; Scouts; Orch; CR (R); Tri-M (Music Honor Society); Steering Committee Member; Goucher College; Towson U

CUMMINGS, EVANGELINE; OXON HILL, MD; OXON HILL HS; (FR); Hi Hnr Roll; Hnr Roll; Perf Att; Pres Sch; St of Mnth; ArtClub; Chrch Yth Grp; Dbte Team; Lib Aide; Ch Chr; Dnce; SP/M/VS; Stg Cre; Cr Ctry (V); Track (V); Nurse; Real Estate Agent; Wesley College; Towson U

CUMMINGS, RAYANN; FORT WASHINGTON, MD; FRIENDLY HS; (SO); Hi Hnr Roll; Otst Ac Ach Awd; Comm Volntr; Peer Tut/Med; Chrch Yth Grp; FTA; Ch Chr; Dnce; Stu Cncl (S); Tass Nominee; President's Education Awards Program; Education Major; Elementary School Teacher; Spelman College; Stanford U

CUNDIFF, JESSICA R; REISTERSTOWN, MD; BALTIMORE LUTHERAN HS; (JR); Ctznshp Aw; DAR; Hnr Roll; Nat Hon Sy; WWAHSS; Chrch Yth Grp; Drma Clb; Emplmnt; FCA; Key Club; Tchrs Aide; Acpl Chr; Chr; SP/M/VS; Sftball (J L); Vllyball (VJCL); Cl Off (T); Maryland Higher Commission Distinguished Scholar; Education; Language; Pepperdine U; Ohio Wesleyan U

CURTIS, BRIAN M; OWINGS, MD; NORTHERN HS; (JR); Ctznshp Aw; Hi Hnr Roll; Hnr Roll; MVP; Otst Ac Ach Awd; Peer Tut/Med; Chrch Yth Grp; DARE; Bskball (V); Peer Mediation in Elementary School; Landscaping; Architecture; Howard U

CYGANOWSKI, ANNA; BALDWIN, MD; NOTRE DAME PREPARATORY SCH; (SO); Hnr Roll; Perf Att; Yth Ldrshp Prog; Peer Tut/Med; Cmptr Clb; Tech Clb; Ch Chr; Cl Off (R); Robotics Club Founder / President; Student Technology Advisors / Stars Club; Electrical Engineering / Computer Science; Neuroscience; Massachusetts Institute of Technology; California Institute of Technology

CZAJKOWSKI, MEGAN A; PASADENA, MD; THE CATHOLIC HS OF BALTIMORE; (JR); Hnr Roll; Nat Hon Sy; Perf Att; St of Mnth; Peer Tut/Med; Lib Aide; SP/M/VS; Stg Cre; Stu Cncl (R); CR (R); President - Library Club; Member - Academic Integrity Committee; Engineering; Medical; Mount St Mary's Emmitsburg MD; Goucher College Towson MD

Curtis, Brian M
Northern HS
Owings, MD

Cooke, Paul J
North Cty SR HS
Glen Burnie, MD

Conteh, Isatu
Friendly HS
Ft Washington, MD

Clark, Elisia M
Charles Herbert Flowers HS
Upper Marlboro, MD

Colliflower, Brittney M
Northern HS
Chesapeake Beach, MD

Cramer, Maegan
Catoctin HS
Frederick, MD

Czajkowski, Megan A
The Catholic HS Of Baltimore
Pasadena, MD

D'ADAMO, NICK; MECHANICSVLLE, MD; CHOPTICAN HS; (FR); Ctznshp Aw; Hnr Roll; Perf Att; Sci Fairs; St of Mnth; DARE; Jzz Bnd; SP/M/VS; Certificate of Achievement / DARE Certificate Award / Outstanding Jazz / Outstanding Achievement-Math; National Physical Fitness Award, Certificate Award-Science/Band Student; Music Major

DALE, ANDREW; OAKLAND, MD; SOUTHERN GARRETT HS; (FR); Hnr Roll; Perf Att; St of Mnth; DARE; Emplmnt; Scouts; Bnd; Jzz Bnd; Mch Bnd; Pep Bnd; Track; Lifeguard, Baseball, Snow Boarding/Skiing; Boy Scouts

DAMBROSIA, JOSEPH; FREDERICK, MD; WALKERSVILLE HS; (SO); Hi Hnr Roll; Otst Ac Ach Awd; Comm Volntr; Red Cr Aide; Chrch Yth Grp; Emplmnt; Key Club; Psychology/Counseling; Nutrition Science

DAMICO, GARY A; BALTIMORE, MD; BALTIMORE POLY TECH INST 403; (SO); Hnr Roll; Peer Tut/Med; It's Academic Member; Biology; Engineering; Johns Hopkins U; Temple U

DANG, LAN; GAMBRILLS, MD; ARUNDEL SR HS; (SR); Hi Hnr Roll; Hnr Roll; Nat Hon Sy; Nat Ldrshp Svc; Sci Fairs; WWAHSS; Yth Ldrshp Prog; Comm Volntr; Peer Tut/Med; Red Cr Aide; DARE; Dbte Team; Emplmnt; FCA; Key Club; Mod UN; NYLC; Clr Grd; Orch; Stg Cre; Chrldg (J); Fld Hky (J); PPSqd (J); Tennis (V L); Track (J); Vsy Clb; Adv Cncl (R); Cl Off (V); Stu Cncl (R); CR (R); Yrbk; Biology; Pre-Med; Pennsylvania State U; U of Maryland College Park

DANKWAH, HOUSLEY L; BELTSVILLE, MD; HIGH POINT HS; (SO); Hnr Roll; Perf Att; St of Mnth; WWAHSS; Comm Volntr; Peer Tut/Med; Chrch Yth Grp; ROTC; Scouts; Drl Tm; Military Order of the Purple Heart; Medicine; Business; Johns Hopkins U; Howard U

D'ANTONI, ERICA; BROOKLYN, MD; NORTH CTY SR HS; (SO); Hnr Roll; Comm Volntr; Sftball (J); Vllyball (J); Physical Therapist; Nurse; U of Florida; U of North Carolina

DARCIS, JESSICA; POTOMAC, MD; THOMAS S. WOOTTON HS; (JR); F Lan Hn Soc; Hnr Roll; Comm Volntr; Peer Tut/Med; Emplmnt; Svce Clb; Lcrsse (J); PP Ftbl (V); Yrbk (E); Psychology Club; Summer Camp Counselor; Communications; Journalism, Publishing; Syracuse U; Miami U (Oxford)

DARR, CATHERINE; BALTIMORE, MD; TOWSON HS; (SO); Pres Sch; Key Club; Mus Clb; Bnd; Mch Bnd; Pep Bnd; SP/M/VS; Sch Ppr (R); Political Science; International Affairs; Georgetown U; American U

DAVENPORT, FELICE; DISTRICT HEIGHTS, MD; CHARLES HERBERT FLOWERS HS; (FR); Ctznshp Aw; Hnr Roll; Otst Ac Ach Awd; Perf Att; Drma Clb; Dnce; SP/M/VS; National Junior Honors Society; Forensic Science; Fashion Design; Princeton U; New York U

DAVIS, ANGELO; BALTIMORE, MD; NEW ERA AC; (SO); Ctznshp Aw; Hi Hnr Roll; Hnr Roll; Otst Ac Ach Awd; Perf Att; Sci/Math Olympn; Chess; Dbte Team; Bsball (V); CR (R); Johns Hopkins U; Florida State U

DAVIS, CARMALIA N; CAPITOL HEIGHTS, MD; CHARLES HERBERT FLOWERS HS; (SO); Hnr Roll; Comm Volntr; Peer Tut/Med; Emplmnt; Mch Bnd; Pre-Med; Information Systems; Johns Hopkins U; Georgetown U

DAVIS, CHRISTOPHER; HAGERSTOWN, MD; SMITHSBURG HS; (SO); Hi Hnr Roll; Hnr Roll; Otst Ac Ach Awd; St of Mnth; WWAHSS; Comm Volntr; Chrch Yth Grp; Ftball (V); Presidential Achievement Award; Weight Lifting Club; Law; Secondary Education / History; U of Miami; U of Virginia

DAVIS, JENNIFER; POCOMOKE CITY, MD; POCOMOKE HS; (FR); Hnr Roll; Perf Att; Sci Fairs; St of Mnth; USMC Stu Ath Aw; Comm Volntr; Hosp Aide; DARE; ROTC; Tchrs Aide; Bowling Team; Taking Over My Dad's Heating, HVAC & Electrical Business; Wor Wic Tech

DAVIS, RYAN J; FORT WASHINGTON, MD; FRIENDLY HS; (SO); Hi Hnr Roll; Hnr Roll; MVP; Perf Att; Sci Fairs; Chess; ROTC; Clr Grd; Drl Tm; Golf (V); Science; Technology; Massachusetts Institute of Technology; United States Naval Academy

DEAN, SIDRA; COLUMBIA, MD; WILDE LAKE HS; (JR); Hi Hnr Roll; Hnr Roll; Nat Mrt LOC; Otst Ac Ach Awd; Perf Att; St of Mnth; Yth Ldrshp Prog; Comm Volntr; Hosp Aide; Peer Tut/Med; Chrch Yth Grp; Drma Clb; Off Aide; Prom Com; Tchrs Aide; Ch Chr; Stg Cre; Adv Cncl (P, R); Stu Cncl (R); CR (R); Make-A-Wish; Pharmacy; Howard County Community College; U of Maryland, Baltimore

DECKER, GREGORY; GAITHERSBURG, MD; WALTER JOHNSON HS; (JR); F Lan Hn Soc; Hnr Roll; Nat Hon Sy; Perf Att; Pres Ac Ftns Aw; Pres Sch; Sci Fairs; St of Mnth; Peer Tut/Med; Sci Clb; Vsity Clb; Cr Ctry (V L); Ice Hky (J); Lcrsse (V L); Sccr; Swmg (J); Track (V L); Marine Corp Marathon, 2003-Youngest Runner; NIH Summer Internship; Biology; Pre-Med

DELAPENHA, ANDREW; ASHTON, MD; SHERWOOD HS; (JR); Hnr Roll; Nat Hon Sy; Chrch Yth Grp; Emplmnt; FBLA; Star Scholarship Award Winner; Pre-Medicine; Business; Johns Hopkins U; U of Maryland

DEL COSTELLO, HEATHER; PORT DEPOSIT, MD; SETON HOME STUDY SCH; (SR); Hnr Roll; Perf Att; St of Mnth; Chrch Yth Grp; Emplmnt; Tchrs Aide; Stu Cncl (P); Master's Degree in Nursing; U of Central Florida

DELOATCH, ROBERT; FORT WASHINGTON, MD; OXON HILL HS; (SO); Hnr Roll; WWAHSS; Comm Volntr; Computer Science; U of Maryland; Virginia Tech

DENSTON, WILLIAM B; POCOMOKE CITY, MD; POCOMOKE HS; (FR); Hi Hnr Roll; St of Mnth; Comm Volntr; ROTC; Bnd; Jzz Bnd; Mch Bnd; Cr Ctry (V); Skt Tgt Sh; Helping Volunteer Fire Company; Business / Engineering; Salisbury U; U of MD Baltimore County

DESPERTT, DONOVAN D; DISTRICT HEIGHTS, MD; FORESTVILLE MILITARY AC; (SO); Ctznshp Aw; Hnr Roll; Sci Fairs; Comm Volntr; Peer Tut/Med; ROTC; Scouts; Tchrs Aide; Ch Chr; Bskball; Graphic Design; Computer Science; U of Maryland; Georgetown U

DIAZ, MICHAEL; COCKEYSVILLE, MD; TOWSON CATHOLIC HS; (SO)

DIAZ, TOMASA C; UPPER MARLBORO, MD; CENTRAL HS; (JR); Hnr Roll; Perf Att; ROTC; Law; Medicine; Prince George's Community College

DICKARD, STEPHANIE; PERRY HALL, MD; BALTIMORE LUTHERAN HS; (JR); Hnr Roll; Yth Ldrshp Prog; Comm Volntr; ArtClub; Photog; Lit Mag (R, P); Honorary Mention in Art Shows; National Young Leaders Conference; Arts Management; Music Business; Goucher College; Long Island U

DI FERDINANDO, DANIELLE; ELLICOTT CITY, MD; RESERVOIR HS; (SR); Hnr Roll; Nat Mrt LOC; St of Mnth; Comm Volntr; Peer Tut/Med; DECA; FBLA; Dnce; Chrldg (J); Ftball (L); Track (J); Yrbk (P); CEO of Danielle Nicole Fashions; 1st Place in Maryland DECA Fashion Merchandising Sales Promotion Plan; Fashion Merchandising; Fashion Design; Fashion Institute of Technology

DIKE, NWAMAKA; LANHAM, MD; ELEANOR ROOSEVELT HS; (SO); Hnr Roll; Comm Volntr; Peer Tut/Med; Chrch Yth Grp; Mus Clb; Clb; Dnce; Orch; Track; Vllyball; Cl Off (R); American Sign Language Club; International Club; Biology / Pre-Med; International Studies; U of North Carolina Chapel Hill; Cornell U

DIPINTO, TORI; ODENTON, MD; ARUNDEL SR HS; (FR); AVID 9; NASA Space Project 5th Grade (Group); Criminal Law; Doctor; U of Maryland; Virginia Tech

DISNEY, RAEYA N; HAGERSTOWN, MD; NORTH HAGERSTOWN HS; (FR); Ctznshp Aw; Otst Ac Ach Awd; WWAHSS; Comm Volntr; Key Club; Pep Squd; Dnce; Orch; Chrldg (J); Cl Off (V); Key Club; Play the Piano for a Year; Psychiatrist; Maryland U

DJER, NAJJAH; CLINTON, MD; SURRATTSVILLE HS; (SO); Ctznshp Aw; Hnr Roll; Sci Fairs; Comm Volntr; Emplmnt; Mus Clb; ROTC; Spanish Clb; Bnd; Mch Bnd; Orch; Member of the Pathfinders Club; Major in Languages (Spanish); Become a Spanish Interpreter; Prince George Community College

DOBSON, SHOSHANA R; BOWIE, MD; BOWIE HS; (SO); Hnr Roll; Nat Hon Sy; St of Mnth; FBLA; Tchrs Aide; Bskball (J); Sccr (J); Law; Psychology, Maryland U, Florida State U

DOCKERY, JO ANNA M; WALKERSVILLE, MD; WALKERSVILLE HS; (SR); F Lan Hn Soc; Hi Hnr Roll; Hnr Roll; Nat Hon Sy; Salutrn; St Schl; WWAHSS; Peer Tut/Med; Chrch Yth Grp; Emplmnt; Quiz Bowl; Tchrs Aide; Chr; Clr Grd; SP/M/VS; PP Ftbl; Sccr (J); Track (V L); Sch Ppr (E); French Honor Society-Vice President; Maryland Distinguished Scholar-Finalist; Harding U

DOHMEIER, SAMANTHA; PARKVILLE, MD; BALTIMORE LUTHERAN HS; (JR); Hi Hnr Roll; Hnr Roll; Nat Hon Sy; Perf Att; Sci Fairs; Comm Volntr; ArtClub; Emplmnt; Quiz Bowl; Sci Clb; SADD; Chr; Ch Chr; SP/M/VS; Fld Hky (L); PP Ftbl (V); Track (L); Lit Mag (R); Treasurer of National Honor Society; Biological Sciences; Pre-Med / Pre-Veterinary; Clemson U; U of SC Columbia

DONHAM, JENNIFER L; OAKLAND, MD; SOUTHERN GARRETT CTY HS; MS; All Am Sch; Hnr Roll; Nat Hon Sy; St of Mnth; USAA; Comm Volntr; Chrch Yth Grp; Emplmnt; Chr; Dnce; Success in School Award; National Mathematics Award; Major in Mathematics; Degree in Education; Frostburg State U

DONOVAN, JENNA; HOLLYWOOD, MD; LEONARDTOWN HS; (SO); Ctznshp Aw; Hnr Roll; Perf Att; Pres Sch; Sci Fairs; St of Mnth; USAA; WWAHSS; Yth Ldrshp Prog; Peer Tut/Med; Spec Olymp Vol; Biology Clb; FBLA; NYLC; Svce Clb; Tchrs Aide; French Clb; Chrldg (V L); Lcrsse (JC); Cl Off (R); Stu Cncl (S); Pre-Med

DORADO, EDUARDO J; BELTSVILLE, MD; GONZAGA COLLEGE HS; (SO); Hnr Roll; Nat Hon Sy; Otst Ac Ach Awd; Pres Sch; Valdctrian; Yth Ldrshp Prog; Comm Volntr; Peer Tut/Med; Chrch Yth Grp; Emplmnt; Lib Aide; Mth Clb/Tm; NYLC; Outdrs Clb; HISPANO Clb; Cr Ctry (J); 2005 Pepco Academic Achievement Award; President of the Hispano Club; Engineer; U of Maryland; Loyola College in Baltimore

DORSEY, ELANDRA G; SUITLAND, MD; SUITLAND HS; (JR); Hnr Roll; Emplmnt; Nursing; Pediatrician; Georgetown U; Maryland U

DORSEY, TERRILL; FORT WASHINGTON, MD; NATIONAL CHRISTIAN AC; (SR); Hnr Roll; Perf Att; Sci Fairs; St of Mnth; Comm Volntr; Peer Tut/Med; Chrch Yth Grp; FCA; Mth Clb/Tm; Off Aide; Tchrs Aide; Vsity Clb; SP/M/VS; Bskball (V); Sch Ppr (E); Yrbk (E); Accounting; Business Management; U of Maryland Eastern Shore; Salisbury State U

DOUGLASS, JOY K; TEMPLE HILLS, MD; FORESTVILLE MILITARY AC; (FR); Ctznshp Aw; Hi Hnr Roll; Hnr Roll; Pres Sch; Sci Fairs; Hosp Aide; Chrch Yth Grp; Emplmnt; Mus Clb; Scouts; Chr; Ch Chr; Dnce; SP/M/VS; PPSqd (L); PP Ftbl (L); Track (L); CR (R); Presidential Award Honor Roll; Citizenship Awards Volunteering; Criminal Justice; Culinary Arts; Maryland U; Georgetown U

DOWNING, YOLANDA; BALTIMORE, MD; BALTIMORE POLY TECH INST 403; (SO); Hnr Roll; Perf Att; Biology Clb; Dnce; Part of SHOUT; Part of a Group at BCCC

DOWTIN, TYRA; DISTRICT HEIGHTS, MD; LARGO SR HS; (SO); Ctznshp Aw; Hi Hnr Roll; Hnr Roll; Perf Att; Sci Fairs; Comm Volntr; Peer Tut/Med; Chess; Drma Clb; Emplmnt; Off Aide; Tchrs Aide; SP/M/VS; Stg Cre; Chrldg (J); Sftball (J); CR (S); Public Relations; Social Work; Spelman College; Howard U

DROZDOVSKA, OKSANA; JOPPA, MD; JOPPATOWNE HS; (FR); Hnr Roll; Chr; Singing; Lawyer; Teacher; Harford Community College

DRUMHELLER, ERIN M; HAMPSTEAD, MD; NORTH CARROLL HS; (JR); Hi Hnr Roll; Hnr Roll; Nat Hon Sy; Perf Att; WWAHSS; Yth Ldrshp Prog; Comm Volntr; Chrch Yth Grp; Drma Clb; Key Club; Lib Aide; Off Aide; Sci Clb; Tchrs Aide; Clr Grd; Dnce; SP/M/VS; Stg Cre; Mar Art; Cardiologist-Pre-Medicine; Johns Hopkins U; U of Maryland

DUARTE, BRIDGETT; NORTH POTOMAC, MD; THOMAS S WOOTTON HS; (JR); Hnr Roll; Sci Fairs; Comm Volntr; Peer Tut/Med; Emplmnt; Svce Clb; SADD; PP Ftbl (V); Yrbk (E, R, P); Honorable Mention for MD Distinguished Homeopathic Doctor's Assistant Scholars; Pre-Medicine or Bio Major; Biochemistry; Wake Forest U; U of Maryland

DU BOIS, NASHATIA; EDGEWOOD, MD; JOPPATOWNE HS; (JR); Hnr Roll; Accounting; Bookkeeping; Morgan State U; U of Maryland

DUCKETT, ROBERT-LEE; UPPER MARLBORO, MD; CHARLES HERBERT FLOWERS HS; (SO); Bnd; Ftball (V); Track (V); Wt Lftg (V); Assisting in Serving the Homeless on Thanksgiving & Received an Award; Business Management; Automotive Work; U of Maryland College Park; Bowie State U

DUCKWORTH, MICHAEL B; OAKLAND, MD; SOUTHERN GARRETT HS; (FR); Hnr Roll; St of Mnth; Scouts; Bnd; Mch Bnd; Garrett Community College; West Virginia U

DUDKIN, ILYA; BURTONSVILLE, MD; (SO); Hnr Roll; Comm Volntr; Bnd; Community Service; Musician; Peabody Conservatory of Johns Hopkins U; George Washington U

DUGHLY, OMAR; MILLERSVILLE, MD; SEVERNA PARK HS; (FR); Hi Hnr Roll; WWAHSS; Key Club; Tennis (J); Peer Helper; Piano - Guild Auditions; Engineering; Biology; Harvard U; U of Pennsylvania

DULIN, MANDY; CORDOVA, MD; EASTON AREA HS; (SR); Hnr Roll; Nat Hon Sy; St of Mnth; WWAHSS; Ntl FFA; Sccr (J); Sftball (JCL); Vllyball (V L); Animal Science; Veterinary Medicine; Montana State U-Bozeman; U of Idaho-Moscow

DUNBAR, DAVID M; JOPPA, MD; JOPPATOWNE HS; (FR); Ctznshp Aw; Hi Hnr Roll; Hnr Roll; MVP; Nat Mrt Fin; Perf Att; Sci/Math Olympn; Chrch Yth Grp; Off Aide; Bsball (J); Ftball (J); Wt Lftg (J); Honor Roll; Law School-Lawyer; U of Maryland; U of Miami

DUNN, SASHA; CLEAR SPRING, MD; CLEAR SPRING HS; (SR); Hi Hnr Roll; Hnr Roll; Nat Hon Sy; St of Mnth; Otst Ac Ach Awd; Red Cr Aide; Emplmnt; Lib Aide; Photog; Bnd; Chr; Cl Off (S); Yrbk (R, P); Maryland Distinguished Scholar - Honorable Mention; Student Council Member of History Club and Academic Team; Law; Psychology; Mount Saint Mary's U

DYE, ARIEL; BALTIMORE, MD; PAUL L DUNBAR HS 414; Ctznshp Aw; Hi Hnr Roll; Hnr Roll; Nat Hon Sy; Otst Ac Ach Awd; Perf Att; Salutrn; Sci Fairs; Peer Tut/Med; Chrch Yth Grp; Lib Aide; Off Aide; Bnd; Chr; Ch Chr; Dnce; Track; BS Degree; Medical Degree; Johns Hopkins U; Meharry Medical School

EARL, CHRISTOPHER T; WINDSOR MILL, MD; MILFORD MILL AC; (SO); All Am Sch; Hnr Roll; Perf Att; Comm Volntr; Chr; Ftball (V L); Cl Off (V); Law; Information Technology / Info Systems Management; Miami U; Boston College

EBB, LATOYA; EDGEWOOD, MD; JOPPATOWNE HS; (JR); Hnr Roll; St of Mnth; Track (V); Nursing; Salisbury State; Towson U

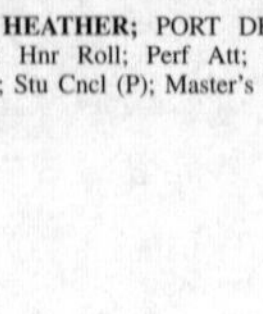
Drozdovska, Oksana
Joppatowne HS
Joppa, MD

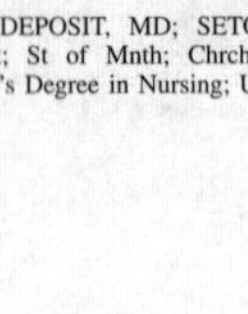
Djer, Najjah
Surrattsville HS
Clinton, MD

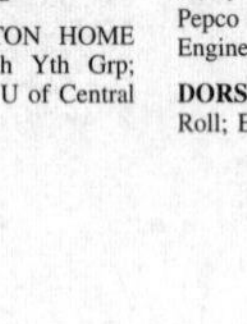
Diaz, Tomasa C
Central HS
Upper Marlboro, MD

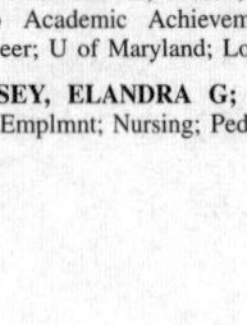
Dean, Sidra
Wilde Lake HS
Columbia, MD

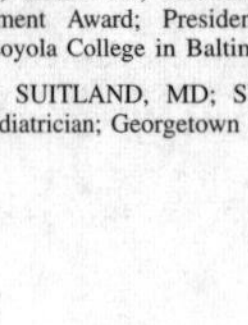
Dale, Andrew
Southern Garrett HS
Oakland, MD

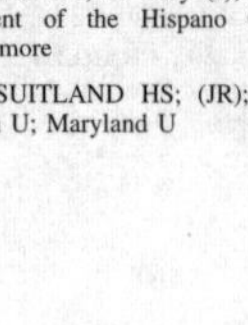
Davis, Christopher
Smithsburg HS
Hagerstown, MD

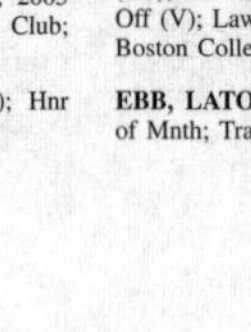
Dipinto, Tori
Arundel SR HS
Odenton, MD

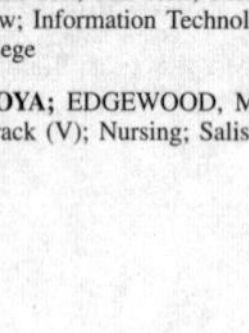
Douglass, Joy K
Forestville Military AC
Temple Hills, MD

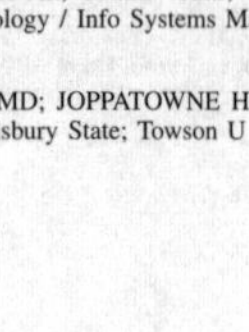
Duckett, Robert-Lee
Charles Herbert Flowers HS
Upper Marlboro, MD

EBBAY, FLORENCE C D; SILVER SPRING, MD; ALBERT EINSTEIN HS; (JR); Hnr Roll; Nat Hon Sy; Nat Mrt Sch Recip; Perf Att; Sci/Math Olympn; WWAHSS; Comm Volntr; Peer Tut/Med; Chrch Yth Grp; Emplmnt; Scouts; Bnd; Chr; Dnce; Mch Bnd; Chrldg (V); Track (V); Vllyball (V); Cl Off (S); Stu Cncl (S); Forensic Science; Criminal Justice; U of New Haven; U of Maryland

EDMONDS, STEPHANIE J; BOWIE, MD; BOWIE HS; (JR); Hi Hnr Roll; Chrch Yth Grp; Emplmnt; Ch Chr; Ladies with Class Organization; United Minds Organization; Social Work; Psychology; U of Maryland College Park; Virginia Commonwealth U

EDWARDS, KARESA; BROOKEVILLE, MD; THE BARRIE SCH; (FR); Hi Hnr Roll; Nat Stu Ath Day Aw; Otst Ac Ach Awd; Pres Ac Ftns Aw; WWAHSS; Yth Ldrshp Prog; Comm Volntr; Peer Tut/Med; Biology Clb; Emplmnt; Off Aide; Sci Clb; Spanish Clb; Acpl Chr; Chr; Hsbk Rdg; Vllyball (V); Pony Club - Jr Council President

EDWARDS, KENDRA A; LUSBY, MD; PATUXENT HS; (SO); Hnr Roll; Otst Ac Ach Awd; Pres Ac Ftns Aw; Sci Fairs; Comm Volntr; Chrch Yth Grp; Emplmnt; GAA (J); Sccr (V L); Swmg (V); Track (V); Law-Criminal Justice

EDWARDS, LAURA J; FORT WASHINGTON, MD; FRIENDLY HS; (SR); Hnr Roll; WWAHSS; Tchrs Aide; National Art Honor Society; Principal's Award; Animation; Game Design; Art Institute of Washington

EHRMANN, AMALIA; HYATTSVILLE, MD; CHARLES HERBERT FLOWERS HS; (FR); Hi Hnr Roll; Dnce; Chrldg (J); Performing Arts; English; Fashion Institute of Technology; U of Maryland College Park

ELLIS, ASHLEY M; ELKTON, MD; BOHEMIA MANOR HS; (JR); Hnr Roll; Comm Volntr; Award for "When Not to Keep a Secret" Story; Registered Nurse; Wilmington College; Cecil Community College

ELLIS, KARA J; BOWIE, MD; BOWIE HS; (SO); Hi Hnr Roll; Hnr Roll; Nat Hon Sy; St of Mnth; Comm Volntr; Chrch Yth Grp; Emplmnt; ROTC; Clr Grd; Drl Tm; Bskball (J); Received the Tuskegee Airmen Award; Graduated from Cadet Officer Leadership Program; To Become an Military Officer; Lawyer; U of Maryland; Liberty U

ELOSHWAY, KIMBERLY; BOWIE, MD; ST. JOHN'S COLLEGE HS; (JR); Hi Hnr Roll; Nat Hon Sy; WWAHSS; Comm Volntr; Peer Tut/Med; Chrch Yth Grp; Bnd; Dnce; SP/M/VS; Vllyball (VJ L); Spanish National Honor Society; Peer Minister; International Affairs Major; Fine Arts-Music Minor; American U; Georgetown U

EMMONS, ANDREA; PARKVILLE, MD; PATAPSCO HS CFA; (SR); Nat Hon Sy; Pres Sch; Acpl Chr; Chr; SP/M/VS; Stu Cncl (S); Tri-M Music Honors Society; MD Distinguished Scholar; Psychology; Music-Vocal Performance; McDaniel College; U of MD, College Park

ENGLISH, CHELSEA; RHODESDALE, MD; NORTH DORCHESTER HS; (SR); Hi Hnr Roll; Nat Hon Sy; St of Mnth; WWAHSS; Comm Volntr; Emplmnt; Key Club; Mus Clb; Bnd; Chr; Mch Bnd; SP/M/VS; Sccr (V CL); Track (V CL); Recording Secretary for National Honor Society; Vice-President Tri-M Honor Society; Pre-Law; Pennsylvania State U

ENGRAM, MARQUITA C; CAPITOL HGTS, MD; LARGO HS; (JR); Nat Sci Aw; Perf Att; Sci Fairs; Spec Olymp Vol; DARE; Law; Georgia State U

ENRIQUEZ, REGINA V; COLUMBIA, MD; WILDE LAKE HS; (SR); Hi Hnr Roll; Hnr Roll; Nat Hon Sy; Comm Volntr; Ntl Beta Clb; Prom Com; SP/M/VS; Stg Cre; Track (J); Adv Cncl (S); Stu Cncl (R); Legion of Scholars Mentorship Program Maryland Youth Action Corps, Student Gov't.; Film Club, Spanish Club; International Marketing; Communications; Boston U, Pennsylvania State U; U of Southern California, U of Virginia

ERHARD, KRISTIN; SPENCERVILLE, MD; PT BRANCH HS; (JR); 4-H; Chr; Swg Chr; Vllyball (V L); Physical Therapy; U of Maryland; Palm Beach Atlantic U

ESTEVES, NICKOLAS N; SILVER SPRING, MD; JAMES H BLAKE HS; (JR); Hnr Roll; Comm Volntr; Hab For Humty Volntr; DARE; Emplmnt; Mus Clb; Scouts; Bnd; Jzz Bnd; Mch Bnd; Pep Bnd; Sccr (J); Classic Soccer Player; Law; Doctorate; American U; Bucknell

EVERETT, PHILIP; CLINTON, MD; GRACE BRETHREN CHRISTIAN SCH; (JR); Hi Hnr Roll; MVP; Nat Hon Sy; Sci Fairs; WWAHSS; Yth Ldrshp Prog; Comm Volntr; Peer Tut/Med; Chrch Yth Grp; Emplmnt; Tchrs Aide; Bsball (V C); Swmg (V); Varsity Baseball Co-MVP; Operation Barnabas International (Missions Trip); Pre-Medicine; United States Naval Academy; United States Air Force Academy

EXUM, ASHLEY N; UPPER MARLBORO, MD; KETTERING MS; (MS); Ctznshp Aw; Hnr Roll; Nat Hon Sy; Otst Ac Ach Awd; Sci Fairs; Comm Volntr; Peer Tut/Med; DARE; Scouts; Tchrs Aide; Dnce; SP/M/VS; Cl Off (R); CR (R); National Junior Honor Society-Treasurer; Ladies of Distinction; Psychology; Interior Design; Maryland U; Spelman College

FADNESS, ALETHEIA; SUITLAND, MD; GRACE BRETHREN CHRISTIAN SCH; (JR); Hi Hnr Roll; MVP; WWAHSS; Scouts; Tchrs Aide; Bskball (C); Sccr (V); Tennis (V); Track (V); Stu Cncl (R); Journalism; Communications; Towson U; Meredith College

FAIRBANK, JORDIN; TILGHMAN, MD; ST MICHAELS JR/SR HS; (MS); Hnr Roll; Nat Hon Sy; Otst Ac Ach Awd; Comm Volntr; Drma Clb; Scouts; Bnd; Mch Bnd; Pep Bnd; SP/M/VS; Community Softball (I Don't Play for the School); Criminal Justice; Environmental; Baylor U

FAIRLEY, BRITTANY; DUNDALK, MD; PATAPSCO HS; (SO); Hi Hnr Roll; Hnr Roll; Nat Hon Sy; Perf Att; Peer Tut/Med; Red Cr Aide; HO'Br Yth Ldrshp; Scouts; SADD; Tchrs Aide; Clb; Bskball (VJC); Sccr (V); Sftball (V); Stu Cncl (R); CR (R); School Selected Women in Engineering Member; Community Hugh O'Brian Youth Leadership Member; Sports Medicine; Mechanical Engineering; Johns Hopkins U; U of Maryland

FAISON, JELANI A; RANDALLSTOWN, MD; WESTERN SCH OF TECH AND ENVIRONMENTAL SCIENCE; (FR); Hnr Roll; Perf Att; Sci Fairs; Chrch Yth Grp; DARE; FCA; Kwanza Clb; Scouts; Bnd; Mch Bnd; Bskball (J); Play Division Basketball; Become a Sports Agent; U of Maryland, College Park; Syracuse U

FAISON, MELINDA M; GWYNN OAK, MD; WOODLAWN HS; (SO); Hnr Roll; St of Mnth; Chrch Yth Grp; Nursing; Cosmetologist/Manicurist; Temple U; Washington College

FALK, JOCELYN P; ROCKVILLE, MD; WALTER JOHNSON HS; (JR); F Lan Hn Soc; Hnr Roll; Nat Hon Sy; WWAHSS; Yth Ldrshp Prog; Comm Volntr; Peer Tut/Med; Emplmnt; Key Club; Off Aide; Tchrs Aide; Sftball (V L); Tennis (V CL); Co-President French Honor Society; Communications: Film; Syracuse U; U of Michigan Ann Arbor

FALLAHKHAIR, YASMIN B; POTOMAC, MD; THOMAS S WOOTTON HS; MS; Ctznshp Aw; Hi Hnr Roll; Hnr Roll; Pres Ac Ftns Aw; St of Mnth; Comm Volntr; Peer Tut/Med; ArtClub; DARE; Lib Aide; Pep Squd; Tchrs Aide; Spanish Clb; Dnce; SP/M/VS; Bdmtn; Chrldg; Sccr; Vllyball; CR (R); Lit Mag (R); Sch Ppr (E, R); SGA Treasurer (Student Government Association); 3 Time Student of the Month Winner; Pre Law; Education; U of California, Berkeley; Columbia U of UCLA (U of California, Los Angeles)

FARLEY, ASHLEAHA S; BRANSON, MD; BILLINGS SCH; (MS); Hi Hnr Roll; Hnr Roll; Otst Ac Ach Awd; Sci Fairs; Sci/Math Olympn; Mth Clb/Tm; Quiz Bowl; Spch Team; Acpl Chr; SP/M/VS; Stg Cre; Bskball (J); Science / Life, Earth, Biology; All Areas of Math; U of MO; Princeton U

FARO, VALERIE A; WOODSBORO, MD; WALKERSVILLE HS; (SO); Hnr Roll; Comm Volntr; Key Club; Photog; Bskball; Fld Hky; Sccr; Veterinarian; Frederick Community College

FARRELL III, THOMAS D; CAPITOL HEIGHTS, MD; CHARLES HERBERT FLOWERS HS; (FR); Ctznshp Aw; Hnr Roll; Nat Hon Sy; Otst Ac Ach Awd; Sci Fairs; St of Mnth; Comm Volntr; Business; Graphic Design; Prince George's County Community College

FAYESE, LAOLU; SILVER SPRING, MD; KEYSTONE NATIONAL HS; (SR); Hnr Roll; Comm Volntr; Lib Aide; A+ Certified; Microsoft Certified Professional; Exercise Sciences; Kinesiology; Montgomery County Community College; George Mason U

FELLOWS, RACHEL; BALTIMORE, MD; PATTERSON SR HS 405; (JR); Hi Hnr Roll; Hnr Roll; Perf Att; Peer Tut/Med; 4-H; Chrch Yth Grp; DARE; Emplmnt; FTA; ROTC; Drl Tm; Skt Tgt Sh (L); Adv Cncl (S); Stu Cncl (S); Sch Ppr (R); Elementary Education; Morgan State U; Coppin State U

FERNANDES, NICOLE; DUNKIRK, MD; NORTHERN HS; (FR); Hi Hnr Roll; Hnr Roll; Otst Ac Ach Awd; Sci Fairs; St of Mnth; Comm Volntr; Emplmnt; Tchrs Aide; Degree in Radio Television & Film; Journalism; U of Maryland; New York U

FERNANDEZ, JARED; COLUMBIA, MD; WILDE LAKE HS; (SO); Hnr Roll; Yth Ldrshp Prog; NYLC; Bsball (JC); Golf (V C); Johns Hopkins Center for Gifted & Talented Youth; JV Baseball Team Captain-2005, Golf Team Captain 2004; Political Science; Business; U of Southern California; Emory U

FERNANDEZ, MONIQUE S; RIVERDALE, MD; FRIENDSHIP-EDISON COLLEGIATE AC; (JR); Hnr Roll; Nat Hon Sy; St Optmst of Yr; WWAHSS; Chrch Yth Grp; Emplmnt; Mus Clb; Tchrs Aide; Ch Chr; Dnce; SP/M/VS; Chrldg (V C); Sch Ppr (R); Forensic Science; Criminal Justice; Clark Atlanta U; Hampton U

FERRARI, ANGELA L; SEVERNA PARK, MD; SEVERNA PARK SR HS; (JR); Hnr Roll; Chrch Yth Grp; Drma Clb; Key Club; Mus Clb; Chr; Yrbk (P); Music; Medicine; U of Maryland

FERRIS, MATTHEW; TOWSON, MD; LOCH RAVEN HS; (JR); F Lan Hn Soc; Hnr Roll; Nat Hon Sy; MuAlphaTh; Lcrsse (V); Sccr (J); Law; Medicine; U of Richmond; Loyola College

FERRON III, ERNEST M; RANDALLSTOWN, MD; RANDALLSTOWN HS; (JR); Hnr Roll; Nat Hon Sy; Perf Att; St of Mnth; WWAHSS; Bnd; Jzz Bnd; Mch Bnd; Pre-Law; Howard U; Georgetown U

FIERS, JESSICA; GWYNN OAK, MD; MILFORD MILL AC; (FR); Ctznshp Aw; Hnr Roll; Perf Att; USMC Stu Ath Aw; ROTC; Drl Tm; Medical Degree / Obstetrician; Acting Minor; Drexel U; Towson U

FIGUEREDO, MARIA; SILVER SPRING, MD; ST JOHN'S COLLEGE HS; (SR); Hnr Roll; Comm Volntr; Sccr (J); Black Belt in Kung Fu; Competed Nationally in Kung Fu and Ranked #3 in the Nation in 2002; College Major-Pre-Med; Prof. Degrees Interested In-Pediatrics; U of Maryland, U of Miami; U of Tampa, Temple U, U of NC Greensboro

FILKINS, KATHRYN; ANNAPOLIS, MD; BROADNECK HS; (SR); Hi Hnr Roll; Hnr Roll; Nat Hon Sy; Nat Ldrshp Svc; St of Mnth; Key Club; Key Club; Annapolis Rowing Club - 4 Years; Penn State; Boston U

FINE, JASON; OWINGS MILLS, MD; OWINGS MILLS HS; (SR); Hnr Roll; Nat Hon Sy; Pres Sch; Yth Ldrshp Prog; Red Cr Aide; Drma Clb; Emplmnt; FBLA; SADD; SP/M/VS; Stg Cre; Stu Cncl (T); CR (R); Yrbk (E); Technical Director, Plays and Musicals; International Business and Management; Political Science; Dickinson College

FITCH, WILLIAM R R; SAINT LEONARD, MD; CALVERT HS; (FR); Hnr Roll; MVP; Otst Ac Ach Awd; Sci Fairs; St of Mnth; Comm Volntr; AL Aux Boys; DARE; Scouts; SADD; Bsball (V L); Golf (V L); American Legion Essay Award; President's Academic Excellence Award; Aeronautics; Mathematics; College of William and Mary; Wake Forest

FLESHER, DARRELL; WALDORF, MD; ST MARY'S RYKEN HS; (SO); 4H Awd; Hi Hnr Roll; Sci Fairs; Comm Volntr; 4-H; DARE; Drma Clb; Mus Clb; Sci Clb; Spanish Clb; Bnd; SP/M/VS; 3rd Black Belt in AAU Tae Kwon Do; Officer in Local 4-H club; Aerospace Engineering; Massachusetts Institute of Technology; U of Maryland

FOBBS, CARINE C N H; COLUMBIA, MD; HOWARD HS; (FR); Hnr Roll; MVP; Otst Ac Ach Awd; Pres Sch; Sci Fairs; St of Mnth; Comm Volntr; Chrch Yth Grp; DARE; P to P St Amb Prg; Scouts; Chr; Sftball (J); Stu Cncl (S); Presidential Award of Excellence; Outstanding Achievement on Maryland State Assessment; Major in International Business; Psychiatry; U of Barcelona Spain; Duke U

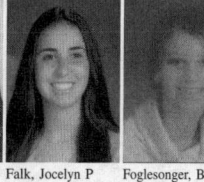

FOGLESONGER, BRITTANY; VIENNA, MD; NORTH DORCHESTER HS; (JR); Hi Hnr Roll; Nat Hon Sy; Emplmnt; Key Club; Prom Com; Chr; Chrldg (J); Sftball (JC); Cl Off (V); Sch Ppr (R); Yrbk (R); Honor Society Vice President; Advertisement Manager (Newspaper & Year Book); Accounting; Medicine; Villa Julie; College of Notre Dame Maryland

FOONG, CHELSEA E; ELKRIDGE, MD; HOWARD HS; (FR); Hi Hnr Roll; Hnr Roll; Pres Ac Ftns Aw; Pres Sch; Sci Fairs; St of Mnth; Comm Volntr; Chrch Yth Grp; Emplmnt; Mth Clb/Tm; Bnd; Mch Bnd; Cr Ctry (V L); Track (J); 2nd Team - All-County Cross Country; Pre-Med

FORD, ARAINA R; SUITLAND, MD; SUITLAND HS; (SR); Hi Hnr Roll; Hnr Roll; Nat Hon Sy; Nat Mrt Sch Recip; Otst Ac Ach Awd; WWAHSS; Comm Volntr; Peer Tut/Med; BPA; Chrch Yth Grp; DARE; Emplmnt; FBLA; Off Aide; Quiz Bowl; Chrldg (V); Cr Ctry (V); Track (V); Sch Ppr (E, R); Yrbk (R); Psychology; Corporate Law; U of Maryland; U of Miami

FORD, QUENTIN; CAPITOL HEIGHTS, MD; BOWIE HS; (FR); Hnr Roll; Nat Hon Sy; Civil Air Pat; Emplmnt; Zoology; Morehouse; Yale

FOREMAN, APRIL M; WESTMINSTER, MD; SOUTH CARROLL HS; (JR); Hi Hnr Roll; Nat Hon Sy; Perf Att; Emplmnt; Key Club; Dnce; PP Ftbl; Key Club Treasurer; Past Honored Queen, International Order of Job's Daughters; English

FORMAN, PHOEBE E; SEVERNA PARK, MD; SEVERNA PARK HS; (SO); Hi Hnr Roll; Nat Hon Sy; Yth Ldrshp Prog; Comm Volntr; Spec Olymp Vol; ArtClub; Emplmnt; Key Club; Photog; Bnd; Fld Hky (J); Member of Annapolis Rowing Club- Crew; Vice President of Key Club; Photography

FOSTER, ADRIANNE; CORDOVA, MD; EASTON HS; (FR); Ctznshp Aw; Hi Hnr Roll; MVP; Otst Ac Ach Awd; Perf Att; St of Mnth; Comm Volntr; Chrch Yth Grp; DARE; Dbte Team; Drma Clb; Lib Aide; Pep Squd; Photog; SADD; Chr; Ch Chr; SP/M/VS; Chrldg (V); Scr Kpr (J); Sftball (J L); Cl Off (P); Stu Cncl (S); NESASC Board Representative; Chesapeake Community College; U of Maryland

FOSTER, ANTHONY; FORT WASHINGTON, MD; FRIENDLY HS; (SO); Ctznshp Aw; Hnr Roll; Perf Att; Sci Fairs; St of Mnth; CARE; Comm Volntr; Peer Tut/Med; Chrch Yth Grp; DARE; Kwanza Clb; ROTC; Ch Chr; International Order of St Vincent; Culinary Arts; Chef/Master Chef; U of Maryland Eastern-Shore

FOSTER, BRODERICK D; BALTIMORE, MD; W E B DUBOIS HS; (JR); Sci Fairs; Bnd; Mar Art (L); Black in Martial Arts (Kempo)

FOURNIER, LYNDSAY; MOUNT AIRY, MD; SOUTH CARROLL HS; (FR); Hi Hnr Roll; Otst Ac Ach Awd; Perf Att; Pres Sch; WWAHSS; Comm Volntr; Peer Tut/Med; Drma Clb; Key Club; P to P St Amb Prg; Scouts; Svce Clb; Tchrs Aide; Chr; Ch Chr; Clr Grd; Orch; Chrldg (J); CR (R); Girl Scout Silver Award, Leadership Award; Community Service Award, 600 Hours; Medicine; Doctor; William and Mary College; Harvard

FOX, SHARIA; BOWIE, MD; CHARLES HERBERT FLOWERS HS; (SO); Ctznshp Aw; Hi Hnr Roll; Hnr Roll; Otst Ac Ach Awd; Pres Sch; Red Cr Aide; Emplmnt; Bnd; Vllyball (J); CR (R); Member of the Sigma Gamma Rho Rhodes; Medicine; International Business; Howard U; U of Maryland

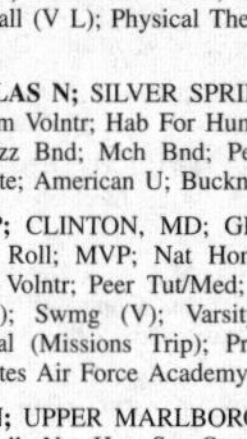

Fellows, Rachel
Patterson SR HS 405
Baltimore, MD

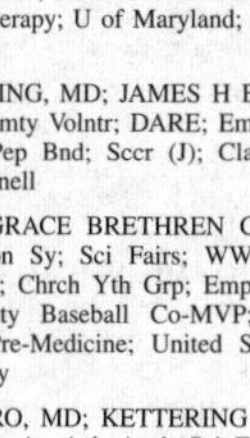

Faison, Melinda M
Woodlawn HS
Gwynn Oak, MD

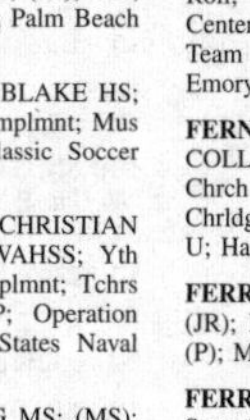

Esteves, Nickolas N
James H Blake HS
Silver Spring, MD

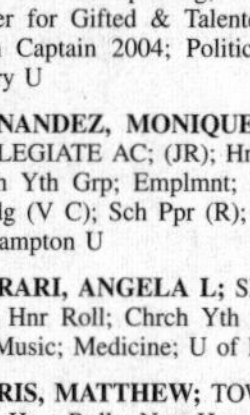

Enriquez, Regina V
Wilde Lake HS
Columbia, MD

National
Honor Roll
Spring 2005

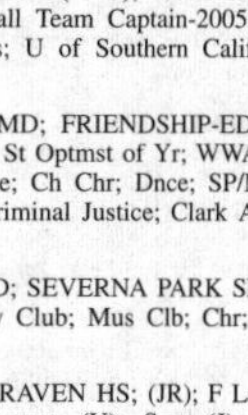

Edwards, Kendra A
Patuxent HS
Lusby, MD

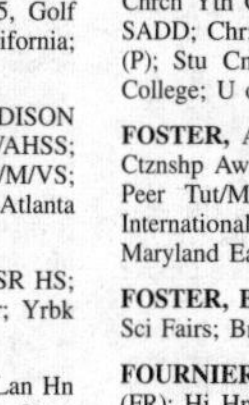

Exum, Ashley N
Kettering MS
Upper Marlboro, MD

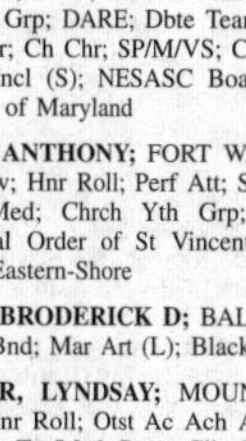

Falk, Jocelyn P
Walter Johnson HS
Rockville, MD

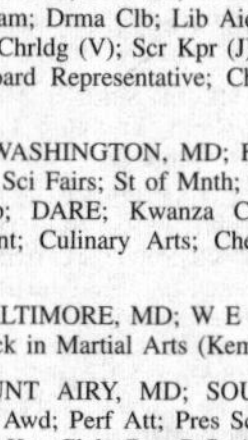

Foglesonger, Brittany
North Dorchester HS
Vienna, MD

FRADKIN, ABIGAIL R; POTOMAC, MD; WINSTON CHURCHILL HS; (SR); DAR; F Lan Hn Soc; Gov Hnr Prg; Hi Hnr Roll; Jr Eng Tech; Nat Hon Sy; Nat Mrt Fin; Nat Mrt Sch Recip; Valdctrian; WWAHSS; Comm Volntr; Peer Tut/Med; Dbte Team; MuAlphaTh; NtlFrnscLg; Dnce; 2004 National Council of Teachers of English Achievement Award in Writing; History; Government / Political Science; Harvard U - Attending Fall 2005

FRALINGER, ALEXANDRA; FREDERICK, MD; TUSCARORA HS; (FR); Hnr Roll; WWAHSS; ArtClub; French Clb; SP/M/VS; French Club; Liberal Arts; Berkeley U; California Institute of the Arts

FRANCOIS, TIFFANY; UPPER MARLBORO, MD; CH FLOWERS HS; (MS); Hnr Roll; Sci/Math Olympn; Comm Volntr; Scouts; Bnd; Editor's Choice Award - Outstanding Achievement in Poetry; Doctor; Lawyer; Columbia U; Frostburg U

FRANSEN, MICHAEL B; BURTONSVILLE, MD; PAINT BRANCH HS; (JR); Hnr Roll; Off Aide; Ice Hky (V C); Track (V L); Become an Automotive Engineer; Physics Major; Boston U; U of Massachusetts-Amherst

FREEMAN, WILLIAM T; WESTERNPORT, MD; WESTMAR HS; (FR); Hnr Roll; MVP; Sci Fairs; St of Mnth; Biology Clb; DARE; FTA; Mth Clb/Tm; Bnd; SP/M/VS; Bsball (J); Ftball (J); Mar Art (V); Skiing (V); CR (R); Yrbk (R); Homecoming Court; 1st Degree Black Belt; Engineering-Chemical; Bucknell U; Yale U

FREEMAN JR, DARYLE L; HYATTSVILLE, MD; FRIENDSHIP-EDISON COLLEGIATE AC; (SR); Ctznshp Aw; Hnr Roll; Perf Att; Sci Fairs; St of Mnth; WWAHSS; Comm Volntr; Drma Clb; Emplmnt; FBLA; Tchrs Aide; French Clb; Bnd; Ch Chr; SP/M/VS; Mar Art; Wt Lftg; Knight Award; Business Management; Business Finance; Johnson C Smith U; Delaware State U

FUNDERBURK, KARNISHIA; HYATTSVILLE, MD; NORTHWESTERN HS; (JR); Hnr Roll; Perf Att; Sci Fairs; Chr; Sftball (J); Peer Mediator; Business Management; U of Maryland; Towson U/Morgan State U

FURLONG, KATHERINE E; LUTHERVILLE TIMONIUM, MD; NOTRE DAME PREPARATORY SCH; (JR); Hnr Roll; Bnd; Jzz Bnd; SP/M/VS; Bdmtn (V); Swmg (V)

GAINES, PHYLLICIA; HAGERSTOWN, MD; NORTH HAGERSTOWN HS; (SO); Hnr Roll; Nat Hon Sy; Comm Volntr; DARE; Drma Clb; Scouts; Bnd; Dnce; Bskball (J); Chiropractor; Lawyer; New York U; U of Illinois

GANG, DAVID; BETHESDA, MD; DE MATHA CATHOLIC HS; (SR); Hnr Roll; Nat Hon Sy; WWAHSS; Comm Volntr; Tmpl Yth Grp; Bnd; Bskball (VJ L); Ftball (V L); Cl Off (T); College of the Holy Cross

GANTT, AMANDA; HYATTSVILLE, MD; DUVAL HS; (JR); Hi Hnr Roll; Hnr Roll; Otst Ac Ach Awd; Perf Att; Pres Ac Ftns Aw; Sci Fairs; Chrldg (VJ); PP Ftbl (J); CR (R); Academic Excellence in World Processing; Medicine (Pediatrics); PhD; North Carolina Agricultural and Technical

GARAY-STANTON, FELICIA; JOPPA, MD; JOPPATOWNE HS; (FR); Hi Hnr Roll; WWAHSS; Comm Volntr; Spanish Clb; Chrldg (V); Track (V L); Attorney; Fashion Design; Ohio State U; Louisiana State U

GARBOCZI, ANNE P; GAITHERSBURG, MD; HOME SCH; (SR); Nat Mrt Fin; Perf Att; Pres Ac Ftns Aw; Pres Sch; Comm Volntr; Peer Tut/Med; Dbte Team; Drma Clb; Emplmnt; Spanish Clb; Ch Chr; SP/M/VS; Stg Cre; Sch Ppr; Perfect SAT Score / Won NRMCA National Essay Contest - 1 Winner Annually; Education / BA; Patrick Henry College - Accepted

GARCIA CESPEDES, STEPHANIE; NOTTINGHAM, MD; PERRY HALL HS; (SO); Hnr Roll; Pres Sch; St of Mnth; Tchrs Aide; Wdwrkg Clb; Bnd; Yrbk; Presidential Award; Yearbook Sales Manager; Certified Nurse; Surgeon; Johns Hopkins U; UMBC

GARG, KEVA; CABIN JOHN, MD; WALK WHITMAN HS; (SO); Dbte Team; Dnce; Swg Chr; Swmg (V); Medical

GASKIN, ADRIAN; SILVER SPRING, MD; HIGH POINT HS; (SR); Hnr Roll; Comm Volntr; Chrch Yth Grp; Emplmnt; Tchrs Aide; Stg Cre; Communications; Bowie State U

GASKINS, COLETTE; BALTIMORE, MD; OVERLEA HS; (SO); Nat Hon Sy; WWAHSS; Comm Volntr; Peer Tut/Med; Chess; DECA; Mod UN; Mus Clb; NYLC; Stg Cre; Vllyball (J); Cl Off (R); CR (R); Sch Ppr (R, P); Having the Chance to Run for Vice-President of the Maryland State Chapter Of DECA; Being Able to Attend the Academy of Finance at Overlea High School.; I Would Like to Be a Successful Chef or Be Able to work in the Finance World (Music Business); I Would Like to Be My Own Boss or Go in Business with Friends and Family.; Lebanon Valley College Annville, PA; Morgan State U Baltimore, Maryland

GBE, HARMONY R; SILVER SPRING, MD; SPRINGBROOK HS; (JR); F Lan Hn Soc; Hnr Roll; WWAHSS; Comm Volntr; Peer Tut/Med; MuAlphaTh; Tchrs Aide; French Clb; Bnd; Dnce; Mch Bnd; Lit Mag (E); National Society of High School Scholars; Star Scholarship; Business; Economics

GELWICKS, BAILLE; HAGERSTOWN, MD; NORTH HAGERSTOWN HS; (JR); All Am Sch; Hi Hnr Roll; WWAHSS; Prom Com; Chr; Dnce; Flg Crps; SP/M/VS; Cum Laude on National Latin Exam; Major in Dance

GEORGE, ALISHA; WESTMINSTER, MD; WINTERS MILL; (JR); Hi Hnr Roll; Nat Hon Sy; Otst Ac Ach Awd; WWAHSS; Yth Ldrshp Prog; Comm Volntr; Peer Tut/Med; Drma Clb; Emplmnt; HO'Br Yth Ldrshp; Key Club; SP/M/VS; Sccr (J); Track (J); CR (R); Sch Ppr (R)

GIBBS, GARID A; DISTRICT HEIGHTS, MD; CHARLES HERBERT FLOWERS HS; (SO); F Lan Hn Soc; Hi Hnr Roll; Hnr Roll; St Optmst of Yr; WWAHSS; Peer Tut/Med; DARE; Quiz Bowl; Schol Bwl; Spanish Clb; Mathematics; Computer Science; U of Maryland; U of Pennsylvania

GIBBS, LINWOOD; BALTIMORE, MD; DIGITAL HARBOR HS 416; (JR); Hnr Roll; Ftball (VJ); Computer Science; Business; Florida State U

GILBERT, ANNE; NORTH EAST, MD; NORTH EAST HS; (SO); Hnr Roll; Peer Tut/Med; 4-H; Civil Air Pat; Bnd; Jzz Bnd; Mch Bnd; Pep Bnd; Track (J); Camp Counselor, 3 Years; Zoology

GILMORE, TIAJUANA; FORT WASHINGTON, MD; GRACE BRETHREN CHRISTIAN SCH; (SO); Hi Hnr Roll; WWAHSS; Comm Volntr; Emplmnt; ROTC; Stg Cre; Pre-Med; Music; Langston U; Temple U

GILMOUR, JONATHAN M; UPPER MARLBORO, MD; GRACE BRETHREN CHRISTIAN SCH; (JR); Hi Hnr Roll; Nat Hon Sy; Sci Fairs; Comm Volntr; Chrch Yth Grp; Emplmnt; Swmg (V L); Yrbk (R, P); Computer/IT; Hood College; Grove City

GILSTRAP, MIA A; FORT WASHINGTON, MD; FRIENDLY HS; (SO); F Lan Hn Soc; Hi Hnr Roll; Hnr Roll; Perf Att; Sci Fairs; Chrch Yth Grp; ROTC; Ch Chr; Dnce; Tennis (V); 1st Place County Science Fair; Mock Trial; Pre-Law; Clark-Atlanta U; Spelman College

GIRALDO, BRITTANY; BALTIMORE, MD; NEW ERA AC; (FR); Hnr Roll; Nat Hon Sy; Comm Volntr; DARE; Dbte Team; Drma Clb; Mus Clb; Latin Clb; Bnd; SP/M/VS; Bsball (J); Bskball (J); Sccr (J); Vllyball (J); Towson Debate Summer Camp Scholarship; Student of the Week; Lawyer; Nurse; Coppin State U; Bob Jones U

GIRI, PUJA; GAITHERSBURG, MD; GAITHERSBURG HS; (SR); Hnr Roll; SP/M/VS; Life Science; Montgomery College; U of Maryland

GLADSTONE, JESSIE; PERRY HALL, MD; PERRY HALL HS; (SO); Hnr Roll; Emplmnt; Chr; Cr Ctry (V); Fld Hky (V); Lcrsse (J); Pediatrician; Nurse; Johns Hopkins U; U of Maryland

GLASCOE, RALLENE V; OXON HILL, MD; OXON HILL HS; (FR); Ctznshp Aw; Hnr Roll; Nat Hon Sy; St of Mnth; Hab For Humty Volntr; Chess; Chrch Yth Grp; Pep Squd; Ch Chr; Dnce; PPSqd (V); Sch Ppr; Veterinarian Medicine; Biology; U of Maryland (College Park); Virginia Tech

GLESSNER, JUSTIN W; RHODESDALE, MD; NORTH DORCHESTER HS; (JR); Hi Hnr Roll; Hnr Roll; Nat Mrt LOC; Comm Volntr; Chrch Yth Grp; Emplmnt; FCA; Key Club; Mus Clb; Prom Com; Tchrs Aide; Bnd; Chr; SP/M/VS; Sccr (VJ L); Tennis (V CL); Firefighter I; Computer Application; Liberty U

GLOVER, MARY M; ELLICOTT CITY, MD; WILDE LAKE HS; (SR); Hi Hnr Roll; Hnr Roll; Nat Hon Sy; Nat Mrt Semif; Amnsty Intl; Comm Volntr; Peer Tut/Med; Emplmnt; Mus Clb; Prom Com; Bnd; Mch Bnd; Sftball (VJ); Vllyball (J), Cl Off (R), Stu Cncl (R); CR (R); Editor of Class Newsletter; Swim Team Member @ Howard CO. YMCA; Biology; Pre Medical; Emory U; Drew U

GLUCK, LAUREN; NORTH POTOMAC, MD; THOMAS S WOOTTON HS; (SO); F Lan Hn Soc; Hi Hnr Roll; Otst Ac Ach Awd; St of Mnth; WWAHSS; Comm Volntr; Spec Olymp Vol; ArtClub; Key Club; Tmpl Yth Grp; Dnce; Ice Sktg (C); CR (R); National Spanish Honor Society; State Senate Stellar Achievement Award; Architecture; Meteorology (Atmospheric Science); Cornell U; Yale U

GODFREY, KRISTAL M; GLENN DALE, MD; BOWIE HS; (JR); Hi Hnr Roll; Hnr Roll; Nat Hon Sy; Sci Fairs; St of Mnth; WWAHSS; Yth Ldrshp Prog; Comm Volntr; Chrch Yth Grp; Prom Com; Tchrs Aide; Dnce; PPSqd (V); Cl Off (R); Secretary of National Honor Society; National Society of High School Scholars; Business / Aviation Science; Political Science; U of Maryland College Park; Penn State

GOETSCH, BRITTANY; GERMANTOWN, MD; NORTHWEST HS; (SO); F Lan Hn Soc; Hi Hnr Roll; Hnr Roll; Nat Hon Sy; Comm Volntr; Emplmnt; P to P St Amb Prg; Quill & Scroll; Scouts; Swmg (V L); Lit Mag (E); Girl Scout Silver Award; Politically Active Women Club; Political Science; Literature; Harvard U; Yale U

GOGGIN JR, MARK A; BOWIE, MD; BOWIE HS; (SO); Hnr Roll; Sci Fairs; Scouts; Chr; Cr Ctry (VJ L); CR (R); Rank of Star - Scout; Game Designer; Culinary Artist; U of Maryland

GOINES, ANGELA; SILVER SPRING, MD; ALBERT EINSTEIN HS; (SR); Hnr Roll; Comm Volntr; Dnce; All-Star Cheerleader; Selected All-American Cheerleader; Psychology; U of Maryland College Park; Temple U

GOLBOURN, MAXINE; BALTIMORE, MD; WALBROOK HS; (SR); Perf Att; Comm Volntr; Hosp Aide; Chrch Yth Grp; Emplmnt; Off Aide; Prom Com; Tchrs Aide; Ch Chr; Mch Bnd; Stg Cre; Barbizon Modeling; Business Administration; Business Management; Baltimore City Community College; Coppin State College

GOLDBERG, ALLISON; GAITHERSBURG, MD; RICHARD MONTGOMERY HS; (JR); Ctznshp Aw; Hi Hnr Roll; Nat Hon Sy; Dbte Team; Scouts; Tmpl Yth Grp; Environmental Science; Mathematics Education

GOLDBERG, EMILY; COLUMBIA, MD; WILDE LAKE HS; (JR); Nat Hon Sy; Yth Ldrshp Prog; Comm Volntr; Hab For Humty Volntr; Chrch Yth Grp; Emplmnt; Photog; Dnce; Sftball (J); Elementary Education; English; Wheaton College (Illinois); U of Mary Washington

GOLDBERG, HELEN; SILVER SPRING, MD; RICHARD MONTGOMERY HS; (JR); F Lan Hn Soc; Nat Hon Sy; Comm Volntr; Peer Tut/Med; Drma Clb; Emplmnt; Key Club; Svce Clb; Spanish Clb; Stg Cre; Fld Hky (J); Played Violin-8 years; International Relations; Public Policy; Princeton U; U of Pennsylvania

GONZALEZ, FIDEL A; ROCKVILLE, MD; WHEATON HS; (FR); Chief Justice; Baseball Player; Maryland; Virginia Tech

GOOD, CASEY J; BALTIMORE, MD; (JR); Hi Hnr Roll; Hnr Roll; Comm Volntr; Peer Tut/Med; Red Cr Aide; Chrch Yth Grp; Tchrs Aide; Ch Chr

GORELIK, MARIYA; GAITHERSBURG, MD; WALTER JOHNSON HS; (JR); Hnr Roll; Nat Hon Sy; WWAHSS; Comm Volntr; Peer Tut/Med; Emplmnt; Sci Clb; Chr; Dnce; Chrldg (VJ); Swmg (J); Play Piano and Keyboard; Pre-Medicine; Financial Management/Business; U of Maryland; Georgetown

GOURDINE, KELLIE S; WINDSOR MILL, MD; MILFORD MILL AC; (JR); Hnr Roll; Perf Att; Emplmnt; Scouts; CR (R); Pre-Med; Howard U; Lincoln U

GRAFF, MEAGAN; HAGERSTOWN, MD; NORTH HAGERSTOWN HS; (FR); Hi Hnr Roll; Hnr Roll; Otst Ac Ach Awd; Comm Volntr; Chrch Yth Grp; FCA; Key Club; Bnd; Dnce; Mch Bnd; Orch; Vllyball (VJ); Numerous Instrumental Music Awards; Numerous Academic Achievement Awards; Engineering; Music; U of Virginia; U of Maryland

GRAHAM, CRYSTAL; TAKOMA PARK, MD; HIGH POINT HS; (SR); Hi Hnr Roll; Hnr Roll; Comm Volntr; Off Aide; Tchrs Aide; Chrldg (V); Best Buddies; I Want to Be a Teacher.; I Also Want to Be a Cosmetologist.; Prince George's Community College

GRAHAM, RACHAEL; WESTMINSTER, MD; SOUTH CARROLL HS; (JR); Hnr Roll; Nat Hon Sy; Otst Ac Ach Awd; WWAHSS; Peer Tut/Med; Key Club; Tchrs Aide; Chr; Fld Hky (V L); Lcrsse (V L); PP Ftbl; Skiing; Track (V); CR (R); Historian of Key Club; Newsletter Editor for Key Club; Nurse Anesthetist; U of Maryland; Florida State U

GRAVES, ALISE; CROFTON, MD; SOUTH RIVER HS; (JR); Hi Hnr Roll; Hnr Roll; Otst Ac Ach Awd; Perf Att; Peer Tut/Med; DARE; Emplmnt; Photog; Spanish Clb; Dnce; Step Team; Psychology; Fashion Design; New York U; Niagara U

GRAVES, KATIE; POCOMOKE CITY, MD; (SR); F Lan Hn Soc; Hi Hnr Roll; Nat Hon Sy; Sci Fairs; St of Mnth; WWAHSS; Peer Tut/Med; Drma Clb; Emplmnt; Key Club; Sci Clb; SADD; Tchrs Aide; Spanish Clb; Chr; SP/M/VS; Hsbk Rdg; Sch Ppr (E, R); Art; Physics; Spanish; Salisbury U; St. Louis U, Madrid Campus

GRAY, BRITTANY; WINDSOR MILL, MD; WOODLAWN HS; (FR); Nat Hon Sy; Otst Ac Ach Awd; Sci/Math Olympn; Comm Volntr; Chrch Yth Grp; Mus Clb; Quiz Bowl; ROTC; Ch Chr; Clr Grd; Drl Tm; Sftball (J); Vllyball (J); Masters Degree; Bachelors Degree; U of Atlanta; U of Maryland

GREEN, AMANDA; RAWLINGS, MD; WESTMAR HS; (FR); Hnr Roll; Office Systems; Medical Coding; Allegany College; Frostburg State

GREEN, JASON L; THURMONT, MD; CATOCTIN HS; (SR); Hnr Roll; Nat Hon Sy; Perf Att; Ntl FFA; Tchrs Aide; Electrician; Frederick Community College

GREER, CHARMINQUE; BALTIMORE, MD; NEW ERA AC; (FR); Hnr Roll; Perf Att; Comm Volntr; Dbte Team; Emplmnt; Ch Chr; Dnce; Stu Cncl (S); Debate Team / Assistant Captain; Honor Roll Student; Pre-Med; Law; Howard U; U of Maryland

GREER, DESIREE; EDGEWOOD, MD; JOPPATOWNE HS; (FR); Ctznshp Aw; Hnr Roll; MVP; Perf Att; St of Mnth; Peer Tut/Med; Bskball (J); Cr Ctry; Track; Perfect Attendance; Going to the Navy

GREGOROWICZ, DANICE V; ABERDEEN PROVING GROUND, MD; ABERDEEN HS; (SR); F Lan Hn Soc; Hnr Roll; Pres Ac Ftns Aw; WWAHSS; Comm Volntr; ArtClub; DARE; Scouts; SADD; French Clb; PP Ftbl (J); Sccr (V L); Sftball (V L); National Art Honor Society; National Society of High School Scholars; Biology; Biomedical Research; Lycoming College

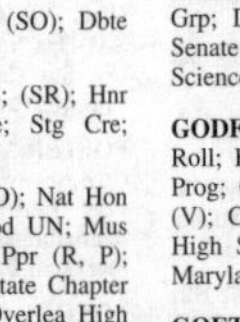

Graham, Crystal
High Point HS
Takoma Park, MD

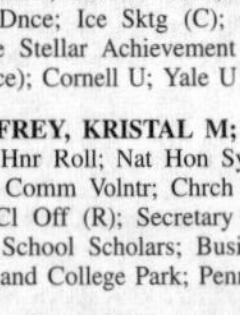

Godfrey, Kristal M
Bowie HS
Glenn Dale, MD

National
Honor Roll
Spring 2005

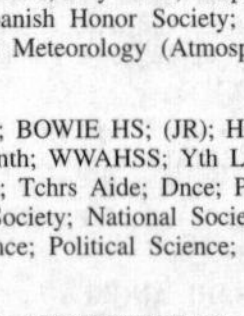

Giri, Puja
Gaithersburg HS
Gaithersburg, MD

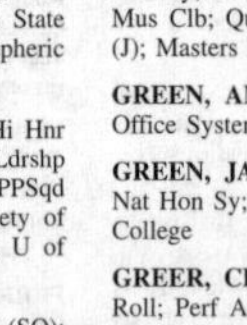

Gregorowicz, Danice V
Aberdeen HS
Aberdeen Proving Ground, MD

GREISLER, JEN; MOUNT AIRY, MD; SOUTH CARROLL HS; (JR); All Am Sch; F Lan Hn Soc; Hnr Roll; Nat Hon Sy; Perf Att; Pres Sch; USAA; WWAHSS; Comm Volntr; Peer Tut/Med; Chrch Yth Grp; Emplmnt; Key Club; Tchrs Aide; Bnd; Dnce; Orch; SP/M/VS; Cr Ctry (V); Track (V); Stu Cncl (R); Chemical Engineering; Spanish Language; U of Maryland-College Park; Johns Hopkins U

GRIFFIN, CANDACE L; FREDERICK, MD; PINE FORGE AC; (SO); Ctznshp Aw; Hi Hnr Roll; Nat Hon Sy; Otst Ac Ach Awd; Valdctrian; Comm Volntr; Peer Tut/Med; Chrch Yth Grp; Emplmnt; Prom Com; Tchrs Aide; Acpl Chr; Chr; Ch Chr; SP/M/VS; Bskball (V); Cr Ctry (V); Cl Off (P); Kappa Alpha Psi Academic Achievement Recognition; Pathfinders; Biochemistry Major; Pre-Med Major; Oakwood College; Howard U

GRIFFITH, ANGELA; SALISBURY, MD; JAMES M BENNETT HS; (SR); Ctznshp Aw; F Lan Hn Soc; Hnr Roll; Otst Ac Ach Awd; St of Mnth; WWAHSS; Yth Ldrshp Prog; DARE; Emplmnt; Photog; Scouts; Sccr (J); Sftball (V); Intern At the Maryland State Police-Barrack "E"; Outstanding Student of the Class-Criminal Justice; Criminal Justice Major; Become a Maryland State Trooper to Become a Detective; U of Maryland Eastern Shore; Delaware Technical of Community College

GRIFFITH, CHANISE A; FORT WASHINGTON, MD; FRIENDLY HS; (SO); Hnr Roll; Nat Hon Sy; Perf Att; Pres Ac Ftns Aw; ROTC; John Casablancas Modeling and Career Center; Culinary Arts; Business Management; Stratford U; Art Institute of Washington

GRIFFITH, RYAN P; COLUMBIA, MD; DE MATHA CATHOLIC; (SR); 4H Awd; Hnr Roll; MVP; Otst Ac Ach Awd; WWAHSS; Comm Volntr; Hosp Aide; Emplmnt; Bskball (J); Ftball (V CL); Lcrsse (J L); Wt Lftg (V); CR (R); Political Science; Weapons & Systems Engineering; United States Naval Academy

GROSS, KRISTINA A; BALTIMORE, MD; DIGITAL HARBOR HS 416; (JR); Hnr Roll; St of Mnth; Comm Volntr; Social Worker; Nurse

GROSS JR, WILLIAM J; FREDERICK, MD; FREDERICK HS; (SR); Hi Hnr Roll; Hnr Roll; MVP; Perf Att; WWAHSS; Comm Volntr; Chrch Yth Grp; Emplmnt; FCA; Lttrmn Clb; Lib Aide; Vsity Clb; SP/M/VS; Bsball (V CL); Ftball (VJ L); Golf (V L); Wt Lftg (VJ); CR (R); Yrbk (E, P); Homecoming Court; Mr. FHS Winner; Sports Management Business; Education Math; Towson U; James Madison U

GRUBB, BRIAN E; OWINGS, MD; NORTHERN HS; (FR); Hnr Roll

GUE, ALEXANDRA; ESSEX, MD; THE CATHOLIC HS OF BALTIMORE; (SO); Hi Hnr Roll; Nat Hon Sy; Perf Att; Photog; Lcrsse (J); Fashion Merchandising; Loyola College; Salisbury U

GUERIN, CHANDA D; DUNKIRK, MD; NORTHERN HS; (SR); Hnr Roll; Nat Hon Sy; BPA; Drma Clb; FBLA; Stg Cre; Business; Towson U

GUY, JEREMIE; BOWIE, MD; LANHAM CHRISTIAN SCH; (JR); Hi Hnr Roll; Hnr Roll; Nat Sci Aw; WWAHSS; Comm Volntr; Chrch Yth Grp; Drma Clb; Emplmnt; SP/M/VS; Bskball (V); Sccr (V L); Physical Therapy; U of Maryland-College Park; Florida State U

HAASS, KOURTNEY E; GREENSBORO, MD; CAROLINE CAREER & TECH CTR; (JR); Hnr Roll; St of Mnth; 4-H; FBLA; Ntl FFA; Chr; 5th Place At FBLA State Competition; Animal Science; Natural Resources; U of Delaware; Delaware State U

HADDAD, JENNIFER; WESTMINSTER, MD; GLENELG CTRY SCH; (MS); Hnr Roll; Perf Att; Comm Volntr; Drma Clb; Chr; Dnce; SP/M/VS; Fld Hky; Gmnstcs; Lcrsse; Sccr; Tennis; Stu Cncl (R); Sch Ppr (E); Yrbk (E); Lawyer; Actress; U of Virginia; Virginia Tech

HADDAD, NATASHA C; ROCKVILLE, MD; WHEATON HS; (FR); F Lan Hn Soc; Hi Hnr Roll; Hnr Roll; St of Mnth; Comm Volntr; Chrch Yth Grp; DARE; Drma Clb; Key Club; French Clb; Chr; Medical School; Language

HAIR, SHENNA; BALTIMORE, MD; BALTIMORE CITY COLLEGE HS; (JR); F Lan Hn Soc; Hnr Roll; Perf Att; WWAHSS; Red Cr Aide; Photog; Pharmacy; Psychology; Quinnipiac U; Mt. St Mary's College

HALL, DARRELL; PIKESVILLE, MD; MILFORD MILL AC; (SR); DARE; Outdrs Clb; Spch Team; Tech Clb; Wdwrkg Clb; Wt Lftg (V); Music; Human Services; Sheffield Institute; Catonsville Community College

HALL, KIM R; PORT REPUBLIC, MD; CALVERT HS; (JR); Ctznshp Aw; Hnr Roll; Otst Ac Ach Awd; Perf Att; St of Mnth; Yth Ldrshp Prog; Peer Tut/Med; P to P St Amb Prg; Vsity Clb; Bskball (V C); Member of Peer Advisory Council; Communications; Writing / Publishing; Delaware State U; U of MD Eastern Shore

HALLBERG, ALYSSA; MANCHESTER, MD; NORTH CARROLL HS; (SR); Hi Hnr Roll; Hnr Roll; Nat Hon Sy; Hab For Humty Volntr; Chrch Yth Grp; ROTC; Svce Clb; Spanish Clb; ROTC Awards; Marine Biology; Eckerd College

HALLEY, CHINELLE; BALTIMORE, MD; NORTHWESTERN HS; (JR); Hnr Roll; Perf Att; St of Mnth; Comm Volntr; Sch Ppr (E, R); Ranked #1 in the Junior Class; Accepted to Young Scholars Program At UMD; Public Relations; Business Administration; U of Maryland, College Park; Fordham U

HAMILTON, JANIA L; PIKESVILLE, MD; RANDALLSTOWN HS; (JR); Comm Volntr; Chrch Yth Grp; Pep Squd; Mch Bnd; PPSqd; Lawyer; Psychologist; Clark Atlanta U; New York U

HAMMER, CONSTANCE; CLINTON, MD; GRACE BRETHREN CHRISTIAN SCH; (JR); Hi Hnr Roll; Hnr Roll; Sci Fairs; Comm Volntr; Peer Tut/Med; Lib Aide; Tchrs Aide; Bnd; Mch Bnd; Pep Bnd; Homeroom Representative (Alternate) (2 Years); National Junior Honor Society; Library Science; U of Maryland

HAMMETT, MORGAN; POOLESVILLE, MD; POOLESVILLE HS; (JR); Hnr Roll; Nat Hon Sy; Comm Volntr; Dbte Team; Emplmnt; Lib Aide; NtlFrnscLg; Sccr (J); Track (V); Minds in Motion Award Recipient; Roots & Shoots Club; English; Humanities; Washington College MD; St Mary's MD

HAMMOND, AVA-DAWN; RANDALLSTOWN, MD; RANDALLSTOWN HS; (SO); Hnr Roll; Spanish Clb; Medicine; Business; U of Maryland; Towson U

HAMMOND III, JOHN R; FORT WASHINGTON, MD; GRACE BRETHREN CHRISTIAN SCH; (JR); Sci Fairs; Comm Volntr; Emplmnt; Bskball (VJ); Cl Off (V); Mission Trip to Costa Rica Spring 2005; Participated in Teen Cotillion; Finance; Sports Management; Elon U; St. Mary's College in Maryland

HANLON, STEPHANIE A; BOWIE, MD; BOWIE HS; (JR); DAR; Hnr Roll; Comm Volntr; Spec Olymp Vol; Emplmnt; Prom Com; Tchrs Aide; Swmg (V L)

HANSON JR, DALLAS A; BALTIMORE, MD; MERVO HS; (JR); Ctznshp Aw; Hnr Roll; Perf Att; Comm Volntr; Outdrs Clb; Wdwrkg Clb; Physical Therapist; Bowie U; U of Southern California

HARAB, JULIE; ROCKVILLE, MD; RICHARD MONTGOMERY HS; (JR); F Lan Hn Soc; Hnr Roll; Nat Hon Sy; Otst Ac Ach Awd; Comm Volntr; Peer Tut/Med; Key Club; Acpl Chr; Bnd; Chr; Jzz Bnd; Bskball (J); Fld Hky (V L); Sftball (V L); CR (R); Sch Ppr (R); Nursing; Education; U of Maryland College Park; Emory U

HARBAUGH, JEREMY; SMITHSBURG, MD; SMITHSBURG HS; (SO); Hi Hnr Roll; Otst Ac Ach Awd; Pres Ac Ftns Aw; WWAHSS; Chess; Cmptr Clb; Orch; Ftball (V); Lcrsse (V); Wrstlg (V); Received Faculty Distinguished Honor Roll Award in 2004-2005; Received STARS Recognition Four Times; Computer Science; Aviation; Princeton U; United States Naval Academy

HARMON, JAMAR; PRINCESS ANNE, MD; WASHINGTON HS; (SR); Hnr Roll; Nat Hon Sy; Otst Ac Ach Awd; St of Mnth; WWAHSS; Bsball (J); Bskball (J); Cr Ctry (VJ); National Honor Society; Business Administration; Accounting; Hampton U; Morgan State U

HAROUN, LOLA O; BOWIE, MD; CHARLES HERBERT FLOWERS HS; (FR); Ctznshp Aw; F Lan Hn Soc; Hnr Roll; Nat Hon Sy; Sci Fairs; Yth Ldrshp Prog; CARE; Comm Volntr; Red Cr Aide; ArtClub; Chrch Yth Grp; Cmptr Clb; Dbte Team; Drma Clb; Scouts; Tchrs Aide; French Clb; Chr; Ch Chr; Dnce; Orch; Bdmtn (J); Bskball (J); GAA (J); Gmnstcs (J); Sccr (V); Tennis (J); Track (J); Vllyball (J); Cl Off (P); Sch Ppr (P); Surgeon; Fashion Designing; Howard U; U of Maryland

HARRACKSINGH, VINDRA T; ESSEX, MD; PERRY HALL HS; (SO); Hnr Roll; Nat Hon Sy; Nat Stu Ath Day Aw; Otst Ac Ach Awd; Perf Att; DARE; SADD; Chr; Bskball (C); Scr Kpr (J); Nurse; Teacher; U of Maryland

HARRILL, OLIVER; OCEAN CITY, MD; STEPHEN DECATUR HS; (FR); Hi Hnr Roll; Hnr Roll; St of Mnth; Comm Volntr; Peer Tut/Med; Chess; Cmptr Clb; Teaching Degree; Master's Degree; Stanford U; Syracuse U

HARRIS, DANAE' I; WALDORF, MD; MC DONOUGH HS; (FR); Hi Hnr Roll; Hnr Roll; WWAHSS; Chrch Yth Grp; Ch Chr; Chrldg (VJ); Praise Dancer at Church; Early Childhood Development; Nursing / Dealing with Premature Babies; U of Maryland College Park; Bowie State U

HARRIS, GEORGE; FORESTVILLE, MD; CHARLES HERBERT FLOWERS HS; (SO); Hi Hnr Roll; Hnr Roll; Chrch Yth Grp; P to P St Amb Prg; Bnd; Dnce; Jzz Bnd; Mch Bnd; Golf (V); Science and Technology Program at Charles Flowers HS; Most Valuable Player for Glenarden Track Club; Engineering; Alabama Agricultural and Mechanical U; Florida Agricultural and Mechanical U

HARRIS, MICHELLE; UPPER MARLBORO, MD; FREDERICK DOUGLASS HS; (SO); Ctznshp Aw; Hnr Roll; Nat Hon Sy; Otst Ac Ach Awd; Perf Att; St of Mnth; USAA; Comm Volntr; ArtClub; Scouts; Sccr (V); Pediatric Surgeon; Auto Engineering; Johns Hopkins U; Columbia U

HARRIS, MORGHEN; ROCKVILLE, MD; SHERWOOD HS; (JR); Hi Hnr Roll; Pres Sch; Sci Fairs; St of Mnth; Comm Volntr; Peer Tut/Med; Chrch Yth Grp; Chr; Bskball; Adv Cncl (R); Podiatry; Criminal Justice; Spelman College; North Carolina A & T U

HART, CHERISH; KITZMILLER, MD; SOUTHERN GARRETT CTY HS; (FR); Hnr Roll; Comm Volntr; DARE; Emplmnt; Bnd; Lit Mag (E); Young Marines - Mountaineer Platoon; Nursing; Garrett Community College; West Virginia U

HARTING, ANDY; BOWIE, MD; BOWIE HS; (JR); Hi Hnr Roll; Hnr Roll; Sci Fairs; WWAHSS; Chrch Yth Grp; Emplmnt; Golf (V); Lcrsse (V); Engineering

HARTMAN, KRISTINA; CATONSVILLE, MD; MT DE SALES AC; (JR); Hnr Roll; Nat Hon Sy; Comm Volntr; Maryland Distinguished Scholar; Law; Psychology; Villa Julie College; Loyola College

HATHAWAY, JERMIAH A; SPRINGFIELD, MD; KICKAPOO HS; (SO); Hnr Roll; Mar Art; Sccr; Medical Field; SMS

HAWKES, FLOYD; WINDSOR MILL, MD; WESTERN SCH OF TECH AND ENVIRONMENTAL SCIENCES; (FR); Hnr Roll; Nat Hon Sy; Otst Ac Ach Awd; Perf Att; WWAHSS; Comm Volntr; P to P St Amb Prg; Bnd; Mch Bnd; Orch; Computer Networking; Computer Repair

HAWKINS, TAMISHA K; FORT WASHINGTON, MD; FRIENDLY HS; (SO); Ctznshp Aw; Hnr Roll; Sci Fairs; Chrch Yth Grp; DARE; ROTC; Sftball (J); Cl Off (S); Pediatrics; Nursing; Howard U

HAYEK, CHRISTINE; SILVER SPRING, MD; MONTGOMERY BLAIR HS; (JR); Hi Hnr Roll; Hnr Roll; Nat Hon Sy; Otst Ac Ach Awd; St Schl; WWAHSS; Comm Volntr; Peer Tut/Med; ArtClub; Vsity Clb; Fld Hky (VJ L); Track; CR (R); Varsity Field Hockey - Most Improved; Organized Student Art Show and Displayed Work; Dartmouth College; Davidson College

HAYES, CHELSEA; SILVER SPRING, MD; JAMES H BLAKE HS; (JR); Hnr Roll; MVP; Nat Hon Sy; Otst Ac Ach Awd; Sci Fairs; Comm Volntr; Emplmnt; Mus Clb; Photog; Scouts; SADD; Tchrs Aide; Vsity Clb; Chr; Dnce; SP/M/VS; Swg Chr; PP Ftbl (V CL); Sccr (V CL); Stu Cncl (T); Honorable Mention in All-Met in 2003; Indoor Soccer - Varsity & Captain; Psychology; Law; Elon U; U of Maryland

HAYES, MALENA; POCOMOKE CITY, MD; POCOMOKE HS; (FR); Hi Hnr Roll; Hnr Roll; Sci Fairs; St of Mnth; Comm Volntr; Peer Tut/Med; Chrch Yth Grp; DARE; ROTC; Scouts; Tchrs Aide; Vsity Clb; Ch Chr; Dnce; Chrldg (V); Yrbk (P); Obstetrician; Pediatrician; Harvard U; Morgan U

HAYES, QUAVIS; POCOMOKE CITY, MD; POCOMOKE HS; (FR); Hi Hnr Roll; Hnr Roll; Bsball (J); Bskball (J); Electronics; Physical Education; U of North Carolina; Maryland College Park

HEINS, PAUL E; ANNAPOLIS, MD; BROADNECK HS; (JR); Hi Hnr Roll; Hnr Roll; Kwnis Aw; Nat Hon Sy; Otst Ac Ach Awd; Yth Ldrshp Prog; Comm Volntr; Peer Tut/Med; DARE; Key Club; Scouts; Foreign Clb; Cr Ctry (J); Lcrsse (J); Track (J); VP of Key Club; Treasurer of Foreign Language Club; Pilot for the US Navy; Lawyer; USNA; Emory Riddle

HENDRICKS, JADE; GWYNN OAK, MD; WESTERN STATES HS; (SR); Hnr Roll; Nat Hon Sy; Perf Att; St of Mnth; Comm Volntr; Emplmnt; Lib Aide; Bskball (J); Lcrsse (V); Sccr (V C); Wrstlg (V C); First Female to Go to MD State Wrestling Tournament; Aerospace Engineering; Virginia Tech; U of Maryland-College Park

HENDRICKSON, LAUREN K; BEL AIR, MD; ALBEMARLE HS; Perf Att; Pres Ac Ftns Aw; WWAHSS; Hab For Humty Volntr; ArtClub; Chrch Yth Grp; Emplmnt; People to People Student Ambassador '03; Gallery Showing / Oils/ - 8/5/05; Architecture / Design; Psychology

HENSON, JOHNNISA N; FRIENDSHIP, MD; SOUTHERN SR HS; (JR); Hnr Roll; Pres Sch; St of Mnth; WWAHSS; Red Cr Aide; Chrch Yth Grp; DECA; Emplmnt; FBLA; HO'Br Yth Ldrshp; Prom Com; Tchrs Aide; Bnd; Chr; Mch Bnd; Cl Off (S); Stu Cncl (S); Pre-Medicine; Pre-Law; U of Maryland College Park; Johns Hopkins U

HEREDIA, KIARA D; GWYNN OAK, MD; BALTIMORE POLY TECH INST 403; (SO); Hnr Roll; Perf Att; WWAHSS; Chrch Yth Grp; Bdmtn (J); Ben Carson Scholarship; Optimist International Outstanding Service; Business; Georgia Institute of Technology; Stevens Institute of Technology

HERNANDEZ, ALEXANDER; WALDORF, MD; ST MARY'S RYKEN HS; (SR); Ctznshp Aw; Hi Hnr Roll; Nat Hon Sy; Otst Ac Ach Awd; Pres Sch; WWAHSS; Comm Volntr; Peer Tut/Med; Drma Clb; FBLA; Key Club; Svce Clb; Bnd; Jzz Bnd; SP/M/VS; Mar Art; Swmg; Vllyball; (XBSS) Xaverian Brothers Sponsored School Steward; Ambassador's Club; Pre-Medicine; Biology; St Mary's College of Maryland; Loyola College in Maryland

HERNANDEZ BAIPES, JENNY; CAPITOL HEIGHTS, MD; CENTRAL HS; (SO); Dnce; Orch; SP/M/VS

HILETEWORK, TSION G; GAITHERSBURG, MD; GAITHERSBURG HS; (SO); Ctznshp Aw; DAR; F Lan Hn Soc; Hi Hnr Roll; Hnr Roll; Nat Hon Sy; Nat Mrt LOC; Otst Ac Ach Awd; Perf Att; Sci Fairs; Comm Volntr; Peer Tut/Med; Chrch Yth Grp; Cmptr Clb; DARE; FCA; Fr of Library; Lib Aide; Mth Clb/Tm; Outdrs Clb; Dnce; SP/M/VS; Stg Cre; Arch (J); Bdmtn (J); Bsball (J); Bskball (J); Fld Hky (J); Sccr (J); Sftball (J); Vllyball (J); Medicine; Law/History; U of Maryland; U of Virginia

Hernandez, Alexander
St Mary's Ryken HS
Waldorf, MD

Hathaway, Jermiah A
Kickapoo HS
Springfield, MD

Harris, Danae' I
Mc Donough HS
Waldorf, MD

Gross, Kristina A
Digital Harbor HS 416
Baltimore, MD

Griffith, Ryan P
De Matha Catholic
Columbia, MD

Griffin, Candace L
Pine Forge AC
Frederick, MD

Griffith, Angela
James M Bennett HS
Salisbury, MD

Hall, Kim R
Calvert HS
Port Republic, MD

Harris, George
Charles Herbert Flowers HS
Forestville, MD

Hayes, Malena
Pocomoke HS
Pocomoke City, MD

Henson, Johnnisa N
Southern SR HS
Friendship, MD

HILL, KEYSIA; BUSHWOOD, MD; (FR); 4H Awd; Ctznshp Aw; Nat Mrt Semif; Otst Ac Ach Awd; Sci Fairs; St Schl; Comm Volntr; Peer Tut/Med; 4-H; Biology Clb; DARE; Drma Clb; Fr of Library; Jr Ach; Sci Clb; Scouts; Ch Chr; Dnce; SP/M/VS; Stg Cre; Chrldg (C); Fld Hky (C); Gmnstcs (C); PPSqd (C); Sccr (C); Swmg (C); Vllyball (JC); Citizenship & Christmas in April; Environmental Science

HILL, LATOYA L; SUITLAND, MD; CENTRAL HS; (JR); Ctznshp Aw; Hnr Roll; MVP; Perf Att; St of Mnth; Spec Olymp Vol; Chrch Yth Grp; DARE; Emplmnt; FTA; Scouts; Tchrs Aide; Psychology; Media/ Communication; Shaw U; College of Notre Dame-Maryland

HINTON, AMBER; MOUNT AIRY, MD; SOUTH CARROLL HS; (JR); Hi Hnr Roll; Nat Hon Sy; Otst Ac Ach Awd; Perf Att; WWAHSS; Drma Clb; Key Club; Chr; Dnce; PP Ftbl (J); Vllyball (J); Mathematics; Computer Science; UMBC; Villa Julie

HINTON, BROOKE L; UPPER MARLBORO, MD; OXON HILL HS; (FR); Hnr Roll; Sci Fairs; Peer Tut/Med; Vllyball (J); MBA, Law; Undergrad: Philosophy; Georgetown U; Stanford U

HIRABAYASHI, SCOTT; GAITHERSBURG, MD; QUINCE ORCHARD HS; (JR); Hnr Roll; Comm Volntr; Chess; Mus Clb; Bnd; Mch Bnd; Pep Bnd; Tri-M Music Honor Society; English Literature / Language; Medical Biology; University of Maryland Baltimore County

HOAG, BRANDI; ELKTON, MD; ST MARK'S HS; (SR); Duke TS; Hi Hnr Roll; Hnr Roll; WWAHSS; Yth Ldrshp Prog; Hab For Humty Volntr; Key Club; Vllyball (J); Mock Trial- State Champs 2004; Biology Major; Coastal Carolina U

HODGES, BRITTANY; HYATTSVILLE, MD; CHARLES HERBERT FLOWERS HS; (JR); Ctznshp Aw; Hi Hnr Roll; Hnr Roll; Nat Hon Sy; Pres Sch; Comm Volntr; ArtClub; Cmptr Clb; DARE; Emplmnt; FBLA; P to P St Amb Prg; Tchrs Aide; Vsity Clb; Dnce; Chrldg (V CL); Gmnstcs (V); Member of the National Academy of Finance; Optometry; Accountant; Penn State U; Duke U

HOFFMAN, ELIZABETH; BOWIE, MD; BOWIE HS; (JR); Ctznshp Aw; Hi Hnr Roll; Hnr Roll; Nat Hon Sy; Otst Ac Ach Awd; St of Mnth; Comm Volntr; AL Aux Girls; Emplmnt; Mod UN; Mus Clb; Svce Clb; Acpl Chr; Chr; SP/M/VS; Stu Cncl (R); Have Been Studying Piano for Seven Years / President of the Tri-M Music Honor Society; Graduation Committee; Engineering; Law and Legal Studies; U of Maryland College Park; Carnegie Mellon U

HOFFMAN, JASON; WALKERSVILLE, MD; WALKERSVILLE HS; (JR); Hi Hnr Roll; Hnr Roll; Kwnis Aw; Comm Volntr; Emplmnt; Key Club; NYLC; Stg Cre; Elected to NCYC Lots of Community Hours; In a Band Play Drums; Business; Music; U of Maryland; James Madison U

HOFFMAN, LEAH; ROCKVILLE, MD; RICHARD MONTGOMERY HS; (JR); Hi Hnr Roll; Otst Ac Ach Awd; St of Mnth; Comm Volntr; Hosp Aide; Drma Clb; Prom Com; Chr; SP/M/VS; Chrldg (J); Stu Cncl (R); CR (R); Nursing; James Madison U; Penn State U

HOLDER, CORI; UPPER MARLBORO, MD; LARGO HS; (SR); Hnr Roll; Kwnis Aw; WWAHSS; Comm Volntr; Chrch Yth Grp; Key Club; ROTC; Ch Chr; I Am a Part of the Entrepreneurship Strand; Acceptance to 2 Colleges; Computer Engineering and Technology, Communications, Capitol College; Norwich U

HOLLEY, JASMINE E; BALTIMORE, MD; DUNBAR HS; (FR); Hnr Roll; Otst Ac Ach Awd; Perf Att; Mus Clb; Tchrs Aide; Bnd; Pediatrics-Nursing; Fashion Medal; Morgan State U; Fashion Institute of Design and Merchandising

HOLT, JENNIFER A; SYKESVILLE, MD; SOUTH CARROLL HS; (SR); Hi Hnr Roll; Hnr Roll; Nat Hon Sy; Nat Stu Ath Day Aw; Otst Ac Ach Awd; Perf Att; St of Mnth; WWAHSS; Yth Ldrshp Prog; Comm Volntr; Peer Tut/ Med; Chrch Yth Grp; Emplmnt; Key Club; NYLC; Ch Chr; Chrldg (V C); PP Ftbl (V); Cl Off (T); Psychology/Education; Master's Degree; McDaniel College

HONG, ANGELA S; PARKVILLE, MD; LOCH RAVEN HS; (FR); Ctznshp Aw; Hnr Roll; Otst Ac Ach Awd; Pres Ac Ftns Aw; Sci Fairs; Comm Volntr; Peer Tut/Med; ArtClub; Chrch Yth Grp; DARE; Mus Clb; Pep Squd; Photog; SADD; Tech Clb; Bnd; Dnce; Stu Cncl (R); Yrbk (E); Historian of Steering Committee; Diversity Club President; Pre-Med; Pre-Law; Carnegie Mellon U; Johns Hopkins U

HOOPER JR, AHMED; PIKESVILLE, MD; MILFORD MILL AC; (SO); Hnr Roll; Perf Att; Comm Volntr; Chess; Bsball (J); Ftball (J); Bachelor's Degree / Programming; Bachelor's Degree / Business; Auburn U; West Virginia U

HOOVER, CHRISTOPHER; DUNDALK, MD; DUNDALK HS; (JR); Hnr Roll; Otst Ac Ach Awd; Perf Att; Pres Ac Ftns Aw; Sci Fairs; Comm Volntr; Peer Tut/Med; Emplmnt; Tech Clb; Bnd; Mch Bnd; Mar Art (J); Wrstlg (V); Principal's List; Tech-Ed Robot Competition Certificate; Psychology; Photography; U of Maryland; U of Towson

HOPSON, BRITTANY; UPPER MARLBORO, MD; GRACE BRETHREN CHRISTIAN SCH; (SO); Hnr Roll; Nat Hon Sy; Salutrn; Sci Fairs; Comm Volntr; Chrch Yth Grp; Emplmnt; Dnce; Flg Crps; Chrldg (J); Scr Kpr (V); Cl Off (P, T); Sophomore Princess; Forensic Science; Chemical Engineering; U of Maryland College Park; Bennett U

HORNICK, LYDIA; JOPPA, MD; FALLSTON HS; (JR); Hnr Roll; Otst Ac Ach Awd; St of Mnth; Comm Volntr; Peer Tut/Med; FBLA; Prom Com; Vsity Clb; Dnce; PPSqd (V); PP Ftbl (V); Sftball (V L); Vsy Clb (V); Sch Ppr (R, P); Yrbk (R, P); JV Softball Sportsmanship Award; Dance Team 4-Years; Communications; Business; U of Maryland College Park; Clemson U

HORNICKEL, JONATHAN M; BRANDYWINE, MD; GRACE BRETHREN CHRISTIAN SCH; (SO); Hi Hnr Roll; Nat Hon Sy; WWAHSS; Chrch Yth Grp; Emplmnt; Sccr (V L); Track (V CL); Criminal Justice; FBI; Maryland U; Liberty U

HORSEMAN, ABBY G; RHODESDALE, MD; NORTH DORCHESTER HS; (JR); Hi Hnr Roll; Nat Hon Sy; WWAHSS; Comm Volntr; AL Aux Girls; Chrch Yth Grp; Emplmnt; Key Club; Prom Com; Scouts; Bnd; Chr; Mch Bnd; Fld Hky (V); Scr Kpr (V); Cl Off (P); National Honor Society Pres.; Girls State; Dentist; Medical

HOTTINGER JR, JOHN A; SMITHSBURG, MD; NORTH HAGERSTOWN HS; (JR); Hi Hnr Roll; Hnr Roll; St of Mnth; WWAHSS; Comm Volntr; Hab For Humty Volntr; Red Cr Aide; Chrch Yth Grp; Drma Clb; Key Club; Prom Com; SP/M/VS; Stg Cre; Psychology; Forensic Anthropology; Syracuse U; U of California, San Diego

HOWARD, MICHAEL; HYATTSVILLE, MD; BLADENSBURG HS; (SO); Hnr Roll; Comm Volntr; Chrch Yth Grp; Bskball (J); Track; Cl Off (R); Law; Communications; George Mason U; Georgetown U

HOWE, PERRY; FORT WASHINGTON, MD; FRIENDLY HS; (SO); Hosp Aide; ROTC; Drl Tm; Bsball; Mar Art; I've Worked At Veterans Administration Hospital As a Volunteer.; Business; Telecommunications; Duke U; Xavier U

HUBER, AMANDA; PARKVILLE, MD; PERRY HALL HS; (SR); Hnr Roll; Emplmnt; Yrbk (E); Networking; Community College of Baltimore County-Essex

HUDDLESTON, JASMINE; BALTIMORE, MD; CARVER VO-TECH HS; (JR); Ctznshp Aw; Hnr Roll; Nat Sci Aw; Perf Att; Dnce; Thurgood Marshall Achievers Society; Fashion Designing; Registered Nurse; Baltimore City Community College; Morgan State U

HUDSON, JENNIFER; DUNDALK, MD; PATAPSCO HS; (SO); Hnr Roll; Perf Att; Yth Ldrshp Prog; Peer Tut/Med; Chr; Stu Cncl (R); CR (R); Girls V Basketball-Manager; Tri-M Music Honor Society; Pre-Law; Pre-Medicine; Pennsylvania State U; U of Maryland College Park

HUDSON, SALLY; COLUMBIA, MD; WILDE LAKE HS; (JR); Hi Hnr Roll; Nat Hon Sy; Perf Att; St of Mnth; Amnsty Intl; Hab For Humty Volntr; Chrch Yth Grp; Emplmnt; Mus Clb; Scouts; French Clb; Chr; SP/M/VS; Fld Hky (VJ L); Tennis (J); Stu Cncl (R); CR (P); Finished At Top of Class in German Gymnasium (Lived in Germany for 4 Years); Language: French/ German/Italian; International Relations; Bowdoin College; Middleburg College

HUFF, STEPHANIE; MILLERSVILLE, MD; OLD MILL HS; (SO); Hi Hnr Roll; Hnr Roll; Nat Hon Sy; Perf Att; Pres Ac Ftns Aw; Comm Volntr; Drma Clb; Emplmnt; SP/M/VS; Gmnstcs (V); Sccr (J); U of Maryland: College Park

HUFF, TISHAWNA; HAVRE DE GRACE, MD; HAVRE DE GRACE HS; (JR); Hi Hnr Roll; Hnr Roll; St of Mnth; WWAHSS; Comm Volntr; Peer Tut/ Med; FTA; Lib Aide; Mth Clb/Tm; Scouts; Bnd; Drl Tm; Mch Bnd; Sccr (L); Track (V); Drill Sergeant for Band; Pre-Law; Delaware State; Temple U

HUGHES, JENNIFER; POCOMOKE CITY, MD; POCOMOKE HS; (FR); Hnr Roll; Perf Att; Sci Fairs; St of Mnth; DARE; Emplmnt; FTA; Lib Aide; Ntl Beta Clb; Sftball (J); Wt Lftg (J); Law; Marine Biology; New York U

HUGHES, ROBERT M; HYATTSVILLE, MD; ELEANOR ROOSEVELT HS; (JR); F Lan Hn Soc; Hi Hnr Roll; Hnr Roll; Nat Hon Sy; Nat Mrt Semif; Otst Ac Ach Awd; Pres Sch; Sci Fairs; St Schl; WWAHSS; Comm Volntr; Peer Tut/Med; Lib Aide; Mth Clb/Tm; Off Aide; Sci Clb; Svce Clb; Tchrs Aide; Spanish Clb; Lcrsse (VJ); Intern at National Institutes of Health - NIH; Junior Acolyte at West Hyattsville Baptist Church; Pre-Med; Chemistry; Harvard U; Johns Hopkins U

HULING, ANTHONY; ABINGDON, MD; BEL AIR HS; (SO); Hnr Roll; Perf Att; Peer Tut/Med; Chrch Yth Grp; FCA; Bsball (V); County Wide Student Art Exhibit II; Student of the Quarter -Spanish; Teaching; English; Arizona State U; U of Maryland

HUNT, DANIELLE; GLEN BURNIE, MD; GLEN BURNIE SR HS; (JR); F Lan Hn Soc; Hnr Roll; Nat Hon Sy; DARE; Emplmnt; Mus Clb; Pep Squd; Prom Com; Spanish Clb; Bnd; Chr; Dnce; Mch Bnd; Bskball (J); PPSqd (V); Tennis (V L); Cl Off (S); American Cancer Society; Pre-Medicine; U of Maryland-College Park; Johns Hopkins U

HUNTER, BRANDON L; BOWIE, MD; CHARLES HERBERT FLOWERS HS; (SO); Hnr Roll; Otst Ac Ach Awd; Perf Att; Comm Volntr; Chrch Yth Grp; Emplmnt; Ch Chr; Bskball; Ftball; Track; Law Enforcement; NCCU; UNC Wilmington

HUNTER, KASEY K; FINKSBURG, MD; WESTMINSTER HS; (SR); Hnr Roll; Nat Hon Sy; 4-H; Sccr (J); Sftball (J); Yrbk (R, P); Rec. Soccer Team; Early Childhood Education; Villa Julie College

HURSEY, KRISTEN; HAMPSTEAD, MD; NORTH CARROLL HS; (SR); Hnr Roll; Nat Hon Sy; Otst Ac Ach Awd; Pres Sch; St Schl; WWAHSS; Comm Volntr; Hosp Aide; Peer Tut/Med; Chrch Yth Grp; Emplmnt; Tchrs Aide; Cr Ctry (V CL); Lcrsse (J); Skiing; Track (V L); Winter and Summer Community Swim Team; Earned CNA from Career & Technology Center; Nursing; Spanish; York College of PA

HURTADO, ELIZABETH; GERMANTOWN, MD; NORTHWEST HS; (JR); Ctznshp Aw; Hnr Roll; Chrch Yth Grp; Quill & Scroll; Spanish Clb; Dnce; SP/M/VS; Yrbk (E, R, P); Journalism; Communications; Hofstra U

HWANG, GRACE; OLNEY, MD; JAMES HUBERT BLAKE HS; (JR); Hi Hnr Roll; Hnr Roll; Nat Hon Sy; Otst Ac Ach Awd; Comm Volntr; Peer Tut/ Med; Fr of Library; Photog; Swmg (V); Tennis (V); Track (V); Piano; Medicine; Mathematics/Biology; U of Maryland, College Park; U of Maryland, Baltimore County

HWANG, SUSAN; GAITHERSBURG, MD; QUINCE ORCHARD HS; (JR); Ctznshp Aw; F Lan Hn Soc; Hi Hnr Roll; Hnr Roll; Nat Hon Sy; Otst Ac Ach Awd; Perf Att; Comm Volntr; Quill & Scroll; Bnd; Mch Bnd; Pep Bnd; SP/M/VS; Track (J); Sch Ppr (E, R); 2005-2006 Newspaper Editor-In-Chief; Tri-M Honor Society; Communications; Business; Northwestern U; Boston U

HYDE, LAUREN M; BRANDYWINE, MD; GWYNN PARK HS; (SR); Ctznshp Aw; Hnr Roll; Otst Ac Ach Awd; Sci Fairs; Peer Tut/Med; Off Aide; Tchrs Aide; Dnce; SP/M/VS; Stg Cre; Cosmetology I & II; Business Degree (Master's); Bowie State U

IMUS, LINDSEY; BETHESDA, MD; WALT WHITMAN HS; (SO); Hnr Roll; Comm Volntr; Chrch Yth Grp; Cr Ctry (V); Tennis (V); Sch Ppr (R); Piano; Biology; Anatomy; Duke U; Davidson College

INAMDAR, PUJA; GLEN BURNIE, MD; GLEN BURNIE HS; (JR); F Lan Hn Soc; Hnr Roll; Nat Hon Sy; St of Mnth; Dbte Team; Emplmnt; Prom Com; Quill & Scroll; Spch Team; Vsity Clb; Tennis (V); Cl Off (R); Sch Ppr (E); Interact Member; Pre-Medicine; U of Maryland, Baltimore County; Towson U

INGRAM, ERIKA M; RIVERDALE, MD; LANHAM CHRISTIAN SCH; (JR); Comm Volntr; Peer Tut/Med; Chrch Yth Grp; DARE; Drma Clb; Tchrs Aide; Dnce; CR (S); Secretary of My Junior Class; Formerly Member of International Studies Program; Law; Business Administration; Howard U; North Carolina

IRELAND, ZOE; BALTIMORE, MD; BALTIMORE POLYTECH INST HS; (SO); Ctznshp Aw; Hi Hnr Roll; Hnr Roll; Perf Att; Pres Ac Ftns Aw; Sci Fairs; Peer Tut/Med; Spec Olymp Vol; Chrch Yth Grp; Chrldg (V); Doctor; Registered Nurse; Duke U; North Carolina A & T

IROANYA, MICHAEL; WOODSTOCK, MD; WESTERN TECH HS; (FR); Hnr Roll; MVP; Nat Hon Sy; Otst Ac Ach Awd; Perf Att; Sci Fairs; St of Mnth; WWAHSS; Yth Ldrshp Prog; CARE; Comm Volntr; Peer Tut/Med; ArtClub; Chrch Yth Grp; Cmptr Clb; DARE; Jr Ach; Mth Clb/Tm; Mus Clb; SADD; Bnd; Orch; Stg Cre; Ftball (J); Lawyer; Doctor; Harvard Law School; Massachusetts Institute of Technology (MIT)

IRWIN, RACHEL; ANDREWS AFB, MD; GRACE BRETHREN CHRISTIAN SCH; (SO); Hi Hnr Roll; Hnr Roll; Nat Hon Sy; WWAHSS; Comm Volntr; Chrch Yth Grp; Orch; Sccr (V); Swmg (V); Track (V); Cl Off (V); Academic Awards-Computer Science; English/Government-Freshman Year

ISAAC, CHRISTENA; GAITHERSBURG, MD; GAITHERSBURG HS; Hnr Roll; Otst Ac Ach Awd; Comm Volntr; Peer Tut/Med; FCA; Chr; Fld Hky; Lcrsse; Accounting, Business Management; Teaching; U of Maryland; U of North Carolina

ISLER, ARMARNI; UPPER MARLBORO, MD; SUITLAND HS; (FR); Ctznshp Aw; Hnr Roll; Scouts; Dnce; Stu Cncl (S); Starpower National 1st Place Dance Award; Showstoppers 1st Place Dance Award; Psychology; Dance; Shenandoah Valley; Temple U

IZEBERE, DAVID B; BOWIE, MD; CHARLES HERBERT FLOWERS HS; (FR); Hnr Roll; Otst Ac Ach Awd; Comm Volntr; Bskball (J); Robotics Engineer; Computer Engineer; Duke U; U of Maryland

JABERI, LEELAH; LUTHVLE TIMON, MD; NOTRE DAME PREP SCH; (JR); Hnr Roll; St Schl; Yth Ldrshp Prog; Peer Tut/Med; ArtClub; Drma Clb; Mth Clb/Tm; Cultural Awareness Club; Pre-Medicine; Dentistry; Johns Hopkins U; Swarthmore College

Ingram, Erika M
Lanham Christian Sch
Riverdale, MD

Huff, Tishawna
Havre De Grace HS
Havre De Grace, MD

Howard, Michael
Bladensburg HS
Hyattsville, MD

National
Honor Roll
Spring 2005

Hodges, Brittany
Charles Herbert Flowers HS
Hyattsville, MD

Huling, Anthony
Bel Air HS
Abingdon, MD

Isler, Armarni
Suitland HS
Upper Marlboro, MD

JACKSON, CHANTARA Z; CAPITOL HEIGHTS, MD; CHARLES HERBERT FLOWERS HS; (FR); 4H Awd; All Am Sch; Ctznshp Aw; Hi Hnr Roll; Hnr Roll; Nat Sci Aw; Otst Ac Ach Awd; Perf Att; Sci Fairs; St of Mnth; Comm Volntr; Hosp Aide; Peer Tut/Med; 4-H; Chrch Yth Grp; Drma Clb; Mth Clb/Tm; Pep Squd; Prom Com; Quiz Bowl; Sci Clb; Ch Chr; Dnce; SP/M/VS; Stg Cre; Arch (J); Bskball (J); Chrldg (J); Cr Ctry (J); PPSqd (J); Scr Kpr (J); Sccr (J); Wt Lftg (J); Cl Off (V); Certificate of Promotion; How Computers Work - Award; Criminal Law; Writing; Spelman College; Howard U

JACKSON, DOMINIQUE M; UPPER MARLBORO, MD; CHARLES HERBERT FLOWERS HS; (SR); Hnr Roll; Perf Att; WWAHSS; Chrch Yth Grp; Tchrs Aide; Chr; Ch Chr; Early Childhood Education; U Maryland Eastern Shore; Morgan State U

JACKSON, TIARA P; FORT WASHINGTON, MD; OXON HILL HS; (FR); Ctznshp Aw; Hi Hnr Roll; Nat Hon Sy; Sci Fairs; Chrch Yth Grp; Ch Chr

JACOB, MEGHA; GLEN BURNIE, MD; OLD MILL HS; (JR); F Lan Hn Soc; Hi Hnr Roll; Hnr Roll; Nat Hon Sy; Nat Mrt Sch Recip; Otst Ac Ach Awd; Perf Att; Comm Volntr; Peer Tut/Med; BPA; Chrch Yth Grp; Emplmnt; FBLA; Key Club; Mth Clb/Tm; Mus Clb; Outdrs Clb; Chr; Ch Chr; SP/M/VS; Stu Cncl (R); CR (R); Music and Spanish Honors Societies; Received Award for Most Talented Singer; Music Therapy; Pharmacy; Berklee Institute of Music; U of Maryland of Baltimore County

JACOBS III, HARRY L; UPPR MARLBORO, MD; LARGO HS; (SO); Hi Hnr Roll; Hnr Roll; Kwnis Aw; Otst Ac Ach Awd; Perf Att; Pres Ac Ftns Aw; Pres Sch; Comm Volntr; Chrch Yth Grp; Civil Air Pat; ROTC; Ftball (V); Civil Air Patrol-Moral Leadership Program; Law Enforcement; Criminal Law; U of Maryland; U of Virginia

JAMISON, KASEY; ARNOLD, MD; BROADNECK HS; (JR); Hnr Roll; Nat Hon Sy; Perf Att; Pres Ac Ftns Aw; USAA; WWAHSS; Comm Volntr; Chrch Yth Grp; Key Club; Mth Clb/Tm; Vsity Clb; Foreign Clb; Stg Cre; Cr Ctry (V CL); Track (V CL); CR (R); County Champion in the Mile; Engineering; Duke U; U of Virginia

JANI, AMIT K; GAITHERSBURG, MD; MAGRUDER HS; (JR); Hnr Roll; Sci Fairs; ArtClub; Chess; Bnd; Mar Art; Pre-Med; Science; U of Maryland; Johns Hopkins U

JARRETT, MELISSA; HAGERSTOWN, MD; NORTH HAGERSTOWN HS; (JR); Hi Hnr Roll; Hnr Roll; Chrch Yth Grp; Tchrs Aide; Chr; Ch Chr; SP/M/VS; Honor Club; Music; Psychology; Hagerstown Community College

JARVIS III, RONALD E; NOTTINGHAM, MD; PERRY HALL HS; (SO); Hnr Roll; Perf Att; Ftball (J); Professional Skate Boarder; Psychiatrist; Johns Hopkins U; U of Southern California

JAWARA, MARIAM; GAITHERSBURG, MD; GAITHERSBURG HS; (SO); Hnr Roll; Perf Att; Comm Volntr; Chrch Yth Grp; DARE; Emplmnt; Photog; Tchrs Aide; Ch Chr; PP Ftbl (J); Track (J); Sch Ppr (R); Boys JV and Varsity Basketball Manager; Journalism; Law; Clark Atlanta U; Howard U

JEFFERYS, ROY; CUMBERLAND, MD; ALLEGANY HS; (SO); Bsball (V); Ftball (V)

JENIFER, BRANDON J L T; UPPER MARLBORO, MD; CHARLES HERBERT FLOWERS HS; (JR); Ctznshp Aw; Hnr Roll; St of Mnth; Peer Tut/Med; Chess; Chrch Yth Grp; DARE; Dnce; Adv Cncl (R); 2005 Teen Cotillion; Surgery; Johns Hopkins U

JENKINS, BRITTANY Y C; SILVER SPRING, MD; PAINT BRANCH HS; (JR); Hnr Roll; Comm Volntr; Hab For Humty Volntr; Chrch Yth Grp; DARE; Emplmnt; Key Club; Chr; Fld Hky (J); Sccr (J); Track (J); Diamond Girl Essay Winner; Journalism; Clemson, U of South Carolina, Elon U, and Clark U

JENKINS, JAMES W; DERWOOD, MD; MAGRUDER HS; (FR); Hnr Roll; Otst Ac Ach Awd; Ftball (J L); Lcrsse (V CL); Engineering; Business; U of Maryland; Johns Hopkins U

JENKINS, TINILLE T; BOWIE, MD; BISHOP MC NAMARA HS; (SO); Ctznshp Aw; Hi Hnr Roll; Hnr Roll; MVP; Perf Att; Sci Fairs; St of Mnth; WWAHSS; Comm Volntr; Hab For Humty Volntr; Peer Tut/Med; Chrch Yth Grp; Emplmnt; Bskball (J); Vllyball (VJ L); Bowling; Orthopedic Doctor; Chiropractor; Xavier U of Louisiana; Florida A & M U

JENSEN, AMANDA K; BOWIE, MD; BOWIE HS; (SO); Hnr Roll; Nat Hon Sy; Sci Fairs; Comm Volntr; Emplmnt; Mod UN; Chr; SP/M/VS; Stu Cncl (R); CR (R); Attending Model UN Conference at Harvard; In Schools Summit Program for Academics; Biology; Marine Biology; UCLA; Columbia U

JEON, HESTER; COLUMBIA, MD; WILDE LAKE HS; (SO); Nat Hon Sy; Chrch Yth Grp; Dbte Team; FBLA; Chr; Orch; Cr Ctry (J); Fld Hky (J); Stu Cncl (R); Leader for Church Dance Group: Expression; International Business; Business; U of Pennsylvania; Brown U

JERNIGAN, TUNISIA G; RANDALLSTOWN, MD; RANDALLSTOWN HS; (SR); Hnr Roll; USAA; WWAHSS; Dnce; SP/M/VS; Bskball (V); Stu Cncl (R); Yrbk (E, P); Accounting; Actuary Science; Delaware State U; U of Maryland Eastern Shore

JETER, KEVIN O; UPPER MARLBORO, MD; GRACE BRETHREN CHRISTIAN SCH; (SO); Hnr Roll; MVP; Nat Hon Sy; Sci Fairs; WWAHSS; Chrch Yth Grp; DARE; Drma Clb; Emplmnt; Off Aide; Tchrs Aide; Bnd; Ch Chr; Drm Mjr; Mch Bnd; Bsball (V); Bskball (VJ); Sccr (J); Track (V); CR (R); PVAC All-Star Basketball Team Player; Harvard U; MIT (Massachusetts Institute of Technology)

JETT, DOMINICK W; GWYNN OAK, MD; ST FRANCES AC; (FR); Perf Att; Sci Fairs; St of Mnth; Bsball (V); Bskball; Ftball (V); Mar Art (V); Lawyer; Video Game Creator

JIA, DAVID; GERMANTOWN, MD; MBHS; (FR); Hnr Roll; Perf Att; Sci Fairs; Comm Volntr; Peer Tut/Med; Chess; Cmptr Clb; DARE; Mth Clb/Tm; Sci Clb; Tech Clb; Orch; Honor Student in Chinese School; Johns Hopkins Talent Search; Biology; Astrophysics

JIMENEZ-RUIZ, SAHIR; HYATTSVILLE, MD; NORTHWESTERN HS; (JR); Hnr Roll; Chrch Yth Grp; ROTC; Clr Grd; Drl Tm; Sccr (V C); ROTC Honor Cadet; Boot Camp Outstanding Cadet Ect; Engineering; Pilot

JOHN, GINA; ELKTON, MD; ELKTON HS; (FR); Hnr Roll; Foreign Language Award; Music Award; Pediatrician; Registered Nurse; Columbia U; U of Delaware

JOHN, ROSI; FT WASHINGTON, MD; SUITLAND HS; (JR); Hnr Roll; Comm Volntr; Chrch Yth Grp; FBLA; ROTC; Vsity Clb; Ch Chr; Ftball (V); Wt Lftg (V); Sports Management; Salisbury U

JOHNS, MEGAN; BOWIE, MD; BOWIE HS; (JR); DAR; Hi Hnr Roll; Nat Hon Sy; Sci Fairs; WWAHSS; Emplmnt; Prom Com; Dnce; Chrldg (C); PPSqd (V CL); Stu Cncl (R); Cheerleading - Not with School; Teacher; Accounting; Salisbury U; Towson U

JOHNSON, APRIL; UPPER MARLBORO, MD; CHARLES HERBERT FLOWERS HS; (SO); Hnr Roll; Perf Att; St of Mnth; Comm Volntr; ROTC; Chrldg (V)

JOHNSON, BRITTANI R; FORT WASHINGTON, MD; FRIENDLY HS; (JR); Hi Hnr Roll; Hnr Roll; Perf Att; St of Mnth; WWAHSS; Comm Volntr; Peer Tut/Med; Chrch Yth Grp; Emplmnt; Off Aide; Scouts; Tchrs Aide; Chr; Ch Chr; SP/M/VS; Adv Cncl (R); Yrbk (E); Medical Doctor; Professional Singer; Johns Hopkins U; U of Virginia

JOHNSON, CHIQUITA S; BALTIMORE, MD; REGINALD F LEWIS HS; (SO); MVP; Otst Ac Ach Awd; Spec Olymp Vol; Chrch Yth Grp; P to P St Amb Prg; Ch Chr; Bskball (V); CR; Second Honors; Law; Medical; Duke U; U of North Carolina Chapel Hill

JOHNSON, ELISHA M; GWYNN OAK, MD; RANDALLSTOWN HS; (JR); Hnr Roll; Nat Hon Sy; Nat Ldrshp Svc; WWAHSS; Yth Ldrshp Prog; Hosp Aide; Chrch Yth Grp; Emplmnt; NYLC; Prom Com; Scouts; 19th Annual Symposium on Career Opportunities in Biomedical Sciences-The James Irvine Ford; BS/MD in Medicine; BS/MSN in Nursing; Howard U; U of Maryland-College Park

JOHNSON, GRACE A; DISTRICT HEIGHTS, MD; SUITLAND HS; (JR); Hnr Roll; Otst Ac Ach Awd; St of Mnth; Peer Tut/Med; Chrch Yth Grp; Emplmnt; Off Aide; Pep Squd; Tchrs Aide; Ch Chr; Dnce; Chrldg (V); PPSqd; Summer in New York with Alvin Ailey Dance Company; Radiography; Business Administration; Towson State U; North Carolina School of the Arts

JOHNSON, JACOB N; ANNAPOLIS, MD; BROADNECK HS; (FR); Hnr Roll; Comm Volntr; Chrch Yth Grp; Key Club; Mus Clb; Scouts; Chr; SP/M/VS; County Recreation Soccer - 11 Years; Group Works Volunteer Mission / Northern Tier Scout Trip; Music Teacher / High School Choral Director; Rock Star; St. Mary's College Maryland

JOHNSON, KATELYN E; FREDERICK, MD; WALKERSVILLE HS; (SR); Hi Hnr Roll; Hnr Roll; MVP; Nat Hon Sy; Otst Ac Ach Awd; WWAHSS; Red Cr Aide; Emplmnt; Key Club; Fld Hky (VJCL); PP Ftbl; Swmg (V L); Track (V L); Sch Ppr (E); MD Distinguished Scholar-Honorable Mention; Mass Communications; Journalism; Salisbury U; Shepherd U

JOHNSON, KIERAN A D; CLINTON, MD; SURRATTSVILLE HS; (SO); Hnr Roll; Comm Volntr; Chrch Yth Grp; Drma Clb; ROTC; Bnd; Ch Chr; Mch Bnd; Bsball (V); Bskball (V); Sports Medicine; Electronics

JOHNSON, KYLE E; BOWIE, MD; BOWIE HS; (SO); Ctznshp Aw; Hnr Roll; Sci Fairs; Comm Volntr; Peer Tut/Med; Bnd; SP/M/VS; Bskball (J); Sccr (J); Timekeeper / Bookkeeper for U 10 Boys Basketball Team; 150 Hrs Community Service; Architecture; Engineering; Hampton U; Morehouse College

JOHNSON, MARILYN S; ANNAPOLIS, MD; (JR); Hnr Roll; Nat Hon Sy; Pres Sch; Comm Volntr; Peer Tut/Med; Chrch Yth Grp; Key Club; Mus Clb; SADD; Tchrs Aide; Foreign Clb; Chr; SP/M/VS; Cultural Heritage Alliance/ Key Club Secretary; Cape St. Claire UMCIMYF President/2001 Strawberry Festival Princess; Math; Teaching/Or Engineer; Music; Bowdoin College/ Messiah College; Colby College

JOHNSON, SEAN; ARNOLD, MD; BROADNECK HS; (SO); Hnr Roll; Perf Att; Comm Volntr; Key Club; Cr Ctry (V); Lcrsse (J); Track (J); Cl Off (T); Who's Who Among Am High School Students

JOHNSON, STEPHANIE; BALTIMORE, MD; DIGITAL HARBOR HS; (JR); Hnr Roll; Perf Att; WWAHSS; Chrch Yth Grp; Dbte Team; Mus Clb; Pep Squd; Drl Tm; Bskball (V); Sccr (V); Sftball (V); Track (V); Vllyball (V); Cl Off (S); Stu Cncl (R); CR (S); Forensic Science; U of Baltimore

JOHNSON, TANYA; LAUREL, MD; RESERVOIR HS; (SO); Hi Hnr Roll; Hnr Roll; Pres Ac Ftns Aw; St of Mnth; Comm Volntr; Chrch Yth Grp; HO'Br Yth Ldrshp; Scouts; Chr; Ch Chr; Dnce; Sccr (JV); Track (VL); Girl Scout Silver Award; President of Black Student Union; Clinical Psychologist; Hampton U; North Carolina A & T U

JOHNSON, TEYANNA; ABINGDON, MD; EDGEWOOD HS; (SR); F Lan Hn Soc; Hnr Roll; WWAHSS; Comm Volntr; Peer Tut/Med; Chrch Yth Grp; Emplmnt; Lttrmn Clb; Tchrs Aide; Vsity Clb; Spanish Clb; Bskball (VJ L); Scr Kpr (V); Sftball (V CL); Vllyball (VJCL); Pre-Law; Morgan State U

JOHNSON, TIFFANY; CHARLOTTE HALL, MD; (SR); Ctznshp Aw; Hnr Roll; Nat Hon Sy; Perf Att; Sci Fairs; St of Mnth; Comm Volntr; DARE; Emplmnt; SADD; Chr; Best Buddies; Child Care; Psychology; College of Southern MD; Penn State

JOHNSON, VERNELL; FORT WASHINGTON, MD; FRIENDLY HS; (JR); Ctznshp Aw; Hnr Roll; Sci Fairs; St of Mnth; Yth Ldrshp Prog; Peer Tut/ Med; Drma Clb; Prom Com; ROTC; Sci Clb; Tchrs Aide; Chr; Dnce; PPSqd (V); Sftball (V); Stu Cncl (S); Nominated to National Young Leaders Conference 2004; Business Administration; Sociology; U of Maryland; Howard U

JONES, ANNTWANNETTE; BALTIMORE, MD; PAUL L DUNBAR HS 414; (JR); Hi Hnr Roll; Hnr Roll; Nat Hon Sy; St of Mnth; Comm Volntr; Hab For Humty Volntr; Hosp Aide; Jzz Bnd; Nursing Program Achiever; Advanced Academic; Masseuse; Geriatric Nurse

JONES, CHARNELE S; SILVER SPRING, MD; WHEATON HS; (FR); Hnr Roll; Comm Volntr; Peer Tut/Med; Chr; Sftball; Pediatrician; Pediatric Nurse; Howard U; Johns Hopkins U

JONES, DERRICK; TEMPLE HILLS, MD; CROSSLAND HS; (MS); Hnr Roll; Drl Tm; Ftball; Iowa State U

JONES, DEVON; RANDALLSTOWN, MD; RANDALLSTOWN HS; (JR); Ctznshp Aw; Hnr Roll; MVP; Perf Att; Comm Volntr; Chrch Yth Grp; Emplmnt; ROTC; Scouts; Bnd; Chr; Ch Chr; Clr Grd; Ftball (VJC); Lcrsse (V C); Track (V); Coaches Award for Football; Sports Medicine; Hampton U; Grambling U

JONES, EUGENIA; BALTIMORE, MD; PATTERSON HS; (SO); Ctznshp Aw; Duke TS; Hi Hnr Roll; Hnr Roll; Nat Hon Sy; Perf Att; Pres Sch; St Schl; St of Mnth; Yth Ldrshp Prog; Amnsty Intl; Comm Volntr; Peer Tut/ Med; ArtClub; Chrch Yth Grp; Dbte Team; Drma Clb; Mod UN; Mus Clb; Prom Com; SADD; Chr; Dnce; SP/M/VS; Stg Cre; CR (P); Vocals/Acting Drama; Skin Doctor/Doctor; Morgan State College; Barbizon Modeling College

JONES, GABRIELLE M; BOWIE, MD; CHARLES HERBERT FLOWERS HS; (SO); Ctznshp Aw; Hi Hnr Roll; Nat Hon Sy; Otst Ac Ach Awd; Perf Att; St of Mnth; Peer Tut/Med; Dbte Team; Lib Aide; Mch Bnd; Tennis; Volunteer for Prince George Police Dept 10 Months out of the Yr for Demo on Drugs / Alcohol; Massage Therapist / Physician; Yale U; A & T U

JONES, INDIA R; FT WASHINGTON, MD; FRIENDLY HS; (FR); Ctznshp Aw; Gov Hnr Prg; Hi Hnr Roll; Hnr Roll; Nat Hon Sy; Otst Ac Ach Awd; Perf Att; Sci Fairs; St of Mnth; Comm Volntr; Peer Tut/Med; Drma Clb; Emplmnt; ROTC; Sci Clb; Scouts; Tchrs Aide; Chr; Dnce; Chrldg; Gmnstcs; Step-Team; Modeling; Lawyer; Business Major; Atlanta U; Harvard U

JONES, JASMINE R; LANHAM, MD; PARKDALE HS; (SO); Hnr Roll; Otst Ac Ach Awd; Perf Att; Sci Fairs; St of Mnth; Comm Volntr; Chrch Yth Grp; DARE; Mus Clb; Spanish Clb; Bnd; Mch Bnd; Chrldg (VJ); Sftball (J); Basketball Award; Business Management; Journalism; Maryland Eastern Shore; North Carolina Art

JONES, SETH H; RHODESDALE, MD; NORTH DORCHESTER HS; (SO); Ctznshp Aw; Hi Hnr Roll; Nat Hon Sy; Sci Fairs; St of Mnth; WWAHSS; Chrch Yth Grp; DARE; Drma Clb; Key Club; Sci Clb; Spanish Clb; Chr; Ch Chr; SP/M/VS; Tennis (V); Key Club Class Representative; Music Teacher- Master's Degree

JONES, SHAAKIRA M; CLINTON, MD; GRACE BRETHREN CHRISTIAN SCH; (JR); Hnr Roll; Sci Fairs; WWAHSS; Comm Volntr; Chrch Yth Grp; Emplmnt; Prom Com; Chr; Dnce; Flg Crps; Scr Kpr (VJ); Tennis (V)

Jones, Seth H
North Dorchester HS
Rhodesdale, MD

Jones, Gabrielle M
Charles Herbert Flowers HS
Bowie, MD

Johnson, Tanya
Reservoir HS
Laurel, MD

Johnson, Sean
Broadneck HS
Arnold, MD

Johnson, Vernell
Friendly HS
Fort Washington, MD

Jones, India R
Friendly HS
Ft Washington, MD

Jones, Shaakira M
Grace Brethren Christian Sch
Clinton, MD

Johnson, Kieran A D
Surrattsville HS
Clinton, MD

Jenkins, Tinille T
Bishop Mc Namara HS
Bowie, MD

Jarvis III, Ronald E
Perry Hall HS
Nottingham, MD

Jacobs III, Harry L
Largo HS
Uppr Marlboro, MD

Jacob, Megha
Old Mill HS
Glen Burnie, MD

National
Honor Roll
Spring 2005

Jackson, Chantara Z
Charles Herbert Flowers HS
Capitol Heights, MD

Jani, Amit K
Magruder HS
Gaithersburg, MD

Jenifer, Brandon J L T
Charles Herbert Flowers HS
Upper Marlboro, MD

John, Gina
Elkton HS
Elkton, MD

John, Rosi
Suitland HS
Ft Washington, MD

JONES, SHANAE; BOWIE, MD; ELEANOR ROOSEVELT HS; (JR); Hnr Roll; Otst Ac Ach Awd; Pres Sch; Sci Fairs; WWAHSS; Comm Volntr; Chrch Yth Grp; DARE; Dbte Team; Lib Aide; Tchrs Aide; Latin Clb; Orch; Stu Cncl (R); CR (R); African-American/Women's Studies; International Relations and Affairs; American U in Washington, DC; Fordham U

JONES, SIERRA S; ESSEX, MD; CHESAPEAKE HS; (SR); Hi Hnr Roll; Hnr Roll; Nat Hon Sy; Otst Ac Ach Awd; St of Mnth; WWAHSS; Peer Tut/Med; Dbte Team; Pep Squd; Scouts; Spanish Clb; Chr; Pep Bnd; Chrldg (C); Principal's Honor Roll; Won Poetry Contest; Clothing Designer; Poetry; Towson U

JONES, TAYDRA; LARGO, MD; CHARLES HERBERT FLOWERS HS; (FR); Hi Hnr Roll; Hnr Roll; Comm Volntr; Chrch Yth Grp; Emplmnt; Mus Clb; Bnd; Orch; Johns Hopkins U Center for Talented Youth; Greater Washington Urban League / National Achievers Society; Bachelor's Degree in Pre-Med / Health Studies; Biochemistry; Spelman College; Massachusetts College of Pharmacy and Health Sciences

JORDAN, LANIKAH; LANHAM, MD; CH FLOWERS HS; (SR); Hnr Roll; Sci Fairs; St of Mnth; WWAHSS; Comm Volntr; Peer Tut/Med; Spec Olymp Vol; Chrch Yth Grp; Civil Air Pat; Pep Squd; Dnce; SP/M/VS; PPSqd (V C); Sccr (V); Sftball (J); Cl Off (T); CR (R); Accounting; Mathematics Education; U of Maryland College Park; Spelman College

JORDAN, SHANNON A; POCOMOKE CITY, MD; POCOMOKE HS; (FR); Hnr Roll; Otst Ac Ach Awd; Pres Sch; Sci Fairs; Comm Volntr; Chrch Yth Grp; Emplmnt; Lib Aide; ROTC; Svce Clb; Bnd; Clr Grd; Mch Bnd; Pep Bnd; Scr Kpr (V); Skt Tgt Sh (V); Vllyball (J); Lit Mag (E, R); USO Volunteer - Dover AFB; Food Bank Volunteer / Humanitarian Aid / Toys 4 Tots; Military Career / Officer; Law Enforcement; Norwich U VT; Naval Academy Annapolis

JOSEPH, JOY; BOWIE, MD; CHARLES HERBERT FLOWERS HS; (FR); Hnr Roll; Otst Ac Ach Awd; St of Mnth; Chrch Yth Grp; Ch Chr; Culinary Arts; Computer Engineering; Towson U; Regent U

JOSEPH, REBEKAH N; BELTSVILLE, MD; ELEANOR ROOSEVELT HS; (JR); F Lan Hn Soc; Hnr Roll; Nat Hon Sy; Comm Volntr; Emplmnt; Tchrs Aide; Indian Clb; Cl Off (T); Stu Cncl (R); CR (R); Yrbk (R); Member of Latin Honor Society; Co-Chair of Membership Committee for NHS; Physical Therapy; Kinesiology; U of Maryland College Park; U of Maryland Baltimore County

JOYNER II, LEMONT; GLENELG, MD; RIVER HILL HS; (JR); Ctznshp Aw; Fut Prb Slvr; Hi Hnr Roll; Hnr Roll; Pres Sch; Yth Ldrshp Prog; Comm Volntr; Red Cr Aide; Chrch Yth Grp; Dbte Team; Emplmnt; FBLA; NYLC; Pep Squd; Prom Com; Svce Clb; Adv Cncl (R); CR (R); Sch Ppr (E, R); Awarded First Place Regional Team for Parliamentary Procedure - FBLA; Selected to Meet with MD Lt Governor; Double Major in English and History; Earn JD in Law School / Become a DA; Cornell U; Emory U

KAAKYIRE, ABENA; POOLESVILLE, MD; QUINCE ORCHARD HS; (SR); Hnr Roll; Otst Ac Ach Awd; WWAHSS; Comm Volntr; Chrch Yth Grp; Lib Aide; Off Aide; Ch Chr; Dnce; Registered Nurse; Accountant; Morgan State University Baltimore; University of Maryland Eastern Shore

KANE, JOSHUA A; BALTIMORE, MD; FOREST PARK HS; (SO); Fut Prb Slvr; Hnr Roll; MVP; Otst Ac Ach Awd; Perf Att; Pres Ac Ftns Aw; Sci Fairs; Sci/Math Olympn; St of Mnth; WWAHSS; Comm Volntr; Peer Tut/Med; Chrch Yth Grp; Dbte Team; Drma Clb; Mth Clb/Tm; NYLC; Off Aide; Outdrs Clb; French Clb; Acpl Chr; Ch Chr; Clr Grd; Bskball (V); Ftball (J); Mar Art (J); Sccr (V); Wt Lftg (V); Wrstlg (C); Adv Cncl (R); Cl Off (R); CR (R); Sch Ppr (E); Pathfinders (Explorer); Teach Sign Choir/Director of Voice Choir; Lawyer; Doctor (Pediatrician); Howard U; U of MD

KAPPERT, MICHAEL; COLUMBIA, MD; WILDE LAKE HS; (SO); Hnr Roll; Nat Hon Sy; USAA; Comm Volntr; Emplmnt; Bnd; Jzz Bnd; Mch Bnd; Pep Bnd; Cr Ctry (J); Track (J); Political Science; Law

KASPER, BRITTANEE; FORT WASHINGTON, MD; FRIENDLY HS; (SO); Hnr Roll; Comm Volntr; ROTC; Chr; Vllyball (J); Children's Medicine; Secondary Teaching; Johns Hopkins U

KEATING, BRETTON; GARRETT PARK, MD; AC OF THE HOLY CROSS; (JR); Hnr Roll; Nat Hon Sy; Comm Volntr; Peer Tut/Med; Emplmnt; P to P St Amb Prg; Spanish Clb; Chr; Dnce; Fld Hky (J); Lcrsse (J); Track (V); Cl Off (V); Sch Ppr (R); Piano; Community Service Award; Communications; Psychology; Elon U

KEEHAN, TERRI; NOTTINGHAM, MD; PERRY HALL HS; (SR); WWAHSS; Spec Olymp Vol; ArtClub; Golf (V); National Art Honor Society; Fine Arts; Psychology; Maryland Institute College of Art; Towson U

KEENAN, MAURA; MOUNT AIRY, MD; SOUTH CARROLL HS; (FR); Hi Hnr Roll; Hnr Roll; Otst Ac Ach Awd; Pres Ac Ftns Aw; WWAHSS; Comm Volntr; Chrch Yth Grp; Key Club; NYLC; Off Aide; Svce Clb; Dnce; Orch; Distinguished Honor Roll; Key Club Member; Early Childhood Education; Dance; Penn State U; U of Maryland

KEENEY, LINDSAY; WALKERSVILLE, MD; WALKERSVILLE HS; (SO); Hnr Roll; Chrch Yth Grp; Clr Grd; Orch; Bskball (J); Cr Ctry (V L); Track (V L); Lit Mag (E, R, P); Environmental Club; Envirothon; Bachelor of Science; Virginia Tech; U of Maryland

KELLER, KENDRA R; HAGERSTOWN, MD; NORTH HAGERSTOWN HS; (SO); Hnr Roll; Comm Volntr; Chrch Yth Grp; Emplmnt; Key Club; Clr Grd; CR (R); Medical Academy; Psychology; Behavioral Therapy

KENION, KIERRA T; ABERDEEN, MD; ABERDEEN MS; (MS); Hi Hnr Roll; Hnr Roll; Perf Att; St of Mnth; Yth Ldrshp Prog; Peer Tut/Med; Chrch Yth Grp; DARE; FTA; Chr; Ch Chr; Elected to - People to People Program; Spanish Teacher; Johns Hopkins U; Towson U

KENNEDY, CAITLYN H; GAITHERSBURG, MD; QUINCE ORCHARD HS; (SR); F Lan Hn Soc; Hi Hnr Roll; MVP; Nat Hon Sy; Quill & Scroll; Cr Ctry (V CL); Fld Hky (V L); Lcrsse (V L); Track (V CL); Sch Ppr (E); Maryland Distinguished Scholar; Journalism/Communication; Lehigh U (Start Fall 2005) (Accepted)

KHAN, NAZIA A; RIVERDALE, MD; BLADENSBURG HS; (JR); Hnr Roll; Honor Roll Since Elementary School; Received the Presidents Award - 8th; Pre-Med; Biology; U of Maryland; Princeton U

KHAN, SOFIYA; CATONSVILLE, MD; WOODLAWN HS; (JR); Hnr Roll; Comm Volntr; Peer Tut/Med; Computer Engineer; Doctor; U of Maryland; Towson State U

KHASTOU, ELNAZ; COLLEGE PARK, MD; PARKDALE HS; (FR); Hnr Roll; WWAHSS; Comm Volntr; Peer Tut/Med; Orch; Cl Off (V); U of Maryland; New York U

KIDD, MELISSA M; WARWICK, MD; ST MARKS HS; (JR); Hnr Roll; Pres Ac Ftns Aw; Sci Fairs; Comm Volntr; DARE; Emplmnt; Key Club; Fld Hky (J); Skiing (J); Honor Roll; Business Class Winner for Stock Market Contest; Doctorate in Psychology; Nursing; Wilmington College; U of Delaware

KIDWELL, JAMIE; HAGERSTOWN, MD; SOUTH HAGERSTOWN HS; (SR); Hi Hnr Roll; Hnr Roll; Nat Hon Sy; Perf Att; WWAHSS; Chrch Yth Grp; Emplmnt; Key Club; Mth Clb/Tm; Off Aide; Photog; Prom Com; Scouts; Clr Grd; Flg Crps; Cr Ctry (J); Track (V); Yrbk (P); Who's Who Americas Schools; Key Club Treasurer; Photography; Finance; Utah State, Lenoir Rhyne; Utah Valley State

KIESSLING, LAURA N; GLEN BURNIE, MD; GLEN BURNIE SR HS; (SO); Hnr Roll; Sci Fairs; St of Mnth; Peer Tut/Med; Chrch Yth Grp; DARE; Mus Clb; SADD; Acpl Chr; Ch Chr; SP/M/VS; Cl Off (P); Harvard Law

KILIBARDA, NATASHA; CABIN JOHN, MD; WALT WHITMAN HS; (SO); Hnr Roll; Nat Ldrshp Svc; Comm Volntr; Peer Tut/Med; DECA; Emplmnt; Key Club; Svce Clb; Vsity Clb; Vllyball (V); Yrbk (E); Rowing-Varsity; Advertising; Digital Art; U of Wisconsin, Madison; Pennsylvania State U

KIM, BO; GLEN ARM, MD; LOCH RAVEN HS; (JR); F Lan Hn Soc; Hnr Roll; Nat Hon Sy; Peer Tut/Med; FTA; Mus Clb; Prom Com; Tchrs Aide; Spanish Clb; Acpl Chr; Orch; SP/M/VS; Foreign Language; Physical Therapy; Towson U; Arizona U

KIM, BRADLEY; COLUMBIA, MD; WILDE LAKE HS; (JR); Hnr Roll; Nat Hon Sy; Perf Att; Sci Fairs; Comm Volntr; Peer Tut/Med; Chrch Yth Grp; Emplmnt; Vsity Clb; Asian Clb; Tennis (V); I Have Won a Couple of Trophies in Karate (Tae Kwon Do); I Have Won A Few Awards in Piano Competitions; Education (Teaching-Teacher/Professor); U of Maryland College Park

KIM, JOAN; PARKVILLE, MD; LOCH RAVEN HS; (JR); Ctznshp Aw; Hnr Roll; Otst Ac Ach Awd; ArtClub; Chrch Yth Grp; MuAlphaTh; Tchrs Aide; Japanese Clb; Ch Chr; Bdmtn (V); Interior Designing

KIM, SAES B; GLEN BURNIE, MD; GLEN BURNIE SR HS; (JR); ArtClub; Mus Clb; Chr; National Honor Art Society; Business; U of Maryland (College Park)

KIMBEL, THOMAS L; DUNDALK, MD; ARCHBISHOP CURLEY HS; (JR); Hnr Roll; St of Mnth; WWAHSS; Comm Volntr; Lcrsse (V L); Freshman Artist of the Year; Towson State U; Villa Julie U

KING, DARRELL A; HYATTSVILLE, MD; CHARLES HERBERT FLOWERS HS; (FR); Ctznshp Aw; Hnr Roll; MVP; Nat Sci Aw; St of Mnth; Yth Ldrshp Prog; Comm Volntr; Peer Tut/Med; Emplmnt; Fr of Library; Lib Aide; Off Aide; SADD; Tchrs Aide; Mch Bnd; SP/M/VS; Stg Cre; Bsball (V); Bskball (C); Ftball (V); Tennis (V); Wrstlg (V); Stu Cncl (T); CR (P); U of Maryland

KING, ERIN; COLLEGE PARK, MD; PARKDALE HS; (JR); Nat Hon Sy; Otst Ac Ach Awd; Sftball (V L); International Baccalaureate; Elementary Education; Education; U of Maryland College Park

KING, MEGAN E; HURLOCK, MD; (SR); Hnr Roll; Nat Hon Sy; WWAHSS; Comm Volntr; FCA; Key Club; Mus Clb; Prom Com; Tchrs Aide; Spanish Clb; Chr; Ch Chr; SP/M/VS; Fld Hky (V); Track (V); Stu Cncl (R); CR (R); Sch Ppr (R, P); Yrbk (P); Tri-M (President); Maryland Distinguished Scholar Semi-Finalist; Music Education; Towson U

KIRBY, KYLE; MT SAVAGE, MD; BEALL HS; (JR); Hnr Roll; Perf Att; Comm Volntr; Emplmnt; Tchrs Aide; Ftball (J); Wt Lftg (J); Extra Effort Award; Game Design; Business Ethics; Art Institute of Penn; DeVry U

KIRMANI, NABEEL S; TOWSON, MD; TOWSON HS; (SR); Ctznshp Aw; Hnr Roll; Kwnis Aw; Otst Ac Ach Awd; Perf Att; Comm Volntr; Peer Tut/Med; Red Cr Aide; Emplmnt; Key Club; Mth Clb/Tm; Vsity Clb; Orch; Tennis (V L); Varsity Tennis Sportsmanship Award; Publication in Yearly School Literary Magazine; Psychology; Sports Medicine; Harvard U; Yale U

KLIMEK, NICOLE E; DUNDALK, MD; SPARROWS POINT HS; (JR); Hi Hnr Roll; Hnr Roll; ArtClub; Yrbk (R, P); National Art Honor Society; Psychology; Business Management; Towson U; Salisbury U

KNESEL, DESTINY R; BRUNSWICK, MD; BRUNSWICK HS; (MS); Hnr Roll; Nat Hon Sy; Perf Att; Sci Fairs; St of Mnth; Comm Volntr; Drma Clb; SP/M/VS; Gmnstcs; Swmg; Ballet; 4 Yrs Junior Pre-High - Cheerleading; Pediatrician; Tulane U Louisiana

KNIGHT, ERIKA; OXON HILL, MD; POTOMAC; (SR); Hnr Roll; Comm Volntr; Chrch Yth Grp; Emplmnt; Off Aide; ROTC; Ch Chr; Professional Model; Bachelor's Degree / Early Childhood Education; Prince George's Community College; Maryland Eastern Shore

KNIGHT, TANIA D; ABINGDON, MD; BALTIMORE POLYTECHNIC INST; (SR); Hnr Roll; WWAHSS; Peer Tut/Med; Chrch Yth Grp; Emplmnt; Dnce; Chrldg (V); Nursing; Dance; Emory U; U of Maryland Baltimore County

KOEPPL, VALERIE; BOWIE, MD; BOWIE HS; (SO); Hi Hnr Roll; Hnr Roll; Otst Ac Ach Awd; Sccr (V L); Who's Who Among High School Athletes Award '03-'04'& '04-'05; Gatorade Rookie of the Year Award Varsity '02-04'; Physical Therapy; Occupational Therapy; Towson U; U of Maryland College Park

KOUAMO, BRANDONE; UPPER MARLBORO, MD; LARGO HS; (SO); F Lan Hn Soc; Hnr Roll; MVP; CARE; Comm Volntr; Hab For Humty Volntr; ArtClub; Cmptr Clb; ROTC; Sci Clb; French Clb; Ch Chr; Drl Tm; Mch Bnd; SP/M/VS; Bskball (L); Cyclg (C); Gmnstcs (J); Hsbk Rdg (L); Mar Art (J); Sccr (V); Tennis (C); Track (L); Science and Technology.; Aviation Engineering; American U; U of Maryland College Park

KRAMER, GILLIAN; HAGERSTOWN, MD; NORTH HAGERSTOWN HS; (FR); Hi Hnr Roll; Nat Hon Sy; Otst Ac Ach Awd; Pres Ac Ftns Aw; Sci Fairs; St of Mnth; WWAHSS; Comm Volntr; Red Cr Aide; DARE; Drma Clb; Key Club; Mus Clb; Tmpl Yth Grp; Bnd; Chr; Dnce; Jzz Bnd; Biology "Star"; Who's Who American High Schools; Accomplished Actress; PhD; Yale U; Oxford U

KRAUSS, JUSTIN; BALTIMORE, MD; TOWSON CATHOLIC HS; (MS); All Am Sch; Ctznshp Aw; Hi Hnr Roll; MVP; Nat Hon Sy; Nat Stu 4th Day Aw; Otst Ac Ach Awd; Perf Att; Yth Ldrshp Prog; Comm Volntr; Chrch Yth Grp; Emplmnt; Fr of Library; Tchrs Aide; SP/M/VS; Stg Cre; Bsball (J); Sccr (J); Swmg (J); Wt Lftg (J); Honors - English / Biology, Musician; CSI Investigator; Towson U; UCLA

KREUTZER, KRISTIN; COCKEYSVILLE, MD; DUNDALK HS; (SR); Hnr Roll; Nat Ldrshp Svc; Yth Ldrshp Prog; Spec Olymp Vol; Chrch Yth Grp; Jr Ach; PP Ftbl; CR (R); Marching Band (Varsity) and (Letter Winner); Criminology; Psychology; Towson U; U of Maryland-Baltimore County

KRIMSKI, MATTHEW; SANDY SPRING, MD; THE BARRIE SCH; (SO); Hi Hnr Roll; Hnr Roll; Pres Ac Ftns Aw; Sci Fairs; WWAHSS; Comm Volntr; Biology Clb; Sci Clb; Tennis (V); Track (V); Lit Mag (E); Sch Ppr (E); Black Belt - Budo Taijutsu Karate; Overall Academic Excellence Award; Law; Humanities

KRISHNAKURUP, PRASAD; BURTONSVILLE, MD; PAINT BRANCH HS; (SO); Hi Hnr Roll; Hnr Roll; Otst Ac Ach Awd; Comm Volntr; Hosp Aide; Key Club; Academic Achievement Award; President's Award for Educational Excellence; Medicine; U of Maryland; Duke U

KUCHEVSKI, IRINA; COLUMBIA, MD; HAMMOND HS; (JR); F Lan Hn Soc; Hi Hnr Roll; Hnr Roll; Otst Ac Ach Awd; Comm Volntr; Peer Tut/Med; WWAHSS; Yth Ldrshp Prog; Comm Volntr; Peer Tut/Med; Emplmnt; Prom Com; Svce Clb; Spanish Clb; Dnce; Stg Cre; Cr Ctry (V CL); Track (V CL); Stu Cncl (R); CR (R); Interact Club (Community Service Club); International Relations; Foreign Languages; U of Maryland; College Park; Towson U

KUREK, ANGELA B; DUNDALK, MD; DUNDALK HS; (SO); Hnr Roll; Dnce; Orch; Chrldg (V L); Church Lector Usher; Honor and GT Classes; Nursing; Villa Julie; Towson State

KURZROK, ADAM D; BETHESDA, MD; SIDWELL FRIENDS; (FR); NYLC; Stg Cre; Bsball (J)

Kim, Bradley
Wilde Lake HS
Columbia, MD

Kidd, Melissa M
St Marks HS
Warwick, MD

Kenion, Kierra T
Aberdeen MS
Aberdeen, MD

Jordan, Shannon A
Pocomoke HS
Pocomoke City, MD

Kappert, Michael
Wilde Lake HS
Columbia, MD

Kidwell, Jamie
South Hagerstown HS
Hagerstown, MD

Knight, Erika
Potomac
Oxon Hill, MD

KURZROK, MARK; BETHESDA, MD; SIDWELL FRIENDS SCH; (JR); MVP; Comm Volntr; Chrch Yth Grp; Mth Clb/Tm; Jzz Bnd; Bsball (V); Sccr (V); Adv Cncl (R); Sch Ppr (E)

KYLE, BRANDON; LONACONING, MD; WESTMAR HS; (FR); Ftball (J); Mar Art (V); Wt Lftg (V); Wrstlg (V); Law Enforcement; Frostburg State U; Penn State

LA BRIOLA, RACHEL; HUNTINGTOWN, MD; NORTHERN HS; (SR); Ctznshp Aw; Hnr Roll; Yth Ldrshp Prog; Comm Volntr; Red Cr Aide; Chrch Yth Grp; DARE; Drma Clb; Emplmnt; FCA; Prom Com; Quill & Scroll; Scouts; Chr; Ch Chr; SP/M/VS; Sftball (J); Adv Cncl (R); Cl Off (R); Broadcasting-Associate Producer; To Be an Investigative Reporter; Anne Arundel Community

LACEY, MICHELLE; MARRIOTTSVILLE, MD; GLENELG HS; (JR); Hi Hnr Roll; Hnr Roll; Nat Hon Sy; Perf Att; Pres Ac Ftns Aw; Pres Sch; St of Mnth; Comm Volntr; Peer Tut/Med; Bnd; Mch Bnd; Pep Bnd; SP/M/VS; Lcrsse (V); Sccr (V); First Place in GLMTA Flute Competition; Honorable Mention in Young Musician's Columbia Orchestra; English; Spanish; Gettysburg College; Lehigh U

LADAS, MICHAEL H; GERMANTOWN, MD; NORTHWEST HS; (MS); Sci/Math Olympn; Johns Hopkins Cty Participant-Gifted & Talented; Riflery Team, Marksman, Soccer Team, Flag Football; Architecture; Medical

LANE, KRISTEN L; EASTON, MD; EASTON AREA HS; (SR); Hi Hnr Roll; Hnr Roll; Emplmnt; Ntl FFA; Vllyball (J); No If's And's or Butt's Club; Accounting Internship; Accounting; Salisbury U; St Mary's College

LANGSTON, AYANA; CLINTON, MD; OXON HS; (FR); Ctznshp Aw; Hi Hnr Roll; Hnr Roll; Otst Ac Ach Awd; Perf Att; Pres Sch; Sci Fairs; Drma Clb; Lib Aide; Prom Com; Dnce; SP/M/VS; PPSqd (V); Cl Off (P); First Place - Medical Science Section of School Science Fair / Cheerleader of the Year; Pre-Med; Hampton U; Howard U

LANTZ, DANIELLE M; SPARROWS POINT, MD; SPARROWS POINT HS; (JR); Hnr Roll; WWAHSS; Emplmnt; Quill & Scroll; Golf (V); Lit Mag; Maryland Athletic Assn Scholar Athlete Award; Baltimore County Varsity All-Academic Team; English

LAPORTE, REENA L; GERMANTOWN, MD; SENECA VALLEY SHS; (JR); Hnr Roll; Peer Tut/Med; Chrch Yth Grp; Ch Chr; Participated in Olympic Quiz - Outside US; AAFAE Nominee; Accounting; Business Management; Cornell U; Florida Southern College

LAPP, JASON B; LUSBY, MD; PATUXENT HS; (SR); Hnr Roll; Nat Hon Sy; Otst Ac Ach Awd; Yth Ldrshp Prog; Peer Tut/Med; Emplmnt; Prom Com; Ftball (J); Track (V); Stu Cncl (R); National Youth Leadership Forum on Medicine; Mentorship in Neurosurgery; Major in Chemistry; Pre-Med; U of Maryland, College Park; UMBC and Villa Julie College

LARMAN, ALAN T; CHESAPEAKE BEACH, MD; NORTHERN HS; (FR); Hnr Roll; MVP; Otst Ac Ach Awd; Perf Att; Pres Ac Ftns Aw; AL Aux Boys; Emplmnt; FCA; Bsball (J); Ftball (J); Architecture; Business; Auburn; South Carolina

LARSON, DORA M; SILVER SPRING, MD; RICHARD MONTGOMERY HS; (JR); F Lan Hn Soc; Hnr Roll; Nat Hon Sy; WWAHSS; Amnsty Intl; Comm Volntr; Peer Tut/Med; Key Club; Lit Mag (E); International Baccalaureate Program; English / Anthropology- Double Major; Law School; U of Maryland College Park; Georgetown U

LATHAM, CRYSTAL; ABERDEEN, MD; ABERDEEN HS; (JR); F Lan Hn Soc; Hnr Roll; Nat Hon Sy; Pres Sch; WWAHSS; Peer Tut/Med; Bnd; Mch Bnd; Pep Bnd; Tri-M Honor Society; Band Section Leader; Astronomer / Astronomy; Physicist/ Physics; Rochester Institute of Technology; U of Maryland

LATULOLA, MARYLAND A; GAITHERSBURG, MD; GAITHERSBURG HS; (FR); Hi Hnr Roll; Hnr Roll; Otst Ac Ach Awd; Sci Fairs; Sci/Math Olympn; Comm Volntr; Chrch Yth Grp; DARE; Mus Clb; Outdrs Clb; Photog; Bnd; Ch Chr; Dnce; Vllyball (J); I Do Cheerleading (Not on School Team).; I Do Softball (Not on School Team).; Master's Degree; Johns Hopkins U; U of Maryland

LAU, JULIANNA R; MOUNT AIRY, MD; GLENELG HS; (JR); Hi Hnr Roll; Hnr Roll; Nat Ldrshp Svc; Nat Mrt Fin; Nat Mrt LOC; Otst Ac Ach Awd; Sci Fairs; St of Mnth; St Optmst of Yr; Yth Ldrshp Prog; Comm Volntr; Peer Tut/Med; Red Cr Aide; Chrch Yth Grp; Drma Clb; NYLC; Photog; Prom Com; Tchrs Aide; French Clb; SP/M/VS; Stg Cre; Fld Hky (J); Scr Kpr (VJ); Stu Cncl (V); Lit Mag (E, R); State Semi-Finalist American Teen Miss; Business Communications; Villa Julie College; Greensboro U

LAWSON, AHLORA; WINDSOR MILL, MD; MILFORD MILL AC; (SO); Hnr Roll; Otst Ac Ach Awd; Comm Volntr; Manager of Boys JV Basketball Team; Architecture; Duke; NC State

LEE, BRITTANY; RANDALLSTOWN, MD; RANDALLSTOWN HS; (JR); Nat Sci Aw; Perf Att; St of Mnth; Peer Tut/Med; Chrch Yth Grp; DARE; FTA; Ch Chr; Chrldg (J); Track (J); Daycare Assistant; FACTS Certificate; Education; Early Childhood; Morgan State; U of Missouri

LEE, GARRETT J; BOWIE, MD; ARCHBISHOP SPALDING HS; (MS); Hnr Roll; Chr; Sccr; Tennis; Cl Off (P)

LEE, JACLYN B; OWINGS, MD; NORTHERN HS; (JR); Ctznshp Aw; Hi Hnr Roll; Hnr Roll; MVP; Nat Hon Sy; Nat Ldrshp Svc; WWAHSS; Yth Ldrshp Prog; Comm Volntr; ArtClub; Chrch Yth Grp; Emplmnt; NYLC; Photog; Vsity Clb; Lcrsse (V L); Swmg (V CL); Vsy Clb; Cl Off (V); Stu Cncl (R); CR (R); Yrbk (E); Washington Post 1st Team Selection-Swimming 9, 10, 11; SMAC 1st Team Selection-Swimming 9th, 10th, 11th; Architecture; North Carolina State U; Syracuse U

LEFFLER, MATT; ARNOLD, MD; BROADNECK; (JR); Hi Hnr Roll; Hnr Roll; Nat Hon Sy; Perf Att; Pres Sch; WWAHSS; Key Club; Tennis (V L)

LEFFNER, LAURA; COLUMBIA, MD; WILDE LAKE HS; (JR); Hi Hnr Roll; Hnr Roll; Nat Hon Sy; St of Mnth; Comm Volntr; Hab For Humty Volntr; Prom Com; Scouts; Chr; Swg Chr; Fld Hky (VJ L); Swmg (V); Stu Cncl (R); Girl Scout Silver Award; Biochemistry; Molecular Biology; Washington College; James Madison U

LEGG, JESSICA; HOLLYWOOD, MD; ST MARY'S RYKEN HS; (SO); Hi Hnr Roll; MVP; Perf Att; Pres Ac Ftns Aw; Comm Volntr; Key Club; Scouts; Bskball (J); Hsbk Rdg; Sccr (JC); Track (V); Sch Ppr (R); Physical Sciences; History; Mount St Mary's; Hood College

LEISHMAN, ALEXANDER B; SILVER SPRING, MD; JAMES H BLAKE HS; (FR); Hi Hnr Roll; Perf Att; Comm Volntr; Quiz Bowl; Scouts; Bnd; Jzz Bnd; Mch Bnd; Pep Bnd; Bsball (J); Scholar Athlete Award; Band Leadership Award; Aerospace Engineering; Instrumental Music; U of Maryland; MIT

LENETSKY, LAUREN E; WESTMINSTER, MD; WINTERS MILL HS; (SR); Hi Hnr Roll; Hnr Roll; Comm Volntr; Key Club; Chr; Nursing

LEON JR, JOSEPH; POTOMAC, MD; CHURCHILL HS; (FR); Hi Hnr Roll; Hnr Roll; MVP; Perf Att; Sci Fairs; Drma Clb; JSA; Mus Clb; Acpl Chr; Chr; Dnce; SP/M/VS; International Relations; Political Science; Georgetown U; Stanford U

LEVEE, BETHANY; MANCHESTER, MD; NORTH CARROLL HS; (JR); Hnr Roll; Nat Hon Sy; Perf Att; Comm Volntr; Chrch Yth Grp; Key Club; Scouts; Dnce; Interior Design

LEVIN, SCOTT M; COLUMBIA, MD; WILDE LAKE HS; (SR); Hnr Roll; MVP; Nat Hon Sy; Peer Tut/Med; Emplmnt; Bnd; Jzz Bnd; Mch Bnd; SP/M/VS; Cr Ctry (V L); Sccr (JC); Track (V L); Wrstlg (J); Stu Cncl (R); Materials Engineering; U of Illinois Champaign-Urbana; Northwestern U

LEVY, MATTHEW; GERMANTOWN, MD; WATKINS MILL HS; (FR); Hi Hnr Roll; Hnr Roll; Perf Att; Ftball (J); Track (J); Wt Lftg (J); Peer Mediator; Flag Football; Architecture; Computer Programming; U of Maryland; Virginia Tech

LEWIS, ASSATA J; BALTIMORE, MD; BALTIMORE POLYTECHNIC INST; (SR); Ctznshp Aw; Hnr Roll; Perf Att; WWAHSS; Yth Ldrshp Prog; Comm Volntr; Peer Tut/Med; ArtClub; Chess; Chrch Yth Grp; Drma Clb; Emplmnt; Mus Clb; Pep Squd; Scouts; Bnd; Dnce; Drm Mjr; Flg Crps; Cl Off (P); CR (R); Baltimore City Council Page; Winner of Fox 45 TV - Champion of Courage; Engineering Degree; Dance Minor; Morgan State U; Howard U

LEWIS, JAZZ M; UPPER MARLBORO, MD; CHARLES HERBERT FLOWERS HS; (SO); Ctznshp Aw; Hnr Roll; MVP; Comm Volntr; ArtClub; Dbte Team; Scouts; Sign Clb; Bnd; Jzz Bnd; Illustration Club; Debate Team; Architecture; U of Maryland College Park; U of Virginia

LEWIS, KEVIN; WINDSOR MILL, MD; (SR); Hnr Roll; Perf Att; Tech Clb; Stg Cre; Cl Off (R); Lit Mag (R); Sch Ppr (R); Mass Communications; Delaware State; Bowie State

LEWIS, TEVIN T; GWYNN OAK, MD; WOODLAWN HS; (SR); Ctznshp Aw; Hnr Roll; MVP; Comm Volntr; Chrch Yth Grp; Emplmnt; FCA; Lttrmn Clb; Bskball (V); Business Admin; Atlanta Clark U; Florida A & M

LI, ERIK; ROCKVILLE, MD; MONTGOMERY BLAIR HS; (JR); Hnr Roll; Nat Hon Sy; Scouts; Dnce; Sch Ppr (E, R); Systems Administrator for Blair High School's Webserver; Extracurricular Activity - Wushu (AKA Kung Fu); Bioengineering; Business; U of Maryland; California Institute of Technology

LI, JUDITH Y; CLARKSVILLE, MD; RIVER HILL HS; (SO); Ctznshp Aw; Duke TS; Hi Hnr Roll; Perf Att; Sci Fairs; St of Mnth; WWAHSS; ArtClub; Photog; Stg Cre; Cr Ctry (J); Track (J); Lit Mag (P); Founder / Founding Member of Honor Council at School; PTSA - Student Executive Board Member; Business Administration / Management and Operations; Design and Visual Communications / Commercial and Advertising Art; Duke U; U of Pennsylvania

LIM, JIYUN; ARNOLD, MD; BROADNECK HS; (JR); Hi Hnr Roll; Hnr Roll; Nat Hon Sy; Perf Att; Comm Volntr; Chrch Yth Grp; Key Club; Journalist; New York U

LINDO, ABIGAIL C U; RANDALLSTOWN, MD; RANDALLSTOWN HS; (JR); Ctznshp Aw; Hi Hnr Roll; Hnr Roll; Sci Fairs; Comm Volntr; ArtClub; Chrch Yth Grp; DARE; Dbte Team; Drma Clb; Mus Clb; Bnd; Chr; Ch Chr; Mch Bnd; Sch Ppr (E); Induction Into High School Honors Choir; Environmental Design; Psychology; Howard U; U of Maryland

LINGG, KAREN M; WESTMINSTER, MD; SOUTH CARROLL HS; (SR); Hnr Roll; WWAHSS; Drma Clb; Emplmnt; Key Club; Dnce; SP/M/VS; Chrldg (VJCL); PP Ftbl (V); Yrbk (R); Job Shadowing; Camp Hashawa Counselor; Nursing; Towson U

LIPPY, MATT; WESTMINSTER, MD; SOUTH CARROLL HS; (SO); Hnr Roll; USAA; WWAHSS; Spec Olymp Vol; Key Club; Lcrsse (JC); Sccr (J); Environmental Science; Virginia Tech; St Mary's College-Maryland

LIPSCOMB, JONATHAN; REISTERSTOWN, MD; CALVERT HALL HS; (SR); Hnr Roll; Nat Hon Sy; Yth Ldrshp Prog; Hab For Humty Volntr; Peer Tut/Med; DARE; Mus Clb; P to P St Amb Prg; Scouts; SADD; Bnd; Jzz Bnd; Mch Bnd; Orch; Lit Mag (R); Sch Ppr (R); Life Boy Scout; Music Performance Major in Jazz Guitar; Berklee School of Music

LISKA, MATTHEW P; PERRY HALL, MD; ARCHBISHOP CURLEY HS; (JR); Hi Hnr Roll; Hnr Roll; Comm Volntr; Chess; Chrch Yth Grp; Emplmnt; FCA; Vsity Clb; Bskball (J); Golf (V); Sccr (V); Soccer- Unsung Hero Award; Physical Therapy; U of Maryland; Towson U

LITTLE, ASHLEY M; WHITE PLAINS, MD; WESTLAKE HS; (SR); All Am Sch; Hi Hnr Roll; Hnr Roll; Otst Ac Ach Awd; Perf Att; St of Mnth; WWAHSS; Drma Clb; FCA; Key Club; Prom Com; SP/M/VS; Stg Cre; Choreographer for School Musicals-3 years.; Dance Student-13 Years Competive Line-7 years; Mass Communications/Broadcast Journalism; Performing Arts; Elon U

LITTLE, ZACHARY M; THURMONT, MD; CATOCTIN HS; (FR); Hi Hnr Roll; Nat Hon Sy; Otst Ac Ach Awd; Perf Att; Comm Volntr; Bsball (J); Bskball (J); Engineering; Architectural Drawing; U of Virginia

LIU, AUSTIN; POTOMAC, MD; WINSTON CHURCHILL HS; (FR); Hnr Roll; Perf Att; Comm Volntr; Cmptr Clb; NYLC; Sci Clb; Chr; Stg Cre; Vllyball (V); First Place in Final Frontiers (The Maryland Space Business Roundtable); Nuclear Engineer; Massachusetts Institute of Technology

LIU, YUE; BETHESDA, MD; WALTER JOHNSON HS; (FR); Hnr Roll; St of Mnth; Comm Volntr; Peer Tut/Med; Cmptr Clb; Dbte Team; Mth Clb/Tm; NtlFrnscLg; Orch; Walter Johnson It's Academic Team; Outstanding Musician Award

LIU, YUHANG; ROCKVILLE, MD; THOMAS S WOOTTON HS; (FR); Hnr Roll; MVP; Comm Volntr; Peer Tut/Med; ArtClub; Chess; Dbte Team; Mth Clb/Tm; Chinese Clb; Bnd; SP/M/VS; Bdmtn (V); Bsball (J); Bskball (J); Ftball (V); Gmnstcs (V); Sccr (V); Swmg (V); Tennis (J); CR (V); Computer Science IT; Business; Johns Hopkins U; Maryland U

LLANO, MATTHEW; ARNOLD, MD; BROADNECK HS; (JR); Ctznshp Aw; Hi Hnr Roll; MVP; Nat Hon Sy; Otst Ac Ach Awd; Perf Att; Pres Ac Ftns Aw; Valdctrian; Comm Volntr; Peer Tut/Med; Emplmnt; Key Club; Mth Clb/Tm; Cr Ctry (V L); Sccr (J); Track (V CL); Cl Off (R); Stu Cncl (R); Yrbk (R); National Honor Society-President & Vice President; Pre-Med; Pre-Vet; U of Richmond; U of Pennsylvania

LOCKATELL, ALLISON; NEW WINDSOR, MD; SOUTH CARROLL HS; (JR); Hi Hnr Roll; Yth Ldrshp Prog; Comm Volntr; Hosp Aide; Emplmnt; Key Club; Scouts; Tchrs Aide; Spanish Clb; Bnd; Sccr (J); Track (V L); National Society of High School Scholars; Health Care-Nursing; Psychology; Widener U; Salisbury U

LOGAN, PAUL W; MC HENRY, MD; NORTHERN GARRETT HS; (JR); Hi Hnr Roll; Hnr Roll; Otst Ac Ach Awd; Sci Fairs; St of Mnth; WWAHSS; Comm Volntr; Chess; Chrch Yth Grp; Emplmnt; Tchrs Aide; Vsity Clb; Chr; SP/M/VS; Bskball (V); Track (V L); Pre-Veterinary Medicine; Animal Sciences; U of Maryland, College Park; West Virginia U

LONG, SHATE'RRA; DUNDALK, MD; DUNDALK HS; (FR); Hnr Roll; Otst Ac Ach Awd; Perf Att; Comm Volntr; ArtClub; Chrch Yth Grp; DARE; Emplmnt; Prom Com; SADD; Dnce; Bdmtn (J); Bskball (J); Sftball (J); Adv Cncl (S); Stu Cncl (S); Captain of the Step Squad; Won $100 Savings Bond from Art Contest; Major in Info. Systems Management; Fine Arts; Howard State U; Virginia Tech U

LOWERY, KAITLIN R M; BOWIE, MD; BOWIE HS; (FR); Comm Volntr; Peer Tut/Med; Chrch Yth Grp; Emplmnt; Svce Clb; Track (VJ); Adv Cncl (R); CR (R); Peer Mentoring; Pharmacist; Columbia U

LUCAS, DANIELLE; CLINTON, MD; SURRATTSVILLE HS; (SO); Hnr Roll; Nat Hon Sy; Comm Volntr; Peer Tut/Med; Emplmnt; Bnd; Ch Chr; Mch Bnd; Sftball (V); Clark-Atlanta U; Virginia State U

LUKE, DENICE S; SUITLAND, MD; GRACE BRETHREN CHRISTIAN SCH; (SO); Hi Hnr Roll; Hnr Roll; Otst Ac Ach Awd; Valdctrian; WWAHSS; Comm Volntr; Chrch Yth Grp; Drma Clb; Dnce; Flg Crps; SP/M/VS; Chrldg (V C); Cl Off (P); Stu Cncl (R); CR (P, R); Finalist in Who's Who Poetry; Lead America Student; Business; Education; Penn State U; U of Georgia

LUTZ, NATASHA C; HAGERSTOWN, MD; SOUTH HAGERSTOWN HS; (JR); Hi Hnr Roll; WWAHSS; Comm Volntr; Emplmnt; FCA; Prom Com; Bskball (J); Cr Ctry (J); Tennis (VJ); Wt Lftg (VJ); Sch Ppr (R); Yrbk (P); Physical Therapy; Sports Medicine; Salisbury U; James Madison U

Liu, Austin, Winston Churchill HS, Potomac, MD | Lindo, Abigail C U, Randallstown HS, Randallstown, MD | Levy, Matthew, Watkins Mill HS, Germantown, MD | Latulola, Maryland A, Gaithersburg HS, Gaithersburg, MD | Latham, Crystal, Aberdeen HS, Aberdeen, MD | La Briola, Rachel, Northern HS, Huntingtown, MD | Lapp, Jason B, Patuxent HS, Lusby, MD | Lau, Julianna R, Glenelg HS, Mount Airy, MD | Lewis, Assata J, Baltimore Polytechnic Inst, Baltimore, MD | Lipscomb, Jonathan, Calvert Hall HS, Reisterstown, MD | Little, Ashley M, Westlake HS, White Plains, MD

LYNCH, ONTARIA W; CLINTON, MD; SUITLAND HS; (SR); Hnr Roll; WWAHSS; Comm Volntr; Hosp Aide; Chrch Yth Grp; Emplmnt; Mod UN; Off Aide; Prom Com; Tchrs Aide; Drm Mjr; Bskball (J); PP Ftbl (V); Sccr (V); Nursing; Norfolk State U; Howard U

LYNCH, SHAKEARA; DUNDALK, MD; DUNDALK HS; (FR); Ctznshp Aw; Hi Hnr Roll; Hnr Roll; Perf Att; St of Mnth; St Optmst of Yr; Comm Volntr; Peer Tut/Med; Chrch Yth Grp; FBLA; Bnd; Dnce; Drm Mjr; Mch Bnd; Chrldg (C); Step Squad (Captain); Dance Team (Captain); Bachelor's-Criminal Justice (Pre-Law); Dance Ballet, Jazz, Hip-Hop, Modern; Maryland U College Park; Clark Atlanta U, U of MO Sch of Law

LYONS, GARY C; CAPITOL HEIGHTS, MD; (SR); Hnr Roll; Perf Att; WWAHSS; Comm Volntr; Peer Tut/Med; Chrch Yth Grp; Mus Clb; Chr; Drl Tm; SP/M/VS; Bskball; Mar Art; Masters in Business Administration; U of MD Eastern Shore; Bowie State College

MABRY, DOMINICK; RIVERDALE, MD; PARKDALE HS; (SO); Ctznshp Aw; Hi Hnr Roll; Hnr Roll; Perf Att; WWAHSS; Comm Volntr; DARE; Mus Clb; Bnd; Drm Mjr; Mch Bnd; Bskball (JC); Ftball (J); Track (V); NBA; NFL; UNO U of Nebraska of Omaha; U of Las Vegas of Nevada

MACKLEY, ANNA P; WESTMINSTER, MD; WINTERS MILL HS; (SR); All Am Sch; Hi Hnr Roll; Kwnis Aw; Nat Hon Sy; Otst Ac Ach Awd; Perf Att; St of Mnth; WWAHSS; Comm Volntr; Peer Tut/Med; Key Club; Prom Com; Tchrs Aide; Lcrsse (V L); Sccr (V CL); Track (V L); Stu Cncl (R); CR (R); MD Distinguished Scholar Honorable Mention; Scholastic Letter; Biology; Biotechnology; Salisbury U

MAC NEIL, THOMAS P; DAVIDSONVILLE, MD; SOUTH RIVER HS; (SO); Hi Hnr Roll; Hnr Roll; MVP; Nat Hon Sy; Otst Ac Ach Awd; Sci Fairs; Sci/Math Olympn; WWAHSS; Comm Volntr; Hab For Humty Volntr; Peer Tut/Med; BPA; Chrch Yth Grp; Civil Air Pat; DECA; FCA; FBLA; Mth Clb/Tm; Spanish Clb; Ch Chr; SP/M/VS; Cr Ctry (V L); Golf (J); Lcrsse (V L); Sccr (JC); Track (V L); Adv Cncl (R); Cl Off (R); Stu Cncl (R); CR (R); US Naval Academy; Duke U

MACVAUGH, REBECCA; TOWSON, MD; TOWSON HS; (JR); Hnr Roll; Kwnis Aw; Nat Hon Sy; Perf Att; Yth Ldrshp Prog; Comm Volntr; ArtClub; Chrch Yth Grp; Key Club; Mod UN; National Art Honor Society; Multiple Essay Contest Awards; Communications; Broadcasting; Towson U; Messiah College

MADISON, MICHELLE; INDIAN HEAD, MD; MC DONOUGH HS; (JR); Ctznshp Aw; Hnr Roll; Otst Ac Ach Awd; WWAHSS; Chess; Chrch Yth Grp; ROTC; Scouts; Tchrs Aide; Drl Tm; Chrldg (VJCL); Pediatrician; Nurse; Morgan U; Howard U

MADYUN, TAHIR S; UPPER MARLBORO, MD; ST JOHN'S COLLEGE HS; (JR); Hnr Roll; Comm Volntr; Hab For Humty Volntr; Emplmnt; Svce Clb; Bskball (J); Ftball (J); Business Management; MBA; Morehouse College; U of Virginia

MAHER, MEGHAN; LEXINGTON PARK, MD; ST MARY'S RYKEN HS; (SO); Hi Hnr Roll; Hnr Roll; Comm Volntr; Chrch Yth Grp; DARE; FBLA; Key Club; SADD; Fld Hky (J L); Lcrsse (J L); Florida State U; South Carolina

MAJOR, LAKIA C; BALTIMORE, MD; PATTERSON SR HS 405; (JR); Hi Hnr Roll; Hnr Roll; Otst Ac Ach Awd; Perf Att; St of Mnth; Criminal Justice; Journalism; New York U; Goucher College

MALICK, RACHEL; PASADENA, MD; CHESAPEAKE SR HS; (JR); Hnr Roll; CARE; Tchrs Aide; Lcrsse (JC); Sccr (VJC); CR (R); Step Leadership Team; Statistician for V/JV Lacrosse; Elementary Education; Towson U; Villa Julie College

MAMAKOS, MALLORY C; SILVER SPRING, MD; JAMES BLAKE HS; (JR); Hnr Roll; Nat Mrt LOC; Otst Ac Ach Awd; Sci Fairs; Comm Volntr; BPA; FBLA; FTA; Chr; Dnce; Chrldg (VJ L); Stu Cncl (R); CR (R); Accounting; PR; U of Maryland College Park; U of Virginia

MANNEH, AYEDEE; GREENBELT, MD; PARKDALE HS; (SO); Hnr Roll; Ch Chr; Pre-Veterinary Medicine; Music

MARKS, SADE; BOWIE, MD; BOWIE HS; (FR); Pres Ac Ftns Aw; Sci Fairs; ROTC; Drl Tm; Bskball; Sftball (J); Law; Doctor; Naval Academy; Yale School of Law

MARROQUIN, ADRIANA; GERMANTOWN, MD; NORTHWEST HS; (SO); Hnr Roll; Photog; Quill & Scroll; Stg Cre; Lit Mag (E); National Latin Exam-Gold Medal; Students Against Destructive Decisions; English; Film Studies; Northeastern U; Northwestern U

MARSH, LAUREN N; CHESAPEAKE BEACH, MD; HUNTINGTOWN HS; (JR); 4H Awd; Hi Hnr Roll; Hnr Roll; Sci Fairs; Comm Volntr; 4-H; Emplmnt; Prom Com; Yrbk (E); Many Through Equestrian Sports; Many Through Skills USA; Restaurant/Hotel Management; Graphic Design; Baltimore International College; U of Maryland

MARSHALL, MARTREZ; GWYNN OAK, MD; WESTERN SCH OF TECH AND ENVIRONMENTAL SCIENCES; (FR); Hnr Roll; Perf Att; Chrch Yth Grp; Mus Clb; Bnd; Mch Bnd; SP/M/VS; Architecture; Graphic Design/Printing; Syracuse U; Princeton U

MARTIN, ANDREW T; HAGERSTOWN, MD; NORTH HAGERSTOWN HS; (JR); All Am Sch; Hi Hnr Roll; Nat Hon Sy; Otst Ac Ach Awd; USAA; WWAHSS; Comm Volntr; Hab For Humty Volntr; Peer Tut/Med; Chrch Yth Grp; Emplmnt; Key Club; P to P St Amb Prg; Cr Ctry (V L); Lcrsse (V L); Sccr (J); Track (V L); Wrstlg (J); Stu Cncl; Scholar Athlete Award; Medicine; Pharmacy

MARTIN, CRYSTAL; BALTIMORE, MD; REGINALD F LEWIS HS; (JR); Nursing; Obstetrics; Towson U; U of Phoenix & Coppin State U

MARTIN, DIAMOND; GWYNN OAK, MD; WOODLAWN HS; (FR); Hnr Roll; Peer Tut/Med; DARE; A Medal for Outstanding Achievement for Law Class @ GRA; I Want to Major in Civil Law; U of Maryland-College Park; Harvard U

MARTIN, DIANA M; WALKERSVILLE, MD; WALKERSVILLE HS; (SO); Hi Hnr Roll; Chrch Yth Grp; Emplmnt; Scouts; Hsbk Rdg; Church Youth Group Leadership; Peer Ministry; Social Work; Psychology; Franciscan U of Steubenville; Ave Maria U

MARTIN, JOHN J; SILVER SPRING, MD; SPRINGBROOK HS; (SO); Hnr Roll; Otst Ac Ach Awd; Sci Fairs; Comm Volntr; Peer Tut/Med; MuAlphaTh; Bnd; Altar Server-St Michael's Catholic Church; Engineering

MARTINEZ, ANGELICA; BALTIMORE, MD; TOWSON HS; (SO); Hi Hnr Roll; Pres Ac Ftns Aw; Hab For Humty Volntr; ArtClub; Key Club; Scouts; Stg Cre; Environmental Club; Towson High Academic Champion; Computer Programming; Visual and Game Programming; Stanford U; The Art Institute of Phoenix

MASON, A'VIA; BALTIMORE, MD; PAUL L DUNBAR HS 414; (JR); Ctznshp Aw; Hnr Roll; Nat Hon Sy; Otst Ac Ach Awd; Perf Att; Comm Volntr; Emplmnt; Bnd; Nursing; Delaware State U; Drexel U

MASON, CHERYL; HYATTSVILLE, MD; CHARLES HERBERT FLOWERS HS; (JR); Ctznshp Aw; Hnr Roll; Perf Att; Comm Volntr; Emplmnt; FBLA; Business; Economics; Virginia State U; Bowie State U

MASON, MYRON; BALTIMORE, MD; REGINALD F LEWIS HS; (JR); Hnr Roll; WWAHSS; Political Science; Astronomy; U of Maryland; Baltimore Community College

MASONE, ADRIAN; SILVER SPRING, MD; BARRIE SCH; (FR); Ctznshp Aw; F Lan Hn Soc; Hnr Roll; Comm Volntr; Spec Olymp Vol; Chess; Bskball (VJCL); Johns Hopkins Cty; Socratic Award for Humanities / Scientific Achievement; Business

MATHIS, CHRISTOPHER R; TRAPPE, MD; EASTON AREA HS; (FR); Scouts; U of Virginia

MAZURKEVICH, JULIE C; SEVERNA PARK, MD; SEVERNA PARK HS; (JR); Hnr Roll; Pres Ac Ftns Aw; Pres Sch; Yth Ldrshp Prog; Comm Volntr; Peer Tut/Med; Spec Olymp Vol; Chrch Yth Grp; DECA; Emplmnt; Key Club; Prom Com; Scouts; French Clb; Track (J); Cl Off (S); Stu Cncl (R); Yrbk (P); Member of the Leadership Institute; Business Administration; Education; College of Charleston; U of Delaware

MC CARTHEY, KELLY; ELLICOTT CITY, MD; WILDE LAKE HS; (SO); Hi Hnr Roll; Hnr Roll; Yth Ldrshp Prog; Amnsty Intl; Hab For Humty Volntr; Red Cr Aide; Dbte Team; HO'Br Yth Ldrshp; French Clb; Chr; Dnce; Stg Cre; Fld Hky (J); Lcrsse (J); Stu Cncl (T); Sch Ppr (E); Student Rep to School Improvement Team; Journalism; Stanford; Columbia U

MC CASKILL, KENNETH L; BALTIMORE, MD; NATIONAL AC FOUNDATION; (SO); Hnr Roll; Hosp Aide; Emplmnt; Bskball (V); Cr Ctry (V); Ftball (V); Honor Roll; Perfect Attendance Award; Computer Software Engineer; Computer Science; Howard U

MC CAUL, ALISON O; WHITE MARSH, MD; PERRY HALL HS; Hnr Roll; Bnd; Performance Artist with Stringling Marionettes (Puppeteer)

MC CAY, WILLIAM P; WALKERSVILLE, MD; WALKERSVILLE HS; (SO); Hi Hnr Roll; Hnr Roll; Comm Volntr; Bsball (V); Golf (V L); Sports Medicine; Physical Therapist; Virginia Polytechnic Institute and State U

MC COY JR, CHRISTOPHER; FINKSBURG, MD; MT ST JOSEPH; (JR); Hi Hnr Roll; Hnr Roll; Sci/Math Olympn; WWAHSS; Yth Ldrshp Prog; Comm Volntr; Drma Clb; Lib Aide; NYLC; Bnd; Mch Bnd; Stg Cre; School Television Station Crew - WMSJ; Music Composition; Mechanical Engineering; Mass Communication; U of Maryland

MC DANIELS, CRYSTAL; BALTIMORE, MD; BALTIMORE CITY COLLEGE HS; (JR); Ctznshp Aw; Hi Hnr Roll; Hnr Roll; Nat Mrt Sch Recip; Perf Att; Sci Fairs; USAA; WWAHSS; Comm Volntr; Hosp Aide; Peer Tut/Med; ArtClub; P to P St Amb Prg; Scouts; Acpl Chr; Chr; Swg Chr; Perfect Attendance; Citizenship; Pre-Law; Nursing; Lincoln U; Howard U

MC DONALD, JASMINE; FORT WASHINGTON, MD; FRIENDLY HS; (SO); Hnr Roll; ROTC; Clr Grd; Drl Tm; Tennis (V); Outstanding NS-1 Award (R.O.T.C.); Outstanding NS-2 Award (R.O.T.C.); Drama; Journalism; Columbia U; Georgetown U

MC FADDEN, CONNOR Q; SILVER SPRING, MD; PRINT BRANCH; (FR); Hnr Roll; Comm Volntr; ROTC; Bnd; Drl Tm; Mch Bnd; Pep Bnd; Naval Academy

MC FARLAND, SCOTT A; WESTMINSTER, MD; CARROLL CHRISTIAN HS; (JR); Hi Hnr Roll; MVP; Perf Att; Yth Ldrshp Prog; Chrch Yth Grp; Emplmnt; HO'Br Yth Ldrshp; Prom Com; Spch Team; Bnd; Mch Bnd; SP/M/VS; Sccr (V C); Cl Off (R); CR (R); Selected to Attend HOBY Leadership Seminar in May, 2004; Biblical Studies / Christian Counseling; Harding U; Ohio Valley College

MC FARLANE, S'ADE; BALTIMORE, MD; THE CATHOLIC HS OF BALTIMORE.; (JR); Hi Hnr Roll; Nat Hon Sy; St of Mnth; WWAHSS; Comm Volntr; Peer Tut/Med; Spec Olymp Vol; Chrch Yth Grp; Pep Squd; Photog; Prom Com; Bnd; Orch; Chrldg (V); PP Ftbl (V); Stu Cncl (R); CR (R); Lit Mag (P); Community Service Awards

MC GAUGHEY, MICHELLE L; ANNAPOLIS, MD; BROADNECK HS; (FR); Hnr Roll; Perf Att; Comm Volntr; Spec Olymp Vol; Key Club; Photog; Chr; Dnce; CR (R); Yrbk (R); Accomplished Bowler; 2D Art; Business; U of Maryland; U of Notre Dame

MC GAULEY, DERIC; HYATTSVILLE, MD; JERICHO CHRISTIAN AC; (SO); All Am Sch; Hnr Roll; MVP; Perf Att; USAA; Chrch Yth Grp; Dbte Team; Ch Chr; Bskball (VJC); Ftball (VJC); Track (V); CR (R); Accounting; Business Management; Georgetown U; East Carolina U

MC GRAW, CHRISTINE L; HYDES, MD; LOCH RAVEN HS; (JR); F Lan Hn Soc; Hnr Roll; Nat Hon Sy; Otst Ac Ach Awd; Comm Volntr; Peer Tut/Med; ArtClub; Chrch Yth Grp; Photog; Prom Com; Spanish Clb; Bnd; Dnce; Mch Bnd; Pep Bnd; Bdmtn (V); Gmnstcs (V); Hsbk Rdg (V); Stu Cncl (R); Roller Skating; Piano Lessons; Foreign Language / Spanish; Medicine; U of Maryland; York College

MC HENRY, ALLISON M; FREDERICK, MD; WALKERSVILLE HS; (SO); Ctznshp Aw; Hnr Roll; Pres Sch; St of Mnth; Comm Volntr; Peer Tut/Med; Red Cr Aide; Chrch Yth Grp; Emplmnt; Key Club; Lib Aide; Scouts; Chr; SP/M/VS; Swmg (L); Elementary Education College Degree; Hood College

MC KOY, INDIA; BALTIMORE, MD; (FR); Ctznshp Aw; Hnr Roll; Otst Ac Ach Awd; Perf Att; Valdctrian; Dbte Team; ROTC; Ch Chr; JROTC; Pediatrician; Essex Community College

MC LENDON, KERRIE J; CLINTON, MD; SURRATTSVILLE HS; (SO); Ctznshp Aw; Hnr Roll; Perf Att; Comm Volntr; Mus Clb; ROTC; Scouts; Bnd; Ch Chr; Mch Bnd; Orch; Homicide Detective; Actress/Veterinarian; Norfolk State U; Florida A & M U

MEACHUM, HILLARY M; MOUNT AIRY, MD; SOUTH CARROLL HS; (FR); Hnr Roll; WWAHSS; Comm Volntr; Chrch Yth Grp; Dbte Team; Drma Clb; Key Club; Lib Aide; Ch Chr; Clr Grd; Dnce; Stg Cre; Elementary Education; Massage Therapy; McDaniel College; Pensacola College

MEADOWS, MICHAEL R; SYKESVILLE, MD; LIBERTY HS; (SO); 4H Awd; Hi Hnr Roll; MVP; Otst Ac Ach Awd; Yth Ldrshp Prog; Comm Volntr; Peer Tut/Med; Spec Olymp Vol; 4-H; Chrch Yth Grp; FCA; Quiz Bowl; Vsity Clb; Chr; Cr Ctry (V L); Track (V L); Vsy Clb (V); CR (R); State Champions Cross Country; Lacrosse National Engineering & Leadership Event; Criminal Justice; Military Service; United States Air Force Academy; United States Naval Academy

MEDCALF JR, DOUGLAS A; FREDERICK, MD; WALKERSVILLE HS; (SO); Hi Hnr Roll; St of Mnth; DARE; Emplmnt; Mus Clb; Scouts; Bnd; Clr Grd; Jzz Bnd; Mch Bnd; Ftball (J); Business/Marketing; Music

MEDINA, KELLY; SILVER SPRING, MD; WHEATON HS; (FR); Hnr Roll; Comm Volntr; Sccr (J); Never Been in Trouble or Misbehaved in School; I Want to Become a Pediatrician; DeVry U; Harvard

MEJIA, SUSAN; SILVER SPRING, MD; JAMES H BLAKE HS; (JR); Hnr Roll; Peer Tut/Med; Mar Art (V); US Capital Open Champion in Tae Kwon Do; Business Marketing and Sales; Business Management and Administration; U of Maryland; Salisbury U

MELENDEZ, SUYAPA; TAKOMA PARK, MD; HIGH POINT HS; (SO); Hnr Roll; Otst Ac Ach Awd; Perf Att; Comm Volntr; Peer Tut/Med; DARE; Emplmnt; ROTC; Scouts; Tchrs Aide; Spanish Clb; Dnce; Sccr (V); Sftball (J); CR (V); Tutoring; Psychology; Teacher; New York U; Maryland U

MELLOCK, TAYLOR A; UPPER MARLBORO, MD; CHARLES HERBERT FLOWERS HS; (FR); 4H Awd; Nat Hon Sy; Dnce; Swmg (V); Adv Cncl (V); MBR of Spanish Club; Pre Medicine; Emory U

Medcalf Jr, Douglas A
Walkersville HS
Frederick, MD

Mc Graw, Christine L
Loch Raven HS
Hydes, MD

Mathis, Christopher R
Easton Area HS
Trappe, MD

Lyons, Gary C
Capitol Heights, MD

National
Honor Roll
Spring 2005

Lynch, Shakeara
Dundalk HS
Dundalk, MD

Mc Gauley, Deric
Jericho Christian AC
Hyattsville, MD

Meachum, Hillary M
South Carroll HS
Mount Airy, MD

Medina, Kelly
Wheaton HS
Silver Spring, MD

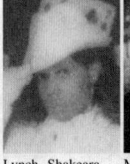

MELTON, LYDIA M; SUITLAND, MD; CROSSLAND HS; (SR); Hi Hnr Roll; Hnr Roll; Nat Hon Sy; Nat Sci Aw; Salutrn; Sci Fairs; USAA; USMC Stu Ath Aw; WWAHSS; Yth Ldrshp Prog; Comm Volntr; Chrch Yth Grp; Emplmnt; Mod UN; Photog; ROTC; Ch Chr; Clr Grd; Dnce; Drl Tm; Bskball (V); Chrldg (V); PPSqd (V); Sccr (V); Track (V); Vllyball (V); CR (R); Yrbk (P); MCJROTC Outstanding Cadet; MCJROTC Scholastic Achievement Award; International Relations; Political Science; Pennsylvania State U-U Park; U of Maryland College Park

MENCH, WHITNEY R; ROCK HALL, MD; KENT CTY HS; (JR); Hi Hnr Roll; Hnr Roll; WWAHSS; Drma Clb; SP/M/VS; Stg Cre; Tennis (V); Sch Ppr (E, R); Journalism; Pottery/Sculpture; Washington College; Villa Julie College

MENTZER, JOSEPH; JOPPA, MD; JOPPATOWNE HS; (SR); Ctznshp Aw; Hnr Roll; Yth Ldrshp Prog; Comm Volntr; Chrch Yth Grp; Emplmnt; Off Aide; Lcrsse (V L); Made Good Sportsmanship Award; Got Gold Medal Achievement Award; Going to Be Chef, Been Accepted in Pittsburgh Culinary School; Pittsburgh Culinary School-PCI

MERCADO, VICTORIA; WHITE PLAINS, MD; HENRY E LACKEY HS; (SR); Hi Hnr Roll; Hnr Roll; Perf Att; Sci Fairs; WWAHSS; Key Club; SADD; Track (V L); Vllyball (V L); CR (R); Business; U of Maryland-College Park; Towson U

MICHNEWICH, DANIEL; SILVER SPRING, MD; PAINT BRANCH HS; (SO); Hnr Roll; Otst Ac Ach Awd; Perf Att; Pres Ac Ftns Aw; Sci Fairs; St of Mnth; Comm Volntr; Chess; DARE; Emplmnt; Mus Clb; ROTC; Scouts; Clr Grd; Drl Tm; SP/M/VS; CR (R); Color Guard Commander 2004-2005; Commanding Officer NJROTC 2005-2006; Engineering; Mathematics; United States Air Force Academy; United States Naval Academy

MIDDLETON, SEAN N; WINDSOR MILL, MD; MILFORD MILL AC; (JR); Hi Hnr Roll; Hnr Roll; Comm Volntr; Chrch Yth Grp; Ch Chr; Business Administration; Criminal Justice; Bowie State U; Keuka College

MILES, MARIA A; BALTIMORE, MD; THE CATHOLIC HS OF BALTIMORE; (SO); Hi Hnr Roll; Hnr Roll; Otst Ac Ach Awd; Perf Att; WWAHSS; Peer Tut/Med; Red Cr Aide; Chrch Yth Grp; Acpl Chr; Chr; Ch Chr; Drl Tm; Bskball (J); Sftball (J); Vllyball (J); Veterinary Degree; Obstetrics Gynecology; Texas A & M U; Howard U

MILLER, CHELSEY; THURMONT, MD; CATOCTIN HS; (FR); Hi Hnr Roll; Hnr Roll; Perf Att; Comm Volntr; Ntl FFA; FFA-Junior Secretary; Received a Foreign Language Credit in Middle School / President's Award for Educational Excellence; Registered Nurse; Frederick Community College; U of Maryland

MILLER, JYNON N; OXON HILL, MD; OXON HILL HS; (FR); Ctznshp Aw; Hi Hnr Roll; Hnr Roll; Comm Volntr; Chrch Yth Grp; Ch Chr; Chrldg; Sftball; Law; Philosophy; Florida State U; U of California

MILLER, MARCIE; GWYNN OAK, MD; CATHOLIC HS OF BALTIMORE; (JR); F Lan Hn Soc; Hi Hnr Roll; Hnr Roll; Nat Hon Sy; Perf Att; St of Mnth; WWAHSS; Comm Volntr; Lib Aide; P to P St Amb Prg; Spanish Clb; Dnce; Chrldg (V); Lcrsse (J); Tennis (V); Lit Mag (R); Yrbk (R, P); 1st Place Poetry Award; Technology Award; Political Science; Pre-Law; Villa Julie College; U of Miami

MILLER, NATHAN T; WALKERSVILLE, MD; WALKERSVILLE HS; (SO); Hi Hnr Roll; MVP; Otst Ac Ach Awd; Pres Ac Ftns Aw; Bsball (J); Ice Hky (V); Rlr Hky; Skiing; Johns Hopkins Talented Youth Search; Mathematics; U of Michigan; United States Air Force Academy

MILLER, ROBIN; GAITHERSBURG, MD; GAITHERSBURG HS; (SR); Hnr Roll; Nat Mrt Sch Recip; Otst Ac Ach Awd; Pres Sch; Peer Tut/Med; Chrch Yth Grp; P to P St Amb Prg; Svce Clb; SP/M/VS; Cr Ctry (C); Track (J); Vllyball (J); Cl Off (S); Stu Cncl (R); CR (R); Kappa Alpha Psi Fraternity; 2005 Diamond Debutante Program; Business Administration; Pre-Medical; Temple U; U of Pittsburgh

MILLER, SHANICE; DISTRICT HEIGHTS, MD; CHARLES HERBERT FLOWERS HS; (SO); Hi Hnr Roll; Hnr Roll; St of Mnth; Comm Volntr; Peer Tut/Med; Emplmnt; Chr; Enrolled in the Science and Technology Program; Computer Science; Computer Engineer; Georgetown U; U of Maryland

MILLER, SHAUNTELLE A; PASADENA, MD; LAKE SHORE CHRISTIAN AC; MS; 4H Awd; Hnr Roll; St of Mnth; Comm Volntr; Chrch Yth Grp; Drma Clb; Spanish Clb; Ch Chr; SP/M/VS; Yrbk; Math-A-Thon; 2nd Place AWANA Grand Prix; Doctor; Missionary; Pensacola Christian College

MILLER, TAMAR; ROCKVILLE, MD; (JR); Hnr Roll; Sci Fairs; Comm Volntr; ArtClub; DARE; Drma Clb; Emplmnt; Key Club; Lib Aide; SP/M/VS; Congressional Art Show; Member of Young Democrats; Art Therapy, Political Science; U of Wisconsin (Madison)

MILLS, ALEXANDRA; KENSINGTON, MD; (FR); Hi Hnr Roll; Hnr Roll; Pep Squd; Quiz Bowl; Scouts; Chrldg (V); Skiing; CR (R); Most Accelerated Reader Points; Bachelor of Science; English Major; U of Louisville; U of Maryland

MILLS, QUADERA; POCOMOKE CITY, MD; POCOMOKE HS; (FR); Hnr Roll; Otst Ac Ach Awd; Sci Fairs; St of Mnth; Peer Tut/Med; Dnce; Psychology; Spelman College; Morgan State U

MINOR, PORSCHE C; SUITLAND, MD; ST VINCENT PALLOTTI HS; (FR); Ctznshp Aw; Hnr Roll; Nat Hon Sy; Sci Fairs; Comm Volntr; Peer Tut/Med; Chrch Yth Grp; SADD; Tchrs Aide; Ch Chr; Dnce; PPSqd (V); Stu Cncl (V); BASU; International Cuisine Club; Dance; Physical Therapy; Spelman College; Bowie State U

MINOR, TYISE; UPPR MARLBORO, MD; (SR); Hi Hnr Roll; Hnr Roll; Perf Att; St of Mnth; Spec Olymp Vol; Off Aide; ROTC; Scouts; Cr Ctry; Track; Morgan State Health Inspector; Bowie State Criminal Law; North Carolina A & T U; Delaware State

MITCHELL, CARRIE; MOUNT AIRY, MD; LINGANORE HS; (MS); Hi Hnr Roll; Sci Fairs; St of Mnth; Chrch Yth Grp; Chr; Dnce; SP/M/VS; Theatre Arts / Musical Theatre; Arts / Communication; Virginia Polytechnic Institute & State U; Towson U

MITCHELL, RENAE C; BALTIMORE, MD; BALTIMORE POLY TECH INST 403; (JR); Ctznshp Aw; Hi Hnr Roll; Hnr Roll; Nat Hon Sy; Otst Ac Ach Awd; Sci/Math Olympn; St Optmst of Yr; Comm Volntr; Peer Tut/Med; Dbte Team; Mth Clb/Tm; Ob/Gyn; Linguistics; Johns Hopkins U; Columbia U

MITCHELL, SHERIE; LAUREL, MD; RESERVOIR HS; (JR); 4H Awd; All Am Sch; Hi Hnr Roll; Hnr Roll; Otst Ac Ach Awd; Perf Att; St of Mnth; Comm Volntr; Chrch Yth Grp; Tech Clb; Vsity Clb; Dnce; SP/M/VS; PPSqd (V); Piano - 5 Yrs; Student of the Month Awards; Mass Communications; Marketing; Hampton U; Spelman College

MOFFETT, STEVE; PARKVILLE, MD; LOCH RAVEN HS; (JR); Hnr Roll; FBLA; MuAlphaTh; SP/M/VS; Ftball (VJ L); PP Ftbl (V); Track (V L); Wt Lftg (V); Interact Club / Math Honor Society; Future Business Leaders of America; Computer Science; Information Technology

MOK, SEEUN; COLUMBIA, MD; WILDE LAKE HS; (JR); Hnr Roll; Nat Hon Sy; Perf Att; St of Mnth; Peer Tut/Med; ArtClub; FBLA; Mth Clb/Tm; Bnd; Mch Bnd; Student Government Association Parliamentarian; Asian Awareness Club President, Secretary Of FBLA; Pre-Med; Architecture; Johns Hopkins U; U of Maryland College Park

MONGELLO, KEVIN; COLUMBIA, MD; WILDE LAKE HS; (SR); Hnr Roll; MVP; Nat Hon Sy; Nat Mrt Sch Recip; St of Mnth; Comm Volntr; Peer Tut/Med; Bnd; Sccr (V); CR (R); Blood Drive Volunteer; Grassroots Volunteer; Business Administration (Marketing Finance); Salisbury U; U of Maryland College Park

MONKOU, DWIGH L J; LANHAM, MD; TAKOMA AC; (FR); Hnr Roll; Chrch Yth Grp; Ch Chr; Bskball; Piano Student; Medicine; Johns Hopkins U; Howard U

MONTEBON, EDROMAN B; BALTIMORE, MD; DIGITAL HARBOR HS 416; (JR); Ctznshp Aw; Scouts; SP/M/VS; Sccr; Play Keyboard; Musician; Pilot (Navy Seal); Baltimore City Community College

MOORE, BRIAN; FORT WASHINGTON, MD; FRIENDLY HS; (SO); F Lan Hn Soc; Hnr Roll; Comm Volntr; ROTC; Drl Tm; ROTC Academic Team; Computer Science; Frostburg State U; U of Maryland

MOORE, JENN; ROCKVILLE, MD; RICHARD MONTGOMERY HS; (SO); Hi Hnr Roll; Hnr Roll; WWAHSS; Comm Volntr; DARE; Emplmnt; Key Club; Prom Com; Scouts; Fld Hky (J); Yrbk (E, R, P); Assistant Football Coach; U of Maryland; Pennsylvania State U

MOORE, TRACIE B; GLEN BURNIE, MD; GLEN BURNIE SR HS; (SO); Hnr Roll; Otst Ac Ach Awd; Sci Fairs; Peer Tut/Med; Chrch Yth Grp; DARE; Emplmnt; Chr; Ch Chr; Dnce; CR (R); Yrbk (P); I Was on the Step Squad; I Am a Debutante; Master's Degree in Business; Major in Business Minor in Communications; Howard U; Bowie State U

MOORHEAD, NINI; CHEVY CHASE, MD; NATIONAL CATHEDRAL; (SO); Comm Volntr; Photog; Vsity Clb; Cr Ctry (V); Ice Hky (V); Track (V); Cl Off (T); Sch Ppr (E); National Spanish Exam High Scorer; Scholastic Art & Writing Award for Photography; International Relations; Brown U; Harvard U

MORAD, SHARIF; ELLICOTT CITY, MD; WILDE LAKE HS; (JR); Hi Hnr Roll; Hnr Roll; Nat Hon Sy; Perf Att; Amnsty Intl; Hab For Humty Volntr; Red Cr Aide; Mus Clb; Bnd; Chr; Jzz Bnd; Mch Bnd; Tennis (V); In Amnesty International (Club); Secretary of Habitat for Humanity (Club); Electrical Engineering; Computer Science; U of Virginia; U of Maryland College Park

MORANT, JAMES E; BALTIMORE, MD; BALTIMORE CITY COLLEGE HS; (SR); Hnr Roll; Chrch Yth Grp; Emplmnt; Chr; Ch Chr; Swg Chr; Stu Cncl (R); Sports Equivalent Letter for Fine Arts; International Business; Law; Temple U; Howard U

MORIN, CHRISTIN M; BROOKLYN, MD; NORTH CTY HS; (FR); Ctznshp Aw; Gov Hnr Prg; Hi Hnr Roll; Nat Hon Sy; Nat Sci Aw; Nat Stu Ath Day Aw; Otst Ac Ach Awd; Pres Ac Ftns Aw; Sci Fairs; St of Mnth; Comm Volntr; Peer Tut/Med; DARE; Sci Clb; Bskball (J); Track (J); Vllyball (J); CR (P); Student of the Month; Maternity Nurse; Pediatrician; U of Miami

MORRIS, LYNAYA; POCOMOKE CITY, MD; POCOMOKE HS; (SO); Hi Hnr Roll; Perf Att; St of Mnth; USAA; WWAHSS; Key Club; Bnd; Mch Bnd; Pep Bnd; Fld Hky (J); Rotary Club 4-Way Test Award Winner; Chemistry; Biology; Drexel U; Towson U

MORRIS JR, DAVID A; BOWIE, MD; CHARLES HERBERT FLOWERS HS; Hnr Roll; Chrch Yth Grp; Chr; Bskball; Yrbk (P); Korean Scholarship Essay Contest Winner; Scholastic Spelling Bee Winner

MOSKIOS, EMILY; LUTHERVILLE TIMONIUM, MD; DULANEY HS; (SO); Hnr Roll; Nat Hon Sy; Comm Volntr; ArtClub; Emplmnt; Key Club; Mus Clb; Fld Hky (J); Second Place Optimist Club Essay Winner; National Honor Society; Education; Counseling; St Mary's College of Maryland; Dickinson College

MOSS, ALEXIS; SILVER SPRING, MD; PAINT BRANCH HS; (JR); Ctznshp Aw; Hi Hnr Roll; Hnr Roll; Otst Ac Ach Awd; WWAHSS; Yth Ldrshp Prog; Comm Volntr; Hosp Aide; Red Cr Aide; Emplmnt; Bnd; Mch Bnd; Sccr (JC); Pre-Med/Biology Major; Education-Minor; Emory U; Mercer U

MOXLEY, BRITTANY T; NEW WINDSOR, MD; SOUTH CARROLL HS; (FR); Hnr Roll; Comm Volntr; 4-H; Key Club; Ntl FFA; Key Club Member (Active); Carroll County Western Circuit (Youth Rep); Dentist; Psychology; College Park; McDaniel

MOZINGO, ERIN; HAGERSTOWN, MD; SMITHSBURG HS; (SO); Hnr Roll; Prom Com; Scouts; Lcrsse (V); Sccr (J); Nuclear Technology

MULLAN, TYLER M; CUMBERLAND, MD; ALLEGANY HS; (JR); Hi Hnr Roll; Hnr Roll; Nat Hon Sy; Sci Fairs; Peer Tut/Med; Emplmnt; French Clb; Bnd; Mch Bnd; National Honor Society - AFS; Ecology Club-State Envirothon Team; Veterinarian; Plastic Surgeon

MULLENNEX, COURTNEY; SABILLASVILLE, MD; CATOCTIN HS; (FR); Hi Hnr Roll; Hnr Roll; Perf Att; Pres Ac Ftns Aw; Sci Clb; Foreign Clb; Sccr (V); Criminal Investigation; Forensic Science; U of Maryland; Mount St Mary's College

MUNNELYN, ASHLEY C; UPPER MARLBORO, MD; RIVERDALE BAPTIST; (FR); Hi Hnr Roll; Sci Fairs; WWAHSS; Yth Ldrshp Prog; Chrch Yth Grp; Scouts; Ch Chr; Dnce; Piano

MURPHY, KAITLYN; MILLERSVILLE, MD; SEVERNA PARK HS; (JR); Hnr Roll; Nat Hon Sy; WWAHSS; Yth Ldrshp Prog; Amnsty Intl; AL Aux Girls; Emplmnt; Sftball (J L); CR (R); Lit Mag (E); Sch Ppr (R, P); Yrbk (E); Mock Trial / Club Swimming / National Merit Qualifier; Teen Court / Weight Lifting Record Holder; Pre-Law; English

MURRAY, ERIN; TOWSON, MD; ANNAPOLIS HS; (SR); Hnr Roll; Nat Hon Sy; Nat Mrt Semif; St of Mnth; WWAHSS; Comm Volntr; Peer Tut/Med; ArtClub; Chrch Yth Grp; Drma Clb; Emplmnt; Off Aide; Photog; Quill & Scroll; Stg Cre; Stu Cncl (S); Sch Ppr (E, R, P); It's Academic Team; Art Club President; Photo Journalism; Advertising; Pacific U

MURTHA, STEPHANIE; STEVENSVILLE, MD; ST MARY'S HS; (SO); Ctznshp Aw; DAR; Hi Hnr Roll; Otst Ac Ach Awd; Pres Sch; WWAHSS; Comm Volntr; Spec Olymp Vol; HO'Br Yth Ldrshp; Lttrmn Clb; Vsity Clb; Bskball (J); Lcrsse (V L); Vsy Clb (V); Vllyball (J); Cl Off (P); Engineering; Johns Hopkins U; Duke U

MUSCHER, PAM; MECHANICSVILLE, MD; CHAPTICON HS; (SR); Ctznshp Aw; Hi Hnr Roll; Nat Hon Sy; St of Mnth; WWAHSS; Comm Volntr; Spec Olymp Vol; Emplmnt; Off Aide; Prom Com; SADD; Tchrs Aide; Bskball (V L); Lcrsse (V L); Sccr (V L); CR; Yrbk (E, P); MD State Finalist in Wendy's Heisman Award; Health Sciences; Human Services; U of Mary Washington

MYERS, ASHLEE; OAKLAND, MD; SOUTHERN GARRETT HS; (FR); St of Mnth; Comm Volntr; Chrch Yth Grp; Svce Clb; SADD; Chr; GAA (J); STEAM; Girls Softball Team/Outside of School; Pediatrician; Sports Physician; Frostburg State U; West Virginia U

MYERS, KRISTIN L; LOTHIAN, MD; SOUTHERN SR HS; (JR); Hi Hnr Roll; Nat Hon Sy; St of Mnth; Yth Ldrshp Prog; Comm Volntr; Hab For Humty Volntr; ArtClub; Chrch Yth Grp; DARE; Dbte Team; Drma Clb; Emplmnt; Mod UN; Quill & Scroll; Acpl Chr; Chr; Ch Chr; SP/M/VS; Sch Ppr (E); All-County Chorus; Treasurer-Church Youth Group; Journalism; Public Policy; Princeton U; U of Maryland

MYLES, SHAYNA D; LAUREL, MD; LAUREL SR HS; (JR); Hnr Roll; MVP; Comm Volntr; Peer Tut/Med; Chrch Yth Grp; DARE; Drma Clb; Emplmnt; Lttrmn Clb; Mus Clb; Scouts; SADD; Ch Chr; Dnce; Jzz Bnd; Orch; Bskball (J); Sccr (V L); Swmg (V L); Lifeguard and First Aid Certification; Restaurant and Hotel Management; U of Maryland Eastern Shore

Murtha, Stephanie
St Mary's HS
Stevensville, MD

Munnelyn, Ashley C
Riverdale Baptist
Upper Marlboro, MD

Myers, Kristin L
Southern SR HS
Lothian, MD

Moss, Alexis
Paint Branch HS
Silver Spring, MD

Morant, James E
Baltimore City College HS
Baltimore, MD

Mitchell, Sherie
Reservoir HS
Laurel, MD

Miller, Shauntelle A
Lake Shore Christian AC
Pasadena, MD

Miller, Marcie
Catholic HS Of Baltimore
Gwynn Oak, MD

Mentzer, Joseph
Joppatowne HS
Joppa, MD

Michnewich, Daniel
Paint Branch HS
Silver Spring, MD

Mitchell, Carrie
Linganore HS
Mount Airy, MD

Montebon, Edroman B
Digital Harbor HS 416
Baltimore, MD

Morin, Christin M
North Cty HS
Brooklyn, MD

Morris Jr, David A
Charles Herbert Flowers HS
Bowie, MD

NABINGER, MATTHEW; BOWIE, MD; BOWIE HS; (JR); Hnr Roll; Nat Hon Sy; Otst Ac Ach Awd; Sci Fairs; St of Mnth; Comm Volntr; Chrch Yth Grp; Mus Clb; Tchrs Aide; Chr; Ch Chr; SP/M/VS; Music Education; Vocal Performance; Towson U; Liberty U

NAMING'ONA, ELINA S; OLNEY, MD; SHERWOOD HS; (SO); Hnr Roll; Sci/Math Olympn; Yth Ldrshp Prog; Comm Volntr; Chrch Yth Grp; Emplmnt; Scouts; Chr; Dnce; African American Festival of Academic Excellence Award; Psychology; Forensic Science; Hampton U; North Carolina A & T U

NANCE, ALANDA; DISTRICT HEIGHTS, MD; LARGO HS; (SO); Ctznshp Aw; Hnr Roll; Nat Hon Sy; Otst Ac Ach Awd; Comm Volntr; Chrch Yth Grp; DARE; ROTC; Dnce; Step Team; Business and Law; Harvard U; U of Maryland Eastern Shore

NAPOLI, KATHRYN; PERRY HALL, MD; PERRY HALL HS; (JR); 4H Awd; Hnr Roll; Sci Fairs; Comm Volntr; Peer Tut/Med; Emplmnt; FCA; Quill & Scroll; Spanish Clb; Chr; Tennis (V L); CR (R); Sch Ppr (E, R, P); Yrbk (E, R, P); Communications; Journalism; Columbia College Chicago; American U

NASH, JOVAN D.; BOWIE, MD; CHARLES HERBERT FLOWERS HS; (SO); Ctznshp Aw; Hnr Roll; Sci Fairs; Yth Ldrshp Prog; Comm Volntr; Peer Tut/Med; ArtClub; Chess; Emplmnt; Jr Ach; Off Aide; Photog; 1st Place County Write-A-Book Festival 2002 / 2003 - Princes Georges County; 2nd Place County Write-A-Book Festival - 2004; Graphic Arts; U of Arts in Philadelphia

NASIR, SYED M; WINDSOR MILL, MD; WOODLAWN HS; (SO); Hnr Roll; Comm Volntr; Peer Tut/Med; Student of the Month in World Literature in 2005; Certificate of Achievement in Essay Competition; Engineering; Medicine; Virginia Tech; Johns Hopkins U

NASTASE, ANGELINA M; ELLICOTT CITY, MD; MOUNT DE SALES AC; (SO); WWAHSS; Comm Volntr; Scouts; Dnce; Fld Hky (VJ); Girl Scout Silver Award; Nominated State Finalist, 2005 Miss MD Jr Teen Pageant; Pre-Med; Air Force-ROTC; U of Nebraska At Lincoln; Colorado State U

NAVALANEY, STAN; CUMBERLAND, MD; ALLEGANY HS; (SO); WWAHSS; Chess; Spanish Clb; Bnd; Mch Bnd; Pep Bnd; Engineering; Notre Dame; Penn State

NEEQUAYE, IRENE; SILVER SPRING, MD; WHEATON HS; (FR); Hnr Roll; Otst Ac Ach Awd; St of Mnth; Comm Volntr; Chrch Yth Grp; Off Aide; Chr; Ch Chr; Dnce; SP/M/VS; Bskball (VJ); Sftball (J); Wrstlg (J); Youth Job Skills Training Program; Obstetrics/Gynecology; Pediatrics; Howard U; U of Maryland, Baltimore County

NEWSOME, JALEESA A; DISTRICT HEIGHTS, MD; CHARLES HERBERT FLOWERS HS; (SO); Hi Hnr Roll; Hnr Roll; Otst Ac Ach Awd; St of Mnth; Chrch Yth Grp; DARE; Dnce; SP/M/VS; Finalist in Pre-Engineering Competition / Power Point Presentation on Homeland Security - 2/05; Psychology; U of Maryland College Park

NGUYEN, ANH KHOA; SILVER SPRING, MD; JOHN F KENNEDY HS; (FR); Hnr Roll; Outdrs Clb; Bdmtn (V); Cr Ctry (V); Sccr (V); Vllyball (J); Computer Engineering; College of Maryland

NGUYEN, THU THI; HURLOCK, MD; NORTH DORCHESTER HS; (JR); Hnr Roll; Nat Hon Sy; St of Mnth; Peer Tut/Med; Key Club; Prom Com; Tchrs Aide; SP/M/VS; Stg Cre; Cl Off (S); Stu Cncl (R); Sch Ppr (E); Yrbk (R); National Honor Society; Accounting; Banking; Salisbury U; Towson U

NICHOLS, LAMAR; RANDALLSTOWN, MD; RANDALLSTOWN HS; (FR); MVP; St of Mnth; DARE; Bnd; Bskball (J); Ftball (JC); Student of the Week; Loyalty Award of the Year; Criminal Justice; Professional Football; Auburn U; U of Maryland

NICHOLS, REBECCA; MECHANICSVILLE, MD; CHOPTICON HS; (JR); All Am Sch; Ctznshp Aw; Hi Hnr Roll; Hnr Roll; Nat Hon Sy; Otst Ac Ach Awd; St of Mnth; WWAHSS; Yth Ldrshp Prog; Comm Volntr; Peer Tut/Med; Spec Olymp Vol; Chrch Yth Grp; FBLA; Quill & Scroll; Tchrs Aide; Chr; Sch Ppr (E, R); Journalism; U of Florida

NICHOLS, SHAWN L; PARKVILLE, MD; PARKVILLE HS; (JR); Hnr Roll; Nat Hon Sy; Chess; DECA; Emplmnt; Quill & Scroll; Bnd; Chr; SP/M/VS; Sch Ppr (E, R); Spanish Honor Society; Computer Science; Computer Engineering; Drexel U; Cornell U

NICHOLSON, DION; BALTIMORE, MD; REGINALD F LEWIS HS; (SR); Comm Volntr; Bskball (J); Ftball (V C); Lcrsse (V); Marketing; Bowie State U; Liberty U

NIGAM, LOKESH; COLUMBIA, MD; ATHOLTON HS; (JR); Hi Hnr Roll; Hnr Roll; St of Mnth; Peer Tut/Med; Ftball (V L); Track (J); Spanish Honor Society

NISAR, BABAR; PASADENA, MD; GLEN BURNIE SR HS; (SO); Perf Att; Sccr; Wt Lftg

NJOKU, JULIANA; RIVERDALE, MD; PARKDALE HS; (JR); Hnr Roll; Perf Att; Sci Fairs; St of Mnth; Comm Volntr; Hosp Aide; Chrch Yth Grp; Vllyball; Surgeon; Medical Doctor

NOACK, LAURA A; WOODBINE, MD; (SO); Hi Hnr Roll; Hnr Roll; Nat Stu Ath Day Aw; Otst Ac Ach Awd; Perf Att; Pres Ac Ftns Aw; Pres Sch; WWAHSS; Comm Volntr; Key Club; Vsity Clb; Lcrsse (J); Sccr (V L); Wellness Club; Zoology; Law

NOEL, CIERRA Y; RANDALLSTOWN, MD; MILFORD MILL HS; (JR); Hnr Roll; Scouts; Chrldg; Medical Doctor; Johns Hopkins U; Villa Julie College

NOEL, JOHANNA L; MOUNT AIRY, MD; SOUTH CARROLL HS; (SO); Hi Hnr Roll; Nat Hon Sy; Nat Stu Ath Day Aw; WWAHSS; Comm Volntr; Hab For Humty Volntr; Drma Clb; Key Club; Prom Com; Scouts; Chr; Fld Hky (J L); Skiing; Track (V L); Cl Off (R); Stu Cncl; Physical Therapy; Speech/Language Therapy; Ithaca College; U of Maryland

NORBERG, MICHAEL; SILVER SPRING, MD; JAMES HUBERT BLAKE HS; (SO); Hnr Roll; ROTC; Clr Grd; Ftball (J); Lcrsse (V L); Wrstlg (V L); Civil War Reenactor; Business; Virginia Military Institute; Ohio State U

NORRINGTON, JANETTE G; GAITHERSBURG, MD; WATKINS MILL HS; (SR); Hnr Roll; Nat Hon Sy; Otst Ac Ach Awd; Peer Tut/Med; Chrch Yth Grp; Stg Cre; Sch Ppr (E); Officer in Best Buddies; Psychology / Pre-Med; Temple U; Syracuse U

NORRIS, RONNISE; BOWIE, MD; ARCHBISHOP CARROLL HS; (JR); Hi Hnr Roll; Hnr Roll; Nat Hon Sy; WWAHSS; Yth Ldrshp Prog; Comm Volntr; Drma Clb; Dnce; SP/M/VS; Chrldg (VJ); Vsy Clb (J); Medicine; Engineering / Law; Florida A & M; Boston College

NORTON, ERIN C V; FOREST HILL, MD; C MILTON WRIGHT HS; (JR); F Lan Hn Soc; Hi Hnr Roll; Hnr Roll; Jr Eng Tech; Comm Volntr; Tech Clb; Bnd; Mch Bnd; Orch; Pep Bnd; PP Ftbl (V); Adv Cncl (R); Lit Mag (R); Member of Political Club; Environmental Science; Environmental Engineering; Brown U; Massachusetts Institute of Technology

NUBLA, ADRIAN; CAMBRIDGE, MD; SOUTHCHESTER HS; (SO); Chess; Computer Specialist; Nurse; New York University; Maryland University

NUTTER, AMBER N; DUNDALK, MD; DUNDALK HS; (SO); Hi Hnr Roll; Hnr Roll; Otst Ac Ach Awd; Perf Att; Comm Volntr; Peer Tut/Med; 4-H; DARE; Emplmnt; Kwanza Clb; Spch Team; Ch Chr; Spelling Bee; Psychology; Yale U; York U

NUTTER, CIERRA; BALTIMORE, MD; NATIONAL AC FOUNDATION; (SO); Perf Att; Chrch Yth Grp; Drma Clb; Ch Chr; Cl Off (S); Information Technology; Medical Field; Morgan State U; Baltimore City Community College

OATES, MONISHA; SILVER SPRING, MD; WHEATON HS; (MS); Ctznshp Aw; Hnr Roll; Perf Att; St of Mnth; Peer Tut/Med; Montgomery College

OBERNEITMANN, EVELYNN M; NEWARK, MD; STEPHEN DECATUR HS; (FR); Hnr Roll; St of Mnth; Comm Volntr; Bnd; Chr; Mch Bnd; Pep Bnd; CR (R); Optimist Oratorical Speech Contest Participant; Air Force Fighter Pilot; Teacher; Air Force Academy

OFOSU, AFUA O; GREENBELT, MD; ELEANOR ROOSEVELT HS; (JR); Ctznshp Aw; Hi Hnr Roll; Hnr Roll; Nat Hon Sy; Otst Ac Ach Awd; Perf Att; Sci Fairs; WWAHSS; Yth Ldrshp Prog; Comm Volntr; Chrch Yth Grp; SP/M/VS; Stg Cre; Lit Mag; Television Productions; Mock Trial; Lawyer; Paralegal; Actress; Magazine Editor; Howard U; Columbia U

OHANIAN, LISA; DERWOOD, MD; MAGRUDER HS; (JR); Hnr Roll; Drma Clb; Key Club; NtlFrnscLg; P to P St Amb Prg; Chr; SP/M/VS; Stg Cre; Forensics Team / SADD / Book Club; Production Staff / Drama, 1st Degree Black Belt; Business Administration; Communications; Mc Daniel; Salisbury

OHLER, MELISSA; NORTH EAST, MD; (FR); Hnr Roll; Otst Ac Ach Awd; St of Mnth; Comm Volntr; Emplmnt; Key Club; Ch Chr; SP/M/VS; Creative Writing Award; Modeling School Certification; Marine Biologist; Ithaca U; U of Delaware

OJESANMI, MODUPE; GREENBELT, MD; ELEANOR ROOSEVELT HS; (JR); Hnr Roll; Comm Volntr; Chrch Yth Grp; Chr; Track (J); Invited to National Student Leadership Conf; Pre-Med; Biochemistry; Johns Hopkins U; Brown U

OKAI, LINDA; LAUREL, MD; ELEANOR ROOSEVELT HS; (SO); Hnr Roll; Perf Att; Sci Fairs; Yth Ldrshp Prog; Comm Volntr; Spec Olymp Vol; Chrch Yth Grp; Tchrs Aide; Ch Chr; National Junior Honor Society; Pre-Med; Medical Degree

OKOJIE, EBOSETALE; LAUREL, MD; LAUREL HS; (JR); Ctznshp Aw; Hnr Roll; USAA; WWAHSS; Emplmnt; Bskball (V); Chrldg (J); Adv Cncl (R); Cl Off (V); Leaders of Promise (Member); Political Science; Public Relations; New York U; Barry U

OKORONKWO, OBIANUJU; BALTIMORE, MD; PAUL L DUNBAR HS 414; (FR); Ctznshp Aw; Hnr Roll; Otst Ac Ach Awd; Perf Att; Pres Sch; Comm Volntr; Spec Olymp Vol; Bnd; Track; Pharmacy or Pharmacy Technician; Dentistry; Johns Hopkins U; College of Maryland

OKUNJI, CHINYERE; SILVER SPRING, MD; PAINT BRANCH HS; (FR); Hnr Roll; Otst Ac Ach Awd; Chrch Yth Grp; Mth Clb/Tm; P to P St Amb Prg; Ch Chr; Clr Grd; Orch; SP/M/VS; Psychology; Medicine-Pediatrics; Johns Hopkins U; U of Maryland

OKUTUGA, ELIZABETH A; SILVER SPRING, MD; SPRINGBROOK HS; (SR); Hi Hnr Roll; Hnr Roll; WWAHSS; Peer Tut/Med; Drma Clb; NtlFrnscLg; Prom Com; Tchrs Aide; SP/M/VS; Stg Cre; Vllyball (V); Psychology; Sociology; North Carolina A & T State U

OLIVER, TYSHIA T; GWYNN OAK, MD; WOODLAWN HS; (FR); Hnr Roll; MVP; Nat Hon Sy; Otst Ac Ach Awd; Perf Att; Sci Fairs; Sci/Math Olympn; St of Mnth; Yth Ldrshp Prog; Comm Volntr; Peer Tut/Med; DARE; ROTC; Sci Clb; SADD; Tchrs Aide; Ch Chr; Cr Ctry (V); Track (V); CR (R); Yrbk (P); ASF American Student Fund; Law (English, Political Science, Journalism); Mass Communication, History; Boston U; Duke U

ONIJALA, GBOYINDE; OLNEY, MD; MAGRUDER HS; (SR); Hnr Roll; Nat Hon Sy; WWAHSS; Peer Tut/Med; Chrch Yth Grp; Key Club; Svce Clb; Bskball (J); Sch Ppr; NAACP Scholar; Horatio Alger Scholar; Towson U; Mass Communication & Political Science; Towson U

ONWUZURUIKE, ADAEZE A; SILVER SPRING, MD; WHEATON HS; (FR); Hnr Roll; Comm Volntr; Chrldg (J); Medicine; Harvard U; Princeton U

ORIOWO, CHRISTANA; UPPER MARLBORO, MD; KETTERING MS; (MS); Ctznshp Aw; Hnr Roll; Perf Att; Comm Volntr; ArtClub; Drma Clb; SP/M/VS; Stg Cre; Juilliard

O'SHEA, MEGAN C; BEL AIR, MD; HARFORD CHRISTIAN SCH; (JR); Hi Hnr Roll; Hnr Roll; Chrch Yth Grp; Chr; Bskball (VJ); Fld Hky (VJ); Sftball (VJC); Yrbk; Mission Trip to West VA to Help Fix Homes; Mission Trip to Brazil with Focus on the Family; Communications; Music

OSTROFSKY, JUSTIN N; MOUNT AIRY, MD; SOUTH CARROLL HS; (SO); Hnr Roll; ArtClub; Drma Clb; Key Club; French Clb; Ftball (J); Winner of Carroll Co Public School Film Contest; Winner of Various Art Contests; Film; Video Production; U of Southern California; Florida State U

OUK, LENA; SILVER SPRING, MD; ALBERT EINSTEIN HS; (JR); Hnr Roll; MVP; Otst Ac Ach Awd; St of Mnth; Comm Volntr; FBLA; Key Club; Chrldg (VJ L); Lcrsse (V); PP Ftbl (J); Sch Ppr (E, R); Zoology; Accounting; Northwood; Penn State

OWENS, CORINNE; DERWOOD, MD; MAGRUDER HS; (JR); Hnr Roll; MVP; Otst Ac Ach Awd; Perf Att; St of Mnth; Yth Ldrshp Prog; Comm Volntr; Chrch Yth Grp; DARE; Vsity Clb; Ch Chr; Bskball (V); African American Achievement Awards; 1st All-League Girls Basketball Team / 2nd Team All-County; Business; Sports Management; Wake Forest U; Villanova U

OWOLABI, MARIAN O; ROSEDALE, MD; OVERLEA HS; (SO); Perf Att; Chrch Yth Grp; DECA; Yrbk (R, P); Medicine; Harvard U; Morgan State U

PABON, TAHLIA; MC DANIEL, MD; ST MICHAELS JR/SR HS; (FR); Hnr Roll; Comm Volntr; Bnd; Dnce; Mch Bnd; Pep Bnd; Trendsetter 8th Grade; SGA 8th Grade; Pediatrician; Dancer; Hope College; U of Akron

PAGELS, REBECCA; HAMPSTEAD, MD; NORTH CARROLL HS; (SR); Hi Hnr Roll; Hnr Roll; Nat Hon Sy; Salutrn; USAA; WWAHSS; Comm Volntr; Peer Tut/Med; ArtClub; Prom Com; Tchrs Aide; Vsity Clb; SP/M/VS; Sccr (V); Sftball (V); Cl Off (P); Stu Cncl (R); Chemical Engineering; U of Delaware

PALMER, NATASHA; SILVER SPRING, MD; SPRINGBROOK HS; (SO); Hnr Roll; ArtClub; Stu Cncl (R); CR (R); Yrbk (R, P); Girls Varsity Basketball Manager; Media Management; Public Relations; Clark Atlanta U; Hampton State U

PANANON, BOOSABA; SILVER SPRING, MD; JOHN F KENNEDY HS; (JR); Hi Hnr Roll; Hnr Roll; Kwnis Aw; Perf Att; Pres Sch; St Schl; St of Mnth; Yth Ldrshp Prog; Comm Volntr; ArtClub; Emplmnt; HO'Br Yth Ldrshp; Mth Clb/Tm; NYLC; ROTC; Tmpl Yth Grp; Dnce; Chrldg (J); Lcrsse (V L); Tennis (V L); Somapa Thai Dance Company; President of Asian-American Day; Business; Psychology; U of Maryland College Park; George Washington U

PARKER, ERICA M; ARNOLD, MD; BROADNECK HS; (SO); Hi Hnr Roll; Hnr Roll; Key Club; Scouts; Foreign Clb; Bnd; Mch Bnd; Russian President of the Foreign Language Club; History; Business; Towson U; Virginia Polytechnic Institute and State U

PARLIS, ALYSIA; DUNDALK, MD; DUNDALK HS; (SO); Hnr Roll; Otst Ac Ach Awd; Perf Att; Peer Tut/Med; Drma Clb; Prom Com; Lcrsse (V L); Sccr (V L); Cl Off (R); Yrbk (E); Lawyer; Nurse; Towson U; U of Maryland Baltimore City

PARNELL, ANDREW; DERWOOD, MD; MAGRUDER HS; (SR); Nat Hon Sy; WWAHSS; Comm Volntr; Chrch Yth Grp; Key Club; Lib Aide; SADD; Dnce; SP/M/VS; Bsball (VJCL); Ftball (J); Cl Off (R); CR (R); Capital District Key Club Governor; High School - Tsunami Relief Coordinator; Biochemistry / MBA; Doctorate; U of Notre Dame - Accepted

Nguyen, Thu Thi
North Dorchester HS
Hurlock, MD

Newsome, Jaleesa A
Charles Herbert Flowers HS
District Heights, MD

Nastase, Angelina M
Mount De Sales AC
Ellicott City, MD

Neequaye, Irene
Wheaton HS
Silver Spring, MD

Owolabi, Marian O
Overlea HS
Rosedale, MD

PATE, JESSICA; PARKVILLE, MD; LOCH RAVEN HS; (JR); Hnr Roll; Perf Att; WWAHSS; Comm Volntr; Peer Tut/Med; Spec Olymp Vol; DARE; Emplmnt; FTA; Key Club; Scouts; Bnd; Working on Gold Award for Girl Scouts; Member of Swim / Dive Teams; Elementary Education; Psychology; Salisbury U; Frostburg U

PATEL, AKSHAL; SILVER SPRING, MD; PT BRANCH HS; (SO); Hnr Roll; Otst Ac Ach Awd; Perf Att; PharmD; Degree in Medicine; Johns Hopkins U; Maryland U

PATEL, RONAK; BELCAMP, MD; ABERDEEN MS; (MS); Hnr Roll; Perf Att; St Schl; DARE; Scouts; Chr; Pre-Med; Engineering; Harvard U; Oxford U

PATEL, RUPA S; ANNAPOLIS, MD; BROADNECK HS; (JR); Hnr Roll; Comm Volntr; Key Club; Foreign Clb; French President for Foreign Language Club; Biology; Optometry; U of Maryland College Park; Drexel U

PATTERSON, ASHLEY; NOTTINGHAM, MD; OVERLEA HS; (SO); Hnr Roll; Kwnis Aw; Perf Att; St of Mnth; WWAHSS; Peer Tut/Med; Lib Aide; Tchrs Aide; Chr; Bskball (J); Scr Kpr; Sftball (V); Vllyball (VJ L); Manager (Wrestling); Architecture; Marine Biology; U of Maryland College Park; U of North Carolina-Chapel Hill

PAUL, STEPHANIE; GAITHERSBURG, MD; MONTGOMERY BLAIR HS; (JR); Hnr Roll; MVP; Nat Hon Sy; Sci Fairs; Sci/Math Olympn; St of Mnth; WWAHSS; Yth Ldrshp Prog; Comm Volntr; Peer Tut/Med; Spec Olymp Vol; FBLA; Key Club; Tmpl Yth Grp; Sign Clb; Sftball (J); Tennis (V CL); Research Project on Wetlands; Tennis Teacher / Editor of Schools Magnet Magazine; Pre-Med; Business / Accounting / Statistics; Duke U; U of Virginia

PAYNE, DAVID A; GWYNN OAK, MD; WOODLAWN HS; (SO); Hi Hnr Roll; Hnr Roll; Perf Att; Comm Volntr; Peer Tut/Med; Emplmnt; ROTC; Tchrs Aide; Flg Crps; Basketball Coach (For Ages 7-8); Speaking French; Engineering; Automechanic Engineer; Morgan U; U of Maryland

PEAK, GLEN; WESTMINSTER, MD; NORTH CARROLL HS; (SR); Hi Hnr Roll; Hnr Roll; St of Mnth; WWAHSS; Emplmnt; Tchrs Aide; Ftball (J); Wrstlg (J); Mechanical Engineering; U of Maryland, Baltimore County

PECK, RACHEL; SEVERNA PARK, MD; SETON KEOUGH HS; (JR); Comm Volntr; Red Cr Aide; Key Club; Outdrs Clb; SP/M/VS; Fld Hky (V C); Lcrsse (J); Track (V); Annapolis Striders / Won Medals for Running; 1st Place in Group; Athletic Training; Opening Gyms Nationwide; UVA; Washington College

PEDDICORD, DANIELLE N; ANNAPOLIS, MD; BROADNECK HS; (FR); Ctznshp Aw; Hnr Roll; Otst Ac Ach Awd; Perf Att; Pres Ac Ftns Aw; WWAHSS; Key Club; Sccr (J); Play Piano; McDaniel College; Anne Arundel Community College

PEGRAM, IAN; CLINTON, MD; SURRATTSVILLE HS; (SR); Hnr Roll; Peer Tut/Med; Computer Science; US History; Morgan State U

PELLER, LINDSEY C; GAITHERSBURG, MD; WOOTTON HS; (SO); F Lan Hn Soc; Hnr Roll; MVP; Perf Att; Sci Fairs; Yth Ldrshp Prog; Comm Volntr; Peer Tut/Med; DARE; Scouts; Tchrs Aide; Tmpl Yth Grp; Spanish Clb; Chr; Dnce; Lcrsse (VJC); Swmg (V C); Cl Off (S); Marine Biology; Law; Cornell U; Emory U

PENG, ELIOT S; COCKEYSVILLE, MD; DULANEY HS; (JR); Sci/Math Olympn; Comm Volntr; Chrch Yth Grp; FCA; FBLA; Orch; Cr Ctry (J); Track (J); Future Business Leader of America-State Competition Desktop Publishing-2nd Place '04 & 05; Music; Computer Science; U of Maryland College Park

PEREZ, ANDREA; HAGERSTOWN, MD; NORTH HAGERSTOWN HS; (FR); Hnr Roll; Otst Ac Ach Awd; Comm Volntr; Drma Clb; Emplmnt; Key Club; Stg Cre; Chrldg (J); Lcrsse (V L); Fashion Club; Marine Biology; U of West Florida, Pensacola, Florida; U of NC at Wilmington

PERROTT, DUSTIN M; HAGERSTOWN, MD; NORTH HAGERSTOWN HS; (SO); Hnr Roll; Pres Ac Ftns Aw; WWAHSS; Comm Volntr; Peer Tut/ Med; Emplmnt; FCA; Acpl Chr; Chr; SP/M/VS; Swg Chr; Bsball (J); Track (J); Stu Cncl (R); National Society of High School Scholars; All-County Chorus; Business Management; Music Teacher; Temple U; U of Miami (Florida)

PERRY, UNIQUE; BALTIMORE, MD; EDMONDSON HS; (FR); Hnr Roll; Comm Volntr; Chrch Yth Grp; Scouts; Ch Chr; SP/M/VS; Dvng; Gmnstcs; Go to School for Nursing for 7 Years; Morgan State U; Baltimore City Cmty College

PERRY III, HAYWOOD L; ACCOKEEK, MD; OXON HILL HS; (FR); Nat Ldrshp Svc; Nat Sci Aw; Sci Fairs; USAA; Peer Tut/Med; FBLA; NYLC; Sci Clb; Bnd; Cr Ctry (J); Track (J); Stu Cncl (V); CR (R); Yrbk (P); 2005 Robert L. Wistort Best Presentation Award; YMCA 2004 Crystal Y Award for Personal Achievement; Bachelor of Architecture; Master of Architecture; Harvard U; Yale U

PERZAN, LAUREN M; NOTTINGHAM, MD; PERRY HALL HS; (JR); Ctznshp Aw; Hi Hnr Roll; Nat Hon Sy; WWAHSS; Comm Volntr; DARE; Emplmnt; Prom Com; Clr Grd; Mch Bnd; Orch; SP/M/VS; Fld Hky (V L); Lcrsse (J); PPSqd (V L); Track (J); Cl Off (S); Peer Mediator; Baltimore County Music Awards; Music; Mathematics; Shenandoah U; Bridgewater College

PETERS, YVONNE N; WORTON, MD; KENT CTY HS; (FR); Ctznshp Aw; Hi Hnr Roll; Hnr Roll; Comm Volntr; Chrch Yth Grp; Emplmnt; Tennis (V); Vllyball (J); CR; Business Management; Telecommunications; U of Maryland College Park; Georgetown U

PETERSON, CORY; BOWIE, MD; ROOSEVELT HS; (JR); Hi Hnr Roll; Hnr Roll; Nat Hon Sy; Sci Fairs; Peer Tut/Med; DARE; Vsity Clb; Ftball (VJCL); Lcrsse (VJ L); Wrstlg (V L); U of Maryland College Park; Georgia Tech U

PFLAUM, KATHERINE; CATONSVILLE, MD; MT DE SALES AC; (JR); Hi Hnr Roll; Hnr Roll; MVP; Comm Volntr; Emplmnt; Vsity Clb; Bnd; PP Ftbl; Sccr (VJ L); Sftball (J); Biology / Science; Math; U of Maryland College Park; Towson State

PHILLIPS, KIMBERLY; ARNOLD, MD; BROADNECK HS; (JR); Hi Hnr Roll; Hnr Roll; Nat Hon Sy; WWAHSS; Key Club; Bnd; Dnce; Mch Bnd; Orch

PICKETT, CHELSEA L; SPARROWS POINT, MD; SPARROWS POINT HS; (JR); Hnr Roll; MVP; Perf Att; Comm Volntr; Peer Tut/Med; Quill & Scroll; Chr; SP/M/VS; Chrldg (V); Yrbk (E); Dance - 2 Years; Piano -10 Years; Journalist; Pianist; Towson U; UMBC

PIETROPAOLI, JENNIFER; OWINGS, MD; NORTHERN HS; (JR); Hi Hnr Roll; Nat Hon Sy; Pres Sch; WWAHSS; Comm Volntr; Emplmnt; Quill & Scroll; French Clb; Chrldg (V CL); Stu Cncl; Yrbk (E); Pre-Med; Foreign Language; U of Pennsylvania; College of the Holy Cross

PILCHARD, L KYLE; POCOMOKE CITY, MD; POCOMOKE HS; (FR); Hi Hnr Roll; Otst Ac Ach Awd; Comm Volntr; U of Maryland College Park; Duke U

PITTS, KORI; POCOMOKE CITY, MD; POCOMOKE HS; (FR); Hi Hnr Roll; Hnr Roll; Perf Att; Key Club; Bskball (J); Sftball (J); Vllyball (VJ); Medical; Child Psychology; U of Maryland College Park; Morgan State U

PLUME, BETH; HAGERSTOWN, MD; NORTH HAGERSTOWN HS; (SO); Ctznshp Aw; Hi Hnr Roll; Hnr Roll; Kwnis Aw; Perf Att; St of Mnth; WWAHSS; Comm Volntr; Peer Tut/Med; Chrch Yth Grp; DARE; Key Club; Quiz Bowl; Bnd; Ch Chr; Jzz Bnd; Mch Bnd; Vllyball (J); Cl Off (R); CR (R); Key Club President (2 Years); Nursing; Criminal Justice/Forensics; U of Maryland

POLANSKY, CHERI J; SYKESVILLE, MD; SOUTH CARROLL HS; (SR); Hi Hnr Roll; Hnr Roll; WWAHSS; Comm Volntr; Drma Clb; Key Club; Mus Clb; Scouts; Tchrs Aide; Bnd; Clr Grd; Jzz Bnd; Mch Bnd; Bskball; Hsbk Rdg; PP Ftbl (VJ); Scr Kpr (VJ); Yrbk (R); Vice President of Key Club; Baltimore's Marching Ravens; Elementary Education; Early Childhood Education; Towson U

PONTER, CHELSEA R; POMFRET, MD; M J MC DONOUGH; (SR); Ctznshp Aw; Hi Hnr Roll; MVP; Nat Hon Sy; Otst Ac Ach Awd; Perf Att; Pres Ac Ftns Aw; Pres Sch; Sci Fairs; St Schl; Hab For Humty Volntr; Peer Tut/Med; ArtClub; Chrch Yth Grp; Emplmnt; Key Club; Photog; Tennis (V L); Yrbk (E, R, P); President of Art Society - 2 Yrs; Envirothon; Illustration Major; Psychology Minor; Towson U

POOLE, KENT; BURTONSVILLE, MD; PAINT BRANCH HS; (SO); Hi Hnr Roll; Hnr Roll; Otst Ac Ach Awd; Perf Att; Comm Volntr; Chrch Yth Grp; Off Aide; Scouts; Mock Trial; Anime Club; U of Maryland, College Park; U of Pennsylvania

PORAMBO, LINDSEY R; BOWIE, MD; BOWIE HS; (SO); Hi Hnr Roll; Nat Hon Sy; Sci Fairs; St of Mnth; Emplmnt; NYLC; Tmpl Yth Grp; Orch; Sftball (J); Stu Cncl (R); CR (R); National Youth Leadership Congress; Chemistry Award; Journalism; Creative Writing; Brown U; Emerson College

POSEY, KARYSSA; CHESAPEAKE BEACH, MD; NORTHERN HS; (SR); Hnr Roll; MVP; Nat Mrt LOC; FBLA; Sftball (J); Academy of Finance; FBLA; Accounting Major; College of Southern MD

POTEET, MIKE; WESTMINSTER, MD; CARROLL CHRISTIAN SCH; (JR); Hnr Roll; Nat Hon Sy; Chr; Pre-Law; Law School; Mc Daniel College; U of Virginia

POWELL, SHANNA; UPPER MARLBORO, MD; FREDERICK DOUGLASS HS; (SR); Ctznshp Aw; Hnr Roll; Nat Ldrshp Svc; St of Mnth; Yth Ldrshp Prog; Spec Olymp Vol; Chrch Yth Grp; FBLA; Off Aide; Prom Com; ROTC; Tchrs Aide; Ch Chr; Bskball (J); Cl Off (P, V); Nursing; Bowie State U

POWERS, BETHANY; HAGERSTOWN, MD; NORTH HAGERSTOWN HS; (SO); Hi Hnr Roll; WWAHSS; Chrch Yth Grp; Emplmnt; Key Club; Tech Clb; Chr; Cl Off (S)

PRADHAN, SUJINA; BURTONSVILLE, MD; PAINT BRANCH HS; (JR); Hnr Roll; Nat Hon Sy; Pres Sch; Yth Ldrshp Prog; Comm Volntr; Emplmnt; Fr of Library; Key Club; Track (V L); Vllyball (VJ L); Stu Cncl (R); CR (R); Yrbk (R, P); Biomedical Engineering; Pre-Medicine; Maryland U; Duke U

PRATT, LATOYE; PRINCE FREDERICK, MD; CALVERT HS; (FR); Hnr Roll; Chrch Yth Grp

PRICE, ABBY; EASTON, MD; ST MICHAELS JR/SR HS; (FR); Hi Hnr Roll; Hnr Roll; Nat Stu Ath Day Aw; Sci Fairs; Comm Volntr; DARE; Bnd; Mch Bnd; Pep Bnd; Fld Hky (J); Swmg (J L); Delmarva Swim Association Championships; C & P Championships; Own My Own Business; Washington College; Salisbury U

PRICE, LENICE D; BALTIMORE, MD; HOMESCHOOL; (SO); Hnr Roll; Perf Att; St of Mnth; Comm Volntr; Red Cr Aide; Spec Olymp Vol; ArtClub; Emplmnt; Tchrs Aide; Ch Chr; SP/M/VS; Bskball (J); Scr Kpr (J); Sch Ppr (E); Graphic Arts; Teacher; Maryland Institute College of Art; Johns Hopkins U

PRICE, NIKITA; WHITEFORD, MD; NORTH HARFORD; (JR); Hnr Roll; WWAHSS; Comm Volntr; 4-H; Tchrs Aide; German Clb; Bnd; Mch Bnd; Pep Bnd; Hsbk Rdg; Veterinary Medicine; U of Virginia; U of Maryland

PRINCE, LAUREN E; POTOMAC, MD; THE BULLIS SCH; (JR); Hnr Roll; MVP; Nat Ldrshp Svc; Yth Ldrshp Prog; Comm Volntr; Peer Tut/Med; Chrch Yth Grp; Drma Clb; JSA; Mod UN; NYLC; SADD; Chr; Dnce; SP/ M/VS; Ftball (V); Sccr (J); Track (V); Adv Cncl (S); Cl Off (R); Citation-Governor Ehrlich Maryland; Proclamation-Maryland State Senate; International Relations/Communication; International Studies; Georgetown U; William & Mary (College Of)

PROCTOR, DESMOND R; WALDORF, MD; WESTLAKE HS; (FR); Hi Hnr Roll; Hnr Roll; Otst Ac Ach Awd; St of Mnth; Comm Volntr; Chrch Yth Grp; DARE; Bnd; SP/M/VS; Bskball; Cr Ctry (L); Track; Wt Lftg; Stu Cncl (R); CR (R); Blackbelt Tae Kwon Do; Law Enforcement; Professional Basketball Player; Duke U; U of Maryland

PROCTOR, PORACHE; RIVERDALE, MD; PARKDALE HS; (JR); Ctznshp Aw; Hi Hnr Roll; Hnr Roll; Perf Att; CARE; Comm Volntr; Spec Olymp Vol; Chrch Yth Grp; Bnd; Chr; Dnce; Ftball (J); Teaching; Lawyer; U of Maryland; Bowie U

PRUZINSKY, AMANDA A; LINTHICUM HTS, MD; NORTH CTY HS; (FR); Hi Hnr Roll; Hnr Roll; Perf Att; Sci Fairs; Peer Tut/Med; Chrch Yth Grp; DARE; Bnd; Chr; Jzz Bnd; Mch Bnd; Bskball (J); Vllyball (J)

PUGH, ASHLEY; WESTMINSTER, MD; WINTERS MILL HS; (SR); Hi Hnr Roll; Hnr Roll; MVP; Nat Hon Sy; St Schl; Comm Volntr; Peer Tut/Med; Emplmnt; Fld Hky (VJCL); Lcrsse (J); Track (V); Yrbk (E, R); Maryland Distinguished Scholar; National Honor Society; International Studies; Salisbury U

PUREC, CHAVI; PIKESVILLE, MD; BAIS YAAKOV HS; (SR); Hnr Roll; Nat Mrt Semif; Comm Volntr; Yrbk (R); Education; Jewish Theological College

PUSEY, TREVER; SNOW HILL, MD; POCOMOKE HS; (SO); Hi Hnr Roll; St of Mnth; WWAHSS; Comm Volntr; Chrch Yth Grp; Emplmnt; Key Club; Mus Clb; P to P St Amb Prg; SADD; Vsity Clb; Bnd; Jzz Bnd; Mch Bnd; Pep Bnd; Bsball (V L); Sccr (JC); Cl Off (P); Straight A's Principal's List; Ministry; Teaching

PUTH, KIAH; UPPER MARLBORO, MD; BOWIE HS; (FR); Ctznshp Aw; Hi Hnr Roll; Hnr Roll; Otst Ac Ach Awd; Perf Att; Sci Fairs; St of Mnth; Comm Volntr; Peer Tut/Med; Photog; Scouts; Bnd; SP/M/VS; Crofton Rockets Soccer Team - Not with School; Highest Achievement in US History; Translator; Anthropology; Georgetown U; Dartmouth College

PYLE, WILLIAM; STEVENSVILLE, MD; KENT ISLAND HS; (JR); Hi Hnr Roll; Hnr Roll; Comm Volntr; Peer Tut/Med; Chess; Emplmnt; Scouts; Computer Science; U of Maryland; Virginia Tech

QUARTEY-PAPAFIO, HENRY K; UPPER MARLBORO, MD; LARGO HS; (JR); Hnr Roll; Hosp Aide; Peer Tut/Med; ROTC; Sccr (V); Aerospace / Aeronautics / Aviation; Realtor / Real Estate; Tuskegee U; U of Maryland

QUASEM, SANJANA; SILVER SPRING, MD; WHEATON HS; (JR); Hnr Roll; Nat Hon Sy; WWAHSS; Comm Volntr; Peer Tut/Med; Emplmnt; Key Club; Lit Mag; Yrbk; Marian Greenblatt Award; 9th Annual Mark Curtis Award; U of Maryland College Park; Georgetown U

QUILES, EILEEN; SEVERN, MD; OLD MILL HS; (SO); F Lan Hn Soc; Hnr Roll; Perf Att; Sci Fairs; Comm Volntr; Peer Tut/Med; ArtClub; Chrch Yth Grp; Mth Clb/Tm; Sci Clb; Scouts; Chr; All County Science Fair-2nd Place; Architecture; Engineering; College Park (U of Maryland); Penn State

RADER, BILL; CHEVY CHASE, MD; GEORGETOWN PREP HS; (JR); Nat Mrt LOC; Peer Tut/Med; Scouts; Bnd; Stg Cre; Cr Ctry (J L); Fncg; Track; Psychology; Politics; Connecticut College; Fairfield U

Quartey-Papafio, Henry K
Largo HS
Upper Marlboro, MD

Pruzinsky, Amanda A
North Cty HS
Linthicum Hts, MD

Quiles, Eileen
Old Mill HS
Severn, MD

Proctor, Desmond R
Westlake HS
Waldorf, MD

Plume, Beth
North Hagerstown HS
Hagerstown, MD

Perry III, Haywood L
Oxon Hill HS
Accokeek, MD

Peak, Glen
North Carroll HS
Westminster, MD

Patel, Ronak
Aberdeen MS
Belcamp, MD

National
Honor Roll
Spring 2005

Pate, Jessica
Loch Raven HS
Parkville, MD

Perez, Andrea
North Hagerstown HS
Hagerstown, MD

Pilchard, L Kyle
Pocomoke HS
Pocomoke City, MD

Polansky, Cheri J
South Carroll HS
Sykesville, MD

Prince, Lauren E
The Bullis Sch
Potomac, MD

RADOMSKY, ALEXANDER J; HYDES, MD; LOCH RAVEN HS; (SR); F Lan Hn Soc; Hnr Roll; Nat Hon Sy; Nat Mrt LOC; WWAHSS; Comm Volntr; Peer Tut/Med; Dbte Team; Emplmnt; Mth Clb/Tm; Mod UN; MuAlphaTh; NtlFrnscLg; Cl Off (T, R); Club Ice Hockey Player; Mock Trial Attorney; Major in Political Science; Major in Russian; Harvard College; Yale U

RAINES, RACHEL; BERLIN, MD; STEPHEN DECATUR HS; (FR); Ctznshp Aw; Hi Hnr Roll; Pres Sch; Sci Fairs; St of Mnth; Comm Volntr; Chrch Yth Grp; FCA; Scouts; Spch Team; Tchrs Aide; Ch Chr; Earth Science; Veterinary Medicine; Salisbury U; U of Maryland College Park

RALLO, BRITTANY P; COCKEYSVILLE, MD; NOTRE DAME PREP SCH; (SR); Comm Volntr; ArtClub; Chrch Yth Grp; Drma Clb; Mus Clb; Tchrs Aide; Bnd; Chr; Cr Ctry (V); Fld Hky (V); Lcrsse (J); Track (V); Cl Off (R); CR (R); Athletic Association At-Large; Magazine Chairperson; Education; Advertisement; College of Notre Dame of Maryland; Towson U

RAMIREZ JR, JUAN R; CLINTON, MD; BISHOP MC NAMARA HS; (SR); Hi Hnr Roll; Hnr Roll; Nat Hon Sy; Otst Ac Ach Awd; Perf Att; Pres Sch; WWAHSS; Peer Tut/Med; Lcrsse (JC); Sccr (V L); Conservative Presidential Honors; Academic Achievement in Web Design; Computer Science; U of Maryland College Park

RANKIN, ARIEL; CAPITOL HEIGHTS, MD; CHARLES W FLOWERS HS; (SR); Ctznshp Aw; Hnr Roll; Perf Att; Sci Fairs; WWAHSS; Comm Volntr; Peer Tut/Med; DARE; Drma Clb; FBLA; Prom Com; Quiz Bowl; Bnd; Mch Bnd; Pep Bnd; Stg Cre; CR (R); Nu Alpha Omega Christian Club; Renaissance; Nursing Administration; Howard U; Florida A & M U

RASHID, SONIA; WINDSOR MILL, MD; WOODLAWN HS; (JR); Hnr Roll; Comm Volntr; Biomedical Engineering; Computer Engineering; U of Maryland; Towson State

RAUM, MELANIE; SALISBURY, MD; BENNETT HS; (JR); Ctznshp Aw; Hi Hnr Roll; Hnr Roll; Otst Ac Ach Awd; Sci Fairs; St of Mnth; Peer Tut/Med; DARE; Emplmnt; Architecture; Savannah College of Art and Design; Spelman College

RAY, LONNETTE L; FORT WASHINGTON, MD; FRIENDLY HS; (SO); Hi Hnr Roll; Hnr Roll; Perf Att; Sci Fairs; St of Mnth; Peer Tut/Med; Chrch Yth Grp; ROTC; Sci Clb; Ch Chr; Cl Off (V); Stu Cncl (V); CR (P); Step Team; Doctor; Lawyer; Johns Hopkins U; Duke U

RAY, OCTAVIA; WINDSOR MILL, MD; MILLFORD MILL AC; (JR); Hnr Roll; St of Mnth; WWAHSS; Comm Volntr; Hosp Aide; Red Cr Aide; Off Aide; Tchrs Aide; Wdwrkg Clb; Chr; SP/M/VS; Scr Kpr (J); Sftball (J); Track (J); Vllyball (J); Leader of the Step Team; Class Leadership Award; Pediatric Surgery; Forensic Science; Spelman College; Clark U

RAYNOR, MARY C; UPPER MARLBORO, MD; CHARLES HERBERT FLOWERS HS; (SO); Hnr Roll; Chrch Yth Grp; Lib Aide; Photog; Bnd; It's Academic Club; Law; Criminal Justice; Texas Southern U Thurgood Marshall School of Law; Lincoln U

REASE, ANTHONY; UPPER MARLBORO, MD; LARGO HS; (SO); Hnr Roll; Perf Att; Sci Fairs; Yth Ldrshp Prog; Comm Volntr; ROTC; Clr Grd; Drl Tm; ROTC - Outstanding Cadet; ROTC - Cadet of Quarter; Military Career; United States Military Academy West Point; South Carolina State U

RECKLEY, SAMANTHA; CUMBERLAND, MD; ALLEGANY HS; (SO); Ctznshp Aw; Hnr Roll; Perf Att; Sci Fairs; Comm Volntr; Peer Tut/Med; Lib Aide; Off Aide; Spanish Clb; Chr; Ch Chr; Stg Cre; Sccr (J); Track (V); SHOP; Peer Helpers; Veterinarian; West Virginia U; Frostburg State U

REDDING, KRISTOPHER; GERMANTOWN, MD; NORTHWEST HS; (SO); Hnr Roll; Yth Ldrshp Prog; Comm Volntr; Ftball (J); Track (J); Member of Students for Montgomery County's Future; Computer Engineering; Penn State U; Maryland U

REEDER, AMANDA; COLUMBIA, MD; WILDE LAKE HS; (JR); Hi Hnr Roll; Nat Hon Sy; Perf Att; Hab For Humty Volntr; Peer Tut/Med; Red Cr Aide; Chrch Yth Grp; Emplmnt; Mus Clb; Chr; Dnce; Lcrsse (J); CR (R); Dance Company Captain; MD Distinguished Scholar of the Arts Nomination; Physical Therapy; U of the Sciences in Philadelphia; James Madison U

REEVES, STANESSA; BOWIE, MD; CHARLES HERBERT FLOWERS HS; (FR); Ctznshp Aw; Hnr Roll; Chrch Yth Grp; Emplmnt; Dnce; Chrldg; Dentistry; Virginia Commonwealth U

REGUERIN, CATALINA; GAITHERSBURG, MD; QUINCE ORCHARD HS; (JR); Hnr Roll; Comm Volntr; Emplmnt; Fr of Library; Lib Aide; Off Aide; Prom Com; Tchrs Aide; Dnce; Fld Hky (J); Yrbk (E); Political Science; Law; U of Maryland; Boston College

REID, KAITLIN; ADELPHIA, MD; HIGH POINT HS; (JR); Hnr Roll; Home Economics; Salisbury U; Towson U

REID, MARGARET; ANNAPOLIS, MD; SEVERN SCH; (JR); Nat Hon Sy; Comm Volntr; Dnce; Tennis; Art Classes - Not with School; Community Service; Interior Design; Fashion Design; Vanderbilt U; U of Virginia

RENNER, JAMAICA; WOODSTOCK, MD; RANDALLSTOWN HS; (FR); Hnr Roll; Perf Att; Comm Volntr; ROTC; Bnd; Drl Tm; Mch Bnd; Bskball (J); Sccr (V); Mathematical Engineering; U.S. Air Force Academy

REPASI, ELIZABETH; HAGERSTOWN, MD; NORTH HAGERSTOWN HS; (JR); Hi Hnr Roll; Hnr Roll; Nat Hon Sy; Perf Att; St Schl; WWAHSS; Comm Volntr; Red Cr Aide; Chrch Yth Grp; DARE; Emplmnt; Prom Com; Acpl Chr; Chr; Dnce; SP/M/VS; Meteorology; Earth Science Teacher; California U of Pennsylvania; Penn State U

REYES, OSCAR; GERMANTOWN, MD; WATKINS MILL HS; (JR); Hnr Roll; Computer Programmer; Software Engineering; Montgomery College

RHABB, CHAVON; HYATTSVILLE, MD; STONE RIDGE CTRY DAY SCH; (JR); Hi Hnr Roll; MVP; Nat Hon Sy; WWAHSS; Comm Volntr; Chrch Yth Grp; Emplmnt; Mus Clb; Photog; Vsity Clb; Chr; SP/M/VS; Stg Cre; Track (V CL); National Latin Exam Award Winner; AAU Summer Track Participant; Pediatrician; Lawyer; Princeton U; Georgetown U

RICE, HEATHER J; THURMONT, MD; CATOCTIN HS; (JR); Hnr Roll; Comm Volntr; P to P St Amb Prg; Prom Com; Dnce; Fld Hky (VJ); Australia/New Zealand People to People Student Ambassador Trip; Nursing; Moravian College, PA; Cedar Crest College, PA

RICE, KYLE; HAGERSTOWN, MD; SOUTH HAGERSTOWN HS; (JR); Hnr Roll; Nat Hon Sy; Perf Att; Comm Volntr; Emplmnt; FBLA; Scouts; Bskball (J); Golf (VJCL); Tennis (V L)

RICHARDSON, BRITTANY; FORT WASHINGTON, MD; FRIENDLY HS; (JR); Hnr Roll; Chrch Yth Grp; DARE; Scouts; Ch Chr; Dnce; Sftball (J); Selected for National Student Leadership Conference; Psychology; Dramatic Arts/Theatre; Virginia Commonwealth U (VCU); Wells College

RICHARDSON, MAGGIE; GIBSON ISLAND, MD; ST MARY'S HS; (SO); Hnr Roll; Emplmnt; Tennis (V); Stu Cncl (R); National American Miss State Finalist; Interior Design; Wedding Planner; Florida State U; Towson U

RICHARDSON, OLIVIA; FORT WASHINGTON, MD; ST MARY'S RYKEN HS; (SO); MVP; Perf Att; Yth Ldrshp Prog; Comm Volntr; Chrch Yth Grp; FBLA; Mth Clb/Tm; Ch Chr; Track (V); Vllyball (J); 3 Time Volleyball MVP; Criminology; Law; U of North Carolina Chapel Hill; Duke U

RICHARDSON, TAMIKA M; LANHAM, MD; CHARLES HERBERT FLOWERS HS; (JR); Hnr Roll; Comm Volntr; Peer Tut/Med; Spec Olymp Vol; Chrch Yth Grp; Prom Com; Chr; Ch Chr; Dnce; Academy of Finance; Music Production; Finance; Spelman College; North Carolina Central U

RIGGIN, JESSICA; SEVERN, MD; ARUNDEL SR HS; (SR); Hnr Roll; Jr Rot; Nat Hon Sy; Nat Mrt LOC; Perf Att; St of Mnth; WWAHSS; Comm Volntr; Peer Tut/Med; Emplmnt; HO'Br Yth Ldrshp; Key Club; Marine Biology; California State U Monterey Bay

RILEY, COLIN P; COLUMBIA, MD; WILDE LAKE HS; (SR); Hi Hnr Roll; Nat Hon Sy; Perf Att; St of Mnth; WWAHSS; Comm Volntr; Peer Tut/Med; Chrch Yth Grp; Drma Clb; Emplmnt; Spch Team; SADD; French Clb; Dnce; SP/M/VS; Stu Cncl (R); Lit Mag (E); President, Shakespeare Club; English, Creative Writing; Drama; Kenyon College, Washington College; Boucher College

RINGLEY, KELLY N; WOODBINE, MD; SOUTH CARROLL HS; (SO); Hnr Roll; MVP; Pres Sch; WWAHSS; Comm Volntr; Chrch Yth Grp; Emplmnt; Key Club; Fld Hky (V); Lcrsse (V)

RISSLER, CANDACE; EMMITSBURG, MD; CATOCTIN HS; (FR); Hnr Roll; Emplmnt; Catoctin Cougars Competition; Cheerleading Squad / Cheerleader in 2005 Hawaii Pro-Bowl / Half-Time and Pre-Game

RITCHEY, CAROLINE M; POCOMOKE CITY, MD; POCOMOKE HS; (SO); Hi Hnr Roll; St of Mnth; Comm Volntr; Hab For Humty Volntr; Peer Tut/Med; Biology Clb; Chrch Yth Grp; Drma Clb; ROTC; Spanish Clb; Ch Chr; SP/M/VS; Cl Off (V); Mission Trips with Church; ROTC Color Guard and Drill; Environmental Science and Forestry; Art, Media, Design / Studio Art; Syracuse U

RIVAS, ASTRID; BOWIE, MD; BOWIE HS; (SO); Hi Hnr Roll; Hnr Roll; Perf Att; Sci Fairs; St of Mnth; Yth Ldrshp Prog; Comm Volntr; Prom Com; ROTC; Clr Grd; Drl Tm; Cr Ctry (J); Stu Cncl (R); Drill Team Commander; Forensic Science; Marketing; Maryland U; Towson U

RIVOLTA, STEFANO M; BURTONSVILLE, MD; PAINT BRANCH HS; (JR); Hnr Roll; Key Club; Bskball (J); Cr Ctry (J); Ftball (VJ L); CPR Certified; First Aid Certified; Film/TV Production; Media; U of Maryland-College Park; U Southern California

RIXHAM JR, J WILLIAM; NOTTINGHAM, MD; PATAPSCO HS; (SO); Hnr Roll; Otst Ac Ach Awd; Perf Att; Yth Ldrshp Prog; Comm Volntr; Emplmnt; Scouts; Bnd; Mch Bnd; Boy Scouts of America; Towson U; U of Maryland

ROBERTS, ANTOINETTE; BALTIMORE, MD; MERGENTHALER VO-TECH HS; (SO); Hnr Roll; MVP; Nat Mrt LOC; Nat Sci Aw; Perf Att; Yth Ldrshp Prog; Comm Volntr; Spec Olymp Vol; Chess; Emplmnt; Ch Chr; Dnce; Mch Bnd; Sccr (V); Wrstlg (V); Modeling; Computer Engineer; Morgan State U; Towson U

ROBERTSON, BRANDY; FORT WASHINGTON, MD; FRIENDLY HS; (SR); Hnr Roll; St Schl; WWAHSS; Peer Tut/Med; Chrch Yth Grp; Off Aide; Tchrs Aide; Dnce; Mch Bnd; Mentoring Program; Tutor; Accounting; Finance; Pennsylvania State U

ROBINSON, ANDREA; BALTIMORE, MD; BALTIMORE POLY TECH INST 403; (SO); Hnr Roll; Prom Com; Bskball (V); Vllyball (V); Cl Off (P); President - Class of 2007; President Prom Committee - Class of 2007; Engineering; Mathematics; Johns Hopkins U; Bucknell U

ROBINSON, CANDACE; GERMANTOWN, MD; NORTHWEST HS; (SR); Hi Hnr Roll; Hnr Roll; WWAHSS; Comm Volntr; Chrch Yth Grp; Chr; Ch Chr; Cr Ctry (V); Track (V); Cl Off (P); Sch Ppr (E)

ROBINSON, CARLYNNE D; COLUMBIA, MD; WILDE LAKE HS; (JR); Ctznshp Aw; Hi Hnr Roll; Hnr Roll; Nat Hon Sy; Otst Ac Ach Awd; Perf Att; Pres Ac Ftns Aw; Sci Fairs; St of Mnth; Yth Ldrshp Prog; Amnsty Intl; Comm Volntr; Hab For Humty Volntr; DARE; Dbte Team; Mod UN; Mus Clb; NYLC; Acpl Chr; Chr; SP/M/VS; Skiing; Theatre; Foreign Language; Yale; Columbia U

ROBINSON, LEAH P; JOPPA, MD; JOPPATOWNE HS; (JR); Hnr Roll; Nat Hon Sy; Nat Mrt Fin; Peer Tut/Med; Chrch Yth Grp; Emplmnt; FBLA; Chr; Ch Chr; SP/M/VS; Journalism; Music; Harvard; Berklee

ROCHESTER, MOLLY E; BURTONSVILLE, MD; PAINT BRANCH HS; (JR); Hnr Roll; Otst Ac Ach Awd; Pres Sch; Comm Volntr; ArtClub; DARE; Emplmnt; Key Club; Lib Aide; P to P St Amb Prg; Photog; Scouts; Cr Ctry (V); Sftball (J); Stu Cncl (S); Yrbk (E, R, P); Gilder Lehrman Scholar

ROCKWELL, STACEY; FREDERICK, MD; GOVERNOR THOMAS JOHNSON HS; (JR); Hnr Roll; Chrch Yth Grp; Drma Clb; Stg Cre; Technical Theatre (Lighting)

RODGERS, CHRISTOPHER; WESTMINSTER, MD; SOUTH CARROLL HS; (FR); Hi Hnr Roll; Hnr Roll; Otst Ac Ach Awd; Perf Att; Pres Sch; WWAHSS; Comm Volntr; Chess; Key Club; Scouts; Bnd; Mch Bnd; Pep Bnd; Acted As a Pro-Life Speaker; Altar Server; Master's in Architecture; U of Notre Dame; U of Miami

ROSARIO, RACHEL; SILVER SPRING, MD; POINT BRANCH HS; (FR); Hnr Roll; WWAHSS; Comm Volntr; Pre-Med; Columbia U; U of Pennsylvania

ROSE, CHELSEA L; LUTHERVILLE TIMONIUM, MD; CARVER CTR FOR ARTS & TECH; (SR); F Lan Hn Soc; Hnr Roll; Nat Hon Sy; St Schl; WWAHSS; Comm Volntr; Chrch Yth Grp; Key Club; Ch Chr; Dnce; SP/M/VS; Religious Studies; U of South Carolina

ROSE, MEAGAN E; GAITHERSBURG, MD; QUINCE ORCHARD HS; (JR); Hnr Roll; Nat Hon Sy; WWAHSS; Comm Volntr; Lttrmn Clb; Prom Com; Tchrs Aide; Vsity Clb; Chr; Bskball (VJ L); Sportsmanship Award; Amateur Athletic Union Basketball Player; Medical Field; Duke U; U of North Carolina

ROSIAK, DANIEL; ROCKVILLE, MD; ROCKVILLE HS; (JR); F Lan Hn Soc; Hnr Roll; Yth Ldrshp Prog; Comm Volntr; Chrch Yth Grp; NYLC; Quill & Scroll; Sccr (V C); Tennis (V C); Track (V); Sch Ppr (E); Foreign Language Honors Society; Honor Roll: 3 Years; Business; Spanish, Villanova U; Fairfield U

ROSSITER, HALEY; ANNAPOLIS, MD; BROADNECK HS; (JR); Hi Hnr Roll; Hnr Roll; Nat Hon Sy; Comm Volntr; Peer Tut/Med; Chrch Yth Grp; Key Club; SADD; Vllyball (JC); Key Club Editor; Sports Management; Law; College of the Southwest; U of Southern California

ROWLAND, SEBASTIAN T; GAITHERSBURG, MD; MAGRUDER HS; (FR); Hnr Roll; St of Mnth; Chrch Yth Grp; Svce Clb; Cr Ctry (J); Track (J); Cty Search - Johns Hopkins; PhD in Environmental Sciences; MIT / Massachusetts Institute of Technology; Harvard U

ROYSTER, CHRISTINA; DERWOOD, MD; MAGRUDER HS; (JR); Hnr Roll; MVP; Perf Att; St of Mnth; Comm Volntr; DARE; Emplmnt; Jr Ach; NYLC; Scouts; Bskball (VJC); Sftball (VJC); Over 210 Hours of Community Service; Guidance Committee; Physical Therapy; Speech -Language Pathology; East Carolina University; University of North Carolina

RUBLE JR, MARK T; DUNDALK, MD; PATAPSCO HS; (SO); Hnr Roll; Comm Volntr; Bnd; Electronic Engineering; Johns Hopkins U

RUECKER, PAIGE L; ANNAPOLIS, MD; BROADNECK HS; (JR); Hnr Roll; Key Club; Dnce; All County Dance; U of Maryland; Towson State U

SACHS, AMBER; OAKLAND, MD; SOUTHERN GARRETT HS; (FR); Hnr Roll; AL Aux Girls; DARE; Bnd; Chr; Mch Bnd; Band Manager; Performing Arts; West Virginia State U; Maryland State U

SAGIN, HANNAH; CUMBERLAND, MD; ALLEGANY HS; (SO); Hi Hnr Roll; Perf Att; Sci Fairs; Comm Volntr; Chrch Yth Grp; Dbte Team; Drma Clb; Mth Clb/Tm; French Clb; Bnd; Mch Bnd; SP/M/VS; Skiing; Swmg; Lawyer; Political

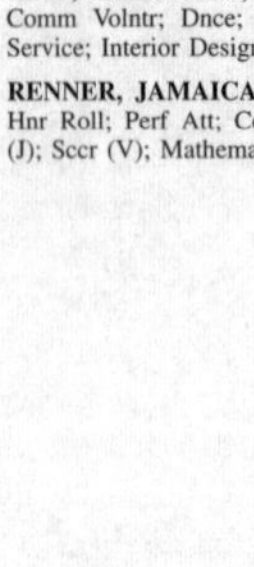
Sachs, Amber
Southern Garrett HS
Oakland, MD

Roberts, Antoinette
Mergenthaler Vo-Tech HS
Baltimore, MD

Richardson, Tamika M
Charles Herbert Flowers HS
Lanham, MD

Rice, Heather J
Catoctin HS
Thurmont, MD

Raynor, Mary C
Charles Herbert Flowers HS
Upper Marlboro, MD

National
Honor Roll
Spring 2005

Ray, Lonnette L
Friendly HS
Fort Washington, MD

Richardson, Brittany
Friendly HS
Fort Washington, MD

Rissler, Candace
Catoctin HS
Emmitsburg, MD

Robinson, Carlynne D
Wilde Lake HS
Columbia, MD

Ruble Jr, Mark T
Patapsco HS
Dundalk, MD

SALATINO, ALEXANDRA C; PARKTON, MD; HEREFORD SR HS; (SO); Hi Hnr Roll; Hnr Roll; MVP; Nat Hon Sy; Comm Volntr; Dbte Team; Bnd; Bskball (J); Sccr (V L); Greater Harford Soccer Club-Div. 2 Champions; Communications; Political Science; Gettysburg College; Dickinson College

SALAZAR, GIANCARLO; HAGERSTOWN, MD; SOUTH HAGERSTOWN HS; (SR); Hnr Roll; WWAHSS; Peer Tut/Med; Chrch Yth Grp; Emplmnt; Tchrs Aide; Dnce; Cr Ctry (J); Sccr (V); Swmg (V); Political Science; Law; Brigham Young U, Provo, UT

SALTIEL, FERNANDO; BETHESDA, MD; WALTER JOHNSON HS; (SO); F Lan Hn Soc; Hi Hnr Roll; Hnr Roll; Nat Hon Sy; Sci/Math Olympn; Peer Tut/Med; Chess; Emplmnt; Soccer Player MSI League-NCSL, Arrived in the US in Jan 04; High Honor Roll Student in Argentina; Economics; Business Administration; U of Maryland/U of Chicago; Harvard U

SANCHEZ, YESLY I; SILVER SPRING, MD; WHEATON HS; (SO); Hi Hnr Roll; Hnr Roll; Yth Ldrshp Prog; Key Club; Tmpl Yth Grp; Dnce; Business Management; Maryland U; Georgetown U

SANDERS, ANISSA C; CLINTON, MD; OXON HILL HS; (FR); Ctznshp Aw; F Lan Hn Soc; Hnr Roll; Sci Fairs; Comm Volntr; Peer Tut/Med; Spec Olymp Vol; Chrch Yth Grp; Emplmnt; Pep Squd; Scouts; Ch Chr; Dnce; SP/M/VS; Chrldg (V); Gmnstcs (L); Forensic Science; New York U

SANDERS, JONOVAN J; CAPITOL HEIGHTS, MD; CHARLES HERBERT FLOWERS HS; (FR); Hnr Roll; St of Mnth; Comm Volntr; Chrch Yth Grp; Bnd; Ch Chr; Mch Bnd; Pep Bnd; National Sr Honor Society; Video Game Designer; Computer Science; Michigan Institute of Technology; U of Maryland

SANDERS, RYAN; DUNDALK, MD; DIGITAL HARBOR HS 416; (SO); Hnr Roll; USAA; WWAHSS; Spec Olymp Vol; Computer Science; Pharmaceutical; Johns Hopkins U

SANDRINE, KOUADIO S; BOWIE, MD; BOWIE HS; (SO); Hnr Roll; Nat Hon Sy; WWAHSS; Georgetown U; Johns Hopkins U

SANFORD-CRANE, CHARLOTTE; ELKTON, MD; BOHEMIA MANOR HS; (SR); 4H Awd; Hnr Roll; Nat Hon Sy; Nat Mrt LOC; Otst Ac Ach Awd; Pres Sch; St Schl; Valdctrian; WWAHSS; Comm Volntr; Peer Tut/Med; 4-H; FBLA; Mth Clb/Tm; Sci Clb; German Clb; Bnd; Mch Bnd; Sccr (V L); Animal Science; Veterinary Medicine; U of Maryland College Park

SAN GABRIEL, GINO; BOWIE, MD; BOWIE HS; (JR); Hnr Roll; Perf Att; Peer Tut/Med; Chess; Chrch Yth Grp; Civil Air Pat; Drma Clb; Prom Com; Sci Clb; SP/M/VS; Film Production; Acting; U of Maryland College Park; North Carolina School of the Arts

SAN JUAN, MARY G; NOTTINGHAM, MD; PERRY HALL HS; (SO); Hi Hnr Roll; Hnr Roll; Perf Att; Peer Tut/Med; Mus Clb; Bnd; Chr; Dnce; Bskball (J); Chamber Choir; Nursing; Towson U

SANTANA, JASMINE; GLEN BURNIE, MD; OLD MILL HS; (SR); Hi Hnr Roll; Hnr Roll; Nat Hon Sy; Nat Mrt LOC; Yth Ldrshp Prog; Peer Tut/Med; ArtClub; Photog; Sci Clb; MESA Club-Treasurer, Trophies; Medal in Mathematics-9th Grade; Microbiology; Astrophysics; U of Michigan-Ann Arbor; Pennsylvania State U-U Park

SARWAR, SHEHARYAR; COLUMBIA, MD; WILDE LAKE HS; (SO); Hi Hnr Roll; Hnr Roll; Pres Sch; Comm Volntr; Peer Tut/Med; French Clb; Lit Mag (E); Best Muslim Student of the Year for 2001 in My Mosque; Published Some Poetry; Medicine; Literature; Yale U; Princeton U

SATTERFIELD, SHAKIRA; DUNDALK, MD; DUNDALK HS; (JR); Fut Prb Slvr; Hi Hnr Roll; Hnr Roll; Otst Ac Ach Awd; Yth Ldrshp Prog; Comm Volntr; Peer Tut/Med; Dbte Team; Fr of Library; Lib Aide; Mth Clb/Tm; Off Aide; Tchrs Aide; Bdmtn (J); Bskball (J); PP Ftbl; Scr Kpr; Wrstlg (C); Stu Cncl (R); CR (V); Sch Ppr (R); Yrbk (E); Tutoring Students After School; Helping W/Organizations in School; Becoming a Doctor; Degree in Medicine; Johns Hopkins U; Maryland U

SAULL, NECHAMA; BALTIMORE, MD; BAIS YAAKOV HS; (SR); Hnr Roll; Nat Mrt LOC; Pres Ac Ftns Aw; Sci Fairs; WWAHSS; Yth Ldrshp Prog; Comm Volntr; Peer Tut/Med; Dbte Team; Emplmnt; Chr; SP/M/VS; Cyclg (V); Stu Cncl (R); Save-A-Life Program; Big Sister-Little Sister Mentoring Program; Psychology; Social Work; U of Maryland Baltimore County; Towson U

SAVERS, SAMANTHA; DUNDALK, MD; DUNDALK HS; (SO); Hi Hnr Roll; Nat Hon Sy; Otst Ac Ach Awd; Perf Att; SADD; Chr; Sftball (J); Track (V); Cl Off (V); Lit Mag (E); Soccer Manager; Liberal Arts; Mount St Mary's; Salisbury U

SAYAN, CLAUDIO; SILVER SPRING, MD; JOHN F KENNEDY HS; (JR); Hi Hnr Roll; Nat Hon Sy; Comm Volntr; Aeronautics; Ophthalmology; Massachusetts Institute of Technology; U of Pennsylvania

SCARLETT, ROBERT J; UPPER MARLBORO, MD; KETTERING FLOWER HS; MS; Ctznshp Aw; Hi Hnr Roll; Hnr Roll; Nat Hon Sy; Otst Ac Ach Awd; Pres Sch; Sci Fairs; Tech Clb; Bnd; Stg Cre; President of National Junior Honor Society; 4.0 GPA Entire Year; Computer Science; Criminal Justice; U of Maryland U College; Clark Atlanta U

SCHECTER, MEIRA; PIKESVILLE, MD; BAIS YAAKOV HS; (SR); Hnr Roll; Pres Ac Ftns Aw; WWAHSS; Dbte Team; Drma Clb; SP/M/VS; Stu Cncl (R); CR (R); National Merit Honorable Mention; Debate Team; Accounting; Towson U

SCHILDWACHTER, RACHEL G; KINGSVILLE, MD; BALTIMORE LUTHERAN HS; (JR); Hi Hnr Roll; Nat Hon Sy; Chrch Yth Grp; Emplmnt; Tchrs Aide; Bskball (V); Cr Ctry (V L); Track (V L); Stu Cncl (V); Vice President of Church Youth Group

SCHLEICHER, LAUREN; SYKESVILLE, MD; LIBERTY HS; (SO); Hi Hnr Roll; Hnr Roll; Pres Sch; Drma Clb; Tech Clb; Stg Cre; CR (R); Food Science; Chemistry; U of Maryland; U of Delaware

SCHMIDT, JUSTIN; GREAT MILLS, MD; ST MARY'S RYKEN HS; (SO); Hnr Roll; MVP; Sci Fairs; DARE; Scouts; Lcrsse (V); Sccr (J); Adv Cncl (R); RC Excellence in Religion 2002-2003; MVP Youth Lacrosse 2001; Business Management

SCHNEIDER, ALEX; COLUMBIA, MD; WILDE LAKE HS; (SO); Hnr Roll; St of Mnth; Emplmnt; Lttrmn Clb; Scouts; Sccr (J); Tennis (V); Wrstlg (J); Yrbk (E); Medical School; Johns Hopkins U; St. Mary's U

SCHRECK, LAUREN; JOPPA, MD; JOPPATOWNE HS; (FR); Hnr Roll; SP/M/VS; Chrldg (V); Actress

SCHRUM, SAMANTHA J; PASADENA, MD; ST. MARYS HS; (JR); Nat Hon Sy; WWAHSS; Comm Volntr; Chrch Yth Grp; FCA; Vsity Clb; Bskball (V); Fld Hky (V); Lcrsse (V); Sccr (V)

SCOTT, JOHN; TEMPLE HILLS, MD; SURRATTSVILLE HS; (SO); Ctznshp Aw; Hnr Roll; Nat Hon Sy; Otst Ac Ach Awd; Sci Fairs; St of Mnth; Yth Ldrshp Prog; Comm Volntr; Peer Tut/Med; ArtClub; Chess; Chrch Yth Grp; Cmptr Clb; FBLA; ROTC; Sci Clb; Tchrs Aide; Bnd; Ch Chr; Mch Bnd; Sccr (V); Cl Off (V); Lit Mag (R); US Army Science Fair Award; American Nuclear Society Award; MBA; Doctorate; Northwestern U; Morehouse U

SENUTA, MIGNON; WALKERSVILLE, MD; WALKERSVILLE HS; (JR); Hnr Roll; Otst Ac Ach Awd; Chrch Yth Grp; Emplmnt; FBLA; Key Club; Sci Clb; Bskball (JC); Sftball (J); Stu Cncl (R); Loyola U; New York U

SEO, SONG; COLUMBIA, MD; OAKLAND MILLS HS; (JR); Hi Hnr Roll; Hnr Roll; Comm Volntr; Chrch Yth Grp; Emplmnt; Ch Chr; Orch; Fld Hky (J); Lcrsse (J); Scr Kpr; Teacher Aide in PACE (Parents And Child ESOL Program) in St. John's Elementary School; Assistant Teacher in Bethel Korean School-2 years; Biology; Business Management; U of Maryland, College Park; Washington College

SEWARD, DANA E; CHESTERTOWN, MD; KENT CTY HS; (JR); Hnr Roll; WWAHSS; Lcrsse (J); Sccr (V L); Swmg (V L); Health Occupations Students of America-Chapter President; Pediatric Nurse; York College of Penn.; Chesapeake College

SEYMORE, COURTNEY T; BALTIMORE, MD; BALTIMORE CITY COLLEGE; MS; Hnr Roll; Nat Hon Sy; Perf Att; Yth Ldrshp Prog; Peer Tut/Med; Spec Olymp Vol; Chrch Yth Grp; FTA; Off Aide; Bnd; Ch Chr; Dnce; SP/M/VS; Bskball (C); Yrbk (E); Vice President of National Jr Honor Society; Special Education Teacher; Special Education Lawyer; Spelman College; St Mary's College

SHAH, KHUSHBU S; WINDSOR MILL, MD; WESTERN SCH OF ENVIR MENTAL SCIENCE AND TECH; (JR); Hnr Roll; Nat Hon Sy; Perf Att; St of Mnth; Bdmtn (V); Tennis (V); Cl Off (R); Stu Cncl (R); CR (R); Oncology (Cancer Research); Biomedicine; U of Baltimore Maryland College; U of Maryland College Park

SHAIBU, BARBARA E; COLLEGE PARK, MD; ELEANOR ROOSEVELT HS; (SO); Hi Hnr Roll; Hnr Roll; Nat Mrt LOC; Otst Ac Ach Awd; Pres Sch; WWAHSS; Comm Volntr; Chrch Yth Grp; President of International Club; Lawyer for Mock Trial; Major in Political Science; Lawyer / Business Law; U of Maryland College Park; Cornell U

SHAKHMAN, MICHAEL; GAITHERSBURG, MD; (JR); Hnr Roll; Bskball; Electrical Engineering; Any State School in Maryland

SHARKEY, DEVIN; ASHTON, MD; ST JOHN'S COLLEGE HS; (JR); Hi Hnr Roll; Hnr Roll; Nat Hon Sy; Perf Att; Comm Volntr; Drma Clb; Emplmnt; ROTC; Scouts; Clr Grd; SP/M/VS; Stg Cre; National Physical Fitness Award; Freshman Football; Business; Forensic Science; U of Maryland; Virginia Military Institute

SHARMA, SONAM; COLUMBIA, MD; WILDE LAKE HS; (FR); Hnr Roll; Biology Clb; FBLA; Vsity Clb; Dnce; SP/M/VS; Fld Hky (V); Tennis (L); Netball, Gymnastics in UK; Yoga and Meditations; Choreography; New York College of Arts

SHEARY, JUDITH; GERMANTOWN, MD; DAMASCUS HS; (JR); Hnr Roll; Nat Hon Sy; Comm Volntr; Chrch Yth Grp; Emplmnt; Bnd; Mch Bnd; Pep Bnd; Track (V); International Club; Pre-Med; U of Maryland Baltimore County; U of Maryland College Park

SHEEHAN, KATIE; ELLICOTT CITY, MD; SETON KEOUGH HS; (SO); Hi Hnr Roll; MVP; Pres Ac Ftns Aw; Comm Volntr; Peer Tut/Med; Spec Olymp Vol; Key Club; Bskball (JCL); Lcrsse (J L); The Thomas Ivey Award; Athletic Coaches Award; Business / Bachelor's Degree / MBA; Engineering / Physics; Elon U; Clemson U

SHERIDAN, KATHRYN T; SEVERNA PARK, MD; SEVERN SCH; (SO); F Lan Hn Soc; Hi Hnr Roll; Perf Att; Yth Ldrshp Prog; Comm Volntr; Peer Tut/Med; Dbte Team; Drma Clb; HO'Br Yth Ldrshp; Mus Clb; Pep Squd; Prom Com; Svce Clb; French Clb; Chr; Ch Chr; Dnce; SP/M/VS; Cr Ctry (V L); Swmg (V L); Sch Ppr (E, R); President of Interact Club / French Club / Dance Classes / Voice Lessons / Mock Trial / Tri-M Music Honor Society; Perform in Regional Theatre; Music / Theatre / Music Theatre / Science; Business; Carnegie Mellon U; Yale U

SHERMAN, LEO; BALTIMORE, MD; TOWSON HS; (SR); F Lan Hn Soc; Hnr Roll; Nat Hon Sy; Nat Mrt LOC; Otst Ac Ach Awd; St Schl; Key Club; Mod UN; Mus Clb; Outdrs Clb; Spanish Clb; Acpl Chr; Chr; Jzz Bnd; Mch Bnd; All-Honors Jazz Ensemble; All-Honors Chorus; Music Composition; International Affairs; George Washington U

SHIFLET, MICHAEL G; PRESTON, MD; WESLEYAN CHRISTIAN SCH; (SR); Ctznshp Aw; Hi Hnr Roll; Hnr Roll; Nat Hon Sy; Otst Ac Ach Awd; Pres Sch; St of Mnth; WWAHSS; Comm Volntr; Chrch Yth Grp; Emplmnt; NYLC; Scouts; Tchrs Aide; Bskball (V); Cl Off (P); Stu Cncl (P); CR (P); Cross Cultural Studies; Toccoa Falls, Georgia

SHIH, DEBORAH C; ROCKVILLE, MD; WALTER JOHNSON HS; (JR); F Lan Hn Soc; Hnr Roll; Nat Hon Sy; WWAHSS; Comm Volntr; Peer Tut/Med; Chrch Yth Grp; FCA; Lib Aide; Mus Clb; Sci Clb; Ch Chr; Lcrsse (J); Vllyball (VJC); National Music Honors Society - Tri-M; Electrical Engineering; Mechanical Engineering; U of Michigan Ann Arbor; U of Illinois Urbana-Champaign

SHRADER, JENNIFER; WESTMINSTER, MD; (SO); Hi Hnr Roll; Hnr Roll; Nat Hon Sy; FCA; Key Club; Fld Hky (J); Skiing; Swmg; Cl Off (R); CR; Education; Towson; Vila Julie

SHRESTHA, DIBESH; GREENBELT, MD; ELEANOR ROOSEVELT HS; (JR); Hnr Roll; Otst Ac Ach Awd; Perf Att; Comm Volntr; Peer Tut/Med; Biology Clb; Cmptr Clb; Sci Clb; Tech Clb; Japanese Clb; Stg Cre; CR (R); Computer Engineering; Business Major; Virginia Tech U; U of Maryland

SHRESTHA, RUCHEE; WOODBINE, MD; GLENELG HS; (SR); Hi Hnr Roll; Hnr Roll; Nat Hon Sy; Nat Mrt LOC; Perf Att; Sci Fairs; WWAHSS; Hosp Aide; Peer Tut/Med; ArtClub; Tchrs Aide; 2004 AP Scholar; Maryland Distinguished Scholar Honorable Mention; Undergraduate Major Biomedical Engineering; Johns Hopkins U

SILK, MEGAN E; SALISBURY, MD; GUAM HS; (JR); Hi Hnr Roll; Hnr Roll; MVP; Nat Hon Sy; Nat Ldrshp Svc; Otst Ac Ach Awd; St Schl; Yth Ldrshp Prog; Peer Tut/Med; Red Cr Aide; Spec Olymp Vol; Chrch Yth Grp; Emplmnt; JSA; Prom Com; ROTC; Svce Clb; Clr Grd; Bskball (V L); Cr Ctry (V CL); Sccr (V CL); Cl Off (P); Youth of the Year-Guam Region; Selected for Summer Seminar USNA & USAFA; Doctor-Pediatrician; Sports Medicine; U North Carolina; United States Naval Academy

SILVAN, ERIN N; CLINTON, MD; SURRATTSVILLE HS; (JR); Hnr Roll; Perf Att; Sci Fairs; St of Mnth; Peer Tut/Med; Dbte Team; Mus Clb; ROTC; Bnd; Chr; Flg Crps; Mch Bnd; Stu Cncl (P); Mock Trial Team; Criminal Justice; Music Education; U of North Carolina; Georgetown U

SILVESTRE, GOLDIE; SILVER SPRING, MD; WHEATON HS; (FR); Hnr Roll; Key Club; AOIT (Academy of Information Technology; Computer Programming; Computer Science; Stanford U; U of California, Los Angeles

SIMMONS, MARIAH; MC DANIEL, MD; ST MICHAELS JR/SR HS; (MS); Hi Hnr Roll; St of Mnth; Comm Volntr; Bnd; Mch Bnd; Yrbk; Interior Design

SIMMS, CEDRIC; BALTIMORE, MD; LAKE CLIFTON #426; (FR); Perf Att; Comm Volntr; Mth Clb/Tm; Ftball (J); Track (V); Stu Cncl (S); (Out Side Activities) Martial Arts; Engineering; Morgan U; U of Maryland

SINGH, DHARAMVEER; NOTTINGHAM, MD; BALTIMORE POLY TECH INST 403; (SO); Hnr Roll; Perf Att; Emplmnt; Mth Clb/Tm; Volunteer at Church; Electrical Engineering; Biomedical Engineering; Johns Hopkins U; Towson U

SINGH, ISHITA; GAITHERSBURG, MD; RICHARD MONTGOMERY HS; (JR); F Lan Hn Soc; Hnr Roll; Nat Hon Sy; Comm Volntr; Peer Tut/Med; Drma Clb; Key Club; Mod UN; Spanish Clb; Chr; Dnce; SP/M/VS; Sch Ppr (E); Have Played Piano - 8 Years; Journalism; Business; U of Penn; U of Maryland

SINGLETON, RENITA J; BALTIMORE, MD; NEW ERA AC; (FR); Hi Hnr Roll; Hnr Roll; Comm Volntr; ArtClub; Drma Clb; SP/M/VS; Stg Cre; CR (T); Sch Ppr (R); Ben Carson Scholarship Award; President's Academic Achievement Award; Actress; Writer; Harvard U; Yale U

Shah, Khushbu S
Western Sch Of Envir Mental Science And Tech
Windsor Mill, MD

Scarlett, Robert J
Kettering Flower HS
Upper Marlboro, MD

San Juan, Mary G
Perry Hall HS
Nottingham, MD

Sanchez, Yesly I
Wheaton HS
Silver Spring, MD

Sanders, Jonovan J
Charles Herbert Flowers HS
Capitol Heights, MD

Seymore, Courtney T
Baltimore City College
Baltimore, MD

Sharma, Sonam
Wilde Lake HS
Columbia, MD

SISLER, MISTY; DUNDALK, MD; DUNDALK HS; (SO); Hnr Roll; Otst Ac Ach Awd; Perf Att; Pres Sch; Comm Volntr; Dnce; I Got and Maintained a Job; Been in Dance 13 Years; Animal Medicine; Veterinary; Virginia Tech; Villa Julie

SISSOM, AMIE; MILLINGTON, MD; CHESTERTOWN CHRISTIAN AC; (SO); Hi Hnr Roll; Hnr Roll; MVP; Sci Fairs; Comm Volntr; Peer Tut/Med; Chrch Yth Grp; Emplmnt; Pep Squd; Bskball (V L); Chrldg (V CL); Sccr (V L); Vllyball (V L); Yrbk (R); Gatorade Player of the Year; Washington College-Business; English; Washington College; Lancaster Bible College

SIZEMORE, KIARA; UPPER MARLBORO, MD; KETTERING MS; (MS); Hnr Roll; Sci Fairs; Comm Volntr; Tchrs Aide; Dnce; SP/M/VS; Honorable Mention in the County Science Fair in the Health & Medicine Category; 1st Place in School Science Fair; Veterinarian; Architect; U of Maryland - College Park, MD

SKIPPER, RACHEL K; OAKLAND, MD; SOUTHERN GARRETT HS; (FR); Hi Hnr Roll; Hnr Roll; Comm Volntr; Chrch Yth Grp; Emplmnt; Svce Clb; Bnd; Ch Chr; Dnce; Cr Ctry; Track; Lit Mag (R); Teaching; Business; Frostburg U

SKIRTA, JANEANN; PATUXENT RIVER, MD; ST MARY'S RYKEN HS; (JR); Hi Hnr Roll; Nat Hon Sy; WWAHSS; Comm Volntr; Key Club; Cr Ctry (V); Sccr (J); Track (V); Architecture & Design; Marymount U; Mount St Mary's College

SMITH, AHKEEM R; UPPER MARLBORO, MD; DUVAL HS; (SR); Hnr Roll; MVP; Nat Hon Sy; Nat Mrt Semif; WWAHSS; Comm Volntr; Red Cr Aide; Emplmnt; Sci Clb; Bsball (J); Bskball (J); Fball (J); Cl Off (P); Al Minnigh Student Achievement Award (04); Peace Project Winner (1st Place); Computer Engineering; Civil Engineering; North Carolina A & T U; Bethune-Cookman College

SMITH, ASHLEY T; ELLICOTT CITY, MD; MT HEBRON HS; (JR); Hi Hnr Roll; Hnr Roll; MVP; Nat Hon Sy; Sci Fairs; St of Mnth; Comm Volntr; Chrch Yth Grp; Emplmnt; FCA; Prom Com; Svce Clb; Cr Ctry (V L); Track (V L); Vllyball (JC); CR (P); Volleyball - Gatorade Rookie of the Year; National Honors Society; Education; James Madison U; Towson U

SMITH, BRITTNEY N; SILVER SPRING, MD; JAMES H BLAKE HS; (JR); Hnr Roll; WWAHSS; Hab For Humty Volntr; Chrch Yth Grp; Fr of Library; Prom Com; Ch Chr; Dnce; PPSqd (V L); Cl Off (S); CR (R); Biology Major; U of North Carolina Greensboro; North Carolina A & T State U

SMITH, CHELSEA R; MOUNT AIRY, MD; SOUTH CARROLL; (FR); F Lan Hn Soc; Hi Hnr Roll; Nat Stu Ath Day Aw; Otst Ac Ach Awd; Key Club; Dnce; Fld Hky (J); Lcrsse (J)

SMITH, KAYLA; BARTON, MD; WESTMAR; (JR); Hnr Roll; Perf Att; WWAHSS; Yth Ldrshp Prog; ArtClub; Emplmnt; Prom Com; Sftball (V); Sch Ppr (R); Forensic Science; Villa Julie; West Virginia U

SMITH, KEVON; BALTIMORE, MD; WOODLAWN HS; (SR); Fut Prb Slvr; Hnr Roll; Sci Fairs; St of Mnth; WWAHSS; Yth Ldrshp Prog; CARE; Comm Volntr; Hosp Aide; ArtClub; Chess; Cmptr Clb; Emplmnt; Lib Aide; Photog; ROTC; Wdwrkg Clb; Chr; Drl Tm; Orch; Pep Bnd; Mar Art (J)

SMITH, LAUREN; CLINTON, MD; ELIZABETH SETON HS; (SR); Hnr Roll; Jr Mshl; MVP; Nat Hon Sy; Otst Ac Ach Awd; Perf Att; Sci Fairs; St of Mnth; Comm Volntr; Hab For Humty Volntr; Spec Olymp Vol; ArtClub; Biology Clb; Drma Clb; Emplmnt; Mth Clb/Tm; Mus Clb; SADD; Vsity Clb; Bnd; Chr; SP/M/VS; Stg Cre; Fld Hky (V L); Tennis (V CL); Lit Mag (R); Yrbk (P); Bio-Medical Science (Researcher); Forensic Science; Salisbury U, Towson U; Temple U, Frostburg State

SMITH, LISA; ESSEX, MD; OVERLEA HS; (JR); Hnr Roll; Peer Tut/Med; DECA; Emplmnt; FBLA; Mod UN; Chrldg (J); Stu Cncl (V); 2005 Academy of Finance Most Involved Junior; Second Place Winner in DECA State Conference; Business Management; Ph.D; Bowie State U; Central Penn

SMITH, MATTHEW; HAGERSTOWN, MD; SOUTH HAGERSTOWN HS; (JR); Nat Hon Sy; Otst Ac Ach Awd; Pres Ac Ftns Aw; Emplmnt; Lttrmn Clb; Schol Bwl; Golf (V); Engineering; Miami; Penn State

SMITH, RIVA-NIGER; OXON HILL, MD; OXON HILL HS; (FR); Ctznshp Aw; Hi Hnr Roll; Hnr Roll; Nat Hon Sy; Comm Volntr; Peer Tut/Med; Chrch Yth Grp; P to P St Amb Prg; ROTC; Ch Chr; Dnce; CR (P); 2nd Place in Prince George's County Walk-A-Thon; Silver Hill Strikers Bowling League; Lawyer; Paralegal; Howard U; Spelman College

SMITH, SEAN E; SMITHSBURG, MD; MIDDLETOWN HS; (SR); Hnr Roll; Automotive / High Performance

SMITH, TIARA; CAPITOL HEIGHTS, MD; CHARLES HERBERT FLOWERS HS; (JR); Hnr Roll; WWAHSS; Comm Volntr; Emplmnt; FBLA; Prom Com; Dnce; PPSqd; Cl Off (S); Science and Tech Program for 4 Years / AP classes for Junior & Senior year; National Academy of Finance; English; Spelman College; Florida A & M University

SMITH, YANNICK; RANDALLSTOWN, MD; RANDALLSTOWN HS; (FR); Hnr Roll; Ftball (J); Sccr (J); Business; Finance; Florida State; U of Miami

SNOWDEN, DIAMOND T K; BALTIMORE, MD; BALTIMORE CITY COLLEGE HS; (SO); Ctznshp Aw; Hi Hnr Roll; Nat Hon Sy; Otst Ac Ach Awd; Peer Tut/Med; Child / Teenage Psychologist; Teacher

SNYDER, SHANNON; BOWIE, MD; (SR); Ctznshp Aw; Hi Hnr Roll; Hnr Roll; MVP; Nat Hon Sy; Otst Ac Ach Awd; Sci Fairs; WWAHSS; Comm Volntr; Peer Tut/Med; Chrch Yth Grp; Civil Air Pat; Emplmnt; Jr Ach; Key Club; Prom Com; ROTC; Clr Grd; Drl Tm; Golf (V); Biotechnology; U of MD-College Park

SOLOMON, EDEN; FORT WASHINGTON, MD; ST MARY'S RYKEN HS; (JR); Hnr Roll; Comm Volntr; Peer Tut/Med; BPA; Chrch Yth Grp; DARE; FBLA; Key Club; P to P St Amb Prg; Latin Clb; Fld Hky (V); Public Relations; International Business; American U; U of Maryland College Park

SPELZ, JUDY; SAINT INIGOES, MD; ST MARY'S RYKEN HS; (JR); Hi Hnr Roll; Hnr Roll; Nat Hon Sy; WWAHSS; Comm Volntr; Peer Tut/Med; DARE; Emplmnt; FBLA; Key Club; Bskball (J); Fld Hky (V); Lcrsse (V); Sftball (J); Xavarian Brothers Honor Society Leadership; Architecture; Real Estate Agent, Chemistry

SPENCER, CANDACE; BOWIE, MD; BOWIE HS; (SO); Hnr Roll; St of Mnth; WWAHSS; Yth Ldrshp Prog; Comm Volntr; Peer Tut/Med; Chrch Yth Grp; Tchrs Aide; Ch Chr; Dnce; Most Outstanding Peer Mediator; Psychology; Business Management; U of Maryland; Howard U

SPENCER, TIFFANY; SILVER SPRING, MD; WHEATON HS; Hnr Roll; Key Club; Chr; Track; Key Club; Pediatrician; TV/Production; UCLA

STAHL, HANNAH; OAKLAND, MD; SOUTHERN GARRETT HS; (SR); Hnr Roll; WWAHSS; Comm Volntr; Ntl FFA; Quiz Bowl; Chr; Mch Bnd; SP/M/VS; Stg Cre; Track; Environmental Science; West Virginia Wesleyan College

STAINES, DANIELLE A.; WOODBINE, MD; SOUTH CARROLL HS; (FR); Hnr Roll; Comm Volntr; Chrch Yth Grp; Key Club; Lib Aide; Scouts; Ch Chr; Orch; Scr Kpr (VJ); Ten Years of Girl Scouts; 200+ Service Hours; Veterinarian; Gemologist

STARKS II, ANTHONY W; BOWIE, MD; BOWIE HS; (SO); Ctznshp Aw; Hnr Roll; Yth Ldrshp Prog; Comm Volntr; Peer Tut/Med; Chrch Yth Grp; Off Aide; Scouts; Ch Chr; Swmg (J); Yrbk (R); Academic Excellence Award; Skiing / Snowboarding Achievement; Aerospace Engineering; Robotics; Carnegie Mellon U; Massachusetts Institute of Technology

STAYMATES, LINDSEY; WESTMINSTER, MD; WESTMINSTER HS; (JR); Chrch Yth Grp; Drma Clb; Spanish Clb; Chr; Dnce; CR (R); Recreational Basketball, Golf, Softball, Ballet.; Business; Psychology, Human Services; Salisbury U; Towson U

ST CLAIR, JASMINE; UPPER MARLBORO, MD; SUITLAND HS; (SO); Hnr Roll; St of Mnth; Comm Volntr; Chrch Yth Grp; Drma Clb; Dnce; SP/M/VS; Dance; Theatre; Marymount College of Fordham U

STEINWEG, STEPHANIE; ARNOLD, MD; BROADNECK HS; (FR); Hnr Roll; Comm Volntr; Chrch Yth Grp; Key Club; Ch Chr; Lcrsse (V); Sccr (J); Principal's Honor Roll; Medical; Business; Duke U; Johns Hopkins U

STEPHENSON, JERASIA; HYATTSVILLE, MD; BLADENSBURG HS; (SO); Hnr Roll; Chr; Dnce; Psychology; Dance; Clark Atlanta U; A & M U

STEVENS, MELANIE R; DISTRICT HEIGHTS, MD; CHARLES HERBERT FLOWERS HS; (FR); Hnr Roll; Drma Clb; Dnce; SP/M/VS; Veterinary Medicine; Master's Degree; Princeton U; Yale U

STEVENS, SCOTT A; HAGERSTOWN, MD; NORTH HAGERSTOWN HS; (SO); Hnr Roll; St of Mnth; WWAHSS; Comm Volntr; Chrch Yth Grp; Key Club; Scouts; Bnd; Mch Bnd; Pep Bnd; Computers; Hagerstown Community College

STEVENSON, BIANCA L; FORT WASHINGTON, MD; FRIENDLY HS; (SO); Ctznshp Aw; Hi Hnr Roll; Hnr Roll; Sci Fairs; WWAHSS; Yth Ldrshp Prog; Scouts; Flg Crps; National Honor Society Nominee; Accounting; Nursing; Hampton U; Florida Agricultural & Mechanical U

STEWART, JESSICA E; SILVER SPRING, MD; JAMES H BLAKE HS; (SO); Hi Hnr Roll; Hnr Roll; MVP; Pres Ac Ftns Aw; Chrch Yth Grp; Tech Clb; Dnce; Fld Hky (J); Lcrsse (V L); Swmg (V); Track (V L); Yrbk (R, P); Received AP Credits in AP Spanish & AP Calc AB as Sophomore; MVP of JV Field Hockey Team / Math Achievements; U of Maryland; U of Virginia

STEWART, KENT; SILVER SPRING, MD; PAINT BRANCH HS; (JR); Hi Hnr Roll; Hnr Roll; Wt Lftg; Academic Honor Rolls; Biology (Life Science); Biotechnology; U of Maryland, College Park; U of Maryland, Baltimore County

STEWART, SHELLEE; HYATTSVILLE, MD; BLADENSBURG HS; (JR); Hnr Roll; Perf Att; Comm Volntr; AL Aux Girls; Chrch Yth Grp; Dbte Team; P to P St Amb Prg; ROTC; Ch Chr; Clr Grd; Drl Tm; Chrldg (V); Sftball (J); CR (R); Criminal Justice; Criminology; Bowie State U; Towson U

STILES, DANIEL L; KITZMILLER, MD; SOUTHERN GARRETT HS; (SO); Hi Hnr Roll; Hnr Roll; Comm Volntr; Chrch Yth Grp; Chr; SP/M/VS; Drama; Secondary Education; Garrett College; Potomac State

STINCHCOMB, SARAH; LINTHICUM HEIGHTS, MD; NORTH CTY SR HS; (SO); Hnr Roll; Peer Tut/Med; Drma Clb; FBLA; Stg Cre; Cl Off (P); CR (P); Marine Biology; Child Psychiatrist; Towson U; U of Maryland

ST LOUIS, AMBER E; FORT WASHINGTON, MD; FRIENDLY HS; (SO); F Lan Hn Soc; Hi Hnr Roll; Hnr Roll; Nat Hon Sy; Otst Ac Ach Awd; WWAHSS; Peer Tut/Med; Emplmnt; Scouts; Chr; Scr Kpr (V); CR (R); National Honor Society; English Honor Society; Business Administration; English; Virginia State U; Belmont Abbey

STONE, CHRISTIE; DUNDALK, MD; PATAPSCO HS; (SO); Hnr Roll; Nat Hon Sy; Perf Att; Comm Volntr; Chrch Yth Grp; Scouts; Chr; Ch Chr; SP/M/VS; Writer (Novelist); Teacher; McDaniel; Lebodan Valley

STONE, MEGAN; DUNDALK, MD; PATAPSCO HS; (SO); Ctznshp Aw; Hnr Roll; Nat Hon Sy; Otst Ac Ach Awd; Perf Att; Sci Fairs; St of Mnth; Comm Volntr; DARE; Quiz Bowl; U of Maryland; U Of Notre Dame

STORCK, MADELINE; ANNAPOLIS, MD; BROADNECK HS; (FR); Hi Hnr Roll; WWAHSS; Comm Volntr; Key Club; Orch; Cl Off (R); Lit Mag (E); Formal Piano Lessons for 10 Years; Volunteer At Maryland Therapeutic Riding Center, Teach French to Elementary Students; Pediatrics-Surgeon / Neonatologist; Obstetrics / Gynecologist; Dartmouth College; U of Virginia

STRAUSBAUGH, DANIEL A; NEW WINDSOR, MD; SOUTH CARROLL HS; (JR); Hi Hnr Roll; Hnr Roll; Nat Hon Sy; Nat Ldrshp Svc; Otst Ac Ach Awd; Yth Ldrshp Prog; Comm Volntr; Peer Tut/Med; Chrch Yth Grp; Dbte Team; Emplmnt; HO'Br Yth Ldrshp; Key Club; Off Aide; Sci Clb; Tech Clb; Skiing; Sccr (VJ); Track (V); Stu Cncl (S); Black Belt-Karate

STUMP, STEVEN R; ANNAPOLIS, MD; BROADNECK HS; (SO); Hnr Roll; Perf Att; Ftball (J); Lcrsse (J); Wrstlg (V L); Criminal Justice; Molecular Genetics; Mount St. Mary's U MD; North Georgia U

STURGEON, BRIAN; LUTHERVILLE TIMONIUM, MD; DULANEY HS; (JR); Hi Hnr Roll; Hnr Roll; Comm Volntr; Peer Tut/Med; Mus Clb; Photog; SADD; Bnd; Put Out 4 CD's with My Band; Out Sold the House Ticket Sales at Reder Theatre; Business Administration; Music; Loyola College; U of Maryland

SUMMERLIN, AMBER; BOWIE, MD; ELEANOR ROOSEVELT HS; (SR); Hnr Roll; Sci Fairs; Chrch Yth Grp; Emplmnt; Scouts; Tchrs Aide; Dnce; PPSqd (V L); Honorable Mention-Science Fair; Political Science/Government; North Park U; U of Maryland College Park

SWARINGEN, ERIKA; TEMPLE HILLS, MD; JERICHO CHRISTIAN AC; (SR); Hnr Roll; Nat Ldrshp Svc; Sci Fairs; USAA; WWAHSS; Dbte Team; Emplmnt; Sci Clb; International Clb; SP/M/VS; Sftball (V); Vllyball (V); Stu Cncl (V); Sch Ppr (R); Yrbk (E, P); Biochemistry; Biophysics

SWEETNEY II, RENNARD P; SILVER SPRING, MD; SPRING BROOK HS; (SO); Hnr Roll; Nat Hon Sy; WWAHSS; Comm Volntr; Chrch Yth Grp; Emplmnt; ROTC; Practice Law; Harvard; Yale

TABOR, SHALAI; WALDORF, MD; THOMAS STONE HS; (JR); Hnr Roll; MVP; Otst Ac Ach Awd; Emplmnt; Chrldg (V L); Sftball (V L); All Conference, All County, All Southern; MD Atlantic Conference, All So MD Extra; Photography-Criminal Investigations; U of Maryland: U of Delaware; U of Maryland Baltimore County

TAFT, ROB; PASADENA, MD; CHESAPEAKE HS; (SO); Hnr Roll; Pres Ac Ftns Aw; German Clb; Bnd; Ftball (JC); Lcrsse (J); Track (V C); Sophomore Scholars; Computer Programming; Game Design; Virginia Tech; Maryland U

TALBERT, ASHLEYIGH; UPPER MARLBORO, MD; ELIZABETH SETON HS; (SO); Ctznshp Aw; Hnr Roll; Pres Ac Ftns Aw; Salutrn; Sci Fairs; Yth Ldrshp Prog; Peer Tut/Med; ArtClub; Chrch Yth Grp; Drma Clb; Pep Squd; Ch Chr; Dnce; SP/M/VS; PPSqd; Stu Cncl (P); CR (P); Lit Mag (E); Sch Ppr (E); History; Performing Arts; Maryland U, College Park; Georgetown U, DC

TALLEY, KATRINA D; BOWIE, MD; BOWIE HS; (SR); Hi Hnr Roll; Hnr Roll; MVP; St of Mnth; Comm Volntr; Pep Squd; Tchrs Aide; Ch Chr; Pianist; Step Team; Business Management; Sociology; Bowie State; Trinity

TARPLEY, CHRISTINA; GERMANTOWN, MD; NORTHWEST HS; (JR); Ctznshp Aw; Hnr Roll; Otst Ac Ach Awd; St of Mnth; WWAHSS; Chrch Yth Grp; Key Club; Scouts; Bskball (JC); Ftball (V); Track (J); Varsity Football Manager (State Champ); Varsity Basketball Manager; Communication TV/Radio Broadcast; Teacher Education; Frostburg State U; North Carolina A & T U

TAYLOR, BROOKE; WILLIAMSPORT, MD; WILLIAMSPORT AREA HS; (SR); Hi Hnr Roll; Hnr Roll; Emplmnt; 2 Yrs First MOD Representative (SGA); Worked All High School Career; Registered Nurse; Licensed Practical Nurse; Hagerstown Community College

Taylor, Brooke
Williamsport Area HS
Williamsport, MD

Stevens, Scott A
North Hagerstown HS
Hagerstown, MD

Snowden, Diamond T K
Baltimore City College HS
Baltimore, MD

Smith, Matthew
South Hagerstown HS
Hagerstown, MD

Smith, Lisa
Overlea HS
Essex, MD

Smith, Ahkeem R
Duval HS
Upper Marlboro, MD

Smith, Lauren
Elizabeth Seton HS
Clinton, MD

Smith, Riva-Niger
Oxon Hill HS
Oxon Hill, MD

Snyder, Shannon
Bowie, MD

Taft, Rob
Chesapeake HS
Pasadena, MD

Talley, Katrina D
Bowie HS
Bowie, MD

TAYLOR, ERIKA N; STREET, MD; HARTFORD TECH; (SO); 4H Awd; Hnr Roll; Perf Att; Ntl FFA; Scouts; Lcrsse (JC); Pony Club-C2 Rating; Vet Tech; Biology; Virginia Technical; Texas A & M U

TAYLOR, JAMIE L; CHESTERTOWN, MD; KENT CTY HS; (JR); Hnr Roll; Nat Hon Sy; St Schl; Emplmnt; Scouts; Sccr (VJCL); Swmg (V L); Pediatrician (MD); Biology; Duke U; U of Maryland

TAYLOR, WAYNE; MONTGOMERY VILLAGE, MD; TAKOMA AC; (JR); Hi Hnr Roll; Hnr Roll; Nat Hon Sy; St of Mnth; WWAHSS; Comm Volntr; Chrch Yth Grp; Emplmnt; Prom Com; Vsity Clb; Ch Chr; Drm Mjr; Bskball (V); CR (R); Bio Medical; Sport Therapist; Oakwood College; Cornell U

TAYLOR, YOTASHIA Y; HYATTSVILLE, MD; CHARLES HERBERT FLOWERS HS; (JR); Hi Hnr Roll; Hnr Roll; Nat Hon Sy; St of Mnth; Yth Ldrshp Prog; Comm Volntr; Peer Tut/Med; Red Cr Aide; Chrch Yth Grp; Drma Clb; Emplmnt; Off Aide; Prom Com; ROTC; SADD; Tchrs Aide; Ch Chr; Dnce; SP/M/VS; CR (T); Completed the Paxen Group, Inc Program; Triple Crown Winner for High School Assessment Test; Business Management; Culinary and Dance; Howard U; Florida A & M

TAYLOR JR, TRAVIS F; EDGEWOOD, MD; JOPPATOWNE HS; (JR); Hnr Roll; Perf Att; Comm Volntr; 4-H; Chrch Yth Grp; Bnd; Orch; Pep Bnd; SP/M/VS; Bskball (J); Ftball (J); Wt Lftg (J)

TEEGARDIN, DENNIS; BERLIN, MD; STEPHEN DECATUR HS; (FR); Hnr Roll; Perf Att; Comm Volntr; Peer Tut/Med; Scholastic Achievement Award; S.T.A.R. Award; Lost Election Close - 2nd Place for President Politics-U.S. Senate, Local Official; Political Science; Georgetown U

THACKER, TAMBRIA; DUNDALK, MD; DUNDALK HS; (FR); Hnr Roll; Comm Volntr; Cl Off (S); Vice President of Step Team; A Member of Step Team; Business Management; U of Maryland

THOMAS, CHANTIL P; TAKOMA PARK, MD; MONTGOMERY BLAIR HS; Ctznshp Aw; Hnr Roll; Sci Fairs; St of Mnth; WWAHSS; Comm Volntr; Peer Tut/Med; DARE; Prom Com; Sci Clb; Svce Clb; Tchrs Aide; Pep Bnd; SP/M/VS; Chrldg (V); Skiing (V); CR (R); Yrbk (E); Mass Communication; Broadcast Journalism; Howard U; Winston-Salem State U

THOMAS, DICHONNE; BALTIMORE, MD; FRANCIS M WOOD ALT HS; (SR); Hnr Roll; Perf Att; CARE; Hosp Aide; Mod UN; Mus Clb; Prom Com; Dnce; Mch Bnd; Mar Art (C); PPSqd (C); Pediatrician; Nursing; Morgan State U; Rutgers U

THOMAS, EMMA K; JARRETTSVILLE, MD; BALTIMORE LUTHERAN HS; (JR); Nat Hon Sy; Comm Volntr; Peer Tut/Med; Chrch Yth Grp; FCA; P to P St Amb Prg; Prom Com; SADD; Tchrs Aide; SP/M/VS; Bskball (JC); Fld Hky (V); Cl Off (V); Leader of Crisis Pregnancy Center Project; Ran 1/2 Marathon; DCE-Cross Cultural Studies; Concordia U

THOMAS, KIEARA; CATONSVILLE, MD; WOODLAWN HS; (JR); Hnr Roll; Nat Hon Sy; Peer Tut/Med; Emplmnt; Prom Com; Tchrs Aide; Cr Ctry (V); Track (V L); Cl Off (V); AVID Program; Steps Program; Math; Business; U of Miami; U of Tampa

THOMAS, LOGAN; FROSTBURG, MD; BEALL HS; (JR); Hi Hnr Roll; Hnr Roll; MVP; Nat Hon Sy; Otst Ac Ach Awd; St of Mnth; Comm Volntr; Peer Tut/Med; Emplmnt; Svce Clb; Bsball (CL); Ftball (CL); Engineering; Psychology; United States Naval Academy; U of Notre Dame

THOMAS, MEG; SYKESVILLE, MD; CENTURY HS; (JR); Hi Hnr Roll; Nat Hon Sy; Otst Ac Ach Awd; WWAHSS; Peer Tut/Med; Bnd; Cr Ctry (V L); Sccr (J); Track (V L); POND - Volunteer Group; York College

THOMAS, TRAYANA; RANDALLSTOWN, MD; RANDALLSTOWN HS; (SO); Hnr Roll; Sci Fairs; St of Mnth; Comm Volntr; Chrch Yth Grp; Dbte Team; Emplmnt; FBLA; SADD; Tchrs Aide; Bnd; Ch Chr; SP/M/VS; Chrldg (J); Sccr (J); Cl Off (R); CR (R); Business Owner; Entrepreneur; Temple U; Clarke U

THOMPSON, ALEXANDER S; WHITE MARSH, MD; PERRY HALL HS; (SR); Hnr Roll; Nat Hon Sy; Emplmnt; Quill & Scroll; Quiz Bowl; Track (VJ); Stu Cncl (R); Yrbk (E, R, P); Top 5% of Class (562 People); Architectural Engineering; Drexel U

THOMPSON, ASHLEY; BALTIMORE, MD; PAUL L DUNBAR HS 414; (FR); Ctznshp Aw; Hnr Roll; Otst Ac Ach Awd; Perf Att; DARE; Bnd; Track (V); Track and Field-Shot Put; Obstetrics; Veterinary Medicine; JHU; Towson U

THOMPSON, CHRISTOPHER; MECHANICSVLLE, MD; CHOPTICAN HS; (SO); Hnr Roll; Nat Hon Sy; DARE; Lcrsse (VJ); Sccr (J); Engineering; Aviation; Syracuse U; College of Southern Maryland

THOMPSON, IMANI; UPPER MARLBORO, MD; DUKE ELLINGTON HS; (FR); Hnr Roll; Otst Ac Ach Awd; Sci Fairs; Comm Volntr; Chrch Yth Grp; Emplmnt; Dnce; SP/M/VS; Chrldg; Stu Cncl (S); 1st Place Science Fair (2004); 1st Place Church Talent Show (2005); Professional Dancer; Lawyer; Howard U; Duke U

THORNTON, SARAH; BOWIE, MD; BOWIE HS; (SO); F Lan Hn Soc; Hi Hnr Roll; Hnr Roll; Nat Hon Sy; Pres Sch; St of Mnth; Yth Ldrshp Prog; Comm Volntr; Chrch Yth Grp; DARE; Emplmnt; Mod UN; Tchrs Aide; Spanish Clb; Bnd; Dnce; Sccr (J); Tennis (V); Cl Off (P); Stu Cncl (P); CR (P); Graduation Committee; U of Maryland Biomedical Jumpstart Program; Pediatric Physical Therapy; Hospital Nursing; U of Maryland; Temple U

TIAN, YUAN; COLUMBIA, MD; WILDE LAKE HS; (JR); Foreign Relations; Teaching (Mathematics, Science, Philosophy); Johns Hopkins U; U of Maryland College Park

TIBBS, SHELBY J; UPPER MARLBORO, MD; CHARLES HERBERT FLOWERS HS; (JR); Hnr Roll; Pres Sch; Sci Fairs; WWAHSS; Comm Volntr; Peer Tut/Med; ArtClub; Chrch Yth Grp; DARE; Quiz Bowl; ROTC; Schol Bwl; Drl Tm; CR (P); Lit Mag (R); Sch Ppr (R, P); Cadet of the Quarter - ROTC; Kitty Hawk Honor Society; Political Science; Zoology; La Salle U; York College

TINNER, NAISHA A; UPPER MARLBORO, MD; LARGO HS; (SR); Ctznshp Aw; Hnr Roll; Otst Ac Ach Awd; St of Mnth; Comm Volntr; DARE; Key Club; Tchrs Aide; Spanish Clb; Received Governor's Award for Outstanding Academic Achievement; Psychology; Lawyer; P C Community College; Bowie State U

TINSLEY, LEANNE M; MECHANICSVLLE, MD; CHOPTICAN HS; (FR); Nat Hon Sy; Otst Ac Ach Awd; Perf Att; Pres Ac Ftns Aw; Pres Sch; St Schl; St of Mnth; Comm Volntr; Chrch Yth Grp; Member of Scholars Program; Student of the Month; Fashion; Fashion Magazine Editor; California

TODD, CEDRIC A; PARKVILLE, MD; BALTIMORE SCH FOR THE ARTS; (SO); Hi Hnr Roll; Hnr Roll; MVP; Nat Hon Sy; Perf Att; WWAHSS; Peer Tut/Med; Chrch Yth Grp; Bnd; Ch Chr; Jzz Bnd; SP/M/VS; Theatre; New York U; Juilliard

TOGBA, ALEXANDER; GWYNN OAK, MD; WOODLAWN HS; (SO); Hnr Roll; Nat Hon Sy; Perf Att; Comm Volntr; ArtClub; DARE; Sccr (V)

TOLSON, DATALLION; UPPER MARLBORO, MD; OXON HILL HS; (FR); Hnr Roll; Pres Ac Ftns Aw; Bskball; Ftball; Engineering; Business; Auburn U; U of Miami

TOOMBS, TAYLOR; LEONARDTOWN, MD; LEONARDTOWN HS; (JR); Hi Hnr Roll; MVP; Nat Hon Sy; Chrch Yth Grp; Prom Com; Scouts; Cr Ctry (V); Sccr (V); Adv Cncl (P); Cl Off (P); Eagle Scout; International Business; Italian; Naval Academy; Eckerd College

TRACEY, ADRIENNE; SMITHSBURG, MD; SMITHSBURG HS; (SO); Ctznshp Aw; Hi Hnr Roll; Hnr Roll; Perf Att; WWAHSS; Chrch Yth Grp; Photog; Latin Clb; Bnd; Mch Bnd; Elementary Education; Early Childhood Education; Frostburg State U; Gettysburg College

TRACEY II, DAVID; HAGERSTOWN, MD; SOUTH HS; (SR); Hnr Roll; Key Club; Off Aide; Stu Cncl (R); Yrbk (P); Massage Therapy; Hagerstown Community College

TRAFTON, KATESSA A; OWINGS MILLS, MD; WESTERN TECH HS; (SR); Hnr Roll; Perf Att; Comm Volntr; Tchrs Aide; Psychology; College of Notre Dame

TRAN, CYNTHIA; HYATTSVILLE, MD; ELEANOR ROOSEVELT HS; (JR); Ctznshp Aw; F Lan Hn Soc; Hi Hnr Roll; Nat Hon Sy; Perf Att; Sci Fairs; WWAHSS; Peer Tut/Med; DARE; Tchrs Aide; Vsity Clb; Tennis (V); CR (R); Pre-Medicine; Chemistry; U of Pennsylvania; U of Maryland College Park

TRAVERS, QUEEN; CLINTON, MD; CENTRAL SR HS; (SO); Hi Hnr Roll; Hnr Roll; Comm Volntr; SP/M/VS; Sccr (V); Member of the Emporer Programs Girl's Advisory Board; Culinary Arts; Business Management; Johnson and Wales U; The Art Institute of New York City

TRUDY, RONNETTA; SILVER SPRING, MD; (FR); Hnr Roll; Nat Mrt Sch Recip; Comm Volntr; Key Club; Mus Clb; Ch Chr; Dnce; Sftball (L); Doctors; Harvard; Howard U

TSAOI, DERICK; COLUMBIA, MD; WILDE LAKE HS; (FR); Hnr Roll; Otst Ac Ach Awd; Hab For Humty Volntr; Emplmnt; Mth Clb/Tm; Orch; Tennis (J); It's Academic; Law; Business; Harvard; Yale

TSAOI, JESSICA; COLUMBIA, MD; WILDE LAKE HS; (JR); Hnr Roll; Nat Hon Sy; Perf Att; Hab For Humty Volntr; Emplmnt; Mth Clb/Tm; Dnce; Orch; SP/M/VS; Tennis (V); Stu Cncl (R); National Honor Society Presidential Candidate; Senior Dance Company Treasurer; Biochemistry; Bioengineering; U of Maryland College Park; U of California Los Angeles

TUCKER, ANTHONY; BURTONSVILLE, MD; PAINT BRANCH HS; (FR); Hnr Roll; Sci Fairs; Peer Tut/Med; Chrch Yth Grp; DARE; Off Aide; Sci Clb; CR (V); Sch Ppr (R); Duke U; New York U

TURAY, ACHMED; ACCOKEEK, MD; OXON HILL HS; (FR); Hnr Roll; Otst Ac Ach Awd; Hosp Aide; Chrch Yth Grp; Bnd; Jzz Bnd; Mar Art

TURNER, AISHA; ABINGDON, MD; JOHN CARROLL SCH; (SR); F Lan Hn Soc; Hi Hnr Roll; Hnr Roll; Nat Hon Sy; WWAHSS; Comm Volntr; Emplmnt; Quill & Scroll; Svce Clb; Spanish Clb; Lit Mag (E); Sch Ppr (E); National Achievement Finalist; Judith Resnick Math/Science Award; Civil Engineering; Public Policy; Duke U

TURNER, MEGAN C; UPPER MARLBORO, MD; CHARLES HERBERT FLOWERS HS; (SR); Hnr Roll; WWAHSS; Comm Volntr; Peer Tut/Med; Chrch Yth Grp; Prom Com; Tchrs Aide; Flg Crps; Business Administration & Management; Virginia Commonwealth U

TURNER, SHARNIESHA; BALTIMORE, MD; BALTIMORE POLY TECH INST 403; (SO); Hnr Roll; Otst Ac Ach Awd; Peer Tut/Med; SP/M/VS; Architectural Design; Fashion Design; Morgan State U

TYLER, KYRA N; GLENN DALE, MD; BOWIE HS; (JR); Hi Hnr Roll; Hnr Roll; Nat Ldrshp Svc; Sci Fairs; St of Mnth; WWAHSS; DARE; Emplmnt; FTA; NYLC; Off Aide; Prom Com; Vsity Clb; Orch; Cr Ctry (V); Ftball; PP Ftbl (V); Track (VJCL); Cl Off (T); Stu Cncl (T, R); Athletic Honor Roll; Business / Marketing; Entrepreneur; Howard U; Florida A & M U

TYSON, NAKEA; CLINTON, MD; GWYNN PARK HS; (SO); Hi Hnr Roll; Nat Mrt Fin; Otst Ac Ach Awd; Perf Att; Pres Sch; Sci Fairs; St of Mnth; Comm Volntr; Emplmnt; FTA; Pep Squd; Quiz Bowl; Scouts; Tech Clb; Chr; Dnce; SP/M/VS; PPSqd (V); CR (R); Member of National Achievers Society of Greater Washington DC Urban League; Meteorology; News Broadcast; Clark-Atlanta U; Florida State U

ULLAH, ARIF; POTOMAC, MD; RICHARD MONTGOMERY HS; (JR); Hnr Roll; DARE; Bskball; Track; Electrical Engineering; Network Security; U of Delaware; U of Maryland

UMOH, EDIDIONG; TOWSON, MD; TOWSON HS; (SO); F Lan Hn Soc; Hnr Roll; Nat Hon Sy; Yth Ldrshp Prog; Comm Volntr; Chrch Yth Grp; Key Club; Spanish Clb; Orch; Bskball (J); Vllyball (J); Sch Ppr (R); Semifinalist for Quest Scholars; Awarded a Superior Title in a Fine Arts; Medicine; Geonomics; Harvard U; Johns Hopkins U

URSIC, MICHAEL; LUSBY, MD; (JR); Hnr Roll; Nat Hon Sy; Perf Att; Sci Fairs; St of Mnth; Comm Volntr; Peer Tut/Med; Chess; Chrch Yth Grp; DARE; Emplmnt; FCA; FBLA; Scouts; Chr; Lcrsse (V L); Swmg (V CL); Stu Cncl (R); CR (R); Coach's Award Swimming All SMAC 1st Team Swimming; Eagle Scout Award; Psychology; History/Political Science; Loyola College Baltimore, Md.; Providence College Providence, R.I

URUBSHUROW, DELGHI; CHEVY CHASE, MD; BETHESDA-CHEVY CHASE HS; (JR); Hnr Roll; MVP; Nat Hon Sy; WWAHSS; ArtClub; Spanish Clb; Swmg (V L); High School All-American Swimmer; Columbia U

VAGENOS, MICHAEL D; DUNDALK, MD; PATAPSCO HS; (JR); Hi Hnr Roll; Hnr Roll; WWAHSS; Comm Volntr; Bnd; Lcrsse (V L); PP Ftbl (V); Wrstlg (J); Mock Trial; Forensic Psychology; Law; Johns Hopkins U

VALCIN, MONIQUE; CLINTON, MD; SURRATTSVILLE HS; (SO); Hnr Roll; WWAHSS; Bnd; Mch Bnd; Bskball (V); Honor Roll; Section Leader; Sound Engineer; Biotechnology Engineer; U of Maryland; Morgan State College

VALENTINE, GREGORY; BALTIMORE, MD; WOODLAWN HS; (SO); Hnr Roll; MVP; Nat Hon Sy; Otst Ac Ach Awd; Perf Att; St of Mnth; Comm Volntr; Peer Tut/Med; Bskball (J); Ftball (V); Business Management; Computer Science; Florida State U; Wake Forest U

VALENTINE, JONTE'; ODENTON, MD; ARUNDEL HS; (SO); Hnr Roll; Pres Sch; Peer Tut/Med; Emplmnt; P to P St Amb Prg; Photog; Maryland State Finalist in National American Miss Jr Teen Pageant; Participated in a One-Day Student Leadership Institute; Broadcast Communications; Journalism; Spelman College; Clarke Atlanta U

VANASDALAN, LINDSAY C; CATONSVILLE, MD; SETON KEOUGH HS; (FR); All Am Sch; Hnr Roll; Nat Hon Sy; Nat Sci Aw; USAA; Comm Volntr; Drma Clb; Chr; Dnce; SP/M/VS; Summer on Stage Theatre Intensive; Concert Chair; Photography/Journalism; Performing Arts; Johns Hopkins U; Loyola College

VARGAS-LICONA, WALTER M; GLEN BURNIE, MD; GLEN BURNIE HS; (FR); Ctznshp Aw; Hi Hnr Roll; Otst Ac Ach Awd; WWAHSS; ROTC; Engineering; Aircraft Maintenance; Maryland U

VENERO, STEPHANY; SILVER SPRING, MD; JAMES H BLAKE HS; (SO); Ctznshp Aw; Hi Hnr Roll; Hnr Roll; Otst Ac Ach Awd; Perf Att; Sci Fairs; Yth Ldrshp Prog; Comm Volntr; Peer Tut/Med; Chrch Yth Grp; Cmptr Clb; Scouts; Tchrs Aide; Spanish Clb; Chr; Ch Chr; Sccr (J/C); CR (V); Attended the National Youth Leadership Forum on Medicine in Washington DC / Georgetown U; Won Class Geography Bee; Architecture and Major in Interior Design; Geriatric Major in Nutrition; University of Maryland; University of Hawaii

Venero, Stephany
James H Blake HS
Silver Spring, MD

Turner, Megan C
Charles Herbert Flowers HS
Upper Marlboro, MD

Tolson, Datallion
Oxon Hill HS
Upper Marlboro, MD

Tibbs, Shelby J
Charles Herbert Flowers HS
Upper Marlboro, MD

Thornton, Sarah
Bowie HS
Bowie, MD

Thomas, Chantil P
Montgomery Blair HS
Takoma Park, MD

Thompson, Imani
Duke Ellington HS
Upper Marlboro, MD

Togba, Alexander
Woodlawn HS
Gwynn Oak, MD

Trudy, Ronnetta
Silver Spring, MD

Tyson, Nakea
Gwynn Park HS
Clinton, MD

Vanasdalan, Lindsay C
Seton Keough HS
Catonsville, MD

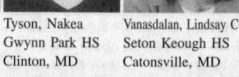

VICHAYAKUL, VANESSA; BROOKEVILLE, MD; SHERWOOD HS; (SR); F Lan Hn Soc; Hnr Roll; St of Mnth; Chrch Yth Grp; Dbte Team; Mod UN; Scouts; Tech Clb; French Clb; Stg Cre; Stu Cncl (V); Sch Ppr (E); Yrbk (R); Commendation for Contribution to International Poetry; Garden International School Honor Student; Freelance Writer; Private Business; U of Maryland; Harvard U

VOSSLER, JESSICA; MOUNT AIRY, MD; SOUTH CARROLL HS; (FR); Hi Hnr Roll; Otst Ac Ach Awd; WWAHSS; Comm Volntr; Chrch Yth Grp; Key Club; Firehouse Volunteer (New Market); PhD; Psychiatry; New York U; Maryland U

VU, THO; BOWIE, MD; BOWIE HS; (JR)

WAGNER, CHRISTOPHER; MOUNT AIRY, MD; SOUTH CARROLL HS; (FR); Hi Hnr Roll; MVP; Comm Volntr; Civil Air Pat; Key Club; Ch Chr; Track (V); Physical Training; Engineering; Rensselaer Polytechnic Institute; Slippery Rock U

WAGNER, JONATHAN M; MOUNT AIRY, MD; SOUTH CARROLL HS; (FR); Hi Hnr Roll; Pres Ac Ftns Aw; WWAHSS; Comm Volntr; Key Club; Chr; Journalism; Sports Broadcasting/Journalism

WALKER, LYDIA M; PIKESVILLE, MD; (JR); Hnr Roll; Pres Ac Ftns Aw; Peer Tut/Med; Chrch Yth Grp; Lib Aide; Photog; Bnd; Chr; Ch Chr; Drl Tm; Yrbk (E); Counselor (School or Teenage); Flight Attendant; Andrews U; Southern Adventist U

WALKER, MAYA; LAUREL, MD; ST VINCENT PALLOTTI HS; (FR); Hnr Roll; Comm Volntr; Chrch Yth Grp; Drma Clb; FCA; Scouts; Tchrs Aide; Bskball (J); Ice Hky (J); Stu Cncl (R); CR (P); I Have Been in Honors Chorus; Qualified for the Johns Hopkins Program; Law/Attorney; Child Development; Hampton; Spelman

WALLACE, LANCE J; BOWIE, MD; BOWIE HS; (SO); Hnr Roll; Perf Att; Comm Volntr; Peer Tut/Med; Spec Olymp Vol; Bnd; Jzz Bnd; Mch Bnd; Cr Ctry (J); Ftball (J); Track (J); Engineering; Entrepreneur; U of Maryland College Park; Howard U

WALLACE JR, ERVIN; POCOMOKE CITY, MD; POCOMOKE HS; (JR); Hnr Roll; St of Mnth; ROTC; Bnd; Jzz Bnd; Mch Bnd; Pep Bnd; National Band Award; Marine Corps JROTC; Political Science; Music; U of Maryland; Syracuse U

WALLENMEYER, JACLYN M S; ROCKVILLE, MD; ROCKVILLE HS; (SR); Hnr Roll; Kwnis Aw; MVP; Nat Hon Sy; Otst Ac Ach Awd; Pres Sch; Sci Fairs; St Schl; Valdctrian; WWAHSS; Comm Volntr; Peer Tut/Med; Chrch Yth Grp; Off Aide; Quill & Scroll; Svce Clb; Tchrs Aide; Tech Clb; Bnd; Ch Chr; Mch Bnd; Pep Bnd; Bskball (V CL); Sch Ppr (E); Gatorade Player of the Year Scholarship; Mark Curtis Humanities Award; Scientific & Medical Writing; Doctorate in Communications; Johns Hopkins U

WALTON, AISHA; RIVERDALE, MD; PARKDALE HS; (SO); Hnr Roll; Perf Att; Comm Volntr; Hosp Aide; Emplmnt; ROTC; Dnce; Bskball; Chrldg; Business Major; Pediatrician; Howard U; U of Maryland

WANG, CINDY; COCKYS HT VLY, MD; DULANEY HS; (SO); Hnr Roll; Nat Hon Sy; Otst Ac Ach Awd; Perf Att; WWAHSS; Comm Volntr; Peer Tut/Med; Biology Clb; Key Club; Mod UN; Orch; Bdmtn (V); Tennis (V); CR (R); Distinction Certificate from Johns Hopkins U - Center for Talented Youth; Biomedical Engineering; Pre-Med; Johns Hopkins U; Brown U

WANTZ, AUBREY E; ABINGDON, MD; JAMES RUN CHRISTIAN SCH; (FR); Nat Hon Sy; St of Mnth; Comm Volntr; Chrch Yth Grp; SADD; Ch Chr; Chrldg; Sccr; Cl Off (R); Sch Ppr (E); Yrbk (R, P); Nursing; Harford Community College

WARD, BEN; CROFTON, MD; ARUNDEL SR HS; (FR); Hnr Roll; MVP; Perf Att; Pres Ac Ftns Aw; Sci Fairs; St of Mnth; Comm Volntr; Chrch Yth Grp; DARE; Vsity Clb; Tennis (V); Archeology; Brigham Young U

WARD, MATT; WESTMINSTER, MD; CARROLL CHRISTIAN HS; (JR); Bsball (V); Bskball (V); Sccr (V); Conduct Honor Roll

WARE, FOLAMI; BALTIMORE, MD; PIKESVILLE SR HS; (JR); Hnr Roll; Yth Ldrshp Prog; Comm Volntr; Peer Tut/Med; Chrch Yth Grp; DARE; Jr Ach; NYLC; Scouts; SADD; Ch Chr; Being on Morning Announcement Team; Being in Minority Awareness; Pre-Law (Bachelor of Science); Law Degree; Syracuse U; Spelman College

WARNER, BENJAMIN; GAITHERSBURG, MD; COL ZADOK MAGRUDER HS; (FR); Hnr Roll; Otst Ac Ach Awd; St of Mnth; Peer Tut/Med; Vsity Clb; Bnd; Ch Chr; Mch Bnd; Pep Bnd; Bsball (J); Swmg (V L); County & State / Solo & Ensemble Festival Winner; Jesse Owens Athletic Award; Aeronautics / Aviation; Music; American U; Indiana U Purdue U Indiana

WARNER, JORDAN; GAITHERSBURG, MD; COL ZADOK MAGRUDER HS; (JR); Hnr Roll; Otst Ac Ach Awd; St of Mnth; Yth Ldrshp Prog; Peer Tut/Med; Emplmnt; Photog; Scouts; Vsity Clb; Ch Chr; Bskball (VJCL); Cl Off (S); Sch Ppr (R); Jesse Owens Athletic Award; African American Festival of Academic Excellence; Elementary Education; Journalism; American U; Emory U

WARNER, PAUL S; HUNTINGTOWN, MD; CALVERT HS; (SR); Ctznshp Aw; F Lan Hn Soc; Hi Hnr Roll; Hnr Roll; Nat Hon Sy; Perf Att; St Schl; USAA; WWAHSS; Chrch Yth Grp; Cmptr Clb; FCA; Schol Bwl; Scouts; Bnd; Swmg (V L); Sch Ppr (E); Urban Studies; Wheaton College Illinois

WARREN, ARIELLE; PIKESVILLE, MD; RANDALLSTOWN HS; (FR); Otst Ac Ach Awd; St of Mnth; Chrch Yth Grp; DARE; Drma Clb; Stg Cre; Yrbk (E); Acting; To Be an Actress

WASHINGTON, LAQUANDA; UPPER MARLBORO, MD; CHARLES HERBERT FLOWERS HS; (SO); Duke TS; Hnr Roll; Perf Att; St of Mnth; WWAHSS; Comm Volntr; Hab For Humty Volntr; Chrch Yth Grp; DARE; Off Aide; ROTC; Tchrs Aide; Spanish Clb; Chr; Drl Tm; Cl Off (R); Judge; Military Science; U Maryland; Penn State U

WASHINGTON, SHAMIKA K; BOWIE, MD; CHARLES HERBERT FLOWERS HS; (JR); Hi Hnr Roll; Hnr Roll; Otst Ac Ach Awd; Perf Att; Pres Sch; St of Mnth; Chrch Yth Grp; Prom Com; Vsity Clb; Chr; Chrldg (J); Gmnstcs (J); Track (V); Stu Cncl (R); CR (R); Most Likely to Succeed; Outstanding Music Award; Fashion Design; Business Administration; Fashion Institute of Design & Merchandising; Fashion Institute of Technology

WASKIEWICZ, KIMBERLY M; TANEYTOWN, MD; FRANCIS SCOTT KEY HS; (SR); 4H Awd; Hi Hnr Roll; Hnr Roll; WWAHSS; Comm Volntr; 4-H; ArtClub; Chrch Yth Grp; DARE; Emplmnt; Ntl FFA; Bnd; Clr Grd; Mch Bnd; Bskball; Sftball; Track (L); Graduate Culinary Program Tech Center; Middle School VP Award/2005 Vol. Award; Culinary Arts; Johnson & Wales-Accepted; Stratford U

WEDDLE, JANET; FREDERICK, MD; BRUNSWICK HS; (SR); Hnr Roll; Perf Att; Emplmnt; Off Aide; Photog; Scouts; SADD; Tchrs Aide; Sftball (J); Vllyball (J); National Honors Society; Marketing; Frederick Community College

WEEMS, SHARESE; PRINCE FREDERICK, MD; CALVERT HS; (FR); Hnr Roll; Red Cr Aide; The Gourmet Club; Nurse; Day Care

WEI, MINTING; GAITHERSBURG, MD; THOMAS S WOOTTON HS; (JR); Hi Hnr Roll; Hnr Roll; Perf Att; St of Mnth; WWAHSS; Comm Volntr; Hosp Aide; ArtClub; Key Club; Chinese Clb; Anime Club Treasurer/Secretary; Piano for 6 Years; Business; Biology; U of Maryland College Park; Georgetown U

WEIKLE, SHANNON E; BOWIE, MD; BOWIE HS; (JR); Hi Hnr Roll; Hnr Roll; MVP; Nat Hon Sy; Comm Volntr; Emplmnt; Mod UN; Prom Com; Vsity Clb; Lcrsse (V CL); Vllyball (VJCL); Stu Cncl (R); President Model UN; National Honor Society; Childhood Education; U of Maryland-College Park; Salisbury State

WEISS, BRIAN; SILVER SPRING, MD; SPRINGBROOK HS; (SR); Hnr Roll; Pres Ac Ftns Aw; WWAHSS; Comm Volntr; Quill & Scroll; Bsball (V L); Ftball (V L); Sccr (J); Sch Ppr (E, R, P); Yrbk (E, R, P); Black Belt in Martial Arts; 7 Years of Piano; Media Arts and Design

WELLS, COURTNI S; WALDORF, MD; WESTLAKE HS; (JR); Hnr Roll; Nat Hon Sy; Otst Ac Ach Awd; Scouts; Vsity Clb; Chrldg (V); Actor; Business; Albany State College; Georgia Southern U

WELLS, MATTHEW; WHALEYVILLE, MD; STEPHEN DECATUR HS; (FR); DARE; Auto Technician; NASCAR Technical Institute

WENG, JIA; CHEVY CHASE, MD; (JR); Hnr Roll; Nat Hon Sy; Sci Fairs; WWAHSS; Comm Volntr; Emplmnt; Mth Clb/Tm; Mus Clb; Quiz Bowl; Sci Clb; Bnd; Pep Bnd; SP/M/VS; Biology; Pre-Med; Johns Hopkins U; Northwestern U

WHITE, AARON; UPPER MARLBORO, MD; CHARLES HERBERT FLOWERS HS; (FR); Hi Hnr Roll; Hnr Roll; Perf Att; Comm Volntr; ROTC; Scouts; Cr Ctry (J); Eagle Scout; Architecture; Engineering; Florida A & M; Penn State U

WHITE, ASHLEY; FREDERICK, MD; WALKERSVILLE HS; (SO); Hi Hnr Roll; MVP; Otst Ac Ach Awd; WWAHSS; Comm Volntr; Bskball; Lcrsse (V L); Sccr (V L); Wt Lftg; Cl Off (S); USA Weight Lifting; Sports Medicine; Orthopedics; Duke; U of Virginia

WHITE, DEANNA M; FT WASHINGTON, MD; GRACE BRETHREN CHRISTIAN SCH; (JR); Hnr Roll; Sci Fairs; Comm Volntr; Peer Tut/Med; Chrch Yth Grp; Drma Clb; Emplmnt; Tchrs Aide; Bnd; Dnce; Flg Crps; Mch Bnd; Vllyball (J); Yrbk (E); Christmas Play Production Cast; Graphic Design; American Literature; Temple U; Pratt Institute

WHITE, MARIE ANTOINETTE; WALKERSVILLE, MD; WALKERSVILLE HS; (SO); Hnr Roll; Perf Att; Yth Ldrshp Prog; Comm Volntr; Peer Tut/Med; Dnce; Have Received Numerous Awards from Kappa Alpha Psi Fraternity for Grades; Masters in Health Care Management; Bachelor in Business Law; Mount St Mary's U; Maryland State U

WHITE, MYRA M; WESTOVER, MD; WASHINGTON HS; (JR); 4H Awd; Hnr Roll; Nat Stu Ath Day Aw; Comm Volntr; Peer Tut/Med; 4-H; DARE; Bskball (J); Sftball (V); Sch Ppr (R)

WHITFIELD, DOMINIQUE D; RANDALLSTOWN, MD; RANDALLSTOWN HS; (JR); Hi Hnr Roll; MVP; Otst Ac Ach Awd; St of Mnth; Peer Tut/Med; Photog; Tchrs Aide; Spanish Clb; PPSqd (V); Sftball (V); Business / Cosmetology; Corporate Lawyer; Atlanta State; Georgia Tech

WHYTE III, WILLIAM M; HAVRE DE GRACE, MD; ABERDEEN HS; (SR); Hi Hnr Roll; Hnr Roll; Nat Mrt Sch Recip; Comm Volntr; Bskball; Ftball (V); Biology; History; Hood College Frederick MD; McDaniel College

WICKLEIN, HANNAH; TOWSON, MD; TOWSON HS; (JR); F Lan Hn Soc; WWAHSS; Comm Volntr; Key Club; Spanish Clb; Bdmtn (V L); Honorable Mention-Jack London Writing Contest; Key Club President (04-05) Lieutenant Governor (05-06); Creative Writing; Ohio Northern U; Emerson U

WILBURN, JESSICA; BOWIE, MD; BOWIE HS; (JR); Hi Hnr Roll; Hnr Roll; Otst Ac Ach Awd; St of Mnth; WWAHSS; CR (R); National Society of High School Scholars; Community Sports / Softball & Volleyball; Mathematics; Mechanical Engineering; U of Maryland; U of North Carolina

WILLIAMS, ALYSSA M S; CLINTON, MD; GRACE BRETHREN CHRISTIAN SCH; (JR); Hi Hnr Roll; Nat Hon Sy; Sci Fairs; WWAHSS; Comm Volntr; Chrch Yth Grp; Emplmnt; Clb; Ch Chr; Dnce; SP/M/VS; Stg Cre; Cl Off (T); Stu Cncl (V); Distinguished Christian High School Student Award; President's Award for Educational Excellence; Business / BS Degree; Graduate Jeweler Gemologist Diploma; Grove City College

WILLIAMS, ASHLEY S; TEMPLE HILLS, MD; LARGO HS; (SO); Hnr Roll; MVP; Sci Fairs; Comm Volntr; Chr; Bskball (V); Ftball (V); Sftball (V); Vllyball (V); Lawyer; U of North Carolina

WILLIAMS, AUTREZZ; BROOKLYN, MD; SOUTHSIDE AC; (FR); Hnr Roll; Otst Ac Ach Awd; Perf Att; Comm Volntr; Bnd; Jzz Bnd; Mch Bnd; SP/M/VS; Bsball; Business and Account; Towson U

WILLIAMS, CHELSEA B; MARRIOTTSVILLE, MD; LIBERTY HS; (FR); Hnr Roll; MVP; Perf Att; Sci Fairs; St of Mnth; Yth Ldrshp Prog; Comm Volntr; Chrch Yth Grp; DARE; Drma Clb; Scouts; Lcrsse (J); Sccr (J); Track (V L); Adv Cncl (R); Cl Off; CR (R); Graphic Design; Lehigh U; Virginia Military Institute

WILLIAMS, KANEESHA D; WALDORF, MD; MC DONOUGH HS; MS; Ctznshp Aw; Hi Hnr Roll; Hnr Roll; Nat Sci Aw; Perf Att; Sci Fairs; St of Mnth; Comm Volntr; DARE; Orch; Cl Off (S); Kickball; Double Dutch League; Medical Lab Technician; Marketing; U of Michigan; Atlanta U

WILLIAMS, KATHERINE; COLUMBIA, MD; WILDE LAKE HS; (SO); Hi Hnr Roll; MVP; Sci Fairs; St of Mnth; Amnsty Intl; Comm Volntr; Hab For Humty Volntr; Chrch Yth Grp; Dbte Team; Mus Clb; Prom Com; Spch Team; French Clb; Orch; Cr Ctry (V L); Lcrsse (J); Track (V L); Stu Cncl (R); CR (R); State Medalist-Cross Country; Excellent Extemporaneous Speaker (Debate); Psychology; Pre-Medicine; Princeton; College of William Mary

WILLIAMS, KOLYAUN J; SALISBURY, MD; JAMES M BENNETT HS; (JR); Hnr Roll; Comm Volntr; Hab For Humty Volntr; Chrch Yth Grp; Chr; Bskball (J); Music; Engineering; Howard U; William Paterson U

WILLIAMS, LESA; ANDREWS AFB, MD; GRACE BRETHREN CHRISTIAN SCH; (JR); Hnr Roll; ArtClub; DARE; FCA; Prom Com; Ch Chr, Bskball (V L); Track (V); Vllyball (V); Award for Art (Highest Honor) Visual; National Art Competition (Scholarship); Surgical Dentistry; Culinary; U of Maryland

WILLIAMS, MATTHEW J; EDGEWOOD, MD; JOPPATOWNE HS; (JR); Hnr Roll; Nat Hon Sy; FBLA; Lttrmn Clb; Mus Clb; Vsity Clb; Bnd; Tennis (V CL); Architectural Engineering; Engineering Graphics; Temple U; Villanova U

WILLIAMS, TIFFANY; CRISFIELD, MD; CRISFIELD HS; (SR); WWAHSS; Comm Volntr; Chrch Yth Grp; Key Club; ROTC; Bnd; Dnce; Drm Mjr; Mch Bnd; Bskball (V); Chrldg (V); Pre-Med; Salisbury U; Temple U

WILLIAMSON, ANTHONY; GREENBELT, MD; KETTERING MS; (MS); Ctznshp Aw; Hi Hnr Roll; Hnr Roll; Otst Ac Ach Awd; Perf Att; Sci Fairs; St of Mnth; Comm Volntr; Chrch Yth Grp; Mus Clb; Chr; Ch Chr; Career in Animation; Career in Singing; Art Institute of Washington

WILLIS JR, MARCUS E; LANHAM, MD; ST VINCENT PALLOTTI HS; (FR); Hi Hnr Roll; Hnr Roll; MVP; Nat Hon Sy; Sci Fairs; Emplmnt; Bskball (JC); Ftball (V L); Track (L); Computer Engineering; U of Maryland; U of Miami

WILLOUGHBY, ALISHA C; DISTRICT HEIGHTS, MD; CENTRAL HS; (JR); Hnr Roll; MVP; Comm Volntr; 4-H; DARE; Dnce; Swmg (V C); Track; Student Service Learning Advisor; Education; Math; Florida A & M U; North Carolina A & T U

WILLS, NIYA M; SUITLAND, MD; FRIENDLY HS; (SO); Ctznshp Aw; Hi Hnr Roll; Hnr Roll; Otst Ac Ach Awd; Sci Fairs; Peer Tut/Med; FBLA; FTA; Mus Clb; ROTC; Bnd; Chr; Clr Grd; Mch Bnd; PPSqd (J); Music Performance/Production; Accounting; Morgan State U; Bethune Cookman College

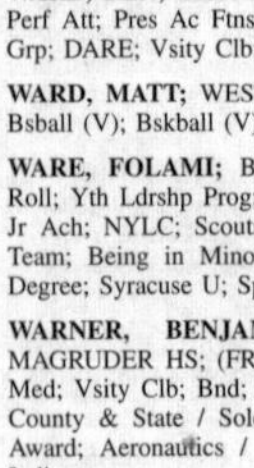
Williams, Kolyaun J
James M Bennett HS
Salisbury, MD

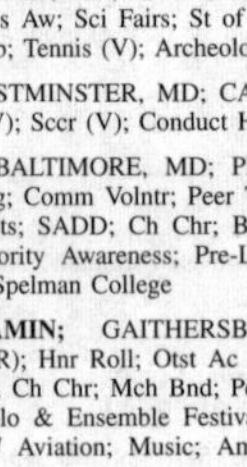
Whyte III, William M
Aberdeen HS
Havre De Grace, MD

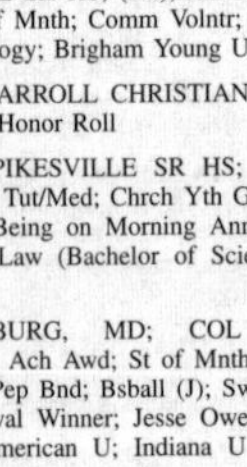
Ware, Folami
Pikesville SR HS
Baltimore, MD

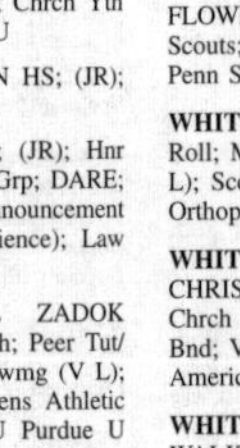
Wallace, Lance J
Bowie HS
Bowie, MD

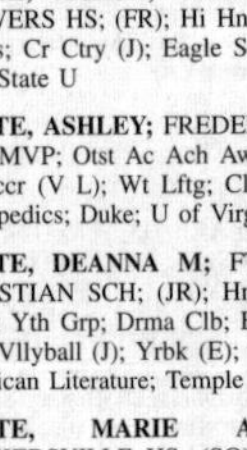
Walker, Maya
St Vincent Pallotti HS
Laurel, MD

National
Honor Roll
Spring 2005

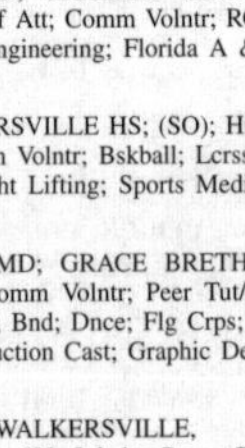
Vu, Tho
Bowie HS
Bowie, MD

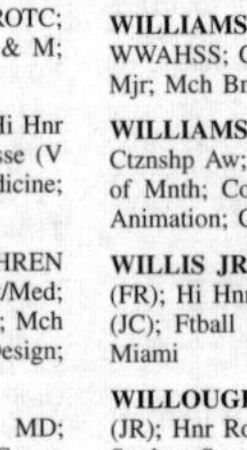
Wallenmeyer, Jaclyn M S
Rockville HS
Rockville, MD

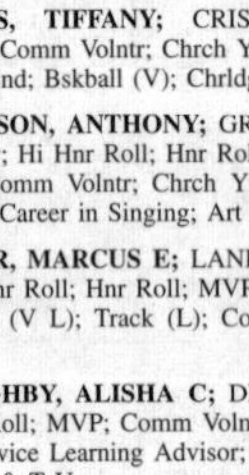
White, Aaron
Charles Herbert Flowers HS
Upper Marlboro, MD

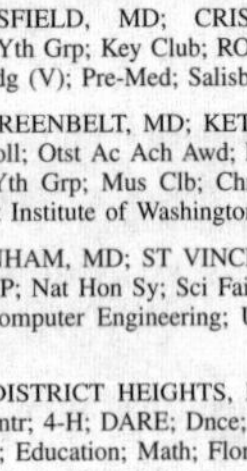
Williams, Chelsea B
Liberty HS
Marriottsville, MD

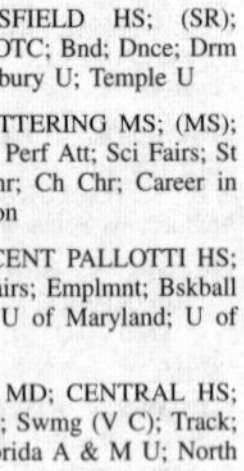
Williams, Kaneesha D
Mc Donough HS
Waldorf, MD

WILSON, CHRISTINA M; BOWIE, MD; BOWIE HS; (JR); Hnr Roll; WWAHSS; Comm Volntr; FBLA; Tchrs Aide; Dnce; Cl Off (R); Business Management; Interior / Fashion Design; Howard U; Hampton U

WILSON, DAMARAH; CAPITOL HEIGHTS, MD; FAIRMONT HEIGHTS HS; (SO); Hnr Roll; MVP; Perf Att; Emplmnt; Spanish Clb; Bskball (V); Cr Ctry (V); Track (V); Cl Off (V); CR (R); Spanish II Award; Lawyer; Bachelor's Degree in Science; Columbia University of Law; Duke U

WILSON, NNENA P; TEMPLE HILLS, MD; FRIENDLY HS; (SR); Hi Hnr Roll; Hnr Roll; Nat Hon Sy; Otst Ac Ach Awd; WWAHSS; Yth Ldrshp Prog; Comm Volntr; Cmptr Clb; Off Aide; Photog; Tchrs Aide; Yrbk; National Honor Society; Journalism; Communications; U of Maryland

WILSON, PAULETTE M; RANDALLSTOWN, MD; RANDALLSTOWN HS; (JR); Hnr Roll; ArtClub; Lit Mag (E, R); Yrbk (R, P); Member of the Student Government Association; Journalism; Communications; Towson U; Coppin State U

WILSON, PHILIP R; OXON HILL, MD; OXON HILL HS; (FR); Hnr Roll; Perf Att; Sci Fairs; Sci/Math Olympn; St of Mnth; Comm Volntr; Peer Tut/Med; Chrch Yth Grp; Emplmnt; Jr Ach; Mus Clb; Acpl Chr; Chr; Ch Chr; Marine Biology; Law; U of Maryland Eastern Shore; Virginia State U

WILSON, SEAN; BERLIN, MD; STEPHEN DECATUR HS; (FR); Ctznshp Aw; Hi Hnr Roll; Hnr Roll; Perf Att; St of Mnth; Comm Volntr; Peer Tut/Med; Chess; CR (R); Wexl; U of Maryland; Wor-Wic Community College

WIMBUSH, CHANTEL; DISTRICT HEIGHTS, MD; SUITLAND HS; (JR); Hnr Roll; Otst Ac Ach Awd; Perf Att; Peer Tut/Med; Pep Squd; Dnce; Chrldg (J); All-Star Cheerleader for Spirit Force; Accounting; Business/Finance; Strayer U

WINFIELD, ELIZABETH; POCOMOKE CITY, MD; POCOMOKE HS; (SR); Hi Hnr Roll; MVP; Nat Hon Sy; St of Mnth; WWAHSS; Chrch Yth Grp; P to P St Amb Prg; Prom Com; SADD; Dnce; SP/M/VS; Vllyball (V CL); Stu Cncl (S); Treasurer of NHS; Rotary 4-Way Test Winner - 2004; Major in Biology; Career in Forensics; Towson U; Frostburg U, Loyola College

WINROW, TAYLOR-SYMONE'; OWINGS MILLS, MD; NEW TOWN HS; (SO); Hnr Roll; WWAHSS; Peer Tut/Med; Red Cr Aide; Drma Clb; NYLC; Photog; Prom Com; Chr; Dnce; SP/M/VS; Chrldg (VJ); Gmnstcs (J); Hsbk Rdg (J); Ice Sktg (V C); Tennis (V); Track (V); Vllyball (V); Cl Off (R); Yrbk (P); Dance Company; Veterinary Medicine; Fashion Design; Spelman College; Duke U

WISNER, HELLEN; FREDERICK, MD; FREDERICK HS; (SR); Hnr Roll; Emplmnt; Off Aide; Tchrs Aide; Cr Ctry (J); Lcrsse (V); Track (J); Future Educators of America Club; Multicultural Experience Club; Criminal Justice; Forensic Science; Mount Saint Mary's College; Frederick Community College

WOLFE, BEN; COCKEYSVILLE, MD; DULANEY HS; (FR); Hnr Roll; Pres Ac Ftns Aw; Peer Tut/Med; BPA; Chess; Emplmnt; Bnd; Mch Bnd; Cr Ctry (JC); Track (J); CR (R); Business; Architecture; Princeton

WOLFGANG, ANGIE; HUNTINGTON, MD; CALVERT HS; (SR); F Lan Hn Soc; Hi Hnr Roll; Nat Hon Sy; Nat Mrt LOC; Perf Att; Pres Sch; St Schl; USAA; Valdctrian; WWAHSS; Comm Volntr; Spec Olymp Vol; AL Aux Girls; Chrch Yth Grp; Emplmnt; FCA; Quiz Bowl; Svce Clb; Bnd; Drm Mjr; Jzz Bnd; Mch Bnd; Tennis (V C); Track (V L); President / Treasurer of Tri-M Honor Society; Team Captain of the Academic Team - Quiz Bowl; Physics; Astronomy; Cornell U

WOLFINGER, ASHLEY; HAGERSTOWN, MD; SMITHSBURG HS; (SO); WWAHSS; Emplmnt; STARS Award for Academic Achievement; Maryland; HCC

WONG, AARON; BURTONSVILLE, MD; JAMES H BLAKE HS; (FR); Hnr Roll; Perf Att; 4-H; DARE; Dbte Team; Tchrs Aide; Bsball (J); CR (R); Kung Fu - Black Belt / Not with School; Soccer; Lawyer; U of Maryland; College of William and Mary

WONGUS, PIERRE; JOPPA, MD; JOPPATOWNE HS; (JR); Hnr Roll; MVP; Perf Att; St of Mnth; Chrch Yth Grp; DARE; Bsball (J); Track (V)

WOOD, STEVEN; PRINCE FREDERICK, MD; CALVERT HS; (MS); Hi Hnr Roll; Hnr Roll; Chrch Yth Grp; Outdrs Clb; ROTC; ROTC; Rec Soccer; Doctor; U of Maryland

WOODARD, FAITH; CLINTON, MD; SURRATTSVILLE HS; (FR); Ctznshp Aw; Hnr Roll; MVP; Perf Att; Sci Fairs; St of Mnth; WWAHSS; CARE; Comm Volntr; Peer Tut/Med; ArtClub; Chrch Yth Grp; ROTC; P St Chr; Clr Grd; Drl Tm; Bskball (J); Who's Who High School; Nestle's Very Best in Youth; Architecture; Engineering; Howard U; Duke U

WOODARD, TIMEKA M; BALTIMORE, MD; MERGENTHALER VOC TECH; (JR); Scouts; Chr; Entrepreneurship; Baltimore International College

WOODWORTH, JAMES D; ELKTON, MD; NORTH EAST HS; (FR); Hnr Roll; Perf Att; Bnd; CTY-Johns Hopkins; Psychology

WOOLEN, MICHELE; CAPITOL HEIGHTS, MD; CENTRAL HS; (JR); Hnr Roll; Educational Talent Search Program; Sophisticated Ladies Club; Education; Psychology; Hood College; Towson University

WU, DOREEN; LUTHERVILLE TIMONIUM, MD; DULANEY HS; (SO); Hnr Roll; Nat Hon Sy; WWAHSS; Comm Volntr; FBLA; Key Club; Journalist (Editor of a Magazine); Public Relations; U of Maryland College Park; New York U

WULFF, EDWARD V; BOWIE, MD; BOWIE HS; (SO); Hnr Roll; Sci Fairs; Comm Volntr; Chrch Yth Grp; ROTC; Drl Tm; Gentlemen's Club; Naval Engineering; Computer Science; Annapolis Naval Academy; Virginia Tech

WYCHE, MARCUS; SILVER SPRING, MD; PAINT BRANCH HS; (JR); Hnr Roll; MVP; Comm Volntr; Scouts; Bskball (JV/L); Track (V/JV); Jesse Owens Student-Athlete Award from Alpha Phi Alpha Fraternity; African-American Festival of Academic Excellence Honoree from Montgomery County, Maryland; Computer Science; Communications; Hampton U; North Carolina A & T U

XIAO, JIN; HAGERSTOWN, MD; SOUTH HAGERSTOWN HS; (JR); Hi Hnr Roll; Hnr Roll; Nat Hon Sy; Otst Ac Ach Awd; Perf Att; WWAHSS; Yth Ldrshp Prog; Comm Volntr; Peer Tut/Med; ArtClub; Vsity Clb; Sccr (VJ); Biotechnology; Engineer; The Clarkson U; Massachusetts Institute of Technology

XU, MATTHEW; SILVER SPRING, MD; (MS); Peer Tut/Med; Chess; Cmptr Clb; Drma Clb; Mth Clb/Tm; Stu Cncl (R); CR (R); Sch Ppr (R); Yrbk (P); Princeton

YANO, ELIZABETH MIKO; SMITHSBURG, MD; SMITHSBURG HS; (JR); Hi Hnr Roll; Hnr Roll; WWAHSS; Comm Volntr; Chrch Yth Grp; Chr; Ch Chr; Track (J); Business Management; Franciscan U Steubenville; U of Dallas

YANOVICH, ELIZAVETA; GAITHERSBURG, MD; (SR); Hnr Roll; Comm Volntr; Peer Tut/Med; Drma Clb; Emplmnt; Mth Clb/Tm; Photog; Tchrs Aide; Russian Clb; Theater Club Outside School; Bally Fitness Club Member; International Law; Foreign Languages; U of Maryland; Ithaca College

YATES, EDWARD W; SILVER SPRING, MD; PAINT BRANCH HS; (JR); Hnr Roll; Pres Ac Ftns Aw; WWAHSS; Stg Cre; Who's Who American High Schools; Paint Branch TV Production; Towson U; U of Maryland

YETTE, LAILA M; SILVER SPRING, MD; JAMES H BLAKE HS; (SO); Hnr Roll; MVP; Perf Att; Yth Ldrshp Prog; Comm Volntr; Chrch Yth Grp; Tchrs Aide; Bskball (J); Chrldg (J); Physical Therapy

YOHANNES, ISEY; HYATTSVILLE, MD; HIGH POINT HS; (SR); Hi Hnr Roll; Jr Eng Tech; Comm Volntr; Tech Clb; SP/M/VS; Bskball (J); Ftball (J); Sccr (J); Stu Cncl (V); Yrbk (P); Awarded for My Excellence in Technology; Was Given a Certificate for Advanced Tech; Business and Management; Accounting; Montgomery Community College; Prince George's Community College

YOO, HA E; MARRIOTTSVILLE, MD; RIVER HILL HS; (JR); Hnr Roll; Nat Hon Sy; Otst Ac Ach Awd; Perf Att; St of Mnth; Comm Volntr; Peer Tut/Med; Chrch Yth Grp; FBLA; Mus Clb; Acpl Chr; Chr; Ch Chr; Orch; Ice Sktg (J); International Club; Students Helping Other People - SHOP; Pediatrics; Dentistry; U of Maryland College Park; Johns Hopkins U

YOUNG, AARON; FT WASHINGTON, MD; SUITLAND HS; (SO); Hnr Roll; WWAHSS; Comm Volntr; Bskball (J); Electrical Engineer; Business; Maryland U

YOUNG, HEATHER; GAITHERSBURG, MD; URBANA HS; (SO); Hnr Roll; Drma Clb; Photog; Dnce; SP/M/VS; Stg Cre; PPSqd (J); Thespian Society Member; Fashion Design; Photography; Boston U; Towson U

YOUNG, JUSTIN A; SALISBURY, MD; DELMAR JR/SR HS; (JR); Ctznshp Aw; Hnr Roll; Nat Hon Sy; Nat Ldrshp Svc; Otst Ac Ach Awd; WWAHSS; Comm Volntr; Chrch Yth Grp; Emplmnt; FCA; FTA; P to P St Amb Prg; Prom Com; Tchrs Aide; Bnd; Drm Mjr; Mch Bnd; Stg Cre; Sccr (JC); Veterinarian; U of MD College Park; VA Tech

YOUNG, SHALISA; DUNDALK, MD; DUNDALK HS; (JR); Hnr Roll; WWAHSS; Comm Volntr; Peer Tut/Med; Chrch Yth Grp; Emplmnt; Photog; Prom Com; SADD; Tchrs Aide; Clr Grd; Dnce; Ice Sktg; Scr Kpr (V); Sccr; Sftball (V); Vllyball (V); Sterling Committee; Early Child Education; Child Care (Development); Morgan State U; Coburn State U

YOUNG JR, WARDELL; BALTIMORE, MD; WALBROOK SR HS; (JR); Hnr Roll; Hab For Humty Volntr; Dbte Team; Emplmnt; FBLA; Prom Com; Ch Chr; Bskball (V); Cl Off (V); Stu Cncl (S); Yrbk (P); To Major in Business Administration; Entrepreneurship

YU, PAUL; BETHESDA, MD; WALT WHITMAN HS; (SO); Hnr Roll; WWAHSS; Chrch Yth Grp; Key Club; Mth Clb/Tm; Bnd; Mch Bnd; Track (J); Outstanding Academic Excellence 2005; Mathematics; Science; Stanford U

YU, TIFFANY A; BETHESDA, MD; WALT WHITMAN HS; (JR); F Lan Hn Soc; Hnr Roll; Otst Ac Ach Awd; WWAHSS; Comm Volntr; Peer Tut/Med; Drma Clb; NtlFrnscLg; Svce Clb; Acpl Chr; Chr; Stg Cre; Cl Off (V); CR; Anti-Tobacco Coalition President; School Idol Creator, Director, Coordinator; Broadcast Journalism; Communications; Oxford U; Harvard U

YUSIF, AHMAD H; HYATTSVILLE, MD; HIGH POINT HS; (SR); Hnr Roll; Nat Mrt LOC; Comm Volntr; Sccr; Swmg; Lawyer; Engineering; U of Maryland College Park; Strayer U

YUTUC, ANGELI N; BURTONSVILLE, MD; PAINT BRANCH HS; (JR); Hnr Roll; Pres Ac Ftns Aw; St Schl; Valdctrian; WWAHSS; Chrch Yth Grp; Key Club; Chr; Ch Chr; Bskball (J); Sftball (J); Stu Cncl (R); Yrbk (E); President's Award for Educational Excellence; Certificate of Academic Excellence for Straight A's; Dentistry; Engineering; U of Maryland College Park; Columbia Union College

ZABECKI, KAYLA M; WALDORF, MD; CTRL KITSAP HS; (SR); Hnr Roll; Nat Hon Sy; Nat Stu Ath Day Aw; Otst Ac Ach Awd; Pres Ac Ftns Aw; WWAHSS; Yth Ldrshp Prog; Comm Volntr; Chrch Yth Grp; Emplmnt; Mth Clb/Tm; Tchrs Aide; French Clb; Track (J); Vllyball (JCL); Destination Imagination Regional; Sports Medicine Athletic Trainer Winner; Dentistry; Accounting; Towson U

ZEIGLER, MELISSA; LUTHERVILLE TIMONIUM, MD; TOWSON HS; (SO); Hnr Roll; Nat Hon Sy; WWAHSS; Yth Ldrshp Prog; Comm Volntr; Peer Tut/Med; Chrch Yth Grp; Drma Clb; Key Club; Bnd; SP/M/VS; Stg Cre; Swmg; Class Steering Committee; Youth Group Student Leader; Communications/Theatre Arts; Psychology; Wheaton College (Illinois); The Johns Hopkins U

ZHANG, SIJUN; GAITHERSBURG, MD; MAGRUDER HS; (FR); Comm Volntr; ROTC; Pharmacist; U of Maryland

ZHANG, XIN; POTOMAC, MD; WINSTON CHURCHILL HS; (JR); 4H Awd; Hnr Roll; Nat Hon Sy; Otst Ac Ach Awd; Pres Sch; Sci Fairs; Yth Ldrshp Prog; Red Cr Aide; 4-H; Biology Clb; DARE; Drma Clb; Emplmnt; Mth Clb/Tm; Sci Clb; Dnce; Stg Cre; Gmnstcs (J); Mar Art (V); Swmg (V L); Vllyball (J); Stu Cncl (R); CR (R); Intern At NIH Transplantation Branch; Science Competition Team; Premedicine Doctor MD PhD; Fashion Merchandising; John's Hopkins U; U of Chicago

ZHUANG, MARY; CLARKSVILLE, MD; RIVER HILL HS; (MS); Hnr Roll; Perf Att; Comm Volntr; Chr; Arch; Bdmtn; Fld Hky; Lcrsse; Vllyball; Stu Cncl (V); CR (R); Harvard U; Stanford U

ZICK, KRISTEN; ARNOLD, MD; BROADNECK HS; (JR); Hnr Roll; Nat Hon Sy; Perf Att; Pres Ac Ftns Aw; Comm Volntr; Peer Tut/Med; Key Club; Lcrsse (V L); Sccr (V L); Business Management; Virginia Tech; U of NC Chapel Hill

Massachusetts

ABDEL-GHAFFAR, YASMEEN; CAMBRIDGE, MA; CAMBRIDGE RINDGE & LATIN HS; (JR); Hnr Roll; Otst Ac Ach Awd; Perf Att; St of Mnth; Yth Ldrshp Prog; Comm Volntr; Hosp Aide; Spec Olymp Vol; Emplmnt; Jr Ach; Mod UN; Pep Squd; Ftball (Mang); Track (V); Leaders In Action Job / Work Force Development Program; Manager of Cambridge High School Falcons Football team; Mass Communications; Temple U; University of Michigan Ann Arbor

ABDELLAS, SAMMY M; CAMBRIDGE, MA; CAMBRIDGE RINDGE & LATIN HS; (SO); Hnr Roll; St of Mnth; Photog; Dvng (V); Swmg (V); Outside Basketball League; GBL's Swim Champs 2005; Business; Boston U; Boston College

ADAMS, MONICA; CHICOPEE, MA; CHICOPEE HS; (SR); Hi Hnr Roll; Hnr Roll; Nat Hon Sy; Comm Volntr; Peer Tut/Med; DARE; Emplmnt; Key Club; SP/M/VS; Stu Cncl (R); Lit Mag (E, P); Rank 23 Out of 285; Pre-Law; Political Science; Northeastern U; Westfield State College

ADUBI, MOSES; HYDE PARK, MA; O'BRYANT SCH OF MATH & SCIENCE; MS; Hnr Roll; St of Mnth; Peer Tut/Med; DARE; Ch Chr; Doctor; Harvard U

AFSAR, YASMIN F; BELMONT, MA; BELMONT HS; (JR); Hi Hnr Roll; Nat Hon Sy; Sci/Math Olympn; Comm Volntr; Peer Tut/Med; Mth Clb/Tm; Sci Clb; Orch; Sch Ppr (R); Mock Trial Team Captain; Philosophy Society Co-Founder, President; Physics; Astronomy; Massachusetts Institute of Technology; Harvard U

AGOLLI, ENIANA; WORCESTER, MA; BANCROFT SCH; (SO); Hi Hnr Roll; Hnr Roll; Comm Volntr; Red Cr Aide; Drma Clb; Tennis (J L); Vllyball (J L); High Honor Roll - 2 Years; Gourmet Club

AGOSTINI, ANDREA; TAUNTON, MA; TAUNTON HS; (SO); Hi Hnr Roll; Hnr Roll; Otst Ac Ach Awd; St of Mnth; SADD; Chr

AGUIRRE, KARINA L; BROCKTON, MA; EDGEWOOD GREATER BOSTON AC; (SO); Hnr Roll; Comm Volntr; Chrch Yth Grp; Orch; Cl Off (R); Church Pathfinder Club (Marching); International Business; Business Administration; Atlantic Union College; Northeastern U

AHMED, SAMIA S; MILFORD, MA; MILFORD HS; (FR); Chr; Fld Hky (J); Science; Mathematics

ALBERTO, ALEXANDRIA R; CONCORD, MA; CONCORD-CARLISLE HS; (SO); Hi Hnr Roll; Otst Ac Ach Awd; Bnd; Pep Bnd; Bskball (J); Cr Ct Ski (V L); Sftball (J); Track (V); Rookie of the Year - Cross Country; Who's Who; European History Major; Business Major; U of North Carolina; Dartmouth College

ALEIXO, RAFAELLA; SOMERVILLE, MA; SOMERVILLE HS; (JR); F Lan Hn Soc; Hi Hnr Roll; Hnr Roll; Nat Hon Sy; Sci Fairs; Yth Ldrshp Prog; Comm Volntr; Peer Tut/Med; Emplmnt; Prom Com; Vllyball (J); Cl Off (P); Peer Leader of Cops and Kids Program; Volunteer At Homeless Shelter; Communications; Business; Boston College; Yale U

ALLARD, RENEE; TEWKSBURY, MA; TEWKSBURY MEMORIAL HS; (SR); Hi Hnr Roll; Hnr Roll; Nat Hon Sy; USAA; Comm Volntr; Peer Tut/Med; DECA; Emplmnt; Sftball (J); Stu Cncl (S); Student Council; ECHO; Business; Marketing; Northeastern U

ALMAN, ASHLEY; NORWELL, MA; NORWELL HS; (SO); Hnr Roll; MVP; Yth Ldrshp Prog; Comm Volntr; Tech Clb; Bskball (JCL); Sccr (JCL); Business; Law; UC Santa Barbara; UC San Diego

ALMEIDA, ALLISON; SOMERSET, MA; SOMERSET HS; (SO); Hi Hnr Roll; Hnr Roll; MVP; Perf Att; Sci Fairs; Sci/Math Olympn; Yth Ldrshp Prog; DARE; Emplmnt; Mth Clb/Tm; Sccr (V); Tennis (V)

ALVAREZ, ALEX; SHREWSBURY, MA; SHREWSBURY HS; (FR); Hnr Roll; MVP; Yth Ldrshp Prog; Comm Volntr; Peer Tut/Med; NYLC; Ftball (V L); Track (V L); Stu Cncl (R); League All-Star Award Winner; Pop Warner Football State Champions - 2002; Business; Hospitality Management; Cornell U; Johnson & Wales U

ALVES, NEILDA; BROCKTON, MA; BROCKTON HS; (SO); Hi Hnr Roll; Kwnis Aw; Nat Hon Sy; WWAHSS; Comm Volntr; Key Club; Leadership and Character; Business; Law; U of Massachusetts; Boston U

AMARO, MELISSA; SOUTH DARTMOUTH, MA; DARTMOUTH HS; (SR); Nat Hon Sy; Emplmnt; Prom Com; Tchrs Aide; Clb; Dnce; CR (R); Accounting; Finance; Bryant U; U of Massachusetts Dartmouth

AMOAH, CLARISE; WALTHAM, MA; WALTHAM HS; (JR); Hnr Roll; Otst Ac Ach Awd; Pres Ac Ftns Aw; USAA; Hosp Aide; Biology Clb; French Clb; Tennis (J); Vllyball (J); Participation in Focus on Math Expo 2005; History Medal Award Nominee 2005; Tufts U; Brown U

ANDERSON, ARIANNA A; BOXFORD, MA; MASCONOMET REG HS; (SO); Hnr Roll; WWAHSS; Comm Volntr; Peer Tut/Med; Ch Chr; Dnce; Chrldg (V L); Political Science / Law; Duke U; North Carolina Chapel Hill

ANDERSON, SHELLONDA; MILTON, MA; MILTON AC; (JR); WWAHSS; Comm Volntr; Spec Olymp Vol; Cmptr Clb; Emplmnt; Dnce; Bskball; Track (V L); Wt Lftg (V); Cl Off (R); Stu Cncl; CR (R); National Society of High School Scholars; Pre-Med; Psychology; Brown U; U of North Carolina Chapel Hill

ANDREW, CLARK L; SOMERSET, MA; SOMERSET HS; (SO); Ctznshp Aw; F Lan Hn Soc; Fut Prb Slvr; Hi Hnr Roll; MVP; Otst Ac Ach Awd; Perf Att; Sci Fairs; Sci/Math Olympn; St of Mnth; Amnsty Intl; Comm Volntr; Peer Tut/Med; Chrch Yth Grp; Dbte Team; Emplmnt; Fr of Library; Key Club; Mth Clb/Tm; Mod UN; Photog; Bnd; Ftball (JC); Skiing (J); Sccr; Wt Lftg; Wrstlg (V L); Adv Cncl (R); Stu Cncl (R); Sch Ppr (R, P); Catholic Youth Group-Speaker; Architect; Engineering; Princeton; U of Pennsylvania

ANTWI, MICHAEL; SPRINGFIELD, MA; HS OF SCIENCE & TECH; (FR); Hnr Roll; Perf Att; St of Mnth; Chrch Yth Grp; Key Club; Scouts; Medicine, Pre-Med; Biology; Harvard Princeton; Amherst College

ARIAS-PINA, CELIA; BOSTON, MA; (FR); F Lan Hn Soc; Hi Hnr Roll; Perf Att; USAA; Comm Volntr; Track; Vllyball; Nominee for the Congressional Youth Leadership Council; USAA International Foreign Language Award Winner; Criminologist; Government/Law; Brown U; Spelman College

ARSENAULT, MACKENZIE H T; ASHFIELD, MA; MOHAWK TRAIL REG HS; (SR); Ctznshp Aw; Hi Hnr Roll; Hnr Roll; Nat Hon Sy; WWAHSS; Hosp Aide; Emplmnt; Lib Aide; Mod UN; Scouts; Tchrs Aide; Chr; Dnce; Swg Chr; Fld Hky (J); Lcrsse (V); Skiing (V); Business; Marketing; Roger Williams U

ASANTE, SHEILA K; WORCESTER, MA; NORTH HS; (SO); Hnr Roll; Perf Att; Sci Fairs; St of Mnth; Comm Volntr; Chrch Yth Grp; Ch Chr; Sccr (V); Vsy Clb (J); Stu Cncl (S); Sch Ppr (R); Several Student of the Month Awards; Perfect Attendance Awards; Biology, Physics, Chemistry; Cancer (Pediatrician); UMass Amherst (College); Northeastern College

ASHLEY, CHRISTOPHER T; DEDHAM, MA; DEDHAM HS; (JR); Hi Hnr Roll; Hnr Roll; Otst Ac Ach Awd; Peer Tut/Med; DARE; Wdwrkg Clb; Wt Lftg; Yrbk; Drummer in My Own Band; Exercise Science; Nutrition; Northeastern U; Boston U

ASOMANING, FELICIA; SOUTHBRIDGE, MA; SOUTHBRIDGE HS; (SR); Hnr Roll; MVP; Nat Hon Sy; Otst Ac Ach Awd; Sci Fairs; St of Mnth; Yth Ldrshp Prog; Comm Volntr; Red Cr Aide; Spec Olymp Vol; Chrch Yth Grp; Dbte Team; Mus Clb; Sci Clb; French Clb; Acpl Chr; Chr; Ch Chr; Sccr (V); Vllyball (V); Perfect Attendance; Science Project Award Winner; Pharmacist; Chemical Engineer

AUGUSTO, ANA C; MARLBOROUGH, MA; MARLBOROUGH HS; (JR); Hi Hnr Roll; Hnr Roll; Comm Volntr; Chrch Yth Grp; Bskball (J), Vllyball (J); Stu Cncl (R); President Achievement Award; Pediatrics; Law / Judge; Nova Southeastern U; Boston U

AVILES, GIOVANNA; LOWELL, MA; GREATER LOWELL TECH HS; (SR); Hnr Roll; St of Mnth; WWAHSS; Emplmnt; Photog; Boston Globe Show Award; Top Ten Freshman Students; Criminal Justice; Photography; U of Mass Lowell; Mount Ida College

AYALA, SELVIN; LYNN, MA; LYNN ENGLISH HS; (FR); French Clb; Beginning Acting; Teacher; UMass; Boston College

BABINO, ALICIA; HANSON, MA; WHITMAN-HANSON REG HS; (JR); Hi Hnr Roll; Nat Hon Sy; Key Club; Dnce; Drl Tm; PP Ftbl; Track (J); Top Ten Paper-32nd Annual State High School History Conference Framingham State Cell Boy; Clinical Laboratory Science; Biochemical Engineering

BAGLEY, ASHLEY; HOPKINTON, MA; HOPKINTON HS; (JR); Hi Hnr Roll; Hnr Roll; Nat Hon Sy; Yth Ldrshp Prog; Comm Volntr; Tennis (J); Sch Ppr (R); National Society of High School Scholars; Various School Clubs and Student Mentoring; Journalism; Film Studies; Boston U; Stonehill College

BAHOSH, JOSHUA T; CLINTON, MA; CLINTON HS; (JR); Hi Hnr Roll; Hnr Roll; Health

BAILEY, MICHAEL B; MENDON, MA; NIPMUC REG HS; (SO); Hi Hnr Roll; Hnr Roll; Comm Volntr; Ftball (V); Community Service; Criminal Science; West Point Academy

BALA, GENCI; ROSLINDALE, MA; MADISON PARK HS; (SR); Hi Hnr Roll; Hnr Roll; Jr Mshl; Nat Hon Sy; Otst Ac Ach Awd; Perf Att; Biology Clb; Drma Clb; Fr of Library; Mth Clb/Tm; Sci Clb; Spch Team; Bskball; Sccr; Tennis; Vllyball; National Dean's List 2001-2004 U Mass Amherst; Biochemistry / Biology; Medical / Pharmacy; U Mass Amherst

BALISE, ALEXANDRA N; EAST LONGMEADOW, MA; WILBRAHAM & MONSON AC; (SR); Hi Hnr Roll; Jr Mshl; MVP; Nat Mrt LOC; Nat Stu Ath Day Aw; Otst Ac Ach Awd; Pres Ac Ftns Aw; Salutrn; Valdctrian; WWAHSS; Comm Volntr; Peer Tut/Med; Emplmnt; Bskball (L); Sccr (J); Tennis (V L); Vllyball (V L); Coach's Award-Tennis; Varsity Riflery; Major-English Spanish; Attending College

BALL, COURTNEY A; CLINTON, MA; CLINTON HS; (JR); Hi Hnr Roll; Hnr Roll; Nat Hon Sy; Otst Ac Ach Awd; Comm Volntr; Peer Tut/Med; DARE; Drma Clb; Emplmnt; Dnce; SP/M/VS; Bskball (JC); Fld Hky (V); Scr Kpr (VJ); Dance Awards- DEC Centre / Clinton; High School History Teacher; Degree in Secondary Education; U of Maine Farmington; Assumption College

BANERJEE, RAHUL; SHREWSBURY, MA; ST JOHN'S HS; (JR); Hi Hnr Roll; Nat Hon Sy; Sci/Math Olympn; Comm Volntr; Peer Tut/Med; Mth Clb/Tm; Mod UN; Schol Bwl; Scouts; Tmpl Yth Grp; French Clb; Orch; Lit Mag (E); Sch Ppr (R); Cultural Dance; Web Master of Online Newsletter; Health Care; Biology

BARBEE, DELANIA C; SPRINGFIELD, MA; HS OF COMMERCE; (JR); Hi Hnr Roll; Hnr Roll; Nat Hon Sy; WWAHSS; Key Club; SP/M/VS; Track (J); Mass YMCA Youth and Government Press Corp; Psychology; Law; American U; Duke U

BARBOUR, JACOB M L; PITTSFIELD, MA; PITTSFIELD HS; (SO); Hnr Roll; French Clb; Bsball (J); Ice Hky (V); Stu Cncl (R); Criminal Justice

BARRETT, JUSTIN B; WAYLAND, MA; WAYLAND HS; (JR); Hi Hnr Roll; MVP; Nat Hon Sy; Pres Sch; WWAHSS; Comm Volntr; Emplmnt; JSA; Mth Clb/Tm; Vsity Clb; Bskball (V CL); Golf (V CL); Food for the Poor; Asset Management

BARRY, CHRIS; HOPKINTON, MA; HOPKINTON HS; (JR); Hi Hnr Roll; Hnr Roll; Nat Hon Sy; Yth Ldrshp Prog; Comm Volntr; Drma Clb; Prom Com; SADD; French Clb; SP/M/VS; Lcrsse (C); Sccr (V); Track (V); Wrstlg (V); Set a New Record for the 4x800m Relay at the Class D State Meet During Winter Track 2005; Captain of My Club Soccer Team; Business; Psychology; The George Washington U, Washington D.C.; Ithaca College, Ithaca, New York

BARRY, STEFANIE L; FRAMINGHAM, MA; MARIAN HS; (JR); Hi Hnr Roll; Hnr Roll; Nat Hon Sy; Otst Ac Ach Awd; Sci Fairs; Amnsty Intl; Comm Volntr; Hosp Aide; Chess; Drma Clb; SP/M/VS; Cr Ctry (J); Ranked No-2 / Freshman-Sophomore Yrs; Local Hospital Volunteer; Biochemistry; Chemistry; Brown U; Tufts U

BARTHOLOMEW, KATE; NAHANT, MA; SWAMPSCOTT HS; (SO); Ctznshp Aw; Hnr Roll; MVP; Pres Ac Ftns Aw; WWAHSS; Comm Volntr; Emplmnt; Spanish Clb; Dnce; SP/M/VS; Cr Ctry (V L); Track (V L); Stu Cncl (S); Competed Internationally for Irish Step Dance; Education

BARTOLIK, ASHLEIGH; HOPKINTON, MA; HOPKINTON HS; (JR); Hnr Roll; Nat Hon Sy; French Clb; Mock Trial; Film; Science

BASKIN, JAMAL; MALDEN, MA; MALDEN HS; (SO); Ctznshp Aw; Fut Prb Slvr; Hnr Roll; Kwnis Aw; Nat Hon Sy; Nat Ldrshp Svc; Perf Att; St of Mnth; Yth Ldrshp Prog; Comm Volntr; Peer Tut/Med; Chess; Cmptr Clb; Emplmnt; NYLC; Off Aide; Wdwrkg Clb; Ch Chr; Bskball (J); Ftball (J, V); Track; Master's Degree; Computer Technology; Boston College; University of North Carolina

BATANGLO, JACKIE L; WINDSOR, MA; WAHCONAH REG; (SR); Hnr Roll; Otst Ac Ach Awd; Emplmnt; Svce Clb; Dnce; Participated in Norman Rockwell Art / Gladys Filmus Art Memorial; Honorable Mention in Sheffield Art / Drafting Award; Interior Design; Graphic Design; U Mass Amherst - Accepted; U of Massachusetts

BATEMAN, KRISTIE; PITTSFIELD, MA; PITTSFIELD HS; (MS); F Lan Hn Soc; Hi Hnr Roll; Hnr Roll; Dnce; Gmnstcs; Tennis; Vllyball; Physical Therapist; Fashion Designer

BAUMAN, BONNIE; DANVERS, MA; DANVERS HS; (FR); Hi Hnr Roll; Hnr Roll; WWAHSS; Key Club; Bskball; Cr Ctry (V); Student of the Month

BEAN, CORINNE R; CHICOPEE, MA; CHICOPEE HS; (SO); Hi Hnr Roll; Otst Ac Ach Awd; Pres Ac Ftns Aw; Yth Ldrshp Prog; Pep Squd; Vsity Clb; Chrldg (V L); MA Star Leadership Conference; Junior National Honor Society; Elementary Education; Nutritionist; Our Lady of the Elms College; Westfield State College

BEHMER, JOHN H; WESTBOROUGH, MA; WESTBOROUGH HS; (JR); Hnr Roll; Otst Ac Ach Awd; Perf Att; Comm Volntr; Peer Tut/Med; Cmptr Clb; Cr Ctry (J); Tennis (V); Track (J); Academic Decathlon; Computer Science/Engineering; Entrepreneurship

Bala, Genci
Madison Park HS
Roslindale, MA

Asante, Sheila K
North HS
Worcester, MA

Alves, Neilda
Brockton HS
Brockton, MA

Alberto, Alexandria R
Concord-Carlisle HS
Concord, MA

National
Honor Roll
Spring 2005

Abdellas, Sammy M
Cambridge Rindge & Latin HS
Cambridge, MA

Amaro, Melissa
Dartmouth HS
South Dartmouth, MA

Ashley, Christopher T
Dedham HS
Dedham, MA

Balise, Alexandra N
Wilbraham & Monson AC
East Longmeadow, MA

BELISLE, ELISABETH S; CHICOPEE, MA; CHICOPEE HS; (FR); Hi Hnr Roll; Comm Volntr; Scr Kpr; Sccr (V); Track (V); Cl Off (P); Physician; Cornell U; Clarkson U

BELL, MERCY L; JAMAICA PLAIN, MA; PHILLIPS AC; (FR); Hi Hnr Roll; Hnr Roll; Nat Hon Sy; Nat Mrt Sch Recip; St Schl; Comm Volntr; Peer Tut/Med; Drma Clb; Svce Clb; Chr; Dnce; SP/M/VS; Fld Hky (V); Stu Cncl (V, R); CR (R); Head of School's (Former School's) Dance Club; Tutor at the Epiphany School; Degree in Business; Degree in Psychology, Behavioral Sciences; Brown U; Dartmouth U

BELLO, LUIS J; CLINTON, MA; CLINTON HS; (JR); Comm Volntr; Chrch Yth Grp; Drma Clb; SP/M/VS; Yrbk (R); Award for Participating at the Lider Organization of the WSC; Civil Engineer; Law; Boston U; Northeastern U

BENOIT, JOANNA; LANCASTER, MA; NASHOBA REG HS; (FR); Hi Hnr Roll; Nat Hon Sy; Otst Ac Ach Awd; Scouts; SP/M/VS; Sch Ppr (R); Yrbk (E); Tennis Lesson; Guitar Lesson

BERGSTROM, KAYLA A; MILLBURY, MA; MILLBURY MEMORIAL JR/SR HS; (SO); Hnr Roll; Nat St Ath Day Aw; Peer Tut/Med; Spec Olymp Vol; Drma Clb; SP/M/VS; Black Belt in Karate; Pediatrician; U Mass Amherst; Fitchburg State College

BERICH, TRICIA; DANVERS, MA; DANVERS HS; (FR); Hnr Roll; St of Mnth; WWAHSS; Comm Volntr; Drma Clb; Key Club; SADD; SP/M/VS; Sch Cre; Volunteer At APC Through Key Club; Special Education Teacher; Actress

BERLIANT, STERLING; SUDBURY, MA; LINCOLN-SUDBURY REG HS; (JR); Hnr Roll; Comm Volntr; Prom Com; Track (V L); CR (P); Business; Communications; Emory U; U of Pennsylvania

BERNARD, JOSHUA M; SHARON, MA; SHARON HS; (SO); Hi Hnr Roll; Hnr Roll; St of Mnth; Comm Volntr; Spec Olymp Vol; Tmpl Yth Grp; Bnd; Pep Bnd; Bsball; Cr Ctry (VJ L); Stu Cncl (R); Mock Trial Team; President-Temple Youth Group; Law

BERTELLI, PETER A; MIDDLEBORO, MA; MIDDLEBOROUGH HS; (SO); Hnr Roll; Sci Fairs; St of Mnth; Comm Volntr; Chrch Yth Grp; Key Club; Svce Clb; SADD; Stu Cncl (R); CR (R); Founder President of Greater Bridgewater Leo Club; Psychiatry; Criminal Justice; Bridgewater State College

BESHAI, MICAH J; WORCESTER, MA; FIRST ASSEMBLY CHRISTIAN AC; (FR); Hi Hnr Roll; Nat Hon Sy; Sci Fairs; Comm Volntr; Mus Clb; Bnd; Graphic Design

BETTY, SOPHIA; BROOKLINE, MA; BROOKLINE HS; (SR); Ctznshp Aw; Hnr Roll; Otst Ac Ach Awd; Comm Volntr; Emplmnt; Pep Squd; Acpl Chr; Ch Chr; Chr; Dnce; PPSqd (C); CR (R); Lit Mag (P); African-American Scholar Program; Captain of Lady Warriors Dance Team; Accounting; Business Management; George Washington U; American U

BEYNON, RICHARD T; EAST WEYMOUTH, MA; WEYMOUTH HS; (FR); Emplmnt; Weymouth Youth Soccer, Weymouth Soccer Club; Freshman HS Soccer, Archery (Outside School); Vocational-Sheet Metal; Military Service

BHAGAT, SAHIL; STOUGHTON, MA; STOUGHTON HS; (SO); Gov Hnr Prg; Hi Hnr Roll; Hnr Roll; Perf Att; Sci Fairs; Comm Volntr; Chess; Sccr (J); Tennis (V CL); Stu Cncl (R); 11th in Nation in National French Contest; Participated in Norfolk Regional Science Fair; Major in Biotechnology; Minor in Computer Science; Boston College; MIT

BIELKEVICIUS, LIANA P; SANDWICH, MA; SANDWICH HS; (JR); Hi Hnr Roll; Hnr Roll; Otst Ac Ach Awd; Peer Tut/Med; Chrch Yth Grp; DECA; Emplmnt; Jr Ach; Pep Squd; Scouts; Clb; Chr; Ch Chr; Chrldg (JC); Graduate - Boston Lithuanian Language School; Law; Business; Stonehill College; U Mass Amherst

BINO, JONELA; WORCESTER, MA; NORTH HS; (JR); Hnr Roll; Nat Hon Sy; Perf Att; St of Mnth; ArtClub; I Have Been a Member of the Art Club; I Would Like to Become an Artist (Professional); Rhode Island School Of Design

BLACK, KEVIN; NORTHBOURGH, MA; ALGONQUIN REG HS; (SR); Comm Volntr; Mus Clb; Photog; Acpl Chr; Bnd; Chr; Jzz Bnd; Skiing (V L); Chemical Engineering; Music; Worcester Polytechnic Institute; Syracuse U

BLAKEMORE, AMY; ASHLAND, MA; ASHLAND HS; (MS); Acpl Chr; Chr; SP/M/VS; Cr Ctry (J); Hsbk Rdg (J); Sftball (J); Track (J); Cl Off (R); Stu Cncl (R); Yrbk (E); Oratory Contest Winner; Science Fair Winner; Law; Social Studies; Yale New York U/Colgate U; Connecticut College/Juilliard U

BLANCHARD, BRITTANY; GLENDALE, MA; MONUMENT MTN REG HS; (SO); Hi Hnr Roll; Hnr Roll; MVP; Otst Ac Ach Awd; Perf Att; Comm Volntr; Emplmnt; Bsball (JC); Scr Kpr; Sftball (V); Vllyball (JC); Yrbk (E, P); Scrabble Tournament; Poem Published; Sports Medicine; Fitness; U of Massachusetts

BLANCHARD, CAITLIN; EAST FALMOUTH, MA; FALMOUTH HS; (SR); Hi Hnr Roll; Hnr Roll; Otst Ac Ach Awd; Pres Ac Ftns Aw; WWAHSS; Comm Volntr; DARE; Emplmnt; Dnce; Ice Hky (V); PP Ftbl; Track (J); Criminal Justice; Northeastern U; Endicott College

BLANCHARD, CAROLYNN M; WEYMOUTH, MA; WEYMOUTH HS; (SR); Hnr Roll; Comm Volntr; DARE; Voc Ind Clb Am; Bnd; Clr Grd; Lcrsse (J); Yrbk (E); I Went from Academic Class to College Prep Class & Honor Class; Psychology; U of Bridgeport, CT

BLINN, THOMAS J; GREEN HARBOR, MA; MARSHFIELD HS; (SO); Hnr Roll; Comm Volntr; Chrch Yth Grp; DARE; Emplmnt; Scouts; Bnd; Mch Bnd; Tennis (VJ); Business / Computers

BLOCKER, KYLA M; WESTFORD, MA; WESTFORD AC; (SO); F Lan Hn Soc; Hi Hnr Roll; Nat Hon Sy; Comm Volntr; Drma Clb; Emplmnt; Mus Clb; Spanish Clb; Chr; Orch; SP/M/VS; CR; Theatre Arts; New York U; Branders U

BLUM, CHRISTOPHER R; WESTON, MA; WESTON HS; (JR); Hnr Roll; Nat Hon Sy; Comm Volntr; Dbte Team; Emplmnt; NtlFrnscLg; Bsball (J); Bskball (JC); Golf (V CL); Math Book Award Winner; Community Service Award; Business; Economics

BOATENG, CRYSTAL O; WILBRAHAM, MA; MINNECHAUG REG HS; (JR); Hi Hnr Roll; Hnr Roll; Nat Hon Sy; Perf Att; WWAHSS; Peer Tut/Med; Emplmnt; Jr Ach; Key Club; Mod UN; ROTC; Chr; Yrbk (P); Political Science; Pre-Law; Brown U; Mt Holyoke College

BOBRAKOV, ROMAN; NORTH ANDOVER, MA; NORTH ANDOVER HS; (JR); Hi Hnr Roll; Hnr Roll; Nat Hon Sy; Sci Fairs; Comm Volntr; Peer Tut/Med; Chess; Chrch Yth Grp; Drma Clb; Mth Clb/Tm; Spanish Clb; Acpl Chr; Chr; Ch Chr; Dnce; Sccr (J); Cl Off (S); Senior Districts & All New England Choir; Performing with New England Classical Singers; Physics Major-Mechanical Engineer; Chemical Engineering/Biochemistry; Worcester Polytechnic Institute; Merrimack College

BOGHOSIAN, RICHARD; WELLESLEY, MA; WELLESLEY HS; (SR); Hnr Roll; Hab For Humty Volntr; Hosp Aide; Key Club; Wdwrkg Clb; Bskball (V); Business; George Washington U

BONDURANT, BENJAMIN; BELMONT, MA; TRINITY CATHOLIC HS; (JR); Hnr Roll; Otst Ac Ach Awd; Sci Fairs; Comm Volntr; Ice Hky (V C); Academic Achievement Award in US History; Received Honorable Mention - 2005 Science Fair; Computer Science; Assumption; Western College of New England

BOSQUET, RICHARDSON; ARLINGTON, MA; EDGEWOOD GREATER BOSTON AC; (JR); Hnr Roll; Nat Hon Sy; Nat Sci Aw; Comm Volntr; Chrch Yth Grp; Bnd; Chrldg (V); Sccr (V C); Cl Off (P); Sch Ppr (R); CR (R); Student Council Award; Minority Leadership Award; Computer Information Technology; International Business; Boston U; Tufts U

BOSSMAN, AMANDA R; LITTLETON, MA; LITTLETON HS; (JR); Hi Hnr Roll; Hnr Roll; Nat Hon Sy; Otst Ac Ach Awd; Pres Sch; St of Mnth; Yth Ldrshp Prog; Peer Tut/Med; Dbte Team; Drma Clb; Mod UN; Prom Com; Sci Clb; Scouts; Sccr (J); Ch Chr; Pep Bnd; Sccr (J); Sftball (V); Adv Cncl (R); Yrbk (R); Silver Award Girl Scouts; Optometrist / Opthamologist; Boston College; College of the Holy Cross

BOURDEAU, CHRISTOPHER; WESTFORD, MA; WESTFORD AC; (SR); Hi Hnr Roll; Hnr Roll; MVP; Otst Ac Ach Awd; Pres Ac Ftns Aw; WWAHSS; Comm Volntr; Spec Olymp Vol; BPA; DECA; Emplmnt; Tchrs Aide; Vsity Clb; Golf (V L); Skiing (V); Sccr (J); Sch Ppr (R); Title 1st Junior PGA Champion; Health Care Management; Accounting; U of Connecticut

BOWE, JEN; NORTH ANDOVER, MA; NORTH ANDOVER HS; (JR); Hi Hnr Roll; MVP; Nat Hon Sy; Pres Ac Ftns Aw; Photog; Tchrs Aide; Chrldg (V C); Lcrsse (V); Sch Ppr (R); Science; Forensics; Duke U; Wake Forest U

BOWLER, LAUREN; TYNGSBORO, MA; TYNGSBORO HS; (SO); Hi Hnr Roll; Hnr Roll; Nat Sci Aw; Comm Volntr; 4-H; Bsball (J); Hsbk Rdg (V); Sccr (V); Track (V); Professional Acting; Physical Therapist; Quinnipiac U; U of New England

BRABAZON, JOSH; QUINCY, MA; NORTH QUINCY HS; (JR); Hi Hnr Roll; MVP; Nat Stu Ath Day Aw; Pres Ac Ftns Aw; St of Mnth; Yth Ldrshp Prog; Comm Volntr; Peer Tut/Med; Spec Olymp Vol; DARE; Emplmnt; Bsball (VJ); Bskball (J); Ftball (J); CR; Peer Mediation; Alliance Against Racism; Sports Management; Coaching Sports; Saint Michael's College; Western New England College

BRADBURY, LAURA; DEDHAM, MA; DEDHAM HS; (JR); Hi Hnr Roll; Nat Hon Sy; WWAHSS; Peer Tut/Med; AL Aux Girls; NYLC; Sccr (V); Track (V); Cl Off (R); Peer Leaders; National Honor Society; Physical Therapy; Boston U; Northeastern U

BRADLEY, CHRISTOPHER; WORCESTER, MA; WORCESTER VOC; (SR); Hi Hnr Roll; Hnr Roll; MVP; Nat Hon Sy; Nat St Ath Day Aw; Voc Ind Clb Am; Ftball (VJCL); Lcrsse (VJ); Massachusetts Vocation Association Outstanding Technical Student Award; Electrical Engineer; Worcester State College

BREA, LLEWELLYN; BOSTON, MA; SNOWDEN INTERNATIONAL SCH; (JR); Hnr Roll; Otst Ac Ach Awd; Perf Att; Sci Fairs; WWAHSS; Comm Volntr; Peer Tut/Med; Emplmnt; Bsball (V); Bskball (V); Boston Area Health Educ Cent Youth Advisory Board; History; Pre-Dental; Dentist; Harvard U; Boston College

BREAULT, TRACEY; CHARLTON, MA; SHEPHERD HILL REG HS; (SR); Hi Hnr Roll; Nat Hon Sy; WWAHSS; Yth Ldrshp Prog; Comm Volntr; Peer Tut/Med; Spec Olymp Vol; Chrch Yth Grp; Emplmnt; Svce Clb; Tchrs Aide; Ch Chr; Sccr (V L); Track (V L); Awarded 4 Yr NROTC Scholarship; Advanced Merit Based Scholarships; Civil Engineering; Norwich U

BRESLOW, AUSTIN J; COHASSET, MA; COHASSET HS; (SO); Hi Hnr Roll; Hnr Roll; Otst Ac Ach Awd; Yth Ldrshp Prog; Comm Volntr; Dbte Team; Drma Clb; Mth Clb/Tm; Photog; SP/M/VS; Stg Cre; Tennis; Sch Ppr (R); MHSDG - Drama Festival Finalist / All-Star Award; Developed Senior Citizen Computer Technology Course

BRETTLER, EZRA; NEWTON CTR, MA; GANN AC; (JR); Nat Mrt LOC; Comm Volntr; Peer Tut/Med; Emplmnt; Svce Clb; Tmpl Yth Grp; Chr; Bskball (V); Tennis (V C); Sch Ppr (E); Doubles Tennis Gold Medal on 2003 Maccabi Games; Volunteer Tutor for Disabled Kids; Sports Medicine; Engineering; U of Pennsylvania; Yale U

BRISTOL, AMANDA; SPRINGFIELD, MA; PUTNAM VOC TECH HS; (SO); Ctznshp Aw; Hnr Roll; ROTC; Computer Technician; Nurse Practitioner

BRITTO, KYLE M; INDIAN ORCHARD, MA; HS OF COMMERCE; (SR); Hnr Roll; Nat Hon Sy; Otst Ac Ach Awd; WWAHSS; Comm Volntr; Chess; DECA; Emplmnt; Quiz Bowl; Cr Ctry (V L); Track (V L); Stu Cncl (R); Mock Trial; Accounting; Johnson & Wales U

BROOKS, DANIEL A; FOXBORO, MA; FOXBOROUGH HS; (SO); Hnr Roll; WWAHSS; Chrch Yth Grp; Sci Clb; Bskball (J); Cr Ctry (V); Track (V); Scholar Athlete Award; 2-Time Massachusetts Interscholastic Athletic Association Sportsmanship Award

BROWN, BETH; WELLESLEY HILLS, MA; WELLESLEY HS; (JR); Hnr Roll; Nat Hon Sy; WWAHSS; Comm Volntr; Hab For Humty Volntr; Key Club; Chr; Cr Ctry (V L); Lcrsse; Sccr; Track (V L); Yrbk (R, P); Anti Defamation League; Sailing Team Varsity & Letter; Engineering

BROWN, JACQUELINE A; SPRINGFIELD, MA; SPRINGFIELD CTRL HS; (SO); Hnr Roll; Otst Ac Ach Awd; Sci Fairs; Sci/Math Olympn; USAA; WWAHSS; Peer Tut/Med; Red Cr Aide; Emplmnt; Mth Clb/Tm; ROTC; Scouts; Clr Grd; Drl Tm; Sftball (C); Yrbk (E); Girl Scout Silver Award; Pre Medicine; U of Miami; Norwich U

BROWN, LAUREN E; WELLESLEY, MA; WELLESLEY HS; (JR); Hnr Roll; WWAHSS; Yth Ldrshp Prog; Comm Volntr; ArtClub; Chrch Yth Grp; Emplmnt; Key Club; Photog; Spanish Clb; Dnce; SP/M/VS; Cr Ctry (L); Lcrsse; Scr Kpr; Sccr; Stu Cncl (R); Manager of X Country Team; Mgr of Wrestling & Lacrosse Teams; Psychology; Creative Writing/Journalism; Davidson College, North Carolina; Wake Forest U NC

BROWN, MICHAEL; BOSTON, MA; MALDEN HS; (SO); Ctznshp Aw; Hnr Roll; Perf Att; St of Mnth; Red Cr Aide; DARE; Mus Clb; Orch (B); Good Citizenship Award; Sports Commentator; Sports Interviewer; Boston U; Northeastern U

BROWN, NICOLE; SPRINGFIELD, MA; CENTRAL HS; (JR); Comm Volntr; DARE; VP -Best Buddies; Child Lawyer; Lawyer; Wheelock U

BROWN, SARAFINA; SPRINGFIELD, MA; PUTNAM VOC TECH HS; (SO); Hnr Roll; Perf Att; DARE; FTA; Chr; Stu Cncl (R); Mass Mutual Achievement Group; Culinary Arts; History; Johnson & Wales U

BROWN-LAVOIE, LAURA L; BROOKLINE, MA; BROOKLINE HS; (JR); Hi Hnr Roll; Acpl Chr; Sftball (VJ L); History; Creative Writing

BUCHARELLI, DEVON J; SOUTHBRIDGE, MA; SOUTHBRIDGE HS; (SR); Nat Hon Sy; Bsball (J); Sccr (V CL); Tennis (V); Southern Worcester League All Star (Soccer); Computer Science; U Mass Dartmouth

BULGER, JODY; DANVERS, MA; DANVERS HS; (FR); Hi Hnr Roll; St of Mnth; Comm Volntr; Key Club; Vsity Clb; Dnce; Stg Cre; Gmnstcs (V); 3rd Place All Around-Level 7 State Champion Gymnastics; U of New Hampshire

BUNKER, MICHAEL; LOWELL, MA; GREATER LOWELL VOC TECH SCH; (SO); Hnr Roll; Perf Att; WWAHSS; Spec Olymp Vol; Voc Ind Clb Am; Cl Off (R); CR (R); Walk America; Walk For Hunger; Food Service Management; Hospitality Management; Johnson and Wales U Providence Rhode island; Boston U Boston Massachusetts

BURKE, ANNA K; NORFOLK, MA; KING PHILIP REG HS; (JR); Hi Hnr Roll; Hnr Roll; Pres Ac Ftns Aw; Sci/Math Olympn; WWAHSS; Comm Volntr; Mth Clb/Tm; Lcrsse (J); Sccr (V L); Track (V L); Stu Cncl; Science National Honor Society; State History Day Finalist; Engineering

Brown, Lauren E
Wellesley HS
Wellesley, MA

Brabazon, Josh
North Quincy HS
Quincy, MA

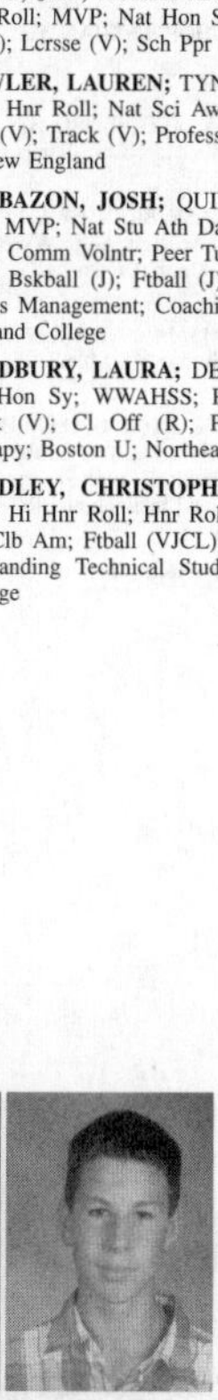

Blinn, Thomas J
Marshfield HS
Green Harbor, MA

National
Honor Roll
Spring 2005

Benoit, Joanna
Nashoba Reg HS
Lancaster, MA

Breslow, Austin J
Cohasset HS
Cohasset, MA

Bulger, Jody
Danvers HS
Danvers, MA

BURNARD, RACHEL A; NEEDHAM, MA; NEEDHAM HS; (SR); Hi Hnr Roll; Hnr Roll; Nat Hon Sy; Amnsty Intl; Comm Volntr; Peer Tut/Med; Emplmnt; Spanish Clb; Chrldg (V CL); Gmnstcs (V L); PP Ftbl; Member of Civil Rights Team; Cheerleading and Gymnastics Coach; Pre-Med (Medicine); Nursing; U of Pennsylvania (Accepted and Will Be Attending)

BURRIS, TIFFANEE; LYNN, MA; LYNN ENGLISH HS; (FR); Ctznshp Aw; Hnr Roll; Comm Volntr; Chrch Yth Grp; French Clb; Ch Chr; Stg Cre; Sftball (J); Volunteer Work with Church & Upward Bound; Doctor; Lawyer; Boston College; Bentley College

BURT, DOMINIQUE; SPRINGFIELD, MA; SCI-TECH; (SO); WWAHSS; Key Club; Dnce; Track (V); Vllyball (J); Mass Mutal; Pre-Med; Dancing; Spelman College; Howard College

BURT, GARRETT; OAK BLUFFS, MA; MARTHAS VINEYARD PUBLIC CHRT; (SR); Comm Volntr; DARE; Founded - International Forum on Freshwater Stingrays / Flat-Fish.com; Marine Biology; Web Design; University of Massachusetts; University of New Hampshire

BYS, SARAH L; SPRINGFIELD, MA; CENTRAL HS; (SO); Hnr Roll; Jr Rot; Spec Olymp Vol; ArtClub; Emplmnt; Key Club; Scouts; Dnce; Sccr (V); Swmg (V); Girl Scouts Silver Award; Key Club; Journalism; Fashion / Costume Design

CABRERA, MARIO O; LYNN, MA; LYNN ENGLISH HS; (SR); St of Mnth; WWAHSS; 4th Place National Spanish Exam; Computer Engineering; Salem State College

CADET, SOSHIMA V; HYDE PARK, MA; BOSTON LATIN AC; (JR); Hnr Roll; Comm Volntr; Hosp Aide; Dbte Team; Golf; Track; Received the Mayors Award; National Latin Exam Award Recipient; International Business; Civil Engineering & Building Engineering; U of McGill; U of New York

CAMARA, ALEXANDRA; SOMERSET, MA; SOMERSET HS; (FR); Hi Hnr Roll; Hnr Roll; WWAHSS; Dbte Team; Key Club; Chrldg (V L); Fld Hky (J); Track

CAMARA, WILLIAM L; SOMERSET, MA; SOMERSET HS; (SR); Hi Hnr Roll; Hnr Roll; Nat Hon Sy; Sci Fairs; Comm Volntr; Peer Tut/Med; Emplmnt; Mod UN; Bnd; Jzz Bnd; Orch; Stg Cre; Golf (V L); Cl Off (V); Biomedical Engineering; Electrical Engineering; U of Connecticut; U of Massachusetts At Dartmouth

CAMERON, KAYLA; HOPKINTON, MA; HOPKINTON HS; (JR); F Lan Hn Soc; Hi Hnr Roll; Hnr Roll; Nat Hon Sy; Sci Fairs; Comm Volntr; Peer Tut/Med; AL Aux Girls; Chrch Yth Grp; Drma Clb; Emplmnt; P to P St Amb Prg; Svce Clb; SADD; SP/M/VS; Stg Cre; Bskball (J); Sccr (JC); Track (J); Published in a Celebration of Young Poets; Third Award-2005 MA State Science Fair; Political Science; Georgetown U; George Washington U

CAMP, BETHANY; E LONGMEADOW, MA; PIONEER VALLEY CHRISTIAN SCH; (SO); Hnr Roll; Comm Volntr; Chrch Yth Grp; Chr; SP/M/VS; Bskball (V); Vllyball (V); Performing Arts; U of California UCSB, Palm Beach Atlantic U; State U of New York, College At Fredonia

CAMPBELL, MELISSA; ATTLEBORO, MA; ATTLEBORO HS; (SO); F Lan Hn Soc; Hi Hnr Roll; Amnsty Intl; Comm Volntr; Spec Olymp Vol; Emplmnt; Quill & Scroll; Lit Mag (R); Sch Ppr (E); Leo Club; Gay-Straight Alliance; Communications / Journalism; Political Science; New York U; U of Massachusetts Amherst

CANAVAN, JOSEPH C; QUINCY, MA; NORTH QUINCY HS; (SO); Ctznshp Aw; Hi Hnr Roll; Hnr Roll; Perf Att; St of Mnth; Yth Ldrshp Prog; Comm Volntr; Peer Tut/Med; Chess; DARE; Drma Clb; FCCLA; Kwanza Clb; SADD; Dnce; Bsball (J); Ice Hky (V); Law, Attorney; Sports Management; Boston College; U of Connecticut

CANDELARIO, ANAIS; WORCESTER, MA; (JR); Nat Hon Sy; Pres Ac Ftns Aw; WWAHSS; Red Cr Aide; Emplmnt; Prom Com; Spanish Clb; Drl Tm; Track; Physical Therapist-Doctorate; Massage Therapist; American International College; Sacred Heart U

CANONICA, ASHLYN; HOPKINTON, MA; HOPKINTON HS; (JR); Hnr Roll; Otst Ac Ach Awd; SADD; Dnce; Fld Hky (V); Biochemistry; Pharmacy; U of Connecticut

CANUTO, WALTER; BROCKTON, MA; BROCKTON HS; (JR); Hi Hnr Roll; Hnr Roll; Perf Att; Amnsty Intl; Comm Volntr; Spec Olymp Vol; Emplmnt; Jr Cls League; Key Club; Mth Clb/Tm; ROTC; Wt Lftg; Wrstlg (V CL); Lit Mag (R); 5th - South Sectional Tournament; 2nd - Cohasset Tournament; Major in Law; Major in Criminal Justice; Boston U; Harvard U

CAPLES, EVAN; BILLERICA, MA; BILLERICA MEM HS; (JR); Hi Hnr Roll; Nat Hon Sy; Nat Mrt LOC; Pres Sch; St of Mnth; Comm Volntr; Peer Tut/Med; Emplmnt; Quiz Bowl; Schol Bwl; Vllyball (V); Lit Mag (E); Pre-Med; Biology; Tufts U; Dartmouth College

CAPPABIANCA, DAVID; SPRINGFIELD, MA; (FR); Hnr Roll; Otst Ac Ach Awd; Comm Volntr; DARE; Chr; Arch (J); Sccr (J); Tennis (J); Basketball for Years Till This Yr; Received the "Barnabus Award"

CAPPELLO, TINA; ATTLEBORO, MA; BISHOP FEEHAN HS; (SO); Hnr Roll; Nat Ldrshp Svc; Comm Volntr; Peer Tut/Med; Chrch Yth Grp; Cmptr Clb; Emplmnt; Photog; Svce Clb; Chr; Track (J); Spanish Honor Society; Science Honor Society; Journalism; Meteorology; Harvard U; Providence College

CARABALLO, JEANNETTE E; LOWELL, MA; GREATER LOWELL VOC TECH SCH; (SO); Hnr Roll; MVP; Sci Fairs; Sci/Math Olympn; Comm Volntr; Peer Tut/Med; DARE; DECA; SADD; Bsball; Bskball; Sftball; Vllyball; Cl Off (S, T); Stu Cncl (R); Math Award; DARE Certificate; Doctor; Pediatrics; U Mass

CARBON, AMY; BELLINGHAM, MA; BELLINGHAM MEM HS; (SO); 4H Awd; Hi Hnr Roll; Hnr Roll; Comm Volntr; Peer Tut/Med; Spec Olymp Vol; 4-H; DARE; SADD; Bskball (J); Fld Hky (V); Sftball (VJ); Adv Cncl; Cl Off (V); Stu Cncl (R); Business; Law; Northeastern U; U Conn

CARDONA LOPEZ, NATHALIE; REVERE, MA; NORTH CAMBRIDGE CATHOLIC HS; (SO); Hi Hnr Roll; Hnr Roll; Otst Ac Ach Awd; Perf Att; Sci Fairs; St of Mnth; Aqrium Clb; ArtClub; Emplmnt; Dnce; Elementary 2nd Valedictorian; Art Award; Marine Biology; Performing Arts; Boston U; Northeastern U

CARDULLO, LAUREN M; HALIFAX, MA; SILVER LAKE REG HS; (SO); Duke TS; Hi Hnr Roll; Hnr Roll; Otst Ac Ach Awd; Pres Sch; St of Mnth; WWAHSS; Comm Volntr; Chrch Yth Grp; DARE; Drma Clb; Emplmnt; Off Aide; Chr; SP/M/VS; Stg Cre; Wt Lftg; Sch Ppr (R); Psychology; Counselor; Columbia U; New York U

CAREAU, NICHOLAS D; LEOMINSTER, MA; LEOMINSTER HS; (SR); Fut Prb Slvr; Hnr Roll; Nat Hon Sy; WWAHSS; Comm Volntr; Peer Tut/Med; Red Cr Aide; AL Aux Boys; Chrch Yth Grp; Emplmnt; Tchrs Aide; Vllyball; USFIRST Robotics Team; Lector; Mechanical Engineering; Chemical Engineering; Worcester Polytechnic Institute; Northeastern U

CAREY, BRITTANY; ANDOVER, MA; NORTH ANDOVER HS; (JR); Hi Hnr Roll; Hnr Roll; Nat Hon Sy; Otst Ac Ach Awd; Comm Volntr; Chrch Yth Grp; Emplmnt; Photog; German Clb; Dnce; Pianist; National Honors Society Member; Performing Arts; Bio Sciences; Boston U; Northeastern U

CARLSON, NICK; GREAT BARRINGTON, MA; MONUMENT MTN REG HS; (SO); Hi Hnr Roll; Hnr Roll; Perf Att; WWAHSS; Scouts; Bnd; Mch Bnd; Golf (V); Eagle Scout Class of 2004; Engineering; Accounting

CARON, SCOTT R; LOWELL, MA; GREATER LOWELL TECH HS; (JR); Hi Hnr Roll; Hnr Roll; Nat Hon Sy; Nat Stu Ath Day Aw; Otst Ac Ach Awd; Perf Att; Sci Fairs; Comm Volntr; Emplmnt; Tchrs Aide; Voc Ind Clb Am; Track (VJ); National Vocational Honor Society; Perfect Attendance (5 Yrs.); Graphic Arts; Computer; Fitchburg State College; Rivier College

CARROLL, ASHLEY A; TYNGSBORO, MA; TYNGSBORO HS; (SR); Otst Ac Ach Awd; Academic Achievement Awards in Unified Arts

CARTER, MARQUIS J; SPRINGFIELD, MA; CATHEDRAL HS; MS; Hnr Roll; MVP; Otst Ac Ach Awd; Perf Att; Chrch Yth Grp; DARE; Emplmnt; Bskball (J); Ftball (V); Sports Medicine; Biology; Syracuse U; U of Virginia Tech

CATLIN, JESSICA; WESTON, MA; WESTON HS; (JR); Hi Hnr Roll; Nat Hon Sy; Comm Volntr; Dbte Team; Drma Clb; Mth Clb/Tm; NtlFrnscLg; Svce Clb; Chr; SP/M/VS; Stg Cre; Chorus and Drama Letters; Various Awards in High School Classes for High Achievement; Doctor-MD or PhD-Pre-Med and Biochemistry; Psychology and French; Yale U; Harvard College

CAVALLO, MARISSA; REVERE, MA; REVERE HS; (JR); Hnr Roll; Nat Hon Sy; Otst Ac Ach Awd; Perf Att; Comm Volntr; Emplmnt; Vsity Clb; Chrldg (V); Sftball (V); Stu Cncl (S); Financing; Chemistry; Northeastern U; Boston U

CAVANAUGH, ANGELA; NORTON, MA; BISHOP FEEHAN HS; (JR); Drma Clb; Photog; SP/M/VS; Swmg (V C); Sch Ppr (P); Theater; Communications; Assumption College; Boston College

CHAMBERLAIN, AMANDA; ATTLEBORO, MA; ATTLEBORO HS; (SR); Hi Hnr Roll; Hnr Roll; Nat Hon Sy; Emplmnt; Lib Aide; Chr; Tennis (J); X Ray Technician; Massasoit College

CHAN, VANIA; EAST BRIDGEWATER, MA; EAST BRIDGEWATER HS; (JR); Hi Hnr Roll; Hnr Roll; Nat Hon Sy; Otst Ac Ach Awd; WWAHSS; Amnsty Intl; Chrch Yth Grp; Key Club; SADD; Dnce; Cr Ctry (V); Track (VJ); Botany; Marine Biology; Brown U; Harvard College

CHANDLER, NICOLLETTE M; NORTH ADAMS, MA; CHARLES H MC CANN TECH HS; (SO); Hnr Roll; Pep Squd; Chrldg (V); Sftball (J); Shop Representative; Accountant; Boston U

CHAPMAN, KATIA; ANDOVER, MA; ANDOVER HS; (FR); DAR; Hi Hnr Roll; Hnr Roll; Pres Ac Ftns Aw; Sci Fairs; St of Mnth; Yth Ldrshp Prog; Hab For Humty Volntr; Chess; Drma Clb; Emplmnt; P to P St Amb Prg; Dnce; SP/M/VS; Stg Cre; Cl Off (V); Government and International Relations; International Study Stream; Clark U; Amherst College

CHAREST, JODI; WEBSTER, MA; (FR); Hnr Roll; Clr Grd; Teachers Degree; Mechanics

CHARLES, MARCKINSON; BOSTON, MA; BOSTON ADULT AC; (SR); F Lan Hn Soc; Fut Prb Slvr; MVP; Otst Ac Ach Awd; Perf Att; Sci Fairs; St of Mnth; St Optmst of Yr; Yth Ldrshp Prog; Cmptr Clb; Drma Clb; Mus Clb; Sci Clb; Vsity Clb; Bnd; Chr; Ch Chr; Dnce; Bskball (J); Ftball (J); Sccr (V); Adv Cncl (P); CR; Yrbk (R); Civil Engineering; Architecture; Massachusetts Institute of Technology; U of Advancing Technology

CHARTIER, JOHN; ANDOVER, MA; ANDOVER HS; (SO); Ctznshp Aw; Hi Hnr Roll; Otst Ac Ach Awd; Pres Sch; St of Mnth; Comm Volntr; Peer Tut/Med; Emplmnt; Tchrs Aide; Adv Cncl (R); Stu Cncl (R); CR (R); Lit Mag (E); Write For Local Newspaper; Play Soccer With The Town; Business; Law

CHEEK, LIA M; HYDE PARK, MA; BROOKLINE HS; (SR); Hnr Roll; Nat Mrt Sch Recip; Comm Volntr; Emplmnt; Photog; Bnd; Ch Chr; Dnce; Orch; Sccr (L); Swmg (J); National Hispanic Merit Scholar; Biology; Doctorate Degree; Oberlin; Duke U

CHEN, DANTONG; BOSTON, MA; O'BRYANT SCH OF MATH & SCIENCE; MS; Hnr Roll; Perf Att; Sci Clb; Bnd; Business; Designer; Boston College; Boston U

CHEN, HSUANFONG; NATICK, MA; WALNUT HILL SCH; (SO); Chr; Orch; Excellent Classical Pianist; Professional Musician-Oboist; The Juilliard School; New England Conservatory

CHEN, JING J; HOPKINTON, MA; HOPKINTON HS; (SO); Hi Hnr Roll; Hnr Roll; Nat Hon Sy; Otst Ac Ach Awd; Perf Att; Comm Volntr; Peer Tut/Med; ArtClub; Svce Clb; Chr; Stu Cncl (R); Piano (Will Be Taking Up to Level 5 Tests); Soccer Referee (Certified-Grade 8); Pre-Medicine; Fashion or Interior Design; Stanford U; U of Los Angeles California

CHEN, YUE-MEI; WELLESLEY HILLS, MA; WELLESLEY HS; (SO); Hnr Roll; Key Club; Mth Clb/Tm; Sci Clb; Biology; Chemistry; Massachusetts Institute of Technology; Boston U

CHILINGERIAN, JOHN; NEWTON, MA; NEWTON NORTH HS; (JR); Hnr Roll; Comm Volntr; Acpl Chr; Chr; Stg Cre; Swmg (V); Play Lead Guitar/Accompanist in Church and School; Sunday School Teacher's Aide; Science; Business; Brandeis U; BC

CHIM, SOCHEATA; NORTH CHELMSFORD, MA; CHELMSFORD HS; (JR); Hi Hnr Roll; Hnr Roll; Nat Mrt LOC; Perf Att; Red Cr Aide; Emplmnt; Off Aide; Supervisor at Work; Psychologist; Pharmacist; Northeastern U; Rivier College

CHIU, CONNIE; QUINCY, MA; FONTBONNE AC; (SO); Hnr Roll; Perf Att; Peer Tut/Med; Key Club; Svce Clb; Ch Chr; International Club; Pharmacy; Association for Diversity in Action; Massachusetts College of Pharmacy; Simmons College

CHOKSI, ISHANI; NORTON, MA; BISHOP FEEHAN HS; (SO); Hi Hnr Roll; Nat Hon Sy; Perf Att; Pres Sch; Sci Fairs; St of Mnth; WWAHSS; CARE; Comm Volntr; Hosp Aide; DARE; Mth Clb/Tm; Scouts; SADD; Tmpl Yth Grp; Dnce; Cr Ctry (J); Track (J); Stu Cncl (R); Lion's Club Youth Speech-Runner Up at District; 2nd Degree Black Belt- Tae Kwon Do; Medicine; Health Science; Brown U; Tufts U

CHOY, SUSAN; MALDEN, MA; MALDEN HS; (SO); Hi Hnr Roll; Comm Volntr; Key Club; Cr Ctry (V); Track (V); Cl Off (S); Lit Mag (E); Sch Ppr (E); I Am Vice President of the Literary Society; I Am the Student Rep. for My Class in Key Club; English Major; History Major; Tufts U

CHU, TIFFANY K; BROOKLINE, MA; BROOKLINE HS; (JR); Hnr Roll; Comm Volntr; Peer Tut/Med; DARE; Scouts; Dnce; Vllyball (JC); Piano; Primary Education; New York U; Boston U

CICCKETTI, BRITTANY; CANTON, MA; CANTON HS; (FR); Hnr Roll; Comm Volntr; Chrch Yth Grp; Drma Clb; Scouts; Chr; SP/M/VS; Track (J); Piano Lessons for 7 Years; Nursing; Journalism; Boston College; Salve Regina U

CIOLKOWSKI, CHELSEY; NORTH ADAMS, MA; CHARLES H MC CANN TECH HS; (SO); Ctznshp Aw; Hnr Roll; St of Mnth; Comm Volntr; Peer Tut/Med; Emplmnt; SADD; Spanish Clb; Adv Cncl (R); Stu Cncl (S); Shop Advisor; Early Childhood Education; History / Teaching; Purdue U; U of Massachusetts Amherst

CISERO, CICELY; SPRINGFIELD, MA; EARLY COLLEGE HS AT HCC; (JR); Hnr Roll; Dbte Team; Dnce; National Rising Achiever; Law; Sociology; Emory College; Morris Brown U

CISERO, MESHAWN; SPRINGFIELD, MA; SCIENCE AND TECH; (FR); Hi Hnr Roll; Hnr Roll; Perf Att; Tech Clb; Track (J); Stu Cncl (V); Aerospace Engineer; Chemical Engineer; Georgia Tech; Massachusetts Institute of Technology

CLARK, AMANDA; CHICOPEE, MA; CHICOPEE HS; (JR); Child Development; Early Childhood Education; Holyoke Community College

CLARK, SAMANTHA; MARION, MA; WAREHAM HS; (JR); Hnr Roll; DECA; Boston U

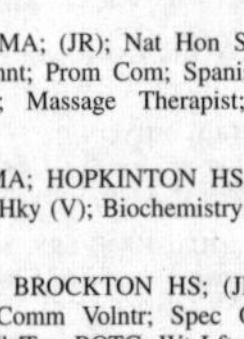
Ciccketti, Brittany
Canton HS
Canton, MA

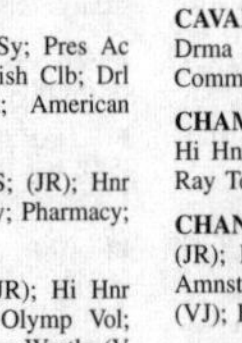
Carter, Marquis J
Cathedral HS
Springfield, MA

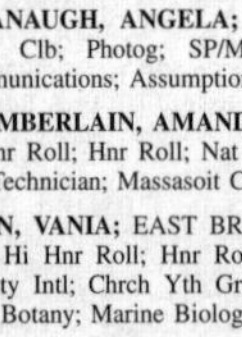
Cardona Lopez, Nathalie
North Cambridge Catholic HS
Revere, MA

National
Honor Roll
Spring 2005

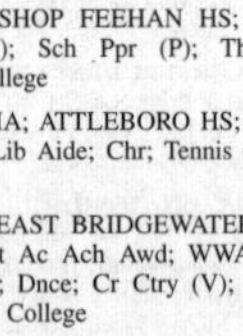
Burris, Tiffanee
Lynn English HS
Lynn, MA

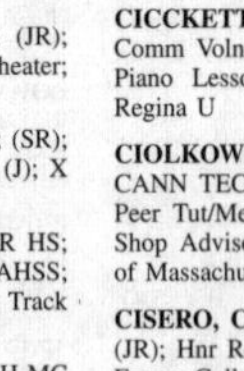
Chilingerian, John
Newton North HS
Newton, MA

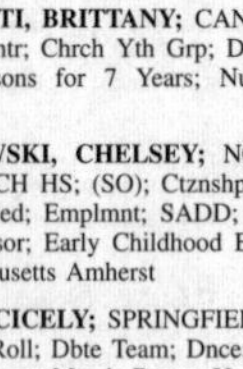
Ciolkowski, Chelsey
Charles H Mc Cann Tech HS
North Adams, MA

CLAUDIO, BRIAN; BOSTON, MA; EDGEWOOD GREATER BOSTON AC; (FR); Comm Volntr; Bnd; Ch Chr; SP/M/VS; Bsball (C); Bskball (C); Sccr (C); Cl Off (V); CR (V); Master's; Doctorate; Boston College; Atlantic Union College

CLEARY, ABBY; YARMOUTH PORT, MA; DENNIS YARMOUTH HS; (JR); Hi Hnr Roll; Hnr Roll; Nat Hon Sy; Pres Sch; Comm Volntr; Hab For Humty Volntr; Key Club; Prom Com; Bskball; Sccr; Tennis (J); Cl Off (P); Stu Cncl; CR (P); Yrbk; Leo Club President; Key Club Secretary; Photography; Leadership; College of William and Mary; Salve Regina U

CLOPPER, ILANA; READING, MA; READING MEMORIAL HS; (JR); Hi Hnr Roll; Nat Hon Sy; Comm Volntr; Spec Olymp Vol; DARE; Sccr (V L); Track (V CL); Track Captain; Business; Law; James Madison U; U Mass Amherst

COBB, MATTHEW A; EAST SANDWICH, MA; SANDWICH HS; (SO); Acpl Chr; Bnd; Jzz Bnd; Mch Bnd; CR (R); Peer Mediation; Leadership Team; Chemistry; Musical Theater; Emerson College; New York U

COGLIANO, JENNIFER L; REVERE, MA; REVERE HS; (SR); Hnr Roll; Comm Volntr; Emplmnt; Chr; Vllyball (J); Elementary Education; Psychology; Rhode Island College

COLE, KATIE; FLORENCE, MA; NORTHAMPTON HS; (SR); Nat Hon Sy; Comm Volntr; Hab For Humty Volntr; Yrbk (E); Zoology/Wildlife Management-BS; PhD-Zoology/Wildlife Management; U of New Hampshire

COLLARD, MATTHEW J; ATTLEBORO, MA; BISHOP FEEHAN HS; (JR); Hnr Roll; WWAHSS; Yth Ldrshp Prog; Comm Volntr; SADD; Track (J); Christian Youth Leadership Award; Business Administration/Management; Johnson & Wales U

COLOMBARI, MEGHAN; PITTSFIELD, MA; PITTSFIELD HS; (SR); Hnr Roll; Nat Hon Sy; Comm Volntr; Hab For Humty Volntr; DARE; Scouts; Dnce; Psychology; Child Education; Massachusetts College of Liberal Arts; Westfield State College

COLON, JAHNILSA; LOWELL, MA; LOWELL HS; (SR); Hnr Roll; Sci Clb; SP/M/VS; Track (V); Homecoming Queen; Fashion Design; Fashion Merchandising; Boston; New York

COMASKEY, MAX; BROOKLINE, MA; BROOKLINE HS; (JR); Hnr Roll; Hab For Humty Volntr; Drma Clb; Mus Clb; Outdrs Clb; Photog; SADD; Acpl Chr; Bnd; Jzz Bnd; SP/M/VS; Yrbk (P); Won a Scholarship to Berklee College of Music; Music Teacher; Recording Tech; The New School; Oberlin College

COMBS, JOSH; CHELMSFORD, MA; CHELMSFORD HS; (JR); Hi Hnr Roll; Hnr Roll; MVP; Comm Volntr; Red Cr Aide; Emplmnt; Ice Hky (J); Stu Cncl (R); Walk for Hunger; Medical Field; Surgeon; Tufts U; U of Connecticut

COMEAU, ALANA; IPSWICH, MA; IPSWICH HS; (FR); Hi Hnr Roll; Hnr Roll; Perf Att; Pres Sch; Comm Volntr; Chrch Yth Grp; DARE; Scouts; Chr; Dnce; Company Dance (Competitive Dance Team); Pre-Competitive Gymnastics; Dance; Law; Tufts U; Endicott College

COMEAU, VINNY; LYNN, MA; ENGLISH HS; (SO); Hnr Roll; Nat Hon Sy; WWAHSS; Comm Volntr; Peer Tut/Med; Emplmnt; FTA; Pep Squd; Tchrs Aide; Ice Hky (J); Nominated for the National Latin Exam; Nominated for the National Technical Honor Society; Computer Science

CONLY, SAMANTHA; AVON, MA; AVON MIDDLE HS; (JR); Hi Hnr Roll; Hnr Roll; Otst Ac Ach Awd; St of Mnth; Chrldg (V); Sftball (V C); Vllyball (V C); Stu Cncl (R); Mayflower League All Star - Volleyball; Brockton Enterprise All-Scholastic -Volleyball; Dental Hygiene; Mount Ida College; Mass. College of Pharmacy & Health Sciences

CONNELLY, PATRICK; MARBLEHEAD, MA; MARBLEHEAD HS; (JR); Hi Hnr Roll; Nat Hon Sy; Comm Volntr; Jzz Bnd; Golf (J); High Performance in English Award; Business; Entrepreneur Programs; Cornell U; Bucknell U

CONNOR, JOSEPH T; MARSHFIELD, MA; MARSHFIELD HS; (SO); Hi Hnr Roll; Otst Ac Ach Awd; Yth Ldrshp Prog; Peer Tut/Med; DARE; Drma Clb; Photog; Prom Com; Chr; SP/M/VS; Ftball; Golf; Tennis; Wt Lftg; Cl Off (P); Stu Cncl; Class President; Enjoys Fishing; Law

CONNORS, STEFHANIE P; BLACKSTONE, MA; NORFOLK CTY AG HS; (JR); Hi Hnr Roll; Hnr Roll; Perf Att; Peer Tut/Med; Ntl FFA; Prom Com; Scouts; SP/M/VS; Stg Cre; Bskball (L); Stu Cncl (V); Sch Ppr (E); Animal Science Agricultural Teacher; U of Massachusetts-Amherst

CONROY, COURTNEY P; CHICOPEE, MA; CHICOPEE HS; (SO); Hi Hnr Roll; Hnr Roll; Yth Ldrshp Prog; Comm Volntr; Emplmnt; Key Club; Scouts; Bnd; Mch Bnd; Scuba Certified / GS Gold Award; Certified Lifeguard; Early Childhood Education

CONSTANTI, ELIZABETH; DEDHAM, MA; DEDHAM HS; (FR); Hnr Roll; Drma Clb; SP/M/VS; Stg Cre; Lawyer; Journalist; Northeastern U; Boston U

CONTANT, SEAN; SPRINGFIELD, MA; CENTRAL HS; (SO); Hi Hnr Roll; Nat Hon Sy; Sci Fairs; WWAHSS; Comm Volntr; Spec Olymp Vol; Drma Clb; Key Club; Bsball (J); Sccr (J); National Honor Society / Work at a Country Club; Played Piano 5 Yrs / Acted in 9th Grade Play; Math; Science

COOKE, CLARE; GREAT BARRINGTON, MA; MONUMENT MTN REG HS; (SO); Hi Hnr Roll; Hnr Roll; Drma Clb; SP/M/VS; Art Major; English Major

COOKE, SARAH; YARMOUTH PORT, MA; DENNIS-YARMOUTH REG HS; (SR); Hnr Roll; Nat Hon Sy; WWAHSS; Comm Volntr; Spec Olymp Vol; AL Aux Girls; Key Club; Prom Com; Scouts; French Clb; Bnd; Bskball (V L); Sccr (V L); Tennis (V L); Academic Leadership Institute; Sportsmanship Award (Soccer and Tennis); Occupational Therapy; U of New England; Sacred Heart U

CORREA, JUSTIN D; SOMERSET, MA; SOMERSET HS; (SR); Hi Hnr Roll; Hnr Roll; Nat Hon Sy; Salutrn; Sci Fairs; St of Mnth; WWAHSS; Comm Volntr; Dbte Team; Sccr (V L); Track (V CL); U of Rochester, Humanities and Social Sciences Award; Air Force Research Award for Outstanding Aeronautics; History, Politics; Law; Brown U

CORREIA, KAYLA; WARE, MA; QUABBIN REG HS; (SO); Hi Hnr Roll; Hnr Roll; WWAHSS; Spanish Clb; President of Spanish Club; Psychology; Literature; Smith College; New York U

CORRIGAN, DEVIN E; WELLESLEY HILLS, MA; BELMONT HILL SCH; (JR); Hi Hnr Roll; Hnr Roll; WWAHSS; Amnsty Intl; Comm Volntr; Chrch Yth Grp; Bnd; Jzz Bnd; Cr Ctry (J); Skiing (J); Sccr (J); Tennis (J); Cl Off (P, V); Sch Ppr (E, R); Asian Studies / Chinese Language & Literature; Princeton U; Georgetown U

CORTES, NATHALIE; SPRINGFIELD, MA; SCIENCE AND TECH; (JR); Hnr Roll; Perf Att; WWAHSS; Chrch Yth Grp; Mus Clb; Photog; Chr; Ch Chr; Jzz Bnd; SP/M/VS; Sccr (V); Sftball (J); Track (J); Jazz / Rock Choir; Chorale Choir; Psychology; Music; Columbia International College; U of South Carolina

COSTA, ASHLEY; SOMERSET, MA; SOMERSET HS; (JR); Hi Hnr Roll; Hnr Roll; Nat Hon Sy; Pres Ac Ftns Aw; St of Mnth; Peer Tut/Med; FTA; Key Club; Prom Com; Sci Clb; Chrldg (V L); Gmnstcs (V L); Track (V L); Stu Cncl (R); CR (R); Big Buddy Program; Hip-Hop Dance Team Co-Captain; Physical Therapy; Engineering; Boston U; U Mass Lowell

COSTELLO, CAROLINA; ATTLEBORO, MA; ATTLEBORO HS; (JR); Hi Hnr Roll; Hnr Roll; Nat Hon Sy; Quill & Scroll; Bskball (J); Sch Ppr (R); Emmanuel College; U of Connecticut

COSTELLO, KAREN A; EAST WEYMOUTH, MA; WEYMOUTH HS; (JR); Hi Hnr Roll; Hnr Roll; St of Mnth; WWAHSS; Comm Volntr; Peer Tut/Med; SADD; Gmnstcs (V); Whose Who in American High Schools; Future Career and Community Leaders of America; Graphic Design; Business Communications

COTA, JESSICA M; WEYMOUTH, MA; WEYMOUTH HS; (JR); Hnr Roll; Perf Att; Comm Volntr; SP/M/VS; Stg Cre; (Club) Future Career and Community Leaders of America; Ultimate Frisbee (School Sport); Psychology; Forensic Science

COTREAU, KEVIN; BILLERICA, MA; BILLERICA MEM HS; (JR); Hnr Roll; Nat Hon Sy; Perf Att; Pres Sch; St of Mnth; Peer Tut/Med; DECA; Sci Clb; Bsball (J); Ftball (J); Track (V); Cl Off (R); Business Management; Accounting; Bryant U; Northeastern U

COUGHLIN, LINDSAY K; LONGMEADOW, MA; LONGMEADOW HS; (JR); Hi Hnr Roll; Nat Hon Sy; Pres Ac Ftns Aw; Yth Ldrshp Prog; Comm Volntr; Peer Tut/Med; Red Cr Aide; ArtClub; Chrch Yth Grp; DARE; Drma Clb; NYLC; Scouts; Vsity Clb; Bnd; Dnce; Orch; SP/M/VS; Sccr (J); Track (V L); 4 X 800 Relay School Record Holder 2003, '05 All-State Relay Team; 1st Choir / 1st Oboe-Recommended for All-State Orchestra, All-West Massachusetts Orchestra 1st Chair Oboe; Science; Medicine; College of William and Mary; College of the Holy Cross MA

COULOMBE, KAYLA A; SWANSEA, MA; EAST GATE CHRISTEN AC; (FR); Hi Hnr Roll; Drma Clb; Ch Chr; Dnce; SP/M/VS; Bskball; Piano/ Violin; Archery; Etymology; Art; Cambridge/Oxford U in England; Boston College

CRANE, BRIANNA N; BILLERICA, MA; ARLINGTON CATHOLIC HS; (FR); Hi Hnr Roll; Kwnis Aw; Sci Fairs; Hosp Aide; Chrch Yth Grp; Spanish Clb; Chrldg (V); Lcrsse (J); Vllyball (J); Doctor; Boston College; Boston U

CROAK, JEFFREY V; CLINTON, MA; CLINTON HS; (JR); Hi Hnr Roll; Hnr Roll; Otst Ac Ach Awd; Comm Volntr; Bskball (J); Accounting; Electrician; U Mass; Worcester State College

CROSSMAN, DEBORAH A; TAUNTON, MA; NEW TESTAMENT CHRISTIAN SCH; (SO); Sci Fairs; Chrch Yth Grp; Drma Clb; Mus Clb; Cl Off (T); Amateur Drama Production; Video Game Design; Acting

CROTTS, KATRINA; DANVERS, MA; DANVERS HS; (SR); F Lan Hn Soc; Hi Hnr Roll; Hnr Roll; Jr Mshl; Nat Hon Sy; Otst Ac Ach Awd; St of Mnth; WWAHSS; Yth Ldrshp Prog; Comm Volntr; Hab For Humty Volntr; Peer Tut/Med; Chrch Yth Grp; FTA; Key Club; Bnd; Ch Chr; Mch Bnd; Bskball (V CL); Sccr (V L); Track (J); Yrbk (R); Danvers Community Council Youth Volunteer of Year 2004; Harvard Book Award 11th Grade; Psychology; Westfield State College; Connecticut College

CULVERHOUSE, MARISA; FORESTDALE, MA; SANDWICH HS; (SR); Hi Hnr Roll; Hnr Roll; Nat Hon Sy; Perf Att; WWAHSS; Comm Volntr; Emplmnt; Key Club; Silver Scholar Award; Secretary of Key Club; Animal Science; Pre-Vet; U of Rhode Island; U of Kentucky

CUNNINGHAM, JOSH; WAYLAND, MA; WAYLAND HS; (JR); Hnr Roll; Ftball (V); Lcrsse (V); Wrstlg (V); Played in Door Lacrosse; 110% Award for JV Lacrosse; Political Science; U of Santa Barbara

CURTIN, MELISSA M; HOPKINTON, MA; HOPKINTON HS; (JR); Hi Hnr Roll; Hnr Roll; MVP; Yth Ldrshp Prog; Comm Volntr; Peer Tut/Med; ArtClub; Emplmnt; SADD; Vsity Clb; Fld Hky (VJ L); Ice Hky (JC); Sftball (VJCL); Academic Award for Wellness; Member of Diversity Club; Criminal Justice; Pre-Law; Northeastern U; U of New Hampshire

DABROWSKI, ALYCIA M; CHICOPEE, MA; CHICOPEE HS; (JR); Hi Hnr Roll; Hnr Roll; Hosp Aide; Outdrs Clb; Cr Ctry (V); Track (V); Raised Money for Breast Cancer; Ecology Club / Bay State Volunteer; Medical Field; American International College; Holyoke Community College

DACEY, DANIEL P; WEST ROXBURY, MA; BOSTON UNIVERSITY AC; (JR); Ctznshp Aw; Fncg (C); Crew; Math Area

DA CRUZ, BRITTANY; LUDLOW, MA; LUDLOW HS; (FR); Hi Hnr Roll; SADD; Biology; Veterinarian; U of Massachusetts

DAGONDON, KATRINA A; BOSTON, MA; O'BRYANT SCH OF MATH & SCIENCE; MS; Hi Hnr Roll; Hnr Roll; SP/M/VS; Headmaster's List; Bridge-Building Club; Law; Interior Design; Harvard Law School; Princeton U

DAIGLE, AARYN; WESTON, MA; WESTON HS; (JR); Hnr Roll; Comm Volntr; ArtClub; P to P St Amb Prg; Chr; Sccr (VJ); Early Childhood Education; Plymouth State U; U of Maine (Orono)

DALZON, MICHELLE G; MALDEN, MA; POPE JOHN XXIII HS; (JR); Hi Hnr Roll; Hnr Roll; MVP; Perf Att; Chrch Yth Grp; Drma Clb; Emplmnt; HO'Br Yth Ldrshp; Lib Aide; Clb; Dnce; Bskball (J); Chrldg (J); Yrbk; Winning Championship for Basketball in Elementary School; Marketing; Accounting; Boston College; Syracuse U

DAM, QUYNH D; BRIGHTON, MA; O'BRYANT SCH OF MATH & SCIENCE; MS; Hi Hnr Roll; Hnr Roll; Otst Ac Ach Awd; Perf Att; St of Mnth; Chrch Yth Grp; Pharmacy; Medical Field; Boston U; UMass Boston

DAMARI, LIAT; CANTON, MA; CANTON HS; (JR); Hi Hnr Roll; Nat Hon Sy; St of Mnth; Comm Volntr; Peer Tut/Med; ArtClub; Dbte Team; Drma Clb; Emplmnt; Mus Clb; NYLC; Scouts; Vsity Clb; Acpl Chr; Chr; SP/M/VS; Stg Cre; Sftball (J); Swmg (V L); Sch Ppr (R); Tri-M Music Honors Society; Lifeguard & CPR Certified; Biotechnology; Genetics / Neurobiology

DAME, MICHELLE; TURNERS FALLS, MA; TURNERS FALLS HS; (SO); Hi Hnr Roll; Otst Ac Ach Awd; St of Mnth; Bnd; Chr; Jzz Bnd; Mch Bnd; Bskball (J); Fld Hky (V); Sftball (J); Stu Cncl (R); CR (R); Law; Forensic Science

DAME, STEPHANIE S; WARREN, MA; QUABOAG MIDDLE HS; (JR); Hnr Roll; Perf Att; Emplmnt; Anthropology; Salve Regina U

D'ANDREA, TINA M; REVERE, MA; REVERE HS; (SR); Hnr Roll; Nat Hon Sy; Yth Ldrshp Prog; Sch Ppr (E, R); Yrbk; Interact Club; AP Scholar; Forensic Science; U of New Haven

DARSCH, NICKOLAUS; KINGSTON, MA; BOSTON COLLEGE HS; (JR); Hi Hnr Roll; Hnr Roll; Yth Ldrshp Prog; Key Club; Mth Clb/Tm; NYLC; Spanish Clb; Sch Ppr (R); Youth and Government / History Club; Business; Psychology; Boston College; Bentley College

DAVIN, MICHAEL; WESTON, MA; WESTON HS; (JR); Ctznshp Aw; Hnr Roll; Pres Ac Ftns Aw; Comm Volntr; Chrch Yth Grp; Emplmnt; Vsity Clb; Chr; Bskball (V L); Track (V L); Sch Ppr (P); Community Service Award; Intergenerational Club; MD; Mathematics (Engineer); Providence College; Boston College

DAVIS, JAYNA L; SWAMPSCOTT, MA; ESSEX AGRICULTURAL HS; (JR); Hi Hnr Roll; Ntl FFA; Bskball (V); Hsbk Rdg; Dramatic/Creative Writing; English; Emerson College; New York U

DE ANGELIS, JOSH; CHELMSFORD, MA; CHELMSFORD HS; (SO); Major League Baseball Player; Boston College

DECKER, ALYSIA M; DANVERS, MA; DANVERS HS; (FR); Spec Olymp Vol; FTA; Key Club; Bnd; Mch Bnd; Track (J)

DEEBLE, ZIPPORAH A; MAYNARD, MA; MAYNARD HS; (JR); Hnr Roll; Comm Volntr; Tchrs Aide; Bskball (J); Sftball (J); WAVM Radio; Musical "The King and I"; Pre-Law; Simon's Rock College of Bard; NYU

D'Andrea, Tina M
Revere HS
Revere, MA

Coulombe, Kayla A
East Gate Christen AC
Swansea, MA

Conly, Samantha
Avon Middle HS
Avon, MA

Comeau, Vinny
English HS
Lynn, MA

National
Honor Roll
Spring 2005

Claudio, Brian
Edgewood Greater Boston AC
Boston, MA

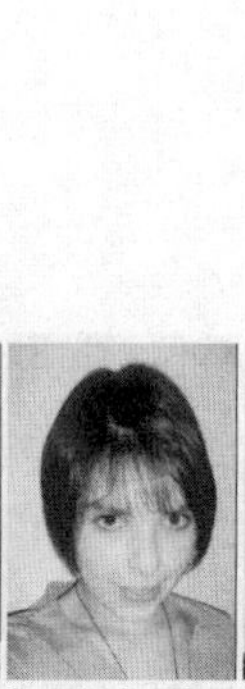
Cota, Jessica M
Weymouth HS
Weymouth, MA

Cunningham, Josh
Wayland HS
Wayland, MA

Davin, Michael
Weston HS
Weston, MA

DEGIROLAMO, TERESA A; BOSTON, MA; SAVIO PREPARATORY HS; (JR); Hi Hnr Roll; Nat Hon Sy; Valdctrian; Comm Volntr; Key Club; Bsball (J); Bskball (J); PP Ftbl (J); Sftball (J); President of Key Club; National Honors Society; Doctor; Northeastern U; Boston U

DELISLE, KAYLA; EAST LONGMEADOW, MA; EAST LONGMEADOW HS; (SO); Hnr Roll; WWAHSS; Comm Volntr; DARE; Spanish Clb; Medical Field

DELL, FELICIA; SHERBORN, MA; DOVER SHERBURN REG HS; (SO); F Lan Hn Soc; Hnr Roll; Otst Ac Ach Awd; Scouts; Tmpl Yth Grp; Clb; Dnce; Lit Mag (E); Sch Ppr (E); French National Exam Award; English Achievement Award; Sociology; Writing; Boston U; U of Miami

DE MELO, NICOLE; NEW BEDFORD, MA; NEW BEDFORD HS; (SR); All Am Sch; WWAHSS; Comm Volntr; DARE; Fld Hky (VJ L); Track (J); Nursing; Psychology; U of Massachusetts, Dartmouth College; Bridgewater State College

DEMPSEY, SARAH; BILLERICA, MA; BILLERICA MEM HS; (JR); Hi Hnr Roll; Hnr Roll; Peer Tut/Med; SADD; Track (J); Civil Engineering

DENNIS, JOSHUA R; BOYLSTON, MA; TAHANTO REG HS; (SO); Hi Hnr Roll; Nat Hon Sy; WWAHSS; Tmpl Yth Grp; Bsball (J); Ftball (J); Skiing (V); Black Belt Karate; Lifeguard; Engineering; U of Vermont; U of Connecticut

DEPTULA, BRITTANY; REVERE, MA; REVERE HS; (JR); Ctznshp Aw; Hi Hnr Roll; Hnr Roll; Nat Hon Sy; Nat Sci Aw; Otst Ac Ach Awd; Perf Att; St Schl; WWAHSS; Comm Volntr; Emplmnt; Fr of Library; Pep Squd; Prom Com; Vsity Clb; Dnce; SP/M/VS; Chrldg (V L); GAA (V); Vsy Clb (V L); Adv Cncl (P); Stu Cncl (R); Sch Ppr (R); State Cheerleading Champ - 2002 & 2003; National Cheerleading Champ - 2004 & 2005; Journalism; Law; New York U; Boston U

DICESARE, JENNA; MARSHFIELD, MA; NOTRE DAME AC; (SR); Hnr Roll; Perf Att; WWAHSS; Comm Volntr; Emplmnt; Key Club; Dnce; Language Honor Society / French; Academic Achievement for Honors US History; Communications; French; Fairfield U

DILLAN, EMILY; SANDWICH, MA; SANDWICH HS; (SO); Hnr Roll; Nat Sci Aw; Pres Ac Ftns Aw; Comm Volntr; Drma Clb; Emplmnt; Mod UN; SP/M/VS; Stg Cre; Swmg (V); CR (R); Published in Local Papers - Writing; Participated in Poetry Slam; English Teacher; Biology; U of New Hampshire

DIMARZIO, JULIANA; LEOMINSTER, MA; LEOMINSTER HS; (SO); Hi Hnr Roll; Hnr Roll; Cr Ctry (V L); Wrstlg (V); I Do Three Phase Events with My Horse and Was Able to Go to the Novice Championships; Chiropractic or Massage Therapy for Horses; Veterinarian or Assistant Veterinary; U of New Hampshire; Vermont Technical College

DIMINO, ALICIA A; WEST SPRINGFIELD, MA; WEST SPRINGFIELD HS; (SO); Hi Hnr Roll; Hnr Roll; P to P St Amb Prg; Dnce; Sccr (J); People-To-People Student Ambassador (2 Tours); Forensic Science; Psychology

DION, JOSEPH; DANVERS, MA; DANVERS HS; Hi Hnr Roll; Hnr Roll; MVP; WWAHSS; Emplmnt; Key Club; Stg Cre; Bsball (V L); Ftball (V L); Cinematography/Film

DIYAOLU, MODUPEOLA; BROCKTON, MA; BROCKTON HS; (JR); Hi Hnr Roll; Nat Hon Sy; Perf Att; Salutrn; Sci Fairs; USAA; Comm Volntr; Chrch Yth Grp; Drma Clb; Key Club; Sci Clb; Tech Clb; SP/M/VS; Stg Cre; Mar Art; Stu Cncl (R); CR (R); Bible Quizzing - Capitan; Medicine / Surgery; EMT; Brown U; New York U

DOLIBER, SARAH R; MARBLEHEAD, MA; MARBLEHEAD HS; (SR); Hnr Roll; MVP; Comm Volntr; Peer Tut/Med; Fld Hky (V); PP Ftbl (V); Sftball (V); CPR / First Aid / Lifeguard Certified; College of Charleston

DOMEGAN, LYNORE A; TEWKSBURY, MA; AC OF NOTRE DAME; (SR); Hnr Roll; Otst Ac Ach Awd; Perf Att; St of Mnth; WWAHSS; Comm Volntr; Spec Olymp Vol; DARE; Emplmnt; Dnce; SP/M/VS; Stu Cncl (T); Biology; Psychology; St Anselm's College; Rivier College

DOMINIQUE, VALERIE; MALDEN, MA; MALDEN HS; (SO); Hnr Roll; Comm Volntr; Chr; Dnce; SP/M/VS; Tennis (J); Step Team; Gospel Choir; Physics; Biology; Boston U; Tufts U

DONAHER, COURTNEY R; TYNGSBORO, MA; TYNGSBORO HS; (SO); Hi Hnr Roll; Hnr Roll; MVP; Otst Ac Ach Awd; Comm Volntr; Lcrsse (J); Sccr (V L); CR (R); Snowboarding Club; Engineering; Architecture

DONALDSON, KATHERINE; TAUNTON, MA; TAUNTON HS; (SO); Fut Prb Slvr; Hi Hnr Roll; Nat Hon Sy; Salutrn; Sci Fairs; Bnd; Bskball (J); Fld Hky; Track; Vllyball (J); Stu Cncl (R); CR (R); Law; Pharmacy; Boston College; Columbia

DONNELLY, KRISTYN D C; ATTLEBORO, MA; BISHOP FEEHAN HS; (JR); Hnr Roll; Comm Volntr; ArtClub; Emplmnt; Photog; Scouts; Vsity Clb; Chr; Swg Chr; Sftball (J); Track (V); Yrbk (R, P); National Art Honor Society; National Spanish Honor Society; Secondary Education; Business Management; Providence College; Stonehill College

DOYLE, TARA; CHICOPEE, MA; CHICOPEE HS; (SO); Hi Hnr Roll; Nat Hon Sy; St of Mnth; Comm Volntr; Peer Tut/Med; Emplmnt; Prom Com; Sccr (V L); Track (V L); Cl Off (S); Stu Cncl (R); Yrbk (E); Several Writing Contest Awards; Journalism; Brown U; U of Massachusetts

DRAYTON, CECELIA G; HAVERHILL, MA; HAVERHILL HS; (JR); Hi Hnr Roll; Hnr Roll; Otst Ac Ach Awd; Perf Att; Sci Fairs; St of Mnth; Yth Ldrshp Prog; Comm Volntr; ArtClub; Chrch Yth Grp; DARE; Key Club; Ntl FFA; Prom Com; Chr; Ch Chr; Dnce; SP/M/VS; Lit Mag (E); Environmental Club President; Pre-Med (Ob/Gyn); Landscape Design; Penn State U; U of Maryland Eastern Shore

DUARTE, RACHEL; TAUNTON, MA; COYLE & CASSIDY HS; (JR); Hi Hnr Roll; Nat Ldrshp Svc; Comm Volntr; Hosp Aide; Peer Tut/Med; Emplmnt; Prom Com; Dnce; Chrldg (J); Yrbk (P); Academic Letters Freshman/Soph & Junior; Leadership Assembly; Marketing; Public Relations; Syracuse U; Bryant U

DUBOIS, SAMANTHA N; SOMERSET, MA; SOMERSET HS; (FR); Hi Hnr Roll; WWAHSS; Amnsty Intl; Key Club; Mth Clb/Tm; Sci Clb; Clr Grd; Orch; Sch Ppr (R); Harvard U; Yale U

DULUDE, JILLIAN R; SOUTHAMPTON, MA; WESTFIELD HS; (FR); Perf Att; Scouts; Dnce; Fashion Design; Graphic Arts; Westfield State College; U of Massachusetts

DUMOND, DIANA P; REVERE, MA; REVERE HS; (JR); Hnr Roll; Comm Volntr; Dbte Team; Emplmnt; Prom Com; Clb; Track (VJ L); Vllyball (J); Stu Cncl (R); CR (R); Pharmacist; Physical Therapist; College of Pharmacy; U Mass Boston

DUNKELLY ALLEN, NIKESHIA; SPRINGFIELD, MA; NEW LEADERSHIP CHARTER SCH; MS; Ctznshp Aw; Hi Hnr Roll; Hnr Roll; Nat Hon Sy; Otst Ac Ach Awd; Perf Att; Sci Fairs; St of Mnth; St Optmst of Yr; Yth Ldrshp Prog; DARE; Drl Tm; Track (V); Medical Doctor; Harvard U; Boston U

DUNKLEY, NECKEISHA; SPRINGFIELD, MA; NEW LEADERSHIP CHART SCH; MS; MVP; Otst Ac Ach Awd; Perf Att; Sci Fairs; Hosp Aide; Chrch Yth Grp; DARE; Ch Chr; Dnce; Orch; Track (V); Pediatrician; Yale U; Temple U

DUPERRE, JUSTIN; BELCHERTOWN, MA; BELCHERTOWN HS; (SO); Hi Hnr Roll; Hnr Roll; Otst Ac Ach Awd; Comm Volntr; Chess; Emplmnt; Vllyball (J); Computer Engineering; Western New England College

DURANT, MARTHA E; LYNNFIELD, MA; PHILLIPS AC-ANDOVER; (JR); Comm Volntr; Peer Tut/Med; Emplmnt; Mod UN; Photog; Prom Com; Stg Cre; Lcrsse (J); Sccr (V L); Yrbk (P); Squash-Junior Varsity; Mathematics; Photography; Brown U; Princeton U

DURGIN, JULIENNE; MASHPEE, MA; MASHPEE HS; (SO); Hnr Roll; Sci Fairs; Comm Volntr; Hab For Humty Volntr; Chrch Yth Grp; DARE; Emplmnt; FBLA; Prom Com; Scouts; SADD; Chr; Ch Chr; Dnce; SP/M/VS; Bskball (J); Cr Ct Ski; Fld Hky (VJ L); Lcrsse (VJ L); PP Ftbl (VJ); Tennis (J); Track (J); Adv Cncl (R); Stu Cncl (R); Relay for Life / Cancer - 2 Yrs; Pro Am Golf Fund Raiser - 3 Yrs; Design; Business; Stonehill College; Wheaton College

DUVAL, DANIELLE L; DOUGLAS, MA; DOUGLAS HS; (JR); Hi Hnr Roll; Hnr Roll; Nat Hon Sy; Sci Fairs; St of Mnth; WWAHSS; Comm Volntr; Peer Tut/Med; DARE; Emplmnt; Jr Ach; Scouts; Chrldg (J); MADD; Broadcasting; Communications; Ithaca; New England

DWORSACK, ALISON M; AYER, MA; AYER HS; Hi Hnr Roll; Comm Volntr; ArtClub; DARE; Emplmnt; Glass Painting; Massachusetts College of Art

EAGLES, JULIANNA; QUINCY, MA; FONTBONNE AC; (JR); Hnr Roll; MVP; Comm Volntr; Peer Tut/Med; Bskball (V CL); Sccr (V CL); Silver Medal National Latin Exam-Freshman Year; Elected Honor Guard Member; Elementary Education/Special Education; Salve Regina, Holy Cross, Anna Maria; Roger Williams

EARLE, KATIE; WESTBOROUGH, MA; WESTBOROUGH HS; (SR); All Am Sch; Hi Hnr Roll; Nat Hon Sy; Nat Ldrshp Svc; Otst Ac Ach Awd; Pres Sch; USAA; WWAHSS; Comm Volntr; Spec Olymp Vol; Mth Clb/Tm; Ice Sktg; Skiing; Sccr; Cl Off (V); Stu Cncl; CR (R)

EARLY, BRITTANY; CHARLTON, MA; BAY PATH REG VOC HS; (FR); Hnr Roll; Civil Air Pat; CR (T); Culinary Arts; Johnson & Wales U

EDOUARD, EVELYN; AVON, MA; AVON HS; (SO); Hnr Roll; Otst Ac Ach Awd; St of Mnth; WWAHSS; Chrch Yth Grp; Emplmnt; Chr; Ch Chr; Dnce; Vllyball (V); Law; Music; Boston College; Berklee College of Music

ELBERT, DENNIS; LEXINGTON, MA; LEXINGTON HS; (SO); Hnr Roll; St of Mnth; DARE; Vsity Clb; Bnd; Ftball (V); Track (J); Received Medal from American Classical; League for National Latin Exam; Professional Football Player; Harvard U; Brown U

EL DAYAA, SALY; NORWOOD, MA; NORWOOD HS; (JR); Ctznshp Aw; F Lan Hn Soc; Hi Hnr Roll; Nat Ldrshp Svc; WWAHSS; Red Cr Aide; SADD; Chr; Ch Chr; Dnce; Book Club; Psychology; Richmond U in London

ENCARNACAO, ELIZABETH B; WINCHESTER, MA; WINCHESTER HS; (JR); F Lan Hn Soc; Hi Hnr Roll; Hnr Roll; MVP; Comm Volntr; SP/M/VS; Fncg (J); Track (J); Elementary School Tutoring; Business; Hotel and Restaurant Management; The College of William and Mary; Wake Forest U

ENGELKING, JARED; WESTBOROUGH, MA; WESTBOROUGH HS; (JR); Hi Hnr Roll; Nat Hon Sy; Nat Stu Ath Day Aw; WWAHSS; Comm Volntr; Peer Tut/Med; Spec Olymp Vol; Bskball (V); Sccr (V); Track (V); National Honor Society Member; State Champions Div. 2 Soccer 2003; Tufts U

ENTEL, STACY; BERKLEY, MA; SOMERSET HS; (JR); Hi Hnr Roll; Nat Hon Sy; Nat Mrt Semif; WWAHSS; Peer Tut/Med; Drma Clb; Emplmnt; Key Club; Mod UN; Acpl Chr; Chr; Ch Chr; SP/M/VS; Bskball; Sftball (V); Track; Vllyball (V C); Cl Off (S); Stu Cncl (R); 5 Years of Piano; Journalist; International Relations; Syracuse U; The American U

EPLER, BRETT; WELLESLEY HILLS, MA; WELLESLEY HS; (SO); Bsball (J); Cr Ctry (J L); Track (J L); Most Improved Player-Cape Cod Baseball; Coach Terners Baseball Camp-Umpire

EPLER, GREG; WELLESLEY HILLS, MA; WELLESLEY HS; (JR); Bsball (J); Cr Ctry (V L); Ftball; Sccr (J); Track (V CL); Stu Cncl; Coach's Award-Indoor Track; Coach's Award-Indoor Track; Coach's Award-Cape COD Baseball

ESTIME, VESMITA; CAMBRIDGE, MA; CAMBRIDGE RINDGE & LATIN HS; (JR); Hnr Roll; Perf Att; St of Mnth; Comm Volntr; Chrch Yth Grp; Emplmnt; Jr Ach; Lib Aide; Ch Chr; Lcrsse (?); Certificate of Invitation from the - National Student Leadership Conference - 2 Received; Certificate of Invitation from the -Congressional Student Leadership Conference - 1 Received; Nursing; Social Work; University of Massachusetts; Simmons College

ETIENNE, STEPHANIE; CAMBRIDGE, MA; CAMBRIDGE RINDGE & LATIN HS; (JR); Hi Hnr Roll; Hnr Roll; Nat Hon Sy; Otst Ac Ach Awd; Comm Volntr; Chrch Yth Grp; Emplmnt; Clb; Ch Chr; Bdmtn (J); Anesthesiology; Harvard U; Yale U

EVANGELISTO, DOMINIQUE K; PITTSFIELD, MA; PITTSFIELD HS; (JR); Hi Hnr Roll; Hnr Roll; Perf Att; Hosp Aide; Spanish Clb; Tae Kwon Do-Green Belt; Radiologist; Johns Hopkins U; U of Massachusetts Dartmouth

EVANS, EMILY; MARSHFIELD, MA; MARSHFIELD HS; (JR); Hi Hnr Roll; Hnr Roll; Nat Hon Sy; Perf Att; Spec Olymp Vol; Chrch Yth Grp; Key Club; Prom Com; Chr; Ch Chr; Swmg (V CL); Track (V); Yrbk (P); Elementary Education; Early Childhood Education; Simmons College; Emmanuel College

EWING, MATT; WELLESLEY HILLS, MA; THE RIVERS SCH; (FR); Hnr Roll; Sci Fairs; WWAHSS; Comm Volntr; ArtClub; Chrch Yth Grp; Emplmnt; Photog; Sci Clb; Tech Clb; Stg Cre; Cyclg; Lcrsse; Track; Wt Lftg; Engineering; Massachusetts Institute of Technology; Worchester Polytechnic Institute

FADRIGALAN, ERRAH; HOLBROOK, MA; HOLBROOK JR/SR HS; (SO); Hnr Roll; St of Mnth; Comm Volntr; Chrch Yth Grp; Dnce; Vllyball; Dance Philippines Performing Arts Company; Medicine, Fashion Designer

FAGAN, CATHERINE; SOUTHBOROUGH, MA; ALGONQUIN REG HS; (JR); Ctznshp Aw; Hnr Roll; Nat Hon Sy; Comm Volntr; Chrch Yth Grp; DARE; Drma Clb; Emplmnt; Key Club; Vsity Clb; French Clb; SP/M/VS; Bskball; Cr Ctry (V L); Sccr (J); Track (L); Vsy Clb; Yrbk (R); Boston Globe Drama Festival Award/3 yrs; Citizenship Award (2 Yrs); Communications/ Drama; U Connecticut, Providence College

FAHEY, KRISTEN L; BURLINGTON, MA; BURLINGTON HS; (JR); Hi Hnr Roll; Hnr Roll; Nat Hon Sy; Otst Ac Ach Awd; Sci Fairs; Comm Volntr; DARE; Emplmnt; Prom Com; SADD; Dnce; Fld Hky; Art Shows; Flute Recital; Psychology; Studio Art; Skidmore College; Colby College

FALLER, JESSE; BURLINGTON, MA; BURLINGTON HS; (JR); Hi Hnr Roll; St Schl; St of Mnth; Comm Volntr; Spec Olymp Vol; Latin Clb; Bnd; Jzz Bnd; Cr Ctry (V CL); Sccr (J); Track (V L); Engineering

FARAGO, MICHAEL A; WESTFORD, MA; WESTFORD AC; (SO); Hnr Roll; Nat Mrt LOC; Pres Sch; Sci Fairs; Peer Tut/Med; DARE; DECA; Emplmnt; Golf (J); Skiing (J); CR (R); Yrbk (R); National DECA Competitor; Business Management; Business Law; Bryant U; Babson College

FARRINGTON, LISA J; WALTHAM, MA; ARLINGTON CATHOLIC; (SR); Hnr Roll; Nat Hon Sy; WWAHSS; Peer Tut/Med; Drma Clb; Key Club; Dnce; SP/M/VS

FASOLINO, ALYSSA M; INDIAN ORCHARD, MA; SPRINGFIELD CTRL HS; (FR); All Am Sch; F Lan Hn Soc; Hnr Roll; Perf Att; WWAHSS; Comm Volntr; DARE; Drma Clb; Key Club; Photog; Dnce; SP/M/VS; Swmg (L); Vllyball (J); Yrbk (R); Psychology; Fashion Marketing; New York U; Columbia

Epler, Greg
Wellesley HS
Wellesley Hills, MA

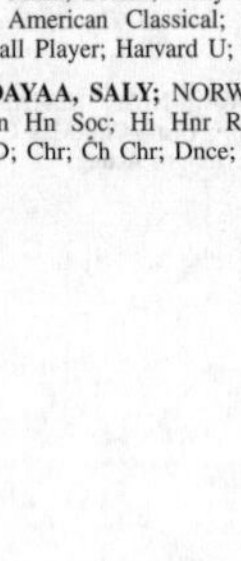

Epler, Brett
Wellesley HS
Wellesley Hills, MA

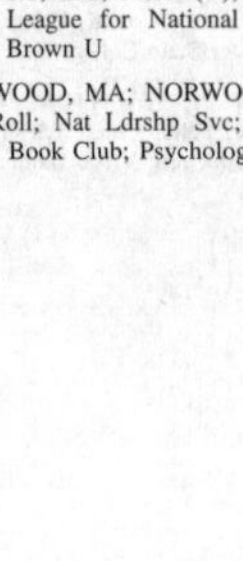

Domegan, Lynore A
AC Of Notre Dame
Tewksbury, MA

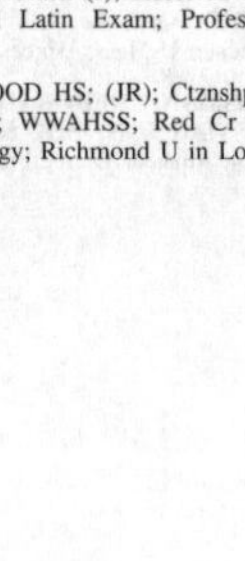

Elbert, Dennis
Lexington HS
Lexington, MA

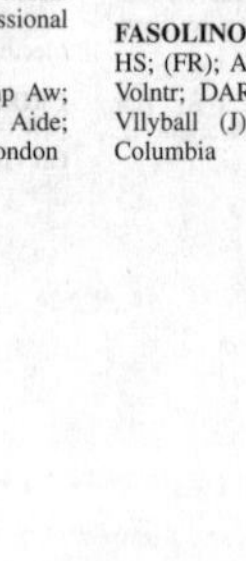

Etienne, Stephanie
Cambridge Rindge & Latin HS
Cambridge, MA

FAUCHER, MATTHEW M; NORTH ANDOVER, MA; N ANDOVER HS; (JR); Hi Hnr Roll; Nat Hon Sy; Comm Volntr; Emplmnt; Wrstlg (V L); Computer Sciences; Computer Tech / Engineering; Northeastern U; Wentworth Institute of Technology

FEDDERSEN, KEITH; TOWNSEND, MA; NASHOBA TECH HS; (SR); Hi Hnr Roll; Nat Hon Sy; Pres Sch; Salutrn; St Schl; Comm Volntr; Spec Olymp Vol; Voc Ind Clb Am; Adv Cncl (R); Dual Enrollment- Received Associate's Degree with Diploma; President of Schools Chapter of the National Tech Honor Society; Pre-Med; Pediatric Medicine; U of Massachusetts Amherst

FERRER, MARIANNE; LEOMINSTER, MA; LEOMINSTER HS; (SO); Registered Nurse; Michigan State; U Mass

FERRI, ANDREA T; DRACUT, MA; DRACUT HS; (JR); Hi Hnr Roll; MVP; Nat Hon Sy; Otst Ac Ach Awd; Yth Ldrshp Prog; Comm Volntr; Peer Tut/Med; Chrch Yth Grp; Emplmnt; Tech Clb; Bnd; Mch Bnd; Bskball (V CL); Sftball (V L); Track; Vllyball (V L); Stu Cncl (R); Sch Ppr (R); Nominated for Who's Who Among High School Students; Mathematics Major

FIALKOV, SHANYN D; MARBLEHEAD, MA; MARBLEHEAD HS; (JR); Hi Hnr Roll; Hnr Roll; Comm Volntr; Lcrsse (V); Sccr (J); Swmg (V); Lifeguard CPR & WSI Certified / LAX MVP & Most Improved; NEC Swimming Champs; Syracuse U; Stony Brook U

FINOCCHIETTI, LISA M; DANVERS, MA; DANVERS HS; (FR); Ctznshp Aw; Hi Hnr Roll; Otst Ac Ach Awd; St of Mnth; Comm Volntr; Emplmnt; Key Club; Prom Com; Svce Clb; Dnce; CR (R); Dance Awards; Baton Awards; Physical Therapy; Business; Mc Gill U; U of Miami

FLAHERTY, RYAN; BILLENZA, MA; BILLERICA MEM HS; (JR); Hi Hnr Roll; Nat Hon Sy; Nat Mrt LOC; Pres Sch; St of Mnth; Comm Volntr; Peer Tut/Med; Dbte Team; DECA; Emplmnt; JSA; Quiz Bowl; Schol Bwl; Sci Clb; Bsball (J); Cr Ctry (J); Vllyball (J); Lit Mag (E); 1st Place; Massachusetts Interscholastic Athletic Assoc. Essay Contest; MBA; Engineering; U of Pennsylvania; Boston College

FLANAGAN, BILLY; LYNN, MA; LYNN ENGLISH HS; (FR); Hnr Roll; Sci Fairs; ROTC; Bsball; Bskball; Golf; Sccr (J); CR (R); Boston Ballet School - 12 Weeks / 3rd Grade; Bowling League 1st Place; Military Science; Computer Science; Air Force Academy; Massachusetts Institute of Technology

FLANAGAN, BRIANNA J; SOUTH YARMOUTH, MA; DENNIS-YARMOUTH REG HS; (SR); Hi Hnr Roll; Hnr Roll; Nat Hon Sy; Otst Ac Ach Awd; WWAHSS; Comm Volntr; Chrch Yth Grp; Emplmnt; Pep Squd; Prom Com; Svce Clb; Dnce; Chrldg (V CL); Gmnstcs; Animal Science, Pre-Vet; U of Massachusetts Amherst

FLOYD, DANIEL W; HANSON, MA; WHITMAN-HANSON REG HS; (JR); Hi Hnr Roll; Hnr Roll; Perf Att; St of Mnth; Comm Volntr; Key Club; SADD; Foreign Clb; Stg Cre; Track; Adv Cncl (R); Personal Achievement Award; Ignite Leadership Academy; Marine Biology; History, U.S.

FLYNN, ERIN A; WILBRAHAM, MA; MINNECHAUG REG HS; (SR); Hnr Roll; Nat Hon Sy; Perf Att; Comm Volntr; Peer Tut/Med; Emplmnt; Key Club; NYLC; Scouts; Tchrs Aide; Tech Clb; Bnd; Mch Bnd; Pep Bnd; Stg Cre; Fld Hky (V); Skiing (V); Tennis (V); Girl Scout Gold Award; PharmD; Massachusetts College of Pharmacy of Health Sciences; Boston

FONTELLIO, CAMILLE; CAMBRIDGE, MA; CAMBRIDGE RINDGE & LATIN HS; (JR); Hi Hnr Roll; Hnr Roll; Nat Mrt LOC; WWAHSS; Peer Tut/Med; Emplmnt; Spanish Clb; Completion of Albert V Scott's Program; Part of School's Step Team; Pre-Med; Harvard U; Temple U

FORSYTH, SARA; WESTFORD, MA; WESTFORD AC; (JR); F Lan Hn Soc; Hi Hnr Roll; Nat Hon Sy; St of Mnth; Spec Olymp Vol; Chrch Yth Grp; Drma Clb; Mus Clb; Chr; Ch Chr; Orch; SP/M/VS; Honorable Mention for National German Exam (2x); Music Education; Librarian; Brigham Young U; U of New Hampshire

FORTE, MICHELLE; HANSON, MA; WHITMAN-HANSON HS; (FR); Hi Hnr Roll; DARE; Key Club; SADD; SADD

FRADKOV, ELENA; BRIGHTON, MA; BOSTON LATIN SCH; (JR); Hi Hnr Roll; Sci Fairs; Drma Clb; Jr Cls League; Lib Aide; French Clb; Dnce; Sch Ppr (R); Gold on National Latin Exam- 2003, 2004; Modern Prize - A Average in All Classes for Year 2003, 2004; College Major / Pre-Med; Professional Degree / MD; Harvard College

FRANCO, MICHELLE N; WILBRAHAM, MA; MINNERHAUG REG HS; (SO); Hi Hnr Roll; Pres Sch; St of Mnth; Comm Volntr; DARE; Key Club; Mod UN; Outdrs Clb; Scouts; Dnce; Cr Ctry (J); Sch Ppr (R); Member of Mock Law / Mock Trial Team; Girl Scout Silver Award

FRYE, CHRISTINE; EAST FALMOUTH, MA; FALMOUTH HS; (FR); 4H Awd; Hnr Roll; Nat Hon Sy; Sci Fairs; St of Mnth; Hosp Aide; 4-H; DARE; Emplmnt; SADD; Wdwrkg Clb; Dnce; Chrldg (V); Veterinarian; Applied Science; U of Florida; U of California, LA

FUNG, PER KING; BOSTON, MA; O'BRYANT SCH OF MATH & SCIENCE; (JR); Hnr Roll; Perf Att; ROTC; NJROTC (Guidon) 2 Years; Boston U; Boston College

FUNG, YUNG; CHELMSFORD, MA; CHELMSFORD HS; (JR); Hi Hnr Roll; Nat Hon Sy; Otst Ac Ach Awd; Comm Volntr; Peer Tut/Med; Dbte Team; Emplmnt; JSA; Mth Clb/Tm; Mod UN; Mus Clb; Sci Clb; Orch; Vllyball (J); CR (R); Chairman and Co-Founder of the Asian Culture Committee; Participated in Northeastern Districts Central Committee; Biomedical Business

GADSON, JACKEE L; SPRINGFIELD, MA; CATHEDRAL HS; (SR); Hnr Roll; Otst Ac Ach Awd; Sci/Math Olympn; Chrch Yth Grp; Emplmnt; Photog; Ch Chr; African-American History - Academic Excellence; Religion-Academic Excellence; Law / Criminal Justice; American International College

GAGE, STEVEN; MIDDLEBORO, MA; MIDDLEBORO HS; (JR); Sci Fairs; St of Mnth; Zoologist / Zoology; U of Rhode Island; Bridgewater State College

GAKPO, AGNES E; BOSTON, MA; O'BRYANT SCH OF MATH & SCIENCE; MS; Hnr Roll; Perf Att; Sci Fairs; Comm Volntr; Peer Tut/Med; Chrch Yth Grp; DARE; Dbte Team; Drma Clb; Jr Ach; Mus Clb; Sci Clb; Chr; SP/M/VS; Stepping Stone Academy (Graduated in 2003); Pediatrician; Bio Tech Engineering; Harvard U; Boston U

GALLUCIO, NICOLE; PEABODY, MA; PEABODY VETERANS MEMORIAL HS; MS; Hnr Roll; St of Mnth; ArtClub; Chr; Ch Chr; Dnce; Yrbk (E, R, P); Professional Photographer; School Teacher; U of Massachusetts; Boston College

GARBER, MELANIE; PEABODY, MA; PINGREE SCH; (SR); Hi Hnr Roll; Hnr Roll; Comm Volntr; Drma Clb; Tchrs Aide; SP/M/VS; Stg Cre; CR (R); Lit Mag (E); Theater Education; Theater Arts; Emerson College

GARBER, MICHAEL; SHARON, MA; SHARON HS; (SO); Hnr Roll; St of Mnth; Yth Ldrshp Prog; Comm Volntr; Peer Tut/Med; Cmptr Clb; Emplmnt; Mod UN; Scouts; Svce Clb; Tmpl Yth Grp; Bnd; Jzz Bnd; Seeds of Peaces Beyond Borders; Ordinary Heroes Project; International Relations; Political Science; American U; George Washington U

GARCIA, LINDA A; MILFORD, MA; MILFORD HS; (SR); Hnr Roll; WWAHSS; Comm Volntr; Hab For Humty Volntr; Chrch Yth Grp; Photog; Prom Com; Spanish Clb; Ch Chr; Dnce; Cr Ctry (J); Track (J); Yrbk (P); Participated In Character Education; Prom Committee / Talent Show / Pep Rally; Professional Actress; Study Languages / Business; Framingham College; Mass B Community College

GAROFOLI, NICOLE; STERLING, MA; WACHUSETT REG HS; (SR); Hi Hnr Roll; Hnr Roll; Nat Mrt Sch Recip; WWAHSS; Comm Volntr; Hosp Aide; Spec Olymp Vol; Emplmnt; Prom Com; Chr; Dnce; Breast Cancer Walk Volunteer; Soup Kitchen Volunteer; High School Teacher; Suffolk U

GASTALL, LAUREN K; SOMERSET, MA; SOMERSET HS; (SR); Hi Hnr Roll; Otst Ac Ach Awd; Bskball (V L); Tennis (J); Vllyball (J); Cl Off (V); Social Work; Physical Education Teaching

GAWLIK JR, PETER A; MARSHFIELD, MA; MARSHFIELD HS; (SO); Hnr Roll; DARE; Bnd; Lcrsse (J); Boston College; Bridgewater State U

GAY, DARA; TAUNTON, MA; TAUNTON HS; (SR); Hnr Roll; Nat Hon Sy; Sci Fairs; WWAHSS; Drma Clb; Prom Com; Portuguese Clb; Bnd; Dnce; Mch Bnd; SP/M/VS; Sccr (V L); Swmg (V CL); Stu Cncl (R); CR (R); Who's Who Among High School Students 03-04; National Honor Society; Civil Engineering; Architecture; Roger Williams U

GIARD, ADAM J; NORTH ANDOVER, MA; NORTH ANDOVER HS; (JR); Hnr Roll; Comm Volntr; Peer Tut/Med; Foreign Language German/ Japanese; Physics and Mathematics

GIENG, DEBBIE; LAWRENCE, MA; NORTH ANDOVER HS; (SR); Nat Hon Sy; WWAHSS; Yth Ldrshp Prog; Comm Volntr; Spec Olymp Vol; Emplmnt; Off Aide; Svce Clb; Tchrs Aide; Track (V); Stu Cncl (R); Interact; Computer Science; Theatre; Northeastern U; U of Massachusetts Amherst

GILLIGAN, TIMOTHY; MEDFORD, MA; MEDFORD HS; (SO); Ctznshp Aw; Hi Hnr Roll; Hnr Roll; Otst Ac Ach Awd; Perf Att; St of Mnth; Yth Ldrshp Prog; Comm Volntr; Chrch Yth Grp; Drma Clb; Emplmnt; Key Club; Bnd; Mch Bnd; Pep Bnd; SP/M/VS; Yrbk (E, P); Theater Arts; Diplomacy; Florida U; New York U

GILLOTTE, KEVIN; TEWKSBURY, MA; TEWKSBURY MEMORIAL HS; (SR); Hi Hnr Roll; Hnr Roll; Nat Hon Sy; Perf Att; Pres Ac Ftns Aw; Yth Ldrshp Prog; Comm Volntr; Peer Tut/Med; Emplmnt; Vsity Clb; Sccr (V); Mechanical Engineering; Chemical Engineering; Loyola Marymount U; U of San Diego

GILOOLY, CAROLYN; MEDWAY, MA; MEDWAY HS; (SO); Hi Hnr Roll; Pres Ac Ftns Aw; Comm Volntr; Emplmnt; Bskball (J); Sccr (J); Track (L)

GIRARD, LEANNE L; DANVERS, MA; DANVERS HS; (SR); F Lan Hn Soc; Hi Hnr Roll; Hnr Roll; Kwnis Aw; Nat Hon Sy; St of Mnth; Peer Tut/Med; Key Club; Photog; SADD; Sccr (V L); Sftball (J); National Honor Society; World Language National Honor Society; Hospitality Management; Business; U of New Hampshire; Bentley College

GLASER, JONATHAN; WESTWOOD, MA; WESTWOOD HS; (JR); Hnr Roll; Comm Volntr; Peer Tut/Med; Key Club; Vsity Clb; Sccr (V L); Track (J); Founder of Critical Analysis of Pop-Culture Club; International Business; Entrepreneurship; Babson College; Wharton School of Finance

GOLDBERG, ALYSSA; WELLESLEY, MA; WELLESLEY HS; (SR); Hnr Roll; Nat Stu Ath Day Aw; Pres Sch; WWAHSS; Yth Ldrshp Prog; Comm Volntr; Emplmnt; Jr Ach; Key Club; Svce Clb; Tchrs Aide; Dnce; Orch; Ice Hky (V L); PP Ftbl (V); Vllyball (V L); Stu Cncl (R); Treasurer of Key Club; Psychology; Medicine; Union College

GOMES, SIERRA M; MALDEN, MA; POPE JOHN XXIII HS; (SR); Hi Hnr Roll; Hnr Roll; Nat Hon Sy; Otst Ac Ach Awd; Yth Ldrshp Prog; Comm Volntr; Peer Tut/Med; Emplmnt; Prom Com; Vsity Clb; Bskball (V C); Scr Kpr (J); Sccr (V C); Sftball (V C); Cl Off (P); CR (R); Yrbk (R); Junior of the Year; Sophomore of the Year; Sports Public Relations; PR; Southern New Hampshire U

GONCALVES, JASON P; PLYMOUTH, MA; PLYMOUTH SOUTH HS; (JR); Hnr Roll; Sci Fairs; Comm Volntr; Peer Tut/Med; ArtClub; Cmptr Clb; Emplmnt; Outdrs Clb; Scouts; Tech Clb; Bskball; Ice Sktg; Sccr; Presently Attending Computer Science Program / Going Toward a Certificate; Computer Science Engineer- / Master's Degree Computer Science; WPI; Wentworth College

GONSALVES, SHAYNA L; NORTH DARTMOUTH, MA; DARTMOUTH HS; (SO); Ctznshp Aw; Hnr Roll; Pres Ac Ftns Aw; Amnsty Intl; Hab For Humty Volntr; Emplmnt; Mus Clb; Orch; SP/M/VS; Track (J); Junior District Orchestra - 8th & 9th Grade; Senior District Orchestra -10th Grade; Music Performance; World History; Boston U; New York U

GOOD, STEVEN; GREEN HARBOR, MA; MARSHFIELD HS; (SO); Hi Hnr Roll; Hnr Roll; Comm Volntr; Ftball (V); Lcrsse (VJ); Cl Off; Boston College

GOODWIN III, DONALD E; REVERE, MA; MALDEN CATHOLIC HS; (SO); Hi Hnr Roll; Hnr Roll; Nat Hon Sy; Pres Sch; Sci Fairs; St of Mnth; Comm Volntr; Track (J); Wt Lftg (J); CR (R); Sch Ppr (R); Andrew Marzilli Scholarship (Most Deserving Freshman); Model Congress / Tutor; Business Administration; Finance; Notre Dame U; Boston College

GORDON, EMILY A; AGAWAM, MA; THE MACDUFFIE SCH; (SR); F Lan Hn Soc; Hi Hnr Roll; Hnr Roll; Kwnis Aw; Nat Hon Sy; Otst Ac Ach Awd; Perf Att; St of Mnth; Comm Volntr; Peer Tut/Med; Emplmnt; Key Club; Mus Clb; Quill & Scroll; Spanish Clb; SP/M/VS; Adv Cncl (R); Sch Ppr (E); Cum Laude / National Piano Competition Awards; Best News Article / Peace Award at HS 2005; Spanish / French Major - Romance Languages; Law / Journalism / International Affairs; Attending in Fall 2005 - U of Maryland

GORDON, JESSE; MANSFIELD, MA; (SR); Hi Hnr Roll; Lcrsse (V); Mechanical Engineering; U of Massachusetts Amherst; U of Massachusetts Dartmouth

GOWELL, KATIE; LUNENBURG, MA; LUNENBURG HS; (SR); Hi Hnr Roll; Hnr Roll; Nat Hon Sy; Otst Ac Ach Awd; St Schl; Comm Volntr; Spec Olymp Vol; Emplmnt; Prom Com; SP/M/VS; Mar Art; Martial Arts Instructor; English / Secondary Education; Lesley College; Brandeis U

GRAHAM, LINDSAY; WESTFORD, MA; WESTFORD AC; (JR); Hnr Roll; DECA; Emplmnt; FCA; Ntl Beta Clb; Dnce; Sftball (V L); DECA President 05-06; Public Relations; Marketing; Boston College; Providence College

GRANT JR, MIKE G; NORTH CARVER, MA; CARVER HS; (JR); Hnr Roll; MVP; Comm Volntr; Peer Tut/Med; Bskball (V); Ftball (V); Track (V); New England Long Jump Champion (2004); 1,000 Yd Rusher - Football; Sports Medicine; Psychology; Boston College; U of Southern California

GRASS, ALEXANDRA; HOLYOKE, MA; MAC DUFFIE HS; (JR); Key Club; Latin Clb; Dnce; Tennis (V); Who's Who; Psychology; American History; College of the Holy Cross; Rollins

GRAVELINE, NICK; PALMER, MA; PALMER HS; (FR); Hi Hnr Roll; Hnr Roll; Bsball (J); Ftball (V); Wt Lftg

GRAVELLESE, JOSEPH J; REVERE, MA; REVERE HS; (JR); Hnr Roll; Nat Hon Sy; WWAHSS; Comm Volntr; Dbte Team; Emplmnt; NtlFrnscLg; Spch Team; Golf (V); Sch Ppr (R); President of Debate Team; 8th in the Country - National French Exam; Communications; Northeastern U; Boston U

GRAVES, EILEEN M; ASHFIELD, MA; MOHAWK TRAIL R. HS; (JR); Hi Hnr Roll; Nat Hon Sy; Sci Fairs; Comm Volntr; Chrch Yth Grp; Emplmnt; Lib Aide; Mus Clb; Chr; Ch Chr; Dnce; SP/M/VS; Track; Vllyball (J)

GRAY, ERIN; GARDNER, MA; GARDNER HS; (JR); Hi Hnr Roll; Nat Hon Sy; WWAHSS; Tech Clb; Swmg (V); Greenwood Memorial Swim Club; Education

GREENE, MARK; LEE, MA; LENOX MEMORIAL; (SO); Hi Hnr Roll; Scouts; French Clb; Cr Ctry (V L); Cr Ct Ski (V L); Hsbk Rdg; United States Pony Clubs-C/Rating As of 5/04; United States Eventing Association-Area1 Beginner Novice Championship Competition 2004; Mechanical Engineering; U of Massachusetts-Amherst; U of New Hampshire

Goodwin III, Donald E
Malden Catholic HS
Revere, MA

Gakpo, Agnes E
O'Bryant Sch Of Math & Science
Boston, MA

Fung, Per King
O'Bryant Sch Of Math & Science
Boston, MA

Floyd, Daniel W
Whitman-Hanson Reg HS
Hanson, MA

Ferrer, Marianne
Leominster HS
Leominster, MA

Flanagan, Brianna J
Dennis-Yarmouth Reg HS
South Yarmouth, MA

Gadson, Jackee L
Cathedral HS
Springfield, MA

Gonsalves, Shayna L
Dartmouth HS
North Dartmouth, MA

Grant Jr, Mike G
Carver HS
North Carver, MA

GREENE, NATIERA; SPRINGFIELD, MA; NEW LEADERSHIP CHARTER SCH; MS; Hi Hnr Roll; Hnr Roll; Nat Sci Aw; Otst Ac Ach Awd; Perf Att; Sci Fairs; DARE; Mar Art (V); Pediatrician; Entrepreneur; U of NC; Atlanta A & T

GREENE, TANISHA M; BOSTON, MA; ECONOMICS AND BUSINESS AC; (SR); Hnr Roll; Nat Hon Sy; Perf Att; Sci Fairs; Comm Volntr; Scouts; Dnce; SP/M/VS; Chrldg (V); Yrbk (E); National Honor Society Member Award; Cheerleading Leadership Award; Business Management; Salem State College; Curry College

GROCHMAL, KYLE C; REHOBOTH, MA; BISHOP FEEHAN HS; (JR); F Lan Hn Soc; Hi Hnr Roll; Hnr Roll; Nat Hon Sy; Sci Fairs; WWAHSS; Comm Volntr; Peer Tut/Med; Emplmnt; Mth Clb/Tm; NYLC; SADD; Cr Ctry (V C); Track (V); Beyond Borders Delegate for "Seeds of Peace" Organization; Business; Arabic; Stanford U; New York U

GROH, CAITLYN; WELLESLEY HILLS, MA; WELLESLEY HS; (SO); MVP; St of Mnth; Comm Volntr; Hab For Humty Volntr; ArtClub; Chrch Yth Grp; Key Club; Lib Aide; Photog; Svce Clb; Spanish Clb; Ice Hky (V L); President of Habitat for Humanity Club; Anti-Deformation League Peer Trainer; Public Interest Law; Civil Rights Studies; Northeastern U; St. Johns U

GROSS, VLADIMIR; NORTH ANDOVER, MA; NORTH ANDOVER HS; (SO); Hnr Roll; Hosp Aide; Bnd; Mch Bnd; Tennis (J); Biology; Tufts U; Boston College

GRZELAK, STEPHANIE J; CHICOPEE, MA; CHICOPEE COMP HS; (JR); F Lan Hn Soc; Fut Prb Slvr; Hi Hnr Roll; Hnr Roll; Nat Hon Sy; Otst Ac Ach Awd; WWAHSS; Yth Ldrshp Prog; Peer Tut/Med; Civil Air Pat; Drma Clb; Emplmnt; Prom Com; SADD; Vsity Clb; Drl Tm; SP/M/VS; Cr Ctry (V); Track (V); Adv Cncl (R); Stu Cncl (R); Civil Air Patrol C/Major; Foreign Language Achievement; Business; Language

GUERIN, MICHELE; CHICOPEE, MA; CHICOPEE HS; Hnr Roll; St of Mnth; Comm Volntr; DARE; Prom Com; Bskball (V L); Sccr (V L); Stu Cncl (R); Athlete of the Month; Criminal Justice

GUILLEMETTE, MICHAEL; TAUNTON, MA; TAUNTON HS; (JR); Hnr Roll; Nat Hon Sy; Sci Fairs; Comm Volntr; Hosp Aide; Peer Tut/Med; DARE; Drma Clb; Key Club; Portuguese Clb; Stu Cncl (R); Sch Ppr (R); Biologist

HABOSIAN, ARMEN; WESTFORD, MA; WESTFORD AC; (SO); Hnr Roll; Comm Volntr; Chess; Ftball (VJ L); Lcrsse (VJCL); Track (V); 2004 Boston College Football Camp MVP; Boston College; U of New Hampshire

HANLON, CHARLES; PILLERICA, MA; BILLERICA MEM HS; (JR); Hi Hnr Roll; Nat Mrt Semif

HARRINGTON, JENNIFER; WESTBOROUGH, MA; WORCESTER AC; (JR); Hi Hnr Roll; Hnr Roll; Amnsty Intl; Comm Volntr; Hab For Humty Volntr; Drma Clb; Emplmnt; Mth Clb/Tm; Mod UN; Chr; Dnce; SP/M/VS; Stg Cre; Lit Mag (R); Humane Society Volunteer; Accomplished Pianist and Guitarist; International Business with French; New York U; Cambridge U

HARRISON, PAIGE; SUTTON, MA; SUTTON HS; (JR); Hi Hnr Roll; Hnr Roll; Nat Hon Sy; Otst Ac Ach Awd; Perf Att; Pres Ac Ftns Aw; Yth Ldrshp Prog; Comm Volntr; Peer Tut/Med; DARE; Emplmnt; NYLC; Bnd; Jzz Bnd; Bskball (VJCL); Sccr (VJCL); Sftball (J); Tennis (V L); Track (V L); Cl Off (T); President Peer Leaders; Massachusetts Olympic Development Soccer; Pre-Med; Tufts U; Boston College

HASTINGS, JEANNINE; FEEDING HILLS, MA; AGAWAM HS; (SR); Ctznshp Aw; F Lan Hn Soc; Hi Hnr Roll; Nat Hon Sy; Otst Ac Ach Awd; Pres Sch; Comm Volntr; Peer Tut/Med; DARE; Emplmnt; FTA; Mth Clb/Tm; Photog; Prom Com; Quill & Scroll; SADD; Chr; Sccr (V L); Track (L); Lit Mag (E); Yrbk (P); Lions Club Scholarship Award; American Legion Award / President's Award; Elementary Education; English; Westfield State College; Franklin Pierce College

HATSTAT, SPENSER A; CLINTON, MA; CLINTON HS; (JR); Hi Hnr Roll; Peer Tut/Med; DARE; Emplmnt; P to P St Amb Prg; Scouts; Bsball (J); Bskball (J); People to People Student Ambassador; Marine Biology; Sports Management; U of Rhode Island; Salem State College

HATZIIOANNOU, VASILIOS; DANVERS, MA; DANVERS HS; (JR); Hi Hnr Roll; Hnr Roll; WWAHSS; Comm Volntr; DARE; Outdrs Clb; Greek Clb; Lcrsse (J); Sccr (V); Track (V); Pre Medical; Biology; McGill (Canada); Boston U

HAY, TEJA D; RANDOLPH, MA; FONTBONNE AC; (JR); Ctznshp Aw; F Lan Hn Soc; Hi Hnr Roll; Sci Fairs; WWAHSS; Emplmnt; Off Aide; Spanish Clb; Sccr (V); Track (V); Peer Education Club; Business Administration, Marketing; Communication; Boston U; Bentley College

HAYCOCK, NICHOLAS W; CAMBRIDGE, MA; CAMBRIDGE RINDGE & LATIN HS; (SR); Hnr Roll; Nat Hon Sy; Nat Mrt LOC; Sci Fairs; Sci/Math Olympn; Comm Volntr; Mus Clb; Jzz Bnd; Cr Ctry (V); Track (V); Yrbk (R, P); National History Day Regional and State; Science Medal Academic Decathlon; Brown U; U of Pennsylvania

HENO-COE, GILLES R; NORTH ADAMS, MA; MT GREYLOCK HS; (SR); Hi Hnr Roll; Hnr Roll; Nat Hon Sy; Nat Mrt Fin; WWAHSS; Comm Volntr; Peer Tut/Med; Emplmnt; Jr Cls League; SP/M/VS; Stg Cre; Stu Cncl (R); Sch Ppr (E); JCL Officer - 4 Years; Film Club President & Co-Founder; Art / Literature / History; Classics / Psychology; Williams College; Brown U

HENRICKSEN, TRISTAN C; LEXINGTON, MA; LEXINGTON HS; (SO); Hnr Roll; St of Mnth; Aviation/Flight Operations; Astronomy; Daniel Webster College

HENRY, PAUL J; NORTHBOROUGH, MA; ST JOHN'S HS; (SO); Hi Hnr Roll; Hnr Roll; Comm Volntr; Lcrsse; Track; History; Boston College; Stanford

HERNANDEZ PEREZ, YANILEE; SPRINGFIELD, MA; PUTNAM VOC TECH HS; (FR); 4H Awd; Hi Hnr Roll; 4-H; DARE; Dbte Team; ROTC; Bsball (V); Vllyball (V); Springfield Technical Community College; American International College

HERRING, TORIN; EAST WEYMOUTH, MA; WEYMOUTH HS; (SR); Hi Hnr Roll; Hnr Roll; Nat Hon Sy; Comm Volntr; Chrch Yth Grp; Emplmnt; Cr Ctry (J); Lcrsse (J); Sccr (VJ); Track (V L); Engineering; Military Fighter Pilot; United States Air Force Academy

HESS, JILLIAN; KINGSTON, MA; SILVER LAKE REG HS; (JR); Hnr Roll; Nat Hon Sy; Nat Stu Ath Day Aw; Otst Ac Ach Awd; Hab For Humty Volntr; Emplmnt; Key Club; Vsity Clb; Sccr (V L); Track (V CL); NHS-Treasurer; Captain Council-President; Physical Therapy; Psychology; Northeastern U; UConn-U of Connecticut

HEWITT, AMANDA; LANCASTER, MA; NASHOBA REG HS; (FR); Hi Hnr Roll; Hnr Roll; Perf Att; Peer Tut/Med; Chr; PP Ftbl (J); Yrbk (R); Pre-Med; Master's Degree; Harvard Medical School; U Of Notre Dame

HIRALDO, MARICRUZ; SALEM, MA; SALEM HS; (SO); Hnr Roll; St of Mnth; Yth Ldrshp Prog; Comm Volntr; Chrch Yth Grp; Cmptr Clb; DARE; Mod UN; Ch Chr; Dnce; Upward Bound Program Salem State College; Union Latina; Salem State College

HOBSON, LORI; BOSTON, MA; BOSTON LATIN AC; (MS); F Lan Hn Soc; Hnr Roll; Otst Ac Ach Awd; Pres Sch; Comm Volntr; Chrch Yth Grp; Emplmnt; Pep Squd; Latin Clb; Chr; Pep Bnd; Summa Cum Laude for National Latin Exam; Interior Designing; Cooking; U of Miami

HOFFMAN, SARAH J; HADLEY, MA; HOPKINS AC; (JR); Hi Hnr Roll; Hnr Roll; Nat Hon Sy; Perf Att; Pres Sch; Sci/Math Olympn; St of Mnth; Comm Volntr; Drma Clb; Mth Clb/Tm; P to P St Amb Prg; Prom Com; Dnce; SP/M/VS; Stg Cre; Yrbk (E, P); Health Advisory Committee; Science; Math; Boston U; New York U

HOGUE, JENNIE; MILLVILLE, MA; BLACKSTONE MILLVILLE REG; (SR); Hi Hnr Roll; MVP; Nat Hon Sy; Nat Stu Ath Day Aw; Otst Ac Ach Awd; Pres Ac Ftns Aw; Sci Fairs; Sci/Math Olympn; WWAHSS; Comm Volntr; Peer Tut/Med; Chrch Yth Grp; DARE; Emplmnt; Bskball (J); Mar Art; Skiing; Sccr (VJCL); Track (VJ L); Vllyball; Cl Off (S); Medical Transcription; Medical Technology; Community College of Rhode Island; Rhode Island College

HOLLAND, CHRISTIAN; BOSTON, MA; CATHOLIC MEMORIAL HS; (JR); Hi Hnr Roll; Hnr Roll; Perf Att; Nat Hon Sy; Comm Volntr; Red Cr Aide; Dbte Team; Emplmnt; NtlFrnscLg; Spch Team; Chr; Ch Chr; Jzz Bnd; Bskball (J); Ftball (V); Track (V); Wt Lftg (V); Campus Ministry; Forensic Team; Business Management; Fashion Mechandising; Howard U; Brown U

HOLMES, KENNETH; SPRINGFIELD, MA; BRIDGE AC; (SO); Hnr Roll; St of Mnth; Peer Tut/Med; DARE; Emplmnt; Off Aide; Tchrs Aide; Business & Computers; Harvard U; Georgia Tech

HOU, TA A; REVERE, MA; REVERE HS; (JR); Hnr Roll; MVP; Otst Ac Ach Awd; Comm Volntr; Hosp Aide; ArtClub; Outdrs Clb; Prom Com; Dnce; SP/M/VS; Stg Cre; Track (V L); Vllyball (V L); Stu Cncl (R); CR (R); Yrbk; Excellence in Social Studies - Award; Cultural Talent Show Coordinator; Chemistry / Pharmacist; Forensic Science; Northeastern U; Boston U

HOUGHTLING, SAMANTHA; PITTSFIELD, MA; TACONIC HS; (JR); Hnr Roll; WWAHSS; Comm Volntr; ROTC; Forensic Psychology; Bay Path College

HOULE, HEATHER L; GRANBY, MA; GRANBY JR/SR HS; (FR); Hnr Roll; Perf Att; Peer Tut/Med; Bskball (J); Doctorate; UConn; UMass

HOWLAND, AMANDA L; MILLBURY, MA; MILLBURY MEMORIAL JR/SR SH; (SO); Hi Hnr Roll; Chrch Yth Grp; DARE; Drma Clb; Emplmnt; Mus Clb; Bnd; Ch Chr; Jzz Bnd; Mch Bnd; Rose Bowl Parade Participant; All State Band & District Band; Music Education; English or History; U Mass Amherst; Westfield State College

HRISULEV, GEORGE; WINCHESTER, MA; WINCHESTER HS; (JR); Hnr Roll; Comm Volntr; Spec Olymp Vol; ArtClub; Drma Clb; Emplmnt; P to P St Amb Prg; Photog; Volunteer At Health South Rehabilitation Center, Woburn MA; Pre-Dentistry; General Dentistry; Tufts U; Clark U

HSU, MICHAEL T; WESTON, MA; WESTON HS; (JR); Hi Hnr Roll; Hnr Roll; MVP; Otst Ac Ach Awd; Comm Volntr; Chrch Yth Grp; Emplmnt; Mth Clb/Tm; Sci Clb; Orch; SP/M/VS; Tennis (V); Cl Off (T); Stu Cncl (P); Yrbk (R); Math Team Co-Captain; Biology, Chemistry; Tufts U; Boston College

HUBACZ, ZACHARY J; NORTH BROOKFIELD, MA; HOMESCHOOL; (SR); WWAHSS; Bskball (VJ); Associate's Degree Completed While in High School; BS in Criminal Justice; Federal Law Enforcement Position; Anna Maria College

HUCKINS-AYLMER, THOMAS; YARMOUTH PORT, MA; DENNIS-YARMOUTH REG HS; (JR); Hi Hnr Roll; Nat Hon Sy; Otst Ac Ach Awd; Peer Tut/Med; Key Club; Tennis (V); Boys State (Massachusetts); Outstanding Achievement in English (10); Entrepreneur; International Finance; Babson College; U of Miami

HUSSEIN, PASIL M; CHELSEA, MA; CHELSEA HS; (JR); Hnr Roll; Nat Hon Sy; Otst Ac Ach Awd; St of Mnth; Comm Volntr; Sci Clb; Sccr (V); Environmental Club; Electronic Club/Multi-Cultural Club; Pre-Med; Biology-Genetics; Boston U; Boston College

IACOVINO, JUSTIN F; PEMBROKE, MA; SACRED HEART HS; (JR); Hi Hnr Roll; Hnr Roll; Nat Hon Sy; Nat Sci Aw; Otst Ac Ach Awd; Sci Fairs; Amnsty Intl; Comm Volntr; Peer Tut/Med; Emplmnt; Prom Com; SADD; Tchrs Aide; Spanish Clb; Pep Bnd; SP/M/VS; Cr Ctry (V CL); Skiing (V L); Track (V CL); Cl Off (V); Sch Ppr (R); Yrbk (R); Spanish / History Award; History / English; Political Science; Brown U; Dartmouth College

INGALLS, ANDREW; WESTFORD, MA; WESTFORD AC; (SO); Hnr Roll; Comm Volntr; Drma Clb; Emplmnt; Mth Clb/Tm; Photog; Sci Clb; SADD; Tech Clb; SP/M/VS; Stg Cre; Vllyball (J); Architect; Cornell U; Rhode Island School of Design

INGRAM, RYAN; COHASSET, MA; COHASSET MIDDLE HS; (SO); Hi Hnr Roll; WWAHSS; Yth Ldrshp Prog; Chrch Yth Grp; Seeds of Peace Beyond Borders; USA Gymnastics - Level 8; International Relations; Middle Eastern Studies; U of North Carolina; Yale U

JABER, HISHAM; AUBURN, MA; BAY PATH REG VOC TECH HS; (SO); Arch; Bsball; Sccr

JACHOWICZ, MEREDITH; SOUTHBOROUGH, MA; ALGONQUIN REG HS; (JR); Hi Hnr Roll; Nat Hon Sy; Nat Mrt Semif; Comm Volntr; Peer Tut/Med; Emplmnt; Prom Com; Scouts; Stg Cre; PP Ftbl; CR (R); Yrbk (E)

JAIKARAN, MIKAIL; JAMAICA PLAIN, MA; BOSTON LATIN AC; (SO); Hnr Roll; Perf Att; WWAHSS; Comm Volntr; Biology Clb; Chrch Yth Grp; Jr Cls League; Lib Aide; Vsity Clb; Bnd; Lcrsse (V); CR (R); State Winner XIII Position in Latin Dramatic Interpretation '05; National Winner XII Place Comics Drawing '04; Lawyer; Criminal Investigator

JANISZEWSKI, DANUTA; SPRINGFIELD, MA; CENTRAL HS; (FR); Ctznshp Aw; Hi Hnr Roll; Hnr Roll; Otst Ac Ach Awd; Perf Att; Sci Fairs; Comm Volntr; Spec Olymp Vol; Key Club; Fld Hky (V); Swmg (V); English / Literature Award of Achievement; American History Achievement Award; Law; Literature Major; Oxford U; U of Stockholm

JEAN, JEFFREY; MALDEN, MA; MALDEN HS; (SO); Hi Hnr Roll; Hnr Roll; Peer Tut/Med; Track (J); In Church Choir; Criminal Law; Business Administration; Boston College; Boston U

JELINEK, MARK; WELLESLEY HILLS, MA; WELLESLEY HS; (SO); Hnr Roll; St of Mnth; Comm Volntr; Chrch Yth Grp; Key Club; Photog; Mass Ski Club; Golf; Business; Boston College; Boston U

JENSEN, MEGAN; CLINTON, MA; CLINTON HS; (JR); Hi Hnr Roll; Hnr Roll; Nat Hon Sy; Comm Volntr; Peer Tut/Med; Emplmnt; Svce Clb; Chr; Flg Crps; Bskball (J); Biology; Mathematics / General; Clark U; Tufts U

JIANG, ALEXANDRA; WELLESLEY, MA; WELLESLEY HS; (SO); Hi Hnr Roll; Hnr Roll; Otst Ac Ach Awd; WWAHSS; Yth Ldrshp Prog; Key Club; Mth Clb/Tm; Sci Clb; Bnd; Chr; Orch; Pep Bnd; Vllyball (J)

JIANG, NING; BOSTON, MA; WOODWARD SCH; (JR); Hnr Roll; Comm Volntr; Emplmnt; Mth Clb/Tm; Dentistry; Environmental Study; Boston College; Clark U

JOBERT, CHET J; NORFOLK, MA; NEW TESTAMENT CHRISTIAN SCH; (FR); Hnr Roll; MVP; Nat Hon Sy; Otst Ac Ach Awd; Sci Fairs; WWAHSS; Comm Volntr; Peer Tut/Med; Chrch Yth Grp; SP/M/VS; Bsball (V); Bskball (V); Volunteer Services to Senior Citizens; 2005 NEMA Eng. Award; Town - Fall, Spring & Summer Baseball; Baseball-Playing; Sports Related

JOHNSON IV, FREDERICK J; FALL RIVER, MA; B M C DURFEE HS; (JR); Hi Hnr Roll; Hnr Roll; Nat Hon Sy; WWAHSS; Comm Volntr; Hosp Aide; Prom Com; Sci Clb; Ftball (VJ); Track (V); Cl Off (P); Mayor's Youth Council; Bible Club; Pre-Med; Sports Medicine; U of New Orleans; Tulane U

JONES, ILYA L O; AMHERST, MA; AMHERST REG HS; (JR); Hnr Roll; Comm Volntr; Chess; Bnd; Chr; Skiing; Sociology / Criminology; Political Science; Bowdoin College; Boston U

Hussein, Pasil M
Chelsea HS
Chelsea, MA

Holland, Christian
Catholic Memorial HS
Boston, MA

Hatziioannou, Vasilios
Danvers HS
Danvers, MA

Hastings, Jeannine
Agawam HS
Feeding Hills, MA

Habosian, Armen
Westford AC
Westford, MA

Harrison, Paige
Sutton HS
Sutton, MA

Hoffman, Sarah J
Hopkins AC
Hadley, MA

Holmes, Kenneth
Bridge AC
Springfield, MA

Jaber, Hisham
Bay Path Reg Voc Tech HS
Auburn, MA

JOSSELYN, BRITTANY E; HOPKINTON, MA; HOPKINTON HS; (SR); Hnr Roll; Sci Fairs; Yth Ldrshp Prog; Comm Volntr; Peer Tut/Med; Emplmnt; Photog; Dnce; Stg Cre; School Sports Manager-3 Years; Samaritans Suicide Volunteer; Sports Management; Saint Leo U, Florida

JULES, MANOUCHECA M; CHELSEA, MA; CHELSEA HS; (SR); F Lan Hn Soc; Fut Prb Slvr; MVP; Otst Ac Ach Awd; Perf Att; St of Mnth; WWAHSS; Yth Ldrshp Prog; Comm Volntr; Hosp Aide; Peer Tut/Med; Chrch Yth Grp; Cmptr Clb; DARE; Drma Clb; Mod UN; Mus Clb; Outdrs Clb; SADD; Bnd; Chr; Dnce; SP/M/VS; Bsball (V); Bskball (V); Chrldg (J); Fld Hky (V); Sftball (V); Track (L); Vllyball (J); CR (R); Bunker Hill Community College; Criminal Justice; U Mass; Northern U

KAHN, JOSHUA D; WAYLAND, MA; WAYLAND HS; (JR); Hnr Roll; Emplmnt; Prom Com; Lcrsse (J); Started Ultimate Frisbee Club; Sport Management; Law; U of New Hampshire; Syracuse

KANE, ALYSSA; WESTON, MA; WESTON HS; (JR); Hnr Roll; Nat Hon Sy; Pres Ac Ftns Aw; Comm Volntr; Chrch Yth Grp; SADD; Drm Mjr; Fld Hky (J); Stu Cncl (R); Nationally Ranked Baton Twirler; Political Science; Communications; U of Miami; U of Connecticut

KASPER, JENELLE; NORTH ANDOVER, MA; NORTH ANDOVER HS; (JR); Hi Hnr Roll; MVP; Comm Volntr; Emplmnt; Cr Ctry (V L); Swmg (V L); Track (V); Exemplary Student; Sports Award; Doctor of Medicine; Law; Northwestern U; Mc Gill

KASSAB, JOHN-CLAUDE; SHREWSBURY, MA; ST. JOHN'S HS; (JR); Nat Hon Sy; WWAHSS; Comm Volntr; Chrch Yth Grp; Mod UN; Track (V); Mechanical Engineer; Electrical Engineer; Drexel; Duke

KATHURIA, ASHNA; NORTH ANDOVER, MA; NORTH ANDOVER HS; (JR); Hi Hnr Roll; Nat Hon Sy; WWAHSS; Comm Volntr; Photog; Tchrs Aide; Sch Ppr (E, R); Black Belt in Tae Kwon Do; Pre-Medicine; Biology; Cornell U; Harvard U

KAUR, GAGANDEEP; BROCKTON, MA; AVON HS; (SO); Hi Hnr Roll; Hnr Roll; Nat Hon Sy; St of Mnth; Amnsty Intl; Comm Volntr; Tech Clb; Bskball (V L); Cl Off (P); Multi-Cultural Committee Member; Student Council Member; Medicine / Pre-Med; Boston U; Northeastern U

KAZENEL, MELANIE R; CANTON, MA; CANTON HS; (JR); Hi Hnr Roll; Hnr Roll; Nat Hon Sy; St of Mnth; Peer Tut/Med; ArtClub; Drma Clb; Mus Clb; Acpl Chr; Chr; Dnce; SP/M/VS; Lit Mag (R); Sch Ppr (R); Creative Writing; Environmental Science; Vassar College; Brown U

KEANE, KAYTIE; ATTLEBORO, MA; ATTLEBORO HS; (JR); All Am Sch; Hnr Roll; Nat Hon Sy; USAA; Peer Tut/Med; Emplmnt; Quill & Scroll; Sch Ppr (R, P); Humanities Major; Master's Degree in Teaching; Bennington College; Clark U

KEIFFER, SADE; ORLEANS, MA; NAUSET HS; (MS); Ctznshp Aw; Hi Hnr Roll; Hnr Roll; MVP; Nat Sci Aw; Nat Stu Ath Day Aw; Sci Fairs; St of Mnth; Peer Tut/Med; Chrch Yth Grp; DARE; Drma Clb; Emplmnt; Lib Aide; Off Aide; Scouts; Wdwrkg Clb; Chr; Ch Chr; SP/M/VS; Stg Cre; Chrldg (V); Sccr (V); Track (V); Stu Cncl (R); National American Miss Pageant '05; John Robert Powers School; Criminal Science; Performing Arts; New York U; Ohio State

KELLEY, COURTNEY R; LEICESTER, MA; NOTRE DAME AC; (SO); Hi Hnr Roll; Hnr Roll; MVP; Nat Ldrshp Svc; Otst Ac Ach Awd; Yth Ldrshp Prog; Comm Volntr; Chrch Yth Grp; DARE; Emplmnt; Scouts; Bskball (J L); Fld Hky (V L); Sftball (V L); Cl Off (V); Nursing; Forensic Sciences; Bridgewater State; Brandeis U

KELLY, CHRISTINE E; GROTON, MA; GROTON-DUNSTABLE HS; (FR); Hi Hnr Roll; Pres Ac Ftns Aw; WWAHSS; DARE; Dnce; Bskball; Irish Step Dancing; Become a Doctor; U of Connecticut

KEMP-FEUDO, ERICA; KINGSTON, MA; SILVER LAKE REG HS; (SR); Hnr Roll; Pres Sch; DARE; Emplmnt; Key Club; CR (T); Yrbk (P); Bachelor's Degree in Nursing; Worcester State College; Curry College

KENNEY, JILLIAN P; ANDOVER, MA; ANDOVER SR HS; (JR); Hi Hnr Roll; Nat Hon Sy; Yth Ldrshp Prog; Comm Volntr; Emplmnt; Svce Clb; Tchrs Aide; National Youth Leadership Forum on Medicine Participant; Member of GLAM (Girls Leadership Action Motivators); Biology; Nursing; Georgetown U; Boston College

KERR, TAYLOR; MARSHFIELD, MA; MARSHFIELD HS; (SO); F Lan Hn Soc; Hi Hnr Roll; Nat Hon Sy; Hnr Roll; Perf Att; Comm Volntr; Bskball (J); Sccr (J); Sftball (J); Nursing; Education; Boston U; Northeastern

KERRIGAN, THERESA; NEEDHAM HEIGHTS, MA; NEEDHAM HS; (JR); Hnr Roll; DARE; Emplmnt; Vsity Clb; Dvng (V CL); Gmnstcs (V CL); Swmg (V CL); Track (J); Psychology; Business Law; American College; George Washington

KHUZEYKINA, YANINA; MALDEN, MA; MALDEN HS; (SO); Hi Hnr Roll; Hnr Roll; Kwnis Aw; Sci Fairs; Peer Tut/Med; Chrch Yth Grp; Cmptr Clb; DARE; Chr; Clb; Bskball (L); Stu Cncl (R); Accepted & Going to Summer Search; Zonta Club Award; Human Resource Manager / Executive; Massage Therapy; U Mass Boston; Salem State

KILCOYNE, LAUREN M; LANCASTER, MA; CLINTON HS; (JR); Hi Hnr Roll; Hnr Roll; Nat Hon Sy; Nat Mrt LOC; Otst Ac Ach Awd; Yth Ldrshp Prog; Comm Volntr; Peer Tut/Med; Red Cr Aide; Drma Clb; Emplmnt; Mth Clb/Tm; NYLC; Prom Com; Svce Clb; SADD; International Clb; Dnce; SP/M/VS; Stg Cre; Bskball (V L); Fld Hky (V L); Tennis (V L); Adv Cncl (R); Cl Off (R); Stu Cncl (S); Sch Ppr (R); Yrbk (P); Vice-President National Honor Society; President Service Club / Excel Club; International Business; Foreign Language; Providence College; College of the Holy Cross

KITAEFF, NICHOLAS R; CAMBRIDGE, MA; CAMBRIDGE RINDGE & LATIN HS; (JR); Hnr Roll; Chrch Yth Grp; DARE; Italian Clb; Ice Hky (V); Sccr (V); Architecture; Engineering; U of Colorado Boulder; George Washington U

KLAPPRODT, SARAH E; WESTFORD, MA; WESTFORD AC; (SO); F Lan Hn Soc; Hi Hnr Roll; Hnr Roll; Otst Ac Ach Awd; Peer Tut/Med; Scouts; SADD; Tchrs Aide; German Clb; SP/M/VS; Fld Hky (JC); Track (V L); International Club; Student Exchange with Germany; Business; Entertainment; Boston U; U of Richmond

KLEBER, EDWARD T; NORWELL, MA; NORWELL HS; (JR); Hnr Roll; Emplmnt; Ftball (V CL); Lcrsse (J); Track (V); Wrstlg (V CL); Lit Mag; Mock Trial-Team Captain; Business

KLINGER, CAITLIN; SUDBURY, MA; LINCOLN-SUDBURY REG HS; (JR); Hnr Roll; Nat Mrt LOC; Pres Sch; Chrch Yth Grp; Mus Clb; French Clb; Acpl Chr; Ch Chr; Dnce; Orch; Hsbk Rdg; Dance Troupe Captain; Ranked 8th National French Test 2004; French Language; Dance; Boston College; George Washington U

KLISIEWICZ, DAVID; NORTH ANDOVER, MA; NORTH ANDOVER HS; (JR); Hnr Roll; Comm Volntr; Chrch Yth Grp; Emplmnt; Photog; Sccr (L); Track (L); Business Administration/Management; Business-General; Assumption College; Hofstra U

KNIGHT, COURTNEY R; PEMBROKE, MA; PEMBROKE HS; (JR); Ctznshp Aw; Hi Hnr Roll; Hnr Roll; Perf Att; Pres Ac Ftns Aw; Pres Sch; Sci Fairs; St of Mnth; Chrch Yth Grp; DARE; Drma Clb; Emplmnt; Off Aide; Chr; Ch Chr; SP/M/VS; Chrldg (J); Track (J); Adv Cncl (R); Cl Off (V); Stu Cncl (R); CR (R); Poetry Contest Winner Many Times; Work with Children 20 Hours a Week; Elementary Education; Early Childhood Education; U of Maine Orono; U of Mass Amherst

KNIGHTON, CHRISTOPHER; SOUTH WEYMOUTH, MA; WEYMOUTH HS; (JR); WWAHSS; Who's Who of America; Computer Science

KOFMAN, MIKE; VLG NAGOG WDS, MA; ABR HS; (JR); Hnr Roll; Civil Air Pat; Ftball (J); Electrical Technician; U of Massachusetts Amherst; Stony Brook

KOMNATNAIA, ANNA; HOPEDALE, MA; MILFORD HS; (JR); Hi Hnr Roll; Hnr Roll; Nat Hon Sy; WWAHSS; Comm Volntr; Emplmnt; Mth Clb/Tm; Cr Ctry (V CL); Tennis (V L); Track (V L); Pre-Dentistry; Economics; U of Massachusetts Amherst; McGill U

KONOPKO, MONIKA; LUDLOW, MA; LUDLOW HS; (FR); Hnr Roll; Comm Volntr; Accounting; Pediatrician; U of Massachusetts; Springfield Technical Community College

KORNETSKY, ADAM B; SHARON, MA; (JR); Hi Hnr Roll; Perf Att; St of Mnth; Comm Volntr; Emplmnt; Tmpl Yth Grp; Spanish Clb; Mock Trial; Community Service Club

KOUSTAS, ARIANA K; TYNGSBORO, MA; TYNGSBORO HS; (JR); Hi Hnr Roll; Nat Hon Sy; Chrch Yth Grp; Bnd; Ch Chr; Mch Bnd; Veterinary Medicine; Tufts U

KOUTSOS, LEXIE; DANVERS, MA; DANVERS HS; (SO); Hi Hnr Roll; Nat Hon Sy; WWAHSS; Comm Volntr; Emplmnt; Key Club; Swmg; Psychologist; Social Worker; Regis College; U of Massachusetts

KROHMER, JESSICA M E; NEWBURY, MA; TRITON REG HS; (SO); Hi Hnr Roll; Nat Hon Sy; Otst Ac Ach Awd; Comm Volntr; Spec Olymp Vol; Chrch Yth Grp; Drma Clb; Emplmnt; Mus Clb; Svce Clb; Bnd; Chr; Ch Chr; Mch Bnd; Track (J); Singer's Award; Science Award

KRYSKO, MATT; FOXBOROUGH, MA; FOXBOROUGH HS; (SO); Ctznshp Aw; Hi Hnr Roll; Hnr Roll; Pres Sch; Comm Volntr; Peer Tut/Med; Emplmnt; Ftball (V); Track (VJ); Foxboro Midget Football Scholar/Athlete; Defensive Player of the Year; Criminal Justice; Sports Medicine; Stonehill College; Northeastern U

KVENVOLD, LAURA; HARVARD, MA; BROMFIELD HS; (SO); Hi Hnr Roll; Nat Hon Sy; Sci Fairs; WWAHSS; Comm Volntr; Quiz Bowl; Biology

KWAK, PETER; WELLESLEY HILLS, MA; WELLESLEY HS; (JR); Hnr Roll; Chrch Yth Grp; Key Club; Sccr; Track (V L); Business Management/ Administration; Psychology; New York U; Georgetown U

LABONTE, HILARY; PEMBROKE, MA; PEMBROKE HS; (JR); Hnr Roll; MVP; Nat Hon Sy; Perf Att; Pres Ac Ftns Aw; St of Mnth; Comm Volntr; Hab For Humty Volntr; DARE; Scouts; Gmnstcs (V CL); Yrbk (E, P); Gymnastics All-Star; Elementary Education; Nursing; Salve Regina U; Wheelock College

LA FLAMME, ANGIE; WINCHENDON, MA; MURDOCK MIDDLE/HS; (FR); Hi Hnr Roll; Hnr Roll; Perf Att; Sci Fairs; St of Mnth; Yth Ldrshp Prog; Comm Volntr; Hosp Aide; Key Club; Mus Clb; Scouts; Chr; Ch Chr; Dnce; SP/M/VS; Ice Sktg; Sccr (J); Track (V); Junior Teen Miss Massachusetts; Interior Design; Prom Dress Designing; Framingham State

LALLY, KATIE H M; DANVERS, MA; DANVERS HS; (FR); Hi Hnr Roll; Pres Ac Ftns Aw; St of Mnth; WWAHSS; Comm Volntr; Chrch Yth Grp; Key Club; Bnd; Ch Chr; SP/M/VS; Gmnstcs (V L); Physical Therapy; Biology; Merrimack College; Eastern Nazarene College

LANDANNO, SHAELYN M; LITTLETON, MA; BROMFIELD HS; (SO); Hnr Roll; Sci Fairs; WWAHSS; Comm Volntr; Bnd; Dnce; Science Fair; Music / Foreign Language; Forensics; Harvard U; Boston U

LAORENZA, SAM; NORTH ANDOVER, MA; NORTH ANDOVER HS; (JR); Hi Hnr Roll; Nat Hon Sy; Pres Ac Ftns Aw; Comm Volntr; Chrch Yth Grp; Bskball (V L); Ftball (V L); Track (V L); Sch Ppr (R); National Honor Society; Journalism; Radio/TV Broadcasting; Syracuse U; Ithaca College

LA RAIA, LAURA; MELROSE, MA; POPE JOHN XXIII HS; (JR); Hi Hnr Roll; Hnr Roll; Nat Hon Sy; Comm Volntr; Peer Tut/Med; Chrch Yth Grp; Emplmnt; Scouts; Chrldg; Cr Ctry (V CL); Tennis (V CL); Vllyball (V L); Yrbk (P); Blessed John XXIII Scholarship; Coaches Award - Tennis; Accounting; Occupational Therapy; Salem State College; Northeastern U

LAREAU, KASEY; CHICOPEE, MA; CHICOPEE HS; (SR); Hi Hnr Roll; Hnr Roll; Nat Hon Sy; WWAHSS; Comm Volntr; Peer Tut/Med; Spec Olymp Vol; Emplmnt; Bskball; Cr Ctry (V CL); Dvng (V); Swmg (V L); Tennis (V CL); Stu Cncl (P, T); Yrbk (R); Nurse Anesthesia; U of New England

LAROCHELLE, JOSHUA R; LOWELL, MA; GREATER LOWELL VOC TECH SCH; (SR); Ctznshp Aw; Hnr Roll; MVP; Otst Ac Ach Awd; Perf Att; St of Mnth; Chrch Yth Grp; DARE; Drma Clb; Emplmnt; Mus Clb; Photog; Chr; Drm Mjr; SP/M/VS; Stg Cre; Bsball (J); Bskball (J); Vllyball (V); License Master Electrician

LAU, EMILY C; WESTON, MA; WESTON HS; (SO); Hi Hnr Roll; Hnr Roll; Comm Volntr; Photog; Yrbk (E); Received National Latin Exam Silver Medal; Received Outstanding Achievement Award in Photography; Biology; Master's Degree; Wellesley College; Harvard U

LAU, JACKSON W; QUINCY, MA; CENTRAL MS; (MS); Hnr Roll; Mth Clb/Tm; Dulcimer; Flute

LAUNA, JANELL; ANDOVER, MA; ANDOVER HS; (JR); Hnr Roll; St of Mnth; Yth Ldrshp Prog; Comm Volntr; Pep Squd; Scouts; Tchrs Aide; Chr; Dnce; Chrldg (V CL); Ice Hockey - Out of Town; Fashion Merchandising / Marketing; Marist College NY; Philadelphia U

LAWRENCE, AMANDA K; SOMERSET, MA; SOMERSET HS; (SR); Hnr Roll; Nat Hon Sy; Amnsty Intl; Comm Volntr; Peer Tut/Med; Drma Clb; Key Club; Sci Clb; Sftball (VJ L); Track (VJCL); Vllyball (VJ L); Participated in Multiple Sclerosis Walk-A-Thon; Participated in Ellegirl's Fashion for a Cause; Psychology; U of New Hampshire; U of Massachusetts-Amherst

LE, NICHOLAS; WORCESTER, MA; DOHERTY MEMORIAL HS; (SO); Computer Engineering; Computer Programming; Worcester Polytech Institute; U Mass Amherst

LEAL, CHRISTINE; CHESHIRE, MA; CHARLES H MC CANN TECH HS; (FR); Hi Hnr Roll; Otst Ac Ach Awd; WWAHSS; SADD; Voc Ind Clb Am; Business; Massachusetts College of Liberal Arts; Williams College

LE BLANC, SEAN; HAVERHILL, MA; HAVERHILL HS; (FR); Hi Hnr Roll; Hnr Roll; WWAHSS; Key Club; Poetry Awards; Photography Awards; Architect; Writer; Georgia Tech; Virginia Tech

LEGROW, DANAE; PEABODY, MA; PEABODY VETERANS MEMORIAL HS; Hnr Roll; WWAHSS; Comm Volntr; Bnd; Emplmnt; Chr; Ch Chr; Missions Studies; Gordon College; Evangel U

LEIGHER, KRISTEN E; ROCHDALE, MA; OXFORD HS; (FR); Hnr Roll; Sci Fairs; St Schl; St of Mnth; WWAHSS; Spec Olymp Vol; Bnd; Dnce; Adv Cncl (R); Stu Cncl (R); 10 Years of Dedicated Dance Award; Student Dance Assistant; Science; Math; Massachusetts Institute of Technology; Harvard

LEMME, MIKE; CHICOPEE, MA; CHICOPEE COMP HS; (FR); Peer Tut/ Med; Emplmnt; SP/M/VS; Bskball (J); National Junior Honor Society - 8th Grade; Writing; History; Columbia U; New York U

LEONARD, AMANDA L; HANSON, MA; WHITMAN-HANSON REG HS; (JR); Hi Hnr Roll; Nat Hon Sy; Otst Ac Ach Awd; Perf Att; Pres Ac Ftns Aw; Peer Tut/Med; Sccr (V L); Track (V L); School Council-Appointed; Math; Science; Boston College; Northeastern U

LEONARD, DONALD; BOSTON, MA; O'BRYANT SCH OF MATH & SCIENCE; (SO); Hnr Roll; Perf Att; Mus Clb; Bnd; Ftball (V); Mar Art (J); Stu Cncl (R); Broadcast Journalism; Business Communications; Emerson College; Boston College

Labonte, Hilary — Pembroke HS — Pembroke, MA
Klapprodt, Sarah E — Westford AC — Westford, MA
Kenney, Jillian P — Andover SR HS — Andover, MA
Kelly, Christine E — Groton-Dunstable HS — Groton, MA
National Honor Roll Spring 2005
Kelley, Courtney R — Notre Dame AC — Leicester, MA
Kerrigan, Theresa — Needham HS — Needham Heights, MA
Krysko, Matt — Foxborough HS — Foxborough, MA
Landanno, Shaelyn M — Bromfield HS — Littleton, MA

LEONARD, ERIN; EAST WEYMOUTH, MA; WOODWARD SCH; (JR); Hi Hnr Roll; Hnr Roll; MVP; Perf Att; Pres Ac Ftns Aw; St of Mnth; Peer Tut/Med; Chrch Yth Grp; Cmptr Clb; DARE; Emplmnt; FCCLA; Jr Cls League; Mth Clb/Tm; Photog; Sftball (V); Cl Off (R); Lit Mag (R); Yrbk (R); Known for Deep Political Thought; Maintained Part Time Job; Forensic Science; Law; U of Texas; Rice U

LEONARD, MARK C; NORTH ANDOVER, MA; NORTH ANDOVER HS; (JR); Hi Hnr Roll; Nat Hon Sy; St of Mnth; Comm Volntr; Chrch Yth Grp; DARE; Photog; Scouts; Vsity Clb; Ice Hky (V L); Lcrsse (V); Sccr (JC); Architectural Engineering; U of Massachusetts At Amherst; U of Connecticut

LEPPER, JOSEPH J; LONGMEADOW, MA; LONGMEADOW HS; (JR); Hnr Roll; Kwnis Aw; WWAHSS; Yth Ldrshp Prog; Comm Volntr; Red Cr Aide; Spec Olymp Vol; Chrch Yth Grp; Dbte Team; Drma Clb; Key Club; Tchrs Aide; SP/M/VS; Golf (V); Lcrsse (J); Vllyball; Wt Lftg; Adv Cncl (R); CR (R); Key Club, New England District Governor; Business Administration; Certified Public Accountant; Bentley College; Babson College

LES, ANDREW; PALMER, MA; LUDLOW HS; (FR); Hi Hnr Roll; Hnr Roll; MVP; Nat Sci Aw; Otst Ac Ach Awd; St of Mnth; Comm Volntr; Emplmnt; Ice Hky (V); BC; U of Maine

LESLIE, ROXANNE; DANVERS, MA; DANVERS HS; (FR); Hi Hnr Roll; Comm Volntr; Key Club; Chr; Chrldg (V L); Cr Ctry (V L); Track (V)

LEVIT, MICHAEL; SWAMPSCOTT, MA; SWAMPSCOTT HS; (SO); Biology; Computer Science

L HEUROX, AMRIT; BELLINGHAM, MA; BELLINGHAM MEM HS; (SO); Engineering; Architecture; U Mass Boston; U Mass Amherst

LI, SIDA; WESTFORD, MA; WESTFORD AC; (SO); F Lan Hn Soc; Hi Hnr Roll; WWAHSS; Peer Tut/Med; Emplmnt; Mth Clb/Tm; Sccr (J); Track (J); Engineering; Architecture

LIN, CORA; MALDEN, MA; MALDEN HS; (SO); Hi Hnr Roll; Nat Hon Sy; Perf Att; Sci/Math Olympn; Comm Volntr; Peer Tut/Med; ArtClub; Key Club; Mth Clb/Tm; Interact Club; Rowing Team; Accountant; Pediatrician; Tufts U; Boston College

LING, JONATHAN; NORFOLK, MA; BOSTON UNIVERSITY AC; (JR); Hi Hnr Roll; Hnr Roll; Nat Mrt LOC; Sci Fairs; Sci/Math Olympn; Comm Volntr; ArtClub; Chess; Cmptr Clb; Mth Clb/Tm; Mus Clb; Sci Clb; Bnd; Chr; SP/M/VS; Bskball (V); Lit Mag; Piano Competition Awards; Art Awards; Bio Engineering; Life Science / Medical Research; Harvard U; Massachusetts Institute of Technology

LINNEHAN, KEVIN T; SPRINGFIELD, MA; (SO); Hi Hnr Roll; Comm Volntr; Key Club; Bsball (V); Sccr (V); Member of Key Club; Mass Mutual Academic Achiever; Video Journalist

LIU, JAMES; LONGMEADOW, MA; LONGMEADOW HS; (JR); Hnr Roll; Nat Hon Sy; Perf Att; Sci Fairs; Sci/Math Olympn; Red Cr Aide; Chrch Yth Grp; Sci Clb; Orch; Swmg (V L); Track (V); Water Polo; Medical Science; Biology

LIU, JING; WORCESTER, MA; NORTH HS; (SO); Hnr Roll; Nat Hon Sy; Perf Att; Biology Clb; Mth Clb/Tm, Dnce

LIU, YUEE; WORCESTER, MA; NORTH HS; (JR); Hnr Roll; Nat Hon Sy; Comm Volntr; Mth Clb/Tm; Tech Clb; Dnce; Winning Scholarship from WPI (Math Meet); Math, Engineer

LIYAUDEEN, MAJIDHA; PITTSFIELD, MA; PITTSFIELD HS; (FR); Hnr Roll; Sch Ppr (R); Bachelor's Degree; Boston College

LIZOTTE, MEGAN E; CHARLTON, MA; SHEPHERD HILL REG HS; (SO); Hi Hnr Roll; Hnr Roll; Nat Hon Sy; Comm Volntr; Peer Tut/Med; P to P St Amb Prg; Dnce; Fld Hky (V L); Skiing; Sftball (J); Track; Cl Off (V); CR (R); Yrbk (P); Superintendent's Advisory Council; Peer Tutor; Marine Biology; Genetics; U of New Hampshire; U of Massachusetts

LOCKE, CRYSTAL D; LINWOOD, MA; UXBRIDGE HS; (JR); Hnr Roll; St of Mnth; 4-H; Chrch Yth Grp; DARE; Emplmnt; Mth Clb/Tm; Mus Clb; Off Aide; Scouts; Bnd; Jzz Bnd; Pep Bnd; Lawyer; Paralegal/Legal Secretary; Worcester State

LOR, SEE; LEOMINSTER, MA; LEOMINSTER HS; (SR); Hnr Roll; Nat Hon Sy; St of Mnth; WWAHSS; Comm Volntr; Peer Tut/Med; Red Cr Aide; Chrch Yth Grp; Emplmnt; FTA; Svce Clb; Ch Chr; Tennis (V); Pharmacy; Massachusetts College of Pharmacy; Northeastern U

LOUKAS, BRITTANI N; WATERTOWN, MA; WATERTOWN HS; (FR); Hnr Roll; Otst Ac Ach Awd; SADD; Dnce; Bskball; Chrldg (V); Track (V); Public Relations; Medical School; U of California, LA; Stanford

LU, ALEXANDRA; WELLESLEY, MA; WELLESLEY HS; (SO); F Lan Hn Soc; Hi Hnr Roll; WWAHSS; Yth Ldrshp Prog; Comm Volntr; DARE; Key Club; P to P St Amb Prg; Latin Clb; Orch; Lcrsse (J); Sccr (V); Track (J); National Latin Exam Gold Medal (Perfect Score); National Spanish Exam (6th Place); Medicine; Law; Yale; Harvard

LUBIN, ALYSSA; NORTH READING, MA; NORTH READING HS; (JR); Hi Hnr Roll; Hnr Roll; Nat Hon Sy; Perf Att; USAA; WWAHSS; Yth Ldrshp Prog; Comm Volntr; Dbte Team; Drma Clb; Emplmnt; Mth Clb/Tm; NYLC; Svce Clb; SADD; Dnce; SP/M/VS; Stu Cncl (T); CR (R); Sch Ppr (P); Yrbk (E); 2005 State Finalist Teen for Miss Massachusetts; Inducted Into National Society of H School Scholars; Become a Successful Veterinarian; Cornell U; Brigham Young U

LUND-WILDE, JOSH; WESTFORD, MA; WESTFORD AC; (SO); Hi Hnr Roll; Nat Hon Sy; Perf Att; DECA; Emplmnt; Jr Cls League; Mth Clb/Tm; Latin Clb; Bnd; Jzz Bnd; Orch; Tennis (V CL); Sch Ppr (R, P); United States Tennis Association Sectional Ranking-30; Coach of Intramural Team Basketball; Business; Journalism

LY, BETTY; BOSTON, MA; O'BRYANT SCH OF MATH & SCIENCE; (MS); Hnr Roll; Perf Att; Sci Fairs; St of Mnth; Comm Volntr; ArtClub; DARE; Chr; CR (P); Science; Business

LYON, BRITTANY; PITTSFIELD, MA; PITTSFIELD HS; (SO); Hi Hnr Roll; Pres Sch; Comm Volntr; DARE; Pep Squd; Italian Clb; Bskball (J); Sccr (V L); Business; Sports Management; Coastal Carolina U

LYTTLE, CORINA; SWAMPSCOTT, MA; SWAMPSCOTT HS; (SO); Hi Hnr Roll; Hnr Roll; Comm Volntr; DARE; Tennis (J); Track (J); Won Certificates in International Poetry Contests; National American Miss Finalist; Business Administration; Psychology; Florida State U; Charleston State

MAC, ROSE; QUINCY, MA; NORTH QUINCY HS; (SR); F Lan Hn Soc; Hi Hnr Roll; Hnr Roll; Nat Hon Sy; WWAHSS; Dbte Team; Mth Clb/Tm; ROTC; Drl Tm; Tennis (V); Track (V); Vllyball (V); Pharmacy; Pre-Med; Northeastern U; Massachusetts College of Pharmacy

MAC DONALD, JAMES; METHUEN, MA; METHUEN HS; (FR); Hi Hnr Roll; Hnr Roll; Comm Volntr; Emplmnt; Ice Hky (V L); Physical Education; Coaching; Plymouth State U; U Rhode Island

MAC DONALD, JESSICA A; MILLBURY, MA; MILLBURY MEMORIAL JR SR HS; (SO); Hi Hnr Roll; Hnr Roll; Perf Att; Sci Fairs; St of Mnth; Drma Clb; SP/M/VS; Sccr (J); Track (V); Fashion Club; Pastry Chef; Chef; Johnson & Wales U; ISA Sydney, Australia

MAC KENZIE, AMANDA; WRENTHAM, MA; KING PHILIP REG HS; (JR); Hnr Roll; DECA; Emplmnt; Prom Com; French Clb; Cr Ctry (J); Fld Hky (V L); Track (V L); CR (R); Yrbk (E, R, P); National French Exam; International Competitor for DECA; Business Administration; Psychology; Clemson U; U of North Florida

MADAUS, WILLIAM O; SHREWSBURY, MA; ST JOHN'S HS; (JR); Hnr Roll; WWAHSS; Yth Ldrshp Prog; Hab For Humty Volntr; Drma Clb; Mod UN; SP/M/VS; Lit Mag (R); Sch Ppr (R); National Youth Leadership Conference; Model UN, Habitat for Humanity Volunteer; English/Political Science; Law; Boston College; Providence College

MAFFEI, DOMINIQUE; EAST FALMOUTH, MA; FALMOUTH HS; (JR); Hi Hnr Roll; Hnr Roll; WWAHSS; Comm Volntr; Emplmnt; Key Club; Mus Clb; P to P St Amb Prg; Prom Com; Acpl Chr; Chr; SP/M/VS; Business (Hospitality); Boston College; Cornell U

MAFUZ, TASHA; SPRINGFIELD, MA; HS OF COMMERCE; (SO); Perf Att; Scouts; Dnce; Business; Stcc, Western Nec, Aic

MAGANZINI, HOLLY; WAKEFIELD, MA; WAKEFIELD HS; (JR); Hnr Roll; Nat Mrt Sch Recip; Nat Mrt Semif; Comm Volntr; DECA; Dnce; Skiing; Tennis (V L); Dancing for 14 Years; Deca Club Member; Business Management; Marketing; Bentley; U of Rhode Island

MAINVILLE, BRYCE J; GREENFIELD, MA; TURNERS FALLS HS; (JR); Hi Hnr Roll; Peer Tut/Med; Aqrium Clb; ArtClub; Chess; Emplmnt; Lib Aide; Tchrs Aide; French Clb; Yrbk (E, R); Recently Nominated for National Honor Society; English/Journalism; Philosophy; U of Massachusetts-Boston; U of Massachusetts-Amherst

MALLOY-WALKER, BRIANA; BOSTON, MA; O'BRYANT SCH OF MATH & SCIENCE; MS; Hnr Roll; Comm Volntr; Chrch Yth Grp; DARE; Chr; Ch Chr; Graduating the Stepping Stone Foundation; Lawyer (Law-Major); Harvard U; Howard U

MALONE, JOHN; WALPOLE, MA; WALPOLE HS; Ctznshp Aw; Hnr Roll; St of Mnth; Peer Tut/Med; Chrch Yth Grp; Emplmnt; Wdwrkg Clb; Latin Clb; Bsball (J); Ftball (V); Law; Medicine; Boston College; Babson College

MALONI, BRANDI E; MONSON, MA; MONSON HS; (JR); Hi Hnr Roll; Hnr Roll; Nat Hon Sy; Drma Clb; Emplmnt; Prom Com; Scouts; Chr; Dnce; SP/M/VS; Stg Cre; Cr Ctry (V C); Track (V); Best Actress, One Act Plays 2002; Drama / Performing Arts; Clark U Worcester

MANGONE, HEATHER; SOUTH WEYMOUTH, MA; WEYMOUTH HS; (SO); Hi Hnr Roll; Hnr Roll; Nat Hon Sy; Peer Tut/Med; ArtClub; DARE; Emplmnt; Dnce; Lit Mag (R); Psychology; Literature; Lesley College; UMass

MANSFIELD, LAUREN; ATHOL, MA; ST. BERNARD'S; (JR); Hi Hnr Roll; Hnr Roll; WWAHSS; Emplmnt; Outdrs Clb; SADD; French Clb; National Latin Exam-Magna Cum Laude; Medusa Mythology Exam-Certificate (Curia Laura); Political Science; Law; Northwestern U; George Washington U

MANTE, THOMAS; WESTFORD, MA; BISHOP GUERTIN HS; (JR); F Lan Hn Soc; Hnr Roll; WWAHSS; Comm Volntr; Peer Tut/Med; Bsball (V L); Bskball (J); Ftball (V L); Sccr (JC); Track (V L); Recipient of the Brothers of the Sacred Heart Scholarship; New Hampshire American Legion Baseball All-Star; Bioengineering; Finance; Duke U; U of Virginia

MARCHIONE, LISA M; STOUGHTON, MA; STOUGHTON HS; (SO); Hi Hnr Roll; Hnr Roll; Otst Ac Ach Awd; Sci Fairs; Yth Ldrshp Prog; Comm Volntr; Peer Tut/Med; DARE; Emplmnt; SADD; Tchrs Aide; Dnce; Sch Ppr (E, R); Co-Founder of Becca's Closet at Stoughton HS; Medicine / Science; Law; Harvard U; Yale U

MARCOUILLIER, SARA; LOWELL, MA; GREATER LOWELL VOC TECH SCH; (SO); Hnr Roll; Comm Volntr; Stu Cncl (R); Altar Server / Youth Lector; Criminology; Forensic Science; Suffolk U; U Mass Lowell

MARKOS, JOHN E; TOPSFIELD, MA; BRIDGTON AC; (SR); Hi Hnr Roll; Otst Ac Ach Awd; Comm Volntr; Peer Tut/Med; Chrch Yth Grp; Emplmnt; SP/M/VS; Ftball (J); Golf (V L); Wrstlg (J L); Suffolk U; Bryant U

MAROKHOVSKY, JON; UPTON, MA; NIPMUC REG HS; (SO); Hi Hnr Roll; Hnr Roll; Perf Att; Comm Volntr; Chrch Yth Grp; Scouts; Bnd; Jzz Bnd; Pep Bnd; Track (V); Science Award; Chemical Engineering; Biological Engineering

MARRYSHOW, STEPHANY; SPRINGFIELD, MA; NEW LEADERSHIP CHARTER SCH; MS; Hnr Roll; Nat Hon Sy; Otst Ac Ach Awd; Pres Ac Ftns Aw; Sci Fairs; Comm Volntr; Chrch Yth Grp; Dbte Team; Tmpl Yth Grp; Drl Tm; Chrldg (JV); Mar Art (JV); Certified CPR Training; Baby-Sitting Training for ages 7 Months-9 Years old; Medicine (Doctor); Science (Scientist)

MARTELLY, FREDERICA; LYNN, MA; LYNN ENGLISH HS; (SO); Hnr Roll; Sci Fairs; Comm Volntr; ArtClub; Mus Clb; Pep Squd; ROTC; French Clb; Physical Training Team; Art Club / French Club; Law / Lawyer; Psychology / Psychologist; Boston U; Brooklyn College

MARTIN, GABRIELLE; NORTHBOROUGH, MA; WORCESTER AC; (JR); Hi Hnr Roll; Hnr Roll; Amnsty Intl; Comm Volntr; Hab For Humty Volntr; Mth Clb/Tm; Dnce; Swmg (V); Naturalist of the Year (2 Times) At Worcester's Ecotarium; Achievement in Dance Award; Biology; Zoology; New York U; Mc Gill U

MARTINEZ, RENNA; WORCESTER, MA; NORTH HS; (SR); Dnce; Secretary; Criminal Justice; John Jay, St. John's U; Bay State

MASCHINO, ALYSSA; PITTSFIELD, MA; TACONIC HS; (SR); Hi Hnr Roll; Hnr Roll; Nat Hon Sy; Comm Volntr; Hosp Aide; Peer Tut/Med; Emplmnt; Prom Com; Italian Clb; Yrbk (E); Interior Design; Business; Bay Path College

MASCIULLI, LAURA; SCITUATE, MA; FONTBONNE AC; (JR); Hnr Roll; WWAHSS; Comm Volntr; 4-H; Emplmnt; Chr; Hsbk Rdg (C); Equestrian Club; Community Volunteer; Psychology; Communications; Suffolk U, U Mass Amherst; U of RI

MATHAISEL JR, BRYAN F; WESTWOOD, MA; WESTWOOD HS; (SR); Hnr Roll; Perf Att; WWAHSS; Bsball (J); Bskball (J); Sport Management Major; Springfield College

MATHIEU-BUSHER, MACKENZIE; NEWBURYPORT, MA; NEWBURY PORT HS; (JR); Ctznshp Aw; Hnr Roll; Comm Volntr; ArtClub; Drma Clb; Emplmnt; Lib Aide; Photog; Ch Chr; Orch; SP/M/VS; Stg Cre; Lit Mag (R, P); State Drama Festival 2004 & 2005 Acting Award; School Freshman Acting Award, Photography; Peace Corps, Theater, Teaching; Boston U; U of Massachusetts-Amherst

MAYOTTE, KEITH; CLINTON, MA; CLINTON HS; (SO); Hi Hnr Roll; Nat Mrt LOC; Otst Ac Ach Awd; Pres Ac Ftns Aw; Sci Fairs; Sci/Math Olympn; WWAHSS; Comm Volntr; Dbte Team; Emplmnt; Mth Clb/Tm; Schol Bwl; Bsball (J); Sccr (V); Track (V)

MC ALPINE, SHAUN R; WESTON, MA; WESTON HS; (JR); Hnr Roll; Perf Att; Comm Volntr; Spec Olymp Vol; Outdrs Clb; Quiz Bowl; Bnd; Jzz Bnd; Mch Bnd; Pep Bnd; Bdmtn; Bskball; Golf (V); Skiing; American Music Abroad; Law; Business; U of Edinburgh; Vanderbilt

MC CABE, JAMIE; MARLBOROUGH, MA; MARLBOROUGH HS; (FR); Hnr Roll; St of Mnth; Emplmnt; Interior Decorator; Psychologist; Cazenovia College; U of Findlay

MC CALL, ALISON E; UXBRIDGE, MA; UXBRIDGE HS; (JR); Hi Hnr Roll; Otst Ac Ach Awd; St of Mnth; WWAHSS; Peer Tut/Med; Emplmnt; Dnce; Jzz Bnd; Chrldg (V); High Honors All Semesters; 2004 Sportsmanship Award for Fall Cheerleading; History; English/Journalism; Brown U

MC CUSHER, SEAN; WESTFORD, MA; WESTFORD AC; (JR); Hi Hnr Roll; Hnr Roll; Nat Hon Sy; WWAHSS; Comm Volntr; Chrch Yth Grp; DECA; Emplmnt; Photog; Svce Clb; SP/M/VS; Bskball (JC); Sccr (VJCL); Track (V L); Stu Cncl (R); CR (R); Coach's Award for Varsity Soccer; New England Championships-Track

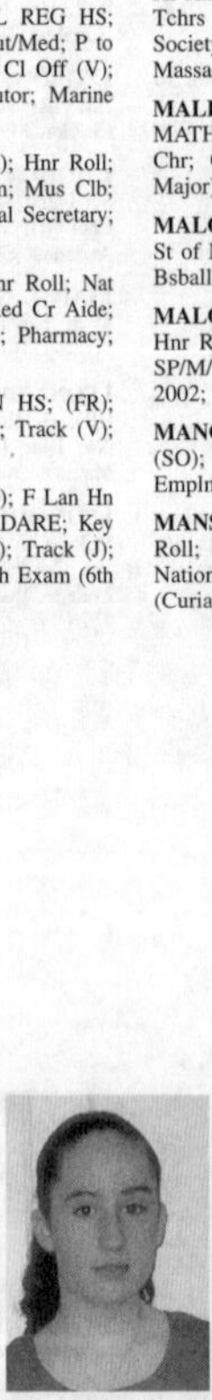

Marcouillier, Sara
Greater Lowell Voc Tech Sch
Lowell, MA

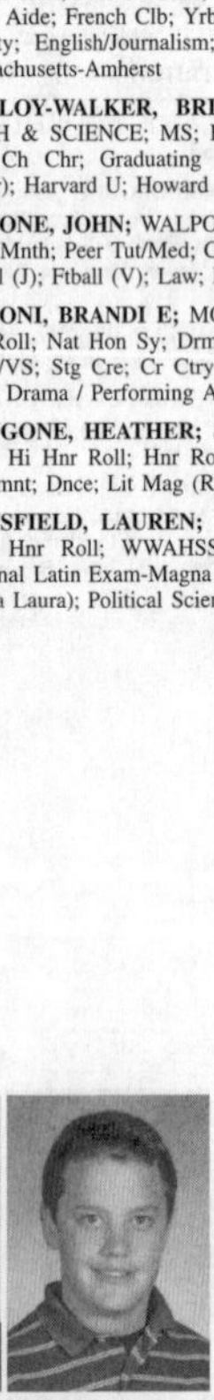

Malone, John
Walpole HS
Walpole, MA

National Honor Roll Spring 2005

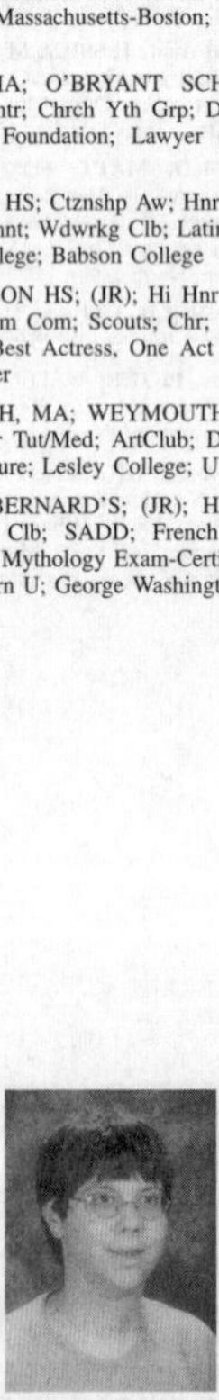

Mainville, Bryce J
Turners Falls HS
Greenfield, MA

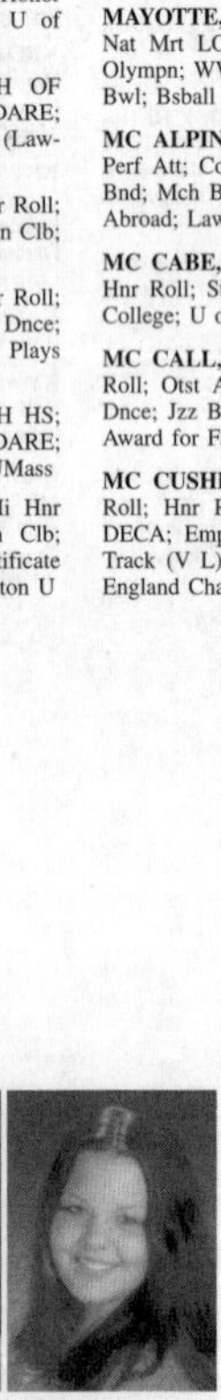

Maschino, Alyssa
Taconic HS
Pittsfield, MA

MC DONALD, MEGAN; AVON, MA; NORFOLK CTY AG HS; (JR); Hnr Roll; MVP; Comm Volntr; Peer Tut/Med; DARE; Ntl FFA; Bskball (V); Sftball (V); Vllyball (V C); Operate & Run Landscape Company; Massachusetts Maritime Academy; Stockbridge School of Agriculture

MC FARLAND, CAITLIN H; KINGFIELD, ME; MT ABRAM HS; (FR); Hnr Roll; Dnce; SP/M/VS; Skiing (V L); Cl Off (P); Public Speaking; Graphic Design; Publishing / Editing; Stanford U; Colby College

MC GRATH, BRITTANY; LYNN, MA; LYNN CLASSICAL HS; (JR); Hi Hnr Roll; Hnr Roll; Sci Fairs; WWAHSS; Peer Tut/Med; Chess; Drma Clb; Emplmnt; Jr Ach; Key Club; Mth Clb/Tm; SP/M/VS; PP Ftbl (L); Track (L); Cl Off (R); CR (R); Bowling League; Journalism; Psychology; UMass Amherst; UMass Lowell

MC GRATH, EDWARD W; BROCKTON, MA; AVON HS; (SR); WWAHSS; Bnd; Play Guitar In Band; Music; Bridgewater State College

MC INTYRE, MICHELLE; PEMBROKE, MA; PEMBROKE HS; (JR); Hi Hnr Roll; Hnr Roll; MVP; Nat Hon Sy; St of Mnth; Peer Tut/Med; Emplmnt; Cr Ctry (V CL); Track (V CL); Sch Ppr (R, P); Peer Mediation; Equine Business Management; Becker College; Cazenovia College

MC KEON, BRITTANY; HOLBROOK, MA; HOLBROOK JR/SR HS; (SO); Hi Hnr Roll; Hnr Roll; Perf Att; Pres Sch; Amnsty Intl; DARE; Lib Aide; Scouts; Cl Off (S); Yrbk (R, P); Journalism; Psychology; U of Massachusetts, Amherst

MC KIM, KEVIN J; NORTH ATTLEBORO, MA; NORTH ATTLEBORO HS; (SR); F Lan Hn Soc; Hi Hnr Roll; Nat Hon Sy; Nat Sci Aw; Sci Fairs; USAA; Comm Volntr; Emplmnt; Tchrs Aide; Cr Ctry (V L); Sccr (V); Track (V CL); Vsy Clb (V); Yrbk (E); National Honor Society; Editor in Chief Yearbook; Marine Biology; Pre-Med; Saint Joe's ME; U Mass Amherst

MC NAMARA, CHRIS; CLINTON, MA; CLINTON HS; (JR); Hnr Roll; Comm Volntr; DARE; Emplmnt; Scouts; Ice Hky (V); Sccr (V); Stetson U; Westfield U

MC PARTLAND, ELIZABETH; ANDOVER, MA; ANDOVER HS; (JR); Hi Hnr Roll; Hnr Roll; Comm Volntr; Peer Tut/Med; Tennis (V)

MEDEIROS, KATYA; FALL RIVER, MA; BMC DURFEE HS; (JR); Hi Hnr Roll; Hnr Roll; Photog; Sci Clb; Video Club; Photographer; Career in Communications; U of Massachusetts; Bridgewater College

MEISNER, AMANDA M; BELLINGHAM, MA; BELLINGHAM MEM HS; (SR); Hi Hnr Roll; Hnr Roll; Nat Hon Sy; Comm Volntr; Emplmnt; Dnce; Cr Ctry (C); Track (C); Environmental Science; U of Rhode Island; Eastern Connecticut State

MELHEM, JOANNA Y; NORWOOD, MA; NORWOOD HS; (JR); Hnr Roll; St of Mnth; Drma Clb; SADD; Business (Fashion); Director/Producer; American U of Beirut; U of Massachusetts

MENDES, EMMANUEL; FALL RIVER, MA; DIMAN REG VOC TECH HS; (SR); Hi Hnr Roll; Hnr Roll; Nat Hon Sy; CARE; Hosp Aide; Peer Tut/Med; Ch Chr; Dnce; Flg Crps; SP/M/VS; Bskball; Cr Ctry; Gmnstcs; Sccr; Adv Cncl (R); Sch Ppr (R, P); Criminal Justice; Us Army; Columbia U; Barnard College

MENDEZ, CARLOS; SPRINGFIELD, MA; PUTNAM VOC TECH HS; (JR); Hnr Roll; Ftball (V); Wrstlg (V); Business

MICHAELS, JENNIE; HARVARD, MA; THE BROMFIELD SCH; (SO); Hnr Roll; Sci Fairs; WWAHSS; ArtClub; Emplmnt; Bskball (J); Sccr (V); Track (V); Spring Track League All Star; Spring Track District All Star; Law; Business Management; U of Massachusetts Amherst; Boston College

MIHAILIDES, ALEXANDRA; REHOBOTH, MA; DIGHTON REHOBOTH REG HS; (SO); Hnr Roll; MVP; Chrch Yth Grp; Prom Com; Spanish Clb; Fld Hky (V L); Track (V L); Cl Off (T); CR (R); Fashion Buying/ Merchandising; U of Rhode Island; U of New Hampshire

MILLER, ASHANTI R; SPRINGFIELD, MA; NEW LEADERSHIP CHARTER SCH; MS; Hi Hnr Roll; Hnr Roll; Otst Ac Ach Awd; Sci Fairs; Yth Ldrshp Prog; Comm Volntr; DARE; Scouts; SADD; Dnce; Drl Tm; Bskball (V); Cr Ctry (V); Track (V); Psychology; Business/Real Estate; U of Connecticut; Tennessee State College

MIRCHANDANI, ROSHNI; WESTFORD, MA; WESTFORD AC; (JR); Hi Hnr Roll; Hnr Roll; MVP; Nat Hon Sy; Otst Ac Ach Awd; Perf Att; Pres Sch; Sci Fairs; WWAHSS; Yth Ldrshp Prog; Comm Volntr; DARE; DECA; Emplmnt; HO'Br Yth Ldrshp; Mth Clb/Tm; Tmpl Yth Grp; French Clb; Dnce; Cr Ct Ski (V CL); PP Ftbl (V); Sccr (J); Vllyball (J); Stu Cncl (R); CR (R); Sch Ppr (R, P); Multimedia Excellence Award (Annual Awards Night); Academic Award (Sports Awards Night); Columbia U, NY; Boston U, MA

MITCHELL, COURTNEY J; FALL RIVER, MA; PORTSMOUTH ABBEY SCH; (JR); WWAHSS; Yth Ldrshp Prog; Comm Volntr; Drma Clb; Mod UN; Mus Clb; Chr; Dnce; Orch; SP/M/VS; Cr Ctry (J); Tennis (V); Stu Cncl (R); Yrbk (R); 2-Time World Affairs Essay Contest Finalist; Most Industrious Student; Psychology; Law; U of Chicago; Georgetown U

MOLLA, DINA; NORTH ANDOVER, MA; NORTH ANDOVER HS; (JR); Hi Hnr Roll; Nat Hon Sy; Comm Volntr; Chrch Yth Grp; Bnd; Ch Chr; Music Education (Violin); Early Childhood Education; Boston U; Boston College

MONSON, LORENZO; SPRINGFIELD, MA; HS OF SCIENCE & TECH; (JR); Ctznshp Aw; F Lan Hn Soc; Hnr Roll; Nat Hon Sy; Perf Att; St of Mnth; Comm Volntr; Jr Ach; Bskball (J); Vllyball (V); Math; Science; U of Massachusettes, Amherst; Boston College

MONTEIRO, JOCELYN M; SOMERSET, MA; SOMERSET HS; (FR); Hi Hnr Roll; Hnr Roll; Perf Att; Amnsty Intl; Red Cr Aide; Chrch Yth Grp; DARE; Emplmnt; Jr Ach; Key Club; Mus Clb; Bnd; Chr; Ch Chr; Drm Mjr; Track (V); Competition Majorettes; Girl Scouts; Pharmacist; Pediatrician; Boston College

MONTOLIO, JORDANA; HYDE PARK, MA; BOSTON LATIN SCH; (JR); Ctznshp Aw; Hnr Roll; Sci Fairs; St of Mnth; Yth Ldrshp Prog; Comm Volntr; Peer Tut/Med; Chrch Yth Grp; Emplmnt; Jr Ach; Pep Squd; Prom Com; Spanish Clb; Chr; Track (V); Adv Cncl (V, S); Cl Off (R); Italian; Business Management; New York U; Columbia U

MONTT, DANIEL A; FORESTDALE, MA; SANDWICH HS; (JR); Ctznshp Aw; Hi Hnr Roll; Hnr Roll; Perf Att; Comm Volntr; Peer Tut/Med; Emplmnt; Jr Ach; Tchrs Aide; Fld Hky; Ftball (J); Sportsman Award; Most Improved Sailor; Oceanography; Northeastern U

MOORE, MIKE; PEMBROKE, MA; PEMBROKE HS; (JR); Hi Hnr Roll; Hnr Roll; MVP; Nat Hon Sy; Perf Att; St of Mnth; Comm Volntr; Vsity Clb; Ftball (V); Wt Lftg (V); Accounting; Business Management; Bentley College; U Mass Amherst

MORALES, RANDY J; WOBURN, MA; WOBURN SR HS; (JR); Hnr Roll; Emplmnt; Ftball (V); Wt Lftg (V); Forensic Sciences; Computer Technology; UMass Amherst; Plymouth State

MORGAN, CHRIS; CHELMSFORD, MA; CHELMSFORD HS; (JR); Hi Hnr Roll; Nat Hon Sy; Peer Tut/Med; Drma Clb; Emplmnt; P to P St Amb Prg; Tech Clb; Stg Cre; Track (J); CR (R); Destination Imagination Participant; Dynamic Quest Participant; Television / Radio; Technical Theatre Arts; Ithaca College; Boston U

MORGAN, JEN; SOUTH YARMOUTH, MA; DENNIS-YARMOUTH REG HS; (JR); Hi Hnr Roll; Hnr Roll; Comm Volntr; Red Cr Aide; ArtClub; Emplmnt; Key Club; Photog; Prom Com; Svce Clb; French Clb; Tennis (J); Stu Cncl (R); Surfing Competitions; Basketball, Volleyball, Tennis Freshman Year; Photography; Performing Arts; U of Massachusetts; Providence U

MORGIEWICZ, BRITTANY; GROTON, MA; GROTON DUNSTABLE REG HS; (SO); Hi Hnr Roll; Hnr Roll; Competitive Cheerleading; Certified Gymnastics Instructor; Business; Boston College; Bentley College

MOURA, THAUANA; MALDEN, MA; NORTH CAMBRIDGE CATHOLIC HS; (JR); MVP; WWAHSS; Comm Volntr; Hab For Humty Volntr; Drma Clb; Key Club; Prom Com; Bnd; Clr Grd; Jzz Bnd; Mch Bnd; Vllyball (V); International Goals; Journalism; U Mass Boston; Northeastern U

MULLIGAN, KARA; TURNERS FALLS, MA; TURNERS FALLS HS; (JR); Ctznshp Aw; Hi Hnr Roll; Hnr Roll; Otst Ac Ach Awd; St of Mnth; DARE; Emplmnt; Photog; Fld Hky (V); Sftball (J); Swmg (V); Yrbk (E); Psychology; Bachelor's Degree

MULROY, MEAGAN L; EAST FREETOWN, MA; APPONEQUET REG HS; (JR); Hi Hnr Roll; Hnr Roll; Nat Hon Sy; Otst Ac Ach Awd; St of Mnth; Hosp Aide; Peer Tut/Med; ArtClub; Emplmnt; P to P St Amb Prg; Photog; Scouts; Vsity Clb; Chr; Hsbk Rdg; Tennis (V); Yrbk (E); Participated / Selected for National History Day "04"; $25.00 Prize for Poetry Contest & Published '02'; Business; Management; U of New Hampshire; Fairfield U Connecticut

MURPHY, JESSICA; EAST WEYMOUTH, MA; WEYMOUTH HS; (JR); Hnr Roll; Otst Ac Ach Awd; St of Mnth; ArtClub; Chrch Yth Grp; Drma Clb; Emplmnt; SP/M/VS; PP Ftbl (J); Skiing; Track (J); AP Art Student; Architecture; Roger Williams U; North Eastern U

MYLES, MEAGHAN; ATTLEBORO, MA; BISHOP FEEHAN HS; (SO); F Lan Hn Soc; Hnr Roll; Comm Volntr; Bskball (J); Cr Ctry (J); Track (J); Medicine; Education; U of Notre Dame; Northeastern U

NAGDA, PRIYA; ANDOVER, MA; SALEM HS; (JR); Hnr Roll; WWAHSS; Yth Ldrshp Prog; Comm Volntr; Hosp Aide; DARE; Mod UN; P to P St Amb Prg; Spanish Clb; Bdmtn (J); Track (J); Class Rep - HOSA; Biology / Pre-Med; U of Massachusetts Amherst; New York U

NAHAR, BEGUM J; CAMBRIDGE, MA; CAMBRIDGE RINDGE & LATIN HS; (JR); Ctznshp Aw; Hnr Roll; Otst Ac Ach Awd; Comm Volntr; Fr of Library; Outdrs Clb; SP/M/VS; Work Study Program; Asian Club; Business; Management; U of Massachusetts Boston; Suffolk U

NAUGHTON, BRIENNA; NORWOOD, MA; URSULINE AC; (JR); Hi Hnr Roll; Nat Hon Sy; Comm Volntr; Peer Tut/Med; Emplmnt; Svce Clb; Greek Clb; Ice Hky (V CL); Sftball (J); Summer Chemistry Intern At Boston College 2004, Magna Cum Laude on the National Latin Exam; Accepted Into National Leadership Medical Forum Boston MD Summer '05; Medicine; Biology; Georgetown U; Boston College

NEW, SAMANTHA; PITTSFIELD, MA; PITTSFIELD HS; (FR); Ctznshp Aw; Hi Hnr Roll; Sci Fairs; WWAHSS; Peer Tut/Med; Chrch Yth Grp; DARE; Scouts; SADD; Spanish Clb; Sccr (J); Tennis (V); Cl Off (R); Altar Serving; Mystery Writing Contest Winner; Accounting/Business; Boston College

NEWLON, ALEXANDRA; WESTFORD, MA; WESTFORD AC; (JR); Hi Hnr Roll; Hnr Roll; Sci Fairs; WWAHSS; Yth Ldrshp Prog; Comm Volntr; Emplmnt; Tmpl Yth Grp; Dnce; Membership VP/Secretary of Temple Youth Group; Peer Counselor, Ballet Choreographer; French; Environmental Science; Sarah Lawrence College; Mc Gill U

NEYLAND, MELANIE A; NORTH ADAMS, MA; CHARLES H MC CANN TECH HS; (JR); Hi Hnr Roll; Hnr Roll; Otst Ac Ach Awd; Sci/Math Olympn; AL Aux Girls; Off Aide; Prom Com; Voc Ind Clb Am; Chr; Adv Cncl (R); Poem Displayed in Norman Rockwell Museum; Outstanding Achievement in Office Technology; Accounting; Business; Berkshire Community College

NG, CHRISTOPHER; WESTFORD, MA; WESTFORD AC; (SO); F Lan Hn Soc; Hi Hnr Roll; Hnr Roll; Otst Ac Ach Awd; Sci/Math Olympn; Peer Tut/Med; Mth Clb/Tm; Bsball (J); Track (J); Student-Athlete Academic All Scholastic Award; Member of the Table Tennis Club; Architecture; Economics; Carnegie Mellon U; Syracuse U

NGARUIYA, WILLIAM; LOWELL, MA; LOWELL HS; (JR); Engineering; Worcester U; Salem State

NGO, MEI L; MALDEN, MA; MALDEN HS; (SO); Hi Hnr Roll; Hnr Roll; Japanese Clb; Psychology; East Asian Studies

NGUYEN, NGOC Y; DORCHESTER, MA; EXCEL HS; (JR); Hi Hnr Roll; Nat Hon Sy; Otst Ac Ach Awd; Perf Att; WWAHSS; Yth Ldrshp Prog; Comm Volntr; ROTC; Dnce; Lit Mag; Doctor of Pharmacy; Pre-Med; Massachusetts College of Pharmacy; Tufts U

NGUYEN, THU H; BRIGHTON, MA; CHARLESTOWN HS; (JR); Hi Hnr Roll; Hnr Roll; Perf Att; St of Mnth; WWAHSS; Comm Volntr; Hosp Aide; Peer Tut/Med; ArtClub; Drma Clb; Mus Clb; Stg Cre; Bdmtn (V); Sftball (V); Vllyball (J); Pediatrician; Business Management; Boston U; Harvard College

NGUYEN, TRI; WORCESTER, MA; ST JOHN'S HS; (SO); Hnr Roll; Nat Hon Sy; Comm Volntr; Mod UN; Cr Ctry ((J)); Joe Lane Scholars; National Student Leadership Conference; Dental; Medicine; Boston U; Holy Cross College

NGUYEN, VINH Q; MALDEN, MA; MALDEN HS; (SO)

NIEDBALA, JULIA; BELLINGHAM, MA; BELLINGHAM MEM HS; (SO); Hnr Roll; Comm Volntr; Chrch Yth Grp; Bnd; Sftball; Yrbk (R); Cable Club; Early Childhood Development; Boston U

NIMMO, KATHLEEN; WELLESLEY HILLS, MA; WELLESLEY HS; (JR); Cr Ctry (V); Lcrsse (V); Yrbk (R)

NITTEL, ALEXANDER P; NORWELL, MA; NORWELL HS; (SO); Ctznshp Aw; F Lan Hn Soc; Hi Hnr Roll; Hnr Roll; Otst Ac Ach Awd; Sci Fairs; Comm Volntr; Hab For Humty Volntr; Chrch Yth Grp; DARE; 5th Place 2004-05 Science Fair; Honorable Mention 2003-2004 Science Fair; Entrepreneurship; Biology; UVM

NOONAN, JULIE M; ABINGTON, MA; SOUTH SHORE VO-TECH HS; (JR); Peer Tut/Med; Outdrs Clb; Prom Com; Dnce; Chrldg (V CL); Cl Off (V); Stu Cncl (V); Made All-Star Cheerleading Team for HS; Won a Chance to Cheer in London New Years Parade; Paralegal; Forensic Scientist; U Mass Amherst; U of Mass Boston

NOWAK, AMANDA; CHICOPEE, MA; CHICOPEE COMP HS; (SO); F Lan Hn Soc; Hi Hnr Roll; Hnr Roll; ArtClub; Bskball (J); Sccr (J L); Psychology; U of Massachusetts Amherst; Boston U

NOYES, KENDRA; DANVERS, MA; DANVERS HS; (SO); F Lan Hn Soc; Hi Hnr Roll; St of Mnth; Comm Volntr; DARE; FTA; Key Club; Outdrs Clb; SADD; Bnd; Mch Bnd; Bskball (JV); Gmnstcs (V); Cancer Walk, AHA Walk, Lupus Walk; Business

NUNES, ALEXANDRA; REVERE, MA; REVERE HS; (SO); Hnr Roll; Sci Fairs; WWAHSS; Comm Volntr; Chrch Yth Grp; Scouts; Fld Hky (V); Stu Cncl (R); Church Youth Group; Criminal Justice; St Anselm College; U of Massachusetts

NUNEZ, DANIEL M; BOSTON, MA; O'BRYANT SCH OF MATH & SCIENCE; MS; Hnr Roll; Otst Ac Ach Awd; Filmmaker; Animator; Harvard U; Stanford U

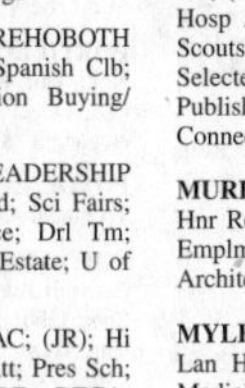

Naughton, Brienna
Ursuline AC
Norwood, MA

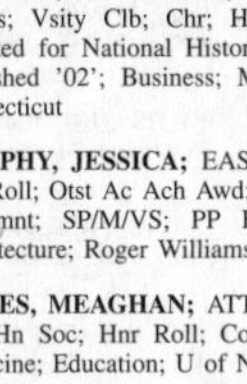

Mc Intyre, Michelle
Pembroke HS
Pembroke, MA

National
Honor Roll
Spring 2005

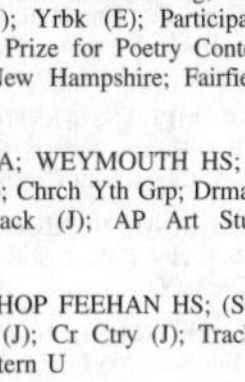

Mc Grath, Brittany
Lynn Classical HS
Lynn, MA

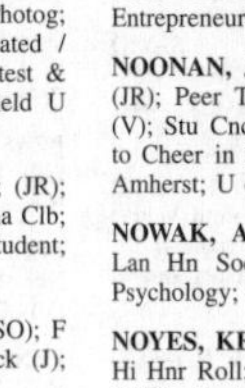

Neyland, Melanie A
Charles H Mc Cann Tech HS
North Adams, MA

NUNEZ, SERGIO A; NORTH ANDOVER, MA; NORTH ANDOVER HS; (JR); Hnr Roll; Stg Cre; Cr Ctry (V); Track (V); Public Access TV Show; History; Foreign Relations; Bentley College; Holy Cross College

NYAIGOTI, MORA; CLINTON, MA; CLINTON HS; (JR); Hi Hnr Roll; Hnr Roll; WWAHSS; Comm Volntr; Peer Tut/Med; Red Cr Aide; Chrch Yth Grp; ROTC; Chr; Sccr; Tennis; Vllyball; Yrbk (E); Excel Club; International Club; PhD in Physical Therapy; Pharmacist; American International College; Northeastern U

O'HARA, SHANNON M; BELLINGHAM, MA; BELLINGHAM MEM HS; (SO); Hnr Roll; Comm Volntr; Chrch Yth Grp; Bnd; Ch Chr; Bskball (J); Fld Hky (J); Scr Kpr (VJ); Sftball; Wrstlg (V); Criminal Investigation; Counseling; Westfield State College; Bridgewater State College

O'KELLY, CATHERINE M; CARLISLE, MA; CONCORD CARLISLE REG HS; (SO); Hi Hnr Roll; Drma Clb; Emplmnt; Bnd; Chr; SP/M/VS; Cr Ctry (J); Track (J); Yrbk (R); Math / English / Spanish Departmental Awards; Performed Classical Guitar at Rivers Contemporary Music Festival; Education; Amherst College; Vassar College

O'LAUGHLIN, ANDRES R; CARLISLE, MA; CONCORD-CARLISLE HS; (SO); Hi Hnr Roll; Hnr Roll; Yth Ldrshp Prog; Comm Volntr; Dbte Team; Emplmnt; JSA; Chr; Semi-Finalist Annual Moot Court Competition; 1st Year Scholar of History Nominee; Law; Political Science; Yale U; Harvard U

OLIVEIRA, ASHLEY R; FALL RIVER, MA; DURFEE HS; (JR); Hnr Roll; St of Mnth; CARE; Comm Volntr; Red Cr Aide; Clb; Nursing Club; Going to College; To Become a RN; U Mass Dartmouth; BCC

OLIVEIRA, MEGAN; SOMERSET, MA; SOMERSET HS; (FR); Hi Hnr Roll; Hnr Roll; Sci/Math Olympn; Amnsty Intl; Comm Volntr; Peer Tut/Med; Drma Clb; Key Club; Mth Clb/Tm; Mus Clb; Sci Clb; Scouts; Bnd; Ch Chr; Mch Bnd; Orch; Fld Hky (J); Track (L); Sch Ppr (R); Coach's Award-Track; Science Field-Medicine; Boston College

OLIVERI, BRANDI; DANVERS, MA; DANVERS HS; (SO); Hi Hnr Roll; Hnr Roll; Nat Hon Sy; St of Mnth; DARE; Outdrs Clb; Spanish Clb; Chr; Gmnstcs (V); Sftball (J); Skiing Every Other Weekend; Psychiatrist; Boston College; Tufts U

OLMSTEAD, SARAH E; HOLYOKE, MA; HOLYOKE HS-GRADE 9/10 HOME SCH-GRADE 11/12; (JR); Hi Hnr Roll; Sci Fairs; WWAHSS; Chrch Yth Grp; Emplmnt; Hsbk Rdg (V); Lit Mag (R); Sch Ppr (E); Certified Pet Care Technician; History Major; Hope for Career As Dog & Horse Trainer; U of Massachusetts At Amherst; Westfield State College

O'MALLEY, SIOBHAN E; TOPSFIELD, MA; MASEONOMET REG HS; (JR); F Lan Hn Soc; Hi Hnr Roll; Nat Hon Sy; Sci Fairs; Comm Volntr; Peer Tut/Med; AL Aux Girls; Drma Clb; Emplmnt; Mus Clb; French Clb; Bnd; Orch; Pep Bnd; SP/M/VS; Bskball (J); Vllyball (J); Cl Off (T); Massachusetts All State Festival Orchestra; Greater Boston Youth Symphony Orchestra; Engineering; Music; Princeton U; Harvard U

ONYEJEKWE, AMECHI; MARLBOROUGH, MA; MARLBORO HS; (JR); Chr; Cr Ctry (J); Ftball (J); Track (V); Wt Lftg (J); Work with Summer Program for Children with Learning Disabilities; Medicine; U of Miami; Lynn U

ORCIUCH, SARAH; WEST FALMOUTH, MA; WORCESTER AC; (JR); Hnr Roll; Otst Ac Ach Awd; St of Mnth; WWAHSS; Comm Volntr; Peer Tut/ Med; DARE; Emplmnt; Key Club; SADD; Spanish Clb; Fld Hky (V CL); Track (V L); CR (R); Ambassador @ Worcester Academy; Big Brother/Big Sister; Medical; Forensics Law; Indiana U Bloomington; Georgetown

ORLANDELLA, CHRISTOPHER; REVERE, MA; SAVIO PREPARATORY HS; (SR); Hnr Roll; Kwnis Aw; Nat Hon Sy; WWAHSS; Yth Ldrshp Prog; Comm Volntr; Key Club; Bsball (V C); Ice Hky (V C); Sccr (V C); Mathematics; Secondary Education; St Anselm College

OUELLETTE, AMY; WESTFORD, MA; WESTFORD AC; (SO); F Lan Hn Soc; Hi Hnr Roll; Hnr Roll; Nat Hon Sy; Otst Ac Ach Awd; Comm Volntr; Drma Clb; Emplmnt; SP/M/VS; Stg Cre; Gmnstcs; Scr Kpr (V); Track (J L); Cl Off (S, T); Stu Cncl (R); Member of W.A.'s Theater Arts Advisory Board; Member of National Honors Society

OUTHUSE, ANDREA; PALMER, MA; PALMER HS; (FR); Hi Hnr Roll; Hnr Roll; Otst Ac Ach Awd; Perf Att; Comm Volntr; Dnce

PAGE, JILLIAN; PEABODY, MA; PEABODY HS; (SR); All Am Sch; Hi Hnr Roll; Hnr Roll; Nat Hon Sy; Nat Sci Aw; Sci Fairs; USAA; WWAHSS; Comm Volntr; Hosp Aide; Peer Tut/Med; FTA; Chr; Dnce; Track (J); Nursing; Nurse Practitioner; Northeastern U

PALLEIRO, LAURA B; LEOMINSTER, MA; LEOMINSTER HS; (FR); Hi Hnr Roll; Hnr Roll; Perf Att; St of Mnth; Comm Volntr; Chrch Yth Grp; DARE; Ch Chr; Give (Community Service); PhD (Pediatrician); Lawyer; Harvard Medical School; Harvard Law School

PALLOS, KRYSTINA L; PITTSFIELD, MA; TACONIC HS; (SR); Hi Hnr Roll; Nat Hon Sy; Otst Ac Ach Awd; Comm Volntr; Hosp Aide; BPA; Prom Com; Italian Clb; Lcrsse (V); Sftball (V); Stu Cncl; National Winner At BPA; Leadership Conference; Accounting; Finance; Western New England College; Bentley College

PANDYA, NIDHI; WILMINGTON, MA; WILMINGTON HS; (SR); Hi Hnr Roll; Hnr Roll; Perf Att; WWAHSS; Comm Volntr; Red Cr Aide; Biology Clb; Drma Clb; Lib Aide; Sci Clb; Acpl Chr; Chr; Dnce; SP/M/VS; Chrldg (J); Track (J); Cl Off (R); Stu Cncl (R); CR (R); Show Choir; Indian Club; Pre-Med; Regis College

PANG, MAGGIE; MALDEN, MA; MALDEN HS; (SO); Hnr Roll; Kwnis Aw; Perf Att; Sci Fairs; Comm Volntr; Drma Clb; Key Club; Track (J); Yrbk (P); Finance / Accounting; Nursing / Doctor; Boston College; Boston U

PARENTEAU, ANDREW J; LANCASTER, MA; NASHOBA REG HS; (JR); Hnr Roll; Nat Hon Sy; Comm Volntr; Chrch Yth Grp; DARE; Emplmnt; Prom Com; Bsball (VJ L); Bskball (VJ L); Golf (V L); Sccr (J); Sports Management-Facilities Mgmt.

PARKER, CALLIE A; WESTFIELD, MA; WESTFIELD HS; (SR); Hi Hnr Roll; Nat Hon Sy; WWAHSS; Comm Volntr; Drma Clb; Bnd; Jzz Bnd; Mch Bnd; Orch; Swmg; Law; Music; Emmanuel College; Framingham State College

PARKHURST, TIFFANY; WINCHENDON, MA; WINCHENDON SCH; (SO); Hi Hnr Roll; Perf Att; WWAHSS; ArtClub; DARE; Scouts; French Clb; Ice Sktg; Vllyball; Interior Design; Fashion Design; New York U; Princeton

PARRELLA, ALEX J; WALTHAM, MA; WALTHAM HS; (JR); Hnr Roll; Yth Ldrshp Prog; Comm Volntr; Hab For Humty Volntr; Chrch Yth Grp; DARE; Emplmnt; Svce Clb; SADD; Italian Clb; SP/M/VS; Lcrsse (J); Skiing (J); Cl Off (R); Freshman Mentor; Communications & Broadcasting; Quinnipiac U; U of Miami

PARRELLA, KEVIN E; WALTHAM, MA; WALTHAM HS; (JR); Hnr Roll; MVP; Yth Ldrshp Prog; Comm Volntr; Hab For Humty Volntr; Chrch Yth Grp; Emplmnt; Svce Clb; SADD; Italian Clb; Bsball (V); Bskball (V); MVP-Basketball; Business-Finance; Fairfield U; Bryant U

PARSONS, EMILY; MARSHFIELD, MA; MARSHFIELD HS; (SO); Ctznshp Aw; Hi Hnr Roll; Hnr Roll; Mas Aw; Otst Ac Ach Awd; Comm Volntr; Red Cr Aide; DARE; Emplmnt; Key Club; Scr Kpr (J); Sccr (J); Adv Cncl (T); Stu Cncl (R); Student Council Member; Bioretention System Citation-Rep Frank Hines; 4 Year College for Biology or Pre-Med; Med School Degree; Boston U; Stonehill College

PATEL, AMIT; EAST WAREHAM, MA; WAREHAM HS; (SR); Hi Hnr Roll; Nat Hon Sy; Perf Att; St of Mnth; Comm Volntr; Chess; Prom Com; ROTC; Schol Bwl; Foreign Clb; Bsball (V); Treasurer of Honor Society; Law; Bentley College

PATEL, JENNY H; SOMERSET, MA; SOMERSET HS; (JR); Hi Hnr Roll; Hnr Roll; Nat Hon Sy; Otst Ac Ach Awd; St of Mnth; Comm Volntr; Peer Tut/Med; DARE; FTA; Key Club; Prom Com; Sci Clb; Peer Leadership-Treasurer; National Honor Society; Nursing; RN; Northeastern U; Massachusetts College of Pharmacy & Health Sciences

PATWIN, SAMUEL C, TAUNTON, MA; TAUNTON HS; (JR); Hi Hnr Roll; Hnr Roll; Chess; Orch; Northwest Talent Search; 7th Grade PSAT; Computer Science; Business (General); Wentworth Institute of Technology; Fitchburg State College

PEARSON, BRITTANY; MILLBURY, MA; MILLBURY MEMORIAL JR/SR HS; (SO); 4H Awd; Hi Hnr Roll; Hnr Roll; MVP; Nat Hon Sy; Pres Ac Ftns Aw; Yth Ldrshp Prog; Comm Volntr; Peer Tut/Med; 4-H; Chrch Yth Grp; Drma Clb; Emplmnt; Quiz Bowl; Bnd; Dnce; Orch; SP/M/VS; Cr Ctry (V L); Track (V L); Stu Cncl (R); Yrbk (R); Veterinarian; Biology Teacher / Zoology; U of Massachusetts; Becker

PEASE, MEGAN; EASTHAM, MA; NAUSET REG HS; (JR); Hnr Roll; Hab For Humty Volntr; Cr Ctry (J); Sccr (J); Restaurant Management; Business; Connecticut College; Franklin Pierce

PELLEGRINO, NICHOLAS W; BOSTON, MA; SAVIO PREP; (JR); Hi Hnr Roll; Hnr Roll; Nat Hon Sy; Yth Ldrshp Prog; Key Club; SADD; Sccr (V); Track (V)

PENA, PEDRIANT; LAWRENCE, MA; LAWRENCE HS; (JR); Hi Hnr Roll; Hnr Roll; MVP; Nat Hon Sy; Otst Ac Ach Awd; Perf Att; Pres Ac Ftns Aw; USAA; Comm Volntr; Peer Tut/Med; Red Cr Aide; Emplmnt; Mth Clb/Tm; ROTC; Sci Clb; Clr Grd; Drl Tm; Cl Off (P); Stu Cncl (P); CR (P); Mathematical Sciences; Physics; Massachusetts Institute of Technology; Worcester Polytechnic Institute

PENEAU, SCOTT; BELLINGHAM, MA; BELLINGHAM HS; (SR); Ctznshp Aw; Hi Hnr Roll; Hnr Roll; Nat Hon Sy; WWAHSS; Comm Volntr; Red Cr Aide; DECA; Emplmnt; Bsball (VJ); Golf (VJC); President - National Honor Society; Bob Purich Memorial Sportsmanship Award; Business Administration; Professional Golf Management; Methodist College

PERCEL RODRIGUEZ, ANDRES A; LYNN, MA; LYNN ENGLISH HS; (SR); St of Mnth; WWAHSS; Comm Volntr; Red Cr Aide; DARE; ROTC; SADD; Spanish Clb; Bsball (VJ); Bskball (J); In Charge of the Recycle Program; Automotive Technology; Benjamin Franklin Institute of Technology

PEREZ, DIANA; LOWELL, MA; LOWELL HS; (SO); Hi Hnr Roll; Hnr Roll; Nat Hon Sy; St of Mnth; DARE; Scouts; Chr; Sch Ppr; Kickball - 2 Years; National Junior Honor Society; Fashion Designer; Nurse; New York U; Boston U

PEREZ, ROSA F; SPRINGFIELD, MA; HS OF COMMERCE; (SO); Hnr Roll; WWAHSS; Yth Ldrshp Prog; Comm Volntr; DARE; ROTC; Scouts; Drl Tm; JROTC; Medical Doctor; Military Services

PERRY, DEIRDRE; DANVERS, MA; DANVERS HS; (FR); Hi Hnr Roll; Hnr Roll; Otst Ac Ach Awd; St of Mnth; Comm Volntr; Chrch Yth Grp; DARE; FTA; Key Club; Chrldg (V L); Lcrsse (J); Cl Off (P); Stu Cncl (R); Key Club Member; Government/Law

PERRY, RUSSELL; NORTH ANDOVER, MA; NORTH ANDOVER HS; (JR); Hi Hnr Roll; Nat Hon Sy; Drma Clb; Chr; SP/M/VS; Stu Cncl (R); Shakespeare & Co. Fall Festival

PETRONE, CATHERINE; MEDFORD, MA; MEDFORD HS; (SO); Hi Hnr Roll; Sci Fairs; St of Mnth; Comm Volntr; Red Cr Aide; Chrch Yth Grp; Key Club; Quiz Bowl; Sch Ppr (E, R); Outstanding Effort Awards; Community Service Award; Nursing; Teaching; Boston College; U Mass Lowell

PHILLIPS, KARI; MARSHFIELD, MA; MARSHFIELD HS; (SO); Hi Hnr Roll; Hnr Roll; Peer Tut/Med; Emplmnt; Key Club; Prom Com; Fld Hky (J); Sftball (J); Sch Ppr (R); Medicine; Medical Tech; U of Vermont

PIERCE, CHRISTINE M; HANSON, MA; WHITMAN HANSON REG HS; (SR); Hnr Roll; Comm Volntr; Key Club; Internship At Brockton Hospital; Nursing; Quincy College

PIERRE, PATRICIA; MALDEN, MA; MALDEN HS; (SR); Hi Hnr Roll; Nat Hon Sy; ArtClub; Chrch Yth Grp; Key Club; Ch Chr; Clr Grd; Dnce; Published Poem; Physician / Pediatrician; Boston College; Emmanuel College

PIERRE, RICHARDSON; MEDFORD, MA; MEDFIELD HS; (JR); Ctznshp Aw; Peer Tut/Med; Chrch Yth Grp; Drma Clb; Emplmnt; Clb; Chr; Ch Chr; Dnce; SP/M/VS; Swmg; Track; Works in an Assisted Living Corporation as a Dietary Aide; In a Dance Group; Business / CPA; Performing Arts; Howard U; Bentley

PIERRE-LOUIS, FELISHA; MEDFORD, MA; MEDFORD HS; (FR); Hi Hnr Roll; Otst Ac Ach Awd; Comm Volntr; Chrch Yth Grp; Scouts; Ch Chr; Silver / Bronze Girl Scout Award; Business; Harvard U; Columbia U

PILOTTE, KARA; WINCHESTER, MA; WINCHESTER HS; (JR); F Lan Hn Soc; Hnr Roll; Yth Ldrshp Prog; Comm Volntr; Hab For Humty Volntr; Peer Tut/Med; Emplmnt; Photog; Prom Com; Chr; Chrldg (V L); Sftball (J); Swmg (V L); Student Delegate to MADD Youth Summit 2004; Marine Biology/Oceanography; Business Administration/Management; U of South Carolina; U of Washington

PINKSTEN, KRISTEN; ANDOVER, MA; ANDOVER SR HS; (SR); Hi Hnr Roll; MVP; Nat Hon Sy; Pres Sch; Yth Ldrshp Prog; Comm Volntr; Peer Tut/ Med; DECA; Emplmnt; NYLC; Pep Squd; Prom Com; SADD; Bskball (J); PP Ftbl (V C); Vllyball (V L); Stu Cncl (P); Prom Queen; International Business; Marketing; Georgetown U; U of Pennsylvania

POLIDO, LIZ; STOW, MA; NASHOBA REG HS; (JR); Hi Hnr Roll; Hnr Roll; MVP; Comm Volntr; Peer Tut/Med; Prom Com; Bskball (V L); Sccr (V CL); Integrity of Character Award; Soccer League All-Star ('03-04), Central Mass All-Star, SE All-Star, Metrowest All-Star; Journalism; Marketing; Middlebury College; Bucknell U

PORTILLO, ANA D; ARLINGTON, MA; ARLINGTON HS; (SO); Hi Hnr Roll; Hnr Roll; Nat Hon Sy; Comm Volntr; Emplmnt; SADD; French Clb; Chr; Dnce; SP/M/VS; Mar Art; Black Belt - Tae Kwon Do; Omni Award For Academic & Community Contribution

POTOCNJAK, JOHN C; ARNOLD, MA; FOX SR HS; (JR); Ranken Technical College

POWELL, DEMAR; BOSTON, MA; BOSTON ENGLISH HS; (SR); Ctznshp Aw; MVP; Perf Att; Sci Fairs; US Army Sch Ath Aw; Comm Volntr; Spec Olymp Vol; Chess; Chrch Yth Grp; Dbte Team; Emplmnt; ROTC; Ch Chr; Bdmtn (V); Fld Hky (C); Ftball (V CL); Track (V); Vllyball (V); Wt Lftg (V); CR (P, R); Business Management; Dean College; Bethune-Cookman College

PRIOR, NIKKIA; HYDE PARK, MA; TECHBOSTON AC; (SO); Hnr Roll; St of Mnth; ArtClub; Vllyball; Art; Graphic Design; Fashion Design; The New England Institute of Art in Brookline, MA; Bay State U in Boston, MA

PUGSLEY, SAMANTHA; MILLBURY, MA; MILLBURY MEMORIAL JR/SR HS; (SO); Hi Hnr Roll; Hnr Roll; Perf Att; WWAHSS; Yth Ldrshp Prog; Spec Olymp Vol; Chrch Yth Grp; Emplmnt; P to P St Amb Prg; Tech Clb; Chr; Ch Chr; Chrldg (V); Modeling / Acting; Gymnastics - Outside of School; Neurologist; Obstetrics and Gynecology; Harvard U; Tufts U

Pinksten, Kristen
Andover SR HS
Andover, MA

Pellegrino, Nicholas W
Savio Prep
Boston, MA

Ouellette, Amy
Westford AC
Westford, MA

Orciuch, Sarah
Worcester AC
West Falmouth, MA

Nunez, Sergio A
North Andover HS
North Andover, MA

O'Laughlin, Andres R
Concord-Carlisle HS
Carlisle, MA

Patel, Amit
Wareham HS
East Wareham, MA

Peneau, Scott
Bellingham HS
Bellingham, MA

Powell, Demar
Boston English HS
Boston, MA

PULTORAK, TANYA; LEE, MA; MONUMENT MTN REG HS; (SR); Hnr Roll; WWAHSS; Key Club; Vllyball (J); Early Childhood Education; Psychology; Massachusetts College of Liberal Arts

PUOPOLO, ANDREW P; WESTWOOD, MA; WESTWOOD HS; (JR); Hnr Roll; Peer Tut/Med; Emplmnt; Photog; SADD; Spanish Clb; Cr Ctry (V); Yrbk (E, P); Secretary of SADD; Vice President of WW Ambassadors; Plastic Surgery; Real Estate; Boston College

PUTNAM, KRISTINA; DANVERS, MA; DANVERS HS; (SO); Hi Hnr Roll; Otst Ac Ach Awd; St of Mnth; WWAHSS; Key Club; Dnce; SP/M/VS; Bskball; College Major-Biology; Career-Physician; St Michael's College

QIU, LILY; QUINCY, MA; NORTH QUINCY HS; (SR); Hi Hnr Roll; Hnr Roll; Emplmnt; Jr Ach; ROTC; Physician's Assistant; Pre-Med; Simmons College; Massachusetts College of Pharmacy

QUINN, KIMBERLY N; ARLINGTON, MA; ARLINGTON HS; (JR); F Lan Hn Soc; Hi Hnr Roll; Hnr Roll; Nat Hon Sy; Peer Tut/Med; DARE; Mth Clb/Tm; Pep Squd; SADD; Latin Clb; Chrldg (V CL); Sftball (J); Most Determined; Unsung Hero; Forensic Science; Radiology; U of New Hampshire; U of Connecticut

QUINN, MEAGHAN; NORWELL, MA; NORWELL HS; (JR); F Lan Hn Soc; Hi Hnr Roll; Nat Hon Sy; Sci Fairs; Comm Volntr; Peer Tut/Med; Chrch Yth Grp; Emplmnt; Jr Cls League; Mus Clb; Vsity Clb; Bnd; Orch; Pep Bnd; SP/M/VS; Bskball (V L); Fld Hky (J); Lcrsse (V L); PP Ftbl (J); Sccr (J); Sch Ppr (R); Peer Education; Young Republicans; Medicine; Business; Boston College; Fordham U

QUINN, MELISSA; DEDHAM, MA; DEDHAM HS; (JR); Hnr Roll; Dnce

RABELO, HIABELLA; MEDFORD, MA; MEDFORD HS; (SO); F Lan Hn Soc; Hi Hnr Roll; Perf Att; Yth Ldrshp Prog; Comm Volntr; Hosp Aide; Chrch Yth Grp; Drma Clb; Mus Clb; Chr; Ch Chr; Orch; SP/M/VS; Mar Art; Translator at Church; Gospel Club; Pre-Law; Languages; Harvard U; Georgetown U

RACZKOWSKI, ADAM J; EAST LONGMEADOW, MA; EAST LONGMEADOW HS; (SR); Hi Hnr Roll; Hnr Roll; Nat Hon Sy; Nat Mrt LOC; Otst Ac Ach Awd; Pres Sch; Salutrn; WWAHSS; Comm Volntr; Peer Tut/Med; 4-H; Chrch Yth Grp; Dbte Team; Key Club; Mth Clb/Tm; Sci Clb; French Clb; Bnd; Jzz Bnd; Mch Bnd; SP/M/VS; Cr Ctry (V); Track (V); Stu Cncl (R); CR (R); Lit Mag (E); Key Club President; Debate Team, Math Team, Science League; Mathematics; Physics; Tufts U (Accepted)

RAHMAN, JOBAIDA; CAMBRIDGE, MA; (SR); Hi Hnr Roll; Hnr Roll; Nat Hon Sy; WWAHSS; Yth Ldrshp Prog; Comm Volntr; Peer Tut/Med; Red Cr Aide; Chrch Yth Grp; Mod UN; Prom Com; Clb; Dnce; Bdmtn (V); Bskball (J); Tennis (J); Track (J); Vllyball (J); Yrbk (E, R, P); I Am the President of the Cultural History Club.; I Am Part of Many Other Clubs.; Dentistry; Pharmacy; Tufts U; Boston U

RAHMAN, SYED A; WRENTHAM, MA; KING PHILIP REG HS; (SO); Hi Hnr Roll; Hnr Roll; Otst Ac Ach Awd; WWAHSS; Yth Ldrshp Prog; Comm Volntr; Ftball (J); Track (V L); Most Dedicated - Track; RYLA - Rotary & Youth Leadership Award; Medical Field; Biomedical; Harvard U; Boston U

RAMASWAMY, VISWANATH; WESTFORD, MA; WESTFORD AC; (SO); Hi Hnr Roll; Hnr Roll; Perf Att; Comm Volntr; Hosp Aide; Mth Clb/Tm; Sci Clb; Track (J); Rivier College Basketball Camp Champion; Kumon Achievement Award; Medicine; Biology; Boston U; Northeastern U

REARDON, JULIANN L; UXBRIDGE, MA; UXBRIDGE HS; (SO); Hi Hnr Roll; Nat Hon Sy; WWAHSS; Chrch Yth Grp; Emplmnt; Mus Clb; Bnd; Chr; Jzz Bnd; Pep Bnd; Mar Art (V L); Skiing; Sccr; Track (V L); Full Scholarship to NASA'S Advanced Space Academy; Engineering; Massachusetts Institute of Technology; Worcester Polytechnic Institute

REGAN, MARCIE A; BUZZARDS BAY, MA; WAREHAM HS; (SR); Otst Ac Ach Awd; WWAHSS; DECA; 04' Mass-DECA Technical Sales Event: 3rd Place; DECA Nationals, Nashville, TN; Fitchburg State College

REY, SAMANTHA; CAMBRIDGE, MA; CAMBRIDGE RINDGE & LATIN HS; (JR); Hnr Roll; Sci Fairs; Emplmnt; Photog; Chr; Dance Academy Awards; Most Improved Student Award; Accountant; Psychologist / Social Worker; U Mass Lowell; Temple U

REYNOLDS, KELLY; LEXINGTON, MA; LEXINGTON HS; (JR); Hi Hnr Roll; Nat Hon Sy; Comm Volntr; Spec Olymp Vol; Chrch Yth Grp; Spanish Clb; Bnd; Dnce; Jzz Bnd; Mch Bnd; Sftball (V)

REYNOLDS, SAMUEL; CHELMSFORD, MA; CHELMSFORD HS; (JR); F Lan Hn Soc; Hi Hnr Roll; Hnr Roll; Jr Rot; Nat Hon Sy; WWAHSS; Yth Ldrshp Prog; Comm Volntr; Peer Tut/Med; Chess; Chrch Yth Grp; Emplmnt; FTA; Mus Clb; Prom Com; Scouts; Bnd; Jzz Bnd; Mch Bnd; Orch; Ftball (V L); Track (J L); Adv Cncl (S, R); CR (R); Member of Merrimack Valley American Athletic Union Basketball Team; Member of Winter Guard International Percussion Ensemble; Chemical Engineering; Music Performance; Cornell U; Harvard College

RICE, ALEXA C; STILL RIVER, MA; THE BROMFIELD SCH; (SO); Hnr Roll; Yth Ldrshp Prog; NYLC; Bnd; Hsbk Rdg (L); Mar Art (L); Black Belt Karate; John Philip Sousa National Honors Band; Psychology; Language (French, Spanish, Italian, German); Occidental College; U of California; Berkeley

RICHARDSON, ASHLEY; SPRINGFIELD, MA; SPRINGFIELD CTRL HS; (JR); Hnr Roll; Yth Ldrshp Prog; Comm Volntr; Spec Olymp Vol; Chrch Yth Grp; Drma Clb; Scouts; Ch Chr; Dnce; SP/M/VS; Yrbk (R, P); Mass Mutual Rising Academic Achiever; Numerous Girl Scout Awards; Child Psychology; Drama; Howard U, Washington DC

RICHARDSON, HANNAH S; CONCORD, MA; CONCORD-CARLISLE HS; (SO); Hi Hnr Roll; Lcrsse (V); Cl Off (R); Stu Cncl (R); Varsity Crew Team - CRI Boston; Neuropsychology; Journalism; Harvard U; Columbia U

RIDDLE, SHANE; TEWKSBURY, MA; TEWKSBURY MEMORIAL HS; (SO); Hi Hnr Roll; Yth Ldrshp Prog; Comm Volntr; Emplmnt; Mth Clb/Tm; Robotics Club, Volunteer At Nursing Homes; Math Team; Robotic Engineering; Mechanical Engineering; U of Vermont; U of New Hampshire

RILEY, MICHAEL; TYNGSBORO, MA; (SO); Hnr Roll; Bnd; Jzz Bnd; Mch Bnd; Lcrsse (J); Sccr (V); Eastern Mass. District Band Participant

RITSKO, ALIZA; NORWELL, MA; NORWELL HS; (FR); F Lan Hn Soc; Hi Hnr Roll; Hnr Roll; JSA; Acpl Chr; Chr; Tennis (V); Have Sung in Ravel's Opera (Noyes Flude); Journalism; Business; U of Pennsylvania; Boston College

RITTENHOUSE, JULIA A; STONEHAM, MA; GREATER BOSTON AC; (JR); Hi Hnr Roll; Nat Hon Sy; USAA; WWAHSS; Comm Volntr; Mus Clb; Ch Chr; Orch; Cl Off (P, V); Yrbk (E); Pre-Med; Music; Southern College, Harvard U; Atlantic Union College

RIVERA, AIMEE F; TAUNTON, MA; TAUNTON HS; (SR); Hnr Roll; Comm Volntr; Portuguese Clb; Yrbk (R); Sunday School Teacher; Spanish Club; Management; Entrepreneurship; Bentley College; Framingham State College

RIVERA, JOCELYN L; LEOMINSTER, MA; LEOMINSTER HS; (SO); Hi Hnr Roll; Hnr Roll; Otst Ac Ach Awd; St of Mnth; Comm Volntr; DARE; Emplmnt; Jr Ach; Tchrs Aide

RIVERS, MARIE; HOPKINTON, MA; HOPKINTON HS; (SR); Hnr Roll; Nat Hon Sy; Pres Sch; Sci Fairs; WWAHSS; Yth Ldrshp Prog; Comm Volntr; Emplmnt; Bnd; Pep Bnd; Chrldg (V CL); Cr Ctry (J); Dvng (V L); Track (J); Rensselaer Medal; Youth Salute Award; Environmental Engineering; U of Delaware

ROBERTS, ROCHELLE; CHELMSFORD, MA; CHELMSFORD HS; (JR); Hi Hnr Roll; Hnr Roll; Otst Ac Ach Awd; Comm Volntr; Peer Tut/Med; Red Cr Aide; DARE; Dnce; Bskball (J); Chrldg (VJ); Gmnstcs (J); Community Service Director; Major in Business; Police Officer; Bedford Middlesex Community College; Tampa U

ROBERTSON, SAMANTHA; PITTSFIELD, MA; TACONIC HS; (SO); Hi Hnr Roll; Nat Hon Sy; Peer Tut/Med; Bnd; Mch Bnd; Tennis (V); Miss Massachusetts Teen America 2003; Western MA Senior District Band with French Horn; Pilot; Aviation Management; Florida Institute of Technology; Jacksonville U

ROBINSON, JADE; MARSHFIELD, MA; MARSHFIELD HS; (SO); Hi Hnr Roll; Hnr Roll; MVP; Nat Hon Sy; Otst Ac Ach Awd; Perf Att; Yth Ldrshp Prog; Peer Tut/Med; Bskball; Sftball (J); Vllyball (J); Cl Off (T); DECA Youth Group; Peer Tutor in Grammar School; Principal's Award

ROBINSON, ROMAN; SPRINGFIELD, MA; NEW LEADERSHIP CHARTER SCH; MS; Hnr Roll; Sci Fairs; Yth Ldrshp Prog; Comm Volntr; BPA; Chrch Yth Grp; Emplmnt; FBLA; Tmpl Yth Grp; Ch Chr; Mar Art (C); Skt Tgt Sh (V); Adv Cncl (R); Business Courses; Theology, Law; World Harvest Bible College; U of Connecticut

ROBINSON, TROY; ROSLINDALE, MA; O'BRYANT SCH OF MATH & SCIENCE; MS; Hnr Roll; Peer Tut/Med; Bskball (J); Went to State Championship; Highest GPA on Basketball Team.; Math; PhD; Duke U; U of North Carolina

RODRIGUEZ, ZAMAYRA; BOSTON, MA; BRIGHTON HS; (JR); Comm Volntr; Peer Tut/Med; Volleyball - Not with School; Best Student in US History Class; Pre-Med; Psychology; Loyola College Maryland; Boston College

ROGERS, ELIZABETH S; MANSFIELD, MA; URSULINE AC; (SR); Hnr Roll; Nat Hon Sy; Comm Volntr; Hab For Humty Volntr; Peer Tut/Med; ArtClub; Chrch Yth Grp; Emplmnt; Mth Clb/Tm; Photog; Prom Com; Svce Clb; SADD; Dnce; Cl Off (P); Stu Cncl (V); Sch Ppr (P); Yrbk (P); Neurobiology; Genetics; Bates College; Colby College

ROGERS, KYLE R; WOBURN, MA; WOBURN SR HS; (SO); Hnr Roll; Ice Hky (J); Skiing; Carpentry; Business; UNH; Northeastern U

ROKHKIND, ANNA; EAST LONGMEADOW, MA; EAST LONGMEADOW HS; (SO); Hnr Roll; Perf Att; St of Mnth; Comm Volntr; BPA; DARE; Latin Clb; Cr Ctry (V); Ice Sktg; Business Major; Graphic Design; Boston U; Boston College

ROMERO, JESSICA M; HAVERHILL, MA; WHITTIER VO-TECH HS; (FR); Hi Hnr Roll; Hnr Roll; WWAHSS; Comm Volntr; Red Cr Aide; Emplmnt; Key Club; Bskball (J); Vllyball (J); Multicultural Club; Key Club Treasurer; Childhood Education-Early; Master's Degree; Northeastern U

ROSENBERG, KAYLA; NORTH ANDOVER, MA; NORTH ANDOVER HS; (JR); Hi Hnr Roll; Hnr Roll; Nat Hon Sy; Hab For Humty Volntr; Spanish Clb; Communications; Psychology; Tufts U; Boston U

ROSENBLATT, AMANDA S; SOUTH ATTLEBORO, MA; ATTLEBORO HS; (SR); Lit Mag (R); Sch Ppr (E, R); Reporter for Local Newspaper - Place Section; Ran Becca's Closet - Free Prom Dresses to Needy; Newspaper Journalist; Columbia College Chicago - Accepted

ROUX, KATIE A; GROTON, MA; GROTON DUNSTABLE REG HS; (SO); Hi Hnr Roll; Hnr Roll; WWAHSS; Comm Volntr; Track (V L); Vllyball (J); Psychology or Physical Therapy; Teaching

RUEDA, ERIK; ESSEX, MA; MANCHESTER ESSEX REG; (SR); Lcrsse (VJ); Private Pilot License; Aeronautical Engineering; Architecture; Embry Riddle

RUIZ, JASON D; BOSTON, MA; O'BRYANT SCH OF MATH & SCIENCE; MS; Hnr Roll; Sci Fairs; Comm Volntr; ArtClub; Cmptr Clb; ROTC; Sci Clb; Tech Clb; Drl Tm; Bsball (V); Sccr (V); CR (R); Graphic Designing; Automotive Design; Northeastern U; Boston College

RUSSELL, BRIANA; PETERSHAM, MA; MAHAR REG HS; (FR); Hnr Roll; Nat Hon Sy; SADD; Fld Hky (J); Track (V); Medical; New York U

RYAN, MEGHAN; NEWBURYPORT, MA; NEWBURYPORT HS; (JR); Hi Hnr Roll; Hnr Roll; Nat Hon Sy; Peer Tut/Med; Chrch Yth Grp; Emplmnt; Key Club; NYLC; Prom Com; Fld Hky (V L); Lcrsse (V L); Cl Off (V); CR (V); Prom Coordinator; Business; College of the Holy Cross; Colby College

SA, PRISCILLA; NEW BEDFORD, MA; NEW BEDFORD HS; (JR); Hi Hnr Roll; Hnr Roll; Perf Att; WWAHSS; Hosp Aide; Chrch Yth Grp; Emplmnt; Key Club; CR (R); Secretary of Medical Careers Club; Registered Nurse; Physician's Assistant; Salve Regina U; U of Massachusetts, Dartmouth College

SADOWSKI, ALLISON; WEBSTER, MA; BAY PATH REG VOC HS; (JR); Hnr Roll; DECA; DECA Member; VICA Skills USA Member; Painting / Fine Arts; Photography; Montserrat College of Art; The Art Institute of Boston - Lesley U

SAGANICH III, ALBERT; SHIRLEY, MA; GDR HS; (SO); Ctznshp Aw; Hnr Roll; Sci Fairs; St of Mnth; Comm Volntr; First Robotics; Prep Cook for Elderly; Engineering; Robotics; Worchester Poly Technical Institute; U of Massachusetts

SAGER, BRIAN; MARION, MA; SUFFIELD AC; (JR); Hnr Roll; WWAHSS; Comm Volntr; Red Cr Aide; Emplmnt; Swmg (V L); 3 Years Water Polo; 2 Years Nantucket Surf Lifeguard; Tufts U; Colby College

SAGUICH, LUIS E; MARLBOROUGH, MA; MARLBOROUGH HS; (FR); Sccr (J); Architecture; Engineering; Drexel U

SAISA, OLIVIA R; CLINTON, MA; NASHOBA REG HS; (FR); Hi Hnr Roll; Hnr Roll; Hosp Aide; DARE; Sftball (V); Stu Cncl (P); Yrbk (E, P); Some Hospice Work; Volunteer Year-Round @ Marlboro E. R.; E. R. Doctor; Homicide Detective; New York U; Boston College

SALTANOVICH, JULIA; PITTSFIELD, MA; PITTSFIELD HS; (SO); 4H Awd; Hi Hnr Roll; Perf Att; Sci Fairs; St of Mnth; Comm Volntr; 4-H; ArtClub; DARE; Drma Clb; Jr Ach; Tmpl Yth Grp; French Clb; Dnce; Vllyball (J); Liberal Arts; Psychology

SANCHEZ, KRYSTIN E; BILLERICA, MA; BILLERICA HS; (SR); Hnr Roll; WWAHSS; Comm Volntr; DARE; DECA; Emplmnt; Dnce; Dance Teacher; Foreign Exchange with Spain; Sports Entertainment Event Management; Johnson & Wales U

SANON, SAMANTHA J; MATTAPAN, MA; BRIGHTON HS; (FR); Hnr Roll; Nat Hon Sy; Otst Ac Ach Awd; St of Mnth; Chrch Yth Grp; Mth Clb/Tm; Ch Chr; Dnce; SP/M/VS; Chrldg; Cr Ctry; Tennis; Track (V); Yrbk (R); Girls Rowing; Computer Technician; Dentist; Georgia Tech; Benjamin Franklin Institute of Tech.

SARGENT, DANIELLE M; DANVERS, MA; NORTH SHORE TECH HS; (SR); Hnr Roll; MVP; Nat Hon Sy; Nat Stu Ath Day Aw; Otst Ac Ach Awd; WWAHSS; Peer Tut/Med; Emplmnt; Key Club; Scouts; SADD; Voc Ind Clb Am; Cr Ctry (V CL); Track (V CL); Bachelor's Degree-Culinary Arts; Associate's-Baking & Pastry Arts; Johnson & Wales U

SARNELLI JR, MICHAEL; CHICOPEE, MA; CHICOPEE HS; (JR); Hnr Roll; WWAHSS; Key Club; Sccr (V L); Track (V L); Stu Cncl; Member of the Renaissance Club; Graduate from College; Elms College; Westfield State College

Rivera, Aimee F
Taunton HS
Taunton, MA

Richardson, Hannah S
Concord-Carlisle HS
Concord, MA

Rice, Alexa C
The Bromfield Sch
Still River, MA

National
Honor Roll
Spring 2005

Reynolds, Samuel
Chelmsford HS
Chelmsford, MA

Ritsko, Aliza
Norwell HS
Norwell, MA

Rosenberg, Kayla
North Andover HS
North Andover, MA

SAUCIER, KATHERINE A; MIDDLEBORO, MA; MIDDLEBORO HS; (SO); Hnr Roll; WWAHSS; Key Club; Quiz Bowl; Chr; Stu Cncl (R); Summer Orchestra First Flute - MHS; MHS Key Club; Psychology; Geology

SAVARIA, MARTHA; SPRINGFIELD, MA; BELCHERTOWN HS; (SR); Hi Hnr Roll; WWAHSS; Peer Tut/Med; Bskball; Audio Production; Emerson College

SAWULA, NICOLE A; NORTHAMPTON, MA; NORTHAMPTON HS; (SO); Hi Hnr Roll; MVP; Perf Att; 4-H; DARE; Drma Clb; Emplmnt; Photog; Wdwrkg Clb; Chr; Dnce; Lcrsse (V L); Sccr (V L); Teaching; Physical Therapy; Wheaton College; Williams College

SCHELIN, DEIDRE; WEST BOYLSTON, MA; WEST BOYLSTON HS; (JR); F Lan Hn Soc; Hi Hnr Roll; Hnr Roll; Nat Hon Sy; St of Mnth; WWAHSS; Comm Volntr; Peer Tut/Med; Chrch Yth Grp; Emplmnt; Foreign Clb; Skiing; Sccr (V L); Tennis (V CL); Awards In-Geometry Pre-Calc, AP Biology, Alg II, Integrated Science, Teens Organized Against Drugs Kaplan Certificate of Mastery; Economics; Pre-Med; Boston College; Brown

SCHILLING, JOYCE; FORESTDALE, MA; SANDWICH HS; (SR); Hi Hnr Roll; Hnr Roll; Otst Ac Ach Awd; Comm Volntr; Wdwrkg Clb; MSPCA Volunteer; Zoology; Nursing; Cape Cod Community College

SCOTT, LAURA E; CHELMSFORD, MA; CHELMSFORD HS; (JR); Hi Hnr Roll; Hnr Roll; Comm Volntr; Dnce; Orch; Skiing (V); Track (V); Vllyball (V); Black Belt in Tae Kwon Do - Studied 9 Years; Most Improved Skier 2003/2004; Business; Marketing; Bentley College; Assumption College

SEPLOW, CANDICE; METHUEN, MA; WHITTIER REG TECH HS; (SR); Hnr Roll; Nat Hon Sy; WWAHSS; Dbte Team; Mod UN; Voc Ind Clb Am; Sccr (V L); Coach's Award-Soccer; VICA; Computer Science; Master's; River College; U-Mass Lowell

SERPE, NICK; WESTFORD, MA; WESTFORD AC; (JR); F Lan Hn Soc; Hi Hnr Roll; Nat Hon Sy; St of Mnth; Amnsty Intl; Emplmnt; Spanish Clb; Orch; SP/M/VS; Cirrus Instructor; National Honor Society Executive Board; Human Rights; Political Science; Columbia U; Brown

SERRA, HEATHER L; MATTAPOISETT, MA; OLD ROCHESTER REG HS; (SR); Dnce; Chrldg; Yrbk (E, P); Bristol Community College; Bridgewater State College

SERRANO, ANTHONY R; NORTH ANDOVER, MA; NORTH ANDOVER HS; (FR); Hi Hnr Roll; Comm Volntr; Hab For Humty Volntr; Bskball (J); Sccr (J); Track (J)

SERRANO, ASHLEIGH A L; NORTH ANDOVER, MA; NORTH ANDOVER HS; (JR); Hi Hnr Roll; Nat Hon Sy; Pres Ac Ftns Aw; Comm Volntr; Hab For Humty Volntr; Peer Tut/Med; Chrch Yth Grp; Emplmnt; Svce Clb; Bskball (J); Lcrsse (V L); Sccr (V L); Track (V L); Stu Cncl; Own a Jewelry Business; Belong to Community Give Back Programs

SERRANO, ITSVA G; BOSTON, MA; BRIGHTON HS; (JR); Hnr Roll; Perf Att; Key Club; Sccr (V); Law; Psychology; Northeastern U; Lesley U

SHACKELTON, AMANDA F; MALDEN, MA; POPE JOHN XXIII HS; (SR); Hnr Roll; SADD; Tchrs Aide; Biology / BS Degree; Salem State

SHACKLETON, SCOTT; WESTFORD, MA; WESTFORD AC; (JR); Hnr Roll; Nat Hon Sy; Perf Att; WWAHSS; Comm Volntr; Bsball (V L); Bskball (V CL); Ftball (V L); Engineering, Graphic Communications

SHAFIRO, ANNA; WINCHESTER, MA; WINCHESTER HS; (JR); Hi Hnr Roll; Hnr Roll; Nat Hon Sy; Sci/Math Olympn; Comm Volntr; Hosp Aide; Dbte Team; Mth Clb/Tm; Photog; Tchrs Aide; Dnce; Cr Ctry (J); Track (J); Sch Ppr (R); USA Math Talent Search: Silver Medal Winner; AIME Qualifier; Math; Finance; Massachusetts Institute of Technology; Yale U

SHAH, ADIT; WESTFORD, MA; WESTFORD AC; (SO); Comm Volntr; Computer Science; Astro Physics; U of Michigan; U of Massachusetts Amherst

SHAHEEN, NICK; WILLIAMSBURG, MA; NORTHAMPTON HS; (MS); Hi Hnr Roll; Bskball (J); Ftball (J); Lcrsse (J)

SHARAF, NEMAT U; NORTH ANDOVER, MA; NORTH ANDOVER HS; (SR); Hi Hnr Roll; Hnr Roll; Tennis (J); Track (J); Long Distance Swimmer; Bilingual; Genetics; Medical; Boston College; U of Connecticut

SHARMA, MEGHA; CAMBRIDGE, MA; CAMBRIDGE RINDGE & LATIN HS; (JR); Hnr Roll; Comm Volntr; Clb; Dnce; Pediatrician; Computer Engineer; Massachusetts Bay College

SHEIKH, IMAD P; CHELMSFORD, MA; CHELMSFORD HS; (JR); Hnr Roll; MVP; Perf Att; St of Mnth; WWAHSS; Comm Volntr; Peer Tut/Med; Drma Clb; Photog; Arabic Clb; Bnd; Jzz Bnd; Bdmtn (J); Bsball (J); Bskball (J L); Ftball (J); Sftball (J L); Tennis (J); Vllyball (J); CR (R); Cricket Team; Pre-Med; Doctor; Boston U; U of Pennsylvania

SHELL, WYATT A; SPRINGFIELD, MA; SPRINGFIELD CTRL HS; (JR); Hi Hnr Roll; Nat Hon Sy; Comm Volntr; Key Club; Sci Clb; Chinese Clb; Mar Art; Lit Mag (E); Award for Best Fictional Writing from AIC and the SPF; Earned the Rank of Black Belt in Tae Kwon Do; Behavioral Science; Brown; Princeton

SHERIDAN, ELISE; SOUTH YARMOUTH, MA; DENNIS-YARMOUTH REG HS; (JR); Hnr Roll; Nat Hon Sy; Hab For Humty Volntr; Emplmnt; Key Club; Prom Com; Sccr (JC); Cl Off (R); Stu Cncl (R); Communications; Art in Advertising; U of Connecticut; U of Massachusetts Amherst

SHILO, ASHLEY B; MILLIS, MA; MILLIS HS; (JR); Hi Hnr Roll; Hnr Roll; Nat Hon Sy; Perf Att; WWAHSS; Comm Volntr; AL Aux Girls; Emplmnt; Prom Com; SADD; Chrldg (V L); PP Ftbl; Track (V L); Cl Off (S); Stu Cncl (R); Sch Ppr (R); Boston Herald Teen Correspondent; National Girls & Women in Sports Day; Journalism; Communications; Syracuse U; Boston U

SHIRKOVA, TERESA; AYER, MA; BOSTON UNIVERSITY AC; (JR); Hi Hnr Roll; Hnr Roll; Nat Mrt Fin; Nat Mrt Semif; Otst Ac Ach Awd; Yth Ldrshp Prog; Comm Volntr; Peer Tut/Med; ArtClub; Emplmnt; Jr Cls League; Mus Clb; NYLC; Outdrs Clb; Tchrs Aide; Wdwrkg Clb; Chr; Ch Chr; Dnce; SP/M/VS; Fncg (V); Tennis (V); International Conference Translator; Fundraising $3,000.00 / Individual Effort; International Relations; Psychology; Princeton U; Johns Hopkins U

SHURTLEFF, MATHEW; MARSTONS MILLS, MA; BARNSTABLE HS; (JR); Hnr Roll; Emplmnt; Mus Clb; Tech Clb; Bnd; Jzz Bnd; Mch Bnd; Pep Bnd; Marchiff Champion 2004; Computer Engineer; Technician; Wentworth U; Northeastern U

SICO, VANESSA H; CAMBRIDGE, MA; CAMBRIDGE RINDGE & LATIN HS; (JR); Hi Hnr Roll; Hnr Roll; Sci Fairs; Red Cr Aide; Emplmnt; Acpl Chr; Chr; Dnce; Chrldg (V); Yrbk; Coaches Award - Cheerleading; Captain of Cheerleading Squad; Forensic Scientist or Dentist; Syracuse University; New York U

SILVA, JACLYN; HAVERHILL, MA; HAVERHILL HS; (JR); Ctznshp Aw; Hi Hnr Roll; Hnr Roll; Nat Hon Sy; Comm Volntr; Key Club; P to P St Amb Prg; Prom Com; Yrbk (E); Social Committee; Marketing; Art

SILVA, JACQUELYN; BROCKTON, MA; BROCKTON HS; (JR); Hi Hnr Roll; Nat Hon Sy; WWAHSS; Yth Ldrshp Prog; Amnsty Intl; Comm Volntr; Chrch Yth Grp; Key Club; Track (V); Vllyball (V); Stu Cncl (R); CR (R); National History Day - 1st Place; Accepted to National Student Leadership Conference - NSLC; Medicine / Health Care; Science Field; Tuffs U

SILVA, JULIE A; MALDEN, MA; ARLINGTON CATHOLIC HS; (JR); Hi Hnr Roll; Kwnis Aw; Nat Hon Sy; Otst Ac Ach Awd; St of Mnth; USAA; WWAHSS; Comm Volntr; Peer Tut/Med; Dbte Team; Sci Clb; Spanish Clb; US Achievement Academy Award; Bachelor's / Master's Degree; Law School; Harvard College; Boston College

SILVIA, MELISSA E; FALL RIVER, MA; BMC DURFEE HS; (SR); Hi Hnr Roll; Hnr Roll; Nat Hon Sy; WWAHSS; Comm Volntr; Off Aide; Prom Com; Fld Hky (V L); Computer Engineering; Northeastern U

SIM, SUSIE; LOWELL, MA; LOWELL HS; (JR); Hnr Roll; Perf Att; St of Mnth; Comm Volntr; Emplmnt; Mth Clb/Tm; Sci Clb; International Clb; Pharmacist; Computers

SIMPSON, KATHLEEN; BELLINGHAM, MA; BELLINGHAM MEM HS; (SR); Hi Hnr Roll; Hnr Roll; Nat Hon Sy; WWAHSS; Comm Volntr; Hab For Humty Volntr; Hosp Aide; Emplmnt; SADD; Bnd; Mch Bnd; Orch; Cr Ctry (V); Track (V); Won St. Michaels Book Award; John and Abigail Adams Scholarship; Biology / Pre-Med; U of Massachusetts Amherst; Syracuse U

SITES, JESSICA; PEMBROKE, MA; PEMBROKE HS; (JR); Ctznshp Aw; Hi Hnr Roll; Hnr Roll; Nat Hon Sy; Otst Ac Ach Awd; Perf Att; Sci Fairs; St of Mnth; Peer Tut/Med; Emplmnt; Key Club; Prom Com; Dnce; Fld Hky (V); Track (V); Adv Cncl (R); Cl Off (P); Stu Cncl (R); Yrbk; Attended Girls State & Mass Star Leadership Camps; Picked - Best & Brightest of Pembroke; Engineering; Lawyer; Massachusetts Institute of Technology; Brown U

SIWILA-SACKMAN, ERICA; LEXINGTON, MA; LEXINGTON HS; (JR); Hnr Roll; Nat Hon Sy; WWAHSS; Comm Volntr; Emplmnt; Svce Clb; Dnce; Fld Hky (J); Sftball (V CL); National Honor Society; French Achievement Award; Science, Pre-Med; Economics

SLATER, BLAKELY J; SOMERSET, MA; SOMERSET HS; (FR); Hi Hnr Roll; Otst Ac Ach Awd; Sci Fairs; DARE; Emplmnt; Pep Squd; SP/M/VS; Cr Ct Ski (J); Gmnstcs (L); Track (J); Cl Off (R); Stu Cncl (R); CR (R); Yrbk (R); Continental Math League-1st Place; Journalism; Law; New York U; Brown

SLATER, BRITTNEY L; SOMERSET, MA; SOMERSET HS; (JR); Hnr Roll; MVP; Nat Hon Sy; Sci Fairs; Comm Volntr; Chrch Yth Grp; DARE; Emplmnt; Pep Squd; Prom Com; Chr; Dnce; Orch; SP/M/VS; Swmg (V); Track (J); Hotel Restaurant Management; Advertising, Marketing; Boston U; New York U

SLEPECKI, KATIE E; LUDLOW, MA; LUDLOW HS; (SO); Hnr Roll; Perf Att; St of Mnth; Comm Volntr; Jr Ach; Scouts; SADD; Dnce; Cr Ctry (V); Track (V); Pharmacy; U of Massachusetts Amherst; Massachusetts College of Pharmacy and Health and Sciences

SLOMIAK, CHRISTOPHER C; BROOKLINE, MA; BROOKLINE HS; (SO); Hnr Roll; Comm Volntr; Peer Tut/Med; Red Cr Aide; Vllyball (V); Education; English; Boston U

SMITH, JAMIE-LYNN; BOSTON, MA; WOODWARD SCH; (JR); Hnr Roll; Nat Hon Sy; Sci Fairs; WWAHSS; Comm Volntr; Chrch Yth Grp; Cmptr Clb; DARE; Drma Clb; Emplmnt; Lttrmn Clb; Lib Aide; Mus Clb; Chr; Ch Chr; SP/M/VS; Stg Cre; Choir Letter-9th Grade; Teaching/Social Work; Youth Ministry; Western New England College; Pine Manor College

SMITH, LASHARIA; SPRINGFIELD, MA; NEW LEADERSHIP CHARTER SCH; (FR); Otst Ac Ach Awd; Comm Volntr; Chrch Yth Grp; Emplmnt; Ch Chr; Dnce; Drl Tm; Teacher; Pediatrician; Spelman College; Howard U

SMITH, PETER; CUMMAQUID, MA; BARNSTABLE HS; (FR); Hnr Roll; MVP; Bsball (J); Bskball (J); Ftball (JC); Wt Lftg (J); Excel In Sports; Excel In Business & Finance; U Mass; Notre Dame

SOARES, JILLIAN; SOMERSET, MA; SOMERSET HS; (SO); Hi Hnr Roll; WWAHSS; Amnsty Intl; Drma Clb; Key Club; Acpl Chr; Mch Bnd; Orch; SP/M/VS; Grand Champion Snow Soloist and Best Female Soloist; 2005 Showtime Idol Finalist, Newton Cultural, (Show Choir)

SOCCI, SHAINA; FRANKLIN, MA; FRANKLIN HS; (SR); Hnr Roll; Nat Hon Sy; WWAHSS; Yth Ldrshp Prog; Hosp Aide; NYLC; Dnce; Orch; Sftball (J); National Honor Society; Biology; Forensic Medicine; Assumption College; Stonehill College

SONTAG, AUBREY; CLINTON, MA; CLINTON HS; (SO); Hi Hnr Roll; Nat Hon Sy; Pres Ac Ftns Aw; St of Mnth; WWAHSS; Peer Tut/Med; Chrch Yth Grp; Emplmnt; Scouts; Gmnstcs; Mar Art; Silver Award in Girl Scouts; Aviation Major; Architecture Major; Air Force Academy; Pratt

SOTO, AISHA; SOUTHBRIDGE, MA; BAY PATH; (SO); Hnr Roll; Sci Fairs; St of Mnth; DARE; SADD; Chrldg (V); Music; Science; Barbizon College

SPADONI, JESSICA; CHICOPEE, MA; CHICOPEE HS; (SO); Hi Hnr Roll; Hnr Roll; SADD; Dvng (V); Sftball (J); Swmg (V); Stu Cncl (R); Surgical Technician; Physician's Assistant; U of Massachusetts Amherst; Elms College

SPECK, CHRISTOPHER J; HOPKINTON, MA; HOPKINTON HS; (JR); Track (V); Business; Marketing; U of Massachusetts Amherst

SPIEGEL, PATRICK; SUDBURY, MA; LINCOLN-SUDBURY REG HS; (JR); Comm Volntr; Hab For Humty Volntr; Chrch Yth Grp; Dbte Team; Ftball (V L); Rugby Team; Sports Management; Business; Syracuse U; U of Connecticut

SPIGEL, LAUREN; FRAMINGHAM, MA; FRAMINGHAM HS; (JR); Hnr Roll; Nat Hon Sy; WWAHSS; Emplmnt; Tchrs Aide; Ice Hky (J); Lcrsse (J); Swmg (V); Relay for Life Captain 2005

SPIRO, EMMA; WELLESLEY HILLS, MA; WELLESLEY HS; (JR); Hnr Roll; MVP; Nat Hon Sy; Nat Ldrshp Svc; Pres Ac Ftns Aw; USAA; Yth Ldrshp Prog; Comm Volntr; DARE; Emplmnt; JSA; Key Club; NYLC; Svce Clb; Tmpl Yth Grp; Vsity Clb; Bskball (V C); Lcrsse (V); Sccr (V C); First Team Bay State All Star-Lacrosse Soph. Yr; NE Lower Lacrosse-Team #2; Law; DNK

STAFFORD, CHELSEA; SPRINGFIELD, MA; SPRINGFIELD CTRL HS; (FR); Hi Hnr Roll; WWAHSS; Comm Volntr; Spec Olymp Vol; Chrch Yth Grp; Key Club

STEIGER, PATRICK; FRAMINGHAM, MA; FRAMINGHAM HS; (JR); Hnr Roll; MVP; Nat Hon Sy; Comm Volntr; Peer Tut/Med; Emplmnt; Tchrs Aide; SP/M/VS; Cr Ctry (V L); Lcrsse (V L); Track (V L); National Honor Society; Engineering; Boston U; Pennsylvania U

STEINBACH, SCOTT T; BOSTON, MA; LATIN AC HS; (JR); Hnr Roll; MVP; Perf Att; Emplmnt; Bsball (V)

STEWART, APRIL; LOWELL, MA; (MS); Hi Hnr Roll; Hnr Roll; St of Mnth; Chrch Yth Grp

STEWART, JENNA M; HOPKINTON, MA; HOPKINTON HS; (SR); F Lan Hn Soc; Hi Hnr Roll; Hnr Roll; Comm Volntr; Peer Tut/Med; 4-H; Chrch Yth Grp; Emplmnt; Prom Com; Radiographic Technology; Quinsigamond Community College

ST MARTIN, DEREK; WESTFORD, MA; WESTFORD AC; (SO); Hi Hnr Roll; Hnr Roll; Otst Ac Ach Awd; Comm Volntr; Emplmnt; Vllyball (J L); Coach Middle School Recreation; Basketball Team; Computer Engineering or Software

STROUSS, SAMANTHA; ESSEX, MA; GOVERNOR DUMMER AC; (FR); Otst Ac Ach Awd; Comm Volntr; Spec Olymp Vol; Chr; Lcrsse (J); Sccr (J); Photography; U of Virginia; Cornell

SUH, SARAH; NORTH ANDOVER, MA; NORTH ANDOVER HS; (JR); Hnr Roll; Otst Ac Ach Awd; Perf Att; St of Mnth; Yth Ldrshp Prog; Hab For Humty Volntr; ArtClub; Chrch Yth Grp; Emplmnt; FCA; Key Club; Spanish Clb; Chr; Ch Chr; Orch; SP/M/VS; Track (J); Piano Competitions; Basketball (Rec. League); Events Coordinator; Therapist/Orthodontist; U of Connecticut; Boston College

Soares, Jillian
Somerset HS
Somerset, MA

Sheikh, Imad P
Chelmsford HS
Chelmsford, MA

Sharma, Megha
Cambridge Rindge & Latin HS
Cambridge, MA

Schelin, Deidre
West Boylston HS
West Boylston, MA

Serra, Heather L
Old Rochester Reg HS
Mattapoisett, MA

Sico, Vanessa H
Cambridge Rindge & Latin HS
Cambridge, MA

Soto, Aisha
Bay Path
Southbridge, MA

SULLIVAN, BRENDAN; TYNGSBORO, MA; TYNGSBORO HS; (SO); Hi Hnr Roll; Hnr Roll; Perf Att; WWAHSS; Comm Volntr; DARE; Emplmnt; Quiz Bowl; Vsity Clb; Cr Ctry (V L); Lcrsse (V); Cl Off (V); Snowboarding; Business; U Mass Amherst; Quinnipiac U

SULLIVAN, CAITLIN M; MARSHFIELD HILLS, MA; MARSHFIELD HS; (SO); Hnr Roll; Pres Ac Ftns Aw; Comm Volntr; DARE; Emplmnt; Key Club; Scouts; Chrldg (J); Gmnstcs (V L)

SULLIVAN, KEVIN M; NEWBURYPORT, MA; NEWBURYPORT HS; (JR); Hi Hnr Roll; MVP; Nat Hon Sy; Sci Fairs; Mth Clb/Tm; NYLC; Bskball (V CL); Ftball (V CL); Lcrsse (V CL); Stu Cncl (R); CR (R); National Honor Society; Junior Honor Scholar; Pre-Med

SUNDER, SINDHUJA; NORTH DARTMOUTH, MA; DARTMOUTH HS; (SR); Nat Hon Sy; Nat Mrt LOC; St Schl; WWAHSS; Amnsty Intl; Lib Aide; Mth Clb/Tm; Spch Team; Chr; SP/M/VS; Mar Art; Swmg; Adv Cncl; Lit Mag (E); Winner of Massachusetts State John & Abigail Adm Scholarship; Physics; Research in Applied Sciences; Harvey Mudd College; Rose Hulman Institute of Technology

SUPERNAW, KIMBERLEE; FLORENCE, MA; NORTHAMPTON HS; (JR); Hnr Roll; MVP; Comm Volntr; Emplmnt; Vsity Clb; Dnce; Bskball (J); PP Ftbl (V); Sccr (J); Sftball (V); Vllyball (V); Stu Cncl (R); CR (R); Yrbk (R, P); Most Spirited Player / 2002 - 2005; Early Childhood Education; Coaching; Westfield State College; Keene State College

SWARTOUT, BEN; UPTON, MA; NIPMUC REG HS; (SO); Hi Hnr Roll; Comm Volntr; DARE; Emplmnt; Scouts; Tmpl Yth Grp; Bnd; Jzz Bnd; Mch Bnd; Ftball (V); Track (J); Engineering; Architecture; Lafayette College; MIT

SWEENEY, ALEXANDRA; NORTH ANDOVER, MA; NORTH ANDOVER HS; (JR); Hi Hnr Roll; Hnr Roll; Nat Hon Sy; Hab For Humty Volntr; Chrch Yth Grp; Mod UN; Photog; Hsbk Rdg; Pre-Law/Law; Journalism; Boston College; Brown U

TAGLIERI, MICHAEL; ARLINGTON, MA; ARLINGTON HS; (JR); Hnr Roll; Sci/Math Olympn; WWAHSS; Chrch Yth Grp; Emplmnt; Latin Clb; Bsball (V L); Wrstlg (J); Sch Ppr (P); Engineering

TAILEB, SABRINA; REVERE, MA; (JR); F Lan Hn Soc; Hnr Roll; Perf Att; Sci Fairs; Comm Volntr; Chess; Cmptr Clb; Dbte Team; Drma Clb; Lib Aide; Mth Clb/Tm; Mus Clb; Sci Clb; SP/M/VS; Stg Cre; Bdmtn (J); Scr Kpr (V); Sccr (C); Tennis (J); Vllyball (C); Cl Off (T); Stu Cncl (V); CR (P); Mathematics; Sciences; Boston College; U of Massachusetts in Amherst

TANG, ANNIE; WAYLAND, MA; WAYLAND HS; (SO); Hnr Roll; Perf Att; Comm Volntr; Spec Olymp Vol; Sci Clb; Clb; Tennis (J); Chinese Folk Dance; Chinese Instrument: Gu-Zheng; Performing Arts; Business; Boston U; U of California Los Angeles

TANG, PHILIP; QUINCY, MA; NORTH QUINCY HS; (FR); Comm Volntr; Wdwrkg Clb

TARA, ROGERS; LOWELL, MA; GREATER LOWELL VOC TECH SCH; (SO); Hnr Roll; Perf Att; Peer Tut/Med; DARE; Vsity Clb; Bskball (V); Sccr (V); Tennis (J); Nursing School; Health Care; U Mass Lowell; U Conn

TARANTINI, DANIELA; LYNN, MA; CLASSICAL HS; (SO); WWAHSS; Comm Volntr; Peer Tut/Med; ArtClub; Scouts; French Clb; Chrldg (J); Martial Arts (Not School Sponsored); Dance (Not School Sponsored); Law; Psychology; Harvard U; Yale U

TAUPIER, BRIAN; CHICOPEE, MA; CHICOPEE COMP HS; (SO); Hnr Roll; Sccr (J); Track (V); National Junior Honor Society; Doctorate in Physical Therapy; Springfield College; Quinnipiac U

TAYLOR, MONICA; BOSTON, MA; ENGLISH HS; (SO); Hnr Roll; Sci Fairs; St of Mnth; WWAHSS; Peer Tut/Med; Emplmnt; SP/M/VS; Bskball (J); CR (P); Sch Ppr (E, R); Law; Business Management; Howard U; U of North Carolina

TEAGUE, ALEXANDRA P; BROOKLINE, MA; BROOKLINE HS; (JR); Comm Volntr; Biology Clb; Svce Clb; Chr; Chrldg (J); PP Ftbl (J); Swmg (J); Varsity Crew; Honors Choir; Political Science; History; Saint Lawrence; Trinity College

TEIXEIRA, AMANDA; FALL RIVER, MA; B M C DURFEE HS; (SO); Hnr Roll; Nat Ldrshp Svc; Otst Ac Ach Awd; Perf Att; St of Mnth; Yth Ldrshp Prog; Chrch Yth Grp; NYLC; Ch Chr; Bskball (J); Sccr (J); Stu Cncl (R); CR (R); Christian Leadership Institution 2004; National Junior Leaders Conference; Law

TETREAULT, VICTORIA; ADAMS, MA; CHARLES H MC CANN TECH HS; (JR); Hi Hnr Roll; Hnr Roll; Comm Volntr; Chrch Yth Grp; Prom Com; Dnce; Accounting; Doctor

THIBOU, OLIVIA K; BOSTON, MA; O'BRYANT SCH OF MATH & SCIENCE; (JR); Hnr Roll; MVP; Sci Fairs; Peer Tut/Med; Chrch Yth Grp; DARE; Pep Squd; ROTC; Tchrs Aide; Ch Chr; Track (V L); All-Scholastic in Boston Globe & Herald; State Champion "B" Long Jump; Pre-Med; Business Management; U of Rhode Island; Syracuse U

THOMAS, ELISHA; LYNN, MA; LYNN VOC TECH; (JR); Social Work; Psychiatry; Boston U; Salem State

THOMAS, JANAY; HAVERHILL, MA; HAVERHILL HS; (JR); Hi Hnr Roll; WWAHSS; Yth Ldrshp Prog; Peer Tut/Med; Chrch Yth Grp; Emplmnt; Key Club; P to P St Amb Prg; Prom Com; Acpl Chr; Chr; SP/M/VS; Stu Cncl (R); Yrbk (R); The National Society of High School Scholars; Marketing; Music Business; Merrimack College; Northeastern U

THOMAS, MATTHEW R; BOYLSTON, MA; ST PETER MARIAN HS; (SO); Hnr Roll; Emplmnt; Mus Clb; Bnd; Bsball (J); Cr Ctry (V); Golf (V); Ice Hky (J); Skiing; International Business; Communications; Northeastern U; U of Massachusetts-Amherst

THOMAS, NATHANIEL; CAMBRIDGE, MA; CAMBRIDGE RINDGE & LATIN HS; (JR); Emplmnt; Top Student in Journalism / Literary Course; Speak Nepalese / Some Chinese / Japanese / and French - No Language Club at School; International Relations; Journalism; Boston University; New York U

THU, JACK T; METHUEN, MA; METHUEN HS; (FR); Hnr Roll; St of Mnth; DARE; Bskball; Mechanical Engineering; Professional Basketball Player; Boston College

THYBERG, HEATHER; NORTH EGREMONT, MA; TACONIC HILLS CTRL HS; (JR); ArtClub; DARE; Emplmnt; Photog; SADD; Training My Horse; Lawyer; Horse Trainer; Marist College; Cornell U

TINNEY, JEANNA L; CHESHIRE, MA; CHARLES H MC CANN TECH HS; (FR); Hi Hnr Roll; Nat Hon Sy; Otst Ac Ach Awd; St of Mnth; Yth Ldrshp Prog; NYLC; Scouts; SADD; Spanish Clb; Bskball (J); Scr Kpr (V); Sftball (V); Nominated to Go to National Young Leaders; Nominated to Go to Australia for Sports Camp / State Conference; Psychologist; Guidance Counselor; Syracuse U; Williams College

TORRISI, CHUCK; NORTH ANDOVER, MA; (JR); Gov Hnr Prg; Hi Hnr Roll; Nat Hon Sy; Otst Ac Ach Awd; WWAHSS; Peer Tut/Med; NYLC; P to P St Amb Prg; Bskball (L); Scr Kpr; Stu Cncl (R); CR (R); Bowling Club; Business; U of Pennsylvania; Georgetown

TRACY, COLLIN; MEDFORD, MA; MEDFORD HS; (SO); Hi Hnr Roll; MVP; Comm Volntr; Ice Hky (V); Lcrsse (V); All Scholastic Hockey; Varsity Hockey MVP; To Make College Hockey and NHL; Also Want to Be an Engineer; Boston U, Harvard U; Boston College

TRAHAN, DANIEL; BURLINGTON, MA; BURLINGTON HS; (JR); Hi Hnr Roll; Hnr Roll; MVP; Pres Ac Ftns Aw; WWAHSS; Comm Volntr; Chrch Yth Grp; Emplmnt; Bskball (V CL); Math; History

TRAN, JENNIFER; SALEM, MA; SALEM HS; (SR); Hi Hnr Roll; Nat Hon Sy; Yth Ldrshp Prog; Comm Volntr; Peer Tut/Med; Emplmnt; Mod UN; Svce Clb; SADD; Spanish Clb; SP/M/VS; Lcrsse (V L); PP Ftbl; Tennis (V CL); Track (V CL); Vllyball; Stu Cncl (R); North Shore Chamber of Commerce Scholar; MCAS High Achievement Award; Pre-Med; Biology; New York U; Tulane U

TRASK, JEFF; SANDWICH, MA; SANDWICH HS; (SO); Duke TS; Hi Hnr Roll; Hnr Roll; Pres Ac Ftns Aw; Red Cr Aide; Chrch Yth Grp; FCA; FBLA; Cr Ctry (VJ L); Ftball (J); Lcrsse (J); Track (J L); Eagle Scout; Member- International Relations Club; Law; Journalism; Duke U; Yale U

TRAVERS, JACQUELINE J; WELLESLEY HILLS, MA; WELLESLEY HS; (JR); Hnr Roll; WWAHSS; Comm Volntr; Emplmnt; Jr Ach; Key Club; Vsity Clb; Ice Hky (V); Lcrsse (J); Sccr (V); Vsy Clb (V); Yrbk (R); Pennsylvania State; College of Charleston; U North Carolina, Wilmington; U Miami

TREMBLAY, ANDREW; SOMERSET, MA; SOMERSET HS; (SO); Hi Hnr Roll; Otst Ac Ach Awd; Sci Fairs; Sci/Math Olympn; St of Mnth; WWAHSS; Chrch Yth Grp; Dbte Team; Jr Ach; Key Club; Bnd; Chr; Drm Mjr; Orch; Sch Ppr (E); Music Education

TREMBLAY, KASINA S; SOUTH EASTON, MA; OLIVER AMES HS; (JR); Hnr Roll; Nat Hon Sy; Comm Volntr; FBLA; Dnce; Presidential Freedom Scholarship; FBLA VP & State Reporter; Green Team BOD; U.S. Natl. TAP Team; IDO World Dance Championships, Reisa Germany (Gold Medal); Boston College; Providence College

TREMBLAY, MEGAN; BEVERLY, MA; NORTH SHORE TECH HS; (JR); Hnr Roll; Nat Hon Sy; Sci Fairs; WWAHSS; Yth Ldrshp Prog; Comm Volntr; Peer Tut/Med; Spec Olymp Vol; Drma Clb; Emplmnt; Prom Com; Vsity Clb; Chrldg (V); Track (V); Cl Off (V); Stu Cncl; Peer Mediation; RYLA; Medical Assistant; LPN; Salem State College; Tufts U

TRUONG, BAO LE; BOSTON, MA; O'BRYANT SCH OF MATH & SCIENCE; MS; Hi Hnr Roll; Hnr Roll; Perf Att; Sci Fairs; St of Mnth; Sci Clb; SP/M/VS; Bdmtn (L); Sccr (L); Stu Cncl (V); O'Bryant School Honor Roll-All Terms 2003-04; Best Conduct & Effort Award; Doctor; Dentist; Harvard U; Massachusetts Institute of Technology

TSAI, TA-WEI; NATICK, MA; WALNUT HILL SCH; (SO); Chr; Orch; SP/M/VS; 1999 Yamaha Piano Competition of Taiwan 1st Prize; Conservatory or Music Institute; Harvard U

TUDEN, FREELAND J; MEDFORD, MA; MEDFORD HS; (SO); Ctznshp Aw; Hi Hnr Roll; Hnr Roll; Sci Fairs; St of Mnth; Comm Volntr; Peer Tut/Med; Emplmnt; Bsball (J); Swmg (V); Highest Batting Aug. on JV Baseball Team; Made Regionals for Swimming; Chemistry Major; Teacher; Massachusetts Institute of Technology; U of Massachusetts (Amherst)

TUMASYAN, VLAD; SPRINGFIELD, MA; NEW LEADERSHIP CHARTER SCH; MS; Otst Ac Ach Awd; DARE; Bskball (J); Swmg (V); Stu Cncl (T); Engineer; Western New England College; American International College

TUROVA, SVETLANA; LINCOLN, MA; LINCOLN-SUDBURY REG HS; (SR); Hnr Roll; WWAHSS; Comm Volntr; Spec Olymp Vol; ArtClub; Emplmnt; Lib Aide; Photog; Quill & Scroll; Tchrs Aide; French Clb; Lit Mag (E, P); Sch Ppr (E, R); Spanish Club; International Connections; Art History; Romance Languages; Boston College

UKO, EKEMINI G; JAMAICA PLAIN, MA; BOSTON LATIN AC; (JR); Hnr Roll; Comm Volntr; Peer Tut/Med; Chrch Yth Grp; Emplmnt; P to P St Amb Prg; Dnce; Tennis (J); Track (J); National Society of High School Scholars; Criminal Justice; Political / Social Science Studies; Columbia U; Boston U

UMBRIANO, RACHAEL; FRANKLIN, MA; FRANKLIN HS; (JR); Ctznshp Aw; Comm Volntr; ArtClub; Dbte Team; P to P St Amb Prg; Prom Com; Schol Bwl; Cr Ctry (J); Lcrsse (J); Track (J); Sch Ppr (E); Yrbk (E, P); Friendship Award; Liberal Arts; Graphic and Web Design

VACHA, ANNA; CLINTON, MA; CLINTON HS; (SO); Hi Hnr Roll; Hnr Roll; Nat Hon Sy; Otst Ac Ach Awd; Pres Sch; St of Mnth; WWAHSS; HO'Br Yth Ldrshp; Mth Clb/Tm; Stg Cre; First - Robotics; MVP - Mentors in Violence Prevention

VACHON, JULIA; EAST FALMOUTH, MA; UPPER CAPE TECH HS; (SR); Hnr Roll; MVP; Hab For Humty Volntr; Prom Com; Vsity Clb; Voc Ind Clb Am; Wdwrkg Clb; Bskball (V CL); Sftball (V CL); Cl Off (T); Business Management; Interior Designer; UMass Dartmouth

VANOSSENBRUGGEN, MAX; CHICOPEE, MA; CHICOPEE HS; (SR); Ftball (V); Lcrsse (J); Track (V L); Army

VARGHESE, SHAINA; BURLINGTON, MA; BURLINGTON HS; (JR); Hi Hnr Roll; Hnr Roll; Nat Hon Sy; St of Mnth; Comm Volntr; Hosp Aide; Chrch Yth Grp; Mod UN; Sci Clb; Latin Clb; Ch Chr; Dnce; Track; Carmel MTC Youth Secretary; Occupational Therapy; Pharmacy; Quinnipiac U; Ithaca College

VARYPATAKIS, GREGORIOS; CHICOPEE, MA; CHICOPEE HS; (JR); Hi Hnr Roll; Hnr Roll; Nat Hon Sy; Pres Ac Ftns Aw; Comm Volntr; Peer Tut/Med; Bskball (J); Sccr (J); Cl Off (P); Business Management; Boston U; U of Miami

VATAN, SHAWDEEN; ARLINGTON, MA; ARLINGTON HS; (FR); Comm Volntr; Bnd; Pep Bnd; Ice Hky (J); Mar Art; Sccr (J)

VAUGHAN, LINWOOD; ORANGE, MA; FRANKLIN CTY TECH SCH; Ctznshp Aw; Hi Hnr Roll; Hnr Roll; MVP; Nat Hon Sy; Otst Ac Ach Awd; St of Mnth; USMC Stu Ath Aw; WWAHSS; Comm Volntr; Peer Tut/Med; Outdrs Clb; Vsity Clb; Bnd; Mch Bnd; Arch (V); Bsball (V L); Ftball (VJCL); Mar Art (VJ); Vsy Clb (V); Wt Lftg (V); Wrstlg (V CL); Adv Cncl (R); CR (R); Chess Club UIL; Environmental Police; Law Enforcement Officer; Unity College

VAZQUEZ, JAVIER; SPRINGFIELD, MA; HS OF COMMERCE; (SO); F Lan Hn Soc; Hnr Roll; Perf Att; St of Mnth; Dnce; Music Production / Hip-Hop; Law Degree; U Mass

VEINOGLOU, AMY; GREAT BARRINGTON, MA; MONUMENT MTN REG HS; (JR); Hi Hnr Roll; Hnr Roll; Nat Hon Sy; Otst Ac Ach Awd; St of Mnth; Comm Volntr; NYLC; Tennis (J); Track (V); Pre-Med; Chemistry

VELAZQUEZ, VERONICA K; SPRINGFIELD, MA; PUTNAM VOC TECH HS; (FR); RN / Nursing; Forensic Nursing; U of Puerto Rico; Fitchburg State College

VELEZ, AMANDA; FALL RIVER, MA; B F TERRY HS; (FR); DAR; Hi Hnr Roll; Hnr Roll; Nat Hon Sy; Nat Sci Aw; Otst Ac Ach Awd; Sci/Math Olympn; St of Mnth; St Optmst of Yr; Yth Ldrshp Prog; Hosp Aide; Red Cr Aide; Spec Olymp Vol; ArtClub; Drma Clb; Fr of Library; Mth Clb/Tm; Mus Clb; SADD; Tmpl Yth Grp; Wdwrkg Clb; Chr; Dnce; Jzz Bnd; SP/M/VS; Bskball (L); GAA (L); Ice Sktg (L); Mar Art (L); Sccr (L); Tennis (L); Vllyball (L); Wt Lftg (L); Cl Off (P); Yrbk (P); Theatre Workshop 2 (E1); Draw and Paint 2 (1,5) (E1); Urban College of Boston; Ricker College

VENTEROSA, ANTHONY W; STOUGHTON, MA; STOUGHTON HS; (SO); Hi Hnr Roll; Hnr Roll; Jr Mshl; MVP; Nat Hon Sy; Perf Att; Pres Ac Ftns Aw; Comm Volntr; Chrch Yth Grp; DARE; Emplmnt; Scouts; SADD; Bnd; Chr; Ch Chr; SP/M/VS; Bsball (J); Cyclg (J); Ftball (J); Sccr (J); Track (V); Wt Lftg (V); Wrstlg (J); Most Valuable Player Baseball 2005; Military Career; Engineering; Coast Guard Academy; Boston College

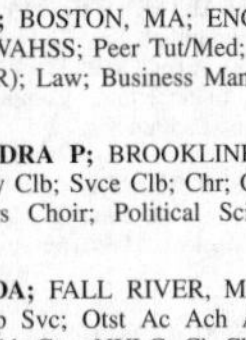
Velazquez, Veronica K
Putnam Voc Tech HS
Springfield, MA

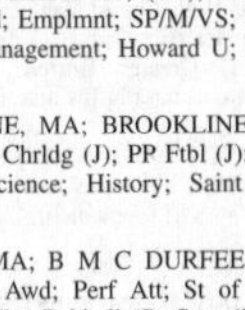
Tremblay, Kasina S
Oliver Ames HS
South Easton, MA

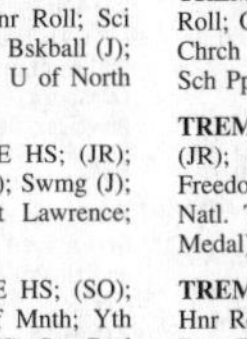
Thyberg, Heather
Taconic Hills Ctrl HS
North Egremont, MA

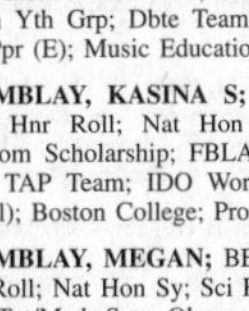
Teague, Alexandra P
Brookline HS
Brookline, MA

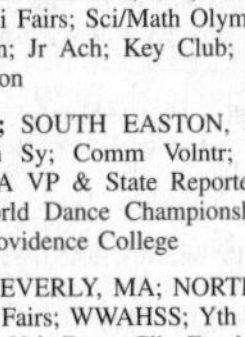
Sullivan, Kevin M
Newburyport HS
Newburyport, MA

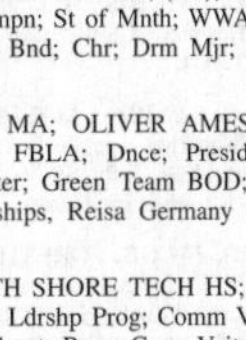
Sweeney, Alexandra
North Andover HS
North Andover, MA

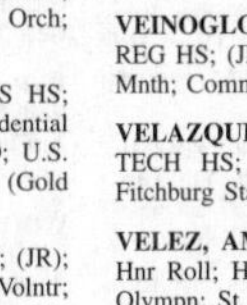
Tinney, Jeanna L
Charles H Mc Cann Tech HS
Cheshire, MA

Truong, Bao Le
O'Bryant Sch Of Math & Science
Boston, MA

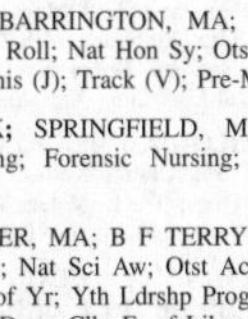
Venterosa, Anthony W
Stoughton HS
Stoughton, MA

VENTO, LAURA M; NORTH ANDOVER, MA; NORTH ANDOVER HS; (JR); Hi Hnr Roll; Hnr Roll; Otst Ac Ach Awd; Comm Volntr; Tchrs Aide; Clr Grd; Dnce; Mch Bnd; Co-Captain, Color Guard, '04-'05; Captain, Color Guard, '05-'06; German Language and Literature; Dance (Minor); Barnard College; Trinity College

VERA, MYDALIS; SPRINGFIELD, MA; PUTNAM VOC TECH HS; (JR); Hi Hnr Roll; St of Mnth; Mth Clb/Tm; Performance Certification in Hospitality; Mass Mutual Achiever / Serv Safe Certified; Business Administration; International Business; Boston U; U Mass

VIERBOOM, YANA C; ARLINGTON, MA; ARLINGTON HS; (SO); F Lan Hn Soc; Hi Hnr Roll; Hnr Roll; MVP; Nat Hon Sy; Sci Fairs; WWAHSS; Yth Ldrshp Prog; Comm Volntr; Emplmnt; NYLC; Orch; Swmg (V); Tennis (J); Lit Mag (E); 2005 Representative for Mass to the Nat. Young Leaders Conf. in D.C.; Language; Foreign Affairs; Tufts U; Harvard U

VIEUX, RALPH; HYDE PARK, MA; EDGEWOOD GREATER BOSTON AC; (JR); Hnr Roll; Yth Ldrshp Prog; Comm Volntr; Emplmnt; Off Aide; Wdwrkg Clb; Bskball (C); Sccr (J); Cl Off (R); Stu Cncl (R); CR (R); Sch Ppr; Construction; Harvard Summer School/MIT Courses; Dental Hygiene; Harvard U; Tufts U

VOSBURG, AMANDA; CLINTON, MA; CLINTON HS; (JR); Hnr Roll; Otst Ac Ach Awd; WWAHSS; Early Childhood Education; Fitchburg State College; Worchester State College

WALCUTT, LEIF E; MARSTONS MILLS, MA; BARNSTABLE HS; (JR); Hnr Roll; Nat Hon Sy; Nat Ldrshp Svc; Comm Volntr; Emplmnt; Key Club; ROTC; Tmpl Yth Grp; Cr Ctry (V); Ftball (J); Cl Off (V, T); Stu Cncl (R); Sch Ppr (E, R, P); Sailing Team - J & V; Journalism Awards; Pre-Med; Journalism; Boston U; McGill U

WALCZAK, LINDSEY M; DUDLEY, MA; SHEPHERD HILL REG HS; (JR); Hnr Roll; Comm Volntr; Criminology; Criminal Profiling; U Mass Amherst

WALKER, SHAQIM K; LEOMINSTER, MA; LEOMINSTER HS; (SR); Hi Hnr Roll; Hnr Roll; MVP; Nat Hon Sy; St of Mnth; WWAHSS; Comm Volntr; Red Cr Aide; AL Aux Boys; Emplmnt; Kwanza Clb; Bnd; Mch Bnd; Orch; Bskball (JC); Mar Art (C); Track (VJ); Youth Venture Program; Business; Engineering; Western New England College

WALSH, ADAM; LEICESTER, MA; LEICESTER HS; (SO); Hi Hnr Roll; Sccr (VJ L); Tennis (V L); Something with Computers

WALSH, ELIZABETH M; MARSHFIELD, MA; MARSHFIELD HS; (JR); Hi Hnr Roll; Nat Hon Sy; WWAHSS; Peer Tut/Med; Spec Olymp Vol; Key Club; Photog; Swmg (V C); Tennis (V); Cl Off (T); Works with Special Olympic Swimmers; Physical Therapy; Wheaton College; St Michael's

WANG, ALAN; BOXBOROUGH, MA; ACTON-BOXBOROUGH REG HS; (SO); Duke TS; F Lan Hn Soc; Hnr Roll; Perf Att; Sci Fairs; USAA; Comm Volntr; Peer Tut/Med; Chess; Mth Clb/Tm; NYLC; Sci Clb; Orch; Track (J); Table Tennis Club; Anime Club; Pre-Med / Medical - MD; Banking and Finance; Johns Hopkins U; U of Pennsylvania

WANG, SHUO; SOMERVILLE, MA; PROSPECT HILL AC CHARTER; (JR); Ctznshp Aw; Hi Hnr Roll; Hnr Roll; Otst Ac Ach Awd; Perf Att; WWAHSS; Yth Ldrshp Prog; Comm Volntr; Peer Tut/Med; ArtClub; Chess; Cmptr Clb; NYLC; Stu Cncl; Lit Mag (E); Charter School Chess Champion; Student Life Club Leader; Math; Graphic Design; MIT; Harvard U

WANKYO, ABIGAIL; FITCHBURG, MA; CLINTON HS; (JR); Hnr Roll; Outdrs Clb; Chr; Drl Tm; Tennis (V); Church Youth Leader; Pathfinder Counselor; Doctor; Occupational Therapist; Andrews U; Columbia U

WARD, ASHLEY H S; WORCESTER, MA; SOUTH HIGH CMTY SCH; (SR); Hnr Roll; Nat Hon Sy; St of Mnth; Amnsty Intl; Comm Volntr; Peer Tut/Med; Chrch Yth Grp; Emplmnt; Mth Clb/Tm; Bnd; Ch Chr; Dnce; SP/M/VS; President of National Honor Society; Recipient of Clark U Book Award; Early Childhood Education; New York U

WARNER, ANNE; NEEDHAM HEIGHTS, MA; URSULINE AC; (JR); Hi Hnr Roll; Nat Hon Sy; Comm Volntr; Peer Tut/Med; Chrch Yth Grp; Emplmnt; Svce Clb; Dnce; Track (V L); Vllyball (L); Irish Step Dancing 4 Years; Piano-8 yrs; Business; Pharmacy; Bentley College; Boston College

WARREN, BENJAMIN C; WEST SPRINGFIELD, MA; WEST SPRINGFIELD HS; (JR); Hi Hnr Roll; Hnr Roll; Nat Hon Sy; WWAHSS; Comm Volntr; Peer Tut/Med; AL Aux Boys; Emplmnt; Outdrs Clb; SP/M/VS; Fld Hky (V L); Ftball (J); Track (V L); Wrstlg (V CL); Sch Ppr (E, R); Boys & Girls Club Volunteer; Art National Honor Society; Communications; Art; Marist College; Massachusetts College of Liberal Arts

WARREN, CAILEIGH; AUBURN, MA; WORCESTER AC; (SR); Hnr Roll; Kwnis Aw; Emplmnt; Photog; Dnce; Bskball (J L); Sccr (V L); Tennis (V); Track (V L); Vllyball (V L); Cl Off (T); Stu Cncl (S); Director of Chapter - Little Things Mean A Lot, Inc; Religious Education Teacher; Engineering / Physics; Accident Reconstruction; Union College

WATKINSON, MELODY; SOMERSET, MA; SOMERSET HS; (FR); Amnsty Intl; Comm Volntr; Chrch Yth Grp; DARE; Drma Clb; Photog; Computer; Dentistry

WEATHERS III, RICHARD G; CAMBRIDGE, MA; CAMBRIDGE RINDGE & LATIN HS; (JR); Hi Hnr Roll; Hnr Roll; Perf Att; Comm Volntr; Chrch Yth Grp; Wdwrkg Clb; Ch Chr; Drm Mjr; No Detention Certificate; Rindge School of Technical Arts Certificate of Excellence; Engineering / Mathematics; Medical Field; Northeastern U; U Mass Boston

WEED, BARRETT S W; CAMBRIDGE, MA; WALNUT HS; (SO); Hi Hnr Roll; Hnr Roll; Amnsty Intl; Comm Volntr; DARE; Drma Clb; Key Club; SADD; Spanish Clb; Acpl Chr; Chr; Ch Chr; Dnce; Bskball; Fld Hky (J); Hsbk Rdg; Ice Hky; Lcrsse (J); Sch Ppr (P); Yrbk (P); Northeastern Junior District Vocal Award; Red Key Student Ambassador; Theater (Major); Director/Producer/Actor; Juilliard School-New York; U of California Los Angeles

WELLS, JOSLIN G; MARSTONS MILLS, MA; BARNSTABLE HS; (SR); WWAHSS; Spec Olymp Vol; Vsity Clb; Fld Hky (V CL); Hsbk Rdg (V CL); Lcrsse (V CL); Voluntary Riding Instructor; Psychology; Marine Biology; U of New Hampshire; Southern Connecticut State U

WEN, TONY; BOSTON, MA; TECH BOSTON AC; (JR); Ctznshp Aw; Hi Hnr Roll; Hnr Roll; Nat Hon Sy; Comm Volntr; Chess; Cmptr Clb; CR (R); Sch Ppr (P); Model Secondary School Project; Semi High Tech U; Architecture; Computer Engineering; Massachusetts Institute Technology; Worcester Polytechnic Institute

WHALLEY, RICH; NORTH ANDOVER, MA; NORTH ANDOVER HS; (JR); Hi Hnr Roll; MVP; Nat Hon Sy; Nat Mrt LOC; Sci Fairs; Yth Ldrshp Prog; Comm Volntr; Peer Tut/Med; Chess; Mth Clb/Tm; NYLC; Photog; Scouts; Tchrs Aide; Sccr (V CL); Track (V L); 12 Years of Piano/Keyboard, Write and Produce Music; Club Soccer W/Seacoast Utd. 3rd 2004 US Club Nationals; Medical Research; Bio-Engineering; Cornell U; U of Chicago

WHEELER, ERIKA; HOPKINTON, MA; HOPKINTON HS; (JR); F Lan Hn Soc; Hi Hnr Roll; Hnr Roll; MVP; Peer Tut/Med; Bnd; Pep Bnd; Bskball (VJ L); Sccr (JC); Track (VJ L); Pit Band for Musical (My Fair Lady); Play Flute in Church; Forensics; Biology; Johns Hopkins U; Cornell U

WILLIAMS, KIYANNA M; SPRINGFIELD, MA; CENTRAL HS; (FR); Hi Hnr Roll; Perf Att; Sci Fairs; Key Club; Mth Clb/Tm; Photog; Chrldg (V); Swmg (V); Tennis (V); Dermatology; Pediatrician; New York U; Yale U

WILLIAMSON, WESTON; SPRINGFIELD, MA; (MS); Hi Hnr Roll; Hnr Roll; Nat Hon Sy; St of Mnth; Bskball (V); Virginia Tech -Football Player-Master's; Georgia Tech - Football Player-Master's; Virginia Technology; Georgia Technology

WILSON, CARRIE; LONGMEADOW, MA; LONGMEADOW HS; (SO); Hi Hnr Roll; Hnr Roll; Comm Volntr; Emplmnt; Key Club; Bnd; Pep Bnd; Lcrsse (JC); Sccr (V L)

WINSLOW, JENNA; EAST WEYMOUTH, MA; WEYMOUTH HS; (JR); Hi Hnr Roll; Hnr Roll; WWAHSS; Comm Volntr; Emplmnt; Sch Ppr (R); Medical Doctor (MD); Psychology; Tulane U (New Orleans)

WINT, RACHEL A; BOSTON, MA; LYNNFIELD HS; (SO); F Lan Hn Soc; Otst Ac Ach Awd; Comm Volntr; Chrch Yth Grp; Fr of Library; Ch Chr; Dnce; Fld Hky (J); Sftball (J); Forensics; Registered Nurse; Boston U; St Anslem College

WONG, ANNA; MEDFIELD, MA; MEDFIELD HS; (SO); F Lan Hn Soc; Perf Att; WWAHSS; Comm Volntr; Drma Clb; SADD; French Clb; Chr; Stg Cre; Harmony Club / Gay Straight Alliance Club; Psychology; McGill U; New York U

WONG, SANDRA; MALDEN, MA; MALDEN HS; (SO); Hi Hnr Roll; Hnr Roll; Nat Hon Sy; Perf Att; Comm Volntr; Hosp Aide; Spec Olymp Vol; ArtClub; Key Club; SP/M/VS; Cr Ctry (V); Swmg (V); Track (V); CR (R); Yrbk (E); Walk for Hunger; Civil Rights Team; Doctor / Nurse; Optometrist

WOOD, JACOB; FORESTDALE, MA; SANDWICH HS; (SO); Ctznshp Aw; Hi Hnr Roll; Otst Ac Ach Awd; Perf Att; Pres Ac Ftns Aw; Pres Sch; Emplmnt; Wdwrkg Clb; Ftball (J); Silver Scholar Award (Top 20 in Class); Criminal Justice; Computer Technology

WOOD-DAVIDSON, RAHAMA; CAMBRIDGE, MA; CAMBRIDGE RINDGE & LATIN HS; (JR); Hnr Roll; Chrch Yth Grp; Ch Chr; Dnce; SP/M/VS; Bdmtn; Lcrsse; Tennis (J); Boston Area Youth Organization Program - BYOP; Psychology; Northeastern U

WRIGHT, NICOLE; BELLINGHAM, MA; BELLINGHAM MEM HS; (SO); Hnr Roll; Mus Clb; Bnd; Jzz Bnd; Mch Bnd; Bskball (J); Sftball (V); Music Education / Performing; Science; Eastman School of Music; U of New Hampshire

WURZEL, BENJAMIN; WEST NEWTON, MA; BEAVER CTRY DAY SCH; (JR); Hi Hnr Roll; Sci/Math Olympn; Comm Volntr; Dnce; SP/M/VS; Tennis (V); Diversity Award; Dance Award - Hip-Hop, Poppin' / Score of 3 on American Invitational Mathematics Examination; Theatre; Ethnic Studies / Economics; Vassar College; Dartmouth College

WUTHRICH, DANIELLE; READING, MA; FELLOWSHIP CHRISTIAN AC; (SR); Ctznshp Aw; Hi Hnr Roll; MVP; Nat Hon Sy; Otst Ac Ach Awd; Salutrn; Sci Fairs; WWAHSS; Chr; SP/M/VS; Bskball (V CL); Sftball (V L); Vllyball (V CL); Cl Off (S); Directed & Acted in School Play; Composer/ Music Education; Bob Jones U

XIAO, ANDREW; ACTON, MA; ACTON-BOXBOROUGH HS; (FR); Hi Hnr Roll; Hnr Roll; Otst Ac Ach Awd; Perf Att; Comm Volntr; Chess; DARE; Dbte Team; Emplmnt; Mus Clb; NtlFrnscLg; Sci Clb; Scouts; Orch; Cr Ctry (L); Stu Cncl (T); Presidential Award for Community Service; Part of the Junior District Orchestra - 3 Years; Law; Medical; Yale; Harvard

YANAKOPULOS, AMBER; MEDFORD, MA; (JR); Hi Hnr Roll; Hnr Roll; MVP; Nat Hon Sy; Otst Ac Ach Awd; St of Mnth; WWAHSS; Emplmnt; Key Club; Vsity Clb; Sccr (V C); Track (V L); Cl Off (S); Girls' Varsity Soccer 4 Year Captain; Girls' Soccer 3 Year GBL All-Star; Tufts U; Merrimack College

YANAKOPULOS, JULIA; MEDFORD, MA; MEDFORD HS; (SO); Hi Hnr Roll; Otst Ac Ach Awd; WWAHSS; Comm Volntr; Emplmnt; Key Club; Vsity Clb; Sccr (V); Track (V); Cl Off (T); Stu Cncl (R); Outstanding Community Service Award; Tufts U; U Mass Amherst

YANOVICH, JACOB; QUINCY, MA; NORTH QUINCY HS; (FR); Hi Hnr Roll; Sci Fairs; Stg Cre; Roy Robertson Award in Microbiology; Margaret Spencer Award for Drama; Forensics; Biology; Boston U; U of New Haven

YELICK, JULIA; CONCORD, MA; CONCORD-CARLISLE HS; (JR); Orch; Cr Ctry (J L); Sftball (J); Works at Local Bakery for - 3 Yrs; Psychology; Literature; Wake Forest U

ZALATORES, KRISTA; WEST BROOKFIELD, MA; QUABOAG REG; (JR); Hi Hnr Roll; Nat Hon Sy; St of Mnth; Valdctrian; WWAHSS; Yth Ldrshp Prog; Comm Volntr; AL Aux Girls; Emplmnt; HO'Br Yth Ldrshp; Mth Clb/Tm; Svce Clb; SADD; Tchrs Aide; Cr Ctry (V); Stu Cncl; Lit Mag (E); Political Science; History; Brown U; Boston U

ZANOLLI, JENNIFER; PLYMPTON, MA; SILVER LAKE REG HS; (SR); Hi Hnr Roll; Hnr Roll; Nat Hon Sy; Otst Ac Ach Awd; Perf Att; WWAHSS; Comm Volntr; Peer Tut/Med; Dbte Team; Drma Clb; Key Club; Bnd; Chr; Dnce; Stg Cre; Key Club Officer; Placement Tap and Jazz; Business Degree

ZENEROVITZ, ALEX; ACTON, MA; ACTON-BOXBOROUGH HS; (JR); Hnr Roll; Comm Volntr; Emplmnt; Sccr (V); Wrstlg (V); Club Soccer, Community Service School, Volunteer, MVP (Mentoring Violence Prevention); Business / International Relations; English / History

ZGURO, JENNIFER L; SPRINGFIELD, MA; MINNECHAUG REG HS; (SR); Hi Hnr Roll; Hnr Roll; St of Mnth; WWAHSS; Comm Volntr; Spec Olymp Vol; DARE; Emplmnt; Jr Ach; Key Club; Tchrs Aide; Sccr (V L); Track (V CL), Physical Education Teacher, Springfield College

ZHANG, LINDA; NORTH READING, MA; NORTH READING HS; (SR); Hi Hnr Roll; Hnr Roll; Perf Att; WWAHSS; Comm Volntr; Hosp Aide; Peer Tut/Med; Emplmnt; Key Club; French Clb; Pharmacy; U of Connecticut-Storrs

ZHANG, TIANYUN; SOUTH DARTMOUTH, MA; DARTMOUTH HS; (JR); Hi Hnr Roll; Comm Volntr; Emplmnt; Key Club; Mth Clb/Tm; Mus Clb; NtlFrnscLg; Sci Clb; Scouts; Tchrs Aide; Orch; Track (V); Youth Symphony Orchestra of Greater Boston; Engineering; Computer/Gaming Software Producer; Massachusetts Institute of Technology

ZICK, DAVID; WEST STOCKBRIDGE, MA; MONUMENT MOUNTAIN REG HS; (SO); Comm Volntr; Stg Cre; Iowa Cable Commissioner; Altar Server for Church; Premedicine; Medical; Massachusetts College of Pharmacy and Health Sciences

ZIEMBA, ASHLEY M; WEST SPRINGFIELD, MA; WEST SPRINGFIELD HS; (JR); Hi Hnr Roll; Hnr Roll; WWAHSS; Comm Volntr; Vsity Clb; Lcrsse (VJ); Sccr (V); Ceili Crew; Renaissance; Physical Therapy; Pre-Medical; U of Massachusetts, Boston; Syracuse U

ZMACZYNSKI, ALYSSA M; FEEDING HILLS, MA; AGAWAM HS; (SR); All Am Sch; F Lan Hn Soc; Hnr Roll; Nat Hon Sy; Nat Ldrshp Svc; Otst Ac Ach Awd; USAA; WWAHSS; Drma Clb; Emplmnt; Quill & Scroll; Quiz Bowl; Tchrs Aide; English Clb; Bnd; Dnce; Mch Bnd; Pep Bnd; Yrbk (E); English Department Award; Dunkin Donuts Scholarship; Secondary Education and English; Elms College

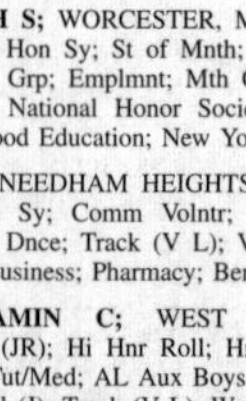
Zguro, Jennifer L
Minnechaug Reg HS
Springfield, MA

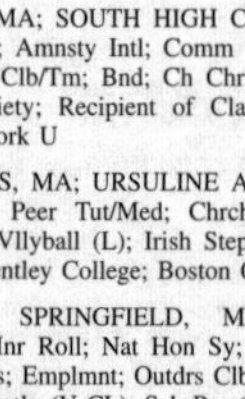
Wood, Jacob
Sandwich HS
Forestdale, MA

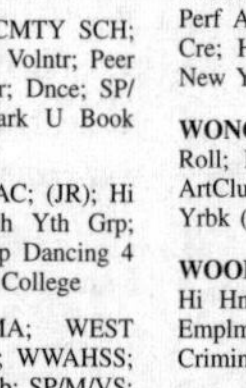
Weed, Barrett S W
Walnut HS
Cambridge, MA

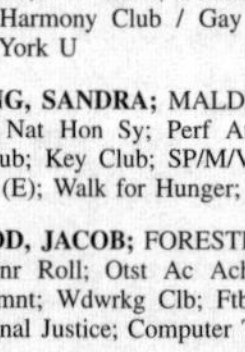
Weathers III, Richard G
Cambridge Rindge & Latin HS
Cambridge, MA

National
Honor Roll
Spring 2005

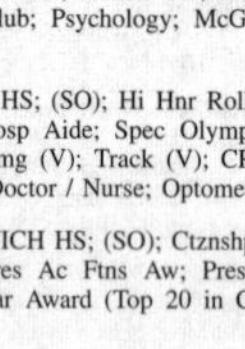
Warren, Benjamin C
West Springfield HS
West Springfield, MA

Whalley, Rich
North Andover HS
North Andover, MA

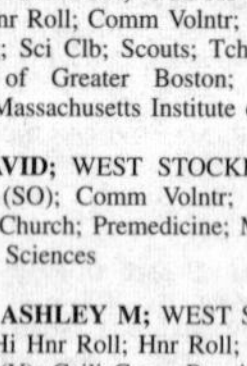
Yanovich, Jacob
North Quincy HS
Quincy, MA

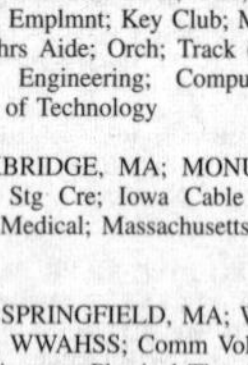
Ziemba, Ashley M
West Springfield HS
West Springfield, MA

New Hampshire

ADAMS, DANE; LEMPSTER, NH; FALL MOUNTAIN REG HS; (JR); Hnr Roll; Perf Att; Peer Tut/Med; Emplmnt; ROTC; Clr Grd; Ftball (V L); Skt Tgt Sh (V); Lit Mag (R); Voice of Democracy Winner for District in NH (2004); Sports Media/Communications; Sports Management

AHEARN, CAITLIN A; RAYMOND, NH; RAYMOND HS; (JR); Hi Hnr Roll; Hnr Roll; Nat Hon Sy; WWAHSS; Bnd; Mch Bnd; Sftball (V L); Vllyball (VJ L); Yrbk (E); Athletic Review; U of Texas Austin; U of New Hampshire Durham

ALBERT, MISTY; CONWAY, NH; KENNETT HS; (SO); Ctznshp Aw; Hnr Roll; St of Mnth; Comm Volntr; 4-H; Key Club; Scouts; Political Science; Childhood Education; U of New Hampshire; U of North Carolina

ALLEY, TIFFANY; SUNCOOK, NH; PEMBROKE AC; (SO); Hi Hnr Roll; Hnr Roll; Sci Fairs; St of Mnth; Comm Volntr; ArtClub; Lib Aide; Art Achievement Award; Secondary Education; Entrepreneurship; Hartwick College; Gettysburg College

AMADI, CRYSTAL; HUDSON, NH; ALVIRNE HS; (JR); Gov Hnr Prg; Hi Hnr Roll; Hnr Roll; Nat Hon Sy; Comm Volntr; Peer Tut/Med; Chrch Yth Grp; Key Club; Mth Clb/Tm; Pharmacy; Medicine

AMLAW, KELLY M; MANCHESTER, NH; MEMORIAL HS; (SO); Hnr Roll; Perf Att; Comm Volntr; Mar Art; Sccr (J); Track (V); Stu Cncl (R); Sch Ppr (E, P); Volunteer at Old Elementary School Fund Raising Events; Volunteer at Martial Arts School for Children's Classes; Physical Therapist; Athletic Trainer

ANDERSON, ANGEL; NORTHFIELD, NH; WINNISQUAM REG HS; (SR); SP/M/VS; Education; Psychology

ARSENAULT, ARIELLE; BERLIN, NH; BERLIN HS; (SO); Hi Hnr Roll; Nat Hon Sy; WWAHSS; Peer Tut/Med; Spec Olymp Vol; Key Club; SADD; Bnd; Bskball (V L); Fld Hky (V L); Sftball (V L); Stu Cncl (R); New Hampshire Teen Institute Staff Member; Pre-Dentistry; DMD Degree; Harvard U; U of Connecticut

ARSENAULT, NICOLE L; MERRIMACK, NH; MERRIMACK HS; (JR); Hi Hnr Roll; Hnr Roll; Nat Hon Sy; Perf Att; DARE; Emplmnt; Interior Design; Computer Graphics; Hesser College; Rivier College

ARUN, ROHAN; NASHUA, NH; NASHUA HS NORTH; (JR); Hi Hnr Roll; Hnr Roll; Perf Att; Mth Clb/Tm; Bnd; Track (V); Computer Science; Electrical Engineering; Massachusetts Institute of Technology; Tufts U

BALINT, DANENE; HUDSON, NH; ALVIRNE HS; (JR); Hi Hnr Roll; Hnr Roll; Nat Hon Sy; Perf Att; WWAHSS; Comm Volntr; Peer Tut/Med; Emplmnt; Key Club; Mth Clb/Tm; Cr Ctry; Fld Hky; Sccr (J); Tennis (V L); Track (J); Vice President for Key Club; Biotechnology; Finance; Boston U; American U

BARKER, MICHELLE; FRANCESTOWN, NH; CONTOOCOOK VALLEY REG HS; (SO); Hi Hnr Roll; Hnr Roll; St of Mnth; Comm Volntr; Sccr (V L); Sch Ppr (R); Furnace Brook Farm Show Team - Horseback Riding; National French Exam 98th Percentile; Medical Doctor / ER or Orthopedics; Brown U; Tufts U

BAUER, MARIANNE; WINDHAM, NH; SALEM HS; (JR); Ctznshp Aw; Hi Hnr Roll; Nat Hon Sy; Otst Ac Ach Awd; Comm Volntr; Peer Tut/Med; Chrch Yth Grp; Key Club; Swmg (V L)

BEAULIEU, DANIELLE A; LONDONDERRY, NH; LONDONDERRY HS; (SR); Ctznshp Aw; Gov Hnr Prg; Hi Hnr Roll; Hnr Roll; Nat Mrt Sch Recip; Otst Ac Ach Awd; St Schl; St of Mnth; Comm Volntr; Peer Tut/Med; Red Cr Aide; Chrch Yth Grp; DARE; Emplmnt; Mus Clb; Off Aide; Quill & Scroll; Tchrs Aide; Vsity Clb; Orch; Chrldg (J L); Skiing; Track (V L); Sch Ppr (E); Biology; Pharmacist; U of New Hampshire; UNH Manchester

BEAULIEU, KRISTIN M; NASHUA, NH; BISHOP GUERTIN HS; (JR); F Lan Hn Soc; Hnr Roll; Comm Volntr; Emplmnt; Pep Squd; Svce Clb; Spanish Clb; Chrldg (J); Track (J); BBGHS 2004 Service Award For 72 Hours; Knights of Columbus Essay Contest Winner; Political Science; Pre-Law

BELCOURT, JAKE; CONTOOCOOK, NH; HOPKINTON HS; (JR); Hi Hnr Roll; Hnr Roll; Otst Ac Ach Awd; Comm Volntr; Chrch Yth Grp; Engineering; Computer Technology; Massachusetts Institute of Technology; Northeastern U

BERNABEO, DOMINIQUE E; NASHUA, NH; NASHUA HS NORTH; (SO); DAR; Fut Prb Slvr; Gov Hnr Prg; Hi Hnr Roll; Hnr Roll; MVP; Nat Hon Sy; Pres Sch; St of Mnth; Comm Volntr; Peer Tut/Med; Spec Olymp Vol; ArtClub; Biology Clb; DARE; Dbte Team; Emplmnt; Jr Ach; JSA; Off Aide; Bskball (J); Sftball (J); Sch Ppr (E); Yrbk (R, P); Published Poet in - Creative Communications; Spokesperson for the Home Health Hospice Center; Master's Degree in Medicine; License to Practice Medicine; Harvard U; Johns Hopkins School of Medicine

BERNARD, ANDY; MANCHESTER, NH; CENTRAL HS; (FR); Hnr Roll; Bnd; Chr; Bskball; Engineering

BINNIE, KELSEY L; GOFFSTOWN, NH; GOFFSTOWN HS; (SO); Hnr Roll; Drma Clb; FBLA; SP/M/VS; Bskball; Scr Kpr (VJ); Sftball; Track (V); Yrbk; Peer Outreach; NH Partnership; Business; Medical; Boston College; Arcadia U

BIRD, ALISON; MONT VERNON, NH; SOUHEGAN COOP HS; (JR); Hi Hnr Roll; Hnr Roll; Comm Volntr; DARE; Chr; Vllyball (J); CR; Earned Black Belt in Kenpo Karate; Earned Coaches' Award on Summer Swim Team; Interior Design; Advertising; U of New Hampshire; Rhode Island School of Design

BOISSY, JONATHAN M; HOOKSETT, NH; CENTRAL HS; (SO); F Lan Hn Soc; Gov Hnr Prg; Hi Hnr Roll; Hnr Roll; Nat Hon Sy; Perf Att; Pres Ac Ftns Aw; St Schl; CARE; Comm Volntr; ArtClub; Cmptr Clb; DARE; Emplmnt; FCCLA; SADD; Wdwrkg Clb; French Clb; Bnd; Ch Chr; Mch Bnd; Stg Cre; Bsball (V); Bskball (J); Cr Ctry (V); Ftball (V); Ice Hky (J); Rlr Hky (J); Track (V); Wt Lftg (V); Adv Cncl (V); Cl Off (S); Stu Cncl (S); CR (R); Lit Mag (P); Sch Ppr (R); Yrbk (P); Plumbing; Carpentry; New Hampshire Cmty Technical College

BONARDI, SAMANTHA E; HUDSON, NH; ALVIRNE HS; (JR); Hnr Roll; WWAHSS; Comm Volntr; Chrldg (V L); Track (J L); National Championship Roller Skating; National Trophy Accordion; Pediatric Nursing

BOONE, DESIRAE C; CONCORD, NH; CONCORD HS; (FR); Hnr Roll; Hosp Aide; Chrldg (J); Gmnstcs; Physician; Dartmouth Medical School

BOSSIO, ANGELA G; MANCHESTER, NH; MEMORIAL HS; (FR); Ctznshp Aw; Hi Hnr Roll; Otst Ac Ach Awd; Pres Ac Ftns Aw; Pres Sch; Valdctrian; Yth Ldrshp Prog; Comm Volntr; Peer Tut/Med; Chrch Yth Grp; DARE; Drma Clb; Mus Clb; Bnd; Ch Chr; Mch Bnd; SP/M/VS; Sftball (L); Stu Cncl (R); Principal's List; Nursing / RN; New Hampshire Community Technical

BOUTIN, DELINA; PELHAM, NH; PELHAM HS; (SR); Hnr Roll; Nat Hon Sy; Otst Ac Ach Awd; Hosp Aide; Peer Tut/Med; DARE; Prom Com; Fld Hky (J); Leadership Team; Health Occupations Students of America; Nursing; Rivier College; Middlesex Community College

BOUTWELL, STEPHEN D; LITTLETON, NH; LITTLETON SR HS; (JR); Hi Hnr Roll; Nat Hon Sy; Pres Sch; WWAHSS; Emplmnt; Mth Clb/Tm; Lawyer; Politics; Georgetown U; Bowdoin College

BROWN, ALICIA; NASHUA, NH; NASHUA HS NORTH; (SO); F Lan Hn Soc; Hi Hnr Roll; Hnr Roll; Pres Sch; WWAHSS; Comm Volntr; ArtClub; Chrch Yth Grp; DARE; Mus Clb; Spanish Clb; Bnd; Chr; Mch Bnd; Orch; Cr Ctry (J); Track (J); Destination Imagination; National History Day

BRUN, JESSICA; HUDSON, NH; ALVIRNE HS; (FR); Hi Hnr Roll; MVP; Sci Fairs; Comm Volntr; ArtClub; Key Club; Sftball (JC); Law School; Business School; Harvard Law School; Brown U

BURNS, GABRIELLE; NORTH HAMPTON, NH; WINNACUNNET HS; (FR); Hi Hnr Roll; MVP; Perf Att; Comm Volntr; Drma Clb; Emplmnt; Mth Clb/Tm; Outdrs Clb; Bnd; Mch Bnd; SP/M/VS; Stg Cre; Vllyball (J); Varsity Math Team; Theater / Acting; Engineering; Worcester Polytechnic Institute; Stanford U

CARGILL, BEN; INTERVALE, NH; KENNETT HS; (FR); F Lan Hn Soc; Hnr Roll; Nat Hon Sy; WWAHSS; Comm Volntr; Key Club; Outdrs Clb; French Clb; Cyclg (V); Skiing (V); Won Honorable Mention in Art Show; Ski Team Won State Championship; Computer Science; Photography; Plymouth State U

CARRON, DESIREE; CONCORD, NH; CONCORD HS; (SO); F Lan Hn Soc; Hi Hnr Roll; USAA; Comm Volntr; Emplmnt; Key Club; German Clb; German Exchange Program / GAPP; Engineering; Teaching; Boston U; U of New Hampshire

CATE, ALEXIS; CONCORD, NH; CONCORD HS; (FR); Hi Hnr Roll; Hnr Roll; Comm Volntr; Key Club; Ice Hky (V); Sccr (J); Tennis (V); Track (J); Education; Journalism; New York U; Stanford U

CERNUDA, CHARLES M; NASHUA, NH; NASHUA HS NORTH; (FR); F Lan Hn Soc; Hnr Roll; Sci Fairs; Hosp Aide; Peer Tut/Med; Scouts; WORLD Clb; CR (R); LAX Blast Team / World Language Club; Amherst Swing Club / 7 Yrs Student of Piano; Global Business; Music; Yale U; St Andrews - Scotland

CHAPUT, KRISTINE; SUNCOOK, NH; PEMBROKE AC; (SO); Hi Hnr Roll; Hnr Roll; Perf Att; Comm Volntr; DARE; Fld Hky (J); Sftball (JC); Captain of Rec Soccer Team - 2 Yrs; Athletic Training; Boston U; Southern New Hampshire U

CIMINI, TARA; PORTSMOUTH, NH; PORTSMOUTH HS; (SO); Hnr Roll; Otst Ac Ach Awd; Yth Ldrshp Prog; Comm Volntr; DARE; Emplmnt; Fld Hky (J); Track; Young Women's Leadership; Interior Design; Marketing; Endicott College; U of New Hampshire

CLARK, EMILY; LITTLETON, NH; LITTLETON SR HS; (SO); Hi Hnr Roll; Hnr Roll; Comm Volntr; Prom Com; Acpl Chr; Bnd; Chr; Dnce; Fld Hky (V L); Tennis (V L); Cl Off (P); Stu Cncl (R); CPR and AED Certified; Psychology; Behavioral Science; U of North Carolina Wilmington

CLEMENTS, CHRISTINA; MANCHESTER, NH; MANCHESTER WEST HS; (SR); Hi Hnr Roll; Nat Hon Sy; WWAHSS; Comm Volntr; Drma Clb; Quill & Scroll; Schol Bwl; Chr; SP/M/VS; Stg Cre; Yrbk (E); Vice President of Gay Straight Alliance; Sergeant of Police Explorer Troop; Theatre; Psychology; Elmira College

CONNELLY, ASHLEY; BERLIN, NH; BERLIN HS; (SO); Comm Volntr; Emplmnt; Key Club; Chr; Tennis (V); Yrbk (R, P); Big Brothers / Big Sisters; Dermatology; Lawyer; U of New Hampshire; Keene State

CORF, ALLISON; LITCHFIELD, NH; CAMPBELL HS; (SR); Hnr Roll; MVP; Nat Hon Sy; WWAHSS; Comm Volntr; Spec Olymp Vol; AL Aux Girls; Emplmnt; Pep Squd; Photog; Prom Com; Tchrs Aide; Vsity Clb; Bnd; Chrldg (V CL); Sftball (JC); Track (V); Sch Ppr (R, P); International Club; Communications; Keene State College

CORNETTE, JESSICA; HOLLIS, NH; HOLLIS/BROOKLINE HS; (JR); Hnr Roll; Comm Volntr; Emplmnt; Spanish Clb; Bnd; Dnce; Yrbk (R); Snowboard Club; Biology; Mathematics

COURTEMANCHE, ALISHA; MERRIMACK, NH; MERRIMACK HS; (JR); Hnr Roll; Emplmnt; Scouts; Bnd; Mch Bnd; Pep Bnd; Yrbk (R); Culinary Arts; Baking and Pastry Arts; New England Culinary Institute; Johnson and Wales U

COVEY, CRYSTAL M; MANCHESTER, NH; MANCHESTER CTRL HS; (SR); Hi Hnr Roll; Hnr Roll; DECA; DECA Member; Attend College-Marketing / Childhood Education; U of New Hampshire; Rivier College

CRANE, ASHLEY A; LACONIA, NH; LACONIA HS; (SO); Ctznshp Aw; Hnr Roll; Otst Ac Ach Awd; St of Mnth; ArtClub; DARE; Scouts; Track; Member of the Art Instructions School for Over a Year; Business Ownership; Art Major

DALEY, KEVIN A; GROVETON, NH; GROVETON HS; (SO); Ctznshp Aw; Hi Hnr Roll; Hnr Roll; Sci Fairs; Sci/Math Olympn; St of Mnth; WWAHSS; Peer Tut/Med; AL Aux Boys; Chess; Mth Clb/Tm; Scouts; Arch; Ice Hky; Mar Art; Sccr; Swmg; Life Scout; Welding-Fabrication; MMI; NHCTC Berlin 2 Yrs Then MMI

DAWALGA, JUSTIN; LOCHMERE, NH; WINNISQUAM REG HS; (FR); Ctznshp Aw; Otst Ac Ach Awd; WWAHSS; Chess; DARE; Vsity Clb; Bsball (VJ); Bskball (VJ); Sccr (VJ); Twin River Babe Ruth Championship; Physical Education. Teacher.; Medical Coach; Boston U; New Hampshire Tech College

DEMEO, DAVE; HOOKSETT, NH; MANCHESTER CTRL HS; Gov Hnr Prg; Hi Hnr Roll; Ftball (V CL); Track (V L)

DEMERS, KELLY H; MERRIMACK, NH; MERRIMACK HS; (JR); Hi Hnr Roll; Hnr Roll; Perf Att; Emplmnt; Svce Clb; Tennis (V L); Yrbk (R); Effort Award / PE Award; 21st Century Award; Physical Education and Coaching Education

Dawalga, Justin
Winnisquam Reg HS
Lochmere, NH

Burns, Gabrielle
Winnacunnet HS
North Hampton, NH

Bonardi, Samantha E
Alvirne HS
Hudson, NH

Beaulieu, Danielle A
Londonderry HS
Londonderry, NH

Arsenault, Nicole L
Merrimack HS
Merrimack, NH

National
Honor Roll
Spring 2005

Albert, Misty
Kennett HS
Conway, NH

Binnie, Kelsey L
Goffstown HS
Goffstown, NH

Boone, Desirae C
Concord HS
Concord, NH

Cernuda, Charles M
Nashua HS North
Nashua, NH

Clements, Christina
Manchester West HS
Manchester, NH

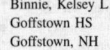

DEVINE, JULIE; MANCHESTER, NH; MANCHESTER CTRL HS; (JR); Hi Hnr Roll; Hnr Roll; Pres Ac Ftns Aw; Sci Fairs; Peer Tut/Med; Emplmnt; Photog; Skiing (V L); Sccr (J); Assistant Rec Soccer Coach; Speech Pathology; Business; U of Vermont; U New Hampshire

DOAK, TYLER; GILMANTON, NH; GILFORD HS; (SO); Hi Hnr Roll; Hnr Roll; Spanish Clb; Pre-Dental; Forensics; Tufts U; U of New Hampshire

DOGUL, AMANDA H; HUDSON, NH; ALVIRNE HS; (FR); Hnr Roll; Nat Hon Sy; Otst Ac Ach Awd; Perf Att; St of Mnth; Key Club; Bnd; Dnce; Mch Bnd; Skiing; Track; Forensic Science; Chemistry; Dartmouth U; Brown U

DOUCETTE, KYLE; CHICHESTER, NH; PEMBROKE AC; (SO); Hnr Roll; MVP; Peer Tut/Med; Chrch Yth Grp; Emplmnt; Jr Ach; Ice Hky (V); Lcrsse (V); Sccr (V); Business; Architecture; UNH; Florida State

DOUIN, JENNIFER; INTERVALE, NH; KENNETT HS; (JR); F Lan Hn Soc; Hi Hnr Roll; Hnr Roll; Nat Hon Sy; Nat Mrt Semif; Otst Ac Ach Awd; WWAHSS; Comm Volntr; Peer Tut/Med; Spec Olymp Vol; Key Club; Cl Off (S); Stu Cncl (S); Yrbk; Sociology; Criminal Law

DROUIN, ALYSSA; GILFORD, NH; GILFORD HS; (SO); 4H Awd; Ctznshp Aw; Hi Hnr Roll; Hnr Roll; Vsity Clb; Spanish Clb; Dnce; Sccr (JC); Vsy Clb (V); Bachelor's; Physical Therapy; Boston College; U of New Hampshire

DUBE, KATHRYN; MANCHESTER, NH; MANCHESTER CTRL HS; (FR); Gov Hnr Prg; 1st Degree Black Belt in Kenpo Karate; Science Field; Medical Field

DU BOIS, JENNIFER L; SOMERSWORTH, NH; SOMERSWORTH HS; (SR); Hi Hnr Roll; Nat Hon Sy; Comm Volntr; Bnd; Chr; Mch Bnd; SP/M/VS; Track (J); Vllyball (V); Stu Cncl; National Honor Society; Interact (President); Biology; Simmons College

EAGLES, KELLY R; LACONIA, NH; PROSPECT MTN HS; (SR); Ctznshp Aw; Hnr Roll; Nat Hon Sy; Otst Ac Ach Awd; Comm Volntr; AL Aux Girls; Chrch Yth Grp; DARE; Emplmnt; HO'Br Yth Ldrshp; SADD; Tech Clb; Bskball (VJ L); Hsbk Rdg (V L); Sccr (V L); Track (V CL); Vllyball (J); Cl Off (T, R); Equestrian Management; Psychobiology; U of New England; U of New Hampshire

ECKSTEIN, VINCENT; NASHUA, NH; NASHUA NORTH HS; (FR); Hnr Roll; Nat Hon Sy; Perf Att; Comm Volntr; Emplmnt; Chr; Sccr (VJ L); Club Soccer Captain and Regional Winner; All State Chorus; Business; Computer Graphics Math

EDES, NICOLE E; SUNCOOK, NH; PEMBROKE AC; (JR); Hnr Roll; Perf Att; Yth Ldrshp Prog; Hab For Humty Volntr; Peer Tut/Med; Red Cr Aide; Emplmnt; Off Aide; Vsity Clb; Orch; SP/M/VS; Bskball (J); Sccr (V C); Sftball (V C); Cl Off (R); American Red Cross - Youth Board; Student Senate; Bachelor's Degree / Nutritionist; Southern New Hampshire U; U of New Hampshire

EDWARDS, LAUREN E; BEDFORD, NH; MANCHESTER HS WEST; (JR); Hi Hnr Roll; Hnr Roll; Perf Att; WWAHSS; Comm Volntr; Chrch Yth Grp; Pep Squd; Quill & Scroll; Dnce; SP/M/VS; Sccr (J); Yrbk (E); Religious Education Teacher; Major in Communications; Elon U; U of North Carolina Greensboro

ELLIOTT, RACHEL; AMHERST, NH; SOUHEGAN HS; (JR); Ctznshp Aw; Hi Hnr Roll; Hnr Roll; WWAHSS; Chrch Yth Grp; DARE; Emplmnt; SADD; Sccr (V L); Swmg (V CL); Physical Therapy; Northeastern U; U of Vermont

ESTES, CAITLIN; OSSIPEE, NH; KINGSWOOD REG; (FR); All Am Sch; Hi Hnr Roll; Nat Hon Sy; Key Club; Cr Ct Ski (V); Fld Hky (V); Lcrsse (V); Middle School Scholar of the Year; Medical Research; Dartmouth; Duke

FIGARELLA, ELIZABETH; NASHUA, NH; NASHUA HS NORTH; (SO); Hnr Roll; Comm Volntr; Emplmnt; FBLA; SADD; Spanish Clb; Stu Cncl; Lit Mag (R); Sch Ppr (R); Business; Medicine; Columbia U; Boston U

FISCHER, ANNA C; PETERBOROUGH, NH; CONTOOCOOK VALLEY REG HS; (SR); DAR; F Lan Hn Soc; Hi Hnr Roll; Otst Ac Ach Awd; Pres Sch; St of Mnth; Emplmnt; German Clb; Lit Mag (R); Yrbk (P); European Sociology Studies; Queen's U Kingston, Ontario

FOWLER, DAN; NASHUA, NH; NASHUA HS NORTH; (JR); Hnr Roll; Comm Volntr; Drma Clb; Emplmnt; SP/M/VS; Chosen Teen; Leader-NH Teen Institute; Music & Arts; Film; Endicott College; Keene State College

FREEMAN, SARAH; CAMPTON, NH; PLYMOUTH REG HS; (SR); Hi Hnr Roll; Hnr Roll; Nat Hon Sy; Nat Mrt LOC; Valdctrian; WWAHSS; Yth Ldrshp Prog; Comm Volntr; Hosp Aide; Outdrs Clb; SADD; Vsity Clb; French Clb; Sccr (V C); Track (V); Stu Cncl (R); CR (R); National Honor Society Secretary; Bausch & Lamb Science Award; Doctor of Veterinary Medicine; Generic Research; Brandeis U

FRISELLA, GINO; RAYMOND, NH; RAYMOND HS; (JR); Hnr Roll; DARE; Emplmnt; Bsball (J); Sccr (V); Track (V)

GALAFASSI, ROBERT; NASHUA, NH; NASHUA HS NORTH; (SO); Hnr Roll; Perf Att; Emplmnt; Breakdancing; Automotive Specialist; Acting; Universal Technical Institute

GALLELLO, MICHELLE N; MILFORD, NH; MILFORD HS; (SR); Hi Hnr Roll; Hnr Roll; Pres Sch; Sci Fairs; Comm Volntr; Hosp Aide; Red Cr Aide; DARE; Prom Com; Spanish Clb; Chrldg (V); Yrbk (R); High Honor Roll All Four Years; Biology / Pre-Med; PhD; U of New Hampshire; Northeastern U

GANGULY, JAVAS; NASHUA, NH; NASHUA HS NORTH; (SO); Hnr Roll; Nat Hon Sy; Comm Volntr; Bnd; Mch Bnd; Sccr (V); Swmg (V); Stu Cncl (P, V); Yrbk (E); Spartans Drum and Bugle Corp.; Computer Programmer; Web Page Design; U of New York; U of Southern California

GAONA, RENEE M; MANCHESTER, NH; MANCHESTER HS WEST; (SR); Hnr Roll; WWAHSS; Comm Volntr; Spec Olymp Vol; Emplmnt; Key Club; Chr; Fld Hky (V); CR; Yrbk; President-Key Club 2004-2005; VP-Key Club 2003-2004; Biology; Law; Villanova U; St Joseph's U

GAUDET, STEPHEN; HUDSON, NH; ALVIRNE; (SO); Hi Hnr Roll; Hnr Roll; MVP; St of Mnth; Key Club; Sccr (V); MVP of the Year for JV Sophomore Year; Business Major; Engineering Major; Boston College; Northeastern

GEORGEVITS, ANDREW P; CONCORD, NH; CONCORD HS; (SR); Ctznshp Aw; Kwnis Aw; MVP; WWAHSS; Yth Ldrshp Prog; Hosp Aide; Chrch Yth Grp; DARE; Emplmnt; HO'Br Yth Ldrshp; Key Club; Prom Com; Svce Clb; Vsity Clb; Bnd; Mch Bnd; Pep Bnd; Stg Cre; Cr Ct Ski (V L); Golf (V); Skiing (V L); Track (V); Vsy Clb (V C); Yrbk (P); Ski Jumping Varsity Captain; New England District Governor Key Club; Marketing; Sales; New Hampshire Technical Institute; St Bonaventure

GILBERT, BRANDON R; BERLIN, NH; BERLIN HS; (JR); Ctznshp Aw; Hnr Roll; Nat Hon Sy; Pres Ac Ftns Aw; WWAHSS; Comm Volntr; DARE; Key Club; Quiz Bowl; Tchrs Aide; Bnd; Bsball (V); Bskball (V); Sccr (J); Work Part Time Job in a Restaurant; Wildlife Management-Conservation; Business; U of New Hampshire

GILMAN, HANNAH; FRANCESTOWN, NH; CONTOOCOOK VALLEY REG HS; (JR); Hi Hnr Roll; Hnr Roll; Pres Sch; St of Mnth; WWAHSS; Comm Volntr; ArtClub; FBLA; Svce Clb; Dnce; Fld Hky; Lit Mag (R)

GLINES, KRISTEN R; LITTLETON, NH; LITTLETON SR HS; (SO); Hi Hnr Roll; Comm Volntr; Hosp Aide; DECA; Prom Com; Bnd; Mch Bnd; Pep Bnd; Bskball (VJ); Sccr (V L); Stu Cncl (R); AAU Basketball; Sports Medicine; Sports Marketing / Advertising; U of New Hampshire; Dartmouth College

GODSAY, VIRAJ; NASHUA, NH; NASHUA HS NORTH; (FR); Bskball (J); Cr Ctry (J); Film Club

GOERGEN, ELIZABETH M; NEW MARKET, NH; WINNACUNNET HS; (FR); Ctznshp Aw; Hnr Roll; Perf Att; St of Mnth; Emplmnt; Lib Aide; ROTC; Chr; Lawyer; Therapist

GOFFINET, ASHLEYMARIE; GOFFSTOWN, NH; GOFFSTOWN AREA HS; (SO); Ctznshp Aw; Hnr Roll; Emplmnt; Photog; Prom Com; Dnce; Lcrsse (J); Peer Outreach; Psychology; Business; Rowan U; U of Texas

GORTON, JAMIE H; HOOKSETT, NH; MANCHESTER HS WEST; (JR); Hi Hnr Roll; Hnr Roll; Nat Hon Sy; WWAHSS; Quill & Scroll; Scouts; Bnd; Mch Bnd; Stu Cncl (R); Sch Ppr (E); Life Scout-Boy Scouts of America; English; Middlebury College; U of New Hampshire

GRACE, HEATHER L; WILMOT, NH; KEARSARGE REG HS; (SR); Hnr Roll; Nat Hon Sy; Pres Sch; WWAHSS; Comm Volntr; Peer Tut/Med; Spec Olymp Vol; Drma Clb; Emplmnt; Mth Clb/Tm; Prom Com; Acpl Chr; Bnd; Chr; SP/M/VS; Sftball (V); Cl Off (T); Wellesley Book Award; Clarinet Choir; Voice Performance; Business; Skidmore College; U of New Hampshire

GUNDLACH, ASHLI; MEREDITH, NH; WINNISQUAM REG HS; (JR); Hnr Roll; St of Mnth; 4-H; DARE; Emplmnt; Ntl FFA; Off Aide; Presidents Award; Most Improved in Grade; Business Degree; Ag Degree; Morrisville State College

HACKETT, KATHLEEN; UNION, NH; FARMINGTON HS; (FR); Gov Hnr Prg; Hnr Roll; Hosp Aide; Spanish Clb; Bskball (J); Spanish Club; Bachelor's Degree in the Science of Nursing; Major in World History; U of New England; New Hampshire Technical Institute

HALBEDEL, BRIANNE; RINDGE, NH; CONANT HS; (SR); Hi Hnr Roll; Hnr Roll; Nat Hon Sy; WWAHSS; Emplmnt; Fr of Library; Dnce; Marine Biology; U of Maine Orono

HALL, CASARRA; COLEBROOK, NH; COLEBROOK AC; (SO); Ctznshp Aw; Comm Volntr; Emplmnt; Key Club; Quiz Bowl; Scouts; SADD; Clb; Chr; Bskball (J); Cl Off (S); Stu Cncl (R); Nationally Recognized for Community Service; Traveled Around the World; Physician's Assistant

HART, KASEY; CONCORD, NH; CONCORD HS; (FR); Hnr Roll; Chrldg (V); Law; Business Management; Fordham U; Northeastern U

HARTENSTEIN, ERIC S; HAMPTON FALLS, NH; WINNACUNNET HS; (SO); Bsball (J); Bskball (J); Ftball (J)

HARUBIN, EMILY E; CTR TUFTONBORO, NH; KINGSWOOD REG HS; (SR); Hi Hnr Roll; Hnr Roll; Nat Mrt Fin; Otst Ac Ach Awd; Pres Sch; WWAHSS; Drma Clb; Key Club; Clb; Bnd; Orch; Pep Bnd; Stg Cre; Hsbk Rdg; Lit Mag (E); Presidential Scholarship from Elmira; Journalism; Business; Attending Elmira College, Elmira, NY

HASKELL, KASSANDRA; MANCHESTER, NH; MANCHESTER CTRL HS; (SO); Gov Hnr Prg; Hi Hnr Roll; Hnr Roll; DARE; Emplmnt; Sccr (J); Media / Visual Communications; Brooks Institute of Photography; Gibbs College Boston

HEATH, WINTER; LITTLETON, NH; LITTLETON SR HS; (SO); Hi Hnr Roll; Hnr Roll; MVP; Nat Hon Sy; Comm Volntr; Emplmnt; Prom Com; Fld Hky (V L); Tennis (V L); Stu Cncl (R); CR (R); Dietitian; Personal Trainer; New England College; Keene State College

HENDERSON, JESS; CONCORD, NH; CONCORD HS; (JR); Hi Hnr Roll; Hnr Roll; MVP; Nat Hon Sy; Comm Volntr; Hosp Aide; Peer Tut/Med; ArtClub; DARE; Key Club; Photog; Tchrs Aide; French Clb; Sch Ppr (R); Yrbk (P); Interior Design; U of Massachusetts Amherst

HENRY, JILLIAN; NASHUA, NH; NASHUA HS NORTH; (SO); Hnr Roll; Nat Hon Sy; WWAHSS; Comm Volntr; Peer Tut/Med; Emplmnt; Junior Honor Society; Obstetrics / Medical; Elmira College; Quinnipiac U

HERGOTT, MATTHEW A; DOVER, NH; DOVER HS; (JR); Hi Hnr Roll; Nat Hon Sy; Otst Ac Ach Awd; Emplmnt; Key Club; Spanish Clb; Golf (J); Scholar Athlete Award; Excellence in Spanish Award; Civil Engineering; Business; Boston College; Northeastern U

HESSLEIN, AMY; CONCORD, NH; CONCORD HS; (FR); Hi Hnr Roll; Hnr Roll; Comm Volntr; Red Cr Aide; Drma Clb; Mus Clb; Acpl Chr; Chr; SP/M/VS; Stg Cre; Golf (V); Swmg (V); National Honors Choir 2005; Music Major

HOGAN, GRACE; MANCHESTER, NH; MEMORIAL HS; (JR); Hi Hnr Roll; Hnr Roll; Drma Clb; Swmg (V); Track; Lit Mag (E); Swim Instructor / Lifeguard at YMCA; Dance - Outside of School; French; Elementary Education; Mc Gill U; Boston College

HORTON III, BENJAMIN M; MANCHESTER, NH; ST DOMINIC HS; (FR); Hi Hnr Roll; Otst Ac Ach Awd; Yth Ldrshp Prog; Comm Volntr; Hosp Aide; Chrch Yth Grp; Mus Clb; Scouts; Bnd; Ch Chr; Ice Hky (J); Lcrsse (J); Sccr (J); Cl Off (R); Stu Cncl (R); Boy Scouts; St Anselm; St Michael's; West Point

HOULE, DANIELLE L; NASHUA, NH; NASHUA HS NORTH; (FR); Hnr Roll; Scouts; Clr Grd; BA / Law; U College Cork Ireland; The U of Dublin / Trinity College Ireland

HOUNSELL, KIRBY; GILFORD, NH; GILFORD HS; (SO); Hi Hnr Roll; WWAHSS; Comm Volntr; Emplmnt; Vsity Clb; French Clb; Skiing (V); Sccr (V); Vsy Clb (V); Hotel Management; Business Management; Cornell U

HUGHSON, JESSICA; BOSCOWEN, NH; MERRIMACK VALLEY HS; (SR); Hi Hnr Roll; Hnr Roll; WWAHSS; Emplmnt; Mth Clb/Tm; Acpl Chr; Chr; SP/M/VS; Early Childhood Education; Plymouth State U

HUMPAL, HANNAH; CORNISH, NH; HARTFORD HS; (JR); Hi Hnr Roll; Hnr Roll; Nat Hon Sy; Otst Ac Ach Awd; Perf Att; Yth Ldrshp Prog; Comm Volntr; Dbte Team; Emplmnt; Prom Com; Tchrs Aide; Bskball (J); Fld Hky (VJ); Sccr (J); Track (VJ); Athletic Council; Law; Sports / Medicine; Boston College; Northeastern U

HUSTED, CLARK H; GILSUM, NH; MONADNOCK REG JR/SR HS; (SO); Hnr Roll; Nat Hon Sy; Pres Ac Ftns Aw; Pres Sch; Comm Volntr; Red Cr Aide; DARE; Emplmnt; Scouts; Bnd; Mch Bnd; Cr Ct Ski (V); Lcrsse (V C); Member Interact - High School Rotary Club; Student Activities Committee Member; Biology; Psychology; UCLA; UNH

JALBERT, ADRIENNE M; HOPKINTON, NH; HOPKINTON HS; (JR); Hi Hnr Roll; Hnr Roll; Nat Hon Sy; WWAHSS; Mth Clb/Tm; Scouts; Bnd; Jzz Bnd; Fld Hky (V L); Track (V L); Aerospace Engineering; Master's Degree; Massachusetts Institute of Technology; Tufts U

Hart, Kasey
Concord HS
Concord, NH

Elliott, Rachel
Souhegan HS
Amherst, NH

Douin, Jennifer
Kennett HS
Intervale, NH

National
Honor Roll
Spring 2005

Dogul, Amanda H
Alvirne HS
Hudson, NH

Galafassi, Robert
Nashua HS North
Nashua, NH

Haskell, Kassandra
Manchester Ctrl HS
Manchester, NH

JAMIESON, SARAH; WEST OSSIPEE, NH; KINGSWOOD REG HS; (FR); Ctznshp Aw; Hi Hnr Roll; Otst Ac Ach Awd; Pres Sch; St of Mnth; WWAHSS; Key Club; Quiz Bowl; Bnd; Pep Bnd; Bskball (J); Sccr (VJ L); Track (V L); I'm Running for Class Representative for Fall 2005

JEPSEN, LAURA; NEW BOSTON, NH; GOFFSTOWN AREA HS; (FR); Hi Hnr Roll; Otst Ac Ach Awd; Pres Sch; Amnsty Intl; Comm Volntr; Red Cr Aide; Bskball (J); Cr Ctry (V); AAU Basketball and 8th Grade Band; Junior Achievement Shadow Day

JETTE, JOANNA; HUDSON, NH; ALVIRNE HS; (SR); Ctznshp Aw; Hnr Roll; Kwnis Aw; Perf Att; St of Mnth; WWAHSS; Comm Volntr; Emplmnt; Jr Ach; JSA; Key Club; Mod UN; Prom Com; Tchrs Aide; Vllyball (JC); Stu Cncl (S); CR (R); Sch Ppr (R); English Major / Education Minor; Salem State College; Plymouth State U

JUNEAU, JEFF; GOFFSTOWN, NH; GOFFSTOWN AREA HS; (SO); Hi Hnr Roll; Hnr Roll; MVP; Nat Mrt LOC; DARE; Emplmnt; Freshman Basketball (2003); Pop-Warner Football (2004); Criminal Justice; Law Enforcement; U of New Hampshire; College of the Holy Cross

KATCHEN, REBECCA; CORNISH, NH; HARTFORD HS; (JR); Hi Hnr Roll; Nat Hon Sy; St of Mnth; WWAHSS; Comm Volntr; Hosp Aide; Mth Clb/Tm; Mus Clb; Clb; Bnd; Pep Bnd; Swmg; International Youth Conference; Mt. Ascutney Hospital Volunteer Award

KAUR, KULBIR; PORTSMOUTH, NH; PORTSMOUTH HS; (SO); Hi Hnr Roll; Hnr Roll; French Clb; Chr; MD / Doctor of Medicine; U of New Hampshire; Dartmouth College

KEENEY, MATT; NASHUA, NH; NASHUA NORTH HS; (FR); Hi Hnr Roll; Hnr Roll; WWAHSS; Scouts; Bsball; Sccr (J); North Carolina; California State

KELLY, BRYCE; HAMPTON, NH; WINNACUNNET HS; (SO); Ctznshp Aw; Hi Hnr Roll; Hnr Roll; Ftball (V L); Business; Meteorology; U of New Hampshire; Boston College

KELLY, JESSICA; DEERFIELD, NH; CONCORD HS; (FR); Hnr Roll; Otst Ac Ach Awd; Mar Art (J)

KIELWEIN, KAYLIN S; HILLSBORO, NH; HILLSBORO DEERING HS; (JR); Hi Hnr Roll; Hnr Roll; Pres Sch; Comm Volntr; DECA; Emplmnt; FBLA; Cl Off (R); DECA Achievement Awards; Video Production; Boston U; New York U

KOCDAL, MARIAL; CONCORD, NH; (FR); Cmptr Clb; Bskball; Sccr

KOVALIK, ALLIE; NORTH CONWAY, NH; KENNETT HS; (FR); Ctznshp Aw; Hnr Roll; Nat Hon Sy; WWAHSS; Comm Volntr; ArtClub; DARE; Key Club; Scouts; Tennis; Yrbk; Graphic Design; U of New Hampshire

LABRECQUE, JOELLE A; LITTLETON, NH; LITTLETON SR HS; (SO); Hi Hnr Roll; Pres Sch; Comm Volntr; Hosp Aide; Peer Tut/Med; Chrch Yth Grp; Emplmnt; Lib Aide; Pep Squd; Prom Com; Bnd; Jzz Bnd; Mch Bnd; Pep Bnd; Fld Hky (J); Cl Off (S); Stu Cncl (R); CR (R); Foreign Language / Spanish; Teaching; Simmons College

LA DIEU, HANNA; HOOKSETT, NH; MANCHESTER CTRL HS; (SR); Hi Hnr Roll; Hnr Roll; Drma Clb; Emplmnt; Stg Cre; Business; Curry College

LAJOIE, MONIQUE; NASHUA, NH; NASHUA NORTH SR HS; (JR); Hi Hnr Roll; Hnr Roll; Nat Hon Sy; WWAHSS; Comm Volntr; Emplmnt; Vllyball (VJ); Freshman Basketball (Captain), Volleyball (Captain), Softball; Youth and Government/House of Representatives; Nursing; Psychology

LA MARCHE, AMANDA; CLAREMONT, NH; STEVENS HS; (JR); Hi Hnr Roll; Hnr Roll; Otst Ac Ach Awd; WWAHSS; Comm Volntr; Chrch Yth Grp; Key Club; Outdrs Clb; Prom Com; Cr Ct Ski (V L); Fncg (V); Early Childhood/Elementary Education; Environmental Science; U of Maine-Machias; Colby-Sawyer

LANGELIER, MEGAN; NASHUA, NH; NASHUA HS NORTH; (FR); Hi Hnr Roll; Hnr Roll; Emplmnt; Sccr (J); REACH - Gifted & Talented Program; Coached a Destination Imagination Team; Art History; Culinary Arts; New England Culinary Institute; Boston U

LA PAGE, CHRISTIAN T; PORTSMOUTH, NH; PORTSMOUTH HS; (JR); Hi Hnr Roll; MVP; Nat Mrt LOC; Comm Volntr; Emplmnt; Ftball (V L); Track (V CL); Snow Science; Outdoor Adventure Recreation; Western State College Colorado; Montana State U

LAWTON, HEATHER L; BEDFORD, NH; MANCHESTER WEST; (SO); Hi Hnr Roll; Hnr Roll; Comm Volntr; Hosp Aide; Spec Olymp Vol; DECA; Emplmnt; Key Club; Hsbk Rdg; Swmg (V); Track (V); Honor Roll; Active Volunteer; Business; Marketing; Boston U; Northwestern U

LEE, JAE K; EXETER, NH; PHILLIPS EXETER AC; (JR); Ctznshp Aw; Hnr Roll; WWAHSS; Yth Ldrshp Prog; Amnsty Intl; Comm Volntr; Hab For Humty Volntr; Chrch Yth Grp; Dbte Team; Emplmnt; JSA; Mth Clb/Tm; P to P St Amb Prg; Photog; Sci Clb; Bdmtn; Hsbk Rdg; Ice Sktg; Tennis; Vllyball (J); Adv Cncl (P); Lit Mag (P); Yrbk (E); Winner (2nd Place) for NSIP; Astrophysics; Princeton U

LESNIAK, ERIKKA; NASHUA, NH; NASHUA HS NORTH; (FR); Lawyer; Chiropractor

LEVELILE, DANIEL; BERLIN, NH; BERLIN HS; (JR); Hnr Roll; Perf Att; Peer Tut/Med; Drma Clb; SP/M/VS; Stg Cre; Graphic Design; Web Design

LEVESQUE, KENDRA; HUDSON, NH; ALVIRNE HS; (JR); Hi Hnr Roll; Hnr Roll; WWAHSS; Key Club; Mth Clb/Tm; Track (V L); Accepted to St. Paul's School Advanced Studies Program; George Washington U

LINDSAY, DANA; LEBANON, NH; LEBANON HS; (FR); Hnr Roll; Perf Att; Fld Hky (J); Track (V); Pre-Med; Doctor of Physical Therapy Degree; Columbia U; Boston U

LINDSAY JR, WILLIAM D; BROOKLINE, NH; HOLLIS/BROOKLINE HS; (FR); 4H Awd; Hi Hnr Roll; MVP; Otst Ac Ach Awd; Pres Ac Ftns Aw; Sci/Math Olympn; Yth Ldrshp Prog; Comm Volntr; 4-H; DARE; Mth Clb/Tm; Mus Clb; NYLC; SADD; French Clb; Bnd; Jzz Bnd; Bskball; Sccr (J); Swmg (V L); Track; Adv Cncl (R); Sch Ppr (P); Johns Hopkins Cty; NHMFA Solo/ Ensemble Festival (Piano); Medical; Legal; Dartmouth U

LINTON, KEVIN D; CONWAY, NH; KENNETT HS; (JR); Ctznshp Aw; Hi Hnr Roll; Hnr Roll; Kwnis Aw; Nat Hon Sy; Otst Ac Ach Awd; Perf Att; St of Mnth; WWAHSS; Comm Volntr; Peer Tut/Med; Chrch Yth Grp; Cmptr Clb; Emplmnt; FTA; Key Club; Mth Clb/Tm; Schol Bwl; Cl Off (P); Lit Mag (R); Sch Ppr (R); Yrbk (R); FCCLA (Future Career and Community Leaders of America); Education (Secondary); Business Administration; U of Colorado At Boulder; Colorado State U

LOGUE, PATRICK; HAMPTON, NH; (JR); Hnr Roll; Jr Rot; Sci Fairs; Emplmnt; Sci Clb; Skiing (J); High Honors Graduate from Biotechnology; Program At SST.; Forensics; Microbiology/Pharmacology; Penn State; U of New Hampshire

LOPES, NICOLE J; TILTON, NH; WINNISQUAM REG HS; (JR); Hnr Roll; Sci Fairs; St of Mnth; Yth Ldrshp Prog; Comm Volntr; Peer Tut/Med; Chrch Yth Grp; DARE; Emplmnt; Clb; Chr; Dnce; CR (R); Step Squad; Elementary School Teacher; Psychologist

LUTER, DIANA; AMHERST, NH; SOUHEGAN HS; (JR); Hnr Roll; MVP; Chr; SP/M/VS; Hsbk Rdg (V); Veterinary; Journalism; Cornell U; Boston U

MAC KENZIE, CHRISTOPHER; CONTOOCOOK, NH; HOPKINTON HS; (SO); Hi Hnr Roll; WWAHSS; Dbte Team; Cr Ctry (V L); Cr Ct Ski (V L); Track (J); Stu Cncl (T); Business; Pre-Law; Syracuse U; Dartmouth

MANCINO, MATTHEW; CLAREMONT, NH; STEVENS HS; (JR); Lcrsse; Mar Art; Business; Florida International U; Florida Atlantic

MANN, MELISSA; LITTLETON, NH; LITTLETON SR HS; (JR); Hi Hnr Roll; MVP; Nat Hon Sy; Otst Ac Ach Awd; Pres Ac Ftns Aw; Comm Volntr; Hosp Aide; Peer Tut/Med; Emplmnt; Photog; SADD; SP/M/VS; Bskball (VJCL); Cr Ctry (V); Sccr (V); Stu Cncl (S); CR (R); Booster Club Female Athlete Award; Coaches' Award - JV Basketball; Dental Hygiene; U of Rhode Island; Forsyth School of Dental Hygiene

MANSUR, LAUREN M; HUDSON, NH; ALVIRNE HS; (FR); Hi Hnr Roll; Sci Fairs; St of Mnth; WWAHSS; Comm Volntr; Emplmnt; Key Club; Bnd; Mch Bnd; Sccr; Sftball (J); Cl Off (R); Stu Cncl (R); Journalism; Education; Harvard; Stanford

MARCEK, BRYAN; BROOKLINE, NH; HOLLIS-BROOKLINE HS; (SO); Nat Sci Aw; Perf Att; Pres Sch; Comm Volntr; Hosp Aide; Sccr (V); Sch Ppr (R); Civil Engineering; Aeronautical Engineering; CU Boulder; UNH

MASON, KATIE S; FRANKLIN, NH; TILTON SCH; (SR); 4H Awd; Hnr Roll; Yth Ldrshp Prog; Peer Tut/Med; Red Cr Aide; 4-H; Emplmnt; Quiz Bowl; Acpl Chr; SP/M/VS; Bskball (V); Fld Hky (V); Sccr (V); Tennis (V); CR (R); Sch Ppr (R); 4-H Events Show Sheep & Diary Cows; Veterinarian; Kansas State U; Colorado State U

MATTA, AMY K; BEDFORD, NH; MANCHESTER HS WEST; (JR); Hi Hnr Roll; Nat Hon Sy; WWAHSS; Yth Ldrshp Prog; Peer Tut/Med; Chrch Yth Grp; Emplmnt; HO'Br Yth Ldrshp; Quill & Scroll; Ch Chr; Dnce; Cr Ct Ski (V); Yrbk (E); Secretary of NHS; Head of Peer Tutoring Program; Nursing; Medical Surgeon; U of Pennsylvania; Boston College

MATUZAS, BRITTNY; NASHUA, NH; NASHUA HS NORTH; (FR); Hnr Roll; Hosp Aide; Drma Clb; Photog; Bskball (J); Lcrsse (V); Coached AAU Basketball Team - Age 10; Journalism; U of Connecticut; Marist College

MC AULIFFE, KIMBERLY; NASHUA, NH; NASHUA HS SOUTH; (JR); Hi Hnr Roll; Hnr Roll; MVP; Nat Hon Sy; Comm Volntr; Emplmnt; Svce Clb; Cr Ctry (V CL); Track (V L); USATF Jr. Olympics National Qualifier; Fitness U Volunteer Coach; Physical Therapy; Nutrition; U of Rhode Island; Framingham State College

MC MANUS, AMANDA C; MANCHESTER, NH; MANCHESTER CTRL HS; (JR); Hi Hnr Roll; Hnr Roll; Nat Hon Sy; Drma Clb; Outdrs Clb; Bnd; Mch Bnd; SP/M/VS; Stg Cre; 8 Yrs of Working on Altar Guild, Acolyte, Eucharistic Minister; Veterinary Medicine; German

MC MANUS, JACOB; CONTOOCOOK, NH; HOPKINTON HS; (SO); Hnr Roll; MVP; WWAHSS; Comm Volntr; Peer Tut/Med; P to P St Amb Prg; Vsity Clb; Bnd; Bsball (V L); Bskball (JC); 3rd Team All State for Baseball Freshman Yr.; Georgia Tech.; Northeastern U

MC NAMARA, BRYANT J; HUDSON, NH; ALAINE HS; (JR); Gov Hnr Prg; Hi Hnr Roll; Hnr Roll; USAA; WWAHSS; Comm Volntr; Hosp Aide; Emplmnt; Key Club; ROTC; Tchrs Aide; Drl Tm; Flg Crps; Lit Mag (R); Acceptance To Air Force Honors Camp - 1 Out Of 600 In US; Established Trick-Drill Team At School; International Studies; Political Science / Government; The Virginia Military Institute; Norwich U

MC NEILL, ASHLEY S; CONTOOCOOK, NH; HOPKINTON HS; (SO); Hi Hnr Roll; Hnr Roll; Otst Ac Ach Awd; Sci/Math Olympn; WWAHSS; Comm Volntr; Dbte Team; Mth Clb/Tm; Ntl Beta Clb; Spch Team; Manager of Math Team; President of Forensics Club; Chemistry; Engineering; Dartmouth College; Mississippi State U

MEDAS, JASON; NASHUA, NH; (JR); Hi Hnr Roll; Hnr Roll; Perf Att; Comm Volntr; Chess; Emplmnt; Aerospace Engineering; Physics

MERLINO, NANCY; HUDSON, NH; ALVIRNE HS; (FR); Gov Hnr Prg; Hi Hnr Roll; Otst Ac Ach Awd; Sci Fairs; St of Mnth; WWAHSS; Comm Volntr; Key Club; Mth Clb/Tm; Tae Kwon Do -(Martial Arts) 2002-Present (Outside School); Guitar 2003-Present (Outside School); Nurse Practitioner; Medical Field; UNH; St. Anselm

MICCOLO, JOSH L; NASHUA, NH; NASHUA HS NORTH; (SO); Hnr Roll; Otst Ac Ach Awd; Comm Volntr; Emplmnt; Mus Clb; Chr; SP/M/VS; Cr Ctry (J L); Track (J); National Junior Honor Society; NH All-State Choir - Fr / Soph Years; Voice Major / Vocal Performance; Chemistry

MILLER, SAMANTHA; HUDSON, NH; ALVIRNE HS; (SO); Bnd; Mch Bnd; Marine Biology; Auburn U Alabama; U of Massachusetts

MOORE, JENNIFER; DUNBARTON, NH; GOFFSTOWN AREA HS; (FR); Hnr Roll; Psychology; Drama/Theatre; Oxford U; NYC

MOQUIN, JUSTINE; CONCORD, NH; CONCORD HS; Hnr Roll; St of Mnth; Drma Clb; SP/M/VS; Sch Ppr (E); Award for Essay About US Flag; Drama Club; Theatre; Interior Design

MORRIS, SHAWN; MANCHESTER, NH; TRINITY HS; (SO); Gov Hnr Prg; Hi Hnr Roll; Hnr Roll; Nat Hon Sy; Nat Ldrshp Svc; Otst Ac Ach Awd; Pres Sch; Yth Ldrshp Prog; Comm Volntr; Chrch Yth Grp; DARE; Mth Clb/Tm; NYLC; P to P St Amb Prg; Prom Com; Bskball (J); Ftball (V); Track (V); Cl Off (T); Stu Cncl (R); National Honor Society; National Jr. Leadership Conference; Doctor; Boston College; Duke

MOSKOWITZ, JEREMY D; NASHUA, NH; NASHUA HS NORTH; (SO); Hi Hnr Roll; Nat Hon Sy; Pres Sch; WWAHSS; Hosp Aide; Chess; Emplmnt; Mth Clb/Tm; Sccr (VJ); Tennis; CR (R); Soccer Referee / Reach Program; Interact Club / Chess Club; Engineering; Biomedicine; Brown U; U of Pennsylvania

MURATOVA, KATIA; HANOVER, NH; HANOVER HS; (JR); Hi Hnr Roll; Comm Volntr; Chrch Yth Grp; Drma Clb; Emplmnt; JSA; Mod UN; Tchrs Aide; SP/M/VS; Ice Sktg; Skiing; Gold Medal At Green Mountain Open (Ice Skating); Treasurer of Model UN and JSA; International Relations; International Business; Columbia U; Dartmouth College

MURPHY, SARAH E; DEERFIELD, NH; THE DERRYFIELD SCH; (SR); DAR; Hi Hnr Roll; Hnr Roll; WWAHSS; Yth Ldrshp Prog; Comm Volntr; Peer Tut/Med; Chrch Yth Grp; Emplmnt; Key Club; Cr Ctry (V L); Lcrsse (VJ L); Wt Lftg; Sch Ppr (E, R); Conservation Club; Sunday School Teacher; Business Management; Elementary/Special Education; American U; U of New Hampshire

NAROLAN, SARAH; HILLSBORO, NH; HILLSBORO DEERING HS; (JR); Hnr Roll; DECA; Emplmnt; Mth Clb/Tm; Cl Off (R); Business Management; Fashion Merchandising; Johnson and Wales U; Southern New Hampshire U

NAVARRO, RYAN; NASHUA, NH; NASHUA HS NORTH; (SO); Hi Hnr Roll; Nat Hon Sy; Sci Fairs; Track (V); Nashua City of Basketball; National History Award; Computer Science; Worcester Polytech Institute; NH Vo Tech

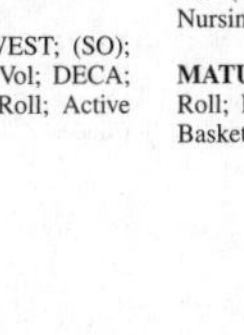

Lawton, Heather L
Manchester West
Bedford, NH

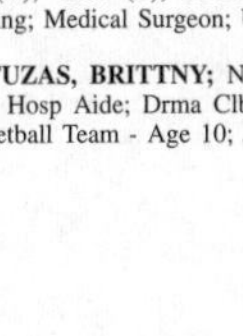

Kocdal, Marial
Concord, NH

National
Honor Roll
Spring 2005

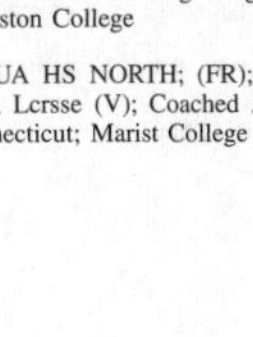

Kaur, Kulbir
Portsmouth HS
Portsmouth, NH

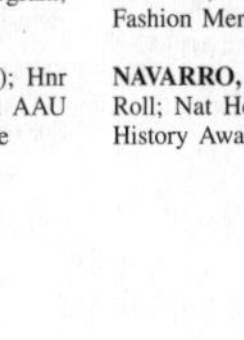

Merlino, Nancy
Alvirne HS
Hudson, NH

NELSON, ERIK; ROCHESTER, NH; (MS); Hi Hnr Roll; Perf Att; Yth Ldrshp Prog; Comm Volntr; Tchrs Aide; Bnd; Skiing; Sccr; Adv Cncl (R)

NEWSOM, SAM; NASHUA, NH; NASHUA HS; (JR); Hi Hnr Roll; Hnr Roll; Nat Hon Sy; Pres Sch; WWAHSS; Comm Volntr; German Clb; Work Part-Time At Sears; Engineering; Construction; Dartmouth College; Wentworth Institute of Tech

NOFTLE, JANELLE; GILMANTON IW, NH; GILFORD HS; (SO); Ctznshp Aw; Hi Hnr Roll; Hnr Roll; Pres Ac Ftns Aw; St of Mnth; DARE; Pep Squd; Scouts; Vsity Clb; German Clb; Vsy Clb (V); Vllyball (J); Youth and Government; Law; Suffolk Law

O'CONNELL, AMANDA; SANBORNTON, NH; WINNISQUAM REG HS; (FR); Ctznshp Aw; Hnr Roll; WWAHSS; Ntl FFA; Bskball (J)

O'ROURKE, HANNAH; DEERFIELD, NH; CONCORD HS; (JR); 4H Awd; Hi Hnr Roll; Hnr Roll; 4-H; 4-H Member; Nursing; U of NH; Colby Sawyer College

OVERDEPUT, MATHEW; SALEM, NH; SALEM HS; (FR); Hi Hnr Roll; Hnr Roll; Chess; Cmptr Clb; Outdrs Clb

PARNAGIAN, JORDAN; HUDSON, NH; ALVIRNE HS; (SR); Kwnis Aw; St of Mnth; Comm Volntr; Chrch Yth Grp; Key Club; SP/M/VS; Stg Cre; Key Club Member of the Month; Graphic Design; Plymouth State U

PARTRIDGE, DAN; CONCORD, NH; CONCORD HS; (FR); Hi Hnr Roll; Hnr Roll; Nat Hon Sy; Wt Lftg (V); Wrstlg (J); Journalism; Pathology; Dartmouth Hitchcock Med-School; U of New Hampshire

PASTORELLO, ADAM R; HUDSON, NH; ALVIRNE HS; (SO); Hnr Roll; St of Mnth; Comm Volntr; Chess; Cmptr Clb; Mth Clb/Tm; Mus Clb; Bnd; Mch Bnd; Belong to Concert Band & Bronco Backers; Video Game Designer; Computers

PATEL, ANISHA; HUDSON, NH; ALVIRNE HS; (SO); Hnr Roll; Comm Volntr; DECA; SADD; SADD Vice President; DECA Member; Hospitality Services; Business Management; U of New Hampshire; Northeastern U

PERREAULT, STEPHANIE; NASHUA, NH; NASHUA HS; (JR); Law

POIRE, MATT; LACONIA, NH; LACONIA HS; (SO); Hnr Roll; Criminal Law; Criminal Science; U of New Hampshire; Southern New Hampshire U

POLLOCK, JENNIFER; SOMERSWORTH, NH; SOMERSWORTH HS; (SR); Hi Hnr Roll; Nat Hon Sy; Otst Ac Ach Awd; USAA; Peer Tut/Med; Spec Olymp Vol; Emplmnt; Mth Clb/Tm; Prom Com; Vsity Clb; Tennis (V); Cl Off (T); Stu Cncl (R); Honorary Member of the Somersworth Woman's Club; National Merit Special Scholarship; Chemistry Major; U of New Hampshire

PRATTE, ASHLEY; MANCHESTER, NH; TRINITY HS; (SO); Hi Hnr Roll; Hnr Roll; MVP; Nat Hon Sy; Perf Att; Pres Sch; Comm Volntr; Peer Tut/Med; Chrch Yth Grp; DARE; Prom Com; Chrldg (VJC); Cr Ctry (V); Scr Kpr (V); Track (V); Adv Cncl (R); Cl Off (P); Stu Cncl (R); CR (P); Yrbk (E); Spirit St Joseph Award; School Service; Adopt-A-Block Project (Community); Forensic Science; Criminal Law; Georgetown U; Princeton U

PRATTE, MORGAN; HOOKSETT, NH; MANCHESTER HS WEST; (JR); Hi Hnr Roll; Hnr Roll; Comm Volntr; ArtClub; Drma Clb; Quill & Scroll; Chr; Sch Ppr (R); National Art Honor Society Member; Capoeira (Outside School); Humanities; Art / Art History; U of New Hampshire Durham; College of the Atlantic

QUEEN, ADAM S; HANCOCK, NH; CONTOOCOOK VALLEY REG HS; (JR); Hnr Roll; Private Pilots License; Aviation Flight Operations; Professional Pilot; Daniel Webster College; Purdue U

REYNOLDS, ASHLEY M; TILTON, NH; WINNISQUAM REG HS; (JR); Ctznshp Aw; Hnr Roll; DARE; Emplmnt; Wdwrkg Clb; Chrldg (V); Sftball (V); Physical Therapy; Occupational Therapy; New England College; U of New Hampshire

RINES, SAM; ROCHESTER, NH; PORTSMOUTH CHRISTIAN AC; (SR); Hi Hnr Roll; Hnr Roll; MVP; Nat Hon Sy; Otst Ac Ach Awd; Perf Att; Sci Fairs; WWAHSS; Comm Volntr; Chrch Yth Grp; Drma Clb; Emplmnt; Scouts; SP/M/VS; Stg Cre; Sccr (V CL); Track (V); Stu Cncl (R); NHSCA All-Scholastic Team - 2003 / 2004; Granite State Conference - All-Conference / '04; Business; Pre-Law; Georgetown U; Roger Williams U

RIVERA, SONJA M; NEWPORT, NH; NEWPORT HS; (SO); Hi Hnr Roll; Peer Tut/Med; Drma Clb; Emplmnt; FBLA; Mod UN; Tchrs Aide; Acpl Chr; Chr; SP/M/VS; Track (V); Youth and Government Participant; Member of Big Brother/Big Sister; International Business; Communications; Harvard U; Georgetown U

ROBERTS, DAVID E; CONTOOCOOK, NH; HOPKINTON HS; (SO); Hnr Roll; Jr Rot; Comm Volntr; Chrch Yth Grp; Cr Ct Ski (J); Lcrsse (V L); Skiing (V L); Sccr (J); 2005 Ski Jumping Sportsmanship Award; 2004 & 2005 Scholar-Athlete Award; Civil Engineering; Bio, Materials, Chemical Engineering; Clarkson U; U of Colorado At Boulder

RODRIGUE, KATHLEEN S; W STEWARTSTWN, NH; CANAAN MEMORIAL HS; (JR); Hi Hnr Roll; Hnr Roll; Nat Hon Sy; WWAHSS; Yth Ldrshp Prog; Comm Volntr; Drma Clb; Emplmnt; Key Club; Outdrs Clb; Prom Com; French Clb; Chr; Bskball (VJC); Sccr (VJ); Sftball (V); Cl Off (P, R); Stu Cncl (T); Leader and Recorder on a Restoration Panel; Volunteered at a Women's Crisis Center; Forensic Science; Wildlife Biology; Keystone; U of New Haven

ROY, JENNIFER; BERLIN, NH; BERLIN HS; (SR); Hi Hnr Roll; Hnr Roll; MVP; Nat Hon Sy; Nat Stu Ath Day Aw; Otst Ac Ach Awd; WWAHSS; Yth Ldrshp Prog; Comm Volntr; Hosp Aide; Peer Tut/Med; Emplmnt; Key Club; Prom Com; Quiz Bowl; SADD; Vsity Clb; Bnd; Bskball (V CL); Fld Hky (V L); Sftball (V CL); Cl Off (R); Stu Cncl (R); CR (R); Yrbk (R, P); Social Work; U of New Hampshire

RUEL, DEVON L; ERROL, NH; COLEBROOK AC; (SO); 4H Awd; Ctznshp Aw; Hi Hnr Roll; Hnr Roll; Kwnis Aw; Otst Ac Ach Awd; Pres Sch; Sci Fairs; WWAHSS; Yth Ldrshp Prog; Comm Volntr; 4-H; Drma Clb; Emplmnt; Fr of Library; HO'Br Yth Ldrshp; Key Club; NYLC; Quiz Bowl; Dnce; SP/M/VS; Cl Off (T); Hugh O'Brian Youth Leadership Rep; Eighth Grade Presidential Scholar; Marine Biology; Nursing; U of Maine Orono; Keene State College

RUSSELL, GINA; HOOKSETT, NH; MANCHESTER CTRL HS; (FR); Hi Hnr Roll; Otst Ac Ach Awd; Peer Tut/Med; Red Cr Aide; Chrch Yth Grp; Stu Cncl (R); Robotics (CHAOS); Sports & Recreational Management; Mass Communication; Franklin Pierce of New Hampshire; New York U

SALTMARSH, DEANNA; WOLFEBORO, NH; KINGSWOOD REG HS; (JR); Hi Hnr Roll; Nat Hon Sy; Otst Ac Ach Awd; St of Mnth; WWAHSS; Comm Volntr; Key Club; Cr Ctry (V CL); Cr Ct Ski (V CL); Track (V CL); CR (R); Sch Ppr (E)

SALVATI, JULIA; NEW BOSTON, NH; GOFFSTOWN AREA HS; (FR); Hi Hnr Roll; Otst Ac Ach Awd; Pres Sch; Comm Volntr; Drma Clb; SP/M/VS; Stg Cre; Writing; English Education; Elmira College N.Y.; St. Anselm's College N.H

SAVAGE, TROY A; GROVETON, NH; GROVETON HS; (FR); Hnr Roll; St of Mnth; Peer Tut/Med; Mth Clb/Tm; Scouts; SP/M/VS; Stu Cncl (T); Graphic Design; Westwood

SCANGAS, JILLIAN D; DURHAM, NH; OYSTER RIVER HS; (JR); F Lan Hn Soc; Gov Hnr Prg; Hi Hnr Roll; Yth Ldrshp Prog; Comm Volntr; DARE; Emplmnt; Spanish Clb; Acpl Chr; Ch Chr; Bskball (V L); National Spanish Honors Society; Ignite Leadership Academy; Duke U; Fordham U

SCHMIDT, LISANNE; GRANTHAM, NH; LEBANON HS; (SO); Hnr Roll; Mus Clb; Quiz Bowl; Vsity Clb; Acpl Chr; Chr; Cr Ct Ski (J); Golf (V L); Law; Business; UNC Chapel Hill; Wake Forest U

SCHNEIDER, PHIL; CLAREMONT, NH; STEVENS HS; (SO); Hi Hnr Roll; WWAHSS; Comm Volntr; Key Club; Quiz Bowl; Sccr (J); Stu Cncl; Lacrosse After School Program; Engineering

SCHWALBE, JADE; MERRIMACK, NH; MERRIMACK HS; (JR); Hi Hnr Roll; Hnr Roll; Bnd; Jzz Bnd; Mch Bnd; Pep Bnd; Gmnstcs (V CL); Swmg (V L)

SCOTT, TITUS; DUNBARTON, NH; TRINITY CHRISTIAN SCH; (SR); Hi Hnr Roll; Hnr Roll; Otst Ac Ach Awd; Perf Att; WWAHSS; Chrch Yth Grp; Civil Air Pat; Chr; Drl Tm; Orch; SP/M/VS; Bskball (V L); Sccr (V CL); Cl Off (V); Yrbk (E, R, P); Science Education; Northland Baptist Bible College

SHI, QINGWEN; BEDFORD, NH; NMH; (JR); Hi Hnr Roll; Hnr Roll; Amnsty Intl; Comm Volntr; Mth Clb/Tm; Chr; SP/M/VS; Cr Ctry (J); Cr Ct Ski (V); Swmg (J); Track (J); Physics; Neurology; Columbia U; Harvard U

SILVA, KEVIN J; HUDSON, NH; ALVIRNE HS; (SO); Hnr Roll; Comm Volntr; Spec Olymp Vol; Chrch Yth Grp; Jr Ach; Ftball (V); Lcrsse; Track (V); Wrstlg (V L); Athletic Training Degree; Certified Personal Trainer; Springfield College; Merrimack College

SIMON, DAVID J; LITTLETON, NH; LITTLETON SR HS; (SO); Hi Hnr Roll; MVP; St of Mnth; Chrch Yth Grp; Bnd; Jzz Bnd; Mch Bnd; Pep Bnd; Bsball (V L); Bskball (V); Sccr (V); Cl Off (R); Stu Cncl (T); CR (R); Philadelphia Biblical U; Liberty U

SMART, KATIE; MILTON, NH; NUTE JR/SR HS; (FR); Hnr Roll; WWAHSS; Comm Volntr; Chrch Yth Grp; Civil Air Pat; Stu Cncl (V); Sch Ppr (R); Daniel Webster College-Nashua NH

SMITH, ERIC; BERLIN, NH; (SR); Hi Hnr Roll; Nat Hon Sy; WWAHSS; Yth Ldrshp Prog; Comm Volntr; Red Cr Aide; Emplmnt; Key Club; Vsity Clb; Golf; Ice Sktg; Rlr Hky; Tennis; Accepted to Dartmouth Health Camp; Plan to Be a Physician's Assistant; U of New England

SOUTHWORTH, HANNAH; DURHAM, NH; OYSTER RIVER HS; (SO); Hi Hnr Roll; Nat Hon Sy; St of Mnth; Comm Volntr; Peer Tut/Med; Spanish Clb; Dnce; Jzz Bnd; SP/M/VS; Stu Cncl (R); Crew/Rowing, Jazz and Plays Trumpet Hip Hop Dance; Graphic Design/Visual Arts; Dance; Lewis and Clark College; U of California

SOUZA, HEMMILLY; SOUTH NASHUA, NH; MERRIMACK HS; (JR); Hi Hnr Roll; Hnr Roll; WWAHSS; Chrch Yth Grp; Chr; Ch Chr; SP/M/VS; Piano Player; Pre-Med; Psychology; Pensacola Christian College

SPRINKLE, LAURA; NASHUA, NH; NASHUA HS NORTH; (SO); Hi Hnr Roll; Hnr Roll; Otst Ac Ach Awd; Yth Ldrshp Prog; Comm Volntr; Spec Olymp Vol; Drma Clb; Emplmnt; P to P St Amb Prg; SP/M/VS; Fld Hky (V L); Swmg (V L); Track (V); Lit Mag (R); Yrbk (E); Non-School Swim Team Lane Captain; International Business; Spanish; Columbia U; New York U

STEARNS, SAMANTHA; LITTLETON, NH; LITTLETON SR HS; (JR); Hi Hnr Roll; Nat Hon Sy; Comm Volntr; Hosp Aide; Peer Tut/Med; DECA; P to P St Amb Prg; Prom Com; Bnd; Mch Bnd; Pep Bnd; Chrldg (V); Cr Ctry (V); Fld Hky (J); Tennis (V); Excellence in English Award (School); Excellence in Spanish Award (School); International Affairs; Pre-Med-Ob/Gyn; United States Coast Guard Academy; Dartmouth College

STEWART, ELIZABETH; HUDSON, NH; ALVIRNE HS; (SO); Hi Hnr Roll; Hnr Roll; Chr; Chrldg (J); Tennis (V); Stu Cncl (R); Medical School / Pediatric Oncology; Dartmouth University; Columbia University

STRAIGHT, ASHLEY; HUDSON, NH; BISHOP GUERTIN HS; (JR); All Am Sch; Hi Hnr Roll; Nat Hon Sy; Otst Ac Ach Awd; Perf Att; Pres Ac Ftns Aw; Pres Sch; St of Mnth; Comm Volntr; Peer Tut/Med; Emplmnt; P to P St Amb Prg; Svce Clb; Tchrs Aide; Spanish Clb; Bskball (J); Scr Kpr (V); Sccr (J); Hand Bell Choir; Coach of Basketball; Holy Cross College

STREBEL, SCOTT A; GREENLAND, NH; GREENLAND CTRL SCH; (MS); 4H Awd; Gov Hnr Prg; Hi Hnr Roll; Perf Att; Comm Volntr; 4-H; Chess; Chrch Yth Grp; DARE; Scouts; Cr Ctry; Skiing; Sccr; Track; Sch Ppr (E); Aerospace Engineering

STUBBLEFIELD, MEGAN; NASHUA, NH; NASHUA HS NORTH; (SO); F Lan Hn Soc; Hi Hnr Roll; Hnr Roll; Perf Att; Comm Volntr; ArtClub; Bnd; Chr; SP/M/VS; Sch Ppr (R); Art Achievement Award; The President's Award for Educational Excellence; Medical Illustration; Creative Writing; Dartmouth; The U of Vermont

SUNDMAN, THOMAS; LITTLETON, NH; LITTLETON SR HS; (JR); Hi Hnr Roll; Nat Hon Sy; Pres Ac Ftns Aw; Comm Volntr; Hosp Aide; Drma Clb; Bnd; Pep Bnd; SP/M/VS; Tennis (V L); Cl Off (T); Sch Ppr (E); Mechanical Engineering; Computer Science; Northeastern U; Rensselaer Polytechnic Institute

SURETTE, HOLLY L; NASHUA, NH; NASHUA HS NORTH; (SO); Hnr Roll; Comm Volntr; Cl Off (P); Stu Cncl (V); Nominee for National Junior Honor Society; Citation of Distinction of Honors; Advertising; Psychology; U of New Hampshire; U of Massachusetts

TAYLOR, ANNA; GLEN, NH; KENNETT HS; (FR); Emplmnt; Key Club; Chr; Dnce; Track (V); French Honors Society

TENNEY, DUSTIN E J; CLAREMONT, NH; STEVENS HS; (SO); Ctznshp Aw; Hi Hnr Roll; Hnr Roll; Mas Aw; MVP; Otst Ac Ach Awd; St of Mnth; WWAHSS; Comm Volntr; Peer Tut/Med; Emplmnt; Key Club; Mod UN; Quiz Bowl; SADD; SP/M/VS; Bskball (V L); Golf (V L); Tennis (V L); CR (R); Lit Mag (R); Sch Ppr (R); Organized (On My Own) to Bring the "Harlem Rockets" to Our School; Criminal Justice Attorney or FBI Agent; Political Science; Wake Forrest U; Duke U

TREMBLAY, ADAM; LEBANON, NH; LEBANON HS; (FR); Hnr Roll; Comm Volntr; Chess; Ftball (V); Ice Hky (J); Lcrsse (V); Wt Lftg (J); Assistant Coach Lacrosse / Hockey; Admiral; Annapolis Naval Academy

TSANG, SABRINA H; MANCHESTER, NH; MANCHESTER HS WEST; (JR); F Lan Hn Soc; Hi Hnr Roll; Jr Mshl; Nat Hon Sy; St of Mnth; WWAHSS; Peer Tut/Med; Red Cr Aide; Jr Cls League; Key Club; Mth Clb/Tm; Quill & Scroll; Latin Clb; Orch; Sch Ppr (R); Book Awards (Cornell); Science Honoring Award; Biology; Psychology; Tufts U; Cornell U

UX, GREG; NASHUA, NH; NASHUA HS SOUTH; (SO); Hi Hnr Roll; Hnr Roll; MVP; Perf Att; Comm Volntr; Emplmnt; Scouts; Ftball (V); Track (V L); CR (R); Aerospace Engineering; U of Michigan At Ann Arbor; Boston College

Surette, Holly L
Nashua HS North
Nashua, NH

National
Honor Roll
Spring 2005

Pratte, Ashley
Trinity HS
Manchester, NH

VAILLANCOURT, EMMA E; PORTSMOUTH, NH; PORTSMOUTH HS; (SO); Hi Hnr Roll; Spec Olymp Vol; Bskball (V); Sccr (V); Track (V); American Legion Award; Athletic Scholar Award

VAN COPPENOLLE, CHARLES R; RAYMOND, NH; RAYMOND HS; (JR); Hnr Roll; Otst Ac Ach Awd; Pres Ac Ftns Aw; USAA; WWAHSS; Comm Volntr; Mth Clb/Tm; Computer Sciences; Film Production

VIOLA, MARISSA G; BEDFORD, NH; MANCHESTER WEST HS; (JR); F Lan Hn Soc; Gov Hnr Prg; Hi Hnr Roll; Kwnis Aw; Nat Hon Sy; Nat Ldrshp Svc; Sci/Math Olympn; WWAHSS; Yth Ldrshp Prog; Comm Volntr; Peer Tut/Med; Red Cr Aide; Key Club; Mth Clb/Tm; Quill & Scroll; Bnd; Drl Tm; Mch Bnd; Lcrsse (V); Track (V); CR (R); Sch Ppr (E); Nacky Loeb School of Writing, Red Cross Blood Drive Organizer for My Sister Who Had Spinal Surgery; M.D., D.D.S or J.D.; Northwestern U, Dartmouth College, Rice U; U of Notre Dame

VIVENZIO, ADRIANNE; HINSDALE, NH; HINSDALE HS; (MS); Ctznshp Aw; Hi Hnr Roll; Hnr Roll; Pres Sch; Yth Ldrshp Prog; Chrch Yth Grp; DARE; Drma Clb; Outdrs Clb; Pep Squd; P to P St Amb Prg; Photog; Scouts; Clr Grd; Dnce; SP/M/VS; Bskball (J); Chrldng (VJ); Fld Hky (VJ); Scr Kpr (J); Sftball (J); Cl Off (P); Stu Cncl (P); Veterinary Medicine; Law; Harvard Law School; Princeton

VO, TRANG T; NASHUA, NH; NASHUA HS NORTH; (SO); Hi Hnr Roll; Hnr Roll; Nat Hon Sy; Otst Ac Ach Awd; Perf Att; Pres Ac Ftns Aw; Comm Volntr; Mth Clb/Tm; Chr; Bskball (J); Track (V); Vllyball (J); National Jr. Honor Society; Ran for Jr. Vice President; Math and Science; Become a General Dentist; Boston College; Brown U

WEBB, BLAIN; MILFORD, NH; HOLLIS-BROOKLINE HS; (JR); Hi Hnr Roll; Hnr Roll; MVP; ArtClub; Emplmnt; Lib Aide; Photog; Bskball (J); Fld Hky (V); Yrbk (P); Published Many Poems; Creative Writing; Journalism; Eckerd College; Northeastern U

WELCH, RILEY; NORTHFIELD, NH; WINNISQUAM REG HS; (FR); Ctznshp Aw; Hi Hnr Roll; Hnr Roll; Peer Tut/Med; Drma Clb; Ntl FFA; Stg Cre; Track (V); Leadership Camps 6, 7, 8; Discovery Degree; Engineering; E.C.A.T.; UNH

WHITNEY, ABBY; HUDSON, NH; ALVIRNE HS; (FR); Hnr Roll; WWAHSS; FBLA; Key Club; Sccr (J L); Track (V); Architecture; Business

WHITNEY, ALYSSA; HUDSON, NH; ALVIRNE HS; (JR); WWAHSS; Comm Volntr; Emplmnt; FBLA; Jr Ach; Key Club; Bnd; Dnce; Mch Bnd; SP/M/VS; Tennis (V); Cl Off (T); Business Management / Translation; Sports Team / Complex Management; Bentley College; Emerson College

WHITNEY, JOSH; NASHUA, NH; NASHUA HS NORTH; (FR); Hnr Roll; Nat Mrt LOC; Comm Volntr; ArtClub; Emplmnt; Off Aide; Wdwrkg Clb; Geography Bee Finalist; Bronze Medalist - State Art Competition; Engineering; Aviation; West Point Military Academy; Embry-Riddle Aeronautical U

WILSON, KRISTINA; HUDSON, NH; ALVIRNE HS; (SO); Hi Hnr Roll; Hnr Roll; MVP; Comm Volntr; FBLA; Mth Clb/Tm; SADD; Sftball (J); Vllyball (V C); Yrbk (R); Finance; Biotechnology; Bentley College; Northeastern U

WOJEWODA, JEFFREY; LONDONDERRY, NH; LONDONDERRY HS; (FR); Hi Hnr Roll; WWAHSS; Spec Olymp Vol; Bsball (J); Bskball (J); Self Taught Guitar; Engineering; Business; Stanford U; Harvard U

WOODBURY IV, PHILIP A; NASHUA, NH; NASHUA HS NORTH; (JR); Hnr Roll; Hosp Aide; Voc Ind Clb Am; Ice Hky (J); Candy Striper 4 Yrs.; Physician's Assistant; Northeastern, Springfield College; Quinnipiac U, U of New England

WYATT, ALEXANDER; NEW DURHAM, NH; KINGSWOOD REG HS; (SO); Hi Hnr Roll; Nat Hon Sy; WWAHSS; Comm Volntr; Drma Clb; Emplmnt; Key Club; Sci Clb; Tchrs Aide; Clb; Bnd; Pep Bnd; SP/M/VS; Stg Cre; Cr Ct Ski (V L); Tennis (V); Cl Off (P); Law/Political Science; Education/Psychology; Rice U; Yale U

XIA, YIYI; HUDSON, NH; ALVIRNE HS; (JR); Hi Hnr Roll; Nat Hon Sy; Perf Att; Valdctrian; WWAHSS; Yth Ldrshp Prog; FBLA; Jr Ach; Key Club; Mth Clb/Tm; Mod UN; Quiz Bowl; Vsity Clb; Tennis (V CL); Track (J); Cl Off (T); CR (R); Academic Decathlon; Piano Player; Business Management; Auditing

YOUNKINS, KATHRYN; LISBON, NH; LISBON REG; (SO); Hi Hnr Roll; WWAHSS; Yth Ldrshp Prog; French Clb; Bskball (V L); Sccr (V L); Cl Off (P); District Attorney; New York U; Columbia

Whitney, Josh
Nashua HS North
Nashua, NH

National Honor Roll Spring 2005

Viola, Marissa G
Manchester West HS
Bedford, NH

New Jersey

ABALOS, CAITLIN; ISELIN, NJ; JOHN F. KENNEDY MEMORIAL; (FR); Hnr Roll; WWAHSS; Key Club; Sccr (J); Sftball (J)

ABDELFATTAH, KAREEM; CARLSTADT, NJ; HENRY P BECTON REG HS; (SR); Hi Hnr Roll; Hnr Roll; Otst Ac Ach Awd; Sci/Math Olympn; ArtClub; Chess; Emplmnt; Photog; Tennis (J); Sch Ppr (R); Photography Club (3 Years); West Point Bridge Design Contest (Top 8%); Business; Engineering, Pharmacology; New Jersey Institute of Technology

ABDULLAH, MAISHA T; TRENTON, NJ; TRENTON CTRL SR HS; (SO); Hnr Roll; Chr; Clr Grd; Mch Bnd; Keystone Leadership Program; Doctorate, Nursing; Bachelor's in Science; Morris Brown College; Alabama State U

ABERMAN, KRYSTAL; NORTHFIELD, NJ; MAINLAND REG HS; (FR); Ctznshp Aw; Hnr Roll; Perf Att; Pres Sch; Scouts; SADD; Fld Hky; Lawyer; Scientist; Harvard U; Princeton U

ABMA, VERONICA; BRICK, NJ; BRICK TWP HS; (SO); Hnr Roll; Otst Ac Ach Awd; Perf Att; Scr Kpr (V); Tennis (J)

ACOSTA, CHRISTOPHER; COLONIA, NJ; COLONIA HS; (JR); Hnr Roll; Nat Hon Sy; St of Mnth; Comm Volntr; Hosp Aide; Peer Tut/Med; Emplmnt; Off Aide; Tchrs Aide; SP/M/VS; Stg Cre; Ftball; Wt Lftg (L); CR (P); Yrbk (R); Medicine; Attorney; Seton Hall U; New York U

ADAMO, JANE; ENGLISHTOWN, NJ; MANALAPAN HS; (JR); F Lan Hn Soc; Hnr Roll; Nat Hon Sy; Otst Ac Ach Awd; Comm Volntr; Spec Olymp Vol; Quill & Scroll; Italian Clb; Lit Mag (E); Excellence in Poetry Award; Enthusiastic Reader Award; Creative Writing; Italian Language; Delaware U; New York U

ADELMAN, SARAH; SUCCASUNNA, NJ; ROXBURY HS; (SO); Hnr Roll; Perf Att; WWAHSS; Comm Volntr; Key Club; Swmg (V); Yrbk (E); Science Major; Villanova U; U of Maryland

AGARWAL, NEHA; FREEHOLD, NJ; FREEHOLD HS; (JR); Gov Hnr Prg; Hi Hnr Roll; Hnr Roll; Nat Hon Sy; Nat Ldrshp Svc; Nat Mrt LOC; Otst Ac Ach Awd; Yth Ldrshp Prog; Comm Volntr; Peer Tut/Med; DARE; Photog; Spanish Clb; Arch; Fld Hky (J); Top 2% of Class; 2330/2400 on New SAT; M.D.; Penn State/Thomas Jefferson U; TCNJ/NJMS

AGNEW, MILAN C; WESTVILLE, NJ; GLOUCESTER CTY INST OF TECH; (JR); Hi Hnr Roll; Hnr Roll; Kwnis Aw; Nat Hon Sy; Nat Ldrshp Svc; WWAHSS; Comm Volntr; Peer Tut/Med; DECA; FBLA; Key Club; Quiz Bowl; Voc Ind Clb Am; Spanish Clb; Dnce; Cl Off (P); Yrbk (P); Junior Dance Company Member; Fellowship to the Alvin Alley American Dance Theatre; Business Administration; Performing Arts: Dance; Fordham U; George Washington U

AGUILERA, CHRISTINE; CLIFTON, NJ; PARAMUS CATHOLIC HS; (JR); F Lan Hn Soc; Nat Hon Sy; WWAHSS; Comm Volntr; Hab For Humty Volntr; Peer Tut/Med; Biology Clb; Chess; DARE; Emplmnt; P to P St Amb Prg; SADD; Spanish Clb; Students Against Violence

AGUIRRE, CLARISSA; BELLEVILLE, NJ; BELLEVILLE HS; (FR); Hnr Roll; Sci Fairs; Hosp Aide; Chrch Yth Grp; DARE; Volunteer at Clara Mass Hospital; Medical Field

AGUTU, LILIAN; JERSEY CITY, NJ; HCST-NORTH HUDSON CTR; (FR); Hnr Roll; Perf Att; Sci Fairs; ArtClub; Cmptr Clb; DARE; Fr of Library; Key Club; Sci Clb; French Clb; Tennis (V); Vllyball (V); Stu Cncl; Yrbk (E); Medicine; Art; New York U; Oxford College

AGYEI, AKOSUA; BROWNS MILLS, NJ; PEMBERTON TOWNSHIP HS; (FR); F Lan Hn Soc; Gov Hnr Prg; Hnr Roll; Nat Hon Sy; Otst Ac Ach Awd; Perf Att; WWAHSS; Yth Ldrshp Prog; Chrch Yth Grp; Bnd; Chr; Ch Chr; Dnce; Bsball; Ftball; Sftball; Tennis; Nursing / BSN; Working with Children

AHERN, KEVIN; SUCCASUNNA, NJ; ROXBURY HS; (FR); Hi Hnr Roll; Comm Volntr; Key Club; Bskball (V); Stu Cncl (R); Basketball Clinic Volunteer; Church Youth Council; Law; Business; U of Pennsylvania; College of William and Mary

AHMED, MAGDY; WILLINGBORO, NJ; WILLINGBORO HS; (FR); Ctznshp Aw; Hi Hnr Roll; Hnr Roll; Nat Hon Sy; St of Mnth; DARE; Mus Clb; Spanish Clb; Bnd; Mch Bnd; Sccr (J); National Junior Honor Society; To Become a Heart Surgeon

AHMED, NAUSHEEN; JERSEY CITY, NJ; DICKINSON HS; (SR); F Lan Hn Soc; Hnr Roll; Nat Hon Sy; Nat Sci Aw; Otst Ac Ach Awd; Perf Att; Sci Fairs; St of Mnth; WWAHSS; Yth Ldrshp Prog; Comm Volntr; Hosp Aide; Red Cr Aide; Key Club; Lib Aide; Mus Clb; Sci Clb; Svce Clb; SADD; Tchrs Aide; Tech Clb; Dnce; Drl Tm; SP/M/VS; Stg Cre; Bdmtn (V); Bskball (V); Chrldg (V); Cyclg (V); Ftball (V); Golf (V); Tennis (V); Cl Off (S); Biology; Pharmacist/Nursing; New Jersey City U; Saint Peter's College

AHMED, NAZNIN; PATERSON, NJ; HARP AC; (SO); Hi Hnr Roll; Perf Att; Pres Sch; Comm Volntr; Peer Tut/Med; Emplmnt; Skiing; Cl Off (P); Stu Cncl (S); Sch Ppr (E); Hoops for Heart Event Organizer; Cardiology; Pharmacy; Johns Hopkins U; Pennsylvania State U

AIYA, UTSAV; SOUTH RIVER, NJ; (JR); Ctznshp Aw; Fut Prb Slvr; Hnr Roll; Nat Hon Sy; Otst Ac Ach Awd; Perf Att; Sci Fairs; St of Mnth; Comm Volntr; Hosp Aide; Spec Olymp Vol; Chess; FTA; JSA; Prom Com; Sci Clb; Wdwrkg Clb; Spanish Clb; Bnd; Bskball (J); Tennis (J); Yrbk (E, P); Law; Medicine; Columbia U

AKINOLA, DAMILOLA; EDISON, NJ; JOHN F STEVENS HS; (SO); Hnr Roll; Yth Ldrshp Prog; Comm Volntr; Pre-Medicine; Journalism; U of Pennsylvania; Cornell U

AKINSANYA, JEMIMA; LANDING, NJ; PARSIPPANY CHRISTIAN SCH; (SO); All Am Sch; Hi Hnr Roll; Sci Fairs; USAA; WWAHSS; Comm Volntr; Chrch Yth Grp; Drma Clb; Emplmnt; Lib Aide; Tchrs Aide; Chr; Ch Chr; Bskball (V CL); Sftball (V); Sch Ppr (R); Ventures Scholar; Science Fair-2nd Place; Physical Therapy; Medicine; Johns Hopkins U; Washington U-St Louis

AKPARANTA, CHRISTINE N; NEWARK, NJ; SCIENCE HS; (SO); Hi Hnr Roll; Hnr Roll; WWAHSS; Drma Clb; Spch Team; SP/M/VS; Stg Cre; I Play the Piano; I Used to Be on a Drill Team.; Obstetrics; Yale; Princeton

AL-AMRANY, HANNY; CLIFTON, NJ; CLIFTON HS; (JR); Ctznshp Aw; Hnr Roll; Comm Volntr; Bskball; Mar Art (V); Wt Lftg; Undercover Police Officer / FBI / CIA; Real Estate; St John's U; Providence U

ALASWAD, ELSA; MONTECLAIR, NJ; MONTCLAIR HS; (JR); Hi Hnr Roll; Nat Hon Sy; Otst Ac Ach Awd; Perf Att; Pres Sch; Sci/Math Olympn; Yth Ldrshp Prog; ArtClub; Chess; Key Club; MuAlphaTh; Mus Clb; Ntl Beta Clb; Quiz Bowl; French Clb; Dnce; Bskball (J); Sccr (V); Track (V L); Yale U; Pratt Institute

ALBANO, NICOLE; MATAWAN, NJ; MATAWAN REG HS; (JR); All Am Sch; F Lan Hn Soc; Hi Hnr Roll; Nat Hon Sy; Peer Tut/Med; Dnce; SP/M/VS; Sccr (V); Yrbk (R); Math Honor Society; Thespian Society / Foreign Language Honor Society; Education; Speech Therapy; Loyola College of Maryland; Seton Hall New Jersey

ALBERTS, CAITLYN; GLASSBORO, NJ; GLASSBORO HS; (SO); 4H Awd; Ctznshp Aw; Hnr Roll; Nat Hon Sy; Perf Att; St of Mnth; Yth Ldrshp Prog; Comm Volntr; Red Cr Aide; Chrch Yth Grp; Drma Clb; Lib Aide; Mus Clb; NYLC; Dnce; Orch; SP/M/VS; Fld Hky; Gmnstcs; Sccr; Sftball; Swmg; Tennis; Stu Cncl (R); Published Poems; Journalism; English

ALCY, JESULA; EAST ORANGE, NJ; EAST ORANGE CAMPUS HS; (SO); F Lan Hn Soc; Hnr Roll; Perf Att; Sci/Math Olympn; St of Mnth; Hosp Aide; Spec Olymp Vol; ArtClub; Cmptr Clb; Drma Clb; Emplmnt; Fr of Library; Mth Clb/Tm; Photog; Tchrs Aide; Bnd; Dnce; Drm Mjr; Jzz Bnd; Bdmtn; Bsball; Bskball; Cyclg; GAA; Gmnstcs; Rqtball; Sccr; Yrbk (P); Doctor or Nurse; Social Worker; Berkeley; Florida Metropolitan U

ALERGANT, BORIS; SADDLE RIVER, NJ; NORTHERN HIGHLANDS REG HS; (SO); Nat Hon Sy; Yth Ldrshp Prog; Comm Volntr; DECA; Fncg (V); 6th Place State-Wide DECA; Finance Bachelor's Degree; Law Master's Degree; Harvard U; Columbia U

ALEXANDER, JESSICA; HEWITT, NJ; WEST MILFORD TWP HS; (JR); Hnr Roll; DECA; Photog; Chrldg (J); Physical Therapy; Culinary; Ramapo Community College; Bergen County Community College

ALEXANDRE, CASSANDRA; ORANGE, NJ; ST MARY OF THE ASSUMPTION HS; (SO); Hnr Roll; WWAHSS; Emplmnt; Drl Tm; Chrldg (V); Stu Cncl (S); CR (R); Psychology; Criminal Justice; William Paterson U; Montclair State U

ALEXANDRE, SAMUEL; EAST ORANGE, NJ; EAST ORANGE CAMPUS HS; (SO); Ctznshp Aw; Hi Hnr Roll; Hnr Roll; Perf Att; St of Mnth; Yth Ldrshp Prog; Comm Volntr; Peer Tut/Med; ArtClub; Chess; Chrch Yth Grp; Dbte Team; Spanish Clb; Ch Chr; SP/M/VS; Bskball (V); Play Piano and Drums; Political Campaign Volunteer; Computer Engineering; Pre-Law; Princeton; New York U

ALFONSO, GEORGINA; JERSEY CITY, NJ; DICKINSON HS; (JR); Otst Ac Ach Awd; St of Mnth; Comm Volntr; Peer Tut/Med; ArtClub; DARE; Drma Clb; FBLA; Mth Clb/Tm; Mus Clb; Schol Bwl; SADD; Acpl Chr; Bnd; Certificate of Achievement; Certificate of Appreciation; Massage Therapy; Nurse (Maternity Ward); Princeton; New Jersey City U

ALFORD JR, WAYNE D; SOMERSET, NJ; FRANKLIN HS; (FR); Perf Att; ArtClub; Chrch Yth Grp; Sci Clb; Future Architects of Tomorrow; R.I.M.E. (Raritan Institute of Minority Engineers); Computer Graphics; Architecture; U of Miami; Howard U

ALLEN, ELIZABETH D; NEWARK, NJ; TECH CAREER CTR; (JR); Hnr Roll; St of Mnth; Comm Volntr; Chr; Belong to HOSA Treasury Position; Allied Health; Yale U; NYU

ALLEN, ELYSE; MARLTON, NJ; CHEROKEE HS; (MS); Hnr Roll; Comm Volntr; Chrch Yth Grp; Bnd; Chr; Ch Chr; Mch Bnd; Church Lector / Church Altar Server; 2nd-8th Grade - Honors English; Broadcasting Journalism; Biology; Assumption College; Boston College

ALMONTE, NABIL; NORTH BERGEN, NJ; AC OF SACRED HEART HS; (JR); Hnr Roll; WWAHSS; Comm Volntr; Peer Tut/Med; Mod UN; French Clb; Dnce; SP/M/VS; Stg Cre; Sccr (V); Yrbk (R); Helped with Fundraisers in School; Business; Behavioral Sciences; Manhattan College

ALMONTE, SALLY; HALEDON, NJ; MANCHESTER REG HS; (JR); Hnr Roll; Perf Att; DARE; Bskball (J); Vllyball (J); Master's Degree; Rutgers U; William Paterson U

ALMONTE, WENDY M; JERSEY CITY, NJ; WILLIAM L DICKINSON HS; (JR); Otst Ac Ach Awd; St of Mnth; Comm Volntr; DARE; Drma Clb; Mus Clb; Business Administration; Education (Grades K-8); Johnson & Whales Rutgers.

ALOISI, JACQLYN; MATAWAN, NJ; OLD BRIDGE HS EAST; (FR); Ctznshp Aw; Hi Hnr Roll; Hnr Roll; Otst Ac Ach Awd; Perf Att; Pres Ac Ftns Aw; Pres Sch; St of Mnth; Comm Volntr; Peer Tut/Med; FBLA; Key Club; Mod UN; Dnce; Lcrsse (J); PP Ftbl; Skiing; Stu Cncl (R); CR (R); Student of the Marking Period in Speech and Drama; PTA Award; Medical School; PTA Award; New York U

AL-OMAISHI, SALAM; TRENTON, NJ; NOTRE DAME HS; (JR); F Lan Hn Soc; Hi Hnr Roll; Hnr Roll; Sci Fairs; Sci/Math Olympn; Comm Volntr; Mth Clb/Tm; Sci Clb; Ftball; High School Leadership Award; 1st Place in Math Team Competition (8th Grd.); Medical Degree; Pharmacy; Rutgers U; Boston College U

ALSTON, JOHN A; PLAINFIELD, NJ; UNION CTY MAGNET HS; (SR); Hnr Roll; WWAHSS; Comm Volntr; Chrch Yth Grp; Prom Com; Bnd; Ch Chr; National Achievement Letter of Commendation; Mini-Med School Participant; Medicine (MD); Music Education; U of Pennsylvania; Duke U

ALSTON, SHALEAH D; EAST ORANGE, NJ; EAST ORANGE CAMPUS 9 HS; (FR); Ctznshp Aw; Hnr Roll; MVP; Nat Hon Sy; Perf Att; Comm Volntr; Svce Clb; Bskball (V); Business Administration; Sports Management; U of Connecticut; Rutgers U

ALTRECHE, TAHELI; JERSEY CITY, NJ; UNIVERSITY AC CHARTER HS; (JR); Perf Att; Pres Sch; WWAHSS; Comm Volntr; Peer Tut/Med; Red Cr Aide; Prom Com; SP/M/VS; CR (R); Social Work; Guidance Counselor; Rutgers U (Newark); New Jersey City U

ALVARADO, CAROLYN; ELIZABETH, NJ; ELIZABETH HS; (JR); Hnr Roll; WWAHSS; Comm Volntr; Dbte Team; Key Club; NtlFrnscLg; Outdrs Clb; Scouts; Sch Ppr (E, R); Yrbk (R); Accounting

ALVARADO, MARISA; FREEHOLD, NJ; FREEHOLD TWP HS; (JR); Hnr Roll; Nat Hon Sy; Perf Att; Comm Volntr; Chrch Yth Grp; Sch Ppr (R, P); Winner-Halloween Window Painting Contest; Arts/Graphic Design; Animation; Georgian Court U; Rutgers U

ALVAREZ, SEBASTIAN; ROSELLE, NJ; ABRAHAM CLARK HS; (SO); Hnr Roll; Nat Hon Sy; Cmptr Clb; DARE; Sccr (J); CR (R); Intergenerational Day Associate - Volunteer; Completed Course Science at UCC; Forensic Scientist/Criminal Justice; Psychologist

AMADOR, TEENA; MANAHAWKIN, NJ; SOUTHERN REG HS; (SO); Hnr Roll; Nat Hon Sy; Otst Ac Ach Awd; Comm Volntr; Hab For Humty Volntr; Peer Tut/Med; ArtClub; Drma Clb; Emplmnt; Lib Aide; Mus Clb; Prom Com; Spch Team; Spanish Clb; Chr; SP/M/VS; PP Ftbl (J); Stu Cncl (R); CR (R); French Academic Award; Best Vocal Award; Child Psychologist; Forensic Scientist; Ramapo College; Roanoke U

AMADOR, VANESSA; SUMMIT, NJ; SUMMIT HS; (FR); MVP; Comm Volntr; Spanish Clb; Sftball (J); Vllyball (J)

AMARAL, ANDREIA; NEWARK, NJ; EAST SIDE HS; (SR); Hi Hnr Roll; Portuguese Clb

AMBUBUYOG, JANINE; JERSEY CITY, NJ; AC ST ALOYSIUS HS; (SO); Hnr Roll; Nat Hon Sy; Perf Att; Yth Ldrshp Prog; Comm Volntr; DARE; Pep Squd; P to P St Amb Prg; Ch Chr; Dnce; Pep Bnd; Tennis; Track; Cl Off (V); Stu Cncl; President's Education Award; Nursing; William Paterson U

AMEEN, ALEX; WANAQUE, NJ; LAKELAND REG HS; (JR); Hi Hnr Roll; Hnr Roll; Nat Mrt Semif; St of Mnth; Cr Ctry (V); Track (J); CR (R); Sch Ppr (R); Activity TV Production Club; Sport Winter Track; Chemistry; Mathematics; U of Pennsylvania; Massachusetts Institute of Technology

Alvarez, Sebastian
Abraham Clark HS
Roselle, NJ

Allen, Elyse
Cherokee HS
Marlton, NJ

Alexandre, Samuel
East Orange Campus HS
East Orange, NJ

Alergant, Boris
Northern Highlands Reg HS
Saddle River, NJ

Agutu, Lilian
Hcst-North Hudson Ctr
Jersey City, NJ

Aberman, Krystal
Mainland Reg HS
Northfield, NJ

Abma, Veronica
Brick Twp HS
Brick, NJ

Alexander, Jessica
West Milford Twp HS
Hewitt, NJ

Alford Jr, Wayne D
Franklin HS
Somerset, NJ

Alston, John A
Union Cty Magnet HS
Plainfield, NJ

Alvarado, Marisa
Freehold Twp HS
Freehold, NJ

AMEVOR, TCHAZ; JERSEY CITY, NJ; UNIVERSITY AC CHARTER HS; (JR); Hi Hnr Roll; Hnr Roll; St of Mnth; Comm Volntr; Cr Ctry (V C); Track (V C); National Student Leadership Conf., History Club; National Youth Forum on Medicine, President's Education Award; Genetic Counselor/ Geneticist; U of Pennsylvania; Pennsylvania State U

AMIN, BHAVIN; ISELIN, NJ; JFK MEMORIAL HS; (JR); Hnr Roll; Nat Hon Sy; WWAHSS; Emplmnt; Key Club; Bnd; Jzz Bnd; Mch Bnd; SP/M/VS; Track (J L); Stu Cncl (R); Marching Band-Section Leader; Marching Band-Secretary & Treasurer; Psychology-PhD; Rutgers U; Boston U

AMMIRATA, JENNIFER; CALDWELL, NJ; JAMES CALDWELL HS; (SR); Hi Hnr Roll; Hnr Roll; Comm Volntr; Emplmnt; Pep Squd; Bnd; Pep Bnd; Gymnastics (Not in School); Cheerleading (Not in School); Physical Therapy; Sports Medicine; Elizabethtown College; Ithaca College

AMODIA, FELIZ M C; EGG HARBOR TOWNSHIP, NJ; EGG HARBOR TOWNSHIP HS; (JR); WWAHSS; Key Club; Photog; Scouts; SADD; Nursing; Veterinarian

AMORIM, MARLENE; HARRISON, NJ; HARRISON HS; (JR); Hnr Roll; Nat Hon Sy; St of Mnth; Yth Ldrshp Prog; Comm Volntr; Peer Tut/Med; Drma Clb; Scouts; Chr; Dnce; SP/M/VS; Peer Leader Member; Vet; Actress/ Musician; New York U; Howard U

ANDERSON, ALICIA M; JERSEY CITY, NJ; AC ST ALOYSIUS HS; (JR); Pres Ac Ftns Aw; WWAHSS; Hosp Aide; Chrch Yth Grp; Civil Air Pat; Photog; Ch Chr; SP/M/VS; Chrldg (J); Track (J); Sch Ppr (R); Civil Air Patrol; Business Management; Finance; Drexel U; Brown U

ANDERSON, BRENT J; CAPE MAY COURT HOUSE, NJ; MIDDLE TWP HS; (SR); Hi Hnr Roll; Hnr Roll; MVP; Nat Hon Sy; Otst Ac Ach Awd; Pres Ac Ftns Aw; Salutrn; Sci Fairs; Sci/Math Olympn; St of Mnth; Comm Volntr; FBLA; Mth Clb/Tm; Sci Clb; Bsball (V CL); Bskball (V CL); CAL Basketball Team; CAL Baseball Team; Medical; Haverford College; College of NJ

ANDERSON, DENA; RAHWAY, NJ; RAHWAY HS; (SR); Hnr Roll; USAA; WWAHSS; Comm Volntr; Peer Tut/Med; Spec Olymp Vol; Svce Clb; Dnce; SP/M/VS; Nominated - National Young Leaders Conference; Peer Leader; Elementary Education; Rutgers U

ANDERSON, HEIDI L; FRANKLIN, NJ; SUSSEX CTY TECH CHARTER SCH; (SO); Hnr Roll; Chess; Stu Cncl (R); Volunteer At a Pet Shelter

ANDERSON, KERRY J; CAMDEN, NJ; WOODROW WILSON HS; (SR); Hnr Roll; Perf Att; Peer Tut/Med; ArtClub; Bskball (J); Vllyball (C); Rutgers; Coppin State U

ANDERSON, MEGAN I; LUMBERTON, NJ; RANCOCAS VALLEY REG HS3; (FR); Hi Hnr Roll; Hnr Roll; St of Mnth; Key Club; Lib Aide; Off Aide; Scouts; Chr

ANDERSON, SAMANTHA T; SOMERSET, NJ; FRANKLIN HS; (SO); Gov Hnr Prg; Hi Hnr Roll; Hnr Roll; Otst Ac Ach Awd; WWAHSS; Comm Volntr; ArtClub; Photog; Psychology; Biology

ANDERSON, TREVOR J; POINT PLEASANT BEACH, NJ; POINT PLEASANT BEACH HS; (SO); Hi Hnr Roll; WWAHSS; Key Club; Vsity Clb; Sccr (V L); Tennis (J); Track (V L); Stu Cncl (R)

ANDRADE, ROSA M; NEWARK, NJ; SCIENCE HS; (SO); Hi Hnr Roll; Hnr Roll; Otst Ac Ach Awd; Perf Att; Pres Sch; WWAHSS; Comm Volntr; Peer Tut/Med; ArtClub; Chrch Yth Grp; Off Aide; Tchrs Aide; Yrbk (E); President's Education Award; 9th Grade Principal's Honor Roll List; Education; Sciences; Princeton U; Yale U

ANDREINI, MARIANNE; RINGWOOD, NJ; LAKELAND REG HS; (SR); All Am Sch; F Lan Hn Soc; Hi Hnr Roll; Hnr Roll; Nat Hon Sy; Nat Stu Ath Day Aw; WWAHSS; Comm Volntr; Hosp Aide; Emplmnt; Vsity Clb; Bskball (V C); PP Ftbl (V C); Sccr (V C); Track (V C); CR; Pharmacy; Albany College of Pharmacy

ANDREJCISK, CHARLES; CARTERET, NJ; AC-SCI MATH ENG TECH HS; (SO); Hnr Roll; Perf Att; Comm Volntr; Sccr (V); Civil Engineering; Rutgers U; Keane U

ANDREOLI, SAMANTHA; VINELAND, NJ; VINELAND HS NORTH; (SO); Hnr Roll; Perf Att; WWAHSS; Scouts; Sign Clb; Culinary Arts; Psychology

ANGLIN, SASHA; TRENTON, NJ; NOTTINGHAM HS; (JR); Ctznshp Aw; Hi Hnr Roll; Hnr Roll; Otst Ac Ach Awd; Salutrn; WWAHSS; DARE; Drma Clb; Emplmnt; FBLA; Key Club; Chr; Ch Chr; Stg Cre; Chrldg (V); Tennis (V); Track (V); CR (R); Pre-Medicine; Howard U; New York U

ANTOINE, NICHOLAS D; PRINCETON, NJ; PRINCETON HS; (SO); Comm Volntr; ArtClub; Chess; DARE; Dbte Team; Fr of Library; Mth Clb/Tm; Mus Clb; Jzz Bnd; Bsball (J); Cr Ctry (J); Minority Student Achievement Network; Princeton U Prep Program Recipient; Music; Politics; Juilliard School of Music; Columbia U

ANTONUCCI, SAMANTHA; LITTLE SILVER, NJ; RED BANK CATHOLIC HS; (FR); Hi Hnr Roll; Hnr Roll; Perf Att; Comm Volntr; Hab For Humty Volntr; ArtClub; Drma Clb; Emplmnt; FBLA; Spanish Clb; SP/ M/VS; CR (R); Yrbk (P); World History; Theology; Boston College; New York U

APOLAYA, KELLY G; UNION CITY, NJ; AC OF ST ALOYSIUS; (JR); Pres Ac Ftns Aw; Comm Volntr; Chrch Yth Grp; Ch Chr; Cr Ctry (J); Track (J); Mission Club; President's Education Awards Program; Forensic Investigation; John Jay College of Criminal Justice; St Leo U

APONTE, AMANDA; LAKEWOOD, NJ; LAKEWOOD ED INST; (SO); Hnr Roll; Comm Volntr; Emplmnt; Cheerleading & Soccer - Not with School; Honor Chorus / Drama - Not with School; Be with Children & Be a Massage Therapist

AQUINO, LETICIA; UNION CITY, NJ; UNION HILL HS; (SO); All Am Sch; F Lan Hn Soc; Hi Hnr Roll; Hnr Roll; Nat Hon Sy; WWAHSS; Comm Volntr; Peer Tut/Med; DARE; FBLA; Key Club; Mus Clb; Off Aide; Clb; Chr; Dnce; Sftball (J)

ARABITG, MICHAEL; CLARK, NJ; A L JOHNSON; (JR); F Lan Hn Soc; Hnr Roll; Nat Hon Sy; WWAHSS; Emplmnt; Key Club; Sch Ppr (R)

ARDUINI, LISA A; LAWRENCEVILLE, NJ; NOTRE DAME HS; (JR); F Lan Hn Soc; Hi Hnr Roll; Nat Hon Sy; Pres Ac Ftns Aw; WWAHSS; Comm Volntr; Peer Tut/Med; Red Cr Aide; Emplmnt; Key Club; Svce Clb; PP Ftbl (J); Honors Algebra 2 and Trigonometry Academic Award; Latin Academic Award; Business Management; General Business; Drexel U; Rutgers U

ARIF, MOHAMMED; WESTVILLE, NJ; GATEWAY REG HS; (SO); Gov Hnr Prg; Hnr Roll; Nat Hon Sy; Otst Ac Ach Awd; Pres Sch; St of Mnth; Peer Tut/Med; Chess; Fr of Library; Outdrs Clb; Tchrs Aide; Bskball (J); Wt Lftg (J); Superintendent's List; Honor Roll

ARIGORAT, ALBERT; PARLIN, NJ; SAYREVILLE WAR MEMORIAL HS; (JR); F Lan Hn Soc; Hnr Roll; FBLA; Mth Clb/Tm; MuAlphaTh; Prom Com; Sci Clb; Tennis (J); Cl Off (S); Sch Ppr (E); 2005-2006 NJ FBLA State Parliamentarian; Economics; Political Science; Stanford U; U of North Carolina

ARNOLD, JAKE; SICKLERVILLE, NJ; TIMBER CREEK REG HS; (SO); Hnr Roll; Otst Ac Ach Awd; St of Mnth; Chrch Yth Grp; Emplmnt; Stg Cre; Cr Ctry (V L); Track (J); 2nd Degree Black Belt in Goju Karate; Aerospace Engineering; Liberty U; York College

ARNOLD, MICHELE S; NEPTUNE, NJ; NEPTUNE HS; (FR); Hnr Roll; Sci Fairs; Yth Ldrshp Prog; Bskball (VJ); State Finalist in NAM Pageant; Certified in First Aid and CPR; Business; Interior Design; LSU; North Carolina U

ARNTZENIUS, MICHAEL R; PRINCETON, NJ; PRINCETON HS; (SO); Hab For Humty Volntr; Peer Tut/Med; Mth Clb/Tm; Orch; Gents Leadership Award; Mathletes / Team; Computer Science; Physics; California Institute of Technology; Massachusetts Institute of Technology

AROTSKY, LUBA; VOORHEES, NJ; EASTERN HS; (JR); Hnr Roll; Comm Volntr; DARE; Dnce; Dance Awards; Biochemist; Management; Rider U; The College of New Jersey

ARRISICATO, ROSALIA; OLD BRIDGE, NJ; OLD BRIDGE HS WEST; (SR); Hnr Roll; St of Mnth; Yth Ldrshp Prog; Peer Tut/Med; Italian Clb; Dnce; Pep Bnd; Sftball; Cosmetology License; Business Administration; Katherine Gibbs-Piscataway NJ

ARSCOTT, MUBIYNA; EAST ORANGE, NJ; EAST ORANGE CAMPUS 9 HS; (FR); Hi Hnr Roll; Hnr Roll; Pres Sch; Comm Volntr; Peer Tut/Med; ArtClub; Mus Clb; Quiz Bowl; Schol Bwl; Svce Clb; Wdwrkg Clb; Chr; SP/ M/VS; PhD in Sports Medicine; Johns Hopkins U; Seton Hall U

ARSHAD, FAIZA; JERSEY CITY, NJ; DICKINSON HS; (JR); Hnr Roll; Comm Volntr; PAKISTANI Clb; Volunteer Work; Medical; Hunter College

ARTZ-GRADZICKYJ, TRAVIS; BAYONNE, NJ; BAYONNE HS; (SO); All Am Sch; Fut Prb Slvr; Hnr Roll; St of Mnth; WWAHSS; Drma Clb; Mus Clb; Quiz Bowl; Schol Bwl; Sci Clb; Bnd; Chr; Dnce; SP/M/VS; Stu Cncl (R); Nomination for Papermill Playhouse; All Boy's Choir; Speech Therapist; Musical Theatre Major; New York U; Montclair U

ASHER, MITSU; TURNERSVILLE, NJ; WASHINGTON TWP HS; (SO); Hi Hnr Roll; Hnr Roll; St of Mnth; Peer Tut/Med; Spec Olymp Vol; DECA; Mth Clb/Tm; SP/M/VS; Tennis (J); Track (J); Stu Cncl; Volunteer in Interact Club Events, Project 540 Leadership Team; 1 Yr Ahead in Math Class; Business and Management; Finance; U of Pennsylvania; New York U, American U

ATLAS, FAZIL; PATERSON, NJ; (SR); Ctznshp Aw; Hnr Roll; Structural Engineering; Architecture; Rutgers College Rutgers U

AUGUSTINE, JOE; BERGENFIELD, NJ; BERGENFIELD HS; (SO); Hi Hnr Roll; Hnr Roll; St of Mnth; Dbte Team; Anatomy; Microbiology

AUMACK, JESSICA; EATONTOWN, NJ; MONMOUTH REG HS; (SO); Hi Hnr Roll; WWAHSS; Hosp Aide; Emplmnt; Key Club; Bnd; Chr; SP/M/VS; Chrldg (V L); Sftball (J); Stu Cncl (R); CR (R); Support the Troops Club; Spanish Honor Society; Pediatrics; Radiology

AVECILLAS, ALIXON; NEWARK, NJ; QUEEN OF PEACE HS; (SO); Hnr Roll; Accounting; Psychology; Rutgers U; Seton Hall

AVENDANO, ANDREW; GUTTENBERG, NJ; (JR); Hnr Roll; WWAHSS; Yth Ldrshp Prog; ArtClub; Key Club; Scouts; Track (J); Wrstlg (J); Pre-Medicine; Rutgers U; Penn State U

AVICHAL, MISHAL P; JERSEY CITY, NJ; DR RONALD MC NAIR AC HS; (SO); Hnr Roll; Perf Att; Sci Fairs; Valdctrian; Comm Volntr; Peer Tut/ Med; Key Club; Mth Clb/Tm; ROTC; Sci Clb; Clr Grd; Drl Tm; Secretary of Key Club; Member of Asian Unity; Biology (Pre-Med); Chemistry; Johns Hopkins U; The College of New Jersey

AYZENBERG, DIMITRY; KEASBEY, NJ; ACAD-SCI MATH ENG TECH HS; (FR); Hi Hnr Roll; Hnr Roll; Nat Sci Aw; Otst Ac Ach Awd; Chess; Mod UN; Computer Science; Chemistry; Massachusetts Institute of Technology; New Jersey Institute of Technology

BAALS, AMY E; SICKLERVILLE, NJ; WINSLOW TWP HS; (SR); Hnr Roll; Nat Hon Sy; St of Mnth; Comm Volntr; Peer Tut/Med; Svce Clb; German Clb; Orch; Chemical Engineering; Rowan U

BABALOLA, OLAKIITAN; PENNSAUKEN, NJ; PENNSAUKEN HS; (JR); F Lan Hn Soc; Hnr Roll; Nat Hon Sy; USAA; WWAHSS; Yth Ldrshp Prog; Comm Volntr; Red Cr Aide; Emplmnt; Prom Com; Vsity Clb; Track (V); Vllyball (V); Adv Cncl (R); Cl Off (V); Ventures Scholar; Pharmacist; St. John's U; U of the Sciences in Philadelphia

BABUCKE, RYAN; PARSIPPANY, NJ; PARSIPPANY HILLS HS; (SR); F Lan Hn Soc; Comm Volntr; Vsity Clb; German Clb; SP/M/VS; Bskball (V L); International Business; Criminal Justice; Florida Gulf Coast U; Johnson & Wales U

BABYNYUK, IRYNA; RARITAN, NJ; BRIDGEWATER-RARITAN HS; (SR); Hnr Roll; Perf Att; St of Mnth; Cmptr Clb; DARE; Emplmnt; Dnce; Business Administration; Early Childhood; Kean U; Rutgers U

BACHMAN, JENIFER L; BELMAR, NJ; WALL HS; (JR); Hnr Roll; Perf Att; WWAHSS; Comm Volntr; Spec Olymp Vol; DARE; Emplmnt; Key Club; Scouts; SADD; Acpl Chr; Chr; Swg Chr; Elementary Special Education; Green Mountain College; Centenary College

BACKUS, KELLY M; PISCATAWAY, NJ; IMMACULATA AC; (JR); F Lan Hn Soc; Hnr Roll; Nat Hon Sy; Otst Ac Ach Awd; WWAHSS; Comm Volntr; Peer Tut/Med; DARE; Off Aide; Prom Com; SADD; Bnd; Chr; Ch Chr; Clr Grd; Top Scholarship 2003-2004; Spartan Spirit Committees; Musical Theater (BFA); Communications; Catholic U; Ithaca College

BACOLA, KATHERINE; NORTH ARLINGTON, NJ; QUEEN OF PEACE HS; (SO); Hi Hnr Roll; Perf Att; WWAHSS; Chrldg (JC); Track (V); Sophomore Honor Society

BACULIS, JESSICA; WATCHUNG, NJ; WHB HS; (SR); Hnr Roll; WWAHSS; Yth Ldrshp Prog; Comm Volntr; Drma Clb; German Clb; SP/ M/VS; Stg Cre; Cr Ctry (V L); Mar Art (J); Track (V L); Vllyball (J); Winter Track Varsity and Letter Winner; Biology; Pre-Med; Widener U; Cedar Crest College

BADAGLIACCA, JOHN; CEDAR GROVE, NJ; CEDAR GROVE HS; (SO); Hi Hnr Roll; Hnr Roll; Otst Ac Ach Awd; WWAHSS; Comm Volntr; Chrch Yth Grp; Emplmnt; Key Club; Sci Clb; Foreign Clb; Golf (V); Sccr (V); Business; Pass Bar Exam; Boston College; Fordham U

BADIANI, AMY; HIGHTSTOWN, NJ; HIGHTSTOWN HS; (SO); Hi Hnr Roll; Hnr Roll; Otst Ac Ach Awd; Red Cr Aide; FBLA; Clb; Dnce; Tennis (J); Volunteered For Three Summers at Twin Rivers Library (Three Months Total).; Recipient of 2 Indian Culture Certificates in Dance and 3 Trophies for Indian Dance.; Pre-Veterinary Medicine; Biomedical Sciences; Georgetown U, Washington D.C.; Princeton U, New Jersey

BAGAROZZA, ELENA C; OAKHURST, NJ; OCEAN TOWNSHIP HS; (SO); Hnr Roll; WWAHSS; Comm Volntr; Dbte Team; SADD; Vsity Clb; Italian Clb; Swmg (V); Vsy Clb; Acting; Journalism; Broadcast News; U of Delaware; Loyola

BAGLINO, COURTNEY; ALLENDALE, NJ; NORTHERN HIGHLANDS HS; (JR); Hnr Roll; Nat Hon Sy; WWAHSS; Comm Volntr; Peer Tut/Med; Red Cr Aide; Chrch Yth Grp; DECA; Italian Clb; Vllyball (V); 1st Place At DECA State Competition; Captain Junior Varsity Volleyball; Science; Business; Wake Forest U; College of William and Mary

BAHOUTH, CHRIS; HASBROUCK HTS, NJ; BERGEN CATHOLIC HS; (JR); Hi Hnr Roll; Nat Hon Sy; Perf Att; WWAHSS; Chess; Cr Ctry (J); Track (J); Pharmacy; Rutgers U

Artz-Gradzickyj, Travis
Bayonne HS
Bayonne, NJ

Arnold, Jake
Timber Creek Reg HS
Sicklerville, NJ

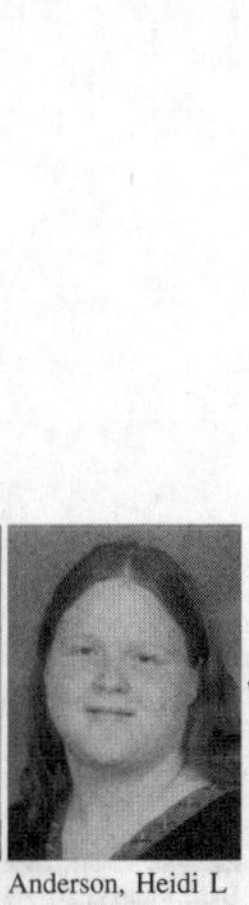
Anderson, Heidi L
Sussex Cty Tech Charter Sch
Franklin, NJ

National
Honor Roll
Spring 2005

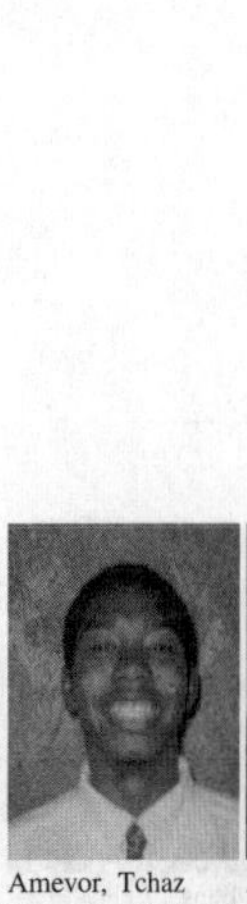
Amevor, Tchaz
University AC Charter HS
Jersey City, NJ

Arrisicato, Rosalia
Old Bridge HS West
Old Bridge, NJ

Augustine, Joe
Bergenfield HS
Bergenfield, NJ

BAILEY, CHARNELLE N; PLAINFIELD, NJ; PLAINFIELD HS; (FR); Nat Hon Sy; Perf Att; Sci Fairs; Chrch Yth Grp; DARE; Ch Chr; Participation in the Laws of Life Essay Contest; Writers Certificate from Youthline USA; Mechanical Engineer (Ph.D); English Teacher (Ph.D); Rutgers State U; Kean U

BAILEY, ELIZABETH A; NEWARK, NJ; PINE FORGE AC; (SO); Ctznshp Aw; Hnr Roll; WWAHSS; Comm Volntr; Chrch Yth Grp; Emplmnt; Lib Aide; Tchrs Aide; Chr; Ch Chr; SP/M/VS; Tennis (V); Cl Off (T); Rutgers U Pre-College Program Summer 2004; Medicine

BAKER, JAMIE; VERNON, NJ; VERNON TOWNSHIP HS; (SO); F Lan Hn Soc; Hi Hnr Roll; Hnr Roll; Perf Att; WWAHSS; Key Club; Mod UN; Sch Ppr; Safety Town; DEER

BAKER, NAZSA S; EAST ORANGE, NJ; EAST ORANGE CAMPUS 9; (FR); Hnr Roll; WWAHSS; Comm Volntr; Mth Clb/Tm; Mch Bnd; Skiing (J); Sccr (J); Sftball (J); Tennis; Wrstlg

BALESTRACCI, DANA; COLONIA, NJ; COLONIA HS; (JR); All Am Sch; Hnr Roll; Nat Hon Sy; Perf Att; Comm Volntr; Peer Tut/Med; Prom Com; Bskball (L); Scr Kpr (L); Track (V); Stu Cncl (R); Yrbk; Interact Club; Football Statistician - Varsity; Psychology; English; Montclair State U; Rider U

BALEVSKI, KRISTINA L; TOTOWA, NJ; PASSAIC VALLEY REG HS; (SR); Hnr Roll; Nat Mrt Sch Recip; Otst Ac Ach Awd; DARE; Emplmnt; FBLA; Scouts; Vsity Clb; Dnce; Chrldg (VJ); PPSqd (J); Employee of the Month (X2); Challenge Award; Bachelor's Degree-Internat'l. Bus.; Bachelor's Degree-Fashion Marketing; Berkeley U

BALL, MELISSA A; BRICK, NJ; BRICK TWP MEMORIAL HS; (SR); Hi Hnr Roll; Hnr Roll; MVP; Pres Ac Ftns Aw; WWAHSS; Comm Volntr; Emplmnt; Svce Clb; Bskball (J); Lcrsse (V C); PP Ftbl; Sccr (VJ); Sftball (L); Elementary Education / Special Education; East Stroudsburg U; Fairleigh Dickinson U

BALLESTEROS, YESENIA; JERSEY CITY, NJ; DICKINSON HS; (JR); Hnr Roll; Perf Att; Comm Volntr; Vsity Clb; Bskball; Hotel Management; Social Work; St Peter's U; Rutgers U (Newark)

BALMAKUND, DEVO; BELLEVILLE, NJ; BELLEVILLE HS; (JR); Hnr Roll; Comm Volntr; Chrch Yth Grp; Mth Clb/Tm; Mus Clb; Prom Com; Quill & Scroll; Ice Hky (V); Forensic Science; Computer Science; Richard Stockton College of New Jersey; Monmouth U

BALTER, EVAN; ROSELAND, NJ; WEST ESSEX REG HS; (JR); Hnr Roll; Pres Ac Ftns Aw; St of Mnth; WWAHSS; Yth Ldrshp Prog; Comm Volntr; Chrch Yth Grp; DARE; Emplmnt; Photog; Tchrs Aide; Wdwrkg Clb; Bnd; Bsball (J L); Bskball (V L); Track (V L); Vllyball (V CL); Yrbk (P); Third Degree Black Belt in Tae-Kwon-Do 11 Years of Study; Finance; Medical Science; Pennsylvania State U; Wake Forest U

BALTZ, EMILY; FLANDERS, NJ; ROXBURY HS; (JR); F Lan Hn Soc; Hi Hnr Roll; Hnr Roll; Nat Hon Sy; Nat Mrt Semif; Comm Volntr; Chrch Yth Grp; Quill & Scroll; Scouts; Vsity Clb; Fld Hky (V L); Lit Mag (R); Sch Ppr (E); English; Communications

BANGS, EVIN; HIGHTSTOWN, NJ; HIGHTSTOWN HS; (JR); Hi Hnr Roll; Chrch Yth Grp; Drl Tm; Track (V L); Track-3rd in Mercer County-Hurdles; Sports Management; Business Management; Florida State U; Montclair State U

BANHALMI, LIZA; EAST BRUNSWICK, NJ; EAST BRUNSWICK HS; (JR); F Lan Hn Soc; Hnr Roll; Otst Ac Ach Awd; Hosp Aide; Peer Tut/Med; Drma Clb; Emplmnt; MuAlphaTh; Prom Com; SP/M/VS; Cr Ctry (VJ); Sccr (J); Track (VJ); Adv Cncl; CR; Sch Ppr (E, R); Outstanding Academic Distinction from UMBC (Honors U in Maryland); Engineering; Economics; Princeton U; New York U

BANISZEWSKI, THOMAS; PASSAIC, NJ; QUEEN OF PEACE HS; (SO); F Lan Hn Soc; Hi Hnr Roll; Perf Att; Salutrn; WWAHSS; Comm Volntr; Peer Tut/Med; DARE; Svce Clb; Tchrs Aide; SP/M/VS; Stu Cncl (R); Sch Ppr (R); Yrbk (R); Lector at Parish / Altar Server; Sophomore Honor Society; Medical Degree; Master's Degree

BAPTISTE, SEAN; DAYTON, NJ; ST JOSEPH'S HS; (JR); MVP; WWAHSS; Clb; Bskball (V C); Home News Student Athlete; 2005 Prime Time Shootout MVP/2005 USA Junior National; Business

BARBARA, GINA M; BEDMINSTER, NJ; BERNARDS HS; (JR); F Lan Hn Soc; Hnr Roll; Comm Volntr; Drma Clb; Emplmnt; Pep Squd; Photog; Vsity Clb; Dnce; SP/M/VS; Chrldg (V L); Fld Hky (J); National Latin Award; Psychology; Nutritionist; Northeastern U; U of Rhode Island

BARBOSA, JULIAN T; ELIZABETH, NJ; ELIZABETH HS; (SO); Hnr Roll; Kwnis Aw; Nat Hon Sy; WWAHSS; Key Club; Outdrs Clb; Sci Clb; Orch; SP/M/VS; Friends of Linden Animal Shelter; Tri-M Music Honor Society; Saint John's College; Princeton U

BARTLETT, NICK; WYCKOFF, NJ; RAMAPO HS; (SO); Yth Ldrshp Prog; Comm Volntr; Stg Cre; Rlr Hky (J); Skiing (J); Underclass Achievement Award; Mechanical Interest

BASH, ASIA M; JERSEY CITY, NJ; UNIVERSITY AC CHARTER SCH; (JR); Bskball (V); Track (V); Sch Ppr (E); National Honor Society; Nursing; Psychology; Rutgers; Morgan State

BASILE, SANDRA; JERSEY CITY, NJ; AC ST ALOYSIUS HS; (JR); Hnr Roll; WWAHSS; Comm Volntr; Emplmnt; SP/M/VS; Multicultural Night; Fashion Show Talent Show; Social Work; All Type of Arts; Rutgers U; Seton Hall U

BASS, KENDELL J; JERSEY CITY, NJ; LINCOLN HS; (SO); Otst Ac Ach Awd; Perf Att; Sci Fairs; Yth Ldrshp Prog; Comm Volntr; Peer Tut/Med; Chess; Chrch Yth Grp; Scouts; Acpl Chr; Chr; Bskball (VJ); Ftball (VJ); Vllyball (VJ); Young Gentleman Club; College Prep.; Law; Business Management; New Jersey City U; Duke U

BASS, SAMANTHA R; MORGANVILLE, NJ; MARLBORO HS; (SO); Hnr Roll; Sci Fairs; Comm Volntr; Emplmnt; JSA; Tmpl Yth Grp; Stg Cre; Swmg (J); Stu Cncl (R); CR (R); Student Exchange Program to Japan; Psychology; History; College of New Jersey; Cornell U

BASSI, NICOLE; NORTH BRUNSWICK, NJ; N BRUNSWICK TWP HS; (JR); Hi Hnr Roll; Hnr Roll; Nat Hon Sy; Pres Sch; Chrch Yth Grp; Ch Chr; Ceramics; Oil Painting; Social Worker; Elementary School Teacher; Rutgers U; Princeton U

BASTARDO, AMANDA M; MANASQUAN, NJ; WALL HS; (JR); Hi Hnr Roll; Hnr Roll; Nat Hon Sy; Yth Ldrshp Prog; Comm Volntr; Peer Tut/Med; FCA; NYLC; SADD; Latin Clb; Bnd; Mch Bnd; Gmnstcs (V L); Swmg (J); National Latin Exam Award; Liberal Arts

BATISTA, ANDREA; CLARK, NJ; ARTHUR L JOHNSON HS; (SO); Hnr Roll; Key Club; Chr; Bskball (J); Sftball; Sch Ppr (P); Karate; Child Development; Law Enforcement

BATTASH, JESSY; EAST WINDSOR, NJ; HIGHTSTOWN HS; (SO); Hnr Roll; Comm Volntr; Emplmnt; NYLC; P to P St Amb Prg; Tmpl Yth Grp; Cr Ctry (V); Karate; Business; Real Estate

BAU, CHRISTINA; HIGHTSTOWN, NJ; HIGHTSTOWN HS; (SO); Hi Hnr Roll; Hnr Roll; Perf Att; Red Cr Aide; Spec Olymp Vol; Biology Clb; Drma Clb; Mus Clb; German Clb; Bnd; Mch Bnd; SP/M/VS; Stg Cre; Arch; Bdmtn; Tennis (J); Yrbk (E); Robotics Team; Ecology Club; Veterinarian; Biology

BAUCOM, GERALD; JERSEY CITY, NJ;; Hnr Roll; Comm Volntr; Hudson County

BAXENDELL, MEGHAN; LANDING, NJ; ROXBURY HS; (FR); Hnr Roll; WWAHSS; Comm Volntr; ArtClub; Drma Clb; Key Club; Mth Clb/Tm; Scouts; Acpl Chr; Chr; SP/M/VS; Stg Cre; Lit Mag (E, R); Silver Award in Girl Scouts; Class Representitive for Choir; Math; Art; Ithaca; Scranton

BAYARD, JEN; GREEN VILLAGE, NJ; MADISON HS; (FR); Hi Hnr Roll; WWAHSS; Hosp Aide; Key Club; Mth Clb/Tm; Italian Clb; Bnd; Stg Cre; Bskball (J); Key Club; Italian Club

BAYINDIR, KAZIM; BURLINGTON, NJ; BURLINGTON TWP HS; (JR); Hi Hnr Roll; Hnr Roll; Perf Att; St of Mnth; WWAHSS; Tennis (VJ); Pre-Med; Medical School

BEARD, JOVONIA; WILLINGBORO, NJ; WILLINGBORO HS; (FR); Hnr Roll; Comm Volntr; Hosp Aide; Chrch Yth Grp; Lib Aide; SP/M/VS; Nursing; Medical; Temple

BEAUVIL, MERLINE; EAST ORANGE, NJ; EAST ORANGE CAMPUS 9 HS; (FR); Hnr Roll; Perf Att; Sci Fairs; WWAHSS; Comm Volntr; ArtClub; Mus Clb; Chr; Stg Cre; Scr Kpr (J); Sftball (J); Tennis (V); 1st Place in the District Science Fair; Mathematics Teacher; Accounting; U of Maryland of Eastern Shore; U of Miami

BECKER, CORINNA; OAK RIDGE, NJ; JEFFERSON TWP HS; (SO); Hnr Roll; Pres Sch; Sci Fairs; WWAHSS; Comm Volntr; Peer Tut/Med; Red Cr Aide; Emplmnt; FBLA; Sftball (V); Teacher; Accountant; Ramapo College; Monmouth U

BECKFORD, KEVIN; VINELAND, NJ; VINELAND HS SOUTH; (SO); Hi Hnr Roll; Hnr Roll; Nat Sci Aw; Otst Ac Ach Awd; Perf Att; Sci Fairs; St Schl; St of Mnth; Comm Volntr; Peer Tut/Med; Red Cr Aide; Chrch Yth Grp; Dbte Team; Emplmnt; FBLA; Svce Clb; Latin Clb; Ch Chr; Lcrsse (J); Adv Cncl (R); Cl Off (P); Stu Cncl (R); CR (P); Sch Ppr (R); NAACP YBC Vice President, Vineland NAACP President, Eagle Publication Alpha & Omega; African Amer Cultural League, National ACT-SO Winner, National Archives Alive, Model Congress; African American Studies; Political Science; Harvard, Yale; Princeton, Columbia

BEEKS, VANESSA A; ROSELLE, NJ; ABRAHAM CLARK HS; (JR); Hi Hnr Roll; Hnr Roll; Otst Ac Ach Awd; St of Mnth; Design; Business Management; Seton Hall U; Rutgers U

BEGUM, KASRAT; PATERSON, NJ; JOHN F KENNEDY HS; (FR); Sci Fairs; Cl Off (V); Pediatrician; Computer Engineer; Rutgers; Ramapo

BEGUM, RUNA; PATERSON, NJ; JOHN F KENNEDY HS; (SR); Hnr Roll; Nat Hon Sy; Sci Fairs; WWAHSS; Comm Volntr; Peer Tut/Med; DARE; Sci Clb; Sch Ppr (R); National History Day; Pre-Med; Biology; Rutgers U

BELFER, SAMY; MANALAPAN, NJ; MARINE AC OF SCI/TECH HS; (FR); Hi Hnr Roll; Jr Eng Tech; Nat Hon Sy; Sci Fairs; St of Mnth; WWAHSS; Yth Ldrshp Prog; Comm Volntr; Hab For Humty Volntr; Drma Clb; Key Club; Mth Clb/Tm; ROTC; Svce Clb; Tech Clb; Tmpl Yth Grp; Acpl Chr; Drl Tm; SP/M/VS; CR (R); 1st Place in TSA State Competition in Prepared Presentation; Promoted to Seaman in NJ ROTC Program; Sciences; Princeton U; U of Pennsylvania

BELL, ATIYA; ATLANTIC CITY, NJ; ATLANTIC CITY HS; (SR); Hnr Roll; Kwnis Aw; Nat Hon Sy; Comm Volntr; Emplmnt; Key Club; Photog; Svce Clb; NJ Senate & General Assembly Citation; John Henry "Pop" Lloyd Youth Award; Nursing; Atlantic Cape Community College

BELL, SADE A; TRENTON, NJ; TRENTON CTRL HS; (SO); Hi Hnr Roll; Hnr Roll; Nat Hon Sy; Otst Ac Ach Awd; WWAHSS; Hosp Aide; DECA; FBLA; Orch; Galloping Gourmet; Princeton Preparatory Program; Pediatrician; Pediatric Nurse; New York U; Princeton U

BELLINGER, TYLER J; BURLINGTON, NJ; BURLINGTON TWP HS; (SR); Hi Hnr Roll; Hnr Roll; Comm Volntr; Emplmnt; Chr; SP/M/VS; TV Commercial; Regional Theatre; Music Theory; New York U; U of the Arts

BELLIZIA, MIRANDA; SOUTH ORANGE, NJ; COLUMBIA HS; (JR); Hnr Roll; Comm Volntr; Peer Tut/Med; ArtClub; Fr of Library; Mth Clb/Tm; Photog; Quiz Bowl; Stg Cre; Sftball; Sch Ppr (R); Tutoring; Quiz Bowl; Advertising; Public Relations; Temple U; Fashion Institute of Technology

BELMONT, SAMANTHA M; CRANFORD, NJ; MOTHER SETON REG HS; (JR); Hi Hnr Roll; Hnr Roll; WWAHSS; Comm Volntr; Peer Tut/Med; Drma Clb; Dnce; Drl Tm; Sch Ppr (R); Tutoring / Organized & Participated in Food Drives; Dance Competitions / Placed; Math or Chemistry; Montclair State; Kean U

BELNAVIS, CAYLA R B; MONTCLAIR, NJ; MONTCLAIR HS; (JR); Hi Hnr Roll; Hnr Roll; Nat Hon Sy; Comm Volntr; Hab For Humty Volntr; Peer Tut/Med; Mod UN; CR (R); Sch Ppr (E, R, P); Respect All Cultures Equally Club - President; Received 3 Community & School Service Awards; Criminal Law; Columbia U; Yale U

BENARBA, FARAH; GLASSBORO, NJ; GLASSBORO HS; (FR); Hi Hnr Roll; Hnr Roll; Perf Att; Sccr (V); Cl Off (T); Photography; Psychology; Syracuse U; New York U

BENCOSME, AMADO; PERTH AMBOY, NJ; CARDINAL MC CARRICK HS; (JR); Hnr Roll; Computer Engineer; Architect; Rutgers; New Jersey Institute of Technology

BENDY, ELSIE R; ATCO, NJ; HAMMONTON HS; (FR); Cooking and Baking; Arts and Crafts At Home; Owning My Own Bakery; Owning My Own Store; Camden County Community College

BENITEZ, GWENDOLYN C; BOGOTA, NJ; BOGOTA HS; (SO); Hnr Roll; Otst Ac Ach Awd; Comm Volntr; Peer Tut/Med; Chrch Yth Grp; Cmptr Clb; Dbte Team; Mth Clb/Tm; Mus Clb; Sci Clb; Tech Clb; French Clb; Bnd; Ch Chr; Dnce; CR (R); Criminology; Computer and System Manager; New Jersey Institute of Technology; John Jay College

BENNETT, JENNIFER; PARSIPPANY, NJ; PARSIPPANY HS; (SR); F Lan Hn Soc; Hi Hnr Roll; Hnr Roll; Nat Hon Sy; Otst Ac Ach Awd; Pres Sch; WWAHSS; Yth Ldrshp Prog; Comm Volntr; Peer Tut/Med; Red Cr Aide; Chrch Yth Grp; Emplmnt; Mth Clb/Tm; Pep Squd; Prom Com; Svce Clb; Vsity Clb; Spanish Clb; Chrldg (V CL); Dvng (V); Gmnstcs; PP Ftbl; Sccr (V CL); Sftball (J L); Vsy Clb (CL); Cl Off (V); CR (R); Yrbk (R); President of Interact Comm. Service Club; Participant in LTC & RYLA; Education of the Developmentally Handicapped; Spanish; The College of New Jersey

BENOIT, CLAUDEEN; WEST ORANGE, NJ; WEST ORANGE HS; (SO); Hnr Roll; St of Mnth; Yth Ldrshp Prog; Comm Volntr; Peer Tut/Med; Chrch Yth Grp; Drma Clb; Key Club; NYLC; French Clb; Ch Chr; Dnce; Drl Tm; SP/M/VS; Stu Cncl (T); Member of the International Thespian Society; Musical Theatre; Business; New York U

BERENATO, SUSANA R; HAMMONTON, NJ; HAMMONTON HS; (JR); Hnr Roll; USAA; WWAHSS; Yth Ldrshp Prog; Comm Volntr; Svce Clb; Chr; SP/M/VS; Stg Cre; Chrldg (V CL); Gmnstcs; Track (V L); Stu Cncl; CR; Leo Club, Pres., VP; Touring Choir; Sports Management/Education

BERFET, SHONTELLE; HILLSIDE, NJ; HILLSIDE HS; (SR); Nat Hon Sy; St of Mnth; Ch Chr; Drl Tm; Track (J); Stu Cncl (P); CR (P); President of Future Doctors of America Organization; Voting with Purpose-Vice President; Pre-Med/Biology; Education; North Carolina Central U; Spelman College

BERGMAN, ANDREW; PRINCETON, NJ; PRINCETON HS; (SO); Sci/Math Olympn; Comm Volntr; Peer Tut/Med; FBLA; Mth Clb/Tm; Sci Clb; Jzz Bnd; Cr Ctry (J); Tennis (V); Sch Ppr (R); President of Compukids - Non-Profit Charity; Johns Hopkins Math & Verbal / State Award; Biomedical Engineering; Engineering; Stanford U; Massachusetts Institute of Technology

BERMUDEZ, CRYSTAL M; FORT LEE, NJ; FORT LEE HS; (JR); Hnr Roll; Otst Ac Ach Awd; Perf Att; WWAHSS; Comm Volntr; Key Club; Dnce; I Am a Member of Key Club; A Member of the Voice; Education; Dance; Kean U; College of New Rochelle

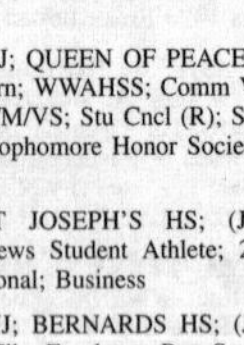
Belnavis, Cayla R B
Montclair HS
Montclair, NJ

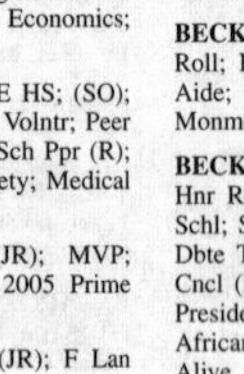
Banhalmi, Liza
East Brunswick HS
East Brunswick, NJ

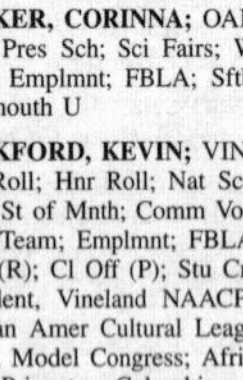
Bangs, Evin
Hightstown HS
Hightstown, NJ

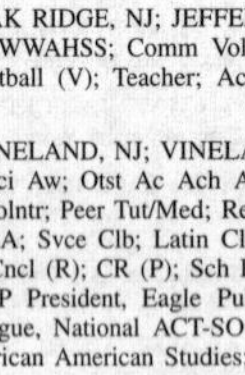
Baker, Nazsa S
East Orange Campus 9
East Orange, NJ

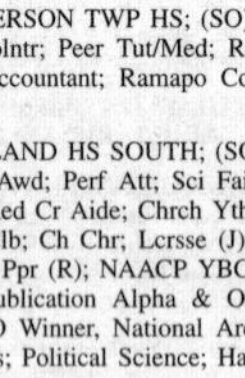
Ball, Melissa A
Brick Twp Memorial HS
Brick, NJ

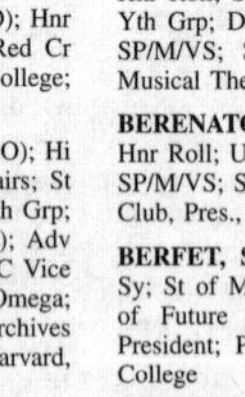
Baptiste, Sean
St Joseph's HS
Dayton, NJ

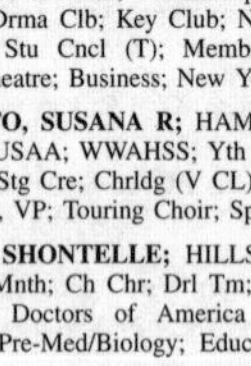
Berenato, Susana R
Hammonton HS
Hammonton, NJ

BERNARD, EVAN; BERKELEY HEIGHTS, NJ; GOVERNOR LIVINGSTON HS; (JR); Hnr Roll; WWAHSS; DARE; Drma Clb; Emplmnt; Mus Clb; SP/M/VS; Stg Cre; Two Bands-Jersey Bound & Inspector Hector; Lo Fi Ink Record Label; Music Industry Major; Drexel U; Northeastern U

BERRY, SAMANTHA E; FLORENCE, NJ; FLORENCE TWP MEM HS; (FR); Hi Hnr Roll; Hnr Roll; St of Mnth; Peer Tut/Med; FTA; Fld Hky (J); Scr Kpr (V); Cl Off (S); Stu Cncl (R); 3rd Place in Burlington County Times Create an Editorial Contest; Dermatology; Psychiatrist; California State U; Princeton U

BERWICK, BENJAMIN W; CLAYTON, NJ; VICTORY CHRISTIAN SCH; (JR); Hi Hnr Roll; Hnr Roll; Nat Hon Sy; Otst Ac Ach Awd; St of Mnth; WWAHSS; Yth Ldrshp Prog; Chrch Yth Grp; Bsball; Bskball; Sccr; Cl Off (R); Sch Ppr (E, R, P); Yrbk (P); Leadership Team in Youth Ministry; Chaplin for My Class; Architecture; Engineering; Bob Jones U; Pensacola Christian College

BESKO, DANIELLE; EASTAMPTON, NJ; RANCOCAS VALLEY REG HS; (JR); Hi Hnr Roll; MVP; Otst Ac Ach Awd; Perf Att; WWAHSS; Emplmnt; Key Club; Tchrs Aide; Sccr (J); Sftball (J); National Art Honor Society; Graphic Arts / Advertising Design; Princeton U; U of the Arts Philadelphia

BESKO, MICHAEL; EAST AMPTON, NJ; RANCOCAS VALLEY REG HS; (FR); Hi Hnr Roll; Hnr Roll; Perf Att; WWAHSS; Emplmnt; Key Club; Scouts

BESNER, ROBERT E; SOUTH AMBOY, NJ; ST JOSEPH'S HS; (JR); Hi Hnr Roll; Hnr Roll; Nat Mrt LOC; Pres Ac Ftns Aw; Sci Fairs; Comm Volntr; DARE; Emplmnt; Fr of Library; Lttrmn Clb; Outdrs Clb; Svce Clb; Vsity Clb; Cr Ctry (J L); Swmg (V CL); Wt Lftg; All County Swimming; Meet of Champions Qualifier-Swimming; Sports Medicine/Athletic Trainer; Neurology; Rowan U; St. Michaels College-Vermont

BEUTE, MARY E; LONG VALLEY, NJ; WEST MORRIS CTRL HS; (JR); Hnr Roll; WWAHSS; Comm Volntr; Peer Tut/Med; Chrch Yth Grp; FTA; Key Club; Scouts; Tchrs Aide; Tennis (J); Cl Off (S); Century Club Award; Spanish National Honors Society; Elementary Education; Special Education; St Francis U; U of Scranton

BEVERLEY, NYISHA; PISCATAWAY, NJ; PISCATAWAY HS; (JR); Hnr Roll; WWAHSS; Track (J); Stu Cncl (R); Peer Mediation; Student Ambassador; Psychology; Morgan State U; Howard U

BHARRAT, SHARI; SOMERSET, NJ; FRANKLIN HS; (JR); Hi Hnr Roll; Hnr Roll; Nat Sci Aw; USAA; WWAHSS; Hosp Aide; Clb; Sccr (J); Pre-Medicine; Medical Degree (MD); Columbia U

BHATT, ISHA; ABSECON, NJ; PLEASANTVILLE HS; (JR); Hnr Roll; Nat Hon Sy; WWAHSS; Yth Ldrshp Prog; Comm Volntr; Hosp Aide; ArtClub; Key Club; Mth Clb/Tm; Sci Clb; SADD; Tech Clb; Cl Off (S); Pre-Med; Biochemistry; Richard Stockton College; Rutgers U New Brunswick

BIANK, FRANK; WHARTON, NJ; ROXBURY HS; (JR); Hi Hnr Roll; Hnr Roll; MVP; Otst Ac Ach Awd; Sci Fairs; Comm Volntr; FBLA; Key Club; Lcrsse (J); Renaissance Award; Junior Class Homecoming Prince; Business/Math Major; Clemson U; College of New Jersey

BICHET, JORDANA F; ABERDEEN, NJ; MATAWAN REG HS; (JR); Nat Mrt LOC; Otst Ac Ach Awd; Peer Tut/Med; Chess; Emplmnt; Tmpl Yth Grp; Ice Sktg; Swmg; Lit Mag (R); Journalist / Writer / Lyricist; Career in Communications; Ramapo College; Montclair State U

BIRCSAK, KRISTIN; HIGHTSTOWN, NJ; HIGHTSTOWN HS; (JR); Hnr Roll; Nat Hon Sy; Pres Ac Ftns Aw; WWAHSS; Comm Volntr; Peer Tut/Med; Red Cr Aide; Chrch Yth Grp; Spanish Clb; Chr; Fld Hky (V C); Track (V); Biology; Medicine; Rutgers U; Arizona State U

BISERTA, PAT; POINT PLEASANT BEACH, NJ; POINT PLEASANT BOROUGH HS; (SO); Bsball (V L); Ftball (V L); All County & All Division Baseball; Wake Forest, Tennessee

BISHOP, ASHLEY; IRVINGTON, NJ; IRVINGTON HS; (FR); Hnr Roll; Perf Att; Sci Fairs; St of Mnth; Hosp Aide; Peer Tut/Med; ArtClub; DARE; Drma Clb; Mod UN; Mus Clb; Scouts; Ch Chr; Dnce; SP/M/VS; Chrldg (V); GAA (V); Swmg (V); Track (V); In a Cheerleading Out Not for School; Private Detector; Investigator; Montclair State U

BLACK, JARED; OAK RIDGE, NJ; JEFFERSON TWP HS; (JR); F Lan Hn Soc; Hi Hnr Roll; Hnr Roll; St of Mnth; WWAHSS; Yth Ldrshp Prog; Comm Volntr; Chess; Emplmnt; Lib Aide; Golf (J); Sccr (J); Youth for Literacy Chairman; Computer Science; Computer Game Programmer; Bethany College; St Marys College of Maryland

BLACK, KAYLEE A; VERNON, NJ; VERNON TOWNSHIP HS; (FR); Hi Hnr Roll; Perf Att; WWAHSS; Comm Volntr; Chrch Yth Grp; Key Club; Dnce; Orch; Tennis (J); Peer Leadership; Music Education; Westminster College; College of New Jersey

BLACK, KEVIN; PARLIN, NJ; SAYREVILLE WAR MEMORIAL HS; (SO); Hi Hnr Roll; Hnr Roll; Sccr (J); Track (V, L); Yrbk (E); Sports Psychology; Teaching; Florida State University; UCLA

BLACKWELL, CHRISTIE L; ROEBLING, NJ; FLORENCE TWP MEM HS; (FR); Hnr Roll; WWAHSS; DARE; Participated in Peer Coaching; Teacher - Bachelor's / Master's Degree; Social Worker / Master's Degree; Rutgers State U; Ramapo

BLAISE, WANDA; SOUTH ORANGE, NJ; COLUMBIA; (SO); Hnr Roll; Comm Volntr; Chrch Yth Grp; Ch Chr; Determined & Hard Working; Registered Nurse; Pediatric Doctor; Rutgers U; Harvard U

BLANC, NATHALIE; JACKSON, NJ; JACKSON MEMORIAL HS; (JR); Hi Hnr Roll; Comm Volntr; Lib Aide; Svce Clb; French Clb; Dnce; Tennis (J); Track (V); Biochemical Engineering; Orthodontics; Rutgers U

BLANCHARD, KATHRYN N; EATONTOWN, NJ; RED BANK CATHOLIC HS; (FR); DAR; Hi Hnr Roll; Hnr Roll; Comm Volntr; Hosp Aide; Chess; DARE; Drma Clb; Mus Clb; Pep Squd; Sci Clb; Bnd; Clr Grd; SP/M/VS; Chrldg (L); Sftball (L); Cl Off (V); Life Club

BLOUNT, ALEXIS M; CARTERET, NJ; MIDDLESEX CO VOC-WOODBRIDGE; (FR); Hnr Roll; Nat Hon Sy; Otst Ac Ach Awd; Perf Att; St of Mnth; Hosp Aide; DARE; Drma Clb; Chr; Dnce; Drl Tm; Bskball (V); Chrldg (J); Track (V); Stu Cncl (P); Doctor / Medical Field; Law / Lawyer; Rutgers U; UCLA

BOARDMAN II, STEPHEN A; PRINCETON, NJ; SOUTH BRUNSWICK HS; (JR); Hosp Aide; DARE; Duke U, Georgia Tech, Syracuse U; Illinois Institute of Technology

BOBEL, AMY; GRENLOCH, NJ; WASHINGTON TWP HS; Yth Ldrshp Prog; Dbte Team; CR (R); Medical Field; U of Penna; Medical College of Penn

BODNAR, LAURA; BRIDGEWATER, NJ; BRIDGEWATER-RARITAN HS; (FR); Hi Hnr Roll; Perf Att; Comm Volntr; Chrch Yth Grp; Key Club; Scouts; Vllyball (J)

BOEHM, ALLISON; SUSSEX, NJ; VERNON TOWNSHIP HS; (SO); F Lan Hn Soc; Hi Hnr Roll; Hnr Roll; Otst Ac Ach Awd; WWAHSS; Comm Volntr; Peer Tut/Med; Chrch Yth Grp; Key Club; Mod UN; Bnd; Dnce; Mch Bnd; Orch; Band Council; In-Town Softball; Meteorology; Elementary Education; Penn State U; Millersville U

BOEHNKE, NATALIE; RANDOLPH, NJ; RANDOLPH HS; (FR); Hnr Roll; Comm Volntr; Scouts; Orch

BOGERTEY, SHARDEY; WILLINGBORO, NJ; BCIT-WESTAMPTON; (SR); Hnr Roll; Hosp Aide; Peer Tut/Med; Emplmnt; Key Club; Tchrs Aide; Nursing; Burlington County College; Helene Fuld College

BOLTON, EMILY A; WOODBURY, NJ; WOODBURY HS; (JR); Hnr Roll; Nat Hon Sy; Otst Ac Ach Awd; WWAHSS; Comm Volntr; Peer Tut/Med; Emplmnt; Key Club; Mth Clb/Tm; Schol Bwl; Svce Clb; Vsity Clb; Spanish Clb; Bnd; Chr; Clr Grd; Cr Ctry (V); Golf (J); Track (V); Vsy Clb (V); Lit Mag (E); Who's Who Among American Poets; Psychology; Sociology

BOLTON, JENNIFER; SOMERVILLE, NJ; SOMERVILLE HS; (SO); Clr Grd; Dnce; Flg Crps; Track (V); CR (R); North Atlantic Duet Baton 1st Place; North Atlantic Trio Baton

BONSANTO, NICHELE R; BORDENTOWN, NJ; BORDENTOWN REG HS; (SR); Hi Hnr Roll; Hnr Roll; Nat Hon Sy; Comm Volntr; Peer Tut/Med; Red Cr Aide; Dbte Team; Emplmnt; Tchrs Aide; Bnd; Chr; Mch Bnd; SP/M/VS; Lit Mag (E, R); Sch Ppr (E, R, P); Olde English B Recipient; Poetry Contest Winner; Journalism; Music Business; Bradley U

BORDEN, TARYN; BRIDGEWATER, NJ; BRIDGEWATER RARITAN HS; (JR); Hnr Roll; MVP; Comm Volntr; Hosp Aide; Spec Olymp Vol; Emplmnt; Vsity Clb; Bskball (JC); Sftball (J); Track (J); Vllyball (VJCL); Marketing; Business Administration; Saint Francis U; Montclair State U

BORUCH, JACLYN; SOUTH AMBOY, NJ; OLD BRIDGE HS; (FR); F Lan Hn Soc; Hnr Roll; St of Mnth; Comm Volntr; Peer Tut/Med; Red Cr Aide; 4-H; FBLA; Mod UN; Hsbk Rdg (L); Swmg (L); CR (R); Certified Interior Designer; Certified Life Guard; Interpreter for the U.N.; Foreign Language; New York U; Columbia-NYU

BOSITS, STEPHANIE; LAKE HIAWATHA, NJ; PARSIPPANY HS; (SO); Hi Hnr Roll; Hnr Roll; MVP; Otst Ac Ach Awd; Pres Sch; Hab For Humty Volntr; Emplmnt; Scouts; Bnd; Bskball (V L); Fld Hky (V L); Sftball (V); Track (V L); Spanish; Environmentalist; U of Virginia; Roanoke

BOVERY, CAITLIN; PARLIN, NJ; SAYREVILLE WAR MEMORIAL HS; (JR); Hi Hnr Roll; Nat Hon Sy; Nat Mrt Semif; AL Aux Girls; Drma Clb; Mus Clb; Pep Squd; Prom Com; Sci Clb; Spanish Clb; Acpl Chr; Chr; Ch Chr; SP/M/VS; Chrldg (V L); Marine Biology; Brown U; College of William & Mary

BOWERS, SEAN L; TOMS RIVER, NJ; TOMS RIVER HS NORTH; (JR); Hnr Roll; Creating Video Games; Become a Policeman; Ocean County College

BOWLING, JANAE N; SOMERSET, NJ; FRANKLIN HS; (FR); Hnr Roll; Comm Volntr; Chrch Yth Grp; Emplmnt; P to P St Amb Prg; Orch; Paul Robeson Scholarship Award; Biology; Howard U; Rutgers U

BOYCE, KANEISHA K; SALEM, NJ; SALEM HS; (FR); Ctznshp Aw; Hi Hnr Roll; Hnr Roll; Otst Ac Ach Awd; Perf Att; Sci Fairs; St of Mnth; Valdctrian; Comm Volntr; Peer Tut/Med; DARE; FBLA; Jr Ach; Ntl FFA; Sci Clb; Tchrs Aide; Dnce; Drm Mjr; SP/M/VS; Sftball (J); National Junior Honor Society; Basketball Championships; Drama; Medicine; Duke U; New York U

BOYLE, CASEY J; CRANBURY, NJ; NOTRE DAME HS; (JR); DAR; F Lan Hn Soc; Hi Hnr Roll; Hnr Roll; Nat Hon Sy; Otst Ac Ach Awd; Pres Ac Ftns Aw; St of Mnth; Amnsty Intl; Peer Tut/Med; Emplmnt; Scouts; Bnd; SP/M/VS; PP Ftbl

BRACAMONTE, NATALIE; PASSAIC, NJ; PASSAIC HS; (SR); F Lan Hn Soc; Hnr Roll; Sci Fairs; Comm Volntr; Peer Tut/Med; AL Aux Girls; Chrch Yth Grp; FTA; Off Aide; Vllyball (J); Cl Off (R); CR (R); Club Latino; Tutoring Children That Need Help; Major-Mathematics; Minor-Chemistry; Rutgers U; William Paterson U

BRADLEY, TAWN M; WESTAMPTON, NJ; RANCOCAS VALLEY REG HS; (SO); Hi Hnr Roll; Hnr Roll; Nat Hon Sy; WWAHSS; Yth Ldrshp Prog; Key Club; Chrldg (J); Tennis (J); Track (V L); Stu Cncl (R); CR (R); Minorities in Engineering Program; Red & White Night Captain

BRANCH, SARNE; PLAINFIELD, NJ; PLAINFIELD HS; (FR); Comm Volntr; Peer Tut/Med; Chrch Yth Grp; DARE; Ch Chr; I Write Poetry.; Lawyer; Psychiatrist; Va. State; Morgan State U, Grambling State U

BRAND, JAMES; METUCHEN, NJ; ST JOSEPH'S HS; (SO); Hi Hnr Roll; Nat Mrt LOC; Chess; Emplmnt; Mth Clb/Tm; Off Aide; Vllyball (J); Advanced Certified SCUBA Diver; Lifeguard (Will Be Certified in April); Business; Engineering (Civil, Mechanical); Lehigh U; Washington U, St Louis

BRANNIGAN, DESTINIE; HOWELL, NJ; HOWELL HS; (JR); All Am Sch; Hi Hnr Roll; Nat Hon Sy; Nat Ldrshp Svc; USAA; WWAHSS; Comm Volntr; Peer Tut/Med; Emplmnt; Prom Com; Clb; Fld Hky (V); Wrstlg (C); Cl Off (R); Stu Cncl (R); Lit Mag (R); National DECA Qualifier; Marketing; Business; Boston U; The College of New Jersey

BRAY, CASSANDRA; TOWNSHIP OF WASHINGTON, NJ; PARAMUS CATHOLIC; (JR); Hnr Roll; Comm Volntr; Peer Tut/Med; Chrch Yth Grp; DARE; Emplmnt; NtlFrnscLg; Outdrs Clb; Photog; French Clb; Hsbk Rdg; Lcrsse; Scr Kpr; Skiing; Sccr

BRECHER, ELISSA R; BRIDGEWATER, NJ; BRIDGEWATER-RARITAN HS; (JR); F Lan Hn Soc; Hi Hnr Roll; Hnr Roll; Nat Hon Sy; Otst Ac Ach Awd; Perf Att; WWAHSS; Comm Volntr; DARE; Emplmnt; Key Club; Svce Clb; Tchrs Aide; Spanish Clb; Chr; Dnce

BRECHER, ERICA L; RANDOLPH, NJ; RANDOLPH HS; (FR); Hnr Roll; Otst Ac Ach Awd; WWAHSS; Emplmnt; Prom Com; Chr; Orch; SP/M/VS; Cyclg; Sccr; Sftball; Cl Off (P); Stu Cncl (S); Sch Ppr (R); Various Literary Awards Including Published Poems and Prose

BREIDENBACH, ANDREW; SPARTA, NJ; SPARTA HS; (JR); F Lan Hn Soc; Hi Hnr Roll; Hnr Roll; Pres Sch; Peer Tut/Med; Emplmnt; NYLC; Scouts; Bnd; Jzz Bnd; Mch Bnd; Pep Bnd; Junior Region Jazz Band-9th Grade; Life Scout Rank-Boy Scouts of America; Communications-Radio and Television; Business Administration; U of Virginia; Wake Forest U

BRIFU, FRANCIS; EAST BRUNSWICK, NJ; EAST BRUNSWICK HS; (JR); Hnr Roll; Nat Ldrshp Svc; St of Mnth; Comm Volntr; Chrch Yth Grp; Bskball (J); Stu Cncl (R); CR (R); Nominated to National Student Leadership Conference; Pediatrician (MD); New York U, Carnegie-Melon, U of Pennsylvania; Temple U, Boston U, State U of New York

BRIGHT, DANIEL; RINGWOOD, NJ; LAKELAND REG HS; (SR); Hi Hnr Roll; Hnr Roll; WWAHSS; Yth Ldrshp Prog; Spec Olymp Vol; Mth Clb/Tm; Scouts; Acpl Chr; Bnd; Chr; Mch Bnd; Cr Ctry (V); Tennis (J); Wrstlg (J); Stu Cncl (R); CR (R); Sch Ppr (R, P); Business Admin; Law School; Rutgers; Ramapo

BROWN, ANGELA; ORANGE, NJ; ORANGE HS; (JR); Hnr Roll; Bnd; Drl Tm; Bskball (VJC); Sftball (V); Vllyball (V); Engineering; U of North Carolina; Fordham U

BROWN, DANIELLE; PITMAN, NJ; PITMAN HS; (FR); Hi Hnr Roll; Hnr Roll; Sci Fairs; St of Mnth; WWAHSS; Comm Volntr; Chrch Yth Grp; Drma Clb; Emplmnt; Jr Ach; Key Club; Photog; SP/M/VS; Stg Cre; Johns Hopkins Gifted & Talented Award/Math & Science

BROWN, IBRAHIM K; NEWARK, NJ; EAST SIDE HS; (SO); Ctznshp Aw; Hnr Roll; Perf Att; St of Mnth; Chess; Dbte Team; Bnd; Do Something - Captain; Yearbook Committee; Law Degree; Computer Science; U of Virginia; Syracuse

BROWN, JESSICA C; CRESSKILL, NJ; CRESSKILL JR/SR HS; (JR); F Lan Hn Soc; Hnr Roll; ArtClub; Dbte Team; Spanish Clb; Chr; Clr Grd; Mch Bnd; Sftball (J L); Vllyball (J L); Interact Club; Scenic Crew; Creative Writing; Journalism; Drew U; Tufts U

BROWN, JESSICA L; RUTHERFORD, NJ; RUTHERFORD HS; (JR); Hi Hnr Roll; Hnr Roll; Comm Volntr; Biology Clb; Emplmnt; FBLA; FTA; Key Club; Yrbk (R); Accounting; U of Delaware; Penn State U

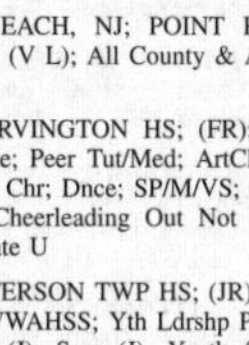
Brown, Ibrahim K
East Side HS
Newark, NJ

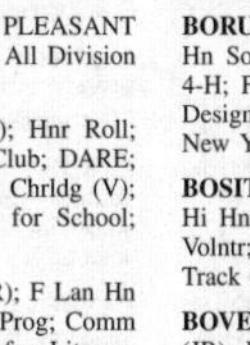
Bracamonte, Natalie
Passaic HS
Passaic, NJ

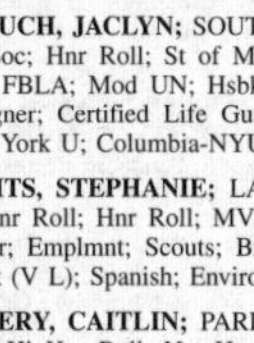
Blount, Alexis M
Middlesex Co Voc-Woodbridge
Carteret, NJ

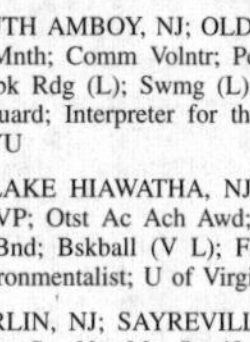
Bichet, Jordana F
Matawan Reg HS
Aberdeen, NJ

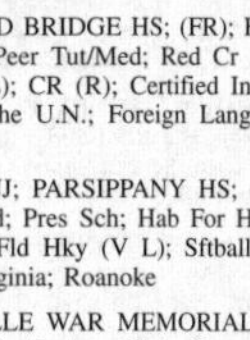
Black, Kevin
Sayreville War Memorial HS
Parlin, NJ

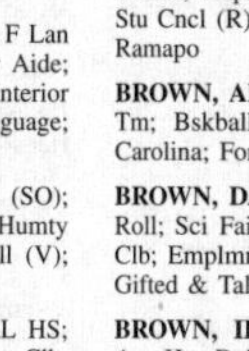
Branch, Sarne
Plainfield HS
Plainfield, NJ

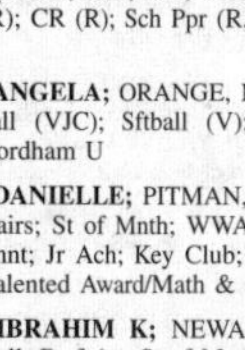
Brown, Jessica L
Rutherford HS
Rutherford, NJ

BROWN, JUSTIN; ROEBLING, NJ; FLORENCE TWP MEM HS; (FR); Hnr Roll; WWAHSS; Bnd

BROWN, LAUREN; SUMMIT, NJ; KENT PLACE SCH; (FR); Hosp Aide; Jr Cls League; Key Club; NYLC; Chr; Cr Ctry (V); Fld Hky (C); Track (J); Vllyball (J); Stu Cncl (R); Yrbk (P); Community Service Award; Cambridge U (UK)

BROWN, MALLORY L; ANNANDALE, NJ; NORTH HUNTERDON HS; (FR); Hi Hnr Roll; Hnr Roll; Otst Ac Ach Awd; Yth Ldrshp Prog; Hosp Aide; Peer Tut/Med; Spec Olymp Vol; Drma Clb; NYLC; P to P St Amb Prg; Svce Clb; French Clb; Chr; Dnce; SP/M/VS; Fld Hky (J); Cl Off (S); Stu Cncl (P); Hunterdon County Distinguished Student; Johns Hopkins Academic Talent Search; Pre-Med; Biology; Duke U; Johns Hopkins

BROWN, MICHAEL T; PHILLIPSBURG, NJ; PHILLIPSBURG HS; (JR); Ctznshp Aw; Hnr Roll; Kwnis Aw; Nat Hon Sy; Perf Att; Yth Ldrshp Prog; Comm Volntr; Chrch Yth Grp; Key Club; NYLC; Bnd; Cr Ctry (V); Cyclg (C); PP Ftbl (C); Swmg (V CL); Track (V L); Wt Lftg (C); Stu Cncl (V, T); CR (R); Key Club President; Acolyte of the Year; Political Science; Pre-Law; USNA; Villanova U

BROWN, RACHEL; CHESTER, NJ; WEST MORRIS MENDHAM HS; (SR); Hi Hnr Roll; Hnr Roll; Comm Volntr; Emplmnt; Photog; Svce Clb; Acpl Chr; Chr; Equestrian Sports; Accounting; Miami U of Ohio

BROWN, VICTORIA L; SICKLERVILLE, NJ; PAUL VI HS; (SO); Hnr Roll; Nat Hon Sy; P to P St Amb Prg; Scouts; Svce Clb; Sccr (J); Sftball (J); Track (J); Hospitality Club; Ambassadors Club; Psychologist

BROWNE, OLIVIA; BRIDGEWATER, NJ; BRIDGEWATER-RARITAN HS; (JR); Hnr Roll; Perf Att; St of Mnth; WWAHSS; Emplmnt; Key Club; Scouts; Italian Clb; Track (V); Girl Scout Silver Award; Graphic Design; Teaching; Cooper Union; Carnegie Mellon

BROWNING, JORDAN E; PRINCETON JUNCTION, NJ; THE HUN SCH OF PRINCETON; (SO); Hi Hnr Roll; WWAHSS; Comm Volntr; Key Club; Prom Com; Dnce; SP/M/VS; Lit Mag (R); Coached a National Pop Warner Cheer Squad; Member of Tri-State Area Dance Team; Creative Writing; Boston College; Duke

BRUCE, KANECIA; MONROE TOWNSHIP, NJ; MONROE TWP HS; (SO); Ctznshp Aw; Hnr Roll; Nat Mrt Sch Recip; Perf Att; St of Mnth; Comm Volntr; Peer Tut/Med; Chrch Yth Grp; DARE; Drma Clb; Bnd; Ch Chr; SP/M/VS; Bskball (V); Cr Ctry (V); Stu Cncl (R); CR (R); Sch Ppr (R); Peer Leadership; Excellence in Botany; Criminal Justice/ Law; Psychology; Yale U; Howard U

BRULATO, AMANDA; BELLEVILLE, NJ; BELLEVILLE HS; (FR); Hnr Roll; WWAHSS; Key Club; Scouts; Bnd; Jzz Bnd; Mch Bnd; SP/M/VS; Track (J); Recreational Softball; Small Ensembles; Architecture; Music; Princeton U; Harvard U

BRULATO, CRYSTAL M; BELLEVILLE, NJ; BELLEVILLE HS; (SO); Hnr Roll; Comm Volntr; Hosp Aide; Spec Olymp Vol; Drma Clb; Key Club; Pep Squd; Scouts; Italian Clb; Jzz Bnd; Mch Bnd; SP/M/VS; Stg Cre; Track (J); Tri-M Music Honors Society; Interact Club; Music Major; Montclair State U

BRUNO, VINCENT A; BLACKWOOD, NJ; HIGHLAND REG HS; (SO); Hi Hnr Roll; Hnr Roll; Perf Att; Pres Sch; St of Mnth; Comm Volntr; Chess; Chrch Yth Grp; Emplmnt; Bnd; Ch Chr; Jzz Bnd; Mch Bnd; Adv Cncl (R); Interact (Community Service); All-State Jazz Band (Trumpet); Political Science; Master's Degree; Brown U; Harvard U

BRUNS, ALYSON; GLASSBORO, NJ; GLASSBORO HS; (MS); Ctznshp Aw; Hi Hnr Roll; Hnr Roll; Otst Ac Ach Awd; St of Mnth; Comm Volntr; DARE; Fr of Library; Scouts; Chrldg (J); Yrbk (E); Writing Awards; Cosmetologist; Pre-School Teacher; Rowan U; Harvard U

BRUNSON, SAMANTHA; RUTHERFORD, NJ; HOMESCHOOL; (FR); Hi Hnr Roll; Pres Ac Ftns Aw; Comm Volntr; ArtClub; Chess; DARE; Drma Clb; Bnd; Dnce; Drl Tm; Mch Bnd; Chrldg (V); Yrbk (R); Acting; Alvin Ailey Summer Intensive; Performing Arts; Education; Spelman College; Hampton U

BRUTUS, TALAMAS; ENGLEWOOD, NJ; DWIGHT MORROW HS; (FR); Hnr Roll; Comm Volntr; Bsball; Businessman; Technology Information; New York U; Columbia U

BUDKIEWICZ, JAMES M; PENNSAUKEN, NJ; PENNSAUKEN HS; (JR); F Lan Hn Soc; Hnr Roll; Nat Hon Sy; WWAHSS; Comm Volntr; Emplmnt; SADD; Spanish Clb; Mch Bnd; Stg Cre; Sch Ppr (R); Yrbk (R); Spanish Honor Society; Law; Psychology; Rutgers U New Brunswick; Villanova U

BUNTING, RYAN; CLEMENTON, NJ; HIGHLAND HS; (SO); Hnr Roll; Perf Att; Swmg (V); Track; Pharmacist; Architect; Princeton U; Drexel U

BURDGE, BROOKE; SPRING LAKE, NJ; COMMUNICATIONS HS; (JR); Hi Hnr Roll; Nat Hon Sy; Otst Ac Ach Awd; Pres Ac Ftns Aw; Comm Volntr; ArtClub; Drma Clb; Emplmnt; Prom Com; SADD; Tech Clb; Dnce; SP/M/VS; Yrbk (E); Television Broadcast Club; Visual Communications Club; Public Relations; Marketing; Fordham U; Ursinus College

BURGAN JR, EVERETT; GLASSBORO, NJ; PAUL VI HS; (SO); Hnr Roll; Perf Att; St of Mnth; Yth Ldrshp Prog; Cmptr Clb; DARE; Emplmnt; Lit Mag (E); Sch Ppr (P); Student of the Week; PhD in Computer Engineering; or PhD in Computer Science; Massachusetts Institute of Technology; New Jersey Institute of Technology

BURGOYNE, KIRA; BAYVILLE, NJ; CTRL REG HS; (JR); Hi Hnr Roll; St of Mnth; Chrch Yth Grp; Quiz Bowl; Volunteered with the Ocean County GOP During 2004 Mayoral Election; Pre-Law; International Relations; New York U; U of Southern California

BURNS, NICHOLAS; WANAQUE, NJ; LAKELAND REG HS; (SR); Hi Hnr Roll; Nat Hon Sy; WWAHSS; Yth Ldrshp Prog; Comm Volntr; Peer Tut/Med; AL Aux Boys; Biology Clb; Chrch Yth Grp; Dbte Team; Drma Clb; Mth Clb/Tm; NYLC; Outdrs Clb; Bnd; Chr; Mch Bnd; SP/M/VS; Bskball (J); Sccr (V L); Tennis (V CL); Track (V L); Stu Cncl (R); CR (R); NJ Governor's School of Engineering & Technology; Management; Bucknell U

BUSKIRK, JAMES; WESTVILLE, NJ; GATEWAY REG HS; (FR); Hnr Roll; Pres Ac Ftns Aw; French Clb; Ftball (J); Wt Lftg (V); Wrstlg (J); Karate-Orange Belt-Aikido; Medical File Clerk-Part Time; Criminal Forensics; Engineer; Stanford U; Penn State U

BUSTAMANTE, JEANPAUL; CEDAR GROVE, NJ; CEDAR GROVE HS; Bnd; Stg Cre; Sch Ppr (R); Tech Crew; Science Club; Electrical Engineer; Biomedical Engineer; UCLA; Cal Tech

BYFIELD, FIONA; WEST ORANGE, NJ; WEST ORANGE HS; (JR); Bnd; Tennis (J); Criminology; Mythology; Montclair State U; Kean U

BYNOE, CORINNE; ISELIN, NJ; JOHN F KENNEDY MEMORIAL HS; (SO); Hnr Roll; Otst Ac Ach Awd; WWAHSS; Comm Volntr; Peer Tut/Med; Chrch Yth Grp; Dbte Team; Emplmnt; Key Club; Pep Squd; P to P St Amb Prg; Tchrs Aide; Chr; Ch Chr; SP/M/VS; Swg Chr; Chrldg (JCL); Track (V); Stu Cncl (R); CR (R); Religious Education Teacher; Education; Theater Arts; Seton Hall U; New York U

BYUEN, EUGENE; BERKELEY HEIGHTS, NJ; GOVERNOR LIVINGSTON HS; (JR); Hnr Roll; Nat Hon Sy; Nat Mrt LOC; Sci/Math Olympn; WWAHSS; Comm Volntr; Hosp Aide; Chess; Chrch Yth Grp; Dbte Team; Mth Clb/Tm; MuAlphaTh; Quill & Scroll; ROTC; Tennis (JC); Sch Ppr (E); Cornell U; Stanford U

CACCIOLA, CATHERINE; PARAMUS, NJ; PARAMUS HS; (FR); Hi Hnr Roll; Comm Volntr; Peer Tut/Med; ArtClub; Chrch Yth Grp; Drma Clb; Off Aide; Scouts; Chr; Ch Chr; SP/M/VS; Vllyball (J); Film Makers Club

CADET, REGINE; ISELIN, NJ; JOHN F KENNEDY MEMORIAL HS; (SO); Hnr Roll; WWAHSS; Key Club; Clb; Nurse; Doctor; Rutgers U; The College of New Jersey

CAGILUS, VLADIMIR; NEWARK, NJ; PINE FORGE AC; (FR); Ctznshp Aw; Hi Hnr Roll; Hnr Roll; Perf Att; Sci Fairs; St of Mnth; Comm Volntr; Chrch Yth Grp; Drma Clb; Ch Chr; SP/M/VS; Stg Cre; Cl Off (R); Business Major; Law; Oakwood College; Columbia Union College

CAHILL, KASEY; EGG HARBOR TOWNSHIP, NJ; EGG HARBOR TWP HS; (SO); Hnr Roll; Otst Ac Ach Awd; Pres Ac Ftns Aw; WWAHSS; Chrch Yth Grp; Drma Clb; Key Club; Scouts; Bnd; Jzz Bnd; Mch Bnd; Orch

CAI, KIMBERLY; RUTHERFORD, NJ; RUTHERFORD HS; (JR); Hi Hnr Roll; Nat Hon Sy; Sci/Math Olympn; WWAHSS; Amnsty Intl; Comm Volntr; Hosp Aide; Biology Clb; FBLA; Key Club; Bnd; Drm Mjr; Mch Bnd; Biology Major; Columbia; NYU

CALDERON, CHRISTIAN; UNION CITY, NJ; UNION HILL HS; (FR); 4H Awd; Ctznshp Aw; Hi Hnr Roll; Hnr Roll; Otst Ac Ach Awd; Perf Att; St of Mnth; WWAHSS; DARE; Key Club; Mus Clb; Sci Clb; Bnd; Jzz Bnd; Mch Bnd; Orch; Swmg (V); Key Club President; Secretary of Science Club; Pediatrics; Computers; Columbia U; Brown

CALHOUN, ASHLEY E; MILLVILLE, NJ; MILLVILLE SR HS; (SR); Hi Hnr Roll; Hnr Roll; Perf Att; WWAHSS; Emplmnt; FTA; Key Club; Off Aide; Prom Com; Scouts; Tchrs Aide; Elementary Education; Paralegal; Cumberland County College; Rowan U

CALLAHAN, JENNIFER; SUMMIT, NJ; SUMMIT HS; (FR); Hi Hnr Roll; Nat Sci Aw; Otst Ac Ach Awd; Pres Ac Ftns Aw; Sci/Math Olympn; Comm Volntr; Peer Tut/Med; DARE; Dbte Team; Key Club; Mth Clb/Tm; NtlFrnscLg; Pep Squd; Sci Clb; Wdwrkg Clb; Bnd; Chr; Dnce; Jzz Bnd; Bsball (J); Bskball; Cr Ctry; Gmnstcs (V); Hsbk Rdg; Sftball (J); Swmg; Wrstlg; Cl Off (R); Stu Cncl (P, V, R); CR (R); Play Guitar, Saxophone, Piano; Volunteer Through Out Community; Criminal Lawyer; Athletic Personal Trainer; Harvard Law School; Yale Law School

CAMPBELL, MICALIA; PATERSON, NJ; JOHN F KENNEDY HS; (SO); Ctznshp Aw; Hnr Roll; Otst Ac Ach Awd; Perf Att; St of Mnth; WWAHSS; Peer Tut/Med; Mus Clb; Outdrs Clb; Prom Com; Bnd; Dnce; Flg Crps; Bskball (J); GAA (V); Sftball (J); CR (V); Sch Ppr (E, P); Criminal Justice Mechanic Engineer; Medical Doctor, Accounting Marketing; Atlanta Georgia; Morgan State U

CAMPBELL, SHANEY; CHERRY HILL, NJ; CHERRY HILL HS EAST; (SO); Hnr Roll; Nat Hon Sy; WWAHSS; Comm Volntr; Chrch Yth Grp; DARE; Chr; Dnce; Track (V L); African-American Club Office; Computer Science; Computer Engineering; Georgia Institute of Technology; Brown U

CAMPBELL, THERESA; WASHINGTON, NJ; WARREN HILLS REG HS; (SO); Hnr Roll; WWAHSS; Spec Olymp Vol; Emplmnt; Key Club; Bnd; Johns Hopkins Talent Search for Talented and Gifted Students; Archaeology; Field in History; Leigh Valley U; South Carolina U

CAMPO, ASHLEY M; TOTOWA, NJ; PASSAIC VALLEY REG HS; (SR); Hnr Roll; Emplmnt; Bskball; PP Ftbl; Girls Show Head of Novelties 2005; Relays 2004; Communications; Bergen Community College

CANALES, CHRISTINA; KEARNY, NJ; QUEEN OF PEACE HS; (SO); Hi Hnr Roll; Perf Att; St of Mnth; Valdctrian; Comm Volntr; Chrch Yth Grp; DARE; Mod UN; Mus Clb; Svce Clb; Ch Chr; SP/M/VS; Stg Cre; Track (V); Vllyball (JCL); Stu Cncl (R); Sch Ppr (E); Yrbk (R); Mock Trial - Attorney for Both Sides; Pre-Law; Pre-Med; New York U; Columbia U

CANNULI, ALYSSA C; HOWELL, NJ; ST. ROSE HS; (JR); All Am Sch; Hi Hnr Roll; Hnr Roll; MVP; Nat Hon Sy; Otst Ac Ach Awd; WWAHSS; Yth Ldrshp Prog; Chrch Yth Grp; Mth Clb/Tm; Prom Com; Svce Clb; Bsball (C); Lcrsse (V L); Sccr (V CL); Sftball (C); Lit Mag (R); Sch Ppr (R); Yrbk (R)

CANOVA, MARISA; CEDAR GROVE, NJ; CEDAR GROVE HS; (JR); Hi Hnr Roll; Nat Hon Sy; WWAHSS; Yth Ldrshp Prog; Key Club; Sci Clb; Foreign Clb; Tennis (V); Track (J); Stu Cncl (R); Sch Ppr (R)

CAO, YONDA; BELLE MEAD, NJ; MONTGOMERY HS; (SO); Hi Hnr Roll; Nat Hon Sy; WWAHSS; Yth Ldrshp Prog; Comm Volntr; Hosp Aide; Chess; Chrch Yth Grp; Drma Clb; Mus Clb; NYLC; Off Aide; Tchrs Aide; Tech Clb; Ch Chr; Stg Cre; Bsball; Bskball (V); Vllyball; CR (R); Sch Ppr (R); Piano - 6 Years; Somerset Medical Center 120+ Hours Volunteering; Pre-Med; Johns Hopkins U; Columbia U

CAPORALE, ANTOINETTE C; HAMMONTON, NJ; HAMMONTON HS; (FR); Hnr Roll; Chrch Yth Grp; Emplmnt; Chr; Ch Chr; Dnce; Psychology; Journalism; New York U; Columbia U

CAPOROSO, JOSEPH; RINGWOOD, NJ; LAKELAND REG HS; (SR); Hi Hnr Roll; Hnr Roll; MVP; Nat Hon Sy; WWAHSS; Comm Volntr; Emplmnt; Bskball (V CL); Ftball (V CL); Track (V L); Sch Ppr (E, R); Writer for Local Paper; 1st Team All-County for Football; Communications; Journalism; Muhlenberg College; Johns Hopkins U

CAPOZZOLI, HOLLY E; SOMERDALE, NJ; STERLING HS; (JR); WWAHSS; Comm Volntr; Peer Tut/Med; Chrch Yth Grp; Italian Clb; Stg Cre; Chrldg (J); Track (V); Youth Group-Our Lady of Grace; Italian Club; Culinary Arts; Television Director; Atlantic County Community College; The Restaurant School

CAPP, DANIEL; EMERSON, NJ; PARAMUS CATHOLIC HS; (JR); Hi Hnr Roll; Hnr Roll; WWAHSS; Chrch Yth Grp; Emplmnt; Bsball (J); Mechanical Engineering; Computer Engineering; Stevens Institute of Technology

CAPRIOLI, SABRINA; DOVER, NJ; DOVER HS; (SR); Hi Hnr Roll; Hnr Roll; Jr Rot; Nat Hon Sy; St of Mnth; WWAHSS; Comm Volntr; Spec Olymp Vol; Drma Clb; Emplmnt; Key Club; Off Aide; Prom Com; Orch; SP/M/VS; Sccr (J); Invited to National Student Leadership Conference; Finalist for Governor's School for Public Issues and the Future of New Jersey; Politics; Sociology; New York U

CAPUTO, BRITTANY; BELLEVILLE, NJ; BELLEVILLE HS; (JR); Hnr Roll; WWAHSS; Hosp Aide; Emplmnt; Pep Squd; Cr Ctry (L); Student Government Org; Mock Trial Captain

CAPUTO, NATALIE S; BELLEVILLE, NJ; BELLEVILLE HS; (SO); WWAHSS; Comm Volntr; Key Club; Cr Ctry (J); Track (L); Fashion Designer / Interior Designer; New York U; Fashion Institute of Technology

CARDEN, MICHELLE N; PLAINFIELD, NJ; PLAINFIELD HS; (SO); Peer Tut/Med; Emplmnt; Chr; Ch Chr; Vllyball; Stu Cncl (R); Nursing or Something in the Medical Field; Teaching; Rutgers U; North Carolina A & T State U

CARDENAS, KATHLEEN; PISCATAWAY, NJ; PISCATAWAY HS; (JR); Modeling Pageant of Trenton; Youth and Child Worker; DeVry U; Caldwell College

CARDENAS, LEONARDO; WESTWOOD, NJ; WESTWOOD REG JR/SR HS; (FR); Hi Hnr Roll; Hnr Roll; MVP; Nat Hon Sy; Comm Volntr; Chess; Chrch Yth Grp; Emplmnt; Bnd; Ftball (J); Wrstlg (J); Software Designer; Ohio State U; U of Notre Dame

CARDUCCI, MICHAEL J; WOODBURY, NJ; GLOUCESTER CATHOLIC HS; (JR); Hnr Roll; Nat Hon Sy; Nat Mrt LOC; WWAHSS; Comm Volntr; Emplmnt; Jr Ach; Schol Bwl; Vllyball (V); Aerospace Engineering; Nuclear Engineering; U of Maryland; Penn State

Capozzoli, Holly E
Sterling HS
Somerdale, NJ

Buskirk, James
Gateway Reg HS
Westville, NJ

Burgan Jr, Everett
Paul VI HS
Glassboro, NJ

Brown, Lauren
Kent Place Sch
Summit, NJ

Brown, Michael T
Phillipsburg HS
Phillipsburg, NJ

Callahan, Jennifer
Summit HS
Summit, NJ

Cardenas, Kathleen
Piscataway HS
Piscataway, NJ

CARELLA, ALEXANDRA; SICKLERVILLE, NJ; TIMBER CREEK REG; (FR); 4H Awd; Hi Hnr Roll; Hnr Roll; Otst Ac Ach Awd; Pres Sch; St of Mnth; Comm Volntr; 4-H; Emplmnt; Swmg (V); Writer for Static in South Jersey Carrier Post; Awarded Most Promising Athlete on Swim Team; Journalism; Broadcast Journalism; New York U; Allegheny U

CAREY, DAKOTA; WESTFIELD, NJ; WESTFIELD HS; (JR); Hnr Roll; Yth Ldrshp Prog; Comm Volntr; Peer Tut/Med; Chrch Yth Grp; NYLC; Tchrs Aide; Cr Ctry (J); Sccr (J); Track (J); Transition Project; Sunday School Teacher; Education; Communications; Rutgers U

CARLSEN, KYLA; PARSIPPANY, NJ; PARSIPPANY HS; (SR); Hi Hnr Roll; Hnr Roll; Nat Hon Sy; St Optmst of Yr; WWAHSS; Comm Volntr; Peer Tut/Med; Dbte Team; Emplmnt; Mth Clb/Tm; Pep Squd; Photog; Prom Com; Svce Clb; Vsity Clb; Chrldg (V C); Gmnstcs; PP Ftbl (V); Scr Kpr (J); Sftball (J); Vsy Clb (V); Cl Off (T); Stu Cncl (R); CR (R); Lit Mag (E); Yrbk (E); Business Management; Fashion Design; U of Delaware

CARR, LATASHA; GLASSBORO, NJ; GLASSBORO HS; (SO); Ctznshp Aw; Hi Hnr Roll; Hnr Roll; Otst Ac Ach Awd; Perf Att; Peer Tut/Med; DARE; Drma Clb; Emplmnt; Pep Squd; Photog; SP/M/VS; Chrldg (V); PP Ftbl (J); Track (V); Photography; Theater; RN; Theater; Howard U; Temple U

CARSON, HUNTER S; SEWELL, NJ; WASHINGTON TWP HS; (SO); Hi Hnr Roll; Hnr Roll; MVP; Otst Ac Ach Awd; St of Mnth; WWAHSS; Chrch Yth Grp; Cmptr Clb; Mth Clb/Tm; Ice Hky (J); Rlr Hky (J); Soccer Ref; Intramural Soccer; Mechanical Engineering; U of Rhode Island

CARSON, JASMINE D; EAST ORANGE, NJ; EAST ORANGE CAMPUS 9 HS; (SO); Hnr Roll; Perf Att; Comm Volntr; Dbte Team; ROTC; Ch Chr; Bskball (J); Track (J); CR (R); English Major; Educational Studies; Seton Hall U; North Carolina A & T

CARTER III, CLINTON D; PITMAN, NJ; PITMAN HS; (JR); Hnr Roll; St of Mnth; WWAHSS; Yth Ldrshp Prog; AL Aux Boys; DARE; Drma Clb; Emplmnt; Jr Ach; Key Club; NYLC; Off Aide; SP/M/VS; Stg Cre; Ftball (V); Track (V); Wrstlg (V); Stu Cncl (R); Boys State Delegate, Kodak Young Leader; Student of the Month, 3 Times, Governor's School; Engineering-US Naval Academy; US Naval Academy; Rutgers U

CARUSO, COURTNEY; MATAWAN, NJ; MATAWAN REG HS; (JR); Ctznshp Aw; Hnr Roll; Nat Hon Sy; Peer Tut/Med; DARE; Photog; Sftball (J); Tennis (J); Yrbk (E, P); Fashion Merchandising; Photography; Philadelphia U; Fashion Institute of Technology

CARUSO, DAVID; BELLEVILLE, NJ; BELLEVILLE HS; (JR); Hi Hnr Roll; Hnr Roll; Nat Hon Sy; WWAHSS; Peer Tut/Med; Emplmnt; Vsity Clb; Bsball (VJ L); Ftball (JC); Conflict Mediator-Pres Nominee; MBA, BS Exercise Science; Massage Therapy; Rowan U; Caldwell College

CASAPULLA, KRISTEN; MOORESTOWN, NJ; MOORESTOWN HS; (JR); Hi Hnr Roll; Hnr Roll; Yth Ldrshp Prog; Comm Volntr; Peer Tut/Med; Emplmnt; NYLC; Photog; Fld Hky (J L); Track (J); Yrbk (R); Honor & Service Society; International Affairs; Political Science; Columbia U; American U

CASEY, KRISTOPHER; NORTH BRUNSWICK, NJ; N BRUNSWICK TWNSHP HS; (JR); Hi Hnr Roll; Hnr Roll; Wdwrkg Clb

CASEY, LANNA; CLAYTON, NJ; GLOUCESTER CTY INST OF TECH; (SO); Hnr Roll; Peer Tut/Med; Chrch Yth Grp; DECA; FBLA; Chr; SP/M/VS; Chrldg (V); Stu Cncl (R); CR (R); Magazine Club (Reporter); Big Brother-Big Sister; Child Psychology; Retail; Pennsylvania State U; Rutgers U

CASINGAL, JENNA M; JERSEY CITY, NJ; CTY PREP HS; MS; Hi Hnr Roll; Hnr Roll; MVP; Otst Ac Ach Awd; Pres Sch; St of Mnth; Peer Tut/Med; Chrch Yth Grp; DARE; Ch Chr; Dnce; SP/M/VS; Bskball; Cr Ctry; Sftball; Track; Vllyball; Stu Cncl (S, R); CR (R); Yrbk (R); Scholastics Olympics English; Freshmen Honor Society; Medical Science / Doctor; Army; Military - West Point; Princeton U

CASSIDY, ELIZABETH; MADISON, NJ; MADISON HS; (JR); Hi Hnr Roll; Hnr Roll; Hab For Humty Volntr; Key Club; Orch; Stu Cncl (R); CR (R); Lit Mag (E); Architecture; Management; Rhode Island School of Design; U of Virginia

CASSIDY, KENNETH; MIDDLETOWN, NJ; MIDDLETOWN HS NORTH; (JR); F Lan Hn Soc; Hi Hnr Roll; Hnr Roll; MVP; Nat Hon Sy; Pres Ac Ftns Aw; 4-H; Emplmnt; FBLA; Spanish Clb; Ftball (JC); Ice Hky (J); Rlr Hky (C); Wt Lftg; Nominated for National Young Leaders Conference; Participated in FBLA Regional Competition; Management / Marketing; Business Concepts; Penn St U; Wake Forest U

CASTILLO, DALILA; RIDGEFIELD, NJ; RIDGEFIELD MEMORIAL HS; (SR); F Lan Hn Soc; Hnr Roll; Nat Hon Sy; Comm Volntr; Spec Olymp Vol; Pep Squd; Italian Clb; Chr; Cr Ctry (J); Track (V); Cl Off (S); Sch Ppr (R); Piano; Intergenerational Club; Nursing; Seton Hall U

CASTILLO, MEGAN; LINDEN, NJ; LINDEN HS; (SR); Hi Hnr Roll; Hnr Roll; Nat Hon Sy; Otst Ac Ach Awd; Pres Sch; Peer Tut/Med; Cmptr Clb; DECA; Drma Clb; Emplmnt; Mus Clb; Prom Com; Vsity Clb; Spanish Clb; Bnd; Dnce; Drm Mjr; Jzz Bnd; Mch Bnd; Sftball (JVL); Cl Off (T); Lit Mag (R); DECA Scholarship Recipient; International Baccalaureate; Management; Fashion Marketing; Johnson & Wales U

CASTILLO JR, JOEL; CHERRY HILL, NJ; CHERRY HILL HS WEST; (SR); Hnr Roll; Nat Hon Sy; Perf Att; Comm Volntr; BPA; DECA; Svce Clb; Spanish Clb; Ftball (J); Mar Art; Stu Cncl (R); CR (R); DECA; BASE; Business; Accounting; Drexel U; Temple U

CAVIEDES, NATALY; NORTH BERGEN, NJ; NORTH BERGEN HS; (FR); Comm Volntr; Key Club; Dnce; North Bergen Federation of Teachers Award; Economy; Psychology

CAWLEY, STEPHANIE; CAPE MAY COURT HOUSE, NJ; MIDDLE TWP HS; (SO); Hi Hnr Roll; Hnr Roll; Otst Ac Ach Awd; St of Mnth; Valdctrian; WWAHSS; Peer Tut/Med; Mth Clb/Tm; Outdrs Clb; Quiz Bowl; Sci Clb; Bnd; Chr; Jzz Bnd; Mch Bnd; Sch Ppr (R); Yrbk (R); Played Piano for 9 Years; NJ State Envirothon; Performance Piano; California Institute of the Arts

CELLS, MEAGHAN; LONG VALLEY, NJ; WEST MORRIS CTRL HS; (JR); F Lan Hn Soc; Hnr Roll; WWAHSS; Spec Olymp Vol; FTA; Key Club; Scouts; Chr; Dnce; SP/M/VS; Chrldg (V C); Track (V); Secondary Education

CENTENO, ASHLEY M; JERSEY CITY, NJ; AC OF SACRED HEART HS; (SO); Hnr Roll; Nat Hon Sy; Comm Volntr; Cmptr Clb; Scouts; Stg Cre; Bskball (V); Sftball (V); Vllyball (V); Stu Cncl (P); Business; Florida State U; Notre Dame

CEPEDA, KARINA; PATERSON, NJ; PATERSON CATHOLIC HS; (FR); Ctznshp Aw; Hi Hnr Roll; Hnr Roll; Nat Hon Sy; Otst Ac Ach Awd; Perf Att; Salutrn; Sci Fairs; St of Mnth; Yth Ldrshp Prog; Comm Volntr; Hosp Aide; DARE; Dbte Team; Mus Clb; Quiz Bowl; Spch Team; Bnd; Chr; Mch Bnd; CR (P); Surgeon (Major Biology); Columbia U

CERDA, WILMER; NORTH BERGEN, NJ; HCST-NORTH HUDSON CTR; (SO); Hi Hnr Roll; Hnr Roll; Sci Fairs; Peer Tut/Med; DARE; Emplmnt; Off Aide; Tchrs Aide; Bsball (V); Stu Cncl (R); CR (R); Math High Honors; Science Fair Awards; Graduate with At Least a Master's Degree; Become Part of National Honor Society; Steven's Institute of Technology; New Jersey Institute of Technology

CERRUTI, CHRISTINE E; RINGWOOD, NJ; LAKELAND REG HS; (JR); Hi Hnr Roll; Hnr Roll; Nat Hon Sy; St of Mnth; WWAHSS; ArtClub; Photog; Dnce; Gmnstcs (V); Student of the Month-Fine Arts/04; Graphic Design/ Advertising; Northeastern; Fordham

CESPEDES, SADIEL; UNION CITY, NJ; UNION HILL HS; (FR); Nat Hon Sy; Lawyer; Engineering; Columbia U; Jersey U

CHAMORRO, OLGAMARIE; NEWARK, NJ; ESSEX CTY VOC-TECH HS; (SO); Hi Hnr Roll; Hnr Roll; St of Mnth; Comm Volntr; Peer Tut/Med; Chrch Yth Grp; Emplmnt; Ch Chr; Religious Education Teacher; Catholic Missions; Math Teacher; Psychology; Seton Hall; Bloomfield College

CHAMPAGNE, TAHKEIA; PATERSON, NJ; ROSA PARKS HS; (FR); Ctznshp Aw; Hi Hnr Roll; Hnr Roll; Nat Hon Sy; Otst Ac Ach Awd; Salutrn; St of Mnth; Comm Volntr; Chrch Yth Grp; Drma Clb; Photog; Bnd; Ch Chr; Dnce; Drl Tm; Bskball (L); Chrldg (L); Sftball (L); Vllyball (L); Stu Cncl (R); CR (R); Yrbk (P); Drama / Acting; Law Degree; Juilliard College of Performing Arts; Howard U

CHAN, CHRISTINE; EATONTOWN, NJ; MONMOUTH REG HS; (SO); Ctznshp Aw; F Lan Hn Soc; Hi Hnr Roll; Hnr Roll; MVP; Otst Ac Ach Awd; Sci/Math Olympn; Comm Volntr; Biology Clb; Key Club; Mus Clb; Sci Clb; Spanish Clb; Acpl Chr; Chr; SP/M/VS; Tennis (J); Cl Off (P); Stu Cncl (P); CR (R); Sch Ppr (E, R); Douglass Science Institute for Women at Rutgers U; Pianist / Guitarist; Princeton U; Columbia U

CHAN, DAVID; ISELIN, NJ; JFK MEMORIAL HS; (SO); Hnr Roll; WWAHSS; Comm Volntr; Chrch Yth Grp; Key Club; Ch Chr; Vllyball; Engineering; New Jersey Institute of Technology; Rutgers U

CHANDRA, AVINASH; JERSEY CITY, NJ; DR RONALD MC NAIR AC HS; (SO); All Am Sch; Nat Hon Sy; Sci Fairs; Comm Volntr; JSA; Mth Clb/Tm; Sci Clb; Track (J); Business Management; Computer Science; U of Pennsylvania; Columbia

CHANG, ANNIE; VOORHEES, NJ; EASTERN REG HS; (SO); Hi Hnr Roll; Hnr Roll; Perf Att; Sci Fairs; St of Mnth; Comm Volntr; Peer Tut/Med; Chrch Yth Grp; Key Club; Scouts; Chr; Ch Chr; SSI-Special Group in St Mary's HS That Requires High Social Skills & Academic Grades; Medical Doctor Degree; Dermatologist; Columbia U in New York; Amherst U in Massachusetts

CHANG, APRIL; PALISADES PARK, NJ; THE AC OF THE HOLY ANGELS; (SR); Hnr Roll; WWAHSS; Yth Ldrshp Prog; Peer Tut/Med; Chrch Yth Grp; Dbte Team; Chr; CR (R); Volunteered At KALCA's Voter Registration Drive; #2 Debater in Bergen County JV Debate; English; Boston College; Boston U

CHANG, CHING-WEN; BRIDGEWATER, NJ; BRIDGEWATER-RARITAN HS; (SR); 4H Awd; Hi Hnr Roll; Hnr Roll; Comm Volntr; 4-H; Key Club; Clb; Bdmtn (V); Cl Off (V); International Hotel & Tourism Management; Johnson & Wales U

CHANG, CHING-YI; BRIDGEWATER, NJ; BRIDGEWATER-RARITAN HS; (SR); 4H Awd; F Lan Hn Soc; Hi Hnr Roll; Hnr Roll; Perf Att; St of Mnth; Comm Volntr; 4-H; Key Club; MuAlphaTh; Bdmtn (V); Volunteer Service Award From Chinese American Cultural Association; Tourism Management; Airline Management; Johnson & Wales U

CHANG, JENNIFER; EDISON, NJ; J P STEVENS HS; (JR); Hnr Roll; Nat Hon Sy; Comm Volntr; Peer Tut/Med; Quill & Scroll; Chr; Orch; Tennis (J); Lit Mag (E); Sch Ppr (R); Yrbk (R); Odyssey of the Mind - Regionals - 2nd Place; Various Awards in Piano; Education; Physical Therapy; Rutgers; The College of New Jersey

CHAO, EDITH; HOLMDEL, NJ; HOLMDEL HS; (JR); F Lan Hn Soc; Hi Hnr Roll; Nat Hon Sy; Nat Mrt LOC; Yth Ldrshp Prog; Comm Volntr; Hosp Aide; Drma Clb; NYLC; Tchrs Aide; French Clb; Chr; Dnce; SP/M/VS; Lcrsse (J); Scr Kpr (J); Yrbk (E); President of Performing Arts Club; Holmdel First Aid EMT; Psychology; Business; Northwestern U; Cornell U

CHAUDHARI, AMIT; EDISON, NJ; JOHN P STEVENS HS; (JR); WWAHSS; Comm Volntr; Hosp Aide; Chess; Cmptr Clb; FBLA; Dnce; Black Belt in Marshal Arts; Pre-Med; Rutgers U; New York U

CHAVIS, J'QUAN; PLAINFIELD, NJ; PLAINFIELD HS; (JR); Hnr Roll; Bskball (J); Ftball (V); Sports Management (Bachelor's); Electrical Engineer (Master's); Clark Atlanta U; Florida A & M U

CHEN, GEORGE; ATLANTIC CITY, NJ; ATLANTIC CITY HS; (FR); Hnr Roll; Key Club; Sch Ppr; History Club; Leo Club; Accounting and Finance; Management Informative Systems

CHEN, HELEN; LEDGEWOOD, NJ; ROXBURY HS; (SO); Ctznshp Aw; F Lan Hn Soc; Hi Hnr Roll; Perf Att; Sci/Math Olympn; St of Mnth; WWAHSS; Comm Volntr; Hosp Aide; Peer Tut/Med; Dbte Team; Fr of Library; HO'Br Yth Ldrshp; Key Club; Mth Clb/Tm; Spch Team; French Clb; Bnd; Mch Bnd; Pep Bnd; Lit Mag (R); Sch Ppr (E, R); Judge for N Consortium for Gifted & Talented Program; Officer / Editor of Key Club - Kiwanis International; Law; Business; Columbia U; Cornell U

CHEN, MING J; PARSIPPANY, NJ; PARSIPPANY HILLS HS; (JR); Hnr Roll; Doctor's Degree; Become a Coach; New Jersey Institute of Technology; New Jersey Medical School

CHEN, MOQIAN; LEDGEWOOD, NJ; (SO); F Lan Hn Soc; Hi Hnr Roll; Hnr Roll; Dbte Team; Key Club; Mth Clb/Tm; Sci Clb; Bnd; Tennis (V); Sch Ppr (P); 1st Dan Black Belt in Tae Kwon Do

CHENEY, MC LAIN; SADDLE RIVER, NJ; NORTHERN HIGHLANDS REG HS; (SO); Hnr Roll; Pres Ac Ftns Aw; Comm Volntr; DARE; Bnd; Ftball (J); Lcrsse (V); EMT; Pre-Med; Georgetown U; Middlebury College

CHENG, CHRISTOPHER; EAST WINDSOR, NJ; HIGHTSTOWN HS; (JR); Hnr Roll; Comm Volntr; Drma Clb; FBLA; Stg Cre; Stu Cncl (R); Business; Boston U

CHENG, FELICIA; ABSECON, NJ; (JR); Hi Hnr Roll; Perf Att; St of Mnth; Comm Volntr; Peer Tut/Med; Key Club; SADD; Chinese Clb; Joined Many Clubs; Accountant; Fashion Merchandising; Drexel U; Lafayette

CHEONG, JESSIE; ISELIN, NJ; JOHN F. KENNEDY MEMORIAL HS; (SO); F Lan Hn Soc; Hnr Roll; WWAHSS; Yth Ldrshp Prog; Peer Tut/Med; FCCLA; Key Club; Lib Aide; Chr; Stg Cre; newspaper: advertising

CHEUNG, KING; EGG HARBOR TOWNSHIP, NJ; EGG HARBOR TWP HS; (JR); Hi Hnr Roll; Hnr Roll; Nat Hon Sy; WWAHSS; Comm Volntr; Chrch Yth Grp; Jr Cls League; Key Club; SADD; Latin Clb; Stu Cncl (R); CR (R); Sch Ppr (E, R, P); Reaching Everyone By Exploring Lies; Academic Team; Economics; Mathematics

CHEUNG, QUEENA W; MONTCLAIR, NJ; MONTCLAIR HS; (JR); Gov Hnr Prg; Hnr Roll; Sci/Math Olympn; Yth Ldrshp Prog; Comm Volntr; Spec Olymp Vol; ArtClub; Chess; Chrch Yth Grp; Dbte Team; DECA; Drma Clb; Lib Aide; Sci Clb; Dnce; Lit Mag (E); Ceramics Artist; International Business Management; Economics and Mathematics / Business; U of Pennsylvania; Harvard U

CHEW, NICHOLAS; SOUTH ORANGE, NJ; COLUMBIA HS; (JR); Hi Hnr Roll; Hnr Roll; WWAHSS; Bnd; Bsball (J); Business; Sports Management; U of Pennsylvania; Wake Forest U

CHHANGAWALA, SAGAR; EDISON, NJ; EDISON HS; (JR); Hi Hnr Roll; Hnr Roll; Perf Att; Comm Volntr; Hosp Aide; Biotechnology; Pre-Medical; Rutgers U, New Brunswick, NJ; Penn State, U Park

CHILAKA, CYNTHIA S; WEST ORANGE, NJ; WEST ORANGE HS; (JR); Comm Volntr; Chrch Yth Grp; Emplmnt; Inducted Into Spanish Honors Society; The National Society of High School Scholars; Somerset Christian College; Seton Hall U

Chan, Christine
Monmouth Reg HS
Eatontown, NJ

Cespedes, Sadiel
Union Hill HS
Union City, NJ

Casingal, Jenna M
County Prep HS
Jersey City, NJ

National
Honor Roll
Spring 2005

Carter III, Clinton D
Pitman HS
Pitman, NJ

Chamorro, Olgamarie
Essex Cty Voc-Tech HS
Newark, NJ

Chilaka, Cynthia S
West Orange HS
West Orange, NJ

CHILDS, ASHLEY M; TRENTON, NJ; HAMILTON EAST/STEINERT; (JR); Hnr Roll; ArtClub; Chrch Yth Grp; FBLA; Mus Clb; Off Aide; ROTC; German Clb; Chr; Ch Chr; Clr Grd; Mch Bnd; High School Education (Teaching); ROTC Instructor; Virginia Tech U

CHILDS, LUCY; TOMS RIVER, NJ; MANCHESTER TWP HS; (FR); Hnr Roll; St of Mnth; ROTC; Bnd; Drl Tm; Mch Bnd; Law; Forensic; Princeton U; Stanford U

CHISELKO, STEPHEN; WARREN, NJ; ST JOSEPH'S HS; (SO); Hnr Roll; Spec Olymp Vol; Chrch Yth Grp; Bnd; Amateur Cyclist; 2002 State Criterium Champion; Engineering; Psychology; Duke U; U of Colorado

CHISHTY, JAVERIA; EAST WINDSOR, NJ; HIGHTSTOWN HS; (JR); Hi Hnr Roll; Hnr Roll; Nat Hon Sy; Otst Ac Ach Awd; St of Mnth; WWAHSS; Comm Volntr; Red Cr Aide; Spec Olymp Vol; FBLA; Latin Clb; Tennis (V); Girl's State Nominee; Doctor of Pharmacy; Biomedical/Chemical Engineering; Princeton U; Rutgers School of Pharmacy

CHMIELEWSKA, IWONA; GARFIELD, NJ; QUEEN OF PEACE HS; (SO); Hi Hnr Roll; USAA; WWAHSS; Comm Volntr; Dbte Team; Stg Cre; Sch Ppr (E); Yrbk (R); Psychology; Military Science; New York U; Columbia U

CHMURA, AGNES; HIGHLAND LAKES, NJ; VERNON TWP HS; (SO); Ctznshp Aw; Hi Hnr Roll; Hnr Roll; Nat Hon Sy; Pres Ac Ftns Aw; St of Mnth; WWAHSS; Peer Tut/Med; Key Club; Mod UN; Scr Kpr; Stu Cncl (R); Elementary Teacher; Montclair U

CHOATE, CHRISTOPHER; BLACKWOOD, NJ; WASHINGTON TWP HS; (JR); Hi Hnr Roll; Nat Hon Sy; Nat Mrt LOC; Otst Ac Ach Awd; St of Mnth; Comm Volntr; Peer Tut/Med; Chess; Dbte Team; DECA; Cr Ctry; Track; President - DECA 2005-2006 School Year; Prosecuting Attorney; Justice; Harvard U; University of Pennsylvania

CHOI, SUNGWON; SADDLE RIVER, NJ; NORTHERN HIGHLANDS REG HS; (SO); Hi Hnr Roll; Comm Volntr; Bnd; SP/M/VS; Bsball (V); Bskball (V); Sccr (V); Concours National De Francois-Laureat National; Multicultural Task Force/Stock Club; Lawyer; CPA; Columbia U; U of Pennsylvania

CHONILLO, KENNETH R; NORWOOD, NJ; NUOT; (JR); Hnr Roll; Comm Volntr; Cr Ctry; Track; Penn State U; Virginia Tech

CHOPRA, CRYSTAL C; CLIFTON, NJ; CLIFTON HS; (SO); Hnr Roll; DARE; Photog; Chr; SP/M/VS; Bskball (L); Nurse; Montclair State U

CHORDIA, APOORVA; PARSIPPANY, NJ; PARSIPPANY HILLS HS; (FR); Hnr Roll; WWAHSS; Comm Volntr; Key Club; Dnce; Bskball (J); Tennis (J); Participated in Dance Competitions; Participated in Johns Hopkins Talent Search; English Literature; Computer Engineer; Columbia U; New York U

CHORMANSKI, CHRISTOPHER; MAYWOOD, NJ; HACKENSACK HS; (SO); Hi Hnr Roll; Otst Ac Ach Awd; WWAHSS; Yth Ldrshp Prog; Chrch Yth Grp; Scouts; Bnd; Golf (V L); Sccr (J); Sales; The College of New Jersey

CHOROMANSKI, STEVEN; BORDENTOWN, NJ; BORDENTOWN REG HS; (JR); Hi Hnr Roll; Otst Ac Ach Awd; Perf Att; WWAHSS; Who's Who Among High School Students 3 Years - 2003, 2004, 2005

CHOUDHRY, AMAD; ELIZABETH, NJ; ELIZABETH HS; (SO); Hnr Roll; Comm Volntr; Hosp Aide; Key Club; Outdrs Clb; Sci Clb; Tennis (J); Med School To Become a Surgeon; Rutgers; Stevens, Penn State

CHOW, LISA; NUTLEY, NJ; QUEEN OF PEACE HS; (SR); Hi Hnr Roll; Nat Mrt LOC; Otst Ac Ach Awd; USAA; WWAHSS; Amnsty Intl; Comm Volntr; Chrch Yth Grp; Mth Clb/Tm; French Clb; Lit Mag (P); Sch Ppr (P); Students Together Opposing Prejudice Club; Tour Guide at School Open Houses; English; Fine Arts; Tufts U

CHRISTIAN, CRYSTAL; OAKHURST, NJ; OCEAN TOWNSHIP HS; (JR); Hi Hnr Roll; Hnr Roll; Hosp Aide; Chrch Yth Grp; Sci Clb; French Clb; Ch Chr; Spartan Scholar Award Recipient; Principal's Commendation List; Corporate Law; Villanova U; The College of New Jersey

CHRISTIE, EILEEN; BRIDGEWATER, NJ; BRIDGEWATER-RARITAN HS; (JR); Hnr Roll; Emplmnt; Key Club; Scouts; Tennis (JC); Stu Cncl (R); Girl Scout Silver Award; U of Delaware; Rutgers, the State U of New Jersey

CHRZANOWSKI, DAVID; MATAWAN, NJ; MATAWAN REG HS; (JR); Ctznshp Aw; Hnr Roll; Nat Hon Sy; Pres Ac Ftns Aw; WWAHSS; Comm Volntr; Chess; Chrch Yth Grp; DARE; Emplmnt; P to P St Amb Prg; SP/M/VS; Ftball; Track; National Society of High School Scholars; Nominated-People to People Student Ambassador; Business; Quinnipiac U; U of Delaware

CHU, DENNIS; RED BANK, NJ; IDDLETOWN HS SOUTH; (FR); Hi Hnr Roll; Comm Volntr; Cmptr Clb; Emplmnt; Svce Clb; Sch Ppr (P); Karate-High Red Belt; Chinese School-8th Grade; Computer Science; Graphics Design; Columbia U; Rochester Institute of Technology

CHU, KRISTINA; EGG HARBOR TOWNSHIP, NJ; EGG HARBOR TOWNSHIP HS; (SR); F Lan Hn Soc; Hnr Roll; Nat Hon Sy; USAA; WWAHSS; Comm Volntr; Peer Tut/Med; Red Cr Aide; Emplmnt; Jr Cls League; Key Club; Sci Clb; SADD; Vsity Clb; Fld Hky (VJ L); Cl Off (P); Stu Cncl (R); CR (R); Sch Ppr (E); Yrbk (R); REBEL-Chairperson, YABBER, Council of 9; Medical Explorers-President; Political Science; Economics; New York U

CHUMBIMUNE, DAVID; EAST NEWARK, NJ; HARRISON HS; (JR); Hnr Roll; St of Mnth; Sccr (J)

CHUNG, CHRISTINE; CRESSKILL, NJ; CRESSKILL JR/SR HS; (JR); F Lan Hn Soc; Hi Hnr Roll; Hnr Roll; Comm Volntr; Peer Tut/Med; ArtClub; Chrch Yth Grp; Tchrs Aide; Spanish Clb; Sftball (J L); Track (J L); Vllyball (V L); Yrbk (E); Scholar Athlete Award/Spanish Club (Treas); International Club & Art Club (Vice President); Pre Medicine; Medical Profession; New York U; Johns Hopkins U

CHUNG, STEPHANIE; SHORT HILLS, NJ; MILLBURN HS; (SO); WWAHSS; Key Club; Mth Clb/Tm; Bnd; Mch Bnd; Orch; SP/M/VS; Track (J); Chamber Orchestra; Johns Hopkins Talent Search; Medicine / Pre-Med; Applied Mathematics; Johns Hopkins U; Georgetown U

CICCHINO, MARLA; EAST HANOVER, NJ; HANOVER PARK HS; (JR); Hi Hnr Roll; Nat Hon Sy; Spec Olymp Vol; Drma Clb; Emplmnt; FBLA; Jr Ach; Key Club; NtlFrnscLg; Prom Com; Acpl Chr; Chr; SP/M/VS; Scr Kpr (V); Sccr (J); Sftball (J); Stu Cncl (V); Lit Mag (R); Sch Ppr (R); Yrbk (R); Camp Fatima Volunteer; Poetry Contest Winner; Marketing; Special Education; Northeastern U; U of Delaware

CIMMET, BRIAN; BELLEVILLE, NJ; BELLEVILLE HS; (JR); Hnr Roll; Nat Hon Sy; WWAHSS; Comm Volntr; Spec Olymp Vol; Bsball (V L); Bskball (V L); Pep Club-Peers Educating Peers Club; Computer Science; New Jersey Institute of Technology; Stevens Institute of Technology

CINTRON, CYNTHIA S; TRENTON, NJ; TRENTON CTRL HS; (JR); Hnr Roll; Perf Att; St of Mnth; WWAHSS; Comm Volntr; Peer Tut/Med; DECA; Drma Clb; Emplmnt; Pep Squd; Tchrs Aide; Chr; Dnce; SP/M/VS; CR (R); Sch Ppr (E, R); Skills USA "VICA", DECA, Gourmet Club; Teen Pep, Peer Leadership; Criminal Justice (BA); Performing Arts (BA); Montclair State U; Rutgers U

CINTRON, JENNIFER; JERSEY CITY, NJ; AC ST ALOYSIUS HS; (SR); Hnr Roll; WWAHSS; Emplmnt; Pep Squd; Bskball (V); Cr Ctry (V); Sftball (V C); Stu Cncl (V, R); Psychology; U of Texas; U of Tampa

CINTRON, MARILIN; JERSEY CITY, NJ; UNIVERSITY AC CHARTER SCH; (JR); Sci Fairs; St of Mnth; Comm Volntr; Sch Ppr (E); Editor in High School Journalism Club; Criminal Justice; Health; Kean U; Temple U

CIOFFI, CHRISTOPHER; HAMMONTON, NJ; HAMMONTON HS; (FR); Hi Hnr Roll; Hnr Roll; St of Mnth; USAA; Emplmnt; Photog; Stg Cre; Yrbk (E); Accounting; Actuarial Science; Rutgers U-Camden NJ; Temple U-Phila. PA

CIPARIS, STEPHANIE; LINDEN, NJ; LHS LINDEN HS; (JR); F Lan Hn Soc; Hi Hnr Roll; Hnr Roll; Nat Hon Sy; Pres Sch; Sci Fairs; St of Mnth; WWAHSS; Comm Volntr; ArtClub; DARE; Lib Aide; Sci Clb; Scouts; German Clb; Clr Grd; Cl Off (R); Stu Cncl (R); CR (S); Girl Scout Silver Award; German National Honor Society; U of Del

CIRIDCO, STEPHANIE; NEWARK, NJ; BARRINGER HS; (FR); Hnr Roll; St of Mnth; Computer Technician; Tourism; Rutgers U; Essex County College

CIRILLO, GINA; LEONIA, NJ; LEONIA HS; (JR); Hi Hnr Roll; WWAHSS; Comm Volntr; Hosp Aide; Chrch Yth Grp; Drma Clb; Mus Clb; Latin Clb; Chr; Ch Chr; Dnce; SP/M/VS; Sings National Anthem for High School Sports; Cantor At Church; Pre Dentistry; Musical Theater

CLANCEY, JESSICA A; PITTSTOWN, NJ; NORTH HUNTERDON HS; (JR); Hi Hnr Roll; Hnr Roll; Pres Sch; Sci Fairs; Comm Volntr; Spec Olymp Vol; Drma Clb; Key Club; Spanish Clb; Cr Ctry (J); Sccr (J); President of Spanish Exchange Club; Spanish Honors Society Member; Psychology; English; College Of William & Mary

CLARK, ALEXANDER; RINGWOOD, NJ; LAKELAND REG HS; (JR); Hi Hnr Roll; Hnr Roll; WWAHSS; Comm Volntr; Emplmnt; Cr Ctry (J L); Track (J); Chemistry; Computer Science; Rutgers U; Drew U

CLARK, DANIEL G; HIGHTSTOWN, NJ; HIGHTSTOWN HS; (JR); Hi Hnr Roll; Hnr Roll; Nat Hon Sy; St of Mnth; Drma Clb; Emplmnt; Scouts; German Clb; Bnd; Mch Bnd; Stg Cre; Cr Ctry (J); Almost Completed Eagle Project; Environmental Science; Journalism; Rutgers U; Bowdoin College

CLARKE, THOMAS; BRIDGEWATER, NJ; BRIDGEWATER-RARITAN HS; (JR); Hi Hnr Roll; Key Club; Prom Com; Bskball (V); Cl Off (R); Stu Cncl (R); Business; Law; U of Virginia; Villanova U

CLASTON, FRANCHESCA; ISELIN, NJ; JOHN F KENNEDY MEMORIAL HS; (FR); Hnr Roll; Chr; Drl Tm; SP/M/VS; Chrldg (J); Gmnstcs; Tennis; Track (V); Stu Cncl; Recreational Aide / Assistant; Journalism / Communications; Medical / Video Technology; NYU; Princeton U

CLAVELLI, ELINA V; RARITAN, NJ; BRIDGEWATER-RARITAN HS; (JR); F Lan Hn Soc; Hi Hnr Roll; WWAHSS; Comm Volntr; FBLA; Mod UN; MuAlphaTh; NtlFrnscLg; Spch Team; Russian Clb; Acpl Chr; Chr; Ch Chr; SP/M/VS; Student of the Year - Somerville Elks; National French "Grand Concours" Champion; Finance; Boston U; U of Pennsylvania

CLAYTON, KENDYLL; EGG HBR TWP, NJ; HOLY SPIRIT HS; (JR); St of Mnth; Yth Ldrshp Prog; Comm Volntr; Hosp Aide; DARE; Sccr (VVVC); Cl Off (V); CR (V); 3 yr varsity member Crew program; League All-Star Soccer 2 Yrs / AC Press All-Star 2 Yrs Soccer; Medical Field; Literary Field

COBOS, JENNIFER M; CLIFFSIDE PARK, NJ; CLIFFSIDE PARK HS; (SO); Hnr Roll; Sccr (J); Marketing; Accounting; New York U; College of New Jersey

COBURN, CHRIS; LINDEN, NJ; LHS LINDEN HS; (SO); Hnr Roll; ROTC; German Clb; Orch; Computer Animation; Computer Programming; State U of New York

COFFEY, MIKE; SPOTSWOOD, NJ; SPOTSWOOD HS; (JR); Cmptr Clb; Mth Clb/Tm; Tennis (V); Engineering; Astronomy; Rutgers; College of New Jersey

COFFEY, YOLANDA; BURLINGTON, NJ; BURLINGTON CITY JHS; MS; Ctznshp Aw; Hi Hnr Roll; Hnr Roll; MVP; Nat Hon Sy; Otst Ac Ach Awd; Perf Att; Pres Ac Ftns Aw; St of Mnth; Comm Volntr; Peer Tut/Med; Chess; Scouts; Bnd; Chr; Bskball (C); Fld Hky (C); Sftball (L); Stu Cncl (R); CR (P); 8th Grade Student of the Week; Very Important Person; Criminal Law; Pre-Med; Princeton U; Harvard U

COHEN, ADRIENNE; SUMMIT, NJ; KENT PLACE SCH; (FR); Ctznshp Aw; F Lan Hn Soc; Yth Ldrshp Prog; Comm Volntr; Hosp Aide; Dbte Team; Jr Cls League; Key Club; Bskball (J); Lcrsse (J); Sccr (J); Cl Off (R); Sch Ppr (R); Traveling Team-Metro Lacrosse; Lead America Inauguration; Political Campaign Volunteer; International Relations; Economics; Brown; Georgetown

COHEN, JANIS; SPRINGFIELD, NJ; JONATHAN DAYTON HS; (SO); Nat Hon Sy; Yth Ldrshp Prog; Comm Volntr; Emplmnt; Tmpl Yth Grp; Spanish Clb; Bskball (J); Sftball (J); Swmg (J); Tennis (J); Ski/Snowboard

COHEN, JUDD E; SOUTH ORANGE, NJ; COLUMBIA HS; (JR); Hnr Roll; WWAHSS; Peer Tut/Med; Chess; Key Club; Tmpl Yth Grp; Sccr (V); Tennis (J)

COLASURDO, DARA N; LEDGEWOOD, NJ; ROXBURY HS; (JR); F Lan Hn Soc; Hi Hnr Roll; Hnr Roll; MVP; Nat Hon Sy; WWAHSS; Comm Volntr; Chrch Yth Grp; Emplmnt; Key Club; Prom Com; Vsity Clb; Dnce; Bskball (J); Lcrsse (V L); PP Ftbl (J); Scr Kpr (V); Sccr (VJCL); Vsy Clb (V); Cl Off (V); Stu Cncl (T); President and Treasurer of Sports; Medicine Club; Biology; Psychology; Johns Hopkins U; Lehigh U

COLASURDO, KATE; HAMMONTON, NJ; HAMMONTON HS; (FR); Hi Hnr Roll; St of Mnth; Emplmnt; Chr; Dnce; Tennis (J); Student Council; Peer Mediation

COLASURDO, SAL; HAMMONTON, NJ; HAMMONTON HS; (JR); Hnr Roll; Perf Att; WWAHSS; Comm Volntr; Emplmnt; Key Club; Bsball (VJ); Bskball (J); Ftball (J); Sccr (J); Honor Roll; Academic Excellence Award

COLDER, KARL; COLUMBUS, NJ; HOLY CROSS HS; (FR); Hnr Roll; Otst Ac Ach Awd; Perf Att; Comm Volntr; Chrch Yth Grp; Chr; Bskball (J L); Ftball (JCL); Track (V); CR (R); Outstanding Seventh Grade Male Runner-Up; Top 8th Grade Math Male Student; Major in Journalism; Meteorology Degree; Florida State U; Temple U

COLEMAN, CHRISTINE; STOCKHOLM, NJ; VERNON TOWNSHIP HS; (JR); F Lan Hn Soc; Hi Hnr Roll; Perf Att; WWAHSS; Comm Volntr; Chrch Yth Grp; Key Club; P to P St Amb Prg; Orch; Tennis (J); Psychology

COLIN, JAKE; FREEHOLD, NJ; ALLENTOWN HS; (JR); Hi Hnr Roll; Hnr Roll; St of Mnth; Peer Tut/Med; Red Cr Aide; Dbte Team; Outdrs Clb; Sci Clb; Bnd; Mch Bnd; Bsball (V L); Sccr (V CL); Stu Cncl; Assistant Athletic Trainer; Gifted and Talented; Pre-Law; Pre-Med; Duke U; U of Pennsylvania

COLLINS, ASHLEY; CAPE MAY COURT HOUSE, NJ; MIDDLE TWP HS; (JR); Hnr Roll; Nat Hon Sy; WWAHSS; Emplmnt; FBLA; Key Club; Bskball; Stu Cncl; Secondary Education; History

COLON, CINDY; ELIZABETH, NJ; ELIZABETH HS; (SO); Hnr Roll; Nat Hon Sy; WWAHSS; Comm Volntr; Chrch Yth Grp; Emplmnt; Key Club; ROTC; Sci Clb; Bnd; Bskball (J); CR (R); Sch Ppr (R, P); Psychology; Biology; Montclair U; Rutgers U

COLON MARCANO, ARACELIS I; DEWAR, NJ; NEWARK VOC HS; (SR); Hnr Roll; Otst Ac Ach Awd; Perf Att; Sci Fairs; St of Mnth; Yth Ldrshp Prog; Comm Volntr; ArtClub; Chrch Yth Grp; DARE; Dbte Team; Drma Clb; Emplmnt; Pep Squd; Scouts; Chr; Ch Chr; Dnce; Drl Tm; Chrldg (J); Teacher; Journalist; Rutgers U; Essex County College

COMPARI, KAITLYN; MILLVILLE, NJ; OUR LADY OF MERCY AC; (SO); Hi Hnr Roll; Perf Att; Yth Ldrshp Prog; Comm Volntr; Hosp Aide; Chrch Yth Grp; Emplmnt; Sccr (V); Congressional Medal Award; Psychology; Princeton U; Brown U

Colder, Karl
Holy Cross HS
Columbus, NJ

Coffey, Mike
Spotswood HS
Spotswood, NJ

Cioffi, Christopher
Hammonton HS
Hammonton, NJ

Chu, Dennis
Iddletown HS South
Red Bank, NJ

Choromanski, Steven
Bordentown Reg HS
Bordentown, NJ

National
Honor Roll
Spring 2005

Chopra, Crystal C
Clifton HS
Clifton, NJ

Cintron, Cynthia S
Trenton Ctrl HS
Trenton, NJ

Clark, Alexander
Lakeland Reg HS
Ringwood, NJ

Coffey, Yolanda
Burlington City JHS
Burlington, NJ

Cohen, Adrienne
Kent Place Sch
Summit, NJ

CONAWAY, WINFIELD D; SALEM, NJ; SALEM HS; (MS); Ctznshp Aw; MVP; Nat Hon Sy; St of Mnth; Chrch Yth Grp; FCA; Ch Chr; Bsball; Bskball; Cyclg; Ftball; Swmg; Computer Tech / Administration; Business or Government; Miami U; Florida State

CONDITO, NICOLE; BELLEVILLE, NJ; BELLEVILLE HS; (SO); Hi Hnr Roll; Hnr Roll; Comm Volntr; Key Club; Track (V L); All Star Competition Cheerleading-Just Cheer; Occupational Therapy; Physical Therapy; Seton Hall U; U of Medicine & Dentistry of NJ

CONNOR, ANTHONY; MERCHANTVILLE, NJ; PENNSAUKEN HS; (JR); Ctznshp Aw; Hnr Roll; Sci Fairs; Bnd; Mch Bnd; Stg Cre; Aerospace Engineering; Computer Engineering; New Jersey Institute of Technology; Rutgers New Brunswick

CONSTANTINE, KRISTEN; BRICK, NJ; MONSIGNOR DONOVAN HS; (SO); Ctznshp Aw; Hi Hnr Roll; Nat Hon Sy; Otst Ac Ach Awd; Pres Ac Ftns Aw; Valdctrian; WWAHSS; Yth Ldrshp Prog; Comm Volntr; Hab For Humty Volntr; Peer Tut/Med; Chrch Yth Grp; Emplmnt; Key Club; P to P St Amb Prg; Photog; Sci Clb; Svce Clb; Bnd; Chr; Jzz Bnd; Pep Bnd; Soccer for Brick / Published Poet; Volunteer for Therapeutic Riding; Art Therapy / Teacher; Vet; St Mary of the Woods College

CONTE, NICOLE; LINCROFT, NJ; MIDDLETOWN HS SOUTH; (JR); Hi Hnr Roll; Emplmnt; Chrldg (V L); PP Ftbl (VJ); Yrbk; Eagles Scholar; Business; Accounting; Seton Hall U; Rowan U

COOPER, AMIRA D L; WILLINGBORO, NJ; WILLINGBORO HS; (FR); Ctznshp Aw; Hnr Roll; Sci Fairs; St of Mnth; Tchrs Aide; Bnd; Mch Bnd; Photo Journalism; Information Technology; U of North Carolina; Hampton U

COOPER, CHAKIRA; JERSEY CITY, NJ; UNIVERSITY AC CHARTER SCH; (SO); Hnr Roll; Nat Hon Sy; Nat Ldrshp Svc; St of Mnth; Comm Volntr; DARE; SP/M/VS; Bskball (V); CR (S); Lit Mag (E); Psychology; Howard

COOPERHOUSE, MICHAEL; MARTINSVILLE, NJ; BRIDGEWATER-RARITAN HS; (JR); Hnr Roll; Nat Hon Sy; WWAHSS; Yth Ldrshp Prog; Hosp Aide; Key Club; Sci Clb; Tmpl Yth Grp; Skiing; Vllyball (J); Fed Challenge; Biological Sciences; Harvard U; Boston U

COPPOLA, JEAN M; HAZLET, NJ; RARITAN HS; (SR); Hi Hnr Roll; Hnr Roll; WWAHSS; Comm Volntr; Vsity Clb; Fld Hky (V L); PP Ftbl; FBI; IRS; John Jay College

CORDERO, XIOMARA; NEWARK, NJ; GLADYS HILLMAN JONES SCH; (MS); Perf Att; Peer Tut/Med; DARE; Dnce; Drl Tm; Bsball (J); Sftball (J); Writer (Author); Actress; Essex County College; Rutgers U

CORDI, SALVATORE M; BLOOMFIELD, NJ; QUEEN OF PEACE HS; (JR); Hnr Roll; St of Mnth; WWAHSS; Bskball (V); Wt Lftg (V); Stu Cncl (R); Principal's Scholarship Recipient; Law; Caldwell College; Seton Hall U

CORLEW, ASHLEY; LINCROFT, NJ; MIDDLETOWN HS SOUTH; (JR); Hi Hnr Roll; Hnr Roll; WWAHSS; Yth Ldrshp Prog; Comm Volntr; FBLA; Bskball; Diversity Day; Regionals for Future Business Leaders; Biology; Pre-Med; Drew U; DeSales U

CORMACK, KIMBERLY A; HIGHTSTOWN, NJ; HIGHSTOWN HS; (SR); Hi Hnr Roll; Hnr Roll; Nat Hon Sy; Otst Ac Ach Awd; WWAHSS; Comm Volntr; Peer Tut/Med; Drma Clb; Emplmnt; Mth Clb/Tm; Off Aide; Outdrs Clb; Stg Cre; Skt Tgt Sh (C); Distinguished Expert in Rifle Marksmanship; Graduated with High Honors; Mechanical Engineering; Aerospace Engineering; Rensselaer Polytechnic Institute

CORNWALL, KASEY-ANN; BRIDGETON, NJ; CUMBERLAND REG HS; (JR); Ctznshp Aw; Hi Hnr Roll; Hnr Roll; Otst Ac Ach Awd; Perf Att; St of Mnth; Comm Volntr; Peer Tut/Med; FCA; FBLA; Off Aide; Tchrs Aide; Ch Chr; Mar Art (J); Skiing; CR (T, R); Yrbk (P); Outstanding Award in Biology; Arts (Fine Arts); Mathematics; Bloomfield; Rowan U

CORPUZ, JESSA J R; JERSEY CITY, NJ; (FR); Hnr Roll; Perf Att; Bdmtn; Bskball; Vllyball; Nursing; Doctor; New Jersey City U; Saint Peter's College

CORRENTE, ANTHONY J; EDISON, NJ; ST JOSEPH'S HS; (JR); Hi Hnr Roll; MVP; Nat Hon Sy; Perf Att; WWAHSS; Comm Volntr; Hab For Humty Volntr; Chrch Yth Grp; Emplmnt; Off Aide; Spanish Clb; Sccr (V); Track (J); Computer Science; Computer Engineering

CORTES, ERICA J; ISELIN, NJ; JOHN F KENNEDY HS; (SO); Ctznshp Aw; Hnr Roll; WWAHSS; Comm Volntr; Emplmnt; Key Club; Chr; Track (J); Stu Cncl (R); CR (R); Nursing; Teaching; Saint Peter's College; Rutgers U

CORTES, MAIDA; KEYPORT, NJ; KEYPORT HS; (MS); Ctznshp Aw; Hnr Roll; St of Mnth; Comm Volntr; DARE; Spch Team; Vsity Clb; Bskball (VJ); Sftball (V); Vsy Clb (V); Cl Off (P); CR (P); Princeton U; U of Maryland

CORTES, NOEL; BELLEVILLE, NJ; BELLEVILLE HS; (JR); WWAHSS; Key Club; Wrstlg (J); Volunteered At Boys and Girls Club Summer of 2003-Received Award; College Major-Literature / English; Career Goal-Professional Wrestler; Montclair State U; Rutgers U

CORUJO, RAVEN D; SAYREVILLE, NJ; SAYREVILLE WAR MEMORIAL HS; (JR); Chr; Varsity Choir, Mixed Choir, Voice Training; Study of the Body; Biology; U of Tampa

COSCA, CARMELA M; ISELIN, NJ; COLONIA HS; (JR); F Lan Hn Soc; Hnr Roll; Comm Volntr; DARE; Emplmnt; FCCLA; Fashion Show; Sewing Club; Fashion Design - Merchandise / Sales; Middlesex County College; Newark College of Arts and Science

COSTALES, MARIA J; SECAUCUS, NJ; AC OF SACRED HEART HS; (SO); F Lan Hn Soc; Hi Hnr Roll; Hnr Roll; Nat Ldrshp Svc; Nat Mrt LOC; Otst Ac Ach Awd; USAA; Peer Tut/Med; ArtClub; DARE; Off Aide; Sccr (V); Vllyball (J); The Scholarship Fund For Inner-City Children; National Youth Leadership on Medicine; Medicine; Architecture; New York U; Rutgers U

COSTE, JORDAN; OCEAN CITY, NJ; OCEAN CITY HS; (JR); Hi Hnr Roll; Comm Volntr; Chrch Yth Grp; Emplmnt; Svce Clb; Sccr (J); Wrstlg (J); Voice of Democracy Essay Winner; Freshmen Coach's Soccer Award; Business Major; The Citadel Military College of SC; Gettysburg College

COSTELLO, KIMBERLY; MT HOLLY, NJ; RANCOCAS VALLEY REG HS; (SO); Hi Hnr Roll; Hnr Roll; WWAHSS; Key Club; Sccr; U of North Carolina

COSTELLO JR, MICHAEL; SAYREVILLE, NJ; CARDINAL MC CARRICK HS; (JR); F Lan Hn Soc; Hnr Roll; MVP; Perf Att; Emplmnt; Scouts; Bskball (V); Cr Ctry (V); Eagle Scout; State Trooper; HS Basketball Coach; Monmouth College; Rutgers U

COTIGNOLA, KAREN; OAK RIDGE, NJ; JEFFERSON TWP HS; (JR); Hnr Roll; Red Cr Aide; Chrch Yth Grp; DARE; Chr; Dnce; SP/M/VS; Stg Cre; Singing; Acting, Dancing; American Music and Dance Academy; New York U

COTIGNOLA, MELISSA; MADISON, NJ; MADISON HS; (FR); Hi Hnr Roll; Hnr Roll; Pres Sch; Yth Ldrshp Prog; Comm Volntr; Red Cr Aide; Key Club; NYLC; Bnd; Volunteer / Coach Town Cheerleading Program; Political Science; History; Georgetown U; American U

COTOULAS, ALEXANDRA; WATCHUNG, NJ; WATCHUNG HILLS REG HS; (SO); Hnr Roll; Comm Volntr; Emplmnt; SADD; Chrldg (V); Lcrsse (J); Film; Journalism; New York U; Syracuse U

COURTNEY, DAVID; MONTCLAIR, NJ; MONTCLAIR HS; (JR); F Lan Hn Soc; Hnr Roll; Nat Hon Sy; Pres Ac Ftns Aw; CARE; Hab For Humty Volntr; Emplmnt; Jr Cls League; Vsity Clb; French Clb; SP/M/VS; Swmg (V CL); Stu Cncl (V); French National Honor Society; Physics

COUSINEAU, LYSSA; ROOSEVELT, NJ; HIGHTSTOWN HS; (JR); Hi Hnr Roll; Hnr Roll; Nat Hon Sy; Otst Ac Ach Awd; WWAHSS; Comm Volntr; Peer Tut/Med; Drma Clb; French Clb; Chr; SP/M/VS; Stg Cre; Mock Trial Team; Schola Cantorum; Anthropology

COX, STEPHANIE; CLIFTON, NJ; QUEEN OF PEACE HS; (SO); Hi Hnr Roll; Hnr Roll; Otst Ac Ach Awd; WWAHSS; Comm Volntr; French Clb; Ch Chr; Dnce; Social Adventures Club; Summer Theater Work Shop NYC; Law; Psychology; Columbia U; Seton Hall U

COYLE, JOSEPH; HIGHTSTOWN, NJ; HIGHTSTOWN HS; (JR); Hnr Roll; Emplmnt; Prom Com; Scouts; German Clb; Cr Ctry (V); Track (J); Cl Off (V); Private Study of Bass Guitar; Eagle Scout Candidate; Criminal Justice; Political Science; Rowan U; York College

COZZARELLI JR, ROBERT; BELLEVILLE, NJ; BELLEVILLE HS; (SO); Hi Hnr Roll; Hnr Roll; Jr Rot; MVP; Pres Ac Ftns Aw; Comm Volntr; Hosp Aide; Spec Olymp Vol; DARE; Drma Clb; FCA; Key Club; Vsity Clb; Italian Clb; Wrstlg (V CL); Team NJ USA Wrestling; Octagon Club Secretary; Physical Therapy; Rehabilitation Medicine; Penn State; U of PA

CRAM, SHIELLA M; RIO GRANDE, NJ; MIDDLE TWP HS; Hnr Roll; Nat Hon Sy; Perf Att; ArtClub; Key Club; Art Club; Major in Computer Science; Full Sail; Philadelphia Art College

CRANFORD, CIARE B; NEWARK, NJ; BARRINGER HS; (FR); Ctznshp Aw; Hi Hnr Roll; Otst Ac Ach Awd; Perf Att; Sci/Math Olympn; St of Mnth; Peer Tut/Med; Chrch Yth Grp; DARE; Dbte Team; Ch Chr; Vllyball; Cl Off (P); Stu Cncl (T); CR (P, T); Bowling; Chef; PhD in Mathematics; Art Institute of New York; Art Institute of PA

CRASTO, EROISHA; JERSEY CITY, NJ; DR RONALD MC NAIR AC HS; (FR); Hnr Roll; Perf Att; Salutrn; Tennis; Journalism; Psychology; Pennsylvania State U; Harvard U

CRAWFORD, ALEXIS N; NEWARK, NJ; MALCOLM X SHABAZZ HS; (SO); Hnr Roll; Cmptr Clb; Emplmnt; FTA; Dnce; SP/M/VS; Stg Cre; Best Friend - Diamond Girl; Most Likely to Succeed / First Honors; Lawyer / Entertainment or Defense; Rutgers U; Florida A & M U

CRAWFORD, SAVANNAHRE' V; JERSEY CITY, NJ; DICKINSON HS; (SO); Hnr Roll; Otst Ac Ach Awd; Perf Att; St of Mnth; Comm Volntr; Peer Tut/Med; DARE; Drma Clb; Quiz Bowl; Schol Bwl; Dnce; SP/M/VS; Stg Cre; Chrldg (V); Stu Cncl (R); Member of College Prep; New Jersey City U Visual Performing; Performing Arts Theatre; Criminal Justice; Rowan U; Michigan State

CRAWFORD, TEMPESTT; ELIZABETH, NJ; ELIZABETH HS; (SR); Ctznshp Aw; Hnr Roll; Perf Att; Comm Volntr; Peer Tut/Med; Chrch Yth Grp; DARE; Emplmnt; Jr Ach; Key Club; Ch Chr; Drl Tm; Network Engineering; Business Administration; Johnson & Wales U

CRELIN, AMANDA L; MIDDLETOWN, NJ; MIDDLETOWN HS NORTH; (JR); F Lan Hn Soc; Hi Hnr Roll; Hnr Roll; Sccr (J); Track (J); Currently Taking Art Instruction Classes; Art Therapy; Fine Arts; Arcadia U; Long Island U

CRENNAN JR, THOMAS J; JACKSON, NJ; JACKSON MEMORIAL HS; (SR); All Am Sch; Sci Fairs; WWAHSS; Comm Volntr; Chess; Chrch Yth Grp; Civil Air Pat; Cmptr Clb; Emplmnt; FBLA; Key Club; ROTC; AFJROTC-Letter/Inspector General; AFJROTC-Sons of American Revolution Award; Certified Flight Instructor; USAF Pilot; Daniel Webster College

CRIQUE, JANISA; PASSAIC, NJ; PASSAIC HS; (SO); Hnr Roll; Elementary Art Teacher; Rutgers U; Bergen Community College

CRIVELLO, CHRISTOPHER M; NESHANIC STATION, NJ; ST JOSEPH'S HS; (SO); Hi Hnr Roll; WWAHSS; Comm Volntr; Chrch Yth Grp; Mth Clb/Tm; Cr Ctry (J L); Scr Kpr (J); Track (J L); Stu Cncl (R); Math League Award; Medical Research; Business/Accounting; PA St U; Johns Hopkins U

CRUZ, ISAIAH; NEWARK, NJ; BARRINGER HS; (SO); Hi Hnr Roll; Hnr Roll; Fr of Library; Bnd; Graphic Arts Design; Brown College

CRUZ, SAMUEL A; UNION CITY, NJ; UNION HILL HS; (FR); Ctznshp Aw; Hi Hnr Roll; Hnr Roll; Otst Ac Ach Awd; Perf Att; WWAHSS; Yth Ldrshp Prog; Peer Tut/Med; Chrch Yth Grp; DARE; Emplmnt; Key Club; Mus Clb; Bnd; Tennis; CR (R); Pathfinder Club; Junior Police; Pastor of My Church; Computer Engineering; Andrews U

CSONTOS, ALEX; MANVILLE, NJ; MANVILLE HS; (SR); Hnr Roll; Stg Cre; Bskball; Ftball; Stu Cncl; Sch Ppr (R); Get a Job; Football; Basketball

CUCCO, ELENA M; MADISON, NJ; MADISON HS; (FR); Hnr Roll; Comm Volntr; Chrch Yth Grp; Key Club; Sci Clb; Bnd; Vllyball (V L); National Invention Convention Winner; PDP Member; Psychology; Education; Villanova; William and Mary

CUCCO, LAURIE A; NEW MILFORD, NJ; AC OF THE HOLY ANGELS; (SR); F Lan Hn Soc; Hi Hnr Roll; Hnr Roll; Comm Volntr; Hosp Aide; ArtClub; Mus Clb; Svce Clb; Chr; Lit Mag; Executive Board of Operation Smile; Eucharistic Minister; BS Nursing; Villanova U; U of Rhode Island

CUCINELLA JR, ROBERT; HACKETTSTOWN, NJ; HACKETTSTOWN HS; (SR); Hi Hnr Roll; Hnr Roll; WWAHSS; Yth Ldrshp Prog; Peer Tut/Med; Drma Clb; Chr; SP/M/VS; Stg Cre; Member of NJ Civic Youth Ballet; Theatre Major; History Major; DeSales U

CUCUNATO, ALYSSA; SOMERDALE, NJ; PAUL VI HS; (SO); Hnr Roll; ArtClub; Italian Clb; Rowan U; Villanova U

CUNNINGHAM, JESSICA M; PHILLIPSBURG, NJ; PHILLIPSBURG HS; (SR); Hi Hnr Roll; Hnr Roll; Comm Volntr; ArtClub; Chr; SP/M/VS; Swg Chr; 2nd Place in Talent Show; Music; Art

CURCIONE, CHRISTINE; SOMERS POINT, NJ; OUR LADY OF MERCY AC; (SO); Hi Hnr Roll; WWAHSS; Comm Volntr; DARE; Photog; SADD; SPAN Clb; Sftball (J); Vllyball (J); Chemistry; Biology

CURRAN, RICHARD; SADDLE BROOK, NJ; PARAMUS CATHOLIC HS; (JR); Hnr Roll; Nat Hon Sy; Otst Ac Ach Awd; Comm Volntr; Biology Clb; Mth Clb/Tm; Bsball (J); Ice Hky (J); Sccr (J); Criminal Justice; Athletic Training; The College of New Jersey; Lehigh U

CURRAN, RYAN; FREEHOLD, NJ; FREEHOLD TWP HS; (SO); Hi Hnr Roll; Hnr Roll; Nat Mrt LOC; Ftball (J); Wt Lftg; Stu Cncl (R); Teaching; Pennsylvania State U; Michigan State U

CURRY, KIMBERLY; PARSIPPANY, NJ; PARSIPPANY HS; (SR); Hnr Roll; WWAHSS; Yth Ldrshp Prog; Comm Volntr; Pep Squd; Vsity Clb; Chrldg (V CL); Track (V L); Jack & Jill of America Inc. Eastern Reg.; Teen Treasurer, Nat'l Youth Forum - Law; Psychology; Public Relations; U of Maryland Eastern Shore

CUSACK, FRANK; TRENTON, NJ; NOTTINGHAM HS; (JR); Nat Hon Sy; Dbte Team; Emplmnt; Tmpl Yth Grp; Bnd; Mch Bnd; Pep Bnd; Stg Cre; Swmg (V L); Academic Letter; National Honor Society; Bachelor in Culinary Arts; The Restaurant School At Walnut Hill College; Johnson & Wales U

Cusack, Frank
Nottingham HS
Trenton, NJ

Cranford, Ciare B
Barringer HS
Newark, NJ

Cotignola, Karen
Jefferson Twp HS
Oak Ridge, NJ

Cornwall, Kasey-Ann
Cumberland Reg HS
Bridgeton, NJ

Cooper, Amira D L
Willingboro HS
Willingboro, NJ

National
Honor Roll
Spring 2005

Constantine, Kristen
Monsignor Donovan HS
Brick, NJ

Costello Jr, Michael
Cardinal Mc Carrick HS
Sayreville, NJ

Cozzarelli Jr, Robert
Belleville HS
Belleville, NJ

Crasto, Eroisha
Dr Ronald Mc Nair AC HS
Jersey City, NJ

Cunningham, Jessica M
Phillipsburg HS
Phillipsburg, NJ

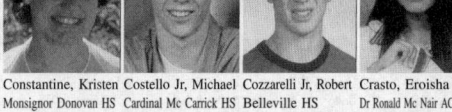

CUSENZA, KRISTINA; EGG HARBOR TOWNSHIP, NJ; EGG HARBOR TOWNSHIP HS; (JR); Hi Hnr Roll; Nat Hon Sy; WWAHSS; Comm Volntr; Red Cr Aide; Chrch Yth Grp; Key Club; Lit Mag (R); Sch Ppr (R); Varsity Rowing; English/Creative Writing/Philosophy; Hope to Be a Novelist/Poet; Mount St Marys; Fairleigh Dickinson U

CZAJKOWSKI, ANTHONY; MILLTOWN, NJ; SPOTSWOOD HS; (SO); Hi Hnr Roll; Hnr Roll; Otst Ac Ach Awd; Perf Att; FBLA; Mth Clb/Tm; Sci Clb; Bnd; Mch Bnd; Pep Bnd; Track (J L); Stu Cncl (R); Accounting

CZERWINSKI, DANA; CLIFTON, NJ; CLIFTON HS; (JR); 4H Awd; Ctznshp Aw; Hi Hnr Roll; Hnr Roll; MVP; Otst Ac Ach Awd; Perf Att; St of Mnth; Yth Ldrshp Prog; Comm Volntr; Chrch Yth Grp; DARE; Emplmnt; Key Club; Psychology; Social Work

DABROWSKA, PAULINA; LINDEN, NJ; LINDEN HS; (JR); F Lan Hn Soc; Hi Hnr Roll; Hnr Roll; Comm Volntr; Emplmnt; FTA; Scouts; German Clb; Orch; Sccr (J); Sftball (J); Psychology; Teaching

DAHDAH, NICOLE A; TOTOWA, NJ; PASSAIC VALLEY HS; (SO); Sci Fairs; Chrch Yth Grp; DARE; Emplmnt; Key Club; Chr; Bskball (J); Fld Hky (V L); Stu Cncl (R); Work at a Day Care Center; Teaching; Mathematics; Fairfield U

DAHL, ALICIA A; HAMBURG, NJ; VERNON TOWNSHIP HS; (SO); Ctznshp Aw; Hnr Roll; Pres Ac Ftns Aw; Pres Sch; WWAHSS; Yth Ldrshp Prog; Comm Volntr; Chrch Yth Grp; Emplmnt; Key Club; Mod UN; Prom Com; Dnce; Cr Ctry (V); Stu Cncl (V); Sch Ppr (E); Presidential Award, French National Honor Society; Prudential Community Service Award

DALPE, JESSICA R; HAMPTON, NJ; (JR); Ctznshp Aw; F Lan Hn Soc; Hi Hnr Roll; Hnr Roll; Otst Ac Ach Awd; Pres Ac Ftns Aw; DARE; Emplmnt; Scouts; Vsity Clb; French Clb; Fld Hky (V CL); Sftball (V L); Who's Who Among American H.S students-Sports Edition; Environmental Science; Engineering

DALY, WILLIAM; SOUTH PLAINFIELD, NJ; SOUTH PLAINFIELD HS; (JR); F Lan Hn Soc; Hi Hnr Roll; Hnr Roll; Comm Volntr; DARE; P to P St Amb Prg; Cr Ctry (V L); Wt Lftg; Wrstlg (VJ L); Recreation Baseball; Electrical Engineering; Masters; Lehigh U; Worcester Polytechnic Institute

D'AMATO, AMANDA M; MT ARLINGTON, NJ; ROXBURY HS; (SR); F Lan Hn Soc; Hi Hnr Roll; Hnr Roll; Nat Hon Sy; Perf Att; ArtClub; Emplmnt; Scouts; Mar Art; PP Ftbl; Sftball (VJ); National Art Honor Society; Guardian Angels; Master's Degree in Biology; PhD in Human Anthropology; Ramapo College of New Jersey

DAMIANO, JESSICA L; FLORENCE, NJ; FLORENCE TWP MEM HS; (FR); Hnr Roll; Bskball (J); Sch Ppr (R); Pediatrician; Writer

D'AMICO, DANIELLE; CRANFORD, NJ; CRANFORD HS; (JR); DAR; Hnr Roll; Otst Ac Ach Awd; Yth Ldrshp Prog; Comm Volntr; Peer Tut/Med; Chrch Yth Grp; Emplmnt; Sci Clb; Svce Clb; Vsity Clb; Latin Clb; Sccr (V L); Sch Ppr (R); 3rd Team Coaches All County, Soccer 2004; Student Athlete of the Week; Political Science; Sports Management; Southeastern College; Messiah College

DAMODARA, NITESH; BERGENFIELD, NJ; ACADEMIES AT ENGLEWOOD; (FR); Hi Hnr Roll; Hnr Roll; St of Mnth; Hab For Humty Volntr; Peer Tut/Med, ArtClub; Chess; Orch; Tennis (J); Sch Ppr (R); Yrbk (E); Mathematics State Award - Talent Search By Johns Hopkins; Writers Achievement Award; Medical Science-Specializing in Endocrinology or Cardiology; Harvard Medical School-Boston; Princeton-New Jersey

DANCER, JON E; NEW EGYPT, NJ; ALLENTOWN HS; (SR); Hnr Roll; St of Mnth; Comm Volntr; Emplmnt; Ntl FFA; Wdwrkg Clb; FFA Outstanding Member; Chapter Star Farmer; Ornamental Horticulture; Agronomy; Delaware Valley College; U of Delaware

DANG, JENNIFER; SUMMIT, NJ; SUMMIT HS; (JR); Hi Hnr Roll; Hnr Roll; Comm Volntr; Hosp Aide; Peer Tut/Med; Emplmnt; P to P St Amb Prg; Orch; Lcrsse (J); Sccr (J); CR (R); Business; Advertisement; Boston College; George Washington U

DANIELS, DAVID; CLEMENTON, NJ; LINDENWOLD HS; (SR); Hnr Roll; WWAHSS; Comm Volntr; Emplmnt; Tchrs Aide; Wdwrkg Clb; Project Seed; Determination Award; Computer Repair; Computer Engineer; Rowan U; Morris Brown U

DANIELS, SHAWN; IRVINGTON, NJ; IRVINGTON HS; (SO); Hnr Roll; St Schl; SP/M/VS; Bskball (V); Ftball (V); Football; School of Law; (UConn) U of Connecticut; Clemson U

DARDEN, SHANTAL M; PERTH AMBOY, NJ; MIDDLESEX CO VOC-WOODBRIDGE; (FR); Hnr Roll; Otst Ac Ach Awd; Peer Tut/Med; ArtClub; Drma Clb; Doctor / Medical Field; Theatre / Drama Communication; New York U; Hampton U

DASIKA, KOUSHIK; BRIDGEWATER, NJ; BRIDGEWATER-RARITAN HS; (SO); Hnr Roll; WWAHSS; Comm Volntr; Chess; FBLA; Key Club; Lib Aide; Mod UN; Tech Clb; Tmpl Yth Grp; Latin Clb; National Society of High School Honors; Small Business Administration; Marketing & Sales; Harvard Business School; Wharton Business School

DA SILVA, PATRICIA; KENILWORTH, NJ; DAVID BREARLEY MIDDLE HS; (JR); Hnr Roll; Otst Ac Ach Awd; Perf Att; Comm Volntr; DARE; Prom Com; Scouts; Portuguese Clb; Gmnstcs (L); Track (J); Tae Kwon Do (Martial Arts) Trophies; Music Merit Awards/Music Metals; Pre-Veterinary Medicine; Norwich U

DAVE, MILI; EDISON, NJ; EDISON HS; (SO); Hi Hnr Roll; Hnr Roll; Amnsty Intl; Comm Volntr; Hosp Aide; Emplmnt; Tennis (J); Stu Cncl (R); CR (R); Medicine

DAVIDSON, BRITTANY A; BLOOMFIELD, NJ; DE PAUL CATHOLIC HS; (JR); Hi Hnr Roll; Nat Hon Sy; Otst Ac Ach Awd; WWAHSS; Comm Volntr; Peer Tut/Med; Key Club; Chrldg (V); Stu Cncl (T); Sch Ppr (R); Yrbk (R); Business (MBA Future); Broadcasting; Marist; Lafayette

DAVIDSON, JESSICA R; WHIPPANY, NJ; WHIPPANY PARK; (JR); Hi Hnr Roll; Nat Hon Sy; Yth Ldrshp Prog; Comm Volntr; Red Cr Aide; Emplmnt; FBLA; FTA; Key Club; NYLC; Off Aide; Sci Clb; Svce Clb; Peer Counseling and Peer Buddy; Health Careers Club

DAVIS, MEREDITH; ALLENDALE, NJ; NORTHERN HIGHLANDS REG HS; (SO); Hi Hnr Roll; Hnr Roll; Nat Ldrshp Svc; Perf Att; Chrch Yth Grp; DARE; DECA; Emplmnt; Scouts; Svce Clb; Spanish Clb; Clr Grd; Dnce; Mch Bnd; Stg Cre; Girl Scout Silver Award; Accounting; Finance

DAVISON, COURTNEY K; TRENTON, NJ; NOTRE DAME HS; (JR); Hi Hnr Roll; Hnr Roll; Otst Ac Ach Awd; Sci Fairs; Ch Chr; Dnce; SP/M/VS; The Teacher's Selection Anthology of Poetry 2002 Edition; Psychology; Nutrition; Charter Carolina U; Rutgers U

DAVISON, DENISE; NORTH BRUNSWICK, NJ; NORTH BRUNSWICK TWP HS; (JR); WWAHSS; DECA; Emplmnt; Off Aide; Dnce; Track (V); Stu Cncl (R); Make a Difference Award; Varsity Dance Team; Finance; Business; U of Delaware; Loyola College

DEANGELIS, TINA; MARLTON, NJ; CAMDEN CATHOLIC HS; (SR); Hi Hnr Roll; Hnr Roll; Peer Tut/Med; Drma Clb; Scouts; Svce Clb; SADD; Sch Ppr (E, R); Yrbk (E); Communications; Adelphi U; Manhattan College

DEANS, CHRISTOPHER; WEST ORANGE, NJ; WEST ORANGE HS; (JR); Hnr Roll; Perf Att; Comm Volntr; Key Club; Bnd; Cr Ctry (J); Business; Rutgers New Brunswick; College of New Jersey

DE BLASI, DEANNA; FAIRFIELD, NJ; QUEEN OF PEACE HS; (JR); 4H Awd; Hi Hnr Roll; Nat Hon Sy; Otst Ac Ach Awd; St of Mnth; WWAHSS; Amnsty Intl; Comm Volntr; Hab For Humty Volntr; 4-H; Chrch Yth Grp; Drma Clb; Emplmnt; Mus Clb; Photog; Prom Com; Scouts; Chr; Ch Chr; SP/M/VS; Stu Cncl (R); Sch Ppr (E); Yrbk (R, P); Third Highest GPA in Junior Class; National Society of High School Scholars; Forensics; Religion / Theatre; College of New Jersey; New York U

DEEN, DAVID V; SICKLERVILLE, NJ; WINSLOW TWP HS; (SR); Hnr Roll; Nat Hon Sy; Lcrsse (V CL); Sccr (V L); National Honor Society; Business Marketing; Stockton; Hofstra

DEE NORWOOD, PATRINA; NEWFIELD, NJ; VINELAND HS; (JR); Hi Hnr Roll; Hnr Roll; Comm Volntr; Red Cr Aide; Emplmnt; Gear Up; School Counts-School To-Careers; Law Enforcement; Child Care; Cumberland; Temple

DEFREECE, KHAYREEDAH; MONTCLAIR, NJ; MONTCLAIR HS; (JR); Hnr Roll; Comm Volntr; Peer Tut/Med; Tchrs Aide; SP/M/VS; Track (J); Poetry Published in "Eternal Portraits"; English; Interior Design; Virginia State U; South Carolina State U

DEGALA, VIRGILIO; HO HO KUS, NJ; (JR); Hi Hnr Roll; Perf Att; Comm Volntr; Emplmnt; Sci Clb; Vsity Clb; Bnd; Mch Bnd; Varsity Marching Band; BS Biology/Pre-Med; Muhlenberg College; Allegheny College

DE GORI, AVA; PITMAN, NJ; PITMAN HS; (SR); Hi Hnr Roll; Hnr Roll; St of Mnth; Comm Volntr; Red Cr Aide; Chrch Yth Grp; Dbte Team; Emplmnt; FCA; JSA; Key Club; Off Aide; Prom Com; SP/M/VS; Bskball (L); Fld Hky (V CL); PP Ftbl; Track (V L); Stu Cncl (R); Major-Finance; Hofstra U Hempstead, NY

DEL AGUILA, CYNTHIA; SPRINGFIELD, NJ; JONATHAN DAYTON HS; (SO); Hnr Roll; Comm Volntr; Spec Olymp Vol; Sci Clb; Alternative Club; Medical Careers Club; Doctorate in Architecture; Mastery in Architecture; Princeton/Harvard; Yale

DE LA ROSA, JOSEPH; NORTH BERGEN, NJ; NORTH BERGEN HS; (FR); Hnr Roll; WWAHSS; Key Club; French Clb; Investment Banker; Certified Public Accountant; Harvard U; NYU

DELEON, ALEXANDER L; MERCHANTVILLE, NJ; PENNSAUKEN HS; (JR); F Lan Hn Soc; Hnr Roll; St of Mnth; Emplmnt; Wdwrkg Clb; Cr Ctry (V); Tennis (V); Wrstlg (V); Criminal Justice; Psychology/Psychological rehabilitation; Long Island U; Drew U

DE LEON, SEBASTIAN; WEST ORANGE, NJ; WEST ORANGE HS; (JR); F Lan Hn Soc; Hnr Roll; Spanish Clb; Sccr (VJ L); Architecture; Essex County; NJIT

DELIBERTI, MATTHEW; HOLMDEL, NJ; HOLMDEL HS; (SO); F Lan Hn Soc; Hi Hnr Roll; Otst Ac Ach Awd; Perf Att; Comm Volntr; Chrch Yth Grp; Italian Clb; Accounting; CPA; Boston College; Seton Hall U

DELLE, SANGU J; HIGHTSTOWN, NJ; PEDDIE HS; (JR); Ctznshp Aw; Hi Hnr Roll; Hnr Roll; Nat Ldrshp Svc; Otst Ac Ach Awd; St of Mnth; Yth Ldrshp Prog; Comm Volntr; Peer Tut/Med; Red Cr Aide; Biology Clb; Dbte Team; Drma Clb; Emplmnt; Jr Ach; Key Club; Mod UN; Svce Clb; SP/M/VS; Stg Cre; Scr Kpr (V); Sccr (C); Vllyball (J); Adv Cncl (P); Cl Off (P); Stu Cncl (P); CR (P); Lit Mag (E); Sch Ppr (E); Yrbk (R); Time Magazine/ Bentley Tomorrow 25; Founded My Own N.G.O.; Double Major-Biology/ Econ.; Medicine/Law; Harvard U; Columbia U

DELVA, AMANDA; ELIZABETH, NJ; ELIZABETH HS; (JR); F Lan Hn Soc; WWAHSS; Comm Volntr; Key Club; Tennis (J); Nursing

DEMPSEY, TIM; NEW PROVIDENCE, NJ; NEW PROVIDENCE HS; (SO); Hnr Roll; Chrch Yth Grp; Emplmnt; Vsity Clb; Wdwrkg Clb; Bsball; Bskball (J L); Ftball (V L); Track (V); Wt Lftg; Bass Guitar Player; Criminal Justice; U of Maryland; Northeastern U

DENISICK, MAGDALENA; MONTCLAIR, NJ; MONTCLAIR HS; (SO); Hi Hnr Roll; Hnr Roll; Nat Hon Sy; WWAHSS; Comm Volntr; Spec Olymp Vol; ArtClub; Key Club; P to P St Amb Prg; Italian Clb; Golf (J); Gmnstcs (V); Tennis (J); CR (S); Boston U; New York U

DENNIS, ZEVENIA S; TEANECK, NJ; TEANECK HS; (SO); Hnr Roll; Nat Hon Sy; Chess; Chrch Yth Grp; DARE; Drma Clb; Emplmnt; Fr of Library; Clr Grd; Dnce; Track (V L); Stu Cncl (S); CR (R); Journalism; Psychology; Spelman College; Brown U

DENNY, ANGELA; MONMOUTH JUNCTION, NJ; SOUTH BRUNSWICK HS; (SO); Otst Ac Ach Awd; Yth Ldrshp Prog; Comm Volntr; Hosp Aide; Emplmnt; P to P St Amb Prg; Prom Com; Scouts; Svce Clb; Vllyball; Congressional Student Leadership Conference, Teenagers Abroad Language Immersion Program; National Junior Leadership Conference; Psychology; Entrepreneurship/Business Management; Georgetown U; Boston U

DE PASQUALE JR, NELSON; BELLEVILLE, NJ; QUEEN OF PEACE HS; (SO); Hi Hnr Roll; Nat Hon Sy; St of Mnth; Amnsty Intl; Comm Volntr; Dbte Team; Drma Clb; Emplmnt; Mod UN; Mus Clb; Italian Clb; Chr; Ch Chr; SP/M/VS; Bsball (J); Stu Cncl; Sch Ppr (E); Queen of Peace Principal's Scholarship; Columbus Citizens Foundation H.S. Scholarship; Communications, Lawyer, Psychiatrist; Drama/Acting; Drew U, Seton Hall U; Fordham U

DE PREE, BRIAN K; RINGWOOD, NJ; LAKELAND REG HS; (JR); Hnr Roll; Nat Hon Sy; Sci Fairs; WWAHSS; Comm Volntr; Chrch Yth Grp; DARE; Emplmnt; Lttrmn Clb; Mod UN; NYLC; Sci Clb; Vsity Clb; Bsball (V L); Ice Hky (V CL); Sccr (V L); Model Congress; Road Show; Communications; Sports Management; U of North Carolina Greensboro; Penn State U

DEPSEE, DIANA N; WEST PATERSON, NJ; PASSAIC VALLEY REG HS; (SR); Hi Hnr Roll; Hnr Roll; WWAHSS; Comm Volntr; DARE; Emplmnt; FBLA; Prom Com; PP Ftbl (VJ); Scr Kpr (J); FBLA President/PVTV (Passaic Valley Television); First Honors; Lawyer; Communications; Passaic County Community College; Caldwell College

DESAI, DHARA; LINDEN, NJ; LHS LINDEN HS; (JR); F Lan Hn Soc; Hi Hnr Roll; Hnr Roll; St of Mnth; WWAHSS; Comm Volntr; Peer Tut/Med; Mth Clb/Tm; ROTC; Sci Clb; German Clb; USAA International Foreign Languages Award; National Youth Leadership Forum; Pediatrics; The College of New Jersey; Rutgers U (New Brunswick)

DESAI, SHIVANI; VOORHEES, NJ; (SR); Gov Hnr Prg; Hi Hnr Roll; Hnr Roll; Nat Hon Sy; Nat Mrt LOC; St Schl; St of Mnth; WWAHSS; Yth Ldrshp Prog; Comm Volntr; Hosp Aide; Peer Tut/Med; Emplmnt; Mod UN; NYLC; Svce Clb; Tmpl Yth Grp; Chr; Dnce; Bdmtn (J); Bskball (J); Stu Cncl (R); Started Club for Students Against Bullying; History & English Student of the Year; Pre-Medicine; U of Maryland in Baltimore County; Rutgers U

DESTRO, DAVID; COLONIA, NJ; COLONIA HS; (JR); F Lan Hn Soc; Hnr Roll; Nat Hon Sy; Perf Att; Comm Volntr; Peer Tut/Med; Chrch Yth Grp; DARE; Emplmnt; Mod UN; Scouts; Acpl Chr; SP/M/VS; Sccr; Stu Cncl (R); Participating in Shakespeare Festival; Spanish and National Honor Societies; Computer Engineering / Electrical Engineering; Computer Science; New Jersey Institute of Technology; Stevens Institute of Technology

DEUTSCH, ERICA; PARSIPPANY, NJ; PARSIPPANY HS; (SO); Hi Hnr Roll; Hnr Roll; MVP; Pres Sch; Bskball (VJC); Scr Kpr (J); Sccr (VJC); Cl Off (S); Stu Cncl (R); Member of Spanish Honor Society; Responsible Enthusiastic Active Leader Award; Business; Nursing; U of Maryland; Boston U

DHABLIWALA, SAPNA; ISELIN, NJ; JFK MEMORIAL HS; (JR); Hnr Roll; Perf Att; Comm Volntr; Peer Tut/Med; DARE; Key Club; Lib Aide; Prom Com; Sci Clb; Chr; Dnce; Orch; Stg Cre; Sccr (J); Sch Ppr (R); Pharmacy; Physical Therapy; Rutgers Pharmacy; Long Island U

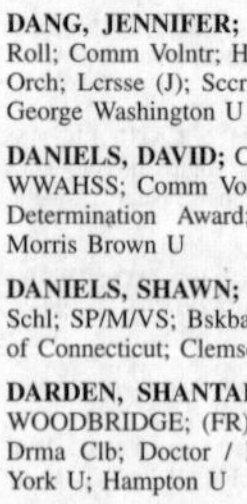
Depsee, Diana N
Passaic Valley Reg HS
West Paterson, NJ

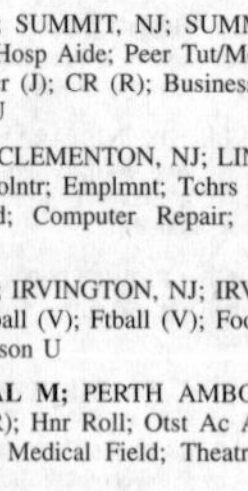
De Gori, Ava
Pitman HS
Pitman, NJ

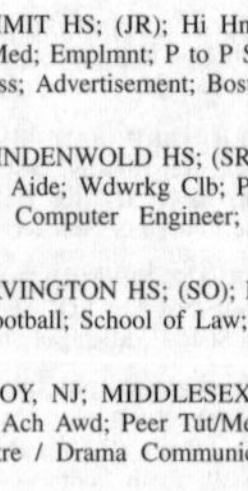
Dasika, Koushik
Bridgewater-Raritan HS
Bridgewater, NJ

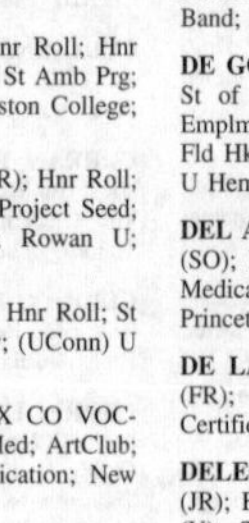
Dang, Jennifer
Summit HS
Summit, NJ

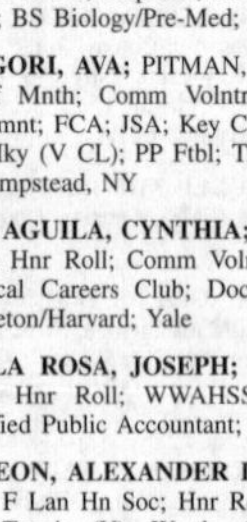
Dancer, Jon E
Allentown HS
New Egypt, NJ

National
Honor Roll
Spring 2005

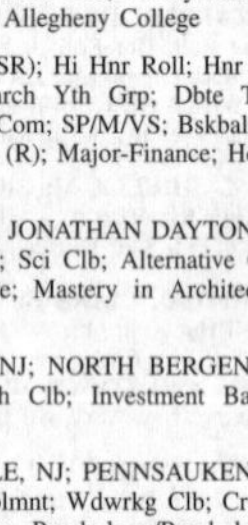
Dabrowska, Paulina
Linden HS
Linden, NJ

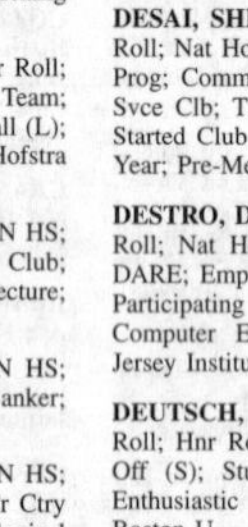
Daniels, David
Lindenwold HS
Clementon, NJ

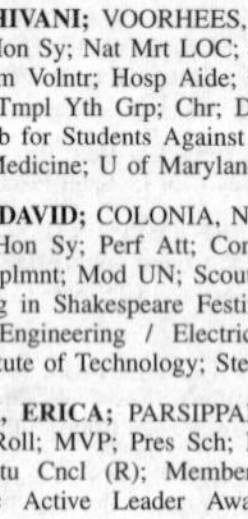
Deans, Christopher
West Orange HS
West Orange, NJ

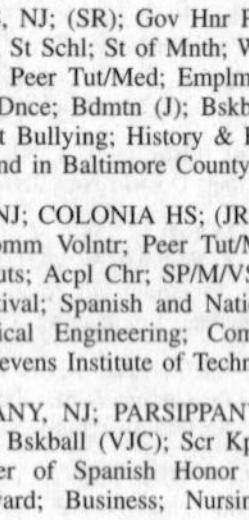
Del Aguila, Cynthia
Jonathan Dayton HS
Springfield, NJ

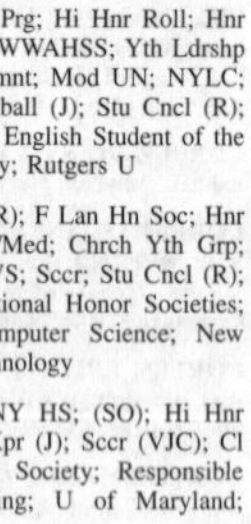
Deliberti, Matthew
Holmdel HS
Holmdel, NJ

DIANA, ANNA; EAST RUTHERFORD, NJ; HENRY P BECTON REG HS; (JR); F Lan Hn Soc; Hnr Roll; Comm Volntr; DARE; Emplmnt; Chrldg (J); Scr Kpr (V); Sftball (J); Cosmetology/Dermatology; Business Administration; Liz Claiborne, Pennsylvania; Montclair U

DIAS, HASANI; HALEDON, NJ; MANCHESTER REG HS; (JR); Hi Hnr Roll; Hnr Roll; WWAHSS; Comm Volntr; Chess; Cmptr Clb; Stg Cre; Cr Ctry (J); Track (V); Business Management; William Paterson U; NYU

DIAS, RICARDO F; HARRISON, NJ; HARRISON HS; (JR); Ctznshp Aw; Hnr Roll; Nat Hon Sy; Perf Att; St of Mnth; Tech Clb; Engineering; Electrician; New Jersey Institute of Technology; Rutgers U-New Brunswick

DIAS-HOLPERIN, JESSICA; KEARNY, NJ; KEARNY HS; (SO); Accounting; Homicide Detective; Jersey City U; Rutgers U

DIAZ, ELIANA; WEST ORANGE, NJ; WEST ORANGE HS; (SR); Hi Hnr Roll; Hnr Roll; St of Mnth; Yth Ldrshp Prog; Comm Volntr; Chess; Cmptr Clb; DARE; Lttrmn Clb; Pep Squd; SADD; Vsity Clb; Wdwrkg Clb; Chrldg (J); PPSqd (V); PP Ftbl (V); Scr Kpr (V); BS; Montclair State U

DIAZ, ERICA; NORTH BERGEN, NJ; AC OF SACRED HEART HS; (JR); Hi Hnr Roll; Hnr Roll; Nat Hon Sy; Otst Ac Ach Awd; Salutrn; Sci Fairs; St Schl; St of Mnth; Yth Ldrshp Prog; Comm Volntr; Hosp Aide; Peer Tut/Med; DARE; Emplmnt; NYLC; Off Aide; Prom Com; Tchrs Aide; Vsity Clb; French Clb; Stg Cre; Bskball (V); Scr Kpr (VJ); Vsy Clb (V); Vllyball (V); Adv Cncl (R); Cl Off (V, T, R); Stu Cncl (V, T, R); CR (V, T, R); Peer Minister; National Honor Society; Education - Secondary / Doctorate; History / Law - Master's / Doctorate; Ramapo College; Northeastern U

DIAZ, GEANNA E; OLD BRIDGE, NJ; OLD BRIDGE HS; (JR); Hi Hnr Roll; Hnr Roll; Perf Att; Comm Volntr; Tchrs Aide; Spanish Clb; Previous Participation In: Soccer, Dance, Cheerleading, Gymnastics, Chorus, and Ice Skating; Communications (Radio and Television); William Paterson U; Rider U

DIAZ, JOEL; NEWARK, NJ; BARRINGER HS; (SO); Hnr Roll; Sci Fairs; WWAHSS; DARE; Key Club; Chr; Stg Cre; Stu Cncl (R); Rutgers U; Montclair State U

DIAZ, SASHA; FRANKLIN LAKES, NJ; INDIAN HILLS HS; (JR); Hi Hnr Roll; Hnr Roll; Otst Ac Ach Awd; Perf Att; Yth Ldrshp Prog; Comm Volntr; Hosp Aide; Peer Tut/Med; Chrch Yth Grp; Dbte Team; Emplmnt; NYLC; Chr; Ch Chr; Bskball (J); Lcrsse (J); PP Ftbl (V); Scr Kpr (J); CR (R); TIGS Program; Peer Leadership Program; Accounting; Tax Attorney; Berkeley College; Miami-U, OH

DIAZ, SELENE; JERSEY CITY, NJ; HCST-NORTH HUDSON CTR; (SO); F Lan Hn Soc; Hi Hnr Roll; Sci/Math Olympn; Peer Tut/Med; Emplmnt; French Clb; Yrbk (E, R, P); Participation in Hudson County, NJ Art Exposition; Graphic Design/Web Design; Studio Art

DICKSON, MATTHEW J; PITMAN, NJ; PITMAN HS; (JR); Hnr Roll; Nat Hon Sy; Otst Ac Ach Awd; St of Mnth; Yth Ldrshp Prog; AL Aux Boys; Chrch Yth Grp; Emplmnt; Key Club; Lib Aide; SADD; Tchrs Aide; Acpl Chr; Chr; Cr Ctry (V); Track (V); Yrbk (E, P); Math Education; West Chester U; Rowan U

DIDONATO, MATTHEW S; HAMMONTON, NJ; HAMMONTON HS; (FR); Hi Hnr Roll; Perf Att; Pres Sch; Sci Fairs; St of Mnth; Comm Volntr; Peer Tut/Med; Chrch Yth Grp; Sci Clb; Tchrs Aide; Bnd; Chr; Mch Bnd; Pep Bnd; First Choir Alto Saxophone in All South Jersey Jazz Ensemble; Kindness Award; Biology; Secondary Education; The College of New Jersey; Princeton U

DIEGUEZ, ALEJANDRO; KEARNY, NJ; QUEEN OF PEACE HS; (JR); MVP; St of Mnth; Comm Volntr; DARE; SADD; Bsball (V L); Bskball (J); Ftball (V L); Track (V L); Stu Cncl (R); Peer Ministry; Sociology / Psychology; Teacher; Felician College; Montclair State U

DIMEN, RACHEL; EAST AMPTON, NJ; RANCOCAS VALLEY REG HS; (FR); Hi Hnr Roll; Hnr Roll; St of Mnth; WWAHSS; Comm Volntr; Key Club; Bnd; Chr; Ch Chr; Stg Cre; Lcrsse; Medicine; Psychology; Penn State; Rutgers U

DI MINO, CHARLES; ANNANDALE, NJ; NORTH HUNTERDON HS; (JR); Hi Hnr Roll; Otst Ac Ach Awd; Perf Att; Sci/Math Olympn; BPA; Cmptr Clb; Svce Clb; Tech Clb; Spanish Clb; Sccr (J); Sch Ppr (E, R); Computer Science; Business; Hofstra U; Drexel U

DIOS, DAVID; KEARNY, NJ; QUEEN OF PEACE HS; (SO); F Lan Hn Soc; Hi Hnr Roll; WWAHSS; Comm Volntr; Peer Tut/Med; Mod UN; P to P St Amb Prg; Clb; Foreign Language Major; International Business and Finance Major; U of Pennsylvania; Georgetown U

DI RENZO, LAURA; CLARK, NJ; ARTHUR L JOHNSON HS; (JR); F Lan Hn Soc; Hi Hnr Roll; Nat Hon Sy; Perf Att; WWAHSS; Comm Volntr; Mth Clb/Tm; Italian Clb; Chr; National Society for High School Scholars / National Young Leaders Conf.; Nominated For Presidential Classroom Scholar; Education / Medicine

DISTURCO, ALYSSA; MILLINGTON, NJ; WATCHUNG HILLS REG HS; (SR); Hi Hnr Roll; Hnr Roll; Nat Hon Sy; Otst Ac Ach Awd; USAA; WWAHSS; Comm Volntr; Hab For Humty Volntr; Peer Tut/Med; Emplmnt; Svce Clb; SADD; Spanish Clb; Stg Cre; Sccr (J); Vllyball (V CL); CR (R); Mock Trial-Attorney; Psychology; International Affairs; The George Washington U; New York U

DIXON, CHRISTOPHER; ENGLEWOOD, NJ; DWIGHT MORROW HS; (SO); Hnr Roll; Sci Fairs; St of Mnth; DARE; Mus Clb; Bskball (J); Sch Ppr (R); Member of the Photo Club; Web Design; Master Chef

DIXON, TANTANIA; PATERSON, NJ; PATERSON CATHOLIC HS; (SO); Hnr Roll; Perf Att; Sci Fairs; St of Mnth; DARE; Emplmnt; SADD; Chrldg (V); Business; Computers; Alabama A & M U; Miami U

DJEKA, ERMAL; RIDGEFIELD, NJ; NEW YORK MILITARY SCH; (SO); Hnr Roll; Nat Ldrshp Svc; Yth Ldrshp Prog; ArtClub; ROTC; Chr; Drl Tm; Bsball (V); Bskball; Ftball (V); Sccr (V); Cl Off (R); Air Force Academy; Be a Pilot; West Point; Air Force Academy of Colorado

DOBARIYA, VARUN; NORTH BERGEN, NJ; NORTH BERGEN HS; (JR); Hi Hnr Roll; Hnr Roll; Comm Volntr; Key Club; Lib Aide; Russian Clb; Stu Cncl (R); Dentist; Eye Specialist; Rutgers U; UMDNJ

DOBSON, LATOYA; TEANECK, NJ; TEDNECK HS; (SO); Hnr Roll; Perf Att; Chr; Fncg (J); Vllyball (J)

DOLLEAR, CORY; CLIFFWOOD, NJ; MATAWAN REG HS; (SO); Hnr Roll; Yth Ldrshp Prog; Emplmnt; Bsball (J); Architecture; Athletic Trainer; Rutgers U; Penn State U

DOMINGUEZ, ANTONIO; CARTERET, NJ; ST JOSEPH'S HS; (JR); Hnr Roll; WWAHSS; Hosp Aide; Emplmnt; Spanish Clb; Bnd

DOMINGUEZ, MATTHEW; NEWARK, NJ; SCIENCE HS; (FR); Hnr Roll; Otst Ac Ach Awd; Sci/Math Olympn; St of Mnth; Bsball (V); Stu Cncl (R); Accounting; U of Miami; U of South Carolina

DONAHUE, PRISCILLA; MAYS LANDING, NJ; OAKCREST HS; (FR); Hi Hnr Roll; Hnr Roll; Nat Hon Sy; Sci Fairs; Comm Volntr; Peer Tut/Med; Emplmnt; Sci Clb; Tech Clb; Chr; GAA (L); Gmnstcs (J); Swmg (J); Stu Cncl (R); Crew=5V Poems Published; Michael H Duberson Memorial Award; Veterinary Medicine; Zoology

DONNELLY, JESSICA; HAMBURG, NJ; WALLKILL VALLEY REG HS; (SO); Nat Hon Sy; Mus Clb; Chr; Chrldg (JC); Big Brother and Big Sister; Cosmetology

DORIO, JESSICA; FLEMINGTON, NJ; HUNTERDON CTRL REG HS; (SO); Hi Hnr Roll; Hnr Roll; Perf Att; Chrch Yth Grp; Emplmnt; Chr; English; Journalism; The College of New Jersey

DORMAN, JENNIFER; CEDAR GROVE, NJ; CEDAR GROVE HS; (SO); Hi Hnr Roll; WWAHSS; Comm Volntr; Peer Tut/Med; Chrch Yth Grp; DARE; Key Club; Dnce; SP/M/VS; Chrldg (V); Sccr (J); Track (V); Dance; Pennsylvania State U; New York U

DORSAINVILLE, JAYELLE; OLD BRIDGE, NJ; OLD BRIDGE HS; (JR); Comm Volntr; Hosp Aide; Peer Tut/Med; Kwanza Clb; Bskball (J); Track (J); African American Club; Asian Pacific Club; Forensic Science; Criminal Justice; John Jay U; Florida State U

DORSETT, ROSEMARY; HAMILTON SQUARE, NJ; THE HUN SCH OF PRINCETON; (SO); Hi Hnr Roll; Comm Volntr; Key Club; Fld Hky (V L); Crew-Varsity Program; Journalism; Psychology; U of Virginia; U of North Carolina-Chapel Hill

DOSHI, PALAK A; UNION CITY, NJ; ST DOMINIC AC; (JR); Hnr Roll; Perf Att; Comm Volntr; Chr; Bdmtn; Bskball; Vllyball; Hospitality Club; Multicultural Club; Law; Seton Hall; Fordham

DOU, NICHOLAS G; DAYTON, NJ; SOUTH BRUNSWICK HS; (FR); Hi Hnr Roll; Comm Volntr; Peer Tut/Med; DARE; JSA; Mth Clb/Tm; Sci Clb; Bnd; Jzz Bnd; SP/M/VS; Tennis (V); 2005 Physics I Award / Top 10% in New Jersey Science League / AMCIO / AIME Participant; Johns Hopkins U-CTY/ National Math Talent Search Score 700-800 SAT I Math Before Age 13

DRAGONETTI, ANTHONY; CHERRY HILL, NJ; CHERRY HILL HS EAST; (JR); Ctznshp Aw; Hnr Roll; Perf Att; Sci Fairs; St of Mnth; Comm Volntr; Stu Cncl (R); Played with Various Bands; Instructor in Karate; Music Production; Business Law; Drexel U; Lebanon Valley College

DREWKE, LAURA M; RIVERSIDE, NJ; RIVERSIDE HS; (FR); Ctznshp Aw; Hnr Roll; Perf Att; St of Mnth; DARE; Drma Clb; Fr of Library; Mth Clb/Tm; Mus Clb; Photog; Spch Team; Tchrs Aide; Chr; Dnce; SP/M/VS; Yrbk (E, R, P); Cheerleading for Bulldogs / Outside of School - Fishtown PA; Veterinary Medicine; Performing Arts; New York U

DUCASSE, ALESSANDRA; MAPLEWOOD, NJ; COLUMBIA HS; (JR); Hi Hnr Roll; Hnr Roll; WWAHSS; Comm Volntr; Hab For Humty Volntr; Chrch Yth Grp; Key Club; Lib Aide; Nursing; Business Manager; Seton Hall U; Rutgers U

DUCILLE, EBONY; SICKLERVILLE, NJ; WINSLOW TWP HS; (JR); Hi Hnr Roll; Hnr Roll; MVP; Nat Mrt LOC; Perf Att; St of Mnth; WWAHSS; Peer Tut/Med; Chrch Yth Grp; Chr; Ch Chr; Drl Tm; Bskball (J); Chrldg; Cr Ctry (J); Scr Kpr; Track (V); Principal's Honor Roll Before Selected Student of the Month; Education; Business and Management; Fordham; D'Youville

DUKE, CHRISTINE L; JERSEY CITY, NJ; AC OF SACRED HEART HS; (JR); Hi Hnr Roll; Hnr Roll; Comm Volntr; Peer Tut/Med; Drma Clb; Emplmnt; Lib Aide; Mus Clb; Chr; Ch Chr; Dnce; SP/M/VS; Fashion Show / Talent Show; Sing At Nursing Homes; Pharmacist; Doctor; Rutgers U in Newark; St Peter's Prep College in NJ

DUKE, SAMANTHA L; JERSEY CITY, NJ; AC OF SACRED HEART HS; (SO); Hi Hnr Roll; Nat Ldrshp Svc; Otst Ac Ach Awd; Perf Att; Sci Fairs; St of Mnth; Yth Ldrshp Prog; Comm Volntr; Hosp Aide; Drma Clb; Mus Clb; Chr; SP/M/VS; Stu Cncl (T); CR (P); Accounting; Nursing

DUMES, KATHLEEN; NORTH BERGEN, NJ; HCST-NORTH HUDSON CTR; (SO); F Lan Hn Soc; Hi Hnr Roll; Hnr Roll; Nat Mrt LOC; Otst Ac Ach Awd; Sci Fairs; St of Mnth; Comm Volntr; Peer Tut/Med; DARE; Emplmnt; Key Club; Mod UN; Off Aide; Sci Clb; Tchrs Aide; Spanish Clb; Chr; Dnce; Bskball (L); Chrldg (L); Vllyball (L); Stu Cncl (P); CR (R); Criminal Justice; Criminology; John Jay College of Criminal Justice

DUNHAM, JAMYE; WILLINGBORO, NJ; WILLINGBORO HS; (FR); Hnr Roll; Chrch Yth Grp; Ch Chr; Bskball; Medical Degree; Virginia Tech

DUNN, CASEY; CEDAR GROVE, NJ; CEDAR GROVE HS; (JR); F Lan Hn Soc; Hi Hnr Roll; Hnr Roll; Nat Hon Sy; Otst Ac Ach Awd; St of Mnth; WWAHSS; Comm Volntr; Peer Tut/Med; Emplmnt; Key Club; Vsity Clb; Italian Clb; Chr; SP/M/VS; Tennis (V); Candidate for Tri-M Honors Society; The National Society of High School Scholars; Elementary Education; English; DeSales U; Susquehanna U

DUNNAN, DIANA; WESTFIELD, NJ; WESTFIELD HS; (JR); Hnr Roll; Comm Volntr; Peer Tut/Med; Emplmnt; Sccr (V L); Sftball (V L); Sch Ppr (E, R, P); Business/Communications; Journalism

DURAC, SHAMUS; BRIDGEWATER, NJ; BRIDGEWATER RARITAN HS; (SO); F Lan Hn Soc; Hi Hnr Roll; Hnr Roll; Yth Ldrshp Prog; JSA; Key Club; NYLC; P to P St Amb Prg; Spanish Clb; Bnd; Jzz Bnd; Mch Bnd; Orch; USSBA Honors Jazz Band; Politics Club; Political Science; International Relations; Georgetown; George Washington U

DURAND, KEVIN C; BRIDGEWATER, NJ; BR HS; (JR); Ctznshp Aw; Hnr Roll; Perf Att; Chess; Key Club; Orch

DURAND, MICHELLE E V; LINDEN, NJ; LINDEN HS; (JR); Hi Hnr Roll; Hnr Roll; MVP; St of Mnth; Comm Volntr; Chrch Yth Grp; Emplmnt; Mus Clb; ROTC; Sci Clb; Vsity Clb; Acpl Chr; Chr; Ch Chr; Orch; Bskball (VJ L); Cr Ctry (V L); Sftball (J); CR (R); Semper Fidelis Award For Musical Excellence; 2004 Div II Miss Jr. Teen Newark - 2nd Runner Up; Business and Finance / Bachelor's Degree; Banking / Associate's or Bachelor's Degree; Rider U; Rutgers U

DURU, DERMAN; PATERSON, NJ; JOHN F. KENNEDY HS; (SR); Ctznshp Aw; Hnr Roll; Nat Hon Sy; WWAHSS; Comm Volntr; Biology Clb; Emplmnt; Sci Clb; Bowling (Varsity); National History Day (NJ Award & 3rd Place); Engineering; Pre-Med; Rutgers U (Accepted and Enrolled); Montclair State U (Accepted)

DUVELSAINT, HERBENSON K; EAST ORANGE, NJ; EAST ORANGE CAMPUS 9 HS; (SO); Mth Clb/Tm; Sccr (V); Track (V); Vllyball; Lawyer; U of Miami; Rutgers U

DWORAK, JULIE M; WOODBRIDGE, NJ; WOODBRIDGE HS; (SR); F Lan Hn Soc; Hnr Roll; Nat Hon Sy; Nat Sci Aw; Otst Ac Ach Awd; Pres Ac Ftns Aw; Yth Ldrshp Prog; Comm Volntr; Peer Tut/Med; Emplmnt; NYLC; Prom Com; Spanish Clb; Bnd; Orch; Stu Cncl (S); Top Twenty; EMT; Food Science; Nutrition; Rutgers U; Drexel U

DWYER-HELMECK, KEITH; JERSEY CITY, NJ; DICKINSON HS; (SR); Comm Volntr; Spec Olymp Vol; DARE; Scouts; Wdwrkg Clb; Bsball; NJCU; Steven's School of Tech

EADDY, MALISSA; ROSELLE, NJ; MOTHER SETON REG HS; (MS); Hnr Roll; Perf Att; Dbte Team; Ch Chr; Dnce; SP/M/VS; First and Second Place Forensic Competition; First Place Winner in Scholastic Olympic; Biological Research Scientist; Interpreter for Japanese; New York U; Princeton U

EARL, DAVID; MIDDLESEX, NJ; MIDDLESEX HS; (SR); Ctznshp Aw; F Lan Hn Soc; Hi Hnr Roll; Hnr Roll; Nat Hon Sy; Pres Sch; Salutrn; St of Mnth; WWAHSS; Yth Ldrshp Prog; Comm Volntr; Peer Tut/Med; Red Cr Aide; AL Aux Boys; Emplmnt; FBLA; HO'Br Yth Ldrshp; Mod UN; Pep Squd; Quiz Bowl; Scouts; Bnd; Jzz Bnd; Pep Bnd; Bskball (V); Cr Ctry (V); Golf (V); Cl Off (P); Stu Cncl (P, S); Sch Ppr (E); Political Journalist; George Washington U

EAST, ROBERT S; PASSAIC, NJ; PASSAIC HS; (FR); Perf Att; Chrch Yth Grp; Wdwrkg Clb; Ch Chr; Ftball (J); Track (V); Pre-Med; Do; U of Tennessee; Virginia Tech U

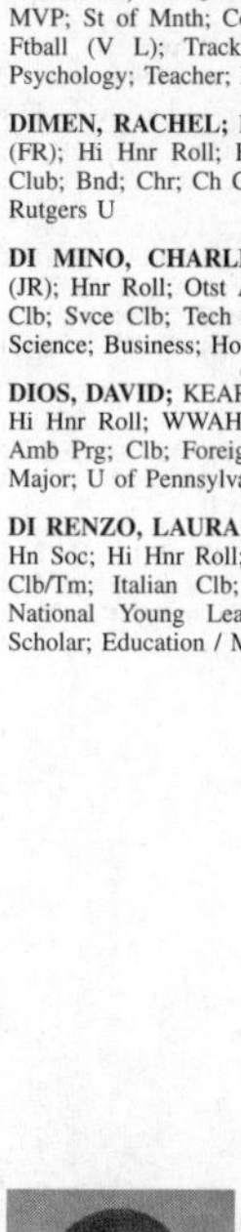
East, Robert S
Passaic HS
Passaic, NJ

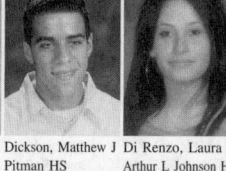

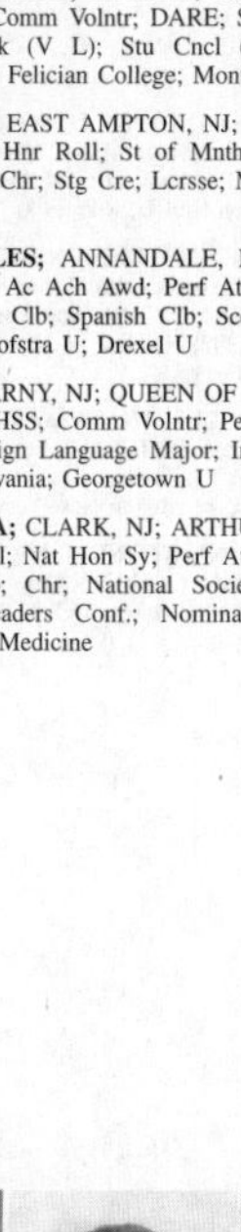
Drewke, Laura M
Riverside HS
Riverside, NJ

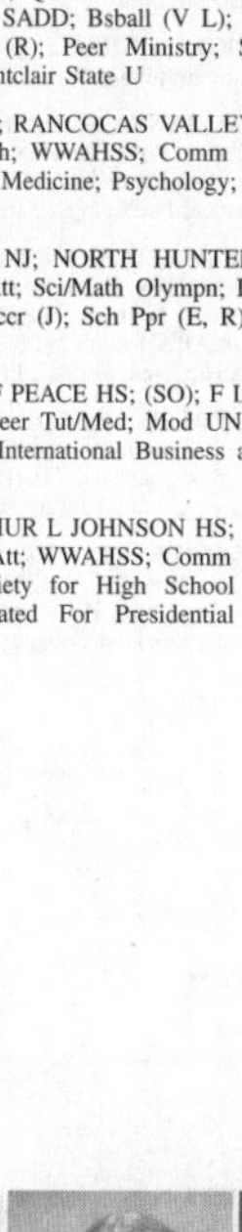
Dorio, Jessica
Hunterdon Ctrl Reg HS
Flemington, NJ

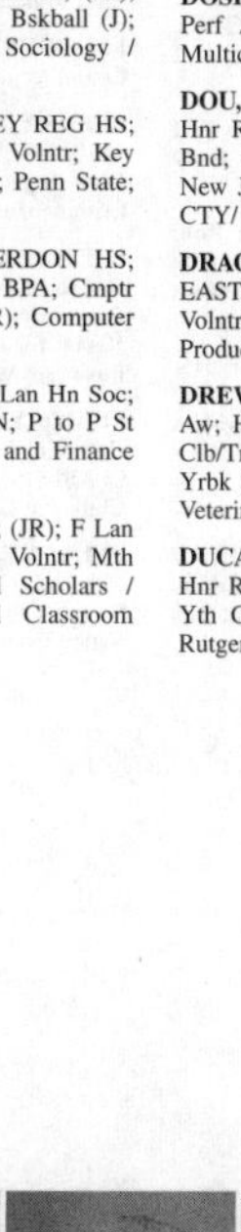
Dollear, Cory
Matawan Reg HS
Cliffwood, NJ

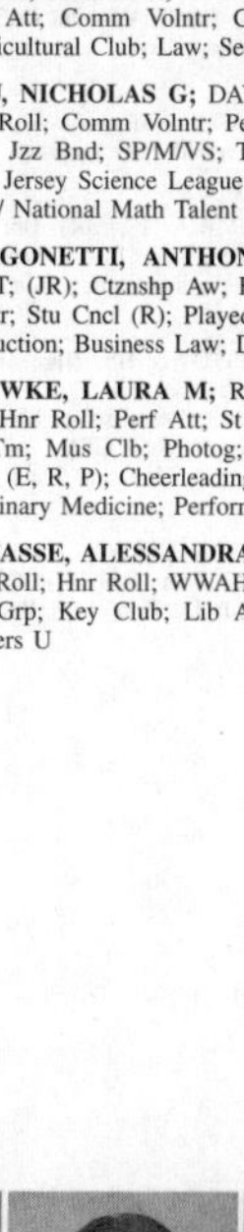
Dobson, Latoya
Tedneck HS
Teaneck, NJ

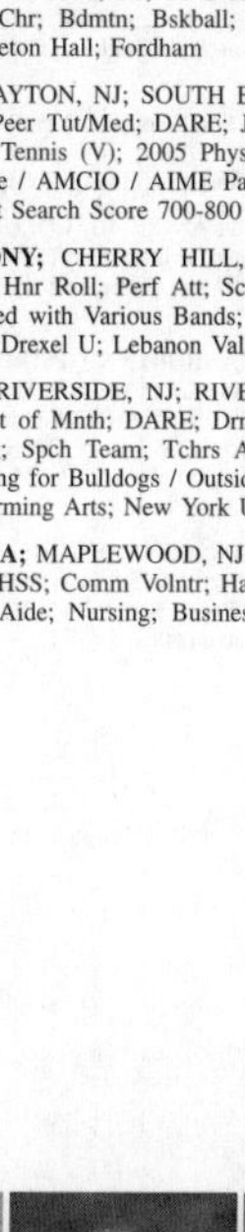
Dickson, Matthew J
Pitman HS
Pitman, NJ

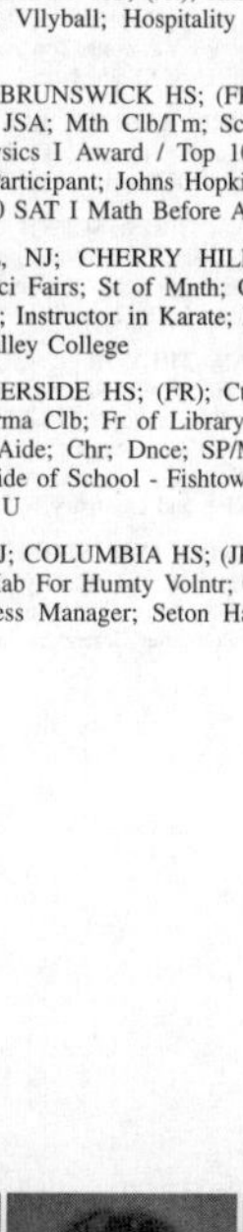
Di Renzo, Laura
Arthur L Johnson HS
Clark, NJ

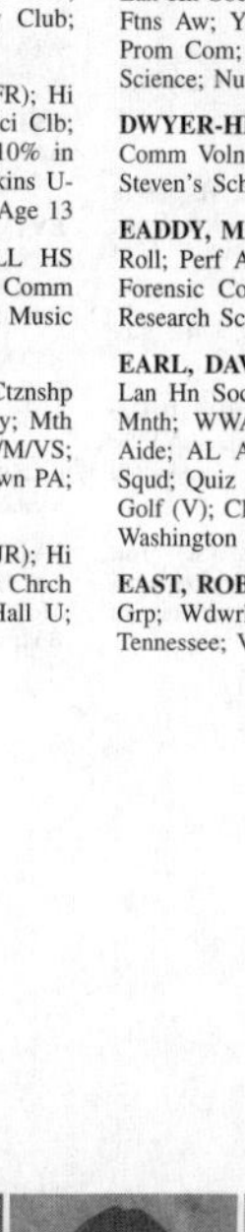
Donahue, Priscilla
Oakcrest HS
Mays Landing, NJ

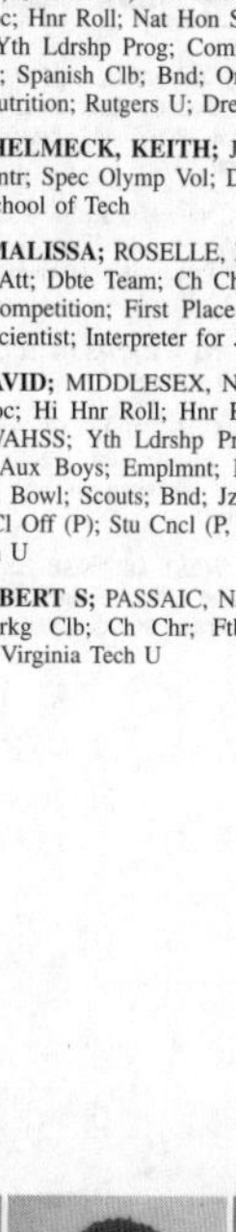
Dorsainville, Jayelle
Old Bridge HS
Old Bridge, NJ

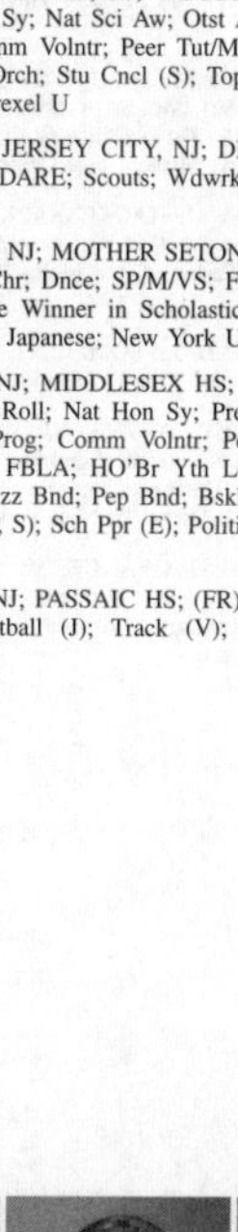
Dworak, Julie M
Woodbridge HS
Woodbridge, NJ

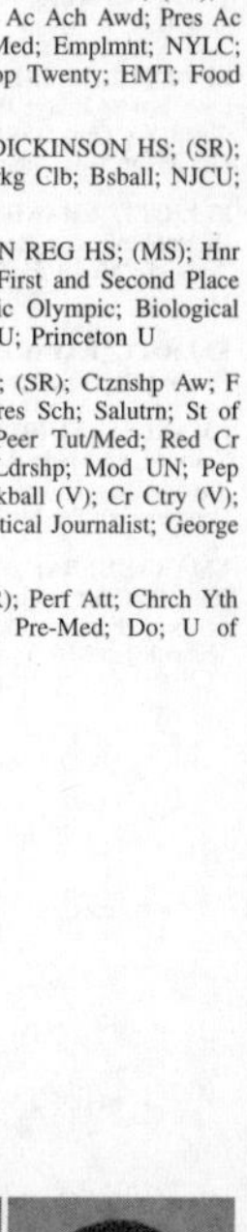
Dwyer-Helmeck, Keith
Dickinson HS
Jersey City, NJ

EBANKS, YASHECA; EAST ORANGE, NJ; CICELY TYSON HS; (SR); Hnr Roll; Nat Hon Sy; Sci Fairs; St of Mnth; WWAHSS; Comm Volntr; Peer Tut/Med; Biology Clb; Chrch Yth Grp; DARE; Drma Clb; Emplmnt; Prom Com; Sci Clb; Tchrs Aide; Acpl Chr; Chr; Ch Chr; SP/M/VS; Cl Off (T); Stu Cncl (R); CR (R); Lit Mag (R); Yrbk (E); Gold Medalist State Competition NAACP; 1st Place Literacy Award; Biology; Writing; U of Hartford; College of St Elizabeth

EDEN, ESKOR; LINDEN, NJ; LINDEN HS; (JR); Comm Volntr; Sccr ((J)); Track ((V)); Assisted with Donations for Homeless Shelters - Union County NJ; Sociology / Pre-Law; Bachelor's Degree / Master's Law; University of Vermont; New York University

EDILLOR, FAYTH Y; BERGENFIELD, NJ; BERGEN CTY AC; (SO); Hi Hnr Roll; Hnr Roll; Otst Ac Ach Awd; Pres Ac Ftns Aw; Sci Fairs; Hosp Aide; Peer Tut/Med; Off Aide; Bskball (J); Stu Cncl (P); Yrbk (P); World Hunger Relief Club; Skills USA; Pharmacy; St John's U; U of Michigan

EDMONDS, JOCELYN; ROSELLE, NJ; ABRAHAM CLARK HS; (JR); Hnr Roll; FTA; Jr Ach; Step Team; Early Childhood Education; Child Psychology; Montclair U; North Carolina A & T State U

EDMONDS, JUSTIN; WILLIAMSTOWN, NJ; WILLIAMSTOWN HS; (SR); Peer Tut/Med; Red Cr Aide; DARE; ROTC; Vsity Clb; Cr Ctry (V); Track (V); Vsy Clb (V); Criminal Justice; Stockton U; U of Delaware

EDSON, AMY E; MOUNT HOLLY, NJ; RANCOCAS VALLEY REG HS; (SR); F Lan Hn Soc; Hi Hnr Roll; Hnr Roll; MVP; Nat Hon Sy; Pres Ac Ftns Aw; WWAHSS; Comm Volntr; Peer Tut/Med; Emplmnt; Key Club; Scouts; Gmnstcs; National Spanish Honor Society; National Art Honor Society; Pre-Med; Ursinus College

EDWARDS, MARQUISHA; NEWARK, NJ; GLADYS HILLMAN JONES SCH; MS; Ctznshp Aw; Hi Hnr Roll; Hnr Roll; Otst Ac Ach Awd; Perf Att; St of Mnth; Comm Volntr; Cmptr Clb; DARE; Mth Clb/Tm; Tech Clb; Spanish Clb; Dnce; Drl Tm; SP/M/VS; Bskball (C); Mar Art (C); Cl Off (P); Stu Cncl (T); Sch Ppr (E, P); Teacher; FBI Agent; Rutgers U; Essex County College

EDWARDS, TENTA; IRVINGTON, NJ; NEWARK TECH HS; (SR); Cr Ctry (J); Sftball (V); Yrbk (E); Get a Degree in Pre-Med; Temple U; NYU

EGAN, MAEVE; ALLENDALE, NJ; NORTHERN HIGHLANDS REG HS; (SO); Hnr Roll; Otst Ac Ach Awd; WWAHSS; Comm Volntr; Dnce; Leader Teen Freedom Corps; Championship Irish Dance (National International Level); Teaching/Education; Medicine; Johns Hopkins U; U of Maryland

EGUINO, MARIA T; UNION CITY, NJ; UNION HILL HS; (JR); F Lan Hn Soc; Hi Hnr Roll; Hnr Roll; Nat Hon Sy; Perf Att; St of Mnth; WWAHSS; Chess; Key Club; MuAlphaTh; Spanish Clb; Sch Ppr (R); Architecture; Civil Engineering; Columbia U; Stevens Institute of Technology

EINEKER, LAUREN; MARLBORO, NJ; MARLBORO HS; (SO); Hi Hnr Roll; Comm Volntr; Emplmnt; JSA; Bskball (V L); Cr Ctry (V L); Published Poet; Active Member Junior Statesmen America; Finance & Business; Chemistry; Colgate U; U of Michigan

ELAMENA, HASSAN; NEWARK, NJ; ESSEX CTY VOC-TECH HS; Ctznshp Aw; Hnr Roll; MVP; Nat Sci Aw; Nat Stu Ath Day Aw; Perf Att; Sci Fairs; St of Mnth; WWAHSS; Yth Ldrshp Prog; CARE; Comm Volntr; Peer Tut/Med; Chess; DARE; Dbte Team; Emplmnt; Photog; Prom Com; Svce Clb; Tech Clb; Flg Crps; Pep Bnd; SP/M/VS; Stg Cre; Bsball (J); Bskball (J); Ftball (J); Scr Kpr (J); Sccr (J); Sftball (J); Track (J); Vllyball (J); CR (T); Yrbk (P); Baseball; Football; Physical Therapy; Massage Therapist; Montclair State U; U of Miami

ELFRANK, KATRINA M; SOMERVILLE, NJ; ST CLARK HS; (SO); Hnr Roll; Nat Hon Sy; Perf Att; St of Mnth; Red Cr Aide; Spec Olymp Vol; Chrch Yth Grp; DARE; Drma Clb; Key Club; Pep Squd; SP/M/VS; Sccr (J); FBI Agent; Psychology; Mizzou; East Central, Texas U

ELLIOTT, AMANDA C; HACKENSACK, NJ; HACKENSACK HS; (SO); Hi Hnr Roll; Nat Hon Sy; Perf Att; Pres Ac Ftns Aw; Peer Tut/Med; Dnce; Track (J); Model for Fashion Club; Biology; Psychology; Georgetown U; U of Maryland

ELLIOTT, RAYMOND L; SOMERSET, NJ; FRANKLIN HS; (JR); Sccr (V); Wrstlg (V); Wrestler, Transportation; Management

EMANUEL, SHIRLEY; WAYNE, NJ; WAYNE HILLS HS; (JR); Hi Hnr Roll; St of Mnth; Dbte Team; Emplmnt; FBLA; Svce Clb; Spanish Clb; Swmg (J); Future Business Leaders of America (Club Membership Coordinator); Pre-Med; Drexel U; New York U

EMARA, HEBA; WEST ORANGE, NJ; WEST ORANGE HS; (SO); Hnr Roll; Perf Att; Comm Volntr; ArtClub; Mod UN; Stu Cncl (R); Computer Science; Foreign Languages) Arabic/Japanese; Massachusetts Institute of Technology; New York U

EMEANA, EZE L; HILLSIDE, NJ; HILLSIDE HS; (SO); All Am Sch; Ctznshp Aw; Hi Hnr Roll; Hnr Roll; MVP; Nat Mrt LOC; Otst Ac Ach Awd; Perf Att; Pres Ac Ftns Aw; Pres Sch; Comm Volntr; Hosp Aide; Peer Tut/Med; Biology Clb; Chess; Chrch Yth Grp; Cmptr Clb; DARE; Dbte Team; Jr Ach; Mth Clb/Tm; Bskball (V); Cr Ctry (V); Ftball (V); Sccr (J); Track (V); Wt Lftg; Stu Cncl (P); Sch Ppr (E); Yrbk (E); Mark Hampton- Athletic / Academic Jr Community Seminar; Dennis Farrall Award - Athletic / Academic; Criminal Attorney in Defense of the Defenseless; Medical Doctor for the Service of Community; Princeton U; U of Connecticut

EMMA, FRANCESCA; KENILWORTH, NJ; DAVID BREARLEY MIDDLE HS; (JR); Hnr Roll; Comm Volntr; Peer Tut/Med; ArtClub; DARE; Emplmnt; Lib Aide; Prom Com; International Clb; Chr; SP/M/VS; Cl Off (R); CR (R); Pre-Veterinary Medicine; Cornell U; Drexel U

ENGLANDER, JEFF; BEDMINSTER, NJ; BERNARDS HS; (JR); Hi Hnr Roll; Hnr Roll; Nat Hon Sy; Otst Ac Ach Awd; Perf Att; WWAHSS; Comm Volntr; Peer Tut/Med; Emplmnt; Key Club; Scouts; Tech Clb; Tmpl Yth Grp; Bnd; Jzz Bnd; Mch Bnd; SP/M/VS; Adv Cncl (R); Stu Cncl (R); CR (R); Eagle Scout; Section Leader / Marching Band; Chemical Engineering; Jazz Studies

ENGSELL, TIFFANY; SEWELL, NJ; GCIT; (JR); Hi Hnr Roll; Hnr Roll; Nat Hon Sy; WWAHSS; Comm Volntr; Key Club; Dnce; Broadcast Journalism; Fordham U; New York U

ENTWISTLE, CLARE; SUMMIT, NJ; UNION CTY MAGNET HS; (FR); Hnr Roll; Yth Ldrshp Prog; Comm Volntr; Chrch Yth Grp; Yrbk (P); Part of an Invent Team for MIT; Part of REBEL (Which Is Like DARE); Math Related; Photography; Georgetown U, Washington DC; Virginia Tech

ERNST, ARTHUR; CRANFORD, NJ; CRANFORD HS; (SR); DAR; Hi Hnr Roll; Hnr Roll; Nat Hon Sy; Perf Att; Pres Sch; Sci Fairs; Comm Volntr; Peer Tut/Med; Emplmnt; Mth Clb/Tm; MuAlphaTh; Mus Clb; Scouts; Acpl Chr; Bnd; Chr; Mch Bnd; Selected for 8 Regional & All-State Festival Choirs; Eagle Scout-BSA; Music Education; The College of New Jersey; Susquehanna U

ESAU, JOSEPH D; MARLBORO, NJ; MARLBORO HS; (FR); Hnr Roll; Pres Sch; Bnd; Ftball; Computer Science / Physics; Communications; Massachusetts Institute of Technology; Stanford U

ESMOND, DAPHNE N; NEWARK, NJ; MALCOLM X SHABAZZ HS; (JR); Hi Hnr Roll; MVP; Nat Hon Sy; Otst Ac Ach Awd; Yth Ldrshp Prog; Peer Tut/Med; DARE; Drl Tm; Bsball (V C); Bskball (J); Sftball (V C); Vllyball (V C); Community Service / Costa Rica '04; Summer Institute - NJIT; Degree in Law; Degree in Medicine; Drew U; Vermont State

ESSINGTON, JONATHAN R; EAST ORANGE, NJ; IMMACULATE CONCEPTION HS; (SR); Hi Hnr Roll; Nat Hon Sy; Pres Sch; St of Mnth; Peer Tut/Med; ArtClub; Emplmnt; Ch Chr; Bsball (VJ); Bskball (VJ); Chrldg (VJ); Cr Ctry (VJ L); Mar Art (V); Yrbk (R); President's Educational Award; New Jersey Scholar Athlete; Anesthesiologist; Dartmouth College

ESTEVEZ, ALBANIA; CAMDEN, NJ; CCTS; (SO); Hnr Roll; Perf Att; Sci Fairs; St of Mnth; FBLA; Lawyer; Criminal Justice Degree; Rutgers U; Rider U

ESTRADA, AILEEN; JERSEY CITY, NJ; AC OF ST ALOYSIUS; (FR); Hnr Roll; Drma Clb; Sftball (V); Mission Club; Nursing; Meteorology

ESTRADA, LISA; TRENTON, NJ; HUN SCH OF PRINCETON; (JR); Hi Hnr Roll; Peer Tut/Med; Key Club; Photog; French Clb; Fencing (J); English/ Literature; Mathematics; Princeton U; New York U

ETTORE, ANTHONY J; BRANCHBURG, NJ; SOMERVILLE HS; (SO); Hnr Roll; WWAHSS; Comm Volntr; Peer Tut/Med; Chrch Yth Grp; DARE; Dbte Team; Emplmnt; Key Club; Pep Squd; Bnd; Ftball (VJ); Stu Cncl (R); Who's Who Among Top American Students; Business Law; Marketing; U of Miami; U of Rhode Island

ETTORE, ASHLEY; KEYPORT, NJ; KEYPORT HS; (SR); Hnr Roll; Perf Att; Chrch Yth Grp; DARE; Track; 10th grade child care program; Early Childhood Education; BrookdaleCommunity College

EVANS, IDRIS; SOUTH ORANGE, NJ; COLUMBIA HS; (SR); Hnr Roll; Comm Volntr; Hab For Humty Volntr; Peer Tut/Med; Key Club; Kwanza Clb; Bnd; Fncg (V CL); National Merit Participant; International Studies; Japanese; Davidson College

EVANS, TREVOR J; CRANBURY, NJ; HIGHSTOWN HS; (JR); Hi Hnr Roll; Hnr Roll; Nat Sci Aw; Otst Ac Ach Awd; Sci/Math Olympn; St of Mnth; Comm Volntr; Red Cr Aide; DARE; Emplmnt; German Clb; SP/M/VS; Cr Ctry (V L); Sccr (L); Track (V L); Cl Off (R); Highest GPA - All A's - 6th-8th Grade; American Legion Award; Pre-Med; Engineering Field; U of Medicine and Dentistry NJ; Rutgers

FAJARDO, CHRISTOPHER; RINGOES, NJ; IMMACULATA HS; (JR); F Lan Hn Soc; Nat Hon Sy; Perf Att; Sci Fairs; Yth Ldrshp Prog; Mth Clb/Tm; Mod UN; Mus Clb; Quiz Bowl; Schol Bwl; Bnd; Jzz Bnd; Mch Bnd; Pep Bnd; Computer Science; Mathematics

FALCO, JOHN R; LINCROFT, NJ; MIDDLETOWN HS SOUTH; (SO); Hi Hnr Roll; Hnr Roll; Pres Ac Ftns Aw; Comm Volntr; Chrch Yth Grp; Emplmnt; FBLA; Track (J); Cl Off (T); Pre-Veterinarian; Rowan U; Rutgers U

FALCO, LAUREN; KEANSBURG, NJ; RED BANK CATHOLIC HS; (FR); Hnr Roll; Bskball (J); Sccr (J); CR (R); Pro-Life Club; Ambassador for School; Mathematics; Computer Science; UCLA; Rutgers U

FALCO, PAUL J; KEANSBURG, NJ; RED BANK CATHOLIC HS; (JR); WWAHSS; Comm Volntr; Svce Clb; Mar Art (V L); Black Belt Karate; Mechanical Engineering; Design

FALLON, SAMANTHA E; LODI, NJ; LODI HS; (JR); Otst Ac Ach Awd; St of Mnth; Yrbk (R); Class Citizenship; Student of the Month - SAT Prep; Elementary Education; Art; Felician College; Montclair State U

FANELLI, MICHAEL; EDISON, NJ; ST JOSEPH'S HS; (JR); Hi Hnr Roll; Hnr Roll; Nat Hon Sy; Perf Att; Comm Volntr; Scouts; Cr Ctry (V CL); Track (V L); Club President, Perfect Attendance High School Through 11th; Letter in Indoor Track; Officer-US Army; Police Officer; United States Military Academy At West Point; Penn State U

FANG, MICHAEL; BERKELEY HEIGHTS, NJ; GOVERNOR LIVINGSTON; (JR); Hnr Roll; Nat Hon Sy; Sci/Math Olympn; WWAHSS; Comm Volntr; Hosp Aide; ArtClub; Chess; Cmptr Clb; Dbte Team; FBLA; JSA; Mth Clb/Tm; Mod UN; Orch; Fncg (V); Tennis (J)

FARINO, SALVATORE J; CLIFTON, NJ; PARAMUS CATHOLIC HS; (JR); Hnr Roll; Comm Volntr; Chrch Yth Grp; Scouts; Track (VJ); Wrstlg (VJ); Stu Cncl (V); Eagle Scout 2004; Engineering; Air Force Academy

FARMER, CHARLES; COLONIA, NJ; JOHN F KENNEDY HS; (FR); Hnr Roll; Perf Att; St of Mnth; WWAHSS; Comm Volntr; Chrch Yth Grp; Key Club; Bnd; Sch Ppr; Mock Trial; Pharmacy; Rutgers U

FARRAJ, AISHA; MATAWAN, NJ; MATAWAN REG HS; (JR); F Lan Hn Soc; Hi Hnr Roll; Hnr Roll; Nat Hon Sy; Otst Ac Ach Awd; Comm Volntr; Peer Tut/Med; Emplmnt; Mth Clb/Tm; ROTC; Track (VJ); Psychology; Criminal Law; Northeastern U; Cornell U

FARRELL, ASHLEY M; COLONIA, NJ; JOHN F KENNEDY HS; (FR); Hnr Roll; Pres Ac Ftns Aw; St of Mnth; Comm Volntr; ArtClub; Chrch Yth Grp; DARE; Emplmnt; Key Club; Scouts; Vsity Clb; Dnce; Chrldg (VJ L); Cr Ct Ski (V); Skiing (J); Track (V); Sch Ppr (P); NJ Heat All Star Cheerleading Team; Gifted and Talented for Visual Arts; Art Teacher (Art Major); Interior Design; Fashion Institute Technology; Florida State U

FARZAN, THOMAS; MIDDLETOWN, NJ; (SO); Hi Hnr Roll; Hnr Roll; Otst Ac Ach Awd; NYLC; Bnd; Jzz Bnd; Mch Bnd; SP/M/VS; Cr Ctry; Tennis (V); Track (J); Sch Ppr (R); Proficient in Three Musical Instruments: Piano, Oboe & Alto Saxophone; Medical Doctor; Business/Finance; Columbia U; Harvard College

FECANIN, CASEY L; STEWARTSVILLE, NJ; BETHLEHEM CATHOLIC HS; (FR); Ctznshp Aw; Hi Hnr Roll; Hnr Roll; WWAHSS; Comm Volntr; Peer Tut/Med; Key Club; Off Aide; Scouts; Tchrs Aide; Bnd; Ch Chr; Mch Bnd; Orch; Biology Achievement Award 2005; Communication Science (Journalism); Art; Lehigh U; Penn State (1 Pane)

FEDERICO, JESSICA L; SOMERVILLE, NJ; SOMERVILLE HS; (SR); Ctznshp Aw; Hi Hnr Roll; Hnr Roll; Nat Hon Sy; Pres Sch; WWAHSS; Comm Volntr; Emplmnt; Off Aide; Sftball (V); Adv Cncl (R); Cl Off (R); National Honor Society; Physical Therapy; East Stroudsburg U

FEDERICO, JULIA M; FLORENCE, NJ; FLORENCE TWP MEM HS; (FR); Hi Hnr Roll; Mus Clb; Scouts; Spanish Clb; Bnd; Chr; Jzz Bnd; Mch Bnd; Music; Astronomy

FEDORENKO, MIKHAIL; FAIR LAWN, NJ; FAIR LAWN HS; (SO); Comm Volntr; Emplmnt; Vsity Clb; Fncg (J); Business; Law; Boston U

FELDER, SU-TANNA C; JERSEY CITY, NJ; UNIVERSITY AC CHARTER SCH; (JR); Hnr Roll; Nat Hon Sy; St of Mnth; WWAHSS; Comm Volntr; Dbte Team; Emplmnt; Bskball (J); Track (J); Lit Mag (R); Yrbk (E, R); Criminal Justice; Psychology; Seton Hall U; Rutgers U

FELDMAN, JARED; WARREN, NJ; WATCHUNG HILLS REG HS; (JR); Hnr Roll; WWAHSS; Yth Ldrshp Prog; Comm Volntr; Spec Olymp Vol; Dbte Team; Emplmnt; NYLC; Svce Clb; CR (R); Sch Ppr (R); Scored in Top 50,000 for PSAT Selection Index 202; National Society High School Scholars; Business; Music; New York U; Emory U

FELIZ, YAFRESIE; LITTLE FALLS, NJ; PASSAIC VALLEY REG HS; (JR); Hnr Roll; Emplmnt; Prom Com; PP Ftbl (V); Scr Kpr (V); Sccr (VJCL); Cl Off (P); Stu Cncl (R); CR (P, R); Student Trainers Club; Spanish/Latino Club; Pre-Law; Criminal Justice; U of Miami; New York U

FELL, HEATHER; TRENTON, NJ; STEINERT HS; (JR); F Lan Hn Soc; Hnr Roll; Nat Hon Sy; WWAHSS; Chrch Yth Grp; P to P St Amb Prg; French Clb; Bnd; Mch Bnd; SP/M/VS; Interact Club; Mathematics; Lebanon Valley College; Stockton College

Falco, Lauren
Red Bank Catholic HS
Keansburg, NJ

Emma, Francesca
David Brearley Middle HS
Kenilworth, NJ

Egan, Maeve
Northern Highlands Reg HS
Allendale, NJ

National
Honor Roll
Spring 2005

Edson, Amy E
Rancocas Valley Reg HS
Mount Holly, NJ

Esau, Joseph D
Marlboro HS
Marlboro, NJ

Farzan, Thomas
Middletown, NJ

FELLMAN, DANIEL; WOODBURY HEIGHTS, NJ; GATEWAY REG HS; (FR); Hnr Roll; St of Mnth; DARE; Bsball (L); Bskball; Renaissance Club; Basketball/Baseball Scholarship; Elementary Education; U of Maryland; Rowan U

FENENBOCK, ADAM; SADDLE RIVER, NJ; NORTHERN HIGHLANDS REG HS; (SO); Hnr Roll; Comm Volntr; DECA; Emplmnt; Latin Clb; Sccr (J); Scholar Athlete; Level I-National Latin Exam-Magna Cum Laude

FEOLA, JACLYN; BELLEVILLE, NJ; BELLEVILLE HS; (JR); WWAHSS; Drma Clb; Emplmnt; Key Club; Clb; Dnce; SP/M/VS; Cr Ctry (V); Track (V); Stu Cncl (S); UIL Honorable Mention for Cross Country - 2 Years; Elementary Education; English; William Paterson U; Kean U

FERIOZZI, ASHLEY; DENNSAUKEN, NJ; CAMDEN CATHOLIC HS; (SR); Hnr Roll; Nat Hon Sy; Perf Att; Comm Volntr; Emplmnt; Svce Clb; SADD; Stg Cre; Yrbk; Medical Research; Drexel U

FERNANDES, RHEA M; PARLIN, NJ; BISHOP GEORGE AHR HS; (FR); Hi Hnr Roll; Otst Ac Ach Awd; Pres Sch; Sci/Math Olympn; St of Mnth; Comm Volntr; Chrch Yth Grp; Cmptr Clb; Drma Clb; French Clb; Chr; Ch Chr; Clr Grd; SP/M/VS; Chrldg (V); Stu Cncl (R); Lit Mag (R); Sch Ppr (E); Poem Published in Anthology of 8th Gr Poetry; VFW Voice of Democracy Essay Contest; Law; Journalism; Harvard U; Villanova U

FERNANDEZ, ALLYSON; BAYONNE, NJ; BAYONNE HS; (JR); Hnr Roll; MVP; Nat Hon Sy; Otst Ac Ach Awd; Pres Ac Ftns Aw; St of Mnth; DARE; Quiz Bowl; Dnce; Cr Ctry (V); Track (V); Stu Cncl (R); Played Basketball As Freshman; Scholars of the House & Anthony Kunishak Award; New York U; Penn State U

FERNANDEZ, CYNTHIA; DUMONT, NJ; DUMONT HS; (JR); Drma Clb; Spch Team; Chr; Dnce; SP/M/VS; Stg Cre; International Thespian Society; New Jersey Drama and Forensics League; Performing Arts; Psychology; U of Southern California; Ithaca College

FERNANDEZ, JAMES; NEWARK, NJ; SCIENCE HS; (SO); Hi Hnr Roll; Hnr Roll; Nat Hon Sy; Sci/Math Olympn; St of Mnth; Valdctrian; Peer Tut/Med; Bsball (V); Track (J); Yrbk (E); Veterinarian; Sports Medicine; Villanova U; Rutgers U

FERNANDO, JAYSON M; ROSELLE, NJ; ABRAHAM CLARK HS; (SR); All Am Sch; Hnr Roll; Nat Hon Sy; Nat Mrt Fin; Nat Mrt LOC; Comm Volntr; Biology Clb; Cmptr Clb; Jr Ach; Photog; Dnce; SP/M/VS; Bskball (VJ); Ice Sktg (L); Stu Cncl (S); Sch Ppr (P); Merit Honor Roll; Biology; Doctor / MD; Montclair State U

FERRARA, CHRISTOPHER; SOUTH AMBOY, NJ; CARDINAL MC CARRICK HS; (JR); Hnr Roll; Nat Hon Sy; Nat Mrt Fin; Nat Mrt LOC; Otst Ac Ach Awd; Perf Att; Comm Volntr; Sci Clb; Scouts; Tchrs Aide; Spanish Clb; Veterans of Foreign Wars Essay Winner; Senate & General Assembly Citation / Knights of Columbus Essay Contest Winner / Christian Awareness Certificate; Chemical Engineering; Rutgers U; Harvard U

FERREIRA, DAISY; LINDEN, NJ; LINDEN HS; (JR); Ctznshp Aw; Hnr Roll; Perf Att; Pres Ac Ftns Aw; Sci Fairs; St of Mnth; Comm Volntr; French Clb; Lit Mag (R); VP of French Club; Head of Media - Diversity Club; Business Management; International Business; Montclair State U; Caldwell College

FERREIRA, VANESSA L; BRIDGEWATER, NJ; BRIDGEWATER-RARITAN HS; (SO); Hi Hnr Roll; Hnr Roll; Pres Ac Ftns Aw; Pres Sch; Comm Volntr; Hab For Humty Volntr; Hosp Aide; Chrch Yth Grp; DARE; Drma Clb; Key Club; Dnce; Stu Cncl (R); Sch Ppr (R); Medicine; Johns Hopkins U; Princeton U

FETTY, TARA M; HAMMONTON, NJ; HAMMONTON HS; (JR); Hnr Roll; Otst Ac Ach Awd; WWAHSS; Comm Volntr; DARE; W.R.A.P program; Journalism/Writing/English; Art

FICKLING, MEGAN V; ENGLEWOOD, NJ; WALDWICK SDA SCH; (FR); Hi Hnr Roll; Hnr Roll; Otst Ac Ach Awd; Pres Sch; Salutrn; Sci Fairs; Comm Volntr; Peer Tut/Med; Chrch Yth Grp; Orch; Cl Off (V); Stu Cncl (R); Yrbk (E); Mission Trip to Peru; Pathfinders Club; Magazine Publisher; Forensics Science; Columbia U; Spelman

FIELDS, MONIQUE'A; PLAINFIELD, NJ; PLAINFIELD HS; (FR); Hnr Roll; MVP; Nat Hon Sy; Otst Ac Ach Awd; St of Mnth; WWAHSS; Peer Tut/Med; Chess; DARE; Emplmnt; Mth Clb/Tm; ROTC; Clr Grd; Bskball (J); Sccr (V); Sftball (J); Business Management; U of Connecticut; Duke

FINK, LAUREN; MORRISTOWN, NJ; (JR); Hi Hnr Roll; Hnr Roll; Nat Ldrshp Svc; Otst Ac Ach Awd; Perf Att; Pres Ac Ftns Aw; Sci Fairs; WWAHSS; Comm Volntr; Peer Tut/Med; Spec Olymp Vol; Chrch Yth Grp; DARE; Key Club; NYLC; Prom Com; Scouts; Tchrs Aide; Vsity Clb; Dnce; Fld Hky (VJ); Ice Sktg (C); Lcrsse (J); Business Major; U of Richmond; U of Virginia, Clemson

FISHBERG, SCOTT; WESTFIELD, NJ; WESTFIELD HS; (SR); F Lan Hn Soc; Hi Hnr Roll; Hnr Roll; Nat Hon Sy; Yth Ldrshp Prog; (Latin & Span.) Clb; Certified EMT-B (Volunteer at the Westfield Volunteer Rescue Squad), AP Scholar; Founder and Captain of a Club Crew Team for Westfield HS Students (Unaffiliated with the School); Biology and Classics (possible college majors); Medical School; Tufts U (accepted E.D)

FISHER, DIEADRE; HALEDON, NJ; MANCHESTER REG HS; (JR); Hnr Roll; Nat Stu Ath Day Aw; Pres Ac Ftns Aw; WWAHSS; Comm Volntr; Chrch Yth Grp; DARE; FCA; Fr of Library; Jr Ach; Prom Com; Ch Chr; Drl Tm; Track (VJ); Nursing; Lab Technician; William Peterson U; Ramapo College

FITZSIMMONS, MARIE T; PARSIPPANY, NJ; (SR); Hnr Roll; MVP; WWAHSS; Emplmnt; Bskball (J); Sccr (J); Swmg (V L); Parsippany Hills Girls Swim Team Scholar-Athlete Award; Art Education; Art Advertising; Seton Hall U, Montclair; U, Marywood U

FIX, CAROLINE; BRICK, NJ; MONSIGNOR DONOVAN HS; (JR); Hi Hnr Roll; Key Club; Track (V L); Drawing Art Award; Fashion Design; Communications; Fashion Institute of Technology; Marist College

FLEM, ROBERT J; WENONAH, NJ; GATEWAY REG HS; (FR); Ctznshp Aw; Hi Hnr Roll; Hnr Roll; Pres Ac Ftns Aw; Sci Fairs; Chrch Yth Grp; DARE; Spanish Clb; Chr; Bsball (L); Ftball (L)

FLORA, ANTHONY J; MILFORD, NJ; DELAWARE VALLEY REG HS; (JR); Ctznshp Aw; Hnr Roll; Perf Att; St of Mnth; DARE; FCA; Wdwrkg Clb; Bsball (JC); Bskball (J); Wt Lftg (J)

FLORES, JAMIE M; FORDS, NJ; MIDDLESEX CO VOC-WOODBRIDGE; (FR); Hi Hnr Roll; Hnr Roll; Otst Ac Ach Awd; Perf Att; St of Mnth; WWAHSS; Hosp Aide; Cmptr Clb; DARE; Mus Clb; Prom Com; Sci Clb; Tchrs Aide; Bnd; Mch Bnd; SP/M/VS; Bskball (V); Comic Book Project; Rebel; Pediatrician; Author; Pennsylvania State U; Princeton U

FLORES, JENNIFER; UNION CITY, NJ; EMERSON HS; (SR); Hi Hnr Roll; Hnr Roll; Perf Att; Spec Olymp Vol; DARE; Key Club; ROTC; Chr; Dnce; SP/M/VS; Chrldg (V); Wrstlg (V); Stu Cncl (R); High Honor Roll; Honor Roll; Nursing; Veterinary Technician; Hudson County Community College

FLOURNOY, CLARISS I; COLONIA, NJ; MIDDLESEX CO VOC-WOODBRIDGE; (FR); Hi Hnr Roll; Hnr Roll; Perf Att; St of Mnth; Hosp Aide; DARE; Ch Chr; Dnce; Orch; SP/M/VS; Bskball (V); Sftball (V); Pediatrician; Doctor's Degree

FONDA, WILLIAM J; MANASQUAN, NJ; MANASQUAN HS; (SO); Hi Hnr Roll; Otst Ac Ach Awd; Perf Att; Yth Ldrshp Prog; ArtClub; DARE; Drma Clb; NYLC; P to P St Amb Prg; Acpl Chr; Chr; SP/M/VS; Stg Cre; Stu Cncl (R); People to People Student Ambassador; All Shore Chorus; Lawyer; Math; Princeton U; Seton Hall U

FONDOULES, GARRETT; HAMILTON, NJ; MARINE AC OF SCI & TECH HS; (JR); Hnr Roll; Comm Volntr; Chess; Chrch Yth Grp; Cmptr Clb; Key Club; ROTC; Tchrs Aide; Tech Clb; French Clb; Drl Tm; Skills USA Gold Winner for NJ; Aeronautical Engineering; Naval Architecture; Rensselaer Polytechnic Institute; Webb Institute

FONSECA, DANNY; NEWARK, NJ; QUEEN OF PEACE HS; (JR); Comm Volntr; Portuguese School; Business; Architecture; Rutgers U; NJIT

FONTANEZ, JOSHUA; BROWNS MILLS, NJ; (FR); Hnr Roll; Perf Att; Comm Volntr; Chrch Yth Grp; DARE; ROTC; Scouts; Clr Grd; Drl Tm; Lcrsse (J); Skt Tgt Sh (V); CR (R); Sch Ppr (E); Peer Mediation, JROTC, Staff, Nation Level Leadership Award; People's Choice Award; US Army JAG Lawyer; Then Politics; Senate/Congress; WestPoint, Harvard Law School; Liberty U

FORD, JYSHARMA M; NEPTUNE, NJ; NEPTUNE HS; (JR); Hnr Roll; Otst Ac Ach Awd; Pres Sch; St of Mnth; Yth Ldrshp Prog; Comm Volntr; Peer Tut/Med; DARE; Drma Clb; Emplmnt; FBLA; Pep Squd; P to P St Amb Prg; SADD; Dnce; Chrldg (V); CR; Junior Debutante for Monmouth County Cotillion; Business Law Attorney; Accounting; Hampton U; Johnson C Smith U

FORD, STEPHEN; SOUTH ORANGE, NJ; DELBARTON SCH; (JR); Ctznshp Aw; Hi Hnr Roll; Hnr Roll; MVP; Otst Ac Ach Awd; Pres Ac Ftns Aw; Yth Ldrshp Prog; Amnsty Intl; Comm Volntr; Peer Tut/Med; Emplmnt; Mod UN; NYLC; Off Aide; P to P St Amb Prg; SADD; Bnd; Bskball (J); Track (V); Adv Cncl (R); Stu Cncl (R); International Relations; Yale U; Georgetown U

FORTNEY, EBONY D; PLAINFIELD, NJ; PLAINFIELD HS; (FR); Nat Hon Sy; Peer Tut/Med; Mch Bnd; Caterer, Bachelor's Degree, 2 Years Culinary Arts; Lawyer Master's, Law School; FMU; Kean U

FRANCESCO, GABRIELLE; SOUTH ORANGE, NJ; COLUMBIA HS; (JR); Hi Hnr Roll; Hnr Roll; Peer Tut/Med; Sch Ppr (E); Foreign Languages for Elementary Students; Achieve Teaching Program; Physical Therapy; Graphic Design; U of Miami; Tufts U

FRANCO, JOAN; UNION CITY, NJ; EMERSON HS; (SO); Medicine

FRANKLIN, JONATHAN; MONROE TWP, NJ; MONROE TWP HS; (JR); Hnr Roll; WWAHSS; Comm Volntr; Peer Tut/Med; Chrch Yth Grp; Bskball (V); Psychology; Photography; Hampton U; Lincoln U

FREDERICKS, STEPHEN; CAPE MAY, NJ; LOWER CAPE MAY REG HS; (SO); Ctznshp Aw; Hnr Roll; Otst Ac Ach Awd; Pres Ac Ftns Aw; St of Mnth; Yth Ldrshp Prog; Comm Volntr; Hosp Aide; Peer Tut/Med; Red Cr Aide; Chrch Yth Grp; DARE; Key Club; NYLC; Vsity Clb; Bnd; Jzz Bnd; SP/M/VS; Stg Cre; Cr Ctry; Swmg; Track; Vsy Clb; Stu Cncl (P); Assistant Principal's Award; Medical / Endocrinology; University of Southern California

FREEMAN, LA'SHAE; TRENTON, NJ; TRENTON CTRL HS; (SO); Hnr Roll; BPA; Bnd; Sch Ppr (R); Elementary Education; RNA Nurse; Rutgers U; Coppin U

FREEMAN, NAKEESHA M; PENNS GROVE, NJ; PENNS GROVE HS; (JR); Hnr Roll; Nat Mrt LOC; Perf Att; St of Mnth; WWAHSS; Yth Ldrshp Prog; Comm Volntr; Bskball (V L); Tennis (V L); Track (V L); Participated in Rising Stars; Selected As a State Delegate in NJ Teen Program; Child Psychology; Temple U; Rider U

FRENEAUX, LAURA D; KENDALL PARK, NJ; SOUTH BRUNSWICK HS; (SO); Hnr Roll; WWAHSS; Key Club; Chr; Dnce; Swmg (V); CR (R); Lacrosse; Key Club

FRIEDRICH, BRIAN; POMPTON PLAINS, NJ; PEQUANNOCK HS; (JR); Hnr Roll; MVP; Yth Ldrshp Prog; Comm Volntr; NYLC; Latin Clb; Sccr (V L); Tennis (V CL); NJ Poet's Award 2003; Business; Medicine; Villanova U; Loyola College

FRITH JR, ANDREW H; TRENTON, NJ; TRENTON CTRL HS WEST; (JR); Hnr Roll; Otst Ac Ach Awd; Perf Att; Sci Fairs; Yth Ldrshp Prog; Hosp Aide; Chrch Yth Grp; Emplmnt; Lib Aide; Sccr (V); Track (V); Broadcast Journalism; Medicine; New York U; Columbia U

FROST, STEPHANIE M; PITMAN, NJ; PITMAN HS; (JR); Hnr Roll; Nat Hon Sy; Otst Ac Ach Awd; WWAHSS; Comm Volntr; Emplmnt; Key Club; Off Aide; SADD; Scr Kpr (V); Yrbk (R); Major-Spanish; Fordham U At Lincoln Center

FULLER, AMANDA T; SOUTH RIVER, NJ; BISHOP GEORGE AHR; (SO); Hi Hnr Roll; Hnr Roll; Hosp Aide; Drma Clb; Outdrs Clb; Quiz Bowl; Tchrs Aide; Sccr (VJ L); Most Promising Freshman - Soccer; Helping Hands Club; Graphic Design; Architecture; North Carolina State U; Penn State

FULTON, CHANELL; HOWELL, NJ; FREEHOLD TWP HS; (JR); Hnr Roll; Nat Hon Sy; Perf Att; Mus Clb; Pep Squd

FUNG, TAK-YIN S; RANDOLPH, NJ; RANDOLPH HS; (FR); Hnr Roll; Pres Ac Ftns Aw; Yth Ldrshp Prog; Hosp Aide; Emplmnt; Mod UN; Scouts; Bnd; Mch Bnd; Pep Bnd; Sccr; Sch Ppr (E); Johns Hopkins Cty Student; Lead America NJLC Alumnus; Pre-Med Biology Major; Biology / Political Science Double Major; Johns Hopkins U; Washington U

FUNICELLO, SARA; CLEMENTON, NJ; SOUTHERN NJ AC OF THE PERF ARTS AT GCIT; (SO); Hnr Roll; Nat Hon Sy; Perf Att; WWAHSS; Comm Volntr; Key Club; Scouts; Dnce; Girl Scout Silver Award; President of Dance Company Organization; Dance; Physical Therapy; Montclair U; Rowan U

FUNK, DANA P; PITMAN, NJ; PITMAN HS; (SR); Ctznshp Aw; Hi Hnr Roll; Kwnis Aw; Nat Hon Sy; Nat Ldrshp Svc; Otst Ac Ach Awd; St of Mnth; WWAHSS; Yth Ldrshp Prog; Comm Volntr; Peer Tut/Med; Red Cr Aide; DARE; Emplmnt; HO'Br Yth Ldrshp; Key Club; Lttrmn Clb; Off Aide; Pep Squd; Prom Com; Fld Hky (V CL); Swmg (V L); Track (V CL); Stu Cncl (T); CR (R); Yrbk (E, P); Communication; Elon U, North Carolina Accepted.

FURZE, MORGAN E; BAY HEAD, NJ; PT PLEASANT BEACH HS; (FR); Hi Hnr Roll; Otst Ac Ach Awd; St of Mnth; USAA; WWAHSS; Comm Volntr; DARE; Drma Clb; Key Club; Sci Clb; SP/M/VS; Bskball (V); Sccr (V); Track (J); Cl Off (V); Medicine; Interior Design

FUSCHETTI, TOM; EATONTOWN, NJ; RED BANK CATHOLIC HS; (FR); Hnr Roll; ArtClub; Italian Clb; Swmg (V); Architecture; Engineering; Copper Union College

GABAUD, ABED; IRVINGTON, NJ; IRVINGTON HS; (JR); Hi Hnr Roll; Hnr Roll; Otst Ac Ach Awd; Perf Att; Chrch Yth Grp; FCA; Bnd; Jzz Bnd; Mch Bnd; SP/M/VS; Cr Ctry (V); Track (J); Concert Band Integrity Achievement; Sigma Beta Club Academic Achievement; Biology; Zoology; Rutgers U; Harvard U

GABAUER, CHERYL A; PRINCETON, NJ; PRINCETON HS; (JR); Hnr Roll; Comm Volntr; Spec Olymp Vol; DARE; Emplmnt; Lib Aide; Quiz Bowl; Scouts; Yrbk (E, R, P); Girl Scout Bronze & Silver Award; Cosmetologist; Mercer County Community College

GAGLIANO, SARAH; WASHINGTON, NJ; WARREN HILLS REG HS; (SR); Hnr Roll; Comm Volntr; Spec Olymp Vol; DARE; Key Club; Chr; Vllyball (J); Secretary & President in Junior Advisory Board; Masters Then Doctoral in Childhood Education; Montclair State U

Ford, Jysharma M
Neptune HS
Neptune, NJ

Ferreira, Vanessa L
Bridgewater-Raritan HS
Bridgewater, NJ

Ferreira, Daisy
Linden HS
Linden, NJ

Fernando, Jayson M
Abraham Clark HS
Roselle, NJ

Ferrara, Christopher
Cardinal Mc Carrick HS
South Amboy, NJ

Fickling, Megan V
Waldwick Sda Sch
Englewood, NJ

Frith Jr, Andrew H
Trenton Ctrl HS West
Trenton, NJ

GALBRAITH, DANNEILLE V; PATERSON, NJ; ROSA PARKS HS; (FR); Ctznshp Aw; Hnr Roll; Otst Ac Ach Awd; St of Mnth; Chrch Yth Grp; Acpl Chr; Chr; Ch Chr; Drl Tm; Stu Cncl (V); Forensic Science; Interior Designing; Pace U

GALLAGHER, KRYSTA A; WEST HAMPTON, NJ; RANCOCAS VALLEY REG HS; (JR); Hi Hnr Roll; Hnr Roll; Peer Tut/Med; Sccr (J); Track (L); Performed an Acrobatics Solo; Volunteered at Church & with Girl Scouts; Major in Elementary Education; Master's Degree; Rowan U; Richard Stockton College of New Jersey

GALLEGOS, DAISY; JERSEY CITY, NJ; DICKINSON HS; (SO); Hnr Roll; MVP; Otst Ac Ach Awd; Perf Att; St of Mnth; Comm Volntr; Peer Tut/Med; Cmptr Clb; Sci Clb; Spanish Clb; Swmg (V); Track (V); Participate in Sports and Clubs / Manage to Achieve High Grades; Magnet - Academy of Information Technology - Have One of the Highest GPA; Computer Engineering; Software Engineering; Rutgers U; New Jersey Institute of Technology

GALLUCCI, CHRISTOPHER; PRINCETON, NJ; MONTGOMERY HS; (SO); Hnr Roll; Otst Ac Ach Awd; TREND; Renaissance Achievement Recognition Award; Science; Spanish; Rutgers U; Rider U

GALVIS, EDGAR S; PATERSON, NJ; PARAMUS CATHOLIC HS; (JR); F Lan Hn Soc; Hi Hnr Roll; Hnr Roll; Nat Hon Sy; Comm Volntr; Peer Tut/Med; DARE; NYLC; Photog; Spanish Clb; Sccr (V); Ophthalmologist; Cornell U; Miami U

GANGULY, TERESA; JERSEY CITY, NJ; ST DOMINIC AC; (JR); Perf Att; WWAHSS; Comm Volntr; Peer Tut/Med; Drma Clb; Emplmnt; Svce Clb; Tchrs Aide; SP/M/VS; Stg Cre; Pre-Law; Criminal Justice; Fordham U; Seton Hall U

GANZ, LYNDSAY; KEYPORT, NJ; RED BANK REG HS; (SR); F Lan Hn Soc; Hi Hnr Roll; Hnr Roll; Nat Hon Sy; Pres Sch; St of Mnth; Yth Ldrshp Prog; Comm Volntr; Peer Tut/Med; Red Cr Aide; DARE; Dbte Team; Emplmnt; FTA; Mth Clb/Tm; Pep Squd; P to P St Amb Prg; Prom Com; Dnce; SP/M/VS; Chrldg (V); Stu Cncl (R); CR (R); Sociology & Philosophy; Law School; Drexel U

GAO, GEORGE; NEW PROVIDENCE, NJ; NEW PROVIDENCE HS; (SO); Hi Hnr Roll; Perf Att; Sci Fairs; Sci/Math Olympn; St of Mnth; Chess; Mth Clb/Tm; Mus Clb; Vsity Clb; Jzz Bnd; Mch Bnd; Orch; Pep Bnd; Bsball (J); Track (V); Lit Mag (R); Member of the New Jersey Youth Symphony Family; Attended Cty (Center for Talented Youth) Program; Astrophysics; Orchestral Conducting; Cornell U; Columbia U

GARCIA, ANGIE; JERSEY CITY, NJ; DR RONALD MC NAIR AC HS; (FR); Ctznshp Aw; Hnr Roll; Sci Fairs; Spanish Clb; Bnd; Jzz Bnd; Cr Ctry (J); Track (J); President's Educational Program (Silver); Spanish Award; Lawyer; Pediatrician; Princeton U; Columbia U

GARCIA, GABRIELA; KEYPORT, NJ; MATAWAN REG HS; (JR); Peer Tut/Med; Chrch Yth Grp; Emplmnt; SADD; Clb; Business Administration

GARGES, COURTNEY; CRANFORD, NJ; CRANFORD HS; (JR); Hnr Roll; Nat Hon Sy; Perf Att; Sci Fairs; Bnd; Dnce; Drm Mjr; Mch Bnd; Psychology; Education; Washington College

GARRETT, ARIEL; MORRISTOWN, NJ; MORRISTOWN HS; (JR); Hnr Roll; WWAHSS; Hosp Aide; Emplmnt; Tmpl Yth Grp; Fld Hky (J); Lcrsse (J); Skiing (V); CR (R)

GASKILL, KATIE; CAPE MAY COURT HOUSE, NJ; MIDDLE TWP HS; (JR); Hi Hnr Roll; Hnr Roll; Nat Hon Sy; Otst Ac Ach Awd; Emplmnt; Lttrmn Clb; Mth Clb/Tm; Prom Com; Quiz Bowl; Sci Clb; Bnd; Mch Bnd; PP Ftbl (J); Track (V L); Medical Research; Chemistry Teacher; College of New Jersey; Drexel U

GATARZ, JEFFREY; PARSIPPANY, NJ; PARSIPPANY HS; (JR); Key Club; Mod UN; Stg Cre; Bskball (J); Skiing; Key Club Class Director; Key Club VP 2005-2006; Marketing; Advertising

GATES, MICHELLE; ROCKAWAY, NJ; MORRIS KNOLLS HS; (JR); F Lan Hn Soc; Hi Hnr Roll; Pres Ac Ftns Aw; WWAHSS; Hab For Humty Volntr; MuAlphaTh; Prom Com; Vsity Clb; Bskball; PP Ftbl (J); Sftball (J); Vllyball (V); Adv Cncl (R); Certified Scuba Diver; Biology; Zoology

GATOULIS, ELIAS; WOODCLIFF LAKE, NJ; PASCACK HILLS HS; (JR); Hi Hnr Roll; Nat Hon Sy; Perf Att; Civil Air Pat; NYLC; Sci Clb; Bnd; Jzz Bnd; Mch Bnd; Sccr (V); Wrstlg (C); Pre-Med; Pharmacy; The College of NJ; The College of William & Mary

GAUDIN, VALERIE; ISELIN, NJ; JOHN F KENNEDY MEMORIAL HS; (SO); Hnr Roll; Perf Att; WWAHSS; Key Club; French Clb; Stu Cncl (R); Pre-Med; Social Worker; Rogers U

GEHR, AMANDA M; BURLINGTON, NJ; BURLINGTON TOWNSHIP HS; (JR); Hnr Roll; Nat Hon Sy; WWAHSS; Comm Volntr; Peer Tut/Med; ArtClub; Emplmnt; Key Club; Sci Clb; Cl Off (T)

GEORGE, ZINDZI; PISCATAWAY, NJ; PISCATAWAY HS; (FR); Hnr Roll; Chrch Yth Grp; Key Club; Ch Chr; Middlesex County Arts High School - Advanced Acting; Dermatology; U of Maryland College Park; Rutgers U

GERALDINO, MASSIEL; PATERSON, NJ; KENNEDY HS; (FR); Ctznshp Aw; Hnr Roll; Perf Att; Earth Day Newspaper Publication; Elected Into Academics; High School Diploma; Master Degrees (Medicine); Stanford; Ramapo College

GERGES, JACELYN; LEONARDO, NJ; MIDDLETOWN HS NORTH; (JR); F Lan Hn Soc; Hi Hnr Roll; Nat Hon Sy; Otst Ac Ach Awd; St of Mnth; WWAHSS; Yth Ldrshp Prog; Comm Volntr; Hosp Aide; Peer Tut/Med; Chrch Yth Grp; Emplmnt; Key Club; NYLC; Spanish Clb; SP/M/VS; Sccr (J); Law; History; Columbia U; Brown U

GERHART, BRENNEN T; MILLTOWN, NJ; SPOTSWOOD HS; (SO); Hi Hnr Roll; Nat Hon Sy; Nat Sci Aw; Otst Ac Ach Awd; Pres Ac Ftns Aw; St of Mnth; USAA; WWAHSS; Comm Volntr; Peer Tut/Med; DARE; Emplmnt; FBLA; SADD; SP/M/VS; Bskball (VJ); Stu Cncl (R); CR (R); Academic Team, Altar Server; Basketball Coach (Youth), Our Lady of Lourdes Falcon; Athletic Association Volunteer; Accounting, Business Marketing; Duke U

GERONIMO, JERICA; BELLEVILLE, NJ; BELLEVILLE HS; (FR); Hi Hnr Roll; Hnr Roll; Perf Att; Drma Clb; Key Club; Orch; SP/M/VS; Sftball; Tennis (J); Crew / Rowing; Medical Field; Princeton U; New York U

GHUNTADARIA, SAGAR O; SUCCASUNNA, NJ; ROXBURY HS; (JR); Hnr Roll; WWAHSS; Hosp Aide; Emplmnt; FBLA; Key Club; Chr; Sccr (J); Track (J); Medicine; Business; Rutgers; Temple

GIAMBATTISTA, EMILY M; RINGWOOD, NJ; LAKELAND REG HS; (JR); Hnr Roll; WWAHSS; Comm Volntr; Scouts; Sccr (J); LEAP (Leadership Council); Road Show; Montclair State U; Ramapo College of New Jersey

GIANETTI, ALANE; BEDMINSTER, NJ; BERNARDS HS; (JR); Hnr Roll; Nat Hon Sy; Vsity Clb; Chrldg (V CL); Vsy Clb (V); UCA All-Star Cheerleader; Won 1st Place In An Art Contest; Art

GIANFRANCESCO, AMANDA; RINGWOOD, NJ; LAKELAND REG HS; (JR); Hnr Roll; Nat Hon Sy; WWAHSS; Comm Volntr; Spanish Clb; Track (J); Vllyball (V); Spanish Honor Society President; Biomedical Engineering; International Business; The College of New Jersey; Boston U

GIARDINA, CHRISTINE; ENGLISHTOWN, NJ; MANALAPAN HS; (SO); Hnr Roll; Sci/Math Olympn; Yth Ldrshp Prog; Comm Volntr; Chrch Yth Grp; DARE; FTA; Tchrs Aide; French Clb; Dnce; Cr Ctry; Sch Ppr; Miss Monmouth County Jr. Teen 2004; Co-Chair Person Manalapan Township Teen Advisory Committee; Broadcast Journalism; Communications; Syracuse U

GIBISON, THOMAS M; WESTVILLE, NJ; GATEWAY REG HS; (FR); Comm Volntr; DARE; Scouts; Ftball (J); Wt Lftg; Boy Scout; Bowling League

GIBSON JR, BENNIE; SOUTH PLAINFIELD, NJ; SOUTH PLAINFIELD HS; (FR); Hnr Roll; Bskball (JC); Ftball; NBA Basketball Player; Lawyer; Duke U; North Carolina U

GICHUKI, EDWIN; LINDEN, NJ; LINDEN HS; Hnr Roll; St of Mnth; Chrch Yth Grp; Outdrs Clb; Ch Chr; Church Youth Leader; Medicine; Rutgers U; Seton Hall U

GIERY, BRIDGETT L; TUCKERTON, NJ; PINELANDS REG HS; MS; All Am Sch; Hi Hnr Roll; Hnr Roll; Nat Hon Sy; Nat Ldrshp Svc; Otst Ac Ach Awd; Pres Ac Ftns Aw; Pres Sch; St Schl; St of Mnth; Chrch Yth Grp; DARE; Emplmnt; SADD; Bnd; Ch Chr; Dnce; Bskball (C); Chrldg (C); Golf; Track (C); Vllyball; President of National Junior Honor Society; Secretary of National Junior Honor Society; BFA in Dance; Montclair State U; Juilliard School

GIKORSKI, MATTHEW; BAYONNE, NJ; BAYONNE HS; (JR); Hi Hnr Roll; Hnr Roll; MVP; Nat Hon Sy; Pres Ac Ftns Aw; Sci Fairs; St of Mnth; Comm Volntr; Clb; Bsball (V); Business / Finance, Accounting; Penn State; Rutgers U

GIL, BRYAN; RAHWAY, NJ; RAHWAY HS; (JR); DECA; Computer Operator/Programmer; Network Engineer; Kean U; Rutgers

GILLIAM, MALIKA; ROSELLE, NJ; ABRAHAM CLARK HS; (JR); Hi Hnr Roll; Hnr Roll; WWAHSS; Comm Volntr; Latin Clb; Drl Tm; Bskball (V); Track (V); Cl Off (T); Peer Leadership; Nursing; Pharmaceuticals; Rutgers U; Pennsylvania State U

GILLIAM, MONICA; BROWNS MILLS, NJ; GUTHRIE HS; (SO); Ctznshp Aw; Hnr Roll; Otst Ac Ach Awd; Perf Att; St of Mnth; Chrch Yth Grp; DARE; FCA; Fr of Library; Ch Chr; Dnce; Drl Tm; Liberty House Student; Honor Roll Mention; Going to Cittone Institute

GILMER, RENEE B; SOUTH ORANGE, NJ; COLUMBIA HS; (SR); Emplmnt; Bnd; Dnce; Sccr (V); Track (V)

GIORDANO, GINA M; MOUNT HOLLY, NJ; RANCOCAS VALLEY REG; (SO); Hi Hnr Roll; Nat Hon Sy; Pres Ac Ftns Aw; WWAHSS; Comm Volntr; Peer Tut/Med; Spec Olymp Vol; Emplmnt; Key Club; Mod UN; Ftball (V); Lcrsse (J); Stu Cncl (R)

GIOVENCO, CAILEIGH R; SAYREVILLE, NJ; SAYREVILLE WAR MEMORIAL HS; (JR); Hi Hnr Roll; Hnr Roll; Nat Hon Sy; WWAHSS; Comm Volntr; Peer Tut/Med; Chrch Yth Grp; Prom Com; Acpl Chr; Chr; Ch Chr; SP/M/VS; Bskball (V L); Sccr (V L); Track (V L); Stu Cncl (R); Peer Leadership; Education; Psychology; Elizabethtown College; St Joseph's

GIRARD, BRITTANY L; SICKLERVILLE, NJ; TIMBER CREEK HS; (SO); Hnr Roll; Otst Ac Ach Awd; Pres Sch; St of Mnth; Comm Volntr; Emplmnt; Prom Com; Latin Clb; PP Ftbl (J); Adv Cncl (R); Cl Off (P); Stu Cncl (R); CR (P); Business Degree; Medical Degree; U of Pennsylvania; Wharton School of Business

GIRGIS, MARINA; MONROE TOWNSHIP, NJ; (JR); Ctznshp Aw; Hi Hnr Roll; Hnr Roll; Nat Hon Sy; Perf Att; Sci Fairs; Comm Volntr; Chrch Yth Grp; Fr of Library; Lib Aide; Mth Clb/Tm; Bnd; Sch Ppr (R); Young Science Achievers Program; Environmental Action Club; Medicine; Physician; Rutgers U; New York U

GIRON, LIGIA A; HARRISON, NJ; HARRISON HS; (SO); Hnr Roll; St of Mnth; Spanish Clb; Bnd; Dnce; Math Rally; Spelling Bee; Forensic Science; Interior Decoration; John Jay College; Art Institute of New York

GIULIANO, ALYSSA; BAYVILLE, NJ; CTRL REG HS; (JR); Hi Hnr Roll; Hnr Roll; MVP; WWAHSS; Comm Volntr; Dnce; Chrldg (V); Pre-Law; Accounting; Rider U; Providence College

GLICK, MICHELLE; SADDLE RIVER, NJ; NORTHERN HIGHLANDS REG HS; (JR); Hi Hnr Roll; Nat Hon Sy; Nat Mrt Semif; Comm Volntr; DECA; Scouts; Tmpl Yth Grp; Franco-Hispanic Clb; Bnd; Chr; SP/M/VS; Cr Ctry (J); Track (J); Sch Ppr (R); Girl Scout Gold Award Recipient, Girl Scout Leadership Award Recipient; Temple Youth Group Social Action Vice President / Book Club Member; Psychology; Pre-Med; Dartmouth College; Amherst College

GLOEDE, REBECCA; ELMWOOD PARK, NJ; PARAMUS CATHOLIC HS; (JR); F Lan Hn Soc; Hi Hnr Roll; Hnr Roll; Nat Hon Sy; Otst Ac Ach Awd; USAA; WWAHSS; Comm Volntr; Hab For Humty Volntr; Peer Tut/Med; Svce Clb; Spanish Clb; Scr Kpr (V); Vllyball (JC); Best Teammate; Elementary Education Major; The College of New Jersey

GODBOLT, TAKINIA; NEWARK, NJ; MALCOLM X SHABAZZ HS; (JR); Ctznshp Aw; Hnr Roll; Nat Hon Sy; Otst Ac Ach Awd; St of Mnth; Valdctrian; WWAHSS; Lib Aide; Ntl Beta Clb; Sci Clb; 8th Grade Valedictorian; Published Poet; Radio / TV Production, Psychology; Iowa State

GODUGU, RASHMI; EDISON, NJ; JOHN P STEVENS HS; (SO); Hnr Roll; MVP; Nat Mrt LOC; Comm Volntr; Hosp Aide; ArtClub; Biology Clb; Cmptr Clb; Key Club; Mth Clb/Tm; Mus Clb; Outdrs Clb; Orch; SP/M/VS; Cr Ctry (L); Sccr (L); Track (L); CR (T); Spelling Bee - Semifinalist; Pediatrician; Engineer; Rutgers U; Kean U

GOITEIN, LAURA D; PENNINGTON, NJ; THE HUN SCH OF PRINCETON; (FR); Hi Hnr Roll; Perf Att; Comm Volntr; Hosp Aide; DARE; Bsball (V); Cr Ctry (V); Sccr (V); Sftball (V); Crew Member; Psychology; Medicine; Bucknell

GOLAS JR, ROBERT; RARITAN, NJ; BRIDGEWATER-RARITAN REG HS; (FR); Hi Hnr Roll; Hnr Roll; MVP; Nat Hon Sy; St of Mnth; WWAHSS; Key Club; Ftball (J); Engineering; Virginia Tech

GOLDBERG, ANDREA; SHORT HILLS, NJ; MILLBURN HS; (JR); Hnr Roll; MVP; WWAHSS; Comm Volntr; Hab For Humty Volntr; Hosp Aide; Key Club; Mus Clb; Tmpl Yth Grp; Vsity Clb; Spanish Clb; Acpl Chr; Chr; Fld Hky (V CL); Swmg (V L); Track (J); Vsy Clb (V); Adv Cncl; Stu Cncl; Sch Ppr (R); Yrbk (E, P); President of Central Hebrew High School; Member of the Student Liaison Committee

GOLDBERG, JONATHAN A; SOMERVILLE, NJ; SOMERVILLE HS; (FR); Sccr (VJ); Track (VJ); 4 Time Honor Roll Student in Freshman Year; Political Science; Business Administration; Rutgers U

GOLDEN JR, RICHARD F; PINE BROOK, NJ; MONTVILLE TWP HS; (JR); Hnr Roll; Comm Volntr; FBLA; Bskball (J); Sccr (JC); Track (V C); Mock Trial; Math; Vet

GOLDFARB, CARL; MARLBORO, NJ; MARLBORO HS; (SO); Hnr Roll; Sci Fairs; Peer Tut/Med; Dbte Team; JSA; Mus Clb; P to P St Amb Prg; French Clb; Bnd; Mch Bnd; Fncg (V); Mar Art (V); Skiing; Tennis; Published Author; Political Science; History; Princeton U; Yale U

GOLDMAN, JON; COLLINGSWOOD, NJ; COLLINGSWOOD SR HS; (SO); Peer Tut/Med; Drma Clb; Emplmnt; Mus Clb; Off Aide; Chr; Dnce; SP/M/VS; Sccr (C); Cl Off (V); Stu Cncl (S); Sch Ppr (E); Yrbk (R); Acting; Performing; U of Delaware; Philadelphia School of Arts

GOMES, JOHN; HARRISON, NJ; HARRISON HS; (JR); Hi Hnr Roll; Hnr Roll; Nat Hon Sy; DARE; Emplmnt; Tech Clb; Sccr (V); Honor Society; Engineering; Doctor; New York U; Rutgers U

GOMEZ, GABRIELLA; ELIZABETH, NJ; ELIZABETH HS; (JR); Key Club; Master's Degree; Doctorate Degree

Giron, Ligia A
Harrison HS
Harrison, NJ

Gilliam, Monica
Guthrie HS
Browns Mills, NJ

Goldfarb, Carl
Marlboro HS
Marlboro, NJ

Giery, Bridgett L
Pinelands Reg HS
Tuckerton, NJ

Giardina, Christine
Manalapan HS
Englishtown, NJ

Geronimo, Jerica
Belleville HS
Belleville, NJ

Ganz, Lyndsay
Red Bank Reg HS
Keyport, NJ

Gallagher, Krysta A
Rancocas Valley Reg HS
West Hampton, NJ

National
Honor Roll
Spring 2005

Galbraith, Danneille V
Rosa Parks HS
Paterson, NJ

Gehr, Amanda M
Burlington Township HS
Burlington, NJ

Gianetti, Alane
Bernards HS
Bedminster, NJ

Gibison, Thomas M
Gateway Reg HS
Westville, NJ

Gichuki, Edwin
Linden HS
Linden, NJ

GONG, HANSON; BERNARDSVILLE, NJ; BERNARD HS; (SO); Hi Hnr Roll; Hnr Roll; Pres Ac Ftns Aw; WWAHSS; Yth Ldrshp Prog; Comm Volntr; DARE; Key Club; Bnd; Jzz Bnd; Mch Bnd; SP/M/VS; Ice Hky (V L); Tennis (V L); Sch Ppr (P); Business Management; International Relations; Princeton U; New York U

GONNELLA, CHRIS; SHORT HILLS, NJ; MILLBURN HS; (JR); Pres Ac Ftns Aw; WWAHSS; Yth Ldrshp Prog; Comm Volntr; Key Club; NYLC; Vsity Clb; SP/M/VS; Bsball (V CL); Sccr (V CL); Stu Cncl (R); Sch Ppr (R); West Point Eisenhower Award of Scholarship; Wendy's High School Heisman Award; Professor; Pomona College; Northwestern U

GONZALEZ, MARIA ELENA; PATERSON, NJ; JOHN F KENNEDY HS; (SO); Ctznshp Aw; Hi Hnr Roll; Hnr Roll; Valdctrian; WWAHSS; Comm Volntr; Peer Tut/Med; Chrch Yth Grp; Emplmnt; FBLA; Photog; Tchrs Aide; Bnd; Sch Ppr (E, R, P); 2005 Youth Peacemaker Award; Pre-Law; English; William Paterson U; Princeton U

GONZALEZ, NATHALIE; JERSEY CITY, NJ; (JR); All Am Sch; Hi Hnr Roll; Nat Hon Sy; WWAHSS; Amnsty Intl; Emplmnt; Prom Com; CR (R); President of the National Honor Society; Marketing; Architecture

GONZALEZ, SHALIMAR Y; JERSEY CITY, NJ; WILLIAM L. DICKINSON HS, (SR); Hnr Roll; Perf Att; WWAHSS; Comm Volntr; DECA; Chrldg (V); Sftball (V); Co-Op; Marketing Business Magnet; Marketing/ Management; Masters (Degree); The College of NJ; William Paterson

GONZALEZ, WINELY; JERSEY CITY, NJ; FERRIS HS; (SO); Hi Hnr Roll; Hnr Roll; Yth Ldrshp Prog; Comm Volntr; DARE; Emplmnt; P to P St Amb Prg; Web Designer; Computer Software Specialist; Rutgers U; New York U

GOOD, JESSICA; LAKEHURST, NJ; MANCHESTER TWP HS; (FR); Ctznshp Aw; Hnr Roll; Nat Hon Sy; Perf Att; Comm Volntr; Chrch Yth Grp; Lib Aide; Scouts; Culinary Arts; Art Institute of New York; Atlantic Cape Community College

GOODIN, JENNIFER; BRIDGEWATER, NJ; BRIDGEWATER-RARITAN HS; (FR); Hnr Roll; WWAHSS; Key Club; Orch; Psychology; U of Pittsburgh; Rutgers U

GOODMAN, ASHLEY; ISELIN, NJ; JOHN F KENNEDY MEMORIAL HS; (SO); Hnr Roll; WWAHSS; Peer Tut/Med; Key Club; Mus Clb; Pep Squd; Chr; Drl Tm; Track (J); Doctorate of Physical Therapy; Rutgers U, New Brunswick, NJ; Arcadia, Penn

GORCHINSKY, THAIZA; ROSELLE, NJ; ABRAHAM CLARK HS; MS; Hi Hnr Roll; Hnr Roll; Nat Sci Aw; Perf Att; St of Mnth; Comm Volntr; DARE; Ch Chr; Chrldg (L); Vllyball (L); Pediatrician; U of South Florida; U of North Carolina

GORDON, LATOYA; EAST ORANGE, NJ; EAST ORANGE CAMPUS 9 HS; (JR); All Am Sch; Ctznshp Aw; Hnr Roll; Nat Hon Sy; Nat Mrt LOC; Otst Ac Ach Awd; Perf Att; Sci Fairs; St Schl; Comm Volntr; Peer Tut/Med; ArtClub; Chrch Yth Grp; Emplmnt; FCA; Ch Chr; SP/M/VS; Elite Club/ Montclair Museum Exhibit; NJPAC Artwork Exhibit for Excellent Art Work; Fine Art; Fashion Design; Parsons; Fashion Institute of Technology

GORDON, TAMEIKA; NORTH BRUNSWICK, NJ; NORTH BRUNSWICK TWP HS; (SR); WWAHSS; Comm Volntr; Peer Tut/Med; Chrch Yth Grp; Emplmnt; Key Club; Chr; Ch Chr; Lit Mag (E); Painted Words Literary Club; Tutoring Programs; Nursing; Dietetics; Marywood U

GORNITZKY, ALEX; TOMS RIVER, NJ; TOMS RIVER HS NORTH; (SO); Hi Hnr Roll; Sci/Math Olympn; Comm Volntr; Hosp Aide; Biology Clb; Emplmnt; FBLA; Mth Clb/Tm; Sci Clb; Scouts; Vsity Clb; Swmg (V); Adv Cncl (R); Boy Scout - Eagle Scout; Pre-Med

GORR, COLLEEN D; JACKSON, NJ; JACKSON MEMORIAL HS; (SO); Hi Hnr Roll; Hnr Roll; Nat Hon Sy; Otst Ac Ach Awd; Pres Ac Ftns Aw; St of Mnth; Key Club; Chr; Sftball (J); Swmg (J)

GOSS, MELISSA; TRENTON, NJ; THE HUN SCH OF PRINCETON; (SO); Hi Hnr Roll; Comm Volntr; Emplmnt; Photog; Asian Clb; Dnce; Fncg (J); Fld Hky (J); Skiing; Upper School Student Council Scholarship Award Winner; Psychology; Philosophy; Princeton U; U of Pennsylvania

GOSSETT, NATALIE R; CAMDEN, NJ; THE LAWRENCEVILLE SCH; (JR); Hi Hnr Roll; Hnr Roll; Nat Hon Sy; Nat Mrt Semif; Otst Ac Ach Awd; WWAHSS; Comm Volntr; Hosp Aide; Chrch Yth Grp; Drma Clb; FBLA; Mod UN; Mus Clb; Quiz Bowl; Scouts; Spanish Clb; Chr; Dnce; Jzz Bnd; SP/ M/VS; Cl Off (V); CR (V); Sch Ppr (R); Future Business Leaders of America - VP; Catholic Students Organization - President; International Law; Entertainment Law; Georgetown U; Princeton U

GOTTSCHALK, KRISTEN; LITTLE FERRY, NJ; BERGEN CTY TECH HS; (JR); Hnr Roll; Nat Hon Sy; WWAHSS; ArtClub; Emplmnt; Prom Com; Chrldg (V); Yrbk (P); Girl Scout Silver Award; Girl Scout Gold Award; Accounting; Business Management; Ramapo College; William Paterson U

GOVERNALE, DAN; JACKSON, NJ; JACKSON MEMORIAL HS; (JR); Hi Hnr Roll; Hnr Roll; Perf Att; WWAHSS; Comm Volntr; Wdwrkg Clb; Bnd; Jzz Bnd; Mch Bnd; Golf (V L); Paint High School Field with School Emblem; Commercial Architectural Engineer; Virginia Technical U

GRABLACHOFF, BRANDON J; ISLAND HEIGHTS, NJ; CTRL REG HS; (SO); Chrch Yth Grp; Emplmnt; Fr of Library; Ch Chr; YMCA- Youth Counselor; Team Member / Toms River - Basketball Team / Basketball Team; Meteorologist

GRABOWSKI, ALEX; SUCCASUNNA, NJ; ROXBURY HS; (FR); Hnr Roll; Pres Ac Ftns Aw; WWAHSS; Comm Volntr; Key Club; Sci Clb; Vsity Clb; Cr Ctry (J); Track (V); Vsy Clb (V); CR (R); New Jersey State Indoor Track Distance Medley Relay Champion & Record Holder

GRACI, KATLYN; TOMS RIVER, NJ; MONSIGNOR DONOVAN HS; (JR); Nat Hon Sy; Perf Att; Pres Ac Ftns Aw; WWAHSS; Sccr (V L); Track (V L); National Honor Society; History Club; Archeology / Anthropology; Psychology; Columbia U; U of Pennsylvania

GRAF, JEAN; BAYVILLE, NJ; CTRL REG HS; (JR); Hi Hnr Roll; Hnr Roll; WWAHSS; Yth Ldrshp Prog; Comm Volntr; Emplmnt; Key Club; Dnce; Doctor; Monmouth U; Rutgers U

GRAHAM, BRITTANY A; MONTCLAIR, NJ; MONTCLAIR HS; (JR); Hnr Roll; Hosp Aide; Chrch Yth Grp; Emplmnt; Pep Squd; Ch Chr; Dnce; Mar Art (J); Stu Cncl (R); Hospital Volunteer - 3 Days Per Week; Business Management; Administrative Nursing; Hampton U; Marymount U

GRAHAM, MEGAN P; WENONAH, NJ; OUR LADY OF MERCY AC; (FR); All Am Sch; Hnr Roll; Nat Ldrshp Svc; St of Mnth; Yth Ldrshp Prog; Comm Volntr; Chrch Yth Grp; Emplmnt; NYLC; Spanish Clb; Bskball (J); Lcrsse (J); National Leadership Merit Award; All-American Scholar Award/ Invited to Congressional Student Leadership Conference; Political Science; Languages

GRAHAM, TREVOR T; MONTCLAIR, NJ; MONTCLAIR HS; (SO); Hi Hnr Roll; WWAHSS; DARE; Ice Hky (J); Lcrsse (VJ); Science; Child Development; McGill U; Edinburgh-Scotland

GRANDA, LEILANI J; GUTTENBERG, NJ; AC OF SACRED HEART HS; (JR); Ctznshp Aw; Hnr Roll; Nat Ldrshp Svc; Perf Att; Sci Fairs; St of Mnth; Cmptr Clb; DARE; Mus Clb; Chr; Dnce; SP/M/VS; Dance; Computers - Web Design; Business; Montclair State U; Berkeley College

GRANDE, CANDACE; PARSIPPANY, NJ; PARSIPPANY HS; (SR); Hi Hnr Roll; Hnr Roll; WWAHSS; Peer Tut/Med; Emplmnt; Pep Squd; Chrldg (V L); Sccr (V L); Track (V L); CR (R); Physical Education and Health; Montclair State U

GRANT, MELISSA M; STEWARTSVILLE, NJ; BETHLEHEM CATHOLIC HS; (FR); Hnr Roll; WWAHSS; Comm Volntr; Chrch Yth Grp; Key Club; Dnce; Participates in Dance Classes; Tap, Jazz, Ballet & Theater Dance; Graphic Design Artist

GRAULAU, KEVIN; PENNSAUKEN, NJ; PENNSAUKEN HS; (SO); F Lan Hn Soc; Hnr Roll; St of Mnth; Yth Ldrshp Prog; Comm Volntr; Chrch Yth Grp; Emplmnt; FCA; Quiz Bowl; Scouts; Ch Chr; Bsball (J); Bskball (J); Ftball (J); Gmnstcs; Swmg; Honor Roll; Business; Rutgers U; Temple U

GRAY, KATIA; ATLANTIC CITY, NJ; ATLANTIC CITY HS; (JR); Ctznshp Aw; Hi Hnr Roll; Hnr Roll; Nat Hon Sy; Otst Ac Ach Awd; Perf Att; St of Mnth; WWAHSS; Yth Ldrshp Prog; Comm Volntr; Red Cr Aide; DARE; Emplmnt; FTA; Key Club; SADD; French Clb; Dnce; Bdmtn (J); Fld Hky (J); Golf (J); Sftball (J); Tennis (J); Stu Cncl (R); CR (P); Sch Ppr (R); I Was a Member of the Z Club; Education; Sociology; Immaculata U; Duquesne U

GRECHKO, VITA; LAKE HIAWATHA, NJ; PARSIPPANY HS; (SO); Hi Hnr Roll; Hnr Roll; Comm Volntr; Italian Clb; Chr; Dnce; Swg Chr; Stu Cncl (R); Surgeon; Translator; Penn State U; Rutgers U

GREEN, DOUGLAS; WILLINGBORO, NJ; BURLINGTON CTY INST OF TECH; (SO); Hnr Roll; Comm Volntr; Chrch Yth Grp; Robotics; Game Programmer; Electronic Game Developer; DeVry University; Duke University

GREEN, GERARD; SAYREVILLE, NJ; SAYREVILLE WAR MEMORIAL HS; (JR); Hnr Roll; Otst Ac Ach Awd; Emplmnt; Bskball (VJC); Business Major; Computer Programming; U of North Carolina; Kansas U

GREEN, MICHAEL R; COLONIA, NJ; COLONIA HS; (JR); Hnr Roll; Nat Hon Sy; WWAHSS; Peer Tut/Med; Prom Com; Tchrs Aide; Chrldg (V L); Ftball (V L); Wrstlg (J); CR; Bob Luban Civic Association Award; Rutgers U; College of New Jersey

GREEN, REBECCA; CALIFON, NJ; WEST MORRIS CTRL HS; (JR); Hnr Roll; Kwnis Aw; Hab For Humty Volntr; Spec Olymp Vol; Emplmnt; Key Club; Lcrsse (V); CR (T); Sch Ppr (E, R, P); Reach Club Member; International Baccalaureate Program; Journalist; Trinity College; Franklin and Marshall

GREEN, TRAI; JERSEY CITY, NJ; (JR); Fut Prb Slvr; Nat Stu Ath Day Aw; Sci Fairs; St of Mnth; Comm Volntr; Peer Tut/Med; Chrch Yth Grp; Dbte Team; FBLA; Dnce; Bskball (V); Stu Cncl (P); CR (V); Marketing Degree Assoc/Masters; Real; St. John's U; Georgetown U

GREENBAUM, AARON; MAPLEWOOD, NJ; COLUMBIA HS; (JR); Hnr Roll; Otst Ac Ach Awd; WWAHSS; Yth Ldrshp Prog; Bnd; Jzz Bnd; Mch Bnd; Biomedical Engineer

GREENE, NISHERRAH D; WILLINGBORO, NJ; WILLINGHORO HS; (FR); Hi Hnr Roll; Hnr Roll; St of Mnth; Comm Volntr; Chrch Yth Grp; Drma Clb; Ch Chr; SP/M/VS; Bskball (J); Cl Off; Yrbk; Middle School Education; Psychologist; Rider U; Rutgers U

GREGORIO, TINAMARIE; JACKSON, NJ; JACKSON MEMORIAL HS; (SR); F Lan Hn Soc; Hi Hnr Roll; Hnr Roll; Nat Hon Sy; Otst Ac Ach Awd; WWAHSS; Comm Volntr; Emplmnt; Stu Cncl; Yrbk (R, P); Yearbook Club; Student Human Relation's Committee; Pediatrician; Physician's Assistant; Richard Stockton College of New Jersey; Rutgers U

GREVE, MEG; MT HOLLY, NJ; RANCOCAS VALLEY REG HS; (JR); F Lan Hn Soc; Hnr Roll; Nat Hon Sy; Pres Ac Ftns Aw; WWAHSS; Peer Tut/ Med; Chrch Yth Grp; Emplmnt; Key Club; Lib Aide; P to P St Amb Prg; Tchrs Aide; Chr; Ch Chr; SP/M/VS; Stg Cre; Sccr; Sftball (J L); Swmg (L); Track (J); Sports Medicine; Duke U; Elon U

GREWAL, HARDEEP; CARTERET, NJ; ST JOSEPH'S HS; (JR); Hi Hnr Roll; Nat Hon Sy; Nat Ldrshp Svc; WWAHSS; Yth Ldrshp Prog; Comm Volntr; Emplmnt; Mth Clb/Tm; Spanish Clb; Bnd; Pre-Med; Biology; Johns Hopkins U; Cornell U

GROOVER, CARLI; NEWTON, NJ; NEWTON HS; (SO); Hnr Roll; Chrch Yth Grp; FCA; Chr; Sccr (J); Journalism; Photojournalism; New York U

GROSS, CHRISTINE K; NEWARK, NJ; EAST SIDE HS; (SO); Hnr Roll; Comm Volntr; Video History Club; Art Animation; Book Author

GROSS, REBECCA; MARGATE CITY, NJ; ATLANTIC CITY HS; (JR); All Am Sch; Hi Hnr Roll; Nat Hon Sy; Nat Mrt LOC; Otst Ac Ach Awd; USAA; Red Cr Aide; Acpl Chr; Chr; Dnce; Swg Chr; American Legion Award; 1999 Atlantic County Spelling Champ; Mathematics Education; Performing Arts; Rutgers U; Princeton

GROSS, VANESSA; WESTWOOD, NJ; PARAMUS CATHOLIC HS; (JR); Hnr Roll; Comm Volntr; Chrch Yth Grp; DARE; Emplmnt; Off Aide; Clb; Bskball (J); Sccr (J); Volunteer Work; Pre-Med; Psychology; New York U; Fairfield U

GRZYBOWSKI, CORINNE; ALLENDALE, NJ; NORTHERN HIGHLANDS REG HS; (JR); Hi Hnr Roll; Nat Mrt Fin; Sci Fairs; WWAHSS; Yth Ldrshp Prog; Comm Volntr; Peer Tut/Med; Dbte Team; Emplmnt; Jr Cls League; Mod UN; P to P St Amb Prg; Sci Clb; Scouts; Latin Clb; Hsbk Rdg; Fed Challenge; Piano; Economics; International Relations; Stanford U; Princeton U

GUERRA, ALEJANDRA; EAST RUTHERFORD, NJ; HENRY P BECTON REG HS; (SO); Hi Hnr Roll; Emplmnt; Vllyball (J); Math Major; Architecture; Rutgers U

GUERRA, LYDIA; NORTH BERGEN, NJ; NORTH BERGEN HS; (SO); Hi Hnr Roll; Hnr Roll; Peer Tut/Med; JSA; Key Club; German Clb; CR (R); Lit Mag (E); Pediatric Medicine; English Literature; Boston U; Princeton U

GUERRA, VANESSA J; ELIZABETH, NJ; ELIZABETH HS; (JR); Ctznshp Aw; Hnr Roll; Nat Hon Sy; Otst Ac Ach Awd; Key Club; Sci Clb; Orch; Tri-M Music Honor Society; Champions for Excellence; Pediatrician; Veterinarian; Rutgers; Seton Hall

GUERRERO DE LUNA, GRACE; LINDEN, NJ; LINDEN HS; (SO); Hi Hnr Roll; Hnr Roll; WWAHSS; Chrch Yth Grp; Bnd; Ch Chr; Accounting; Physical Therapy; Rutgers U; Seton Hall U

GUICHINA, DELIYA; SPRINGFIELD, NJ; JONATHAN DAYTON HS; (JR); F Lan Hn Soc; Hi Hnr Roll; Nat Hon Sy; St of Mnth; Comm Volntr; Peer Tut/Med; Spec Olymp Vol; Emplmnt; Key Club; Mth Clb/Tm; Svce Clb; Spanish Clb; Cr Ctry (V L); Track (V L); Sch Ppr (R); Peer Leadership; Alternatives Club; Business Management; Entrepreneurship; U of Pennsylvania; Amherst College

GUMASTE, PRIYANKA; CRESSKILL, NJ; CRESSKILL JR/SR HS; (JR); Hnr Roll; WWAHSS; Comm Volntr; Hosp Aide; Jr Cls League; Mod UN; Svce Clb; Dnce; Chrldg (V); Cl Off (S); Stu Cncl (S); Lit Mag (E); Sch Ppr (R); Interact (Service Club Affiliated with Rotary)-President; Model UN-Won Best Speaker, Delegation 1st Position Paper; Medicine

GUO, LAWRENCE; HACKENSACK, NJ; HACKENSACK HS; (SO); Hi Hnr Roll; Hnr Roll; Perf Att; Pres Sch; Sci Fairs; St of Mnth; WWAHSS; Peer Tut/Med; ArtClub; Chess; DARE; FBLA; Lib Aide; Mth Clb/Tm; Quiz Bowl; Schol Bwl; Bnd; Jzz Bnd; Tennis (J); Cl Off (R); CR (R); Psychology; Architecture; Yale U; Princeton U

GUPTA, INDIRA; NORTH BERGEN, NJ; HCST NORTH HUDSON CTR; (SO); Hi Hnr Roll; Comm Volntr; Peer Tut/Med; DARE; Key Club; Sci Clb; Bnd; Chr; Chrldg (L); Skiing; Swmg (L); Tennis; Stu Cncl (P)

GUTIERREZ, ARASELI; PATERSON, NJ; J F KENNEDY HS; (SO); Hi Hnr Roll; Hnr Roll; Chr; Medical Assisting; Graphic Design and Animation; Passaic County Community College; Gibbs College

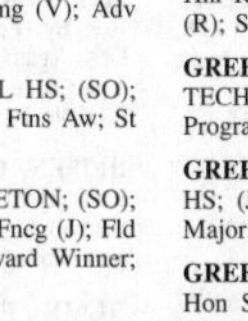
Gupta, Indira
Hcst North Hudson Ctr
North Bergen, NJ

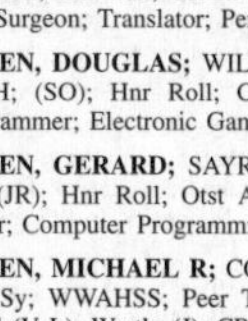
Greene, Nisherrah D
Willinghoro HS
Willingboro, NJ

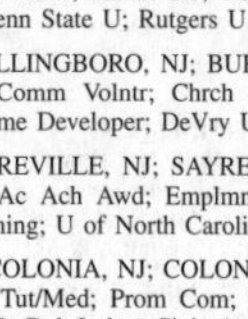
Gorchinsky, Thaiza
Abraham Clark HS
Roselle, NJ

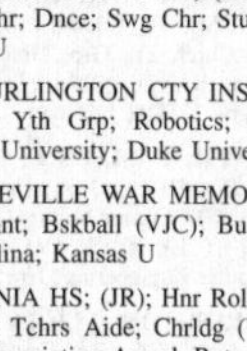
Graulau, Kevin
Pennsauken HS
Pennsauken, NJ

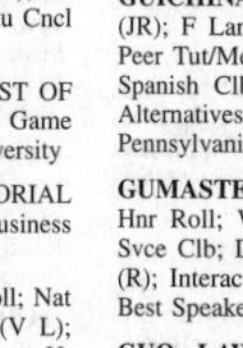
Gutierrez, Araseli
J F Kennedy HS
Paterson, NJ

GUTIERREZ, BRUCE R; ELIZABETH, NJ; ELIZABETH HS; (SO); Ctznshp Aw; Hnr Roll; Otst Ac Ach Awd; Perf Att; St of Mnth; Valdctrian; Comm Volntr; Peer Tut/Med; Chrch Yth Grp; DARE; Key Club; Mod UN; Outdrs Clb; ROTC; Drl Tm; Cl Off (P); JROTC Air Rifle Team; Psychology; Pre-Medicine; New York U; Richmond U (London)

GUTIERREZ, KIMBERLY A; MAPLEWOOD, NJ; COLUMBIA HS; (SO); Hnr Roll; Peer Tut/Med; Chrch Yth Grp; DARE; Mth Clb/Tm; Quiz Bowl; Track (J); Teaching; Law; Northeastern U; Northwestern U

GUTIERREZ JR, RADAME; CLARK, NJ; ARTHUR L JOHNSON HS; (SR); Ctznshp Aw; F Lan Hn Soc; Hi Hnr Roll; Hnr Roll; Nat Sci Aw; Otst Ac Ach Awd; Sci Fairs; Sci/Math Olympn; St of Mnth; WWAHSS; Peer Tut/Med; Emplmnt; Mth Clb/Tm; Mus Clb; Sci Clb; Tchrs Aide; Spanish Clb; Bnd; SP/M/VS; Stg Cre; Bsball; Outstanding Music Student - Private Lessons; Sound Engineering; William Paterson U; Monmouth U

GUZMAN, MARC P Q; HACKENSACK, NJ; HACKENSACK HS; (JR); All Am Sch; Ctznshp Aw; F Lan Hn Soc; Jr Rot; Nat Hon Sy; Nat Ldrshp Svc; Nat Mrt Sch Recip; USAA; WWAHSS; Yth Ldrshp Prog; Comm Volntr; Hab For Humty Volntr; Hosp Aide; AL Aux Boys; Chrch Yth Grp; Mus Clb; Off Aide; Schol Bwl; Svce Clb; Tchrs Aide; French Clb; Bnd; Chr; Drm Mjr; Mch Bnd; Vllyball (V); Adv Cncl (R); Cl Off (P, T); Stu Cncl (R); CR (T); Lit Mag (R); Sch Ppr (R, P); Yrbk (P); Dwight D Eisenhower Leadership West Point Award; Presidential Freedom Leadership Award; Biology; Genetics; U of Pennsylvania; Princeton U

GYSBERS, BRENDAN J; BROWNS MILLS, NJ; GUTHRIE HS; (SO); Hnr Roll; Sci Fairs

HA, CATHERINE J; WARREN, NJ; WATCHUNG HILLS REG HS; MS; Ctznshp Aw; Hi Hnr Roll; Otst Ac Ach Awd; Yth Ldrshp Prog; Peer Tut/Med; ArtClub; Chrch Yth Grp; DARE; Dbte Team; Photog; Quiz Bowl; Bnd; Mch Bnd; Orch; Vllyball (J); Stu Cncl (P); Sch Ppr (R); Member of the New Jersey Youth Symphony for 6 Years; Recipient of the President's Education Award; Concert Violinist; Marine Biologist; Harvard U; Yale U

HACKETT, LAUREN; RINGWOOD, NJ; LAKELAND REG HS; (FR); Comm Volntr; Acpl Chr; Bnd; Chr; Ch Chr; President of 8th Grade Band; Secretary of 8th Grade Choral; Music Education; Vocal Performance; Berkley College of Music; William Paterson U

HADDAD, SANDRA; MATAWAN, NJ; MATAWAN REG HS; (JR); Hi Hnr Roll; Nat Hon Sy; Nat Ldrshp Svc; Otst Ac Ach Awd; Perf Att; Comm Volntr; Emplmnt; Key Club; Fld Hky (J); Track (V); Cl Off (S); Dwight D Eisenhower Leadership Award; Pre-Law; Public Administration; New York U; Drexel U

HAFEEZ, HANNAH; ISELIN, NJ; AC-SCI MATH ENG TECH HS; (FR); Hnr Roll; Otst Ac Ach Awd; Perf Att; Sci Fairs; St of Mnth; Comm Volntr; Hosp Aide; DARE; Drma Clb; P to P St Amb Prg; Sci Clb; Stg Cre; Stu Cncl (R); President's Award-Outstanding Academic-2004 Excellence; Doctorate in Biomedical; 2002 Best of the Year Award/Scholarship-ICNA; UMDNJ; Rutgers

HAHN, KATIE; BLACKWOOD, NJ; GLOUCESTER CATHOLIC HS; (JR); Hnr Roll; Comm Volntr; Svce Clb; Chr; Swmg (V); CR (R); Elementary Education; Rowan U

HAIDER, HIRA F; PRINCETON JCT, NJ; WWPHS SOUTH; (JR); Amnsty Intl; CARE; Comm Volntr; Dbte Team; Emplmnt; Mod UN; ROTC; Schol Bwl; Founded a Club: Mirth; Pre Medical; Barnard; Rutgers

HAJJAR, MARC J; CRESSKILL, NJ; DWIGHT-ENGLEWOOD HS; (SO); Hnr Roll; Peer Tut/Med; ArtClub; Cr Ctry (J); Cr Ct Ski (J); Track (J); Cl Off (R); Yrbk (P); Poster Club Member; Pre-Med; Architecture; Georgetown U; New York U

HALIKERE, APOORVA; EAST BRUNSWICK, NJ; EAST BRUNSWICK HS; (SO); Ctznshp Aw; F Lan Hn Soc; Hnr Roll; Perf Att; Hosp Aide; Drma Clb; Fr of Library; Scouts; French Clb; Stg Cre; Sch Ppr (R); Active Member of Girl Scouts; Active Volunteer at Hospital; Biochemistry; Radiology; Princeton U; Rutgers U

HALL, ANDRE; JERSEY CITY, NJ; UNIVERSITY AC CHARTER SCH; (FR); Hi Hnr Roll; Hnr Roll; Perf Att; St of Mnth; Comm Volntr; Peer Tut/Med; Chrch Yth Grp; Drma Clb; Emplmnt; Mus Clb; Bnd; Chr; Ch Chr; Drm Mjr; Bskball; Cr Ctry; Ftball; Track (VJCL); Business; Engineering; Howard U; Georgia Tech

HALLIGAN-CEBULKO, COURTNEY; OCEANPORT, NJ; SHORE REG; (SO); Hi Hnr Roll; Otst Ac Ach Awd; St of Mnth; Peer Tut/Med; DARE; Drma Clb; Emplmnt; FCA; Mod UN; NYLC; Acpl Chr; Chr; Dnce; SP/M/VS; Chrldg (V CL); Stu Cncl; National Junior Honor Society President; Major in Business / Marketing; Minor in Musical Theatre; Ithaca College; UNC Chapel Hill

HALUSKA, CORY M; FLORENCE, NJ; FLORENCE TWP MEM HS; (FR); Hi Hnr Roll; Hnr Roll; Sci Clb; Bsball (VJ); Sccr (V L); Astronomy; Rutgers State U; Florida State U

HAMILTON, AMANDA; WILLINGBORO, NJ; WILLINGBORO HS; (FR); Hnr Roll; Pres Ac Ftns Aw; Sci Fairs; St of Mnth; ArtClub; Chrch Yth Grp; DARE; Scouts; Chr; Ch Chr; Dnce; SP/M/VS; Lawyer; Child Psychologist

HAMILTON, GINO; PATERSON, NJ; (SO); Ctznshp Aw; Cr Ctry

HAMILTON, JENNIFER; PT PLEASANT BEACH, NJ; PT PLEASANT BORO HS; (SR); F Lan Hn Soc; Hi Hnr Roll; Hnr Roll; Nat Hon Sy; Otst Ac Ach Awd; Pres Ac Ftns Aw; WWAHSS; Comm Volntr; ArtClub; Emplmnt; FBLA; Key Club; Mth Clb/Tm; Prom Com; Bskball (V L); Ice Hky (V); PP Ftbl; Scr Kpr (V L); Sccr (J L); Track (V L); Stu Cncl (R); CR (R); Certified Lifeguard; PharmD Degree; U of Connecticut Storrs

HAND, JANE; HIGHLAND PARK, NJ; HIGHLAND PARK HS; (FR); Hi Hnr Roll; WWAHSS; Spec Olymp Vol; Chrch Yth Grp; P to P St Amb Prg; Chr; Ch Chr; Orch; Track (J); Cl Off (V); AFG Student Representative; Sunday School Teacher; Medicine; Biology; Yale U; Columbia U

HANKE, KAYLA; ALLENHURST, NJ; OT HS; (SO); Hnr Roll; Pres Sch; Comm Volntr; Chrch Yth Grp; Key Club; Scouts; Vsity Clb; Spanish Clb; Cr Ctry (V CL); Swmg (V CL); Track (V L); Vsy Clb (V); Nutrition Science; U of North Carolina-Chapel Hill; U of Delaware

HANLEY, RACHEL L; RANDOLPH, NJ; RANDOLPH HS; (SO); Hnr Roll; Comm Volntr; Emplmnt; Key Club; Lcrsse (J); Sccr (J)

HANNA, MARIAN; JERSEY CITY, NJ; AC ST ALOYSIUS HS; (JR); Perf Att; Sci Fairs; Yth Ldrshp Prog; Comm Volntr; Peer Tut/Med; Chrch Yth Grp; Emplmnt; Ch Chr; Chrldg (J); Cr Ctry (J); Pre-Medical Honors Program At UMDNJ; Pre-Med; Biology; Rutgers; Fairleigh Dickinson U

HANNA, MENA; BAYONNE, NJ; BAYONNE HS; (JR); Red Cr Aide; Ch Chr; Tennis (J); Biology, Chemistry, Mathematics and Physics; PhD Degree Biology; Harvard U; Columbia U

HANNA, YOUSTINA E; MILLTOWN, NJ; SPOTSWOOD HS; (SO); Hi Hnr Roll; Hnr Roll; Perf Att; Sci/Math Olympn; St of Mnth; Comm Volntr; Chrch Yth Grp; DARE; Drma Clb; Chr; Ch Chr; Tennis (J); Yrbk (E, P); Community Service; Dentistry; Eye Doctor; Rutgers U; NJIT

HANNAH, MARISSA; CLEMENTON, NJ; GLOUCESTER CATHOLIC HS; (SR); Key Club; Mus Clb; Bnd; Mch Bnd; Track; Stu Cncl (V); CR (V); Sch Ppr (R); Cardiology; U of Miami; Ursinus College

HANSEN, KATIE; NEPTUNE, NJ; (JR); Hnr Roll; WWAHSS; Swmg (V); MVP - High School Swim Team; National Art Society

HARARI, JOE; W LONG BRANCH, NJ; HILLEL YESHIVA HS; (SO); Hi Hnr Roll; Comm Volntr; Peer Tut/Med; ArtClub; Emplmnt; Tmpl Yth Grp; Wdwrkg Clb; French Clb; Stu Cncl (R); CR (R); Lit Mag; Sch Ppr (E); Selected to Attend Ematai Leadership Conference; Chairman of the American History Fair; Summer Reading Committee; Bachelor's in Culinary Arts; Journalism / Communications; Culinary Institute of America, Hyde Park, NY; New York U, New York, NY

HARBECK, JACLYN; MILLTOWN, NJ; SPOTSWOOD HS; (JR); Hi Hnr Roll; Hnr Roll; Nat Hon Sy; Comm Volntr; DECA; FBLA; Svce Clb; Bnd; Pep Bnd; Sftball (J); Tennis (V CL); Stu Cncl (R); CR (R); Sch Ppr (R); Yrbk (R); DECA Nationals Participant; Marketing; Business; Montclair State U; The College of New Jersey

HARDY, SAMANTHA A; CLIFFSIDE PARK, NJ; PARAMUS CATHOLIC HS; (JR); Comm Volntr; Emplmnt; Photog; Scouts; Ambassador of Paramus Catholic; Business Administration MBA; Global Intelligence/Criminal Justice; Embry-Riddle Aeronautical U; C.W. Post Long Island U

HARP, LONDYN; MONTCLAIR, NJ; MONTCLAIR HS; (JR); F Lan Hn Soc; Gov Hnr Prg; Hi Hnr Roll; Hnr Roll; Nat Hon Sy; St of Mnth; WWAHSS; Yth Ldrshp Prog; Comm Volntr; Hab For Humty Volntr; Peer Tut/Med; Chrch Yth Grp; Dbte Team; Drma Clb; Emplmnt; Pep Squd; Sci Clb; Scouts; SADD; SP/M/VS; Stg Cre; CR (P); Crew - Rowing; Pre-Med; Biology; UCLA; Fordham U

HARPER, DAMAUS F; HAINESPORT, NJ; RANCOCAS VALLEY REG HS; (JR); Hi Hnr Roll; Hnr Roll; Nat Hon Sy; Otst Ac Ach Awd; Perf Att; WWAHSS; Comm Volntr; Chrch Yth Grp; Key Club; Tchrs Aide; Bskball (L); Ftball (J L); Track (VJ L); Lockheed Martin Minorities in Engineering; Computer Engineering; North Carolina A & T U; Drexel U

HARRINGTON, ALICIA D; MILLVILLE, NJ; VINELAND HS; (JR); Hnr Roll; Chrch Yth Grp; Emplmnt; Tchrs Aide; Spanish Clb; Ch Chr; Dnce; Stu Cncl (R); Social Worker; Degree in Early Childhood Development.; Winston Salem State U; Temple U

HARRIRAM, NOORI S; JERSEY CITY, NJ; WILLIAM DICKINSON HS; (JR); Hnr Roll; Otst Ac Ach Awd; Perf Att; St of Mnth; Hosp Aide; Peer Tut/Med; DECA; Off Aide; Prom Com; Tchrs Aide; Bdmtn (J); Cr Ctry (J); CR (R); Lit Mag (R); Sch Ppr (R); Yrbk (P); Rotary Award 2005; Criminal Justice; Marketing; John Jay College; Rutgers U

HARRIS, JANELL; PISCATAWAY, NJ; PISCATAWAY HS; (SO); Hi Hnr Roll; Hnr Roll; WWAHSS; Peer Tut/Med; Key Club; Yrbk (E); Peer Mediation; Tutor; Lawyer; Culinary Arts

HARRIS, SAMANTHA C; SALEM, NJ; SALEM HS; (FR); Hnr Roll; Chrch Yth Grp; Ch Chr; Chorus; Drama; Pensacola Christian College

HARRIS, STEPHANIE; SOMERSET, NJ; SOMERSET CHRISTIAN AC; (JR); Ctznshp Aw; Hi Hnr Roll; Hnr Roll; MVP; Otst Ac Ach Awd; Pres Ac Ftns Aw; Pres Sch; WWAHSS; Comm Volntr; Hab For Humty Volntr; Chrch Yth Grp; Emplmnt; Mus Clb; Prom Com; Tchrs Aide; Vsity Clb; Chr; SP/M/VS; Bsball (V); Bskball (V L); Scr Kpr (VJ); Sccr (V CL); Sftball (V CL); Vllyball; Cl Off (T); CR (R); 5 Year Member of the Somerset County Youth Council; Worship Leader (Minister of Music); Sports Management

HARRIS-BLEVIN, ANNACLER; PARSIPPANY, NJ; PARSIPPANY HILLS HS; (JR); F Lan Hn Soc; Nat Hon Sy; Chrch Yth Grp; Key Club; Tech Clb; Dnce; Fld Hky (V); Track (J); Stu Cncl (R); Girl Scouts Gold Award; Lehigh U; Northeastern U

HARRISON, ROBERT J; BAYONNE, NJ; BAYONNE HS; (SO); Doctor; Lawyer; Rutgers U; Boston U

HARTMAN, LAUREN; MANASQUAN, NJ; WALL HS; (JR); Hnr Roll; Nat Hon Sy; St of Mnth; Comm Volntr; DARE; Emplmnt; Key Club; NYLC; Scouts; SADD; Spanish Clb; Chrldg (JC); International Business / Finance; Spanish; U of Miami; Flagler College

HARTMAN, REGINA B; VINELAND, NJ; SACRED HEART HS; (SR); F Lan Hn Soc; Jr Rot; Nat Hon Sy; Pres Ac Ftns Aw; Comm Volntr; Peer Tut/Med; Spec Olymp Vol; HO'Br Yth Ldrshp; Acpl Chr; SP/M/VS; Stg Cre; Sccr; Swmg; Yrbk; Congressional Gold Medal for Youth; Certified EMT; Medicine; U of PA; Columbia U

HASKINS, KATHRYN; MONTVILLE, NJ; MONTVILLE TWP; (SR); F Lan Hn Soc; Hnr Roll; Nat Hon Sy; Nat Stu Ath Day Aw; US Army Sch Ath Aw; WWAHSS; Comm Volntr; Peer Tut/Med; Emplmnt; Key Club; Photog; SADD; Vsity Clb; WORLD Clb; Sftball (V CL); Shop Rite Athlete of the Month / STAR; Kinesiology; Shenandoah U

HASPEL, ROBERT F; LINCROFT, NJ; MIDDLETOWN SOUTH HS; (JR); F Lan Hn Soc; Hi Hnr Roll; Hnr Roll; WWAHSS; Yth Ldrshp Prog; Emplmnt; FBLA; Vsity Clb; Spanish Clb; Bsball (V C); Bskball (V); Ftball (V C); Eagle Scholar Award 9, 10 & 11; Rookie of the Year Varsity Baseball -10; Physical Therapy; Business Management; Lafayette U; Bucknell U

HATULAN, MICAH; LINDEN, NJ; LINDEN HS; (SR); F Lan Hn Soc; Hi Hnr Roll; St of Mnth; Chrch Yth Grp; Emplmnt; Lib Aide; German Clb; Orch; Tennis (V); GAPP - German Exchange Program; Pharmacy; Rutgers U; St John's U

HAYES, EDEN; ATCO, NJ; HAMMONTON HS; (FR); Hnr Roll; St of Mnth; Comm Volntr; German Clb; Renaissance Award Recipient; Car Technician; U of the Arts At Philadelphia

HAZEL, KRISTEN L; WEST ORANGE, NJ; WEST ORANGE HS; (JR); Hnr Roll; Peer Tut/Med; Emplmnt; FTA; Spanish Clb; Orch; Stg Cre; Sccr (J); Sch Ppr (R); Spanish SALE: Teach Spanish to Children; Education; Communications; Seton Hall U; Montclair State U

HEID, KATLYN; SEASIDE HEIGHTS, NJ; CTRL REG HS; (SO); Hi Hnr Roll; Hnr Roll; Perf Att; Pres Ac Ftns Aw; Off Aide

HEILMANN, CRAIG; HO HO KUS, NJ; (JR); Pres Ac Ftns Aw; Yth Ldrshp Prog; Comm Volntr; Peer Tut/Med; Cr Ctry (V L); Track (V L); Architecture; Pratt Institute; Rensselaer

HEIMRICH, JASON; HIGHLAND LAKES, NJ; VERNON TOWNSHIP HS; (SR); Ctznshp Aw; F Lan Hn Soc; Gov Hnr Prg; Hi Hnr Roll; Hnr Roll; Nat Hon Sy; Perf Att; WWAHSS; Comm Volntr; Red Cr Aide; Chrch Yth Grp; Dbte Team; Emplmnt; Key Club; Mod UN; NtlFrnscLg; Spch Team; Tchrs Aide; Bnd; Mch Bnd; Cr Ctry (V); Swmg (L); Tennis (L); Mock Trial; English; Pre-Law; U of Chicago; U of Scranton

HEISEN, GREGORY; PRINCETON, NJ; PRINCETON HS; (JR); Hi Hnr Roll; Hnr Roll; MVP; Hab For Humty Volntr; Peer Tut/Med; Vsity Clb; Bskball (J); Golf (V L); All-County Golf - #2; Political Science; Economics; Vanderbilt U; Wake Forest U

HELOU, RANA; PATERSON, NJ; JOHN F KENNEDY HS; (FR); Ctznshp Aw; Hnr Roll; Nat Hon Sy; Perf Att; Lib Aide; Mod UN; Bskball (V); Sch Ppr; Safety Patrol

HENDERSON, ALTAMER; NEWARK, NJ; (FR); Hnr Roll; Otst Ac Ach Awd; Perf Att; Yth Ldrshp Prog; Chrch Yth Grp; DARE; ROTC; Bskball (V); Cl Off (P); Veterinarian; Seton Hall

HERING, DANIELLE; HIGHLAND LAKES, NJ; VERNON TWP HS; (SO); Ctznshp Aw; Hnr Roll; Kwnis Aw; Pres Sch; WWAHSS; Yth Ldrshp Prog; Comm Volntr; Spec Olymp Vol; ArtClub; Emplmnt; Key Club; Prom Com; Scr Kpr (V); CR (R); Sch Ppr (P); Vice President of Key Club; Education/Special Education; Math; Ramapo U; College of New Jersey

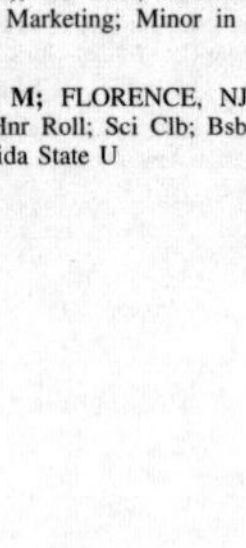
Haspel, Robert F
Middletown South HS
Lincroft, NJ

Hanley, Rachel L
Randolph HS
Randolph, NJ

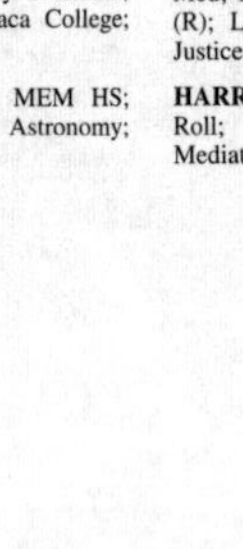
Hall, Andre
University AC Charter Sch
Jersey City, NJ

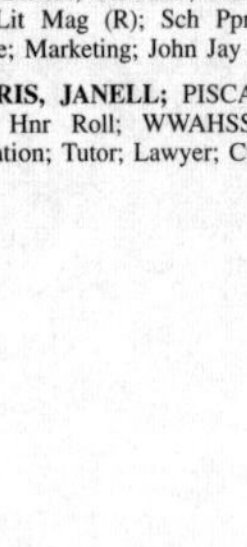
Halikere, Apoorva
East Brunswick HS
East Brunswick, NJ

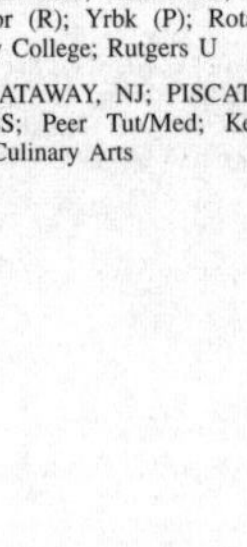
Gutierrez, Kimberly A
Columbia HS
Maplewood, NJ

Ha, Catherine J
Watchung Hills Reg HS
Warren, NJ

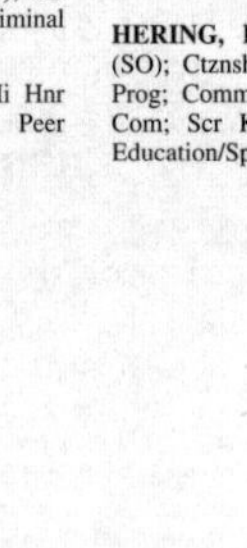
Hamilton, Jennifer
Pt Pleasant Boro HS
Pt Pleasant Beach, NJ

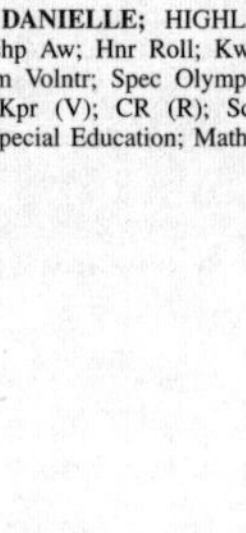
Hartman, Lauren
Wall HS
Manasquan, NJ

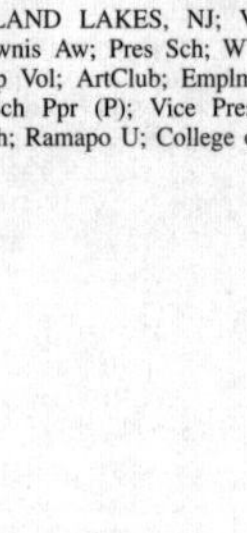
Heisen, Gregory
Princeton HS
Princeton, NJ

HERNANDEZ, ABIGAIL; GLASSBORO, NJ; GLASSBORO HS; (SR); Hi Hnr Roll; Hnr Roll; Otst Ac Ach Awd; Pres Ac Ftns Aw; St of Mnth; Comm Volntr; Chrch Yth Grp; Emplmnt; Prom Com; Svce Clb; Spanish Clb; Cl Off (R); Stu Cncl (R); CR (R); Glassboro Bulldog Spirit Award - 3 Times; Excellence in Honors - Childhood; Degree in International Business; Degree in Teaching; Temple U Ambler Campus

HERNANDEZ, YASMIN; PASSAIC, NJ; PASSAIC HS; (FR); Duke TS; Fut Prb Slvr; Hnr Roll; Sci Fairs; St of Mnth; Yth Ldrshp Prog; CARE; Hosp Aide; Red Cr Aide; ArtClub; Cmptr Clb; Fr of Library; Mth Clb/Tm; ROTC; Schol Bwl; Spch Team; SADD; Clr Grd; Dnce; Drl Tm; Mch Bnd; Arch (V); Chrldg (V); GAA (V); Gmnstcs (V); Mar Art (V); Sftball (C); Tennis (V); Vllyball (L); Adv Cncl (P); Cl Off (R); Stu Cncl (R); CR (R); Lit Mag (E); Sch Ppr (E); Yrbk (P); Secretary of Hospitals; Teacher for HS; Rutgers U

HESINGTON, CORINNE C; HAMMONTON, NJ; HAMMONTON HS; (JR); Comm Volntr; Emplmnt; Clr Grd; Dnce; Teaching Degree

HIBBERT, CAIECA; PLAINFIELD, NJ; NORTH PLAINFIELD HS; (JR); F Lan Hn Soc; WWAHSS; Comm Volntr; Chrch Yth Grp; Dbte Team; ROTC; WORLD Clb; Drl Tm; Sch Ppr (R); Political Science; Biology; Spelman College; Temple U

HICKEY, ERIN; OCEANPORT, NJ; RED BANK CATHOLIC HS; (FR); Hi Hnr Roll; Hnr Roll; Otst Ac Ach Awd; St of Mnth; Comm Volntr; ArtClub; Chrch Yth Grp; Emplmnt; FBLA; Svce Clb; Bnd; Mch Bnd; Swmg (V); American Legion Award

HICKS, ANEISA J; ASBURY PARK, NJ; AC CHARTER HS; (JR); Hi Hnr Roll; Hnr Roll; Perf Att; WWAHSS; Yth Ldrshp Prog; Comm Volntr; Peer Tut/Med; Chrch Yth Grp; Mus Clb; Photog; Scouts; Tech Clb; Ch Chr; Chrldg (J); CR (R); Gymnastics Outside of School; Psychology; Nurse Practitioner; College of New Jersey; Seton Hall

HICKS, CHARLES; WOODBRIDGE, NJ; WOODBRIDGE HS; (JR); F Lan Hn Soc; Hnr Roll; Nat Hon Sy; WWAHSS; Emplmnt; Cr Ctry (V L); Track (J); Stu Cncl (R); CR (R); Bowling-V-L; Computer Science/Math/Business; Education

HIGGS, CEDRICA; PATERSON, NJ; ROSA PARKS HS; (FR); Hi Hnr Roll; Hnr Roll; Otst Ac Ach Awd; Pres Sch; St of Mnth; Yth Ldrshp Prog; Peer Tut/Med; Chrch Yth Grp; Chr; Mch Bnd; Cl Off (T); CR (P); Music Education; Math Teacher; Morgan State U; Florida Memorial College

HIGHAM, SUSAN; RINGWOOD, NJ; LAKELAND REG HS; (SR); F Lan Hn Soc; Hi Hnr Roll; Nat Hon Sy; St of Mnth; WWAHSS; Comm Volntr; Svce Clb; Bnd; Mch Bnd; Fncg (V); Tennis (V); Student of the Month Scholastics; International Business; Spanish; Dickinson College (Attending Fall 2005)

HILL, TIFFANY M; IRVINGTON, NJ; IRVINGTON HS; (SR); Ctznshp Aw; Hnr Roll; Nat Ldrshp Svc; Perf Att; St of Mnth; Yth Ldrshp Prog; Comm Volntr; Drma Clb; Mod UN; ROTC; Scouts; Dnce; Drl Tm; Bskball (L); Sccr (L); Track (L); Wt Lftg (L); Modeling Career Goal; Business Management, Electronic Engineering; Essex County College

HINDS, LA SHAWNA; PASSAIC, NJ; PASSAIC HS; (FR); Bskball (J); Cr Ctry (J); CR (P, R); Recreation Softball; Lunch Aid, Lunch Period "7"; Publicist; New York U

HOAGLAND, TIMOTHY G; LINDEN, NJ; DAVID BREARLEY MIDDLE HS; (JR); Hi Hnr Roll; Hnr Roll; Nat Hon Sy; Perf Att; WWAHSS; Emplmnt; NYLC; Pep Squd; Chr; SP/M/VS; Sccr (V L)

HOAHNG, KRISTI L; EATONTOWN, NJ; (SR); Ctznshp Aw; Hi Hnr Roll; Hnr Roll; Nat Hon Sy; WWAHSS; Comm Volntr; Chrch Yth Grp; DARE; Emplmnt; Key Club; Photog; Prom Com; Tchrs Aide; Chr; Stg Cre; Cl Off (V); Yrbk (R); Pom Pom Football; Child Psychology; Teaching; Rutgers U; Montclair State U

HOFFMAN, ERICA; BELFORD, NJ; MIDDLETOWN NORTH HS; (JR); Hnr Roll; WWAHSS; Comm Volntr; Emplmnt; Scouts; Voc Ind Clb Am; Bskball (V L); PP Ftbl; CR (R); Vocational School for Law Enforcement; Criminal Justice; Sports; Quinnipiac U; Caldwell College

HOFFMAN, MATILDE V; SUMMIT, NJ; SUMMIT SR HS; (SO); Hnr Roll; US Army Sch Ath Aw; Yth Ldrshp Prog; Red Cr Aide; Dnce; Track (J); Selected for the National Youth Leadership Forum on Medicine in Washington DC; Biology (Medical School); Genetic Research; Fordham U; Fairleigh Dickinson U

HOFFMAN, TIFFANY L; LUMBERTON, NJ; RANCOCAS VALLEY REG HS; (JR); Ctznshp Aw; Hi Hnr Roll; Hnr Roll; Otst Ac Ach Awd; Pres Ac Ftns Aw; St of Mnth; Comm Volntr; Emplmnt; Key Club; Photog; Gmnstcs (J); Psychology; Business Management; U of South Carolina; Loyola U

HOGAN, ALLISON; BELLEVILLE, NJ; BELLEVILLE HS; (FR); Hnr Roll; Spec Olymp Vol; Drma Clb; Scouts; Bnd; Jzz Bnd; Mch Bnd; SP/M/VS; Sftball; Track (V L); Sch Ppr (R); Marching Band-Letter Winner & Officer; Psychology; Law; College of William & Mary

HOGAN, BRIANNA F; HACKETTSTOWN, NJ; MORRIS CATHOLIC HS; (JR); Hnr Roll; Pres Ac Ftns Aw; CARE; Comm Volntr; DARE; Emplmnt; Tchrs Aide; Dnce; SP/M/VS; Bskball (J); Chrldg (V); Sccr (J); Stu Cncl (R); CR (R); Model - Actor in NYC / Mission Club; Seventeen Model in New York; Business Management; Dance; Penn State U; William Patterson U

HOGAN, JESSICA; LINDEN, NJ; LINDEN HS; (SR); Hnr Roll; St of Mnth; Emplmnt; HOSA Youth of United Ways; President of United Ways; Nursing; Charles E Gregory School of Nursing; Muhlenberg College

HOLDER, AMETHYST; PARSIPPANY, NJ; PARSIPPANY HS; (FR); Hi Hnr Roll; Hnr Roll; Chrch Yth Grp; Key Club; Bskball (J); Track (V); Vllyball (J); Student Athlete; Medical; Business; U of Pennsylvania; Stanford U

HOLDER, GREGORY; NEWARK, NJ; (JR); MVP; Nat Hon Sy; Nat Stu Ath Day Aw; Perf Att; St of Mnth; Comm Volntr; 4-H; Bsball (J); Bskball (V); Ftball (V); Track (V); Sports and Management; Rutgers New Brunswick; Saint Peters

HOLDER, MICHAEL; SOUTH ORANGE, NJ; COLUMBIA HS; (JR); Hnr Roll; WWAHSS; Comm Volntr; Key Club; Track (V); Business Management; Mechanical Engineering; U of Maryland-College Park; Lafayette College

HOLLADAY, CHRISTINA; PENNSVILLE, NJ; PENNSVILLE MEMORIAL HS; (SR); Hnr Roll; Nat Hon Sy; Pres Ac Ftns Aw; WWAHSS; Yth Ldrshp Prog; Comm Volntr; Hab For Humty Volntr; Peer Tut/Med; AL Aux Girls; Emplmnt; FBLA; Jr Ach; Lib Aide; NYLC; Prom Com; Svce Clb; PP Ftbl (V C); Sccr (V L); Sftball (V L); Stu Cncl (R); CR (R); Criminal Justice; Psychology; Western Carolina U

HOLMES, CURTIS; WILLINGBORO, NJ; WILLINGBORO HS; (FR); Hnr Roll; Bskball (J); Ftball (J); Duke

HOLST, AMANDA; TOMS RIVER, NJ; MONSIGNOR DONOVAN HS; (JR); Hi Hnr Roll; Nat Hon Sy; Otst Ac Ach Awd; Pres Ac Ftns Aw; WWAHSS; Comm Volntr; Emplmnt; Key Club; Prom Com; SADD; PP Ftbl (V); Sftball (L); Track (J); Cl Off (S); Lifeguard and CPR Certified; Secretary of Interact Club; Biology; Psychology; Cornell U; Swarthmore College

HOLSTEIN, ASHLEY; DAYTON, NJ; SOUTH BRUNSWICK HS; (SO); Hnr Roll; Perf Att; WWAHSS; Emplmnt; NYLC; Chr; Dnce; Attended Lead America Conference

HOMER, ZACK; VOORHEES, NJ; EASTERN REG HS; (JR); Hi Hnr Roll; Hnr Roll; Otst Ac Ach Awd; Sci Fairs; Sci/Math Olympn; St of Mnth; Yth Ldrshp Prog; Comm Volntr; DARE; Dbte Team; Emplmnt; Photog; Sci Clb; Svce Clb; JEWISH Clb; Bnd; SP/M/VS; Stg Cre; Bskball; Tennis (J L); Adv Cncl (S); Completed 8 Years of Religious Education-Leader & Graduate; Table Tennis Champion-2 Tournaments; Creative Writing; Psychology; Syracuse U; Tufts U

HOMICILLADA, KATHLEEN; CEDAR GROVE, NJ; CEDAR GROVE HS; (SO); Hi Hnr Roll; Otst Ac Ach Awd; WWAHSS; Comm Volntr; DARE; Mth Clb/Tm; SADD; Foreign Clb; Sch Ppr (R); Interact Club; TIGS (Teens in the Garden State); Nursing; Fashion Design; U of South Florida; William Patterson U

HOOVER, ASHLEY; LANOKA HARBOR, NJ; LACEY TOWNSHIP HS; (JR); Sccr (JC); Ocean County College

HOPKINS, JEFF; PITMAN, NJ; PITMAN HS; (FR); Ctznshp Aw; St of Mnth; Comm Volntr; Peer Tut/Med; Key Club; SADD; Chr; SP/M/VS; Stg Cre; Bsball (J); Sccr (J); Sportsmanship Award

HOPKINS, JESSICA; ANNANDALE, NJ; NORTH HUNTERDON HS; (JR); F Lan Hn Soc; Hi Hnr Roll; Hnr Roll; Otst Ac Ach Awd; St of Mnth; Amnsty Intl; Comm Volntr; Chrch Yth Grp; Drma Clb; Emplmnt; Mth Clb/Tm; French Clb; Chr; Ch Chr; SP/M/VS; Swmg (V); Tennis Lessons, International Thespian Society; Church Youth Bible Study Group; Psychology; Marketing; Villanova U; James Madison U

HOPKINS, LAUREN M; TOMS RIVER, NJ; TOMS RIVER NORTH; (SR); Hi Hnr Roll; Hnr Roll; Fld Hky (V); Sftball (J)

HOPPEL, DAWN; BRIDGEWATER, NJ; BRIDGEWATER-RARITAN HS; (JR); Hnr Roll; WWAHSS; Comm Volntr; Hosp Aide; Spec Olymp Vol; Key Club; Ice Sktg; Swmg; Track (VJ L); Interior Design; Marymount U; Philadelphia U

HORNER, ASHLEY M; HAINESPORT, NJ; RANCOCAS VALLEY REG HS; (SO); Hi Hnr Roll; Nat Hon Sy; Otst Ac Ach Awd; Perf Att; WWAHSS; Comm Volntr; Chrch Yth Grp; Key Club; Lib Aide; Off Aide; Photog; Svce Clb; Lcrsse (L); Student Athletic Trainer; Team Mega; Law; Psychology; Rowan U; Rutgers U

HOROWITZ, CARYN H; BRIDGEWATER, NJ; BRIDGEWATER RARITAN; (JR); F Lan Hn Soc; Gov Hnr Prg; Hi Hnr Roll; Hnr Roll; Nat Hon Sy; WWAHSS; Comm Volntr; Peer Tut/Med; FBLA; Key Club; Scouts; Tmpl Yth Grp; Orch

HOUSER, KENDRA; JERSEY CITY, NJ; UNIVERSITY AC CHARTER SCH; (JR); Hi Hnr Roll; Hnr Roll; Sci Fairs; St of Mnth; WWAHSS; DARE; Emplmnt; Acpl Chr; Chrldg (V); Track; Sch Ppr (R); February Student of the Month; High Honor Roll; Elementary Education; News and Media; Hudson Community College; U of South Carolina (Orangeburg)

HOUZE, DOMINIQUE; TEANECK, NJ; TEANECK HS; (SO); Hi Hnr Roll; Hnr Roll; Nat Hon Sy; Yth Ldrshp Prog; Peer Tut/Med; DARE; Emplmnt; Off Aide; Dnce; Flg Crps; Mch Bnd; SP/M/VS; Stu Cncl (V); Teaneck High School Terpsichoreans; Medicine; Law; Duke U; Spelman

HU, COLIN; RAMSEY, NJ; RAMSEY HS; (SR); Gov Hnr Prg; Hi Hnr Roll; Hnr Roll; MVP; Nat Hon Sy; Nat Mrt LOC; Pres Sch; Sci/Math Olympn; St Schl; Yth Ldrshp Prog; Comm Volntr; Peer Tut/Med; Emplmnt; JSA; Mth Clb/Tm; Mod UN; NYLC; Outdrs Clb; Quiz Bowl; Sci Clb; Chr; SP/M/VS; Sccr (J); CR (R); SAT I 1500; NJ Governor's School on the Environment; Biology / Pre-Med; Environmental Studies; Emory U

HU, DEBORA; BEDMINSTER, NJ; BERNARDS HS; (JR); Hi Hnr Roll; Nat Hon Sy; WWAHSS; Yth Ldrshp Prog; Comm Volntr; Chess; Key Club; Chr; Swmg (J); Track (J); Cl Off (S); Stu Cncl (V, R); Chemistry Team; Economics; Philosophy; Yale U; Williams College

HU, JUNG; NORTH BRUNSWICK, NJ; N BRUNSWICK TWNSHP HS; (JR); Hi Hnr Roll; Hnr Roll; Nat Hon Sy; St of Mnth; WWAHSS; Comm Volntr; Hosp Aide; Chess; Chrch Yth Grp; Key Club; Mus Clb; Tmpl Yth Grp; Chr; High Honor Rolls, Honor Rolls; Who's Who Among American High School Student; Law School; Math, Pre Law; Rutgers College; New York U

HUA, NELSON; ASBURY, NJ; WARREN HILLS HS; (SO); Hi Hnr Roll; WWAHSS; Chess; Dbte Team; FBLA; Key Club; Tennis (J); 1st Place FBLA State Comp. (International Business); 1st Place WCCC Math Competition in Geometry; Architecture; Astrophysics; Princeton U; MIT

HUANG, EDWARD; PRINCETON, NJ; PRINCETON HS; (JR); Sci/Math Olympn; Comm Volntr; Mod UN; Orch; Sch Ppr (R); Captain - Ultimate Frisbee; Princeton Chinese Language School Cultural Teacher; Lawyer; College Professor; Stanford U; U of Pennsylvania

HUDAK, CAROLYN; OLD BRIDGE, NJ; CARDINAL MC CARRICK HS; (JR); Hnr Roll; Comm Volntr; Sci Clb; Track (L); Certified EMT; Nursing; Doctor; Fairleigh Dickinson U

HUFF, ZACHARY; ISELIN, NJ; JOHN F KENNEDY MEMORIAL HS; (JR); Hnr Roll; Perf Att; WWAHSS; Key Club; School Stone (Assistant Manager); Education; History; Kean U; Rutgers U

HUGHES, JOHN; EGG HARBOR CY, NJ; HOLY SPIRIT HS; (SO); Hnr Roll; St of Mnth; Bskball (J); Crew-JV; Mock Trial; Liberal Arts; Economics; U of Pennsylvania; Princeton U

HUGHES, KRISTEN; SICKLERVILLE, NJ; OUR LADY OF MERCY AC; (SO); Hnr Roll; WWAHSS; Peer Tut/Med; Pep Squd; French Clb; Dnce; Chrldg (V L); Cr Ctry (V L); Lcrsse (V L); Yrbk (P); Cheerleading Competition Volunteer; Psychology; Mathematics; Cabrini College

HUGHES, SARAH; MILLBURN, NJ; MILLBURN HS; (SR); Hnr Roll; Nat Hon Sy; Nat Mrt LOC; Chr; SP/M/VS; Swmg (V); Science League; Student Liaison Committee; English/Writing; Vassar

HUNT, FRANCHESCA; SOUTH ORANGE, NJ; COLUMBIA HS; (JR); Hnr Roll; WWAHSS; Chrch Yth Grp; Key Club; Chr; Ch Chr; Dnce; Tele- A-Height Organization; Elementary Education

HUNT, TAMMY L; PEDRICKTOWN, NJ; SALEM CTY VOC TECH CAREER CTR HS; (JR); Hnr Roll; St of Mnth; Bskball (V C); Sftball (J); Stu Cncl (R); CR (R); Breast Cancer Walk 2004; Relay for Life 2005; Diagnostic Medical Sonographer; Gloucester Community College

HUNT, VALENCIA C; IRVINGTON, NJ; ESSEX CTY VOC-TECH HS; (JR); Hnr Roll; Otst Ac Ach Awd; Perf Att; St of Mnth; Comm Volntr; Chess; DARE; Emplmnt; FBLA; Drl Tm; Bskball (J); Chrldg (V); Cr Ctry (V); Vice Pres for FBLA-PB1; Business Administrations; Accounting; Montclair State U; Rutgers U

HUQ, SANA S; ROEBLING, NJ; FLORENCE TWP MEM HS; (FR); Hnr Roll; Pediatrician; Rutgers U; The College of New Jersey

HURLEY, MEGAN; JERSEY CITY, NJ; SAINT DOMINIC AC; (SO); F Lan Hn Soc; Amnsty Intl; Comm Volntr; Chrch Yth Grp; Cmptr Clb; Emplmnt; Off Aide; P to P St Amb Prg; Prom Com; Svce Clb; Dnce; Chrldg (V); PPSqd (V); School Spirit Award; Executive Board - Dominican Youth in Action Club; Dance / Acting / Singing; Teaching - Dance / Choreographer; New York U; Wagner College

HWANG, STEFANIE; ROBBINSVILLE, NJ; ALLENTOWN HS; (FR); Hi Hnr Roll; Perf Att; Sci Fairs; Sci/Math Olympn; St of Mnth; USAA; NYLC; P to P St Amb Prg; Sci Clb; Bskball; Sch Ppr (E, R); NJ State Teen Arts Festival; NJ Science League; Medical Doctor; Eye Doctor; Johns Hopkins U; Stanford U

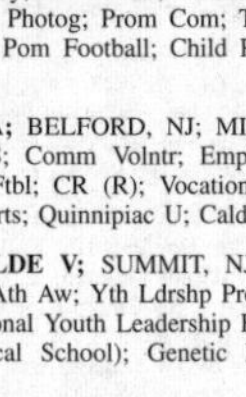
Hunt, Franchesca
Columbia HS
South Orange, NJ

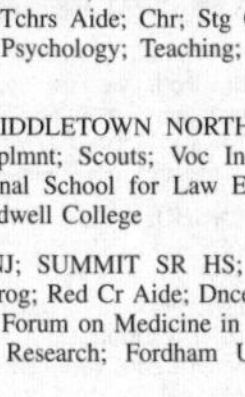
Huang, Edward
Princeton HS
Princeton, NJ

Hoffman, Matilde V
Summit SR HS
Summit, NJ

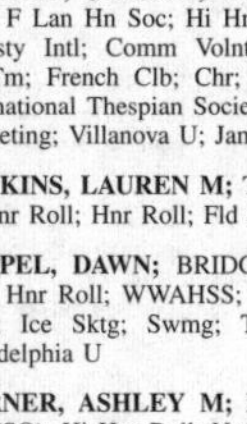
Hill, Tiffany M
Irvington HS
Irvington, NJ

National
Honor Roll
Spring 2005

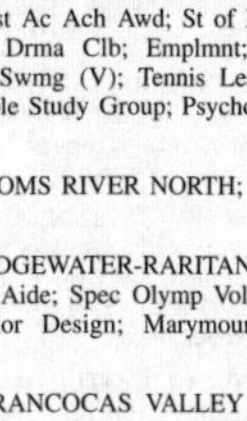
Hernandez, Abigail
Glassboro HS
Glassboro, NJ

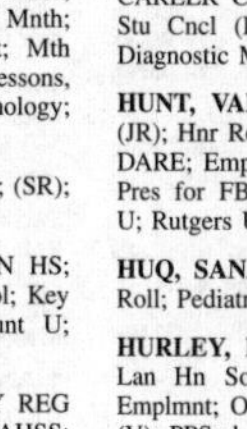
Horner, Ashley M
Rancocas Valley Reg HS
Hainesport, NJ

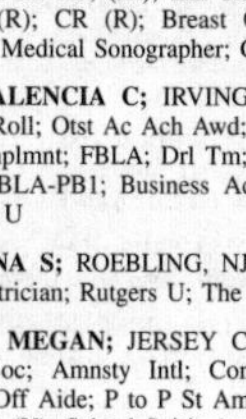
Hudak, Carolyn
Cardinal Mc Carrick HS
Old Bridge, NJ

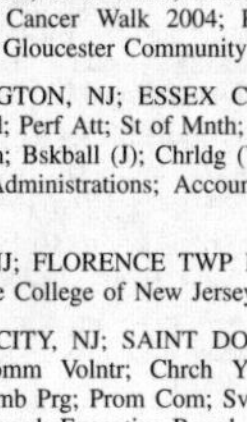
Hurley, Megan
Saint Dominic AC
Jersey City, NJ

HYNES, ASHLEY; CRANFORD, NJ; CRANFORD HS; (JR); Hnr Roll; Nat Hon Sy; Pres Ac Ftns Aw; Comm Volntr; DARE; Emplmnt; Mth Clb/Tm; Sci Clb; Svce Clb; Vsity Clb; PP Ftbl (V); Sccr (V); Vsy Clb (V); Yrbk (R, P); Education Early Childhood; Elementary; Montclair U; Rutgers U

IBARRA, EMILY; KEARNY, NJ; KEARNY HS; (SO); Ctznshp Aw; Hnr Roll; MVP; St of Mnth; DARE; Emplmnt; Mth Clb/Tm; Outdrs Clb; French Clb; Chr; Bskball (J); Mar Art (L); Sccr (J); Sftball (VJC); Vllyball (VJ); Stu Cncl (S); CR (R); Thistle Soccer U-17 / Science Award; Traveling Soccer U-16; Accounting; Business; Pace U; Rutgers U

IBRAHIM, TAOFEEK; LINDEN, NJ; LINDEN HS; (JR); Hi Hnr Roll; Hnr Roll; Nat Sci Aw; Pres Sch; St of Mnth; Comm Volntr; DARE; Drma Clb; Tech Clb; Bskball (VJ); Sccr (J); Learn and Serve / CAS Program; Master's / Mechanical Engineering; Minor / Law and Music; Princeton U; Fairleigh Dickinson U

IBRAMIM, OMAR; HOLMDEL, NJ; WARDLAW HARTRIDGE SCH; (JR); Nat Ldrshp Svc; Yth Ldrshp Prog; Comm Volntr; Hab For Humty Volntr; Hosp Aide; Key Club; Off Aide; Svce Clb; Bskball (J); Ftball (V); Sccr (J); Research in the Medical Field; Medical Field; George Washington; New York U

ILEWSKI, MICHAL; CLARK, NJ; ARTHUR L JOHNSON HS; (SO); Hi Hnr Roll; WWAHSS; Comm Volntr; Hab For Humty Volntr; ArtClub; Dbte Team; Key Club; Photog; Sci Clb; French Clb; Lit Mag (E); Sch Ppr (E, R); Yrbk (R); Volunteering at Nursing Home; Polish School; Medicine; History; Princeton U; U of Virginia

ILOGIENBOH, OFURE R; WEST ORANGE, NJ; WEST ORANGE HS; (JR); F Lan Hn Soc; Hnr Roll; Nat Hon Sy; Pres Ac Ftns Aw; Sci Fairs; Yth Ldrshp Prog; Comm Volntr; Peer Tut/Med; Chrch Yth Grp; Mus Clb; Spanish Clb; Chr; Ch Chr; Track (V L); New Jersey Region Choir; New Jersey Governor's School; Major in Biology or Chemistry; Pre-Med; Lehigh U; U of Pennsylvania

IMBESI, ALEXANDRIA; ESTELL MANOR, NJ; OUR LADY OF MERCY AC; (SO); Hi Hnr Roll; Nat Hon Sy; ArtClub; Biology Clb; DARE; Svce Clb; SADD; French Clb; Lcrsse (J); Swmg (V); Vllyball (J); U of Penn

IMPERATO, GINA; NEWFIELD, NJ; OUR LADY OF MERCY AC; (SO); All Am Sch; Hi Hnr Roll; Nat Hon Sy; Otst Ac Ach Awd; Yth Ldrshp Prog; DARE; Drma Clb; Spanish Clb; Dnce; Chrldg (V); Lcrsse (J); Yrbk; Business and Marketing; Law

INFERRERA, JAMIE; HAMMONTON, NJ; GLOUCESTER CTY INST OF TECH; (JR); Hi Hnr Roll; Nat Hon Sy; WWAHSS; Comm Volntr; Red Cr Aide; Key Club; SADD; Dnce; SP/M/VS; National Society of High School Scholars; Dance; Education; Point Park U; Columbia U

INGLESE, ANNETTE; BELFORD, NJ; MIDDLETON HS NORTH; (JR); Hi Hnr Roll; Hnr Roll; Nat Hon Sy; Comm Volntr; Spec Olymp Vol; Chrch Yth Grp; Prom Com; Scouts; Dnce; Chrldg (V); Junior Council; Special Education / Autistic Students; Elementary Education; U of Delaware; Rowan

INIZARRY, VANESSA; PATERSON, NJ; PATERSON CATHOLIC HS; (FR); Hi Hnr Roll; Hnr Roll; Otst Ac Ach Awd; Perf Att; Sci Fairs; Sci/Math Olympn; St of Mnth; Hosp Aide; DARE; Dnce; Former Cheerleader At P.S. 21; Medical Arts; Nursing Degree; Ramapo College of New Jersey; William Paterson U

IRVINE, BRITTANY; BRICK, NJ; BRICK; (FR); Hi Hnr Roll; Hnr Roll; Perf Att; St of Mnth; Comm Volntr; Emplmnt; Svce Clb; Dnce; Chrldg (V)

IRWIN, CHANTAL N; EGG HARBOR TOWNSHIP, NJ; EGG HARBOR TOWNSHIP HS; (JR); All Am Sch; Hi Hnr Roll; Hnr Roll; Nat Hon Sy; Pres Sch; USAA; WWAHSS; Comm Volntr; Chrch Yth Grp; DARE; Key Club; Ch Chr; Dnce; Bskball (J); Track (V); CR (S); National Honor Society; Who's Who Among American HS Students; Engineering/Mathematics; Business; Rutgers U (New Brunswick); Drexel U

ISSA, AMR E; OLD BRIDGE, NJ; OLD BRIDGE HS; (JR); Hnr Roll; Comm Volntr; Bskball (J); Cr Ctry (J); Track (J); Volunteer Work At Raritan; Bay Medical Center; Occupational Therapist; NYU-Rutgers-Kane

ITRI, DANIELLE; ATCO, NJ; HAMMONTON HS; (FR); Hnr Roll; Nat Hon Sy; Cr Ctry (J); Track (J); Art; Nutritionist; Penn State U; Temple U

JABER, ALAA; JERSEY CITY, NJ; WILLIAM DICKINSON HS; (JR); Hnr Roll; Perf Att; St of Mnth; Comm Volntr; BPA; DECA; Bskball (V); Business Educator; New Jersey City U

JABER, ALISSAR; HOWELL, NJ; FREEHOLD TWP HS; (JR); Hnr Roll; Nat Hon Sy; Peer Tut/Med; Emplmnt; Chr; PP Ftbl; Sccr (J); Track (J); Cl Off (R); International Relations; Global Languages; Georgetown U; New York U

JACINTO, JEANNE; UNION CITY, NJ; AC OF SACRED HEART HS; (JR); Hi Hnr Roll; Hnr Roll; Salutrn; Comm Volntr; Peer Tut/Med; Emplmnt; Lib Aide; Mus Clb; French Clb; Dnce; Sccr (V); Vllyball (V); Yrbk (E); Pre-Law; Seton Hall U; New York U

JACKSON, HEIDI L; SOMERVILLE, NJ; SOMERVILLE HS; (JR); Hi Hnr Roll; Nat Hon Sy; WWAHSS; Yth Ldrshp Prog; Hosp Aide; Peer Tut/Med; Red Cr Aide; ArtClub; Emplmnt; Key Club; Photog; French Clb; Cr Ctry (V L); Track (J); Stu Cncl (R); Yrbk (R); Outward Bound Youth Leadership Award; Peer Leadership

JACKSON, JOSEPH; VINELAND, NJ; VINELAND HS; (SO); Tmpl Yth Grp; Ftball; Townsend U; Rowan

JACKSON, KHIRY; LONG BRANCH, NJ; LONG BRANCH HS; (FR); Track (J); English; Business; UCLA; Rutgers

JACOB, APRIL G; NORTH BERGEN, NJ; HCST-NORTH HUDSON CTR; (JR); Gov Hnr Prg; Hi Hnr Roll; MVP; Nat Ldrshp Svc; Nat Mrt Sch Recip; Nat Sci Aw; Otst Ac Ach Awd; Pres Sch; Valdctrian; WWAHSS; Peer Tut/Med; Drma Clb; Mus Clb; Prom Com; Sci Clb; Tchrs Aide; Chr; Sftball (V); Stu Cncl (R); CR (R); Lit Mag (R); Phat Club (Environment); Spanish Honor Society; M.D.; Princeton U; Drew U

JACOB, ASHLEY L; SUSSEX, NJ; VERNON TWP HS; (SR); F Lan Hn Soc; Hi Hnr Roll; Nat Hon Sy; Otst Ac Ach Awd; Perf Att; Pres Sch; Salutrn; Sci/Math Olympn; WWAHSS; Yth Ldrshp Prog; Comm Volntr; Peer Tut/Med; DARE; Emplmnt; Mod UN; Prom Com; Quiz Bowl; Vsity Clb; Bnd; Bskball (VJ L); Sftball (VJ L); Vsy Clb (V L); Stu Cncl (R); CR (R); Sch Ppr (E, R); Biology; Psychology; Mary Washington U

JAGO, MEGAN; MONMOUTH JUNCTION, NJ; SOUTH BRUNSWICK HS; (JR); Nat Hon Sy; Comm Volntr; Peer Tut/Med; Bnd; SP/M/VS; Cr Ctry (V); PP Ftbl (V); Track (V); CR (R); Homecoming Princess; Marine Biology; Animal Behavior; U of North Carolina; Coastal Carolina U

JAGRUP, YASHMINI; JERSEY CITY, NJ; DR RONALD MC NAIR AC HS; (SO); All Am Sch; Hnr Roll; Perf Att; WWAHSS; Comm Volntr; Key Club; ROTC; Spanish Clb; Ch Chr; Clr Grd; Drl Tm; Tennis (J); International Culture Club; Accounting; Business Management; Stern School of Business; Rutgers University

JAKUBASZEK, MARCIN; MAPLE SHADE, NJ; MAPLE SHADE HS; (JR); Hnr Roll; Perf Att; Sci Fairs; St of Mnth; Red Cr Aide; Cmptr Clb; DARE; Emplmnt; Photog; Tech Clb; Bskball (V L)

JALA, THOMAS L; BRIDGEWATER, NJ; BRIDGEWATER-RARITAN HS; (JR); Hnr Roll; Nat Hon Sy; WWAHSS; DARE; Emplmnt; Key Club; Sci Clb; Scouts; French Clb; Senior Patrol Leader - Boy Scouts; Culinary Arts; Culinary Institute of America; Johnson & Wales U

JAMES, HOLLY C; BELLEVILLE, NJ; BELLEVILLE HS; (SR); Hnr Roll; Comm Volntr; Emplmnt; Key Club; Prom Com; Sftball (J); Track (J); Vllyball (J); Yrbk (E); Interact Club; Prom Committee; Business; Montclair State U

JAMES, LINDSAY J; HACKENSACK, NJ; HACKENSACK HS; (SO); Hi Hnr Roll; Hnr Roll; Nat Sci Aw; Otst Ac Ach Awd; Pres Ac Ftns Aw; Salutrn; WWAHSS; Comm Volntr; Chrch Yth Grp; DARE; Emplmnt; Pep Squd; Ch Chr; Dnce; Drl Tm; Stu Cncl (T); Veterinary Medicine; Performing Arts-Dance; Seton Hall U; Hampton U

JAMES, MONIQUE; EAST ORANGE, NJ; EAST ORANGE CAMPUS 9 HS; (FR); Ctznshp Aw; Hi Hnr Roll; Hnr Roll; Perf Att; Sci Fairs; Comm Volntr; Emplmnt; Svce Clb, Stg Cre; Swmg; President's Award for Educational Excellence; Member of East Orange Street Team; Law Major, Master's Degree; Seton Hall U; Morgan State U

JANANSKY, MATT; EGG HARBOR TOWNSHIP, NJ; EGG HARBOR TOWNSHIP HS; (FR); Hnr Roll; Otst Ac Ach Awd; Sci Fairs; WWAHSS; Jr Cls League; Key Club; Scouts; Latin Clb; SP/M/VS; Bskball

JANANSKY, STEVE; EGG HARBOR TOWNSHIP, NJ; EGG HARBOR TWP; (JR); Gov Hnr Prg; Hnr Roll; Nat Hon Sy; WWAHSS; Jr Cls League; Key Club; Scouts; SP/M/VS

JANECKI, BRITTANY; MILLVILLE, NJ; MILLVILLE SR HS; (JR); Hnr Roll; Sci Fairs; St of Mnth; Drma Clb; Key Club; Lib Aide; Scouts; SP/M/VS; Varsity Academic Letter, Silver Award Girls Scout & Bowling Club, Symposium of Arts; A Writer

JANKOWY, JACLYN; MANVILLE, NJ; MANVILLE HS; (SR); Hi Hnr Roll; Hnr Roll; Nat Hon Sy; Perf Att; WWAHSS; Comm Volntr; Peer Tut/Med; Chrch Yth Grp; Emplmnt; FBLA; Key Club; Lttrmn Clb; Vsity Clb; Sftball (VJCL); Yrbk (R, P); Scholar Athlete Award; Education; Business; Monmouth U

JANNUCCI, CAITLIN A; LAKE HAPATRONG, NJ; MORRIS CATHOLIC HS; (SO); Hi Hnr Roll; Nat Hon Sy; Otst Ac Ach Awd; Comm Volntr; Peer Tut/Med; ArtClub; Ntl Beta Clb; Scr Kpr (V); Track; Lit Mag (R); Short Story Published in Literature Magazine at Morris Catholic; Journalism; Brown U; Seton Hall U

JANSSEN, MATT S; PITTSTOWN, NJ; DELAWARE VALLEY HS; (SO); Hnr Roll; St of Mnth; DARE; Bnd; Ftball (J); Scr Kpr (V L); Track (V L); Midget "A" Travel Ice Hockey; Local Band; Music Degree; Audio Engineering Degree; Lebanon Valley College; Massachusetts Institute of Technology

JANUSZ, KRYSTI; LINDEN, NJ; LINDEN HS; (SO); Hi Hnr Roll; Hnr Roll; Sci Fairs; St of Mnth; Lib Aide; Scouts; Dnce; Cr Ctry (V L); Swmg (V L); Track (V L); Cl Off (V); Forensic Pathology; Medical Degree; Harvard U; UCLA

JARAMILLO CHAMORRO, DIANA L; NEWARK, NJ; SCIENCE HS; (FR); Perf Att; Sci Fairs; Peer Tut/Med; Outdrs Clb; Swmg (J); Vllyball (J); Certificate of Participation; Safety Patrol Club; Interior Designer; Business; Rutgers U; New York U

JARED, ALLIE; SALEM, NJ; SALEM HS; (FR); Hi Hnr Roll; Sci Fairs; WWAHSS; Comm Volntr; Chrch Yth Grp; Drma Clb; FCA; Chr; Ch Chr; Sccr (J); Students Move Against Cancer- SMAC Club; Ambassador Club; Pulmonologist Degree in Medicine; U of Pennsylvania; Albright College

JARILLO, MARIA; EGG HARBOR TOWNSHIP, NJ; EGG HARBOR TOWNSHIP HS; (JR); Hi Hnr Roll; Hnr Roll; Nat Hon Sy; WWAHSS; Yth Ldrshp Prog; Key Club; SADD; Varsity Scholar; Reaching Everyone By Exposing Lies (REBEL); Cinema and Photography; Writing; Richard Stockton College of New Jersey; CW Post Campus of Long Island U

JARRI, NAOMI A; NEWARK, NJ; BARRINGER HS; (SO); Hi Hnr Roll; Hnr Roll; Sci/Math Olympn; St of Mnth; WWAHSS; Spec Olymp Vol; Chrch Yth Grp; Drma Clb; FTA; Mth Clb/Tm; Spch Team; Bnd; Mch Bnd; Orch; SP/M/VS; Vllyball; Wt Lftg (J); Medical Doctor; Sanford Brown - Institute Diagnostic; Medical College

JASAN, STEPHANIE; LANOKA HARBOR, NJ; KEYSTONE NATIONAL HS; (JR); Hi Hnr Roll; Hnr Roll; Nat Hon Sy; Otst Ac Ach Awd; Chrch Yth Grp; Mus Clb; Dnce; Special Education Teacher; Occupational Therapy; Richard Stockton College of New Jersey; Montclair State U

JAWOROWSKI, BREANN; BAYVILLE, NJ; CTRL REG HS; (JR); Hi Hnr Roll; Hnr Roll; Nat Hon Sy; Peer Tut/Med; Drma Clb; Emplmnt; Mus Clb; Outdrs Clb; Bnd; Clr Grd; Dnce; Jzz Bnd; Fld Hky (J); Yrbk (P); Renaissance Award; Student of the Marking Period; Culinary Arts; Bakery / Pastry Arts; Drexel U; Paul Smith's College

JEAN, LOUIS C; NEWARK, NJ; CENTRAL HS; (SR); Chrch Yth Grp; Ch Chr; International Business; Fashion Merchandising

JEAN, MARIE M; JERSEY CITY, NJ; AC ST ALOYSIUS HS; (SO); Hnr Roll; Otst Ac Ach Awd; Perf Att; Sci Fairs; St of Mnth; ArtClub; Chess; DARE; Interior Designer; Graphic Designer; New Jersey City U; Manhattan College

JEAN-CHARLES, CYNTHIA; MONTCLAIR, NJ; MONTCLAIR HS; (JR); Hi Hnr Roll; Hnr Roll; Yth Ldrshp Prog; Emplmnt; Peer Leadership; Pediatric Doctor; Fairleigh Dickinson U; Montclair State U

JEAN-LOUIS, PHYLICIA; PLAINFIELD, NJ; UNION CATHOLIC HS; MS; Ctznshp Aw; Hnr Roll; Otst Ac Ach Awd; St of Mnth; Yth Ldrshp Prog; Comm Volntr; Peer Tut/Med; Dbte Team; Emplmnt; Pep Squd; Dnce; SP/M/VS; Chrldg (V); Cl Off (P); Stu Cncl (R); CR (P); Yrbk (R); 2004 National All American Pre Teen; New Jersey Senate Award; Education; Performing Arts; U of North Carolina; Spelman College

JEAN-SIMON, MELISSA; IRVINGTON, NJ; IRVINGTON HS; (FR); Hnr Roll; Nat Hon Sy; Otst Ac Ach Awd; Perf Att; St of Mnth; Comm Volntr; Mus Clb; P to P St Amb Prg; Wdwrkg Clb; Bnd; Chr; Chrldg; Pediatrics; Psychology; Rutgers U College

JEFFERSON, SHALET; WILLINGBORO, NJ; WILLINGBORO HS; (JR); F Lan Hn Soc; Hnr Roll; Jr Eng Tech; Nat Hon Sy; Nat Sci Aw; Otst Ac Ach Awd; Perf Att; Sci Fairs; WWAHSS; Hosp Aide; Peer Tut/Med; Chrch Yth Grp; DARE; Emplmnt; Latin Clb; Chr; Chrldg (V); Lcrsse (V L); Sccr (V L); Stu Cncl (P); Young Ladies of Excellence; NSBE JR; Medical Engineering; Chemistry & Physics Major; Rutgers New Brunswick; Temple U

JEON, SAE-MI; MT LAUREL, NJ; LENAPE HS; (JR); F Lan Hn Soc; Hi Hnr Roll; Hnr Roll; Nat Hon Sy; Otst Ac Ach Awd; WWAHSS; Yth Ldrshp Prog; Comm Volntr; Emplmnt; Lib Aide; Svce Clb; Spanish Clb; Ch Chr; Fld Hky (J); Tennis (J); Track (J); Sch Ppr (E); Environmental Club President; Asian Club Treasurer; Medicine; Psychology; Johns Hopkins U; Princeton U

JIANG, PENGBO; BRIDGEWATER, NJ; BRIDGEWATER RARITAN HS; (SO); Duke TS; F Lan Hn Soc; Gov Hnr Prg; Hnr Roll; Nat Sci Aw; Otst Ac Ach Awd; Perf Att; Sci Fairs; Sci/Math Olympn; St of Mnth; Amnsty Intl; Comm Volntr; Hosp Aide; Biology Clb; Cmptr Clb; Emplmnt; FBLA; Key Club; Mod UN; MuAlphaTh; Sci Clb; Tennis (V); Track (J); Cl Off (T); CR (R); 1st Team All Area for Tennis At 1st Singles; Vice President At Amnesty Int'l Club; Medical; Pre-Med/Pre Dentist; Johns Hopkins U; Northwestern U

JIMENEZ, ELVIA; HARRISON, NJ; HARRISON HS; (SO); Hnr Roll; St of Mnth; Yth Ldrshp Prog; Chrch Yth Grp; Spanish Clb; Dnce; SP/M/VS; Sccr (J); Sftball (J); Spanish Club-Treasurer; Choreography; US History; Kane U; Princeton U

JIMENEZ, STEPHANIE; ELIZABETH, NJ; ELIZABETH HS; (JR); Nat Sci Aw; Otst Ac Ach Awd; Perf Att; St of Mnth; Comm Volntr; Hosp Aide; Chrch Yth Grp; Key Club; Outdrs Clb; Ch Chr; Dnce; Sccr (J); Swmg (J); Track (J); Marketing; Dental School; NJIT; Rutgers

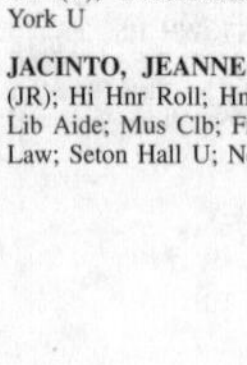
Jimenez, Stephanie
Elizabeth HS
Elizabeth, NJ

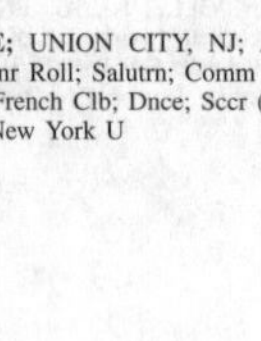
Jean-Charles, Cynthia
Montclair HS
Montclair, NJ

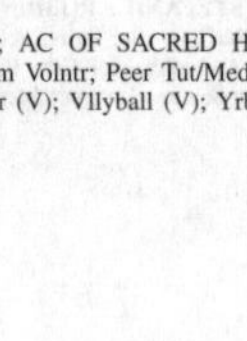
Jarri, Naomi A
Barringer HS
Newark, NJ

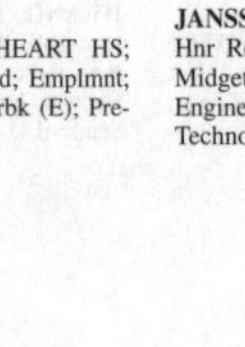
Jackson, Heidi L
Somerville HS
Somerville, NJ

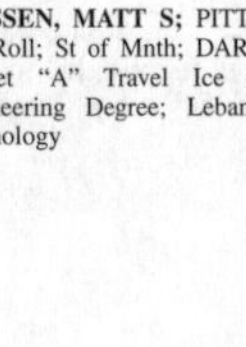
Ibramim, Omar
Wardlaw Hartridge Sch
Holmdel, NJ

National
Honor Roll
Spring 2005

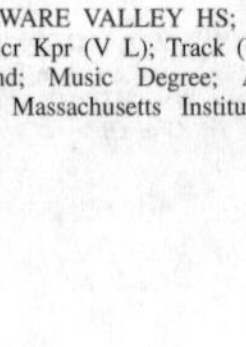
Hynes, Ashley
Cranford HS
Cranford, NJ

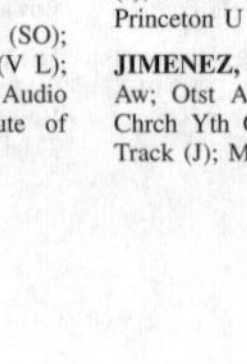
James, Monique
East Orange Campus 9 HS
East Orange, NJ

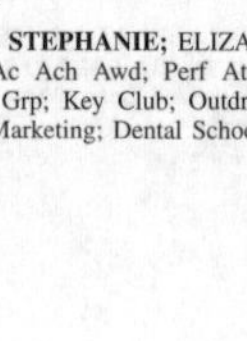
Jean, Marie M
AC St Aloysius HS
Jersey City, NJ

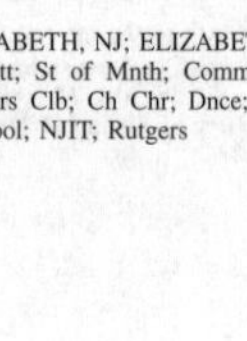
Jean-Louis, Phylicia
Union Catholic HS
Plainfield, NJ

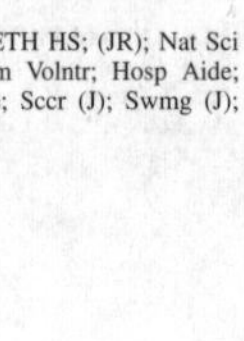
Jeon, Sae-Mi
Lenape HS
Mt Laurel, NJ

JIN, YUTING; BERKELEY HEIGHTS, NJ; GOVERNOR LIVINGSTON HS; (JR); Hi Hnr Roll; Hnr Roll; Nat Hon Sy; Perf Att; WWAHSS; Comm Volntr; Dbte Team; Drma Clb; Emplmnt; Quill & Scroll; Quiz Bowl; French Clb; SP/M/VS; Stg Cre; Tennis (J); Track (J); Lit Mag (E); Published Poet / Author; Governor's Award Finalist; English Lang & Lit; U of Chicago; Northwestern

JOHN, ELIZABETH S; BELLEVILLE, NJ; BELLEVILLE HS; (FR); Ctznshp Aw; Hi Hnr Roll; MVP; Otst Ac Ach Awd; Perf Att; Yth Ldrshp Prog; Peer Tut/Med; Chrch Yth Grp; DARE; Dbte Team; Drma Clb; Emplmnt; FCA; FBLA; Mth Clb/Tm; Chr; Ch Chr; Orch; SP/M/VS; Bskball (L); Vllyball (L); Stu Cncl (R); Public Speaker; Solo Singer; Neurologist; Lawyer / Medical Attorney

JOHN, SHIRLEY; HARRISON, NJ; HARRISON HS; (SO); Hi Hnr Roll; Hnr Roll; Nat Hon Sy; Otst Ac Ach Awd; St of Mnth; DARE; Medicine; Law; Columbia U; Duke U

JOHNS, PATRICK; SOMERS POINT, NJ; MAINLAND REG HS; (JR); Ctznshp Aw; Fut Prb Slvr; Hi Hnr Roll; Hnr Roll; MVP; Otst Ac Ach Awd; Sci Fairs; St of Mnth; Comm Volntr; Emplmnt; Key Club; Street Hockey All Stars; Peer Mediator; Business; Architecture; Stockton College; Rowan U

JOHNSEN, KAITLIN; MATAWAN, NJ; MATAWAN REG HS; (SO); Ctznshp Aw; WWAHSS; Key Club; Scouts; Bnd; Fld Hky (L); Cl Off (R); Cadette Girl Scout Silver Award; Douglass Science Institute Participant; Equine Science

JOHNSON, ALICIA M; EGG HARBOR TOWNSHIP, NJ; EGG HARBOR TOWNSHIP HS; (SR); Hnr Roll; Otst Ac Ach Awd; WWAHSS; Comm Volntr; Chrch Yth Grp; Emplmnt; Key Club; Ch Chr; Dnce; Track (J); Stu Cncl (R); CR (R); Sch Ppr (R); African American Society; Interact Club; Social Work; Stockton State College

JOHNSON, ASHLEY N; LINDEN, NJ; LINDEN HS; (SR); Fut Prb Slvr; Chr; Student Counseling; Lawyer; Legal Secretary; Clark Atlanta U; UCLA

JOHNSON, BONIFIA; WILLINGBORO, NJ; WILLINGBORO HS; (FR); Hnr Roll; Comm Volntr; Emplmnt; Pep Squd; Drl Tm; CR; Won 3rd Runner Up in Glamour Pageants; Models; Plastic Surgeon; Communications; U of Atlanta; New York U

JOHNSON, BRITTANY; ABSECON, NJ; ABSEGAMI HS; (SO); Hi Hnr Roll; Hnr Roll; Otst Ac Ach Awd; St of Mnth; WWAHSS; Comm Volntr; Drma Clb; Emplmnt; Key Club; Mus Clb; Photog; Chr; Dnce; SP/M/VS; Stg Cre; Sccr (J); Lit Mag (R); #9 in Class of 575; In Anytown Club (Against Racial Comments); Psychologist/ Child Counselor; Princeton; Rutgers U New Brunswick

JOHNSON, BRITTANY A; LINDEN, NJ; LINDEN HS; (FR); Hi Hnr Roll; St of Mnth; St Optmst of Yr; Comm Volntr; Chrch Yth Grp; Emplmnt; Scouts; Chr; Ch Chr; Track (J); Science; Rutgers U; Delaware State

JOHNSON, CARMELLA A L; SOUTH AMBOY, NJ; OLD BRIDGE HS; (JR); Hnr Roll; Nat Hon Sy; DARE; John Jay College NYC; Delaware U Delaware

JOHNSON, CLIFFORD; PT PLEASANT BEACH, NJ; PT PLEASANT BOROUGH HS; (JR); Hnr Roll; Comm Volntr; Chess; DARE; Key Club; Bowling Team; Business; Law; East Carolina U

JOHNSON, JUSTIN; SOMERVILLE, NJ; ST JOSEPH'S HS; (JR); 4H Awd; Hi Hnr Roll; MVP; Otst Ac Ach Awd; Pres Ac Ftns Aw; Sci Fairs; St of Mnth; Comm Volntr; Peer Tut/Med; 4-H; DARE; Outdrs Clb; Ice Hky (J L); Skiing; Travel Hockey for 6 Years

JOHNSON, KANDACE C; HAZLET, NJ; RARITAN HS; (FR); Hi Hnr Roll; Hnr Roll; DARE; Bskball (V); Track (V); CR (P, R); Presidential Athletic Fitness Award; Dentist / Orthodontics; WNBA; Rutgers U

JOHNSON, KIA; CAMDEN, NJ; CAMDEN HS; (FR); SP/M/VS; Bskball (VJ); Psychology; University of Maryland; Howard University

JOHNSON, ROBERT M; FORKED RIVER, NJ; LACEY TOWNSHIP HS; (JR); Hi Hnr Roll; Hnr Roll; MVP; Nat Hon Sy; Otst Ac Ach Awd; Peer Tut/ Med; Emplmnt; Mus Clb; Bnd; Chr; Drm Mjr; Pep Bnd; Ocean County Vocational Technical School; Audio Electronic Media-NAES; Audio Technology Recording; Music-Media; Berkeley; Juilliard

JOHNSON, STEPHANIE; FLORHAM PARK, NJ; BAYLEY-ELLARD HS; (JR); All Am Sch; Gov Hnr Prg; Hi Hnr Roll; Hnr Roll; Otst Ac Ach Awd; Sci Fairs; St of Mnth; USAA; WWAHSS; Comm Volntr; Drma Clb; Emplmnt; Svce Clb; French Clb; Dnce; SP/M/VS; Stg Cre; Chrldg (V C); Cr Ctry (C); Cl Off (V, T); Yrbk (P); Finalist for the Governor's School of the Arts; Dance Competition Student for 8 Years; Dance / BFA; Dance / Education Major; Fordham U; New York U

JOHNSON JR, JEFFREY L; MONTCLAIR, NJ; MONTCLAIR HS; (SO); Hnr Roll; MVP; Chrch Yth Grp; Chr; Ch Chr; Bskball (J); CR (R); All-American Scholar Award Winner

JOHNSTON, LINDSAY; MIDDLETOWN, NJ; MIDDLETOWN HS SOUTH; (JR); Hi Hnr Roll; Hnr Roll; Comm Volntr; Career in Art

JONES, HEATHER A; PENNSVILLE, NJ; PENNSVILLE MEMORIAL HS; (FR); Hi Hnr Roll; Hnr Roll; Sci Fairs; Chrch Yth Grp; DARE; Spanish Clb; Bnd; Sccr (J); Sftball (J); Medicine; 4-Year-College

JONES, KYLA R; LUMBERTON, NJ; RANCOCAS VALLEY REG HS; (SR); F Lan Hn Soc; Hi Hnr Roll; Nat Hon Sy; WWAHSS; Comm Volntr; Chrch Yth Grp; Emplmnt; Lib Aide; P to P St Amb Prg; ROTC; Tchrs Aide; Bnd; Ch Chr; Mch Bnd; SP/M/VS; City of Hope Summer Intern; Edward V Bloustein Distinguished Scholar; Elementary Education; Rehabilitation Services; Penn State U

JONES, TAMIRA; TRENTON, NJ; (SR); Hnr Roll; WWAHSS; Yth Ldrshp Prog; Comm Volntr; Chrch Yth Grp; Mus Clb; Vsity Clb; Acpl Chr; Chr; Ch Chr; Dnce; Chrldg (JCL); Lcrsse (JC); Who's Who Among High Sch. Students; Eastern U; Kean U

JONES-MC BURROWS, SHANEA; WILLIAMSTOWN, NJ; OUR LADY OF MERCY AC; (SO); Hnr Roll; Perf Att; Comm Volntr; Photog; SADD; Spanish Clb; Yrbk (P); Fashion Design/Merchandising; Business Management; Drexel U; Fashion Institute of Technology

JOO, HYE Y; FORT LEE, NJ; FORT LEE HS; (SO); Cmptr Clb; Key Club; French Clb; Mch Bnd; Regional Chorus; County Chorus; Music Education; Pastry Chef

JORDAN, KAITLIN; MONROE TOWNSHIP, NJ; MONROE TOWNSHIP HS; (FR); Hnr Roll; St of Mnth; Comm Volntr; Pep Squd; Clr Grd; Major in Law; Harvard U

JORDAN, SHAKIRA; JERSEY CITY, NJ; DR RONALD MC NAIR AC HS; (SO); Hi Hnr Roll; Hnr Roll; Kwnis Aw; Otst Ac Ach Awd; Perf Att; Pres Sch; St of Mnth; Valdctrian; WWAHSS; Comm Volntr; DARE; Emplmnt; Key Club; Scouts; Dnce; SP/M/VS; Gmnstcs (J); Sftball (J); Swmg (J); Track (J); Cl Off (T); CR (R); Yrbk (P); Bowling Junior Varsity; Accountant, Finance/ Banking; International Business; Spelman

JOSEPH, STANLEY; ASBURY PARK, NJ; ASBURY PARK HS; (SR); Hnr Roll; Nat Mrt Sch Recip; Perf Att; St of Mnth; Comm Volntr; Peer Tut/Med; Chrch Yth Grp; Cmptr Clb; Drma Clb; Key Club; Mus Clb; Off Aide; Vsity Clb; French Clb; Ch Chr; Dnce; Sccr (V); CR (R); Most Improved Player - Soccer; Editor's Choice Award In Poetry; Business / Finance; International Business; Montclair State U

JOSEPH, WALTER; WESTWOOD, NJ; WESTWOOD HS; (JR); F Lan Hn Soc; Hi Hnr Roll; Nat Hon Sy; Nat Ldrshp Svc; WWAHSS; Yth Ldrshp Prog; Comm Volntr; Peer Tut/Med; DECA; Drma Clb; Emplmnt; HO'Br Yth Ldrshp; Mth Clb/Tm; NYLC; Acpl Chr; Drm Mjr; Mch Bnd; SP/M/VS; Sftball (J); Tennis (V L); Cl Off (P); County Humanity Award; Dwight D. Eisenhower Leadership Award; Biology; Medicine; Dartmouth College; Stanford U

JUMAN, SHANICE; BELLEVILLE, NJ; BELLEVILLE HS; (FR); Good Grades; Veterinary; Cartoonist; New York U College; Columbia U

JUSINSKI, GREGORY; PISCATAWAY, NJ; PISCATAWAY HS; (JR); Hi Hnr Roll; Nat Hon Sy; WWAHSS; Comm Volntr; Red Cr Aide; DARE; Key Club; ROTC; Clr Grd; Drl Tm; Track (J); 2005-2006 Group Commander for JROTC; Awarded the Air Force Association Award; Study Neuroscience; Become a Neurologist; Barry U; Drew U

JUST, JESSICA; SECAUCUS, NJ; SECAUCUS HS; (SR); F Lan Hn Soc; Hi Hnr Roll; Hnr Roll; MVP; Nat Hon Sy; Sci/Math Olympn; USAA; WWAHSS; Comm Volntr; Emplmnt; MuAlphaTh; Mus Clb; Tech Clb; Vsity Clb; Bnd; Chr; Ch Chr; Drm Mjr; Cr Ctry (V); Track (V CL); National Leadership and Service Award; All-American Scholar; Elementary Education; Music Performance; Millersville U

KABACHEK, SOFYA; MT LAUREL, NJ; LENAPE HS; (JR); Comm Volntr; Tennis; Received a Certificate of Distinction for 9th grade; Reached Outstanding Academic Level in a Foreign Country; Astrophysics Major; Aerospace Engineering Major; Boston U; Massachusetts Institute of Technology

KAHRER, LEANN; HAZLET, NJ; MARINE AC OF SCIENCE & TECH; (SO); F Lan Hn Soc; Hi Hnr Roll; Hnr Roll; Pres Sch; WWAHSS; Yth Ldrshp Prog; Comm Volntr; Key Club; ROTC; Tchrs Aide; French Honor Society; Law; The College of New Jersey; Ursinus

KAI, SUEGATHA; TRENTON, NJ; TRENTON CTRL HS; (FR); Hi Hnr Roll; Hnr Roll; Nat Stu Ath Day Aw; Otst Ac Ach Awd; St of Mnth; USAA; Chrch Yth Grp; Drma Clb; Ch Chr; Sccr (J); Cl Off; Vice Principal National Club; Pediatrician; Theater Performance; Princeton U; Columbia U

KALOLA, RUTIKA; OLD BRIDGE, NJ; OLD BRIDGE HS; (SR); Hi Hnr Roll; Hnr Roll; Otst Ac Ach Awd; St of Mnth; WWAHSS; Comm Volntr; Hosp Aide; Sci Clb; Tmpl Yth Grp; 7 Yrs. of Indian Classical Dance; 2 Awards from Gov't of Gujral (India); Dentistry; Physical Therapist; Middlesex County College; Rutgers U

KAM, VINCENT; BELLEVILLE, NJ; BELLEVILLE HS; (SR); Hi Hnr Roll; Hnr Roll; Nat Hon Sy; Nat Mrt LOC; Perf Att; WWAHSS; Comm Volntr; Peer Tut/Med; Cmptr Clb; FBLA; Mth Clb/Tm; Orch; Tennis (VJCL); Stu Cncl (R); Bausch and Lomb Honorary Science Award; Cornell U

KANG, ASHLEY; FORT LEE, NJ; FORT LEE HS; (SO); Hi Hnr Roll; Perf Att; WWAHSS; Yth Ldrshp Prog; Peer Tut/Med; Chrch Yth Grp; Dbte Team; Drma Clb; Key Club; Mod UN; Mus Clb; Sci Clb; Svce Clb; Chr; Mch Bnd; Orch; Stg Cre; Pharmacy; Dental/Medical; Columbia U; New York U

KANG, BRIAN J; EGG HARBOR TOWNSHIP, NJ; EGG HARBOR TOWNSHIP HS; (JR); Hnr Roll; Nat Hon Sy; Comm Volntr; Peer Tut/Med; Key Club; Cr Ctry (J); Track (J); CR (R); Mathematics and Verbal Talent Search: State Award; National Honor Society; Financial Engineering; Mathematician; Massachusetts Institute of Technology; Chicago U

KANTANAS, CHARLENE E; SOUTH AMBOY, NJ; SAYREVILLE WAR MEMORIAL HS; (SR); Hnr Roll; Otst Ac Ach Awd; Comm Volntr; DECA; Prom Com; SADD; Stu Cncl (R); Yrbk (E); Teaching; Business; Kean U; Seton Hall U

KANWAL, JASMEEN; HOLMDEL, NJ; HOLMDEL HS; (SR); F Lan Hn Soc; Nat Hon Sy; Nat Mrt Fin; Nat Mrt Semif; Peer Tut/Med; ArtClub; Dbte Team; Emplmnt; JSA; Key Club; Mus Clb; Sci Clb; Spanish Clb; Plays Drums (4 Years); President of Spanish Honor Society; Physics; Philosophy; Oxford U (Accepted); Columbia U (Accepted)

KAPADIA, DHAWAL M; PARLIN, NJ; SAYREVILLE WAR MEMORIAL HS; (JR); Hi Hnr Roll; Sci/Math Olympn; WWAHSS; Yth Ldrshp Prog; Comm Volntr; Hab For Humty Volntr; Hosp Aide; AL Aux Boys; Chess; Dbte Team; FBLA; Mth Clb/Tm; MuAlphaTh; NYLC; Sci Clb; Tennis (V); Track (J); Sch Ppr (E); Founder of My Own Tsunami Relief Fund and Website; Internship with District Assemblyman Wisniewski; Finance; Economics; U of Pennsylvania; Georgetown U

KAPADIA, POONAM; JERSEY CITY, NJ; DICKINSON HS; (SR); WWAHSS; Key Club; Quill & Scroll; SP/M/VS; Lit Mag (E); Sch Ppr (E); FCCLA-Secretary; Teen Ink National Teen Magazine; Biochemistry; Radiology; Montclair State U

KAPLAN, MAX A; CRANFORD, NJ; CRANFORD HS; (JR); Hnr Roll; Nat Hon Sy; Otst Ac Ach Awd; Emplmnt; Mth Clb/Tm; Mus Clb; Photog; Bowling Team; Engineering; Physics; Brown U; Lehigh U

KAPUR, ARJUN; MONTVILLE, NJ; MONTVILLE TOWNSHIP HS; (SO); 4H Awd; F Lan Hn Soc; Hi Hnr Roll; MVP; Nat Ldrshp Svc; Otst Ac Ach Awd; Yth Ldrshp Prog; Comm Volntr; Peer Tut/Med; Chess; DARE; Dbte Team; DECA; FBLA; Key Club; NYLC; Sci Clb; Sccr (V); Stu Cncl (T); CR (S); Sch Ppr (E); Invited & Attended the National Student Leadership Conference in Washington DC; Law; Stock Trading; Stanford; UCLA

KARAM, SABINE; KENDALL PARK, NJ; SOUTH BRUNSWICK HS; (JR); F Lan Hn Soc; Hi Hnr Roll; Nat Hon Sy; Comm Volntr; Peer Tut/Med; ArtClub; Tchrs Aide; Wdwrkg Clb; SP/M/VS; George Brabson Memorial Award

KARAS, JAMIE; PINE HILL, NJ; OVERBROOK HS; (SO); Hnr Roll; Otst Ac Ach Awd; ArtClub; Chrch Yth Grp; DARE; Drma Clb; Stg Cre; Tennis (J); Art; Animation 3-D; Philadelphia Art Institute

KARCHER, KEVIN; VILLAS, NJ; LOWER CAPE MAY REG HS; (FR); Hnr Roll; Pres Ac Ftns Aw; Bsball; Peer to Peer Leader - 8th Grade; Teacher; Stanford U

KARPINSKI, ERIC; SOMERVILLE, NJ; (MS); Hi Hnr Roll; Hnr Roll; WWAHSS; Comm Volntr; Key Club; Bsball (J); Bskball (J); Ftball (J); Stu Cncl (R); Engineering

KATRONETSKY, ILANA; KENDALL PARK, NJ; SOUTH BRUNSWICK HS; (JR); Nat Hon Sy; WWAHSS; Yth Ldrshp Prog; Comm Volntr; Peer Tut/ Med; Emplmnt; Mus Clb; NYLC; Off Aide; Tchrs Aide; Tmpl Yth Grp; Bnd

KATZ, LISA M.; CAPE MAY COURT HOUSE, NJ; MIDDLE TWP HS; (FR); Key Club; Chr; Atlantic Cape Community College

KEELEN, KYLE; KEANSBURG, NJ; KEANSBURG HS; (JR); Hi Hnr Roll; Hnr Roll; Nat Hon Sy; Perf Att; St of Mnth; WWAHSS; Yth Ldrshp Prog; Comm Volntr; FCA; Key Club; Mus Clb; SADD; Clb; Bnd; Chr; Jzz Bnd; Pep Bnd; Bsball (V L); Bskball (VJC); Ftball (V L); Cl Off (T); Stu Cncl (T); Mayor for Student Government Day; Mathematics; Penn State; Virginia Tech

KEENAN, MICHAEL A; CLARK, NJ; ARTHUR L JOHNSON HS; (FR); Hi Hnr Roll; Nat Hon Sy; WWAHSS; Emplmnt; Key Club; Italian Clb; Bnd; Tennis (V); Meteorology; Languages

KEHOE, CAROLINE; HOPEWELL, NJ; THE HUN SCH OF PRINCETON; (JR); Hi Hnr Roll; Comm Volntr; Drma Clb; Key Club; Chr; Dnce; SP/M/VS; Track (L); Adv Cncl (R); Stu Cncl (R); CR (R); Lit Mag (R); Yrbk; American Repertory Ballet Workshop Member; Peer Leadership Program; Dance; English; Barnard College; Connecticut College

KELLY, BRITTANY S; STEWARTSVILLE, NJ; BETHLEHEM CATHOLIC HS; (FR); Hi Hnr Roll; Perf Att; WWAHSS; Key Club; Spanish Clb; Cr Ctry (J); CR (R); Spanish Clb; Goods for Soldiers in Iraq Organization; Journalism; Lawyer; Notre Dame; Princeton U

Kapur, Arjun
Montville Township HS
Montville, NJ

Jusinski, Gregory
Piscataway HS
Piscataway, NJ

Jones, Heather A
Pennsville Memorial HS
Pennsville, NJ

Johnson, Stephanie
Bayley-Ellard HS
Florham Park, NJ

Johnson, Brittany A
Linden HS
Linden, NJ

Johnson, Robert M
Lacey Township HS
Forked River, NJ

Jones, Tamira
Trenton, NJ

Kang, Brian J
Egg Harbor Township HS
Egg Harbor Township, NJ

Karam, Sabine
South Brunswick HS
Kendall Park, NJ

KELLY, CRISTINA M; PITMAN, NJ; PITMAN HS; (FR); Hnr Roll; Pres Ac Ftns Aw; Sci Fairs; WWAHSS; Peer Tut/Med; Key Club; SADD; Bnd; Chr; Bskball; Fld Hky; Scr Kpr; Sftball; Adopt a Grandparent; Meteorology

KELLY, LAUREN T; BRICK, NJ; MONSIGNOR DONOVAN HS; (JR); Bnd; Orch; Bskball (J); Lcrsse (V L); Swmg (V L); Tennis (V L); Stu Cncl (R); CR (R); Urban Challenge Recital; Key Club / Project GO; Accounting; Business / Finance; Villanova U; Clemson U

KELOKATES, AMANDA M; MERCHANTVILLE, NJ; PENNSAUKEN HS; (JR); Hi Hnr Roll; Hnr Roll; Otst Ac Ach Awd; Perf Att; Peer Tut/Med; ArtClub; DARE; Sci Clb; Scouts; IRISH Clb; Stg Cre; Fld Hky (VJ); Sftball; Medical; Nursing; Camden County; Our Lady of Lords

KENDALL, KRYSTLE M; SHREWSBURY, NJ; RED BANK REG HS; (JR); F Lan Hn Soc; Hnr Roll; Yth Ldrshp Prog; Comm Volntr; Hab For Humty Volntr; Chrch Yth Grp; DARE; Emplmnt; FCA; FTA; Chr; Lit Mag (E); Dominican Republic Missions Trip; Creative Writing Major in Visual; Psychology / Literature; Ramapo College of New Jersey; Monmouth U

KENNEY, RACHAEL; TINTON FALLS, NJ; MONMOUTH REG HS; (SO); Duke TS; F Lan Hn Soc; Fut Prb Slvr; Hi Hnr Roll; Nat Mrt Semif; Nat Sci Aw; Otst Ac Ach Awd; Valdctrian; WWAHSS; Comm Volntr; Chrch Yth Grp; DARE; Emplmnt; Key Club; Mod UN; Scouts; French Clb; Bnd; Swmg (V); Cl Off (S); Stu Cncl (R); Christ Church Leadership Team; Architectural Engineer

KENNY, EVE; MONTCLAIR, NJ; MONTCLAIR HS; (JR); F Lan Hn Soc; Hi Hnr Roll; Hnr Roll; Nat Hon Sy; Otst Ac Ach Awd; Pres Ac Ftns Aw; Comm Volntr; Spec Olymp Vol; Vsity Clb; Spanish Clb; Dnce; Skiing; CR; President of Dance Company; Active Volunteer of Special Olympics; Business; Communication; Fairfield U; U of Loyola Maryland

KERTUS, JONATHAN; CALDWELL, NJ; WEST ESSEX REG HS; (JR); F Lan Hn Soc; Hi Hnr Roll; Nat Hon Sy; Comm Volntr; Peer Tut/Med; Emplmnt; FBLA; Italian Clb; Cr Ctry (V); Vllyball (V); Sch Ppr (E); National Youth Leadership Forum; National Honor Society; Doctor; Emory U; Vanderbilt U

KESSIG, MICHAEL; MIDDLETOWN, NJ; MIDDLETOWN SOUTH HS; (SO); Hnr Roll; Comm Volntr; Peer Tut/Med; Emplmnt; Scouts; Vsity Clb; Bsball (J); Sccr (V L); Get a Good Job; Start a Good Family; Ramapo U; Duquesne U

KETTY, KRISTEN M; HIGHTSTOWN, NJ; HIGHTSTOWN HS; (JR); Ctznshp Aw; Hi Hnr Roll; Hnr Roll; Nat Hon Sy; WWAHSS; Yth Ldrshp Prog; Comm Volntr; Red Cr Aide; Spec Olymp Vol; Drma Clb; Emplmnt; Mus Clb; NYLC; Chr; Dnce; SP/M/VS; Stg Cre; Fld Hky (J); Sftball (J); Swmg (J); Book Club President; Forensic Science; Sociology; Boston U

KEYASKO, NICHOLAS; GREEN BROOK, NJ; WATCHUNG HILLS REG HS; (SO); F Lan Hn Soc; Hi Hnr Roll; Nat Hon Sy; Pres Sch; Comm Volntr; Chrch Yth Grp; Svce Clb; Swmg (J); Stu Cncl (R); Sch Ppr (R); New York U; Boston College

KEYES, NARIAH; JERSEY CITY, NJ; UNIVERSITY AC CHARTER SCH; (FR); Hnr Roll; Peer Tut/Med; Scouts; Drl Tm; Stu Cncl (R); Fashion Design (Merchandising); A Professional Event Planner, Fashion Institute of New York; West Virginia State U

KHALID, YASER S; EGG HARBOR TOWNSHIP, NJ; EGG HARBOR TOWNSHIP HS; (FR); Ctznshp Aw; F Lan Hn Soc; Gov Hnr Prg; Hi Hnr Roll; Hnr Roll; St Schl; Valdctrian; WWAHSS; Yth Ldrshp Prog; Comm Volntr; Hab For Humty Volntr; Hosp Aide; Biology Clb; Chess; DARE; Dbte Team; Jr Ach; Jr Cls League; Key Club; P to P St Amb Prg; SP/M/VS; Stg Cre; Swmg (V); Tennis (V); Cl Off (R); Stu Cncl (R); CR (R); Sch Ppr (R); Academic Excellence; Physician; Surgeon; Harvard U; Princeton U

KHALIL, EMY; CEDAR GROVE, NJ; CEDAR GROVE HS; (FR); Hi Hnr Roll; Hnr Roll; Nat Hon Sy; Otst Ac Ach Awd; WWAHSS; Yth Ldrshp Prog; Comm Volntr; ArtClub; Chrch Yth Grp; DARE; Mus Clb; P to P St Amb Prg; Ch Chr; Clr Grd; SP/M/VS; Gmnstcs (J); Swmg (J); Tennis (J); Sch Ppr (R); Medical School; Major in Biology; Yale; Harvard

KHALIL, MERIAM; CEDAR GROVE, NJ; CEDAR GROVE HS; (SO); All Am Sch; Ctznshp Aw; F Lan Hn Soc; Hi Hnr Roll; Hnr Roll; Nat Hon Sy; Otst Ac Ach Awd; WWAHSS; Yth Ldrshp Prog; Comm Volntr; Peer Tut/Med; Chrch Yth Grp; DARE; Mus Clb; P to P St Amb Prg; Photog; SADD; Tchrs Aide; Foreign Clb; Acpl Chr; Chr; Ch Chr; SP/M/VS; Dvng (J); Golf (J); Gmnstcs (J); Ice Sktg (J); Skiing (J); Sccr (J); Swmg (J); Vllyball (J); Sch Ppr (R); Biology; Medical School; Harvard College; Yale

KHAN, ARSHEEN; JERSEY CITY, NJ; DICKINSON HS; (SO); Hnr Roll; Otst Ac Ach Awd; Perf Att; Sci Fairs; Key Club; Sci Clb; Tennis (J); CR (R); Sch Ppr; Mock Trial; Medicine

KHAN, HIRA; RANDOLPH, NJ; RANDOLPH HS; (SO); Hnr Roll; Perf Att; Sci Fairs; Peer Tut/Med; Red Cr Aide; Biology Clb; DARE; Key Club; Mod UN; Sch Ppr (R); Dance; Biomedical Engineering; U of Toronto; Johns Hopkins U

KHAN, NAZIA; ISELIN, NJ; JFK MEMORIAL HS; (JR); F Lan Hn Soc; Hnr Roll; Nat Hon Sy; Perf Att; WWAHSS; Comm Volntr; Peer Tut/Med; Dbte Team; Key Club; Mth Clb/Tm; French Clb; Stu Cncl (R); Lit Mag (E); Ranked #3 in Class; Pre-Medicine; Pre-Law; New York U; Rutgers U

KHANGOORA, KARAMBIR S; CRANBURY, NJ; HIGHTSTOWN HS; (JR); Hi Hnr Roll; Nat Mrt Fin; Perf Att; Valdctrian; Yth Ldrshp Prog; Comm Volntr; Peer Tut/Med; Red Cr Aide; Chess; Emplmnt; Mth Clb/Tm; Off Aide; Sci Clb; Tmpl Yth Grp; Ch Chr; Finalist in Quest Scholars Program; Teach Children at Temple; Biomedical Engineering; Bioinformatics; Cornell U; Princeton U

KHATTAB, AMANDA; BAYONNE, NJ; BAYONNE HS; (JR); Hi Hnr Roll; Hnr Roll; Nat Hon Sy; Valdctrian; WWAHSS; FBLA; Mth Clb/Tm; Sci Clb; Spanish Clb; Green Belt In Tae Kwon Do; Pharmacy; Rutgers U

KHATUN, SAFIA; PATERSON, NJ; JOHN F KENNEDY HS; (FR); Ctznshp Aw; Hi Hnr Roll; Hnr Roll; Nat Hon Sy; Doctor; Engineer; Montclair State U; Rutgers

KHOMUSI, ZAINAB A; HIGHTSTOWN, NJ; HIGHTSTOWN HS; (JR); Hnr Roll; Red Cr Aide; Clb; Honor Roll; Girls Scouts; Pediatrics; Art (Interior Designing); Rutgers U; Princeton U

KHONA, SHERIN; SHORT HILLS, NJ; MILLBURN HS; (SO); Hnr Roll; WWAHSS; Yth Ldrshp Prog; Comm Volntr; Chrch Yth Grp; Emplmnt; Key Club; Svce Clb; Tchrs Aide; Bnd; Pep Bnd; Fncg (J); Sch Ppr (R); New Jersey Science League Participant; Le Grand Concours French National Exam Participant; Nutrition and Food Science; Culinary / Pastry Arts; Cornell U

KHONG, VINCENT; JERSEY CITY, NJ; CTY PREP HS; (JR); Ctznshp Aw; Hnr Roll; Perf Att; St of Mnth; Sci Clb; HOSA; Internship At Hospital (Volunteer); Medical Science; Business; Rutgers-New Brunswick; Montclair U

KHOROSHENKO, IRINA V; TRENTON, NJ; HAMILTON HS WEST; (JR); Hnr Roll; Otst Ac Ach Awd; WWAHSS; Yth Ldrshp Prog; Chrch Yth Grp; Ch Chr; Orch; Academic Awards; Church Youth Group; Nurse; Emergency Physician; The College of New Jersey; Rider U

KHOURSHED, MAY E; LINDEN, NJ; GILL ST BERNARD'S SCH; (JR); Hi Hnr Roll; Hnr Roll; Peer Tut/Med; Mod UN; Quill & Scroll; French Clb; Chr; Lit Mag (E, R); Sch Ppr (R); Participated in Votes As President of a Party; Political Science

KHOUZAM, MARIA; CEDAR GROVE, NJ; CEDAR GROVE HS; (SO); Hnr Roll; Otst Ac Ach Awd; Tennis (V)

KIERNAN, MARY; LITTLE SILVER, NJ; THE PEDDIE SCH; (JR); WWAHSS; Hab For Humty Volntr; Photog; Fld Hky (V); Yrbk (P); Crew-JV; Operation Smile; Business; Bio-Chemistry; U of Pennsylvania

KIJPATANASILP, NATE; NORTH BERGEN, NJ; NORTH BERGEN HS; (SO); Hi Hnr Roll; Hnr Roll; Otst Ac Ach Awd; Perf Att; WWAHSS; Peer Tut/Med; Spec Olymp Vol; DARE; JSA; Key Club; SADD; French Clb; Golf (J); Mar Art (J); Tennis (JC); Principal's Academic Awards; P.E.A.K. Art Achievement; Doctor of Dental Surgery; Rutgers (UMDNJ) State U; Columbia U

KIKI, ABRAHAM; FAIRVIEW, NJ; CLIFFSIDE PARK HS; (SO); Hi Hnr Roll; Hnr Roll; Nat Hon Sy; Pres Sch; St of Mnth; WWAHSS; Comm Volntr; Peer Tut/Med; DARE; Bskball; Forensic Science; Congressman; Princeton U; Columbia U

KILLI, KRISTEN A; WANAQUE, NJ; LAKELAND REG HS; (SR); Hi Hnr Roll; Hnr Roll; Nat Hon Sy; St of Mnth; USAA; WWAHSS; Drma Clb; Chr; SP/M/VS; Stg Cre; Sch Ppr; Voice of Democracy Winner; Communications; The College of New Jersey

KIM, ERIC; MORRIS PLAINS, NJ; PARSIPPANY HILLS HS; (JR); F Lan Hn Soc; Hnr Roll; Nat Mrt LOC; Sci/Math Olympn; Comm Volntr; Hosp Aide; FBLA; Key Club; Pre-Medicine; Radiology; Cornell U; Columbia U

KIM, EUN J; PALISADES PARK, NJ; PALISADES PARK HS; (SR); Hnr Roll; Nat Hon Sy; St Schl; WWAHSS; Comm Volntr; Peer Tut/Med; Chrch Yth Grp; MuAlphaTh; Tennis (V); Yrbk (E); Edward J Bloustein Distinguished Scholar (NJ); Nursing; Physician's Assistant; Rutgers U

KIM, HANNAH; WYCKOFF, NJ; RAMAPO HS; (FR); Hi Hnr Roll; Otst Ac Ach Awd; Comm Volntr; Peer Tut/Med; Chrch Yth Grp; Mod UN; Latin Clb; Acpl Chr; Bnd; Ch Chr; Orch; Lcrsse (J); Mar Art (J); Vllyball (J); Cl Off (R); Gold Prize in the Korean-English / English-Korean Translation Contest; Environmental Club; Pharmacist / PhD; Business; UCLA; Princeton U

KIM, JENNA; RANDOLPH, NJ; RANDOLPH HS; (JR); F Lan Hn Soc; Hnr Roll; Perf Att; Comm Volntr; Hab For Humty Volntr; Chrch Yth Grp; Key Club; French Clb; Ch Chr; Orch; Yrbk (E); Appointed Seat in Pre-School Volunteer Service; Martial Arts Outside of School; Law; Business; U of Michigan; Boston College

KIM, SOOJIN; RIVER EDGE, NJ; PARAMUS CATHOLIC HS; (JR); Hi Hnr Roll; Hnr Roll; Comm Volntr; ArtClub; Outstanding Student Award for Basic Elements of Design; The Scholastic Art or Writing Awards of 2004-5; Doctor of Fine Art; Owning an Art/Animation Firm; Rhode Island School of Design; New York U

KIM, SOOK; MORRISTOWN, NJ; MORRISTOWN HS; (FR); Hi Hnr Roll; Hosp Aide; Chrch Yth Grp; 1st Place - Awarded on Poster Contest; Planner in Church Youth Group; Designer; Boston College; Penn State College

KING, CYNDALL N; MORRISTOWN, NJ; MORRISTOWN HS; (SO); 4H Awd; Ctznshp Aw; Hnr Roll; Perf Att; St of Mnth; 4-H; Chrch Yth Grp; DARE; Scouts; Bskball (J); Track (J); U of North Carolina; Rutgers U

KING, DAVID; PARSIPPANY, NJ; PARSIPPANY HS; (SR); Hi Hnr Roll; Hnr Roll; Nat Hon Sy; Otst Ac Ach Awd; Chrch Yth Grp; Emplmnt; Bsball (J); Bskball (V CL); CR (R); School of Business-Accounting; Villanova and Syracuse U; U of Connecticut and U of Maryland

KING, JONATHAN M; MATAWAN, NJ; MATAWAN REG HS; (SO); SP/M/VS; Stg Cre; Bskball (J); Sccr (VJ); Sftball (J); Track (J); Vllyball (J); Wt Lftg (J); Physical Therapy; U of North Carolina Charlotte; Duke U

KING, KRISTEN; CARTERET, NJ; CARTERET HS; (JR); Hnr Roll; WWAHSS; FTA; Spanish Clb; Bnd; Mch Bnd; Pep Bnd; Stg Cre; Elementary Education; Psychology; Kean U; Montclair U

KING, LAUREN; MORRISTOWN, NJ; MORRISTOWN HS; (SR); Hi Hnr Roll; Hnr Roll; Nat Hon Sy; Comm Volntr; Spec Olymp Vol; Chrch Yth Grp; Emplmnt; Prom Com; Lcrsse (J); Swmg (V C); COAP - Christian Outreach Appalachian People; Interior Design; Philadelphia U

KING, MARK; MAPLEWOOD, NJ; COLUMBIA HS; (SO); Perf Att; Comm Volntr; Peer Tut/Med; Chrch Yth Grp; Mus Clb; Ch Chr; Orch; SP/M/VS; Bskball (J); Lcrsse (J); Swmg (J); Vllyball (J); Wt Lftg (J); Engineer Mechanical / Electrical

KING, PETER; GLADSTONE, NJ; BERNARDS HS; (JR); Hi Hnr Roll; Hnr Roll; Nat Hon Sy; WWAHSS; Comm Volntr; Peer Tut/Med; Chess; Lib Aide; Golf (J); President & Founder Chess Club; Astro Physics; Animation

KING, PHOEBE A; MAPLEWOOD, NJ; COLUMBIA HS; (JR); Hnr Roll; Sci Fairs; St of Mnth; Comm Volntr; Chrch Yth Grp; Emplmnt; Key Club; Dnce; Drl Tm; Vllyball (J); Ballet Since 4 Yrs Old; Performed in Church Plays; Dance / Choreography Double Major; Sociology / Criminology Double Major; Temple U; Rutgers New Brunswick

KINHOFER, KAYLYNN; ASBURY PARK, NJ; OCEAN TWP HS; (SO); All Am Sch; Hi Hnr Roll; Hnr Roll; Perf Att; Yth Ldrshp Prog; DARE; Key Club; SADD; Vsity Clb; Bskball (J); GAA (V); Sftball (J); Vsy Clb (V); Cl Off (R); Spartan Scholar, Leadership Award; Principal's Focus Group; Pre-Med; Teaching

KINNEY, JEFFREY; TRENTON, NJ; HAMILTON HS EAST; (SO); Hi Hnr Roll; Hnr Roll; MVP; Otst Ac Ach Awd; St of Mnth; Comm Volntr; Spec Olymp Vol; Chrch Yth Grp; DARE; FBLA; Svce Clb; Tchrs Aide; Bskball (J L); Tennis (J L); I Play AAU Basketball.; I've Made Honor Roll All Through High School.; Business Management; Stockbroker; U Of Delaware; U of Pennsylvania

KINTALI VENKATA, MANOJ K; WOODBRIDGE, NJ; JOHN F KENNEDY MEMORIAL HS; (JR); Hnr Roll; Nat Hon Sy; WWAHSS, Comm Volntr; Peer Tut/Med; Chess; Key Club; Mth Clb/Tm; Sci Clb; Tech Clb; Wdwrkg Clb; Tennis (V); Sch Ppr (R); Yrbk (R); Engineering, Mathematics Comp Science; Penn State U; U of Michigan

KIRCHER, ROBERT J; CLARK, NJ; ARTHUR L JOHNSON HS; (SO); Hi Hnr Roll; WWAHSS; Chrch Yth Grp; Bnd; Cl Off (V); Mathematics

KIRKLAND, RICHARD; PATERSON, NJ; PASSAIC CTY TECH INST; (SO); Hi Hnr Roll; WWAHSS; Comm Volntr; Key Club; Vsity Clb; Bskball (V); Ftball (V C); Track (V); Criminal Justice

KIRSHENBAUM, MICHAEL; FREEHOLD, NJ; FREEHOLD TWP HS; (SO); Hnr Roll; Getting Into Peer Leadership; Creative Writing; English

KIRUPAHARAN, PRADHAB; NORTH BRUNSWICK, NJ; N BRUNSWICK TWP HS; (JR); F Lan Hn Soc; Hnr Roll; Nat Hon Sy; Pres Sch; Sci/Math Olympn; Yth Ldrshp Prog; Comm Volntr; Peer Tut/Med; DARE; French Clb; Stu Cncl (R); CR (R); National Honors Society; National French Honors Society; Liberal Arts; Pre-Law / Law; U of North Carolina; Duke U

KISH, KATHRYN M; PISCATAWAY, NJ; PISCATAWAY HS; (JR); Hnr Roll; Comm Volntr; Drma Clb; Emplmnt; Tchrs Aide; Vsity Clb; Vsy Clb (V); Secondary Education; Nursing; Kean U; Rutgers U

KITZMILLER, AMANDA P; MINE HILL, NJ; MORRIS CATHOLIC HS; (SO); Hi Hnr Roll; Nat Hon Sy; Comm Volntr; Chrch Yth Grp; Ntl Beta Clb; Prom Com; Scouts; Bsball; Bskball (V L); Sccr (V L); Track (V L)

KIVET, ERIC; CEDAR GROVE, NJ; CEDAR GROVE HS; (JR); Hi Hnr Roll; Hnr Roll; Chrch Yth Grp; Mth Clb/Tm; Sci Clb; Scouts; Stg Cre; Sccr (J); Mechanical Engineering; German; Lehigh U; Purdue U

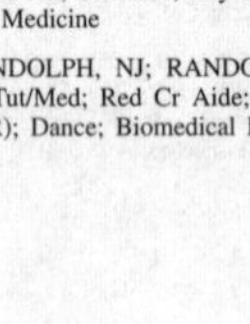
King, Peter
Bernards HS
Gladstone, NJ

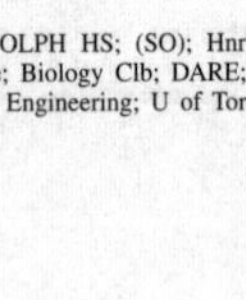
Kim, Soojin
Paramus Catholic HS
River Edge, NJ

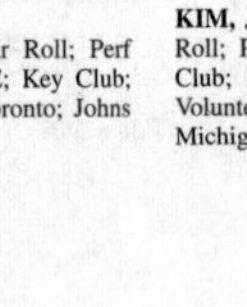
Keyes, Nariah
University AC Charter Sch
Jersey City, NJ

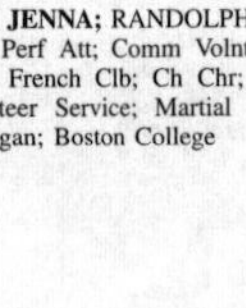
Kelly, Lauren T
Monsignor Donovan HS
Brick, NJ

National
Honor Roll
Spring 2005

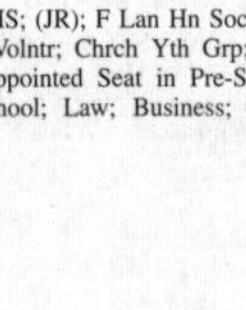
Kelly, Cristina M
Pitman HS
Pitman, NJ

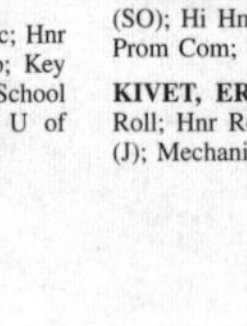
Kiki, Abraham
Cliffside Park HS
Fairview, NJ

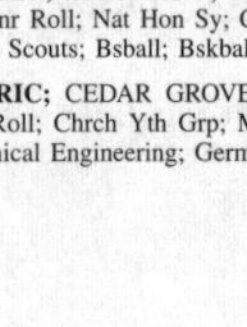
King, Jonathan M
Matawan Reg HS
Matawan, NJ

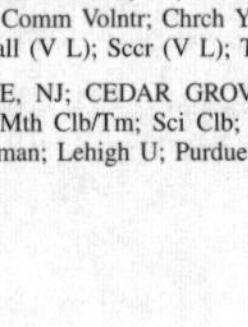
Kirupaharan, Pradhab
N Brunswick Twp HS
North Brunswick, NJ

KLEEF, RAELYN V; COLONIA, NJ; COLONIA HS; (JR); F Lan Hn Soc; Hnr Roll; Nat Hon Sy; Yth Ldrshp Prog; Peer Tut/Med; Emplmnt; Mod UN; Prom Com; Clr Grd; Dnce; SP/M/VS; Swg Chr; Scr Kpr (V); Adv Cncl (R); Stu Cncl (R); Lit Mag; An Evening with Young Writers; Close Up; Journalism; Creative Writing; The College of New Jersey; Princeton U

KLINEK, KATHERINE; STANHOPE, NJ; LENAPE VALLEY REG HS; (JR); F Lan Hn Soc; Hi Hnr Roll; Hnr Roll; Nat Hon Sy; Otst Ac Ach Awd; WWAHSS; Yth Ldrshp Prog; Comm Volntr; Peer Tut/Med; AL Aux Girls; Chrch Yth Grp; Lttrmn Clb; Quill & Scroll; Scouts; Svce Clb; Vsity Clb; German Clb; Chrldg (V L); Track (V L); CR (R); Sch Ppr (E, R); Reporter for the Daily Record; Journalism; Law; U of Maryland; Villanova U

KLOPACZ, DOUGLAS; HASBROUCK HTS, NJ; ST JOSEPH REG HS; (JR); Hnr Roll; Comm Volntr; Ftball (V); Track (V C); MVP Athlete in Soph. Class; MVP Track Athlete Fresh, Soph. Year; Business; Athletic Field; Penn State; Maryland

KLUMPP, ERICA; CLAYTON, NJ; CLAYTON HS; (SO); Hnr Roll; Kwnis Aw; St of Mnth; WWAHSS; Comm Volntr; Key Club; Prom Com; SADD; WORLD Clb; Chr; Bskball (V L); Fld Hky (V L); Track (J); Stu Cncl (T); Sch Ppr (R); SURE Club; Film; Journalism

KNAUB, DANIELLE N; PEMBERTON, NJ; PEMBERTON TWP HS; (FR); Ctznshp Aw; Hnr Roll; Chrch Yth Grp; Drma Clb; Chr; SP/M/VS; Fld Hky (J); Swmg (J); Cl Off (V); Stu Cncl (R); Education; Science Field (Medical/ Forensics); Rutgers U; College of New Jersey

KNOTT, WILLIE; NEWARK, NJ; WESTSIDE HS; (SO); Hnr Roll; MVP; Comm Volntr; Bnd; Mch Bnd; Orch; Bsball (V); Ftball (V); Wrstlg (V C); Police Officer; Fire Fighter; Ohio State; Morehouse

KOBERNICK, IAN; GLEN RIDGE, NJ; GLEN RIDGE HS; (JR); F Lan Hn Soc; Hi Hnr Roll; Nat Mrt LOC; Perf Att; Comm Volntr; Peer Tut/Med; Emplmnt; Vsity Clb; Spanish Clb; Bskball (V L); Ftball (V L); Adv Cncl (T); Yrbk (R); Business; Economics; Carnegie Mellon U; Emory U

KODARE, SANDRAMA; NEWARK, NJ; BARRINGER HS; (JR); Hi Hnr Roll; Hnr Roll; Perf Att; Hosp Aide; Lib Aide; Sftball; Yrbk; Medical Field; Business; Montclair U; Rough's

KOHAN, JONATHAN A; ASBURY, NJ; NORTH HUNTERDON HS; (JR); Hnr Roll; Otst Ac Ach Awd; Yth Ldrshp Prog; Comm Volntr; AL Aux Boys; Chess; Emplmnt; JSA; Mod UN; NYLC; P to P St Amb Prg; German Clb; Lcrsse (J); Seeds of Peace-International Ambassador to Jordan for the Beyond Borders Program; Presidential Classroom; Political Science; Law Degree; Georgetown U; American U

KOLVITES, CASEY; FRENCHTOWN, NJ; DELAWARE VALLEY REG HS; (SO); Hi Hnr Roll; Hnr Roll; MVP; Comm Volntr; Chrch Yth Grp; DARE; Scouts; SADD; Chr; Ch Chr; Skiing; Sccr (F); Sftball (F); Track (J); Girl Scout Silver Award; Math Teacher; Pilot in the United States Air Force; U of Colorado; Air Force Academy

KOMURA, STEPHANIE; NUTLEY, NJ; NUTLEY HS; (JR); F Lan Hn Soc; Hi Hnr Roll; Hnr Roll; Nat Hon Sy; WWAHSS; Peer Tut/Med; Key Club; Svce Clb; Spanish Clb; Bnd; Mch Bnd; Orch; Stg Cre; Cr Ctry; Sccr; Track; Cl Off; Stu Cncl; Yrbk; Varsity Letter / Key Club / NHS; VP of Claw Club / Spanish Honor Society; Economics / Architectural Engineer; International Relations; Georgetown U; Yale U

KONG, JOYCE; ISELIN, NJ; JFK MEMORIAL HS; (JR); F Lan Hn Soc; Hnr Roll; Nat Hon Sy; Nat Mrt LOC; WWAHSS; Comm Volntr; Peer Tut/ Med; Chrch Yth Grp; Dbte Team; Emplmnt; Key Club; Sci Clb; Svce Clb; Chr; Ch Chr; Stg Cre; Skiing (J); Sccr (J); Stu Cncl (R); Lit Mag (E); Sch Ppr (R); Performed Piano Solo/Duet At Carnegie Hall; Treasurer of Ecology Club; Accounting; Finance; U of Pennsylvania; Columbia U

KONOPKA, KRZYSZTOF; FRANKLIN, NJ; WALLKILL VALLEY REG HS; (SR); Hnr Roll; Sccr (J); Teen Arts; TSA (Technology Students Association); Computer Programming; Art; Sussex County Community College; County College of Morris

KOONCE, KELLI; BELLEVILLE, NJ; ESSEX CTY VOC-TECH HS; (JR); Hi Hnr Roll; Hnr Roll; Nat Hon Sy; Otst Ac Ach Awd; Yth Ldrshp Prog; Comm Volntr; Emplmnt; Pep Squd; Ch Chr; Pep Bnd; Yrbk (R); Medicine; Seton Hall U; Rutgers

KOPENSKI, SCHYLER B; KEARNY, NJ; QUEEN OF PEACE HS; (FR); Hnr Roll; WWAHSS; Comm Volntr; Chrch Yth Grp; DARE; Emplmnt; Dnce; Bskball; Vllyball (V)

KORKES, WILLIAM; WAYNE, NJ; WAYNE VALLEY HS; (SR); Hnr Roll; Pres Ac Ftns Aw; Comm Volntr; Spec Olymp Vol; Chrch Yth Grp; DARE; Chr; Track (J); Police Officer; Automotive; County College of Passaic; Lincoln Tech

KORNWEISER, GENNA; FORT LEE, NJ; FORT LEE HS; (SR); Hnr Roll; Comm Volntr; Emplmnt; FTA; Key Club; P to P St Amb Prg; SADD; Tmpl Yth Grp; Dnce; Stu Cncl (R); Lit Mag; Public Relations; Quinnipiac U; American U

KOROTKY, KANDYCE; TOMS RIVER, NJ; TOMS RIVER HS NORTH; (JR); Hi Hnr Roll; Hnr Roll; Nat Hon Sy; Perf Att; Valdctrian; Yth Ldrshp Prog; Comm Volntr; Peer Tut/Med; AL Aux Girls; Key Club; P to P St Amb Prg; Svce Clb; Hsbk Rdg; Lit Mag (R); Published in Best Poems & Poets of 2003 (And 2004); Attended Rotary Youth Leadership Academy; Law; Political Science; Boston U; Lebanon Valley College

KORSGAARD, LIZZIE; RIDGEFIELD, NJ; BERGEN CTY AC; (SO); F Lan Hn Soc; Hi Hnr Roll; Hnr Roll; Otst Ac Ach Awd; Amnsty Intl; Comm Volntr; Hab For Humty Volntr; FBLA; Off Aide; Spanish Clb; Chr; Dnce; Stg Cre; Yrbk (E); NJ Business Idea Competition Semi-Finalist; Golf & Tennis & Piano; Business; Law; Harvard College; The Wharton School of the U of Pennsylvania

KOSH, JENN; BRICK, NJ; BRICK TWP MEMORIAL HS; (JR); Hnr Roll; Sci Fairs; Comm Volntr; Peer Tut/Med; ArtClub; Emplmnt; Cr Ctry (V C); PP Ftbl (V); Track (V); Lit Mag (R); Biochemistry; Marine Biology; North Carolina State U; York College

KOSZEL, JUSTINE; CLARK, NJ; ARTHUR L JOHNSON HS; (SO); Hi Hnr Roll; Hnr Roll; ArtClub; Key Club; Vllyball (J); SPEL YAC For Teen Institute; REBEL (County) Prevention Links; Physical Therapy

KOWALEWSKI, AMY; MATAWAN, NJ; MATAWAN REG HS; (SO); Hi Hnr Roll; Hnr Roll; St of Mnth; Chrch Yth Grp; Stg Cre; Fld Hky (J); Sch Ppr (R); Yrbk (R); Battle of the Books State Champions 2002-2003; Scientist; Teacher; Rutgers U; Seton Hall U

KOYFMAN, REGINA; MADISON, NJ; MADISON HS; (FR); Hi Hnr Roll; Hnr Roll; Pres Ac Ftns Aw; Comm Volntr; DARE; Key Club; Orch; Lcrsse (J); Tennis (J); Lawyer; Doctor; Boston U

KOZIOL, VICTORIA R; KINNELON, NJ; KINNELON HS; (SO); Hnr Roll; Comm Volntr; Hab For Humty Volntr; Peer Tut/Med; Chrch Yth Grp; Emplmnt; Scouts; Vsity Clb; Latin Clb; Bskball (V); Vllyball (V); Girl Scout Silver Award; Girl Scout Senior Challenge-Leadership Awards; Veterinarian; Boston College; Marist College

KRAEMER, ANTHONY; TRENTON, NJ; HAMILTON HS EAST; (SO); Hnr Roll; Comm Volntr; Italian Clb; People to People Award; Marine Biology; Business Law; Rutgers U; Delaware State U

KRMPOTIC, TATIANA; MAPLEWOOD, NJ; COLUMBIA HS; (JR); Hnr Roll; Peer Tut/Med; Swmg (V L); Tennis (V L); Pre-Med; Biochemistry; Yale U; Brown U

KROIS, HOLLY; SOUTH ORANGE, NJ; COLUMBIA HS; (JR); Comm Volntr; SP/M/VS; Chrldg (V); Lcrsse (J); Sccr (JC); Sch Ppr (R)

KROLIKOWSKI, MICHELLE; TRENTON, NJ; NOTTINGHAM HS; (SR); 4H Awd; Ctznshp Aw; Hnr Roll; Perf Att; St of Mnth; WWAHSS; Yth Ldrshp Prog; Comm Volntr; Peer Tut/Med; 4-H; Emplmnt; Key Club; Photog; Tech Clb; Clr Grd; Flg Crps; Mch Bnd; Stg Cre; Yrbk (R, P); Independent Study/ Graphic Arts; Psychology; Child Development; Rowan U; Monmouth U

KUBERNAC, ROBERT J; WILLIAMSTOWN, NJ; GLOUCESTER CO INST OF TECH; (JR); Hnr Roll; Perf Att; Comm Volntr; DARE; Emplmnt; Outdrs Clb; Scouts; SADD; Spanish Clb; Stg Cre; Sccr (V); Swmg (V); Yrbk (R)

KUCHER, ORYSIA; LITTLE FALLS, NJ; COLLEGIATE SCH; (SO); Hnr Roll; Otst Ac Ach Awd; WWAHSS; Comm Volntr; Hosp Aide; Peer Tut/Med; Drma Clb; Key Club; Quiz Bowl; Dnce; SP/M/VS; Stg Cre; Bskball; Chrldg; Sftball; Vllyball; Community Theatre; Theatre Arts / Psychology / Pre-Law; English; New York U; UCLA

KUCHUKULLA, DEEKSHITA; BRIDGEWATER, NJ; BRIDGEWATER-RARITAN HS; (SO); Hi Hnr Roll; Hnr Roll; Pres Sch; St of Mnth; Comm Volntr; Hosp Aide; Key Club; Orch; Lit Mag (E, R); Yrbk (R, P); Doctor / Scientist; Journalist / Writer; Princeton U; Yale U

KURLANDER, MICHAEL J; BURLINGTON, NJ; LIFE CTR AC; (SR); Hi Hnr Roll; Hnr Roll; Nat Hon Sy; WWAHSS; Yth Ldrshp Prog; Comm Volntr; Hab For Humty Volntr; Chess; Chrch Yth Grp; Sci Clb; SP/M/VS; Bsball (V L); Bskball (J L); Sccr (V CL); Cl Off (V); Lit Mag; Sch Ppr (E); Student Leadership Conference 2002-04; Psychology; Business Management; Seton Hall U; The College of New Jersey

KUSHWAHA, ROLI; BELLEVILLE, NJ; BELLEVILLE HS; (SO); Hi Hnr Roll; Hnr Roll; Otst Ac Ach Awd; Hosp Aide; Lttrmn Clb; Vsity Clb; Clb; Dnce; Cr Ctry (V L); Track (V L); Participated in a Beauty Pageant; Community Service at Town Hospital; Advanced Biology; Cardiologist; Boston U; New York U

KUSI, EUGENIA; ROSELLE, NJ; ABRAHAM CLARK HS; (JR); Hi Hnr Roll; Nat Hon Sy; Otst Ac Ach Awd; Sci Fairs; St of Mnth; WWAHSS; Comm Volntr; Peer Tut/Med; Drma Clb; Sci Clb; Vsity Clb; Chr; SP/M/VS; Tennis (V); CR (R); Outstanding Academic Achievement Award; Pre-Med; Pre-Pharmacy; Temple U; Drexel U

KWITNICKI, LAURA; SUMMIT, NJ; (SO); Hi Hnr Roll; Hnr Roll; St of Mnth; WWAHSS; Yth Ldrshp Prog; Comm Volntr; Hab For Humty Volntr; Peer Tut/Med; Chrch Yth Grp; DARE; Emplmnt; Key Club; Mus Clb; Svce Clb; Vsity Clb; Acpl Chr; Chr; Hsbk Rdg (V); Skiing (V); Tennis (V); Lit Mag (R); Sch Ppr (R); Tennis-Junior Instructor; Babysitter; Possibly Medical Doctor; Georgetown U; Trinity College

LACKLAND-TOLEITO, SAVANNAH; EGG HARBOR TOWNSHIP, NJ; EGG HARBOR TOWNSHIP HS; (SR); Hnr Roll; Nat Hon Sy; USAA; WWAHSS; Comm Volntr; Emplmnt; Key Club; Svce Clb; Sch Ppr (R); Pre-Med; Biology; Richard Stockton College of NJ

LACTAOEN, KATHERINE; HAINESPORT, NJ; RANCOCAS VALLEY REG HS; (SO); Hi Hnr Roll; Hnr Roll; Key Club; Ch Chr; Color Blind - Club; Asian Pacific - Hula Dancer; Culinary Arts; Business Management; The Art Institute of Philadelphia; Heald College - School of Business & Technology

LAING, ALICIA; HIGHTSTOWN, NJ; HIGHTSTOWN HS; (SO); Hi Hnr Roll; Hnr Roll; Otst Ac Ach Awd; Red Cr Aide; Chrch Yth Grp; Spanish Clb; Chr; Ch Chr; Pediatrics; Nursing; Columbia U; Temple U

LAINO, JACKIE; PINE HILL, NJ; GCIT; (SO); Hi Hnr Roll; Hnr Roll; St of Mnth; DARE; Key Club; Spanish Clb; Dnce; SP/M/VS; Chrldg (V); Pharmaceutical; Dance; Rutgers

LAL, SHAAN; BAYONNE, NJ; STATEN ISLAND AC; (SR); F Lan Hn Soc; Hi Hnr Roll; Hnr Roll; Nat Hon Sy; Nat Mrt LOC; Sci/Math Olympn; Emplmnt; Mod UN; Quill & Scroll; Quiz Bowl; Spanish Clb; Orch; Bsball (V); Bskball (V); Sch Ppr (E); Yrbk (E); National Honor Society; First Honor Roll; Business Administration; U of Pennsylvania; New York U

LAM, MARITA S; MERCHANTVILLE, NJ; PENNSAUKEN HS; (JR); F Lan Hn Soc; Hnr Roll; Nat Hon Sy; Perf Att; WWAHSS; Hab For Humty Volntr; Chrch Yth Grp; Emplmnt; Off Aide; Chr; Business; Engineering; U of Georgia; New York U

LAM, PAULINA; NORTH BERGEN, NJ; NORTH BERGEN; (FR); Hnr Roll; Perf Att; WWAHSS; Key Club

LAM, THANH; ATLANTIC CITY, NJ; ATLANTIC CITY HS; (SR); Ctznshp Aw; Hi Hnr Roll; Hnr Roll; Nat Hon Sy; Otst Ac Ach Awd; Perf Att; St of Mnth; WWAHSS; Comm Volntr; Key Club; Bnd; Mch Bnd; Orch; Sch Ppr (E, R); AP Scholar; Pharmacy; U of the Sciences Philadelphia

LAMICHHANE, DEEPTA; BERNARDSVILLE, NJ; BERNARDS HS; (JR); Hnr Roll; Comm Volntr; Chrldg (V); Communications; Business; U of Massachusetts Amherst; U of Delaware

LAMONICA, MICHAEL; BEACHWOOD, NJ; TOMS RIVER HS SOUTH; (JR); Hnr Roll; Bsball (V L); Ftball (V L); Engineering; Rutgers U

LAMPERT, KAITLIN; SUSSEX, NJ; VERNON TOWNSHIP HS; (JR); Hi Hnr Roll; Hnr Roll; Nat Hon Sy; USAA; WWAHSS; Emplmnt; Key Club; Photog; Bnd; Orch; SP/M/VS; Key Club Corresponding Secretary; Biotechnology

LANCLOS, JARON; AVENEL, NJ; COLONIA HS; (JR); Hi Hnr Roll; Hnr Roll; Perf Att; St of Mnth; Peer Tut/Med; BPA; Chrch Yth Grp; DARE; Emplmnt; FBLA; Mth Clb/Tm; Ch Chr; CR (R); Mathematics; Accounting

LANDAU, DAVID J; CRANFORD, NJ; CRANFORD HS; (JR); Hi Hnr Roll; Hnr Roll; Nat Hon Sy; WWAHSS; Comm Volntr; ArtClub; Emplmnt; FBLA; JSA; Mth Clb/Tm; Sci Clb; Tech Clb; Tmpl Yth Grp; SP/M/VS; Mar Art; Sccr (J); Tennis (V); Wt Lftg; Wrstlg (J); Junior Statesman/Invited to Republican & Democratic 2004 Presidential Conventions; Attended Brandeis U Genesis 2004 Program

LANGAN, MICHAEL P; KEYPORT, NJ; KEYPORT HS; (JR); Hnr Roll; DARE; Emplmnt; Bnd; Business; Sports Management; Richard Stockton College of NJ; Rutgers

LANZEROTTI, SAMANTHA L; WOOD RIDGE, NJ; WOOD-RIDGE HS; (JR); Hnr Roll; MVP; Nat Hon Sy; WWAHSS; Comm Volntr; Drma Clb; Emplmnt; Prom Com; Scouts; Vsity Clb; SP/M/VS; Sccr (V CL); Sftball (V); Track (J); Cl Off (T); CR (R)

LAOYE, SAMUEL; MAPLEWOOD, NJ; COLUMBIA HS; (SR); Hnr Roll; WWAHSS; Chr; Ch Chr; Sccr (J); Track (J); Play Piano for 2 Churches; Economics; Music; Columbia U; Penn State

LARNED, KIMBERLY; EGG HARBOR TOWNSHIP, NJ; EGG HARBOR TOWNSHIP HS; (SO); All Am Sch; Hnr Roll; Otst Ac Ach Awd; Chrch Yth Grp; Key Club; Lib Aide; Bnd; Mch Bnd; Symphony WMO's (Performing Art)

LA ROSE, ASHLEY; RINGWOOD, NJ; LAKELAND REG HS; (JR); Hi Hnr Roll; Hnr Roll; Nat Hon Sy; Pres Ac Ftns Aw; Emplmnt; Acpl Chr; Chr; CR (R); Sang in Carnegie Hall W/Chorus in NHS and Road Show; Psychology; Communications; Princeton; The College of New Jersey

Krolikowski, Michelle
Nottingham HS
Trenton, NJ

National
Honor Roll
Spring 2005

Korsgaard, Lizzie
Bergen Cty AC
Ridgefield, NJ

LARSON, SCOTT J; PITMAN, NJ; PITMAN HS; (JR); WWAHSS; Comm Volntr; Red Cr Aide; Cmptr Clb; Dbte Team; Drma Clb; Key Club; Mth Clb/Tm; SADD; SP/M/VS; Stg Cre; Ftball (V); Track (V C); Wrstlg (V C); Engineering; US Naval Academy; Drexel U

LASSITER, FRANKIE O; ORANGE, NJ; ORANGE HS; (FR); Hnr Roll; Perf Att; ArtClub; Chess; SP/M/VS; Bskball (J); Ftball (J); Track (J); Professional Football Player; Actor; Florida State U

LATHAM, HELENA A; PRINCETON, NJ; NOTRE DAME HS; (JR); F Lan Hn Soc; Hi Hnr Roll; Hnr Roll; Nat Hon Sy; Otst Ac Ach Awd; Perf Att; WWAHSS; Comm Volntr; Peer Tut/Med; Red Cr Aide; Key Club; NYLC; P to P St Amb Prg; Svce Clb; Vsity Clb; French Clb; Lcrsse (VJCL); PP Ftbl; Sccr (J); Business Administration; Marketing/Finance/Sports Management; U of Notre Dame

LATORRE, JOHAN; HACKENSACK, NJ; HACKENSACK HS; (SO); Hi Hnr Roll; Hnr Roll; Pres Ac Ftns Aw; French Clb; Sccr (V); Tennis (V); CR (R); Medicinal Chemist; Geneticist; Harvard U; Cornell U

LAU, KEVIN; EGG HARBOR TOWNSHIP, NJ; EGG HARBOR TWP; (JR); Hnr Roll; Nat Hon Sy; WWAHSS; Chrch Yth Grp; FCA; Key Club; SADD; Swmg (J); Tennis (V L); Sch Ppr (R)

LAU, PEGGY; MATAWAN, NJ; MATAWAN REG HS; (JR); F Lan Hn Soc; Hi Hnr Roll; Hnr Roll; Nat Hon Sy; Prom Com; Sccr (V CL); Track (V CL); Most Dedicated / Maroon and Steal Award; All-Around Award; Physical Therapy; Athletic Training; Northeastern U; Ithaca College

LAU, VIVIAN; EGG HARBOR TOWNSHIP, NJ; EGG HARBOR TOWNSHIP HS; (JR); WWAHSS; Key Club; Pre-Med; Chemistry; C

LAUDANO, KRYSTLE L; BAYVILLE, NJ; CTRL REG HS; (JR); Hnr Roll; St of Mnth; WWAHSS; Chr; Mar Art; Chosen for Student of Marking Period; Given Renaissance Award; Master's Degree; Registered Nurse; New York U; Brooklyn College

LAURETI, JOSEPH; BORDENTOWN, NJ; FLORENCE TWP MEM HS; (FR); Hi Hnr Roll; Hnr Roll; Peer Tut/Med; Mth Clb/Tm; Bskball (J); Sccr (V L); Track (V L); Academic Award-Freshman History; Teaching; Engineering; The College of New Jersey; Rutgers U

LAUTE, JILLIAN E; WATERFORD WORKS, NJ; HAMMONTON HS; (JR); Hnr Roll; St of Mnth; Comm Volntr; Tennis (V); CCD Teacher (1st Grade Religious Education(, Academic Excellence Award, Options Award for Tennis; Varsity Letter Renaissance Award; Elementary Education; Richard Stockton; Rowan

LAUTERHAHN, ERIN; WANAQUE, NJ; LAKELAND REG HS; (JR); Hi Hnr Roll; Hnr Roll; Nat Hon Sy; St of Mnth; WWAHSS; Comm Volntr; DARE; Emplmnt; SADD; Vsity Clb; Dnce; Bskball (JC); Chrldg (VJCL); PP Ftbl; Sftball (VJCL); Stu Cncl (R); CR (R); Yrbk (E); Psychology; Education; William Paterson U; Quinnipiac U

LAVIN, YERI; PATERSON, NJ; PARAMUS CATHOLIC HS; (SR); Cmptr Clb; Drma Clb; SADD; Dnce; SP/M/VS; Stg Cre; Mar Art (L); Swmg (V); Track (J); Yrbk (P); NJ Athlete of the Year, 2001; Competitor of the Year 2001, 2002; Computer Information Systems; Florida Southern College; Barry U

LAWLESS, ERIC P; BARNEGAT, NJ; SO REG HS; (JR); All Am Sch; Hi Hnr Roll; Hnr Roll; MVP; Nat Hon Sy; Nat Mrt Fin; Chess; Mth Clb/Tm; Golf (V); Sccr (V); 1st Place AMC Math Council; Computer Science / Engineering; Mathematics; The College of New Jersey; Princeton U

LAWSON, JELISA B; WEST ORANGE, NJ; WEST ORANGE HS; (JR); Hnr Roll; Chrch Yth Grp; FCCLA; Prom Com; Chr; Ch Chr; Breast Cancer Walk Volunteer; NJIT Pre College Summer Program; Mechanical Engineer; Computer Technician; New Jersey Institute of Technology; New York U

LAZARTE, VERONICA; BRIDGEWATER, NJ; BRIDGEWATER-RARITAN HS; (JR); Hi Hnr Roll; Nat Hon Sy; Comm Volntr; Key Club; French Clb; Track (J); Member of Ski Club; Member of Key Club; Architecture; Cornell U; Northeastern U

LE, VICTORIA; RUTHERFORD, NJ; RUTHERFORD HS; (SO); Hi Hnr Roll; Hnr Roll; Comm Volntr; Biology Clb; Key Club; French Clb; Tennis (J); Track (J); Physical Therapy; Pharmacist

LEDER, JAMIE; MONTCLAIR, NJ; MONTCLAIR HS; (SO); Vllyball (JC); National Spanish Society

LEE, ALEX; LAKE HIAWATHA, NJ; PARSIPPANY HS; (SO); Hi Hnr Roll; Hnr Roll; Perf Att; Pres Ac Ftns Aw; Comm Volntr; Chess; DARE; Lib Aide; Scouts; Cr Ctry; Golf; Skiing; Portfolio Experience Project; Computer Science; Pre-Law

LEE, ALISON Y; BRIDGEWATER, NJ; BRIDGEWATER-RARITAN HS; (SO); Hnr Roll; Sci/Math Olympn; Comm Volntr; FBLA; Lib Aide; Mod UN; Scouts; Tchrs Aide; Chinese Clb; Orch; SP/M/VS; Student Teacher At Chinese School (Volunteer); Pre-Black in Tae Kwon Do, Assistant Instructor; Psychology; Philosophy; Rutgers U; Stanford U

LEE, ANDY; WARREN, NJ; WATCHUNG HILLS REG HS; (FR); Hi Hnr Roll; Hnr Roll; Perf Att; St of Mnth; Comm Volntr; Peer Tut/Med; Chess; FBLA; P to P St Amb Prg; Bsball; Sch Ppr (R); National Student Leadership Conference (NSLC); Business; Medicine; Duke U; Cornell U

LEE, BO MI; VOORHEES, NJ; EASTERN HS; (SO); Hi Hnr Roll; Hnr Roll; Nat Hon Sy; Perf Att; Pres Sch; St of Mnth; WWAHSS; Comm Volntr; Peer Tut/Med; Chrch Yth Grp; Mth Clb/Tm; Mod UN; Orch; SP/M/VS; Member in Tri-M Music Honor Society; Steering Committee of World Affairs Club; Radiology; Architecture; Johns Hopkins U; Harvard U

LEE, CAROLYN; BRIDGEWATER, NJ; BRIDGEWATER RARITAN HS; (SO); F Lan Hn Soc; Hi Hnr Roll; Otst Ac Ach Awd; Sci/Math Olympn; Hosp Aide; Chrch Yth Grp; MuAlphaTh; Orch; Sch Ppr (E); Certificate of Merit for National German Test; Junior Black Belt for Tae Kwon Do; Medicine; Harvard U; U of Pennsylvania

LEE, CHRISTOPHER S; BAYVILLE, NJ; CTRL REG HS; (SR); Hnr Roll; Nat Hon Sy; WWAHSS; Comm Volntr; Chess; Emplmnt; Scouts; Track; Vllyball; Fire Prevention Poster Contest; Eagle Scout Candidate; Art; Savannah College of Art & Design; Art Institute of Philadelphia

LEE, DANIEL D; PARSIPPANY, NJ; PARSIPPANY HILLS HS; (SR); Hi Hnr Roll; Hnr Roll; Nat Hon Sy; Nat Mrt LOC; WWAHSS; Hosp Aide; Chess; FBLA; Key Club; Mth Clb/Tm; German Clb; Track (J); Biomedical Engineering; Electrical Engineering; Will Attend Duke U 9/2005

LEE, HANNAH; HACKENSACK, NJ; HACKENSACK HS; (SO); Ctznshp Aw; Hi Hnr Roll; Comm Volntr; Peer Tut/Med; Emplmnt; Tchrs Aide; Scr Kpr (V); Vllyball (J); Sch Ppr (E, R); Ranked #3 in Class Out of 504; 3.8 GPA; Journalism/Communications; English; Columbia U; Cornell U

LEE, JAMES; EGG HARBOR TOWNSHIP, NJ; EGG HARBOR TOWNSHIP HS; (JR); Hi Hnr Roll; Hnr Roll; Nat Hon Sy; Otst Ac Ach Awd; Perf Att; WWAHSS; Biology Clb; Key Club; Sci Clb; SADD; Bskball; Stu Cncl (R); CR (R); Sch Ppr (E); Engineering; Carnegie, Melon U; U of Maryland

LEE, JOOMI; EAST RUTHERFORD, NJ; HENRY P BECTON REG HS; (JR); Hi Hnr Roll; Hnr Roll; MVP; Amnsty Intl; Comm Volntr; Peer Tut/Med; ArtClub; Chrch Yth Grp; Key Club; Mth Clb/Tm; Mus Clb; Off Aide; Vsity Clb; Bnd; SP/M/VS; Cr Ctry (V); Tennis (V); Track (V); Cl Off (R); Stu Cncl; Lit Mag (E); Yrbk (P); Education; Business; Boston College; U of Michigan

LEE, LANA; EGG HARBOR TOWNSHIP, NJ; EGG HARBOR TOWNSHIP HS; (SR); Hi Hnr Roll; Hnr Roll; Key Club; Computer Engineer; Computer Science

LEE, MEGAN C; MAYWOOD, NJ; HACKENSACK HS; (SO); Hi Hnr Roll; Hnr Roll; Perf Att; Chrldg (V L); Cl Off (T); Education

LEE, SAMANTHA C; NEW PROVIDENCE, NJ; SUMMIT SR HS; (SO); Hi Hnr Roll; MVP; Sci Fairs; Drma Clb; Bnd; Chr; Mch Bnd; SP/M/VS; Sccr (V); Track (V); Cl Off (S); CR (R); 1st Team All County (Union) Track; Top "20" North II Region Soccer; Medical; Georgetown; Princeton

LEE, TIARRA H; NEWARK, NJ; SCIENCE HS; (SO); Ctznshp Aw; Hi Hnr Roll; Hnr Roll; Otst Ac Ach Awd; Sci Fairs; Sci/Math Olympn; WWAHSS; DARE; FBLA; Do Something Team Captain; Best Friends Girl; Psychologist; Pediatrician; Princeton U, Howard U

LEE, WILLIAM K; CAMDEN, NJ; DR BRIMM MEDICAL ARTS HS; (FR); Hnr Roll; Otst Ac Ach Awd; Sci Fairs; St of Mnth; Valdctrian; Comm Volntr; Peer Tut/Med; Chrch Yth Grp; Dbte Team; Drma Clb; Emplmnt; Scouts; Spch Team; Ch Chr; SP/M/VS; Track (J); Stu Cncl (R); CR (R); Political Science/Law; Business Management; Morehouse College; Howard U

LEFKOWITZ, MATTHEW; SADDLE RIVER, NJ; NORTHERN HIGHLANDS REG HS; (SO); Hi Hnr Roll; WWAHSS; Dbte Team; Tennis (J); Debate Club; Business Club; History Business; Medicine; Cornell U; Duke U, Colgate U

LEGASPI, DON PREM L; BELLEVILLE, NJ; BELLEVILLE HS; (JR); Hnr Roll; Nat Hon Sy; WWAHSS; Novice Crew; C.L.A.M.P. Secretary; Nursing/Medicine/Physical Therapy; Fine Arts/Culinary Arts; Felician College; Kean U

LEGER, KAITLYN M; BRIDGEWATER, NJ; IMMACULATA; (SR); MVP; Peer Tut/Med; Emplmnt; Scouts; SADD; Bskball (J); Sccr (V CL); Sftball (V CL); Girl Scouts Gold Award; Physical Therapy; College Misericordia

LEON, EULALIA; TEANECK, NJ; TEANECK HS; (SO); F Lan Hn Soc; Hi Hnr Roll; Hnr Roll; Nat Hon Sy; Otst Ac Ach Awd; Perf Att; Sci Fairs; Comm Volntr; ArtClub; DARE; Drma Clb; Jr Ach; Lib Aide; Mus Clb; Scouts; Spanish Clb; Chr; Dnce; Orch; SP/M/VS; Chrldg (V); Mar Art (V); Tennis (V); Drama Achievement; President's Educational Awards; Doctor; Business Field; St Joseph's College; Rutgers U

LEONARD, CHRISTOPHER; HACKENSACK, NJ; HACKENSACK HS; MVP; St of Mnth; Comm Volntr; Chrch Yth Grp; Mus Clb; Wdwrkg Clb; Spanish Clb; Chr; Ch Chr; Bskball (J); Ftball (L); Sccr (V); Track (L); Stu Cncl (R); CR (R); Helping to Feed the Homeless; Business Administration

LERNER, ALEXANDRIA; MAPLEWOOD, NJ; COLUMBIA HS; (SO); Hi Hnr Roll; Hnr Roll; Comm Volntr; Hab For Humty Volntr; Peer Tut/Med; Key Club; Svce Clb; Lcrsse (J); Fundraising for Juvenile Diabetes; Education or Psychology; Business Management

LESKO, KRZYSZTOF; LINDEN, NJ; LINDEN HS; (JR); Hi Hnr Roll; Hnr Roll; Nat Hon Sy; WWAHSS; Peer Tut/Med; Chrch Yth Grp; Emplmnt; Off Aide; ROTC; Tchrs Aide; Drl Tm; Skt Tgt Sh (J); Electrical Engineer; Stevens Institute of Technology; New Jersey Institute of Technology

LESSER, RACHEL O; ALLENDALE, NJ; NORTHERN HIGHLANDS REG HS; (SO); 4H Awd; Comm Volntr; 4-H; ArtClub; DARE; Dbte Team; Drma Clb; Emplmnt; Photog; Scouts; Stg Cre; Scr Kpr; Lit Mag (E, R); 2nd Place Award-Creative Writing; Publication of Art Piece in Literacy Mag., Published in Literacy Magazine & Newspaper Recognition; Art; Journalism; Rutgers U; Rhode Island School of Art Design

LESTE, NEPHTALY; TRENTON, NJ; HAMILTON HS WEST; (SO); Hnr Roll; Hosp Aide; Chrch Yth Grp; Ch Chr; Sccr; Computer Science; Dance; College of New Jersey; Thomas Edison College

LETSON, JESSE; EGG HARBOR TOWNSHIP, NJ; EGG HARBOR TOWNSHIP HS; (FR); Hnr Roll; Nat Hon Sy; Comm Volntr; Chess; DARE; Key Club; SADD; Varsity Scholar; Police Athletic League Volunteer Food Bank Volunteer; Engineering/Computers; Business/Advertising; Princeton; MIT

LEVESQUE JR, DAVID S; WESTWOOD, NJ; WESTWOOD REG JR/SR HS; (FR); Hnr Roll; Nat Hon Sy; Yth Ldrshp Prog; Comm Volntr; Peer Tut/Med; Chrch Yth Grp; Bnd; Ch Chr; Jzz Bnd; Tennis (V L); Stu Cncl (R); Yrbk; Music; Ministry; Gordon College; Messiah College

LEVINE, ERICA H; HARRINGTON PARK, NJ; NORTHERN VALLEY REG AT OLD TAPPAN; (JR); Hnr Roll; Nat Hon Sy; WWAHSS; Peer Tut/Med; Off Aide; Multi-Cultural Club; Peer Mentor; TV/Radio Production; Syracuse U; Ithaca College

LEVINS, CAITLIN; PITMAN, NJ; PITMAN HS; (JR); Hnr Roll; Nat Hon Sy; Comm Volntr; Key Club; SADD; Bskball (J); Cr Ctry (V L); Sccr (J); Track (V L); Stu Cncl (V); Yrbk (E, R, P); Indoor Track Captain; Communications; Marketing; The College of New Jersey; U of Delaware

LEW, THOMAS; OCEAN, NJ; (SO); Hnr Roll; Comm Volntr; Chess; Classical Piano; Guitar; Business; Health Field

LEWANDOSKI, LAUREN; RINGWOOD, NJ; LAKELAND REG HS; (JR); Hnr Roll; WWAHSS; Emplmnt; Photog; Fncg (V L); CR (R); Student Culture Club; Road Show

LEWIE-CEPERO, KRISTA J J; SUSSEX, NJ; VERNON TWP HS; (SR); Ctznshp Aw; DAR; F Lan Hn Soc; Hnr Roll; MVP; Pres Ac Ftns Aw; Sci Fairs; WWAHSS; Comm Volntr; Hab For Humty Volntr; Peer Tut/Med; Chrch Yth Grp; Dbte Team; Emplmnt; Key Club; Mod UN; Mus Clb; NYLC; Tech Clb; Acpl Chr; Ch Chr; Clr Grd; Dnce; Chrldg (C); Cr Ctry; Golf (V); Mar Art; Cl Off (R); Stu Cncl (R); CR (R); Have Worked W/Congressman E Scott, Garrett for 5 Years; Model U.N outstanding Delegate Award; Law; I Want to Go Into Politics; The Kings College, NY; George Washington U Law School

LEWIS, ANDREW; HACKENSACK, NJ; HACKENSACK HS; (JR); Hi Hnr Roll; Hnr Roll; Peer Tut/Med; DARE; Bnd; Bsball (J); Ftball (J); Astrology; Engineering; Siena U; Temple U

LEWIS, CONNOR A; TRENTON, NJ; NOTRE DAME HS; (JR); F Lan Hn Soc; Hnr Roll; Nat Hon Sy; Yth Ldrshp Prog; Peer Tut/Med; Emplmnt; SP/M/VS; Bskball (J); Sccr (JC); CR (R); Student Development Team; Business/Marketing; Business/Management; U of Maryland; U of North Carolina

LEWIS, DUSTIN D C; HIGHTSTOWN, NJ; HIGHTSTOWN HS; (JR); Hi Hnr Roll; Hnr Roll; Red Cr Aide; Chrch Yth Grp; Dnce; Drl Tm; Stg Cre; Scr Kpr (V); Track (V); Marketing; Accounting; College of New Jersey; Hampton U

LEWIS, JACQUELYN; JACKSON, NJ; JACKSON MEMORIAL HS; (JR); Hi Hnr Roll; Hnr Roll; St of Mnth; Nutrition/Dietician; Rutgers; Stockton

LI, JACQUELINE; METUCHEN, NJ; JOHN F KENNEDY MEMORIAL HS; (SO); F Lan Hn Soc; Hnr Roll; Perf Att; WWAHSS; Yth Ldrshp Prog; Comm Volntr; Peer Tut/Med; Emplmnt; Key Club; Bnd; Chr; Mch Bnd; Cl Off (P); Stu Cncl (R); Sch Ppr (R); Yrbk (E); Mock Trial; Chinese School; New York U; Boston U

LI, JESSICA; PARSIPPANY, NJ; PARSIPPANY HILLS HS; (JR); F Lan Hn Soc; Hnr Roll; Nat Hon Sy; WWAHSS; DECA; FBLA; Key Club; Vsity Clb; Fld Hky (V L); CR (R); 2nd Place DECA Regionals (Hospitality); 3rd Place DECA States (Hospitality); Marketing Management; Public Relations; NYU; U of Michigan

LI, LUCY; WATCHUNG, NJ; WATCHUNG HILLS REG HS; (MS); Hi Hnr Roll; Hnr Roll; Nat Mrt LOC; DARE; Bnd; Stg Cre; Sch Ppr (R); Plays Piano; PhD, MD; PhD in Biology; Harvard U

LIANG, ALEX; DENVILLE, NJ; PARSIPPANY HILLS HS; (FR); Hi Hnr Roll; Hnr Roll; WWAHSS; Comm Volntr; FBLA; Key Club; Bnd; Mch Bnd; Business; Engineer; Penn State U; Rutgers U

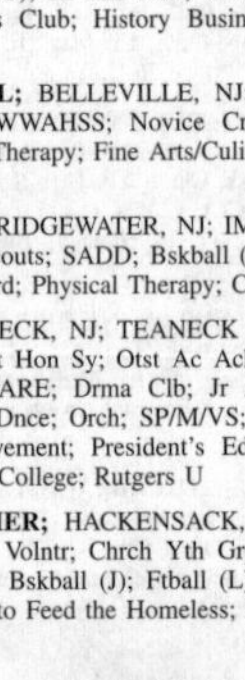

Li, Lucy
Watchung Hills Reg HS
Watchung, NJ

Lewis, Dustin D C
Hightstown HS
Hightstown, NJ

Leon, Eulalia
Teaneck HS
Teaneck, NJ

Lee, Alison Y
Bridgewater-Raritan HS
Bridgewater, NJ

Lazarte, Veronica
Bridgewater-Raritan HS
Bridgewater, NJ

Lawson, Jelisa B
West Orange HS
West Orange, NJ

Lassiter, Frankie O
Orange HS
Orange, NJ

Latorre, Johan
Hackensack HS
Hackensack, NJ

Leder, Jamie
Montclair HS
Montclair, NJ

Lee, Andy
Watchung Hills Reg HS
Warren, NJ

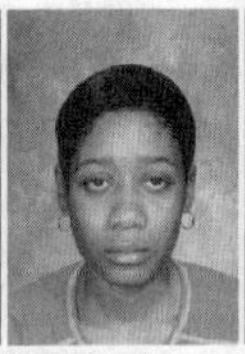

Leste, Nephtaly
Hamilton HS West
Trenton, NJ

Lewie-Cepero, Krista J J
Vernon Twp HS
Sussex, NJ

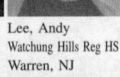

LIANG, ERICK; LIVINGSTON, NJ; LIVINGSTON HS; (SO); Hnr Roll; Nat Hon Sy; Perf Att; WWAHSS; Comm Volntr; Lib Aide; Track; CR (R); Game Design; Journalism

LIMA, FLAVIA; EAST BRUNSWICK, NJ; EAST BRUNSWICK HS; (FR); Ctznshp Aw; Hnr Roll; Perf Att; St of Mnth; Chrch Yth Grp; DARE; Drma Clb; Emplmnt; Scouts; Chr; Dnce; Yrbk (P); Graphic Design; Computer Engineering; Rutgers; Princeton

LIN, JENNIFER; MORRIS PLAINS, NJ; PARSIPPANY HILLS HS; (JR); F Lan Hn Soc; Hnr Roll; Nat Hon Sy; Comm Volntr; Peer Tut/Med; DECA; Emplmnt; FBLA; Key Club; Spanish Clb; Orch; SP/M/VS; Fld Hky (V); Mar Art; FBLA Vice President; Key Club Secretary; Finance; Marketing; New York U; Cornell U

LIN, TED; BRIDGEWATER, NJ; BRIDGEWATER-RARITAN HS; (JR); Hi Hnr Roll; Nat Hon Sy; Nat Mrt Semif; USAA; Yth Ldrshp Prog; Comm Volntr; AL Aux Boys; Key Club; MuAlphaTh; French Clb; Orch; Track (V L); American Legion Boy's State; County Track 4 X 200 in Champions; Business; Engineering; Harvard U; Cornell U

LIN, TIFFANY; ROBBINSVILLE, NJ; NOTRE DAME HS; (JR); F Lan Hn Soc; Hi Hnr Roll; Hnr Roll; Nat Hon Sy; Otst Ac Ach Awd; Comm Volntr; Peer Tut/Med; Chrch Yth Grp; Emplmnt; Mus Clb; Svce Clb; Tchrs Aide; Vsity Clb; French Clb; Bnd; Tennis (VJ L); President of Notre Dame Exchange Club; Chemistry; PhD; Boston U; Columbia U

LIND, SAMANTHA; KEARNY, NJ; ST MARY HS; (JR); Comm Volntr; Emplmnt; Yrbk; Science; Education; Ramapo; William Paterson

LINDER, GARRETT; SOUTH RIVER, NJ; SOUTH RIVER HS; All Am Sch; Fut Prb Slvr; Hnr Roll; Nat Hon Sy; WWAHSS; Comm Volntr; Prom Com; German Clb; Bsball (V L); Bskball (V L); Ftball (V L); Stu Cncl (T); Yrbk (R); History Teacher; Rutgers U

LINDER, SAMANTHA; ALLENDALE, NJ; NORTHERN HIGHLANDS REG HS; (SO); Hi Hnr Roll; Comm Volntr; ArtClub; Chrch Yth Grp; DARE; Italian Clb; Bnd; Mch Bnd; Food Science; Psychology; Cornell U; Siena College

LINDGREN, JASON B; BELFORD, NJ; MIDDLETOWN HS NORTH; (JR); Hi Hnr Roll; Hnr Roll; Comm Volntr; FBLA; Key Club; Scouts

LIPNICK, MICHAEL C; TOWNSHIP OF WASHINGTON, NJ; WESTWOOD REG JR/SR HS; (FR); Ctznshp Aw; Perf Att; Pres Sch; Comm Volntr; Chrch Yth Grp; DARE; Emplmnt; Mus Clb; Bnd; Jzz Bnd; Mch Bnd; Orch; Tennis (J); Johns Hopkins; Music Education/Business; Sports Broadcasting; U of Delaware; Syracuse U

LIRA, IRVING; LINDEN, NJ; LINDEN HS; (SO); Hnr Roll; Perf Att; Comm Volntr; Bsball (J); Scr Kpr (VJ); Sccr (J); Concert Band - 6 Years; Teacher; Architecture; Princeton U; Rutgers U

LIU, EMERSON; BRIDGEWATER, NJ; BRIDGEWATER-RARITAN HS; (FR); Gov Hnr Prg; Hi Hnr Roll; Hnr Roll; Nat Ldrshp Svc; Nat Sci Aw; Otst Ac Ach Awd; Pres Ac Ftns Aw; Sci/Math Olympn; WWAHSS; Comm Volntr; Peer Tut/Med; Chess; Emplmnt; FCA; FBLA; Key Club; Mth Clb/Tm; Mus Clb; Latin Clb; Jzz Bnd; Orch; SP/M/VS; Yrbk (P); 4th Place-Young Artist's International Piano Competition; 4th Chair 1st Violin- NJ All-State Orchestra; Bioengineering; Aerospace Engineering; Harvard U; Princeton U

LIU, LUCY; SPRINGFIELD, NJ; JONATHAN DAYTON HS; (SO); Hi Hnr Roll; ArtClub

LIU, XUAN; MORGANVILLE, NJ; MARLBORO HS; (SO); Hnr Roll; Otst Ac Ach Awd; Perf Att; Mod UN; Mathematics and Verbal Talent Speech - Johns Hopkins U; Finance; Business; New York U - Stern; Pennsylvania State U (Wharton)

LLEONART, DANIEL; BELLEVILLE, NJ; BELLEVILLE HS; (SR); WWAHSS; Key Club; P to P St Amb Prg; Stg Cre; Mock Trial, Octagon Club, FCCLA; Psychology / Law; Fairleigh Dickinson U

LLOJA-MACKENZIE, LAUREN; RIVERSIDE, NJ; DELRAN HS; (SR); Hnr Roll; Nat Hon Sy; Peer Tut/Med; Red Cr Aide; Emplmnt; Scouts; Spanish Clb; Bnd; Chrldg (J); Lcrsse (J); Scr Kpr (V); Sccr; Stu Cncl (R); CR; Girl Scout Board of Directors; Girl Scout Gold Award; Spanish; Business; Rutgers U; American U

LLONTOP, JENIFER M; ELIZABETH, NJ; ELIZABETH HS; (JR); F Lan Hn Soc; Hnr Roll; Nat Hon Sy; WWAHSS; Key Club; ROTC; Drl Tm; Vllyball (V); Accounting; Business Management; Montclair U; Rutger U

LLOYD, DENNISE L; JERSEY CITY, NJ; DICKINSON HS; (SR); MVP; Comm Volntr; ArtClub; Cmptr Clb; DARE; Emplmnt; Svce Clb; Tchrs Aide; Ch Chr; Bskball (V); Sftball (V); Vllyball (V); Yrbk (E); Old Dominion

LOBODA, LINDSAY; LAKE HIAWATHA, NJ; PARSIPPANY HS; (FR); Hnr Roll; MVP; Bskball (VJ L); Sccr (J); Track (J); Education; Physical Therapy; Rutgers U; Temple U

LOIODICE, ANNA; SUCCASUNNA, NJ; ROXBURY HS; (JR); F Lan Hn Soc; Hi Hnr Roll; Hnr Roll; MVP; Peer Tut/Med; Emplmnt; Key Club; Vsity Clb; Lcrsse (V L); Sccr (JC); Biomedical Engineering; Biotechnology; Lafayette College; Bucknell U

LOMBARDI, JOHN W; RINGWOOD, NJ; LAKELAND REG HS; (SR); All Am Sch; Hnr Roll; Yth Ldrshp Prog; Comm Volntr; Chrch Yth Grp; DARE; DECA; Vllyball (VJCL); Latin Award; Homer S. Pace Medal Award; Forensic Accounting; Law; College of New Jersey

LOMBARDO, ANDREW; OAKHURST, NJ; OCEAN TOWNSHIP HS; (SO); Hnr Roll; WWAHSS; Chrch Yth Grp; Emplmnt; Key Club; Sccr (J); Spartan Scholar Award; Who's Who Among American HS Students; Medical; Business; U Of Notre Dame

LONG, FEI; ALLENDALE, NJ; NORTHERN HIGHLANDS REG HS; (SO); Hi Hnr Roll; WWAHSS; ArtClub; Dbte Team; DECA; Mth Clb/Tm; Sci Clb; Scouts; Bnd; Chr; Mch Bnd; Fncg (V); Sch Ppr (E, R); Bergen County Chorus; NJ All-State Choir; Wharton; U of Pennsylvania; Columbia U

LONG, NATNAIEL C; WEST ORANGE, NJ; NEW YORK MILITARY AC; (SO); Hnr Roll; ArtClub; Wrstlg (V); Achieved Rank of Corporal; Won Art Contest in School; Writer/Novelist

LOPEZ, ANGIE P; ELIZABETH, NJ; ELIZABETH HS; (JR); F Lan Hn Soc; Comm Volntr; Key Club; Outdrs Clb; French Clb; Swmg (V); International Business; Chef; Montclair U; Berkeley U

LOPEZ, HANS; FLORENCE, NJ; FLORENCE TWP MEM HS; (FR); Hnr Roll; Comm Volntr; DARE; Sccr (J); Tennis (J); Stu Cncl (R); Yrbk (E, P); Electrical Engineer

LOPEZ, MARIA F; GARFIELD, NJ; PARAMUS CATHOLIC HS; (JR); F Lan Hn Soc; Hi Hnr Roll; Hnr Roll; Otst Ac Ach Awd; Perf Att; Comm Volntr; Hab For Humty Volntr; Peer Tut/Med; Chrch Yth Grp; DARE; Emplmnt; Svce Clb; Spanish Clb; Ch Chr; CR (R); Psychology; Social Work; Seton Hall U; Western New England College

LORD, JAMES R; TURNERSVILLE, NJ; WASHINGTON TWP HS; (SR); Hnr Roll; Nat Hon Sy; Otst Ac Ach Awd; St Schl; St of Mnth; Peer Tut/Med; Bnd; Mch Bnd; Marching Band Field Manager; Successful Poet; Zoology; Rutgers, the State U of New Jersey

LOSIER, NANDY; ROSELLE, NJ; ABRAHAM CLARK HS; (JR); Hnr Roll; Perf Att; Comm Volntr; Track (J); School Government; Engineering; NYU; NJIT

LOTZ, GRIFFIN; MONTCLAIR, NJ; MONTCLAIR HS; (JR); Hi Hnr Roll; Hnr Roll; Nat Hon Sy; USAA; WWAHSS; Comm Volntr; Emplmnt; Key Club; Ice Hky (J); Lcrsse; Yrbk (E); Photography; Graphic Design; Middlebury College

LOUIE, CYNTHIA; TOMS RIVER, NJ; TOMS RIVER HS NORTH; (SR); Hi Hnr Roll; Hnr Roll; Nat Hon Sy; Nat Sci Aw; Otst Ac Ach Awd; Yth Ldrshp Prog; Comm Volntr; Hab For Humty Volntr; Peer Tut/Med; Mth Clb/Tm; Sci Clb; French Clb; Orch; SP/M/VS; Stu Cncl (R); TEAM (Together Everyone Achiever More); PAWS (Promotion of Animal Welfare Society); Computer Engineering; Cornell U; U of California-Berkeley

LOURENCO, KIMBERLY M; CLARK, NJ; ARTHUR L JOHNSON HS; (JR); F Lan Hn Soc; Hi Hnr Roll; Hnr Roll; Nat Hon Sy; WWAHSS; Comm Volntr; Sci Clb; Vsity Clb; Spanish Clb; Sccr (V L); History Club Vice President; Peer Leader; Environmental Ecology / Policy; Environmental Sciences; Ithaca College; Colgate U

LOVE, DAVID; WAYNE, NJ; WAYNE VALLEY HS; (SR); Hnr Roll; Sci Fairs; WWAHSS; Hab For Humty Volntr; Chrch Yth Grp; Emplmnt; Scouts; Bnd; Ch Chr; Mch Bnd; Pep Bnd; Sch Ppr (E, R); Eagle Scout (BSA); Math; Computer Science; Rensselaer Polytechnic

LOVE, JOI; LONG BRANCH, NJ; LONG BRANCH HS; (FR); Hi Hnr Roll; Hnr Roll; St of Mnth; Latin Clb; Bnd; Jzz Bnd; Retail Industry; Journalism; Rutgers U; Penn State

LOVRENSKY, LACEY M; LINDEN, NJ; LINDEN HS; (SR); Hnr Roll; Perf Att; FTA; Prom Com; Yrbk (E, R); High School Teacher; High School Administrator; Kean U; Union County College

LOWERY, STEVEN J; BUTLER, NJ; BUTLER HS; (SR); F Lan Hn Soc; Hi Hnr Roll; Hnr Roll; Nat Hon Sy; St of Mnth; WWAHSS; Peer Tut/Med; Red Cr Aide; AL Aux Boys; Chrch Yth Grp; DARE; Drma Clb; Emplmnt; Key Club; Photog; SP/M/VS; Track (V L); Stu Cncl (R); Psychology; Theatre Arts; Ithaca College

LUCAS, SONIA; SAYREVILLE, NJ; CARDINAL MC CARRICK HS; (JR); Hi Hnr Roll; Hnr Roll; Nat Hon Sy; Perf Att; DARE; P to P St Amb Prg; Prom Com; SP/M/VS; Stg Cre; Sccr (V); Track (V); CR (R); Played with Church Band - Drums; History / Teaching; Music; Rider U; Fordham U

LUCCA, CHRISTY; HAMMONTON, NJ; HAMMONTON HS; (FR); Chrldg; Stu Cncl (R)

LUCCA, LAURA; SEWELL, NJ; GLOUCESTER CATHOLIC HS; (JR); Hi Hnr Roll; Nat Hon Sy; St of Mnth; WWAHSS; Hab For Humty Volntr; Peer Tut/Med; Emplmnt; Lib Aide; NtlFrnscLg; Prom Com; Scouts; Spanish Clb; Chr; Ch Chr; SP/M/VS; Scr Kpr (VJ); Track (J); Vllyball (J); Stu Cncl (R); Sch Ppr (E, R); Yrbk (R, P); Silver Award, Gold Leadership Award (Girl Scouts); Scholarship-ASM Materials Engineering Camp; Materials Science and Engineering; Penn State U; Harvard

LUCERO, SANDRA; CALDWELL, NJ; WEST ESSEX SR HS; (SO); F Lan Hn Soc; Hi Hnr Roll; Comm Volntr; Spec Olymp Vol; Key Club; P to P St Amb Prg; French Clb; Chr; Vllyball (J); Sch Ppr (R); Stage Crew; Neurosurgeon; Columbia U

LUCIANO, JOSEF; RIVERSIDE, NJ; DELRAN HS; (SO); Hnr Roll; Peer Tut/Med; Chrch Yth Grp; Cmptr Clb; Drma Clb; Emplmnt; Quill & Scroll; Scouts; Tech Clb; German Clb; SP/M/VS; Stg Cre; Lit Mag (R); Music Recording with own Band; Vocal Training / A / V Club; Movie Directing / Film; Script Writing; LaSalle U; Rutgers U

LUCIDONIO, JOE; GLASSBORO, NJ; GLASSBORO HS; (JR); Ctznshp Aw; Hnr Roll; Hnr Roll; Nat Hon Sy; Nat Stu Ath Day Aw; St of Mnth; Peer Tut/Med; DARE; Vsity Clb; Ftball (V); Track (V); CR (R); Business; Rutgers New Brunswick

LUI, BRIAN; BRIDGEWATER, NJ; BRIDGEWATER RARITAN HS; (FR); Hnr Roll; Comm Volntr; Key Club; Chinese Clb; Lcrsse (J); Mar Art (C); Black Belt in Tae Kwon Do; The College of New Jersey; Princeton U

LUKASIAK, RICHARD J; PENNSAUKEN, NJ; PENNSAUKEN HS; (JR); Bsball (V); Sccr (V); Sports Medicine; Athletic Sports Trainer; Rowan U

LUMBSDEN, DWAYNE; BLOOMFIELD, NJ; PINE FORGE SDA AC; (SR); Hi Hnr Roll; Nat Hon Sy; Peer Tut/Med; Drma Clb; SP/M/VS; Sch Ppr (R); Student Council Sergeant-At-Arms; Dorm Head RA; Business Management; Social Work; Morehouse College

LUNGREN, THEADOUR; SOUTH HACKENSACK, NJ; HACKENSACK HS; (SO); Hnr Roll; Otst Ac Ach Awd; Perf Att; Sci Fairs; St of Mnth; Comm Volntr; Chrch Yth Grp; DARE; Mus Clb; Scouts; Chr; Ch Chr; Dnce; SP/M/VS; Sccr (J); Vllyball (J); Stu Cncl (V); Volunteer At Boys & Girls Club of Paterson; Political Science & Government; Bachelor's, Master's; Georgia State U; Harvard Law School

LURIE, DANIEL; SAYREVILLE, NJ; SAYREVILLE WAR MEMORIAL HS; (JR); Hnr Roll; Yth Ldrshp Prog; Comm Volntr; FBLA; Sci Clb; Alternate for New Jersey Boy's State; Composed and selected to read an essay on an episode of Dateline dedicated to September 11th, 2001.; Law; Psychology; New York University; The College of New Jersey

LUZBET, STEPH; HARRISON, NJ; HARRISON HS; (SO); Hnr Roll; St of Mnth; Spanish Clb; Bskball (VJ); Sftball (J)

LY, MAI; SICKLERVILLE, NJ; TIMBER CREEK REG HS; (SO); Hi Hnr Roll; Hnr Roll; Perf Att; Sci Fairs; WWAHSS; Hosp Aide; ArtClub; Lib Aide; Mth Clb/Tm; Sci Clb; Spanish Clb; Science Club President 9th-10th Grade; Dentist

LYNCH, CHRISTINE R; MT HOLLY, NJ; RANCOCAS VALLEY REG HS; (JR); F Lan Hn Soc; Hi Hnr Roll; Nat Hon Sy; WWAHSS; Comm Volntr; Emplmnt; Key Club; P to P St Amb Prg; Sccr; Tennis (J); Key Club; Critical Care Pediatrician; Temple U; U of Delaware

LYNCH, JENNIFER; RANDOLPH, NJ; RANDOLPH HS; (JR); Hnr Roll; Peer Tut/Med; Chrch Yth Grp; Emplmnt; Vsity Clb; Chr; Bskball (J); Sccr (V L); Track (V L); Pre-Law; Psychology / Clinical Psychologist; U of Maryland; U of Richmond

LYNCH, SHANNON; SECAUCUS, NJ; SECAUCUS HS; (SO); Ctznshp Aw; Hi Hnr Roll; Hnr Roll; St of Mnth; WWAHSS; Peer Tut/Med; Fr of Library; JSA; Mth Clb/Tm; MuAlphaTh; Sftball (J); Vllyball (J); Yrbk (E); JSA; Pre-Law; English; Notre Dame U; Boston College

LYONS, MARGARET A; WAYNE, NJ; WAYNE VALLEY HS; (SR); Hnr Roll; Nat Hon Sy; Comm Volntr; AL Aux Girls; Chrch Yth Grp; Emplmnt; NYLC; Svce Clb; SADD; Tchrs Aide; Spanish Clb; Bnd; Chr; Ch Chr; Chrldg (V L); Fld Hky (J); Swmg (V L); Track (J); Spanish Club President; Chorus Vice President; Psychology; Engineering; Annapolis Naval Academy; U of Southern California

LYTLE, MAGGIE; BOUND BROOK, NJ; BRIDGEWATER-RARITAN HS; (FR); Hnr Roll; Comm Volntr; Chrch Yth Grp; Key Club; Scouts; Orch; First Aid Certified; Musician; Writer; Penn State

MA, JESSICA; EAST WINDSOR, NJ; HIGHTSTOWN HS; (JR); Hnr Roll; Comm Volntr; German Clb; Bnd; Mch Bnd; Cr Ctry (J); Track (J); Highest Distinction Mark for ABRSM-May 2003 Exam NJ, DE, PA; 2nd Place-Anna B. Stokes Lions Club Competition-2004; Law School; History; New York U; Columbia U

Lucero, Sandra
West Essex SR HS
Caldwell, NJ

Lovrensky, Lacey M
Linden HS
Linden, NJ

Losier, Nandy
Abraham Clark HS
Roselle, NJ

Lopez, Maria F
Paramus Catholic HS
Garfield, NJ

Lopez, Hans
Florence Twp Mem HS
Florence, NJ

Lindgren, Jason B
Middletown HS North
Belford, NJ

Long, Natnaiel C
New York Military AC
West Orange, NJ

Lord, James R
Washington Twp HS
Turnersville, NJ

Love, Joi
Long Branch HS
Long Branch, NJ

Lucas, Sonia
Cardinal Mc Carrick HS
Sayreville, NJ

Lucca, Laura
Gloucester Catholic HS
Sewell, NJ

MACALUSO, LISA M; LEDGEWOOD, NJ; ROXBURY HS; (SO); Ctznshp Aw; Hi Hnr Roll; Hnr Roll; Otst Ac Ach Awd; Sci Fairs; St of Mnth; Yth Ldrshp Prog; Comm Volntr; Hab For Humty Volntr; Chrch Yth Grp; Fr of Library; Scouts; SADD; Tchrs Aide; Bnd; Chr; Ch Chr; Stg Cre; Skiing; Tennis (J); Sch Ppr (E); Yrbk (E); Psychology; Nursing; Pennsylvania State; Marywood U

MAC KENZIE, SARA; CRANBURY, NJ; PRINCETON HS; (SO); Comm Volntr; Dnce; Tae Kwon Do; Irish Dance Prize Winner; Japanese; History; U of St Andrews

MACLEARIE, JACQUELINE; TINTON FALLS, NJ; RED BANK CATHOLIC HS; (FR); Hnr Roll; MVP; Pres Ac Ftns Aw; St of Mnth; Comm Volntr; ArtClub; Svce Clb; Bskball; Fld Hky; Lcrsse; Volunteer in Special Ed Classroom; Help at Food Bank; Physical Therapist

MADURUH, BRIAN; LINDEN, NJ; LINDEN HS; (JR); Hi Hnr Roll; Hnr Roll; Perf Att; Cmptr Clb; Tech Clb; Lit Mag (E, R, P); Learn and Serve; Computer Programming; Computer Science; New Jersey Institute of Technology

MAGALLANES, ROSE; COLONIA, NJ; COLONIA HS; (JR); Hnr Roll; Emplmnt; Prom Com; Chr; Chrldg (J); Cl Off (P); Criminal Justice

MAGBIRO, ALBERT; BERGENFIELD, NJ; BERGENFIELD HS; (SO); Hnr Roll; Perf Att; Wdwrkg Clb; Nursing; Engineering

MAHABIR, SHANE; JERSEY CITY, NJ; WILLIAM L DICKINSON HS; (SR); Hnr Roll; Nat Hon Sy; Sci Fairs; WWAHSS; Comm Volntr; Spec Olymp Vol; FCCLA; Key Club; Sci Clb; Swmg (V); Key Club (Secretary/Treasurer); Science Research (Gold Winner); Biochemistry; Chemistry; Rutgers U: New Brunswick

MAHMOUD, OMAR; JERSEY CITY, NJ; CTY PREP HS; Sci Fairs; Comm Volntr; Key Club; Photog; Sci Clb; Scouts; Bskball (L); American Heart Assn - CPR Layperson Certified; Pre-Med; Pre Dental; Rutgers-New Brunswick; Montclair

MAHMUD, SYED; EAST WINDSOR, NJ; HIGHTSTOWN HS; (JR); Hnr Roll; Pres Ac Ftns Aw; St of Mnth; Comm Volntr; Peer Tut/Med; Red Cr Aide; DARE; Emplmnt; Fr of Library; Mth Clb/Tm; Mus Clb; Photog; Tchrs Aide; Spanish Clb; Tennis (J); Stu Cncl (R); Yrbk (R); Mechanical/Electrical Engineering; Business; Massachusetts Institute of Technology; Drexel U

MAHON, DEIRDRE; PRINCETON, NJ; PRINCETON HS; (SO); Italian Clb; Fld Hky (V L); Ice Hky (V CL); Sftball (V L); Chemistry; English; Columbia U; Georgetown U

MAJEWSKI, ALEXANDER; WEST CALDWELL, NJ; JAMES CALDWELL HS; (JR); Hi Hnr Roll; Nat Hon Sy; WWAHSS; Orch; SP/M/VS; Juilliard Pre-College; New York Youth Symphony; Concert Violinist; Violin Teacher; The Juilliard School; Royal College of Music, London

MAK, STEPHANIE; EGG HARBOR TOWNSHIP, NJ; EGG HARBOR TWP HS; (SO); ArtClub; Key Club; Pharmacy; Temple U; Rutgers U

MALCHENKOU, DMITRI; JERSEY CITY, NJ; DR RONALD MC NAIR AC HS; (SO); Perf Att; Sci Fairs; Comm Volntr; Emplmnt; Spanish Clb; Swmg (V); Vllyball (J); Merit Roll; Psychology; Law; Rutgers U; Seton Hall U

MALDONADO, ERICK; SECAUCUS, NJ; (JR); Nat Hon Sy; Perf Att; Mth Clb/Tm; MuAlphaTh; Stevens Institute of Technology

MALDONADO, JEREMIA A; TRENTON, NJ; NOTTINGHAM HS; (FR); WWAHSS; Chrch Yth Grp; Key Club; Bnd; Anesthesiologist; Stanford School of Medicine; Minneapolis School Of Anesthesia

MALDONADO, JONATHAN; CAMDEN, NJ; WOODROW WILSON HS; (SR); Hnr Roll; Nat Hon Sy; USAA; WWAHSS; Chrch Yth Grp; ROTC; Clr Grd; Drl Tm; Edward T. Bloustein Distinguished Scholar; Hospitality Management; Studio Art/Music; Richard Stockton College; Montclair State U

MALIK, SAAD M; MONMOUTH JCT, NJ; SOUTH BRUNSWICK HS; (JR); Comm Volntr; Peer Tut/Med; Emplmnt; Outdrs Clb; Prom Com; Lcrsse (J); Tennis (J); Volunteer at Religious Centre; Cricket Team Captain; MD; Investment Banker; SUNY Stony Brook; NYU

MALLON, ASHLEY N; CLAYTON, NJ; VICTORY CHRISTIAN SCH; (JR); Hnr Roll; MVP; Nat Hon Sy; Sci Fairs; Comm Volntr; Peer Tut/Med; Chrch Yth Grp; Photog; Prom Com; Bskball (V CL); Cr Ctry (V); Sccr (V L); Sftball (V L); Track (V); Sch Ppr (R, P); Yrbk (R, P); Sculpture; Readers Theatre; Sports Medicine; Forensic Science; Liberty U; Eastern U

MALONE, TAMARA L; CHERRY HILL, NJ; CHERRY HILL HS WEST; (SR); Hnr Roll; Comm Volntr; Chrch Yth Grp; DECA; Off Aide; Ch Chr; Psychology; Spanish

MAMMONE, SARA; ROCHELLE PARK, NJ; HACKENSACK HS; (JR); Hnr Roll; Pres Ac Ftns Aw; Comm Volntr; Chrch Yth Grp; Emplmnt; Tchrs Aide; Mar Art; Sccr (V CL); Destination Imagination (DI); Art/Education; Sports-Soccer; Montclair State U; William Paterson U

MANCINI, GIOVANNI; HASKELL, NJ; LAKELAND REG HS; (JR); Duke TS; F Lan Hn Soc; Hi Hnr Roll; Hnr Roll; Nat Hon Sy; Otst Ac Ach Awd; WWAHSS; Comm Volntr; AL Aux Boys; Quiz Bowl; Bsball (V L); Sccr (V L); Cl Off (V); Stu Cncl (R); Varsity Quiz Bowl; Business Management; Bio Medical Engineering; U of North Carolina Greensboro; U of Tampa

MANCUSO, KAITLIN; EGG HARBOR TOWNSHIP, NJ; EGG HARBOR TOWNSHIP HS; (FR); Hi Hnr Roll; Peer Tut/Med; Key Club; Sci Clb; Dnce; Chrldg (J); Sccr (J); Cl Off (V); Varsity Scholar; Interact Club; Physical Therapy

MANGAL, KUSH; PRINCETON JCT, NJ; WWPHS NORTH; (JR); Fut Prb Slvr; Sci/Math Olympn; WWAHSS; Yth Ldrshp Prog; Comm Volntr; Hab For Humty Volntr; Red Cr Aide; Dbte Team; Mth Clb/Tm; Mod UN; P to P St Amb Prg; Sci Clb; Lcrsse; Sccr (J); Track (J); CR (R); Pre-Med; Pre-Science; Cornell; Columbia

MANGIAPANE, SARA; LONG VALLEY, NJ; WEST MORRIS CTRL HS; (JR); F Lan Hn Soc; Hi Hnr Roll; WWAHSS; Yth Ldrshp Prog; Comm Volntr; Chrch Yth Grp; Key Club; NYLC; Bnd; Mch Bnd; Mar Art; Trinity College Piano Grade 5; International Baccalaureate Program

MANLEY, MARLENA E; BAYVILLE, NJ; CTRL REG HS; (JR); All Am Sch; Ctznshp Aw; Salutrn; Sci Fairs; Sci/Math Olympn; Comm Volntr; Peer Tut/Med; Chrch Yth Grp; DARE; Key Club; Svce Clb; Lcrsse (J); Sccr (J); President of Ocean Club; Most Improved Player Award - Soccer; Elementary Education; English; Oneonta State U; Hartwick U

MANN, KRISTINA; PISCATAWAY, NJ; PISCATAWAY HS; (SR); Hnr Roll; WWAHSS; Peer Tut/Med; Key Club; Mar Art; National Honors Society; National Art Honors Society; Visual Arts; Rutgers U; Kent U

MANOCCHIO, JEFF S; SHORT HILLS, NJ; MILLBURN HS; (JR); Comm Volntr; Hab For Humty Volntr; Peer Tut/Med; Red Cr Aide; Key Club; Chr; Sccr (J); President of the Key Club; Pre-Med; Finance; Fordham; Fairfield U

MANTILLA, JOYMARIE C; LAKE HIAWATHA, NJ; MORRIS CATHOLIC HS; (SO); Hi Hnr Roll; Nat Hon Sy; Otst Ac Ach Awd; Perf Att; Pres Ac Ftns Aw; Salutrn; Sci Fairs; Sci/Math Olympn; Comm Volntr; Peer Tut/Med; Chrch Yth Grp; DARE; Drma Clb; HO`Br Yth Ldrshp; Mth Clb/Tm; Mus Clb; Ntl Beta Clb; NtlFrnscLg; Bnd (S); Chr; Ch Chr; Dnce; Mar Art; Tennis (L); Track (L); Vllyball; Stu Cncl (S); CR (R); Morris Catholic H.S. Scholarship of 2000 Year; Doctorate in Pharmaceuticals; Music Major; Rutgers U; Massachusetts College of Pharmacy and Health Sciences

MANZO, JACQUELINE A; MATAWAN, NJ; MATAWAN REG HS; (JR); Ctznshp Aw; F Lan Hn Soc; Hi Hnr Roll; Hnr Roll; Kwnis Aw; Nat Hon Sy; Nat Stu Ath Day Aw; WWAHSS; Comm Volntr; DARE; Key Club; Prom Com; SADD; Fld Hky (V L); Sftball (J); Stu Cncl (R); Varsity Wrestling Manager; Key Club Treasurer and Secretary

MAQSUDI, FEEROZ; MONTVILLE, NJ; (SO); Otst Ac Ach Awd; DECA; Track (J); Neurosurgeon; Chemist; Duke U; U of Virginia

MARCANO, MICHAEL; LODI, NJ; LODI HS; (SR); Hnr Roll; Nat Hon Sy; Bnd; Jzz Bnd; Mch Bnd; SP/M/VS; Music Performance; Physics; William Peterson U; Montclair State U

MARCINO, CHRISTIE; RAHWAY, NJ; RAHWAY HS; (SO); Hi Hnr Roll; Hnr Roll; WWAHSS; Drma Clb; Key Club; Outdrs Clb; Chr; Dnce; SP/M/VS; Stg Cre; PP Ftbl (V); Swmg (J); Vllyball (V); The U of North Carolina; U of Maryland

MARCUCCI, JENNIFER; NEWPORT, NJ; BRIDGETON HS; (JR); Hi Hnr Roll; Hnr Roll; Jr Rot; Nat Hon Sy; Peer Tut/Med; Lib Aide; Off Aide; Lit Mag (R); Sch Ppr (E, R); Student Government; HOSA; Master's Degree in Social Work; Monmouth U

MARCUS, JOY ELIZABETH; OLD BRIDGE, NJ; OLD BRIDGE HS; (JR); Hnr Roll; Comm Volntr; ArtClub; DARE; Emplmnt; FBLA; Tmpl Yth Grp; Chr; English; Law; Monmouth U

MARIANI, JAMIE A; TRENTON, NJ; NOTRE DAME HS; (SO); Hi Hnr Roll; Yth Ldrshp Prog; Comm Volntr; Peer Tut/Med; Chrch Yth Grp; DARE; Drma Clb; Svce Clb; Acpl Chr; Ch Chr; SP/M/VS; Fld Hky (J); Youth Leadership Forum on Medicine Participant; Peer Leader; Medicine/Pediatrician; Psychology; Georgetown U; Brown U

MARIDUENA, STEFANIE; RAHWAY, NJ; RAHWAY HS; (FR); Hi Hnr Roll; WWAHSS; Comm Volntr; Chrch Yth Grp; Chr; Major in Fashion; Major in Psychology; Princeton U; Fashion Institute of Technology

MARIN, ANDREA D; MORRIS PLAINS, NJ; PARSIPPANY HILLS HS; (FR); Hi Hnr Roll; Hnr Roll; Pres Ac Ftns Aw; ArtClub; Key Club; Bskball (JC); Cr Ctry (J); Sftball (JC); Track (VJ); Nursing

MARIN, MARIA E; BRIDGEWATER, NJ; BRIDGEWATER-RARITAN HS; (JR); F Lan Hn Soc; Hi Hnr Roll; Hnr Roll; Comm Volntr; Key Club; Spanish Clb; Biology; Boston U; U of Virginia

MARINEZ, CHRISTOPHER; KEARNY, NJ; QUEEN OF PEACE HS; (SO); Hnr Roll; Comm Volntr; Chrch Yth Grp; DARE; Photog; Scouts; Clr Grd; Drl Tm; Mar Art; Pathfinder of the Year - Church Club; Violin Player; Doctor; Architect; Columbian Union College; Princeton U

MARINEZ, DENISE; HARRISON, NJ; HCST-NORTH HUDSON CTR; (SO); Hi Hnr Roll; Hnr Roll; WWAHSS; Comm Volntr; Key Club; Sci Clb; SP/M/VS; Stg Cre; Instrumental Music; Pathfinders-Church Organization; Medicine-Pediatrician; Fashion Designer; U of Medicine and Dentistry of New Jersey; Loma Linda U, California

MARK, LAUREN M; MAYWOOD, NJ; HACKENSACK HS; (FR); Hnr Roll; Svce Clb; Montclair State U; Bergen Community College

MARKRIOUS, CHARLES; CLIFFWOOD, NJ; MATAWAN REG HS; (JR); Hi Hnr Roll; Hnr Roll; Jr Eng Tech; Nat Hon Sy; Nat Ldrshp Svc; Pres Sch; Sci/Math Olympn; St of Mnth; Comm Volntr; Hosp Aide; Peer Tut/Med; Cmptr Clb; Key Club; Mth Clb/Tm; NYLC; Sci Clb; Tech Clb; Spanish Clb; Fld Hky (V); Cl Off (V); Sccr (V); Tennis (V); Cl Off (T); Treasurer of Spanish Club; Key Club; Medical Science / Medicine; Computer Science; New Jersey Medical School; Rutgers U

MARKS, CALVIN; NEWARK, NJ; BARRINGER HS; (SO); Hnr Roll; MVP; Otst Ac Ach Awd; St of Mnth; Mth Clb/Tm; Sccr (VJC); CR (P); Aircraft Mechanics; Aviation; Spartan College of Technology and Aeronautics; Westwood College of Aviation Technology

MAROTTA, JOSEPH; MADISON, NJ; MADISON HS; (JR); Hi Hnr Roll; MVP; Pres Ac Ftns Aw; Emplmnt; Key Club; Bnd; Jzz Bnd; Pep Bnd; SP/M/VS; Bskball (JC); Track (V L); Vllyball (V); Stu Cncl (R); Sch Ppr (R); MSS Student Council Award 2002-2003; MSS Athlete of the Year Award 2003; Political Science; Doctorate / United States History; Pennsylvania State U; U of Michigan

MARQUEZ, BIANCA; NORTH BERGEN, NJ; AC OF SACRED HEART HS; (SO); Hi Hnr Roll; Nat Hon Sy; Perf Att; Comm Volntr; ArtClub; SP/M/VS; Vllyball (V); Yrbk; 1st Place Winner of School Spelling Bee; Poetry Published in School Paper; Pediatrician; Professional Photographer; Rutgers U; New York U

MARQUEZ, KIMBERLY; HEWITT, NJ; WEST MILFORD TWP HS; (JR); F Lan Hn Soc; Hi Hnr Roll; Hnr Roll; Nat Hon Sy; WWAHSS; Peer Tut/Med; 4-H; Emplmnt; Photog; Quiz Bowl; Schol Bwl; Vsity Clb; Spanish Clb; Gmnstcs (V CL); Vsy Clb (V); Criminal Justice; Psychology; Seton Hall

MARQUEZ, NATALIE; WILLIAMSTOWN, NJ; WILLIAMSTOWN HS; (JR); Nat Hon Sy; Pres Sch; CARE; Comm Volntr; DARE; Prom Com; Svce Clb; Vsity Clb; Dnce; SP/M/VS; Fld Hky (V L); Swmg (J); Track (V); Vsy Clb (VJ L); Cl Off (P); Stu Cncl (R); CR (P); Cheerleading Coach, Monroe Twp, Braves; Miss New Jersey Teen Participant; Anatomy; Nursing; Stockton College; Rowan U

MARRERO, AMANDA L; ENGLEWOOD CLIFFS, NJ; CRESSKILL JR/SR HS; (JR); Hnr Roll; Comm Volntr; Yrbk (E, R); Created a Drug & Alcohol Awareness Club; Also a Non-Smoking Club; Psychologist; U of California-Berkeley; U of California-San Diego

MARRERO, ANGEL; EGG HARBOR TOWNSHIP, NJ; EGG HARBOR TOWNSHIP HS; (SO); Hnr Roll; Perf Att; Pres Ac Ftns Aw; St of Mnth; WWAHSS; ArtClub; Vsity Clb; Sccr (J); Vsy Clb (L); National Junior Honor Society; Who's Who Among American High School Students; Engineering

MARRERO, ASHLEY; NORTH ARLINGTON, NJ; NORTH ARLINGTON HS; (SO); Ctznshp Aw; Hnr Roll; St of Mnth; WWAHSS; Comm Volntr; Chrch Yth Grp; Civil Air Pat; Drma Clb; Emplmnt; Mus Clb; French Clb; Bnd; Chr; Ch Chr; Drl Tm; Sftball (V L); Vllyball (V L); Band President; Masters in History; Masters in Music; California U At Long Beach; Penn State

MARSTON, ELLEN; TENAFLY, NJ; AC OF THE HOLY ANGELS; (FR); F Lan Hn Soc; Hnr Roll; Dbte Team; French Clb; Fncg (V); Golf (V); Yrbk (R); 5 on French Language AP Exam; Nationally Ranked-National French Exam; International Business; Interior Design

MARTE, JENICE; CARTERET, NJ; BISHOP GEORGE AHR HS; (JR); Hi Hnr Roll; Hnr Roll; Nat Hon Sy; WWAHSS; Yth Ldrshp Prog; Comm Volntr; Peer Tut/Med; Chrch Yth Grp; Prom Com; Svce Clb; Spanish Clb; Ch Chr; Tennis (VJ L); Cl Off (V S, T); CR (R); National Honors Society; Congressional Youth Leadership Council; Bio Medical Engineering; Pharmaceuticals; Yale U; U of Miami

MARTE, RUBEN; JERSEY CITY, NJ; SNYDER HS; (SO); Pep Bnd; Bsball (V); Ftball (V); Computer Technician; Ramapo College

MARTIN, CATHY; LANDING, NJ; ROXBURY HS; (JR); Comm Volntr; Aqrium Clb; DARE; Emplmnt; Key Club; Scouts; Tchrs Aide; Skiing (V C); Swmg (V L); Girl Scout Silver Award / Key Club; Freshman Volleyball & Softball; Elementary Education; Special Education; Rowan U; Montclair U

MARTIN, RACHEL S; PT PLEASANT, NJ; PT PLEASANT BORO HS; (JR); Hnr Roll; Nat Hon Sy; Comm Volntr; Emplmnt; Tmpl Yth Grp; Bnd; Clr Grd; Teacher; Grad School

MARTIN, SEANETTE A; IRVINGTON, NJ; IRVINGTON HS; (JR); Comm Volntr; Hosp Aide; Law Degree; Seton Hall Prep

MARTINEZ, ALEJANDRA; NORTH BERGEN, NJ; NORTH BERGEN HS; (JR); F Lan Hn Soc; Hi Hnr Roll; Hnr Roll; Nat Hon Sy; WWAHSS; Cmptr Clb; Key Club; Lib Aide; Italian Clb; Track; Stu Cncl; CR; Secretary and Webmaster of the Italian Club; Accounting (CPA)

MARTINEZ, BRENDA L; CLIFTON, NJ; PASSAIC CTY TECH INST; (SR); Architect

MARTINEZ, CHRISTOPHER; UNION CITY, NJ; EMERSON HS; (FR); Hnr Roll; Perf Att; CARE; Comm Volntr; Peer Tut/Med; DARE; Dbte Team; Key Club; Mth Clb/Tm; Mus Clb; ROTC; Sci Clb; Spanish Clb; Pep Bnd; Cl Off (V); Algebra Club; Lawyer (Law); Rutgers U

MARTINEZ, EVELIN; ELIZABETH, NJ; ELIZABETH HS; (JR); Ctznshp Aw; F Lan Hn Soc; Hi Hnr Roll; Hnr Roll; Nat Hon Sy; WWAHSS; Yth Ldrshp Prog; Comm Volntr; Chrch Yth Grp; DARE; Emplmnt; Key Club; Outdrs Clb; Sftball (V); Vllyball (V); Cl Off (T); Lit Mag (E); Confirmation, Roman Catholic; Lawyer; English Teacher; Rutgers U; Kean U

MARTINEZ, JENNIFER; NEW BRUNSWICK, NJ; NEW BRUNSWICK HS; (JR); Hnr Roll; Nat Hon Sy; Sci Fairs; St of Mnth; Comm Volntr; Chrch Yth Grp; DARE; Drma Clb; Mus Clb; Chr; Ch Chr; Drl Tm; SP/M/VS; Child Psychology; Music; Douglass College-Rutgers; Rutgers U

MARTINEZ, JOAN B; BELLEVILLE, NJ; BELLEVILLE HS; (JR); Hnr Roll; Peer Tut/Med; Chrch Yth Grp; Drma Clb; Emplmnt; Tchrs Aide; Tmpl Yth Grp; Wdwrkg Clb; Ch Chr; Ftball (V); Baptismal; Sound Engineering; Paralegal; William Paterson; Seton Hall

MARTINEZ, JULIE; NORTH BERGEN, NJ; NORTH BERGEN HS; (SO); Hi Hnr Roll, WWAHSS; Comm Volntr; Key Club; Chr; Track; Cl Off (S); CR (R); Plastic Surgery; Columbia U

MARTINEZ, MADELINE; NEWARK, NJ; MALCOLM X SHABAZZ HS; (JR); Hi Hnr Roll; Hnr Roll; Nat Hon Sy; St of Mnth; WWAHSS; DARE; Dbte Team; Sftball; Stu Cncl

MARTINEZ, MARTIKA; KEARNY, NJ; KEARNY HS; (FR); Comm Volntr; Chrch Yth Grp; Outdrs Clb; Tmpl Yth Grp; Ch Chr; Baby Sitting; Play in My School Band with Love; Summer Program for Needy Kids; RN Nursing; Harvard U..; Kean College

MARTINEZ, PRISCILLA M; UNION CITY, NJ; UNION HILL HS; (SO); F Lan Hn Soc; Hi Hnr Roll; Hnr Roll; Perf Att; WWAHSS; Comm Volntr; Key Club; MuAlphaTh; Italian Clb; Chr; Bskball (VJ); Cr Ctry (V); Scr Kpr (V); Sftball (J); Track (V); Stu Cncl (R); Won Medals in Track and Cross-Country; Nursing; Elementary Education; Boston U; Bloomfield College

MARTINEZ, STEVEN; HARRISON, NJ; HARRISON HS; (SO); Hnr Roll; Drma Clb; Bnd; Pep Bnd; Stg Cre; Wt Lftg; Computer Engineer; NJIT, New Jersey Institute of Tech; New Jersey City U

MARTINEZ, WALESKA; PLAINFIELD, NJ; PLAINFIELD HS; (SO); Hnr Roll; St of Mnth; WWAHSS; Chr; Dnce; Business; Medical; Saint John's U; Rutgers U

MARTINO, KELLI L; WOODBINE, NJ; MIDDLE TOWNSHIP HS; (SO); Hnr Roll; Nat Sci Aw; Sci Fairs; Peer Tut/Med; Chrch Yth Grp; Key Club; Mth Clb/Tm; Sci Clb; Sftball (V L); Swmg (V L); Math League; Science League; Engineering; Music; Rowan U; Rutgers U

MARTORELL, MATTHEW; KEANSBURG, NJ; KEANSBURG HS; (SO); Hnr Roll; ArtClub; Art Honors Society; Animation; New York U

MARVIN, JAMES M; BRICK, NJ; BRICK TWP MEMORIAL HS; (SR); Hi Hnr Roll; Hnr Roll; St of Mnth; DARE; Key Club; Bsball (VJC); Bskball (JC); Skiing; CR; Sch Ppr; Life Guard- 4 Years; Major in Mathematics Education; U Delaware Rowan; College of New Jersey

MARZIGLIANO, BRIANNA N; LINCROFT, NJ; MIDDLETOWN HS SOUTH; (JR); DAR; F Lan Hn Soc; Hi Hnr Roll; Hnr Roll; Nat Hon Sy; WWAHSS; Comm Volntr; Peer Tut/Med; Spec Olymp Vol; Emplmnt; Prom Com; Svce Clb; Spanish Clb; Fld Hky (V CL); Sftball (J); CR (R); The National Society of HS Scholars; Communications; Math / Spanish; College of New Jersey; U of Maryland

MARZOCCA, STEPHANIE; SOMERSET, NJ; FRANKLIN HS; (JR); Hnr Roll; St of Mnth; WWAHSS; Hosp Aide; Jr Cls League; Sccr (V L); Track (V L); Biology; Rowan U; Rutgers U: Cook College

MASCO, MICHAEL; OAKHURST, NJ; OCEAN TOWNSHIP HS; (JR); Nat Hon Sy; Comm Volntr; DARE; DECA; Emplmnt; Key Club; Lib Aide; Sci Clb; Wdwrkg Clb; Italian Clb; Stg Cre; Bdmtn (L); Cyclg (L); Ftball (L); Skiing (L); Swmg (L); Wt Lftg (L); Cl Off (R); Sch Ppr (R); Everyday Hero of the Month; Broadcasting; Meteorology; Western Connecticut

MASHEEB, ZAHRAH; BOGOTA, NJ; BERGEN CTY AC; (JR); F Lan Hn Soc; Hi Hnr Roll; Nat Mrt Semif; Pres Ac Ftns Aw; Yth Ldrshp Prog; Amnsty Intl; Peer Tut/Med; ArtClub; Chess; Prom Com; French Clb; Chr; Vllyball (V L); Cl Off (V); Stu Cncl (R); Vice President of Amnesty International Chapter; Selected Peer Leader in Spark Program; Physics; Medicine; Columbia U; New York U

MATASSA, DAN; SADDLE BROOK, NJ; PARAMUS CATHOLIC HS; (SR); F Lan Hn Soc; Hi Hnr Roll; Hnr Roll; Nat Hon Sy; Comm Volntr; Mth Clb/Tm; Spanish Clb; Bowling, JV; Medical Doctor (PhD); LaSalle U; Lehigh U

MATERA, CHRISTINE F; MOORESTOWN, NJ; CAMDEN CATHOLIC HS; (SO); Hnr Roll; Bskball (V L); Two Time AAU National Basketball Champion 2002 / 2004; Medicine; Coaching; Princeton U; Duke U

MATHANGANI, JEFF; PISCATAWAY, NJ; PISCATAWAY HS; (SR); Hnr Roll; Comm Volntr; Red Cr Aide; Scouts; Bskball (J); Sccr (J); Wt Lftg (VJ); Volunteered for Global Literacy Project; Making the National Honor Roll; Automotive Technology; Middlesex County College; Rutgers U

MATHENY, NICOLE; KEANSBURG, NJ; KEANSBURG HS; (SR); Hnr Roll; Otst Ac Ach Awd; Forensic Scientist; Monmouth U; Rutgers U

MATHEWS, KRYSSA L; MANCHESTER TOWNSHIP, NJ; MANCHESTER TWP HS; (FR); Hi Hnr Roll; Hnr Roll; Otst Ac Ach Awd; Pres Ac Ftns Aw; Comm Volntr; DARE; Emplmnt; Fr of Library; Pep Squd; Scouts; Spanish Clb; GS - Bronze Award; Graduated Barbizon Modeling School; Law; Chef; Harvard U; Princeton U

MATIAS, MELANIE A; BELLEVILLE, NJ; BELLEVILLE HS; (SO); Hnr Roll; WWAHSS; Comm Volntr; Key Club; Vsity Clb; Clb; Bskball (VJ); Cr Ctry (V L); Member At-Large - Student Government; Secondary Education; Culinary Arts

MAURO, JAMES; MILFORD, NJ; DELAWARE VALLEY REG HS; (SO); Hi Hnr Roll; Perf Att; Comm Volntr; Chess, DARE; Key Club; Sci Clb; Bnd; Amateur Radio Operator; Cherryville Reporter Assn; Scientist-Chemist/ Biology; Engineering; Rutgers U

MAXON, SEAN; TOWNSHIP OF WASHINGTON, NJ; WESTWOOD REG JR/SR HS; (FR); Hi Hnr Roll; Hnr Roll; Moguts Inc. (School Store); Relay for Life Cancer Walk; Computer Science; Criminal Justice; Fairleigh Dickinson U

MAY, TARA R; RAHWAY, NJ; RAHWAY HS; (FR); Hi Hnr Roll; Hnr Roll; Otst Ac Ach Awd; Pres Ac Ftns Aw; DARE; Drma Clb; ROTC; Chr; SP/M/VS; Sftball (J); Sch Ppr (E, R); Rahway MC JROTC; Forensic Science; Culinary Arts; Drexel U; Rutgers U

MAYA, MELISSA; HAWTHORNE, NJ; HAWTHORNE HS; (JR); F Lan Hn Soc; Gov Hnr Prg; Hi Hnr Roll; Hnr Roll; Nat Hon Sy; Perf Att; WWAHSS; Yth Ldrshp Prog; Comm Volntr; Hosp Aide; Peer Tut/Med; Biology Clb; Chrch Yth Grp; DARE; Emplmnt; Lib Aide; NYLC; Off Aide; Spanish Clb; Stg Cre; Sccr (J); Tennis (J); Track (J); Wt Lftg (J); Cl Off (R); Stu Cncl (S); CR (R); National Youth Leadership Forum on Medicine; Biology Major; Pre-Med

MAYER, COLLEEN E; EGG HARBOR TOWNSHIP, NJ; EGG HARBOR TOWNSHIP HS; (FR); Hi Hnr Roll; Hnr Roll; WWAHSS; Peer Tut/Med; Jr Cls League; Sch Ppr (R); Academic Challenge Club Member; Varsity Scholar; Engineering; Law; U of Pennsylvania; Dartmouth College

MAYER, KATHERINE; ALLENTOWN, NJ; ALLENTOWN HS; (JR); Hi Hnr Roll; St of Mnth; Comm Volntr; Chrch Yth Grp; Emplmnt; Latin Clb; Chr; SP/M/VS; Tennis (J); Stu Cncl (R); CR; Lit Mag (R); Yrbk (R); Optimist Club; Grammar Club

MAZLAGIC, SANDRA; MONTCLAIR, NJ; MONTCLAIR HS; (JR); F Lan Hn Soc; Hi Hnr Roll; Nat Hon Sy; Nat Ldrshp Svc; Pres Ac Ftns Aw; Sci Fairs; Sci/Math Olympn; St of Mnth; Comm Volntr; ArtClub; Emplmnt; Mth Clb/Tm; Mod UN; Mus Clb; Spanish Clb; Bnd; Jzz Bnd; Mch Bnd; Vllyball (V L); Cl Off (P); Sch Ppr (R); School Musical Pit Band; Community Band; Mathematics

MAZUR, JOSEPH J; BRIDGEWATER, NJ; BRIDGEWATER-RARITAN HS; (JR); F Lan Hn Soc; Hi Hnr Roll; Hnr Roll; Nat Hon Sy; St of Mnth; Red Cr Aide; FBLA; Key Club; Italian Clb; Jzz Bnd; Orch; Bowling Awards; Piano Awards; Business; Princeton U; New York U

MAZZEO, KAMI; HAMMONTON, NJ; VICTORY CHRISTIAN SCH; (JR); Hnr Roll; Sci Fairs; Chr; Bskball (V CL); Cr Ctry (V); Sccr (V L); Sftball (V L); Track (V); Cl Off; Music Education; Music Performance; U of the Arts; West Chester U

MC CALL, KIMAYA; HILLSIDE, NJ; HILLSIDE HS; (FR); Hnr Roll; Chrch Yth Grp; Ch Chr; Dnce; SP/M/VS; Chrldg (V)

MC CARTHY, CAROLINE; EAST WINDSOR, NJ; HIGHTSTOWN HS; (JR); Hi Hnr Roll; Hnr Roll; Nat Hon Sy; Comm Volntr; Peer Tut/Med; Red Cr Aide; Emplmnt; Off Aide; French Clb; Track (J); Sch Ppr (R); Philosophy Club-06 President; Mock Trial Team; Neuroscience; Pre-Med; Vanderbilt U; U of Rochester

MC CARTHY IV, JOHN J; KEARNY, NJ; ST BENEDICT'S PREP HS; (SR); Hi Hnr Roll; Nat Hon Sy; Sci Fairs; Comm Volntr; Peer Tut/Med; Emplmnt; Track (V L); Wt Lftg (V); Wrstlg (J); CR (R); Lit Mag (R, P); Outstanding Engineer Award-NSBE; NJIT Communications Award, Pres. National Honor Society; English; U of Scranton

MC CLINTOCK, KYLE; SEWELL, NJ; WASHINGTON TWP HS; (SO); Sccr (J); Track (V L); Accounting; Marketing

MC CRIMMON, MARISA; BAYONNE, NJ; BAYONNE HS; (JR); Hnr Roll; St of Mnth; WWAHSS; Hosp Aide; Peer Tut/Med; ArtClub; Chrch Yth Grp; DARE; Emplmnt; FBLA; Jr Ach; Lib Aide; Photog; Ch Chr; Vllyball (C); Wt Lftg (L); Wrstlg (L); CR (R); Yrbk (P); Art Club

MC CUSKER, MEGHAN; SEWELL, NJ; GLOUCESTER CATHOLIC HS; (JR); Hnr Roll; MVP; Comm Volntr; Hab For Humty Volntr; Emplmnt; Prom Com; Svce Clb; Sccr (V CL); Track (V); CR (R); Yrbk (R); CCD Teacher; Community Service; Sports Management; Education; Stockton College, NJ; Monmouth U

MC DONNELL, JACLYNN N; TOMS RIVER, NJ; MONSIGNOR DONOVAN HS; (SO); Hnr Roll; Sci Fairs; Comm Volntr; DARE; Lttrmn Clb; Pep Squd; Svce Clb; SADD; Chr; Ch Chr; Chrldg (VJ L); Gmnstcs (V); Scr Kpr (VJ L); Graduate of Barbizon Modeling; Contestant National American Miss Pageant; Veterinarian; Princeton U; U of Miami

MC GOVERN, RYAN T; RIVER EDGE, NJ; RIVERDELL REG HS; (JR); WWAHSS; Comm Volntr; Ftball (V L); Swmg (V); Track (J); Stu Cncl (T); President's Award; Volunteer Basketball Coach for Special Stars / Volunteer to Feed the Homeless in NJ

MC GREGOR, MATTHEW C; TEANECK, NJ; RUTGERS PREP SCH; (JR); Hi Hnr Roll; Hnr Roll; Comm Volntr; Hosp Aide; Chrch Yth Grp; Emplmnt; FBLA; Prom Com; Chr; Ch Chr; Swmg (V L), Yrbk (R); Advanced Ceramics; Work Submitted for National Competition; Law Degree; Liberal Arts Major (Undergrad); Columbia U; Fordham U

MC GWIER, MEGHAN S; HIGHTSTOWN, NJ; THE PEDDIE SCH; (JR); Hi Hnr Roll; Hnr Roll; Comm Volntr; Emplmnt; Mth Clb/Tm; Scouts; Svce Clb; Spanish Clb; Chr; Dnce; Bskball (V); Sccr (V L); Track (V); Stu Cncl (R); CR (R); Commented List for Biology and Spanish; Honorable Mention for All-Prep Soccer 2003; Pre-Medical (MD); Biology; Brown U, John's Hopkins U; The U of Pennsylvania

MC INTYRE, AMANDA; TRENTON, NJ; HAMILTON HS EAST; (SO); Red Cr Aide; Scouts; Swmg (J); Architecture; Engineering; Penn State U

MC KENZIE, SOPHIA; JERSEY CITY, NJ; LINCOLN HS; (JR); Nat Hon Sy; Comm Volntr; Peer Tut/Med; Chess; Chrch Yth Grp; Cmptr Clb; DARE; Key Club; Clr Grd; Drl Tm; Sch Ppr (R); Certificate of Appreciation From Columbia University–s School of Public Health, Young Poets of America; American Cancer Society Breast Cancer Walk, Casper After School Program, Rebel Anti-Drug Program; Computer Science / Computer & Software Engineering; Computer / Information Science; Clark Atlanta University; New Jersey Institute of Technology

MC KERNAN, JOHN F; OAK RIDGE, NJ; JEFFERSON TWP HS; (FR); Comm Volntr; Lcrsse (J); Culinary Institute

MC KINNEY, SEAN-ERIK; MORRISTOWN, NJ; MORRISTOWN HS; (FR); Hnr Roll; Nat Mrt LOC; Disc Jockey for High School Radio Station; Communications; Graphic Design; U of Buffalo; Canisius College

MC LENDON, RAHSHAN; NEWARK, NJ; ESSEX CTY VOC-TECH HS; (SO); Hnr Roll; Yth Ldrshp Prog; Comm Volntr; Chrch Yth Grp; DARE; Emplmnt; Tchrs Aide; Tmpl Yth Grp; Ch Chr; SP/M/VS; President of Cooking Ministry At Church.; Business; Law; Montclair State U; New York U

MC MILLAN, BRIANNE; BRICK, NJ; MONSIGNOR DONOVAN HS; (JR); Hnr Roll; Otst Ac Ach Awd; Perf Att; Sci Fairs; St of Mnth; Hab For Humty Volntr; Peer Tut/Med; DARE; Drma Clb; Emplmnt; Key Club; SADD; Dnce; SP/M/VS; Stg Cre; Lit Mag (R); Mentor for Big Brother Big Sister; Member of Thespian Society; Psychology; Villanova U; Monmouth U

MC MORRIN, YASMINE-IMANI; SOUTH ORANGE, NJ; COLUMBIA HS; (JR); Hnr Roll; Sci Fairs; Comm Volntr; Peer Tut/Med; Chrch Yth Grp; Ch Chr; Dnce; Orch; Golf; Scr Kpr (J); Track (J); Vllyball (J); Cl Off (S); Sch Ppr (R); Pre-Law; Fashion Merchandising; Spelman College; Columbia U

MC PHAIL, ARTESIA S; PLAINFIELD, NJ; PLAINFIELD HS; (FR); Hnr Roll; Chrch Yth Grp; Bnd; Ch Chr; Dnce; Mch Bnd; Sftball (J); Swmg (V); Mechanical Engineering; Interior Architect; Clark Atlanta U; Florida A & M U

MC PHERSON, BENJAMIN; MILFORD, NJ; DELAWARE VALLEY REG HS; (SO); Hi Hnr Roll; Hnr Roll; Perf Att; Sci Fairs; Comm Volntr; 4-H; DARE; Emplmnt; Vsity Clb; Bnd; Jzz Bnd; Mch Bnd; Pep Bnd; Track (V L); Vsy Clb (L); Drumline; Animation/Special FX; Academy of Art U; Art Institute of Philadelphia

MC PHERSON, TIFFANY L; EGG HARBOR TOWNSHIP, NJ; EGG HARBOR TOWNSHIP HS; (JR); MVP; Pres Ac Ftns Aw; WWAHSS; Comm Volntr; Peer Tut/Med; Chrch Yth Grp; FCA; Key Club; Prom Com; Svce Clb; Ch Chr; Dnce; Bskball (VJ); Sccr (V); Sftball (J); Track (V); Cl Off (R); Athlete of the Month May 2005; Broadcast Journalism/Film & Studio Production; Business Management; New York U; U of Maryland

Mc Pherson, Tiffany L
Egg Harbor Township HS
Egg Harbor Township, NJ

Mc Pherson, Benjamin
Delaware Valley Reg HS
Milford, NJ

Mc Carthy IV, John J
St Benedict's Prep HS
Kearny, NJ

Mazlagic, Sandra
Montclair HS
Montclair, NJ

Matera, Christine F
Camden Catholic HS
Moorestown, NJ

Martino, Kelli L
Middle Township HS
Woodbine, NJ

Martinez, Jennifer
New Brunswick HS
New Brunswick, NJ

Martinez, Martika
Kearny HS
Kearny, NJ

Mathangani, Jeff
Piscataway HS
Piscataway, NJ

Mazur, Joseph J
Bridgewater-Raritan HS
Bridgewater, NJ

Mc Donnell, Jaclynn N
Monsignor Donovan HS
Toms River, NJ

Mc Morrin, Yasmine-Imani
Columbia HS
South Orange, NJ

MC QUISTON, NICOLA; WARREN, NJ; OAK KNOLL SCH; (JR); F Lan Hn Soc; Hi Hnr Roll; Hnr Roll; Pres Ac Ftns Aw; Chrch Yth Grp; Drma Clb; Mus Clb; Scouts; Chr; Bskball (V C); Sccr (V); Vllyball (V C); Sch Ppr (R); I Have Founded a Non-For-Profit Organization Named Curequest.; French; Journalism; The U of Notre Dame; The U of Michigan

MC RAE, RASHANDA M A A; TRENTON, NJ; TRENTON CTRL HS; (JR); Ctznshp Aw; Hnr Roll; Nat Hon Sy; Perf Att; St of Mnth; WWAHSS; Peer Tut/Med; Mod UN; Photog; ROTC; Clr Grd; Dnce; Drl Tm; SP/M/VS; Bskball (J); Sccr (J); Sftball (V); Cl Off (P); Stu Cncl (S); CR (S); Lit Mag (E); Law; Nursing; Georgia State; Temple U

MC RIMMON, KIARA; MONTCLAIR, NJ; MONTCLAIR HS; (SO); Hnr Roll; Perf Att; Spec Olymp Vol; Chr; Cr Ctry (J); Track (V L); CR (R); Sch Ppr (R); In Teen Pep; Major in Biology; PhD; UCLA; Stanford U

MEDINA, DINORAH; WEST NEW YORK, NJ; MEMORIAL HS; (JR); Sci Fairs; Peer Tut/Med; DARE; Emplmnt; Acpl Chr; Chrldg (L); Swmg (L); Vllyball (J); Cl Off (T); Model Professionally for an Agency; Business; Psychology; Monmouth U; Montclair State College

MEDULME, CLAUSERLINE; EAST ORANGE, NJ; EAST ORANGE CAMPUS HS; (SO); F Lan Hn Soc; Hnr Roll; Perf Att; NATIONAL C Clb; National Caribbean Club; I Was Caught Being Positive; Nurse; Bachelor Degree; Kean U

MEHRING, LINDSEY; ANNANDALE, NJ; NORTH HUNTERDON HS; (FR); Hnr Roll; Otst Ac Ach Awd; Yth Ldrshp Prog; Comm Volntr; Chrch Yth Grp; Drma Clb; Emplmnt; Scouts; Bnd; Dnce; Mch Bnd; SP/M/VS; Bskball; Cr Ctry; Lcrsse; Sftball; Vllyball; Girl Scout Silver Award; Johns Hopkins Talent Search; Education; Environmental Science; Flagler College; Lafayette College

MEHROTRA, PRIYANKA; MORRIS PLAINS, NJ; PARSIPPANY HILLS HS; (FR); Hi Hnr Roll; Hnr Roll; WWAHSS; Comm Volntr; Hab For Humty Volntr; Key Club; Mth Clb/Tm; Tmpl Yth Grp; Dnce; Bskball (J); Track (J); Indian Dance Competition; Pediatrician; Psychologist; Columbia U

MEI, BRITTANY H; MAYWOOD, NJ; HACKENSACK HS; (JR); Hnr Roll; Hosp Aide; Chrch Yth Grp; Emplmnt; Prom Com; Tchrs Aide; Chrldg (V L); Cr Ctry (J L); Track (J L); CR (R); Nursing RN; Ramapo College; Holy Name

MEI, GRAYCE; PRINCETON JCT, NJ; WWPHS SOUTH; (JR); Nat Mrt LOC; WWAHSS; Comm Volntr; Hosp Aide; BPA; FBLA; Mth Clb/Tm; Sci Clb; Chinese Clb; Orch; Track (J); Silver Satori in Talent Network; Concert Mistress; Investment Banker; Banker; Princeton U; Harvard U

MEJIA, JEASON; UNION CITY, NJ; UNION HILL HS; (JR); Hi Hnr Roll; Hnr Roll; Nat Hon Sy; Otst Ac Ach Awd; Perf Att; Sci Fairs; St of Mnth; WWAHSS; Comm Volntr; Key Club; Tchrs Aide; Social Studies Honor Society; Who's Who Among American High School Students; Computer Graphics; NYIT

MEKITA, MEGAN; LAKE HIAWATHA, NJ; PARSIPPANY HS; (SR); F Lan Hn Soc; Hi Hnr Roll; Hnr Roll; Nat Hon Sy; St of Mnth; WWAHSS; Comm Volntr; Peer Tut/Med; Chrch Yth Grp; Dbte Team; Emplmnt; Key Club; Mth Clb/Tm; Bnd; Drm Mjr; Mch Bnd; Track (V C); Sch Ppr (E); International Relations; Attending the College of New Jersey

MELE, MELISSA; PARSIPPANY, NJ; PARSIPPANY HS; (JR); F Lan Hn Soc; Hnr Roll; Perf Att; St of Mnth; WWAHSS; Comm Volntr; AL Aux Girls; Chrch Yth Grp; Emplmnt; Prom Com; ROTC; Vsity Clb; Italian Clb; Dnce; PP Ftbl; Scr Kpr (V L); Sftball (V); Vsy Clb; Vllyball (V); Cl Off (T, R); Stu Cncl (R); CR (R); Yrbk (R, P); Executive Board of Interact Club; Education; The College of New Jersey; Montclair U

MELILLO, TARA N J; MIDDLETOWN, NJ; MIDDLETOWN HS NORTH; MS; Hi Hnr Roll; Hnr Roll; Sci Fairs; St of Mnth; Peer Tut/Med; Spec Olymp Vol; Mus Clb; Outdrs Clb; Scouts; SADD; Bnd; Clr Grd; Skiing; Sailing; Nursing; Brookdale

MENA, ALEXANDER; LINDEN, NJ; LINDEN HS; (SO); Hnr Roll; Sci Fairs; St of Mnth; WWAHSS; Chrch Yth Grp; Bsball (V); Wt Lftg (V); Electronics Master's Degree; Miami U

MENDOZA, EDSON; BAYONNE, NJ; BAYONNE HS; (JR); Hnr Roll; Perf Att; Sci Fairs; St of Mnth; Comm Volntr; Peer Tut/Med; Photog; Sccr (L); Sch Ppr (P); Law Enforcement; Teacher; Rutgers

MENESES, GISSELLE; ELIZABETH, NJ; ELIZABETH HS; (FR); Comm Volntr; Drma Clb; Key Club; Acpl Chr; Ch Chr; Dnce; SP/M/VS; Bsball (J); Bskball (C); Sccr (J); Sftball (J); CR (R); Bachelor's Degree and Master's Degree; U of South Florida State; Rutgers U

MENGISTU, ABNET; EAST BRUNSWICK, NJ; EAST BRUNSWICK HS; (SO); Hnr Roll; Emplmnt; Svce Clb; Public Health/Medicine; International Relations; Boston College; Lehigh U

MENINO, LAUREN J; SHORT HILLS, NJ; MILLBURN HS; (SO); WWAHSS; Yth Ldrshp Prog; Key Club; Vsity Clb; Spanish Clb; Fld Hky (J); PP Ftbl (J); Sftball (V); Science Team

MENSCHING, DAVID; GARWOOD, NJ; ARTHUR L JOHNSON HS; (JR); Nat Hon Sy; WWAHSS; Emplmnt; Key Club; Italian Clb; Bsball (V); Bskball (J); Sch Ppr (E); Statistics; Civil Engineering; U of FL; GA Tech

MENSCHING, ZOEI B; GARWOOD, NJ; ARTHUR L JOHNSON HS; (FR); WWAHSS; Key Club; Italian Clb; Scr Kpr; Sftball; Sch Ppr (P); Teaching; Psychology; U of Miami; U of FL

MERCEDES, CARLOS; BAYONNE, NJ; BAYONNE HS; (FR)

MERISIER, CARLINE; ORANGE, NJ; ORANGE HS; (FR); Hnr Roll; Perf Att; Chrch Yth Grp; DARE; Mus Clb; Chr; Ch Chr; Dnce; CR (R); Lawyer; Doctor; Harvard Law; Montclair U

MEYER, LINDA; TRENTON, NJ; NOTTINGHAM HS; (SO); Hnr Roll; Sci Fairs; St of Mnth; WWAHSS; Chrch Yth Grp; Emplmnt; Key Club; Scouts; Chr; SP/M/VS; Scr Kpr (V); Sccr (J); Key Club; Vocal Music Education; Westminster Choir College

MEYERS, CASSANDRA R; KEANSBURG, NJ; KEANSBURG HS; (SO); Hnr Roll; WWAHSS; Comm Volntr; ArtClub; Key Club; Clb; Bnd; Tennis; Sch Ppr; Nat'l Society of High School Scholars; Nat'l Art Honor Society; Japanese Studies; Creative Writing; Gettysburg College

MEYERS, ERIC; RANDOLPH, NJ; RANDOLPH HS; (JR); Hnr Roll; Otst Ac Ach Awd; Yth Ldrshp Prog; Comm Volntr; Key Club; Lib Aide; Mod UN; NtlFrnscLg; NYLC; Quill & Scroll; Svce Clb; Spch Team; Bnd; SP/M/VS; Sch Ppr (E, R, P); Forensics-State Finalist, Degree of Special Distinction; School Newspaper-Editor-In-Chief, Leadership Awards; Journalism; Syracuse U; Boston U

MEYERS, KEVIN; LINDEN, NJ; LINDEN HS; (SO); Hi Hnr Roll; Hnr Roll; DARE; ROTC; German Clb; Math; Science

MIAN, HUMAYUN; SUMMIT, NJ; SUMMIT SR HS; (SO); Hi Hnr Roll; Hnr Roll; MVP; Sci Fairs; Comm Volntr; Hosp Aide; Peer Tut/Med; Cmptr Clb; DARE; Emplmnt; Key Club; Mth Clb/Tm; Photog; Bdmtn (J); Bskball (J); Honor Roll; Doctor; Medicine; Rutgers; Duke U

MICELI, MELISSA; EATONTOWN, NJ; MONMOUTH REG HS; (JR); Hnr Roll; Nat Hon Sy; WWAHSS; Yth Ldrshp Prog; Comm Volntr; DECA; Drma Clb; Emplmnt; FBLA; Key Club; Prom Com; Spanish Clb; Cl Off (P); Yrbk (P); Marketing; International Business; Montclair State U; Ramapo College

MICHEL, CHRISTINE; WEST ORANGE, NJ; ESSEX CTY VOC-TECH HS; (SO); Hnr Roll; Scouts; Dnce; Bskball (J); Mar Art (V); Track (J); Law; Psychology; Monclair State U; Rutgers U

MICKENS, LATASHA; JERSEY CITY, NJ; WM. C DICKINSON HS; (JR); Hnr Roll; Perf Att; St of Mnth; WWAHSS; Yth Ldrshp Prog; Comm Volntr; Hosp Aide; Peer Tut/Med; Chrch Yth Grp; Dbte Team; Drma Clb; FBLA; Pep Squd; Prom Com; Scouts; Tchrs Aide; Ch Chr; Dnce; Drl Tm; SP/M/VS; GAA; Cl Off (V); Stu Cncl (V); CR (V); Yrbk (E); Vice President of Student Council; Honor Society; Business and Management; Business and Computer Management; Fairleigh Dickinson; Florida State

MILLAR, DAVID; CLIFTON, NJ; QUEEN OF PEACE HS; (JR); Hi Hnr Roll; Nat Hon Sy; Nat Sci Aw; St of Mnth; Valdctrian; WWAHSS; Yth Ldrshp Prog; Amnsty Intl; Comm Volntr; Peer Tut/Med; Chess; Dbte Team; Emplmnt; Mod UN; Tech Clb; Ch Chr; Stu Cncl (R); Yrbk (E); President of Model United Nations Team; Lead America Alumni; International Diplomacy / Studies; Asian Studies; Haverford College; Boston College

MILLER, LISA M; MERCHANTVILLE, NJ; PENNSAUKEN HS; (JR); All Am Sch; F Lan Hn Soc; Hnr Roll; Peer Tut/Med; SADD; German Clb; Lcrsse (V L); Sccr (V L); CR (R); Ll-American Scholar Award; Forensic Science; Biochemistry or Criminal Justice; Long Island U; Pittsburgh U

MILLS, MARY; PISCATAWAY, NJ; PISCATAWAY HS; (JR); Hnr Roll; Comm Volntr; Key Club; Scouts; Stg Cre; Swmg (L); Volunteered Read & Lead to Kids; Marine Biology; Marine Mammal Science; Stockton College

MILWARD, TARA L; PITMAN, NJ; PITMAN HS; (FR); Hi Hnr Roll; Hnr Roll; Key Club; PP Ftbl; Sccr; Sftball; Key Club; Honor Roll All Year; Criminal Investigation; Law/Journalism

MINAYA, CATHERINE; PERTH AMBOY, NJ; MIDDLESEX CTY VOC SCH-WOODBRIDGE; (FR); 4H Awd; Hi Hnr Roll; Hnr Roll; Otst Ac Ach Awd; Perf Att; St of Mnth; Comm Volntr; ArtClub; Chrch Yth Grp; Cmptr Clb; DARE; Emplmnt; Fr of Library; Pep Squd; Sign Clb; Acpl Chr; Chr; Ch Chr; Dnce; Chrldg (V); Gmnstcs (V); Stu Cncl (P); Sch Ppr (R); Peace Maker-4 times; Best Student Award; Nursing/Doctor; Business; Columbus U; Harbor U

MINEO, CONCETTA; SEWELL, NJ; WASHINGTON TOWNSHIP HS; (SR); Hnr Roll; Nat Hon Sy; St of Mnth; Comm Volntr; Peer Tut/Med; Emplmnt; FTA; Tchrs Aide; Chr; SP/M/VS; Mar Art; PP Ftbl; Yrbk (E); Writer for Courier-Post (Statistics Section); Recipient of Acceptance and Understanding Scholarship Award; Psychology with Pre-Medical Concentration; Rowan U

MINITELLI, THERESA A; CRANFORD, NJ; CRANFORD HS; (JR); Hnr Roll; Nat Hon Sy; Comm Volntr; Peer Tut/Med; Emplmnt; Photog; Sci Clb; Vsity Clb; Spanish Clb; Bskball (V CL); PP Ftbl (V); Sccr (VJ L); Yrbk (R, P); Business and Marketing; Graphic Design; U of Maryland; James Madison U

MIRANDA, CYNTHIA C; HILLSIDE, NJ; HILLSIDE HS; (FR); Lawyer Major in History

MIRANDA, JENNIFER; PISCATAWAY, NJ; PISCATAWAY HS; (SR); Hnr Roll; Chrch Yth Grp; DECA; Emplmnt; FBLA; Key Club; Photog; Prom Com; Dnce; SP/M/VS; Graphic Design; Kean U

MITCHELL, DANIEL B; BRIDGEWATER, NJ; BRIDGEWATER-RARITAN HS; (SO); Hnr Roll; Pres Ac Ftns Aw; WWAHSS; Key Club; French Clb; Orch

MITCHELL, TYNEISHA; EGG HARBOR TOWNSHIP, NJ; EGG HARBOR TOWNSHIP HS; (SO); Hnr Roll; Nat Hon Sy; WWAHSS; Comm Volntr; Hosp Aide; Chrch Yth Grp; Key Club; Off Aide; Svce Clb; Bnd; Mch Bnd; Chardon/Karate; Pharmacy; Rutgers U

MOAVEN, AURASCH; SHORT HILLS, NJ; MILLBURN HS; (FR); Hnr Roll; Key Club; Orch; Swmg (V L); Tennis (J); 3rd Degree Black Belt in Martial Arts; Life Scout in the Boy Scouts of America; Sports Medicine; Psychology; U of Pennsylvania; Yale U

MOGIRE, EMMANUEL; JERSEY CITY, NJ; ST PETER'S PREP; (SR); Ctznshp Aw; Gov Hnr Prg; Hnr Roll; WWAHSS; Yth Ldrshp Prog; Chrch Yth Grp; Prom Com; SADD; Ch Chr; Yrbk; Pharmacy; Villanova U; Providence College

MOHAN, BHARATH; BASKING RIDGE, NJ; DELBARTON SCH; (JR); Ctznshp Aw; Hi Hnr Roll; Perf Att; Sci Fairs; St of Mnth; Amnsty Intl; Comm Volntr; Chess; Cmptr Clb; DARE; Dbte Team; Lib Aide; Mth Clb/Tm; Sci Clb; Spch Team; Chr; Orch; Cyclg; Hsbk Rdg; NASA Funded - Summer Research Project in Nanotechnology at the U Arkansas / Planning to Publish a Paper; South Indian Classical Music Singer - Won Several Competitions; Computer Science; Business Administration / MBA; Princeton U; Carnegie Mellon U

MOJICA, CHRISTINA M; HOBOKEN, NJ; AC OF SACRED HEART HS; (SO); Hnr Roll; Nat Ldrshp Svc; Nat Mrt Sch Recip; Nat Stu Ath Day Aw; Yth Ldrshp Prog; Comm Volntr; DARE; Drma Clb; Mus Clb; NYLC; Acpl Chr; Chr; Ch Chr; SP/M/VS; Bskball (J); Vllyball (J); National Junior Honor Society; Master's in Criminal Justice; Master's in Law and Society; John Jay College of Criminal Justice; New York U

MOLINA, GUIDO A; WEST NEW YORK, NJ; HCST-NORTH HUDSON CTR; (SO); Hi Hnr Roll; Hnr Roll; MVP; Perf Att; Pres Ac Ftns Aw; St of Mnth; Peer Tut/Med; DARE; Bskball (V); Stu Cncl (R); Biology; Architect; Princeton U; Rutgers U

MOLINA, KEVIN; BELLEVILLE, NJ; ESSEX CTY VOC-TECH HS; (SO); Ctznshp Aw; Fut Prb Slvr; Hi Hnr Roll; Hnr Roll; MVP; Otst Ac Ach Awd; Perf Att; St of Mnth; WWAHSS; Yth Ldrshp Prog; Cmptr Clb; Emplmnt; Mth Clb/Tm; Bnd; Orch; SP/M/VS; Stg Cre; Bsball (L); Bskball (L); Sccr (J); Swmg (L); Tennis (L); Vllyball (L); Cl Off (S); CR (S); Business; Engineering; Miami U Hamilton; Montclair State U

MOLINA, PRISCILLA; ELIZABETH, NJ; ELIZABETH HS; (JR); F Lan Hn Soc; Hi Hnr Roll; Nat Hon Sy; Valdctrian; WWAHSS; Comm Volntr; Peer Tut/Med; Chrch Yth Grp; Emplmnt; Key Club; P to P St Amb Prg; Sci Clb; Stu Cncl (P, S); CR (R); Science League Award; (3) Piano Certificates; Science Field; Career in Medicine; Rutgers U; New York U

MOLINA JR, RICHARD; BELLEVILLE, NJ; ST BENEDICT'S PREP; (JR); Hi Hnr Roll; Hnr Roll; Nat Hon Sy; Yth Ldrshp Prog; Peer Tut/Med; Chess; NYLC; Quill & Scroll; Bsball (J); Fncg (V C); Stu Cncl (P); Sch Ppr (E, R, P); Honor Code Committee; Physics/Astronomy; Journalism; Notre Dame; Florida Institute of Technology

MOLLOY, BRITTANY A; ISELIN, NJ; JOHN F. KENNEDY MEMORIAL HS; (SO); Ctznshp Aw; Hnr Roll; Otst Ac Ach Awd; Pres Sch; St of Mnth; WWAHSS; Comm Volntr; DARE; Drma Clb; Key Club; Chr; SP/M/VS; Swg Chr; Chrldg (V CL); Sftball (J); Stu Cncl (R); Coaching Grammar School Cheerleading; Recreational Swim Team; Dramatic Arts; Biology; Columbia U; Rutgers U

MOLNER, MICHAEL J; PT PLEASANT BEACH, NJ; PT PLEASANT BEACH HS; (SR); MVP; WWAHSS; Emplmnt; Key Club; Wdwrkg Clb; Bsball (V CL); Ftball (V L); CR (R); Helped Organize - Breast Cancer Fundraiser; Montclair State U

MONACO, DEANNA; MT HOLLY, NJ; RANCOCAS VALLEY REG HS; (SO); Hi Hnr Roll; Hnr Roll; St of Mnth; WWAHSS; Comm Volntr; Spec Olymp Vol; Chrch Yth Grp; Key Club; Scouts; Italian Clb; Chr; National Honors of HS Scholars; Teacher / Pre-K - 8th Grade; Music

MONBRUN, FEGGENS M; RAHWAY, NJ; RAHWAY HS; (SO); Spec Olymp Vol; Chrch Yth Grp; Cmptr Clb; Outdrs Clb; ROTC; Bnd; Jzz Bnd; Mch Bnd; Pep Bnd; Rutgers U

Molloy, Brittany A
John F. Kennedy Memorial HS
Iselin, NJ

Mojica, Christina M
AC Of Sacred Heart HS
Hoboken, NJ

Mineo, Concetta
Washington Township HS
Sewell, NJ

Merisier, Carline
Orange HS
Orange, NJ

National
Honor Roll
Spring 2005

Mele, Melissa
Parsippany HS
Parsippany, NJ

Moaven, Aurasch
Millburn HS
Short Hills, NJ

Molina Jr, Richard
St Benedict's Prep
Belleville, NJ

Monaco, Deanna
Rancocas Valley Reg HS
Mt Holly, NJ

MONCHER, ERIC; MULLICA HILL, NJ; CLEARVIEW REG HS; (FR); Hi Hnr Roll; Hnr Roll; Key Club; NYLC; Latin Clb; Johns Hopkins - Center for Talented Youth; Medical Field; Business Field; Penn State U; Arizona State U

MONCION, JEFRY; JERSEY CITY, NJ; JAMES E FERRIS HS; (SO); Hnr Roll; Perf Att; Sci Fairs; St of Mnth; Peer Tut/Med; Mus Clb; Vsity Clb; French Clb; Drm Mjr; Bsball; Bskball (J); Dvng (J); Sftball (J); Swmg (V); Cl Off (V); Computer Designer; Computer Programmer; Boston College; Rutgers U

MONCRIEFFE, TIFFANY; JERSEY CITY, NJ; DR RONALD MC NAIR ACADEMIC HS; (FR); Hnr Roll; Otst Ac Ach Awd; Perf Att; DARE; Mod UN; Schol Bwl; Bnd; Bskball (J); Sccr (V); Sftball (J); President's Education Award for Academic Achievement; Law; Business and Finance; Harvard U School of Law; Howard U

MONROE, JULIE; BROWNS MILLS, NJ; PEMBERTON TWP HS; (SO); MVP; St of Mnth; Comm Volntr; Peer Tut/Med; DARE; Clb; Bnd; Stg Cre; Sftball (VLJ); Full Year Community Service in the School Building; Varsity and Junior Varsity Bowling Team; Historian; Professional Softball Player

MONTALVAN, CYNTHIA; RAHWAY, NJ; RAHWAY HS; (SR); Hnr Roll; USAA; WWAHSS; French Clb; Vllyball (V); Architecture; Interior Design; New Jersey Institute of Technology; New York Institute of Technology

MONTAQUE, MIKHALE; EAST ORANGE, NJ; CAMPUS HS; (FR); Perf Att; Chess; Mar Art (J); Computer & Designer; Coast Guard; Essex County College; Florida State University

MONTECINOS, LENIDYT; MADISON, NJ; MADISON HS; (JR); F Lan Hn Soc; Hi Hnr Roll; Hnr Roll; Comm Volntr; Hab For Humty Volntr; Key Club; Spanish Clb; Tennis (VJ); Yrbk (E); Frederick Douglass Scholar Program; Political Science; Engineering; Boston College; Columbia U

MOORE, DOROTHY A; PRINCETON, NJ; PRINCETON HS; (SO); Scouts; Svce Clb; Major Contributor to School Literary Magazine; Johns Hopkins Scholar; English / Poetry or Literary Criticism; Peace Studies; Rutgers U

MOORE, JENNIFER; PARAMUS, NJ; PARAMUS HS; (JR); F Lan Hn Soc; Hi Hnr Roll; Hnr Roll; Nat Hon Sy; Otst Ac Ach Awd; Pres Ac Ftns Aw; Pres Sch; WWAHSS; Yth Ldrshp Prog; Comm Volntr; DARE; Drma Clb; Emplmnt; Mus Clb; Pep Squd; Photog; Scouts; Svce Clb; Chr; Dnce; SP/M/VS; Chrldg (VJCL); Pre-Veterinary Medicine; Ithaca College; Colgate U

MOORE, ROBERT T; RAHWAY, NJ; RAHWAY HS; (SO); Hi Hnr Roll; Hnr Roll; WWAHSS; Yth Ldrshp Prog; Comm Volntr; HO'Br Yth Ldrshp; Key Club; Mod UN; SP/M/VS; Cr Ctry (L); Tennis; Track (J); Cl Off (P); Stu Cncl; CR; Economics; Chemistry; Brown U; Dartmouth College

MORALES, BARBARA I; TRENTON, NJ; TRENTON CTRL HS; (JR); Hi Hnr Roll; Hnr Roll; Otst Ac Ach Awd; St of Mnth; Yth Ldrshp Prog; Comm Volntr; Peer Tut/Med; Chrch Yth Grp; Emplmnt; Sccr (VJCL); Sftball (J); Swmg; I'm a Microsoft Office Specialist; Culinary Arts; Mercer County Community College

MORENO, RAUL; JERSEY CITY, NJ; MC NAIR ACADEMIC SCH; (FR); Hnr Roll; Perf Att; Salutrn; Sci Fairs; St of Mnth; WWAHSS; Comm Volntr; Spanish Clb; Mock Trial Team; Psychiatrist; Lawyer; Harvard U; Yale U

MORESTON, ANTHONY; CHERRY HILL, NJ; CHERRY HILL HS WEST; (JR); Cr Ctry (V); Track (V); ROTC-Vice Committee; Criminal Justice; San Jose State; William Patterson

MORETTI, JOSEPH; BLOOMFIELD, NJ; QUEEN OF PEACE HS; (SO); WWAHSS; Comm Volntr; Drma Clb; Mus Clb; SP/M/VS; Music Club Member; Video Games Designer; Graphic Arts

MORGAN, ELIZABETH A; WILLIAMSTOWN, NJ; WILLIAMSTOWN HS; (FR); Hnr Roll; Excellent Student; Computer Technician; Typist; Gloucester County College; Camden County College

MORGAN-ARHIN, KWESI; ROSELLE, NJ; ROSELLE CATHOLIC HS; (JR); Hnr Roll; Comm Volntr; Vsity Clb; Bskball (J); Track (V); Medicine; Pharmacy; Seton Hall U; Rutgers U

MORGUNOFF, DIANA; BRIGANTINE, NJ; HOLY SPIRIT HS; (MS); Hnr Roll; MVP; Perf Att; Sci Fairs; Comm Volntr; Aqrium Clb; ArtClub; Chrch Yth Grp; DARE; Emplmnt; Mus Clb; Bnd; Chr; Orch; SP/M/VS; Bdmtn (V); Ice Sktg (V); Sftball (V); Swmg (CL); 3 Year Band Award; Jr. Coach/Aide Award; Interior Design; Modeling; UCLA -U of California Los Angeles; NYU-New York U

MORILLA, JENNIFER; CLIFFSIDE PARK, NJ; CLIFFSIDE PARK HS; (SO); Comm Volntr; Hosp Aide; Red Cr Aide; Outdrs Clb; Dnce; Stg Cre; Track (V); Vllyball (J); Part of Student Council; Part of Class Council; Medicine; Doctor; New York U; Cornell U

MORIN, JACLYN M; FAIRVIEW, NJ; AC OF SACRED HEART HS; (SO); Hnr Roll; Nat Hon Sy; Comm Volntr; Peer Tut/Med; Tchrs Aide; Spanish Clb; Bskball (V C); Sftball (V); Vllyball (V); Physical Therapy; Fairleigh Dickinson U; Felician College

MOROWITZ, DAN; ALLENDALE, NJ; NORTHERN HIGHLANDS REG HS; (SO); Hnr Roll; Perf Att; Quiz Bowl; Italian Clb; Fncg (V); Doctor

MOROWITZ, MATT; ALLENDALE, NJ; NORTHERN HIGHLANDS REG HS; (SO); Hnr Roll; WWAHSS; Photog; Quiz Bowl; Italian Clb; Fncg (J); Major in Archaeology; Doctorate in Archaeology; Columbia U; George Washington U

MORRISON, BRITTANY K; MONTCLAIR, NJ; MONTCLAIR HS; (JR); Ctznshp Aw; Hnr Roll; St of Mnth; Yth Ldrshp Prog; Comm Volntr; DARE; Emplmnt; Lib Aide; Off Aide; Pep Squd; Prom Com; Svce Clb; SADD; Chr; Ch Chr; Clr Grd; SP/M/VS; Bsball; Bskball; Jr Usher Board President; Senior Youth Group Sergeant; Criminal Justice; Computer Technology

MORROBEL, DIANA L; NEWARK, NJ; GLADYS HILLMAN JONES SCH; MS; Ctznshp Aw; Hi Hnr Roll; Hnr Roll; Otst Ac Ach Awd; Perf Att; Sci Fairs; St of Mnth; St Optmst of Yr; ArtClub; Chrch Yth Grp; Cmptr Clb; Drma Clb; Mus Clb; Scouts; Spch Team; Tech Clb; Bnd; Ch Chr; Dnce; SP/M/VS; Bskball (V); Stu Cncl (V); CR (P); Yrbk (E); I Want to Be the Best Singer Ever.

MOSER, ANDREW R; FLEMINGTON, NJ; HUNTERDON CHRISTIAN AC; (JR); Hi Hnr Roll; Hnr Roll; Sci Fairs; Comm Volntr; Chess; Chrch Yth Grp; Cmptr Clb; Drma Clb; Spch Team; SP/M/VS; Stg Cre; Bskball (V C); Sccr (V); Sftball (VJ); Yrbk (R, P); Theology; Law Enforcement; Houghton College; Hartford U

MOSLEY, ASHLEY; NEWARK, NJ; BARRINGER HS; (JR); Hi Hnr Roll; Hnr Roll; MVP; Nat Sci Aw; Otst Ac Ach Awd; Perf Att; Sci Fairs; St of Mnth; Comm Volntr; Hosp Aide; ArtClub; Dbte Team; Drma Clb; Mus Clb; Ntl Beta Clb; Spch Team; Bnd; Clr Grd; Dnce; Pep Bnd; Bskball (J); Cr Ctry (J); Mar Art (C); Track (J); Wt Lftg (J); Stu Cncl (S); Chemistry / Master's Degree; Pharmacy / Chemistry / Master's Degree; Washington State U; Michigan State U

MOSLEY, TANNIA N; MONTCLAIR, NJ; MONTCLAIR HS; (JR); Hnr Roll; Peer Tut/Med; Spec Olymp Vol; Drl Tm; Bskball (L); Track (J); Law; Child Psychology; Howard U; Florida A & M U

MOSS, DE'NITA M; IRVINGTON, NJ; IRVINGTON HS; (SO); Hi Hnr Roll; Hnr Roll; Perf Att; WWAHSS

MOUNT JR, JOHN G; EDISON, NJ; ST JOSEPH'S HS; (JR); Hi Hnr Roll; Nat Hon Sy; WWAHSS; Chess; Mth Clb/Tm; French Clb; Bsball (J); Sccr; Track (J); 2005 Trophy 1st Place JV Board #2 NJSCF Journal; 2004 Cert. Algebra 2 First Place Math Fax League; Engineering/Business; Law/Medicine; U of Pennsylvania; Villanova

MOZIA, MICHAEL V; HACKENSACK, NJ; HACKENSACK HS; (SO); Hnr Roll; Pres Ac Ftns Aw; Hosp Aide; Cmptr Clb; Emplmnt; Sci Clb; Ftball (V); Track (J); CR (R); Science League Contestant; Mechanical Engineering; Electrical Engineering; Syracuse U; NJIT

MUHAMMAD, MALCOLM A; RAHWAY, NJ; RAHWAY HS; (JR); Hnr Roll; Hosp Aide; Chrch Yth Grp; Community Sports; Baseball & Basketball; Architecture; Engineering; New Jersey Institute of Technology

MULLEN, JEFFREY; MARLTON, NJ; CHEROKEE HS; (SR); Bskball (J); Cr Ctry (J); Sccr (J); Tennis (V CL); Adv Cncl (R); Stu Cncl (R); National Honor Society; Quantitative Finance; Economics; James Madison U (Admitting and Attending)

MULLER, ERICA; CLARK, NJ; ARTHUR L JOHNSON HS; (SO); F Lan Hn Soc; Hi Hnr Roll; WWAHSS; Yth Ldrshp Prog; Peer Tut/Med; Key Club; Photog; Prom Com; Sftball; Swmg (J); Yrbk (R); Spanish Honor Society; Key Club Award; Mathematics Education; Boston U; Drew U

MULROONEY, BRIANNA; SOMERVILLE, NJ; SOMERVILLE HS; (FR); 4H Awd; Ctznshp Aw; Hi Hnr Roll; Otst Ac Ach Awd; WWAHSS; 4-H; Key Club; Mth Clb/Tm; Stg Cre; Yrbk (R); Chemical Engineering; Biomedical Engineering

MUNOZ, MARIA A; NEWARK, NJ; EAST SIDE HS; (JR); Hi Hnr Roll; Hnr Roll; Perf Att; WWAHSS; Comm Volntr; Peer Tut/Med; Chrch Yth Grp; FBLA; Vsity Clb; Ch Chr; Tennis (V); Psychology; Rutgers New Brunswick

MUNOZ, VANESSA; UNION CITY, NJ; AC OF SACRED HEART HS; (SO); Sccr (J); Sftball (J); Swmg (C); Vllyball (J); Stu Cncl (P); CR (P); Pediatrician; Physical Therapist; Montclair U; Rutgers College (Newark)

MURPHY, ALLIE; WESTWOOD, NJ; WESTWOOD REG HS; (SR); Hi Hnr Roll; Hnr Roll; WWAHSS; Yth Ldrshp Prog; Peer Tut/Med; DARE; Drma Clb; Off Aide; SADD; Vsity Clb; Spanish Clb; Chr; Ch Chr; Dnce; SP/M/VS; Chrldg (V L); Track (V L); Vsy Clb (V); Stu Cncl (R); CR (R); Yrbk (P); Ski Club; Criminology-FBI/CIA Agent; Psychology; Florida State U

MUSTAFA, MANAL; TRENTON, NJ; ASSUNPINK CTR; (SR); Hnr Roll; Cooking; Nursing; College of New Jersey

MUSTAFA, RAWAN M; JERSEY CITY, NJ; DICKINSON HS; (SO); Sci Fairs; WWAHSS; Comm Volntr; Emplmnt; Key Club; Sci Clb; Bnd; Sccr (J); Completed FAX ST Summer Program At UMDNJ; Completed SYP Summer Program At UMDNJ; Marine Biology; Molecular Biology; U of Pennsylvania; Boston College

MUZAFFAR, ZARA; MONTVALE, NJ; PASCACK HILLS HS; (SR); Comm Volntr; Emplmnt; Photog; Spanish Clb; Lit Mag (E); Yrbk (E); Medicine; Pharmacy; Long Island U; Bergen Community College

MUZASHVILI, IRAKLI; SOUTH AMBOY, NJ; ST JOSEPH'S HS; (SO); Hi Hnr Roll; Hnr Roll; Perf Att; Mth Clb/Tm; Math League; Robotics Club Flag Football; Engineering; Computers, Medicine

MYERS, STEVEN S; LAKE HIAWATHA, NJ; PARSIPPANY HS; (SO); Hnr Roll; Yth Ldrshp Prog; Comm Volntr; AL Aux Boys; Jr Cls League; P to P St Amb Prg; Scouts; Latin Clb; Ftball (J); Track (J); Wt Lftg (VJ); Fencing At South Mountain Martial Arts (Madison); Psychology; Teaching; Drew U; Arizona State U

NAIK, PAIYANKU; NORTH BERGEN, NJ; NORTH BERGEN HS; (SO); Key Club; Bdmtn (V); Bsball (V); Bskball (V); Ftball (V); Sccr (V); Tennis (V); Wt Lftg (V); Medical Line; Nurse; N.J.I.T.

NAJJAR, SARAH; TRENTON, NJ; NOTRE DAME HS; (JR); F Lan Hn Soc; Hi Hnr Roll; Hnr Roll; Otst Ac Ach Awd; Yth Ldrshp Prog; Comm Volntr; AL Aux Girls; Chrch Yth Grp; Emplmnt; Key Club; Svce Clb; Vsity Clb; French Clb; Bnd; Orch; SP/M/VS; Stg Cre; Sccr; Swmg (V L); Track; Campus Ministry-Retreat Facilitator; Psychology Major; PhD in Psychology; Hampshire College; Bard College

NAQVI, RUQAIYA; LIVINGSTON, NJ; LIVINGSTON HS; (JR); Hnr Roll; Comm Volntr; Peer Tut/Med; ArtClub; Sci Clb; Stu Cncl (R); Yrbk (E); Pharmacy; Chemist; Rutgers U; Montclair State U

NARANJO, GALO; UNION CITY, NJ; UNION HILL HS; (JR); Hnr Roll; Nat Hon Sy; Chrch Yth Grp; Key Club; MuAlphaTh; Ch Chr; Bsball (VJ); Bskball (J); Member of the Sea Cadet Corps; Computer Technology; Intelligence; The Naval Academy

NASCHER, CAITLIN; OLD BRIDGE, NJ; CARDINAL MC CARRICK HS; (JR); F Lan Hn Soc; Hi Hnr Roll; Hnr Roll; Emplmnt; Lit Mag (E); Fiction Writing Club - Work in Progress - Founder; National Novel Writing Month; Publishing; Creative Writing; Emerson College; Rider U

NASH, DENISHA S; JERSEY CITY, NJ; UNIVERSITY AC CHARTER SCH; (JR); Hnr Roll; Nat Hon Sy; St of Mnth; Yth Ldrshp Prog; Comm Volntr; Peer Tut/Med; Prom Com; Chr; Sch Ppr (E); Dean's List; Science Award; Nursing; Corrections/Law; Harvard U; U of Hawaii

NATALE, JESSICA F; NORTH BERGEN, NJ; NORTH BERGEN HS; (SO); Comm Volntr; Key Club; German Clb; Chrldg (V); Gmnstcs; Sftball (J); Key Club Treasurer

NAVARRO, CRYSTAL; PASSAIC, NJ; PASSAIC HS; (SO); Hnr Roll; Perf Att; Sci Fairs; Comm Volntr; Chrch Yth Grp; Dnce; Orch; Skiing; Track (J); Vllyball (J); Bowling-Varsity; Letter Winner, Ski Club; Z-Club, National Jr. Honor Society; Culinary Arts, Education, Law; Business, Fashion, Medicine; Princeton U, Yale U; Harvard U

NAVIA, AIXA; SUMMIT, NJ; SUMMIT SR HS; (SO); Hnr Roll; Comm Volntr; Spec Olymp Vol; Dbte Team; Drma Clb; Key Club; Pep Squd; Photog; Clr Grd; Dnce; SP/M/VS; Stg Cre; Bskball (J); Mar Art (L); Honor Biology, AP Chemistry; Honors Pre-Calculus; Medicine, Pre-Med; Princeton; Columbia

NAYAK, AMITH; GREAT MEADOWS, NJ; HACKETTSTOWN HS; (JR); Hi Hnr Roll; Nat Hon Sy; Comm Volntr; Peer Tut/Med; Mth Clb/Tm; Mus Clb; Quill & Scroll; Bnd; SP/M/VS; Fncg (V); Stu Cncl (R); Sch Ppr (E, R); Engineering-Computer; History; Columbia U; Cornell U

NAZARECHUK, CAITLIN; RINGWOOD, NJ; LAKELAND REG HS; (SR); Hi Hnr Roll; Hnr Roll; MVP; Nat Hon Sy; St of Mnth; Comm Volntr; Emplmnt; Scouts; Vsity Clb; Bskball (V CL); Sccr (V CL); Sftball (V CL); Sch Ppr (E, R); Girl Scout-Silver Award; Selected for the SYI/ODP National Soccer Team; Childhood/Special Education; Marist College

NEAS, DANIEL; BORDENTOWN, NJ; FLORENCE TWP MEM HS; (FR); Hnr Roll; Spec Olymp Vol; Chess; Bsball (J); Computers; Accounting; Rutgers State U; Burlington County College

NEDD, ASHLEY L; LONG VALLEY, NJ; GILL ST BERNARD'S SCH; (JR); Hnr Roll; Comm Volntr; Drma Clb; Emplmnt; Mod UN; Quill & Scroll; Chr; Dnce; SP/M/VS; Chrldg (V L); Tennis (V L); Yrbk (E, P); Model UN; Mock Trial; Pre-Med; Columbia U; Brown U

NELSON, ANNE; CLARK, NJ; ARTHUR L JOHNSON REG HS; (FR); Hi Hnr Roll; Hnr Roll; Sci/Math Olympn; WWAHSS; Comm Volntr; Biology Clb; Key Club; Track (V); Passion Play with the Church Youth Organization; Business; Forensics; U of Notre Dame; Rutgers U

NENTEBOOM, MATTHEW; BLACKWOOD, NJ; WASHINGTON TWP HS; (FR); St of Mnth; Hosp Aide; FBLA; Placed 1st in FBLA Regional Competition for Visual Basic Programming; Placed 5th in FBLA State Competition for Visual Basic Programming; Computer Programming; Business Degree

NERO, VANELLE S; ROSELLE, NJ; ABRAHAM CLARK HS; (JR); Hnr Roll; Otst Ac Ach Awd; St of Mnth; Peer Tut/Med; ArtClub; Stg Cre; Tennis (V); Yrbk (P); Broadcasting; Nursing; Temple; Kean U

Nero, Vanelle S
Abraham Clark HS
Roselle, NJ

Nelson, Anne
Arthur L Johnson Reg HS
Clark, NJ

Nash, Denisha S
University AC Charter Sch
Jersey City, NJ

Naqvi, Ruqaiya
Livingston HS
Livingston, NJ

Muhammad, Malcolm A
Rahway HS
Rahway, NJ

Mount Jr, John G
St Joseph's HS
Edison, NJ

Moreston, Anthony
Cherry Hill HS West
Cherry Hill, NJ

Morrobel, Diana L
Gladys Hillman Jones Sch
Newark, NJ

Najjar, Sarah
Notre Dame HS
Trenton, NJ

Nascher, Caitlin
Cardinal Mc Carrick HS
Old Bridge, NJ

Navarro, Crystal
Passaic HS
Passaic, NJ

Nazarechuk, Caitlin
Lakeland Reg HS
Ringwood, NJ

NETO, CARLOS; NEWARK, NJ; EAST SIDE; (SO); ArtClub; Chess; Dbte Team; Mth Clb/Tm; Bskball; Sccr (J)

NEWELL, JA'VAE; ENGLEWOOD, NJ; PARAMUS CATHOLIC HS; (JR); Hi Hnr Roll; Hnr Roll; Otst Ac Ach Awd; Yth Ldrshp Prog; Comm Volntr; DARE; Emplmnt; Scouts; Pre-Med; Hampton U; Spelman U

NEWENHOUSE, TIFFANY; W LONG BRANCH, NJ; SHORE REG; (SO); Hi Hnr Roll; Perf Att; WWAHSS; Emplmnt; Mth Clb/Tm; Svce Clb; Bskball (J); Lcrsse (J); Sccr (V L); Track (J); Adv Cncl (R); Rookie of the Year - Soccer 2003; Children International - Sponsor; Teaching

NEWKIRK, JOSH; SPARTA, NJ; SUSSEX CTY TECH CHARTER SCH; (FR); DARE; Vsity Clb; Wdwrkg Clb; Bnd; Bsball (J); Sccr (V L); Vsy Clb (V); Indiana U

NEWMAN, AARON P; MAHWAH, NJ; MAHWAH HS; (SO); Hi Hnr Roll; Emplmnt; Sci Clb; Tmpl Yth Grp; Ice Hky (J); Tennis (J); Thunder Bird Scholar

NGUYEN, CONGKHANH P; BRIDGEWATER, NJ; BRIDGEWATER-RARITAN HS; (JR); Ctznshp Aw; Hi Hnr Roll; Hnr Roll; Perf Att; Pres Ac Ftns Aw; Comm Volntr; Key Club; Mar Art; Balancing Part Time Job; Business; Sales / Marketing; Boston U; Rutgers U

NGUYEN, LILLIAN K; WILLINGBORO, NJ; BURLINGTON CTY INST OF TECH; (SO); Hnr Roll; Otst Ac Ach Awd; Perf Att; Pres Sch; St of Mnth; Peer Tut/Med; DARE; Chrldg (J); Yrbk (E); Registered Nurse; Respiratory Therapist; Temple U

NGUYEN, LISA N; EGG HARBOR TOWNSHIP, NJ; EGG HARBOR TOWNSHIP HS; (JR); Hnr Roll; Nat Hon Sy; WWAHSS; Drma Clb; Key Club; Prom Com; SADD; Dnce; SP/M/VS; Tennis (J); Stu Cncl (R); Secretary of Key Club; REBEL (Reaching Everyone By Exposing Lies); Pharmacy; Pediatrician; Rutgers U; Temple U

NGUYEN, MAI T; EGG HARBOR TOWNSHIP, NJ; EGG HARBOR TOWNSHIP HS; (JR); Comm Volntr; Drma Clb; Key Club; Dnce; SP/M/VS; Bskball (J); Fld Hky (J); Tennis (J); Nurse; Performing Arts (Dance); Richard Stockton College; Rutgers U

NI, TEDDY; MORRIS PLAINS, NJ; PARSIPPANY HILLS HS; (FR); Hi Hnr Roll; Hnr Roll; Hab For Humty Volntr; Chess; FBLA; Key Club; Mth Clb/Tm; Cr Ct Ski (V); Princeton U

NICHOLS, MARCUS; SALEM, NJ; SALEM HS; (SO); Hnr Roll; Otst Ac Ach Awd; Pres Ac Ftns Aw; Sci/Math Olympn; St of Mnth; Peer Tut/Med; ArtClub; Chess; FBLA; Lib Aide; Mth Clb/Tm; Bsball (J); Ftball (V L); Track (V L); Wt Lftg (V L); Business Manager; Landscape Architecture; U of Southern California; Stanford U

NICHOLSON, EDWARD Y C R; JERSEY CITY, NJ; UNIVERSITY AC CHARTER HS; (SO); Ctznshp Aw; Hi Hnr Roll; Hnr Roll; Nat Ldrshp Svc; Nat Sci Aw; Otst Ac Ach Awd; Perf Att; Sci Fairs; St Schl; St of Mnth; Peer Tut/Med; Drma Clb; Mth Clb/Tm; Pep Squd; Photog; Schol Bwl; Tchrs Aide; Pep Bnd; SP/M/VS; Bskball (L); Cr Ctry (L); Ftball (J); Sftball (L); Swmg (L); Track (L); Wt Lftg (J); Wrstlg (L); CR (R); Best of the Best Awards; Principal/Asst. Principal Awards; Movie Director and Writer; Business Owner; New York U; Harvard U

NICKTERN, ADAM E; WILLIAMSTOWN, NJ; WILLIAMSTOWN HS; (FR); Nat Hon Sy; WWAHSS; Comm Volntr; Chrch Yth Grp; Civil Air Pat; ROTC

NICOLAS, JHONNY F; HILLSIDE, NJ; HILLSIDE HS; (FR); Chess; DARE; Drma Clb; Mth Clb/Tm; Sci Clb; Spch Team; Bnd; Chr; Jzz Bnd; SP/M/VS

NICOLOSI, SELINA; PHILLIPSBURG, NJ; BETHLEHEM CATHOLIC HS; (FR); Peer Tut/Med; Key Club; Tennis (V); Sports Administration; Fashion Merchandising; U of Miami; U of Texas

NIEVES, STEPHANIE; BELLEVILLE, NJ; BELLEVILLE HS; (FR); Hnr Roll; Dnce; SP/M/VS; Bsball (J); Bskball (V); Cl Off (V); Yrbk; Modeling

NIEWINSKA, PAULINA; NEWTON, NJ; NEWTON HS; (JR); Hnr Roll; ArtClub; French Clb; Interact Club; Art Honor Society; Psychology; Art; Syracuse U; Pace U

NINI, JESSICA A; TRENTON, NJ; ALLENTOWN HS; (JR); F Lan Hn Soc; Hnr Roll; Otst Ac Ach Awd; St of Mnth; St Optmst of Yr; Peer Tut/Med; Emplmnt; Ntl FFA; Prom Com; Dnce; Chrldg (V L); PP Ftbl (L); CR (R); Ebase Academy; Optimist Club; Business Management; International Business; Lehigh U; American U

NISIVOCCIA, ANGELA; FREEHOLD, NJ; FTHS; (SR); Hnr Roll; Yth Ldrshp Prog; Peer Tut/Med; DECA; Pep Squd; Vsity Clb; Chr; Dnce; Chrldg (V); Accounting; Business; Monmouth U

NITZAN, LIRAN; TRENTON, NJ; ASSUNPINK CTR; (SR); Hnr Roll; Otst Ac Ach Awd; Emplmnt; Stg Cre; Cl Off (S); Sociology; Nursing; Temple U

NOCERA, PASQUALE F; TRENTON, NJ; NOTRE DAME HS; (JR); WWAHSS; Peer Tut/Med; Dbte Team; Drma Clb; French Clb; Chr; SP/M/VS; Stg Cre; Tennis (J); Wt Lftg; Communications; Computer & Arts; Stockton College; U of Delaware/Montclair

NOEL, BRITTINI; PLAINFIELD, NJ; PLAINFIELD HS; (SO); Otst Ac Ach Awd; Peer Tut/Med; Chrch Yth Grp; Mus Clb; Scouts; Ch Chr; SP/M/VS; Bsball (J); Sftball (J); Studio Time At School Studio; Law and Order; Business; Drexel U; St. Peter's College

NOEL, WATSON; IRVINGTON, NJ; IRVINGTON HIGHSCHOOL; (SO); Hnr Roll; Nat Hon Sy; Sccr

NOGUEIRA, JULIE; CLARK, NJ; ARTHUR L JOHNSON HS; (SO); Hnr Roll; Comm Volntr; Key Club; Spanish Clb; Stg Cre; Teaching Master's Degree; Rutgers U

NORMIL, CHRISTOPHER; PEMBERTON, NJ; BURLINGTON INST TECH MEDFORD HS; (SR); Hnr Roll; MVP; Otst Ac Ach Awd; St of Mnth; Comm Volntr; ArtClub; Chrch Yth Grp; Drma Clb; Emplmnt; Vsity Clb; Bskball (V); Cr Ctry (V); Stu Cncl (R); Graphic Communications; Drama; Keene State; Rutgers

NOSOVA, RAISA A; LITTLE FALLS, NJ; PASSAIC VALLEY REG HS; (JR); ArtClub; Drma Clb; Mth Clb/Tm; Sci Clb; Chr; Dnce; SP/M/VS; Stg Cre; Fld Hky (J); Nominee for Presidential Classroom; Delegate to Represent the State of NJ At 2005 National Student Leadership Conference; Fine Arts; Foreign Language; Cooper Union; Fashion Institute of Technology

NOVELLI, STEPHANIE; HOWELL, NJ; HOWELL HS; (SR); F Lan Hn Soc; Hnr Roll; MVP; Nat Hon Sy; Otst Ac Ach Awd; St of Mnth; Yth Ldrshp Prog; Comm Volntr; Peer Tut/Med; Emplmnt; NYLC; Svce Clb; Gmnstcs (V C); Lit Mag (R); Lead Attorney on Mock Trial Team; Vice President of National Honors Society; Political Science; Law School; Villanova U; Syracuse U

NOWICKI, DANIEL; EAST BRUNSWICK, NJ; EAST BRUNSWICK HS; (JR); F Lan Hn Soc; Hnr Roll; Nat Hon Sy; WWAHSS; Comm Volntr; Peer Tut/Med; Dbte Team; Mod UN; NtlFrnscLg; Tmpl Yth Grp; Spanish Clb; Bnd; Vllyball (J); Spanish Honor Society President; Best Representative Model Congress Award; International Relations; Georgetown; Tufts

NUNES JR, AGEU; HARRISON, NJ; HARRISON HS; (JR); Hi Hnr Roll; Nat Hon Sy; Otst Ac Ach Awd; St of Mnth; ROTC; Ftball (L); Record 5 Students of the Cycle in 1 Semester; Computer Science; Computer Engineering; Virginia Polytechnical (VA Tech); Rutgers

NWAZIRI, ALEXIA; SAYREVILLE, NJ; CARDINAL MC CARRICK HS; (SO); Hnr Roll; Perf Att; Chrch Yth Grp; DARE; Ch Chr; Dnce; Track (J); Lit Mag (R); Latin Award; Pre Medicine; Princeton U; Rutgers U

OCAL, ANIL; HACKENSACK, NJ; HACKENSACK HS; (SR); ArtClub; Drma Clb; Emplmnt; Dnce; SP/M/VS; Cl Off (V); CR (P); Being an Architect; Syracuse U; Penn State U

OCASIO, SARAH; PATERSON, NJ; HARP AC; (JR); Comm Volntr; Hosp Aide; Chrch Yth Grp; Tchrs Aide; Dnce; CR (R); Major-Biology (Pre-Med); Degree-Doctorate; Oral Roberts U; Grove City College

O CONNOR, KELLY; CEDAR GROVE, NJ; CEDAR GROVE HS; (SO); Hi Hnr Roll; WWAHSS; Key Club; Sci Clb; Foreign Clb; Scr Kpr (VJ); Sccr (V); Sftball (V); Interact Club, Steering Committee; Psychology; Accounting; Drew U; Boston U

OFFEMARIA, KEVIN; PARLIN, NJ; SAYREVILLE WAR MEMORIAL HS; (SR); Perf Att; Chess; Cmptr Clb; Mth Clb/Tm; Chess - Varsity; Accounting; Marketing; Middlesex County College; Rutgers U

OFOSU-APPIAH, DAVID; WILLIAMSTOWN, NJ; WILLIAMSTOWN HS; (FR); Hi Hnr Roll; Hnr Roll; Nat Hon Sy; Nat Sci Aw; Perf Att; Peer Tut/Med; Chrch Yth Grp; DARE; Drma Clb; Mus Clb; SP/M/VS; Bskball (J); Ftball (L); NASA Mars Student Imaging Award; Renaissance Group Member; Computer Engineer; Chief Information Officer; Princeton U; Harvard U

OGONOWSKI, MATTHEW; LINDEN, NJ; LINDEN HS; (JR); F Lan Hn Soc; Hi Hnr Roll; Hnr Roll; Nat Hon Sy; WWAHSS; Yth Ldrshp Prog; Peer Tut/Med; Chrch Yth Grp; Drma Clb; Mus Clb; NYLC; Scouts; German Clb; Acpl Chr; Bnd; Chr; Ch Chr; Cl Off (P); CR (R); Sch Ppr (R); National Young Leaders Conference; Music Business; International Business; New York U; The College of New Jersey

OGULE, KEVIN M; MONROE TOWNSHIP, NJ; MONROE TWP HS; (JR); Hnr Roll; Comm Volntr; DARE; Emplmnt; Scouts; Rlr Hky; Culinary Arts; U of Pittsburgh

OH, AMY; BLOOMINGDALE, NJ; BUTLER HS; (FR); Hnr Roll; Perf Att; Sci Fairs; Comm Volntr; Chrch Yth Grp; DARE; Emplmnt; Key Club; Scouts; Ch Chr; Fld Hky (J); Girl Scouts Award - Humanitarian Award; Cheerleading Trophies; Teacher; Baker; Rutgers; Princeton U

OH, BRIAN; DENVILLE, NJ; MORRIS KNOLLS HS; (JR); Ctznshp Aw; Hi Hnr Roll; Hnr Roll; Comm Volntr; Dbte Team; Drma Clb; Emplmnt; JSA; Pep Squd; Prom Com; SP/M/VS; Adv Cncl (R); Cl Off (R); Stu Cncl (R); CR (R); Member of SGA; Film; Political Science; New York U

OH, SARAH; FORT LEE, NJ; FORT LEE HS; (SO); Ctznshp Aw; Hnr Roll; Perf Att; St of Mnth; Peer Tut/Med; Chrch Yth Grp; Key Club; Off Aide; Orch; Cr Ctry (J); Track (V L); Stu Cncl (T); Pediatrician; Teacher-English; New York U; Columbia U

O'HANLON-RODRIGUEZ, RACHEL; TEANECK, NJ; TEANECK HS; (JR); Hi Hnr Roll; Hnr Roll; Nat Sci Aw; St of Mnth; Peer Tut/Med; DARE; Drma Clb; Emplmnt; Dnce; SP/M/VS; Lit Mag (R); Sch Ppr (R); Performing Arts Major; Fine Arts Major; Rutgers U; New York U

OJUTALAYO, ABAYOMI; NEWARK, NJ; MALCOLM X SHABAZZ HS; (JR); Hi Hnr Roll; Hnr Roll; Jr Eng Tech; Nat Hon Sy; Nat Sci Aw; Otst Ac Ach Awd; Sci Fairs; St of Mnth; Yth Ldrshp Prog; Hosp Aide; Peer Tut/Med; Red Cr Aide; Biology Clb; Chrch Yth Grp; Dbte Team; Emplmnt; FCA; Mth Clb/Tm; Mus Clb; Sci Clb; Ch Chr; Dnce; Drl Tm; SP/M/VS; Bskball (C); Scr Kpr (J); Sccr (C); Wt Lftg (J); Wrstlg (J); Cl Off (P); Stu Cncl (P); CR (T); Lit Mag (P); Sch Ppr (P); Yrbk (P); Physical Therapy; Virginia Commonwealth U

OKATOR, EMEKA T; LINDEN, NJ; LINDEN HS; (SR); Hi Hnr Roll; MVP; Nat Mrt LOC; Nat Mrt Semif; St of Mnth; Biology Clb; Chess; Emplmnt; Bskball (J); Golf (V); Tennis (J); Track (V); Orthopedist; Neurologist; New York U; Rutgers U

OKOSI, TED; KEYPORT, NJ; MATAWAN-ABERDEEN REG; (JR); Hnr Roll; MVP; Nat Stu Ath Day Aw; Otst Ac Ach Awd; Perf Att; Pres Ac Ftns Aw; St of Mnth; Yth Ldrshp Prog; Comm Volntr; Chrch Yth Grp; Emplmnt; FCA; Vsity Clb; Ch Chr; Bskball (J); Ftball (V L); Track (V CL); Pre-Med; Pharmacy; Columbia U; Georgetown U

OKPARAEKE, IVEOMA A; JACKSON, NJ; JACKSON MEMORIAL HS; (JR); Hi Hnr Roll; Hnr Roll; Perf Att; WWAHSS; Hosp Aide; Chrch Yth Grp; Emplmnt; Lib Aide; French Clb; Fld Hky (J); Creator/Founder of 3-D Animation Series; Sunday School Teacher; Ophthalmology; Duke U; Northwestern U

OKSENIUK, ROMINA; SPRINGFIELD, NJ; JONATHAN DAYTON HS; (JR); F Lan Hn Soc; Hnr Roll; Comm Volntr; Spec Olymp Vol; Emplmnt; Lib Aide; Bnd; Dnce; Gmnstcs (C); Skiing (V); Tennis (C); Volunteer Tutoring-Volunteer Club; Volunteer At the Public Library; Biology; Medicine; Union Country College-Robert Wood Johnson; Sam Percy College Medical School

OLAZO, ALLISON; KENDALL PARK, NJ; SOUTH BRUNSWICK HS; (JR); F Lan Hn Soc; Nat Hon Sy; Key Club; Clr Grd

OLDER, MICHELLE A; BERKELEY HEIGHTS, NJ; GOVERNOR LIVINGSTON HS; (JR); F Lan Hn Soc; Nat Hon Sy; Chrch Yth Grp; Emplmnt; MuAlphaTh; Spanish Clb; Chr; Sftball (J); Track (J); Lit Mag (R); Elementary Education; Journalism; Temple U; Arcadia U

OLENCHAK, JASON; EDISON, NJ; ST JOSEPH'S HS; (JR); Hi Hnr Roll; Hnr Roll; Nat Hon Sy; Pres Ac Ftns Aw; Comm Volntr; Emplmnt; Mus Clb; Prom Com; Bnd; Track (J); Stu Cncl (R); CR (R); Audio Production; Music Management; U of Hartford; U of Scranton

OLIVEIRA, KELLY G R; FORT LEE, NJ; FORT LEE HS; (SR); Chrch Yth Grp; Key Club; Prom Com; Ch Chr; Sccr (V); Sftball (V); Stu Cncl; Lit Mag; President of the Youth Group; Pharmacy; Real Estate Broker; William Patterson U; Rutgers U

OLIVEIRA, STEPHANIE; LINDEN, NJ; LINDEN HS; (JR); Hnr Roll; Yth Ldrshp Prog; Hosp Aide; ArtClub; ROTC; Peer Leader; Physical Team (ROTC); Architect; Environmental or Naval Engineer; Stevens Institute of Tech; NJIT

OLIVERI, AMANDA; MT HOLLY, NJ; RANCOCAS VALLEY REG HS; (SO); Hi Hnr Roll; Comm Volntr; Emplmnt; Key Club; Bnd; Fld Hky (J L); Wrestling Manager - L; Culinary School; Art

OLSAVSKY III, PAVOL; LINDEN, NJ; LHS LINDEN HS; (SO); Hi Hnr Roll; Hnr Roll; ArtClub; Chess; Cmptr Clb; German Clb; Sccr (J); Track (J); Wt Lftg (V); Won Art Contests; Poems Were Published; History; Art; College of New Jersey; Princeton

O'MALLEY, ETHAN D; SPRING LAKE, NJ; RED BANK CATHOLIC HS; (FR); Hnr Roll; Perf Att; Pres Ac Ftns Aw; Comm Volntr; FBLA; Bskball; Ftball; Golf; Varsity Academic Letter

O'MALLEY, KATIE; HAINESPORT, NJ; RANCOCAS VALLEY REG HS; (FR); Chr; Track (L); Key Club; Business / Marketing; Fashion Design; Temple U; Yale U

OMOREGIE, NOSAWARU; MAPLEWOOD, NJ; COLUMBIA HS; (JR); Ctznshp Aw; Hnr Roll; Comm Volntr; Photog; SP/M/VS; Ftball (V); Track (V); Played Varsity Football Since Sophomore Year; Biology Major; Doctor; U of North Carolina; U of Pennsylvania

OMUSO, INARA; BURLINGTON, NJ; BURLINGTON TWP HS; (JR); Hi Hnr Roll; MVP; Nat Hon Sy; Perf Att; Pres Ac Ftns Aw; St of Mnth; Comm Volntr; Emplmnt; Chr; SP/M/VS; Bskball (V); Sccr (V); Track (V); Sch Ppr (R); Pediatrics; Biology; Drexel U; Johns Hopkins U

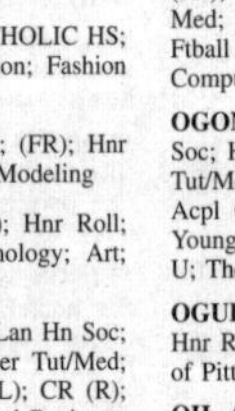
O'Malley, Ethan D
Red Bank Catholic HS
Spring Lake, NJ

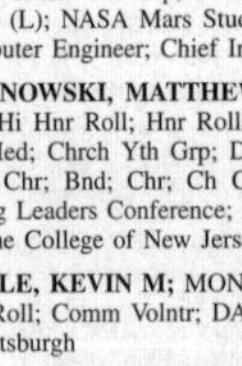
Okparaeke, Iveoma A
Jackson Memorial HS
Jackson, NJ

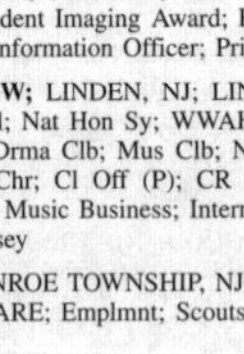
Okosi, Ted
Matawan-Aberdeen Reg
Keyport, NJ

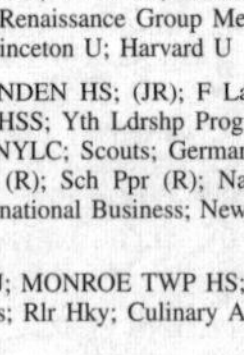
Olsavsky III, Pavol
Lhs Linden HS
Linden, NJ

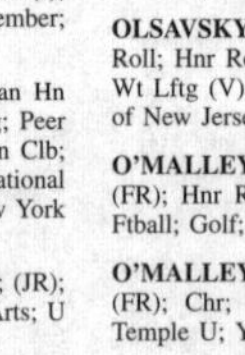
Omuso, Inara
Burlington Twp HS
Burlington, NJ

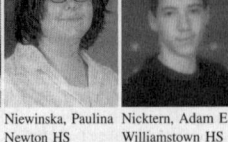

Ogule, Kevin M
Monroe Twp HS
Monroe Township, NJ

Offemaria, Kevin
Sayreville War Memorial HS
Parlin, NJ

Nogueira, Julie
Arthur L Johnson HS
Clark, NJ

Niewinska, Paulina
Newton HS
Newton, NJ

Nicktern, Adam E
Williamstown HS
Williamstown, NJ

National
Honor Roll
Spring 2005

Nguyen, Congkhanh P
Bridgewater-Raritan HS
Bridgewater, NJ

Nocera, Pasquale F
Notre Dame HS
Trenton, NJ

Ocal, Anil
Hackensack HS
Hackensack, NJ

Ofosu-Appiah, David
Williamstown HS
Williamstown, NJ

Ogonowski, Matthew
Linden HS
Linden, NJ

O'NEIL, MALLORY; MARLTON, NJ; CHEROKEE HS; (JR); DAR; Hnr Roll; St of Mnth; Comm Volntr; Chrch Yth Grp; DARE; Drma Clb; Emplmnt; FCA; FTA; SADD; Spanish Clb; Chr; Dnce; Orch; SP/M/VS; Chrldg (JC); PP Ftbl (V); Scr Kpr (V L); Adv Cncl (R); Stu Cncl (R); CR (R); Dance Company National Champions; Communications; Acting; Fordham U; Emerson College

ORHO, ORHAN; BRIDGEWATER, NJ; BRIDGEWATER-RARITAN HS; (JR); Hnr Roll; WWAHSS; FBLA; Key Club; Wdwrkg Clb; Swmg (VJ); Medical Field; St John's U; Montclair State U

ORTEGA, EMILY; PATERSON, NJ; PATERSON CATHOLIC HS; (SO); Hnr Roll; I Am Proud that I'm Still in HS; I Maintain Good Grades.; Film Production; Script Writer; New York U; Parsons School of Fashion Design

ORTIZ, ALVIN J; LANDISVILLE, NJ; BUENA REG; (JR); Ftball (J); Wt Lftg; Wrstlg (J)

ORTIZ, MELODEE; BELLEVILLE, NJ; BELLEVILLE HS; (SO); Hi Hnr Roll; WWAHSS; Comm Volntr; Chrch Yth Grp; Key Club; Ch Chr; Vllyball (J); Member of Family, Career, Community Leaders of America; Gold / Silver Medal for Patchwork and Poster Competition; Major in Criminal Justice / Criminology; U of Richmond VA; Rutgers U

ORTIZ, NATASHA; BELLEVILLE, NJ; BELLEVILLE HS; (FR); Hnr Roll; WWAHSS; Comm Volntr; Chrch Yth Grp; DARE; Key Club; Ch Chr; Vllyball (J); Family Career Community Leaders of America Member; Won 2 Silver Medals for Patchwork and Poster Competition; Major in Advertising; Culinary Arts; Rutgers U; Montclair State U

ORTIZ, SOPHIA; CAMDEN, NJ; (SO); Hnr Roll; Perf Att; Sci Fairs; St of Mnth; Comm Volntr; Cmptr Clb; FBLA; Mth Clb/Tm; Banking & Financing; Health Aide; Rutgers U; Camden County College

OSEI-FRIMPONG, JENNIFER; NEWARK, NJ; BARRINGER HS; (SO); 4H Awd; Hi Hnr Roll; Hnr Roll; Sci/Math Olympn; St of Mnth; Peer Tut/Med; 4-H; Chrch Yth Grp; Drma Clb; FTA; Mth Clb/Tm; Spch Team; Bnd; Vllyball (J); Medical Doctor; Dental Doctor; St Patrick's College; Holy Cross College

OSORIO, LAURA S; ENGLEWOOD, NJ; DWIGHT MORROW HS; (FR); Hnr Roll; Computer Communication; Technology; Penn State; Columbia U

OTA, YU; FORT LEE, NJ; FORT LEE HS; (JR); Hnr Roll; WWAHSS; Comm Volntr; Peer Tut/Med; Chrch Yth Grp; FTA; Key Club; Photog; Chr; Ch Chr; Stg Cre; Bskball (VJ); Sftball (J); Yrbk (P); POST; Pediatrician; Forensic Scientist; Rutgers New Brunswick; Boston U

OTERO, JENNIFER; NEWARK, NJ; ESSEX CTY VOC-TECH HS; (FR); Ctznshp Aw; Hi Hnr Roll; Hnr Roll; Otst Ac Ach Awd; Perf Att; DARE; Tech Clb; Psychology; Medicine; Princeton; New Jersey Institute of Technology

OTERO, ROGELIO; NEWARK, NJ; GLADYS HILLMAN JONES SCH; MS; Ctznshp Aw; Hnr Roll; Perf Att; Cmptr Clb; Mus Clb; Tech Clb; Bnd; Computer Repair; Criminal Justice; New Jersey Institute of Technology; Stevens Institute of Technology

OTTE, ASHLEY; ELMWOOD PARK, NJ; IMMACULATE CONCEPTION HS; (SO); All Am Sch; Hnr Roll; Nat Hon Sy; Perf Att; Pres Sch; WWAHSS; P to P St Amb Prg; Chrldg (V); Ambassador

OTTINO, JUSTIN K; LITTLE FALLS, NJ; PASSAIC VALLEY REG HS; (SO); Hi Hnr Roll; WWAHSS; DARE; FBLA; Tennis (V L); Track (J)

OUMA JR, RICHARD O; TRENTON, NJ; (SR); Hnr Roll; Chrch Yth Grp; Emplmnt; Clb; Bnd; Mch Bnd; Lcrsse (V); Sccr (V); Drexel U; Stockton College

OUYANG, JENNY; EGG HARBOR TOWNSHIP, NJ; EGG HARBOR TOWNSHIP HS; (SO); Ctznshp Aw; Hi Hnr Roll, Hnr Roll; Nat Hon Sy; Otst Ac Ach Awd; Perf Att; St of Mnth; Red Cr Aide; ArtClub; Cmptr Clb; Key Club; Off Aide; Bnd; Mch Bnd; Orch; Vllyball; Stu Cncl (R); Sch Ppr (R); Journalist; Architect; Columbia U; Princeton U

OVERMIRE, JAMES D; HAMBURG, NJ; SUSSEX CTY TECH CHARTER SCH; (FR); Hi Hnr Roll; Hnr Roll; Nat Hon Sy; Otst Ac Ach Awd; St of Mnth; Yth Ldrshp Prog; Voc Ind Clb Am; Wdwrkg Clb; Bsball (V); Sccr (V); Carpentry-High Achievement Award; Sussex County Cmty College

OWENS, ASHLEY N; TOMS RIVER, NJ; MANCHESTER TWP HS; (FR); Hi Hnr Roll; Pres Ac Ftns Aw; Comm Volntr; Lib Aide; Scouts; Spanish Clb; Library Service and Achievement; Peers; Teacher; Georgian Court U

OYELOLA, TAIWO A; ROSELLE, NJ; ABRAHAM CLARK HS; (JR); Hi Hnr Roll; Hnr Roll; DARE; Bskball; Sftball; Tennis; Business Management; U Conn; Villanova

OZIMEK, ROMAN C; WOOD RIDGE, NJ; BERGEN CTY ACADEMIES; (SR); Hnr Roll; WWAHSS; Comm Volntr; AL Aux Boys; FBLA; Vllyball (VJ); Multicultural Taskforce, Leadership Board; 8th Place Mr. FBLA At State Competition; Business; Pre-Law; Lehigh U; George Washington U

PACHUTA, LINDSEY; EAST BRUNSWICK, NJ; EAST BRUNSWICK HS; (SR); Hnr Roll; MVP; Sftball (V L); Nursing; Education; U of Scranton

PACKOWSKI, MELISSA K C; WOOD RIDGE, NJ; PARAMUS CATHOLIC HS; (SO); Hi Hnr Roll; Hnr Roll; Perf Att; Pres Sch; Sci Fairs; St of Mnth; WWAHSS; Comm Volntr; Peer Tut/Med; Spec Olymp Vol; Drma Clb; Emplmnt; NYLC; P to P St Amb Prg; Quiz Bowl; Scouts; Tchrs Aide; Italian Clb; SP/M/VS; Top 20 in 2003 National American Miss Pageant Essay Contest; Top 10 in Nation for American Dreams; Journalism Science & History; English & World History Teacher; Ramapo College; Montclair State U

PAGAN, AARON; BERGENFIELD, NJ; BERGENFIELD HS; (SO); Hnr Roll; Nat Hon Sy; DECA; Ftball (J); Wrstlg (V L); National Youth Forum on Medicine; National Human Society on Foreign Language; West Point; Study Abroad

PAGENKOPF, DALE; LUMBERTON, NJ; RANCOCAS VALLEY RHS; (SO); F Lan Hn Soc; Hi Hnr Roll; WWAHSS; Comm Volntr; Chrch Yth Grp; Emplmnt; Key Club; Tchrs Aide; Bnd; Clr Grd; Mch Bnd; Fld Hky (J L); Lcrsse (V L); Track (V)

PALLATTA, ALYSSA; BRIDGEWATER, NJ; BRIDGEWATER-RARITAN HS; (FR); Hnr Roll; Comm Volntr; Hab For Humty Volntr; Key Club; Prom Com; Scouts; Stg Cre; Habitat for Humanity; Johns Hopkins U; Rutgers U

PALMER, AMBER F; BRIDGETON, NJ; BRIDGETON HS; (SR); Hi Hnr Roll; Hnr Roll; Nat Hon Sy; Peer Tut/Med; AL Aux Girls; Chrch Yth Grp; Emplmnt; Bnd; Ch Chr; Jzz Bnd; Mch Bnd; Fld Hky (V L); Cl Off (R); Sch Ppr (R); Yrbk (E); Cumberland County Mock Trial Champion; Member of NJREBEL - Youth Led Tobacco Prevention Program; Business Management Major; The College of New Jersey

PALMERI, ALICIA; SADDLE BROOK, NJ; SADDLE BROOK HS; (JR); Hnr Roll; Comm Volntr; Spanish Clb; Chrldg (V C); Sch Ppr (R); Interact Club; Spanish Club; Psychology

PALMISANO, CRAIG; CRANFORD, NJ; CRANFORD HS; (FR); Hnr Roll; Spanish Clb; Bnd; Mch Bnd; Tennis (V); Stu Cncl (R); Intramural Basketball and Baseball; Business/Marketing; Sports Administration/Management; Rutgers U; U of Maryland

PALMUCCI, JULIANNE; COLONIA, NJ; COLONIA HS; (JR); Hnr Roll; Nat Hon Sy; DARE; Scouts; Bnd; Stg Cre; Sftball (J); National Honor Society; Nursing; Psychology; Rutgers U; Middlesex County College

PANDOLFO, CHRISTINE C; HOWELL, NJ; HOWELL HS; (SR); Hi Hnr Roll; Hnr Roll; MVP; Nat Hon Sy; St of Mnth; WWAHSS; CARE; Comm Volntr; Peer Tut/Med; Chrch Yth Grp; DECA; Prom Com; Chrldg (J); Lcrsse (V L); Sccr (V L); Adv Cncl (R); Stu Cncl (P); CR (R); Distinguished Rebel Scholar; Scholar Athlete; Secondary Education-Mathematics; The College of New Jersey; U of Delaware

PANZER, RIMIDA; WESTWOOD, NJ; WESTWOOD HS; (JR); F Lan Hn Soc; Hi Hnr Roll; Nat Hon Sy; Peer Tut/Med; ArtClub; Cmptr Clb; Mth Clb/Tm; P to P St Amb Prg; SADD; Spanish Clb; Tennis (V); Sch Ppr (R); Academic Decathlon Team Leader; Biology; Photography; Amherst College; Boston College

PAOLIN, MELISSA; MERCHANTVILLE, NJ; PENNSAUKEN HS; (JR); Hnr Roll; Nat Hon Sy; St of Mnth; Comm Volntr; DARE; SADD; Sccr (V); Cl Off (P); National Honor Society; Spanish National Honor Society; Education; Rowan U; Rider U

PAOLINI, PAUL; MERCHANTVILLE, NJ; PENNSAUKEN HS; (JR); Hnr Roll; Chess; Dbte Team; JSA; Vsity Clb; French Clb; SP/M/VS; Tennis (V); Sch Ppr (R); Pennsauken Pathfinder; Business Degree; Automotive Technician; Rutgers, Camden, New Jersey; Stockton U

PAPENDICK, HANNAH; BUTLER, NJ; KINNELON HS; (SO); F Lan Hn Soc; Hnr Roll; Emplmnt; Vsity Clb; French Clb; Bnd; Sftball (J L); Swmg (V L); College of Charleston

PAPETTI, ANTHONY G; RANDOLPH, NJ; SETON HALL PREPARATORY SCH; (SO); F Lan Hn Soc; Hi Hnr Roll; Nat Hon Sy; Otst Ac Ach Awd; Comm Volntr; Peer Tut/Med; Chess; Chrch Yth Grp; Emplmnt; NtlFrnscLg; NYLC; Spch Team; Spanish Clb; Bnd; Stu Cncl (R); CR (P); Math Honors Society; Tutor Elementary School Kids; Pre-Med / Biochemistry; Pre-Vet; Boston College; Harvard U

PARIKH, KEYUR; CLIFTON, NJ; CLIFTON HS; (SO); Hi Hnr Roll; Nat Hon Sy; Otst Ac Ach Awd; Yth Ldrshp Prog; Hosp Aide; Asian Clb; Track (J); Tae Kwon Do at YMCA - Black Belt; Pharmacy / Medicine; Rutgers U

PARIKH, MONISHA; ELIZABETH, NJ; ELIZABETH HS; (JR); F Lan Hn Soc; Hnr Roll; Nat Hon Sy; Comm Volntr; Hosp Aide; Key Club; Mod UN; Sci Clb; Dnce; Pre-Medicine; New York U; Rutgers U

PARIKH, PRACHI; HASBROUCK HTS, NJ; HASBROUCK HEIGHTS HS; (SO); F Lan Hn Soc; Hnr Roll; Nat Hon Sy; Yth Ldrshp Prog; Comm Volntr; Key Club; Spanish Clb; Sftball (J); Tennis (J); Sch Ppr (E, R); Peer-Leader; Pre-Med; Rutgers Pre-Med; Johns Hopkins U

PARISI, JENNIFER L; PITMAN, NJ; PITMAN HS; (SO); Hi Hnr Roll; St of Mnth; WWAHSS; Comm Volntr; Chrch Yth Grp; Key Club; SADD; Tchrs Aide; PP Ftbl (V); Sccr (V L); Swmg (J); Track (V L); Stu Cncl (R); Sch Ppr (E, R); Communications; College of William and Mary; U of Pennsylvania

PARK, ANGELA; CARLSTADT, NJ; HENRY P BECTON REG HS; (FR); Hi Hnr Roll; Chrch Yth Grp; Key Club; Scouts; Dnce; Bskball (V); Chrldg (V); Sftball (V); Stu Cncl (R); Business; Pharmacy; Rutgers Pharmacy; New York U

PARK, CHEON-IL; CLIFFSIDE PARK, NJ; CLIFFSIDE PARK HS; (SR); Hnr Roll; Comm Volntr; Chrch Yth Grp; Emplmnt; Tennis (J); Yrbk (P); Pharmacy / Pharmacist; Missionary; SUNY Buffalo

PARK, GINA; FORT LEE, NJ; FORT LEE HS; (FR); Hnr Roll; FBLA; Key Club; Mod UN; Yrbk; Economics; New York U Stern's School of Business; Boston College

PARKER, CHANTELLE L; PLAINFIELD, NJ; PLAINFIELD HS; (FR); Hi Hnr Roll; Perf Att; Comm Volntr; Red Cr Aide; DARE; Ch Chr; Chrldg (V); Track (V); Pediatrician; Psychology; Florida State U; Spelman College

PARKER, CIERA; GLASSBORO, NJ; GLASSBORO HS; (SR); Hnr Roll; Otst Ac Ach Awd; Perf Att; St of Mnth; Comm Volntr; Chrch Yth Grp; Ch Chr; Unity Day Poster Winner (1st Place); Theater; Music; City U of New York; Alabama State U

PARKER JR, CRAIG; LAKE HIAWATHA, NJ; PARSIPPANY HS; (FR); Hi Hnr Roll; Hnr Roll; WWAHSS; Italian Clb; Bnd; Jzz Bnd; Mch Bnd; Orch; Stu Cncl (R); CR (R); Sch Ppr (P); Italian Honors Society Jr. Member; History; Music

PARLOW, BRITTANY J; PT PLEASANT BEACH, NJ; PT PLEASANT BEACH HS; (SR); Hi Hnr Roll; MVP; Nat Hon Sy; Nat Mrt Semif; Pres Ac Ftns Aw; Sci/Math Olympn; WWAHSS; Comm Volntr; Peer Tut/Med; AL Aux Girls; Chrch Yth Grp; DARE; Drma Clb; HO'Br Yth Ldrshp; Key Club; Prom Com; Sci Clb; Chr; Stg Cre; Bskball (V CL); Cr Ctry (V CL); Sftball (V CL); Cl Off (S); Stu Cncl (R); Lit Mag (R); Yrbk (R, P); Girl Scouts; Medical School; Practicing Physician; Bucknell U

PASAPERA, GLADYS S; WEST NEW YORK, NJ; HCST-NORTH HUDSON CTR HIGH TECH HS; (JR); F Lan Hn Soc; Hi Hnr Roll; Hnr Roll; Pres Sch; Comm Volntr; ArtClub; Off Aide; Tchrs Aide; French Clb; Chr; SP/M/VS; Stg Cre; Studio Arts Major; Fashion Show Participant; Studio Arts Major in College; Culinary School After 4 Year College; New York U; Moore College of Art and Design

PASELA, MEGAN; TRENTON, NJ; HAMILTON HS WEST; (SR); Hnr Roll; Nat Hon Sy; WWAHSS; Comm Volntr; Biology Clb; Emplmnt; Key Club; Sci Clb; Scouts; Ch Chr; Stg Cre; Tennis (V CL); Biology/Pre-Med

PASS, R J; CAPE MAY COURT HOUSE, NJ; MIDDLE TWP HS; (JR); Hnr Roll; MVP; Nat Hon Sy; Sci Fairs; St of Mnth; WWAHSS; Comm Volntr; Prom Com; Cr Ctry (V L); Track (V L); Stu Cncl (R); Indoor Track Varsity Letter; Education; Chiropractics; Boston College; Rutgers U

PATEL, CHIRALI; ISELIN, NJ; JOHN F KENNEDY MEMORIAL HS; (SO); Hnr Roll; St of Mnth; Comm Volntr; Key Club; Chr; JD; Business Management; Emory U; Duke U

PATEL, DEEP; DUMONT, NJ; DUMONT HS; (JR); F Lan Hn Soc; Hi Hnr Roll; Nat Hon Sy; Valdctrian; Comm Volntr; Hosp Aide; Peer Tut/Med; Dbte Team; Emplmnt; Mth Clb/Tm; Spanish Clb; CR (R); Sch Ppr (R); Economics/ Mathematics

PATEL, DEVAN; DAYTON, NJ; SOUTH BRUNSWICK HS; (SO); Ctznshp Aw; Hnr Roll; Hosp Aide; Cmptr Clb; Bskball (L); Tennis (L); MBA; Rutgers NJ; Temple PA

PATEL, HEENA; PARSIPPANY, NJ; PARSIPPANY HILLS HS; (JR); F Lan Hn Soc; Hi Hnr Roll; Hnr Roll; WWAHSS; Yth Ldrshp Prog; Hab For Humty Volntr; Hosp Aide; Drma Clb; Jr Cls League; Key Club; Latin Clb; Stu Cncl (R); Secretary of Key Club; NJ State Officer of the JCL; Nursing; Psychology; New York U; Washington U

PATEL, JAY; ROCKAWAY, NJ; MORRIS HILLS HS; (SO); F Lan Hn Soc; Hi Hnr Roll; Otst Ac Ach Awd; Perf Att; Sci/Math Olympn; Yth Ldrshp Prog; Comm Volntr; Peer Tut/Med; Emplmnt; FBLA; Mth Clb/Tm; Schol Bwl; Sci Clb; Scouts; Tech Clb; Bnd; Mch Bnd; Fncg (V); BU Engineering Design Competition Finalist; NJSCF Tech Category winner; Biomedical Engineering; Psychology; MIT; Johns Hopkins U

PATEL, JIGISHA; PARSIPPANY, NJ; PARSIPPANY HILLS HS; (SR); Hnr Roll; Chemistry; Pharmacy; County College of Morris

PATEL, LATISHA; JERSEY CITY, NJ; WILLIAM L. DICKINSON; (SO); Nat Hon Sy; Comm Volntr; Spec Olymp Vol; Chess; Key Club; Tech Clb; Technology Magnet; Architect; Archeology; New Jersey Institute of Technology

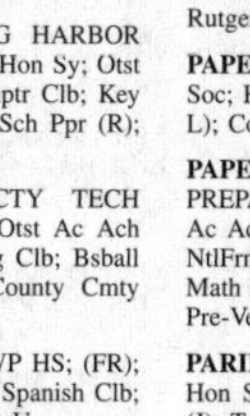
Papetti, Anthony G
Seton Hall Preparatory Sch
Randolph, NJ

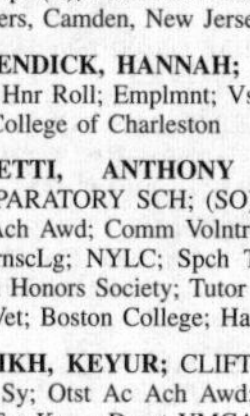
Otero, Rogelio
Gladys Hillman Jones Sch
Newark, NJ

National
Honor Roll
Spring 2005

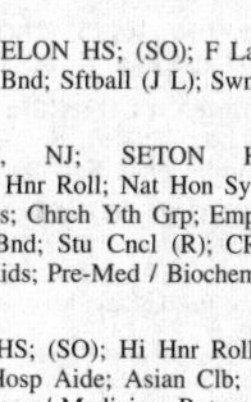
Osei-Frimpong, Jennifer
Barringer HS
Newark, NJ

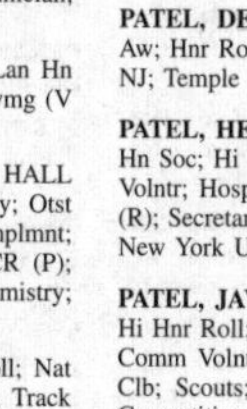
Parker, Chantelle L
Plainfield HS
Plainfield, NJ

PATEL, MEGHA; JERSEY CITY, NJ; AC OF ST ALOYSIUS; (JR); Hnr Roll; Nat Hon Sy; Otst Ac Ach Awd; Perf Att; WWAHSS; Peer Tut/Med; Mth Clb/Tm; Svce Clb; Bskball (V); Cr Ctry (J); Tennis (V); CR (R); Presidential Award; Multicultural Club; Pre-Med; Bio-Chemistry; Cornell U; New York U

PATEL, MITESH; ISELIN, NJ; JOHN F KENNEDY HS; (SO); Hi Hnr Roll; Otst Ac Ach Awd; Comm Volntr; Key Club; Sci Clb; Tech Clb; Sccr (J); Accepted in Science Research Program; Special Awards in Biology; Pre-Med; Pharmacy; Johns Hopkins; Rutgers

PATEL, NIRALI; UNION, NJ; UNION HS; (JR); F Lan Hn Soc; Hnr Roll; Nat Hon Sy; Otst Ac Ach Awd; Hosp Aide; ArtClub; Spanish Clb; Optimist Club; Ecology Club; Pharmacy; Rutgers U; U of the Sciences in Philadelphia

PATEL, NIYATI; PISCATAWAY, NJ; PISCATAWAY HS; (SR); Comm Volntr; Key Club; Nursing; Middlesex County College

PATEL, PRASHANT; PISCATAWAY, NJ; PISCATAWAY HS; (SR); Hnr Roll; Nat Hon Sy; JSA; Cr Ctry (V); Pre-Pharmacy; PhD; Rutgers U-Newark; Rutgers U-New Brunswick

PATEL, PRITEN; SADDLE BROOK, NJ; SADDLE BROOK HS; (SO); Hi Hnr Roll; Hnr Roll; WWAHSS; Yth Ldrshp Prog; Comm Volntr; Drma Clb; Cr Ctry (J); Track (V); Medicine / Doctor; Dentist; U of Pennsylvania

PATEL, PRITESH; KENDALL PARK, NJ; SOUTH BRUNSWICK HS; (SO); Hnr Roll; Perf Att; Cr Ctry (J); Track (J); Business; Computer; Rutgers U

PATEL, SAGAR; LINDEN, NJ; LINDEN HS; (SO); Hi Hnr Roll; Kwnis Aw; Nat Sci Aw; Perf Att; Pres Sch; Sci Fairs; Sci/Math Olympn; St of Mnth; Yth Ldrshp Prog; Comm Volntr; Hosp Aide; Peer Tut/Med; Biology Clb; Cmptr Clb; Key Club; Mth Clb/Tm; Sci Clb; Svce Clb; Tech Clb; Spanish Clb; Bnd; Bskball (J); Cyclg (V); Fncg (V); Mar Art (V); Tennis (V); Track (J); Wt Lftg (V); Lit Mag (R); Yrbk (R); Pharmacy; Rutgers U; New York U

PATEL, SAMTA; JERSEY CITY, NJ; WILLIAM L. DICKINSON; (SR); Hnr Roll; Nat Hon Sy; Perf Att; Sci Fairs; St of Mnth; WWAHSS; Yth Ldrshp Prog; Comm Volntr; Peer Tut/Med; Chess; Emplmnt; Key Club; Lib Aide; Mth Clb/Tm; Tmpl Yth Grp; Ch Chr; Dnce; Tennis (V); Stu Cncl (S); Sch Ppr (E); BAPS-Balika-Kishori Karykar Adhiveshon; BAPS-Balika-Kishori Convention; Pharmacist; Bio-Medical Engineering; Montclair State U; Steven Institute of Technology

PATEL, SANI; NORTH BERGEN, NJ; NORTH BERGEN HS; (FR); All Am Sch; Hi Hnr Roll; Hnr Roll; Perf Att; WWAHSS; Comm Volntr; Hosp Aide; Key Club; Tennis (J); Stu Cncl (R); Bowling (Varsity); Environmental Club; Pharmacist MD; Mechanical Engineer; Rutgers U (New Brunswick); Drexel U

PATEL, SKETA; JERSEY CITY, NJ; DICKINSON HS; (JR); Perf Att; Sci Fairs; Comm Volntr; Key Club; Lib Aide; Tmpl Yth Grp; Dnce; Stu Cncl (R); Criminal Psychology; Biomedical Engineering; Rutgers U; Penn State

PATEL, TULSHI; EGG HARBOR TOWNSHIP, NJ; EGG HARBOR TOWNSHIP HS; (SO); Hnr Roll; Hosp Aide; Key Club; Dnce; Medical Explorers Officer (Secretary); Varsity Scholar Award; Medicine; Psychology; Rutgers State U; Columbia U

PATEL, VANESSA; PARSIPPANY, NJ; PARSIPPANY HILLS HS; (JR); F Lan Hn Soc; Hnr Roll; Nat Hon Sy; Perf Att; Pres Sch; WWAHSS; Hab For Humty Volntr; Hosp Aide; Peer Tut/Med; Chrch Yth Grp; Key Club; Track (V); CR (R); Sch Ppr (R); End Racism & Sexism Everywhere (ERASE); Indian Cultural Club, FCCLA; Pediatrics (PhD, Master's); Rutgers U (RU); U of Sciences of Philadelphia

PATEL, VILOKI; JERSEY CITY, NJ; (SR); Hnr Roll; Nat Mrt Fin; Perf Att; WWAHSS; Red Cr Aide; Key Club; Dnce; Bachelor Science Nursing; Registered Nurse (RN) Master's; FDU, NJCU, HCCC

PATEL, YASHVI; LODI, NJ; LODI HS; (SO); Hi Hnr Roll; Perf Att; Pres Sch; St of Mnth; WWAHSS; Comm Volntr; Hosp Aide; Peer Tut/Med; FTA; Foreign Clb; Pre Medicine; Biomedical Engineering; Cornell U; Duke U

PATRICK, MADELINE; BRIDGEWATER, NJ; BRIDGEWATER RARITAN HS; (JR); Hi Hnr Roll; Hnr Roll; Nat Hon Sy; WWAHSS; Comm Volntr; AL Aux Girls; Drma Clb; NtlFrnscLg; SP/M/VS; Sftball (J); CR (R); Captain of Forensic Team; International Studies; Boston U; U of Miami

PAUL, JOHANN; IRVINGTON, NJ; IRVINGTON HS; (FR); Hnr Roll; MVP; Perf Att; St of Mnth; USAA; Comm Volntr; Hosp Aide; Drma Clb; Fr of Library; Key Club; Lib Aide; Mod UN; Mus Clb; Pep Squd; Scouts; Bnd; Chr; Clr Grd; Dnce; Bskball (J); Modeling; Lawyer; Harvard U; Seton Hall

PAULINO, CINDY; FAIR LAWN, NJ; FAIR LAWN HS; (JR); Nat Hon Sy; Comm Volntr; Doctor; Nurse

PAULINO, KATHERINE; NORTH BERGEN, NJ; NORTH BERGEN HS; (JR); Hi Hnr Roll; Hnr Roll; Nat Hon Sy; Nat Mrt LOC; Nat Mrt Sch Recip; WWAHSS; ArtClub; DARE; Interior Design; Photography; Fashion Institute of Technology; Art Institute of New York

PAYNE, TYLER; BROWNS MILLS, NJ; PEMBERTON TOWNSHIP HS; (FR); Sci Fairs; Comm Volntr; Emplmnt; Lcrsse; Swmg (J); Vllyball; Culinary Arts; Law; Oklahoma U; Princeton U

PAZCOGUIN, LAUREN; CLOSTER, NJ; NORTHERN VALLEY REG HS (DEMAREST); (JR); Hi Hnr Roll; Hnr Roll; Perf Att; CARE; Hosp Aide; 4-H; DARE; Pep Squd; Japanese Clb; Bnd; Dnce; Stg Cre; Skiing (J); Track (J); Yrbk (E); Band Award; Carnegie Hall Concert Award; Pharmacy; Pharmacology; Rutgers U; St. John's U

PEARCE, TARA; RINGWOOD, NJ; LAKELAND REG HS; (SO); Hnr Roll; Comm Volntr; Peer Tut/Med; Chrch Yth Grp; Emplmnt; SADD; Lcrsse (J); PP Ftbl (J); Sccr (J); Track (J); Leaders Encouraging Adolescent Progress; Student Cultural Club; Developmental Psychology; Pediatrics; Florida Atlantic U; Florida State

PEARSON, CHRISTIAN; MONTCLAIR, NJ; MONTCLAIR HS; (JR); Hnr Roll; Nat Hon Sy; WWAHSS; Comm Volntr; Peer Tut/Med; ArtClub; Chrch Yth Grp; Emplmnt; Sci Clb; Fncg (V); CR (R); Yrbk (P); Weston Science Scholars; Philosophy; U of Pennsylvania; Morehouse College

PECK, ALLISON E; CAPE MAY, NJ; LOWER CAPE MAY REG HS; (SR); Hi Hnr Roll; Hnr Roll; Nat Hon Sy; Nat Ldrshp Svc; Otst Ac Ach Awd; Pres Ac Ftns Aw; St of Mnth; WWAHSS; Comm Volntr; Chrch Yth Grp; Emplmnt; Mus Clb; Bnd; Chr; Dnce; Mch Bnd; CR (R); Yrbk (E); U of the Sciences in Philadelphia

PECK, KRISTEN; WOODBURY, NJ; DEPTFORD HS; (SO); Hnr Roll; Perf Att; Comm Volntr; ArtClub; Chrch Yth Grp; Scouts; Yrbk (E); Girl Scout Silver Award; Veterinary Medicine

PECORINO, CHRISTINE M; SUCCASUNNA, NJ; ROXBURY HS; (SO); F Lan Hn Soc; Hnr Roll; Pres Ac Ftns Aw; St of Mnth; WWAHSS; Key Club; Scouts; National Gymnast; Psychology; Nutrition; Drew U; Princeton

PELLEGRINO, STEPHEN; BEDMINSTER, NJ; BERNARDS HS; (JR); Ctznshp Aw; Hi Hnr Roll; Hnr Roll; WWAHSS; Hab For Humty Volntr; Mod UN; NtlFrnscLg; Scouts; SP/M/VS; Sccr (VJC); Tennis (VJ); Winner of Comedic Duet-South American Competition; Engineering-Mechanical / Civil; Bucknell U; Carnegie Mellon

PELTZ, TETYANA; VINELAND, NJ; VINELAND HS; (JR); Nat Hon Sy; Chess; Mth Clb/Tm; German Clb; Ch Chr; Dnce; Vllyball (V)

PENA, LUISA; UNION CITY, NJ; EMERSON HS; (SO); Hnr Roll; ArtClub; Spanish Clb; SP/M/VS; Vllyball (V); Pediatrics; Pre-Chiropractic; Saint Peter's College; Jersey City U

PENA, YADELIN; ELIZABETH, NJ; ELIZABETH HS; (SR); F Lan Hn Soc; Hi Hnr Roll; Hnr Roll; Nat Hon Sy; Otst Ac Ach Awd; WWAHSS; Comm Volntr; Peer Tut/Med; Key Club; NtlFrnscLg; SP/M/VS; Biology; Kean U

PENG, KATHY; LEDGEWOOD, NJ; (SO); F Lan Hn Soc; Hi Hnr Roll; Hnr Roll; Otst Ac Ach Awd; WWAHSS; Comm Volntr; Key Club; Mth Clb/Tm; Sci Clb; Chr; Environmental Science; Architect/Interior Design; U of Pennsylvania; Cornell U

PENNY, ANTHONY; MOUNT LAUREL, NJ; LENAPE HS; (JR); Ctznshp Aw; Hnr Roll; Jr Eng Tech; MVP; St of Mnth; WWAHSS; Comm Volntr; Vsity Clb; Spanish Clb; Bskball (VJ); Track (VJC), Student of the Month; Athletic Achievement Award; Architectural Engineering; Civil Engineering; Drexel; U of Delaware

PEPE, ELIOT; MAPLEWOOD, NJ; COLUMBIA HS; (SO); Hi Hnr Roll; Hnr Roll; Comm Volntr; Key Club; Photog; Chr; Tennis (J); Lit Mag (P); Computer Graphics / Advertising; Graphic Arts; Rhode Island School of Design; Parsons School of Design

PERAZZONE, KYLE; CEDAR GROVE, NJ; CEDAR GROVE HS; (JR); Hi Hnr Roll; Hnr Roll; WWAHSS; Bnd; Sccr (VJ); Tennis (VJC)

PERCHMENT, CHANICE; PARAMUS, NJ; COLUMBIA HS; (SO); Comm Volntr; Peer Tut/Med; Key Club; Ch Chr; Newark Lightbearers / Pathfinder Club Youth Group; Nursing; Real Estate; New York U; Hunter College

PERCONTINO, TONI A; HOBOKEN, NJ; HOBOKEN HS; (JR); Perf Att; WWAHSS; Comm Volntr; Drma Clb; Emplmnt; Pep Squd; Italian Clb; Chrldg (VJ); Sccr (VJ); Yrbk (P); Nominated for Governor's School Award; IB Program; Psychology; Management; American U of Rome; Montclair State U

PEREIRA, UEREQUENIA; NEWARK, NJ; EAST SIDE HS; (SO); Hnr Roll; MVP; Nat Stu Ath Day Aw; ArtClub; Cmptr Clb; DARE; Mus Clb; Vsity Clb; Portuguese Clb; Bnd; Drm Mjr; Mar Art (V L); Swmg (V); Vllyball (V); FBI; Trainer; Penn State; Hawaii

PEREZ, AARON D; JERSEY CITY, NJ; ST ALOYSIUS HS; (SR); Hnr Roll; Bsball (VJ L); Sccr (V); Track (VJCL); Sch Ppr (E); Yrbk (R, P); Criminal Justice; Business; John Jay College of Criminal Justice; Seton Hall U

PEREZ, NAOMI A; PATERSON, NJ; PCTI; (SR); Emplmnt; ROTC; Voc Ind Clb Am; Clr Grd; Drl Tm; NJROTC; Criminal Justice; New Jersey City U; Rutgers U

PEREZ, PLICELIANY; PATERSON, NJ; LOOMIS CHAFFEE SCH; MS; Ctznshp Aw; Hi Hnr Roll; Hnr Roll; Nat Hon Sy; Otst Ac Ach Awd; Pres Sch; Salutrn; Sci Fairs; St Schl; St of Mnth; Bnd; Dnce; Bskball (J); Sccr (J); Vllyball (J); Stu Cncl (R); Sch Ppr (R); Art's Highest Achievement Award; GEPA - Advanced Proficient Award / All Areas; Veterinarian; PhD Degree; Princeton U; Columbia U

PEREZ, STEPHANIE; ROCKAWAY, NJ; MORRIS HILLS HS; (FR); Hi Hnr Roll; Hnr Roll; Chr; National Physical Fitness Award; Beautician; Pre School Teacher

PERI, ALEXANDRA; HASKELL, NJ; LAKELAND REG HS; (JR); Hi Hnr Roll; Valdctrian; WWAHSS; Quiz Bowl; Latin Clb; Book Club, Latin Club; Fed Challenge; Bio Tech; WPU

PERILLO IV, JAMES L; STIRLING, NJ; WATCHUNG HILLS REG HS; (SO); Hnr Roll; Nat Hon Sy; Comm Volntr; Hab For Humty Volntr; Chrch Yth Grp; Lcrsse (VJ); Stu Cncl (R); CR (R); Rutgers

PERRONE, JOHN A; EATONTOWN, NJ; AC OF ALLIED HEALTH; (JR); Red Cr Aide; Mth Clb/Tm; Ftball (V); CR (R); HOSA, Fitness and Math Club; MD; U of Pennsylvania; The College of New Jersey

PETERSON, RYAN A; LAKE HOPATCONG, NJ; JEFFERSON TWP HS; (FR); Hnr Roll; MVP; Otst Ac Ach Awd; Pres Ac Ftns Aw; St of Mnth; DARE; Emplmnt; Wdwrkg Clb; Stg Cre; Bskball (J); Cr Ctry (J); Ftball (J); Track (J); Technology; New Jersey Institute of Technology

PETOUKHOFF, CHRISTOPHER E; HADDON HEIGHTS, NJ; PAUL VI HS; (SO); Hi Hnr Roll; Hnr Roll; WWAHSS; Comm Volntr; Peer Tut/Med; Chess; Lib Aide; Scouts; Bowling Club; Pharmacology; Medicine; U of Pennsylvania; New York U

PHEAN, BOPHA; TRENTON, NJ; TRENTON CTRL HS; (FR); Nat Hon Sy; St of Mnth; Pep Squd; Business; Lawyer; Harvard; Princeton

PHILIP, LIJIN; AVENEL, NJ; COLONIA HS; (SO); Gmnstcs (V); Pharmacy; Rutgers State U; William Paterson U

PHILIPPE, DINA; ELIZABETH, NJ; ELIZABETH HS; (JR); Hnr Roll; Nat Hon Sy; Nat Mrt LOC; Nat Sci Aw; Otst Ac Ach Awd; Perf Att; WWAHSS; Comm Volntr; Key Club; Outdrs Clb; HAITIAN Clb; Lit Mag; I Did Community Services; I Did Community Services At YMCA; Major in Nursing; Montclair U; Rutgers U

PIECZONKA, MICHAL; KEARNY, NJ; HCST-NORTH HUDSON CTR; (SO); Hnr Roll; Peer Tut/Med; Emplmnt; Bsball (V); Sccr (V); Second Team-All County-Soccer; .472 Batting Average-Sophomore Year; Business; Cinematography; Pennsylvania State U; New York U

PIEDADE, IZABELY; BELLEVILLE, NJ; BELLEVILLE HS; (JR); Kwnis Aw; Comm Volntr; Key Club; Dnce; Track (J)

PIERRE, JENNIFER; RINGWOOD, NJ; IMMACULATE HEART AC; MS; Hnr Roll; Nat Hon Sy; Pres Sch; Comm Volntr; Peer Tut/Med; DARE; P to P St Amb Prg; Tchrs Aide; Chr; Ch Chr; Dnce; SP/M/VS; Mar Art; Stu Cncl (P); Yrbk (E); Distinguished Scholar in Johns Hopkins Talent Search; Language Arts & Christian Service Award; Literature; Communications; Harvard; Princeton

PIERRE, NOAH; WILLINGBORO, NJ; BCIT; (JR); Hnr Roll; Nat Hon Sy; St of Mnth; Comm Volntr; FBLA; Accounting; Statistics; Boston U; Penn U

PIERRE, WOODLINE; ELIZABETH, NJ; ELIZABETH HS; (JR); Hnr Roll; WWAHSS; Comm Volntr; Chrch Yth Grp; Key Club; Outdrs Clb; Chr; CR (R); New York U; Columbia U

PIETRO, NATALIE A; PT PLEASANT BEACH, NJ; PT PLEASANT BEACH HS; (SR); Hi Hnr Roll; Hnr Roll; Nat Hon Sy; Peer Tut/Med; Drma Clb; Key Club; Sci Clb; Chr; Chrldg (V L); Stu Cncl (R); CR (R); Yrbk (E, R); Founder of Sailing Team & Captain; Psychology; Boston College

PIETRZAK, MONIKA; LINDEN, NJ; MILLBURN HS; (SR); Hi Hnr Roll; Nat Mrt LOC; Sci Fairs; Comm Volntr; Emplmnt; Sci Clb; Chr; Dnce; Part of Modern Issues Club; Miss Polonia of Linden; Pre-Law; Psychology; New York U

PINTO, KYIESHA M; CAMDEN, NJ; CAMDEN CTY TECH SCH; (FR); Hnr Roll; Perf Att; Comm Volntr; Peer Tut/Med; Tchrs Aide; Dnce; Drl Tm; Stg Cre; Nurse for Infants; Teaching; Fayetteville State U; Delaware State U

PINTO, MELISSA; LITTLE FALLS, NJ; MARY HELP OF CHRISTIANS AC; (JR); Hnr Roll; Nat Hon Sy; Otst Ac Ach Awd; Pres Sch; WWAHSS; Hosp Aide; Lttrmn Clb; SP/M/VS; GAA; Vllyball (J L); Cl Off (S); National Youth Leadership Forum on Medicine; Pre-Med; Pre-Dental; Fordham U; Seton Hall U

PIOTROWICZ, KLAUDIA; KEANSBURG, NJ; PERTH AMBOY HS; (SR); 4H Awd; Hi Hnr Roll; Hnr Roll; Perf Att; St of Mnth; WWAHSS; Yth Ldrshp Prog; Comm Volntr; Emplmnt; SADD; WORLD Clb; Chr; Bskball (VJCL); CR (S); Heroes and Cool Kids; Elementary Education; Kean U; Montclair State U

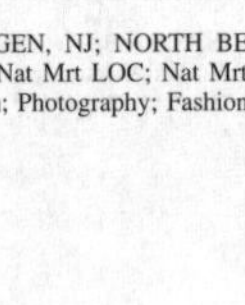
Pieczonka, Michal
Hcst-North Hudson Ctr
Kearny, NJ

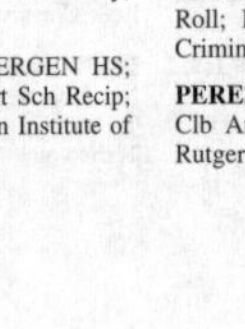
Penny, Anthony
Lenape HS
Mount Laurel, NJ

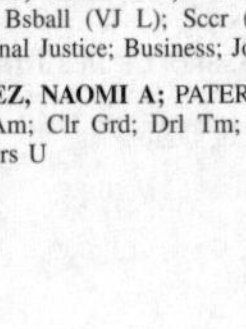
Pena, Luisa
Emerson HS
Union City, NJ

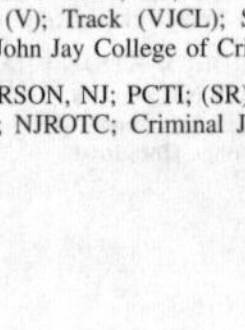
Patel, Niyati
Piscataway HS
Piscataway, NJ

Peck, Allison E
Lower Cape May Reg HS
Cape May, NJ

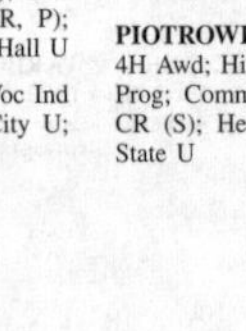
Perez, Pliceliany
Loomis Chaffee Sch
Paterson, NJ

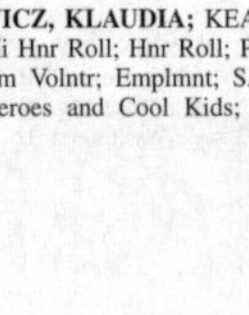
Pierre, Jennifer
Immaculate Heart AC
Ringwood, NJ

PISCITELLI, GRACE; JERSEY CITY, NJ; AC OF SACRED HEART HS; (SO); Hnr Roll; Comm Volntr; ArtClub; SP/M/VS; Bskball (V); Sccr (J); Sftball (V); Yrbk (R); 2005 Softball All Star; Architecture; Criminal Justice; New York U; Seton Hall U

PIWINSKI, KAREN E; LEBANON, NJ; NORTH HUNTERDON HS; (JR); Hnr Roll; Otst Ac Ach Awd; Comm Volntr; Spanish Clb; Stg Cre; Hsbk Rdg; President's Volunteer Service Award

PLANTIER, CHRIS; MERCERVILLE, NJ; NOTTINGHAM-HAMILTON HS NORTH; (JR); Hnr Roll; WWAHSS; Chrch Yth Grp; Emplmnt; FBLA; Key Club; Stg Cre; Who's Who / 2004 & 2005 Edition; Accounting & Finance; Criminal Justice; Richard C Stockton U; Rowan U

PLASENCIA, CEIDA; JERSEY CITY, NJ; CTY PREP HS; (FR); Hi Hnr Roll; Hnr Roll; Perf Att; Sci Fairs; Peer Tut/Med; Chess; Chrch Yth Grp; DARE; Drma Clb; Key Club; Mth Clb/Tm; Dnce; Chrldg (J); Mar Art (V); Track (J); Best Model Award; 1st Place At Karate Tournament; Sociology; Business Management for a Fashion Industry; Fashion Institute of Technology; New York U

PLASKET, NICOLE; GLASSBORO, NJ; GLASSBORO HS; (SR); All Am Sch; Hnr Roll; Sci Fairs; USAA; Comm Volntr; Hab For Humty Volntr; Chrch Yth Grp; DARE; Drma Clb; Scouts; Chr; Clr Grd; SP/M/VS; USAA National Honor Student; Honor Roll; Medical Administrative Assistant; Cittone Institute-Mt Laurel, NJ

PLAZA, RONALD; NORTH BERGEN, NJ; NORTH BERGER HS; (FR); Hnr Roll; Spec Olymp Vol; Key Club; Volunteer At Salvation Army; Volunteer At Special Olympics; Computer Teacher; Saint Peter's College-Jersey City New Jersey

PLEASANTS JR, DELON; MONTCLAIR, NJ; MONTCLAIR HS; (JR); WWAHSS; Comm Volntr; Peer Tut/Med; Ftball (J); Wt Lftg (J); Avid; Gear Up; Education; Mathematics; Kean U; Boston College

PLOSTINS, INTA; MADISON, NJ; MADISON HS; (SO); Hi Hnr Roll; Comm Volntr; Peer Tut/Med; Drma Clb; JSA; Key Club; French Clb; SP/M/VS; Stg Cre; Latvian Summer High School; Key Club President; International Relations; Peace and War Studies; Pomona College; New York U

POAT, AMANDA E; NEWFOUNDLAND, NJ; WEST MILFORD TWP HS; (JR); Hnr Roll; Comm Volntr; Spec Olymp Vol; Chrch Yth Grp; Dbte Team; Drma Clb; Emplmnt; Mod UN; Svce Clb; Tech Clb; Italian Clb; Bnd; Drm Mjr; Mch Bnd; SP/M/VS; Track (J); Yrbk (R); Paramedic; Criminal Justice; Edinboro U of Pennsylvania; U of Connecticut

PODOLSKI, PETER M; NEW PROVIDENCE, NJ; NEW PROVIDENCE HS; (JR); Hnr Roll; Comm Volntr; Mth Clb/Tm; Japanese Clb; Cr Ctry; Track; Lit Mag (R); Social Studies Award; Volunteer At International Night; Filmography; Psychology; Rutgers U; U of California, Los Angeles

PODRAZA, ELAINE; SPOTSWOOD, NJ; SPOTSWOOD HS; (JR); Hi Hnr Roll; Hnr Roll; Comm Volntr; DECA; Dnce; Stu Cncl (R); Sch Ppr (R); DECA Chapter President (2005-2006); Elementary Education; The College of New Jersey; Rowan U

POLANCO, BYRON; PATERSON, NJ; PATERSON CATHOLIC HS; (SO); Hnr Roll; Bsball (J); Baseball State Champs (Traveling Team)

POLITE, JEROME; NEWARK, NJ; WEST SIDE HS; (SO); Perf Att; Bnd; Music Scholarship; Selling, Police Officer and Acting; Essex County College; Montclair State

POON, THERESA; ATLANTIC CITY, NJ; ATLANTIC CITY HS; (SR); Hnr Roll; Nat Hon Sy; Comm Volntr; FBLA; Key Club; P to P St Amb Prg; Photog; Sch Ppr (P); Sociology; Rider U; Georgian Court U

PORCELLINI, CONNIE; LANOKA HARBOR, NJ; MONSIGNOR DONOVAN HS; (SO); Hi Hnr Roll; Hnr Roll; Key Club; SADD; Dnce; Bskball (J); Johns Hopkins CTY's Talent Search; Forensic Scientist; Criminal Justice

PORTELLI, JOSEPH; WAYNE, NJ; WAYNE VALLEY SR HS; (JR); Ctznshp Aw; F Lan Hn Soc; Hi Hnr Roll; Nat Hon Sy; Otst Ac Ach Awd; Comm Volntr; Emplmnt; Jr Cls League; Latin Clb; Ftball (V); Track (V); Vice President of Latin Club; Minds in Motion Awards-4.0 GPA W/ Varsity Letter; Architecture; U of Virginia; Drexel U

PORTER, ASHLEY; PATERSON, NJ; EASTSIDE HS; (SO); Hnr Roll; Nat Hon Sy; Chrch Yth Grp; Real Estate; Real Estate College

PORTER, SKYLAR; ROCKAWAY, NJ; THE AC OF ST ELIZABETH; (JR); Hnr Roll; Emplmnt; Chr; Dnce; SP/M/VS; Sccr (V); CR; Gymnastics-Nat'l Team Outside School Before Knee Surgery; Commercials

PORTILLO, ERIKA; BAYONNE, NJ; BAYONNE HS; (SO); Hnr Roll; Emplmnt; CR (R); Psychologist; Doctor / Pediatrician; Seton Hall U; NJCU

PRAKASH, NICK; SADDLE RIVER, NJ; NORTHERN HIGHLANDS REG HS; (SO); Hnr Roll; Perf Att; Pres Ac Ftns Aw; Comm Volntr; DARE; DECA; Vsity Clb; Cr Ctry (V L); Track (V L); Medical; New York U

PRAKRIYA, DIVYA; PLAINSBORO, NJ; WEST WINDSOR PLAINSBORO HS SOUTH; (FR); Hi Hnr Roll; Red Cr Aide; Lib Aide; Orch; Stg Cre; Track; Yrbk (P); Officer of Watts (Women Achieving Triumphs in Technology and Science)-Authorization As Non-Profit Organization Pending; Volunteer At Library; Marine Biology; Criminal Justice & Law Enforcement; U of Chicago; Yale

PRICE, TREVOR; PLAINFIELD, NJ; PLAINFIELD HS; (JR); Hnr Roll; Red Cr Aide; BPA; Cmptr Clb; Emplmnt; FBLA; Scouts; Dnce; Stg Cre; Swmg (V); CR (R); Lifeguard-Certified; Word & Excel-Certified; Business Management; Culinary Arts; Schiller Int'l U; NYU

PRYBELLA, AMANDA; SOUTH PLAINFIELD, NJ; SOUTH PLAINFIELD HS; (SR); F Lan Hn Soc; Hi Hnr Roll; Hnr Roll; Nat Hon Sy; Pres Ac Ftns Aw; Salutrn; Hab For Humty Volntr; Scouts; SADD; Spanish Clb; Dnce; Yrbk (E, R, P); Unsung Hero Award, Bloustein Distinguished Scholar; Silver Award & Gold Award in Girl Scouts; Secondary Education; Chemistry; The College of New Jersey

PUGH, NYKIMA L; ASBURY PARK, NJ; ASHBURY PARK HS; (FR); Hnr Roll; Otst Ac Ach Awd; Perf Att; St of Mnth; Comm Volntr; Chrch Yth Grp; Emplmnt; Key Club; Scouts; Ch Chr; Chrldg (J); Vllyball (J); CR (V); Health and Medicine

PUKL, CASEY M; RINGWOOD, NJ; LAKELAND REG HS; (SR); Hi Hnr Roll; Hnr Roll; Nat Hon Sy; St of Mnth; Dbte Team; Drma Clb; Mus Clb; Acpl Chr; Bnd; Chr; Jzz Bnd; Scr Kpr (V); Vllyball (J); Sch Ppr (R); President Choral Program (2 Years); Vice President of Band; Music Production & Engineering; Songwriting; Berklee College of Music

QUA, MICHAEL; SKILLMAN, NJ; NOTRE DAME HS; (JR); Hi Hnr Roll; Hnr Roll; Nat Hon Sy; Sci/Math Olympn; Comm Volntr; ArtClub; Mus Clb; Sci Clb; Bnd; Jzz Bnd; Piano; 3rd Degree Black Belt Tae Kwon Do; Business; Engineering; Villanova U; Lehigh U

QUICHUA, DWIGHT V; SOUTH PLAINFIELD, NJ; SOUTH PLAINFIELD HS; (SR); F Lan Hn Soc; Hi Hnr Roll; Hnr Roll; Nat Hon Sy; Pres Ac Ftns Aw; Yth Ldrshp Prog; Hab For Humty Volntr; Peer Tut/Med; Emplmnt; SADD; Vsity Clb; French Clb; Sccr (V CL); Track (V); Stu Cncl (R); CR (R); Criminal Justice; Sociology; York College of Pennsylvania; Rutgers U

QUIMOYOG, ANDREA; CLIFTON, NJ; QUEEN OF PEACE HS; (JR); Hi Hnr Roll; Comm Volntr; Peer Tut/Med; Chess; Emplmnt; Quiz Bowl; Chr; Yrbk (R); Biochemistry / Biophysics; Pediatric Medical; Rutgers U New Brunswick; New York U

QUINN, JUSTIN T P; MONROEVILLE, NJ; GLOUSTER CTY INST OF TECH; (JR); Hnr Roll; WWAHSS; Comm Volntr; Key Club; Scouts; SP/M/VS; Stg Cre; (Boy Scouts) Assistant Senior Patrol Leader; S.A.D.D. Club and R.E.B.E.L. Club; Theatre; Television, Film; New York U; West Point

QUINONES, YVONNE M; FREEHOLD, NJ; COMMUNICATIONS HS; (SR); WWAHSS; Comm Volntr; Chrch Yth Grp; Quill & Scroll; Sch Ppr (E); Yrbk (R); Journalism; English; Wagner College; U of Delaware

QUINTELA, ROBERT; NORTH BERGEN, NJ; NORTH BERGEN HS; (JR); F Lan Hn Soc; Hi Hnr Roll; Otst Ac Ach Awd; WWAHSS; Comm Volntr; Key Club; Principal's Academic Award; Nomination for the National Honor Society; Mechanical Engineering; Electrical Engineering; Stevens Institute of Technology; Columbia U

QUINTERO, ERIC; ENGLEWOOD, NJ; ACADEMIES AT ENGLEWOOD; (JR); Hi Hnr Roll; Hnr Roll; St of Mnth; Comm Volntr; ArtClub; DARE; Emplmnt; Mus Clb; Bnd; Mch Bnd; Bsball (J); Bskball (L); Wt Lftg; Illustration; Animation; School of Visual Arts

RAAB, STELLA T; WENONAH, NJ; OUR LADY OF MERCY AC; (SO); Hi Hnr Roll; Hnr Roll; Otst Ac Ach Awd; Sci Fairs; Hab For Humty Volntr; Red Cr Aide; ArtClub; Drma Clb; Pep Squd; Sci Clb; Scouts; SADD; Spanish Clb; Sftball (J); Vllyball (J); Stu Cncl (T); Played Piano for 8 Years; Received an Achievement Scholarship; Marine Biology; Mathematics; Arcadia U; Rutgers U

RABINOVICH, REMY; MORGANVILLE, NJ; MARLBORO HS; (SO); Comm Volntr; Hosp Aide; Dbte Team; FBLA; Ice Hockey; Pre-Med; MD; New York U; Boston U

RAFEL, DARREN A; EAST HANOVER, NJ; HANOVER PARK HS; (JR); Hnr Roll; Comm Volntr; Emplmnt; Tennis (V); E.R.A.S.E. Club; Peer Counselor; Criminal Attorney; U of Massachusetts At Amherst; U of Florida

RAFFERTY, KRISTIN; BELVIDERE, NJ; BELVIDERE HS; (FR); Hi Hnr Roll; Hnr Roll; Nat Hon Sy; Pres Sch; Photog; Chr; Cl Off (R); Stu Cncl (R); CR (R); National American Miss Pageants; Handbell Choir; Professional Model

RAHBARI, STEVEN; NORTH BERGEN, NJ; HIGH TECH HS; Hnr Roll; Otst Ac Ach Awd; DARE; Key Club; Bsball (V); Marine Biology; Medical Doctor; Miami State U

RAJARAM, STEPHANIE M; JERSEY CITY, NJ; DR RONALD MC NAIR AC HS; (FR); Perf Att; Sci Fairs; Hosp Aide; Outdrs Clb; Spanish Clb; Cr Ctry; Track; Yrbk (E); Science Four Award Grammar School; Rotary Award-Grammar School; Pharmacist; Teacher; Rutgers U; New York U

RAJU, PREETHI; BRIDGEWATER, NJ; BRIDGEWATER-RARITAN HS; (SO); Hi Hnr Roll; Hnr Roll; Otst Ac Ach Awd; Yth Ldrshp Prog; Comm Volntr; Hosp Aide; Spec Olymp Vol; ArtClub; Key Club; MuAlphaTh; Chr; Dnce; Track (J); Yrbk (R, P); Active Member of the Indian Association of Somerset County; Member of the National Society of High School Scholars; Architecture; Engineering; Massachusetts Institute of Technology; New York Institute of Technology

RALLY, PRIYA; JERSEY CITY, NJ; DICKINSON HS; (FR); Perf Att; Sci Fairs; Comm Volntr; Key Club; Dnce; SP/M/VS; Bskball; Swmg; Vllyball; Cl Off; Award from City Hall

RAMCHARITAR, NALINI; JERSEY CITY, NJ; DICKINSON HS; (JR); Medical; Nursing; Rutgers College

RAMEY, JESSICA; ANNANDALE, NJ; GILL ST BERNARD'S SCH; (JR); Ctznshp Aw; Hi Hnr Roll; Hnr Roll; WWAHSS; Comm Volntr; Emplmnt; Quill & Scroll; Dnce; SP/M/VS; Tennis (V); Sch Ppr (E); French Honor Society; Academic League; Business Management; Architecture; Lafayette; Villanova U

RAMEY, SHADAYA S; BAYONNE, NJ; BAYONNE HS; (FR); Hi Hnr Roll; Hnr Roll; Chrch Yth Grp; DARE; Ch Chr; Drl Tm; Stepping; African American Studies; Pediatrics; Hampton U; Clark Atlanta U

RAMIREZ, CINDY; MORRISTOWN, NJ; MORRISTOWN HS; (SR); Hi Hnr Roll; Hnr Roll; St of Mnth; Dnce; Bskball (V); Criminal Justice; Police Officer; Boston College; U Miami

RAMIREZ, FRANCES M; PARLIN, NJ; SAYREVILLE WAR MEMORIAL HS; (SR); All Am Sch; F Lan Hn Soc; Hi Hnr Roll; Hnr Roll; Nat Hon Sy; Peer Tut/Med; AL Aux Girls; Mth Clb/Tm; MuAlphaTh; Pep Squd; Chr; Drl Tm; SP/M/VS; Cl Off (R); Stu Cncl (V, T, R); Lead America - CSI; History Club / Teen Institute of Garden State - TIGS; Forensic Science Major; George Washington U

RAMNANAN, TIFFANY; MONTCLAIR, NJ; (JR); Hnr Roll; St of Mnth; Yth Ldrshp Prog; Comm Volntr; Peer Tut/Med; Red Cr Aide; Chrch Yth Grp; Emplmnt; Fr of Library; Key Club; Bskball; Tennis (L); Track (L)

RAMOS, NICHOLAS K; OAKLAND, NJ; BARNSTABLE AC; (JR); Hi Hnr Roll; Nat Hon Sy; WWAHSS; Yth Ldrshp Prog; Emplmnt; HO'Br Yth Ldrshp; CR (P); Computer Animation / Graphics and Design; World History; Fordham U; California Institute of Technology.

RAMOS, SAMANTHA; BELLEVILLE, NJ; BELLEVILLE HS; (FR); Hnr Roll; Comm Volntr; Key Club; Sftball (V C); Vllyball (V L); Stu Cncl (R); Key Club; Octagon Club; Psychology; Master's Degree; Rutgers U; St Peter's College

RANA, MITALI; TRENTON, NJ; STEINERT HS; (SO)

RAO, HARI; RARITAN, NJ; BRIDGEWATER-RARITAN HS; (JR); Hnr Roll; Hosp Aide; Emplmnt; FBLA; Key Club; NYLC; Prom Com; Mar Art (V); Cl Off (P); Stu Cncl (R); 4 Years of Private Lessons - Guitar; Community Battle of Bands - Final 3; Psychology; Biomedical Engineering; Boston College; Duke U

RAPPOPORT, JULIA; MONTCLAIR, NJ; MONTCLAIR HS; (JR); F Lan Hn Soc; Hi Hnr Roll; Nat Hon Sy; Comm Volntr; Hab For Humty Volntr; Peer Tut/Med; Biology Clb; Mth Clb/Tm; Italian Clb; Skiing; Civics and Government Institute; Biochemistry; Doctor; U of Pennsylvania; Tufts U

RASMUSSEN, KATE; PRINCETON, NJ; SOUTH BRUNSWICK HS; (SO); Hnr Roll; Perf Att; Comm Volntr; Prom Com; Tchrs Aide; CR (R); VFW Voice of Democracy Essay Contest Local Winner; Homecoming Committee; Liberal Arts and Sciences

RASTOGI, RAHUL; LONG VALLEY, NJ; WEST MORRIS CTRL HS; (JR); F Lan Hn Soc; Hi Hnr Roll; Nat Hon Sy; Nat Mrt LOC; Comm Volntr; Spec Olymp Vol; FBLA; Key Club; Mth Clb/Tm; Sci Clb; Track (J); National Honor Society; AP Scholar with Honor; Engineering-Industrial & Operations; Business-Management & Finance; U of Michigan-Ann Arbor; Cornell U

RASTOGI, TANVI; BRIDGEWATER, NJ; BRIDGEWATER-RARITAN HS; (JR); F Lan Hn Soc; Hi Hnr Roll; Nat Hon Sy; Comm Volntr; Hab For Humty Volntr; Peer Tut/Med; FBLA; MuAlphaTh; Scouts; 1st Degree Black Belt in Tae Kwon Do; Mensa Member; Bio Chemistry; Harvard College; U of Pennsylvania

RAY, CHELSEA-LEE J; WILLIAMSTOWN, NJ; WILLIAMSTOWN HS; (JR); F Lan Hn Soc; Hi Hnr Roll; Nat Hon Sy; St of Mnth; WWAHSS; Comm Volntr; Chrch Yth Grp; Drma Clb; Key Club; NYLC; Ch Chr; SP/M/VS; Tennis (V L); National Honor Society Secretary; Fencing (Sport); Law; Political Science; The College of New Jersey; The College of William and Mary

Rajaram, Stephanie M
Dr Ronald Mc Nair AC HS
Jersey City, NJ

Prybella, Amanda
South Plainfield HS
South Plainfield, NJ

Porcellini, Connie
Monsignor Donovan HS
Lanoka Harbor, NJ

National
Honor Roll
Spring 2005

Piscitelli, Grace
AC Of Sacred Heart HS
Jersey City, NJ

Raab, Stella T
Our Lady Of Mercy AC
Wenonah, NJ

Ramcharitar, Nalini
Dickinson HS
Jersey City, NJ

REAP, COLETTE A; WANAQUE, NJ; LAKELAND REG; (JR); Hnr Roll; Nat Hon Sy; Pres Sch; WWAHSS; Yth Ldrshp Prog; Comm Volntr; ArtClub; Chrch Yth Grp; Emplmnt; GAA (J); Sftball (J); CR (R); Sch Ppr (R); Yrbk (E); Art; Biology; State U of New York; The College of New Jersey

REBMANN, REBECCA; CAPE MAY COURT HOUSE, NJ; CAPE MAY CTY TECH; (SR); 4H Awd; All Am Sch; Ctznshp Aw; Gov Hnr Prg; Hi Hnr Roll; Nat Hon Sy; Nat Ldrshp Svc; Otst Ac Ach Awd; Pres Sch; St Schl; Comm Volntr; Peer Tut/Med; 4-H; Emplmnt; Mus Clb; Ntl FFA; Outdrs Clb; Schol Bwl; Orch; Sch Ppr (R); President-National Honors Society; President FFA / Community Band; Veterinarian; Delaware Valley College

REDMOND, TIMOTHY; WENONAH, NJ; GATEWAY REG HS; (SO); Hnr Roll; Comm Volntr; Chrch Yth Grp; Mus Clb; Scouts; German Clb; Cr Ctry (V); Swmg (V); Track (V); In the Fall Season of 2003 I Broke the School Record for the 5K in Cross Country.; Art & Creative Writing (Double Major); I Hope to Go Into Teaching.

REED JR, CHARLES S; JERSEY CITY, NJ; DR RONALD MC NAIR AC HS; (SO); All Am Sch; Hi Hnr Roll; Hnr Roll; Nat Ldrshp Svc; Otst Ac Ach Awd; St of Mnth; USAA; Valdctrian; WWAHSS; Comm Volntr; Chrch Yth Grp; Lib Aide; Mod UN; Dnce; SP/M/VS; Stg Cre; Bskball (V); Sch Ppr (R); Certificate of Merit Awards; Certificate of Achievement Award; Business Management; Lawyer; Old Dominion U; Harvard U

REEVE, ALISON; PISCATAWAY, NJ; PISCATAWAY HS; (JR); Gov Hnr Prg; Hi Hnr Roll; Nat Hon Sy; Pres Ac Ftns Aw; WWAHSS; Comm Volntr; Peer Tut/Med; Drma Clb; Key Club; Scouts; Vsity Clb; Stg Cre; Gmnstcs (V); Scr Kpr (V); Swmg (V); Governor's School of Environmental Science; Environmental Science; Penn State U; U of Connecticut

REEVES, ANTHONY L; LUMBERTON, NJ; RANCOCAS VALLEY REG HS; (SO); Hi Hnr Roll; Hnr Roll; St of Mnth; Ftball (V); Wrstlg (J); Criminal Law; Justice; Drexel U; Villanova U

REGAN, EMILY E; BERKELEY HEIGHTS, NJ; GOVERNOR LIVINGSTON HS; (JR); F Lan Hn Soc; Nat Hon Sy; Emplmnt; MuAlphaTh; Photog; Quill & Scroll; Chr; Swmg (V L); Lit Mag; Scholar Athlete Award; English Language & Literature / General; Lafayette; U of Delaware

REGGI, JUSTIN; TRENTON, NJ; STEINERT HS; (FR); Hnr Roll; Nat Sci Aw; Otst Ac Ach Awd; Pres Sch; Sci Fairs; Comm Volntr; Dbte Team; Drma Clb; Italian Clb; SP/M/VS; Skiing; Sccr; Track (V L); Poetry Published In Local College Publication; Architecture; Acting

REGIS, JESSE; HACKETTSTOWN, NJ; WEST MORRIS CTRL HS; (SO); WWAHSS; Key Club; P to P St Amb Prg; Bsball (J); People to People Student Ambassador; Teen Writer-Morris County Daily Record; Photo Journalist; New York U; Boston U

REID, ANTON C; NEWARK, NJ; PINE FORGE AC; (FR); Hnr Roll; Comm Volntr; Chrch Yth Grp; Mus Clb; Acpl Chr; Bnd; Ch Chr; CR (P); Industrial Design; Business; La Sierra U CA

REID, DANIELLE; IRVINGTON, NJ; FRANK H MORRELL HS; (SO); Ctznshp Aw; Hnr Roll; St of Mnth; Mus Clb; Chr; Dnce; Art; Fashion Design; Singing

REILLY, MEGAN; ATLANTIC HIGHLANDS, NJ; RED BANK CATHOLIC HS; (FR); Hi Hnr Roll; Hab For Humty Volntr; ArtClub; Chrch Yth Grp; Vsity Clb; Ch Chr; SP/M/VS; Swmg (V); Sch Ppr (R); Yrbk (P); Providence College

REILLY, PADEN; WHITEHOUSE STATION, NJ; HUNTERDON CHRISTIAN AC; (SO); Hi Hnr Roll; Hnr Roll; Perf Att; Sci Fairs; Yth Ldrshp Prog; Comm Volntr; Peer Tut/Med; Chess; Dbte Team; Drma Clb; Emplmnt; Scouts; Bnd; SP/M/VS; Bsball (J); Skiing (J); Bagpipe Band; Drama; Drama School; Writer

REINGLE, TRICIA; MATAWAN, NJ; ST JOHN VIANNEY HS; (SR); Ctznshp Aw; Hnr Roll; MVP; Perf Att; Comm Volntr; Key Club; SADD; PP Ftbl (V); Sftball (V L); Yrbk (R, P); Varsity Bowling; Gatorade Softball Player of the Year; Special Education

REINOSO, YESENIA; FORT LEE, NJ; FORT LEE HS; (JR); Hi Hnr Roll; Hnr Roll; Perf Att; WWAHSS; Key Club; Lib Aide; Svce Clb; Invited to National Student Leadership Conference; International Business; Marketing; Rice U; St. John's U

REISCH, KEVIN G; RINGELON, NJ; MORRIS CATHOLIC HS; (FR); Comm Volntr; Peer Tut/Med; Chess; Chrch Yth Grp; DARE; Emplmnt; Scouts; Chr; Ch Chr; SP/M/VS; Bsball (J); Bskball (J); Sccr (J); Track (V L); Cl Off (R); Sch Ppr (R); Eagle Scout; NBA; Computer Science; U of Maryland; U North Carolina

REISEN, DYANA; WANAQUE, NJ; LAKELAND REG HS; (SR); Ctznshp Aw; Hi Hnr Roll; Hnr Roll; Nat Hon Sy; Valdctrian; WWAHSS; Yth Ldrshp Prog; Comm Volntr; Chrch Yth Grp; Emplmnt; SADD; Vllyball (VJCL); Summa Award (High Honor Roll All 4 Marking Periods); LEAP (Leaders Encouraging Adolescent Progress); Biology; The College of New Jersey (Attending); Lafayette College

REITER, HEATHER; MORRIS PLAINS, NJ; PARSIPPANY HILLS HS; (SR); F Lan Hn Soc; Hnr Roll; Nat Hon Sy; Otst Ac Ach Awd; St of Mnth; WWAHSS; DECA; German Clb; Bnd; Mch Bnd; Pep Bnd; Finance BA; Economics; Rutgers U Newark

REMY, MARIALA; IRVINGTON, NJ; IRVINGTON HS; (FR); Hnr Roll; Svce Clb

RENATA, TELY O; HOBOKEN, NJ; AC OF SACRED HEART HS; (SO); Gov Hnr Prg; Hi Hnr Roll; Hnr Roll; Nat Hon Sy; Nat Sci Aw; Comm Volntr; Peer Tut/Med; ArtClub; Drma Clb; Emplmnt; SP/M/VS; Vllyball (J); Fashion Show; Soccer Intramural; Foreign Languages & Literatures; Area, Ethnic, and Cultural Studies; New York U; Columbia U

RENAUDO, ANDRE; IRVINGTON, NJ; FRANK H MORRELL HS; (SO); Hnr Roll; WWAHSS; Comm Volntr; Emplmnt; Track (J); Urban Youth Coalition; Sigma Beta Club; Business Administration; Marketing; Princeton U; Montclair U

RENDEIRO, KAITLIN; CEDAR GROVE, NJ; CEDAR GROVE HS; (SO); Hi Hnr Roll; Otst Ac Ach Awd; WWAHSS; Comm Volntr; Chrch Yth Grp; DARE; Key Club; Sci Clb; Foreign Clb; Dnce; PP Ftbl; Sccr (V); Sftball (V); Track; Certified Lifeguard; Certified USSF Referee; Accounting; Law

RENNA, ASHLEY; CLARK, NJ; ARTHUR L. JOHNSON; (FR); Hnr Roll; Chrch Yth Grp; Key Club; Sccr (J); Track (J)

REVOLUS, MARIE; TRENTON, NJ; TRENTON CTRL HS; (SO); Ctznshp Aw; Hi Hnr Roll; Perf Att; Comm Volntr; Hosp Aide; Peer Tut/Med; French Clb; Sftball (J); College of New Jersey

REXON, LISA; CLEMENTON, NJ; OVERBROOK HS; (SO); Hnr Roll; Mar Art (V); Track (J); Leo Club; Sportsmanship Award; Physical Therapy; Psychology; U of Pennsylvania; Duke U

REYES, HECTOR A; DOVER, NJ; MORRIS CATHOLIC HS; (SO); MVP; Pres Ac Ftns Aw; Chrch Yth Grp; Bskball (JC); Lcrsse (V L); Sccr (V); Stu Cncl (R); Received Academic Scholarship to Morris Catholic; Athlete of the Year Winner; Physical Therapy; Sports Medicine; Ithaca; Drew U

REYES, JEFFREY; BRIDGEWATER, NJ; BRIDGEWATER-RARITAN HS; (JR); F Lan Hn Soc; Hnr Roll; Nat Hon Sy; Perf Att; Chrch Yth Grp; Key Club; Latin Clb; Swmg (V L); Summa Cum Laude on National Latin Exam; Psychology; Journalism; U of Michigan; U of North Carolina Chapel Hill

REYNOLDS, CRAIG S; SICKLERVILLE, NJ; WINSLOW TWP HS; (SO); Hnr Roll; St of Mnth; DARE; I Play Roller Hockey for a Tournament Team; I Play Guitar and Base Guitar; Business Management; Engineering; Hood College; Temple U

RHODES, BIANCA R; SPRINGFIELD, NJ; JONATHAN DAYTON HS; (JR); F Lan Hn Soc; Hi Hnr Roll; Comm Volntr; Mth Clb/Tm; Sci Clb; SADD; Spanish Clb; Vllyball (V L); NJIT Women in Technology Leadership Award; Johns Hopkins Talent Search; Computer Engineering; Electrical Engineering; Cornell U; Carnegie Mellon U

RHODES, EDWIN; ELMER, NJ; PENNS GROVE HS; (SO); Hnr Roll; St of Mnth; WWAHSS; Comm Volntr; Peer Tut/Med; Chrch Yth Grp; Emplmnt; P to P St Amb Prg; Student Ambassador-People to People Member; U.S.A.F.; Rowan U; New Jersey Institute of Technology

RIANO, RICHARD; CARTERET, NJ; MIDDLESEX CO VOC-PISCATAWAY; (SR); Hnr Roll; Perf Att; St of Mnth; Bsball; Graphic Arts; Middlesex County College

RICH, ASHLEY J; TRENTON, NJ; HAMILTON HS EAST; (SO); Hnr Roll; Comm Volntr; Key Club; Italian Clb; Fld Hky (V L); Psychology; Education; Delaware U; Boston U

RICHA, VERA; NEW BRUNSWICK, NJ; RUTGERS PREP SCH; (JR); Hi Hnr Roll; Nat Hon Sy; Otst Ac Ach Awd; Sci Fairs; Comm Volntr; Peer Tut/Med; Chrch Yth Grp; DARE; Emplmnt; Key Club; MuAlphaTh; Quiz Bowl; Vsity Clb; Spanish Clb; Ch Chr; Dnce; SP/M/VS; Bskball (J); Sccr (V L); Sftball (V L); Swmg (V); Cl Off (P); Stu Cncl (R); CR (R); Yrbk (P); Varsity Soccer Prep B All-State Winners; Mu Alpha Theta Member; Communications; International Affairs; New York U; George Washington U

RICHARDS, CHAD; MAPLEWOOD, NJ; COLUMBIA HS; (SO); Hnr Roll; Perf Att; Chess; Chrch Yth Grp; Lib Aide; Magic Club; Animation Club; Computer Engineering; New York Institute of Technology; Massachusetts Institute of Technology

RICHARDS, GRACE P; EGG HARBOR TOWNSHIP, NJ; EGG HARBOR TWP HS; (FR); Ctznshp Aw; Hnr Roll; Otst Ac Ach Awd; Comm Volntr; Chrch Yth Grp; FCA; Key Club; Chr; Ch Chr; Academic Scholar; Lawyer; Prosecutor (District Attorney); Grace U; Penn State U

RIEGEL, JESSICA; WESTFIELD, NJ; WESTFIELD HS; (SO); Hi Hnr Roll; Hnr Roll; WWAHSS; Comm Volntr; Mod UN; NYLC; Svce Clb; Tmpl Yth Grp; Spanish Clb; Dnce; Stg Cre; Cl Off (P); Lit Mag (R); Journalism; Political Science; George Washington U; U of Pennsylvania

RIGBY, CAITLIN E; MADISON, NJ; MADISON HS; (FR); Hi Hnr Roll; Hnr Roll; MVP; Nat Hon Sy; WWAHSS; Emplmnt; Key Club; Chr; Bskball (J); Chrldg (J); Sccr (J); Sftball (VJ); Stu Cncl (S)

RIGGS, KIMBERLY; SWEDESBORO, NJ; CLEARVIEW REG; (SR); Hi Hnr Roll; Hnr Roll; Nat Hon Sy; Nat Mrt Sch Recip; Pres Ac Ftns Aw; Comm Volntr; DECA; Jr Cls League; Latin Clb; Fld Hky (J); Scr Kpr (V); Sftball (J); Stu Cncl (R); CR (R); Received Scholarship from Policeman's Benovolent Association of New Jersey; Business; Pre-Law; Syracuse U

RIMMAUDO, GABRIELLE; CLARK, NJ; ARTHUR L JOHNSON HS; (FR); Hi Hnr Roll; Hnr Roll; WWAHSS; Key Club; NtlFrnscLg; Sci Clb; Italian Clb; Bnd; SP/M/VS; Music Education; Italian; Syracuse; Stanford

RINKER, ALLISA; BAYONNE, NJ; BAYONNE HS; (FR); Hnr Roll; Nat Hon Sy; Bskball; Track; Accounting; New Jersey City U

RIOS, BIANCA; NEWARK, NJ; SCIENCE HS; (FR); Hi Hnr Roll; Hnr Roll; Nat Hon Sy; St of Mnth; Peer Tut/Med; Chr; Lawyer; Nurse; Rutgers U; Harvard U

RIOTTO, LUCIA G; STEWARTSVILLE, NJ; BETHLEHEM CATHOLIC HS; (JR); 4H Awd; Hnr Roll; Perf Att; WWAHSS; Yth Ldrshp Prog; Comm Volntr; 4-H; Emplmnt; HO'Br Yth Ldrshp; Key Club; Pep Squd; SADD; German Clb; Dnce; SP/M/VS; Chrldg (V L); Gmnstcs; Hsbk Rdg; Sccr (V L); New Jersey Delegate-National 4-H Congress, Have Held Offices in 4-H Clubs; T.R.A.I.L. Trip to Russia; International Business

RISOLA, CHRISTOPHER; COLONIA, NJ; JFK MEMORIAL HS; (SO); Hnr Roll; Otst Ac Ach Awd; Comm Volntr; Chrch Yth Grp; Key Club; Bskball; Masters; Rutgers; Montclair

RIVAS, NATHALY; NORTH BERGEN, NJ; NORTH BERGEN HS; (JR); F Lan Hn Soc; Hnr Roll; Otst Ac Ach Awd; JSA; Key Club; Italian Clb; Tae Kwon Do Instructor-Belt: Semi-Black; Doctorate Degree; Princeton U; Columbia U

RIVERA, JANINE; METUCHEN, NJ; JOHN F KENNEDY MEMORIAL HS; (SO); Hnr Roll; Otst Ac Ach Awd; Comm Volntr; Key Club; Spanish Clb; Stg Cre; Sccr (V); Track (J); Cl Off (P); Stu Cncl (R)

RIVERA, JOHANNA; NORTH BERGEN, NJ; NORTH BERGEN HS; (FR); Ctznshp Aw; Hnr Roll; Sci Fairs; WWAHSS; Comm Volntr; DARE; Key Club; Dnce; Forensic Scientist; Columbia U; NYU

RIVERA, KATHLEEN; PENNSAUKEN, NJ; PENNSAUKEN HS; (SO); Hnr Roll; Carpentry; Professional Writing; Fordham U; New York U

RIVERA, MARTHA; BAYONNE, NJ; BAYONNE HS; Hi Hnr Roll; Hnr Roll; Vllyball; Boston U; New York U

RIVERA, VICTOR; BURLINGTON, NJ; BURLINGTON TWP HS; (SR); All Am Sch; Ctznshp Aw; Perf Att; WWAHSS; Comm Volntr; Hosp Aide; Peer Tut/Med; DARE; Emplmnt; Ntl FFA; ROTC; Vsity Clb; Wdwrkg Clb; Cr Ctry (V CL); Ftball (V L); Track (V CL); Wt Lftg (J); Police Explorers - Buena; Jr Member Landisville Vol Fire Co; Criminal Justice; Sports Medicine; New York U; Rider U

RIVEROS, ELISA P; ELIZABETH, NJ; ELIZABETH HS; (JR); All Am Sch; Hi Hnr Roll; Hnr Roll; Kwnis Aw; Nat Hon Sy; Nat Stu Ath Day Aw; Otst Ac Ach Awd; Pres Sch; WWAHSS; Yth Ldrshp Prog; Comm Volntr; Dbte Team; Drma Clb; Key Club; Mus Clb; NtlFrnscLg; Outdrs Clb; Dnce; SP/M/VS; Stg Cre; Dvng (J); Sftball (J); Swmg (J); Tennis (J); Track (J); Vllyball (V); Adv Cncl (R); Cl Off (R); Stu Cncl (R); Sch Ppr (E); Law; Criminology; Rutgers; Princeton

ROBAK, GARRETT; TRENTON, NJ; HAMILTON HS EAST; (SO); Hnr Roll; Emplmnt; Stg Cre; Track (L); Yearbook in 8th Grade; Pre-Medicine; St. Leo U

ROBALINO, PAMELA; JERSEY CITY, NJ; AC OF SACRED HEART HS; (JR); Hnr Roll; St of Mnth; Drma Clb; Spanish Clb; Yrbk (E); Resident's Education Awards Program; Achievement Award for Computer Applications; Web Design; Accounting; St Peter's College; Fordham U

ROBERTS, KIMBERLY A; RINGWOOD, NJ; LAKELAND REG HS; (SR); Hi Hnr Roll; Hnr Roll; Nat Hon Sy; WWAHSS; Yth Ldrshp Prog; Comm Volntr; Drma Clb; Emplmnt; Pep Squd; Vsity Clb; Dnce; Drl Tm; SP/M/VS; Chrldg (V); Stu Cncl (T); CR (R); Sch Ppr (E, R); Dance Team Captain; Garden State Champs; Business-Finance & Marketing; U of Connecticut

ROBINSON, JOUELLE; SUCCASUNNA, NJ; ROXBURY HS; (JR); Hnr Roll; MVP; Perf Att; WWAHSS; Comm Volntr; Peer Tut/Med; Emplmnt; Key Club; Vsity Clb; Chr; Fld Hky (V); Renaissance; TGIF - Volunteer Group; Pre-Med; U of Connecticut; U of North Carolina Chapel Hill

ROBINSON, TAYLOR; CAPE MAY COURT HOUSE, NJ; MIDDLE TWP HS; (JR); Ctznshp Aw; Hnr Roll; Nat Hon Sy; Otst Ac Ach Awd; Sci Fairs; St of Mnth; Comm Volntr; Emplmnt; Key Club; French Clb; Fld Hky (V L); Lcrsse (V L); Sportsmanship Award (Field Hockey); National Youth Leadership Forum-Med; Physical Therapy (PhD); Biology; Washington College, MD; College Misericordia, PA

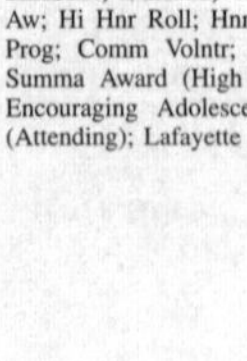
Rivera, Martha
Bayonne HS
Bayonne, NJ

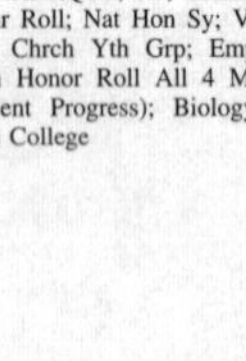
Rhodes, Bianca R
Jonathan Dayton HS
Springfield, NJ

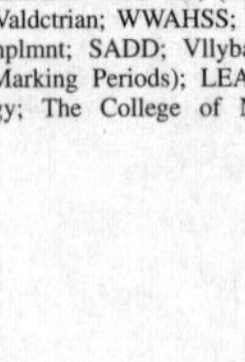
Rexon, Lisa
Overbrook HS
Clementon, NJ

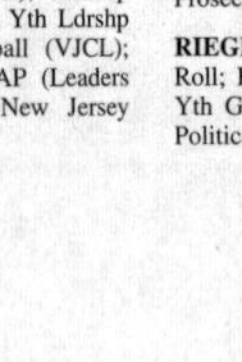
Reinoso, Yesenia
Fort Lee HS
Fort Lee, NJ

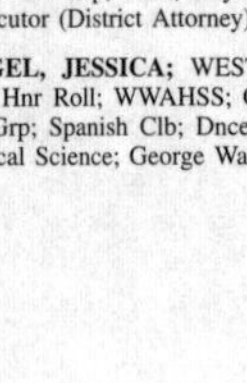
Reid, Anton C
Pine Forge AC
Newark, NJ

National
Honor Roll
Spring 2005

Reed Jr, Charles S
Dr Ronald Mc Nair AC HS
Jersey City, NJ

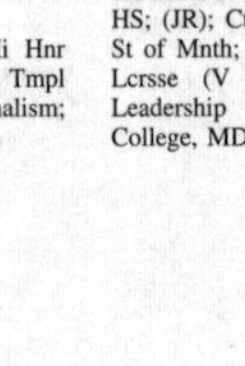
Reisch, Kevin G
Morris Catholic HS
Ringelon, NJ

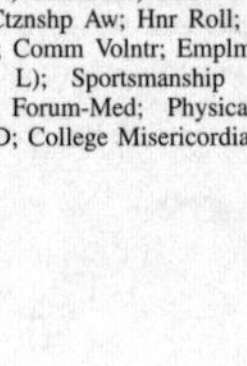
Reynolds, Craig S
Winslow Twp HS
Sicklerville, NJ

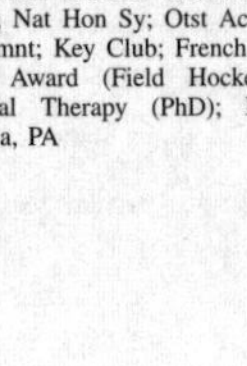
Riano, Richard
Middlesex Co Voc-Piscataway
Carteret, NJ

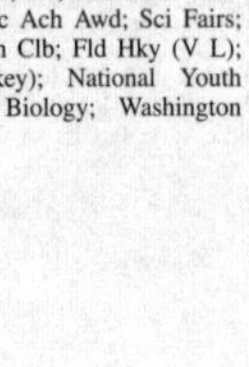
Riotto, Lucia G
Bethlehem Catholic HS
Stewartsville, NJ

ROBINSON, TRACY; MULLICA HILL, NJ; CLEARVIEW REG HS; (SR); Hi Hnr Roll; Hnr Roll; Nat Hon Sy; St of Mnth; USAA; WWAHSS; DECA; NYLC; SADD; Swmg (L); CR; Mock Trial; Renaissance; International Relations; Architecture; U of Miami FL - Attending

ROBLES, WILLIAM; ROSELLE PARK, NJ; ROSELLE PARK HS; (SO); Comm Volntr; ArtClub; Chrch Yth Grp; Spanish Clb; Tennis (V L); Architecture; Computer Science; U of Florida; U of South Florida

ROCCA, GLENN; WESTWOOD, NJ; WESTWOOD REG JR/SR HS; (JR); F Lan Hn Soc; Hi Hnr Roll; Nat Hon Sy; Comm Volntr; Peer Tut/Med; Chrch Yth Grp; NYLC; Vsity Clb; Clb; Ftball (V); Vsy Clb; The National Society of High School Scholars; Medicine; Finance; Princeton Univ.; Yale

ROCCO, ANGELA; FREEHOLD, NJ; RED BANK CATHOLIC HS; (FR); Hnr Roll; Freshman Softball

ROCCO, LISA; DAYTON, NJ; (SR); F Lan Hn Soc; Hnr Roll; Nat Hon Sy; Otst Ac Ach Awd; WWAHSS; Yth Ldrshp Prog; Comm Volntr; Hosp Aide; Peer Tut/Med; Emplmnt; JSA; Key Club; Mod UN; Off Aide; Svce Clb; Tchrs Aide; Acpl Chr; Bnd; Chr; Ch Chr; Special Education (Severe Disabilities); Attending-Boston U

ROCK, DEBORAH A; IRVINGTON, NJ; IRVINGTON HS; (SR); Hnr Roll; WWAHSS; Comm Volntr; Chrch Yth Grp; Key Club; Yrbk (R); Criminal Justice; Fairleigh Dickinson U

ROCKFORD, ADRIANNA; GARFIELD, NJ; BERGEN CTY ACADEMIES; (SO); Hnr Roll; Yth Ldrshp Prog; Comm Volntr; JSA; Mod UN; Acpl Chr; Chr; Dnce; SP/M/VS; Sccr (J); Pre-Law; Fordham U; Seton Hall U

RODGERS, IESHA N; PENNSAUKEN, NJ; PINE FORGE AC; (FR); Ctznshp Aw; Hi Hnr Roll; Hnr Roll; Otst Ac Ach Awd; Perf Att; Pres Ac Ftns Aw; Sci Fairs; St of Mnth; Yth Ldrshp Prog; Comm Volntr; Peer Tut/Med; Chrch Yth Grp; Drma Clb; Emplmnt; Outdrs Clb; Scouts; Tchrs Aide; Ch Chr; SP/M/VS; Chrldg; Gmnstcs; Sch Ppr (E); Poetry Contests Winner-Poetry.Com; Member of Christian Writer's Club; Nursing; Journalism; Oakwood College-Huntsville, AL; Loma Linda U

RODGERS, MICHAEL J; RAYONNE, NJ; HORACE MANN EL SCH; MS; Hnr Roll; St of Mnth; St Optmst of Yr; DARE; Emplmnt; Photog; Bnd; Lcrsse; Vllyball; Stu Cncl (P, V, R); Yrbk (P); Captain-Bayonne Lacrosse Team; Floor Hockey; Mechanical Engineer; Car Designer; Johns Hopkins U; West Point Military Academy

RODRIGO, KEVIN; SECAUCUS, NJ; HUDSON CATHOLIC REG HS; (JR); Hnr Roll; Nat Hon Sy; Perf Att; Amnsty Intl; Peer Tut/Med; Biology Clb; Chess; Cmptr Clb; Pep Squd; Prom Com; Svce Clb; Tech Clb; Ice Hky (V L); Sccr (V L); Track (V L); Cl Off (S); Stu Cncl (S); Yrbk (E); Leader of Lasallian Youth Corps; Civil Engineering; Drexel U; Rensselaer Polytechnic Institute

RODRIGUES, RAQUEL A; MOUNTAINSIDE, NJ; GOVERNOR LIVINGSTON HS; (JR); Hnr Roll; Otst Ac Ach Awd; Perf Att; Comm Volntr; Chrch Yth Grp; Drma Clb; Photog; Prom Com; Quill & Scroll; Scouts; Svce Clb; Chr; Ch Chr; Dnce; SP/M/VS; Track (V); Lit Mag (R); Sch Ppr (R); 9 Yrs Priggs Piano Academy; Advertising / Business; Fashion Design; New York U; Fordham U

RODRIGUES, TRACY; ELIZABETH, NJ; ELIZABETH HS; (SO); Hi Hnr Roll; Hnr Roll; Nat Hon Sy; Perf Att; Salutrn; St of Mnth; Key Club; Mod UN; Outdrs Clb; Dnce; Chrldg (C); Sch Ppr (E); French Honor Society; Journalism; Georgetown U; New York U

RODRIGUEZ, ERIC K; EGG HARBOR TOWNSHIP, NJ; EGG HARBOR TOWNSHIP HS; (SO); All Am Sch; Hnr Roll; Nat Hon Sy; WWAHSS; Comm Volntr; Key Club; Vsy Clb (J); JV Crew/Rowing; ARCH Riding Center for Handicapped; Mechanical Engineer; U of Pennsylvania; Johns Hopkins U

RODRIGUEZ, JANICE A; JERSEY CITY, NJ; JAMES J FERNS HS; (SR); 4-H; Chrch Yth Grp; Co-Op Program; Early Childhood Education; New Jersey City U

RODRIGUEZ, JENIFFER; ELIZABETH, NJ; ELIZABETH HS; (JR); F Lan Hn Soc; Comm Volntr; Key Club; Mod UN; Outdrs Clb; Cr Ctry (V); Gmnstcs (J); Swmg (V); CR (P); Did Model UN; Psychology; Miami U; U of Tampa

RODRIGUEZ, MARY E; UNION CITY, NJ; EMERSON HS; (SO); Hnr Roll; Perf Att; St of Mnth; Peer Tut/Med; DARE; Svce Clb; Bskball (J); Teacher; Nurse; Florida State U; Connecticut State U

RODRIGUEZ, RAFAEL; HARRISON, NJ; HARRISON HS; (JR); Hnr Roll; St of Mnth; Comm Volntr; Emplmnt; Bskball (V L); Ftball (V L); Student of the Cycle for Algebra 2; Student of the Cycle for HSPA Math Strategies; Business Administration; Criminal Justice; Rutgers U; Berkeley College

RODRIGUEZ, REYNALDO; IRVINGTON, NJ; IRVINGTON HS; (FR); Hi Hnr Roll; Key Club; Bsball (J)

RODRIGUEZ, RUBEN; HARRISON, NJ; HARRISON HS; (JR); Bsball (V); Bskball (V); Business Management; Accounting; Rutgers U (New Brunswick); Kean

RODRIGUEZ, VANESSA; ELIZABETH, NJ; ELIZABETH HS; (JR); Hnr Roll; WWAHSS; Chrch Yth Grp; Key Club; Mod UN; Cr Ctry (V); Track (V); Indoor Track; Criminal Justice; Law

RODRIQUEZ, JASMIN; PLAINFIELD, NJ; PLAINFIELD HS; (SO); Hnr Roll; Perf Att; St of Mnth; 4-H; DARE; Sccr (V); Vllyball (V); I Really Want to Have a PhD In Medicine.; I Would Like to Have a Degree In Criminal Justice.; Sacred Heart U Fairfield, Connecticut; Union County College Plainfield, New Jersey

ROGERS, CHRISTINA M E; WILLINGBORO, NJ; HOLY CROSS HS; (FR); Hnr Roll; Comm Volntr; Chrch Yth Grp; Dnce; SP/M/VS; Chrldg (J); Track (J); Stu Cncl (V); CR (R); Sch Ppr (R); R.E.B.E.L. II; Truth Campaign; Political Science; Psychology; Yale U; New York U

ROH, ALBERT; RUTHERFORD, NJ; BERGEN CTY ACADEMIES; (JR); Hnr Roll; Nat Mrt Fin; Red Cr Aide; Chrch Yth Grp; DECA; FBLA; Mod UN; Vsity Clb; Orch; Ftball (J); Golf (V)

ROJAS, MELISSA; PATERSON, NJ; PATERSON CATHOLIC HS; (SO); Perf Att; Sci Fairs; St of Mnth; Comm Volntr; Peer Tut/Med; Red Cr Aide; ArtClub; JSA; Mod UN; Off Aide; Photog; Prom Com; Pep Bnd; Sftball (J); Vllyball (J); Adv Cncl (S); Stu Cncl (T); CR (S); Lit Mag (R); Sch Ppr (R); Yrbk (R); Montclair State U; Princeton U

ROLDAN, ESTEBAN C; ELIZABETH, NJ; ELIZABETH HS; (JR); All Am Sch; Hnr Roll; Nat Hon Sy; Valdctrian; WWAHSS; Comm Volntr; Chrch Yth Grp; Emplmnt; Key Club; Mus Clb; Bnd; Tennis (V); Track (J); CR (R); 1st Place in Mural Art Contest for School; Graphic Arts; Audio Engineering; New York U; New Jersey Technical School

ROLLE, ROBERTA L; BRIDGETON, NJ; FAIRFIELD MS; Ctznshp Aw; Hnr Roll; Otst Ac Ach Awd; Perf Att; Sci Fairs; St of Mnth; Comm Volntr; Peer Tut/Med; Spec Olymp Vol; Aqrium Clb; Chrch Yth Grp; Drma Clb; Off Aide; Photog; Tchrs Aide; Ch Chr; Dnce; Drl Tm; SP/M/VS; Bsball (J); Chrldg (J); Fld Hky (J); Scr Kpr (J); Sccr (J); Sftball (J); Track (J); Vllyball (J); CR (P, R); Yrbk (P); Yearbook Committee First-Aid Club; A Pediatrician; A Lawyer; Virginia Union U

ROMANO, DANA; PARSIPPANY, NJ; PARSIPPANY HS; (JR); Hi Hnr Roll; Hnr Roll; MVP; Nat Hon Sy; Otst Ac Ach Awd; St of Mnth; WWAHSS; Comm Volntr; Svce Clb; PP Ftbl; Sccr (V L); Sftball (V L); Stu Cncl (R); CR (R); Spanish Honors Society; Langenscheidt Award for Excellence in Spanish; Physical Therapy; Teaching; Rowan U; U of Delaware

ROMANO, SAMSON; WAYNE, NJ; WAYNE VALLEY HS; (SO); Sci Fairs; DARE; Photog; Sci Clb; Tech Clb; Wdwrkg Clb; 2001 Site 1st Place; 2002 Site 1st Place; Engineer; Montclair State U; William Patterson U

ROMERO, BRYAN P; ASBURY PARK, NJ; OCEAN TOWNSHIP HS; (JR); Hnr Roll; Comm Volntr; French Clb; Bskball (J); Character Club-Secretary; Focus Group; Biomedical, Medical, Business; Bachelor's Degree, Master's Degree; Maryland U; Virginia Tech

ROMERO, JILLIAN A; EDISON, NJ; JOHN P STEVENS; (JR); Hnr Roll; WWAHSS; Hab For Humty Volntr; DARE; Emplmnt; Lcrsse (J); Stu Cncl (R)

ROMERO, MYLEDY; NORTH BERGEN, NJ; NORTH BERGEN HS; (JR); F Lan Hn Soc; Hnr Roll; Perf Att; Peer Tut/Med; Key Club; German Clb; Chr; SP/M/VS; Bskball (L); Track (L); Yrbk (R); History Award; Psychologist/Masters Degree; BFA\Drama, Astronomy/Masters; Penn State, Montclair, Rutgers

RONCAL, EDUARDO A; ELIZABETH, NJ; ELIZABETH HS; (JR); Ctznshp Aw; Hi Hnr Roll; Hnr Roll; Nat Hon Sy; WWAHSS; Comm Volntr; Key Club; Cr Ctry (V); Track (V); Superintendent's Scholar, Principal's Scholar; Member of the National Honor Society; Electrical Engineering; Computer Engineering; NJIT New Jersey Institute of Technology; Rutgers

ROSARIO, LAURA; KEARNY, NJ; KEARNY HS; (JR); Hnr Roll; Sci Fairs; Chrch Yth Grp; Scouts; Tmpl Yth Grp; Ch Chr; History Teacher; Lawyer; New Jersey City U; Rutgers the State U of NJ

ROSAS, RONNIE; ABSECON, NJ; ABSEGAMI HS; (JR); Hi Hnr Roll; Nat Hon Sy; WWAHSS; Hosp Aide; NYLC; Sccr (J); Track (J); Class Rank: 4/527; Attended Johns Hopkins Center For Talented Youth - Summer Course; Pre-Med

ROSENBERG, MICHELLE; SUCCASUNNA, NJ; ROXBURY HS; (JR); Hnr Roll; St of Mnth; Yth Ldrshp Prog; Comm Volntr; Drma Clb; Emplmnt; Key Club; NYLC; Dnce; Sch Ppr (R); Volunteer - Work with Autistic Children; Temple Work; Lawyer; Psychologist; Boston U; U of Maryland

ROSENBLOOM, JENNIFER I; HIGH BRIDGE, NJ; VOORHEES HS; (SR); Hnr Roll; ArtClub; Chrch Yth Grp; Clr Grd; Dnce; SP/M/VS; Global Business; Rider U

ROSENFELDER, MATTHEW; SOUTH ORANGE, NJ; NEW YORK MILITARY AC; (JR); Hi Hnr Roll; Hnr Roll; Nat Mrt LOC; WWAHSS; Amnsty Intl; Emplmnt; ROTC; Cr Ctry (J); Fncg (V L); Track (VJ L); Promoted to the Rank of Cadet Lieutenant and Given Position of Battalion (Master Development; Officer and Honor Representative); Mechanical Engineering; Military; United States Military Academy; United States Naval Academy

ROSENSTRAUCH, KARA; SOUTH ORANGE, NJ; COLUMBIA HS; (SO); Hnr Roll; Sci Fairs; Peer Tut/Med; Chrch Yth Grp; Scouts; Fld Hky (J); Lcrsse (J); Education; Art; Alfred U; Syracuse U

ROSZKOWSKA, KAROLINA; LINDEN, NJ; LINDEN HS; (SR); Chess; Emplmnt; Key Club; Sci Clb; Polish Clb; Accounting; Kean U

ROTH, MELISSA A; JACKSON, NJ; LAKEWOOD PREP; (FR); Hi Hnr Roll; Hnr Roll; Scouts; SP/M/VS; Stu Cncl (V); Piano; Bowling Team; English/Languages; History

ROTUNDO, AMANDA; NORTH BERGEN, NJ; NORTH BERGEN HS; (JR); Hi Hnr Roll; MVP; Nat Hon Sy; Nat Mrt Sch Recip; WWAHSS; Comm Volntr; Red Cr Aide; Key Club; Italian Clb; Sftball (JC); Vllyball (JC); Stu Cncl (R); CR (R); Yrbk (R); Wrestling Manager; Accounting; Massage Therapy; Monmouth U; St. Peter's College

ROYAL, BENJAMIN; LEBANON, NJ; NORTH HUNTERDON HS; (JR); Hi Hnr Roll; Hnr Roll; St of Mnth; Comm Volntr; DARE; Drma Clb; Scouts; German Clb; Stg Cre; Ftball (V); Volunteer Firefighter; Military; Engineering; United States Naval Academy

ROZENBLAT, NICOLE; HIGHTSTOWN, NJ; HIGHSTOWN HS; (JR); Hnr Roll; Red Cr Aide; FBLA; PP Ftbl; Stu Cncl (R); Elementary Education; West Chester U; East Strausburg U

ROZYNSKI, BRIAN A; LAKE HIAWATHA, NJ; PARSIPPANY HS; (SO); Hnr Roll; MVP; Comm Volntr; Chrch Yth Grp; P to P St Amb Prg; Bskball (J); Rlr Hky (V); Sccr (J); Track (V); Bowling; Sports Ambassador; Sports Medicine; Business Management; Boston U; Duke U

RUBINO, ALEXANDRA; SADDLE RIVER, NJ; NORTHERN HIGHLANDS REG HS; (SO); Hi Hnr Roll; Otst Ac Ach Awd; Perf Att; Sci/Math Olympn; DARE; Dbte Team; Lib Aide; Hispanic Clb; Acpl Chr; Chr; Dnce; Lit Mag (R); Mathematics Award in Middle School; Spanish Award in Middle School; Mathematics Major; Theatre Major; Yale U; Princeton U

RUBIO, ANJELICA C; ROSELLE PARK, NJ; ROSELLE PARK HS/ UNION CTY VOC TECH SCH; (SR); Hnr Roll; Nat Hon Sy; Perf Att; St of Mnth; WWAHSS; Comm Volntr; Chrch Yth Grp; DARE; Emplmnt; Ntl FFA; Off Aide; Tchrs Aide; Chr; Ch Chr; Dnce; SP/M/VS; Cl Off (V); Dietetic / Nutritionist / Bachelor's Degree; Performing Arts; Rutgers U; Middlesex County College

RUDNICKI, VICTORIA; BROOKLAWN, NJ; GLOUCESTER HS; (JR); Hnr Roll; Perf Att; Comm Volntr; ArtClub; Drma Clb; Mus Clb; SP/M/VS; Stg Cre; Yrbk (R); Hussian School of Art; Rutgers U

RUDOWSKY, LUKE; CLARK, NJ; ARTHUR L JOHNSON HS; (FR); Hi Hnr Roll; Hnr Roll; WWAHSS; Key Club; Bsball; Ftball; Track; Wt Lftg; Johns Hopkins State Award; Continental Math League Award

RUHNKE, KRISTINE G; TINTON FALLS, NJ; MONMOUTH REG HS; (SO); Hnr Roll; WWAHSS; Spec Olymp Vol; Key Club; Scouts; SP/M/VS; Cl Off (T); Elementary Education; College of New Jersey; Brookdale College

RULAND, SARAH B; HAMBURG, NJ; WALLKILL VALLEY REG HS; (JR); Hi Hnr Roll; Hnr Roll; Pep Squd; Tech Clb; Spanish Clb; Chrldg (V L); Track (J); Architectural Design; Art History; U of Florida, Drexel; Temple, U of Miami

RUSH, CANDACE; MEDFORD, NJ; SHAWNEE HS; (JR); Hnr Roll; Comm Volntr; Emplmnt; Svce Clb; French Clb; Fld Hky (J); Lcrsse (V); CR (P); LDTV Award; Friendliness Award; Communications; TV / Broadcasting; Rutgers U; College of Charleston

RUSINQUE, FAIDY; ELIZABETH, NJ; ELIZABETH HS; (SR); Hnr Roll; Nat Hon Sy; St of Mnth; WWAHSS; Comm Volntr; Chrch Yth Grp; FTA; Jr Ach; Key Club; Outdrs Clb; Spanish Clb; Dnce; Sccr (V); Swmg (J); Track (J); National Honor Society; Spanish Honor Society; Pharmaceutical Degree; Union County College; Rutgers

RUSSO, LAWRENCE; WYCKOFF, NJ; RAMAPO HS; (JR); Hi Hnr Roll; Hnr Roll; Comm Volntr; Chess; Emplmnt; SADD; Vsity Clb; Spanish Clb; Bnd; Lcrsse (V); Sccr (JC); English; History; Villanova U; College of New Jersey

RYAN, CAITLYN; SADDLE BROOK, NJ; PARAMUS CATHOLIC HS; (JR); F Lan Hn Soc; Hi Hnr Roll; Nat Hon Sy; WWAHSS; Comm Volntr; Peer Tut/Med; DARE; NYLC; P to P St Amb Prg; Prom Com; SADD; Dnce; Chrldg (V); Yrbk (P); Occupational Therapist; Quinnipiac U; The College of New Jersey

Rubio, Anjelica C	Rodrigo, Kevin	Rodgers, Michael J	Robinson, Tracy	Rockford, Adrianna	Rogers, Christina M E	Rusinque, Faidy
Roselle Park HS/Union Cty Voc Tech Sch	Hudson Catholic Reg HS	Horace Mann El Sch	Clearview Reg HS	Bergen Cty Academies	Holy Cross HS	Elizabeth HS
Roselle Park, NJ	Secaucus, NJ	Rayonne, NJ	Mullica Hill, NJ	Garfield, NJ	Willingboro, NJ	Elizabeth, NJ

RYAN, WHITNEY; BRIDGEWATER, NJ; BRIDGEWATER-RARITAN HS; (SR); Hi Hnr Roll; MVP; Nat Hon Sy; WWAHSS; Peer Tut/Med; Chrch Yth Grp; Drma Clb; Key Club; Mus Clb; Prom Com; Spanish Clb; Acpl Chr; Orch; SP/M/VS; Sccr (J); Track (J); CR (R); Student Rep for Waksman Student Scholars Program; Psychology / Counseling Psychologist; Lehigh U

RYMER, CARLOS; UNION CITY, NJ; UNION HILL HS; (SR); F Lan Hn Soc; Hi Hnr Roll; Hnr Roll; Nat Hon Sy; Perf Att; Sci Fairs; St of Mnth; USAA; WWAHSS; Comm Volntr; Key Club; MuAlphaTh; Schol Bwl; Sci Clb; Spanish Clb; SP/M/VS; Track (V); Lit Mag (R); Sch Ppr (R); Student of the Marking Period; Environmental Club President; Environmental Studies; Cornell U

SAAB, ASHLEY M; WILLINGBORO, NJ; BCIT/MEDFORD CAMPUS; (JR); Hi Hnr Roll; Hnr Roll; Otst Ac Ach Awd; Perf Att; St of Mnth; Comm Volntr; Chrch Yth Grp; Emplmnt; Scouts; Ch Chr; Dnce; SP/M/VS; Chrldg (J); Cl Off (P); Stu Cncl (P); Principal's Honor; Medical Doctor; Registered Nurse; Rider U; Rutgers U

SABATURA, RACHEL; BOUND BROOK, NJ; BRIDGEWATER-RARITAN HS; (SO); F Lan Hn Soc; Hi Hnr Roll; Hnr Roll; Comm Volntr; Peer Tut/Med; Emplmnt; MuAlphaTh; Italian Clb; Chr; Clr Grd; Colorguard Captain; Winter Guard Section Leader; Medicine; Veterinary

SACKIE, MELANIE F; SOMERVILLE, NJ; SOMERVILLE HS; (SO); Hi Hnr Roll; Hnr Roll; WWAHSS; Comm Volntr; Emplmnt; Key Club; Scouts; Chr; Ch Chr; Fld Hky (J); Lcrsse (V); Silver Award Girl Scouts

SACKS, JUSTINE A; BRIDGEWATER, NJ; BRIDGEWATER-RARITAN HS; (SR); Hi Hnr Roll; Nat Hon Sy; WWAHSS; Spec Olymp Vol; Emplmnt; FBLA; Key Club; Tmpl Yth Grp; Fld Hky (V); Scr Kpr (V); Track (J); Wt Lftg (J); Hospitality Management; Food and Beverage Management; Johnson & Wales U

SACKS, ROBYN A; BRIDGEWATER, NJ; BRIDGEWATER-RARITAN HS; (FR); Hnr Roll; St of Mnth; WWAHSS; Key Club; Clr Grd; Certificate of Achievement for Participation in Bands of America Regional Championship Tropicana Field-Florida 10/04

SACTA, MARIA A; UNION CITY, NJ; UNION HILL HS; (SR); Hi Hnr Roll; Nat Hon Sy; Sci Fairs; St of Mnth; Valdctrian; WWAHSS; Comm Volntr; Key Club; MuAlphaTh; Quiz Bowl; Sci Clb; Italian Clb; Stu Cncl (R); SEED Scholarship Recipient; National Junior Humanities and Science Delegate; Chemical Engineering; U of Pennsylvania; Cornell U

SADDA, ARAM; BERGENFIELD, NJ; BERGENFIELD HS; (JR); Gov Hnr Prg; Hnr Roll; Sci/Math Olympn; Peer Tut/Med; Tchrs Aide; Ftball (V); Wt Lftg (J); National Chemistry Olympiads; National Chemistry Nomenclature; Heart Surgeon; Maxillofacial Surgeon; New York U; Rutgers U

SAEZ, ROGER; CARLSTADT, NJ; HENRY P BECTON REG HS; (SR); F Lan Hn Soc; Hi Hnr Roll; Hnr Roll; Perf Att; Chess; Photog; Sccr (V); Spanish Honor Society; Electrical Engineering; Computer Science; NJIT (New Jersey Institute of Technology)

SAFARPOUR, YELENA; PRINCETON, NJ; PRINCETON HS; (JR); Lit Mag (E); Numina Gallery Publicity Director; Gay-Straight Alliance; Brown U; UC Berkeley

SAFRAN, JOSHUA; EDISON, NJ; JOHN P STEVENS HS; (JR); Hnr Roll; MVP; Nat Hon Sy; Comm Volntr; Emplmnt; Vsity Clb; Cr Ctry (V CL); Sccr (J); Tennis (V L); Track (V); Vsy Clb (V C); National Honor Society; Walk for Hope/Find a Cure for Cancer) Board Member; Advertising; Psychology; Boston U; Claremont Mc Kenna College

SAHU, SIMI; BELLEVILLE, NJ; BELLEVILLE HS; (SO); Hnr Roll; WWAHSS; Comm Volntr; Cmptr Clb; FCCLA; Key Club; Mth Clb/Tm; WORLD Clb; Cr Ctry (V); Sch Ppr (R); Officer in State Executive Council, FCCLA, NJ -VP of National Programs; Law; MBA; Harvard U; Seton Hall U

SAID, LOURO; BAYONNE, NJ; BAYONNE HS; (FR); Fut Prb Slvr; Hi Hnr Roll; Nat Ldrshp Svc; Perf Att; Sci Fairs; Sci/Math Olympn; St of Mnth; Comm Volntr; Peer Tut/Med; DARE; Quiz Bowl; Cl Off (R); CR (R); Culinary Chef; Federal Agent; Cornell U; New York U

SALA, VICTORIA; BRICK, NJ; BRICK TWP MEMORIAL HS; (SO); Hi Hnr Roll; Hnr Roll; Nat Hon Sy; Comm Volntr; Dnce; Cl Off (R); Speech Theraphy; Journalism

SALABRITAS, LISA; MARLTON, NJ; CHEROKEE HS; (JR); F Lan Hn Soc; Hnr Roll; Emplmnt; Spanish Clb; Sftball (J); Journalism; Paralegal; Montclair State U; York College of Pennsylvania

SALEEM, MADASER; JERSEY CITY, NJ; HCST-NORTH HUDSON CTR; (FR); All Am Sch; Hnr Roll; Red Cr Aide; Chess; Mth Clb/Tm; SP/M/VS; Bsball; Bskball; Ftball; Mar Art; Vllyball; Medical Science; Computer Technician; Harvard U; Yale U

SALLAM, NADIA; HACKENSACK, NJ; HACKENSACK HS; (SO); Hi Hnr Roll; Hnr Roll; WWAHSS; Comm Volntr; Hosp Aide; Tchrs Aide; Cr Ctry (J); Track (J); Interact Club; Medical; Finance; Columbia U; Princeton U

SALPELDER, KATHRYN E; FAIR LAWN, NJ; FAIR LAWN HS; (SR); F Lan Hn Soc; Hi Hnr Roll; Jr Mshl; Nat Hon Sy; Nat Mrt LOC; Sci/Math Olympn; St Schl; WWAHSS; Comm Volntr; Biology Clb; Emplmnt; Mth Clb/Tm; Tchrs Aide; Bnd; Jzz Bnd; Mch Bnd; SP/M/VS; Classical Pianist-12yrs-Awards/Prizes; Varsity Lettered Marching Band; Music Composition; Will Attend: New England Conservatory

SALTER, KEVIN; PLAINFIELD, NJ; PLAINFIELD HS; (JR); Hi Hnr Roll; Hnr Roll; Drma Clb; SP/M/VS; Bsball (V); Bskball (J); Ftball (V); Placed 3rd At the NJS Governor's Awards for Performing Arts; Performing Arts; Science, Sports Medicine; Morgan U; Virginia Union

SALZMANN, BRIELLE; SOMERVILLE, NJ; SOMERVILLE HS; (SO); Hnr Roll; WWAHSS; Yth Ldrshp Prog; Hosp Aide; Key Club; Lcrsse (V); Tennis (V L); CR (R); Mock Trial; Nursing; College of New Jersey; Richard Stockton College

SALZMANN, SUZANNE; SOMERVILLE, NJ; SOMERVILLE HS; (MS); WWAHSS; Hosp Aide; Chrldg (J); Lcrsse (J); CR (R); Mock Trial; Public Relations; Teaching; Rutgers; The College of New Jersey

SANCHEZ, CRIS; UNION CITY, NJ; EMERSON HS; (SO); Sci Fairs; Comm Volntr; Hosp Aide; Chrch Yth Grp; DARE; Chr; Ch Chr; Dnce; Criminal Justice; The U of Phoenix in Florida

SANCHEZ, DIANA; WEST NEW YORK, NJ; NORTH BERGEN HS; (FR); Hi Hnr Roll; Hnr Roll; Sci Fairs; St of Mnth; Comm Volntr; Chrch Yth Grp; FCCLA; Off Aide; Stu Cncl (S); CR (R); Outstanding Service in the Ministry; Lawyer; Doctor; New York U; Harvard U

SANCHEZ, GINO; NEWARK, NJ; SCIENCE HS; (SO); Hnr Roll; St of Mnth; WWAHSS; Hosp Aide; Bnd; Sch Ppr (R); UMDNJ - Mini Med Program; UMDNJ - Pre-Med Honors Program; Medical Physician; Oncologist; U of Medicine and Dentistry of New Jersey; Yale U

SANCHEZ, JESULIE A; RAHWAY, NJ; RAHWAY HS; (SR); WWAHSS; Comm Volntr; Peer Tut/Med; Drma Clb; Emplmnt; Key Club; Prom Com; ROTC; Clr Grd; Dnce; SP/M/VS; PP Ftbl; Vllyball; Forensic Psychologist; Montclair State U; St Peter's College

SANCHEZ, NICOLE; BRIDGEWATER, NJ; BRIDGEWATER-RARITAN HS; (JR); Ctznshp Aw; Hi Hnr Roll; Hnr Roll; Otst Ac Ach Awd; Sci Fairs; St of Mnth; Yth Ldrshp Prog; Comm Volntr; Chrch Yth Grp; DARE; Drma Clb; Emplmnt; Key Club; Mus Clb; Prom Com; Scouts; Chr; Dnce; Stu Cncl (R); Business; Teaching; St. Joseph's U; Villanova U

SANCHEZ, REBECCA; MATAWAN, NJ; OLD BRIDGE HS WEST; (SO); Hi Hnr Roll; Hnr Roll; PP Ftbl; Track

SANCHEZ ANGON, VANESSA; NEWARK, NJ; ESSEX CTY VOC-TECH HS; (SO); Hnr Roll; Perf Att; St of Mnth; Ch Chr; CR (R); Student of the Month October 2002; Highest GPA World History 2004; Graphic Design; Writing; Gibbs College; Essex County College

SANDERS, KEVIN G; LUMBERTON, NJ; RANCOCAS VALLEY REG HS; (SO); DAR; F Lan Hn Soc; Hi Hnr Roll; Hnr Roll; Pres Sch; WWAHSS; Comm Volntr; Key Club; Tchrs Aide; Chr; SP/M/VS; Yrbk (R); Babe Ruth Baseball / Tournament Team, Education; History; U of Maryland; San Diego State U

SANDFORD, MICHAEL; BRIDGEWATER, NJ; BRIDGEWATER-RARITAN HS; (JR); F Lan Hn Soc; Hi Hnr Roll; Nat Hon Sy; Yth Ldrshp Prog; Hab For Humty Volntr; Spec Olymp Vol; AL Aux Boys; Chrch Yth Grp; DARE; Emplmnt; FBLA; Key Club; Vsity Clb; Wdwrkg Clb; Cr Ctry (V); Track (V); Winter Track Varsity; Mechanical Engineering; Biomechanical Engineering; Lehigh U; Rensselaer Polytechnic Institute

SANICHAR, DAVINDRA; JERSEY CITY, NJ; DICKINSON HS; (SO); Master Degree; Automotive Technician; New York City U; New Jersey City U

SANTA, STEPHANY; HARRISON, NJ; HARRISON HS; (JR); Hnr Roll; Comm Volntr; Drma Clb; Prom Com; Chr; SP/M/VS; Scr Kpr (V); Vllyball (V); Stu Cncl; Varsity Bowling Team; Medical Assistant; Dramatic Arts; Montclair U; Rutgers New Brunswick

SANTAMARIA, AMANDA; CRANBURY, NJ; PRINCETON HS; (SO); Pres Ac Ftns Aw; Yth Ldrshp Prog; Comm Volntr; Peer Tut/Med; NYLC; Chr; Bskball (V); Fld Hky (V); Track (J)

SANTANA, BIANCA; ASBURY PARK, NJ; AC CHARTER HS; (JR); Hi Hnr Roll; Nat Ldrshp Svc; WWAHSS; Peer Tut/Med; Adv Cncl (P); Cl Off (P); CR (P); President of Women's Studies Club; Graphic Makeup Artist; Relationship Counselor

SANTANA, NICAURY; JERSEY CITY, NJ; AC ST ALOYSIUS HS; (JR); Otst Ac Ach Awd; Perf Att; Pres Sch; St of Mnth; WWAHSS; Comm Volntr; ArtClub; Drma Clb; Prom Com; Dnce; SP/M/VS; Stg Cre; Scr Kpr (V); Tennis (J); Cl Off (R); CR (R); Sch Ppr (P); Performing Arts; Communication; Rutgers U; Richmond American International U of London

SANTANGELO, VINCENT; SICKLERVILLE, NJ; GLOUCESTER CATHOLIC HS; (JR); MVP; Nat Hon Sy; Pres Ac Ftns Aw; St of Mnth; USMC Stu Ath Aw; Red Cr Aide; Emplmnt; Bsball (J); Ftball (V L); Stu Cncl (R); CR (R); Gatorade Player of Year; Business Management; Law Enforcement; Hofstra U; Syracuse U

SANTUCCI, NANCY; TOMS RIVER, NJ; TOMS RIVER HS EAST; (SO); Hi Hnr Roll; Otst Ac Ach Awd; WWAHSS; Comm Volntr; Svce Clb; Spanish Clb; Dnce; Psychology; Journalism; Princeton U

SAPANARA, AMANDA; SOMERVILLE, NJ; SOMERVILLE HS; (SO); Hnr Roll; MVP; WWAHSS; Comm Volntr; ArtClub; Chrch Yth Grp; Drma Clb; Key Club; Mod UN; Photog; French Clb; Chr; SP/M/VS; Fncg (J); Sftball (JC); Yrbk (R); Film Directing; Photography; New York U

SARABIA, LENARD; CLARK, NJ; ARTHUR L JOHNSON HS; (JR); Hi Hnr Roll; WWAHSS; Comm Volntr; Hab For Humty Volntr; Key Club; Sci Clb; Sccr (J); Sch Ppr (R); Science League; Computer Science; Engineering; Rutgers U; NJ Institute of Technology

SARABU, KIRAN; TOWACO, NJ; MONTVILLE TOWNSHIP HS; (JR); F Lan Hn Soc; Otst Ac Ach Awd; Yth Ldrshp Prog; Comm Volntr; Peer Tut/Med; DECA; Emplmnt; Svce Clb; Tmpl Yth Grp; Chr; Cr Ctry (J); Sch Ppr (R); Yrbk (R, P); Vice President of Earth Club; Co-Founder of Fed Challenge Chapter; Pre-Law; Economics/Business; U of Michigan-Ann Arbor; Case Western Reserve

SARKAR, SUPRIYA; PENNINGTON, NJ; NOTRE DAME HS; (JR); Hi Hnr Roll; Hnr Roll; MVP; Nat Hon Sy; Spec Olymp Vol; Key Club; Mod UN; Lcrsse (L); Tennis (V L); Peer Leadership Vice President; Junior Portfolio Award; Management Information Systems; Business Management; New York U; U of Pennsylvania

SARODE, SUDHA; EDISON, NJ; EDISON HS; (JR); F Lan Hn Soc; Hi Hnr Roll; Nat Hon Sy; Otst Ac Ach Awd; Perf Att; Pres Ac Ftns Aw; WWAHSS; Comm Volntr; Peer Tut/Med; French Clb; SP/M/VS; CR (R); Lit Mag (R); Sch Ppr (R); Rotary Interact Club - President; Peacock Society - Club / Co-Chair - 2 Years; Rutgers U; The College of New Jersey

SARPONG, TRACEY N Y; MAPLEWOOD, NJ; MILTON HERSHEY SCH; (SR); Hi Hnr Roll; Hnr Roll; Emplmnt; FCA; FBLA; Lib Aide; Prom Com; Ch Chr; Dnce; SP/M/VS; Track (V); Wt Lftg (V); Communications; UNC Charlotte - Accepted; Georgetown U

SASSANO, NINA; PT PLEASANT BEACH, NJ; PT PLEASANT BEACH HS; (JR); Hi Hnr Roll; Hnr Roll; Sci Fairs; Sci/Math Olympn; St of Mnth; WWAHSS; Aqrium Clb; Chess; DARE; Drma Clb; Emplmnt; Key Club; Mus Clb; Sci Clb; Bnd; Jzz Bnd; Mch Bnd; Pep Bnd; Golf; Tennis; Stu Cncl (R); CR (R); Sch Ppr (R); Yrbk (E); Volunteer Coach - Volleyball Team; Sailing Team; Marine Biology; Teaching Certificate; Fairleigh Dickinson U; U of Maine Bar Harbor

SASTRE, DANIELLE; NORTH BERGEN, NJ; NORTH BERGEN HS; (JR); F Lan Hn Soc; Hnr Roll; WWAHSS; Yth Ldrshp Prog; Drma Clb; Emplmnt; Key Club; Spanish Clb; Dnce; Track (V); Veterinarian

SAUERWALD, MAEGAN; PEMBERTON, NJ; PEMBERTON TWP HS; (SO); Hnr Roll; Emplmnt; SADD; Tchrs Aide; Football, Basketball Manager; Early Childhood Education; U of South Carolina; Colgate U

SAVADELIS, ANDREA J; BELLE MEAD, NJ; MONTGOMERY HS; (JR); Hnr Roll; Emplmnt; Tchrs Aide; Vsity Clb; Bnd; Mch Bnd; SP/M/VS; Hsbk Rdg; Swmg (V L); Live Historians Club - Rockingham Association; History Major / Master's Degree; History Teacher; Boston U; College of William and Mary

SAVINO, AMANDA; HOWELL, NJ; FREEHOLD TOWNSHIP; (SR); Hnr Roll; Peer Tut/Med; DECA; Lcrsse (V L); Sccr (J); Yrbk (E, P); Peer Leadership President; Secondary Education; U of Rhode Island

SCALERA, GREGORY; COLONIA, NJ; COLONIA HS; (JR); Hnr Roll; DARE; Bnd; Jzz Bnd; Mch Bnd; Orch; Sch Ppr (E); Wrote Various Articles for the "Teen Scene" for a Local Newspaper; Journalism; Music; Rutgers U

SCERBO, JENNIFER L; BRICK, NJ; BRICK TOWNSHIP HS; (SO); Hnr Roll; WWAHSS; Comm Volntr; Emplmnt; Scouts; Track (J)

SCHAFFER, GIL; TRENTON, NJ; HAMILTON HS EAST; (SO); Nat Hon Sy; Pres Ac Ftns Aw; Ice Hky (V); Academic Presidential Award; All Through School; Sports Administration; Physical Therapy; Rider U; Rutgers U

SCHAPPELL, SETH; YARDVILLE, NJ; STEINERT HS; (FR); Red Cr Aide; Chrch Yth Grp; Key Club; Scouts; Ftball; Track; Junior Leadership Training; Red Cross Lifeguard Certification; Teacher; Physical Therapist; The College of New Jersey; Rowan U

SCHAPPERT, CASEY L; WYCKOFF, NJ; RAMAPO HS; (JR); Comm Volntr; Hab For Humty Volntr; Hosp Aide; Sccr (VJ L); Sftball (V L)

SCHMIDT, TIFFANY; HIGHTSTOWN, NJ; HIGHTSTOWN HS; (JR); Hi Hnr Roll; Hnr Roll; Nat Hon Sy; Comm Volntr; Red Cr Aide; Drma Clb; Emplmnt; Scouts; German Clb; Clr Grd; SP/M/VS; Sch Ppr (E, R, P); Journalism; Criminal Law

Schappell, Seth
Steinert HS
Yardville, NJ

Savino, Amanda
Freehold Township
Howell, NJ

Sarpong, Tracey N Y
Milton Hershey Sch
Maplewood, NJ

Sarabia, Lenard
Arthur L Johnson HS
Clark, NJ

Santana, Bianca
AC Charter HS
Asbury Park, NJ

Sarkar, Supriya
Notre Dame HS
Pennington, NJ

Sauerwald, Maegan
Pemberton Twp HS
Pemberton, NJ

Schaffer, Gil
Hamilton HS East
Trenton, NJ

Schmidt, Tiffany
Hightstown HS
Hightstown, NJ

Sanichar, Davindra
Dickinson HS
Jersey City, NJ

Sanchez, Jesulie A
Rahway HS
Rahway, NJ

Saleem, Madaser
Hcst-North Hudson Ctr
Jersey City, NJ

Sacks, Robyn A
Bridgewater-Raritan HS
Bridgewater, NJ

Sacks, Justine A
Bridgewater-Raritan HS
Bridgewater, NJ

National
Honor Roll
Spring 2005

Saab, Ashley M
Bcit/Medford Campus
Willingboro, NJ

Sahu, Simi
Belleville HS
Belleville, NJ

Sanchez, Gino
Science HS
Newark, NJ

Sanchez, Nicole
Bridgewater-Raritan HS
Bridgewater, NJ

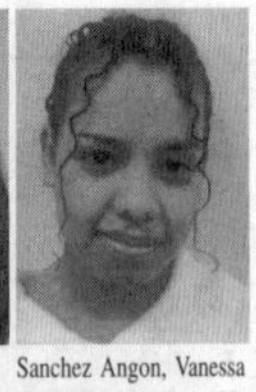
Sanchez Angon, Vanessa
Essex Cty Voc-Tech HS
Newark, NJ

SCHNEIDER, KELSEY; AUDUBON, NJ; PAUL VI HS; (SO); Hi Hnr Roll; Comm Volntr; Ch Chr; Fld Hky (J); Teen Style Squad; Environmental Club; Interior Design, Marketing; Law; Monmouth U; New York U

SCHOMP, NICOLE; CRANFORD, NJ; CRANFORD HS; (FR); Bskball (J); Vllyball (J); Gourmet Club and Sign Language Club; Girl Scout Silver Award; Teaching; Psychologist; New York U; College of New Jersey

SCHRAMM, THERESA M E; ALLENDALE, NJ; NORTHERN HIGHLANDS REG HS; (SO); Hi Hnr Roll; Comm Volntr; Chrch Yth Grp; DECA; Spanish Clb; Cr Ctry (V L); Sccr; Track (V L); Sch Ppr (R); Earned 'Superior' Rating for Piano in the National Federation of Music 'Clubs' 4 Years in a Row; 2nd Place DECA Instructional Area Award at State Conference

SCHULDE, SARAH; GLASSBORO, NJ; GLASSBORO HS; (SO); Hi Hnr Roll; Hnr Roll; MVP; Otst Ac Ach Awd; Pres Ac Ftns Aw; Chrch Yth Grp; DARE; Emplmnt; Theatrical Arts; Law; UCLA; NYU

SCHWARZBERG, ADAM; SPRINGFIELD, NJ; JONATHAN DAYTON HS; (SO); Hnr Roll; Perf Att; Sci/Math Olympn; WWAHSS; Hosp Aide; Mth Clb/Tm; Quiz Bowl; Sci Clb; Tmpl Yth Grp; Spanish Clb; Sccr (J); Tennis (J); Track (V L); Martial Arts Student for 4 Yrs, Blue Stripe; Confirmation Graduate; Architecture; Engineering; York College; Temple U

SCOTT, BRITTNEY K; MAPLEWOOD, NJ; COLUMBIA HS; (SO); Nat Hon Sy; St of Mnth; Comm Volntr; Peer Tut/Med; Chrch Yth Grp; Chr; Dnce; High Honor Roll - Gotha Middle School; Teacher; Rutgers U; Jersey City State College

SCOTT, DARREN; HACKENSACK, NJ; HACKENSACK HS; (SO); Hnr Roll; St of Mnth; Comm Volntr; Chess; Sci Clb; Svce Clb; Outstanding Academic Achievement; Science; History

SCOTT, KATRINA; MAYS LANDING, NJ; OUR LADY OF MERCY AC; (SO); MVP; Pep Squd; SADD; Chr; SP/M/VS; Bskball (V L); Sftball (V L); Interior Decorator; Marine Biologist; Cabrini College; Drexel U

SCOTT, LINDSEY A; PRINCETON, NJ; THE HUN SCH OF PRINCETON; (SO); Hi Hnr Roll; Nat Mrt LOC; Peer Tut/Med; Chrch Yth Grp; Key Club; Asian Clb; SP/M/VS; Bskball (J); Sccr (V); Ski Club; Race for the Cure; Journalism; Duke U

SEEBALD, ALLISON C; BERKELEY HTS, NJ; THE PINGRY SCH; (SR); Hnr Roll; Nat Mrt Fin; Valdctrian; Comm Volntr; Emplmnt; Svce Clb; Chr; Dnce; SP/M/VS; Cr Ctry (J); Sftball (J); Tennis (J); NJ Governor's School on the Environment / Cum Laude Society; Appalachian Service Project / Celiac Disease Research; Molecular Biology / Biochemistry; Biomedical Research; Princeton U - Will Be Attending

SEELEY, KIMBERLY A; NORTH ARLINGTON, NJ; KEARNY HS; (SR); Ctznshp Aw; Hi Hnr Roll; Hnr Roll; Perf Att; Sci/Math Olympn; St of Mnth; WWAHSS; Comm Volntr; Hosp Aide; Peer Tut/Med; ArtClub; DARE; Emplmnt; Lib Aide; Off Aide; Prom Com; Tchrs Aide; Stu Cncl (R); CR (R); Early Childhood Education; Elementary Education; New Jersey City U; Kean U

SEIBERT, ISADORA; MILLBURN, NJ; MILLBURN HS; (JR); Hnr Roll; WWAHSS; Comm Volntr; Peer Tut/Med; Key Club; Tmpl Yth Grp; Chr; Dnce; Vllyball (V L); Cl Off (S); Education; Spanish; Ramapo College of New Jersey; College of New Jersey

SEIXAS, FREDERIK M; MAPLEWOOD, NJ; COLUMBIA HS; (SR); Hi Hnr Roll; Hnr Roll; Otst Ac Ach Awd; Sci Fairs; WWAHSS; Yth Ldrshp Prog; Comm Volntr; Dbte Team; Key Club; Sci Clb; Stg Cre; Wrstlg (V); CR (R); 3rd Place at Princeton Moot Court 2005; 2nd Place Columbia High School Science Fair; Biomedical Engineer; Classics; Rutgers U

SELBY, FELICITY D; MONTCLAIR, NJ; MONTCLAIR HS; (JR); All Am Sch; F Lan Hn Soc; Hi Hnr Roll; Hnr Roll; Nat Hon Sy; Nat Mrt Sch Recip; USAA; Peer Tut/Med; Chrch Yth Grp; Drma Clb; Key Club; Italian Clb; Chr; Ch Chr; Stg Cre; Treasurer of RACE Club; Doctor; Teacher

SELLARS, TANEESHA; NEWARK, NJ; BARRINGER HS; (SO); Hnr Roll; Otst Ac Ach Awd; Perf Att; St of Mnth; Bnd; Dnce; Stu Cncl (S); CR (P); Business Woman; Fashion Designer; Virginia State U

SEME, GRACE; MARTINSVILLE, NJ; BRIDGEWATER-RARITAN HS; (FR); Hi Hnr Roll; Hnr Roll; Perf Att; Pres Sch; St of Mnth; Comm Volntr; Peer Tut/Med; Chrch Yth Grp; Key Club; Mod UN; Scouts; Dnce; Yrbk (R); Silver Award for Girl Scouts; Business; Mathematics; Brown U; Cornell

SEMUS, CHRISTOPHER W J; MILMAY, NJ; ST AUGUSTINE PREP; (FR); Hi Hnr Roll; Pres Ac Ftns Aw; St of Mnth; Yth Ldrshp Prog; Comm Volntr; Chess; P to P St Amb Prg; Cyclg; Ice Hky (J); Science / Business; Boston College; College Providence

SENDEROFF, ANDREA; CHERRY HILL, NJ; CHERRY HILL HS EAST; (JR); Hnr Roll; MVP; Comm Volntr; Hab For Humty Volntr; BPA; DECA; Key Club; Prom Com; Lcrsse (J); Sccr (J); Track (V); Wrstlg (J); Cl Off (P); Stu Cncl (T); CR (R); Sch Ppr (R); President/Founder of Club TEENS-Volunteer Club; 1st Place DECA States/President of Sr Class; Marketing, Broadcasting; Fashion Marketing/Fashion Design; U of Maryland; North Eastern U

SENDLER, ALYSSA; STRATFORD, NJ; STERLING HS; (JR); Hnr Roll; WWAHSS; Comm Volntr; Dbte Team; Emplmnt; Tech Clb; Stg Cre; Mar Art (V); Tennis (VJ L); Sch Ppr (R); Yrbk (E, P); Project Graduation, Morning News; Freshman Mentor; Communication (Film/Video); Middle School Education; Rowan U, La Salle; Rutgers

SEPULVEDA, FRANCESCA; KEARNY, NJ; KEARNY HS; (MS); Ctznshp Aw; Hi Hnr Roll; Hnr Roll; Pres Ac Ftns Aw; Chrch Yth Grp; DARE; Chr; Clr Grd; Dnce; SP/M/VS; Bskball; Chrldg; Sccr; Stu Cncl (P); Sch Ppr; Singing; Acting; Teaching; Performing; The Juilliard School; Jersey City State College

SERAPHIM, ASHLEY; PARSIPPANY, NJ; PARSIPPANY HS; (JR); F Lan Hn Soc; Hnr Roll; Nat Hon Sy; WWAHSS; Comm Volntr; Svce Clb; French Clb; Dnce; Secretary of French Honor Society; Director of Service and Charities for Interact-Community Service Club; Elementary Education; Montclair State U; Rowan U

SEREBRANSKY, LAUREN; SEWELL, NJ; WASHINGTON TWP HS; (FR); Hnr Roll; Jr Rot; St of Mnth; Comm Volntr; Peer Tut/Med; Drma Clb; Mus Clb; Scouts; Svce Clb; Tmpl Yth Grp; Chr; SP/M/VS; Volunteer At the YMCA; Involved in Peer Outreach for Special Need Kids; Music Therapy; Special Ed. Teacher; George Washington U; The College of New Jersey

SERKO, RON; ALPINE, NJ; TENAFLY HS; (FR); Hi Hnr Roll; Hnr Roll; Sci/Math Olympn; Valdctrian; Comm Volntr; DARE; Mth Clb/Tm; Quiz Bowl; Bnd; Bskball; Sch Ppr (E); Recipient of 15 Awards for Excellence in Academics (Various Subject); First Chair, First Clarinet Section in 8th Grade Band; Juris Doctor (JD); Master's in Business Administration (MBA); Harvard U; Princeton U

SEVENTKO, JUSTIN; GARFIELD, NJ; BERGEN CTY AC; (SO); Pres Sch; St of Mnth; Valdctrian; Comm Volntr; Chrch Yth Grp; DECA; Emplmnt; FBLA; Mod UN; Dean's List; Federal Reserve Challenge; Finance; History; New York U (Nyu); Rutgers

SHAE, PATRICK; HAINESPORT, NJ; RANCOCAS VALLEY REG HS; (SO); Hnr Roll; Otst Ac Ach Awd; Perf Att; Comm Volntr; Spec Olymp Vol; Emplmnt; Vsity Clb; Cr Ctry (V); Track (J); Vsy Clb (V); Winter Track Junior Varsity; Homecoming Member; Business and Management; Hotel Management; New York U; UCLA

SHAEQUE, MOHAMMAD T; NEWARK, NJ; SCIENCE HS; (FR); Ctznshp Aw; Hi Hnr Roll; Hnr Roll; Otst Ac Ach Awd; Sci/Math Olympn; St of Mnth; Cmptr Clb; Tech Clb; Bnd; Chr; Bskball (J); Cl Off (P); CR (P); Sch Ppr (R); Defensive Player of the Year in Basketball; Bioinformatics; Medical School; U of Connecticut

SHAFER, JESSY; MONROEVILLE, NJ; SALEM CO VOC TECH CAREER CTR; (SR); Hnr Roll; Pres Ac Ftns Aw; Chrch Yth Grp

SHAH, ARPITA; JERSEY CITY, NJ; WILLIAM L DICKINSON HS; (SR); Hi Hnr Roll; Hnr Roll; Nat Hon Sy; Nat Mrt Semif; Otst Ac Ach Awd; Perf Att; Pres Sch; Valdctrian; WWAHSS; Yth Ldrshp Prog; Comm Volntr; Hosp Aide; Peer Tut/Med; Chess; Emplmnt; Fr of Library; Key Club; Lib Aide; Mth Clb/Tm; Sci Clb; Tchrs Aide; Tennis (J); Stu Cncl (P); Sch Ppr (R); Topical Winner in 7th Annual High School Poetry Contest; Elks National Foundation Scholarship Recipient; Pharmacy; Pre-Medicine Research; Rutgers U-School of Pharmacy; Stanford U

SHAH, KRISHNA; ROSELLE PARK, NJ; ROSELEE PARK HS; (SO); Hi Hnr Roll; Perf Att; Pres Sch; St of Mnth; Hosp Aide; DARE; Spanish Clb; Tennis (J); Track (J); Future Health Career Club; Club- HUE / Straight-Gay Alliance; Pharmacy; Medicine; Rutgers U; Brown U

SHAH, KRISTEN J; LINCOLN PARK, NJ; BUTLER HS; (SO); Peer Tut/Med; Key Club; Judicial Mentoring; Law and Public Safety Academy; Pre-Law; NYU School of Law; Georgetown Law Center

SHAH, MANTHAN; CLIFTON, NJ; CLIFTON HS; (SR); 4H Awd; Gov Hnr Prg; Hi Hnr Roll; MVP; Nat Hon Sy; Otst Ac Ach Awd; Perf Att; Yth Ldrshp Prog; Comm Volntr; Hosp Aide; Peer Tut/Med; 4-H; Chess; Chrch Yth Grp; Cmptr Clb; Emplmnt; Mth Clb/Tm; Outdrs Clb; ROTC; Clr Grd; Dnce; Bskball (J); Wt Lftg (J); Stu Cncl (R); CR (R); Sch Ppr (P); Yrbk (P); 4-Year Honor Roll; Tutoring at Boys & Girls Club; Criminal Justice; Business; Quinnipiac U

SHAH, NIYATI U; PISCATAWAY, NJ; PISCATAWAY HS; (SR); Hi Hnr Roll; Hnr Roll; Nat Hon Sy; WWAHSS; Comm Volntr; Hosp Aide; Peer Tut/Med; Key Club; Mth Clb/Tm; Sch Ppr (P); Ping Pong Player; Pharmacist; Rutgers U

SHAH, ROSHNI J; STANHOPE, NJ; LENAPE VALLEY REG HS; (JR); Duke TS; Salutrn; WWAHSS; Hosp Aide; Spec Olymp Vol; Key Club; Sci Clb; German Clb; Stu Cncl (R); Yrbk (E); German Honor Society; Gifted and Talented

SHAH, RUCHI; NORTH BERGEN, NJ; NORTH BERGEN HS; (JR); Hi Hnr Roll; Nat Hon Sy; Otst Ac Ach Awd; Salutrn; WWAHSS; Red Cr Aide; ArtClub; DARE; Dbte Team; DECA; Key Club; Lib Aide; Mth Clb/Tm; Quiz Bowl; Tennis (V); Track (V); Lit Mag (R); Environmental Club; Rebel (Anti Smoking)

SHAH, SAJEL; BEDMINSTER, NJ; BERNARDS HS; (JR); Hnr Roll; Nat Hon Sy; WWAHSS; Comm Volntr; Hosp Aide; Key Club; Photog; Orch; Swmg (VJC); Sch Ppr (E, R, P); Yrbk (R); National Honor Society; Hospital Volunteer; Medicine; Business; U of Michigan

SHAH, SAMAR; EDISON, NJ; JOHN P STEVENS HS; (JR); Nat Hon Sy; Otst Ac Ach Awd; Sci/Math Olympn; Comm Volntr; Peer Tut/Med; Spec Olymp Vol; Biology Clb; Key Club; Mth Clb/Tm; Mod UN; Sci Clb; Scouts; Svce Clb; Sch Ppr; Webmaster of Key Club 2004-2005; Winner of 2 best delegation: ILMUNC (Ivy League MUN) and WMHSMUN (William and Mary High School MUN); Biomedical Engineering; Pre-med into Doctor; U of Pennsylvania (UPENN); Cornell U

SHAHZAD, SHAWN F; COLONIA, NJ; COLONIA HS; (JR); Ctznshp Aw; Hi Hnr Roll; Hnr Roll; Nat Hon Sy; St of Mnth; Yth Ldrshp Prog; Comm Volntr; Hosp Aide; Chrch Yth Grp; Mth Clb/Tm; Mus Clb; NYLC; Off Aide; Sci Clb; Yrbk (E); MD / Cardiologist; Rutgers U; Johns Hopkins Institute of Tech

SHANKAR, JAVAS P; SOMERSET, NJ; FRANKLIN HS; (SO); Hnr Roll; Sch Ppr (R); Karate Black Belt; Tennis Lessons; Game Programming; Elon U; Lafayette College

SHARMA, NISHA; JERSEY CITY, NJ; SAINT DOMINIC AC; (FR); Pres Sch; WWAHSS; Comm Volntr; SADD; First Honors; Pre Medicine; New York U

SHARMA, RESHMA; JERSEY CITY, NJ; AC OF SACRED HEART HS; (JR); Hi Hnr Roll; Hnr Roll; Nat Hon Sy; Nat Sci Aw; Otst Ac Ach Awd; Comm Volntr; Peer Tut/Med; Cmptr Clb; Schol Bwl; Tchrs Aide; Sccr; Track; Principal's List; Excellence Awards; Pre-Med / Computer-Related; Mathematics; New York U; College of St Elizabeth

SHARMA, VIKRAM; JERSEY CITY, NJ; DICKINSON HS; (SO); Hnr Roll; Perf Att; St of Mnth; Comm Volntr; Peer Tut/Med; Biology Clb; Cmptr Clb; Indian Clb; Stu Cncl (R); CR (R); Volunteer Work-Community Service; Business and Management; MBA; Berkeley College; Rutgers

SHARPE, ELISABETH; EGG HARBOR TOWNSHIP, NJ; EGG HARBOR TWP HS; (FR); Hnr Roll; WWAHSS; Comm Volntr; Chrch Yth Grp; Key Club; Scouts; Bnd; Chr; Dnce; Mch Bnd; Cr Ctry (V); Track (J); Pediatric Occupational Therapy; Arcadia U

SHAW, SHEAMA J; ATCO, NJ; HAMMONTON HS; (FR); Hnr Roll; Chrch Yth Grp; DARE; Mus Clb; Ch Chr; Drl Tm; Awards for Track First Place; Youth Student Award (Church); Pediatrics; Princeton U; Temple U

SHEEDER, KATELYNN; MT HOLLY, NJ; RANCOCAS VALLEY REG HS; (FR); Hi Hnr Roll; WWAHSS; Comm Volntr; Chrch Yth Grp; Key Club; Lcrsse (C); Sccr (J); Freshmen Girl Captain for Spirit Organizations; Church Youth Group

SHEIKH, AQSA S; ELIZABETH, NJ; ELIZABETH HS; (JR); Hi Hnr Roll; Hnr Roll; Nat Mrt Sch Recip; Perf Att; Sci/Math Olympn; Comm Volntr; Hosp Aide; Peer Tut/Med; Key Club; Sci Clb; Representative of Physics League of CHS; Medical Mentors; Pre-Medical; New York U; U of Medicine & Dentistry of New Jersey

SHEIKHZADEH, SHAHAB; JACKSON, NJ; JACKSON MEMORIAL HS; (SR); Perf Att; WWAHSS; Comm Volntr; Computer Science; Web Page Design; Princeton, Princeton, New Jersey; California Institute of Technology, Pasadena, California

SHELTON, JUSTIN; SOUTH PLAINFIELD, NJ; SOUTH PLAINFIELD HS; (SR); F Lan Hn Soc; Hi Hnr Roll; Hnr Roll; Perf Att; Chess; Spanish Clb; Academic Letter, Academic Pin, Gold Card; Academic Team Silver Medalist; Criminal Justice; Sociology; Rutgers U; St Peters U

SHEPPARD, JAMEL; SCOTCH PLAINS, NJ; SCOTCH PLAINS-FANWOOD HS; (JR); DARE; Bskball (J); Ftball (J); Bachelor's Degree / Computer Science; Georgia Institute of Technology; Virginia Institute of Technology

SHERIDAN, BETHANY F; TOMS RIVER, NJ; MANCHESTER TWP HS; (FR); Hi Hnr Roll; ROTC; Dnce; Drl Tm; Fld Hky (J); Lcrsse (J); Track (J); Jr. ROTC Petty Officer - 3rd Class; Law; Medicine; U of Pennsylvania; Rutgers U

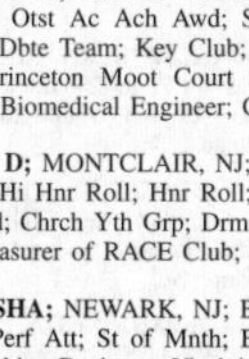
Shaw, Sheama J
Hammonton HS
Atco, NJ

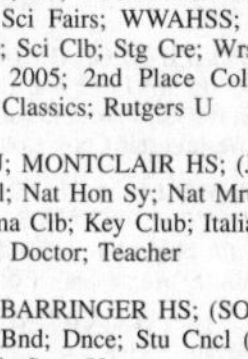
Selby, Felicity D
Montclair HS
Montclair, NJ

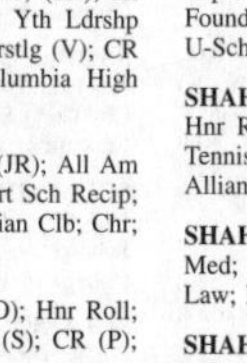
Scott, Lindsey A
The Hun Sch Of Princeton
Princeton, NJ

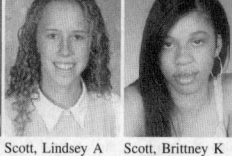

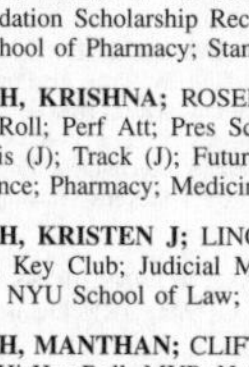
Scott, Brittney K
Columbia HS
Maplewood, NJ

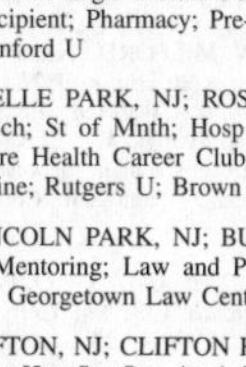
Schneider, Kelsey
Paul VI HS
Audubon, NJ

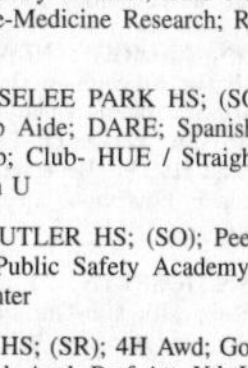
Schramm, Theresa M E
Northern Highlands Reg HS
Allendale, NJ

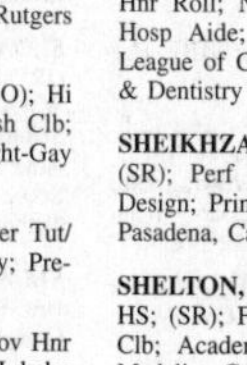
Seebald, Allison C
The Pingry Sch
Berkeley Hts, NJ

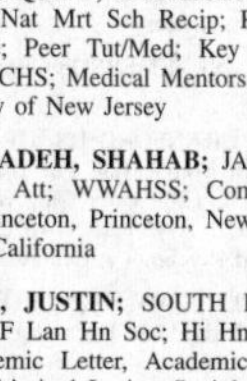
Sharma, Vikram
Dickinson HS
Jersey City, NJ

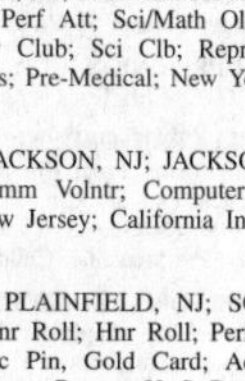
Sheridan, Bethany F
Manchester Twp HS
Toms River, NJ

SHERMAN, LAUREN; PT PLEASANT BEACH, NJ; PT PLEASANT BORO HS; (SR); Hnr Roll; MVP; Comm Volntr; DARE; Emplmnt; Prom Com; PP Ftbl (V); Sftball (J L); Yrbk (P); Project Graduation Committee; Student / Teacher Switch Day; Bachelor's Degree / Real Estate; Bachelor's Degree / Interior Design; Florida Atlantic U; U of Hawaii Manoa

SHETH, SHIVANI; GLASSBORO, NJ; GLASSBORO HS; (FR); Ctznshp Aw; Hi Hnr Roll; Otst Ac Ach Awd; Perf Att; Comm Volntr; ArtClub; Svce Clb; Tennis (J L); Cl Off (P); Renaissance Club; Student Government; Business; Pharmacy; U of Pennsylvania; Princeton U

SHI, YINGTING; BRIDGEWATER, NJ; BRIDGEWATER-RARITAN HS; (SO); Hi Hnr Roll; Comm Volntr; FBLA; Key Club; French Clb; Business and Management; Fashion Merchandise; New York U

SHIKITINO, TAYLOR; GLASSBORO, NJ; G C I T; (JR); Ctznshp Aw; Hi Hnr Roll; Hnr Roll; Otst Ac Ach Awd; Perf Att; WWAHSS; Comm Volntr; Chrch Yth Grp; Emplmnt; Key Club; Spanish Clb; Dnce; Chrldg (V); Principal's List; Outstanding Student Award; Nursing RN

SHIN, JIWOONG J; CHERRY HILL, NJ; CHERRY HILL HS WEST; (JR); Hnr Roll; Comm Volntr; Chrch Yth Grp; Tchrs Aide; Tennis (V); Sch Ppr (R); Spanish Honor Society; Law; Medicine; Princeton U; U of Pennsylvania

SHISHMANIAN, HAIG; ALLENDALE, NJ; NORTHERN HIGHLANDS REG HS; Hnr Roll; WWAHSS; Comm Volntr; Chrch Yth Grp; Emplmnt; FCA; Jr Cls League; Latin Clb; Bnd; Chr; Ch Chr; Mch Bnd; Track (J); Executive Committee Member of Church Youth Organization; Magna Cum Laude Award on National Latin Exam; Mechanical Engineering; Law; Stevens Institute of Technology; Massachusetts Institute of Technology

SHOCKLEY, VALERIE N; SOMERDALE, NJ; PAUL VI HS; (SO); Hi Hnr Roll; Hnr Roll; Yth Ldrshp Prog; Comm Volntr; DARE; Drma Clb; Scouts; Psychology; Vet. Med.; Villanova U; Rutgers New Brunswick

SHOLAKH, NATASHA H; FAIR LAWN, NJ; PARAMUS CATHOLIC HS; (JR); Hi Hnr Roll; Hnr Roll; MVP; Nat Hon Sy; Otst Ac Ach Awd; Pres Ac Ftns Aw; Pres Sch; Sci/Math Olympn; WWAHSS; Yth Ldrshp Prog; Comm Volntr; Hab For Humty Volntr; Peer Tut/Med; Biology Clb; Cmptr Clb; Mth Clb/Tm; NYLC; P to P St Amb Prg; SADD; Tchrs Aide; Vsity Clb; Chr; Dnce; SP/M/VS; Bsball (V C); Bskball (V CL); Sccr (V CL); Vsy Clb (V CL); Cl Off (R); Stu Cncl (P, V, S); CR (T, R); Sch Ppr (R); Yrbk (R, P); Ambassadors Club; Represented School in Leadership & Management Conference; Athletic Training/Sports Medicine; Professor Secondary Education; Columbia U; Princeton U

SHORT, LATOYA S; EAST ORANGE, NJ; EAST ORANGE CAMPUS 9 HS; (FR); Ctznshp Aw; Hnr Roll; Nat Mrt LOC; Otst Ac Ach Awd; Perf Att; WWAHSS; Comm Volntr; DARE; Emplmnt; ROTC; Stu Cncl (T); Street Team; Nursing; Child Care; U of Maryland; U of Delaware

SHOWALTER, MASON A; SADDLE RIVER, NJ; NORTHERN HIGHLANDS REG HS; (SO); Hi Hnr Roll; Hnr Roll; Sci Fairs; Comm Volntr; Peer Tut/Med; Cr Ctry (J); Track (J); Architect; Aerospace Engineer; Purdue U; U of Illinois

SHULER, JASON M P; LONG BRANCH, NJ; LONG BRANCH HS; (JR); Hi Hnr Roll; Hnr Roll; Perf Att; St of Mnth; Chrch Yth Grp; Emplmnt; FCA; Vllyball (J); Martial Arts Yellow / White Belt Awards, Christian Studies; Veterinary Studies; Monmouth U; Rutgers U

SHULMAN, MICHAEL; HIGHLAND PARK, NJ; HIGHLAND PARK HS; (JR); Hnr Roll; WWAHSS; Yth Ldrshp Prog; Comm Volntr; Peer Tut/Med; Biology Clb; Bskball (J); Mar Art (L); Chemistry; Pharmacy; Rutgers U

SIEGEL, NAOMI B; ENGLISHTOWN, NJ; MANALAPAN HS; (SR); F Lan Hn Soc; Hi Hnr Roll; Hnr Roll; Nat Hon Sy; WWAHSS; Comm Volntr; Prom Com; Vsity Clb; Cr Ctry (V C); Track (V C); Cl Off (V); Stu Cncl (R); Biology; Marine Biology; College of William & Mary

SIERRA, GAUDALUPE; UNION CITY, NJ; EMERSON HS; (JR); Hnr Roll; Comm Volntr; ROTC; Chr; Track

SIGMUND, RACHEL; CRANFORD, NJ; CRANFORD HS; (JR); Hnr Roll; Jr Rot; Sci Fairs; Yth Ldrshp Prog; Comm Volntr; Hab For Humty Volntr; Chrch Yth Grp; Mth Clb/Tm; Sci Clb; Svce Clb; Vsity Clb; Wdwrkg Clb; Spanish Clb; Dnce; SP/M/VS; Gmnstcs (V CL); Gymnastics-All County Team 2; All-Around Member; Pre-Medicine; Child Psychology; Lehigh U; Boston U

SILBER, BECKY; BELFORD, NJ; MIDDLETOWN HS NORTH; (JR); Hnr Roll; WWAHSS; Drma Clb; Emplmnt; Bnd; Mch Bnd; Stg Cre; Music Production; Music Management; Berklee College of Music; Full Sail

SILVERMAN, BRITTANY; MAHWAH, NJ; MAHWAH HS; (SO); Hi Hnr Roll; Comm Volntr; Emplmnt; Tmpl Yth Grp; Bnd; Chr; Track; Pediatrician / Minor in Teaching; Lawyer

SILVERMAN, MARC D; HIGHTSTOWN, NJ; HIGHTSTOWN HS; (JR); Golf; Ice Hky (V CL); Lcrsse (J); Sccr (J); Aeronautical Engineering/ Business; Boston U, U of Maryland; U of Michigan

SILVERSHEIN, ANDREW; UPPER SADDLE RIVER, NJ; NORTHERN HIGHLANDS REG HS; (SO); Hi Hnr Roll; Nat Hon Sy; Pres Ac Ftns Aw; DECA; Golf (V); Tennis (J); Stu Cncl; Political Science; Business/Marketing

SILVESTRI, KRISTINE; FLEMINGTON, NJ; HUNTERDON CTRL REG HS; (JR); F Lan Hn Soc; Gov Hnr Prg; Hi Hnr Roll; Hnr Roll; MVP; WWAHSS; Comm Volntr; NYLC; Off Aide; Spanish Clb; Sftball (J); PAWS Club (Animal Rights)-President; Kindness and Justice Award; Political Science; Government; Wellesley; Tufts U

SIMEONI, MATTHEW; MONTCLAIR, NJ; MONTCLAIR HS; (SO); Ctznshp Aw; F Lan Hn Soc; Hi Hnr Roll; Hnr Roll; Otst Ac Ach Awd; Pres Ac Ftns Aw; Pres Sch; St of Mnth; Comm Volntr; Emplmnt; Jr Cls League; Tmpl Yth Grp; Latin Clb; Bnd; Mch Bnd; SP/M/VS; Stg Cre; Ice Hky (V L); Lcrsse (J); Rabbi Search Committee; Hammer / Coaches Award; Economics; Management; Middlebury College; Boston U

SIMMONS, QIYDAAR; NEWARK, NJ; MALCOLM X SHABAZZ HS; (FR); Hnr Roll; Chess; Chrch Yth Grp; Emplmnt; Ch Chr; Stg Cre; Track (L); Stu Cncl (T); Law; Virginia Technical

SIMS, NAHZIRAH B M; TRENTON, NJ; TRENTON CTRL HS; (JR); Hi Hnr Roll; Hnr Roll; Nat Hon Sy; Nat Stu Ath Day Aw; Perf Att; WWAHSS; DARE; DECA; FBLA; P to P St Amb Prg; Prom Com; Scouts; Sftball (V); Cl Off (R); Stu Cncl (S); CR (R); Child-Development; Accountant; Drew U; Clarkson U

SINCK, MICHAEL A; BRIDGEWATER, NJ; BRIDGEWATER-RARITAN HS; (JR); F Lan Hn Soc; Hnr Roll; Nat Hon Sy; WWAHSS; Chrch Yth Grp; Emplmnt; Key Club; Swmg (V L); Psychology; Religion; Gettysburg College; The College of New Jersey

SIRRAH, ARJUN; PENNINGTON, NJ; HOPEWELL VALLEY CTRL HS; (SO); Hi Hnr Roll; Hnr Roll; Otst Ac Ach Awd; Pres Ac Ftns Aw; St of Mnth; Comm Volntr; DARE; DECA; Mod UN; Quiz Bowl; Bsball; Club-Consumer Bowl Champion; Finance; Economics; U of Pennsylvania; U of Chicago

SITAL, KRYSTAL A; BAYONNE, NJ; BAYONNE HS; (SR); All Am Sch; F Lan Hn Soc; Hnr Roll; Nat Hon Sy; Nat Mrt LOC; Perf Att; WWAHSS; Comm Volntr; FBLA; Photog; Vsity Clb; Spanish Clb; Fncg (V C); Scr Kpr (V C); Vsy Clb (V C); Stu Cncl (R); Sch Ppr (R); Yrbk (R); Literature; William Paterson U

SKARZYNSKI, BEN; BERNARDSVILLE, NJ; BERNARDS HS; All Am Sch; Ctznshp Aw; F Lan Hn Soc; Fut Prb Slvr; Gov Hnr Prg; Hi Hnr Roll; MVP; Nat Hon Sy; Nat Ldrshp Svc; Nat Mrt LOC; Comm Volntr; Hab For Humty Volntr; Peer Tut/Med; Biology Clb; BPA; Dbte Team; Fr of Library; Key Club; Lttrmn Clb; Mth Clb/Tm; Mod UN; Bnd; Chr; Orch; Ftball (V C); Lcrsse (V C); Wt Lftg (V); Cl Off (P); Lit Mag (R); Sch Ppr (R); Yrbk (R); Attorney; Georgetown U; Bowdoin College

SKINNER, KENNETH; IRVINGTON, NJ; ST BENEDICT'S PREP SCH; (SO); Hi Hnr Roll; Nat Hon Sy; Perf Att; Pres Sch; St of Mnth; WWAHSS; Comm Volntr; Peer Tut/Med; Red Cr Aide; Chess; NYLC; Spch Team; Cr Ctry (V L); Track (V L); Lit Mag (E); Sch Ppr (E); Made All-State Prep in Cross Country; Certified in First Aid; MD; Biology; Yale; Harvard

SKRIVANIC, JULIE; GUTTENBERG, NJ; HCST-NORTH HUDSON CTR HS; (SO); Hi Hnr Roll; Otst Ac Ach Awd, Pres Sch; St of Mnth; Valdctrian; Peer Tut/Med; Stu Cncl (R); National Spanish Honor Society; Architecture; Business; NJIT-New Jersey Institute of Technology; Steven's Institute of Technology

SLAUGHTER, KEVIN; LINDEN, NJ; LINDEN HS; (SO); Hnr Roll; Otst Ac Ach Awd; Perf Att; Sci Fairs; Cmptr Clb; Lib Aide; Mth Clb/Tm; Sci Clb; Stg Cre; CR (R); Engineering; Aeronautics Engineering; Massachusetts Institute of Technology; Howard U

SLOAN, ANDREW; NEW MILFORD, NJ; PARAMUS CATHOLIC HS; (JR); F Lan Hn Soc; Hi Hnr Roll; Hnr Roll; Nat Hon Sy; Pres Ac Ftns Aw; WWAHSS; Comm Volntr; Peer Tut/Med; Emplmnt; Quiz Bowl; Scouts; Spanish Clb; Lcrsse (V L); Swmg (V L); Aquinas Scholar, Who's Who American HS; Fr. Benedict Achievement Scholarship; Mechanical Engineer; Secondary Education Degree; Manhattan College; Stevens Institute of Technology

SLOAN, JOSELYN; ALLENHURST, NJ; OCEAN TOWNSHIP HS; (JR); Hnr Roll; Mth Clb/Tm; French Clb; Stg Cre; Lit Mag (R); Engineering; Comparative Literature; Yale U; Emory U

SLOCUM, JEFF; JACKSON, NJ; JACKSON MEMORIAL HS; (SR); Gov Hnr Prg; Hi Hnr Roll; Hnr Roll; Nat Hon Sy; Otst Ac Ach Awd; St of Mnth; Emplmnt; NYLC; Bskball (J); CLSC (Congressional Leaders Student Conference); Sports Medicine/Exercise Science; Florida State U

SMALL, CHINYERE; JERSEY CITY, NJ; DR RONALD MC NAIR AC HS; (SO); Hnr Roll; Otst Ac Ach Awd; Perf Att; Peer Tut/Med; Chrch Yth Grp; DARE; Emplmnt; ROTC; Drl Tm; Swmg (VJ); Vllyball (VJCL); Stu Cncl (V); President's Award; Medicine; Photography; Pennslyvania State U; Seton Hall U

SMART, WHITNEY N; JERSEY CITY, NJ; UNIVERSITY AC CHARTER SCH; Hi Hnr Roll; Hnr Roll; MVP; Otst Ac Ach Awd; Perf Att; Sci Fairs; St of Mnth; WWAHSS; Yth Ldrshp Prog; Comm Volntr; Hosp Aide; Red Cr Aide; Chrch Yth Grp; DARE; Dbte Team; Drma Clb; Mus Clb; Prom Com; Tchrs Aide; Bnd; Chr; Ch Chr; Dnce; Chrldg (L); Stu Cncl (V); CR (V); Lit Mag (P); Sch Ppr (R); Musical Theatre/Acting; Singing; U of Arts (Philadelphia); Lock Haven U (Pennsylvania)

SMAY, REBEKAH; LANDING, NJ; (JR); Hnr Roll; WWAHSS; Comm Volntr; Hab For Humty Volntr; Chrch Yth Grp; Bnd; Mch Bnd; SP/M/VS; NJ State Champions; Group 11A Marching Band; Lawyer, Political Sci. or Eng.; Wellesley College; Georgetown U

SMITH, BRIDGETTE; CRANBURY, NJ; PRINCETON HS; (JR); Duke TS; Hnr Roll; Sci Fairs; WWAHSS; Comm Volntr; Chrch Yth Grp; Emplmnt; P to P St Amb Prg; Ch Chr; Orch; Chrldg (V); Sftball (V); Track (V); Co-President of Cooking Club; Teacher of Children's Liturgy of the Word - Church; Social Work; Religious Ministry

SMITH, ELYSE S; COLUMBUS, NJ; NORTHERN BURLINGTON CTY HS; MS; Hi Hnr Roll; Hnr Roll; Otst Ac Ach Awd; St of Mnth; DARE; Pep Squd; Chr; Chrldg (C); Teaching; Psychology

SMITH, JAMIE E; SICKLERVILLE, NJ; TIMBER CREEK REG HS; (JR); Hnr Roll; Nat Hon Sy; Pres Sch; St of Mnth; WWAHSS; Comm Volntr; Peer Tut/Med; Spec Olymp Vol; AL Aux Girls; Emplmnt; Latin Clb; Bskball (L); Chrldg (JC); PP Ftbl (V); Sftball (JC); Cl Off (P); Yrbk (E); People's Choice Award Winner; Student of the Month; Nursing; Education/Psychology Counseling; Drexel U; La Salle U

SMITH, MARCUS D; EAST ORANGE, NJ; MARIST HS; (JR); Hnr Roll; Chess; Civil Engineering; Computer Sciences

SMITH, MAUREN; CRANBURY, NJ; PRINCETON HS; (JR); MVP; WWAHSS; Chrch Yth Grp; FBLA; P to P St Amb Prg; Fld Hky (J); Sftball (V); Track (V); Most Prepared Player - Field Hockey '04; Co-President of Cooking Club

SMITH, REBECCA M; ISELIN, NJ; MOTHER SETON REG HS; (SO); Hi Hnr Roll; Otst Ac Ach Awd; Pres Ac Ftns Aw; Sci/Math Olympn; Comm Volntr; Peer Tut/Med; Cmptr Clb; DARE; Mth Clb/Tm; Scouts; Tech Clb; Bowling League - Varsity; National Math League / Seton Leadership Team; Math Major; Science Minor; Seton Hall U; Rutgers U

SMITH, SHANE; EAST WINDSOR, NJ; HIGHTSTOWN HS; (JR); Hi Hnr Roll; Hnr Roll; FBLA; NYLC; Bsball (V L); Bskball (J); 1st and 2nd Year Honors Award Winner; Nominated - National Volunteers Conference / Boys State; Medical Degree; Law Degree; U of California Berkeley; Rutgers U New Brunswick

SMITH, SHANE; HACKENSACK, NJ; HACKENSACK HS; (SO); Hi Hnr Roll; Hnr Roll; Yth Ldrshp Prog; Comm Volntr; Peer Tut/Med; DARE; Emplmnt; Sci Clb; SP/M/VS; Ftball (V); Track (V); Wt Lftg; Stu Cncl (P); Master's Degree-Chemistry; PhD; Howard U; Penn State U

SMITH, SHANICE S; JERSEY CITY, NJ; YACHS; (SO); Hi Hnr Roll; Hnr Roll; Otst Ac Ach Awd; Perf Att; St of Mnth; Comm Volntr; Peer Tut/Med; Chrch Yth Grp; Pep Squd; Chr; Dnce; Drl Tm; Chrldg; Yrbk; Dance Major; Business Administration; Clark U; Benedict College

SMITH, TASHA M; WILLINGBORO, NJ; WILLINGBORO HS; (FR); Hnr Roll; Perf Att; Comm Volntr; Chr; Sccr; Child Psychiatry; Nuclear Medicine Tech.; Howard U; Rutgers U

SMULDERS, ASHLEY M; HOBOKEN, NJ; AC OF SACRED HEART HS; (JR); Hnr Roll; Comm Volntr; Peer Tut/Med; ArtClub; Drma Clb; SP/M/VS; Chrldg (V); Gmnstcs (V); Yrbk (P); Lawyer; Business; John Jay College of Criminal Justice

SNOW, CHRISTINE; GLADSTONE, NJ; BERNARDS HS; (JR); Hnr Roll; Nat Hon Sy; Nat Mrt LOC; Yth Ldrshp Prog; Chrch Yth Grp; Drma Clb; Chr; Ch Chr; SP/M/VS; Peer Leader; Church Youth Retreat Leader; Music Education; Westminster Choir College

SOLAN JR, WILLIAM M; PINE BEACH, NJ; CTRL REG HS; (SO); Hi Hnr Roll; Hnr Roll; WWAHSS; Emplmnt; Key Club; Swmg (V); Athletic Scholar Award; Student Role Model; Forensic Science; Criminal Justice; York College of PA; St Augustine's College NC

SOLANKI, HETALSINH M; JERSEY CITY, NJ; WILLIAM L DICKINSON HS; (SR); Hi Hnr Roll; Perf Att; WWAHSS; Comm Volntr; Peer Tut/Med; Spec Olymp Vol; Drma Clb; Key Club; Mth Clb/Tm; SP/M/VS

SOMERA, CHRISTOPHER; PERTH AMBOY, NJ; ACAD-SCI MATH ENG TECH HS; (SO); Hnr Roll; Otst Ac Ach Awd; Perf Att; Pres Sch; Yth Ldrshp Prg; Chess; Mth Clb/Tm; Mod UN; Tech Clb; Clb; Cl Off (T); National Student Leadership Conference; Finance; Business Administration; University of Pennsylvania; New York University

SOOFI, SHERAZ; JERSEY CITY, NJ; DICKINSON HS; (SR); Hnr Roll; Cmptr Clb; MULTICULTR Clb; Accounting; Finance; Bergen County Community College; Rutgers U

Smith, Tasha M
Willingboro HS
Willingboro, NJ

Smith, Rebecca M
Mother Seton Reg HS
Iselin, NJ

Skinner, Kenneth
St Benedict's Prep Sch
Irvington, NJ

Sims, Nahzirah B M
Trenton Ctrl HS
Trenton, NJ

Shuler, Jason M P
Long Branch HS
Long Branch, NJ

Sholakh, Natasha H
Paramus Catholic HS
Fair Lawn, NJ

Short, Latoya S
East Orange Campus 9 HS
East Orange, NJ

Sital, Krystal A
Bayonne HS
Bayonne, NJ

Smith, Elyse S
Northern Burlington Cty HS
Columbus, NJ

Smith, Shane
Hackensack HS
Hackensack, NJ

Smith, Shanice S
YACHS
Jersey City, NJ

SORRENTINO, CHRISTOPHER; MONROE TOWNSHIP, NJ; AC-SCI MATH ENG TECH HS; (SO); Hi Hnr Roll; Hnr Roll; Sci/Math Olympn; Peer Tut/Med; Biology Clb; Chess; Drma Clb; Mth Clb/Tm; Sci Clb; Scouts; Rqtball; Skiing; Science League; Princeton; Stevens Institute of Technology

SOSKEY, LAURA; NESHANIC STATION, NJ; SOMERVILLE HS; (JR); Hi Hnr Roll; Nat Hon Sy; Nat Mrt LOC; Nat Mrt Sch Recip; Valdctrian; Peer Tut/Med; Chrch Yth Grp; Drma Clb; Key Club; Spanish Clb; Bnd; SP/M/VS; Sccr (V); Sftball (J); Swmg (J); CR (R); Played Piano and Taken Private Lessons for 10 Yrs; Biology Major; Spanish Minor; Amherst College; Gettysburg College

SOTELO, KATHRYN; PISCATAWAY, NJ; (SR); DAR; Hi Hnr Roll; Nat Hon Sy; Pres Sch; WWAHSS; Comm Volntr; Peer Tut/Med; Chrch Yth Grp; DARE; Drma Clb; Emplmnt; Photog; Svce Clb; Dnce; SP/M/VS; Lit Mag (R); Fine Arts; Graphic Design; The U of the Arts; The Cooper Union for the Advancement of Science and Art

SOUMAR, ROMAN; PISCATAWAY, NJ; PISCATAWAY HS; (SR); Hnr Roll; Sci/Math Olympn; Chess; Key Club; Mth Clb/Tm; Mod UN; Sci Clb; Electrical Engineering; Commercial Airline Pilot; Rutgers U

SOWELL, JEFF; BRICK, NJ; POINT PLEASANT BEACH HS; (FR); Hi Hnr Roll; Hnr Roll; Otst Ac Ach Awd; Pres Ac Ftns Aw; Comm Volntr; Peer Tut/Med; Key Club; Vsity Clb; Golf (V); Ice Hky (L); Track (V L); Sch Ppr (R); Junior Commodore-Metedeconk River Yacht Club (2005); Commercial Airline Pilot

SOWELL, KATELYN; SICKLERVILLE, NJ; GCIT HS; (FR); Hnr Roll; Otst Ac Ach Awd; Yth Ldrshp Prog; Key Club; Dnce; SP/M/VS; Dance; Dance; Journalism; U of the Arts; U of Pennsylvania

SPAIN, DOMINIQUE; PLAINFIELD, NJ; PLAINFIELD HS; (FR); Ctznshp Aw; Hnr Roll; Peer Tut/Med; Chr; Dnce; Drl Tm; Track (J); Stu Cncl (R); CR (R); Lit Mag (R); Sch Ppr (E); Performing Arts; Business Management; North Carolina Central U; Kean U

SPANARKEL, MEGAN; TINTON FALLS, NJ; RED BANK CATHOLIC HS; (FR); Hnr Roll; Nat Stu Ath Day Aw; Comm Volntr; Emplmnt; Bskball (J); Junior National Honor Society; Athletic Amateur Union - Basketball; Marine Biology; Sports Education

SPAR, DANIELLE; SHORT HILLS, NJ; MILLBURN HS; (JR); Hi Hnr Roll; MVP; Nat Hon Sy; Nat Mrt Semif; Comm Volntr; Peer Tut/Med; Key Club; Lib Aide; Off Aide; Vsity Clb; Bnd; Mch Bnd; Orch; Pep Bnd; Fld Hky (V); Yrbk (P); 8-Yrs Winner of PTSA Piano Competitions; Region I Orchestra & Wind Ensemble / Clarinet; Television; Business; Yale U; Tufts U

SPARACO, THERESA M; WAYSIDE, NJ; OCEAN TOWNSHIP HS; (FR); Hi Hnr Roll; Hnr Roll; WWAHSS; Yth Ldrshp Prog; Comm Volntr; Hosp Aide; Chrch Yth Grp; Key Club; Vsity Clb; Chr; Bsball (V); Bskball (V); Lcrsse (J); Sccr (V); Quinnipiac, CT

SPARGO, KATHERINE; RINGWOOD, NJ; LAKELAND REG HS; (JR); Hnr Roll; Nat Hon Sy; Pres Ac Ftns Aw; WWAHSS; Emplmnt; Bnd; Mch Bnd; Pep Bnd; Vllyball (VJ L); Patriotism Award; Road Show, Gifted and Talented; Sociology; Communications; The Pennsylvania State U; Montclair State U

SPEARMAN, JESSICA N; RAHWAY, NJ; TIMOTHY CHRISTIAN SCH; (JR); Hi Hnr Roll; Hnr Roll; Perf Att; Comm Volntr; Chrch Yth Grp; Emplmnt; Ch Chr; Clr Grd; Drl Tm; Yrbk (P); Seventh Day Adventist Church Pathfinder Club Member and Counselor; Psychology; Business Management; Howard U; Spelman College

SPENCE JR, NORMAN O; LAKE HOPATCONG, NJ; PINE FORGE AC; (JR); Hi Hnr Roll; Comm Volntr; Peer Tut/Med; Chrch Yth Grp; Stg Cre; Bsball (J); Bskball (J); Ftball (J); Sccr (J); Black Belt-Karate; Medical Doctor; U of Delaware; Rutgers U

SPINELLI, ANTHONY; CLIFFSIDE PARK, NJ; PARAMUS CATHOLIC HS; (JR); F Lan Hn Soc; Hi Hnr Roll; Nat Hon Sy; USAA; Comm Volntr; Mod UN; Quiz Bowl; Bnd; Track; Mechanical Engineering; Physics; Rutgers U; Carnegie Mellon U

SPIRIDOROV, ALEXANDER; MATAWAN, NJ; MARINE AC OF SCI AND TECH HS; (SO); Hi Hnr Roll; Hnr Roll; WWAHSS; Key Club; ROTC; Tech Clb; Drl Tm; 1st Place State for TSA Competition; Top Ten (Finalist) for National TSA Competition; Physics; Business

SPIZZUCO, MIKE; EGG HARBOR TOWNSHIP, NJ; EGG HARBOR TOWNSHIP HS; (FR); Hnr Roll; Otst Ac Ach Awd; WWAHSS; Peer Tut/Med; Key Club; Bnd; National Black Belt League World Champion; 3rd Degree Black Belt; Law; Harvard U; Princeton U

SPRAGUE, IRIS; BELLEVILLE, NJ; BELLEVILLE HS; (JR); Hnr Roll; Nat Mrt LOC; Perf Att; Comm Volntr; Peer Tut/Med; Vsity Clb; Cr Ctry (V L); Golf (J); Track (V L); Crew JV; Pediatrician / Medical; Biology / Zoology; Rutgers New Brunswick; Keane U

SPRINGER, CAITLIN; PT PLEASANT BEACH, NJ; PT PLEASANT BOROUGH HS; (JR); 4H Awd; Hnr Roll; Perf Att; 4-H; ArtClub; Emplmnt; Bnd; Chr; Dnce; Drm Mjr; Swmg (VJ L); 4-H Jr Leader; Governor's School for the Arts Nominee; Music Education; Mount Holyoke College; U of Massachusetts Amherst

SQUIER, JENNIFER L; NESHANIC STA, NJ; SOMERVILLE HS; (SR); Hnr Roll; Comm Volntr; ArtClub; Mus Clb; Photog; Scouts; Acpl Chr; Bnd; Ch Chr; Clr Grd; Bskball (J); Sftball (J); President of Venture Crew; Silver Award (Girl Scouts); Art (Photography); Music (Choral or Band); Rutgers; Fairleigh Dickinson U

SQUITIERI, MALORIE P; GUTTENBERG, NJ; PARAMUS CATHOLIC HS; (SR); Hnr Roll; Comm Volntr; Drma Clb; Photog; Lcrsse (V); Second Honors; U of CO At Boulder

STANLAW, NICHOLAS J; BAYONNE, NJ; BAYONNE HS; (FR); Ctznshp Aw; Hi Hnr Roll; Hnr Roll; MVP; Otst Ac Ach Awd; Perf Att; St of Mnth; WWAHSS; Comm Volntr; Chess; Cmptr Clb; DARE; Mth Clb/Tm; Quiz Bowl; Mar Art (V); Stu Cncl (R); CR (R); Character Educational Award

STAR, ELISABETH; MONTCLAIR, NJ; MONTCLAIR HS; (JR); F Lan Hn Soc; Hi Hnr Roll; Nat Hon Sy; WWAHSS; Comm Volntr; Spec Olymp Vol; Jr Cls League; Sccr (V); Track (V L); Fed Challenge Team

STARCEVICH, JOHN; PENNSVILLE, NJ; PENNSVILLE HS; (FR); ArtClub; Mus Clb; Orch; Ftball (V); Golf (J); Wrstlg (V L); Stu Cncl (R); CR (P); Weight Lifting; 1,000 Lbs, Club; Notre Dame U

STARK, JESSICA A; TURNERSVILLE, NJ; WASHINGTON TWP HS; (SR); Hnr Roll; Nat Hon Sy; Otst Ac Ach Awd; WWAHSS; Comm Volntr; Peer Tut/Med; Emplmnt; FCCLA; P to P St Amb Prg; Tchrs Aide; Spanish Clb; PP Ftbl (VJ); Renaissance; Honor Roll; Nursing; Gloucester County College; Neumann College

STASISHYN, STEPHEN; JERSEY CITY, NJ; FERRIS HS; (FR); Hnr Roll; Perf Att; Sci Fairs; St of Mnth; Chess; Cmptr Clb; DARE; Jr Ach; Sci Clb; Swmg; Track; Business Lawyer; Computer Programmer; Princeton U; Georgetown U

STAVRINOU, ANGELICA; CLIFTON, NJ; CLIFTON HS; (JR); Hnr Roll; WWAHSS; Emplmnt; Key Club; Chr; Psychology / Teaching; Health Care Professional; Montclair State U; Rutgers U

STEELE, EBONY D; NEWARK, NJ; GLADYS HILLMAN JONES SCH; (MS); Ctznshp Aw; Hi Hnr Roll; Hnr Roll; Otst Ac Ach Awd; Perf Att; Sci Fairs; Sci/Math Olympn; St of Mnth; Comm Volntr; ArtClub; Cmptr Clb; DARE; Mth Clb/Tm; Sci Clb; Tech Clb; Spanish Clb; Drl Tm; Bskball (C); Stu Cncl (S); Law Degree; Criminal Justice; Seton Hall U; Montclair U

STEINBACH, ALEXANDRIA; WEST BERLIN, NJ; G C I T; (SO); Ctznshp Aw; Hnr Roll; Comm Volntr; Chrch Yth Grp; DARE; Drma Clb; Key Club; Scouts; Spanish Clb; Dnce; Dance Competitions; Student Teaching (Dance); Elementary Education; BA; Rowan U; Camden County College

STEPHEN, JOSEPH; RANDOLPH, NJ; RANDOLPH HS; (SO); Hnr Roll; Perf Att; Sci Fairs; WWAHSS; Biology Clb; Chess; Lib Aide; Mth Clb/Tm; Sci Clb; Clr Grd; Bdmtn (L)

STEPHENSON, CHRISTINA N; SICKLERVILLE, NJ; PAUL VI HS; (SO); Hnr Roll; Stg Cre; Schools of Nursing

STERLING, TRUDY ANN; ELIZABETH, NJ; ELIZABETH HS; (SO); Hnr Roll; St of Mnth; WWAHSS; Key Club; Sch Ppr (R); Dance Out of School Netball (Jamaica); Reading Track & Field (Jamaica); Pediatrician; MBA Master's; Colombia; Yale

STERN-CHARLES, BRANDON; SPRINGFIELD, NJ; JONATHAN DAYTON HS; (JR); Hi Hnr Roll; Hnr Roll; MVP; Nat Ldrshp Svc; Pres Ac Ftns Aw; St of Mnth; Yth Ldrshp Prog; Comm Volntr; Peer Tut/Med; AL Aux Boys; BPA; Chess; Dbte Team; FBLA; JSA; Mth Clb/Tm; NYLC; Bsball (V L); Wrstlg (V L); Johns Hopkins Talent Search; Political Science; Finance; Rice U; Tufts U

STEVENS, CANDICE; CHERRY HILL, NJ; CHERRY HILL HS WEST; (SR); DAR; Hnr Roll; Comm Volntr; Emplmnt; Photog; ROTC; Chr; Dnce; Drl Tm; Psychology; Temple U; Delaware State U

STEWART, DANIEL B; CRANBURY, NJ; PRINCETON HS; (JR); Comm Volntr; Spec Olymp Vol; Emplmnt; Mus Clb; Sci Clb; SADD; Bnd; Jzz Bnd; Eagle Scout - 8/05; Major Engineering; Minor Music; Duke U; Rochester Institute of Technology

STIHI, ANDRE; PITTSTOWN, NJ; NORTH HUNTERDON HS; (JR); Ctznshp Aw; Hnr Roll; Comm Volntr; Mth Clb/Tm; Tech Clb; Swmg (L); Biomedical Engineering; Mechanical Engineering; Rutgers; Rensselaer Polytechnic Institute

STINSON, KELLY J; TURNERSVILLE, NJ; WASHINGTON TOWNSHIP HS; (JR); Hnr Roll; Nat Hon Sy; WWAHSS; Comm Volntr; Dbte Team; Emplmnt; Scouts; Orch; SP/M/VS; National Honor Society; Girl Scout Silver Awards; English/Library Science; Wheaton College; Gordon College

STONE, DARRELL; MILLINGTON, NJ; WATCHUNG HILLS REG HS; (FR); Sccr (J); Volunteer Time Building Houses in Mexico; Business Economics Major; Becoming a Lawyer; Duke U; Wake Forest U

STONE, KEVIN T; GLASSBORO, NJ; GLASSBORO HS; (JR); Perf Att; DECA; Business Management; Marketing; Penn State U; Florida State U

STRATTON, NICHOLAS; ORADELL, NJ; DON BOSCO PREP HS; (JR); F Lan Hn Soc; Hnr Roll; Comm Volntr; Clb; Track; Plan to Pursue a Degree in Archaeology; Dickinson College

STRAYHORN, BRITTANI; HOMMONTON, NJ; OUR LADY OF MERCY AC; (SO); All Am Sch; Hnr Roll; Nat Hon Sy; Nat Ldrshp Svc; WWAHSS; Hab For Humty Volntr; Biology Clb; SADD; Spanish Clb; Bskball (J L); Vllyball (J); Marine Biology; Brown U

STREEKS, NICOLE; DELRAN, NJ; DELRAN HS; (SR); Hi Hnr Roll; Hnr Roll; Nat Hon Sy; Otst Ac Ach Awd; Pres Sch; Sci Fairs; St of Mnth; Comm Volntr; Peer Tut/Med; Spec Olymp Vol; AL Aux Girls; Chrch Yth Grp; Drma Clb; Emplmnt; Mus Clb; Prom Com; Quill & Scroll; Sci Clb; Bnd; Ch Chr; Drm Mjr; Jzz Bnd; Track (V); Cl Off (T); Yrbk (E); Treasurer of Spanish Club/Ventures Scholar; Secretary of Thespian Society; Pediatric Medicine (Pediatric Doctor); Attending Rutgers U (New Brunswick)

STUCKEY, IYANA A; JERSEY CITY, NJ; UNIVERSITY AC CHARTER SCH; (FR); Hi Hnr Roll; Hnr Roll; MVP; Nat Hon Sy; Sci Fairs; Sci/Math Olympn; St of Mnth; Chrch Yth Grp; Dbte Team; Scouts; Ch Chr; Bskball (J); Vllyball (J); Criminal Investigation; Doctor; U of South Carolina; U of Clemson

STUTZBACH, MELISSA; PITMAN, NJ; PITMAN HS; (FR); Hi Hnr Roll; Hnr Roll; Otst Ac Ach Awd; Pres Ac Ftns Aw; Sci Fairs; St of Mnth; Amnsty Intl; Comm Volntr; DARE; Key Club; Svce Clb; Chr; SP/M/VS; Sccr (J); Track (V L); Quixote Quest (Volunteer Organization); Something That Involves Helping People

SUBOL, JAMIE; JERSEY CITY, NJ; AC ST ALOYSIUS HS; (SO); Hnr Roll; Otst Ac Ach Awd; Perf Att; St of Mnth; WWAHSS; Comm Volntr; Chess; DARE; Svce Clb; SP/M/VS; Track; CR (R); Lit Mag (E); Presidential Award; Fine Arts/Performing Arts; Psychiatry; Rutgers; Oxford

SUGGETT, MARY E; STOCKHOLM, NJ; WALLKILL VALLEY REG HS; (JR); Hnr Roll; Chrch Yth Grp; FBLA; SADD; Orch; Sftball; Vllyball; Biology; Psychology; U of Washington

SULLIVAN, DEVIN; BRIDGEWATER, NJ; BRIDGEWATER-RARITAN HS; (SO); Hnr Roll; Nat Ldrshp Svc; Comm Volntr; Peer Tut/Med; 4-H; Chrch Yth Grp; DARE; Emplmnt; Off Aide; French Clb; Lcrsse (VJ); Skiing (V); Sccr (J); Stu Cncl (R); Sch Ppr (R); Play Piano and Guitar; Active Player in Club Soccer; Journalism; Teacher; U of Virginia; William and Mary College

SULTON, LATRICE G; BRIDGETON, NJ; BRIDGETON HS; (JR); Hi Hnr Roll; Hnr Roll; Nat Hon Sy; Otst Ac Ach Awd; Perf Att; WWAHSS; 4-H; ROTC; Svce Clb; Bskball (V); Stu Cncl (R); Health Occupational Student of America; Youth Alive; Psychology; Business Management

SUNGA, IMMANUEL; BELLEVILLE, NJ; BELLEVILLE HS; (FR); Hi Hnr Roll; Hnr Roll; Chess; Chrch Yth Grp; Mus Clb; Bnd; Orch; Pep Bnd; SP/M/VS; Sccr (L); Vllyball (J); Computer Engineering / Science; Civil Engineering; Rutgers U Newark

SUNIAZ, JOSE L W S; HARRISON, NJ; HARRISON HS; (JR); Hnr Roll; MVP; St of Mnth; Sccr (V); Swmg (V C); Vllyball (V C)

SUTHERLAND, MAKEDA; PLAINFIELD, NJ; BISHOP LOUGHLIN M HS; (FR); Ctznshp Aw; Gov Hnr Prg; Hi Hnr Roll; Hnr Roll; MVP; Nat Hon Sy; Nat Ldrshp Svc; Nat Stu Ath Day Aw; Otst Ac Ach Awd; Perf Att; Comm Volntr; Biology Clb; Chrch Yth Grp; Cmptr Clb; Dbte Team; Mus Clb; Outdrs Clb; Svce Clb; Spch Team; Bnd; Ch Chr; Dnce; Drm Mjr; Cr Ctry; Dvng; GAA; Gmnstcs; Swmg; Track; Stu Cncl (S); CR (V); Sch Ppr (R); Yrbk (E); Leadership Council; Lasallian Youth; Criminal Law; Business Law; Cornell U; Harvard U

SWAMINATHAN, SUNDAR; SWEDESBORO, NJ; ARCHMERE AC; (JR); Hi Hnr Roll; Nat Hon Sy; Hosp Aide; Chess; Mth Clb/Tm; Quiz Bowl; Sccr (J); Black Belt in Karate; Medicine; Biomedical Engineering; U of Pennsylvania; UC Berkeley

SWAN, DIA K; WILDWOOD, NJ; WILDWOOD HS; (SO); Hnr Roll; WWAHSS; Peer Tut/Med; Drma Clb; Emplmnt; Photog; Prom Com; Vsity Clb; SP/M/VS; Stg Cre; Chrldg (V L); CR (P); Yrbk (E); Peer Leader; Business; Accounting; Rutgers; Penn State

SWANSON, KELSEY; SOMERDALE, NJ; STERLING HS; (JR); Hnr Roll; Nat Hon Sy; Perf Att; St of Mnth; Comm Volntr; SADD; Dnce; Bskball (J); Vllyball (V); Yrbk; Theater/Performing Arts; Marine Biology; Sacred Heart U; Lynn U

SWATEK, ALLISON; MAYWOOD, NJ; HACKENSACK HS; (SO); Hi Hnr Roll; Comm Volntr; Red Cr Aide; Fld Hky (V L); Cl Off (S); Sch Ppr (E, R); Journalism; Brown U; New York U

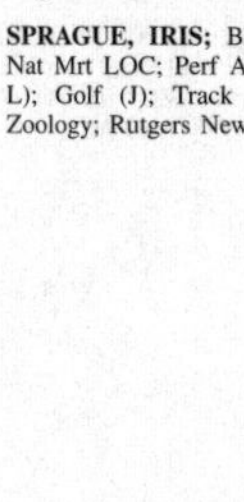
Swanson, Kelsey
Sterling HS
Somerdale, NJ

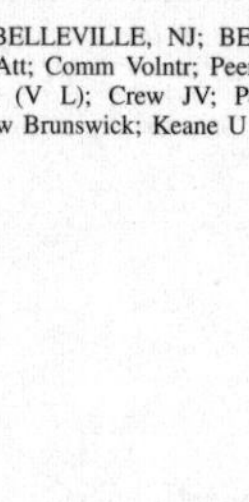
Sunga, Immanuel
Belleville HS
Belleville, NJ

Stuckey, Iyana A
University AC Charter Sch
Jersey City, NJ

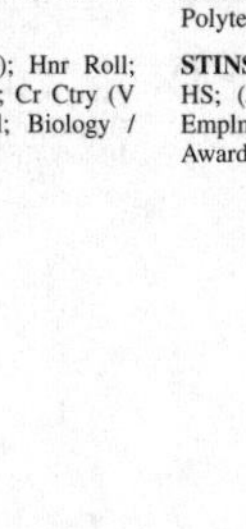
Squitieri, Malorie P
Paramus Catholic HS
Guttenberg, NJ

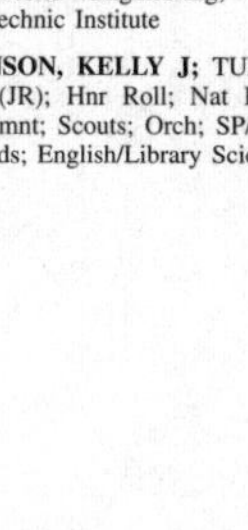
Sprague, Iris
Belleville HS
Belleville, NJ

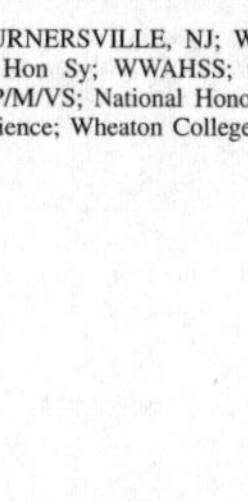
Spearman, Jessica N
Timothy Christian Sch
Rahway, NJ

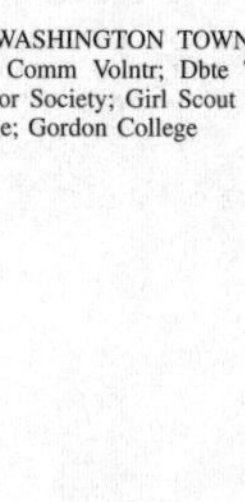
Spinelli, Anthony
Paramus Catholic HS
Cliffside Park, NJ

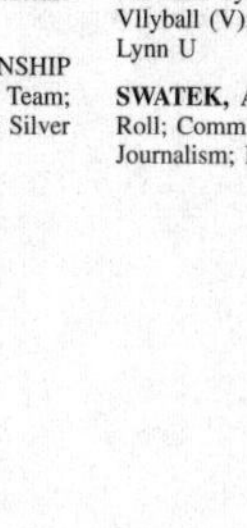
Stihi, Andre
North Hunterdon HS
Pittstown, NJ

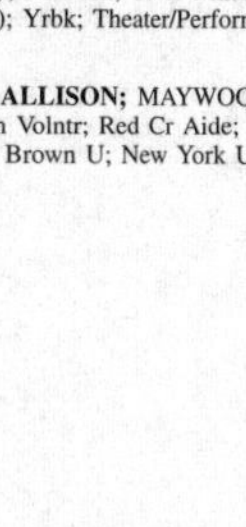
Subol, Jamie
AC St Aloysius HS
Jersey City, NJ

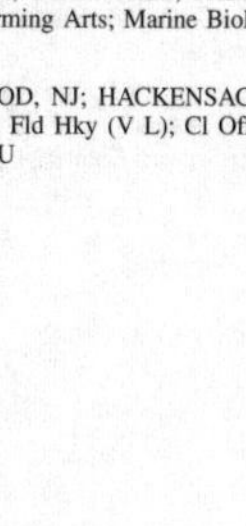
Sutherland, Makeda
Bishop Loughlin M HS
Plainfield, NJ

Swaminathan, Sundar
Archmere AC
Swedesboro, NJ

SWEENEY, DANIELLE; COLONIA, NJ; COLONIA HS; (JR); Hnr Roll; Peer Tut/Med; DARE; Mth Clb/Tm; Mod UN; Prom Com; Scouts; Clr Grd; Flg Crps; Stg Cre; Lit Mag (R); Sch Ppr (R); Close-Up on Washington DC; Student Advisory Committee; Journalism; Fashion Merchandising; Kean College; Rutgers U

SYMBER, CONRAD M; SOUTH AMBOY, NJ; CARDINAL MC CARRICK HS; (JR); Hi Hnr Roll; Hnr Roll; Comm Volntr; Emplmnt; Sccr (V); Business; Stockton; Rider

SZAFRANSKI, JULIE; STRATFORD, NJ; STERLING HS; (JR); Hnr Roll; Pres Ac Ftns Aw; WWAHSS; Comm Volntr; DARE; Emplmnt; Track; Yrbk; All Star Cheerleading; Interact Club; Marine Biologist; Zoology; U of Delaware

SZELC, ALICIA; HELMETTA, NJ; CARDINAL MC CARRICK HS; (JR); Hi Hnr Roll; Hab For Humty Volntr; Prom Com; Tennis (V); Stu Cncl (R); Business Management; New York U; Pennsylvania State College

SZULEWSKI, ERIN A; WILLIAMSTOWN, NJ; WILLIAMSTOWN HS; (SO); Hnr Roll; Comm Volntr; Prom Com; Vsity Clb; Cr Ctry (V); Track (V L); Vllyball (J); VFW Voice of Democracy Contest-3rd Place; Poem Published in Literary Grounds Magazine; English; Communications; New York U; Villanova

TAHIR, SALMAN; JERSEY CITY, NJ; FERRIS HS; (JR); Hi Hnr Roll; Hnr Roll; Salutrn; Sci Fairs; St of Mnth; Yth Ldrshp Prog; Chess; Schol Bwl; Bskball (J); Lawyer; Doctor; St Peter's College; Rutgers

TAKYI, SELORM; WEST ORANGE, NJ; WEST ORANGE HS; (JR); Hnr Roll; Comm Volntr; AL Aux Boys; Track (J); Works at a Doctor's Office; Pre-Med; PhD; Rutgers U; U of the Sciences in Philadelphia

TALAGA, PAWELL; LINDEN, NJ; LHS LINDEN HS; (JR); F Lan Hn Soc; Hi Hnr Roll; Hnr Roll; Pres Sch; St of Mnth; Yth Ldrshp Prog; Comm Volntr; Red Cr Aide; Spec Olymp Vol; Biology Clb; Chess; Chrch Yth Grp; Dbte Team; Emplmnt; FCCLA; Key Club; Sci Clb; Ch Chr; SP/M/VS; Stg Cre; Golf (V CL); Swmg (V CL); Cl Off (P); CR (R); Key Club/FCCLA President; Mini-Med School @ UMDNJ /IB.; Pre-Med (Biology); MD/Phd; NYU; Cornell

TALOTTA, BRITTNEY; CLEMENTON, NJ; OVERBROOK HS; (FR); Hnr Roll; Nat Hon Sy; Comm Volntr; Dbte Team; Mod UN; P to P St Amb Prg; Scouts; Bnd; Chr; Ch Chr; SP/M/VS; Chrldg (J); Gmnstcs (J); Sftball (J); Tennis (J); Stu Cncl (R); CR (R); Yrbk (E, P); Girl Scouts 7 Years

TANG, MICHELLE; FORT LEE, NJ; FORT LEE HS; (JR); Hnr Roll; Perf Att; St of Mnth; Yth Ldrshp Prog; Comm Volntr; Peer Tut/Med; Cmptr Clb; Fr of Library; Key Club; Spanish Clb; Chr

TANGANELLI, CRISTINA; ROSELLE, NJ; ABRAHAM CLARK HS; (JR); Hi Hnr Roll; Hnr Roll; Otst Ac Ach Awd; St of Mnth; WWAHSS; Peer Tut/Med; Emplmnt; Scouts; Track (V); Peer Leadership; Health Occupations; Pre-Med; Pediatrician; New York U; Columbia U

TANGARIFE, MARISA; LANDING, NJ; ROXBURY HS; (SO); F Lan Hn Soc; Hi Hnr Roll; WWAHSS; Peer Tut/Med; Spec Olymp Vol, DARE; Key Club; P to P St Amb Prg; Clb; Chrldg (JCL); National Spanish Honor Society; 2000 US Roller Skating Dance Champion; Marine Biology; International Finance / Business

TAPAL, SAFIA; MILLBURN, NJ; MILLBURN HS; (JR); WWAHSS; Comm Volntr; Key Club; Latin Clb; Bnd; Chr; Mch Bnd; Cr Ctry (J); Fld Hky (J); Track (V L); National Latin Exam 2004-3rd Place; National Latin Exam 2005-Cum Laude; International Relations; Foreign Languages; Tufts U

TARANTINO, NICOLE L; JACKSON, NJ; JACKSON MEMORIAL HS; (SO); Hi Hnr Roll; Pres Ac Ftns Aw; Yth Ldrshp Prog; Emplmnt; Key Club; Photog; Fld Hky (J); Lcrsse (J); Chemistry; Pharmacy; Villanova

TASKOY, EVIN; CALDWELL, NJ; COLLEGIATE SCH; (SO); All Am Sch; Hi Hnr Roll; Hnr Roll; Nat Hon Sy; USAA; WWAHSS; Comm Volntr; Hosp Aide; Key Club; Dnce; Sccr (V); Sftball (V); Vllyball (V); Stu Cncl (R); CR (R); Medicine; Health; New York U; St Joseph U

TATE, ASHLEY; NEWARK, NJ; IRVINGTON HS; (FR); Hnr Roll; Comm Volntr; Emplmnt; ROTC; Ch Chr; Biology & Nursing; Kings U; Rutgers U

TATE, ERIN; CLARK, NJ; ARTHUR L JOHNSON HS; (SR); F Lan Hn Soc; Hi Hnr Roll; Hnr Roll; WWAHSS; Comm Volntr; Key Club; Photog; Spanish Clb; Lit Mag (R); Union County Teen Arts Festival; New Jersey State Teen Arts Festival; Chemistry; Forensic Science; Kean U

TAYLOR, CORNELIUS; MONTCLAIR, NJ; MONTCLAIR HS; (SO); Hnr Roll; WWAHSS; Emplmnt; Mechanical Engineering; Technology; Essex County; Montclair State

TAYLOR, DEON; JERSEY CITY, NJ; UNIVERSITY AC CHARTER SCH; (FR); Hi Hnr Roll; Hnr Roll; Perf Att; Sci Fairs; Yth Ldrshp Prog; Emplmnt; French Clb; Computer Science; Culinary Arts

TAYLOR, MAI; TRENTON, NJ; NOTTINGHAM HS; (SR); Comm Volntr; Chrch Yth Grp; Emplmnt; Key Club; Ch Chr; Cl Off (T); Honor Roll At Mercer County Tech; My Career Goal (Major) Is Nursing; Mercer County Community College; Mercer County Technical School

TAYLOR, MATTHEW K; MONTCLAIR, NJ; MONTCLAIR HS; (SO); Hnr Roll; Yth Ldrshp Prog; Comm Volntr; Chrch Yth Grp; DARE; Scouts; Bnd; Ch Chr; Jzz Bnd; Mch Bnd; Ftball (J); Track (J); Architect; Engineer; Hampton U; Michigan U

TAYLOR, VICTOR A; SOUTH ORANGE, NJ; COLUMBIA HS; (SR); Hnr Roll; Perf Att; WWAHSS; Chrch Yth Grp; Key Club; Sccr (J); Medicine; Accounting

TENENBAUM, MARCUS; FLORHAM PARK, NJ; NEW YORK MILITARY AC; (SO); Hi Hnr Roll; Hnr Roll; MVP; Pres Ac Ftns Aw; Comm Volntr; Hab For Humty Volntr; Hosp Aide; Dbte Team; Emplmnt; Key Club; ROTC; Tmpl Yth Grp; Flg Crps; Sccr (C); Aviation; United States Air Force Academy

TENORE, CHRISTINA; MILLBURN, NJ; MILLBURN HS; (SO); Hi Hnr Roll; Perf Att; Yth Ldrshp Prog; Peer Tut/Med; Chrch Yth Grp; Emplmnt; Key Club; Italian Clb; Bnd; Chr; Dnce; Pep Bnd; Fncg (V); Track (V); Peer Leader-Officer; Student Steering Committee; Education

TERON, ERICA; IRVINGTON, NJ; IRVINGTON HS; (FR); Comm Volntr; Peer Tut/Med; Emplmnt; Chr; Bskball; Sftball; Stu Cncl (R); Teacher (Kindergarten); Pediatrician; Kean U; Rutgers U

TERRY JR, DARRELL K; SOUTH ORANGE, NJ; COLUMBIA HS; (JR); Bskball (V C); Lcrsse; Sccr; CR (R); Sports Management; U of Vermont; U of Maryland

THAI, JENNIFER; BELLEVILLE, NJ; BELLEVILLE HS; (JR); Hi Hnr Roll; Hnr Roll; Perf Att; WWAHSS; Hosp Aide; Mus Clb; Bnd; SP/M/VS; Vllyball (V CL); Stu Cncl (V); Student Director of Clarinet Ensemble; Physical Therapy; Ramapo College; Seton Hall U

THAI, JONATHAN; BELLEVILLE, NJ; BELLEVILLE HS; (JR); Hi Hnr Roll; Perf Att; WWAHSS; Comm Volntr; Emplmnt; Mth Clb/Tm; Orch; Ftball (L); Tennis (V); Chamber Orchestra; Octagon Club; Elementary Education; Math Science / Teacher Education; Kean U; Seton Hall U

THOMA, ALYSSA J; SUSSEX, NJ; HIGH POINT REG; (JR); Hnr Roll; Chrch Yth Grp; Accounting

THOMAS, ALBERT G; WEST ORANGE, NJ; WEST ORANGE HS; (JR); Hnr Roll; Jr Mshl; WWAHSS; Yth Ldrshp Prog; Comm Volntr; Hosp Aide; Peer Tut/Med; Chrch Yth Grp; Key Club; NYLC; Prom Com; Svce Clb; Cl Off (V, S); CR (V, S); Volunteer, Unity Club Treasures; C Youth Group, Make a Wish-Peer Assistant; Pre-Med; Business/Accounting

THOMAS, AMIRAH K; EAST ORANGE, NJ; EAST ORANGE CAMPUS 9 HS; (FR); Hnr Roll; Yth Ldrshp Prog; Comm Volntr; Hab For Humty Volntr; DECA; Emplmnt; Dnce; Drl Tm; Medical; Law; Rutgers U; Seton Hall U

THOMAS, BARBIE S; ELIZABETH, NJ; ELIZABETH HS; (JR); Hnr Roll; WWAHSS, Comm Volntr; Chrch Yth Grp; Key Club; Ch Chr; Cr Ctry (J); Swmg (J); Track (J); Vllyball (V); Yrbk (E); Child Psychology; Computer System Information; Rutgers U; Seton Hall U

THOMAS, CHAUNTE; LINDEN, NJ; LINDEN HS; (JR); Hnr Roll; Perf Att; St of Mnth; Comm Volntr; Peer Tut/Med; DARE; Dnce; SP/M/VS; Learn and Serve Member; Rebel Member; Teaching; Business Management; Brown U

THOMAS, JASMINE; NEWARK, NJ; NORTH 13TH STREET; (FR); Hi Hnr Roll; Perf Att; Yth Ldrshp Prog; Comm Volntr; Emplmnt; Dnce; Cyclg; Swmg; Vllyball; North Jersey Youth Club; Business; Accounting; New Jersey Institute Of Technology; New York U

THOMAS, KELLY L; BRIDGEWATER, NJ; BRIDGEWATER RARITAN HS; (SO); Hi Hnr Roll; WWAHSS; Comm Volntr; Emplmnt; NYLC; Scouts; Lcrsse (J); Scr Kpr; Skiing; Sccr (J); Obtained Silver Award in Girl Scouts; Attended National Youth Leadership Forum on Medicine; Business; Biology; Dartmouth College; Duke U

THOMAS, O'NEIL; LINDEN, NJ; LINDEN HS; (JR); Hnr Roll; MVP; Comm Volntr; Ch Chr; Bskball (V L); Ftball (V CL); Track (V CL); CR (R); Business Management; Math Teacher; U of Virginia; Syracuse U

THOMAS, TIARA A; TRENTON, NJ; NOTRE DAME HS; (JR); Hnr Roll; Otst Ac Ach Awd; Perf Att; Pres Sch; WWAHSS; Yth Ldrshp Prog; Comm Volntr; Chrch Yth Grp; NYLC; Ch Chr; Chrldg (J); PP Ftbl (J); Peer-Leadership Club; African American Student Union; Business/Accounting; Seton Hall U; La Salle U

THOMPSON, CAROLINE E; OCEAN, NJ; OCEAN TWP HS; (FR); Hi Hnr Roll; Hnr Roll; WWAHSS; Comm Volntr; DARE; Emplmnt; Key Club; P to P St Amb Prg; Sftball (J); A.S.A. Softball Pitcher; Psychology; English Literature

THOMPSON, LILY; MILLBURN, NJ; MILLBURN HS; (JR); Chr; Ch Chr; Lcrsse; Swmg

THOMPSON, PATRICE M; PLAINFIELD, NJ; PLAINFIELD HS; (SR); Hnr Roll; WWAHSS; Comm Volntr; Emplmnt; Pep Squd; P to P St Amb Prg; Mch Bnd; College Prep. Program; NYLAG; Nursing; Early Childhood Education; Kean U; Medgar Evers College

THOMPSON, PATRICK; HAMILTON, NJ; NOTRE DAME HS; (SO); Hi Hnr Roll; Otst Ac Ach Awd; Yth Ldrshp Prog; Mth Clb/Tm; Mod UN; NYLC; Cr Ctry (J); Track (J); Stu Cncl (R); Peer Leader; Model Congress; Business; Criminal Justice; Duke U; U of Notre Dame

THOMSEN, DANA; BRICK, NJ; MONSIGNOR DONOVAN HS; (JR); Hi Hnr Roll; Nat Hon Sy; Perf Att; Comm Volntr; Emplmnt; Key Club; P to P St Amb Prg; Svce Clb; SADD; Vsity Clb; Sccr (V L); National Society of High School Scholars; Club / Traveling Soccer Team; Physical Therapy; Athletic Trainer; U of Delaware; Quinnipiac U

THORNE, MEGHAN; SOMERSET, NJ; FRANKLIN HS; (JR); Hi Hnr Roll; Hnr Roll; MVP; Nat Hon Sy; Comm Volntr; Chrch Yth Grp; Tchrs Aide; Bnd; Fld Hky (L); Bowling Team-Letter Winner; Fashion Merchandising; Fashion Design; Drexel U; Art Institute of Philadelphia

THREADGILL, JASMINE; TRENTON, NJ; TRENTON CTRL HS; (SO); Ctznshp Aw; Hnr Roll; Perf Att; Sci Fairs; St of Mnth; Comm Volntr; Hab For Humty Volntr; Peer Tut/Med; DARE; Emplmnt; MuAlphaTh; Chr; Business Administration; Criminal Justice; Spelman College; Alabama State U

THURMOND, JAQUASA; PASSAIC, NJ; PATERSON CATHOLIC HS; (SO); Hnr Roll; Chrldg (V); Criminal Justice; Business Management; Montclair State U; Howard U

TILLER, JOSEPH T; PLAINFIELD, NJ; PLAINFIELD HS; (FR); Volunteer/Faith Tab Church Food Bank; Audio Assistance in Faith Tab Church; Sound Engineering-Producer; Business Administration; Georgia U; Miami U

TIMMICK, JEFF; BRIDGEWATER, NJ; BRIDGEWATER RARITAN REG HS; (JR); Duke TS; Hnr Roll; Nat Hon Sy; WWAHSS; Emplmnt; Key Club; Wrstlg (V)

TIRUCHANUR, PRASANTH; PRINCETON JCT, NJ; WEST-WINDSOR PLAINSBORO NORTH HS; (JR); Nat Hon Sy; Perf Att; Comm Volntr; Hosp Aide; Red Cr Aide; Fr of Library; Key Club; Lib Aide; Mth Clb/Tm; Mod UN; ROTC; Sci Clb; Tmpl Yth Grp; Drl Tm; Bdmtn (C); Mar Art (J); National Young Leadership Conference; National Honors Society; Surgeon (General); Doctor; Drexel U; U of Medicine & Dentistry of New Jersey

TISCIA, SUSAN; WEST PATERSON, NJ; PASSAIC VALLEY REG HS; (SR); F Lan Hn Soc; Hnr Roll; WWAHSS; Quill & Scroll; Dvng (V); Thought Club (Secretary One Year, Vice President the Other); 8th Grade Presidential Scholar and My School's Ursula Seal Award for Writing; Radiology (MRI); Creative Writing; Massasoit Community College

TITUS, ROCHELLE; GLEN RIDGE, NJ; GLEN RIDGE HS; (JR); Hosp Aide; Track; Screenwriter; Singing; Howard U

TODD JR, CALVIN; SOMERSET, NJ; TIMOTHY CHRISTIAN SCH; (JR); Hnr Roll, WWAHSS; Yth Ldrshp Prog; Comm Volntr; Peer Tut/Med; Chrch Yth Grp; Emplmnt; Lib Aide; Wdwrkg Clb; Chr; Bskball (V L); Sccr (V L); Business Sports Management; U Maryland; U Pennsylvania

TOMEO, SARA; HACKETTSTOWN, NJ; HACKETTSTOWN HS; (JR); Peer Tut/Med; Emplmnt; Key Club; Quill & Scroll; Stu Cncl (R); Sch Ppr (R); Yrbk (E); Social Work; Journalism; U of Rhode Island; Roger Williams College

TOM WOLVERTON, MATTHEW; NESHANIC STATION, NJ; IMMACULATA HS; (JR); Nat Hon Sy; Peer Tut/Med; Mth Clb/Tm; Mod UN; Mus Clb; Quiz Bowl; Schol Bwl; Bnd; Chr; Jzz Bnd; Mch Bnd; Math Major; The College of New Jersey

TONELLI, JAMIE; MILLBURN, NJ; MILLBURN HS; (JR); Amnsty Intl; Comm Volntr; Peer Tut/Med; Key Club; Italian Clb; Chr; Golf (V); PP Ftbl (V); Tennis (V); Lit Mag (R); Katherine Marketta Award for Outstanding Community Service; Ranked USTA Tennis Player; Mathematics; Science

TONG, CINDY Y; JERSEY CITY, NJ; DR RONALD MC NAIR AC HS; (FR); Gov Hnr Prg; Hi Hnr Roll; Otst Ac Ach Awd; Perf Att; Pres Sch; Sci Fairs; Sci/Math Olympn; St of Mnth; Valdctrian; Comm Volntr; Peer Tut/Med; DARE; Dbte Team; SP/M/VS; Stu Cncl (P); Yrbk (E); Johns Hopkins Search for Talented Youth; Marist Bowl; Law; Banking; Princeton; Columbia

TONINI, VALERIE; MORRIS PLAINS, NJ; MORRIS CATHOLIC HS; (SO); Hi Hnr Roll; Comm Volntr; Scouts; Cr Ctry (V L); Track (V L); Teach Sunday School; Education; English; St Elizabeth; Stetson U

TOOMEY, DANIEL; HOLMDEL, NJ; HOLMDEL HS; (JR); Hnr Roll; Sci Fairs; St of Mnth; Yth Ldrshp Prog; Comm Volntr; Peer Tut/Med; Chrch Yth Grp; Emplmnt; FBLA; Key Club; NYLC; Scouts; Track (V); President of History Club; History; Business; College of New Jersey; Loyola (Maryland)

Thurmond, Jaquasa
Paterson Catholic HS
Passaic, NJ

Tate, Ashley
Irvington HS
Newark, NJ

Tangarife, Marisa
Roxbury HS
Landing, NJ

Szelc, Alicia
Cardinal Mc Carrick HS
Helmetta, NJ

Tahir, Salman
Ferris HS
Jersey City, NJ

Thompson, Patrice M
Plainfield HS
Plainfield, NJ

Toomey, Daniel
Holmdel HS
Holmdel, NJ

TORRES, CHELSEA A; DEMAREST, NJ; NORTHERN VALLEY REG HS; (FR); Hnr Roll; WWAHSS; Yth Ldrshp Prog; Comm Volntr; Chrch Yth Grp; DARE; Drma Clb; Pep Squd; Scouts; Chr; Dnce; Chrldg (JC); Dance Competitions; State Pageant; Drama; Women's Studies; Columbia U; Fordham

TORRES, DARIO; UNION CITY, NJ; UNION HILL HS; (SR); F Lan Hn Soc; Hi Hnr Roll; Hnr Roll; Nat Hon Sy; Perf Att; Sci Fairs; WWAHSS; Comm Volntr; Chess; Key Club; MuAlphaTh; Cr Ctry (J); Track (V); Computer Engineering; Electrical Engineering; Stevens Institute of Technology (Accepted)

TORRES, JONATHAN; NORTH BERGEN, NJ; HCST-NORTH HUDSON CTR; (JR); Hi Hnr Roll; Hnr Roll; Nat Hon Sy; Sci Fairs; Valdctrian; Yth Ldrshp Prog; Peer Tut/Med; Tchrs Aide; Bnd; Chr; SP/M/VS; Pre-Medicine; Pharmacy; Columbia U; New York U

TORRES, JOSE; PATERSON, NJ; PATERSON CATHOLIC HS; (SR); Ctznshp Aw; Hnr Roll; Yth Ldrshp Prog; Comm Volntr; Chrch Yth Grp; Tmpl Yth Grp; Christmas Dinner for the Elderly; Halloween Children's Bash; Pharmaceutical (PHMD); Child Psychology; Valley Forge; New York U

TORRES, LUIS A; HILLSIDE, NJ; HILLSIDE HS; (JR); Hnr Roll; DARE; Emplmnt; ROTC; Scouts; Bsball (V); Computer Programming; Rutgers U; Kean U

TORRES, STEPHANIE; BAYONNE, NJ; BAYONNE HS; (SO); Hi Hnr Roll; Hnr Roll; WWAHSS; Chrch Yth Grp; Mus Clb; Pep Squd; Chr; Chrldg (V); Stu Cncl (R); The College of New Jersey; New York U

TORRES, TROY; MIDDLETOWN, NJ; MIDDLETOWN HS NORTH; (JR); F Lan Hn Soc; Hi Hnr Roll; Nat Hon Sy; St of Mnth; Comm Volntr; Hab For Humty Volntr; Peer Tut/Med; Chess; Jr Cls League; Key Club; Scouts; Latin Clb; League of Women Voters Internship Award; Architecture; Political Science; Princeton U

TOSCANO, TAYLOR; LAVALLETTE, NJ; PT PLEASANT BEACH HS; (SO); Hi Hnr Roll; Hnr Roll; WWAHSS; Comm Volntr; Hosp Aide; Chess; Emplmnt; Key Club; Sccr (V); Sftball (J); Volunteer At Hospital; Law; Business

TOWNSEND JR, NASH; PLAINFIELD, NJ; PLAINFIELD HS; (JR); Sccr (V C); Swmg (V); Vllyball (V); Cl Off (V); CR (V); Engineering; Master's Degree; St Peter's College; Seton Hall U

TRAVERS, AMANDA; SUCCASUNNA, NJ; ROXBURY HS; (SO); F Lan Hn Soc; Hnr Roll; MVP; Pres Sch; St of Mnth; WWAHSS; Comm Volntr; Chrch Yth Grp; Emplmnt; Key Club; Sci Clb; Spch Team; Bnd; Lcrsse (J L); Sccr (J L); Sch Ppr (R); 1989 Olympic Development Soccer Program; Johns Hopkins Talent Search; Princeton U; Columbia U

TREMARK JR, JOHN W; PISCATAWAY, NJ; PISCATAWAY HS; (JR); F Lan Hn Soc; Hi Hnr Roll; Hnr Roll; Nat Hon Sy; WWAHSS; Emplmnt; FBLA; Key Club; Odyssey of the Mind; Business; Ramapo College of New Jersey; Rider U

TRINH, FELICE; LINDEN, NJ; LINDEN HS; (FR); Hi Hnr Roll; Hnr Roll; Otst Ac Ach Awd; Sci Fairs; St of Mnth; Key Club; Sci Clb; Tennis (V); Tennis - 3rd Rank in Counties Freshman Year; Law; New York U; Seton Hall U

TRIVEDI, JAY R; JERSEY CITY, NJ; HUDSON CATHOLIC HS; (JR); Hi Hnr Roll; Hnr Roll; Nat Hon Sy; Emplmnt; Tech Clb; Scholars Program; Business Management; NYU-New York U; Rutgers (New Brunswick)

TRUMBETTI, FRANK J; ALLENDALE, NJ; NORTHERN HIGHLANDS REG HS; (SO); Hnr Roll; Emplmnt; Italian Clb; Mch Bnd; Fncg (V L); Ice Hky (V L); Lcrsse (V L); Sccr (J); Teen Freedom Corps; Culinary; Entrepreneur; Johnson & Wales U; Georgetown U

TSUI, TIFFANY S; PARSIPPANY, NJ; PARSIPPANY HS; (SO); Perf Att; Comm Volntr; Chrch Yth Grp; Spanish Clb; Ch Chr; Mch Bnd; Sftball (J); Swmg (V L); National Academic All-American Team Scholar Award Silver Level; Forensic Scientist; Ob/Gyn; Rutgers; Cornell U

TUCKER, SIMON; MILLBURN, NJ; MILLBURN HS; (JR); Hnr Roll; Nat Mrt LOC; Comm Volntr; Hab For Humty Volntr; Peer Tut/Med; Emplmnt; Key Club; Tmpl Yth Grp; Bskball (VJ L); Business & Management; Marketing; Cornell U; Washington U St. Louis

TUGADE-ELIASI, MIKHAEL; JERSEY CITY, NJ; UNIVERSITY AC CHARTER SCH; (SO); F Lan Hn Soc; Hi Hnr Roll; Hnr Roll; Sci Fairs; St of Mnth; Comm Volntr; Peer Tut/Med; Chess; Chrch Yth Grp; Dbte Team; FCA; Lib Aide; Mus Clb; Sci Clb; SADD; Chr; Ch Chr; SP/M/VS; Stg Cre; Bskball; Mar Art; Track; CR; Science Fair Winner; Bowling; Lawyer; Harvard U; Yale U

TULLO, MICHAEL; LITTLE FALLS, NJ; PASSAIC VALLEY REG HS; (JR); Hnr Roll; Chrch Yth Grp; Bskball (J); Track (VL); Business Management; Education; U of North Carolina at Chapel Hill; Rowan U

TUMSON, JUDLINE; NEWARK, NJ; ARTS HS; (JR); Hi Hnr Roll; Hnr Roll; Perf Att; USAA; WWAHSS; ArtClub; Chrch Yth Grp; Ch Chr; Dnce; Cr Ctry (V); Track (V); Art; Business; Montclair U; Duke U

TURRO, SEMELE; LAVALLETTE, NJ; PT PLEASANT BEACH HS; (JR); Hnr Roll; Nat Hon Sy; Chess; Chrch Yth Grp; DARE; Emplmnt; Key Club; P to P St Amb Prg; Stg Cre; Sccr (V L); Play Technical Crew - Lighting; Various Clubs; International Relations; History / Art History

TYLER, JENNIFER; NEWARK, NJ; MALCOLM X SHABAZZ HS; (SR); Perf Att; St of Mnth; Yth Ldrshp Prog; Peer Tut/Med; DARE; FCCLA; Off Aide; Outstanding Academic Performance; Criminal Justice; Business; Katherine Gibbs College; Kean U

UBAID, SYED; JERSEY CITY, NJ; WILLIAM DICKINSON HS; (JR); Hnr Roll; Comm Volntr; Spec Olymp Vol; Tennis; Law; Medical; New York U (NYU); Pace U

ULAJ, SIBORA; WARREN, NJ; WATCHUNG HILLS REG HS; (SO); Hi Hnr Roll; Nat Hon Sy; Vllyball (V); Stu Cncl (R); Princeton U; NYU

UMMARINO, MIKE; MARMORA, NJ; OCEAN CITY HS; (SR); Hi Hnr Roll; Hnr Roll; WWAHSS; ArtClub; Drma Clb; Emplmnt; Sci Clb; Scouts; SP/M/VS; Ftball (L); Track (V L); Stu Cncl (R); Eagle Scout; Interactive Development and Game Design; Animation; Champlain College

UPADHYAYA, VANDAN; ISELIN, NJ; JFK MEMORIAL HS; (FR); Hnr Roll; WWAHSS; Comm Volntr; DARE; Key Club; French Clb; Bnd; Mch Bnd; Track (J); Engineering; Columbia U; MIT

URBINA, ELYN M; UNION CITY, NJ; EMERSON HS; (FR); Hnr Roll; Perf Att; Peer Tut/Med; Chrch Yth Grp; DARE; Drma Clb; Ch Chr; Dnce; CR (R); Business Executive (NBA); Choreographer; New York U; Montclair U

URREGO, AILICEC; PATERSON, NJ; JOHN F KENNEDY HS; (FR); Hi Hnr Roll; Valdctrian; Quiz Bowl; Principal's List All 3 Marking Periods; Law; Optometry; Rutgers U; William Paterson U

USKOVA, EUGENIA; ATLANTIC HIGHLANDS, NJ; MARINE AC OF SCIENCE & TECH; (SO); F Lan Hn Soc; Hi Hnr Roll; Otst Ac Ach Awd; St of Mnth; Comm Volntr; Peer Tut/Med; Key Club; Mth Clb/Tm; ROTC; French Clb; Drl Tm; Fncg; Business/Law; Diplomacy; Harvard; Yale

UTLEY, CHANTEL N; BURLINGTON, NJ; BURLINGTON TWP HS; (JR); Gov Hnr Prg; Hi Hnr Roll; Hnr Roll; St of Mnth; Comm Volntr; Chrch Yth Grp; FBLA; Key Club; Photog; Ch Chr; Bskball (J); Tennis (J); Psychology; Chemistry; Temple U; Howard U

UY, ABRAHAM; BURLINGTON, NJ; BURLINGTON TWP HS; (JR); Hnr Roll; Ftball (J); Track (V); Football Player; Game Designer

UZZELL, BRIANNA; NEWARK, NJ; SCIENCE HS; (SO); Hnr Roll; MVP; Otst Ac Ach Awd; Perf Att; St of Mnth; WWAHSS; Yth Ldrshp Prog; Peer Tut/Med; Chrch Yth Grp; Mus Clb; Pep Squd; Vsity Clb; Ch Chr; Dnce; SP/M/VS; Sftball (V); Stu Cncl (R); CR (R); Bowling - Varsity; Law; Medicine; Howard U; Princeton U

VACCHIANO, LUANNE; MADISON, NJ; MADISON HS; (FR); Hnr Roll; Comm Volntr; Hab For Humty Volntr; DARE; Key Club; Mus Clb; Quiz Bowl; Scouts; Orch; Tennis (J L); National Leader Conference; College

VALERIO, YASMILKA; UNION CITY, NJ; EMERSON HS; (SO); SP/M/VS; CR (S); Psychology; Nurse; Saint Peter's College; Jersey City U

VALLESPIN, QUIRINA; WANAQUE, NJ; LAKELAND REG HS; (JR); F Lan Hn Soc; Hi Hnr Roll; WWAHSS; Comm Volntr; Peer Tut/Med; P to P St Amb Prg; SADD; French Clb; Fncg (V); Track (J); Vllyball (V); Sch Ppr (R); 1st Place Spanish Poetry Recitation Contest; Pre-Med to Be an Ob-Gynecologist; Columbia U; New York U

VANDENBERGH, JESSE; CRESSKILL, NJ; CRESSKILL JR/SR HS; (SO); Hi Hnr Roll; Hnr Roll; Hosp Aide; ArtClub; Biology Clb; Bnd; Mch Bnd; SP/M/VS; Stg Cre; Wrstlg (J); Sch Ppr (P); Founder of the "Improv Club" (Cartoonist); Clubs: Art, Interact, Communities, Horticulture, Improv; Film; English-(comedy Writing); New York U; U of Delaware

VAN DEN BROECK, MARILYN C; JERSEY CITY, NJ; DR RONALD MC NAIR AC HS; (JR); Nat Hon Sy; WWAHSS; Peer Tut/Med; Mth Clb/Tm; ROTC; Spanish Clb; Drl Tm; Cr Ctry (V); Track (V); Stu Cncl (R); International Culture Club; Chemistry; Rutgers U; New York Institute of Technology

VANETTI, JENNIFER L; RINGWOOD, NJ; LAKELAND REG HS; (SR); Hi Hnr Roll; Hnr Roll; Nat Hon Sy; WWAHSS; Hab For Humty Volntr; Peer Tut/Med; Chrch Yth Grp; French Clb; PP Ftbl; Sftball; Vllyball; Stu Cncl (S, T); Sch Ppr (E); Nursing; Villanova U

VAN GROVER, ADAM; RIDGEWOOD, NJ; RIDGEWOOD HS; (SO); F Lan Hn Soc; Hi Hnr Roll; Nat Hon Sy; Pres Sch; Dbte Team; DECA; P to P St Amb Prg; Tmpl Yth Grp; Business; U of Pennsylvania; U of Michigan

VAN LENTEN, ERIC; ALLENDALE, NJ; NORTHERN HIGHLANDS REG HS; (JR); Hab For Humty Volntr; Chrch Yth Grp; Emplmnt; Jzz Bnd; Cr Ctry (J); Ice Hky (V); Church Youth Group Work; Homeless Shelter / Habitat for Humanity; Engineering; Teaching; Rutgers U; Lehigh U

VARGAS, ANTHONY; CLARK, NJ; (FR); Hnr Roll; Comm Volntr; Key Club; SP/M/VS; Ftball (VJ); Track (V)

VASQUEZ, ARIELLA; TEANECK, NJ; TEANECK HS; (JR); Acpl Chr; Stu Cncl (R); CR (R); Vice President of Cancer-Awareness Club; Bachelor's in Web Design; Westwood U

VECCHIO, JULIANNE E; CEDAR KNOLLS, NJ; MORRISTOWN-BEARD SCH; (FR); Hnr Roll; Comm Volntr; Hab For Humty Volntr; Chrch Yth Grp; Drma Clb; Emplmnt; Svce Clb; Chr; Dnce; SP/M/VS; Stg Cre; Bskball (V L); Sccr (V L); Sftball (V L); Community Service Awards; Pre-Law / Law; Rutgers U / Rutgers Law School; U of Pennsylvania

VEGA, JUAN; JERSEY CITY, NJ; DICKISON HS

VEGA, MARANGELLE; BRIDGEWATER, NJ; BRIDGEWATER-RARITAN HS; (SO); F Lan Hn Soc; Hi Hnr Roll; Hnr Roll; WWAHSS; Comm Volntr; Chrch Yth Grp; Drma Clb; FCA; Tchrs Aide; French Clb; Ch Chr; SP/M/VS; Stg Cre; Stu Cncl (R); CR (R); Audio / Visual Technician at Church; The National Society of High School / Scholars; Marketing; Psychology; Columbia U; New York U

VELAGALETI, SARATH C; PRINCETON, NJ; WWPHS; (JR); Fut Prb Slvr; Hnr Roll; Otst Ac Ach Awd; Perf Att; Pres Ac Ftns Aw; Pres Sch; Sci Fairs; Sci/Math Olympn; St of Mnth; WWAHSS; Comm Volntr; Chess; Cmptr Clb; Dbte Team; Mth Clb/Tm; Sci Clb; Tennis (J); Track (J); Vllyball (J); CR (R); Yrbk (R); Theobald Smith Award; Math and Astronomical Studies; Scientific Research; Princeton U; Stanford U

VELASQUEZ, STEPHANIE; PASSAIC, NJ; PASSAIC HS; (SR); Hnr Roll; Nat Hon Sy; Yth Ldrshp Prog; Comm Volntr; Peer Tut/Med; FTA; CR (R); Piano Recital 2004; Youth in City Government Day; Early Childhood Education; Montclair State U; Boston U

VELEZ, ALEXIS; BELLEVILLE, NJ; BELLEVILLE HS; (SO); Drma Clb; Key Club; SP/M/VS

VELEZ, MICHELLE; JERSEY CITY, NJ; CTY PREP HS; (SR); Hi Hnr Roll; Hnr Roll; Nat Hon Sy; St of Mnth; WWAHSS; Comm Volntr; Chess; Chrch Yth Grp; DARE; Emplmnt; Sci Clb; Dnce; SP/M/VS; Cr Ctry (V); Track (V); Arts Achievement Award; Athletic Award; Acting; Journalism; New Jersey City U; Rutgers U New Brunswick

VENTRONE, MARIE N; TOMS RIVER, NJ; MONSIGNOR DONOVAN HS; (SO); Hi Hnr Roll; Hnr Roll; Pres Ac Ftns Aw; Comm Volntr; Peer Tut/Med; Chrch Yth Grp; Drma Clb; Key Club; Acpl Chr; Chr; Ch Chr; Dnce; Stu Cncl (R); Principal's Honor Roll; Key Club Vice President - Director Sophomore; Musical Theater; Education; Ithaca College; Chicago College of Performing Arts

VENTURA, THOMAS J; SCOTCH PLAINS, NJ; SCOTCH PLAINS FANWOOD HS; (JR); Hi Hnr Roll; Hnr Roll; Perf Att; Pres Ac Ftns Aw; Comm Volntr; DECA; Mus Clb; ROTC; Vsity Clb; Bnd; Jzz Bnd; Orch; Ftball (V L); Track (V L); Wt Lftg (V); Usher in My Church; DECA / SMAC - Accomplished Track Runner; Business Management; Law and Government; Northeastern U; Penn State

VENUTO, SAMANTHA T; STRATFORD, NJ; STERLING REG HS; (FR); Hnr Roll; Sci Fairs; Comm Volntr; Peer Tut/Med; DARE; SADD; Chrldg (V); Stu Cncl (R); Teaching; Art

VERDEL, DANIEL N; TRENTON, NJ; NOTRE DAME HS; (JR); Hi Hnr Roll; Hnr Roll; Yth Ldrshp Prog; Chess; Emplmnt; Sccr (V); Track (V); CR; Soccer-Competitive Super Y League, Region I (MASA Grizzlies); State Cup Finalist, Qtr. Finalist '04 & '05 Boys State; Political Science/Government; Law School; Penn State U; U of Vermont

VERGARA, ALICIA; PATERSON, NJ; JOHN F KENNEDY HS; (SR); Hi Hnr Roll; Hnr Roll; Nat Hon Sy; Vsity Clb; Vllyball (VJCL); Computer Engineering; NJIT

VERMA, BHAVNA; EATONTOWN, NJ; MONMOUTH REG; (JR); Nat Hon Sy; Comm Volntr; ArtClub; Key Club; Lib Aide; Photog; Prom Com; Spanish Clb; Drl Tm; President of Spanish Club; Captain of Step Team; Pre-Med; Rutgers U New Brunswick

VERO, AMANDA; MATAWAN, NJ; MATAWAN REG HS; (SO); Hi Hnr Roll; Hnr Roll; Scouts; Dnce; Stg Cre; Stage Crew; Environmental Club

VESPERMAN, KATIE; MAHWAH, NJ; PARAMUS CATHOLIC HS; (JR); F Lan Hn Soc; Hi Hnr Roll; Hnr Roll; Nat Hon Sy; Chrch Yth Grp; Outdrs Clb; Spanish Clb; Sftball (J)

VICK, CHANELL M; CLEMENTON, NJ; OVERBROOK HS; (SO); Hi Hnr Roll; Hnr Roll; Otst Ac Ach Awd; Svce Clb; Chr; SP/M/VS; CR (R); Leo Club, Style Squad, Shooting Star Award; Successfully Recovering from Back Surgery; Retailing & Merchandising; Business; Atlanta U, Clark College; Morris Brown College

VIDAL, ALEXANDRA; UNION CITY, NJ; UNION HILL HS; (SR); Ctznshp Aw; F Lan Hn Soc; Hi Hnr Roll; Hnr Roll; Kwnis Aw; Nat Hon Sy; Nat Sci Aw; Sci Fairs; St of Mnth; Valdctrian; Comm Volntr; Hosp Aide; Emplmnt; Key Club; MuAlphaTh; Photog; Sci Clb; Tchrs Aide; Yrbk (E); Theta Delta XI; Edward J Bloustein; Political Science (Ambassador); Architecture; Rutgers U; New Jersey City U

Vidal, Alexandra
Union Hill HS
Union City, NJ

Velez, Michelle
County Prep HS
Jersey City, NJ

Velasquez, Stephanie
Passaic HS
Passaic, NJ

Ummarino, Mike
Ocean City HS
Marmora, NJ

Tumson, Judline
Arts HS
Newark, NJ

Travers, Amanda
Roxbury HS
Succasunna, NJ

Tremark Jr, John W
Piscataway HS
Piscataway, NJ

Utley, Chantel N
Burlington Twp HS
Burlington, NJ

Velez, Alexis
Belleville HS
Belleville, NJ

Ventrone, Marie N
Monsignor Donovan HS
Toms River, NJ

Vick, Chanell M
Overbrook HS
Clementon, NJ

VIJA, KAI; JACKSON, NJ; OCEAN CTY VOC TECH SCH; (JR); Photography; Management; Brookdale Community College

VIJAY, PRIYANKA; EDISON, NJ; J.P. STEVENS HS; (FR); Hnr Roll; St of Mnth; Comm Volntr; ArtClub; Drma Clb; Spanish Clb; Dnce; Stg Cre; Cl Off (R); Stu Cncl (R); National Spanish Exam (One of the Best Scores); Odyssey of the Mind; Fashion Design; Business and Marketing; Fashion Institute of Technology (NY); Wharton School, U of Pennsylvania

VILLALONA, SARAH; NORTH BERGEN, NJ; NORTH BERGEN HS; (JR); F Lan Hn Soc; Hi Hnr Roll; USAA; WWAHSS; Comm Volntr; Key Club; French Clb; President of the French Club; Business; Economics

VILLANUEVA, JOY; JERSEY CITY, NJ; HCST-NORTH HUDSON CTR; (SO); Key Club; Chr; Dnce; Tennis (V); Athlete of the Month-Tennis; Most Improved Player-Tennis; Nursing; Physical Therapist; Stevens Institute of Technology; New York U

VINASCO, ANGELA M; OLD HARBOR TWP, NJ; ATLANTIC CITY HS; (SR); DECA; ROTC; Clr Grd; Dnce; Drl Tm; Nursing; Child Psychology; Montclair State U; Rowan U

VITAL, YOLA; UNION, NJ; (JR); Ctznshp Aw; WWAHSS; Comm Volntr; Dbte Team; Emplmnt; Fr of Library; FBLA; Clr Grd; Mch Bnd; Orch; Track (VJ); Stu Cncl (R); CR (R); Lit Mag (R); Author of "Words of a Child" Book of Poetry, Maud Carroll Music Scholarship Foundation; Who's Who Among American High School Students; Law; Writing/Journalism; U of Bridgeport; Seton Hall

VITYUK, VICTORIA; ENGLISHTOWN, NJ; MANALAPAN HS; (SR); Hi Hnr Roll; Hnr Roll; MVP; Nat Hon Sy; WWAHSS; JSA; Photog; Quill & Scroll; Russian Clb; Bskball (J); Tennis (V C); Track (V); Sch Ppr (E); Most Improved Award; Coach's Award; Business; Russian; Lehigh U

VIVAS, BELINDA; SAYREVILLE, NJ; SWM HS; (SO); Hi Hnr Roll; Hnr Roll; Nat Hon Sy; Comm Volntr; FBLA; Mth Clb/Tm; Spanish Clb; Academic Excellence; Business; Clinical Sciences; Columbia U; New York U

VIZZI, JARED L; BELLEVILLE, NJ; BELLEVILLE HS; (SO); Hi Hnr Roll; WWAHSS; Cmptr Clb; Key Club; WORLD Clb; Bnd; Mch Bnd; Stg Cre; Tennis (J); Psychology; Commercial Arts; Boston U

VOGEL, TOMMY; ALLENDALE, NJ; NORTHERN HIGHLANDS REG HS; (SO); Nat Hon Sy; Peer Tut/Med; Tmpl Yth Grp; Bsball (J); Coached Youth Basketball; Umpired Youth Baseball; Business; Law; U of Delaware; UMass

VOGT, CHRISTINA M; TURNERSVILLE, NJ; WOODBURY JR/SR HS; (SO); Ctznshp Aw; F Lan Hn Soc; Hi Hnr Roll; Otst Ac Ach Awd; Pres Sch; Sci Fairs; St of Mnth; USAA; WWAHSS; Comm Volntr; Peer Tut/Med; Emplmnt; Key Club; Mod UN; Quiz Bowl; Sci Clb; Scouts; Svce Clb; French Clb; Scr Kpr (VJ); Tennis (VJ); Cl Off (R); Stu Cncl (R); CR (R); Sch Ppr (R); Girl Scout Silver Award; West Point Society of Phila Leader Award; Pre-Law; Pre-Med

VOGT, JESSICA; VERNON, NJ; VERNON TWP HS; (JR); F Lan Hn Soc; Hnr Roll; Nat Hon Sy; WWAHSS; Yth Ldrshp Prog; Comm Volntr; Peer Tut/Med; Chrch Yth Grp; DECA; Emplmnt; Key Club; Svce Clb; Sccr; Track (VJ); Sch Ppr (E, P); Key Club President-DECA NJ; State Officer-DECA Jr. Class Office; Forensic Psychology; Criminal Justice; College of NJ; Boston College

VOORHEES, DANIELLE; ASBURY PARK, NJ; OCEAN TOWNSHIP HS; (FR); Hi Hnr Roll; Hnr Roll; WWAHSS; Key Club; SADD; Tmpl Yth Grp; Spanish Clb; Dnce; Competition Dance Team

VRANJES, IVANA; TRENTON, NJ; LAWRENCE HS; (JR); Hi Hnr Roll; Hnr Roll; Otst Ac Ach Awd; Perf Att; Yth Ldrshp Prog; Comm Volntr; Peer Tut/Med; DECA; Drma Clb; Emplmnt; Dnce; Stg Cre; Track (J); Yrbk (E, P); 7th Annual Ira Silverman Teen Leadership Conference-Award, Honor for Leadership Ability; Acting (Film/TV); Business; New York U; Columbia U, NY

WACHTLER, PAIGE; HASKELL, NJ; LAKELAND REG HS; (SR); Hi Hnr Roll; Hnr Roll; Nat Hon Sy; WWAHSS; Comm Volntr; Dbte Team; Emplmnt; Chr; Fncg (J); Vllyball (V L); Marine Biology; Florida Institute of Technology

WADE, JANAI; PLAINFIELD, NJ; PLAINFIELD HS; (FR); Nat Hon Sy; WWAHSS; Hosp Aide; Emplmnt; Ch Chr; Bskball (J); Sftball (J); Journalism and Mass Communication; Education; Elizabeth City State U; North Carolina Central

WALKER, JANAY M; WILLIAMSTOWN, NJ; VICTORY CHRISTIAN SCH; (JR); Perf Att; Cr Ctry (J); Sccr (J); Sftball (J); Early Childhood Education; Journalism; Messiah College; Rowan U

WALKER, JASMINE C; NEWARK, NJ; MALCOLM X SHABAZZ HS; (JR); Hi Hnr Roll; Hnr Roll; Otst Ac Ach Awd; Perf Att; St of Mnth; Cmptr Clb; DARE; Bnd; Business Management; Hair Stylist

WALKER, JEROME; NEWARK, NJ; WESTSIDE HS; (SO); Hnr Roll; Perf Att; St of Mnth; Peer Tut/Med; ArtClub; Mth Clb/Tm; Tchrs Aide; Stg Cre; Bskball (J); Ftball (J); Track (J); Bowling-Varsity; Computer Technician; Masters Degree; Art, Designs; Parson School of Design; Pratt Institute

WALKER, LINDSAY; RINGWOOD, NJ; LAKELAND REG HS; (JR); Comm Volntr; Chrch Yth Grp; Law Degree; Social Services

WALLACE, RANDI L; CHERRY HILL, NJ; CAMDEN CTY TECH; (JR); Hnr Roll; Nat Hon Sy; Perf Att; St of Mnth; Peer Tut/Med; Chrch Yth Grp; DARE; Emplmnt; Prom Com; Scouts; Voc Ind Clb Am; Bnd; Sccr; Sftball; Cl Off (S); Culinary Arts; Johnson and Wales U; Atlantic Cape Community College

WALSH, DAN; CEDAR GROVE, NJ; CEDAR GROVE HS; Hi Hnr Roll; Hnr Roll; WWAHSS; Comm Volntr; Chrch Yth Grp; Mod UN; Quiz Bowl; SP/M/VS; Track (V); EMT on Volunteer Rescue Squad; Film; U of Southern California; Emerson College

WALSH, MARY F J; WALDWICK, NJ; PARAMUS CATHOLIC HS; (SO); Hi Hnr Roll; Hnr Roll; Comm Volntr; 4-H; Chess; Chrch Yth Grp; Drma Clb; Emplmnt; Mod UN; Off Aide; Orch; Ftball Clb; SP/M/VS; Creative Writing; Mathematics; Wellesley College; Princeton U

WALTERS, LAUREN C; POINT PLEASANT BEACH, NJ; PT PLEASANT BEACH HS; (JR); Hi Hnr Roll; Hnr Roll; Nat Hon Sy; Comm Volntr; Peer Tut/Med; Chess; DARE; Drma Clb; Key Club; Mus Clb; Prom Com; Clb; Bnd; Chr; Drm Mjr; Jzz Bnd; Bskball (V); Chrldg (J); Cr Ctry (V); Track (V); Yrbk (R, P); Competitive Horseback Riding; Volunteer At Veterinary Office; Veterinary Medicine; Equine Studies; Cornell U; U of Pennsylvania

WALTERS, RACHEL; MILLTOWN, NJ; SPOTSWOOD HS; (SR); Hi Hnr Roll; Hnr Roll; MVP; Nat Hon Sy; St of Mnth; DECA; Drma Clb; FBLA; Mth Clb/Tm; Outdrs Clb; SP/M/VS; Chrldg (VJCL); CR; Vice President DECA; National Honor Society; Business; Lehigh U

WANG, CUICUI; LEONIA, NJ; LEONIA HS; (JR); Hi Hnr Roll; Nat Hon Sy; Jr Ach; French Clb; Bnd; Chr; Bdmtn (C); Vllyball (C); Cl Off (P); Stu Cncl (V); CR (V, T); National Olympic Contest of English-First Prize (In China); Dentistry; Pre-Med; Binghamton U

WANG, DAMON; FORT LEE, NJ; BERGEN CTY AC; (SO); Hi Hnr Roll; Yth Ldrshp Prog; Mth Clb/Tm; Mod UN; Act 36, One of 3 in State and 82 in the Nation; Accepted to Columbia U's Science Honors Program; Medicine; Molecular Biology; Columbia U

WANG, HAOWEI; TENAFLY, NJ; TENAFLY HS; (JR); Comm Volntr; Hosp Aide; Mth Clb/Tm; Chinese Clb; Bnd; Mch Bnd; Emergency Medical Trainer EMT; Medical (Doctor); Business; New York U; U of Pennsylvania

WANG, JASPER; MONTVILLE, NJ; MONTVILLE TOWNSHIP HS; (JR); F Lan Hn Soc; Gov Hnr Prg; Hi Hnr Roll; Nat Hon Sy; Valdctrian; Comm Volntr; Peer Tut/Med; DECA; FBLA; HO'Br Yth Ldrshp; Key Club; Mth Clb/Tm; Quiz Bowl; Sci Clb; Orch; Bsball (J); Cr Ctry (L); Adv Cncl (P, V); Stu Cncl (P, V, S); Sch Ppr (E); Business; Biology; Harvard; Yale

WANG, KAN; ATLANTIC CITY, NJ; ATLANTIC CITY HS; (JR); Hnr Roll; Nat Mrt LOC; USAA; WWAHSS; Comm Volntr; Chrch Yth Grp; DARE; Key Club; Photog; Ch Chr; Dnce; Yrbk (P); Bioengineering; Pre-Med; New Jersey Institute of Technology; U of the Sciences in Philadelphia

WANG, MARLENE D; MADISON, NJ; MADISON HS; (SO); Hi Hnr Roll; Perf Att; Pres Ac Ftns Aw; WWAHSS; Peer Tut/Med; Key Club; Scouts; Bnd; Chr; Cr Ctry (V); Fld Hky (J L); Sftball (J L); 10 Years of Piano Training; 7 Years of Clarinet Training; Biology

WANG, WEICHENG; EDISON, NJ; JOHN P STEVENS HS; (SO); Hi Hnr Roll; Hnr Roll; Perf Att; Key Club; Track (J); Medical; Technology; Harvard; Massachusetts Institute of Technology

WANG, XIN; PLAINFIELD, NJ; NORTH PLAINFIELD HS; (JR); Hnr Roll; WWAHSS

WASEEM, IHTSHAM; LITTLE FERRY, NJ; RIDGEFIELD PARK; (SR); Hnr Roll; WWAHSS; Comm Volntr; Bsball; Bskball; Cr Ctry (V); Mar Art; Track; Wt Lftg

WASHINGTON, JELISSA; ORANGE, NJ; ORANGE HS; (JR); Hnr Roll; WWAHSS; Nursing; Pediatrician; U of Georgia

WASHINGTON, SHEREKA D; JERSEY CITY, NJ; HCST-NORTH HUDSON CTR; (SO); F Lan Hn Soc; MVP; Perf Att; Chrch Yth Grp; Ch Chr; Dnce; SP/M/VS; Stg Cre; Bskball (V); Chrldg (V); Tennis (V); Forensic Science; Dance; New York U; Spelman College

WASHUTA, REBECCA; KENILWORTH, NJ; UNION CTY MAGNET HS; (JR); Hi Hnr Roll; Hnr Roll; St Optmst of Yr; WWAHSS; Yth Ldrshp Prog; DARE; Prom Com; Svce Clb; Chrldg (VJCL); PP Ftbl (V); CR (R); Lit Mag (R); Sch Ppr (P); Yrbk (R); Political Science; U of Miami; Wake Forest

WASTI, ATIF; TRENTON, NJ; THE HUN SCH OF PRINCETON; (SO); Hi Hnr Roll; Hnr Roll; Otst Ac Ach Awd; Pres Sch; St of Mnth; Hab For Humty Volntr; Peer Tut/Med; Key Club; Mth Clb/Tm; Fncg (J); Public Relations Manager of Diversity Club; Member of My Masque's Youth Group; Engineering; Math; Massachusetts Institute of Technology; Villanova U

WATSON, MACKENZIE; ASBURY, NJ; NORTH HUNTERDON HS; (JR); F Lan Hn Soc; Hi Hnr Roll; Hnr Roll; Spec Olymp Vol; Chrch Yth Grp; Emplmnt; Svce Clb; SADD; French Clb; Clr Grd; Fncg (J); Stu Cncl (R); Academic Achievement Society; Interact/Able Club; Marketing; Psychology; Boston College

WEBER, CHRISTOPHER R; FREEHOLD, NJ; FREEHOLD BOROUGH HS; (SR); Fut Prb Slvr; Hnr Roll; Perf Att; WWAHSS; Chrch Yth Grp; Emplmnt; P to P St Amb Prg; Sci Clb; Bsball (J L); Swmg (J L); Participated in People to People Sports Ambassador for Baseball; Criminal Justice; Rutgers U

WEEKS, WILLIAM; HOWELL, NJ; FREEHOLD TWP HS; (JR); Hi Hnr Roll; Hnr Roll; Nat Hon Sy; Yth Ldrshp Prog; Peer Tut/Med; ArtClub; DECA; JSA; Mth Clb/Tm; Scouts; Tech Clb; Bskball (J); Cr Ctry (V); Ftball (J); Ice Hky (J); Track (V C); Wt Lftg; Sch Ppr (E); Peer Leadership; Sports Psychology; Physical Therapy; Rutgers U; U of Maryland

WEHRLEN, EMMA M; BRICK, NJ; MONSIGNOR DONOVAN HS; (JR); Hnr Roll; WWAHSS; Yth Ldrshp Prog; Hosp Aide; Svce Clb; PP Ftbl; Skiing; Track (VJ L); History Club; Nursing; Health Related Careers; U of Northern Colorado; U of Vermont

WEISENBACH, LUKE W; BARRINGTON, NJ; PAUL VI HS; (JR); Nat Hon Sy; WWAHSS; Comm Volntr; Chrch Yth Grp; DARE; Emplmnt; Mus Clb; Pep Squd; Bnd; Jzz Bnd; Pep Bnd; Vllyball; Wt Lftg; Wrstlg; Sch Ppr (R); National Honor Society; English Teacher

WEISS, ARIELLE J; CHERRY HILL, NJ; CHERRY HILL HS WEST; (FR); Hnr Roll; Comm Volntr; Fr of Library; Lib Aide; Sch Ppr (R); Peace Club; Horseback Riding; Writing; Communications; Adelphi U; Boston U

WEISS, DAVID F; TITUSVILLE, NJ; NOTRE DAME HS; (JR); Hnr Roll; Comm Volntr; Cmptr Clb; Writing Award; BS Computer Programming; College of New Jersey; Rutgers U

WEKESA, AUDREY N; MATAWAN, NJ; MATAWAN REG HS; (JR); Hi Hnr Roll; Hnr Roll; WWAHSS; SADD; Chr; Interact Club; Teen Mentor; Sociology; Social Work; Ramapo College of New Jersey; Georgian Court U

WELSH, ASHLEY; CAPE MAY, NJ; LOWER CAPE MAY REG HS; (SR); Hi Hnr Roll; Hnr Roll; Nat Hon Sy; Perf Att; St of Mnth; WWAHSS; Comm Volntr; Peer Tut/Med; Red Cr Aide; Chrch Yth Grp; Emplmnt; Prom Com; Spanish Clb; Chr; Cl Off (V); Stu Cncl (R); Yrbk (E); Psychology; College of Charleston; Wake Forest U

WERNEKE, BRIAN M; LAVALLETTE, NJ; PT PLEASANT BEACH HS; (SR); Gov Hnr Prg; Hi Hnr Roll; Nat Hon Sy; Pres Ac Ftns Aw; USAA; Valdctrian; WWAHSS; Chess; Drma Clb; Key Club; Mth Clb/Tm; Sci Clb; SADD; Bnd; Jzz Bnd; Mch Bnd; SP/M/VS; Sccr (V); Tennis (V); Track (V); Cl Off (V); Stu Cncl (R); American Chemical Society Chemistry Award; Engineering; Product Design and Innovation; Rensselaer Polytechnic Institute

WHALEN IV, TERENCE V; BAYONNE, NJ; BAYONNE HS; (SO); Hi Hnr Roll; Hnr Roll; Perf Att; Pres Sch; WWAHSS; Comm Volntr; Stg Cre; Wt Lftg; Wrstlg; Stu Cncl (R); Criminal Justice; Drew U; Rutgers U

WHITAKER, JALEESA C; NEWARK, NJ; MALCOLM X SHABAZZ HS; (JR); Hnr Roll; Perf Att; St of Mnth; ROTC; Bnd; Dnce; Flg Crps; Mch Bnd; Track (V); Pre-Med; Nurse / Pediatrician; Ramapo College; Rutgers U

WHITE, BRYAN; WOODBURY, NJ; WOODBURY HS; (JR); F Lan Hn Soc; Hi Hnr Roll; Hnr Roll; Kwnis Aw; Nat Hon Sy; St of Mnth; Yth Ldrshp Prog; Comm Volntr; AL Aux Boys; Emplmnt; HO'Br Yth Ldrshp; Key Club; Mth Clb/Tm; Schol Bwl; French Clb; Chr; Bsball (V); Bskball (J); Cr Ctry (V); Scr Kpr (V); Stu Cncl (R); CR (R); Kodak Young Leaders Award; Sports Management; U of Bowling Green, OH; Seton Hill U, NJ

WHITE, JENTORA A; NEWARK, NJ; SCIENCE HS; (SO); Hi Hnr Roll; Hnr Roll; MVP; Perf Att; Pres Sch; St of Mnth; WWAHSS; Peer Tut/Med; Pep Squd; Scouts; Chrldg (J); Cr Ctry (J); Track (V); Creative Writing-English; Art-Drawing

WHITE, WHITNEY O; LUMBERTON, NJ; RANCARAS VALLEY REG HS; (FR); Hi Hnr Roll; Comm Volntr; Key Club; Ch Chr; Fld Hky (L); Piano Lessons; Yeagers Teens; Biochemistry; U of Pennsylvania; Johns Hopkins U

WHITTY, LESLIE; CRANFORD, NJ; CRANFORD HS; (JR); Hi Hnr Roll; Comm Volntr; Mth Clb/Tm; Sci Clb; Swmg (V); Volunteer-Children's Hospital-Scotch Plains, NJ; Lawyer; Criminal Psychologist; U of Mass At Amherst; U of Connecticut

WIEN, MITCHELL; ALLENTOWN, NJ; HAMILTON HS EAST; (SO); Hi Hnr Roll; Hnr Roll; MVP; Sci Fairs; St of Mnth; WWAHSS; Comm Volntr; Peer Tut/Med; Biology Clb; Emplmnt; Mus Clb; NtlFrnscLg; Sci Clb; Wdwrkg Clb; Stg Cre; Ice Hky (V); Doctor; Forensic Scientist; Maine U; Princeton U

WILBURN, NEAH; CLEMENTON, NJ; OVERBROOK HS; (JR); Hnr Roll; Perf Att; Comm Volntr; DARE; Teen Counselor (Summer Camp); Member of African-American Culture Club; Communications Major; Retail Management; Georgia State U; Kennesaw State U

Wien, Mitchell — Hamilton HS East — Allentown, NJ
Wekesa, Audrey N — Matawan Reg HS — Matawan, NJ
Wang, Damon — Bergen Cty AC — Fort Lee, NJ
Vogt, Christina M — Woodbury JR/SR HS — Turnersville, NJ
Vivas, Belinda — SWM HS — Sayreville, NJ
Vijay, Priyanka — J.P. Stevens HS — Edison, NJ
Vital, Yola — Union, NJ
Walters, Rachel — Spotswood HS — Milltown, NJ
Weiss, David F — Notre Dame HS — Titusville, NJ
Whalen IV, Terence V — Bayonne HS — Bayonne, NJ
White, Jentora A — Science HS — Newark, NJ

WILLIAMS, AKIL; LINDEN, NJ; LINDEN HS; (JR); Comm Volntr; Peer Tut/Med; Key Club; Chemistry Major; Pharmacology; Rutgers U New Brunswick; Montclair State U

WILLIAMS, ANDREW; BOGOTA, NJ; BOGOTA HS; (SR); Hnr Roll; Perf Att; Sci Fairs; St of Mnth; WWAHSS; Hab For Humty Volntr; Hosp Aide; Red Cr Aide; Cmptr Clb; Dbte Team; Emplmnt; Fr of Library; Off Aide; Outdrs Clb; Photog; Tchrs Aide; Stg Cre; Ftball (V); Lit Mag (R); Major in Small Business; Auto Repair; Berkeley College; Delaware State

WILLIAMS, CAMILLE; MT HOLLY, NJ; RANCOCAS VALLEY REG HS; (FR); Hi Hnr Roll; Key Club; Lcrsse (J); Meteorology; Psychology; College of New Jersey; Rutgers U

WILLIAMS, DANIELLE; EAST ORANGE, NJ; EAST ORANGE CAMPUS 9 HS; (FR); Hnr Roll; Nat Mrt Fin; Perf Att; Pres Sch; Comm Volntr; Peer Tut/Med; Chrch Yth Grp; Mus Clb; Off Aide; Svce Clb; Chr; SP/M/VS; Mar Art; Stu Cncl (T); Pride in Public Education Award; Math Fair Award; Economics; Finance; Spelman College

WILLIAMS, FRANCISCA; ASBURY PARK, NJ; AC CHARTER HS; (JR); Hi Hnr Roll; Perf Att; St of Mnth; Peer Tut/Med; Chr; Sccr (J); Sftball (V L); Cl Off (T); Post Liaison in Medical Explorers; Treasurer in the Elizabethan Club; Pre-Med; Master's Degree; Rutgers U in Newark; Howard U

WILLIAMS, JERRELL; PLAINFIELD, NJ; DUNELLEN HS; (JR); Hnr Roll; DARE; Bsball; Ftball (J); Wrstlg (VJ); Delaware State; Maryland State College

WILLIAMS, JOHN; PITMAN, NJ; PITMAN HS; (FR); Hnr Roll; Kwnis Aw; St of Mnth; Yth Ldrshp Prog; Peer Tut/Med; Key Club; Ftball (J); Swmg (V L); Track (V L); Stu Cncl (R); Kiwanis Leadership Award; Diversity Conference-Rowan. U.; English/Writing

WILLIAMS, KAITI; CHERRY HILL, NJ; CAMDEN HS; (JR); Hnr Roll; Sci Fairs; Dbte Team; REBEL club; Volunteer as Food Giver to Homeless; English; History; New York University; University of Chicago

WILLIAMS, KEVIN; SECAUCUS, NJ; SECAUCUS HS; (FR); Hi Hnr Roll; Hnr Roll; MVP; Nat Hon Sy; Nat Ldrshp Svc; Nat Sci Aw; Otst Ac Ach Awd; Perf Att; Sci Fairs; St of Mnth; Comm Volntr; Peer Tut/Med; DARE; Emplmnt; Mth Clb/Tm; MuAlphaTh; Mus Clb; P to P St Amb Prg; Sci Clb; Svce Clb; Bnd; Chr; Bskball (J); Cr Ctry (V); Track (V); Cl Off (T); Stu Cncl (T); Founder & Pres of PTPI- Go International For Tomorrow and Wrap 4A Smile Organization; Medicine & Health Care; International Affairs; Georgetown U; Johns Hopkins U

WILLIAMS, PHYLICIA D; WILLINGBORO, NJ; WILLINGBORO HS; (FR); Hnr Roll; St of Mnth; Emplmnt; ROTC; Bskball (CL); Lcrsse (J L); Stu Cncl (R); CR (R); Delta Sigma Theta Teen Bowling H Game Series; Temple U/Rec League Most Improved Defensive Player, All Star Sportsmanship; Pediatric Medicine; Sports Medicine; Temple U; Rutgers U

WILLIAMS III, FRANKLIN; OCEAN CITY, NJ; OCEAN CITY HS; (JR); Bsball (J); Sccr (J); Tennis (J); Wrstlg (V L); Dentistry; Penn State U

WILLIAMSON, RHETT; EGG HARBOR TOWNSHIP, NJ; EGG HARBOR TOWNSHIP HS; (FR); Hnr Roll; WWAHSS; Red Cr Aide; Biology Clb; Key Club; Sci Clb; Sccr (J); Yi's Martial Art Association 2nd Degree Black Belt; Forensic Chemist; Spanish Professor; Princeton U; Thomas Jefferson U

WILLIAMSON, TIARA; MONTCLAIR, NJ; MONTCLAIR HS; (JR); Hi Hnr Roll; Hnr Roll; Nat Hon Sy; Otst Ac Ach Awd; Sci Fairs; Sci/Math Olympn; WWAHSS; Yth Ldrshp Prog; Comm Volntr; Hab For Humty Volntr; Hosp Aide; AL Aux Girls; Chrch Yth Grp; DECA; Emplmnt; Jr Cls League; Lib Aide; NYLC; ROTC; Clr Grd; Dnce; Fncg (J); Cl Off (R); CR (R); Founder & President of the Teen Read Book Club; Cum Laude for National Latin Exam; Biomedical Engineering; Molecular Biology; Johns Hopkins U; Rutgers U New Brunswick

WILSON, ASHLEY; MARTINSVILLE, NJ; BRIDGEWATER-RARITAN HS; (FR); Hi Hnr Roll; Hnr Roll; Otst Ac Ach Awd; Pres Sch; Comm Volntr; Hab For Humty Volntr; Peer Tut/Med; Chrch Yth Grp; Emplmnt; Key Club; Chr; Ch Chr; Dnce; SP/M/VS; Yrbk (R); Trenton Area Soup Kitchen Volunteer; JD-Juris Doctorate; U of Pennsylvania; Yale U

WILSON, JULIA; ORADELL, NJ; AC OF THE HOLY ANGELS; (JR); F Lan Hn Soc; Hnr Roll; Comm Volntr; Hab For Humty Volntr; Dbte Team; Mod UN; Scouts; French Clb; SP/M/VS; Captain of Debate Team; President and Founder of Foreign Film Club; Lawyer; Broadcast Journalist; Pomona College; Williams College

WINDER, JULIA; PRINCETON, NJ; PRINCETON HS; (SO); MVP; Perf Att; Comm Volntr; Sftball (J); Swmg (V L); Kids 4 Kids - Community Service; Teen Advisory Board; Architecture; Political Science; Kenyon College; Princeton U

WINKLER, TRAVIS; MORGANVILLE, NJ; MARLBORO HS; (SO); Hnr Roll; Otst Ac Ach Awd; Yth Ldrshp Prog; Chess; Emplmnt; FBLA; NYLC; Tennis (V); Cl Off (P); Started Own Website Design Studio-Theandsign.Com; Manager of Band-The Company Calls; Finance Major; MBA; U of Pennsylvania; Columbia U

WINTER, WARREN; KEYPORT, NJ; CHRISTIAN BROTHERS AC; (JR); F Lan Hn Soc; Hi Hnr Roll; Hnr Roll; Nat Mrt LOC; Yth Ldrshp Prog; Comm Volntr; Peer Tut/Med; ArtClub; Emplmnt; FBLA; Jr Cls League; JSA; Mod UN; Off Aide; Photog; Fncg (C); Wt Lftg; Lit Mag (E, R, P); Sch Ppr (R); Published Fictions Author; Entered Holmdel Fencing Into National League; Industrial / Organizational Psychology; Political Science; Brown U; Amherst College

WINTERS, LARISSA; RINGWOOD, NJ; LAKELAND REG HS; (JR); Hi Hnr Roll; Hnr Roll; Nat Hon Sy; Pres Sch; WWAHSS; Yth Ldrshp Prog; Hosp Aide; Peer Tut/Med; Emplmnt; HO'Br Yth Ldrshp; Mod UN; NYLC; Bskball (J); Chrldg (V); PP Ftbl (V); Scr Kpr (V); Sccr (V); Sftball (V); Adv Cncl (P); Cl Off (P); Stu Cncl (R); CR (P); Yrbk (E); National Honor Society; Speak with a Peer (SWAP); Pre-Medicine; Public Relations; Villanova U; Quinnipiac U

WISHNIA, ROBERT; RANDOLPH, NJ; RANDOLPH HS; (SO); Hnr Roll; MVP; Comm Volntr; Chrch Yth Grp; Bnd; SP/M/VS; Ftball (J); Wrstlg (J); Acting / Comedy / Body-Building; Drums; BA / Business; New York U; Monmouth U

WITHERSPOON, ELLEN M; TRENTON, NJ; NOTTINGHAM HS; (FR); Hi Hnr Roll; Hnr Roll; Perf Att; St of Mnth; Chrch Yth Grp; Key Club; Ch Chr; Track (J); Yrbk (P); Master's in Nursing; Pediatrician; Princeton U; Montclair U

WITKOWSKI, JENNIFER; CLIFTON, NJ; CLIFTON HS; (SR); F Lan Hn Soc; Hi Hnr Roll; Nat Hon Sy; Chrch Yth Grp; Svce Clb; President - Botany Club; Church Assistant Pianist - Volunteer; Education / Teacher; School Guidance Counselor; Montclair State U

WOLF, CATHLEEN; CEDAR GROVE, NJ; CEDAR GROVE HS; (SO); Hi Hnr Roll; Otst Ac Ach Awd; Yth Ldrshp Prog; HO'Br Yth Ldrshp; Svce Clb; Dnce; SP/M/VS; Tennis (V); Track (J)

WONG, ETHAN; ALLENDALE, NJ; NORTHERN HIGHLANDS REG HS; (SO); Hi Hnr Roll; WWAHSS; Yth Ldrshp Prog; Comm Volntr; Dbte Team; DECA; Mod UN; Bnd; Mch Bnd; Sch Ppr (E); Honors At William Patterson Piano Competition; History; Medical Field; Columbia U

WONG, OLIVIA; NORTH BRUNSWICK, NJ; N BRUNSWICK TWNSHP HS; (JR); Hi Hnr Roll; Hnr Roll; Nat Hon Sy; Otst Ac Ach Awd; St of Mnth; WWAHSS; Comm Volntr; Key Club; Tchrs Aide; You Made a Difference Award; Pre-Med; Early Childhood Education; Rutgers U; New York U

WONG, RICHARD S; ISELIN, NJ; JFK MEMORIAL HS; (JR); Hnr Roll; Nat Hon Sy; Comm Volntr; Key Club; Mth Clb/Tm; French Clb; Tennis (J); Yrbk (E); Business; Computer Science; New York U; Carnegie Mellon U

WOOD, LAUREN; SALEM, NJ; SALEM HS; (FR); Ctznshp Aw; Hnr Roll; Otst Ac Ach Awd; St of Mnth; Chrch Yth Grp; DARE; Bnd; Mch Bnd; Blac Bottom Band Music Award; Mathematics; Salem Community College; Rowan U

WOODEN II, JOSEPH E; PENNSAUKEN, NJ; PENNSAUKEN HS; (SO); Hi Hnr Roll; Hnr Roll; St of Mnth; Comm Volntr; Chrch Yth Grp; Svce Clb; Asian Clb; Bnd; Bsball (J); Bskball (J); Ftball (VJ); Wrstlg (V); Cl Off (T); Stu Cncl (R); 2003 National Junior Olympics (Hurdles); Become a Doctor Pre-Med; Engineer; U of North Carolina Chapel Hill; Duke U

WOODS, RYAN J; HARRISON, NJ; HOST-NORTH HUDSON CTR; (SO); Ctznshp Aw; Hnr Roll; MVP; Nat Sci Aw; Comm Volntr; Biology Clb; P to P St Amb Prg; Sci Clb; Bnd; Skiing; Sccr (V); Stu Cncl (P); CR (R); Grade 3 Competition Bagpiper; People to People Student Ambassador Alumnus; Motion Picture Production; Architecture; U of Southern California; School of Visual Arts

WORTSMANN, JAIME; ISELIN, NJ; JOHN F KENNEDY MEMORIAL HS; (SO); Hnr Roll; WWAHSS; Comm Volntr; Key Club; Sch Ppr; Scuba Certified; Tutoring

WORTSMANN, JESSICA; ISELIN, NJ; JOHN F KENNEDY MEMORIAL HS; (SR); Hnr Roll; Perf Att; WWAHSS; Comm Volntr; Emplmnt; Key Club; Prom Com; Cr Ctry (V L); Track (V); Black Belt Karate; Speech Pathology; Penn State; U of Massachusetts

WRIGHT, CHAUNTEL V; BROWNS MILLS, NJ; PEMBERTON TWP HS; (SO); Hi Hnr Roll; Hnr Roll; Otst Ac Ach Awd; Perf Att; Pres Sch; WWAHSS; Peer Tut/Med; 4-H; Scouts; Bnd; Chr; Dnce; Chrldg (V L); Track (J); Youth of the Year Nominee; Attended National Youth Leadership Forum; Pediatrician; Clemson U

WRIGHT, CHENEISE; BROWNS MILLS, NJ; PEMBERTON TOWNSHIP HS; (FR); 4H Awd; Hnr Roll; WWAHSS; 4-H; DARE; Scouts; Dnce; Chrldg (V); Lawyer; Professional Dancer; Duke U

WU, MINGDI; UNION, NJ; UNION HS; (SR); Hnr Roll; DECA; Biography Have Been Selected By Who's Who Among American Students; Marketing; Education; CUNY-Hunter College; CUNY-Branch College

WUTKE, JAMIE; BRIDGEWATER, NJ; BRIDGEWATER-RARITAN HS; (FR); Hi Hnr Roll; Hnr Roll; WWAHSS; Peer Tut/Med; DARE; Key Club; Scouts; Chr; Presidential Award; Bronze and Silver Awards in Girl Scouts; Teaching (Elementary); Interior Design; Oneonta State (NY)

WYNN, JULIUS M; PENNSAUKEN, NJ; PENNSAUKEN HS; (JR); F Lan Hn Soc; Hnr Roll; Spanish Clb; Ftball (V); Track (J)

XIE, JIMMY; BRIDGEWATER, NJ; BRIDGEWATER-RARITAN HS; (JR); Hnr Roll; Nat Mrt LOC; Comm Volntr; Hosp Aide; FBLA; Key Club; French Clb; Business; Marketing; Pennsylvania State U; New York U

YABLON, GARY D; SUCCASUNNA, NJ; ROXBURY HS; (JR); Ctznshp Aw; Hnr Roll; Perf Att; Yth Ldrshp Prog; DARE; Emplmnt; Mus Clb; Photog; Vsity Clb; Bnd; Cr Ctry (J L); Tennis (V CL); Track (J L); Yrbk (E, P); Attorney General of the 2005 PYLC - Lead America Conference; Renaissance Member; History; Law; U of Kentucky; U of Connecticut

YAN, MICHAEL C; CHERRY HILL, NJ; CHERRY HILL HS EAST; (SO); Hnr Roll; MVP; Otst Ac Ach Awd; Comm Volntr; Chess; Tchrs Aide; Chr; Sccr (J); Tennis (J); Engineering; Massachusetts Institute of Technology; Rutgers U

YANG, ASHLEY; EGG HARBOR TOWNSHIP, NJ; EGG HARBOR TOWNSHIP HS; (FR); Hnr Roll; WWAHSS; Key Club; Tennis (V); Track (J)

YANG, DEVON; LEDGEWOOD, NJ; ROXBURY HS; (JR); Hi Hnr Roll; Hnr Roll; Nat Mrt LOC; Perf Att; Pres Ac Ftns Aw; WWAHSS; Comm Volntr; Hosp Aide; Emplmnt; Key Club; Mth Clb/Tm; Quiz Bowl; Sci Clb; Vsity Clb; Bnd; Jzz Bnd; Mch Bnd; Pep Bnd; Cr Ctry (J); Track (V); Vsy Clb (V); Computer Engineering; U of California Berkeley; Carnegie Mellon U

YANG, PAMELA; GREEN BROOK, NJ; WATCHUNG HILLS REG HS; (FR); All Am Sch; Hi Hnr Roll; Hnr Roll; St of Mnth; Comm Volntr; Peer Tut/Med; 4-H; Chrch Yth Grp; French Clb; Ch Chr; Orch; Stg Cre; Science League; President's Award; Pharmacy; Business; U of California San Diego; U of Pennsylvania

YANNI, JASON; ISELIN, NJ; JOHN F KENNEDY HS; (FR); Key Club; Sccr (V); Track (J); Business; Sports Management; Rutgers

YASMIN, WARDA; JERSEY CITY, NJ; FERRIS HS; (FR); Perf Att; Sci Fairs; St of Mnth; CARE; Comm Volntr; Hosp Aide; ArtClub; Cmptr Clb; DARE; Drma Clb; Spanish Clb; Stg Cre; Swg Chr; Bskball; Pediatrician; Business; Rutgers U; New Jersey City U

YAURE, CAITLIN; EGG HARBOR TOWNSHIP, NJ; ATLANTIC CHRISTIAN SCH; (FR); ArtClub; Chrch Yth Grp; Dnce; 2004-2005 Compensatory Education Winner for Gloucester County Special Service; Finalist in Creative Communications; Performing Arts Drama / Dance; Child Development; Philadelphia School of Performing Arts

YE, JASON; WAYNE, NJ; WAYNE VALLEY HS; (SO); Nat Hon Sy; Comm Volntr; Cmptr Clb; DARE; FBLA; Vllyball (VJ); Presidential Award (Academic); Pre-Med; Pre-Law; NYU; Columbia

YEAMANS, KARLA J; CLIFTON, NJ; CLIFTON HS; (SO); Hi Hnr Roll; WWAHSS; Drma Clb; French Clb; Chr; SP/M/VS; Swmg (V); Optimist International Oratorical Scholarship Winner; VFW - Voice of Democracy Essay Winner; Vocal Performance; Business Administration

YEARWOOD, SARAH; RAHWAY, NJ; AC ST ALOYSIUS HS; (JR); Hnr Roll; Otst Ac Ach Awd; Pres Sch; Chrch Yth Grp; Ch Chr; Vllyball (J); Pre-Med; Paramedics; Rutgers U; U of Medicine and Dentistry

YERO, STEPHANIE; FORT LEE, NJ; FORT LEE HS; (JR); Hnr Roll; FBLA; Mod UN; French Clb; Clr Grd; Stg Cre; Stu Cncl (R); Political Science; Pre-Law

YERRAMILLI, PALLAVI; KENDALL PARK, NJ; SOUTH BRUNSWICK HS; (SO); Otst Ac Ach Awd; Hosp Aide; Mod UN; MuAlphaTh; Sci Clb; Bnd; Private Vocal Lessons; New Jersey Science League (I Received a Plaque in Chemistry I); Medicine; Biophysics; Princeton U; Columbia U

YILMAZ, OZLEM; TUCKERTON, NJ; PINELANDS REG; (SO); Hnr Roll; Perf Att; Spanish Clb

YIP, MANG H; EGG HARBOR TOWNSHIP, NJ; (SR); Hnr Roll; WWAHSS; Comm Volntr; Chrch Yth Grp; Key Club; Stu Cncl (R); CR (R); Sch Ppr (R); Counseling; Rutgers U

YONG, SAMANTHA C; STIRLING, NJ; WATCHUNG HILLS REG HS; (SR); Hnr Roll; Yth Ldrshp Prog; Comm Volntr; Chrch Yth Grp; Mod UN; NYLC; SADD; Ch Chr; SP/M/VS; Stu Cncl (R); CR (P); Yrbk (R); Journalism; New York U; Penn State U

YOO, DANIEL; EGG HARBOR TOWNSHIP, NJ; EGG HARBOR TOWNSHIP HS; (JR); Gov Hnr Prg; Hi Hnr Roll; Hnr Roll; Nat Hon Sy; USAA; WWAHSS; Comm Volntr; Hosp Aide; Peer Tut/Med; Biology Clb; FCA; Key Club; Mth Clb/Tm; Sci Clb; Tennis (V L); Sch Ppr (R, P); New Jersey State Teen Arts Finalist: Piano; Varsity Scholar; Biomedical Engineering; Pre-Medicine; Georgetown U; Columbia U

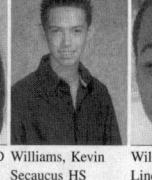

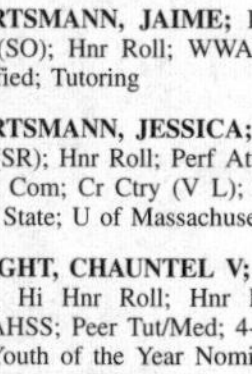
Yearwood, Sarah
AC St Aloysius HS
Rahway, NJ

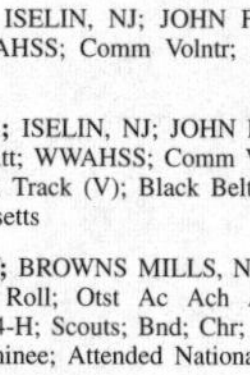
Ye, Jason
Wayne Valley HS
Wayne, NJ

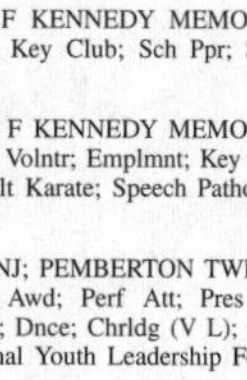
Yerramilli, Pallavi
South Brunswick HS
Kendall Park, NJ

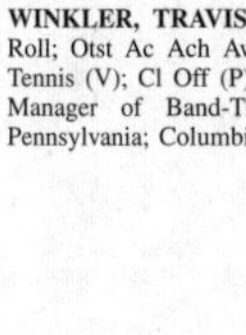
Yaure, Caitlin
Atlantic Christian Sch
Egg Harbor Township, NJ

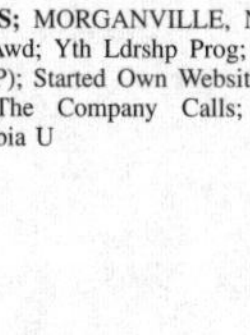
Wood, Lauren
Salem HS
Salem, NJ

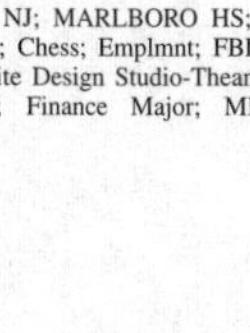
Wishnia, Robert
Randolph HS
Randolph, NJ

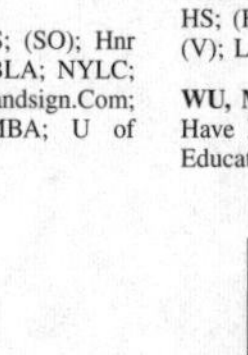
Williams, Phylicia D
Willingboro HS
Willingboro, NJ

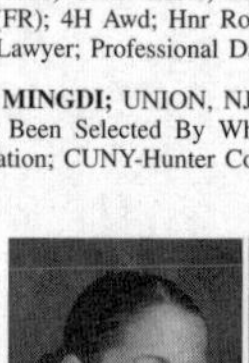
Williams, Kevin
Secaucus HS
Secaucus, NJ

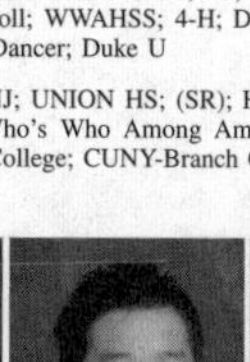
Williams, Akil
Linden HS
Linden, NJ

Williams, Danielle
East Orange Campus 9 HS
East Orange, NJ

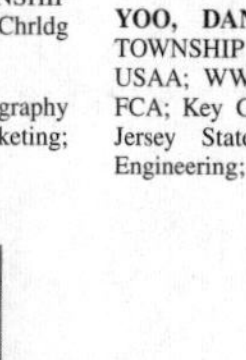
Williamson, Tiara
Montclair HS
Montclair, NJ

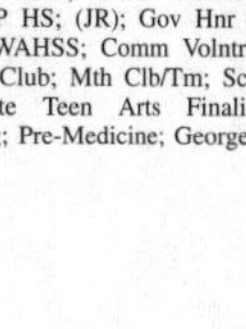
Witherspoon, Ellen M
Nottingham HS
Trenton, NJ

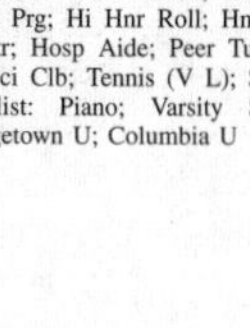
Wooden II, Joseph E
Pennsauken HS
Pennsauken, NJ

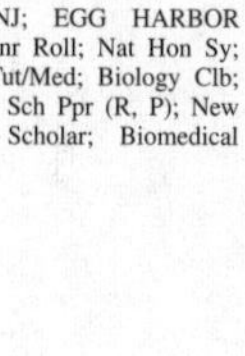
Yablon, Gary D
Roxbury HS
Succasunna, NJ

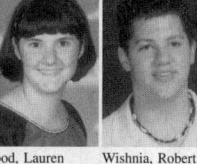

YOU, XUE; BRIDGEWATER, NJ; BRIDGEWATER-RARITAN HS; (SO); Hnr Roll; WWAHSS; Comm Volntr; Chrch Yth Grp; Key Club; Chinese Clb; Chr; Dnce; Pharmacy; Accounting

YOUNG, DANIELLA; BLOOMFIELD, NJ; BLOOMFIELD MS; (MS); Ctznshp Aw; Hi Hnr Roll; Nat Hon Sy; Otst Ac Ach Awd; Comm Volntr; ArtClub; Spch Team; Dramatic Arts; Psychology; Stanford University; Yale University

YOUSSEF, MATTHEW; BAYONNE, NJ; HCST-NORTH HUDSON CTR; (JR); F Lan Hn Soc; Perf Att; WWAHSS; Comm Volntr; Chrch Yth Grp; Drma Clb; Mus Clb; Bnd; Jzz Bnd; Mch Bnd; Orch; Ftball (V); Mar Art (V); Biology; Physics; Rutgers U; Drexel U

YOUSSEF, SIMONE; ELMWOOD PARK, NJ; BERGEN CTY AC; (JR); Hi Hnr Roll; Hnr Roll; WWAHSS; Amnsty Intl; Red Cr Aide; Yrbk (E); Hackensack Hospital Volunteer; Spanish Honor Society; Anatomy; Biology

YUAN, BRIAN; MORGANVILLE, NJ; MARLBORO HS; (SO); Hnr Roll; Comm Volntr; Hosp Aide; Peer Tut/Med; Key Club; Mod UN; Bnd; Mch Bnd; Fncg (V); Tennis (J); Track (J); Wrstlg (J); Cl Off (V); Yrbk (E, R); Local Tournament Winner - Fencing; Law; Business; Cornell U; New York U

YUN, HEIDI; MOUNT LAUREL, NJ; LENAPE HS; (FR); Hi Hnr Roll; Hnr Roll; Yth Ldrshp Prog; Comm Volntr; ArtClub; Chrch Yth Grp; NYLC; Orch; Tennis (J); Interior Architecture; U of Pennsylvania; New York U

ZACCONE, KRISTINE; SECAUCUS, NJ; (JR); Comm Volntr; Key Club; Photog; Chr; Bskball (V); Sftball (V); Vllyball (J); Writing/English; Journalism; Rutgers; FDU

ZAKRZEWSKI, MEGAN L; SOUTH AMBOY, NJ; SAYREVILLE WAR MEMORIAL HS; (JR); F Lan Hn Soc; Hi Hnr Roll; Hnr Roll; MVP; Nat Hon Sy; Otst Ac Ach Awd; Comm Volntr; Biology Clb; Emplmnt; Mth Clb/Tm; Prom Com; Sci Clb; Vsity Clb; Spanish Clb; Bskball (V L); Cr Ctry (V L); Lit Mag (E, R); Sch Ppr (E, R); Interact / All-Star for Hawk's; Float Committee Basketball League; Journalism; Business; Montclair State U; Rowan U

ZAMORSKI, MARK J; CRANFORD, NJ; CRANFORD HS; (JR); Hnr Roll; Nat Hon Sy; Comm Volntr; Mth Clb/Tm; MuAlphaTh; Ntl Beta Clb; Bnd; Jzz Bnd; Ftball (V L); Lcrsse (V C); Stu Cncl (T, R); Scholars Circle; Engineering; Forensic Science

ZATORSKI, ALEXANDRA; RAHWAY, NJ; RAHWAY HS; (SO); Chr; Chrldg (V L); Gmnstcs (V); Skiing (V); Swmg (V); Yrbk (E); Member of Jr National Honor Society; Recipient of President's Award; Law / PhD; Politics / PhD; Harvard U; U of Texas

ZATTA, JILLIAN; BERKELEY HEIGHTS, NJ; GOVERNOR LIVINGSTON HS; (JR); F Lan Hn Soc; Hnr Roll; WWAHSS; Comm Volntr; Peer Tut/Med; ArtClub; Emplmnt; Jr Cls League; Prom Com; Quill & Scroll; Italian Clb; Fld Hky (JC); PP Ftbl (J); Swmg (J); Lit Mag (E); Sch Ppr (R); Yrbk (R)

ZEISWEISS, JAMES; MT HOLLY, NJ; RANCOCAS VALLEY REG HS; (SO); Hi Hnr Roll; Nat Hon Sy; Pres Ac Ftns Aw; Comm Volntr; Hosp Aide; Spec Olymp Vol; Key Club; Sci Clb; French Clb; Bnd; Cr Ctry (V); Track (V); Cl Off (S); Stu Cncl (S); Key Club VP; Salutatorian - As of Spring Sophomore Year; Law; Political Science

ZERPA, ELIANY; EAST RUTHERFORD, NJ; BECTON REG HS; (JR); Hnr Roll; Nat Stu Ath Day Aw; Pres Ac Ftns Aw; St of Mnth; Comm Volntr; Hosp Aide; Peer Tut/Med; Chrch Yth Grp; Emplmnt; Key Club; Photog; Ch Chr; Track (J); Lit Mag (E); Pharmacist; Physician's Assistant; Rutgers U; U of Southern California

ZEVALLOS, CHRISTOPHER M; NORTH BERGEN, NJ; NORTH BERGEN HS; (FR); Hnr Roll; Perf Att; Comm Volntr; Peer Tut/Med; Key Club; French Clb; Computer Engineering; Marine Biology; Rutgers U

ZHANG, LISA; MORGANVILLE, NJ; FREEHOLD BOROUGH HS; (SO); Hi Hnr Roll; Hnr Roll; Perf Att; St of Mnth; Yth Ldrshp Prog; Comm Volntr; Hosp Aide; Mus Clb; NYLC; Svce Clb; French Clb; Dnce; Dance Competition, Art Drawing; Piano ABRSM Certificate Level 4; Medicine; Law; U of Pennsylvania; Cornell U

ZHANG, SUSAN; NEW PROVIDENCE, NJ; NEW PROVIDENCE HS; (SO); Hi Hnr Roll; Hnr Roll; Perf Att; Peer Tut/Med; ArtClub; FTA; Tchrs Aide; French Clb; Bnd; Mch Bnd; Pep Bnd; Stg Cre; Vllyball (J); Ophthalmologist; Veterinary; Columbia U; U of Michigan

ZHU, ANGELA J; MORGANVILLE, NJ; FREEHOLD BOROUGH HS; (SO); Hi Hnr Roll; Hnr Roll; Perf Att; Comm Volntr; Emplmnt; Orch; Lit Mag (R); Sch Ppr (R); Published Poet; Internal Medicine; Princeton U; U of Pennsylvania

ZHU, SHELLY; LIVINGSTON, NJ; LIVINGSTON HS; (SR); Hi Hnr Roll; Hnr Roll; Nat Hon Sy; Hosp Aide; Bnd; Biomedical Sciences; Law

ZIA, JAVAIRIA; JERSEY CITY, NJ; HCST-NORTH HUDSON CTR; (SO); All Am Sch; Hi Hnr Roll; Hnr Roll; Nat Sci Aw; Salutrn; Sci Fairs; St of Mnth; USAA; Comm Volntr; Peer Tut/Med; ArtClub; DARE; Drma Clb; Key Club; Mth Clb/Tm; Mod UN; Schol Bwl; Sci Clb; SP/M/VS; Stg Cre; Stu Cncl (P, S, R); CR (P, S, R); Sch Ppr (R); President's Award for Educational Excellence; National Science League; Psychiatry; Political Science; Princeton U; Harvard U

ZIEGLER, ASHLEY E; WILDWOOD, NJ; GLOUCESTER CTY INST OF TECH; (JR); Hnr Roll; Nat Hon Sy; WWAHSS; Comm Volntr; Emplmnt; Key Club; Dnce; Performed in Disney World; Dance; Adelphi U

ZULUAGA, JOHULIN; WEST NEW YORK, NJ; MEMORIAL HS; (SO); Hnr Roll; Vllyball (J); Private Investigator / Police Officer; Anthropologist; New York City U; Columbia U

ZYCH, SOFIA A; GLASSBORO, NJ; OUR LADY OF MERCY AC; (SO); Hi Hnr Roll; Photog; Scouts; Spanish Clb; Dnce; Stg Cre; Track (V); Culinary Arts; Business Management; Johnson and Wales U

Zhang, Lisa
Freehold Borough HS
Morganville, NJ

National Honor Roll Spring 2005

Zeisweiss, James
Rancocas Valley Reg HS
Mt Holly, NJ

New York

AARON, ROGER; STATEN ISLAND, NY; ST PETER'S BOYS HS; (JR); Hnr Roll; Nat Hon Sy; St of Mnth; WWAHSS; Hosp Aide; Chess; Dnce; Bskball (J); Track (J); Stu Cncl (R); 2nd Place At Apollo Theatre; 1st Place in High Jump Competition; Business; Finance; U of Maryland; Fordham U

ABBOTT, KIRSTIE; ENDICOTT, NY; UNION ENDICOTT HS; (SO); Hi Hnr Roll; Otst Ac Ach Awd; Sci Fairs; St of Mnth; WWAHSS; Comm Volntr; Spec Olymp Vol; Chrch Yth Grp; Key Club; Mus Clb; French Clb; Chr; Ch Chr; SP/M/VS; Sang with Tri-Cities Opera; Vice President of Leo's Club; Music Therapy; Opera; Berklee College of Music; East Carolina U

ABDULRAHMAN, ROZAN; BRONX, NY; BARD HS EARLY COLLEGE; (SO); Gov Hnr Prg; Hi Hnr Roll; Otst Ac Ach Awd; Salutrn; St of Mnth; Comm Volntr; Off Aide; Bskball (J); Sch Ppr (R); Player to Access Graduate - Hostos Community College; State Winner of Essay Writing About Sports; PhD Medicine; Master's in Psychology; Columbia U; Harvard U

ABDULSATTAR, RAMZY; BROOKLYN, NY; FT HAMILTON HS; (JR); St of Mnth; Jr Ach; Mus Clb; Orch; Pilot; Engineer; New York U; Pace U

ABITANTE, LISA; BROOKLYN, NY; BISHOP KEARNEY HS; (JR); Hnr Roll; MVP; Nat Hon Sy; WWAHSS; Peer Tut/Med; Tchrs Aide; Dnce; Bskball (VJC); Founder of Dance Club and Captain; Peer Intervention Program; Veterinarian; Psychology; Michigan State U; Clemson U

ABO-ALI, EHAB M; ELMHURST, NY; RAZI HS; (SR); Hi Hnr Roll; Hnr Roll; Nat Hon Sy; Otst Ac Ach Awd; Perf Att; Sci Fairs; St of Mnth; Valdctrian; Comm Volntr; Peer Tut/Med; Cmptr Clb; Dbte Team; Drma Clb; Tchrs Aide; SP/M/VS; Adv Cncl (P); Stu Cncl (R); Sch Ppr (E); Yrbk (E); Principal's Honor Roll; Attended UNIS-UN Youth Conference; Biochemistry Major; Pediatric Medicine; New York U - Accepted Via E.D.

ABRAHAM, FLORINE; ELMSFORD, NY; ALEXANDER HAMILTON HS; (SR); Hi Hnr Roll; Kwnis Aw; Nat Hon Sy; Nat Ldrshp Svc; Salutrn; WWAHSS; Yth Ldrshp Prog; Comm Volntr; Peer Tut/Med; Emplmnt; Key Club; Mth Clb/Tm; NYLC; SADD; Track (V CL); Yrbk; Key Club - President; SADD - Vice President; Pre-Dental; New York U

ABRAHAM, SHERIN; ELMSFORD, NY; ALEXANDER HAMILTON; (SO); Hi Hnr Roll; Nat Hon Sy; Comm Volntr; Key Club; SADD; Sftball (V); Track (V); Vllyball (JCL); CR (R)

ABREU, JESUS; BRONX, NY; WALTON HS; (FR); Hi Hnr Roll; Hnr Roll; Perf Att; Criminal Justice

ABREU, LILIANA; OZONE PARK, NY; AC FOR AMERICAN STUDIES; (FR); Hnr Roll; Chr; SP/M/VS; Stu Cncl (R); Columbia U; Princeton U

ACEVEDO, VIANNEY J; NEW YORK, NY; LOUIS D BRANDEIS HS; (SO); Hnr Roll; Nat Hon Sy; Comm Volntr; Hosp Aide; ArtClub; BPA; Cmptr Clb; Tech Clb; Spanish Clb; Bsball (J); Gmnstcs (J); Vllyball (J); Wt Lftg (J); Pediatrician; Secretary; Columbia U; Hunter College

ACOSTA, GABRIELA; BRONX, NY; AC OF MT ST URSULA; (JR); WWAHSS; Sch Ppr (R); Biology; Pre-Veterinary Medicine; Lehman College; Cornell U

ACOSTA, JONATHAN; BRONX, NY; ALFRED E SMITH VOC HS; (SO); Hnr Roll; Emplmnt; Ftball (C); Went to Bronx High School of Science for Prep for Prep; Electrician

ADAMCHICK, MATTHEW; AMSTERDAM, NY; AMSTERDAM HS; (SR); Hi Hnr Roll; Hnr Roll; MVP; Nat Hon Sy; WWAHSS; Yth Ldrshp Prog; Peer Tut/Med; Chess; Key Club; Mth Clb/Tm; Mus Clb; NYLC; Bnd; Jzz Bnd; Mch Bnd; Pep Bnd; Sccr (V CL); Tennis (V CL); American League Boys State of New York; Aeronautical Engineering; Applied Math; Clarkson U; U of Virginia

ADAMCZAK, RYAN; DUNKIRK, NY; DUNKIRK HS; (SR); Hnr Roll; Nat Hon Sy; WWAHSS; Comm Volntr; Spec Olymp Vol; Emplmnt; Key Club; SADD; French Clb; Hsbk Rdg (J); Sccr (J); Yrbk; Major in Graphic Design and Become a Car Designer; SUNY Fredonia

ADAMCZYK, ANTHONY; OGDENSBURG, NY; LISBON CTRL SCH; (SO); Hi Hnr Roll; Nat Hon Sy; Otst Ac Ach Awd; Mod UN; NtlFrnscLg; Photog; Stu Cncl (R); CR (R); Construction Engineering Tech; Building Construction; SUNY Canton College of Technology; Clarkson U

ADAMITEY, MICHAEL; STATEN ISLAND, NY; NEW DORP HS; (JR); St of Mnth; Comm Volntr; Chrch Yth Grp; Ch Chr; Track (J); Cl Off (S); Stu Cncl; Computer Repair; Computer Programming; Saint John's College; College of Staten Island

ADAMS, CARON L; LIMA, NY; LIMA CHRISTIAN SCH; (SO); Hi Hnr Roll; Chrch Yth Grp; Bnd; Chr; Dnce; Mch Bnd; Education Services

ADAMS, PETER; SCARSDALE, NY; SUMMIT SCH; (JR); Yth Ldrshp Prog; Comm Volntr; Peer Tut/Med; Red Cr Aide; Chrch Yth Grp; FBLA; Key Club; Clb; Bnd; SP/M/VS; Ftball (J); Sccr (J); Tennis (J); Track (V); Jack and Jill of America; Black Awareness Club; PPE College at Oxford University; Oxford U; Duke U

ADARKWAH, STEPHEN; BRONX, NY; MARBLE HILL HS FOR INTERNATIONAL STUDIES; (SO); Hi Hnr Roll; Hnr Roll; Otst Ac Ach Awd; Perf Att; Sci Fairs; St of Mnth; Yth Ldrshp Prog; Chrch Yth Grp; Cmptr Clb; Dbte Team; Emplmnt; Mus Clb; NYLC; Off Aide; Outdrs Clb; Ch Chr; Drm Mjr; Jzz Bnd; SP/M/VS; Sccr (V); Track (V); CR (P); MD / Medical Doctor; Master's Degree; New York U; Yale U

ADEWUYI, ADENIKE A; ELMONT, NY; SEWANHAKA HS; (SR); F Lan Hn Soc; Hi Hnr Roll; Nat Hon Sy; Nat Mrt Fin; Nat Mrt Sch Recip; Sci Fairs; Sci/Math Olympn; St of Mnth; Valdctrian; WWAHSS; Peer Tut/Med; Chrch Yth Grp; Key Club; Mth Clb/Tm; Quiz Bowl; SADD; Foreign Clb; Ch Chr; Tennis (V L); Cl Off (S); Stu Cncl (P, V, T, R); Sch Ppr; National Ventures Scholar; Math Fair Gold Medal Winner; Biomedical Engineering; Medical Science; Harvard U

ADJEI-BAAFUOR, PRISCILLA; BRONX, NY; AC OF MT ST URSULA; (JR); Hnr Roll; Comm Volntr; Chrch Yth Grp; Emplmnt; Kwanza Clb; Stg Cre; Pre-Med / Psychology; Actuarial Science; Columbia U; Boston U

ADUSEI, SAMUEL K; ARVERNE, NY; BEACH CHANNEL HS; (SR); Hi Hnr Roll; Hnr Roll; Comm Volntr; Sccr (V); Pharmacy; SUNY Buffalo

AFRIYIE, LOUISA; BRONX, NY; MARBLE HILL HS FOR INTERNATIONAL STUDIES; (SO); Perf Att; Comm Volntr; Chrch Yth Grp; Drma Clb; Ch Chr; Dnce; SP/M/VS; Sccr; Track; Pediatrician; Nursing; Penn State U; Buffalo U

AFROZ, SURAIYA; WOODSIDE, NY; HS FOR HEALTH PROFESSION AND HUMAN SERVICES; (JR); Ctznshp Aw; Duke TS; Hi Hnr Roll; Hnr Roll; Nat Hon Sy; Otst Ac Ach Awd; Perf Att; Pres Sch; Sci Fairs; St of Mnth; Comm Volntr; Peer Tut/Med; Red Cr Aide; Biology Clb; Cmptr Clb; Dbte Team; Emplmnt; Mod UN; NYLC; Sci Clb; Svce Clb; Dnce; SP/M/VS; Cr Ctry (V); Track (V); Vllyball (J); CR (P); Sch Ppr (R); Member of United Nations Club, Harlem Children Society's Summer Research Program; Radiology: Giving Back to New York Essay Winner (3rd Prize) New York Science and Engineering Fair's Awards; Pre-Med, Biology, Chemistry, Liberal Arts; M.D., PhD; Columbia U; Cornell U

AFSANA, SURAIYA; JAMAICA, NY; HILLCREST HS; (JR); Nat Hon Sy; Comm Volntr; Dbte Team; MD; JD

AGARONOV, ALEN; BROOKLYN, NY; JAMES MADISON HS; (SO); Hnr Roll; Sci/Math Olympn; Key Club; Certificate of Distinction for Science 2004; Certificate of Distinction for Science 2005; Medical Science; MD; New York U; Pace U

AGEN, QUINN; UTICA, NY; (JR); Hi Hnr Roll; Hnr Roll; Sci Fairs; Emplmnt; Golf (V L); Ice Hky (V L); Sccr (V L); CR (S); 1st Team All-Star for Hockey; Law; Art; New York U; Boston U

AGGARWAL, NEHA; FLORAL PARK, NY; FRANCIS LEWIS HS; (SO); Hi Hnr Roll; Hnr Roll; Nat Hon Sy; Sci Fairs; Comm Volntr; Hosp Aide; Lib Aide; Mth Clb/Tm; Tchrs Aide; Medicine; Pharmacy; New York U; Sophie Davis School of Biomedical Education

AGGARWAL, PAYAL; KEW GARDENS, NY; BRONX HS OF SCIENCE; (SO); Hnr Roll; Otst Ac Ach Awd; Valdctrian; WWAHSS; Comm Volntr; Red Cr Aide; Biology Clb; Key Club; Spch Team; Dnce; Organizer of Tsunami Relief Dance in School; Member of Indian Dance Club; Medicine; New York U; Johns Hopkins U

AGHIMSON, KANDU E; MANORVILLE, NY; (JR); Hnr Roll; Bskball (V); Ftball (V); Scr Kpr (J); Wt Lftg (V); Sports Medicine; Radiologist; The College of Saint Rose (Albany, NY); Saint Joseph College (Patchogue, NY)

AGIUS, ALEXANDRA; FLUSHING, NY; BRONX HS OF SCIENCE; (SR); Nat Hon Sy; Dbte Team; Jr Ach; Bnd; Stg Cre; Varsity Member of Lincoln-Douglas Debate Team; Law; Politics; New York U - Attending

AGUILAR, OMAR; STATEN ISLAND, NY; NEW DORP HS; (SO); Hnr Roll; Perf Att; St of Mnth; Lawyer; Doctor; Yale U; Harvard U

AGYAPON, KWEKA A; ELDRED, NY; ELDRED CTRL SCH; (JR); Hnr Roll; Chrch Yth Grp; Bskball (V); Sccr (V); Obtaining a PhD in Astrophysics; Massachusetts Institute of Technology; Georgetown U

AGYEMANG, SERWAA; BRONX, NY; HEALTH OPPORTUNITIES HS; (SO); Hi Hnr Roll; Hnr Roll; Nat Hon Sy; Otst Ac Ach Awd; Perf Att; Peer Tut/Med; Red Cr Aide; ArtClub; Chrch Yth Grp; Cl Off (P); CR (P); National Junior Honor Society; American Red Cross; Ob/Gyn; Registered Nurse / RN; SUNY Binghamton; SUNY Stony Brook

AHMAD, SARAH Q; ASTORIA, NY; AC FOR AMERICAN STUDIES; (FR); Ctznshp Aw; Hi Hnr Roll; Hnr Roll; Nat Hon Sy; Otst Ac Ach Awd; Perf Att; Sci Fairs; Tchrs Aide; Chr; Stg Cre; Yrbk (E, R, P); Nomination For Cambridge Prep Experience; Academy of American Studies-Eagle Award; Stony Brook U; New York U

AHMAD, ZARAH; EAST AURORA, NY; IROQUOIS HS; (SO); Hnr Roll; Pres Sch; WWAHSS; Comm Volntr; Jr Ach; Key Club; Mth Clb/Tm; Mod UN; Spanish Clb; Bnd; Mch Bnd; Pep Bnd; Stu Cncl (R); Sch Ppr (E, R); NY State Scholar Athlete-Bowling V; Mock Trial; Lawyer; Journalist; Columbia U; Cornell U

AHMED, JABBER; LITTLE NECK, NY; BENJAMIN CARDOZO HS; (JR); Hnr Roll; Comm Volntr; FBLA; Key Club; Bnd; SP/M/VS; CR (R); Recipient of the Lions Club Award for Community Service; On the Tech Team / Treasurer of the Muslim Student Association; Business Administration; Pharmacy; SUNY Stony Brook; Cornell U

AHMED, LILA; FARMINGVILLE, NY; SACHEM HS EAST; (SO); F Lan Hn Soc; Hnr Roll; Otst Ac Ach Awd; Sci Fairs; Sci/Math Olympn; Comm Volntr; Peer Tut/Med; ArtClub; DARE; Drma Clb; French Clb; Bnd; SP/M/VS; Stg Cre; Swmg (VJC); Master's Degree; Columbia U; Hofstra U

AHMED, SABA; NANUET, NY; NANUET HS; (JR); Hnr Roll; Nat Hon Sy; WWAHSS; Peer Tut/Med; Emplmnt; MuAlphaTh; Sch Ppr (R); Editors' Choice Award from Poetry.Com; Pharmacy; Albany College of Pharmacy; St John's U

AHMED, SANA; ENDICOTT, NY; UNION-ENDICOTT HS; (SR); Hi Hnr Roll; Nat Hon Sy; Otst Ac Ach Awd; WWAHSS; Comm Volntr; Peer Tut/Med; Biology Clb; Key Club; SADD; Tennis (V); Spanish Club; History Club; Biochemistry; Biology; Binghamton U

AHMED, SHARMIN; FLUSHING, NY; FRANCIS LEWIS HS; (JR); Hnr Roll; Perf Att; Comm Volntr; Key Club; Lib Aide; Mth Clb/Tm; Off Aide; Dnce; Lit Mag (E, R, P); Barnard-Columbia U; New York U

AHMED, TOFAYALE; QUEENS, NY; FRANKLIN K LANE HS; (SR); Hnr Roll; Otst Ac Ach Awd; Perf Att; Sci Fairs; Comm Volntr; Chess; Sci Clb; SP/M/VS; Sccr (V); Arista Member; Professional Pilot; Engineering; Farmingdale State College

AHNERT, JORDAN; MASSENA, NY; MASSENA CTRL HS; Hnr Roll; St of Mnth; Comm Volntr; Bskball (JC); Ftball (JCL); Tourney Sports USA; Athletic Trainer; Marine Biologist; Miami U

AHSAN, MOHAMMAD AZAZ; JAMAICA, NY; in 7th grade not in eight graduate in 2010 not 2009; MS

AIKEN, ALICIA; CINCINNATUS, NY; CINCINNATUS; (JR); Ctznshp Aw; Hnr Roll; St of Mnth; Comm Volntr; Prom Com; Spanish Clb; SP/M/VS; Chrldg (V); Sccr (C); CR (R); Involved in Various Clubs

AIMALETOINOVA, INARA; FOREST HILLS, NY; FIORELLO H LA GUARDIA HS; (SR); Hnr Roll; Nat Hon Sy; WWAHSS; Comm Volntr; Peer Tut/Med; Drma Clb; Emplmnt; Lib Aide; Off Aide; Photog; Dnce; SP/M/VS; Track (L); Arista (The National Honor Society); French and Russian Languages; Acting; Boston U; U of Pennsylvania

AITKEN, ANDREA M; WAPPINGERS FALLS, NY; ROY C KETCHAM HS; (SO); DAR; Hi Hnr Roll; Perf Att; Pres Ac Ftns Aw; Sci Fairs; St of Mnth; USAA; WWAHSS; Comm Volntr; Drma Clb; Mod UN; Stg Cre; Mar Art; Yrbk (E); Black Belt in Tang Soo Do (1st Degree); Won Bowling League Title Twice; Medical Research; Environmental Studies; Cornell U; Johns Hopkins U

AJDINOULE, AMELA; UTICA, NY; THOMAS R PROCTOR HS; (JR); Hi Hnr Roll; Perf Att; St of Mnth; WWAHSS; Hosp Aide; Principal's List Awards for High Average & Highest Achievement; Physical Therapy

AKBAR, ANISAH I; BRONX, NY; BRONX SCH OF LAW & FINANCE; (SO); Hnr Roll; St of Mnth; ArtClub; Jr Ach; Latin Clb; Ch Chr; Tennis (L); Secretary of the Latin / Roman Club; Won Second Place in a Mock Trial Tournament - 2005; Journalist/Writer or Business Lawyer; Major in Journalism and the Arts or Business Law; Smith College; Grambling State

AKHTAR, RUBENA; BRONX, NY; MARBLE HILL HS; (FR); Hi Hnr Roll; New York U; Princeton U

AKHUEMOKHAN, AKHERE; BRONX, NY; DEWITT CLINTON HS; (JR); Hi Hnr Roll; Hnr Roll; MVP; Perf Att; Sci Fairs; Comm Volntr; Chrch Yth Grp; Bnd; SP/M/VS; Bskball (V); Ftball (V); Track (V); Wrstlg (V); Stu Cncl (V); Audio Engineering; Dentistry; Binghamton U (SUNY); Alfred U/Syracuse U

Ahsan, Mohammad Azaz
In 7th Grade Not In Eight Graduate In 2010 Not 2009
Jamaica, NY

Agyemang, Serwaa
Health Opportunities HS
Bronx, NY

Abo-Ali, Ehab M
Razi HS
Elmhurst, NY

Adusei, Samuel K
Beach Channel HS
Arverne, NY

Akhuemokhan, Akhere
DeWitt Clinton HS
Bronx, NY

AKRUWALA, RAJSHI; PT JEFFERSON STATION, NY; COMSEWOGUE HS; (SO); Hi Hnr Roll; Hosp Aide; FBLA; Key Club; Quiz Bowl; Spanish Clb; Tennis - Not with School; Law Club & Wise; MD - Opthamologist; MD - Cardiovascular Anesthesiologist; Columbia U; NYU

AKUAMOA, REYNOLDS; BROOKLYN, NY; MIDWOOD HS; (JR); Hnr Roll; Perf Att; St of Mnth; WWAHSS; Comm Volntr; Ftball (V); Optometry

AKUAMOAH-BOATENG, MAXWELL; SYRACUSE, NY; NOTTINGHAM HS; (SR); Hnr Roll; MVP; Nat Hon Sy; Sci Fairs; Sci/Math Olympn; St of Mnth; WWAHSS; Yth Ldrshp Prog; Comm Volntr; Dbte Team; Sci Clb; Lcrsse (V CL); Pre Medicine; Hamilton College

ALBA, CHERYLL; KEW GARDENS, NY; FRANCIS LEWIS HS; (SO); Hnr Roll; Off Aide; Dnce; Volunteer for Jehovah's Witnesses Organization; Dance Club; Registered Nurse/Doctor; Chef; New York U; Columbia U

ALBA, CRISTINA; BRONX, NY; JOHN F KENNEDY HS; (JR); Ostst Ac Ach Awd; Perf Att; Svce Clb; Regent Review; Student of the Month; At John Jay Criminal Justice; Administrative Assistant; John Jay Criminal of Justice; Fordham U

ALBERT, JENNIFER S; NANUET, NY; IMMACULATE HEART AC; (FR); Hi Hnr Roll; Pres Sch; Valdctrian; CARE; Comm Volntr; DARE; Drma Clb; Quiz Bowl; Sci Clb; Dnce; Orch; SP/M/VS; Cty Talent Search; Fashion Merchandising; Law; Stanford U; Fashion Institute of Technology

ALBERT, VANNA; BROOKLYN, NY; MIDWOOD HS; (SR); Hnr Roll; Pres Sch; Comm Volntr; Peer Tut/Med; Clr Grd; Drl Tm; Track (V); Pianist; Nutrition; Medical Degree; Cornell U

ALBERTO, MARIELA; BROOKLYN, NY; WASHINGTON IRVING HS; (SO); Ctznshp Aw; Hnr Roll; Perf Att; St of Mnth; Peer Tut/Med; Stg Cre; Sftball; CR (P); Become a Teacher; Hunter College

ALCIN, DOMINIQUE; SPRING VALLEY, NY; SPRING VALLEY HS; (FR); WWAHSS; Comm Volntr; Key Club; Dnce; SP/M/VS; Bskball (J); Vsy Clb; Fashion Club; Ladies & Men Club; Pediatric Nurse; Cosmetologist

ALDARONDO, JESSICA; LARCHMONT, NY; MAMARONECK HS; (SO); Chrch Yth Grp; DARE; Chr; Ch Chr; Dnce; SP/M/VS; Sccr (J&V); Track; Travel Soccer team, Play in NY and Out of State / Soccer Ref Cert; Talent Shows, Wrote Song, Choreograph Dances, Sing Solos in Church, Draw Japanese Anime; Math Major / Math Teacher; Computer Animation; SUNY Purchase; Iona College New Rochelle

ALDEN, RACHAEL; ENDICOTT, NY; UNION ENDICOTT HS; (JR); Hi Hnr Roll; Hnr Roll; Perf Att; Pres Ac Ftns Aw; Sci Fairs; Comm Volntr; Chrch Yth Grp; DARE; Key Club; Sci Clb; Spanish Clb; Bnd; Chr; Mch Bnd; SP/M/VS; Stu Cncl (R); Medical; New York U; Penn State

ALDERMAN, SHAUNA; PETERSBURG, NY; BERLIN JR/SR HS; (SO); Ctznshp Aw; Hi Hnr Roll; Hnr Roll; Nat Hon Sy; St of Mnth; DARE; Drma Clb; Prom Com; Scouts; Chr; Chrldg (V); Sccr (J); Girl Scouts; National Honor Society; Interior Design; Arts; Syracuse U; Siena College

ALDI, ANTHONY N; STILLWATER, NY; STILLWATER CTRL HS; (JR); Hi Hnr Roll; Nat Hon Sy; Sci/Math Olympn; WWAHSS; Peer Tut/Med; Emplmnt; Sci Clb; Ftball (J)

ALEJALDRE, JUAN; PT CHESTER, NY; PT CHESTER HS; Ctznshp Aw; Hi Hnr Roll; Hnr Roll; MVP; Nat Hon Sy; Otst Ac Ach Awd; Perf Att; Sci Fairs; Comm Volntr; DARE; Mus Clb; Quiz Bowl; Tech Clb; French Clb; Bnd; Chr; Mch Bnd; SP/M/VS; Cr Ctry (V); Sccr (J); Track (V); Computer / Electrical or Circuit Engineer

ALEXANDER, ALECIA; MT VERNON, NY; MT VERNON HS; (FR); Hnr Roll; Comm Volntr; FCCLA; Scouts; Chr; Swg Chr; Medical; Culinary; New York U; Florida U

ALEXANDER, ALLEN T; NEW HYDE PARK, NY; HERRICKS HS; (SO); Perf Att; Yth Ldrshp Prog; Comm Volntr; Hosp Aide; Chrch Yth Grp; Emplmnt; Lib Aide; Tchrs Aide; Tech Clb; Vsity Clb; CULTURAL CLB; Bnd; Chr; Ch Chr; Mch Bnd; Bskball; Ftball; Mar Art; Adv Cncl; Sch Ppr; Church Youth Activities; Physical Therapy; Master's Degree; Doctorate; Colleges That Provide Physical Therapy

ALEXANDER, AMANDA L; BROOKLYN, NY; BOYS & GIRLS HS; (JR); Hnr Roll; Nat Hon Sy; WWAHSS; Yth Ldrshp Prog; Comm Volntr; Chrch Yth Grp; Off Aide; Ch Chr; Forensic Science; John Jay College

ALEXANDER, AYANNA; NEWBURGH, NY; (SO); Ctznshp Aw; Hi Hnr Roll; Otst Ac Ach Awd; Pres Sch; St of Mnth; Peer Tut/Med; Chrch Yth Grp; DARE; Emplmnt; Mth Clb/Tm; Bnd; Orch; Cr Ctry (J); Yrbk (P); Accounting; Business Management; New York U; Harvard U

ALEXANDER, DYLAN; FALLSBURG, NY; FALLSBURG HS; (JR); Hi Hnr Roll; Hnr Roll; Kwnis Aw; Nat Hon Sy; Nat Ldrshp Svc; Perf Att; Sci/Math Olympn; Yth Ldrshp Prog; Comm Volntr; Peer Tut/Med; Red Cr Aide; DARE; Drma Clb; Emplmnt; FBLA; Key Club; Mth Clb/Tm; NYLC; Prom Com; Mar Art; Skiing (V); Track (V); Wt Lftg; Stu Cncl (R); CR (R); Sch Ppr (E); Second Degree Black Belt; National Honor Society Member; Biology; Medicine

ALEXANDER, MALACHI; BRONX, NY; CELIA CRUZ BRONX HS OF MUSIC; (FR); Hi Hnr Roll; Hnr Roll; Perf Att; Bnd; Computer Graphics; Band; New York U; Duke U

ALEXANDER, SHANNON; EAST AURORA, NY; EAST AURORA HS; (JR); Hnr Roll; Sci/Math Olympn; WWAHSS; Key Club; Mod UN; Sci Clb; Chr; Jzz Bnd; SP/M/VS; Fld Hky (J); Participating Member of Piano Guild; Vocal Performance; Singer; Ithaca College; State U of New York Fredonia

ALEXIS, JEFF; BROOKLYN, NY; CANARSIE HS; (SO); Hosp Aide; Peer Tut/Med; Chrch Yth Grp; Emplmnt; FCA; Fr of Library; Outdrs Clb; Ch Chr; Clr Grd; SP/M/VS; Bskball; Bskball; Ftball; Scr Kpr; To Study Law; Business; St John's U; Syracuse U

ALFORD, TRINESHA; JAMAICA, NY; MAGNET SCH LAW/GOVERN; (FR); Otst Ac Ach Awd; Perf Att; Sci Fairs; St of Mnth; CARE; DARE; Chr; Dnce; Georgetown U

ALGER, KRYSTAL; BOONVILLE, NY; ADIRONDACK HS; (JR); Ctznshp Aw; Hnr Roll; Otst Ac Ach Awd; Emplmnt; Chr; Baby-sit Every Night After School; Construction Management; Architectural Engineering; Clarkson U; Milwaukee School of Engineering

ALI, HASSAN; BRONX, NY; (FR); Hnr Roll; Stu Cncl (V); Being A Doctor & Scientist & Comp.; Lehman College

ALICKAJ, ANITA; YONKERS, NY; SAUNDERS HS; (JR); Hi Hnr Roll; Hnr Roll; Nat Hon Sy; Perf Att; Comm Volntr; Hab For Humty Volntr; Peer Tut/Med; Drma Clb; Key Club; Spch Team; SADD; Dnce; Won a 2nd Place Trophy for Skills USA; Opening & Closing Team; Psychology; Fordham U; Manhattan College

ALIE, AMIL A; JAMAICA, NY; GATEWAY TO HEALTH SCIENCES SCH; (SO); Hnr Roll; Yth Ldrshp Prog; Comm Volntr; Cmptr Clb; Emplmnt; Tech Clb; Stu Cncl (T); CR (R); Sch Ppr (E, P); Selected to Represent Queens Gateway in 2004; Medicine; Doctorate-MD; Columbia U; New York U

ALIMARAS, JUSTIN; OAKLAND GARDENS, NY; BENJAMIN CARDOZO HS; (JR); Hnr Roll; Nat Hon Sy; USAA; WWAHSS; Comm Volntr; Peer Tut/Med; Emplmnt; Key Club; Off Aide; Sci Clb; Secretary, Arista; Black Belt Candidate For Tae Kwon Do

ALIYU, KARIM O; BALDWIN, NY; BALDWIN HS; (SO); Ctznshp Aw; Hnr Roll; Otst Ac Ach Awd; Perf Att; Mus Clb; Sci Clb; Tchrs Aide; Bskball (J); Lcrsse (J); Track (V); Stu Cncl (R); Lyricist-Poetry & Creative Writing; Perfect Attendance / Attendance Room Asst.; Law Degree / Criminal Justice; Adelphi U; NYU

ALLEGRETTO, DAN; ELMIRA, NY; THOMAS A EDISON HS; (JR); Hi Hnr Roll; Jr Rot; Nat Hon Sy; WWAHSS; Key Club; SADD; French Clb; Tennis (V); Cl Off (T); Ski Club; Elmira College Ethics Bowl Winner; NYU; Fordham

ALLEN, BRADLEY; BERKSHIRE, NY; NEWARK VALLEY HS; (JR); Hi Hnr Roll; Hnr Roll; WWAHSS; Emplmnt; Stg Cre; Bsball; Bskball; Ftball; Albany College of Pharmacy

ALLEN, SHANNON; ROCHESTER, NY; JOHN MARSHALL HS; (FR)

ALLER, AMANDA; GLENDALE, NY; CHRIST THE KING HS; (JR); Hi Hnr Roll; Hnr Roll; Perf Att; St of Mnth; WWAHSS; Peer Tut/Med; Drma Clb; Key Club; Spch Team; Chr; SP/M/VS; Tennis (V L); Treasurer / VP of Key Club; Psychology; Film / Production; Hofstra U; SUNY Oneonta

ALLEY, CHRISTINE; LAGRANGEVILLE, NY; ARLINGTON HS; (JR); Hnr Roll; Nat Hon Sy; Hosp Aide; Biology Clb; Chrch Yth Grp; SADD; Bnd; Mch Bnd; Biology; SUNY Stony Brook; Marist College

ALMEIDA, BYANCA; ASTORIA, NY; INTERNATIONAL HS AT LAGUARDIA; (SO); St of Mnth; ArtClub; Drma Clb; Emplmnt; Tech Clb; SP/M/VS; Swmg; CR (R); Sch Ppr (E); Science Medal; Student Government

ALMENDINGER, JULIE A; LANCASTER, NY; LANCASTER HS; (SO); Hnr Roll; Perf Att; Comm Volntr; DECA; Skiing (J); Vllyball (J); Youth Court Volunteer; Health Awareness Volunteer; Master's Degree in Teaching; Elementary School Teacher; U of Buffalo

ALMER, BRIANA K; PLEASANT VALLEY, NY; ARLINGTON HS; MS; Hi Hnr Roll; Nat Hon Sy; Otst Ac Ach Awd; Perf Att; St of Mnth; Comm Volntr; ArtClub; Perf Att; Sci Fairs; Comm Volntr; Jr Ach; Mus Clb; Tchrs Aide; Dnce; Orch; SP/M/VS; Yrbk; Art Shows & Awards; Violin Student for Years; Lawyer; Teacher / Accountant; Marist College; Vassar College

ALONSO, KARLA; FAR ROCKAWAY, NY; BEACH CHANNEL HS; (JR); Ctznshp Aw; Hi Hnr Roll; Hnr Roll; Nat Hon Sy; Otst Ac Ach Awd; Perf Att; St of Mnth; USAA; Valdctrian; Yth Ldrshp Prog; Comm Volntr; Peer Tut/Med; Drma Clb; Emplmnt; Jr Ach; Mus Clb; Photog; Bnd; Chr; Bskball (L); Fld Hky (C); Tennis (L); Vllyball (L); Stu Cncl (R); CR (S)

ALOSI, MERIDEANA; BROOKLYN, NY; SHEEPSHEAD BAY HS; (FR); Chess; P to P St Amb Prg; SP/M/VS; Sch Ppr (R); Artist / Cartooning

ALSTON, DAVID; STILLWATER, NY; STILLWATER CTRL HS; (JR); Hi Hnr Roll; MVP; Otst Ac Ach Awd; Pres Sch; WWAHSS; Comm Volntr; Peer Tut/Med; Emplmnt; Mth Clb/Tm; P to P St Amb Prg; Vsity Clb; Bskball (V CL); Golf (V L); Peer Leader; WAVE Trainer (Working Against Violence Everywhere); Sports Administration/Management; Business; Williams College; Lemoyne College

ALTAMORE, JOSEPH; SHIRLEY, NY; LONGWOOD HS; (SR); Hi Hnr Roll; Hnr Roll; Won National Event in Orlando for Paintbook; Police Officer; School Teacher; John Jay School of Criminal Justice; Suffolk Community College

ALTMAN, ARIEL; FOREST HILLS, NY; AC FOR AMERICAN STUDIES; (SO); Hnr Roll; Comm Volntr; Tmpl Yth Grp; Politician; Lawyer; Binghamton U; Albany U

ALVARADO, JASMINE; WOODHAVEN, NY; FRANCIS LEWIS HS; (SO); F Lan Hn Soc; Hi Hnr Roll; Nat Hon Sy; St of Mnth; Comm Volntr; Key Club; Tchrs Aide; Bdmtn (V); Lit Mag (R); Hispanic Achievement Award; Columbia U; Cornell U

ALVAREZ, PILAR; STATEN ISLAND, NY; CURTIS HS; (JR); Hnr Roll; WWAHSS; Comm Volntr; Peer Tut/Med; Emplmnt; Key Club; Kwanza Clb; Bskball; Vllyball; Wt Lftg; Sch Ppr (E); Key Greeter; Nursing; Hunter College; Kingsborough Community College

ALVORD, ASHLEY N; GREENFLD CTR, NY; NEWPORT HS; (SO); Hi Hnr Roll; Hnr Roll; Otst Ac Ach Awd; Perf Att; St of Mnth; DARE; Drma Clb; Key Club; Scouts; SADD; Chr; Dnce; Publication in Poetry Anthology Book "Sublime Remembrance"; Psychiatry; Music

AMARA, FIONIA; BRONX, NY; HARRY S TRUMAN HS; (JR); Hnr Roll; Perf Att; St of Mnth; USAA; Comm Volntr; Peer Tut/Med; Dbte Team; P to P St Amb Prg; Chr; Dnce; SP/M/VS; Chrldg (J); Yrbk (P); Law Team; Psychology; Hunter College (CUNY); Lehman College

AMATO, GABRIELLA; FRANKLIN SQUARE, NY; H FRANK CAREY HS; (JR); F Lan Hn Soc; Hi Hnr Roll; Nat Hon Sy; Comm Volntr; Peer Tut/Med; SADD; Vsity Clb; Italian Clb; Bnd; Chr; Mch Bnd; Sccr (VJC); Homecoming Queen; Irish-Literature Award; Medical Doctor (Pre-Med); Attorney (Pre-Law); New York U; Columbia U

AMATO, LAUREN N; FAIRPORT, NY; FAIRPORT HS; (JR); Hnr Roll; St of Mnth; WWAHSS; Chrch Yth Grp; Emplmnt; Ch Chr; Tennis (J); Education; Monroe Community College

AMENT, IAN; NEW YORK, NY; ABRAHAM JOSHUA HERSCHEL HS; (SO); Hnr Roll; Comm Volntr; Hosp Aide; English Honors; Medicine/Medical Research; Columbia U

AMES, TASHANNA; BROOKLYN, NY; PAUL ROBESON HS; (SO)

AMINI, ELIZABETH A; NIAGARA FALLS, NY; NIAGARA FALLS HS; (JR); Hnr Roll; Perf Att; Sci Fairs; Comm Volntr; Drma Clb; Emplmnt; Key Club; Mus Clb; Acpl Chr; Chr Chr; SP/M/VS; Bskball (J); Vllyball (J); Yrbk (P); Business Internship; Child Development; Teacher's Degree; Niagara U

AMMAN, IAN; QUEENS VILLAGE, NY; WHITESTONE AC; (SR); WWAHSS; Accounting; Psychology; Molloy College; C W Post

AMOAKO, THERESA; BRONX, NY; RICHARD R GREEN HS; (JR); Hnr Roll; Nat Ldrshp Svc; Perf Att; WWAHSS; Chrch Yth Grp; Sch Ppr; Science / Doctor; U Penn; NYU

AMODEO, COURTNEY; NEW HYDE PARK, NY; GREAT NECK SOUTH HS; (SO); Hi Hnr Roll; Hnr Roll; WWAHSS; Comm Volntr; Key Club; SP/M/VS; Scr Kpr (J); Vllyball (VJ); Peer Aids Educator Club; Communications Degree; Journalism; New York U; Hofstra U

AMUSA, TAWAKALITU; CTRL ISLIP, NY; CTRL ISLIP HS; (JR); Ctznshp Aw; Hnr Roll; Perf Att; St of Mnth; Yth Ldrshp Prog; Comm Volntr; Hab For Humty Volntr; Peer Tut/Med; BPA; DARE; FBLA; Vsity Clb; Chr; Dnce; Stg Cre; Chrldg (V); Vsy Clb (V); Stu Cncl (R); CR (R); Sch Ppr (E); Medical Field; Pre-Law; Cornell U; Buffalo U

AMY, DAPHNE M; FARMINGVILLE, NY; SACHEM HS EAST; (SO); Sci/Math Olympn; Chrch Yth Grp; Pep Squd; P to P St Amb Prg; Ch Chr; Dnce; Swmg; Dance Trophy; Singing Award; 50 Zigzag Relay Ribbon

AN, SARAH; FRESH MEADOWS, NY; THE BRONX HS OF SCIENCE; (SO); Comm Volntr; Key Club; Bnd; Spanish; Smith College

ANASA, MICHELLE S; LITTLE NECK, NY; BENJAMIN CARDOZO HS; (SO); Hnr Roll; Perf Att; Comm Volntr; Chrch Yth Grp; Key Club; Tennis (V); Forensic Medicine; Psychiatry

ANBINDER, DAVID; BROOKLYN, NY; LEON M GOLDSTEIN HS SCIENCES; (SO); Hi Hnr Roll; Hnr Roll; MVP; Perf Att; Sci Fairs; WWAHSS; Hosp Aide; Chess; Sci Clb; Vsity Clb; Tennis (V C); Volunteer At a Hospital; Won 3rd Place in Junior Division Tournament in Tennis; Medicine; Psychology; Cornell U; New York U

An, Sarah — The Bronx HS Of Science — Fresh Meadows, NY
Alvord, Ashley N — Newport HS — Greenfld Ctr, NY
Alongi, Briana K — Arlington HS — Pleasant Valley, NY
Alexander, Ayanna — Newburgh, NY
Alcin, Dominique — Spring Valley HS — Spring Valley, NY
National Honor Roll Spring 2005
Alberto, Mariela — Washington Irving HS — Brooklyn, NY
Alexis, Jeff — Canarsie HS — Brooklyn, NY
Altamore, Joseph — Longwood HS — Shirley, NY
Amara, Fionia — Harry S Truman HS — Bronx, NY
Amato, Gabriella — H Frank Carey HS — Franklin Square, NY

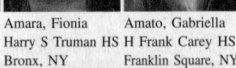

ANDERSEN, LAUREN E; BLUE POINT, NY; BAYPORT BLUE POINT HS; (SO); Hi Hnr Roll; Hnr Roll; Nat Sci Aw; St of Mnth; Comm Volntr; Mus Clb; Orch; SP/M/VS; Lcrsse (J); Tennis (J); Track (J); Cl Off (T); Lit Mag (R); Concert Orchestra, Best in Class Math Award; National Junior Honor Society; Child Education Teacher; Columbia U

ANDERSON, ANDRE; SPRINGFIELD GARDENS, NY; QUEENS HS FOR THE SCIENCES; (SO); Hnr Roll; Valdctrian; FBLA; Mth Clb/Tm; Sci Clb; Chr; Sch Ppr (E); Astronomy Club; Medicine; Biology; Columbia U; New York U

ANDERSON, DORRANT; BRONX, NY; COLUMBUS HS; (FR); Lawyer; Law Enforcement; John Jay College of Criminal Justice; New York U

ANDERSON, JAMIE L; EAST AURORA, NY; EAST AURORA HS; (SR); Hi Hnr Roll; Hnr Roll; Otst Ac Ach Awd; WWAHSS; Yth Ldrshp Prog; Amnsty Intl; Comm Volntr; Peer Tut/Med; DARE; DECA; Emplmnt; NYLC; Svce Clb; SADD; Lit Mag (R); Yrbk (P); National Student Leadership Conference; Youth Leadership Erie County; Child Psychologist; Psychology; St Bonaventure U; Denison U

ANDERSON, JASON; ROCKVILLE CENTRE, NY; MALVERNE HS; (JR); Hnr Roll; Perf Att; Comm Volntr; DARE; Emplmnt; Bnd; Ftball (V); Track; Wt Lftg; Mechanical Engineering; Aerospace Engineering; U of Southern California; Drexel U

ANDERSON, KATRINA; BUFFALO, NY; MC KINLEY VOC TECH HS; (FR); Perf Att; Cmptr Clb; ROTC; Dnce; Bskball (J); Dance; Dental; Clark Academy

ANDERSON, LANDEL; BRONX, NY; HARRY S TRUMAN HS; (JR); Hnr Roll; Working; Pre-Law; Lawyer; Howard U; Siena College

ANDERSON, LATASHA N; BROOKLYN, NY; BENJAMIN BANNEKER AC; (FR); Hnr Roll; Salutrn; Sci Fairs; St of Mnth; Valdctrian; Peer Tut/Med; Dbte Team; Mth Clb/Tm; Dnce; Sch Ppr; 14 Double Dutch Trophies; 2 Story Telling/Speech Trophies; Cryptology - Code Breaking; Chemistry - Medicine / Pediatrician; Norfolk State; Hampton U

ANDRE, JENNIFER; WEST HAVERSTRAW, NY; NORTH ROCKLAND HS; (FR); Hnr Roll; MVP; Perf Att; Sci Fairs; St of Mnth; Peer Tut/Med; Chrch Yth Grp; DARE; Drma Clb; FTA; ROTC; Scouts; Bnd; Ch Chr; Clr Grd; Dnce; Gmnstcs; Scr Kpr; Track; Vllyball; Stu Cncl (R); CR (R); RN; Ob/Gyn-Doctor; Westchester U; St. Dominique

ANDREWS, SHANNA L; DUNDEE, NY; DUNDEE CTRL SCH; (SR); Hi Hnr Roll; MVP; Nat Hon Sy; Perf Att; Pres Sch; Salutrn; St of Mnth; WWAHSS; Comm Volntr; AL Aux Girls; Drma Clb; Bnd; Chr; Mch Bnd; SP/M/VS; Sccr (V C); Track (V); Cl Off (T); Stu Cncl (P); Bowling; All County Band & Chorus; Physical Therapy; Ithaca College

ANKUMAR, SEEMA; HOLLISWOOD, NY; TOWNSEND HARRIS HS; (JR); All Am Sch; Ctznshp Aw; F Lan Hn Soc; Hnr Roll; Nat Hon Sy; Otst Ac Ach Awd; Perf Att; Salutrn; Sci Fairs; St Schl; Comm Volntr; Peer Tut/Med; Mth Clb/Tm; MuAlphaTh; Tchrs Aide; Chr; Dnce; Pre-Med

ANNABI, SAMIRA; EAST ELMHURST, NY; TOWNSEND HARRIS HS; (SR); Hnr Roll; Nat Hon Sy; Nat Mrt LOC; Otst Ac Ach Awd; Perf Att; WWAHSS; Comm Volntr; Hosp Aide; Peer Tut/Med; Chess; Emplmnt; Off Aide; Tchrs Aide; SP/M/VS; Bskball (V); Vllyball (J); CR (R); Lit Mag (E); Sch Ppr (R); New York State Science Honor Society Inductee; National Ventures Scholar; Pre-Medicine Major; Biochemistry Major; Sophie Davis School of Biomedical Education; New York U

ANTHONY, RASHIDA A; BROOKLYN, NY; JOHN DEWEY HS; (JR); Hnr Roll; Nat Hon Sy; Otst Ac Ach Awd; Perf Att; WWAHSS; Yth Ldrshp Prog; Comm Volntr; Peer Tut/Med; Chess; Chrch Yth Grp; DARE; Emplmnt; Jr Ach; Ntl Beta Clb; Off Aide; Tchrs Aide; Bnd; Ch Chr; Dnce; Stg Cre; CR (R); Academy of Finance; Pre-Med/Biology; Dance; U of Maryland; U of Pennsylvania

ANTIPENKO, CHRISTINA; STATEN ISLAND, NY; SUSAN E WAGNER HS; (SO); Hnr Roll; Nat Hon Sy; Sci Fairs; Hosp Aide; Tchrs Aide; Russian Clb; Dentist; Orthodontist; New York U; Columbia U

ANTOINE, CHANTE; FREEPORT, NY; FREEPORT HS; (JR); Hi Hnr Roll; Hnr Roll; Nat Hon Sy; Otst Ac Ach Awd; Chrch Yth Grp; Journalism; Social Work

ANTOUN, MIRA; YONKERS, NY; CHARLESE GORTON HS; (JR); Hi Hnr Roll; Hnr Roll; Perf Att; WWAHSS; Comm Volntr; Red Cr Aide; Emplmnt; Quiz Bowl; French Clb; Sccr (VJ); Sch Ppr (R); Yrbk (P); Active Member of Community Wellness Center; Completed Many College Courses; Pre-Med; Pharmacy; New York U; St John's U

ANUSZEWSKI, HEATHER R; SALEM, NY; GREENWICH CTRL SCH; (JR); Hnr Roll; Pres Ac Ftns Aw; Pres Sch; St of Mnth; WWAHSS; ArtClub; DARE; Emplmnt; Lttrmn Clb; Mus Clb; Prom Com; SADD; Vsity Clb; Chr; Tennis (V); Wt Lftg (V); Prom Committee; Fundraising Committee; Pre-Med; Pediatrician/Nursing; Clarkson U; SUNY Schools

AQUILINA, COURTNEY R; STONY BROOK, NY; WARD MELVILLE HS; (SO); F Lan Hn Soc; Hi Hnr Roll; Nat Hon Sy; Comm Volntr; Chrch Yth Grp; Drma Clb; Mus Clb; Scouts; Bnd; Chr; Ch Chr; Jzz Bnd; Cr Ctry (J); Stu Cncl (R); NYSSMA-Piano Clarinet, Vocal Solo; Chamber Choir-9th Grade; Brown U

AQUINO, JOSE; FREEPORT, NY; FREEPORT HS; (JR); Hnr Roll; Comm Volntr; Science Research Class; Engineering; Technician in Cars; Nassau Community College

ARACENA, ANDRES A; NEW YORK, NY; SEWARD PARK HS; (JR); F Lan Hn Soc; Hnr Roll; Otst Ac Ach Awd; Perf Att; St Optmst of Yr; Comm Volntr; Hab For Humty Volntr; ArtClub; Jr Ach; Schol Bwl; Sci Clb; Tech Clb; Flg Crps; Bsball (J); CR (R); Law Related Field; Design Art; John Jay College; Hunter College

ARAUJO, KATHERINE; EAST MEADOW, NY; EAST MEADOW HS; (SO); Hnr Roll; Salutrn; Sci Fairs; Sci/Math Olympn; WWAHSS; Comm Volntr; Chrch Yth Grp; Dbte Team; Drma Clb; Key Club; Bnd; Mch Bnd; SP/M/VS; Stg Cre; Tennis (J); World Hunger Action Club; Children's Theatre; Medicine; Law; New York U; Pennsylvania State U

ARCHER, DANIEL; COLD SPRING, NY; HALDANE SCH; (JR); Hi Hnr Roll; Nat Hon Sy; WWAHSS; Drma Clb; Emplmnt; Chr; SP/M/VS; Stg Cre; Lit Mag (R); International Club Member; Mentoring Program Member; Creative Writing; English; Carnegie Mellon U; SUNY Purchase

ARCHETTO, BIANCA; BROOKLYN, NY; ST EDMUND PREP HS; (JR); Hnr Roll; Sci Fairs; Prom Com; Scouts; Foreign Clb; Bskball (J); Chrldg (JC); Working Part Time; Business Management; Business of Fashion; Adelphi College; Delhi

ARCOS, MARIA; NEW YORK, NY; HS FOR MEDIA & COMMUNICATIONS; (SR); Jr Eng Tech; US Army Sch Ath Aw; WWAHSS; Comm Volntr; Hab For Humty Volntr; Peer Tut/Med; ArtClub; Chrch Yth Grp; Cmptr Clb; Fr of Library; Mth Clb/Tm; Mus Clb; Prom Com; ROTC; Dnce; Drl Tm; Bskball (J); Sccr (J); Sftball (J); Vllyball (J); Wt Lftg (J); Yrbk (P); Attended to JROTC; Helping the Counselor; Architecture; Technology in Graphics; City College; Queensborough

ARENA, NANCY D; BRONX, NY; BX HS OF LAW AND COMM SER; (FR); Hnr Roll; Otst Ac Ach Awd; Perf Att; Sci Fairs; Criminal Justice; Politics; Harvard U; Princeton U

ARGENNA, KAYLEE; MOUNT MORRIS, NY; LIMA CHRISTIAN SCH; (SO); Hi Hnr Roll; Pres Ac Ftns Aw; Drma Clb; Emplmnt; Bnd; Chr; Jzz Bnd; Mch Bnd; Bskball (J); Sccr (V); Cl Off (R); 16 Community Theater Plays; Music/Voice; Houghton; Kansas State

ARGJENDARI, OLSI; BROOKLYN, NY; FORT HAMILTON HS; (SR); Hnr Roll; Nat Hon Sy; Otst Ac Ach Awd; Sci Fairs; St of Mnth; Comm Volntr; Peer Tut/Med; Chess; Cmptr Clb; Mth Clb/Tm; Sci Clb; Vsity Clb; Vllyball (V); Sch Ppr (R); Finalist in 2002 Japan Society History Day Competition; Polytechnic U Principal's Scholar Certificate; Biological Sciences; Biochemistry; Columbia U; New York U

ARJUNE, RICKY; BRONX, NY; LOUIS D BRANDEIS HS; (SO); Hnr Roll; Health

ARMES, ELIZABETH; HAMLIN, NY; BROCKPORT HS; (FR); Hi Hnr Roll; Hnr Roll; Sci Fairs; Comm Volntr; Chrch Yth Grp; Emplmnt; Outdrs Clb; Tchrs Aide; Bnd; Dnce; Mch Bnd; Sccr (J); Education; Counselor / Psychologist; SUNY Geneseo; SUNY Fredonia

ARMIJO, HEATHER M; BYRON, NY; NOTRE DAME HS; (JR); Ctznshp Aw; Hi Hnr Roll; Nat Hon Sy; St Schl; WWAHSS; Comm Volntr; Drma Clb; SADD; Chr; Dnce; SP/M/VS; Sccr (V L); Yrbk (P); Dance Scholarship; Scholar Athlete; Theatre; Theology; Fordham U; Northeastern U in Boston

ARNONE, JAMES; MERRICK, NY; CALHOUN HS; (JR); F Lan Hn Soc; Hnr Roll; Nat Hon Sy; WWAHSS; Comm Volntr; Peer Tut/Med; Emplmnt; Key Club; Mus Clb; Sci Clb; Bnd; Jzz Bnd; Mch Bnd; Pep Bnd; Cr Ctry (VJ L); Rlr Hky (J); Track (VJ L); All-County Band

ARROYO PENA, QUEMUEL; NEW YORK, NY; BRONX EXPEDITIONARY LEARNING; (FR); Ctznshp Aw; Fut Prb Slvr; Hnr Roll; Otst Ac Ach Awd; Perf Att; Comm Volntr; Peer Tut/Med; ArtClub; Dbte Team; Emplmnt; Mth Clb/Tm; Outdrs Clb; Tech Clb; Stu Cncl (P); CR (P); Sch Ppr (E); Yrbk (R); Newspaper Club - First Editor; Intern at Merrill Lynch; Business / Finance; Marine Biology; Cornell U; Yale U

ARTIS, NADJA M; BUFFALO, NY; CLEVELAND HILL HS; (SR); Hnr Roll; Nat Hon Sy; Comm Volntr; Peer Tut/Med; Chrch Yth Grp; Emplmnt; Chr; Ch Chr; Dnce; SP/M/VS; Peer Mediation; Diversity Club; Clinical Psychology / PhD; Canisius College; SUNY Buffalo

ASARE, KINGSFORD; BRONX, NY; MARBLE HILL HS FOR INTERNATIONAL STUDIES; (FR); Hnr Roll; Perf Att; Dbte Team; Drma Clb; Mod UN; SP/M/VS; Medicals

ASH, CAITLIN E; STRYKERSVILLE, NY; HOLLAND HS; (JR); 4H Awd; Hi Hnr Roll; Hnr Roll; Otst Ac Ach Awd; Pres Ac Ftns Aw; St of Mnth; WWAHSS; Comm Volntr; Red Cr Aide; 4-H; Drma Clb; Key Club; Photog; Acpl Chr; Chr; Ch Chr; Dnce; Stu Cncl; Veterinary Technician (Technology); Medville College

ASHFORD, THERESA; WATERTOWN, NY; WATERTOWN HS; (FR); Hnr Roll; Pres Sch; Peer Tut/Med; Chrch Yth Grp; Key Club; Bnd; Chr; Ch Chr; SP/M/VS; Vllyball (J); NYSMAA Vocal & Instrumental; Music Education; Choral Directing

ASHLAW, VALERIE; SODUS, NY; SODUS JR/SR HS; (SO); Hi Hnr Roll; Hnr Roll; Sci Fairs; St of Mnth; Comm Volntr; DARE; SADD; Bnd; Chr; Mch Bnd; Pep Bnd; Select Choir; All-County Choir; Nursing; Music Therapy; Nazareth; Fredonia

ASHLINE, TANNER; WILLSBORO, NY; WILLSBORO CTRL SCH; (FR); Hnr Roll; Nat Hon Sy; Spanish Clb

ASHRAF, SUFIA; EAST MEADOW, NY; EAST MEADOW HS; (FR); 4H Awd; Ctznshp Aw; Hi Hnr Roll; Hnr Roll; Otst Ac Ach Awd; Perf Att; Pres Sch; Sci Fairs; Sci/Math Olympn; St of Mnth; WWAHSS; Comm Volntr; Peer Tut/Med; FBLA; Key Club; Mth Clb/Tm; Sci Clb; Tennis (J); Track (J); Sch Ppr (R); Honorary Mention From The Math Teams; Honorary Recognition From Toshiba Exploravision; Studying Medicine; Cardiologist; Yale U; Brown U

ASIF, NABEEL; STATEN ISLAND, NY; PT RICHMOND HS; (SR); Hi Hnr Roll; Nat Hon Sy; Sci/Math Olympn; Comm Volntr; DARE; Math Olympiads - Spring 2002; Toast Masters; Accounting; Business Management; Baruch College; Pace U

ASIGHIERI, STEPHANIE; SEAFORD, NY; SEAFORD HS; (SR); Hi Hnr Roll; Hnr Roll; WWAHSS; Comm Volntr; Emplmnt; Key Club; Mth Clb/Tm; Mus Clb; SADD; Chr; Yrbk (E); Graphic Design; Dowling College

ASTACIO, DARLENE; BRONX, NY; HEALTH OPPORTUNITIES HS; (FR); Hnr Roll; Nat Hon Sy; Nat Ldrshp Svc; Otst Ac Ach Awd; Perf Att; Yth Ldrshp Prog; NYLC; Bsball (V); Tennis (V); Vllyball (V); Medical College / Doctor

ASUQUO-ASANG, NSEMEKE; BRONX, NY; EVANDER CHILDS HS; (JR); Hnr Roll; Perf Att; Comm Volntr; Chrch Yth Grp; Ch Chr; Gmnstcs; Sccr; Vllyball; Principal's Honor Roll; Perfect Attendance; Engineering; Columbia U, New York; New York U

ATEHORTUA, CAROL S; ASTORIA, NY; HILLCREST HS; Hi Hnr Roll; Hnr Roll; Nat Hon Sy; Sci Fairs; St of Mnth; Peer Tut/Med; DARE; Emplmnt; Fr of Library; Photog; SADD; Bnd; Chr; Flg Crps; Stg Cre; Sftball (L); Vllyball (J); Adv Cncl (R); Stu Cncl (V); CR (T); Yrbk (R, P); Arista Member; Student Government Leader; Ancient Languages; Egyptologist; Brown U; Wellesley U

ATHANASIOU, VICKY; WHITESTONE, NY; ST FRANCIS PREP HS; (JR); Hnr Roll; MVP; Otst Ac Ach Awd; Perf Att; St of Mnth; St Optmst of Yr; Comm Volntr; Drma Clb; Greek Clb; Dnce; Bskball; Gmnstcs; Mar Art; Sccr; Swmg; Track; Stu Cncl (P); Piano-The Sports Listed Above Are Not Part Of School But In Another League; Pharmacy; Psychology; New York U; St John's U

ATKINSON, DEVAUGHN; NEW YORK, NY; RICE HS; (SR); Hi Hnr Roll; Hnr Roll; WWAHSS; Comm Volntr; Peer Tut/Med; Emplmnt; Off Aide; Bskball (J); Office Worker in the Congressional Democratic Party - Fall 2004 / City Councilman - Fall 2003; Volunteer at Maxwell Day Care - Summer 2004 / Toys For Tots - Christmas 2003; Business Management; SUNY New Paltz

ATTONITO, PAIGE; ELMONT, NY; SEWONHAKA HS; (JR); Hi Hnr Roll; Hnr Roll; MVP; Nat Hon Sy; St of Mnth; WWAHSS; FBLA; Key Club; Mod UN; Mus Clb; SADD; Bnd; Jzz Bnd; Mch Bnd; Stg Cre; Bskball (J); Lcrsse (V); Sccr (VJ); Stu Cncl (P, V, R); CR (R); Sch Ppr (E, R, P); Yrbk (R)

ATZROTT, JOSH; BUFFALO, NY; CLEVELAND HILL HS; (SO); Hnr Roll; Chess; Ftball (J); Swmg (V); Track (J); Scholar Athlete; Architect; Engineer; U of Buffalo; Canisius College

AU, KARMEN; BROOKLYN, NY; BRONX HS OF SCIENCE; (SO); Hi Hnr Roll; Sci/Math Olympn; St of Mnth; Comm Volntr; Red Cr Aide; Key Club; Cardiologist; Cornell U; Carnegie Mellon

AUBRECHT, AMY; EAST AURORA, NY; NARDIN AC; (JR); Hnr Roll; Otst Ac Ach Awd; St of Mnth; WWAHSS; Peer Tut/Med; Emplmnt; Mth Clb/Tm; Outdrs Clb; Prom Com; Scouts; Bskball (J); Lcrsse (J); Skiing (V); Cl Off (P); Volunteer At Lothlorien Therapeutic Riding CRT; Altar Server At Church; Education; Communications; Cornell U; College of William & Mary

AUGUSTE, MOLLIE; SPRING VALLEY, NY; WALDWICK SDA SCH; (JR); Ctznshp Aw; Hi Hnr Roll; Hnr Roll; Otst Ac Ach Awd; St of Mnth; Comm Volntr; Peer Tut/Med; Chrch Yth Grp; Off Aide; French Clb; Ch Chr; Orch; Stu Cncl (V, T); Yrbk (R); Pre-Medicine; New York U; Columbia U

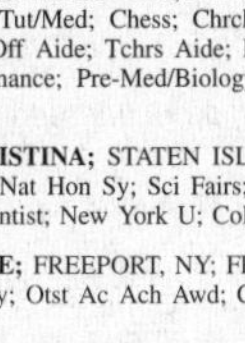

Asif, Nabeel
Pt Richmond HS
Staten Island, NY

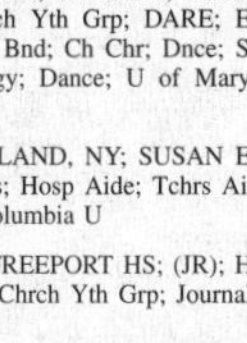

Archetto, Bianca
St Edmund Prep HS
Brooklyn, NY

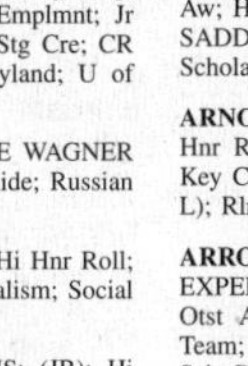

Antoun, Mira
Charlese Gorton HS
Yonkers, NY

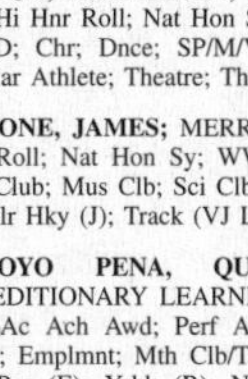

Antoine, Chante
Freeport HS
Freeport, NY

National
Honor Roll
Spring 2005

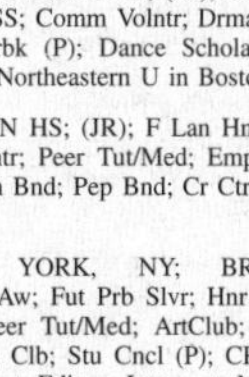

Antipenko, Christina
Susan E Wagner HS
Staten Island, NY

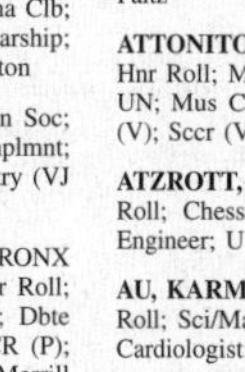

Aquilina, Courtney R
Ward Melville HS
Stony Brook, NY

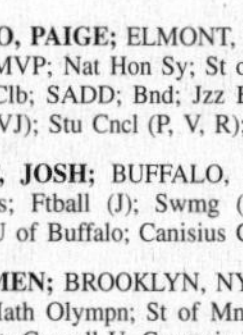

Asare, Kingsford
Marble Hill HS For International Studies
Bronx, NY

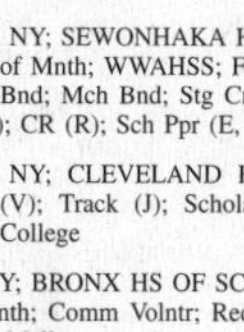

Asuquo-Asang, Nsemeke
Evander Childs HS
Bronx, NY

AUGUSTIN, PRINCESS M; BROOKLYN, NY; PAUL ROBESON HS; (SO); Hnr Roll; Otst Ac Ach Awd; Pres Sch; FBLA; Mth Clb/Tm; Mus Clb; Chr; Adv Cncl (P); Cl Off (V); Stu Cncl (P); CR (T); Business Administration; Accounting; UC Berkeley

AULETTA, REGINA; BROOKLYN, NY; ST EDMUND PREP HS; (JR); Gov Hnr Prg; Hnr Roll; Pres Sch; Emplmnt; Bowling

AUQUI, KATHERINE; NEW YORK, NY; LOUIS D BRANDEIS HS; (JR); Hnr Roll; St of Mnth; Comm Volntr; Dnce; Global Teacher / Master's Degree; Doctor; City College; John Jay

AURICCHIO, AIMEE; CAMDEN, NY; CAMDEN HS; (SO); Hnr Roll; ArtClub; Cr Ctry (V); Track (V); Auto-Body Repair; Pathologist; Mohawk Valley Community College

AUSTIN, ARICA M; FREEPORT, NY; FREEPORT HS; (JR); Hi Hnr Roll; Nat Hon Sy; Pres Sch; St of Mnth; WWAHSS; Yth Ldrshp Prog; Comm Volntr; Chrch Yth Grp; DECA; Emplmnt; SADD; Chr; Ch Chr; Dnce; Bdmtn (V); Track (V); Vllyball (V); Medicine; Crime Scene Investigator; New York U; Stony Brook

AVERY, GILLIAN; WHITESTONE, NY; ARCHBISHOP MOLLOY; (JR); Comm Volntr; NYLC; SADD; Italian Clb; Yrbk (R); Varsity Basketball Team: Manager; International Studies; History; American U; Drew U

AVERY, LORI; BROOKLYN, NY; NEW UTRECHT HS; (JR); Hnr Roll; Sci Fairs; Lib Aide; Social Work; Hunter College; College of Staten Island

AVETSIUK, PIETRO; UTICA, NY; THOMAS R PROCTOR HS; (FR); 4H Awd; Hi Hnr Roll; Nat Hon Sy; Perf Att; St of Mnth; Comm Volntr; 4-H; Chrch Yth Grp; DARE; Scouts; Ch Chr; Young Scholars; Artist; Illustrator; Mohawk Valley Community College; Utica College

AVILES, JOHN; ROCKAWAY PARK, NY; ST EDMUND PREP HS; (SO); Hnr Roll; Bskball (J); Computer Engineering; U of Connecticut; Rutgers U

AVRUSEVICH, NADEZHDA; UTICA, NY; THOMAS R PROCTOR HS; (SO); Hi Hnr Roll; Hnr Roll; Otst Ac Ach Awd; Perf Att; St of Mnth; Ch Chr; Tennis; Physician; Physiotherapist

AYEO, KIMBERLY; YONKERS, NY; MARIA REGINA HS; (SO); Hi Hnr Roll; Drma Clb; Key Club; Dnce; SP/M/VS; Sch Ppr (R); Pre-Med; Biology; New York U; Hofstra U

AYLSWORTH, JENNIFER L; CORFU, NY; PEMBROKE JR/SR HS; (JR); Hnr Roll; WWAHSS; Peer Tut/Med; FTA; Key Club; Tchrs Aide; German Clb; Secretary of Future Teachers of America; Accounting; Business Management; SUNY Brockport; Clarkson U

AYOOB, NILAB; LITTLE NECK, NY; BENJAMIN CARDOZO HS; (FR); Hnr Roll; WWAHSS; Key Club; Off Aide; Dnce; Participated in Mock Trial Semi-Finals; International Club (Middle-Eastern); Medicine; Liberal Arts; New York U

AYOUB, HUSSEIN; ASTORIA, NY; BACCALAUREATE SCH; (FR); Stu Cncl (V); CR (V); Pre-Med; Medicine MD; Saint John's U; New York U

AZIZ, ASAD; LITTLE NECK, NY; BENJAMIN CARDOZO HS; (JR); Hnr Roll; German Clb; Bnd; Orch; Biology; History; New York U; Stony Brook U

AZOR, STEWART A; ARVERNE, NY; CHRIST THE KING HS; (JR); 4H Awd; Ctznshp Aw; Hi Hnr Roll; Hnr Roll; Kwnis Aw; Otst Ac Ach Awd; Perf Att; St of Mnth; WWAHSS; Comm Volntr; 4-H; ArtClub; Chrch Yth Grp; Cmptr Clb; DARE; Emplmnt; FBLA; Jr Ach; Bsball (VJ); Scr Kpr (J); Sftball (J); Track (V); Vllyball (J); Lit Mag (E, R, P); Sch Ppr (E, R, P); Academic Achievement Award; 5 Time Silver Honor Roll List; Communications; Sports Management; St John's U

BABUSHKIN, ANTON; BROOKLYN, NY; LAGUARDIA ARTS HS; (JR); F Lan Hn Soc; Hi Hnr Roll; Hnr Roll; Nat Hon Sy; Otst Ac Ach Awd; Sci Fairs; St of Mnth; Comm Volntr; Peer Tut/Med; Cmptr Clb; DARE; Dbte Team; Drma Clb; Emplmnt; Off Aide; Svce Clb; Tchrs Aide; Bnd; Jzz Bnd; Orch; SP/M/VS; Bskball (V L); Mar Art; Vllyball (V CL); COC 1st Place Forms Winner 3x in a Row; Participant in Around Long Island Regatta '04; Pre-Medicine/Biology; Music-Masters; SUNY College At Geneseo; Cornell U

BACK, MELODIE; WOODSIDE, NY; QUEENS HS FOR SCIENCES AT YORK; (FR); Hnr Roll; Nat Hon Sy; Perf Att; Comm Volntr; Chrch Yth Grp; Key Club; Mth Clb/Tm; Photog; Tchrs Aide; Bnd; Dnce; Jzz Bnd; Psychology; Sociology; Brown U; Sophie Davis School

BACON, TRACI; MASSENA, NY; MASSENA SR HS; (SO); F Lan Hn Soc; Hi Hnr Roll; MVP; Nat Hon Sy; Otst Ac Ach Awd; Perf Att; Pres Ac Ftns Aw; St Schl; St of Mnth; Comm Volntr; Peer Tut/Med; DARE; Lib Aide; Off Aide; Prom Com; Spanish Clb; Bnd; Mch Bnd; Pep Bnd; SP/M/VS; Bskball (V L); Sccr (V L); Sftball (J); Track (V L); Stu Cncl (R); Yrbk (P); Physical Therapist

BADAL, CHAYA; BROOKLYN, NY; AUGUST MARTIN HS; (SO); Hnr Roll; Nat Hon Sy; Otst Ac Ach Awd; Perf Att; Comm Volntr; Key Club; Dnce; SP/M/VS; Business; Communications

BADALI, SALVATORE J; STATEN ISLAND, NY; ADELPHI AC; (SO); Hnr Roll; Sci Fairs; WWAHSS; Dbte Team; Emplmnt; Photog; Tech Clb; Bnd; Stg Cre; Rlr Hky (J); Yrbk (P); Dean's List; Computer Science; 3-D Graphics Design; Wagner College; College of Staten Island

BADAMI, ROSILLA G; NEW PALTZ, NY; OAKWOOD FRIENDS SCH; (JR); Hi Hnr Roll; Hnr Roll; MVP; Perf Att; Sci Fairs; Comm Volntr; Hab For Humty Volntr; Peer Tut/Med; DARE; Emplmnt; Photog; Bnd; Chr; Dnce; Jzz Bnd; Bsball (J); Bskball (V); Sftball (VJC); Vllyball (V C); 5 Logged Flying Hours At Embry Riddle Summer Camp; Aeronautical Sciences; Aeronautical Engineering; Embry Riddle Aeronautical U; Daniel Webster College

BADGLEY, NICOLE L; JAMESTOWN, NY; JAMESTOWN HS; (FR); Hnr Roll; ArtClub; Intramural Lacrosse (Girls); Psychology; Forensics; Cornell

BADIA, LEONARDO; NEW YORK, NY; MANHATTAN CTR FOR SCIENCE AND MATH; (SR); Hnr Roll; Peer Tut/Med; Emplmnt; Outdrs Clb; Svce Clb; U of Vermont

BAGCHI, ATRISH; BROOKLYN, NY; STUYVESANT HS; (JR); Kwnis Aw; Nat Hon Sy; Nat Mrt LOC; Nat Mrt Semif; WWAHSS; Comm Volntr; Peer Tut/Med; Drma Clb; Key Club; Mod UN; Svce Clb; Bnd; Chr; SP/M/VS; Adv Cncl (R); CR (R); Lit Mag (R); Sch Ppr (R); Key Club Lt. Governor; Multicultural Queen Allies Secretary; Medicine, Physics; Comparative Literature; Yale U; Brown U

BAGUE, SAMANTHA N; SYRACUSE, NY; HENNINGER HS; (JR); Hnr Roll; Pre-Medicine; Criminal Justice; Buffalo State U; St. John Fisher

BAI, LAURA Y; HOLTSVILLE, NY; (JR); F Lan Hn Soc; Hnr Roll; Nat Hon Sy; Pres Sch; Sci/Math Olympn; St of Mnth; WWAHSS; Comm Volntr; Peer Tut/Med; ArtClub; Sci Clb; French Clb; Dnce; Orch; Lit Mag (E); NYSSMA Level 6 A+/Associated Board of Royal School of Music; American Chemical Society Award; College Professor; Massachusetts Institute of Technology; Cornell U

BAIDO, EDWIN L A; BROOKLYN, NY; ERASMUS HALL HS; (SR); Hnr Roll; Nat Hon Sy; Otst Ac Ach Awd; Perf Att; Sci Fairs; WWAHSS; Comm Volntr; Chess; Cmptr Clb; Off Aide; Adv Cncl (R); Stu Cncl (R); Sch Ppr (R); Yrbk (R); Crochet Club; Mentor Club; Mathematician; Pediatrician Cardiologist; SUNY-Stony Brook U; New York U

BAILEY, CHANTEL; WYANDANCH, NY; HALF HOLLOW HILLS HS; (FR); Hi Hnr Roll; Hnr Roll; Perf Att; Sci Fairs; Sci/Math Olympn; Comm Volntr; Peer Tut/Med; Spec Olymp Vol; Cmptr Clb; DARE; Scouts; French Clb; Ch Chr; Dnce; Orch; SP/M/VS; Chrldg (J); Track (J); Poetry Club / Girl Scout Silver Award; 2nd Place in French Competition / Principal's Award; Medical Research & Development; Doctorial Degree in Medicine; Harvard U; Stanford U

BAILEY, EMILY; ALLEGANY, NY; ALLEGANY-LIMESTONE CTRAL; (SR); 4H Awd; Hi Hnr Roll; Hnr Roll; Nat Hon Sy; Otst Ac Ach Awd; WWAHSS; Yth Ldrshp Prog; Comm Volntr; Peer Tut/Med; 4-H; Chr; SP/M/VS; Hsbk Rdg; Yrbk (R); Bowling County Champions; Level 1 Parelli Natural Horse-Man-Ship Certified; Veterinarian / DVM; Riding Stable and Horse Trainer; U of Findlay

BAILEY, TRALINA; ITHACA, NY; ITHACA HS; (JR); Hi Hnr Roll; Hnr Roll; Comm Volntr; Peer Tut/Med; Emplmnt; Dnce; Track (J); Champion of the Month @ Work KFC; Volunteer Work in the Community; Business Management; Johnson & Wales U; Syracuse U

BAINS, JASLEEN K; PHOENIX, NY; C W BAKER HS; (JR); Hi Hnr Roll; Nat Hon Sy; Otst Ac Ach Awd; WWAHSS; Amnsty Intl; Hab For Humty Volntr; Emplmnt; Key Club; Vsity Clb; Orch; Golf (V); Mar Art; 1st Degree Black Belt in Karate; Played for Syracuse Symphony Youth String Orchestra; Architecture; Interior Design; Cornell U; Syracuse U

BAIRD, MEGAN E; NEW HAMPTON, NY; MINISINK VALLEY HS; (JR); Hnr Roll; MVP; Pres Ac Ftns Aw; St of Mnth; Key Club; Lib Aide; Mod UN; Vsity Clb; Cr Ctry (V); Track (V); Vsy Clb (V); OCIAA High Jump-1st Place

BAISDEN-FOLKES, AKEEM; STATEN ISLAND, NY; FIORELLO H LA GUARDIA HS; (SO); Hnr Roll; Nat Sci Aw; Sci Fairs; Valdctrian; WWAHSS; Drma Clb; Dnce; Stg Cre; I Was a Volunteer At Brooklyn Public Library; PhD in Psychology and Mental Health Studies; Minor in the Theatrical Arts; New York U; U of Pennsylvania

BAJAJ, NEHA; GARNERVILLE, NY; NORTH ROCKLAND HS; (JR); Hi Hnr Roll; Hnr Roll; Nat Hon Sy; WWAHSS; Comm Volntr; Peer Tut/Med; Key Club; MuAlphaTh; Quiz Bowl; Svce Clb; Cr Ctry (J); Track (J); Dental Major; Business Minor; Stony Brook U

BAJJAJ, ALI; WEST HEMPSTEAD, NY; MALVERNE HS; (JR); Hi Hnr Roll; Hnr Roll; MVP; Nat Hon Sy; St of Mnth; WWAHSS; Amnsty Intl; Comm Volntr; Cmptr Clb; Mod UN; Quiz Bowl; Arabic Clb; Lcrsse (V); Sccr (V C); Track (V C); Computer Systems Analysis; Farmingdale State College

BAKER, AMY M; LISBON, NY; MADRID-WADDINGTON CTRL SCH; (SO); 4H Awd; 4-H; Chrch Yth Grp; Dbte Team; Drma Clb; Emplmnt; Key Club; Spch Team; Spanish Clb; Bnd; Mch Bnd; Stg Cre; Hsbk Rdg (V); Dairy Court - Candidate for Princess; Mock Trial; Lawyer; Radiologist; North Country Community College

BAKER, DAWN; MIDDLETOWN, NY; MIDDLETOWN HS; (JR); Hnr Roll; MVP; Otst Ac Ach Awd; Sci Fairs; St of Mnth; Peer Tut/Med; ArtClub; DARE; Drma Clb; Emplmnt; Prom Com; Tchrs Aide; Bnd; Dnce; SP/M/VS; Bskball (J); PP Ftbl (VJ); Physical Therapy; Social Worker / Working With People / Children

BAKER, KELSEY; HAMMONDSPORT, NY; HAVERLING HS; (JR); Hi Hnr Roll; Jr Rot; Otst Ac Ach Awd; Pres Sch; Peer Tut/Med; Red Cr Aide; P to P St Amb Prg; French Clb; Hsbk Rdg; Mar Art; Skiing; Swmg (V CL); Tennis; President of Rotary Club; Major in Pre-Med; Minor in Sociology; Binghamton U; U At Buffalo

BAKER, VALERIE R; OAKFIELD, NY; OAKFIELD-ALABAMA JR/SR HS; MS; Hi Hnr Roll; Perf Att; Pres Sch; Sci Fairs; Mth Clb/Tm; Chr; Sccr (C); Sftball (J); Honorable Mention in Science Fair; Real Estate

BAKERT MICELI, ADREANA C; ROCKAWAY PARK, NY; BIRCH WATHEN LENOX SCH; (JR); Ctznshp Aw; Hi Hnr Roll; MVP; Otst Ac Ach Awd; Comm Volntr; Hab For Humty Volntr; Peer Tut/Med; ArtClub; Dbte Team; Emplmnt; Prom Com; Svce Clb; Vsity Clb; Dnce; Bskball (V); Track (V); Vllyball (V L); Yrbk (E); Avid Community Service; W/The 92nd St. 4 Over 100 Hrs.; Architecture; Medicine; UW Madison; Brown

BALBI, YESFANIN; NEW YORK, NY; A PHILIP RANDOLPH HS; (SR); Hnr Roll; WWAHSS; Comm Volntr; Chrch Yth Grp; Off Aide; Tchrs Aide; Stg Cre; Sch Ppr (R); Yrbk (R); Advertising; Hotel Management; Syracuse U; Lehigh U

BALDE, IBRAHIMA; BRONX, NY; BRONX AEROSPACE AC; (JR); Hi Hnr Roll; Hnr Roll; Perf Att; Comm Volntr; Peer Tut/Med; Mod UN; Outdrs Clb; ROTC; Sci Clb; Vsity Clb; Drl Tm; Sccr (V); Stu Cncl (R); Sch Ppr (R); Anti-Deformation League Peer Tutor / Summer Leadership Instructor; Astronomy; Aerospace Engineering; Columbia U; Staten Island College

BALDUZZI, KARA; SYRACUSE, NY; SOLVAY HS; (SR); DAR; Hi Hnr Roll; Hnr Roll; Nat Hon Sy; Otst Ac Ach Awd; WWAHSS; Comm Volntr; ArtClub; Emplmnt; Key Club; Off Aide; Photog; Italian Clb; Track (V); Stu Cncl (V, T); Yrbk (R); Member of Ski Club; President of Key Club; Pharmacy; Northeastern U

BALIDEMAJ, DAFINA; BRONX, NY; ST RAYMOND HS; (JR); Bnd; Clr Grd; Drl Tm; Mch Bnd; CR (V); Pro-Life; Amnesty International; Fordham U; St Lawrence U

BALL, BRADLEY; WILLSBORO, NY; WILLSBORO CTRL SCH; (FR); Hi Hnr Roll; Hnr Roll; Kwnis Aw; Nat Hon Sy; WWAHSS; Comm Volntr; Peer Tut/Med; DARE; Tchrs Aide; Spanish Clb; Bnd; Bsball (J); Sccr (J); Vice President of National Junior Honor Society; High School Science Teacher

BALL, JACQUELINE M; SAUGERTIES, NY; SAUGERTIES HS; (SR); Hi Hnr Roll; Nat Hon Sy; Valdctrian; WWAHSS; Comm Volntr; Emplmnt; Key Club; Mth Clb/Tm; SP/M/VS; Lcrsse (V C); Sccr (VJ); Track (V); NY State Scholar Athlete

BANG, JOOWON; FRESH MEADOWS, NY; BENJAMIN CARDOZO HS; (FR); Hnr Roll; Otst Ac Ach Awd; Perf Att; Sci Fairs; Comm Volntr; Peer Tut/Med; Key Club; Mth Clb/Tm; SP/M/VS; Performance in Annual Piano Concerts Since '00; Honors on AME Math Tests; Medical Degree; Biology Major; Columbia U; Princeton U

BANKER, MICHELE; OZONE PARK, NY; CHRIST THE KING HS; (JR); Nat Hon Sy; Sci Fairs; WWAHSS; Yth Ldrshp Prog; Peer Tut/Med; Dbte Team; Drma Clb; Emplmnt; Sci Clb; Spch Team; SP/M/VS; Humane Society Award; Major in Secondary Education; Psychology; St Joseph's; St John's U

BAPTISTE, JENNELLE C; BROOKLYN, NY; MIDWOOD HS; (JR); Hnr Roll; Perf Att; Valdctrian; Comm Volntr; Key Club; Svce Clb; Chr; Sch Ppr (R); Arista Honor Society, Participated in Angel Tree Foundation Prison-Ministry at Church; Film Club / Ventures Scholar; Pharmacy; Chemistry; Rutgers U; Columbia U

BAPTISTE, RENEE S; ROOSEVELT, NY; ROOSEVELT HS; (FR); Ctznshp Aw; Hnr Roll; Sci Fairs; Spec Olymp Vol; Dnce; Drl Tm; Fashion Design; Psychology; Fashion Institute of Design & Merchandise

BAQUE, EDUARDO A; BROOKLYN, NY; JAMES MADISON HS; (SO); Peer Tut/Med; Bnd; Stg Cre; Ftball (J); Wt Lftg (J); Business Administration; Brooklyn College; NYU

BARAHAT, AHMAD; BROOKLYN, NY; SHEEPSHEAD BAY HS; (SO); Comm Volntr; Stg Cre; Criminal Justice; Police Officer; John Jay College

BARATTO, LAUREN E; LATHAM, NY; SHAKER HS; (SO); Hi Hnr Roll; Hnr Roll; Otst Ac Ach Awd; Perf Att; St of Mnth; Comm Volntr; Hosp Aide; Key Club; Cr Ctry (J); Track (J); Global & Humanities May Student of the Month; Communications; Journalism; Northeastern College Boston

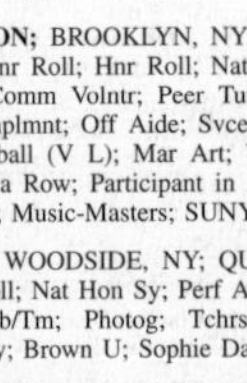
Bailey, Emily
Allegany-Limestone Ctrl
Allegany, NY

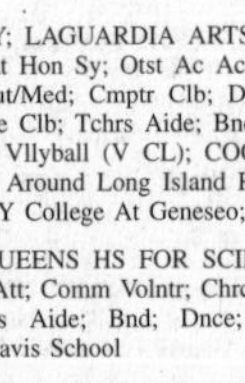
Bague, Samantha N
Henninger HS
Syracuse, NY

Badami, Rosilla G
Oakwood Friends Sch
New Paltz, NY

Badali, Salvatore J
Adelphi AC
Staten Island, NY

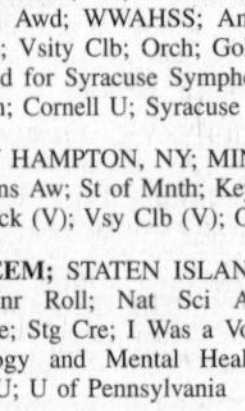
Aviles, John
St Edmund Prep HS
Rockaway Park, NY

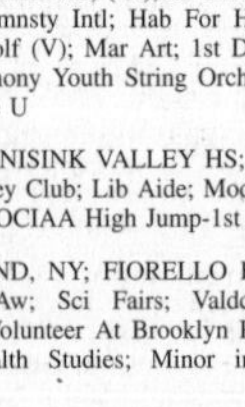
Badal, Chaya
August Martin HS
Brooklyn, NY

Badgley, Nicole L
Jamestown HS
Jamestown, NY

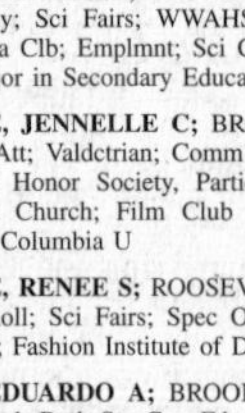
Bailey, Chantel
Half Hollow Hills HS
Wyandanch, NY

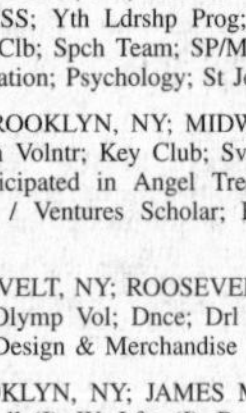
Bains, Jasleen K
C W Baker HS
Phoenix, NY

BARBER, MARK; TICONDEROGA, NY; TICONDEROGA HS; (JR); Hi Hnr Roll; Perf Att; Sci Fairs; St of Mnth; Comm Volntr; Peer Tut/Med; Red Cr Aide; Drma Clb; Emplmnt; Key Club; Outdrs Clb; French Clb; Bnd; Chr; Jzz Bnd; SP/M/VS; Cr Ctry (V); Track (V); Stu Cncl (R); Yrbk (P); Newspaper Carrier of the Month; Student Intern of the Month; Medical; U of Rochester, Rochester, New York; U of Albany, Albany, New York

BARBOUTEV, ILIA; WALLKILL, NY; WALLKILL HS; (SO); Hnr Roll; Emplmnt; Tennis (V); Lit Mag (E); Law

BARCENA, JOSE; BRONX, NY; DEWITT CLINTON HS; (JR); Ctznshp Aw; Hnr Roll; Nat Hon Sy; Otst Ac Ach Awd; Salutrn; St of Mnth; WWAHSS; Comm Volntr; Peer Tut/Med; Tchrs Aide; National Society of High School Scholars; Membership to Aspira; Engineering; Economics; Yale U; Stanford U

BARLOW, CORI D; BUFFALO, NY; WEST SENECA EAST SR HS; (FR); Perf Att; Comm Volntr; Chrch Yth Grp; DARE; Key Club; Scouts; Girl Scout Silver Award; Fashion Design; Art

BARNAS, KARA; HOLLAND, NY; HOLLAND HS; (FR); Hi Hnr Roll; WWAHSS; Chrch Yth Grp; Key Club; Lib Aide; Chr; Ch Chr; Fncg (J); Fld Hky (J); Varsity Bowling; Pre-Law; Canisius College

BARNETT, ARIC A; MOHAWK, NY; JARVIS HS; (JR); Ctznshp Aw; Hi Hnr Roll; Hnr Roll; Nat Hon Sy; Nat Ldrshp Svc; Perf Att; USAA; Comm Volntr; FBLA; French Clb; Bnd; Adv Cncl (R); Cl Off (V); Stu Cncl (R); Founder/Organizer of MHS Gay Straight Alliance; National Honor Society; Sociology; Boston U

BARNETT, TIMOTHY T; SCIO, NY; SCIO CTRL SCH; (SO); Hnr Roll; DARE; Computer

BARONE, KARLA; LITTLE FALLS, NY; LITTLE FALLS HS; (FR); Hnr Roll; Bnd; Fld Hky (J); Sftball (V); Stu Cncl (R); Magazine Journalism; Public Relations; New York U; Hofstra U

BARONE, KRISTY M; ELMIRA HTS, NY; THOMAS A EDISON HS; (SO); Hi Hnr Roll; Hnr Roll; Key Club; Chr; Clr Grd; Teacher

BARONE, MARGARET A; HUNTINGTON, NY; HUNTINGTON HS; (FR); Hi Hnr Roll; Otst Ac Ach Awd; Pres Ac Ftns Aw; Hab For Humty Volntr; Spec Olymp Vol; Emplmnt; Svce Clb; Tchrs Aide; Bnd; Jzz Bnd; Mch Bnd; Crew-Varsity Coxswain; Drummer in Rock Band, St. John's U Women in Science Award; Law; Government

BARRANCOTTA, DANIEL; LOCKPORT, NY; LOCKPORT HS; (SO); Hi Hnr Roll; MVP; Otst Ac Ach Awd; Perf Att; Pres Sch; WWAHSS; Comm Volntr; Peer Tut/Med; Jr Ach; Tchrs Aide; Vsity Clb; Bsball (JC); Ftball (JC); Golf; Ice Hky (V); Rlr Hky; Swmg; Wt Lftg (J); Niagara County Youth Court; Criminal Justice; Secondary Education; SUNY Fredonia; SUNY Buffalo

BARRATT, RAECHEL E; LAWTONS, NY; NORTH COLLINS HS; (SR); Hnr Roll; Nat Hon Sy; Perf Att; St of Mnth; WWAHSS; Comm Volntr; Peer Tut/Med; Biology Clb; Chrch Yth Grp; Emplmnt; Photog; Tchrs Aide; Vsity Clb; Spanish Clb; Bnd; SP/M/VS; Bskball (J); Sccr (VJCL); Vsy Clb (V); Cl Off (V); Stu Cncl (R); Yrbk; First Team All-Star Soccer, AP Courses; Scholastic Achievement Award; Major in Biology; Canisius College

BARRETT, AKEETA; JAMAICA, NY; BISHOP LOUGHLIN MEMORIAL HS; (SR); WWAHSS; Peer Tut/Med; ArtClub; Bskball (V); Forensic; Corrections; Temple U; John Jay

BARRETT, JESSICA; STATEN ISLAND, NY; NEW DORP HS; (SO); Hnr Roll; Otst Ac Ach Awd; St of Mnth; Drma Clb; HO'Br Yth Ldrshp; SP/M/VS; Vllyball (V); CR (R); Sch Ppr (R); Business; Psychology; Baruch College; UC Berkeley

BARRIE, FATOUMATA K; BRONX, NY; EVANDER CHILDS HS; (SO); F Lan Hn Soc; Hnr Roll; Otst Ac Ach Awd; Perf Att; ArtClub; Fr of Library; Mus Clb; Communication (News on TAP); Lawyer

BARRY, CHRISTINA; WEST ISLIP, NY; WEST ISLIP HS; (JR); Hi Hnr Roll; Otst Ac Ach Awd; St of Mnth; WWAHSS; Yth Ldrshp Prog; Peer Tut/Med; Spec Olymp Vol; Emplmnt; Mth Clb/Tm; NYLC; Outdrs Clb; Prom Com; Lcrsse (VJC); Sccr (J); Track (V); Cl Off (V); Yrbk (E); Student of the Month in Chemistry and English; National Honors Society; Pre-Med; Doctorate

BARTHELEMY, JONATHAN; NORTH BABYLON, NY; HALF HOLLOW HILLS EAST; (SR); Hi Hnr Roll; Hnr Roll; MVP; St Schl; WWAHSS; Comm Volntr; Spec Olymp Vol; FBLA; Key Club; Vsity Clb; Spanish Clb; Chr; Bskball (J); Sccr (V); Track (V); County Champion in Track; Scholar Athlete Award; Pre-Med; Penn State U Altoona

BARTHELEMY, PASCALE; NEW CITY, NY; PARAMUS CATHOLIC HS; (JR); Hi Hnr Roll; Hnr Roll; Nat Mrt Fin; Nat Mrt LOC; Comm Volntr; Hosp Aide; Biology Clb; P to P St Amb Prg; Clb; Tennis (J); Pharmacy; Biology; State U of New York At Stony Brook; St. Johns U-Penn State U

BARTLEY, ASHA A; MIDDLETOWN, NY; PINE BUSH HS; (JR); Ctznshp Aw; Hi Hnr Roll; Hnr Roll; Nat Hon Sy; Otst Ac Ach Awd; Perf Att; Peer Tut/Med; Chrch Yth Grp; Drma Clb; Photog; Sch Ppr (R, P); Internship @ American Museum of Natural History; Journalism; Acting and Directing/ Theatre; Temple U; Penn State U

BARTMAN, NATHAN; AMSTERDAM, NY; AMSTERDAM HS; (JR); Hi Hnr Roll; Nat Hon Sy; Otst Ac Ach Awd; Comm Volntr; Peer Tut/Med; 4-H; Chrch Yth Grp; HO'Br Yth Ldrshp; P to P St Amb Prg; Quiz Bowl; SADD; Tech Clb; Jzz Bnd; Cr Ctry (V); Track (V); Stu Cncl (R); Captain of School Envirothon Team; Peer Leadership; Exercise Physiology

BARTOLUCCI, ERIKA M; GREENWICH, NY; GREENWICH CTRL HS; (JR); 4H Awd; Hi Hnr Roll; Hnr Roll; Nat Hon Sy; Otst Ac Ach Awd; WWAHSS; Comm Volntr; 4-H; ArtClub; Emplmnt; FCCLA; Chr; Chrldg (V L); Math Education

BARTON, ANNAMARIA; AUBURN, NY; AREA OCCUPATIONAL CTR; (JR); Hi Hnr Roll; Hnr Roll; Sci Fairs; St of Mnth; Prom Com; Scouts; Chr; Vllyball (JC); CR (R); Sch Ppr (R); Yrbk (P); Skills USA; Business Management; Administrative Assistant; Morrisville; Bryant & Stratton College

BARTUMIOLI, DIANA N; GREENLAWN, NY; ST ANTHONY'S HS; (JR); Hnr Roll; Nat Hon Sy; Comm Volntr; Peer Tut/Med; Emplmnt; Svce Clb; Dnce; Chrldg (J); Cr Ctry (J); Skiing; Sccr; Track (J); Duns Scotus Award (2 Years); National Honor Society Member; Business Marketing; Pre-Medical or Forensics; Fordham U; Loyola College of Maryland

BASCHNAGEL, BRETT M; SAUGERTIES, NY; SAUGERTIES HS; (JR); Hi Hnr Roll; Nat Hon Sy; Otst Ac Ach Awd; Comm Volntr; AL Aux Boys; Emplmnt; Key Club; Prom Com; Vsity Clb; Chr; Bsball (V CL); Mar Art; Cl Off (R); Morris Salkino Earth Science Award; MHAL Sports Scholar; Physical Therapy; U of Buffalo; U of Connecticut

BASS, ROBERT K; DIX HILLS, NY; HALF HOLLOW HILLS HS EAST; (JR); Hi Hnr Roll; Nat Hon Sy; Nat Stu Ath Day Aw; WWAHSS; Comm Volntr; Spec Olymp Vol; Key Club; Bsball (V L); Track (V L); Vllyball (J L); Key Club-Vice President; Spanish Honor Society; Architecture

BASSETT, ASHLEE; WHITEHALL, NY; WHITEHALL JR SR HS; (SO); Ctznshp Aw; Hi Hnr Roll; Hnr Roll; MVP; Nat Hon Sy; Nat Stu Ath Day Aw; WWAHSS; Yth Ldrshp Prog; CARE; Comm Volntr; Hosp Aide; ArtClub; Chrch Yth Grp; DARE; Drma Clb; Fr of Library; Lib Aide; Scouts; Tchrs Aide; Bnd; Chr; Mch Bnd; SP/M/VS; Bsball (VJ); Bskball (VJ); Chrldg (VJ); PPSqd (J); Scr Kpr (J); Sccr (J); Sftball (VJ); Track (J); Cl Off (T); Stu Cncl (R); CR (R); Drama; Criminal Justice; Adirondack Community College

BASTEDO, AMANDA M; MASSENA, NY; MASSENA SR HS; (SO); Hnr Roll; St of Mnth; Comm Volntr; French Clb; Sccr (J); Track (J); Played Hockey in 7th Grade / Most Improved UB Upward Bound 2004; Outstanding Student in State History / Current Events; Science / Math Major; Albany College of Pharmacy; Albany U

BASTIEN JR, FRED; MASSAPEQUA PARK, NY; AMES-MASSAPEQUA HS; (FR); Hi Hnr Roll; WWAHSS; Comm Volntr; ArtClub; Key Club; French Clb; Psychology; Biology; Harvard University; Princeton

BATAILLE, MERRY; ROSEDALE, NY;; Hnr Roll; Otst Ac Ach Awd; Perf Att; St of Mnth; Peer Tut/Med; Chrch Yth Grp; Drma Clb; Fr of Library; Mus Clb; Tchrs Aide; Chr; Dnce; SP/M/VS; Bskball; Scr Kpr; Vllyball; CR; Yrbk; Singing; Dancing Acting; Doctor; Basketball; Harvard, Princeton

BATES, ALLYSON S; DELANSON, NY; BERNE KNOX JR/SR HS; (FR); Hnr Roll; 4-H; Bnd; Chr; Bskball (J); Sccr (J); Track (V); Eric Stempel Soccer Award

BATTAGLIA, SARAH; ORCHARD PARK, NY; ORCHARD PARK HS; (SO); Hnr Roll; MVP; Otst Ac Ach Awd; Comm Volntr; Photog; Vllyball (JCL); Yrbk (R); U of Buffalo

BAUER, KATHERINE; BUFFALO, NY; WEST SENECA EAST SR HS; (SO); Hnr Roll; Perf Att; St of Mnth; WWAHSS; Comm Volntr; ArtClub; Key Club; Sci Clb; Vsity Clb; Cr Ctry (V L); GAA (V); Track (V); CR (R); Yrbk (P); Black Belt in Tae Kwon Do

BAUMGARTNER, AMANDA; CAMILLUS, NY; WEST GENESEE HS; (SR); Hi Hnr Roll; Nat Hon Sy; Nat Mrt Sch Recip; Comm Volntr; DARE; Emplmnt; Orch; Hsbk Rdg; Skiing; Bowling Team-2 varsity Letters; Equine Science; SUNY Morrisville; Cazenovia College

BAXTER, THERESA; BRONX, NY; HARRY S TRUMAN HS; (JR); Dnce; Pediatrician (Doctor)

BAYONA, JULIA; NEW YORK, NY; BROOKLYN TECH HS; (JR); Hnr Roll; CARE; Comm Volntr; Ntl Beta Clb; Orch; Juilliard's Music Advancement Program Graduate; Young Reviewers for the Best Children's Books

BAYRAMOVA, MARINA; LIVERPOOL, NY; LIVERPOOL HS; (SO); Hnr Roll; WWAHSS; Comm Volntr; Peer Tut/Med; ArtClub; Chrldg (V); Yoga, Art Club, Global Exchange Club; Psychologist; Interior Designer

BEAM, JENNIFER; SILVER CREEK, NY; SILVER CREEK HS; (SR); Hi Hnr Roll; Hnr Roll; Nat Hon Sy; WWAHSS; Comm Volntr; Emplmnt; Key Club; Mus Clb; Prom Com; SADD; French Clb; Bnd; Chr; SP/M/VS; Stu Cncl (P); Key Club Lt Governor; President of Video Yearbook; U of Albany

BEAMON, SHATINA R; BROOKLYN, NY; METROPOLITAN CORPORATE AC; (SR); Ctznshp Aw; Hnr Roll; Nat Ldrshp Svc; Nat Mrt Sch Recip; Nat Sci Aw; Otst Ac Ach Awd; St of Mnth; USAA; Yth Ldrshp Prog; Comm Volntr; Emplmnt; Jr Ach; Prom Com; Stu Cncl; Yrbk (E, R, P); Consistency in Academic Performance Award; Semi-Finalist - JP Morgan Chase Scholarship; Communications - Radio & Television; Business - Promotions & Marketing; Clark Atlanta U; SUNY Albany

BEARD, DAVID; COLD SPRING, NY; (JR); Ctznshp Aw; MVP; Nat Hon Sy; Nat Stu Ath Day Aw; Pres Ac Ftns Aw; St of Mnth; Red Cr Aide; Bnd; Ftball (V L); Lcrsse (V L); Wrstlg (V L); Fly Helicopters for Coast Guard; US Coast Guard Ac

BEARD, SONJA; WALLKILL, NY; WALLKILL SR HS; (JR); Hi Hnr Roll; Nat Hon Sy; Otst Ac Ach Awd; Comm Volntr; Chrch Yth Grp; Drma Clb; Mth Clb/Tm; Bnd; Jzz Bnd; SP/M/VS; Stg Cre; Teen Leader in Youth Group; Doctorate in Music Education; Jazz Doctorate; SUNY Fredonia; Ithaca College

BEARDSLEY, KAYLA; DALTON, NY; KESHEQUA MIDDLE HS; (MS); Hi Hnr Roll; MVP; Nat Hon Sy; Otst Ac Ach Awd; Chr; Bskball (C); Sccr (C); Sftball (L); Nursing; Photography; Syracuse U; Houghton College

BEATRICE, TESS; SAUGERTIES, NY; SAUGERTIES HS; (FR); Hi Hnr Roll; Otst Ac Ach Awd; Key Club; Spanish Clb; Chr; Tennis (V); Teaching; Music; Brown U; Berklee School of Music

BEATRICE, TYLER; SAUGERTIES, NY; SAUGERTIES HS; (JR); Hnr Roll; Nat Hon Sy; Chess; Key Club; Chr; SP/M/VS; Lcrsse (V); Tennis (V); Music; Berklee College of Music; Hampshire

BEATTY, TIAVISHA; MT VERNON, NY; MT VERNON HS; (FR); Hi Hnr Roll; Hnr Roll; Nat Hon Sy; Sci/Math Olympn; Chr; National Junior Honor Society; Lawyer

BEAUBRUN, MIKERONALD; SPRING VALLEY, NY; NEW YORK MILITARY AC; (JR); Hnr Roll; MVP; Perf Att; Yth Ldrshp Prog; Comm Volntr; DARE; Quiz Bowl; ROTC; Scouts; Spanish Clb; Clr Grd; Drl Tm; Bskball (V L); Ftball (V CL); Track (V CL); CR (P); National Youth Leadership Forum on Medicine; Sports Medicine; Orthopedist; Penn State U; Eastern Pennsylvania College

BEAUDOIN, KEVIN; MASSENA, NY; MASSENA CTRL HS; (FR); Hnr Roll; Scouts; Mch Bnd; Pep Bnd; Wrstlg (V); Computer Engineer

BEAUDOIN, MATTHEW; CHEEKTOWAGA, NY; EAST SR WEST SENECA HS; (SO); Kwnis Aw; Key Club; SP/M/VS; Stg Cre; Mechanic & Detail; Wyo Tech

BEAVERS, ANGELA T; ROME, NY; ROME FREE AC; (SO); Hnr Roll; Nat Hon Sy; Nat Sci Aw; Nat Stu Ath Day Aw; Perf Att; Sci Fairs; St of Mnth; WWAHSS; Red Cr Aide; Chrch Yth Grp; DARE; Emplmnt; Lib Aide; P to P St Amb Prg; ROTC; Ch Chr; Drl Tm; Orch; Bskball; Sccr; Track (V); Vllyball; CR (R); Lit Mag (E); Black History Club; Step Team; Gynecologist; Syracuse U; Princeton U

BECERRA, MICHELLE A; WEST HEMPSTEAD, NY; CATHEDRAL HS; (JR); Comm Volntr; Peer Tut/Med; Emplmnt; Vllyball (V); Town Swim Team; Traveling Soccer Team; Pre-Law Major; Psychology Minor; Hawaii OH U; Florida State U

BECHARD, BRIANNE; QUEENSBURY, NY; LAKE GEORGE HS; (SO); Hi Hnr Roll; Perf Att; Key Club; Bnd; Bskball (JC); Fld Hky (V L)

BECHARD, JESSICA; ROUSES POINT, NY; NORTHEASTERN CLINTON CTRL SCH; (JR); Hi Hnr Roll; Nat Hon Sy; WWAHSS; Drma Clb; Key Club; Mod UN; Quiz Bowl; Scouts; Cr Ctry (V); Track (V); Church Lector; Girl Scouts Silver Award; Literature; Linguistics; Harvard U; Columbia U

BECHOR, SARRAH; QUEENS VILLAGE, NY; FRANCIS LEWIS HS; (JR); Hi Hnr Roll; Hnr Roll; WWAHSS; Off Aide; Photog; Tmpl Yth Grp; Hebrew Clb; Swmg (V); Sch Ppr (R, P); Semi-finalist in Bayer/National Science Foundation Award; Writer; Journalism; New York U; Fordham U

BECKER, KALEIGH K; LAKE PLACID, NY; NORTHWOOD SCH; (SR); Hnr Roll; Nat Hon Sy; WWAHSS; CARE; Emplmnt; Prom Com; Tchrs Aide; Cr Ctry (V L); Ice Hky (V L); Swmg (V L); CR (R); Yrbk (E); Resident Assistant; Communications; Government; Lake Forest; Quinnipiac U

BECKER, LAURA A; ELMIRA, NY; WAVERLY JR/SR HS; (SR); Jr Rot; Nat Hon Sy; WWAHSS; Comm Volntr; Prom Com; Bnd; Mch Bnd; Vllyball (VJCL); Who's Who Among American High School Students for 2 Yrs; Physical Therapy; Graphic Design; Daemen College

BECKERMAN, BERNARD M; NEW YORK, NY; FIORELLO H LA GUARDIA HS; (SR); Nat Mrt Fin; Nat Mrt Semif; Otst Ac Ach Awd; Sci/ Math Olympn; Peer Tut/Med; Chess; Mth Clb/Tm; Mus Clb; Bnd; Jzz Bnd; Mathematics; Music-Jazz; New York U

Beard, Sonja
Wallkill SR HS
Wallkill, NY

Bastien Jr, Fred
Ames-Massapequa HS
Massapequa Park, NY

Bartumioli, Diana N
St Anthony's HS
Greenlawn, NY

Barthelemy, Pascale
Paramus Catholic HS
New City, NY

National
Honor Roll
Spring 2005

Barone, Kristy M
Thomas A Edison HS
Elmira Hts, NY

Bass, Robert K
Half Hollow Hills HS East
Dix Hills, NY

Beam, Jennifer
Silver Creek HS
Silver Creek, NY

Beavers, Angela T
Rome Free AC
Rome, NY

BECKFORD, NATASHA; ROSEDALE, NY; FRANCIS LEWIS HS; (JR); Hnr Roll; Comm Volntr; Drma Clb; Dnce; Pediatrics, Performing Arts; Miami U; Florida State U

BECKLEY, AMY E; LIBERTY, NY; LIBERTY HS; (JR); Hi Hnr Roll; Hnr Roll; Comm Volntr; 4-H; Emplmnt; Scouts; SP/M/VS; Stg Cre; Animal Husbandry; Arts; Pratt Institute; SUNY Delhi

BECKSTEAD, RYAN D; GARDEN CITY, NY; GARDEN CITY HS; (FR); Hi Hnr Roll; Comm Volntr; FBLA; Key Club; Bskball (J L); Sccr (J L)

BECKTOLD, AMBER; GLEN COVE, NY; GLEN COVE HS; (JR); Hi Hnr Roll; Nat Hon Sy; WWAHSS; Comm Volntr; Dbte Team; DECA; Drma Clb; Emplmnt; Key Club; Pep Squd; Prom Com; SP/M/VS; Stg Cre; Scr Kpr (V); Tennis (C); Yrbk (E); Peer Aids Club; Plastic Surgeon; Business; New York U

BEDDOE, NARISSA; SOUTH OZONE PARK, NY; BENJAMIN N CARDOZO HS; (JR); Nat Hon Sy; Sci Fairs; WWAHSS; Comm Volntr; Peer Tut/Med; Chrch Yth Grp; Emplmnt; Tchrs Aide; Ch Chr; Youth Leader Council Member (Presbyterian); Editor's Choice Award from PoetryCom; Child Psychology; Physical Therapist; New York U; Queens College

BEDELL, RACHEL A; OWEGO, NY; OWEGO FREE AC; (SR); Hi Hnr Roll; WWAHSS; Chrch Yth Grp; Emplmnt; Key Club; Chr; Hsbk Rdg; Sccr; Youth Group Helper; Elementary Education Teacher; Liberty U

BEESON, CHRYSTAL; SOUTH OZONE PARK, NY; FLUSHING HS; (JR); Perf Att; Sci Fairs; St of Mnth; Yth Ldrshp Prog; Red Cr Aide; Chrch Yth Grp; Bnd; Dnce; SP/M/VS; Swmg (V); Track (V); I Plan to Work in the Field of Forensic Science; Become a Professional Actor; John Jay Criminal Justice; Hampton U

BEGEAL, MATTHEW; NORTHVILLE, NY; WELLS CTRL SCH; (JR); Hi Hnr Roll; Hnr Roll; MVP; Nat Hon Sy; Pres Ac Ftns Aw; Bsball (V L); Bskball (V CL); Sccr (V CL); Cl Off (V); Stu Cncl

BEGHO, ITSE; SPRNGFLD GDNS, NY; COLLEGIATE SCH; (SO); Cr Ctry (V L); Track (V L); Medicine; Law; Yale U; Duke U

BEGUM, AKHI; BROOKLYN, NY; NEW UTRECHT HS; (JR); Hnr Roll; Otst Ac Ach Awd; Perf Att; Yth Ldrshp Prog; Comm Volntr; DARE; Fr of Library; SADD; Tchrs Aide; URDU Clb; Dnce; SP/M/VS; Physical Therapist; LIU-Long Island U

BEGUM, NILUFA; ASTORIA, NY; AL-MADINAH SCH; (JR); Fut Prb Slvr; Hi Hnr Roll; Hnr Roll; MVP; Otst Ac Ach Awd; Sci Fairs; St of Mnth; St Optmst of Yr; WWAHSS; Yth Ldrshp Prog; Hab For Humty Volntr; Hosp Aide; Peer Tut/Med; ArtClub; Dbte Team; Drma Clb; Mth Clb/Tm; Mus Clb; Off Aide; Spch Team; BANGLA Clb; Chr; Dnce; SP/M/VS; Stg Cre; Bdmtn (J); Bskball (J); GAA (V); Ice Sktg (J); Mar Art (V); Track (C); Vllyball (V); Wrstlg (V); Stu Cncl (P); Sch Ppr (E); 1st Place Winner of School Wide Speech Camp; Lead Singer of High School; Medical Field; Journalism; New York U; Yale

BEHETTE, DANIELLE; BROOKLYN, NY; BISHOP KEARNEY HS; (SO); All Am Sch; Hi Hnr Roll; Nat Hon Sy; Otst Ac Ach Awd; Sci Fairs; USAA; Valdctrian; WWAHSS; Peer Tut/Med; Mth Clb/Tm; Prom Com; Clb; Swmg (V); Tennis (V); Cl Off (P); Yrbk; Summa Cum Laude on National Latin Exam; Business and Finance; Law; Boston College; Georgetown U

BEHLER, MONICA; PT JEFFERSON STATION, NY; COMSEWOGUE HS; (SO); Hnr Roll; Comm Volntr; Orch; Vllyball (J); Long Island String Festival Association; Suffolk County Music Educators Association; Public School Music Teacher; Private Music Teacher / Performer; Ithaca College; Hartt School of Music

BEIKIRCH, KEVIN J; BROCKPORT, NY; BROCKPORT HS; (SO); Bsball (J); Ftball (J); Sports Journalism; Syracuse U; SUNY Oswego

BEJARANO, MICHELLE; UNIONDALE, NY; UNIONDALE HS; (SO); Hi Hnr Roll; Sci Fairs; St of Mnth; WWAHSS; Key Club; Mus Clb; Photog; Sci Clb; Spanish Clb; Orch; Public Relations Officer of Science Honor-Society (Club Publications); Liberal Arts; Sociology

BEKTESHI, MEGI; BROOKLYN, NY; (FR); Ctznshp Aw; F Lan Hn Soc; Hnr Roll; Jr Mshl; Red Cr Aide; FCA; Fr of Library; Lib Aide; Outdrs Clb; Bskball; GAA; Vllyball; Columbia U; Brooklyn College

BELGRAIER, ALYSON; MERRICK, NY; CALHOUN HS; (FR); Hnr Roll; Comm Volntr; Emplmnt; Key Club; Tmpl Yth Grp; Chr; SP/M/VS; Cr Ctry (L); Track (L); Hebrew High School

BELGRAIER, LAUREN; MERRICK, NY; (FR); Hnr Roll; Comm Volntr; Emplmnt; Key Club; Tmpl Yth Grp; Dnce; Cr Ctry (L); Track (L); Hebrew HS; Psychologist

BELL, BENJAMIN; TONAWANDA, NY; KENMORE WEST SR HS; (FR); F Lan Hn Soc; Hnr Roll; Nat Hon Sy; Nat Mrt Fin; Nat Mrt Sch Recip; Sci Fairs; St of Mnth; Comm Volntr; Chess; Mus Clb; Sci Clb; Scouts; Tech Clb; Wdwrkg Clb; Chr; Merit Roll; Quarter Back on a Football Team or Computer Software/Games Designer

BELL, JAZMINE; BUFFALO, NY; RIVERSIDE SCH OF TECH; (FR); Ctznshp Aw; Hnr Roll; Perf Att; St of Mnth; Clb; Bskball (V); Cr Ctry (V); Track (V); Veterinarian; UCLA

BELL, MODESTINA M; BROOKLYN, NY; EDWARD R MURROW HS; (JR); Hi Hnr Roll; Yth Ldrshp Prog; Chrch Yth Grp; Emplmnt; Mus Clb; Tchrs Aide; Chr; Ch Chr; Clr Grd; Dnce; Psychology; Cornell U Ithaca; Hamilton College

BELL, TASHEENA; JAMAICA, NY; ST AGNES ACADEMIC HS; (FR); Hnr Roll; Hosp Aide; Peer Tut/Med; ArtClub; Clb; Bnd; Ch Chr; Stu Cncl; CR (R); Medicine; Psychology; U of Connecticut; U of Columbia

BELOUS, VIKTORIYA; BROOKLYN, NY; NEW UTRECHT HS; (SO); Perf Att; Lib Aide; Mod UN; Dnce; SP/M/VS; Bskball (J); Sccr (J); Vllyball (J); Handball Team, Fashion Show; Business; New York U; Long Island U

BELTON, TANAYA; BROOKLYN, NY; JAMES PETER SINNOTT MAGNET SCH; Perf Att; Hosp Aide; Quiz Bowl; Dnce; Bskball (J); Cl Off (V); Sch Ppr (R); Stepping; Law; Doctor; Brooklyn Colleges; Saint John Colleges

BENAVIDES, KRYSTINA M; BROOKLYN, NY; JOHN DEWEY HS; (SO); Hi Hnr Roll; Perf Att; Comm Volntr; Aqrium Clb; Chrch Yth Grp; Photog; Sci Clb; Scouts; Tchrs Aide; Dnce; Stu Cncl (V); Sch Ppr (R); Dermatology; New York U; Columbia U

BENION, DAISJA; MIDDLE ISLAND, NY; LONGWOOD HS; (SO); Hi Hnr Roll; Bnd; Craft and Artisanry; Bachelor's Degree; New York U

BENIS, MAX; SPRING VALLEY, NY; SPRING VALLEY HS; (JR); F Lan Hn Soc; Hnr Roll; Perf Att; Pres Sch; St of Mnth; Chess; Emplmnt; Key Club; Cr Ctry (V CL); Sccr (J); Track (V L); Computer Science, Graphic Design, Computer Programming; Binghamton U

BENJAMIN, LEA; ENDICOTT, NY; UNION ENDICOTT HS; (SO); Hi Hnr Roll; Hnr Roll; Peer Tut/Med; DARE; Emplmnt; Key Club; Scouts; Spanish Clb; Track (V); Yrbk (P); Radiology; Keystone College; Rochester Institute of Technology

BENNETT, CHARLEEN J; BROOKLYN, NY; SPRINGFIELD GARDENS HS; (JR); WWAHSS; Comm Volntr; 4-H; Lib Aide; Dnce; Sccr; Biology; Zoology; SUNY Potsdam; SUNY Oswego

BENNETT, SHANA; BRONX, NY; PRESTON HS; (JR); Hnr Roll; Nat Hon Sy; WWAHSS; Comm Volntr; Drma Clb; Emplmnt; P to P St Amb Prg; Spanish Clb; Drl Tm; Cl Off (V); Stu Cncl (R); Yrbk (E); National Honors Society; Spanish Honors Society; Psychology; Writer; Brown U; Cornell U

BENNINGER, ERIKA M; SCHOHARIE, NY; SCHOHARIE HS; (FR); Hi Hnr Roll; MVP; Perf Att; Pres Ac Ftns Aw; WWAHSS; Comm Volntr; Hosp Aide; Peer Tut/Med; Chrch Yth Grp; FBLA; FCCLA; French Clb; Bskball (J); Sftball (J); Vllyball (J); Cl Off (T); Stu Cncl (R); CR (T, R); Part of a County Wide Student Government; Law; Business/Therapy

BENSOUDA, TARIKA; BRONX, NY; BRONX PREPARATORY CHARTER SCH; MS; Hnr Roll; Nat Hon Sy; Otst Ac Ach Awd; Sci Fairs; Sci/Math Olympn; St of Mnth; Peer Tut/Med; Dbte Team; Mth Clb/Tm; Mod UN; Spch Team; Chr; Stu Cncl (R); Sch Ppr (E, R); Piano; Lawyer; Scientist; Harvard U; Massachusetts Institute of Technology

BENTLEY, CHELSEA; BATH, NY; HAVERLING HS; (JR); Hi Hnr Roll; Nat Hon Sy; Comm Volntr; AL Aux Girls; Chrch Yth Grp; Drma Clb; Prom Com; Spanish Clb; Chr; SP/M/VS; Stg Cre; Yrbk (R, P); Serving Witnessing, and Training Team; 2 Summer Mission Trips; Missions/Bible; English; Indiana Wesleyan U; Bob Jones U

BENTLEY, CHRISTOPHER L; WARRENSBURG, NY; WARRENSBURG HS; (SO); Hnr Roll; MVP; Perf Att; St of Mnth; Red Cr Aide; Chrch Yth Grp; Key Club; SADD; Vsity Clb; Arch; Bsball (J); Ftball (V); Wt Lftg; Stu Cncl (R); Culinary Arts; Masters in Culinary Arts/Hospitality; Johnson and Wales U; Culinary Institute America

BENWAY, CARRIE A; SPENCERPORT, NY; SPENCERPORT HS; (JR); Hi Hnr Roll; Hnr Roll; Nat Hon Sy; Chrch Yth Grp; Criminal Justice-Legal; Spanish-Translator; Bryant U; Niagara U

BERBERICH, KURT H; BROOKLYN, NY; ST EDMUND PREP HS; (SO); Hnr Roll; St of Mnth; Comm Volntr; Chess; Emplmnt; Bskball; Doctor; Lawyer; Brooklyn College; NYU

BERDS, MELODY; LEWISTON, NY; LEWISTON-PORTER HS; (SR); Hi Hnr Roll; Nat Hon Sy; WWAHSS; Comm Volntr; AL Aux Girls; Chrch Yth Grp; Emplmnt; SADD; Yrbk (E); Bowling; Traditions Club; Chemical Engineering; Rensselaer Polytechnic Institute

BERDYNAJ, DRILON; YONKERS, NY; SAUNDERS HS; (SR); All Am Sch; Ctznshp Aw; F Lan Hn Soc; Fut Prb Slvr; Hi Hnr Roll; Hnr Roll; Otst Ac Ach Awd; Perf Att; Pres Ac Ftns Aw; St of Mnth; Comm Volntr; Hosp Aide; Peer Tut/Med; ArtClub; BPA; DARE; Emplmnt; FBLA; Jr Ach; Key Club; Off Aide; Dnce; SP/M/VS; Fld Hky (J); Ftball (VJ); Lcrsse (J); PP Ftbl (J); Rlr Hky (J); Scr Kpr (J); Sccr (J); Swmg (V); Lit Mag (P); High Honor Roll; Architecture Open House Winner; Architecture; Real Estate; Syracuse U; Westchester Community College

BERG, REISA; HUNTINGTON, NY; HUNTINGTON HS; (SO); Hnr Roll; Sci/Math Olympn; St of Mnth; Key Club; Mth Clb/Tm; Mus Clb; Scouts; Dnce; Cl Off (T); Stu Cncl (T); Crew Team (Rowing) Varsity; Teaching; Interior Design; Boston U

BERG, SHANALEE; MONSEY, NY; MANHATTAN HS; (JR); Hi Hnr Roll; Nat Hon Sy; Nat Ldrshp Svc; Otst Ac Ach Awd; Comm Volntr; Acpl Chr; Chr; SP/M/VS; Sch Ppr (R); Arista National Honor Society - All Semesters of HS; National Student Leadership Conference; Health Therapies; Speech Therapy & Physical Therapy; Hunter College Honors/Cuny Honors; Touro College

BERGER, YEVGENIY; NANUET, NY; CLARKSTOWN SOUTH HS; (JR); Otst Ac Ach Awd; Comm Volntr; Peer Tut/Med; DECA; Orch; Stg Cre; Engineering; Business; Massachusetts Institute of Technology; Harvard U

BERKMAN, KEITH; MASSAPEQUA, NY; ST ANTHONY'S HS; (JR); Hi Hnr Roll; Hnr Roll; MVP; Pres Ac Ftns Aw; Comm Volntr; Prom Com; Chr; Tennis (J); Yrbk (R); Varsity Bowling; Baseball Outside of School; Communications; Business; Cornell U; SUNY Binghamton

BERKOVICH, NICOLE; BROOKLYN, NY; EDWARD R MURROW HS; (JR); Nat Hon Sy; WWAHSS; Wdwrkg Clb; Stg Cre; Mock Trial; Tutor; Economics; Law

BERLINGIERI, CHRISTOPHER; BELLE HARBOR, NY; EDWARD R MURROW HS; (JR); Hi Hnr Roll; Otst Ac Ach Awd; Sci Fairs; Comm Volntr; Peer Tut/Med; Emplmnt; Mus Clb; Tchrs Aide; Chr; Music Teachers Association Certificate of Merit; Intel-Science; Pharmacy (Pharmaceutical Degree); Medical Degree (Radiologist); St John's U; New York U

BERNADIN, FARAH K; BROOKLYN, NY; JOHN DEWEY HS; (SO); Hnr Roll; Comm Volntr; Chrch Yth Grp; Tchrs Aide; Ch Chr; Step Club; Liturgical Dance; Medical Field; Lawyer; New York U; Columbia U

BERNARDEZ, ANDREW C; FREEPORT, NY; FREEPORT HS; (JR); Hi Hnr Roll; Hnr Roll; Nat Hon Sy; Nat Sci Aw; Pres Sch; Sci/Math Olympn; Comm Volntr; Chrch Yth Grp; Drma Clb; Mth Clb/Tm; Mus Clb; Vsity Clb; Bnd; Chr; Jzz Bnd; Mch Bnd; Swmg (V L); Tennis (V L); Freeport High School Select Chorale 11th Grade Representative; Freeport High School Wood Ensemble Trumpet Section Leader; Music Performance/Jazz; Engineering; Ithaca College; Cincinnati Christian U

BERNSTEIN, ELANA; BROOKLYN, NY; LEON GOLDSTEIN HS; (JR); Hnr Roll; ArtClub; Pep Squd; Spanish Clb; Scr Kpr; STEP Squad; Fashion Design; Architecture; Columbia U; Cooper Union

BERNSTEIN, TAYLOR S; BROOKLYN, NY; MARKTWAIN Is 239; Nat Hon Sy; Dnce; Sccr

BESCH, ABIGAIL; ALDEN, NY; ALDEN HS; (SO); Hnr Roll; St of Mnth; WWAHSS; Drma Clb; Key Club; Spanish Clb; Bnd; Dnce; Mch Bnd; Pep Bnd; Swmg (V); Medical; Business

BESLER, BESIANA A; BRONX, NY; AC OF MT ST URSULA; (JR); Gov Hnr Prg; Hi Hnr Roll; Hnr Roll; Otst Ac Ach Awd; Perf Att; Sci Fairs; St of Mnth; St Optmst of Yr; WWAHSS; Yth Ldrshp Prog; Comm Volntr; ArtClub; DARE; Drma Clb; Lib Aide; NYLC; Asian Clb; SP/M/VS; Tennis; Yrbk (R); National Education Development Test; Youth Con; International Relations; Political Science; American U; U of Notre Dame

BETANCES, ROYSA; NEW YORK, NY; HS FOR MEDIA & COMMUNICATIONS; (JR); Hnr Roll; Otst Ac Ach Awd; ArtClub; Chrch Yth Grp; Academic Excellence; Early Childhood Education; Master's Degree; Buffalo State College; Hunter College

BETANCOURT, SAMANTHA; BRONX, NY; HEALTH OPPORTUNITIES HS; (FR); Ctznshp Aw; Hnr Roll; Sci Fairs; Peer Tut/Med; Bsball; Vllyball; Yrbk; Teaching Degree; Doctors Degree; N.Y.U; Hunter College

BETIT, NICOLE L; COSSAYUNA, NY; GREENWICH CTRL SCH; (JR); Hnr Roll; Otst Ac Ach Awd; Perf Att; St of Mnth; WWAHSS; Ntl FFA; Tennis (V); 3 Years on Who's Who Among Am. HS Students; Social Work

BEYDOUN, AMEEN; FOREST HILLS, NY; THE KEW-FOREST SCH; (SO); Ctznshp Aw; F Lan Hn Soc; Hnr Roll; Perf Att; WWAHSS; Chess; Dbte Team; Outdrs Clb; Bsball (V); Sch Ppr (R)

BHAMRA, RITU; HICKSVILLE, NY; HICKSVILLE HS; (FR); Hi Hnr Roll; Hnr Roll; Drma Clb; Mus Clb; Chr; Ch Chr; All-County; NYSSMA; Singer; Lawyer; The Juilliard School

BHARDWAJ, MEERA; MONSEY, NY; HACKLEY SCH; (JR); Hnr Roll; WWAHSS; Yth Ldrshp Prog; Comm Volntr; Bnd; Fld Hky (V); Lit Mag (P); Free the Children Co-President & Co-Chapter Founder, Black & Gray Key Club (Helps Out At School Events); Volunteer At Good Samaritan Hosp. & Tarrytown Life Center Tutor, Nominated for People to People, Art Awards, JV Squash Capt-2 Yrs., Invited to See Pres. Inaugural; Doctor, Scientist; Artist (Visual Artist)

BHIR, AKASH; PT JEFFERSON STATION, NY; COMSEWOGUE HS; (FR); Hi Hnr Roll; Comm Volntr; Mth Clb/Tm; Svce Clb; Sccr (J); Tennis (V); Mechanical / Automotive Engineering; Architecture; Cooper Union; U of Michigan

Besler, Besiana A
AC Of Mt St Ursula
Bronx, NY

Berberich, Kurt H
St Edmund Prep HS
Brooklyn, NY

Bekteshi, Megi
Brooklyn, NY

Begum, Nilufa
Al-Madinah Sch
Astoria, NY

Beckford, Natasha
Francis Lewis HS
Rosedale, NY

Begho, Itse
Collegiate Sch
Sprngfld Gdns, NY

Bell, Tasheena
St Agnes Academic HS
Jamaica, NY

Bernstein, Elana
Leon Goldstein HS
Brooklyn, NY

Bhamra, Ritu
Hicksville HS
Hicksville, NY

BIAGIOTTI, KATHERINE; DELMAR, NY; BETHLEHEM CTRL HS; (JR); Hi Hnr Roll; Otst Ac Ach Awd; Perf Att; Pres Sch; Sci/Math Olympn; St of Mnth; Peer Tut/Med; DARE; Emplmnt; Prom Com; Sccr; Sftball; Track (VJ L); Stu Cncl (R); Russell Ellers Award; Law School; New York U; Boston College

BIALZA, LESLIE A; STATEN ISLAND, NY; PORT RICHMOND HS; (SO); Hi Hnr Roll; Nat Hon Sy; Otst Ac Ach Awd; St of Mnth; Italian Clb; Sccr (V); Track (J); Vllyball (J); National Honor Society; High Honor Roll; Nursing; Hunter College (CUNY); Columbia (NY)

BIAN, WENAN; FOREST HILLS, NY; (JR); Hnr Roll; WWAHSS; Comm Volntr; Peer Tut/Med; Red Cr Aide; Chrch Yth Grp; Key Club; Mth Clb/Tm; Ch Chr; SP/M/VS; Yrbk (E); Business; New York U; Amherst

BIANCHI, ANDREA; CLAY, NY; BISHOP LUDDEN HS; (SO); Hi Hnr Roll; Nat Hon Sy; Comm Volntr; Peer Tut/Med; Jr Ach; NYLC; P to P St Amb Prg; Chr; Sccr (J); Vllyball (J); Nominated for People to People (Seeds of Peace); Psychology; English or Language Major

BIENKOWSKI, JILLYAN A; SEAFORD, NY; SEAFORD HS; (JR); Hnr Roll; Emplmnt; Key Club; Bnd; Chr; Cr Ctry (V); Sccr (V); Sftball (J); Track (V); Academic All Stars; Interior Design; Fashion Institute of Technology; Philadelphia U

BIGNALL, ZOE; BRONX, NY; HARRY S TRUMAN HS; (JR); F Lan Hn Soc; Hi Hnr Roll; Hnr Roll; Nat Hon Sy; Otst Ac Ach Awd; Perf Att; Sci Fairs; Yth Ldrshp Prog; Peer Tut/Med; Chrch Yth Grp; Mth Clb/Tm; Mus Clb; ROTC; Italian Clb; Chr; Ch Chr; Dnce; Drl Tm; Chrldg (C); Gmnstcs (V); Ice Sktg; Sccr; Swmg; Track; Cl Off (P); Stu Cncl (S); CR (R); Double Dutch Team; Pediatrician; Math H.S. Teacher/College; Hofstra U; N.Y.U.

BIGNELL, LISA; LEWISTON, NY; LEWISTON PORTER HS; (JR); Hnr Roll; Nat Hon Sy; Nat Mrt LOC; Sci Fairs; St of Mnth; Chrch Yth Grp; Dbte Team; Emplmnt; Key Club; Dnce; Track (V); Certificate of Achievement Award for Jazz at the Lewiston Dance Studio; Pharmacology / Pharmacy; Spanish; SUNY Buffalo; Niagara U

BIGTREE, TORRY; ROOSEVELTOWN, NY; MASSENA CTRL HS; (FR); Hnr Roll; MVP; Perf Att; Ice Hky (V); Architecture

BILLY, KATERRA; JAMAICA, NY; BAYSIDE HS; (JR); Ctznshp Aw; Hnr Roll; Peer Tut/Med; Chrch Yth Grp; Emplmnt; Mus Clb; Prom Com; Vsity Clb; Chr; Ch Chr; Drl Tm; SP/M/VS; Chrldg (V); Stu Cncl (S); Judged By NYSSMA (Music-Prestige) 93 of 100; Invited to Participate in Youth Pageant of America; Go Into Public Relations and Entertainment Law; Music/History Teacher; Morgan State U; Hampton U

BIN, DANNY; RICHMOND HILL, NY; BROOKLYN TECH HS; (JR); Hnr Roll; Perf Att; Sci Fairs; Comm Volntr; Hosp Aide; Mth Clb/Tm; Chr; Lit Mag (E); New York City Math Team Winner; Management; Engineering; Cornell U; New York U

BING, EVELYN C; SAUGERTIES, NY; SAUGERTIES HS; (FR); Hi Hnr Roll; Otst Ac Ach Awd; WWAHSS; Dbte Team; Key Club; French Clb; Bnd; Chr; Dnce; Skiing (V); Track (V); All County Jr. High Band; All County Jr. High Chorus; Become a Successful Lawyer; Harvard U; Bates College

BINNIE, BRITTANY; MIDDLETOWN, NY; MIDDLETOWN HS; (JR); Hi Hnr Roll; Hnr Roll; Bskball (V CL); PP Ftbl (V); Award Won for Basketball; Meteorology; Child Psychology; Wesleyan U; LaSalle U

BINSACK, CHRISTOPHER; OYSTER BAY, NY; ST DOMINIC HS; (SO); Hnr Roll; Pres Ac Ftns Aw; WWAHSS; Comm Volntr; Spec Olymp Vol; Bsball (J); Sports Management; Forensic Science; New York U; Miami U

BIONDI, DOMINIQUE; BRONX, NY; FIORELLO H LA GUARDIA HS; (JR); Perf Att; Comm Volntr; ArtClub; Emplmnt; Italian Clb; Dnce; Wt Lftg (V); Perfect Attendance from Kindergarten-Now; Trained Habilitator for Autistic Children; Art (Commercial Art, Architecture); Marine Biologist; State U of New York At New Paltz; State U of New York At Purchase

BIRCHMORE, WARREN J; BROOKLYN, NY; BENJAMIN BANNEKER AC; (SO); Hnr Roll; Otst Ac Ach Awd; Perf Att; Comm Volntr; Hosp Aide; Peer Tut/Med; Mth Clb/Tm; Outdrs Clb; Tchrs Aide; Tech Clb; Dnce; Sch Ppr (R); Mario De Falco Award- Community Service and Academic Achievement; Music; Accountant; Howard U; Long Island U

BIRD, LIANNE; MOUNT KISCO, NY; FOX LANE HS; (SO); Hi Hnr Roll; St of Mnth; Comm Volntr; Orch; Chrldg (J); Fld Hky (J); Sccr (JC)

BIRD, MEREDITH S L; WEST LEYDEN, NY; ADIRONDACK HS; (SO); Hi Hnr Roll; Hnr Roll; Comm Volntr; Mod UN; Bnd; SP/M/VS; Cr Ctry (J); Vllyball (J); Cl Off (S); Play Violin and Piano Outside of School; Social Sciences; History; Oberlin College; Macalester College

BISENIUS, DAVID; CHEEKTOWAGA, NY; WEST SENECA EAST SR HS; (FR); Hnr Roll; WWAHSS; Key Club; Orch; Buffalo Bicycling Club; Masterminds; Aeronautical Engineer; U of Minnesota; Rochester Institute of Technology

BISHARAH, JENNIFER; BOHEMIA, NY; ST JOHN THE BAPTIST HS; (JR); F Lan Hn Soc; Hi Hnr Roll; Nat Hon Sy; WWAHSS; Hosp Aide; Dbte Team; Emplmnt; Svce Clb; Tech Clb; Vsity Clb; Sccr (V); Track (V); Peace and Justice Club; Nassau-Suffolk Catholic High School Girls Athletic Assn. All Academic; Medical Field, MD; Psychology; Marist College; Cornell U

BISOGNO, BRIANNA R; FRANKLIN SQ, NY; SEWANHAKA HS; (JR); F Lan Hn Soc; Hi Hnr Roll; Nat Hon Sy; Nat Mrt Sch Recip; Otst Ac Ach Awd; Sci Fairs; Sci/Math Olympn; St of Mnth; WWAHSS; Yth Ldrshp Prog; Comm Volntr; Peer Tut/Med; BPA; FBLA; Key Club; Lttrmn Clb; Mod UN; Quiz Bowl; Spanish Clb; Bnd; Mch Bnd; Bskball (J); Lcrsse (V); Tennis (V); Stu Cncl; CR; Lit Mag (E); Sch Ppr (E); Yrbk (P); St John's U Woman of Science Award; Key Club Vice President; Nuclear Physics; Mortuary Science; Boston U; Columbia U

BIZZARRO, VALERIE A; YORKTOWN HEIGHTS, NY; YORKTOWN HS; (JR); Hi Hnr Roll; Comm Volntr; DARE; Scouts; Dnce; Track (VJ); Sch Ppr (E, R, P); Destination Imagination; Visual Arts; Creative Writing

BLAAKMAN, MICHAEL; FAIRPORT, NY; FAIRPORT HS; (SR); F Lan Hn Soc; Hi Hnr Roll; Nat Hon Sy; Nat Mrt LOC; WWAHSS; Drma Clb; Emplmnt; Scouts; Bnd; Chr; Ch Chr; SP/M/VS; Cl Off (P, T); Stu Cncl (T); Ultimate Frisbee; Sailing; History; Political Science; The College of William and Mary

BLACK, KALILAH; BRONX, NY; LA GUARDIA ARTS HS; (JR); Ctznshp Aw; Comm Volntr; Chrch Yth Grp; Drma Clb; Emplmnt; Ch Chr; Dnce; SP/M/VS; Stg Cre; Stu Cncl (R); Performing Artist; Spelman U; U of North Carolina A&T

BLACKWELL, SHANTE; NYACK, NY; NYACK HS; (JR); F Lan Hn Soc; Hi Hnr Roll; Hnr Roll; Nat Hon Sy; WWAHSS; Comm Volntr; DARE; Emplmnt; FBLA; Bnd; Interact Club; Black Achievements Award / Senior Mentor Program; Accounting; Pace U; St John's U

BLACKWOOD, TERRELL; BROOKLYN, NY; GRAPHIC COMMUNICATION OF ARTS HS; (SR); Hnr Roll; ArtClub; Emplmnt; Photog; Chr; Bsball; Bskball; Ftball; Sccr; Vllyball; Stu Cncl (R); Sch Ppr (P); Yrbk (P); Photography Award; Region 9 Arts 2005 Award for Graphics; Criminology; SUNY at Old Westbury

BLADES, SHELLY; BRONX, NY; EVANDER CHILDS HS; (SO); Hi Hnr Roll; Nat Hon Sy; Nat Ldrshp Svc; Otst Ac Ach Awd; Yth Ldrshp Prog; CARE; Peer Tut/Med; Chrch Yth Grp; Dbte Team; Drma Clb; FCA; Mus Clb; NYLC; Outdrs Clb; Ch Chr; Dnce; SP/M/VS; Stg Cre; Bskball (J); Chrldg (J); Gmnstcs (J); Scr Kpr (J); Track (J); Vllyball (J); Cl Off (S, T); Stu Cncl; Creative Writing Club; Youth Focus Group; Lawyer, Social Worker; Harvard, Columbia U; Princeton

BLAKAJ, GRANIT; BRONX, NY; MARBLE HILL HS FOR INTERNATIONAL STUDIES; (FR); Hnr Roll; MVP; ArtClub; Bskball; Architecture; Business; Syracuse College; St John's

BLAKE, MALLAREE; JAMESTOWN, NY; SOUTHWESTERN HS; (SR); Nat Hon Sy; St of Mnth; WWAHSS; Comm Volntr; Peer Tut/Med; Prom Com; SADD; Dnce; SP/M/VS; Vllyball (J); Cl Off (S); Stu Cncl (R); Sch Ppr (R); Lakewood Area Junior Miss; Ophelia Mentor-Team Leader; Global Studies Teacher; History/Sec Education/Anthropology; U of Dayton

BLASS, JENNIFER D; PORT CHESTER, NY; MARIA REGINA HS; (FR); Hnr Roll; St of Mnth; DARE; Key Club; Scouts; Track (J)

BLEMEL, KYLE; WESTPORT, NY; WESTPORT CTRL SCH; (FR); 4H Awd; Hi Hnr Roll; Hnr Roll; Comm Volntr; 4-H; DARE; Bnd; Dnce; Stg Cre; Bsball; Golf; Sccr; Vehicle Design; Engineering

BLOCK, MELANIE; MASTIC BEACH, NY; WILLIAM FLOYD HS; (JR); F Lan Hn Soc; WWAHSS; Comm Volntr; Emplmnt; French Clb; Dnce; Tennis (VJ); Youth & Government; Psychology; Political Science; Boston U; Loyola College

BLODGETT, TOM; OSWEGO, NY; OSWEGO HS; (SR); Hi Hnr Roll; Hnr Roll; Perf Att; Emplmnt; Swmg (V L); Scholar Athlete Award; Marine Biology; Florida Institute of Technology

BLUM, CAMILLE; ALDEN, NY; ALDEN CTRL HS; (SO); Hi Hnr Roll; St of Mnth; WWAHSS; Yth Ldrshp Prog; Comm Volntr; Hab For Humty Volntr; Peer Tut/Med; Chrch Yth Grp; Key Club; Sci Clb; SADD; Spanish Clb; Bnd; Bskball (V); Sccr (V); Track (V); Cl Off (P); Biology

BOCCI, ALEXANDRA; EAST NORWICH, NY; OYSTER BAY HS; (JR); Hi Hnr Roll; Nat Hon Sy; Otst Ac Ach Awd; WWAHSS; Comm Volntr; Emplmnt; Prom Com; Svce Clb; SADD; Tchrs Aide; Bnd; Chr; Pep Bnd; Sftball (VJ L); Vllyball (VJCL); Cl Off (R); Stu Cncl (R); CR (R); Renaissance Award (Academic); 2004 New York State Final Four Softball Class C; English; Law; Stanford U; Georgetown U

BODANZIO, MANDIE; RONKONKOMA, NY; CONNETQUOT HS; (SR); Ctznshp Aw; Hi Hnr Roll; Nat Hon Sy; Nat Stu Ath Day Aw; Otst Ac Ach Awd; Pres Sch; St of Mnth; WWAHSS; Spec Olymp Vol; ArtClub; Emplmnt; Photog; Vsity Clb; Orch; Sftball (V); President's Honor Roll- Every Quarter; President's Education Award; Elementary Education; St Joseph's College - Suffolk

BODO, ALEXANDRA; SCARSDALE, NY; EDGEMONT HS; (JR); Hi Hnr Roll; Hnr Roll; Otst Ac Ach Awd; Perf Att; WWAHSS; Comm Volntr; Red Cr Aide; Chrch Yth Grp; DARE; Key Club; Schol Bwl; Scouts; SADD; Dnce; Track (J); Medicine (MD); Duke; Cornell

BOEKELMAN, JACKIE; BUFFALO, NY; WILLIAMSVILLE SOUTH HS; (JR); Hi Hnr Roll; Nat Hon Sy; Otst Ac Ach Awd; Pres Sch; Sci/Math Olympn; WWAHSS; Peer Tut/Med; Bnd; Mch Bnd; Chrldg (J); Tennis (V L); Poetry.Com-Poem Published for Spoken/Written Collection; Kodak Young Leaders Certificate; International Studies; Education; U of Rochester-Rochester, NY; Amherst College

BOELTER, CHRISTINA; MASSENA, NY; MASSENA CTRL HS; (FR); Hnr Roll; Pres Ac Ftns Aw; St of Mnth; Comm Volntr; ArtClub; Chrch Yth Grp; Drma Clb; Photog; Spanish Clb; Stg Cre; Track (J); 2003-3rd Place All American Soap Box Poetry Rally; 2002-7th Place All Amer Soap Box Derby Champ; Fine Arts; Photography/Journalism; RIT; SUNY/Binghamton

BOGHAERT, HENDRIK; MONROE, NY; MONROE-WOODBURY HS; (SO); Hi Hnr Roll; Comm Volntr; Peer Tut/Med; Quiz Bowl; Bnd; Sccr (J); Wrstlg (J); Engineering; Cooper Union for the Advancement of Art and Science

BOGUMIL, MICHELLE M; ROCHESTER, NY; GREECE ATHENA HS; (JR); Hi Hnr Roll; Hnr Roll; Comm Volntr; Chrch Yth Grp; Dnce; Active in Church Youth Group At Hope Lutheran Church; Meteorology; Mass Communication/Broadcasting; Valparaiso U; Florida Institute of Technology

BOLAN, SAMANTHA A; ENDWELL, NY; SETON CATHOLIC CTRL HS; (SO); Hi Hnr Roll; Sci Fairs; Sci/Math Olympn; Yth Ldrshp Prog; Comm Volntr; Hosp Aide; Spec Olymp Vol; Drma Clb; Lib Aide; Mod UN; Svce Clb; SADD; Chr; SP/M/VS; Stu Cncl (R); CR (R); President's Volunteer Service Award; College Credit for Intermediate French & AP World History; Journalism; Fashion; Cornell U; New York U

BONACASA, GABRIELA; CORAM, NY; NEWFIELD HS; (JR); Hnr Roll; Perf Att; St of Mnth; Hosp Aide; DARE; Lib Aide; St. Joseph College (Education)

BOND III, EDISON; BROOKLYN, NY; XAVIERIAN HS; (JR); Ctznshp Aw; Hnr Roll; MVP; Sci Fairs; Comm Volntr; Chrch Yth Grp; Emplmnt; Mus Clb; Pep Squd; Bnd; Chr; Ch Chr; Jzz Bnd; Traveled to Japan on Jazz Tour; President of Jack & Jill of America Sr Team; Music; Music Business; Berklee College of Music; Harvard U

BONILLA, HEIDI J; FREEPORT, NY; FREEPORT HS; (JR); Hi Hnr Roll; Otst Ac Ach Awd; Comm Volntr; Peer Tut/Med; Emplmnt; Key Club; Prom Com; Vsity Clb; Italian Clb; Bnd; Mch Bnd; Tennis (V); Odyssey of the Mind; Peer Leadership; Biology; Liberal Arts; Columbia U; U Penn U of Pennsylvania

BONNER, BIANCA A; BRONX, NY; BLESSED SACRAMENT HS; (JR); Hi Hnr Roll; Hnr Roll; Nat Hon Sy; Nat Ldrshp Svc; Nat Sci Aw; Nat Stu Ath Day Aw; Perf Att; St of Mnth; WWAHSS; Yth Ldrshp Prog; Comm Volntr; Hosp Aide; Peer Tut/Med; Biology Clb; Drma Clb; Fr of Library; FCCLA; Prom Com; Sci Clb; Svce Clb; SADD; Dnce; Drl Tm; Stg Cre; Cr Ctry (V); Gmnstcs (J); Sccr (V); Sftball (V); Tennis (J); Track (V); Vsy Clb (V); Vllyball (V); Psychology; Biology / Biological Sciences; Hampton U; Spelman College

BORCILO, SADO; NORWICH, NY; NORWICH HS; (SO); Hi Hnr Roll; Hnr Roll; Perf Att; ArtClub; Bnd; Swg Chr; Bskball (J); Dvng; Sccr (V L); Swmg (J); Track; Stu Cncl (R); CR (R)

BORKOSKI, KATHLEEN; SOUTHAMPTON, NY; SOUTHAMPTON HS; (SR); F Lan Hn Soc; Hi Hnr Roll; Jr Rot; Nat Hon Sy; Pres Sch; Comm Volntr; Emplmnt; Mth Clb/Tm; Latin Clb; Tennis (VJ); Cl Off (T); Stu Cncl (S, R); Lions Club Student of the Month; School & Community Health Education; Towson U

BORODINA, LYUBA; STATEN ISLAND, NY; STATEN ISLAND TECH HS; (JR); Hi Hnr Roll; Hnr Roll; Nat Hon Sy; WWAHSS; Comm Volntr; Peer Tut/Med; ArtClub; Drma Clb; Dnce; SP/M/VS; Stg Cre; Sch Ppr (R); Pre-Law; New York U; Columbia U

BORON, MELANIE; LOCKPORT, NY; LOCKPORT HS; (FR); Hi Hnr Roll; WWAHSS; Yth Ldrshp Prog; Comm Volntr; Hosp Aide; Key Club; SADD; Spanish Clb; Yrbk (R, P)

BORST, TRACY; LEVITTOWN, NY; DIVISION AVE HS; (FR); Hi Hnr Roll; USAA; WWAHSS; Key Club; Mth Clb/Tm; Scouts; Bnd; Ch Chr; Mch Bnd; Key Club Treasurer; Doctor; Physical Therapist

BOSAH, NWANDO; WESTBURY, NY; W TRESPER CLARKE HS; (SR); F Lan Hn Soc; Hnr Roll; Nat Hon Sy; Perf Att; Peer Tut/Med; ArtClub; Chrch Yth Grp; Photog; Scouts; Tchrs Aide; Spanish Clb; Bnd; Ch Chr; Dnce; SP/M/VS; Sch Ppr (R); Multicultural Club; National Art Honor Society; Law; Mass Communication; Saint John's U; Yale U

BOSCO, KAYLA; SYRACUSE, NY; HENNINGER HS; (JR); Hi Hnr Roll; Nat Hon Sy; Perf Att; Sci Fairs; Peer Tut/Med; Emplmnt; SP/M/VS; Stg Cre; Bskball; Sftball (J); Vllyball; Lit Mag (E); Spanish and Italian; Advertising; Canisius College; Boston College

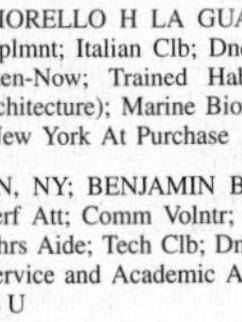
Borkoski, Kathleen
Southampton HS
Southampton, NY

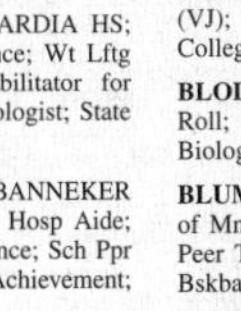
Bolan, Samantha A
Seton Catholic Ctrl HS
Endwell, NY

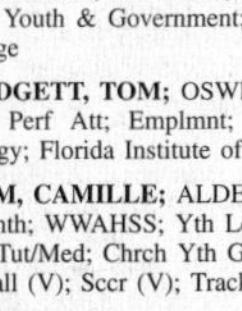
Bodo, Alexandra
Edgemont HS
Scarsdale, NY

National
Honor Roll
Spring 2005

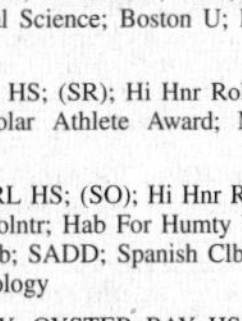
Billy, Katerra
Bayside HS
Jamaica, NY

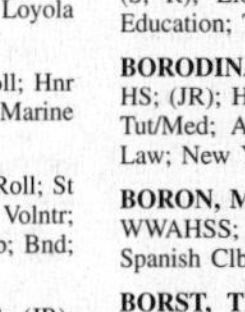
Bonner, Bianca A
Blessed Sacrament HS
Bronx, NY

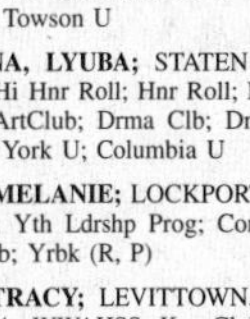
Bosah, Nwando
W Tresper Clarke HS
Westbury, NY

BOTTE, JOHN; SMITHTOWN, NY; SMITHTOWN HS; (SO); Hnr Roll; St of Mnth; Comm Volntr; Peer Tut/Med; DECA; Mus Clb; Bnd; State and International DECA Competitions; Smithtown HS DECA Officer / Web Master; Computer Science; Web Design; Rochester Institute of Technology; Worcester Polytechnic Institute

BOTTORFF, STEPHANIE V; LA FAYETTE, NY; LAFAYETTE JR SR HS; (FR); Hnr Roll; Perf Att; Comm Volntr; DARE; Chr; Lcrsse (V); Sccr (V); Yrbk; Art; Firefighter; Syracuse U

BOU, LYSA; BRONX, NY; CHRISTOPHER COLUMBUS HS; (FR); Hnr Roll; Comm Volntr; DARE; Outdrs Clb; Clr Grd; Golf (C)

BOUKAS, ALEXANDER P; JAMAICA, NY; TOWNSEND HARRIS HS; (JR); Perf Att; St of Mnth; Valdctrian; Comm Volntr; Chess; Chrch Yth Grp; Tchrs Aide; Bnd; Drl Tm; Volunteer Ambulance First Responder; Medicine; Navy Officer; St John's U; Annapolis Naval Academy

BOUTIN, RACHEL; AU SABLE FORKS, NY; AU SABLE VALLEY HS; (JR); Hi Hnr Roll; Otst Ac Ach Awd; WWAHSS; Comm Volntr; Red Cr Aide; Spec Olymp Vol; Drma Clb; Key Club; Prom Com; SADD; French Clb; Bnd; Jzz Bnd; SP/M/VS; Stu Cncl (R); Yrbk (P); Nursing; Biology Education; Clinton Community College; SUNY Plattsburgh

BOWEN, MARIA G; STATEN ISLAND, NY; SUSAN E WAGNER HS; (JR); Ctznshp Aw; Hi Hnr Roll; Hnr Roll; Perf Att; St of Mnth; Comm Volntr; DARE; Emplmnt; Dnce; Business Institute Program Award; International Business; Columbia U; Wagner College

BOWKER III, TRACY; SARATOGA SPRINGS, NY; F DONALD MYERS ED CTR; (SR); Ftball (J); Wrstlg (J); Heavy Equipment Operation & Maintenance; Heavy Equipment Operator; US Army; Universal Technical Institute

BOYCE, CHRISTOPHER W; MONROE, NY; MONROE-WOODBURY HS; (FR); Hnr Roll; MVP; Comm Volntr; Hab For Humty Volntr; Orch; Ftball (J); Track (J); Freshman Football- MVP / Defense; Professional Football Player; Sports Management/Entertainment; U of Florida; Louisiana State U

BOYCE, PATRICK J; MONROE, NY; MONROE-WOODBURY HS; (JR); Hnr Roll; Hab For Humty Volntr; Emplmnt; Vsity Clb; Bsball (V); Bskball (V); Ftball (J); Lcrsse (V C); Vsy Clb (V); Lacrosse- MVP; Business; Criminal Justice; Iona College; Manhattan College

BOYER, ANGELIQUE; MASSAPEQUA, NY; ST JOHN THE BAPTIST HS; (SO); Hnr Roll; WWAHSS; Chrch Yth Grp; Cmptr Clb; Mus Clb; Sci Clb; SADD; Bnd; Mch Bnd; SP/M/VS; Yrbk (R); Tri M-Modern Music Master's Society; Pre Medicine; Yale; Harvard

BRACCIA, ROBERT A; LEVITTOWN, NY; ISLAND TREES HS; (SR); Hi Hnr Roll; Hnr Roll; Otst Ac Ach Awd; Sci/Math Olympn; WWAHSS; Comm Volntr; Spec Olymp Vol; Emplmnt; Key Club; Sci Clb; Tech Clb; Regional and State Medals-State Science Olympiad Comp; Mechanical Engineering; Binghamton; Hofstra

BRACE, RIGELSA; ALBANY, NY; ALBANY HS; Hi Hnr Roll; Hnr Roll; WWAHSS; Comm Volntr; Key Club; Stu Cncl (R); Vice President of International Club; Competed in Mock Trial/Certificate of Appreciation; Criminal Justice; JD; Siena College

BRADLEY JR, JOHN A; BUFFALO, NY; (FR); Hnr Roll; Perf Att; Comm Volntr; Chess; DARE; Dbte Team; Stu Cncl (R); CR (R); Degrees Up to Masters; Syracuse U; Illinois U

BRAILOUSKY, TANYA; BROOKLYN, NY; ABRAHAM LINCOLN HS; (SO); Hnr Roll; Perf Att; Sci Fairs; Emplmnt; Kumon Math and Reading Center; Billing / Accounting; Culinary Arts; Fordham U; Columbia U New York

BRANCH, JADE; BROOKLYN, NY; BENJAMIN BENNEKER AC; (JR); Ctznshp Aw; Hnr Roll; Nat Hon Sy; Perf Att; WWAHSS; Comm Volntr; Chess; Chrch Yth Grp; DARE; Emplmnt; Vsity Clb; Ch Chr; Stg Cre; Bskball (V); Tennis (V); CR (R); Psychology; Business Administration; Virginia State U; Lincoln U

BRAND, DIANDRA; NEW YORK, NY; SCH OF THE FUTURE; (SO); Comm Volntr; ArtClub; Biology Clb; Mus Clb; Off Aide; Photog; Svce Clb; Tchrs Aide; Tmpl Yth Grp; Chr; Tennis; Stu Cncl (R); Black Belt-Tae Kwon Do, Have Own Jewelry Business; Youth Civics Program with State Senator Lil Krueger; Work in Medicine with People; Empower Others to Be Healthy; NYU

BRANDT, MATT; SAUGERTIES, NY; (FR); WWAHSS; Drma Clb; Key Club; Lib Aide; French Clb; Bnd; SP/M/VS; Performing Arts

BRANIGIN, BRITTANY R; WALTON, NY; WALTON HS; (JR); Hi Hnr Roll; Hnr Roll; Otst Ac Ach Awd; Perf Att; Sci Fairs; St of Mnth; Hosp Aide; DARE; Emplmnt; P to P St Amb Prg; Scouts; Bnd; Chr; Mch Bnd; Pep Bnd; Poetry Published; BSN (Nursing); Pediatrics; D'Youville (Buffalo, NY); Hunter College

BRATCHER, SHAYNA; MOUNT VERNON, NY; MT VERNON HS; (JR); Hnr Roll; Photog; Certificate of Special Commendation; US Military Soldier; Teacher; New York U; Military Academy

BRAUNER, DAVE; CORFU, NY; PEMBROKE JR/SR HS; (SR); Hi Hnr Roll; Hnr Roll; MVP; Nat Hon Sy; WWAHSS; Key Club; Scouts; Vsity Clb; German Clb; Cr Ctry (V); Ftball (J); Swmg (V C); Track (V); Chemical Society Award; Pre-Optometry; SUNY Oswego

BRAWDY, JESSICA L; NORTH TONAWANDA, NY; NIAGARA ED CTR; (JR); Hnr Roll; Nat Hon Sy; Vsity Clb; Chrldg (J); Cr Ctry (V); Hsbk Rdg; Sccr (J); Track (V); Stu Cncl (S); RN, Nurse; Eventually NP; D'Youville College; U At Buffalo

BRAXTON, NAKIMEEA; STATEN ISLAND, NY; PORT RICHMOND HS; (FR); Ctznshp Aw; Hnr Roll; Otst Ac Ach Awd; Perf Att; Sci Fairs; St of Mnth; Yth Ldrshp Prog; Comm Volntr; ArtClub; Chrch Yth Grp; Drma Clb; FBLA; Mth Clb/Tm; ROTC; Sci Clb; Scouts; Ch Chr; Clr Grd; Dnce; SP/M/VS; Bdmtn (J); Bskball (V); Chrldg (C); Ftball (J); Scr Kpr (C); Sccr (J); Vllyball (V); Wt Lftg (V); Stu Cncl (S); Sch Ppr (P)

BRAYMER, DAVID F; CAMBRIDGE, NY; GREENWICH CTRL; (JR); Hi Hnr Roll; Hnr Roll; WWAHSS; Emplmnt; Wdwrkg Clb; Bsball (J); Ftball (V); Skiing (V)

BREHL, REBECCA E; NEW CITY, NY; (SR); F Lan Hn Soc; Hi Hnr Roll; Nat Hon Sy; Nat Mrt Fin; Nat Mrt Sch Recip; Otst Ac Ach Awd; St of Mnth; WWAHSS; Comm Volntr; Hab For Humty Volntr; Chrch Yth Grp; Mod UN; MuAlphaTh; Scouts; Chr; Ch Chr; Sch Ppr (E); Board of Directors Rockland County Girl Scouts; Gold Award Girl Scouts; Journalism; History; U of Chicago; Cornell

BREMNER, THOMAS; MASSAPEQUA, NY; FARMINGDALE HS; (JR); F Lan Hn Soc; Hi Hnr Roll; Hnr Roll; Nat Hon Sy; Comm Volntr; Peer Tut/Med; Spec Olymp Vol; Emplmnt; Key Club; SADD; Vsity Clb; Sccr (VJC); Vsy Clb (V); Vllyball (VJ); Sch Ppr (R); Business; Villanova; Marist

BRENNAN, NATALIA; MASTIC, NY; WILLIAM FLOYD HS; (SO); Ctznshp Aw; F Lan Hn Soc; Hnr Roll; Otst Ac Ach Awd; St of Mnth; Comm Volntr; Chrch Yth Grp; Italian Clb; Chr; Ch Chr; Stu Cncl (R); Maternity Nursing; Wedding Planner; Stony Brook U

BRENNER, TIFFANY; LIBERTY, NY; LIBERTY HS; (SO); Hi Hnr Roll; Hnr Roll; USAA; Peer Tut/Med; Drma Clb; Mth Clb/Tm; Mus Clb; Scouts; Acpl Chr; Bnd; Jzz Bnd; Mch Bnd; Sccr (J); Senior Girl Scout

BRETSCHER, RACHELE; CAMDEN, NY; CAMDEN HS; (FR); Hi Hnr Roll; Hnr Roll; Nat Hon Sy; Otst Ac Ach Awd; Perf Att; Spec Olymp Vol; ArtClub; Chrch Yth Grp; Chr; Sccr (J); Architect; Artist

BRIGHAM, DREW; LOCKPORT, NY; (SO); Hi Hnr Roll; Comm Volntr; Key Club

BRILL, JONAH B; CATSKILL, NY; SAUGERTIES HS; (SO); Hi Hnr Roll; Kwnis Aw; WWAHSS; Comm Volntr; Emplmnt; Key Club; Spanish Clb; Bskball (V L); Golf (V); Tennis (V); Stu Cncl (R); CR (R); Yrbk (R); Exchange Student with AFS in Spain; Founder of Students Against Racism Club; Law; Stanford U; Cornell U

BRINK, JENNIFER; OWEGO, NY; OWEGO FREE AC; (JR); Hnr Roll; Nat Hon Sy; Comm Volntr; Drma Clb; Key Club; Vsity Clb; Stg Cre; Tennis (V L); Sch Ppr (R, P); Key Club Secretary; Sports Media; Special Education; Ithaca College; Syracuse College

BRISCOE, LASHANTE' M; BRONX, NY; BRONX SCH OF LAW & FINANCE; (SO); Ctznshp Aw; Hnr Roll; Dbte Team; Emplmnt; Jr Ach; Latin Clb; Dnce; SP/M/VS; Sftball (VJCL); Interned at Personal Injury Firm; Open a Public Relations Firm; Psychologist; Columbia U; NYU

BRISSETT, ANDRE M; BROOKLYN, NY; ENY TRANSIT TECH HS; (SR); Ctznshp Aw; Hnr Roll; Nat Hon Sy; Otst Ac Ach Awd; Perf Att; St of Mnth; Yth Ldrshp Prog; Comm Volntr; Chrch Yth Grp; Dbte Team; FCA; Photog; Ch Chr; SP/M/VS; Bowling Team; Take Part in "Walk of America"; Biomedical Science; Hunter College; Long Island U

BRITO, JOSE; BROOKLYN, NY; COBBLE HILL SCH OF AMERICAN STUDIES; (SO); All Am Sch; Hi Hnr Roll; Hnr Roll; MVP; Nat Hon Sy; Nat Ldrshp Svc; Otst Ac Ach Awd; Perf Att; Sci Fairs; St of Mnth; WWAHSS; Comm Volntr; Hab For Humty Volntr; Hosp Aide; Peer Tut/Med; Chrch Yth Grp; Cmptr Clb; DARE; Dbte Team; Emplmnt; Fr of Library; FBLA; Jr Ach; Mod UN; Outdrs Clb; Sci Clb; Bnd; Chr; Bsball (J); Ftball (J); Vllyball (J); Yrbk (P); National Society of High School Scholars; Enrolled in Honors Classes; Pre-Med; Biology; Ivy League Colleges

BRITTON, KATHLEEN; PORT LEYDEN, NY; SOUTH LEWIS HS; (SR); Hnr Roll; Voc Ind Clb Am; President of Skills USA VILA; Medical Concentration Specialist; Syracuse U; Utica School of Commerce

BROADUS, TIONA P; BUFFALO, NY; LEONARDO DA VINCI HS; (SO); Ctznshp Aw; Hi Hnr Roll; Hnr Roll; Nat Hon Sy; Otst Ac Ach Awd; Perf Att; St of Mnth; DARE; Emplmnt; Dnce; Jesse Ketchum Memorial Fund $100 Savings Bond; Bronze Medal 2002-2003 Award; Computer Engineering; Culinary Arts; Chicago Institute; Orlando Culinary Academy

BROBERG, DIANA K; LEVITTOWN, NY; DIVISION AVE HS; (SO); Hi Hnr Roll; Hnr Roll; Nat Hon Sy; WWAHSS; Comm Volntr; Chrch Yth Grp; Drma Clb; Key Club; Chr; Ch Chr; Clr Grd; Dnce; Track (V); NYS School Music Awards-Vocal & Violin; All County Chorus Participant; Drama; Music

BROD, CARLY A; MERRICK, NY; JOHN F KENNEDY HS; (FR); Hnr Roll; Nat Hon Sy; Otst Ac Ach Awd; St of Mnth; Key Club; Tmpl Yth Grp; Bnd; Track; Annually Participate in the Lupus Walk; Active Member of the Key Club; Teaching; Biology; Cornell U; Pennsylvania State U

BRODY, SPENCER T; MOUNT KISCO, NY; FOX LANE HS; (JR); Hi Hnr Roll; WWAHSS; Chess; Cmptr Clb; Drma Clb; Emplmnt; Outdrs Clb; Tech Clb; Chr; SP/M/VS; Stg Cre; Amer. Comp. Sci. League Award; AMC 10 Award; Computer Science; Lighting Design (Theater); Carnegie Mellon U; Harvard U, SUNY Binghamton

BROLLOSY, LEILA; MERRICK, NY; CALHOUN HS; (FR); Ctznshp Aw; Hnr Roll; Nat Hon Sy; Pres Sch; Sci Fairs; Comm Volntr; Chrch Yth Grp; Key Club; French Clb; Finalist in LI Science Fair; Urban Planning; Ethnic Studies; Columbia U; Harvard U

BRONSON, KEVIN W; CONSTABLEVILLE, NY; SOUTH LEWIS HS; (FR); Hi Hnr Roll; WWAHSS; Comm Volntr; Emplmnt; Vsity Clb; Bnd; Bskball; Cr Ctry (V L); Track (V L); Vsy Clb; Major Achievement Program (MAP); History Professor; State Trooper; St Lawrence; Edinboro U

BROOKS, BRANDON T; BOONVILLE, NY; ADIRONDACK HS; (SO); Ctznshp Aw; Hi Hnr Roll; Hnr Roll; Nat Hon Sy; Otst Ac Ach Awd; Pres Sch; WWAHSS; Comm Volntr; Peer Tut/Med; Emplmnt; Mth Clb/Tm; Bnd; Chr; Jzz Bnd; SP/M/VS; Ftball (V); Sccr (J); Track (V L); President's Award for Educational Excellence; NYS Mathematics Honor Society; Criminal Justice; Mohawk Valley Community College; Utica College

BROOKS, CAITLIN E; GLEN HEAD, NY; NORTH SHORE HS; (SR); Hi Hnr Roll; Hnr Roll; WWAHSS; Comm Volntr; FCCLA; Key Club; Track (V); Early Childhood Education; SUNY Oneonta

BROOKS, DARREN Q; MASSAPEQUA, NY; AMITYVILLE MEMORIAL HS; (JR); Hi Hnr Roll; Nat Hon Sy; WWAHSS; Peer Tut/Med; Emplmnt; Mth Clb/Tm; Bnd; Cr Ctry (V); Track (V); Business

BROOKS, OLANA; BROOKLYN, NY; INST FOR SECONDARY ED; Sci Fairs; Emplmnt; Sch Ppr (R, P); Piano Lessons; Flamenco Classes; Physical Therapist; Stony Brook

BROOKS JR, JOSHUA; BRONX, NY; JOHN F KENNEDY HS; (JR); Hnr Roll; Nat Hon Sy; Otst Ac Ach Awd; Perf Att; St of Mnth; WWAHSS; Chrch Yth Grp; DARE; Vsity Clb; Ch Chr; Drm Mjr; Ftball (V); Track (J); Sch Ppr (R); Member of National Arista Society; Penn State U; Syracuse U

BROSIUS, TONI; JAMESTOWN, NY; JAMESTOWN HS; (JR); St of Mnth; Chr; Dnce; Cosmetology; Spanish Award-Best Effort; Doctor; Lawyer; Jamestown Community College

BROUILLET, JEN; LEVITTOWN, NY; DIVISION AVE HS; (JR); MVP; Comm Volntr; Hosp Aide; Emplmnt; Key Club; Vsity Clb; Bskball (V L); Sccr (V); President Key Club; Nursing; Sports Medicine; Shepherd U; East Stroudsburg U

BROUNEUS, AMY; PAINTED POST, NY; CORNING-PAINTED POST WEST HS; (JR); Hi Hnr Roll; Nat Hon Sy; WWAHSS; Scouts; Tchrs Aide; Sftball (VJ); Yrbk (E); Business

BROWN, AIKEEMA; BROOKLYN, NY; PAUL ROBESON HS; (SO); Nat Hon Sy; Comm Volntr; Chrldg (J); Business Law; Computer Tech; Mississippi State U; Harvard U

BROWN, ALYNA; MOUNT VERNON, NY; MT VERNON HS; (SO); 4H Awd; Hi Hnr Roll; Hnr Roll; Nat Hon Sy; WWAHSS; Comm Volntr; Peer Tut/Med; Off Aide; A Member of the TSTT (Today's Students Tomorrow's Teachers Program); Accounting; Marketing; Howard U

BROWN, BIANCA; WILLISTON PARK, NY; MINEOLA HS; (FR); Hi Hnr Roll; St of Mnth; Drma Clb; Emplmnt; Svce Clb; Bnd; Clr Grd; SP/M/VS; Lcrsse (J); Track (V); Adv Cncl; Cl Off (S); CR

BROWN, GINA L; MACHIAS, NY; PIONEER CTRL SCH; (SR); 4H Awd; Nat Hon Sy; 4-H; Ntl FFA

BROWN, KIMBERLY A; SUFFERN, NY; SUFFERN HS; (JR); F Lan Hn Soc; Hi Hnr Roll; Hnr Roll; Nat Hon Sy; WWAHSS; Comm Volntr; DECA; Drma Clb; Emplmnt; Spch Team; Chr; Dnce; SP/M/VS; Yrbk (E); History Honor Society-Executive Board Public Relations Officer; English Honor Society; Politics & Government; Theater; Harvard U; Boston U

BROWN, KRISTA; ALDEN, NY; ALDEN HS; (SR); Hi Hnr Roll; Nat Hon Sy; St of Mnth; WWAHSS; Comm Volntr; Emplmnt; Key Club; Tchrs Aide; Foreign Clb; Swmg (V L); Scholar Athlete Award; Childhood Education Grades 1-6; Genesee Community College

BROWN, LAUREN B; GLOVERSVILLE, NY; GLOVERSVILLE HS; (SO); Hi Hnr Roll; WWAHSS; Yth Ldrshp Prog; Comm Volntr; Chrch Yth Grp; HO'Br Yth Ldrshp; Key Club; NYLC; SP/M/VS; Stg Cre; Vllyball (J); Cl Off (T); Stu Cncl (P); Engineering

Brod, Carly A
John F Kennedy HS
Merrick, NY

Brailousky, Tanya
Abraham Lincoln HS
Brooklyn, NY

Boyce, Christopher W
Monroe-Woodbury HS
Monroe, NY

Boukas, Alexander P
Townsend Harris HS
Jamaica, NY

Botte, John
Smithtown HS
Smithtown, NY

Bou, Lysa
Christopher Columbus HS
Bronx, NY

Boyce, Patrick J
Monroe-Woodbury HS
Monroe, NY

Broadus, Tiona P
Leonardo Da Vinci HS
Buffalo, NY

Brooks Jr, Joshua
John F Kennedy HS
Bronx, NY

BROWN, NICOLA R; SPRING VALLEY, NY; EAST RAMAPO HS; (SR); Hnr Roll; Nat Mrt LOC; Otst Ac Ach Awd; Perf Att; St of Mnth; Comm Volntr; Hosp Aide; Peer Tut/Med; DARE; Prom Com; Bskball (J); Track (VJ); Cl Off (T); Nursing / MSN; Bowie State U

BROWN, NICOLE C; EAST NORWICH, NY; OYSTER BAY HS; (JR); MVP; Pres Sch; Yth Ldrshp Prog; Comm Volntr; Hosp Aide; ArtClub; Chrch Yth Grp; Drma Clb; Emplmnt; Pep Squd; SADD; Tchrs Aide; Vsity Clb; Chr; Dnce; SP/M/VS; Chrldg (VJ); Swmg (V); Track (V); I Would Like to Become a Lawyer.; I Also Want to Work in a Dance Studio.; Georgia Tech U; Hampton U

BROWN, SHANNON R; SOUTH OZONE PARK, NY; WASHINGTON IRVING HS; (JR); Otst Ac Ach Awd; Yth Ldrshp Prog; Comm Volntr; Hosp Aide; Peer Tut/Med; Chrch Yth Grp; Emplmnt; Mus Clb; Off Aide; Tchrs Aide; Bnd; Chr; Ch Chr; Dnce; Business; Health; Duke U; Stanford U

BROWN, TED D; BUFFALO, NY; EMERSON SCH OF HOSPITALITY; (SR); Hnr Roll; Comm Volntr; DARE; CR (R); Voted Most Likely to Succeed; Voted Best Cook in My Class; To Become a Master Chef; To Open My Own Restaurant; Erie Community College; Culinary Institute of America

BROWN II, ROBERT P; STATEN ISLAND, NY; CURTIS HS; (SO); Hnr Roll; Perf Att; WWAHSS; Ftball (V); Mar Art (V); Track (V); Entertainment; Business Law; Hampton U; Howard U

BROWNING, JOSEPH O; LAKE VIEW, NY; FRONTIER CTRL HS; (JR); Hnr Roll; WWAHSS; Comm Volntr; Chrch Yth Grp; Cr Ctry (V); Track (V); Scholar Athlete; Architecture; Buffalo State College; U At Buffalo

BROWN JR, CARL; LAURELTON, NY; NEW CANAAN HS; (JR); Hi Hnr Roll; Hnr Roll; Pres Sch; Comm Volntr; Spec Olymp Vol; Chess; Mus Clb; Tech Clb; Bnd; Jzz Bnd; SP/M/VS; Bskball (J); Ftball (V); Track (V L); Ranked 5th in Track FCIAC Championship; Ranked 6th in Track CIAC Championship; Engineering; Mathematics; Columbia U; Lehigh U

BRUEFACH, ALLAHNA L; STONY BROOK, NY; WARD MELVILLE SCH; MS; Hi Hnr Roll; Hnr Roll; ArtClub; Drma Clb; SP/M/VS; Art; Music; New York U; Florida State

BRUMLEY, SAMANTHA; AMSTERDAM, NY; AMSTERDAM HS; (JR); Hi Hnr Roll; Hnr Roll; Nat Hon Sy; USAA; Comm Volntr; Peer Tut/Med; Emplmnt; Key Club; Mus Clb; Bnd; Mch Bnd; SP/M/VS; Chrldg (V C); Stu Cncl (P); Sch Ppr (R); Rotary Summer Program Exchange Student - Finland 2004; Medical Explorers / Community Service; Psychology; Psychiatry; Colgate U; Columbia U

BRUNNER, ZACHARY D; HARRISON, NY; HARRISON HS; (SO); Acpl Chr; Chr; SP/M/VS; Cr Ctry (J); Track (J); Lit Mag (R); Film Director; Actor; UCLA; New York U

BRUNO, GAEL; YONKERS, NY; LINCOLN HS; (SO); Hnr Roll; Perf Att; St of Mnth; Ch Chr; Bskball; Basketball (For College); Syracuse; U of Connecticut

BRYAN, ELEANOR S; JEFFERSONVILLE, NY; SULLIVAN WEST LAKE HUNTINGTON HS; (JR); F Lan Hn Soc; Hi Hnr Roll; Kwnis Aw; Nat Hon Sy; Otst Ac Ach Awd; Perf Att; Valdctrian; Comm Volntr; Peer Tut/Med; Lib Aide; Tchrs Aide; Bnd; Jzz Bnd; Pep Bnd; Cr Ctry (V L); Sccr (J L); Track (V L); Cl Off (S); Indoor Track-Varsity-Jetta Winner; English; Creative Writing; Hamilton College; Board College

BRYAN, OMAR; JAMAICA, NY; MARTIN VAN BUREN HS; (SR); Hnr Roll; Emplmnt; Acting; Law / Criminal Justice; SUNY Purchase; SUNY Old Westbury

BRYANT, LATANYA S; MIDDLETOWN, NY; MIDDLETOWN HS; (JR); Hi Hnr Roll; Hnr Roll; Nat Hon Sy; Otst Ac Ach Awd; St of Mnth; WWAHSS; Comm Volntr; Peer Tut/Med; DARE; Dbte Team; Emplmnt; Off Aide; Tchrs Aide; Drl Tm; PP Ftbl; Adv Cncl (P); CR (R); Community Service / Abstinence Program; President of Health and Fitness Academy; Lawyer / Psychology Minor; Lawyer / Business Minor

BRYANT, WILLIAM; BROOKLYN, NY; ST EDMUND PREP HS; (JR); Hnr Roll; Comm Volntr; Peer Tut/Med; ArtClub; Chrch Yth Grp; Emplmnt; Key Club; Mus Clb; Pep Squd; Prom Com; Sci Clb; Bnd; Jzz Bnd; Pep Bnd; Stg Cre; CR (R); Attended SOM Architectural (Skidmore Owings Merrill); A Member of the Junior Committee; Civil Engineer; Physical Therapist; City College; Hunter College

BRZEZINSKI, GENNI; SEAFORD, NY; SEAFORD HS; (FR); Hi Hnr Roll; Comm Volntr; Emplmnt; Key Club; Scouts; Vsity Clb; Bnd; Mch Bnd; Sftball (V)

BUCCHERI, SONJA L; UTICA, NY; T R PROCTOR HS; (SR); DAR; Hi Hnr Roll; Hnr Roll; St of Mnth; WWAHSS; Comm Volntr; Hab For Humty Volntr; Red Cr Aide; Chrch Yth Grp; Emplmnt; ROTC; Ch Chr; Orch; American Legion Silver Medal for Scholastic Excellence; Honor Cadet; Pre-Medicine; Roberts Wesleyan College

BUCK, ELIZABETH; PINE CITY, NY; SOUTHSIDE HS OF ELMIRA; (SO); 4H Awd; Hi Hnr Roll; Perf Att; Pres Ac Ftns Aw; Comm Volntr; 4-H; Chrch Yth Grp; Emplmnt; Key Club; Mus Clb; Vsity Clb; Bnd; Mch Bnd; Orch; Pep Bnd; Sccr (V); Track (V L); Sch Ppr (E); Cornell U

BUCK, KELLY A; LODI, NY; SOUTH SENECA HS; (JR); Ctznshp Aw; Hi Hnr Roll; Hnr Roll; St of Mnth; Amnsty Intl; Scouts; Sftball (J); Early Childhood Education; Tompkins Cortland Community College; Cortland College

BUCK, MELISSA; ORISKANY, NY; ORISKANY CTRL SCH; (JR); Hi Hnr Roll; Nat Hon Sy; St of Mnth; WWAHSS; Spec Olymp Vol; Key Club; Mth Clb/Tm; Sci Clb; SADD; Vsity Clb; French Clb; Bnd; Sccr (V); Track (V); Stu Cncl (T); Teen Aids Task Force

BUCKMASTER, KRISTINA; ALMOND, NY; HORNELL HS; (JR); Hi Hnr Roll; Hnr Roll; Nat Hon Sy; WWAHSS; AL Aux Girls; Chrch Yth Grp; SADD; Spanish Clb; Bnd; Chr; Clr Grd; Dnce; Cr Ctry (V L); Sccr (J); Track (V L); Alfred U Student Orchestra; School Play of Footloose and Wizard of Oz; Accounting; Dance; Roberts Wesleyan; Air Force

BUELL, CODY; SCHENECTADY, NY; BURNT HILLS-BALLSTON LAKE HS; (SO); Hi Hnr Roll; MVP; Nat Hon Sy; Otst Ac Ach Awd; FBLA; SADD; Cr Ctry (V); Track (V); Church Youth Group; Study Circles / County Embraces Diversity Organization; Biology / Sports Medicine; Criminal Justice; Hofstra U

BUKOLT, AMY; HANNIBAL, NY; HANNIBAL SR HS; (SR); Ctznshp Aw; Hi Hnr Roll; Hnr Roll; MVP; Nat Hon Sy; Otst Ac Ach Awd; Perf Att; St of Mnth; WWAHSS; Comm Volntr; Chess; Chrch Yth Grp; Key Club; Mus Clb; Prom Com; Sci Clb; French Clb; Chr; Ch Chr; SP/M/VS; Sccr (VJCL); Sftball (VJ L); Vllyball (VJCL); Cl Off (P); Stu Cncl (T); Yrbk (E, P); First Team All League-Volleyball; Select Chorus; Broadcasting; SUNY Oswego

BUKSOV, MIKHAIL; BROOKLYN, NY; LEON M GOLDSTEIN HS SCIENCES; (SO); Comm Volntr; Sci Clb; Swmg (V); Medicine; Law; Columbia U; New York U

BUMP, KARI E; HORSEHEADS, NY; HORSEHEADS HS; (SR); Hnr Roll; St of Mnth; Chrch Yth Grp; Emplmnt

BUNIAK, WILLIAM; FAYETTEVILLE, NY; MANLIUS PEBBLE HILL SCH; (FR); Pres Ac Ftns Aw; DARE; Scouts; Bnd; Dnce; Sccr (J); Swmg (J); Track (J); Zoology; Pre-Med; Cornell U; Le Moyne College

BUONO, JOANNA; SAUGERTIES, NY; SAUGERTIES HS; (FR); Bnd; Dnce; Chrldg (J)

BURGHER, TAJ; CTRL ISLIP, NY; CTRL ISLIP HS; (JR); Hi Hnr Roll; Hnr Roll; Peer Tut/Med; ArtClub; FBLA; FTA; Mth Clb/Tm; Tchrs Aide; Bskball (V L); Cl Off (T); Stu Cncl (R); CR (R); Sch Ppr (E, P); Graphic Design; Journalism / Mass Communications; St John's U; Georgia Tech U

BURGOS, RAIDELYS; BRONX, NY; MARBLE HILL HS FOR INTERNATIONAL STUDIES; (SO); Hnr Roll; Perf Att; St of Mnth; Comm Volntr; Peer Tut/Med; Chess; Tchrs Aide; Tech Clb; Biologist; Accounting; Columbia U

BURGOS, STEVE; BRONX, NY; COLUMBUS HS; (FR); Bsball (J); Lawyer; Professional Baseball Player

BURLESON, SARAH; BETHPAGE, NY; ISLAND TREES HS; (SO); Hnr Roll; Otst Ac Ach Awd; WWAHSS; Key Club; Mth Clb/Tm; Svce Clb; SADD; Vsity Clb; Bnd; Mch Bnd; Orch; Pep Bnd; Lcrsse (V); Scr Kpr (V); Sccr (V L)

BURLEY, SHANNON M; LISBON, NY; LISBON CTRL SCH; (SO); Hnr Roll; Perf Att; Comm Volntr; Emplmnt; NtlFrnscLg; Photog; Tech Clb; Science Major; Math Major; SUNY Canton College of Technology

BURNBAUM, JENNA; HUNTINGTON, NY; OUR LADY OF MERCY AC; (JR); Hnr Roll; Nat Hon Sy; Drma Clb; Mus Clb; Off Aide; Prom Com; Chr; SP/M/VS; Stu Cncl; CR (P); Law; Communications

BURNHAM, RASHIDA; BRONX, NY; AC OF MT ST URSULA; (JR); Hnr Roll; Nat Mrt Semif; St of Mnth; WWAHSS; Comm Volntr; Lib Aide; Dnce; Chrldg (V); St. John's U Math and Science Award; National Latin Exam - Maxima Cum Laude; Business / MBA; Bentley College; SUNY New Paltz

BURROUGHS, AMBER L; TICONDEROGA, NY; TICONDEROGA HS; (SO); Hi Hnr Roll; Hnr Roll; Perf Att; Pres Ac Ftns Aw; Comm Volntr; Peer Tut/Med; DARE; Key Club; French Clb; Bnd; Chr; Yrbk (E, R); Teaching; Early Childhood Development; Saint Rose; Cobleskill (SUNY)

BURT-MILLER, JAVIER; MOUNT VERNON, NY; MT VERNON HS; (JR); Hi Hnr Roll; Hnr Roll; Nat Hon Sy; Otst Ac Ach Awd; Perf Att; WWAHSS; Yth Ldrshp Prog; Chrch Yth Grp; Key Club; ROTC; Drl Tm; Accounting; Masters Degree; U of Connecticut; St John's

BURVEE, GRACE; WILLET, NY; CINCINNATUS; (JR); Hi Hnr Roll; Nat Hon Sy; WWAHSS; Comm Volntr; Red Cr Aide; Prom Com; Spanish Clb; Bskball (V); Sccr (J); Cl Off (T)

BUSH, JEFF; BROCKPORT, NY; BROCKPORT HS; (JR); Hi Hnr Roll; Kwnis Aw; Nat Hon Sy; Perf Att; WWAHSS; Yth Ldrshp Prog; Comm Volntr; Emplmnt; HO'Br Yth Ldrshp; Foreign Clb; Ftball (V L); Golf (V L); Stu Cncl (P); CR (P); Winning the Top Junior Award in 2005; Bentley College; Georgetown U

BUSS, MICHAEL T; WESTFIELD, NY; WESTFIELD AC & CTRL SCH; (JR); Hi Hnr Roll; Hnr Roll; Pres Ac Ftns Aw; Sci Fairs; WWAHSS; Comm Volntr; Chrch Yth Grp; Emplmnt; Tchrs Aide; Sccr (VJ L); Tennis (V L); Vllyball (VJ L)

BUSSETTI, CHRIS; STATEN ISLAND, NY; ST PETER'S BOYS HS; (SO); Perf Att; Comm Volntr; Emplmnt; Lib Aide; Scouts; Cyclg (C); Mar Art (V); Eagle Scout 2005; Purple Belt Karate; Industrial Engineering; Cooper Union College; St John's U

BUSSING, JULIE; GREENWICH, NY; GREENWICH CTRL SCH; (JR); Hi Hnr Roll; Nat Hon Sy; Otst Ac Ach Awd; Perf Att; Pres Ac Ftns Aw; Comm Volntr; ArtClub; Chrch Yth Grp; Emplmnt; Prom Com; Fld Hky (VJ); Track (VJ L); Stu Cncl (R); Yrbk

BUTLER, AMBER; SOUND BEACH, NY; MILLER PLACE HS; (JR); Ctznshp Aw; Hnr Roll; St of Mnth; WWAHSS; Hab For Humty Volntr; Peer Tut/Med; ArtClub; Chess; Drma Clb; Emplmnt; Key Club; P to P St Amb Prg; Chr; Dnce; SP/M/VS; Cr Ctry (J); Track (J); Adv Cncl (R); Cl Off (P); Stu Cncl (P); CR (R); 2001 & 2002 Nominee for Poet of the Year; Bronze Medal - NYSSMA Festival; Psychology; Medicine; Columbia U; Brown U

BUTT, HAROON A; BROOKLYN, NY; INST FOR SECONDARY ED; (SO); Hnr Roll; Sci Fairs; St of Mnth; Peer Tut/Med; Chess; CR (R); Lit Mag (E); Sch Ppr (E); Lawyer; Author; Harvard U; Princeton U

BUTTER, ERIC E; VESTAL, NY; SETON CATHOLIC CTRL HS; (SO); Hi Hnr Roll; Pres Ac Ftns Aw; Sci Fairs; WWAHSS; Comm Volntr; Spec Olymp Vol; Chess; DARE; Key Club; Mod UN; Quiz Bowl; SADD; French Clb; Orch; Bskball; Lcrsse (V); Sccr (VJ); Wt Lftg (V); Violin; Acting (Plays Over Summer); Pre-Med; Biomedical Engineering; Cornell U; Wake Forest

BUTTON, KAYLYN M; ONTARIO, NY; WAYNE CTRL (J.A.B); (FR); Hi Hnr Roll; Otst Ac Ach Awd; Perf Att; St of Mnth; Comm Volntr; Peer Tut/Med; Key Club; Scouts; Bnd; Jzz Bnd; Bskball (J); Sccr (J); Sftball (J); Stu Cncl (R)

BUZOVETSKY, OLGA; NEW YORK, NY; THE BEACON SCH; (JR); Hnr Roll; Perf Att; Sci Fairs; WWAHSS; Bskball (J); Vllyball; Lit Mag; Ultimate Frisbee; Community Service/College Courses

BUZZOLANI, SAMANTHA; EAST ROCKAWAY, NY; EAST ROCKAWAY JR/SR HS; (SO); Hi Hnr Roll; Kwnis Aw; St of Mnth; Comm Volntr; Mth Clb/Tm; Sci Clb; SADD; Foreign Clb; Chr; Orch; SP/M/VS; Sccr (J); Track (V); The Young Artist Orchestral Program At Law Post; Natural Sciences (Forensics)

BYER, AVA; DELMAR, NY; BETHLEHEM CTRL HS; (JR); Hi Hnr Roll; Sci/Math Olympn; WWAHSS; Yth Ldrshp Prog; Comm Volntr; Hab For Humty Volntr; Emplmnt; Key Club; NYLC; Photog; Svce Clb; Vsity Clb; Spanish Clb; Swmg (V C); Mentor Club; Business; Fordham U; Fairfield U

BYRD, TIFFANY J; BRONX, NY; HEALTH OPPORTUNITIES HS; (SO); Hnr Roll; Perf Att; Yth Ldrshp Prog; Comm Volntr; Mus Clb; Dnce; Arch (L); Swmg (V); Doctor's Assistant; Nursing; American U; NYU

BYRNE, JAMES; VALLEY COTTAGE, NY; NYACK HS; (SR); Hi Hnr Roll; Nat Hon Sy; Perf Att; Sci Fairs; WWAHSS; Yth Ldrshp Prog; Comm Volntr; Peer Tut/Med; Biology Clb; Chrch Yth Grp; Emplmnt; Scouts; Eagle Scout

BYRNE, KELLY V; LEWISTON, NY; LEWISTON-PORTER HS; (SO); Hi Hnr Roll; Hnr Roll; Nat Hon Sy; Otst Ac Ach Awd; WWAHSS; Comm Volntr; DARE; Drma Clb; Fr of Library; Lib Aide; Pep Squd; Scouts; SADD; Foreign Clb; Bnd; Chr; Dnce; Orch; PPSqd (JC); Sch Ppr (R); First in Class for Spelling, Math and Science.

BYRNE, MEGAN; MONROE, NY; MONROE-WOODBURY HS; (SO); Hnr Roll; MVP; DARE; Emplmnt; Chr; Chrldg (V); Cheerleader of the Year; Financing; Physical Therapy; U of Connecticut; Manhattan College

CABALLERO, MELISSA A; EAST MEADOW, NY; EAST MEADOW HS; (SO); Hnr Roll; Nat Hon Sy; Perf Att; Sci Fairs; WWAHSS; Comm Volntr; Emplmnt; Key Club; Bnd; Dnce; Mch Bnd; Master's Degree; Cornell U; Syracuse U

CACCAMO, SIMONE A; STATEN ISLAND, NY; STATEN ISLAND TECH; (SO); Hnr Roll; Key Club; Vsity Clb; SP/M/VS; Sccr (V)

CACCHILLO, LEAH; SAUGERTIES, NY; SAUGERTIES HS; (FR); Hi Hnr Roll; Hnr Roll; Otst Ac Ach Awd; Comm Volntr; DARE; FCCLA; Key Club; Bnd; Chr; SP/M/VS; Mar Art; Sftball; Education; Music

Caballero, Melissa A, East Meadow HS, East Meadow, NY
Burgos, Raidelys, Marble Hill HS For International Studies, Bronx, NY
Buniak, William, Manlius Pebble Hill Sch, Fayetteville, NY
Buck, Melissa, Oriskany Ctrl Sch, Oriskany, NY
Brumley, Samantha, Amsterdam HS, Amsterdam, NY
Brown II, Robert P, Curtis HS, Staten Island, NY
Browning, Joseph O, Frontier Ctrl HS, Lake View, NY
Buell, Cody, Burnt Hills-Ballston Lake HS, Schenectady, NY
Burgher, Taj, Central Islip HS, Central Islip, NY
Butt, Haroon A, Institute For Secondary Ed, Brooklyn, NY
Butter, Eric E, Seton Catholic Ctrl HS, Vestal, NY

CACCIOTTI, ALDEN; HORSEHEADS, NY; HORSEHEADS HS; (JR); Hi Hnr Roll; Nat Hon Sy; Otst Ac Ach Awd; Yth Ldrshp Prog; Comm Volntr; Peer Tut/Med; Chrch Yth Grp; Drma Clb; Emplmnt; NYLC; P to P St Amb Prg; Scouts; French Clb; Acpl Chr; Chr; Ch Chr; Dnce; Chrldg (VJ L); Vllyball (JCL); Show Choir; Treasurer of Drama Club; Psychology; Medicine; Liberty U; Baptist Bible College

CACERES, CATHERINE; BRONX, NY; ST CATHARINE AC; (SR); F Lan Hn Soc; Hnr Roll; Nat Hon Sy; Perf Att; WWAHSS; Comm Volntr; ArtClub; Chrch Yth Grp; Yrbk (E); Management Operations; Journalism; Baruch College

CACERES, CINTHYA A; PEEKSKILL, NY; PEEKSKILL HS; (JR); Ctznshp Aw; SADD; Latin Clb; Pediatrician or Chef; New York U Medical School; The Culinary Academy of Long Island

CACERES, NATALIE; WHITE PLAINS, NY; WHITE PLAINS HS; (SO); Hnr Roll; Nat Sci Aw; Comm Volntr; Chrch Yth Grp; NYLC; Off Aide; Scouts; Svce Clb; Clb; Bnd; Mch Bnd; Fld Hky (V, JV); Lcrsse (JV); Sccr (JV); Stu Cncl (R); Yrbk (E, P); Highest Community Service Award (Two Consecutive Years); Certificate of Participation in the National Geographic Bee; Social Worker

CADEAU, PIERRE R; BROOKLYN, NY; SAMUEL J TILDEN HS; (JR); Hnr Roll; Perf Att; Comm Volntr; Chrch Yth Grp; Tchrs Aide; Tmpl Yth Grp; Italian Clb; SP/M/VS; Swmg (L); First Place in Contest / Honor By the President of the Borough College / Host of a Show; Teaching; Political Science; Brooklyn College; Medgar Evers College

CADET, VANIA; NEW YORK, NY; WASHINGTON IRVING HS; (SO); Bskball; Cr Ctry (V); Sccr; Sftball; Tennis; Track (V); Pediatrician; Nursing; Columbia U; Hunter College

CAHILL, SOPHIA; WESTBURY, NY; CARLE PLACE HS; (SR); F Lan Hn Soc; Nat Hon Sy; WWAHSS; Peer Tut/Med; AL Aux Girls; Key Club; MuAlphaTh; Bnd; Chr; Orch; SP/M/VS; Tennis (V); Track (V); Stu Cncl (V); Sch Ppr (E); Yrbk (R)

CAIN, MARILEE E; EAST ELMHURST, NY; ST MICHAEL AC; (JR); Hnr Roll; Nat Mrt Fin; Nat Mrt Sch Recip; Nat Mrt Semif; Otst Ac Ach Awd; St of Mnth; Peer Tut/Med; DARE; P to P St Amb Prg; Chr; Chrldg (V); New York U; Columbia U

CAINE, RONCALLA; BROOKLYN, NY; PAUL ROBESON HS; (FR); Achieve Mastery; Old Westbury U; Cooper Union U

CAITO, SHARON A; GENEVA, NY; GENEVA HS; (FR); Hi Hnr Roll; Hnr Roll; USAA; WWAHSS; Bnd; Jzz Bnd; Mch Bnd; Pep Bnd; Teach 2nd Grade Religion

CALA, STEVEN M; STATEN ISLAND, NY; ST. PETERS HS FOR BOYS; (JR)

CALDARA, ALICIA R; SCHENECTADY, NY; SCHALMONT HS; (FR); Ctznshp Aw; Hi Hnr Roll; Nat Hon Sy; St of Mnth; WWAHSS; Comm Volntr; Peer Tut/Med; Chrch Yth Grp; Key Club; Sci Clb; SADD; International Clb; Bnd; Chr; Dnce

CALDERON, SOFIA; BROOKLYN, NY; ST EDMUND PREP HS; (SO); Hi Hnr Roll; Hnr Roll; Sci Fairs; Comm Volntr; Mus Clb; Quiz Bowl; Chr; SP/M/VS; Bskball (J); Altar Service; Pharmacy; Interpreter / Languages; LIU; St John's U

CALLEJA, JOSEPH A; NEW YORK, NY; MANHATTAN CTR FOR SCI & MATH; (SO); Hi Hnr Roll; Stu Cncl (R); Boxing; Technology; Math Teacher; The Marines; Hunter College

CAMARENA, LETICIA A; SYRACUSE, NY; HENNINGER HS; (FR); Hnr Roll; Perf Att; Pediatrician; Pre-School Teacher; Onondaga Community College; Syracuse U

CAMERON, JACLYN; CORNWALL ON HUDSON, NY; CORNWALL CTRL HS; (JR); Hi Hnr Roll; MVP; Nat Hon Sy; Otst Ac Ach Awd; St of Mnth; WWAHSS; Comm Volntr; Peer Tut/Med; Emplmnt; Key Club; Spanish Clb; Bskball (VJ L); Tutor / Coach Basketball; Education / Speech Pathology / Audiology; Medical / Science / Physical Therapy

CAMERON, KATIE L; MASSENA, NY; MADRID-WADDINGTON CTRL SCH; (FR); Ctznshp Aw; Hi Hnr Roll; WWAHSS; Comm Volntr; Peer Tut/Med; Red Cr Aide; Dbte Team; Drma Clb; Fr of Library; Key Club; Lib Aide; P to P St Amb Prg; Spch Team; French Clb; Bnd; Jzz Bnd; Mch Bnd; SP/M/VS; Sftball (J); Vllyball (J); Mock Trial; Law; St John's U; Albany Law School

CAMPBELL, AMANDA; ERIN, NY; HORSEHEADS HS; (JR); Hi Hnr Roll; Hnr Roll; Nat Hon Sy; Otst Ac Ach Awd; Perf Att; St of Mnth; Yth Ldrshp Prog; Comm Volntr; Scouts; Chr; Ob-Gyn Doctor; Elmira College; Wells College

CAMPBELL, CODY D; HAMLIN, NY; BROCKPORT HS; (SO); Bsball (J); Ice Hky (V); Vsy Clb (V); Wt Lftg (V); Select Hockey Team in Europe 7/05; Technology; Engineering

CAMPBELL, ISAIAH; MT VERNON, NY; MT VERNON HS; (FR); Ctznshp Aw; Hi Hnr Roll; Hnr Roll; Nat Hon Sy; St of Mnth; Comm Volntr; Tech Clb; Bnd; Jzz Bnd; Entrepreneurial Studies; Creative Writing; Boston College; New York U

CAMPBELL, JAMILA; YONKERS, NY; LINCOLN HS; (JR); Hnr Roll; Nat Hon Sy; Red Cr Aide; Emplmnt; Photog; Dnce; Vllyball (J); Helping Plan and Organize the Junior Banquet; African-American Club; International Business; Fashion Marketing; Johnson and Wales; Jacksonville U

CAMPBELL, TYLEEA; NEW YORK, NY; M L K HS OF ARTS & TECH; (JR); Ctznshp Aw; Hi Hnr Roll; Hnr Roll; Perf Att; WWAHSS; Comm Volntr; Chrch Yth Grp; Vsity Clb; Ch Chr; Bskball (V); Pre-Law; Business; Hostos Community College; Morgan State

CAMPISI, JOSEPH B; FLORAL PARK, NY; CHAMINADE HS; (JR); Hnr Roll; Chess; Emplmnt; Bskball; Sccr; Town Baseball Team for 10 Years; Dentist; Fordham U; Boston College

CAMPOS, STEPHANIE; CTRL ISLIP, NY; CTRL ISLIP HS; (SO); Hi Hnr Roll; Hnr Roll; USAA; Yale U; Saint John's U

CANNIZZARO, ANDREW; NEW YORK, NY; BRONX HS OF SCIENCE; (JR); Comm Volntr; Cmptr Clb; Stg Cre; Advanced Explainer - NY Botanical Garden; Film Crew Internships; Filmmaking; Creative Writing; New York U; SUNY Purchase

CANTILLO, FREDDY; ROOSEVELT, NY; (FR); Hnr Roll; Nat Hon Sy; Sci Fairs; St of Mnth; DARE; Chr; Ftball (J); Honor Roll; Law; Medicine; U of Utah; Florida U

CANTOR, PAMELA; EAST MEADOW, NY; EAST MEADOW HS; (SO); Hnr Roll; Otst Ac Ach Awd; Sci/Math Olympn; WWAHSS; Comm Volntr; Peer Tut/Med; ArtClub; FTA; Key Club; Mth Clb/Tm; Tchrs Aide; Tmpl Yth Grp; Bnd; Mch Bnd; Lit Mag (R); Selected & Played in All County (2005); Founded Future Educators of America in My School; Mathematics; Education; The College of New Jersey; Binghamton U (SUNY)

CANTORAL, KELLY; CORONA, NY; LA GUARDIA PERF ARTS HS; (SR); Bnd; Orch; SP/M/VS; School of Orchestral Studies NYSSMA; Music; Composition; Potsdam U; Adelphi U

CANTRES, AWILDA; BRONX, NY; HS OF FASHION IND; (FR); Comm Volntr; Drma Clb; Emplmnt; Off Aide; International Clb; Dnce; Playing Sports - Not with School; Math Honors; Criminal Justice; Journalism; Salem State College; Clark University

CANTUNA, JANE D; BRONX, NY; ST PIUS V HS; (JR); Hnr Roll; Comm Volntr; Dnce; Modeling-Barbizon School; Acting Barbizon School; Performing Arts; Finance; NYU; FIT

CAO, STEVEN; STATEN ISLAND, NY; STUYVESANT; (FR); Key Club; Track; Vsy Clb (J)

CAPECELATRO, ALEX; BREWSTER, NY; BREWSTER HS; (JR); Skiing (V); Sch Ppr (P); Yrbk (E, P); PhD in Chemistry; Cal Tech; UCLA

CAPORALI, MICHELE; ENDICOTT, NY; UNION ENDICOTT HS; (SO); Hi Hnr Roll; Hnr Roll; WWAHSS; Biology Clb; DARE; Emplmnt; Key Club; Vsity Clb; Orch; Tennis (V, L); Stu Cncl (R); CR (R); Sch Ppr (R); New York State Scholar Athlete-2 Years; Medicine; Johns Hopkins U; Cornell U

CARBONE, KRISTIN N; AQUEBOGUE, NY; RIVERHEAD HS; (SR); F Lan Hn Soc; Hi Hnr Roll; MVP; Nat Hon Sy; St of Mnth; Comm Volntr; Peer Tut/Med; ArtClub; Emplmnt; Photog; SADD; Bskball; Chrldg (C); Vllyball; Lit Mag (E); Yrbk (E, R); Latin National Honor Society; Pre-Law Program; Math; Sacred Heart U; Quinnipiac U

CARCACHE, IRENE; ALBANY, NY; ALBANY HS; (JR); Hi Hnr Roll; Hnr Roll; WWAHSS; Key Club; French Clb; Tennis (J); Track (V); Sch Ppr (R); Architecture; Sociology; Cornell U; Rensselaer Polytechnic Institute

CARDENAS, ELIZA; MASSENA, NY; MASSENA SR HS; (SO); Pres Ac Ftns Aw; Chrch Yth Grp; Photog; Scouts; French Clb; President's Education Awards Program; Reading Award; Marine Biology; Photography; U of NYC

CARDILLO, KIDD; MASSAPEQUA, NY; PLAINEDGE HS; (JR); Hi Hnr Roll; Hnr Roll; MVP; Peer Tut/Med; Mth Clb/Tm; Ftball (J); Vllyball (V CL); Tutoring Math; Accounting; Math Teacher; Syracuse U; St. Joseph U

CARDONE, MARIA A; BROOKLYN, NY; BISHOP KEARNEY HS; (JR); Hi Hnr Roll; WWAHSS; Cmptr Clb; Lib Aide; Off Aide; Tchrs Aide; Italian Clb; Bnd; Mch Bnd; Lit Mag (R); Sch Ppr (R); St John's Award for Excellence in Math / Biology; St John's Award for Excellence in Math / Chemistry; History; Journalism

CAREY, AUTUMN B; GLOVERSVILLE, NY; GLOVERSVILLE HS; (FR); Hi Hnr Roll; Nat Hon Sy; Perf Att; St of Mnth; Chrch Yth Grp; Drma Clb; Scouts; Bnd; Chr; Ch Chr; SP/M/VS; Swmg (V); Student Government Association (SGA); Child Education/Teacher; Drama, Music and Acting; St. Rose; Fulton Montgomery Community College

CARIDAD, ALVARO L; YONKERS, NY; SAUNDERS TRADES & TECH HS; (SR); Hi Hnr Roll; Hnr Roll; Peer Tut/Med; School Bowling Team; Business Degree; Computer Engineer; Westchester Community College

CARL, COURTNEY; HUNTINGTON, NY; HUNTINGTON HS; (SO); Hi Hnr Roll; Hnr Roll; Perf Att; Pres Ac Ftns Aw; Sci Fairs; St of Mnth; Comm Volntr; Scouts; Bnd; Ftball (C); Sccr (J); Yrbk; VMCA Travel Soccer Program; Journalism; Graphic Design

CARLIN, MEGHAN; EAST MEADOW, NY; EAST MEADOW HS; (SO); Hnr Roll; Kwnis Aw; Nat Hon Sy; WWAHSS; Peer Tut/Med; Chrch Yth Grp; Key Club; Off Aide; Photog; Chr; Stg Cre; Bskball (JC); Fld Hky (JC); Sftball (J); Engineering

CARLISLE, DANIELLE M; LEWISTON, NY; LEWISTON PORTER HS; (JR); Hi Hnr Roll; Hnr Roll; Sci Fairs; St of Mnth; Comm Volntr; Off Aide; Scouts; Tchrs Aide; Silver Award - Girl Scouts; Early Childhood Education; Special Education; Trocaire College; D'youville College

CARLSON, JAMIE L; WEST COXSACKIE, NY; COLUMBIA-GREENE ED CTR; (JR); Hnr Roll; MVP; Nat Hon Sy; WWAHSS; Comm Volntr; Chrch Yth Grp; Emplmnt; P to P St Amb Prg; Prom Com; Ch Chr; Fld Hky (JCL); Lit Mag (E, R, P); Business / MBA; Highest Degree Possible; Endicott College; U of Bridgeport

CARLSON, JEREMIE; SCHENECTADY, NY; SCHENECTADY HS; (SO); F Lan Hn Soc; Hi Hnr Roll; Hnr Roll; Nat Hon Sy; Otst Ac Ach Awd; USAA; WWAHSS; Comm Volntr; Chrch Yth Grp; DARE; French Clb; Ch Chr; Orch; Track (J); Crew; National Fine Arts Festival Place First for NY State; Medical Doctor (Pediatrics); Architecture; Harvard U; Union College

CARMAN, DANIEL; MONSEY, NY; SPRING VALLEY HS; (SO); Hnr Roll; Otst Ac Ach Awd; Bnd; Jzz Bnd; Mch Bnd; Stg Cre; Bsball (J); Bskball (J); Ftball (V); Wt Lftg (VJ); Student of the Month/English; Athletic Training; U of Miami; Syracuse U

CARMAN, KATYA; WATERTOWN, NY; WATERTOWN HS; (JR); Hnr Roll; Nat Hon Sy; Sci/Math Olympn; Comm Volntr; Hosp Aide; Key Club; Mth Clb/Tm; Mod UN; Quiz Bowl; Sci Clb; SADD; Acpl Chr; Bnd; Chr; Ch Chr; Lcrsse (V); Swmg (V); Cl Off (S); Stu Cncl (R); Ukrainian Dancing; President of Jr. Veterinarian Orthodox League; Business; Boston College; Case Western Reserve

CARPENTIER, MEGHAN R; ALTAMONT, NY; GUILDERLAND HS; (JR); Hnr Roll; Nat Hon Sy; Otst Ac Ach Awd; Perf Att; St of Mnth; WWAHSS; Emplmnt; Key Club; Prom Com; Chr; Ch Chr; Dnce; Chrldg (J); Cl Off (R); Sing National Anthem At Sporting Events; Mathematics-Education; Vassar College; Williams College

CARR, BRIANA; MASSENA, NY; MASSENA CTRL HS; (FR); Hi Hnr Roll; Hnr Roll; Otst Ac Ach Awd; Comm Volntr; Chr; Reality Check; Teaching; Occupational Therapy; Clarkson U; Potsdam State

CARRIES, OLGA; CTRL ISLIP, NY; (JR); Hnr Roll; Chess; Chrch Yth Grp; Emplmnt; Photog; Sci Clb; SADD; Orch; Stg Cre; Sftball (L); Yrbk (P); Music Honor Society; Medical Degree - Ob/Gyn; Adelphi U; SUNY Albany

CARRIGAN, SHAYLYN; CLAY, NY; CBA HS; (FR); Hnr Roll; Comm Volntr; Emplmnt; Bnd; Dvng (V); Vllyball (J); Competitive Figure Skating; Sunday School Teacher; Ob/Gyn; Neonatal Nurse; Castleton State College; Le Moyne College

CARROLL, TANNER; WESTPORT, NY; WESTPORT CTRL SCH; (FR); Hnr Roll; MVP; Yth Ldrshp Prog; Comm Volntr; DARE; Drma Clb; Scouts; Jzz Bnd; Stg Cre; Bskball (V); Golf (V); Sccr (V); Athletic Trainer; History; Duke U; UVM

CARROW, CHRISTOPHER; WEST FALLS, NY; EAST AURORA HS; (SO); Hnr Roll; Otst Ac Ach Awd; St of Mnth; DARE; SADD; Bdmtn (L); Math Honoree; Criminal Justice; Erie Community College

CARSON, DANIEL J; SINCLAIRVILLE, NY; CASSADAGA VALLEY MHS; (JR); Hnr Roll; St of Mnth; Emplmnt; Tech Clb; Stu Cncl (T); MBA; Architectural Design; Canisius College; Alfred State College

CARTER, CHRISTI; APALACHIN, NY; OWEGO FREE AC (OFA); (SR); Ctznshp Aw; Hi Hnr Roll; Nat Hon Sy; WWAHSS; Comm Volntr; Peer Tut/Med; Chrch Yth Grp; DARE; Emplmnt; Key Club; Mth Clb/Tm; SADD; Ch Chr; Fld Hky (V C); Lcrsse (V); Violin (Private Lessons); Member of the Month for Key Club; Social Work; Mansfield U

CARTER, KRISTEN; BUFFALO, NY; LEONARDO DA VINCI HS; (FR); Hnr Roll; Red Cr Aide; Dnce; Swmg (V); Battle of the Books Champion (2004)

CARTER, MICHELLE A; STATEN ISLAND, NY; PT RICHMOND HS; (SR); Hnr Roll; Nat Hon Sy; Perf Att; Comm Volntr; Spec Olymp Vol; Emplmnt; Mus Clb; Prom Com; ROTC; Bnd; Clr Grd; Jzz Bnd; Mch Bnd; Swmg (J); Vllyball (V); Criminal Justice; Psychology; Pennsylvania State U; U of Miami

CARVAJAL, DANIEL; WOODSIDE, NY; FOREST HILLS HS; (SR); Comm Volntr; Cr Ctry (V); Sccr (V); Track (V); Wrstlg (V); Outstanding Office Monitor; United States Marine Corps; Culinary Arts

Campbell, Jamila
Lincoln HS
Yonkers, NY

Calleja, Joseph A
Manhattan Ctr For Sci & Math
New York, NY

Caceres, Cinthya A
Peekskill HS
Peekskill, NY

Caine, Roncalla
Paul Robeson HS
Brooklyn, NY

Cantuna, Jane D
St Pius V HS
Bronx, NY

CARVALHO, MARION; BALDWINSVILLE, NY; CW BAKER HS; (SO); Hi Hnr Roll; Hnr Roll; Comm Volntr; Chrch Yth Grp; DARE; Key Club; P to P St Amb Prg; Photog; Scouts; Dnce; Sccr (L); Tennis (J L); Vllyball (L); Yrbk (R, P); Literary Writing Award; Dance Awards & NYSSMA-Vocal; Sports & Entertainment Marketing; Advertising; UNC Chapel Hill; Laboratory Institute of the Arts NY

CASCIO, DANIELLE; STATEN ISLAND, NY; MOORE CATHOLIC HS; (JR); Yth Ldrshp Prog; Comm Volntr; Stu Cncl (R); Day Care Center Volunteer; Student Council; Accounting; Rider U; College of Staten Island

CASCO, JAN M; BELLMORE, NY; JOHN F KENNEDY HS; (FR); Comm Volntr; Mth Clb/Tm; Orch; Ftball (J); Vllyball (JC); Orchestra; Biology; Penn State U

CASE, ARI; ARVERNE, NY; ENY TRANSIT TECH HS; (SR); F Lan Hn Soc; Hnr Roll; Perf Att; USAA; Arista Award; Computer Engineering; Polytechnic U; Stony Brook U

CASE, NICOLE; BOONVILLE, NY; ADIRONDACK HS; (SO); Ctznshp Aw; Hi Hnr Roll; Nat Hon Sy; WWAHSS; Comm Volntr; Spec Olymp Vol; Chrch Yth Grp; DARE; Dnce; Sccr (V); Yrbk (P); National Honor Society, Math; Honor Society; Business Management; Penn State; U of California, Los Angeles

CASEY, JONATHAN; COHOES, NY; SHAKER HS; (SO); Bsball (J L); Member of Town of Colonie Youth Court; Physics; Material Science; Boston College; RPI

CASEY, THOMAS; STUYVESANT, NY; ICHABOD CRANE HS; (JR); Hi Hnr Roll; Hnr Roll; Perf Att; Comm Volntr; DARE; Emplmnt; Off Aide; Prom Com; SADD; Wdwrkg Clb; Sch Ppr; ITT Tech; Columbia Greene Cmty College

CASPER, RACHEL A; DELANSON, NY; DUANESBURG JR/SR HS; (JR); Hi Hnr Roll; Hnr Roll; Nat Hon Sy; Otst Ac Ach Awd; Comm Volntr; Spec Olymp Vol; Chrch Yth Grp; Drma Clb; Emplmnt; Mus Clb; Prom Com; Svce Clb; Chr; Ch Chr; SP/M/VS; Cl Off (S); Sch Ppr (R)

CASSIMORE, JEREMY; ERIN, NY; HORSEHEADS HS; (JR); Hnr Roll; Perf Att; Comm Volntr; Chrch Yth Grp; Emplmnt; Wdwrkg Clb; Ftball (J); Stu Cncl (R); Horse Heads Youth Bureau; Super Saturday; Business; Culinary Arts; Paul Smith's College; Alfred State, NY

CASTAGNO, NICOLE; STATEN ISLAND, NY; PT RICHMOND HS; (SR); Bskball (V C); Sftball (V C); Vllyball (V C); Physical Education Teacher; Kean U

CASTANOS, JUAN; BRONX, NY; SAMUEL GOMPERS HS; (JR); Nat Hon Sy; Comm Volntr; Cmptr Clb; Emplmnt; Computer Technology/Technician; Communications; Binghamton U; SUNY Morrisville

CASTEL, LIZZIE; BRONX, NY; FREDERICK DOUGLASS AC; (JR); Hi Hnr Roll; Hnr Roll; Perf Att; Pres Ac Ftns Aw; Pres Sch; Sci Fairs; St of Mnth; WWAHSS; Yth Ldrshp Prog; Comm Volntr; Peer Tut/Med; ArtClub; Chess; Cmptr Clb; DARE; Dbte Team; Emplmnt; FBLA; Mus Clb; Bnd; Dnce; SP/M/VS; Stg Cre; Bskball (L); Track (L); Vllyball (L); CR (P); Sch Ppr (R); One Major Achievement I've Made Is a Drawing Which Was Made Into a Carousel; Law; Business; Spelman College; Bryant College

CASTELLANO, MATTHEW W; PEARL RIVER, NY; BERGEN CATHOLIC; (JR); Hnr Roll; Comm Volntr; Emplmnt; NYLC; Prom Com; Svce Clb; Ftball (V); Track (V); Cl Off (S); Sch Ppr (E); Peer Minister; West Point Leadership Award USMA; Fordham U; LaSalle U

CASTIGLIA, ROBERT; EAST NORTHPORT, NY; ELWOOD-JOHN H GLENN HS; (JR); Hi Hnr Roll; Hnr Roll; Nat Hon Sy; Nat Stu Ath Day Aw; Yth Ldrshp Prog; Comm Volntr; Hab For Humty Volntr; AL Aux Boys; Svce Clb; Chr; Bsball; Ftball; Lcrsse; Wt Lftg; Wrstlg; National Scholar Athlete; Owning An Accounting Firm; Law; U of Maryland; SUNY Binghamton

CASTLES, RYAN A; BETHPAGE, NY; ST DOMINIC HS; (SO); Otst Ac Ach Awd; Comm Volntr; FBLA; Sccr (V); Swmg (V); Track (V); Sacred Heart; Hofstra U

CASTRO, VALERIE; SPRING VALLEY, NY; SPRING VALLEY HS; (JR); Hnr Roll; Comm Volntr; Peer Tut/Med; Key Club; Chr; Ch Chr; Zeta Phi Beta Sorority Inc Youth Group; Mock Trial-County Champions; Education K-6; Psychology; New York U; Barnard College

CATAPANO, MICHAEL; LEVITTOWN, NY; ISLAND TREES HS; (SO); Hi Hnr Roll; Hnr Roll; Peer Tut/Med; Cl Off (P)

CATARELLI, SAMANTHA; SHIRLEY, NY; WILLIAM FLOYD HS; (JR); Hnr Roll; WWAHSS; Mth Clb/Tm; Bnd; Pep Bnd; Cr Ctry (J L); Track (V L); Chemistry; Environmental Sciences

CATTOI, DEREK; ALDEN, NY; ALDEN CTRL HS; (JR); Hi Hnr Roll; Hnr Roll; WWAHSS; Comm Volntr; Emplmnt; Key Club; Off Aide; Wdwrkg Clb; Electrician; Erie Community College

CATTRY, DEEPIKA; SYOSSET, NY; OYSTER BAY HS; (JR); Ctznshp Aw; Hi Hnr Roll; Hnr Roll; Nat Hon Sy; Perf Att; Comm Volntr; Peer Tut/Med; Sftball (J); Tennis (V L); Vllyball (J); Cl Off (T); Stu Cncl (R); CR (R); Human Relations-Treasurer; Drama Club-Stage Manager; Pre-Medicine/Pre-Medical Studies; Language-Spanish; Villanova U, Syracuse U; Cornell U, Boston U

CAYETANO, ANDRES; MOUNT VERNON, NY; MT VERNON HS; (SO); F Lan Hn Soc; Hi Hnr Roll; Hnr Roll; Nat Hon Sy; Otst Ac Ach Awd; Perf Att; St of Mnth; Emplmnt; Sccr (J); Computer Engineer; Web Design; Westchester College; Fordham U

CEBALLOS, BRYAN; BRONX, NY; ALFRED E SMITH VOC HS; (FR); Hnr Roll; St of Mnth; WWAHSS; Attending Freshman Honors Classes; Lawyer

CECILIO, ESPERANZA; BRONX, NY; DEWITT CLINTON HS; (SR); Hnr Roll; Perf Att; Comm Volntr; Emplmnt; Have Worked After School from 10th to 12th Grade; Teacher; Hunter; City College

CEJA, CLAUDIA; PORT CHESTER, NY; MARIA REGINA; (FR); Hnr Roll; Key Club; Dnce; Track

CELIO, JACKLYN; WOODHAVEN, NY; FRANKLIN K LANE HS; (SR); Hnr Roll; Nat Hon Sy; Perf Att; WWAHSS; Comm Volntr; Drma Clb; Emplmnt; Off Aide; Tchrs Aide; Sftball (V); Vllyball (V); Sch Ppr (E); Yrbk (E); Arista; TV Sports Broadcasting; Mount St. Mary College

CELLA, ALYSSA; FARMINGDALE, NY; FARMINGDALE HS; (JR); F Lan Hn Soc; Hi Hnr Roll; Nat Hon Sy; Nat Sci Aw; Otst Ac Ach Awd; USAA; WWAHSS; Peer Tut/Med; Key Club; Pep Squd; Vsity Clb; Bnd; Dnce; PPSqd (V L); Kickline-V

CENTURIONI, DOMINICK A; MECHANICVILLE, NY; STILLWATER CTRL HS; (JR); Hi Hnr Roll; Hnr Roll; Nat Hon Sy; Nat Sci Aw; Otst Ac Ach Awd; Pres Sch; Sci/Math Olympn; WWAHSS; Yth Ldrshp Prog; Comm Volntr; Peer Tut/Med; Red Cr Aide; AL Aux Boys; ArtClub; DARE; Emplmnt; Key Club; Mth Clb/Tm; NYLC; P to P St Amb Prg; Bsball (VJ); Bskball (J); Ftball (VJCL); Wt Lftg (VJ); Cl Off (R); Stu Cncl (P); CR (P); Bausch & Lomb Medal Winner; Clarkson Leadership Scholarship; Pre-Med; Chemical Engineering; Clarkson U; Colgate U

CERCHIONE, NIKKI; BROOKLYN, NY; LEON M GOLDSTEIN HS; (SO); Hi Hnr Roll; Nat Hon Sy; Otst Ac Ach Awd; Comm Volntr; Chrch Yth Grp; NYLC; Dnce; SP/M/VS; Adv Cncl (S); New York U; State U

CEREOLA, PATRICK; RIDGE, NY; LONGWOOD HS; (JR); Hi Hnr Roll; Otst Ac Ach Awd; Pres Ac Ftns Aw; Comm Volntr; Emplmnt; Tchrs Aide; Cl Off (P); CR (P); Sch Ppr (R); Yrbk (E); Travel Ice Hockey - Silver Medalist, Team Captain; 2002 Nationals, 2004 Long Island Champions, 2004 Silver Medalist NY State Championship; Physical Therapy; Foreign Language / Spanish; U of Maryland; U of Connecticut

CERNE, CARLIE; NORTH COLLINS, NY; NORTH COLLINS HS; (SO); Hnr Roll; MVP; Otst Ac Ach Awd; Pres Sch; WWAHSS; Chrch Yth Grp; FTA; Tchrs Aide; Vsity Clb; Spanish Clb; Chr; Sftball (V C); Vsy Clb (V C); Vllyball (V C); MVP Varsity Volleyball; Section 6 Class D First Team All Star (Volleyball); Northeastern U; U of Notre Dame

CESAR, ASHA A; CTRL ISLIP, NY; CTRL ISLIP HS; (SO); Ctznshp Aw; Hnr Roll; Nat Hon Sy; Perf Att; Sci Fairs; St of Mnth; Yth Ldrshp Prog; Comm Volntr; Chrch Yth Grp; Drma Clb; Pep Squd; Scouts; SADD; Tmpl Yth Grp; Spanish Clb; Acpl Chr; Chr; Ch Chr; Dnce; Chrldg (V); Gmnstcs (J); Tennis (J); Track (V); Published Literature; Performed with A cappella Choir at Disney Honors; Communications; Business Management; New York U; Columbia U

CESSANT, CYNTHIA; BRONX, NY; HEALTH OPPORTUNITIES HS; (JR); Hi Hnr Roll; Perf Att; St of Mnth; WWAHSS; Red Cr Aide; Empire Promise Nurse Opportunity Corps EMT 1st Aide; Exchange Makes Change Club; Master's Degree; Molecular Biophysics and Biochemistry; Yale U; Columbia U

CETIN, OZLEM; BELLEROSE, NY; MARTIN VAN BUREN HS; (JR); Hnr Roll; Comm Volntr; Drma Clb; Emplmnt; Off Aide; Svce Clb; Tchrs Aide; SP/M/VS; Adv Cncl (R); Stu Cncl (R); I Plan to Join Leaders Gym, Soccer and Volleyball in My Senior Year; Business and Management; Baking and Pastry Arts; Stony Brook U; Adelphi U

CHABLA, LUIS; ELMONT, NY; SEWANHAKA HS; (SR); F Lan Hn Soc; Hi Hnr Roll; Hnr Roll; Nat Hon Sy; St of Mnth; WWAHSS; Comm Volntr; Emplmnt; Key Club; Mth Clb/Tm; Sch Ppr (R); Yrbk (R); AP Scholar; Biology

CHADHA, GULSHEEN K; LITTLE NECK, NY; BENJAMIN CARDOZO HS; (FR); Ctznshp Aw; Hnr Roll; Perf Att; Comm Volntr; Peer Tut/Med; Key Club; Chr; Chrldg (V); Stu Cncl (T); PTA Award, President's Education Award; Attorney General's Triple C Award; Medicine; Business; New York U; Columbia U

CHALIK, GARY; STATEN ISLAND, NY; STUYVESANT HS; (JR); Nat Hon Sy; Nat Mrt LOC; WWAHSS; Key Club; Ftball (VJ); Swmg (V); Tennis (V); Adv Cncl (R); CR; Business; Political Science; U of Pennsylvania; Georgetown U

CHAMBERLAIN, BRANDYN; UNIONDALE, NY; UNIONDALE HS; (SO); F Lan Hn Soc; Hi Hnr Roll; Nat Hon Sy; Otst Ac Ach Awd; Sci Fairs; Peer Tut/Med; 4-H; Chrch Yth Grp; Drma Clb; FBLA; Key Club; Mus Clb; P to P St Amb Prg; Orch; SP/M/VS; Stg Cre; Swmg (V); Cl Off (T); Biology Biomedical, Marine Biology; Dartmouth U; Cornell U

CHAN, CHRYSTINA P; OAKLAND GARDENS, NY; BENJAMIN CARDOZO HS; (SO); 4H Awd; Hnr Roll; Nat Hon Sy; WWAHSS; FBLA; Key Club; Sci Clb; Bnd; Chr; Rank 4 in Da Vinci Science (Chem) Class; AP Global As Sophomore; Pre-Law; Trial Attorney; Cornell U; Harvard U

CHAN, JOYCE; BROOKLYN, NY; MIDWOOD HS; (JR); Comm Volntr; Chrch Yth Grp; Emplmnt; Key Club; Ch Chr; Clr Grd; Orch; Archon; Early Education; Psychology; Binghamton University; University of Connecticut

CHAN, JOYCE; NEW YORK, NY; BARD HS EARLY COLLEGE; (FR); Hi Hnr Roll; Hnr Roll; Nat Hon Sy; Comm Volntr; Dnce; Hsbk Rdg (V); Track (J); Medical Sciences

CHAN, NANCY; LEVITTOWN, NY; DIVISION AVE HS; (FR); F Lan Hn Soc; Hi Hnr Roll; Otst Ac Ach Awd; Perf Att; Sci Fairs; Sci/Math Olympn; St of Mnth; WWAHSS; Comm Volntr; Key Club; Mth Clb/Tm; Sci Clb; Chr; Stg Cre; Sch Ppr (R); Yrbk (P); President's Education Awards Program; National History Day-Outstanding Achievement; Education; Nursing; Hofstra U; Molloy College

CHAN, TRACEY; GREAT NECK, NY; GREAT NECK NORTH HS; (SO); F Lan Hn Soc; MVP; Pres Ac Ftns Aw; Hab For Humty Volntr; Spec Olymp Vol; Pep Squd; Fld Hky (J); Vllyball (J); Presidential Award for Physical Fitness; National Award for French Level 3; Magazine Editor; Doctor; Yale U; Columbia U

CHAN, WILLIAM; CEDARHURST, NY; LAWRENCE HS; (FR); Hnr Roll; Kwnis Aw; WWAHSS; Comm Volntr; Peer Tut/Med; Emplmnt; Key Club; SADD; Bnd; Mch Bnd; Mar Art (J); Metropolitan Opera-Children's Chorus (Met); All-County Wind Ensemble (Band) 2005; Chef; Doctor; Princeton; Le Cordon Bleu

CHAN, WINNIE; NEW YORK, NY; STUYVESANT HS; (JR); F Lan Hn Soc; Nat Hon Sy; Comm Volntr; Peer Tut/Med; Key Club; Spch Team; SP/M/VS; Lit Mag (R); Sch Ppr (R); Political Science; Psychology; U of Pennsylvania; New York U

CHANDLER, TYRELL; NANUET, NY; SPRING VALLEY HS; Key Club; Tchrs Aide; Bskball (V); Track (V); Key Club; Connecticut; Duke

CHANDRABOS, CEENA; YONKERS, NY; MARIA REGINA HS; (SO); Hi Hnr Roll; Nat Hon Sy; Otst Ac Ach Awd; Sci Fairs; St of Mnth; Valdctrian; Emplmnt; Key Club; Svce Clb; Dnce; The National Society of High School Scholars; Congressman Eliot Engel Achievement Award

CHANG, ALEX; FLUSHING, NY; BENJAMIN CARDOZO HS; (JR); Hnr Roll; Otst Ac Ach Awd; Perf Att; Sci Fairs; Sci/Math Olympn; Yth Ldrshp Prog; Comm Volntr; Peer Tut/Med; Chess; Jr Ach; Key Club; Mth Clb/Tm; Orch; SP/M/VS; Bdmtn; Lcrsse (V); Vsy Clb (C); Chinese Youth Corp of New York Orchestra / Concert Master & Student Body Vice President; Math Team Captain; Engineering; Management / Hotel or other Areas; Massachusetts Institute of Technology; Cornell U

CHANG, ALICE; BROOKLYN, NY; NEW UTRECHT HS; (FR); Perf Att; St of Mnth; Comm Volntr; DARE; Emplmnt; Tmpl Yth Grp; Pharmacy; Engineering; St. John's U; Cooper Union

CHANG, CATHERINE; FLUSHING, NY; STUYVESANT HS; (JR); Duke TS; F Lan Hn Soc; Hnr Roll; Nat Hon Sy; Nat Mrt LOC; Otst Ac Ach Awd; Sci Fairs; Valdctrian; Amnsty Intl; Comm Volntr; Peer Tut/Med; Red Cr Aide; Emplmnt; Key Club; Mth Clb/Tm; Mus Clb; NtlFrnscLg; Off Aide; Spch Team; Wdwrkg Clb; Chr; Orch; Lit Mag; Sch Ppr; The Merrill Lynch Young Business Leaders Summer Institute at Baruch College; Economics; Finance/Banking; Harvard; U of Pennsylvania, Philadelphia

CHANG, GARY; BROOKLYN, NY; MIDWOOD HS; (SO); Hnr Roll; Nat Hon Sy; Key Club; Mth Clb/Tm; Bnd; Ch Chr; Jzz Bnd; Mch Bnd; Sftball; Midwood Handball Team; Cornell U; U of Pennsylvania

CHANG, JAEWON; ALBANY, NY; SHAVER HS; (SR); Hi Hnr Roll; Hnr Roll; Nat Hon Sy; Comm Volntr; Peer Tut/Med; Key Club; Lcrsse (V L); Sccr (J L); Track (V L); Pre-Med; Biochemistry; Case Western Reserve; Cornell U

CHANG, PHILIP; FLUSHING, NY; STUYVESANT HS; (FR); Hnr Roll; Nat Hon Sy; Otst Ac Ach Awd; Perf Att; WWAHSS; Comm Volntr; Peer Tut/Med; Lib Aide; Mth Clb/Tm; Off Aide; Svce Clb; Chr; SP/M/VS; Stg Cre; CR (P); Sch Ppr (E); Acceptance Into Magnet Class; Art Award; Pediatrician; Pharmacist; Cornell; Johns Hopkins

Cereola, Patrick
Longwood HS
Ridge, NY

Cella, Alyssa
Farmingdale HS
Farmingdale, NY

Celio, Jacklyn
Franklin K Lane HS
Woodhaven, NY

Case, Ari
Eny Transit Tech HS
Arverne, NY

Cattry, Deepika
Oyster Bay HS
Syosset, NY

Cerchione, Nikki
Leon M Goldstein HS
Brooklyn, NY

Chan, Nancy
Division Ave HS
Levittown, NY

CHANG, WEN H; JAMAICA, NY; BRONX HS OF SCIENCE; (FR); Hnr Roll; Perf Att; St of Mnth; Key Club; Photog; Orch; Fncg (J); Junior Arista Honor Society; Excellence in Science; Economics; Music / Art; Princeton U; Columbia U

CHAPMAN, CANDACE; BRASHER FALLS, NY; MASSENA CTRL HS; (SO); Hi Hnr Roll; Hnr Roll; Chr; Dnce; Chrldg (V); Math; English

CHARITABLE, JESSICA; BRONX, NY; GRACE DODGE HS; (FR); Perf Att; Chrch Yth Grp; Tchrs Aide; Tmpl Yth Grp; Ch Chr; Participated in Charity; Medical Doctor; New York U; Columbia U

CHARLES, COURTNEY; LAKEWOOD, NY; SOUTHWESTERN HS; (FR); Hnr Roll; Nat Hon Sy; Chrch Yth Grp; Photog; SADD; Chr; Ch Chr; SP/M/VS; Sccr; Sftball; Yrbk (P); Private Guitar Lessons; Journalism; Veterinarian; St Bonaventure U; Princeton

CHARLES, CRYSTAL; BROOKLYN, NY; MIDDLE COLLEGE HS; (SO); Ctznshp Aw; Hi Hnr Roll; Hnr Roll; Otst Ac Ach Awd; Perf Att; St of Mnth; WWAHSS; Peer Tut/Med; Chess; DARE; Drma Clb; Jr Ach; Ch Chr; Sch Ppr (R); Nurse / Pediatrician; Journalism / Performing Arts

CHARLES, JOSEPH C; MONSEY, NY; HIGHLAND HS; (SO); Perf Att; Sci Fairs; St of Mnth; Comm Volntr; Peer Tut/Med; Chrch Yth Grp; Emplmnt; Fr of Library; Sci Clb; Ch Chr; Mch Bnd; Bskball; Ice Sktg (L); Mar Art (V); Skiing (L); Swmg (J); Medical Doctor; Columbia U; Cornell U

CHARLES, SAFIYA; YONKERS, NY; LINCOLN HS; (SR); Hnr Roll; WWAHSS; Comm Volntr; Peer Tut/Med; Jr Ach; Prom Com; Mch Bnd; Cr Ctry (J); Track (VJCL); Child Psychology; Forensics; SUNY Albany; Hampton U

CHASE, DAVID; BELLMORE, NY; KELLENBERG MEMORIAL HS; (SR); Hnr Roll; Nat Hon Sy; Nat Mrt LOC; P to P St Amb Prg; Quiz Bowl; Sch Ppr (R); Academic Quiz Bowl Participant; Vassar College; Boston U

CHASKIN, JASON D; BELLMORE, NY; W C MEPHAM HS; (JR); F Lan Hn Soc; Hnr Roll; Sci Fairs; WWAHSS; Comm Volntr; Peer Tut/Med; Drma Clb; Key Club; Tmpl Yth Grp; Bnd; Mch Bnd; SP/M/VS; Cl Off (S); Lit Mag (R); Outstanding Achievement in Chemistry; Science Mentorship (Research); Binghamton-State; U of New York

CHASSE, ROBERT; HOPEWELL JCT, NY; ARLINGTON HS; (JR); Hi Hnr Roll; Bnd; Skiing (V); Town Sports Basketball / Roller Hockey / Care Member Rock Band; Black Belt & Tae Kwon Do; High School Science Teacher / Master's Degree; Minor HS Global Science; Duchess Community College; Marist College

CHAU, MICHELLE; FLUSHING, NY; STUYVESANT HS; (FR); Hnr Roll; Otst Ac Ach Awd; Perf Att; WWAHSS; Comm Volntr; Key Club; Mth Clb/Tm; Bnd; Ch Chr; Doctor; Accountant; Cornell; Princeton

CHAU, STEPHANIE; JACKSON HEIGHTS, NY; STUYVESANT HS; (FR); Peer Tut/Med; Key Club; Acpl Chr; Chr; Psychologist; Cornell

CHEANOGUZ, MIKHAIL; BROOKLYN, NY; ABRAHAM LINCOLN HS; (FR); Hnr Roll; Nat Hon Sy; Perf Att; Sci Fairs; Cmptr Clb; Sccr (J); Tennis (V); Science Fair 3rd Place; Information Technology; Boston U; New York U

CHEN, AMY; OCEANSIDE, NY; OCEANSIDE HS; (SO); Hi Hnr Roll; Hnr Roll; Comm Volntr; Hab For Humty Volntr; Peer Tut/Med; ArtClub; Emplmnt; Key Club; SADD; Art Award 7-9 Grade; Induction Into National Junior Honor Society; Psychology; Education (Teaching); Columbia; NYU

CHEN, BECKY; JACKSON HEIGHTS, NY; BRONX HS OF SCIENCE; (JR); Nat Hon Sy; WWAHSS; Comm Volntr; Peer Tut/Med; Key Club; Mth Clb/Tm; Off Aide; Tchrs Aide; Volunteer - Rehab & Health Care Center; Business; Engineering; New York U - Stern Business School

CHEN, BRYANT; BROOKLYN, NY; FDR; (SO); St of Mnth; WWAHSS

CHEN, CLARA; WOODSIDE, NY; WILLIAM CULLEN BRYANT HS; (SR); Nat Hon Sy; Sci Fairs; WWAHSS; Comm Volntr; Spec Olymp Vol; Key Club; Track (V C); Sch Ppr (E); John Jay College of Criminal Justice

CHEN, DAISY; FRESH MEADOWS, NY; STUYVESANT HS; (FR); Hnr Roll; Perf Att; Mth Clb/Tm; Svce Clb; Chr; Journalism; Law; NYU; Columbia

CHEN, DANIEL; WOODHAVEN, NY; STUYVESANT HS; (SO); Nat Hon Sy; WWAHSS; Key Club; Photog; Swmg (V); Sch Ppr (P); Rookie of the Year; Most Improved Swimmer; Biology; Medicine; Cornell; New York U

CHEN, GUAN; BROOKLYN, NY; BRONX HS OF SCIENCE; (SO); Hi Hnr Roll; Hnr Roll; Key Club; Fncg (J); Ecology; Economics; Stanford U; Cornell U

CHEN, JENNY; SCHENECTADY, NY; SCHENECTADY HS; (FR); All Am Sch; Ctznshp Aw; Hi Hnr Roll; Hnr Roll; Nat Hon Sy; Nat Sci Aw; Otst Ac Ach Awd; Perf Att; Sci Fairs; St of Mnth; ArtClub; DARE; Emplmnt; Mth Clb/Tm; Tchrs Aide; Chinese Clb; Orch; Yrbk (E, P); President's Award for Educational Excellence; Certificate of Academic Recognition for Life Science; Pharmacy; Pre-Med; Albany College of Pharmacy; Massachusetts College of Pharmacy

CHEN, KATEY; OAKLAND GARDENS, NY; BENJAMIN CARDOZO HS; (FR); Hnr Roll; Perf Att; Chrch Yth Grp; Key Club; Bnd; Ch Chr; Criminal Justice; Therapist; Cornell U; Buffalo U

CHEN, LEWIS; OAKLAND GARDENS, NY; BENJAMIN CARDOZO HS; (FR); Hi Hnr Roll; Hnr Roll; Perf Att; WWAHSS; Comm Volntr; Hosp Aide; Key Club; Scouts; Economics; Business

CHEN, MENGSHA; FLUSHING, NY; BRONX HS OF SCIENCE; (SO); Ctznshp Aw; Nat Hon Sy; WWAHSS; Comm Volntr; Key Club; Mth Clb/Tm; Medicine; Psychology; Columbia U; Cornell U

CHEN, NINA; BROOKLYN, NY; MIDWOOD HS; (JR); F Lan Hn Soc; WWAHSS; Hosp Aide; Emplmnt; Key Club; Orch; Track (L); Sch Ppr (R); Pre-Med; Investment Banking; Hunter College; Cornell U

CHEN, ROGER; OAKLAND GARDENS, NY; BENJAMIN CARDOZO HS; (SO); Hi Hnr Roll; Hnr Roll; Nat Hon Sy; Perf Att; WWAHSS; Comm Volntr; Peer Tut/Med; ArtClub; Biology Clb; Chess; Key Club; Mth Clb/Tm; Mus Clb; Sci Clb; Scouts; Bnd; Clr Grd; Jzz Bnd; Orch; Track (V); Yrbk (E); Pharmacist; Cornell; St John's U

CHEN, SHUAN-HAN; LOCKPORT, NY; LOCKPORT HS; (FR); Hi Hnr Roll; Otst Ac Ach Awd; Perf Att; St of Mnth; WWAHSS; Comm Volntr; Red Cr Aide; Chrch Yth Grp; Key Club; Latin Clb; President's Award for Educational Achievement; National Junior Honor Society; Science; Education; SUNY Binghamton; Cornell U

CHEN, TONY; OAKLAND GARDENS, NY; BENJAMIN CARDOZO HS; (SO); Perf Att; WWAHSS; Comm Volntr; Chess; Key Club; Lib Aide; Off Aide; Tchrs Aide; Tennis (J); Track (J); Intern for Homebase Networks; Chemistry; Computer Science; Columbia U; Cornell U

CHEN, VIRGINIA; BROOKLYN, NY; MIDWOOD HS; (JR); Ctznshp Aw; Hnr Roll; Otst Ac Ach Awd; Perf Att; WWAHSS; Yth Ldrshp Prog; Comm Volntr; Peer Tut/Med; Key Club; P to P St Amb Prg; Svce Clb; Bnd; Mch Bnd; SP/M/VS; Stg Cre

CHEN, XIAO; WOODSIDE, NY; WILLIAM CULLEN BRYANT HS; (SR); F Lan Hn Soc; Hnr Roll; Nat Hon Sy; Key Club; Chinese Clb; Fashion Merchandising; Fashion Institute of Technology

CHEN, YEN J; LOCKPORT, NY; LOCKPORT HS; (SO); Hi Hnr Roll; Otst Ac Ach Awd; Perf Att; WWAHSS; Comm Volntr; Red Cr Aide; Chrch Yth Grp; Key Club; National Junior Honor Society; Academic L Award; Science; Technology; SUNY Stony Brook; UC Berkeley

CHEN, YIFAN; SLINGERLANDS, NY; GUILDERLAND HS; (FR); Hi Hnr Roll; Otst Ac Ach Awd; Perf Att; WWAHSS; Comm Volntr; Hosp Aide; Key Club; Mth Clb/Tm; Bnd; Dnce; Orch; Tennis (J); Track (V); Sch Ppr (E); Indoor Track Rookie of the Year; Medical; Engineering; Dartmouth College; Stanford U

CHENG, ASHLEY; NEW YORK, NY; STUYVESANT HS; (FR); Hnr Roll; Salutrn; Comm Volntr; Key Club; Bnd; English; Psychology

CHENG, ZHI A; YONKERS, NY; BRONX HS OF SCIENCE; (SO); Hi Hnr Roll; Kwnis Aw; Nat Hon Sy; Nat Ldrshp Svc; Otst Ac Ach Awd; Sci Fairs; Sci/Math Olympn; WWAHSS; Yth Ldrshp Prog; Comm Volntr; Red Cr Aide; Biology Clb; Chess; Key Club; Lib Aide; Svce Clb; Tchrs Aide; Stg Cre; Fncg (J); Golf (J); Tennis (J); Vllyball (J); Level 6 Piano Test Passed; MD; Medicine; Brown U

CHENMIAN, ZOU; FRESH MEADOWS, NY; FRANCIS LEWIS HS; (JR); Play Piano in the Cell Group of the Church; Biomedical Engineer; Doctor; New York U; Columbia U

CHERIYAN, JISA; MINEOLA, NY; MINEOLA HS; (FR); Hi Hnr Roll; Hnr Roll; Nat Hon Sy; Perf Att; St of Mnth; Comm Volntr; Hosp Aide; Chrch Yth Grp; Dbte Team; Drma Clb; Jr Ach; Lib Aide; NYLC; Photog; Bnd; Track (V); CR

CHERRY, NICOLE K; CRITTENDEN, NY; ALDEN HS; (SR); Hnr Roll; Red Cr Aide; ArtClub; Art; Music; Buffalo State; Elk Community College

CHERY, ROSEDELLE A; FAR ROCKAWAY, NY; MAGNET SCH LAW/ GOVERN; (FR); Hi Hnr Roll; Hnr Roll; Perf Att; Chrch Yth Grp; Ch Chr; Lawyer; Child Psychologist; Stony Brook U; St John's U

CHESTNUT, DELAVIA; WATERTOWN, NY; INDIAN RIVER HS; (JR); Hnr Roll; Otst Ac Ach Awd; Emplmnt; Key Club; SADD; Spanish Clb; Bskball (J); Track (V); Community Service Award for Ft Washington; Medical; Designer; Duke; Benedict

CHEUNG, CONNIE; SCHENECTADY, NY; SCHENECTADY HS; (SO); F Lan Hn Soc; Hnr Roll; Perf Att; WWAHSS; Foreign Clb; Lcrsse (J); Law; Pharmacy

CHEUNG, JENNIFER; BROOKLYN, NY; FORT HAMILTON HS; (SR); Hnr Roll; Nat Hon Sy; Perf Att; Comm Volntr; Peer Tut/Med; ArtClub; Emplmnt; Off Aide; Stg Cre; Pharmacy; Chemistry; Rutgers, State U of New Jersey; New York U

CHEUNG, JOYCE; EAST ELMHURST, NY; FRANCIS LEWIS HS; (SR); Hnr Roll; Nat Hon Sy; Sci Fairs; WWAHSS; Comm Volntr; Hab For Humty Volntr; Peer Tut/Med; Spec Olymp Vol; Key Club; ROTC; Sci Clb; Lit Mag (E); Semi-finalist: the NY Science & Engineering Fair and the Junior Science & Humanities Symposium; Environmental Engineering; Biology; Smith College, Northampton MA; Tufts U, Medford MA

CHEUNG, JOYCE; JACKSON HEIGHTS, NY; FRANCIS LEWIS HS; (SR); Nat Hon Sy; Sci Fairs; Comm Volntr; Peer Tut/Med; Spec Olymp Vol; Key Club; ROTC; Sci Clb; Lit Mag (E); St. John's U Women in Science Award; Environmental Engineering; Tufts U; Smith College

CHEUNG, THOMAS; WHITESTONE, NY; BENJAMIN N. CARDOZO; (JR)

CHIAFFITELLA, CHRISTINA; MERRICK, NY; CALHOUN HS; (SO); Hnr Roll; Comm Volntr; Key Club; SADD; Sftball (JC); Teacher; Advertisement; NYU; Boston U

CHIANG, BELINDA; SCARSDALE, NY; SCARSDALE HS; (JR); Hnr Roll; Nat Hon Sy; Nat Mrt LOC; Pres Ac Ftns Aw; Sci Fairs; Sci/Math Olympn; St of Mnth; Valdctrian; Comm Volntr; Peer Tut/Med; ArtClub; Chess; Dbte Team; Drma Clb; Mth Clb/Tm; NYLC; Quiz Bowl; Spch Team; Dnce; Orch; SP/M/VS; Stu Cncl (R); Lit Mag (E, R); Sch Ppr (E); Tae Kwon Do Red Belt; Officer of Six School Clubs; Harvard U; Yale U

CHIARELLO, JACQUELINE; MERRICK, NY; CALHOUN HS; (JR); ArtClub; Key Club; Dentistry; SUNY New Paltz; Albany U

CHIKVASHVILI, IRINA; FLUSHING, NY; THE KEW-FOREST SCH; (JR); Hnr Roll; Comm Volntr; DARE; Spanish Clb; Martial Arts (2nd Degree Black Belt); Tae Kwon Do; Medicine; NYU, Pace, Boston College

CHIN, BRIAN; YORKTOWN HEIGHTS, NY; YORKTOWN HS; (JR); Hi Hnr Roll; Nat Hon Sy; Sci Fairs; Yth Ldrshp Prog; Comm Volntr; Emplmnt; Track (V); Sch Ppr; WESEF 2005-Society for In-Vitro Biology Award; Boston College; Boston U

CHIN, BRITTANY; EAST GREENBUSH, NY; COLUMBIA HS; (JR); Ctznshp Aw; Hi Hnr Roll; Nat Hon Sy; Otst Ac Ach Awd; St of Mnth; WWAHSS; Yth Ldrshp Prog; Peer Tut/Med; DARE; Emplmnt; Prom Com; SADD; Bnd; Dnce; Fld Hky (J); Stu Cncl (P, R); Physical Therapy; Quinnipiac U; Russell Sage College

CHIN, GREG; WANTAGH, NY; SEAFORD HS; (SR); Hi Hnr Roll; Hnr Roll; St of Mnth; WWAHSS; Comm Volntr; Peer Tut/Med; Drma Clb; Key Club; Bnd; Drm Mjr; Mch Bnd; Tennis; Cl Off (S); Yrbk (E, R, P); Homecoming King; Tri-M Music Honor Society; Business Management; Quinnipiac U

CHIN, STACEY; WANTAGH, NY; SEAFORD HS; (SO); Hi Hnr Roll; Otst Ac Ach Awd; WWAHSS; Comm Volntr; Peer Tut/Med; Chrch Yth Grp; Drma Clb; Key Club; Scouts; Bnd; Mch Bnd; SP/M/VS; Chrldg (J L); NYSSMA Flute Solo Levels 1-5; Marching Band Fronts Squad - Silks / Swing Flags / Poms; Communications Major; New York U; Quinnipiac U

CHIN-KING, KATHY ANN; BROOKLYN, NY; MIDDLE COLLEGE HS; (SO); Ctznshp Aw; Hnr Roll; Otst Ac Ach Awd; Perf Att; St of Mnth; Emplmnt; Jr Ach; Stu Cncl (P); CR (R); Medical / Pediatrician; Columbia U; New York U

CHIO, TAK I; BROOKLYN, NY; NEW UTRECHT HS; (JR); Nat Hon Sy; Comm Volntr; Key Club; Medical Science; Pharmacy; Boston U; Cornell U

CHIO, UN S; BROOKLYN, NY; STUYVESANT HS; (SO); Hi Hnr Roll; Nat Hon Sy; Perf Att; Salutrn; St of Mnth; USAA; WWAHSS; Key Club; Mth Clb/Tm; Off Aide; Tchrs Aide; Bnd; SP/M/VS; Ultimate Frisbee; Medicine; Engineering; Massachusetts Institute of Technology; Stanford

CHIRIBOGA, SILEN; DIAMOND POINT, NY; LAKE GEORGE HS; (JR); Ctznshp Aw; F Lan Hn Soc; Hi Hnr Roll; Hnr Roll; Otst Ac Ach Awd; St of Mnth; Yth Ldrshp Prog; Chrch Yth Grp; DARE; Emplmnt; Key Club; Outdrs Clb; Prom Com; Scouts; Spanish Clb; Bnd; Chr; Ch Chr; Dnce; Chrldg (V); Track (V L); Cl Off (P); Stu Cncl (V); Degree in Teaching/Early Childhood Development; English; Brigham Young U

CHISLOM, COURTNEY; NEW YORK, NY; (JR); Hnr Roll; Nat Ldrshp Svc; Peer Tut/Med; FCA; Bnd; Bsball (L); Mar Art (J); Sftball (J); Wt Lftg (J); Computer Science; Computer Engineer; City College/Duke U; St John's U

CHIU, EMILY; FLUSHING, NY; (SO); St of Mnth; Comm Volntr; Peer Tut/Med; Chrch Yth Grp; DARE; Drma Clb; Emplmnt; Lib Aide; Off Aide; Photog; Tchrs Aide; Bnd; Dnce; SP/M/VS; Tennis; Dragon Boat Racing; PAL "Stories My Grandparents Told Me" Writing Contest; Writing; Pediatrician; Sarah Lawrence; Brown U

CHIU, KATHY; BROOKLYN, NY; MIDWOOD HS; (JR); Hnr Roll; Kwnis Aw; Perf Att; Comm Volntr; Hosp Aide; Chess; Emplmnt; Key Club; Off Aide; Tchrs Aide; Russian Clb; Track (J); Archon; Girls Varsity Bowling Team; Business Management; Administrative / Secretarial Services; SUNY Binghamton; Berkeley College

Chikvashvili, Irina
The Kew-Forest Sch
Flushing, NY

Chen, Bryant
Fdr
Brooklyn, NY

Chen, Amy
Oceanside HS
Oceanside, NY

National
Honor Roll
Spring 2005

Charles, Joseph C
Highland HS
Monsey, NY

Cherry, Nicole K
Alden HS
Crittenden, NY

Chiriboga, Silen
Lake George HS
Diamond Point, NY

CHIU, SUNG; ELMHURST, NY; BRONX HS OF SCIENCE; (JR); Comm Volntr; Peer Tut/Med; Chrch Yth Grp; Lib Aide; Off Aide; Tchrs Aide; Clr Grd; Pianist for Children's Worship at Church; Mathematics; Teacher / Education; New York U; Columbia U

CHIU, TIFFANY; NORTH MASSAPEQUA, NY; FARMINGDALE HS; (SO); F Lan Hn Soc; Hi Hnr Roll; Hnr Roll; Perf Att; Sci/Math Olympn; WWAHSS; Comm Volntr; Spec Olymp Vol; Key Club; Lib Aide; Photog; Sci Clb; Svce Clb; Vsity Clb; Orch; Tennis (J); Track (V); Vsy Clb (V); Archeology; Astronomy; Pennsylvania State U; New York U

CHLOSTA, KATHRYN; HAMBURG, NY; HAMBURG HS; (FR); Hi Hnr Roll; St of Mnth; Comm Volntr; DARE; DECA; Emplmnt; Vsity Clb; Bnd; Dnce; Mch Bnd; Tennis (V); DECA Member of the Year; Physical Anthropology; General Dentistry; U of Buffalo; Tufts U

CHO, ALEXANDER; ASTORIA, NY; BROOKLYN TECH HS; (JR); Hi Hnr Roll; Hnr Roll; Track (V); Leader in Seekers Club; Guitar Player; Pharmacy; Chemistry; St John's U; Albany College of Pharmacy

CHO, CHRISTINA; ELMHURST, NY; BRONX HS OF SCIENCE; (JR); Hi Hnr Roll; Otst Ac Ach Awd; Pres Sch; Salutrn; Sci/Math Olympn; St of Mnth; Comm Volntr; Hosp Aide; Chrch Yth Grp; Lib Aide; Off Aide; Tchrs Aide; Ch Chr; Orch; SP/M/VS; Lit Mag (R); Alternate Class Senator; Medical Physician; Pharmacist; CUNY Sophie Davis Biomed; Brown U Medical Program

CHOATE, MEGHAN; BROCKPORT, NY; BROCKPORT HS; (SO); Hnr Roll; St of Mnth; Chr; Track (V); Gold Card Student in 8th Grade; Criminal Justice; Rape, Homicide, Abuse Detective; U of Nevada in Reno; State U of New York

CHOI, AHLOOM; SUNNYSIDE, NY; BRONX HS OF SCIENCE; (FR); Hnr Roll; Nat Hon Sy; Comm Volntr; Key Club; Lib Aide; Mth Clb/Tm; Photog; Tchrs Aide; Fncg (J); Mar Art (J); Osteopathy; Psychiatry; Columbia U; Johns Hopkins U

CHOI, BAN; PAINTED POST, NY; CPP WEST HS; (JR); Hi Hnr Roll; Nat Hon Sy; Perf Att; Comm Volntr; Chrch Yth Grp; Bskball (J); Sccr (VJC); Tennis (V); Track (V); Architecture; Interior Design; Ohio State U Columbus; Kent State U

CHOI, ESTHER; WHITESTONE, NY; LA GUARDIA HS; (JR); WWAHSS; Yth Ldrshp Prog; Comm Volntr; Hab For Humty Volntr; Chrch Yth Grp; Emplmnt; Mus Clb; Outdrs Clb; Korean Clb; Bnd; Chr; Orch; SP/M/VS; CR (P, V); Piano Concerts, Competition Winner; Accompanying; Music; Education; Juilliard School; Columbia U

CHOI, MAY-YEE; FOREST HILLS, NY; STUYVESANT HS; (SO); Nat Hon Sy; WWAHSS; Comm Volntr; Red Cr Aide; Key Club; Mth Clb/Tm; Off Aide; Chinese Clb; SP/M/VS; Sch Ppr (R); Biology; Education; Princeton; Columbia

CHONG, KAYUE; BROOKLYN, NY; NEW UTRECHT HS; (JR); Medicine; Psychology; Boston U; Tufts U

CHONG, LAWRENCE; JAMAICA, NY; STUYVESANT HS; (JR); Hnr Roll; Nat Mrt LOC; Comm Volntr; Hosp Aide; Key Club; Bnd; Ftball (V); Wt Lftg (V); Korean Heritage Essay Winner Award; Cardiology; Boston College; Middlebury College

CHOUDHARY, NIRAS; CTRL ISLIP, NY; CTRL ISLIP HS; (SO); Hnr Roll

CHOUDHRY, ISMAIL; BROOKLYN, NY; WASHINGTON IRVING HS; (SR); Ctznshp Aw; Nat Hon Sy; Perf Att; WWAHSS; CARE; Comm Volntr; Peer Tut/Med; Chess; Cmptr Clb; Stu Cncl (S); Rev Martin Luther King Jr. Living the Dream Award; Project Smart - Academic Achievement; Computer Engineering; B- Tech; Polytechnic U; City Tech

CHOUDHURY, TANIMA; BRONX, NY; COLUMBUS HS; (JR); F Lan Hn Soc; Hnr Roll; Otst Ac Ach Awd; Perf Att; ArtClub; Biology Clb; Cmptr Clb; Mth Clb/Tm; Mus Clb; Outdrs Clb; Sci Clb; Clb; Chr; Ch Chr; SP/M/VS; Swg Chr; Bskball (J); Ftball (J); Gmnstcs (J); Sccr (J); Sftball (J); Track (J); Vllyball (J); Wt Lftg (J); Multicultural Club; Accounting; Psychology; Hunter College; Baruch College

CHOUDHURY, TYIEBAH; NEW YORK, NY; RAZI SCH; (JR); Hnr Roll; Sci Fairs; WWAHSS; Hosp Aide; Peer Tut/Med; Dbte Team; Drma Clb; Off Aide; Sci Clb; Bskball (L); Fncg (V); Ice Hky (V); Vllyball; Dentistry; Computer Engineering; New York U

CHOUDRI, CHRISTINE M; FAIRPORT, NY; PENFIELD HS; (FR); Hi Hnr Roll; WWAHSS; Mod UN; Scouts; Chr; Tennis (J); Rifle & Pistol Shooting with Genesee Conservation League; Silver Medal-National Latin Exam (Latin I)

CHOW, JAELENE; DEER PARK, NY; DEER PARK HS; (JR); Hnr Roll; Nat Hon Sy; Perf Att; Comm Volntr; Hab For Humty Volntr; Peer Tut/Med; DECA; Emplmnt; Jr Ach; Prom Com; Scouts; Svce Clb; Chr; SP/M/VS; Chrldg (J); Cr Ctry (V); Sccr (JC); Sftball (J); Track (V); Adv Cncl (R); Cl Off (P); Stu Cncl (R); CR (R); Yrbk (E); Girl Scout Silver Award; DECA State Medal/Trophy Winner; Special Education; Elementary Education; Hunter College; St Joseph's

CHOW, MAY; BROOKLYN, NY; MIDWOOD HS; (JR); F Lan Hn Soc; Hnr Roll; Perf Att; Key Club; Off Aide; Tchrs Aide; Nursing; Teaching; Binghamton U; Stony Brook U

CHOWDHURY, KOWNINE; BRONX, NY; COLUMBUS HS; (SO); Hnr Roll; Comm Volntr; Peer Tut/Med; Mus Clb; Ftball; Peer Mediator; Leadership; Engineering; Medicine; Lehigh U; Cooper Union

CHRESOMALES, PAUL E; LYNBROOK, NY; MALVERNE HS; (SR); Hi Hnr Roll; Hnr Roll; Nat Hon Sy; WWAHSS; Cmptr Clb; Mth Clb/Tm; Outdrs Clb; Photog; Scouts; Bsball (VJ L); Lcrsse (V L); Yrbk (P); Varsity Bowling - Captain; Scholastic Athlete Award

CHRISANTHOPOULOS, VALERIE; BAYSIDE, NY; BENJAMIN CARDOZO HS; (JR); Hnr Roll; Nat Hon Sy; Chrch Yth Grp; Emplmnt; Jr Ach; Dnce; Bskball (C); Member of Saint Nicholas GOYA - Greek Orthodox Youth Association; Played Basketball For GOYA; Pre-Med; Pre-Law; New York U; Queens College

CHU, EUNICE; WHITESTONE, NY; BAYSIDE HS; (SR); Nat Hon Sy; Comm Volntr; Peer Tut/Med; Chrch Yth Grp; Key Club; Mth Clb/Tm; Photog; Tchrs Aide; Bnd; Track (J); Lit Mag (R); Sch Ppr (R); Hunter College; Binghamton U

CHU, JENNIFER; FLUSHING, NY; TOWNSEND HARRIS HS; (JR); Hnr Roll; Nat Hon Sy; Perf Att; Mth Clb/Tm; SP/M/VS; Foreign Language; Business; New York U; Carnegie Mellon U

CHUDY, NICHOLAS; ORCHARD PARK, NY; ORCHARD PARK HS; (JR); Hnr Roll; FBLA; Scouts; Orch; Tennis (V L); Business Administration; Economics; Cornell U; Saint Michael's College

CHUKWUMA, BRADLEY; VALLEY STREAM, NY; ELMONT MEMORIAL HS; (JR); Hnr Roll; Otst Ac Ach Awd; Perf Att; Sci Fairs; St of Mnth; Comm Volntr; FBLA; SADD; Lcrsse (J); Sccr (JC); Track (J); Business Honor Society; AP Student; Pre-Law; Business Administration; Columbia U; Cornell U

CHUNG, HA YOUNG; WOODSIDE, NY; STUYVESANT HS; (SO); Hnr Roll; Nat Hon Sy; Valdctrian; Hosp Aide; Red Cr Aide; Chrch Yth Grp; Key Club; Off Aide; Tchrs Aide; Bnd; SP/M/VS; Yrbk; Lawyer; Columbia U; U of Pennsylvania

CHUNG, JENNY; BROOKLYN, NY; BROOKLYN TECH HS; (SR); Hnr Roll; WWAHSS; Key Club; Svce Clb; Tchrs Aide; Pharmacy; St John's U; Rutgers U

CHURCHILL, JAIME; SAUGERTIES, NY; SAUGERTIES HS; (JR); 4H Awd; Hi Hnr Roll; Nat Hon Sy; WWAHSS; 4-H; Key Club; Education

CHWAN, ELISE M; WARWICK, NY; WARWICK VALLEY HS; (SO); Hi Hnr Roll; Hnr Roll; Comm Volntr; DARE; Architect; Pharmacist; Morrisville State College; SUNY Buffalo

CIAMPA, KAREN; FAIRPORT, NY; FAIRPORT HS; (FR); Hi Hnr Roll; Hnr Roll; Otst Ac Ach Awd; Yth Ldrshp Prog; Comm Volntr; Chrch Yth Grp; NYLC; Prom Com; Chr; Stu Cncl (S); Yrbk (P); Olde English F Award; President of Dance Committee; Elementary Education; Geneseo State; Nazareth

CIANFRIGLIA, STEPHANIE C; ENDICOTT, NY; UNION-ENDICOTT HS; (SO); Hnr Roll; Perf Att; Sci Fairs; Hosp Aide; Bnd; Lit Mag (E); MASH Camp 2003; Johns Hopkins Institute; Occupational Therapist; Speech Therapist; Broome Community College; Binghamton U

CIESLEWICZ, TYLER; DUNKIRK, NY; DUNKIRK HS; (FR); Hi Hnr Roll; Otst Ac Ach Awd; Perf Att; Comm Volntr; Key Club; Lttrmn Clb; French Clb; Chr; Ch Chr; SP/M/VS; Ftball (J); Tennis (L); CR (V); Accomplished Guitarist; Letter Winner in Bowling; Masters in Business Administration; U of Columbia; New York U

CIPOLLA, LEANNE M; HAWTHORNE, NY; WESTLAKE HS; (SR); F Lan Hn Soc; Hi Hnr Roll; Hnr Roll; MVP; Nat Hon Sy; St of Mnth; WWAHSS; Comm Volntr; Peer Tut/Med; Drma Clb; Mus Clb; Scouts; Tchrs Aide; Vsity Clb; Chr; SP/M/VS; Swg Chr; Swmg (V CL); Track (V L); Girl Scout Gold & Silver Award, Rotary Student of the Month; Humanities & Social Science Award; Elementary Education; Marist College

CIRILO, DAVID; BROOKLYN, NY; TRANSIT TECH HS; (SR); Otst Ac Ach Awd; Perf Att; Comm Volntr; Business Administration; Computer Science; Penn State U; Syracuse U

CISLARSKI, ANNA C; GRAND ISLAND, NY; GRAND ISLAND HS; (SO); Hnr Roll; WWAHSS; Orch; Yrbk; Teaching Degree

CISU, TUDOR; MANLIUS, NY; FAYETTEVILLE-MANLIUS HS; (SO); Hi Hnr Roll; Hnr Roll; Sci/Math Olympn; Comm Volntr; Hosp Aide; Peer Tut/Med; Chess; Dbte Team; Jr Cls League; JSA; Mth Clb/Tm; Mod UN; Sci Clb; Svce Clb; Tennis (V); CR (R); Pre-Med; Mathematics; Cornell U; Brown U

CLARK, AARON J; GRAND ISLAND, NY; GRAND ISLAND HS; (JR); Ctznshp Aw; Otst Ac Ach Awd; Interact Club; Technology; Science Field

CLARK, DANIELLE; WELLSVILLE, NY; HEBRON CTR CHRISTIAN SCH; (SR); Hi Hnr Roll; Hnr Roll; MVP; WWAHSS; Chrch Yth Grp; Spch Team; Wdwrkg Clb; Sign Clb; Bnd; Vllyball (C); Yrbk (E); Social Services; Missions; Lancaster Bible College

CLARK, SARAH; MILTON, NY; OAKWOOD FRIENDS SCH; (SO); Hnr Roll; Comm Volntr; Drma Clb; Chr; Jzz Bnd; Orch; SP/M/VS; Cr Ctry (V); Swmg (V); Theater; Music; Vassar College

CLARK, STEPHANIE E; BUFFALO, NY; MC KINLEY VOC TECH HS; (FR); Comm Volntr; Peer Tut/Med; Chrch Yth Grp; ROTC; Bnd; Winner of Bronze Medal Jesse Ketchum Award; Winner of Steven B Moskal Mathematics Award; Work for Prevention of Animal Cruelty; Astronomy; Penn State U; New York U

CLARK, ZACHARY; NORWOOD, NY; NORWOOD-NORFOLK JR/SR HS; (FR); Hi Hnr Roll; Nat Hon Sy; St of Mnth; WWAHSS; Comm Volntr; Spec Olymp Vol; Emplmnt; Key Club; Photog; Sci Clb; Spanish Clb; Bnd; Sccr (J L); Track (J L); Yrbk (E, R, P); Forensic Science; Criminal Justice

CLARKE, ERICA; BRONX, NY; EVANDER CHILDS HS; (SO); Hnr Roll; Sci Fairs; St of Mnth; Peer Tut/Med; Dbte Team; Drma Clb; Chr; Cr Ctry (V); Track (V); Cl Off (V); Stu Cncl (R); CR (R); Sch Ppr (R); SLT (School Leadership Team); Neonatologist; Supreme Court Justice; Howard U; Clarke Atlanta U

CLARKE, HOPE; LEVITTOWN, NY; DIVISION AVE HS; (SO); F Lan Hn Soc; Hi Hnr Roll; Hnr Roll; Nat Hon Sy; WWAHSS; Drma Clb; Key Club; Kwanza Clb; Chr; Dnce; SP/M/VS; Stg Cre; Drama / Theatre; Childhood Education; New York U

CLARKE, ROBERT J; KIRKVILLE, NY; CHITTENANGO HS; (JR); Hi Hnr Roll; Nat Hon Sy; Otst Ac Ach Awd; Sci/Math Olympn; St of Mnth; USAA; WWAHSS; Yth Ldrshp Prog; Comm Volntr; Peer Tut/Med; Chrch Yth Grp; DARE; Drma Clb; Emplmnt; Sci Clb; Bnd; Chr; SP/M/VS; Bsball (J); Bskball (J); Cr Ctry (V); Tennis (V); Track (V); President of Local Church Youth Group; Select All-County Choir; Computer Science; Mathematics; Roberts Wesleyan College; Rochester Institute of Technology

CLARKE, SADE; BRONX, NY; HARRY S TRUMAN HS; (SO); 4H Awd; Hnr Roll; Nat Mrt LOC; Perf Att; St of Mnth; 4-H; ArtClub; Dbte Team; Drma Clb; Key Club; Mus Clb; Sci Clb; Chr; Dnce; SP/M/VS; Chrldg; Sccr; Sftball; Track; Vllyball; Stu Cncl (P); CR (S); Netball; Teacher/Teaching; Pediatrician; New York City U; Hunter College

CLAUSEN, CASEY; ITHACA, NY; ITHACA HS; (JR); Hnr Roll; Comm Volntr; Emplmnt; Cr Ctry (J); Track (V); English; Political Science; Cornell U; Reed College

CLAUSEN, SARA L; BEACON, NY; BEACON HS; (SO); Hi Hnr Roll; Hnr Roll; Nat Hon Sy; Varsity Bowling-Since 7th Grade; Communications / Journalism; Marist College; Quinnipiac College

CLAY, JOSEPH; MACEDON, NY; EASTERN MONROE CAREER CTR; (JR); Hnr Roll; Perf Att; Lcrsse (V); Criminal Justice; Park Services; SUNY Brockport; Penn State

CLAYTON, KATHERINE; HEWLETT, NY; G W HEWLETT HS; (SO); Hi Hnr Roll; Otst Ac Ach Awd; WWAHSS; ArtClub; Key Club; Mus Clb; Orch; 3 R Award; Architect; Parson's School of Design

CLEMENT, ASHLEY; JAMAICA, NY; SPRINGFIELD GARDENS HS; (SO); Hnr Roll; Perf Att; Comm Volntr; Chrch Yth Grp; Ch Chr; Bskball (J); Track (J); Marine Biologist; U of Maryland

CLEVELAND, ROBERTA C; CAMPBELL, NY; CAMPBELL-SAVONA HS; (SR); Hi Hnr Roll; Hnr Roll; Nat Hon Sy; Perf Att; WWAHSS; Emplmnt; FBLA; Photog; Japanese Clb; Tennis (V L); Vllyball (VJCL); Yrbk (E, P); Captain of Winter Guard / In Winter Guard for 6 Years; History; Archival; Drexel U

CLIFT, LISA M; GLENMONT, NY; BETHLEHEM CTRL HS; (SO); Hnr Roll; Comm Volntr; Hosp Aide; ArtClub; Dnce; Chrldg (V); CR (R); Fashion Designer; Fashion Merchandise; Fashion Institute of Technology; UCLA

COELHO, ISRAEL; TROY, NY; HEATLY SCH; (JR); St of Mnth; Drma Clb; Spanish Clb; Stg Cre; Bskball (V); Sccr (V); Medicine; Biotechnology; U of Miami; Siena College

COFFIN, MICHELLE; TICONDEROGA, NY; TICONDEROGA HS; (JR); Hnr Roll; St of Mnth; WWAHSS; Chrch Yth Grp; Key Club; Prom Com; Sccr (J); Sftball (VJ); Cl Off (R); CR (R); Yrbk (E, R, P); Prom Court; Dental Hygiene; Farmingdale U; Boston College, Pharmacy & Health Sciences

COHEN, COREY J; HUNTINGTN STA, NY; HALF HOLLOW HILLS HS WEST; (SO); F Lan Hn Soc; Hi Hnr Roll; Comm Volntr; Peer Tut/Med; Spec Olymp Vol; DECA; FBLA; Key Club; SADD; Vllyball (J); Sch Ppr (E, R); Suffolk County DECA Regional Finalist; AASO; Sports Agent; Writer; Brown U; NYU

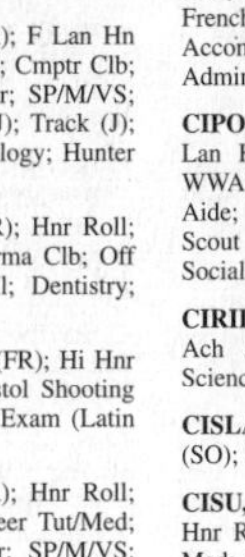

Clark, Stephanie E
Mc Kinley Voc Tech HS
Buffalo, NY

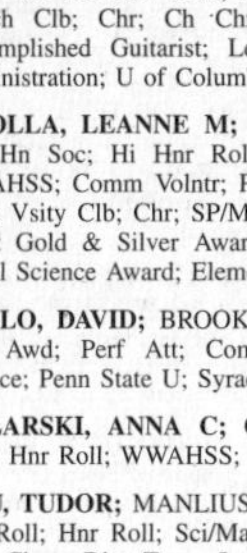

Clark, Aaron J
Grand Island HS
Grand Island, NY

National
Honor Roll
Spring 2005

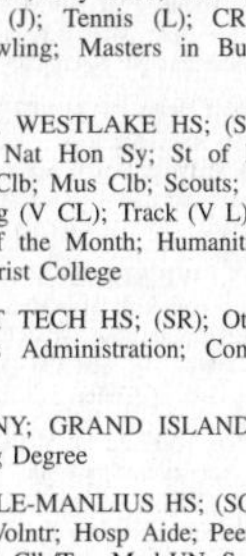

Chresomales, Paul E
Malverne HS
Lynbrook, NY

Clement, Ashley
Springfield Gardens HS
Jamaica, NY

COHEN, HARRIE; EAST MEADOW, NY; EAST MEADOW HS; (JR); F Lan Hn Soc; Hi Hnr Roll; Nat Hon Sy; Perf Att; Sci/Math Olympn; USAA; WWAHSS; Comm Volntr; Hab For Humty Volntr; FBLA; Key Club; Mth Clb/Tm; Prom Com; SADD; Bnd; Mch Bnd; Cl Off (T); Putney Community Service-Alaska; Visions Community Service-Virgin Islands; Business

COHEN, JORDAN; BROOKLYN, NY; LEON M GOLDSTEIN HS SCIENCES; (SO); Ctznshp Aw; F Lan Hn Soc; Hi Hnr Roll; Nat Sci Aw; Otst Ac Ach Awd; Perf Att; Sci Fairs; St of Mnth; Comm Volntr; Peer Tut/Med; DARE; Dbte Team; Jr Ach; Photog; Chr; Stu Cncl (V); Sch Ppr (R); Project Hope; Walk for Breast Cancer; Columbia; Hofstra

COHN, ADAM H; EAST SETAUKET, NY; ST ANTHONY'S HS; (JR); Hi Hnr Roll; Hnr Roll; Pres Ac Ftns Aw; Yth Ldrshp Prog; Spanish Clb; Chr; Bsball (J); Business (MBA); Finance; St. Johns U

COKER, MADISON C; ROCHESTER, NY; PENFIELD HS; (JR); Hnr Roll; Perf Att; St of Mnth; WWAHSS; Comm Volntr; Peer Tut/Med; Chrch Yth Grp; DARE; Emplmnt; Mus Clb; Pep Squd; Foreign Clb; Chr; Dnce; Orch; SP/M/VS; Black Student Union; Pre-Law; Psychology; Howard U; Buffalo U

COLE, MATTHEW; BALDWINSVILLE, NY; CW BAKER HS; (SR); Hi Hnr Roll; Nat Hon Sy; WWAHSS; Amnsty Intl; Comm Volntr; Red Cr Aide; ArtClub; Emplmnt; Photog; Skiing; Sch Ppr; Volunteered & Participated in Amnesty International; My Band Is Releasing a Record on Vulture Records; Political Science; Philosophy; SUNY Buffalo

COLE, PETER C; OSSINING, NY; OSSINING HS; (SO); Nat Hon Sy; Comm Volntr; Mus Clb; Bnd; Orch; Sch Ppr; Computer Animation; Game Design; Rensselaer Polytechnic Inst.

COLE, SHEVENE L; MT VERNON, NY; MT VERNON HS; (FR); Hi Hnr Roll; Hnr Roll; Nat Hon Sy; St of Mnth; Chrch Yth Grp; DARE; Lib Aide; ROTC; Ch Chr; Drl Tm; Cl Off (V); Major in Medicine; Law; Harvard U; Yale U

COLLERAN, KATIE T; OSSINING, NY; OSSINING HS; (SR); F Lan Hn Soc; Hi Hnr Roll; Nat Hon Sy; WWAHSS; Comm Volntr; Chrch Yth Grp; Emplmnt; SADD; Track (V); Communications; St. Michael's College; Boston College

COLLEY, APRIL C; MILLBROOK, NY; MILLBROOK JR/SR HS; MS; Hi Hnr Roll; Hnr Roll; Otst Ac Ach Awd; Bnd; Chr; Dnce; Chrldg; Fld Hky; Gmnstcs; Skiing; Sccr

COLLIER, KYLE; HICKSVILLE, NY; HICKSVILLE HS; (JR); Hnr Roll; Otst Ac Ach Awd; St of Mnth; Emplmnt; Bnd; Jzz Bnd; AP & Honors Classes; Soccer Player for Hicksville; Forensics; Sciences/Chemistry/Biology; John Jay College; CW Post-Hofstra

COLLINS, ALEXANDRA; EVANS MILLS, NY; INDIAN RIVER HS; (SR); Hnr Roll; WWAHSS; Comm Volntr; Key Club; Orch; SP/M/VS; CR (R); Yrbk; Area All State

COLLINS, BRITTANY; HAMPTON BAYS, NY; HAMPTON BAYS JR/SR HS; (SR); Hi Hnr Roll; Hnr Roll; Comm Volntr; Key Club; SADD; Bnd; Mch Bnd; Fld Hky (V); Sftball (J); Tennis (J); Nursing; Early Education; Sacred Heart U

COLLINS, CAILEEN M; SEAFORD, NY; ISLAND TREES HS; (JR); Hi Hnr Roll; Nat Hon Sy; WWAHSS; Comm Volntr; Peer Tut/Med; Drma Clb; Key Club; Mus Clb; Prom Com; SADD; Bnd; Chr; Mch Bnd; Pep Bnd; Track (V); Cl Off (S); Social Worker; Lawyer; Adelphi; Ford

COLLINS, JULIEN; UNIONDALE, NY; UNIONDALE HS; (SO); 4H Awd; Hi Hnr Roll; Hnr Roll; MVP; Nat Hon Sy; Nat Sci Aw; Otst Ac Ach Awd; Pres Ac Ftns Aw; Pres Sch; Sci Fairs; Comm Volntr; Peer Tut/Med; 4-H; Jr Ach; Key Club; Mth Clb/Tm; Ntl FFA; Sci Clb; Chr; Bsball (J); Ftball (J); Uniondale Science Research Awards/Winner; Spanish/And Science National Honor Society; Ph.D astronomy; Major Business and Marketing; Columbia U; Cornell U

COLLINS, KELLY L; MONSEY, NY; SPRING VALLEY HS; (SR); Hnr Roll; Nat Hon Sy; Nat Sci Aw; Otst Ac Ach Awd; Comm Volntr; Peer Tut/Med; Chrch Yth Grp; Drma Clb; FTA; Key Club; Photog; Sci Clb; Scouts; SP/M/VS; Stg Cre; Lit Mag (P); Sch Ppr (P); Yrbk (P); Women's Recognition Presented By NAACP; Silver Award for Girl Scouting; Professor; Childhood Education; SUNY New Paltz (State U of New York)

COLLINS, LESLIE S; BRONX, NY; ALFRED E SMITH VOC HS; (FR); Hnr Roll; St of Mnth; Peer Tut/Med; ArtClub; Chess; Cmptr Clb; Ftball (V); Track (V); Wt Lftg (V); Bronx Community College; Hunter College

COLLYER, TRICIA; STATEN ISLAND, NY; PORT RICHMOND HS; (JR); Hnr Roll; Otst Ac Ach Awd; St of Mnth; Comm Volntr; Chrch Yth Grp; DARE; Emplmnt; Fr of Library; Outdrs Clb; Scouts; SADD; Tchrs Aide; Bnd; Sch Ppr (E); Model/Actor; Teacher or Into Law; John Jay; Caldwell Catholic U.

COLON, JEANELLE; MIDDLETOWN, NY; MIDDLETOWN HS; (JR); Hnr Roll; Comm Volntr; Cmptr Clb; ROTC; Track; Martial Arts-Not Within the School; Heart Surgeon; General Surgery; Boston U; Binghamton U

COLON, WARLENY; BROOKLYN, NY; FRANKLIN K LANE HS; (JR); Hnr Roll; Nat Hon Sy; Otst Ac Ach Awd; Perf Att; Sci Fairs; Hab For Humty Volntr; Peer Tut/Med; Off Aide; Sci Clb; Tennis (V); Track; CR (R); Arista Honor Society; Bowling Team; Medicine; Dermatologist; Columbia U; Princeton U

COLONEL, JEFF; POUGHQUAG, NY; ARLINGTON HS; (JR); Hi Hnr Roll; Hnr Roll; Otst Ac Ach Awd; St of Mnth; WWAHSS; Comm Volntr; Peer Tut/Med; ArtClub; Dbte Team; Mod UN; Mus Clb; NtlFrnscLg; Spch Team; SP/M/VS; Utopian Club

COLON JR, HECTOR; BRONX, NY; FREDERICK DOUGLASS AC; (JR); Hi Hnr Roll; Hnr Roll; Otst Ac Ach Awd; Comm Volntr; DARE; Drma Clb; Emplmnt; Tchrs Aide; Vsity Clb; Drl Tm; Mch Bnd; Pep Bnd; SP/M/VS; Cr Ctry (V); Ftball (V); Track (L); Vsy Clb (L); Theatre Arts; Drama and Communications; Temple U; Georgia State U

COLOT, NATALY; BROOKLYN, NY; SHEEPSHEAD BAY HS; (JR); Hnr Roll; Comm Volntr; Emplmnt; Vllyball (V); Angels Club; Health Professions; Doctoral Degree; SUNY Stony Brook; Hunter College

CONEYS, TESSA; HUNTINGTON, NY; HUNTINGTON HS; (SO); Hi Hnr Roll; Dnce; Orch; PPSqd; Yrbk (R); Crew-Team; Positive Action Committee; Elementary Education

CONKLIN, JEFFREY W; BLOOMINGBURG, NY; PINE BUSH HS; (JR); Hi Hnr Roll; Nat Hon Sy; Perf Att; Comm Volntr; Emplmnt; Bsball (J); Sccr (J); Tennis (V); Travel Soccer 6 Yrs.-Present; Guitar Lessons-1 Yr.; Meteorology; Stony Brook U; Pennsylvania State U

CONLIN, MEGAN; YORKTOWN HEIGHTS, NY; YORKTOWN HS; (JR); Hi Hnr Roll; Otst Ac Ach Awd; Comm Volntr; Emplmnt; Key Club; NYLC; Scouts; Dnce; Chrldg (J); Sch Ppr (R); Yrbk (R); Student Senate; Religious Education Instructor; Communications; Business

CONNERTON, ROBERT; BINGHAMTON, NY; BINGHAMTON HS; (SR); Hi Hnr Roll; Hnr Roll; Pres Sch; WWAHSS; Yth Ldrshp Prog; Comm Volntr; Emplmnt; SADD; Ftball (VJ L); Wrstlg (VJ L); Binghamton Athletes Care (BAC); Citizen Action; Secondary Education of History; Psychology; U of Albany; U of Buffalo

CONNORS, MADDIE; MANCHESTER, NY; CANANDAIGUA; (JR); Hi Hnr Roll; MVP; Nat Hon Sy; Comm Volntr; Emplmnt; Lcrsse (V); History; PhD; West Point; Naval Academy

CONROY, KATELYN; NORTH BABYLON, NY; NORTH BABYLON HS; (JR); Hi Hnr Roll; Hnr Roll; Comm Volntr; ArtClub; Spanish Clb; Dnce; SP/M/VS; Track (J); Lit Mag (R); Fashion Design; Merchandising; Fashion Institute of Technology; The Fashion Institute of Design & Merchandising

CONSALRI, MARISSA L; CANDOR, NY; CANDOR HS; (JR); Hi Hnr Roll; Nat Hon Sy; Comm Volntr; Chrch Yth Grp; Emplmnt; Bskball (V); Sftball (J); Track (V); Education; SUNY Cortland; Tompkins Cortland Community College

CONSIGLIO, CHRISTOPHER M; BUFFALO, NY; HOMESCHOOL; (SR); Hi Hnr Roll; Comm Volntr; Chrch Yth Grp; Emplmnt; Jzz Bnd; Pianist-Church; AAA Traffic Safety Poster Contest Winner; Government/Political Science; Performing Arts/Music; Oral Roberts U

CONSTANTINE, LISA; CHESTNUT RIDGE, NY; SPRING VALLEY HS; (JR); WWAHSS; Comm Volntr; Chrch Yth Grp; SADD; Ch Chr; Orch; Sftball; Academic Excellence Award; Medicine-Pediatrician

COOK, VIRGINIA A; ASHLAND, NY; WINDHAM ASHLAND JEWETT CTRL SCH; (JR); Hi Hnr Roll; Nat Hon Sy; St of Mnth; USAA; WWAHSS; Comm Volntr; Peer Tut/Med; Drma Clb; Prom Com; Tchrs Aide; Spanish Clb; Bnd; Jzz Bnd; Mch Bnd; SP/M/VS; Bskball (VJ); Sftball (VJ); President of Prom Committee; Secondary Education English

COOK I, KEVIN J; BUFFALO, NY; MC KINLEY VOC TECH HS; (FR); Ctznshp Aw; Hnr Roll; Nat Ldrshp Svc; Perf Att; Salutrn; St of Mnth; Peer Tut/Med; Quiz Bowl; Stg Cre; Stu Cncl (V); The Sherman F Feyler Award; Perfect Attendance Award; Law Degree; Master's Degree; UCLA; North Carolina

COON, WILLIAM; SCHUYLERVILLE, NY; STILLWATER CTRL HS; (JR); Hi Hnr Roll; Hnr Roll; Otst Ac Ach Awd; Perf Att; WWAHSS; ArtClub; DARE; Emplmnt; Outdrs Clb; ROTC; Bnd; Chr; Drl Tm; Arch (J); Bskball (VJ); Ftball (J); Track (V); Wt Lftg (VJ); Wrstlg (J); New York National Guard Corp of Cadets; Criminal Justice; Architecture; Norwich U; SUNY

COONS, FAYLA; CLAVERACK, NY; HUDSON HS; (JR); Hi Hnr Roll; Hnr Roll; Amnsty Intl; Comm Volntr; Peer Tut/Med; Emplmnt; Prom Com; Chr; Chrldg (V); Scr Kpr (J); Sftball (J); Track (V L); History (World and American); Secondary Education; Hartwich; College of St. Joseph in Vermont

COONS, JOSHUA; ELLENBURG DEPOT, NY; NORTH ADIRONDACK JR/SR HS; (SO); All Am Sch; Hi Hnr Roll; Nat Hon Sy; Pres Sch; USAA; Comm Volntr; Lib Aide; Spanish Clb; Bnd; Tennis (V); School Website Designer

COOPER, ANN; MASSENA, NY; MASSENA SR HS; (SO); F Lan Hn Soc; Hi Hnr Roll; Hnr Roll; Comm Volntr; French Clb; Orch; Psychology; Foreign Language; U of Massachusetts Amherst

COOPER, CAITLIN D; MERRICK, NY; CALHOUN HS; (JR); Hi Hnr Roll; Hnr Roll; WWAHSS; Comm Volntr; ArtClub; DECA; Emplmnt; Key Club; Outdrs Clb; Prom Com; Scouts; Elementary Education

COOPER, NOAH; POPLAR RIDGE, NY; CAYUGA-ONONDAGA AREA OCCUPATIONAL CTR; (JR); Ntl FFA; Sch Ppr (R); Senior FFA Reporter; National Technical Honor Society; Computer Animation

COPELAND, ALICIA T; HEMPSTEAD, NY; HEMPSTEAD HS; (FR); Hnr Roll; Kwnis Aw; St of Mnth; Chrch Yth Grp; Chr; Child Psychiatrist; Pediatrician; Harvard U; George Washington U

COPENHAVER, JESSICA A; MONROE, NY; WASHINGTONVILLE HS; (SR); Hi Hnr Roll; Nat Hon Sy; Comm Volntr; Sftball (J); National Honor Society; Elementary Education; U of Albany; CW Post

COPPA, DANIELA; PORT CHESTER, NY; MARIA REGINA HS; (JR); Ctznshp Aw; F Lan Hn Soc; Hi Hnr Roll; Nat Hon Sy; Otst Ac Ach Awd; Valdctrian; WWAHSS; Emplmnt; Key Club; Italian Clb; Fairfield U Book Award; Rensselaer Polytechnic Institute Math & Science Award; Major in Biology; Fairfield U; Sacred Heart U

CORDERO, ALISIA V; YONKERS, NY; MONSIGNOR SCANLAN HS; (SR); Sci Fairs; Comm Volntr; Drma Clb; Emplmnt; Mus Clb; Prom Com; Svce Clb; Chr; Dnce; SP/M/VS; Sch Ppr (R); Stock Broker; Nursing; College of New Rochelle; Pace U

CORDERO, ESMERALDA; BRONX, NY; HS COMMUNICATION GRAPHIC ART; (SO); Hi Hnr Roll; Hnr Roll; Otst Ac Ach Awd; Yth Ldrshp Prog; Peer Tut/Med; Chrch Yth Grp; Scouts; Chr; Dnce; SP/M/VS; Drawing; Mathematics; Commercial Art; Business Administration; Columbia U; New York U

CORLETTA, MICHAEL; WESTTOWN, NY; MINISINK VALLEY HS; (FR); Hi Hnr Roll; Hnr Roll; Pres Ac Ftns Aw; St of Mnth; WWAHSS; Comm Volntr; Key Club; Bsball (J); Cr Ctry (V L); Wrstlg (V L); Architecture; U of Connecticut

CORLETTA, SUSAN; WESTTOWN, NY; MINISINK VALLEY HS; (JR); Hi Hnr Roll; Nat Hon Sy; Nat Ldrshp Svc; Pres Sch; Sci Fairs; WWAHSS; Comm Volntr; Hosp Aide; Peer Tut/Med; AL Aux Girls; Emplmnt; Key Club; Off Aide; Latin Clb; Dnce; Tennis (V L); Girl's State Representative; Pharmacy; Wilkes U; U of the Sciences in Philadelphia

CORREA, DAVID; FREEPORT, NY; FREEPORT HS; (JR); Hi Hnr Roll; Hnr Roll; Nat Hon Sy; Comm Volntr; Chrch Yth Grp; Scouts; Vsity Clb; Bnd; Jzz Bnd; Mch Bnd; Pep Bnd; Ftball (V); Lcrsse (V); Track (V); Physical Therapist; Brigham Young U; Albany U

CORRERA, ALLIE; SCHENECTADY, NY; SCHALMONT HS; (SO); Hnr Roll; MVP; St of Mnth; ArtClub; DARE; Drma Clb; Key Club; Chr; Bskball (J L); Sccr (J L); Sftball (J L); Track (V L); Varsity Girls Bowling; Child Psychology; Teacher; Syracuse U; Sienna College

CORTES, ADRIANA; FLORAL PARK, NY; (JR); F Lan Hn Soc; Hnr Roll; Nat Hon Sy; Perf Att; WWAHSS; Comm Volntr; Spec Olymp Vol; ArtClub; Key Club; Photog

CORTES, ANA; WOODSIDE, NY; CATHEDRAL HS; (SO); Hnr Roll; Nat Hon Sy; Perf Att; Sci Fairs; St of Mnth; WWAHSS; Yth Ldrshp Prog; Hosp Aide; ArtClub; Emplmnt; Mth Clb/Tm; Bnd; Dnce; Sftball (J); Sch Ppr (R); Medical Field / Pediatrics; Columbia U; Cornell U

CORTES OREA, MANELI N; HAVERSTRAW, NY; NORTH ROCKLAND HS; (FR); Hnr Roll; Otst Ac Ach Awd; St of Mnth; Emplmnt; Fr of Library; Studio in Art; Fashion Designer; Floral Designer; Marist College; Fashion Institute of Technology

CORTORREAL, RONNY; NEW YORK, NY; HS FOR MEDIA & COMMUNICATIONS; (FR); Otst Ac Ach Awd; Perf Att; Sci/Math Olympn; USMC Stu Ath Aw; Hosp Aide; ROTC; Sci Clb; Tmpl Yth Grp; Drl Tm; Bsball (V); Bskball (V); Cyclg (V); Dvng (V); Ftball (V); Sccr (V); Swmg (V); Track (V); CR (V); Astronaut; Detective; John Jay College

CORWIN, SARA M; ENDICOTT, NY; UNION ENDICOTT HS; (FR); Hi Hnr Roll; Lcrsse (V L); Swmg (V L); Vllyball (J); Key Club; Science Olympiad

COSCIA, LISA; OAKDALE, NY; CONNETQUOT HS; (SR); F Lan Hn Soc; Hi Hnr Roll; Pres Ac Ftns Aw; St of Mnth; WWAHSS; Hab For Humty Volntr; Peer Tut/Med; Spec Olymp Vol; DECA; Bskball (L); Sccr (V C); Track (V); Vllyball (J); CR (S); Yrbk (E); Criminal Justice; Forensics; U of New Haven

COSME, JUAN; BRONX, NY; MONROE AC FOR VISUAL ARTS; (FR); Hnr Roll; Chrch Yth Grp; Dnce; SP/M/VS; Bsball (J); Bskball (J); Swmg (V); Computer Science; Electrical Engineering; NYU; Fordham U

Cooper, Noah
Cayuga-Onondaga Area Occupational Ctr
Poplar Ridge, NY

Colonel, Jeff
Arlington HS
Poughquag, NY

Colley, April C
Millbrook JR/SR HS
Millbrook, NY

Cole, Matthew
CW Baker HS
Baldwinsville, NY

National
Honor Roll
Spring 2005

Cohen, Jordan
Leon M Goldstein HS Sciences
Brooklyn, NY

Collier, Kyle
Hicksville HS
Hicksville, NY

Coon, William
Stillwater Ctrl HS
Schuylerville, NY

Cortorreal, Ronny
HS For Media & Communications
New York, NY

COSTA, MICHAEL; MERRICK, NY; CALHOUN HS; (JR); F Lan Hn Soc; Hnr Roll; Nat Hon Sy; Peer Tut/Med; Drma Clb; Emplmnt; Key Club; Prom Com; Bnd; Chr; Jzz Bnd; SP/M/VS

COSTANTINO, MICHELLE; GLEN COVE, NY; GLEN COVE HS; (SR); Ctznshp Aw; Hi Hnr Roll; Jr Rot; Kwnis Aw; Nat Hon Sy; Otst Ac Ach Awd; Pres Sch; Salutrn; St of Mnth; WWAHSS; Comm Volntr; Peer Tut/Med; Red Cr Aide; Dbte Team; DECA; Drma Clb; Emplmnt; Key Club; Prom Com; Svce Clb; Italian Clb; Lcrsse (VJ L); Tennis (VJ L); Cl Off (P); Lit Mag (E); Sch Ppr (E); Prom Princess; Homecoming Court; Pre-Law; Education; Fordham U - Class of 2009

COSTANZO, DANIELLE; WANTAGH, NY; WANTAGH HS; (SO); Hi Hnr Roll; Key Club; Bnd; Dnce; Lcrsse (J); Law; Accounting; SUNY Binghamton; SUNY Geneseo

COSTANZO, MICHAEL T; TONAWANDA, NY; TONAWANDA HS; (JR); All Am Sch; Hi Hnr Roll; Otst Ac Ach Awd; Perf Att; WWAHSS; P to P St Amb Prg; SP/M/VS; Stg Cre; Sccr (V L); Track (V L); Chemistry Major; Chemical and Physical Engineering Degree; Cornell U; U At Buffalo

COSTELLO, LARRY; GLOVERSVILLE, NY; GLOVERSVILLE HS; (FR); Hnr Roll; Chess; Sccr (J); Track (J); ACIS Trip to Greece and Italy; Saxophone 3 Years

COSTELLO, PAMELA A; MASSAPEQUA, NY; MASSAPEQUA HS; (FR); Hnr Roll; WWAHSS; Key Club; Scouts; Orch; Girl Scout Silver Award; NYU; St John's U

COTHREN, CHRISTA; VERPLANCK, NY; JOHN F KENNEDY CATHOLIC HS; (JR); Hnr Roll; St of Mnth; WWAHSS; Comm Volntr; DARE; Emplmnt; SADD; Sccr (J); Criminal Justice; Accounting; St. Thomas Aquinas College

COTTO, ELIZABETH; NEW YORK, NY; ST JEAN BAPTISTE HS; (SO); Hi Hnr Roll; Hnr Roll; Valdctrian; WWAHSS; Amnsty Intl; Comm Volntr; Cmptr Clb; Jr Ach; Photog; Sch Ppr (R); Hunter College; Fordham U

COTTO, TANA; MT VERNON, NY; MT VERNON HS; F Lan Hn Soc; Hnr Roll; WWAHSS; Comm Volntr; Prom Com; Yrbk (E); Lawyer; Criminal Justice

COUGHLAN, RYAN P; HUNTINGTON, NY; HUNTINGTON HS; (SO); Hi Hnr Roll; Hnr Roll; Nat Hon Sy; Nat Ldrshp Svc; Nat Sci Aw; Otst Ac Ach Awd; Sci Fairs; Sci/Math Olympn; WWAHSS; Comm Volntr; Hab For Humty Volntr; DARE; Orch; Bskball; Ftball; Lcrsse (J L); Mar Art (J); Vllyball; Honor Society; Habitat for Humanity; Computer Science; Business Degree

COVELL, CARLEEN; NEWFANE, NY; NEWFANE SR HS; (JR); Hi Hnr Roll; Hnr Roll; Nat Stu Ath Day Aw; WWAHSS; Comm Volntr; Peer Tut/Med; Chrch Yth Grp; Drma Clb; Emplmnt; Lttrmn Clb; Vsity Clb; Chr; SP/M/VS; Stg Cre; Swg Chr; Swmg (V L); Track (V L); Vllyball (JC); Master's in Business; Baruch College; U of Buffalo

COVELLI, ANTHONY; OCEANSIDE, NY; OCEANSIDE HS; (SO); Hi Hnr Roll; Hnr Roll; Otst Ac Ach Awd; Pres Ac Ftns Aw; Pres Sch; Sci Fairs; Sci/Math Olympn; Yth Ldrshp Prog; Peer Tut/Med; Mus Clb; NtlFrnscLg; Sci Clb; Bnd; Jzz Bnd; Orch; SP/M/VS; Golf; Rlr Hky (V); Sccr; Finger Printer in 2005 Forensic Competition; Most Outstanding Musician in Jazz Band / Band Ensemble; Forensic Major / Criminalistics; Music Education / Music Teacher; John Jay College of Criminal Justice; Juilliard School

COWAN, SEAN D; FRANKLIN SQUARE, NY; H F CAREY HS; (JR); F Lan Hn Soc; Hi Hnr Roll; Hnr Roll; Nat Hon Sy; St of Mnth; WWAHSS; Comm Volntr; Peer Tut/Med; FBLA; Mch Bnd; Pep Bnd; Karate; Pre-Med; Education & Computer Science; Adelphi U, St. Johns U; Hofstra U

COX, KRYSTAL L; CATTARAUGUS, NY; PINE VALLEY CTRL SCH; (FR); Hnr Roll; Pres Ac Ftns Aw; Sci Fairs; St of Mnth; WWAHSS; Comm Volntr; ArtClub; Chrch Yth Grp; Golf (V); I Am A Mentor; Law; Arts; St Bonaventure

COX, MARCUS J; AVON, NY; LIMA CHRISTIAN SCH; (SO); Hi Hnr Roll; WWAHSS; Comm Volntr; Chrch Yth Grp; Emplmnt; Bnd; Bskball (J); Cr Ctry (J); Golf (V); Sccr (J); Swmg (V); Cl Off (P); Stu Cncl (T); Sprint Tri Athletic; Sunday School Volunteer; Medicine

COX, STEPHANIE; ROME, NY; ROME FREE AC; (JR); Hi Hnr Roll; Hnr Roll; Comm Volntr; Chess; Chrch Yth Grp; Emplmnt; ROTC; Bnd; 4 Yrs - RFA Girls Bowling Team / 3 Yrs J / Last Yr V; Broadcast Technology; Brigham Young University Idaho; Southern Virginia University

CRAFT, CHRISTINA; KINGSTON, NY; SAUGERTIES HS; (FR); Hi Hnr Roll; St of Mnth; WWAHSS; Dbte Team; Key Club; Bnd; Lcrsse (V); Sccr (J); 54 Key Club Hours; Health and Fitness Teacher; Colgate U

CRAYTON, LERICE N; UNIONDALE, NY; UNIONDALE HS; (JR); Hnr Roll; WWAHSS; Comm Volntr; Peer Tut/Med; Chrch Yth Grp; Key Club; SADD; Chr; Ch Chr; Orch; Junior Firefighter; Participated in the Long Island Strings Festival; Nursing; SUNY Stony Brook; Nassau Community College

CREIGHTON, RICARDO J A; YONKERS, NY; YONKERS HS; (JR); All Am Sch; Hi Hnr Roll; USAA; WWAHSS; Peer Tut/Med; Chrch Yth Grp; Ftball (V L); Business; Computers; Harvard U; Princeton

CRISCONE, AMBER N; ALTAMONT, NY; GUILDERLAND HS; (FR); Hi Hnr Roll; Hnr Roll; Nat Hon Sy; Perf Att; Comm Volntr; Key Club; Skiing (C); Presidential Award for Academic Achievement; Broadcast Journalism; Communications; Fordham U; Syracuse U

CROCCIA, NICOLE; CORAM, NY; (SR); Gov Hnr Prg; Hi Hnr Roll; Hnr Roll; Chr; Flg Crps; Marine Biology; Education; Central Florida Community

CROCE IV, LOUIS; GARDEN CITY, NY; FRIENDS AC; (FR); Hi Hnr Roll; Comm Volntr; Dbte Team; Drma Clb; Mth Clb/Tm; Mus Clb; P to P St Amb Prg; Bnd; Mch Bnd; Pep Bnd; SP/M/VS; Bsball (J); Ftball (J)

CROSBY, JAIME; LAURENS, NY; LAURENS CTRL SCH; (JR); Hi Hnr Roll; Nat Hon Sy; Nat Stu Ath Day Aw; WWAHSS; Red Cr Aide; Drma Clb; Key Club; Prom Com; Tchrs Aide; Spanish Clb; Bnd; Jzz Bnd; Mch Bnd; Stg Cre; Bskball (V L); Sccr (V L); Track (V L); Cl Off (P, V); SADD; Mathematics; Houghton College

CROSBY, LAURA; LAURENS, NY; LAURENS CTRL SCH; (SR); Hi Hnr Roll; Hnr Roll; Nat Hon Sy; WWAHSS; Red Cr Aide; ArtClub; Drma Clb; Key Club; Tchrs Aide; Spanish Clb; Chr; SP/M/VS; Bskball (V); Sccr (V); Track (V); Anthropology; History; Houghton College; SUNY Oneonta

CROSSLEY, NATHANIEL G; GOSHEN, NY; GOSHEN CTRL HS; (SR); Hi Hnr Roll; Hnr Roll; Nat Hon Sy; Nat Sci Aw; Perf Att; Sci/Math Olympn; Emplmnt; Sci Clb; Scouts; French Clb; Bnd; Cr Ctry (V C); Track (V); International Business and Relations; New York U

CROWE, DANIEL J; BUFFALO, NY; KENMORE WEST SR HS; (SR); Hi Hnr Roll; Nat Hon Sy; Perf Att; Comm Volntr; Chrch Yth Grp; Dbte Team; Stg Cre; WNYFLEC Award in German Ranked #1 in All of NY; Physics Major; Foreign Languages; St. Louis U Madrid Spain; Canisius College Buffalo New York

CROWLEY, RONAL; STILLWATER, NY; STILLWATER CTRL HS; (JR); Hi Hnr Roll; Hnr Roll; Perf Att; AL Aux Boys; DARE; Key Club; Outdrs Clb; Sci Clb; Bnd; Jzz Bnd; Mch Bnd; SP/M/VS; Bsball (V L); Ftball (V L); NYSMMA; All County; Engineering; Medical; Siena; SUNY Oswego

CRUZ, ELAINE-MARIE; RICHMOND HILL, NY; WASHINGTON IRVING HS; (JR); Hnr Roll; Perf Att; Peer Tut/Med; Spec Olymp Vol; Key Club; Chr; Dnce; SP/M/VS; Honor Roll in Academic Contests; Musical Theatre/Dance; Fashion Designing/Business; New York U; Fashion Institute of Technology

CRUZ, ERICA; SODUS, NY; SODUS JR/SR HS; (SO); Ctznshp Aw; Hi Hnr Roll; Hnr Roll; MVP; Sci Fairs; Chrch Yth Grp; Drma Clb; Emplmnt; Chr; SP/M/VS; Chrldg (V); Sftball (V)

CRUZ, GLADYBELLE R; ALBANY, NY; ALBANY HS; (SR); Hnr Roll; Otst Ac Ach Awd; WWAHSS; Yth Ldrshp Prog; Comm Volntr; Emplmnt; P to P St Amb Prg; Puerto Rican Hispanic Youth Leadership Institute Participant; Lieutenant John F. Finn Community Service Award; Pharmacist; Albany College of Pharmacy; U DE Puerto Rico

CRUZ, JESSICA; UNIONDALE, NY; UNIONDALE HS; (JR); Hnr Roll; DARE; Scouts; Latinos Unidos Club; Real Estate

CRUZ, LORENA; BAYVILLE, NY; LOCUST VALLEY HS; (SR); F Lan Hn Soc; Hi Hnr Roll; Nat Hon Sy; St of Mnth; WWAHSS; Comm Volntr; Emplmnt; Lit Mag (E); Triple "C" Award 8th Grade - 2001; Scholastic Award / Rotary July 2000; Accounting; Finance; SUNY Old Westbury; SUNY Farmingdale

CRUZ, TABITHA N; BRONX, NY; MONSIGNOR SCANLAN HS; (JR); Hnr Roll; Nat Hon Sy; Perf Att; Peer Tut/Med; Drma Clb; Mus Clb; P to P St Amb Prg; German Clb; Chr; Psychology; Cornell U; New York U

CRUZ, TIFFANY; MIDDLETOWN, NY; PINE BUSH HS; (SO); Hnr Roll; Yth Ldrshp Prog; Comm Volntr; Emplmnt; Bnd; Chr; Dnce; Youth Leadership and Service Council; MA in Theater; Long Island U (C.W. Post Campus); Siena College

CRYTZER, ASHLEY; OLEAN, NY; HINSDALE CTRL SCH; (FR); Hi Hnr Roll; Hnr Roll; St of Mnth; Comm Volntr; Peer Tut/Med; Spec Olymp Vol; ArtClub; Chrch Yth Grp; DARE; Emplmnt; Scouts; SADD; Tchrs Aide; Vsity Clb; Chr; Clr Grd; Bskball (J); Sccr (VJ L); Sftball (VJ); Vsy Clb (L); Cl Off (P); Sch Ppr (R); Applying for SADD & School Paper Next Year; No Weights Team - I Lift Optionally; Education; Psychology; Alfred U

CSAKANY, RACHEL E; SCHENECTADY, NY; SCHENECTADY HS; (FR); Hi Hnr Roll; Hnr Roll; Pres Sch; ArtClub; Bnd; Mch Bnd; Bskball (V); Sftball (J); New York State Athletic Award; Interior Design; Newspaper / Magazine Writer

CSIZMAR, JAMIE-LEIGH; GLENFIELD, NY; SOUTH LEWIS HS; (JR); Hi Hnr Roll; Nat Hon Sy; Nat Ldrshp Svc; Otst Ac Ach Awd; WWAHSS; DARE; Emplmnt; NYLC; Prom Com; SADD; Bnd; Chr; SP/M/VS; Sccr; Track; Cl Off (P, V, S); Stu Cncl (R); Yrbk (P)

CUBERO, SHEYLA; LIBERTY, NY; LIBERTY HS; (JR); Hi Hnr Roll; Nat Hon Sy; WWAHSS; Chrch Yth Grp; Chr; Early Childhood Education; Nyack College; Niagara U

CUEBAS, SALVADOR; BRONX, NY; ENY TRANSIT TECH HS; (SR); F Lan Hn Soc; Hnr Roll; MVP; Nat Hon Sy; Otst Ac Ach Awd; Perf Att; USAA; Comm Volntr; Emplmnt; Scouts; Tchrs Aide; Bsball (VJC); CR (R); Yrbk (E, P)

CUI, JOHNSON; BROOKLYN, NY; BROOKLYN TECH HS; (JR); Comm Volntr; Emplmnt; Off Aide; Pharmacy/Pharmacology; Doctorate; Princeton U; Columbia U

CULKIN, LAURIE; REXFORD, NY; SHENENDEHOWA HS; (MS); Hi Hnr Roll; Hnr Roll; ArtClub; Chrch Yth Grp; DARE; Pep Squd; Dnce; Stu Cncl (R); Yrbk (P); Lettered in Academics; Interior Design

CULVER, SARAH E; FREWSBURG, NY; FREWSBURG CTRL HS; (SR); 4H Awd; Ctznshp Aw; Hi Hnr Roll; Nat Hon Sy; Otst Ac Ach Awd; Perf Att; Sci Fairs; Valdctrian; WWAHSS; Comm Volntr; 4-H; Biology Clb; Chrch Yth Grp; Emplmnt; HO'Br Yth Ldrshp; Lib Aide; Quiz Bowl; Spch Team; Chr; Ch Chr; SP/M/VS; Bskball (JC); Skiing (V); Track (V); Cl Off (T); Stu Cncl (T); Yrbk (E); National Society for High School Scholars; Biology/Pre-Vet; Environmental Studies; Allegheny College

CURIEL, GISSELLE; BRONX, NY; JANE ADDAMS HS; (JR); Hnr Roll; Lawyer; Business Management; Lehman College, Monroe College; NYU

CURRIE, CARISSA A; PATCHOGUE, NY; PATCHOGUE-MEDFORD HS; (JR); F Lan Hn Soc; Hi Hnr Roll; Comm Volntr; Hosp Aide; Photog; Fld Hky (V); Track (V); Yrbk (R); Criminal Justice; Forensic Science; C.W. Post, Long Island U

CURRY, AKIE N; JAMAICA, NY; MARTIN VAN BUREN HS; (JR); Hnr Roll; St of Mnth; CARE; Hosp Aide; Red Cr Aide; DARE; Scouts; Spch Team; Chr; Dnce; Flg Crps; Stg Cre; Tennis (V); Wt Lftg (V); Stu Cncl (S); NYPD Police Academy; Medical Assistant; Psychology; New York U; Savannah College of Art & Design

CURTIS, STEPHANIE; GLEN COVE, NY; GLEN COVE HS; (JR); Hi Hnr Roll; Hnr Roll; Nat Hon Sy; WWAHSS; Comm Volntr; Dbte Team; DECA; Drma Clb; Emplmnt; Key Club; Mth Clb/Tm; Pep Squd; Bnd; Mch Bnd; Pep Bnd; SP/M/VS; Chrldg (V); Track (V); Biology; Barnard College; Boston U

CUSHING, CARLY; CORNING, NY; CORNING-PAINTED POST WEST HS; (SO); Hi Hnr Roll; Hnr Roll; Perf Att; Comm Volntr; Chr; Sftball (VJCL); Stu Cncl (R); Veterinarian; Cornell; SUNY Canton

CUSIMANO, DEREK H; PANAMA, NY; PANAMA CTRL SCH; (SR); Hnr Roll; MVP; Nat Hon Sy; Otst Ac Ach Awd; Perf Att; Pres Ac Ftns Aw; St of Mnth; Comm Volntr; Peer Tut/Med; Emplmnt; Ftball (VJCL); Skt Tgt Sh (VJ); Tennis (V); Wrstlg (VJCL); Land Surveying; Automotive; Alfred State (SUNY); Morrisville (SUNY)

CYRUS, WHITNEY R; SYRACUSE, NY; (JR); Hnr Roll; Perf Att; Pres Ac Ftns Aw; DARE; Drma Clb; Emplmnt; Chr; Drl Tm; Stg Cre; Tennis (V); Track (V); Stu Cncl (R); Technology, Athletic Awards; Volunteer Big Brother Big Sister Program; Elementary Education; Mathematics; Design; Clothing or Stage; Charlotte North Carolina State; LeMoyne College-Syracuse, NY

CZESAK, AMANDA M; CHAFFEE, NY; PIONEER HS; (SR); 4H Awd; F Lan Hn Soc; Hi Hnr Roll; Nat Hon Sy; Perf Att; Pres Sch; WWAHSS; Comm Volntr; Spec Olymp Vol; 4-H; Chrch Yth Grp; Emplmnt; Ntl FFA; French Clb; Orch; U.S. Air Force Math and Science Award; Dairy Production and Management; State U of New York At Cobleskill

CZORA, RACHEL S; BLISS, NY; LETCHWORTH CTRL HS; (SR); Hi Hnr Roll; Nat Hon Sy; WWAHSS; Comm Volntr; Peer Tut/Med; Red Cr Aide; Drma Clb; FBLA; Mod UN; Prom Com; Vsity Clb; Bnd; SP/M/VS; Sccr (V); Swmg (V L); Track (V L); Stu Cncl (S); Yrbk (P); Pre-Law; Psychology; Niagara U

CZUMAK, ASHLEY; WESTBURY, NY; W T CLARKE HS; (SR); Hnr Roll; Nat Hon Sy; St of Mnth; Comm Volntr; Hosp Aide; Peer Tut/Med; Emplmnt; Key Club; Scouts; Voc Ind Clb Am; Dnce; Pep Bnd; SP/M/VS; Lcrsse (VJ); Gymnastics, Karate, Dance; Skills USA, Key Club, NTHS; Education; Fashion; Nassau Community College

DABROWNY, SONYA; WEBSTER, NY; OUR LADY OF MERCY HS; (SO); Hnr Roll; Comm Volntr; Scouts; Dnce; Cr Ctry; Track; CR (R); Law Explorers; Pianist; Law; Medicine; U of Rochester; Harvard U

DADDEZIO, RACHEL; ENDICOTT, NY; UNION-ENDICOTT HS; (SR); Hi Hnr Roll; Hnr Roll; Kwnis Aw; Nat Hon Sy; WWAHSS; Peer Tut/Med; Drma Clb; Emplmnt; Key Club; Prom Com; Italian Clb; Chr; SP/M/VS; Swg Chr; Italian and Arabic Translation/Interpretation; Vocal Performance; SUNY Binghamton

DADSON, OSWALD A; BROOKLYN, NY; LEON M GOLDSTEIN HS; (SO); Sci/Math Olympn; Hosp Aide; Peer Tut/Med; Mth Clb/Tm; Sccr (V); Best of Brooklyn Award; Arista / Archon; Pharmacy; Medicine; St John's U; Long Island U

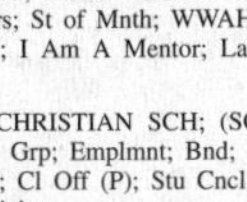
Dabrowny, Sonya
Our Lady Of Mercy HS
Webster, NY

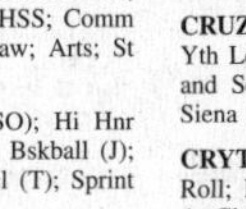
Currie, Carissa A
Patchogue-Medford HS
Patchogue, NY

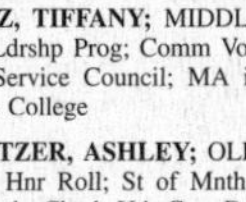
Curiel, Gisselle
Jane Addams HS
Bronx, NY

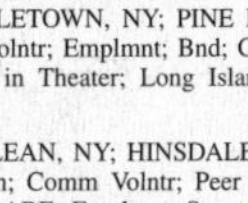
Creighton, Ricardo J A
Yonkers HS
Yonkers, NY

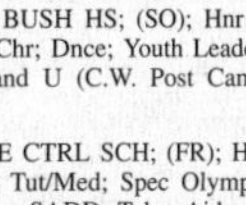
Cruz, Tabitha N
Monsignor Scanlan HS
Bronx, NY

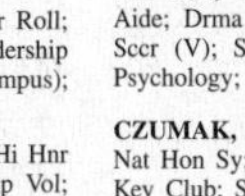
Cusimano, Derek H
Panama Ctrl Sch
Panama, NY

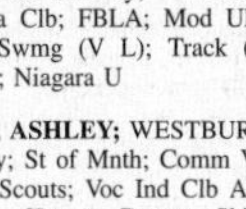
Dadson, Oswald A
Leon M Goldstein HS
Brooklyn, NY

DAHAR, JENNIE; HINSDALE, NY; HINSDALE CTRL HS; (SR); All Am Sch; Ctznshp Aw; Hi Hnr Roll; MVP; Nat Hon Sy; Nat Mrt LOC; Nat Stu Ath Day Aw; Pres Sch; USAA; Valdctrian; Comm Volntr; Peer Tut/Med; AL Aux Girls; Chrch Yth Grp; Dbte Team; Emplmnt; Jr Ach; P to P St Amb Prg; Tchrs Aide; Vsity Clb; Chr; Ch Chr; SP/M/VS; Sccr (V CL); Cl Off (V); President of the National Honor Society; Bausch & Lomb Honorary Science Award; Pre-Veterinary Medicine; Veterinary Medicine; Cornell U; Saint Bonaventure U

DAHLGREN, LISA; SCHENECTADY, NY; BURNT HILLS-BALLSTON LAKE HS; (FR); Hnr Roll; DARE; Chr; DARE Award; Physical Therapy; Teacher; U of Albany; Siena College

DAIGLE, CODY P; STILLWATER, NY; STILLWATER CTRL HS; (JR); Hi Hnr Roll; Hnr Roll; MVP; WWAHSS; Comm Volntr; Chrch Yth Grp; DARE; Emplmnt; Vsity Clb; Bskball (V); Golf (V); Vsy Clb (V); 2005 Wasaren League Basketball MVP; 2005 Wasaren League Golf MVP; Physical Education; Sports Management; Siena College; St Rose

DALE, JOEL S; WYANDANCH, NY; WYANDANCH MEM. HS; (JR); Comm Volntr; Chrch Yth Grp; Drma Clb; Ch Chr; Sccr (V); Track (V); Neurology; Florida U; Long Island U

DALEY, DARNELL; BROOKLYN, NY; BENJAMIN BANNEKER AC; (FR); Hi Hnr Roll; Hnr Roll; Otst Ac Ach Awd; Comm Volntr; Dbte Team; Drma Clb; Mth Clb/Tm; Mus Clb; Sci Clb; Bnd; Chr; Ch Chr; SP/M/VS; Bsball (V); Bskball (V); Cr Ctry (V); Ftball (V); Track (V); Pre-Med; Media; Duke U; Cornell U

D'ALLURA, CHRIS; CORAM, NY; LONGWOOD HS; (JR); Hi Hnr Roll; Hnr Roll; DARE; Mus Clb; Bnd; Jzz Bnd; Mch Bnd; Orch; Tri-M Music Honor Society; Music Education; Music Performance; Ithaca College; Crane School of Music

D'AMICO, CHRISTIAN; LEVITTOWN, NY; ISLAND TREES HS; (SO); Hi Hnr Roll; Kwnis Aw; Otst Ac Ach Awd; WWAHSS; Comm Volntr; Hosp Aide; Key Club; Medical; Biological; Cornell; Stony-Brook

D'AMIGO, PETER; BINGHAMTON, NY; JOHNSON CITY HS; (JR); Hi Hnr Roll; Hnr Roll; Comm Volntr; Drma Clb; Key Club; Mus Clb; Bnd; Chr; Jzz Bnd; SP/M/VS; Cl Off (V, S); Stu Cncl (V); All State Mixed Chorus; Pharmacy; Dentistry

DANGOL, ASMIKA R; WOODSIDE, NY; ROBERT F WAGNER JR; (SO); Hnr Roll; Nat Hon Sy; Perf Att; Photog; Mar Art; Track; CR; Sch Ppr (E); United Student Organization; School Leadership Team; Journalism; Criminal Law; Columbia U; Brown U

DANIEL, MAKIA; BROOKLYN, NY; JAMES MADISON HS; (FR); Hnr Roll; Tchrs Aide; Lawyer; Chemical Engineering; Howard U

DANIEL, NYEESHA I; BROOKLYN, NY; A PHILIP RANDOLPH HS; (SR); Nat Stu Ath Day Aw; Perf Att; St of Mnth; Peer Tut/Med; Emplmnt; Scouts; Tennis (J); Vllyball (VJ); National Student Athlete Day Certificate; Winner of Oral Presentation Competition; Biology; Psychology; SUNY Binghamton

DANKO, JAIME; ELMIRA, NY; NOTRE DAME HS; (SO); Hi Hnr Roll; Hnr Roll; Comm Volntr; Hab For Humty Volntr; Chrch Yth Grp; Key Club; Mth Clb/Tm; Mus Clb; Bnd; Jzz Bnd; Mch Bnd; Orch; Skiing (J); Cl Off (T); Pathology; Mathematics; Binghamton SUNY; Boston U

DANOFF, JACLYN; GREAT NECK, NY; NORTH SHORE HEBREW AC HS; (JR); Hnr Roll; Nat Hon Sy; Pres Sch; Sci Fairs; Sci/Math Olympn; WWAHSS; Comm Volntr; Hosp Aide; Peer Tut/Med; Emplmnt; NYLC; SADD; Tennis (V); Vllyball (V); Lit Mag (E); Sch Ppr (E); President SADD; NYSSMA-Violin; Dentistry; Boston U 7 Yr. Dental Program

DARCY, KAYLA A; BUFFALO, NY; SOUTH PARK HS; (SO); Bsball; Chrldg; Sftball

DARIS, MEGHAN; NORTH BALDWIN, NY; BALDWIN HS; (SR); F Lan Hn Soc; Hi Hnr Roll; Nat Hon Sy; WWAHSS; Comm Volntr; ArtClub; Sci Clb; Tchrs Aide; Spanish Clb; Science; Stony Brook U

DARLINA IV, R CLEMENT; DELMAR, NY; DOANE STUART SCH; (SR); Hi Hnr Roll; Nat Hon Sy; Yth Ldrshp Prog; Drma Clb; Acpl Chr; Chr; Jzz Bnd; SP/M/VS; Bskball (V); Sccr (V); Tennis (V); Cl Off (R); Lit Mag (E); Sch Ppr (E, R); Film & Cinema Studies; NYU; USC

DARNELL, MADALYN; GREAT NECK, NY; GREAT NECK SOUTH HS; (SO); Kwnis Aw; Pres Sch; Sci Fairs; WWAHSS; Comm Volntr; Key Club; Vsity Clb; Tennis (V L); Tennis-All County; Science Research Fair-3rd Place

DAS, AMRITA K; MERRICK, NY; SANFORD H CALHOUN HS; Hnr Roll; WWAHSS; Comm Volntr; Spec Olymp Vol; ArtClub; Key Club; Orch; Stu Cncl (R); Sch Ppr (R); Art Club; World of Difference; Pre-Med; Drama / Theatre; NYU; Princeton U

DA SILVA JOHRDEN, JONATHAN; HICKSVILLE, NY; ST MARY'S COLLEGE PREP HS; (JR); Hi Hnr Roll; Hnr Roll; Nat Hon Sy; Otst Ac Ach Awd; Sci Fairs; Sci/Math Olympn; Comm Volntr; Spec Olymp Vol; Cmptr Clb; National Scholar Institute; Kempo (Martial Arts) and Intern Teaching; Electrical Engineering, Electronic Engineer; Computers, Business; Cooper Union U, MIT, Columbia U; Cornell U, Yale, Princeton, Carnegie Mellon

DAVE, SHAILEE; BRIARCLIFF MANOR, NY; BRIARCLIFF HS; (FR); Hi Hnr Roll; DARE; Scouts; Black Belt in Tae Kwon Do; Pianist / Indian Dancing; Pediatrician; Biology Major; Columbia U; New York U

DAVIDS, RACHEL; BETHPAGE, NY; ISLAND TREES HS; (SR); Hnr Roll; Sci/Math Olympn; Chrch Yth Grp; Drma Clb; Emplmnt; Key Club; SP/M/VS; Sccr (J); Vllyball (J); Pre-Medicine; Northeastern U

DAVIDSON, JASMINE; POUGHKEEPSIE, NY; POUGHKEEPSIE HS; (FR); Hi Hnr Roll; Hnr Roll; Sci Fairs; St of Mnth; Peer Tut/Med; Chrch Yth Grp; DARE; Ch Chr; Dnce; Yrbk (R); Alpha Gamma Ro Step Team; Teaching; Law; Vassar College; Drexel U

DAVIS, BRITNEY D; BUFFALO, NY; SENECA COMP HS; (JR); Otst Ac Ach Awd; Chrch Yth Grp; DARE; Emplmnt; Forensics; Nursing Field

DAVIS, HOLLY E; GREENE, NY; GREENE HS; (FR); Bskball (J L); Fld Hky (V L); Track (V L); Cl Off (S); Stu Cncl (P, R); CR (R); Teacher of Physical Education; Division I Track Scholarship

DAVYDOV, YURI; FRESH MEADOWS, NY; FRANCIS LEWIS HS; (SR); Hnr Roll; Nat Stu Ath Day Aw; Perf Att; Peer Tut/Med; Vsity Clb; Wrstlg (V C); I Was a City Champ in Swimming (1998) 2nd & 3rd Place.; I Was a City Champ in Wrestling (2004) 5th Place.; Pharmacy; Dentistry; St. Johns U; Brooklyn College

DAWIDOWICZ, ALAN I; NEW YORK, NY; YESHIVA UNIVERSITY HS FOR BOYS; (SO); Hnr Roll; Dbte Team; Mod UN; Photog; Tmpl Yth Grp; Mar Art (V); Wt Lftg (J)

DAWSON, LINDSAY; MONROE, NY; MONROE-WOODBURY HS; (JR); Hi Hnr Roll; Nat Mrt Semif; Pres Sch; Comm Volntr; Hosp Aide; Emplmnt; Svce Clb; Bnd; Jzz Bnd; Pep Bnd; Track (J); Clarkson Leadership Award; Biological Sciences; Pre-Med; Lehigh U; Columbia U

DAYAL, AKSHANDEEP; TUCKAHOE, NY; EASTON AREA HS; (FR); Hi Hnr Roll; Nat Hon Sy; Otst Ac Ach Awd; Sci Fairs; USAA; Comm Volntr; Italian Clb; Rank of 7 in 8th Grade; Highest Average in 8th Grade Science; Medicine; Law; Harvard U; Princeton U

DAYE, KMOY; FAR ROCKAWAY, NY; SPRINGFIELD GARDENS HS; (JR); Hnr Roll; Otst Ac Ach Awd; Perf Att; Comm Volntr; Peer Tut/Med; Chess; Drma Clb; Mod UN; Stu Cncl (R); Think Quest New York Finalist; Aerospace Engineering; Business-Management/Administration; Rensselaer Polytechnic U; Boston U

DEAN, CORBIN; PETERSBURG, NY; (SO); Hnr Roll; Sci Fairs; Sci/Math Olympn; Comm Volntr; Chrch Yth Grp; Emplmnt; Scouts; Cyclg; Skt Tgt Sh; Boy Scouts - Life Scout Working Toward Eagle; Snow Boarding

DE BIASE, TARA; SAUGERTIES, NY; (FR); Hi Hnr Roll; Hnr Roll; WWAHSS; Comm Volntr; DARE; Key Club; Bnd; Dnce; SP/M/VS; Chrldg (V); Travel; Lawyer; U of Massachusetts; U of Rhode Island

DEBONIS, LAUREN; SAUGERTIES, NY; SAUGERTIES HS; (FR); Hi Hnr Roll; Hnr Roll; Otst Ac Ach Awd; St of Mnth; Comm Volntr; DARE; Key Club; Spanish Clb; Chr; Sccr (J); Journalism; Forensics

DE BONIS, NICHOLAS; SAUGERTIES, NY;; Hi Hnr Roll; Hnr Roll; Nat Hon Sy; Pres Ac Ftns Aw; Comm Volntr; Key Club; Spanish Clb; Chr; Golf (V); Lcrsse (V); Play Guitar; Have a Job; Psychology; Business; Florida State U; Air Force

DECKER, ERIC; CHEMUNG, NY; WAVERLY HS; (SR); Hi Hnr Roll; Hnr Roll; Nat Hon Sy; Drma Clb; Mus Clb; Chr; SP/M/VS; Ftball (VJCL); Track (V L); Wrstlg (VJ L); Cl Off (P); Pre-Medicine; SUNY Oneonta

DEDA, ROBERT; BROOKLYN, NY; ST EDMUND PREP HS; (JR); All Am Sch; Hnr Roll; Nat Hon Sy; Otst Ac Ach Awd; Sci Fairs; St of Mnth; Comm Volntr; ArtClub; Emplmnt; Skiing; Vllyball; Wt Lftg; Community Service; Finance; U of Michigan; Hofstra U

DEDJA, ERION; STATEN ISLAND, NY; NEW DORP HS; (SO); Nat Mrt Sch Recip; Quill & Scroll; Orch; Swg Chr; Lcrsse (J); Skiing (L)

DEE, DANIEL J; ALDEN, NY; ALDEN CTRL HS; (JR); Hnr Roll; Nat Hon Sy; Perf Att; St of Mnth; Comm Volntr; Chess; Chrch Yth Grp; Emplmnt; Key Club; Schol Bwl; Svce Clb; Tech Clb; Stg Cre; Seminary; Concordia U Ann Arbor; Canisius College

DEES, BREANNA; EAST BERNE, NY; BERNE-KNOX-WESTERLO HS; (SO); Hi Hnr Roll; Hnr Roll; Sci Fairs; 4-H; Key Club; Chr; SP/M/VS; Sccr (VJC); Cl Off; Stu Cncl; All County Select Chorus; Natural Helpers

DE FORREST, ALLISON; HERKIMER, NY; HERKIMER HS; (FR); Perf Att; St of Mnth; Comm Volntr; Peer Tut/Med; Pep Squd; Chr; Stg Cre; Fld Hky (J); Sftball (J); Vllyball (J); Forensic Science; Math

DEGAN, LINDSAY; LOCKPORT, NY; LOCKPORT HS; (SO); Hi Hnr Roll; Perf Att; St of Mnth; WWAHSS; Key Club; Latin Clb; Tennis (V L); Key Club; Latin Club; History Major; U of Buffalo; Niagara U

DE GELNOR, TIFFANY; INWOOD, NY; LAWRENCE HS; (SO); Hi Hnr Roll; WWAHSS; Comm Volntr; Peer Tut/Med; Chrch Yth Grp; Drma Clb; Key Club; Scouts; Chr; SP/M/VS; Track (J); Who's Who Among High School Students; State Finalist in Miss Teen NY; Pre-Med; Biology; U of Miami; U of Los Vegas

DE GRAAFF, AUDREY; POUGHQUAG, NY; ARLINGTON HS; (JR); Nat Hon Sy; Comm Volntr; Chrldg (J); Hsbk Rdg (V); Marketing; Business; Skidmore College; Cornell

DE JESUS, ERIKA; HAVERSTRAW, NY; NORTH ROCKLAND HS; (JR); Hnr Roll; Comm Volntr; Photog; Dnce; Chrldg (J); CR (V); Business; Fordham U

DE JOSEPH, ALLIE; WATERVLIET, NY; (SO); Hnr Roll; Comm Volntr; Key Club; Fld Hky (J); Key Club Secretary; Psychology; Teaching

DEJULIO, NICOLE; STATEN ISLAND, NY; SUSAN E WAGNER HS; (FR); Ctznshp Aw; Hi Hnr Roll; Hnr Roll; Nat Hon Sy; Nat Mrt LOC; Perf Att; St of Mnth; Comm Volntr; Peer Tut/Med; ArtClub; DARE; Drma Clb; Key Club; Mus Clb; Photog; Scouts; Vsity Clb; Bnd; Chr; Dnce; SP/M/VS; Chrldg; Cr Ctry (V); Track (V); Vsy Clb; Arista; Church Volunteer; Fashion; Forensic Science; Princeton U; Iona

DE LA CRUZ, HECTOR A; BRONX, NY; BRONX HS OF BUSINESS; (SO); Hi Hnr Roll; Hnr Roll; Bskball; Stu Cncl (R); CR (P); Student of the Week; Princeton U; Bronx Community College

DELACRUZ, JOSEPH; BRONX, NY; JACQUELINE KENNEDY ONASSIS HS; (FR); Perf Att; Comm Volntr; Chrch Yth Grp; Cmptr Clb; Mus Clb; Bnd

DELAHOZ, CATALINA; QUEENS VILLAGE, NY; QUEENS HS OF TEACHING; (SO); Hi Hnr Roll; Hnr Roll; Nat Hon Sy; Nat Ldrshp Svc; Otst Ac Ach Awd; Comm Volntr; Peer Tut/Med; Chrch Yth Grp; Dbte Team; Off Aide; Scouts; Tchrs Aide; Vsity Clb; Ch Chr; SP/M/VS; Bskball (J); Sccr (V); Adv Cncl (R); Cl Off (R); CR (P); Hispanic Achievement Award; English Teacher; Business Administration; Columbia U; New York U

DELAPO, MICHELLE; FLORAL PARK, NY; FLORAL PARK MEMORIAL HS; (JR); Hnr Roll; Spec Olymp Vol; ArtClub; Key Club; Photog; Bnd; Jzz Bnd; Mch Bnd; Fld Hky (V); Mar Art (V); Art Work Has Been Published And Won; United States Coast Guard; United States Coast Guard Academy

DE LAS NUECES, ANDY; BRONX, NY; ALFRED E SMITH VOC HS; (SO); Hi Hnr Roll; Hnr Roll; Nat Hon Sy; Otst Ac Ach Awd; Perf Att; St of Mnth; Comm Volntr; DARE; Master's Degree; City College

DELBRIDGE, CHANAI; HEMPSTEAD, NY; KELLENBERG MEMORIAL HS; (JR); Hnr Roll; Nat Hon Sy; Comm Volntr; Mth Clb/Tm; Scouts; Dnce; Danced At Alvin Ailey; Danced At Richmond Ballet; Dance/Theatre Arts; Pharmacy; New York U; Marymount Manhattan College

DELEA, ASHLEY L; BROOKLYN, NY; BISHOP KEARNEY HS; (JR); All Am Sch; Hi Hnr Roll; Hnr Roll; Comm Volntr; Peer Tut/Med; ArtClub; SP/M/VS; Vllyball (VJCL); National Society HS Scholars; Creative Arts; Cooper Union

DELEON, GENESIS V; BRONX, NY; ST PIUS V HS; (FR); Hi Hnr Roll; Otst Ac Ach Awd; Sci Fairs; St of Mnth; Comm Volntr; ArtClub; DARE; Drma Clb; Mus Clb; Chr; SP/M/VS; CR (P); 1st Place in Science Fair 3 Times in a Row; Student Ambassador in 7th and 8th Grade; Music; Business Administration; Harvard U; New York U

DELGADO, CLARISSA N; EAST ELMHURST, NY; THE MARY LOUIS AC; (JR); Hi Hnr Roll; Hnr Roll; Nat Hon Sy; Nat Ldrshp Svc; Nat Sci Aw; Pres Sch; St of Mnth; Comm Volntr; Chrch Yth Grp; Emplmnt; Mus Clb; NYLC; Tchrs Aide; Spanish Clb; Acpl Chr; Chr; Ch Chr; Cl Off (P); Women in Science-St John's U; Science Medal 8th Grade; English; Music; New York U; Columbia U

DELISI, FRANCESCA; RIDGEWOOD, NY; THE MARY LOUIS AC; (JR); Hnr Roll; WWAHSS; Comm Volntr; Emplmnt; Clb; Law; Political Science; Fordham U; Marist U

DELMORE, LISA; FARMINGDALE, NY; FARMINGDALE HS; (SO); Comm Volntr; Peer Tut/Med; Emplmnt; Key Club; Off Aide; Tmpl Yth Grp; Social Work; Psychology; Boston U; Hofstra U

DELOSH, JAMES; MELVILLE, NY; WALT WHITMAN HS; (JR); Hi Hnr Roll; Hnr Roll; Emplmnt; Bnd; Participated in the New York State School Music Association festival up to sophomore year(NYSSMA); Aeronautical Engineering; Computer Science; Penn State U; U of Tennessee, Knoxville, Tennessee

DE LOS SANTOS, MICHELLE; BRONX, NY; HOSTOS HS; (SR); Hnr Roll; Comm Volntr; Hosp Aide; DARE; Emplmnt; Skiing; Yrbk (P); Stainglass; Volleyball; English/Teacher Education; Psychology; Daemen College; Morrisville College

De Gelnor, Tiffany
Lawrence HS
Inwood, NY

Decker, Eric
Waverly HS
Chemung, NY

Davidson, Jasmine
Poughkeepsie HS
Poughkeepsie, NY

Darlina IV, R Clement
Doane Stuart Sch
Delmar, NY

National
Honor Roll
Spring 2005

Dale, Joel S
Wyandanch Mem. HS
Wyandanch, NY

Dayal, Akshandeep
Easton Area HS
Tuckahoe, NY

De Forrest, Allison
Herkimer HS
Herkimer, NY

Delea, Ashley L
Bishop Kearney HS
Brooklyn, NY

DEL ROSARIO, DIANA; NEW YORK, NY; HEALTH OPPORTUNITIES HS; (FR); Nat Mrt Sch Recip; Perf Att; Dnce; Junior Fellow Class of 2005; Truama Surgeon; Doctor; City College; Community College

DEL VALLE, EMILY A; BAY SHORE, NY; ISLIP HS; (FR); Hsbk Rdg; Have Been Horseback Riding Since 7 Years Old; Fashion Design; Stetson U

DEL VALLE, JESSICA; ELMHURST, NY; NEWTOWN HS; (JR); Hi Hnr Roll; Hnr Roll; Nat Hon Sy; Peer Tut/Med; Emplmnt; Jr Ach; Services; Veterinary; Cornell U, NYS College of Veterinary Medicine; State U College of Technology

DE MAIO, RICKY; GOSHEN, NY; JOHN S BURKE CATHOLIC HS; (JR); Hi Hnr Roll; Hnr Roll; Nat Hon Sy; Drma Clb; Photog; Vsity Clb; Bnd; SP/M/VS; Stg Cre; Tennis (V)

DE MARIA, KAREN; FLORAL PARK, NY; FLORAL PARK MEMORIAL HS; (FR); Hi Hnr Roll; Kwnis Aw; Nat Hon Sy; Perf Att; WWAHSS; Comm Volntr; Peer Tut/Med; Key Club; Scouts; Swmg (V L); Cl Off (R); Pre-Med

DEMBKOWSKI, EVAN J; CICERO, NY; CHRISTIAN BROTHERS AC; (SR); Ctznshp Aw; Hnr Roll; Otst Ac Ach Awd; Yth Ldrshp Prog; Comm Volntr; Peer Tut/Med; Chrch Yth Grp; Svce Clb; Bskball (VJC); Cr Ctry (J); Sccr (J); Track (V); Sch Ppr (E, R); Optimist Club Award; Peer Ministry; Marketing; Sport Management; U of Miami; Syracuse U

DEMERS, ANDREW; TUPPER LAKE, NY; TUPPER LAKE HS; (JR); Hnr Roll; Perf Att; Wdwrkg Clb

DENG, ELLEN; BROOKLYN, NY; MIDWOOD HS; (JR); Perf Att; Comm Volntr; Peer Tut/Med; Red Cr Aide; Biology Clb; DARE; Key Club; Off Aide; Tchrs Aide; Bnd; Accounting; Pharmacy; Stony Brook U; SUNY Binghamton

DENIS, DANIELA; OSSINING, NY; OSSINING HS; (FR); DARE; Drma Clb; Scouts; Vllyball (J); Wrstlg (V); Sch Ppr (R); Acting; Psychology/ Sociology; New York U; Boston U

DENIS, EMMANUELLA; UNIONDALE, NY; UNIONDALE HS; (SO); Hnr Roll; Peer Tut/Med; Chrch Yth Grp; Mus Clb; Acpl Chr; Chr; Ch Chr; SP/M/VS; Medical; Adelphi U; Hofstra U

DENIS-MACK, JORDAE; BRONX, NY; BRONX HS FOR THE VISUAL ARTS; (SO); Hnr Roll; Perf Att; Sci Fairs; St of Mnth; Comm Volntr; Peer Tut/Med; Dbte Team; Drma Clb; Emplmnt; Outdrs Clb; Spanish Clb; Bnd; Ch Chr; Dnce; Bsball; Sccr; Sftball; Track; CR (R); UFT Award - National Federation of Teachers; Outstanding Stepper Award; Fashion and Merchandising; Business; Fashion Institute of Design and Merchandising; Fashion Institute of Technology

DENMARK, MICHAEL; ROCK STREAM, NY; DUNDEE CTRL SCH; (JR); Hi Hnr Roll; Hnr Roll; Perf Att; WWAHSS; Cmptr Clb; Chr; CR (R); Varsity Bowling (V); A Bachelor's Degree in Computer Science; Corning Community College; Norwich U

DENNIS, CURTIS; PELHAM, NY; BLESSED SACRAMENT HS; (JR); MVP; Perf Att; Chess; Vsity Clb; Bskball (V); Vsy Clb (V); Wt Lftg (V); 90's Club in St. Raymond; Engineering; Physical Education; Florida International U; U of Louisville

DENNO, BEN; HAGUE, NY; TICONDEROGA HS; (FR); Bskball (J); Ftball (J); Culinary Arts

DENNY, DIONNE C; HOLLIS, NY; HILLCREST HS; (JR); Hnr Roll; Comm Volntr; Peer Tut/Med; Ch Chr; Dnce; Nursing; NYU-New York U

DENONCOURT, JOE; OGDENSBURG, NY; OGDENSBURG FREE AC; (FR); Hi Hnr Roll; Otst Ac Ach Awd; Perf Att; St of Mnth; WWAHSS; Comm Volntr; ArtClub; Key Club; Bnd; Mch Bnd; Pep Bnd; Stg Cre; Sccr (J); Track (V); Cl Off (V); Yrbk (P); Key Club Lt. Governor; Pharmacy; Law; Albany College of Pharmacy; Harvard Law School

DENTON, HEATHER E; LEWIS, NY; WESTPORT CTRL SCH; (FR); 4H Awd; Hnr Roll; Comm Volntr; 4-H; Chrch Yth Grp; DARE; Mod UN; Bnd; Bsball (J); Bskball (J); Hsbk Rdg; Sccr (J); Veterinarian; Equine Science Management; SUNY Morrisville; Cornell U

DENUNZIO, MIKE; WOODSIDE, NY; ARCHBISHOP MOLLOY HS; (JR); Ctznshp Aw; Hi Hnr Roll; Hnr Roll; Otst Ac Ach Awd; Mus Clb; Italian Clb; Bnd; SP/M/VS; Cr Ctry (V); Track (V); Wt Lftg (V); Principal's List Award; Law; Politics; St John's U; New York U

DEOCHAN, MATTHEW; SOUTH OZONE PARK, NY; GEORGE WASHINGTON CARVER HS; (FR); Hnr Roll; Bskball (J); Pharmaceuticals; St. Johns U; LIU

DEOLEO, CHRISTOPHER; BRONX, NY; (JR); Hnr Roll; Otst Ac Ach Awd; Perf Att; St of Mnth; Emplmnt; Mock Trial Participant; Psychology; Law; New York U; Long Island U

DEOLIVEIRA, ELEN; HUNTINGTON, NY; HUNTINGTON HS; (SO); Hi Hnr Roll; Hnr Roll; St of Mnth; ArtClub; Chrch Yth Grp; DARE; Drma Clb; Photog; Bnd; Ch Chr; Dnce; Mch Bnd; PPSqd (V); Cl Off (S); Stu Cncl (S); CR (S); Yrbk (R, P); Spanish Award-Test; English-Writing

DEOPAUL, KARMELA; BROOKLYN, NY; JAMES MADISON HS; (JR); Hnr Roll; Nat Hon Sy; Salutrn; Sci Fairs; Comm Volntr; Key Club; Off Aide; Prom Com; Sci Clb; Svce Clb; Tchrs Aide; Stg Cre; CR (R); Yrbk (E, R); Arthur Ashe Science Institute.; Pharmacy; Pre-Med; St. Johns U; New York U

DE PENA, NATALIA; BROOKLYN, NY; EDWARD R MURROW HS; (SO); Otst Ac Ach Awd; Perf Att; ArtClub; Chrch Yth Grp; DARE; Mth Clb/Tm; Ch Chr; Dnce; SP/M/VS; CR (T); Art Award; Fashion Designing; Computer Animation; State U of New York; City U of New York

DERN, MARC; VALLEY STREAM, NY; (JR); Hnr Roll; St of Mnth; Comm Volntr; Mus Clb; Vsity Clb; Bnd; Mch Bnd; Orch; Pep Bnd; Bsball (V); Bskball (V); Vsy Clb (V); Coach's Award (Baseball); Sports Management & Training; Business Administration; Sacred Heart U; Saint Johns U

DESIDERIO, JENNA; BUFFALO, NY; KENMORE WEST HS; (JR); Ctznshp Aw; Hi Hnr Roll; Hnr Roll; Nat Hon Sy; Nat Ldrshp Svc; Otst Ac Ach Awd; Perf Att; Pres Ac Ftns Aw; St of Mnth; WWAHSS; Comm Volntr; Peer Tut/Med; Spec Olymp Vol; Chrch Yth Grp; DARE; Emplmnt; Pep Squd; SADD; Bnd; Dnce; SP/M/VS; Chrldg (V); Cl Off (R); Stu Cncl (R); CR (R); Sch Ppr (R); Yrbk (E); Working; Elementary Education; Communications; Northeastern; Boston

DE SIMONE, MARISSA; STATEN ISLAND, NY; STATEN ISLAND TECH HS; (JR); Hnr Roll; Nat Hon Sy; WWAHSS; Comm Volntr; Red Cr Aide; Key Club; SP/M/VS; Stg Cre; Piano Player 4 1/2 Months In Russia; Ronald S Lauder Student Exchange Program VP of National Honor Society; Boston U; New York U

DE SOUZA, AMANDA; YONKERS, NY; MARIA REGINA HS; Hi Hnr Roll; Hnr Roll; Key Club; Kwanza Clb; Dnce; Criminal Justice Club; African American Club; Psychology; Telecommunications; Clarke U; Mt St Vincent

D'ESPOSITO, GREGORY; SMITHTOWN, NY; SMITHTOWN HS; (SR); Hnr Roll; Comm Volntr; Peer Tut/Med; DECA; Mus Clb; Bnd; Chr; Jzz Bnd; Orch; Bsball; Golf; Vllyball; DECA - National Finalist / NYS 2nd Place; SUNY Oneonta; Marist College

DESSAINT, GABRIELLE-RENE; GRANVILLE, NY; HARTFORD CTRL SCH; (SO); 4H Awd; Ctznshp Aw; Otst Ac Ach Awd; St of Mnth; WWAHSS; Comm Volntr; 4-H; DARE; Emplmnt; Key Club; Mus Clb; Outdrs Clb; Scouts; French Clb; Bnd; Chr; Mch Bnd; Horse Showing (Barrel Racing); Team Running; Law; Crime Scene Analysis; Siena College; Harvard U

DESTEFANO, GINA; HUNTINGTON, NY; OUR LADY OF MERCY AC; (JR); F Lan Hn Soc; Hi Hnr Roll; Hnr Roll; Nat Hon Sy; Perf Att; Yth Ldrshp Prog; Amnsty Intl; Comm Volntr; Peer Tut/Med; DARE; Dbte Team; Emplmnt; Mus Clb; NYLC; Svce Clb; Vsity Clb; Spanish Clb; Chr; Ch Chr; Dnce; SP/M/VS; CR (R); Lit Mag (R); Sch Ppr (R); Varsity Mock Trial; Dance Company; Pre-Law Major; English / Education; Fordham U; St John's U

DETWEILER, EDWARD; WEST HEMPSTEAD, NY; WEST HEMPSTEAD HS; (FR); Hi Hnr Roll; Sci/Math Olympn; Peer Tut/Med; Key Club; Mth Clb/Tm; Italian Clb; Cr Ctry (J); Lcrsse (J); Sccr (J); Track (J); Medical Degree

DE VITO, CHRISTOPHER; MOUNT VERNON, NY; ARCHBISHOP STEPINAC HS; (SO); Bsball (J L); Sch Ppr (R); Multiple Nominations to Who's Who Among American High Schools, Nat'l Math Award; Engineering Manhattan College; Villanova U; Manhattan College; Villanova U

DE VITO, DANIELLE; NEW YORK, NY; FIORELLO H LA GUARDIA HS; (SR); Hnr Roll; Nat Ldrshp Svc; Yth Ldrshp Prog; Comm Volntr; Drma Clb; Mus Clb; NYLC; Italian Clb; Acpl Chr; Chr; Ch Chr; Dnce; Cr Ctry (J); Track (J); Knight of Columbus Award for Service to Community; Theatre/ Musical Theater; Journalism; Northwestern U; The Boston Conservatory

DEWI, NIDYA; ELMHURST, NY; NEWTOWN HS; (SR); Pres Sch; Comm Volntr; Hosp Aide; Dbte Team; Key Club; Clb; Tennis (V); Pharmacy; Interior Design; SUNY At Buffalo; St. John's U

DHALLA, ZIANA; EAST MEADOW, NY; EAST MEADOW HS; (FR); Hnr Roll; Perf Att; Pres Sch; St of Mnth; Comm Volntr; ArtClub; Key Club; Special Recognition in English; Lawyer; CSI; New York U

DHAVAL, PARIKH; EAST ROCKAWAY, NY; EAST ROCKAWAY JR/SR HS; (JR); Hi Hnr Roll; Hnr Roll; St of Mnth; St Optmst of Yr; WWAHSS; Comm Volntr; Hab For Humty Volntr; Key Club; Latin Club Clb; Bsball (V); Wrote An Article For Newsday; Help to feed the hungry people in local community; Engineering; Pharmacy; Boston University, Boston, MA; New York University, New York, NY

DIA, FERDUSY; ELMHURST, NY; NEWTOWN HS; (JR); Hnr Roll; Yth Ldrshp Prog; Comm Volntr; Peer Tut/Med; Emplmnt; MuAlphaTh; Dnce; Bowling; Pre-Med; Medicine; SUNY Stony Brook; Binghamton U

DIALLO, SADIALIOU; BROOKLYN, NY; SAMUEL J TILDEN HS; (SR); Hnr Roll; Perf Att; St of Mnth; Cmptr Clb; Vsity Clb; Sccr (JC); Computer / Mechanical Engineering; Medicine; Rochester Institute of Technology; New York City College

DIAMOND, JOSH; WEST BABYLON, NY; WEST BABYLON SR HS; (JR); Hi Hnr Roll; Hnr Roll; WWAHSS; Mth Clb/Tm; Scouts; Chr; Computers; Mathematics

DIAZ, ANGELICA; NEW YORK, NY; MANHATTAN VILLAGE AC; (SO); Hnr Roll; Otst Ac Ach Awd; Perf Att; WWAHSS; Comm Volntr; Chrch Yth Grp; Drma Clb; Jr Ach; Bnd; Bskball (V); Stu Cncl (R); Cooking Club; Radio Club; Music Producer; New York U; Columbia U

DIAZ, DAVID; JACKSON HEIGHTS, NY; CHRIST THE KING HS; (SO); Hi Hnr Roll; Hnr Roll; Otst Ac Ach Awd; Perf Att; St of Mnth; Comm Volntr; Peer Tut/Med; Chrch Yth Grp; Emplmnt; Mth Clb/Tm; Mus Clb; Bnd; Stu Cncl (R); Full 4-Year Scholarship to Christ the King HS; Excellence Certificate; Music Engineering; Film Major; Cornell U; Boston U

DIAZ, DENISE; BRONX, NY; JANE ADDAMS HS; (SR); Otst Ac Ach Awd; Perf Att; Forensic Science; John Jay for Criminal Justice

DIAZ, DENNIS; ELMONT, NY; CARDINAL HAYES HS; (JR); Hnr Roll; Comm Volntr; Emplmnt; Latin Clb; SP/M/VS; Sch Ppr (R); Latin Society; Music; Business Management; Five Towns College; Bloomfield U

DIAZ, GREYLIS; BRONX, NY; SCH FOR EXCELLENCE; (JR); ArtClub; Chrch Yth Grp; Drma Clb; Emplmnt; Dnce; SP/M/VS; Vllyball; Cl Off (P); CR (P); Sch Ppr (E); Hospital Aide / Volunteer / Community Service; Graphic Designer; Professional Dancer / Choreographer; Columbia U; Juilliard

DIAZ III, L MICHAEL; STATEN ISLAND, NY; CURTIS HS; (JR); All Am Sch; Hnr Roll; Nat Ldrshp Svc; St of Mnth; USAA; WWAHSS; Yth Ldrshp Prog; Bsball (V); Pre-Med, Pro Baseball; Architecture; Miami U; SFU

DIAZ MELENDEZ, ANA Y; NEW YORK, NY; CATHEDRAL HS; (FR); Comm Volntr; Chrch Yth Grp; Off Aide; Writing; Spanish; Fordham U; Columbia College

DIBELLO, LEO; FAIRPORT, NY; FAIRPORT HS; (SO); F Lan Hn Soc; Hi Hnr Roll; Hnr Roll; WWAHSS; Yth Ldrshp Prog; Comm Volntr; Peer Tut/ Med; Chrch Yth Grp; Drma Clb; Fr of Library; Lib Aide; Scouts; Vsity Clb; Spanish Clb; Chr; SP/M/VS; Crew Team Varsity; Forensics; Acting / Film Making; Niagara U; Syracuse U

DIEHL, JESSICA L; WATERFORD, NY; WATERFORD HS; (SO); Hnr Roll; Nat Hon Sy; Pres Ac Ftns Aw; St of Mnth; Comm Volntr; Chrch Yth Grp; Mth Clb/Tm; Photog; SADD; Bnd; Mch Bnd; Bskball (V); Sccr (V); Sftball (V); Cl Off (P); Stu Cncl (P); Ranked 6th Academically in My Class; Completed American Red Cross Lifeguard Swimming and Water Safety Instruction Courses; Masters Degree; Law School; SUNY Albany; Sienna College

DIFO BURGOS, MIRLENIA S; BRONX, NY; JOHN F KENNEDY HS; (JR); Hnr Roll; Otst Ac Ach Awd; Perf Att; Comm Volntr; Drma Clb; Photog; Dnce; SP/M/VS; Cinematography/Film; Dramatic Arts; Lehman College; Fordham U

DI GIULIO, ALFRED V; CLIFTON PARK, NY; SHENENDEHOWA HS; (SO); Hi Hnr Roll; Sci Fairs; Hab For Humty Volntr; Chrch Yth Grp; Bnd; CR (R); College of the Holy Cross; Dartmouth College

DIKKERS, CAROLIEN; PELHAM, NY; PELHAM MEMORIAL HS; (JR); Hi Hnr Roll; Nat Hon Sy; Yth Ldrshp Prog; CARE; Hab For Humty Volntr; Peer Tut/Med; Emplmnt; Sci Clb; SADD; French Clb; Sccr (J); Tennis (VJ L); Pelham Community Rowing Association-Novice 4

DIMAGGIO, KIMBERLY; CROTON ON HUDSON, NY; CROTON HARMON HS; (SR); Hi Hnr Roll; Nat Hon Sy; Comm Volntr; Peer Tut/Med; Chrch Yth Grp; DARE; Drma Clb; Jr Ach; Mus Clb; Prom Com; Chr; SP/M/VS; Bskball (VJC); Golf (V); Vllyball (VJ); NYS Scholar Athlete Award; Television/Film/Broadcast; Broadcast Journalism; Syracuse U; Binghamton U

DI MARTINO, SARA; BROOKLYN, NY; NEW UTRECHT HS; (SR); Hnr Roll; Nat Hon Sy; WWAHSS; Comm Volntr; Hosp Aide; Emplmnt; CR (V); Sch Ppr (E); Business Education Honor Society; Kingsborough Community College

DIMARTINO, SHANNON; W HEMPSTEAD, NY; WEST HEMPSTEAD HS; (SO); F Lan Hn Soc; Hi Hnr Roll; MVP; Otst Ac Ach Awd; Pres Sch; Sci Fairs; Sci/Math Olympn; WWAHSS; Yth Ldrshp Prog; Comm Volntr; Hosp Aide; Key Club; Quiz Bowl; Sci Clb; Scouts; Italian Clb; Bnd; Mch Bnd; Pep Bnd; Sftball (J); Tennis (V); Member of Nassau County Youth Council; Girl Scout Silver Award; Pre-Med; Surgeon; College of William and Mary; Boston U

DI MATTEO, SHAYNA; GRAND ISLAND, NY; GRAND ISLAND HS; (SR); Hi Hnr Roll; Hnr Roll; Nat Hon Sy; WWAHSS; Comm Volntr; Chrch Yth Grp; Bnd; Bskball (J); Vllyball (V); Elementary Education; Geneseo State U; Niagara U

DI NAPOLI, SARA; MANORVILLE, NY; MOUNT SINAI HS; (SO); Hi Hnr Roll; St of Mnth; WWAHSS; Spec Olymp Vol; Emplmnt; Mth Clb/Tm; Scr Kpr (L); Tennis (V); Women in Science & Engineering Research Team; National Ocean Science Bowl-Team Regional Champions; Molecular Biology; Swarthmore College; Mt Holyoke College

De Souza, Amanda
Maria Regina HS
Yonkers, NY

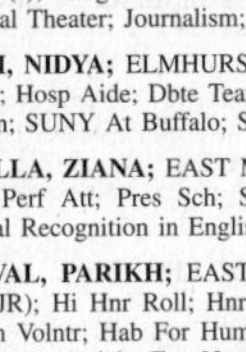
Dern, Marc
Valley Stream, NY

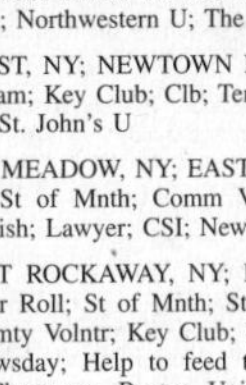
Dennis, Curtis
Blessed Sacrament HS
Pelham, NY

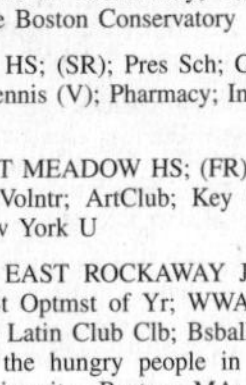
Denoncourt, Joe
Ogdensburg Free AC
Ogdensburg, NY

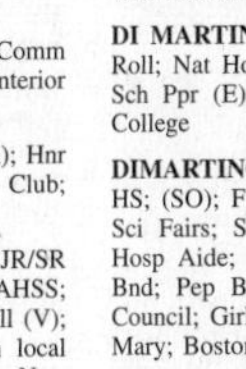
Diaz III, L Michael
Curtis HS
Staten Island, NY

DINGMAN, TAYLOR M; FONDA, NY; FONDA FULTONVILLE CTRL SCH; (FR); Hnr Roll; St of Mnth; Key Club; Bsball (J); Bskball (J); Ftball (J); Stu Cncl (R); Law Enforcement; Zoology

DIPALERMO, LUCIANO; WANTAGH, NY; SEAFORD HS; (SR); Ctznshp Aw; Hi Hnr Roll; Nat Hon Sy; Otst Ac Ach Awd; St of Mnth; WWAHSS; Yth Ldrshp Prog; Comm Volntr; Peer Tut/Med; AL Aux Boys; Cmptr Clb; Key Club; Mth Clb/Tm; Bnd; Cr Ctry (V); Track (V); CR (P); International Relations; Foreign Languages; Dickinson College

DIXON, CRYSTAL; BROOKLYN, NY; CANARSIE HS; (JR); Hnr Roll; St of Mnth; Peer Tut/Med; Emplmnt; Vsity Clb; SP/M/VS; CR (R); NYU - Saturday Sessions; Interior Design; Culinary Arts; Howard U; FIT

DIXON, GENA; MT VERNON, NY; MT VERNON HS; (SR); F Lan Hn Soc; Hi Hnr Roll; Hnr Roll; Nat Hon Sy; WWAHSS; Comm Volntr; Peer Tut/Med; Chrch Yth Grp; Cmptr Clb; Emplmnt; Lib Aide; Ntl Beta Clb; Quiz Bowl; French Clb; Ch Chr; Sccr; Undergraduate Award in French & History; Certificate for Competing in NEC; Pediatric Nurse; Dentist; Oakwood College; Hunter College

DIXON JR, DEVON M; CAMBRIA HEIGHTS, NY; BROOKLYN TECH HS; (JR); Hnr Roll; WWAHSS; Comm Volntr; Chrch Yth Grp; Drma Clb; Emplmnt; Mus Clb; Chr; Ch Chr; SP/M/VS; NYS Church of God Keyboard & Organ- Solo 1st Place; Chemistry; Biology; New York U; Massachusetts Institute of Technology

DIZON, JILLIAN; BALDWIN, NY; BALDWIN HS; (JR); F Lan Hn Soc; Hi Hnr Roll; Kwnis Aw; Sci Fairs; WWAHSS; Yth Ldrshp Prog; Comm Volntr; Peer Tut/Med; Chrch Yth Grp; Key Club; SADD; Acpl Chr; Chr; Ch Chr; Dnce; Chrldg (VJ); Fld Hky (VJC); GAA; Lcrsse (J); Stu Cncl; Scholar Athlete Award; Intramural Nite Captain; Physical Therapy

DJAHA, BRETT; EAST ISLIP, NY; EAST ISLIP HS; (JR); Hnr Roll; Nat Mrt Semif; WWAHSS; Peer Tut/Med; Sci Clb; Vsity Clb; Ftball (V); Lcrsse (V)

DLENICK, CHRISTINA; BRONX, NY; HORACE MANN SCH; (JR); Hnr Roll; WWAHSS; Comm Volntr; Japanese Clb; Mar Art; Sftball (V L); Vllyball (V CL); Lit Mag (R); Prep for Prep Alumnus; Japanese Language; Arabic Language; Georgetown U

DMYTRIV, KRISTINA; SUNNYSIDE, NY; FRANCIS LEWIS HS; (SO); Ctznshp Aw; Hnr Roll; Peer Tut/Med; Medicine; Microbiology; New York U; Columbia U

DOBERSTEIN, RYAN J; HOLLAND, NY; HOLLAND HS; (SO); Hi Hnr Roll; MVP; Otst Ac Ach Awd; Pres Ac Ftns Aw; Pres Sch; WWAHSS; Comm Volntr; Emplmnt; Key Club; SADD; Vsity Clb; Bnd; Jzz Bnd; Mch Bnd; Bsball (VJCL); Vllyball (JCL); Cl Off (V); Stu Cncl (R); National Junior Honor Society, Varsity Captain or Bowling Team; J.V. Captain on Baseball Team for 2 Years; Specific Chiropractic Care; Earth Science Teacher; Palmer College of Chiropractics, Iowa; U of Buffalo

DOBRINI, ANTHONY; LEVITTOWN, NY; ISLAND TREES HS; (SR); Hi Hnr Roll; Kwnis Aw; Nat Hon Sy; WWAHSS; Peer Tut/Med; Spec Olymp Vol; Drma Clb; Emplmnt; Key Club; Prom Com; Chr; SP/M/VS; Lcrsse (V); Sch Ppr (R); Communications, Radio, TV and Music Management; Nassau Community College

DODD, JESSICA; SAUGERTIES, NY; ULSTER CAREER & TECH CTR; (JR); Hi Hnr Roll; Hnr Roll; Perf Att; Emplmnt; SP/M/VS; Sftball (J); Business Management

DODGE, SARAH R; GANSEVOORT, NY; SARATOGA SPRINGS HS; (JR); Hi Hnr Roll; Key Club; Vllyball (J); Engineering; RPI; Clarkson U

DOLCE, LAURA C; JACKSON HEIGHTS, NY; THE MARY LOUIS AC; (JR); Hnr Roll; Nat Hon Sy; Nat Mrt LOC; Mth Clb/Tm; Sci Clb; Italian Clb; Sccr (V C); Secretary of Italian Club

DOLOGAN, CHRISTINA; CORNING, NY; CORNING-PAINTED POST WEST HS; (JR); Hi Hnr Roll; Hnr Roll; WWAHSS; Pre-Med; Biology

DOMBROWSKI, KAITLYN M; GENEVA, NY; GENEVA HS; (FR); 4H Awd; Ctznshp Aw; Hnr Roll; St of Mnth; WWAHSS; Yth Ldrshp Prog; Comm Volntr; Spec Olymp Vol; 4-H; Chrch Yth Grp; DARE; Key Club; Youth Group-Retreat Leader; Early Childhood Education; Child & Adolescent Counselor

DOMINIANNI, ALEXANDRA; FRESH MEADOWS, NY; MS 158; Hnr Roll; Nat Hon Sy; Perf Att; Chrch Yth Grp; Scouts; Tchrs Aide; Dnce; Swmg; Stu Cncl (R); CR (P); Dance Production; Talent Show; Medical; Law; Pepperdine U; Harvard U

DONG, MENG Y; CORONA, NY; FIORELLO H LA GUARDIA HS; (JR); Hnr Roll; ArtClub; Chrch Yth Grp; Lib Aide; Tchrs Aide; Architecture; Children's Book Illustration/Illustrations Related; NYU

DONNELLY, BRIDGET; ROME, NY; ROME FREE AC; (JR); Hi Hnr Roll; Hnr Roll; Nat Hon Sy; Comm Volntr; Red Cr Aide; Spec Olymp Vol; Chrch Yth Grp; Key Club; Mus Clb; Prom Com; Bnd; Orch; SP/M/VS; Cr Ctry (V); Lcrsse (V); Sccr (J); Tennis (V); NYSSMA in Violin & Piano; NYSPHS Scholar Athlete; Biology; Medicine; Canisius Buffalo NY; St John Fischer Rochester

DORFMAN, AMY; WOODBURY, NY; SYOSSET HS; (SR); F Lan Hn Soc; Comm Volntr; Hab For Humty Volntr; Hosp Aide; Emplmnt; Tmpl Yth Grp; Russian Clb; Lit Mag (R); President of Gay-Straight Alliance; President of Martin Luther King Club; Political Science; Sociology; George Washington U

DORFMAN, ANTON; BUFFALO, NY; KENMORE WEST SR HS; (SO); Hnr Roll; Cmptr Clb; Dbte Team; Bnd; Sccr (J); Tennis (V); Yrbk (R); Dale Carnegie Leadership Program; Biology; Business; U of Buffalo; U of Rochester

DORING, ASHLEY; YOUNGSTOWN, NY; LEWISTON-PORTER HS; (FR); Hnr Roll; Otst Ac Ach Awd; Comm Volntr; Drma Clb; Clb; Dnce; Sftball (J); Tennis (J); Track (J); National Junior Honor Society; Home interior design & clothing design; Business; Duke U; Yale U

DORSAINVIL, SASHA N; BROOKLYN, NY; MIDWOOD HS; (SR); Hnr Roll; WWAHSS; Yth Ldrshp Prog; Comm Volntr; Peer Tut/Med; NYLC; Prom Com; Dnce; 2005 -Youth Service Award from the Black and Puerto Rican Legislators; Child Development; Child Psychologist; Duke U; Florida State U

DORSEY, MARQUIS L; BUFFALO, NY; CLEVELAND HILL HS; (SO); Comm Volntr; Ftball (V); Track (V); Wt Lftg (V); Architecture; Mathematics; Texas U; U of Auburn

DORVIL, WALDO; JAMAICA, NY; JOHN ADAMS HS; (SR); St Optmst of Yr; Mth Clb/Tm; French Clb

DOUBRAVA, JACOB P; MIDDLETOWN, NY; MINISINK VALLEY HS; (JR); Hi Hnr Roll; Nat Hon Sy; Otst Ac Ach Awd; St of Mnth; Yth Ldrshp Prog; Comm Volntr; DARE; Key Club; NYLC; SADD; Vsity Clb; Ftball (VJ); Golf (V L); Vsy Clb; Wt Lftg; Volunteer Fireman

DOUCET, KRISTINA; WANTAGH, NY; WANTAGH HS; (JR); F Lan Hn Soc; Hnr Roll; Nat Hon Sy; WWAHSS; Comm Volntr; Hab For Humty Volntr; Chrch Yth Grp; Drma Clb; Emplmnt; French Clb; Stg Cre; Cr Ctry (J); Track (J); Environmental Science; SUNY Environmental Science & Forestry

DOUGAN, KOUAKOU; NEW YORK, NY; FREDERICK DOUGLASS AC; (JR); Hi Hnr Roll; Hnr Roll; MVP; Nat Hon Sy; Perf Att; Peer Tut/Med; Spec Olymp Vol; Chess; DARE; Emplmnt; Off Aide; Tchrs Aide; Vsity Clb; Bskball (VJ); Mar Art; Scr Kpr; Sccr (V); Tennis (V); Vsy Clb; Wt Lftg; Stu Cncl (R); CR (P); Electrical Engineering, Petroleum Eng.; Electronic Engineering, Chemical Eng.; U of Connecticut; Duke U

DOUGHERTY, BRENDEN; BURNT HILLS, NY; BURNT HILLS-BALLSTON LAKE HS; (JR); Hi Hnr Roll; Nat Hon Sy; Otst Ac Ach Awd; Pres Ac Ftns Aw; St of Mnth; WWAHSS; Comm Volntr; Chrch Yth Grp; DARE; Drma Clb; Mus Clb; Vsity Clb; Acpl Chr; Chr; Ch Chr; SP/M/VS; Swmg (V L); Tennis (V L); Lead in School Play; Unit Winner - We the People / Competition; History; Princeton U; Williams U

DOUGHERTY, CHRISTINE; LINDENHURST, NY; LINDENHURST HS; (JR); Hi Hnr Roll; Hnr Roll; Nat Hon Sy; Perf Att; Pres Ac Ftns Aw; WWAHSS; Peer Tut/Med; Key Club; Vsity Clb; Chr; Fld Hky (V L); Lcrsse (V L); Track (V L); Scholar Athlete Award; Ski Club; Criminal Law / Lawyer; English; Boston U; Boston College

DOUGLAS, JOVANNES; BROOKLYN, NY; SPRINGFIELD GARDENS HS; (JR); Hnr Roll; Comm Volntr; Vsity Clb; Sccr (V); Track (V); Medical Field; Computer Technology; Queens College; John Jay College

DOUGLAS, SERIKA; BRONX, NY; EVANDER CHILDS HS; (SR); Hnr Roll; Nat Hon Sy; Otst Ac Ach Awd; Perf Att; St of Mnth; WWAHSS; Yth Ldrshp Prog; Comm Volntr; Peer Tut/Med; Chrch Yth Grp; Off Aide; Prom Com; Tchrs Aide; Cl Off (S, T); Stu Cncl (S); CR (S, T); Accounting; Dental Hygiene; U of New Haven

DOUSUAH, WROSEOYEA; BRONX, NY; MARBLE HILL HS FOR INTERNATIONAL STUDIES; (FR); Hi Hnr Roll; Hnr Roll; Otst Ac Ach Awd; Perf Att; Yth Ldrshp Prog; Chrch Yth Grp; Drma Clb; Drl Tm; Mch Bnd; Track (L); Certificate of Merit / Medals / Ribbon for Track; Attendance Award / Citizenship Award; Medicine; PhD; Iowa College; Columbia U

DOW, JAMES; GANSEVOORT, NY; F DONALD MYERS ED CTR; (SR); Hnr Roll; Perf Att; Comm Volntr; Bnd; Auto/Diesel Technician; Also Will Become a Paramedic; Universal Technical Institute

DOYLE, KRISTINA A; BUFFALO, NY; NICHOLS SCH; (SR); F Lan Hn Soc; Hnr Roll; Comm Volntr; Hosp Aide; Chrch Yth Grp; Mth Clb/Tm; Chr; Ch Chr; SP/M/VS; Scr Kpr (V); Lit Mag (R); Yrbk (E); Varsity Squash Player; Captain/Founder of Fencing Team; Pre-Med; Pre-Vet; Going to Attend U of Rochester

DRAGO, MADELINE J; LAKEWOOD, NY; SOUTHWESTERN HS; (SR); Hi Hnr Roll; Nat Hon Sy; Comm Volntr; Peer Tut/Med; Key Club; Prom Com; SADD; Chrldg (V C); Vllyball (V C); Cl Off (S); Yrbk (E); Ophelia/Peer Mentor; Business First "First Honors"; Elementary Education; Saint Bonaventure U

DRAKE, JESSICA; ISLAND PARK, NY; WEST HEMPSTEAD HS; (SO); Hi Hnr Roll; Nat Hon Sy; Otst Ac Ach Awd; Sci Fairs; Comm Volntr; ArtClub; Drma Clb; Scouts; Spanish Clb; SP/M/VS; Stg Cre; Cl Off (T); Travel Soccer Team; Piano, Swimming, Guitar Lessons; Visual & Motion Effects; Journalism; Pennsylvania State U; Columbia College Chicago

DRAKE, KELLIE L; ELMIRA, NY; THOMAS A EDISON HS; (SR); Hi Hnr Roll; Nat Hon Sy; WWAHSS; Comm Volntr; DARE; Emplmnt; Key Club; SADD; French Clb; Chr; Sftball (VJCL); Business Marketing; West Virginia U

DRENNAN, MEGHAN; ESSEX, NY; WESTPORT CTRL SCH; (FR); Hi Hnr Roll; Hnr Roll; Otst Ac Ach Awd; Comm Volntr; Bnd; Sccr (J); Sftball (J); Sch Ppr (R, P); Education; Foreign Affairs; Mc Gill U; Concordia U

DROBNJAK, ALEKSANDAR; SCHENECTADY, NY; COLONIE CTRL HS; (JR); Nat Hon Sy; St of Mnth; WWAHSS; Yth Ldrshp Prog; Comm Volntr; Peer Tut/Med; Bnd; Pep Bnd; Vllyball (J); Albany Swim Club; International Business; Engineering

DROZ, MARY T; WHITESBORO, NY; HOLY CROSS AC; (SR); Hi Hnr Roll; MVP; Nat Hon Sy; Nat Mrt LOC; Nat Stu Ath Day Aw; WWAHSS; Peer Tut/Med; ArtClub; Drma Clb; Emplmnt; Photog; Bnd; Ch Chr; SP/M/VS; Swg Chr; Bskball (V C); Sccr (V C); Stu Cncl (S); Yrbk (R); High Honors in Guild (Piano Competition); All-Star (Basketball, 4 Years); Math Education; Christian Singer; Franciscan U of Steubenville

DROZDOWSKI, CASSIE; CASTILE, NY; LETCHWORTH CTRL HS; (SO); Hi Hnr Roll; Otst Ac Ach Awd; St of Mnth; 4-H; Ntl FFA; Chr; Veterinarian; Psychologist; Cornell U; U of North Carolina

DRUMMOND, DAMARLEY D; ELMONT, NY; THOMAS EDISON; (FR); Hi Hnr Roll; Hnr Roll; Perf Att; St of Mnth; Peer Tut/Med; FBLA; Lib Aide; Mus Clb; Off Aide; Tchrs Aide; Track (C); Participation in NAMISS Pageant; NAMISS-National American Miss; Ph.D in Medicine; Ph.D in Psychology; Stony Brooke; Yale

DRYDEN, KIMBERLY C; BALDWINSVILLE, NY; CW BAKER HS; (SR); Hi Hnr Roll; Nat Hon Sy; WWAHSS; Amnsty Intl; Comm Volntr; Emplmnt; Key Club; Prom Com; Stu Cncl (R); People to People Student Ambassador; AP Scholar; Anthropology; Archaeology; SUNY Albany

DUAN, HUDSON H; ALBANY, NY; SHAKER HS; (SO); Ctznshp Aw; Hi Hnr Roll; MVP; Otst Ac Ach Awd; Perf Att; Pres Ac Ftns Aw; Sci Fairs; Sci/Math Olympn; St of Mnth; WWAHSS; Comm Volntr; Hab For Humty Volntr; Peer Tut/Med; Dbte Team; HO'Br Yth Ldrshp; Key Club; Mth Clb/Tm; Mus Clb; Spch Team; Bnd; Jzz Bnd; Mch Bnd; SP/M/VS; Bskball (J); Sccr (VJ L); Swmg (V L); Track (VJ L); Cl Off (R); Stu Cncl (P); Sch Ppr (E); Foreign Language Scholarship 2004; Biology; Economics; Harvard U; U of Pennsylvania

DUARTE, SYLVIA M; OZONE PARK, NY; FOREST HILLS HS; (SR); Hnr Roll; Perf Att; St of Mnth; Comm Volntr; Peer Tut/Med; Emplmnt; Spanish Clb; Fashion Merchandising Management; Business Management; Fashion Institute of Technology

DUCKWORTH, KIERA D; CASSADAGA, NY; CASSADAGA VALLEY MHS; (JR); Hnr Roll; Nat Hon Sy; Pres Sch; St of Mnth; WWAHSS; Comm Volntr; Chrch Yth Grp; Emplmnt; Key Club; NYLC; Photog; Prom Com; Tchrs Aide; French Clb; Bnd; Chr; Mch Bnd; Bskball (L); Sftball (J); Track (L); Vllyball (L); Cl Off (T); Coach of - Little Hoopers -Youth Basketball Program; Engineering; Aquatic / Marine Biology; U of Connecticut; Hofstra U

DUDA, STACIE; SAUGERTIES, NY; SAUGERTIES HS; (JR); Hi Hnr Roll; Nat Hon Sy; WWAHSS; Comm Volntr; Spec Olymp Vol; Key Club; Spanish Clb; Dnce; SP/M/VS; Tennis (V); Track (V); CR (R); Who's Who Among American HS Students; Special Education; Spanish Professor; College of St. Rose; SUNY Albany

DUENO, DAVID; UNIONDALE, NY; BARRY TECH CTR-WESTBURY; (SR); Comm Volntr; Peer Tut/Med; Spec Olymp Vol; 4-H; DARE; Emplmnt; Hofstra U Teen Advisory Board Service Award; Hofstra U Teen Advisory Board Community Service Award; Auto Technician; Universal Technical Institute

DUGGAN, ALLISON M; HUNTINGTON STATION, NY; HUNTINGTON HS; (SO); Ctznshp Aw; Hi Hnr Roll; Hnr Roll; WWAHSS; Comm Volntr; Peer Tut/Med; Drma Clb; Mus Clb; Scouts; Tmpl Yth Grp; Bnd; Chr; Clr Grd; Jzz Bnd; Fncg (VJ); Track (J); Lit Mag (R); A World of Difference, Positive Action Committee; Gay/Straight Alliance; Music, Business; English; Syracuse U, NY; Potsdam, Crane School

DUMAIN, KATE; SAUGERTIES, NY; SAUGERTIES HS; (FR); Comm Volntr; Lcrsse (JC); Sccr (J); Physical Education Teacher; Physical Therapist; SUNY Cortland

Drummond, Damarley D
Thomas Edison
Elmont, NY

Dorsainvil, Sasha N
Midwood HS
Brooklyn, NY

Dominianni, Alexandra
MS 158
Fresh Meadows, NY

National
Honor Roll
Spring 2005

Dixon, Crystal
Canarsie HS
Brooklyn, NY

Dousuah, Wroseoyea
Marble Hill HS For International Studies
Bronx, NY

Dueno, David
Barry Tech Ctr-Westbury
Uniondale, NY

DUMAS, NDIJA; BRONX, NY; ST BARNABAS HS; (JR); Hnr Roll; FTA; Chr; SP/M/VS; Bdmtn (J); Chrldg (J); Track (J); CR (P); Faith Sharing; Bridge Building / Right-To-Life Society; Teaching / Early Childhood Education; Manhattan College; Adelphi U

DUMMETT, IAN; SAINT ALBANS, NY; QUEENS HS FOR SCIENCES AT YORK; (FR); Nat Hon Sy; Sci Fairs; Sci/Math Olympn; St of Mnth; Peer Tut/Med; Mth Clb/Tm; Sci Clb; Svce Clb; Swmg (L); Governor's Committee on Scholastic Achievement; Math Academic Achievement Award; Harvard U; Princeton U

DUNCKLE, ALLISON; GREENE, NY; GREENE CTRL HS; (SO); Hi Hnr Roll; WWAHSS; Emplmnt; Scouts; Bnd; Chr; Jzz Bnd; Mch Bnd; Swmg (V)

DUNN, ALYSSA; GUILDERLAND CTR, NY; GUILDERLAND HS; (FR); Hnr Roll; Cl Off (T); Journalism; Criminal Justice; Michigan State

DUTCHER, DAYLE L; OTEGO, NY; LAURENS CTRL SCH; (FR); 4H Awd; Ctznshp Aw; Hi Hnr Roll; Nat Hon Sy; Otst Ac Ach Awd; Pres Sch; WWAHSS; Comm Volntr; 4-H; Chrch Yth Grp; Drma Clb; Key Club; Spanish Clb; Bnd; Chr; Mch Bnd; SP/M/VS; Bskball (JC); Sccr (JC); Stu Cncl (R); CR; Foreign Language Teacher; Translator

DUVA, JOSEPH A; CUTCHOGUE, NY; MERCY HS; (SO); USAA; Emplmnt; Bnd; National Society of HS Scholars

DUVAL, CHRISTINE; ROCHESTER, NY; SPENCERPORT HS; (SR); Hi Hnr Roll; Hnr Roll; Nat Hon Sy; WWAHSS; Red Cr Aide; Drma Clb; SADD; Chr; SP/M/VS; Sch Ppr (R); Yrbk (R); Scholastic Achievement Society; Major in Theatre; SUNY Oswego

DWYER, CHARLENE; WATERVLIET, NY; SHAKER HS; (JR); WWAHSS; Jr Ach; SADD; SP/M/VS; African American and Cultural Club; Hispanic Culture Club; Acting; Directing and Production; SUNY Purchase; New School University NY

DWYER, DENISE; BRONX, NY; ST BARNABAS HS; (JR); F Lan Hn Soc; Hi Hnr Roll; Hnr Roll; Nat Hon Sy; Peer Tut/Med; Lib Aide; Mth Clb/Tm; Scouts; Sch Ppr (E, R); Yrbk (E); Creative Writing Club; First Grade CCD Teacher; Astronautical / Aeronautical Engineering; Law; United States Air Force Academy; New York U

DYKEMAN, BRITTA A; HOOSICK FALLS, NY; HOOSICK FALLS CTRL SCH; (JR); Hi Hnr Roll; Hnr Roll; Drma Clb; Emplmnt; Ch Chr; Stg Cre; Stu Cncl (R); Creative Writing Club; 2 Poems Published in Anthology; Education (Secondary & Elementary); English; Cedarville U; Appalachian Bible College

EAGEL, BRETT J J; YONKERS, NY; SAUNDERS TRADES & TECH HS; (SR); Hi Hnr Roll; Hnr Roll; Chess; Key Club; Scouts; Bowling Team; Business Marketing; Business Advertising; Adelphi U; Fairfield U

EASTMAN, ASHLEY M; COPAKE, NY; TACONIC HILLS CTRL HS; (JR); Hi Hnr Roll; Hnr Roll; Nat Hon Sy; Perf Att; Emplmnt; Accounting; Real Estate; Columbia Green; College of Saint Rose

EBANGWESE, ABANEH; ROCHESTER, NY; PITTSFORD SUTHERLAND HS; (JR); Hnr Roll; Otst Ac Ach Awd; Pres Sch; St of Mnth; Hab For Humty Volntr; Peer Tut/Med; Dbte Team; DECA; Emplmnt; Prom Com; Vsity Clb; Chr; Orch; Bskball (J); Track (VJ L); Cl Off (V, R); CR; Think About Teaching Award; Student Mediator Award; Sciences (Biology); Foreign Languages (French and Spanish); SUNY Colleges (State of New York); U of Rochester

ECCLESTON, SIERRA S; ODESSA, NY; ODESSA MONTOUR JR SR HS; (JR); Hnr Roll; Perf Att; Sci Fairs; WWAHSS; Comm Volntr; Spec Olymp Vol; Chrch Yth Grp; Emplmnt; Prom Com; Scouts; Chr; Ch Chr; Dnce; Bskball (V CL); Sccr (V L); Track (V L); Vllyball (J L); Cl Off (T); Stu Cncl (R); Law; English; Albany U; U At Buffalo

ECHEVARRIA, LETISHA N; FREDONIA, NY; FREDONIA HS; (SR); Hi Hnr Roll; Hnr Roll; Kwnis Aw; Otst Ac Ach Awd; St of Mnth; Comm Volntr; Spec Olymp Vol; Key Club; Sch Ppr (E); Secretary for Key Club; Business Manager & Advertising Editor; Marketing / Business; Business Management; Jamestown Business College

ECKLEY, CHERI; SILVER CREEK, NY; SILVER CREEK HS; (SR); Chrch Yth Grp; Key Club; Bnd; Chr; SP/M/VS; Chrldg (V C); Yrbk (R, P); VP of Key Club; VP of SADD

EDDINGTON, BETHANNE; SENECA FALLS, NY; MYNDERSE AC HS; (SO); Hi Hnr Roll; Hnr Roll; St of Mnth; Comm Volntr; Mod UN; Scouts; Bnd; Mch Bnd; Cr Ctry (V); Track (V)

EDGE, SHANECE B; HEMPSTEAD, NY; HEMPSTEAD HS; (SO); Hi Hnr Roll; Hnr Roll; WWAHSS; Comm Volntr; Chrch Yth Grp; Emplmnt; Key Club; P to P St Amb Prg; Ch Chr; Regents Scholar; Business Management; Accounting; Clark Atlanta U

EDMONDSON, ALISHA M; ITHACA, NY; ITHACA HS; (SR); Hnr Roll; Comm Volntr; Peer Tut/Med; DARE; Key Club; Dnce; Stu Cncl (R); Education; International Relations; SUNY Albany; Florida International U

EDONA, ZARIQI; BRONX, NY; MARBLE HILL SCH; (JR); MVP; Comm Volntr; Scouts; Vllyball (V); Wt Lftg (V); Stu Cncl; Sch Ppr (R); Fordham U; Hunter College

EDOUARD, REBECCA M; QUEENS VILLAGE, NY; THOMAS A EDISON HS; (SR); Hnr Roll; Nat Hon Sy; Perf Att; USAA; WWAHSS; Comm Volntr; Peer Tut/Med; Chrch Yth Grp; Emplmnt; Lib Aide; Track (V); 4 Time National Certificate Winner for Playing Piano; Biology; Doctor (Surgeon); Hunter College; Hofstra U

EDWARDS, JASON; BROOKLYN, NY; BRONX HS OF SCIENCE; (JR); WWAHSS; Comm Volntr; Drma Clb; SP/M/VS; Track (V); National Society of High School Scholars; Biochemistry; Cornell U; Duke U

EDWARDS, LAUREN; CORNING, NY; WEST HS; (SO); Hi Hnr Roll; Otst Ac Ach Awd; Perf Att; Sci Fairs; Bnd; Chr; Bskball (J); Cr Ctry (J); Teaching; Drama; Corning Community College

EDWARDS, SHANNON; BALDWIN, NY; HOLY TRINITY HS; (JR); Hi Hnr Roll; Nat Hon Sy; Quill & Scroll; Orch; Swmg (V); Yrbk (E); Entertainment Lawyer; Public Relations; U of Southern California; Stanford U

EHRLICH, ZACK; MERRICK, NY; BELLMORE JFK HS; (SO); Hi Hnr Roll; Hnr Roll; Nat Hon Sy; WWAHSS; BPA; Emplmnt; FBLA; Key Club; Helping Unfortunate Families By Purchasing Them Homes; Business; Real Estate; Binghamton; New York U

EICHELBERGER, IMANI; ALBANY, NY; NOTRE DAME BISHOP GIBBONS HS; (SO); Hi Hnr Roll; Nat Hon Sy; Comm Volntr; Peer Tut/Med; Chrch Yth Grp; Ch Chr; Stg Cre; Vllyball (J); Yrbk (E, P); Student Ambassador; Air Force Award for Math and Science; MD (Pediatrician); Hampton U

EINBINDER, ALLYSON; ALBANY, NY; GUILDERLAND HS; (JR); Hi Hnr Roll; Hnr Roll; Nat Hon Sy; Otst Ac Ach Awd; Perf Att; Pres Sch; Amnsty Intl; Comm Volntr; Red Cr Aide; ArtClub; Dbte Team; Emplmnt; Key Club; Scouts; Svce Clb; SADD; Tmpl Yth Grp; Dnce; Sch Ppr (R); Vice President of Albany Chapter Now; Delegate on 2005 Border-Witness Mexico Trip; Psychology; Women's Studies; Vassar College; Tufts U

EINERMAN, GARRETT; LEVITTOWN, NY; DIVISION AVE HS; (SO); F Lan Hn Soc; Hi Hnr Roll; Hnr Roll; Perf Att; St of Mnth; Key Club; Sccr (V); Wt Lftg (J); National Honor Society - Secretary; Business; Law

EISELE, TRAVIS E; LOCKPORT, NY; LOCKPORT HS; (FR); Hi Hnr Roll; Otst Ac Ach Awd; St of Mnth; Comm Volntr; Key Club; Off Aide; French Clb; Volunteer Service for the Lockport Monday Night Cruise Optimist Club; Law Degree; Master's Degree; Harvard Law School; Buffalo U

EISENBACH, CASEY; PLEASANT VALLEY, NY; ARLINGTON HS; (JR); Hnr Roll; St of Mnth; Comm Volntr; Peer Tut/Med; Drma Clb; Tmpl Yth Grp; Orch; Sccr; Track; Sch Ppr (R); Volunteered - To Help Homeless; Volunteered At Nursing Homes; Teacher / Secondary Education Chemistry; High School Principal; Long Island U; Vassar College

ELA, JOSHUA M; BUSKIRK, NY; BLUE MOUNTAIN AC; (SO); Hi Hnr Roll; Pres Ac Ftns Aw; Comm Volntr; 4-H; Chrch Yth Grp; Mus Clb; Photog; Yrbk (P); Engineering; Architecture; Walla Walla College

ELDREDGE, CRYSTAL; SENECA FALLS, NY; MYNDERSE AC HS; (SO); Hi Hnr Roll; Hnr Roll; Otst Ac Ach Awd; Pres Sch; St of Mnth; Comm Volntr; Mod UN; Pep Squd; French Clb; Chrldg (JCL); Tennis (J L)

ELIE, STEPHANIE; FRESH MEADOWS, NY; FRANCIS LEWIS HS; (JR); MVP; Perf Att; Comm Volntr; Key Club; Off Aide; Dnce; Tennis (V C); Lit Mag (R); Communications (Broadcaster); Philosophy; Brown U; Colorado State U

ELIEN, SANDRA; WEST BABYLON, NY; WEST BABYLON SR HS; (JR); F Lan Hn Soc; Hi Hnr Roll; Hnr Roll; Nat Mrt Semif; Nat Sci Aw; Otst Ac Ach Awd; Perf Att; Sci Fairs; St of Mnth; Comm Volntr; Red Cr Aide; Spec Olymp Vol; ArtClub; Chrch Yth Grp; Cmptr Clb; Emplmnt; Prom Com; Sci Clb; Svce Clb; International Clb; Principal's Achievement Award; Certificat De Merit; MD; PhD; U of Rochester; State U of New York

ELIEZER, MICHELLE; BROOKLYN, NY; SHULAMITH HS FOR GIRLS; (JR); Sci/Math Olympn; Comm Volntr; Peer Tut/Med; Mth Clb/Tm; Stg Cre; Lit Mag (R); Sch Ppr (P); Head of Weekend - Shabbaton; Business Head in Production; Psychology; Brooklyn College; Barnard U

ELISCAR, VALERIE; ROSEDALE, NY; QHST; (SO); Hnr Roll; Comm Volntr; Hosp Aide; Emplmnt; Scouts; SP/M/VS; CR (R); Girl Scouts Silver Award; Pediatrician; Computer; New York Institute of Technology; CW Post

ELKIND, ZACHARY; BROOKLYN, NY; FIORELLO H LA GUARDIA HS; (FR); Ctznshp Aw; Hnr Roll; Nat Hon Sy; Pres Sch; Comm Volntr; Drma Clb; SP/M/VS; Drama, History, Biology; New Paltz, Binghamton, Purchase; U Mass-Amherst

ELLING, LAURA; ALTAMONT, NY; GUILDERLAND HS; (FR); Hnr Roll; Comm Volntr; Key Club; I Am on Navis Crew.; I Went to a Horizons Program At Clarkson U.; I'm Interested in Math & Science.; I Am Also Interested in Technology.; Clarkson U

ELLIS, SHERI; WEST HEMPSTEAD, NY; MALVERNE HS; (SR); Hi Hnr Roll; Hnr Roll; MVP; Nat Hon Sy; Otst Ac Ach Awd; St of Mnth; WWAHSS; Chrch Yth Grp; Chr; Ch Chr; Tennis (V); Girls Bowling Scholar Athlete (2003-2004); Member of NAACP Youth Council; Business; Music Production; St John's U; Hofstra U

EL-TOURKY, AMANDA; MASTIC BEACH, NY; CLONLARA HS; (SO); 4H Awd; Ctznshp Aw; Nat Mrt LOC; Sci Fairs; Comm Volntr; Hab For Humty Volntr; 4-H; Chrch Yth Grp; Emplmnt; Quiz Bowl; Scouts; Ch Chr; Clr Grd; Orch; SP/M/VS; Gmnstcs (J); Mar Art (J); Rlr Hky (J); Sftball (J); Swmg (V); Stu Cncl (P, V, S); Yrbk (P); National American / Miss NY Junior Teen Finalist; Early Education / Music Instructor; Fashion Designer; Savannah College of Art and Design; North Carolina School of the Arts

EL-TOURKY, SHAREIN; MASTIC BEACH, NY; CLONLARA HS; (JR); 4H Awd; Nat Hon Sy; Nat Mrt Semif; WWAHSS; Comm Volntr; Peer Tut/Med; 4-H; Chrch Yth Grp; Dbte Team; Emplmnt; Mus Clb; Quiz Bowl; Spanish Clb; Ch Chr; Dnce; Orch; SP/M/VS; Swmg (V); Sch Ppr (E, R, P); Yrbk (E, P); Suffolk County Clerk's Certificate of Merit; The Big Exposition Senior Division Llama Show Grand Champion; Marine Biology; Physics; Roger Williams U; Duke U

EMERY, NIKKI; RENSSELAER, NY; RENSS MIDDLE HS; (JR); Hnr Roll; Nat Hon Sy; Otst Ac Ach Awd; Perf Att; St of Mnth; WWAHSS; Key Club; SADD; Chr; Vllyball (J)

EMKE, DARYN C; NORTH COLLINS, NY; NORTH COLLINS HS; (SR); Hi Hnr Roll; Hnr Roll; Nat Hon Sy; WWAHSS; Comm Volntr; Red Cr Aide; Bsball (J); Sccr (VJ L); Sch Ppr (R); National Honor Society; I Want to Be a Mathematics Teacher.; St. Bonaventure; Canisius College

EMMONS, CORY M; MARTVILLE, NY; HANNIBAL CTRL SCH; (SR); Hi Hnr Roll; Nat Hon Sy; Perf Att; Pres Sch; Valdctrian; Comm Volntr; Peer Tut/Med; AL Aux Boys; Chess; Emplmnt; Key Club; Photog; Prom Com; SP/M/VS; Cr Ctry (V L); Tennis (V CL); Cl Off (P); Yrbk (E, P); Oswego County Academic Youth League; Engineering (Civil, Chemical); Neuroscience; SUNY Oswego; Clarkson U

EMPEY, JESSICA; CANTON, NY; MADRID-WADDINGTON HS; (SO); St of Mnth; Red Cr Aide; DARE; Chr; Sftball (V); Track (V); Yrbk; Bachelor's; Potsdam; Ithaca

EMPTAGE, JACQUELINE; AMAGANSETT, NY; EAST HAMPTON HS; (SO); Hi Hnr Roll; Hnr Roll; Pres Ac Ftns Aw; Pres Sch; WWAHSS; Comm Volntr; DARE; Key Club; Tennis (JC); Track (V); Education (Elementary); Psychology; Lafayette

EMURIAN, LAUREL; GLOVERSVILLE, NY; GLOVERSVILLE HS; (SO); Hi Hnr Roll; Otst Ac Ach Awd; Perf Att; WWAHSS; Comm Volntr; Bnd; Ch Chr; Pep Bnd; Odyssey of the Mind; Fulton County Youth Bureau Member; Mathematics; Hobart and William Smith Colleges

ENAW, SAMANTHA; HUNTINGTON STATION, NY; ST ANTHONY'S HS; (JR); Hi Hnr Roll; Hnr Roll; Amnsty Intl; Comm Volntr; Peer Tut/Med; Dbte Team; DECA; Emplmnt; SADD; Foreign Clb; Chr; Stg Cre; Swg Chr; Fld Hky (J); Yrbk (R); Forensic Science; Accounting; Western New England College; Bentley College

ENDRES, KATIE; GRAND ISLAND, NY; GRAND ISLAND HS; (SO); Hnr Roll; Comm Volntr; Emplmnt; Scouts; Svce Clb; Bnd; Chrldg (VJ L); Yrbk; Wind Ensemble Band Member; Interact Member (Division of Rotary); Pharmacist; French Teacher; U of Buffalo; U of Rochester

ENG, CHRISTOPHER D; FREEPORT, NY; FREEPORT HS; (JR); Hi Hnr Roll; Hnr Roll; Perf Att; Mth Clb/Tm; Mus Clb; Bnd; Mch Bnd; Software Engineering; Cornell U; Brown U

ENGELBRECHT, CAROL; WEST LEYDEN, NY; ADIRONDACK HS; (SO); Hi Hnr Roll; MVP; Nat Hon Sy; Mod UN; Prom Com; Bnd; Stg Cre; Cr Ctry (V L); Track (V L); Cl Off (R); Stu Cncl (T); Math Honor Society

ENGLEHARDT, STEPHANIE A; SEAFORD, NY; SEAFORD HS; (JR); Hi Hnr Roll; Nat Hon Sy; Pres Sch; WWAHSS; Comm Volntr; Hosp Aide; Peer Tut/Med; Emplmnt; Key Club; SADD; Chr; Chrldg (V C); Stu Cncl (R); Scholar Athlete Award; Coaches Award; Nursing; Medicine; Columbia U; SUNY Stony Brook

ENGLISH, ASHLEY; ROCHESTER, NY; EDISON TECH HS; (JR); Otst Ac Ach Awd; WWAHSS; Comm Volntr; Chrch Yth Grp; Drma Clb; SP/M/VS; Bskball (V); Golf (V); Tennis (V); Sch Ppr (E); Who's Who Among American High Schools; Editor (Journalism); Radio & AIR; Central State U; Clark U-Clark Atlanta U

ENGWER, HEATHER; LAKE GEORGE, NY; LAKE GEORGE HS; (JR); F Lan Hn Soc; Hnr Roll; Nat Hon Sy; St of Mnth; WWAHSS; Comm Volntr; ArtClub; Chrch Yth Grp; Emplmnt; Key Club; Prom Com; Scouts; SADD; Spanish Clb; Chr; SP/M/VS; Chrldg (L); Vllyball (J); Yrbk; Bowling Team Varsity; Spanish/Education; Art; Potsdam NY; Castleton VA

EPOLITO, ZACHARY R; ROCHESTER, NY; WEST IRONDEQUOIT HS; (JR); Hnr Roll; Nat Hon Sy; Sci/Math Olympn; Cmptr Clb; Emplmnt; Mth Clb/Tm; Scouts; Rochester Institute of Technology

Elien, Sandra
West Babylon SR HS
West Babylon, NY

Ela, Joshua M
Blue Mountain AC
Buskirk, NY

Ebangwese, Abaneh
Pittsford Sutherland HS
Rochester, NY

Edwards, Jason
Bronx HS Of Science
Brooklyn, NY

Emmons, Cory M
Hannibal Ctrl Sch
Martville, NY

EPPS, ALEXANDER I; BRONX, NY; BRONX HS OF SCIENCE; (JR); F Lan Hn Soc; Nat Hon Sy; Sci/Math Olympn; Peer Tut/Med; Chess; Mth Clb/Tm; Off Aide; Quiz Bowl; Sci Clb; Arista Honors Society; Math Team / Oceanography Team; Math / Physics; Engineering; U of Pennsylvania; Massachusetts Institute of Technology

ERFANI, SINA; WHITESTONE, NY; BRONX HS OF SCIENCE; (SO); Mth Clb/Tm; Math Team; Law; Medical; Columbia U; U of Chicago

ERICKSON, M D; INTERLAKEN, NY; SOUTH SENECA JR SR HS; (JR); Hi Hnr Roll; Hnr Roll; Otst Ac Ach Awd; Comm Volntr; Peer Tut/Med; Emplmnt; Ftball (V L); Wrstlg (V L); CR; Physics; Theology; Cornell U

ESDELLE, RENEE D; SPRINGFIELD GARDENS, NY; QUEENS GATEWAY HS; (SR); Hnr Roll; Nat Sci Aw; Sci Fairs; WWAHSS; Comm Volntr; Chrch Yth Grp; Emplmnt; Prom Com; Tchrs Aide; Lit Mag (R); Sch Ppr (R); Yrbk (R, P); Published Poet Entitled Goodbye; Physical / Occupational Therapy; Psychology; SUNY Stony Brook; York College

ESLICK, XOBERT; OLD BETHPAGE, NY; PLAINVIEW JFK HS; (JR); F Lan Hn Soc; Hi Hnr Roll; Nat Hon Sy; Perf Att; Yth Ldrshp Prog; Comm Volntr; Peer Tut/Med; Spec Olymp Vol; Dbte Team; DECA; Emplmnt; Mod UN; Ntl Beta Clb; NYLC; P to P St Amb Prg; Bsball; Cr Ctry; Ftball; Wrstlg; Started 501 C3 Not-for-Profit Kids Way, Inc / DBA Kids Helping Kids Raised $500,000 ++ Since 1997; Business Honor Society / Scholar Athlete Award / National Youth Leadership Forum on Law; Business; Law; NYU; Boston College

ESTEROW, DANIELLE; MASSAPEQUA, NY; MASSAPEQUA HS; (SO); Hi Hnr Roll; Hnr Roll; Otst Ac Ach Awd; WWAHSS; Emplmnt; Key Club; Svce Clb; SADD; French Clb; Bnd; Dnce; Jzz Bnd; Mch Bnd; Cr Ctry (L); Tri-M Music Honor Society & NYSMMA; Dance Company; Dance; Music; SUNY Purchase College; Regis College

ETIENNE, EDWINE; BROOKLYN, NY; MIDWOOD HS; (SR); Hnr Roll; Nat Hon Sy; Otst Ac Ach Awd; Perf Att; Sci Fairs; WWAHSS; Comm Volntr; Emplmnt; Off Aide; Svce Clb; Tchrs Aide; Orch; Nursing / RN; Nursing Master's Degree / Nurse Practitioner or Doctorate; Hunter College

ETIENNE, SANAA; CHESTNUT RIDGE, NY; RAMAPO HS; (JR); Hnr Roll; Nat Hon Sy; Otst Ac Ach Awd; WWAHSS; Comm Volntr; Peer Tut/Med; Chrch Yth Grp; Drma Clb; Emplmnt; Key Club; MuAlphaTh; Mus Clb; Scouts; SADD; Ch Chr; Dnce; Orch; SP/M/VS; Vllyball (J); Cl Off (T); Silver Award - Girl Scouts; Marian Medal; Pre-Med; Elementary Education; SUNY Stony Brook; Hofstra U

ETIENNE-PARKINSON, ASHLEY; BROOKLYN, NY; SHEEPSHEAD BAY HS; (FR); Hnr Roll; Pre-Med

EUSDEN, CAITLIN; BIG FLATS, NY; HORSEHEADS HS; (JR); Hi Hnr Roll; Nat Hon Sy; Comm Volntr; AL Aux Girls; P to P St Amb Prg; Quiz Bowl; Svce Clb; Bnd; Sccr (V); Track (V); Ski Club; Williams College; Amherst College

EVAN SOTO, CODY J; BALDWIN, NY; BALDWIN HS; (JR); Hnr Roll; MVP; Nat Hon Sy; St of Mnth; Yth Ldrshp Prog; Comm Volntr; Red Cr Aide; ArtClub; Emplmnt; Key Club; Off Aide; Scouts; Ftball (V L); Lcrsse (V L); Track (V L); Art Award; David Rogers Award; Sports Medicine; Art; Adelphi U; SUNY Cortland

EVBUOMWAN, OSARIEME; SPRINGFIELD GARDENS, NY; GATEWAY TO HEALTH SCIENCES SCH; (SO); Hi Hnr Roll; Hnr Roll; Comm Volntr; Hosp Aide; Peer Tut/Med; Chrch Yth Grp; Bnd; SP/M/VS; Bskball (J); Sccr (J); Honor Roll; Medicine

EVERICH, AMANDA; BRONX, NY; AC OF MOUNT SAINT URSULA; (SO); Hnr Roll; Photog; 2 Years of Photo Club; Safety Patrol in Grade 8; Journalism; Photography; Columbia U; NYU

EVERTS, SAMANTHA; HUDSON, NY; HUDSON HS; (SO); Hi Hnr Roll; Hnr Roll; Amnsty Intl; Chr; SP/M/VS; Swmg (V); School Mock Trial Team; Pre Law; Psychology; Harvard; Union

EVOY, PAULINA A; LOCKPORT, NY; LOCKPORT HS; (FR); Hi Hnr Roll; Nat Hon Sy; St of Mnth; WWAHSS; Drma Clb; Key Club; Latin Clb; Chrldg (J); Stu Cncl (R); Interfaith; Marine Biology; Dentistry; Syracuse U

EXANTUS, NEDJIE; ITHACA, NY; ITHACA HS; (SR); Hnr Roll; Perf Att; St of Mnth; Comm Volntr; Hab For Humty Volntr; Peer Tut/Med; Emplmnt; Nursing; Counseling; Tompkins Community College; Wells College

FABEL, KAITLIN M; WEBSTER, NY; WEBSTER THOMAS HS; (JR); F Lan Hn Soc; Hi Hnr Roll; Nat Hon Sy; Otst Ac Ach Awd; WWAHSS; Comm Volntr; Spec Olymp Vol; Emplmnt; Key Club; Ntl Beta Clb; Scouts; Spanish Clb; Orch; Rotary Club; Gold Award (Girl Scouts); Elementary Education; State U of New York At Oswego; State U of New York At Oneonta

FABI, PARIS D; WEST HARRISON, NY; WHITE PLAINS HS; (SO); Hnr Roll; Comm Volntr; Chrch Yth Grp; DARE; Emplmnt; NYLC; Bnd; Ch Chr; Dnce; SP/M/VS; CR (R); Sch Ppr (E, R, P); DARE; Nominated By the National Youth Leaders Conference; Music / Dance; Criminal Law; Berklee School of Music; SUNY

FABIANO, MARK; SAUGERTIES, NY; SAUGERTIES HS; (JR); Hi Hnr Roll; Hnr Roll; MVP; Nat Hon Sy; WWAHSS; Emplmnt; Key Club; Bsball (VJ); Bskball (J); Cl Off (T)

FABIG, STEPHANIE; PATCHOGUE, NY; BAYPORT BLUE POINT HS; (SO); Hi Hnr Roll; Hnr Roll; St of Mnth; Dnce; Orch; Chrldg (J); Track (J); The Carl Friedrich Gouss Award; Dance; Music; St Joseph's; New York U

FAGAN, SARA K; ELMIRA, NY; NOTRE DAME HS; (SR); Hi Hnr Roll; Nat Hon Sy; Comm Volntr; Hab For Humty Volntr; Peer Tut/Med; Chrch Yth Grp; Drma Clb; Emplmnt; Key Club; Spanish Clb; SP/M/VS; Bdmtn (V); Bskball (V); Sccr (V); CR (R); Hands of Christ Award; IAC Soccer All-League Honorable Mention; Biology; Canisius College; Cornell U

FALCE, CHRISTINE; LEVITTOWN, NY; ISLAND TREES HS; (FR); Hi Hnr Roll; Hnr Roll; Otst Ac Ach Awd; WWAHSS; Comm Volntr; Chrch Yth Grp; Drma Clb; Key Club; Mus Clb; Chr; Ch Chr; SP/M/VS; Swg Chr; Stu Cncl (R); CR (R); Lit Mag (E, R); Human Awareness Club; NYSSMA; Music; Art

FALISI, ANGELA L; WHITE PLAINS, NY; MARIA REGINA HS; (FR); Hi Hnr Roll; Otst Ac Ach Awd; Perf Att; Sci Fairs; Valdctrian; WWAHSS; Comm Volntr; Peer Tut/Med; Chrch Yth Grp; Drma Clb; Emplmnt; Key Club; Scouts; Svce Clb; Tchrs Aide; Bnd; Chr; Ch Chr; SP/M/VS; Ice Sktg; Swmg; Tennis; Stu Cncl; Sch Ppr (R); Yrbk (R); Italian Language Honor Awards; Most Promising Young Scientist-Manhattanville College; International Relations; Journalism / Political Science; Yale U; Cornell U

FALKOWITZ, JASON E; BROOKLYN, NY; JAMES MADISON HS; (JR); Hnr Roll; Yth Ldrshp Prog; Comm Volntr; NYLC; Outdrs Clb; Tchrs Aide; Tmpl Yth Grp; Vsity Clb; SP/M/VS; Stg Cre; Tennis (V C); Yrbk (R)

FALLICK, ASHLEY; GREAT NECK, NY; GREEN NECK SOUTH HS; (JR); F Lan Hn Soc; DECA; Emplmnt; Key Club; SADD; Sccr (J); Adv Cncl (R); CR (R); Four (4) Years Class Programming; President B'nai B'rith Youth Assn; Management; Journalism; Emory College; Cornell U

FALLON JR, ROBERT; BOONVILLE, NY; ADIRONDACK HS; (JR); Perf Att; Emplmnt; Scouts; French Clb; Sccr (V L); Track (V); Published Writer; Forensic Science; Criminal Justice; Fordham U; Mohawk Community College

FANA, DIANDRA M; CORONA, NY; THE MARY LOUIS AC; (FR); MVP; Nat Sci Aw; Nat Stu Ath Day Aw; Otst Ac Ach Awd; Perf Att; Pres Ac Ftns Aw; Sci Fairs; Sci/Math Olympn; St of Mnth; Comm Volntr; Peer Tut/Med; ArtClub; Emplmnt; FCA; Photog; Prom Com; Scouts; SADD; Tech Clb; Chr; Ch Chr; Dnce; SP/M/VS; Bsball; Chrldg; Cr Ctry; GAA; Gmnstcs; Mar Art; Scr Kpr; Track (J); Cl Off (P); Stu Cncl (R); Educational Intensive Award; Pediatrician; Navy Seal; Nova Southeastern U; West Point Military Academy

FANFAN, STEPHANIE; BROOKLYN, NY; EDWARD R MURROW HS; (SR); Hnr Roll; Perf Att; SP/M/VS; One of My Poems Was Published in the April 11, 2005 Brooklyn Skyline; Science, Chemistry or Writing or Psychology; Polytechnic U

FARMER, SABRINA; MASSAPEQUA, NY; AMITYVILLE MEMORIAL HS; (SO); Hi Hnr Roll; Hnr Roll; Nat Hon Sy; Nat Mrt LOC; Otst Ac Ach Awd; WWAHSS; Key Club; Bnd; Lit Mag (R); Tri-M: National Music Honor Society; Editor's Choice Award from International Library of Poetry; Columbia U: Columbia College; New York U

FARNHAM, KIMBERLY; MONTAUK, NY; EAST HAMPTON HS; (JR); Hi Hnr Roll; Nat Hon Sy; St of Mnth; Peer Tut/Med; AL Aux Girls; Key Club; Fld Hky (VJC); Sftball (J); Track (V); International Law/Political Science; Teaching; Georgetown; Middlebury

FARNHAM, LINDA N; WESTFIELD, NY; WESTFIELD AC AND CTRL SCH; (JR); Hi Hnr Roll; Hnr Roll; MVP; Nat Hon Sy; Otst Ac Ach Awd; Perf Att; Pres Sch; St of Mnth; WWAHSS; Yth Ldrshp Prog; Comm Volntr; Hab For Humty Volntr; Chrch Yth Grp; DARE; Drma Clb; FCA; French Clb; Acpl Chr; Chr; Ch Chr; SP/M/VS; Tennis (V); Forensic Chemistry; Waynesburg College; St Andrews College

FAROOQUI, AFRIN; FRESH MEADOWS, NY; (MS); Hnr Roll; St of Mnth; Hosp Aide; Mus Clb; Tchrs Aide; Voc Ind Clb Am; Bnd; Chr; Dnce; SP/M/VS; Bdmtn (J); Cyclg (V); Ftball (V); Scr Kpr (V); Sccr (V); Sftball (V); Swmg (J); Vllyball (V); St John's U

FARR, ASHLEY J; BRANTINGHAM, NY; SOUTH LEWIS HS; (SO); Hi Hnr Roll; WWAHSS; Peer Tut/Med; ArtClub; Scouts; Chr; Stg Cre; Cr Ctry (V); GAA (V); Track (V); Vllyball (JC); Yrbk (E); Mathematics; Computer Science; Lemoyne; Cornell

FARSAKH, SHAFEEKA; BROOKLYN, NY; NEW UTRECHT HS; (SO); Hnr Roll; Perf Att; St of Mnth; Yth Ldrshp Prog; Comm Volntr; Peer Tut/Med; Emplmnt; Mod UN; Sci Clb; Sccr (J); Cl Off (P); Toast Masters; Travel and Hospitality Academy; Physical Therapy; Dentistry (Orthodontist); New York U; Columbia U

FATADE, AYOBAMI; BROOKLYN, NY; IS 218 JAMES PETER SINNOTT MS; Hnr Roll; Perf Att; St of Mnth; Peer Tut/Med; Red Cr Aide; Chess; Chrch Yth Grp; Dbte Team; Quiz Bowl; Bsball; Bskball; Ftball; Sftball; Swmg; Wt Lftg; Lit Mag; Aeronautic Engineering; Pre-Med Sciences; Stony Brook U NY

FAUST, TYLER J; MIDDLETOWN, NY; MINISINK VALLEY HS; (FR); Hi Hnr Roll; Pres Sch; St of Mnth; Chrch Yth Grp; Emplmnt; Key Club; Scouts; Sccr (J); Tennis (J); Life Scout; Sports Writer; Sports Medicine; Duke; SUNY Binghamton

FAVILLE, MATTHEW D; CLINTON, NY; CLINTON SR HS; (SR); Hi Hnr Roll; Amnsty Intl; Comm Volntr; Chrch Yth Grp; Bnd; Mch Bnd; Orch; Computer Engineering; Business Management; Utica College; Syracuse U

FAWCETT, TAYLOR M; MT KISCO, NY; MARIA REGINA HS; (FR); Hi Hnr Roll; Hnr Roll; Comm Volntr; Chrch Yth Grp; Key Club; Mus Clb; Acpl Chr; Bnd; Chr; Ch Chr; Sch Ppr (R); Key Club; Mission Outreach; Sports Announcer - For Baseball; Sports Writer; New York U

FEDER, ARIELLE; BELLMORE, NY; JOHN F KENNEDY HS; (FR); Ctznshp Aw; Hi Hnr Roll; Hnr Roll; Nat Hon Sy; Comm Volntr; Peer Tut/Med; Key Club; Tmpl Yth Grp; Honor Roll; Key Club and Freshman Club

FEINMAN, ROSS; EAST MEADOW, NY; EAST MEADOW HS; (SO); Hnr Roll; Peer Tut/Med; HO'Br Yth Ldrshp; Key Club; NYLC; P to P St Amb Prg; Sci Clb; SADD; Tmpl Yth Grp; Bnd; Jzz Bnd; Mch Bnd; Sccr (J); Vllyball (J, C); Selected to Attend People to People Student Ambassadorship As Well As NYLC in Washington DC; Alternate for HOBY Award (Hugh O'Brian Youth Leadership); Forensic Science; Criminology; Syracuse U; Binghamton U

FEINSOT, STACY; NORTH WOODMERE, NY; LAWRENCE HS; (SO); Hi Hnr Roll; Nat Sci Aw; Perf Att; Sci Fairs; Sci/Math Olympn; Valdctrian; WWAHSS; Peer Tut/Med; Key Club; Mus Clb; Sci Clb; Orch; Bdmtn (V); Yrbk (E); Interning At a Lab At the U of Pennsylvania; Pre Medicine

FELDER, SHARAIA; SHIRLEY, NY; WILLIAM FLOYD HS; (SO); FBLA; Key Club; Orch; Music; Vet.

FELDMAN, VALERIE B; ALBANY, NY; GUILDERLAND HS; (JR); All Am Sch; Hi Hnr Roll; Hnr Roll; MVP; Nat Hon Sy; Otst Ac Ach Awd; Perf Att; Sci Fairs; Sci/Math Olympn; Yth Ldrshp Prog; Amnsty Intl; Comm Volntr; Peer Tut/Med; ArtClub; BPA; DARE; FBLA; Key Club; Mth Clb/Tm; Vsity Clb; Spanish Clb; Ice Hky (VJC); Lcrsse (VJCL); Sccr (VJCL); Cl Off (R); Stu Cncl (R); CR (R); Hospitality Administration/Management; Cornell U; UMass-Endicott

FELDMAN, YULIYA; BROOKLYN, NY; STUYVESANT HS; (FR); Hnr Roll; Otst Ac Ach Awd; St of Mnth; Key Club; Lib Aide; Mth Clb/Tm; Bnd; Yrbk (R); I Helped Make Costumes for SING; Business Lawyer; International Business; Columbia U; New York U

FELICIANO, NICOLE E; WESTBURY, NY; W TRESPER CLARKE HS; MS; Hnr Roll; Otst Ac Ach Awd; Sci Fairs; ArtClub; Orch; Fld Hky (L); Track (L); Vllyball (L); Lit Mag (E); President's Award for Education Excellence; Merit Award Towards Writing Literature; Law; Psychology; Harvard U; NYU

FELICIONE, KRISTEN; MERRICK, NY; SANFORD H CALHOUN HS; (JR); Ctznshp Aw; F Lan Hn Soc; Hnr Roll; Nat Hon Sy; WWAHSS; Peer Tut/Med; DECA; Key Club; MuAlphaTh; SADD; Clb; Dnce; Kickline Varsity- Will Be Captain Next Year; Orthodontist; Colgate U; Bucknell U

FELIZ, YANNERIS; BRONX, NY; HEALTH OPPORTUNITIES HS; (FR); Hi Hnr Roll; Hnr Roll; ArtClub; Medical Degree; Professional Doctor; Columbia U

FENG, JENNIFER; BAYSIDE, NY; FRANCIS LEWIS; (SO); F Lan Hn Soc; Hi Hnr Roll; Nat Hon Sy; Perf Att; Sci Fairs; Comm Volntr; Peer Tut/Med; Lib Aide; Off Aide; ROTC; Tchrs Aide; Clr Grd; Sch Ppr (R); NYAS Expo Member; Project Liberty Diversity Team; Law; Medicine; Saint Johns U; New York U

FERNANDEZ, ALVARO; PT JEFFERSON STATION, NY; COMSEWOGUE HS; (FR); Ctznshp Aw; Hi Hnr Roll; Hnr Roll; Nat Hon Sy; Perf Att; St of Mnth; Comm Volntr; Hab For Humty Volntr; Key Club; Svce Clb; Spanish Clb; Hofstra U

FERNANDEZ, MARIBEL; NEW YORK, NY; SAINT JEAN BAPTISTE HS; (JR); Hnr Roll; Amnsty Intl; Drma Clb; Dnce; SP/M/VS; Stu Cncl (R); CR (R); Psychology; Engineering; Skidmore College; Columbia U

FERNANDEZ, ROSALIE; BROOKLYN, NY; NORMAN THOMAS HS; (JR); Hi Hnr Roll; Hnr Roll; Perf Att; St of Mnth; Vllyball (J); Hotel Management; Business Administration; College of New Rochelle; New York U

FERRANTE, ALYSSA; BAYSIDE, NY; ST FRANCIS PREP; (JR); F Lan Hn Soc; Hi Hnr Roll; WWAHSS; Comm Volntr; Biology Clb; Scouts; Italian Clb; Dnce; Stg Cre; Retreat Leader; St Vincent De Paul Society; Fashion Industry; Business; Hofstra U; St John's U

FERRANTI, STACEY M; ROCHESTER, NY; BRIGHTON HS; (JR); Hnr Roll; MVP; Comm Volntr; Hosp Aide; Peer Tut/Med; Chrch Yth Grp; DARE; DECA; FBLA; Off Aide; Photog; Prom Com; Scouts; Bskball (V); Sccr (J); Sftball (V); Scholar Athlete - Basketball/Softball; NYS - Class AA Softball All Tournament Team; Communication; Business Administration; U of Dayton; U of Tampa

Feliciano, Nicole E
W Tresper Clarke HS
Westbury, NY

Fana, Diandra M
The Mary Louis AC
Corona, NY

Everts, Samantha
Hudson HS
Hudson, NY

Evan Soto, Cody J
Baldwin HS
Baldwin, NY

Epps, Alexander I
Bronx HS Of Science
Bronx, NY

Esdelle, Renee D
Queens Gateway HS
Springfield Gardens, NY

Fallon Jr, Robert
Adirondack HS
Boonville, NY

Fatade, Ayobami
IS 218 James Peter Sinnott
Brooklyn, NY

Ferranti, Stacey M
Brighton HS
Rochester, NY

FERRARA, FRANK J; COPIAGUE, NY; ST ANTHONY'S HS; (JR); Hnr Roll; MVP; Nat Hon Sy; Nat Mrt Sch Recip; Otst Ac Ach Awd; Perf Att; Pres Ac Ftns Aw; Sci Fairs; WWAHSS; Yth Ldrshp Prog; Comm Volntr; Peer Tut/Med; Chrch Yth Grp; Emplmnt; FBLA; Chr; Bsball (VJ L); Skiing (VJ); Wt Lftg (VJ); National Honor Society, Duns Scolus; Homer S Pace Business Award St Benuento; Business Major; Accounting; Pace U; Stony Brook U

FERREIRA, AMANDA; YONKERS, NY; YONKERS MIDDLE HS; (SO); Ctznshp Aw; Hi Hnr Roll; Hnr Roll; Comm Volntr; Chrch Yth Grp; Bnd; Mch Bnd; Veterinarian; Psychology; Marymount College of Fordham U

FERRETTI, ALEXANDRA R; POUGHKEEPSIE, NY; FRANKLIN DELANO ROOSEVELT HS; (JR); Hnr Roll; Nat Hon Sy; Sci Fairs; WWAHSS; Peer Tut/Med; Prom Com; Chr; Bskball (V L); Sccr (V); Vllyball (V); Cl Off (S); Stu Cncl (R); Will to Win Athlete Scholar Athlete; MHAL-All-Star Honorable Mention; Psychology; Journalism; Niagara U; Plattsburgh

FESTA, JESSICA D; FARMINGVILLE, NY; SACHEM HS EAST; (SR); Hnr Roll; Nat Hon Sy; Nat Ldrshp Svc; Comm Volntr; Peer Tut/Med; Spec Olymp Vol; 4-H; DARE; Drma Clb; Emplmnt; Tchrs Aide; Foreign Clb; Dnce; Sch Ppr (R); Presidential Student Service Award; Vice President of Volunteer Center; Communications / Public Relations; Communications / Journalism; Quinnipiac U - Accepted / Attending

FETILI, BENNY; BRONX, NY; MARBLE HILL HS FOR INTERNATIONAL STUDIES; (FR); Ctznshp Aw; Hi Hnr Roll; Hnr Roll; Nat Sci Aw; Otst Ac Ach Awd; Perf Att; Sci Fairs; Sci/Math Olympn; St Schl; St of Mnth; Comm Volntr; Hosp Aide; Mod UN; SP/M/VS; Sccr; Literacy; Social Studies; Medical Doctor / Ob/Gyn; Actress

FETILI, DAISY; BRONX, NY; BRONX INTERNATIONAL HS; (JR); Ctznshp Aw; Hnr Roll; Perf Att; Sci/Math Olympn; USAA; Yth Ldrshp Prog; SADD; Dnce; Bskball; Adv Cncl (R); Stu Cncl (S); Internship in a Law Firm; Essay About IMF and World Bank; Law; Criminal Justice; John Jay; Baruch

FETUS, MOHWANAH G; BROOKLYN, NY; ST EDMUND PREP HS; (SO); Hnr Roll; St of Mnth; Comm Volntr; Key Club; Foreign Clb; Chr; Yrbk (R); Writing; Pre-Med; Creative Writing/Journalism; New York U; Howard U

FEYEN, DIANA; CORNWALL, NY; CORNWALL CTRL HS; (JR); Hnr Roll; Comm Volntr; Hab For Humty Volntr; Key Club; Prom Com; Sccr (J); Sch Ppr (R); Yrbk (R); Sociology; Journalism

FEYGIN, ALEXANDER; BROOKLYN, NY; JAMES MADISON HS; (JR); Pres Ac Ftns Aw; Peer Tut/Med; Off Aide; Tchrs Aide; New York U; Columbia U

FIELDS, AKEEM; BROOKLYN, NY; BENJAMIN BANNEKER AC; (FR); Hnr Roll; Nat Stu Ath Day Aw; Otst Ac Ach Awd; Peer Tut/Med; Outdrs Clb; Tchrs Aide; Bnd; Chr; SP/M/VS; Bskball (J); CR (R); Associate's Degree; Master's Degree; Howard U; Florida's U

FIGUEROA, ALAINA; PT CHESTER, NY; PT CHESTER HS; (FR); Hi Hnr Roll; Hnr Roll; Otst Ac Ach Awd; Peer Tut/Med; Cmptr Clb; SADD; Chr; Clr Grd; Dnce; Wt Lftg; Stu Cncl (S); CR (R); Sch Ppr (E, R, P); EMT Training; Winter Guard; Pediatrician; Actress; Harvard U; Yale U

FIGUEROA, PATRICIA; SOUTH RICHMOND HILL, NY; JOHN ADAMS HS; (SO); Hnr Roll; Nat Hon Sy; Chrch Yth Grp; DARE; Swmg; Track; For Presenting an Outstanding Report on Africa; St Johns U; Queens College

FILIPPONE, ASHLEE B; BUFFALO, NY; CITY HONORS SCH; (JR); Hi Hnr Roll; Hnr Roll; Nat Hon Sy; Perf Att; Pres Sch; WWAHSS; DARE; Dbte Team; DECA; Emplmnt; Bnd; Cr Ctry (V L); Sftball (V L); Vllyball (V L); Lit Mag (R); College Prospects of America Participant; Forensics; Psychology; U of Pittsburgh; U of Syracuse

FINCH, ANDREW J; PENN YAN, NY; EMMANUEL BAPTIST AC; (JR); Hi Hnr Roll; Hnr Roll; Perf Att; Chrch Yth Grp; Emplmnt; SP/M/VS; Word of Life Bible Institute; Cedarville U/Indiana Wesleyan

FINCH, STEVEN R; ONEIDA, NY; ONEIDA HS; (SR); St of Mnth; Chrch Yth Grp; Emplmnt; Lib Aide; Mar Art; Near Perfect Attendance; Computer Science; Mohawk Valley Community College

FINDLATOR, JANELLE C; MEDFORD, NY; BELLPORT HS; (JR); Hi Hnr Roll; Hnr Roll; St of Mnth; Comm Volntr; Peer Tut/Med; DARE; FBLA; Key Club; Ch Chr; Peer Leadership- President; Honor Society-Vice President; International Business; Pre-Law

FINKENAGEL, AMANDA R; MIDDLE ISLAND, NY; LONGWOOD HS; (SR); Hnr Roll; Otst Ac Ach Awd; Hab For Humty Volntr; Chrch Yth Grp; Emplmnt; Photog; Bnd; Chr; Ch Chr; Dnce; Secondary Education; Photography; Dowling College; St Joseph's College

FINNEGAN, MARY E; HUNTINGTON, NY; ST DOMINIC HS; (SO); Hi Hnr Roll; Hnr Roll; Sci Fairs; Comm Volntr; Emplmnt; Off Aide; Svce Clb; SADD; IRISH Clb; Chr; Tennis (V L); Cl Off (V); Stu Cncl (V); Music Honor Society; Jensen Spirit Award; Education; Business; Fairfield U; Siena College

FISCHBACH, RUDOLF; WHITESTONE, NY; QUEENS HS FOR SCIENCES AT YORK; (FR); Hi Hnr Roll; Cmptr Clb; DARE; Merit Roll; Biochemical Engineering / PhD; Computer Engineering; Massachusetts Institute of Technology; Johns Hopkins U

FISCHER, ASHLEY L; SAUGERTIES, NY; SAUGERTIES HS; (FR); Hi Hnr Roll; Comm Volntr; Peer Tut/Med; ArtClub; Key Club; Spanish Clb; Bnd; Chr; Music Production; Art & Architecture; Berklee School of Music; Juilliard School of Music

FISCO, TINAMARIE; SAUGERTIES, NY; SAUGERTIES HS; (FR); Hi Hnr Roll; Otst Ac Ach Awd; WWAHSS; Comm Volntr; Peer Tut/Med; Chrch Yth Grp; FCCLA; Key Club; French Clb; Bnd; Chr; Dnce; Tennis (V); Created a Garden for Cancer Patients / Honor By Assembly Congress / County; International Law; Foreign Language; Cornell U; New York U

FISHER, BRIAN M; RIPLEY, NY; RIPLEY CTRL SCH; (JR); Hnr Roll; Comm Volntr; Chrch Yth Grp; DARE; Key Club; Scouts; Bnd; Sccr (V L); Meteorology; Jamestown Community College

FITTIPALDI, JANINE; NEW YORK, NY; ST MICHAEL AC; (SR); Hi Hnr Roll; Nat Hon Sy; Nat Mrt LOC; Otst Ac Ach Awd; St of Mnth; Valdctrian; WWAHSS; Peer Tut/Med; Biology Clb; Drma Clb; Prom Com; Tchrs Aide; Dnce; SP/M/VS; Stu Cncl (P, R); Yrbk (E); Scholarship for NYU's "Looking for Shakespeare 2004"; Scholarship for "Dr. Glay's Youth Theatre"; Medicine; Theatre Studies; SUNY Stony Brook; Columbia U

FITZGERALD, CHELSEA; MERRICK, NY; CALHOUN HS; (SO); Hnr Roll; Nat Hon Sy; WWAHSS; Comm Volntr; DECA; Key Club; Bdmtn (V); Tae Kwon Do -Brown Belt; Dance-10 Years

FITZMAURICE, SHANE G; HICKSVILLE, NY; HICKSVILLE HS; (FR); Hnr Roll; Kwnis Aw; Pres Ac Ftns Aw; Comm Volntr; Chrch Yth Grp; Scouts; Ch Chr; Cr Ctry (J); Ftball (J); Lcrsse (J); Wrstlg (J); Youth Work Camp Volunteer (Christian Based); Architecture

FITZPATRICK, RACHAEL; MASPETH, NY; CHRIST THE KING HS; (SO); Hnr Roll; Nat Hon Sy; St of Mnth; WWAHSS; Key Club; SADD; Sch Ppr (R); Early Childhood Education; Queens College; St John's U

FLANNIGAN, HEATHER; MONSEY, NY; RAMAPO HS; (JR); Hnr Roll; Nat Hon Sy; St of Mnth; Comm Volntr; Emplmnt; Key Club; Chr; Vllyball (J); Bowling - Varsity; Boy Scouts of America Volunteer / Lifeguard; History; Childhood Development; College of Saint Rose; Rockland Community College

FLEMING, AYLA V; BALLSTON LAKE, NY; TROY HS; (SR); Hi Hnr Roll; Hnr Roll; Nat Hon Sy; WWAHSS; Comm Volntr; Drma Clb; Emplmnt; Key Club; Mus Clb; Svce Clb; Tchrs Aide; Chr; Track (V L); Co-Member/ Founder of Students for Peace; Co-Vice Pres. of Environmental Club; Anthropology; Forensic Science; State U of New York At New Paltz

FLINT, BRITTANY G; AMSTERDAM, NY; AMSTERDAM HS; (JR); Hi Hnr Roll; Hnr Roll; Nat Hon Sy; Otst Ac Ach Awd; Comm Volntr; Peer Tut/ Med; Drma Clb; Emplmnt; Prom Com; Bnd; Dnce; Mch Bnd; SP/M/VS; Bskball (J); Tennis (V); Cl Off (S)

FLINT, GABRIELLA; GLOVERSVILLE, NY; GLOVERSVILLE HS; (SO); Hi Hnr Roll; WWAHSS; Chr; D.A.R.E. Award; Psychology; Psychology Professor

FLITT, DENNINE M; SILVER CREEK, NY; SILVER CREEK HS; (SO); Hnr Roll; WWAHSS; Comm Volntr; Peer Tut/Med; Chrch Yth Grp; Key Club; Sci Clb; Spanish Clb; Chr; SP/M/VS; Vllyball (J); Key Club Lt Governor; Business Administration

FLORES, FLORA; ELMHURST, NY; WASHINGTON IRVING HS; (FR); Hnr Roll; Perf Att; St of Mnth; St Optmst of Yr; Hosp Aide; Peer Tut/Med; ArtClub; Off Aide; Tchrs Aide; Spanish Clb; Chr; Dnce; Bskball (V); Gmnstcs (V); Sccr (V); Vllyball (V); Cl Off (P); CR (P); Yrbk (P); Dentist; Administrator; LaGuardia Community College

FLORES, JULIE; GREAT NECK, NY; (JR); Ctznshp Aw; Perf Att; WWAHSS; Comm Volntr; Emplmnt; Key Club; Photog; SADD; Chr; SP/ M/VS; Stg Cre; Fncg (J); Fld Hky (J); Ice Sktg (V)

FLORES, KARINA; UNIONDALE, NY; UNIONDALE HS; (SO); Ctznshp Aw; F Lan Hn Soc; Hi Hnr Roll; Nat Hon Sy; Sci Fairs; Comm Volntr; Emplmnt; Key Club; Bnd; Mch Bnd; 1st Place Science Fair 2004-2005

FLORES, PABLO; FAR ROCKAWAY, NY; FAR ROCKAWAY HS; (JR); Hi Hnr Roll; Hnr Roll; Nat Hon Sy; Perf Att; WWAHSS; Peer Tut/Med; Sccr (V); Wrstlg (V); Computer Engineering; Business Management; City U of New York: City College; City U of New York: Baruch College

FLORES, ROXANNA; HICKSVILLE, NY; HICKSVILLE HS; (FR); Hnr Roll; Comm Volntr; Hosp Aide; Mth Clb/Tm; Clr Grd; Chrldg (V); Lawyer; Culinary Arts

FLORES, VAL; STORMVILLE, NY; CARMEL HS; (SO); Hi Hnr Roll; Hnr Roll; Perf Att; FBLA; Skiing (V); Freshman Baseball; Engineering; Meteorology; Villanova U; Penn State U

FLORIO, CHRISTINE; BROOKLYN, NY; BISHOP KEARNEY HS; (FR); Hi Hnr Roll; Comm Volntr; Peer Tut/Med; Key Club; Italian Clb; Chr; Dnce; Speech Therapy; Psychology; New York U; Yale

FOCER, ASHLEY N; OZONE PARK, NY; ST MARY'S HS; (SR); Hnr Roll; Nat Hon Sy; WWAHSS; Comm Volntr; Drma Clb; Emplmnt; Mus Clb; Scouts; Svce Clb; Chr; Dnce; SP/M/VS; 2004 American Coed NY Teen; 2004 American Coed NY Cover Girl; Graphic Design; Musical Theatre; U of Central Florida; Fordham U

FODERA, MICHAEL O; CLIFTON PARK, NY; SHENENDEHOWA HS; (JR); Hi Hnr Roll; Hnr Roll; Pres Ac Ftns Aw; Comm Volntr; Peer Tut/Med; DARE; Emplmnt; FBLA; Skiing (V); Sccr (V); Legal; Business; U of Rochester; Boston College

FOGLIETTA, JORDAN; QUEENSBURY, NY; QUENNSBURY HS; (SR); Hi Hnr Roll; Nat Hon Sy; Perf Att; Comm Volntr; USAA National Art Award Winner; National Honor Society; Education; English; SUNY Potsdam; SUNY Oneonta

FOKAS, HOPE; DIX HILLS, NY; ST ANTHONY'S HS; (JR); Hi Hnr Roll; CARE; Comm Volntr; Quill & Scroll; SADD; Chr; Cr Ctry (VJ); Track (VJ); Sch Ppr (R); Yrbk (E); Pre-Law; U of North Carolina-Chapel Hill; U of Virginia

FOLARON, SARAH E; ELMA, NY; IROQUOIS HS; (JR); Hi Hnr Roll; Kwnis Aw; Nat Hon Sy; St of Mnth; Comm Volntr; Peer Tut/Med; Chrch Yth Grp; Key Club; Vsity Clb; French Clb; Sccr (V L); Track (J); Vsy Clb (V); Science; Mathematics

FOLCHETTI, WILLIAM G; PATTERSON, NY; CARMEL HS; (SR); Ctznshp Aw; WWAHSS; Comm Volntr; NYLC; SADD; Italian Clb; Chr; SP/ M/VS; Putnam County Youth Service Award; Communication/Public Relations; Business; Baruch College; Hunter College

FOLKES, DUKEN O; BROOKLYN, NY; JAMES MADISON HS; (FR); Ctznshp Aw; Hi Hnr Roll; Hnr Roll; Jr Eng Tech; MVP; Nat Hon Sy; Perf Att; Pres Sch; Sci Fairs; St of Mnth; Peer Tut/Med; Spec Olymp Vol; Biology Clb; Cmptr Clb; DARE; Jr Ach; Mth Clb/Tm; Mus Clb; Sci Clb; Bnd; Bskball (J); Track (J); Stu Cncl (V); Technology; Medical; Baruch College; Brooklyn College

FOON, CHRISTOPHER T; BROOKLYN, NY; STUYVESANT HS; (SO); Key Club; Mth Clb/Tm; Stg Cre

FORBES, ASHLEY M; RYE BROOK, NY; BLIND BROOK HS; (SO); Comm Volntr; Peer Tut/Med; Red Cr Aide; DARE; Scouts; Svce Clb; SADD; Tmpl Yth Grp; Sccr (V); CR (R); Sch Ppr (R); Yrbk (R, P); Horseback Rider for 12 Years; Interior Design; European History; New York U; Syracuse U

FORCIONE, BRITTANY; CHITTENANGO, NY; CHITTENANGO HS; (JR); Hi Hnr Roll; Nat Hon Sy; St of Mnth; WWAHSS; Chrch Yth Grp; Drma Clb; Emplmnt; Chr; Orch; SP/M/VS; Sccr (C); Track (V); Vllyball (C); Cl Off (P); Business; Spa/Massage Therapy

FORD, SHARON; BRONX, NY; AQUINAS HS; (JR); Hnr Roll; Sci Fairs; St of Mnth; Comm Volntr; Chrch Yth Grp; Emplmnt; SADD; Stu Cncl (R); CR (R); Modeling School; Modeling Association of America International - Winner-Runway 2003 / Make-Up 2004; Political Science; Law; New York U; Columbia U

FORD III, REUBEN; BRONX, NY; ST RAYMOND HS; (SO); Hnr Roll; Comm Volntr; Emplmnt; Pathways for Youth Scholastic Excellence; English Award; Lawyer; Law Enforcement; Howard U; Albany U

FORETTE, AMANDA; MOOERS FORKS, NY; NORTHEASTERN CLINTON CTRL SCH; (JR); Hnr Roll; Outdrs Clb; 4 Years of Spanish; 3 Years of Art; Major in Design; Art Degree; Plattsburg State; Clinton Community

FORNARI, MARCI J; GREAT NECK, NY; GREAT NECK SOUTH HS; (FR); Hnr Roll; Lcrsse (J); Swmg (V); Doctor (MD); Colgate U; U of Penn

FORTUNE, CLAUDIA; BROOKLYN, NY; SHEEPSHEAD BAY HS; (JR); Hnr Roll; Perf Att; Clr Grd; Vllyball (V); Pediatric Surgeon; Pediatrician

FOSBURG, KRISTIN; GERRY, NY; CASSADAGA VALLEY MHS; (JR); Hnr Roll; Nat Hon Sy; St of Mnth; WWAHSS; Yth Ldrshp Prog; Peer Tut/ Med; Chrch Yth Grp; Key Clb; Off Aide; Photog; Prom Com; SADD; Tchrs Aide; Spanish Clb; Chr; Chrldg (VJ L); Stu Cncl (R); Accounting; Business; U of Southern California; UCLA

FOWLER, SARA L; BLOSSVALE, NY; CAMDEN HS; (FR); Hnr Roll; Comm Volntr; 4-H; Chrch Yth Grp; Drma Clb; Mus Clb; Scouts; Chr; SP/ M/VS; Tennis (J); Stu Cncl (R); CR (R); Silver Project for Girl Scout; Crime Scene Investigation; Teacher; SUNY Buffalo; Mohawk Valley Community College

FOX, LINA; SOMERS, NY; JOHN JAY HS; (JR); Hnr Roll; Nat Hon Sy; WWAHSS; Comm Volntr; Chrch Yth Grp; Bnd; Competitive Gymnastics (USA); Biology Major; Doctor of Veterinary Medicine; State of New York At Geneseo; State of New York At Binghamton

Folchetti, William G
Carmel HS
Patterson, NY

Focer, Ashley N
St Mary's HS
Ozone Park, NY

Fischer, Ashley L
Saugerties HS
Saugerties, NY

Fetus, Mohwanah G
St Edmund Prep HS
Brooklyn, NY

National
Honor Roll
Spring 2005

Ferrara, Frank J
St Anthony's HS
Copiague, NY

Fisco, Tinamarie
Saugerties HS
Saugerties, NY

Foglietta, Jordan
Quennsbury HS
Queensbury, NY

Fowler, Sara L
Camden HS
Blossvale, NY

FOZARD, JESSICA; THORNWOOD, NY; WESTLAKE HS; (SR); F Lan Hn Soc; Hnr Roll; Nat Hon Sy; Comm Volntr; Peer Tut/Med; Dbte Team; Emplmnt; JSA; Spanish Clb; Tennis (J); Sch Ppr (E); Political Science; Languages/Translator; Binghamton U

FRAGOSO, JEVON C; WHITESTONE, NY; HOLY TRINITY MS; (MS); Hnr Roll; Perf Att; Comm Volntr; Biology Clb; Chr; SP/M/VS; Sch Ppr (E); Study Piano for Six Years; Law; Engineering; Columbia U; Berkeley U

FRANCIS, KERSIAND; BRONX, NY; ALFRED E SMITH VOC HS; (FR); Perf Att; Chess; Mth Clb/Tm; Mus Clb; Ftball (J); Master's Degree; Florida State

FRANCIS, KORI J; NORTH COLLINS, NY; NORTH COLLINS HS; (SR); Hnr Roll; Nat Hon Sy; Comm Volntr; 4-H; ArtClub; Chrch Yth Grp; DARE; Drma Clb; Emplmnt; FTA; Photog; Bnd; Chr; Ch Chr; SP/M/VS; Sftball (J); Vsy Clb (V); Vllyball (VJ); Cl Off (T); Yrbk (E, R, P); Future Educators of America Officer; Mass Media/Communications Major; Calvin College

FRANCIS, SHANAGAE; BRONX, NY; HARRY S TRUMAN HS; (JR); Hnr Roll; Otst Ac Ach Awd; Perf Att; CARE; Comm Volntr; Peer Tut/Med; Chrch Yth Grp; Tmpl Yth Grp; Chr; Ch Chr; Dnce; SP/M/VS; Chrldg (J)

FRANCIS, SHAUNA A; MT VERNON, NY; MT VERNON HS; (SO); Hi Hnr Roll; Hnr Roll; Perf Att; WWAHSS; Hab For Humty Volntr; Drma Clb; Mth Clb/Tm; Chr; Sch Ppr (E); Participated in ACTSO - Poetry Competition-Received a Certificate; Nursing / Singing; Theatre; Harvard U; Miami U

FRANCO, RAISSA; MAMARONECK, NY; MAMARONECK HS; (FR); Hi Hnr Roll; Hnr Roll; Nat Hon Sy; Sci/Math Olympn; St of Mnth; Valdctrian; Comm Volntr; Chrch Yth Grp; DARE; Key Club; Bskball; Stu Cncl; Guitar; Science Major; PhD / Pediatrics; New York U; Columbia U

FRANCOIS, ALGESTE; QUEENS VILLAGE, NY; SPRINGFIELD GARDENS HS; (JR); Nat Hon Sy; Dnce; Bskball; Vllyball; Veterinarian-Animal Doctor; SUNY-State U of New York

FRANK, MICHELE; SKANEATELES, NY; SKANEATELES HS; (JR); Hnr Roll; Yth Ldrshp Prog; Comm Volntr; Peer Tut/Med; Red Cr Aide; DARE; Emplmnt; Mus Clb; Scouts; SADD; French Clb; Acpl Chr; Chr; Lit Mag (R); Silver Award in Girl Scouts; Religious Award in Girl Scouts; Fashion Merchandising; Music History Major; Boston U; Syracuse U

FRANKEL, BRITTNEY; HEWLETT, NY; G W HEWLETT HS; (FR); Hi Hnr Roll; St of Mnth; WWAHSS; Key Club; Chr; Dnce; Chrldg (J); Sch Ppr (R); Journalism; Medical Degree; Duke U; Cornell U

FRANKLIN, JESSICA P; BRONX, NY; THE AC OF MOUNT SAINT URSULA; (JR); Ctznshp Aw; Comm Volntr; Peer Tut/Med; ArtClub; Emplmnt; Lib Aide; Photog; SADD; Ch Chr; Hsbk Rdg (J); Swmg (J); Lit Mag (E); Sch Ppr (E, P); Church Youth Council President; Parks and Recreation Volunteer; Mass Communications; Pre-Dentistry; Tulane U; New York U

FRANKLIN, MATTHEW L; SYOSSET, NY; SYOSSET HS; (SO); Hnr Roll; Nat Hon Sy; Sci Fairs; Comm Volntr; DECA; Spanish Clb; Bnd; Sccr (J); Track (J); Winner of 2004 Stock Market LI Game; 2004 Career Day Participant; CPA; Lawyer; U of Binghamton; U of Maryland

FRASER, EBONY; FAR ROCKAWAY, NY; SPRINGFIELD GARDENS HS; (JR); Hnr Roll; WWAHSS; Peer Tut/Med; Emplmnt; Off Aide; Scouts; Svce Clb; Dnce; Sch Ppr (R); Yrbk (E); Psychology; Nursing; CW Post; SUNY Plattsburgh

FRASER, LEETROY; FAR ROCKAWAY, NY; THOMAS EDISON HS; (FR); Nat Stu Ath Day Aw; Perf Att; St of Mnth; Peer Tut/Med; Emplmnt; Stg Cre; Bskball (C); Tennis (C); Stu Cncl (R); Lit Mag (R); Computer Technology; Georgia Tech, New York Tech Inst; Connecticut U

FRAZER, TAYSHA; BROOKLYN, NY; CATHERINE MC AULEY HS; (JR); F Lan Hn Soc; Nat Ldrshp Svc; Nat Sci Aw; Otst Ac Ach Awd; Perf Att; Yth Ldrshp Prog; Comm Volntr; Hosp Aide; ArtClub; Chrch Yth Grp; Mth Clb/Tm; Prom Com; Tchrs Aide; Tmpl Yth Grp; Spanish Clb; Acpl Chr; Chr; Ch Chr; Dnce; Bskball; Yrbk (E); St Charles Luwalga / NY Young Black Achievers Award - Boro Hall; Criminal Justice; Paralegal; Saint Leo U; St John's U

FREEMAN, ADAM M; CUBA, NY; CUBA RUSHFORD MIDDLE HS; (SO); Emplmnt; Wdwrkg Clb; Skiing (VJ); Community Baseball, 2 Part Time Jobs

FREY, MARIELLE R; PATCHOGUE, NY; BAYPORT BLUE POINT HS; (JR); Hi Hnr Roll; Hnr Roll; Pres Sch; Sci Fairs; St of Mnth; Yth Ldrshp Prog; Comm Volntr; Chrch Yth Grp; DARE; Emplmnt; Chr; Sftball (J); Connetquot Tournament / Travel Softball Team; Bachelor's Degree; RN / Teaching; Stony Brook U; Oneonta State College

FRIEDLIN, ELYSE B; LITTLE NECK, NY; BENJAMIN N CARDOZO HS; (SO); Hnr Roll; Sci Fairs; Key Club; Mus Clb; Chr; USY; Journalism; English; State U At New Paltz

FRIEDMAN, CHLOE; CANDOR, NY; SPENCER-VAN ETTEN HS; (FR); Hi Hnr Roll; Hnr Roll; Otst Ac Ach Awd; USAA; WWAHSS; Key Club; Bnd; Jzz Bnd; SP/M/VS; Sccr (J); Cl Off (S); USAA Nominee; Who's Who Among American HS Students Nominee; Photography; Teaching

FRIEDMAN, JENNA; GREAT NECK, NY; GREAT NECK SOUTH HS; (SO); MVP; Pres Ac Ftns Aw; St of Mnth; Peer Tut/Med; DECA; Fr of Library; Key Club; Pep Squd; Tmpl Yth Grp; Dnce; Chrldg (C); Yrbk (P)

FRIEDMAN, SAMANTHA; WOODMERE, NY; G.W. HEWLETT HS; (SO); Hi Hnr Roll; WWAHSS; ArtClub; Key Club; Sccr (V); CR (R); Sch Ppr (R)

FRIEDSON, JORDAN S; MONROE, NY; MONROE-WOODBURY HS; (JR); Hi Hnr Roll; Pres Ac Ftns Aw; Peer Tut/Med; DARE; Drma Clb; Emplmnt; SP/M/VS; Wt Lftg; Formed Improvisational Group; Business; Theater; Syracuse U; New York U

FRONCZAK, KELLY M; ATTICA, NY; ATTICA SR HS; (SO); Hnr Roll; Perf Att; Yth Ldrshp Prog; Comm Volntr; Spec Olymp Vol; Chrch Yth Grp; Drma Clb; Emplmnt; Fr of Library; Lib Aide; Bnd; Chr; Mch Bnd; SP/M/VS; Swmg (V CL); Cl Off (V); Sch Ppr (P); Early Childhood; Teaching Degree; SUNY Geneseo; SUNY Brockport

FROUDE, JACK; MALDEN ON HUDSON, NY; SAUGERTIES HS; (FR); Hi Hnr Roll; Spec Olymp Vol; Dbte Team; Key Club; Spanish Clb; Chr; Lcrsse (V); Skiing; Sccr; Psychology; Engineering; Stanford U; Cambridge U

FU, KENNETH; TONAWANDA, NY; SWEET HOME HS; (JR); Hnr Roll; Nat Hon Sy; FBLA; French Clb; Chr; French Honor Society; Accounting; Cornell U; CUNY-Baruch College

FUENTECILLA, MONINA-FREYA; ELMHURST, NY; THE MARY LOUIS AC; (JR); All Am Sch; Hi Hnr Roll; Hnr Roll; Nat Hon Sy; Nat Sci Aw; WWAHSS; Comm Volntr; Sci Clb; Latin Clb; International Business; The American International U in London-Richmond

FUENTES, BERNADETTE; HICKSVILLE, NY; HOLY TRINITY DIOCESAN HS; (SO); Hnr Roll; Pres Ac Ftns Aw; Sftball (V); Vllyball (JC); National Junior Honor Society; Forensics; Loyola U; Boston U

FULLEM, ZOE; ALBANY, NY; ALBANY HS; (SO); Hi Hnr Roll; WWAHSS; Yth Ldrshp Prog; Hab For Humty Volntr; ArtClub; Drma Clb; Key Club; Stg Cre; Track (V); Crew-Varsity; Lifeguard - Red Cross Certified; Social Work; Spanish; Northwestern U; Stanford U

FULLER, CHARLES R; HASTINGS, NY; TECH CAREER CTR; (SR); Hnr Roll; Natef Brakes / Electrical / Engine / Suspension Outstanding Effort Award; Diesel Technologies; SUNY Cobleskill

FULTON, KENESHA R; HEMPSTEAD, NY; HEMPSTEAD HS; (SO); Hi Hnr Roll; Hnr Roll; Nat Hon Sy; Sci/Math Olympn; WWAHSS; Emplmnt; Chr; Nursing; Business Communications; North Carolina A & T U; Howard U

FUNG, MANDY; BROOKLYN, NY; JAMES MADISON HS; (JR); Hnr Roll; Nat Hon Sy; St of Mnth; WWAHSS; Comm Volntr; Red Cr Aide; Emplmnt; Off Aide; Svce Clb; Tchrs Aide; Chr; Science Honor Society; Forensic Pathologist; Pharmacist; Cornell; Binghamton

FURMAN, CHAD; DELANSON, NY; DUANESBURG JR/SR HS; (JR); Cmptr Clb; Drma Clb; SP/M/VS; Wt Lftg (V); Lit Mag (R); Rock Climbing; School Web Design; Particle Physics; Software Engineer; Rochester Polytechnical Engineer; Rensselaer Polytechnic Institute

FURTADO, COURTNEY M; CHITTENANGO, NY; CHITTENANGO HS; (JR); F Lan Hn Soc; Hi Hnr Roll; Nat Hon Sy; St of Mnth; WWAHSS; Comm Volntr; AL Aux Girls; Chrch Yth Grp; Emplmnt; Chr; Sccr (V); Track (V); Biology

FUSCO, ANDREW; BALDWINSVILLE, NY; CW BAKER HS; (JR); Hi Hnr Roll; WWAHSS; Comm Volntr; Dbte Team; Key Club; Off Aide; Bnd; CR (R); Perfect Average Club - 8th Grade Social Studies; Economics; Binghamton U; SUNY Albany

FUSCO, JONATHAN; STATEN ISLAND, NY; CURTIS HS; (JR); Hi Hnr Roll; Hnr Roll; Nat Hon Sy; Comm Volntr; Emplmnt; Mus Clb; Bnd; Chr; Drm Mjr; Jzz Bnd; Arista; Jazz Ensemble; Law

GABBEY, JENNIFER; CORFU, NY; PEMBROKE JR/SR HS; (JR); Hi Hnr Roll; Hnr Roll; MVP; Nat Hon Sy; WWAHSS; Comm Volntr; Chrch Yth Grp; Key Club; Vsity Clb; German Clb; Bskball (V); Scr Kpr (VJ); Track (V C); Vllyball; Physical Therapy; Daemen College; Brockport

GABBEY, KIM; CORFU, NY; PEMBROKE JR/SR HS; (SO); Hi Hnr Roll; Chrch Yth Grp; Key Club; Vsity Clb; Bskball (J); Track (V); Vllyball (J); Wt Lftg; Bible Club; Accounting

GACHE, DANIELLE N; FREEPORT, NY; FREEPORT HS; (JR); Hi Hnr Roll; Hnr Roll; Nat Hon Sy; Sci Fairs; Comm Volntr; Peer Tut/Med; Drma Clb; Emplmnt; Key Club; Mus Clb; Off Aide; Acpl Chr; Chr; Dnce; Orch; CR (R); Hofstra U; Adelphi U

GADDIS, SHEENA D; SPRING VALLEY, NY; SPRING VALLEY HS; (SR); Hnr Roll; Otst Ac Ach Awd; St of Mnth; Chrch Yth Grp; Emplmnt; Key Club; Ch Chr; Orch; SP/M/VS; Chrldg (V); Track (V); Vllyball; Stu Cncl (R); NAACP Assistant Secretary; Nursing/Child Health; Pace U; SUNY Plattsburgh

GAETA, MERISSA; KIRKWOOD, NY; WINDSOR HS; (JR); Hnr Roll; MVP; WWAHSS; DARE; Vsity Clb; French Clb; Bskball (V); Sccr (V); All Metro Basketball Selection; All Star/Conference for Bball; Sports Management; Sports Medicine; Bucknell; Albany

GAETANO, MICHAEL C; UTICA, NY; NOTRE DAME JR/SR HS; (FR); Hi Hnr Roll; St of Mnth; Bsball (J); Ftball (J); Utica Falcons Baseball; Engineer; Pharmacist; Albany

GAFOOR, NATASHA; S RICHMOND HL, NY; RICHMOND HILL HS; (SR); Hnr Roll; Peer Tut/Med; Off Aide; Tchrs Aide; Bdmtn (L); Yrbk (R); Trained Peer Negotiator; Trained Peer Mediator; Bachelor's Degree in Business Administration; Queens College; Lehman College

GAFUR, GIBRAN N; BRONX, NY; WALTON HS; (FR); Perf Att; Bskball; Vllyball; Fitness; Engineer; Hostos College

GAGLIO, JAMES T; WEBSTER, NY; WEBSTER SCHROEDER HS; (SO); Hi Hnr Roll; Sci/Math Olympn; WWAHSS; Emplmnt; Key Club; Mod UN; Orch; Rochester Scholars; Alfred U Summer Institute in Science & Engineering; Computer Science; Robotics; Rensselaer Polytechnic Institute; Carnegie Mellon U

GAGLIONE, JESSICA L; VALLEY STREAM, NY; CENTRAL HS; (JR); F Lan Hn Soc; Hi Hnr Roll; Nat Hon Sy; Comm Volntr; Peer Tut/Med; Emplmnt; Mus Clb; Photog; Prom Com; Chr; Dnce; Orch; SP/M/VS; Tri-M Music Honor Society; Foreign Language Honor Society; Education; Music

GAINES, SULEKA; BROOKLYN, NY; METROPOLITAN CORPORATE AC; (JR); Nat Ldrshp Svc; Perf Att; Comm Volntr; Emplmnt; Chr; Ch Chr; Cl Off (T); Sch Ppr (E); Perfect Attendance; Public Color; Law; Writing; John Jay College

GAITHER, CECILY N; BRONX, NY; CELIA CRUZ BRONX HS OF MUSIC; (FR); Hnr Roll; Perf Att; Sci Fairs; Mus Clb; Chr; Currently Learning Piano; Got an Excellent in 1st NYSSMA Solo; English; Psychiatry; New York U; Columbia U

GALANOPOULOS, STAUROULA; WHITESTONE, NY; FRANCIS LEWIS HS; (JR); Ctznshp Aw; Hnr Roll; Nat Hon Sy; Perf Att; Valdctrian; Comm Volntr; Peer Tut/Med; DARE; Emplmnt; Lib Aide; Photog; Tchrs Aide; Greek Clb; Ch Chr; Clr Grd; The Three Hierarchs Award of Excellence; Comptroller's Award; Psychology and Philosophy Major; Master's in English and History; New York U

GALARZA, ALEX A; MIDDLETOWN, NY; MIDDLETOWN HS; (JR); Hnr Roll; WWAHSS; Tchrs Aide; Bsball (V); Ftball (V); Track (V); Math Education; Physical Education; Florida State U; U of Miami

GALATIOTO, CATHERINE M; MARGARETVILLE, NY; MARGARETVILLE CTRL SCH; (JR); Hi Hnr Roll; Hnr Roll; Nat Hon Sy; Comm Volntr; Drma Clb; Emplmnt; Mus Clb; Prom Com; SADD; Acpl Chr; Chr; Ch Chr; SP/M/VS; Bskball (J); Chrldg (V); Sccr (VJCL); Sftball (VJ L); Cl Off (P); American Music Abroad; Education; English; Oneonta State; Albany State

GALKOWSKI, JEFF; ENDICOTT, NY; UNION-ENDICOTT HS; (SO); Hi Hnr Roll; Otst Ac Ach Awd; Sci/Math Olympn; WWAHSS; Peer Tut/Med; Key Club; Mth Clb/Tm; Sci Clb; SADD; Gmnstcs (V); Lit Mag (E); Piano; Programming Team; Chemistry; Engineering

GALLO, CONNOR; TROY, NY; LANSINGBURGH HS; (FR); Ctznshp Aw; F Lan Hn Soc; Hi Hnr Roll; St of Mnth; Chr; Swg Chr; Bskball (J); Ftball (J); Wt Lftg (J); Yrbk (R)

GALYUTINA, YELENA; STATEN ISLAND, NY; BENJAMIN CARDOZO HS; (SO); Sci Fairs; St of Mnth; WWAHSS; Comm Volntr; Chrch Yth Grp; Key Club; Ch Chr; Dnce; Psychiatrist; Teaching; Pace U; Baruch College

GAMACHE, NICK; SYRACUSE, NY; HENNINGER HS; (SO); Hi Hnr Roll; Hnr Roll; Perf Att; ArtClub; Veterinarian

GANAS, JOYCE; INWOOD, NY; LAWRENCE HS; (JR); Hnr Roll; Nat Hon Sy; Hosp Aide; ArtClub; Key Club; Prom Com; Bnd; Mch Bnd; Pep Bnd; Cl Off (V); CR (V); National Art Honor Society; Pre-Med; New York U

GANDHI, ANU; NEW HYDE PARK, NY; SEWANHAKA HS; (SR); Hi Hnr Roll; Hnr Roll; Nat Hon Sy; St of Mnth; Yth Ldrshp Prog; Comm Volntr; Peer Tut/Med; Emplmnt; FBLA; Key Club; Mth Clb/Tm; Mod UN; Prom Com; SADD; Dnce; Orch; Bskball (J, L); Sccr (VJCL); Sftball (JL); Cl Off (T); CR (R); Sch Ppr (R); Yrbk (R); Summer Internships at Cold Spring Harbor Laboratory and Mount Sinai School of Medicine; Varsity Girls Soccer Student Scholar Athlete 2004-2005; Major - Biochemistry; Professional Degree Programs - Medical Degree / Pre-Med; Accepted / Attending SUNY Stony Brook Class of 2009

GANETIS, SARA; JAMESPORT, NY; MERCY HS; (SO); Hi Hnr Roll; WWAHSS; Comm Volntr; Photog; Tennis (V); Stu Cncl (V); National Latin Award; Latin Neclematio Winner; Meteorology

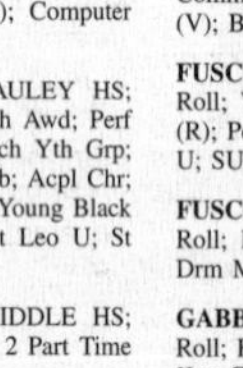
Gache, Danielle N
Freeport HS
Freeport, NY

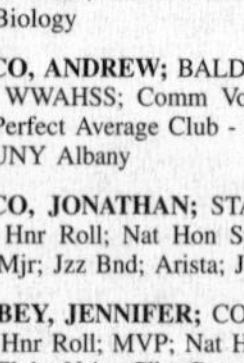
Frazer, Taysha
Catherine Mc Auley HS
Brooklyn, NY

National
Honor Roll
Spring 2005

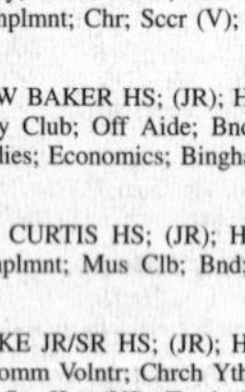
Frank, Michele
Skaneateles HS
Skaneateles, NY

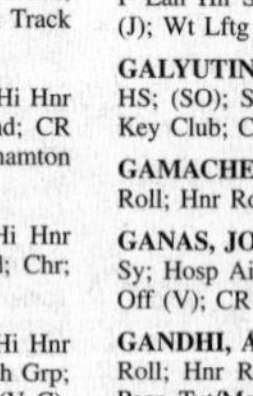
Gaddis, Sheena D
Spring Valley HS
Spring Valley, NY

GANGONE, LIZ; NEW HYDE PARK, NY; SEWANHAKA HS; (JR); Hi Hnr Roll; Hnr Roll; Nat Hon Sy; Otst Ac Ach Awd; Sci/Math Olympn; WWAHSS; Key Club; Mus Clb; Chr; Tennis (V L); Sch Ppr (R); Science Research Paper and Internship; Physics Major; Medical Degree; Northwestern U; College of William and Mary

GANNON, CIARA; BRONX, NY; DEWITT CLINTON HS; (FR); Ctznshp Aw; Hnr Roll; Perf Att; Yth Ldrshp Prog; Peer Tut/Med; Chess; DARE; Key Club; Adv Cncl (R); Stu Cncl (R); CR (R); Sch Ppr (E, R); Yrbk (R); Summer Mediation Program; Teaching; Columbia U; Fordham U

GAO, JING; FLUSHING, NY; FRANCIS LEWIS HS; (SO); Hnr Roll; Perf Att; Doctor; Lawyer; U of Pennsylvania; Dartmouth U

GAO, YING L; STATEN ISLAND, NY; TOTTENVILLE HS; (JR); Hnr Roll; Nat Hon Sy; Nat Mrt Fin; Nat Mrt LOC; Otst Ac Ach Awd; Perf Att; Sci Fairs; USAA; WWAHSS; ArtClub; Fr of Library; Asian Clb; Sccr; Vllyball; Asian Club; Science Fair; Medical Field; Architecture

GARAY, STEPHANIE; FLUSHING, NY; CATHEDRAL HS; (FR); Otst Ac Ach Awd; Perf Att; St of Mnth; Mus Clb; Acpl Chr; Bnd; Chr; Ch Chr; 1st Place Singing Award; 1st Place Dancing Award; Veterinarian; Soprano Singer; U of New Haven; Rosemont College

GARCIA, ALYSSA I; YONKERS, NY; SAUNDERS TRADES & TECH HS; (SO); F Lan Hn Soc; Hnr Roll; Comm Volntr; Hosp Aide; Due to Medical Condition Certain Action and Sports Have Not Been Accomplished; Fashion Design; Fashion Merchandise; Parsons; Fashion Institute of Technology

GARCIA, FRANKIE; NEW YORK, NY; FIORELLO H LA GUARDIA HS; (JR); Hnr Roll; Comm Volntr; Chrch Yth Grp; Mus Clb; Dnce; Orch; Bsball (V); Accounting; Culinary Arts; Manhattan College; Art Institute of New York City

GARCIA, JEANETTE; BRONX, NY; HS FOR MEDIA AND COMMUNI; (SO); Hi Hnr Roll; Hnr Roll; Otst Ac Ach Awd; Perf Att; Pres Ac Ftns Aw; St of Mnth; Comm Volntr; Peer Tut/Med; DARE; Drma Clb; Emplmnt; Mod UN; SADD; Stu Cncl (R); CR (R); HIV/AIDS Internship; Minds Matter Prep Program; Business/Fashion Design; TV Production; Yale U; Columbia U

GARCIA, JESSICA; BROOKLYN, NY; SHEEPSHEAD BAY HS; (FR); Hnr Roll; Perf Att; Comm Volntr; Drma Clb; Dnce; Mch Bnd; SP/M/VS; Stg Cre; Bsball (V); Hsbk Rdg (V); Mar Art (V); Scr Kpr (V); Sftball (V); Tennis (V); Track (V); Psychologist; Acting; Brooklyn College; Harvard U

GARCIA, KEVYN; JAMAICA, NY; GATEWAY TO HEALTH SCIENCES SCH; (SO); Pres Ac Ftns Aw; Yth Ldrshp Prog; Comm Volntr; Chrch Yth Grp; Cmptr Clb; Emplmnt; Mus Clb; Bnd; Ch Chr; Clr Grd; SP/M/VS; Lit Mag (E); Member of School Website Committee; Computer Engineer; Architecture; ITT Technical Institute; Arizona State U

GARCIA, TIRZA; BRONX, NY; HOSTOS HS; (JR); Duke TS; Perf Att; St Optmst of Yr; Yth Ldrshp Prog; Comm Volntr; Red Cr Aide; Emplmnt; Lib Aide; Off Aide; Tchrs Aide; Bnd; Dnce; Orch; Chrldg (V); Ftball (V); Gmnstcs (l); Sccr (V); Tennis (l); Lit Mag (R); Yrbk (R); architect; teacher; City U of New York; Georgia Tech

GARDNER, ABIGAIL; BROOKLYN, NY; STATEN ISLAND TECH HS; (JR); Hnr Roll; Sci Fairs; St of Mnth; Valdctrian; WWAHSS; Comm Volntr; Chrch Yth Grp; Drma Clb; Emplmnt; Ch Chr; Cr Ctry (J); History; Interior Design; Indiana Wesleyan U; Messiah College

GARLAN, KEVIN C; JACKSON HEIGHTS, NY; ARCHBISHOP MOLLOY HS; (JR); Gov Hnr Prg; Hnr Roll; Bskball (V); Cr Ctry (J); Skiing (L); Track (J); CR (R); Business; Law; Bentley College; SUNY Binghamton

GARLITOS, EMMANUEL A; PT JEFFERSON STATION, NY; COMSEWOGUE HS; (SO); F Lan Hn Soc; Hi Hnr Roll; WWAHSS; Comm Volntr; Spec Olymp Vol; Chrch Yth Grp; Key Club; Photog; Scouts; Svce Clb; French Clb; Orch; SP/M/VS; Lit Mag (P); Grade of 98 on NYSSMA for Piano - 2004; Biology; Medicine; Stanford U; Columbia U

GARLOCK, KELSEY; HAMLIN, NY; BROCKPORT HS; (FR); Hi Hnr Roll; Hnr Roll; Nat Sci Aw; Otst Ac Ach Awd; Sci Fairs; Comm Volntr; Chrch Yth Grp; Mod UN; Tchrs Aide; Swmg (J L); Stu Cncl (R); CR (R); Ice Hockey for Club Outside School; Political Science; Writing; Brown U, Northwestern, Stanford

GARNER, DOMINIQUE D; BRONX, NY; FREDERICK DOUGLASS SEC SCH; (SO); Hnr Roll; Otst Ac Ach Awd; Perf Att; Pres Sch; WWAHSS; Peer Tut/Med; Chrch Yth Grp; Emplmnt; Ch Chr; Clr Grd; Dnce; Flg Crps; Psychology; Medicine; Temple U; Pennsylvania State U

GARNETT, EURAIYA; BRONX, NY; ST PIUS V HS; (JR); Hnr Roll; Comm Volntr; Dnce; Robotics Club/Beta Club; Animation; Video Game Programming; New York U; Savannah College of Art & Design

GARRAWAY, MAYA; BRONX, NY; JOHN F KENNEDY HS; (SO); Perf Att; Comm Volntr; Chrch Yth Grp; Ch Chr; Track (V); Biology; Education

GARRY, LAURA; WATERTOWN, NY; WATERTOWN HS; (SO); Hnr Roll; St of Mnth; WWAHSS; Comm Volntr; Chrch Yth Grp; Key Club; Photog; Fld Hky (J); Track (VJ); Vllyball (VJC); Who's Who Among American High School Students; Film; San Diego State U; U of Washington

GARRY, MATTHEW; EAST MEADOW, NY; EAST MEADOW HS; (SO); Hnr Roll; Perf Att; Peer Tut/Med; Key Club; Mus Clb; Tmpl Yth Grp; Bnd; Jzz Bnd; Mch Bnd; Rlr Hky (V); Sccr (J); Cl Off (T); CR (T); All County Band 2004; Law; Criminology

GARTMAYER, KRISTI; LOCUST VALLEY, NY; OUR LADY OF MERCY AC; (SO); Hnr Roll; WWAHSS; Comm Volntr; Peer Tut/Med; Drma Clb; Pep Squd; Svce Clb; Spanish Clb; Drl Tm; SP/M/VS; Stg Cre; Hsbk Rdg (V); Rowing Team (Crew); Fashion Merchandising; Fashion Institute of Tech

GARWAI WU, DIANA; NEW YORK, NY; BRONX HS OF SCIENCE; (SR); Nat Hon Sy; Sci Fairs; WWAHSS; Comm Volntr; Mth Clb/Tm; Engineering; Cornell U

GARY, KELLI; PARISHVILLE, NY; PARISHVILLE-HOPKINTON CTRL; (FR); Hi Hnr Roll; Hnr Roll; Otst Ac Ach Awd; Perf Att; Pres Ac Ftns Aw; DARE; Photog; Scouts; Sccr (J); Sch Ppr (R, P); Yrbk (R, P)

GARZIA, MICHELLE; EAST MEADOW, NY; EAST MEADOW HS; (FR); Hnr Roll; WWAHSS; Emplmnt; Orch; Chrldg (J); New York U

GASBY, LARAIDA; FAR ROCKAWAY, NY; BEACH CHANNEL HS; (JR); Hnr Roll; Yth Ldrshp Prog; Comm Volntr; Emplmnt; Dnce; Tennis (V); Track (V); Completion of Toastmasters Youth Leader Program; Journalism Communications; Psychology; Hampton U Morgan State; Virginia State, North Carolina Central

GASKIN, TIMOTHY; HEMPSTEAD, NY; HEMPSTEAD HS; (FR); Hi Hnr Roll; Hnr Roll; MVP; Nat Hon Sy; St of Mnth; Comm Volntr; ArtClub; Chess; DARE; Mus Clb; Scouts; Bnd; Mch Bnd; Bskball (J); Ftball (J); Lcrsse (V); Medical Doctor; Sports; Florida State U; Johns Hopkins U

GATLING, IYESHA; BROOKLYN, NY; PAUL ROBESON HS; (MS); Hnr Roll; Perf Att; Business Management; Business Administration; Albany State U; U of Illinois

GATTO, BIANCA; LOCKPORT, NY; LOCKPORT HS; (SO); Hi Hnr Roll; WWAHSS; Comm Volntr; Key Club; Pep Squd; French Clb; Bnd; Dnce

GAUDIOSO, MOLLY; WEBSTER, NY; WEBSTER THOMAS HS; (SO); F Lan Hn Soc; Hi Hnr Roll; Hnr Roll; Otst Ac Ach Awd; Sci Fairs; Comm Volntr; Chrch Yth Grp; Key Club; Mod UN; Ntl Beta Clb; Scouts; French Clb; Ch Chr; Clr Grd; Dnce; SP/M/VS; Stu Cncl (R); CR (R); My Ceramic Piece Was Chosen for a Rep. in Town Village.; Law Using Foreign Language; Chemistry/Physics; New York U

GAVRIYELOVA, SONYA; FOREST HILLS, NY; FOREST HILLS HS; (JR); Hnr Roll; Nat Hon Sy; Perf Att; Sci Fairs; St of Mnth; Yth Ldrshp Prog; Comm Volntr; Hosp Aide; Peer Tut/Med; Drma Clb; Fr of Library; Mth Clb/Tm; Mus Clb; Photog; Sci Clb; SADD; Spanish Clb; Bnd; Chr; Dnce; SP/M/VS; Cr Ct Ski (V L); Dvng (J); Hsbk Rdg (J); Ice Sktg (J); Skiing (C); Sftball (J); Swmg (J); Lit Mag (E); Yrbk (E, P); Hebrew Club/Volunteer in Forest Hills Community House; Congregation Machane Chodosh; Dentistry; Doctor in Pharmacy; St. Johns U; Long Island U

GEKONGE, DISMUS; ALBANY, NY; ALBANY HS; (JR); Hi Hnr Roll; Hnr Roll; Yth Ldrshp Prog; Red Cr Aide; Chrch Yth Grp

GENTLES, LARRY L; CAMBRIA HEIGHTS, NY; JOHN BOWNE HS; (JR); Hnr Roll; Perf Att; Drma Clb; Key Club; Mus Clb; Bnd; Chr; Sccr (V); Tennis (J); Track (J); CR (P); Lawyer; John Jay College; New York U

GEORGE, ALEXANDRA; EAST SETAUKET, NY; (MS); Orch; SP/M/VS; Swmg (C); Tennis; Cl Off (P); CR (P); Sch Ppr (E); Concert Mistress Long Island Strings; Festival for 2 Years; Harvard-Medicine MD; Yale-Medicine MD; Princeton U; Brown U

GEORGE, ALPHENA A; BROOKLYN, NY; NORTHEASTERN AC; (SO); Ctznshp Aw; Hi Hnr Roll; Hnr Roll; Jr Mshl; Perf Att; Sci Fairs; Valdctrian; Comm Volntr; Chrch Yth Grp; Drma Clb; Quiz Bowl; Scouts; Sign Clb; Acpl Chr; Ch Chr; Clr Grd; Drl Tm; Yrbk (R, P); Adventist Youth Leader At My Church; Pathfinder Counselor in Pathfinder Club; Medicine (Pediatrician); Andrews U in Michigan; Loma Linda U in California

GEORGE, MERIL; MEDFORD, NY; PATCHOGUE-MEDFORD HS; (JR); F Lan Hn Soc; Hi Hnr Roll; Hnr Roll; Nat Hon Sy; Otst Ac Ach Awd; Perf Att; Pres Sch; Sci Fairs; Comm Volntr; Hab For Humty Volntr; Hosp Aide; Chrch Yth Grp; Emplmnt; Off Aide; Tchrs Aide; Tech Clb; Spanish Clb; Chr; Stu Cncl (R); Sch Ppr (E, R, P); Yrbk (E, P); Interact Club, Anchor Club; National Junior Honor Society; Combined BA/MD Program; 7-8 Pre-Medical Program & Medical Program; Stony Brook U; City U of New York

GERACI-YEE, SABRINA; FREEPORT, NY; FREEPORT HS; (JR); Fut Prb Slvr; Hi Hnr Roll; Nat Hon Sy; Pres Sch; Sci Fairs; Sci/Math Olympn; WWAHSS; Yth Ldrshp Prog; Comm Volntr; Peer Tut/Med; Mth Clb/Tm; Mus Clb; Prom Com; Sci Clb; Bnd; Chr; Jzz Bnd; Orch; Sftball (V L); Swmg (V L); Cl Off (P); Stu Cncl (R); CR (R); Yrbk; All-State Mixed Chorus; Best Categorical Project-Long Island Science Congress; Biology; Behavioral Science; Case Western Reserve U; U of Pennsylvania

GERAGHTY, LENA; SARATOGA SPRINGS, NY; SARATOGA SPRINGS HS; (FR); Hi Hnr Roll; Otst Ac Ach Awd; Comm Volntr; Sccr (J); Swmg; Historical Preservation Society Writing Award; Architecture; McGill U

GERGELIS, KRISTYN N; EAST AMHERST, NY; WILLIAMSVILLE EAST HS; (JR); Hi Hnr Roll; MVP; Nat Hon Sy; Nat Mrt Fin; St of Mnth; Yth Ldrshp Prog; Comm Volntr; Hosp Aide; Chrch Yth Grp; DARE; Emplmnt; Prom Com; SADD; Latin Clb; Swmg (J L); Cl Off (P); Varsity Bowling; Physician; Journalism; Canisius; Grove City

GERMANO, CHRISSIE; MASSENA, NY; MASSENA SR HS; (SO); F Lan Hn Soc; Hi Hnr Roll; Hnr Roll; Nat Hon Sy; Perf Att; Pres Ac Ftns Aw; Pres Sch; St of Mnth; Comm Volntr; Red Cr Aide; Chrch Yth Grp; DARE; Mus Clb; Scouts; French Clb; Chr; Ch Chr; Mch Bnd; Pep Bnd; Swmg (V); Vllyball (J); Yrbk (E, P); Marine Biology; Criminal Law

GERVASE, ADAM; GETZVILLE, NY; WILLIAMSVILLE NORTH HS; (SO); Hi Hnr Roll; Hnr Roll; MVP; Otst Ac Ach Awd; Pres Sch; Comm Volntr; Peer Tut/Med; DECA; Emplmnt; Mth Clb/Tm; Ice Hky (J); Sccr (VJ); 1st Place in DECA State Competition; Math Honor Society; Medical; Business; Cornell U; Brown U

GETCHELL, ALISON R; WHITESBORO, NY; ORISKANY JR/SR HS; (SR); Hi Hnr Roll; MVP; Nat Hon Sy; St of Mnth; St Optmst of Yr; WWAHSS; Comm Volntr; Peer Tut/Med; Emplmnt; Key Club; Prom Com; Scouts; SADD; Vsity Clb; French Clb; Chr; SP/M/VS; Bskball (V C); Chrldg (V); Cr Ctry (V L); Sftball (V); Cl Off (P, T); Sch Ppr (E, R); Yrbk (E); Center State Conference Division III All-Star Basketball; Childhood Education; Theatre; Niagara U

GHELLI, CLARISSA; NEW YORK, NY; BARD HS EARLY COLLEGE; (FR); Perf Att; Comm Volntr; Hosp Aide; Italian Clb; Bnd; Cr Ctry (J); Swmg (V); Pre-Med; Archaeology; Princeton U; Vassar College

GHODUSY, JANELLE; FRESH MEADOWS, NY; FRANCIS LEWIS HS; (JR); Ctznshp Aw; Hi Hnr Roll; Hnr Roll; Nat Hon Sy; WWAHSS; Biology Clb; Cmptr Clb; Svce Clb; Dnce; Biology Club/Computer Club, Volunteer Sunday School Teacher; Plenty of School Service Accomplished; Optometry; Accounting

GHORBANDI, SAJJAD A; FAIRPORT, NY; FAIRPORT HS; (SO); Hi Hnr Roll; Hnr Roll; Pres Ac Ftns Aw; Comm Volntr; Peer Tut/Med; Clb; Sccr (J); Medical Doctor; Harvard; U of Rochester

GHOSH, DWITIYA; ELMONT, NY; SEWANHAKA HS; (SR); F Lan Hn Soc; Hi Hnr Roll; Kwnis Aw; Nat Hon Sy; Otst Ac Ach Awd; Pres Sch; Salutrn; Sci/Math Olympn; St of Mnth; Yth Ldrshp Prog; Comm Volntr; Peer Tut/Med; Chess; Dbte Team; Emplmnt; FBLA; Key Club; Mth Clb/Tm; Mod UN; SADD; Chr; Dnce; SP/M/VS; Stu Cncl (R); CR (R); Sch Ppr (R); Yrbk (R, P); New York Academy of Sciences - Research; Legislator Lisanne Altmann's Office-Internship; Bachelor's Degree / Economics; Law; New York U; Boston U

GIAMBELLUCA, MARISSA; BETHPAGE, NY; ISLAND TREES HS; (SO); Ctznshp Aw; Hi Hnr Roll; Hnr Roll; Nat Hon Sy; Nat Ldrshp Svc; Nat Sci Aw; Otst Ac Ach Awd; Pres Ac Ftns Aw; Sci/Math Olympn; USAA; Comm Volntr; Peer Tut/Med; Spec Olymp Vol; ArtClub; Dbte Team; Drma Clb; Emplmnt; Key Club; Mus Clb; Svce Clb; SADD; Bnd; Chr; Dnce; Mch Bnd; Bdmtn (J); Gmnstcs (J); Scr Kpr (J); Sftball (J); Stu Cncl (R); CR (R); Lit Mag (E, R); PAWS for Parkinson's; Walks for Cancer; English Major; Actress/Drama Major; NYU New York U

GIANACA, STEVEN T; FREEPORT, NY; FREEPORT HS; (JR); Hi Hnr Roll; Nat Hon Sy; Perf Att; Sci Fairs; Sci/Math Olympn; WWAHSS; Yth Ldrshp Prog; Comm Volntr; Peer Tut/Med; Key Club; Mth Clb/Tm; NYLC; Scouts; Bnd; Jzz Bnd; Mch Bnd; Orch; Skt Tgt Sh (V)

GIANCHANDANI, DINA; ALBANY, NY; (JR); Hi Hnr Roll; Nat Hon Sy; Sci Fairs; WWAHSS; Comm Volntr; Dbte Team; Key Club; Orch; Tennis (V); Track (J); Key Club Lieutenant Governor '05-'06; Secretary of Debate Club; Psychology; Industrial Relations; Cornell U

GIBBONS, STACEY T; JAMAICA, NY; SAMUEL J TILDEN HS; (JR); Hnr Roll; Perf Att; Sci Fairs; St of Mnth; Yth Ldrshp Prog; Comm Volntr; Hosp Aide; Peer Tut/Med; Sccr; Vllyball; Cricket; Nursing; SUNY Plattsburgh; Long Island U CW Post

GIBSON, LYDIA; UNIONDALE, NY; UNIONDALE HS; (SO); F Lan Hn Soc; Hi Hnr Roll; Nat Hon Sy; Sci Fairs; WWAHSS; Comm Volntr; Chrch Yth Grp; Drma Clb; Key Club; Sci Clb; Chr; Orch; SP/M/VS; Venture Scholar

GIGLIO, ALYSIA; MILLERTON, NY; WEBUTUEK; Hnr Roll; Peer Tut/Med; Bnd; Bskball (VJC); Fld Hky (J); Skiing (J); Sccr (V)

GIGLIO, JENNIFER; WESTBURY, NY; WT CLARKE HS; (SR); Hnr Roll; Kwnis Aw; Otst Ac Ach Awd; St of Mnth; Red Cr Aide; Key Club; Mus Clb; Pep Squd; Prom Com; Chr; Chrldg (V); Sccr (V); Sftball (JC); Fashion Merchandising and Marketing; Delaware U; FIT

GIL, NATHALI; BRONX, NY; BRONX LEADERSHIP AC; (JR); St of Mnth; WWAHSS; Comm Volntr; Jr Ach; French Clb; Forensic Scientist; FBI Detective; John Jay U; NYU

GILBERT, ERIN; LEVITTOWN, NY; DIVISION AVE HS; (JR); F Lan Hn Soc; Hi Hnr Roll; Hnr Roll; WWAHSS; Key Club; Scouts; SADD; Bnd; Stg Cre; Sch Ppr (R); SADD; Veterinarian; U of Maryland; Cornell U

Getchell, Alison R
Oriskany JR/SR HS
Whitesboro, NY

George, Meril
Patchogue-Medford HS
Medford, NY

Garry, Matthew
East Meadow HS
East Meadow, NY

Garlitos, Emmanuel A
Comsewogue HS
Pt Jefferson Station, NY

Garay, Stephanie
Cathedral HS
Flushing, NY

Garcia, Jessica
Sheepshead Bay HS
Brooklyn, NY

George, Alexandra
East Setauket, NY

Germano, Chrissie
Massena SR HS
Massena, NY

Gibson, Lydia
Uniondale HS
Uniondale, NY

GILBERT, KRISTINA J; FREEPORT, NY; FREEPORT HS; (JR); Hi Hnr Roll; Peer Tut/Med; Emplmnt; Key Club; Italian Clb; Bnd; Chr; Jzz Bnd; Mch Bnd; Tennis (J); Part of Johns Hopkins Center for Talented Youth; Psychology; Early Childhood Education; Brown U; Syracuse U

GILLIAM, KAYLA; BROCKPORT, NY; BROCKPORT HS; (FR); Hi Hnr Roll; Nat Hon Sy; Nat Sci Aw; Comm Volntr; Chrch Yth Grp; Bnd; Mch Bnd; Sccr; Mission Trip; Dance Marathon for Strong Hospital; Elementary Education; Nursing; SUNY Geneseo; SUNY Brockport

GILLIGAN, BRITTANY L; KINGSTON, NY; SAUGERTIES HS; (FR); Hi Hnr Roll; Pres Ac Ftns Aw; WWAHSS; Spec Olymp Vol; DARE; Dbte Team; Key Club; Bskball (J); Lcrsse (V); Sccr (J); Cl Off (T); Stu Cncl (R); Varsity Lacrosse MNAL -2 team in 9th Grade; Doctor-Surgeon

GIMONDO, NANCY C; LATHAM, NY; SHAKER HS; (SR); Hi Hnr Roll; Nat Hon Sy; Nat Mrt LOC; Otst Ac Ach Awd; Perf Att; St of Mnth; Valdctrian; Comm Volntr; Hab For Humty Volntr; Peer Tut/Med; Chrch Yth Grp; Key Club; Scouts; French Clb; Bnd; Mch Bnd; Pep Bnd; Stg Cre; Key Club Secretary; National Honor Society Secretary; Elementary School Math Teacher; College of Saint Rose

GINZBURG, YELENA; BROOKLYN, NY; JAMES MADISON HS; (JR); Sci/Math Olympn; Comm Volntr; ArtClub; Mth Clb/Tm; Svce Clb; Dnce; Drl Tm; SP/M/VS; Vllyball (J); College Now Program; Math Honor Society; Medicine; Physical Therapy, Pharmacy; Columbia U in Manhattan; Long Island U in Brooklyn

GIRGENTI, SAM; HUNTINGTON STATION, NY; HALF HOLLOW HILLS HS; (SR); F Lan Hn Soc; Hi Hnr Roll; Nat Hon Sy; Comm Volntr; Hosp Aide; Spec Olymp Vol; Emplmnt; Key Club; Quiz Bowl; Tmpl Yth Grp; Spanish Clb; Cr Ctry (J); Track (V); Criminal Justice; SUNY Binghamton; Syracuse U

GIROLAMO, ANTHONY N; NORTHPORT, NY; NORTHPORT HS; (FR); Otst Ac Ach Awd; Pres Ac Ftns Aw; Sci Fairs; Peer Tut/Med; Emplmnt; Key Club; Scouts; Bskball; Sccr (J)

GIRON, GABRIELLE A; UNIONDALE, NY; UNIONDALE HS; (SO); Hi Hnr Roll; WWAHSS; Comm Volntr; Peer Tut/Med; ArtClub; Chrch Yth Grp; Dbte Team; Emplmnt; Key Club; Mus Clb; P to P St Amb Prg; Acpl Chr; Bnd; Chr; Dnce; Bdmtn (J); Chrldg (C); United States Choral/String & Wind Ensemble; Zoology; Performing Arts; SUNY Oswego; Juilliard

GITTENS, ABIOLA; JAMAICA, NY; GATEWAY TO HEALTH SCIENCES SCH; (JR); Ctznshp Aw; Fut Prb Slvr; Otst Ac Ach Awd; Perf Att; St of Mnth; Hosp Aide; Chrch Yth Grp; Drma Clb; Emplmnt; FCA; Mus Clb; Ch Chr; Dnce; SP/M/VS; Veterinary Science; Purdue U; CUNY

GIUSTINO, ANTHONY; RONKONKOMA, NY; SACHEM HS EAST; (JR); Hnr Roll; Nat Hon Sy; Perf Att; Comm Volntr; DARE; Emplmnt; Vsity Clb; Bnd; Ftball (V); Track (V); Vsy Clb (V); Wt Lftg (V); Scholar Athlete; NYSSMA / Piano Solo; Business; Marketing; SUNY Stony Brook; New York U

GIWA, NADINE K; MEDFORD, NY; ST JOHN THE BAPTIST HS; (JR); F Lan Hn Soc; Hi Hnr Roll; Hnr Roll; Nat Hon Sy; Pres Sch; St of Mnth; WWAHSS; Comm Volntr; Bnd; Mch Bnd; Pep Bnd; Bdmtn (V); Tennis (V); Member of Tri-M Music Honor Society; Participant in Dolan DNA Learning Center; Veterinarian Medicine; Biology; Princeton U; Columbia U

GIZZI, ALEXIS; PINE BUSH, NY; PINE BUSH HS; (SO); Hi Hnr Roll; Hnr Roll; Nat Hon Sy; Comm Volntr; Emplmnt; Scouts; Chr; Dnce; Chrldg (J); History; Performing Arts

GLOGOWSKI, NICK; SARATOGA SPRINGS, NY; SARATOGA SPRINGS HS; (FR); Hi Hnr Roll; Hnr Roll; Nat Hon Sy; Sci Fairs; Comm Volntr; Chrch Yth Grp; DARE; Anthology of Young American Poets; Engineering; Sienna College

GLUCK, LAUREN; MERRICK, NY; SANFORD H CALHOUN HS; (JR); F Lan Hn Soc; Hi Hnr Roll; Hnr Roll; Nat Hon Sy; Nat Mrt Semif; Pres Sch; Peer Tut/Med; Dbte Team; Key Club; MuAlphaTh; Prom Com; SADD; Vsity Clb; Orch; Tennis (V L); Cl Off (T); Neuroscience; Medical Degree; Tufts U; Wesleyan U

GOARD, JEREMY J; TROY, NY; TAMARAC HS; (SR); Hi Hnr Roll; Otst Ac Ach Awd; Perf Att; WWAHSS; Yth Ldrshp Prog; Comm Volntr; Hab For Humty Volntr; Peer Tut/Med; Emplmnt; Key Club; NYLC; Prom Com; Spanish Clb; Stu Cncl (R); Mock Trial Participant; Rising Star Internship Winner; Meteorology; Doctorate; Florida Institute of Technology

GOH, JING M; NEW YORK, NY; ST JEAN BAPTISTE HS; (SR); Hnr Roll; Nat Hon Sy; Perf Att; Pres Sch; Scouts; Yrbk (R); Girl Scouts' Patrol Leader; Peer Support Leader; Psychology; Psychiatry; New York U; St John's U

GOHL, CASSIE; SAUGERTIES, NY; SAUGERTIES HS; (FR); Hi Hnr Roll; Comm Volntr; Chrch Yth Grp; Emplmnt; Key Club; Spanish Clb; Bnd; Track (J L); Early Elementary Teaching

GOLAND-VAN RYN, MATTHEW L; SLINGERLANDS, NY; GUILDERLAND HS; (SR); Hi Hnr Roll; Nat Hon Sy; Nat Mrt LOC; Otst Ac Ach Awd; St Schl; WWAHSS; Comm Volntr; Emplmnt; Fr of Library; Key Club; SADD; Tmpl Yth Grp; Vsity Clb; Chr; Stg Cre; Golf (J); Tennis (V L); Guilderland Library Board Student Rep.; Doctor; Business; Cornell U

GOLD, HEATHER; NEW YORK, NY; FIORELLO H LA GUARDIA HS; (SR); All Am Sch; Nat Hon Sy; Comm Volntr; Off Aide; Photog; Svce Clb; Tmpl Yth Grp; Lit Mag (P); Awarded Scholastic Gold Key for Photography; Member of Art Honor League; U of Chicago

GOLDBACH, ALYSSA; MIDDLE VILLAGE, NY; ARCHBISHOP MOLLOY HS; (SO); Sftball (J L); Swmg (V L); Lifeguard; Volunteer At Lantern; The Field of Medicine; Maryland State; Georgetown

GOLDEN, SARA S; ELMIRA, NY; NOTRE DAME HS; (SO); Hi Hnr Roll; Pres Sch; WWAHSS; Comm Volntr; Scouts; French Clb; Chrldg (V L); CR (R); National Society of High School Scholars; Who's Who-Sports Edition; Law; Education

GOLDENBERG, HILARY; WHITE PLAINS, NY; WESTCHESTER HEBREW HS; (JR); Otst Ac Ach Awd; Yth Ldrshp Prog; Hosp Aide; Red Cr Aide; DARE; Emplmnt; Mod UN; Tmpl Yth Grp; Bsball (VJ); Bskball (VJ); Gmnstcs (J); Sccr (V); Sftball (V); Lit Mag (R, P); Sch Ppr (R); Yrbk (E, P); Connecticut Writing Award; Outstanding Achievement in English; Political Science Major; Journalism; SUNY Binghamton

GOLD-PARKER, ARYEH; NYACK, NY; NYACK HS; (FR); Bnd; Jzz Bnd; Tennis (J)

GOLDSTEIN, JACOB; GREAT NECK, NY; GREAT NECK SOUTH HS; (JR); Nat Mrt LOC; Comm Volntr; Key Club; Lib Aide; Outdrs Clb; Photog; Yrbk (E); Key Club Lieutenant Governor; History; Education; U of Rochester; Brandeis U

GOLEBIEWSKA, SYLVIA; BROOKLYN, NY; HS FOR ENVIRONMENTAL STUDIES; (SO); Ctznshp Aw; Hnr Roll; Perf Att; Sci Fairs; St of Mnth; ArtClub; Emplmnt; Tchrs Aide; Bnd; Chr; Dnce; SP/M/VS; Bsball (J); Chrldg (J); Ice Sktg (J); Sccr (J); Sftball (J); Swmg (J); Tennis (J); Vllyball (J); Teacher; Interpreter; Hunter College

GOLEMBIEWSKI, AMBER; EAST OTTO, NY; CATTARAUGUS-LITTLE VALLEY; (FR); Hi Hnr Roll; Chrch Yth Grp; Bnd; Chr; Track (V)

GOLLINGER, WHITNEY; HERMON, NY; EDWARDS-KNOX CTRL SCH; (SO); Ctznshp Aw; Hi Hnr Roll; Hnr Roll; Otst Ac Ach Awd; WWAHSS; ArtClub; DARE; Prom Com; Spanish Clb; Bnd; Chr; Clr Grd; Mch Bnd; Chrldg (C); Cosmetology; Accounting; SUNY Canton; SUNY Potsdam

GOLUB, MARISSA; SEAFORD, NY; SEAFORD HS; (JR); Hi Hnr Roll; Hnr Roll; Nat Hon Sy; Pres Sch; WWAHSS; Yth Ldrshp Prog; Comm Volntr; Peer Tut/Med; Dbte Team; Emplmnt; Key Club; Mus Clb; NYLC; Svce Clb; Bnd; Jzz Bnd; Mch Bnd; SP/M/VS; Bskball (V); Fld Hky (V); Lcrsse (V); Lit Mag (R); National Honor Society, Tri M Music Honor Society; Peer Leader, NYS Rep. At Presidential Inauguration.; Political Science; Pre-Law; George Washington U; Northeastern U

GOMES, TANIA; MT VERNON, NY; BLESSED SACRAMENT HS; (JR); Gov Hnr Prg; Hnr Roll; Nat Ldrshp Svc; Dnce; Sccr (V); Stu Cncl (R); Yrbk (P); International Business; Teacher / Radiology; Mt Saint Vincent; Dominican College

GOMEZ, EMILY; STATEN ISLAND, NY; CURTIS HS; (SO); Ctznshp Aw; F Lan Hn Soc; Hi Hnr Roll; Hnr Roll; Otst Ac Ach Awd; St of Mnth; WWAHSS; Comm Volntr; Chrch Yth Grp; Photog; Swmg; Sch Ppr (R, P); Yrbk (E, P); Poetry Club - President; Film Club - Video; Journalism; English; New York U, New York; Columbia U, New York

GOMEZ, MAOLY; STATEN ISLAND, NY; PORT RICHMOND HS; (FR); Hnr Roll; Otst Ac Ach Awd; Perf Att; Sci Fairs; St of Mnth; Comm Volntr; Hosp Aide; Emplmnt; Chr; Dnce; SP/M/VS; Greatest Singer Solo Award; I Won a TV in School for Perfect Attendance; Business-MBA; Baruch

GONCALVES, STEVEN; MINEOLA, NY; MINEOLA HS; (FR); Hosp Aide; Sci Clb; Bnd; Mch Bnd; Golf (V); Medical Degree; Columbia U; New York U

GONYO, ASHLEY M; SHARON SPRINGS, NY; (JR); Hnr Roll; Pres Sch; WWAHSS; Emplmnt; Physical Therapy; Pre-Law; Clarkson U; Russell Sage College

GONZALES, ELIZA; WHITE PLAINS, NY; ALEXANDER HAMILTON HS; (SR); Hi Hnr Roll; Hnr Roll; MVP; Nat Hon Sy; WWAHSS; Yth Ldrshp Prog; Comm Volntr; Emplmnt; Key Club; Lttrmn Clb; Mus Clb; Pep Squd; Prom Com; SADD; Vsity Clb; Bnd; Dnce; Chrldg (V); Sftball (V L); Track (V); Vsy Clb (V); Vllyball (V L); Cl Off (R); CR (R); Yrbk (R); Pharmacy; Long Island U Brooklyn Campus; U of the Sciences in Philadelphia

GONZALEZ, GABRIELLE; SCHENECTADY, NY; BURNT HILLS BALLSTON LAKE SHS; (JR); Ctznshp Aw; Hi Hnr Roll; Hnr Roll; WWAHSS; Drma Clb; Emplmnt; Stg Cre; Chrldg (J); All Star Cheerleading (Competition); Fashion Design; Fashion Institute of Technology; Katharine Gibbs

GONZALEZ, LEO; BROOKLYN, NY; SHEEPSHEAD BAY HS; (JR); Ctznshp Aw; Hi Hnr Roll; Hnr Roll; Nat Hon Sy; Otst Ac Ach Awd; Sci Fairs; St Schl; Valdctrian; WWAHSS; Bdmtn; Ftball; Sccr; Vllyball; Cl Off (R); International Business Administration; Film; New York U; U of Southern California

GONZALEZ, TRINITA; JAY, NY; AUSABLE VALLEY CTRL HS; (JR); Hi Hnr Roll; Hnr Roll; WWAHSS; Comm Volntr; Prom Com; Vsity Clb; Bskball (J L); Vsy Clb (V); Vllyball (VJ L); Yrbk (R, P); Accounting; Trinity College Connecticut

GONZALEZ, VERONICA; BRONX, NY; WALTON HS; (JR); Hnr Roll; Veterinary Science; Computer Science; Cedar Crest College; Edinboro U

GOODHEART, SCOTT; NORTH COLLINS, NY; NORTH COLLINS HS; (JR); Hnr Roll; Comm Volntr; Stg Cre; Bsball (V); Bskball (V); Academic Athlete; All-Star Athlete; Teaching; Accounting; Buffalo State; U of Buffalo

GOODINE, JESSICA; CLAYTON, NY; THOUSAND ISLAND HS; (FR); Hi Hnr Roll; Nat Hon Sy; St of Mnth; Bnd; Sccr (J); Sftball (J); Vllyball (V); Academics Certificate of Achievement; Forensic Lab Technician; Bachelor Degree Involving Forensic Science; John Jay College of Criminal Justice; U of New Haven

GOODING, ROBBIE; BEACON, NY; BEACON HS; (MS); Comm Volntr; Scouts; Golf; Law Enforcement Explorer Program; Law Enforcement; Fire Protection

GOODMAN, WILLIAM J; SCHENECTADY, NY; NOTRE DAME-BISHOP GIBBONS HS; (JR); Hnr Roll; Perf Att; St of Mnth; WWAHSS; Comm Volntr; Drl Tm; Bskball (J); Ftball (V); Track (V); Computer Science; Business; Cornell U; Hartford College

GOOSSENS, EMERY; ELMIRA, NY; NOTRE DAME HS; (SR); Hi Hnr Roll; WWAHSS; Comm Volntr; Hab For Humty Volntr; Chrch Yth Grp; Key Club; Bnd; Mch Bnd; Stg Cre; Bdmtn (V); Ftball (V); Lcrsse (VJ); Sccr (J); Track (VJ); Hands of Christ Rochester Diocese.; Business; U of Albany; Hobart & William Smith College

GORAYA, SUNEET; WHITE PLAINS, NY; ALEXANDER HAMILTON HS; (JR); Hi Hnr Roll; Hnr Roll; Nat Hon Sy; WWAHSS; Yth Ldrshp Prog; Comm Volntr; Hosp Aide; Emplmnt; Key Club; SADD; Vsity Clb; Dnce; Pediatrician; Dentist; Pennsylvania State U; Boston U

GORBENKO, CHRISTINA; LAKE PLACID, NY; LAKE PLACID HS; (SR); Hi Hnr Roll; Hnr Roll; MVP; Nat Hon Sy; Perf Att; WWAHSS; Comm Volntr; Red Cr Aide; Drma Clb; Emplmnt; Scouts; Vsity Clb; Bnd; Chr; Ch Chr; SP/M/VS; Ice Hky (V L); Sccr (V L); Track (V CL); Vllyball (V L); Sectional High Jump Champion; (Volunteer) Head Camp Counselor-Scout; Business-Marketing/Advertising; U of Connecticut; U of Albany

GORE, DANIEL; STATEN ISLAND, NY; STATEN ISLAND TECH HS; (JR); Hnr Roll; Nat Hon Sy; Perf Att; WWAHSS; Yth Ldrshp Prog; Comm Volntr; Hosp Aide; Emplmnt; Mth Clb/Tm; Tchrs Aide; Stg Cre; Stu Cncl (R); Handball Team; Pre-Med; Physician

GORE, RENA T; BRONX, NY; BRONX HS OF BUSINESS; (SO); Hi Hnr Roll; Hnr Roll; Nat Hon Sy; Otst Ac Ach Awd; Sci Fairs; Yth Ldrshp Prog; Comm Volntr; Chrch Yth Grp; Mus Clb; Ch Chr; SP/M/VS; Sch Ppr (E, R, P); National Junior Honor Society; National Foundation for Teaching Entrepreneurship; Business Management; Culinary Arts; Rutgers U; Columbia U

GORGONE, MATTHEW J; MONROE, NY; (JR); Hi Hnr Roll; Comm Volntr; Orch; Wrstlg (J)

GORRELL, ANTHONY J; BOSTON, NY; HAMBURG HS; (JR); Hi Hnr Roll; Hnr Roll; MVP; Perf Att; Sci/Math Olympn; St of Mnth; Comm Volntr; Bsball (V); Ftball (V); Secretary of Power Club; Math Student of the Year; Mechanical Engineering; Pennsylvania State U; Clarkson U

GOSSERT, NICOLE; MERRICK, NY; JOHN F KENNEDY HS; (SO); F Lan Hn Soc; Hi Hnr Roll; Hnr Roll; Nat Hon Sy; Otst Ac Ach Awd; Comm Volntr; Emplmnt; Key Club; SADD; Tmpl Yth Grp; Chrldg (JC); CR (R); Education; Binghamton U; Maryland U

GOTTLIEB, ERIC; SYOSSET, NY; COLD SPRING HARBOR HS; (JR); Hnr Roll; Nat Hon Sy; Yth Ldrshp Prog; Comm Volntr; Peer Tut/Med; Spec Olymp Vol; Dbte Team; Drma Clb; Emplmnt; NtlFrnscLg; Latin Clb; Bnd; Jzz Bnd; Pep Bnd; Lit Mag (P); Debate Captain / Certified Underwater Photographer; Certified Scuba Diver; Law Degree; Political Science; Emory U; New York U

GRABOWSKI, CRYSTAL; NORTH COLLINS, NY; NORTH COLLINS HS; (SO); Hnr Roll; Nat Hon Sy; Otst Ac Ach Awd; Perf Att; Comm Volntr; Drma Clb; Chr; SP/M/VS; Battle of the Books @ Library; Short Story Published in Newspaper; Art Education; Creative Writing; Flagler College; Allegheny College

GRABY, MARYCAROL; CHURCHVILLE, NY; CHURCHVILLE-CHILI HS; (SR); Hi Hnr Roll; Nat Hon Sy; WWAHSS; Bnd; Chr; Lcrsse (V); Sccr (V); Top 20 of Class of 2005; Biology / Chemistry; Pre-Med; Union College

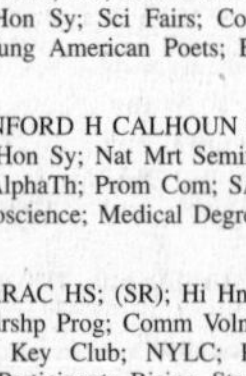

Goldenberg, Hilary
Westchester Hebrew HS
White Plains, NY

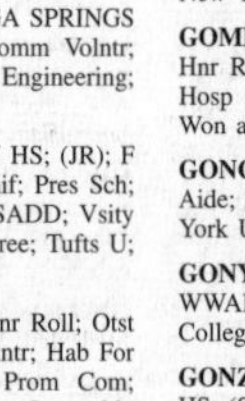

Goard, Jeremy J
Tamarac HS
Troy, NY

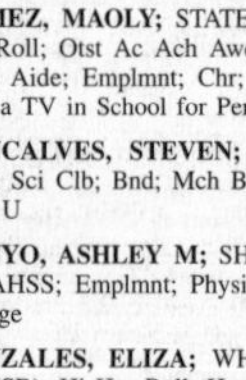

Gluck, Lauren
Sanford H Calhoun HS
Merrick, NY

National
Honor Roll
Spring 2005

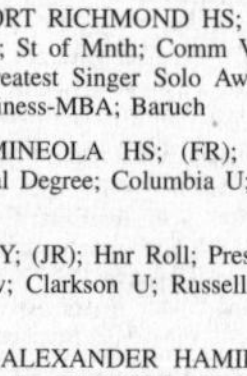

Giustino, Anthony
Sachem HS East
Ronkonkoma, NY

Goldbach, Alyssa
Archbishop Molloy HS
Middle Village, NY

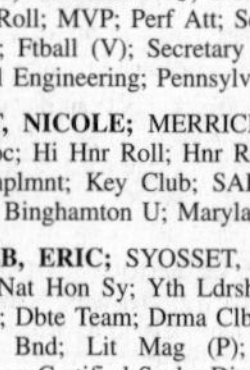

Gore, Rena T
Bronx HS Of Business
Bronx, NY

HARRIS, LOUISE M; HEMPSTEAD, NY; HEMPSTEAD HS; (JR); Ctznshp Aw; Hi Hnr Roll; Hnr Roll; Nat Hon Sy; Sci Fairs; WWAHSS; Comm Volntr; Chess; DARE; Key Club; Photog; Dnce; Orch; Bdmtn (VJ); Bskball (V); Cr Ctry (V); Track (V); Adv Cncl (R); Cl Off (R); Stu Cncl (R); CR (R); Theatre Media Arts/Drama; Hofstra U; NYU

HARRIS, MONIQUE; NORTH COLLINS, NY; NORTH COLLINS HS; (JR); Hnr Roll; Nat Hon Sy; Perf Att; St of Mnth; WWAHSS; Comm Volntr; Peer Tut/Med; ArtClub; Photog; Spanish Clb; SP/M/VS; Stg Cre; Wt Lftg (VJ L); Yrbk (P); Merit Award from Drexel (Photography); Bioinformatics; Biochemistry; Rochester Institute of Technology; Canisius College

HARRISON, SARAH A; SPENCER, NY; SPENCER-VAN ETTEN HS; (SR); Hi Hnr Roll; Nat Hon Sy; Otst Ac Ach Awd; St of Mnth; Valdctrian; WWAHSS; Yth Ldrshp Prog; Comm Volntr; Peer Tut/Med; Dbte Team; Emplmnt; Key Club; Mod UN; Photog; Prom Com; Quiz Bowl; Schol Bwl; Chr; Stg Cre; Cl Off (V, S); Yrbk (E, P); Major: Political Science; Bucknell U

HARTMAN, KARISSA; SELDEN, NY; NEWFIELD HS; (SR); Hi Hnr Roll; Hnr Roll; Otst Ac Ach Awd; WWAHSS; Comm Volntr; Peer Tut/Med; Drma Clb; Emplmnt; FTA; Photog; Quill & Scroll; Scouts; Foreign Clb; Acpl Chr; Chr; SP/M/VS; Stg Cre; Fncg (V); Sch Ppr (E, P); Yrbk (P); Early Childhood Education; Therapeutic Psychology; Suffolk Community College; Virginia Military Institute

HARTZELL, ANNETTE; BINGHAMTON, NY; CHENANGO FORKS HS; (JR); Hi Hnr Roll; Nat Hon Sy; Perf Att; St of Mnth; USAA; WWAHSS; Hosp Aide; Prom Com; Sci Clb; Tennis (V); CR (R); Mock Trial; Envirothon Competition; Food Science; U of Delaware; Penn State

HARVEY, FIONA D; CAMBRIA HEIGHTS, NY; MARTIN LUTHER HS; (SO); Hi Hnr Roll; Hnr Roll; Nat Hon Sy; Comm Volntr; Hosp Aide; Peer Tut/Med; Chrch Yth Grp; DARE; Key Club; Off Aide; P to P St Amb Prg; Tchrs Aide; Spanish Clb; Dnce; Tennis (V); Track (V); Stu Cncl (P); Yrbk (E); Pre-Med; Drama; Cornell U; Johns Hopkins U

HARVIN, ATIA; NEWBURGH, NY; (MS); Mas Aw; Pres Ac Ftns Aw; St of Mnth; Comm Volntr; Peer Tut/Med; Chrch Yth Grp; DARE; Drma Clb; Kwanza Clb; Photog; SADD; Chr; Dnce; Bskball (J); Chrldg (J); Track (J); Vllyball (J); CR (R); Yrbk (R); Howard U; Hampton U

HARVIN-BRATHWAITE, TARAMIA; BROOKLYN, NY; EDWARD R MURROW HS; (JR); Hnr Roll; Hosp Aide; Lit Mag (R); Major in Art (Screened Art Student); Beginner in Piano; Pre-Med; Fashion Illustration; Stony Brook U (SUNY); Temple U

HASSAN, NAFEEZA; NANUET, NY; SPRING VALLEY HS; (JR); Hi Hnr Roll; Hnr Roll; WWAHSS; Comm Volntr; Key Club; Orch; Stu Cncl (P, T); Business; Computers

HASSAN, REHAM; STATEN ISLAND, NY; ST JOHN VILLA AC; (SO); Hi Hnr Roll; Hnr Roll; Nat Hon Sy; Otst Ac Ach Awd; Perf Att; Sci Fairs; St of Mnth; Valdctrian; WWAHSS; Comm Volntr; Peer Tut/Med; JSA; Mth Clb/Tm; Stu Cncl (V, R)

HASSELBECK, EMILY A; GRAND ISLAND, NY; GRAND ISLAND HS; (SO); Hnr Roll; Otst Ac Ach Awd; Pres Sch; St Optmst of Yr; Comm Volntr; Chrch Yth Grp; DARE; Emplmnt; Chr; Ch Chr; SP/M/VS; Lcrsse (J); Skiing (V); Piano, American Red Cross; Babysitting Class; Ophthalmologist; Dentist; Grove City; Oral Roberts U

HASSMAN, KATHERINE E R; DANSVILLE, NY; ARKPORT CTRL HS; (SR); Ctznshp Aw; DAR; Hi Hnr Roll; Nat Hon Sy; Perf Att; Pres Sch; Valdctrian; WWAHSS; Comm Volntr; Peer Tut/Med; ArtClub; Chrch Yth Grp; DARE; Drma Clb; Emplmnt; Quiz Bowl; Tchrs Aide; Chr; Ch Chr; Clr Grd; Dnce; Stu Cncl (T); CR (R); Yrbk (E); Library Council-Vice-President; Steuben All-County Chorus Participant; Forensic Science; D'Youville College

HASTWELL IV, JOHN; BOONVILLE, NY; SOUTH LEWIS HS; (JR); Ctznshp Aw; Hi Hnr Roll; Nat Hon Sy; Nat Ldrshp Svc; Otst Ac Ach Awd; St of Mnth; WWAHSS; Comm Volntr; Peer Tut/Med; Spec Olymp Vol; Chrch Yth Grp; DARE; Scouts; French Clb; Bnd; Pep Bnd; SP/M/VS; Mar Art (V); CR; Yrbk (E); Who's Who; SAVE; Mathematics; Science; Jefferson Community College; Utica College

HATHAWAY, CHASE P; STILLWATER, NY; STILLWATER CTRL HS; (FR); Hi Hnr Roll; Nat Hon Sy; Perf Att; Comm Volntr; Peer Tut/Med; Bnd; Bsball (J); Sccr (V)

HATTER, JOE; PHOENIX, NY; JOHN C BIRDLEBOUGH HS; (FR); Hi Hnr Roll; Hnr Roll; Perf Att; Peer Tut/Med; Wrstlg (J); Graphic Design; Computer Graphics; MIT; UCLA

HAU, CHUI Y; COLLEGE POINT, NY; FRANCIS LEWIS HS; (SR); Nat Hon Sy; Comm Volntr; Peer Tut/Med; Cmptr Clb; Lib Aide; Off Aide; Tchrs Aide; Chinese Clb; SP/M/VS; Lit Mag (E); CAHSEE Award from the S.T. E.M. Program; The Principal's List; Engineer; Polytechnic U; Rochester Institute of Technology

HAWKINS, SARAH; CATO, NY; CATO MERIDIAN HS; (SO); Hnr Roll; Scouts; CR (R); Registered Nurse; Physical Therapist; Cayuga Community College

HAWRYSCHUK II, PETER J; SENECA FALLS, NY; MYNDERSE AC HS; (SO); Hnr Roll; St of Mnth; Ftball (V); Lcrsse (JC); Homecoming Court; Business; Entertainment; Yale U; Johns Hopkins U

HAYDEN, FRANCIS E; SEAFORD, NY; SEAFORD HS; (JR); Hi Hnr Roll; Nat Hon Sy; WWAHSS; Peer Tut/Med; Key Club; Mth Clb/Tm; Bnd; Jzz Bnd; Mch Bnd; Tri-M Music Honor Society; History; Brown U; Georgetown U

HAYES, REBECCA; BOONVILLE, NY; SOUTH LEWIS HS; (SO); Hi Hnr Roll; Hnr Roll; Comm Volntr; Spec Olymp Vol; Chrch Yth Grp; Scouts; Stg Cre; Chrldg (J); GAA (V); Sccr (J); Yrbk (P); Community Service Organization; Physician's Assistant; Nursing; Lemoyne; Upstate Medical U

HAYES, SCOTT; LAKE GEORGE, NY; LAKE GEORGE HS; (SR); Ctznshp Aw; F Lan Hn Soc; Nat Hon Sy; Otst Ac Ach Awd; Perf Att; Pres Sch; St of Mnth; Valdctrian; WWAHSS; Yth Ldrshp Prog; Comm Volntr; Peer Tut/Med; AL Aux Boys; Chrch Yth Grp; Emplmnt; HO'Br Yth Ldrshp; Key Club; Mod UN; Quiz Bowl; Scouts; Bnd; Chr; Jzz Bnd; SP/M/VS; Tennis (V L); Cl Off (S); Stu Cncl (P, T, R); Sch Ppr (E); Biological Engineering/Biology; Biomedical Engineering; Cornell U Arts and Sciences

HAYMES, BEN; ROCHESTER, NY; BRIGHTON HS; (SR); Hnr Roll; MVP; Comm Volntr; DECA; FBLA; Bsball (V CL); Bskball (V CL); Basketball 1st Team All-County; 3rd in NYS DECA Competition; Business Management; Syracuse U

HAYRE, SATINDERJIT; RICHMOND HILL, NY; HEALTH PROF & HUMAN SERV HS; (SO); Hi Hnr Roll; Hnr Roll; Nat Hon Sy; Otst Ac Ach Awd; Perf Att; Sci Fairs; St of Mnth; Peer Tut/Med; Sci Clb; Tchrs Aide; Tmpl Yth Grp; Ch Chr; Dnce; SP/M/VS; Sch Ppr (R); Arista Society Award; Part of Science Research Class and Liberty Partnership Program; Bachelor of Science (BS); Doctor of Medicine (M.D.); Cornell U; The Sophie Davis School of Biomedical Education

HE, ANTHONY; BROOKLYN, NY; HSES; (FR); Hi Hnr Roll; Hnr Roll; Nat Mrt LOC; Nat Sci Aw; Perf Att; St of Mnth; Comm Volntr; Bnd; Chr; SP/M/VS; Bsball (V); Bskball; Sccr (V); Stu Cncl (T); Sch Ppr (E); Business Degree; Computer Science Degree; Harvard U; California Institute of Technology

HEALEY, ELIZABETH; ITHACA, NY; ITHACA HS; (JR); Hi Hnr Roll; Hnr Roll; MVP; Chess; Lcrsse (VJ L); Sccr (VJCL); Yrbk (E, P); Scholar Athlete Award (Lacrosse and Soccer); Soccer-All Conference Award Southern Tier Athletic Conference All-Conference Award (Varsity Soccer); Business; Education; Cornell U; Boston U

HEALEY, MAUREEN; ITHACA, NY; ITHACA HS; (JR); Hi Hnr Roll; Hnr Roll; Emplmnt; Lcrsse (VJ L); Sccr (VJCL); Stu Cncl (R); Yrbk (E, P); Scholar Athlete Award in Lacrosse and Soccer; All-Conference Award in Soccer; Anthropology; Marine Biology; Cornell U; Boston U

HEANEY, PATRICK D; STATEN ISLAND, NY; SUSAN E WAGNER HS; (SO); Hnr Roll; WWAHSS; Swmg (V); Track (V); Cl Off (V); Rider U; Wagner College

HEARN, KAITLYN; LITTLE FALLS, NY; LITTLE FALLS HS; (FR); Hnr Roll; Comm Volntr; Chrch Yth Grp; DARE; Drma Clb; FBLA; Scouts; Svce Clb; French Clb; Chr; SP/M/VS; Sccr (J); Dietitian; X-Ray Lab Technician; Herkimer County Community College; Hamilton College

HEATH, JODI-ANN; HEMPSTEAD, NY; HEMPSTEAD HS; (SO); Hi Hnr Roll; Hnr Roll; Nat Hon Sy; Otst Ac Ach Awd; WWAHSS; Yth Ldrshp Prog; Hosp Aide; Chrch Yth Grp; Ch Chr; Cr Ctry (J); Track (J); Master's Degree in Medicine; Career in Obstetrics

HEATH, NICOLA; BRONX, NY; COLUMBUS HS; (SO); Hnr Roll; College Now Program; Pediatrician; Georgetown U; New York U

HECTOR, EMMANUEL; BROOKLYN, NY; BENJAMIN BANNEKER AC; (JR); Hnr Roll; MVP; WWAHSS; Peer Tut/Med; Chrch Yth Grp; Drma Clb; Vsity Clb; Ch Chr; SP/M/VS; Stg Cre; Cr Ctry (V); Mar Art (V); Scr Kpr (V); Sccr (C); Track (C); Cl Off (S); CR (R); Yrbk (R); Girls Soccer Team Manager; Sunday School Teacher; Psychology; Pre-Med; Adelphi U; Howard U

HEIDCAMP, DANIELLE; SAUGERTIES, NY; (SR); Hi Hnr Roll; Hnr Roll; Nat Hon Sy; WWAHSS; Comm Volntr; Peer Tut/Med; Dbte Team; Key Club; Quiz Bowl; Chr; SP/M/VS; Ice Sktg; Skiing; Sccr (J); Track (J); Stu Cncl (P); Studio Vivace (Vocal Training); Business Management; Education; Oneonta State U; Plattsburgh

HEIGHTS, TAFEISHA; WYANDANCH, NY; WYANDANCH MEM. HS; (FR); Hnr Roll; Otst Ac Ach Awd; Comm Volntr; Cmptr Clb; Tchrs Aide; SP/M/VS; Bskball (J); Women of the Future Club; Ob/Gyn-Pediatrician; Computer Programmers; D'Youville College; Long Island U

HEIMANN, HEATHER M; NEW ROCHELLE, NY; NEW ROCHELLE HS; (JR); Hi Hnr Roll; Hnr Roll; Peer Tut/Med; Pep Squd; Chrldg (VJ L); Mentor Program for Freshmen; Communication

HELD II, THOMAS J; WEST SENECA, NY; W. SENECA EAST SR HS; (FR); Hi Hnr Roll; Hnr Roll; Comm Volntr; DARE; Emplmnt; Key Club; Stg Cre; Engineering

HELLER, CALLIE; FOREST HILLS, NY; BRONX HS OF SCIENCE; (JR); Duke TS; Hi Hnr Roll; Hnr Roll; Nat Hon Sy; Nat Ldrshp Svc; WWAHSS; Comm Volntr; Peer Tut/Med; NYLC; Off Aide; Vsity Clb; Cr Ctry (V); Track (V); Language Dept Aide, National Student Leadership Council; Arista Applicant, Leadership Council Center For Talented Youth; Classics Major, European Studies Major; Humanities Major, History Major; Swarthmore College; Haverford College

HELLER, DANIEL; SMITHTOWN, NY; SMITHTOWN HS; (JR); Hnr Roll; Emplmnt

HELMS, AMANDA; MACEDON, NY; GANANDA CTRL SCH; (FR); Hnr Roll; Otst Ac Ach Awd; Perf Att; Pres Ac Ftns Aw; St of Mnth; Peer Tut/Med; Drma Clb; Mod UN; SADD; Acpl Chr; Chr; SP/M/VS; Vllyball (J); Yrbk; Model UN; Psychology; Social Work

HELOWICZ, JOSEPH; BUFFALO, NY; CLARENCE HS; (SR); Hnr Roll; Nat Hon Sy; WWAHSS; Yth Ldrshp Prog; Comm Volntr; Spec Olymp Vol; Emplmnt; P to P St Amb Prg; Vsity Clb; Latin Clb; Golf (V L); Academic Varsity Letter; Scholar Athlete; Science / Health Profession; Baldwin-Wallace College

HEMMER, CHARISSA; STATEN ISLAND, NY; MOORE CATHOLIC HS; (JR); Hnr Roll; Nat Hon Sy; St of Mnth; Comm Volntr; Psychologist; Biologist; Hunter College; Pace U

HENDERSON, CASSANDRA; ELLISBURG, NY; BELLEVILLE HENDERSON; (JR); Ctznshp Aw; Hnr Roll; Perf Att; St of Mnth; WWAHSS; Peer Tut/Med; ArtClub; Chrch Yth Grp; DARE; Emplmnt; Scouts; Tchrs Aide; Foreign Clb; Bnd; Chr; SP/M/VS; Scr Kpr (VJ); Sccr (VJCL); Sftball (V); Vllyball (VJCL); Yrbk (P); President of Foreign Language Club; Sports Medicine; Chemistry; Syracuse U; Oswego U

HENDRICK, EDEN; STILLWATER, NY; STILLWATER CTRL HS; (JR); Hi Hnr Roll; Nat Hon Sy; Pres Sch; WWAHSS; Comm Volntr; Chrldg (V C); Accounting; Teaching; Sierra College; U At Albany

HENEVELD, HEATH L; EAST HAMPTON, NY; EAST HAMPTON HS; (SO); Ctznshp Aw; Hi Hnr Roll; Otst Ac Ach Awd; Pres Ac Ftns Aw; Sci Fairs; Sci/Math Olympn; WWAHSS; Comm Volntr; Peer Tut/Med; Emplmnt; Key Club; Mth Clb/Tm; Ftball (J); Rlr Hky (V L); Tennis (V L); Track (V L); Harvard Model Congress-Army Chief of Staff; Youth Court-Prosecuting Attorney; Engineering; US Naval Academy; US Military Academy-West Point

HENRIQUEZ, YOMARIS; GARNERVILLE, NY; NORTH ROCKLAND HS; (JR); F Lan Hn Soc; Hnr Roll; Yth Ldrshp Prog; Comm Volntr; Emplmnt; Secretary of the ASPIRA Club; Graduate of Rockland Teen Leadership Program; Education Major; English/Literature Minor; Fordham U; Pace U

HENRY, HILARIE L; ELMA, NY; IROQUOIS CTRL HS; (JR); Hi Hnr Roll; Nat Hon Sy; Otst Ac Ach Awd; Perf Att; Pres Sch; St of Mnth; WWAHSS; Yth Ldrshp Prog; Comm Volntr; Peer Tut/Med; Emplmnt; Key Club; Vsity Clb; Bnd; Chr; Dnce; Jzz Bnd; Bskball (V); Sccr (V); American Legion School Award; Law; Yale U; Tufts U

HENRY, JHONELLE; BRONX, NY; EVANDER CHILDS HS; (SR); Ctznshp Aw; Hnr Roll; Perf Att; St of Mnth; Comm Volntr; Peer Tut/Med; DARE; Drma Clb; Mus Clb; Photog; Prom Com; ROTC; Chr; Ch Chr; Drl Tm; SP/M/VS; Cr Ctry (V); Sccr (V); Sftball (V); Tennis (C); Track (V); Stu Cncl (R); Yrbk (E, P); Nursing; Surgical Technology; Littman; Hostos

HENRY, KHADIJAH; BROOKLYN, NY; BISHOP LOUGHLIN MEMORIAL HS; (JR); Hnr Roll; Chrch Yth Grp; Ch Chr; Dnce; Pre-Med; Psychology; Clark Atlanta U; Virginia Union U

HERETH, MICHAEL J; BUFFALO, NY; WEST SENECA EAST SR HS; (SO); Hi Hnr Roll; Hnr Roll; Kwnis Aw; Otst Ac Ach Awd; Perf Att; WWAHSS; Chess; Chrch Yth Grp; Emplmnt; Key Club; Spanish Clb; Orch; Arch; Sch Ppr (E); Foreign Language Award of Excellence; Foreign Language-Related Careers; Music; Wittenberg U

HERNANDEZ, EMMANUEL; PT CHESTER, NY; PT CHESTER HS; (FR); Hi Hnr Roll; Otst Ac Ach Awd; Comm Volntr; Chrch Yth Grp; DARE; P to P St Amb Prg; Chr; Ch Chr; Mch Bnd; SP/M/VS; Surgeon; Aeronautics

HERNANDEZ, REYES; FREEPORT, NY; FREEPORT HS; (JR); Hnr Roll; French Clb; Orch; Electronic Engineer

HERNANDEZ, YENNIFER; BRONX, NY; BARD HS EARLY COLLEGE; (FR); Hi Hnr Roll; Hnr Roll; Chr

HERR, MEGAN; TONAWANDA, NY; KENMORE EAST SR HS; (SR); Hi Hnr Roll; Nat Hon Sy; Perf Att; Pres Sch; St of Mnth; Comm Volntr; Emplmnt; Scouts; French Clb; Bnd; Orch; Cr Ct Ski; Fld Hky (V L); Lcrsse (C); Track (J); French Club Treasurer; Softball - Recreational; Physical Therapy; Daemen College

Heller, Callie
Bronx HS Of Science
Forest Hills, NY

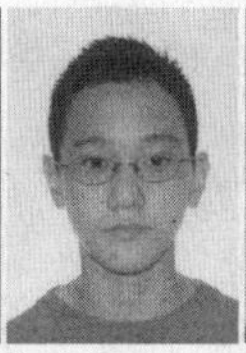

He, Anthony
HSES
Brooklyn, NY

Hau, Chui Y
Francis Lewis HS
College Point, NY

National
Honor Roll
Spring 2005

Hassman, Katherine E R
Arkport Ctrl HS
Dansville, NY

Heidcamp, Danielle
Saugerties, NY

Henry, Jhonelle
Evander Childs HS
Bronx, NY

HERRERA, MARIO; BROOKLYN, NY; BUSHWICK HS; (SR); Hnr Roll; Perf Att; Sci Fairs; St of Mnth; Vsity Clb; Bsball (C); Bskball (V); Track (V); Stu Cncl (R); Computer Engineering; Business; Berklee College; CUNY Brooklyn College

HESS, ROBINE J; SCHENECTADY, NY; NISKAYUNA HS; (JR); Hi Hnr Roll; Nat Hon Sy; Sci/Math Olympn; St of Mnth; Comm Volntr; DARE; Scouts; SADD; Spanish Clb; Dnce; Hsbk Rdg; Volunteer in 3 Senate Campaigns; Psychology; Literature; SUNY Geneseo NY; Champlain College UT

HEUSNER, GRACE E; BUFFALO, NY; WILLIAMSVILLE NORTH HS; (JR); Hi Hnr Roll; Hnr Roll; Nat Mrt LOC; WWAHSS; Yth Ldrshp Prog; DECA; Emplmnt; HO'Br Yth Ldrshp; Prom Com; French Clb; Cr Ctry (V C); Skiing; Track (V); Stu Cncl (R); CR (R); Yrbk (R); National Merit Commended Scholar; DECA International Conference Qualifier; Juris Doctorate; Law; U of Chicago; Washington U

HEYLIGER, ANTHONY; JAMAICA, NY; JOHN ADAMS HS; (JR); Hnr Roll; Nat Hon Sy; St of Mnth; Emplmnt; Off Aide; P to P St Amb Prg; Tchrs Aide; Bskball (V); Cl Off (P); Safety Council; Accounting; Business Administration; U of Pennsylvania; U of Chapel Hill

HEYMAN, CALEB; HARTSDALE, NY; ARDSLEY HS; (SO); Hnr Roll; Amnsty Intl; Hab For Humty Volntr; Chrch Yth Grp; Tmpl Yth Grp; Latin Clb; Tennis (V); Latin Club / Habitat for Humanity; Amnesty International Club; Political Science; English; U of Michigan; U of Wisconsin Madison

HICKEY, APRIL; FISHKILL, NY; OUR LADY OF LOURDES HS; (SO); Hi Hnr Roll; Nat Hon Sy; Pres Ac Ftns Aw; Sci Fairs; Comm Volntr; ArtClub; Emplmnt; Mus Clb; Vsity Clb; Bnd; Jzz Bnd; Sccr (JC); Assistant Coach of a Lacrosse Team.; Goalie for a Local Travel Soccer Team; Marine Biology; Chemistry; U of Rhode Island; Hawaii State

HICKS, ERICA; NEW YORK, NY; FREDERICK DOUGLASS SEC SCH; (SO); Ctznshp Aw; Hi Hnr Roll; Hnr Roll; Otst Ac Ach Awd; Perf Att; St of Mnth; Yth Ldrshp Prog; Comm Volntr; Peer Tut/Med; Chrch Yth Grp; Cmptr Clb; DARE; Dbte Team; Drma Clb; Emplmnt; Jr Ach; Lttrmn Clb; Chr; Ch Chr; Dnce; Bsball (L); Bskball (L); Ftball (L); Vllyball (L); Cl Off (R); CR (R); Hope for Kids; Journalist/Communication; Psychologist

HICKSON, ISHA D; BROOKLYN, NY; HARRY VAN ARSDALE HS; (JR); Nat Sci Aw; Sci Fairs; St of Mnth; DARE; Stu Cncl (V); Won the National Science Fair; Dentist Assistant; Early Education; Medgar Evers; York College

HIDALGO, ELIZABETH; STATEN ISLAND, NY; PORT RICHMOND HS; (FR); Hnr Roll; Perf Att

HIGGINBOTHAM, NATE; SCHENECTADY, NY; SCHENECTADY HS; (FR); Hnr Roll; Ftball; Wt Lftg; Photography; Football; Virginia Tech

HIGGINS, CHRISTOPHER; WADDINGTON, NY; MADRID-WADDINGTON CS HS; (JR); Hi Hnr Roll; WWAHSS; Dbte Team; Drma Clb; Key Club; Prom Com; Spch Team; French Clb; Bnd; Chr; SP/M/VS; Swg Chr; Yrbk (E); All-State and All-Eastern Choir; Vice President of Drama Club; Acting; Vocal Performance; U of the Arts (PA, USA); CW Post (Long Island, NY)

HILDENBRAND, SARAH; SAUGERTIES, NY; SAUGERTIES; (SO); Hi Hnr Roll; Hnr Roll; WWAHSS; Comm Volntr; HO'Br Yth Ldrshp; Key Club; Sccr (V L); Track (V); Cl Off (R); Stu Cncl (R)

HILL, LEAH; BALLSTON LAKE, NY; BURNT HILLS-BALLSTON LAKE HS; (JR); Hi Hnr Roll; Nat Hon Sy; WWAHSS; Comm Volntr; 4-H; Chrch Yth Grp; Civil Air Pat; Dbte Team; Emplmnt; Orch; Hsbk Rdg; Vllyball (J); VP of 4-H Club; In CAP; Engineering; West Point; RPI

HILL, TALITHA; BRONX, NY; HARRY S TRUMAN HS; (SR); DAR; Hnr Roll; Comm Volntr; Emplmnt; Photog; ROTC; Drl Tm; Tennis (V); Physical Therapist; Master's Degree or Doctorate; Pennsylvania State U

HILMY, HESHAM H; ENDICOTT, NY; UNION ENDICOTT HS; (JR); Hnr Roll; Nat Hon Sy; St of Mnth; Comm Volntr; Peer Tut/Med; DARE; Emplmnt; Key Club; Pep Squd; Prom Com; Svce Clb; SADD; Vsity Clb; Chrldg (V); Gmnstcs; Tennis (V L); Cl Off (S); Stu Cncl (P); CR (P); Yrbk (P); 200 Hours Community Service; Scholars Athlete; Masters in Business MBA; Foreign Languages; Ohio State U; SUNY Binghamton

HIMES, ERIN; PITTSFORD, NY; PITTSFORD MENDON HS; (JR); Hi Hnr Roll; Nat Hon Sy; Otst Ac Ach Awd; WWAHSS; Dbte Team; Mod UN; French Clb; Dnce; Fld Hky (V L); Skiing (J); Sccr (V L); Scholar Athlete Award; Association of Teen-Age Diplomats; Political Science; Law; Boston College; Tufts U

HIMPELE, MICHAEL R; CLIFTON PARK, NY; BURNT HILLS-BALLSTON LAKE HS; (FR); Hi Hnr Roll; Nat Hon Sy; Comm Volntr; Bsball (J); Sccr (JC); Wrstlg (V L); Presidential Fitness Award; Computer Technology; Marietta College; Slippery Rock U

HINES, CORETTA; BRONX, NY; EVANDER CHILDS HS; (JR); Peer Tut/Med; Chrch Yth Grp; Dbte Team; Emplmnt; Fr of Library; I Am Currently on the Debating Team; Accounting; Entrepreneurship; Johnson and Wales U; New York U

HINRICHS, KRISTEN; LEVITTOWN, NY; DIVISION AVE HS; (FR); Hi Hnr Roll; Sci Fairs; St of Mnth; WWAHSS; Comm Volntr; Key Club; Dnce; Tutoring / Community Service Through Key Club; Made the Kickline Team; Lawyer; Harvard U; Yale U

HITCHCOCK, SHANNA E; ONEONTA, NY; LAURENS CTRL SCH; (SR); Ctznshp Aw; DAR; WWAHSS; Yth Ldrshp Prog; Comm Volntr; ArtClub; Chrch Yth Grp; Emplmnt; Key Club; Prom Com; Scouts; SADD; Bskball (V L); Sccr (J); Sftball (V L); Cl Off (T); Yrbk (E); Dar Award, Leadership Award, Braille-; Presidential Excellence Award; Radiology Technician; Mohawk Valley Comm. College

HO, ANGELA; NEW YORK, NY; BRONX SCIENCE HS; (SO); Perf Att; St of Mnth; Drma Clb; Key Club; NtlFrnscLg; Photog; Spch Team; Magna Cum Laude on the National Latin Exam; History

HO, ERIC; MIDDLE ISLAND, NY; LONGWOOD SR HS; (SO); Hi Hnr Roll; Hnr Roll; Nat Mrt LOC; St of Mnth; Yth Ldrshp Prog; Peer Tut/Med; DARE; Brookhaven Youth Court

HO, STEVE; BROOKLYN, NY; NEW UTRECHT HS; (JR); Computer Repairing

HOBLER, AMANDA; HORSEHEADS, NY; HORSEHEADS HS; (JR); Hnr Roll; Nat Hon Sy; Yth Ldrshp Prog; Comm Volntr; Chrch Yth Grp; Emplmnt; NYLC; Ch Chr; Mch Bnd; Secondary Education; Spanish; State U of New York At Fredonia; Colgate U

HOBLIN, KARA; BLUE POINT, NY; BAYPORT BLUE POINT HS; (SO); Hi Hnr Roll; Hnr Roll; Nat Hon Sy; Otst Ac Ach Awd; St of Mnth; WWAHSS; Comm Volntr; Hab For Humty Volntr; Peer Tut/Med; ArtClub; Chrch Yth Grp; Emplmnt; Tchrs Aide; Fld Hky (J); Lcrsse (J); Track (J); Lit Mag (R); 3rd Place in BAFFA Art Show; Fashion Design; Business Communications; Fashion Institute of Technology; Columbia U

HOCHHEIM, PISIE; SCHENECTADY, NY; SCHENECTADY HS; (FR); Hi Hnr Roll; Otst Ac Ach Awd; Amnsty Intl; Comm Volntr; Chrch Yth Grp; Drma Clb; Outdrs Clb; Ch Chr; Dnce; SP/M/VS; Stg Cre; Stu Cncl (R); Piano; Law; Journalism; Harvard U; Vassar College

HODGE, SABRINA; NEW YORK, NY; SAINT MICHAEL AC; (SO); Chr; Ch Chr; Dnce; SP/M/VS; Veterinary Field; Journalism; Columbia U; New York U

HOERBELT, CHRISTOPHER V; LANCASTER, NY; ALDEN HS; (JR); Hi Hnr Roll; Hnr Roll; Perf Att; St of Mnth; WWAHSS; Comm Volntr; Emplmnt; Key Club; Golf (V); Cl Off (T); Stu Cncl (R); Computer Engineering; Law; Rensselaer Polytechnic Institute; Carnegie Mellon U

HOFFMANN, KYLE P; ENDICOTT, NY; UNION-ENDICOTT HS; (FR); Hi Hnr Roll; WWAHSS; Key Club; Bnd; Bsball; Sccr (J)

HOILETTE, CAHSHIRIA; STATEN ISLAND, NY; PT RICHMOND HS; (JR); Hnr Roll; Perf Att; Sci Fairs; Peer Tut/Med; DARE; Certificate for Microsoft Excel Power Point; Business; Computers; College of Staten Island; New York U

HOLDEN, DANIEL; SAUGERTIES, NY; SAUGERTIES HS; (SR); Hi Hnr Roll; Nat Hon Sy; Nat Mrt Sch Recip; Otst Ac Ach Awd; WWAHSS; Comm Volntr; Chess; Key Club; English; Film & Media Arts; Ithaca College; SUNY Geneseo

HOLLANDER, ORI; GREAT NECK, NY; GREAT NECK SOUTH HS; (SO); Hi Hnr Roll; Hnr Roll; Peer Tut/Med; DECA; Bskball (J); Stu Cncl (R); CR (T, R); Model Congress Club; Business; Law; U of Pennsylvania; Duke U

HOLLINGSHEAD, ASHLEY; BROOKLYN, NY; MIDWOOD HS; (SO); Comm Volntr; Key Club; Biomedical Engineering; Forensic Psychology; New York U; City College

HOLLINGSHEAD, MICHAEL; ROCHESTER, NY; CORNERSTONE CHRISTIAN AC; (SR); Hi Hnr Roll; Valdctrian; Chrch Yth Grp; Emplmnt; National Student Leadership Forum; Tutoring in School; Pre-Law / Political Science; Economics; Houghton College

HOLLMAN, TAKEYA; ROCHESTER, NY; JOHN MARSHALL HS; (SR); Hi Hnr Roll; Hnr Roll; St of Mnth; Peer Tut/Med; Chrch Yth Grp; Chr; Ch Chr; Dnce; Drl Tm; Bskball (V); Chrldg (V); Cr Ctry (J); GAA (V); Gmnstcs (V); Sftball (V); Track (V); Vllyball (V); Lawyer; Judge; Florida State; Texas A & M

HOLODAR, MICHELLE A; ISLAND PARK, NY; WEST HEMPSTEAD HS; (FR); Hi Hnr Roll; Hnr Roll; Nat Hon Sy; WWAHSS; Key Club; Chr; Dnce; Orch; SP/M/VS; Social Worker

HOMAYOON, SHERI; BAYPORT, NY; BAYPORT BLUE POINT HS; (SO); Hi Hnr Roll; Comm Volntr; Drma Clb; Scouts; Orch; Bskball (J); Sccr (V CL); Track (V L); Vllyball (J); State Qualifier For 2004 Spring Track; Teaching / Business; U of Miami; Duke

HORAN, SARAH E; NEWBURGH, NY; NEWBURGH FREE AC; (JR); F Lan Hn Soc; Hi Hnr Roll; Nat Hon Sy; Otst Ac Ach Awd; Comm Volntr; Chrch Yth Grp; Emplmnt; Outdrs Clb; Photog; Lit Mag (R, P); Foreign Exchange-Venezuela (YFU); NYSSA Summer Art Program-SUNY Brockport; Photography; International Studies

HORTON, AMY; PAINTED POST, NY; CORNING-PAINTED POST WEST HS; (JR); Hi Hnr Roll; Nat Hon Sy; Perf Att; St of Mnth; Comm Volntr; Dbte Team; JSA; Svce Clb; Tchrs Aide; French Clb; Chr; SP/M/VS; CR (R); Yrbk (R); Peace Corps

HOSEIN, SARA; QUEENS VILLAGE, NY; JAMAICA HS; (SR); F Lan Hn Soc; Hnr Roll; Nat Hon Sy; WWAHSS; Comm Volntr; Key Club; Lib Aide; Bdmtn (L); Sccr (V); Tennis (V); Lit Mag (R); Sch Ppr (R); Yrbk (P); Journalism; Management; Brooklyn College; Hunter College

HOSIE, TORY; CONESUS, NY; LIVONIA HS; (JR); 4H Awd; Hnr Roll; 4-H; Quiz Bowl; Chr; Hsbk Rdg (V); Sccr (J); Swmg (J); Criminal Justice; SUNY Oswego; Canton U

HOSLER, STEPHANIE R; CHAZY, NY; CHAZY CTRL RURAL SCH; (FR); Hi Hnr Roll; Comm Volntr; Emplmnt; Key Club; French Clb; Bnd; Chr; Ch Chr; Mch Bnd; Bskball (J); Sftball (JC); Stu Cncl (R); All-County Chorus; All State Chorus-Women's Chorus; Physician's Assistant; Registered Nurse; SUNY Plattsburgh

HOSSAIN, DERRICK; JAMAICA, NY; ST JOHN'S PREP HS; (SO); Hnr Roll; St of Mnth; Comm Volntr; Bnd; Cr Ctry (J); Tennis (V); Track (V); Stu Cncl (R); CR (R); Doctor; Career in Entertainment; New York U; College of Los Angeles

HOSSAIN, NAZMUL; OZONE PARK, NY; JOHN ADAMS HS; (SR); F Lan Hn Soc; Otst Ac Ach Awd; Perf Att; St of Mnth; Chrch Yth Grp; Scouts; Ch Chr; Vllyball (V); ESL Academic Award; Mathematical Academic Award; Medical Science; Teacher; Queens College; Hunter College

HOSSAIN, RAFAT; JACKSON HEIGHTS, NY; WILLIAM C BRYANT HS; (JR); F Lan Hn Soc; Hi Hnr Roll; Hnr Roll; MVP; Nat Hon Sy; Perf Att; Pres Ac Ftns Aw; WWAHSS; Comm Volntr; Peer Tut/Med; ArtClub; Chess; Key Club; Lib Aide; Photog; Svce Clb; Tchrs Aide; Foreign Clb; SP/M/VS; Cr Ctry (V); Track (V); Key Club Member; Library Volunteer; Pharmacy; Computer Science; St John U; Long Island U

HOSSAIN, SAZZAD; JACKSON HEIGHTS, NY; RENAISSANCE CHARTER SCH; (JR); Hnr Roll; Nat Hon Sy; Sci Fairs; WWAHSS; Yth Ldrshp Prog; Comm Volntr; Peer Tut/Med; ArtClub; Cmptr Clb; DARE; Dbte Team; Emplmnt; Jr Ach; NYLC; Photog; Bnd; SP/M/VS; Stg Cre; Bsball (V); Track (V); Adv Cncl (R); Stu Cncl (R); Sch Ppr (R, P); Yrbk (E, R, P); Graphic/Website Designer for School Sites; Masters in Computer Engineering; New York U; Pena State

HOU, ANDREW; FOREST HILLS, NY; STUYVESANT HS; (MS); Peer Tut/Med; Scouts; Tchrs Aide; Bnd; SP/M/VS; Stg Cre; Biological Sciences; Music; Yale U; Massachusetts Institute of Technology

HOULE, KRISTEN E; COHOES, NY; COHOES HS; (SR); Hnr Roll; Comm Volntr; Emplmnt; Prom Com; Svce Clb; Chr; Bskball (J); Lcrsse (VJ); Sccr (VJ); Yrbk (R); Speech Pathologist; Nutrition; SUNY Oneonta; SUNY Cortland

HOUSER, CHARLES; AVOCA, NY; AVOCA CTRL HS; (SR); Hi Hnr Roll; Hnr Roll; Nat Sci Aw; Scouts; Wdwrkg Clb; Clb; Prom King- 2005; Third In Senior Class Standings; Engineering Sciences; Construction Site Management; Monroe Community College Rochester NY

HOUSLEY, DANA M; BINGHAMTON, NY; SUSQUEHANNA VALLEY SR HS; (JR); Hi Hnr Roll; Hnr Roll; Otst Ac Ach Awd; Pres Ac Ftns Aw; St of Mnth; Comm Volntr; Hab For Humty Volntr; Chrch Yth Grp; DARE; Emplmnt; Scouts; Tech Clb; French Clb; Track (V); Wrstlg (J); Equestrian for 7 Years; Excite Club; Forensics; Criminal Justice; Cortland U; Ithaca U

HOUTMAN, ALEXANDER D; SAUGERTIES, NY; SAUGERTIES HS; (SO); Hi Hnr Roll; Otst Ac Ach Awd; WWAHSS; Comm Volntr; Spec Olymp Vol; DARE; Emplmnt; Key Club; Sccr (V L); Track (V L); Wrstlg (J L); Commercial Airline Pilot; Sports Medicine

HOWARD, CRYSTAL; BUFFALO, NY; MC KINLEY HS; (SO); Hnr Roll; Perf Att; Peer Tut/Med; ROTC; Bnd; Chr; Drl Tm; Sftball (L); Veterinarian; Photographer; Buffalo State College

HOWARD, LINDSAY M; BUFFALO, NY; MC KINLEY VOC TECH HS; (FR); Hnr Roll; Nat Hon Sy; Comm Volntr; DARE; ROTC; Swmg; Teens Taking Charge - Delavan Grider Center; Merit Roll Scholarship Award; Nurse Anesthetist / Bachelor's Degree; Lawyer; D'youville College; SUNY

HOWARD, SARAH; SAUGERTIES, NY; SAUGERTIES HS; (FR); Hi Hnr Roll; St of Mnth; WWAHSS; Comm Volntr; DARE; Dbte Team; Key Club; Scouts; Spanish Clb; Bnd; Lcrsse (J); Sch Ppr (R); Key Club International; Journalism; English; Boston U; Syracuse U

Hosler, Stephanie R
Chazy Ctrl Rural Sch
Chazy, NY

Hinrichs, Kristen
Division Ave HS
Levittown, NY

Herrera, Mario
Bushwick HS
Brooklyn, NY

Hines, Coretta
Evander Childs HS
Bronx, NY

Houle, Kristen E
Cohoes HS
Cohoes, NY

HOWELL, BRYANT; MT VERNON, NY; MT VERNON HS; (JR); Sci Fairs; Comm Volntr; Hosp Aide; Red Cr Aide; Chrch Yth Grp; Emplmnt; ROTC; Scouts; Mount Vernon Baseball; Yonkers Basketball; Business; Military; New York State Schools

HOWELL, DESTINY; BROOKLYN, NY; PAUL ROBESON HS; (SR); Fashion Management; Fashion Institute Of Technology; UC Berkeley

HOWELL, LAMAR; BRONX, NY; CARDINAL HAYES HS; (JR); ArtClub; Emplmnt; Bnd; Jzz Bnd; Mathematics

HOWELL, RACHEL; HUNT, NY; KESHEQUA HS; (SR); Hi Hnr Roll; Nat Hon Sy; WWAHSS; 4-H; Drma Clb; Key Club; Photog; Bnd; Chr; Mch Bnd; SP/M/VS; Sftball (V); Vllyball (V); Cl Off (S); Yrbk (E); 4-H; Nursing; Photography; SUNY Alfred

HOY JR, ALCIDES; BROOKLYN, NY; LA SALLE AC; (JR); Ctznshp Aw; Hi Hnr Roll; Hnr Roll; Nat Ldrshp Svc; Otst Ac Ach Awd; Perf Att; St of Mnth; WWAHSS; Peer Tut/Med; BPA; Chrch Yth Grp; FBLA; Bskball (J); Track (V); Stu Cncl (R); CR (R); Business; Marketing; Penn State Abington; Pennsylvania U

HRABKO, ROBYN L; ROCHESTER, NY; EASTRIDGE SR HS; (SR); Hi Hnr Roll; Hnr Roll; MVP; Comm Volntr; Peer Tut/Med; Emplmnt; Scouts; Varsity Bowling; Equine Business Major; U of Findlay

HRYNKIW, ANNASTASIA; ELMIRA, NY; THOMAS A EDISON HS; (SO); Hi Hnr Roll; Chrch Yth Grp; Key Club; Chr; Ch Chr; SP/M/VS; Track (V); Stu Cncl; NYSSMA Solo Festival; ACDA Eastern Division Honors Choir; Music Education; Psychology; Berkeley in Boston; Fredonia

HSU, LYDIA; ITHACA, NY; ITHACA HS; (SO); Hi Hnr Roll; Sci Fairs; Chrch Yth Grp; Bnd; Orch; Education; Music; Northwestern U; Cornell U

HU, KAREN; FRESH MEADOWS, NY; FRANCIS LEWIS HS; (SO); Hnr Roll; Nat Hon Sy; St of Mnth; WWAHSS; Comm Volntr; Peer Tut/Med; ArtClub; Chrch Yth Grp; Emplmnt; Bnd; Orch; Yrbk (R); Junior Arista; Nizma (Piano); Creative Writing; Journalism; U of Richmond; U of Vermont

HU, LEYDA; NEW YORK, NY; MANHATTAN CTR FOR SCI & MATH; (SR); Hnr Roll; Perf Att; Comm Volntr; Chrch Yth Grp; FCA; Counselor for University Settlement; Engineering; SUNY Binghamton; SUNY Stony Brook

HU, SHIRLEY; REGO PARK, NY; STUYVESANT HS; (SO); Hnr Roll; Perf Att; St of Mnth; Comm Volntr; Red Cr Aide; Emplmnt; Key Club; Mth Clb/Tm; Mod UN; Svce Clb; Dnce; Stg Cre; Yrbk (E, R); Math Fair; Art Awards (Drawing); Medicine; Arts (Architecture, Graphic Design); Columbia U; Massachusetts Institute of Technology

HUANG, AMY; BROOKLYN, NY; STUYVESANT HS; (SO); Nat Hon Sy; Perf Att; WWAHSS; Yth Ldrshp Prog; Key Club; Mth Clb/Tm; Sci Clb; Tchrs Aide; Bnd; Track (L); The National Society of High School Scholars Member; Best of Brooklyn Award; Pre-Medicine; Surgery; Harvard U; Yale U

HUANG, DANIEL; EAST ELMHURST, NY; AC FOR AMERICAN STUDIES; (FR); Hnr Roll; MVP; Perf Att; Sci Fairs; St of Mnth; Bnd; Vllyball (V); CR (R); MVP - New York Junior Tennis League; Master's Degree; Teacher; Queens College; New York U

HUANG, JENNY J; SOUTH SETAUKET, NY; WARD MELVILLE HS; (SR); F Lan Hn Soc; Hi Hnr Roll; Nat Hon Sy; Otst Ac Ach Awd; WWAHSS; Hab For Humty Volntr; Hosp Aide; Spec Olymp Vol; Pep Squd; Quill & Scroll; Svce Clb; Clr Grd; Orch; Cl Off (S); Sch Ppr (E); Women of the Moose Community Service Award; Political Science; Law; SUNY Stony Brook

HUANG, LINGQIN; WOODSIDE, NY; WILLIAM C BRYANT HS; (SO); Off Aide; Tchrs Aide; Chinese Clb; Architecture; Environmental/Architecture Design; The Cooper Union

HUANG, MARY; BROOKLYN, NY; MIDWOOD HS; (JR); Hnr Roll; Nat Hon Sy; Perf Att; Sci Fairs; St of Mnth; WWAHSS; Comm Volntr; Hosp Aide; Peer Tut/Med; Chrch Yth Grp; Key Club; Off Aide; Photog; Orch; Sch Ppr; Piano- Grade 5 Associated Board of Music; Psychology; Child Education; Binghamton U; New York U

HUANG, SOFIE S; BROOKLYN, NY; STUYVESANT HS; (SO); Sci Fairs; WWAHSS; Comm Volntr; Key Club; Mod UN; Sci Clb; Chinese Clb; Chr; SP/M/VS; Adv Cncl (R)

HUANG, WENDY; BROOKLYN, NY; STUYVESANT HS; (SO); Hnr Roll; Salutrn; Comm Volntr; Key Club; Mth Clb/Tm; SP/M/VS; Business/ Marketing; Fashion Design; Princeton U; Harvard U

HUBERMAN, ROBERT; BROOKLYN, NY; JAMES MADISON HS; Hnr Roll; Otst Ac Ach Awd; Sci Fairs; Comm Volntr; Raising Money for JDRF in an Academic Setting; Increased Public Awareness and Helped To Expand Public Outreach; Political Science; Cornell, Boston U, NYU; Columbia, Vassar, Princeton

HUDLIN, MIKHAIL A; BRENTWOOD, NY; BRENTWOOD HS; (JR); Otst Ac Ach Awd; St of Mnth; Comm Volntr; Chrch Yth Grp; Drma Clb; Mus Clb; ROTC; Acpl Chr; Chr; Clr Grd; Drl Tm; Tennis (V); Track (V); Stu Cncl (R); CR (R); Yrbk (R); Martin Luther King Jr Poem 1st Place / 10th Grade; NAACP Vice President / 9th-10th Grade; Aviation - Air Traffic Controlling / Engineering; Music - Performance / Production / Recording; Vaughn College of Aeronautics; Embry Riddle Aeronautical U

HUDSON, CHEYENNE N; BRONX, NY; GRACE H DODGE VOC HS; (JR); Hnr Roll; St of Mnth; Comm Volntr; Chrch Yth Grp; Emplmnt; Mock Trial Program; Handball - School Sports; Forensic Science; Criminal Justice; U of New Haven; Iona College

HUDSON, MONIQUE; BALDWIN, NY; BALDWIN HS; (FR); Hnr Roll; St of Mnth; Dnce; Hofstra U; NYU

HUDSON, SHANIKA S; SOUTH OZONE PARK, NY; ST FRANCIS PREP SCH; (SR); F Lan Hn Soc; Nat Hon Sy; Comm Volntr; Off Aide; Chr; Liturgical Ensemble; National Science Honor Society; Biology; MD; Boston U

HUESER, ANDREW; HAMLIN, NY; BROCKPORT HS; (FR); Ctznshp Aw; Hi Hnr Roll; Comm Volntr; Vllyball (J); Church Usher; Flying Club Member; Mechanical Engineering; Rochester Institute of Technology; Clarkson U

HUGHES, KAITLIN A; PATCHOGUE, NY; BELLPORT HS; (FR); Hi Hnr Roll; MVP; Nat Hon Sy; WWAHSS; Comm Volntr; Peer Tut/Med; Chrch Yth Grp; Drma Clb; Key Club; Outdrs Clb; French Clb; Bnd; Chr; Mch Bnd; Orch; Sftball (J); Bowling-Varsity; Altar Server; Neurosurgeon; Neurologist; Boston U; Northeastern U

HUI, IVANA; LITTLE NECK, NY; BRONX HS OF SCIENCE; (FR); Hnr Roll; Nat Hon Sy; Comm Volntr; Emplmnt; Key Club; Animal Sciences; Asian History; New York U; Cornell U

HULL, STACEY; ROCHESTER, NY; GATES CHILI HS; (JR); Hi Hnr Roll; Hnr Roll; Nat Hon Sy; WWAHSS; Yth Ldrshp Prog; Comm Volntr; Chrch Yth Grp; Emplmnt; Mth Clb/Tm; Ch Chr; Tennis (V); Stu Cncl (R); CR (R); Academic Varsity Letter; Young Women of Distinction Award; Forensic Sciences; Genetic Research; U of Rochester; Cedar Crest College

HULL, TIMOTHY; BUFFALO, NY; WILLIAMSVILLE SOUTH; (JR); Hnr Roll; Nat Hon Sy; WWAHSS; Comm Volntr; Hab For Humty Volntr; Emplmnt; Bnd; Ftball (V L); Wrstlg (L)

HUMPHREY, JASON A; ITHACA, NY; ITHACA HS; (SR); Hnr Roll; Comm Volntr; Red Cr Aide; FBLA; Math Department Award-10th Grade; Hotel Management; Johnson & Wales U

HUNT, EVAN; SAUGERTIES, NY; (JR); Hnr Roll; WWAHSS; Key Club; Mus Clb; Vsity Clb; Chr; SP/M/VS; Stg Cre; Ftball (V L); Lcrsse (V L); Sccr (VJ L); Tennis (V L); Play Guitar-Recorded CD; Business; Music

HUNT, J ERIC; INTERLAKEN, NY; SOUTH SENECA HS; (SR); 4H Awd; Ctznshp Aw; DAR; Hi Hnr Roll; Nat Hon Sy; Otst Ac Ach Awd; Sci/Math Olympn; St of Mnth; Valdctrian; WWAHSS; Comm Volntr; Red Cr Aide; AL Aux Boys; Chrch Yth Grp; Emplmnt; Bnd; Bsball (VJ L); Bskball (VJ L); Adv Cncl (R); Cl Off (V, S); Stu Cncl (R); Biological & Environmental Engineering; Cornell U

HUNTER, FELICIA R; ELMONT, NY; FLORAL PARK MEMORIAL HS; (SR); Hnr Roll; Nat Hon Sy; Nat Mrt Fin; Nat Mrt Sch Recip; Nat Mrt Semif; St of Mnth; WWAHSS; Comm Volntr; Hab For Humty Volntr; Peer Tut/Med; Emplmnt; P to P St Amb Prg; SADD; Orch; Vllyball (J); Sch Ppr (R); President of Big Brother/Big Sister; Accounting; Bernard Baruch College; New York U

HUNTER, JESSICA L; SCHENECTADY, NY; SCHENECTADY HS; (SO); Hnr Roll; Otst Ac Ach Awd; Perf Att; Chrch Yth Grp; Drma Clb; Foreign Clb; Acpl Chr; Ch Chr; Dnce; SP/M/VS; Stu Cncl (R); Umoja African Dance Troupe; Participation in Science Olympiads; Biochemical Engineering; Physics

HUNTER, LAURA A; CASSADAGA, NY; CASSADAGA VALLEY MHS; (JR); Hi Hnr Roll; Nat Hon Sy; Pres Ac Ftns Aw; St of Mnth; WWAHSS; Comm Volntr; Cmptr Clb; Emplmnt; Key Club; Prom Com; SADD; Tchrs Aide; Spanish Clb; Bnd; Chr; Jzz Bnd; SP/M/VS; Bskball (VJ L); Track (V L); Vllyball (VJ L); Pre-Med; Psychology; Cornell U; Penn State U

HUNTINGTON, CAITLYN E; GANSEVOORT, NY; SOUTH GLENS FALLS SR HS; (JR); Ctznshp Aw; DAR; F Lan Hn Soc; Hi Hnr Roll; Hnr Roll; Nat Hon Sy; Pres Sch; Emplmnt; Key Club; Bnd; Fld Hky (VJ); Lcrsse (J); Stu Cncl (V, S); Young Kodak Leaders Award; Political Science; Pre-Law; Hamilton; U of Rochester

HURTADO, CAROL; WOODSIDE, NY; INTERNATIONAL HS AT LAGUARDIA; (SO); Ctznshp Aw; St of Mnth; Drma Clb; Dnce; CR (R); Theatre/Performing Arts; NYU; Columbia U

HUSSAIN, RAAFAE; HIGHLAND MILLS, NY; MW HS; (SO); Hnr Roll; Nat Hon Sy; Comm Volntr; Cmptr Clb; Drma Clb; Mth Clb/Tm; NYLC; P to P St Amb Prg; Sci Clb; Jzz Bnd; SP/M/VS; Track (V); Vsy Clb (J); Radiologist MD; Genetic Research (Biology)

HUSSEIN, NAFISA; YONKERS, NY; SAUNDERS TRADES & TECH HS; (SO); Hi Hnr Roll; Nat Hon Sy; Perf Att; Comm Volntr; Peer Tut/Med; Spec Olymp Vol; Key Club; SADD; Pre-Med in College; Doctor; New York U; SUNY Stony Brook

HUTCHINSON, PRINCESS; MONROE, NY; MONROE-WOODBURY HS; (SO); Hnr Roll; St of Mnth; Drma Clb; FTA; Mus Clb; Dnce; Orch; Sch Ppr (R); Journalism; Mass Communications; Virginia State U; Virginia Union U

HYMAN, SHALISIA; BROOKLYN, NY; ACORN HS FOR SOCIAL JUSTICE; (SO); Hi Hnr Roll; Hnr Roll; Otst Ac Ach Awd; Perf Att; Sci Fairs; DARE; Sci Clb; Dnce; Law; Florida State U; Georgia Tech U

IACONO, MATTHEW; JEWETT, NY; WINDHAM ASHLAND JEWETT CTRL SCH; (SO); Hi Hnr Roll; Hnr Roll; Nat Hon Sy; Nat Stu Ath Day Aw; St of Mnth; WWAHSS; Comm Volntr; Peer Tut/Med; Red Cr Aide; Chrch Yth Grp; Emplmnt; Mus Clb; Spanish Clb; Bnd; Jzz Bnd; Bsball (V L); Bskball (J); Sccr (V L); Cl Off (P); All-Star Athlete (Baseball); Outstanding Community Service (Red Cross); Sports Medicine; Law; St. John's U

IBRAHEEM, AFAF; BROOKLYN, NY; JAMES MADISON HS; (SO); Hi Hnr Roll; Sci Fairs; Comm Volntr; Hosp Aide; Peer Tut/Med; DARE; Key Club; Mth Clb/Tm; Off Aide; Outdrs Clb; Quiz Bowl; Stu Cncl (R); CR (V); Bio-Chemistry, Medicine; Pediatrics; Columbia U; New York U

IBRAHIM, AZIZA; YONKERS, NY; LINCOLN HS; (JR); Hnr Roll; Perf Att; WWAHSS; ArtClub; Dnce; Vllyball (J); In Who's Who Tenth Grade Year; Real Estate; Business; Mercy College; Pace U

IBRAHIM, OMAR; SYRACUSE, NY; WARDLAW HARTRIDGE SCH; (JR); St of Mnth; Yth Ldrshp Prog; Comm Volntr; Hab For Humty Volntr; Hosp Aide; BPA; Key Club; Off Aide; Bskball (V); Ftball (J); Tennis (JV); Wrstlg (JV); Riverview Med Ctr Research (The Relation Between Obesity & Early Miscarriage in Hispanic Women); Volunteer for Tryout Marathon for Breast Cancer Research, Youth Coordinator for EPIC Organization; Biology / Science; Healthcare; New York U; Villanova U

IBRAHIM, SHAMIRA; NEW YORK, NY; BRONX HS OF SCIENCE; (SO); Dbte Team; NtlFrnscLg; Stu Cncl (R); 97th Percentage in PSATS; Law; Politics; Columbia U; Vassar College

IERVESE, BRIANNA; WADING RIVER, NY; SHOREHAM-WADING RIVER HS; (JR); Hi Hnr Roll; Hnr Roll; Otst Ac Ach Awd; Perf Att; St of Mnth; Comm Volntr; Hab For Humty Volntr; Peer Tut/Med; Chrch Yth Grp; Emplmnt; Mth Clb/Tm; Tchrs Aide; Ch Chr; Dnce; Orch; Sch Ppr (E, R, P); English; Education; St John's U; Columbia U

IFILL, XAVIER J; BROOKLYN, NY; BENJAMIN BANNEKER AC; (JR); Ctznshp Aw; Hnr Roll; Nat Hon Sy; St of Mnth; WWAHSS; Yth Ldrshp Prog; Comm Volntr; Peer Tut/Med; ArtClub; Dbte Team; Mth Clb/Tm; Prom Com; Tchrs Aide; SP/M/VS; Stg Cre; Track (V); Adv Cncl (R); Cl Off (R); Stu Cncl (R); CR (R); Yrbk (E); Finance; Mechanical Engineering; Florida State U; Morehouse College

IGNAT, ANDREI; BRONX, NY; HUNTER COLLEGE HS; (JR); Nat Mrt LOC; Peer Tut/Med; Chess; Emplmnt; Mth Clb/Tm; Scouts; Swmg (V); Film Maker; Columbia U; Pomona College

IJAZ, YASREEN; BROOKLYN, NY; NEW UTRECHT HS; (SO); Hnr Roll; Fr of Library; Stg Cre; Bskball (J); Ftball (J); Vllyball (J); Fashion Designer; Law School; Brooklyn College; NYU

ILIN, YELENA; STATEN ISLAND, NY; STATEN ISLAND TECH HS; (SO); Ctznshp Aw; Hi Hnr Roll; Hnr Roll; Kwnis Aw; Otst Ac Ach Awd; Perf Att; Sci Fairs; Sci/Math Olympn; St of Mnth; Valdctrian; Comm Volntr; Hosp Aide; Key Club; Mth Clb/Tm; SP/M/VS; Track (J); Stu Cncl (R); Participation in Various School Assemblies; Participant in Regional Level Social Studies Fair; Architecture; Business Administration; Cooper Union; Yale U

ILLUZZI, CHRISTINA; STATEN ISLAND, NY; ST PETER'S HS FOR GIRLS; (FR); Hi Hnr Roll; Nat Sci Aw; Valdctrian; Comm Volntr; Lib Aide; Clb; Stg Cre; General Excellence Award; High Honor Roll; Law; Teaching; Wagner College; St Joseph's College, St John's U

ILUKOWICZ, JESSICA; LEVITTOWN, NY; ISLAND TREES HS; (FR); Hi Hnr Roll; Hnr Roll; Sci Fairs; Comm Volntr; Key Club; Scouts; Bnd; Jzz Bnd; Mch Bnd; Sccr (J); Island Trees Soccer Club.; Bronze and Silver Award; Optometrist; Dermatologist

IMBER, ANDREW G; MERRICK, NY; JOHN F KENNEDY HS; (FR); Hnr Roll; Sci/Math Olympn; Comm Volntr; Key Club; Mth Clb/Tm; Chr; Sccr (J); Cl Off (R); Stu Cncl (R); Chosen to Take American High School Math Exam & National Spanish Exam; Placed 9th in Math Competition At SUNY

IMBODY, KELLEY; SCHENECTADY, NY; SCHENECTADY HS; (SO); F Lan Hn Soc; Hi Hnr Roll; Hnr Roll; WWAHSS; Comm Volntr; French Clb; Sccr (V); Track (V); Stu Cncl (R); English Education; English Literature; York College; Drexel U

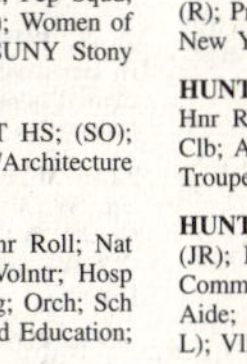

Ilin, Yelena
Staten Island Tech HS
Staten Island, NY

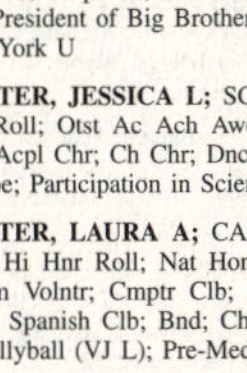

Hutchinson, Princess
Monroe-Woodbury HS
Monroe, NY

National
Honor Roll
Spring 2005

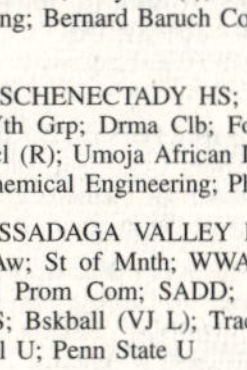

Humphrey, Jason A
Ithaca HS
Ithaca, NY

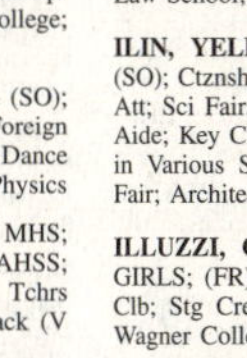

Illuzzi, Christina
St Peter's HS For Girls
Staten Island, NY

INFANTE, ROSEANNE; HOWARD BEACH, NY; LEON M GOLDSTEIN HS SCIENCES; (SO); F Lan Hn Soc; Hnr Roll; Nat Hon Sy; Sci Fairs; Comm Volntr; Mus Clb; Photog; Chr; Clr Grd; Dnce; SP/M/VS; Tennis (V); CR (R); International Foreign Language Award; Teacher; New York U (NYU); Columbia U

INGRAHAM, GRETCHEN; EARLVILLE, NY; VALLEY HEIGHTS CHRISTIAN AC; (SO); Hi Hnr Roll; Nat Hon Sy; Sci Fairs; WWAHSS; Comm Volntr; Chrch Yth Grp; Lib Aide; Chr; Ch Chr

INHOFF, MARIKA; ENDICOTT, NY; UNION ENDICOTT HS; (JR); Hi Hnr Roll; Hnr Roll; Otst Ac Ach Awd; Sci Fairs; WWAHSS; Amnsty Intl; Comm Volntr; Key Club; Vsity Clb; French Clb; Dnce; Tennis (V); Psychology; Medicine; New York U; Boston College

INNES, SABRINA; SHIRLEY, NY; WILLIAM FLOYD HS; (JR); F Lan Hn Soc; Hnr Roll; Sci Fairs; WWAHSS; Comm Volntr; ArtClub; Key Club; Mth Clb/Tm; French Clb; Hsbk Rdg; Swmg (V); Art; Math; New York U; U of the Arts

INOA, NATHALY; BRONX, NY; EVANDER CHILDS HS; (SR); Hnr Roll; Otst Ac Ach Awd; Perf Att; Emplmnt; ROTC; Vllyball (C); Criminal Justice; Business Management; John Jay Criminal Justice; Lehman College

INZINNA, CONCETTA; LIMA, NY; LIVONIA HS; (SR); 4H Awd; Hi Hnr Roll; Nat Hon Sy; WWAHSS; Comm Volntr; Peer Tut/Med; Spec Olymp Vol; 4-H; Key Club; Photog; Prom Com; Spanish Clb; Bnd; Jzz Bnd; Mch Bnd; SP/M/VS; Bskball (J); Track (V L); Vllyball (V L); Cl Off (V); Stu Cncl (V); Yrbk (R); Broadcasting Communications; SUNY Oswego

IOVINO, JESSICA R; OAKDALE, NY; ST ANTHONY'S HS; (JR); Hnr Roll; Pres Ac Ftns Aw; Sci Fairs; Yth Ldrshp Prog; Peer Tut/Med; DARE; Off Aide; Pep Squd; Svce Clb; Chr; Dnce; PPSqd (V); Track; Psychology; Education; Geneseo U; Binghamton U

IP, JESSICA; FRESH MEADOWS, NY; FRANCIS LEWIS HS; (JR); Mus Clb; Chr; Psychology; Harvard U; Stanford U

IPPOLITO, KIESHA R S; AMSTERDAM, NY; BROADALBIN-PERTH HS; (JR); Hnr Roll; WWAHSS; ArtClub; Drma Clb; Key Club; Prom Com; Dnce; SP/M/VS; Key Club, Art Club, and Drama Club; Fashion Design; Fashion Merchandising; Fashion Institute of Technology; The Pratt Institute

IQBAL, MOHAMMAD T; BALDWINSVILLE, NY; CW BAKER HS; (JR); Ctznshp Aw; Hnr Roll; Nat Mrt LOC; Otst Ac Ach Awd; Perf Att; Pres Ac Ftns Aw; Pres Sch; Sci/Math Olympn; Comm Volntr; Hosp Aide; Peer Tut/Med; 4-H; Mth Clb/Tm; Ntl Beta Clb; Ftball (V); Track (V); Boys State of New York-American Legion; MD; Biology; Boston U; Cornell

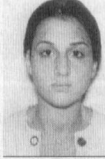

ISAAKOVA, JULIA; BROOKLYN, NY; JAMES MADISON HS; (SO); Hnr Roll; Kwnis Aw; Nat Hon Sy; Perf Att; Sci Fairs; Sci/Math Olympn; Comm Volntr; Peer Tut/Med; Key Club; Lib Aide; Off Aide; Sci Clb; Svce Clb; Jewish Club; Research Club; Degree in Medicine; Optometrist or Pediatrician; New York U; School of Optometry

ISHAM, CAITLIN; MERRICK, NY; CALHOUN HS; (SO); F Lan Hn Soc; Hnr Roll; WWAHSS; Peer Tut/Med; DECA; Emplmnt; Key Club; NYLC; Chrldg (V); Lcrsse (JC); Cl Off (T); Stu Cncl (R); Math Fair Semi-Finalist; National DECA Competitor; Business; Finance

ISKAROS, JOHN; STATEN ISLAND, NY; NEW DORP HS; (JR); Hnr Roll; Nat Hon Sy; Nat Sci Aw; Otst Ac Ach Awd; St of Mnth; St Optmst of Yr; Comm Volntr; Peer Tut/Med; Biology Clb; Emplmnt; NtlFrnscLg; Ch Chr; Stg Cre; CR (V); Medicine; Forensics; New York U

ISLAM, AYSHA; BROOKLYN, NY; BARD HS EARLY COLLEGE; (SO); Hnr Roll; Perf Att; WWAHSS; Comm Volntr; Hosp Aide; Peer Tut/Med; Mus Clb; Bnd; Clr Grd; Skiing (J); Track (J); Propagandist of Current Events Club; Biology; Columbia U; New York U

ISLAM, AZHARUL; BROOKLYN, NY; IS 218 JAMES PETER SINNOTT; MS; Hnr Roll; Sci Fairs; St of Mnth; Chess; Mth Clb/Tm; Sccr (J); Sftball (V); Track (V); Doctor; Lawyer; Columbia U; NYU

ISLAM, MAINUL; ELMHURST, NY; NEWTOWN HS; (SO); Hnr Roll; Perf Att; Wt Lftg (J); Astronomy; Engineering

ISRAEL, RUBEN; ELMHURST, NY; NEWTOWN HS; (SO); Perf Att; St of Mnth; Chrch Yth Grp; Ch Chr; Medical Doctor; Forensic Science; Any Private College

ITOKA, RANEK; ROSEDALE, NY; NEW YORK MILITARY AC; (SO); Hnr Roll; Perf Att; USAA; Comm Volntr; Red Cr Aide; DARE; Drma Clb; P to P St Amb Prg; ROTC; Chr; Clr Grd; Drl Tm; Lcrsse (J); Sccr (J); Track (V L); Leo's Club; Pharmacy; Lab Technician; Xavier U of Louisiana; U of Chicago

JAACKS, LINDSAY; WATERTOWN, NY; WATERTOWN HS; (JR); Hnr Roll; MVP; Nat Hon Sy; Pres Sch; WWAHSS; Comm Volntr; Red Cr Aide; Chrch Yth Grp; Emplmnt; Key Club; Sci Clb; Ch Chr; Sccr; Track; Vllyball (V); Cl Off (P); CR (P); Mission Trip to Tijuana, Mexico; Chemical Nanotechnology; Biomedical Engineering; Duke U; North Carolina State

JAACKS, MEGHAN; WATERTOWN, NY; WATERTOWN HS; (SR); Hi Hnr Roll; Jr Rot; MVP; Nat Hon Sy; Otst Ac Ach Awd; Pres Ac Ftns Aw; Comm Volntr; Peer Tut/Med; Red Cr Aide; Chrch Yth Grp; Emplmnt; Key Club; Mth Clb/Tm; Vsity Clb; Bnd; Chr; Mch Bnd; SP/M/VS; Lcrsse (V L); Sccr (V CL); Track (V CL); Vllyball (V CL); Cl Off (T); Stu Cncl (S); CR (R); Yrbk (E); National Honor Society Executive Board Member; Key Club President; Major in Business Administration; Northeastern U

JACK, ALISHA M; CANISTEO, NY; CANISTEO-GREENWOOD CTRL HS; (SO); Hi Hnr Roll; Chrch Yth Grp; Spanish Clb; Bnd; Mch Bnd; Pep Bnd; Bskball (J); Sccr (V); Track (V); Cl Off (P); CR (P); Sch Ppr (R); Elementary Education; Law; Syracuse University; Boston College

JACKSON, BRIANNA; BUFFALO, NY; BUFFALO AC FOR VISUAL AND PERF ARTS HS; (FR); Ctznshp Aw; Hnr Roll; Otst Ac Ach Awd; Perf Att; Sci Fairs; St of Mnth; Comm Volntr; Chrch Yth Grp; DARE; Jr Ach; Mth Clb/Tm; Sci Clb; Scouts; Acpl Chr; Bnd; Chr; Ch Chr; Dnce; Mch Bnd; Gmnstcs; Mar Art; Scr Kpr; University of Buffalo Pre-Collegiate Summer Program; National Youth Sports Programs; Business Administration; Cosmetology; Howard U; Canisius College

JACKSON, ELIZABETH A; CHITTENANGO, NY; CHITTENANGO HS; (JR); Hi Hnr Roll; Hnr Roll; St of Mnth; Peer Tut/Med; DARE; Emplmnt; Pep Squd; Chrldg (VJ); Air Traffic Controller

JACKSON, LISHAN; FREEPORT, NY; FREEPORT HS; (JR); Hi Hnr Roll; Hnr Roll; Sci Fairs; St of Mnth; Comm Volntr; Peer Tut/Med; DECA; FBLA; Key Club; Mod UN; Bskball (V); Tennis (V); New York State Scholar-Athlete Team; Top 10 of the NY DECA State Competition for Category; Pre-Medicine; Cornell U; SUNY Binghamton U

JACKSON, TIANA; BUFFALO, NY; MC KINLEY VOC TECH HS; (FR); Hi Hnr Roll; Hnr Roll; Nat Hon Sy; St of Mnth; Peer Tut/Med; Dnce; Cl Off (V); Stu Cncl (T); Computer Technology; Printing; Canisius College; U of Buffalo

JACKSON, TINA M; BROOKLYN, NY; (FR); Hnr Roll; Perf Att; Sci Fairs; St of Mnth; Dnce

JACOB, ALBY; GLEN OAKS, NY; BRONX HS OF SCIENCE; (SO); WWAHSS; Chrch Yth Grp; Jr Cls League; Key Club; Svce Clb; Dnce; Indian Cultural Assembly; National Student Leadership Conference; Doctor; Pharmacy; Boston U; St John's U

JACOBS, ANDRE L; PEEKSKILL, NY; PEEKSKILL HS; (JR); Ctznshp Aw; Hnr Roll; Otst Ac Ach Awd; Yth Ldrshp Prog; Comm Volntr; DARE; Emplmnt; Kwanza Clb; SP/M/VS; Bskball (VJ); Ftball (V); Lcrsse (V); Leadership/Personal Growth; Acme; Engineering; Florida A & M U; Morehouse U

JACOBS, MITCHELL; GROTON, NY; GROTON HS; (SO); Hi Hnr Roll; Comm Volntr; Chrch Yth Grp; Emplmnt; Bnd; Jzz Bnd; Cl Off (T); Karate; Aerospace Engineering; Software Engineering; Syracuse U; Rochester Institute of Technology

JACOBSEN, TYLER M; HIGHLAND MILLS, NY; MONROE-WOODBURY HS; (FR); Hi Hnr Roll; Comm Volntr; Chrch Yth Grp; Bnd; Mch Bnd; Ftball (J); Martial Arts- 6 Years / Black Belt

JAGNANAN, DEVIKA; SPRING VALLEY, NY; RAMAPO HS; (JR); Hnr Roll; Peer Tut/Med; ArtClub; Sccr (V); Yrbk (R); Psychology; Photography; Marlboro College; SUNY Fredonia

JAIME, NOEMI R; BROOKLYN, NY; TRANSIT TECH HS; (JR); Hnr Roll; Nat Hon Sy; Otst Ac Ach Awd; St of Mnth; Vsity Clb; Sftball (V); Sch Ppr (R); Yrbk (P); Community Service Awards; Psychology; Hunter College; Long Island U

JAIN, PREETI; STATEN ISLAND, NY; (MS); Ctznshp Aw; Perf Att; St of Mnth; Mus Clb; Bnd; Dnce; SP/M/VS; Stg Cre; Swmg; Tennis; Track; Recognized for Achievement on Nat'l Latin Exam; Won a Scholarship to Summer Studio Program; Pediatrics/MD

JAIN, SEJAL; FOREST HILLS, NY; STUYVESANT HS; (JR); Hi Hnr Roll; Nat Hon Sy; Otst Ac Ach Awd; Comm Volntr; Key Club; Tmpl Yth Grp; Dnce; SP/M/VS; President of Indian Culture Club; Volunteer for Rajasthan Association of N America; Pre-Med; Johns Hopkins; Columbia U

JAIRAM, ROMMEL; SOUTH OZONE PARK, NY; JOHN ADAMS HS; (SR); Hnr Roll; MVP; Nat Hon Sy; Otst Ac Ach Awd; Sci Fairs; St of Mnth; WWAHSS; Comm Volntr; Peer Tut/Med; Biology Clb; Key Club; Mth Clb/Tm; Off Aide; Prom Com; Sci Clb; Bnd; SP/M/VS; Track (J); CR (R); National Honor Society; Math & Science Institute; Computer Engineer; Architect; St. John's U; New York Institute of Technology

JAISINGH, JAVID R; JAMAICA, NY; HILLCREST HS; (JR); Hnr Roll; ROTC; Bsball; Bskball; Sccr; Track; Participated in R.O.T.C. for 1 Yr.; Aeronautics Engineering; Optometry; Baruch College (CUNY); New York U

JANAK, TAYLOR C; BOSTON, NY; IMMACULATA AC; (SO); Hi Hnr Roll; USAA; WWAHSS; Comm Volntr; Drma Clb; SP/M/VS; Yrbk (R); Helen Keller Scholarship; Immaculata Academy Scholarship; Canisius College

JANNEH, KARALANG; BRONX, NY; MONROE AC FOR BUSINESS & LAW; (FR); Ctznshp Aw; Gov Hnr Prg; Nat Mrt LOC; Otst Ac Ach Awd; Perf Att; Pres Ac Ftns Aw; Pres Sch; St of Mnth; USAA; Yth Ldrshp Prog; Amnsty Intl; Comm Volntr; Spec Olymp Vol; BPA; Emplmnt; FBLA; Mth Clb/Tm; NYLC; P to P St Amb Prg; Spch Team; SADD; Bnd; Ch Chr; Mch Bnd; SP/M/VS; Bsball; Bskball; Cyclg; Lcrsse; PP Ftbl; Sccr; Swmg; Vllyball; Stu Cncl (S); Sch Ppr; Student of the Month; Lawyer; Doctor; Hunter College; John Jay College

JAO, PAMELA; LITTLE NECK, NY; STUYVESANT HS; (FR); Comm Volntr; Drma Clb; Key Club; Lib Aide; Mus Clb; Bnd; SP/M/VS; Yale U; New York U

JAQUEZ, KARINA; BRONX, NY; WALTON HS; (SO); Hnr Roll; Otst Ac Ach Awd; Perf Att; Peer Tut/Med; DARE; Emplmnt; Mth Clb/Tm; Off Aide; Tchrs Aide; Dnce; SP/M/VS; Stu Cncl (S); Law-Criminal Justice, Publicity Manager; Education-Teacher; John Jay

JAQUITH, MAT; LOCKE, NY; AREA OCCUPATIONAL CTR; (JR); Hi Hnr Roll; Otst Ac Ach Awd; Computer Programmer; Web-Page Designer

JARECKI, EMILY; CLAYVILLE, NY; SAUQUOIT VALLEY HS; (FR); Hnr Roll; Comm Volntr; Bskball (J); Fld Hky (V L); Sftball (V L); Massage Therapy; Utica College; Duke U

JARRETT, ERIKA; RICHMOND HILL, NY; MATH SCIENCE RESEARCH TECH HS; (SO); Hnr Roll; Perf Att; Chrch Yth Grp; DECA; Off Aide; Stg Cre; Bskball (V); Forensic Science; Environmental Science; U of Connecticut; Rutgers U

JARVIS, NICHOLAS; SYRACUSE, NY; ONONDAGA JR/SR HS; (FR); Hi Hnr Roll; Hnr Roll; Spanish Clb; Bnd; Bskball (J); Ftball (V); Lcrsse (V); Wt Lftg; National Junior Honor Society

JASINSKI, CARLY; NORTH TONAWANDA, NY; NORTH TONAWANDA; (JR); MVP; Nat Hon Sy; Nat Mrt LOC; Perf Att; WWAHSS; Comm Volntr; Peer Tut/Med; Vsity Clb; Bnd; PP Ftbl (V); Sccr (V CL); Vsy Clb (V L)

JAVAID, MASOOMA; STATEN ISLAND, NY; STATEN ISLAND TECH HS; (SO); Hi Hnr Roll; Otst Ac Ach Awd; Sci Fairs; WWAHSS; Comm Volntr; Hosp Aide; ArtClub; Key Club; Mth Clb/Tm; Tchrs Aide; Stg Cre; CR (R); Lit Mag; Sch Ppr; ACE Mentor Program; Bowling; Engineering; Architecture; New York U; Rutgers U

JAVID, SUMAYYA; MONSEY, NY; SPRING VALLEY HS; (SO); Hnr Roll; Otst Ac Ach Awd; Peer Tut/Med; Key Club; Orch; Sch Ppr (R); Dentistry; MBBS; Johns Hopkins; Harvard U

JAVIER, DAVID; FRESH MEADOWS, NY; FRANCIS LEWIS HS; (JR); Hnr Roll; Perf Att; Comm Volntr; Peer Tut/Med; Biology Clb; Key Club; Mth Clb/Tm; ROTC; Mch Bnd; Chemical Engineering; New York U

JAWIN, ERICA; WAINSCOTT, NY; EAST HAMPTON HS; (SO); Hi Hnr Roll; WWAHSS; Comm Volntr; Emplmnt; HO'Br Yth Ldrshp; Key Club; Mus Clb; Bnd; Jzz Bnd; Mch Bnd; SP/M/VS; Tennis (J); Lit Mag (E); Teaching Sunday School; Summer Institute for the Gifted Academic Camp; Chemistry; Physics; New York U; Columbia U

JAYAKUMAR, MOGANA V; YONKERS, NY; SAUNDERS HS; (FR); Ctznshp Aw; Hi Hnr Roll; Nat Hon Sy; Otst Ac Ach Awd; Sci/Math Olympn; WWAHSS; Comm Volntr; Hosp Aide; Emplmnt; Key Club; Mth Clb/Tm; Mus Clb; Quiz Bowl; Sci Clb; Voc Ind Clb Am; Bnd; Jzz Bnd; Mch Bnd; Stg Cre; Bowling Team Member; 1st Degree Brown Belt in Kenpo Karate; Ophthalmology; Pharmacy; Columbia; NYU

JEAN, FRANCESKA M R; MT VERNON, NY; MT VERNON HS; (FR); Hi Hnr Roll; Hnr Roll; Nat Hon Sy; Otst Ac Ach Awd; Perf Att; St of Mnth; Comm Volntr; Chrch Yth Grp; DARE; Drma Clb; Emplmnt; Ch Chr; Dnce; Pediatrician; Singer; Berkeley; Atlanta U

JEAN-MARY, CATHELINE; BROOKLYN, NY; SHEEPSHEAD BAY HS; (JR); Hnr Roll; Nat Hon Sy; Perf Att; Sci Fairs; Comm Volntr; Peer Tut/Med; Chrch Yth Grp; Jr Ach; Tchrs Aide; SP/M/VS; Stg Cre; Cr Ctry (V); Track (V); Sch Ppr (R); Yrbk (E); Nursing; Pharmacy; SUNY Stony Brook; Long Island U

JEFFORDS, BRITTANY; BUFFALO, NY; AMHERST CTRL HS; (JR); Hnr Roll; MVP; Comm Volntr; Hosp Aide; Emplmnt; Bnd; Dnce; Pep Bnd; Bskball (VJ L); Fld Hky (VJCL); Sftball (VJ L); CR (R); Softball- ECIC Div II Team; Field Hockey - ECIC Honorable Mention; St Lawrence U; U of Mary Washington

JEMISON, MISHA; SAINT ALBANS, NY; TOWNSEND HARRIS HS; (JR); Hnr Roll; Nat Hon Sy; Comm Volntr; Hosp Aide; Chrch Yth Grp; Emplmnt; Bnd; Ch Chr; SP/M/VS; Stg Cre; Stu Cncl (R); CR (R); Martin Luther King Speech Contest Winner; Achievement Award in Piano; Journalism; Psychology; American U; Vassar

JENKINS, JOSEPH R; BROCKPORT, NY; BROCKPORT HS; (SO); Hi Hnr Roll; Hnr Roll; Perf Att; St of Mnth; Comm Volntr; Scouts; Bsball (J); Bskball (J); Vllyball (V); Criminal Law; Engineering; U of South Carolina; U of Illinois

Jaquith, Mat
Area Occupational Ctr
Locke, NY

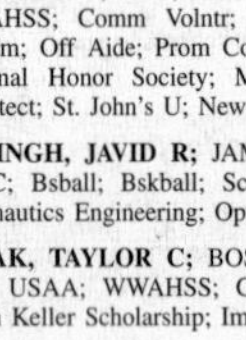
Janneh, Karalang
Monroe AC For Business & Law
Bronx, NY

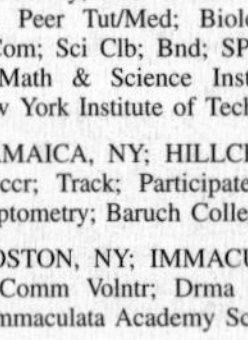
Isaakova, Julia
James Madison HS
Brooklyn, NY

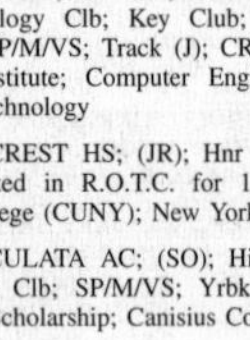
Itoka, Ranek
New York Military AC
Rosedale, NY

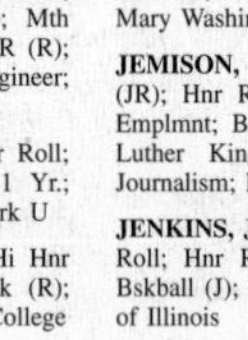
Jeffords, Brittany
Amherst Ctrl HS
Buffalo, NY

JENNINGS, PATRICK; ELMIRA, NY; NOTRE DAME HS; (JR); Ctznshp Aw; Hi Hnr Roll; Nat Hon Sy; USAA; WWAHSS; Comm Volntr; Red Cr Aide; Prom Com; Chr; Ftball (VJ L); Golf (V CL); Skiing; Cl Off (T); Stu Cncl (R); CR (R); Elmira Youth Court; Red Cross Youth Council Finance Director; Business; Sciences; Dartmouth College; Princeton U

JEON, HWAJEONG; BAYSIDE, NY; (SR); F Lan Hn Soc; Hnr Roll; Perf Att; Comm Volntr; Chess; Cmptr Clb; NtlFrnscLg; Korean Clb; Ch Chr; Bdmtn (J); Mar Art (J); Swmg (V); Track (J); Lit Mag (E)

JEREMIAH, NATASHA A; HEMPSTEAD, NY; HEMPSTEAD HS; (JR); Hi Hnr Roll; Hnr Roll; Nat Hon Sy; WWAHSS; Comm Volntr; Peer Tut/Med; Chrch Yth Grp; Key Club; Scouts; Chr; Stu Cncl (R); PhD in Psychology; U of Chicago; New York U

JETTY, SANKARSH N; CLARENCE CTR, NY; (SO); Comm Volntr; Emplmnt; Tech Clb; Stg Cre; Top 10 in Class; School President; Medical Field; Cornell U; Yale U

JEUNE, AUBREY F; BERNE, NY; BERNE-KNOX-WESTERLO HS; (FR); 4H Awd; Hi Hnr Roll; Hnr Roll; Otst Ac Ach Awd; Pres Sch; WWAHSS; Comm Volntr; 4-H; Chrch Yth Grp; Key Club; Chr; Sftball (L); Vllyball (L); Stu Cncl (T); Forensic Medical Examiner; Criminal Science; Baylor U Texas; U of New Haven Connecticut

JEUNE, RICHARD; ELMONT, NY; SEWANHAKA HS; (JR); Hnr Roll; Otst Ac Ach Awd; Perf Att; St of Mnth; Comm Volntr; Stg Cre; Stu Cncl (R); Pre-Law; Biology; St John's U; Adelphi U

JHA, ANTONIO; FLUSHING, NY; BENJAMIN CARDOZO HS; (SR); Hnr Roll; Perf Att; Sci Fairs; Comm Volntr; Peer Tut/Med; ArtClub; Chess; Chrch Yth Grp; Emplmnt; Lib Aide; Mth Clb/Tm; Tchrs Aide; Chinese Clb; Bnd; Ch Chr; Arista; Worship Leader in Church; Bio-Medical Engineering; Architecture; Cornell U; Carnegie Mellon U

JIA, HERAN; NEW CITY, NY; CLARKSTOWN HS NORTH; (SO); Hnr Roll; Perf Att; St of Mnth; Peer Tut/Med; Cmptr Clb; Mth Clb/Tm; MuAlphaTh; Computer Science; Mathematics; Connell U; Princeton U

JIANG, JEFFREY; FRESH MEADOWS, NY; STUYVESANT HS; (JR); Hnr Roll; WWAHSS; Hosp Aide; Emplmnt; FBLA; SP/M/VS; Yrbk (P); Pre-Med; Biology; Cornell U; Johns Hopkins U

JIJON, JESSENIA V; UNIONDALE, NY; UNIONDALE HS; (JR); F Lan Hn Soc; Hnr Roll; Nat Hon Sy; WWAHSS; Peer Tut/Med; Drma Clb; Key Club; Mus Clb; Latinos Clb; Chr; Ch Chr; Orch; SP/M/VS; Interior Design; Fashion Institute of Technology; Pratt Institute

JOACHIM, TRENTON; MIDDLETOWN, NY; MIDDLETOWN HS; (JR); Hnr Roll; Comm Volntr; Hosp Aide; Key Club; Golf (J); Pre-Med; Pre-Dentistry; Pepperdine U; Miami State U

JOCK, CATHERINE N; HOGANSBURG, NY; MASSENA SR HS; (SO); Hnr Roll; Perf Att; Sci Fairs; Comm Volntr; Emplmnt; Prom Com; French Clb; Bnd; Chr; Ice Sktg; Sftball; Vllyball (JC); Stu Cncl (R); 85+ Club; Graphic Design; Culinary Arts; American Intercontinental U

JOHANSEN, KATHERINE; WEST HEMPSTEAD, NY; WEST HEMPSTEAD HS; (SO); Hi Hnr Roll; Hnr Roll; MVP; Nat Hon Sy; Pres Ac Ftns Aw; Sci Fairs; Sci/Math Olympn; Comm Volntr; Chrch Yth Grp; Dbte Team; Emplmnt; Key Club; Mth Clb/Tm; Quiz Bowl; Scouts; Vsity Clb; Bnd; Mch Bnd; Bskball (V L); Sccr (V L); Sftball (V L); Stu Cncl (R)

JOHN, AMIRAH; BROOKLYN, NY; FRANKLIN K LANE HS; (SR); Hnr Roll; Nat Hon Sy; Nat Mrt Fin; Otst Ac Ach Awd; Perf Att; WWAHSS; Comm Volntr; Peer Tut/Med; Cmptr Clb; Key Club; Prom Com; Tchrs Aide; Tech Clb; Dnce; Wt Lftg (J); Stu Cncl (T); CR (R); Sch Ppr (E, R, P); Digital Media; Media and Communication; Polytechnic U

JOHN, GIJU; FRESH MEADOWS, NY; JAMAICA HS; (JR); Hnr Roll; Perf Att; Comm Volntr; Chrch Yth Grp; Cmptr Clb; Emplmnt; Ch Chr; SP/M/VS; Bdmtn; Bskball (C); Cyclg; Ftball; Sccr (C); Tennis; Vllyball; Wt Lftg; CR (R); Yrbk; Physician Assistant; Saint John's U

JOHN, KIMBERLY A; FREEPORT, NY; FREEPORT HS; (JR); Pres Ac Ftns Aw; WWAHSS; DECA; Italian Clb; Tennis (V); Cl Off (T); Varsity Rifle Team; Caribbean Club; Business Marketing; Drexel U; U of Pennsylvania

JOHN, KRISTEN; DELMAR, NY; BETHLEHEM CTRL HS; (SO); Hnr Roll; Pres Sch; Comm Volntr; Chrch Yth Grp; Jr Ach; P to P St Amb Prg; Bskball (J); Mar Art (L); Wt Lftg (V); Yrbk (E); Physician; Lawyer; Union College; Rensselaer Poly Institute

JOHN, STANLEY; SPRING VALLEY, NY; RAMAPO HS; (JR); Comm Volntr; Hosp Aide; Vsity Clb; Chr; Ch Chr; Bsball (VJ); Varsity Bowling; Mechanical Engineering; New York U; SUNY Canton

JOHNSON, ASHLEY P; HUNTINGTON STATION, NY; HUNTINGTON HS; (SO); Hi Hnr Roll; Pres Sch; Sci/Math Olympn; St of Mnth; Comm Volntr; Hab For Humty Volntr; Chrch Yth Grp; Key Club; Scouts; Bnd; Ch Chr; Jzz Bnd; Mch Bnd; Bskball (J); Cr Ctry (J); Fncg (V); Mar Art (J); Sccr (J); Sftball (J); Track (V); Vllyball (V); Girl Scout Silver Award; Johns Hopkins U, Mathematics and Verbal Talent Search; Computer Engineering; Secondary Education; Washington U At Saint Louis; Clemson U

JOHNSON, CHRISTOPHER; BRONX, NY; EVANDER CHILDS HS; (SO); Hnr Roll; Ftball (V); Business; Engineering; NYU; Fordham U

JOHNSON, CORY; ELMHURST, NY; CATHEDRAL PREP SEMINARY; (SR); Hnr Roll; Pres Ac Ftns Aw; WWAHSS; Ch Chr; Ice Hky; Most Improved Student Award - '03-'04; Educational Incentive Award - '04-'05; Computer Science; Queens College

JOHNSON, HEIDI M; JAMESTOWN, NY; JAMESTOWN HS; (SO); St of Mnth; ArtClub; Chrch Yth Grp; Drma Clb; Clb; Chr; Student of the Month (Randolph); 1st Plane for Cheerleading in 97 & 98; Japanese; Music; North Park U; Tokyo U

JOHNSON, KARI A; SENECA CASTLE, NY; DE SALES HS; (SO); All Am Sch; Hi Hnr Roll; Otst Ac Ach Awd; Pres Ac Ftns Aw; WWAHSS; Comm Volntr; Peer Tut/Med; FCA; Key Club; SADD; Bskball (VJ); PP Ftbl (VJ); Sccr (V L); Sftball (J); Cl Off (R); Stu Cncl (R); CR (R); Lit Mag (R); Key Club / International Club / SADD; Working Part Time; Teaching; Speech

JOHNSON, KAYANN T; WYANDANCH, NY; WYANDANCH MEM. HS; (FR); Hi Hnr Roll; Otst Ac Ach Awd; St of Mnth; Comm Volntr; Spec Olymp Vol; Chrch Yth Grp; Emplmnt; ROTC; Ch Chr; Track (J); Teaching (Elementary Education); Dowling College

JOHNSON, KELSEY; MARION, NY; MARION JR/SR HS; (JR); Hnr Roll; Nat Hon Sy; WWAHSS; Peer Tut/Med; Emplmnt; Photog; Spanish Clb; Bnd; Chr; Mch Bnd; Stg Cre; Sccr (J); Track (J); Vllyball (VJ); Yrbk (R, P); Journalism; St John Fisher; Cazenovia College

JOHNSON, LAUREN; ELMONT, NY; ELMONT MEMORIAL HS; (JR); Ctznshp Aw; F Lan Hn Soc; Hi Hnr Roll; Hnr Roll; Nat Hon Sy; Otst Ac Ach Awd; Perf Att; Sci Fairs; St of Mnth; Comm Volntr; Chrch Yth Grp; FBLA; Key Club; SADD; Ch Chr; Orch; SP/M/VS; Lcrsse (J); Sch Ppr (R); Major in Education; Become a Lawyer; Binghamton U; Temple U

JOHNSON, MARISSA; SPRING VALLEY, NY; SPRING VALLEY HS; (SO); Nat Hon Sy; St of Mnth; Peer Tut/Med; Chrch Yth Grp; DARE; Key Club; Chr; Ch Chr; Fashion Designer; Plus Size Model

JOHNSON, MATTHEW F; BUFFALO, NY; ST JOSEPH'S COLLEGIATE INST; (SO); Hi Hnr Roll; MVP; Otst Ac Ach Awd; Perf Att; Pres Sch; St of Mnth; Comm Volntr; Bsball (J); Vllyball (V); Collegiate Scholar: Art Show Honorable Mention; Academic Scholarship Award Recipient; Psychology; English & Literature; Professional Baseball; Boston College: Stanford U; Notre Dame: Duke

JOHNSON, MICHELLE; WELLSVILLE, NY; WELLSVILLE HS; (SO); Hi Hnr Roll; Hnr Roll; Peer Tut/Med; Chrch Yth Grp; Bskball (J); Vllyball (JCL)

JOHNSON, NICHOLAS; SAUGERTIES, NY; SAUGERTIES HS; (SR); All Am Sch; Hi Hnr Roll; MVP; Nat Hon Sy; Otst Ac Ach Awd; Pres Sch; WWAHSS; Comm Volntr; Key Club; NYLC; Bnd; Bskball (VJCL); Sccr (VJCL); Track (V CL); Stu Cncl (R); National Honor Society - Treasurer; 2005 Scholar-Athlete; Aviation Management / Pilot; Daniel Webster College; Florida Institute of Technology

JOHNSON, SETH R; SAUGERTIES, NY; SAUGERTIES HS; Hnr Roll; WWAHSS; Comm Volntr; Key Club; Bnd; Sccr (VJC); Track (V L); Wrstlg (J); US Maritime Academy

JOHNSON, STACEY L; SHARON SPRINGS, NY; SHARON SPRINGS CTRL SCH; (SO); Ctznshp Aw; Hi Hnr Roll; Hnr Roll; MVP; Nat Hon Sy; Otst Ac Ach Awd; Pres Sch; Sci Fairs; WWAHSS; Emplmnt; FBLA; Bnd; Chr; Bskball (V); Sccr (V); Stu Cncl; CIA; Accounting; Pace U

JOHNSON, TERRY; POUGHKEEPSIE, NY; POUGHKEEPSIE HS; (SO); Hi Hnr Roll; Hnr Roll; Otst Ac Ach Awd; Perf Att; St of Mnth; Chr; Ch Chr; Dnce; Drm Mjr; Ftball (J); Master's Degree; Architect; Marist College; Vassar College

JOHNSTON, CHRISTOPHER; CARMEL, NY; CARMEL HS; (JR); Hi Hnr Roll; Hnr Roll; MVP; Perf Att; Pres Sch; Comm Volntr; Sci Clb; Vsity Clb; Bnd; Bsball (V); Bskball (L); Presidential Award; Engineering; Arizona U

JOHNSTONE, KATIA; NEW YORK, NY; FLORELLO H LA GUARDIA HS; (FR); 4H Awd; Hi Hnr Roll; Otst Ac Ach Awd; Comm Volntr; Stu Cncl (S); Lit Mag (E); Won A Young Play Wrights Inc Award For A Play I Wrote In 7th Grade

JOINER, SHERRIS N; AMITYVILLE, NY; AMITYVILLE MEMORIAL HS; (SO); Hi Hnr Roll; Hnr Roll; Nat Hon Sy; Nat Sci Aw; WWAHSS; Spec Olymp Vol; Chrch Yth Grp; Dbte Team; Emplmnt; Key Club; Mth Clb/Tm; Bnd; Ch Chr; Jzz Bnd; Mch Bnd; Track (J); Vllyball (J); CR (R); Oncologist; Psychologist; Brown U; Xavier U

JOKAYTYS, ELIZABETH A; BOONVILLE, NY; ADIRONDACK HS; (JR); Ctznshp Aw; Hnr Roll; MVP; Nat Hon Sy; WWAHSS; Comm Volntr; Bnd; Chr; SP/M/VS; GAA; Sftball (V L); Swmg (V L); Vllyball (V L); Volleyball League All-Star & MVP; Physical Therapist; Psychologist

JONES, GABRIELLA; YONKERS, NY; OUR LADY OF VICTORY; (SO); Hnr Roll; Nat Hon Sy; Nat Sci Aw; St of Mnth; Drma Clb; Ch Chr; SP/M/VS; Sftball (J); Vllyball (V); CR (P)

JONES, JESSICA A M; WATERVLIET, NY; SHAKER HS; (SR); Hi Hnr Roll; Hnr Roll; Nat Hon Sy; Emplmnt; SADD; Chr; President of the Gay, Lesbian, and Straight Society; National Achievement Scholarship Semi-Finalist; Acting; Minister; Pace U; New York U

JONES, JUSTIN; BUFFALO, NY; LEONARDO DA VINCI HS; (JR); Hi Hnr Roll; WWAHSS; Track (V); Journalism; Film Directing; Morehouse College; Spelman College

JONES, KRISTINA; BUFFALO, NY; MCKINLEY HS; (SO); Hnr Roll; Perf Att; Chr; Ch Chr; Orch; Bskball

JONES, LATOYA K; BROOKLYN, NY; EDWARD R MURROW; (JR); Ctznshp Aw; MVP; Nat Sci Aw; Perf Att; Sci Fairs; St of Mnth; Peer Tut/Med; ArtClub; Chrch Yth Grp; DARE; Drma Clb; Fr of Library; Mus Clb; Prom Com; Scouts; Stu Cncl (V)

JONES, SEUN; UNIONDALE, NY; UNIONDALE HS; (JR); Hi Hnr Roll; Nat Hon Sy; WWAHSS; Comm Volntr; Hosp Aide; Chrch Yth Grp; FBLA; Key Club; Bnd; Ch Chr; Mch Bnd; Tennis (V); Stu Cncl (R); Pre-Med; Pharmacy; Sophie Davis School of Biomedical Education

JONES, SHADAVIA; BROOKLYN, NY; BENJAMIN BANNEKER AC; (SO); Hi Hnr Roll; Hnr Roll; Nat Hon Sy; Otst Ac Ach Awd; Perf Att; Sci Fairs; St of Mnth; Peer Tut/Med; DARE; Emplmnt; Ntl Beta Clb; Dnce; SP/M/VS; Stu Cncl (P); CR (R); Step Team; Psychology; Business; Princeton U; Duke U

JONES, SHARMAINE; BROOKLYN, NY; CLARA BARTON; (SO); Chrch Yth Grp; Ch Chr; Track (V); Stewart Bashkoff Recognition Award - Is 218; Math Scholarship / Award PS 260; Forensic Science; Pediatrician; Columbia U; Hunter College

JONES, SHAUNA Y; MIDDLETOWN, NY; MIDDLETOWN HS; (JR); Hnr Roll; Fashion Degree; Marketing; Berkeley College; AI College

JOPSON, ASHLEY; GENESEO, NY; LIVONIA HS; (FR); Hi Hnr Roll; St of Mnth; WWAHSS; Spec Olymp Vol; Key Club; Chr; National Jr. Honors Society; Student Council Member; Journalism; U of Arizona

JORALEMON, JESSICA L; SCHENECTADY, NY; GUILDERLAND CTRL HS; (SR); Nat Hon Sy; Otst Ac Ach Awd; Perf Att; WWAHSS; Comm Volntr; Hosp Aide; Peer Tut/Med; Emplmnt; Key Club; Mus Clb; Svce Clb; Tchrs Aide; Chr; National Honor Society; Executive Committee for Peer Mentor Program; Communications; Advertising; Western New England College

JORDAN, ERIK R; LEVITTOWN, NY; DIVISION AVE HS; (SR); F Lan Hn Soc; Hi Hnr Roll; Nat Hon Sy; Nat Mrt Sch Recip; Perf Att; Pres Sch; Sci/Math Olympn; St Schl; WWAHSS; Comm Volntr; Peer Tut/Med; Dbte Team; Emplmnt; Key Club; Mod UN; Photog; Tchrs Aide; Orch; Tennis (V); Yrbk (P); Officer-Tri-M Honor Society; Photography; Psychology; Rochester Institute of Technology; Hofstra U

JORDON, SUNEIL H; BRONX, NY; LAGUARDIA HS; Hnr Roll; Nat Hon Sy; Perf Att; Sci Fairs; St of Mnth; Peer Tut/Med; Cmptr Clb; Tech Clb; Acpl Chr; Chr; 1st Place Science Fair; Management; Computer Technician; Pennsylvania State U; Howard U

JOSEPH, JESSY; SYOSSET, NY; SYOSSET HS; (SR); F Lan Hn Soc; Hi Hnr Roll; Nat Hon Sy; Otst Ac Ach Awd; Sci Fairs; Yth Ldrshp Prog; Comm Volntr; Hosp Aide; Spec Olymp Vol; DECA; French Clb; Sch Ppr (R); Pre-Medicine; Psychology; New York U

JOSEPH, MELISSA; BROOKLYN, NY; PAUL ROBESON HS; (JR); Ctznshp Aw; Hnr Roll; Nat Hon Sy; Nat Ldrshp Svc; Perf Att; St of Mnth; Yth Ldrshp Prog; Comm Volntr; Peer Tut/Med; Chrch Yth Grp; Emplmnt; Mod UN; Pep Squd; Ch Chr; Chrldg; Morgan State U; Temple U

JOSEPH, SOPHIA H; BROOKLYN, NY; ST EDMUND PREP HS; (JR); Ctznshp Aw; Hnr Roll; Perf Att; Sci Fairs; St of Mnth; ArtClub; DARE; Key Club; Photog; Sci Clb; Stg Cre; Yrbk (P); Learning to Play Bagpipes; Doctor; Nurse; U of Bridgeport; Pace U

JOSEPH, STEPHANIE; BROOKLYN, NY; MIDWOOD HS; (FR); Hnr Roll; Perf Att; St of Mnth; Comm Volntr; Key Club; Svce Clb; Chr; Rising Star Award; Arista Honors; Genetics / Neurology, Cardiology; Creative Writing / Mythology; Harvard Medical Institute; New York U

JOSEPH, TINA; ELMONT, NY; SEWANHAKA HS; (FR); Hnr Roll; WWAHSS; Comm Volntr; Peer Tut/Med; Chrch Yth Grp; FBLA; FCCLA; Key Club; Mth Clb/Tm; Sci Clb; Chr; Dnce; SP/M/VS; Pharmacist; Dentist; Hofstra U; St John's U

JOSEPH, TRESA; YONKERS, NY; GORTON HS; (JR); Hi Hnr Roll; Hnr Roll; Otst Ac Ach Awd; Perf Att; St of Mnth; Yth Ldrshp Prog; Comm Volntr; Hab For Humty Volntr; Hosp Aide; Peer Tut/Med; Chrch Yth Grp; Emplmnt; Sci Clb; SADD; Wdwrkg Clb; Clb; Chr; Ch Chr; Dnce; Stg Cre; Nursing; Physician's Assistant; Pace U; St. John's U

JOSEPHS, KEVIN; BROOKLYN, NY; BROOKLYN TECH HS; (SO); Chr; Psychology; Duke U; Howard U

Josephs, Kevin
Brooklyn Tech HS
Brooklyn, NY

Jordon, Suneil H
LaGuardia HS
Bronx, NY

Johnson, Marissa
Spring Valley HS
Spring Valley, NY

Johnson, Christopher
Evander Childs HS
Bronx, NY

John, Kristen
Bethlehem Ctrl HS
Delmar, NY

Jeune, Aubrey F
Berne-Knox-Westerlo HS
Berne, NY

John, Giju
Jamaica HS
Fresh Meadows, NY

Johnson, Cory
Cathedral Prep Seminary
Elmhurst, NY

Joralemon, Jessica L
Guilderland Ctrl HS
Schenectady, NY

Joseph, Sophia H
St Edmund Prep HS
Brooklyn, NY

Joseph, Stephanie
Midwood HS
Brooklyn, NY

JOSHUA, JALISA; DEER PARK, NY; DEER PARK HS; (SO); Hi Hnr Roll; Sci Fairs; St of Mnth; WWAHSS; Comm Volntr; Peer Tut/Med; Chrch Yth Grp; DARE; DECA; Emplmnt; Kwanza Clb; Dnce; SP/M/VS; Chrldg (JCL); Scr Kpr (J); DECA; A World of Difference; Psychiatrist; Entrepreneur; Hofstra U; St John's U

JOYNER, JESSICA; MIDDLETOWN, NY; PINE BUSH HS; (JR); Hnr Roll; Outdrs Clb; Prom Com; Svce Clb; Chr; Bskball (J); Track (V); Biology Major; Dentistry; Florida State U; Florida A & M U

JOYNER JR, ROY L; SYRACUSE, NY; HERKIMER CMTY COLLEGE HS; (JR); 4H Awd; US Army Sch Ath Aw; 4-H; Scouts; Bnd; Chr; Ch Chr; Flg Crps; Bskball (J); Swmg (J); Wrstlg (J); LPN-Army; Accountant; RIT; Herkimer Comm. College

JULIANO, JOSEPH M; PATCHOGUE, NY; BELLPORT HS; (SR); Hi Hnr Roll; Hnr Roll; Nat Hon Sy; Nat Ldrshp Svc; Pres Sch; Comm Volntr; Spec Olymp Vol; Chrch Yth Grp; Emplmnt; FBLA; Outdrs Clb; Tchrs Aide; Bsball (VJCL); Bskball (J); Sccr (VJ L); Wt Lftg (V); Stu Cncl (R); Scholar Athlete, Baseball, JV and V; Leadership Team; Accounting; Law; Fairfield U; Fordham U

JULSON, REGINE; QUEENS VILLAGE, NY; FLUSHING HS; (SR); Hi Hnr Roll; Nat Hon Sy; Nat Mrt Fin; WWAHSS; Yth Ldrshp Prog; Comm Volntr; Peer Tut/Med; Mus Clb; Outdrs Clb; Photog; Chr; Track (V); Sch Ppr (R, P); Nursing; Pre-Med; Liberty U; Morgan State U

JUNG, ALYSSA; ALBANY, NY; ALBANY HS; (JR); Hi Hnr Roll; MVP; WWAHSS; Comm Volntr; Key Club; Cr Ctry (V CL); Track (V L); Private Piano Lessons / Recitals-11 Years; Communications / Journalism / Media

JUREK, JILLY; ALDEN, NY; ALDEN HS; (SO); Hnr Roll; Comm Volntr; Drma Clb; Key Club; Spanish Clb; Chr; SP/M/VS; Cl Off (S); Music Teacher

KACZMARSKY, JASON Z; FULTONVILLE, NY; FONDA FULTONVILLE CTRL SCH; (SO); Hi Hnr Roll; Hnr Roll; Chr; Accelerated Art; Computer Graphics; ITT Tech

KADIAN, EISHA; BELLEROSE, NY; BENJAMIN CARDOZO HS; (SR); Hnr Roll; Nat Hon Sy; Otst Ac Ach Awd; Sci Fairs; WWAHSS; Comm Volntr; Hosp Aide; Key Club; Lib Aide; Tchrs Aide; Sch Ppr (R, P); National Society of High School Scholars; Public Advocate Award; Pharmacy / PharmD D; Long Island U Brooklyn Campus

KADRIC, SAMIR; BRONX, NY; DEWITT CLINTON HS; (JR); Ctznshp Aw; Hi Hnr Roll; Hnr Roll; Salutrn; Sci Fairs; Comm Volntr; Mod UN; Lit Mag (R); Playwriting Class; Medicine

KAIBA, JETO; BROOKLYN, NY; FRANKLIN K LANE HS; (SR); Hnr Roll; Perf Att; Computer Technology; Business Management; Hunter College; Braircliffe College

KAIM, LOGAN; CHAPPAQUA, NY; HORACE GREELEY HS; (SR); Comm Volntr; Outdrs Clb; Cr Ctry (J); Boy Scouts-Life Rank

KAKOLEWSKI, CHRISTOPHER; SAUGERTIES, NY; SAUGERTIES HS; (SR); Hi Hnr Roll; Hnr Roll; Nat Hon Sy; WWAHSS; Comm Volntr; AL Aux Boys; Emplmnt; Key Club; Quiz Bowl; Spanish Clb; SP/M/VS; Stg Cre; Stu Cncl (V); Key Club Sergeant at Arms; History Club; Earth Science; Business; Ulster County Community College

KALECHMAN, HENRY; BROOKLYN, NY; JAMES MADISON HS; (JR); St of Mnth; WWAHSS; Peer Tut/Med; Tchrs Aide; Tmpl Yth Grp; Swmg (V); PSAL Swimming 3rd Place 500 Yds-3rd Place; Internship Mount Sinai Med. School (Summer '04); Medicine; City College of New York, Sophie Davies School; Brooklyn College, BA MD Program

KAMAL, MOHAMMAD; BROOKLYN, NY; JAMES MADISON HS; (SO); Peer Tut/Med; Mth Clb/Tm; MBA; CPA / Certified Public Accountant; Harvard U; New York U

KAMINSKY, ALEXA J; EAST ROCKAWAY, NY; LYNBROOK HS; (FR); Hnr Roll; Sci/Math Olympn; Comm Volntr; Spec Olymp Vol; Mth Clb/Tm; Svce Clb; SADD; SP/M/VS; Bdmtn (V L); Tennis (V L); National Junior Honor Society; Biology; Cornell U; U of Michigan

KAMPNICK, ANTHONY J; THERESA, NY; INDIAN RIVER HS; (FR); JCC

KANE, JESSE W; BROOKLYN, NY; NEW UTRECHT HS; (SO); JV Bowling Team; Math Degree; St. John's U; Brooklyn College

KANG, BYUNGUN; FRESH MEADOWS, NY; BRONX HS OF SCIENCE; (SO); Comm Volntr; Chess; Mth Clb/Tm; Tchrs Aide; Aerodynamics; Astrophysics; Massachusetts - Institute of Technology; Cornell

KANTOR, ADA; BROOKLYN, NY; MIDWOOD HS; (SO); Hi Hnr Roll; Hnr Roll; Perf Att; St of Mnth; Chr; Knitting Club; School Library Monitor; Working in a Publishing House; Business; Columbia U; Pace U

KAPLAN, JENNIFER; LARCHMONT, NY; MAMARONECK HS; (SR); Hnr Roll; MVP; Nat Hon Sy; Comm Volntr; DARE; Emplmnt; Svce Clb; Tchrs Aide; Track (V CL); Psychology; Social Work; Skidmore College - Attending

KAPLON, CHRISTINE; STATEN ISLAND, NY; MOORE CATHOLIC HS; (JR); Hi Hnr Roll; Nat Hon Sy; Nat Ldrshp Svc; Yth Ldrshp Prog; Comm Volntr; Mth Clb/Tm; Lit Mag (R); Yrbk (R, P); Respect Life Club; JDRF Mega Dance Club; Journalism; English; St John's U; California State U LA

KAPLUN, EUGENE; BROOKLYN, NY; ST EDMUND PREP HS; (JR); WWAHSS; Comm Volntr; Cmptr Clb; Lib Aide; Off Aide; Business; Engineering; Pace U; City U of NY: Baruch College

KARAKONSTANTIS, STEVEN; FRANKLIN SQUARE, NY; THE WALDORF SCH OF GARDEN CITY; (JR); WWAHSS; Comm Volntr; ArtClub; SP/M/VS; Bskball (V); Lcrsse (V); Mar Art; Gabriel Kane Spirit of Athletics Award; Kenpo Martial Arts 11th Annual Invitational Tournament-3rd Place 2004; Law; Computer Engineering; Fordham U; Saint John's U

KARAVIAS, GEORGE; BROOKLYN, NY; JAMES MADISON HS; (JR); Comm Volntr; Mechanical Engineer; Business Manager; Polytechnical U; New York Institute of Technology

KARIM, SHADIA A; OZONE PARK, NY; STUYVESANT HS; (FR); Ctznshp Aw; Hi Hnr Roll; Hnr Roll; Nat Hon Sy; Nat Mrt LOC; Otst Ac Ach Awd; Perf Att; Sci Fairs; St of Mnth; Yth Ldrshp Prog; Peer Tut/Med; ArtClub; Mth Clb/Tm; P to P St Amb Prg; Scouts; Tchrs Aide; Bnd; Chr; Stg Cre; Scr Kpr (J); Swmg (V); CR (R); Sch Ppr (R); Continental Mathematics League, Spelling Bee; Scholastic Writing Award, Storytelling Contests, Advanced Regents Program; Master's Degree; Medical Sciences; Harvard U; New York U

KARSKI, GAVIN X; GENEVA, NY; DE SALES HS; (SO); All Am Sch; Ctznshp Aw; Hi Hnr Roll; Otst Ac Ach Awd; Perf Att; Pres Ac Ftns Aw; Pres Sch; USAA; WWAHSS; Yth Ldrshp Prog; Comm Volntr; Emplmnt; FCA; HO'Br Yth Ldrshp; Key Club; Photog; Quiz Bowl; Vsity Clb; Bskball (VJ L); Cr Ctry (V L); Ftball (V L); Lcrsse (J); Vsy Clb; Cl Off (R); Stu Cncl (R); Geneva Area Soccer League; Triathlon Club; Business and Public Policy; Engineering; U of Notre Dame; US Air Force Academy

KARSKI, NICHOLAS J; ELMIRA, NY; THOMAS A EDISON HS; (SO); Hi Hnr Roll; WWAHSS; Comm Volntr; Key Club; SADD; French Clb; Bnd; Mch Bnd; Pep Bnd; Bsball (J); Little League "Challenger Division" Assistant

KASNECI, OLA; YONKERS, NY; ST BARNABAS HS; (JR); Nat Hon Sy; Key Club; Internship - 2 Months Albanian Embassy; Hospital Volunteer; International Relations; Journalism; Georgetown U; Columbia U

KASSNER, ALYSSA L; CORAM, NY; LONGWOOD HS; (JR); F Lan Hn Soc; Hi Hnr Roll; Hnr Roll; Nat Hon Sy; Comm Volntr; Chrch Yth Grp; Emplmnt; Mus Clb; P to P St Amb Prg; Chr; Dnce; Orch; Bskball (J); Lcrsse (JC); Tennis (J); American Cancer Society Volunteer; Gospel For Asia Child Sponsor; Psychology; Sociology; Hartwick College; Monmouth U

KATZ, DAVID L; BROOKLYN, NY; JAMES MADISON HS; (JR); Hnr Roll; MVP; Comm Volntr; Ice Hky (C); Rlr Hky (C); High Achievement in Math Award; High Achievement in Science Award

KATZ, JASON R; BROOKLYN, NY; JAMES MADISON HS; (JR); Hnr Roll; MVP; Comm Volntr; Ice Hky (C); Rlr Hky (C); High Achievement in English Award

KATZ, TIMOTHY E P; FREEPORT, NY; FREEPORT HS; (JR); Hnr Roll; Nat Hon Sy; Chrch Yth Grp; Bskball (V L); Cr Ctry (V L); Lcrsse (V CL); Penn State U; Ohio State U

KAUFMAN, DAVID P; HUNTINGTON, NY; HUNTINGTON HS; (SO); Ctznshp Aw; Hi Hnr Roll; Sci Fairs; Sci/Math Olympn; Hab For Humty Volntr; Spec Olymp Vol; Mth Clb/Tm; Svce Clb; Stg Cre; Tennis (J); Environmental Science; Computer; Cornell; Tufts

KAUR, GURJOT; SPRING VALLEY, NY; SPRING VALLEY HS; (SO); Hi Hnr Roll; Hnr Roll; St of Mnth; WWAHSS; DARE; Key Club; Dnce; 10th Grade Representative for Health and Human Development; Multicultural Club, Participant in Multicultural Day; Gynecology

KAUR, HARJOT; SOUTH OZONE PARK, NY; SPRINGFIELD GARDENS HS; (FR); Hnr Roll; Perf Att; Chess; Member of Student Government; Doctor MD; Doctor PhD; Cornell; Harvard

KAUR, HARPINDER; LEVITTOWN, NY; DIVISION AVE HS; (JR); Hi Hnr Roll; Hnr Roll; WWAHSS; Comm Volntr; Peer Tut/Med; Emplmnt; Key Club; Mth Clb/Tm; French Clb; Bdmtn (V); Business Honor Society; Foreign Language Honor Society; Nursing; Physician's Assistant or Physician; SUNY Stony Brook

KAUR, NAVJOT; YONKERS, NY; SAINT BARNABAS HS; (JR); Hi Hnr Roll; Hnr Roll; Nat Hon Sy; Comm Volntr; Mth Clb/Tm; First Honors / Second Honors; Pharmacy; Psychology; Manhattanville; St John's U

KAWSAR, TASLIM; BROOKLYN, NY; IS 218 JAMES PETER SINNOTT; MS; Hnr Roll; Otst Ac Ach Awd; Perf Att; St of Mnth; Quiz Bowl; Computer Engineer

KAYHAREE, VICKCHAND; S RICHMOND HL, NY; QUEENS VOC & TECH HS; (JR); Sci Fairs; DARE; Emplmnt; Mth Clb/Tm; Tech Clb; Certificate of Achievement in Mathematics; Excellence in Technology; Computer Science; SUNY Stony Brook; New York U

KAZNOWSKI, KARA; BUFFALO, NY; BUFFALO AC FOR VISUAL AND PERF ARTS HS; (JR); Hnr Roll; Perf Att; Chr; Biology; U of Buffalo

KEATON, JESSICA; BALDWINSVILLE, NY; CHARLES W BAKER HS; (JR); Hi Hnr Roll; Nat Hon Sy; Hab For Humty Volntr; DARE; Emplmnt; Key Club; Sccr (VJ L); Track (V L); SUNY Buffalo

KEEGAN, AMANDA; CORNING, NY; WEST HS; (JR); Hi Hnr Roll; Hnr Roll; Otst Ac Ach Awd; Emplmnt; Tchrs Aide; Work with Children for Child Development Class; Veterinarian; Accountant

KEENE, ANDREW; SYRACUSE, NY; HENNINGER HS; (JR); Hnr Roll; Perf Att; Photog; Ftball (V); Law Enforcement; OCC

KEENE, CHRISTINE M; FREEPORT, NY; KELLENBERG MEMORIAL HS; (JR); Hnr Roll; Nat Hon Sy; Perf Att; St of Mnth; Hosp Aide; Peer Tut/Med; Chrch Yth Grp; Drma Clb; Emplmnt; Lib Aide; Chr; Dnce; SP/M/VS; Stg Cre; Physical Therapy; Psychiatry; U of Scranton; Fordham

KELLER, ALICIA; CORFU, NY; PEMBROKE JR/SR HS; (FR); 4H Awd; Ctznshp Aw; Hi Hnr Roll; Kwnis Aw; Perf Att; St of Mnth; WWAHSS; Comm Volntr; Hosp Aide; Peer Tut/Med; 4-H; DARE; DECA; Drma Clb; FTA; Key Club; Lib Aide; Scouts; Dnce; Swmg (V); Tennis (J); Track (V); Stu Cncl (V); Yrbk (E); Venturing

KELLER JR, JOHN M; SCHENECTADY, NY; GUILDERLAND HS; (SO); Hi Hnr Roll; Otst Ac Ach Awd; Perf Att; WWAHSS; Comm Volntr; Chrch Yth Grp; Key Club; French Clb; Cr Ctry (J); Board of Education; Athlete Scholar Award & Black Belt Tae Kwon Do; Government/Political Science; History

KELLEY, KRISTENE; STILLWATER, NY; STILLWATER CTRL HS; (FR); Hi Hnr Roll; WWAHSS; Peer Tut/Med; French Clb; Chr; Sftball (J); Cl Off (V); Top Six; Obstetrician; Union College (Schenectady)

KELLY, ANNELISE; GREENWICH, NY; GREENWICH CTRL HS; (SO); Hi Hnr Roll; Hnr Roll; MVP; Otst Ac Ach Awd; Pres Sch; ArtClub; Spanish Clb; Bskball (JC); Sccr (V L); Cl Off (V); Yrbk (P); Club Sports; Comm.; Architecture/Interior Design; Art/Art Education

KELLY, BLANE; ROCHESTER, NY; SCH OF THE ARTS; (JR); Hi Hnr Roll; Hnr Roll; Comm Volntr; Chess; Cr Ctry (V); Tennis (V); Sch Ppr (R); Play Bass Guitar / Ultimate Frisbee; Brighton Rowing Club; Literature / Writing; Music; Ithaca College; SUNY Fredonia

KELSEY, KARRIE; JAMESTOWN, NY; JAMESTOWN HS; (FR); 4H Awd; Hnr Roll; Kwnis Aw; St of Mnth; 4-H; ArtClub; Scouts; Criminal Justice; Sciences; U of Buffalo; Fredonia State

KEMP, HARRY R; ALBANY, NY; ALBANY HS; (JR); Hi Hnr Roll; Pres Sch; Comm Volntr; Key Club; Scouts; Bsball (V L); Cr Ctry (V L); Track (V L); Secondary Education; Physics; U of Delaware; Clemson U

KENEALY, ELYSE K; MASSAPEQUA, NY; MASSAPEQUA HS; (SR); Hi Hnr Roll; Hnr Roll; Nat Hon Sy; Nat Mrt LOC; WWAHSS; CARE; AL Aux Girls; Key Club; P to P St Amb Prg; French Clb; AP Scholar with Honors; Major-Biochemistry; Profession-Pediatric Neurologist; U of Richmond

KENNEDY, ATHENA; AMHERST, NY; SACRED HEART AC; Comm Volntr; Peer Tut/Med; Biology Clb; DARE; Skiing; Law School

KENNEDY, CATHERINE R; TROY, NY; TROY HS; (FR); All Am Sch; Hi Hnr Roll; Hnr Roll; MVP; WWAHSS; ArtClub; Jr Ach; Key Club; Svce Clb; Vsity Clb; Spanish Clb; Chr; Flg Crps; Mch Bnd; Swmg (V L); Fordham; Tulane

KENNEDY, ELIZABETH M; BROOKLYN, NY; MOORE CATHOLIC HS; (JR); Hi Hnr Roll; Hnr Roll; MVP; Nat Hon Sy; Comm Volntr; Peer Tut/Med; ArtClub; Tchrs Aide; Bskball (V); Sftball (VJ); Swmg (V); Lit Mag (R); Yrbk (P); TCM - Religious Education Teacher; Physical Therapy; Journalism; SUNY Stony Brook; Marist College

KENNEY JR, ROBERT D; STATEN ISLAND, NY; PT RICHMOND HS; (SR); Hnr Roll; Sci Fairs; WWAHSS; Comm Volntr; Peer Tut/Med; Chrch Yth Grp; Emplmnt; Scouts; Vsity Clb; SP/M/VS; Bsball (V); Electrical Engineering; Polytechnic U

KENTOURIS, THOMAS; ROCKAWAY PARK, NY; ST EDMUNDS PREP HS; (JR); Hi Hnr Roll; MVP; Nat Stu Ath Day Aw; Perf Att; Comm Volntr; Chrch Yth Grp; Emplmnt; Off Aide; Vsity Clb; Italian Clb; SP/M/VS; Bsball (V); Bskball (V); Scr Kpr (V); Wt Lftg; CR (R); Lit Mag (R); Foreign Language Club- Italian; Business Management; Canisius College; Iona College

KENYON, BRITTANY; MOHAWK, NY; JARVIS HS; (JR); Hnr Roll; Nat Stu Ath Day Aw; Perf Att; Peer Tut/Med; Sci Clb; Tchrs Aide; French Clb; Bskball (V); Sccr (V); Sftball (V); Stu Cncl (R); All Star and MVP for Soccer; Honorable Mention and MVP for Basketball and Softball; Sports Medicine; Springfield College

KERN, MARK; GASPORT, NY; ROYALTON HARTLAND HS; (FR); 4H Awd; Hi Hnr Roll; Hnr Roll; Comm Volntr; 4-H; Scouts; Cr Ctry (V); Track (V); Decathlon Age Group Winner; History; Fordham U

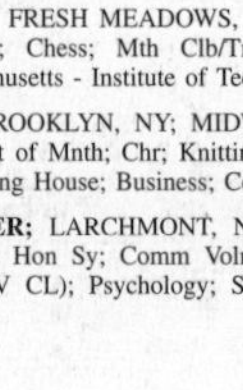
Kelley, Kristene
Stillwater Ctrl HS
Stillwater, NY

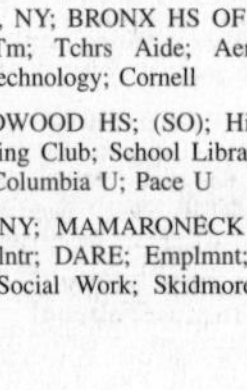
Kassner, Alyssa L
Longwood HS
Coram, NY

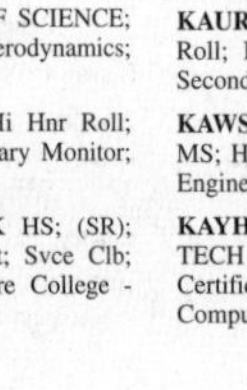
Karim, Shadia A
Stuyvesant HS
Ozone Park, NY

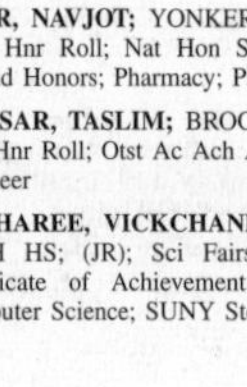
Kaplan, Jennifer
Mamaroneck HS
Larchmont, NY

National
Honor Roll
Spring 2005

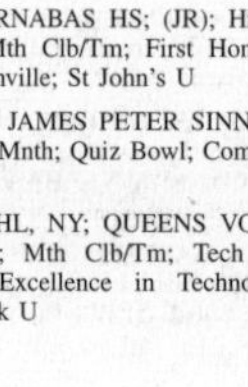
Kadian, Eisha
Benjamin Cardozo HS
Bellerose, NY

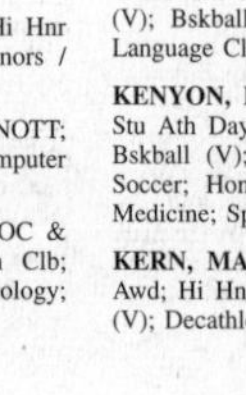
Kasneci, Ola
St Barnabas HS
Yonkers, NY

Kayharee, Vickchand
Queens Voc & Tech HS
S Richmond Hl, NY

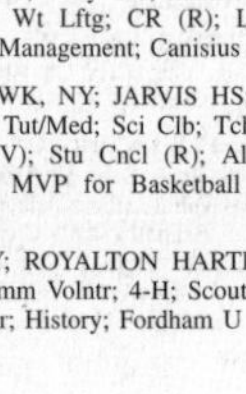
Kentouris, Thomas
St Edmunds Prep HS
Rockaway Park, NY

KERR, TONYA; FINE, NY; CLIFTON-FINE CTRL SCH; (FR); Hi Hnr Roll; Hnr Roll; Scr Kpr (VJ); Sccr (V); Track (V); Cl Off (P); National Junior Honor Society; Physical Education Student Leadership Award; Psychology / Behavioral Sciences; Radiological Sciences / Technology; Long Island U / CW Post; Niagara U

KESELMAN, SVETLANA; BROOKLYN, NY; MIDWOOD HS; (SR); WWAHSS; Emplmnt; Key Club; Off Aide; P to P St Amb Prg; Lit Mag (E); Summa Cum Laude National Latin Exam Awards; Arista; Baruch Honors

KESSELRING JR, CARL R; SPENCERPORT, NY; CORNERSTONE CHRISTIAN AC; (SO); Ctznshp Aw; Hi Hnr Roll; Hnr Roll; St of Mnth; Comm Volntr; Chrch Yth Grp; Ch Chr; Jzz Bnd; Sccr (J); High School Chapel Band; Youth Volunteer in Inner City Church; Culinary Arts; Business Management; Culinary Institute of America; SUNY Brockport

KETTRICK, TESSA B; WATERTOWN, NY; WATERTOWN HS; (JR); Hi Hnr Roll; Nat Hon Sy; Otst Ac Ach Awd; Perf Att; Pres Ac Ftns Aw; WWAHSS; Comm Volntr; Chrch Yth Grp; Emplmnt; Key Club; Bnd; Chr; SP/M/VS; Swmg (V); Track (V); Vllyball (VJC); Yrbk (R); Church Youth Group Mission Trips to Mexico and TN; Handbell Choir; Education; Mathematics; SUNY Geneseo

KHALID, RABYA; ELMONT, NY; SEWANHAKA HS; (JR); Ctznshp Aw; F Lan Hn Soc; Hi Hnr Roll; Hnr Roll; Nat Hon Sy; Sci Fairs; St of Mnth; WWAHSS; Comm Volntr; Peer Tut/Med; Fr of Library; Key Club; Lib Aide; Voc Ind Clb Am; Community Service; School Service; Pre-Med / Medical School / Biology; MD; The Sophie Davis School of Biomedical Education; SUNY Stony Brook

KHALID, WAJIHA; BROOKLYN, NY; JAMES MADISON HS; (SO); Hnr Roll; Nat Hon Sy; Sci Fairs; St of Mnth; Comm Volntr; Peer Tut/Med; Key Club; Mth Clb/Tm; Sci Clb; Was in Intermediate Band; Bio-Med Student in High School; Pre-Med; Sciences and the Liberal Arts; Columbia U; Fordham U

KHALILI-GILEAD, REBECCA R; HOLLIS, NY; YESHIVA UNIVERSITY HS FOR GIRLS; (JR); Hnr Roll; Nat Hon Sy; WWAHSS; Peer Tut/Med; Chess; Tmpl Yth Grp; Optometrist; New York U; Cornell U

KHALIQUE, YEASMINE; EAST ELMHURST, NY; LA GUARDIA HS; (JR); Red Cr Aide; ArtClub; Photog; Cr Ctry (J); Track (J); Art Gallery; Architecture; Syracuse U; Cooper Union

KHAN, FARIZA; BRONX, NY; HS OF AMERICAN STUDIES AT LEHMAN COLLEGE; (JR); Comm Volntr; Peer Tut/Med; Drma Clb; Key Club; Mod UN; Dnce; SP/M/VS; Sftball (V); Sch Ppr; Yrbk (E); Honored At Baitul Aman Blamis Center; Corporate Law; History; U of California-Los Angeles; U of Miami

KHAN, HIRA U; JACKSON HEIGHTS, NY; WILLIAM CULLEN BRYANT HS; (SR); F Lan Hn Soc; Hnr Roll; Nat Hon Sy; Sci Fairs; Sci/Math Olympn; St of Mnth; WWAHSS; Comm Volntr; Peer Tut/Med; DARE; Lib Aide; Off Aide; Sci Clb; Svce Clb; Tchrs Aide; Chr; Tennis (L); Vllyball (C); Cl Off (R); Sch Ppr (R); Nominated for Youth Leadership Program; People to People Sports Ambassador; Pharmacy; Forensics; Long Island U; Albany College of Pharmacy

KHAN, MARINA A; VALLEY STREAM, NY; VALLEY STREAM CTRL HS; (SO); Hnr Roll; WWAHSS; Peer Tut/Med; ArtClub; Drma Clb; Photog; Scouts; SADD; Clb; Chr; Dnce; SP/M/VS; Bdmtn (J); Chrldg (J); Sccr (J); Track (C); Stu Cncl (S); Lit Mag (R); Sch Ppr (R); Yrbk (P); Psychology; Business; Fordham U; SUNY Stony Brook

KHAN, NIEM; SOUTH OZONE PARK, NY; FRANCIS LEWIS HS; (JR); Nat Hon Sy; Cardiology; Surgery; Columbia U; Princeton U

KHAN, PALWASHA; BROOKLYN, NY; MIDWOOD HS; (JR); Hnr Roll; Amnsty Intl; Comm Volntr; Red Cr Aide; Emplmnt; Key Club; Lib Aide; Off Aide; PhD; New York U; Columbia U

KHAN, SABOOH U; BUFFALO, NY; SWEET HOME HS; (SO); Hi Hnr Roll; Hnr Roll; Otst Ac Ach Awd; Pres Ac Ftns Aw; Chess; Lib Aide; Tennis (V L); Computer IT; Civil Services; Yale U; Cornell U

KHAN, SARA; YONKERS, NY; SAUNDERS HS; (JR); Ctznshp Aw; Hi Hnr Roll; Hnr Roll; Nat Hon Sy; Comm Volntr; Jr Ach; Key Club; SADD; Bdmtn (J); Tennis (VJ); Wt Lftg (J); Sch Ppr (R)

KHAN, SHAHEEN; EAST MEADOW, NY; EAST MEADOW HS; (JR); F Lan Hn Soc; Hi Hnr Roll; Hnr Roll; Nat Hon Sy; Otst Ac Ach Awd; Perf Att; Sci Fairs; Sci/Math Olympn; WWAHSS; Yth Ldrshp Prog; Comm Volntr; Hosp Aide; Peer Tut/Med; Cmptr Clb; Dbte Team; Emplmnt; Fr of Library; FBLA; Key Club; Lib Aide; Sci Clb; Chr; Bdmtn (V); Mock Trial; Most Active Member; Computer Science; Business Management; Hofstra U; New York U

KHANIS, IGOR; BROOKLYN, NY; SHEEPSHEAD BAY HS; (JR); Hnr Roll; Comm Volntr; ArtClub; Biology Clb; Tchrs Aide; Sccr (J); Yrbk (P); Accounting; Business Management; Hunter College; Brooklyn College

KHANNA, ARTI; ROCHESTER, NY; PITTSFORD SUTHERLAND HS; (SO); Hnr Roll; Comm Volntr; Mod UN; Adv Cncl; Treasurer of School MUN Club; Winner of Two Awards At Model UN Conference; Chemistry; Psychology; Syracuse U; Swarthmore College

KHANUM, HIRA; BROOKLYN, NY; (FR); Ctznshp Aw; Hi Hnr Roll; Hnr Roll; Pres Ac Ftns Aw; Pres Sch; Salutrn; Sci Fairs; St of Mnth; Comm Volntr; Peer Tut/Med; Biology Clb; Emplmnt; Key Club; Off Aide; P to P St Amb Prg; Sci Clb; Tchrs Aide; Bnd; Stg Cre; Cr Ctry (L); Track (L); Cl Off (R); CR (R); Lit Mag (R); Student Ambassador to China; Medicine (Cardiology); Geneticist; Columbia U; Brown U

KHARMATS, ANNA; BROOKLYN, NY; (SO); Hi Hnr Roll; Comm Volntr; JSA; Mth Clb/Tm; FBI Explorers Program Since 2005 (January); Completed SSA Summer School (2 College Courses); Psychology; Forensic Psychology; Columbia U; Cornell U

KHEMSUWAN, PANPAPHAT; WOODSIDE, NY; HARRY VAN ARSDALE HS; (SO); Hnr Roll; Nat Hon Sy; Otst Ac Ach Awd; Perf Att; Sci Fairs; St of Mnth; Cmptr Clb; Mth Clb/Tm; Sci Clb; Computer Science; Computer Engineering

KHO, IRENE G; OAKLAND GARDENS, NY; STUYVESANT HS; (FR); Perf Att; Sci/Math Olympn; Valdctrian; Key Club; Bnd; Chr; Sch Ppr (R); Medicine; Novelist; Columbia U

KHOURY, HEATHER A; CTRL ISLIP, NY; CTRL ISLIP HS; (SO); Hi Hnr Roll; Pres Sch; Hosp Aide; DARE; Emplmnt; Vsity Clb; Spanish Clb; Bnd; Ch Chr; Dnce; Mch Bnd; Swmg (V); Manager of Softball Team; Forensic Science; Nursing; St John's U (Rome, Italy); UCLA

KHRISHCHANOVICH, LYUBAVA; BROOKLYN, NY; BROOKLYN STUDIO SCH; (SR); Hnr Roll; Nat Hon Sy; Otst Ac Ach Awd; Valdctrian; WWAHSS; Comm Volntr; Tchrs Aide; Gold Medal in Art & Math; Award for Valedictorian; Pre-Med; New York U

KHURSHID, AMMAR; STATEN ISLAND, NY; NEW DORP HS; (SO); Hnr Roll; Perf Att; St of Mnth; Sccr; Student of the Month; Law; Computer Engineering; Wagner College; Howard U

KIEFER, KIMBERLY; ORISKANY, NY; ORISKANY JR/SR HS; (SR); Hi Hnr Roll; Nat Hon Sy; Sci/Math Olympn; St of Mnth; WWAHSS; Comm Volntr; Peer Tut/Med; Spec Olymp Vol; Emplmnt; Key Club; Mth Clb/Tm; Prom Com; Sci Clb; Scouts; SADD; Spanish Clb; Chr; SP/M/VS; Vllyball (V); Stu Cncl (R); Yrbk; Regional Program of Excellence; Whitestown Optimist Student of the Month; Fine Arts; Biology; U of Buffalo

KILLEEN, NICOLE H; PETERSBURG, NY; BERLIN JR/SR HS; (SO); Hi Hnr Roll; Hnr Roll; Comm Volntr; Chrch Yth Grp; Drma Clb; Emplmnt; Prom Com; SP/M/VS; Stg Cre; Sccr (V L); All-American Soccer Team (Played in Sweden); Olympic Development Program - Soccer; Kindergarten Teacher

KILLIANSKI, CAROLINE; MASPETH, NY; ARCHBISHOP MOLLOY HS; (JR); All Am Sch; Ctznshp Aw; Hi Hnr Roll; Hnr Roll; Nat Hon Sy; Nat Sci Aw; Pres Sch; Sci Fairs; Sci/Math Olympn; St of Mnth; Comm Volntr; Peer Tut/Med; ArtClub; Chrch Yth Grp; DARE; Lib Aide; Mth Clb/Tm; Off Aide; Scouts; Dnce; SP/M/VS; Sftball (V); CR (P); Lit Mag (R); Valedictorian 2002; Nursing Home Volunteer; Architecture; Philosophy; Fordham U; Hunter College

KIM, ANNA; GREAT NECK, NY; GREAT NECK SOUTH HS; (JR); Comm Volntr; Peer Tut/Med; Chess; Chrch Yth Grp; Fr of Library; Key Club; Lib Aide; Mus Clb; Svce Clb; Bnd; Chr; Ch Chr; SP/M/VS; Bdmtn (JV); Fld Hky (JV); Tennis (L); Wt Lftg (etc); All-State Voice in NYSSMA; Volunteer at NSAL (North Shore Animal League); Biology; Architecture

KIM, DANIEL J; WEBSTER, NY; WEBSTER SCHROEDER HS; (SO); Hi Hnr Roll; Pres Ac Ftns Aw; Comm Volntr; Chrch Yth Grp; Key Club; Mus Clb; Bnd; Ftball (J); Key Club; Volunteer Hours; Business; Medical; Cornell U; U of Michigan

KIM, DIANNA N; ITHACA, NY; ITHACA HS; (SO); Hi Hnr Roll; Hnr Roll; Nat Hon Sy; Sci Fairs; Hosp Aide; Chrch Yth Grp; Prom Com; Tchrs Aide; Ch Chr; Bskball (V); Stu Cncl (S); Sch Ppr (R); Yrbk (R); Harvard, Stanford, Cornell

KIM, ELLIOT; MONROE, NY; MONROE-WOODBURY; (SO); Hi Hnr Roll; Nat Hon Sy; Perf Att; Comm Volntr; Chrch Yth Grp; Mth Clb/Tm; Mus Clb; Bnd; Mch Bnd

KIM, HANNAH; WOODSIDE, NY; TOWNSEND HARRIS HS; (SO); Gov Hnr Prg; Hi Hnr Roll; Perf Att; WWAHSS; Comm Volntr; ArtClub; Chess; Mth Clb/Tm

KIM, RICHARD; OAKLAND GARDENS, NY; QUEENS HS FOR THE SCIENCES; (FR); Hnr Roll; Peer Tut/Med; Chess; Chrch Yth Grp; DARE; Key Club; Orch; Arista; Peer Mediation - Spark; Architecture; Medicine; Poly Tech; NYU

KIM, SCOTT; GUILDERLAND, NY; GUILDERLAND HS; (SO); Hnr Roll; Comm Volntr; Hosp Aide; Chrch Yth Grp; Sccr (J); Track (V); Architect; Pilot; U.C.L.A; U. Penn

KIM, SO HEE; FLUSHING, NY; FRANCIS LEWIS HS; (JR); Comm Volntr; Chrch Yth Grp; Mth Clb/Tm; Korean Clb; Bnd; Serving At Korean Voters Council; Biochemistry; Stony Brook U

KIM, SOYEAN; BROOKLYN, NY; WASHINGTON IRVING HS; (SR); Hnr Roll; Nat Hon Sy; Perf Att; Comm Volntr; Peer Tut/Med; ArtClub; Chrch Yth Grp; Emplmnt; Key Club; Mus Clb; SUNY @ Stonybrook

KIM, YEON; BROOKLYN, NY; HEALTH PROF & HUMAN SERV HS; (SO); Hnr Roll; Perf Att; ArtClub; Chess; Chrch Yth Grp

KIM, YOOLA; BAYSIDE, NY; STUYVESANT HS; (FR); Hosp Aide; Key Club; Lib Aide; Mth Clb/Tm; Off Aide; Bnd; Sch Ppr; Medicine; Architecture; Cornell U; Brown U

KIM, YOUN HUN; FLUSHING, NY; STUYVESANT HS; (FR); Ctznshp Aw; Hnr Roll; Otst Ac Ach Awd; Perf Att; Key Club; Mth Clb/Tm; Bnd; KMSO Korean Math Olympiad; Handicap Volunteer, Sign Language; Engineering; Massachusetts Institute of Technology; Columbia U of New York

KING, ASHLEY; HOLLEY, NY; WEMECO BOCES-CAREER TECH CTR; (SR); Hnr Roll; Yrbk (R); LPN (Nursing); BN (Nursing); Monroe Community College; BOCES

KING, CORDERO; BROOKLYN, NY; BROOKLYN TECH HS; (SR); Hnr Roll; Nat Hon Sy; WWAHSS; Peer Tut/Med; Ftball (VJ); Track (V); Robotics Team; Electrical Engineering; Computer Engineering; Buffalo State College

KING, SARAH A; ORCHARD PARK, NY; SWEET HOME HS; (SO); Hi Hnr Roll; Hnr Roll; Otst Ac Ach Awd; Comm Volntr; Chrch Yth Grp; Emplmnt; Softball - Not with School; Forensic Scientist; U of Buffalo

KING JR, RONALD; BRONX, NY; CELIA CRUZ BRONX HS OF MUSIC; (FR); Hi Hnr Roll; Nat Hon Sy; Otst Ac Ach Awd; Perf Att; Sci Fairs; St of Mnth; Drma Clb; Mth Clb/Tm; Pep Squd; Bnd; Jzz Bnd; Orch; Cl Off (T); Law; Music; Harvard U; The Juilliard School

KIRK, TYLER; GLOVERSVILLE, NY; GLOVERSVILLE HS; (SO); Hi Hnr Roll; Pres Sch; WWAHSS; Yth Ldrshp Prog; Comm Volntr; Chess; Quiz Bowl; Bnd; Jzz Bnd; Mch Bnd; Pep Bnd; Golf (V L); Cl Off (P, R); NYSSMA Solo Festival (10th); History; Medicine

KIRSCHMAN, DANIEL; FONDA, NY; FONDA FULTONVILLE CTRL SCH; (FR); Hi Hnr Roll; Comm Volntr; Chrch Yth Grp; Lttrmn Clb; Sci Clb; Ftball (J); Track (VJ); NOAH; Church Youth Group; Science

KISSANE, CAROLINE; NEW YORK, NY; UNITED NATIONS INTL SCH; (JR); MVP; Yth Ldrshp Prog; Chrch Yth Grp; Drma Clb; Emplmnt; Mod UN; Mus Clb; Pep Squd; Scouts; Voc Ind Clb Am; Acpl Chr; Chr; Ch Chr; SP/M/VS; Bskball (JC); Dvng (V); Fld Hky (J); Skiing (J); Sccr (V); CR (R); Medicine; Advertising; Vassar College; Brown U

KITZEN, KRISTINA E; HUNTINGTON, NY; HUNTINGTON HS; (JR); Hi Hnr Roll; Hnr Roll; Otst Ac Ach Awd; Perf Att; St of Mnth; Comm Volntr; Peer Tut/Med; DARE; Emplmnt; Mus Clb; Svce Clb; Orch; Science and Math Pride Awards; Positive Action Committee Member; History; International Affairs; SUNY Fredonia; U of Vermont

KIZIS, JODY J; PAINTED POST, NY; CORNING-PAINTED POST WEST HS; (JR); Hi Hnr Roll; Perf Att; Pres Ac Ftns Aw; Emplmnt; Ftball (V L); Math Achievement from Corning Inc; 2nd Place Ribbon - Art Show; Architecture; Law Enforcement; Ohio State U; Penn State U

KLANG, BRIENA B; BROOKLYN, NY; BNOS YAKOV PUPA; (SR); Hi Hnr Roll; Otst Ac Ach Awd; Perf Att; Salutrn; Valdctrian; Comm Volntr; Peer Tut/Med; Cmptr Clb; Dbte Team; Fr of Library; Mth Clb/Tm; Spch Team; Tchrs Aide; Tmpl Yth Grp; Acpl Chr; Chr; SP/M/VS; Stg Cre; Chrldg (V); PPSqd (V); Adv Cncl (V); CR (P); Sch Ppr (E); Yrbk (R); Senior Dinner-Chairperson; School Chair Director; Lawyer; Mathematician; Touro College; New York U

KLEBANOV, YANA; PITTSFORD, NY; RUSH-HENRIETTA HS; (SO); Ctznshp Aw; F Lan Hn Soc; Hi Hnr Roll; Nat Hon Sy; St of Mnth; WWAHSS; Comm Volntr; DECA; Emplmnt; Mod UN; French Clb; Adv Cncl (R); Cl Off (V); Stu Cncl (R); CR (R); Unity Club Treasurer; Student Rep on Board of Education; International / Communications / Business; Boston U; Bentley U

KLEIN, ALEX; CARMEL, NY; CARMEL HS; (FR); Hi Hnr Roll; Hnr Roll; Comm Volntr; Tchrs Aide; Neurologist; Engineer; Massachusetts Institute of Technology; Princeton U

KLEIN, ALYSSA V; MERRICK, NY; CALHOUN HS; (FR); Hi Hnr Roll; WWAHSS; CARE; Comm Volntr; Chrch Yth Grp; Emplmnt; Key Club; SADD; Bnd; Bskball (J L); Sftball (J L); Vllyball (J L); Teacher; Doctor; New York U; Columbia U

KLEIN, JACKIE; PT WASHINGTON, NY; SCHREIBER HS; (JR); Hnr Roll; St of Mnth; Comm Volntr; Peer Tut/Med; Emplmnt; Fr of Library; Key Club; Chr; Swmg (V); Helen Keller National Center Volunteer; Criminal Justice / Protective Service; American Sign Language; Northeastern U; Rochester U

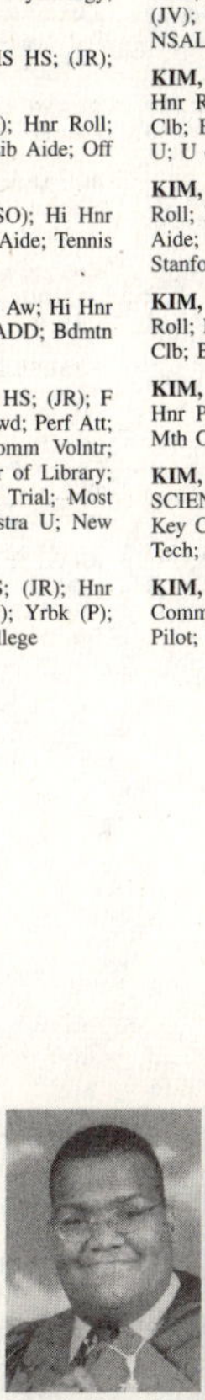
King Jr, Ronald
Celia Cruz Bronx HS Of Music
Bronx, NY

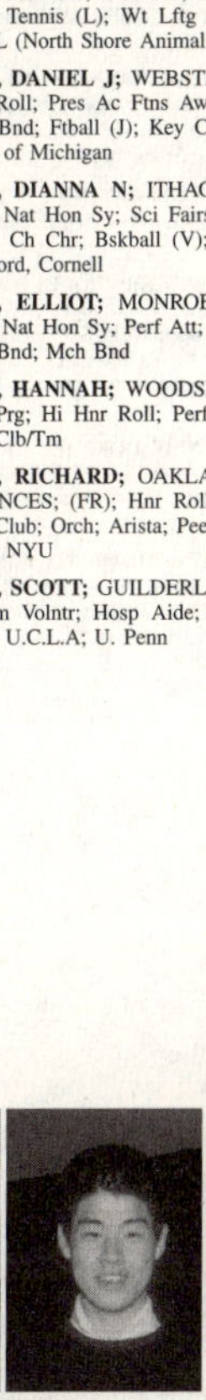
Kim, Scott
Guilderland HS
Guilderland, NY

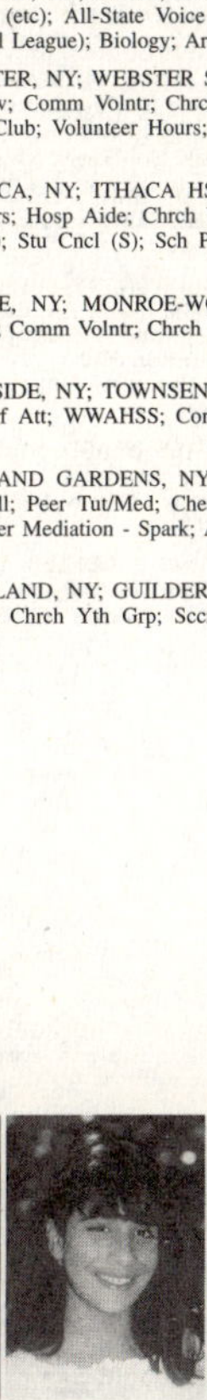
Khalili-Gilead, Rebecca R
Yeshiva University HS For Girls
Hollis, NY

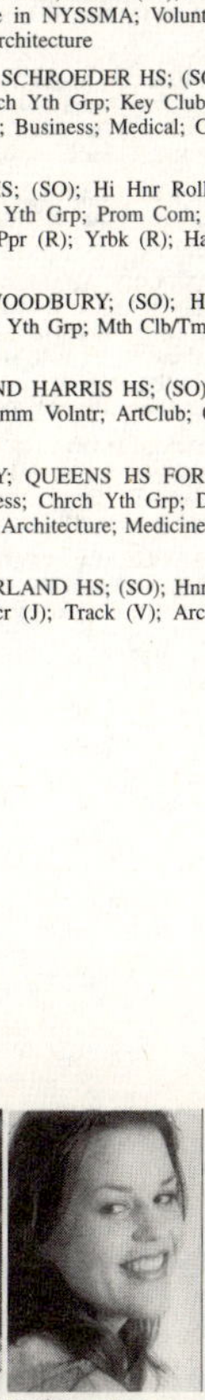
Khrishchanovich, Lyubava
Brooklyn Studio Sch
Brooklyn, NY

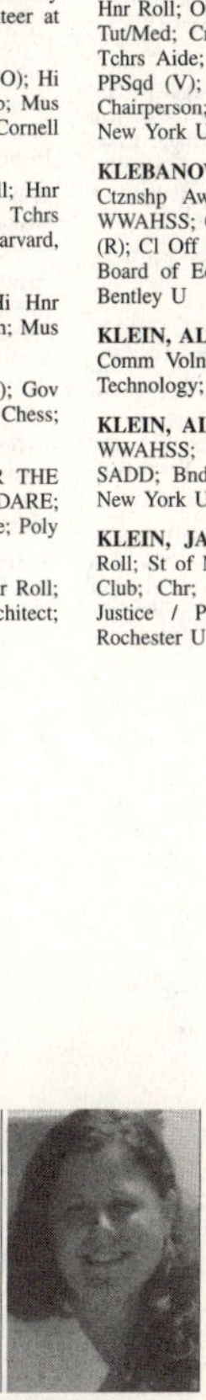
Klein, Jackie
Schreiber HS
Pt Washington, NY

KLEIN, JAKE; MERRICK, NY; JOHN F KENNEDY HS; (FR); Hi Hnr Roll; Sci/Math Olympn; Comm Volntr; Mth Clb/Tm; Tmpl Yth Grp; Chr; Bsball (J); Bskball (J); Sccr (J)

KLEPFER, KATY; BINGHAMTON, NY; SETON CATHOLIC; (SR); Hnr Roll; Sci Fairs; Sci/Math Olympn; Comm Volntr; DARE; Drma Clb; Emplmnt; Mth Clb/Tm; Pep Squd; Scouts; SADD; Spanish Clb; Rotary Exchange Student to Thailand for 1 Year; Nursing; College of New Rochelle

KLIMA, JESSICA; MERRICK, NY; SANFORD H CALHOUN; (JR); F Lan Hn Soc; Hnr Roll; Kwnis Aw; Nat Hon Sy; Perf Att; WWAHSS; Yth Ldrshp Prog; Peer Tut/Med; DECA; Emplmnt; Key Club; Mth Clb/Tm; SADD; Bdmtn (V); Tennis (V); Math Honors Society; Scholar Athlete, Athletic Achievement Award; Nursing; Business Administration; Clemson U; U of Virginia

KLIMAS, CHRISTOPHER; FREEPORT, NY; FREEPORT HS; (JR); Hi Hnr Roll; Hnr Roll; Perf Att; Pres Ac Ftns Aw; Comm Volntr; Chess; Mth Clb/Tm; Bnd; Mch Bnd; Wrstlg (J); Engineering; Mathematics; Columbia U; MIT

KLIMECZKO, JANINE; BUFFALO, NY; MT MERCY AC; (JR); Hnr Roll; Perf Att; SADD; Sftball (J); Swmg (V); Mortuary Science; Massage Therapy; Finger Lake School of Massage; SUNY Canton

KLINE, SARAH A; ENDICOTT, NY; UNION ENDICOTT HS; (FR); Hi Hnr Roll; Otst Ac Ach Awd; Sci Fairs; WWAHSS; DARE; Key Club; Spanish Clb; CR (R); CYO Basketball; Completion of the Medical Explorers Program; A Career As a Medical Doctor; Notre Dame; Boston College

KNAPP, CHRIS; HUDSON FALLS, NY; SOUTHERN ADIRONDACK ED CTR; (JR); Hnr Roll; Perf Att; WWAHSS; Swmg; Track; Sch Ppr; Auto Tech; UTI

KNAPP, JENNIFER L; INTERLAKEN, NY; SOUTH SENECA HS; (JR); Hnr Roll; Otst Ac Ach Awd; 4-H; Chr; Early Childhood; Tompkins Cortland Community College

KNAPP, SARA L; KIRKVILLE, NY; CHITTENANGO HS; (JR); Hnr Roll; St of Mnth; Comm Volntr; FBLA; Bskball (VJC); Lcrsse (VJ); Sccr (J); FBLA-Attending Senior Year-2006; Criminal Law; Business; U At Albany; U At Buffalo

KNAPP, SHELBY; LAURENS, NY; LAURENS CTRL SCH; (SR); Hi Hnr Roll; Hnr Roll; Kwnis Aw; Nat Hon Sy; Otst Ac Ach Awd; Red Cr Aide; Chrch Yth Grp; Drma Clb; Emplmnt; Key Club; Mus Clb; NtlFrnscLg; Prom Com; Tchrs Aide; Chr; Ch Chr; Mch Bnd; SP/M/VS; Sccr (V L); Track (V L); Yrbk (P); Secondary Education; Youth Ministry; Roberts Wesleyan College

KNAPTON, ZACHARY; STANLEY, NY; EMMANUEL BAPTIST AC; (SR); Hnr Roll; Chrch Yth Grp; Ch Chr; Bskball (VJCL); Sccr (V L); Vllyball (V L); Cl Off (P); Yrbk (E, R); Youth Pastor; Police Officer; Word of Life Bible Institute; Pensacola Christian College

KNEESSY, NICOLE; BAYPORT, NY; BAYPORT BLUE POINT HS; (SO); Hnr Roll; Pres Ac Ftns Aw; St of Mnth; Comm Volntr; DARE; Emplmnt; Orch; Fld Hky (J); Track (J); Cl Off (T); Stu Cncl (T); CR (R); Law Degree; U of North Carolina; Boston U

KNIES, KATHERINE; PURDYS, NY; NORTH SALEM HS; (JR); Hi Hnr Roll; MVP; Nat Hon Sy; Otst Ac Ach Awd; St of Mnth; USAA; WWAHSS; Yth Ldrshp Prog; Comm Volntr; Hosp Aide; Peer Tut/Med; Chrch Yth Grp; DARE; Emplmnt; Photog; Scouts; SADD; Sftball (VJCL); Tennis (V CL); Track (V); Psychology

KNOWLTON, HEATHER; MONTROSE, NY; HENDRICK HUDSON HS; (SO); Hi Hnr Roll; Nat Sci Aw; Otst Ac Ach Awd; St of Mnth; Comm Volntr; Hab For Humty Volntr; DARE; FBLA; Outdrs Clb; Photog; Dnce; Sccr (V); Track (V); Member of Cortlandt Soccer Club on Vipers Team for 4 Years; Received Business Education Award from the College of Westchester; Marine Biology/Oceanography; Photography/Film; Princeton U; Yale U

KNUTH, VINCENT; SCHOHARIE, NY; SCHOHARIE HS; (FR); Hnr Roll; Scouts; Drum Instructor; Berkeley

KOBAN, MICHELLE; ENDICOTT, NY; UNION ENDICOTT HS; (SO); Hi Hnr Roll; Chr; SP/M/VS; Education; Music; SUNY Cortland; Ithaca College

KOBIELSKI, LOUIS J; SHERMAN, NY; SHERMAN CTRL SCH; (SR); Hi Hnr Roll; Nat Hon Sy; Perf Att; WWAHSS; Comm Volntr; Emplmnt; Ntl FFA; Schol Bwl; Skt Tgt Sh (C); U of Rochester Kodak Young Leader Award; NYS FFA Empire Degree; Mechanical Engineering; Penn State Behrend

KOCH, KARINA M; BUFFALO, NY; KENMORE WEST SR HS; (SO); Hnr Roll; Perf Att; St of Mnth; Comm Volntr; ArtClub; Emplmnt; P to P St Amb Prg; Photog; Clb; Stg Cre; Tennis (V); Stu Cncl (R); Lit Mag (R); Head of Schools Creative Writing Club; Architecture; Graphic Design; U of Buffalo; The Savannah College of Art and Architecture

KOEHLER, ELIZABETH M; JAMESTOWN, NY; SOUTHWESTERN HS; (JR); Hnr Roll; Nat Hon Sy; Comm Volntr; Peer Tut/Med; DECA; Emplmnt; Key Club; Photog; Prom Com; French Clb; Chr; Dnce; SP/M/VS; Chrldg (J); Sccr (J); Cl Off (S); Sch Ppr (R); Top 10 Finalist in Competitive Event at 2005 International Career Development Conference; Ranked 2nd in Class; Communications; Broadcast Journalism; Ithaca College; Emerson College

KOKARAM, VICTOR; STATEN ISLAND, NY; FRANCIS SCH; (JR); Hnr Roll; St of Mnth; Yth Ldrshp Prog; P to P St Amb Prg; Ftball (J); Computer Science; Political Science; New York U; Oxford U

KOLESOVA, ANNA; SUNNYSIDE, NY; BE'ER HAGOLAH INST; (JR); Hi Hnr Roll; Hnr Roll; Sci Fairs; Comm Volntr; ArtClub; Cmptr Clb; Mth Clb/Tm; Mus Clb; Chr; Dnce; Bskball; Lit Mag (E); Sch Ppr (E); Yrbk (R); Dermatologist; Hunter College; Stern U

KOLISNYK, LYUDMYLA; BROOKLYN, NY; JAMES MADISON HS; (SO); Hnr Roll; Biology Clb; Vllyball (V); Part Time Work in Medical Office; Optometrist; Journalist; Columbia U; College of Communication

KOLLER, MICHAEL; VALHALLA, NY; VALHALLA HS; (SO); Hi Hnr Roll; Perf Att; Pres Sch; Comm Volntr; Hosp Aide; DARE; Emplmnt; P to P St Amb Prg; SADD; Tchrs Aide; Vsity Clb; Spanish Clb; Stg Cre; Cr Ctry (V); Tennis (V); Sch Ppr (R); Helping Hands Club, Spanish Club; VIF Club-High Honor Roll; Engineering, Marketing; NYU; Fordham U

KOLODZIEJCZYK, NICOLE C; CONSTANTIA, NY; PAUL V MOORE HS; (SR); Hi Hnr Roll; Hnr Roll; Nat Hon Sy; WWAHSS; Prom Com; Bskball (V L); Lcrsse (V L); Utica College

KOME, MISPA M; HEMPSTEAD, NY; HEMPSTEAD HS; (SO); Hi Hnr Roll; Hnr Roll; Perf Att; Bdmtn (J); Vllyball (J); In Worst 2 First (A Community Service Activity); Scientist Majoring in Genetics; Biochemist; Columbia U; Yale U

KONADU, ANTHONY; YONKERS, NY; IONA PREP SCH; (MS); Hi Hnr Roll; Nat Sci Aw; Otst Ac Ach Awd; Perf Att; Pres Ac Ftns Aw; WWAHSS; Comm Volntr; Hosp Aide; Chrch Yth Grp; Cmptr Clb; DARE; Off Aide; Tchrs Aide; Bskball (V); Ftball (V); Cty Johns Hopkins U Talent Search; Pathways to College; Business Administration; Nanotechnology; Harvard U; Massachusetts Institute of Technology

KONDELKA, CASEY; BLOOMINGBURG, NY; PINE BUSH HS; (JR); Lcrsse (V); Sccr (V L); Sftball; CR; Education; Engineering

KONSTANTAKOPOULOS, MARINA-SOTIRIA; YONKERS, NY; ST DEMETRIOS HS OF ASTORIA; (JR); WWAHSS; Comm Volntr; ArtClub; Dnce; Chrldg (J); Vllyball (V); Teacher of Math; Accounting; Hunter College; Fordham U

KOOP, SARAH; EAST QUOGUE, NY; WESTHAMPTON BEACH HS; (JR); Hi Hnr Roll; Hnr Roll; Otst Ac Ach Awd; Sci Fairs; St of Mnth; Hab For Humty Volntr; Emplmnt; Key Club; Mus Clb; Bnd; Chr; Jzz Bnd; Orch; Independent Competitive Horseback Riding; Psychology; Music Performance; Columbia U; Amherst College

KOPKO, ADAM; FLORAL PARK, NY; FLORAL PARK MEMORIAL HS; (SO); Perf Att; Key Club; Computer Repair; Briarcliffe; Hunter Business & Technical Programs

KOPKO, ANDREW; FLORAL PARK, NY; FLORAL PARK MEMORIAL HS; (FR); Comm Volntr; Key Club; Aviation; Dowling College Brookhaven Campus

KOPP, AMANDA; MASSAPEQUA, NY; (JR); Hnr Roll; CARE; Vllyball (V)

KOSOVSKAYA, MALKY; BROOKLYN, NY; JAMES MADISON HS; (SO); Hi Hnr Roll; Kwnis Aw; Nat Hon Sy; Comm Volntr; Peer Tut/Med; Key Club; Mth Clb/Tm; Adv Cncl (S); Secretary of Science Honor Society; Arista Honor Roll; Major in Biology; Med School; NYU; Stony Brook

KOSS, NICHOLAS; SCHENECTADY, NY; GUILDERLAND HS; (FR); Hnr Roll; Comm Volntr; Key Club; SADD; Ice Hky (V); Lcrsse (J); Engineering; Business

KOSTRINSKY, ADAM; SUFFERN, NY; SUFFERN HS; (JR); Hi Hnr Roll; Hnr Roll; Sci Fairs; WWAHSS; Amnsty Intl; Comm Volntr; Hosp Aide; Dbte Team; DECA; Emplmnt; Key Club; Mod UN; MuAlphaTh; Sci Clb; SADD; Bnd; Drm Mjr; Jzz Bnd; Mch Bnd; Ftball (J); Lcrsse (J); Skiing (V); Stu Cncl (R); CR (P); Area-All State Concert Band; The United States Wind Ensemble; Law; Business; Harvard; Yale

KOTSONIS, MARIA; STATEN ISLAND, NY; NEW DORP HS; (JR); Hnr Roll; Nat Hon Sy; Nat Ldrshp Svc; Otst Ac Ach Awd; Chrch Yth Grp; Dnce; Stu Cncl (T); Greek Regent / Regents Diploma; Law Degree; Physical Therapy; Fordham U; Pace U

KOTTYARSKAYA, YELENA; BROOKLYN, NY; MIDWOOD HS; (JR); Hnr Roll; Sci Fairs; WWAHSS; Key Club; Chr; SP/M/VS; Sch Ppr (R); Key Club President; Director of the Democratic Club; English; Columbia U; Cornell U

KOTZ, KRISTEN N; ELMA, NY; IROQUOIS CTRL HS; (SR); Hnr Roll; Nat Hon Sy; Perf Att; St of Mnth; WWAHSS; Emplmnt; Scouts; Chr; Skiing; Track; Sch Ppr (E); Presidential Classroom Program 2/2004; Western New York Business Student of the Month; Journalism; Syracuse U; Kent State

KOUFFMAN, ARIELLE; EAST HAMPTON, NY; EAST HAMPTON HS; (JR); Hi Hnr Roll; Hnr Roll; Nat Hon Sy; Nat Ldrshp Svc; Otst Ac Ach Awd; WWAHSS; Comm Volntr; Hab For Humty Volntr; Peer Tut/Med; ArtClub; DARE; Emplmnt; HO'Br Yth Ldrshp; Key Club; Mod UN; Off Aide; Photog; Lcrsse (J); Tennis (J); Adv Cncl (V, R); Cl Off (R); Stu Cncl (V, R); CR (R); Lit Mag (P); WSI Instructor; CPR Instructor, Youth Court Member; PhD, MD, Psychology; Art History, Photography, Biology, Literature; Brown U; Wesleyan U; Tufts U

KOURTIS, STERIANI M; FLUSHING, NY; FRANCIS LEWIS HS; (JR); Ctznshp Aw; F Lan Hn Soc; Hnr Roll; Peer Tut/Med; Chrch Yth Grp; Drma Clb; Greek Clb; Ch Chr; Dnce; SP/M/VS; Adv Cncl (R); Stu Cncl (V); Psychology; Stony Brook U

KOWALSKI, ADAM; BUFFALO, NY; AMHERST HS; (JR); Hnr Roll; Nat Hon Sy; WWAHSS; Comm Volntr; Hab For Humty Volntr; Peer Tut/Med; Chrch Yth Grp; Emplmnt; Bnd; Jzz Bnd; SP/M/VS; Lcrsse (VJ L); Sccr (VJ L); Board of Deacons, Westminster Presbyterian Church; Red Cross Life Guard; Chemistry

KOYA, RACHANA; NEW HYDE PARK, NY; HERRICKS HS; (JR); Hnr Roll; Sci/Math Olympn; St of Mnth; Comm Volntr; Hab For Humty Volntr; Hosp Aide; Dbte Team; Mth Clb/Tm; Mus Clb; P to P St Amb Prg; Chr; Dnce; SP/M/VS; Bskball (J); Sftball (J); Track (J); Stu Cncl (R); CR (R); Lit Mag (E); VFW Honorable Mention; Johns Hopkins Program (CTY); Pre-Med; Ophthalmology; NYU-New York U; Temple U

KOZIORZEBSKA, KAREN; BROOKLYN, NY; ARCHBISHOP MOLLOY HS; (JR); Hi Hnr Roll; Hnr Roll; Comm Volntr; SADD; Cr Ctry (V); Track (V); Eastern European Club; Children Education; Speech Therapy; Boston College; New York U

KRAEGER, SCOTT; CONSTABLEVILLE, NY; SOUTH LEWIS HS; (JR); Ctznshp Aw; Hi Hnr Roll; Hnr Roll; MVP; Sci Fairs; Sci/Math Olympn; St of Mnth; WWAHSS; Comm Volntr; Hab For Humty Volntr; Peer Tut/Med; Spec Olymp Vol; Dbte Team; Emplmnt; Quiz Bowl; Scouts; Vsity Clb; Bsball (VJ L); Bskball (VJ L); Ftball (VJCL); Golf (J L); Vsy Clb (VJ); Wt Lftg (VJ); Adv Cncl (V); Cl Off (P); Sch Ppr (R, P); Mock Trial-NYS Lewis Cty Champions; Local Newspaper Reporter/Photographer; Business/History/Computers; St John Fisher; Hamilton

KRAFT, EMILY E; SENECA FALLS, NY; MYNDERSE AC; (JR); Hnr Roll; St of Mnth; WWAHSS; Comm Volntr; Chrch Yth Grp; DARE; P to P St Amb Prg; Won the International School Cooking Contest (1st); Biology; Photography; Syracuse U; Colgate U

KRAFT, LIOR; REGO PARK, NY; FRANCIS LEWIS HS; (JR); Hnr Roll; Nat Hon Sy; Comm Volntr; Drma Clb; Mth Clb/Tm; Math Team; Medical; Business; Binghamton U; U of Buffalo

KRAJOVAN, MELANIE; ONEONTA, NY; LAURENS CTRL SCH; (SR); Hi Hnr Roll; Nat Hon Sy; Pres Sch; WWAHSS; Comm Volntr; Peer Tut/Med; Red Cr Aide; Emplmnt; Key Club; NtlFrnscLg; Bnd; Chr; Jzz Bnd; Mch Bnd; Bskball (V); Sccr (VJC); Track (J); Psychology (DR); The College of Saint Rose

KRAMER, COREY J; RIPLEY, NY; RIPLEY CTRL SCH; (FR); Hnr Roll; Perf Att; Bsball (V); CR (R); Academic Merit Roll; National Physical Fitness Award; Video Game Programmer

KRAMER, LEAH R; SOUTH LIMA, NY; LIVONIA HS; (FR); Hi Hnr Roll; Pres Ac Ftns Aw; Sci Fairs; St of Mnth; WWAHSS; Yth Ldrshp Prog; Comm Volntr; Spec Olymp Vol; Drma Clb; Emplmnt; Key Club; Bnd; Mch Bnd; Orch; SP/M/VS; Lcrsse (JC); Sccr (JC); Stu Cncl (R); Sch Ppr (R); National Jr Honor Society / Executive Council; Student Leadership Conference "Leadership in Motion"

KRATZER, JESSICA; CORNING, NY; CORNING-PAINTED POST WEST HS; (JR); Hi Hnr Roll; Hnr Roll; Nat Hon Sy; Chrch Yth Grp; Quiz Bowl; Schol Bwl; Youth Ministry; Indiana Wesleyan U

KRAUSE, AIMEE; RAYMONDVILLE, NY; NORWOOD-NORFOLK CTRL; (JR); F Lan Hn Soc; Hi Hnr Roll; Hnr Roll; Nat Hon Sy; Nat Mrt Fin; Sci/Math Olympn; St of Mnth; WWAHSS; Yth Ldrshp Prog; Amnsty Intl; Comm Volntr; Spec Olymp Vol; Dbte Team; HO'Br Yth Ldrshp; Key Club; Mth Clb/Tm; Prom Com; Sci Clb; French Clb; Bnd; Jzz Bnd; Mch Bnd; SP/M/VS; Track (J); Cl Off (P); Sch Ppr (R, P); Mock Trial; Local Library Volunteer; International Business; McGill U

KRAVET, SARA; MELVILLE, NY; HALF HOLLOW HILLS HS EAST; (JR); F Lan Hn Soc; Hi Hnr Roll; Nat Hon Sy; WWAHSS; Comm Volntr; Peer Tut/Med; Spec Olymp Vol; BPA; DECA; FBLA; SADD; Spanish Clb; Sch Ppr (E)

Konadu, Anthony
Iona Prep Sch
Yonkers, NY

Kome, Mispa M
Hempstead HS
Hempstead, NY

National
Honor Roll
Spring 2005

Koban, Michelle
Union Endicott HS
Endicott, NY

Koop, Sarah
Westhampton Beach HS
East Quogue, NY

KRELL, JESSICA; BAYSIDE, NY; BENJAMIN CARDOZO HS; (JR); Hi Hnr Roll; Nat Hon Sy; Perf Att; Sci Fairs; Comm Volntr; Peer Tut/Med; Emplmnt; FBLA; Key Club; Off Aide; Photog; Tchrs Aide; Dnce; Explore! Program; Merit Certificate In Spanish

KRENZER, MELISSA; HUNT, NY; KESHEQUA CTRL SCH; (SR); Hi Hnr Roll; Nat Hon Sy; Pres Ac Ftns Aw; Red Cr Aide; 4-H; Emplmnt; Key Club; Prom Com; Sccr (V); Sftball (V); Member of Section V Division III Softball Team; Business Management: Administration; SUNY Fredonia

KRISHNAN, NISHA V; ELMONT, NY; SEWANHAKA HS; (JR); F Lan Hn Soc; Hi Hnr Roll; Kwnis Aw; Nat Hon Sy; Perf Att; St of Mnth; WWAHSS; Peer Tut/Med; Key Club; Lib Aide; Foreign Clb; Chr; Cl Off (R); Stu Cncl (V, S); CR (R); Sch Ppr (R); Science Research Program; Nursing; Pharmacy; Molloy College; St John's U

KRISTEL, VICTORIA V; SCHENECTADY, NY; SCHENECTADY HS; (FR); Hi Hnr Roll; Hnr Roll; Otst Ac Ach Awd; Perf Att; St of Mnth; Peer Tut/Med; DARE; Cl Off (V); Stu Cncl (V); CR (V); Pediatric Doctor; Pediatric Nurse; SUNY Albany; Union College

KRIVITSKI, MARGARITA; FOREST HILLS, NY; STUYVESANT HS; (SO); Nat Hon Sy; Key Club; SP/M/VS; Gmnstcs (V); Tennis (V); Medicine; Biology/Chemistry Research; Princeton U; Yale U

KROOPNICK, ADAM; ALBANY, NY; ALBANY HS; (JR); Cr Ctry (V); Track (V); Sch Ppr (R); Founder / President Badminton Club; Journalism; Creative Writing; Cornell U; Hamilton College

KRUPIN, CHRISTINE; SEAFORD, NY; SEAFORD HS; (SR); Hi Hnr Roll; Nat Hon Sy; Otst Ac Ach Awd; Pres Sch; Sci Fairs; WWAHSS; Yth Ldrshp Prog; Comm Volntr; Peer Tut/Med; Emplmnt; Key Club; NYLC; Prom Com; Yrbk; Business; Marketing; U of Maryland

KRUPP, CORINNE; SAUGERTIES, NY; SAUGERTIES HS; (FR); Hnr Roll; Chrch Yth Grp; Key Club; Tennis (V); Cl Off (S)

KRUTER, BRANDON; BELLMORE, NY; JOHN F KENNEDY HS; (JR); MVP; Nat Hon Sy; Comm Volntr; 4-H; Vsity Clb; Bskball (VJC); Lcrsse (VJC); Sccr (J); Basketball Rookie of the Year on Varsity; Finance/Banking; Computer Science; New York U; Hamilton College

KUEI, EVAN; MIDDLE VILLAGE, NY; LAGUARDIA HS OF ARTS & PERF ARTS; (SO); Hnr Roll; MVP; Nat Hon Sy; Perf Att; Pres Ac Ftns Aw; St of Mnth; Comm Volntr; Hosp Aide; Peer Tut/Med; Dbte Team; Lib Aide; Mus Clb; Tchrs Aide; Bnd; Clr Grd; Jzz Bnd; SP/M/VS; Bsball (V); Bskball (L); Ftball (L); Scr Kpr (L); Vllyball (C); Stu Cncl (R); CR (R); Yrbk (R, P); Won Numerous Prizes for the Piano; Played in Carnegie and Kennedy Hall (Piano); Business Degree; Music Degree; Columbia U of New York; Juilliard (Music College)

KUFFOUR, DERRICK; BRONX, NY; CARDINAL HAYES HS; (JR); Hnr Roll; Otst Ac Ach Awd; WWAHSS; Peer Tut/Med; Chess; Chrch Yth Grp; Ch Chr; Sch Ppr (R); Crotanu Achievement Program - PSD; Pre-Med; Engineering; SUNY Buffalo; The U of Chicago

KUHLMAN, HANNAH G I; OWEGO, NY; TIOGA CTR CHRISTIAN SCH; (SR); 4H Awd; Hi Hnr Roll; Hnr Roll; Sci Fairs; WWAHSS; Yth Ldrshp Prog; Comm Volntr; Peer Tut/Med; 4-H; Chrch Yth Grp; Emplmnt; Spch Team; Tchrs Aide; Chr; Ch Chr; SP/M/VS; Stu Cncl (P); Sch Ppr (R); Yrbk (R); Attended Congressional Student Leadership Conference; Tioga County Alternate Dairy Princess; Political Science; Communications (Public Relations); Liberty U

KUHN, DESERA; ELMIRA HEIGHTS, NY; THOMAS A EDISON HS; (FR); 4H Awd; Hi Hnr Roll; Hnr Roll; Kwnis Aw; Sci Fairs; St of Mnth; WWAHSS; Comm Volntr; Hosp Aide; 4-H; DARE; Fr of Library; Key Club; Clr Grd; Mch Bnd; SP/M/VS; Cl Off (S); Thomas A Edison High School Award of Excellence; Mash Camp At Arnot Ogden Medical Center Award; Doctor; Occupational Therapy

KUMBARCE, SHPETIME; BROOKLYN, NY; FRANKLIN DELANO ROOSEVELT HS; (SR); Nat Hon Sy; WWAHSS; Book Club; Speaks Albanian, English, Italian; Business; Legal Studies; CUNY Hunter College; CUNY Baruch College

KUMPEL, SARAH; BURNT HILLS, NY; BURNT HILLS-BALLSTON LAKE HS; Hi Hnr Roll; Hnr Roll; WWAHSS; Emplmnt; Accounting; Utica College; U of Albany

KUNJU, JOMY Y; NEW ROCHELLE, NY; NEW ROCHELLE HS; (SR); Hi Hnr Roll; Hnr Roll; Nat Hon Sy; Sci Fairs; Comm Volntr; Hab For Humty Volntr; Hosp Aide; Chrch Yth Grp; DARE; Lib Aide; Mus Clb; SADD; Acpl Chr; Chr; Ch Chr; Dnce; Bdmtn (L); Bsball (C); Bskball (C); Sftball (L); Tennis (L); Vllyball (L); Stu Cncl (R); CR (R); Prose/Poetry Writing; Physician's Assistant; St. John's U (Queens Campus); Long Island U (Brooklyn Campus)

KUNTZ, ANDREW; WESTPORT, NY; WESTPORT CTRL SCH; (FR); Hi Hnr Roll; Otst Ac Ach Awd; Sci/Math Olympn; Mth Clb/Tm; Bnd; Bskball (J); Sccr (J); Cl Off (V)

KUPISZEWSKA, BARBARA; MATTITUCK, NY; HARRY B WARD TECH CTR; (JR); Hi Hnr Roll; Hnr Roll; St Schl; St of Mnth; WWAHSS; Yth Ldrshp Prog; Comm Volntr; Mth Clb/Tm; ROTC; Ch Chr; Chrldg (J); Track (V); Medicine; Business

KURIAKOSE, BETSY; CARLE PLACE, NY; SAINT DOMINIC HS; (JR); F Lan Hn Soc; Hi Hnr Roll; Hnr Roll; Nat Hon Sy; Otst Ac Ach Awd; Sci Fairs; St of Mnth; WWAHSS; Comm Volntr; Hosp Aide; Peer Tut/Med; FBLA; Mod UN; NYLC; Dnce

KURIAN, BETHANY A; HUNTINGTON STATION, NY; WALT WHITMAN HS; (JR); Hi Hnr Roll; Hnr Roll; Nat Hon Sy; Otst Ac Ach Awd; St of Mnth; Peer Tut/Med; Chrldg (J L); Business Major; Law Degree; U of North Carolina; New York U

KURIAN, JENIE; EAST ELMHURST, NY; STUYVESANT HS; (JR); Hnr Roll; Otst Ac Ach Awd; Perf Att; Sci Fairs; St of Mnth; Comm Volntr; Hosp Aide; Peer Tut/Med; Biology Clb; Chrch Yth Grp; Key Club; Mth Clb/Tm; Prom Com; Sci Clb; Tchrs Aide; Bnd; Ch Chr; Dnce; Mastery Level on Physics Regents; Medicine School; Pharmacy; Columbia U; Boston U

KURIAN, MERCY; ELMONT, NY; SEWANHAKA HS; (FR); Hi Hnr Roll; Hnr Roll; Nat Hon Sy; Perf Att; Peer Tut/Med; Chrch Yth Grp; Key Club; Lib Aide; Sci Clb; Orch; Cr Ctry (V)

KURIAN, RUBY; ELMONT, NY; SEWANHAKA HS; (JR); F Lan Hn Soc; Hi Hnr Roll; Nat Hon Sy; Perf Att; WWAHSS; Hosp Aide; Peer Tut/Med; Chrch Yth Grp; Key Club; Lib Aide; Sci Clb; Foreign Clb; Orch; Lit Mag (E); Sch Ppr (E); Pharmacy; Nursing; St John's U; Adelphi U

KURIAN, TITUS; PORT CHESTER, NY; ARCHBISHOP STEPINAC HS; (SO); Ctznshp Aw; Hi Hnr Roll; Hnr Roll; Otst Ac Ach Awd; Comm Volntr; Hab For Humty Volntr; Chrch Yth Grp; FCA; Bnd; Ch Chr; Jzz Bnd; Mch Bnd; Irish Band-Drummer.; Community Service, Church-Sunday School Vocational Bible School; Pharm D; Physical Therapy; Iona College New Rochelle NY; U of Science in Philadelphia, St John's

KURLANDER, AYALA; BROOKLYN, NY; SHULAMITH HS FOR GIRLS; (JR); Hnr Roll; MVP; Nat Hon Sy; Yth Ldrshp Prog; Comm Volntr; Peer Tut/Med; Red Cr Aide; ArtClub; Dbte Team; Emplmnt; Mth Clb/Tm; Chr; SP/M/VS; Bskball (J); Sftball (J); Sch Ppr (R, P); Head of Jewish Affairs Committee / Hebrew Magazine; Debate Team Math Team / Art Club / President of Honor Society; Architecture / Business Woman; Pediatric Dentist; Yeshiva U Stern College for Women; Columbia U

KURTZNER, CHRISTINE A; ALBANY, NY; COLONIE CTRL HS; (JR); Hi Hnr Roll; WWAHSS; Comm Volntr; Bnd; Pep Bnd; Scr Kpr (VJ); Sftball (L); Stu Cncl (R); CR (R); Kept Score for Wrestling Since 8th Grade - Through JV and Varsity Wrestling; Varsity Soccer Score Keeping / Freshman Soccer / JV Lacrosse; Pre-Med; SUNY Albany; Johns Hopkins U

KURYLO, JOANNA; MASPETH, NY; CHRIST THE KING REG HS; (SO); Hnr Roll; Nat Hon Sy; Key Club; SADD; Sch Ppr (R)

KUSI, KWAME; BRONX, NY; COLUMBUS HS; (JR); Hnr Roll; Perf Att; Aviation Flight Science; Western Michigan U; Embry-Riddle Aeronautical U

KUZMACK, ASHLEY N; ROME, NY; ROME CATHOLIC HS; (FR); Hnr Roll; Sci Fairs; DARE; Bskball (J); Sccr (J)

KWIATKOWSKI, BRANDON; ELMA, NY; IROQUOIS HS; (JR); Hnr Roll; Nat Hon Sy; St of Mnth; Comm Volntr; Emplmnt; Scouts; Bnd; Jzz Bnd; Orch; SP/M/VS; Ftball (J); Eagle Scout; Honor Band; Criminal Justice; Fire & Emergency Services; Hilbert College; Medaille College

KWIATKOWSKI, KATHRYN; EAST AURORA, NY; EAST AURORA HS; (SO); Hi Hnr Roll; Hnr Roll; Otst Ac Ach Awd; Pres Ac Ftns Aw; Amnsty Intl; Comm Volntr; DARE; DECA; Drma Clb; SADD; Vsity Clb; Chr; Clr Grd; Mch Bnd; SP/M/VS; Gmnstcs; Hsbk Rdg; Mar Art; PP Ftbl; Tennis (V); Stu Cncl (R); CR (R); Girl Scout; Volunteer for SABAH (Skating Assn for the Blind and Handicapped); Veterinary Medicine; U of Miami; Georgetown

KWIATKOWSKI, KRISTA; ALBANY, NY; GUILDERLAND HS; (SO); Comm Volntr; Key Club; Bnd; Pep Bnd; Taking Guitar Lessons; Volunteer At Guilderland Library in Summer

KWONG, RYAN; NEW YORK, NY; HEALTH PROF & HUMAN SERV HS; (SO); Hnr Roll; Comm Volntr; Pre-Medical; Computer Science; New York U; Pace U

KWUN, JENNY H; OAKLAND GARDENS, NY; STUYVESANT HS; (FR); Hnr Roll; Perf Att; Sci/Math Olympn; St of Mnth; WWAHSS; Peer Tut/Med; Key Club; Mth Clb/Tm; Off Aide; Tchrs Aide; Orch; Arch; Business; Math; U Penn; MIT

KYDD, TRISH-ANN; BROOKLYN, NY; PAUL ROBESON HS; (SO); Hnr Roll; Otst Ac Ach Awd; Mth Clb/Tm; Psychologist; PhD/Doctorate; Harvard U; Howard U

LAAUSER, KYLE C; DELHI, NY; DELAWARE AC; (JR); Hi Hnr Roll; Hnr Roll; Nat Hon Sy; Perf Att; Drma Clb; Emplmnt; Mus Clb; Scouts; Spanish Clb; Chr; SP/M/VS; Stg Cre; Sccr (VJ L); Tennis (V L); Yrbk (E, R, P); National Honor Society; FCCLA; Graphics Design; Web Page Design; SUNY Delhi; Rochester Institute of Tech

LABELLA, JAIMIE; BAYVILLE, NY; LOCUST VALLEY HS; (JR); F Lan Hn Soc; Hnr Roll; Jr Rot; Otst Ac Ach Awd; St of Mnth; WWAHSS; Comm Volntr; ArtClub; Mus Clb; Photog; Prom Com; SADD; Spanish Clb; Bnd; Dnce; Flg Crps; Mch Bnd; Chrldg (V); Golf (V); Scr Kpr (V); CR (R); Yrbk (E); Relay for Life Team Captain (Walk for Cancer); Interact Club, Anthology of Poetry; Villanova; Quinnipiac

LABRANCHE, STANLEY J; EAST NORWICH, NY; OYSTER BAY HS; (SR); Hi Hnr Roll; Hnr Roll; Perf Att; Chr; Cl Off (R); Mock Trial; Accounting; Computer; State U of New York-The College At Old Westbury

LAFRANCA, PETER; HOWARD BEACH, NY; ARCHBISHOP MOLLOY HS; (JR); Hi Hnr Roll; Hnr Roll; Otst Ac Ach Awd; Perf Att; St of Mnth; Valdctrian; Peer Tut/Med; Mth Clb/Tm; Bsball (V); Sports Medicine; Engineering; Marist College; Manhattan College

LAGOON, SYED; ASTORIA, NY; STUYVESANT HS; (FR); 4H Awd; Hi Hnr Roll; Hnr Roll; Otst Ac Ach Awd; Perf Att; Sci Fairs; Sci/Math Olympn; St of Mnth; Yth Ldrshp Prog; Comm Volntr; ArtClub; Chess; Dbte Team; Key Club; Lib Aide; Tchrs Aide; Ch Chr; Flg Crps; SP/M/VS; Stg Cre; Bskball (J); Scr Kpr (V); Swmg (J); Vllyball (J); Stu Cncl (T); Sch Ppr (R); Harvard Law School; Yale

LAHNEN II, PATRICK J; BROCTON, NY; BROCTON CTRL SCH; (SR); Off Aide; Prom Com; Quill & Scroll; Ftball (VJ L); Automotive Mechanics; High-Performance Automotive; U of Northwestern Ohio

LAI, CHRISTINE; BAYSIDE, NY; STUYVESANT HS; (JR); Hnr Roll; Nat Hon Sy; Perf Att; Salutrn; Sci/Math Olympn; USAA; WWAHSS; Hosp Aide; Key Club; Mth Clb/Tm; Sci Clb; Chinese Clb; Orch; SP/M/VS; Stg Cre; Sch Ppr (E); Independent Science Research; Junior Olympic Archery Development Program; Chemistry; Chemical Engineering

LAI, HOLLY; STATEN ISLAND, NY; HEALTH PROF & HUMAN SERV HS; (SO); Hnr Roll; Comm Volntr; Science; Forensics; Columbia U; New York U

LAI, JEFFREY W; BRONX, NY; (JR); Hnr Roll; Nat Hon Sy; Comm Volntr; Drma Clb; Key Club; Mus Clb; Scouts; Bnd; Chr; Orch; Pep Bnd; Bsball (J); Bskball (J); Golf (J); Sccr (J); Swmg (J); Track (J); Wt Lftg (J); Adv Cncl (T); Stu Cncl (T); CR (T); Accounting-CPA; Attorney; New York U; Boston College

LAING, VANESSA N; BRONX, NY; EVANDER CHILDS HS; (JR); Hnr Roll; Perf Att; Peer Tut/Med; Dbte Team; Drma Clb; Tchrs Aide; Dnce; Stu Cncl (P); Junior Student Council President; Library Monitor; English; Harvard U; Howard U

LAINO, JENNIFER; BROOKLYN, NY; NEW UTRECHT HS; Hnr Roll; Sci Fairs; WWAHSS; Comm Volntr; Key Club; Chr; Stg Cre; Teacher BA & Master's; Brooklyn College; College of Staten Island

LAKOW, ALIXANDRA; WOODBURY, NY; SYOSSET HS; (JR); F Lan Hn Soc; Hnr Roll; Nat Hon Sy; Bskball (J); Tennis (VJ); Physical Therapy; Business; Ithaca College; U of North Carolina

LALITE, CARLA M; BRENTWOOD, NY; BRENTWOOD HS; (SR); Nat Hon Sy; Otst Ac Ach Awd; Sci/Math Olympn; Comm Volntr; Spec Olymp Vol; ArtClub; Emplmnt; Mus Clb; Sci Clb; Svce Clb; Bnd; Jzz Bnd; Mch Bnd; Fncg (J L); Boston U Design Competition Finalist; Forensic Science; Chemistry; Siena College; Long Island U CW Post

LALL, SOPHIA V; RICHMOND HILL, NY; FLUSHING HS; (JR); Nat Hon Sy; Comm Volntr; Chrch Yth Grp; DARE; Bnd; Dnce; 1st Place Bible Quizzer-NYC/LI Section; Sociology; Psychology; New York U; Fordham U

LALOO, MICHELLE S; S OZONE PARK, NY; JOHN ADAMS HS; (SR); Nat Hon Sy; Otst Ac Ach Awd; Perf Att; St of Mnth; Valdctrian; WWAHSS; Comm Volntr; Peer Tut/Med; Key Club; Mth Clb/Tm; Prom Com; Sci Clb; Tchrs Aide; Yrbk (P); Valedictorian; Finance; Accounting; St John's U

LAM, ALEX; RIVERHEAD, NY; MERCY HS; (SO); Hi Hnr Roll; Pres Ac Ftns Aw; Bskball (J); Biology; Dentistry; Columbia U; Baltimore U

LAM, GORETTI; FRESH MEADOWS, NY; FRANCIS LEWIS HS; (SR); Hnr Roll; Nat Hon Sy; Comm Volntr; Tech Clb; Chinese Clb; SP/M/VS; Stg Cre; Lit Mag (R); Outward Bound Program; Scholarship Committee; MBA; Marketing; City U of New York: Baruch College

LAM, NANCY; BROOKLYN, NY; JOHN DEWEY HS; (SO); Hnr Roll; Perf Att; Salutrn; Sci Fairs; St of Mnth; Comm Volntr; Key Club; Lib Aide; Photog

LAM, VAN; REGO PARK, NY; HS FOR MATH, SCI AND ENGINEERING@CCNY; (JR); Hi Hnr Roll; Nat Hon Sy; WWAHSS; Comm Volntr; Peer Tut/Med; Red Cr Aide; Emplmnt; Key Club; Mth Clb/Tm; MuAlphaTh; Vllyball (V); Vice President of Key Club; Mu Alpha Theta Member/Honors Society; Mechanical Engineering; Aerospace, Aeronautical and Astronautical; Carnegie Mellon; Massachusetts Institute of Technology

LAMB, VERONICA; ASTORIA, NY; ST VINCENT FERRER HS; (SR); WWAHSS; Scouts; Bskball (J); Vllyball (V); Forensic Science; John Jay College of Criminal Justice

Lakow, Alixandra
Syosset HS
Woodbury, NY

Lagoon, Syed
Stuyvesant HS
Astoria, NY

Kurylo, Joanna
Christ The King Reg HS
Maspeth, NY

Kurtzner, Christine A
Colonie Ctrl HS
Albany, NY

Kuhn, Desera
Thomas A Edison HS
Elmira Heights, NY

Kumpel, Sarah
Burnt Hills-Ballston Lake HS
Burnt Hills, NY

Labranche, Stanley J
Oyster Bay HS
East Norwich, NY

Lahnen II, Patrick J
Brocton Ctrl Sch
Brocton, NY

Lamb, Veronica
St Vincent Ferrer HS
Astoria, NY

LAMBERTA, GABRIELLE; OYSTER BAY, NY; OUR LADY OF MERCY AC; (JR); Hnr Roll; Nat Hon Sy; Nat Ldrshp Svc; Nat Mrt Fin; Nat Mrt LOC; Otst Ac Ach Awd; Perf Att; Pres Ac Ftns Aw; Yth Ldrshp Prog; Comm Volntr; Hosp Aide; Peer Tut/Med; Off Aide; Pep Squd; Prom Com; Svce Clb; Dnce; SP/M/VS; Cr Ctry (J); Sccr (V); Track (V); Stu Cncl (R); Journalism; Law; Fordham U; George Washington U

LAMI, ELYERTA; BROOKLYN, NY; JOHN DEWEY HS; (FR); Hnr Roll; St of Mnth; Comm Volntr; Peer Tut/Med; ArtClub; DARE; Lib Aide; Photog; Dnce; Bdmtn (C); Bskball (L); Fld Hky (L); Sccr (L); Cl Off (S); In Arista 7th & 8th Grade; Won Math Bee & Story Telling Contest; Psychology; New York U, Pace U; Columbia U

LAM-LOI, SUSAN; BROOKLYN, NY; MIDWOOD HS; (SO); Perf Att; Key Club; Tennis; Pre-Med; Cornell U; SUNY

LANDY, TRACI; SEAFORD, NY; SEAFORD HS; (JR); Hnr Roll; MVP; Otst Ac Ach Awd; St of Mnth; WWAHSS; Peer Tut/Med; Key Club; Scouts; SADD; Bnd; Mch Bnd; Bskball (V CL); Lcrsse (V CL); Sccr (V L); Award for Playing - 3 Varsity Sports & Staying on Honor Roll; English; Education; Notre Dame U; Boston U

LANESE, MARISSA; JEFFERSONVILLE, NY; SULLIVAN WEST HS; (JR); F Lan Hn Soc; Hi Hnr Roll; Nat Hon Sy; Otst Ac Ach Awd; Pres Ac Ftns Aw; Comm Volntr; Peer Tut/Med; Chrch Yth Grp; DARE; Photog; Vllyball (VJCL); Church Eucharistic Minister; Major in English; Plan to Get Master's Degree; Sierra College; Saint Rose College

LANG, KATRINA G; LEVITTOWN, NY; DIVISION AVE HS; (FR); St of Mnth; WWAHSS; Dbte Team; Key Club; Bnd; Dnce; Chrldg (VJC); Lcrsse (J); Sccr (J); Adv Cncl (R); Cl Off (P); Stu Cncl (V); CR (R); All-American Scholar Award; High Honor Roll

LANGER, KEVIN; ENDICOTT, NY; UNION ENDICOTT HS; (JR); Hi Hnr Roll; Hnr Roll; Nat Hon Sy; Sci Fairs; WWAHSS; Mus Clb; Bnd; Jzz Bnd; Mch Bnd; SP/M/VS; Science; Math; Siena; SUNY Albany

LANTIN, PETER A; WHITE PLAINS, NY; IOWA PREP SCH; (SO); Hnr Roll; Comm Volntr; Spec Olymp Vol; ArtClub; Chess; Asian Clb; Swmg (V); Rated By National Scholastic Chess Foundation; Physician-Medicine; Lawyer Law; Cornell U; Boston U

LA PIEDRA, NOELLE M; STATEN ISLAND, NY; SUSAN E WAGNER HS; (SO); F Lan Hn Soc; Otst Ac Ach Awd; Comm Volntr; Chrch Yth Grp; Drl Tm; Mch Bnd; Winner of Staten Island Spelling Bee Championship; Journalism; Foreign Languages; St John's U

LAPINSKA, JOLANTA; BROOKLYN, NY; MARTIN LUTHER HS; (SO); Hi Hnr Roll; MVP; St of Mnth; Comm Volntr; Key Club; Chr; Ch Chr; Bskball (JC); Criminal Justice; Business; Columbia U; Duke U

LA PLANTE, MATTHEW D; NORFOLK, NY; NORWOOD-NORFOLK JR/SR HS; (SR); All Am Sch; Hi Hnr Roll; Nat Hon Sy; St of Mnth; USAA; WWAHSS; Comm Volntr; Red Cr Aide; Mth Clb/Tm; Quiz Bowl; Golf (V L); Scr Kpr (V); Sccr (VJ L); Indoor Soccer-Varsity; Computer Engineering; Computer Networking; Clarkson U

LAPOMPE, YVETTE; BROOKLYN, NY; INTERNATIONAL STUDIES; (JR); Hi Hnr Roll; Nat Hon Sy; Salutrn; St of Mnth; Peer Tut/Med; Emplmnt; Scouts; Spanish Clb; Stg Cre; Track (V); Yrbk (E); Peer to Peer Tutoring; Business; Psychology; Princeton U; Duke U

LARA, GISELLE; WOODHAVEN, NY; CHRIST THE KING; (SO); Hi Hnr Roll; Nat Hon Sy; WWAHSS; Peer Tut/Med; Columbia U; Yale U

LARIOS, NICOLE M; MERRICK, NY; SANFORD H CALHOUN HS; (SO); Hnr Roll; WWAHSS; Key Club; Dnce; Bdmtn (J); Bronze Math Fair Winner

LARMOND JR, ORRETT; BRONX, NY; HARRY S TRUMAN HS; (JR); Hnr Roll; MVP; Perf Att; WWAHSS; Comm Volntr; Peer Tut/Med; Chrch Yth Grp; Key Club; Ch Chr; Bskball (L); Cr Ctry; Ftball (J); Track (C); Business Management

LA ROCCA, THOMAS; WEST BABYLON, NY; WEST BABYLON SR HS; (SO); Hi Hnr Roll; Hnr Roll; St of Mnth; WWAHSS; Comm Volntr; Drma Clb; Emplmnt; SADD; Jzz Bnd; Mch Bnd; Pep Bnd; Stg Cre; Golf (V); Lcrsse (J); Vice President of Band; Officer in Mock Trial; Music Education

LARRAZABAL, DULCE; NEW YORK, NY; WASHINGTON IRVING HS; (FR); Ctznshp Aw; Hi Hnr Roll; Hnr Roll; Nat Hon Sy; Nat Ldrshp Svc; Perf Att; Pres Sch; St of Mnth; Comm Volntr; Peer Tut/Med; Chr; Ch Chr; Clr Grd; Orch; Be a Teacher; Be a Pediatrician

LARSEN, STEVEN; STATEN ISLAND, NY; (SR); Peer Tut/Med; Emplmnt; Culinary Arts Class; History Education; English Education; Albany U; Oswego U

LASSALA, GEORGINA; BRONX, NY; COLUMBUS HS; (SR); Hi Hnr Roll; Hnr Roll; WWAHSS; Comm Volntr; Secretary of Aspira; Law Degree; Master's Degree

LATTA, CHELSEA; LOCKPORT, NY; LOCKPORT HS; (SO); Hi Hnr Roll; Otst Ac Ach Awd; WWAHSS; Key Club; Bnd; Dnce; SP/M/VS; National High School Scholars Member

LAU, ELSA; OAKLAND GARDENS, NY; LA GUARDIA HS OF MUSIC & ART; (JR); Hi Hnr Roll; Hnr Roll; Nat Hon Sy; Perf Att; Sci Fairs; Comm Volntr; ArtClub; Scouts; Tchrs Aide; Yrbk (E); Art Honor League; Arista (Academic and Community Achievement); Psychology; Fashion Design; Mount Holyoke College; Amherst

LAU, JOYCE; BROOKLYN, NY; STUYVESANT HS; (SR); Nat Hon Sy; Key Club; Photog; Vice President of AIDS Awareness Club; Coordinator of Interschool Film Forum; Psychology; Photographer; Stony Brook U

LAU, RAYMOND; BROOKLYN, NY; MIDWOOD HS; (SO); Perf Att; St of Mnth; Hab For Humty Volntr; Red Cr Aide; Aqrium Clb; Lib Aide; Chr; Stg Cre; Swmg; CR (P, V); Citation of Honor Award; Sports Medicine; Computer Programming; Boston U; U of Pennsylvania

LAU, YING Y; BROOKLYN, NY; MIDWOOD HS; (JR); WWAHSS; Comm Volntr; Peer Tut/Med; Emplmnt; Key Club; Off Aide; Tchrs Aide; Sign Clb; Board of Committees - Key Club; Asian Society Member; Pharmacist; Nutritionist; Cornell U; New York U

LAUDER, STEPHANIE S; BUFFALO, NY; WEST SENECA WEST SR HS; (JR); Ctznshp Aw; F Lan Hn Soc; Hi Hnr Roll; Hnr Roll; Kwnis Aw; Chrch Yth Grp; DARE; Drma Clb; SADD; French Clb; Bnd; Chr; Ch Chr; Mch Bnd; PhD; Doctor/Surgeon; Clarkson U; Saint John Fisher College

LAURENT, KAREN; EAST ELMHURST, NY; ST JOHN'S PREP HS; (JR); Hi Hnr Roll; MVP; Perf Att; WWAHSS; Comm Volntr; Peer Tut/Med; Drma Clb; Bnd; Chr; SP/M/VS; Tennis (V); Stu Cncl (R); Nursing; Education; College of Mount Saint Vincent; Stony Brook (State U of New York)

LAURENT, PAUL H; ELMONT, NY; SEWANHAKA HS; (SR); Ctznshp Aw; Perf Att; Comm Volntr; Chrch Yth Grp; Tchrs Aide; Ch Chr; Nursing; Youth Pastor; Nassau Community College; Hofstra U

LAURIA, LISA; STATEN ISLAND, NY; PORT RICHMOND HS; (SO); Hnr Roll; Sci Fairs; DARE; Photog; Scouts; Tchrs Aide; Stg Cre

LAUTERSTEIN, DANA E; ROCKVILLE CENTRE, NY; (SO); Hi Hnr Roll; Hnr Roll; Pres Ac Ftns Aw; Hosp Aide; French Clb; Chr; BBYO; Volunteer At South Nassau Hospital; Psychology; English; Boston U; SUNY Binghamton

LAWLER, ALICIA; DEXTER, NY; GENERAL BROWN HS; (JR); 4H Awd; Ctznshp Aw; Hnr Roll; Nat Hon Sy; Perf Att; Comm Volntr; 4-H; DARE; Drma Clb; Spanish Clb; Chr; SP/M/VS; Vllyball (VJCL); Spanish Club Treasurer; Psychology; Photography; Niagara U; SUNY Oswego

LAWRENCE, LAURA; WINDHAM, NY; WINDHAM ASHLAND JEWETT CTRL SCH; (FR); Ctznshp Aw; Hi Hnr Roll; Nat Hon Sy; Otst Ac Ach Awd; Peer Tut/Med; DARE; Emplmnt; Tchrs Aide; Sccr (V); After School Reading Program; Elementary Education; Special Education

LAWRENCE, SACHET; BRONX, NY; ASTOR COLLEGIATE AC; (SO); Hi Hnr Roll; Hnr Roll; Otst Ac Ach Awd; Perf Att; Salutrn; St of Mnth; Comm Volntr; Peer Tut/Med; Chrch Yth Grp; Off Aide; P to P St Amb Prg; Ch Chr; Vllyball (V); Sch Ppr (E); English; American Literature; Columbia U; Hunter College

LAWSON, JOEL; WATERTOWN, NY; WATERTOWN HS; (FR); Hnr Roll; St of Mnth; WWAHSS; Comm Volntr; Key Club; Bnd; Bskball (J); Lawyer/Attorney; Saint John's U

LAWTON, BENJAMIN M; OGDENSBURG, NY; LISBON CTRL SCH; (SO); Hi Hnr Roll; Nat Hon Sy; Sccr (V); Clarkson U

LAWTON, RAMONA; ROCHESTER, NY; JOSEPH C. WILSON MAGNET HS; (SO); Hi Hnr Roll; Hnr Roll; Salutrn; Sccr (V); Engineering; U of Rochester; Rochester Institute of Technology

LAWTON, REGINA; ST ALBANS, NY; AUGUST MARTIN HS; (JR); Emplmnt; Communications / Media; Criminal Lawyer

LEACH, KEVIN; MERRICK, NY; SANFORD H CALHOUN HS; (JR); Bnd; Mch Bnd; Lcrsse (V); U of Albany

LEAHEY, MEGAN; BALDWINSVILLE, NY; BAKER HS; (SO); Hi Hnr Roll; Pres Ac Ftns Aw; WWAHSS; Peer Tut/Med; Chr; Cr Ctry (V); Track (V); Kids Who Care - Award; Jenna's Mentor's Program; Psychology; Education; Cornell U

LEAHY, SHAWN M; SAUGERTIES, NY; (FR); Hi Hnr Roll; Otst Ac Ach Awd; Pres Ac Ftns Aw; Sci Fairs; Comm Volntr; Peer Tut/Med; DARE; Key Club; French Clb; Bnd; Lcrsse (V); Sccr (V); Cl Off (T)

LECLERE, TALIA; LARCHMONT, NY; MAMARONECK HS; (JR); Comm Volntr; Hab For Humty Volntr; Chrch Yth Grp; JSA; Mod UN; Svce Clb; French Clb; Chr; Dnce; SP/M/VS; Stg Cre; Bskball (J); PP Ftbl (V); International Relations; International Law; Georgetown U; Tufts U

LE COGUIC, MARION E; BROOKLYN, NY; FIORELLO H LA GUARDIA HS; (SO); F Lan Hn Soc; Perf Att; Comm Volntr; Peer Tut/Med; Drma Clb; Tchrs Aide; Vsity Clb; Spanish Clb; Ch Chr; Dnce; SP/M/VS; Stg Cre; Bskball (V); Sport: Crew; Forensic Science; Drama; New York U-Tisch; Yale

LEDESMA, ARTURO M; YONKERS, NY; CHARLES E GORTON HS; (SR); F Lan Hn Soc; Hnr Roll; St of Mnth; Comm Volntr; Hab For Humty Volntr; Cmptr Clb; Emplmnt; Vsity Clb; Spanish Clb; Dnce; Bsball (V C); 2004-2005 Gear Up Program; Baseball - All League Award; Criminal Justice; Manhattan College; John Jay College

LEE, ALEX; NEW YORK, NY; NEW YORK MILITARY SCH; (JR); Hi Hnr Roll; Hnr Roll; Perf Att; Sci Fairs; St of Mnth; Comm Volntr; ArtClub; ROTC; Tchrs Aide; Tennis (V); Stu Cncl (V); P.H.D; M.B.A; New York U; Binghamton U

LEE, CAROLINE M; NEW HYDE PARK, NY; HERRICKS HS; (MS); Hnr Roll; Comm Volntr; Orch; Tennis (J); Vllyball (J); National Piano Playing Auditions (Intermediate 2004); Business; Architecture; Columbia U; Princeton U

LEE, CHRIS; BROOKLYN, NY; BRONX HS OF SCIENCE; (SO); Comm Volntr; Peer Tut/Med; Key Club; Photog; Handball Team - Varsity; Attended Architecture/Photography Class; Architecture; Interior Designer; Cornell U; New York U

LEE, CINDY; BROOKLYN, NY; STUYVESANT HS; (SO); Nat Hon Sy; WWAHSS; Comm Volntr; Peer Tut/Med; Key Club; Lib Aide; Mth Clb/Tm; Mus Clb; Off Aide; Bnd; SP/M/VS; Lit Mag (R, P); Sch Ppr (R); Toshiba NSTA Exploravision Awards Participant; Invitation to National Student Leadership Confer; Finance; Accounting; U of Pennsylvania-The Wharton School; New York U-Stern School of Business

LEE, ELIZABETH; OAKLAND GARDENS, NY; BENJAMIN CARDORO HS; (SO); Hnr Roll; Perf Att; Sci/Math Olympn; Key Club

LEE, GINA; LITTLE NECK, NY; MIDWOOD HS; (SO); Otst Ac Ach Awd; Perf Att; Sci Fairs; Valdctrian; Comm Volntr; Peer Tut/Med; Chrch Yth Grp; FCA; Key Club; Ch Chr; Stg Cre; ARISTA / Archon; School Leadership Award; Pre-Med; Architecture; Harvard U; New York U

LEE, JENNIFER J; WHITESTONE, NY; FRANCIS LEWIS HS; (JR); Comm Volntr; Mch Bnd; Pharmacy; Buffalo U

LEE, JESSICA; BROOKLYN, NY; JOHN DEWEY HS; (JR); Otst Ac Ach Awd; Perf Att; Sci Fairs; Comm Volntr; Hosp Aide; Peer Tut/Med; DARE; Key Club; Kwanza Clb; Chr; SP/M/VS; Dvng (V); Swmg (J); Vllyball (V); Nursing; Medical Technology

LEE, JIN C; FLUSHING, NY; FRANCIS LEWIS HS; (JR); Hi Hnr Roll; Hnr Roll; Perf Att; Comm Volntr; Chrch Yth Grp; Emplmnt; Mth Clb/Tm; Off Aide; ROTC; Ch Chr; Bskball (V); Currently Serving Church As the Pianist; Participated in American Mathematics Contest 10 Year (2004); Professional Basketball Player; Business (MBA); Harvard U; Columbia U

LEE, JOANE; REGO PARK, NY; BRONX HS OF SCIENCE; (FR); Ctznshp Aw; Hnr Roll; Perf Att; St of Mnth; Emplmnt; Key Club; Lib Aide; Tchrs Aide; Fncg (J)

LEE, LAURA; BROOKLYN, NY; BRONX HS OF SCIENCE; (JR); Perf Att; WWAHSS; Comm Volntr; Key Club; Off Aide; Photog; Lit Mag; Pharmacy; St. John's U; Rutgers- State U of New Jersey

LEE, LOUISE; BAYSIDE, NY; BENJAMIN CARDOZO HS; (JR); F Lan Hn Soc; Hnr Roll; Nat Hon Sy; Perf Att; Sci Fairs; WWAHSS; Comm Volntr; Peer Tut/Med; ArtClub; Emplmnt; Key Club; Svce Clb; Tchrs Aide; German Clb; National Honor Society - Arista; Pharmacy / Health Field; St John's U

LEE, MAXINE; NEW HYDE PARK, NY; HERRICKS SR HS; (JR); Hnr Roll; St of Mnth; WWAHSS; Hosp Aide; Peer Tut/Med; Chrch Yth Grp; Key Club; Mus Clb; P to P St Amb Prg; Spanish Clb; Orch; Cr Ctry (V); Yrbk (E); Student Athletic Trainer; Pharmacist; Physical Therapist; Saint John's U; U of Buffalo

LEE, MICHELLE; BROOKLYN, NY; MIDWOOD HS; (JR); Comm Volntr; Emplmnt; Key Club; Lib Aide; Off Aide; Svce Clb; Tchrs Aide; Stg Cre; Brooklyn Public Library Computer Coach Award; Prospect Park Zoo Discovery Guide

LEE, NANCY; ASTORIA, NY; LONG ISLAND CITY HS; (SR); Hnr Roll; Nat Hon Sy; Perf Att; WWAHSS; Yth Ldrshp Prog; Comm Volntr; Emplmnt; Lib Aide; Mth Clb/Tm; Mod UN; Tchrs Aide; Spanish Clb; Chr; Drl Tm; Cr Ctry (V); Vllyball (J); Arista National Honor Society Secretary; Childhood Education; Nursing; Hunter College; St John's U

LEE, SANDY; CORINTH, NY; CORINTH CTRL SCH; (SO); Hi Hnr Roll; Nat Hon Sy; Otst Ac Ach Awd; Perf Att; St of Mnth; DARE; FTA; P to P St Amb Prg; Quiz Bowl; Scouts; Chr; Dnce; Fld Hky (J); Cl Off (S); Stu Cncl (R); CR (S); Student Ambassador to Brazil in 2004; Pre-Med; Doctorate Degree; Cornell U; Siena College

Le Coguic, Marion E
Fiorello H La Guardia HS
Brooklyn, NY

Lauterstein, Dana E
Rockville Centre, NY

Laurent, Paul H
Sewanhaka HS
Elmont, NY

Lantin, Peter A
Iowa Prep Sch
White Plains, NY

Larrazabal, Dulce
Washington Irving HS
New York, NY

Lawton, Ramona
Joseph C. Wilson Magnet HS
Rochester, NY

Ledesma, Arturo M
Charles E Gorton HS
Yonkers, NY

LEE, SARA; ASTORIA, NY; STUYVESANT HS; (JR); Peer Tut/Med; Key Club; Svce Clb; Sch Ppr (R); 2 Magna Cum Laude Certificates for Newspaper Business Staff; Selected to Participate in the Merrill Lynch Business Program; Law/Lawyer; Business; Columbia U; Harvard U

LEE, THOMAS; HUNTINGTON, NY; HUNTINGTON HS; (SO); F Lan Hn Soc; Hi Hnr Roll; Pres Ac Ftns Aw; Pres Sch; Sci Fairs; Yth Ldrshp Prog; Mus Clb; Prom Com; Quiz Bowl; Vsity Clb; Bnd; Mch Bnd; SP/M/VS; Golf (V L); Tennis (V L); Track (V); Cl Off (R); Sch Ppr (R); Business

LEE, WILLA; BROOKLYN, NY; STUYVESANT HS; (JR); ArtClub; Key Club; I Volunteer in P.S. 89.; Veterinary Medicine; Architecture; U of Pennsylvania; Cornell

LEE, WINNIE; BROOKLYN, NY; STUYVESANT HS; (JR); All Am Sch; MVP; Nat Hon Sy; Perf Att; USAA; WWAHSS; Comm Volntr; Peer Tut/Med; Key Club; Mth Clb/Tm; Off Aide; Tech Clb; Chinese Clb; Bnd; Sch Ppr (E); Business: Marketing and Management; Health Management; U of Pennsylvania: Wharton Undergraduates; Johns Hopkins U

LEEBER, STEPHEN J; TOMKINS COVE, NY; NORTH ROCKLAND HS; (SO); Hnr Roll; Nat Hon Sy; Comm Volntr; Key Club; Quiz Bowl; Lcrsse (J); Wrstlg (V); History, Gov't.; Engineering; Dartmouth College; Bowdoin College

LEFEVER, SARA; WESTFIELD, NY; WESTFIELD AC AND CTRL SCH; (SR); Hi Hnr Roll; USAA; WWAHSS; Speech and Language Disabilities; State U of New York At Fredonia

LE GAULT, RACHEL L; AMHERST, NY; SWEET HOME HS; (SR); Hnr Roll; Nat Hon Sy; Nat Mrt Sch Recip; Nat Sci Aw; Pres Ac Ftns Aw; Comm Volntr; Drma Clb; Emplmnt; Prom Com; Chr; Dnce; SP/M/VS; Swg Chr; Adv Cncl (R); Sch Ppr (R); Yrbk (E, P); National Honor Society; Criminology/ Law; Biology; U of Buffalo

LEGROS, ARMANDY; POMONA, NY; NORTH ROCKLAND HS; (SO); Hnr Roll; Kwnis Aw; Perf Att; Sci Fairs; St of Mnth; WWAHSS; Yth Ldrshp Prog; Comm Volntr; Chrch Yth Grp; DARE; Drma Clb; Emplmnt; Jr Ach; Key Club; Off Aide; Sci Clb; Chr; Ch Chr; Orch; SP/M/VS; Bskball (J); Vllyball (V); Pediatrician; Doctor; Princeton U; Yale U

LEGUN, PHILIP M; STATEN ISLAND, NY; TOTTENVILLE HS; (JR); Hi Hnr Roll; Nat Hon Sy; Sci Fairs; Sci/Math Olympn; Comm Volntr; Peer Tut/ Med; Jr Ach; Key Club; Lib Aide; Mth Clb/Tm; Tchrs Aide; Stg Cre; Math Team; Library Aide; Mechanical Engineering; Chemical Engineering; Brooklyn Polytechnic U; Cooper Union

LEHMANN, ELIZABETH; PLEASANT VALLEY, NY; ARLINGTON HS; (JR); Duke TS; Hi Hnr Roll; Hnr Roll; Comm Volntr; Chrch Yth Grp; Scouts; Svce Clb; Bnd; Mch Bnd; Pep Bnd; Swimming in Summer League

LEHNE, BRET; BROOKLYN, NY; LEGACY HS; (JR); Pres Ac Ftns Aw; Sci Fairs; ArtClub; Chess; Drma Clb; Emplmnt; Mus Clb; Prom Com; Wdwrkg Clb; SP/M/VS; Stg Cre; Sccr (V); Sftball (V); Yrbk (E); Student Speaker At Ground Breaking Ceremony; Have Completed 2 (Two) Summer College Courses; Film Making (General Arts); Film Industry (Technical); U of Southern California; Brooklyn College

LEIPFERT, ROBERT; WHITEHALL, NY; WHITEHALL JR SR HS; (SO); Hnr Roll; Drma Clb; Mus Clb; Schol Bwl; Chr; SP/M/VS; Tennis (V L); Track (V L); All-Cty Chorus 2003, 2004; All-New England Chorus 2004; Music Career; Plymouth State

LEISTMAN, JOSEPH M; FLUSHING, NY; ROBERT F KENNEDY; (SO); Hnr Roll; Nat Hon Sy; Nat Mrt LOC; Comm Volntr; Bowling Team; Business and Finance; Lawyer; Columbia U; Baruch College

LEMOINE, CHRISTOPHER; QUEENS VILLAGE, NY; BAYSIDE HS; (SO); Chrch Yth Grp; Emplmnt; Mus Clb; Acpl Chr; Chr; Ch Chr; Bskball (V); Chorus Section Leader; Mathematics; Computer Engineering; Penn State U; Northeastern U

LEMONTE, DEBBIE-JEAN; BROOKLYN, NY; FRANKLIN K LANE HS; (SR); Hnr Roll; Nat Hon Sy; Otst Ac Ach Awd; Perf Att; WWAHSS; Yth Ldrshp Prog; Comm Volntr; Chrch Yth Grp; Drma Clb; Off Aide; Prom Com; SADD; Vsity Clb; Ch Chr; Dnce; SP/M/VS; Vllyball (VJC); Stu Cncl (R); Sch Ppr (R); Biology; Pre-Med; Brooklyn College-CUNY

LEONARD, CLAIRE; SOUTHOLD, NY; SOUTHOLD HS; (SR); Hi Hnr Roll; Nat Hon Sy; WWAHSS; Comm Volntr; Peer Tut/Med; Spec Olymp Vol; DARE; Emplmnt; Photog; Prom Com; Chr; Hsbk Rdg (V); Yrbk (P); FIRST Robotics Team Treasurer; Communications; Elon U; U of Rochester

LEUNG, CAROLINE; FOREST HILLS, NY; FRANCIS LEWIS HS; (JR); Hnr Roll; Nat Hon Sy; Nat Ldrshp Svc; Comm Volntr; Key Club; Mth Clb/Tm; Photog; Vsity Clb; Bnd; Sftball (J); Psychology; Economics; Columbia U; Brigham Young U

LEUNG, CHRISTINE Y Y; FLUSHING, NY; FRANCIS LEWIS HS; (JR); Ctznshp Aw; Hnr Roll; Nat Hon Sy; Comm Volntr; Peer Tut/Med; Lib Aide; Chinese Clb; Business; Design; New York U; Columbia U

LEUNG, CINDI; BROOKLYN, NY; BROOKLYN TECH HS; (JR); Hnr Roll; Yth Ldrshp Prog; Comm Volntr; Spec Olymp Vol; Chrch Yth Grp; Emplmnt; Ntl Beta Clb; Bnd; Architecture; Interior Design; Syracuse U; Penn State-U. Park

LEVERENZ, TESS; NEW YORK, NY; FIORELLO H LA GUARDIA HS; (SO); Hi Hnr Roll; Hnr Roll; Tmpl Yth Grp; Chr; Sccr; Teaching; Cantorial Soloist; Columbia U; Barnard College

LEVERICH, MEREDITH G; SAUGERTIES, NY; SAUGERTIES HS; (SO); Hi Hnr Roll; Otst Ac Ach Awd; St of Mnth; Peer Tut/Med; Chrch Yth Grp; DARE; HO'Br Yth Ldrshp; Key Club; Prom Com; Bnd; Dnce; Bskball; Scr Kpr; Skiing; Cl Off (V, S); Sch Ppr (E, R); Volunteered At a Soup Kitchen in Maine; Editor of the Newspaper As A Sophomore; Journalism; English; Columbia U

LEVIN, DANIEL; BROOKLYN, NY; MIDWOOD HS; (SO); St of Mnth; Peer Tut/Med; Vsity Clb; Bskball (J); Lcrsse (J); Swmg (V); Pharmacy; Long Island U

LEVITIN, ALEXANDER; BROOKLYN, NY; JAMES MADISON HS; (SR); Science Honor Society; Arista Honor Society; Pre Medicine; Medical Degree; Penn State; Rutgers

LEVY, SIOBHAN; HIGHLAND, NY; NORTH INT HS; (FR); Hnr Roll; Perf Att; St of Mnth; ArtClub; Chrch Yth Grp; DARE; Drma Clb; French Clb; Ch Chr; Dnce; SP/M/VS; Stg Cre; Piano 4 Years; Pop Warner Cheerleading 1 Yr.; Choreographer; Doctor-Neurologist; Spelman College; Yale U

LEWIN, SHENEA; BROOKLYN, NY; JAMES MADISON HS; (JR); Hnr Roll; Sci Fairs; Peer Tut/Med; ArtClub; Off Aide; Tchrs Aide; Member of the National Academy of Finance; College Major-International Economics; Professional Degree-Masters; Syracuse U; U At Buffalo

LEWIS, KYANNA A; BROOKLYN, NY; BROOKLYN TECH HS; (FR); Ctznshp Aw; Hnr Roll; Otst Ac Ach Awd; Perf Att; Sci Fairs; St of Mnth; Peer Tut/Med; ArtClub; Biology Clb; Chrch Yth Grp; Mus Clb; Photog; Tchrs Aide; SP/M/VS; Track; Triple C Award; Chancellor's Roll of Honor; Culinary Arts; Bio Med; Culinary Institute of America; New York Institute

LEWIS, MARTIN; MECHANICVILLE, NY; (JR); Bakery Chef

LEWIS, ROBIN J; UNIONDALE, NY; UNIONDALE HS; (JR); Hi Hnr Roll; Hnr Roll; Peer Tut/Med; 4-H; AL Aux Boys; Tennis (V); Yrbk (P); Peer Mediator; Psychiatry; Psychology; U of Miami (Florida); Nova South Eastern U Florida

LEWIS, SARAH; MERRICK, NY; CALHOUN HS; (FR); Hnr Roll; Otst Ac Ach Awd; WWAHSS; Yth Ldrshp Prog; Comm Volntr; Peer Tut/Med; Key Club; SADD; Tmpl Yth Grp; Acpl Chr; Chr; Dnce; Chrldg (J); Track (V); Lit Mag (R); Sch Ppr (R); Math Award; Newspaper Award; Medicine; Law; University of Pennsylvania; Princeton U

LEZAMA, STEPHANIE; FLORAL PARK, NY; FLORAL PARK MEMORIAL HS; (FR); Hi Hnr Roll; Kwnis Aw; Nat Hon Sy; Perf Att; Sci Fairs; WWAHSS; Comm Volntr; Peer Tut/Med; FBLA; Key Club; A Top Scorer in National Spanish Examination; Secretary of National Junior Honor Society; Advertising-Visual Arts; Journalism and Media Studies; New York U; Columbia U

LI, ADORA; TAPPAN, NY; TAPPAN ZEE HS; (JR); F Lan Hn Soc; Hi Hnr Roll; Nat Hon Sy; Otst Ac Ach Awd; Perf Att; Comm Volntr; Peer Tut/Med; MuAlphaTh; Svce Clb; Piano Awards; Spanish Honor Society; Pharmacy; Business; Binghamton; Cornell

LI, ALAN; NEW YORK, NY; INST FOR SECONDARY EDUC; (SO); Hi Hnr Roll; Hnr Roll; MVP; Nat Ldrshp Svc; Otst Ac Ach Awd; Perf Att; Sci Fairs; St of Mnth; St Optmst of Yr; Yth Ldrshp Prog; Amnsty Intl; Comm Volntr; Peer Tut/Med; ArtClub; BPA; Chess; Lib Aide; Mus Clb; Off Aide; Outdrs Clb; Photog; Chr; Dnce; SP/M/VS; Stg Cre; Bdmtn (V); Bsball (V); Cyclg (V); Fncg (J); Fld Hky (J); Golf (V); Gmnstcs (V); Mar Art (V); Adv Cncl (P); Cl Off (P); Stu Cncl (S); CR (P); Lit Mag (E); Sch Ppr (E); Yrbk (E); Business Manager; Accountant; U of Pennsylvania (Wharton); U of Michigan-Ann Arbor

LI, GRACE; BROOKLYN, NY; MIDWOOD HS; (MS); Sci Fairs; Bnd; Yrbk (P); Citation Honor

LI, HOLMAN; OAKLAND GARDENS, NY; FIORELLO H LA GUARDIA HS; (SO); Comm Volntr; DARE; Scouts; SP/M/VS; Vllyball (V); Architecture; Visual and Performing Arts; Cooper Union; Cornell U

LI, HUI W; BROOKLYN, NY; FORT HAMILTON HS; (JR); Nat Hon Sy; Asian Clb; Chr; Tennis (V); Bowling Team-Varsity; Virtual Enterprise; Pharmacist; Dermatology; New York U; St. John's U

LI, IRENE; BROOKLYN, NY; BROOKLYN TECH HS; (SR); Hnr Roll; Key Club; Chr; Dnce; SP/M/VS; Merit Award for Biology; Merit Award for Health Education; Certified Public Accounting; SUNY Binghamton

LI, LIBO; WEST HEMPSTEAD, NY; WEST HEMPSTEAD HS; (FR); Hi Hnr Roll; MVP; Nat Hon Sy; Perf Att; Pres Ac Ftns Aw; Sci Fairs; St of Mnth; Comm Volntr; Spec Olymp Vol; Key Club; Mth Clb/Tm; Quiz Bowl; French Clb; Orch; Cr Ctry (V); Lcrsse (J); Track (V); Wrstlg (V); Violin Level 5 in NYSSMA Tarts; Architecture; Graphic Design; Massachusetts Institute of Technology; Union for the Advancement of Science and Art

LI, LILY; FRESH MEADOWS, NY; FRANCIS LEWIS HS; (JR); Hnr Roll; Perf Att; St of Mnth; Comm Volntr; ArtClub; ROTC; Clr Grd; SP/M/VS; Gmnstcs (L); Mar Art (L); Swmg (L); Nutritionist; Nurse; SUNY Stony Brook; New York U

LI, PETER; ELMHURST, NY; NEWTOWN HS; (SO); Hnr Roll; Nat Hon Sy; Perf Att; DARE; Emplmnt; Medical

LI, SANDY YIN; FRESH MEADOWS, NY; FRANCIS LEWIS HS; (JR); Nat Hon Sy; Perf Att; Comm Volntr; Spec Olymp Vol; ROTC; Clr Grd; Dnce; Horticulture Club-President; Business; Law; Brown U; Penn State U Park

LI, XIAO Y; JACKSON HTS, NY; FRANCIS LEWIS HS; (SO); Hi Hnr Roll; Nat Hon Sy; Perf Att; Sci Fairs; Comm Volntr; Chinese Clb; PhD Programs; Psychology Degrees; Sophie Davis School; Columbia U

LI, XINGXING; BRONX, NY; MARBLE HILL HS FOR INTERNATIONAL STUDIES; (SO); Hnr Roll; Comm Volntr; Chess; Massachusetts Institute of Technology; Harvard U

LI, XIYI; OAKLAND GARDENS, NY; THE MARY LOUIS AC; (JR); 4H Awd; All Am Sch; DAR; Hi Hnr Roll; Hnr Roll; Nat Hon Sy; Otst Ac Ach Awd; St Schl; WWAHSS; Yth Ldrshp Prog; Comm Volntr; Peer Tut/Med; Red Cr Aide; ArtClub; Cmptr Clb; Jr Ach; Mth Clb/Tm; Mus Clb; NYLC; Sci Clb; Svce Clb; Chr; Jzz Bnd; Orch; SP/M/VS; Golf (L); Mar Art (L); Swmg (L); Master Degree in Architecture; Study Theater Design; New York U; Cornell U

LIA, JULIETTE; WESTTOWN, NY; MINISINK VALLEY HS; (FR); Chr; Swmg (V); Journalism

LIAN, JENNIFER; BROOKLYN, NY; MIDWOOD HS; (JR); Hnr Roll; Perf Att; Comm Volntr; Red Cr Aide; Key Club; SP/M/VS; Optometry; Speech Therapy

LIANG, EDWIN; NEW YORK, NY; BRONX HS OF SCIENCE; (SO); Comm Volntr; Chess; Cr Ctry (V); Track (V); Mathematics; Computer Science; Princeton U; U of California Berkeley

LIANG, RAYMOND; BROOKLYN, NY; JAMES MADISON; Orch

LIBERATORE, MELISSA L; TONAWANDA, NY; (SO); Hnr Roll; Otst Ac Ach Awd; Amnsty Intl; Emplmnt; Scouts; Stu Cncl (S); Political Science; Molecular Genetics; Boston U; Dartmouth College

LIBERTI, MARIA C; LEVITTOWN, NY; DIVISION AVE HS; (FR); F Lan Hn Soc; Hi Hnr Roll; Kwnis Aw; Nat Hon Sy; Otst Ac Ach Awd; Perf Att; Sci Fairs; Sci/Math Olympn; St of Mnth; Comm Volntr; Peer Tut/Med; Key Club; Mth Clb/Tm; Sci Clb; Scouts; Orch; Bdmtn (V); Tennis; CR (R); Biochemist; Biology Teacher; Cornell U; Stony Brook U

LIBOUS, STEPHANIE; ENDWELL, NY; UNION-ENDICOTT HS; (FR); Hi Hnr Roll; St Schl; WWAHSS; Comm Volntr; Hab For Humty Volntr; Hosp Aide; Biology Clb; Chrch Yth Grp; Key Club; Sci Clb; Vsity Clb; Italian Clb; Acpl Chr; SP/M/VS; Tennis (V L); Track (V L); Vsy Clb (V L); Stu Cncl (R); CR (R); NYS Scholar-Athlete Award; Political Science; Pre-Law & Law School; Union College, Schenectady, NY

LICORI, MEGAN E; AMITYVILLE, NY; ST ANTHONY'S HS; (JR); Hi Hnr Roll; WWAHSS; Cr Ctry (V); Swmg (V); Track (V C)

LIEBERMAN, LYNNE; BROOKLYN, NY; JAMES MADISON HS; (SO); Hnr Roll; Sch Ppr (E); Psychiatry; Psychology; New York U; Albany State U

LIEBERMAN, PAIGE R; MERRICK, NY; JOHN F KENNEDY HS; (FR); Hi Hnr Roll; Hnr Roll; Nat Hon Sy; Sci/Math Olympn; Comm Volntr; Dbte Team; FBLA; Mth Clb/Tm; Mus Clb; Bnd; Dnce; Jzz Bnd; Pep Bnd; National and Local French Contests-Honorable Mention; NYSSA-Oboe & Piano-5 years; Communications/Music; Languages; U of Pennsylvania; Princeton

LIEW, KENNETH; RIDGEWOOD, NY; THE BRONX HS OF SCIENCE; (JR); WWAHSS; Yth Ldrshp Prog; Comm Volntr; Peer Tut/Med; DARE; Key Club; Mth Clb/Tm; Tchrs Aide; Lit Mag (R, P); American Classical League Latin Exam Gold Medalist; 1st Place Regional Winner of Plastics Essay Contest; Architectural Engineering; Massachusetts Institute of Technology; Princeton U

LILES, JORDAN; PAINTED POST, NY; NOTRE DAME HS; (JR); Hi Hnr Roll; Hnr Roll; Nat Hon Sy; Perf Att; Yth Ldrshp Prog; Comm Volntr; Red Cr Aide; AL Aux Boys; Chrch Yth Grp; Drma Clb; Emplmnt; FCA; NYLC; Prom Com; Chr; SP/M/VS; Bskball (J); Golf (V L); Sccr (VJCL); Cl Off (P); Bowling Club; Finance; Business Management; James Madison U; Northeastern U

Libous, Stephanie
Union-Endicott HS
Endwell, NY

Li, Xiyi
The Mary Louis AC
Oakland Gardens, NY

Lewis, Kyanna A
Brooklyn Tech HS
Brooklyn, NY

Lewin, Shenea
James Madison HS
Brooklyn, NY

National
Honor Roll
Spring 2005

Lee, Thomas
Huntington HS
Huntington, NY

Li, Sandy Yin
Francis Lewis HS
Fresh Meadows, NY

Liang, Edwin
Bronx HS Of Science
New York, NY

Liles, Jordan
Notre Dame HS
Painted Post, NY

LIM, JENNIFER; NEW YORK, NY; THE BREARLEY SCH; (FR); Comm Volntr; Dbte Team; Mth Clb/Tm; Mod UN; Vsity Clb; Latin Clb; Orch; Tennis (V); Vllyball (J); CR (P); Sch Ppr (R); School Dance Team; Numerous Awards for Film Making; Harvard U; Yale U

LIM, KATIE; BROOKLYN, NY; STUYVESANT HS; (SO); Hnr Roll; Otst Ac Ach Awd; USAA; WWAHSS; Comm Volntr; ArtClub; Emplmnt; Key Club; Off Aide; Dnce; Stg Cre; Orthodontistry; Pharmaceuticals; New York U; Buffalo U

LIM, NELSON; FLUSHING, NY; BRONX HS OF SCIENCE; (FR); Chess; DARE; Mth Clb/Tm; Scouts; Tchrs Aide; Track (J); Astronomy; Zoology; Columbia U; Harvard U

LIMA, COLLEEN S; STATEN ISLAND, NY; MOORE CATHOLIC HS; (JR); Hnr Roll; Nat Hon Sy; Pres Sch; WWAHSS; Comm Volntr; Peer Tut/Med; Red Cr Aide; AL Aux Girls; Drma Clb; Emplmnt; Mth Clb/Tm; Off Aide; Prom Com; Clb; Dnce; SP/M/VS; Stg Cre; Sccr (V); Stu Cncl (R); CR (R); Yrbk (E); Empire Girls State Attorney General; International Law and Diplomacy; Georgetown U

LIMA, NAOMI; SAUGERTIES, NY; SAUGERTIES HS; (SO); Hnr Roll; WWAHSS; Key Club; Spanish Clb; Chr; Track (J); Law; Biology; Ulster College; Marymount Manhattan

LIMERICK, CHRIS; MIDDLETOWN, NY; MIDDLETOWN HS; (JR); Hnr Roll; Perf Att; Comm Volntr; Bskball (V); Sccr (V); Culinary Arts & Baking & Pastry; Restaurant Management; Johnson & Wales

LIN, FAY; FLUSHING, NY; BAYSIDE HS; (SO); Perf Att; WWAHSS; Chess; Teacher; Pharmacist; Columbia U; New York U

LIN, JING; BUFFALO, NY; WEST SENECA EAST SR HS; (JR); Hi Hnr Roll; Hnr Roll; St of Mnth; ArtClub; Emplmnt; Key Club; Bdmtn; Skiing; Track; International Club; Key Club; Nursing; International Business; Abington Memorial Hospital School of Nursing; Augustana College in Korea

LIN, LING; CORONA, NY; MANHATTAN CTR FOR SCI & MATH; (FR); Hi Hnr Roll; Nat Hon Sy; Perf Att; Gmnstcs; Biology; Math

LIN, MAI; BROOKLYN, NY; FT HAMILTON HS; (JR); Hnr Roll; Otst Ac Ach Awd; Perf Att; Nursing; Medical Coding; Hunter College; The City College

LIN, MICHAEL; LITTLE NECK, NY; BRONX HS OF SCIENCE; (JR); Duke TS; Hnr Roll; Sci Fairs; Sci/Math Olympn; WWAHSS; Yth Ldrshp Prog; Comm Volntr; Red Cr Aide; Chrch Yth Grp; Mth Clb/Tm; Off Aide; Tchrs Aide; Chr; Orch; Tennis (V); Sch Ppr (E); Metropolitan Math Fair; Intel Lab Search; Pre-Med; Marine Science; Columbia U; Johns Hopkins U

LIN, MING; NEW YORK, NY; LA GUARDIA HS; (SO); Amnsty Intl; Hab For Humty Volntr; ArtClub; Dnce; Lit Mag (E); Co -Founder of Arts Magazine; Fine Arts; Language Major

LIN, XIN; NEW YORK, NY; HEALTH PROF & HUMAN SERV HS; (JR); Hnr Roll; Pharmacy; Surgical; Columbia U; New York U

LINDENAU, CHRISTOPHER; ROCHESTER, NY; GREECE ARCADIA HS; (SR); Hi Hnr Roll; Nat Hon Sy; Otst Ac Ach Awd; Pres Sch; WWAHSS; Scouts; Ftball (V); Track (V); Wt Lftg (V); Eagle Scout; Computer Science; Rochester Institute of Technology

LINDORE, TAMEKA; BROOKLYN, NY; HARRY VAN ARSDALE HS; (SO); Hnr Roll; Perf Att; Emplmnt; Mus Clb; Dnce; Tennis (V); Computer Technology; Business Management; Florida State U; New York U

LINEHAN, RACHEL C; S GLENS FALLS, NY; SOUTH GLENS FALLS SR HS; (SO); Hi Hnr Roll; Hnr Roll; HO'Br Yth Ldrshp; Key Club; Bskball (J); Sccr (J); Sftball (J); HOBY Ambassador; Teaching; Science; Notre Dame; College of St Rose

LING, TERRESA; OZONE PARK, NY; STUYVESANT HS; (SR); Kwnis Aw; Salutrn; WWAHSS; Comm Volntr; ArtClub; Key Club; Lib Aide; Photog; Chr; Yrbk (E); Big Sib; President of SM@CK IT! Ping Pong Club; Math; Business/Accounting

LINSENBIGLER, ALANA J; ALDEN, NY; ALDEN HS; (SO); Hi Hnr Roll; St of Mnth; WWAHSS; Yth Ldrshp Prog; Comm Volntr; ArtClub; Key Club; Scouts; Spanish Clb; Chr; SP/M/VS; Track (V); Vllyball (JC); Fashion Merchandising; Journalism; Fashion Institute of Technology; SUNY Oneonta

LIPITZ, BRADLEY A; WOODMERE, NY; LAWRENCE HS; (SR); Hi Hnr Roll; Nat Hon Sy; Sci Fairs; Sci/Math Olympn; Comm Volntr; Peer Tut/Med; Spec Olymp Vol; DECA; Emplmnt; Key Club; Mth Clb/Tm; SADD; Vsity Clb; Orch; Cr Ctry (V); Tennis (V); Sch Ppr (R); Yrbk (R); Accounting; Binghamton U (SUNY)

LIPSKY, KATIE; BAYPORT, NY; BAYPORT BLUE POINT HS; (SO); St of Mnth; Hosp Aide; Chr; Chrldg (J); Cr Ctry; Track; Childhood Education

LIQUORI, ELISE; NEDROW, NY; ONONDAGA JR/SR HS; (FR); Hi Hnr Roll; Nat Hon Sy; Spanish Clb; Chr; Bskball (J); Sccr (J); Sftball (J); Cl Off (V); Stu Cncl; Yorker Club; Psychiatrics; Health Medicine

LITTLE, ASIA U; BRONX, NY; HEALTH OPPORTUNITIES HS; (FR); Hnr Roll; Yth Ldrshp Prog; Biology; Pre-Med; Hobart and William Smith Colleges; SUNY Albany

LIU, GUANG Y; NEW YORK, NY; LOWER EAST SIDE PREP SCH; (SR); Nat Hon Sy; Otst Ac Ach Awd; St of Mnth; Comm Volntr; Peer Tut/Med; Cmptr Clb; Emplmnt; Tchrs Aide; Chinese Clb; Bskball; President of Chinese Culture Club; Electronic Engineering; Binghamton U

LIU, JENNY; STATEN ISLAND, NY; STUYVESANT HS; (SO); Nat Hon Sy; Perf Att; Salutrn; Sci Fairs; Sci/Math Olympn; ArtClub; Key Club; Stg Cre; Key Club-Art Committee Head; Architect; Art Director

LIU, KATHY; FLUSHING, NY; HS OF AMERICAN STUDIES @ LEHMAN COLLEGE; (JR); Hi Hnr Roll; Nat Hon Sy; Perf Att; Emplmnt; Key Club; Bnd; Yrbk (R); Spanish Honor Society (Vice Pres); Arista (Vice Pres); Business; Pre-Law

LIU, LIMIN; FREDONIA, NY; FREDONIA HS; (FR); Hnr Roll; St of Mnth; ArtClub; Key Club; Mth Clb/Tm; Chr; Tennis; Interior Design; Lawyer; U of Buffalo

LIU, XIAO M; ELMHURST, NY; FOREST HILLS HS; (JR); WWAHSS; Comm Volntr; FBLA; Key Club; Off Aide; Bnd; Bskball (V); Junior Achievement; Psychologist; Veterinarian; Binghamton U

LIU, ZHAONAN; BROOKLYN, NY; STUYVESANT HS; (SO); Comm Volntr; Peer Tut/Med; Chess; Key Club; Mth Clb/Tm; Tchrs Aide; Regional Winner in the 2005 Toshiba/NSTA; Exploravision Awards Program

LIVERANO, ANTHONY R; STATEN ISLAND, NY; PT RICHMOND HS; (SO); Hi Hnr Roll; Hnr Roll; St of Mnth; Emplmnt; Off Aide; ROTC; Received a Public Speaking Award; Law and Justice; Business Administration; New York U; Baruch College

LIVERMAN, NATASHA; LONG ISLAND CITY, NY; ST JOHN'S PREP HS; (JR); Hnr Roll; St of Mnth; Chr; Dnce; Step Team; Computer Technology; Law; St John's U; City College of New York

LIVERMORE, KATHLEEN; SAUGERTIES, NY; SAUGERTIES HS; (JR); Hi Hnr Roll; Nat Hon Sy; Comm Volntr; Emplmnt; Key Club; Prom Com; Dnce; Math; Engineer; SUNY Albany; SUNY Binghamton

LOBIANCO, ANTHONY; BROOKLYN, NY; ST EDMUND PREP HS; (JR); Ctznshp Aw; ArtClub; Cmptr Clb; Sci Clb; Bnd; Jzz Bnd; Pep Bnd; Visual Art Design and Graphics; Animation in Film; Pace U; Marymount Manhattan College

LOCK, JEFFREY; FLUSHING, NY; STUYVESANT HS; (JR); Jr Eng Tech; Nat Hon Sy; Comm Volntr; Hosp Aide; Peer Tut/Med; Key Club; Mth Clb/Tm; Tchrs Aide; Orch; Swmg (V); Sch Ppr (R); Stuyvesant HS Honor Roll (Arista); Junior Engineering Technical Society Regional Teams Champions; Engineering; Medicine; Columbia U; Yale U

LOCKHART, DIANE M; BROOKLYN, NY; W E B DU BOIS HS; (SO); Hnr Roll; Perf Att; St of Mnth; Hosp Aide; Chrch Yth Grp; Emplmnt; Off Aide; Tchrs Aide; Ch Chr; Cl Off (V); Yearly Child Care Education; Cosmetics / Hair Styles; U of Maryland; Long Island U

LOCOTETA, NICOLE; CEDARHURST, NY; LAWRENCE HS; (SO); Hi Hnr Roll; Comm Volntr; Emplmnt; Key Club; Lit Mag (R); Yrbk (E); Government in Action; Religious Ed. Asst. Teacher; Law

LOESCH, ROBIN A; STATEN ISLAND, NY; ST AGNES ACADEMIC HS; (FR); Hi Hnr Roll; Hnr Roll; Nat Hon Sy; Hosp Aide; SADD; The Staten Island Federation of Parent Teacher Associations; Law; Forensics; John Jay College of Criminal Justice; New York U

LOFT, JENNIFER; BUFFALO, NY; MT MERCY AC; (JR); Hi Hnr Roll; Hnr Roll; Nat Hon Sy; Otst Ac Ach Awd; Comm Volntr; Peer Tut/Med; ArtClub; Vsity Clb; Dnce; Lit Mag (E); Varsity Bowling; League Bowling; Creative or Professional Writing; Psychology; Niagara U; Syracuse U

LOFTUS, DAVID; MANLIUS, NY; NATIONAL SPORTS AC; (FR); Bnd; Cyclg (V); Skiing (V); Sccr (V); Stu Cncl (R); Johns Hopkins Center for Talented Youth, Sally Davis Scholar Athlete; Thomas Vonn Most Improved J3 Skier in NY, 3rd Place Junior Olympics GS 2003-4, 4th Place S6; 8th Place GS Empire State Games 2004-5

LOKEN, TIFFANY K; LEVITTOWN, NY; ISLAND TREES HS; (SO); Hi Hnr Roll; WWAHSS; Comm Volntr; Peer Tut/Med; Spec Olymp Vol; Chrch Yth Grp; Key Club; Mth Clb/Tm; Mus Clb; Pep Squd; Scouts; Vsity Clb; Spanish Clb; Bnd; Dnce; Mch Bnd; Bdmtn (J); Lcrsse (J); PPSqd (V); Stu Cncl (R); Girl Scouts Silver Award; National Physical Fitness Award; Astronomy; Forensic Science; St. John's U; Hofstra U

LOMBARDO, ERICA; LEVITTOWN, NY; (JR); Nat Hon Sy; Key Club; Nursing; Medical Administration; Nassau Community; Hunters, Molloy, Briarcliffe College

LONDON, MATTHEW; BROOKLYN, NY; SHEEPSHEAD BAY HS; (JR); Chrch Yth Grp; Mus Clb; Bnd; Jzz Bnd; Orch; SP/M/VS; Sccr; 3 Time Semi Finalist - Fine Arts Festival; Music Production; Music Production & Engineering; Professional Music; Berklee College of Music; Juilliard Music College

LONG, MEGAN M; HUNTINGTON, NY; HUNTINGTON HS; (SO); DAR; F Lan Hn Soc; Hi Hnr Roll; Nat Hon Sy; Pres Ac Ftns Aw; Comm Volntr; Hosp Aide; Spec Olymp Vol; Emplmnt; Prom Com; Svce Clb; Orch; Bskball (J L); Cr Ctry (V); Sccr (J L); Track (V L); Adv Cncl (R); Cl Off (S); Stu Cncl (V); CR (R); Make-A-Wish Foundation; Advisory Board-Huntington Youth Bureau; Political Science, Law; Spanish; U of Virginia; Loyola College-Maryland

LONGENDYKE, SARAH W; GLASCO, NY; SAUGERTIES HS; (JR); Hi Hnr Roll; Hnr Roll; Nat Hon Sy; WWAHSS; Comm Volntr; Peer Tut/Med; Spec Olymp Vol; Key Club; Vsity Clb; Bskball (V L); Sftball (VJCL); Vllyball (VJCL); Elementary Education; Physical Education Teacher; SUNY Cortland; Western New England College

LONGOBUCCO, AMANDA M; SEA CLIFF, NY; NORTH SHORE HS; (SR); All Am Sch; Hi Hnr Roll; Hnr Roll; MVP; WWAHSS; Comm Volntr; Emplmnt; Key Club; Prom Com; Scouts; Vsity Clb; Bskball (VJCL); Fld Hky (VJ L); Lcrsse (V CL); CR (R); Sch Ppr (E, R, P); All-American, Honorable Mentor, Lacrosse; Summa Cum Laude, Nat'l. Latin Exam 2X; Journalism; (Penn State) Pennsylvania State U

LOOFT, LAUREN E; STATEN ISLAND, NY; CURTIS HS; (SO); Ctznshp Aw; Hi Hnr Roll; Otst Ac Ach Awd; Sci/Math Olympn; St of Mnth; WWAHSS; Comm Volntr; Peer Tut/Med; Key Club; Off Aide; Tchrs Aide; Tennis; Vllyball; Stu Cncl (R); Sch Ppr (R, P); Yrbk (R, P); Key Club; Women's Awareness Club; Journalism; Biology; Columbia U; Barnard College

LOOMIS, COLIN S; WADDINGTON, NY; MADRID-WADDINGTON CTRL SCH; (FR); Hi Hnr Roll; Comm Volntr; 4-H; Chrch Yth Grp; Dbte Team; Drma Clb; Emplmnt; Key Club; NtlFrnscLg; Spch Team; Bnd; Chr; Jzz Bnd; Mch Bnd; Golf (V); Riding- NY State Fair Winner; Attorney; Veterinarian; St Lawerence U; Cornell U

LOPEZ, ESTELA; STATEN ISLAND, NY; PT RICHMOND HS; (JR); Nat Mrt LOC; Hospitality & Tourism Program; Courses in Parsons New School; Fashion Merchandising; Marketing; Fashion Institute of Technology; New School U

LOPEZ, IVELISSE; BRONX, NY; JANE ADDAMS HS; (SR); Hnr Roll; Perf Att; Chrch Yth Grp; SP/M/VS; Poetry Club; Physical Therapy; Lehman College; City College

LOPEZ, JOSHUA; BRONX, NY; ENY TRANSIT TECH HS; (SR); Hnr Roll; Perf Att; Comm Volntr; Vsity Clb; Stg Cre; Bsball (J); Vllyball (V); Sch Ppr (E); Theater Arts; Sociology; Hunter College

LOPEZ, KERIANN; ELMONT, NY; SEWANHAKA HS; (FR); Hi Hnr Roll; Kwnis Aw; Nat Mrt LOC; Otst Ac Ach Awd; Sci Fairs; Sci/Math Olympn; WWAHSS; Comm Volntr; Peer Tut/Med; Red Cr Aide; Key Club; Quiz Bowl; Schol Bwl; Dnce; Sftball; Vllyball; Fundraising for the LI Lightning Wheelchair Basketball Team; TAG -Poetry Publications; Medical; Physical Therapy; New York U; SUNY Stony Brook

LOPEZ, STEPHANIE; BRONX, NY; AC MT ST URSULA; (JR); Comm Volntr; Peer Tut/Med; Spanish Clb; Nursing; Hunter College; Lehman College

LORENZANA, AMY; BRONX, NY; ALFRED E SMITH VOC HS; (FR); Hi Hnr Roll; Hnr Roll; Perf Att; Mus Clb; Tchrs Aide

LORENZO, RITA YADIRA; BRONX, NY; EVANDER CHILDS HS; (JR); Hnr Roll; Nat Hon Sy; Perf Att; WWAHSS; Sftball (V); Vllyball (V); Stu Cncl (R); Former Director of Marketing Department in School Firm "World Class Travel"; Nominated to take part in Business Plan Competition; Journalism; Interior Design/Fashion Design; Boston U; New York U

LOSEY, JACOB P; MASSENA, NY; MASSENA CTRL HS; (SO); Hnr Roll; Otst Ac Ach Awd; Perf Att; Pres Ac Ftns Aw; WWAHSS; DARE; Bsball (J L); Sccr (J L); Track (VJ L); Spanish Club, Junior Golf League; Snowboarding, Hunting, Fishing, Ski Club; Engineering; Clarkson U; SUNY Potsdam

LOUEY, JONATHAN; AMAGANSETT, NY; EAST HAMPTON HS; (SO); Hi Hnr Roll; Otst Ac Ach Awd; Pres Ac Ftns Aw; WWAHSS; Amnsty Intl; Comm Volntr; Key Club; Bsball (V L); Bskball (V CL); Stu Cncl (R); CR (R); High Honor Roll

LOUIS, MARIE S; BROOKLYN, NY; ABRAHAM LINCOLN HS; (FR); Hnr Roll; Nat Hon Sy; Perf Att; Drma Clb; Ch Chr; Dnce; SP/M/VS; Sftball (VJ); Medicine; Teaching; CCNY; Brooklyn College

LOUIS, RACHELE E; BROOKLYN, NY; STUYVESANT HS; (SR); Hnr Roll; USAA; WWAHSS; Comm Volntr; Chrch Yth Grp; Bnd; Ch Chr; Dnce; SP/M/VS; Architecture (Residential); Cooper Union; Rensselaer Polytechnic Institute

Lorenzo, Rita Yadira
Evander Childs HS
Bronx, NY

Lin, Xin
Health Prof & Human Serv HS
New York, NY

Lin, Jing
West Seneca East SR HS
Buffalo, NY

Lin, Michael
Bronx HS Of Science
Little Neck, NY

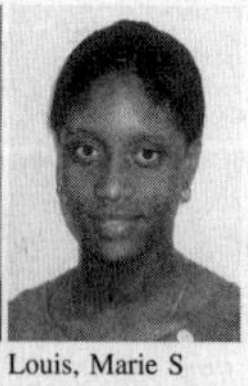

Louis, Marie S
Abraham Lincoln HS
Brooklyn, NY

LOVELESS, KERRI; GREAT VALLEY, NY; ELLICOTTVILLE HS; (SO); 4H Awd; Hi Hnr Roll; Hnr Roll; WWAHSS; Comm Volntr; 4-H; Quiz Bowl; Spanish Clb; Chr; Hsbk Rdg (V); Cl Off (P); Horse Trainer; Nurse; Cornell U; Alfred State

LOVELL, REBECCA; MERRICK, NY; CALHOUN HS; (JR); Hnr Roll; Nat Hon Sy; WWAHSS; Comm Volntr; DECA; Emplmnt; Key Club; Mus Clb; Photog; Tmpl Yth Grp; Bnd; Dnce; Mch Bnd; Pep Bnd; Lit Mag (R); Key Club Historian and Division Secretary; Hebrew Culture Club Public Relations Officer; Communications; Film; Ithaca College; SUNY Geneseo

LOW, SIMON; NEW YORK, NY; HUMANITIES HS; (JR); DARE; Jr Ach; Mathematics; Teaching; Baruch College; Saint John's U

LU, CAROLINE; QUEENS VILLAGE, NY; BENJAMIN CARDOZO HS; (FR); Hnr Roll; Perf Att; Pres Sch; WWAHSS; Key Club; Economics; Forensic Science; New York U

LU, CHIH-CHI; BROOKLYN, NY; MIDWOOD HS; (JR); Hnr Roll; Perf Att; WWAHSS; Comm Volntr; Red Cr Aide; Key Club; Lib Aide; Off Aide; Business Management; Pharmacy; Cornell U; New York U

LU, ISABELLE; OAKLAND GARDENS, NY; BENJAMIN CARDOZO HS; (JR); Hnr Roll; Perf Att; Sci Fairs; Comm Volntr; Chrch Yth Grp; Drma Clb; Mus Clb; Svce Clb; Tchrs Aide; Bnd; Ch Chr; Mch Bnd; Pep Bnd; English; Liberal Arts; Queens College; Hunter College

LU, KATHERINE; OAKLAND GARDENS, NY; STUYVESANT HS; (SO); F Lan Hn Soc; Hi Hnr Roll; Hnr Roll; Nat Hon Sy; WWAHSS; Comm Volntr; Key Club; Mod UN; Mus Clb; Off Aide; P to P St Amb Prg; Scouts; German Clb; Orch; SP/M/VS; Scr Kpr (V); Swmg (V); Stuyvesant String Quartet - Violin; Chamber Orchestra-Concert Mistress; Neurosurgeon; Corporate Lawyer; Yale U; Princeton U

LU, MARY; BROOKLYN, NY; HSMSE @ CCNY; (JR); Hnr Roll; Nat Hon Sy; Perf Att; WWAHSS; Peer Tut/Med; Red Cr Aide; Emplmnt; JSA; Key Club; Mod UN; MuAlphaTh; Yrbk (P); "Toaster in the Tub" (Media Production); Soccer Team (Developmental); International Business; Business Management; Columbia U; Baruch College

LUCHKIV, KRISTINA; ELMIRA, NY; THOMAS A EDISON HS; (FR); Ctznshp Aw; Hi Hnr Roll; Pres Sch; St of Mnth; WWAHSS; Key Club; Chr; Tennis (V); Stu Cncl (R); New York U; Cornell U

LUCKIE, SHARAE C; BRONX, NY; HARRY TRUMAN HS; (JR); Hnr Roll; Comm Volntr; Five of My Poems Have Been Published; Psychology; English; New York U; Fordham U

LUCKINBILL, NICOLE; SENECA FALLS, NY; MYNDERSE AC HS; (SR); Hnr Roll; WWAHSS; Comm Volntr; Peer Tut/Med; Red Cr Aide; Chrch Yth Grp; DARE; Emplmnt; Prom Com; Scouts; Chr; Ch Chr; Dnce; Chrldg (JC); Sccr (VJ L); Religious Education Teacher; Reality Check; English; Education; Monroe Community College; SUNY Brockport

LUDOVICI, ERIC M; LYONS FALLS, NY; SOUTH LEWIS HS; (JR); Hi Hnr Roll; WWAHSS; Yth Ldrshp Prog; Spec Olymp Vol; Chrch Yth Grp; DARE; Emplmnt; Vsity Clb; Bnd; Ch Chr; Jzz Bnd; Mch Bnd; Ftball (V CL); Track (V L); Electrical Engineering; Rochester Institute of Technology; Rensselaer Polytechnic Institute

LUMLEY, ADRIAN; BAYSHORE, NY; SANDERLING BRENTWOOD HS; (SO); Hi Hnr Roll; Hnr Roll; Nat Stu Ath Day Aw; Pres Ac Ftns Aw; St of Mnth; Fncg (J); Wrstlg (J); Master's Degree in Business Administration; Harvard Business School; New York U

LUND, GAVIN; PT JEFFERSON STATION, NY; COMSEWOGUE HS; (JR); F Lan Hn Soc; Hi Hnr Roll; Otst Ac Ach Awd; Pres Sch; Sci/Math Olympn; Yth Ldrshp Prog; Comm Volntr; Peer Tut/Med; Chrch Yth Grp; Emplmnt; FBLA; Mth Clb/Tm; NYLC; Quiz Bowl; Schol Bwl; Sci Clb; Skiing; Tennis (V); AP Scholar Award; Highest Average Awards - Computers / Sci / Physics / Chem / Sequential Math III; Computer Engineering; Computer Science; Princeton U; Stevens Institute of Technology

LUNDI, DAPHNE; BROOKLYN, NY; CLARA BARTON HS; (JR); Hnr Roll; Nat Hon Sy; Perf Att; St of Mnth; WWAHSS; Yth Ldrshp Prog; Comm Volntr; Hosp Aide; ArtClub; Emplmnt; Off Aide; Tchrs Aide; Reporter for Health Newspaper; Citation from Arthur Ashe Institute; Physics; Biochemistry; Wellesley College; Vassar College

LUNDY, MARY; HUDSON FALLS, NY; HUDSON FALLS HS; (JR); Key Club; Kwanza Clb; Chrldg (J); Track (J); Lit Mag (R); I Do Horseback Riding, Enjoy Volleyball, and Gymnastics.; Culinary Arts; Associates; Adirondack Community College; New England Culinary Insitute

LUPO, MATTHEW S; CTRL ISLIP, NY; CTRL ISLIP HS; (SO); Hi Hnr Roll; Hnr Roll; MVP; Nat Hon Sy; Otst Ac Ach Awd; Perf Att; Pres Sch; St of Mnth; Comm Volntr; ArtClub; Chess; Cmptr Clb; DARE; Emplmnt; Lib Aide; Tchrs Aide; Tech Clb; Bsball (J); Yrbk (E); Bowling Trophies; Construction; Baseball

LUPO, MICHAEL; PORT CHESTER, NY; PORT CHESTER HS; (FR); Hnr Roll; Perf Att; Bsball (J); Ftball (J)

LUU, VIVIAN; OAKLAND GARDENS, NY; STUYVESANT HS; (FR); Hi Hnr Roll; Sci Fairs; Red Cr Aide; Key Club; Mth Clb/Tm; Off Aide; Chr; Columbia U

LY, MICHELE; WOODSIDE, NY; STUYVESANT HS; (FR); Hi Hnr Roll; Nat Hon Sy; St of Mnth; Key Club; Photog

LY, MICHELLE; POMONA, NY; RAMAPO HS; (JR); Hnr Roll; MVP; WWAHSS; Peer Tut/Med; Key Club; MuAlphaTh; Dnce; Orch; Chrldg (V); Chemical Engineering; Performing Arts / Acting; Cornell U; Fordham U

LYNCH, MEHALEYA S; BUFFALO, NY; LAFAYETTE HS; (FR); Hnr Roll; Nat Hon Sy; Perf Att; USAA; Chrch Yth Grp; DARE; Scouts; Dnce; Academy of Finance; Law; Education; Harvard; Buffalo State U

LYONS, SHAAKIRA; SAINT ALBANS, NY; MAGNET SCH LAW/ GOVERNMENT; (FR); Photog; Dnce; Lawyer; Harvard; Howard U

LYONS, STEPHEN; SCHENECTADY, NY; GUILDERLAND HS; (SO); Hnr Roll; WWAHSS; Comm Volntr; Key Club; Wdwrkg Clb; Track (J); Psychology; Philosophy

LYSETSKA, NATALIA; BROOKLYN, NY; ST VINCENT FERRER HS; (SR); F Lan Hn Soc; Hi Hnr Roll; Hnr Roll; Nat Hon Sy; Nat Ldrshp Svc; Nat Sci Aw; Sci Fairs; St of Mnth; Yth Ldrshp Prog; CARE; Comm Volntr; Hosp Aide; ArtClub; Biology Clb; Chrch Yth Grp; Dbte Team; Drma Clb; Emplmnt; Lib Aide; Mod UN; Bnd; Chr; Ch Chr; Dnce; Vllyball (J); Adv Cncl (R); Sch Ppr (R); Diploma / Award for International Theater; Ukrainian Dance Ensemble / Syzokryli; Law / Government; Political Science; John Jay College of Criminal Justice; Fordham U

LYTE, BRITTANY; CLIFTON PARK, NY; SHENENDEHOWA HS; (SR); Ctznshp Aw; Hi Hnr Roll; Nat Hon Sy; Nat Sci Aw; WWAHSS; Comm Volntr; Peer Tut/Med; DARE; Drma Clb; Emplmnt; P to P St Amb Prg; Prom Com; Scouts; SADD; Acpl Chr; Bnd; Chr; Orch; PP Ftbl; Skiing; Track; Vllyball; Cl Off (S); Sch Ppr (R); Journalism

MA, STELLA S; MIDDLE VILLAGE, NY; CHRIST THE KING HS; (JR); Hi Hnr Roll; Hnr Roll; Kwnis Aw; Nat Hon Sy; Nat Sci Aw; Otst Ac Ach Awd; Sci Fairs; WWAHSS; Yth Ldrshp Prog; Comm Volntr; Peer Tut/Med; Key Club; Mth Clb/Tm; SAG and AFTRA Member / Advanced Research Program; Piano Since 6 Yrs Old; Pre-Law; Science; New York U; Columbia U

MABOWITZ, BOBBY; BREWSTER, NY; THE GROVE SCH/NORTH SALEM HS; (SR); Hi Hnr Roll; Hnr Roll; MVP; Nat Hon Sy; Otst Ac Ach Awd; St of Mnth; Comm Volntr; Peer Tut/Med; Emplmnt; Mus Clb; Prom Com; Vsity Clb; Chr; Dnce; SP/M/VS; Bsball (VJC); Ice Hky (V); Skiing (V); Vsy Clb (V); Wt Lftg (VJ); Stu Cncl (R); BA Music Industry Technology; Film/Video/Music Production; College of St Rose-Albany, NY; Mercy College-White Plains, NY

MABRY, TAYSHAWN R; NEW YORK, NY; ST MICHAEL'S AC; (SR); Hi Hnr Roll; Hnr Roll; Nat Hon Sy; St of Mnth; WWAHSS; Peer Tut/Med; Emplmnt; Off Aide; P to P St Amb Prg; Prom Com; Ch Chr; SP/M/VS; Stu Cncl (R); PACE Club; Speech Pathology; Pediatrics; Temple U; Long Island U CW Post

MACALUSO, KATRINA G; MARION, NY; MARION HS; (SR); Chr; Sccr (V); Yrbk (E); Tech Support at Teen Outreach Christian Group; Interior Design; Monroe Community College

MAC CHEYNE, CAYLA; INTERLAKEN, NY; SOUTH SENECA JR SR HS; (JR); Ctznshp Aw; Hi Hnr Roll; Nat Hon Sy; Otst Ac Ach Awd; Perf Att; St of Mnth; WWAHSS; Red Cr Aide; AL Aux Girls; Emplmnt; Fr of Library; Spanish Clb; Sccr (V); Sftball (V C); CR (R); Computer Science; U of Pennsylvania; Cornell U

MAC DONAGH, COLIN; BLUE POINT, NY; BAYPORT BLUE POINT HS; (JR); Hi Hnr Roll; Hnr Roll; Perf Att; Pres Ac Ftns Aw; Sci/Math Olympn; WWAHSS; Yth Ldrshp Prog; Comm Volntr; DARE; Emplmnt; Sci Clb; Vsity Clb; Jzz Bnd; Orch; SP/M/VS; Cr Ctry (V); Sccr (J); Track (V); Athletes Helping Athletes Representative; Chamber Orchestra; Engineering; Providence, RI; SUNY Binghamton

MACHAJ, VERONICA; WESTBURY, NY; CARLE PLACE HS; (JR); F Lan Hn Soc; Hnr Roll; Nat Hon Sy; Otst Ac Ach Awd; WWAHSS; Comm Volntr; Emplmnt; Key Club; MuAlphaTh; SADD; Chr; Tennis (V); Sch Ppr (R, P); Ensemble Singing Group; Tri-M Music Honor Society; Education-Secondary Biology; Psychology; U of North Carolina Chapel Hill

MACIASZ, MARTHA; JACKSON HEIGHTS, NY; DOMINICAN AC; (JR); Ctznshp Aw; Hnr Roll; ArtClub; Photog; Sci Clb; Svce Clb; Dnce; SP/M/VS; Track (J); Cl Off (T); Stu Cncl (R)

MACK, ROBERT; CANANDAIGUA, NY; CANANDAIGUA AC; (JR); Hi Hnr Roll; Hnr Roll; MVP; Pres Ac Ftns Aw; Peer Tut/Med; DARE; Emplmnt; Vsity Clb; Ftball (V L); Wrstlg (V L); NY State Representative for Wrestling; Natural Helpers; Dental Science; Health / Medical Field; American U; Villanova U

MAC MANNIS, KAITLYN E; CHAZY, NY; CHAZY CTRL RURAL SCH; (FR); Cl Off (T); Stu Cncl (R); Yrbk (R, P); Key Club / Youth Court; Yearbook; Pre-Law; Diplomacy; American U; College of William & Mary

MADDOX, KENNETH S; NEW YORK, NY; FREDERICK DOUGLASS AC; (JR); Hnr Roll; Perf Att; Yth Ldrshp Prog; Comm Volntr; Peer Tut/Med; Chrch Yth Grp; DARE; Emplmnt; Off Aide; Tchrs Aide; Vsity Clb; Cr Ctry (V); Fncg (V); Ftball (V); Mar Art; Track (V); Vsy Clb (V); Math Certificates; PAL; Computer Engineering; Electronics

MAGARIN, MABIEL; OZONE PARK, NY; JAMAICA HS; (JR); F Lan Hn Soc; Hnr Roll; Nat Hon Sy; Chrch Yth Grp; Spanish Clb; Ch Chr; Dnce; Drl Tm; SP/M/VS; Bsball (V); Golf (V); Rqtball (V); Sccr (V); Swmg (J); Tennis (V); Track (V); Vllyball (J); Stu Cncl (S); Volunteer in a Church; Psychology; Queens College

MAGLI, AMANDA R; GLEN HEAD, NY; NORTH SHORE HS; (SR); Ctznshp Aw; DAR; F Lan Hn Soc; Hi Hnr Roll; Nat Hon Sy; Nat Ldrshp Svc; Nat Mrt LOC; Pres Ac Ftns Aw; Pres Sch; St of Mnth; Comm Volntr; Hosp Aide; Peer Tut/Med; Emplmnt; Key Club; Mth Clb/Tm; MuAlphaTh; NYLC; Prom Com; Scouts; Svce Clb; Lcrsse (V L); Tennis (V CL); Track (V L); Cl Off (P); CR (S); Coca Cola Scholar 2005; AP Scholar W/Honor; International Health; Duke U

MAGNO, SAMANTHA A; FRESH MEADOWS, NY; ST FRANCIS PREP HS; (JR); Hnr Roll; Comm Volntr; Hosp Aide; Chrch Yth Grp; Emplmnt; Key Club; Yrbk (E); National Piano Playing Auditions (NGPT); Swimming (YMCA); Neurologist; Psychiatrist; New York U; Hunter College

MAHFOOZ, ATTIA; BROOKLYN, NY; MIDWOOD HS; (FR); Comm Volntr; Peer Tut/Med; Key Club; Member of City Council; New York U; Brooklyn College

MAHLSTADT, ERIK; HUNTINGTON, NY; WALT WHITMAN HS; (JR); Hi Hnr Roll; Hnr Roll; MVP; Nat Hon Sy; Otst Ac Ach Awd; St of Mnth; Comm Volntr; Hab For Humty Volntr; Peer Tut/Med; Chrch Yth Grp; DECA; Emplmnt; Key Club; Photog; Cr Ctry (V CL); Ice Hky (JC); Lcrsse (J); Track (V L); CR (R); Lit Mag (P); Town of Huntington Certificate of Recognition; E-Mentoring/Career Shadowing Participant; Business; Marketing; Boston U; Northeastern U

MAHMOOD, HUMA; FLUSHING, NY; FRANCIS LEWIS HS; (SR); Hnr Roll; Nat Hon Sy; St of Mnth; DARE; Key Club; Mod UN; Off Aide; Tchrs Aide; Key Club/Model U.N.; Pace U

MAHONEY, ALYSSA; CTRPORT, NY; ST ANTHONY'S HS; (JR); Cr Ctry; Lcrsse; Track

MAHONEY, EMILY; TROY, NY; TROY HS; (SR); Hi Hnr Roll; Hnr Roll; Nat Hon Sy; WWAHSS; Chrch Yth Grp; Emplmnt; Key Club; Mus Clb; French Clb; Chr; Stg Cre; Sccr (VJCL); Stu Cncl; French Club Vice President; Key Club Vice President; English; Journalism; New York U

MAHUNIK, ALYSHA; PENNELLVILLE, NY; JOHN C BIRDLEBOUGH HS; (JR); Hi Hnr Roll; Nat Hon Sy; Perf Att; Sci Fairs; WWAHSS; Yth Ldrshp Prog; Comm Volntr; Peer Tut/Med; DARE; Emplmnt; HO'Br Yth Ldrshp; SADD; Bnd; Dnce; Orch; Adv Cncl (R); Cl Off (S); Stu Cncl (R); CR (R); Presidential Gold Award; Area All State Band; Speech & Language Pathology; Psychology

MAISONAVE, MICHELE N; STATEN ISLAND, NY; PT RICHMOND HS; (FR); Ctznshp Aw; Sci Fairs; Chef / Veterinarian

MAITLAND, JAMES T; PINE CITY, NY; ELMIRA SOUTHSIDE HS; (SR); Hi Hnr Roll; Nat Hon Sy; Otst Ac Ach Awd; WWAHSS; AL Aux Boys; Emplmnt; Key Club; P to P St Amb Prg; Quiz Bowl; Orch; Elmira City Youth Court; Mark Twain Scholar; Visual Effects & Motion Graphics; Art Institute of Pittsburgh

MAK, CHOI S; BROOKLYN, NY; STUYVESANT HS; (FR); Key Club; Mth Clb/Tm; Track (V)

MAKLER, JACOB; HILLSDALE, NY; TACONIC HILLS HS; (SO); Hi Hnr Roll; Hnr Roll; Cmptr Clb; DARE; Mod UN; NYLC; Schol Bwl; Scouts; Bnd; Sccr (J); Track (V); Cl Off (R); CR (R); Yrbk (P); Rotary Youth Leadership Award; Accounting; Psychology; New York U; Boston College

MALAVE, LUIS J; FREEPORT, NY; FREEPORT HS; (JR); Hnr Roll; Perf Att; WWAHSS; Comm Volntr; Chess; Emplmnt; Mth Clb/Tm; Spanish Clb; Chess Club, Martial Arts Student; Sinfonietta Honors; Engineering; Computer Tech

MALCOLM, NATASHIA; ELMONT, NY; SEWANHAKA HS; (JR); Hnr Roll; Perf Att; WWAHSS; Comm Volntr; Chrch Yth Grp; SADD; Chr; Dnce; Track (V L); Stu Cncl (R); CR (R); Math; Accountant; Northeastern U; Utica College

MALCOLM, TARA R; BRONX, NY; PINE FORGE AC; (FR); Hi Hnr Roll; St of Mnth; Valdctrian; WWAHSS; Chrch Yth Grp; Ch Chr; SP/M/VS; MD (Ob/Gyn)

MALDONADO, JULIANA; LEVITTOWN, NY; ISLAND TREES HS; (JR); Hi Hnr Roll; Hnr Roll; Pres Ac Ftns Aw; Prom Com; SADD; Chr; Dnce; PPSqd (V); Chemistry; Lawyer; U of Miami; Florida International U

Malave, Luis J
Freeport HS
Freeport, NY

Machaj, Veronica
Carle Place HS
Westbury, NY

Lynch, Mehaleya S
Lafayette HS
Buffalo, NY

Lysetska, Natalia
St Vincent Ferrer HS
Brooklyn, NY

Malcolm, Tara R
Pine Forge AC
Bronx, NY

MALDONADO, LUIS; HAVERSTRAW, NY; NORTH ROCKLAND HS; (FR); Hi Hnr Roll; Hnr Roll; St of Mnth; Peer Tut/Med; Ftball (J); Computer Tech.

MALDONADO, MELIDA; BRONX, NY; MARBLE HILL HS FOR INTERNATIONAL STUDIES; (SO); Hnr Roll; Otst Ac Ach Awd; Perf Att; Salutrn; Comm Volntr; Dnce; Bskball (J); Cr Ctry (VJ); Mar Art; School Program - Traveling to China; Foreign Language Major; Interpreting; Albany State U; Teikyo Post U

MALDONADO, YARIELY G; UNIONDALE, NY; UNIONDALE HS; (SO); Hnr Roll; Otst Ac Ach Awd; Perf Att; St of Mnth; ArtClub; Cmptr Clb; DARE; Mth Clb/Tm; Spanish Clb; Bnd; Chr; Dnce; Sccr (L); Swmg (J); Art (Like to Draw); Fashion Designer; Doctor (Pediatrician); Teacher; Nassau Community College

MALGIERI, NICHOLAS; SAUGERTIES, NY; SAUGERTIES HS; (JR); Hi Hnr Roll; Nat Hon Sy; WWAHSS; Peer Tut/Med; Emplmnt; Key Club; Spanish Clb; Bnd; Cl Off (T); Yrbk (R); Law; Union College; Cornell U

MALIK, SULEMAN; EAST MEADOW, NY; EAST MEADOW HS; (SO); Hnr Roll; WWAHSS; Yth Ldrshp Prog; Comm Volntr; Hosp Aide; Peer Tut/Med; FBLA; HO'Br Yth Ldrshp; Key Club; Mod UN; Outdrs Clb; Sci Clb; SADD; Bskball (J); Vllyball (J); HOBY; New York State Science Honor Society; Corporate Law

MALIVERT, NERLINE; BROOKLYN, NY; JAMES MADISON HS; (JR); Hnr Roll; Nat Sci Aw; Sci Fairs; WWAHSS; Comm Volntr; Hosp Aide; Peer Tut/Med; Chrch Yth Grp; Emplmnt; Key Club; Mth Clb/Tm; Off Aide; Photog; Sci Clb; Tchrs Aide; Bnd; Ch Chr; Dnce; Chrldg (V); Science and Math Honor Society; The Bio-Med Program (Prestigious); Ob/Gyn (Biology); Physics; Columbia U; City College (Sophie Davis Program)

MALLORY, KATHLEEN; SPRING VALLEY, NY; SPRING VALLEY HS; (SO); Hi Hnr Roll; MVP; Comm Volntr; Biology Clb; Emplmnt; Key Club; Sci Clb; Scouts; Bnd; Dnce; Mch Bnd; Track (V); Arista Treasurer; Girl Scout Silver Award; Pharmacy; Zoology; Rutgers

MALLOW, JESSICA L; ELMIRA, NY; THOMAS A EDISON HS; (JR); Hi Hnr Roll; Jr Rot; Nat Hon Sy; WWAHSS; Yth Ldrshp Prog; Key Club; Bnd; Dnce; Mch Bnd; Pep Bnd; Yrbk; Band President; Junior Rotarian; Rensselaer Polytechnic Institute; Emerson College

MALLOY, AUSTIN; BRONX, NY; HEALTH OPPORTUNITIES HS; (FR); Emplmnt; Off Aide; Bskball (V); Vllyball (V); Working in Comm Center with Kids; Working in My Schl; I Would Like to Be a Veterinarian; Also Interested in Law; Pace U; Columbia U

MAMAY, ELIZABETH; EAST HAMPTON, NY; EAST HAMPTON HS; (FR); Hi Hnr Roll; Hnr Roll; Otst Ac Ach Awd; Sci/Math Olympn; Comm Volntr; Emplmnt; Scouts; Bnd; Chr; Dnce; Jzz Bnd; Bskball (L); Cr Ctry (V L); Fld Hky (L); Scr Kpr; Track (V L); Vllyball (L); Sch Ppr (R); Yrbk (E, P); NYSSMA for Sax & Piano; SCEMA -Choral; Elementary School Teacher; Music Teacher; Geneseo (SUNY)

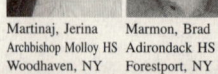

MAN, BERNICE Y; SEAFORD, NY; SEAFORD HS; (SO); Hi Hnr Roll; Otst Ac Ach Awd; Perf Att; Pres Sch; Comm Volntr; Peer Tut/Med; Drma Clb; Key Club; Scouts; Bnd; SP/M/VS; Stg Cre; Tennis (V); Stu Cncl (R); NYSSMA - All-State Participant

MAN, IVANA L; SEAFORD, NY; SEAFORD HS; (SR); Hi Hnr Roll; Nat Hon Sy; Otst Ac Ach Awd; Perf Att; Pres Sch; St of Mnth; WWAHSS; Yth Ldrshp Prog; Comm Volntr; Peer Tut/Med; Drma Clb; Key Club; NYLC; Scouts; SADD; Chr; SP/M/VS; Stg Cre; Tennis (V); Yrbk (R, P); NYSSMA Participant; Tri-M Music Honor Society - Secretary; Child Psychology; George Mason U

MAN, LILY; NEW YORK, NY; FIORELLO H LA GUARDIA HS; (FR); Hi Hnr Roll; Hnr Roll; Otst Ac Ach Awd; Perf Att; Sci Fairs; Comm Volntr; ArtClub; Chess; Prom Com; SP/M/VS; Yrbk (E, R, P); I Won the Art Award; Excellence Award for the Winning Writers' Yearbook Project; Philosophy; Fashion Classes; Yale U; New York U

MANCILLA, ANTONIO; STATEN ISLAND, NY; CURTIS HS; (JR); Hnr Roll; Nat Ldrshp Svc; Ftball (VJ); Track (J); National Student Leadership Conference; Sports Medicine; Sports Management; Saint John's U/Staten Island; Syracuse U

MANCINI, ALICIA; CORNWALL, NY; CORNWALL CTRL HS; (SO); Hi Hnr Roll; Comm Volntr; Emplmnt; Key Club; Biology; Psychiatrist; Boston U; North Carolina U

MANDRIS, META E; ALDEN, NY; ALDEN HS; (JR); Hnr Roll; WWAHSS; Comm Volntr; Chrch Yth Grp; Drma Clb; Emplmnt; Key Club; Outdrs Clb; Scouts; Tchrs Aide; Chr; Dnce; SP/M/VS; Swg Chr; Drama Club Officer; Church Youth Group Officer; Musical Theatre; U of Buffalo

MANGINO, MARISSA; ISLAND PARK, NY; WEST HEMPSTEAD HS; (JR); Hnr Roll; WWAHSS; Emplmnt; Key Club; Orch; Chrldg (V); Track (J); Tri-M music Honor Society; Performing Arts; Journalism; SUNY New Paltz; U of Pittsburgh

MANGONAS, GANAVIAVA; SPRING VALLEY, NY; FT PIERCE WESTWOOD HS; (JR); Hnr Roll; Sci Fairs; St of Mnth; Yth Ldrshp Prog; Comm Volntr; Chrch Yth Grp; Key Club; Scouts; Chr; Ch Chr; Dnce; SP/M/VS; Track (V); Vllyball (J); Captain of the Dance Team; Law Degree (Criminal Justice); Arts (Dancing); New York U; Columbia U

MANGRAVITE, GINA M; FARMINGDALE, NY; HALF HOLLOW HILLS HS EAST; (FR); Hi Hnr Roll; Otst Ac Ach Awd; Comm Volntr; Peer Tut/Med; Key Club; Scouts; Tchrs Aide; Dnce; Girl Scout Silver Award; H.H.H. East Key Club Treasurer; Teaching; Law; Boston U; Princeton U

MANIACI, KRISTINA; BROOKLYN, NY; BISHOP KEARNEY HS; (JR); Hi Hnr Roll; Hnr Roll; Nat Hon Sy; WWAHSS; Comm Volntr; Peer Tut/Med; Drma Clb; Mth Clb/Tm; SP/M/VS; Tennis; Basketball; Part Time Employment

MANNION, JACOB M; GREENFIELD CTR, NY; SARATOGA SPRINGS HS; (SO); 4H Awd; Hnr Roll; Comm Volntr; Dbte Team; Skiing; Sccr (J); Tennis (J); Engineering; Technology

MANOWAR, PERVEEN; CORONA, NY; BRONX HS OF SCEINCE; (JR); WWAHSS; Yth Ldrshp Prog; Red Cr Aide; Key Club; Off Aide; Tchrs Aide; Computer Science; Web Design; New York U; U of Texas Austin

MANZO, MICHELE; BRONX, NY; COLUMBUS INST FOR MATH & SCI; (MS); Ctznshp Aw; Biology Clb; Prom Com; SP/M/VS; Stg Cre; Yrbk (E, R, P); Church Basketball Team Cheerleading; Veterinary Studies; Mercy College

MAO, JEFFERSON Y; FLUSHING, NY; STUYVESANT HS; (JR); Nat Hon Sy; Nat Mrt Semif; Comm Volntr; Hosp Aide; Peer Tut/Med; Cmptr Clb; Key Club; Mth Clb/Tm; Quiz Bowl; Tchrs Aide; Track (V); Sch Ppr (R); Psychology; Business; Stanford U; Columbia U

MAPES, RACHEL; SPRING VALLEY, NY; (JR); F Lan Hn Soc; Hi Hnr Roll; Hnr Roll; Nat Hon Sy; WWAHSS; Comm Volntr; Chrch Yth Grp; Drma Clb; Key Club; Mth Clb/Tm; Mus Clb; NYLC; Sci Clb; Spanish Clb; Ch Chr; Orch; SP/M/VS; Stg Cre; Sccr (L); Cl Off (T); Bowling; Child Psychiatry; Columbia U; Johns Hopkins U, Gordon College

MARADIAGA, DORA; RIPLEY, NY; RIPLEY CTRL SCH; (SO); F Lan Hn Soc; Amnsty Intl; Hab For Humty Volntr; Drma Clb; P to P St Amb Prg; German Clb; Orch; SP/M/VS; Arch (J); Sccr (J); Swmg (J); Tennis (J); CR (P); Master's Degree

MARBLE, JESSICA R; WELLSVILLE, NY; WELLSVILLE HS; (SO); Hnr Roll; Perf Att; St of Mnth; Comm Volntr; Red Cr Aide; DARE; Emplmnt; Key Club; Prom Com; French Clb; Bskball (J L); Sccr (VJC); Track (V L); Cl Off (S); Stu Cncl (R); CR (R); Sch Ppr (R, P); Yrbk (R, P); Pres./treasurer of International Club in Key Club, Leos Club, SADD; Physical Therapy, OCC Therapy; Physical Therapy; D'Youville; Nazareth

MARCH, SHENNIKA A; BROOKLYN, NY; SPRINGFIELD GARDENS HS; (JR); Hnr Roll; St of Mnth; Vllyball (J); RN; Doctor; SUNY Stony Brook; SUNY Oswego

MARCHEGIANI, ALESSIO V; WESTBURY, NY; CLARKE HS; (JR); Hnr Roll; Nat Hon Sy; Sci/Math Olympn; Peer Tut/Med; Key Club; Sccr (V); Tennis (V); Track (V); Wrstlg (V); NJHS; LOTE Honor Society; Pre-Med; Bio Major; SUNY Binghamton; SUNY Geneseo

MARCOLINA, HEATHER; MIDDLETOWN, NY; MINISINK VALLEY HS; (SO); Hi Hnr Roll; Hnr Roll; St of Mnth; WWAHSS; Chrch Yth Grp; Drma Clb; Key Club; Bnd; Chr; Dnce; SP/M/VS; Student Choreographer for High School Musical; Member of Disney Honors Winning Chorus; Dance; Music; SUNY Brockport; Belhaven College-Mississippi

MARCUCCI, LAURA; STATEN ISLAND, NY; CURTIS HS; (JR); Hnr Roll; Sci Fairs; Comm Volntr; Spec Olymp Vol; Emplmnt; Key Club; Mth Clb/Tm; Bnd; Mch Bnd; Chrldg (V); Yrbk (R, P); Yearbook Section Editor; Communications; Fashion Merchandising; Oneonta; Fashion Institute of Technology

MARCUS JR, KENNY I; NEW YORK, NY; ALFRED E SMITH VOC HS; (FR); Ctznshp Aw; Perf Att; St of Mnth; Comm Volntr; Clb; Bskball; Vllyball; Wt Lftg; Honor Roll Student; Engineering

MARIDUENA, CATHERINE D; UNIONDALE, NY; UNIONDALE HS; (SR); All Am Sch; Hi Hnr Roll; Nat Hon Sy; Otst Ac Ach Awd; Salutrn; Sci Fairs; WWAHSS; Peer Tut/Med; 4-H; Chrch Yth Grp; Key Club; Mth Clb/Tm; P to P St Amb Prg; Sci Clb; Scouts; Spanish Clb; Bnd; Mch Bnd; Sftball (V CL); Swmg (V L); President's Award for Educational Excellence; US Air Force & Navy Science Awards; Physician; The City College of New York/Sophie Davis Biomedical Program

MARION, V KENNETH; ENDICOTT, NY; (JR); Hnr Roll; Comm Volntr; Key Club; SP/M/VS; Mar Art (V); Track (V); Lit Mag; Sch Ppr; Black Belt, CYO Varsity B-Ball; Received Awards in Drawing Contests; Pratt, RIT, Cal Arts; Cartoonist, Animator; Pratt Institute; Rochester Institute of Technology

MARJI, MELISSA; YONKERS, NY; CHARLES E GORTON HS; (SR); Ctznshp Aw; DAR; Hi Hnr Roll; Nat Hon Sy; Otst Ac Ach Awd; Perf Att; St of Mnth; WWAHSS; Yth Ldrshp Prog; Comm Volntr; Red Cr Aide; Spec Olymp Vol; Chrch Yth Grp; Emplmnt; Jr Ach; Lib Aide; Prom Com; SADD; Italian Clb; Ch Chr; Bskball (J); Sccr (V); Vllyball (V); Stu Cncl (R); Honor Society Treasurer, Scholar Athlete Award; Best All Around Student; Pre-Med; Psychology; New York U

MARKOVICH, ALEX; BROOKLYN, NY; NEW UTRECHT HS; (JR); Hnr Roll; MVP; WWAHSS; CARE; Comm Volntr; Peer Tut/Med; Key Club; Schol Bwl; Vsity Clb; Chr; SP/M/VS; Swmg (V L); Tennis (V L); PSAL Champion / Indoor Tennis; PSAL Finalist Outdoor Tennis; Pharmacy; Medicine; SUNY Binghamton; SUNY Stony Brook

MARKS, CASEY; ENDICOTT, NY; UNION ENDICOTT HS; (SO); Hi Hnr Roll; Hnr Roll; Nat Stu Ath Day Aw; WWAHSS; Key Club; Scouts; French Clb; Sccr (J); Track (V); Journalism; Pharmacy; New York U; New York State U At Albany

MARKS, NICOLE; BELLEROSE, NY; MARTIN VAN BUREN HS; (SR); Hnr Roll; MVP; Nat Hon Sy; WWAHSS; Comm Volntr; Drma Clb; Emplmnt; Jr Ach; Tchrs Aide; Vsity Clb; SP/M/VS; Stg Cre; Hsbk Rdg (V); Tennis (V L); Vllyball (V C); Doctorate in Psychology; Parapsychology; Queens College; New York U

MARMON, BRAD; FORESTPORT, NY; ADIRONDACK HS; (JR); Ctznshp Aw; Hnr Roll; MVP; Perf Att; Pres Ac Ftns Aw; St of Mnth; Emplmnt; Bnd; Jzz Bnd; SP/M/VS; Bskball (VJ L); Ftball (VJ L); Cl Off (R); CR (R)

MARRA, MARCELLA; FARMINGDALE, NY; FARMINGDALE HS; (JR); Ctznshp Aw; F Lan Hn Soc; Hi Hnr Roll; Hnr Roll; Nat Hon Sy; Otst Ac Ach Awd; Sci Fairs; Sci/Math Olympn; St of Mnth; Yth Ldrshp Prog; Comm Volntr; DARE; DECA; Key Club; Prom Com; Sci Clb; SADD; Tech Clb; Cl Off (T); Finance; Economics; Northeastern U; Boston U

MARS, PHILIP; BROOKLYN, NY; LEON M GOLDSTEIN HS; (SO); Hnr Roll; Otst Ac Ach Awd; Sci/Math Olympn; Peer Tut/Med; Chr; SP/M/VS; Citation of Honor Award; Medicine; Law; New York U; Princeton U

MARSAN, CESCA E; POMONA, NY; RAMAPO HS; (SO); Hnr Roll; MVP; Sci Fairs; Peer Tut/Med; DARE; Outdrs Clb; Photog; Scouts; Bskball (J); Golf (J); Tennis (J); Jack and Jill Youth Organization; Visual Arts / Photography Club; Medicine / Pre-Med; Law / Pre-Law; Columbia U; Cornell U

MARSHALL, JA'LESSA; NEWBURGH, NY; NEWBURGH FREE AC; (JR); Ctznshp Aw; Hnr Roll; Pres Ac Ftns Aw; WWAHSS; Comm Volntr; Peer Tut/Med; Chrch Yth Grp; Ch Chr

MARSICOVETERE, SHEILA; EAST QUOGUE, NY; ST ANTHONY'S HS; (JR); Hi Hnr Roll; Nat Hon Sy; WWAHSS; Comm Volntr; NYLC; Track (V)

MARTIN, ELAYNA; EAST HAMPTON, NY; EAST HAMPTON HS; (SR); Ctznshp Aw; Hi Hnr Roll; Hnr Roll; WWAHSS; Comm Volntr; Emplmnt; Key Club; Photog; Prom Com; Bskball (JC); Fld Hky (VJ); Track (V); Yrbk (E); Scholar Athlete (90+ Avg While on a Sports Team); Candidate for National Honor Society; Elementary Education; Minor in Spanish; SUNY New Paltz

MARTIN, ELIZABETH A; MADRID, NY; MADRID WADDINGTON CTRL SCH; (JR); Hi Hnr Roll; Nat Hon Sy; WWAHSS; Comm Volntr; Peer Tut/Med; Chrch Yth Grp; Dbte Team; Drma Clb; Emplmnt; Key Club; Spch Team; Spanish Clb; Bnd; Chr; Jzz Bnd; Mch Bnd; Chrldg (V); Sccr (J); Sftball (V); Cl Off (V); Stu Cncl (R); St Lawrence County Dairy Princess 2004-2005; Communications; Business; Hamilton; St Lawrence U

MARTIN, KAYLA; MILTON, NY; MARLBORO CTRL HS; (SO); Perf Att; WWAHSS; Comm Volntr; Sccr (V); Law; Psychology

MARTINAJ, JERINA; WOODHAVEN, NY; ARCHBISHOP MOLLOY HS; (SO); Hi Hnr Roll; Otst Ac Ach Awd; Perf Att; Sci Fairs; Peer Tut/Med; Biology Clb; Track (J); Vllyball (J); Principal's List Award; JV - Volleyball Diocesan Finalist Award; Law; Engineering; Columbia U; New York U

MARTINEZ, ANGELINA C; BROOKLYN, NY; ABRAHAM LINCOLN HS; (SO); St of Mnth; Peer Tut/Med; Liberal Arts; Criminal Justice

MARTINEZ, BEATRIZ; BRONX, NY; ST PIUS V HS; (SR); Nat Hon Sy; Perf Att; Comm Volntr; Peer Tut/Med; Dnce; Sftball; Stu Cncl; Yrbk (E); National Honor Society - President 2005; Criminal Justice; Forensic Science; John Jay College / Criminal Justice

MARTINEZ, CAROLINA; BRONX, NY; MARBLE HILL HS FOR INTERNATIONAL STUDIES; (FR); Hi Hnr Roll; Hnr Roll; St of Mnth; Yth Ldrshp Prog; Peer Tut/Med; DARE; Jr Ach; Architecture; Law and Finance; Columbia U; Harvard U

MARTINEZ, VICTOR; RIDGEWOOD, NY; AUTOMOTIVE HS; (FR); Hnr Roll; Sci Fairs; St of Mnth; Comm Volntr; Ftball (J); Vllyball (J); Sports Analyst; Journalism; U of South Carolina; Syracuse U

MARTINO, MARISA; MASSENA, NY; MASSENA HS; (FR); Hi Hnr Roll; Otst Ac Ach Awd; Comm Volntr; Hab For Humty Volntr; Bnd; Chr; Mch Bnd; Pep Bnd; Cr Ctry (J); Sftball (J)

Martinaj, Jerina
Archbishop Molloy HS
Woodhaven, NY

Marmon, Brad
Adirondack HS
Forestport, NY

Marcolina, Heather
Minisink Valley HS
Middletown, NY

Mapes, Rachel
Spring Valley, NY

National
Honor Roll
Spring 2005

Mamay, Elizabeth
East Hampton HS
East Hampton, NY

Marji, Melissa
Charles E Gorton HS
Yonkers, NY

Martin, Elayna
East Hampton HS
East Hampton, NY

Martinez, Carolina
Marble Hill HS For International Studies
Bronx, NY

MARTINS, VANESSA; MINEOLA, NY; MINEOLA HS; (FR); Hi Hnr Roll; Nat Hon Sy; Perf Att; St of Mnth; Clr Grd; Mch Bnd; Lcrsse (J); Christa McAuliffe Award; Drama Club Graduate Award; Photography; Culinary Arts; New York U

MARTYNYUK, ALEKSEY M; BROOKLYN, NY; HS FOR ENVIRONMENTAL STUDIES; (JR); Gov Hnr Prg; Nat Hon Sy; WWAHSS; Chess; Cmptr Clb; Drma Clb; Mth Clb/Tm; Outdrs Clb; Sci Clb; Bnd; Stg Cre; Dvng (V); Gmnstcs (V); Sccr (V); Vllyball (V); Princeton U; Columbia U

MARUSSICH, CHRISTINA B; COMMACK, NY; SAINT ANTHONYS HS; (SR); Hnr Roll; CARE; Emplmnt; Photog; Quill & Scroll; Yrbk (R); Secondary Education; High School English Teacher; St Joseph's College; Hofstra U

MARZEC, JENNA; MASSAPEQUA PARK, NY; MASSAPEQUA HS; (JR); Hi Hnr Roll; Nat Hon Sy; Otst Ac Ach Awd; Pres Ac Ftns Aw; Sci Fairs; CARE; Comm Volntr; 4-H; Emplmnt; Key Club; SADD; Bnd; Mch Bnd; Lcrsse (VJ); Sccr (J); 1st Place Travel Soccer Tournaments; Lacrosse Nassau County Champion 2005; Secondary Education; Business; SUNY Binghamton; Marist

MARZIOTTO, NICHOLAS; LEVITTOWN, NY; MAC ARTHUR HS; (JR); Sci Fairs; St of Mnth; Key Club; Jr Black Belt in Karate; Sun Devils Paintball Team; Culinary Arts; Johnson & Wales U; New York Institute of Tech

MASHKULLI, MEDIJE; BROOKLYN, NY; JOHN DEWEY HS; (JR); Hnr Roll; Sci Fairs; St of Mnth; Lib Aide; Tchrs Aide; Former Drum Corps Member; Dentist; Medical Assistant; Long Island U, Brooklyn Campus; CUNY College of Technology

MASLANKOWSKI, MICHAEL; STATEN ISLAND, NY; PT RICHMOND HS; (SO); Ctznshp Aw; Hi Hnr Roll; Hnr Roll; St of Mnth; ROTC; Video Production; Video Graphics; New York U

MASLIN, ELLA; RHINEBECK, NY; OAKWOOD FRIENDS SCH; (SO); ArtClub; SP/M/VS; Stg Cre; Sccr (V); Tennis (V); Violin Student for Nine Years; Regular Community Service; Fashion Design; Fine Arts Degree; Bard College; New York U

MASON, ANDREA L; BALDWINSVILLE, NY; CW BAKER HS; (SR); Hi Hnr Roll; Nat Hon Sy; WWAHSS; Comm Volntr; Emplmnt; Key Club; Orch; Lcrsse (V L); Tennis (V L); SUNY Geneseo

MASON, DONNIE; MASTIC, NY; WILLIAM FLOYD HS; (FR); Hi Hnr Roll; Hnr Roll; Sci Fairs; Comm Volntr; Peer Tut/Med; Chrch Yth Grp; DARE; Mth Clb/Tm; Sci Clb; Bnd; Ch Chr; Jzz Bnd; Mch Bnd

MASON, SARAH E; BROOKLYN, NY; BISHOP KEARNEY HS; (FR); Hi Hnr Roll; Nat Sci Aw; Sci Fairs; Sci/Math Olympn; St of Mnth; Valdctrian; Comm Volntr; Peer Tut/Med; Sftball (J); Swmg (J); Yrbk (P); Softball / Swimming - Coach / Helper; Aquinas Club; Business Degree; Architecture; Syracuse U

MASONE, JACLYN; LEVITTOWN, NY; DIVISION AVE HS; (JR); F Lan Hn Soc; Hi Hnr Roll; Hnr Roll; MVP; Nat Hon Sy; Sci Fairs; St of Mnth; Emplmnt; Key Club; Mth Clb/Tm; Bskball (JC); Vllyball (VJC); All Conference-Volleyball; Pre-Med

MASSAMBA, RUDY; BRONX, NY; WALTON HS; (SR); Otst Ac Ach Awd; Perf Att; CR (P); Biology; Medicine; Harvard U; Princeton U

MASSEY, SARAH; JACKSON HEIGHTS, NY; CATHEDRAL HS; (FR); Hnr Roll; Comm Volntr; Hosp Aide; Ch Chr; SP/M/VS; Tennis; Vocal; Piano; Medicine / Biology; Dentistry; New York U; Sophie Davis School of Biomedical Education

MASSOBIR, FATHEMA L; FLUSHING, NY; BAYSIDE HS; (SO); Hnr Roll; St of Mnth; The United Federation of Teachers Award; President's Education Award Program; Pediatrician; Teacher of Biology; St John's U; New York U

MASTIN, CHRISTINA; WELLSVILLE, NY; WELLSVILLE HS; (SO); Hnr Roll; Sci Fairs; Comm Volntr; Scouts; SADD; International Clb; Chr; Sccr (V); Track (V); Wt Lftg; Stu Cncl (R); Odyssey of the Mind; International Club; Get Bachelor or Masters Degree in Law Enforcement; Psychology

MASTRANGELO, AMANDA; ROCKAWAY PARK, NY; LEON M GOLDSTEIN HS; (JR); Hnr Roll; Emplmnt; Photog; Stg Cre; Swmg; 2005 Discovery Award-Arts Connection

MASTRANTONIO, ANGELA; FARMINGDALE, NY; FARMINGDALE HS; (JR); F Lan Hn Soc; Hi Hnr Roll; Nat Hon Sy; Otst Ac Ach Awd; Comm Volntr; Hab For Humty Volntr; FTA; Key Club; Chrldg (V); Sch Ppr (E); Cheerleading Coach for Elementary School Age Girls; Pre-Med, Journalism; Pre-Dental; Hofstra U; Long Island U

MASTROCCO, ALYSSA; LEVITTOWN, NY; DIVISION AVE HS; (SO); F Lan Hn Soc; Hi Hnr Roll; Otst Ac Ach Awd; St of Mnth; WWAHSS; HO'Br Yth Ldrshp; Key Club; Orch; Sftball (VJ); Cl Off (V); Hugh O'Brian Youth Leadership Award Nominee; Attorney; Columbia U; New York U

MASTROIANNI, NICHOLAS M; SOMERS, NY; NORTH SALEM HS; (SO); Hi Hnr Roll; Otst Ac Ach Awd; WWAHSS; Comm Volntr; Chess; Mth Clb/Tm; Sci Clb; Bsball (V); Ice Hky (V); Math Honor Society; All League Ice Hockey Winner; Bio; Pre-Med; Boston College; Northeastern

MATHESON, PAUL; SEAFORD, NY; SEAFORD HS; (SO); All Am Sch; Hi Hnr Roll; Hnr Roll; WWAHSS; Cmptr Clb; Key Club; Bnd; Mch Bnd

MATHEW, JINCY; MERRICK, NY; SANFORD H CALHOUN HS; (SR); Hnr Roll; Comm Volntr; ArtClub; Chrch Yth Grp; Key Club; Sci Clb; Chr; Ch Chr; Bdmtn (V); Nursing; Molloy College

MATHEW, JUBIL; BROOKLYN, NY; MURRY BERGTRAUM HS; (JR); Hosp Aide; Chrch Yth Grp; Drma Clb; Bskball; Vllyball; Wt Lftg; Member, Deaf Education Empowerment & Friendship (DEAF Club); Accounting; Manhattan Community College

MATHEW, STANLEY; NEW HYDE PARK, NY; HERRICKS HS; (JR); MVP; Comm Volntr; Hosp Aide; Chrch Yth Grp; Bnd; Chr; Ch Chr; Mch Bnd; Bskball (J); Scr Kpr (J); Track (J); Outstanding Percussionist; Physician's Assistant; Pharmacy; Saint Johns U, Queens; Stony Brook U, Long Island

MATI, BLERONA; STATEN ISLAND, NY; SUSAN E WAGNER HS; (SO); Ctznshp Aw; Hi Hnr Roll; Hnr Roll; Sci Fairs; SP/M/VS; Writer/Publicist/ Publisher/News Editor; Business; New York U; Columbia U

MATOTT, VICKI; WESTERLO, NY; BERN-KNOX-WESTERLO HS; (SO); Otst Ac Ach Awd; Perf Att; Sci Fairs; St of Mnth; Comm Volntr; Peer Tut/ Med; ArtClub; DARE; Emplmnt; Key Club; Outdrs Clb; Photog; Prom Com; Sci Clb; Chr; Clr Grd; Stg Cre; Sccr (J); Yrbk (P); Psychiatric Nurse; Hudson Valley Community; Cobleskill Community College

MATOUK, KAREEN M; BROOKLYN, NY; BISHOP KEARNEY HS; (FR); Hi Hnr Roll; Otst Ac Ach Awd; Comm Volntr; Hosp Aide; Peer Tut/Med; DARE; Key Club; Mth Clb/Tm; Photog; Scouts; Chr; SP/M/VS; Chrldg (J); Skiing (J); Sftball (J); Triple "C" Award-Elliot Spitzer, Essay Contest Winner; Merit Scholarship Winner, Religion Fair, Spanish Award; Pediatrician; Medical Field; New York U; Yale

MATUSZEWKSI, AGNIESZKA; MONSEY, NY; SPRING VALLEY HS; (FR); Hnr Roll; WWAHSS; Key Club; Chr; Sccr (J); Psychology; Law; New York U

MAVUMKAL, MARY; YORKTOWN HEIGHTS, NY; YORKTOWN HS; (JR); Hi Hnr Roll; Hnr Roll; Nat Hon Sy; WWAHSS; Comm Volntr; Chrch Yth Grp; Track (V); Pharmacy; Pre-Medicine; Union College; St. John's U

MAYA, RICHARD; ELMHURST, NY; AVIATION HS; (JR); Aircraft Maintenance Technician; Vaughn College of Aeronautics

MAYBERRY, JAN; CATSKILL, NY; CATSKILL HS; (SO); Ctznshp Aw; Hi Hnr Roll; Hnr Roll; St of Mnth; Chrch Yth Grp; Excellence in a Foreign Language; Newspaper Journalism; Writing; New York U; Princeton U

MAYKISH, COLIN R; SHERBURNE, NY; VALLEY HEIGHTS CHRISTIAN AC; (FR); Nat Mrt LOC; Sci Fairs; 2nd Place Flight B Men's Archery League @ on the Spot Archery

MAYNUS, JULIANNE; COEYMANS HOLLOW, NY; RAVENA COEYMANS SELKIRK HS; (JR); Hi Hnr Roll; Hnr Roll; Nat Hon Sy; Chrldg (J); Mar Art; Track (V L); Winner of Times Union Holiday Art Contest; Passed Figure Drawing At Russell Sage; German Language & Culture; Conceptual Art; Rhode Island School of Design; Bridgewater State U

MAYO, JESSICA; ELMIRA, NY; SOUTHSIDE HS; (SR); Hi Hnr Roll; Hnr Roll; Otst Ac Ach Awd; Perf Att; Comm Volntr; Red Cr Aide; DARE; Key Club; Lib Aide; Vsity Clb; Bnd; Chr; Sccr (VJ); Track (V L); Vsy Clb (V); Treasure of Varsity Club; Early Childhood Development/Bachelor's; Corning Community College

MAZE, MELISSA; SILVER CREEK, NY; SILVER CREEK CTRL HS; (JR); Hi Hnr Roll; Hnr Roll; Nat Hon Sy; WWAHSS; Yth Ldrshp Prog; Comm Volntr; Red Cr Aide; 4-H; DECA; Emplmnt; Key Club; P to P St Amb Prg; Prom Com; Scouts; Vsity Clb; Bnd; Chr; SP/M/VS; Scr Kpr (V); Swmg (V CL); Track (V L); Vsy Clb (V); Cl Off (V); Yrbk (P); Athlete of the Week; Who's Who; Aerospace Engineering; Engineering; U of North Carolina; Ohio State U

MAZUR, CASSANDRA L; ITHACA, NY; ITHACA HS; (JR); Hi Hnr Roll; Hnr Roll; ArtClub; Photog; Track (V); Student of the Quarter in the Fine Arts Dept.; Master of Fine Arts; To Be an Artist; School of the Museum of Fine Arts, Boston; School of Visual Arts, New York, NY

MAZZARA, JOSEPH H; UTICA, NY; THOMAS R PROCTOR HS; (SO); Hi Hnr Roll; St of Mnth; St Optmst of Yr; WWAHSS; Emplmnt; Key Club; Bnd; Bsball (J); Who's Who American HS Students 2005 # 2004, American Legion Baseball; Engineering; Rochester Inst. Technology; Clarkson

MAZZONE, STEPHANIE; BUFFALO, NY; KENMORE WEST HS; (SR); Hnr Roll; WWAHSS; Spec Olymp Vol; Svce Clb; Bnd; Dnce; Social Working; Daemen College; Buffalo State College

MC ALLISTER, PAUL; GARNERVILLE, NY; NORTH ROCKLAND HS; (JR); Hi Hnr Roll; Hnr Roll; Key Club; Medicine; New York U; Yale U

MCATEER, GINA; FLORIDA, NY; SS SEWARD; (SO); Hi Hnr Roll; WWAHSS; Yth Ldrshp Prog; Comm Volntr; Emplmnt; Fr of Library; Prom Com; French Clb; Bnd; Chr; Dnce; Chrldg (V C); Cr Ctry

MC CABE, KRISTOPHER; KINGSTON, NY; (SO); Hi Hnr Roll; Hnr Roll; WWAHSS; Yth Ldrshp Prog; Comm Volntr; DARE; Key Club; NYLC; Cr Ctry (V); Swmg (V); Track (V); Teach Swim Lessons At YMCA; Teaching; Boston U; Boston College

MC CALL, MICHAEL; EAST HAMPTON, NY; EAST HAMPTON HS; (JR); Hi Hnr Roll; Hnr Roll; Key Club; Kwanza Clb; Golf (J); Tennis (VJ); Engineering

MC CARTHY, MAUREEN; BUFFALO, NY; WILLIAMSVILLE EAST; (SO); Hnr Roll; MVP; Perf Att; WWAHSS; Peer Tut/Med; Chrch Yth Grp; Drma Clb; Mod UN; Prom Com; Scouts; Dnce; Lcrsse (J); Scr Kpr (J); Sccr (JC); Track (V L); Cl Off (S); Rookie of the Year in Soccer; 13th Place on the National Spanish Exam; Medical Doctor; Bio Medical Researcher; U of Southern California; Northeastern U

MC CONNELL, ALICIA; BREWERTON, NY; PAUL V MOORE HS; (JR); Hi Hnr Roll; Hnr Roll; Comm Volntr; ArtClub; Cmptr Clb; Emplmnt; Photog; Scouts; Chr; Yrbk (P); Conflict Mediation; Top 99 Club; Arts; Math; Oswego Community College; U of Manchester

MC CORMACK, STEVEN; KINGSTON, NY; SAUGERTIES HS; (FR); Hi Hnr Roll; Hnr Roll; Otst Ac Ach Awd; Sci Fairs; Comm Volntr; Key Club; French Clb; Bskball (J); Sccr (J); Babe Ruth All-Star; French Club / Key Club; Physical Education Teacher; The College of St Rose; SUNY New Paltz

MC CORMICK, NICK; FREDONIA, NY; FREDONIA HS; (FR); Hi Hnr Roll; Chrch Yth Grp; Key Club; Mod UN; Quiz Bowl; Bnd; Chr; Dnce; Pep Bnd; Ftball (J); Track (J); Wrstlg (JC); Stu Cncl (R); Youth for Understanding Scholarship Winner; International Business; Linguistics; Fordham U; Rochester U

MC CRAY, ANDRE M D; BUFFALO, NY; RIVERSIDE HS; (SO); Hnr Roll; St of Mnth; Yth Ldrshp Prog; Comm Volntr; Chrch Yth Grp; Cmptr Clb; DARE; Photog; Chr; Ch Chr; Cr Ctry (V); Track (V); Sch Ppr (P); Business / Master's Degree; Social Science / Master's Degree; D'Youville College; Daemen College

MC CROBIE, WILLIAM; BUFFALO, NY; KENMORE WEST SR HS; (FR); Jr Rot; Nat Hon Sy; Perf Att; Comm Volntr; BPA; FBLA; Scouts; Skiing; Business Interact Club; Lawyer; Culinary Artist; Harvard Law School; UB

MC CUTCHEON, MANDI; BROCKPORT, NY; BROCKPORT HS; (FR); Hi Hnr Roll; Hnr Roll; Chrch Yth Grp; Chr; Ch Chr; Lcrsse (J); Track (J); Stu Cncl (R); CR (R); Masterminds Club; Law; Nurse; Pensacola Christian College; Stanford U

MC CUTCHEON, NATHAN; WESTFIELD, NY; RIPLEY CTRL SCH; (FR); F Lan Hn Soc; Hi Hnr Roll; Hnr Roll; Pres Ac Ftns Aw; Pres Sch; DARE; Bsball (JC); Ftball (J); Cl Off (P)

MC DONALD, ERIKA; ALTAMONT, NY; BERNE KNOX JR/SR HS; (FR); Ctznshp Aw; Hi Hnr Roll; Hnr Roll; Otst Ac Ach Awd; Comm Volntr; Chr; Sccr (J); Traveling Soccer Team; Orthopedics; Forensic Science

MC DONELL, MATTHEW R; WEST FALLS, NY; EAST AURORA HS; (SR); Hnr Roll; MVP; Comm Volntr; Red Cr Aide; DARE; Emplmnt; Outdrs Clb; Vsity Clb; Vllyball (V CL); National Technical Honor Society; Computer Information Systems; U At Buffalo; Erie Community College

MC DONNOUGH, JAMIELA; HEMPSTEAD, NY; SOUTHSIDE HS; (SO); Ctznshp Aw; Hi Hnr Roll; MVP; Nat Hon Sy; Sci Fairs; St of Mnth; Peer Tut/Med; Drma Clb; Photog; Sci Clb; Scouts; Tech Clb; Spanish Clb; Chr; Ch Chr; Chrldg (V); Track (C); Stu Cncl (V); Martial Arts Outside of School; National Institute of Health Program; Pre-Medicine; Spanish; Georgetown U; Columbia U

MC DOWL, DIANA M; MASPETH, NY; CHRIST THE KING HS; (SR); Hi Hnr Roll; Hnr Roll; Nat Hon Sy; Yth Ldrshp Prog; Comm Volntr; Drma Clb; Tchrs Aide; Dnce; CR (T); Elementary Education; Dance / Performing Arts; Queens College; Hunter College

MC ELRATH, MATTHEW J; SAUGERTIES, NY; SAUGERTIES HS; (SR); Hi Hnr Roll; Nat Hon Sy; Comm Volntr; Spec Olymp Vol; ArtClub; Emplmnt; Key Club; Prom Com; Tchrs Aide; SP/M/VS; Stg Cre; Cr Ctry (V CL); Sccr (J L); Track (V CL); Cl Off (V); Stu Cncl; Contributed the Most Award / Cross County Track 11th & 12th; Announcer of High School Daily Morning Announcements; SUNY Ulster County Community College; Joint Admissions Program with SUNY & New Paltz

MC ELROY, MYRTLE M; JAMAICA, NY; AUGUST MARTIN HS; (FR); Hnr Roll; Perf Att; St of Mnth; Key Club; BA Degree; MA Degree; New York U; Pace U

MC FADDEN, ESU; NEW YORK, NY; BEACON; (JR); Hnr Roll; Sccr (V)

Mc Cutcheon, Mandi
Brockport HS
Brockport, NY

Matouk, Kareen M
Bishop Kearney HS
Brooklyn, NY

Massamba, Rudy
Walton HS
Bronx, NY

Marziotto, Nicholas
Mac Arthur HS
Levittown, NY

Martins, Vanessa
Mineola HS
Mineola, NY

Marussich, Christina B
Saint Anthonys HS
Commack, NY

Massey, Sarah
Cathedral HS
Jackson Heights, NY

Mc Connell, Alicia
Paul V Moore HS
Brewerton, NY

Mc Elroy, Myrtle M
August Martin HS
Jamaica, NY

MC FADDEN, KRISTIE; BUFFALO, NY; WEST SENECA EAST SR HS; (SO); Hnr Roll; Kwnis Aw; Otst Ac Ach Awd; Pres Sch; St of Mnth; WWAHSS; Comm Volntr; DECA; Key Club; Lttrmn Clb; Lib Aide; Quill & Scroll; Quiz Bowl; Sci Clb; Clb; Bnd; Orch; Swmg (J); Stu Cncl (R); CR (R); Outstanding Musician; String Quartet; Biology; Music; U of Buffalo

MC FARLANE, CHRISSA; BRONX, NY; THE BRONX HS OF SCI; (SO); Hi Hnr Roll; Nat Ldrshp Svc; Salutrn; St of Mnth; Yth Ldrshp Prog; Chrch Yth Grp; Dbte Team; Off Aide; Tchrs Aide; Ch Chr; Dnce; Chrldg (V); Fncg (J); CR (P); Secretary of Black Organization of Student Strength; Member of the Pre-Med Club; Pre-Medicine; Cornell U; Emory U

MC FARLANE, DOMILA; SHIRLEY, NY; WILLIAM FLOYD HS; (JR); F Lan Hn Soc; Hi Hnr Roll; Hnr Roll; Nat Hon Sy; Otst Ac Ach Awd; Sci Fairs; WWAHSS; Comm Volntr; Hab For Humty Volntr; Spec Olymp Vol; DECA; Mth Clb/Tm; Quiz Bowl; Flg Crps; Track (V); Vllyball (J); Chief Justice Position in the N.Y. State Youth and Government Conference; Treasurer in Interact Club; Pre-Law; Business Administration; Yale U; New York U

MC GANN, TARYN; JAMESVILLE, NY; JAMESVILLE-DEWITT HS; (SO); Hi Hnr Roll; WWAHSS; Comm Volntr; Key Club; Scouts; Dnce; Scholastic Art Gold Award; Scholastic Art Silver Award

MC GEE, NAJIA M; ROCHESTER, NY; EDISON TECH SCH OF BUSINESS; (JR); Hnr Roll; WWAHSS; Comm Volntr; Hosp Aide; Chrch Yth Grp; Dbte Team; Ch Chr; Cr Ctry (V); Track (V); All League Award 55-60 Mtr Dash; 3rd Place in Monroe Cty High School Debate Competition; Criminal Justice/Law; Business/Accounting; U of Buffalo; Syracuse U

MC GOWAN, CHELSEA; CATSKILL, NY; SAUGERTIES HS; (FR); Hi Hnr Roll; Comm Volntr; Chrch Yth Grp; Emplmnt; Key Club; French Clb; Attended Band College Archaeology; Class Grade A; Archaeology; History; William and Mary; Cornell

MC GRANN, JAMES; STATEN ISLAND, NY; ST PETERS BOYS HS; (JR); Hi Hnr Roll; Otst Ac Ach Awd; Sci Fairs; Yth Ldrshp Prog; Comm Volntr; Hosp Aide; NYLC

MC GUIGAN, DENISE; HUNTINGTON, NY; HUNTINGTON HS; (SO); Hi Hnr Roll; Nat Hon Sy; Pres Sch; Hab For Humty Volntr; Key Club; Tennis (J); CR (R); Crew Team; Natural Helpers (Club); Architecture; Marine Biologist

MC HUGH, CAITLIN M; NORTH BABYLON, NY; NORTH BABYLON HS; (JR); Hi Hnr Roll; Hnr Roll; Nat Hon Sy; Hosp Aide; SADD; Lcrsse (J); Tennis (J); Students for a Better World; Student Advisory; Culinary Arts

MC INTOSH, DOMINIQUE H; SAINT ALBANS, NY; BROOKLYN TECH HS; (JR); Ctznshp Aw; Hnr Roll; Perf Att; Salutrn; St of Mnth; Chrch Yth Grp; Drma Clb; Off Aide; Ch Chr; SP/M/VS; Seekers Christian Club; Nursing; Teaching

MC INTOSH, MONIQUE; W HEMPSTEAD, NY; WEST HEMPSTEAD HS; (SO); Hnr Roll; WWAHSS; FBLA; Key Club; SADD; Chr; Track (J); Awarded for NYSSMA Solo; Biology

MC INTYRE, BREANNA; LAUREL, NY; MC GANN MERCY; (JR); Prom Com; Bskball (V); Sccr (V); Track (V); Vsy Clb (V); Cl Off (P); Stu Cncl (R); CR (P)

MC INTYRE, FANTASIA; MOUNT VERNON, NY; A B DAVIS MS; (MS); Ctznshp Aw; Hnr Roll; Sci Clb; Scouts; Fashion Designing; Stockbroker; Miami U; Katharine Gibbs School

MC INTYRE, KRISTEN; LOCKPORT, NY; ROYALTON HARTLAND; (SR); Ctznshp Aw; Hi Hnr Roll; MVP; Nat Hon Sy; WWAHSS; Comm Volntr; Red Cr Aide; Prom Com; Vsity Clb; Bnd; Bskball (V CL); Fld Hky (V CL); Sftball (V CL); Yrbk (R); First Team All-League Basketball & Field Hockey; 2nd Team All Western New York-Field Hockey; Mathematics Major; Nazareth - Attending

MC KAY, MELISSA; BRONX, NY; BRONX LEADERSHIP AC II; (JR); Hi Hnr Roll; Yth Ldrshp Prog; DARE; Mus Clb; Scouts; Acpl Chr; Dnce; Stu Cncl (P); Pre-Med / MD; Vocal Music / Performance; SUNY Binghamton; Spelman College

MC KENNA, SUZANNE M; GARDEN CITY, NY; SACRED HEART AC; (JR); Nat Hon Sy; WWAHSS; Hosp Aide; Emplmnt; Mth Clb/Tm; Spanish Clb; Ch Chr; Tennis; Track

MC KENZIE, DYLAN; STONY BROOK, NY; ST ANTHONY'S HS; (JR); Nat Hon Sy; Peer Tut/Med; Chr; Ice Hky (J); Sch Ppr (P); Psychology; Film; New York U; Stanford

MC KENZIE, HUGH S; BROOKLYN, NY; DANIEL HAND HS; (JR); Hnr Roll; Salutrn; Comm Volntr; Peer Tut/Med; Chrch Yth Grp; DARE; Emplmnt; Ch Chr; Bskball (J); Sccr (VJ); Track (VJ); Cl Off (R); Stu Cncl (R); Most Improved Soccer Player Award; Science Award; Business Administration/Law; Pre-Med/Pediatrics; Georgetown U; Washington U

MCKINNEY, LAUREN; WATERTOWN, NY; WATERTOWN HS; (JR); Hi Hnr Roll; MVP; Key Club; P to P St Amb Prg; Sftball (V); Swmg (V); Vllyball (V); Physical Therapy; St Francis U

MC KOY, NAKEBA; BROOKLYN, NY; NAZARETH REG HS; (FR); Hi Hnr Roll; Hnr Roll; Nat Mrt LOC; Sci Fairs; Yth Ldrshp Prog; Comm Volntr; Emplmnt; Lib Aide; Photog; Sci Clb; French Clb; Sftball (J); Stu Cncl (R); CR (R); School Choir, Leadership Program, Principal's List; Accepted in the HCPI Program At Downstate Center; Veterinary Sciences or Marine Biology/ Math; Master's and PhD-Real Estate; Stanford U/Brooklyn College; Tuskegee College

MC LAUGHLAN, SEAN; SAYVILLE, NY; SAYVILLE HS; (JR); Hi Hnr Roll; Hnr Roll; Nat Hon Sy; Otst Ac Ach Awd; Pres Ac Ftns Aw; Amnsty Intl; Comm Volntr; DARE; FBLA; Key Club; Quiz Bowl; Bskball (VJ); Mar Art; Sccr (VJ); MBA; Education; U of North Carolina; Boston U

MC LAUGHLIN, DANIELLE; STATEN ISLAND, NY; MOORE CATHOLIC HS; (JR); All Am Sch; MVP; Nat Hon Sy; USAA; Comm Volntr; ArtClub; Emplmnt; Prom Com; Bskball (V L); Sccr (V L); Stu Cncl (R); Yrbk (R); Congressional Award Silver Medal & Bronze Medal; 2003 Presidential Service Award; Physical Therapy; Education; Loyola College; Wagner College

MC LAUGHLIN, SAMANTHA; BROOKLYN, NY; NEW UTRECHT HS; (SO); Tchrs Aide; Bnd; Mch Bnd; Chrldg (V); Stu Cncl (R); Basketball (Outside of School); Piano Classes; Law; Harvard Law School; Benedict College

MC LEAN, BROOK; STATEN ISLAND, NY; CURTIS HS; (SO); Otst Ac Ach Awd; St of Mnth; Comm Volntr; Chrch Yth Grp; Ch Chr; Cr Ctry (J); Track (J); Indoor & Outdoor Track; Black Achievement Award; Lawyer (Criminal Law); Contract Law; Howard U; Spelman College

MC LEAN, CHRISTINA; POUGHKEEPSIE, NY; POUGHKEEPSIE HS; (JR); 4H Awd; Hi Hnr Roll; Hnr Roll; Otst Ac Ach Awd; Perf Att; Double Major - Doctor / Lawyer; New York U

MC LEAN, FATIMA J E L; BROOKLYN, NY; BUSHWICK HS; (SR); Hnr Roll; Comm Volntr; Chrch Yth Grp; Emplmnt; Jr Ach; Ch Chr; Dnce; Veterinarian Medicine; LaGuardia College

MC LEAN, JEAME; BRONX, NY; HARRY S TRUMAN HS; (FR); Hnr Roll; Chr; Bdmtn; Vllyball; Criminal Law; Psychology; NYU; Princeton U

MC LEOD, JOEDIA; BRONX, NY; EVANDER CHILDS HS; (SO); Gov Hnr Prg; Hnr Roll; Nat Hon Sy; Otst Ac Ach Awd; Perf Att; Peer Tut/Med; 4-H; ArtClub; Chrch Yth Grp; Emplmnt; Mus Clb; English Clb; Ch Chr; Dnce; Chrldg (V); Fld Hky (J); Vllyball (J); Cl Off (P); Sch Ppr (E); Nursing; Teaching; Monroe College; Lehman College

MC MAHON, AMANDA; COLLINS, NY; GOWANDA HS; (SR); Hi Hnr Roll; Hnr Roll; Comm Volntr; Emplmnt; Lib Aide; Prom Com; French Clb; Wrstlg (VJ); French Club Secretary; Model Office Student; Business Administration; Houghton College

MC NAMARA, SHANNON; LEVITTOWN, NY; ST ANTHONY'S HS; (JR); Hi Hnr Roll; Nat Hon Sy; CARE; Comm Volntr; Emplmnt; Svce Clb; Orch; SP/M/VS; Secretary Of The Orchestra; Secondary Education; English; College of William and Mary; Fordham U

MC NEAL, JANELLE; BROOKLYN, NY; SHEEPSHEAD BAY HS; (JR); Hnr Roll; WWAHSS; Peer Tut/Med; Mth Clb/Tm; Bnd; Dnce; Medicine Sciences

MC NEIL, CANDICE; BINGHAMTON, NY; BINGHAMTON HS; (JR); Hnr Roll; Emplmnt; FTA; Outdrs Clb; Sci Clb; SADD; Chr; Track (V); Stu Cncl (R); Sister 2 Sister, Dance Club, Yes Club; Dollars 4 Scholars, Adopt a Family (Christmas); Film Directing / Screen Writing; Fashion Design; Scripps College; Bryn Mawr College

MC PHILLIPS, KATE; LAKE GEORGE, NY; LAKE GEORGE HS; (FR); Ctznshp Aw; Hi Hnr Roll; Nat Hon Sy; Comm Volntr; Key Club; Bskball (J); Vllyball (J); Junior National Honor Society; Volunteer At Double H Hole in the Woods for 3 Years; Criminal Psychology; Education; Simmons College; Northeastern U

MC READY, KEVIN; MIDDLE VILLAGE, NY; CHRIST THE KING HS; (SR); Hnr Roll; Chrch Yth Grp; Graphic Design; Briarcliffe College

MC TIERNAN, SARAH P; SCHENECTADY, NY; SCHENECTADY HS; (FR); Hi Hnr Roll; Hnr Roll; Hosp Aide; Dnce; Vllyball (C); SUNY Albany

MEAD, ALLISON; FARMINGDALE, NY; FARMINGDALE HS; (SR); F Lan Hn Soc; Hi Hnr Roll; Nat Hon Sy; Nat Sci Aw; Pres Sch; Sci Fairs; Sci/ Math Olympn; St of Mnth; WWAHSS; Comm Volntr; Emplmnt; Key Club; Mus Clb; Sci Clb; Vsity Clb; French Clb; Dnce; Orch; SP/M/VS; Swmg (V CL); Intel STS Semi-Finalist; Intel ISEF County Semi-Finalist; Medical-Ophthalmology; Will Be Attending Adelphi U Honors College

MEADE, ALISON; WAPPINGERS FALLS, NY; ROY C KETCHAM HS; (JR); Hi Hnr Roll; Hnr Roll; Sci Fairs; Drma Clb; Scouts; Tmpl Yth Grp; Vsity Clb; Bnd; Chr; SP/M/VS; Stg Cre; Gmnstcs (V L); Acting; Film / Television; New York U

MECEVIC, NINO; WEBSTER, NY; WEBSTER THOMAS; (SO); F Lan Hn Soc; Hi Hnr Roll; Nat Hon Sy; Ski and Snowboard Club; Film Production; Computer Science; Rochester Institute of Technology; U of Rochester

MEDELLIN, JESSICA A; BETHPAGE, NY; ISLAND TREES HS; (JR); Hnr Roll; Comm Volntr; Emplmnt; Key Club; Photog; Prom Com; Scouts; Chr; Bdmtn (V); Poem Published 2000; Primary Education Teacher; Physical Therapist; Manhattenville; C W Post

MEDINA, JEFRIE; BRONX, NY; COLUMBUS HS; (SO); Perf Att; Comm Volntr; Ftball (J); Chappaqua Summer Scholarship Program; Syracuse U; Brown U

MEDITZ, ERICA; MERRICK, NY; CALHOUN HS; (JR); Hnr Roll; Nat Mrt LOC; Comm Volntr; Hosp Aide; Key Club; Outdrs Clb; Bnd; Mch Bnd; Cr Ctry (V); Track (V); Played Piano for 8 Years

MEEHAN, SAMUEL R; CHAZY, NY; CHAZY CTRL RURAL SCH; (SR); Bnd; Mch Bnd; SP/M/VS; Stg Cre; Bsball (V L); Sccr (VJCL); Cl Off (V); Stu Cncl (V); CR (R); NY Boys State; American Legion Oratory; Physics; Pre-Med; U of New Hampshire

MEEKS, SADE'; BRONX, NY; CATHEDRAL HS; (FR); Hnr Roll; Nat Mrt LOC; Perf Att; Sci Fairs; Comm Volntr; Chess; DARE; Tchrs Aide; Ultra Sound Technologist; Fashion Designer; Long Island U; Pennsylvania State U

MEHTA, HINAL; ELMHURST, NY; BRONX HS OF SCIENCE; (SO); Hnr Roll; Nat Hon Sy; Otst Ac Ach Awd; Sci Fairs; WWAHSS; Comm Volntr; Peer Tut/Med; Key Club; Lib Aide; Mth Clb/Tm; Off Aide; Tchrs Aide; Tmpl Yth Grp; Won Writing and Art Competitions; Won Silver Medal in Math Fair Competition; Medicine; New York U; Columbia U

MEHTA, ISHA; WHITESTONE, NY; QUEENS HS FOR THE SCIENCES; (JR); Hnr Roll; Nat Hon Sy; Sci Fairs; WWAHSS; Comm Volntr; Jr Ach; Key Club; Mth Clb/Tm; Sch Ppr (E, R); Yrbk; President of Key Club and Arista-National Honor Roll; Recipient of Presidential Award for Excellence.; Pre-Medicine; History; U of Pennsylvania; Sophia Davis School of Bioengineering At City College

MEJIA, RICHARD; BELLEROSE, NY; ST MARY'S HS; (JR); Hi Hnr Roll; Hnr Roll; Comm Volntr; Peer Tut/Med; Cmptr Clb; Drma Clb; Spanish Clb; Skiing (V); Shepard - Help Underclassmen / Act as Role Model; Freshmen Camp Leader; Computer Sciences; Physics / Chemistry; New York Institute of Technology

MELENDEZ, LEYDA E; UNIONDALE, NY; UNIONDALE HS; (SO); Hi Hnr Roll; St of Mnth; FBLA; Key Club; Red Cross Club Member; Science Honor Society Member; Education; Dowling College

MELENDY, MORGAN; ELMIRA, NY; ELMIRA FREE AC; (JR); Hi Hnr Roll; Nat Hon Sy; Comm Volntr; Drma Clb; Key Club; Stg Cre; Dvng (V); Sccr (J); Track (V)

MELINDO, CHARLENE; SARATOGA SPGS, NY; SARATOGA SPRINGS JR HS; MS; Hi Hnr Roll; Hnr Roll; Otst Ac Ach Awd; Pres Ac Ftns Aw; Mus Clb; Dnce; Orch; Tennis (J); Stu Cncl

MELKUN, STEPHANIE E; SEAFORD, NY; SEAFORD HS; (JR); Hi Hnr Roll; Hnr Roll; WWAHSS; Key Club; Bnd; Mch Bnd; Sccr (V); Sftball (V); All-Star Athletic Award; Physical Education; Coaching; Manhattan College; Adelphi U

MELUZIO, JACQUELYN; LYNBROOK, NY; LYNBROOK SR HS; (JR); Hi Hnr Roll; Hnr Roll; MVP; Nat Hon Sy; Peer Tut/Med; ArtClub; Chrch Yth Grp; P to P St Amb Prg; SADD; Vsity Clb; Spanish Clb; SP/M/VS; Bskball (V); Sccr (V); Track (V); Sch Ppr (E); Athletes Creating Excellence; All Class A-Soccer; Art Education; Physical Education; Adelphi U; SUNY New Paltz

MENARD, ALYSSA; HAVERSTRAW, NY; NORTH ROCKLAND HS; (JR); Hnr Roll; Otst Ac Ach Awd; WWAHSS; Key Club; SADD; Key Club Bulletin Editor and Secretary; Black Achievement Award Recipient; Public Relations; Sports & Marketing; Syracuse U; Fordham U

MENDELSON, STEPHANIE T; LEVITTOWN, NY; ISLAND TREES HS; (SR); Hi Hnr Roll; Nat Hon Sy; USAA; WWAHSS; Comm Volntr; Drma Clb; Emplmnt; Key Club; Tmpl Yth Grp; Bnd; Dnce; Jzz Bnd; Mch Bnd; Ftball (J); Skt Tgt Sh (VJ); Adv Cncl (P); Cl Off (V); Stu Cncl (P, V); Lit Mag (R); Yrbk; Congressional Youth Leadership Council National Scholar.; Tri-M-Musical Honor Society; Architecture; Rensselaer Polytechnic Institute

MENDEZ, CASSANDRA L; CARMEL, NY; CARMEL HS; (SR); Hi Hnr Roll; Hnr Roll; WWAHSS; Emplmnt; Spanish Clb; Yrbk; Step Team; Biochemistry; Engineering; SUNY Albany; Pace U

MENDEZ, DANNY; RIDGEWOOD, NY; MURRY BERGTRAUM HS BUSINESS; (FR); All Am Sch; Ctznshp Aw; Hi Hnr Roll; Hnr Roll; MVP; Nat Hon Sy; Otst Ac Ach Awd; St of Mnth; WWAHSS; Yth Ldrshp Prog; Comm Volntr; Peer Tut/Med; Red Cr Aide; Aqrium Clb; Biology Clb; Chess; Chrch Yth Grp; Emplmnt; FCA; Mus Clb; Outdrs Clb; Ch Chr; Clr Grd; Drl Tm; Flg Crps; Bdmtn (V); Bsball (V); Bskball; Ftball (J); Gmnstcs (V); Sccr (V); Sftball (V); Swmg (V); Cl Off (R); Yrbk (R); Lawyer; Baseball Player; Harvard School; NYU College

Mead, Allison
Farmingdale HS
Farmingdale, NY

Mc Gowan, Chelsea
Saugerties HS
Catskill, NY

Mc Gee, Najia M
Edison Tech Sch Of Business
Rochester, NY

National
Honor Roll
Spring 2005

Mc Farlane, Chrissa
The Bronx HS Of Sci
Bronx, NY

Mc Kenzie, Hugh S
Daniel Hand HS
Brooklyn, NY

Melindo, Charlene
Saratoga Springs JR HS
Saratoga Spgs, NY

MENDEZ, LLOYD; BROOKLYN, NY; NEW UTRECHT HS; (SR); 4H Awd; Nat Hon Sy; Nat Ldrshp Svc; Nat Sci Aw; Otst Ac Ach Awd; Sci Fairs; Comm Volntr; Hosp Aide; Peer Tut/Med; 4-H; Outdrs Clb; Svce Clb; SP/M/VS; Bsball (V); CR (R); Business Administration; Professional Pilot Program; Baruch College; Brooklyn College & Pace U

MENDS, JULIANA A; YONKERS, NY; LINCOLN HS; (SO); Hi Hnr Roll; Hnr Roll; Perf Att; Comm Volntr; Dbte Team; Outdrs Clb; Schol Bwl; Bskball (J); Ftball (C); Sftball (J); Nominated in Who's Who Among American HS Students; Made Principals List (Freshman Year); Law Major; Business; Harvard; Yale

MENSAH, ASHLEY; NEW CITY, NY; CLARKSTOWN HS NORTH; (JR); Hnr Roll; MVP; Nat Mrt LOC; WWAHSS; Comm Volntr; Hosp Aide; Peer Tut/Med; Chrch Yth Grp; Emplmnt; Vsity Clb; Spanish Clb; Chr; Ch Chr; Dnce; SP/M/VS; Vsy Clb (V); Black Achievement Award; Honors Showcase (For Mathematics); Pre-Med; Business; New York U; Stony Brook U

MENSAH, DESIREE A; BRONX, NY; WALTON HS; (JR); F Lan Hn Soc; Perf Att; Comm Volntr; Hosp Aide; Red Cr Aide; Tchrs Aide; Vsity Clb; Bskball (J); Cr Ctry (V); Cr Ct Ski (J); Tennis (J); Track (V); Vllyball (J); Wt Lftg (V); Associates Degree in Nursing; Bachelor in Respiratory Therapy

MENZIES, MARC; LEVITTOWN, NY; ISLAND TREES HS; (JR); Hi Hnr Roll; Hnr Roll; Nat Hon Sy; WWAHSS; Drma Clb; Mus Clb; Scouts; Tech Clb; Wdwrkg Clb; Orch; SP/M/VS; Honor Society (Keter Tarah); Tri-M Music Honor Society; Physics Major; Music Minor

MERCADO, DANIELLE; RIDGEWOOD, NY; ARCHBISHOP MOLLOY HS; (JR); Hi Hnr Roll; Hnr Roll; Comm Volntr; Emplmnt; Prom Com; Vsity Clb; Swmg (VJ); Pre-Med; Biochemistry

MERCADO, LEISY; NEW YORK, NY; HS FOR MEDIA & COMMUNICATIONS; (JR); Comm Volntr; Peer Tut/Med; Ch Chr; Bskball; Gmnstcs; Doctor; Psychologist

MERCHANT, AKEEL; BROOKLYN, NY; ABRAHAM LINCOLN HS; (SR); F Lan Hn Soc; Hi Hnr Roll; Kwnis Aw; Nat Hon Sy; Nat Sci Aw; Otst Ac Ach Awd; Pres Sch; Sci Fairs; Valdctrian; WWAHSS; Comm Volntr; Hosp Aide; Peer Tut/Med; Biology Clb; Cmptr Clb; Dbte Team; Emplmnt; Lib Aide; Mth Clb/Tm; Outdrs Clb; Sci Clb; Bnd; SP/M/VS; Bskball (J); Swmg (J); Tennis; Vllyball (J); Lit Mag (R); Sch Ppr (E); AP Scholar with Distinction Award; 5th Place Finalist in Junior Humanities Symposium Regional Science Fair; Biology; Rensselaer Polytechnic Institute

MERO, CLAIRE E; WILLSBORO, NY; WILLSBORO CTRL SCH; (FR); Hi Hnr Roll; Hnr Roll; Chrch Yth Grp; Bskball (J); Sccr (J); Sftball (J); Catholic Youth Ministry

MESHCHERYAKOVA, MARIYA; BROOKLYN, NY; NEW UTRECHT HS; (FR); Hnr Roll; Comm Volntr; Peer Tut/Med; ArtClub; Key Club; Off Aide; Chr; Stg Cre; Outside Volleyball Club; Manages/Owns Collaborative Writing Site; Business; Law; New York U; Columbia U

MESONERO, CHRIS; LEVITTOWN, NY; DIVISION AVE HS; (SO); F Lan Hn Soc; Hi Hnr Roll; WWAHSS; Key Club; Sccr; Wt Lftg; Consistently Meeting Honor Grade Status; Harvard; Princeton U

MESSINA, MELINDA K; ALTAMONT, NY; GUIDERLAND HS; (JR); Nat Hon Sy; Comm Volntr; Peer Tut/Med; Drma Clb; Key Club; Chr; Stg Cre; Junior National Honor Society; Academic Achievements; Theatre Arts/Acting; English; Emerson College; Drew U

MESSINA, NICOLE; STATEN ISLAND, NY; ST JOHN VILLA AC; (JR); Otst Ac Ach Awd; St of Mnth; Comm Volntr; ArtClub; Cmptr Clb; Drma Clb; Emplmnt; JSA; Photog; Prom Com; SP/M/VS; Yrbk (E, P); Education; Art

MESSMER, PETE; INTERLAKEN, NY; SOUTH SENECA JR/SR HS; (JR); Hi Hnr Roll; Hnr Roll; MVP; Otst Ac Ach Awd; AL Aux Boys; Drma Clb; Bnd; Jzz Bnd; Stg Cre; Ftball (V); 2005 Boy's State Delegate; Football Team Captain; Music; Medicine; St John's U; Middlebury College

MEUCCI, SARAH E; BALDWINSVILLE, NY; CHARLES W BAKER HS; (SO); Hi Hnr Roll; WWAHSS; Key Club; Mth Clb/Tm; Scouts; Bnd; Mch Bnd; Yrbk (P); Key Club; Wood Wind Ensemble; Pharmacy

MEYER, ALYSHIA; ATTICA, NY; ATTICA SR HS; (SO); Comm Volntr; Drma Clb; Emplmnt; SP/M/VS; Stg Cre; Stu Cncl (R); Drama Club Treasurer; United Schools In Action Member - 4 Years; Law; Criminal Justice / Forensics; SUNY Buffalo; SUNY Geneseo

MEYER, CATHERINE; BUFFALO, NY; KENMORE WEST SR HS; (FR); Hnr Roll; Jr Rot; Perf Att; St of Mnth; Comm Volntr; Hosp Aide; Peer Tut/Med; Chrch Yth Grp; Svce Clb; Bnd; Mch Bnd; Pep Bnd; Major in Computers; Erie Community College; U of Buffalo

MEYER, CHRISTINA; BUFFALO, NY; WILLIAMSVILLE EAST HS; (SR); Hi Hnr Roll; Hnr Roll; Nat Hon Sy; Comm Volntr; Prom Com; CR (R); BS in Elementary Education; SUNY At Geneseo

MEYER, LINDSAY; SHIRLEY, NY; WILLIAM FLOYD HS; (JR); F Lan Hn Soc; Hi Hnr Roll; Hnr Roll; Nat Hon Sy; Sci Fairs; WWAHSS; Yth Ldrshp Prog; Comm Volntr; Peer Tut/Med; DECA; Mth Clb/Tm; NYLC; Quiz Bowl; Spanish Clb; Chr; Bskball (J); Lcrsse (J L); VP of FLHS (Foreign Language Honor Society); VP of NYS, MHS (NYS Math Honor Society); Corporate Law; Mathematics; Fordham U; Columbia U

MEYERS, ALLYSE D; WATERTOWN, NY; WATERTOWN HS; (JR); Hnr Roll; WWAHSS; Comm Volntr; Emplmnt; Off Aide; PP Ftbl (J); CR (R); Clark-Atlanta U; U of North Carolina-Chapel Hill

MIAN, SUMRA G; NEW YORK, NY; DOMINICAN AC; (JR); All Am Sch; Hnr Roll; Perf Att; Sci Fairs; St of Mnth; USAA; WWAHSS; Comm Volntr; Red Cr Aide; Biology Clb; Lib Aide; Outdrs Clb; Sci Clb; Svce Clb; Stg Cre; Yrbk (E)

MICELI, CRISTINA; NEW HYDE PARK, NY; GREAT NECK SOUTH HS; (JR); Perf Att; Comm Volntr; Key Club; Bnd; Chrldg (VJC); Lcrsse (J); CR (R); Participant in 2005 NCTE Writing Contest; Attended 2004 Leadership Conference; Medicine

MICHAEL, NICOLE M.; LAWRENCE, NY; LAWRENCE HS; (JR); Hnr Roll; St of Mnth; WWAHSS; Comm Volntr; Spec Olymp Vol; ArtClub; Chrch Yth Grp; Emplmnt; Key Club; Off Aide; Tchrs Aide; Stg Cre; Forensic-Criminology; Marine Biology, Elementary Ed.

MICHAUD, ELIZABETH; HOLLIS, NY;; Hnr Roll; Otst Ac Ach Awd; Perf Att; Sci Fairs; St of Mnth; Comm Volntr; Chrch Yth Grp; Emplmnt; Jr Ach; Mus Clb; Scouts; Chr; Ch Chr; Pathfinder Club; Law / Criminal Law; Harvard U Law

MICHEL, MARIE F; BROOKLYN, NY; EDWARD R MURROW HS; (FR); Nat Mrt LOC; Hosp Aide; Mus Clb; Tchrs Aide; French Clb; Dnce; Sccr (V); Doctor; Nurse; Brooklyn College; Hunter College

MICHEL, REGINE S; HEMPSTEAD, NY; HEMPSTEAD HS; (JR); Hnr Roll; Nat Hon Sy; Nat Mrt LOC; Nat Stu Ath Day Aw; Otst Ac Ach Awd; Sci Fairs; St of Mnth; Hosp Aide; ArtClub; Chrch Yth Grp; Pep Squd; Chr; Ch Chr; Dnce; Bdmtn (V); Swmg (J); Step Team Captain; I Would Like to Major in Pre-Med.; Howard U; Yale U

MICHELS, JULIE R; EAST NASSAU, NY; COLUMBIA HS; (SO); 4H Awd; Hi Hnr Roll; Hnr Roll; WWAHSS; Comm Volntr; 4-H; ArtClub; DARE; Key Club; Sci Clb; SADD; Chr; Dnce; Stg Cre; Sch Ppr (R); Science Olympiad; Forensic Science; Hudson Valley Community College

MICHEVA, NORA; CTREACH, NY; WARD MELVILLE HS; (JR); Hi Hnr Roll; Nat Hon Sy; Nat Mrt LOC; Sci Fairs; Sci/Math Olympn; Comm Volntr; Mth Clb/Tm; Mus Clb; Sci Clb; Chr; Dnce; Sch Ppr (R); Intel ISEF Finalist; Fluent in English, Bulgarian and Japanese; Chemistry; International Relations; Massachusetts Institute of Technology; Columbia U

MIELNICKI, MELISSA; MOUNTAIN DALE, NY; FALLSBURG HS; (SO); Hi Hnr Roll; Key Club; Mth Clb/Tm; Bnd; Tennis (V); Cl Off (R); Stu Cncl (R); President of Key Club; Financial Administrator; Accountant; Stanford; Southwest Florida College

MIGDEL, DAINA L S; MONROE, NY; MONROE-WOODBURY HS; (FR); Hi Hnr Roll; Hnr Roll; Nat Ldrshp Svc; Otst Ac Ach Awd; Perf Att; Yth Ldrshp Prog; Comm Volntr; Peer Tut/Med; Red Cr Aide; Drma Clb; FBLA; Pep Squd; Scouts; Tmpl Yth Grp; Bnd; Chr; Ch Chr; Jzz Bnd; Girl Scout Silver and Bronze Award Recipient; Soccer Goalie / Basketball Team; Paralegal

MIKOLINACZ, ANDREW; BRONX, NY; BLESSED SACRAMENT SAINT GABRIEL; (JR); Hnr Roll; Comm Volntr; Sci Clb; Stu Cncl (R)

MILES, ALANA; SCHENECTADY, NY; SCHENECTADY HS; (SO); Hnr Roll; WWAHSS; Chrch Yth Grp; Ch Chr; Foreign Language Merit Society; Education; Howard U; Spelman College

MILES, AMANDA M; FRANKFORT, NY; FRANKFORT-SCHUYLER CTRL HS; (JR); DAR; Hi Hnr Roll; Nat Hon Sy; WWAHSS; Yth Ldrshp Prog; Comm Volntr; Peer Tut/Med; AL Aux Girls; Chrch Yth Grp; DARE; Emplmnt; FBLA; HO'Br Yth Ldrshp; Key Club; Mus Clb; Chr; SP/M/VS; Swg Chr; Bskball (V L); Yrbk (E, R, P); Secondary Education; Psychology; Syracuse U; U of Massachusetts

MILES, HANNIBAL; BALDWIN, NY; LONG ISLAND SCH FOR GIFTED; (FR); Otst Ac Ach Awd; Sci/Math Olympn; Peer Tut/Med; DARE; Dbte Team; Key Club; Mth Clb/Tm; Tchrs Aide; Bskball; Sftball; Stu Cncl; Yrbk (E); Athletic Awards 2004 / 2005; Science Award; Law; Business; Harvard U; Yale U

MILKS, KRISTALYN N; SILVER CREEK, NY; SILVER CREEK HS; (JR); Hnr Roll; Comm Volntr; Peer Tut/Med; DECA; Key Club; Photog; Prom Com; Vsity Clb; French Clb; Chr; SP/M/VS; Skiing (VJ); Vllyball (VJ); Key Club Member / Officer - 3 Yrs; Commercial Photography; Musician; The Art Institute of Philadelphia; U of the Arts Philadelphia

MILLER, ANTONETTE R; NEW YORK, NY; HS FOR MEDIA & COMMUNICATIONS; (SR); Hnr Roll; Lib Aide; Yrbk (P); Journalist-Writer; A B; Brooklyn College; Lehman College

MILLER, CHRISTINA R; JAMESVILLE, NY;; Hi Hnr Roll; WWAHSS; Comm Volntr; Hosp Aide; Chrch Yth Grp; Key Club; Scouts; CR; Sunny Sensational Kid

MILLER, CHRISTOPHER D; HUNTINGTN STA, NY; COMMACK HS; (JR); Comm Volntr; Spec Olymp Vol; Cougar Athletics - Sports Club Assistant; Psychology; Film; Columbia U; New York U

MILLER, DANIEL G; SLINGERLANDS, NY; CHRISTIAN BROTHERS AC; (JR); Hnr Roll; WWAHSS; Chrch Yth Grp; ROTC; Golf; Skiing

MILLER, ERIC; SAUGERTIES, NY; SAUGERTIES HS; (SO); Hi Hnr Roll; Otst Ac Ach Awd; Sci Fairs; St of Mnth; WWAHSS; Comm Volntr; Peer Tut/Med; Key Club; Mth Clb/Tm; Spanish Clb; Bnd; Golf (V L); Ice Hky (J); Lcrsse (V L); Tennis (V L); Black Belt in Tae Kwon Do; 1170 on SAT in 9th Grade; Computer Sciences; Engineering; Yale U

MILLER, ERIN M; STATEN ISLAND, NY; FIORELLO H LA GUARDIA HS; (JR); Hi Hnr Roll; Hnr Roll; Pres Sch; Sci Fairs; ArtClub; Photog; Vsity Clb; GAA (V); Sftball (V); My Art Work Has Been Exhibited in the Schools Gallery; I Won the Coaches' Award for Softball; Graphic Design; Fashion Design; U of the Arts; School of the Museum of Fine Arts

MILLER, JACQUELINE A; MASTIC, NY; WILLIAM FLOYD HS; (SO); Ctznshp Aw; Hnr Roll; Nat Hon Sy; Sci Fairs; St of Mnth; Student of the Quarter; Science Fair Award; Culinary Institute of New York

MILLER, JEREMY R; SYRACUSE, NY; ONONDAGA JR/SR HS; (FR); Hnr Roll; Comm Volntr; ArtClub; Chess; Drma Clb; Mus Clb; German Clb; Chr; SP/M/VS; Track (V); Lit Mag (E); Founder of the Comic Book Club; Business Owner of a Record Co.; Work for Marvel Comics; UCLA

MILLER, LAUREN A; MASSAPEQUA, NY; LONG ISLAND LUTHERAN HS; (SO); F Lan Hn Soc; Hi Hnr Roll; Nat Hon Sy; Chrch Yth Grp; SADD; Spanish Clb; Bnd; Ch Chr; Spanish Honor Society; Childhood Education; Pediatrician; Columbia; New York U

MILLER, MICHAEL; PLAINVIEW, NY; PLAINVIEW OLD BETHPAGE JFK HS; (JR); Hi Hnr Roll; Hnr Roll; Nat Sci Aw; Otst Ac Ach Awd; Perf Att; Sci Fairs; Sci/Math Olympn; Comm Volntr; Cmptr Clb; Tmpl Yth Grp; Tennis (J); Track (J); Independent Research; Held Steady Job for Past 3 Years; Psychology; PhD in Medicine; Florida; Binghamton U

MILLER, PHYLICIA; NIAGARA FALLS, NY; NIAGARA FALLS HS; (JR); Hi Hnr Roll; Hnr Roll; Nat Hon Sy; WWAHSS; Hosp Aide; Cmptr Clb; Bnd; Mch Bnd; Pep Bnd; Stu Cncl; LPN; Pediatrician; U of Buffalo; U of Rochester

MILLER, RACHELLE N; BUFFALO, NY; KENMORE WEST SR HS; (SR); Hi Hnr Roll; Hnr Roll; MVP; Nat Hon Sy; Perf Att; Pres Ac Ftns Aw; Yth Ldrshp Prog; Comm Volntr; Hab For Humty Volntr; Peer Tut/Med; DARE; Lttrmn Clb; NYLC; Off Aide; Prom Com; Scouts; Tchrs Aide; Bskball (J); PP Ftbl (V); Track (V C); Vllyball (V C); Wt Lftg (V C); Cl Off (V); Stu Cncl (V); CR (R); National Congressional Student Leadership Conference Lotas College/Credit; Forestry/Wild Rescue; Crime Scene Investigator; Colorado State U

MILLER, SHANTEL; ALBANY, NY; ALBANY HS; (SR); Hnr Roll; Perf Att; WWAHSS; Comm Volntr; Emplmnt; Key Club; P to P St Amb Prg; Yrbk; High School Achiever of Color; McCall Institute-Drill; Education / Engineering; Medical Assistant; Wilkes U; Bryant and Stratton College

MILLER, STEPHANIE A; GARNERVILLE, NY; NORTH ROCKLAND HS; (SO); Hi Hnr Roll; MVP; Otst Ac Ach Awd; Perf Att; St of Mnth; Comm Volntr; Hosp Aide; Peer Tut/Med; Key Club; MuAlphaTh; Sci Clb; Bnd; Sccr (J); Received Black Achievement Awards; Travel Soccer Player (Disney Cup 2005); Pre-Med Program; Nursing; Cornell U; New York U

MILLER, THOMAS E; NUNDA, NY; KESHEQUA MIDDLE HS; (MS); Hi Hnr Roll; Hnr Roll; Perf Att; Sci Fairs; ArtClub; Chrch Yth Grp; DARE; Emplmnt; Scouts; Chr; Bskball; Member of Page Turners; Law Enforcement; Syracuse U; SUNY Geneseo

MILLER, YAVONIE; FAR ROCKAWAY, NY; BEACH CHANNEL HS; (JR); Hi Hnr Roll; Hnr Roll; Nat Hon Sy; Nat Ldrshp Svc; Perf Att; Sci Fairs; St of Mnth; WWAHSS; Hosp Aide; Peer Tut/Med; Emplmnt; Tennis (V); Sch Ppr (R); Accountant; CUNY Baruch College

MILLERD, JENNIFER; SENECA FALLS, NY; MYNDERSE AC HS; (SO); Hnr Roll; Pres Sch; St of Mnth; P to P St Amb Prg; Dnce; Hsbk Rdg; Telecommunication; Retail Management or Pharmaceuticals; Cazenovia; U of Buffalo

MILLIEN, MARIELLA; BROOKLYN, NY; JAMES MADISON HS; (SO); St of Mnth; Biology Clb; Honors for Science; Honors for Global; Doctor - MD / Medical Degree; Cornell U; Columbia U

MILLINGTON, KIMBERLY; BRONX, NY; ST BARNABAS HS; (JR); Hnr Roll; Nat Hon Sy; WWAHSS; Peer Tut/Med; Ntl Beta Clb; Dnce; Stu Cncl (V); CR (V); Step Team; Fashion Design; Interior Design

MILLNER, ALICE; BROOKLYN, NY; (FR); Hnr Roll; Sci Fairs; St of Mnth; Peer Tut/Med; Chess; Dbte Team; Cl Off (T); Computer Science; Forensics; John Jay College

Miller, Rachelle N
Kenmore West SR HS
Buffalo, NY

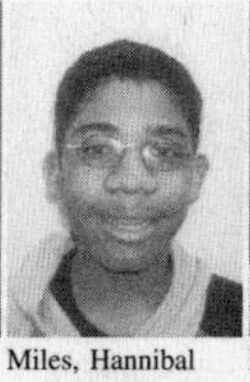
Miles, Hannibal
Long Island Sch For Gifted
Baldwin, NY

Michaud, Elizabeth
Hollis, NY

Meyer, Lindsay
William Floyd HS
Shirley, NY

National
Honor Roll
Spring 2005

Mesonero, Chris
Division Ave HS
Levittown, NY

Michel, Regine S
Hempstead HS
Hempstead, NY

Milks, Kristalyn N
Silver Creek HS
Silver Creek, NY

Millerd, Jennifer
Mynderse AC HS
Seneca Falls, NY

MILLS, GREG; MERRICK, NY;; Hnr Roll; Nat Hon Sy; Key Club; Bsball (J); Swmg (J); Vllyball (J)

MINARIK, BECCA; SCHENECTADY, NY; SCHENECTADY HS; (MS); Hi Hnr Roll; Hnr Roll; Sci Fairs; WWAHSS; ArtClub; DARE; Mth Clb/Tm; Mus Clb; P to P St Amb Prg; Sci Clb; Chr; Orch; Stu Cncl (R); Yrbk (E, R, P); Forensic Science; Engineering; Siena College; Union College

MINCK, AMANDA M; WHITE PLAINS, NY; WHITE PLAINS HS; (JR); Hi Hnr Roll; Hnr Roll; Nat Hon Sy; St of Mnth; Comm Volntr; Peer Tut/Med; Emplmnt; FTA; Mus Clb; NYLC; Prom Com; Chr; Presidents Excellence Award; Community Service Award; Teaches; New York U; Binghamton U-SUNY

MINEO, ANDREW; SYRACUSE, NY; HENNINGER HS; (JR); Hnr Roll; Jr Eng Tech; Chrch Yth Grp; Emplmnt; SP/M/VS; Bsball (J); Bskball (J); Fball (V C); Lcrsse (V); Full Length Album Release Through SU; Sammy Award Winning CD (Syracuse Award); Audio Engineering (Recording Studio); Sound Board Editor for Movies; Full Sail U; Syracuse U

MININNI, STEPHANIE A; STATEN ISLAND, NY; NEW DORP HS; (JR); Hnr Roll; Nat Hon Sy; Perf Att; DARE; FTA; Off Aide; Tchrs Aide; Dnce; SP/M/VS; College Courses; Early Childhood Education; Speech Pathology; Saint John's U; Wagner College

MINKOWITZ, JENNIFER A; GREAT NECK, NY; GREAT NECK SOUTH HS; (FR); Hi Hnr Roll; Hnr Roll; Nat Hon Sy; Perf Att; Sci Fairs; Sci/Math Olympn; WWAHSS; Comm Volntr; Peer Tut/Med; ArtClub; Dbte Team; Key Club; Mth Clb/Tm; Mus Clb; NtlFrnscLg; P to P St Amb Prg; Sci Clb; Orch; SP/M/VS; Sch Ppr (E); Ecybermission Finalist; All County/LISFA; Princeton U; Columbia U

MINNEHAN, CHRISTA; LIVONIA, NY; LIVONIA HS; (SO); Hi Hnr Roll; MVP; Nat Hon Sy; Otst Ac Ach Awd; Pres Ac Ftns Aw; Spec Olymp Vol; Chrch Yth Grp; Key Club; Vsity Clb; Bnd; Mch Bnd; Bskball (V L); Lcrsse (J); Sccr (JC); Childhood Education; Biology

MINOQUE, KATIE; MIDDLE VILLAGE, NY; DOMINICAN AC; (SO); Hnr Roll; WWAHSS; Comm Volntr; Drma Clb; Mus Clb; Chr; SP/M/VS; Stg Cre; Sftball (J); Stu Cncl (R); Sch Ppr (R); National Latin Exam-Cum Laude; New York U; Fordham U

MINOTT, TAMARA P; BROOKLYN, NY; ABRAHAM LINCOLN HS; (SO); Hnr Roll; St of Mnth; Peer Tut/Med; Key Club; Chr; Dnce; Social Work; Psychiatry; St. John's U; Hofstra

MINTO, JAMES; BALLSTON LAKE, NY; BURNT HILLS BALLSTON LAKE SHS; (SO); Hi Hnr Roll; WWAHSS; Dvng (V); Ice Hky (V)

MINUNNI, DERRIN; COHOES, NY; SHAKER HS; (JR); Hnr Roll; Comm Volntr; Dbte Team; Key Club; German Clb; Sftball (VJ); Track (V); Travel Softball All Over US; Technology/Industrial Arts Education; Rider U; Georgetown U

MIRANDA, ADRIANA; NEW YORK, NY; WADLEIGH SECONDARY; (SR); Hnr Roll; Comm Volntr; Dbte Team; Off Aide; Prom Com; Mar Art; PPSqd; CR (V); Lit Mag (R); Sch Ppr; Criminal Justices; Montclair State U; Seton Hall U

MIRANDA, JONISE; BRONX, NY; (SO); Hnr Roll; Perf Att; Sci Fairs; St of Mnth; Amnsty Intl; Comm Volntr; Chrch Yth Grp; DARE; Drma Clb; Fr of Library; Lib Aide; Mth Clb/Tm; Off Aide; P to P St Amb Prg; Bnd; Chr; Ch Chr; Dnce; Bskball; Chrldg; Scr Kpr (V); Cl Off (P); Lit Mag (R, P); Sch Ppr (E, R); Yrbk (P); Computer Science Award; Chemistry (Chemist); Psychology (Psychologist)

MIROCHNIK, MICHAEL; BROOKLYN, NY; MIDWOOD HS AT BROOKLYN COLLEGE; (SO); Hnr Roll; Sci Fairs; Peer Tut/Med; Dbte Team; Key Club; Mth Clb/Tm; Tmpl Yth Grp; SP/M/VS; Stg Cre; Swmg (V); Archon Honor Society; Part of the Social Science Intel Program; Law; Political Science; Harvard U; Columbia U

MIRVILLE, JEAN; BRONX, NY; COLUMBUS HS; (SR); WWAHSS; Vsity Clb; SP/M/VS; Sccr (V); Nursing; Pace U; Adelphi U

MIRZA, FATIMA; FRESH MEADOWS, NY; FRANCIS LEWIS HS; (SO); Hnr Roll; Kwnis Aw; Nat Hon Sy; St of Mnth; Peer Tut/Med; Lib Aide; Off Aide; Tchrs Aide; Vice President of the Muslim Student Association; Silver Honor Roll; Pre-Medicine; Psychology; Johns Hopkins U; Cornell U

MIRZA, SANIA Y; NEW YORK, NY; THE INDEPENDENT SCH; (SR); Hi Hnr Roll; Hnr Roll; Comm Volntr; Hosp Aide; Peer Tut/Med; Drma Clb; Emplmnt; Latin Clb; Stg Cre; Lit Mag (R); William Inge 24-Hour Playwright Festival; New York U - Accepted

MIRZA, TANYA H; PAINTED POST, NY; WEST SCH; (FR); 4H Awd; Hi Hnr Roll; Nat Hon Sy; Otst Ac Ach Awd; Pres Sch; St of Mnth; Comm Volntr; Hab For Humty Volntr; Red Cr Aide; 4-H; Dbte Team; JSA; Lib Aide; Mus Clb; SADD; Bnd; Chr; Dnce; Flg Crps; Track (J); Cl Off (S); Stu Cncl (R); CR (R); Marching Band; Interact - Community Service Group; Law; Foreign Services; Columbia U; Duke U

MISH, ADAM; LAURENS, NY; LAURENS CTRL SCH; (FR); Hi Hnr Roll; Hnr Roll; Otst Ac Ach Awd; WWAHSS; Peer Tut/Med; Red Cr Aide; Drma Clb; Key Club; Mus Clb; NYLC; Spanish Clb; Bnd; Chr; Jzz Bnd; Mch Bnd; Scr Kpr (VJ); Sccr (V L); Track (V L); Cl Off (P); CR (P); Outward Bound-11 Day Camping Trip; Did Karate for 5 Years; Music; Math; Hartwick College; U of Connecticut

MISHIYEV, MICHAEL; BROOKLYN, NY; ADELPHI AC; (JR); Hnr Roll; Sci Fairs; Dbte Team; Sci Clb; Vllyball (V); Lit Mag (R); Sch Ppr (R); Yrbk (R)

MITACEK, MEGAN; BAYSIDE, NY; MARYMOUNT HS; (JR); Hnr Roll; Nat Hon Sy; Pres Ac Ftns Aw; Sci/Math Olympn; St of Mnth; Comm Volntr; Hab For Humty Volntr; Peer Tut/Med; DARE; Drma Clb; P to P St Amb Prg; Scouts; Lcrsse; Swmg (V); Vllyball (V); Lawyer in Mock Trial; Pre-Law; Psychology

MITCHELL, NICOLE; BRONX, NY; HEALTH OPPORTUNITIES HS; (JR); Hnr Roll; Comm Volntr; Lib Aide; Honor Roll Every Year of HS; Television and Radio Production; Business Management; New York U; Syracuse U

MITCHELL, RICHELLE; WEBSTER, NY; RL THOMAS HS; (JR); Hi Hnr Roll; Hnr Roll; Nat Hon Sy; Otst Ac Ach Awd; Comm Volntr; Peer Tut/Med; Drma Clb; Mod UN; Outdrs Clb; SADD; Chr; SP/M/VS; Lcrsse (V); Volunteer at a Camp for the Blind; SADD / Students Against Drunk Driving; Speech Pathology; History Teacher; Nazareth College; U of Buffalo

MITCHELL, SHEVONNE M; SOUTH OZONE PARK, NY; JOHN ADAMS HS; (JR); Nat Hon Sy; Sci Fairs; St of Mnth; Key Club; Mth Clb/Tm; Sci Clb; Sch Ppr (R); First Robotics; History Club; Accounting; Banking; Baruch College; Hofstra U

MITCHELL JR, ROBERT; FARMINGDALE, NY; PINE FORGE AC; (SR); Hi Hnr Roll; Nat Hon Sy; WWAHSS; Chrch Yth Grp; Emplmnt; Ch Chr; Bsball (V); Bskball (J); Cr Ctry (V); Architecture; Electrical Engineer; Andrews U; Florida State U

MIZEL, HOWARD J; OCEANSIDE, NY; OCEANSIDE HS; (SO); Ctznshp Aw; Hi Hnr Roll; Pres Sch; Comm Volntr; Dbte Team; DECA; Mod UN; P to P St Amb Prg; Bnd; Stu Cncl (R); CR (R); Pre-Dental; Orthodontist; U of Pennsylvania; Emory U

MOBLEY, JANINE; BROOKLYN, NY; HS FOR MATH, SCI AND ENGINEERING@CCNY; (JR); Hnr Roll; Pres Ac Ftns Aw; St of Mnth; WWAHSS; Peer Tut/Med; Emplmnt; JSA; Key Club; Photog; SP/M/VS; Stu Cncl (P); Architecture, Construction, and Engineering (ACE) Program; Mount Sinai Biotechnology Program; Pre-Law; English Literature; Duke U; Georgetown U

MOCH, KAREN; OWEGO, NY; OWEGO FREE AC; (JR); Ctznshp Aw; Hi Hnr Roll; Nat Hon Sy; Key Club; Chr; SP/M/VS; Swmg (V C); Yrbk (P); Coach Swimming; Major in Biology & Education; SUNY Potsdam; Le Moyne College

MOCHIDO, RYO; HARTSDALE, NY; WOODLANDS HS; (FR); 4H Awd; Hnr Roll; WWAHSS; Comm Volntr; Spec Olymp Vol; 4-H; Jr Ach; Key Club; Italian Clb; Stg Cre; Cr Ctry (V); Sccr (V); Yrbk (P); Bowling-Varsity; Greco-Asian Club; Athletic Training/Sports Medicine; Business/Sports Marketing; U of Hawaii @ Manoa; Johns Hopkins U

MODESTIN, SHAMIR N; BROOKLYN, NY; W E B DU BOIS HS; (SO); Hnr Roll; Perf Att; Yth Ldrshp Prog; Comm Volntr; Peer Tut/Med; DARE; Emplmnt; Photog; Scouts; Svce Clb; SADD; Clr Grd; Drl Tm; Mch Bnd; Stg Cre; Fball (J); Wt Lftg (J); Law Enforcement / Criminal Justice; Criminology; John Jay College of Criminal Justice; Hunter College

MOE, AVERY; JAMAICA, NY; AUGUST MARTIN HS; (JR); Hnr Roll; Perf Att; Civil Air Pat; Emplmnt; NYLC; Bskball (J); Professional Pilot; Vaughn College of Technology; Bowling College

MOELLER, AMANDA; LOCKPORT, NY; LOCKPORT HS; (SO); Ctznshp Aw; Hi Hnr Roll; Hnr Roll; Otst Ac Ach Awd; Comm Volntr; Chrch Yth Grp; Key Club; Quiz Bowl; Schol Bwl; Scouts; SADD; French Clb; SP/M/VS; Stu Cncl (R); Academic Honor I Award; German Foreign Language Award; Psychology; Pre-Law; New York U; Michigan State U

MOFFETT, LAURA; CHURCHVILLE, NY; LIMA CHRISTIAN SCH; (SO); 4H Awd; Comm Volntr; 4-H; Chrch Yth Grp; Chr; Clr Grd; Mch Bnd; Physical Therapy; Dental Hygienist; Roberts Wesleyan College

MOGLE, LINDSAY; CLINTON, NY; CLINTON SR HS; (SR); Hnr Roll; Pres Ac Ftns Aw; Sci Fairs; ArtClub; Chrch Yth Grp; Photog; Prom Com; Bnd; Clr Grd; Flg Crps; Mch Bnd; Fball (V); Field Band Coach; Public Relations; Journalism; SUNY Buffalo; Utica College

MOHAMED, ANGELINA; BRONX, NY; EVANDER CHILDS HS; (JR); Dnce; Wt Lftg (V); A Business College

MOHAMED, NIKEISHA; SAINT ALBANS, NY; JAMAICA HS; (JR); F Lan Hn Soc; Hnr Roll; Bnd; SP/M/VS; Bdmtn; Wt Lftg; Lit Mag (R); Business Management; Queens College-Cuny; Berkeley

MOHAMED, SHAFECK; JAMAICA, NY; FRANKLIN K LANE HS; (SR); Hnr Roll; Nat Hon Sy; Nat Mrt Sch Recip; Otst Ac Ach Awd; Perf Att; USAA; WWAHSS; Comm Volntr; Spec Olymp Vol; ArtClub; Emplmnt; Key Club; Lib Aide; Off Aide; Photog; ROTC; Tchrs Aide; Bnd; Clr Grd; Drl Tm; Flg Crps; Adv Cncl (R); Stu Cncl (R); Sch Ppr (R); Queens College Presidential Award; National Sojourners Award; Mathematics Teacher; Hotel Management; Colby College-ME; New York U

MOHAN, GANESH; BRONX, NY; COLUMBUS HS; (JR); Hnr Roll; MVP; Perf Att; Comm Volntr; Hab For Humty Volntr; Peer Tut/Med; ArtClub; Chess; Cmptr Clb; Emplmnt; Photog; Sci Clb; Svce Clb; Dnce; SP/M/VS; Stg Cre; Bsball; Bskball; Cyclg; Mar Art; Scr Kpr; Sccr; Vllyball; Wt Lftg; Cricket Club; Most Improved Player; Associate's Degree; Bachelor's Degree; Polytechnic U; Georgia U

MOHINUDDIN, TWAFIQA F; BROOKLYN, NY; EDWARD R MURROW HS; (JR); Hnr Roll; St of Mnth; WWAHSS; Comm Volntr; ArtClub; Lib Aide; Tchrs Aide; Collected Money For Tsunami Relief And Fight Against AIDS; English; Environmental Science; New York U; Brooklyn College (CUNY)

MOISE, MARC H; UNIONDALE, NY; GREATER NY AC; (JR); Ctznshp Aw; Hnr Roll; Nat Sci Aw; Perf Att; Sci Fairs; St of Mnth; Yth Ldrshp Prog; Comm Volntr; Hosp Aide; Chrch Yth Grp; Drma Clb; Fr of Library; FCCLA; Mus Clb; Scouts; SADD; Tchrs Aide; Bnd; Chr; Ch Chr; Clr Grd; Bsball (L); Bskball (L); Gmnstcs (V); Hsbk Rdg (V); Sccr (V); Sftball (V); Swmg (V); CR (R); Pharmacy; Psychology; Andrew U; Stony Brock

MOKEY, REBECCA B; BROOKLYN, NY; STORM KING SCH; (JR); Hi Hnr Roll; Nat Hon Sy; Sci/Math Olympn; Peer Tut/Med; Drma Clb; Photog; Sci Clb; SP/M/VS; Cr Ctry; Track; Yrbk (P); Editor Math Science Magazine 2004; Resident (Student) Advisor; Journalism; Science, Theater; Columbia U; New York U

MOLINA, KATHERINE; BROOKLYN, NY; ABRAHAM LINCOLN HS; (SO); Hnr Roll; Perf Att; St of Mnth; Hosp Aide; Peer Tut/Med; Key Club; Off Aide; Photog; Scouts; Dnce; SP/M/VS; Bskball; Ice Sktg; Swmg; Tennis; Vllyball; Yrbk (P); Veterinarian; Pediatrician; New York U; Cornell U

MOLINA, RUTH A; NEW YORK, NY; WASHINGTON IRVING HS; (FR); Hnr Roll; Otst Ac Ach Awd; St of Mnth; Comm Volntr; Peer Tut/Med; ArtClub; Drma Clb; Tchrs Aide; SP/M/VS; Won a 75 Dollar Savings Bond; Bachelor Degree; Lehman College; Princeton

MOLINARO, KAYLA; KINGSTON, NY; KINGSTON HS; (SO); F Lan Hn Soc; Hi Hnr Roll; Yth Ldrshp Prog; Dvng (V); Gmnstcs (V); Track (V); CR (R); Law

MOLNAR, SHALYN M; MADRID, NY; MADRID-WADDINGTON CTRL SCH; (SO); Hnr Roll; Nat Hon Sy; WWAHSS; AL Aux Girls; DARE; Dbte Team; Key Club; Spch Team; Spanish Clb; Chr; Bskball (J); Sccr (J); Vllyball (V); People to People Sports Ambassador; Law; Syracuse U; St Lawrence U

MONACO, BETHANY; OWEGO, NY; (SO); Hnr Roll; WWAHSS; Chrch Yth Grp; Key Club; Chr; Ch Chr; Zoology; Wildlife Biology; Oswego SUNY; Syracuse SUNY

MONCADA, JOSEPH; ELMONT, NY; ELMONT MEMORIAL HS; (MS); Perf Att; Sci Fairs; Sci/Math Olympn; Comm Volntr; Peer Tut/Med; Sci Clb; Tech Clb; Bnd; Cr Ctry (J); Track (J); NYSSMA; Advanced Placement; College Majors; Music; College Majors: Engineering; Queens College; NYU

MONCAYO, JORGE A; KEW GARDENS, NY; FRANCIS LEWIS HS; (SO); Hnr Roll; Nat Hon Sy; Perf Att; Scouts; Bnd; Track (J); Automotive Design; Mechanical Engineering Technology; Academy of Art U; Penn State Erie College

MONCION, KATHERINE; NEW YORK, NY; (FR); Hi Hnr Roll; Hnr Roll; Comm Volntr; Hosp Aide; Dnce; Bskball (J); Track (J); CR (P); Be a Doctor and Professional Model; Go to College; St John's U

MONDAY, AUDREY; BRONX, NY; LEGACY HS; (SO); Gov Hnr Prg; Hi Hnr Roll; Hnr Roll; Nat Hon Sy; Otst Ac Ach Awd; Perf Att; Sci/Math Olympn; WWAHSS; Yth Ldrshp Prog; Comm Volntr; Hab For Humty Volntr; Peer Tut/Med; Chrch Yth Grp; Dbte Team; Drma Clb; Mth Clb/Tm; Tchrs Aide; Ch Chr; SP/M/VS; Wt Lftg (V); Adv Cncl (P); Stu Cncl (V); CR (P); Participated in Mathaton Competitions; Selected Personality of the Year in School; Bio/Chemistry; Pre-Med, Political Science; Princeton; U of Connecticut

MONGROO, RANA; SOUTH OZONE PARK, NY; TOWNSEND HARRIS HS; (JR); Hnr Roll; Nat Hon Sy; Nat Sci Aw; Otst Ac Ach Awd; Perf Att; St Schl; WWAHSS; Comm Volntr; Peer Tut/Med; ArtClub; Photog; Bnd; Ophthalmology; Biomedical Research; New York U; St. John's U

MONKS, VINCENT J; GREENWICH, NY; GREENWICH CTRL HS; (JR); F Lan Hn Soc; Hi Hnr Roll; MVP; Nat Hon Sy; Otst Ac Ach Awd; Pres Ac Ftns Aw; WWAHSS; Comm Volntr; Peer Tut/Med; Acpl Chr; Chr; SP/M/VS; Bskball (J); Fball (V CL); Lcrsse (V C); All-Star Football Class C Section; Middle Linebacker; Yale U, Holy Cross College

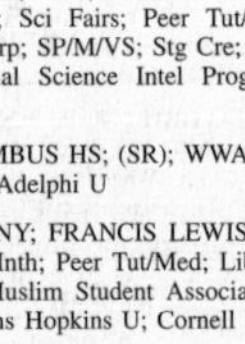
Moise, Marc H
Greater NY AC
Uniondale, NY

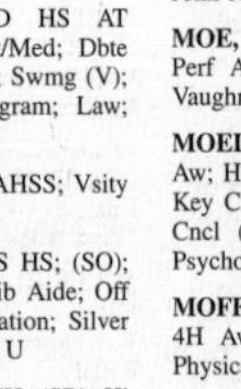
Mizel, Howard J
Oceanside HS
Oceanside, NY

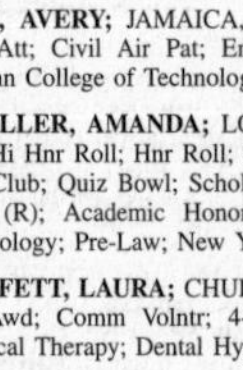
Mirza, Tanya H
West HS
Painted Post, NY

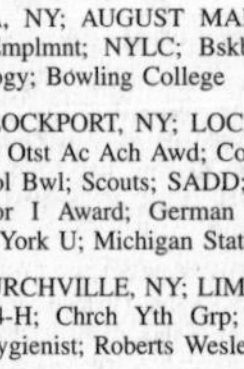
Minck, Amanda M
White Plains HS
White Plains, NY

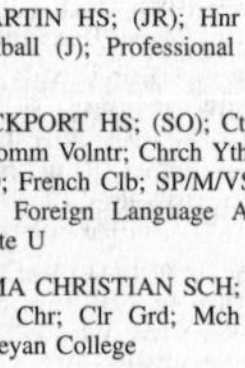
Mirville, Jean
Columbus HS
Bronx, NY

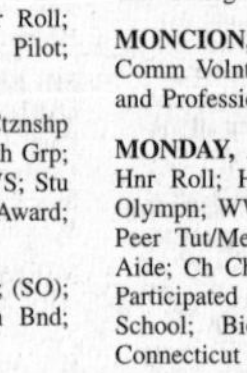
Moe, Avery
August Martin HS
Jamaica, NY

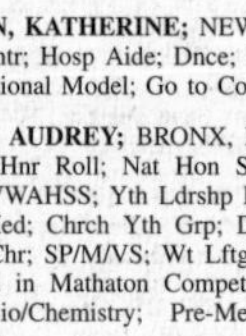
Monday, Audrey
Legacy HS
Bronx, NY

MONTAQUE, TERRY-ANN; UNIONDALE, NY; UNIONDALE HS; (SO); Ctznshp Aw; Hi Hnr Roll; Hnr Roll; Perf Att; St of Mnth; Comm Volntr; Key Club; Chr; Ch Chr; Clr Grd; Drl Tm; Track; King's Daughter Award; Vice President of Senior Junior High Class; Medicine; Child Development; Andrews U; Oakwood College

MONTEFUSCO, DANIELLE; VALLEY STREAM, NY; VALLEY STREAM NORTH; (JR); F Lan Hn Soc; Hi Hnr Roll; Hnr Roll; Sci Fairs; Biology Clb; Bnd; Chr; Interact Club; SPO Club; Science; Accounting

MONTELEONE, SAMANTHA; STONY BROOK, NY; WARD MEWILLE HS; (JR); Hi Hnr Roll; Otst Ac Ach Awd; Pres Sch; Drma Clb; Emplmnt; Mus Clb; Acpl Chr; Chr; Dnce; SP/M/VS; Fld Hky (J); CR (R); Theatre Major; New York U; U of Miami

MONTGOMERY, ALLISON; BALLSTON LAKE, NY; BHBL HS; (JR); Hnr Roll; USAA; WWAHSS; Fld Hky (J); Skiing (V); Sch Ppr (R); Enjoys Writing and Working W/Children

MONTMARQUET, JOCELYN R; AMHERST, NY; SWEET HOME HS; (JR); Hi Hnr Roll; Nat Hon Sy; Comm Volntr; Prom Com; Vsity Clb; Orch; Fld Hky (VJCL); Skiing; Sftball (JC); Track (V); Stu Cncl (R); Who's Who Among American High School Students; EAC All Academic Team; Interior Design; Business

MOOKLAL, MARISKA; HOLLIS, NY; MARTIN VAN BUREN HS; (SR); Ctznshp Aw; F Lan Hn Soc; Hi Hnr Roll; Hnr Roll; Nat Hon Sy; Nat Ldrshp Svc; Nat Mrt Fin; Otst Ac Ach Awd; Sci Fairs; WWAHSS; Comm Volntr; Peer Tut/Med; Dbte Team; Jr Ach; Mth Clb/Tm; Off Aide; Svce Clb; Tchrs Aide; CR (R); Treasurer of Leaders Organization; President of Math Honor Society; Political Science Major; Lawyer; Queens College

MOON, AIMEE J; COLLEGE POINT, NY; BRONX HS OF SCIENCE; (SR); Nat Hon Sy; WWAHSS; Comm Volntr; Peer Tut/Med; Chrch Yth Grp; Key Club; Photog; Orch; Gmnstcs (V); Stu Cncl (V); Yrbk (E); Dartmouth College

MOORE, AUDREY; FREEVILLE, NY; GROTON CTRL SCH; (JR); Hi Hnr Roll; Hnr Roll; MVP; Nat Hon Sy; WWAHSS; Comm Volntr; Hab For Humty Volntr; ArtClub; Chrch Yth Grp; Drma Clb; Emplmnt; Mth Clb/Tm; Mus Clb; French Clb; Bnd; Chr; Ch Chr; Clr Grd; Cr Ctry (V C); Track (V C); Adv Cncl (V); Both Track/Cross Country Scholar Athlete; Elementary Education; Houghton College; Roberts Wesleyan College

MOORE, JAMEKA; BUFFALO, NY; BENNETT HS; (SR); Yth Ldrshp Prog; Comm Volntr; Chrch Yth Grp; Emplmnt; Dnce; Stg Cre; Community Service; Internship; Pre-Med; Niagara U; St. John Fisher College

MOORE, KAREN M; FREDONIA, NY; FREDONIA HS; (JR); Hi Hnr Roll; Hnr Roll; WWAHSS; Comm Volntr; Chrch Yth Grp; Emplmnt; Key Club; Bnd; Chr; Chrldg (V); PP Ftbl; Swmg; Sch Ppr (R); Yrbk (E); Most Improved Player-Cheerleading; Swimming Manager

MOORE, MALCOLM; ROOSEVELT, NY; (SR); Hnr Roll; Yth Ldrshp Prog; Comm Volntr; Bskball; Ftball (V); Track (C); Cl Off (S); Stu Cncl (R); Business Administration; Teacher; Virginia State Albany; Morgan State, Tuskegee

MORABITO, DOMONIQUE C; MASTIC, NY; WILLIAM FLOYD HS; (SO); F Lan Hn Soc; Hi Hnr Roll; Hnr Roll; Comm Volntr; Peer Tut/Med; Biology Clb; Emplmnt; Key Club; Foreign Clb; Chr; Lit Mag (R); Biology Lab; Veterinarian Medicine; Wingate U; LaGrange College

MORABITO, ROSA; MASPETH, NY; CHRIST THE KING REG HS; (SO); F Lan Hn Soc; Hi Hnr Roll; Hnr Roll; Peer Tut/Med; ArtClub; Emplmnt; Italian Clb; Acpl Chr; Chr; Dnce; SP/M/VS; Sch Ppr (E); Psychology; Pediatrician; St John's U; Nassau CC

MORA JR, ABRAHAM; NEW YORK, NY; MURRY BERGTRAUM HS; (SR); DAR; Hi Hnr Roll; Hnr Roll; MVP; St of Mnth; Comm Volntr; Peer Tut/Med; Jr Ach; Bnd; Bsball (V); Gmnstcs; Boys' Club Baseball; Business Administration; Marketing Management & Law; SUNY Binghamton; SUNY Stony Brook

MORALES, NEFTALI; ROCHESTER, NY; JOHN MARSHALL HS; (JR); Ctznshp Aw; Hi Hnr Roll; MVP; US Army Sch Ath Aw; WWAHSS; Comm Volntr; Red Cr Aide; Cmptr Clb; Emplmnt; FCA; ROTC; Clr Grd; Drl Tm; Wrstlg (V); ASAR Award (Exemplary Stud. of Sch.); Law- Lawyer Major; Psychologist Minor; Harvard U; Pennsylvania State U

MORARU, ALINA; CHAUMONT, NY; GENERAL BROWN HS; (SR); Hnr Roll; Fr of Library; Lib Aide; Chr; I Want to Be a Nurse when I graduate from General Brown HS.; Pediatrician; Jefferson Community College in Watertown, New York

MORBY, CHELSEA; MECHANICVILLE, NY; STILLWATER HS; (FR); Hi Hnr Roll; Nat Hon Sy; WWAHSS; Comm Volntr; Hab For Humty Volntr; Peer Tut/Med; Drma Clb; Emplmnt; P to P St Amb Prg; Scouts; French Clb; Bnd; Jzz Bnd; SP/M/VS; Stg Cre; Cl Off (S); Masterminds; Actuarial Science; State U of New York; Simon's Rock College of Bard

MOREHOUSE, JEFFERY M; WARRENSBURG, NY; WARRENSBURGH JR/SR HS; (SR); Ctznshp Aw; Hnr Roll; MVP; Perf Att; St of Mnth; WWAHSS; Comm Volntr; DARE; Emplmnt; Key Club; Scouts; Stg Cre; Bsball (VJ L); Bskball (J L); Ftball (J); NY State Prostart Culinary Arts Comp-2nd Place; Skills USA (VICA) Local Baking Comp-2nd Place; Bakery Pastry Chef AOS; New England Culinary Institute; Culinary Institute of America

MOREIRA, CHRISTOPHER; LEVITTOWN, NY; DIVISION AVENUE HS; (SO); Ctznshp Aw; Hnr Roll; Kwnis Aw; St of Mnth; WWAHSS; Comm Volntr; Bnd; Mch Bnd

MORETT, ARVILLA M; SARATOGA SPRINGS, NY; F DONALD MYERS ED CTR; (SR); Hi Hnr Roll; Hnr Roll; Perf Att; Peer Tut/Med; Red Cr Aide; Chrch Yth Grp; Emplmnt; Photog; Voc Ind Clb Am; Ch Chr; Sch Ppr (R); 2nd Place in Regional Competition for Job Skills Demo, 2nd Place for Local Competition; Graphic Designer (BFA); Teaching (Master's); Cazanovia College; Alfred U

MORGAN, BRIAN G; STATEN ISLAND, NY; TOTTENVILLE HS; (JR); Hi Hnr Roll; Nat Hon Sy; WWAHSS; Emplmnt; Tchrs Aide; Bskball (J); Lcrsse (VJC); Track (J); Medical; Business Management; State U of New York

MORGAN, KADINA E; SPRNGFLD GDNS, NY; FRANCIS LEWIS HS; (JR); Ctznshp Aw; Hnr Roll; Perf Att; Comm Volntr; Chrch Yth Grp; Emplmnt; Svce Clb; Tech Clb; Ch Chr; Dnce; Stg Cre; Sch Ppr (E); English Major; Psychology Major; Yale U; Spelman U

MORGAN, TOMOYA; BRONX, NY; WALTON HS; (SO); Perf Att; Comm Volntr; Red Cr Aide; Chrch Yth Grp; Vsity Clb; Chr; Ch Chr; Chrldg (V); Stu Cncl (S); Master Degree (Education); College of New Rochelle

MORILLO, JOHNNY; CTRL ISLIP, NY; (JR); Hi Hnr Roll; Hnr Roll; Perf Att; St of Mnth; Valdctrian; Key Club; Kwanza Clb; Ftball (V); Football Player; Bachelor Degree; Syracuse U; West Virginia State

MORING, KATIE; ENDICOTT, NY; UNION-ENDICOTT HS; (SR); Hi Hnr Roll; Nat Hon Sy; Pres Sch; WWAHSS; Comm Volntr; 4-H; Emplmnt; Key Club; Spanish Clb; Hsbk Rdg; Science; Psychology/Sociology; Elmira College

MORINI, THERESA C; AMSTERDAM, NY; AMSTERDAM HS; (FR); Chr; Bskball; Tennis (V); Track (V)

MORRILL, CRYSTAL; TICONDEROGA, NY; TICONDEROGA HS; (FR); Hnr Roll; DARE; Math Major; 4-Year Degree / 6-Year Degree; West Point College; UNH

MORRIS, AILEEN; LINDENHURST, NY; LINDENHURST HS; (JR); Hi Hnr Roll; Nat Stu Ath Day Aw; Otst Ac Ach Awd; WWAHSS; Yth Ldrshp Prog; Drma Clb; Key Club; Mus Clb; Spanish Clb; Acpl Chr; Chr; Clr Grd; Dnce; Bdmtn (V); Sftball (J L); Tennis (V); Track (V); Founders Day Performance Awards; NYSSMA; Musical Theater; Health / Nutrition

MORRIS, GABRIELLE; MT VERNON, NY; MT VERNON HS; (FR); Hnr Roll; Nat Hon Sy; Comm Volntr; Fashion Designer; Pediatrician; Bowie State U; NYU College

MORRIS, JAMAL; WARWICK, NY; WVHS; (JR); Hi Hnr Roll; WWAHSS; Comm Volntr; Chrch Yth Grp; P to P St Amb Prg; Ftball (V); Wrstlg (V)

MORRISON, MATTHEW; MODENA, NY; WALLKILL SR HS; (SR); Hi Hnr Roll; Hnr Roll; DARE; Emplmnt; Architecture; Ulster County Community College

MORROW, CALIE; MERRICK, NY; JOHN F KENNEDY HS; (FR); Hnr Roll; MVP; Pres Ac Ftns Aw; Sci Fairs; Comm Volntr; Mth Clb/Tm; SADD; Tchrs Aide; Tmpl Yth Grp; Bnd; Jzz Bnd; Cr Ctry (V L); Track (V L); Vllyball (J L); Stu Cncl (V); Sch Ppr (R); Participant in Al Ralfus Long Island Math Fair; Participant in El Examen Nacional De Espanol; Cardio Vascular Surgeon; Michigan Medical Science

MOSKALENKO, ELIZABETH; DEER PARK, NY; ST ANTHONY'S HS; (JR); Hi Hnr Roll; Nat Hon Sy; Peer Tut/Med; ArtClub; Emplmnt; Svce Clb; Stg Cre; Bdmtn; Scr Kpr (V); Skiing; Cl Off (T); Sch Ppr (R)

MOSSER, KATHERINE; EAST AURORA, NY; EAST AURORA HS; (SO); Hnr Roll; Otst Ac Ach Awd; St of Mnth; WWAHSS; Comm Volntr; Peer Tut/Med; Chrch Yth Grp; Key Club; Bnd; Jzz Bnd; Mch Bnd; SP/M/VS; Cr Ctry (V L); Sccr (J); Track (V L); Cl Off (S); Lit Mag (E); A Poem Published in Next Newspaper Apr 05; NYSSMA Sax Solo Grade 5, 100 May '05; Spanish; Biology

MOTEN, TROY; OAKLAND GARDENS, NY; BENJAMIN CARDOZO HS; (SR); Perf Att; WWAHSS; Emplmnt; SP/M/VS; Lcrsse (V); National Ventures Scholar; Engineering; U of Maryland

MOTT, BRITTANY E; MORAVIA, NY; MORAVIA HS; (JR); Hi Hnr Roll; Otst Ac Ach Awd; Perf Att; WWAHSS; Comm Volntr; Prom Com; Bskball (VJCL); Fld Hky (VJCL); Sftball (VJCL); Cl Off (T); Sch Ppr (R); Doctor; Criminal Profiling; Boston College; SUNY Albany

MOTTA, MARIA; WOODSIDE, NY; HEALTH PROF & HUMAN SERVICES HS; (JR); Hnr Roll; Nat Hon Sy; Comm Volntr; Peer Tut/Med; Major in Biology.; Professional Degree in the Field of Medicine; New York U, NY, NY; Yale University, New Haven, CT

MOXHAM, CHANCE; FULTONVILLE, NY; FONDA FULTONVILLE CTRL SCH; (FR); Hi Hnr Roll; Hnr Roll; Drma Clb; Stg Cre

MOY, ALICE; NEW YORK, NY; TOWNSEND HARRIS HS; (SO); Hnr Roll; Nat Hon Sy; WWAHSS; Yth Ldrshp Prog; Comm Volntr; ArtClub; Lib Aide; Off Aide; Dnce; Stg Cre; Fncg (V); CR (R); First Place for Individual Exhibit on NYC History Day; Business/Economics; Law; U of Pennsylvania

MOYNIHAN, KIRBY; LAKEWOOD, NY; SOUTHWESTERN HS; (SR); Hnr Roll; Nat Hon Sy; Pres Ac Ftns Aw; WWAHSS; Comm Volntr; Peer Tut/Med; Spec Olymp Vol; DARE; Prom Com; Vsity Clb; Chrldg (V); Gmnstcs (V); Yrbk (R); Journalism; Law; U At Albany; St John Fischer College

MUCHIN, BRYN D; MASPETH, NY; MARTIN LUTHER HS; (JR); Hi Hnr Roll; Nat Hon Sy; Emplmnt; Tchrs Aide; Chr; Bskball (J); Cr Ctry (V); Tennis (V); Track (V); Women in Science Award from St John's U; Pharmacy; Pharmaceutical Chemistry; SUNY New Paltz; SUNY Stony Brook

MUCHNIK, EDUARD; BROOKLYN, NY; ABRAHAM LINCOLN HS; (SO); Hnr Roll; Perf Att; Sci Fairs; St of Mnth; Comm Volntr; Key Club; Lib Aide; Mth Clb/Tm; Stu Cncl (T); Engineering; Architecture; Massachusetts Institute of Technology; Columbia U

MUELLER, JESSICA; SAUGERTIES, NY; SAUGERTIES HS; (SR); Hi Hnr Roll; Nat Hon Sy; WWAHSS; Emplmnt; Key Club; Vsity Clb; Sccr (V); Key Club - Editor; Yearbook-Treasurer; Psychology; American Sign Language; U of Rochester

MUFUTE, FALLON; HOLLIS, NY; JAMAICA HS; (JR); Ctznshp Aw; F Lan Hn Soc; Hi Hnr Roll; Hnr Roll; Otst Ac Ach Awd; Comm Volntr; Peer Tut/Med; Chrch Yth Grp; Drma Clb; Emplmnt; Key Club; Lib Aide; Svce Clb; Chr; Ch Chr; SP/M/VS; Stg Cre; Lit Mag (E); Law Team/Mock & Moot Trials; Law Team Award; Psychology/Educator; Law; Columbia U; Cornell U

MUKOMOLOVA, GALINA; BROOKLYN, NY; FIORELLO H LA GUARDIA HS; (SR); Hnr Roll; Amnsty Intl; Comm Volntr; Peer Tut/Med; ArtClub; DARE; Photog; Lit Mag (E, P); Art Gallery Show, Honorary Poetry Mention; Museum Internship; Women's Studies; Poetry; Going to Hobart & William Smith

MULCAHY, MICHAEL A; BELLPORT, NY; BELLPORT HS; (SO); Hi Hnr Roll; Hnr Roll; Nat Hon Sy; Perf Att; St of Mnth; Comm Volntr; ArtClub; Chess; Cmptr Clb; Emplmnt; Outdrs Clb; P to P St Amb Prg; Bnd; Jzz Bnd; Mch Bnd; SP/M/VS; Karate-Green Belt

MULE', CHRISTINA; BETHPAGE, NY; ISLAND TREES HS; (SO); Hi Hnr Roll; Sci/Math Olympn; WWAHSS; Peer Tut/Med; Spec Olymp Vol; Drma Clb; Key Club; Mus Clb; Sci Clb; SADD; Bnd; Mch Bnd; SP/M/VS; Lit Mag (R); Sch Ppr (R); I Am an All-County Flutist; I Am the Treasurer of My Key Club; Journalism; Entertainment Law; New York U; Marymount Manhattan College

MULHALL, JAMIE L; GLOVERSVILLE, NY; GLOVERSVILLE HS; (FR); Hi Hnr Roll; Comm Volntr; Bskball (V L); Sccr (V L); Scholar/Athlete Award-Soccer; Scholar/Athlete Award-Basketball; Psychology Major; Fulton-Montgomery (Senior Year); Boston College

MULLEN, KURTIS J; CANISTEO, NY; CANISTEO-GREENWOOD CTRL HS; (JR); Hnr Roll; Chrch Yth Grp; DARE; Emplmnt; Mus Clb; Stg Cre; Bsball (VJ L); Bskball (VJ L); Sch Ppr (P); 100 Percent Award in English - 10th Grade; 100 Percent Award in Math - 10th Grade; Computer Arts & Designs; SUNY College of Tech

MULLEN, TARA; ROCKAWAY PARK, NY; BISHOP KEARNEY HS; (FR); Hi Hnr Roll; Hnr Roll; MVP; Nat Hon Sy; Pres Sch; Comm Volntr; Peer Tut/Med; Spec Olymp Vol; ArtClub; Drma Clb; Emplmnt; Chr; SP/M/VS; Cr Ctry (V); Sccr (V); Track (V); Emerald Society 2004 Scholarship Award; Medical Field; Law; Loyola College; Boston College

MULLIGAN, ALFRED; BRONX, NY; HEALTH OPPORTUNITIES HS; (FR); Hi Hnr Roll; Hnr Roll; Otst Ac Ach Awd; Perf Att; St of Mnth; ArtClub; Emplmnt; Mus Clb; Schol Bwl; Tchrs Aide; Bskball (J); Bachelor's Degree; Hunter College; New York U

MULLIGAN, CHASE; NEW WINDSOR, NY; NEWBURGH FREE AC; (JR); Ctznshp Aw; Hnr Roll; Comm Volntr; Peer Tut/Med; Scouts; Orch; Snowboarding; Boy Scouts; Veterinary Medicine; U of Maine

MULVEY, MEGAN; WANTAGH, NY; WANTAGH HS, GC TECH; (JR); Hnr Roll; Nat Hon Sy; Comm Volntr; Peer Tut/Med; Emplmnt; Key Club; Religion Teacher; NYS Art Teacher Award-Distinguished 2003, 2004; Elementary Education; Math; Hofstra U; Molloy College

MUNDERVILLE, EVAN G; SCHENECTADY, NY; GUILDERLAND CTRL HS; (JR); Hnr Roll; WWAHSS; Yth Ldrshp Prog; Comm Volntr; Emplmnt; Key Club; Tchrs Aide; Chr; Cr Ct Ski (J); Track (J); Sanctioned Soccer Referee; Mathematics; St. Lawrence U; Hobart College

Mulhall, Jamie L
Gloversville HS
Gloversville, NY

Muchin, Bryn D
Martin Luther HS
Maspeth, NY

Moreira, Christopher
Division Avenue HS
Levittown, NY

Morehouse, Jeffery M
Warrensburgh JR/SR HS
Warrensburg, NY

National
Honor Roll
Spring 2005

Montgomery, Allison
BHBL HS
Ballston Lake, NY

Morris, Jamal
WVHS
Warwick, NY

Mufute, Fallon
Jamaica HS
Hollis, NY

Mullen, Kurtis J
Canisteo-Greenwood Ctrl HS
Canisteo, NY

MUNIZ, CHRISTINA M; BRONX, NY; ST BARNABAS HS; (JR); F Lan Hn Soc; Hnr Roll; WWAHSS; ArtClub; Sci Clb; Spanish Clb; Catechist / CCD; Criminal Lawyer; John Jay College of Criminal Justice; Fordham U

MUNNLYN, SHAVONNE T; BROOKLYN, NY; SCIENCE SKILLS CTR HS; (SR); All Am Sch; Hnr Roll; Nat Hon Sy; Otst Ac Ach Awd; USAA; Emplmnt; Off Aide; Tchrs Aide; Lit Mag (R); Poem - "Positive Leads to Negative" Was Published; Poem - "Hopeless" Is a Semifinalist on Poetry.Com; Social Work; Psychology; York College of Pennsylvania; SUNY Oswego

MUNOZ, FENDI; NEW YORK, NY;; Sci Fairs; Yth Ldrshp Prog; Drma Clb; Mus Clb; Svce Clb; Acpl Chr; Chr; Ch Chr; Dnce; Salvation Army Choir; Law; Columbia U; Fordham U

MUNOZ, WILLIAM; NEW YORK, NY; WASHINGTON IRVING HS; (FR); Hnr Roll; Bnd; Bskball; Hudson Guild Beacon Summer Memorial Classic 16-Under 1st Place; Florida State U; Hunter College

MURACO, STEPHANIE; MELVILLE, NY; ST ANTHONY'S HS; (JR); Hi Hnr Roll; Hnr Roll; Nat Hon Sy; CARE; Comm Volntr; Peer Tut/Med; DECA; Emplmnt; SADD; Fashion Merchandiser; Fashion Buyer; New York U; Fashion Institute of Technology

MURAWSKI, MEGAN; LOCKPORT, NY; (SO); Hnr Roll; Comm Volntr; ArtClub; Chrch Yth Grp; DARE; Drma Clb; Key Club; SADD; Bnd; Pep Bnd; Lawyer; New York U

MURDAKHAYEVA, INESSA; CORONA, NY; BE'ER HAGOLAH INST; (JR); Hi Hnr Roll; Hnr Roll; Valdctrian; Comm Volntr; ArtClub; Mth Clb/Tm; Chr; Dnce; Bskball; CR (V); Sch Ppr (R); Yrbk (E); Pharmacist; Long Island U; St John's U

MURDOCK, KATHERINE; SCHENECTADY, NY; GUILDERLAND HS; (SO); Hnr Roll; Otst Ac Ach Awd; Pres Sch; Comm Volntr; Key Club; Skiing; Sccr (J L); Track (V L); Cl Off (T); Business; Engineering-Architectural

MURPHY, DAVID J; BOONVILLE, NY; ADIRONDACK HS; (SO); Ctznshp Aw; Hi Hnr Roll; Otst Ac Ach Awd; Perf Att; Pres Sch; Comm Volntr; Peer Tut/Med; Chrch Yth Grp; Emplmnt; Mth Clb/Tm; Ftball (J); Wt Lftg (V); National Junior Honor Society; In Process of Making Confirmation; Science and Math; Pharmacist; Syracuse U; SUNY College of Technology Utica / Rome

MURPHY, KATHERINE M; SYRACUSE, NY; JAMESVILLE-DEWITT HS; (SO); Hi Hnr Roll; Comm Volntr; Key Club; Dnce; Sch Ppr (R); Interior Design / Architecture; Genetics

MURPHY, TAMARA F; BRONX, NY; HEALTH OPPORTUNITIES HS; (SO); F Lan Hn Soc; Hi Hnr Roll; Hnr Roll; Otst Ac Ach Awd; Perf Att; Comm Volntr; Chrch Yth Grp; Emplmnt; Chr; Dnce; Swmg (V); Stu Cncl (S); Writer; Psychology; New York U; Harvard U

MURRAY, AMANDA E; CHITTENANGO, NY; CHITTENANGO HS; (JR); F Lan Hn Soc; Hi Hnr Roll; Nat Hon Sy; St of Mnth; WWAHSS; Comm Volntr; Peer Tut/Med; Mth Clb/Tm; Mus Clb; French Clb; Bnd; Orch; SP/M/VS; Stg Cre

MURRAY, AMANDA R; LEVITTOWN, NY; DIVISION AVE HS; (JR); Ctznshp Aw; Hnr Roll; MVP; St of Mnth; Yth Ldrshp Prog; Comm Volntr; Key Club; NYLC; SADD; SP/M/VS; Lcrsse (VJCL); Sccr (VJCL); Cl Off (V); CR (R); Yrbk (R); Honor Roll, Junior Year; Skills USA 2nd Place-Speech; Medical Assistant

MURRAY, ELENA; ALTAMONT, NY; GUILDERLAND HS; (SO); F Lan Hn Soc; Hi Hnr Roll; Hnr Roll; Nat Hon Sy; WWAHSS; Comm Volntr; Peer Tut/Med; ArtClub; Key Club; Pep Squd; P to P St Amb Prg; Dnce; Jzz Bnd; Pep Bnd; Cr Ctry (J); Scr Kpr; Skiing; Track (J); Wt Lftg; Piano Lessons; English; Mathematics

MURRAY, JENNIFER; NEW PALTZ, NY; NEW PALTZ HS; (SR); Hnr Roll; Nat Hon Sy; Nat Mrt LOC; Otst Ac Ach Awd; Sci Fairs; St of Mnth; Comm Volntr; Emplmnt; FBLA; NYLC; Photog; Voc Ind Clb Am; Sftball (J); CR (S); Skills USA; National Technical Honor Society; Hotel Management; Cosmetology; Johnson & Wales U; Western New England College

MURRELL, JALEESA; BROOKLYN, NY; CHOATE ROSEMARY HALL HS; (JR); Nat Hon Sy; WWAHSS; Peer Tut/Med; Chrch Yth Grp; Emplmnt; Photog; Vsity Clb; Dnce; Bskball; Track (V L); Adv Cncl (R); Georgetown U; Smith College

MYERS, MELISSA A; PULASKI, NY; PULASKI JR/SR HS; (SO); Hnr Roll; St of Mnth; Chr; Chrldg (V); Track (J); Writing / Poetry; Master's Degree / Writing; Simon's Rock College

MYFTIU, EGLIND; RIDGEWOOD, NY; FRANCIS LEWIS HS; (SO); Peer Tut/Med; Architectural Engineering; Columbia U; Cornell U

MYINT, MELISSA; CORONA, NY; STUYVESANT HS; (JR); Nat Hon Sy; Valdctrian; WWAHSS; Comm Volntr; Peer Tut/Med; Emplmnt; Key Club; Bnd; Student Environmental Advocate; Caring Animal-Loving Friends; Chemistry; Astronomy; Yale U; U of Connecticut

MYLES, SHARANDA; CORAM, NY; BROOKHAVEN TECH & ACADEMIC CTR; (JR); Hnr Roll; Otst Ac Ach Awd; Perf Att; Pres Ac Ftns Aw; Sci Fairs; Comm Volntr; ArtClub; Chrch Yth Grp; Jr Ach; Ch Chr; Dnce; SP/M/VS; Stg Cre; Cr Ctry (V); Track (V); Students Against Racism; Varsity Step Squad; Associate's Degree; Bachelor's Degree; Laboratory Institute Merchandising

MYRIE, SABRINA L; BRONX, NY; HARRY S TRUMAN; (JR); Hi Hnr Roll; Hnr Roll; Nat Hon Sy; St of Mnth; WWAHSS; Comm Volntr; Chrch Yth Grp; Drma Clb; Mus Clb; Chr; Ch Chr; Dnce; Bskball; Sccr; Vllyball; Was Elected Into the National Honor Society in Junior High School; Community Health Educator; Sociology; Hunter College; Bernard Baruch College

NACE, ASHLEY; PORT EWEN, NY; ULSTER CAREER & TECH CTR; (JR); Hnr Roll; Comm Volntr; Emplmnt; Vllyball (L); Teacher; Cosmetologist; Dutchess; SUNY Ulster

NAFZIGER, MARCI; LOWVILLE, NY; CLONLARA SCH; (JR); WWAHSS; Comm Volntr; Peer Tut/Med; Chrch Yth Grp; Emplmnt; Lib Aide; National Latin Exam - Perfect Score; The Medusa Mythology Exam - Silver Medal; English; Humanities; Columbia U; New York U

NAIR, AJIT S; STATEN ISLAND, NY; PT RICHMOND HS; (SR); Hnr Roll; St of Mnth; Hosp Aide; Chess; Lib Aide; Tech Clb; SP/M/VS; Stg Cre; Adv Cncl (S); Yrbk (P); President of the Asian/European Association; Member of the Robotics Team and Class Champion; Physician's Assistant; Pre-Med; St John's U; Pace U

NALLY, MEAGAN; BURNT HILLS, NY; BURNT HILLS BALLSTON LAKE SHS; (SO); Hi Hnr Roll; Hnr Roll; Yth Ldrshp Prog; ArtClub; Chrch Yth Grp; P to P St Amb Prg; Lcrsse (J); Sccr (J); Stu Cncl (R); Teaching; Art

NANDA, AMANDEEP; S RICHMOND HL, NY; JOHN ADAMS HS; (SR); Hi Hnr Roll; Hnr Roll; ArtClub; Quiz Bowl; Dnce; Bsball (J); Bskball (C); CR (P); Yrbk; Accounting; Business Management; Harvard College; Yale U

NANDALALL, NATASHA; BRONX, NY; TRUMAN HS; (JR); Hnr Roll; Comm Volntr; DARE; Dnce; Accounting; Iona College; Mount Saint Vincent

NAPARSTEK, RACHEL; SCHENECTADY, NY; NISKAYUNA HS; (SO); F Lan Hn Soc; Amnsty Intl; Comm Volntr; Key Club; Tmpl Yth Grp; Sch Ppr (R); President's Volunteer Service Award (Gold); Brandeis U; New York U

NAPPO, A J; WESTTOWN, NY; MINISINK VALLEY HS; (JR); Ctznshp Aw; Hi Hnr Roll; Nat Hon Sy; St of Mnth; WWAHSS; Comm Volntr; AL Aux Boys; Emplmnt; Jr Cls League; Schol Bwl; Latin Clb; Bnd; Drm Mjr; Jzz Bnd; Mch Bnd; Bsball (J); Lcrsse (V L); National Honor Society - President; Interact Club; Education; Law

NAPPO, DEANNA; WEST ISLIP, NY; AC OF ST JOSEPH; (JR); Hi Hnr Roll; Hnr Roll; USAA; Comm Volntr; Hab For Humty Volntr; ArtClub; Photog; Dnce; Orch; Bdmtn (V); Current Member of Free the Children; Current Member of ACES and Habitat for Humanity; Psychology; Criminal Justice; New York U; Boston U

NARAINE, JEREMY; BRONX, NY; B KELLY CMTY LEARNING CTR; (JR); Hnr Roll; Perf Att; Sci Fairs; St of Mnth; ArtClub; Chrch Yth Grp; Fr of Library; Spch Team; Wdwrkg Clb; Chr; Ch Chr; Dnce; SP/M/VS; Bsball; Bskball; Ftball; Gmnstcs; Sftball; Vllyball; Art; Business; Lehman College; Monroe College

NASCA, LISA; ELMA, NY; NARDIN AC; (SO); Hnr Roll; Otst Ac Ach Awd; Sci/Math Olympn; Bskball (J); Engineer; Architect

NASIR, ARAIB; CTRL ISLIP, NY; CTRL ISLIP HS; (SO); Hi Hnr Roll; Hnr Roll; WWAHSS; Comm Volntr; Mth Clb/Tm; Track (J); Computer Engineering; Stanford U

NASR, JOHN; MONROE, NY; WASHINGTONVILLE HS; (JR); Nat Hon Sy; Chrch Yth Grp; Mth Clb/Tm; Tennis (V); Sojourner Truth Award; Certificate of Excellence in Living Environment; Medicine; Computer Science

NAT, NAVINDER K; MERRICK, NY; SANFORD H CALHOUN HS; (SO); Hi Hnr Roll; WWAHSS; Yth Ldrshp Prog; Amnsty Intl; Comm Volntr; Key Club; Chr; Bdmtn (J); Track (V L); Participated in Neurobiology Research At Cornell Medical College; Biology Major; New York U; Cornell U

NATAL, SAMANTHA; STATEN ISLAND, NY; PT RICHMOND HS; (SR); Hnr Roll; Drma Clb; Emplmnt; Chr; SP/M/VS; Stg Cre; Robotics Club; Nurse; Law Consultant; SUNY Buffalo; Binghamton U

NATHAN, ERICA N; HAVERSTRAW, NY; NORTH ROCKLAND HS; (SO); Hnr Roll; Drma Clb; Key Club; Chr; Dnce; Bskball (J); For Class Representative I Was Elected Historian; Music (Piano); Business (Lawyer)

NATHOO, CRISTEE; RIDGEWOOD, NY; FLUSHING; Dnce

NATWORA, ASHLEY; ANTWERP, NY; GOUVERNEUR CTRL SCH; (SR); Hi Hnr Roll; Hnr Roll; Nat Hon Sy; Perf Att; WWAHSS; Comm Volntr; Chrch Yth Grp; Emplmnt; Key Club; Prom Com; Sccr (J L); Vllyball (VJ L); Cl Off (S); Stu Cncl (R); Yrbk (E); Biology; Utica College; Keuka College

NAUROTH, SHEILEENA A; GLOVERSVILLE, NY; GLOVERSVILLE HS; (SO); Hi Hnr Roll; Hnr Roll; Otst Ac Ach Awd; Comm Volntr; Outdrs Clb; Bnd; Scr Kpr (V); Sccr (J); Vllyball (J); Veterinary Medicine; Animal Sciences; Cornell U

NEANG, RATHMONY; UTICA, NY; THOMAS R PROCTOR HS; (FR); Hi Hnr Roll; Hnr Roll; Otst Ac Ach Awd; Perf Att; St of Mnth; Business; Boston College

NEAR, KYLE; PHILMONT, NY; TACONIC HILLS CTRL HS; (JR); Hnr Roll; Perf Att; DARE; Emplmnt; Ftball (VJ); Vllyball (V); Carpentry; Construction; SUNY Delhi

NECHAMKIN, CHARLES; JACKSON HEIGHTS, NY; FIORELLO H LA GUARDIA HS; (SO); Hnr Roll; Nat Hon Sy; SP/M/VS; Sch Ppr (R); Participates in Drama Program At La Guardia High School; Acting/Drama; Writing/Journalism; Yale U (For Performing Arts); Carnegie Melon Conservatory (Performing Arts)

NEELY, BRITTANY; MERRICK, NY; SANFORD H CALHOUN HS; (SO); Hi Hnr Roll; Nat Hon Sy; Sci/Math Olympn; Comm Volntr; Peer Tut/Med; DECA; Key Club; Mth Clb/Tm; SADD; Vsity Clb; Chr; Chrldg (V C); French Honor Society; Math Honor Society; Math; Psychology; Boston College; U of North Carolina At Chapel Hill

NEGRON, KRYSTAL; BRONX, NY; CHRISTOPHER COLUMBUS HS; (SO); Ctznshp Aw; Hi Hnr Roll; Hnr Roll; Otst Ac Ach Awd; Chess; Tchrs Aide; Yrbk (P); (Dec 2003) Editor Choice Award for Poetry; (Dec 2004) Editor Choice Award for Poetry

NELSON, DREW; MANLIUS, NY; FAYETTEVILLE-MANLIUS HS; (JR); Hi Hnr Roll; WWAHSS; Emplmnt; Bsball (V); Le Moyne College; St John Fisher College

NELSON, JENNIFER L; STEPHENTOWN, NY; BERLIN JR/SR HS; (SO); Hi Hnr Roll; DARE; Prom Com; Chr; Sccr (J); Taconic Valley Soccer Club; Pediatric Oncologist; Pediatrician; Hawaii Pacific U; SUNY Albany

NELSON, NICHOLE; LEVITTOWN, NY; DIVISION AVE HS; (SO); F Lan Hn Soc; Hi Hnr Roll; Nat Hon Sy; St of Mnth; WWAHSS; Dbte Team; HO'Br Yth Ldrshp; Key Club; SADD; Spanish Clb; Orch; Tri M Music Honor Society; Editor of Tri-M Newsletter; Law Degree; Columbia U; Howard U

NELSON-FINK, CHRISTOPHER; MARATHON, NY; MARATHON CTRL SCH; (JR); Ctznshp Aw; Hi Hnr Roll; Nat Hon Sy; Otst Ac Ach Awd; St of Mnth; Comm Volntr; Wrstlg (VJ); Cl Off (T); Tutor Students; Computer Science; Rochester Institute of Technology; SUNY Oneonta

NER, OLIVIA; MASPETH, NY; ARCHBISHOP MOLLOY HS; (JR); Hi Hnr Roll; Salutrn; St of Mnth; Comm Volntr; Peer Tut/Med; Emplmnt; Lib Aide; Mod UN; Scouts; Sch Ppr (R); Yrbk (R); St. John's Women In Science Society Award Recognition Award; Washington DC - Alumni Scholarship; Communications and Media / Journalism; Marymount Manhattan College; St John's U

NERIS, EMMANUEL A; BRENTWOOD, NY; BRENTWOOD HS SONDERLING CTR; (JR); Hnr Roll; Perf Att; WWAHSS; Cmptr Clb; ROTC; Clr Grd; Dnce; Drl Tm; Orch; Cr Ctry (V); Track (V); Chamber Orchestra; NYSSMA Level 5; Bachelor's of Computer Science

NESBITT, JARED S; BROOKLYN, NY; BROOKLYN TECH HS; (JR); Hnr Roll; Ftball (VJ); Biomedical Sciences; Biomedical Engineering; Duke U; Northwestern U

NETH, BRYAN; CORFU, NY; PEMBROKE HS; (SO); Hi Hnr Roll; Otst Ac Ach Awd; Sci Fairs; WWAHSS; Key Club; Mth Clb/Tm; Bnd; Jzz Bnd; Mch Bnd; SP/M/VS; Ftball (V); Wt Lftg (V); American Chemical Society; Neurology; Spanish; Washington U; Johns Hopkins

NETH, MATTHEW; CORFU, NY; PEMBROKE HS; (SO); Hi Hnr Roll; Kwnis Aw; Otst Ac Ach Awd; WWAHSS; Emplmnt; Key Club; Bnd; Jzz Bnd; Mch Bnd; Pep Bnd; Bsball (J); American Chemical Society; Pharmacy; Spanish; Texas (U Of); Washington U

NEWELL, LASHAY; TROY, NY; DOYLE MS; (MS); Hnr Roll; Nat Hon Sy; Peer Tut/Med; Chrch Yth Grp; DARE; Bnd; Dnce; Drl Tm; Jzz Bnd; Track; Stu Cncl (R); Yrbk (P); Doctor; Model; Harvard U; RPI

NEWMAN, JAMIE L; CATTARAUGUS, NY; CATTARAUGUS-LITTLE VALLEY; (FR); Hi Hnr Roll; 4-H; Emplmnt; Bnd; Chr; Jzz Bnd; Bskball (J); Track (V); Vllyball (J); Cl Off (S); Captain of Flute Ensemble; Musical

NEWMAN, MARISA; LEVITTOWN, NY; DIVISION AVE HS; (JR); Hnr Roll; Mas Aw; Nat Hon Sy; Comm Volntr; Red Cr Aide; Drma Clb; Key Club; Scouts; Chr; SP/M/VS; Key Club; Student Ambassador; Veterinary Science; Business; SUNY Stony Brook; Nassau CC

NEWMAN, MESERETE; BRONX, NY; ST JEAN BAPTISTE HS; (JR); Hi Hnr Roll; Hnr Roll; MVP; Otst Ac Ach Awd; Pres Ac Ftns Aw; St of Mnth; Yth Ldrshp Prog; Comm Volntr; Peer Tut/Med; Chrch Yth Grp; Emplmnt; Bskball (V); Track (V); Stu Cncl (R); CR (R); Youth of the Year Nomination for a Keystone Convention; Temple U; U of Georgia

Neris, Emmanuel A
Brentwood HS Sonderling Ctr
Brentwood, NY

Neely, Brittany
Sanford H Calhoun HS
Merrick, NY

Myrie, Sabrina L
Harry S Truman
Bronx, NY

Murray, Amanda R
Division Ave HS
Levittown, NY

National
Honor Roll
Spring 2005

Murphy, David J
Adirondack HS
Boonville, NY

Naparstek, Rachel
Niskayuna HS
Schenectady, NY

Nelson, Nichole
Division Ave HS
Levittown, NY

Newell, Lashay
Doyle MS
Troy, NY

NEWMARK, MICHELLE; WOODRIDGE, NY; FALLSBURG HS; (JR); Hi Hnr Roll; Hnr Roll; Nat Hon Sy; WWAHSS; Comm Volntr; Emplmnt; Key Club; English; Law; SUNY New Paltz; Marist

NEWTOWN, MEGAN; MADRID, NY; MADRID-WADDINGTON CTRL SCH; (SO); Hi Hnr Roll; Nat Hon Sy; WWAHSS; Comm Volntr; Chrch Yth Grp; Drma Clb; Emplmnt; Key Club; NtlFrnscLg; French Clb; Bnd; Chr; Jzz Bnd; Stg Cre; New York District Key Club Treasurer; Mock Trial; Forensic Science

NG, COURTNEY M; BROOKLYN, NY; STUYVESANT HS; (SO); Hnr Roll; Nat Hon Sy; Sci/Math Olympn; St of Mnth; Valdctrian; Comm Volntr; Hosp Aide; Peer Tut/Med; Key Club; Off Aide; Adv Cncl (R); Junior Fellows Program; Spelling Bee NYC Finalist; Doctor; Teacher (History); Yale; U of Chicago

NG, LISAMARIE; BROOKLYN, NY; MIDWOOD HS; (SR); WWAHSS; Key Club; Off Aide; Prom Com; Bnd; SP/M/VS; Sch Ppr (E); Yrbk (E); National Latin Exam - Gold Merit; Helping Out Poverty Stricken People; City U of New York Hunter

NICHOLAS, BRANDON; POUGHKEEPSIE, NY; POUGHKEEPSIE HS; (SO); Hnr Roll; St of Mnth; Comm Volntr; Ch Chr; Dnce; Track; Stu Cncl (R); Psychologist; Lawyer

NICHOLS, BRANNA A; CAZENOVIA, NY; CAZENOVIA JR/SR HS; (FR); Comm Volntr; Chrch Yth Grp; Ntl FFA; Stg Cre; Snowboarding; Skateboarding; Journalism; Music; New York U

NICHOLS, JENNA L; BATAVIA, NY; ALEXANDER CTRL SCH; (SR); Hi Hnr Roll; Hnr Roll; Nat Hon Sy; Perf Att; Pres Sch; WWAHSS; ArtClub; Photog; Scouts; Bnd; Sccr (VJ L); Swmg (V L); Tennis (VJ L); Sch Ppr (E); Graphic Design; Art Therapy; Nazareth U; Alfred U

NICHOLS, STEVEN; BURNT HILLS, NY; BURNT HILLS-BALLSTON LAKE HS; (SO); Hi Hnr Roll; Ice Hky (V); Lcrsse (J); CR (R); Roller Hockey - Not with School

NICKELSEN, ASHLEY M; STATEN ISLAND, NY; STATEN ISLAND TECH HS; (JR); Hi Hnr Roll; Nat Hon Sy; Nat Sci Aw; Otst Ac Ach Awd; Perf Att; Sci Fairs; WWAHSS; Comm Volntr; Peer Tut/Med; Biology Clb; Drma Clb; Jr Ach; Key Club; Mth Clb/Tm; Sci Clb; Tchrs Aide; Dnce; SP/M/VS; 14 Science Fair Awards; Team Captain Community Chapter-Leukemia Society; Biology; Environmental Studies; Princeton U; Johns Hopkins U

NICKOLOFF, ANDREA; ORANGEBURG, NY; TAPPAN ZEE HS; (SR); F Lan Hn Soc; Kwnis Aw; Nat Hon Sy; Otst Ac Ach Awd; Pres Sch; USAA; Comm Volntr; Peer Tut/Med; Chrch Yth Grp; French Clb; Veterinarian; Delaware Valley College

NICKOLOFF JR, EDWARD; ORANGEBURG, NY; BERGER CATHOLIC HS; (SO); Hi Hnr Roll; WWAHSS; Comm Volntr; Hosp Aide; Chrch Yth Grp; Svce Clb; Ice Hky (J); Sch Ppr (R); High Honor Roll; Sports Management; Business Or/Law; U of Miami; U of Michigan

NIEFFER, ANNA C; SAUGERTIES, NY; SAUGERTIES HS; (SO); Hi Hnr Roll; WWAHSS; Yth Ldrshp Prog; Comm Volntr; Chrch Yth Grp; Emplmnt; Key Club; Bnd; Chr; Lcrsse (V); Vllyball (J); Yrbk (R); Foreign Language Teacher; Middlebury College Vermont

NIEFFER, NATE; SAUGERTIES, NY; SAUGERTIES HS; (SO); Ctznshp Aw; DAR; Hi Hnr Roll; Hnr Roll; Nat Hon Sy; Otst Ac Ach Awd; Perf Att; St of Mnth; WWAHSS; Comm Volntr; Peer Tut/Med; Emplmnt; Key Club; Mth Clb/Tm; Spanish Clb; Bnd; Ch Chr; Ftball (J L); Lcrsse (V CL); Wrstlg (J L); Cl Off (P); Manager of Varsity Lacrosse; Mathematics; Business/Accounting; Syracuse U

NIEWADOMSKI, GABRIELLE M; RIVERHEAD, NY; MERCY HS; (SO); Hi Hnr Roll; Hnr Roll; Pres Sch; WWAHSS; Yth Ldrshp Prog; Comm Volntr; DARE; Emplmnt; Photog; Stu Cncl (R); Baking Club; Homecoming Committee; Law; Psychiatry; Yale U; U of Rhode Island

NIU, JENNIFER; FLUSHING, NY; BRONX HS OF SCIENCE; (JR); Nat Mrt LOC; Comm Volntr; Peer Tut/Med; Mth Clb/Tm; Off Aide; Tchrs Aide; Dnce; Orch; SP/M/VS; Swmg (J); Cl Off (T); Stu Cncl (R); CR (T); Yrbk (P); Pharmacy; Business Administration; SUNY Buffalo; Rutgers

NIYAZOV, DIMASH; STATEN ISLAND, NY; NEW DORP HS; (SO); Hnr Roll; Perf Att; WWAHSS; Sccr (V); 2004 USKBA Champion; Dentist; MD; NYU, New York U; Staten Island College

NJOO, SHELLY; BROOKLYN, NY; STUYVESANT HS; (JR); Perf Att; WWAHSS; Comm Volntr; ArtClub; Svce Clb; Stg Cre; Dvng (L); Ice Sktg; Swmg (L); Lit Mag (R); Perfect Score on National Latin Exam; Mastery Level Academic Performance in Chemistry; Art and Design; Chemistry; Columbia U; New York U

NOBILE, ALANA; LEVITTOWN, NY; DIVISION AVE HS; (SO); F Lan Hn Soc; Hi Hnr Roll; Hnr Roll; Kwnis Aw; St of Mnth; Key Club; Chrldg (V); Lcrsse (JC); Teaching Degree; Nassau Community College

NOGUEIRA, ANTHONY; FLUSHING, NY; BRONX HS OF SCIENCE; (SR); Pres Sch; Comm Volntr; Key Club; Bnd; Fncg (J); Psychology; English; SUNY Stony Brook; SUNY Binghamton

NOH, SAM; BAYSIDE, NY; BRONX HS OF SCIENCE; (JR); Dbte Team; Mth Clb/Tm; Cr Ctry (J); Track (V); Physical Science; Economics; Columbia U; MIT

NOLAN, PHALON S; KEESEVILLE, NY; AUSABLE VALLEY MIDDLE HS; (FR); Ctznshp Aw; Hi Hnr Roll; Otst Ac Ach Awd; Pres Sch; Sci Fairs; St of Mnth; Yth Ldrshp Prog; Comm Volntr; DARE; Scouts; French Clb; Sccr (VJ); Vllyball (JC); Biologist; Medical Lab Technician; Cornell U

NOLAN, SEAN M; BROOKHAVEN, NY; BELLPORT HS; (SO); Hi Hnr Roll; Nat Hon Sy; Otst Ac Ach Awd; Sci Fairs; St of Mnth; Comm Volntr; Peer Tut/Med; Emplmnt; Outdrs Clb; Bnd; Golf (V L); Scr Kpr (J); Scholar Athlete for Golf Team; Math Education; History Education

NOONAN, TREVOR; MOHAWK, NY; JARVIS HS; (JR); WWAHSS; DARE; Emplmnt; Prom Com; Bskball (VJ L); Ftball (VJCL); Track (V L); Cl Off (P); Empire State Games-Track

NORAY, JENNA; BROOKLYN, NY; SHEEPSHEAD BAY HS; (JR); St of Mnth; Comm Volntr; Vllyball (V); Nursing / Associate's Degree; Pre-Med; SUNY Delhi College of Technology; Framingham State College

NORMAN, CORTNEY; FARMINGDALE, NY; FARMINGDALE HS; (SO); Hi Hnr Roll; Nat Hon Sy; WWAHSS; Peer Tut/Med; ArtClub; Emplmnt; Key Club; Photog; Scouts; Spanish Clb; Sftball (V); Vllyball (J); National Honor Society

NORTON, JAMIE; EAST AURORA, NY; EAST AURORA HS; (SO); Hnr Roll; Comm Volntr; Peer Tut/Med; Chrch Yth Grp; Key Club; Scouts; Fld Hky (J); Sftball (J); CR (R); Yrbk (R, P); Youth Court; American Legion Scholar Award

NOTTER, ISABELLE; NEW YORK, NY; TREVOR DAY SCH; (FR); MVP; Peer Tut/Med; Chr; SP/M/VS; Stg Cre; Bskball (V); Sccr (V); Sftball (J); Swmg (J); Tennis (V); Sch Ppr (R); Athletics Trophies in Basketball and Tennis; Multiple Community Service Projects; Psychology; Teaching (Early Education or Special Needs); New York U; Columbia U

NOTZ, MICHAEL J; BUFFALO, NY; KENMORE WEST SR HS; (JR); Hnr Roll; MVP; Nat Hon Sy; Pres Ac Ftns Aw; Pres Sch; St of Mnth; WWAHSS; Comm Volntr; Peer Tut/Med; 4-H; Cmptr Clb; DARE; Emplmnt; SADD; Ch Chr; Yrbk (E, R, P); Bowling Team (School) Captain; Letter Winner; Electrical Engineer; U of Buffalo; RIT

NSU, NINA; NEW YORK, NY; SCH OF THE FUTURE; (SO); Biology Clb; Outdrs Clb; Mar Art (L); Tennis (L); Zoology; Marine Biology

NUCKEL, BRIAN; LEVITTOWN, NY; DIVISION AVE HS; (JR); Ftball (VJ L); Lcrsse (VJ L); Greg Kiska '03/Jerry Jewel '04 Football; Rising Junior '04 for Lacrosse; Physical Education; Hofstra U

NUGENT, EAMON; YONKERS, NY; IONA PREP; (JR); Comm Volntr; Bskball (V); I Play the Bagpipes

NUNEZ, BLESSIERHEA R; ELMONT, NY; SEWANHAKA HS; (FR); Hi Hnr Roll; Nat Hon Sy; Perf Att; Sci Fairs; Sci/Math Olympn; St of Mnth; WWAHSS; Comm Volntr; ArtClub; FBLA; Key Club; Quiz Bowl; Published in Celebrate! - Young Poets Speak Out; Doctor / Pediatrician; New York U; SUNY Stony Brook

NUTT, STEPHANIE; SHIRLEY, NY; WILLIAM FLOYD HS; (JR); Hnr Roll; St of Mnth; WWAHSS; Yth Ldrshp Prog; Comm Volntr; Peer Tut/Med; Emplmnt; Mth Clb/Tm; Italian Clb; Lcrsse (JC); Adv Cncl (S); CR (R); Pre-Medicine; Teaching; Buffalo State U; Sacred Heart U

NWAKEZE, CHIAMAKA L; NEW ROCHELLE, NY; RYE CTRY DAY SCH; (JR); Sci Fairs; WWAHSS; Yth Ldrshp Prog; Comm Volntr; Hab For Humty Volntr; Peer Tut/Med; Chess; Chrch Yth Grp; Drma Clb; Emplmnt; Lib Aide; NYLC; Sci Clb; Stg Cre; Bskball (JC); Lcrsse (V); Sccr (J); Cl Off (S); Stu Cncl (S); CR (S); Biology; Neuroscience; Yale U; Williams College

NWAOGU, EZINNE; JAMAICA, NY; BROOKLYN TECH HS; (JR); Hnr Roll; Nat Hon Sy; Comm Volntr; Emplmnt; Dnce; Orch; SP/M/VS; Stg Cre; Track (V); Lit Mag (R); Is 59 and Brooklyn Tech Honor Roll; Who's Who; Journalism; Corporate Law; Brown U; New York U

NWASIKE, ONYINYE; BROOKLYN, NY; CANARSIE HS; (SR); Hnr Roll; Nat Hon Sy; Nat Ldrshp Svc; Nat Mrt Semif; Otst Ac Ach Awd; Perf Att; Sci Fairs; St of Mnth; Yth Ldrshp Prog; Comm Volntr; Peer Tut/Med; Chrch Yth Grp; NYLC; Off Aide; Svce Clb; Sccr (J); Stu Cncl (V); Pre-Med; Biology; SUNY Stony Brook

NYAMEKYE, LISA A; QUEENS VILLAGE, NY; MARTIN VAN BUREN HS; (SO); Hnr Roll; Otst Ac Ach Awd; Sci Fairs; St of Mnth; WWAHSS; Peer Tut/Med; Off Aide; Svce Clb; Tchrs Aide; SP/M/VS; Stg Cre; Bskball (V); Psychology; Physical Therapy; Columbia U; St John's U

OBASUYI, EMMANUEL; BRONX, NY; MARBLE HILL HS FOR INTERNATIONAL STUDIES; (FR); Hnr Roll; Perf Att; ArtClub; Sci Clb; Ch Chr; Sccr; Track; Stu Cncl; CR (R); Medical Degree; Bachelor's Degree; NYU School of Medicine; Harvard Medical School

OBASUYI, JOY; BRONX, NY; MARBLE HILL HS FOR INTERNATIONAL STUDIES; (SO); Hnr Roll; Perf Att; St of Mnth; Comm Volntr; Hosp Aide; ArtClub; Biology Clb; Sci Clb; Ch Chr; Sccr; Tennis; Track; CR (R); Yrbk (E); Student of the Month / Community Service; Medicine / Nurse; Bachelor's Degree; NYU School of Medicine; U of Washington School of Nursing

OBER, TERESA; ITHACA, NY; ITHACA HS; (JR); Hi Hnr Roll; WWAHSS; Comm Volntr; Chrch Yth Grp; DARE; Emplmnt; Key Club; Vsity Clb; German Clb; Varsity Rowing Team; Psychology

OBEROI, GUPREET; QUEENS VILLAGE, NY; BAYSIDE HS; (SO); Hnr Roll; Nat Hon Sy; Nat Ldrshp Svc; Peer Tut/Med; Key Club; Mus Clb; Clb; Bnd; Bskball (J); Varsity Bowling Team, Mathematics Research; Bhangra Club; Business; Doctor; NYU; Columbia U

O'BRIAN, MAC KENZIE; LISBON, NY; LISBON HS; (SO); Ctznshp Aw; Hnr Roll; Jr Rot; Otst Ac Ach Awd; Comm Volntr; Lib Aide; Mod UN; Photog; Quiz Bowl; Spanish Clb; Clr Grd; Flg Crps; Chrldg (V); PPSqd (V); Sccr (V); Sftball (V); Cl Off (P); CR; Mock Trial; Interact; RN; Doctor; Albany State

OCAMPO, ANGELA; WHITE PLAINS, NY; WHITE PLAINS HS; (JR); Hi Hnr Roll; Hnr Roll; Nat Hon Sy; Otst Ac Ach Awd; Sci Fairs; WWAHSS; Comm Volntr; Peer Tut/Med; Emplmnt; Dnce; PPSqd (J); Youth Good Samaritan from Red Cross; STEP Academic Excellence; International Relations; Sociology; Yale U; Columbia U

OCEAN, MARSHA; QUEENS VILLAGE, NY; MATH SCIENCE RESEARCH TECH HS; (JR); Hnr Roll; Perf Att; WWAHSS; Sccr (V); Track (V); Medicine; SUNY Stony Brook

OCHLER II, GARY R; GOWANDA, NY; GOWANDA HS; (SO); Hnr Roll; St of Mnth; Bnd; Mch Bnd; Pep Bnd; SP/M/VS; Bsball (JCL); Bskball (J L); Cr Ctry (V L); Business Owner; Penn State U; U of California

O'CONNELL, CAITLIN; NEW YORK, NY; MARYMOUNT SCH; (JR); Hi Hnr Roll; Nat Hon Sy; Nat Mrt LOC; WWAHSS; Comm Volntr; Peer Tut/Med; Quill & Scroll; Swmg (V L); Sch Ppr (E, R); Piano Player - 10 Years; Book Club President; Journalist / Journalism; Columbia U

O'CONNELL, CHRISTINA; NEW YORK, NY; BRONX HS OF SCIENCE; MS; Hnr Roll; MVP; Perf Att; Pres Ac Ftns Aw; Sci Fairs; Comm Volntr; Chess; Drma Clb; Mth Clb/Tm; Mod UN; Mus Clb; Scouts; Tchrs Aide; Tech Clb; SP/M/VS; Swmg (V); Stu Cncl (R); CR (P, R); ICG (International Children's Games); Broadcasting; Medicine; Yale U; Columbia U

O'CONNOR, BRANDI R; VALLEY STREAM, NY; VALLEY STREAM CTRL; Oregon State; Montana State

O'CONNOR, GREG; SARATOGA SPRINGS, NY; BLACK HAWK HS; (SR); Hnr Roll; Perf Att; Comm Volntr; Cmptr Clb; Emplmnt; Fr of Library; Key Club; Mth Clb/Tm; Off Aide; Photog; Arch; Skt Tgt Sh; Webmaster Key Club, 2 Years; Blacksmithing Basic I - Complete; Computer Programming; Adirondack Community College; Sage College of Albany

OCTAVE, LAILA; BRONX, NY; HOSTOS LINCOLN AC OF SCI; (SO); Ctznshp Aw; Hi Hnr Roll; Hnr Roll; Nat Hon Sy; Otst Ac Ach Awd; Comm Volntr; Hosp Aide; Peer Tut/Med; Dbte Team; Tchrs Aide; Debate; Black Student Union-Vice President; Business; Forensic Science; Cornell; Harvard

ODOBASIC, JESSICA; TUCKAHOE, NY; EASTCHESTER HS; (JR); DAR; Hnr Roll; Yth Ldrshp Prog; Hosp Aide; Emplmnt; Dnce; Orch; Stg Cre; Cl Off (V); Leo Club President; Pre-Med; Brown U; U of Rhode Island

ODURO, AISSA; BUFFALO, NY; (SO); F Lan Hn Soc; Hi Hnr Roll; Yth Ldrshp Prog; Amnsty Intl; Emplmnt; Spanish Clb; Chr; SP/M/VS; Stu Cncl (R); CR (R); Finalist in Amherst Teen Idol & Buffalo Idol; Principal's Award; Pre-Med / Pediatrician; Linguistics; Columbia U; Yale U

OELSNER, ALISSA; CORTLANDT MANOR, NY; HENDRICK HUDSON HS; (FR); Hi Hnr Roll; Otst Ac Ach Awd; Pres Sch; St of Mnth; Drma Clb; NYLC; Bnd; Mch Bnd; Pep Bnd; Math; Science

OEST, LAURA; YONKERS, NY; LINCOLN HS; (SO); Hi Hnr Roll; Hnr Roll; Nat Mrt LOC; Accountant-Accounting; New York U

OESTRICHER, CHRISTIAN; BROOKLYN, NY; JOHN DEWEY HS; (JR); Hnr Roll; Nat Ldrshp Svc; WWAHSS; Yth Ldrshp Prog; Red Cr Aide; Dbte Team; Emplmnt; Jr Ach; Key Club; Ftball (J); Adv Cncl (V); Stu Cncl (V); Culinary Arts; Football; SUNY Albany-State U of Albany; California Culinary Arts School

OFUYA, TEMISANREN; BALDWIN, NY; BALDWIN HS; (JR); Hnr Roll; Kwnis Aw; Perf Att; ArtClub; Bskball; Ftball (V); Track (V); Principal Award For Summer Reading; Most Improved Student Award; Lawyer; Mechanical Engineer; Georgetown U; Wake Forest U

OGUNLOWO, MORADEKE S; ELMONT, NY; SEWANHAKA HS; (JR); Hnr Roll; WWAHSS; Comm Volntr; Chrch Yth Grp; Key Club; Pep Squd; Ch Chr; Dnce; SP/M/VS; Chrldg (C); Stu Cncl (R); CR (R); Manager of B-Ball Team; Biology / Pre-Med; Child Psychology / Development; Virginia Commonwealth U; Clark Atlanta U

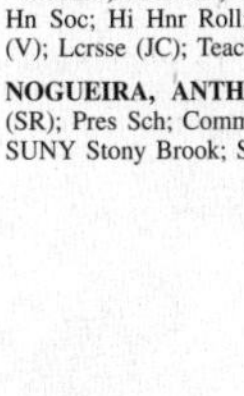

Oest, Laura
Lincoln HS
Yonkers, NY

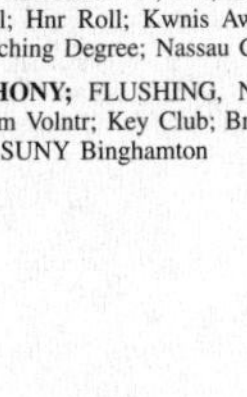

Nwasike, Onyinye
Canarsie HS
Brooklyn, NY

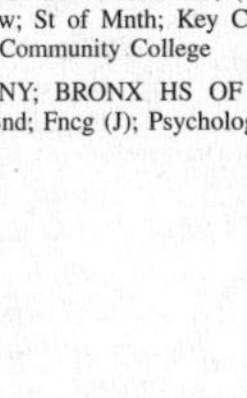

Nolan, Phalon S
Ausable Valley Middle HS
Keeseville, NY

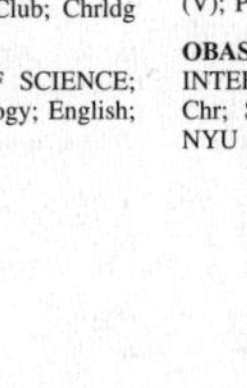

Nichols, Branna A
Cazenovia JR/SR HS
Cazenovia, NY

Ng, Lisamarie
Midwood HS
Brooklyn, NY

National
Honor Roll
Spring 2005

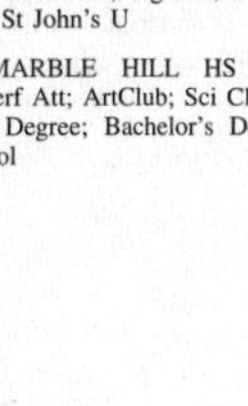

Newtown, Megan
Madrid-Waddington Ctrl Sch
Madrid, NY

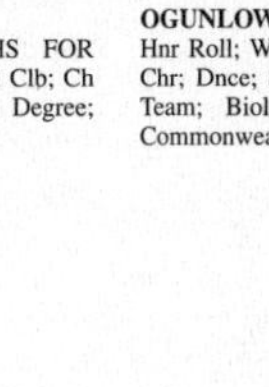

Niyazov, Dimash
New Dorp HS
Staten Island, NY

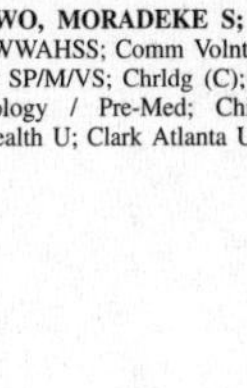

Nunez, Blessierhea R
Sewanhaka HS
Elmont, NY

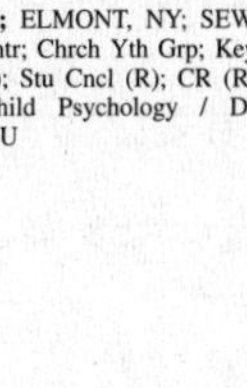

Nyamekye, Lisa A
Martin Van Buren HS
Queens Village, NY

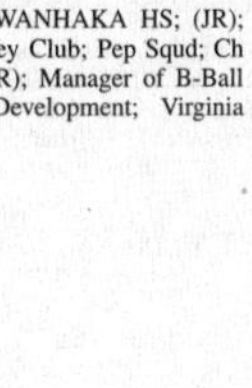

Odobasic, Jessica
Eastchester HS
Tuckahoe, NY

O'HARA, AMY; EAST AURORA, NY; EAST AURORA HS; (SO); Comm Volntr; Bnd; SP/M/VS; Fld Hky (JC); Lit Mag (R); Synchronized Swimming (6 Years); SADD (2 Years); Education; Journalism; Penn State U; Keuka College

O'HERRON, KACEY; ELMIRA, NY; SOUTHSIDE HS; (SR); Hi Hnr Roll; Nat Hon Sy; WWAHSS; Comm Volntr; Key Club; Chr; SP/M/VS; Yrbk (E); Mock Trial; Elementary Education; Lock Haven U

OLIVER, DAVID; MEDINA, NY; CORNERSTONE CHRISTIAN AC; (SR); 4H Awd; Hi Hnr Roll; MVP; Salutrn; 4-H; Chrch Yth Grp; Emplmnt; Ch Chr; Bskball (V); Sccr (C); Engineer; Chemist

OLIVERI, DIANA R; BROOKLYN, NY; NEW UTRECHT HS; (JR); Hnr Roll; Academy; Bowling Team (Varsity); Health Education; Counseling; Brooklyn College; Saint Francis College

OLIVERI, GIOVANNI; BETHPAGE, NY; ISLAND TREES HS; (JR); Hi Hnr Roll; Hnr Roll; Key Club; Prom Com; Tech Clb; Vsity Clb; Spanish Clb; Bnd; Jzz Bnd; Mch Bnd; Lcrsse (VJC); Sccr (VJC); Sch Ppr (R); Coach's Award, Jump Rope for Heart.; Salvation Army for Key Club, Altar Boy.; Architecture; Construction; Bryant College; New York Institute of Technology

OLSEN, ELIZABETH E; SAUGERTIES, NY; SAUGERTIES HS; (FR); Hi Hnr Roll; Hnr Roll; WWAHSS; Key Club; Lacrosse Club; Journalism

OLSON, AMBER; ALBANY, NY; GUILDERLAND HS; (JR); Emplmnt; FBLA; Hsbk Rdg; Swmg (V); Stu Cncl (T); Varsity Crew; 6th Place in NYS FBLA Banking & Finance; Business Management; Marketing; Babson College; Bryant U

O'MEALIA, KEELEY; ROCHESTER, NY; SPENCERPORT HS; (JR); Hi Hnr Roll; Hnr Roll; Perf Att; WWAHSS; Comm Volntr; Svce Clb; Chrldg (VJ L); Yrbk (R); Education; SUNY Fredonia; Niagara U

OMEZI, STEPHANIE; ROSEDALE, NY; FLUSHING HS; (FR); Hi Hnr Roll; Hnr Roll; Perf Att; Sci Fairs; St of Mnth; Comm Volntr; Chrch Yth Grp; Dbte Team; Emplmnt; Off Aide; Tchrs Aide; Ch Chr; Dnce; Swmg (L); Track (J); Stu Cncl (R); Law Major; Social Work Major; Harvard U; Yale U

OMIDIJI, DEBORAH; NEW YORK, NY; (JR); Hnr Roll; Ch Chr; Track; Psychology Classes; Psychology; Nursing; U of Pennsylvania

OMOREBOKHAE, GRACE; BRONX, NY; LA GUARDIA HS; (JR); Hnr Roll; Nat Hon Sy; Otst Ac Ach Awd; Perf Att; St Optmst of Yr; WWAHSS; Yth Ldrshp Prog; Comm Volntr; Peer Tut/Med; Chrch Yth Grp; Drma Clb; Mus Clb; Outdrs Clb; Photog; Tchrs Aide; Chr; Ch Chr; Dnce; SP/M/VS; Vllyball (J); Been a Back Up Singer for Josh Graban; Walked for Breast Cancer.; Business Administration; Marketing; Harvard U; New York U

O'NEIL, ELIZABETH; SYRACUSE, NY; (SR); Ctznshp Aw; Hnr Roll; MVP; Nat Ldrshp Svc; Yth Ldrshp Prog; Comm Volntr; Peer Tut/Med; Chrch Yth Grp; Prom Com; Vsity Clb; Chr; Ch Chr; Bskball (V C); Lcrsse (V CL); Mar Art; Sccr (V); Jr. Black Belt in Karate; Criminal Justice; Attending Mercyhurst College

O'NEILL, SHANNON; CORFU, NY; PEMBROKE JR/SR HS; (FR); Hi Hnr Roll; WWAHSS; Comm Volntr; DECA; Drma Clb; FTA; Key Club; Outdrs Clb; SADD; Vsity Clb; Spanish Clb; SP/M/VS; Hsbk Rdg; Mar Art; Skiing; Swmg (V L); Track (V L); Vsy Clb; Yrbk (E); Scholar Athlete Award; Blue Belt in Kenpo Karate, Orange Belt in Judo; Pre-Med MD (Psychiatry); Bucknell U; Brown U

O'NOLL, DESIRAE K; GLEN COVE, NY; GLEN COVE HS; (JR); Hi Hnr Roll; Otst Ac Ach Awd; Pres Sch; St of Mnth; Comm Volntr; Peer Tut/Med; Key Club; Pep Squd; Prom Com; SADD; Chr; Bskball (V C); Sftball (V); Cl Off (V); CR (V); Recipient of Princeton Award for Language; Student of the Month from Knights of Columbus; Adolescent Psychology; Binghamton U; Cortland U

ONYEKABA, ANDY; BRONX, NY; COLUMBUS HS; (JR); Hnr Roll; Perf Att; Svce Clb; Swg Chr; Sccr (V); Civil Engineer; U of Vermont

OPPICI, CHRISTOPHER; SHARON SPRINGS, NY; SHARON SPRINGS CTRL SCH; (SO); Hi Hnr Roll; Hnr Roll; MVP; Perf Att; Sci Fairs; WWAHSS; BPA; FBLA; Vsity Clb; Spanish Clb; Bnd; Chr; Jzz Bnd; Mch Bnd; Bsball (V); Bskball (JC); Sccr (V); Vsy Clb (V); Stu Cncl (R); EPGY - Stanford U- Summer 2004 - For Geometry; Architectural Engineering; Law / Criminal Justice; Harvard U; RPI - Troy

ORANGE, INDIA N; WHITE PLAINS, NY; WHITE PLAINS HS; (SO); Hnr Roll; Perf Att; Comm Volntr; Emplmnt; Off Aide; Adolescent Vocational Exploration Program; Reach for Success; Veterinarian; Law Enforcement; North Carolina State U; U of Pennsylvania

ORELLANA, JESSE J; SWAIN, NY; KESHEQUA MIDDLE HS; (MS); Hi Hnr Roll; Hnr Roll; Bnd; Mch Bnd; Skiing; Stu Cncl (R); CR (R); Science; Engineering; Alfred State College of Technology; U of Phoenix

ORMSBY, DENICIA; JAMAICA, NY; SPRINGFIELD GARDENS HS; (JR); Hi Hnr Roll; Hnr Roll; WWAHSS; Bnd; Bskball (V); Sftball (V); Vllyball (V); Queens College Presidential Award for Top Junior Student; Biochemistry; Physics; SUNY New Paltz; Susquehanna U

ORNSTEIN, DOUGLAS P; MAHOPAC, NY; YORKTOWN HS; (JR); Hi Hnr Roll; Hnr Roll; Nat Hon Sy; Comm Volntr; Key Club; Ftball (V); Skiing (V); Sch Ppr (R); Business; Law; Washington and Lee U; St. Lawrence U

ORTEGA, SONIA C; BELLMORE, NY; W C MEPHAM HS; (JR); Hnr Roll; Otst Ac Ach Awd; St of Mnth; Comm Volntr; Emplmnt; Photog; Vsity Clb; Chr; Italian; Criminal Justice; St. John's U; C W Post-Long Island U

ORTIZ, DIANA P; BROOKLYN, NY; FIORELLO H LA GUARDIA HS; (JR); Comm Volntr; Emplmnt; Off Aide; Tchrs Aide; Gmnstcs (J); Sccr (J); Vllyball (J); Certificate of Recognition; NSLC Certificate of Invitation; Linguistic Studies; Fine Arts; Syracuse U; New York U

ORTIZ, DIANNA; BOONVILLE, NY; ADIRONDACK HS; (SO); Ctznshp Aw; Hi Hnr Roll; Hnr Roll; Comm Volntr; Chrch Yth Grp; Scouts; Mythology; Archaeology; Cornell U

ORTIZ, DIANNA; NEWBURGH, NY; NEWBURGH FREE AC; (SR); Ctznshp Aw; Hi Hnr Roll; Hnr Roll; Nat Hon Sy; Nat Ldrshp Svc; Perf Att; WWAHSS; Comm Volntr; DARE; Emplmnt; Prom Com; ROTC; French Clb; Dnce; SP/M/VS; AFJROTC; French Club; Psychology Major; French; Dutchess Community College; SUNY New Paltz

ORTIZ, IVELLISSE M; BUFFALO, NY; HUTCH-TECH HS; (SR); Hnr Roll; Perf Att; Chrch Yth Grp; BEAM Club; Computer Science; U of Buffalo

ORTIZ, JASMINE; BROOKLYN, NY; SECONDARY SCH FOR RESEARCH; (JR); Ctznshp Aw; Hnr Roll; Otst Ac Ach Awd; Peer Tut/Med; Good Citizenship in Advisory; Chef; Professional Dancing; Miami U; Baruch College

OSCEOLA, ANNA; BROOKLYN, NY; LAUREL SPRINGS HS; (JR); Hi Hnr Roll; WWAHSS; Emplmnt; Professional Model and Actress; Journalism; Acting

OSDOBY, SAMANTHA M; PLAINVIEW, NY; PLAINVIEW OLD BETHPAGE JOHN F KENNEDY HS; (JR); Hi Hnr Roll; Hnr Roll; Nat Hon Sy; Comm Volntr; DECA; Sci Clb; Spanish Clb; SP/M/VS; Sccr (V); Sftball (V); Soccer-Junior Varsity-Captain; DECA-Senior Board/DECA-Junior Board; Business; Accounting-Certified Public Accountant; Pennsylvania State U; U of Delaware

OSEI-SRAHA, GABRIEL; BALDWIN, NY; BALDWIN HS; (JR); Hnr Roll; Off Aide; Sccr (V); Architecture; Civil Engineering; Princeton U; Syracuse U

OSHODI, BEATRICE F; BRONX, NY; (SO); All Am Sch; Hnr Roll; Jr Eng Tech; Perf Att; Yth Ldrshp Prog; Comm Volntr; Peer Tut/Med; ArtClub; DARE; Dbte Team; Mus Clb; SP/M/VS; Stg Cre; Bdmtn (V); Bskball (L); Swmg (L); Track (L); Vllyball (J); Adv Cncl (P); Cl Off (V); Stu Cncl (P); CR (P); Yrbk (E, P); My Photography Was Bought By Jim Carey; Photography; Music Video Direction; New York U; Cornell U

OSORIA, REYNALDO; BROOKLYN, NY; MIDDLE COLLEGE HS; (SO); Fut Prb Slvr; Hi Hnr Roll; Hnr Roll; Otst Ac Ach Awd; Perf Att; St of Mnth; St Optmst of Yr; Hosp Aide; Chrch Yth Grp; Cmptr Clb; DARE; Emplmnt; Jr Ach; Scouts; Svce Clb; SADD; Ch Chr; Vsy Clb (V); CR (R); Sch Ppr (E, R); Bowling - Boys Varsity; Basketball - Coach of Students Vs. Teachers Games; Sports Journalism; Finance / Business Ownership; Medgar Evers College; New York U

O'STEEN, JOCELYN; BUFFALO, NY; (JR); Hnr Roll; St of Mnth; WWAHSS; Yth Ldrshp Prog; ROTC; Clr Grd; Bskball (V C); Cr Ctry (V); Track (V); Mass Communications; Journalism; Miami U of Ohio; U of Michigan At Flint

OSTOYICH, NICOLE; HANNACROIX, NY; GREENVILLE HS; (MS); Hi Hnr Roll; Otst Ac Ach Awd; Pres Sch; St of Mnth; Yth Ldrshp Prog; Comm Volntr; ArtClub; Chrch Yth Grp; Emplmnt; P to P St Amb Prg; Scouts; Bnd; Chr; Stg Cre; Chrldg; Gmnstcs; Current Events League; Interior Design, Computer Graphics; Forensic Science

O'TOOLE, HANNAH; MADRID, NY; MADRID-WADDINGTON CTRL SCH; (FR); Hi Hnr Roll; Nat Hon Sy; Otst Ac Ach Awd; DARE; Dbte Team; Drma Clb; Emplmnt; Key Club; Spch Team; Spanish Clb; Bnd; Chr; Dnce; Jzz Bnd; GAA (V); Sccr (J); Track (V); NYSSMA - New York State Scholastic Music Association; All County Band; Fashion Designing; Web Designing; Rhode Island School of Design; Cornell U

OUTAR, TIFFANY; SOUTH OZONE PARK, NY; JOHN ADAMS HS; (JR); Hnr Roll; Nat Hon Sy; Perf Att; WWAHSS; Comm Volntr; Peer Tut/Med; Chrch Yth Grp; Key Club; Prom Com; Bdmtn; Lawyer; Nursing; Stony Brook U; Hunter College

OUTLEY II, STEVEN; BATH, NY; HAVERLING HS; (SO); Hi Hnr Roll; Comm Volntr; Spanish Clb; Chr; Track (V); Volunteer to Help Veterans @ VA Hospitals; Computer Engineer; Lawyer; Duke U, North Carolina State; U of North Carolina. U-Conn.

OVERBAUGH, ASHLEE M; BERNE, NY; BERNE-KNOX-WESTERLO HS; (SO); Hnr Roll; MVP; Comm Volntr; Drma Clb; Key Club; Chr; SP/M/VS; Stg Cre; Vllyball (J); Sch Ppr (R); Yrbk (E); Varsity Bowling Team; Martial Arts (Outside of School); Teaching K-3; U SC Clemson; USC Furman

OWAID, SARMED; STATEN ISLAND, NY; (JR); Hi Hnr Roll; Hnr Roll; Perf Att; Emplmnt; Part-Time Job; Doctor; New York U (NYU); Rochester Institute of Technology

OWENS, NAADIA; HIGHLAND MILLS, NY; MONROE-WOODBURY HS; (JR); Hi Hnr Roll; Yth Ldrshp Prog; Comm Volntr; Drma Clb; Lib Aide; NYLC; Chr; SP/M/VS; Sch Ppr (R); Junior Prom Committee; Volunteer Swim Teacher at YWCA - New Windsor, NY; Broadcasting Journalism; Musical Theatre; New York University; George Washington University

OWENS, TURIA; NEW YORK, NY; WADLEIGH HS; (SR); Drma Clb; Pep Squd; Photog; Prom Com; Scouts; Tchrs Aide; Chr; Dnce; SP/M/VS; Bskball (V); Chrldg (V); Yrbk (P); Valley Dance Program; NY Art School of Institute; N.Y.U

OWUSU, MAXINE; MIDDLETOWN, NY; MIDDLETOWN HS; (JR); Ctznshp Aw; Hi Hnr Roll; Chrch Yth Grp; Off Aide; Prom Com; Tchrs Aide; Ch Chr; Bskball (J); Track (V); Step / Dance Group in School; Mission Trip to Russia to Help the Children; Doctor / Pediatrician; Physical Therapist; New York U; Columbia U

PABON, ANDRES; INWOOD, NY; LAWRENCE HS; (JR); Hnr Roll; Comm Volntr; ArtClub; Key Club; Stg Cre; Sccr (J); Track (V); Electrical Engineering; Computer Engineering; New York Institute of Technology; Hofstra U

PACE, ERIK M; BAY SHORE, NY; (FR); Hnr Roll; Nat Sci Aw; St of Mnth; Comm Volntr; Chrch Yth Grp; Emplmnt; Quiz Bowl; Chr; Physician

PACZKOWSKI, ALICIA; BELLMORE, NY; JOHN F KENNEDY HS; (FR); Hi Hnr Roll; Hnr Roll; Nat Hon Sy; Comm Volntr; ArtClub; Drma Clb; SP/M/VS; Completion of LOTE (Polish) W/ Regents (Passed); Forensic Science; Criminal Law; Binghamton U; New York U

PADDOCK, BRITTANY; CALCIUM, NY; INDIAN RIVER HS; (SO); Ctznshp Aw; Hnr Roll; Perf Att; St of Mnth; Peer Tut/Med; Chrch Yth Grp; Key Club; SADD; Chr; Sccr (J); Masters Degree in Teaching; Bachelors Degree in Teaching; Jefferson Community College; SUNY Potsdam

PADDOCK, WENDY; MAYVILLE, NY; CHAUTAUQUA LAKE CTRL HS; (SR); Hi Hnr Roll; Nat Hon Sy; St of Mnth; WWAHSS; Comm Volntr; Emplmnt; Prom Com; Bnd; Chr; Scr Kpr (V); Sccr (V); Track (V L); Stu Cncl (R); Yrbk (E); Reach Award; Rensselaer Medal; Psychology; Spanish; Allegheny College; Alfred U

PAGAN, STEPHANIE; AMITYVILLE, NY; AMITYVILLE MEMORIAL HS; (SR); Hi Hnr Roll; Nat Hon Sy; Salutrn; Sci/Math Olympn; WWAHSS; Comm Volntr; Peer Tut/Med; Spec Olymp Vol; ArtClub; HO'Br Yth Ldrshp; Key Club; Mth Clb/Tm; Mus Clb; Orch; SP/M/VS; President of Music Honor Society & Honor Society; Vice President; Psychology; Columbia U

PAIGE, TANISHA M; JAMAICA, NY; SPRINGFIELD GARDENS HS; (JR); Perf Att; Peer Tut/Med; Emplmnt; Off Aide; Dnce; Chrldg (V); PPSqd (V); Cl Off (T); Sch Ppr (R); Law; John Jay; U of Albany

PAL, SAMANTHA; HUNTINGTN STA, NY; COMMACK HS; (JR); Ctznshp Aw; Hi Hnr Roll; Hnr Roll; Nat Hon Sy; Pres Ac Ftns Aw; Comm Volntr; Hosp Aide; Spec Olymp Vol; Emplmnt; Mus Clb; Spanish Clb; Bnd; Mch Bnd; Sccr (J); Medical Field; Dentistry; New York U; SUNY Stony Brook

PALACIOS, GERALDINE; FLUSHING, NY; FLUSHING HS; (JR); Comm Volntr; Sftball (J); Track (J); Business Management; Accounting; Queensborough Community College; Hunter College

PALAGUACHI, ANGELICA; BROOKLYN, NY; NEW UTRECHT HS; (SO); Perf Att; St of Mnth; Yth Ldrshp Prog; Chrch Yth Grp; Wdwrkg Clb; Dnce; Sccr (J); Traveling Tourism; Toastmaster; Accounting; Nurse; NYU; Brooklyn College

PALATHRA, ELIZABETH C; RONKONKOMA, NY; ST ANTHONY'S HS; (JR); Hnr Roll; Peer Tut/Med; DECA; Drl Tm; SP/M/VS; DECA (2002-Present), Vice President DECA (2004-Present); DECA Regional Finalist; Social Work; Psychology; U of California-Berkeley; U of Illinois-Chicago

PALERMO, JEFFREY T; LYNBROOK, NY; LYNBROOK HS; (JR); Hnr Roll; MVP; Perf Att; Comm Volntr; Emplmnt; Bnd; Bsball (VJC); Engineering; Police Science; Syracuse U; Hofstra U

PALERMO, NICOLE M; WHITESTONE, NY; ST. FRANCIS PREP SCH; (SO); Hi Hnr Roll; St of Mnth; Comm Volntr; Key Club; Italian Clb; SP/M/VS; Sch Ppr (E); Arista (National Junior Honor Society); Consistently on Principal's List (95+GPA); Law; Business Management; Fordham U; Columbia U

PALING, ADRIAN A; BRONX, NY; HS OF ENVIRONMENTAL STUDIES; (SR); St of Mnth; Comm Volntr; Peer Tut/Med; Emplmnt; Mus Clb; Spanish Clb; Keyboard Performance; Psychology; Biology; State U New York Stony Brook

PALKO, AMANDA; PT JERVIS, NY; PT JERVIS HS; (JR); Hi Hnr Roll; Hnr Roll; MVP; Pres Sch; St of Mnth; Comm Volntr; Chrch Yth Grp; Emplmnt; Spanish Clb; Ch Chr; Sftball (V); Childhood Education; Wesley College; U of Delaware

Paczkowski, Alicia
John F Kennedy HS
Bellmore, NY

Pabon, Andres
Lawrence HS
Inwood, NY

Ostoyich, Nicole
Greenville HS
Hannacroix, NY

Osei-Sraha, Gabriel
Baldwin HS
Baldwin, NY

Ortiz, Diana P
Fiorello H La Guardia HS
Brooklyn, NY

Orange, India N
White Plains HS
White Plains, NY

Omezi, Stephanie
Flushing HS
Rosedale, NY

Oppici, Christopher
Sharon Springs Ctrl Sch
Sharon Springs, NY

Ortiz, Dianna
Newburgh Free AC
Newburgh, NY

Osoria, Reynaldo
Middle College HS
Brooklyn, NY

Outley II, Steven
Haverling HS
Bath, NY

Overbaugh, Ashlee M
Berne-Knox-Westerlo HS
Berne, NY

PALLAS, CHRISTINE M; WANTAGH, NY; SEAFORD HS; (SO); Hi Hnr Roll; Pres Sch; WWAHSS; Peer Tut/Med; Key Club; Scouts; Bnd; Mch Bnd; Education

PALLISTER, JENNIFER J; STATEN ISLAND, NY; MOORE CATHOLIC HS; (JR); Hi Hnr Roll; Nat Hon Sy; Sci Fairs; Sci/Math Olympn; Valdctrian; WWAHSS; Yth Ldrshp Prog; Comm Volntr; Peer Tut/Med; Emplmnt; HO'Br Yth Ldrshp; Mth Clb/Tm; NYLC; Prom Com; Bnd; Jzz Bnd; Stu Cncl (R); Lit Mag (R); Sch Ppr (R); Biology

PALMA, ALYSSA; MINEOLA, NY; MINEOLA HS; (FR); Hnr Roll; Comm Volntr; Emplmnt; Mus Clb; Bnd; Mch Bnd; Orch; Ice Hky; Ice Sktg; Rlr Hky; Skiing; Sccr; Sftball (J); Swmg; Vllyball (J); Journalism; Education; New York U; St Joseph's College

PALMATEER, PATRISHA N; SARATOGA SPRINGS, NY; SARATOGA SPRINGS HS; (SR); Hnr Roll; Perf Att; Red Cr Aide; DARE; Emplmnt; French Clb; Chr; Dnce; Fashion Design; Forensics; Adirondack Community College; Schenectady County Community College

PALMER, HEATHER M; MIDDLETOWN, NY; PINE BUSH HS; (SR); Hnr Roll; Otst Ac Ach Awd; Perf Att; Comm Volntr; Chrch Yth Grp; DARE; Emplmnt; Off Aide; P to P St Amb Prg; Photog; Tchrs Aide; Arch; Chrldg; PP Ftbl; Sccr; Yrbk; Forensics; John Jay College; SUNY

PALMER, KIMBERLY M; WHITEHALL, NY; WHITEHALL JR/SR HS; (SO); Hi Hnr Roll; Hnr Roll; SADD; Bnd; Mch Bnd; Chrldg (J); Sccr (J); Track (V); Sch Ppr (R); Varsity Indoor Track; Equine Science; SUNY Morrisville

PALMIERO, GIORGIO; BRONX, NY; BLESSED SACRAMENT HS; (JR); Hi Hnr Roll; Hnr Roll; Nat Hon Sy; Medical Sciences; Biotechnology; St John's U; Hunter College CUNY

PAMPALONE, NADIA; RIDGEWOOD, NY; TOWNSEND HARRIS HS; (JR); Hnr Roll; Nat Hon Sy; Perf Att; Salutrn; WWAHSS; Comm Volntr; Peer Tut/Med; ArtClub; Emplmnt; Lib Aide; Mod UN; MuAlphaTh; Off Aide; Tchrs Aide; Chr; St. John's University Women in Science; New York State Science Honor Society; Education; Biology/Mathematics; St. John's U; New York U

PANAGIOTATOS, SANDI; FARMINGTON, NY; CANANDAIGUA AC; (JR); Hi Hnr Roll; Hnr Roll; Comm Volntr; Part Time Job Auntie Anne's; Part Time Job Blissful Times; Psychology; Doctor; Syracuse U; NYU

PANDOLFO, DANIELLE; STATEN ISLAND, NY; ST JOHN VILLA AC; (JR); Nat Hon Sy; Otst Ac Ach Awd; St of Mnth; WWAHSS; Comm Volntr; Hosp Aide; Saint John's U Women in Science Award; National Honor Society; Nursing; Law Enforcement; U of Las Vegas Nevada; U of San Francisco

PANNELL, GENEVIEVE L; SMITHTOWN, NY; ST ANTHONY'S HS; (JR); Hi Hnr Roll; Nat Hon Sy; Yth Ldrshp Prog; Comm Volntr; Lcrsse (VJ); Tennis (VJCL); Speech Pathologist; Spanish Education; Emerson New Paltz; Boston U America U

PANTER, NASTASSIA; SAINT ALBANS, NY; FLUSHING HS; (SO); Hnr Roll; Comm Volntr; Tchrs Aide; Bnd; Law; Foreign Languages; Oxford U; Howard U

PAONESSA, GABRIELLE; LEWISTON, NY; LEWISTON PORTER HS; (SO); Ctznshp Aw; Hnr Roll; Perf Att; St of Mnth; Comm Volntr; Bskball (JC); Sftball (J); Cl Off (P); Elementary Education; Law; Niagara U; U of Buffalo

PAPADOPOULOS, ALEXANDROS; JERICHO, NY; JERICHO HS; (JR); WWAHSS; Hosp Aide; Key Club; Pep Squd; Photog; Orch; Vllyball (V); Bowling; Computer Science; Stony Brook U; Adelphi U

PAQUIN, MEAGHAN; MASSENA, NY; (FR); Hnr Roll; Hosp Aide; Photog; Dnce; Bskball; Chrldg; Gmnstcs; Cl Off (R); CR (R); Cosmetology; Novelist; New York U

PAREDES, MAYRA; CTRL ISLIP, NY; CTRL ISLIP HS; (SO); Hi Hnr Roll; Hnr Roll; Comm Volntr; ArtClub; Dnce; Sccr (V); Track (V); Vllyball (J); Art Award; Computer Designing; Art

PAREDES, RICARDO A; BRONX, NY; HS FOR MEDIA & COMMUNICATIONS; (JR); Ctznshp Aw; Hnr Roll; Perf Att; St of Mnth; Yth Ldrshp Prog; Mus Clb; Outdrs Clb; ROTC; Mathematics Honors; Computer Engineering; Computer Science; Columbia U; Buffalo U

PARENTE, LEONARDA; STATEN ISLAND, NY; MOORE CATHOLIC HS; (JR); Hnr Roll; Nat Hon Sy; Yth Ldrshp Prog; Comm Volntr; Peer Tut/Med; ArtClub; Scouts; Vllyball (V); Stu Cncl (R); CR (R); Sch Ppr (R, P); Yrbk (R); Respect Life; Religious Education Teacher; Nursing; Teaching; Rutgers; College of Staten Island

PARENTE, MARIA; STATEN ISLAND, NY; MOORE CATHOLIC HS; (JR); Ctznshp Aw; Hi Hnr Roll; Nat Hon Sy; Nat Ldrshp Svc; Otst Ac Ach Awd; Comm Volntr; Peer Tut/Med; ArtClub; Emplmnt; Scouts; Tchrs Aide; Vllyball (V); Stu Cncl (R); CR (R); Sch Ppr (R); Yrbk (E, R, P); Respect Life; Religious Education Teacher; Pre-Med; Rutgers; College of State Island

PARISI, DANIELLE; POMONA, NY; NORTH ROCKLAND HS; (JR); F Lan Hn Soc; Hi Hnr Roll; Hnr Roll; Comm Volntr; FTA; Key Club; MuAlphaTh; Prom Com; Bnd; Sftball (V); Sch Ppr (E); Yrbk (R); Secretary of the Youth Against Cancer; Active Member of Math, Science, and Foreign Lang. Honor Society; Physical Therapy; Speech/Language Pathology/Audiology; Boston U

PARISIS, DIMITRIA; MERRICK, NY; CALHOUN HS; (SO); Hnr Roll; Amnsty Intl; Comm Volntr; Chrch Yth Grp; Drma Clb; Key Club; Vsity Clb; Chr; Dnce; SP/M/VS; Swg Chr; PPSqd (V); Kickline Junior Varsity and Varsity

PARKER, CHANIQUA; MOUNT VERNON, NY; BLESSED SACRAMENTO GABRIEL; (JR); Hnr Roll; Nat Hon Sy; WWAHSS; Comm Volntr; Peer Tut/Med; Ch Chr; Dnce

PARKER, KIRSTEN; CHAZY, NY; CHAZY CTRL RURAL SCH; (FR); Hi Hnr Roll; Peer Tut/Med; Key Club; French Clb; Bskball (J); Sccr (J); Stu Cncl (R); Forensic Science

PARKER, SARAH; POTSDAM, NY; POTSDAM CTRL HS; (SO); Hi Hnr Roll; Nat Hon Sy; Comm Volntr; DARE; Emplmnt; Mus Clb; Photog; Chr; Cl Off (P); Stu Cncl (R); Miss St Lawrence Cty Teenager 2003; Business Administration; Dentistry; Siena; Clarkson

PARMAR, PRIYA; FAIRPORT, NY; FAIRPORT HS; (JR); F Lan Hn Soc; Hi Hnr Roll; Hnr Roll; WWAHSS; Comm Volntr; Emplmnt; Tennis (VJ); Scholar Athlete Award; Youth Asset Building Volunteer; Pharmacy; U At Buffalo; Albany College of Pharmacy

PARRIS, CHANTEL; BRONX, NY; HEALTH OPPORTUNITIES HS; Hnr Roll; Emplmnt

PARSEKIAN, STEPHANIE; LEVITTOWN, NY; DIVISION AVE HS; (SO); F Lan Hn Soc; Hi Hnr Roll; Hnr Roll; Nat Hon Sy; Perf Att; Comm Volntr; Key Club; Scouts; Creative Writing; Music; New England College; Hofstra U

PARSONS, AMANDA K; SAUGERTIES, NY; SAUGERTIES HS; (FR); Hi Hnr Roll; WWAHSS; Peer Tut/Med; Dbte Team; Emplmnt; HO'Br Yth Ldrshp; Key Club; French Clb; Bnd; Chr; Dnce; CR (T)

PARYLO, SARA; BUFFALO, NY; MT MERCY AC; (JR); Hi Hnr Roll; Nat Hon Sy; Perf Att; WWAHSS; Comm Volntr; Peer Tut/Med; Svce Clb; SADD; Spanish Clb; Dale Carnegie Leadership Training

PASSUCCI, LINDA; BUFFALO, NY; MT MERCY AC; (JR); Hnr Roll; Nat Hon Sy; WWAHSS; Yth Ldrshp Prog; Comm Volntr; Peer Tut/Med; Chess; Emplmnt; Prom Com; SADD; Bskball (J); Golf (V); Scr Kpr; CR (R); Yrbk (E); Rugby; Student Athlete Award; Accounting; Teacher; U of Buffalo; Canisius College

PASTINA, KATIE; ROCKAWAY PARK, NY; ARCHBISHOP MOLLOY HS; (JR); Hnr Roll; Comm Volntr; Spec Olymp Vol; Bskball (VJCL); Cr Ctry (J); Sccr (J); Occupational Therapy

PATEL, KRISHAN K S; LATHAM, NY; SHAKER HS; (SR); Hi Hnr Roll; Hnr Roll; MVP; Nat Hon Sy; St of Mnth; Comm Volntr; Peer Tut/Med; BPA; Dbte Team; Emplmnt; FBLA; Key Club; Off Aide; Photog; Tmpl Yth Grp; Tennis (J); Medicine; Business; Cornell U; New York U

PATEL, KRUPA; NEW HYDE PARK, NY; NEW HYDE PARK MEMORIAL JR/SR HS; (JR); Hi Hnr Roll; Otst Ac Ach Awd; Perf Att; Sci Fairs; WWAHSS; Comm Volntr; Mth Clb/Tm; P to P St Amb Prg; Stu Cncl (V); Plan on Attending Medical School

PATEL, KUSH; GLEN OAKS, NY; BENJAMIN CARDOZO HS; (JR); Hi Hnr Roll; Hnr Roll; Nat Hon Sy; Perf Att; WWAHSS; Key Club; Off Aide; Sci Clb; Tchrs Aide; Gold Medalist at the New York Metropolitan Math Fair; Pre-Med; New York U; Boston U

PATENAUDE, BRITTANY; WATERTOWN, NY; WATERTOWN HS; (FR); Ctznshp Aw; Hi Hnr Roll; Perf Att; St of Mnth; WWAHSS; Chrch Yth Grp; Key Club; Chr; Bskball (V); Sccr (J); Sftball (V); Cl Off (T); Triple C Award; Physical Therapy; Teaching; Syracuse U; Ithaca College

PATRICE, KRYSTELLE; BROOKLYN, NY; (JR); Hnr Roll; MVP; Sci Fairs; Comm Volntr; Chrldg (V); Track (VJC); Best of Brooklyn Award; Pre-Med; Education; Cornell; U of Pennsylvania

PATRICK, VERNON H; JAMAICA, NY; LAGUARDIA HS; (JR); MVP; Perf Att; Scouts; Fncg (V C); Tennis (V C); Stu Cncl (P); Yrbk (E); Animation; Social Psychology; School of Visual Arts; Cooper Union

PATTERSON, ERIC S; BUFFALO, NY; WEST SENECA EAST SR HS; (SO); Key Club; Chr; Member Southline Fire District Explorer Program; Health Care; EMT Training; Erie Community College

PATTERSON, SHAQUANDA M; FREEPORT, NY; ROOSEVELT JR/SR HS; (FR); Hi Hnr Roll; Hnr Roll; St of Mnth; Dnce; Drl Tm; Chrldg (J); Drill Team; Criminal Justice; Cosmetology; Jackson U; Florida State

PAUL, JEANETTE; HAWTHORNE, NY; MT VERNON HS; (FR); Hi Hnr Roll; Nat Hon Sy; Otst Ac Ach Awd; Comm Volntr; Law; International Business; Columbia U; New York U

PAUL, MAKEDA A; BROOKLYN, NY; (JR); Yth Ldrshp Prog; Comm Volntr; ArtClub; Chrch Yth Grp; Emplmnt; Tchrs Aide; Bskball (J); Scr Kpr (J); Stu Cncl (R); CR (R); Yrbk (P); Major Representative; Prefect Representative; Corporate Lawyer; U At Buffalo; Hofstra

PAUL, MATTHEW R; FAR ROCKAWAY, NY; BEACH CHANNEL HS; (JR); Hnr Roll; Nat Hon Sy; Perf Att; St of Mnth; Business; Medicine; Georgetown U; Duke U

PAUL, MEAGHAN; STATEN ISLAND, NY; CURTIS HS; (SO); Hi Hnr Roll; Hnr Roll; Nat Hon Sy; Otst Ac Ach Awd; Perf Att; WWAHSS; Chrch Yth Grp; Drma Clb; Emplmnt; Key Club; Scouts; Dnce; SP/M/VS; Stg Cre; Swmg (V); Member of Women's Awareness; Newman Club

PAULINO, EMILY S; SILVER CREEK, NY; SILVER CREEK HS; (SR); 4H Awd; Nat Hon Sy; St of Mnth; WWAHSS; 4-H; DECA; Emplmnt; DECA President & Region President; Business and Marketing Honor Society; Business Administration Culinary; Thiel College

PAULINO, JOEL; FLUSHING, NY; MARTIN LUTHER HS; (JR); Chr; Bsball (J); Bskball (J); Stu Cncl (R); CR (R); Perfect Attendance; US Marshall; Penn State

PAULINO, MELODY; BROOKLYN, NY; JANE ADDAMS HS; (SO); Hnr Roll; Comm Volntr; Chrch Yth Grp; DARE; Mus Clb; Chr; Ch Chr; Dnce; SP/M/VS; Lit Mag; Was Anita in West Side Story Play; Law; Vocal Music/Musical Theater

PAYAMPS DELGADO, BEYRE A; ROCHESTER, NY; JOHN MARSHALL HS; (JR); Ctznshp Aw; Hi Hnr Roll; Hnr Roll; Otst Ac Ach Awd; Sci Fairs; St of Mnth; Yth Ldrshp Prog; Comm Volntr; Peer Tut/Med; ArtClub; Chrch Yth Grp; Cmptr Clb; Drma Clb; Administration; Business; U of Rochester; RIT

PAYANOFF, ANA; FORESTPORT, NY; ADIRONDACK HS; (SO); Hnr Roll; Perf Att; Pres Ac Ftns Aw; ArtClub; Drma Clb; Emplmnt; Schol Bwl; Scouts; French Clb; Acpl Chr; Bnd; SP/M/VS; Stg Cre; Sccr (JC); Sftball (J); Track (J); Vllyball (JC); Psychiatrist; Interior Decorating

PEARCE, JOSE R; CORAM, NY; LONGWOOD HS; (SR); Hi Hnr Roll; Hnr Roll; Computer Science; Computer Information Systems; St John's U; Alfred State U

PECK, JONATHEN; HOLBROOK, NY; SACHEM HS NORTH; (SO); Hnr Roll; Comm Volntr; Emplmnt; Lawyer

PECK, LINDSEY; WILLIAMSON, NY; WILLIAMSON SR HS; (SR); Hnr Roll; Nat Hon Sy; St of Mnth; Comm Volntr; Prom Com; Scouts; Svce Clb; Tchrs Aide; Vsity Clb; Spanish Clb; Chr; Stg Cre; Cr Ctry (V CL); Track (V CL); Vsy Clb (V CL); Stu Cncl (S); Yrbk (E, P); Early Childhood Education; Keuka College

PECORELLA, LYNNE M; UNADILLA, NY; SIDNEY HS; (SR); Hnr Roll; FTA; Ntl FFA; Future Teachers of America; FFA; Early Childhood; BA / Master's Degrees; SUNY Cobleskill

PEDLAR, MARITZA T; CHESTNUT RIDGE, NY; SPRING VALLEY HS; (SO); Hnr Roll; Nat Hon Sy; Otst Ac Ach Awd; Pres Sch; St of Mnth; Comm Volntr; Peer Tut/Med; Key Club; Orch; Swmg (V); Black Achievement Award; Legal Career; Colgate U; Hofstra U

PEERZADA, NEELAM; FLUSHING, NY; BENJAMIN CARDOZO HS; (JR); Hnr Roll; Key Club; Yoga; Doctor; Business; St John's U; NYU

PEGUERO, MIGUEL A; NEW YORK, NY; HS FOR MEDIA & COMMUNICATIONS; (SR); Hnr Roll; Perf Att; St of Mnth; ArtClub; Chess; Chrch Yth Grp; Cmptr Clb; Bsball; Bskball; St. Johns/Criminal Justice; John Jay/Law; St. Johns; John Jay

PELIA, HARPREET; NEW HYDE PARK, NY; HERRICKS HS; (JR); Hnr Roll; Comm Volntr; Hosp Aide; ArtClub; Off Aide; Dnce; Lit Mag (R); National Art Honor Society; Law; Business; New York U; Hofstra U

PELOQUIN, DEREK M; WATERTOWN, NY; CARTHAGE CTRL HS; (SO); Hi Hnr Roll; Sci/Math Olympn; USAA; WWAHSS; Hab For Humty Volntr; Key Club; French Clb; Bnd; Chr; Jzz Bnd; SP/M/VS; Chemistry; Cornell U

PELOQUIN, MATTHEW R; FORT DRUM, NY; CARTHAGE CTRL HS; (SO); Hi Hnr Roll; Sci/Math Olympn; USAA; WWAHSS; Hab For Humty Volntr; Key Club; French Clb; Bnd; Mch Bnd; Mathematics; Cornell U

PENA, CHRISTOPHER; NEW YORK, NY; MEDIA & COMMUNICATIONS HS; (SR); Hnr Roll; Perf Att; Pres Sch; St of Mnth; Peer Tut/Med; Lib Aide; Lit Mag (R); Student Management Services; Computer Engineering; Computer Programming; New York Institute of Technology

PENA, KATHERTEZ; NEW YORK, NY; HS FOR MEDIA & COMMUNICATIONS; (SR); Hnr Roll; Perf Att; Mth Clb/Tm; Spch Team; Dnce; Cardiology; City U of New York; State U of New York

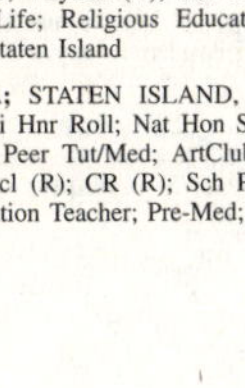
Paul, Matthew R
Beach Channel HS
Far Rockaway, NY

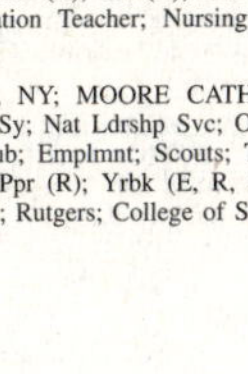
Patrick, Vernon H
LaGuardia HS
Jamaica, NY

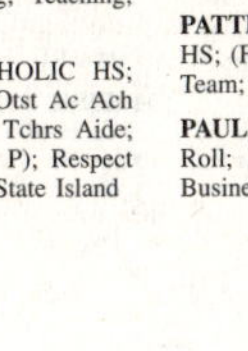
Paonessa, Gabrielle
Lewiston Porter HS
Lewiston, NY

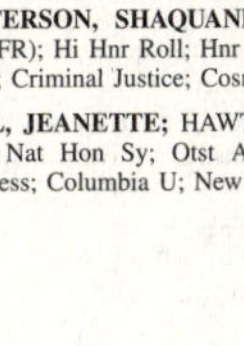
Pandolfo, Danielle
St John Villa AC
Staten Island, NY

National
Honor Roll
Spring 2005

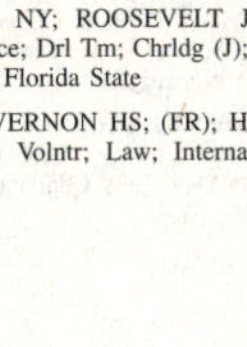
Palmer, Heather M
Pine Bush HS
Middletown, NY

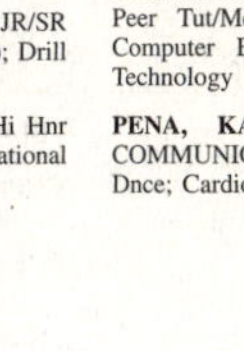
Parker, Kirsten
Chazy Ctrl Rural Sch
Chazy, NY

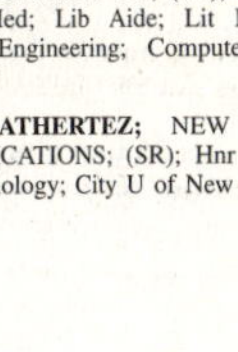
Paul, Makeda A
Brooklyn, NY

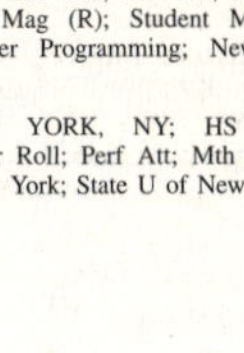
Paul, Meaghan
Curtis HS
Staten Island, NY

PENA, KAYSER; BRONX, NY; HS FOR EXCELLENCE; (JR); Hnr Roll; Perf Att; Peer Tut/Med; Chess; Bsball (V C); Bskball (J); CR (R); Sch Ppr (R); Yrbk (P); Captain of School Baseball Team.; Civil Engineering; Business; U of Miami; St John's U

PENA, LINET; CORONA, NY; AC FOR AMERICAN STUDIES; (FR); F Lan Hn Soc; Hnr Roll; Perf Att; Pres Ac Ftns Aw; Pres Sch; St of Mnth; Peer Tut/Med; Photog; Spanish Clb; Dnce; SP/M/VS; CR (R); Law; John Jay College; Harvard U

PENA, LISA M; HAVERSTRAW, NY; NORTH ROCKLAND HS; (FR); Ctznshp Aw; Hnr Roll; CARE; Comm Volntr; Chrch Yth Grp; DARE; P to P St Amb Prg; Scouts; SADD; Dnce; SP/M/VS; Bskball (J); Vsy Clb (V); Vllyball (V); CR (R); Yrbk (E); Teaching; Computer Science; U of Florida; U of Miami

PENA, PALOMA; BRONX, NY; EVANDER CHILDS HS; (SO); Hnr Roll; Otst Ac Ach Awd; Perf Att; Master's in Psychology; The College of New Rochelle; Manhattan College

PENA, VICTORIA; BRONX, NY; AC OF MT ST URSULA; (JR); Hi Hnr Roll; Perf Att; Sci/Math Olympn; WWAHSS; Comm Volntr; Peer Tut/Med; Emplmnt; Pep Squd; Chrldg (V); Swmg (C); Yrbk (R); Actuarial Science; Business; Long Island U; New York U

PENA ROMAN, VICTOR U; NEW YORK, NY; HS FOR MEDIA & COMMUNICATIONS; (JR); MVP; Yth Ldrshp Prog; Comm Volntr; Cmptr Clb; Emplmnt; Outdrs Clb; Ch Chr; Bsball (V); Bskball (V); Cl Off (R); Sch Ppr (P); Outward Bound; Computer Science; Computer Engineer; Utica College; John Fisher College

PENDLETON, MICHAEL; TRUXTON, NY; DERUYTER CTRL HS; (FR); Hi Hnr Roll; Hnr Roll; Otst Ac Ach Awd; Perf Att; St of Mnth; DARE; Lawyer; Architect; U of Florida; UCLA

PEONE, LORAINE; SAUGERTIES, NY; SAUGERTIES HS; (JR); Hi Hnr Roll; St of Mnth; Comm Volntr; ArtClub; Key Club; French Clb; Chr; 1st Place Winner of Women's Club Art Show; Political Science Major; George Washington U; Northeastern U

PEOPLE, JERARD A; JAMAICA, NY; NEWTOWN HS; (SO); Hnr Roll; Perf Att; St of Mnth; ArtClub; DARE; Dbte Team; Scouts; Cl Off (P); CR (V); Yrbk (P); Computer Engineer; Electrical Engineer; Boston U; NYU

PEPLOWSKI, SAMANTHA; TROY, NY; CATHOLIC CTRL HS; (SR); Hnr Roll; St of Mnth; Comm Volntr; Chrch Yth Grp; DARE; Emplmnt; FBLA; FTA; Key Club; P to P St Amb Prg; Scouts; Bnd; Dnce; Ice Sktg (J); Vllyball (J); Elementary Education; St. Rose College; Maria College

PERDOMO, MARIELY; YONKERS, NY; LINCOLN HS; (SO); Hnr Roll; WWAHSS; ArtClub; Jr Ach; Latino Clb; Drl Tm; Tutor Elementary Students; Visit Mentally & Physically Disabled People; Business-Communications; Lehman College; Berkeley College

PEREA, GABRIELLE; SAUGERTIES, NY; ULSTER CAREER & TECH CTR HS; (JR); Hi Hnr Roll; Hnr Roll; Otst Ac Ach Awd; Comm Volntr; Peer Tut/Med; DARE; Emplmnt; Adv Cncl (R); Cl Off (S); Stu Cncl (S, R); CR (S); Yrbk (R, P); Representative to County Youth Council; Business; Law

PEREYRA, CARLOS; BROOKLYN, NY; ENY TRANSIT TECH HS; (SR); 4H Awd; Hi Hnr Roll; Hnr Roll; Nat Hon Sy; Nat Ldrshp Svc; Otst Ac Ach Awd; Perf Att; St Schl; St of Mnth; Comm Volntr; Peer Tut/Med; Red Cr Aide; 4-H; Drma Clb; Fr of Library; Lib Aide; Mus Clb; Off Aide; Photog; Chr; SP/M/VS; Yrbk (P); Peer-Mediator; Step-Team; Business Administration; Film/Video; Baruch College; Five Towns College

PEREZ, CATHERINE; BRONX, NY; BRONX HS OF BUSINESS; (SO); Hi Hnr Roll; Perf Att; St of Mnth; Dnce; Bdmtn; Sftball; Track; Vllyball; Stu Cncl (T); Architecture; Construction; Hunter College; Lehman College

PEREZ, JISLEYNI; BRONX, NY; F L A G S; (SR); Hi Hnr Roll; Hnr Roll; Nat Sci Aw; Otst Ac Ach Awd; Perf Att; Comm Volntr; Peer Tut/Med; Biology Clb; Chrch Yth Grp; Dbte Team; Sci Clb; Svce Clb; English Clb; Acpl Chr; Ch Chr; Dnce; Flg Crps; Bdmtn (C); Bsball (L); Bskball (C); Gmnstcs (L); Vllyball (C); Adv Cncl (P); Cl Off (T); CR (V); Veterinarian Medicine; Podiatrist; St Francis College; Long Island U (LIU)

PEREZ, KARLA; FLUSHING, NY; BRONX HS OF SCIENCE; (SO); Mod UN; Spch Team; Student Government - Senator; Seeds of Peace - Beyond Borders; International Relations; Political Science; New York U

PEREZ, YVONNE; BRONX, NY; BARD HS EARLY COLLEGE; (FR); F Lan Hn Soc; Hnr Roll; Nat Hon Sy; Sci/Math Olympn; Comm Volntr; Hab For Humty Volntr; Peer Tut/Med; Emplmnt; Tchrs Aide; Chr; Dnce; Drm Mjr; SP/M/VS; 90% and Above in Five Major Subjects; Completed a 2 Week DUA Workshop; Neurosurgery; Forensic Scientist; Cornell U; New York U

PERITORE, JOHNATHAN; DALTON, NY; KESHEQUA MIDDLE HS; (MS); Hi Hnr Roll; Hnr Roll; Comm Volntr; Chrch Yth Grp; DARE; Bskball (J); Stu Cncl (R); Military; Army; West Point

PEROOKUNNEL, SILVIYA; ELMONT, NY; SEWANHAKA; (FR); Hi Hnr Roll; Hnr Roll; Hosp Aide; FBLA; Key Club; Mod UN

PERRICK, REBECCA; EAST MEADOW, NY; EAST MEADOW HS; (JR); F Lan Hn Soc; Hnr Roll; Nat Hon Sy; Sci Fairs; Comm Volntr; Peer Tut/Med; Emplmnt; FBLA; Key Club; Mth Clb/Tm; Mod UN; Pep Squd; Scouts; Tmpl Yth Grp; Bnd; Clr Grd; Flg Crps; Mch Bnd; Chrldg (V); Gmnstcs; Skiing; Currently Teach & Coach Gymnastics; Community Service-Tutor; U of Maryland; U of Delaware-U of Florida

PERSAUD, CHANDANI; HOWARD BEACH, NY; THOMAS A EDISON HS; (SO); All Am Sch; Ctznshp Aw; Hi Hnr Roll; Hnr Roll; Nat Ldrshp Svc; Nat Sci Aw; Otst Ac Ach Awd; Perf Att; Salutrn; Sci Fairs; DARE; Jr Ach; Lib Aide; Mth Clb/Tm; Mod UN; NYLC; Sci Clb; Svce Clb; Dnce; Stu Cncl (V); CR (P); City Tech College

PERSAUD, JAYSON; BELLEROSE, NY; BAYSIDE HS; (SR); Hnr Roll; Nat Hon Sy; Perf Att; WWAHSS; Comm Volntr; Golf (V L); Cl Off (R); Stu Cncl (R); CR (R); Lit Mag (R); Yrbk (R); Pre-Med; Sophie Davis School of Biomedical Education; St John's U

PERSAUD, KRISTEN; BRONX, NY; MARIA REGINA HS; (SO); Hnr Roll; Nat Hon Sy; WWAHSS; Comm Volntr; Key Club; Spanish Clb; Stu Cncl (R); Engineering; Business; Quinnipiac; Temple

PERSAUD, NYRON; BRONX, NY; BRONX HS OF SCIENCE; (SO); Hi Hnr Roll; Hnr Roll; Perf Att; Valdctrian; Chess; Cmptr Clb; Lib Aide; Mth Clb/Tm; Mod UN; Sci Clb; Tchrs Aide; Bskball; Mar Art; Pre-Med; Cornell; NYU

PETERSON, JESSICA; GERRY, NY; CASSADAGA VALLEY MHS; (JR); Hnr Roll; Nat Hon Sy; Otst Ac Ach Awd; WWAHSS; Yth Ldrshp Prog; Chrch Yth Grp; Emplmnt; Photog; Quiz Bowl; Spanish Clb; Bnd; Sccr (V L); Photography; Rochester Institute of Technology

PETILLO, BRITTNEY; BELLPORT, NY; BELLPORT HS; (SR); Hi Hnr Roll; Hnr Roll; Nat Hon Sy; Sci Fairs; WWAHSS; Comm Volntr; Spec Olymp Vol; Chrch Yth Grp; DECA; Emplmnt; Outdrs Clb; Scouts; Chrldg (VJ); Cr Ctry (J); Lcrsse (VJCL); PPSqd (VJ); CR (R); Unsung Hero - Lacrosse; Athletic Helping Others; Psychology; Education; SUNY Cortland

PETIT, FRANCENE E; WOODHAVEN, NY; THE MARY LOUIS AC; (SR); Hi Hnr Roll; Hnr Roll; Nat Hon Sy; Nat Sci Aw; WWAHSS; Comm Volntr; Emplmnt; Spanish Clb; Dnce; CR (R); Principal's List; First Honors; Pre-Medicine; Business Management; St Joseph's College; Queens College

PETRENKO, SVITLANA; BROOKLYN, NY; SHEEPSHEAD BAY HS; (JR); WWAHSS; Comm Volntr; ArtClub; Emplmnt; Off Aide; Tchrs Aide; SP/M/VS; Criminology; Forensic Science

PETRIZZI, JENNIFER; STATEN ISLAND, NY; PT RICHMOND HS; (JR); Hnr Roll; Perf Att; St of Mnth; WWAHSS; Emplmnt; Chr; Sccr (V); Vllyball (V); 100% Attendance During Entire School Career / Arista; Nation Society of High School Scholars; Early Childhood Education; Creative Writing; Wagner College; College of Staten Island

PETROPOULEAS, ANGELIQUE; JAMAICA, NY; HS OF AMERICAN STUDIES @ LEHMAN COLLEGE; (SO); F Lan Hn Soc; Hi Hnr Roll; WWAHSS; Comm Volntr; Key Club; Mod UN; Bnd; Tennis (V); Sch Ppr (E); Princeton; New York U

PETTIFORD, KATRINA; JAMAICA, NY; FIORELLO H LA GUARDIA HS; (JR); Ctznshp Aw; F Lan Hn Soc; Hnr Roll; Nat Hon Sy; St of Mnth; Dnce; Professional Dance; Law and Government

PETTUS, MELANIE; KINGSTON, NY; SAUGERTIES HS; (JR); Hi Hnr Roll; Nat Hon Sy; Salutrn; Valdctrian; Key Club; Prom Com; Spanish Clb; Chr; SP/M/VS; Sccr (J); Tennis (V); Cl Off (S); Stu Cncl (R); Foreign Language / Spanish; Business

PETZKE, ALEX; PINE CITY, NY; SOUTHSIDE HS; (SO); Hi Hnr Roll; Comm Volntr; Chrch Yth Grp; Key Club; Tech Clb; Bnd; Jzz Bnd; Mch Bnd; Pep Bnd; National Junior Honor Society; Environmental Science; Corning Community College; SUNY Cortland

PFEIFFER, ELIZABETH; SAUGERTIES, NY; SAUGERTIES HS; (JR); Dnce; Chrldg (J); Lcrsse (V); Tennis (V); Cl Off (P, V); Yrbk (E); Girls State Nominee and Alternate; Advertising; Public Relations; Manhattan College

PFITZINGER, LEAH; NORTH COLLINS, NY; NORTH COLLINS HS; (SO); Hi Hnr Roll; Hnr Roll; Nat Hon Sy; Perf Att; St of Mnth; 4-H; Chrch Yth Grp; Drma Clb; Mus Clb; Photog; Scouts; Spanish Clb; Bnd; Jzz Bnd; SP/M/VS; Class Treasurer 2005; Interior Design/Architecture

PHAM, AMY; ALBANY, NY; ALBANY HS; (JR); Hi Hnr Roll; WWAHSS; Principal's List; Journalism- Writing in Magazines

PHILIPPE, ROBINE; BROOKLYN, NY; ST EDMUND PREP HS; (SO); Hnr Roll; Nat Hon Sy; Nat Mrt Fin; Nat Sci Aw; Otst Ac Ach Awd; Perf Att; Sci Fairs; St of Mnth; Comm Volntr; Hosp Aide; ArtClub; DARE; Emplmnt; Key Club; Photog; Sci Clb; Dnce; Gmnstcs (J); Sccr (J); Stu Cncl (S); Social Worker; Nursing-Med.

PHILLIP, CHRISTINA; BRONX, NY; BLESSED SACRAMENT ST GABRIEL; (JR); Hnr Roll; Nat Hon Sy; Comm Volntr; Peer Tut/Med; Sftball (V); Pre-Med; Early Childhood Education; Lincoln U; Penn State

PHILLIPS, LA TOYA L.; HEMPSTEAD, NY; HEMPSTEAD HS; (FR); Ctznshp Aw; Hi Hnr Roll; Hnr Roll; Nat Hon Sy; Nat Sci Aw; Nat Stu Ath Day Aw; Otst Ac Ach Awd; Perf Att; Sci Fairs; St of Mnth; CARE; Peer Tut/Med; 4-H; ArtClub; DARE; Key Club; Mus Clb; Prom Com; ROTC; Clb; Clr Grd; Drl Tm; Orch; Sftball (V); Vllyball (V); Lit Mag (R); Sch Ppr (R); Parliamentarian of Law Club; Winner of Renaissance Award; Doctorate; Study to be Judge's Advocate; Columbia U; U of Los Angeles (UCLA)

PHILLIPS, NICK; FULTONVILLE, NY; FONDA FULTONVILLE CTRL SCH; (FR); Hi Hnr Roll; Hnr Roll; Sci Fairs; ArtClub; Chess; Drma Clb; Key Club; Bnd; Jzz Bnd; Mch Bnd; Pep Bnd; Wt Lftg (J L); Bachelor's Degree; Master's Degree; Rochester U; Syracuse U

PHILLIPS, SARAH; MANLIUS, NY; FAYETTEVILLE-MANLIUS HS; (SO); Hi Hnr Roll; Hnr Roll; Comm Volntr; Chrch Yth Grp; Emplmnt; Pep Squd; Photog; Sci Clb; Bnd; Dnce; Pep Bnd; SP/M/VS; CR (P); Honorable Mention in Scholastic Art Competition; Placed 10th Percentile in National French Exam; Communications/Advertising; Public Relations; Boston U; St Lawrence U

PICKERING, STACEY; SODUS, NY; SODUS JR/SR HS; (SO); F Lan Hn Soc; Hi Hnr Roll; Otst Ac Ach Awd; Pres Ac Ftns Aw; Sci Fairs; Chrch Yth Grp; DARE; Emplmnt; FCA; Lib Aide; Pep Squd; Sci Clb; French Clb; Chr; Dnce; Drl Tm; Chrldg (V L); Cr Ctry (V); Hsbk Rdg; Track (V); Vllyball (J); Yrbk (R); Therapeutic Riding Instructor; Nurse/Sports Doctor

PIECORA, CHRISTINA; BROOKLYN, NY; CHRIST THE KING HS; (SO); Ctznshp Aw; Hi Hnr Roll; Nat Hon Sy; Otst Ac Ach Awd; St of Mnth; Peer Tut/Med; Tchrs Aide; International Clb; CR (R); Lit Mag (R); Medicine; Journalism; New York U; St John's U

PIEDMONT, LOREN; VICTOR, NY; ALLENDALE COLUMBIA; (JR); Hnr Roll; Dbte Team; Photog; Stg Cre; Sftball (C); Swmg (V C); Lit Mag (E); Yrbk (E, R); Junior Forum; Communications; Film; Emerson College; New York U

PIEKARZ, JEANNIE; CARMEL, NY; CARMEL HS; (JR); 4H Awd; F Lan Hn Soc; Hi Hnr Roll; Nat Hon Sy; Otst Ac Ach Awd; Comm Volntr; 4-H; Chrch Yth Grp; Emplmnt; FBLA; Clb; Lit Mag (E); Engineering; Spanish; Rensselaer Polytechnic Institute; Clarkson U

PIERCE, EMILY; OGDENSBURG, NY; LISBON CTRL SCH; (SO); Hi Hnr Roll; Nat Hon Sy; Valdctrian; Bnd; Cr Ctry (V L); Track (V L); Academic All Northern Athletic Conference; First Team All NAC - Track / Cross Country; Psychology; Health and Fitness; Grove City College; Ithaca College

PIERCE, JESSICA; SHERIDAN, NY; SILVER CREEK HS; (JR); Key Club; FBI Profiling; Design Technology; Jamestown Community College; Fredonia State

PIERCE, JESSICA N; BATAVIA, NY; BATAVIA HS; (JR); Perf Att; ArtClub; Chrch Yth Grp; Chr; Ch Chr; Sch Ppr (R); All-County Choir; All-County Solo Festival; History Adolescence Education; Interior Design; Fordham U; Brigham Young U

PIERCE, JULIAN N; SHERIDAN, NY; SILVER CREEK HS; (JR); Hnr Roll; Comm Volntr; Peer Tut/Med; Key Club; Prom Com; Spanish Clb; President of Spanish Club; Accounting; Psychology; JCC; Canisius College

PIERRE, DARREN; MEDFORD, NY; ST ANTHONY'S HS; (JR); Ctznshp Aw; Hnr Roll; Nat Hon Sy; Otst Ac Ach Awd; Perf Att; Sci Fairs; Comm Volntr; Peer Tut/Med; Emplmnt; Fr of Library; SADD; Sccr (JC); Piano; Soccer (Travel Club); Physical Therapy; Psychology; State U of New York/Albany; Binghamton U/State U of NY

PIERRE, SAMUEL R; BRENTWOOD, NY; BRENTWOOD ROSS HS; (JR); Hnr Roll; Otst Ac Ach Awd; Perf Att; Pres Sch; Comm Volntr; Law Major; Law Degree & PhD; U of Yale; U of Harvard

PIERRE, THIERRY J; BROOKLYN, NY; ST EDMUND PREP HS; (JR); Hnr Roll; Otst Ac Ach Awd; St of Mnth; USAA; Comm Volntr; Peer Tut/Med; ArtClub; Cmptr Clb; Emplmnt; Sci Clb; Sch Ppr (R); Yrbk (E); National Society of High School Scholars; National History and Government Award; Physician Assistant; Physical Therapy; Georgia State U; St John U

PIERRE-LOUIS, JESSICA; BROOKLYN, NY; ST EDMUND PREP HS; (JR); Hnr Roll; Comm Volntr; ArtClub; Emplmnt; Sci Clb; Drl Tm; High School Internship Program; National Leadership Forum; Physical Therapy; Psychology; St Francis College; Brooklyn College

PIERRE-LOUIS, VLADIMIR; SPRING VALLEY, NY; RAMAPO HS; (JR); Hnr Roll; Sci/Math Olympn; Comm Volntr; Hosp Aide; Red Cr Aide; Chrch Yth Grp; Cmptr Clb; Sci Clb; Svce Clb; Bnd; Jzz Bnd; Stg Cre; Ftball (VJ); Track (VJ); Wt Lftg (VJ); Community Action Club; Spring Hill Volunteer Ambulance Corps; Medicine; Child Psychology; SUNY Stony Brook; Howard U

PIERRE-PAUL, MANOUSCCA; COPIAGUE, NY; WALTER G O'CONNELL HS; (SO); St of Mnth; Peer Tut/Med; Chrch Yth Grp; DARE; Emplmnt; Off Aide; Chr; Dnce; SP/M/VS; Bskball (J); Chrldg (J); Track (V); I Want to Go into Law (Lawyer)

Pierre, Samuel R
Brentwood Ross HS
Brentwood, NY

Pfitzinger, Leah
North Collins HS
North Collins, NY

Persaud, Kristen
Maria Regina HS
Bronx, NY

Pendleton, Michael
Deruyter Ctrl HS
Truxton, NY

Perez, Catherine
Bronx HS Of Business
Bronx, NY

Piekarz, Jeannie
Carmel HS
Carmel, NY

Pierre-Paul, Manouscca
Walter G O'Connell HS
Copiague, NY

PIERSON, KALI; MT MARION, NY; SAUGERTIES HS; (SR); Hi Hnr Roll; Nat Hon Sy; WWAHSS; Comm Volntr; Emplmnt; Key Club; Spanish Clb; Bskball (J); PP Ftbl (J); Scr Kpr (J); Skiing (VJ); Business Major; Ulster Community College

PIETRUSIK, MARK; ORCHARD PARK, NY; ORCHARD PARK HS; (SO); F Lan Hn Soc; Hnr Roll; Sci/Math Olympn; Comm Volntr; Cmptr Clb; Mth Clb/Tm; Sci Clb; Orch; Cr Ctry (J L); Track (J L); Piano Competition Award; All-State Orchestra; Math/Science; Computer

PIKE, KEVIN; SCHENECTADY, NY; SCHENECTADY HS; (FR); Nat Hon Sy; Ftball (J); Wt Lftg (J); NFL - Professional Football Player; Buffalo State; SUNY Buffalo

PIKOVSKAYA, OLGA; BROOKLYN, NY; MIDWOOD HS; (SR); Hnr Roll; Nat Hon Sy; Otst Ac Ach Awd; Sci Fairs; Valdctrian; WWAHSS; Comm Volntr; Peer Tut/Med; Mus Clb; Off Aide; Sci Clb; Dnce; Orch; Intel Science Talent Search Finalist; Rhythmic Gymnast; Biomedical Researcher - MD/PhD; Columbia College - Accepted

PINA, ANDY; BRONX, NY; CELIA CRUZ BRONX HS OF MUSIC; (FR); Hnr Roll; Comm Volntr; Mus Clb; Bnd; Jzz Bnd; Bsball (J); Baseball Player; Miami U

PINA JR, JOSE F; UTICA, NY; THOMAS R PROCTOR HS; (SO); Hi Hnr Roll; Hnr Roll; Otst Ac Ach Awd; St of Mnth; Comm Volntr; Chess; ROTC; Drl Tm; Ftball; Sccr; Honor Guard (ROTC); Mechanical Engineering; Navy; Harvard U; Utica College

PINDT, PAUL A; HILLSDALE, NY; TACONIC HILLS HS; (SO); Hi Hnr Roll; Hnr Roll; Perf Att; Red Cr Aide; SADD; Bnd; Jzz Bnd; Mch Bnd; SP/M/VS; Sccr (J); Blood Donor; SADD Member; English Literature; Creative Writing

PINEDA, ERICK; BRONX, NY; MARBLE HILL HS FOR INTERNATIONAL STUDIES; (JR); Hnr Roll; Perf Att; St of Mnth; WWAHSS; Comm Volntr; Cmptr Clb; Cl Off (R); CR (V); PhD; Medicine; Columbia U; Brandeis U

PINEDA, ROSEMARY; BRONX, NY; MARBLE HILL HS FOR INTERNATIONAL STUDIES; (FR); Hnr Roll; Chrch Yth Grp; Tennis (L); Lehman College

PINKHASOVA, VALERIYA; BROOKLYN, NY; MIDWOOD HS; (SO); WWAHSS; Comm Volntr; Biology Clb; DARE; Key Club; Mod UN; Chr; Intel Science Program; Model Congress; Dermatologist / MD; Neuroscience Major; New York U; SUNY Geneseo

PINNOCK, SAMANTHA; BROOKLYN, NY; SHEEPSHEAD BAY HS; (SO); Hnr Roll; Otst Ac Ach Awd; Perf Att; Sci Fairs; St of Mnth; Valdctrian; Yth Ldrshp Prog; Comm Volntr; Peer Tut/Med; Spec Olymp Vol; Chess; Chrch Yth Grp; DARE; Mth Clb/Tm; Mus Clb; Outdrs Clb; Prom Com; SADD; Ch Chr; Clr Grd; Dnce; SP/M/VS; Chrldg (J); Gmnstcs; Ice Sktg; Swmg; Track; Vllyball; Wt Lftg; CR (V); Yrbk (P); Author's Day Award - Participation; Student of the Week; Pediatrician; Physician

PIRACHA, BENISH; STATEN ISLAND, NY; ST JOSEPH HILL AC; (SO); Hi Hnr Roll; Hnr Roll; Perf Att; Comm Volntr; Peer Tut/Med; Cmptr Clb; Italian Clb; Young Christian Society; Pre-Medicine/Psychology; Nursing; New York U; Columbia

PIRK, SAMANTHA C; HUNTINGTON, NY; ST ANTHONY'S HS; (JR); Hi Hnr Roll; Nat Hon Sy; Sci Fairs; Chr; Ch Chr; Medaled in Sectional; USFA Fencing Tournaments Not Associated with School; Biology; English; Princeton U; New York U

PIROGOV, ROMAN; BROOKLYN, NY; ADELPHI AC; (JR); Dbte Team; Drma Clb; Emplmnt; Sci Clb; Vsity Clb; SP/M/VS; Stg Cre; Sccr (L); Swmg (V); Vllyball (V); Wrstlg (V); Cl Off (V); Engineering Medal from G Washington U; Certificate for Excellence in Math and Art History; Business Administration; Management; New York U; CUNY Baruch College

PISANO, BIANCA; GLEN COVE, NY; GLEN COVE HS; (SO); Hnr Roll; DECA; Pep Squd; Sccr (J L); Sftball (J L); DECA

PISANO, CHRISTINA; BROOKLYN, NY; ST EDMUND PREP HS; (SO); Hi Hnr Roll; Hnr Roll; Otst Ac Ach Awd; Peer Tut/Med; Drma Clb; Tchrs Aide; Vsity Clb; Chr; SP/M/VS; Stg Cre; Chrldg (V); Gmnstcs (J); Published Poetry; Major Roles in School Plays; Art; Fashion; Fashion Institute of Technology; School of Visual Arts

PISCIONERE, TAYLOR A; RYE, NY; RYE HS; (SO); Hi Hnr Roll; Comm Volntr; Hab For Humty Volntr; Bnd; Chr; Dnce; Jzz Bnd; Chair of the Rye Youth Advisory Committee; Vice President of Mock Trial / 12 Yrs Dance; Law; Business; Yale U; U of Pennsylvania

PITTARELLI, MARC; SYRACUSE, NY; KEY WEST HS; (FR); Hi Hnr Roll; Hnr Roll; Otst Ac Ach Awd; Pres Sch; Chrch Yth Grp; Drma Clb; Bnd; Jzz Bnd; SP/M/VS; Sccr; Math; Science

PITTS, OLANDO; HOLLIS, NY; MATH SCIENCE RESEARCH TECH HS; (SO); Perf Att; Hosp Aide; Emplmnt; Dnce; Tennis (V); Yrbk (P); English Achievement Award; Electronic/Computer Engineering; Software Programming; Florida State U; Miami U

PLACIDE, SEBASTIAN G; BROOKLYN, NY; BENJAMIN BANNEKER AC; (FR); Ctznshp Aw; Gov Hnr Prg; Hi Hnr Roll; Hnr Roll; Otst Ac Ach Awd; Salutrn; Sci Fairs; St of Mnth; Comm Volntr; Peer Tut/Med; Chess; Cmptr Clb; Dbte Team; Emplmnt; Jr Ach; Off Aide; Tchrs Aide; Bskball (J); Golf (J); Mar Art (J); CR (P); Excellence in Computer Applications; Publication in - Teacher's Selection Anthology of Poetry; Medicine; Computer Tech; New York U; Columbia U

PLANISNEK, PAMELA J; LIBERTY, NY; LIBERTY HS; (JR); Ctznshp Aw; Hi Hnr Roll; Otst Ac Ach Awd; Pres Sch; USAA; WWAHSS; Comm Volntr; Peer Tut/Med; ArtClub; DARE; Emplmnt; Mth Clb/Tm; P to P St Amb Prg; Scouts; Bnd; Dnce; SP/M/VS; Triple C Award; Architectural Engineering; Architecture; Columbia U; Pennsylvania State U

PLATEK, MARK; SCHENECTADY, NY; GUILDERLAND HS; (SO); WWAHSS; Key Club; Bnd; Cr Ctry (J); Architecture

PLEICKHARDT, CORINNE; FARMINGDALE, NY; FARMINGDALE HS; (SO); Hnr Roll; WWAHSS; Comm Volntr; Emplmnt; Key Club; Vsity Clb; Bnd; Dnce; Mch Bnd; PPSqd (V); Kickline Team; Elementary School Teacher

PLUMMER, BIANCA; BUFFALO, NY; HOLY ANGELS AC; (MS); Hnr Roll; St of Mnth; Peer Tut/Med; Chrch Yth Grp; DARE; Jr Ach; Scouts; Ch Chr; Dnce; Drl Tm; SP/M/VS; Bskball (J); Chrldg (J); Swmg (V); Track (V); Stu Cncl (R); Yrbk (R, P); Drill Team-Captain; Teaching-Reading; Lawyer; Howard U; Yale U

POCHECO, DANNY; STATEN ISLAND, NY; CURTIS HS; (JR); Hi Hnr Roll; WWAHSS; Hosp Aide; Spanish Clb; Bnd; Mch Bnd; Graphic Design / Illustration; Visual Communication; New York U; U of Miami

PODRASKY, CINDY; LEVITTOWN, NY; ISLAND TREES HS; (FR); Ctznshp Aw; Hi Hnr Roll; Kwnis Aw; Nat Hon Sy; Otst Ac Ach Awd; WWAHSS; Comm Volntr; Key Club; Scouts; SADD; Chr; SP/M/VS; Track (V); Stu Cncl (R); Yrbk; Guitar Club; Girl Scouts' Silver Award

POGUE-SMALLS, JESSICA; BRONX, NY; BLESSED SACRAMENT ST GABRIEL; (JR); Hnr Roll; Chrch Yth Grp; Ch Chr; Dnce; Vsy Clb (J); Basketball Championship; Psychology; Child Psychology; Clark Atlanta U; Saint John's U

POLANCO, CONNIE; NEW YORK, NY; GEORGE WASHINGTON HS; (JR); Hnr Roll; Comm Volntr; Lit Mag (P); Fashion Design; Interior Decoration; Columbia U; Parsons School of Design

POLANCO, EDWIN S; JAMAICA, NY; JAMAICA HS; (SO); F Lan Hn Soc; Perf Att; St of Mnth; Chrch Yth Grp; Emplmnt; I Have Received a Nomination for the NYLD; I Was Meritory Student At Dominican Rep; Law; Psychology; Harvard U (Boston); St. Johns (NYC)

POLICASTRO, ALEXANDER; MASSAPEQUA, NY; MASSAPEQUA HS; (SO); Hnr Roll; Sci Fairs; WWAHSS; Comm Volntr; Key Club; Sci Clb; SADD; Skiing; Track (L); Volunteer at the Guide Dog Institute; Volunteer at Local Parish; PhD Robotics and Engineering; Carnegie Mellon University; University of Michigan Ann Arbor

POLIDORA, CHRISTINA; MASSAPEQUA PARK, NY; MASSAPEQUA HS; (JR); Hi Hnr Roll; Hnr Roll; Otst Ac Ach Awd; Sci Fairs; WWAHSS; Amnsty Intl; Chrch Yth Grp; Key Club; Scouts; SADD; Acpl Chr; Chr; Lit Mag (E, R); Psychology; Law; SUNY Stony Brook; Hofstra U

POLISANO, ADRIANA; ELMA, NY; IROQUOIS HS; (SO); Kwnis Aw; St of Mnth; WWAHSS; Comm Volntr; Drma Clb; Key Club; Mod UN; Mus Clb; Scouts; Chr; Orch; Stg Cre; Church Orchestra; National Youth Forum on Medicine (July 2005); Pre-Medicine; Pediatrics; Case Western Reserve U, Cleveland, Ohio; Johns Hopkins U, Maryland

POLLACK, AMANDA; ELMIRA, NY; THOMAS A EDISON HS; (SR); Hi Hnr Roll; Jr Rot; Nat Hon Sy; Pres Sch; Salutrn; USAA; WWAHSS; Comm Volntr; Peer Tut/Med; Red Cr Aide; Chrch Yth Grp; Drma Clb; Emplmnt; Key Club; Prom Com; SADD; Bnd; Mch Bnd; Pep Bnd; SP/M/VS; Swmg (V CL); Cl Off (T); Stu Cncl (T); Aerospace Engineering; Worcester Polytechnic Institute

POLLACK, DONNA; BRONX, NY; FIORELLO H LA GUARDIA HS; (SO); Peer Tut/Med; Dnce; Hebrew Language Certificate; Business (Management); Interior Design; New York U; Columbia U

POLLACK, JESSICA; ELMIRA, NY; THOMAS A EDISON HS; (JR); Hi Hnr Roll; Jr Rot; Nat Hon Sy; Sci Fairs; WWAHSS; Comm Volntr; Key Club; SADD; Bnd; Ch Chr; Pep Bnd; SP/M/VS; Swmg (V L); Tennis (V L); Primary Education; Tropical Medicine; Elmira College

POLLACK, JOSEPH; STATEN ISLAND, NY; STATEN ISLAND TECH HS; (JR); Hi Hnr Roll; Hnr Roll; Nat Hon Sy; Perf Att; WWAHSS; Comm Volntr; Off Aide; Vsity Clb; Stg Cre; Golf (V); Adv Cncl (R); Cl Off (T); Stu Cncl (R); Architecture; Business

POLTINNIKOV, ANAR; BROOKLYN, NY; JAMES MADISON HS; (JR); Hi Hnr Roll; Hnr Roll; Sci Fairs; Comm Volntr; Peer Tut/Med; ArtClub; Key Club; Mth Clb/Tm; Chr; Dnce; Mar Art; Peer Mediator; Actuary; Doctor; Columbia U; New York U

POMALES, ELDA C; YONKERS, NY; SAUNDERS TRADES & TECH HS; (SO); Hnr Roll; WWAHSS; Key Club; ROTC; SADD; Dnce; Tennis (J); Softball League; Architecture

POMBO, RACHEL O; LATHAM, NY; ALPHA OMEGA AC; (JR); Hi Hnr Roll; Nat Hon Sy; Comm Volntr; Peer Tut/Med; Chrch Yth Grp; Emplmnt; Lib Aide; Tchrs Aide; Chr; Ch Chr; Leader of Youth Group Worship Team; Intern at Local Radio Station / Part of ACT Activies Council Team; Communications; Public Relations; Cedarville U; Spring Arbor U

PORCARO, COURTNEY; HOLBROOK, NY; SACHEM HS NORTH; (SO); Hnr Roll; St of Mnth; Spec Olymp Vol; Dnce; Chrldg (J L); Lcrsse (J); Law; Business; New York U

PORTILLO, MICHELLE; WHITE PLAINS, NY; WHITE PLAINS HS; (SO); Hi Hnr Roll; Hnr Roll; Comm Volntr; Key Club; Scouts; French Clb; Bnd; Ch Chr; Sftball (JC); Sch Ppr (R); Basketball for Recreation; Physician; Mathematics Teacher; Yale U; Harvard U

POSADA, PRISCILLA; OAKLAND GARDENS, NY; BAYSIDE HS; (JR); Hi Hnr Roll; Nat Hon Sy; Nat Mrt LOC; Nat Sci Aw; Sci Fairs; WWAHSS; Peer Tut/Med; Emplmnt; Photog; Prom Com; Tchrs Aide; Spanish Clb; Dnce; SP/M/VS; Track (V); Lit Mag (R); Yrbk (E); National Spanish Award 3rd Place Nationally; New York Science and Engineering Finalist; Communications; Advertising and Marketing; Syracuse U; SUNY Baruch College

POSILLICO, CHRISTINA; FARMINGDALE, NY; HS EAST; (SO); Hi Hnr Roll; Peer Tut/Med; Key Club; Italian Clb; Dnce; Chrldg (V); High Honor Roll; Loyola College; Psychology; Loyola; Boston U

POTRIKUS, LINDSEY; COOPERSTOWN, NY; COOPERSTOWN CTRL SCH; (JR); Bskball (J L); Sccr (V L); Tutor for Elementary Students 3 Times Weekly; Communications; Business; Virginia Tech; SUNY Geneseo

POTTER, REGGINA; MOUNT VERNON, NY; BLESSED SACRAMENT ST GABRIEL; (JR); Hi Hnr Roll; Nat Hon Sy; Peer Tut/Med; Emplmnt; Pep Squd; Tchrs Aide; Vsity Clb; SP/M/VS; Chrldg (V); PPSqd (V); Sftball (V); Track (V); Elementary Education; Minor-Cosmetology; Manhattanville College; Iona College

POTTS-COVAN, TAMARA; NEW YORK, NY; ST JEAN BAPTISTE HS; (JR); Nat Hon Sy; WWAHSS; Comm Volntr; Chrch Yth Grp; Drma Clb; SP/M/VS; Stg Cre; Childhood Education; Psychology; Arcadia U; Geneva U

POWERS, ADAM; CLAYTON, NY; THOUSAND ISLAND HS; (FR); Ctznshp Aw; Hi Hnr Roll; Nat Hon Sy; St of Mnth; Comm Volntr; Emplmnt; Dnce; Ftball (V); Law Enforcement

POZNANSKI, ALEX; HOWARD BEACH, NY; BEACH CHANNEL HS; (JR); All Am Sch; Hnr Roll; Nat Hon Sy; Perf Att; Salutrn; Sci Fairs; St of Mnth; Off Aide; Bnd; Jzz Bnd; Mch Bnd; Physics; Engineering

PRAYMAN, KEVIN; SOUTH RICHMOND HILL, NY; JOHN ADAMS HS; (SO); Perf Att; Sccr (J); Law Degree; Medical Degree; Princeton U; Oxford U

PRENDERGAST, MAGGIE; NEW YORK, NY; (SO); Hnr Roll; Amnsty Intl; Comm Volntr; Hab For Humty Volntr; Dnce; Started an Art Magazine in School; Fine Arts; Business; Cornell U; Rhode Island School of Design

PRESSLEY, ALAINA; CHURCHVILLE, NY; CHURCHVILLE-CHILI HS; (FR); Hi Hnr Roll; Hnr Roll; Perf Att; ArtClub; Yrbk (P); Accelerated Math; Like to Help Children with School; Doctor / Medical Field; Actor; Yale U; Harvard U

PRESTON, MARIKATE M; PLATTSBURGH, NY; CHAZY CTRL RURAL SCH; (JR); Hi Hnr Roll; Pres Sch; WWAHSS; Comm Volntr; Chrch Yth Grp; Emplmnt; Key Club; Mth Clb/Tm; Prom Com; SADD; Vsity Clb; Bnd; Ch Chr; Sccr (V); Cl Off (V, T); Sch Ppr (R); Key Club Treasurer; Started Vegetable Garden for Community at Church; Math-Accounting / Finance; Business; SUNY Potsdam New York; Clarkson U

PRESTON, SHARI N; BROOKLYN, NY; BENJAMIN BANNEKER AC; (FR); Hnr Roll; Otst Ac Ach Awd; Perf Att; Comm Volntr; Chrch Yth Grp; Emplmnt; Tchrs Aide; Ch Chr; Dnce; Bsball; Bskball; Sftball (J); NY U Science Entry Program; Citation of Honor; Pre-Med; Engineering; North Carolina A & T U; Spelman U

PREVETE, DAVID; SHIRLEY, NY; WILLIAM FLOYD HS; (JR); Ctznshp Aw; Hi Hnr Roll; Hnr Roll; MVP; Otst Ac Ach Awd; Sci Fairs; Sci/Math Olympn; WWAHSS; Comm Volntr; Peer Tut/Med; Chess; DARE; Lib Aide; Mth Clb/Tm; Mus Clb; P to P St Amb Prg; Tchrs Aide; Bnd; Chr; Jzz Bnd; Mch Bnd; Sccr (V L); Track (V); Cl Off (R); Stu Cncl (R); CR (R); Mechanical Engineering; Mathematics Education

PRIOR, LAURA E; W HEMPSTEAD, NY; WEST HEMPSTEAD HS; (SO); Hnr Roll; Chrch Yth Grp; Key Club; Scouts; Tennis (V); Track (V); Volunteer At West Hempstead Public Library for Summer Reading Program; Interior Design; New York Institute of Technology

PRIORE, ANDREW J; UTICA, NY; NOTRE DAME JR/SR HS; (JR); Hi Hnr Roll; WWAHSS; Comm Volntr; Drma Clb; Chr; SP/M/VS; Stg Cre; Bsball; Bskball; Ftball (V L); Wt Lftg; Adv Cncl (V, S)

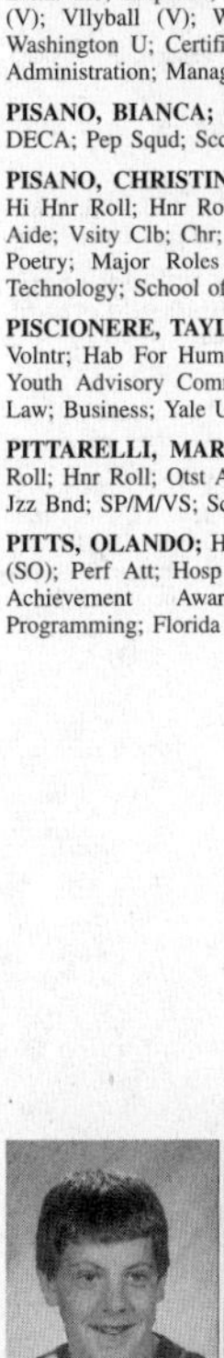
Powers, Adam
Thousand Island HS
Clayton, NY

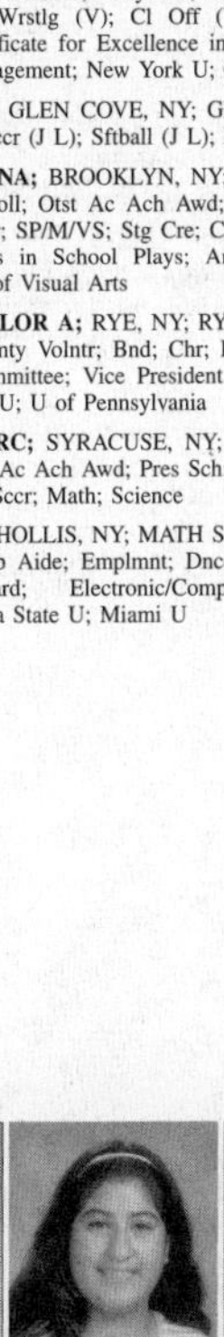
Portillo, Michelle
White Plains HS
White Plains, NY

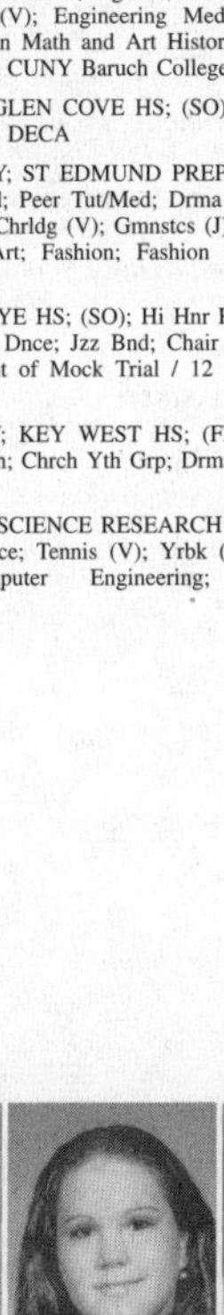
Polidora, Christina
Massapequa HS
Massapequa Park, NY

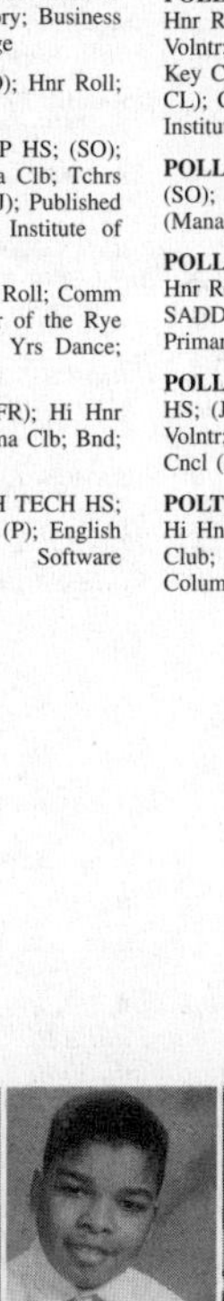
Placide, Sebastian G
Benjamin Banneker AC
Brooklyn, NY

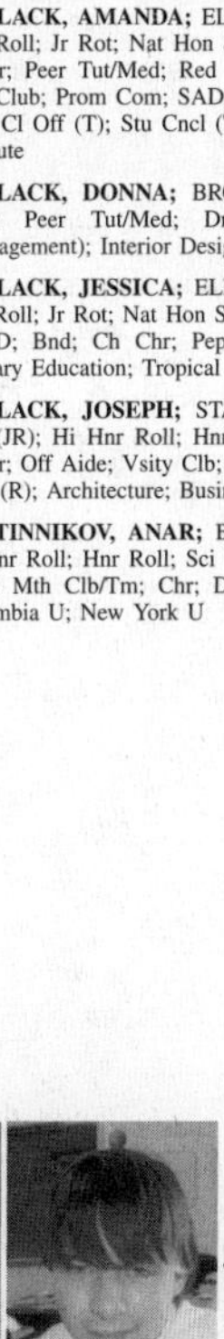
Pirogov, Roman
Adelphi AC
Brooklyn, NY

National
Honor Roll
Spring 2005

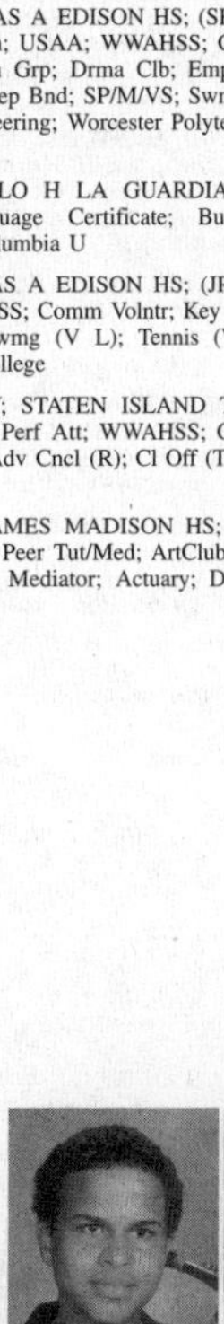
Pina, Andy
Celia Cruz Bronx HS Of Music
Bronx, NY

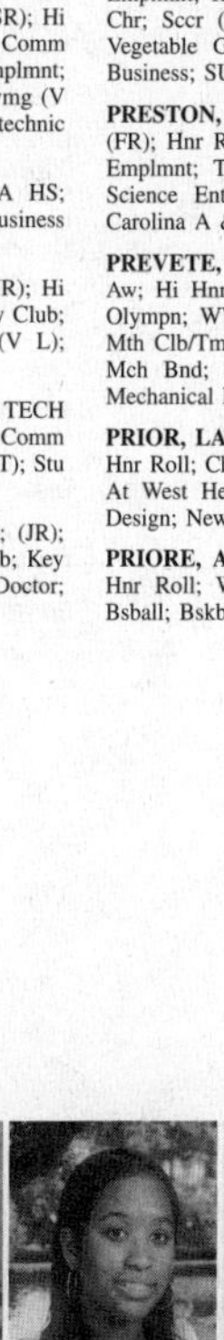
Plummer, Bianca
Holy Angels AC
Buffalo, NY

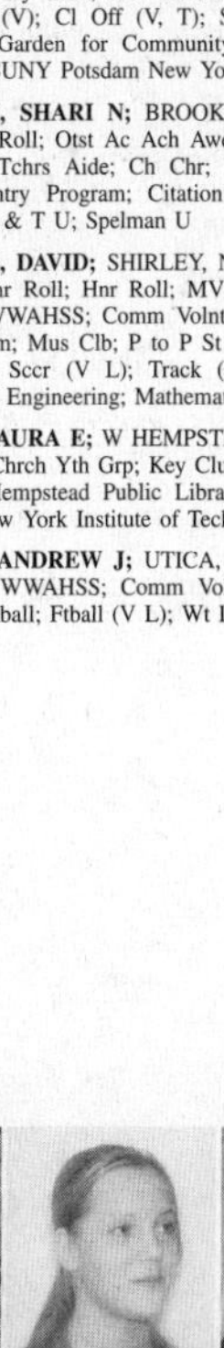
Pollack, Donna
Fiorello H La Guardia HS
Bronx, NY

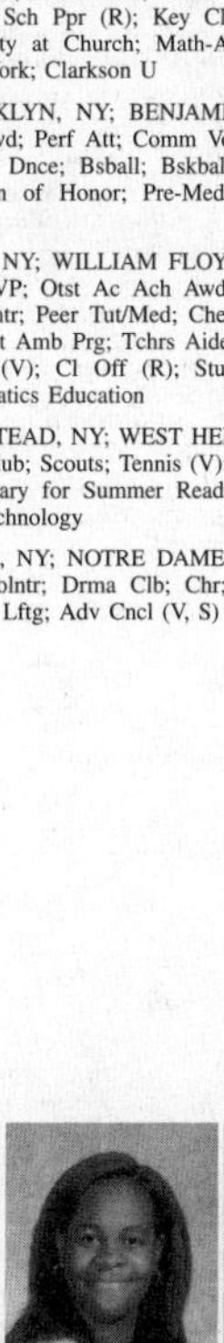
Potter, Reggina
Blessed Sacrament St Gabriel
Mount Vernon, NY

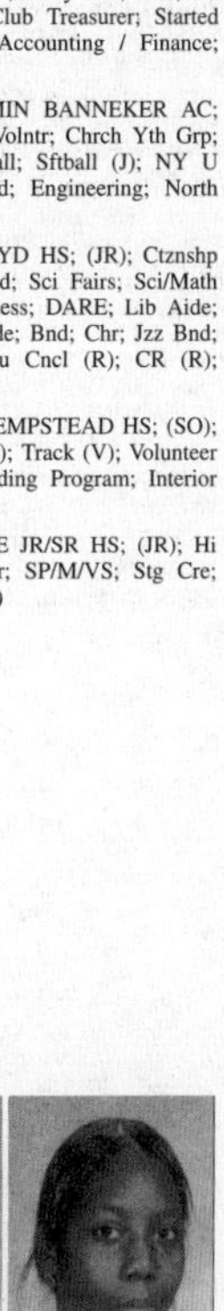
Potts-Covan, Tamara
St Jean Baptiste HS
New York, NY

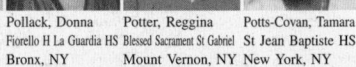

PRISCIANDARO, GABRIELA; BROOKLYN, NY; BISHOP KEARNEY HS; (FR); Hi Hnr Roll; Hnr Roll; MVP; Nat Sci Aw; Perf Att; Pres Sch; Salutrn; Sci Fairs; St of Mnth; Comm Volntr; DARE; Emplmnt; Lib Aide; Chr; Dnce; Bdmtn (J); Cr Ctry (J); Swmg (J); Track (J); Women in Science Award; St John's U Science Award; Public Relations; Advertising; Columbia U; Georgetown U

PRISCO, TUCKER; LYNBROOK, NY; LYNBROOK HS; (FR); Hnr Roll; Perf Att; Peer Tut/Med; ArtClub; Stg Cre; Cr Ctry; Track; Yale U; Johns Hopkins U

PRYOR JR, ALFRED; BRONX, NY; EVANDER CHILDS HS; (SO); MVP; Ftball (V); Track; Photography; Computer Technology; Miami U; Syracuse

PRZYBYLOWICZ, RYLE W; WEBSTER, NY; WEBSTER THOMAS HS; (SO); F Lan Hn Soc; Hi Hnr Roll; Nat Hon Sy; Otst Ac Ach Awd; Comm Volntr; Dbte Team; Ntl Beta Clb; NtlFrnscLg; Svce Clb; Bnd; Sccr (J); Tennis (J); Lawyer; Engineer; U of Notre Dame; Cornell U

PULIDO, BIANCA; LEVITTOWN, NY; ISLAND TREES HS; (SO); Hi Hnr Roll; Kwnis Aw; MVP; Nat Hon Sy; Sci/Math Olympn; WWAHSS; Comm Volntr; Peer Tut/Med; Emplmnt; Key Club; Kwanza Clb; Mth Clb/Tm; Mus Clb; Sci Clb; Tchrs Aide; Bnd; Jzz Bnd; Mch Bnd; Sccr (J); Lit Mag (E); Participation in NYSSMA; Coach's Award-Soccer; Chemistry; English; Georgetown U; Columbia U

PUNZALAN, MAICA; NIAGARA FALLS, NY; NIAGARA-WHEATFIELD SR HS; (SO); Hi Hnr Roll; Hnr Roll; MVP; Nat Hon Sy; Perf Att; Comm Volntr; ArtClub; Dbte Team; Outdrs Clb; French Clb; Tennis (J); Track (J); Sch Ppr (R); Accounting; Nursing; U of Buffalo; Niagara County Community College

PUOPOLO, MICHAEL; NEW YORK, NY; REGIS HS; (SO); F Lan Hn Soc; Hi Hnr Roll; Perf Att; Pres Ac Ftns Aw; WWAHSS; Yth Ldrshp Prog; Peer Tut/Med; Chess; Dbte Team; Emplmnt; Mod UN; NtlFrnscLg; P to P St Amb Prg; Latin Clb; Sccr (JC); Tennis (V L); National Latin Exam-Gold Key / Summa Cum Laude; Lincoln-Douglas Debater -Finalist; Classics / Latin Scholar

PURCELL, ERIN; SOMERS, NY; SOMERS HS; (JR); F Lan Hn Soc; Hi Hnr Roll; Hnr Roll; Hab For Humty Volntr; SADD; French Clb; Chrldg (J); Human Rights Club; Psychology; Accounting

PUTTACHI, ARUN; ALBANY, NY; SHAKER HS; (SO); All Am Sch; Hi Hnr Roll; Pres Ac Ftns Aw; Sci Fairs; Sci/Math Olympn; St Schl; St of Mnth; USAA; WWAHSS; Comm Volntr; Hosp Aide; HO'Br Yth Ldrshp; Jr Cls League; Key Club; Mth Clb/Tm; Tmpl Yth Grp; French Clb; Jzz Bnd; Tennis (V CL); Vllyball (V); Cl Off; Stu Cncl (R); Yrbk (R); US Army Microbiology Research Award; National Latin Exam Gold Medal Winner; Pre-Med; Engineering

QELLO, FLORIDA; STATEN ISLAND, NY; CURTIS HS; (JR); All Am Sch; Hi Hnr Roll; USAA; WWAHSS; Yth Ldrshp Prog; Comm Volntr; Cr Ctry (J); Track (J); Sch Ppr (P); Yrbk (E, P); I'm Going to Be Photography Editor for The Year Book in 12th Grade; Pharmacist; Dentist; Northeastern; New York U

QIAN, JACK; SLINGERLANDS, NY; GUILDERLAND HS; (SO); Hnr Roll; Perf Att; WWAHSS; Key Club; Mth Clb/Tm; Mus Clb; Orch; SP/M/VS; Tennis (J); Sch Ppr; Math/Science Department Award; Member of Empire State Youth Orchestra; Medicine; Computer Science

QIN, XIN; FLUSHING, NY; STUYVESANT HS; (JR); F Lan Hn Soc; Hnr Roll; Nat Hon Sy; Peer Tut/Med; DARE; Emplmnt; Key Club; NtlFrnscLg; Spch Team; Orch; SP/M/VS; Lit Mag (E, P); Business; Law; New York U; U of Pennsylvania

QIROLLARI, ANGELA; ASTORIA, NY; ST DEMETRIOS HS OF ASTORIA; (JR); Hnr Roll; Comm Volntr; ArtClub; Dnce; Bskball (J); Chrldg (J); Vllyball (V); Pharmacist; Teacher; Hunter College; St John's U

QIU, CONNIE; BROOKLYN, NY; MIDWOOD HS; (SO); Hnr Roll; Perf Att; Sci Fairs; St of Mnth; Comm Volntr; Key Club; Tchrs Aide; Yrbk (R); Achievement Award NYCBEC; Pharmacy; New York U; Cornell U

QUACH, LUCY; WHITESTONE, NY; BAYSIDE HS; (SO); Hnr Roll; Amnsty Intl; Comm Volntr; Hosp Aide; Key Club; Off Aide; Tchrs Aide; Ice Sktg (L); Swmg (L); Binghamton U

QUAIL, BRITTANY M; BABYLON, NY; WEST BABYLON HS; (JR); Ctznshp Aw; F Lan Hn Soc; Hi Hnr Roll; Hnr Roll; Nat Hon Sy; Nat Ldrshp Svc; Otst Ac Ach Awd; Pres Ac Ftns Aw; Sci/Math Olympn; St of Mnth; Comm Volntr; Hab For Humty Volntr; Peer Tut/Med; Mth Clb/Tm; NYLC; Prom Com; Quiz Bowl; Scouts; SADD; Vsity Clb; Clb; Dnce; Orch; Tennis (J); Track (V); Vsy Clb (V); Cl Off (R); Stu Cncl (V); Yrbk (R); Foreign Policy; Government; George Washington; American U

QUANSAH, PRISCILLA; CORONA, NY; AC FOR AMERICAN STUDIES; (FR); Hnr Roll; Salutrn; Chrch Yth Grp; Cinematography Club; Medicine; Journalism; Yale U; Harvard U

QUARTERS, TARA; ARGYLE, NY; ARGYLE CTRL SCH; (SO); Perf Att; St of Mnth; DARE; Emplmnt; Ntl FFA; Chr; Business Achievement Award

QUATTROCIOCCHI, PERRI C; ENDICOTT, NY; UNION-ENDICOTT HS; (JR); Ctznshp Aw; Hi Hnr Roll; Nat Hon Sy; WWAHSS; Comm Volntr; Peer Tut/Med; Biology Clb; Chrch Yth Grp; Emplmnt; Key Club; Vsity Clb; Italian Clb; Sccr (V L); Lit Mag (E, R); Captain of Girls JV Soccer; Volunteer with UEHS Marching Band; Marine Mammal Pathobiologist; Marine Biologist; Florida Institute of Technology; State U of New York At Stony Brook

QUENCER, MELISSA; CHAUMONT, NY; THOUSAND ISLAND HS; (FR); Hi Hnr Roll; Hnr Roll; St of Mnth; Comm Volntr; Chrch Yth Grp; Mus Clb; Bnd; Ch Chr; Jzz Bnd; Mch Bnd; Sccr (J); Chemistry; Physics; Saint Lawrence U; Clarkson U

QUIARA, RACHELLE; CASTLETON, NY; COLUMBIA HS; (JR); Hi Hnr Roll; Hnr Roll; Otst Ac Ach Awd; Perf Att; WWAHSS; Amnsty Intl; Peer Tut/Med; Drma Clb; Emplmnt; Key Club; Mth Clb/Tm; Mus Clb; Prom Com; Scouts; Chr; Dnce; Orch; SP/M/VS; Vllyball (JC); Congressional Student Leadership Conference; Invitational Award; Dance Education / Choreography; Music Education; New York U; Columbia U

QUIGLEY, AILEEN E; CORNWALL ON HUDSON, NY; CORNWALL CTRL HS; (SO); Hnr Roll; Ch Chr; Chrldg (JC); Interpreter

QUINN, BRITTNY; GLEN HEAD, NY; OUR LADY OF MERCY AC; (JR); F Lan Hn Soc; Hnr Roll; Comm Volntr; Peer Tut/Med; Key Club; Off Aide; Prom Com; Svce Clb; Tennis (V); Track (V); Yrbk (R); Community Service; Fashion Merchandising, Language; Loyola, Old Dominian, U of MD; U of Delaware

QUINN, RYAN A; NORTH COLLINS, NY; NORTH COLLINS HS; (SR); Hnr Roll; WWAHSS; Hosp Aide; Chrch Yth Grp; DARE; Spanish Clb; Bnd; National Vocational Technical Honor Society; Criminal Justice-County Sheriff; Hilbert College

QUINONES-NOVOA, JESSICA; BROOKLYN, NY; HEALTH PROF & HUMAN SERV HS; (SO); F Lan Hn Soc; Hnr Roll; Perf Att; Sci/Math Olympn; St of Mnth; Comm Volntr; Peer Tut/Med; Chess; Chrch Yth Grp; Emplmnt; Mus Clb; Off Aide; Scouts; SADD; Tchrs Aide; Bnd; Chr; Mch Bnd; Science Research Program (High School); Medicine; Nursing; New York U; Long Island U

QUINONEZ, EDGARDO; NEWBURGH, NY; (SO); Nat Hon Sy; Comm Volntr; Chess; Biologist (Wild Life Expert); Web Designer; Marist College; Vermont U

QUINTANA, KATHERINE S; MILLER PLACE, NY; MILLER PLACE HS; (SR); All Am Sch; F Lan Hn Soc; Hi Hnr Roll; Nat Hon Sy; Otst Ac Ach Awd; Spec Olymp Vol; Emplmnt; Prom Com; SADD; Vsity Clb; Lcrsse (VJ L); Track (V); Vsy Clb (V L); Stu Cncl (R); CR (R); Business Management; MBA; Adelphi U; Bryant U

QUINTERO-MEJIA, ADRIANA; JACKSON HEIGHTS, NY; SAINT MICHAEL AC; (JR); Hnr Roll; Peer Tut/Med; Dbte Team; Drma Clb; Emplmnt; Vsity Clb; SP/M/VS; Vllyball (V); CR (R); Yrbk (P); Debate Team; Decorating School; Business Management; History Major; Pace U; Georgetown U

QUIST, EVELYN E; FAR ROCKAWAY, NY; FAR ROCKAWAY HS; (JR); Hi Hnr Roll; Hnr Roll; Perf Att; Sci Fairs; St of Mnth; WWAHSS; Dbte Team; Key Club; Sftball (V); Vllyball (V); Arista; Perfect Attendance; Pre-Med; Biology; Columbia U; C W Post - Long Island U

QURESHI, ABBAS; HICKSVILLE, NY; HICKSVILLE HS; (JR); Sccr (J); Worked in School Store; Accounting; MBA; Baruch CUNY; NYU

QURESHI, ASAD; EAST AMHERST, NY; CLARENCE HS; (JR); Ctznshp Aw; Duke TS; Hi Hnr Roll; Hnr Roll; Nat Hon Sy; Sci Fairs; Sci/Math Olympn; St of Mnth; Valdctrian; WWAHSS; Comm Volntr; Hosp Aide; Peer Tut/Med; ArtClub; Jr Ach; Lib Aide; Schol Bwl; SADD; Bskball (J); Track (V); Stu Cncl (R); Lit Mag (R); Sch Ppr (R, P); Biochemistry; Physics; Cornell U; Rice U

QURESHI, MEHWASH; ASTORIA, NY; AC FOR AMERICAN STUDIES; (FR); Ctznshp Aw; Hi Hnr Roll; Otst Ac Ach Awd; Perf Att; Sci Fairs; St of Mnth; Comm Volntr; CR (P); Summa Cum Lade - 95% Overall Average; Eagle Award and PTA Achievement Award; Laboratory Sciences; Stock Market; Albany U

RAFOL, ELAINE C Y; FLORAL PARK, NY; BRONX SCIENCE HS; (FR); Hi Hnr Roll; Nat Hon Sy; Otst Ac Ach Awd; Perf Att; Sci Fairs; Sci/Math Olympn; Comm Volntr; Chrch Yth Grp; Key Club; Mth Clb/Tm; Filipino Clb; Dnce; CR (R); Accounting; Journalism; Binghamton U; New York U

RAGINSKAYA, ANNA; BROOKLYN, NY; BROOKLYN TECH HS; (SO); Hnr Roll; WWAHSS; Comm Volntr; Ntl Beta Clb; Dnce; Piano- 7 Years; Attended Stony Brook U - Biotechnology Summer Camp; Pre-Med; Orthodontics; New York U; Honors Program-Hunter College

RAGOTSKIE, LYNNE; BALLSTON SPA, NY; NEWPORT HS; (SO); Comm Volntr; Peer Tut/Med; Pep Squd; Clr Grd; Dnce; Flg Crps; SP/M/VS; Chrldg (V L); Gmnstcs (V); PPSqd (V); Sch Ppr (R); Many 1st & 2nd Place Individual Achievements for Cheerleading; Early Childhood; Writer

RAGUNAUTH, RAYMON G; QUEENS VILLAGE, NY; QUEENS HS FOR SCIENCES AT YORK; (FR); Hi Hnr Roll; Hnr Roll; MVP; Nat Hon Sy; Peer Tut/Med; Drma Clb; SP/M/VS; CR (P); Played in Little League Baseball All-Star Game; Sports Medicine; Biological and Environmental Engineering; Columbia U; Cornell U

RAHMAN, NADIA; JAMAICA, NY; BENJAMIN CARDOZO HS; (JR); Hnr Roll; St of Mnth; Yth Ldrshp Prog; Comm Volntr; Peer Tut/Med; Emplmnt; Tchrs Aide; Ftball (L); GAA (L); Sccr (L); Sftball (L); Vllyball (L); Cl Off (R); CR (R); Explorer of New York Law Enforcement; Master's Degree Or / And Law Degree; Hunter College; Pace U

RAIS, JENNIFER; GLEN COVE, NY; GLEN COVE HS; (SR); Hi Hnr Roll; Nat Mrt Sch Recip; Otst Ac Ach Awd; CARE; Comm Volntr; DECA; Drma Clb; Emplmnt; Mus Clb; Pep Squd; Photog; French Clb; Bnd; Chr; Jzz Bnd; Pep Bnd; Bskball (VJ); Lcrsse (VJ); Tennis (JC); Sch Ppr (R); Varsity Kickline; Law; Business; St John's U (NY)

RAJAB, SALAH; YONKERS, NY; YANKEES HS; (JR); Hi Hnr Roll; Nat Hon Sy; Jr Ach; Dnce; SP/M/VS; Swmg (J); Tennis (V); Club 90 Bronze and Silver Awards; Rochester College Science Project Award; Medical Career; Research Career; NYU; Brown

RAJU, NOOR M; BRONX, NY; MARBLE HILL HS FOR INTERNATIONAL STUDIES; (JR); Ctznshp Aw; Hnr Roll; Perf Att; Sci Fairs; St of Mnth; Comm Volntr; ArtClub; Chess; Drma Clb; SP/M/VS; Sch Ppr (R); Currently Taking An Internship; Pre-Med; Pre-Law

RALSTON, KEVIN S; POMONA, NY; RAMAPO HS; (JR); Hnr Roll; Nat Hon Sy; WWAHSS; Comm Volntr; Emplmnt; Key Club; Chr; Bskball (JCL); Cr Ctry (VJ L); Sccr (JC); Track (VJ L); Yrbk (E, P); Key Club / Financial Sec & Treasurer Distinguished Key Club; Sports / Training; UNC Chapel Hill; Middle Tennessee State

RAMAGLIA, MARIA G; BROOKLYN, NY; E R MURROW HS; (JR); Hnr Roll; St of Mnth; Hosp Aide; Peer Tut/Med; Emplmnt; Off Aide; Tchrs Aide; Italian Clb; Chr; Dnce; Italian National Merit Exam; Nutrition & Food Science; Pre-Law / Law Degree; U of Miami; Florida State U

RAMCHARAN, DANIELLE J; BRENTWOOD, NY; BRENTWOOD HS SONDERLING CTR; (SO); Hi Hnr Roll; Hnr Roll; Nat Hon Sy; Pres Ac Ftns Aw; Peer Tut/Med; Spec Olymp Vol; Drma Clb; FCCLA; Bnd; Clr Grd; SP/M/VS; Stg Cre; Cr Ctry (V); PPSqd (C); Local Community Service Awards; Recognition By the Board of Education; Linguistics; Foreign Languages; U of California San Diego; Louisiana State U

RAMDENE, JESTINA A G; BRONX, NY; BLESSED SACRAMENT ST GABRIEL; (JR); Nat Ldrshp Svc; Nat Mrt LOC; St of Mnth; Peer Tut/Med; Off Aide; Outdrs Clb; Tchrs Aide; Bskball (V); Sccr (V); Sftball (V); Internal Medicine; Forensic Science; Florida State U; Universal of Central Florida

RAMIC, ELVIS; ALBANY, NY; ALBANY HS; (SO); Ctznshp Aw; Hi Hnr Roll; Hnr Roll; Otst Ac Ach Awd; Perf Att; WWAHSS; Comm Volntr; Chess; DARE; Key Club; Sccr (J); Law; Business; Boston College; Cornell

RAMIREZ, ELIZA; FREEPORT, NY; FREEPORT HS; (JR); Hi Hnr Roll; Hnr Roll; St of Mnth; Yth Ldrshp Prog; Comm Volntr; Chrch Yth Grp; DECA; Emplmnt; Spanish Clb; Ch Chr; Dnce; Vllyball (J); Renaissance Award; Music Production and Technology; Performance Arts; New York U; U of Hartford

RAMIREZ, KELVIN; STATEN ISLAND, NY; NEW DORP HS; (SO); Ctznshp Aw; Hnr Roll; Sci Fairs; St of Mnth; Hab For Humty Volntr; ArtClub; Chess; Cmptr Clb; Drma Clb; FTA; Outdrs Clb; Tech Clb; Clb; Chr; Ch Chr; Clr Grd; Dnce; Bsball (V); Bskball (V); Golf (V); Ice Sktg (V); Lcrsse (V); Track; Wt Lftg (V); CR (P); Play Productions; School Production; Math; Science; Wagner College

RAMIREZ, MAYRA; BRONX, NY; BRONX SCH FOR LAW GOVT AND JUSTICE; (SO); Red Cr Aide; Lawyer; Criminal Justice

RAMKISSOON, ARIEL; BRONX, NY; LOUIS D BRANDEIS HS; (FR); Hnr Roll; Perf Att; Psychology; Criminal Lawyer; Ithaca College; Pace U

RAMNARINE, GANESH J; JAMAICA, NY; STUYVESANT HS; (JR); Nat Mrt Semif; WWAHSS; Yth Ldrshp Prog; Peer Tut/Med; Emplmnt; Key Club; Tchrs Aide; Mathematics; Physics; Massachusetts Institute of Technology; Harvard College

RAMOS, JASLEIN; NEW YORK, NY; HS FOR MEDIA & COMMUNICATIONS; (JR); Hnr Roll; Perf Att; Journalism; Nursing; Stony Brook U; Quinnipiac U

RAMOS, RICHIE; BROOKLYN, NY; ST EDMUND PREP HS; (SO); Hnr Roll; Sci Fairs; Comm Volntr; Emplmnt; Prom Com; SADD; Bsball; Bskball; Ftball; Played with the Brooklyn Bulldogs Baseball Team In-House & Travel Team for 8 years; Sports Medicine; Business Administration; Miami State; Georgia Tech

Ramdene, Jestina A G
Blessed Sacrament St Gabriel
Bronx, NY

Qureshi, Mehwash
AC For American Studies
Astoria, NY

Quintana, Katherine S
Miller Place HS
Miller Place, NY

National
Honor Roll
Spring 2005

Pryor Jr, Alfred
Evander Childs HS
Bronx, NY

Raju, Noor M
Marble Hill HS For International Studies
Bronx, NY

Ramirez, Kelvin
New Dorp HS
Staten Island, NY

RAMSAROEP, LENNIE A; ROCKVILLE CENTRE, NY; MALVERNE HS; (JR); Ctznshp Aw; F Lan Hn Soc; Hi Hnr Roll; Nat Hon Sy; Otst Ac Ach Awd; Perf Att; Pres Sch; St of Mnth; WWAHSS; Yth Ldrshp Prog; Comm Volntr; Hosp Aide; Peer Tut/Med; Emplmnt; Mod UN; Off Aide; Quiz Bowl; Bskball (J); Cl Off (V); Sch Ppr (R, P); Yrbk (R, P); President and Founder of Model UN at School; Law; Business / Entrepreneurship; New York U; Princeton U

RAMSAROOP, CANDICE; FLORAL PARK, NY; FLORAL PARK MEMORIAL HS; (JR); F Lan Hn Soc; Hnr Roll; Nat Hon Sy; Comm Volntr; Chrch Yth Grp; School Step Team; Foreign Language Honor Society; Law; Hofstra U; Fordham U

RAMSAWAK, KERI-ANNE; S OZONE PARK, NY; JOHN ADAMS HS; (SR); Hnr Roll; Nat Hon Sy; Comm Volntr; Key Club; Member of National Honor Society; Member of Key Club; Communication Arts; Master's Degree; Queens; NYIT

RAMSAYWAK, RANDY; BRONX, NY; BRONX HS OF SCIENCE; (SO); Gov Hnr Prg; Hi Hnr Roll; Hnr Roll; Nat Hon Sy; Perf Att; Aikido Gokyu; Taijutsu Sankyu; Pre-Med; Biology; Columbia U; Brown U

RAMSEY, DOUGLAS; MASTIC BEACH, NY; WILLIAM FLOYD HS; (JR); Hi Hnr Roll; Hnr Roll; Nat Hon Sy; WWAHSS; Hab For Humty Volntr; Peer Tut/Med; Key Club; Bsball (J); Bskball (J); Stu Cncl (R); Distinguished Key Club Member Award; Mathematics

RAMULIC, EDVIN; BUFFALO, NY; KENMORE WEST HS; (FR); Hnr Roll; Perf Att; Bskball (V); Ftball (V); Mathematics

RANALLETTI, PHILLIP; ROCHESTER, NY; SPENCERPORT HS; (JR); Hi Hnr Roll; Nat Hon Sy; Perf Att; St of Mnth; WWAHSS; Yth Ldrshp Prog; Svce Clb; Vsity Clb; Sccr (V L); Boys State 2005 Delegate; Business Student of the Month; Business; Accounting; U of Buffalo; Syracuse U

RANCIER, KELLY; PATTERSON, NY; CARMEL HS; (FR); Hi Hnr Roll; Pres Ac Ftns Aw; Tchrs Aide; Bnd; Chrldg (V); Gymnastics- Level 9 NYS Balance Beam Champion; Gymnastics

RANDAZZO, HELEN; ELMONT, NY; KELLENBERG MEMORIAL; (JR); Hnr Roll; Nat Hon Sy; Perf Att; Svce Clb; Chr; Lit Mag (E); Sch Ppr (R)

RANEOUR, STEVE; BALLSTON SPA, NY; SARATOGA SPRINGS HS; (FR); Hnr Roll; Perf Att; Comm Volntr; Chrch Yth Grp; Bnd; Track (J); Helped Raise 7 Dogs for Guiding Eyes For The Blind; Aerospace Engineer; Automotive Technician; Hudson Valley Community College; Rensselaer Polytechnic Institute

RANKIN, HANNAH; KENDALL, NY; CORNERSTONE CHRISTIAN AC; Hnr Roll; Perf Att; St of Mnth; Chrch Yth Grp; Drma Clb; FCA; SP/M/VS; Stg Cre; Sccr (V L); Journalism; Business Management; Kent State

RASHID, ADEEL; JAMAICA, NY; JAMAICA HS; (SR); MVP; Otst Ac Ach Awd; WWAHSS; Comm Volntr; ArtClub; Cmptr Clb; Key Club; Mus Clb; Dnce; Bskball (C); Cyclg (C); Swmg (C); CR (P); Getting 100% Marks in Math Regents; High School Senior Award; Accounting; BBA; Baruch College (CUNY)

RASHID, JAWAD; HARTSDALE, NY; ARDSLEY HS; (JR); Hnr Roll; Nat Hon Sy; Mth Clb/Tm; Cr Ctry (V); Track (V); Pre-Med

RASMUSSEN, SEAN A; HORNELL, NY; HORNELL HS; (JR); Hi Hnr Roll; Nat Hon Sy; Otst Ac Ach Awd; Pres Sch; WWAHSS; Comm Volntr; Peer Tut/Med; ArtClub; Chrch Yth Grp; Emplmnt; Photog; Schol Bwl; Scouts; Mch Bnd; Orch; SP/M/VS; Stg Cre; Cr Ctry (VJ L); Ftball (J); Skiing (V CL); Track (V L); Stu Cncl (R); Yrbk (E, P); Section 5 Small School Slalom Ski Racing Champion for NY; Engineering; Graphic Arts; Alfred State College; NYS College of Ceramics At Alfred

RASOULINEJAD, ALI; NEW YORK, NY; SCH OF THE FUTURE; (SO); Chess; Emplmnt; Mus Clb; Vsity Clb; SP/M/VS; Bsball (V); Adv Cncl (R); Stu Cncl (P); CR (R); Mastery With Distinction on Religion and Politics; Founder of Republican Club At High School; Law; Journalism; Rutgers U; Stony Brook U

RATTAN, BRIAN; FREEPORT, NY; BALDWIN HS; (SR); Ctznshp Aw; Hnr Roll; Otst Ac Ach Awd; St of Mnth; WWAHSS; Comm Volntr; Emplmnt; P to P St Amb Prg; Track (V); Wrstlg (V); Student Ambassador Program; NASA Space Program; Culinary Arts Major; Restaurant Management; Johnson & Wales U; New England Culinary Institute

RAUCHFUSS, HANNAH E; ELMONT, NY; (SR); Hi Hnr Roll; MVP; Nat Hon Sy; St of Mnth; WWAHSS; Peer Tut/Med; Chrch Yth Grp; Key Club; Quiz Bowl; Bnd; Jzz Bnd; Mch Bnd; Orch; Sftball (V CL); Sch Ppr (E); Brown U Brown Beck Award; English; Secondary Education; Eastern Nazarene College; Fordham U

RAULLI, STEPHEN; BALDWINSVILLE, NY; BAKER HS; (JR); Hi Hnr Roll; Hnr Roll; Nat Hon Sy; Otst Ac Ach Awd; Perf Att; Pres Sch; DARE; Key Club; Key Club; English; Spanish; Keuka College; Le Moyne College

RAVERT, ALICIA; PINE CITY, NY; SHS; (SO); Hi Hnr Roll; Hnr Roll; Comm Volntr; Hab For Humty Volntr; Key Club; Chr; Track (V); Key Club; Counseling; Corning Community College; Mansfield U

RAY, RASHIDA; BROOKLYN, NY; TEACHERS PREP HS; (JR); Hnr Roll; Perf Att; St of Mnth; ArtClub; Drma Clb; Emplmnt; Chrldg; CR (S); Mentorship Program; Attend College Now At Mercer Evers; Pediatrician; Culinary Arts; U of New Haven; U of South Carolina

RAZA, SYED T; FRESH MEADOWS, NY; BENJAMIN CARDOZO HS; (SR); MVP; St of Mnth; Comm Volntr; Hab For Humty Volntr; Peer Tut/Med; Key Club; Captain of Jamaica Estates Little League Baseball - 6 Straight Years; Worked at Carvel, Burger King, Taco Bell, Pizza Hut and at a Law Internship.; Lawyer; Computer Programming; St John's U; Fordham University

REAGAN, ELIZABETH; YONKERS, NY; DOMINICAN AC; (JR); All Am Sch; Hi Hnr Roll; MVP; Nat Hon Sy; Otst Ac Ach Awd; Perf Att; Valdctrian; Comm Volntr; Peer Tut/Med; P to P St Amb Prg; Sci Clb; Dnce; Ice Hky (C); Ice Sktg; Mar Art; Scr Kpr; Track; Vllyball (V); Cl Off (R); National Latin Exam Perfect Score Summa Cum Laude; The American Association of U Women Science Merit Award; Medical Degree; Biology Master's; Yale U

REARDON, ELIZABETH A; BINGHAMTON, NY; BINGHAMTON HS; (SR); Hi Hnr Roll; Nat Hon Sy; WWAHSS; Red Cr Aide; Chrldg (V L); Swmg (J); Childhood Education; Math Education; SUNY Binghamton - Accepted; SUNY Cortland

REBOLLAR, ESTEPHANY; NEW YORK, NY; FIORELLO H LA GUARDIA HS; (JR); Ctznshp Aw; F Lan Hn Soc; Hi Hnr Roll; Hnr Roll; Nat Mrt Sch Recip; Perf Att; Sci Fairs; St of Mnth; Valdctrian; Comm Volntr; Peer Tut/Med; DARE; Participation in Annual La Guardia Fashion Show; Semi Annual Art Show (Piece in Gallery); Fashion Merchandising; Aircraft Operations (Flight); Fashion Institute of Technology; College of Aeronautics

RECHIN, DAVE; NORTH TONAWANDA, NY; NORTH TONAWANDA SR HS; (SR); Gov Hnr Prg; Hi Hnr Roll; Hnr Roll; Perf Att; WWAHSS; Comm Volntr; Spec Olymp Vol; Chrch Yth Grp; Emplmnt; Vsity Clb; Bskball (J); Ftball (V L); Lcrsse (V L); Scr Kpr (V); Secretary of Powerlifting Team; Football Scholar Athlete; Sports Medicine; Orthopedic Surgery; St. John Fisher; Buffalo State U

RECHIN, MEGAN A; SILVER CREEK, NY; SILVER CREEK HS; (SO); Hi Hnr Roll; Hnr Roll; MVP; WWAHSS; Comm Volntr; Peer Tut/Med; Chess; Chrch Yth Grp; Key Club; Mus Clb; Quiz Bowl; Sci Clb; Spanish Clb; Chr; SP/M/VS; Bskball (J); Ftball (J); PP Ftbl (J); Sftball (JC); President of Key Club; Member of the Winning Chautauqua County Mock Trial Team; Marine Biology; Neurology; New York State U; Oregon State U

REDDINGER, MICHELLE; BALDWINSVILLE, NY; CW BAKER HS; (JR); Hi Hnr Roll; Nat Hon Sy; Otst Ac Ach Awd; Perf Att; Comm Volntr; Emplmnt; Key Club; Scouts; Bskball (VJCL); Tennis (JCL); Track (V L); Yrbk (E, P); Knitting Club; Engineering

REDDIX, NICOLE; ALBANY, NY; ALBANY HS; (JR); Hi Hnr Roll; Hnr Roll; MVP; Perf Att; Comm Volntr; Emplmnt; Off Aide; Bskball (JC); Vllyball (V CL); Coaches' Award; Criminal Justice; SUNY Albany; SUNY Oneonta

REDMAN, JASON; SAUGERTIES, NY; SAUGERTIES HS; (JR); Hi Hnr Roll; MVP; Nat Hon Sy; WWAHSS; Yth Ldrshp Prog; Comm Volntr; Peer Tut/Med; Chess; DARE; Dbte Team; Key Club; Mth Clb/Tm; Vsity Clb; Spanish Clb; Bnd; SP/M/VS; Stg Cre; Mar Art; Skiing; Tennis (V CL); CR (R); Mathematician; Electrical Engineering Studies; Northeastern U; SUNY New Paltz

REDMOND, MARQUS V; BUFFALO, NY; CHEEKTOWAGA HS; (FR); Ctznshp Aw; Nat Mrt Fin; Sci Fairs; Yth Ldrshp Prog; Comm Volntr; Chrch Yth Grp; Emplmnt; FCA; Tech Clb; Bskball (VJ); Computer Technology; English / Literacy; Cincinnati U; North Carolina U

REED, ALEXIS M; ROCHESTER, NY; SUTHERLAND HS; (JR); Ctznshp Aw; Hnr Roll; St of Mnth; WWAHSS; Yth Ldrshp Prog; Emplmnt; Mod UN; NYLC; Chr; Tennis (V); CR (R); Lit Mag (R); Sch Ppr (R); Wrestling Crew; Gift of Sight Initiative; Medicine; Columbia U

REED, ARIEL; MECHANICVILLE, NY; STILLWATER HS; (FR); Hi Hnr Roll; Pres Sch; WWAHSS; Comm Volntr; Peer Tut/Med; Drma Clb; P to P St Amb Prg; Scouts; Bnd; SP/M/VS; Chrldg (J); Sccr (C); Cl Off (R); President's Award for Student Service; Making a Difference Award; Political Science

REED, LAUREN M F; CORTLAND, NY; CORTLAND JR/SR HS; (JR); Hi Hnr Roll; WWAHSS; Yth Ldrshp Prog; Comm Volntr; P to P St Amb Prg; French Clb; Acpl Chr; Bnd; Chr; Mch Bnd; Lcrsse (VJ L); Swmg (V CL); Treasurer: French Club

REEDER, AMBER M; GENEVA, NY; GENEVA HS; (JR); Hi Hnr Roll; Hnr Roll; Otst Ac Ach Awd; Comm Volntr; Emplmnt; Key Club; P to P St Amb Prg; Sftball (J); Vllyball (VJ); Scholar Athlete Award; National Society of High School Scholars; Pharmacy; Business; U of Florida; Albany State College, New York

REENS, DAVID; SYOSSET, NY; SYOSSET HS; (JR); F Lan Hn Soc; Hi Hnr Roll; Nat Hon Sy; Peer Tut/Med; Mus Clb; Vsity Clb; Orch; Bdmtn; Bsball (VJ); Track (J); National Festival Orchestra At Carnegie Hall

REESE, MIRANDA; NEWARK VALLEY, NY; NEWARK VALLEY HS; (JR); Chrldg (J); Law; Art

REGAN, PATRICK M; BROOKLYN, NY; ST EDMUND PREP HS; (SO); Comm Volntr; ArtClub; Art; Court Officer; X-Ray Tech; Kingsborough Community College; Brooklyn College

REGRAGUI, CHAIMA; WOODHAVEN, NY; FRANKLIN K LANE HS; (JR); F Lan Hn Soc; Hi Hnr Roll; Hnr Roll; Perf Att; St of Mnth; Peer Tut/Med; Outdrs Clb; Tchrs Aide; Chr; National History Day; Worked on a Documentary Project With Children; Psychiatrist; OT Occupational Therapy; Queens College; St. Johns College

REHAC, CARLY; BUFFALO, NY; CLEVELAND HILL HS; (SO); Hnr Roll; Sci Fairs; WWAHSS; Comm Volntr; Hosp Aide; Peer Tut/Med; ArtClub; DARE; Acpl Chr; Bnd; Chr; Jzz Bnd; Pep Bnd; SP/M/VS; Swmg (V L); Track (V L); Yrbk (E, P); Play Concert Piano / Saxophone for 7 Yrs; Bassoon - 2 Yrs; Medical Doctor / Emergency Room; SUNY Buffalo

REHMAN, HINA; STATEN ISLAND, NY; SUSAN E WAGNER HS; (FR); Hnr Roll; Bnd; Medicine; Pharmacology; New York U; Rutgers U

REHMAN, PARISA; BRONX, NY; FRANCIS LEWIS HS; (JR); Hnr Roll; St of Mnth; Hosp Aide; Emplmnt; Dnce; Pre-Med; Psychology; NYU; St. John's U

REICH, JENNIFER; MONTAUK, NY; EAST HAMPTON; (FR); Ctznshp Aw; Hi Hnr Roll; Hnr Roll; MVP; Pres Ac Ftns Aw; St of Mnth; Yth Ldrshp Prog; Emplmnt; Key Club; Acpl Chr; Bnd; Chr; Ch Chr; Fld Hky (J); Track (V); CR (R)

REICHHART, BETH; WATERTOWN, NY; WATERTOWN HS; (FR); Hi Hnr Roll; Perf Att; WWAHSS; Key Club; Bnd; Chr; SP/M/VS; Fld Hky (J); Lcrsse (J); Vllyball (J); Joan M. Jones Award; CARE Award; Teacher; Psychologist

REICHMANN, ERICH J; HICKSVILLE, NY; HICKSVILLE HS; (JR); Hnr Roll; MVP; Nat Hon Sy; Nat Sci Aw; Pres Ac Ftns Aw; Sci Fairs; Emplmnt; Wdwrkg Clb; Lcrsse (V); Sccr (V L); Wt Lftg (V); Business Overseas; Accounting; Pennsylvania State U; Duke U

REID, DINEKA L; BROOKLYN, NY; MIDDLE COLLEGE HS; (JR); Chrch Yth Grp; Jr Ach; Ch Chr; Chrldg (V); Cr Ctry (V); Track (V); Church Volunteer; School Volunteer; Nursing; Business; Pennsylvania State U; Hunter College

REILLY, MICHAEL P; CARMEL, NY; CARMEL HS; (FR); Bnd; Ice Hky (V)

REILLY, TIM; CORNING, NY; CORNING-PAINTED POST WEST HS; (JR); Hnr Roll; Perf Att; Comm Volntr; Chrch Yth Grp; Scouts; Lcrsse (V); Pilot; Middle Tennessee State U; Maryland U

REIMER, MICHAEL; BUFFALO, NY; BUFFALO AC FOR VISUAL AND PERF ARTS HS; (FR); Stg Cre; School Morning Show; Bowling Team; Political Science; Communication Arts; New York U; SUNY Buffalo

REIMERS, ERIC; SAUGERTIES, NY; SAUGERTIES HS; (SO); Hnr Roll; Pres Ac Ftns Aw; Comm Volntr; Spec Olymp Vol; DARE; Key Club; Bnd; Bsball (J); Cr Ctry (J); Sccr (J); History Teacher; Physical Education Teacher; Ulster Community College; Cortland College

REMI, RENEE; MASSAPEQUA, NY; MASSAPEQUA HS-AMES CAMPUS; (FR); Ctznshp Aw; Hi Hnr Roll; Comm Volntr; Dbte Team; Key Club; Scouts; French Clb; Orch; Sftball (J); Character Education Committee; NYSSMA - A; Education; Sports Marketing; Hofstra U; U of Connecticut

RENAUD, ASHLEY; ALDEN, NY; ALDEN HS; (SO); Hnr Roll; Perf Att; WWAHSS; Comm Volntr; Key Club; Off Aide; Sci Clb; French Clb; Bnd; Mch Bnd; Pep Bnd; National Junior Honor Society

RENE, DAVID; BROOKLYN, NY; ST EDMUND PREP HS; (SO); Hnr Roll; Perf Att; Comm Volntr; ArtClub; Sci Clb; Stg Cre; Sch Ppr (R); Business; Law; St John's U; Fordham U

RENTAS, NATALIE; RIDGEWOOD, NY; WASHINGTON IRVING HS; (SR); Hi Hnr Roll; Hnr Roll; Nat Hon Sy; Otst Ac Ach Awd; St of Mnth; Comm Volntr; Chrch Yth Grp; Emplmnt; Mod UN; Sci Clb; President's Education Award; Business Management; Psychology; St. John's U; Briar Cliff College

RESNICK, GREG S; MASSAPEQUA PARK, NY; MASSAPEQUA HS; (JR); Hnr Roll; Perf Att; Comm Volntr; DECA; Emplmnt; Key Club; NYLC

RESNICK, KERRI; SYOSSET, NY; SYOSSET HS; (SR); F Lan Hn Soc; Hi Hnr Roll; Hnr Roll; Nat Hon Sy; Comm Volntr; Peer Tut/Med; ArtClub; Spanish Clb; Dnce; Communication Major; NYU (New York U)

RESSLER, HEIDI; PHOENIX, NY; CHARLES W BAKER HS; (JR); Hi Hnr Roll; Nat Hon Sy; Comm Volntr; Key Club; Bnd; Mch Bnd; 200 Hours of Volunteer Work at St Camillus; Secondary Education; State U of Oswego; Syracuse U

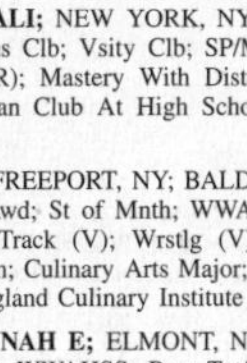
Reichmann, Erich J
Hicksville HS
Hicksville, NY

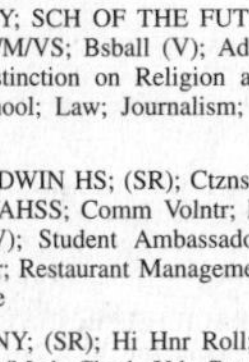
Reeder, Amber M
Geneva HS
Geneva, NY

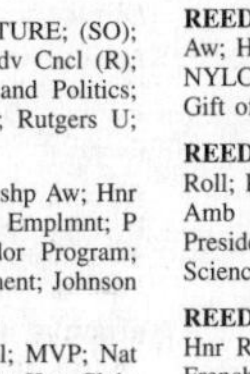
Raza, Syed T
Benjamin Cardozo HS
Fresh Meadows, NY

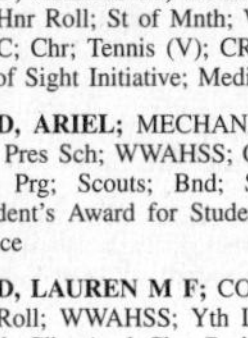
Rattan, Brian
Baldwin HS
Freeport, NY

National
Honor Roll
Spring 2005

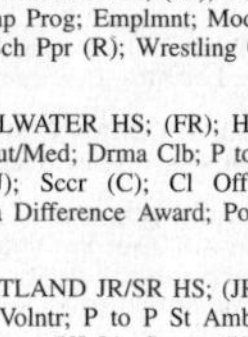
Rasoulinejad, Ali
Sch Of The Future
New York, NY

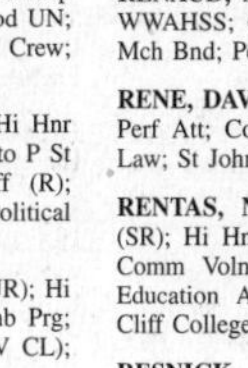
Rebollar, Estephany
Fiorello H La Guardia HS
New York, NY

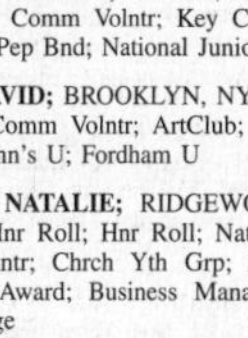
Regan, Patrick M
St Edmund Prep HS
Brooklyn, NY

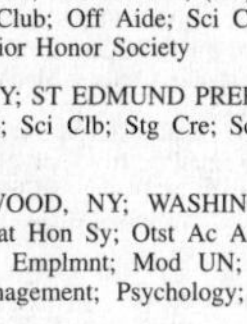
Rene, David
St Edmund Prep HS
Brooklyn, NY

RESTITUYO, VIRGINIA; BRONX, NY; HS COMMUNICATION GRAPHIC ART; (SO); Hi Hnr Roll; Hnr Roll; Perf Att; Comm Volntr; Hosp Aide; Peer Tut/Med; ArtClub; Chrch Yth Grp; Emplmnt; Fr of Library; Lib Aide; P to P St Amb Prg; Photog; SADD; Ch Chr; Dnce; Swg Chr; Arch (V); Bsball (V); CR (P)

RESTIVO, LAUREN; HICKSVILLE, NY; HICKSVILLE HS; (JR); Hnr Roll; MVP; Perf Att; Comm Volntr; Emplmnt; Bskball (V); Photog; Prom Com; SADD; Bskball (V); Sccr (V); Sftball (V); CR (R); Yrbk (P); Vice President of Art Honor Society for 06; Nutrition/Health; Teaching; Cortland U; Long Island U

RESTREPO, ANA; MONTAUK, NY; EAST HAMPTON HS; (SO); Ctznshp Aw; Hi Hnr Roll; Hnr Roll; St of Mnth; Comm Volntr; DARE; Chr; Fld Hky (J); Track (V); National Junior Honor Society; President's Education Awards Program; Art History; Physical Therapy; New York U; Oxford U

RETANA, MARICRUZ; MONTICELLO, NY; MONTICELLO HS; (SO); F Lan Hn Soc; Hi Hnr Roll; Hnr Roll; Nat Hon Sy; St of Mnth; Comm Volntr; DARE; Jr Ach; Schol Bwl; Stg Cre; Sccr (J); Academy of Finance; International Relations & Affairs; Cornell U; New York U

RETTA, CHRISTINE; MINEOLA, NY; MINEOLA HS; (FR); Hi Hnr Roll; Hnr Roll; Nat Hon Sy; Pres Sch; Dbte Team; Drma Clb; Photog; Scouts; Orch; SP/M/VS; Mock Trial; Winner of Essay Contest - Brown Vs Board of Education 50th Anniversary; Lawyer; History Teacher; New York U; Adelphi U

REY, JENNIFER; ASTORIA, NY; ST JOHN'S PREP SCH; (SR); Hi Hnr Roll; Nat Hon Sy; Perf Att; WWAHSS; Comm Volntr; Peer Tut/Med; Photog; National Honor Society; Mathematics; Spanish; Manhattan College

REYES, ALEXANDER; THOMPSON RIDGE, NY; PINE BUSH HS; (SO); Hi Hnr Roll; Hnr Roll; MVP; Perf Att; Pres Ac Ftns Aw; Yth Ldrshp Prog; Peer Tut/Med; Chess; DARE; FBLA; NYLC; Bsball (J); Ftball (J); Mar Art; Track (V); Wt Lftg (V); Yrbk (R, P); Business/Finance; Pre-Med; Florida State U; Binghamton U

REYES, BELI; NEW YORK, NY; WASHINGTON IRVING HS; (JR); Perf Att; CARE; Peer Tut/Med; Chess; DARE; Key Club; Photog; Chr; Dnce; Bsball (J); Bskball (J); Chrldg (J); Ice Sktg (J); Mar Art (J); Sccr (J); Sftball (V); Yrbk (R); Math Award; Psychology (Science); PhD Degree; Hofstra U/ New York U; St. Johns U

REYES, CYNTHIA M; BRONX, NY; MARBLE HILL SCH FOR INTERNATIONAL STUDIES; (SO); Hnr Roll; Nat Hon Sy; St of Mnth; Comm Volntr; Peer Tut/Med; Chess; Chrch Yth Grp; Drma Clb; Japanese Clb; SP/M/VS; Mar Art (L); CR (V); Accepted to Take 2 Year Course At Lebanon College; President of BWB; I Want to Be a Pathologist and Have a Biology Major; I Also Want to Major in Psychology; Manhattan College; Barnard

REYES, ELIZABETH; BRONX, NY; HEALTH PROF & HUMAN SERV HS; (SO); Hi Hnr Roll; Hnr Roll; Perf Att; Valdctrian; Hosp Aide; Lib Aide; Tchrs Aide; Ch Chr; Humanities/Humanitarian Award; Student of the Week Award; Pediatrician; Surgeon; Harvard Medical School; Columbia U

REYNOLDS, COLLEEN M; BALDWINSVILLE, NY; CW BAKER HS; (SO); Hi Hnr Roll; Pres Sch; WWAHSS; Key Club; Mus Clb; Bnd; Ch Chr; Jzz Bnd; Mch Bnd; National Junior Honor Society; Tri-M Music Honor Society; Music Major; Onondaga Community College

REYNOLDS, JEREMY A; WEST CHAZY, NY; CHAZY CTRL; (SO); Hnr Roll; St of Mnth; Comm Volntr; Peer Tut/Med; Key Club; Scouts; French Clb; Bnd; Jzz Bnd; Mch Bnd; SP/M/VS; Sccr (V)

REYNOLDS, JESSICA M; CORFU, NY; PEMBROKE JR/SR HS; (JR); Hnr Roll; DECA; Key Club; Bnd; Clr Grd; Cr Ctry (V C); Swmg (V C); Radiology Technology; Nursing; Trocaire College; Monroe Community College

REYNOSO, FRANNY; BROOKLYN, NY; WASHINGTON IRVING HS; (JR); Ctznshp Aw; Gov Hnr Prg; Hnr Roll; Nat Hon Sy; Nat Ldrshp Svc; Otst Ac Ach Awd; Perf Att; St of Mnth; ArtClub; DARE; Drma Clb; Key Club; SP/M/VS; GAA; Gmnstcs; Interior Design, Photography, Drama, Psychology, Chef

RHEM, DIJON Y; BRONX, NY; ST CATHERINE'S AC; (JR); Hnr Roll; WWAHSS; Comm Volntr; Chrch Yth Grp; Dnce; Step Team (Captain); Pre-Medicine; Psychiatry; Syracuse U; Stony Brook U (SUNY)

RHO, ELIZABETH; BAYSIDE, NY; FRANCIS LEWIS HS; (JR); Perf Att; Comm Volntr; Chrch Yth Grp; Emplmnt; Key Club; Chr; Ch Chr; Korean Christian Fellowship Club, Seekers Club; Piano; Dentistry; Boston U; Johns Hopkins U

RHOADS, CHRIS; HORSEHEADS, NY; (JR); Hi Hnr Roll; Nat Hon Sy; WWAHSS; Yth Ldrshp Prog; DARE; Key Club; Golf (V); Skiing; Sccr (V C); Stu Cncl (R); Key Club Treasurer; Aerospace Engineering; Clarkson; U At Buffalo

RHODEN, ALEXANDRIA; HEMPSTEAD, NY; UNIONDALE HS; (SO); Ctznshp Aw; Hi Hnr Roll; Hnr Roll; MVP; Otst Ac Ach Awd; Pres Sch; Sci Fairs; Comm Volntr; Peer Tut/Med; Chrch Yth Grp; Drma Clb; FTA; Key Club; Mus Clb; Off Aide; SADD; Tchrs Aide; Clr Grd; Orch; SP/M/VS; Stg Cre; Dvng (V L); Scr Kpr (J); Sftball (J L); Swmg (V CL); Track (V L); Vllyball (J L); Adv Cncl (P); Cl Off (S); CR (S); Yrbk (E, P); Psychology (Child Psychology); Education; Cornell U; Fordham U

RIBACK, ELIZABETH; HOLLIS, NY; YESHIRA UNIVERSITY HS FOR GIRLS; (JR); Hi Hnr Roll; Nat Hon Sy; Pres Ac Ftns Aw; WWAHSS; Comm Volntr; Peer Tut/Med; Biology Clb; Dbte Team; Mth Clb/Tm; Mod UN; Mus Clb; Quiz Bowl; Orch; SP/M/VS; Lit Mag (R); Musical Director for School Play; Musical Accompaniment and Arrangements for Spring Festival; English Teacher; High School Principal; Columbia College; U of Pennsylvania

RICCIO-ACKERMAN, GIO; MONROE, NY; MONROE-WOODBURY HS; Hi Hnr Roll; Hnr Roll; Jr Eng Tech; Sci Fairs; WWAHSS; Yth Ldrshp Prog; Comm Volntr; ArtClub; Chess; DARE; Scouts; Chr; Ch Chr; Black Belt - Tae Kwon Do; Gold Medal at NYSTKD Comp in Forms / Silver in Sparrow; Surgeon / Double Major of Art & Pre-Med; Major of Art & Pre-Med; Cornell U; NYU

RICH, SARAH A; SHERIDAN, NY; SILVER CREEK HS; (SR); Hnr Roll; Nat Hon Sy; Salutrn; Sci/Math Olympn; Comm Volntr; Key Club; Pep Squd; Photog; Prom Com; SADD; Vsity Clb; French Clb; Chr; Dnce; SP/M/VS; Chrldg (V); Sccr (V); Vsy Clb (V); Stu Cncl (V); Yrbk (R, P); Elementary Education; Dance Therapy; SUNY Geneseo; Fredonia State

RICHARDS, LEWIN; SUFFERN, NY; NEW YORK MILITARY AC; (SO); Hnr Roll; Nat Su Ath Day Aw; Perf Att; ROTC; Bnd; Mch Bnd; Bskball (V); Sccr (V); Track (V); Science & Mathematics; Engineering; Duke U; Cornell U

RICHARDS, SEAN M; CAMILLUS, NY; WEST GENESEE HS; (SR); Hi Hnr Roll; Nat Hon Sy; Pres Ac Ftns Aw; Sci Fairs; St of Mnth; WWAHSS; Comm Volntr; ArtClub; Chrch Yth Grp; Emplmnt; Outdrs Clb; Photog; Scouts; Spanish Clb; Ftball (VJ L); Track (V CL); Wrstlg (V L); CR (R); Lit Mag (P); Yrbk (E, P); Honorable Mention @ 2004 Scholastic Art Competition; 2004/5 AP Scholar with Honor; Neuroscience; Biological Studies; Cornell U; U of Rochester

RICHARDSON, MERRISHEL I; BRONX, NY; ST BARNABAS HS; (JR); Hnr Roll; Comm Volntr; Mth Clb/Tm; Chr; Dnce; Bskball; Track; Journalism; Creative Writing; Oral Roberts U; Quinnipiac U

RICHARDSON, NICOLE; SAUGERTIES, NY; SAUGERTIES HS; (SO); Hi Hnr Roll; WWAHSS; Key Club; Bnd; Chr; Sccr (J); Veterinary Science-Marine Animals; SUNY Stony Brook; Cornell U

RIDDELL, CHRIS-KAY; BRONX, NY; WALTON HS; (SR); Hi Hnr Roll; Hnr Roll; Nat Hon Sy; Perf Att; St of Mnth; WWAHSS; Comm Volntr; Chr; Tennis (V); Track (V); Stu Cncl (V); #1 Bowling Team; Step Team; Fordham U; New York U

RIEDMAN, SCOTT; MERRICK, NY; CALHOUN HS; (JR); Ctznshp Aw; F Lan Hn Soc; Hi Hnr Roll; Nat Hon Sy; Otst Ac Ach Awd; Perf Att; Sci/Math Olympn; WWAHSS; Yth Ldrshp Prog; Comm Volntr; Peer Tut/Med; Biology Clb; DECA; HO'Br Yth Ldrshp; Key Club; MuAlphaTh; Outdrs Clb; Sci Clb; Acpl Chr; Cl Off; Wrestling Manager; Spanish Honor Society President; Psychology; Cognitive Science; Wesleyan U; U of Pennsylvania

RIEGEL, KRISTIN E; BATAVIA, NY; PEMBROKE HS; (JR); F Lan Hn Soc; Hi Hnr Roll; Nat Hon Sy; Otst Ac Ach Awd; St of Mnth; WWAHSS; Yth Ldrshp Prog; Comm Volntr; Peer Tut/Med; ArtClub; DECA; FTA; HO'Br Yth Ldrshp; Key Club; Scouts; SADD; Vsity Clb; Ch Chr; Sccr (VJCL); Sftball (J); Swmg (V CL); Track (V); Lit Mag (R); Yrbk (E, R, P); GCASA Dove Youth Award Recipient; Student of the Year in 7, 9, & 11th Grade; English; Law; Yale U; Stanford U

RIGGIO, MICHAEL J; MASSAPEQUA, NY; ST ANTHONY'S HS; (JR); Hnr Roll; Comm Volntr; Emplmnt; Psychology; Social Work; SUNY Schools

RIGGS, DANIELLE M; SYRACUSE, NY; FOWLER HS; (SO); Hnr Roll; Otst Ac Ach Awd; Perf Att; DARE; Off Aide; Photog; Swmg; Presidential Achievement Award; Perfect Attendance; Law; Government Official; Syracuse U; Le Moyne College

RIGNEY, KAYLA M; FEURA BUSH, NY; BETHLEHEM CTRL HS; (JR); Hnr Roll; WWAHSS; Comm Volntr; DARE; Emplmnt; Pep Squd; Wdwrkg Clb; Chrldg (VJCL); Yrbk (R); Kickboxing; Psychology; Culinary Arts; State U of New York

RILEY, EMMA G; EAST HAMPTON, NY; EAST HAMPTON HS; (JR); All Am Sch; Hi Hnr Roll; Kwnis Aw; Nat Hon Sy; Nat Ldrshp Svc; Nat Mrt Sch Recip; Otst Ac Ach Awd; Pres Sch; WWAHSS; Comm Volntr; Spec Olymp Vol; Chrch Yth Grp; DARE; Emplmnt; Key Club; NYLC; Scouts; French Clb; Bnd; Dnce; Mch Bnd; SP/M/VS; Lcrsse (J); Sccr (J); Track (V); Lit Mag; Dance Team 9th, 10th Grade

RIORDAN, CHRISTINE M; LORRAINE, NY; SOUTH JEFFERSON HS; (SR); Hnr Roll; Nat Hon Sy; Perf Att; Sci Fairs; Comm Volntr; Ntl FFA; Spanish Clb; Chr; New York State FFA Secretary 2004-2005; State Science Fair First Place in Biochemistry; Veterinarian (Large Animal); Agricultural Educator; State U of New York Cobleskill College

RITTER, BRYAN M; ELMA, NY; IROQUOIS HS; (SR); Hi Hnr Roll; Hnr Roll; MVP; Nat Hon Sy; Comm Volntr; Emplmnt; Bskball (VJ L); Lcrsse (J); Vllyball (VJCL); Power Station Volleyball Club; Accounting; Criminal Justice; Mercyhurst College; Niagara U

RITTER, G T; BATH, NY; HAVERLING HS; (JR); Hi Hnr Roll; Hnr Roll; Perf Att; Yth Ldrshp Prog; Comm Volntr; Peer Tut/Med; Chrch Yth Grp; Fr of Library; Jr Cls League; Lib Aide; Prom Com; Scouts; Tchrs Aide; Latin Clb; Chr; Stg Cre; PP Ftbl (J); Latin Club VP; Forensic Chemist; Corning Community College; John Jay Criminology College

RIUS, LAUREN; STATEN ISLAND, NY; BROOKLYN TECH HS; (SO); Hnr Roll; Peer Tut/Med; Ntl Beta Clb; Scouts; Tchrs Aide; Wdwrkg Clb; 3rd Place Winner of Dr. Martin Luther King Jr. Essay Contest; Child & Adolescent Psychiatry; MD; Yale U; SUNY-Stony Brook

RIVERA, DALILAH D; STATEN ISLAND, NY; BISHOP KEARNEY HS; (JR); F Lan Hn Soc; Hi Hnr Roll; Hnr Roll; Comm Volntr; Lib Aide; Pep Squd; National Latin Exam-Cum Laude; Bowling Club; Nursing; Hunter College; New York U

RIVERA, GABRIELA; BRONX, NY; FASHION INDUSTRIES; (FR); Fut Prb Slvr; Hnr Roll; MVP; Nat Hon Sy; Perf Att; Sci Fairs; WWAHSS; Valdctrian; WWAHSS; Yth Ldrshp Prog; CARE; Hosp Aide; Peer Tut/Med; Chess; Chrch Yth Grp; DARE; Dbte Team; Mth Clb/Tm; Sci Clb; SADD; Tchrs Aide; Chr; Ch Chr; Clr Grd; SP/M/VS; Bskball (V); Rlr Hky (L); Scr Kpr (L); Sftball (L); Swmg (L); Track (L); Vllyball (L); Stu Cncl (R); CR (P); Yrbk (P); Student of the Year; Fashion Designer; New York U; Princeton U

RIVERA, GABRIELA; WOODMERE, NY; LAWRENCE HS; (FR); Ctznshp Aw; Hi Hnr Roll; Comm Volntr; Spec Olymp Vol; Key Club; Orch; Teacher; Adolescence Psychology; Molloy College; Old Westbury U

RIVERA, MICHAEL; BRONX, NY; CELIA CRUZ BRONX HS OF MUSIC; (FR); Comm Volntr; Bnd; Jzz Bnd; SP/M/VS; Mar Art (V); Lawyer; Harvard U; NYU

RIVERA, NICHOLAS L; BROOKLYN, NY;; Hnr Roll; Otst Ac Ach Awd; Perf Att; Sci Fairs; St of Mnth; Peer Tut/Med; ArtClub; Chess; Photog; Vllyball (J); CR (R); Stu Cncl (V); Sch Ppr (R); Culinary Arts; Culinary Arts; Architectural; Harvard Law School; Princeton U

RIVERA, SHARAI M; NEW YORK, NY; MILLENNIUM HS; (FR); Hnr Roll; Nat Hon Sy; Otst Ac Ach Awd; Perf Att; Sci Fairs; St of Mnth; Yth Ldrshp Prog; Comm Volntr; Peer Tut/Med; Cmptr Clb; DARE; Pep Squd; SP/ M/VS; Stu Cncl (R); CR (R); Developmental Assets Group; National Leadership Conference; Forensic Science; Actuarial Science; Harvard U; New York U

RIZKALLA, BRIDGETTE; BROOKLYN, NY; FONTBONNE HALL AC; (JR); Hi Hnr Roll; Hnr Roll; Nat Hon Sy; Perf Att; WWAHSS; Comm Volntr; Peer Tut/Med; Drma Clb; FBLA; Lib Aide; Photog; Svce Clb; SADD; Spanish Clb; Stg Cre; Bravo Volunteer Ambulance; Law; Psychology; Boston College; New York U

ROA, CARLOS; NEW YORK, NY; MARBLE HILL HS FOR INTERNATIONAL STUDIES; (JR); Perf Att; St of Mnth; Comm Volntr; ArtClub; Emplmnt; Wt Lftg (V); Sch Ppr (P); Computer Engineering; FBI; John Jay

ROACH, ADAM J; OGDENSBURG, NY; OGDENSBURG FREE AC; (SO); Hi Hnr Roll; Kwnis Aw; Nat Hon Sy; Otst Ac Ach Awd; St of Mnth; WWAHSS; Key Club; Academic Banquet; Fish and Wildlife Technology; Paul Smiths College

ROACH, TARA; CANANDAIGUA, NY; CANANDAIGUA AC; (JR); Hi Hnr Roll; Hnr Roll; Nat Hon Sy; Peer Tut/Med; Key Club; Chr; Clr Grd; Mch Bnd; Enjoyed Tutoring My Friends and Student Peers So They Could Succeed; Double Majoring in Physical Sciences and Math; U of Buffalo

ROBBINS, RACHAEL E; CLYDE, NY; CLYDE-SAVANNAH JR/SR HS; (JR); Hi Hnr Roll; Hnr Roll; Nat Hon Sy; Chess; Chrch Yth Grp; DARE; Bskball (J); Sftball (JC); Vllyball (VJC); Stu Cncl (V); Winner of Gatorade Award; Veterinary - Major; Graphic Designer - Minor; Gallaudet U; Valdosta State U

ROBINSON, CHERYL; BRONX, NY; MT ST URSULA HS; (JR); Hi Hnr Roll; Hnr Roll; MVP; Otst Ac Ach Awd; Perf Att; Sci Fairs; St of Mnth; Valdctrian; WWAHSS; Comm Volntr; Peer Tut/Med; Emplmnt; Kwanza Clb; Prom Com; Spanish Clb; Dnce; Tennis; Track (V CL); Yrbk (R); Poems Published in Young Anthology:2002; Scored a 4 on AP American History Exam; Political Science/Government; African American or American Studies; Howard U; Delaware State U

Rivera, Nicholas L
Brooklyn, NY

Riccio-Ackerman, Gio
Monroe-Woodbury HS
Monroe, NY

Rivera, Gabriela
Fashion Industries
Bronx, NY

ROBLEDO, CAROLYN; BRONX, NY; FIORELLO H LA GUARDIA HS; (JR); Hnr Roll; Sccr (V); Vllyball (J); I Am an Art Major-My Works Have Been Displayed; I Was in Philosophy and Fashion Club; Liberal Arts; Politics; Columbia U; New York U

ROBLES, GLADYS; BRONX, NY; JANE ADDAMS HS; (SR); Yth Ldrshp Prog; Comm Volntr; Peer Tut/Med; I'm Engage in the Peer Leaders Hip Council; I Want to Become a Register Nurse; U At Buffalo; New Paltz

RODNEY, ESTAN; BROOKLYN, NY; GEORGE W WINGATE HS; (SR); Perf Att; Vllyball (J); United States Coast Guard Academy; NYC Technical College

RODRIGUEZ, ALLYSON; BRONX, NY; HS OF AMERIAN STUDIES; (SO); F Lan Hn Soc; Hi Hnr Roll; Nat Hon Sy; Otst Ac Ach Awd; WWAHSS; Chrch Yth Grp; Emplmnt; Key Club; Ch Chr; Bskball (J); Best Athlete for Freshman Girls in the High School of American Studies; Fashion Design; Psychology; Laboratory Institute of Merchandising; Johns Hopkins U

RODRIGUEZ, AMELFIS M; BRONX, NY; HEALTH OPPORTUNITIES HS; (FR); Perf Att; Gmnstcs; Nurse; Doctor; Mercy College; SUNY College

RODRIGUEZ, GIOVANNI L; BRONX, NY; ALFRED E SMITH VOC HS; (FR); Sci Fairs; St of Mnth; Comm Volntr; Peer Tut/Med; Chrch Yth Grp; Off Aide; Bsball; Bskball; Gmnstcs; Wrstlg; Architect; Fordham U

RODRIGUEZ, IDELSA; BRONX, NY; BRONX EXPEDITIONARY LEARNING HS; (FR); F Lan Hn Soc; Comm Volntr; Mth Clb/Tm; Outdrs Clb, Chr, Dnce; Lit Mag (R); Yrbk (R); Salutatorian- PS 200 - JHS -2004; Attorney; Columbia U; CCNY

RODRIGUEZ, KATHERINE; YONKERS, NY; LINCOLN HS; (SO); Ctznshp Aw; Hnr Roll; Otst Ac Ach Awd; Perf Att; St of Mnth; Comm Volntr; DARE; Emplmnt; Tchrs Aide; Dnce; SP/M/VS; Sftball (JC); Teacher; Cosmotology; Columbia U; Florida U

RODRIGUEZ, LILLIAN; BRONX, NY; HS OF AMERICAN STUDIES; (SO); Hnr Roll; Drma Clb; Key Club; SP/M/VS; Black Belt in Tae Kwon Do (Outside of School); Law; Acting

RODRIGUEZ, NEISHA; BRONX, NY; HS OF FASHION INDUSTRIES; (SR); Hnr Roll; Otst Ac Ach Awd; Salutrn; St of Mnth; WWAHSS; Peer Tut/Med; DECA; Mus Clb; Tchrs Aide; Bsball (V); Bskball (V); Ftball (V); Cl Off (P); I Have Won Art Contest; Won the Young Noble Peace Prize; Masters in Business MBA; Barnard Baruch College; Pace U

RODRIGUEZ, STEPHANIE; CORONA, NY; FRANCIS LEWIS HS; (SO); Perf Att; Hosp Aide; Chrch Yth Grp; Bskball (JV); Child Psychology; Computer Management

RODRIQUEZ JR, ELIAS S; BRONX, NY; HSGCA; (JR); Hnr Roll; Otst Ac Ach Awd; Perf Att; ArtClub; Chrch Yth Grp; DARE; Emplmnt; Mus Clb; Photog; Tchrs Aide; Chr; Ch Chr; Dnce; SP/M/VS; Bsball; Bskball; Lcrsse; Sccr; Sftball; Vllyball; Web Page Design; Photography; School of Visual Art; Art Institute of California - LA

ROE, SANDRA; ROCHESTER, NY; JOHN MARSHALL HS; (SO); Hi Hnr Roll; Hnr Roll; Perf Att; Comm Volntr; ArtClub; Lib Aide; Mth Clb/Tm; Mod UN; Outdrs Clb; ROTC; Drl Tm; Yrbk (R); JROTC; Fashion Design; Fine Arts; U of Tampa; Monroe Community College

ROGERS, ASHLEY; MECHANICVILLE, NY; STILLWATER HS; (FR); DAR; Hi Hnr Roll; Hnr Roll; MVP; Nat Hon Sy; St of Mnth; DARE; Emplmnt; Bskball; Scr Kpr; Cl Off (R); National Junior Honor Society; Psychiatry; Pediatrician; Siena; U of Albany

ROGERS, COLLEEN; WESTERLO, NY; (SO); 4H Awd; Hnr Roll; Comm Volntr; Peer Tut/Med; 4-H; Chrch Yth Grp; DARE; Emplmnt; Key Club; Hsbk Rdg (VJCL); Yrbk (E); Qualified for World Champion of NBHA; Computer Science; Computer Programming; College of Saint Rose; Junior College of Albany

ROGERS, LEAH; CARMEL, NY; CARMEL HS; (SO); St of Mnth; Sccr (J); 1st Place Photograph at Mill Street Loft; Photographer

ROGERS, SERENA A; BROOKLYN, NY; MIDDLE COLLEGE HS; (SR); Hnr Roll; Nat Hon Sy; St of Mnth; WWAHSS; Comm Volntr; Peer Tut/Med; Mus Clb; Ch Chr; Dnce; Spanish Honors; Poetry Club; Sociology; Spanish; Hunter College; College of New Rochelle

ROGERS, TONILYN; ROCHESTER, NY; GREECE OLYMPIA HS; (JR); Hi Hnr Roll; MVP; Nat Hon Sy; Otst Ac Ach Awd; Pres Sch; WWAHSS; Comm Volntr; Peer Tut/Med; Emplmnt; Mus Clb; Quill & Scroll; Vsity Clb; Bnd; Orch; SP/M/VS; Stg Cre; Bskball (V CL); Sccr (V CL); Cl Off (R); Stu Cncl (T, R); Sch Ppr (E); AP Scholar; NHS Treasurer: Band Officer; Sports Management; Math

ROHATGI, ABHINAV; GARDEN CITY, NY; GARDEN CITY HS; (SO); Hi Hnr Roll; Nat Hon Sy; Sci/Math Olympn; WWAHSS; Chess; Mth Clb/Tm; Tennis (J); MD; Boston U; Columbia U

ROLDAN, THERESA I; BROOKLYN, NY; STUYVESANT HS; (FR); Key Club; Sch Ppr; Newspaper Layouts; Financial Business; New York U; Columbia U

ROLL, JACQUELINE; SEAFORD, NY; SEAFORD HS; (JR); Hi Hnr Roll; Hnr Roll; Nat Hon Sy; WWAHSS; Peer Tut/Med; ArtClub; Chrch Yth Grp; Emplmnt; Key Club; Pep Squd; Vsity Clb; Bnd; Clr Grd; Mch Bnd; SP/M/VS; Chrldg (VJ); Tennis (V); Graphic Design; Animator; Fashion Institute of Technology; SUNY New Paltz

ROLL, VALERIE A; ALDEN, NY; ALDEN HS; (SO); Hnr Roll; Peer Tut/Med; DARE; Drma Clb; FTA; Key Club; Svce Clb; French Clb; Bnd; Mch Bnd; Pep Bnd; SP/M/VS; Journalist; Teacher; Wells College; U At Buffalo

ROMAIN, KEVIN; JAMAICA, NY; (MS); St of Mnth; Comm Volntr; Sch Ppr (E, R, P); Yrbk (E, R, P); Computer Tech; Florida U; Maryland U

ROMAN, EMILY H; BEDFORD, NY; THE HARVEY SCH; (JR); Hi Hnr Roll; Otst Ac Ach Awd; Comm Volntr; Peer Tut/Med; Spec Olymp Vol; Emplmnt; SADD; Ice Sktg (L); Sch Ppr (R); Martin Luther King Humanitarian Award; Outstanding Spanish Language Student Award; Sports Medicine Physician

ROMANO, CRISTINA; SOMERS, NY; (JR); F Lan Hn Soc; Hi Hnr Roll; Otst Ac Ach Awd; Comm Volntr; SADD; Spanish Clb; Cr Ctry (V); Track (V); Yrbk (R, P); Lifeguarding; Boston U; U of Rhode Island

RONEY, ANDREA-LYNN; ALDEN, NY; ALDEN HS; (JR); F Lan Hn Soc; Hnr Roll; Otst Ac Ach Awd; Perf Att; WWAHSS; Yth Ldrshp Prog; ArtClub; Biology Clb; Emplmnt; FTA; HO'Br Yth Ldrshp; Key Club; Mus Clb; Prom Com; Bnd; Mch Bnd; Pep Bnd; SP/M/VS; PP Ftbl (J); Sftball (J); Swmg (V); Tennis (V L); Cl Off (P); CR (R); Student Ex Scholar Winner; Triple 'C' Award; Int'l Studies (Relations); Studio Music Performance; SUNY Fredonia; Syracuse U

ROOSEVELT, TIFFANY A; MONGAUP VALLEY, NY; MONTICELLO CTRL HS; (SO); Nat Hon Sy; Comm Volntr; Chrch Yth Grp; DARE; Chr; Orch; Music Engineering; Early Childhood Education; Cortland U; Penn State

ROSADO, CASSANDRA; GLASCO, NY; SAUGERTIES HS; (SO); Hi Hnr Roll; WWAHSS; Yth Ldrshp Prog; Comm Volntr; Peer Tut/Med; Chrch Yth Grp; Emplmnt; HO'Br Yth Ldrshp; Key Club; Mth Clb/Tm; Scouts; Spanish Clb; Acpl Chr; Chr; Ch Chr; Track (V); Vllyball (JC); All-County Chorus 2004-2005; Silver Award; Spanish; Teaching

ROSADO, CRYSTAL M; BRONX, NY; HEALTH OPPORTUNITIES HS; (SO); Hnr Roll; Yth Ldrshp Prog; Comm Volntr; Chrch Yth Grp; Mus Clb; Svce Clb; Nora Feury Award; Nursing; Social Services; Pace U; Boston U

ROSALEZ, ERICA; BROOKLYN, NY; FLORELLO H LA GUARDIA HS; (FR); Medicine; Arts; New York U; Columbia U

ROSARIO, AURA C; BRONX, NY; SAMUEL GOMPERS HS; (JR); Hi Hnr Roll; Perf Att; St of Mnth; Valdctrian; Hosp Aide; Dnce; Student of the Month - Freshman Year; Desktop Publishing; Business Administration; Columbia U; New York U

ROSARIO, JENNIFER M; WATERFORD, NY; WATERFORD HS; (SO); Hi Hnr Roll; St of Mnth; Comm Volntr; Emplmnt; Fr of Library; Pep Squd; SP/M/VS; Stg Cre; Chrldg (V); Vllyball (V); Working Part Time As a Service Clerk; Masters of Business Administration; Masters of Sports Management; U of California Los Angeles; Siena College

ROSARIO, RACHELL; NEW YORK, NY; MANHATTAN HUNTER SCI SCH; (SO); Hi Hnr Roll; Nat Ldrshp Svc; Nat Sci Aw; Nat Stu Ath Day Aw; Otst Ac Ach Awd; Perf Att; Sci Fairs; St of Mnth; Yth Ldrshp Prog; Comm Volntr; Peer Tut/Med; Biology Clb; DARE; Drma Clb; Mth Clb/Tm; Mus Clb; NYLC; Photog; Vsity Clb; Clb; Dnce; Pep Bnd; SP/M/VS; Stg Cre; Bskball; Cr Ctry; Fncg; GAA; Scr Kpr; Sftball; Track; Vllyball; Stu Cncl (R); National American-Israel Friendship League; Psychology / Drama; Help in the Community; Brown U; Yale U

ROSEKOWSKI, MAREK; BROOKLYN, NY; CHRIST THE KING HS; (SO); Hi Hnr Roll; Hnr Roll; Swg Chr; Teaching; Law Enforcement; New York U; Columbia U

ROSEN, MARLENE; W HEMPSTEAD, NY; WEST HEMPSTEAD HS; (FR); Hi Hnr Roll; Pres Ac Ftns Aw; Sci/Math Olympn; Spec Olymp Vol; Key Club; Mth Clb/Tm; Quiz Bowl; Bnd; Chr; Mch Bnd; Cr Ctry (V); Track (V); Lit Mag (E)

ROSEN, SAMANTHA; TROY, NY; TROY HS; (SO); Hnr Roll; Nat Hon Sy; WWAHSS; Key Club; Vsity Clb; Sccr (V); Track (V); Key Club

ROSENBERG, SARAH; GARDEN CITY, NY; SEWANHAKA HS; (FR); F Lan Hn Soc; Hi Hnr Roll; Hnr Roll; Nat Hon Sy; Otst Ac Ach Awd; St of Mnth; Comm Volntr; Key Club; Quiz Bowl; Scouts; Chr; Stg Cre; Stu Cncl (R); Talented and Gifted (TAG); Key Club-Secretary; Photography; Psychology; New York U; Iona College

ROSENTHAL, DANIELLE S; MERRICK, NY; CALHOUN HS; (JR); Hnr Roll; Comm Volntr; Chrch Yth Grp; DECA; Drma Clb; Key Club; Pep Squd; Scouts; SADD; Drl Tm; SP/M/VS; Stg Cre; Chrldg (VJ); Lcrsse (VJ); Charity for Kids with Cancer; Criminal Law; Dance Arts; New York U; Miami U

ROSENTSVEYG, JULIANA; BROOKLYN, NY; LEON M GOLDSTEIN; (JR); Hi Hnr Roll; Sci Fairs; Peer Tut/Med; Emplmnt; Key Club; Lib Aide; Sci Clb; SP/M/VS; Cl Off (T); Sch Ppr (R)

ROSINSKI, CODY; FORESTPORT, NY; ADIRONDACK HS; (SO); Hnr Roll; Nat Stu Ath Day Aw; WWAHSS; Emplmnt; Vsity Clb; Sccr (V L); Track (V); Vsy Clb; Law Enforcement; Architectural Engineering

ROSKA, SAMANTHA P; SILVER CREEK, NY; SILVER CREEK HS; (JR); Comm Volntr; Key Club; Prom Com; Vsity Clb; French Clb; Chrldg (J); Track (V L); Vsy Clb (V); Cl Off (V); Natural Helper; Psychology; Teaching; U of Arizona; U of Buffalo

ROSMAN, JAIME; VICTOR, NY; VICTOR CTRL HS; (SR); Hi Hnr Roll; Hnr Roll; WWAHSS; Chrch Yth Grp; Chrldg (J); Tennis (J); Biology; Pre-Med; Nazareth College; U of Rochester

ROSS, MEGAN M; CONESUS, NY; LIVONIA HS; (SR); Hi Hnr Roll; Kwnis Aw; Nat Hon Sy; Comm Volntr; AL Aux Girls; Emplmnt; Key Club; Quill & Scroll; Bnd; Mch Bnd; Sftball (J); Track (V); Vllyball (V); Lit Mag (E)

ROTA, MICHAEL; STATEN ISLAND, NY; ST JOSEPH BY THE SEA HS; (JR); Hnr Roll; MVP; WWAHSS; Comm Volntr; Cr Ctry (V); Track (V C); Sch Ppr (R); Staten Island U Hospital Volunteer Award; Degree in Law; Degree in Physics; New York U; Wagner College

ROTELLA, KRYSTYNA; CHITTENANGO, NY; CHITTENANGO HS; (JR); F Lan Hn Soc; Hi Hnr Roll; Hnr Roll; Nat Hon Sy; Otst Ac Ach Awd; Perf Att; Sci Fairs; St of Mnth; USAA; Comm Volntr; Peer Tut/Med; ArtClub; Mth Clb/Tm; Bskball (VJ); Cr Ctry (V); Sftball (VJ); Invitation Into 2005 National Student Leadership Conference; United States Achievement Academy 2002 National Awards; Marine Biology; Psychology; U of Miami; Florida State U

ROTH, JAMES J; GARDEN CITY, NY; GARDEN CITY HS; (FR); Hnr Roll; Pres Ac Ftns Aw; Comm Volntr; SADD; Ftball (J); Lcrsse (J); Wrstlg (V); Criminal Justice; Forensic Science; Tuft Prep School; Hofstra U

ROTHBARD, MICHAEL; SPRING VALLEY, NY; SPRING VALLEY HS; (JR); Hi Hnr Roll; Hnr Roll; Nat Hon Sy; WWAHSS; Comm Volntr; Peer Tut/Med; Key Club; MuAlphaTh; Tmpl Yth Grp; Vsity Clb; Bnd; Jzz Bnd; Mch Bnd; SP/M/VS; Tennis (V L); Sch Ppr (E); Key Club Editor/Public Relations; Marching Band Vice President; Architecture/Engineering; Music; U of Maryland; Penn State

ROTUNNO, RINA; YORKTOWN HEIGHTS, NY; YORKTOWN HS; (JR); Hi Hnr Roll; Hnr Roll; Comm Volntr; Red Cr Aide; Emplmnt; Prom Com; SADD; Vsity Clb; Bnd; Chr; Dnce; SP/M/VS; Fld Hky (J); Lcrsse (J); Track (V); Yrbk; Volunteer Ambulance Corp; Student Senate; Forensic Psychology; Criminalistics; Syracuse; John Jay (CUNY) College

ROURKE, MAGGIE; MIDDLETOWN, NY; MIDDLETOWN HS; (SR); Hi Hnr Roll; Nat Hon Sy; WWAHSS; Comm Volntr; Peer Tut/Med; Drma Clb; Key Club; Prom Com; Chr; Dnce; SP/M/VS; Cl Off (V); Public Relations; Nutrition; Syracuse U; U of Connecticut

ROWE, KRYSTAL; YONKERS, NY; LINCOLN HS; (FR); Hi Hnr Roll; Hnr Roll; Perf Att; WWAHSS; Hab For Humty Volntr; Chrch Yth Grp; DARE; Svce Clb; SADD; Acpl Chr; Chr; Ch Chr; Cr Ctry (J); Track (J); Honor Roll; Nursing; Vocal Music

ROWE, TALBERT A; BROOKLYN, NY; CANARSIE HS; (JR); WWAHSS; Business; Advertisement; U of Hartford; SUNY Stony Brook

ROWLAND, KAYLA E; BLUE POINT, NY; BAYPORT BLUE POINT HS; (JR); Hi Hnr Roll; Pres Ac Ftns Aw; Sci/Math Olympn; St of Mnth; WWAHSS; Comm Volntr; Hab For Humty Volntr; Key Club; Prom Com; SADD; Bnd; Mch Bnd; Orch; Fld Hky (VJ); Lcrsse (VJ); Track (V); Cl Off (P); Stu Cncl; CR; Yrbk (E); Treasurer-Key Club, Habitat for Humanity; Participant in Science Olympiad; Medicine / Doctor

ROXAS, ANDREA; PLAINVIEW, NY; PLAINVIEW OLD BETHPAGE JFK HS; (JR); F Lan Hn Soc; Hi Hnr Roll; Nat Hon Sy; Nat Mrt Semif; Otst Ac Ach Awd; Comm Volntr; DECA; Emplmnt; Vllyball (VJ); Sch Ppr (R); Yrbk (E); President-Community Service Club; NCTE Writing Contest Participant; Business; Journalism (English); Columbia U; Yale U

ROXAS, MARY G; NANUET, NY; SORING VALLEY HS; (FR); Hi Hnr Roll; Hnr Roll; Key Club; Bnd

ROZEWICZ, MICHAEL P; SILVER CREEK, NY; SILVER CREEK HS; (JR); Hnr Roll; Nat Hon Sy; Otst Ac Ach Awd; WWAHSS; AL Aux Boys; Chrch Yth Grp; DECA; Key Club; Bnd; Jzz Bnd; Bsball (J); Ice Hky (VJC); Lcrsse (VJC); 2005 Boys State Recipient; AAA / AA Travel Hockey League; Computer Engineer; Armed Forces of United States; West Point; Rochester U

ROZINA, TAMARA; BROOKLYN, NY; MIDWOOD HS; (JR); Nat Hon Sy; Comm Volntr; Biology Clb; Key Club; Off Aide; Swmg (V); Sch Ppr (E, R); Quality of Life Competition Borough Leader; Cultural Diversity Club; Law; Cornell; New York U

ROZOV, ALEKSONDER; BRONX, NY; CRISTOPHER COLUMBUS HS; (SR); WWAHSS; Comm Volntr; Emplmnt; Off Aide; Tchrs Aide; Bdmtn; Mar Art; Sccr; Vllyball; Financing; Economics; Pace U; Baruch College-CUNY

Roosevelt, Tiffany A
Monticello Ctrl HS
Mongaup Valley, NY

Roman, Emily H
The Harvey Sch
Bedford, NY

Rodriguez, Giovanni L
Alfred E Smith Voc HS
Bronx, NY

Rodriguez, Idelsa
Bronx Expeditionary Learning HS
Bronx, NY

Rosario, Aura C
Samuel Gompers HS
Bronx, NY

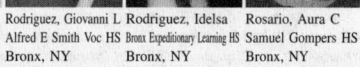

RUBINSTEIN, MICHELLE; CORAM, NY; LONGWOOD HS; (SR); Hi Hnr Roll; Hnr Roll; Comm Volntr; Drma Clb; Photog; Orch; Stg Cre; Private Art Lessons -1 Yr; Film / TV Production; Photography; Suffolk Community College

RUBIO, KARIA; RIDGEWOOD, NY; AC FOR AMERICAN STUDIES; (JR); Hnr Roll; Perf Att; Highest GPA of Freshman Class; Political Sciences; Archaeology; New York U; Columbia U

RUFINO, JOHN; NEW YORK, NY; HS FOR MEDIA & COMMUNICATIONS; (FR); MVP; Otst Ac Ach Awd; DARE; Bsball (J); Bskball (J); Academic Excellence (Passed All Classes); Major League Baseball Player; Astronomy, Law; Syracuse

RUHLMAN, ASHLEE; NASSAU, NY; COLUMBIA HS; (FR); Hnr Roll; Key Club; Bnd

RUHM, BAYLEIGH; ROME, NY; ORISKANY CTRL HS; (SO); Hi Hnr Roll; Otst Ac Ach Awd; Perf Att; St of Mnth; WWAHSS; Comm Volntr; Key Club; French Clb; Cr Ctry (V); English Major

RUIBA, DESIREA; FRANKLINVILLE, NY; TEN BROECK AC; (JR); Hnr Roll; Otst Ac Ach Awd; Perf Att; St of Mnth; Peer Tut/Med; Emplmnt; Ntl FFA; SADD; Vsity Clb; Dnce; Chrldg (V L); Scr Kpr (J); Sccr (V); Sftball (V); Vllyball (J); Stu Cncl (R); Yrbk (E); Cosmetology; U of Cosmetology

RUIZ, KARIN; MASPETH, NY; CHRIST THE KING HS; (JR); Nat Hon Sy; WWAHSS; ArtClub; Key Club; Strive; American Cancer Society; Teacher for Mentally Impaired Children; Journalist; Columbia U; Baruch College

RUIZ, PAUL; BRONX, NY; BLESSED SACRAMENT ST GABRIEL HS; (JR); Comm Volntr; Paint Ball; Drawing; Networking; Programming; U of Honolulu; U of Hawaii

RUMAYOR, ADRIANNA M; BROOKLYN, NY; BISHOP KEARNEY HS; (FR); Hnr Roll; MVP; Otst Ac Ach Awd; Comm Volntr; Chr; Golf (J); Sftball (J); The Mark Hindy Award; Nursing; Education; Miami U; New York U

RUNGE, LORIE; SINCLAIRVILLE, NY; CASSADAGA VALLEY MHS; (JR); Hi Hnr Roll; Nat Hon Sy; Otst Ac Ach Awd; St of Mnth; WWAHSS; Comm Volntr; Emplmnt; Key Club; NYLC; Pep Squd; Prom Com; Sci Clb; SADD; Tchrs Aide; Chr; Chrldg (VJCL); Cheerleading Treasurer; Education; Business; Syracuse U

RUPERT, JONATHAN; ALDEN, NY; ALDEN HS; (JR); Hnr Roll; Nat Hon Sy; USAA; WWAHSS; Comm Volntr; Key Club; Bnd; Mch Bnd; Sccr (J); Swmg (V); Tennis (V); Veterinary; Education

RUSSELL, DOMINIQUE; MT VERNON, NY; SATELLITE ACAD; (SR); Hnr Roll; Perf Att; Pres Ac Ftns Aw; Sci Fairs; Sci/Math Olympn; St of Mnth; Yth Ldrshp Prog; Amnsty Intl; Comm Volntr; Peer Tut/Med; ArtClub; Cmptr Clb; DARE; Dbte Team; Emplmnt; Mus Clb; Photog; Prom Com; Svce Clb; Tchrs Aide; SP/M/VS; Scr Kpr (V); Vllyball (J); Youth Leader of Community Based Group; School Representative Who Travels to other States; Political Science; Law; Monroe College; New York U

RUSSELL, JOELLE; SYRACUSE, NY; ONONDAGA JR/SR HS; (FR); Hi Hnr Roll; Hnr Roll; Comm Volntr; ArtClub; Key Club; German Clb; Bskball (J); Sccr (J); Sftball (J); Cl Off (V); Psychology; Law School; Penn State U

RUSSELL, TYLER; LIVONIA, NY; LIVONIA HS; (FR); Ctznshp Aw; Hi Hnr Roll; Hnr Roll; MVP; Nat Hon Sy; Otst Ac Ach Awd; Perf Att; Pres Ac Ftns Aw; Sci Fairs; Sci/Math Olympn; Comm Volntr; Red Cr Aide; Spec Olymp Vol; DARE; Key Club; Vsity Clb; Ice Hky (V); Lcrsse (JC); Vsy Clb (V); Adv Cncl (R); Stu Cncl (R); Student Council; Play Many Sports Outside of School; Business Management; Sports Management; Syracuse U; Princeton U

RUSSO, CHRISTINA; CORAM, NY; LONGWOOD HS; (JR); Hnr Roll; Pre-Law; History; St Johns' U; St Joseph's College

RUSSO, ROSALBA; RIDGEWOOD, NY; CHRIST THE KING HS; (SO); Hnr Roll; Otst Ac Ach Awd; Perf Att; Peer Tut/Med; ArtClub; DARE; Emplmnt; Dnce; Chrldg (C); STRIVE Leader; Dancing School; Pediatrician; Fashion Merchandise / Magazine Editor; New York U; Boston U

RUSTEMI, MASOOD; MINEOLA, NY; MINEOLA HS; (FR); Hi Hnr Roll; Nat Hon Sy; Perf Att; Sci/Math Olympn; Comm Volntr; Hosp Aide; Mth Clb/Tm; Sci Clb; Bnd; Sccr (J); Sch Ppr (R); Increase the Peace Club; Doctor; Harvard U; Columbia U

RYAN, KIMOY J; BROOKLYN, NY; PAUL ROBESON HS; (JR); WWAHSS; Sccr (V); Youth Venture; Accounting; Sociology; U of Tennessee; Clark Atlanta U

RYAN, MICHAEL J; BUFFALO, NY; CARDINAL O'HARA HS; (SR); Hnr Roll; MVP; Nat Hon Sy; Perf Att; St of Mnth; WWAHSS; Yth Ldrshp Prog; Comm Volntr; Chrch Yth Grp; Emplmnt; HO'Br Yth Ldrshp; Jr Ach; Prom Com; Quiz Bowl; Sci Clb; Spanish Clb; Bsball (V L); Bskball (V CL); Ftball (V CL); Cl Off (V); Yrbk (R); 1st Team All WNY-All Academic Football Team; Defensive Player of the Year "A" League - Football; Business; SUNY Brockport; Allegheny College

RYDER, SAMANTHA L; MORAVIA, NY; AREA OCCUPATIONAL CTR; (JR); Hnr Roll; Nat Hon Sy; Chrch Yth Grp; DARE; Drma Clb; Mus Clb; Prom Com; Chr; SP/M/VS; Chrldg (VJ); Sccr (V); Sftball (J L); CR (V); Medical Assistant; Lincoln Technology PA

RYU, MARISOL; MANHASSET, NY; MANHASSET HS; (JR); F Lan Hn Soc; Hi Hnr Roll; Jr Rot; Kwnis Aw; Nat Hon Sy; Otst Ac Ach Awd; Sci Fairs; St of Mnth; WWAHSS; Yth Ldrshp Prog; Comm Volntr; Hosp Aide; Peer Tut/Med; Emplmnt; JSA; Key Club; Spanish Clb; Orch; Adv Cncl (P); Cl Off (P); Stu Cncl (P); CR (P); ISEF Intel Finalist; Long Island Science Congress 1st Place; Environmental Scientist; Biology; Stanford U; Harvard College

SAAVEDRA, ISABEL; AMAGANSETT, NY; (JR); Hi Hnr Roll; Hnr Roll; Nat Hon Sy; WWAHSS; Yth Ldrshp Prog; Comm Volntr; Chrch Yth Grp; Key Club; NYLC; Spanish Clb; Cr Ctry (V); President Spanish Club; Nominated for Girls State; Law School; NYU; U of Florida

SABETFARD, MATTHEW; GREAT NECK, NY; JLM-GREAT NECK NORTH HS; (JR); Hi Hnr Roll; Hnr Roll; Comm Volntr; Peer Tut/Med; Mod UN; Hebrew Clb; SP/M/VS; Stg Cre; Swmg (V L); Wrstlg (J L); All Conference Swimmer; Wrestling Novice Tournament Semi Final; Business Management; Accounting; Cornell U; New York U

SABIKI, AMBKA; HUNTINGTON STATION, NY; HALF HOLLOW HILLS HS WEST; (JR); F Lan Hn Soc; Hi Hnr Roll; Nat Hon Sy; Comm Volntr; Peer Tut/Med; Key Club; Spanish Clb; Chr; Team Tutoring (Tutoring Club); Pre-Medical; SUNY College At Stony Brook

SABOURI, MONNA; FOREST HILLS, NY; AC OF AMERICAN STUDIES; MS; Hnr Roll; Nat Hon Sy; Perf Att; Sci Fairs; St of Mnth; Red Cr Aide; Drma Clb; Fr of Library; Mus Clb; Chr; Clr Grd; Dnce; SP/M/VS; Bskball (V); Sccr (V); Tennis (V); Vllyball (V); Acting / Performing Arts; Dental Field; New York U; St John's U

SACHMAN, KATIE; OWEGO, NY; OWEGO FREE AC; (SR); Ctznshp Aw; Hi Hnr Roll; Hnr Roll; Nat Hon Sy; Chrch Yth Grp; Key Club; Schol Bwl; Vsity Clb; Bnd; Chr; SP/M/VS; Stg Cre; Tennis (V); Vllyball (J); National Honor Society; Biology; Veterinary Medicine; U of Albany

SADLER, JACLYN A; ROCHESTER, NY; CHURCHVILLE-CHILI HS; (FR); Hi Hnr Roll; Nat Hon Sy; Comm Volntr; Chrch Yth Grp; Emplmnt; Scouts; Bnd; Chr; Dnce; SP/M/VS; Swmg (V); Recipient of the Coveted Silver Award - Girls Scouts; Junior High All-County Band; English Major / Communications; Performing Arts; Azusa Pacific U; Grove City College

SAFFIOTI, DANIELLA-JESSIC; LAWRENCE, NY; LAWRENCE HS; (SR); Hi Hnr Roll; Hnr Roll; Nat Hon Sy; WWAHSS; Red Cr Aide; Spec Olymp Vol; ArtClub; Drma Clb; Key Club; Chr; Stg Cre; Psychology; Elementary Education; State U of New York, New Paltz

SAIERS, DESIRAE; ONTARIO, NY; WAYNE CTRL HS; (FR); Ctznshp Aw; Hnr Roll; Otst Ac Ach Awd; St of Mnth; Comm Volntr; Peer Tut/Med; Drma Clb; Key Club; SP/M/VS; Sch Ppr (R); New York State Attorney General Triple "C" Award; Psychology; Politics; U of Buffalo; U of Syracuse

SAINVIL, SHAREENA; BROOKLYN, NY; ST EDMUND PREP HS; (SO); Hnr Roll; MVP; Yth Ldrshp Prog; Comm Volntr; Chrch Yth Grp; DARE; Chr; Ch Chr; Dnce; Drl Tm; Chrldg (C); Biology; Pre-Med; Duke U; Florida State U

SALEH, MATTHEW; SCHENECTADY, NY; SCHENECTADY HS; (JR); 4H Awd; F Lan Hn Soc; Hi Hnr Roll; Hnr Roll; MVP; Nat Hon Sy; Nat Sci Aw; Otst Ac Ach Awd; Perf Att; Sci Fairs; Comm Volntr; Peer Tut/Med; 4-H; Chess; Cmptr Clb; Dbte Team; Emplmnt; Jr Ach; Key Club; Lttrmn Clb; Cr Ctry (V); Track (V); Wt Lftg (V); Cl Off (P); Stu Cncl (P); Degree in International Business; Degree in Advanced / Applied Mathematics; Cornell U; Rochester Polytechnic Institute

SALEK-RAHAM, JOHN; YOUNGSTOWN, NY; ST JOSEPHS COLLEGIATE INST; (SR); Hnr Roll; Yth Ldrshp Prog; Hosp Aide; Photog; Chr; Sccr (J); Dale Carnegie Youth Character Development; MVP Varsity Crew Team; Pre-Med/Pre Health Professional; U of Delaware; Cornell U/U of Buffalo

SALEM, KRYSTAL; YONKERS, NY; GORTON HS; (JR); Hnr Roll; Comm Volntr; Hab For Humty Volntr; Cmptr Clb; Arabic Clb; Dnce; SP/M/VS; SMART Program; S.T.A.C.K.; Computers; Graphics; Iona College; Mercy College

SALERNO, KATHERINE; STATEN ISLAND, NY; ST JOHN VILLA AC; (JR); Comm Volntr; Chrch Yth Grp; Chosen to be a Youth Role-Model; Business Management; Teaching; College of Staten Island; Baruch College

SALERNO, LISA M; SCHENECTADY, NY; NISKAYUNA HS; (JR); Yth Ldrshp Prog; Comm Volntr; Peer Tut/Med; Chrch Yth Grp; Emplmnt; Prom Com; Spanish Clb; Youth Court; Vice President of Women's Group; School Psychologist; Social Worker; Manhattan College; Drew U

SALICKRAM, SAJNETA D; MASTIC, NY; WILLIAM FLOYD HS; (JR); F Lan Hn Soc; Hnr Roll; Nat Hon Sy; Sci Fairs; WWAHSS; Comm Volntr; DECA; FBLA; Mth Clb/Tm; French Clb; Chr; CR; Vice President of Foreign Language Honor Society; Junior Treasurer of Business Honor Society; Mathematical Engineer; Business Finance; New York U; SUNY Stony Brook

SALMON, ANDREW B; W HENRIETTA, NY; HOMESCHOOL; (SR); Hi Hnr Roll; Nat Mrt LOC; Valdctrian; Comm Volntr; Peer Tut/Med; Chrch Yth Grp; Emplmnt; Scouts; Tchrs Aide; Chinese Clb; SP/M/VS; Stg Cre; Bsball; Fncg; Sccr (V); Swmg; Yrbk (R); Mission Trip to China & 12 Credits College and Chinese Language; Member of the Circle-Writer's Association Chinese Language; English-Writing; Linguistics; Bryan College; Rochester Institute of Technology

SALVATORE, SARAH; WHITEHALL, NY; WHITEHALL JR/SR HS; (SO); Hnr Roll; St of Mnth; WWAHSS; Chrch Yth Grp; Drma Clb; Emplmnt; Bnd; Chr; Ch Chr; SP/M/VS; Chrldg (JC); Sccr (J); Track (V); Cl Off (S); Physical Therapy; Massage Therapy

SAM, NANCY; GLEN OAKS, NY; TOWNSEND HARRIS HS; (MS); Hi Hnr Roll; Hnr Roll; Nat Hon Sy; Otst Ac Ach Awd; Perf Att; Pres Sch; Sci Fairs; St of Mnth; Comm Volntr; ArtClub; Chrch Yth Grp; Lib Aide; Mth Clb/Tm; Off Aide; Tchrs Aide; Spanish Clb; Chr; Ch Chr; Clr Grd; Bdmtn; Bskball; Vllyball; CR (R); Sch Ppr (R); Presidential Outstanding Academic Excellence; Johns Hopkins U Award for Being Among the Highest Scoring Participant in New York on the SAT I; Biology; Cardiology; Columbia U; New York U

SAMA, CHRISTINA; HOWARD BEACH, NY; CHRIST THE KING HS; (JR); Hnr Roll; Kwnis Aw; Nat Hon Sy; St of Mnth; Peer Tut/Med; Chrch Yth Grp; Key Club; SADD; Bskball (J); Tennis (V); Stu Cncl (V); Management; Business; St Vincent College; Seton Hall U

SAMAROO, SARAH; BRONX, NY; LIFE SCIENCES SECONDARY SCH; (JR); Ctznshp Aw; Hnr Roll; Yth Ldrshp Prog; Comm Volntr; ArtClub; Dbte Team; Tchrs Aide; Tmpl Yth Grp; Ch Chr; Dnce; SP/M/VS; CR (V); Pediatrician; Forensic Scientist; Lehman College; Hunter College

SAMEK, ALYSSA; SCHENECTADY, NY; SCHENECTADY HS; (FR); Hnr Roll; Mus Clb; Orch; Writing Profession; Orchestral Performer; New York City School of Fine Arts; Union College

SAMMS, SHANNETTE; BRONSE, NY; MT VERNON HS; (JR); Hi Hnr Roll; Hnr Roll; Otst Ac Ach Awd; Perf Att; St of Mnth; WWAHSS; Yth Ldrshp Prog; Chrch Yth Grp; Ch Chr; Dnce; High School Undergraduate Recognition; Dance; Psychologist; Emory U; Augusta State U

SAMPUGNARO, VICTORIA R; WHITE PLAINS, NY; WHITE PLAINS HS; (SO); Hnr Roll; Nat Hon Sy; WWAHSS; Yth Ldrshp Prog; Hab For Humty Volntr; Emplmnt; Mus Clb; Photog; Bnd; Jzz Bnd; Mch Bnd; Pep Bnd; Photography/Worked Part Time in Bakery for 1 Year; Psychology/ Advertising; Boston U; Philadelphia

SAMREEN, TABINDA; JAMAICA, NY; MATH SCIENCE RESEARCH TECH HS; (JR); Hi Hnr Roll; Hnr Roll; Nat Hon Sy; Nat Mrt Sch Recip; Nat Sci Aw; Otst Ac Ach Awd; Sci Fairs; Sci/Math Olympn; St of Mnth; WWAHSS; Comm Volntr; Peer Tut/Med; Chess; DARE; Jr Ach; Mth Clb/Tm; Sci Clb; SADD; Bnd; Clr Grd; Orch; SP/M/VS; Bdmtn; Bsball; Bskball; Cyclg; Sccr; Tennis; Track; Vllyball; CR (P); Yrbk (P); Pharmacy; Medicine; Columbia U; St John's U

SAMUCHA, JOSHUA; FREDONIA, NY; FREDONIA HS; (FR); Hnr Roll; WWAHSS; Comm Volntr; Key Club

SAMUEL, JOYCE; SYOSSET, NY; OUR LADY OF MERCY AC; (JR); F Lan Hn Soc; Hnr Roll; Perf Att; Yth Ldrshp Prog; Hosp Aide; Chrch Yth Grp; Off Aide; Ch Chr; Bdmtn (V C); Yrbk (R); 2003 Northeast Region Competition - 1st Place for English Solo; Nursing; Pharmacy; College of New Rochelle; Long Island U Brooklyn Campus

SAMUELS, RONEN; BRONX, NY; RAMAZ; (JR); Comm Volntr; Peer Tut/ Med; SADD; Bskball (V); Sccr (V); Medicine; SUNY Binghamton; U of Maryland

SANCHEZ, ALEXANDRA; NEW YORK, NY; CATHEDRAL HS; (FR); Hnr Roll; WWAHSS; Dbte Team; Mth Clb/Tm; Clr Grd; Mch Bnd; Tennis (J); Perfect Attendance at Exploring Program; Award for Raising Grade 82 Points Higher; Pharmacist; Lawyer; St John's U; Temple U

SANCHEZ, MARIO; BRONX, NY; COLUMBUS HS; (SO); Hnr Roll; Perf Att; St of Mnth; Emplmnt; Bnd; Chr; SP/M/VS; Accepted in College Now; International Law; Veterinary Science; Pace U; Hunter College

SANCHEZ, MATTHEW; BRONX, NY; CELIA CRUZ BRONX HS OF MUSIC; (FR); Hnr Roll; Perf Att; St of Mnth; Comm Volntr; Mus Clb; Bnd; Bskball (V); Wt Lftg (V); The Juilliard School - MAP Program; Symphonic Band at Celia Cruz HS; Global History; Band

SANCHEZ, NELSON J; BROOKLYN, NY; AUGUST MARTIN HS; (JR); Hnr Roll; Tech Clb; Bsball (J); Sccr (J); Flight Training; Flight Instructor; Commercial Pilot; Daniel Webster U; SUNY Farmingdale

Samaroo, Sarah
Life Sciences Secondary Sch
Bronx, NY

Salvatore, Sarah
Whitehall JR/SR HS
Whitehall, NY

Salek-Raham, John
St Josephs Collegiate Inst
Youngstown, NY

National
Honor Roll
Spring 2005

Saleh, Matthew
Schenectady HS
Schenectady, NY

Sam, Nancy
Townsend Harris HS
Glen Oaks, NY

Sanchez, Matthew
Celia Cruz Bronx HS Of Music
Bronx, NY

SANCHICK, DANIELLE; SOUTH SALEM, NY; JOHN JAY HS; (SR); F Lan Hn Soc; Hnr Roll; Nat Hon Sy; Comm Volntr; Peer Tut/Med; Mth Clb/Tm; Vsity Clb; French Clb; Lcrsse (J); Vllyball (VJC); National Honor Society Treasurer; Future Problem Solvers Director (Asst); Architecture; Art; Cornell U; Tulane U

SANDAU, ASHLEY J; RIPLEY, NY; BITBURG AMERICAN HS; (JR); Hi Hnr Roll; Nat Hon Sy; Otst Ac Ach Awd; Sci/Math Olympn; Comm Volntr; Emplmnt; Mod UN; Prom Com; Sccr (VJ); Swmg (VJCL); Cl Off (T); Lit Mag (E); Yrbk (E, R, P); Journalism; Communications; Ithaca College; Vassar College

SANDFORD, KIMBERLY; GLOVERSVILLE, NY; GLOVERSVILLE HS; (SO); Hi Hnr Roll; Nat Hon Sy; Perf Att; Pres Ac Ftns Aw; WWAHSS; Spec Olymp Vol; Emplmnt; Scouts; Bnd; Mch Bnd; Bskball (V L); Sccr (V L); Sftball (V L); Cl Off (S); CR (S); Students Solve Program; Lawyer; Medical Examiner; Clarkson U; Albany Medical U

SANDHER, BHUPINDERJIT; STATEN ISLAND, NY; PT RICHMOND HS; (FR); Ctznshp Aw; Otst Ac Ach Awd; Perf Att; Pres Sch; Sci Fairs; St of Mnth; Comm Volntr; ArtClub; Chrch Yth Grp; Cmptr Clb; DARE; Drma Clb; Mth Clb/Tm; Photog; Svce Clb; Bnd; Chr; Clr Grd; Dnce; Business; Management / Marketing; Wagner College; St John's U

SANDOVAL, VICTOR; PT CHESTER, NY; PT CHESTER HS; (FR); Ctznshp Aw; Hi Hnr Roll; Hnr Roll; Perf Att; St of Mnth; Chrch Yth Grp; French Clb; Bnd; Mch Bnd; Engineer; Lawyer

SANGANI, DIMPLE A; LIVERPOOL, NY; CICERO-NORTH SYRACUSE; (JR); Hnr Roll; WWAHSS; Hosp Aide; Chrch Yth Grp; Emplmnt; Fr of Library

SANICOLA, NICOLE; STATEN ISLAND, NY; ST JOHN VILLA AC; (SO); Hnr Roll; WWAHSS; Comm Volntr; ArtClub; Chrch Yth Grp; Spanish Clb; Dnce; The American Legion Student Volunteer Award; Psychologist

SANON, MANOUCHKA; SPRING VALLEY, NY; RAMAPO HS; (JR); Ctznshp Aw; Hnr Roll; MVP; Nat Hon Sy; Otst Ac Ach Awd; Pres Sch; St of Mnth; Comm Volntr; Peer Tut/Med; Mth Clb/Tm; MuAlphaTh; Chr; Dnce; Bskball (J); Track (V); Vllyball (V); Black Achievement Award; Haitian-American Award; Teaching / Mathematics; Speech Pathology; Fordham U; Long Island U

SANSONE, CHRISTOPHER M; LAKE GROVE, NY; ST ANTHONY'S HS; (SO); Hi Hnr Roll; Hnr Roll; Otst Ac Ach Awd; Perf Att; Comm Volntr; Emplmnt; Bnd; Fbtall (J); Computer Science; Michigan State U; Syracuse U

SANTAMARIA, JORGE; STATEN ISLAND, NY; (FR); Journalism; Law; Wagner College

SANTANA, JOSE; BRONX, NY; FIORELLO H LA GUARDIA HS; (JR); Hnr Roll; Perf Att; St of Mnth; Drma Clb; Vsity Clb; SP/M/VS; Stg Cre; Fball; Latin Achievement Award; Drama; Law

SANTELISES, RAFAEL; NEW YORK, NY; HUMANITIES HS; (SO); MVP; Sci Fairs; St of Mnth; Comm Volntr; Emplmnt; Scouts; Clr Grd; Bsball (V); Bskball (J); International Business; Marketing; International Business; NBA

SANTER, RICKIE; LEVITTOWN, NY; DIVISION AVE HS; (FR); All Am Sch; Hi Hnr Roll; Otst Ac Ach Awd; Sci Fairs; Sci/Math Olympn; WWAHSS; Comm Volntr; Drma Clb; Key Club; Mth Clb/Tm; Sci Clb; SP/M/VS; Sch Ppr (R); National History Day-Best in School Medal-Superior Rating; Molloy College Science Fair-High Honors; Engineering; Education; Hofstra U; Molloy College

SANTERAMO, LISA; NEW ROCHELLE, NY; MARIA REGINA HS; (SR); F Lan Hn Soc; Hi Hnr Roll; Hnr Roll; Nat Hon Sy; Perf Att; WWAHSS; Key Club; Italian Clb; Chrldg (V C); USA Gymnastics Team Member - Level 5; National Italian Honor Society - Vice President; Fordham U

SANTIAGO, ANISSA; FLUSHING, NY; JOHN BOWNE HS; (FR); Comm Volntr; Dnce; Whitestone Bowling League; Volunteer Westchester Triathlon-Leukemia Foundation; Veterinary Science; U of Bridgeport; Stony Brook

SANTISTEBAN, YOLANDA M; NEW YORK, NY; EDWARD R MURROW HS; (SR); WWAHSS; SP/M/VS; Psychology; Education; Adelphia U; New York U

SANTOS, A KATIE; PINE CITY, NY; SOUTHSIDE HS; (SR); Hi Hnr Roll; Hnr Roll; Nat Hon Sy; Key Club; Vsity Clb; Orch; Sccr (VJ); Track (V); Vsy Clb (V L); Chemistry; Rochester Institute of Technology

SANTOS, ASHLEY; BRONX, NY; HEALTH OPPORTUNITIES HS; (FR); Hnr Roll; Perf Att; St of Mnth; Comm Volntr; Red Cr Aide; Chess; Fr of Library; Lib Aide; Tchrs Aide; Bnd; Dnce; Vllyball (V); CR (V); Associate/ Teaching; Master Degree/Business; Walden U; Minnesota School of Business

SANTOS, RAMON; NEW WINDSOR, NY; NFA NEWBURGH FREE AC; (FR); Ctznshp Aw; Hi Hnr Roll; Hnr Roll; WWAHSS; Comm Volntr; Chrch Yth Grp; Bnd; Bsball; Bskball; Fball; Mar Art; CR (R); Computer Engineering; Business Management; Columbia U; Massachusetts Inst of Technology

SANTULLI, MEGAN; SCHENECTADY, NY; GUILDERLAND HS; (SR); Hnr Roll; Yth Ldrshp Prog; Comm Volntr; Key Club; Tennis (VJ L); Key Club; Community Service; Child Psychology; Siena College

SANZO, MEGAN; RENSSELAER, NY; COLUMBIA; (SO); Hi Hnr Roll; Hnr Roll; Sci/Math Olympn; Key Club; Scouts; Chr; Lit Mag (R); Key Club Secretary; Liberal Arts; Hudson Valley Community College; Cazenovia College

SANZONE, JAMIE; TROY, NY; TROY HS; (JR); Hi Hnr Roll; Nat Hon Sy; WWAHSS; Comm Volntr; Key Club; Outdrs Clb; German Clb; Chr; Swmg (V L); Vice President for Key Club; Science Researcher; Russell Sage College

SANZONE, JILLIAN; WATERTOWN, NY; WATERTOWN HS; (FR); Nat Sci Aw; WWAHSS; Comm Volntr; ArtClub; Chrch Yth Grp; Key Club; Bskball (J); Fld Hky (J); Lcrsse (J); Cl Off (T); CR (T); USAA Scholarship Awards Program; Orthopedic Surgeon; Chef; Northeastern U; Johns Hopkins U

SAPADIN, JOSH; BRONX, NY; MS/HS 141 STEIN RIVERDALE AC; (FR); Ctznshp Aw; Hi Hnr Roll; Hnr Roll; Kwnis Aw; Nat Hon Sy; Comm Volntr; Peer Tut/Med; Biology Clb; Lib Aide; Mth Clb/Tm; Mod UN; Sci Clb; Bsball (J); Bskball (J); Sccr (J); Vllyball (J); Wt Lftg (J); CR (R); Physical Fitness Achievement Award - Gold; Book Review Club; Medical Physician; PhD / Medicine Field; Stanford U; Brown U

SARACINO, ALYSSA; SEAFORD, NY; ISLAND TREES HS; (SO); Hi Hnr Roll; Hnr Roll; Otst Ac Ach Awd; Perf Att; Pres Ac Ftns Aw; Comm Volntr; Peer Tut/Med; Key Club; Mth Clb/Tm; Prom Com; Spanish Clb; Dnce; Orch; Bdmtn (V); Bskball (J); Lcrsse (J); PPSqd (C); Scr Kpr (J); Sftball (J); Captain of Junior Varsity Kickline Team; Physical Fitness Award (Presidential); Meteorology; Teacher

SARDONE, DAVID M; FAIRPORT, NY; FAIRPORT HS; (JR); Ctznshp Aw; Hnr Roll; Nat Hon Sy; Nat Ldrshp Svc; Otst Ac Ach Awd; Pres Sch; Yth Ldrshp Prog; Comm Volntr; Chrch Yth Grp; Mth Clb/Tm; NYLC; Scouts; Tmpl Yth Grp; Spanish Clb; Bnd; Jzz Bnd; Mch Bnd; Pep Bnd; Lcrsse (V); Skiing; Sccr; Wt Lftg; Asset Building Representative School; National Young Leaders Conf Rep Washington DC; Political Science History; Cornell U, Penn State U Park; SUNY Geneseo, SUNY Binghamton, Michigan SU

SARRATORI, CHARLES M; GENEVA, NY; GENEVA HS; WWAHSS; Key Club; Dvng (V L); Lcrsse (J); Skiing; Carpentry Engineering; Alfred State U

SARRATORI, SALVATORE P; GENEVA, NY; GENEVA HS; (SR); Hi Hnr Roll; Hnr Roll; Perf Att; Pres Ac Ftns Aw; WWAHSS; Key Club; Cr Ctry (V L); Lcrsse (J); Skiing; Bowling Varsity Letter; Sponsored Skateboarder; Business Management; Ithaca College

SASHA, ROMERO; BROOKLYN, NY; BUSHWICK HS; (JR); Sci Fairs; St of Mnth; Dnce; Vllyball (V); CR (V); Yrbk (P); Fashion Designer; Lawyer; Brooklyn College; NYU

SATCHER, MILAN; MONGOMERY, NY; VALLEY CTRL HS; (JR); F Lan Hn Soc; Hi Hnr Roll; Hnr Roll; Nat Hon Sy; Sci/Math Olympn; Comm Volntr; Peer Tut/Med; ArtClub; Mth Clb/Tm; Photog; Sci Clb; Lit Mag (P); Elected secretary for National Honor Society; Conducted Original Research on Williams Syndrome; BA in Biology and International Relations; Medical Degree (Surgery); U of Vermont; Brown U

SATURNI, FIORALBA; BROOKLYN, NY; NEW UTRECHT HS; (MS); Peer Tut/Med; Master's Degree in Law; New York U; College of Staten Island

SAULPAUGH, MICHAEL S; SAUGERTIES, NY; SAUGERTIES HS; (JR); Hnr Roll; Nat Hon Sy; WWAHSS; Key Club; SP/M/VS; Stg Cre; Tennis (V L); Wrstlg (J L); Stu Cncl (P); CR (S); Sch Ppr (E); History / Education; Marketing; St Thomas Aquinas College

SAVAGE, PETER J; CHURCHVILLE, NY; LIMA CHRISTIAN SCH; (JR); Hi Hnr Roll; Hnr Roll; Nat Hon Sy; Red Cr Aide; Chrch Yth Grp; Drma Clb; Emplmnt; Photog; Bnd; Chr; Ch Chr; Jzz Bnd; Bskball (J); Sccr (JC); Cl Off (V); Stu Cncl (P, R); Political Science; Pre-Law; Messiah College; Roberts Wesleyan

SAVORY, MICHELE M; SODUS, NY; SODUS JR/SR HS; (SO); Hi Hnr Roll; Hnr Roll; Sci Fairs; USAA; Chrch Yth Grp; Bnd; Jzz Bnd; Mch Bnd; Biology; Zoology; Monroe Community College; Syracuse U

SAVVA, NICOLE N; EAST ELMHURST, NY; ARCHBISHOP MOLLOY HS; (JR); Hi Hnr Roll; Hnr Roll; Nat Ldrshp Svc; Yth Ldrshp Prog; Comm Volntr; Peer Tut/Med; Emplmnt; Mod UN; NYLC; Pep Squd; Svce Clb; SADD; Spanish Clb; Swmg (J); Stu Cncl (R); School Sport - Step Team-Varsity; Business; Communications; New York U; Stony Brook U

SAWYER, TANJA; MADRID, NY; MADRID-WADDINGTON HS; (SO); Hi Hnr Roll; Nat Hon Sy; Pres Ac Ftns Aw; St of Mnth; WWAHSS; Key Club; Scouts; French Clb; Bnd; Chr; Bskball (J); GAA (V); Sccr (J); Track (V); Police Officer; Forensics

SAYWACK, PRIAM; SOUTH OZONE PARK, NY; ARCHBISHOP MOLLOY HS; (SO); Gov Hnr Prg; Hi Hnr Roll; St of Mnth; Valdctrian; Comm Volntr; Biology Clb; Cmptr Clb; Dbte Team; Sci Clb; Chr; CR (R); Sch Ppr (R); Yrbk (R); 1st Place in Essay Competition; Women in Science Award; Journalism / Law; New York U; Columbia U

SCAGLIONI, JASON; BROOKLYN, NY; ST EDMUND PREP HS; (SO); Hnr Roll; Perf Att; Pres Ac Ftns Aw; St of Mnth; Perfect Attendance; Law; Wagner College; Brooklyn College

SCALIA, JOHN N; LEVITTOWN, NY; LEVITTOWN DIVISION HS; (JR); F Lan Hn Soc; Hi Hnr Roll; Nat Hon Sy; Perf Att; Pres Ac Ftns Aw; Sci Fairs; St of Mnth; WWAHSS; Comm Volntr; Key Club; Sci Clb; Tchrs Aide; Cr Ctry (V L); Lcrsse (VJCL); Sccr (VJ L); Stu Cncl (R); Honor Society; Foreign Lang Honor Society; Biology; Chemistry; West Point; Binghamton

SCANLON, ANDREW P; LITTLE FALLS, NY; LITTLE FALLS HS; (FR); Hnr Roll; Perf Att; St of Mnth; Comm Volntr; Hab For Humty Volntr; ArtClub; DARE; Cr Ctry (J); Sccr (V); Vllyball (J); Herkimer County Community College; SUNY Utica

SCANLON, SAMANTHA; SCHENEVUS, NY; MILFORD CTRL SCH; (FR); Hi Hnr Roll; Hnr Roll; Sci Fairs; DARE; Mus Clb; Spanish Clb; Bnd; Mch Bnd; SP/M/VS; Sccr (J); Lawyer; Mechanic; Harvard Law School

SCAVONE, ANTHONY; SARATOGA SPRINGS, NY; SARATOGA SPRINGS HS; (SO); Hnr Roll; Skiing (V); Track (J); Scholar Athlete; Education, Architecture; Polytechnic Institute (RPI); Rochester Institute of Technology

SCHACHT, JORDANA; WOODMERE, NY; HEWLETT HS; (FR); Hi Hnr Roll; Hnr Roll; Comm Volntr; Peer Tut/Med; Red Cr Aide; Emplmnt; Key Club; Tmpl Yth Grp; Bnd; Chr; Mch Bnd; Pep Bnd; Gmnstcs (V); NYSSMA (Piano); President's Award At Temple; Veterinarian; Cornell U

SCHAEFFER, ELYSSA B; COOPERSTOWN, NY; COOPERSTOWN CTRL SCH; (SO); Hnr Roll; St of Mnth; Yth Ldrshp Prog; Peer Tut/Med; ArtClub; Dnce; SP/M/VS; Swmg; Vsy Clb; CR (R); Ballet - 10 Yrs; Physician; Artist; Cornell U; McGill U

SCHAGER, ALICIA; WESTERLO, NY; BERNE-KNOX-WESTERLO HS; (FR); Ctznshp Aw; Hnr Roll; Otst Ac Ach Awd; Chrch Yth Grp; DARE; Key Club; Chr; Historian; Archivist; Duke U; Yale U

SCHANELY, TERESA L; BLACK RIVER, NY; CARTHAGE CTRL HS; (SR); Ctznshp Aw; Hi Hnr Roll; Nat Hon Sy; Salutrn; St of Mnth; WWAHSS; Comm Volntr; Hab For Humty Volntr; FBLA; HO'Br Yth Ldrshp; Key Club; Mth Clb/Tm; Bnd; Mch Bnd; Pep Bnd; Swmg (V L); Track (V L); Congressional Youth Leadership Conference; Business Administration; Bentley College

SCHEEMAKER, JOSHUA R; HASTINGS, NY; BISHOP GRIMES HS; (SR); Hnr Roll; Nat Hon Sy; WWAHSS; Emplmnt; Scouts; Sccr (V CL); Track (V CL); Wt Lftg (V); Forestry / Conservation; Paul Smith's College - Accepted

SCHIANO III, VICTOR; MASTIC, NY; WILLIAM FLOYD HS; (FR); F Lan Hn Soc; Hi Hnr Roll; Emplmnt; Physicist; Engineer; New York Institute of Technology; New York U

SCHIAVONE, SARA A; SYRACUSE, NY; (JR); Hi Hnr Roll; Nat Hon Sy; Otst Ac Ach Awd; WWAHSS; Comm Volntr; Chrch Yth Grp; Emplmnt; Sftball (V); Tennis (V); Vllyball (V); Yrbk (E); Many Academic Awards; National Honor Society Member (Scholar Athlete)

SCHIFFERLE, LAUREN; EAST AURORA, NY; EAST AURORA HS; (JR); Hnr Roll; Kwnis Aw; Emplmnt; Key Club; Mod UN; Sci Clb; Scouts; Mch Bnd; SP/M/VS; Stg Cre; PP Ftbl; Swmg (V CL); Track (V L); Synchronized Swimming (Made Nationals); AFS Member; Environmental Policy; Political Science

SCHILLACI, EMILY; GENEVA, NY; DE SALES HS; (JR); USAA; WWAHSS; Comm Volntr; Key Club; SADD; Sftball (V); Cl Off (S); Yrbk (R); Fashion Merchandising/Marketing

SCHIMMER, KATE; LINDENHURST, NY; LINDENHURST HS; (SR); Hi Hnr Roll; Nat Hon Sy; Nat Mrt LOC; Pres Sch; WWAHSS; Peer Tut/Med; Yrbk (E); Tulane U

SCHIMPF, LENI; SMITHTOWN, NY; SMITHTOWN HS EAST; (SO); F Lan Hn Soc; Hnr Roll; Nat Hon Sy; Comm Volntr; DARE; DECA; Emplmnt; Tmpl Yth Grp; Bnd; Varsity Kickline - National Champs; NYSMEA Flute Competition; Marketing; Dentistry; SUNY Binghamton; Babson College

SCHINDLER, MALORIE K; GOWANDA, NY; GOWANDA HS; (SR); Hnr Roll; Nat Hon Sy; Comm Volntr; ArtClub; Chrch Yth Grp; Emplmnt; SADD; Tchrs Aide; Vsity Clb; French Clb; Chr; Bskball (J); Sccr (V); French; International Business; Buffalo State U; Erie Community College

SCHLEGEL, DESIREE A; SAUGERTIES, NY; SAUGERTIES HS; (FR); Hi Hnr Roll; Hnr Roll; Perf Att; WWAHSS; Comm Volntr; Peer Tut/Med; DARE; Dbte Team; Key Club; French Clb; Bnd; Yrbk; Psychology; Interior Design; New York U; U of Massachusetts

Scaglioni, Jason
St Edmund Prep HS
Brooklyn, NY

Santisteban, Yolanda M
Edward R Murrow HS
New York, NY

Santer, Rickie
Division Ave HS
Levittown, NY

National
Honor Roll
Spring 2005

Sandher, Bhupinderjit
Pt Richmond HS
Staten Island, NY

Santulli, Megan
Guilderland HS
Schenectady, NY

Scanlon, Andrew P
Little Falls HS
Little Falls, NY

SCHLENDORF, LAUREN; MERRICK, NY; S H CALHOUN; (JR); F Lan Hn Soc; Hi Hnr Roll; Hnr Roll; Nat Hon Sy; Comm Volntr; Peer Tut/Med; Emplmnt; Key Club; Vsity Clb; Lcrsse (V L); Track (V L); Vllyball (V L)

SCHMID, LAUREN; SCHENECTADY, NY; SCHENECTADY HS; (FR); Hi Hnr Roll; Nat Hon Sy; Perf Att; Comm Volntr; Peer Tut/Med; Chrch Yth Grp; Mus Clb; Chr; Ch Chr; Lit Mag (E); Yrbk (E); Psychology; SUNY Oneonta; Sienna College

SCHMIDLE, CHRISTINE; EAST SETAUKET, NY; SUFFOLK CTY CC; (SR); Hnr Roll; Nat Hon Sy; St Optmst of Yr; WWAHSS; Comm Volntr; Hosp Aide; Peer Tut/Med; ArtClub; Drma Clb; SP/M/VS; Stg Cre; Student of the Year; Who's Who Among HS Students; Theatre-Acting; Theatre-Directing; Cornell U; Point Park U

SCHMITT, TARA L; OWEGO, NY; OWEGO FREE AC; (SO); Ctznshp Aw; Hnr Roll; WWAHSS; Hosp Aide; Peer Tut/Med; Chrch Yth Grp; Key Club; Stu Cncl (R); Yrbk (P); Elementary Education

SCHNEIDER, KIMBERLEE; SYRACUSE, NY; CORCORAN HS; (SR); Hi Hnr Roll; Nat Hon Sy; Otst Ac Ach Awd; Pres Ac Ftns Aw; WWAHSS; Lcrsse; Skiing; Tennis; Cl Off (S); Stu Cncl (R); Yrbk (E); Psychology & Inclusive Education; Nazareth College; Mercyhurst College

SCHNOPP, AMANDA; SELDEN, NY; NEWFIELD HS; (FR); Ctznshp Aw; Hi Hnr Roll; Perf Att; St of Mnth; WWAHSS; Comm Volntr; DARE; Drma Clb; Emplmnt; Scouts; Bnd; Mch Bnd; SP/M/VS; Stg Cre; Bskball (J); Fld Hky (J); Yrbk (P); A Poem in a Celebration of Young Poets; Pediatric Physical Therapy; Teaching; New York U

SCHNUR, KIMBERLY; BRONX, NY; ST CATHARINE AC; (SR); F Lan Hn Soc; Hi Hnr Roll; Nat Hon Sy; Perf Att; USAA; WWAHSS; Comm Volntr; ArtClub; Chrch Yth Grp; Prom Com; Asian Clb; Ch Chr; Lit Mag (E); Sch Ppr (R); Church Lector; Mentoring Program; Psychology; College of Mount Saint Vincent

SCHOELL, CHRISTOPHER J; OCEANSIDE, NY; OCEANSIDE HS; (JR); Hi Hnr Roll; Nat Hon Sy; Otst Ac Ach Awd; Comm Volntr; Peer Tut/Med; Key Club; Svce Clb; Bnd; Orch; SP/M/VS; Sccr (VJ); National Honor Society; Award for #1 Fresh / Soph; Math / Business; Medicine; Yale U; U Penn

SCHOER, MATTHEW; BROOKLYN, NY; LEON M GOLDSTEIN HS; (SO); Hi Hnr Roll; Sci/Math Olympn; Comm Volntr; Emplmnt; Lib Aide; Off Aide; Tchrs Aide; Acpl Chr; Chr; Junior Arista Society; Archon Society

SCHOLTZ, PAUL A; BINGHAMTON, NY; BINGHAMPTON HS; (JR); Hi Hnr Roll; Nat Hon Sy; Comm Volntr; Cmptr Clb; Drma Clb; Bnd; Chr; Dnce; SP/M/VS; Skiing

SCHORR, SAMANTHA; MASSAPEQUA, NY; MASSAPEQUA HS; (SR); F Lan Hn Soc; Hi Hnr Roll; Nat Hon Sy; St of Mnth; WWAHSS; CARE; Comm Volntr; Peer Tut/Med; Key Club; P to P St Amb Prg; SADD; Tchrs Aide; Completion of Work-Experience Program; Attorney; Tulane U

SCHOWALTER, SEAN L; LATHAM, NY; SHAKER HS; (JR); All Am Sch; Hi Hnr Roll; Otst Ac Ach Awd; Pres Sch; Sci/Math Olympn; Bnd; Played Ice Hockey for Troy Academy Youth Hockey for 11 Years - Age 5 to 15; Medicine

SCHRADER, ERIK A; WEBSTER, NY; WEBSTER CHRISTIAN HS; (FR); Hi Hnr Roll; Hnr Roll; Chess; Chr; Cl Off (P); Adolescent Education; Meteorology; Monroe Community College; Roberts Wesleyan College

SCHRAVER, ROBERT L; SCHENECTADY, NY; MOHONASEN HS; (JR); Chrch Yth Grp; Bnd; Jzz Bnd; Mch Bnd; Orch; Capital Area Honors Youth Wind Ensemble; Music; UC Berkeley; Ithaca College

SCHREIBER, GILLIAN E; CEDARHURST, NY; LAWRENCE HS; (SO); Gov Hnr Prg; Hnr Roll; WWAHSS; DECA; Emplmnt; Key Club; Mus Clb; Tmpl Yth Grp; Jzz Bnd; Orch; SP/M/VS; Lit Mag (E); Yrbk (R); Lawrence Phil Harmonic; Law; History; Michigan/Brown; Princeton

SCHREIBER, KATHERINE E; NEW YORK, NY; THE CALHOUN SCH; (JR); Otst Ac Ach Awd; Peer Tut/Med; French Clb; SP/M/VS; Claudia Curfman Castellana Award; Nutritional Science/Human Ecology; Biology; Cornell U; Columbia U

SCHRENK, LAURENE; WILLIAMSVILLE, NY; WILLIAMSVILLE EAST HS; (FR); Hnr Roll; Perf Att; Yth Ldrshp Prog; Comm Volntr; Drma Clb; Mus Clb; Vsity Clb; Bnd; Jzz Bnd; SP/M/VS; Swmg (J); Track (V); Stu Cncl (R); CR (R); Lit Mag (R); Shakesperiment; Mock Trial; Writing; Journalism; New York U; Boston U

SCHROEDER, CLARK; ROCHESTER, NY; GREECE ARCADIA HS; (JR); Hnr Roll; Comm Volntr; Scouts; Bnd; Cr Ctry (J); Track (J); Eagle Scout; Heavy Construction Equipment Operator; Penn College of Technology

SCHULTZ, SAMANTHA C; BUFFALO, NY; MT MERCY AC; (SR); Hnr Roll; Nat Hon Sy; WWAHSS; Comm Volntr; ArtClub; Emplmnt; SADD; Spanish Clb; Dnce; Skiing (J); Swmg (VJC); Stu Cncl (R); CR (R); Yrbk (E); Red Cross Life Saving & First Aid; Eucharistic Minister; Political Science; Law Degree; Canisius College; SUNY Buffalo

SCHWARTZ, CHRISTOPHER; SLINGERLANDS, NY; GUILDERLAND HS; (SO); Pres Sch; Sci/Math Olympn; WWAHSS; Peer Tut/Med; Chrch Yth Grp; Key Club; French Clb; Cr Ctry (J); Swmg (V); Longmuir Chemistry Competition Winner; Treasurer of Key Club; Software Engineer; Business Accountant; Cornell U; Swarthmore College

SCIACCA, JUSTINE A; MASPETH, NY; CHRIST THE KING HS; (SO); Hi Hnr Roll; Hnr Roll; Pres Ac Ftns Aw; Italian Clb; Chr; Dnce; Mental Health Professional

SCIARA, CARLO J; WEST BABYLON, NY; WEST BABYLON SR HS; (JR); F Lan Hn Soc; Hi Hnr Roll; Nat Hon Sy; St of Mnth; Yth Ldrshp Prog; Comm Volntr; Peer Tut/Med; Spec Olymp Vol; Mus Clb; NYLC; Prom Com; SADD; Bnd; Jzz Bnd; Mch Bnd; SP/M/VS; Ftball (V); Tennis (V); Track (V); Cl Off (T); Sch Ppr (R); National Honor Society; Tri-M Officer 04-05; International Business; Political Science/Physical Therapy; Clemson U; U of South Carolina

SCIMECA, KRISTA; FORT EDWARD, NY; SOUTH GLENS FALLS SR HS; (SO); DAR; F Lan Hn Soc; Hi Hnr Roll; Perf Att; Pres Sch; St of Mnth; Chrch Yth Grp; Key Club; French Clb; Dnce; Orch; SP/M/VS; Fld Hky (JCL); Principal Roles in Dance Productions; Top Ten in Class; Dance; Psychology, Forensics, Science; Marymount Manhattan College

SCOTT, COURTNEY; SMALLWOOD, NY; MONTICELLO HS; (SR); Hi Hnr Roll; Kwnis Aw; Nat Hon Sy; WWAHSS; Yth Ldrshp Prog; Comm Volntr; Emplmnt; Prom Com; Chr; SP/M/VS; Sccr (J); Track (V L); Honor Award for St. Jude Children's Hospital Fundraiser; CSLC - Medicine and Health Care; Pre-Med; Communication Sciences; Syracuse U; Fordham U-Transfer

SCOTT, PHILLIP; BROOKLYN, NY; EAST NEW YORK FAMILY AC; MS; Hnr Roll; MVP; Perf Att; St of Mnth; Comm Volntr; Chess; Chrch Yth Grp; Emplmnt; FCA; Mus Clb; Bnd; Ch Chr; Dnce; Bskball (JC); Ftball; Swmg; CR (P); Youth Employment At NYC Farms; Basketball Tournament and Vocal Competition; Forensic Science; Law Basketball Player; U of South Carolina; Duke U

SCOTT, TYREEK; YONKERS, NY; LINCOLN HS; (SO); Ctznshp Aw; Hnr Roll; MVP; Nat Stu Ath Day Aw; Otst Ac Ach Awd; Perf Att; Sci Fairs; St of Mnth; WWAHSS; Yth Ldrshp Prog; CARE; Comm Volntr; Hosp Aide; ArtClub; Chess; Dbte Team; Drma Clb; FCA; FBLA; Mth Clb/Tm; Mus Clb; Ch Chr; Dnce; Mch Bnd; SP/M/VS; Bskball (J); Ftball (J); Track (J); Wt Lftg (J); Architect; Computer Technology

SCOTTI, CHRISTINA; BROOKLYN, NY; CHRIST THE KING HS; (SO); Hi Hnr Roll; Hnr Roll; Otst Ac Ach Awd; Salutrn; Sci Fairs; St of Mnth; Drma Clb; Chef; Johnson & Wales U; St Francis College

SCULLEN, BRITTANY E; SANDY CREEK, NY; SANDY CREEK HS; (SO); Hnr Roll; Perf Att; St of Mnth; Comm Volntr; DARE; Scouts; Tchrs Aide; Spanish Clb; Scr Kpr (J); Vsy Clb (J); Vllyball (J L); Wt Lftg (J); Award for Most Dedicated - Volleyball; Global Studies Teacher; U of Oswego; Jefferson Community College

SCULLY, CAITLIN A; RIPLEY, NY; RIPLEY CTRL SCH; (FR); Hi Hnr Roll; Hnr Roll; Yth Ldrshp Prog; Comm Volntr; Peer Tut/Med; Chrch Yth Grp; DARE; Emplmnt; Chr; Dnce; Chautauqua Children's Chorale - 7 Yrs; CASS; Criminal Justice; Social Work; Notre Dame U; SUNY Fredonia

SEAHORN, CHRISTINA L; SARATOGA SPRINGS, NY; SARATOGA HS; (SO); Hi Hnr Roll; Otst Ac Ach Awd; Pres Ac Ftns Aw; Chrch Yth Grp; Bnd; Jzz Bnd; Orch; SP/M/VS; Bskball (J); Forensic Science / Pathology; Crime Scene Investigator; John Jay College of Criminal Justice; SUNY Albany

SEALY, BENJAMIN D; SENECA FALLS, NY; MYNDERSE AC HS; (SO); Hi Hnr Roll; St of Mnth; Chrch Yth Grp; Emplmnt; Bnd; Chr; Ch Chr; Jzz Bnd; Bsball (J); Bskball (J)

SEDDO, JOSHUA; BROOKLYN, NY; BROOKLYN TECH HS; (JR); Hnr Roll; Sci Fairs; St of Mnth; Comm Volntr; Peer Tut/Med; Chrch Yth Grp; Dbte Team; Bnd; Clr Grd; Bsball; Bskball; Swmg; Track; Wt Lftg; Award for Excellence in Music / Attorney General Award; Assistant Principal Award / Controller of NY Special Award; Government and Law; Medical Physics; Columbia U; Princeton U

SEHNE, LARA; FRANKLIN SQUARE, NY; SEWANHAKA HS; (FR); Hi Hnr Roll; Kwnis Aw; Nat Hon Sy; Otst Ac Ach Awd; Sci/Math Olympn; St of Mnth; WWAHSS; Comm Volntr; FBLA; Key Club; Quiz Bowl; SADD; Chr; Dnce; SP/M/VS; Chrldg (J); Sftball (J); Hofstra U

SEIFTER, ALLISON; MELVILLE, NY; HALF HOLLOW HILLS HS EAST; (SO); Hi Hnr Roll; Key Club; Chr; Sftball (J); Peer Aids Educators; Job Mentoring Program At Cancer Care; Marine Biologist; Marine Mammal Vet; Duke U; Stanford U

SELKE, GREGORY M; NORTH CHILI, NY; CHURCHVILLE-CHILI HS; (FR); Hi Hnr Roll; Perf Att; Scouts; Sccr; Boy Scouts; Travel Soccer; Meteorologist; Soccer; UCLA; U of Miami

SELLERS, VICTORIA; STATEN ISLAND, NY; MOORE CATHOLIC HS; (JR); Chrch Yth Grp; Emplmnt; Tchrs Aide; Vsity Clb; Bskball (V); Sccr (V); Yrbk (P); Coaches Award Soccer; Forensics; Criminal Justice; John Jay College; Monmouth U

SENA, ALLISON; YORKTOWN HEIGHTS, NY; YORKTOWN HS; (JR); Hi Hnr Roll; Hnr Roll; Nat Hon Sy; WWAHSS; Comm Volntr; Emplmnt; Pep Squd; Prom Com; Chrldg (V); Track (V)

SEO, BONG-KYO; NEW YORK, NY; UNITED NATIONS INTL SCH; (JR); Hnr Roll; Comm Volntr; Hosp Aide; Chess; Cmptr Clb; Mth Clb/Tm; Sci Clb; Tech Clb; Chinese Clb; Bnd; Vllyball (V); Principal's Award Academic Excellence Honors; Principal's Academic Commendation; To Study Science; Biomedical; New York U; Georgetown U

SEPTIMO, JACQUELINE; WOODSIDE, NY; FRANCIS LEWIS HS; (SO); Hnr Roll; Perf Att; Sci Fairs; St of Mnth; Chr; Track (J); Arista Award; Nursing; Veterinarian; New York U; Hunter College

SEQUEIRA, JESSICA; BRONX, NY; LOUIS D BRANDEIS HS; (SO); Hnr Roll; Perf Att; Law; Master's Degree; Harvard U; Yale U

SERGISON, TREVOR E; SAYVILLE, NY; SAYVILLE HS; (JR); Hi Hnr Roll; Hnr Roll; Nat Hon Sy; Sci Fairs; St of Mnth; Comm Volntr; Hab For Humty Volntr; Peer Tut/Med; DARE; Emplmnt; FBLA; Jr Ach; Key Club; Mth Clb/Tm; Mus Clb; Svce Clb; Bnd; Jzz Bnd; Orch; SP/M/VS; Cr Ctry (V); Track (V); Anchor Club Vice President; Geology 121 Student; Premedicine; New York U; George Washington U

SERIO, VINNY; SPENCER, NY; SPENCER-VAN ETTEN HS; (SR); Ctznshp Aw; F Lan Hn Soc; Hi Hnr Roll; Hnr Roll; MVP; Nat Hon Sy; Nat Ldrshp Svc; Otst Ac Ach Awd; St of Mnth; Comm Volntr; Peer Tut/Med; 4-H; Emplmnt; Key Club; Mus Clb; Tech Clb; Vsity Clb; Chr; SP/M/VS; Swg Chr; Bsball (VJ L); Bskball (VJ L); Skiing; Sccr (VJCL); Track (VJ L); Vsy Clb; Cl Off (T); BA of Business; Cayuga Community College; Ithaca College

SERPA, MANUELLA S; AUBURN, NY; TYBURN AC; (JR); Bskball (V); Sccr (V); Vllyball (V); Stu Cncl (T); CR (T)

SERRANO, ASHLEY; REGO PARK, NY; FIORELLO H LA GUARDIA HS; (JR); Hi Hnr Roll; Hnr Roll; Otst Ac Ach Awd; Peer Tut/Med; Emplmnt; Off Aide; Scouts; Tchrs Aide; Bnd; Chr; Clr Grd; SP/M/VS; Bskball; Sftball (C); Yrbk (E); Art Major; Bowling Champion; Gold Presidential Academic Award; Pre Law-Law; Criminal Justice; Columbia U; Princeton U

SERRANO, SHAVON I; BRONX, NY; ST PIUS V HS; (JR); Hi Hnr Roll; Hnr Roll; Nat Hon Sy; Perf Att; Comm Volntr; Peer Tut/Med; ArtClub; Ntl Beta Clb; Tchrs Aide; Chr; Teacher

SETERA, KARISSA; GLASCO, NY; SAUGERTIES HS; (SO); Hi Hnr Roll; Otst Ac Ach Awd; St of Mnth; WWAHSS; Comm Volntr; Emplmnt; Key Club; Bnd

SEVILLA, GERARDO A; RICHMOND HILL, NY; STUYVESANT HS; (FR); Hi Hnr Roll; Hnr Roll; St of Mnth; DARE; Fortiter et Recte Award; Architecture; Comic Book Artist; New York U; Cooper Union; Columbia

SEWELL, AMBER; UTICA, NY; T R PROCTOR HS; (JR); Hi Hnr Roll; Hnr Roll; Nat Hon Sy; Perf Att; Sci Fairs; St of Mnth; Comm Volntr; Peer Tut/Med; Red Cr Aide; Chrch Yth Grp; Dbte Team; Drma Clb; Emplmnt; Off Aide; ROTC; Spch Team; Bnd; Chr; Clr Grd; Drl Tm; Track (J); Stu Cncl (T); CR (R); Sch Ppr (E); Neurology; Radiologist; Penn State U; New York U

SHADE, AKEEM; MIDDLETOWN, NY; MIDDLETOWN HS; (JR); All Am Sch; Hnr Roll; Nat Hon Sy; Otst Ac Ach Awd; Perf Att; Sci Fairs; WWAHSS; Hab For Humty Volntr; Peer Tut/Med; Red Cr Aide; Spec Olymp Vol; Chess; Fr of Library; Lib Aide; Tchrs Aide; Chr; Ch Chr; Bskball; Ftball; PP Ftbl; Sccr; Tennis; Wt Lftg; Oceanographer; Acting; Maine State University

SHAFIR, OMRI; SUNNYSIDE, NY; (JR); Hnr Roll; Pres Sch; St of Mnth; Comm Volntr; Emplmnt; Mathematics; Genetics, Biochemistry; California Institute of Technology; New York U

SHAH, ADITY; WESTBURY, NY; W T CLARKE HS; (SR); F Lan Hn Soc; Hnr Roll; Nat Hon Sy; Sci/Math Olympn; Comm Volntr; Peer Tut/Med; Red Cr Aide; Emplmnt; JSA; Key Club; Mth Clb/Tm; Quiz Bowl; Sci Clb; Tmpl Yth Grp; SP/M/VS; Bdmtn (V); Vice President of National Honor Society; Biomedical Engineering; Medicine; Yale U; Boston U

SHAH, BHAVIK; HICKSVILLE, NY; WESTBURY HS; (SR); Ctznshp Aw; Hi Hnr Roll; Kwnis Aw; Nat Hon Sy; Nat Mrt Sch Recip; USAA; WWAHSS; Comm Volntr; Peer Tut/Med; FBLA; Lib Aide; Photog; Sch Ppr (E); Varsity Bowling Team; International Business; St John's U

SHAH, MEHAL; CORTLAND, NY; CORTLAND JR/SR HS; (JR); Hi Hnr Roll; Hnr Roll; Nat Hon Sy; Sci/Math Olympn; Peer Tut/Med; Chess; Dbte Team; Emplmnt; JSA; Lib Aide; Quiz Bowl; Foreign Clb; CR (R); Yrbk (E, R); Zonta Club; Architecture; Landscape Architecture; Cornell U; U of Pennsylvania

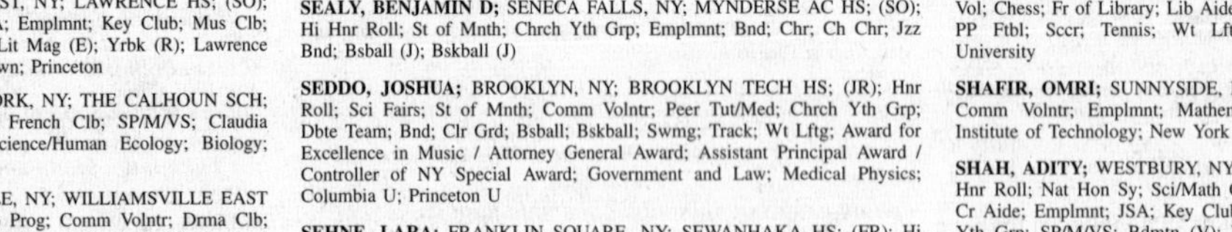

Seo, Bong-Kyo · United Nations Intl Sch · New York, NY
Seddo, Joshua · Brooklyn Tech HS · Brooklyn, NY
Seahorn, Christina L · Saratoga HS · Saratoga Springs, NY
Schoell, Christopher J · Oceanside HS · Oceanside, NY
Scott, Phillip · East New York Family AC · Brooklyn, NY
Selke, Gregory M · Churchville-Chili HS · North Chili, NY
Sequeira, Jessica · Louis D Brandeis HS · Bronx, NY

SHAH, MOHAMMAD A; BRONX, NY; JOHN F KENNEDY HS; (JR); Hi Hnr Roll; Hnr Roll; Sci Fairs; Comm Volntr; Peer Tut/Med; ArtClub; Chess; Cmptr Clb; Emplmnt; Fr of Library; Jr Ach; Lib Aide; Mth Clb/Tm; Bnd; Clr Grd; Drl Tm; Flg Crps; Bdmtn (J); Ftball (J); Sccr (V); Tennis (V); Wt Lftg (V); CR (V); Sch Ppr (R, P); Received Heany Medal in Arts; Semifinalist in Web Designing Contest; PhD in Computer Programming; Fordham U; Baruch College

SHAH, SHRUTI; JAMAICA, NY; JAMAICA HS; (JR); F Lan Hn Soc; Hnr Roll; Perf Att; St of Mnth; Svce Clb; Dnce; SP/M/VS; Bdmtn (L); Sftball (J); Swmg (L); Tennis (L); Sch Ppr (R); School Honor Roll Society for Foreign Lang.; Art; Fashion Institution of Technology

SHAH, SONAM; ALBERTSON, NY;; Chr; SP/M/VS; Gmnstcs; CR; Classical Dance/For the Love of Dance; Naya Andaz 2005 Perform on National SONY Television; Medicine; Health Science; Ivy League

SHAHA, MANISH A; GREAT NECK, NY; GREAT NECK NORTH HS; (JR); Hnr Roll; Nat Hon Sy; Otst Ac Ach Awd; Sci/Math Olympn; St of Mnth; Yth Ldrshp Prog; Peer Tut/Med; Chess; Dbte Team; DECA; Mth Clb/Tm; Mod UN; Bnd; Jzz Bnd; Orch; Fncg (V); Tennis (V); Cl Off (V); Lit Mag (R); Sch Ppr (R); Model Congress Awards Honorable Mention; 2nd Place Junior Fencing Competition; Bio Chemistry Major (Want to Cure Cancer); Head and Neck Cancer Surgeon; Cornell U; Dartmouth U

SHAHINIAN, ERIC; OSSINING, NY; OSSINING HS; (JR); Hi Hnr Roll; Jr Rot; Nat Hon Sy; Otst Ac Ach Awd; Sci Fairs; Comm Volntr; Mod UN; Cr Ctry (V L); Tennis (V L); Track (V CL); Stu Cncl (P, V, R); Interact Club (Public Relations, President); Fundamentals of Science Research; Finance; Economics; U of Pennsylvania; Babson College

SHAN, MINGYANG; MERRICK, NY; (SO); Ctznshp Aw; F Lan Hn Soc; Hnr Roll; Sci Fairs; Sci/Math Olympn; St of Mnth; WWAHSS; Comm Volntr; Peer Tut/Med; ArtClub; Cmptr Clb; Key Club; Mth Clb/Tm; Sci Clb; SADD; Tech Clb; Bnd; Mch Bnd; Stg Cre; MBA; Accounting; Columbia U; New York U

SHANKS, JAYDA M; QUEENS VILLAGE, NY; BENJAMIN BANNEKER AC; (SO); Ctznshp Aw; Hnr Roll; Otst Ac Ach Awd; Peer Tut/Med; Chrch Yth Grp; Drma Clb; Ch Chr; Dnce; SP/M/VS; Trey Whitfield Foundation Award; Most Christ-Like Award; Degree in Criminal Psychology; Law Degree; Temple U; Howard U

SHARGAL, IDO; KEW GARDENS, NY; BARD HS EARLY COLLEGE; (JR); Hi Hnr Roll; Nat Hon Sy; Nat Mrt LOC; Perf Att; St of Mnth; Yth Ldrshp Prog; Comm Volntr; ArtClub; Chess; Cmptr Clb; Dbte Team; Mus Clb; Photog; Scouts; French Clb; Bnd; Chr; Orch; SP/M/VS; Bsball; Bskball; Tennis (V); Cultural Project -Many Faces Of China & Trip To China; Write on For Israel / Journalism Advocacy; Medicine / Science; Politics; Columbia U; Harvard

SHARIFF, BIBI S; SOUTH RICHMOND HILL, NY; JOHN ADAMS HS; (JR); Perf Att; Key Club; Foreign Clb; Chr; Vllyball (J); CR (P); Nursing; Hunter College; York College

SHARIFI, KIANA; NEW YORK, NY; BARUCH COLLEGE CAMPUS HS; (SR); Hi Hnr Roll; Hnr Roll; Pres Sch; WWAHSS; Comm Volntr; Red Cr Aide; French Clb; Chr; SP/M/VS; Sch Ppr (R); Creative Community Poetry Contest (Published Poem); NYSSMA Vocal Contest (Score: 19); Bachelor of Arts-Communications or Theatre; Media Studies; U of California-Berkeley

SHARMA, JYOTI; BRONX, NY; BRONX HS OF SCIENCE; (JR); Nat Hon Sy; Sci/Math Olympn; Peer Tut/Med; Red Cr Aide; Biology Clb; Mth Clb/Tm; Off Aide; SP/M/VS; Stu Cncl (R); Sch Ppr (R); President of Pre-Medical Club; Psychology; Columbia U; New York U

SHARMA, POOJA; FLUSHING, NY; BENJAMIN CARDOZO HS; (FR); Perf Att; St of Mnth; Peer Tut/Med; Key Club; Tae Kwon Do (Black Belt) At Lee's Tae Kwon Do; Medical; Science; St John's U; Stony Brook U

SHARP, HANNAH L; VICTOR, NY; VICTOR HS; (JR); Hnr Roll; St of Mnth; Comm Volntr; Hab For Humty Volntr; Peer Tut/Med; Chrch Yth Grp; DARE; Drma Clb; Emplmnt; Key Club; Mus Clb; Photog; Ch Chr; Dnce; Orch; SP/M/VS; Sccr (J); Sftball (J); Select Choir; NYSSMA Vocal Solo Fest All-State; Performing Arts; Nazareth U; Fredonia

SHARPE, BROOKE A; MADRID, NY; MADRID-WADDINGTON CTRL SCH; (SO); Hi Hnr Roll; MVP; Nat Hon Sy; Otst Ac Ach Awd; Pres Ac Ftns Aw; WWAHSS; Comm Volntr; Red Cr Aide; DARE; Key Club; French Clb; Bnd; Chr; Mch Bnd; SP/M/VS; Bskball (V L); GAA (V); Sccr (V L); Sftball (V L); Track (V); AAU Basketball; Show Choir; Fashion Designer; Broadcasting / Sport Management; Vermont U; Purdue U

SHATTUCH, BENJAMIN; CORINTH, NY; CORINTH CTRL SCH; (SO); Hi Hnr Roll; Hnr Roll; Perf Att; SADD; Bsball (V); Bskball (J); Culinary Arts; College of Saint Rose; Hartwick College

SHAW, ELIZABETH F; ELMIRA, NY; SOUTHSIDE HS; (JR); Hi Hnr Roll; Nat Hon Sy; WWAHSS; Chrch Yth Grp; Key Club; Bnd; Chr; Ch Chr; Mch Bnd; Sftball (VJ); Swmg (V); Sch Ppr (R); Bible Club; Bible Quizzing; Religion Major-Doctorate Degree; Trevecca Nazarene U; Eastern Nazarene College

SHEA, ERIN; ROSLYN, NY; HERRICKS HS; (JR); Hnr Roll; St of Mnth; WWAHSS; Amnsty Intl; Comm Volntr; Peer Tut/Med; ArtClub; Key Club; Dnce; Chrldg (VJCL); Track (V L); Student of the Month; Religious Ed. Teacher; Advertising; Psychology; Northeastern U; Boston U

SHEAHAN, EMILY; LINDENHURST, NY; LINDENHURST HS; (JR); Hi Hnr Roll; Nat Hon Sy; Otst Ac Ach Awd; WWAHSS; Yth Ldrshp Prog; Comm Volntr; Peer Tut/Med; Emplmnt; Vsity Clb; Fld Hky (VJC); Lcrsse (VJ); Vsy Clb; CR (R); Pre-Med; Business Management; Boston U; Johns Hopkins U

SHEARD, TARISHA; SYRACUSE, NY; HENNINGER HS; (JR); Comm Volntr; Hosp Aide; Volunteer Through High School; Work Part Time Since 10th Grade; Master's Degree

SHEEHAN, KATIE; WHITE PLAINS, NY; WHITE PLAINS HS; (FR); Hi Hnr Roll; Hnr Roll; Bnd; Cr Ctry (V L); Track (V L); Lit Mag (R); Poet's Club, New York State Scholar Athlete Award; Advocates for the Earth National Junior Honor Society; English and Biology; Veterinarian; Cornell

SHELDEN, SARAH; SILVER CREEK, NY; SILVER CREEK HS; (JR); 4H Awd; Hnr Roll; Nat Hon Sy; Comm Volntr; 4-H; Key Club; Prom Com; Tchrs Aide; French Clb; Chr; Ch Chr; Dnce; Chrldg (VJ); French- Vice President; Early Childhood Education

SHEN, STEPHANIE; BRONX, NY; ST CATHARINE AC; (FR); Hi Hnr Roll; MVP; Otst Ac Ach Awd; Perf Att; Pres Ac Ftns Aw; Pres Sch; Sci/Math Olympn; St of Mnth; USAA; Valdctrian; Peer Tut/Med; ArtClub; Chess; Dbte Team; Drma Clb; Jr Ach; Mth Clb/Tm; Pep Squd; Scouts; Bnd; Chr; Jzz Bnd; SP/M/VS; Bskball (J); Chrldg (J); Scr Kpr (J); Tennis (J); Vllyball (J); Cl Off (R); Stu Cncl (R); CR (R); Lit Mag (R); Sch Ppr (R, P); Yrbk (P); SAT Score 1220; Northwestern CTD Spectrum Resident; Actuarial Sciences; Business Law; Harvard U; Northwestern U

SHEPARD, ABROM; STATEN ISLAND, NY; PT RICHMOND HS; (SO); Ctznshp Aw; Hi Hnr Roll; Hnr Roll; Otst Ac Ach Awd; Comm Volntr; DARE; Lib Aide; Off Aide; Ftball (VJ); Honor Roll 2003-2004; Pennsylvania State U; Florida State U

SHEPHERD, SEAN; CORAM, NY; NEWFIELD HS; (JR); Hnr Roll; MVP; WWAHSS; Yth Ldrshp Prog; Comm Volntr; Peer Tut/Med; Chrch Yth Grp; DARE; Emplmnt; Prom Com; Scouts; SADD; Bskball (V); Ftball (V); Track (VJ); Business Management; Business Finance; Clark Atlanta U; Virginia State U

SHERIFF, ASHLEY; LATHAM, NY; SHAKER HS; (SR); Comm Volntr; Peer Tut/Med; Emplmnt; Key Club; Scouts; Spanish Clb; Chr; Track; Girl Scout Silver Award; Girl Scout Gold Award; Graphic Design; Education; Alfred U

SHERIFF, OMAR; FARMINGDALE, NY; FARMINGDALE HS; Hnr Roll; Perf Att; Pres Ac Ftns Aw; St of Mnth; Peer Tut/Med; DECA; Wdwrkg Clb; Bnd; Mch Bnd; Track (J); Cl Off; Business

SHERPALAMA, SALEENA; FOREST HILLS, NY; BROOKLYN TECH HS; (SO); Hnr Roll; Nat Hon Sy; WWAHSS; Comm Volntr; Hosp Aide; Lib Aide; Outreach Club; Leadership Club; Medical Field; Doctor; Cornell U

SHERPALAMA, TENJING; FOREST HILLS, NY; STUYVESANT HS; (JR); Hnr Roll; Nat Hon Sy; WWAHSS; Red Cr Aide; Key Club; Mth Clb/Tm; Pre-Medicine; Johns Hopkins U; U of Pennsylvania

SHERRILLS, JEFFREY J; BRONX, NY; THOMAS JEFFERSON HS; (FR); Hnr Roll; Perf Att; ArtClub; Chrch Yth Grp; DARE; FCA; Bnd; Ch Chr; Bskball; Wt Lftg; Lit Mag (P); Art; Music; Syracuse College, or an Out of State College for Music/Art

SHI, DOROTHY; ROSLYN HEIGHTS, NY; MINEOLA HS; (FR); Hi Hnr Roll; Nat Hon Sy; Otst Ac Ach Awd; Sci/Math Olympn; St of Mnth; Emplmnt; Mth Clb/Tm; Mus Clb; Orch; Track (V); Vllyball

SHIEH, MARIA; OAKLAND GARDENS, NY; STUYVESANT HS; (SR); Nat Mrt LOC; Perf Att; Comm Volntr; Hosp Aide; Peer Tut/Med; Chrch Yth Grp; Mth Clb/Tm; Mus Clb; Chinese Clb; Bnd; Dnce; Adv Cncl (R); Lit Mag (R); MBA and BS in Business; JD; New York U

SHILLINGFORD, PAUL; BROOKLYN, NY; MIDDLE COLLEGE HS; (JR); St of Mnth; Comm Volntr; Chrch Yth Grp; Jr Ach; SP/M/VS; Architecture; Business Management; Hampton U; Syracuse U

SHLAFMAN, IRINA; BROOKLYN, NY; MIDWOOD HS; (JR); Hnr Roll; Perf Att; Salutrn; Sci Fairs; Comm Volntr; Peer Tut/Med; Emplmnt; Jr Ach; Key Club; Lib Aide; Off Aide; Tchrs Aide; SP/M/VS; Stg Cre; Sch Ppr (E, R); Pre-Law; Financial Law; New York U; Columbia U

SHORB, KIM; GANSEVOORT, NY; SARATOGA SPRINGS HS; (SO); Hnr Roll; Bnd; Bskball (V L); Dvng (V); Sccr (J)

SHORT, KELLI A; NAPANOCH, NY; TRI-VALLEY HS; (SR); Ctznshp Aw; Hi Hnr Roll; MVP; Nat Hon Sy; Otst Ac Ach Awd; St of Mnth; Comm Volntr; Chrch Yth Grp; Emplmnt; Tchrs Aide; Bnd; Bskball (J); Chrldg (V); Sftball (V); President FCCLA-11th & 12th; MVP-Team Captain JV Softball; Physical Therapy; Mount Saint Mary College

SHORT, LYNDSIE; WHITEHALL, NY; WHITEHALL JR/SR HS; (SO); Hi Hnr Roll; Hnr Roll; Perf Att; Drma Clb; Bnd; Chr; Jzz Bnd; Mch Bnd; Presidents Education Awards Program for Academic Excellence; Veterinary Medicine; Cornell U; Niagara U

SHUAN, YURIKO; SCHENECTADY, NY; SCHENECTADY HS; (SO); Perf Att; Automobile Mechanic; Boston College

SHUGERTS, STACIE; NIAGARA FALLS, NY; NIAGARA FALLS HS; (JR); Hi Hnr Roll; Hnr Roll; WWAHSS; Comm Volntr; Red Cr Aide; Emplmnt; Key Club; Prom Com; Cl Off (V, S); Stu Cncl (R); CR (R); Ski Club; Marketing-Advertising; International Relations; Canisius College; SUNY Cortland

SHULYAK, MARGARITA; BROOKLYN, NY; FORT HAMILTON HS; (JR); Otst Ac Ach Awd; Emplmnt; Chr; Criminal Psychology; History Teacher; Baruch College; Hunter College

SHUM, KATHRYN; NEW YORK, NY; BRONX HS OF SCIENCE; (SR); Nat Hon Sy; WWAHSS; Emplmnt; Mth Clb/Tm; Off Aide; Sci Clb; Dnce; Yrbk (R); Girls Varsity Handball Team; Journalism Publication (Children's Pressline); Business; Astrophysics; City U of New York-Honors Baruch

SHUTRAN, MAX; SCARSDALE, NY; SCARSDALE HS; (JR); F Lan Hn Soc; Hnr Roll; Nat Mrt Semif; Sci/Math Olympn; Comm Volntr; Sci Clb; Tmpl Yth Grp; Bnd; Mch Bnd; Orch; Cr Ctry (J); Track (V); Independent Science Research; Signifer Honor Society; Pre-Med; Brown U; Columbia College

SIBRIAN, DAVID; JAMAICA, NY; AC FOR AMERICAN STUDIES; (FR); Hnr Roll; St of Mnth; Dbte Team; Physical Education Major; St. John's U

SICARD, SASHA; WOODSIDE, NY; WILLIAM CULLEN BRYANT HS; (JR); F Lan Hn Soc; Hi Hnr Roll; Hnr Roll; Nat Hon Sy; Perf Att; St of Mnth; WWAHSS; Comm Volntr; Peer Tut/Med; Dbte Team; Drma Clb; Lib Aide; Tchrs Aide; Chr; Dnce; SP/M/VS; Chrldg (V); Dance Classes and Dance Teams Outside of School; Performances-Dance, Act, Sing; Pre-Law; Philosophy; Fordham U; NYU

SICILIANO, ELLEN; COMMACK, NY; COMMACK HS; (JR); F Lan Hn Soc; Hi Hnr Roll; WWAHSS; Emplmnt; FTA; Bnd; Dnce; Mch Bnd; Varsity Cougarettes - National Champs; History Honor Society / English Honor Society/ Science Honor Society; Pre-Med / Biology; Psychology; SUNY Binghamton; Fordham U

SIDDONS, MEGHAN A; BROCKPORT, NY; BROCKPORT HS; (SO); Hi Hnr Roll; Hnr Roll; St of Mnth; Comm Volntr; Chrch Yth Grp; Emplmnt; SADD; Tennis (J); Excelsior Society; Medical; Dermatology; New York U; Penn State

SIEGEL, ALISON R; IRVINGTON, NY; IRVINGTON HS; (SR); Hi Hnr Roll; Hnr Roll; Nat Mrt LOC; St of Mnth; Peer Tut/Med; Emplmnt; Tchrs Aide; Latin Clb; Swmg (V); Lit Mag (E); Writing; Alfred U

SIEGEL, DANIEL; CHESTER, NY; MONROE-WOODBURY HS; (SO); Hi Hnr Roll; Sci Fairs; Comm Volntr; DARE; Emplmnt; Key Club; Tmpl Yth Grp; Chr; Orch; Mar Art (L); Tennis (J); Principal's Award; Engineering; Law

SIEGEL, JORDAN; BROOKLYN, NY; LEON M GOLDSTEIN HS SCIENCES; (SO); F Lan Hn Soc; Peer Tut/Med; SP/M/VS; Sccr (V); Walked the Three Mile Walk for Cancer; Business; Advertisement; Princeton U; Yale U

SIKES, MATTHEW C; FLORAL PARK, NY; FLORAL PARK MEMORIAL HS; (SR); MVP; Yth Ldrshp Prog; Comm Volntr; Hab For Humty Volntr; Peer Tut/Med; Chrch Yth Grp; Cmptr Clb; DARE; Emplmnt; Key Club; Scouts; Voc Ind Clb Am; Ch Chr; Vllyball (V); Volleyball MVP; Youth Ministry; Psychology; West Virginia Wesleyan

SILK, TARIK; TROY, NY; SHAKER HS; (JR); Hi Hnr Roll; Nat Hon Sy; WWAHSS; Comm Volntr; Drma Clb; Key Club; Mus Clb; SP/M/VS; President of Mock Trial; Boy Scout - Eagle by Year's End; Pre-Med; Law; Boston College

SILVESTRI, KATARINA N; LEWISTON, NY; LEWISTON PORTER HS; (JR); Hi Hnr Roll; Nat Hon Sy; Otst Ac Ach Awd; St of Mnth; WWAHSS; Peer Tut/Med; Drma Clb; Mus Clb; Chr; Jzz Bnd; Orch; Swg Chr; Berklee College of Music Jazz Fest - Judges Choice Award / '04 -'05; Tri-C Jazz Fest - Most Outstanding Performer; Music Education; Recording Industry; SUNY Fredonia; Berklee College of Music

SIMENSKY, MICHELE; WOODMERE, NY; LAWRENCE HS; (SO); Hi Hnr Roll; WWAHSS; Comm Volntr; Key Club; Tmpl Yth Grp; Chr; Lit Mag (E); Focus on Helping America (FHA) Club; Step Team; Psychiatry; New York U

SIMMONS, GWEN M; ALTAMONT, NY; GUILDERLAND HS; (JR); Hnr Roll; MVP; Nat Hon Sy; Otst Ac Ach Awd; Perf Att; Yth Ldrshp Prog; Comm Volntr; Peer Tut/Med; NYLC; Sftball (VJCL); Vllyball (VJCL); Mathematics; Chemistry; Hamilton College; Connecticut College

Siegel, Jordan
Leon M Goldstein HS Sciences
Brooklyn, NY

Sheehan, Katie
White Plains HS
White Plains, NY

Sharma, Jyoti
Bronx HS Of Science
Bronx, NY

Shah, Mohammad A
John F Kennedy HS
Bronx, NY

Shargal, Ido
Bard HS Early College
Kew Gardens, NY

Shulyak, Margarita
Fort Hamilton HS
Brooklyn, NY

Sikes, Matthew C
Floral Park Memorial HS
Floral Park, NY

SIMMONS, REBECCA A; SARANAC LAKE, NY; NATIONAL SPORTS AC; (SO); Hnr Roll; Pres Ac Ftns Aw; St of Mnth; Comm Volntr; Cr Ctry (V); Ice Hky (V); Yrbk (E, R, P); Speed Skating (National); Soccer (Travel); Veterinary Science; Criminal Justice; Cornell U; Minnesota

SIMMONS IV, HARVEY O; SKANEATELES, NY; CHRISTIAN BROTHERS AC; (SO); Hi Hnr Roll; MVP; Pres Ac Ftns Aw; Yth Ldrshp Prog; Amnsty Intl; Comm Volntr; HO'Br Yth Ldrshp; Scouts; Bskball (J); Ftball (J); Golf (J); Cl Off (V); Stu Cncl (V); Johns Hopkins - Talented Youth Program; Math Tutor; Medicine

SIMON, KATHERINE E; NEW YORK, NY; BARUCH COLLEGE CAMPUS HS; (SO); Nat Hon Sy; Perf Att; Yth Ldrshp Prog; Comm Volntr; Red Cr Aide; Emplmnt; Prom Com; Track (V); Master Scuba Diver; Fencer (Not a School Sport); Doctor; Marine Biology

SIMPSON, FRANCINE; NEW YORK, NY; WASHINGTON IRVING HS; (JR); Perf Att; Sci Fairs; DARE; Emplmnt; Dnce; Cl Off (V); Criminal Justice; Law; Georgia State U; Columbus State U

SIMUEL, KIJANA A; HEMPSTEAD, NY; UNIONDALE HS; (MS); Ctznshp Aw; Hi Hnr Roll; Hnr Roll; Nat Hon Sy; Otst Ac Ach Awd; Pres Sch; St of Mnth; Chrch Yth Grp; Drma Clb; Chr; Dnce; SP/M/VS; Sccr (C); Track; Cl Off (P); Stu Cncl (P); Most Improved Award-Rhythmettes (Dance); Major Service Award & Green Belt in Goji Ryu Karate; Actress/Drama; Business Advertisement; Gibbs, North Carolina A & T, Howard U; Morgan State, Florida A & M, NYU

SINACORI, JACQUELINE; WANTAGH, NY; WANTAGH HS; (SO); Hi Hnr Roll; Nat Hon Sy; Peer Tut/Med; Spec Olymp Vol; Prom Com; Orch; Tennis (V); Cl Off (T); Painting Sent to Art Show in Buffalo, NY; Physical Education Leaders Club Sports Night Captain; Architecture; Villanova; Wake Forest

SINGER, MAX; MALVERNE, NY; HOLY TRINITY DIOCESAN HS; (SO); Hi Hnr Roll; Nat Hon Sy; Perf Att; Sci Fairs; St of Mnth; Comm Volntr; 4-H; ArtClub; P to P St Amb Prg; SP/M/VS; Sch Ppr (R); Yrbk (R); Principal's List; Journalism; Yale University; Hofstra University

SINGH, CAMILLE; JAMAICA, NY; BENJAMIN CARDOZO HS; (JR); Hnr Roll; Nat Hon Sy; Nat Sci Aw; Perf Att; St of Mnth; WWAHSS; Comm Volntr; Hosp Aide; Key Club; Arista; Leaders Program, Law Program; Pharmacy, Nutrition & Food Science; Accounting, Business, Paralegal; St. John's U; New York U

SINGH, CHRISTOPHER Y; BROOKLYN, NY; STUYVESANT HS; (SO); WWAHSS; Key Club; Tmpl Yth Grp; Adv Cncl (R); Volunteer at Hindu Sanatan Mandir Church; Pre-Medicine; Mathematics; Columbia U; New York U

SINGH, DAVINDER; HICKSVILLE, NY; HICKSVILLE HS; (JR); Hnr Roll; Perf Att; Pres Ac Ftns Aw; Key Club; Orch; NYSSMA Festival; Interact Club; Business Administration; Health Care Administration; C.W. Post-Long Island U; St. John's U

SINGH, MANDEEP; SOUTH RICHMOND HLL, NY; BENJAMIN CARDOZO HS; (SR); Hi Hnr Roll; Sci Fairs; Sci/Math Olympn; WWAHSS; Comm Volntr; Key Club; Mth Clb/Tm; Sci Clb; CR (P); Team Captain for the School's NYC Envirothon Team - 4 Years; Won Silver Medal At the Greater Metropolitan Math Fair 2002; PhD / Medicine; Master's in American History; SUNY Binghamton

SINGH, MANPREET; MIDDLETOWN, NY; MIDDLETOWN HS; (JR); Hnr Roll; Sci Fairs; ROTC; Tchrs Aide; Ftball (V); Tennis (V)

SINGH, NEETU; SOUTH RICHMOND HILL, NY; JOHN ADAMS HS; (JR); Hnr Roll; Perf Att; Sci Fairs; Key Club; Mth Clb/Tm; Chr; Ch Chr; Orch; Sch Ppr (R); Secretary of Robotics Club; Accounting; Teaching; Hunter College; Queens College

SINGH, SARINA S; JAMAICA, NY; MARTIN LUTHER KING HS; (JR); Ctznshp Aw; Hi Hnr Roll; Hnr Roll; Perf Att; Pres Ac Ftns Aw; Salutrn; Chrch Yth Grp; Drma Clb; Key Club; Acpl Chr; SP/M/VS; Cl Off (V); Sch Ppr (R); Yrbk (R); Business Administration; Business Law; Baruch; Queens

SINGH, VIKRAM; SYOSSET, NY; SYOSSET HS; (SO); Hnr Roll; Comm Volntr; Bsball (J); Sch Ppr (E); Future Leaders of America; Interact Club; Medicine

SINGLETARY, LA TRENDA C; BROOKLYN, NY; WASHINGTON IRVING HS; (JR); Perf Att; St of Mnth; Key Club; Photog; Scouts; Dnce; Sch Ppr (R); Fitness/Work Out; Bowling; Business Administration/Public Relations; Broadcast Journalism; Binghamton U; Syracuse U

SIRACUSA, STEPHANIE E; STATEN ISLAND, NY; A BEKA AC- HOME SCH; MS; Hi Hnr Roll; Hnr Roll; Sci Fairs; St of Mnth; Chrch Yth Grp; Emplmnt; Mus Clb; Scouts; Italian Clb; Bnd; Dnce; Bskball; Mar Art; Tennis; Psychology; Law; Princeton U; Harvard U

SIU, CHING J; BAYSIDE, NY; BRONX HS OF SCIENCE; (SO); Hnr Roll; Nat Hon Sy; Valdctrian; WWAHSS; Comm Volntr; Mth Clb/Tm; Vsity Clb; Golf (V); Track (V); Inwan Altman Award for Excellence in Education; The Associated Board of Royal Schools of Music

SIVAKOVA, LUBA; SCHENECTADY, NY; DOANE STUART SCH; (SO); Comm Volntr; Drma Clb; French Clb; Acpl Chr; SP/M/VS; Stg Cre; Fncg; Tennis; Stu Cncl; Yrbk; Music Theater; Musical Theater, Languages

SKINNER, SHANNON M; BERNE, NY; BERNE-KNOX WESTERLO HS; (SO); Hi Hnr Roll; Hnr Roll; Otst Ac Ach Awd; Perf Att; WWAHSS; Yth Ldrshp Prog; Comm Volntr; Peer Tut/Med; Key Club; SADD; Chr; Track (V); Cl Off (S); Stu Cncl (R); BMX Racing; 2005 Guilderland YMCA Student Community Service Award; Psychology; Neurology; Colgate U; U of Albany

SKIPPER, TAMEKA L; BRONX, NY; JANE ADDAMS HS; (SR); Hnr Roll; Perf Att; Comm Volntr; ArtClub; FBLA; Yrbk (P); Wild Life Conservation Achievement Award; HOSA 3 Year Attendant; Pre-Dentistry; Endodontist; City College of NY (CUNY)

SKORPUT, MILTON; BRONX, NY; MARBLE HILL HS FOR INTERNATIONAL STUDIES; (FR); Perf Att; Sccr; Business; Sports

SLIZSKAYA, SVETLANA; BROOKLYN, NY; MIDWOOD HS; (SO); All Am Sch; Hnr Roll; Key Club; Lib Aide; Off Aide; Dnce; Covenant Dance Theatre Apprentice; Asian Society / Knitting Circle; Archaeology; Anthropologist

SLOAN, DOMINIQUE N; CTRL ISLIP, NY; CTRL ISLIP HS; (JR); Hnr Roll; WWAHSS; Peer Tut/Med; Emplmnt; Off Aide; Bnd; Clr Grd; Chrldg (V); Mar Art; Step Team; Law; Music; Clark U; Spelman College

SLOTHOWER, JEN; SCHROON LAKE, NY; MOUNTAINSIDE CHRISTIAN AC; (SR); Hi Hnr Roll; Hnr Roll; Salutrn; WWAHSS; Chrch Yth Grp; Photog; Chr; SP/M/VS; Bskball (V C); Scr Kpr (V); Vllyball (V C); Stu Cncl (V, S, R); Sch Ppr (E); Yrbk (E, P); Arts Award 2005 and 2004; Sportsmanship Award Basketball 2005; Journalism; Photography; Northeastern U; Syracuse U

SMALL, JESSICA S; FREEPORT, NY; FREEPORT HS; (JR); Hi Hnr Roll; Hnr Roll; Nat Hon Sy; Nat Sci Aw; Perf Att; Sci Fairs; Comm Volntr; Peer Tut/Med; Red Cr Aide; ArtClub; Chrch Yth Grp; Photog; Bnd; Mch Bnd; Bdmtn (V); Tennis (V); Yrbk (P); I Was on the Varsity Bowling Team; Part of HHMI Research Program; Pre-Med (To Become an M.D.); Major in Physics (I Love It); New York U; Cornell U

SMITH, ALESA K; RIPLEY, NY; RIPLEY CTRL SCH; (FR); Ctznshp Aw; Hnr Roll; Pres Ac Ftns Aw; Chrch Yth Grp; Key Club; Scouts; Bnd; Chr; Bskball (V); Gmnstcs; Sftball (J); Vllyball (J); Stu Cncl; Handbells

SMITH, ALYSSA L; BAY SHORE, NY; BRENTWOOD HS; (JR); Hi Hnr Roll; Hnr Roll; Nat Hon Sy; Otst Ac Ach Awd; Perf Att; Pres Ac Ftns Aw; Comm Volntr; Peer Tut/Med; Spec Olymp Vol; Emplmnt; Mus Clb; Photog; Svce Clb; Bnd; Mch Bnd; Sftball; Swmg (J); Vllyball; Stu Cncl (R); Sch Ppr (R); Newspaper Journalist; Photographer; Dowling College

SMITH, AMANDA; SCHENECTADY, NY; MOHONASEN HS; (JR); Hi Hnr Roll; Sci/Math Olympn; WWAHSS; Comm Volntr; Key Club; Sci Clb; Region 7 Odyssey of the Mind 1st Place-X 2 Years; Key Club / Science Honor Society / Science Club; Marine Biology; TBD

SMITH, ANDREW; ALBANY, NY; LA SALLE INST; (SO); Hi Hnr Roll; Emplmnt; Cr Ctry (J); Track (J); Sch Ppr; National Junior Honor Society; Valedictorian of Middle School Class

SMITH, BRADLEY E; ELMIRA, NY; THOMAS A EDISON HS; (SR); Ctznshp Aw; Hi Hnr Roll; Hnr Roll; Emplmnt; Pep Squd; Bnd; Pep Bnd; SP/M/VS; Stg Cre; Tennis (V); Stu Cncl (R); CR (R); National Technical Honor Society; Outstanding Student in Band; Diesel Equipment Technology; Morrisville State College

SMITH, BRITTANY N; ROCHESTER, NY; INTERNAL FINANCE AT FRANKIN HS; (FR); Hi Hnr Roll; Nat Hon Sy; Peer Tut/Med; Chrch Yth Grp; Drma Clb; Emplmnt; Mth Clb/Tm; Chr; Bsball (J); Bskball (J); Chrldg (V); Starred in a Play, Kapa; Psychology; RN; Princeton; Penn State

SMITH, CLAIRE T; SILVER CREEK, NY; SILVER CREEK HS; (FR); Hnr Roll; WWAHSS; Key Club; Spanish Clb; Bnd; Pep Bnd; Track (V); Archeology; Criminal Psychology; State U Buffalo; Canisius College

SMITH, CRAIG R; CORNING, NY; CPP WEST HS; (JR); Hi Hnr Roll; Hnr Roll; Perf Att; Sci Fairs; Chrch Yth Grp; Emplmnt; Scouts; Ftball (V CL); Lcrsse (V CL); History Teacher; Cortland; Mansfield

SMITH, DANAR; FREEPORT, NY; (FR); Ctznshp Aw; Bskball (J); Ftball (J); Doctor; Lawyer; Harvard; Hofstra

SMITH, ISAKE K A; BROOKLYN, NY; EDWARD R MURROW HS; (SO); Hnr Roll; Comm Volntr; Chrch Yth Grp; Emplmnt; Acpl Chr; Chr; Clr Grd; Dnce; Psychiatry (PhD); Music; Case Western Reserve; New York U

SMITH, JOSELYN C; RIVERHEAD, NY; HARRY B WARD TECH CTR; (SR); Perf Att; DARE; Emplmnt; Scouts; Ch Chr; Drl Tm; SP/M/VS; I Released a CD In 2003.; I Danced As Well.; Cert. Nurse's Asst.; Singing/Dancing; Suffolk County Community College

SMITH, JOSHUA J; FREDONIA, NY; FORESTVILLE HS; (SR); Hi Hnr Roll; Hnr Roll; Otst Ac Ach Awd; Sci/Math Olympn; WWAHSS; Comm Volntr; Peer Tut/Med; Red Cr Aide; AL Aux Boys; Chrch Yth Grp; Mth Clb/Tm; Vsity Clb; Spanish Clb; Bskball (V CL); Ftball (V L); Scr Kpr (V); Track (V); Vsy Clb (V); Cl Off (S, T); Economics Stock Trading Award; Business Challenge Seminar Award; Master's in Finance; Degree in Hospitality Management; Fredonia State (SUNY); Duquesne U

SMITH, KERRY-ANN; WHITE PLAINS, NY; WOODLANDS HS; (SR); St of Mnth; Comm Volntr; Dnce; Cr Ctry (V); Track (V); Nursing; College (Nursing); Hunter College; Bronx Community College

SMITH, KODY A; CORNING, NY; CPP WEST HS; (JR); Hi Hnr Roll; Hnr Roll; MVP; St of Mnth; Scouts; Bskball (V); Ftball (V); Wt Lftg (V); Criminal Law; Georgetown U; Duke U

SMITH, LEONARD; BRONX, NY; EVANDER CHILDS HS; (JR); Yth Ldrshp Prog; Peer Tut/Med; Ftball (V C); Computer Tech; Business; Georgia Tech; Virginia Tech

SMITH, MEAGHAN A; PLEASANT VALLEY, NY; ARLINGTON HS; (JR); Hnr Roll; Nat Hon Sy; Pres Ac Ftns Aw; St of Mnth; WWAHSS; Yth Ldrshp Prog; Comm Volntr; Emplmnt; NYLC; Off Aide; Prom Com; Scouts; Tchrs Aide; Vsity Clb; Orch; Cr Ctry (V CL); Track (V CL); Adv Cncl; Stu Cncl (R); Yrbk; Empire State Games - 10,000M Bronze Medal; Pre-Med / Physical Therapy

SMITH, NICOLE E; MADRID, NY; MADRID-WADDINGTON CTRL SCH; (JR); Hi Hnr Roll; Nat Hon Sy; Pres Ac Ftns Aw; WWAHSS; Comm Volntr; DARE; Drma Clb; Key Club; Off Aide; Vsity Clb; French Clb; Bnd; Chr; Jzz Bnd; SP/M/VS; GAA (V); Ice Sktg (V C); Sccr (V); Track (V); Cl Off; NHS, Key Club, Drama Club; Dental Hygiene, Physical/Occupational; Therapy, Speech Pathology; Ithaca Utica, Cortland, Nazareth; Clarkson

SMITH, QUADAZIA S; HELLPORT, NY; WILLIAM FLOYD HS; (SO); Hi Hnr Roll; Hnr Roll; ROTC; Passing Regents; Returning to School After Almost 2 Years; Criminal Justice; Pediatrician; New York U; Virginia Commonwealth U

SMITH, SAMANTHA H; WINDHAM, NY; WINDHAM ASLAND JEWETT CTRL SCH; (FR); All Am Sch; Hi Hnr Roll; Hnr Roll; Pres Sch; St of Mnth; Emplmnt; Tchrs Aide; Bnd; Chrldg (V); Sccr (V)

SMITH, SHANA; MASSENA, NY; MASSENA SR HS; (SO); F Lan Hn Soc; Hi Hnr Roll; Otst Ac Ach Awd; Pres Ac Ftns Aw; Comm Volntr; Red Cr Aide; ArtClub; DARE; Swmg (V); Volunteer Work Lector - Church / PTA Reflection Program Winner (Visual Arts); National Honor Society / Various Art Awards / Mizerack Biology Award; Art; Science

SMITH, TYLER J; ROCHESTER, NY; WEBSTER CHRISTIAN; (FR); Sccr (V)

SMITH, WYAN; BROOKLYN, NY; EDWARD R MURROW HS; (JR); Hnr Roll; WWAHSS; Yth Ldrshp Prog; Chrch Yth Grp; Emplmnt; P to P St Amb Prg; Spanish Clb; Bnd; Mock Trial; Hip Hop Dance; JD/MBA Compound Degree; Cornell U; SUNY of Albany

SMITH JR, DARRELL E; STATEN ISLAND, NY; FIORELLO H LA GUARDIA HS; (JR); Peer Tut/Med; Bnd; Jzz Bnd; Orch; SP/M/VS; Volunteer Student Teacher; NJPAC Program; Phd in Music; Professional Musician; Manhattan School of Music; Juilliard School of Music

SNYDER, EMILY F; BROOKLYN, NY; EDWARD R MURROW HS; (MS); Hnr Roll; Perf Att; Comm Volntr; Hosp Aide; Chess; Lib Aide; Tchrs Aide; Psychology; Florida Atlantic U

SOCHA, PAWEL; BROOKLYN, NY; STUYVESANT HS; (SO); Hi Hnr Roll; Nat Hon Sy; St Schl; WWAHSS; Comm Volntr; Chrch Yth Grp; Key Club; Sci Clb; Bnd; Pep Bnd; Fncg (J); Track (J); Performing in Carnegie Hall with the Brooklyn Wide Band; Mathematics and Verbal Talent Search State Award from JHU; Chemical Engineering; Biochemistry; MIT Massachusetts Institute of Technology; NYU New York U

SODA, DANIELLE T; TRUMANSBURG, NY; CHARLES O'DICKERSON HS; (JR); Hi Hnr Roll; Hnr Roll; Nat Hon Sy; Perf Att; St of Mnth; Comm Volntr; Chrch Yth Grp; Drma Clb; Emplmnt; Off Aide; Prom Com; Tchrs Aide; French Clb; Chr; SP/M/VS; Sccr (J); Early Childhood Education; SUNY Oneonta; Niagara U

SOHM, MICHAEL J; STONE RIDGE, NY; RUNDOUT VALLEY HS; (SR); Hnr Roll; Perf Att; Comm Volntr; Drma Clb; Emplmnt; Bnd; Chr; Skiing (V C); Sccr (VJ); Tennis (V); Firefighter; Lifeguard / Swim Instructor; Criminal Justice; Ulster County Community College

SOKOL, JULIA; BRONX, NY; BRONX HS OF SCIENCE; (JR); Nat Mrt Semif; WWAHSS; Key Club; Several Commendation Letters From The School Principal; Engineering; Harvard College; Columbia College

SOLLY, STEVEN J; LOCKPORT, NY; LOCKPORT HS; (JR); Hi Hnr Roll; Hnr Roll; WWAHSS; Yth Ldrshp Prog; Peer Tut/Med; Key Club; Scouts; Boy Scouts, Key Club, Volunteer Church Aide; Church Sr. Youth Group President; Computer Science; Rochester Institute of Technology; U of Buffalo

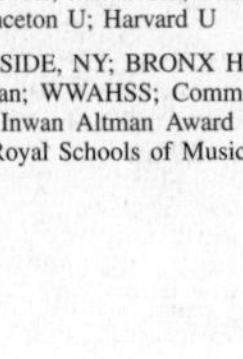
Smith, Joselyn C
Harry B Ward Tech Ctr
Riverhead, NY

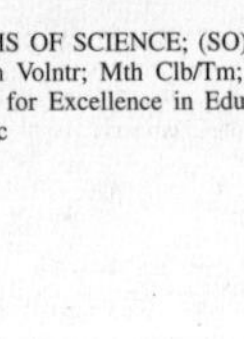
Singh, Sarina S
Martin Luther King HS
Jamaica, NY

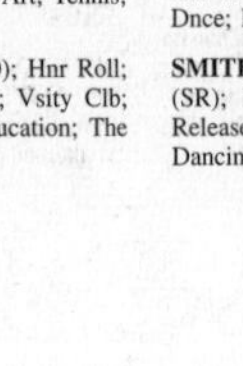
Singh, Davinder
Hicksville HS
Hicksville, NY

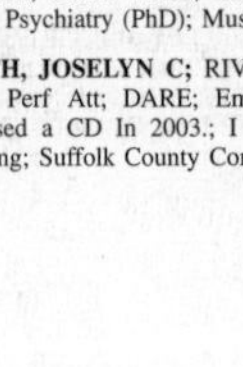
Simuel, Kijana A
Uniondale HS
Hempstead, NY

National
Honor Roll
Spring 2005

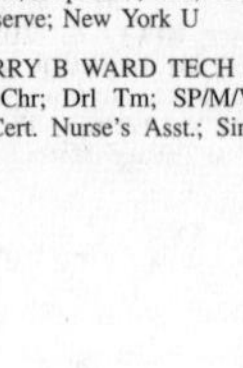
Simmons IV, Harvey O
Christian Brothers AC
Skaneateles, NY

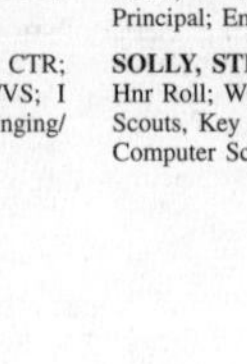
Singh, Neetu
John Adams HS
South Richmond Hill, NY

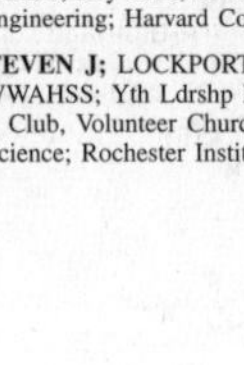
Singh, Vikram
Syosset HS
Syosset, NY

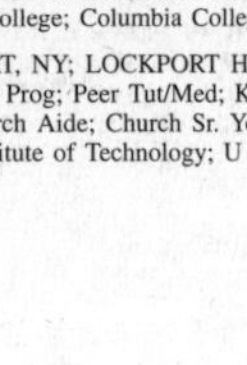
Sohm, Michael J
Rundout Valley HS
Stone Ridge, NY

SOLODOKIN, LEAH J; BROOKLYN, NY; SHULAMITH HS FOR GIRLS; (JR); Hnr Roll; Nat Hon Sy; Nat Ldrshp Svc; Otst Ac Ach Awd; Perf Att; Pres Sch; Sci Fairs; St of Mnth; Valdctrian; Yth Ldrshp Prog; Comm Volntr; Peer Tut/Med; Dbte Team; Drma Clb; Emplmnt; Mth Clb/Tm; NYLC; Tmpl Yth Grp; SP/M/VS; Stg Cre; Scr Kpr (V); Swmg; Stu Cncl; Lit Mag (E, R); Sch Ppr (R); NYS Bar Association Award - Mock Trial; US Senator - Carl Kruger Award / Ran for in VP Elementary Sch / Treasurer in HS; Pharmacy / Chemistry / Biology; Medicine; Arnold & Marie Schwartz College of Pharmacy - LIU College of Pharmacy

SOLOFF, TOM; MC DONOUGH, NY; OXFORD AC HS; (SR); Nat Hon Sy; Ftball (J)

SOLOMON, ERIKA C; ST ALBANS, NY; BENJAMIN CARDOZO HS; (JR); Sci Fairs; Tchrs Aide; Accounting; Business Management; New York U

SOLOMON, JARYD; WEST NYACK, NY; CLARKSTOWN SOUTH HS; (JR); Hi Hnr Roll; Hnr Roll; Nat Hon Sy; Nat Stu Ath Day Aw; Otst Ac Ach Awd; Sci/Math Olympn; Comm Volntr; Peer Tut/Med; Spec Olymp Vol; DECA; Emplmnt; FBLA; JSA; Mth Clb/Tm; MuAlphaTh; Spanish Clb; Skiing (V L); Tennis (V L); Skiing-All-League - Honorable Mention for 2004 & 2005; Tennis - 2nd Team / All-League 2005; Business Management; Law; Cornell U; Duke U

SOLOMON, ROSS; WEST NYACK, NY; CLARKSTOWN SOUTH HS; (JR); Hi Hnr Roll; Hnr Roll; Nat Hon Sy; Nat Stu Ath Day Aw; Otst Ac Ach Awd; Sci/Math Olympn; Comm Volntr; Spec Olymp Vol; DECA; Emplmnt; FBLA; JSA; Mth Clb/Tm; MuAlphaTh; Spanish Clb; Skiing (V L); Tennis (V L); Lit Mag (E); Skiing-All-League - Honorable Mention; Tennis-2004 & 2005 League Champions - Team; Mathematics; Business Administration; U of Pennsylvania; Washington U St Louis

SOLTANI, AZITA; HARTSDALE, NY; WESTCHESTER MAGNET AC; (JR); Hnr Roll; Yth Ldrshp Prog; Comm Volntr; Spec Olymp Vol; DARE; Emplmnt; Svce Clb; Sccr (V); Tennis (J); Psychology; Pre-Med; Boston U; New York U

SOMAN, EBEY P; ELMONT, NY; SEWANHAKA HS; (SO); F Lan Hn Soc; Hi Hnr Roll; Hnr Roll; Nat Hon Sy; Otst Ac Ach Awd; Perf Att; Comm Volntr; Chess; Chrch Yth Grp; Cmptr Clb; Lib Aide; Mth Clb/Tm; Mod UN; Off Aide; Photog; Bnd; Ch Chr; SP/M/VS; Scr Kpr (VJ L); Sccr (J L); Track (V); Vllyball (J L); Model UN - Conference Best Honors Delegate; Math Fair / Pi Day Participant; Business Administration; Computer; Yale U; Oxford U

SON, JENNIFER; STATEN ISLAND, NY; EDWARD R MURROW HS; (JR); F Lan Hn Soc; Nat Hon Sy; Sci Fairs; WWAHSS; Comm Volntr; Red Cr Aide; ArtClub; Chrch Yth Grp; Mth Clb/Tm; Tchrs Aide; Bnd; SP/M/VS; Step 1st Place Science Project; Sing! 2004 & 2005; Pre-Medicine; Pharmacy; Vassar College; U of Virginia

SONG, GLORIA; ELMSFORD, NY; ALEXANDER HAMILTON HS; (JR); Hi Hnr Roll; Hnr Roll; Nat Hon Sy; Otst Ac Ach Awd; WWAHSS; Yth Ldrshp Prog; Comm Volntr; Hosp Aide; Chrch Yth Grp; Cmptr Clb; Key Club; Outdrs Clb; P to P St Amb Prg; SADD; Tchrs Aide; Bnd; Stg Cre; Track (V); Lit Mag (E, R); Sch Ppr (R); Lab Technician; Band Director Award; Film Production; Pediatrician; Northeastern U; Brown U

SONG, KELLY M; EAST MEADOW, NY; EAST MEADOW HS; (SO); Hnr Roll; Hosp Aide; Education; Accounting; SUNY Stony Brook; SUNY Binghamton

SONG, SHUCHEN; BUFFALO, NY; AMHERST CTRL HS; (SO); Hi Hnr Roll; Sci/Math Olympn; WWAHSS; Yth Ldrshp Prog; Comm Volntr; FBLA; French Clb; Orch; Tennis (V); Lit Mag (E); Gifted Math Program At SUNY Buffalo; Lead-America Conference; Computer Science; Philosophy; Massachusetts Institute of Technology; Princeton U

SOPP, JOSEPH; BLUE POINT, NY; BAYPORT BLUE POINT HS; (JR); Hi Hnr Roll; Pres Ac Ftns Aw; Sci/Math Olympn; St of Mnth; Yth Ldrshp Prog; Hab For Humty Volntr; Peer Tut/Med; Sci Clb; Science Olympiad Gold Medal Winner; RYLA Scholarship Winner; Medical Degree; Fine Arts; Cornell U; Cooper Union

SORIA, DANTE; NEW YORK, NY; JOHN F KENNEDY HS; (SR); Hnr Roll; Nat Hon Sy; Perf Att; St of Mnth; DARE; Bnd; Chr; Mch Bnd; SP/M/VS; Bskball; Mar Art (V); Liberal Arts, Criminal Justice; Music Industry; John Jay; Acting Schools

SORIANO CAMPOS, ARACOLI; YONKERS, NY; ROOSEVELT HS; (SO); Ctznshp Aw; Hi Hnr Roll; Hnr Roll; Otst Ac Ach Awd; Perf Att; St of Mnth; Comm Volntr; Emplmnt; Off Aide; Prom Com; Tchrs Aide; Italian Clb; SP/M/VS; Cyclg (V); Dvng (V); Fld Hky (V); Gmnstcs (V); Ice Hky (V); Lcrsse (C); Rlr Hky (C); Scr Kpr; CR (R); Anthropology / Archeology; Engineering; Cornell U; New York U

SOSA, JOVAN; YONKERS, NY; SAUNDERS HS; (SO); Hi Hnr Roll; Hnr Roll; Nat Mrt LOC; Otst Ac Ach Awd; Perf Att; Pres Sch; Salutrn; St of Mnth; Comm Volntr; Emplmnt; Key Club; Certificate of Merit from the Dominican Republic; Computer Engineer; Master Business Degree / MBA; MIT / Massachusetts Institute of Technology; Harvard U

SOSINSKI, MELANIE R; MONTAUK, NY; EAST HAMPTON HS; (JR); Hi Hnr Roll; Nat Hon Sy; St of Mnth; WWAHSS; Emplmnt; Key Club; Quiz Bowl; Fncg (V); Fld Hky (JCL); Lcrsse (VJCL); Track (V L); Scholar Athlete 4 Times; Social Sciences; Wellesley College; Boston College

SOSNOWSKI, AMANDA; BELLMORE, NY; CALHOUN HS; (JR); Hnr Roll; Nat Hon Sy; WWAHSS; Yth Ldrshp Prog; Comm Volntr; Chrch Yth Grp; Drma Clb; Key Club; NYLC; SP/M/VS; Stg Cre; Bskball (J); Youth Elder of Bellmore Presbyterian Church; Member of Bellmore's Jr Fire Department; Philosophy; Law; George Washington U; Boston U

SOTO, JASMINE L; BROOKLYN, NY; SHEEPSHEAD BAY HS; (JR); Emplmnt; Forensic Scientist; Biology Degree; John Jay College; Gibbs College

SOTO, KRYSTAL; FLUSHING, NY; FRANCIS LEWIS; (JR); Otst Ac Ach Awd; Comm Volntr; Key Club; Chr; Lit Mag (P); College Now Classes; Volunteer of the Month; Childhood Education; Hunter College; Queens College

SOUFFRANT, PHARA; BROOKLYN, NY; BENJAMIN BANNEKER AC; (SO); Hnr Roll; WWAHSS; Comm Volntr; Peer Tut/Med; Chess; Chrch Yth Grp; Dbte Team; Drma Clb; Ntl Beta Clb; Photog; Chr; Ch Chr; Dnce; Jzz Bnd; Mar Art (V); Tennis (V); Delta Sigma Theta Oratorical Winner; Biochemistry; Spelman College; New York U

SOUTHWICK, BRITTANY N; MASSENA, NY; MASSENA CTRL HS; (FR); Ctznshp Aw; Hi Hnr Roll; Hnr Roll; ArtClub; Chrch Yth Grp; SP/M/VS; Stg Cre; Ice Sktg (V); Citizenship Award; Writing Award; English; Art / Photography; Boston U; U of Maine

SPANO, JOSEPH; LARCHMONT, NY; MAMARONECK HS; (JR); Hnr Roll; Yth Ldrshp Prog; Comm Volntr; ArtClub; FBLA; Mth Clb/Tm; Svce Clb; Track (J); President of AIDS / HIV Awareness Club; President - Walks For The Care Club; Business Finance; Advertising; Boston U; American U

SPELLMAN, DOMONIGUE S; RIVERHEAD, NY; RIVERHEAD HS; (FR); Nat Hon Sy; FBLA; Chr; Orch; Gospel Choir - After School Activity; Bible Club - After School Activity; Philosophy / History; Political Science / Performing Arts; Columbia U; New York U

SPINKS, BILSON S; BRONX, NY; COLUMBUS HS; (SR); Perf Att; Chrch Yth Grp; Ch Chr; Drm Mjr; Track (V); Medicine; Law; Columbia U; City College New York

SPOONER, BRIDGET M; CANTON, NY; H C WILLIAMS HS; (SR); Ctznshp Aw; Hi Hnr Roll; MVP; Nat Ldrshp Svc; Otst Ac Ach Awd; St of Mnth; WWAHSS; Yth Ldrshp Prog; Comm Volntr; Peer Tut/Med; Spec Olymp Vol; Chrch Yth Grp; Drma Clb; Emplmnt; Prom Com; Bnd; Chr; Ch Chr; Dnce; Lcrsse (V L); Sccr (V L); Track (V L); Adv Cncl (R); Cl Off (P); Stu Cncl (R); Pee Wee Association-Student Member; 1st Team All Northern-Soccer-Academic All-Northern; Business; Clarkson U

SPRAKER, LINDA; BALDWINSVILLE, NY; CW BAKER HS; (JR); Hnr Roll; Chrch Yth Grp; Key Club; Student Council; Respiratory Therapist; Nursing

SQUIRES, TERYN A; SAUGERTIES, NY; SAUGERTIES HS; (FR); Hi Hnr Roll; Hnr Roll; WWAHSS; Comm Volntr; Chrch Yth Grp; Emplmnt; Key Club; P to P St Amb Prg; Spanish Clb; Bnd; Sccr; Track; Medical Doctorate-Pediatrician

SROGA, JOANNA; LEVITTOWN, NY; ISLAND TREES HS; (FR); Hi Hnr Roll; WWAHSS; Hab For Humty Volntr; Peer Tut/Med; Chrch Yth Grp; Key Club; Mus Clb; Dnce; Orch; Member of Student Council; Altar Server; Communications; Pre-Med; Columbia U; New York U

STACY, VICTORIA; LEVITTOWN, NY; ISLAND TREES HS; (SO); Hnr Roll; Sci/Math Olympn; WWAHSS; Key Club; Mus Clb; Sci Clb; Tmpl Yth Grp; Bnd; Dnce; Mch Bnd; Lit Mag; Astronomy; Music; Worchester Polytechnic Institute; Stonybrook

STAHLER, ANDREW; LAWRENCE, NY; DRS HS FOR BOYS; (JR); Chrch Yth Grp; ROTC; Sch Ppr (R); Doctor; New York U; Columbia U

STAIANA, JAYD; SAUGERTIES, NY; ULSTER CAREER & TECH CTR; (JR); Hnr Roll; St of Mnth; Comm Volntr; DARE; Outdrs Clb; Dnce; Received A Savings Bond At 6th Grade Graduation For Being The Friendliest & Kindest; Cosmetologist In Make-up Business Such As Actors/Actresses In Movies; New York City Beauty School

STALEY, RASHANNA C; MT VERNON, NY; MT VERNON HS; (FR); FBLA; Bnd; Chrldg; Business Degree; Law & Business; U of South Carolina; Harvard Law School

STALLINGS, BRITTANY A; FRESH MEADOWS, NY; FRANCIS LEWIS HS; (JR); Nat Hon Sy; WWAHSS; Comm Volntr; Drma Clb; Mus Clb; Outdrs Clb; Acpl Chr; Chr; SP/M/VS; Founder of Teens Against Animal Abuse Club; Honor Choir-District 6-G.A.; Liberal Arts; Performing Arts; Pennsylvania State U; Boston U

STALLINGS, TANYA A; BROOKLYN, NY; PAUL ROBESON HS; (SO); Ctznshp Aw; Hnr Roll; Otst Ac Ach Awd; St of Mnth; Peer Tut/Med; Chrch Yth Grp; Cmptr Clb; Dbte Team; Off Aide; Outdrs Clb; Tchrs Aide; Chr; Ch Chr; Clr Grd; SP/M/VS; Cl Off (P); Most Improved Student; Pediatrician; Broadcasting Televisions/News Reporter

STANAT, MICHAEL; NEW YORK, NY; UNITED NATIONS INTERNATIONAL SCH; (JR); Hab For Humty Volntr; FBLA; NtlFrnscLg; P to P St Amb Prg; French Clb; Sch Ppr (E); Author of Published Book; International Business; Asian Studies; Harvard U; Princeton U

STANGEL, BREANNA; STEPHENTOWN, NY; BERLIN CTRL HS; Hi Hnr Roll; Hnr Roll; Dnce

STANKIEWICZ, JOANNA; LINDENHURST, NY; LINDENHURST HS; (JR); Nat Hon Sy; USAA; WWAHSS; Yth Ldrshp Prog; Comm Volntr; Chrch Yth Grp; DECA; HO'Br Yth Ldrshp; Key Club; German Clb; Chrldg (J); Adv Cncl (R); Cl Off (P, V, S); Stu Cncl (P); Sch Ppr (E); 9th Grade Secretary, 10th Grade VP, 11th Grade Pres, 12th Student Council Pres; International Business; Columbia U; Tufts U

STARGENSKY, STEVEN; WATERFORD, NY; WATERFORD HS; (SO); Bskball (V); Golf (V); Tennis (V); Stu Cncl (R); Black Belt in Tae Kwon Do; Volunteer At Homeless Shelters; Get Masters Degree; Biology Major; Duke U; Penn State

STARR, MARSHALL; PLAINVIEW, NY; JOHN F KENNEDY HS; (SR); Hnr Roll; Perf Att; Comm Volntr; DECA; Emplmnt; Photog; Tchrs Aide; Bsball (J); Yrbk; I Work Many Hrs Per Week At MC Donald's; Accounting; Hofstra

ST DENNIS, KATIE L; SYRACUSE, NY; CICERO NORTH SYRACUSE HS; (JR); Hnr Roll; Nat Hon Sy; Perf Att; ArtClub; Emplmnt; Key Club; Lit Mag (E); Yrbk (P); Verizon Scholastic Art Competition Silver Key Winner; Art Education; Alfred U

STEARNS, MIKALA C; ERIEVILLE, NY; CAZENOVIA JR/SR HS; (JR); Comm Volntr; Chrch Yth Grp; Emplmnt; Wdwrkg Clb; Chr; Dnce; Hsbk Rdg (V); Track (V L); Trained for Interior Volunteer Fire Fighting; Culinary Arts

STEFANIK, NADIA; NEW YORK, NY; HUNTER COLLEGE HS; (JR); Comm Volntr; Peer Tut/Med; Key Club; Outdrs Clb; Tchrs Aide; Swg Chr; Bskball (V C); GAA; Sftball (V); Vllyball (V C); Yrbk (R); Attend Mannes Music School-Guitar (11 Yrs); Member of Term Council (4 Yrs); Exercise Science; Graphic Design

STEIN, CASSANDRA M; LEWISTON, NY; NICHOLS SCH; (FR); Hnr Roll; MVP; Pres Ac Ftns Aw; St of Mnth; Comm Volntr; NYLC; Ice Hky (J); Lcrsse (J); Sccr (V); 7th in Country for Girls Hockey; Michigan State U; Boston College

STEIN, MICHELLE R; ROCHESTER, NY; GREECE ARCADIA HS; (JR); Hi Hnr Roll; Yrbk (P); German National Honor Society; Teaching; SUNY-Geneseo; SUNY-Brockport

STEIN, REBECCA; LAWRENCE, NY; HAFTR HS; (JR); Hnr Roll; Yth Ldrshp Prog; Comm Volntr; Peer Tut/Med; Dbte Team; Emplmnt; Tmpl Yth Grp; Sftball (V); Adv Cncl (R); Lit Mag (E); Coordinator of a Charity Fashion Show (Raised $5,000); Secretary of the Law Institute; Industrial Labor Relations; Labor Law; Cornell U; Brandeis U

STEINMETZ, BRIAN D; EAST MEADOW, NY; EAST MEADOW HS; (JR); F Lan Hn Soc; Nat Hon Sy; Pres Sch; Sci Fairs; Sci/Math Olympn; WWAHSS; Comm Volntr; Peer Tut/Med; Emplmnt; Key Club; Mth Clb/Tm; Sci Clb; Svce Clb; Tmpl Yth Grp; Orch; Vllyball (V); Metropolitan Youth Orchestra Cellist; Chazak Divisional President of USY; Biomedical Engineering

STEINMEYER, NICOLE; HUNTINGTON STATION, NY; ST ANTHONY'S HS; (SO); Hi Hnr Roll; Hnr Roll; Nat Hon Sy; CARE; Quill & Scroll; Dnce; Yrbk (E); Won a $200 Scholarship from the Catholic Daughters of America; Speech Pathology; Fairfield U; Holy Trinity

STEINMULLER, CORI; SAUGERTIES, NY; SAUGERTIES HS; (SO); Hi Hnr Roll; Hnr Roll; Otst Ac Ach Awd; Chrch Yth Grp; Key Club; Yrbk (E); Piano Lessons for Seven Years; Poetry Awards & Writer

STEMPKOWSKI, GINA M; HOLLAND, NY; HOLLAND CTRL HS; (JR); Hi Hnr Roll; Kwnis Aw; Perf Att; Pres Ac Ftns Aw; St of Mnth; WWAHSS; Comm Volntr; Peer Tut/Med; Red Cr Aide; 4-H; Chrch Yth Grp; Drma Clb; Key Club; Lib Aide; Prom Com; Scouts; Vsity Clb; Bnd; Chr; Mch Bnd; SP/M/VS; PP Ftbl (V); Swmg (V); Track (V); Vsy Clb; Cl Off (S); Stu Cncl (R); CR (S); Yrbk (P); Junior Firefighting; BOCES Swim Aid; Chemistry; Earth Science; Canisius College; U of Rochester

STENSON, MICHAEL; BRONX, NY; JOHN F KENNEDY HS; (FR); Otst Ac Ach Awd; St of Mnth; ArtClub; Wt Lftg (J); Triple "C" Award; Larry B Seabrook Award; Bachelors Degree; Law and Finance; Lehman College; Florida State U

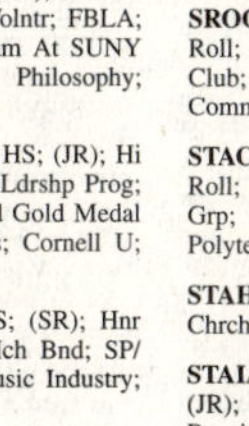

Stefanik, Nadia
Hunter College HS
New York, NY

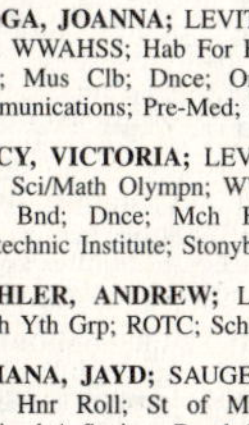

Stallings, Tanya A
Paul Robeson HS
Brooklyn, NY

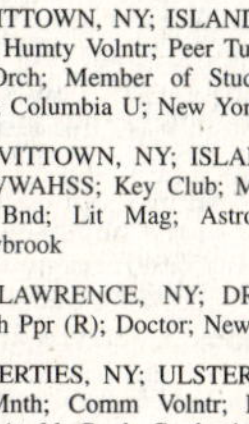

Southwick, Brittany N
Massena Ctrl HS
Massena, NY

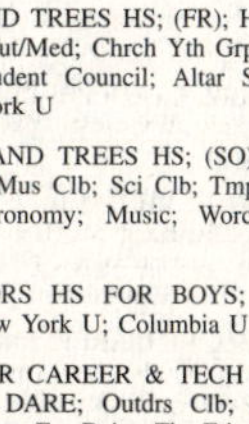

Spellman, Domonigue S
Riverhead HS
Riverhead, NY

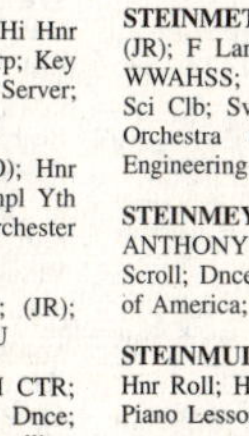

Stempkowski, Gina M
Holland Ctrl HS
Holland, NY

STEPHENS, CLARISSA V; SOUTH OZONE PARK, NY; CAMPUS MAG HS; (SR); Hnr Roll; Otst Ac Ach Awd; Perf Att; Pres Sch; WWAHSS; Comm Volntr; Emplmnt; Ch Chr; Dnce; Vllyball (V); Wt Lftg (V); Drummer in Church; Writer - 4 Year Schooling

STEPHENS, DANIELLE; CALVERTON, NY; RIVERHEAD HS; (SR); Hnr Roll; Comm Volntr; Peer Tut/Med; Emplmnt; Outdrs Clb; Pep Squd; Photog; Tchrs Aide; Vsity Clb; Dnce; Chrldg (C); Track (V); Sch Ppr (R); Poet of the Year - 2004-Feb / 2005-March; Criminal Justice; Mechanic Repair; Virginia Union U; Coppin State U

STERR, ETHAN C; MELVILLE, NY; HALF HOLLOW HILLS HS EAST; (SO); Hi Hnr Roll; Perf Att; WWAHSS; Yth Ldrshp Prog; Comm Volntr; Peer Tut/Med; Red Cr Aide; Chess; Dbte Team; NtlFrnscLg; Spch Team; Tmpl Yth Grp; French Clb; Bnd; Mch Bnd; Sch Ppr (R); Competed in the State Debate Championship

STEVENS, FELICA; BROOKLYN, NY; BENJAMIN BANNEKER AC; (SO); Hnr Roll; Otst Ac Ach Awd; Sci Fairs; St of Mnth; Valdctrian; Peer Tut/Med; Ch Chr; Hsbk Rdg; 90% Above Club; Pre-Med; Plastic Surgery; Georgetown U; Northeastern U

STEVENS, MEGAN; SARATOGA SPRINGS, NY; SARATOGA SPRINGS HS; (JR); Hi Hnr Roll; Nat Hon Sy; Emplmnt; Sccr (V L); Honorable Mentions for Varsity Soccer; 2nd Team for Varsity Soccer; Civil Engineering / Architecture; Chemistry; Fairleigh Dickinson U; Purdue U

STEVENS III, JAKE; BROOKLYN, NY; XAVERIAN HS; (SR); Hnr Roll; St of Mnth; Comm Volntr; Mus Clb; NYLC; SP/M/VS; Bskball (V C); Business Finance; Sports Management; Norfolk State U

STEWART, SHANICE Y; MOUNT VERNON, NY; MT VERNON HS; (FR); Hnr Roll; Nat Hon Sy; St of Mnth; FBLA; Scouts; French Clb; Bskball (J); Cr Ctry (V); Tennis (V); Track (V)

STEWART, TAIAMAL; BRONX, NY; ENY TRANSIT TECH HS; (SR); Hnr Roll; Nat Hon Sy; Perf Att; Comm Volntr; Red Cr Aide; Emplmnt; Wdwrkg Clb; SP/M/VS; Track (V); Sch Ppr (R); Electrical Engineering Technology; Railway Specialists; The City College of Technology; City College

STITT, LEWIS K; ALBANY, NY; ALBANY HS; (JR); Hi Hnr Roll; Otst Ac Ach Awd; WWAHSS; Yth Ldrshp Prog; Comm Volntr; Peer Tut/Med; Chrch Yth Grp; Key Club; NYLC; P to P St Amb Prg; Scouts; Latin Clb; Orch; National Latin Exam - Summa Cum Laude; The National Society of High School Scholars; Electrical Engineering; Columbia U; Cornell U

STOKER, SHELBY L; WILLSBORO, NY; WILLSBORO CTRL SCH; (FR); Hnr Roll; Nat Hon Sy; Comm Volntr; Medicine (Pediatrician); Art, Teaching; Harvard U; U of Vermont

STOLARSKI, ELLEN; ELMA, NY; IROQUOIS HS; (FR); Hnr Roll; Perf Att; WWAHSS; Comm Volntr; Drma Clb; Key Club; Lib Aide; Mth Clb/Tm; Mus Clb; Bnd; Mch Bnd; SP/M/VS; Sftball (J); Swmg (J); Yrbk (R); 2nd Place Battle of the Books Team; Championship EMW Softball Team; Teacher; Business.

STONE, ELIZABETH; CORNING, NY; CORNING-PAINTED POST WEST HS; (SO); 4H Awd; Hi Hnr Roll; Hnr Roll; Nat Stu Ath Day Aw; Perf Att; Pres Ac Ftns Aw; Comm Volntr; 4-H; Mus Clb; Chr; Lcrsse (J L); Sccr (JCL); Track (VJ); Cl Off (R); Stu Cncl (R); CFA Scholar Medal; President's Education Award; Elementary School Teacher; Social Services

STONE, GEORGE; CARTHAGE, NY; CARTHAGE HS; (SR); Hi Hnr Roll; Comm Volntr; Key Club; Mth Clb/Tm; Ch Chr; Golf (V); Sccr (J); Engineer; Jefferson Community College

STOTT, CYNTHIA L; STILLWATER, NY; STILLWATER CTRL HS; (JR); Hi Hnr Roll; Hnr Roll; Nat Hon Sy; Sci Fairs; DARE; SADD; Bnd; Chr; Gmnstcs; Computer Sciences; Psychology; Hudson Valley Community College; Schenectady County Community College, Adirondack Community College

STOYKA, CHRISTINE; BRONX, NY; BLESSED SACRAMENT HS; (JR); Hnr Roll; Sci Fairs; Dnce; Business Management / Marketing; Psychology; College of New Rochelle; Hofstra U

STRACQUODAINE, CATHERINE; MERRICK, NY; SANFORD H CALHOUN HS; (SR); Hnr Roll; Kwnis Aw; Nat Hon Sy; St of Mnth; Comm Volntr; Emplmnt; Key Club; SADD; National Art Honor Society; Accounting; Investment Banking; SUNY Binghamton U; SUNY Albany

STRAIGHT, NATALIE M; CASSADAGA, NY; CASSADAGA VALLEY MS; (JR); Hnr Roll; Nat Hon Sy; St of Mnth; WWAHSS; Drma Clb; Quiz Bowl; French Clb; Bnd; Chr; Jzz Bnd; SP/M/VS; Sccr (V CL); Sftball (J L); Track (V L); Cl Off (P, V); Sch Ppr (R, P); Marine Biology; Music Education; Boston U; U of Maine

STRAIL, KYLE; MC CONELSVILE, NY; CAMDEN HS; (JR); Hi Hnr Roll; Hnr Roll; Nat Hon Sy; WWAHSS; Golf (VJ L); Business Management; Technology

STREAM, SARA E; NEW HYDE PARK, NY; GREAT NECK SOUTH HS; (JR); Nat Mrt Semif; Otst Ac Ach Awd; Sci Fairs; WWAHSS; Comm Volntr; Emplmnt; Key Club; Sci Clb; Sign Clb; Bnd; Mch Bnd; Orch; SP/M/VS; Tennis (V); 2004 National French Exam 11th Place; Physical Sciences

STRIEFLER, KIMBERLY; NEW HAMPTON, NY; MINISINK VALLEY HS; (SO); 4H Awd; Hi Hnr Roll; Hnr Roll; MVP; Otst Ac Ach Awd; Perf Att; St of Mnth; WWAHSS; Comm Volntr; Peer Tut/Med; Red Cr Aide; 4-H; Chrch Yth Grp; FBLA; Key Club; Lib Aide; P to P St Amb Prg; Quiz Bowl; Schol Bwl; Chr; Ch Chr; Cr Ctry (JCL); Track (VJ L); Yrbk (E, R, P); SADD Participant; International Business; Minor French / Russian; Richmond International U London; Cambridge U

STRIGGLES, PATRICIA; BRONX, NY; WALTON HS; (FR); Hi Hnr Roll; Hnr Roll; Perf Att; Comm Volntr; Chrch Yth Grp; DARE; Chr; Clr Grd; Dnce; Sch Ppr (R); Voluntary Work; Teacher; Interior Decorator; Syracuse U; Fordham U

STRIPP, CHRIS; UTICA, NY; HOLLAND PATENT HS; (SR); Hi Hnr Roll; Hnr Roll; Yth Ldrshp Prog; Comm Volntr; Drma Clb; Emplmnt; Prom Com; SP/M/VS; Bskball (L); Ftball (V C); Track (V C); Wt Lftg; Wrstlg (L); Stu Cncl (P); Pre-Law (Lawyer); Hobart and William Smith Colleges; St. John Fisher College

STROBLE JR, WADE A; LINDENHURST, NY; LINDENHURST HS; (JR); Ctznshp Aw; Hi Hnr Roll; Nat Hon Sy; Pres Ac Ftns Aw; St of Mnth; WWAHSS; Peer Tut/Med; Chrch Yth Grp; NYLC; Vsity Clb; Ch Chr; Lcrsse (V L); Mar Art; Rqtball; Wt Lftg; Adv Cncl (R); Stu Cncl (R); Yrbk (R); Lacrosse- Man of the Year - Defense; Citizenship Award, President's Award Scholastic Achievement

STROUBOS, LEMONIA; WHITESTONE, NY; TOWNSEND HARRIS HS; (JR); Ctznshp Aw; Hi Hnr Roll; Hnr Roll; Perf Att; WWAHSS; Comm Volntr; Peer Tut/Med; Mod UN; Dnce; SP/M/VS; Lit Mag (R); Member of Moot Court/Mock Trial Team; Speak Greek Fluently; Political Science; World Affairs; New York U; Brown U

ST SURIN, KLEEDY M; BROOKLYN, NY; BISHOP KEARNEY HS; (JR); Hnr Roll; Nat Hon Sy; Nat Stu Ath Day Aw; Perf Att; WWAHSS; Comm Volntr; Key Club; Dnce; SP/M/VS; CR (R); Yrbk; Boosters-Captain; Pre-Med; Saint Joseph College Brooklyn

STUBER, AARON; SYRACUSE, NY; HENNINGER HS; (JR); Hi Hnr Roll; Hnr Roll; Nat Hon Sy; Comm Volntr; Red Cr Aide; Emplmnt; Lcrsse (V L); Sccr (V CL); Presidential Award for Educational Excellence.; Engineering; Chemistry; Syracuse U; Colorado School of Mines

STUDGEON, NATHAN I; CONKLIN, NY; SUSQUEHANNA VALLEY SR HS; (SR); Hnr Roll; MVP; Otst Ac Ach Awd; Perf Att; Pres Ac Ftns Aw; St of Mnth; WWAHSS; Yth Ldrshp Prog; Comm Volntr; Peer Tut/Med; Chrch Yth Grp; DARE; Emplmnt; Prom Com; SADD; Ch Chr; Bsball (VJC); Bskball (J); Skiing (VJ); Sccr (VJCL); Vllyball (V); Social Work; Psychology; Keuka College

STUDLEY, JEWELLEE; CATTARAUGUS, NY; CATTARAUGUS-LITTLE VALLEY; (FR); Hi Hnr Roll; Hnr Roll; Mus Clb; Quiz Bowl; Bnd; Jzz Bnd; Mch Bnd; Sccr (V); Track (V); Cl Off (T)

STURM, RYAN M; HOLBROOK, NY; CHAMINADE HS; (JR); Hnr Roll; Chess; Emplmnt; Photog

STUTZ, NICOLE; SYOSSET, NY; SYOSSET HS; (JR); Hi Hnr Roll; Hnr Roll; Nat Hon Sy; Sci Fairs; Yth Ldrshp Prog; Comm Volntr; Peer Tut/Med; Sccr (V CL); Soccer All Class AA Division (2004); New York U

SUAREZ, CAROLYN; STATEN ISLAND, NY; ST JOSEPH HILL AC; (JR); Hnr Roll; WWAHSS; Comm Volntr; Bskball (V); Vllyball (V); Speech Pathology

SUAREZ, RICHARD A; MIDDLE VILLAGE, NY; BRONX HS OF SCIENCE; (SO); Nat Hon Sy; Perf Att; Salutrn; Emplmnt; Bowling Team Varsity; Rowing / Crew - Team Varsity; Aerospace Engineering; Biochemistry; Massachusetts Institute of Technology; United State Naval Academy

SUAZO, KIMBERLY; BRONX, NY; AC OF MT ST URSULA; (JR); Gov Hnr Prg; Hi Hnr Roll; Hnr Roll; Pres Sch; Sci Fairs; Spanish Clb; National Junior Honor Society; Math League; Business Administration; International Business; Fordham U

SULLIVAN, ASHLEY; HOLLAND, NY; HOLLAND CTRL HS; (SO); Hi Hnr Roll; Hnr Roll; Sci Fairs; WWAHSS; Comm Volntr; Chrch Yth Grp; Key Club; Mus Clb; Tchrs Aide; Vsity Clb; Bnd; Ch Chr; Mch Bnd; Bskball (J); Fld Hky (VJ L); Vsy Clb; Stu Cncl; Early Childhood; Geneseo; Syracuse

SULLIVAN, BREANA T; WALDEN, NY; VALLEY CTRL HS; (SR); F Lan Hn Soc; Hi Hnr Roll; Nat Hon Sy; Yth Ldrshp Prog; Comm Volntr; Peer Tut/Med; Dbte Team; Drma Clb; Mth Clb/Tm; MuAlphaTh; NYLC; Scouts; Chr; Ch Chr; SP/M/VS; Bskball (VJCL); Cr Ctry (VJ); Skiing (V C); Yrbk (R, P); Vice President of French Honor Society; Participation in Lead America; Dual Major in French and Theatre; State U of New York Geneseo

SULLIVAN, KERRY; STATEN ISLAND, NY; SAINT JOHN VILLA AC; (SO); Hnr Roll; Nat Hon Sy; WWAHSS; Comm Volntr; Hosp Aide; Peer Tut/Med; DARE; Jr Ach; Ch Chr; Dnce; Excellence in Science Award; Excellence in Religion; Psychology; Forensics; Wagner College; Villanova U

SULLIVAN, LEANNA R; BOONVILLE, NY; ADIRONDACK HS; (JR); Ctznshp Aw; Hi Hnr Roll; Hnr Roll; Nat Hon Sy; Perf Att; Comm Volntr; Hab For Humty Volntr; Peer Tut/Med; Emplmnt; Mth Clb/Tm; Mus Clb; Scouts; French Clb; Bnd; Chr; Jzz Bnd; SP/M/VS; Bskball (V); Cr Ctry (L); GAA (V); Sftball (L); Scholar Athlete; All-County Orchestra; Forensic Science; Pre-Med; U of New Haven; SUNY Canton

SULLIVAN, NICOLE; LIVERPOOL, NY; LIVERPOOL HS; (JR); Hi Hnr Roll; Otst Ac Ach Awd; Pres Ac Ftns Aw; Sci Fairs; WWAHSS; Yth Ldrshp Prog; Peer Tut/Med; Emplmnt; HO'Br Yth Ldrshp; Key Club; Swmg (V L); Advertising Graphic Design; Marketing; Rochester Institute of Technology; New York U

SULLIVAN, ROBERT W; STATEN ISLAND, NY; NEW DORP HS; (JR); Ctznshp Aw; St of Mnth; Mod UN; Bsball (V); Cl Off (P); Stu Cncl (P); Sch Ppr (R); Silver Service Award (Over 50 Service Credits); Leadership Award, Varsity Baseball, Fire Explorer; Law; Social Studies; John Jay Criminal Justice CUNY; St. John's U

SULMERS, CHRISTINE; NEW YORK, NY; HEALTH PROF & HUMAN SERVICES HS; (JR); F Lan Hn Soc; Hi Hnr Roll; Hnr Roll; Nat Hon Sy; WWAHSS; Comm Volntr; Hosp Aide; Peer Tut/Med; Dnce; SP/M/VS; Stu Cncl (R); CR (R); Yrbk; Biology, B.S.; Doctoral Degree; Sophie Davis School of Biomedical; Brooklyn College

SUN, AN P; ELMHURST, NY; BRONX HS OF SCIENCE; (FR); F Lan Hn Soc; Hnr Roll; Perf Att; Sci Fairs; St of Mnth; WWAHSS; Comm Volntr; Key Club; Bnd; 2002 World Journal Chinese English Competition - 2nd Place; Interior Designer; New York U; Columbia U

SUNG, NAMI; FLUSHING, NY; STUYVESANT HS; (SR); Nat Hon Sy; Nat Mrt LOC; Comm Volntr; Peer Tut/Med; Emplmnt; Photog; Lit Mag (E); Yrbk (R); Cheese Club President; Docent At Museum of City of NY & NY Historical Society; History; Communications Writing, Publishing, Editing; Harvard College

SUNPITAKSAREE, NATTHA; BRONX, NY; AC OF MT ST URSULA; (JR); Hnr Roll; Lib Aide; Sci Clb; French Clb; Chrldg (J); Track (J); Language Studies

SUPONYA, NIKITA; BROOKLYN, NY; EDWARD R MURROW HS; (JR); Sci Fairs; Sci/Math Olympn; Hosp Aide; Peer Tut/Med; Chess; Mth Clb/Tm; Photog; Sci Clb; Chess Team-Murrow Team Won Nationals Last 2 Years; Won 1st Place Math a Contest; Physics; Business; New York U

SUPPA, ANTONINA; RIDGEWOOD, NY; CHRIST THE KING HS; (SO); Hi Hnr Roll; Perf Att; Comm Volntr; International Clb; Chr; Principal's List at CK; Ranked # 3 as of Sophomore Year; St John's U; New York U

SUROWIEC, SAMANTHA; STATEN ISLAND, NY; NEW DORP HS; (JR); Hnr Roll; Nat Hon Sy; Otst Ac Ach Awd; Sci Fairs; Comm Volntr; Emplmnt; Svce Clb; Dnce; SP/M/VS; Stu Cncl (R); Merit in American and Legal Studies; Honor Roll Society; Master's in Child Psychology; Law Degree; St. John's U; U of Central Florida

SUSSMAN, JONATHAN M; WESTBURY, NY; W.T. CLARKE HS; (SO); F Lan Hn Soc; Hnr Roll; WWAHSS; SP/M/VS; Sccr (JC); Lit Mag (R); Sch Ppr (R); Travel Team Soccer; Assistant Teacher Sunday School

SUTCH, JESSICA; LEVITTOWN, NY; DIVISION AVE HS; (SR); Hnr Roll; Otst Ac Ach Awd; USAA; WWAHSS; Comm Volntr; Key Club; Bnd; Dnce; Lcrsse (VJ); Sccr (VJC); Harriet Lavnick Award; US Achievement Academy Award; Special Education; SUNY Cortland

SUTTMEIER, EMILY; SAUGERTIES, NY; SAUGERTIES HS; (JR); Hi Hnr Roll; Nat Hon Sy; WWAHSS; Comm Volntr; Peer Tut/Med; Chrch Yth Grp; DARE; Key Club; Spanish Clb; Bnd; Chr; SP/M/VS; Bskball (VJCL); Track (V L); Vllyball (VJCL); Secretary of Key Club and National Honor Society; Vice President of Spanish Club; Film Production; Biology / Genetics; Ithaca College; U of Southern California

SUTTON, JAMES; YONKERS, NY; IONA PREP; (JR); Hnr Roll; Sci Fairs; Yth Ldrshp Prog; Amnsty Intl; Comm Volntr; Hosp Aide; I Do Boxing Three to Five Days a Week; I Work As a Bus Boy in a Restaurant; Criminalistics; Physics; The Citadel; Fordham U

SUWANRUT, PORNCHOMPOO; ASTORIA, NY; HEALTH PROF & HUMAN SERV HS; (SO); Ctznshp Aw; Gov Hnr Prg; Hi Hnr Roll; Otst Ac Ach Awd; Perf Att; Sci Fairs; St of Mnth; Valdctrian; Sci Clb; Tchrs Aide; Sch Ppr (R); Active Member of the Liberty Partnership Program Affiliated with Pace U; Science Research Class Affiliated with SUNY; Bachelor of Biological Sciences; Doctor of Medicine; Cornell U; New York U

SUZUKI, HANAKO M; NEW YORK, NY; STUYVESANT HS; (FR); Hnr Roll; Sci Fairs; WWAHSS; Key Club; Mod UN; Japanese Clb; Orch; Physician; Fashion Designer; Harvard U; New York U

Suppa, Antonina
Christ The King HS
Ridgewood, NY

Stone, Elizabeth
Corning-Painted Post West HS
Corning, NY

Stitt, Lewis K
Albany HS
Albany, NY

National
Honor Roll
Spring 2005

Stevens III, Jake
Xaverian HS
Brooklyn, NY

Studgeon, Nathan I
Susquehanna Valley SR HS
Conklin, NY

Suzuki, Hanako M
Stuyvesant HS
New York, NY

SVEREIKA, SAMANTHA M; HANNIBAL, NY; HANNIBAL HS; (JR); Bnd; Chr; Ch Chr; Jzz Bnd; Bskball (V L); Cr Ct Ski (J); Sccr (V L); Sftball (V L); Track (V L); Vllyball (J); Stu Cncl (R); Girl Scout Gold Award; Venture Crew President; Teaching; Ministry; State U of NY At Oswego; Keuka College

SVYATETS, KSENIYA; NEW YORK, NY; SPENCE SCH; (JR); Hi Hnr Roll; Sci Fairs; Yth Ldrshp Prog; Amnsty Intl; Comm Volntr; Emplmnt; Lib Aide; NYLC; Off Aide; Photog; Sci Clb; Svce Clb; Vsity Clb; Dnce; SP/M/VS; Stg Cre; Swmg (V); Lit Mag (R); Competitive Ballroom Dancing; Medicine, Biology; Columbia College, New York U

SWANN, KIAH N; NYACK, NY; WALDWICK SDA SCH; (FR); Ctznshp Aw; Hi Hnr Roll; Hnr Roll; Perf Att; Sci Fairs; St of Mnth; Valdctrian; Comm Volntr; Chrch Yth Grp; DARE; Chr; Ch Chr; Orch; SP/M/VS; Stu Cncl (S); Yrbk (E, P); Medical; Music; Oakwood; NYU

SWEENEY, KHANDI-KAE; BRONX, NY; BLESSED SACRAMENT ST GABRIEL; (JR); Hnr Roll; Nat Hon Sy; Otst Ac Ach Awd; Perf Att; Sci Fairs; Peer Tut/Med; Chrch Yth Grp; Dbte Team; Drma Clb; Key Club; Sci Clb; Spch Team; Chr; Ch Chr; Dnce; SP/M/VS; Chrldg (J); Sccr (J); Sftball; Tennis (C); Track (V); Wt Lftg (L); Stu Cncl (T); SUNY Stony Brook; New York U

SWENSON, BETH; CORTLAND, NY; HOMER CTRL HS; (JR); Hnr Roll; Comm Volntr; Drma Clb; Bnd; Chr; SP/M/VS; Swg Chr; Tennis (V); Sch Ppr (E); Clarinet Quartet Member; The Arts; Education

SWIFT, SHAKEYIA; MIDDLETOWN, NY; MIDDLETOWN HS; (JR); Perf Att; St of Mnth; DARE; Emplmnt; Dnce; Academy of Finance; Teaching Master's Degree; Master's Degree in Chemistry / Biology; Yale U

SWINTON, AKASHIA; HOGUE, NY; (SO); Hi Hnr Roll; Hnr Roll; Nat Hon Sy; St Optmst of Yr; WWAHSS; Comm Volntr; DARE; Emplmnt; Key Club; Scouts; Bnd; Chr; Bskball (J); National Honor Society; Spanish Club Secretary; Spanish Education; Photography or Fashion Design; Hofstra U; Ithaca College

SWINTON, ALANNA M; HAGUE, NY; TICONDEROGA HS; (FR); Hnr Roll; Perf Att; Sci Fairs; St of Mnth; Comm Volntr; DARE; Emplmnt; Mth Clb/Tm; Bnd; Chr; Jzz Bnd; Stg Cre; Yrbk (E); On the Varsity Bowling Team; Auto Mechanics; Professional Bartender; New York U

SYED, IMRAN; BUFFALO, NY; KENMORE WEST SR HS; (FR); Hnr Roll; MVP; Nat Ldrshp Svc; Pres Ac Ftns Aw; Sci Fairs; Sci/Math Olympn; St of Mnth; Hosp Aide; Peer Tut/Med; DARE; FBLA; Outdrs Clb; Sci Clb; Tech Clb; Vsity Clb; Spanish Clb; Chr; SP/M/VS; Bsball (J); Cr Ctry (J); Ftball (V); Ice Hky (JC); Rlr Hky (V C); Wrstlg (J); Cl Off (V); Yrbk (E); Doctor; Computer Engineer; Stanford U; Boston U

SYLVAIN, GEORGE; HUNTINGTN STA, NY; HALF HOLLOW HILLS HS WEST; (JR); Hnr Roll; Clb; Track (J); Freshman Basketball; African American Students Organization Treasurer; Business Law; Sports Management; Rutgers U; Seton Hall U

SYLVAN, RODANY S; BROOKLYN, NY; BRENTWOOD ROSS HS; (SO); Hnr Roll; Clr Grd; Major in Drama /Communications; NYU

SYMNS, MILLIE; BROOKLYN, NY; JAMES MADISON HS; (MS); Hnr Roll; Sci Fairs; WWAHSS; Peer Tut/Med; Chr; Professional Degree in Music / Performing Arts

SYRJALA, HEATHER; EAST BRANCH, NY; DOWNSVILLE CTRL HS; (FR); Hi Hnr Roll; DARE; Scouts; Chr; Clr Grd; History Teacher; English Teacher; Binghamton U

SZCZEPANIAK, DANA K; GRAND ISLAND, NY; GRAND ISLAND HS; (JR); Hi Hnr Roll; Hnr Roll; Nat Hon Sy; Nat Ldrshp Svc; Perf Att; WWAHSS; Yth Ldrshp Prog; Comm Volntr; Peer Tut/Med; Chrch Yth Grp; Pep Squd; Vsity Clb; Bnd; Jzz Bnd; Pep Bnd; Bskball (VJC); Skiing; Sccr (VJ); Sftball (JC); Community Band; Physical Education; Medical School; U of California @ Santa Barbara; U of California @ Berkeley

SZEKELY, AKOS; HUNTINGTON, NY; HUNTINGTON HS; (SO); Hi Hnr Roll; Hnr Roll; Perf Att; Peer Tut/Med; Drma Clb; Emplmnt; Orch; Cr Ctry (J); Fncg; Sch Ppr; National History Day Award; Psychiatry; Pediatrics

SZEKLEY, CSILLA; NEW YORK, NY; FLUSHING HS; (SR); Hnr Roll; WWAHSS; Comm Volntr; Chrch Yth Grp; Drma Clb; Fr of Library; Scouts; Tchrs Aide; Vsity Clb; Ch Chr; Dnce; Sccr (V); Lit Mag (R); Sch Ppr (E, R, P); Vice President of the Kossuth Friendship Circle.; International Affairs; European Studies; New York U; Fordham U

SZTUK, MICHAEL; BUFFALO, NY; SWEET HOME HS; (SO); Hi Hnr Roll; Hnr Roll; STARS - Students That Are Really Special; Ski / Snowboard Club; Computer Technology; Rochester Institute of Technology

SZYMANIAK, JON; OWEGO, NY; OWEGO FREE AC; (JR); Ctznshp Aw; Hi Hnr Roll; Hnr Roll; Nat Hon Sy; WWAHSS; Hab For Humty Volntr; Chrch Yth Grp; Emplmnt; Key Club; Bnd; Jzz Bnd; Golf (V L); Lcrsse (VJ L); Skiing; Student Programmer for Owego School District; Computer Engineering; Electrical Engineering; Rochester Institute of Technology; Clarkson U

TAFFANY, ALEXANDRA C; CLIFTON PARK, NY; SHENENDEHOWA HS; (JR); Hi Hnr Roll; Pres Ac Ftns Aw; WWAHSS; Yth Ldrshp Prog; Comm Volntr; Hosp Aide; Drma Clb; Mus Clb; Scouts; Acpl Chr; Chr; Ch Chr; Dnce; Girl Scouts Silver Award; Tri-M Music Honor Society; Dramatic Arts / Theatre; New York U

TAI, CAROLYN C; BROOKLYN, NY; STUYVESANT HS; (JR); F Lan Hn Soc; Hnr Roll; Kwnis Aw; Nat Hon Sy; Comm Volntr; Peer Tut/Med; Aqrium Clb; ArtClub; Key Club; Kwanza Clb; Lib Aide; Off Aide; Pep Squd; Svce Clb; Dnce; SP/M/VS; Stg Cre; Sch Ppr (R); Art Talent Award-2nd Place; Business-Marketing; Business-Accounting; Cornell U

TAL, ODED; JAMAICA, NY; FIORELLO H LA GUARDIA HS; (SO); Hnr Roll; Nat Hon Sy; Nat Mrt LOC; Perf Att; Peer Tut/Med; Chess; Cmptr Clb; Jr Ach; Work Entered in Art Gallery; Medical Degree; Computer Graphics; Binghamton; Columbia

TALABACU, KATHERINE; MIDDLE VILLAGE, NY; STUYVESANT HS; (FR); St of Mnth; WWAHSS; Comm Volntr; Peer Tut/Med; Chrch Yth Grp; Key Club; Lib Aide; Mth Clb/Tm; Tchrs Aide; Chr; Writer for "The Locksmith"; Physics Lab Squad; Business Major; Law School; Columbia U; New York U

TALLMAN, KATHRYN L; BLOSSVALE, NY; CAMDEN HS; (SO); Hnr Roll; Emplmnt; Schol Bwl; Tennis (J L); Bowling Varsity; Real Estate Business; Hotel Management

TAM, WINNIE; BROOKLYN, NY; NEW UTRECHT HS; (JR); Perf Att; Sci Fairs; St of Mnth; Comm Volntr; Peer Tut/Med; DARE; Pep Squd; Vsity Clb; Chr; Chrldg (V); Vllyball (V); Music; Automobile Design; Wagner College; College of Staten Island

TAMAZASHVILI, TAMARA; BROOKLYN, NY; MIDWOOD HS; (SO); Nat Hon Sy; Comm Volntr; Peer Tut/Med; Biology Clb; Off Aide; Sci Clb; Svce Clb; Stu Cncl (R); CR (R); Sch Ppr (R); Archon Service League; The National Society of High School Scholars; Biology; Chemistry; Hunter College; Long Island U

TAMOL, JESSICA; LANCASTER, NY; LANCASTER HS; (SO); Hnr Roll; DECA; Vsity Clb; Bnd; Cr Ctry (V L); Track (V); Sch Ppr (R); Leadership Award Winner; DECA Officer - Regional Representative; Business and Communications; U of Pittsburgh

TAN, ANALYSA; BROOKLYN, NY; MIDWOOD HS; (SO); Hnr Roll; Nat Hon Sy; Sci Fairs; St of Mnth; Comm Volntr; Key Club; Off Aide; Tchrs Aide; Orch; SP/M/VS; Yrbk (P); In Advanced Placement Classes; Lawyer; Harvard U; Princeton U

TAN, EUGENE M; NEW HYDE PARK, NY; HERRICKS HS; (SR); Hi Hnr Roll; Hnr Roll; Nat Hon Sy; Nat Mrt Fin; Nat Mrt Sch Recip; Nat Mrt Semif; Otst Ac Ach Awd; Salutrn; Sci Fairs; Sci/Math Olympn; Comm Volntr; Hosp Aide; Mth Clb/Tm; Mus Clb; Sci Clb; Orch; Tennis (J); Track (J); Sch Ppr (E); Siemens-Westinghouse Semifinalist 2004; Best Buy Children's Foundation Awards Scholarship; Biology Major / MD; Business Management Minor; SUNY Stony Brook / Scholars for Medicine

TAN, MIN Y; BROOKLYN, NY; BARUCH COLLEGE CAMPUS HS; (JR); WWAHSS; Comm Volntr; Peer Tut/Med; ArtClub; Chrch Yth Grp; Orch; Sch Ppr (E, R); Psychologist; Stony Brook U

TAN, WENNY; FRESH MEADOWS, NY; FRANCIS LEWIS HS; (JR); Hnr Roll; Perf Att; Peer Tut/Med; Key Club; Vllyball (J); Varsity Bowling Team

TANNER, ROBERT J; SPENCERPORT, NY; CHURCHVILLE-CHILI HS; (JR); Hnr Roll; WWAHSS; Emplmnt; Lcrsse (J); Skiing (V); Sccr (VJCL); Tennis (J); Inventors Award; MIP Soccer Award - JV; Engineering; Physical Education Teacher

TANTILLO, STEPHANIE A.; NORTHPORT, NY; NORTHPORT HS; Comm Volntr; Emplmnt; Students for 60,000 (Raise Money for the Poor); Louis J. Acompora Foundation; International Lawyer; U of Pisa; U of Florence

TARIQ, NIDA; OZONE PARK, NY; CLARA MUHAMMAD SCH; (JR); Hnr Roll; St of Mnth; WWAHSS; Comm Volntr; Peer Tut/Med; Stu Cncl (R); Lit Mag (R); President of Student Activities; Principal's Honor Roll; Gynecology; Business Administration and Communications; New York U; Lincoln U

TARNEJA, NITYA; FAIRPORT, NY; FAIRPORT HS; (SO); Hi Hnr Roll; WWAHSS; Comm Volntr; ArtClub; Yrbk (E); Spanish Honor Society; Scholastic Art Show; Medical; Cornell

TARQUINIO, ALESSANDRO; SCHENECTADY, NY; SCHALMONT HS; (FR); Hi Hnr Roll; Hnr Roll; Pres Ac Ftns Aw; Comm Volntr; Chrch Yth Grp; Emplmnt; Key Club; Quiz Bowl; Bnd; Sccr (J L); High Honor Roll; Honors Math

TARQUINIO, LISA A; SCHENECTADY, NY; SCHALMONT HS; (SO); Hi Hnr Roll; MVP; Otst Ac Ach Awd; St of Mnth; WWAHSS; Peer Tut/Med; Biology Clb; Key Club; Sci Clb; Chr; Sccr (V); Track (V); Stu Cncl (R); CR; 4 Year ODP Soccer; RPI - Scholarship Recipient Through Johns Hopkins Organization

TARRANT, SHANEL; HEMPSTEAD, NY; HEMPSTEAD HS; (SO); Hnr Roll; Otst Ac Ach Awd; St Schl; Hosp Aide; Dbte Team; Ch Chr; Bdmtn (V); Sch Ppr (R); Certificate of Completion of the L.I. Regional (Nutritional Program); Medicine; Performing Arts; Harvard U; Yale U

TASIELLO, CATHERINE; MALVERNE, NY; MALVERNE HS; (JR); Hnr Roll; St of Mnth; Drma Clb; Outdrs Clb; SADD; Bnd; Clr Grd; Mch Bnd; SP/M/VS; Sftball (V); Yrbk (P); Color Guard Captain; Photography; Journalism; k2306

TATAJ, ERVIS; BRONX, NY; JOHN F KENNEDY HS; (JR); Hnr Roll; Otst Ac Ach Awd; Perf Att; WWAHSS; Peer Tut/Med; Sci Clb; Stg Cre; Bskball (J); Sftball (J); Vllyball (J); Sch Ppr (R); Summer School Award; Acting Army or Navy Real Estate Agent; Basketball Coach; Niagara College Etc

TATARYNOWICZ, JACK; BROOKLYN, NY; ARCHBISHOP MOLLOY HS; (SO); Hnr Roll; Cmptr Clb; Emplmnt; Bskball (J); Scr Kpr; Stu Cncl (R); Member of Investment Club; Sports Business; U of Connecticut; U of Syracuse

TATUSKO, KENDRA; MIDDLETOWN, NY; MIDDLETOWN HS; (JR); Hi Hnr Roll; Nat Hon Sy; Perf Att; Comm Volntr; Peer Tut/Med; ArtClub; Dbte Team; Emplmnt; Photog; Adv Cncl (R); Stu Cncl (R); Biology

TAVAREZ, SINDY V; BRONX, NY; ST PIUS V HS; (JR); Hi Hnr Roll; St of Mnth; Yth Ldrshp Prog; Comm Volntr; Drma Clb; Emplmnt; Cl Off (V); Stu Cncl (S); CR (P); Business Administration; Computer Technology; Stony Brook U; New York U

TAVERAS, MANUELA; BRONX, NY; ST JEAN BAPTISTE HS; (JR); WWAHSS; ArtClub; Emplmnt; SP/M/VS; Student Sponsor Partner Scholarship; Computer Science; Japanese; Fordham U; St John's U

TAYLOR, RANDY; ALBANY, NY; THE ALBANY AC; (SO); Hnr Roll; Comm Volntr; Bskball (J); Gmnstcs (V); Sccr (V); Track (V); Platoon Leader; Physical Education; Public Relations

TEAL, RICKY; PORT LEYDEN, NY; SOUTH LEWIS HS; (FR); Gov Hnr Prg; Hi Hnr Roll; St of Mnth; Comm Volntr; Emplmnt; Vsity Clb; Bsball (J); Ftball (J); Wrstlg (V L); Cl Off (P)

TEDESCO, MELODY; ALDEN, NY; ALDEN HS; (SO); Hi Hnr Roll; Hnr Roll; Perf Att; St of Mnth; Comm Volntr; Peer Tut/Med; 4-H; ArtClub; DARE; Key Club; Spanish Clb; Chr; HELP Camp; U of Buffalo

TEDONE, ASHLEY; TUCKAHOE, NY; THE URSULINE SCH; (JR); Hi Hnr Roll; Nat Hon Sy; Comm Volntr; Hab For Humty Volntr; Peer Tut/Med; Emplmnt; Italian Clb; Dnce; Psychology; Forensics; Georgetown U; Boston U

TEITELBAUM, DAVID; WEST NYACK, NY; CLARKSTOWN HS S; (SO); F Lan Hn Soc; Hi Hnr Roll; Hnr Roll; Otst Ac Ach Awd; Hosp Aide; Emplmnt; FBLA; Mth Clb/Tm; MuAlphaTh; Tennis (J); Science; Dentistry

TEJOVIC, SUZANNA; RIDGEWOOD, NY; FOREST HILLS HS; (SR); Hi Hnr Roll; Hnr Roll; Comm Volntr; Drma Clb; Emplmnt; Mus Clb; Chr; Dnce; Medicine; Education; Hunter College; Pace U

TELESCO, AMANDA; CARMEL, NY; CARMEL HS; (FR); Hi Hnr Roll; Hnr Roll; St of Mnth; Peer Tut/Med; Drma Clb; Clr Grd; SP/M/VS; Honor Roll; Law; Performing Arts; New York Film Academy; Yale U

TELFORD, TIFFANY; SAINT ALBANS, NY; MATH SCIENCE RESEARCH TECH HS; (JR); Hnr Roll; Otst Ac Ach Awd; Pres Ac Ftns Aw; St of Mnth; WWAHSS; Chrch Yth Grp; Tchrs Aide; Ch Chr; Service Award; Pre-Med-Biology; Psychology; Houghton College

TELGHEDER, ZACHARY L; PORT JERVIS, NY; MINISINK VALLEY HS; (SO); Hi Hnr Roll; Hnr Roll; Perf Att; Pres Ac Ftns Aw; St of Mnth; WWAHSS; Comm Volntr; Key Club; Bsball (V); Sccr (V); Engineering; Medical

TELLER, SCOTT V; GRANVILLE, NY; GRANVILLE JR/SR HS; (SR); DAR; Hi Hnr Roll; Nat Hon Sy; Nat Mrt Semif; WWAHSS; Comm Volntr; Chrch Yth Grp; Drma Clb; Emplmnt; FBLA; Mth Clb/Tm; Prom Com; Quiz Bowl; Scouts; Bnd; Jzz Bnd; Mch Bnd; Bskball (VJ L); Golf (J); Sccr (VJ L); Tennis (VJCL); Cl Off (T); Sch Ppr (R); Sports Management; Business Management; Endicott College; Colby-Sawyer College

TEMPERATO, LISA; CONESUS, NY; LIMA CHRISTIAN SCH; (SO); Bnd; Chr; Ch Chr; Clr Grd; Bskball (J); Sftball (J); Cosmetology; Sociology

TENASCO, TIFFANY A; ELMIRA, NY; THOMAS A EDISON HS; (SO); Hnr Roll; ArtClub; Key Club; French Clb; Stg Cre; Chrldg (J); Track (J); Degree in Art; Corning Community College; Art Institute of Pittsburgh

TERRILLION, ROBYN; LEVITTOWN, NY; DIVISION AVE HS; (JR); F Lan Hn Soc; Hi Hnr Roll; Hnr Roll; Nat Hon Sy; Perf Att; WWAHSS; Comm Volntr; Key Club; Mth Clb/Tm; Mod UN; Photog; Lcrsse (VJC); Vllyball (VJ); National Honor Society; Secretary of Spanish Honor Society; Forensics/Criminal Justice; Psychology; Villanova; Loyola

TERRILLION, TIMOTHY; LEVITTOWN, NY; DIVISION AVE HS; (SO); Hi Hnr Roll; Hnr Roll; Nat Hon Sy; Key Club; Lcrsse (VJC); Key Club; Business Marketing/Management; Syracuse; Johns Hopkins

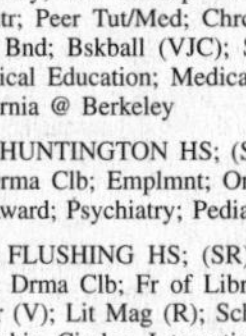
Telesco, Amanda
Carmel HS
Carmel, NY

Tataj, Ervis
John F Kennedy HS
Bronx, NY

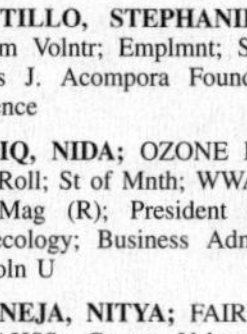
Szekely, Akos
Huntington HS
Huntington, NY

National
Honor Roll
Spring 2005

Syed, Imran
Kenmore West SR HS
Buffalo, NY

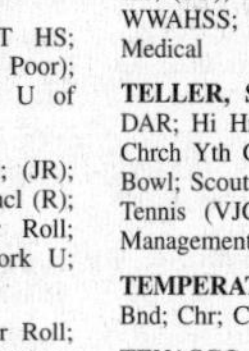
Tejovic, Suzanna
Forest Hills HS
Ridgewood, NY

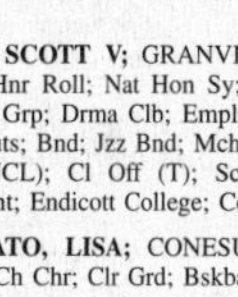
Temperato, Lisa
Lima Christian Sch
Conesus, NY

TERRY, OCTAVIA; SYRACUSE, NY; HENNINGER HS; Hnr Roll; Nat Hon Sy; Comm Volntr; Peer Tut/Med; Emplmnt; Ch Chr; Lcrsse (J); Track (V); Vice President of Teen Aids Task Force; Big Brother Big Sister; Medicine (Pediatrician); Teacher; Syracuse U; Buffalo U

TERZINO, ANTHONY E; REGO PARK, NY; LAFAYETTE HS; (JR); 4H Awd; All Am Sch; Hi Hnr Roll; Hnr Roll; Nat Hon Sy; Perf Att; Salutrn; Sci Fairs; St of Mnth; Comm Volntr; Peer Tut/Med; 4-H; ArtClub; Chrch Yth Grp; Cmptr Clb; DARE; Ntl Beta Clb; Tech Clb; Chinese Clb; Clr Grd; SP/M/VS; Stu Cncl (R); Lit Mag (E); Yrbk (E); Upward Bound Math and Science Center; Cooper Union Research Internship Program; Engineering/Architecture; Accounting; Cooper Union; Columbia U

TERZINO, CAROLINE; REGO PARK, NY; LAFAYETTE HS; (JR); 4H Awd; Nat Hon Sy; Perf Att; St of Mnth; Yth Ldrshp Prog; Comm Volntr; 4-H; ArtClub; Chrch Yth Grp; Cmptr Clb; DARE; Ntl Beta Clb; NYLC; Chinese Clb; Yrbk; Altar Service; Bible Camp; Journalism; Teacher; Queens College

TESSMER, LINDSEY; GOWANDA, NY; GOWANDA HS; (SO); Hi Hnr Roll; Hnr Roll; Otst Ac Ach Awd; DARE; Lib Aide; Mus Clb; French Clb; Bskball (J); Scr Kpr (J); Sftball (J); Vllyball (J); Computer Science; Arts

TESTA, NICHOLAS; FRANKFORT, NY; FRANKFORT-SCHUYLER CTRL HS; (JR); Hi Hnr Roll; Nat Hon Sy; AL Aux Boys; Spanish Clb; Bsball (V); Bskball (V); Ftball (V); Wt Lftg (V); Sports Medicine; Pharmacy; Buffalo U; Ithaca College

THAI, YEN; JACKSON HEIGHTS, NY; FOREST HILLS HS; (JR); Perf Att; Sci Fairs; WWAHSS; Red Cr Aide; Key Club; Lib Aide; Mus Clb; SADD; Tchrs Aide; French Clb; Cr Ctry (V); Track (V); 2nd Place in Chemistry Science Fair; French; Syracuse U; Tufts U

THANCHAN, CHARLES; BEACON, NY; BEACON HS; (JR); Hi Hnr Roll; Hnr Roll; Nat Hon Sy; Otst Ac Ach Awd; Yth Ldrshp Prog; Chrch Yth Grp; DARE; Schol Bwl; Scouts; Boy Scouts, Youth Group; Karate; Architecture; Computer Engineer

THAQI, EGZON; BRONX, NY; MT ST MICHAEL AC; (JR); Hnr Roll; Perf Att; JSA; Spanish Clb; Ftball (J); Lcrsse (VJC); Stu Cncl (R); Spanish Honor Society Club; President of Junior States of America Club; Law and Legal Studies; New York U; Columbia U

THEBAUD, ANDREW; QUEENS VILLAGE, NY; MARTIN VAN BUREN HS; (JR); Hnr Roll; Nat Hon Sy; Perf Att; Comm Volntr; Jr Ach; Bnd; Bsball (V); Arista; Pre-Law / Major; MD / Degree; New York U; Binghamton U

THEBERT, NICHOLE; WILLIAMSON, NY; WILLIAMSON SR HS; (FR); Hi Hnr Roll; Hnr Roll; Otst Ac Ach Awd; Perf Att; Pres Ac Ftns Aw; St of Mnth; Comm Volntr; Spec Olymp Vol; Mus Clb; Bnd; Jzz Bnd; Mch Bnd; Cr Ctry (J); Track (J); Horse Back Riding Won Many Awards; All-County Band Award; Law/Lawyer; Anything with Horses (Not Vet)

THENGONE, DANIEL J; STATEN ISLAND, NY; SUSAN E WAGNER HS; (SO); F Lan Hn Soc; Hi Hnr Roll; Hnr Roll; Nat Hon Sy; Nat Sci Aw; Perf Att; Comm Volntr; Hosp Aide; Peer Tut/Med; Chrch Yth Grp; Emplmnt; Off Aide; Outdrs Clb; Svce Clb; Tchrs Aide; Vsity Clb; Bnd; Chr; Ch Chr; Orch; Cr Ctry (V); Track (V); Winner of NASA Space Flight Contest; 1st Place "Grandparents' Essay" Contest; MD; Harvard; Princeton

THOMAS, CAITLIN A; GENEVA, NY; GENEVA HS; (JR); Hi Hnr Roll; Hnr Roll; WWAHSS; Comm Volntr; Key Club; Bnd; Mch Bnd; Sftball (J); Swmg (V); Track (V); Sectional Qualifier for Swimming Past 3 Yrs.; State Qualifier for Swimming (MCA) Past 5 Yrs.; Teaching/Coaching; Trainer; Lemoyne-Owen College; Saint Lawrence U

THOMAS, CYRIL; STATEN ISLAND, NY; STUYVESANT HS; (SO); Hnr Roll; Nat Hon Sy; Perf Att; Sci Fairs; WWAHSS; Chess; Chrch Yth Grp; Key Club; Mth Clb/Tm; SP/M/VS; Stg Cre; Sch Ppr (R); Yrbk (R); Winner of Kali Prabha Award-Annual Award Handed Out By My Church; Attended Art Classes in the Fall of 2004; Architecture; Engineering; Massachusetts Institute of Technology; Cooper Union

THOMAS, DAWN; OWEGO, NY; OWEGO FREE AC; (SO); Hi Hnr Roll; MVP; Otst Ac Ach Awd; St of Mnth; WWAHSS; Yth Ldrshp Prog; Comm Volntr; Emplmnt; Chr; Fld Hky (JCL); Track (V L); Member of ADSIP (Alcohol Drug Student Info Program), Member of Youth Court; Member of Interact Club (Jr. Kiwanis Club); Pre-Law; Criminal Justice; Oneonta State U

THOMAS, ELEKTRA I; GLENMONT, NY; BETHLEHEM CTRL HS; (JR); Hnr Roll; Comm Volntr; ArtClub; Emplmnt; P to P St Amb Prg; Photog; Prom Com; Vsity Clb; Chrldg (J); Vllyball (VJ L); Stu Cncl (R); CR (R); Sch Ppr (P); Yrbk (R, P); Youth Court Juror; Charter President-Drawing Club; Photography; Visual Arts; Spelman College; Skidmore College

THOMAS, ERROL; ROSEDALE, NY; SPRINGFIELD GARDENS HS; (FR); Ctznshp Aw; St of Mnth; Chess; Emplmnt; FBLA; Bskball (J); Wt Lftg (J); Computers

THOMAS, JASON; JAMAICA, NY; PT WASHINGTON CHRISTIAN SCH; (FR); Hi Hnr Roll; Hnr Roll; Perf Att; ArtClub; Chess; Photog; Ch Chr; SP/M/VS; Track (J); Yrbk (R); The Presidential Active Lifestyle Award; Robotics; Paleontologist; Bob Jones U

THOMAS, JEEVAN; FARMINGVILLE, NY; SACHEM HS EAST; (SO); Ctznshp Aw; Hi Hnr Roll; Hnr Roll; MVP; Nat Hon Sy; Otst Ac Ach Awd; Perf Att; Sci/Math Olympn; St of Mnth; Yth Ldrshp Prog; Comm Volntr; Peer Tut/Med; Chrch Yth Grp; DARE; Drma Clb; Pep Squd; Sci Clb; Svce Clb; Spanish Clb; Ch Chr; Dnce; SP/M/VS; Bskball (J); Vllyball (J); Cl Off (P); CR (P); Homecoming Royalty- Duke; Martial Arts - 2nd Degree Blackbelt; Pediatrician; Surgeon; Columbia U; SUNY Stony Brook

THOMAS, JERRY; YONKERS, NY; GORTON HS; (SO); Ctznshp Aw; Nat Hon Sy; St of Mnth; Valdctrian; Comm Volntr; Hab For Humty Volntr; Red Cr Aide; Chrch Yth Grp; Spanish Clb; Bnd; Ch Chr; Principal's List / Club; Medical Magnet of Gorton Member; Medicine; Pharmacy; New York U; Columbia U

THOMAS, RYAN C; CORNING, NY; CORNING-PAINTED POST WEST HS; (SO); Hi Hnr Roll; Hnr Roll; Otst Ac Ach Awd; Pres Ac Ftns Aw; Comm Volntr; Peer Tut/Med; Chess; Drma Clb; Mus Clb; Acpl Chr; Bnd; Chr; Mch Bnd; Skiing; Music Performance; Computer Programming; Florida State U; U of North Carolina Charlotte

THOMAS, SHENIELLE; BROOKLYN, NY; ABRAHAM LINCOLN HS; (FR); Doctor / Physician; Biochemist; New York U

THOMAS, SHERVON B; BRONX, NY; BRONX SCH FOR LAW GOVT AND JUSTICE; (SO); Hnr Roll; Comm Volntr; Ch Chr; Dnce; Chrldg; Yrbk (R, P); Step Team; Honors Graphic Arts; Cinematography / Filming; Journalism; Bethune-Cookman College

THOMAS, STENNY; ELMONT, NY; SEWANHAKA HS; (JR); Hnr Roll; WWAHSS; Comm Volntr; Chrch Yth Grp; Voc Ind Clb Am; Chr; Ch Chr; Track (V); Physical Therapy; Optometry; New York U; New York Institute of Technology

THOMAS, WILLIAM A; ASHVILLE, NY; PANAMA CTRL SCH; (SR); Hnr Roll; MVP; Nat Hon Sy; Perf Att; St of Mnth; Comm Volntr; Emplmnt; Prom Com; Bskball (V CL); Ftball (V CL); Track (V CL); Cl Off (P); Stu Cncl (R); Computer Engineering; Rensselaer Polytechnic Institute; Rochester Institute of Technology

THOMAS JR, MICHAEL D; BROOKLYN, NY; SOUTH SHORE HS; (SR); Perf Att; Yth Ldrshp Prog; Comm Volntr; Chrch Yth Grp; Emplmnt; Vsity Clb; Bsball (V); Golf (V); Sccr (V C); Goal of the Year (Soccer) (Undefeated Brooklyn Champs); Most Helpful Award (Job) Most Improved; Communication, Journalism; TV and Radio Broadcasting; Lemoyne; Seton Hill

THOMPSON, ALEXIS M; YOUNGSTOWN, NY; LEWISTON PORTER HS; (JR); Nat Hon Sy; Hosp Aide; Peer Tut/Med; Emplmnt; Track (J); Junior Counselor at YMCA Summer Camp; Guidance Counselor; Political Advisor; Washington U

THOMPSON, ALISHA; STATEN ISLAND, NY; CURTIS HS; (SO); Hnr Roll; Perf Att; WWAHSS; Comm Volntr; Peer Tut/Med; Chr; SP/M/VS; Arista Honor Society; Leadership Award; Master's; Bachelor's; Harvard; New York U

THOMPSON, JASON M; NEWBURGH, NY; STEWART AC; (JR); Hi Hnr Roll; Hnr Roll; Otst Ac Ach Awd; Comm Volntr; DARE; Lib Aide; Tchrs Aide; Tech Clb; Chr; Business Law; US History and Government; Mount St Mary's; Yale U

THOMPSON, KEVIN; NEW YORK, NY; FREDERICK DOUGLASS SEC SCH; (FR); Ctznshp Aw; Hi Hnr Roll; Otst Ac Ach Awd; Perf Att; St of Mnth; Valdctrian; Comm Volntr; Peer Tut/Med; Chess; Dbte Team; Drma Clb; Photog; Scouts; Bnd; Chr; Clr Grd; Stg Cre; Bsball (J); Dvng (J); Ftball (V); Mar Art (L); Sccr (J); Swmg (V); Tennis (L); Cl Off (P); Stu Cncl (T); CR (R); Greatest Amount of Hours in Community Service; Become an Attorney; A Degree in Field Of Law; Harvard Law School; Yale U

THOMPSON, LINDSEY; WADDINGTON, NY; MADRID-WADDINGTON CTRL SCH; (SO); Hi Hnr Roll; Hnr Roll; Nat Hon Sy; WWAHSS; Comm Volntr; Red Cr Aide; Chrch Yth Grp; Key Club; French Clb; Bnd; Chr; Mch Bnd; Stg Cre; GAA (V); Sftball (V); Master's Degree

THOMPSON, MARY; FRESH MEADOWS, NY; FLUSHING HS; (SR); Ctznshp Aw; St of Mnth; Chrch Yth Grp; Emplmnt; Off Aide; Chr; SP/M/VS; Cr Ctry; Track; The Queens County District Attorney Award; Invitation to National Student Leadership Conference; Law; Physical Therapy; U of Central Florida; U of South Carolina

THOMPSON, OLIVIA; BLUE POINT, NY; BAYPORT BLUE POINT HS; (SO); Hnr Roll; Nat Hon Sy; Perf Att; Pres Ac Ftns Aw; St of Mnth; Chess; Track (V); Stu Cncl (R); Sch Ppr (R); Medicine; New York U; Oxford U

THOMPSON, SARA M; STATEN ISLAND, NY; SUSAN E WAGNER HS; (FR); Ctznshp Aw; Hi Hnr Roll; MVP; Sci Fairs; St of Mnth; Drma Clb; Sci Clb; Svce Clb; Tmpl Yth Grp; Chr; SP/M/VS; Swmg (V L); Quality of Life Program-Borough Leader; Forensic Science; West Chester U; The College of New Jersey

THOMPSON, SHAKISHA; NEW YORK, NY; WASHINGTON IRVING HS; (FR); Hnr Roll; Perf Att; St of Mnth; Comm Volntr; Peer Tut/Med; DARE; CREATIVE Clb; Chr; Dnce; Bskball; Chrldg; Track; Stu Cncl (R); Teacher; Nurse; John Jay; NYU New York U

THOMPSON, TEMESHA A; MT VERNON, NY; BLESSED SACRAMENT HS; (JR); Hnr Roll; Nat Hon Sy; Perf Att; Pres Ac Ftns Aw; St of Mnth; Ch Chr; Bskball (V); Sftball (V); National Junior Honor Society; Accounting; Law; U of Central Florida; U of South Florida

THORESON, AMBIKA; BROOKLYN, NY; LAGUARDIA ARTS HS; (JR); Nat Hon Sy; Comm Volntr; ArtClub; Off Aide; Art Honor League-Member; Art History; Anthropology

THORNELL, LISA M; SEAFORD, NY; SEAFORD HS; (SR); Ctznshp Aw; Hi Hnr Roll; Nat Hon Sy; Otst Ac Ach Awd; St of Mnth; Comm Volntr; Peer Tut/Med; 4-H; ArtClub; Emplmnt; Fr of Library; Key Club; Lib Aide; Schol Bwl; SADD; Track (J); Vllyball (VJ L); Cl Off (S); Lit Mag (E); Sch Ppr (R); Yrbk (R); National Honor Society - Secretary; All-County Art Achievement Award - 2005; Pre-Law; Art History; Marist College; The College of New Jersey

THORNER, TIFFANY J; CALVERTON, NY; RIVERHEAD HS; (JR); F Lan Hn Soc; Hi Hnr Roll; Otst Ac Ach Awd; Sci Fairs; Peer Tut/Med; AL Aux Girls; ArtClub; Emplmnt; Fr of Library; Mus Clb; ROTC; Scouts; Chr; Clr Grd; Drl Tm; Cl Off (V); Sch Ppr (E); NJROTC; WISE; English; Business; SUNY Stony Brook

THORNTON, DAKITA; JAMAICA, NY; GATEWAY TO HEALTH SCIENCES SCH; (JR); Hnr Roll; Comm Volntr; Spanish Clb; Dnce; Drl Tm; Sccr; Vllyball; Yrbk (R); National Award for Most Improved in Math; MBA in Business; Business Management; St. John's U; Baruch College

THORNTON, KATHARINE; SAUGERTIES, NY; SAUGERTIES HS; (SR); Hi Hnr Roll; Hnr Roll; Nat Hon Sy; WWAHSS; Comm Volntr; Drma Clb; Key Club; Scouts; Spanish Clb; SP/M/VS; Bskball (J); Sftball (JC); Track (V); Vllyball (VJC); Stu Cncl (S); Yrbk (E); Girl Scout Silver Award; 2003-2004 Varsity Volleyball Sportsmanship Award; Atmospheric Science; Education; U of Albany; Florida Institute of Technology

THORP, NATALIE N; GEORGETOWN, NY; OTSELIC VALLEY; (SR); Hi Hnr Roll; Hnr Roll; Nat Hon Sy; Otst Ac Ach Awd; Perf Att; St of Mnth; Comm Volntr; Drma Clb; Emplmnt; Prom Com; SADD; Chr; SP/M/VS; Chrldg (VJ L); Sccr (VJ L); Cl Off (V, S); Cosmetology; Massage Therapy

TIERNEY, EAIN; TICONDEROGA, NY; TICONDEROGA HS; (FR); Hnr Roll; Perf Att; Pres Ac Ftns Aw; Scouts; Cr Ctry (V); Golf (V); Track (V); Stu Cncl (R); Order of the Arrow in Boy Scouts - Life Scout

TIERNEY, MICHELLE L; WANTAGH, NY; SEAFORD HS; (SR); Hi Hnr Roll; Hnr Roll; Nat Hon Sy; Comm Volntr; Peer Tut/Med; 4-H; Drma Clb; Key Club; SADD; Bnd; Clr Grd; Dnce; Mch Bnd; Fld Hky (VJC); Track (V C); Vllyball (V); Tri-M Music Honor Society; Accounting; Business Management; Manhattan College

TING, MICHELLE; FOREST HILLS, NY; HUNTER COLLEGE HS; (JR); Nat Mrt LOC; Sci Fairs; Comm Volntr; Peer Tut/Med; Chrch Yth Grp; Emplmnt; Key Club; Chr; Cr Ctry (J, V); Track (J, V); Sch Ppr (R); Received Writing Awards such as the Scholastic Writing Gold Key; Am Currently Co-president of a Film and Theater Club, and the Key Club at My School; Biology; English; Columbia U, New York, NY; Dartmouth College, Hanover, NH

TITILAWO, GOODNESS; BROOKLYN, NY; IS 218 JAMES PETER SINNO; (SR); Hnr Roll; Otst Ac Ach Awd; Perf Att; St of Mnth; Comm Volntr; ArtClub; Chrch Yth Grp; Cmptr Clb; Dbte Team; Photog; Svce Clb; Tech Clb; Bnd; Chr; Ch Chr; SP/M/VS; Lit Mag (E, R); Yrbk (E, R, P); Making School Promotional Videos; Making School Website

TITILAWO, MERCY; BROOKLYN, NY; IS 218 JAMES PETER SINNO; (SR); Hnr Roll; Otst Ac Ach Awd; Perf Att; St of Mnth; Comm Volntr; Chrch Yth Grp; Cmptr Clb; Photog; Tech Clb; Bnd; Chr; Ch Chr; SP/M/VS; Lit Mag (E, R); Yrbk (E, R, P); Making Promotional Videos

TLATELPA, BEATRICE; MT VERNON, NY; MT VERNON HS; (FR); 4H Awd; Ctznshp Aw; F Lan Hn Soc; Hi Hnr Roll; Hnr Roll; Nat Hon Sy; Otst Ac Ach Awd; Perf Att; Sci Fairs; St of Mnth; Peer Tut/Med; Bnd; Mch Bnd; Pep Bnd; Cl Off (R); Stu Cncl (R); Pediatrician; Child Psychologist; Columbia U; New York U

TOALA, ASHLEY; MERRICK, NY; CALHOUN HS; (SO); Hnr Roll; Comm Volntr; DECA; Emplmnt; Key Club; Photog; Scouts; Lcrsse; DECA Regional Winner; Marketing; Fashion

TOM, JENNIFER; FLUSHING, NY; BENJAMIN CARDOZO HS; (SO); F Lan Hn Soc; Hi Hnr Roll; Perf Att; Sci Fairs; WWAHSS; Key Club; Sci Clb; Sch Ppr (R); Metropolitan New York Math Fair-Silver Medal

TONETTI, LAUREN; FAIRPORT, NY; FAIRPORT HS; (JR); Hnr Roll; Nat Hon Sy; St Schl; St of Mnth; Comm Volntr; Emplmnt; Skiing (V L); Track (J); National Honor Society; Rochester Skating Club; Biology; Cornell U; Syracuse U

TONG, EVAN; AMHERST, NY; JAMES MADISON HS; (SR); Hnr Roll; WWAHSS; Mth Clb/Tm; MuAlphaTh; Sci Clb; Math Honor Roll; Pharmacy; U of Buffalo

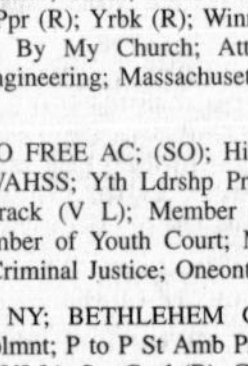

Thompson, Mary
Flushing HS
Fresh Meadows, NY

Thomas, Elektra I
Bethlehem Ctrl HS
Glenmont, NY

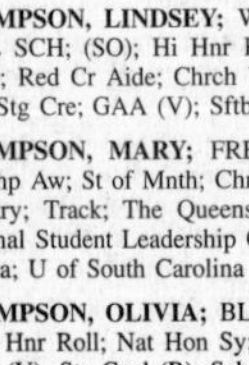

Thomas, Caitlin A
Geneva HS
Geneva, NY

National
Honor Roll
Spring 2005

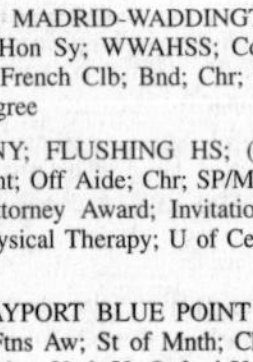

Thebert, Nichole
Williamson SR HS
Williamson, NY

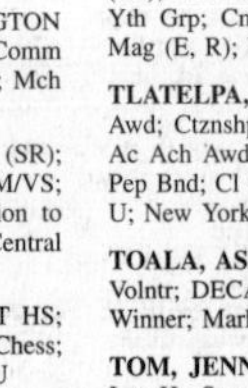

Thomas, Jeevan
Sachem HS East
Farmingville, NY

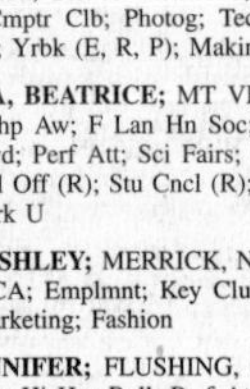

Thorp, Natalie N
Otselic Valley
Georgetown, NY

TOPOROWSKI, AMY K; SAUGERTIES, NY; SAUGERTIES HS; (JR); All Am Sch; Hi Hnr Roll; Nat Hon Sy; Otst Ac Ach Awd; Pres Ac Ftns Aw; Pres Sch; WWAHSS; Yth Ldrshp Prog; Peer Tut/Med; Key Club; Lcrsse (V C); Sccr (V C); Track (V); Key Club, Ski Club; Pre-Med; MD; St. John Fisher, Skidmore College; Elizabeth College

TORKIVER, ARTHUR G; GREAT NECK, NY; GREAT NECK SOUTH HS; (JR); Hnr Roll; Otst Ac Ach Awd; DECA; Emplmnt; Russian Clb; Bnd; Jzz Bnd; DECA States Finalist in Role Play; Law; Psychiatry; Cornell U; New York U

TOROSJAN, SABINA; BROOKLYN, NY; LAGUARDIA HS; (JR); Jzz Bnd; Orch; SP/M/VS; Recipient of Children Found for the Arts Grant; 2nd Place (Violin) in Warner College Competition; Instrumental Solo Performance (Violin); Music-Classical; Juilliard College of Music; Manhattan School of Music

TORRES, AMANDA; WARWICK, NY; WARWICK VALLEY; (SO); Ctznshp Aw; Hnr Roll; St of Mnth; Peer Tut/Med; Pep Squd; P to P St Amb Prg; Chr; Track (V); Cl Off (R); Stu Cncl (R); Sojourner Truth Award; Law; U of Connecticut; Oswego State

TORRES, HAYDEE; UTICA, NY; THOMAS R PROCTOR HS; (JR); ArtClub; Chrch Yth Grp; DARE; Scouts; Tmpl Yth Grp; Fashion Illustrator; Artist; Fashion Institute of Technology; Utica College

TORRES, JASMIN; UNIONVILLE, NY; MINISINK VALLEY HS; (SO); ArtClub; Drma Clb; Key Club; Chr; SP/M/VS; Thespian Troupe 5169; Drug and Alcohol Poster Contest Honorable Mention; Art; Architecture

TORRES, KATHERINE; YONKERS, NY; LINCOLN HS; (SO); Hnr Roll; Perf Att; WWAHSS; Comm Volntr; Hosp Aide; Peer Tut/Med; Jr Ach; Tchrs Aide; Dnce; Over 500 Hrs of Volunteer Services; Medicine; Surgery; North Carolina U; New York U

TRACEY, BRIANNA; CHESTER, NY; MONROE-WOODBURY HS; (SO); Hi Hnr Roll; Pres Ac Ftns Aw; Comm Volntr; Emplmnt; Lib Aide; Mth Clb/Tm; Photog; Vsity Clb; Chr; Bskball (J); Cr Ctry (J L); Track (V L); Scholar Athlete Award; Education; Visual Art; Siena College; U of Miami

TRAMP, CHRISTOPHER; FLUSHING, NY; HOLY CROSS HS; (FR); Hi Hnr Roll; Otst Ac Ach Awd; WWAHSS; Comm Volntr; Tchrs Aide; Sch Ppr (R); National Junior Honor Society (Arista); Columbus Citizens Foundation Scholarship; Mathematics; Journalism

TREMBLAY, ERIKA L; BREWSTER, NY; BREWSTER HS; (SO); Hi Hnr Roll; Drma Clb; Chr; Dnce; SP/M/VS; Vllyball (J); Performing Arts; Law; Boston U; New York U

TREMBLAY, LAURA A; MIDDLE GROVE, NY; SARATOGA SPRINGS HS; (FR); 4H Awd; Hi Hnr Roll; 4-H; DARE; Drma Clb; Mus Clb; Ch Chr; Orch; SP/M/VS; Tennis (J); Saratoga Springs Youth Orchestra Member; Medicine; Business; New York U; Cornell U

TRESIDDER II, ROGER A; EDWARDS, NY; EDWARDS-KNOX CTRL SCH; (JR); Hi Hnr Roll; Hnr Roll; Nat Hon Sy; WWAHSS; Chrch Yth Grp; DARE; Mus Clb; Prom Com; Scouts; Vsity Clb; Bnd; Mch Bnd; Bsball (J); Bskball (VJ); Sccr (VJ); Wt Lftg (VJ); Cl Off (V); Yrbk

TREZEVANT, BRIAN; BROOKLYN, NY; ABRAHAM LINCOLN HS; (SO); All Am Sch; Fut Prb Slvr; Hi Hnr Roll; Nat Ldrshp Svc; Nat Stu Ath Day Aw; Otst Ac Ach Awd; Perf Att; Sci Fairs; St of Mnth; Yth Ldrshp Prog; CARE; Comm Volntr; Peer Tut/Med; Cmptr Clb; Dbte Team; Drma Clb; FTA; Lttrmn Clb; Mus Clb; NYLC; Off Aide; Chr; Clr Grd; Dnce; SP/M/VS; Cr Ctry; Golf; Track; Vllyball; Wt Lftg; Cl Off; Stu Cncl; CR; President of Leadership Program; Teaching; Law; John Jay College; Brooklyn College

TRIANTAFILIS, CHRIS; MERRICK, NY; JOHN F KENNEDY HS; (FR); Hnr Roll; FBLA; Ice Hky (J); Business; Economics; Cornell; Boston U

TRIGO, FRANCINE N; BROOKLYN, NY; CHRIST THE KING REG HS; (SO); Hnr Roll; Nat Hon Sy; Otst Ac Ach Awd; Peer Tut/Med; Chrch Yth Grp; Pep Squd; Chr; Ch Chr; Chrldg (V); Stu Cncl (R); CR (R); Ob/Gyn Field / Medical; Master's Degree; New York U; SUNY Stony Brook

TRIPI, ALICIA; BUFFALO, NY; CHEEKTOWAGA HS; (SO); Hnr Roll; Nat Hon Sy; Comm Volntr; Peer Tut/Med; DARE; Emplmnt; FTA; Jr Ach; Tchrs Aide; SP/M/VS; Vllyball (J); Cl Off (V); Stu Cncl (R); Future Teachers; Elementary Teacher; Canisius College; Buffalo State College

TROFIMENKO, ISAIAH; SCHENECTADY, NY; SCHENECTADY HS; (FR); Swmg (J); Tennis (J); Piano; Russian / Slavonic Languages; Schenectady Community College

TRUELSON, JENA; HAMLIN, NY; HILTON HS; (JR); Hi Hnr Roll; Hnr Roll; Nat Hon Sy; Comm Volntr; 4-H; Emplmnt; FBLA; Mth Clb/Tm; Chr; Dnce; Swmg; Business Management; Finance; U of Central Florida

TRUFFI, AMANDA; WESTTOWN, NY; (SO); Hi Hnr Roll; Hnr Roll; Drma Clb; Key Club; Photog; Latin Clb; Chr; Bskball; I Am in SADD.; Honors Classes (English, Math); Architecture and Design; Engineering

TRUMMER, ANDREA; GLEN OAKS, NY; ST FRANCIS PREP SCH; (JR); Perf Att; Comm Volntr; Key Club; Journalism; International Studies; New York U; Northeastern U

TRUONG, SANDY; BROOKLYN, NY; BENJAMIN BANNEKER AC; (SO); Ctznshp Aw; F Lan Hn Soc; Hnr Roll; Nat Hon Sy; Otst Ac Ach Awd; Perf Att; St of Mnth; Valdctrian; Comm Volntr; Peer Tut/Med; Fr of Library; Lib Aide; Off Aide; Tchrs Aide; Clr Grd; CR (R); Principal's Award; Arista & Archon Awards; Pre-Med; New York U; Harvard U

TSAI, ANDREW S; BAYSIDE, NY; STUYVESANT HS; (JR); Hnr Roll; Nat Mrt LOC; Comm Volntr; Chrch Yth Grp; Emplmnt; Key Club; Svce Clb; Vsity Clb; French Clb; Bnd; Chr; SP/M/VS; Stg Cre; Golf (V); Vsy Clb (VJ); Lit Mag (E); Gold Medal At 2003 Math Fair; Mastery Level Certificates in Regents Chemistry/Physics; Pre-Medicine; Biomedical Engineering; Duke U; Dartmouth College

TSANG, RAVANA; STATEN ISLAND, NY; CURTIS HS; (SR); Amnsty Intl; Comm Volntr; Peer Tut/Med; Chrch Yth Grp; Key Club; Mth Clb/Tm; Prom Com; Bnd; Ch Chr; Drm Mjr; Mch Bnd; Swmg (V); Cl Off (R); Stu Cncl (R); Lit Mag (E, R); Sch Ppr (R, P); Yrbk (E, R, P); National Honor Society; Leadership Team Member; International Business; Marketing; New York U

TSATSKIN, MICHAEL; BROOKLYN, NY; JOHN DEWEY HS; (FR); Hnr Roll; MVP; Bdmtn; Fld Hky; Sccr; Wt Lftg; Business; Professional Hockey Player; Boston U; Michigan State U

TSO, JENNY; BROOKLYN, NY; MIDWOOD HS; (SO); Hi Hnr Roll; Perf Att; St of Mnth; Comm Volntr; Key Club; Lib Aide; Off Aide; Stg Cre; Archon Honor Society; Social Science; Pharmacy; SUNY Stony Brook; SUNY Binghamton

TUCHRELO, MACKENZIE; WILLIAMSON, NY; WILLIAMSON CTRL HS; (JR); Hnr Roll; Nat Hon Sy; St of Mnth; WWAHSS; Comm Volntr; Peer Tut/Med; Chrch Yth Grp; Emplmnt; Prom Com; Bnd; Chr; Drm Mjr; Mch Bnd; Sccr (J); Studied Dance for 12 Years; Won Awards for Dance; Theater & Dance; Teaching

TULL, SHEILA; SYRACUSE, NY; HENNINGER HS; (FR); Sci Fairs; Chrch Yth Grp; Tennis (J); Merit Roll; Pediatrician

TUMAY, KELLY; FLORAL PARK, NY; FLORAL PARK MEMORIAL HS; (JR); F Lan Hn Soc; Hi Hnr Roll; Hnr Roll; WWAHSS; Yth Ldrshp Prog; Peer Tut/Med; Scouts; Chr; SP/M/VS; Chrldg (VJCL); Dvng (VJ); Fld Hky (V); Ftball (V); Swmg (C); CR (T); Pharmacist; St John's U

TUN, SANDY; NEW YORK, NY; BRONX HS OF SCIENCE; (SO); Hi Hnr Roll; Hnr Roll; Nat Hon Sy; Sci Fairs; Valdctrian; Comm Volntr; ArtClub; Key Club; Lib Aide; Off Aide; Spch Team; Tchrs Aide; Sch Ppr (R); LEAP - League of Environmental and Animal Protection; Lunar New Year Production; Doctor's Degree; Business Management; Cornell U; Columbia U

TUOHY, LAUREN; SEAFORD, NY; SEAFORD HS; (JR); Hi Hnr Roll; Nat Hon Sy; Otst Ac Ach Awd; Comm Volntr; Emplmnt; FCA; Key Club; SADD; Knights of Columbus Squirettes; Pre-Med; Forensic Science

TURAY, MEMUNATU; BROOKLYN, NY; EAST NEW YORK FAMILY AC; (FR); Comm Volntr; ArtClub; Chrch Yth Grp; Dbte Team; Vllyball (J); Academic Award; National Honor Roll; Medical Field

TURCOANE, CHRISTINA; MIDDLE VILLAGE, NY; CHRIST THE KING HS; (SO); Hi Hnr Roll; Nat Hon Sy; Sci Fairs; Emplmnt; Key Club; Vllyball (J); Stu Cncl (R); PDHP Member; International Club Member; Attorney; Real Estate Broker; St John's U; Columbia U

TURKEL, ANNI; NEW CITY, NY; CLARKSTOWN NORTH; (SR); F Lan Hn Soc; WWAHSS; Yth Ldrshp Prog; Comm Volntr; Emplmnt; Photog; Tmpl Yth Grp; Dnce; Cr Ctry (V); Sftball (J); Track (C); Sch Ppr (R); English Honor Society; Social Studies Honor Society; English Major; Public Relations Major; Bryn Mawr College

TUROSE, ALYSSA; AUBURN, NY; SKANEATELES HS; (JR); Hi Hnr Roll; Nat Hon Sy; Salutrn; Comm Volntr; Chr; Bskball (VJ); Cr Ctry (J); Sftball (VJ); Lit Mag (E); Princeton U; Middlebury College

TUROWSKI, KRYSTIAN; FAR ROCKAWAY, NY; CHRIST THE KING HS; (JR); ArtClub; Key Club

TUSHAR, MOHAMMED; BRONX, NY; BROOKLYN FRIENDS ACAD; (JR); Perf Att; Sci Fairs; Sci/Math Olympn; Comm Volntr; Hab For Humty Volntr; Peer Tut/Med; Chess; Dbte Team; Mth Clb/Tm; Mod UN; Off Aide; Prom Com; Tchrs Aide; Vsity Clb; Chr; SP/M/VS; Bskball (V); Cr Ctry (V); Scr Kpr; Sccr (V); Cl Off (S); Yrbk; Medicine: Doctor; Johns Hopkins University; Columbia U

TYLER, MALLORY M; WESTPORT, NY; WESTPORT CTRL HS; (JR); 4H Awd; Hnr Roll; Nat Hon Sy; Otst Ac Ach Awd; Sci Fairs; Comm Volntr; 4-H; DARE; Drma Clb; Emplmnt; Prom Com; Scouts; SP/M/VS; Bskball; Sccr; Sftball; Cl Off (P, S); Dentistry

TYNER, ELAIDA; MONROE, NY; MONROE-WOODBURY HS; (JR); Hi Hnr Roll; Hnr Roll; Nat Hon Sy; Otst Ac Ach Awd; Perf Att; WWAHSS; Comm Volntr; Emplmnt; Fr of Library; Orange-Ulster BOCES (Health/Nursing); Nursing (RN/MSN); Westchester Community College

UBALDO, LIZBETH E; BROOKLYN, NY; ABRAHAM LINCOLN HS; (SO); Hnr Roll; Perf Att; Sci Fairs; St of Mnth; Peer Tut/Med; Emplmnt; Key Club; Teacher; Doctor; Brooklyn College; New York U

UDDIN, KABIR; BROOKLYN, NY; FRANKLIN K LANE HS; (SO); Hi Hnr Roll; Hnr Roll; Nat Hon Sy; Otst Ac Ach Awd; Perf Att; St of Mnth; Comm Volntr; Peer Tut/Med; Lib Aide; Tchrs Aide; Arista Membership; Math Honors; Master's-Law; Doctorate-Business Law; St. Johns U; New York U

UDDIN, RAFIA; SUNNYSIDE, NY; NEWTOWN HS; (JR); Sci Fairs; WWAHSS; Comm Volntr; Peer Tut/Med; ArtClub; Key Club; Photog; Svce Clb; Tchrs Aide; Stg Cre; Member of Mock Trial/Moot Court; Achievement in I-Net Computers Stock Exchange from the N.Y. Stock Exchange; Master's in Business Administration; Bachelor's in Marketing; City U of New York Baruch; State U of New York Binghamton

UDHO, VICKRAM; BROOKLYN, NY; ENY TRANSIT TECH HS; (SR); Hi Hnr Roll; Hnr Roll; Otst Ac Ach Awd; Perf Att; St of Mnth; Comm Volntr; Bsball (V); Bskball (V); Wt Lftg (V); Electrical Engineering; Construction Management; New York City College of Technology; York College

UPCHURCH, PAIJAH A; JAMAICA, NY; MATH SCIENCE RESEARCH TECH HS; (SR); Otst Ac Ach Awd; Perf Att; Sci Fairs; Sci/Math Olympn; St of Mnth; Peer Tut/Med; Chrch Yth Grp; Off Aide; Prom Com; Sch Ppr (E, R); Yrbk (R); Criminal Justice; Forensics; St John's U; John Jay College of Criminal Justice

URAGA DOMINGUEZ, FERNANDO JR; BRONX, NY; COLUMBUS HS; (FR); Hnr Roll; Sci Fairs; St of Mnth; Chess; DARE; Tchrs Aide; Dnce; Sftball (JCL); CR (P); City Council Awards

URBAN, KELSEY R G; GENEVA, NY; GENEVA HS; (FR); Hnr Roll; WWAHSS; Comm Volntr; Emplmnt; Key Club; Chr; Ch Chr; Dnce; Sccr (J); Cl Off (T)

URO, AHMED; POUGHKEEPSIE, NY; ROY C KETCHAM HS; (JR); Drma Clb; SP/M/VS; Stg Cre; Bskball; Business Co-Opp; Genetics; Forensic Science; St John's U; Marist College

USCHAKOW, DENISE K; LEVITTOWN, NY; DIVISION AVE HS; (JR); Hi Hnr Roll; Hnr Roll; WWAHSS; Peer Tut/Med; Emplmnt; Key Club; Photog; Bskball (J); Sccr (J); Sftball (VJC); Has a Job as a Cashier; Plays Two Softball Leagues; Psychology; Education; State U of New York; Iona College

UY, CATHERINE; NEW YORK, NY; THE BREARLEY SCH; (FR); Comm Volntr; Hosp Aide; Chr; Dnce; Gmnstcs (V); Lcrsse (V); Vllyball (J); Kuntz Art Collection Award; Coaches Award - Volleyball; Medicine; Science; Princeton U; Yale U

VAICIUNAS JR, MICHAEL J; LEVITTOWN, NY; MAC ARTHUR HS; (SR); Hnr Roll; Perf Att; St of Mnth; Comm Volntr; Chess; Emplmnt; Key Club; Off Aide; Sci Clb; President - Garden Club; To Open a Martial Arts Studio; Nassau Community College; SUNY Farmingdale

VAIDYA, KHUSHBOO J; STATEN ISLAND, NY; PT RICHMOND HS; (FR); Hnr Roll; Perf Att; Yth Ldrshp Prog; Comm Volntr; Fr of Library; Lib Aide; Tchrs Aide; Swmg; Track; Asian Culture Club; Pediatrician / Doctor; Chemistry; Harvard U; Princeton U

VALDEBENITO, EVA; FLUSHING, NY; THE MARY LOUIS AC; (SO); F Lan Hn Soc; Hi Hnr Roll; Hnr Roll; WWAHSS; Comm Volntr; Hosp Aide; Drma Clb; French Clb; Stg Cre; Cr Ctry (J); Scr Kpr (J); Tennis; Track (J); CR (R); All in JCL National Latin Outstanding; Medical Doctor; Columbia U; New York U

VALENTINE, JOHN C; ISLAND PARK, NY; WEST HEMPSTEAD HS; (SR); F Lan Hn Soc; Hi Hnr Roll; Hnr Roll; Nat Hon Sy; St of Mnth; WWAHSS; Dbte Team; Emplmnt; Key Club; Quiz Bowl; Orch; Vllyball (V); Mechanical Engineering; Carnegie Mellon U

VALERIO, ALISON R; GENEVA, NY; GENEVA HS; (JR); Hi Hnr Roll; Hnr Roll; Nat Hon Sy; WWAHSS; Comm Volntr; Peer Tut/Med; Red Cr Aide; Emplmnt; Key Club; Prom Com; Vsity Clb; Bnd; Mch Bnd; Pep Bnd; Bskball (V); GAA (V); Lcrsse (V); PP Ftbl (V); Sccr (V); Stu Cncl (R); CR (R); Yrbk (R); Education-High School Teacher; History; Dickinson College; Loyola College

VALONE, BRADLY; SILVER CREEK, NY; SILVER CREEK HS; (JR); 4H Awd; Hnr Roll; Nat Hon Sy; WWAHSS; Peer Tut/Med; 4-H; Spanish Clb; Secondary Teacher / Math; Mathematician; Indiana Wesleyan U; Jamestown Community College

VAN BRAMER, ALYSABETH; SCHENECTADY, NY; SCHENECTADY HS; (SO); F Lan Hn Soc; Hi Hnr Roll; Hnr Roll; Otst Ac Ach Awd; USAA; WWAHSS; Comm Volntr; Hosp Aide; DARE; Emplmnt; Schol Bwl; Spanish Clb; Bskball; Mar Art (L); Bowling-Varsity; Rowing Crew-JV; PhD Psychology-Criminology; Medical Doctor-Psychiatrist

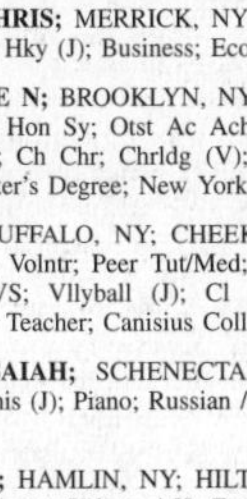
Upchurch, Paijah A
Math Science Research Tech HS
Jamaica, NY

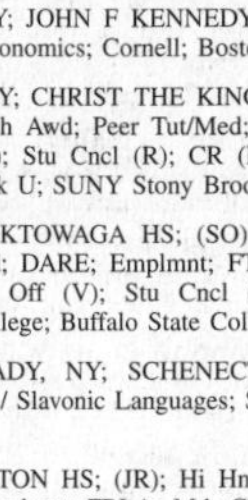
Turowski, Krystian
Christ The King HS
Far Rockaway, NY

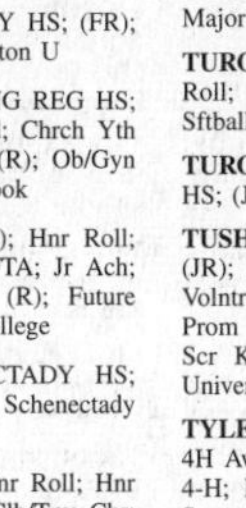
Tremblay, Erika L
Brewster HS
Brewster, NY

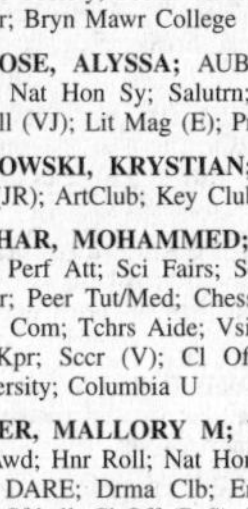
Tramp, Christopher
Holy Cross HS
Flushing, NY

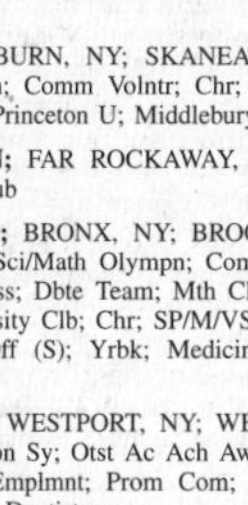
Torkiver, Arthur G
Great Neck South HS
Great Neck, NY

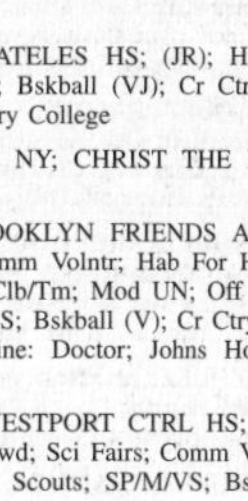
Torres, Amanda
Warwick Valley
Warwick, NY

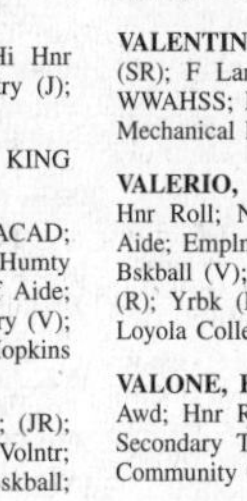
Turay, Memunatu
East New York Family AC
Brooklyn, NY

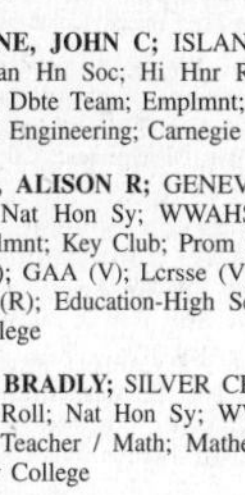
Udho, Vickram
ENY Transit Tech HS
Brooklyn, NY

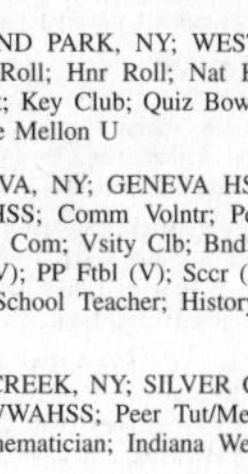
Uraga Dominguez, Fernando Jr
Columbus HS
Bronx, NY

VAN DERWERKEN, CEMI; ESPERANCE, NY; SCHOHARIE HS; (JR); Ctznshp Aw; F Lan Hn Soc; Hi Hnr Roll; Otst Ac Ach Awd; Perf Att; Pres Ac Ftns Aw; Pres Sch; St of Mnth; WWAHSS; Peer Tut/Med; 4-H; Chrch Yth Grp; Drma Clb; Emplmnt; Key Club; MuAlphaTh; Mus Clb; Prom Com; Bnd; Chr; Ch Chr; Dnce; Bskball (VJ); Cr Ctry (V); Gmnstcs; Skiing (J); Sccr (J); Track (VJC); Vsy Clb (V); Cl Off (T); Stu Cncl (V); CR (R); Secretary of Key Club; Secretary of Band; Music Ed./CMP Piano; Psychology; Brigham Young U

VAN DE WATER, COURTNEY K; KINGSTON, NY; SAUGERTIES HS; (SO); Ctznshp Aw; Hi Hnr Roll; Hnr Roll; Kwnis Aw; Otst Ac Ach Awd; WWAHSS; Comm Volntr; Spec Olymp Vol; Key Club; Scouts; Chr; Cr Ctry (V); Girl Scout Silver Award; Cooking; Business; Culinary; Johnson & Wales U

VANEENWYK, EMILY; BENGEN, NY; CORNERSTONE CHRISTIAN AC; (JR); Hi Hnr Roll; Comm Volntr; Chrch Yth Grp; Chr; SP/M/VS; Sccr (V); Elementary Education; Houghton College

VANETTEN, TRINITY B; LODI, NY; SOUTH SENECA HS; (JR); Hnr Roll; Otst Ac Ach Awd; Red Cr Aide; FTA; Pep Squd; Tchrs Aide; Wdwrkg Clb; Dnce; Chrldg (J); Leadership Award in Spanish; Most Improved Student Award; Child Development; Teacher; Ithaca College; Albany U

VAN LAM, KEVIN; POUGHKEEPSIE, NY; POUGHKEEPSIE HS; (SO); Hi Hnr Roll; Sci/Math Olympn; Hosp Aide; Mth Clb/Tm; Bnd; SP/M/VS; Tennis (V); Arts

VAN OMMEREN, MIRANDA; UNIONDALE, NY; UNIONDALE HS; (SO); Hi Hnr Roll; Hnr Roll; Otst Ac Ach Awd; Pres Sch; Comm Volntr; Peer Tut/Med; Chrch Yth Grp; Emplmnt; FBLA; Key Club; Scouts; Svce Clb; Spch Team; Bnd; Ch Chr; Mch Bnd; Sftball (J); Math Honor Society; Pre-Medicine; Doctorates Degree; Cornell U

VAN TYNE, ROBERT J; ROCHESTER, NY; RUSH-HENRIETTA HS; (SR); Hi Hnr Roll; Hnr Roll; Nat Hon Sy; Otst Ac Ach Awd; St of Mnth; Comm Volntr; Spanish Clb; Bnd; Tennis (VJCL); Computer Engineering; Software Engineering; Monroe Community College; Rochester Institute of Technology

VAN WAGENEN, CHRISTOPHER T; ALBANY, NY; GUILDERLAND HS; (JR); Sccr; Track (J); Yrbk (E); Key Club Officer; Physical Science; Engineering

VAN WART, TRACIE-LYNN; CORAM, NY; LONGWOOD HS; (SR); Hi Hnr Roll; MVP; Pres Ac Ftns Aw; Hab For Humty Volntr; Peer Tut/Med; Spec Olymp Vol; ArtClub; DARE; Emplmnt; Fr of Library; FTA; Photog; Scouts; Chr; Orch; SP/M/VS; Sccr; Track (V L); Internship; Secondary Education / Biology; St Joseph's College

VAREIKAITE, SIMONA; BRONX, NY; BRONX SCH FOR LAW GOVT AND JUSTICE; (SO); Dbte Team; Scouts; Vsity Clb; Bskball (V); Sftball (V C); Jeter's Leaders; Knockout-Challenge - Runner Up; Criminal Justice; Psychology; St John's U; U of Vermont

VARER, MARGARITA D; HUNTINGTON, NY; HUNTINGTON HS; (JR); Hi Hnr Roll; Hnr Roll; Nat Hon Sy; Sci Fairs; Yth Ldrshp Prog; Hab For Humty Volntr; Drma Clb; Emplmnt; Sci Clb; SP/M/VS; Track (V L); Several Ribbons and Merits for Equestrian Sport Women in Science Award; Pre-Med; Doctor; New York U; Johns Hopkins U

VARGAS, ERICK; NEW YORK, NY; MARBLE HILL SCH FOR INTERNATIONAL STUDIES; (FR); Hi Hnr Roll; Hnr Roll; St of Mnth; Comm Volntr; Peer Tut/Med; Chess; Drma Clb; Mod UN; Svce Clb; SP/M/VS; Gmnstcs (J)

VARGAS, JESSICA; FLUSHING, NY; ST FRANCIS PREP SCH; (JR); Hnr Roll; Perf Att; Peer Tut/Med; Off Aide; Spanish Clb; Drm Mjr; SP/M/VS; Forensic Psychology; Corporate Lawyer; John Jay College; Columbia U

VARGHESE, BETSY; FRANKLIN SQUARE, NY; H FRANK CAREY HS; (JR); F Lan Hn Soc; Hnr Roll; Nat Hon Sy; Otst Ac Ach Awd; Perf Att; Sci Fairs; St of Mnth; Comm Volntr; Chrch Yth Grp; FBLA; LIBEC-Business Edu. Contest-3rd Place; Pediatrician; Business Management; Sophie Davis School of Biomedical Education; Arcadia U

VARGHESE, SUSAN; GLEN OAKS, NY; FRANCIS LEWIS HS; (JR); Hnr Roll; Nat Hon Sy; Otst Ac Ach Awd; Perf Att; WWAHSS; Comm Volntr; Hosp Aide; Peer Tut/Med; Biology Clb; Chrch Yth Grp; Key Club; Off Aide; Tchrs Aide; Chr; Dnce; Journalism; Education; New York U; Binghamton U

VARTIGIAN, JESSICA A; CLIFTON PARK, NY; CAPITAL REG CAREER & TECH SCH; (SR); Ctznshp Aw; Hnr Roll; Peer Tut/Med; ArtClub; DECA; Emplmnt; Photog; CR (R); Sch Ppr (R); Yrbk (P); Peer Mediator; Student Ambassador; Forensic Psychology; Photography; Hudson Valley Community College; Oswego State U

VARVARO, JIMMY L; W HEMPSTEAD, NY; WESTHEMPSTEAD HS; (FR); F Lan Hn Soc; Hi Hnr Roll; WWAHSS; Spec Olymp Vol; Key Club; Quiz Bowl; Sci Clb; French Clb; Bnd; Mch Bnd; Stu Cncl; French Honor Society; Key Club Secretary; Computer Programming; Chemistry; Massachusetts Institute of Technology

VARY, RACHAEL; CARTHAGE, NY; CARTHAGE CTRL HS; (FR); Hi Hnr Roll; Otst Ac Ach Awd; USAA; WWAHSS; Hab For Humty Volntr; FBLA; Key Club; Bnd; Jzz Bnd; Mch Bnd; Pep Bnd; Scr Kpr; Cl Off (T); CR (R); Math League; Forensics; Pharmacy; Yale U; Marlboro College

VASQUEZ, ALEXANDRA; NEW YORK, NY; DEERFIELD AC; (FR); Hi Hnr Roll; Otst Ac Ach Awd; Perf Att; St of Mnth; St Optmst of Yr; Valdctrian; Comm Volntr; ArtClub; Chess; Mth Clb/Tm; Mus Clb; Off Aide; Dnce; Bskball (J); Fld Hky (J); Stu Cncl (S); Prep for Prep 9 Alumni; Columbia U; U of Pennsylvania

VASQUEZ, ERICA; SYRACUSE, NY; CICERO NORTH SYRACUSE HS; (SR); Hnr Roll; Otst Ac Ach Awd; Perf Att; WWAHSS; Comm Volntr; Emplmnt; Off Aide; Tchrs Aide; Drl Tm; Treasurer of OMOJA - Multicultural Group; Chiropractor / PhD; Optometrist; Wagner College; SUNY Stony Brook

VASQUEZ, JOHN C; BRONX, NY; ALFRED E SMITH VOC HS; (JR); Bsball; Bskball; Computer Technician; Electrical Engineer

VASQUEZ, SONIA; GLEN COVE, NY; GLEN COVE HS; (SO); Gov Hnr Prg; Hi Hnr Roll; Hnr Roll; Nat Ldrshp Svc; Sci Fairs; St of Mnth; Yth Ldrshp Prog; Amnsty Intl; Hab For Humty Volntr; Red Cr Aide; ArtClub; DARE; Emplmnt; FCA; Jr Ach; Mth Clb/Tm; Photog; Spanish Clb; Ch Chr; Arch (V); Bsball (J); Ice Hky (V); Sccr (V); Sftball; Vllyball (V); Nassau College

VASQUEZ LEON, JESSICA J.; BROOKLYN, NY; LOUIS D BRANDEIS HS; (JR); Hnr Roll; Nat Hon Sy; Perf Att; Sci Fairs; WWAHSS; Comm Volntr; Lib Aide; Mus Clb; Off Aide; Tchrs Aide; Vsity Clb; Bnd; SP/M/VS; Sccr (V); Sch Ppr (E); Artista; Spelling Bee Contest Award; Pediatrician; Drexel U; Stanford U

VASSALLO, ATTILIO; FLUSHING, NY; MONSIGNOR MC CLANCY MEMORIAL HS; (SR); F Lan Hn Soc; Hnr Roll; WWAHSS; Chrch Yth Grp; Tchrs Aide; Italian Clb; Italian Club President; Italian Honor Society; Computer Programming; DeVry Institute of Technology

VAUGHAN, KARLEENA M; LEWIS, NY; WESTPORT CTRL SCH; (FR); Hnr Roll; Perf Att; Sci Fairs; Comm Volntr; 4-H; Drma Clb; Emplmnt; Mus Clb; Quiz Bowl; Vsity Clb; Bnd; SP/M/VS; Stg Cre; Arch (J); Bsball (C); Bskball (VJ); Golf (J); Hsbk Rdg (V); Skiing (J); Sccr (V); Sftball (JC); Cl Off (T); Sch Ppr (E, R, P); Several Awards in Horsemanship and Show Jumping.; Animal Rescue; Horseback Riding; Drexel; Briarcliffe

VAUGHN, BRENDEQUA; BRONX, NY; DEWITT CLINTON HS; (SO); WWAHSS; (RN) Nursing; (MD) Obstetrics/Midwife; Yale; Harvard

VAUGHN, JUSTIN; QUEENSBURY, NY; SOUTHERN ADIRONDACK ED CTR; (JR); Hnr Roll; Perf Att; Emplmnt; 2nd Place Skills USA 2005 Championships Conservation; Conservationist; Self Employed Logger Or Grounds Keeper

VAZQUEZ, JASON; OZONE PARK, NY; FRANCIS LEWIS HS; (JR); Hi Hnr Roll; Hnr Roll; Peer Tut/Med; ArtClub; Chess; Drma Clb; Key Club; SP/M/VS; Doctor, Medical; Paramedic; Stony Brook U; Long Island U: Brooklyn

VEGA, JOHANA; BUFFALO, NY; MC KINLEY VOC TECH HS; (FR); Ctznshp Aw; Hnr Roll; Nat Sci Aw; Otst Ac Ach Awd; Perf Att; St of Mnth; DARE; Jr Ach; Mus Clb; Vsity Clb; Chr; SP/M/VS; Stg Cre; Track (J); Vllyball (J); Stu Cncl (R); CR (R); National Junior Honor Society; Math Awards; Scientist; Archaeologist; Yale U; Stanford U

VEKSLER, MARLAND M; BROOKLYN, NY; LEON M GOLDSTEIN HS SCIENCES; (SO); F Lan Hn Soc; Hi Hnr Roll; Hnr Roll; Nat Hon Sy; Sci Fairs; Sci/Math Olympn; Peer Tut/Med; DARE; Photog; Quiz Bowl; Schol Bwl; SP/M/VS; Doctor (Physician); Lawyer; New York U; Columbia U

VELASQUEZ, MINDY J; BRONX, NY; ST PIUS V HS; (JR); Hnr Roll; Nat Hon Sy; Perf Att; Comm Volntr; Tchrs Aide; Vsity Clb; Dnce; Track (V); Adv Cncl (R); Business Management; Magazine Editor; St. John's U (Queens); Fairleigh Dickinson (Teaneck, NJ)

VELASQUEZ, RAMON; CATSKILL, NY; CATSKILL HS; (MS); F Lan Hn Soc; Hnr Roll; Otst Ac Ach Awd; Perf Att; Spanish Clb; Chr; Bskball (J); Sccr (V); Track (V); CR (T); Ran the Turkey Trot Mile in 5 Minutes-Fastest Time; Play Basketball; Georgetown U

VELASQUEZ, SHERI; BRONX, NY; SCH FOR EXCELLENCE; (JR); Hi Hnr Roll; Hnr Roll; Hab For Humty Volntr; Spch Team; Bskball (V); Adv Cncl (R); Lit Mag (E); Have Won Several Awards for Writing Poetry; Political Science; Creative Writing; Eugene Lang College

VELAZQUEZ, ANTHONY R; MEDFORD, NY; BELLPORT HS; (SR); Hnr Roll; Nat Hon Sy; Comm Volntr; Spanish Clb; Wt Lftg; General Automotive Mechanic; Business Administrator; Suffolk Community College

VELAZQUEZ, DIANA M; EAST ELMHURST, NY; ST FRANCIS PREP HS; (JR); Ctznshp Aw; Hnr Roll; Comm Volntr; Hosp Aide; Key Club; Spanish Clb; Business Major; Corporate Lawyer; Manhattan College; Baruch College

VELEZ, LISA; CONGERS, NY; NEW YORK SCH FOR THE DEAF; (SR); Hi Hnr Roll; Hnr Roll; Chrldg (C); Vllyball (C); Cl Off (P); Yrbk (R, P)

VELIC, MENSUR; UTICA, NY; THOMAS R PROCTOR HS; (MS); Nat Hon Sy; St of Mnth; Comm Volntr; Ftball (L); Mar Art (L); Wt Lftg (L); Wrstlg (L); I Want to Be a Professional Wrestler; Graduate As a Lawyer; MUCC

VENDITTO, NICOLE; OSSINING, NY; GOOD COUNSEL AC; (JR); Comm Volntr; Dbte Team; Italian Clb; Sccr (V); Swmg (V); Track (V); Recruitment Club; Advanced Placement Spanish; Psychology; Providence College; Fairfield U

VERA, PAULA; NEW YORK, NY; F H LAGUARDIA HS; (SR); WWAHSS; Peer Tut/Med; Emplmnt; Jr Ach; Mus Clb; Off Aide; Tchrs Aide; Chr; Fncg (J); Cl Off (P); National Hispanic Merit Finalist (2004-2005); Lawyer; Ambassador; Boston U; New York U

VERDELL, DANA C; FREEPORT, NY; FREEPORT HS; (JR); Hnr Roll; Nat Hon Sy; Otst Ac Ach Awd; DECA; Emplmnt; Tennis (V); Pre-Med; Business; Pace U, Hunter College, Barnard College; Rutgers U, Fordham U

VERDESOTO, DIANA; RIDGEWOOD, NY; HEALTH PROF & HUMAN SERV HS; (SO); Hnr Roll; Otst Ac Ach Awd; Perf Att; Salutrn; St of Mnth; Comm Volntr; Emplmnt; Pediatrics; Cardiology; New York U; Cornell U

VERGARA, ELIZABETH; WOODSIDE, NY; FIORELLO H LA GUARDIA HS; (JR); F Lan Hn Soc; Hnr Roll; MVP; Nat Hon Sy; Perf Att; Yth Ldrshp Prog; Comm Volntr; Peer Tut/Med; Spec Olymp Vol; ArtClub; Chess; Emplmnt; Mth Clb/Tm; Off Aide; Outdrs Clb; Photog; Spanish Clb; Ch Chr; Dnce; Gmnstcs; Mar Art; Swmg; Vllyball; Sch Ppr (R); Yrbk (P); Journalism Achievement Award; Many 1st and 2nd Place Awards in Tae Kwon Do - Sparring and Forms; Interior Design; Fashion Design; Fashion Institute of Technology; Parson's School of Design

VERLEY, DANIEL; JAMAICA, NY; MARTIN LUTHER HS; (JR); Hi Hnr Roll; Hnr Roll; Nat Hon Sy; Nat Stu Ath Day Aw; Otst Ac Ach Awd; Pres Ac Ftns Aw; WWAHSS; Comm Volntr; Chrch Yth Grp; Key Club; Tchrs Aide; French Clb; Chr; Bskball (JC); Track (V); Cl Off (P); Stu Cncl (P); Medicine; Anatomy / Biology; SUNY Stony Brook; Cornell U

VERNIEU, TYLER W; LATHAM, NY; SHAKER HS; (JR); Ctznshp Aw; Comm Volntr; DARE; Scouts; Bskball (J); Ftball (J); Track (V); Liberal Arts; UNLV

VERNOLA, COLLEEN; LEVITTOWN, NY; DIVISION AVE; (SO); F Lan Hn Soc; Hi Hnr Roll; Nat Hon Sy; WWAHSS; Comm Volntr; Key Club; Scouts; Bnd; Mch Bnd; Bskball (J); Cl Off (V); Silver Award; Trim Music Honor Society; Psychiatrist

VESPO, KIMBERLY; BETHPAGE, NY; PLAINEDGE HS; (JR); F Lan Hn Soc; Hi Hnr Roll; Nat Hon Sy; Emplmnt; Key Club; Mus Clb; Scouts; Spanish Clb; Bnd; Drm Mjr; Jzz Bnd; SP/M/VS; Music Education; Music General Performance; U of Massachusetts-Lowell; Boston U

VETTER, BRITTANY; PAINTED POST, NY; CORNING-PAINTED POST WEST HS; (JR); Hi Hnr Roll; Hnr Roll; Nat Hon Sy; Perf Att; Comm Volntr; Chrch Yth Grp; Drma Clb; Scouts; Tchrs Aide; Bnd; Chr; Ch Chr; Mch Bnd; Joined Teen Friends (Like Friends of the Library); CPA / Certified Public Account

VETTICHIRA, BICKY; YONKERS, NY; MARIA REGINA HS; (SO); Hnr Roll; Nat Hon Sy; WWAHSS; Chrch Yth Grp; Drma Clb; Key Club; Sci Clb; Ch Chr; Dnce; SP/M/VS; Medicine; Lawyer

VICKERS, MARISSA; MASSENA, NY; MASSENA SR HS; (SO); Hnr Roll; Perf Att; Comm Volntr; Emplmnt; Photog; Scouts; Spanish Clb; Chr; Ch Chr; Sccr; Sftball; Two Time Essay Winner - Dare & Fire Prevention; League Softball and Soccer Player; Public Relations / Journalism; Criminal Investigation; Virginia Wesleyan College; Arizona State U

VICTORIA, SUJEY; NEW YORK, NY; HS FOR MEDIA & COMMUNICATIONS; (JR); Perf Att; DARE; Drma Clb; ROTC; Spch Team; Clb; Dnce; SP/M/VS; Stg Cre; Swg Chr; Sch Ppr (P); Singer; Monroe College; Lehman College

VICUNA, DORIS; FLUSHING, NY; JOHN BOWNE HS; (JR); Hi Hnr Roll; Hnr Roll; Photog; Sccr (V); Vllyball (V); Helped Do Blankets and Pillows for a Shelter in Queens; Doctorate; Veterinarian or Nurse; New York U

VIDAL, MIGUEL; BRONX, NY; RICE HS; (SO); All Am Sch; Hnr Roll; Nat Hon Sy; Nat Sci Aw; Perf Att; USAA; WWAHSS; Comm Volntr; Bsball; Robotics Team; Medical Doctor; Math Teacher; Syracuse U; Miami U

VIDLER, HANNAH E; NORWICH, NY; VALLEY HEIGHTS CHRISTIAN AC; (FR); 4H Awd; Ctznshp Aw; Hi Hnr Roll; Hnr Roll; Perf Att; Sci Fairs; USAA; 4-H; Chrch Yth Grp; Bskball (V); Sccr (V); AAU Basketball

VIKAS, RUCHI; BROOKLYN, NY; JAMES MADISON HS; (JR); Hnr Roll; Kwnis Aw; Comm Volntr; Key Club; Sci Clb; Chr; SP/M/VS; Best Writers Award; Medical Doctor; Writer; HYIT; George Washington U

VILLANE, NATASHA; CANANDAIGUA, NY; CANANDAIGUA AC; (JR); Hi Hnr Roll; Hnr Roll; Nat Hon Sy; Comm Volntr; Key Club; SADD; Vsity Clb; Chr; Vllyball (VJC); Club Volleyball - 3 Years / Year Round; Pharmaceutical; Teaching / Second Choice; SUNY Buffalo; Wingate U

Vidal, Miguel
Rice HS
Bronx, NY

Victoria, Sujey
HS For Media & Communications
New York, NY

Vikas, Ruchi
James Madison HS
Brooklyn, NY

Vetter, Brittany
Corning-Painted Post West HS
Painted Post, NY

Venditto, Nicole
Good Counsel AC
Ossining, NY

Velazquez, Anthony R
Bellport HS
Medford, NY

Vaughn, Brendequa
DeWitt Clinton HS
Bronx, NY

Vasquez Leon, Jessica J.
Louis D Brandeis HS
Brooklyn, NY

Vartigian, Jessica A
Capital Reg Career & Tech Sch
Clifton Park, NY

Vasquez, Erica
Cicero North Syracuse HS
Syracuse, NY

Vega, Johana
Mc Kinley Voc Tech HS
Buffalo, NY

Velazquez, Diana M
St Francis Prep HS
East Elmhurst, NY

Vergara, Elizabeth
Fiorello H La Guardia HS
Woodside, NY

Verley, Daniel
Martin Luther HS
Jamaica, NY

VILLANUEVA VARGAS, ANDERSON; NEW YORK, NY; HS FOR MEDIA & COMMUNICATIONS; Computer Information System; Computer Technology; New York City Tech; Borough of Manhattan Community College

VILLARES, GISELE; BROOKLYN, NY; FT HAMILTON HS; (JR); Hnr Roll; Dnce; 1st Degree Black Belt in Tae Kwon Do; Green Sash in Jeet Kune Do; Entrepreneur; Music Technology; New York U; Brooklyn College

VINNIKOV, ANATOLIY; BROOKLYN, NY; NEW UTRECHT HS; (JR); Hnr Roll; Comm Volntr; Member of Academy of Hospitality and Tourism; NYPD Explorer; Urban Design; Graphic Arts and Industrial Design; Hunter College; New York Institute of Technology

VINNIKOVA, ANNA; BROOKLYN, NY; NEW UTRECHT HS; (SR); Gov Hnr Prg; Perf Att; WWAHSS; Comm Volntr; Dnce; NYPD Explorer; Accounting; Brooklyn College; Hunter College

VINTI, NICOLE M; MASPETH, NY; MARTIN LUTHER HS; (JR); Hi Hnr Roll; Kwnis Aw; WWAHSS; Comm Volntr; Peer Tut/Med; Key Club; Chr; Chrldg (C); Sftball (V); Pre-Med

VISONE, EMILY G; W HEMPSTEAD, NY; WEST HEMPSTEAD HS; (JR); Hi Hnr Roll; Hnr Roll; MVP; Nat Hon Sy; Sci Fairs; Comm Volntr; ArtClub; Chrch Yth Grp; Drma Clb; Emplmnt; Key Club; Mod UN; Quiz Bowl; Scouts; Stg Cre; Vllyball (VJC); Cl Off (P); Athletes Helping Athletes; National Youth Leadership Conf. Law; Legal Profession; Geneseo; Boston U

VITALE, STEPHEN; GARDEN CITY, NY; GARDEN CITY HS; (JR); Hi Hnr Roll; Comm Volntr; Key Club; Italian Clb; Bnd; Jzz Bnd; Bsball (J); Track (V); President of Jump Start Club

VIZZIO, PAUL J; NEW HYDE PARK, NY; HERRICKS HS; (JR); Nat Hon Sy; Sci Fairs; St of Mnth; BPA; DECA; Bnd; Science

VO, AN T; BRONX, NY; HS OF AMERICAN STUDIES @ LEHMAN COLLEGE; (SO); Hi Hnr Roll; Hnr Roll; Nat Hon Sy; ArtClub; Key Club; Photog; Spanish Clb; Dnce; Bskball (J); Sch Ppr (P); National Spanish Honors Society; Psychology; Boston U

VO, THUY; UTICA, NY; THOMAS B PROCTOR HS; (JR); Ctznshp Aw; Hi Hnr Roll; Hnr Roll; Nat Hon Sy; Perf Att; Pres Sch; Sci Fairs; St of Mnth; WWAHSS; Comm Volntr; Peer Tut/Med; Emplmnt; Mus Clb; Chr; Orch; Stu Cncl (R); CR (R); Young Scholars Liberty Partnership Program; Medical; Colgate U; Hamilton College

VOELKLE, RACHEL; MARILLA, NY; IROQUOIS HS; (JR); Ctznshp Aw; Hi Hnr Roll; Nat Hon Sy; St Schl; St of Mnth; WWAHSS; Comm Volntr; Peer Tut/Med; Chrch Yth Grp; Key Club; Schol Bwl; Vsity Clb; Orch; SP/M/VS; Track (J); Stu Cncl (V); CR (R); Varsity Bowling; Chamber Orchestra; Denison U

VOGEL, RYAN; LITTLE NECK, NY; BENJAMIN CARDOZO HS; (JR); Perf Att; Sci/Math Olympn; Comm Volntr; Emplmnt; Tmpl Yth Grp; German Clb; Wt Lftg; Physical Science Research; Da Vinci Program; Architecture; Mechanical / Electrical Engineering; Florida International U; Florida Atlantic U

VOLLMER, SHANNON; SEAFORD, NY; ST ANTHONY'S HS; (JR); Hnr Roll; Yth Ldrshp Prog; CARE; 4-H; ArtClub; Key Club; Svce Clb; SADD; Foreign Clb; Chr; Hsbk Rdg (V); Yrbk (R); Softball Team (Out of School); Swimming (CVO), Part Time Job; Psychology; Business; U of Tampa; Florida State U

VOLMY, DARLENE; LOCKPORT, NY; LOCKPORT HS; (FR); Hi Hnr Roll; Nat Hon Sy; Otst Ac Ach Awd; Perf Att; St of Mnth; Valdctrian; Yth Ldrshp Prog; Comm Volntr; Hosp Aide; Peer Tut/Med; Chrch Yth Grp; DARE; Drma Clb; Emplmnt; Key Club; Lib Aide; Off Aide; Prom Com; Chr; Ch Chr; Dnce; SP/M/VS; Cl Off (P); Stu Cncl (T); CR (V); Yrbk (P); National American Miss / Pageant; Student of the Month Throughout School Career; Obstetrician; Pediatrician; SUNY Buffalo; Harvard U

VOLMY, DONNA; LOCKPORT, NY; LOCK PORT HS; (SO); Ctznshp Aw; Hnr Roll; Nat Hon Sy; Otst Ac Ach Awd; Perf Att; St of Mnth; Comm Volntr; Red Cr Aide; Chrch Yth Grp; Key Club; French Clb; Bnd; Chr; Dnce; SP/M/VS; Chrldg (J); Stu Cncl (S); French Club, Foreign Exchange Club; Key Club, Student Council; Pediatrician; Medical; U of Buffalo; Buffalo State College

VOLOSHINA, ELLA; BROOKLYN, NY; MIDWOOD HS; (JR); Hnr Roll; Nat Mrt Fin; Nat Mrt LOC; Sci Fairs; Comm Volntr; ArtClub; DARE; Emplmnt; Dnce; Science Fair Winner (Intel); Pre-Med; Pre-Law; Vassar; Cornell

VOLPE, JESSICA A; JAMESTOWN, NY; SOUTHWESTERN HS; (SR); DAR; Hi Hnr Roll; MVP; Nat Hon Sy; Otst Ac Ach Awd; Pres Ac Ftns Aw; St of Mnth; Comm Volntr; Peer Tut/Med; Spec Olymp Vol; Key Club; Prom Com; SADD; Vsity Clb; Chrldg (V L); Cr Ctry (V L); Sccr (VJCL); Track (V CL); Cl Off (P); Yrbk (R); National Honor Society President; Community Service Award By Business First Magazine; Art Education; Graphic Design; SUNY Geneseo; Washington & Jefferson College

VOS, STEPHANIE C; APALACHIN, NY; OWEGO FREE AC; (JR); All Am Sch; Hi Hnr Roll; Nat Hon Sy; USAA; WWAHSS; Emplmnt; Key Club; Spanish Clb; Chr; Drl Tm; Swmg (V L); Tennis (V L); Track (V L); Astronomy

VUKOVIC, SEMIN; UTICA, NY; THOMAS R PROCTOR HS; (FR); Ctznshp Aw; Hi Hnr Roll; Nat Hon Sy; Perf Att; St of Mnth; Comm Volntr; Master's Degree; Utica College

VUONG, SUONG T; UTICA, NY; THOMAS R PROCTOR HS; (SO); Psychology; Photography; Cedar Crest

WACENSKE, QUINN; ROCHESTER, NY; GATES CHILI HS; (SO); Hi Hnr Roll; Hnr Roll; Otst Ac Ach Awd; Perf Att; Pres Ac Ftns Aw; Pres Sch; St of Mnth; Chrch Yth Grp; P to P St Amb Prg; Scouts; Italian Clb; Bsball (J); Ftball (J); Wt Lftg (J); Firefighter Explorer Program; Business/Technology; Science

WACLAWSKI, JOSHUA; BROCTON, NY; BROCTON CTRL SCH; (SR); MVP; St of Mnth; Comm Volntr; Emplmnt; FBLA; French Clb; Bsball (J L); Bskball (VJCL); Sccr (VJCL); Vllyball (V L); Wendy's Heisman Scholar Athlete Principal's Award; Sports Management; Medaille College

WADDELL, BRIAN D; SCHENECTADY, NY; SCHALMONT HS; (SO); Hi Hnr Roll; Perf Att; St of Mnth; WWAHSS; Comm Volntr; Chrch Yth Grp; Emplmnt; Key Club; Bnd; Stg Cre; Cr Ctry (J); Cl Off (V); Stu Cncl (V, R); CR (V); Key Club- Sergeant at Arms & Public Relations Officer; Business Management; Psychology

WADHWA, KRITTIKA; POUGHKEEPSIE, NY; POUGHKEEPSIE HS; (SO); Hnr Roll; Yth Ldrshp Prog; HO'Br Yth Ldrshp; Bnd; Sccr (V); Track (V); Vllyball (V); Medical; Journalism; Trinity College; St Louis Medical College

WAGNER, STEPHEN N; GENEVA, NY; GENEVA HS; (SO); Hi Hnr Roll; WWAHSS; Chrch Yth Grp; Key Club; Bnd; Mch Bnd; Pep Bnd; Lcrsse (J); Sccr (JC)

WAGONBLOTT, ANGEL; DEPEW, NY; DEPEW HS; (SO); Hi Hnr Roll; Mus Clb; French Clb; Bnd; SP/M/VS; GAA; Flute Choir; Music

WAHAD, ANWAR; NEW YORK, NY; BEACON HS; (SO); Hnr Roll; Comm Volntr; Lit Mag (R); Democratic Leader; Syracuse; Yale

WAHID, RUTH; SOUTH OZONE PARK, NY; JOHN ADAMS HS; (JR); Hnr Roll; Nat Hon Sy; Comm Volntr; Peer Tut/Med; Drma Clb; Key Club; Prom Com; French Clb; Yrbk (P); Commendation Award

WALAS, CARLY; GLEN HEAD, NY; OUR LADY OF MERCY AC; (JR); Hnr Roll; Perf Att; Comm Volntr; Hosp Aide; Peer Tut/Med; ArtClub; Emplmnt; Off Aide; Svce Clb; Dnce; Drl Tm; SP/M/VS; Stg Cre; Bdmtn (JL); Sftball (J); Tennis (J); Yrbk (P); Dedicated Sports Night Involvement for Four Years on Stripe Cheer Team; Strong volunteer outside and inside school.; Fashion Major; Business Major / Small Business; Loyola College in Maryland; University of North Carolina

WALAWENDER, MICHAEL; ORCHARD PARK, NY; ORCHARD PARK HS; Ctznshp Aw; Hnr Roll; Comm Volntr; Emplmnt; Bsball (J); Golf; Skiing; Wt Lftg; Stu Cncl (R); MBA; Law Degree

WALINSKI, RICHARD; BRONX, NY; ENVIRONMNETAL STUDIES; (SR); Emplmnt; SGA Conservation Leader; Journalism; Journalism; CUNY City College

WALKER, KAYLEE C; LIVONIA, NY; LIVONIA HS; (FR); St of Mnth; Comm Volntr; Spec Olymp Vol; Cmptr Clb; DARE; Key Club; Scouts; Bskball; Swmg (V); Vllyball; Ballooning; Girl Scout Camp Aide

WALKER, RENAE; MOUNT VERNON, NY; MT VERNON HS; (SO); Hnr Roll; Nat Hon Sy; Otst Ac Ach Awd; St of Mnth; Comm Volntr; Peer Tut/Med; Chrch Yth Grp; Ch Chr; Stg Cre; Vllyball (J); Neonatology; New York U; Emory U

WALKER-GRAY, RYAN; EAST SYRACUSE, NY; EAST SYRACUSE MINOA HS; (JR); DAR; Hi Hnr Roll; Nat Hon Sy; Otst Ac Ach Awd; Perf Att; Pres Ac Ftns Aw; Yth Ldrshp Prog; Comm Volntr; DECA; Drma Clb; Emplmnt; FCA; Jr Ach; Bnd; Stg Cre; GAA; Sccr (V); Track (V); MDA Camp Counselor; 2nd Place- DECA Nationals; U of Rochester; Hamilton College

WALLACE, HEATHER; PEEKSKILL, NY; PEEKSKILL HS; (SR); Hi Hnr Roll; Hnr Roll; Nat Hon Sy; WWAHSS; Comm Volntr; Peer Tut/Med; Chrch Yth Grp; Yrbk (R); Mathematics Honor Society; Exchange Club; Elementary Education; The College of New Rochelle

WALLACE, TAKAMMA; YONKERS, NY; LINCOLN HS; (SR); Hi Hnr Roll; Hnr Roll; St of Mnth; WWAHSS; Comm Volntr; DARE; Emplmnt; Stg Cre; Bskball (VJ); Cr Ctry (VJC); Track (VJC); Sch Ppr (E, R, P)

WALSH, PHELESHA; BRONX, NY; BRONX REG HS; (SR); Hnr Roll; WWAHSS; Chrch Yth Grp; Drma Clb; Mus Clb; Chr; Ch Chr; Dnce; SP/M/VS; Adv Cncl (P); Stu Cncl; Elected President- 2003-2004 / Chancellor's Honor Roll; Music Education; Early Childhood Education; SUNY Purchase; Hofstra U

WALTERS, CASSANDRA R; SCHENECTADY, NY; SCHENECTADY HS; (SO); Hnr Roll; Otst Ac Ach Awd; WWAHSS; Comm Volntr; P to P St Amb Prg; CR (R); Lit Mag (R); I Recently Went to China with PTP Student Ambassador; My Poems Have Been Published in the Schools Literary Magazine; English; History; Union College; Colgate U

WALZER, JASON; BLOOMFIELD, NY; LIMA CHRISTIAN SCH; (SO); Hi Hnr Roll; Chrch Yth Grp; Emplmnt; Sccr (V CL); Cl Off (P, V); Civil Engineering; RIT

WANG, CHRISTINE; FLUSHING, NY; LAGUARDIA HS; (JR); Comm Volntr; Lib Aide; Mth Clb/Tm; Off Aide; Tchrs Aide; Tmpl Yth Grp; Fncg; Ace Mentoring Program; Architecture Club; Architecture; Education

WANG, DONNA; BROOKLYN, NY; JAMES MADISON HS; (JR); WWAHSS; Comm Volntr; Red Cr Aide; Key Club; Tchrs Aide; Stg Cre; Math Honor Society; Science Honor Society; Business Administration; Psychology; New York U; U of California-Los Angeles

WANG, GORDON; FRESH MEADOWS, NY; FRANCIS LEWIS HS; (SR); Nat Hon Sy; USAA; Peer Tut/Med; Bnd; Dentistry

WANG, JULIA; FOREST HILLS, NY; STUYVESANT HS; (FR); Hnr Roll; Nat Hon Sy; Perf Att; Comm Volntr; Key Club; Mth Clb/Tm; Medical Doctor; PhD; New York U; Harvard U

WANG, RUI; FAIRPORT, NY; FAIRPORT HS; (SO); F Lan Hn Soc; Hi Hnr Roll; Otst Ac Ach Awd; Sci Fairs; Sci/Math Olympn; St of Mnth; Comm Volntr; Red Cr Aide; Emplmnt; Mth Clb/Tm; Schol Bwl; Sci Clb; Svce Clb; Orch; Track (J L); AMC 8 Perfect Score; AMC 12 School Winner (Score III); Second Place in State (WA) Knowledge Bowl Team Competition; Medicine; Harvard U; Cornell U

WANG, THERESA; GREAT NECK, NY; GREAT NECK SOUTH HS; (FR); Hi Hnr Roll; Hnr Roll; Otst Ac Ach Awd; St of Mnth; Comm Volntr; Key Club; Quiz Bowl; Schol Bwl; Dnce; Bdmtn (J); Scr Kpr; Swmg (J); CR (R); Sch Ppr (R); Piano Study; Performance in the China Expo's Fair of 2004; Doctor of Jurisprudence (JD); History Major; Stanford U; Columbia U

WAPSHARE, MELISSA; BUFFALO, NY; IMMACULATA AC; (SR); Hnr Roll; Comm Volntr; Chess; Chrch Yth Grp; P to P St Amb Prg; SADD; Acpl Chr; Chr; Sccr (V); Sftball (J); Been Officer of SADD for Two Years, President '03-'04 School Year and Treasurer '04-'05 School Year; President of The Franciscan Club - Its the school's youth group; Elementary Education Teacher; Green Mountain College, attending in Fall 2005

WARD, KYLE; ULSTER PARK, NY; KINGSTON HS; (JR); Hi Hnr Roll; Peer Tut/Med; Quiz Bowl; Spanish Clb; Mathematics; Physics/Astronomy; Massachusetts Institute of Technology; Rutgers U

WARING, EUNIQUE; BRONX, NY; COLUMBUS HS; (JR); Ctznshp Aw; F Lan Hn Soc; Hi Hnr Roll; Nat Hon Sy; Perf Att; St of Mnth; Yth Ldrshp Prog; Chrch Yth Grp; DARE; Scouts; Svce Clb; Ch Chr; Bskball (V); Sftball (V); Stu Cncl (R); CR (P); Women of the Year Award - Kips Bay Club; Pediatrician; Lawyer; Harvard U; Syracuse U

WARREN, NEFERTITI; BRONX, NY; TREVOR DAY SCH; (SR); Nat Hon Sy; Comm Volntr; Hab For Humty Volntr; Peer Tut/Med; Dbte Team; Drma Clb; Emplmnt; Prom Com; Chr; Dnce; SP/M/VS; Track (V); Vllyball (J); CR (P); Step Team; M.I.O.W (Club-Multiple Identities, One World); Theatre; Business Management; Northeastern U (Enrolled)

WARREN, RENEE E; BROCKPORT, NY; BROCKPORT HS; (SR); Hi Hnr Roll; Hnr Roll; St of Mnth; Vsity Clb; Bnd; Chrldg (VJ); Early Childhood Education; SUNY Fredonia

WASHBURN, KATIE L; ELMIRA, NY; EDISON HS; (FR); Hi Hnr Roll; Sci Fairs; Comm Volntr; 4-H; Emplmnt; Key Club; Bnd; Mch Bnd; Pep Bnd; Bskball (J); Cr Ctry (J); Youth Court; Youth Council; Counseling; Criminal Justice; Pace U in the Adirondacks; North Carolina U

WASSEF, CHRISTINE; REGO PARK, NY; FOREST HILLS HS; (JR); Hnr Roll; Perf Att; Tchrs Aide; Art Show Activities; Liberal Arts; Computer Science; Harvard U; Baruch College

WATERMAN, ASHLEY; DUNKIRK, NY; DUNKIRK HS; (FR); Hi Hnr Roll; Hnr Roll; Comm Volntr; Key Club; Bnd; Chr; Jzz Bnd; Mch Bnd; Student Ambassador Vice President; English; Drama; SUNY Fredonia

WATERMAN, RAYMOND; BRENTWOOD, NY; BRENTWOOD HS; (SO); Hnr Roll; Perf Att; Comm Volntr; Chrch Yth Grp; Emplmnt; Ch Chr; Bskball; Vllyball; Wt Lftg; Electrician; Mechanics; Suffolk Community College; Nassau Community College

WATKINS, SHATAQUA; BROOKLYN, NY; W E B DU BOIS HS; (SO); Comm Volntr; Chrch Yth Grp; Cmptr Clb; Outdrs Clb; Ch Chr; Dnce; Wt Lftg (V); Math; Science; John Jay College

WATSON, HARRY T S; LIVINGSTON MANOR, NY; LIVINGSTON MANOR CS; (FR); Hnr Roll; St of Mnth; DARE; Emplmnt; Scouts; Former Scout, Former Hockey Player; Placed with Distinction Johns Hopkins Talent Search; Science Master's Degree; Math Master's Degree; Albany College of Nanoscale Science and Engineering

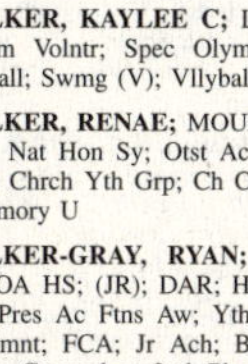

Watson, Harry T S
Livingston Manor CS
Livingston Manor, NY

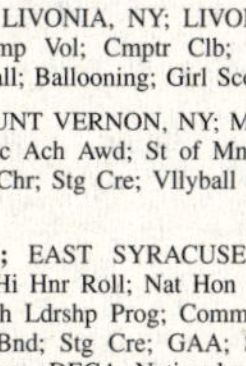

Villanueva Vargas, Anderson
HS For Media & Communications
New York, NY

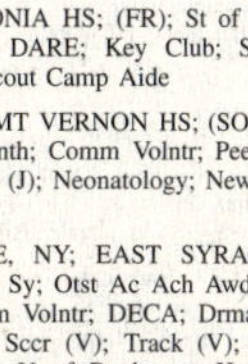

Vinti, Nicole M
Martin Luther HS
Maspeth, NY

WATSON, LEONA; PAINTED POST, NY; CPP WEST HS; (SO); Sci Fairs; Chrch Yth Grp; Scouts; Chr; Corning Cinderella Softball; Bachelor's Degree of Science; Police Officer / Law Enforcement; Corning Community College; Elmira College

WATSON, MICHAEL; BRONX, NY; EVANDER CHILDS HS; (SO); Hnr Roll; MVP; Otst Ac Ach Awd; Perf Att; Sci Fairs; St of Mnth; Valdctrian; Yth Ldrshp Prog; Comm Volntr; Chrch Yth Grp; DARE; Drma Clb; Emplmnt; Lib Aide; Mus Clb; Pep Squd; Spch Team; Bnd; Ch Chr; Dnce; Mch Bnd; Arch; Vllyball (V)

WATSON, SHARDAE; BRONX, NY; THE AC OF MOUNT SAINT URSULA; (JR); Perf Att; Valdctrian; WWAHSS; Tennis; City Council Citation Speaker's Achievement Award; Mechanical Engineering; Psychology; Columbia U; The Massachusetts Institute of Technology

WAY, KRISTEN E; CHITTENANGO, NY; CHITTENANGO HS; (JR); F Lan Hn Soc; Hi Hnr Roll; Hnr Roll; Nat Hon Sy; Otst Ac Ach Awd; Perf Att; St of Mnth; WWAHSS; Comm Volntr; Red Cr Aide; Drma Clb; FBLA; Mod UN; Vsity Clb; International Clb; Chr; Dnce; SP/M/VS; Chrldg (VJ); Track (V L); Yrbk (E, P); Law / Criminal Justice; New York U

WECKENMANN, ELYSIA A.; RONKONKOMA, NY; JERICHO HS; (SR); F Lan Hn Soc; Hi Hnr Roll; Hnr Roll; Nat Hon Sy; Otst Ac Ach Awd; Pres Ac Ftns Aw; Hosp Aide; Mus Clb; Italian Clb; Bnd; Clr Grd; Mch Bnd; Orch; Lcrsse (V L); Sccr (J L); Jericho Band Award; Tri-M Music Honor Society; Chemistry Major; Health Sciences; SUNY Stony Brook

WEDDERBURN, SHERNA L; FAR ROCKAWAY, NY; FAR ROCKAWAY HS; (JR); Hnr Roll; Perf Att; Comm Volntr; Chrch Yth Grp; Dbte Team; Emplmnt; Key Club; Dnce; Bskball (V); Sftball (V); Track (V); Vllyball (V); Social Work-BA; Chemistry-BA, MD, PhD; Binghamton U (SUNY); U of Michigan

WEHR, SAMANTHA; SAUGERTIES, NY; SAUGERTIES HS; (SR); Hi Hnr Roll; Nat Hon Sy; WWAHSS; Comm Volntr; Key Club; Quiz Bowl; Scouts; Spanish Clb; Bnd; Dnce; SP/M/VS; Stg Cre; Lcrsse (J); Track (V L); Vllyball (VJ L); Yrbk (P); History Major; U of Buffalo

WEIHRICH, EMILY; SYRACUSE, NY; JAMESVILLE-DEWITT HS; (JR); F Lan Hn Soc; Hi Hnr Roll; Nat Hon Sy; Sci/Math Olympn; WWAHSS; Key Club; Mth Clb/Tm; Pep Squd; Bnd; Pep Bnd; Bskball (VJ L); Cr Ctry (V L); Mar Art; Sccr (J); Track (V); Sch Ppr (E, P); NYSSMA/All County Clarinet; 4 AP Classes/Tests As of 5/2005; Graphic Design/Animation; Computer Science; Carnegie Melon U; Cornell U

WEILS, ASHLEY; FORT ANN, NY; HARTFORD CTRL SCH; (SR); Hnr Roll; Nat Hon Sy; Otst Ac Ach Awd; Perf Att; Valdctrian; WWAHSS; Key Club; Mth Clb/Tm; Prom Com; Sci Clb; SADD; Foreign Clb; Bnd; Mch Bnd; SP/M/VS; Bskball (J); Sftball (J); Vllyball (JC); Cl Off (S); Treasurer-Key Club, National Honor Society; President-Language (Foreign) Club; Forensic Science; Psychology; Bay Path College

WEILS, PAIGE; FORT ANN, NY; HARTFORD CTRL SCH; (SO); Hnr Roll; WWAHSS; 4-H; Key Club; French Clb; Chr; Bskball (J); Vice President of Key Club; Wildlife Rehabilitation; Wildlife Management

WEINER, SAM; WHITE PLAINS, NY; WHITE PLAINS HS; (FR); Hi Hnr Roll; Hnr Roll; MVP; Nat Hon Sy; Hab For Humty Volntr; Peer Tut/Med; Dbte Team; Cr Ctry (V L); Wrstlg (V L); Scholar/Athlete; Latin Award; Education; Law; Columbia; NYU

WEINTRAUB, DANIEL; MERRICK, NY; CALHOUN HS; (FR); Hnr Roll; Comm Volntr; Emplmnt; Key Club; Tmpl Yth Grp; Chr; Track (J); Lawyer; MBA

WEISS, JACQUELINE; EAST MEADOW, NY; EAST MEADOW HS; (JR); Hnr Roll; St of Mnth; Comm Volntr; Peer Tut/Med; Drma Clb; Mus Clb; Tmpl Yth Grp; Bnd; Clr Grd; Mch Bnd; SP/M/VS; Tennis (J); Student Teaching (Religious School), World Hunger Action Club (School Club); Model Congress (School Club); Marketing/Advertising; Fashion; SUNY Albany; Hunter College

WEISSMANN, ALEXANDRA; MERRICK, NY; CALHOUN HS; (FR); Hnr Roll; WWAHSS; Key Club; Dnce; Cr Ctry (J L); Track (J L); Jr Scope Club; Psychology

WELCH, AMY; PINE CITY, NY; SOUTHSIDE HS; (SR); Hi Hnr Roll; Nat Hon Sy; Nat Ldrshp Svc; WWAHSS; Yth Ldrshp Prog; Comm Volntr; Red Cr Aide; Emplmnt; Key Club; Prom Com; Vsity Clb; Chr; Sccr (V L); Swmg (V L); Track (V L); Cl Off (T); PAL Program; Varsity Club; Physical Education; Spanish Education; SUNY Brockport

WELCH, BRENDAN; WESTPORT, NY; WESTPORT CTRL SCH; (FR); Hi Hnr Roll; Hnr Roll; Nat Hon Sy; Otst Ac Ach Awd; Perf Att; Comm Volntr; Mus Clb; Pep Squd; Bnd; Jzz Bnd; Mch Bnd; Orch; Chrldg (J); Yrbk (P); Band, Be Part of An Orchestra; Duke U; Middlebury

WELLS, ASHLEY A; MADRID, NY; MADRID-WADDINGTON CTRL SCH; (JR); Hi Hnr Roll; Hnr Roll; Nat Hon Sy; WWAHSS; Comm Volntr; Hosp Aide; Chrch Yth Grp; DARE; Mus Clb; Prom Com; Bnd; Chr; Stg Cre; Scr Kpr; Sccr (J); Adv Cncl (P); CR (R); Photography

WEN, FEI; KEW GARDENS, NY; STUYVESANT HS; (FR); Comm Volntr; Key Club; Mth Clb/Tm; Off Aide; Law; Business; Yale U; Columbia U

WENG, LONG; COLLEGE POINT, NY; STUYVESANT HS; (SO); F Lan Hn Soc; Hnr Roll; Nat Ldrshp Svc; Yth Ldrshp Prog; Comm Volntr; Peer Tut/Med; Red Cr Aide; Civil Air Pat; Emplmnt; Key Club; NYLC; Off Aide; Svce Clb; Bnd; Dnce; SP/M/VS; Stg Cre; Bdmtn; Bsball; Swmg (J L); Adv Cncl (R); CR (R); Sch Ppr (R); National Junior Classical League Honorable Merit; American Red Cross Certified Lifeguard; Economics; Business Administration; Columbia U; Stanford U

WERNER, ERIN; HAGAMAN, NY; GALWAY JR/SR HS; (JR); Hnr Roll; Perf Att; Comm Volntr; Emplmnt; Vsity Clb; Sftball (VJ); Vllyball (J); Foreign Language-Linguistics; Education; U of California, San Diego; U of California Los Angeles

WERNER, KIMBERLY; WAPPINGERS FALLS, NY; ROY C KETCHAM HS; (SR); Hi Hnr Roll; Nat Hon Sy; St of Mnth; WWAHSS; Peer Tut/Med; Drma Clb; Emplmnt; Mus Clb; Bnd; Jzz Bnd; Orch; SP/M/VS; Mar Art; Sch Ppr; All State Clarinet; Music Education; New York U; SUNY Potsdam

WERTHEIM, ERICA; PLAINVIEW, NY; PLAINVIEW OLD BETHPAGE JOHN F KENNEDY HS; (SO); Hi Hnr Roll; Hnr Roll; DECA; Svce Clb; Dnce; Business; Marketing/Public Relations; George Washington U; New York U

WESOLOWSKI, MARK; ALDEN, NY; ALDEN CTRL HS; (FR); Hnr Roll; Otst Ac Ach Awd; Perf Att; Pres Ac Ftns Aw; Drma Clb; Key Club; Spanish Clb; Bnd; SP/M/VS; Ftball (J); Track (V L); Cl Off (V); Modified Swim Team / Played Rec Basketball; Love to Snowboard; Master's Degree in Law; History; U of Buffalo; Cornell

WEST, CHRISTINE; BUFFALO, NY; WEST SENECA EAST SR HS; (JR); Hi Hnr Roll; Hnr Roll; Pres Sch; WWAHSS; Comm Volntr; DECA; Sci Clb; Spanish Clb; Orch; Track (VJ); Member of National Academy of Finance; Member of Project Lead the Way; Biomedical Engineering; Business; Syracuse U; Rochester Institute of Technology

WEST, KATHRINA; SYRACUSE, NY; HENNINGER HS; (JR); Hi Hnr Roll; Hnr Roll; Business Law; Cosmetology; Herkimer County Community College

WEST, LISA M; LEVITTOWN, NY; DIVISION AVE HS; (SR); Hnr Roll; Kwnis Aw; Nat Hon Sy; Perf Att; Sci Fairs; St of Mnth; Comm Volntr; AL Aux Girls; Chrch Yth Grp; DARE; Dbte Team; Emplmnt; Key Club; Mod UN; SADD; Yrbk (E, R); Key Club (04-05); Culinary Arts Class; Air Force; Nurse; Culinary Institute of America

WESTCOTT, JULIA; SCHENECTADY, NY; SCHENECTADY HS; (SO); Hi Hnr Roll; Hnr Roll; Nat Hon Sy; St of Mnth; USAA; WWAHSS; CARE; Comm Volntr; P to P St Amb Prg; Acpl Chr; Chr; Ch Chr; School Run Haunted House - Staging and Tickets; Moose Lodge - Community Services / MS Telethon; Arts; Teaching; UCLA

WHALEY, TYSHEEMA; JAMAICA, NY; GEORGE WASHINGTON CARVER HS; (SO); Bskball (J); Sftball (V); Vllyball (J); Obstetrician; Delaware College; Hunter College

WHAREAM, WINSTON; JAMAICA, NY; SPRINGFIELD GARDENS HS; (FR); Gov Hnr Prg; Hi Hnr Roll; MVP; Nat Stu Ath Day Aw; Otst Ac Ach Awd; Perf Att; Pres Ac Ftns Aw; St of Mnth; Yth Ldrshp Prog; Comm Volntr; Peer Tut/Med; Spec Olymp Vol; 4-H; Chess; Chrch Yth Grp; Emplmnt; Key Club; Ntl FFA; Outdrs Clb; SADD; Dnce; Drl Tm; SP/M/VS; Stg Cre; Bsball (J); Bskball (J); Ftball (V); Gmnstcs (J); Sccr (V); Track (J); Vllyball (C); CR (R); Soccer Award; Business Administration; Berkeley College

WHEELER, BRITTANY; WELLSBURG, NY; ELMIRA SOUTHSIDE HS; (SO); Hi Hnr Roll; St of Mnth; WWAHSS; Comm Volntr; Chrch Yth Grp; Key Club; Bnd; Chr; Ch Chr; Mch Bnd; Vllyball (J); Cl Off; Sch Ppr (R); Mission Trip to Honduras; Bible Club; Law; Psychiatry/Psychology

WHEELER, SABRINA J; COHOES, NY; COHOES HS; (SR); Hi Hnr Roll; Hnr Roll; Perf Att; St of Mnth; Yth Ldrshp Prog; Chrch Yth Grp; DARE; Scouts; Tmpl Yth Grp; Ch Chr; Beauty Pageants; Conway Sisters Gymnastics; Criminal Law; Forensics; Hudson Valley Community College; Syracuse U

WHIPPLE, IAN W; CATTARAUGUS, NY; CATTARAUGUS-LITTLE VALLEY; (FR); Hi Hnr Roll; Scouts; Bnd; Sccr (V L); Track (V L); Lifeguard / BSA; Engineering; Syracuse U; Rensselaer Polytechnic Institute

WHITBREAD, KATHLEEN S; BUFFALO, NY; WEST SENECA EAST SR HS; (JR); Hi Hnr Roll; Kwnis Aw; Nat Hon Sy; Pres Sch; St of Mnth; Comm Volntr; Chrch Yth Grp; Emplmnt; P to P St Amb Prg; French Clb; Bnd; Dnce; Mch Bnd; Vice-President of International Club; Biology; Premedicine; Lemoyne College; College of William and Mary

WHITE, ANNA M; BROOKLYN, NY; GEORGE WESTINGHOUSE HS; (FR); Hnr Roll; Perf Att; St of Mnth; Yth Ldrshp Prog; Peer Tut/Med; Chrch Yth Grp; Dbte Team; Mus Clb; P to P St Amb Prg; Bnd; Ch Chr; Tennis (J); Adv Cncl (R); Cl Off (R); Stu Cncl (P, R); CR (P); Full Sail U; LaGuardia Community College

WHITE, BRITNEY; LITTLE VALLEY, NY; CATTARAUGUS-LITTLE VALLEY HS; (FR); Hi Hnr Roll; Sci Clb; Bnd; Chr; Jzz Bnd; Bskball (J); Sftball (J); Track (V L); Vllyball (JC); Double Major-Psychology and Criminal Law; Criminal/Forensic Psychologist; Syracuse U; Brandeis U

WHITE, CRYSTAL; POUGHKEEPSIE, NY; POUGHKEEPSIE HS; (FR); Hi Hnr Roll; Hnr Roll; Perf Att; Pres Ac Ftns Aw; St of Mnth; DARE; Bnd; Vllyball (J); Teaching; Nursing

WHITE, NICOLE L; GLOVERSVILLE, NY; HERITAGE CHRISTIAN AC; (SO); Sci Fairs; St of Mnth; Hosp Aide; Peer Tut/Med; Chrch Yth Grp; Drma Clb; Prom Com; Scouts; Chr; Ch Chr; Dnce; Cr Ctry (J); Vllyball (J); Stu Cncl (V); Yrbk (E); Paramedic; Registered Nurse Trauma Emergency Room; Hudson Valley Community College

WHITEHORN, CAMILLE P; HUNTINGTON, NY; JOHN H GLENN HS; (JR); All Am Sch; Hi Hnr Roll; Hnr Roll; Nat Hon Sy; Perf Att; Sci Fairs; Yth Ldrshp Prog; Comm Volntr; Chrch Yth Grp; Svce Clb; Chr; Dnce; Orch; Sccr (V); Track (V); SCMEA (All-County Vocal); NYSSMA (Vocal)

WHITEHOUSE, RYAN E; NEWARK, NY; DE SALES HS; (JR); Hi Hnr Roll; Hnr Roll; Nat Hon Sy; Pres Sch; USAA; WWAHSS; Comm Volntr; Peer Tut/Med; Key Club; Bnd; Golf (V L); Varsity Bowling, New York State Scholar Athlete; Finger Lakes Scholar

WHITE-MASSERIA, MICHAEL J; BUFFALO, NY; KENMORE WEST HS; (SO); Hnr Roll; Chrch Yth Grp; Recording Engineering; Computer Science; Rochester Institute of Technology; Harvard

WHITEY, ERNEST; MIDDLETOWN, NY; MIDDLETOWN HS; (JR); Hnr Roll; DARE; ROTC; SP/M/VS; Bskball; Ftball; Wt Lftg; CR (R); Computer Engineering; Football; Florida State U; U Of Miami Sports

WHITING, LATOSHA; SOUTH OZONE PARK, NY; GLOBAL STUDIES HS; (SR); Ctznshp Aw; Hi Hnr Roll; Hnr Roll; Otst Ac Ach Awd; Perf Att; Salutrn; Comm Volntr; Peer Tut/Med; Emplmnt; Mth Clb/Tm; Sci Clb; CR (R); Biology; Forensic Science; Francis Marion U; Paul Smiths College

WHITTEMORE, AMBER; EAST QUOGUE, NY; WESTHAMPTON BEACH HS; (JR); Ctznshp Aw; Hi Hnr Roll; Hnr Roll; Yth Ldrshp Prog; Comm Volntr; Peer Tut/Med; DARE; Drma Clb; NYLC; Chr; Sccr (J); Rotary Interact Secretary; Political Science; Prelaw; Clemson U

WHITTON, LAUREN E; MASSENA, NY; MASSENA SR HS; (SO); F Lan Hn Soc; Hi Hnr Roll; Comm Volntr; DARE; Drma Clb; Chr; Stg Cre; Swmg (V); Tennis

WIEDERMANN, RACHEL T; NEW YORK, NY; THE CALHOUN SCH; (JR); Comm Volntr; Peer Tut/Med; Bnd; SP/M/VS; Yrbk (R); Summer Program Planning Committee; French Award for Academic Achievement; Mathematics; MD And/PhD; Harvard U; Yale U

WIELGUS, LAUREN; LEVITTOWN, NY; ISLAND TREES HS; (SO); Hi Hnr Roll; Sci/Math Olympn; WWAHSS; Key Club; Mth Clb/Tm; Mus Clb; Sci Clb; Bnd; Jzz Bnd; Mch Bnd; Bdmtn (V); Sccr (JC)

WIEMANN, KATHRYN; HUNTINGTON STATION, NY; WALT WHITMAN HS; (SR); Ctznshp Aw; Hnr Roll; St Schl; St of Mnth; WWAHSS; Yth Ldrshp Prog; Comm Volntr; Peer Tut/Med; DARE; Emplmnt; NYLC; Prom Com; Svce Clb; Vsity Clb; Fld Hky (VJ L); GAA (V C); PP Ftbl (V); Sftball (VJ L); Track (V L); Stu Cncl (R); CR (R); Aids Peer Education (Treasurer); New York State Lottery Scholarship; Education; Communications; The College of Saint Rose

WIENER, WENDI; LITTLE NECK, NY; BENJAMIN CARDOZO HS; (JR); F Lan Hn Soc; WWAHSS; Comm Volntr; Peer Tut/Med; Tmpl Yth Grp; French Clb; CR (V); Yrbk (E, P); Club - Breast Cancer Awareness (Pink Ribbons Club); Child Psychology; Teaching; Adelphi U; St John's U

WIERS, KATELYN; COLD BROOK, NY; POLAND CTRL HS; (SO); Ctznshp Aw; Hnr Roll; MVP; Otst Ac Ach Awd; Perf Att; Photog; Vsity Clb; Bskball (JC); Cr Ctry (V L); Vsy Clb (V); Poem Published 2003 - Anthology of Poetry; All State Conference List - Cross Country '04-'05; Law Enforcement; Cosmetology; Syracuse U; Herkimer College

WIGDERSON, JENNIFER; WEBSTER, NY; WEBSTER THOMAS HS; (JR); Hi Hnr Roll; Nat Hon Sy; Nat Mrt LOC; Otst Ac Ach Awd; WWAHSS; Peer Tut/Med; Key Club; Mth Clb/Tm; Spanish Clb; Bnd; Orch; SP/M/VS; Swmg (J); Hochstein Scholarship Flute Choir; Hochstein Youth Wind Symphony; Music Performance; Music Education; SUNY Fredonia; SUNY Potsdam

WIGGS, JESSICA M; BROOKLYN, NY; ERASMUS HALL HS; (JR); Perf Att; Peer Tut/Med; English; African Literature; Florida U; Hartford U

WIGLE, AMANDA J; WILLIAMSON, NY; SODUS JR/SR HS; (SO); Hi Hnr Roll; Perf Att; Sci Fairs; DARE; Scouts; Bnd; Chr; Dnce; Jzz Bnd; Sccr (J); Sftball (J); Girl Scout Silver Award; Pharmacist; Culinary Arts

WIGNALL, LOREN; LEVITTOWN, NY; ISLAND TREES HS; (SO); Hnr Roll; WWAHSS; Yth Ldrshp Prog; Comm Volntr; Peer Tut/Med; HO'Br Yth Ldrshp; Key Club; SADD; Stg Cre; PPSqd; Scr Kpr; Track; Cl Off (S); Stu Cncl (S)

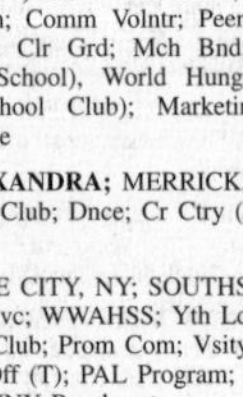
Wiedermann, Rachel T
The Calhoun Sch
New York, NY

Whitehorn, Camille P
John H Glenn HS
Huntington, NY

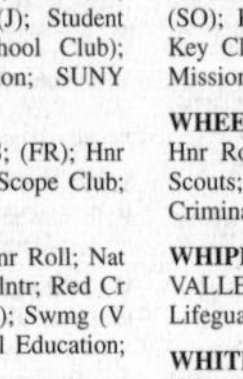
West, Lisa M
Division Ave HS
Levittown, NY

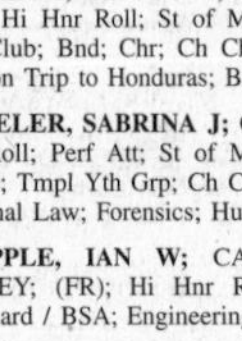
Werner, Kimberly
Roy C Ketcham HS
Wappingers Falls, NY

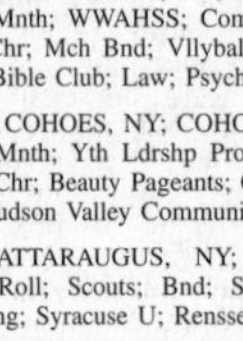
Weckenmann, Elysia A.
Jericho HS
Ronkonkoma, NY

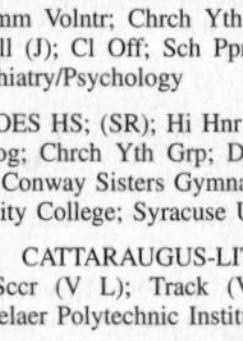
Weng, Long
Stuyvesant HS
College Point, NY

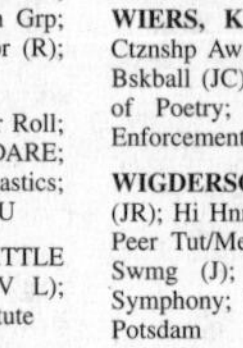
Wheeler, Sabrina J
Cohoes HS
Cohoes, NY

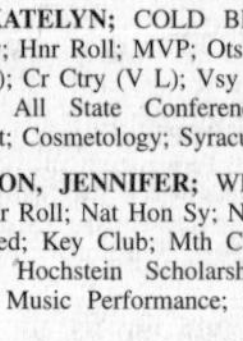
Whitton, Lauren E
Massena SR HS
Massena, NY

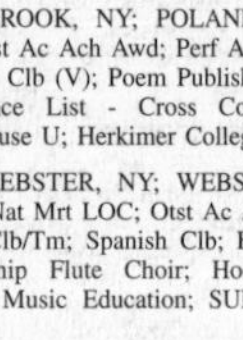
Wiers, Katelyn
Poland Ctrl HS
Cold Brook, NY

WILBUR, KRISTI L; SOUTH NEW BERLIN, NY; VALLEY HEIGHTS CHRISTIAN AC; (SO); Hi Hnr Roll; Hnr Roll; Comm Volntr; Chrch Yth Grp; Chr; Ch Chr; SP/M/VS; Bskball (V); Chrldg (V); Stu Cncl (S); Veterinary Medicine; Music; Christian Colleges

WILBURN, ANDREA C; ROCHESTER, NY; EAST RIDGE HS; (SO); Hnr Roll; Chrch Yth Grp; Ch Chr; Paralegal; Rochester Business Institute

WILCOX, ERIC; BINGHAMTON, NY; CHENANGO VALLEY HS; (JR); Hnr Roll; Nat Hon Sy; Peer Tut/Med; Chrch Yth Grp; Drma Clb; Emplmnt; Bnd; Jzz Bnd; Orch; Pep Bnd; Lcrsse (JC); Sccr (V); Swmg (V); NYSSMA / NGPTA; All-County and All State; History; Philosophy; Le Moyne College; Ithaca College

WILCOX, KRISTEN E; ENDICOTT, NY; (FR); Ctznshp Aw; Hnr Roll; WWAHSS; Comm Volntr; Key Club; Spanish Clb; Bskball (J); Endicott Teener League

WILKEY, BRENT; CATTARAUGUS, NY; CATTARAUGUS-LITTLE VALLEY; (FR); Hi Hnr Roll; Scouts; Bnd; Jzz Bnd; Psychology; Graduate Degree; St Bonaventure U; SUNY Buffalo

WILKINSON, KELSIE M; BAYPORT, NY; BAYPORT BLUE POINT HS; (JR); Hi Hnr Roll; St of Mnth; Comm Volntr; Emplmnt; Key Club; Prom Com; Vsity Clb; Bnd; Lcrsse (V); Cl Off (R); Stu Cncl (R); Presidential Physical Fitness Award; Elementary Education; Guidance Counselor

WILKOW, MATTHEW R; DEER PARK, NY; DEER PARK HS; (SR); Fut Prb Slvr; Hi Hnr Roll; Hnr Roll; Nat Hon Sy; Otst Ac Ach Awd; Pres Sch; St of Mnth; Amnsty Intl; Peer Tut/Med; Chrch Yth Grp; Emplmnt; Stg Cre; Tennis (V); Track (V); President's Education Awards Program; Captain of Academic Team, Breakfast of Champions; Law; Political Science; Temple U; U of Buffalo

WILKS, JESSICA T; HEMPSTEAD, NY; UNIONDALE HS; (JR); Hi Hnr Roll; Hnr Roll; Nat Hon Sy; Otst Ac Ach Awd; Sci Fairs; St of Mnth; Comm Volntr; Peer Tut/Med; ArtClub; Chrch Yth Grp; Emplmnt; Key Club; Lib Aide; Photog; Scouts; Bnd; SP/M/VS; Swmg; Track; Sch Ppr (P); Math Honor Society; Science Honor Society; Pre-Med; BSC; Biology Major; Cornell U; SUNY At Binghamton

WILLIAMS, ALISA; CAMBRIA HEIGHTS, NY; ROBERT WAGNER JR; (JR); Ctznshp Aw; Hnr Roll; Perf Att; Sci Fairs; St of Mnth; WWAHSS; Yth Ldrshp Prog; Comm Volntr; Peer Tut/Med; Biology Clb; Cmptr Clb; Emplmnt; Photog; Tech Clb; Spanish Clb; Dnce; Sftball (J); Cl Off (S); Yrbk (E); New York Cares Day-Volunteer; Education; Mathematics; Adelphi U; SUNY Stony Brook

WILLIAMS, ASHLEY; BRONX, NY; AC OF MT ST URSULA; (SO); Hnr Roll; Peer Tut/Med; Scouts; Italian Clb; Track (J); Sch Ppr (E); Creative Writing; Temple U

WILLIAMS, ASHLEY R; CANAAN, NY; COLUMBIA GREENE ED CTR; (SR); Hi Hnr Roll; Hnr Roll; St of Mnth; Emplmnt; Chr; Business Management / Administration; Cosmetology; Sage College of Albany

WILLIAMS, DESMOND; BOONVILLE, NY; ADIRONDACK HS; (SO); Hnr Roll; Nat Hon Sy; Nat Mrt LOC; Comm Volntr; Bskball (J); Ftball (J); Track (J)

WILLIAMS, JAMIE; HAMBURG, NY; FRONTIER CTRL HS; (SR); F Lan Hn Soc; Hi Hnr Roll; Hnr Roll; Nat Hon Sy; WWAHSS; Comm Volntr; Emplmnt; Svce Clb; Spanish Clb; Yrbk (E, P); Psychology; Biology; Canisius College

WILLIAMS, JEFFREY; BRONX, NY; WASHINGTON IRVING HS; (FR); Hnr Roll; Nat Hon Sy; Sci Fairs; DARE; Off Aide; SP/M/VS; Bskball; Ftball; Mar Art; Swmg; Wt Lftg; Sch Ppr; Pediatrician-Doctor's Degree; Veterinarian

WILLIAMS, JESSICA A; HIGHLAND MILLS, NY; MONROE-WOODBURY HS; (JR); Hnr Roll; MVP; Pres Ac Ftns Aw; Comm Volntr; Emplmnt; Outdrs Clb; Bnd; Bskball (VJ L); Mar Art; Sftball (VJ L); Orange County Community College Athletic Awards; St Patrick's Church Altar Server; Criminal Justice; Physical Education; Delaware Valley College; U of North Carolina Charleston

WILLIAMS, JESSICA R; ROCHESTER, NY; BRIGHTON HS; (JR); Ctznshp Aw; Duke TS; Hnr Roll; Otst Ac Ach Awd; Perf Att; Comm Volntr; Red Cr Aide; Chrch Yth Grp; DECA; Emplmnt; FBLA; Mth Clb/Tm; Prom Com; Vsity Clb; Spanish Clb; Sftball (VJ L); Bowling- V / C / L; Marketing; General Business; UNC Chapel Hill; American U

WILLIAMS, NICOLE; MIDDLETOWN, NY; MINISINK VALLEY HS; (JR); Perf Att; WWAHSS; Key Club; Scouts; Dnce; Bskball (J); Speech Therapist; Hampton U; Howard U

WILLIAMS, TIFFANY S; ROSEDALE, NY; BROOKLYN TECH HS; (JR); Hnr Roll; Otst Ac Ach Awd; St of Mnth; ArtClub; DARE; Chr; Gospel Chorus- 3 Years; City Council Speakers Achievement Award; Forensic Science; Biotechnology; CUNY-John Jay College; SUNY-Buffalo State

WILLIAMS-MONTALVO, KAYLA; BROOKLYN, NY; BROOKLYN SECONDARY SCH OF COLLABORATIVE STUDIES; MS; Hnr Roll; ArtClub; Chrch Yth Grp; Yrbk; Art Club; Silver and Gold Honor Rolls

WILLIAMSON, ADRIAN; YONKERS, NY; LINCOLN HS; Hi Hnr Roll; Hnr Roll; Nat Hon Sy; Perf Att; Comm Volntr; Chess; Key Club; Sccr (V); Wrstlg (V); Accounting; NYU; Wake Forest

WILLIAMSON, ASHLEY; HOLLIS, NY; FRANCIS LEWIS HS; (SR); Hnr Roll; Sci Fairs; St of Mnth; WWAHSS; Yth Ldrshp Prog; Comm Volntr; Peer Tut/Med; Red Cr Aide; Chrch Yth Grp; Cmptr Clb; Emplmnt; Mth Clb/Tm; Off Aide; P to P St Amb Prg; Prom Com; Scouts; Ch Chr; Dnce; Mch Bnd; Tennis; Track; Vllyball; Wt Lftg; Yrbk (E, R, P); Published Own Book from School called: "Express"; Was the Editor-in-chief.; Recipient of Poetry.Com- for Outstanding Achievement in Poetry; Psychology, Forensic Psychology; Business Administration- Plan to Take Double Major; Hofstra U, New York /St. John's U, New York ($8,000 Scholarship); Morgan State U-Baltimore, MD /Coppin State U-Baltimore, MD

WILLIAMSON, JASON J; RIDGEWOOD, NY; CHRIST THE KING HS; (JR); Hnr Roll; WWAHSS; Bnd; Bsball (J); Pitched 2004- All-Star Game at Shea Stadium '04; Computer Science; Meteorology; Arizona State U; SUNY Binghamton

WILLIS, CURTIS A; BROOKLYN, NY; TRANSIT TECH HS; (SO); Hnr Roll; Perf Att; Comm Volntr; Chrch Yth Grp; Emplmnt; Ch Chr; Drl Tm; SP/M/VS; Mechanic; Economics; Duke U; Virginia State U

WILLSEY, TERESA M; CORNING, NY; CORNING-PAINTED POST WEST HS; (FR); Hi Hnr Roll; Hnr Roll; Chr; Chrldg (J); Pediatrician; Animal Medical; Buffalo State U

WILSEY, KARIN M; SAUGERTIES, NY; SAUGERTIES HS; (SR); Hi Hnr Roll; Nat Hon Sy; Pres Ac Ftns Aw; Pres Sch; St of Mnth; WWAHSS; Comm Volntr; AL Aux Girls; Emplmnt; Key Club; Mus Clb; Scouts; Bnd; Chr; Dnce; SP/M/VS; Bskball (J L); Sccr (VJCL); Sftball (VJCL); Girl Scout Silver & Gold / League of Women's Voters; Inside Albany Representative / Pride of Ulster County; Marine Biology; Coastal Carolina U

WILSON, ANGELIQUE S.; BROOKLYN, NY; ABRAHAM LINCOLN HS; (SO); Hi Hnr Roll; Hnr Roll; Nat Hon Sy; Hosp Aide; Chrch Yth Grp; Key Club; Tchrs Aide; Chr; Arista Honor Society / Gilder Lehman Honors Program / National Student's Leadership; Archon Honor Society/ United States Achievement Academy; Doctor / Pediatrician; Medical Law; NYU; U of Maryland

WILSON, DESTINY SHALONE; BROOKLYN, NY; W E B DU BOIS HS; (JR); Hnr Roll; Otst Ac Ach Awd; Yth Ldrshp Prog; Prom Com; Dnce; SP/M/VS; Part of a Pride Documentary on Teen Issues; Real Estate Lawyer; New York U; Spelman College

WILSON, FANASIA; BRONX, NY; CELIA CRUZ BRONX HS OF MUSIC; (FR); Hnr Roll; Comm Volntr; Chrch Yth Grp; Bnd; Ch Chr; Music Education; Liberal Arts; New York U; Lehman College

WILSON, REBEKAH; JAMAICA, NY; GATEWAY TO HEALTH SCIENCES SCH; (JR); Yth Ldrshp Prog; Peer Tut/Med; Chrch Yth Grp; DARE; Tchrs Aide; Chr; Dnce; SP/M/VS; Radiological Sciences; Radiology; Howard U; Clark Atlanta U

WILSON, SHAINA E; CTR MORICHES, NY; CTR MORICHES HS; (JR); Hnr Roll; Otst Ac Ach Awd; WWAHSS; Comm Volntr; Chrch Yth Grp; DECA; Drma Clb; Prom Com; Bnd; Chr; Ch Chr; Jzz Bnd; Sccr (V); Cl Off (P); Yrbk (P); Manager of JV Soccer & Softball; Elementary Education; Music; Utica College; Messiah College

WILSON, STEPHANIE E; SEAFORD, NY; SEAFORD HS; (FR); Hnr Roll; WWAHSS; Comm Volntr; Drma Clb; Key Club; Svce Clb; Chr; SP/M/VS; Stg Cre; 2005 Nassau All-County Art-Exhibition; Art; Music

WINCKELMANN, BRADLEY J S; CHITTENANGO, NY; CHITTENANGO HS; (JR); F Lan Hn Soc; Hi Hnr Roll; Nat Hon Sy; St of Mnth; WWAHSS; Peer Tut/Med; Drma Clb; Mod UN; French Clb; Bnd; Jzz Bnd; Orch; SP/M/VS

WINSTON, MOLLY; ELMIRA, NY; NOTRE DAME HS; (JR); All Am Sch; Ctznshp Aw; Hi Hnr Roll; Kwnis Aw; Nat Hon Sy; Nat Ldrshp Svc; Pres Ac Ftns Aw; St of Mnth; USAA; WWAHSS; Comm Volntr; Peer Tut/Med; Red Cr Aide; Key Club; Lttrmn Clb; Mod UN; NYLC; Pep Squd; Prom Com; Vsity Clb; French Clb; Jzz Bnd; Mch Bnd; Orch; Pep Bnd; Sccr (VJ); Cl Off (P, R); Stu Cncl (R); CR (R); Head Judge Youth Court; Girl's State; Law; International Relations

WINTERFELDT, ALYSSA; MERRICK, NY; SANFORD H CALHOUN; (JR); Hnr Roll; Nat Hon Sy; Key Club; Sci Clb; SADD; Lcrsse (VJ)

WINTERS, DANIELLE; LISBON, NY; LISBON CTRL SCH; (SO); All Am Sch; Hi Hnr Roll; Hnr Roll; Outdrs Clb; Bskball (JCL); Sccr (V L); Sftball (V L); St Lawrence U; SUNY Canton College of Technology

WOLFANGER, KATHERINE R; BERGEN, NY; BYRON-BERGEN HS; (SR); Hi Hnr Roll; Comm Volntr; Peer Tut/Med; Emplmnt; Scouts; Spanish Clb; Bnd; Mch Bnd; Swmg (V L); Track (J); Vllyball (JC); CR (R); Sch Ppr (R, P); Girl Scout Silver Award; President of Kids for the Community; American Sign Language Interpreter; Nation Technical Institute for the Deaf; Rochester Institute of Technology

WOLFLING, ERICA; EAST AURORA, NY; EAST AURORA HS; (SR); Hnr Roll; Nat Hon Sy; St of Mnth; WWAHSS; DECA; Emplmnt; Scouts; Chr; SP/M/VS; Lcrsse (V); PP Ftbl (V); Sccr (J); Stu Cncl (T); Lit Mag (E); All County Chorus; Area All State Chorus; Music Education; Music Business; SUNY Fredonia; Eastman School of Music

WONG, ANTONIO; BROOKLYN, NY; JAMES MADISON HS; (SO); Hnr Roll; Perf Att; Comm Volntr; Peer Tut/Med; Key Club; Mth Clb/Tm; MuAlphaTh; Mus Clb; Off Aide; Sci Clb; Tchrs Aide; Bnd; Jzz Bnd; Mch Bnd; Biology; Mathematics; Columbia U; Stanford

WONG, CATHERINE; EAST ELMHURST, NY; THE MARY LOUIS AC; (JR); Hi Hnr Roll; Nat Hon Sy; WWAHSS; Lcrsse (V); Vllyball (V C); Fashion Designer; Fashion Institution of Technology; Syracuse U

WONG, ELIZA; OAKLAND GARDENS, NY; BENJAMIN CARDOZO HS; (JR); Perf Att; WWAHSS; Comm Volntr; Key Club; Lib Aide; Off Aide; Tchrs Aide; Stg Cre; Fncg (V); Vllyball (J); CR (R); Key Club Secretary; Safe Club; Business; Aviation

WONG, JANE; FRESH MEADOWS, NY; TOWNSEND HARRIS HS; (JR); Hi Hnr Roll; Nat Hon Sy; Perf Att; Sci Fairs; WWAHSS; Peer Tut/Med; Chrch Yth Grp; Fr of Library; Mth Clb/Tm; Stg Cre; Semi-Finalist in NYCSEF (New York City Science Engineering Fair); Gold Medal in the National Latin Exam; Pharmacy; Business

WONG, JANICE; BROOKLYN, NY; NEW UTRECHT HS; (SR); Nat Hon Sy; Nat Ldrshp Svc; Pres Ac Ftns Aw; Sci Fairs; Comm Volntr; Emplmnt; Key Club; Vsity Clb; Bskball (J); Sccr (V); Sftball (J); Vllyball (V); Yrbk (P); Internship At Maimonides Hospital; Teaching Assistant At Angel's Learning Center; Athletic Training; Physician's Assistant; Stony Brook U of New York; Hunter College

WONG, JENNESA; SOUTH OZONE PARK, NY; JOHN ADAMS HS; (JR); Hi Hnr Roll; Hnr Roll; Nat Hon Sy; Comm Volntr; Tchrs Aide; Health Occupation Students of America; Pre-Medical Studies; PhD

WONG, JENNIFER; BROOKLYN, NY; STUYVESANT HS; (FR); Hnr Roll; Nat Hon Sy; Perf Att; Peer Tut/Med; Photog; Orch; Architecture; Mechanical Engineering; MIT (Massachusetts Institute of Technology); Columbia U

WONG, KELVIN; BROOKLYN, NY; STUYVESANT HS; (SO); Gov Hnr Prg; Hnr Roll; WWAHSS; Comm Volntr; Hosp Aide; Key Club; Mth Clb/Tm; SP/M/VS; Medicine; Harvard U; Princeton U

WONG, LINDA S; ELMHURST, NY; AC FOR AMERICAN STUDIES; (JR); Hnr Roll; Nat Hon Sy; Perf Att; WWAHSS; Comm Volntr; Emplmnt; Lib Aide; Photog; International Business; Foreign Affairs; Niagara U; Binghamton U

WONG, LISA; NEW YORK, NY; STUYVESANT HS; (FR); WWAHSS; Comm Volntr; Key Club; Bnd

WONG, PO TING; BROOKLYN, NY; BROOKLYN TECH HS; (SR); All Am Sch; WWAHSS; Red Cr Aide; Jr Ach; Tchrs Aide; Vsy Clb (V); Envirothon 2004 - 2nd Place Winner; Envirothon 2005- 5th Place; Wildlife Biology; Veterinary Medicine; SUNY Environmental Science and Forestry

WOODARD, CHELSEA G; ELMIRA, NY; SOUTHSIDE HS; (FR); Hnr Roll; USAA; Chrch Yth Grp; Key Club; Chr; National Junior Honor Society; Psychology; Teacher

WOODAREK, MERCEDES; SOUTH DAYTON, NY; PINE VALLEY CTRL HS; (FR); Perf Att; St of Mnth; Comm Volntr; Peer Tut/Med; Chrch Yth Grp; DARE; Chrldg (J L); Cl Off (T); Yrbk (E); Teacher Aide for Vacation Bible School; Coaches Award for Cheerleading; Registered Nurse; Photography; SUNY Fredonia; D'youville College

WOODWARD, ROBERT; WELLS, NY; WELLS CTRL SCH; (FR); Hi Hnr Roll; Drma Clb; FBLA; SADD; Bnd; Jzz Bnd; Mch Bnd; Stg Cre; Sccr (J); Cl Off (V); Stu Cncl (R); Secondary Education; State U of New York-Oswego; State U of New York-Geneseo

WOOSTER, TIMOTHY; FULTONVILLE, NY; FONDA FULTONVILLE CTRL SCH; (JR); Hnr Roll; Nat Hon Sy; Perf Att; WWAHSS; Peer Tut/Med; Chrch Yth Grp; Cmptr Clb; Dbte Team; Drma Clb; Emplmnt; Mod UN; Ntl Beta Clb; Ntl FFA; Drl Tm; SP/M/VS; Bsball (J L); Bskball (V); Ftball (JC); Wt Lftg (J); Wrstlg (J); Bachelor of Science; Engineering; Air Force Academy; Florida State U

WORRELL, ERICA; BROOKLYN, NY; LOUIS D BRANDEIS HS; (SO); Hnr Roll; Otst Ac Ach Awd; Peer Tut/Med; Scouts; Asphalt Green Health Gym Intern; Mount Sinai Medical Center Intern; Business; Adult Psychology; Columbia U; Duke U

WOUDENBERG, REBEKAH; PENN YAN, NY; EMMANUEL BAPTIST AC; (SO); DAR; Hi Hnr Roll; Otst Ac Ach Awd; Peer Tut/Med; Chrch Yth Grp; Cmptr Clb; Drma Clb; Chr; Dnce; SP/M/VS; Bskball (V); Sccr (V); Vllyball (V); Cl Off (P); Yrbk (E, R, P); Fine Arts Competitions; Nursing Home Ministry; Language Studies; English; Word of Life Bible Institute

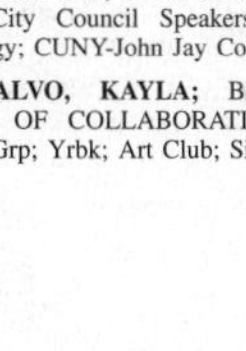

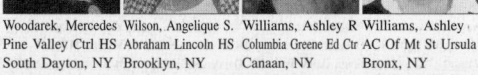

Woodarek, Mercedes
Pine Valley Ctrl HS
South Dayton, NY

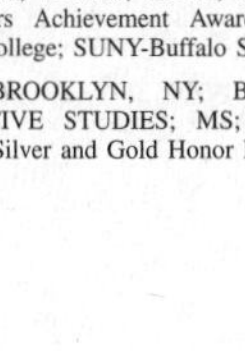

Wilson, Angelique S.
Abraham Lincoln HS
Brooklyn, NY

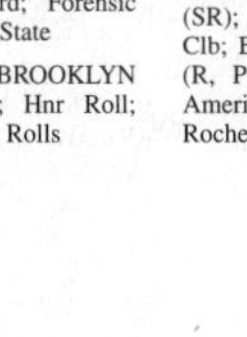

Williams, Ashley R
Columbia Greene Ed Ctr
Canaan, NY

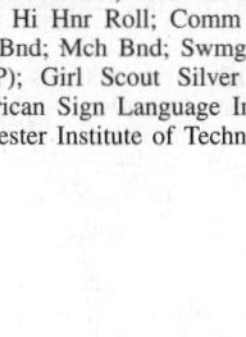

Williams, Ashley
AC Of Mt St Ursula
Bronx, NY

National
Honor Roll
Spring 2005

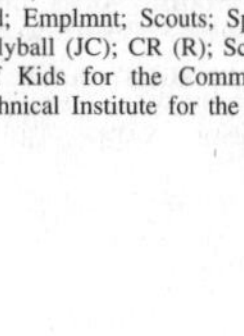

Wilkow, Matthew R
Deer Park HS
Deer Park, NY

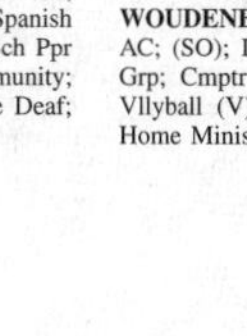

Williamson, Adrian
Lincoln HS
Yonkers, NY

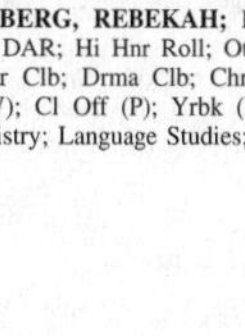

Wilson, Shaina E
Center Moriches HS
Center Moriches, NY

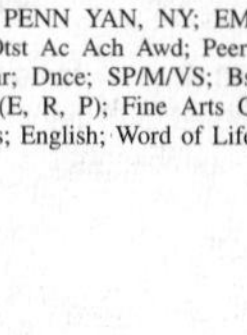

Woudenberg, Rebekah
Emmanuel Baptist AC
Penn Yan, NY

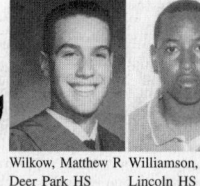

WRIGHT, ALEXANDER; NEW YORK, NY; WASHINGTON IRVING HS; (SO); Ctznshp Aw; Hnr Roll; Otst Ac Ach Awd; Bskball; Mathematics; Computer Technology; U of Maryland; U of Pittsburgh

WRIGHT, JAMES A; FAR ROCKAWAY, NY; BEACH CHANNEL HS; (JR); Hi Hnr Roll; Hnr Roll; Comm Volntr; Spec Olymp Vol; ArtClub; Chrch Yth Grp; Off Aide; Bnd; Jzz Bnd; Mch Bnd; Swmg; Tennis; SUNY Binghamton; U of Delaware

WRIGHT, KEVIA; SAUGERTIES, NY; SAUGERTIES HS; (JR); Hi Hnr Roll; Hnr Roll; Nat Hon Sy; Perf Att; Comm Volntr; Key Club; Prom Com; French Clb; Bskball (VJ); Cr Ctry (V); Lcrsse (V); Track (V); Vllyball (J); Cl Off (V); History Club; Ski Club; Sports Management; Communications & Journalism; Stony Brook U; St John's U

WRIGHT, REBECCA; BROCKPORT, NY; BROCKPORT HS; (FR); Hi Hnr Roll; Hnr Roll; Otst Ac Ach Awd; St of Mnth; Comm Volntr; Chrch Yth Grp; Golf (V L); Stu Cncl (R); CR (R); Brockport Excelsior Society; Student Council Representative Award; Culinary Arts; Forensic Science; Alfred State; Roberts Wesleyan College

WRIGHT, SHAMAR; BRONX, NY; ALFRED E SMITH VOC HS; (FR); Nat Hon Sy; Perf Att; USMC Stu Ath Aw; Chrch Yth Grp; Emplmnt; Tech Clb; Ch Chr; Ftball (J); Tennis (J); Track (J); Wt Lftg (J); Wrstlg (J); Electrical Engineer; Columbia U of Engineering; Syracuse U

WRIGHT, SHANTEL J; NANUET, NY; SPRING VALLEY HS; (JR); Otst Ac Ach Awd; WWAHSS; Comm Volntr; Chrch Yth Grp; Emplmnt; Key Club; Lib Aide; Chr; Ch Chr; Dnce; SP/M/VS; Sch Ppr (R); Bowling Team (Varsity Letters); Reflections Writing Award; Speech Therapy; Physical Therapy; Montclair U; Long Island U

WRIGHTSON, LAURA; HOLLAND, NY; HOLLAND HS; (FR); All Am Sch; Hi Hnr Roll; MVP; Pres Ac Ftns Aw; WWAHSS; Comm Volntr; Peer Tut/Med; Drma Clb; Key Club; Bnd; Chr; Dnce; Jzz Bnd; Golf; Skiing; Sccr (J); Cl Off (T); Sch Ppr (R); Pre-Law; Lawyer; Stanford U; Cornell U

WROBEL, JESSICA; NIAGARA FALLS, NY; NIAGARA FALLS HS; (SO); Hnr Roll; Perf Att; Bnd; Mch Bnd; Track (J); Guitar Club; Math Major; English Major; Penn State U; Niagara U

WRYK, SARAH; EAST AURORA, NY; EAST AURORA HS; (SO); Hnr Roll; Nat Hon Sy; Otst Ac Ach Awd; Perf Att; Sci Fairs; St of Mnth; Comm Volntr; Peer Tut/Med; Emplmnt; Mth Clb/Tm; Outdrs Clb; Dnce; Flg Crps; Orch; Stg Cre; PP Ftbl (V); Swmg (V L); Track (V L); Scholar Athlete Award; Marine Biology; Photography; Florida State; Geneseo

WU, ALICE; BROOKLYN, NY; STUYVESANT HS; (FR); Nat Hon Sy; Perf Att; Salutrn; St of Mnth; Peer Tut/Med; Key Club; Mth Clb/Tm; Chr; Track (J); Sch Ppr (P); Psychology; Journalism; Columbia U; Princeton U

WU, AMANDA; LITTLE NECK, NY; BENJAMIN CARDOZO HS; (SO); Hnr Roll; Comm Volntr; Peer Tut/Med; Key Club; Psychology; Pharmacy; New York U; SUNY Buffalo

WU, ANDRIA; ELMHURST, NY; STUYVESANT HS; (FR); Hnr Roll; Kwnis Aw; Perf Att; Sci Fairs; WWAHSS; Comm Volntr; Key Club; Mth Clb/Tm; Acpl Chr; Chr; Dnce; Psychology; Business

WU, HELEN; BROOKLYN, NY; STUYVESANT HS; (SO); Nat Hon Sy; Key Club; Off Aide; Tchrs Aide; Tai Chi Club; Gu Zheng (Chinese Zither)

WU, IRENE; FOREST HILLS, NY; BRONX HS OF SCIENCE; (SR); F Lan Hn Soc; Hi Hnr Roll; Nat Hon Sy; Nat Ldrshp Svc; Nat Mrt Semif; Otst Ac Ach Awd; Sci Fairs; Red Cr Aide; Key Club; Clb; Bnd; Lit Mag; Journalist; Historian; Bryn Mawr College

WU, JANICE; BROOKLYN, NY; JAMES MADISON HS; Hnr Roll; Nat Sci Aw; Perf Att; St of Mnth; Comm Volntr; Peer Tut/Med; DARE; Key Club; Mth Clb/Tm; Sci Clb; Bnd; Chr; Dnce; Orch; Medical Field; Long Island U; New York U

WU, KEVIN J; ELMHURST, NY; STUYVESANT HS; (JR); Hnr Roll; Nat Hon Sy; Yth Ldrshp Prog; Comm Volntr; FBLA; Mth Clb/Tm; Bnd; Stg Cre; Track (V); AIME Math Competition Participant Twice; Math Fair Semifinalist; Biology; Business; Columbia U; Johns Hopkins U

WU, MELISSA; REGO PARK, NY; STUYVESANT HS; (SO); Hnr Roll; Sci Fairs; Peer Tut/Med; Red Cr Aide; Key Club; Mth Clb/Tm; Off Aide; Bnd; Dnce; Adv Cncl (R); Sch Ppr (E); Lawyer; Business Manager; Harvard U; Yale U

WU, NICOLE; FLUSHING, NY; FRANCIS LEWIS HS; (JR); Comm Volntr; Emplmnt; HIP Intern At Washington Mutual Bank; Grade 8 for the Associated Board of Royal Schools of Music; Criminologist; Pharmacist; Cornell U; U of Binghamton

WU, TAMMY; BROOKLYN, NY; MIDWOOD HS; (JR); Hnr Roll; Perf Att; Comm Volntr; Key Club; Off Aide; Accounting; Pharmacy / Chemistry; Columbia U; New York U

WYCHE, RASHIDA K; BRONX, NY; ST PIUS V HS; (JR); Hnr Roll; Nat Ldrshp Svc; Otst Ac Ach Awd; Yth Ldrshp Prog; Comm Volntr; Peer Tut/Med; Chrch Yth Grp; Emplmnt; Lib Aide; Off Aide; Scouts; Tchrs Aide; Bnd; Ch Chr; Dnce; SP/M/VS; Fashion Merchandising; Early Childhood Education; Clark Atlanta U; New York U

XU, KATHERINE; EAST ELMHURST, NY; STUYVESANT HS; (SO); Hi Hnr Roll; Kwnis Aw; Sci Fairs; WWAHSS; Comm Volntr; Peer Tut/Med; Red Cr Aide; Chrch Yth Grp; FCA; Key Club; Mth Clb/Tm; Mod UN; Off Aide; Tchrs Aide; Dnce; SP/M/VS; Bskball (L); Ice Sktg (L); Sccr (L); Swmg (L); Track (L); Vllyball (L); Wt Lftg (L); Yrbk (R); Participation in Salvation Army Star Search-Piano Level 4, 1st Place; Participation in NYSSMA-Piano Level 6-A+; Medical Science; Ivy League

XUE, ANDREW; STATEN ISLAND, NY; CURTIS HS; (JR); All Am Sch; Hi Hnr Roll; USAA; WWAHSS; Comm Volntr; Key Club; Mth Clb/Tm; Vllyball (V); President of Asian American Club; Computer Engineer; Business; Columbia; Cornell

YAM, MAYLING; VALLEY STREAM, NY; LAWRENCE HS; (SR); F Lan Hn Soc; Hi Hnr Roll; Hnr Roll; Nat Hon Sy; WWAHSS; Comm Volntr; Peer Tut/Med; Spec Olymp Vol; ArtClub; Emplmnt; Key Club; Mus Clb; SADD; French Clb; Orch; Bdmtn (V C); Vllyball (VJC); Yrbk (E); Tri-M music Honor Society; U At Albany; Maryland U, College Park

YAMIN, DANIELLE E; TROY, NY; TROY HS; (SO); Hi Hnr Roll; Hnr Roll; WWAHSS; Comm Volntr; Chrch Yth Grp; Key Club; French Clb; Stu Cncl; Photography; Arts

YAN, MEI Y; NEW YORK, NY; UNIVERSITY NEIGHBORHOOD HS; (JR); F Lan Hn Soc; Hnr Roll; Perf Att; Pres Ac Ftns Aw; Comm Volntr; Drma Clb; Vsity Clb; Chr; Dnce; Jzz Bnd; Tennis (V); Bowling; Education; Fashion Design; New York U

YAN, SOPHIA; FLUSHING, NY; BENJAMIN CARDOZO HS; (SO); Hnr Roll; Perf Att; Comm Volntr; Hosp Aide; Chrch Yth Grp; Mth Clb/Tm; Svce Clb; Orch; Business Woman; Dentist; Boston College; New York U

YANG, JENNY; GREENLAWN, NY; (JR); Hnr Roll; Otst Ac Ach Awd; St of Mnth; WWAHSS; Dnce; SP/M/VS; Lit Mag (E); Attending Presidential Classroom; Student of the Month; Business; Accounting; Cornell U; CW Post

YANG, NINA; FRESH MEADOWS, NY; STUYVESANT HS; (FR); Hnr Roll; Perf Att; Hosp Aide; Peer Tut/Med; Tchrs Aide; Bnd; Chr; Track (V); Sch Ppr (R, P); Played Piano for 8 Years; Passed Level 6 of Associated Board of Royal Schools of Music; Bachelor's Degree for Psychology; Pediatrics/Oncology; Colombia U; Cornell U

YANKE, TSEWANG; ASTORIA, NY; RENAISSANCE CHARTER SCH; (JR); Yth Ldrshp Prog; Comm Volntr; Photog; Prom Com; Vsity Clb; SP/M/VS; Bskball (V); Sftball (V); Vllyball (V); Stu Cncl; Yrbk (P); Won a Scholarship for New York; City Outward Bound Center.; Anthropology; Social Work; Green Mountain College; Truman State U

YAO, STEPHANIE; FRESH MEADOWS, NY; STUYVESANT HS; (SO); Hnr Roll; Otst Ac Ach Awd; Perf Att; WWAHSS; Comm Volntr; Red Cr Aide; Key Club; Svce Clb; SP/M/VS; Life Sciences; Social Sciences

YARDE, CAROLYN; ARVERNE, NY; BEACH CHANNEL HS; (JR); Hnr Roll; ArtClub; Drma Clb; Ch Chr; Dnce; Tennis; Painter / Pianist - Hobby; International Trade and Marketing; Fashion Institute of Technology

YASSIN, IMRAN; SOUTH OZONE PARK, NY; QUEENS HS FOR THE SCIENCES; (FR); Hnr Roll; Comm Volntr; Drma Clb; Key Club; Mth Clb/Tm; Tchrs Aide; SP/M/VS; Sch Ppr (R); Psychiatry; U of Toronto; New York U

YAZZETTI JR, ERNEST A; YONKERS, NY; CARDINAL SPELLMAN HS; (SR); Hi Hnr Roll; First Honors; Law; Elizabethtown College; St John's U

YE, XIANYI; BARRYTOWN, NY; RED HOOK HS; (SO); Ctznshp Aw; Hi Hnr Roll; Hnr Roll; MVP; Otst Ac Ach Awd; Perf Att; St of Mnth; Yth Ldrshp Prog; Comm Volntr; Peer Tut/Med; ArtClub; Chrch Yth Grp; Cmptr Clb; Drma Clb; FCA; Fr of Library; Mus Clb; Outdrs Clb; Bnd; Ch Chr; Bdmtn; Bskball; Ftball (J L); Lcrsse; Mar Art; Swmg; Track (V L); Wt Lftg; Cl Off (P); Achievement for Reading; Superstar of the Drama Club; Techno Design; Art; Harvard U; DeVry U

YEE, KIMBERLY; COLUMBUS CIRCLE STATION, NY; STUYVESANT HS; (SO); Ctznshp Aw; Hnr Roll; Nat Hon Sy; Perf Att; Pres Sch; Sci Fairs; St Schl; St of Mnth; Valdctrian; WWAHSS; Comm Volntr; Peer Tut/Med; JSA; Key Club; Off Aide; Svce Clb; Tchrs Aide; SP/M/VS; Stg Cre; Architecture; Columbia U; New York U

YEH, JONATHAN; SCHENECTADY, NY; GUILDERLAND HS; (SO); Perf Att; WWAHSS; Drma Clb; Key Club; SADD; Student Government; Conservative Students Association (CSA)

YEH, JUSTIN Y; GUILDERLAND, NY; GUILDERLAND HS; (FR); Perf Att; WWAHSS; Key Club; SADD; Orch; Chamber Orchestra; 9th Grade Representative-SADD

YEUNG, HOWA; BROOKLYN, NY; STUYVESANT HS; (SR); Kwnis Aw; WWAHSS; Key Club; Off Aide; Photog; Sci Clb; Dnce; SP/M/VS; Key Club Distinguished Club Treasurer's Award; Medicine; Sophie Davis School of Biomedical Education

YEUNG, KEVIN; FRESH MEADOWS, NY; STUYVESANT HS; (JR); Nat Hon Sy; WWAHSS; Comm Volntr; Hosp Aide; Peer Tut/Med; AL Aux Boys; Chess; Emplmnt; Key Club; Mth Clb/Tm; Off Aide; Tchrs Aide; Chr; Mar Art; Tennis; American Legion Aux - Boys State County Judge; Civil Engineering; Cooper Union; Rensselaer Polytechnic Institute

YEUNG, SUNG; JAMAICA, NY; GATEWAY TO HEALTH SCIENCES SCH; (SO); 4H Awd; Hnr Roll; Perf Att; Comm Volntr; Peer Tut/Med; 4-H; ArtClub; Cmptr Clb; Sci Clb; Vllyball (J); Engineer; Cornell U

YIN, SUE S; NEW YORK, NY; STUYVESANT HS; (SR); Hi Hnr Roll; Nat Mrt LOC; Perf Att; WWAHSS; Comm Volntr; Peer Tut/Med; Spec Olymp Vol; ArtClub; Biology Clb; Emplmnt; Key Club; Mod UN; Mus Clb; Tchrs Aide; Wdwrkg Clb; Acpl Chr; Ch Chr; Dnce; SP/M/VS; Lit Mag (E); Sch Ppr; Yrbk; AP Scholar; The National Society of High School Scholars; Biology; Music (Vocal)

YIP, JESSICA; JACKSON HEIGHTS, NY; VERONA HS; (SR)

YIP, WILLIAM; NEW YORK, NY; BROOKLYN TECH HS; (JR); Comm Volntr; Chess; Emplmnt; Plays for the Rockets - NY Basketball Team; Accounting; SUNY Binghamton; CUNY Baruch

YOM, TIANA; BETHPAGE, NY; BETHPAGE HS; (JR); Ctznshp Aw; Hi Hnr Roll; Hnr Roll; Nat Hon Sy; Nat Mrt Sch Recip; Perf Att; Pres Sch; Sci Fairs; Sci/Math Olympn; Yth Ldrshp Prog; Comm Volntr; Hosp Aide; Peer Tut/Med; Chrch Yth Grp; Mth Clb/Tm; Mus Clb; Sci Clb; SADD; Vsity Clb; Spanish Clb; Mch Bnd; Orch; Pep Bnd; Bdmtn (V L); Scr Kpr (V L); Tennis (V L); Stu Cncl (R); Lit Mag (R); Yrbk (R); 2005 Amateur Poet Winner; Pre-Medicine; Become a Pediatrician; Yale U; Columbia U

YOO, JINNY; WEST HEMPSTEAD, NY; WEST HEMPSTEAD HS; (SO); Hi Hnr Roll; Hnr Roll; Nat Hon Sy; WWAHSS; Comm Volntr; Peer Tut/Med; ArtClub; Chrch Yth Grp; Key Club; Mth Clb/Tm; Mus Clb; Orch; SP/M/VS; Tennis (V); Kickline; LISFA and All-county / Metropolitan Youth Group Orchestra; biology and chemistry; Double Major in Music; Boston College; Colgate U

YORK, KRISTY; ELMIRA, NY; THOMAS A EDISON HS; (FR); Hi Hnr Roll; Hnr Roll; Sci Fairs; WWAHSS; Peer Tut/Med; 4-H; ArtClub; Chrch Yth Grp; Key Club; Kwanza Clb; Scouts; Chr; Clr Grd; Stg Cre; Vet Tech; Artist

YORK, RACHEL E; GLASCO, NY; SAUGERTIES HS; (FR); Hi Hnr Roll; WWAHSS; Key Club; Vsity Clb; French Clb; Bnd; Stg Cre; Lcrsse (V); Sccr (J L)

YORK, SARAH; GLASCO, NY; SAUGERTIES HS; (JR); Hi Hnr Roll; Nat Hon Sy; WWAHSS; Hosp Aide; Emplmnt; Fr of Library; Key Club; Prom Com; Spanish Clb; Sccr (J); Cl Off (R); History Club - President; U of North Carolina Chapel Hill; U of Virginia

YOUNG, CHRIS; BAYPORT, NY; BAYPORT BLUE POINT HS; (SO); Hi Hnr Roll; Hnr Roll; St of Mnth; Chess; Photog; Scouts; SADD; Bnd; Orch; Cr Ctry (J); Track (J); Teacher

YOUNG, HEATHER; SAUGERTIES, NY; SAUGERTIES HS; (SO); Hi Hnr Roll; Pres Ac Ftns Aw; WWAHSS; Comm Volntr; DARE; Key Club; Vsity Clb; Sftball (V); Vllyball (JC); NYS Bowling Youth Leader; Teaching / Math or Physical Education; Veterinarian; Marist College; SUNY New Paltz

YOUNG, HILLARY; BIG FLATS, NY; HORSEHEADS HS; (FR); Hi Hnr Roll; Nat Hon Sy; Otst Ac Ach Awd; St of Mnth; Comm Volntr; Quiz Bowl; Bnd; Jzz Bnd; Completion of NYSSMA; Pioneering to Reach Others About the Bible; Business/Accounting; Corning Community College; Elmira Business Institute

YOUNG, JENNIFER; BROOKLYN, NY; MIDWOOD HS; (SO); Hi Hnr Roll; Nat Mrt LOC; Perf Att; Valdctrian; Red Cr Aide; Key Club; Vsity Clb; Bnd; Ch Chr; Vsy Clb (V); Archon Honor Society; Best of Brooklyn Award; Physical Therapy; Hunter College Honors; SUNY Binghamton

YOUNG, JEROME; BROOKLYN, NY; SAMUEL J TILDEN HS; (SR); Hnr Roll; Chr; Sccr; Vllyball; Nursing; New York Institute of Technology

YOUNG, KASHANA; ELMONT, NY; FRANK SINATRA HS; (JR); Hosp Aide; Chr; Lit Mag (R); Accepted for Summer Course At Columbia; National Student Leadership Conference; Law; English; New York U; Columbia U

YOUNG, MATTHEW; HUDSON FALLS, NY; HUDSON FALLS HS; (SR); Hi Hnr Roll; Hnr Roll; Perf Att; St of Mnth; Comm Volntr; DARE; Emplmnt; Key Club; Quiz Bowl; Bsball (V); Cr Ctry (V); Ftball (VJ L); Track (J); Stu Cncl (R); CR (R); Culinary Institute of America

YOUNG, OLIVER; SENECA FALLS, NY; MYNDERSE AC HS; (FR); Hnr Roll; St of Mnth; Comm Volntr; Peer Tut/Med; Scouts; Skiing (V); Tennis (V); Yrbk (E)

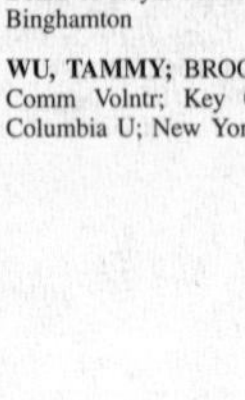
Young, Hillary
Horseheads HS
Big Flats, NY

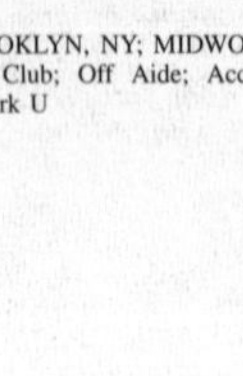
Yee, Kimberly
Stuyvesant HS
Columbus Circle Station, NY

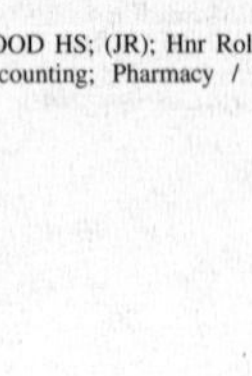
Yazzetti Jr, Ernest A
Cardinal Spellman HS
Yonkers, NY

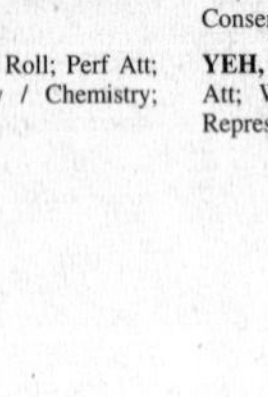
Xu, Katherine
Stuyvesant HS
East Elmhurst, NY

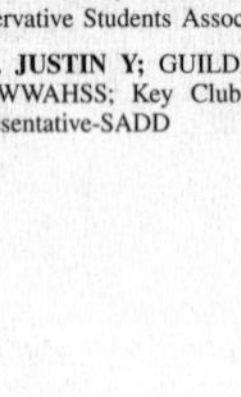
Wu, Alice
Stuyvesant HS
Brooklyn, NY

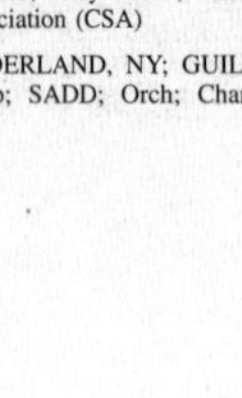
Wright, Kevia
Saugerties HS
Saugerties, NY

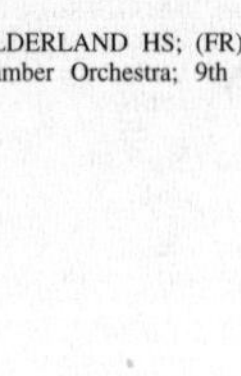
Wright, Shantel J
Spring Valley HS
Nanuet, NY

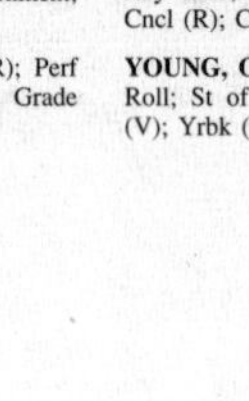
Yassin, Imran
Queens HS For The Sciences
South Ozone Park, NY

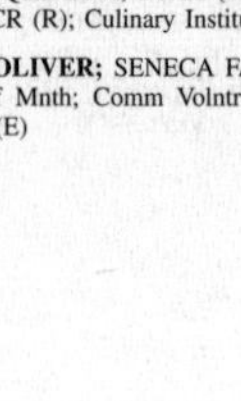
Ye, Xianyi
Red Hook HS
Barrytown, NY

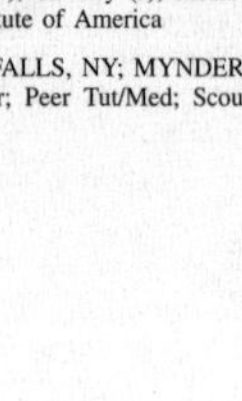
Yip, Jessica
Verona HS
Jackson Heights, NY

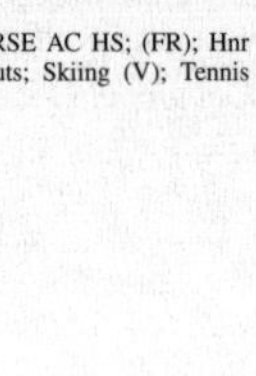
Young, Heather
Saugerties HS
Saugerties, NY

YOUSAF, MUHAMMAD A; EAST ELMHURST, NY; MONSIGNOR MC CLANCY HS; (JR); F Lan Hn Soc; Hnr Roll; Nat Hon Sy; Otst Ac Ach Awd; Comm Volntr; Peer Tut/Med; ArtClub; Chess; Cmptr Clb; Mth Clb/Tm; Sci Clb; Medical; Sophie Davis School; St John's U

YOUSSUFF, TANZIB; JAMAICA, NY; GATEWAY TO HEALTH SCIENCES SCH; (SO); Hnr Roll; Perf Att; Peer Tut/Med; Chess; Sci Clb; Tchrs Aide; Bnd; Dnce; Sch Ppr (R); New York Regional Brain Bee Participant; Arm Wrestling Silver Medalist; Neuroscience; Neurology; Stony Brook U; New York U

YOUSUF, WAQAR; BROOKLYN, NY; ABRAHAM LINCOLN HS; (FR); Hi Hnr Roll; Hnr Roll; Jr Mshl; Otst Ac Ach Awd; Perf Att; St of Mnth; Peer Tut/Med; Chrch Yth Grp; DARE; Emplmnt; Key Club; Off Aide; SADD; Tchrs Aide; Wdwrkg Clb; Bsball (J); Bskball (J); Baseball; Medical Degree; Hunter College; Kingsborough Community College

YU, CARMEN; FLUSHING, NY; FRANCIS LEWIS HS; (JR); Comm Volntr; Science; Art; Cornell U; Stony Brook U

YU, JENNY; BROOKLYN, NY; MIDWOOD HS; (SR); Emplmnt; Key Club; Business / Accounting; Finance; SUNY Stony Brook; SUNY Binghamton

YU, PING X; QUEENS, NY; FRANKLIN K LANE HS; (JR); Hnr Roll; Perf Att; Comm Volntr; Peer Tut/Med; Mth Clb/Tm; Tchrs Aide

YU, YI-JIN; JAMAICA, NY; THE BRONX HS OF SCIENCE; (JR); WWAHSS; Comm Volntr; Key Club; Off Aide; Sch Ppr (R); Journalism; Urban Studies; St John's U; SUNY New Paltz (State U of New York)

YUN, JUDY; BAYSIDE, NY; F H LAGUARDIA HS; (SO); Hnr Roll; Nat Hon Sy; Comm Volntr; Hosp Aide; Peer Tut/Med; Chrch Yth Grp; Emplmnt; Lib Aide; Japanese Clb; Ch Chr; Cartooning/Animation; Graphic Novelist; School of Visual Arts; Cooper Union

YUN, SARA S; OAKLAND GARDENS, NY; BENJAMIN CARDOZO HS; (JR); WWAHSS; Comm Volntr; Key Club; Bnd; Volunteer in Children Day Care Center; Volunteer in an Elementary School; Early Childhood Education; CUNY Queens College; CUNY Hunter College

YUZYNKO, DIANNA C; LATHAM, NY; SHAKER HS; (JR); Ctznshp Aw; Hi Hnr Roll; Hnr Roll; Salutrn; St of Mnth; Comm Volntr; Peer Tut/Med; Key Club; Spanish Clb; Spanish & Latin Clubs; The American Legion Citizenship Award; English / Literature; Elementary Education; SUNY Binghamton; SUNY Oneonta

ZACHARCZYK, LAUREN R; HIGHLAND MILLS, NY; MONROE-WOODBURY HS; (SO); Ctznshp Aw; Hi Hnr Roll; Comm Volntr; ArtClub; Chr; Orch; Honor Roll; NYSSMA - NY State School Music Association

ZACHARIAH, JEENA; ELMSFORD, NY; WOODLANDS HS; (SO); Hi Hnr Roll; Hnr Roll; Perf Att; St of Mnth; WWAHSS; Comm Volntr; Chrch Yth Grp; P to P St Amb Prg; Ch Chr; Basketball outside of school; Piano; Teacher; Physicians Assistant; SUNY College of Stony Brook

ZAIKA, NATALYA; MERRICK, NY; SANFORD H CALHOUN HS; (SO); Ctznshp Aw; F Lan Hn Soc; Hi Hnr Roll; Nat Hon Sy; St of Mnth; Comm Volntr; Peer Tut/Med; ArtClub; Key Club; SADD; Yrbk; New York State Science Honor Society; Mu Alpha Theta Math Honor Society; Ph.D. in Psychology; Brandeis U; Johns Hopkins U

ZAK, SAMUEL; BROOKLYN, NY; ZDR AC; (JR); Neurologist; Dermatologist; Brooklyn College

ZANGWIO, SWEBA; BRONX, NY; COLUMBUS HS; (SR); Hnr Roll; Nat Hon Sy; Perf Att; Comm Volntr; Peer Tut/Med; Aqrium Clb; Off Aide; Svce Clb; Vsity Clb; Cr Ctry (V); Sccr (V); College of New Rochelle; U of Vermont

ZAREMSKI, SARAH E; ALTAMONT, NY; GUILDERLAND HS; (JR); Hnr Roll; Comm Volntr; Peer Tut/Med; Key Club; Pep Squd; Yrbk (E); Mechanical Engineering; Chemical Engineering; U of Miami; California Polytechnic Institute

ZASSMAN, ROBERT; MERRICK, NY; JOHN F KENNEDY HS; (FR); Hnr Roll; FBLA; Key Club; Swg Chr; CR (T, R); Accepted Into the Intel Advanced Science Research Program; Scientist; Entrepreneur; Harvard; Yale

ZAVALA, ELSA; EAST ELMHURST, NY; FLUSHING HS; (FR); St of Mnth; Drma Clb; Bnd; Fashion Design; Law; Queens College; Harvard U

ZEHR, JESSICA L; CANASTOTA, NY; CANASTOTA HS; (SR); DAR; Hi Hnr Roll; Nat Hon Sy; Valdctrian; WWAHSS; Comm Volntr; Peer Tut/Med; Red Cr Aide; ArtClub; Drma Clb; Emplmnt; Photog; Prom Com; Acpl Chr; Bnd; Chr; Mch Bnd; Fld Hky (J); Scr Kpr (V); Track (V); Cl Off (R); Sch Ppr (R, P); Yrbk (R, P); President of National Honor Society; Honorable Mention in Scholastics Art Awards; Communications; Cornell U; Boston U

ZEIGLER, JESSICA; MIDDLETOWN, NY; PINE BUSH HS; (FR); Ctznshp Aw; Hnr Roll; Perf Att; St of Mnth; Hosp Aide; Peer Tut/Med; Chrch Yth Grp; Emplmnt; Mth Clb/Tm; P to P St Amb Prg; Sci Clb; SADD; Chr; Stg Cre; Mar Art; Scr Kpr; Track; Stu Cncl (R); CR (R); Sch Ppr (R); Sojourner Truth Award; Duke U

ZELWIAN, ERIKA D; BROOKLYN, NY; FLORELLO H LA GUARDIA HS; (SO); Hnr Roll; Mus Clb; Acpl Chr; Chr; Ch Chr; SP/M/VS; Bskball (V); Psychology; Mathematics; U of California Los Angeles; Berkeley College

ZEMBER, ERIC; SYOSSET, NY; SYOSSET HS; (JR); F Lan Hn Soc; Hnr Roll; Nat Hon Sy; Sci Fairs; Peer Tut/Med; Red Cr Aide; DECA; Mus Clb; Prom Com; SADD; Tmpl Yth Grp; Spanish Clb; Acpl Chr; Chr; Cyclg (J); Stu Cncl (V); 3rd Place School Science Fair; All State Chorus; Business-Finance; Psychology-Human Development; Cornell U; U of Emory

ZENGERSKI, ANDREA; BUFFALO, NY; WEST SENECA EAST SR HS; (FR); Ctznshp Aw; Perf Att; Comm Volntr; Key Club; Scouts; Spanish Clb; Orch; Bowler of the Year; 200 Hrs Community Service; Business; U of Buffalo; Erie Community College

ZENGERSKI, ASHLEY; BUFFALO, NY; WEST SENECA EAST SR HS; (JR); Ctznshp Aw; Hi Hnr Roll; Hnr Roll; Kwnis Aw; Nat Hon Sy; Perf Att; Pres Sch; St of Mnth; WWAHSS; Comm Volntr; Emplmnt; Key Club; Scouts; SADD; Spanish Clb; Bnd; Jzz Bnd; Orch; Stu Cncl (R); President of Key Club; Community Orchestras; Music Education; Music Performance; State U of New York At Fredonia; Baldwin-Wallace

ZEPHIR, LARYSSA M C; BROOKLYN, NY; SAMUEL J TILDEN HS; (SR); F Lan Hn Soc; Hi Hnr Roll; Hnr Roll; MVP; Nat Hon Sy; Otst Ac Ach Awd; Perf Att; WWAHSS; Peer Tut/Med; Red Cr Aide; Off Aide; Vsity Clb; Ch Chr; Dnce; SP/M/VS; Bskball (V); Vllyball (V); Cl Off; Biology / Pre-Med; Doctor / Obstetrician Nurse; SUNY Binghamton; CUNY Hunter

ZERBA, MEGAN; MOUNT MARION, NY; SAUGERTIES HS; (SO); Hi Hnr Roll; St of Mnth; WWAHSS; Chrch Yth Grp; Key Club; French Clb; Bnd; Tennis (V); Held Offices in FCCLA As Secretary and Vice President; Actively Participated in FCCLA, Key Club & French Club; Biology/Marine Biology; Zoology; Purdue U

ZHANG, ANNIE; BRONX, NY; STUYVESANT HS; (FR); Gov Hnr Prg; Hi Hnr Roll; Nat Hon Sy; Sci Fairs; WWAHSS; Peer Tut/Med; Key Club; Mth Clb/Tm; Svce Clb; Acpl Chr; Stg Cre; Stu Cncl (S); Sch Ppr (R); Ph.D; MD; Harvard U; Columbia U

ZHANG, ZHIHANG; BRONX, NY; (FR); Gov Hnr Prg; Hi Hnr Roll; Hnr Roll; Nat Hon Sy; Perf Att; Pres Ac Ftns Aw; WWAHSS; Comm Volntr; Peer Tut/Med; Cmptr Clb; Key Club; Mth Clb/Tm; Mod UN; Bnd; SP/M/VS; Yrbk (E); Neurologist; Surgeon; Princeton U; Yale U

ZHAO, FANNY; BROOKLYN, NY; MIDWOOD HS; (FR); Comm Volntr; Peer Tut/Med; Emplmnt; Key Club; Lib Aide; Off Aide; Tchrs Aide; Mch Bnd; Winter Concert Usher; HOPS

ZHAO, LONG; ELMHURST, NY; NEWTOWN HS; (FR); Perf Att; Bskball (V); Ftball (V); Sccr (V); BA Degree; BS Degree; New York U; Pace U

ZHAO, SUSAN; BROOKLYN, NY; MIDWOOD HS; (SO); Hi Hnr Roll; Otst Ac Ach Awd; Perf Att; Comm Volntr; Red Cr Aide; Emplmnt; Key Club; Mth Clb/Tm; Off Aide; Bnd; Mch Bnd; Pre-Med; New York U; Columbia U

ZHARNITSKY, ELLIOT; GREAT NECK, NY; GREAT NECK SOUTH HS; (JR); Hnr Roll; MVP; Otst Ac Ach Awd; Peer Tut/Med; DECA; Emplmnt; Mod UN; Russian Clb; Bskball (J); Tennis (V); Vllyball (V); Stu Cncl (R); CR (R); Sch Ppr (E, R); President of the Russian Club; Vice President of the Government Club; Sports Marketing or Management; Dentistry; U of Pennsylvania; Michigan U

ZHEN, MARIAN; NEW YORK, NY; MIDWOOD HS; (SO); Sci Fairs; WWAHSS; Comm Volntr; Peer Tut/Med; Red Cr Aide; Key Club; Off Aide; Tchrs Aide; Swmg; Key Club Board of Directors; Asian Society President; Neurosurgeon; Columbia U; Yale U

ZHENG, MEIHAO; BOONVILLE, NY; ADIRONDACK HS; (JR); Ctznshp Aw; Hi Hnr Roll; Nat Hon Sy; Otst Ac Ach Awd; Perf Att; Pres Sch; Sci/Math Olympn; WWAHSS; Comm Volntr; Peer Tut/Med; Emplmnt; French Clb; Scr Kpr (J); Top Ten Award #1; Elliot Spitzer Triple C Award; Business Management; General Studies; Cornell U; Princeton U

ZHENG, RUI H; FLUSHING, NY; FRANCIS LEWIS HS; (SO); Nat Hon Sy; Comm Volntr; Emplmnt; Sci Clb; Tchrs Aide; Bskball; Writer Workshop; Pre-Medical; Engineering; Cornell U; State U of New York At Binghamton

ZHENG, ZHENGLANG; CARMEL, NY; CARMEL HS; (SO); Accountant; Mechanic

ZHERKA, NADIRE; BRONX, NY; CATHEDRAL HS; (FR); Hnr Roll; DARE; Drma Clb; Chr; SP/M/VS; Sftball (J); CR (R); Drama Club; Actress; Lawyer; Harvard U; NYU

ZHOU, JOANNA; BROOKLYN, NY; STUYVESANT HS; (SO); Pres Sch; Salutrn; St of Mnth; WWAHSS; Comm Volntr; Peer Tut/Med; Emplmnt; Key Club; Off Aide; Stg Cre; Yrbk (E); Medicine; Business

ZHOU, LINDA; MERRICK, NY; W.C. MEPHAM HS; (SO); F Lan Hn Soc; Hnr Roll; Sci Fairs; WWAHSS; Peer Tut/Med; ArtClub; Key Club; SP/M/VS; Lit Mag; Volunteer At Long Island Riding for the Handicapped Assoc.; Semifinalist in the 2005 Quest Leadership Program; Medicine; Business; Columbia U

ZHOU, RACHEL; BROOKLYN, NY; STUYVESANT HS; (SO); Hnr Roll; Pres Sch; St of Mnth; Comm Volntr; Hosp Aide; Key Club; Lib Aide; Mth Clb/Tm; Off Aide; Svce Clb; Tchrs Aide; Sch Ppr (R); Pediatric/Medicine; Columbia U; U of Pennsylvania

ZHOU, ROBIN; EAST AMHERST, NY; WILLIAMSVILLE EAST HS; (SR); Hi Hnr Roll; Hnr Roll; Nat Hon Sy; Nat Mrt LOC; Sci/Math Olympn; Comm Volntr; Hab For Humty Volntr; Drma Clb; Emplmnt; FBLA; Mod UN; Svce Clb; Orch; SP/M/VS; Tennis (V); Yrbk (E, R, P); Unity in Diversity Club - Vice President; Cooking Club - Co-Founder; Biological Sciences; Cornell U

ZHOU, SUZANNA; BROOKLYN, NY; MIDWOOD HS; (SO); Nat Hon Sy; WWAHSS; Yth Ldrshp Prog; Amnsty Intl; Red Cr Aide; Key Club; Lib Aide; Off Aide; Tchrs Aide; Accounting; Business; New York U; St John's U

ZHU, NANCY; NEW YORK, NY; STUYVESANT HS; (FR); Hi Hnr Roll; Nat Hon Sy; Sci Fairs; WWAHSS; Key Club; Mth Clb/Tm; Bnd; Arista; Pediatrician; Yale; Columbia

ZHU, PETER; SLINGERLANDS, NY; GUILDERLAND HS; (SO); Hi Hnr Roll; Otst Ac Ach Awd; WWAHSS; Peer Tut/Med; Emplmnt; Key Club; Mth Clb/Tm; Mus Clb; Prom Com; Orch; SP/M/VS; Cr Ctry (J); Tennis (JC); Sch Ppr (E); 3rd Place: Anthony R. Stetzn Scholarship Competition; Empire State Youth Orchestra; Columbia U; Yale U

ZHUCHENYA, TATYANA; UTICA, NY; THOMAS R PROCTOR HS; (FR); Hi Hnr Roll; Hnr Roll; DARE; Ch Chr

ZHUSHMA, ARTHUR; HERKIMER, NY; HERKIMER HS; (FR); Hi Hnr Roll; Hnr Roll; St of Mnth; Chrch Yth Grp; Emplmnt; FBLA; Bsball (J); Bskball (J); Ftball (V); Cl Off (V); North Carolina; Miami

ZIA, IRFAN; MINEOLA, NY; MINEOLA HS; (FR); Hi Hnr Roll; Nat Hon Sy; Pres Ac Ftns Aw; Sci/Math Olympn; St of Mnth; Comm Volntr; AL Aux Boys; Mth Clb/Tm; Chr; CR (P); Volunteer Mineola Junior Firefighter; President of National Junior Honor Society

ZIPPO, SAMANTHA M; YONKERS, NY; LINCOLN HS; (SO); Hnr Roll; DARE; Emplmnt; Preschool/Daycare Volunteer; Child Psychiatrist/ Psychologist; Teaching; Sacred Heart U; Fairfield U

ZUCCONI, LAUREN M; CHESTNUT RIDGE, NY; SPRING VALLEY HS; (JR); Hnr Roll; MVP; St of Mnth; WWAHSS; Comm Volntr; Emplmnt; Key Club; Sci Clb; Bnd; Dvng (V CL); Vice President Key Club; Education; College of New Jersey/Seton Hall; Marist

ZUCKERMAN, MICHAEL; SYOSSET, NY; SYOSSET HS; (JR); Hnr Roll; Nat Hon Sy; Otst Ac Ach Awd; DECA; Emplmnt; Spanish Clb; Bnd; Mch Bnd; MBA; Finance; U of Michigan-Ann Arbor; Lehigh U

ZULAUF, CHLOE; BROCKPORT, NY; BROCKPORT HS; (FR); Hi Hnr Roll; Hnr Roll; St of Mnth; Yth Ldrshp Prog; Dnce; Business; SUNY Brockport

ZULAUF, RAY; HOPEWELL JCT, NY; CANTERBURY SCH; (JR); Hnr Roll; Comm Volntr; Emplmnt; Golf (J); Ice Hky (J); Sccr (J); Cl Off (V); Volunteer Fireman; Business; Salve Regina University; Quinnipiac University

ZUMBO, MARISSA A; SCHENECTADY, NY; NISKAYUNA HS; (SR); Comm Volntr; Chrch Yth Grp; DECA; Emplmnt; Key Club; Pep Squd; Prom Com; Dnce; Lcrsse (V); Sccr (J); Cl Off (P); DECA Competition 1st Place Winner; Athletic Scholar; Pre-Med; Fordham U; New York U

ZUMMO, KRYSTEN; PATCHOGUE, NY; BAYPORT BLUE POINT HS; (SO); Hi Hnr Roll; Hnr Roll; Nat Hon Sy; St of Mnth; Yth Ldrshp Prog; Drma Clb; Chr; Jzz Bnd; SP/M/VS; Stg Cre; Yrbk (P); Talent Show X - 3 Yrs; Helped Organize Local Fund Raiser; Lawyer; ASPCA; Harvard U; Columbia U

ZURLO, JESSICA; STILLWATER, NY; STILLWATER CTRL HS; (JR); Hi Hnr Roll; Nat Hon Sy; Sci/Math Olympn; Comm Volntr; Peer Tut/Med; Key Club; Mth Clb/Tm; Sci Clb; SADD; Bnd; Mch Bnd; Track (V); Cl Off (S); Pre-Medicine

ZYCH, AMANDA; DOBBS FERRY, NY; MARIA REGINA HS; (JR); Hnr Roll; Nat Hon Sy; ArtClub; Key Club; Svce Clb; Italian Clb; Chrldg (V); Track (V); Secretary of Mission Outreach; Youth Cart Member (Greenburgh); Biology; Science Research; York College; Marist College

Yuzynko, Dianna C / Shaker HS / Latham, NY — Yousaf, Muhammad A / Monsignor Mc Clancy HS / East Elmhurst, NY — Yousuf, Waqar / Abraham Lincoln HS / Brooklyn, NY

North Carolina

ABASHIAN, MICHAEL D; CARY, NC; CARY HS; (SO); Perf Att; WWAHSS; Emplmnt; Scouts; Bskball (VJCL); Veterinarian; Sports Medicine; UNC Chapel Hill; UNC Wilmington

ABDELAZIZ, AHMED A; LUMBERTON, NC; LUMBERTON HS; (FR); Hnr Roll; Perf Att; Bskball; Ftball; CR (P)

ABRAHAM, MUNAZZA; JACKSONVILLE, NC; WHITE OAK HS; (MS); Hnr Roll; Nat Hon Sy; Comm Volntr; Bnd; Mch Bnd; Pep Bnd; Bskball; National Junior Honor Society; Sunburst Beauty-Model Search Pageant; Bachelor of Science; PhD; Howard U; Clark Atlanta U

ABRAMS, MATTHEW; SPRING HOPE, NC; SOUTHERN NASH HS; (JR); Hnr Roll; Perf Att; St of Mnth; ArtClub; Track (V); Wrstlg (V L); Master's Degree in Art; East Carolina U

ABUKAR, SULEKHA; CHARLOTTE, NC; EAST MECKLENBURG HS; (SO); Ctznshp Aw; Hi Hnr Roll; Hnr Roll; Nat Hon Sy; Otst Ac Ach Awd; Perf Att; Sci Fairs; St of Mnth; Comm Volntr; Peer Tut/Med; DARE; Jr Ach; Svce Clb; Stu Cncl (R); Sch Ppr (E); Diversity Club; IB Service Club; Pediatrician / Medicine; Nurse; UNC Chapel Hill; Duke U

ACEVEDO, LILLY C; CONOVER, NC; ST STEPHENS HS; (SR); Spanish Clb; Dnce; Engineer; Architecture; U of North Carolina At Charlotte; Appalachian State U

ACHESON-ADAMS, EMILY M; NEWLAND, NC; CROSSNORE AC; (FR); Hi Hnr Roll; Otst Ac Ach Awd; Pres Sch; St of Mnth; WWAHSS; Comm Volntr; Hab For Humty Volntr; Chrch Yth Grp; Cmptr Clb; Drma Clb; Emplmnt; Jr Cls League; Mus Clb; Outdrs Clb; Photog; Skiing (J)

ADAME, ARISBETT; REIDSVILLE, NC; REIDSVILLE HS; (FR); Hnr Roll; DARE; Bnd; Have Helped Non-Speaking English Students with Work; Psychology; Photographer; U of North Carolina

ADAMS, ANGEL L; LUMBERTON, NC; LUMBERTON HS; (SR); Chr; SP/M/VS; Stg Cre; Local Hospital Volunteer; Volunteer Teen Court; Study Marine Biology; PhD Oceanology & Marine Biology; UNC Wilmington; Roberson Community College

ADAMS, DANIELLE M; JACKSONVILLE, NC; NORTHSIDE HS; (FR); Hi Hnr Roll; Hnr Roll; Otst Ac Ach Awd; Chrch Yth Grp; Ch Chr; Drl Tm; Orch; Bskball (J); Sftball; Track; Vllyball (J); Cardiology; Cosmetology; U of North Carolina At Chapel Hill; East Carolina U

ADAMS, KRYSTEN; GASTON, NC; NORTHAMPTON CTY-WEST HS; (SR); Hi Hnr Roll; Hosp Aide; Chrch Yth Grp; Bnd; Ch Chr; Drl Tm; Mch Bnd; Drum Major; Currently in the SEM Program at Chapel Hill U; Medicine

ADAMS, LAURA; FAIRVIEW, NC; A C REYNOLDS HS; (FR); Hnr Roll; Perf Att; Comm Volntr; Spec Olymp Vol; Chrch Yth Grp; ROTC; Clr Grd; Drl Tm; Swmg (V); Pastry Arts Chef; Lawyer; Culinary Institute of Long Island; Art Institute of New York

ADAMS, LORI B; CLAYTON, NC; WEST JOHNSTON HS; (JR); Hi Hnr Roll; Hnr Roll; St of Mnth; Hab For Humty Volntr; Dbte Team; Drma Clb; SADD; Clb; SP/M/VS; Communication Skills Award; Communications; Theater; UNC Wilmington; Appalachian State

ADAMS, RYAN D; BURLINGTON, NC; WALTER WILLIAMS HS; (JR); Hnr Roll; MVP; Perf Att; WWAHSS; Comm Volntr; AL Aux Boys; Chrch Yth Grp; DARE; FCA; Lttrmn Clb; Pep Squd; SADD; Vsity Clb; Bsball (V); Vsy Clb (V); 03-04 All Conference Player; Education; Sports Trainer; Elon U; Wingate U

ADAMS, THOMAS; EDEN, NC; MOREHEAD JHS; (SO); Hnr Roll; Nat Hon Sy; Perf Att; WWAHSS; CARE; Hosp Aide; Spec Olymp Vol; Biology Clb; DARE; Mth Clb/Tm; ROTC; Tech Clb; Bskball (J); Ftball (L); Track (L); Duke; Carolina; Wake Forest; Georgia Tech

ADCOCK, JAMES L; BULLOCK, NC; J F WEBB HS; (JR); All Am Sch; Hnr Roll; Jr Eng Tech; Nat Hon Sy; Perf Att; Sci Fairs; Comm Volntr; DARE; Emplmnt; Ntl FFA; FFA Sentinel; Engineering; N.C. State

ADEFOLALU, OLALEKAN; GREENSBORO, NC; PAGE HS; (JR); Hi Hnr Roll; Hnr Roll; Chrch Yth Grp; DARE; Bnd; Mch Bnd; Wrstlg (V CL); 135 lb. Metro 4A Conference Champion (Wrestling); Psychology; Religion; The U of North Carolina At Chapel Hill; The U of North Carolina At Pembroke

ADKINS, TIARA M; RICHLANDS, NC; RICHLANDS HS; (JR); DAR; Hi Hnr Roll; Hnr Roll; Nat Hon Sy; Otst Ac Ach Awd; Pres Sch; WWAHSS; Yth Ldrshp Prog; Comm Volntr; Red Cr Aide; Ntl Beta Clb; NYLC; Cr Ctry (V L); PP Ftbl; Scer (V L); Track (V L); Stu Cncl (V, R); Psychology Major; Sociology Minor; Wesleyan College in North Carolina

AGATHON, LUISA; CHARLOTTE, NC; OLYMPIC HS; (JR); Hnr Roll; Jr Mshl; Nat Hon Sy; Perf Att; WWAHSS; Comm Volntr; Peer Tut/Med; Key Club; Ntl Beta Clb; ROTC; Vsity Clb; French Clb; Clr Grd; Drl Tm; Sccr (V CL); Science Honor Society; French Honor Society; Psychology; Choreographer; UNC @ Charlotte; Central Community College

AGOR, UCHE J; CHARLOTTE, NC; PROVIDENCE HS; (SO); Hnr Roll; WWAHSS; Comm Volntr; Red Cr Aide; Chr; Ch Chr; Vllyball (J); MD Degree; Science Major; UNC Chapel Hill; Duke U

AGUON, MARLEE M; HAVELOCK, NC; HAVELOCK HS; (JR); Hi Hnr Roll; Hnr Roll; Otst Ac Ach Awd; Perf Att; WWAHSS; DARE; Emplmnt; Scouts; Bnd; Mch Bnd; Attorney; Vet; Harvard U; UNC Chapel Hill U of North Carolina

AIKEN, RICHARD J; ROSMAN, NC; ROSMAN HS; (SO); Duke TS; Hi Hnr Roll; Nat Hon Sy; Perf Att; Sci Fairs; WWAHSS; Comm Volntr; Peer Tut/Med; Emplmnt; Ntl FFA; P to P St Amb Prg; Voc Ind Clb Am; Bsball (J); Wrstlg (V L); Clemson U; North Carolina State U

AIKENS, CAMERON; KERNERSVILLE, NC; (JR); Hnr Roll; Perf Att; WWAHSS; Yth Ldrshp Prog; Comm Volntr; Peer Tut/Med; Ftball (V); Track (V); Wt Lftg (V); CR (V); BA Degree in Computer Animation; BA Video Game Design; NC State, NC School of Arts; UNC Chapel Hill, Winston Salem State

AKINS, NISA N; JACKSONVILLE, NC; SOUTHWEST HS; (SR); Hnr Roll; MVP; Spanish Clb; Bnd; Bskball (V); Sccr (V C); 2004-2005 Homecoming Queen; All-Conference (Soccer) 2003, 2004; Physical Therapist; Athletic Trainer; High Point U, Mount Olive College; U of North Carolina Greensboro

ALADENIYI, DAYO; CHARLOTTE, NC; NORTH MECKLENBURG HS; (JR); Hnr Roll; Nat Hon Sy; St of Mnth; WWAHSS; Ch Chr; Track; Lit Mag (E); Who's Who American Student; French Club; Law; Physical Therapy; U of North Carolina Chapel Hill; Elon U

ALADENIYI, FUNMI; CHARLOTTE, NC; NORTH MECKLENBURG HS; (SR); Hnr Roll; Nat Sci Aw; St of Mnth; WWAHSS; Yth Ldrshp Prog; Comm Volntr; Chrch Yth Grp; Emplmnt; Voc Ind Clb Am; Chr; Ch Chr; National Technical Honor Society; Chemistry (Major); I Want to Become a Pediatrician.; U of North Carolina At Chapel Hill

ALBEA, MEG; ETOWAH, NC; WEST HENDERSON HS; (JR); All Am Sch; Ctznshp Aw; Hi Hnr Roll; Hnr Roll; Jr Mshl; Kwnis Aw; MVP; Nat Hon Sy; Otst Ac Ach Awd; Pres Ac Ftns Aw; Comm Volntr; Peer Tut/Med; Chrch Yth Grp; DARE; FCA; Key Club; Lib Aide; Ntl Beta Clb; Quill & Scroll; Bnd; Jzz Bnd; Swmg (V CL); Cl Off (V); Stu Cncl (T); Sch Ppr (E); Swimmer of the Year / AP Biology Award / French Award / Brevard College Book Award / Chief Marshall Western Highland Amateur Finalist; Biology; Math; Furman U; UNC Chapel Hill

ALBERGHINI, HOLLYN; STANFIELD, NC; WEST STANLY HS; (JR); Bskball (V); Tennis (V); Business Major; UNCC U of North Carolina Charlotte; U of North Carolina Wilmington

ALBERTSON, LOREN A; ELIZABETH CTY, NC; PASQUOTONK HS; (SO); 4H Awd; Ctznshp Aw; Hnr Roll; Perf Att; Comm Volntr; 4-H; Chrch Yth Grp; Drma Clb; SP/M/VS; Sch Ppr (E, R); Journalism; English; U of North Carolina: Wilmington; North Carolina State U

ALDEN, JOSHUA; CORNELIUS, NC; HOPEWELL HS; (JR); Hnr Roll; Comm Volntr; DARE; Scouts; Stg Cre; Film; Art; Appalachian State

ALEXANDER, AARON T; SHELBY, NC; CREST HS; (FR); Hnr Roll; Comm Volntr; ArtClub; Chrch Yth Grp; DARE; Ntl Beta Clb; Commercial Artist; Cartoonist; Gardner-Webb U; UNC/Chapel Hill

ALEXANDER, SYMONE C; ASHEVILLE, NC; A C REYNOLDS HS; (JR); Gov Hnr Prg; Hnr Roll; WWAHSS; Comm Volntr; Peer Tut/Med; Chrch Yth Grp; FCA; Chr; Dnce; Drm Mjr; SP/M/VS; Track (V); Major in Education; Doctorate Degree; UNC Chapel Hill; UNC Greensboro

ALISCA, CHRISTINA M; CHARLOTTE, NC; BUTLER HS; (JR); Hnr Roll; Nat Hon Sy; WWAHSS; Comm Volntr; Peer Tut/Med; Emplmnt; Key Club; Mus Clb; Scouts; Svce Clb; Orch; SP/M/VS; CR (R); Girl Scout Gold & Silver Awards; Charlotte Symphony Youth Orchestra; Education; U of North Carolina Greensboro; U of North Carolina Wilmington

ALLDER, ALYSSA; IRON STATION, NC; EAST LINCOLN HS; (SO); Hnr Roll; WWAHSS; Comm Volntr; ArtClub; Svce Clb; Clb; Sccr (V); Psychology; U of North Carolina At Wilmington; U of North Carolina At Chapel Hill

ALLEN, AMY L; WILMINGTON, NC; E A LANEY HS; (JR); Hnr Roll; Sci Fairs; Ntl Beta Clb; Ch Chr; SP/M/VS; Golf (V L); Meteorology; Atmospheric Sciences

ALLEN, ANDREW B; SILER CITY, NC; JORDAN MATTHEWS HS; (FR); Hi Hnr Roll; Chrch Yth Grp; Chr

ALLEN, ELAINE R; CREEDMOOR, NC; SOUTH GRANVILLE SCH OF HEALTH SCIENCES; (FR); Ctznshp Aw; Duke TS; Hnr Roll; Sci Fairs; DARE; Scouts; Sftball (V L); Vllyball (V L); Stu Cncl (R); Student of Merit; NCHSAA Scholar-Athlete; Sports Medicine; Physical Therapy; U of North Carolina At Chapel Hill; East Carolina U

ALLEN, KATELYN B; KITTY HAWK, NC; FIRST FLIGHT HS; (JR); Duke TS; Hi Hnr Roll; Nat Hon Sy; Yth Ldrshp Prog; Comm Volntr; Peer Tut/Med; Emplmnt; Key Club; Spanish Clb; Phi Theta Kappa Spring Inductee; Service Learning Award; Pediatric Oncologist; Neurobiology; Pennsylvania State U At U Park; U of North Carolina At Chapel Hill

ALLEN, SARA; HOPE MILLS, NC; SOUTH VIEW HS; (JR); Hnr Roll; WWAHSS; Comm Volntr; Chrch Yth Grp; Key Club; Lib Aide; Ntl Beta Clb; Bnd; Clr Grd; Dnce; CR (R); Key Club President-South View HS; Elementary Education; UNC Wilmington; East Carolina U

ALLEN, VICTORIA; LEXINGTON, NC; NORTH DAVIDSON HS; (SO); Hnr Roll; WWAHSS; Chrch Yth Grp; Emplmnt; FCA; FTA; Foreign Clb; Ch Chr; Swmg (V L); Sch Ppr (R, P); Highest Average in All Geometry Classes; Journalism; Radio/Television Broadcasting; U of North Carolina @ Wilmington; U of Miami

ALLEY, BRETT N; CLAREMONT, NC; BUNKER HILL HS; (JR); Hnr Roll; WWAHSS; ArtClub; Chrch Yth Grp; Emplmnt; Sci Clb; Spanish Clb; National Society of High School Scholars; Leadership Conference; Internet Technologies; Catawba Valley Community College; Appalachian State U

ALLIGOOD, CASEY; WASHINGTON, NC; NORTHSIDE HS; (FR); Duke TS; Hi Hnr Roll; Hnr Roll; MVP; Perf Att; Sci/Math Olympn; WWAHSS; Hosp Aide; DARE; FBLA; Key Club; Mth Clb/Tm; Sci Clb; Dnce; Bskball (V); Sftball (V); Science Olympiad B Medals in 9th Grade; Business Management; U North Carolina At Chapel-Hill

ALLISON, JUSTIN; MONROE, NC; METROLINA CHRISTIAN AC; (JR); Hnr Roll; Sci Fairs; Sci/Math Olympn; Yth Ldrshp Prog; Comm Volntr; Chrch Yth Grp; Ntl Beta Clb; NYLC; Bnd; Chr; Orch; Pep Bnd; Various Community Service Projects; Beta Club / College Classes / Art Award; Attorney; Business Major; U of North Carolina

ALLISON, JUSTIN; PILOT MTN, NC; EAST SURRY HS; (JR); Hnr Roll; WWAHSS; Peer Tut/Med; 4-H; Emplmnt; Photog; Scouts; Spanish Clb; Ftball (V); Sch Ppr (E); Civil Engineering; Anthropology; North Carolina State U

ALLISON, LESLIE; HIGH POINT, NC; J.B. DUDLEY HS; (SO); Hnr Roll; Comm Volntr; Peer Tut/Med; Biology Clb; Chrch Yth Grp; Scouts; Latin Clb; Dnce; CR (R); Biology; Pre Medicine; Georgetown U

ALLISON, LESLIE M; SOUTHPORT, NC; SOUTH BRUNSWICK HS; (SO); Hnr Roll; Pres Sch; Comm Volntr; Hab For Humty Volntr; Peer Tut/Med; Chrch Yth Grp; Tmpl Yth Grp; Dnce; Veterinarian; Physical Therapist; North Carolina State U; U of North Carolina in Wilmington

ALSTON, ERICA S; ROCKY MOUNT, NC; SOUTHERN NASH HS; (JR); Perf Att; DARE; SADD; Teen Court; Major in Law; Carolina U

ALSTON, LENA; DURHAM, NC; SOUTHERN HS; (FR); Ctznshp Aw; Hnr Roll; Perf Att; St of Mnth; Comm Volntr; DARE; NYLC; Chrldg (J); Cl Off (R); HOSA, Medical Programs; Church Usher; PhD in Psychology; Medical Degree; U of North Carolina-Chapel Hill; East Carolina U

ALSTON, MYRISSA; HENDERSON, NC; NORTHERN VANCE HS; (SO); Hnr Roll; WWAHSS; Comm Volntr; DARE; Key Club; Bnd; Mch Bnd; Stu Cncl (R); United States Achievement Academy; Who's Who*Among American High School Students; Doctor; Lawyer; Hampton U; U of Georgia

ALSTON, TIMOTHY; NASHVILLE, NC; NASH CTRL HS; (FR); Hi Hnr Roll; Hnr Roll; Nat Hon Sy; Perf Att; Bskball (J); Track (J); Engineering Degree; Business Degree; Duke U; Wyotech Technical College

ALTHOFF, AMANDA D; WAKE FOREST, NC; WAKE FOREST-ROLESVILLE HS; (JR); Hnr Roll; Nat Hon Sy; Otst Ac Ach Awd; Pres Ac Ftns Aw; WWAHSS; Yth Ldrshp Prog; Comm Volntr; Hab For Humty Volntr; AL Aux Girls; Chrch Yth Grp; DARE; DECA; Emplmnt; FBLA; Key Club; Lttrmn Clb; Chrldg (V L); PP Ftbl (V); Sccr (VJ L); Cl Off (V); Stu Cncl (V); Yrbk (R, P); Business; Marketing & Directing; North Carolina State U; U of North Carolina

AMAN, JENNY; ZEBULON, NC; SMITHFIELD-SELMA HS; (JR); Hnr Roll; Nat Hon Sy; Nat Stu Ath Day Aw; WWAHSS; Spec Olymp Vol; Chrch Yth Grp; HO'Br Yth Ldrshp; Key Club; Prom Com; Tchrs Aide; PP Ftbl; Sftball; Tennis; Cl Off (R); CR (R); Criminal Justice; UNC Wilmington; Elon U

Allison, Justin
Metrolina Christian AC
Monroe, NC

Allen, Elaine R
South Granville Sch Of Health Sciences
Creedmoor, NC

Allison, Leslie M
South Brunswick HS
Southport, NC

Allen, Amy L
E A Laney HS
Wilmington, NC

Akins, Nisa N
Southwest HS
Jacksonville, NC

Adkins, Tiara M
Richlands HS
Richlands, NC

Adame, Arisbett
Reidsville HS
Reidsville, NC

Acevedo, Lilly C
St Stephens HS
Conover, NC

National
Honor Roll
Spring 2005

Abukar, Sulekha
East Mecklenburg HS
Charlotte, NC

Adams, Lori B
West Johnston HS
Clayton, NC

Aikens, Cameron
Kernersville, NC

Alexander, Aaron T
Crest HS
Shelby, NC

Alisca, Christina M
Butler HS
Charlotte, NC

AMBROSE, MADISON; KILL DEVIL HILLS, NC; FIRST FLIGHT HS; (SO); Hi Hnr Roll; WWAHSS; Comm Volntr; Drma Clb; Key Club; SP/M/VS; Sccr (V); Law; Marketing; U of North Carolina At Chapel Hill; William and Mary

AMICK, JENNIFER; WASHINGTON, NC; WASHINGTON HS; (SR); Duke TS; Hnr Roll; Peer Tut/Med; Spec Olymp Vol; Chrch Yth Grp; Emplmnt; FCA; Ntl FFA; Mch Bnd; Americorps Project Heart Member; FFA Vice-President & President; N C State B.S. Degree in Agriculture Education; North Carolina State U

ANDERSON, DA KENYA L; THOMASVILLE, NC; THOMASVILLE HS; (SR); Hnr Roll; WWAHSS; Comm Volntr; Hosp Aide; Chrch Yth Grp; FBLA; Bnd; Flg Crps; Chrldg; Stu Cncl (R); Eng II Award; Who's Who; Nursing; Child Development; East Carolina U; Winston-Salem State U

ANDERSON, ERICA; GREENSBORO, NC; NORTHWEST GUILFORD HS; (MS); Hnr Roll; Comm Volntr; ArtClub; DARE; Bnd; Art Club-Anime; Art or Fashion Merchandising

ANDERSON, GENEVA; ROCKY MOUNT, NC; ROCKY MOUNT SR HS; (FR); Duke TS; Hnr Roll; Bnd; Ch Chr; Clr Grd; Mch Bnd; Scr Kpr (V); Law; Physical Therapy; North Carolina State; Norfolk State

ANDERSON, JESSICA L; WILKESBORO, NC; WEST WILKES HS; (JR); Duke TS; Hnr Roll; Jr Mshl; WWAHSS; Red Cr Aide; Chrch Yth Grp; FCA; Key Club; Ntl Beta Clb; Prom Com; PP Ftbl (V); SWAT Team (Students Working Against Tobacco; Psychology; Genetics; NC State U; UNC Wilmington

ANDERSON, KRYSTAL; JACKSONVILLE, NC; NORTHSIDE HS; (FR); 4H Awd; Hi Hnr Roll; Hnr Roll; Otst Ac Ach Awd; Perf Att; Sci Fairs; Sci/Math Olympn; St of Mnth; Peer Tut/Med; 4-H; Chrch Yth Grp; Chr; Ch Chr; Dnce; SP/M/VS; Chrldg (J); Track (V); Distinguished Scholar in English; Doctor's Degree in Child Psychology; Master's Degree in Family Psychology; Florida State U; U of Miami

ANDERSON, LECHELLE M; LEXINGTON, NC; (JR); Sci Fairs; Comm Volntr; Chrch Yth Grp; Key Club; Chr; Chrldg (J); Business; Child Care; Dudley's College; Winston Salem State

ANDREWS, MARKESHIA N; HALIFAX, NC; LAS VEGAS HS; (JR); Hnr Roll; Nat Hon Sy; Comm Volntr; Red Cr Aide; DARE; Ntl Beta Clb; Ntl FFA; Bnd; Ch Chr; Dnce; Mch Bnd; Chrldg (J); Cl Off (V); Stu Cncl (V); Sch Ppr; Fashion; Medical; U of Chapel Hill; Agricultural and Technical U

ANEJA, SAURABH P; RALEIGH, NC; CARY AC; (SR); Hnr Roll; MVP; Yth Ldrshp Prog; Comm Volntr; Peer Tut/Med; Cmptr Clb; Emplmnt; Key Club; NYLC; Off Aide; Tech Clb; Tmpl Yth Grp; Bnd; Jzz Bnd; Sccr (V L); Tennis (V L); Stu Cncl (R); International Studies; Political Studies; Kenyon College; NCSU

ANIDES, ALMA L; WAKE FOREST, NC; WAKE FOREST-ROLESVILLE HS; (JR); Hi Hnr Roll; Nat Hon Sy; WWAHSS; Comm Volntr; Key Club; Clr Grd; Dnce; Activities Cochair of National Achievers; Communications; International Relationship

ANINKURA, NEWMAN K; GREENVILLE, NC; FARMVILLE CTRL HS; (SO); Hnr Roll; Wdwrkg Clb; Bskball; Sccr; Wt Lftg; Cl Off; Received Gym Award in Grade 7; Played on Basketball Teams Grade 5-8; Business; Business Management; NC State; UNC Chapel Hill

ANNAS, STACY; GRANITE FALLS, NC; SOUTH CALDWELL HS; (SO); Hnr Roll; Yth Ldrshp Prog; Comm Volntr; ArtClub; DARE; Dbte Team; Emplmnt; Mod UN; Ntl Beta Clb; P to P St Amb Prg; People to People Student Ambassador Program; Criminal Justice; Psychology; UNCW

ANTHONY, CHRISTEL Y; WINSTON SALEM, NC; GLENN HS; (SO); Ctznshp Aw; Hi Hnr Roll; Hnr Roll; MVP; Perf Att; Peer Tut/Med; Chrch Yth Grp; DARE; Scouts; Bskball; Track; Yrbk; Pre-Veterinary Science; U of Connecticut; High Point U

ANTONIO, ELIZABETH; GODWIN, NC; MIDWAY HS; (FR); Hnr Roll; Sampson Community College

ARCHAMBO, ANJELICA G; ELIZABETH CITY, NC; RIVER ROAD MS; MS; Hi Hnr Roll; Hnr Roll; Perf Att; Pres Ac Ftns Aw; Sci Fairs; St of Mnth; Hab For Humty Volntr; Peer Tut/Med; Drma Clb; Emplmnt; P to P St Amb Prg; Spanish Clb; Chr; Dnce; SP/M/VS; Bskball; Sftball (C); Tennis; Vllyball; Wt Lftg; Cl Off (P); CR (P); Yrbk (R); Peer Mediation; Criminal Justice; Lawyer; North Carolina State U; South Carolina State U

AREY, SAMUEL H; KERNERSVILLE, NC; EAST FORSYTH HS; (JR); F Lan Hn Soc; Hnr Roll; Jr Mshl; Jr Rot; MVP; Nat Hon Sy; Otst Ac Ach Awd; Perf Att; Sci Fairs; WWAHSS; Hab For Humty Volntr; Peer Tut/Med; Spec Olymp Vol; Chrch Yth Grp; Emplmnt; Jr Cls League; Key Club; Mth Clb/Tm; Svce Clb; Latin Clb; Ch Chr; Cr Ctry (V L); Tennis (V L); Track (V L); Vice President of Crosby Scholars; Gold Medalist on National Latin Exam; Medicine; Veterinary Medicine; U of North Carolina At Chapel Hill; Wake Forest U

ARIAS, JAIME; STATESVILLE, NC; STATESVILLE HS; (SO); Chrch Yth Grp; DARE

ARMON, ALEX; SPRING LAKE, NC; PINE FOREST HS; (FR); Hi Hnr Roll; Hnr Roll; Perf Att; Comm Volntr; Peer Tut/Med; French Clb; Bnd; Mch Bnd; Pep Bnd; Dental Lab Technician; East Carolina U

ARMSTRONG, KIMYATTA; LAURINBURG, NC; (SR); Hi Hnr Roll; Hnr Roll; Nat Hon Sy; USAA; WWAHSS; Peer Tut/Med; ArtClub; Chess; FBLA; Mch Bnd; Bsball (J); Bskball (VJ); Sccr (VJ); Sftball (VJ); Track (V); Who's Who Among American High School Students; Minority Leadership Award; Accounting; Business; NC A & T State U

ARMWOOD, PORSCHA; CLAYTON, NC; CLAYTON HS; (FR); Hnr Roll; Otst Ac Ach Awd; Perf Att; Pres Ac Ftns Aw; St of Mnth; DARE; FBLA; Ntl Beta Clb; Vsity Clb; Bskball (V); Stu Cncl (V); CR (P); 1st Place in Public Speaking I - FBLA; Sportsmanship Award or Basketball Scholar Athletes; Play College & WNBA Basketball; Master's Degree / Doctorate; Duke U; Carolina / UNC

ARTEMISIO, HOLLY; MAGNOLIA, NC; EAST DUPLIN HS; (JR); Hi Hnr Roll; Hnr Roll; Otst Ac Ach Awd; Chrch Yth Grp; Bnd; Mch Bnd; Chrldg (V L); Tri-M music Honor Society

ASBURY, SHANE; WESTFIELD, NC; SOUTH STOKES HS; (SR); Hnr Roll; WWAHSS; Emplmnt; ROTC; Clr Grd; Drl Tm; Automotive Technology; Heavy Equipment Technology; Wilson Technical College; Nashville Auto Diesel College

ASHBY, TAYLOR L; MEBANE, NC; EASTERN ALAMANCE HS; (JR); Hi Hnr Roll; Otst Ac Ach Awd; St of Mnth; WWAHSS; Chrch Yth Grp; Emplmnt; Key Club; Prom Com; Ch Chr; Ftball (J); Tennis (V); Wrstlg (V); Lt Governor for Key Club; National Society for Academic Scholars; Engineering; Financial Planning; North Carolina State; Appalachian State

ASHE, ROSHANA M; HENRICO, NC; NORTHAMPTON WEST HS; (FR); Hnr Roll; Perf Att; WWAHSS; Stu Cncl (R); CR (R); Most Voracious Reader; Nursing / Child Care; Computer Programming; North Carolina A & T State U; Hampton U

ASHLEY, CORTNEY; COLUMBUS, NC; POLK CTY HS; (SR); Ctznshp Aw; Duke TS; Hnr Roll; Jr Mshl; Kwnis Aw; Nat Hon Sy; Pres Sch; St of Mnth; WWAHSS; Yth Ldrshp Prog; Comm Volntr; Peer Tut/Med; Spec Olymp Vol; FCA; Key Club; Ntl Beta Clb; SADD; Spanish Clb; Bskball (VJ); Chrldg (J); Stu Cncl (R); CR (R); Yrbk (E, P); Spanish Club - Publicity Chairman; Key Club - Active Member / 4 Yrs; Communications Degree; Winthrop U

ASKEW, LAURA A; EURE, NC; RIDGECROFT SCH; (JR); Ctznshp Aw; Hnr Roll; Jr Mshl; Perf Att; St of Mnth; WWAHSS; Chrch Yth Grp; Ntl Beta Clb; SADD; Bnd; Pep Bnd; Cl Off (P); Accounting; East Carolina U

ASSELSTINE, DAZEL; WILMINGTON, NC; E A LANEY HS; (FR); Hnr Roll; Yth Ldrshp Prog; Comm Volntr; Dnce; SP/M/VS; Stu Cncl (R); YMCA Leadership; Pediatrician; Oxford U London; Duke U

ATKINSON, BRITTANY R; ASHEBORO, NC; ASHEBORO HS; (JR); Hi Hnr Roll; Jr Mshl; Jr Rot; Nat Hon Sy; Otst Ac Ach Awd; Sci Fairs; Yth Ldrshp Prog; Comm Volntr; ArtClub; Chrch Yth Grp; Dbte Team; HO'Br Yth Ldrshp; Key Club; Ntl Beta Clb; ROTC; Svce Clb; Clr Grd; SP/M/VS; Stg Cre; $500 Service Award from Project Smile; President of Art Club; Technical Theater (Stage Management, Set Design, Costuming, Makeup); Ithaca; State U of New York

ATKINSON, JALESA L; GOLDSBORO, NC; EASTERN WAYNE HS; (JR); Ctznshp Aw; Hnr Roll; MVP; Hosp Aide; Foreign Clb; Bnd; Mch Bnd; Pep Bnd; Bskball (V); Medical Science-Dentistry; Associates; U of North Carolina-Charlotte; U of North Carolina-Chapel Hill

ATKINSON, NELTONIA; RALEIGH, NC; WAKEFIELD HS; (JR); 4H Awd; Hi Hnr Roll; Hnr Roll; MVP; Nat Hon Sy; Perf Att; WWAHSS; Comm Volntr; Peer Tut/Med; 4-H; Chrch Yth Grp; FCA; Key Club; Ch Chr; Bskball (VJCL); PP Ftbl; Sftball (J); National Achievers Society; Kappa Scholars Program; Law; Business

ATKINSON JR, TERRENCE L; HUNTERSVILLE, NC; HARDING U HS; (FR); Hnr Roll; Comm Volntr; Chrch Yth Grp; Ch Chr; Bskball (J); Ftball (J); Track (J); Bowling; Swimming; Engineering; Computer Engineering; Harvard U, Stanford U; UNC-Chapel Hill, Duke U

AUSLEY, ASHLEY; ANGIER, NC; HARNETT CTRL HS; (SO); F Lan Hn Soc; Hi Hnr Roll; Hnr Roll; Nat Hon Sy; Perf Att; Sci/Math Olympn; St of Mnth; Comm Volntr; Peer Tut/Med; FCA; Key Club; Mth Clb/Tm; Ntl Beta Clb; Photog; Quiz Bowl; Schol Bwl; Foreign Clb; Chr; SP/M/VS; Sftball (J); Adv Cncl (R); Stu Cncl (R); CR (R); Yrbk (E); Third in State History Bowl Competition; Who's Who Among American High School Students Nominee; Business Major; Interior Design; U of North Carolina at Wilmington; U of North Carolina at Greensboro

AUSTIN, ELIZABETH L; FUQUAY VARINA, NC; FUQUAY-VARINA HS; (JR); Hnr Roll; Kwnis Aw; Pres Sch; WWAHSS; Key Club; Tchrs Aide; Bnd; Chr; Athletic Trainer for Wrestling and Football (Sports Medicine); Black Belt in Tae Kwon Do-2004 State Champion; Pre-Med; Athletic Training

AUTRY, HANNAH; STEDMAN, NC; CAPE FEAR HS; (JR); DAR; Hi Hnr Roll; Jr Mshl; Otst Ac Ach Awd; WWAHSS; Hab For Humty Volntr; Hosp Aide; Chrch Yth Grp; Emplmnt; Ntl Beta Clb; Quill & Scroll; Sftball (V L); Sch Ppr (E); Highest GPA of Class; Offensive Player of Year (Varsity Softball); Journalism; Mass Communication; U of North Carolina At Chapel Hill; U of North Carolina At Wilmington

AVATO, DESIREE; ASHEBORO, NC; ASHEBORO HS; (SO); WWAHSS; Comm Volntr; 4-H; Key Club; Spanish Clb; Golf (V); Teacher; North Carolina State; Wilmington U

AVENT, STEPHANIE L; SANFORD, NC; LEE CTY SR HS; (JR); Hnr Roll; WWAHSS; Chrch Yth Grp; Ntl FFA; Who's Who Among American High School Students; National Technical Honor Society; Agriculture Science/ Landscaping; Nursing; North Carolina State U; U of North Carolina-Wilmington

AVERETTE, JORDAN; ROUGEMONT, NC; PERSON HS; (FR); Hi Hnr Roll; Hnr Roll; Perf Att; Sci Fairs; St of Mnth; Chrch Yth Grp; Bnd; Jzz Bnd; Mch Bnd; Pep Bnd; Bskball (J); Sccr (J); Student of Merit; Lawyer; Accounting; Duke U; U of North Carolina At Chapel Hill

AVERY, KATE E; DUNN, NC; CAPE FEAR CHRISTIAN AC; (FR); Hi Hnr Roll; Hnr Roll; Otst Ac Ach Awd; Sci/Math Olympn; WWAHSS; Comm Volntr; Chrch Yth Grp; Ntl Beta Clb; Quiz Bowl; Chr; Dnce; SP/M/VS; Piano / Violin - Accomplished in Both; 2nd Place at NATS Voice Competition - For Category; Piano & Voice Performance; Theatre Arts; Westminster Choir College; Juilliard School

AVILA, ANDRES P; GREENSBORO, NC; PAGE HS; (JR); Hi Hnr Roll; Hnr Roll; Chess; French Clb; Sccr (V); Computer Science; Mathematics; U of North Carolina Chapel Hill

AVILES, KAYLA R; CHARLOTTE, NC; HARDING U HS; (SO); Ctznshp Aw; Hnr Roll; Yth Ldrshp Prog; Comm Volntr; Hosp Aide; Peer Tut/Med; Chrch Yth Grp; DARE; Drma Clb; Emplmnt; FBLA; Mus Clb; Off Aide; Photog; Ch Chr; Dnce; Orch; SP/M/VS; Chrldg (J); Scr Kpr (VJ); Sftball (VJ); CR (R); Sch Ppr (R, P); "A-B" Honor; Business Management; Cosmetology; U of North Carolina At Chapel Hill; Florida State U

AWADALLAH, MONEERA H; GREENVILLE, NC; FARMVILLE CTRL HS; (SO); 4H Awd; WWAHSS; Hosp Aide; 4-H; FBLA; Cl Off (V); Stu Cncl (V); CR (V); HOSA (Club), Certificate of Achievement; ICE (Club), Nominated for Student Ambassador Prog; Nursing; EMT; East Carolina U; Duke U

AYCOTH, SARA; MATTHEWS, NC; SUN VALLEY HS; (MS); Hnr Roll; Comm Volntr; Pep Squd; Scouts; Dnce; Yrbk (P); Dance Teacher; Travel and Be in Shows; East Carolina

AYERS, DEBORAH; HOPE MILLS, NC; SOUTHVIEW HS; (SR); All Am Sch; F Lan Hn Soc; Hnr Roll; Jr Mshl; MVP; Nat Hon Sy; Nat Mrt Fin; WWAHSS; Comm Volntr; Hab For Humty Volntr; Red Cr Aide; Chrch Yth Grp; Cmptr Clb; Emplmnt; FCA; Key Club; Ntl Beta Clb; Tmpl Yth Grp; Foreign Clb; Arch (V); Bskball (V); Cr Ctry (V); PP Ftbl (V); Sccr (V); Cl Off (V); CR (R); Daryll Crabtree Award, Academy Of Scholars; Spanish Honor Society of Scholars; Forensics; Elementary Education; U of North Carolina-Wilmington; U of North Carolina-Chapel Hill

AYERS, REBECCA; SPRUCE PINE, NC; MITCHELL HS; (JR); Hnr Roll; Nat Hon Sy; WWAHSS; Yth Ldrshp Prog; FBLA; Chr; Elementary Education; Western Carolina U; Appalachian State U

AZAROVA, NATALIA; WINSTON-SALEM, NC; REYNOLDS HS; (JR); Hnr Roll; Perf Att; Comm Volntr; DECA; Spanish Clb; Martial Arts with Japan Karate Institute; Industrial Engineering / Design; Medicine; U of North Carolina Chapel Hill; North Carolina State U

BAE, KEON; RALEIGH, NC; WAKE FIELD HS; (SO); 4H Awd; Hi Hnr Roll; Comm Volntr; Chrch Yth Grp; Key Club; Sci Clb; Ch Chr; Dvng (V); Student of US EPH Research Apprenticeship Program; Aeronautic Engineer; Astronaut; Massachusetts Institute of Technology

BAGGETT, BRITTANY J; FAYETTEVILLE, NC; TERRY SANFORD HS; (FR); ROTC; Real Estate; RN; Fayetteville State U; Campbell U

BAGINSKI, MICHELLE; KERNERSVILLE, NC; EAST FORSYTH HS; (SO); Duke TS; Hnr Roll; Nat Hon Sy; Comm Volntr; Spec Olymp Vol; Emplmnt; Svce Clb; French Clb; Dnce; Sftball (J); Crosby Scholars; Lawyer; Medicine; North Carolina State U; U of North Carolina At Chapel Hill

BAGLEY, DANIELLE; DURHAM, NC; CJC AC; (SR); Hnr Roll; Jr Mshl; Nat Hon Sy; Valdctrian; WWAHSS; Comm Volntr; Ntl Beta Clb; Stg Cre; Cl Off (P, R); Stu Cncl (T); Yrbk (E); Engineering Technology; U of North Carolina Charlotte

BAGLEY, DAVID M; DURHAM, NC; NORTHERN HS; (FR); Hi Hnr Roll; Hnr Roll; MVP; Nat Ldrshp Svc; Otst Ac Ach Awd; Sci Fairs; St of Mnth; Comm Volntr; Spec Olymp Vol; ArtClub; Key Club; Scouts; SADD; Spanish Clb; Bsball; Bskball; Ftball; Golf; Lcrsse (VJC); Swmg; Baseball All-Star Team; BSA Top Program Salesman for 3 Years; Accounting; Radiology; Bowie State U; Pacific Union College

Aviles, Kayla R
Harding U HS
Charlotte, NC

Ashby, Taylor L
Eastern Alamance HS
Mebane, NC

Archambo, Anjelica G
River Road MS
Elizabeth City, NC

Andrews, Markeshia N
Las Vegas HS
Halifax, NC

Aninkura, Newman K
Farmville Ctrl HS
Greenville, NC

Atkinson, Jalesa L
Eastern Wayne HS
Goldsboro, NC

Aycoth, Sara
Sun Valley HS
Matthews, NC

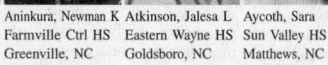

BAGLEY, JUSTIN L; FARMVILLE, NC; FARMVILLE CTRL HS; (SO); Sci Fairs; WWAHSS; Chrch Yth Grp; DARE; Emplmnt; SADD; Bsball (VJ); Cl Off (P); Defensive & Offensive Baseball Award; East Carolina U; Pitt Community, Barton

BAILES, KATHERINE E; MONCURE, NC; ST MARY'S SCH; (JR); Duke TS; Hi Hnr Roll; Sci/Math Olympn; WWAHSS; Yth Ldrshp Prog; Comm Volntr; Hab For Humty Volntr; Chrch Yth Grp; FCA; Key Club; Mth Clb/Tm; Ntl Beta Clb; NYLC; Tchrs Aide; Orch; Sccr (V); Nursing; U of North Carolina Chapel Hill; U of North Carolina Greensboro

BAILEY, BETHANY; BURNSVILLE, NC; MTN HERITAGE HS; (JR); Hi Hnr Roll; Hnr Roll; Nat Hon Sy; Perf Att; Chrch Yth Grp; DARE; Emplmnt; FCCLA; Ntl Beta Clb; Bnd; Ch Chr; Jzz Bnd; Mch Bnd; Track; Member of FCCLA, World History Award; Fitness & Nutrition; Western Carolina; Mars Hill

BAILIFF, VICTORIA L; PFAFFTOWN, NC; MT TABOR HS; (JR); F Lan Hn Soc; Hnr Roll; Nat Hon Sy; WWAHSS; Comm Volntr; Chrch Yth Grp; Key Club; French Clb; Bnd; Mch Bnd; Presidential Award for Academic Excellence; North Carolina State U; U of North Carolina Chapel Hill

BAKER, BRITTNEY D; RALEIGH, NC; SOUTHEAST RALEIGH MAGNET HS; (SO); Hnr Roll; Comm Volntr; Peer Tut/Med; Chrch Yth Grp; Key Club; Scouts; Ch Chr; Child Psychology; Spelman U; U of Greensboro

BAKER, CHASITY; HOPE MILLS, NC; GRAY'S CREEK HS; (SO); Nat Hon Sy; Comm Volntr; Chrch Yth Grp; Key Club; Prom Com; SP/M/VS; Tennis (V L); Cl Off (V); I Am Also a Member of the Senior Adult Committee At My Church; Psychology Major; Pediatric Medicine; U of North Carolina (Chapel Hill); Duke U

BAKER, DANIELLE L; MARIETTA, NC; FAIRMONT HS; (JR); Perf Att; St of Mnth; Comm Volntr; Peer Tut/Med; FBLA; Ntl Beta Clb; Tchrs Aide; SP/M/VS; Psychology; Graphic Design; Duke U; Chapel Hill U

BAKER, JESSICA N; APEX, NC; MIDDLE CREEK HS; (SO); Hnr Roll; Comm Volntr; Chrch Yth Grp; Emplmnt; Ch Chr; Bskball (VJCL); Track (V); Yrbk (P); Offensive Player of the Year; Church National Essay Contest Winner; Biology; Animal Science; High Point U; U North Carolina Pembroke

BAKER, JOSHUA; RALEIGH, NC; MILLBROOK HS; (SO); Duke TS; Hnr Roll; Chrch Yth Grp; Dbte Team; Drma Clb; SP/M/VS; Stg Cre; Working with Millbrook News Crew; Induction Into National Achievers Society; Doctor of Pharmacy; Doctor of Medicine; Massachusetts College of Pharmacy and Health Sciences; Duke U

BAKER, JUSTIN B; AULANDER, NC; RIDGECROFT SCH; (SO); Key Club; Ntl Beta Clb; Bsball (V); Bskball (V); Sccr; MVP Baseball 8th / 9th Grade; Criminology / FBI; Vet; North Carolina State U; U of North Carolina

BAKER, KIARA; ROCKY MOUNT, NC; NASH CTRL HS; (FR); Hnr Roll; Comm Volntr; Chrldg (J); Cl Off (T); CR (T); SGA; Health Team; BSN Nursing; A & T Georgia Tech; North Carolina State U

BAKER, KRISTEN M; CLEMMONS, NC; WEST FORSYTH HS; (FR); Hnr Roll; Nat Hon Sy; Sci Fairs; Bnd; Chr; Dnce; Chrldg (J); Pediatrics; Veterinarian

BAKER, SADARA R; ROWLAND, NC; SOUTH ROBESON HS; (FR); 4H Awd; Hnr Roll; Nat Hon Sy; Perf Att; St of Mnth; Yth Ldrshp Prog; Comm Volntr; 4-H; Chrch Yth Grp; FCCLA; Lttrmn Clb; Scouts; Ch Chr; Scr Kpr (V); Track (V); Wt Lftg (V); Advertising Sales; Marketing; Drexel U

BAKER, SARAH M; SILER CITY, NC; JORDAN MATTHEWS HS; (FR); Spanish Clb; Sch Ppr (E, R, P); Interior Decorator; Psychologist; Sandhills Community College; U of North Carolina At Charlotte

BALDWIN, ARRISSA C; TROY, NC; WEST MONTGOMERY HS; (FR); WWAHSS; Peer Tut/Med; Stu Cncl (R); Pediatrics; U North Carolina Charlotte

BALDWIN, EMILY; CHARLOTTE, NC; OLYMPIC HS; (FR); Duke TS; Hi Hnr Roll; Hnr Roll; Perf Att; Pres Sch; Sci/Math Olympn; Comm Volntr; Peer Tut/Med; Key Club; Mth Clb/Tm; MuAlphaTh; Bnd; Mch Bnd; Pep Bnd; Yrbk (E); Battle of the Books; Engineering; Architectural Design; Massachusetts Institute of Technology

BALDWIN, LISA; CHARLOTTE, NC; COVENANT DAY SCH; (JR); Duke TS; Hi Hnr Roll; MVP; Nat Hon Sy; Nat Mrt LOC; Otst Ac Ach Awd; Perf Att; Pres Sch; WWAHSS; Peer Tut/Med; Chrch Yth Grp; Emplmnt; Jr Ach; Spanish Clb; Sccr (V); Tennis (V L); Stu Cncl (V); Math Teacher; History Teacher; Grove City College; Calvin College

BALDWIN, WHITLEY; RED SPRINGS, NC; HOKE CTY HS; (SO); 4H Awd; Hnr Roll; Nat Sci Aw; Otst Ac Ach Awd; St of Mnth; CARE; DARE; Off Aide; Cl Off (V); RN; Duke U; North Carolina State U

BALI, KARAN S; CHAPEL HILL, NC; EAST CHAPEL HILL HS; (SO); Duke TS; F Lan Hn Soc; Hnr Roll; MVP; Nat Hon Sy; Perf Att; St of Mnth; Comm Volntr; Hab For Humty Volntr; Hosp Aide; Spanish Clb; Bnd; Dnce; Mch Bnd; Track (V); Business Management; Science; Duke U; Wake Forest

BALLANCE, DE ANNA L; ELIZABETH CITY, NC; PASQUOTANK CTY HS; (SR); Hi Hnr Roll; Hnr Roll; Jr Mshl; Nat Hon Sy; Otst Ac Ach Awd; Perf Att; Yth Ldrshp Prog; Comm Volntr; Chrch Yth Grp; Lttrmn Clb; Ntl FFA; ROTC; Vsity Clb; Chr; Tennis (V L); Commander of Raider Team AFJROTC; Nursing; Vet; East Carolina State U; Carolina Coastal Community College

BANKS, JASMINE; FAYETTEVILLE, NC; MASSEY HILL CLASSICAL HS; (JR); Hnr Roll; Nat Hon Sy; Perf Att; WWAHSS; Chr; Dnce; SP/M/VS; Yrbk (P); Dance; Computer Science; U of NC Greensboro; East Carolina U

BANNAN, CHRISTY; NORTH WILKESBORO, NC; NORTH WILKES HS; (FR); Comm Volntr; Scouts; Teacher; Certified Nursing Assistant; Meredith College; U of North Carolina Greensboro

BANNER, TASHAMA T; BLADENBORO, NC; WEST BLADEN HS; (JR); Hnr Roll; MVP; Pres Ac Ftns Aw; Spec Olymp Vol; Chrch Yth Grp; Emplmnt; Scouts; French Clb; Ch Chr; Arch (V); Bskball (V); GAA (V); Sftball (V); Track (V); Youth of the Year-2004-Church; Praise Dance Team-Church; Physical Education; WNBA; UNC Chapel Hill; UNC State U

BANNERMAN, JEREMY T; BURGAW, NC; PENDER HS; (FR); Duke TS; Hnr Roll; USAA; Comm Volntr; Chrch Yth Grp; NYLC; Bnd; Mch Bnd; Bskball (L); Sccr (V); Track (V); Yrbk (E, R, P); Rocame Club; International Business/Economics; Culinary Arts; Duke U; UNC Greensboro

BANNISTER, HILLABY A; HIGH POINT, NC; DUDLEY HS; (SO); Hnr Roll; Otst Ac Ach Awd; Perf Att; Comm Volntr; Hosp Aide; Chrch Yth Grp; Emplmnt; Scouts; Ch Chr; Orch; Class Steering Committee; Top Teens of America; Psychology; Physical Therapy; Spelman College; East Carolina U

BARAHONA, DAVID; WAKE FOREST, NC; WAKE FOREST-ROLESVILLE HS; (JR); DECA; Emplmnt; District & State Finalist @ DECA Competitions; Honorable Merit in National Latin Examination; Business Management; Law; U of North Carolina-Chapel Hill; North Carolina State U

BARBEE, RACHEL M; SALISBURY, NC; WEST ROWAN HS; (FR); Hnr Roll; Otst Ac Ach Awd; Perf Att; Peer Tut/Med; DARE; Sci Clb; Chr; Track; Math; Appalachian U

BARBOUR, BRANDON L; HILLSBOROUGH, NC; ORANGE HS; (JR); Hi Hnr Roll; Hnr Roll; Perf Att; St of Mnth; WWAHSS; Comm Volntr; Spec Olymp Vol; FCA; Ntl Beta Clb; SP/M/VS; Stg Cre; Wrstlg (V CL); Stu Cncl (R); North Carolina Governor's School West Attendee; International Relations; Business; UNC Chapel Hill; Duke U

BARBOUR, JASON; GARNER, NC; WEST JOHNSTON HS; (JR); Duke TS; Hnr Roll; Perf Att; WWAHSS; Peer Tut/Med; Chrch Yth Grp; Emplmnt; FCA; Ch Chr; Ftball (V L); Track (V L); Wt Lftg (V); Web Master (Youth Group); Media Ministry; Pharmacy; Ministry; Campbell U; Wingate U

BAREFOOT, JONATHAN D; DUNN, NC; SOUTH JOHNSTON HS; (SO); Duke TS; Hnr Roll; Kwnis Aw; WWAHSS; Peer Tut/Med; Red Cr Aide; FCA; Mth Clb/Tm; Ntl Beta Clb; Bsball (J); Wrstlg (J); Physical Therapy; Physical Education

BAREFOOT, WILLIAM J; BENSON, NC; SOUTH JOHNSTON HS; (SO); Ctznshp Aw; Hnr Roll; Kwnis Aw; MVP; Perf Att; Pres Ac Ftns Aw; St of Mnth; DARE; Emplmnt; FCA; Ntl Beta Clb; Ntl FFA; Ftball (JC); Wt Lftg; Wrstlg (V L); Major in Agriculture; North Carolina State U

BARLOW, KEVIN W; SHELBY, NC; CREST HS; (SO); Hi Hnr Roll; WWAHSS; Comm Volntr; BPA; Chrch Yth Grp; FCA; FBLA; Sci Clb; Spanish Clb; Highest Average Earth & Environmental Science; Engineering; Marine Biology; U of North Carolina Chapel Hill

BARNES, BRIAN; PLYMOUTH, NC; LAWRENCE AC; (SO); Duke TS; Hnr Roll; MVP; Nat Hon Sy; Otst Ac Ach Awd; USAA; Yth Ldrshp Prog; Comm Volntr; Chrch Yth Grp; DARE; HO'Br Yth Ldrshp; Ntl Beta Clb; P to P St Amb Prg; SADD; Arch (VJC); Skt Tgt Sh (VJ); Yrbk (R, P); National Youth Leadership Forum- Defense / Intelligence and Diplomacy Security Studies; Hoyt National Shooting Staff; International Politics / Joint Degree BS Foreign Service / MA Security Studies; Georgetown U; American U

BARNES, KOLIAK; CHARLOTTE, NC; GARRINGER HS; (SR); Hnr Roll; Perf Att; WWAHSS; Comm Volntr; ArtClub; Chrch Yth Grp; DARE; Emplmnt; Mus Clb; Outdrs Clb; Photog; ROTC; Chr; SP/M/VS; Bskball (J); ROTC; Church Choir, YAMS; Chef (Cook); Music; Johnson & Wales U; A T & T U

BARNES, NIKKI; HOLLY SPRINGS, NC; MIDDLE CREEK HS; (JR); Hnr Roll; Kwnis Aw; St of Mnth; Comm Volntr; Spec Olymp Vol; Emplmnt; Chr; Work in After School Summer Camp Program (K-8 grade); Lettered in Chorus; Social Worker; Western Carolina U; The U of North Carolina Greensboro

BARNES, TRAVIS; WILSON, NC; (SO); Hi Hnr Roll; Hnr Roll; Perf Att; St of Mnth; Chrch Yth Grp; Ch Chr; Ftball (J); Wrstlg (J); Usher At Church; Attend Sunday School; Electrical Engineering; Owning My Own Business; North Carolina State U; North Carolina A & T

BARNETT, LISA; LUMBERTON, NC; (SO); 4-H; DARE; Bnd; Clr Grd; Sftball; Wrstlg; Volunteer At Teen Court; Junior Hospital Volunteer; Psychology; Social Work; Central; UNCCI

BARNETT, TREVOR; FRANKLIN, NC; FRANKLIN HS; (SO); Hnr Roll; US Army Sch Ath Aw; Chrch Yth Grp; Sccr (V); Track (V); Culinary Arts; Outdoor Guide; Southwestern Community College; Western Community College

BARNETTE, AMANDA M; GOLDSBORO, NC; EASTERN WAYNE HS; (JR); Duke TS; Hnr Roll; Jr Mshl; Nat Hon Sy; Sci Fairs; St of Mnth; WWAHSS; Comm Volntr; Peer Tut/Med; ArtClub; FTA; Mth Clb/Tm; Chrldg (VJCL); Job Shadowing; Education, Elementary; Middle-School Education; East Carolina U; U of North Carolina-Wilmington

BARNETTE, MEREDITH R; CORNELIUS, NC; NORTH MECKLENBURG HS; (JR); Hnr Roll; Comm Volntr; Scouts; Gold Award-Girl Scouts-2005

BARRICK, JACOB; HILLSBOROUGH, NC; CEDAR RIDGE HS; (SO); Hnr Roll; Ntl Beta Clb; SP/M/VS; Sccr (V L); Brain Game Club; Rank of Life in the BSA; American History & Government; Education; U of North Carolina Chapel Hill; Duke U

BARRON, FELICIA; MIDLAND, NC; PIEDMONT HS; (FR); Hnr Roll; Perf Att; St of Mnth; Amnsty Intl; Comm Volntr; DARE; Lttrmn Clb; Ntl Beta Clb; Tech Clb; Stu Cncl; Yrbk; Academic Letter; Amnesty International; Psychology; Journalism; U of California-Berkeley; U of California-San Diego

BARTLETT, JOSEPH; REIDSVILLE, NC; REIDSVILLE HS; (FR); Chrch Yth Grp; DARE; ROTC; Wdwrkg Clb; ROTC; Engineering Technology; Small Business / Entrepreneur; U of North Carolina; North Carolina State

BARTO, JENNA C; SOUTHERN PINES, NC; PINECREST HS; (SO); Ctznshp Aw; Hnr Roll; Nat Hon Sy; Sci/Math Olympn; WWAHSS; Comm Volntr; Hab For Humty Volntr; Peer Tut/Med; Chrch Yth Grp; Dbte Team; Emplmnt; FCA; Key Club; Ntl Beta Clb; Scouts; Spanish Clb; Chr; Ch Chr; Chrldg (J); PP Ftbl (V); Silver Award in Girl Scouts; All-County Chorus Member; Education (K-6); English (Writing); U of North Carolina At Chapel Hill; U of Georgia

BARYLA, MORGAN E; CARY, NC; ATHENS DRIVE HS; (SO); Hnr Roll; Jr Mshl; MVP; Perf Att; Pres Ac Ftns Aw; WWAHSS; FCCLA; Key Club; PP Ftbl (J); Scr Kpr (J); Piano - 5 Years; Recreation Softball - 6 Years; UNC Chapel Hill; UNC Wilmington

BASINGER, KYLIE; CONCORD, NC; MT PLEASANT HS; (FR); Ctznshp Aw; Hnr Roll; Perf Att; Chrch Yth Grp; DARE; Ntl Beta Clb; Spanish Clb; Dnce; Impact Through Education; Teacher; Business; U of North Carolina Charlotte; Pfeiffer U

BASKETT II, WILTON E; MIDDLEBURG, NC; NORTHERN VANCE HS; (SO); Hnr Roll; Chrch Yth Grp; Quiz Bowl; Bnd; Ch Chr; Mch Bnd; Track (V); Medical Degree; Legal; U of North Carolina At Chapel Hill; Saint Augustine's College

BASS, MEGHAN C; FAYETTEVILLE, NC; GRAY'S CREEK HS; (JR); Hi Hnr Roll; Jr Mshl; Nat Hon Sy; WWAHSS; Yth Ldrshp Prog; Comm Volntr; Hab For Humty Volntr; Chrch Yth Grp; Drma Clb; Key Club; Mus Clb; Scouts; Foreign Clb; Chr; Ch Chr; Clr Grd; SP/M/VS; Vllyball (JC); Sch Ppr (E); Girl Scout Gold Award; Academy of Scholars; Business Administration; Business W/ Concentration in Resort Mngmt.; UNC At Chapel Hill; USC At Columbia

BASSETT, MICHAEL A; SWANNANOA, NC; CHARLES D OWEN HS; (SR); Hnr Roll; Nat Hon Sy; WWAHSS; Emplmnt; Jr Ach; Ntl Beta Clb; Off Aide; Tchrs Aide; French Clb; CR (R); Business Administration; U of North Carolina Charlotte; U of North Carolina Greensboro

BATTLE, DOMENICK; ROCKY MOUNT, NC; NASH CTRL HS; (FR); Hi Hnr Roll; Perf Att; Pres Sch; St of Mnth; DARE; Ch Chr; Medical Doctor; Laboratory Technician; East Carolina U; U of Chapel Hill

BATTLE, KIS' WANNA L; ROBERSONVILLE, NC; ROANOKE HS; (FR); Hnr Roll; St Schl; Peer Tut/Med; Spec Olymp Vol; Chrch Yth Grp; Bnd; Ch Chr; Mch Bnd; Pep Bnd; Jr Beta Club; 3.535 Grade Point Average; Child Development / Family Relations; Early Childhood Education; North Carolina Central U; East Carolina U

BAUGHAN II, THOMAS G; FAYETTEVILLE, NC; (SR); Hnr Roll; WWAHSS; Chrch Yth Grp; Chr; Bsball (V L); Bskball (V CL); Sccr (V L); Homecoming King 2005; Culinary Arts; Aeronautics; Clearwater Christian College; Air Force Academy

BAUMGARTEN, ELIJAH L; PINEVILLE, NC; SOUTH MECKLENBURG HS; (SR); Hnr Roll; WWAHSS; Yth Ldrshp Prog; Comm Volntr; Peer Tut/Med; Biology Clb; Chrch Yth Grp; DARE; DECA; Emplmnt; Sci Clb; Latin Clb; SP/M/VS; Bsball (V); Bskball (C); Wt Lftg; Odyssey of the Mind; Youth Advisory Leader; Bachelor of Science; Medicine (MD); Wofford College; U of North Carolina

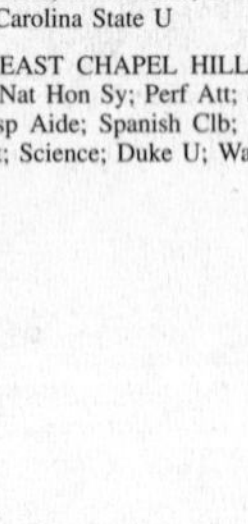

Barron, Felicia
Piedmont HS
Midland, NC

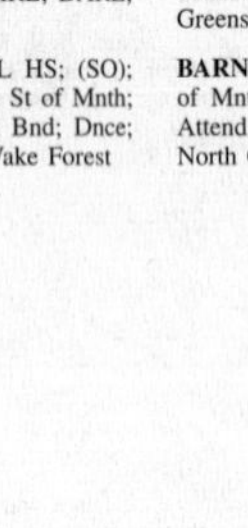

Barnes, Koliak
Garringer HS
Charlotte, NC

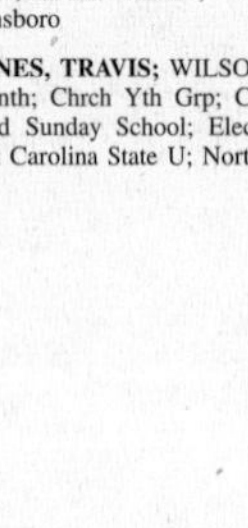

Barbour, Jason
West Johnston HS
Garner, NC

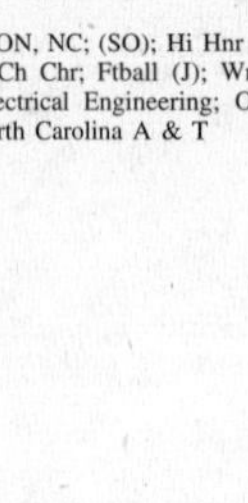

Baker, Joshua
Millbrook HS
Raleigh, NC

Baldwin, Emily
Olympic HS
Charlotte, NC

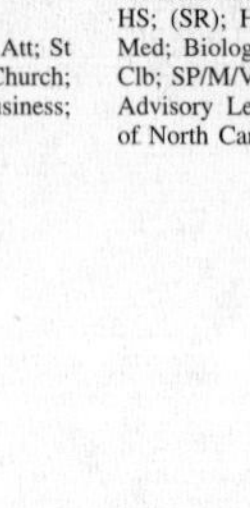

Barrick, Jacob
Cedar Ridge HS
Hillsborough, NC

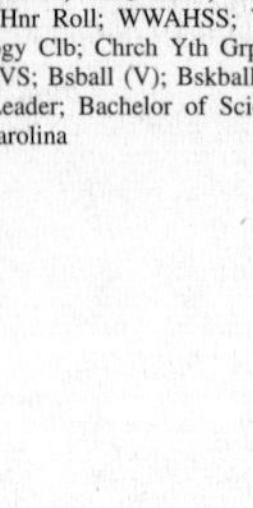

Battle, Domenick
Nash Ctrl HS
Rocky Mount, NC

BAWDEN, JAMES; RALEIGH, NC; MILLBROOK HS; (SR); Hnr Roll; Chrch Yth Grp; Drma Clb; Emplmnt; SP/M/VS; Stg Cre; Lit Mag (R); Anchor on Morning News; Nominated for Governors School; Communications; Theatre; Appalachian State

BAXTER, MAYA L; JACKSONVILLE, NC; WHITE OAK HS; (MS); Hnr Roll; Nat Hon Sy; Perf Att; Bnd; Mch Bnd; Pep Bnd; Music; East Carolina U; U of North Carolina, Chapel Hill

BAXTER, SAMUEL J; KNIGHTDALE, NC; SOUTHEAST RALEIGH HS; (SR); Hnr Roll; MVP; Pres Ac Ftns Aw; Sci Fairs; WWAHSS; Comm Volntr; Peer Tut/Med; Chrch Yth Grp; DARE; SADD; Bskball (JC); Ftball (VJCL); Track (V CL); Sports Management; East Carolina U; Western Carolina U

BAYNES, DASHELLE D; MONROE, NC; MONROE HS; (SO); Hnr Roll; Chrch Yth Grp; Pep Squd; Dnce; SP/M/VS; Chrldg (JC); Sch Ppr (R); Yrbk (R); Journalism / Communications; Teaching; South Piedmont Community; Howard U

BEACHAM, ANDY; CHAPEL HILL, NC; EAST CHAPEL HILL HS; (SO); Chr; SP/M/VS; Stg Cre; Chrldg (V); Actor; Interior Decorator; U of California, Los Angeles; U of Southern California

BEACHAM, CHASE; RALEIGH, NC; NORTH RALEIGH CHRISTIAN AC; (SR); Duke TS; Hnr Roll; MVP; Pres Ac Ftns Aw; Yth Ldrshp Prog; Comm Volntr; Hab For Humty Volntr; Spec Olymp Vol; Chrch Yth Grp; DARE; Dbte Team; Emplmnt; FCA; Key Club; Lttrmn Clb; Off Aide; Bnd; Bskball (J); Lcrsse (V); Sccr (V CL); Track (V); Cl Off (V); Sch Ppr (R); Yrbk (R); Coach's Award; Over 1000 Community Service Hours; Political Science; Philosophy; U of North Carolina Charlotte

BEACHUM, NICOLE; NORWOOD, NC; SOUTH STANLY HS; (FR); Hi Hnr Roll; Hnr Roll; Nat Hon Sy; Perf Att; Sci Fairs; WWAHSS; Chr; Scr Kpr (J); U of North Carolina-Chapel Hill; Art Institute of Charlotte

BEASLEY, LAURA F; FUQUAY VARINA, NC; HILLTOP CHRISTIAN SCH; (SR); Hnr Roll; MVP; Nat Hon Sy; WWAHSS; Chrch Yth Grp; Chr; Bskball (V L); Vllyball (V C); Yrbk (R); Psychology; Liberty U

BEATTY, ARDRIENNA; JACKSONVILLE, NC; NORTHSIDE HS; (FR); Ctznshp Aw; Hi Hnr Roll; Hnr Roll; Nat Hon Sy; Otst Ac Ach Awd; Perf Att; St of Mnth; WWAHSS; Yth Ldrshp Prog; Comm Volntr; Peer Tut/Med; Mth Clb/Tm; ROTC; Tchrs Aide; Spanish Clb; Sftball (V L); Vllyball (J); Stu Cncl (S, R); Sch Ppr (R); Yrbk; Harvard U Law School

BEAUDRY, KARIN A; BRYSON CITY, NC; SWAIN CTY HS; (FR); 4H Awd; Hnr Roll; Peer Tut/Med; 4-H; Emplmnt; SADD; Hsbk Rdg; Track (V); Vllyball (J); Yrbk (R); Business Management; Lawyer; Wake Forest U

BEAVER, AMANDA L; MATTHEWS, NC; WEDDINGTON HS; (JR); Hi Hnr Roll; Comm Volntr; Chrch Yth Grp; DECA; Key Club; Ntl Beta Clb; Pep Squd; Spanish Clb; Swmg (V); Tennis; Invited to National Student Leadership Conference 2005; Architecture; Design; North Carolina State U; Clemson U

BEAVER, JAMES T; SALISBURY, NC; SALISBURY HS; (SO); Duke TS; Hi Hnr Roll; Otst Ac Ach Awd; WWAHSS; Comm Volntr; Chrch Yth Grp; Drma Clb; Key Club; Quiz Bowl; Scouts; French Clb; Bnd; Ch Chr; Mch Bnd; SP/M/VS; Eagle Scout-2004; Tri-M Musical Honor Society; Geology; Paleontology; Lenoir-Rhyne College; North Carolina State U

BEBBER, BRITTANY; ANGIER, NC; CAPE FEAR CHRISTIAN AC; (SO); Hnr Roll; Yrbk; Veterinary; Criminal Justice; North Carolina State U; Campbell U

BECHER, DAVID T; CHARLOTTE, NC; N MECKLENBURG HS; (SO); Duke TS; Hnr Roll; Nat Hon Sy; Comm Volntr; Chrch Yth Grp; Scouts; Bnd; Technical Theatre Classes; Karate; Engineering; Law

BECK, AARON; WILMINGTON, NC; NEW HANOVER HS; (FR); Hnr Roll; Forensics; Chemistry; UNCW-U North Carolina Wilmington; North Carolina State U

BECKER, JAMIE L; ASHEBORO, NC; SOUTHWESTERN RANDOLPH HS; (SR); Ctznshp Aw; Hnr Roll; Jr Eng Tech; Otst Ac Ach Awd; Yth Ldrshp Prog; Ntl Beta Clb; Ntl FFA; Future Farmers of America President, Treasurer; Beta Club Member; Animal Science/Pre-Veterinary Medicine; North Carolina State U

BELCHER, STEFFANY M; WINSTON SALEM, NC; ROBERT B GLENN HS; (JR); Hnr Roll; Perf Att; Mus Clb; Chr; Choral Competitions, Elite Ladies Club, Ebony Society, Trim Club; Education, Psychology; Elon U, U of North Carolina; Greensboro, High Point U

BELL, BRADLEY K; LENOIR, NC; WEST CALDWELL HS; (SO); Ctznshp Aw; Hnr Roll; Perf Att; WWAHSS; Comm Volntr; FCA; FBLA; Key Club; P to P St Amb Prg; SADD; Spanish Clb; Bnd; Ftball (J); Wt Lftg (J); Awarded Citizenship Award; Real Estate Broker; Business Degree; Appalachian State U; Caldwell Community College

BELL, BRANDON C; GREENSBORO, NC; SOUTHWEST GUILFORD HS; (JR); Hnr Roll; WWAHSS; Comm Volntr; Peer Tut/Med; Chrch Yth Grp; Prom Com; Bnd; Mch Bnd; Pep Bnd; Ftball (J); Track (VJ L); Most Improved in Men's Track - Sophomore Year; Culinary Arts / Pastry; Computer Programming; UNC Chapel Hill; Johnson & Wales U

BELL, CARLETTE R; ROCKY MOUNT, NC; SOUTHWEST EDGECOMBE HS; (JR); Ctznshp Aw; Hnr Roll; Jr Mshl; Nat Hon Sy; Otst Ac Ach Awd; Pres Ac Ftns Aw; WWAHSS; Hosp Aide; 4-H; DARE; Emplmnt; FBLA; Mth Clb/Tm; Vsity Clb; Chr; Ch Chr; Mch Bnd; Bskball (V L); Track (V L); Vllyball (V L); All-Conference in Track; Secretary/Treasurer of Monogram Club; Computer Engineering; Computer Science; North Carolina State U; East Carolina U

BELL, CLARENCE; GARYSBURG, NC; NORTHAMPTON WEST HS; (JR); Hnr Roll; Nat Hon Sy; Comm Volntr; Peer Tut/Med; Chess; DARE; Ntl Beta Clb; Who's Who American High School Students; Beta Club; Computer Technician; Pre-Law; North Carolina A & T State U; Fayetteville State U

BELL, JENNIFER L; ELIZABETH CITY, NC; PERQUIMANS HS; (JR); Hnr Roll; Perf Att; DARE; Yrbk (E); Child Care; Dance; East Carolina U; U of North Carolina

BELL, JOSH; DUNN, NC; TRITON HS; (FR); Mus Clb; Bnd; Accounting; Culinary; CUNCW

BELL, KRISTEN P; GASTONIA, NC; FORESTVIEW HS; (FR); Hi Hnr Roll; Hnr Roll; St of Mnth; Comm Volntr; Drma Clb; Dnce; SP/M/VS; Doctor; Professional Ballerina; Wake Forest U; Duke U

BELL, NICOLE; CANDLER, NC; ENKA HS; (JR); Hnr Roll; Nat Hon Sy; St Schl; Chrch Yth Grp; Ch Chr; Chrldg (VJ L); Interior Design; Criminology; Western Carolina U

BELSANTE, MICHELLE M; MATTHEWS, NC; PROVIDENCE SR HS; (SO); Hnr Roll; WWAHSS; Yth Ldrshp Prog; HO'Br Yth Ldrshp; Jr Cls League; Key Club; Bnd; Jzz Bnd; Mch Bnd; SP/M/VS; Fncg (J); Stu Cncl (R)

BENGE, JENNY; MT AIRY, NC; MT AIRY HS; (FR); Duke TS; Otst Ac Ach Awd; Sci Fairs; St of Mnth; Comm Volntr; Spec Olymp Vol; Chrch Yth Grp; FCA; Key Club; Chr; SP/M/VS; Sftball (V); Stu Cncl (R); CR (R); Yrbk (P); Principal's Leadership Award; Marketing / Advertising; NC State; UNC Chapel Hill

BENNETT, DYLAN; MOUNT AIRY, NC; MT AIRY HS; (FR); Hnr Roll; St of Mnth; Chrch Yth Grp; Drma Clb; Key Club; P to P St Amb Prg; SP/M/VS; Veterinarian; Lawyer; Washington State U; Harvard

BENNETT, KENNETH S; LAURINBURG, NC; SCOTLAND HS; (JR); Hi Hnr Roll; Jr Mshl; MVP; Nat Hon Sy; Otst Ac Ach Awd; Pres Ac Ftns Aw; Sci Fairs; WWAHSS; Comm Volntr; Hosp Aide; Chrch Yth Grp; Ntl Beta Clb; Sci Clb; Tech Clb; Stg Cre; Golf (V CL); Mid-Southwestern 4-A Men's Golf All Conference; 26th Class Rank Out of 372 Students; BSN-Anesthesiology; Pharmacy; U of South Carolina, Columbia; Francis Marion U

BENNETT, MARLI T; PILOT MTN, NC; EAST SURRY HS; (SO); Duke TS; Hi Hnr Roll; MVP; Otst Ac Ach Awd; Pres Ac Ftns Aw; USAA; WWAHSS; Hab For Humty Volntr; Peer Tut/Med; Chrch Yth Grp; FCA; Photog; SADD; Ch Chr; Dnce; Bskball (V L); Track (V L); Vllyball (V L); Cl Off (V); Stu Cncl (S); Sch Ppr (R); Athlete-Of-The-Year Basketball; Pre-Dentistry; Dentistry; North Carolina State U; Winston-Salem State U

BENNETT JR, WILLIAM J; LEWISTON, NC; BERTIE HS; (JR); All Am Sch; Hnr Roll; Perf Att; WWAHSS; Vsity Clb; Bskball (J); Ftball (VJ); Track (V); Computer Engineering; North Carolina A & T State

BENTLEY, LINDSAY; MOCKSVILLE, NC; DAVIE HS; (MS); Hnr Roll; Perf Att; Comm Volntr; Chess; Chrch Yth Grp; FCA; Pep Squd; Chr; Ch Chr; Dnce; SP/M/VS; Chrldg (V); PPSqd (V); Scr Kpr; Track; 2005 State Finalist Jr Miss NC Teen Pageant; Nursing; Wake Forest U; NC State

BENTON JR, RAYMOND C; GREENSBORO, NC; DUDLEY HS; (FR); Ctznshp Aw; WWAHSS; Chrch Yth Grp; DARE; Ntl Beta Clb; Pep Squd; Bnd; Ch Chr; Drl Tm; Jzz Bnd; Cl Off (R); CR (R); Panthers of Christ; Pre-Med; Howard U (Washington, DC)

BERKOH, ANITA A; GREENSBORO, NC; DUDLEY HS; (JR); Hnr Roll; St of Mnth; Yth Ldrshp Prog; CARE; Comm Volntr; Chrch Yth Grp; Emplmnt; Chr; Ch Chr; Tennis; Volunteer Work Achievements; Registered Nurse / Bachelor's Degree; Queens College; Winston-Salem State U

BERLING, SONJA E; CHARLOTTE, NC; SOUTH MECKLENBURG HS; (FR); Duke TS; Hnr Roll; Comm Volntr; HOSA Club; Journalism; Pre Medicine; U of Georgia; New York U

BERMUDEZ, BRENDA N; CLAYTON, NC; CLAYTON HS; (FR); FBLA; Master's Degree; NC State; Duke

BERNARDI, RAECHEL; DENVER, NC; NORTH LINCOLN HS; (SR); Emplmnt; Mus Clb; Ntl Beta Clb; Bnd; Mch Bnd; Aeronautical Engineering; Aerospace; North Carolina State U; DeVry Institute

BERO, JOSEPH; GOLDSBORO, NC; EASTERN WAYNE HS; (JR); Hnr Roll; Perf Att; Vsity Clb; Sccr (V); Pharmacy; U of North Carolina; North Carolina State U

BERRY, BEN; HOLLY SPRINGS, NC; (SO); Duke TS; Hnr Roll; Comm Volntr; Chrch Yth Grp; Key Club; Tech Clb; Stg Cre; Computer Science; IT; North Carolina State U; U of North Carolina At Greensboro

BERRY, S CHANDLER; CHARLOTTE, NC; HICKORY GROVE BAPTIST CHRISTIAN; Duke TS; Hi Hnr Roll; Hnr Roll; Nat Hon Sy; Perf Att; WWAHSS; Comm Volntr; Peer Tut/Med; Biology Clb; Chrch Yth Grp; DARE; Dbte Team; Emplmnt; Ntl Beta Clb; Quiz Bowl; Svce Clb; Golf (V); Adv Cncl (V); Sports Medicine Intern for Football Team; Leadership Clubs; Sports Medicine and Med School / Orthopedics; Wake Forest U; UNC Chapel Hill

BERRYMAN, NICOLE; JONESVILLE, NC; STARMOUNT HS; (SO); Hnr Roll; Jr Mshl; Otst Ac Ach Awd; Hosp Aide; Chrch Yth Grp; Emplmnt; Bnd; Chrldg (J); Stu Cncl (R); Academic Award-For Foods & Nutrition; I Lettered in Academics; I Plan to Be An RN; Wake Forest U; UNC Chapel Hill

BESSOIR, NICOLE; HILLSBOROUGH, NC; CEDAR RIDGE HS; (JR); F Lan Hn Soc; Kwnis Aw; Spec Olymp Vol; ArtClub; Drma Clb; Tennis (V); National Spanish Honors Society; Medical Field; North Carolina State U; Appalachian State U

BEST, ALI; WILSON, NC; FIKE HS; (JR); Hnr Roll; Nat Hon Sy; Perf Att; Comm Volntr; Chrch Yth Grp; Emplmnt; Svce Clb; SADD; French Clb; Sch Ppr (R); Journalism; U of North Carolina Chapel Hill

BETHEA, STEPHANIE; GREENSBORO, NC; (SR); Ctznshp Aw; Hnr Roll; MVP; Nat Hon Sy; Perf Att; Sci Fairs; USAA; WWAHSS; Yth Ldrshp Prog; Chrch Yth Grp; DARE; Drma Clb; Emplmnt; FCA; Jr Ach; Lttrmn Clb; Pep Squd; Bnd; Bsball (V L); Chrldg (V CL); GAA (V CL); Hsbk Rdg; Mar Art; PPSqd (V); Skiing; Sftball (V CL); Yrbk (E, P); Pre-Med / Ophthalmologist; Doctor; Phifer College

BETTS, MATTHEW P; APEX, NC; APEX HS; (JR); MVP; Comm Volntr; DECA; Sccr (V CL); State and Region III ODP - Olympic Development Program; Adidas ESP Camp - 2 Yrs

BEVERLY, ELLEN B; DURHAM, NC; JORDAN; (JR); WWAHSS; Key Club; Chr; Sccr (V L)

BHAKTA, ANJALI G; RALEIGH, NC; WAKEFIELD HS; (JR); F Lan Hn Soc; Hnr Roll; Otst Ac Ach Awd; Yth Ldrshp Prog; Amnsty Intl; Comm Volntr; Hosp Aide; DARE; Key Club; Lib Aide; NYLC; Pep Squd; SADD; Tmpl Yth Grp; Spanish Clb; Dnce; Mar Art (L); PP Ftbl (L); Stu Cncl (R); CR (R); Miss India NC Pageant-3rd Runner Up; Winner of Many Dance Competitions.; Engineering, Computer Science; Pharmacy; North Carolina State U; U of North Carolina-Chapel Hill

BIALEK, ALEXANDRA; GREENSBORO, NC; PAGE HS; (MS); Hnr Roll; Kwnis Aw; Sci Fairs; St of Mnth; Comm Volntr; Chrch Yth Grp; DARE; Emplmnt; Orch; Computer Programmer; Forensic Scientist; UNC Chapel Hill; Duke U

BIAS, AMBER D; KITTY HAWK, NC; FIRST FLIGHT HS; (JR); Hi Hnr Roll; Hnr Roll; Otst Ac Ach Awd; DARE; Scr Kpr (VJCL); Fashion Merchandising Award; High Merit for Young Poets Contest 2005; Fashion Designing; Business Ownership; The Art Institute of Charlotte

BIGGS, ETHAN; MATTHEWS, NC; SUN VALLEY HS; (FR); Hi Hnr Roll; Hnr Roll; Jr Rot; Chrch Yth Grp; Mus Clb; Bnd; Mch Bnd; SPEC Summer Camp At Pfeiffer U; Union Regional Medical Center Med Professions Summer Camp At Union Regional Med Center; Physical Therapy; Drexel U; Duke U

BILES, ASHLEY; NORWOOD, NC; SOUTH STANLY HS; (SR); Hnr Roll; Otst Ac Ach Awd; Perf Att; St Schl; WWAHSS; Chrch Yth Grp; Spanish Clb; Ch Chr; Clr Grd; Bskball (J); NC Scholar; Renaissance Card Holder; Special Education; Elementary Education; U of North Carolina Greensboro

BILLINGS, LORI D; TRAPHILL, NC; NORTH WILKES HS; (FR); Hnr Roll; Otst Ac Ach Awd; Pres Ac Ftns Aw; Chrch Yth Grp; DARE; Scouts; Ch Chr; Dnce; Christian Youth Organization; Doctor; Nursing; Wilkes Community College

BIRMINGHAM, DAVID L; CONCORD, NC; JAY M ROBINSON HS; (JR); Hi Hnr Roll; Hnr Roll; Emplmnt; Sccr (J); Honor Roll; Veterinarian Medicine; Wingate U; Catawba College

BISOGNE, STEPHANIE M; TOBACCOVILLE, NC; NORTH FORSYTH HS; (JR); Duke TS; Hnr Roll; Nat Hon Sy; Comm Volntr; Red Cr Aide; ArtClub; Emplmnt; Photog; Prom Com; Scouts; Bnd; Mch Bnd; National Honor Society; FCCLA/Crosby Scholars/Salvation Army; Culinary Arts; Business Management; Johnson & Wales U

BITAR, TARA M; HOLLY SPRINGS, NC; MIDDLE CREEK HS; (SO); Hi Hnr Roll; Hnr Roll; Nat Hon Sy; WWAHSS; Comm Volntr; Chrch Yth Grp; Piano; Law / Teaching English; U of North Carolina; Duke U

BIVENS, MARIAN J D; GREENSBORO, NC; PAGE HS; (JR); Nat Mrt LOC; DARE; Chr; Ch Chr; Track; Acolyte in Church; Counselor in Bible School; Nursing; Howard U; Winston-Salem State U

BLACK, BRITTANY N; ELLENBORO, NC; CHASE HS; (JR); Hnr Roll; Nat Hon Sy; Comm Volntr; Hab For Humty Volntr; Hosp Aide; Chrch Yth Grp; Dbte Team; Emplmnt; FCA; FBLA; Pep Squd; Spch Team; Ch Chr; SP/M/VS; Communications; Law; U of North Carolina (Chapel Hill); U of North Carolina (Charlotte)

Bhakta, Anjali G
Wakefield HS
Raleigh, NC

Bell, Kristen P
Forestview HS
Gastonia, NC

Beaudry, Karin A
Swain Cty HS
Bryson City, NC

Beacham, Chase
North Raleigh Christian AC
Raleigh, NC

Baxter, Maya L
White Oak HS
Jacksonville, NC

Baxter, Samuel J
Southeast Raleigh HS
Knightdale, NC

Bebber, Brittany
Cape Fear Christian AC
Angier, NC

Bermudez, Brenda N
Clayton HS
Clayton, NC

Bialek, Alexandra
Page HS
Greensboro, NC

BLACK, JAMIAL; RALEIGH, NC; WAKE FOREST HS; (JR); Hnr Roll; Otst Ac Ach Awd; WWAHSS; Hab For Humty Volntr; Peer Tut/Med; Emplmnt; FBLA; P to P St Amb Prg; Ftball (V); Member of National Achievers Society; Law; Psychology; Howard U; Central U

BLACK, TIFFANY; CHARLOTTE, NC; INDEPENDENCE HS; (JR); Hnr Roll; Emplmnt; Photog; Dnce; Swmg (V); Dance and Work As Well; Chapel Hill; Wilmington

BLACKMAN, DARREN; CARY, NC; GREEN HOPE HS; (FR); Hnr Roll; Nat Hon Sy; Perf Att; St of Mnth; Comm Volntr; Emplmnt; Scouts; Fld Hky; NC State U

BLACKMON, MEGAN S; LOCUST, NC; WEST STANLY HS; (JR); Hi Hnr Roll; Hnr Roll; Peer Tut/Med; Chrch Yth Grp; FCA; FBLA; Mth Clb/Tm; Ntl Beta Clb; Photog; Tchrs Aide; Ch Chr; Scr Kpr (J); Track (V); Sch Ppr (E, R, P); Yrbk (E, R, P); Physical Therapy; Early Childhood Education; Wingate; U of North Carolina At Charlotte

BLACKSURE, LATORIA L P; WADESBORO, NC; ANSON HS; (FR); 4H Awd; Ctznshp Aw; Hi Hnr Roll; Hnr Roll; Perf Att; Chrch Yth Grp; DARE; Ch Chr; Stu Cncl (P); CR (P); Bearcat Battalion; Excellence Award; Doctorate; Music; Fayetteville U; North Carolina State

BLACKWELL, ASHLEY E; MILL SPRING, NC; POLK CTY HS; (JR); Ctznshp Aw; Hnr Roll; MVP; Nat Hon Sy; Yth Ldrshp Prog; Chrch Yth Grp; Emplmnt; FCA; Key Club; Ntl Beta Clb; Prom Com; Spanish Clb; Chr; Chrldg (V); PP Ftbl (J); Track (V); Cl Off (P); Stu Cncl (R); Extra Miler Award; Physical Therapy; Psychology; U of North Carolina Charlotte

BLACKWELL, BRITTANY; RALEIGH, NC; CARY AC; (SO); Hnr Roll; MVP; Perf Att; Chrch Yth Grp; Emplmnt; Key Club; P to P St Amb Prg; Ch Chr; Dnce; Bskball (V CL); PP Ftbl (V); Scr Kpr; Sftball (V L); Track (V L); Accounting; IT Support; Wake Forest U; U of North Carolina Chapel Hill

BLACKWELL, CAYLEIGH; KILL DEVIL HILLS, NC; (SO); Ctznshp Aw; Hnr Roll; Perf Att; Pres Ac Ftns Aw; St of Mnth; 4-H; Chrch Yth Grp; DARE; Emplmnt; Key Club; Outdrs Clb; Bskball (J); Sftball (V); Vllyball (J); PTA Citizenship Award; Veterinarian; Appalachian State U

BLAKELY, KADEE; CHARLOTTE, NC; NORTH MECKLENBURG SR HS; (JR); Duke TS; Hnr Roll; WWAHSS; Comm Volntr; Chrch Yth Grp; Ntl FFA; SADD; Clr Grd; CR (R); Yrbk (R); Member of "Who's Who"; 2nd Place in NC Writer's Network Poetry Contest; Journalism; Creative Writing; UNC At Wilmington; UNC At Chapel Hill

BLAKLEY, CATHRYN G; DURHAM, NC; NORTHERN HS; (JR); Hnr Roll; Nat Hon Sy; Yth Ldrshp Prog; Comm Volntr; Jr Cls League; Latin Clb; CR (R); All-Star Cheerleading; Nurse Anesthetist, Forensic Science; Biochemistry, Chemistry; North Carolina State U; UNC-Chapel Hill

BLALOCK, WILLIAM L B; HOPE MILLS, NC; FAYETTEVILLE CHRISTIAN SCH; (SO); Hi Hnr Roll; WWAHSS; Yth Ldrshp Prog; Peer Tut/Med; Chr; Bsball (J); Ftball (VJCL); Sch Ppr (R, P); Law; Political Journalism; Duke; Georgia U

BLEVINS, AMANDA; MILLERS CREEK, NC; WEST WILKES HS; (JR); Hi Hnr Roll; Hnr Roll; WWAHSS; Comm Volntr; Hab For Humty Volntr; Peer Tut/Med; Chrch Yth Grp; Emplmnt; FCA; Key Club; Mod UN; Ntl Beta Clb; Chr; Ch Chr; Samaritan's Kitchen; Elementary Education; Nursing; Wilkes Community College; Appalachian State U

BLOUNT, DESEREE; GREENSBORO, NC; NORTHEAST HS; (SO); F Lan Hn Soc; Ch Chr; Dnce; PP Ftbl (V); Track (V); U of North Carolina (Greensboro)

BLOUNT, DOMINIQUE; GREENSBORO, NC; NORTHEAST HS; (SR); Perf Att; Ch Chr; Track (V); Early Childhood Education; U of North Carolina At Greensboro; Guilford Technical Community College

BLUE, KWAME T; LUMBERTON, NC; LUMBERTON SR HS; (SO); Comm Volntr; Emplmnt; Ch Chr

BOATWRIGHT, MATTHEW S; SHELBY, NC; BURNS HS; (JR); Duke TS; F Lan Hn Soc; Hi Hnr Roll; Hnr Roll; Jr Mshl; Nat Hon Sy; Salutrn; St of Mnth; Yth Ldrshp Prog; Comm Volntr; Chrch Yth Grp; Emplmnt; Ntl Beta Clb; Prom Com; Scouts; Sccr (V); Cl Off (V); Stu Cncl (V); Assistant Junior Marshall; Civil Engineering; North Carolina State U

BOAZ, BRADLEY A; GASTONIA, NC; FORESTVIEW HS; (FR); Duke TS; Chr; SP/M/VS; National Honor Choir 2003, 2005; N.C. State Honor Choir 2003, 2004, 2005; Education; Law; Juilliard; Appalachian State U

BODNER, RACHEL V; CANDLER, NC; MT PISGAH AC; (JR); Hnr Roll; Perf Att; Sci Fairs; St of Mnth; Comm Volntr; ArtClub; Chrch Yth Grp; Acpl Chr; Chr; Optometry; Photography; Southern Adventist U

BOGGS, JESSICA; GARNER, NC; WEST JOHNSTON HS; (JR); Hi Hnr Roll; Hnr Roll; Nat Hon Sy; WWAHSS; Chrch Yth Grp; Emplmnt; FCA; FTA; Key Club; Photog; Sch Ppr (R, P); Education; Social Services; U of North Carolina At Wilmington; Appalachian State U

BOGUE JR, ALVIN C; ELIZABETH CITY, NC; NORTHEASTERN HS; (SR); Hnr Roll; Perf Att; WWAHSS; Comm Volntr; Red Cr Aide; Spec Olymp Vol; Emplmnt; Lttrmn Clb; Lib Aide; Mus Clb; Off Aide; ROTC; Bnd; Ch Chr; Jzz Bnd; Mch Bnd; Stu Cncl (R); Outstanding Band Student (02-04); East Carolina U

BOLER, JEREMY; CHARLOTTE, NC; PROVIDENCE HS; (SR); Hnr Roll; Nat Ldrshp Svc; Yth Ldrshp Prog; Comm Volntr; Chrch Yth Grp; FCA; FBLA; NYLC; ROTC; Vsity Clb; SP/M/VS; Track (V); Wt Lftg (V); JROTC - Chief Petty Officer; Congressional Student Leadership - CSLC; Business; Gardner Webb U

BOLTON, ZAVIER K; JAMESTOWN, NC; RAGSDALE HS; (FR); Hnr Roll; Chrch Yth Grp; Ftball (J); Wt Lftg (J); Cinematography; Musical Arts; French National Film Academy; Morehouse College

BOND, ERVIN R; AULANDER, NC; BERTIE HS; (SR); Hnr Roll; Perf Att; Comm Volntr; Peer Tut/Med; Chrch Yth Grp; Drma Clb; Bnd; Chr; Ch Chr; Mch Bnd; Upward Bound; Criminal Justice; Elementary Education K-6; Johnson & Wales U

BOONE, NICALAS; MURFREESBORO, NC; HERTFORD CTY MS; (MS); Perf Att; DARE; Bsball (J); Ftball (J); Elizabeth City State U

BOONE, NYKESHIA; WAKE FOREST, NC; WAKE FOREST ROLESVILLE HS; (JR); Hi Hnr Roll; Hnr Roll; Otst Ac Ach Awd; WWAHSS; Peer Tut/Med; Chrch Yth Grp; Sci Clb; Svce Clb; Pediatrician-Medicine; East Carolina U; U of North Carolina-Chapel Hill

BOONE, PARIS A; MONROE, NC; SUN VALLEY MS; (MS); Hnr Roll; Otst Ac Ach Awd; Perf Att; Comm Volntr; Peer Tut/Med; Chess; Chrch Yth Grp; Ch Chr; Basketball for YMCA; Rec Basketball; Medical Field; Doctor; Duke U; UNC Tarheel

BOONE, RACHEL A; INDIAN TRAIL, NC; METROLINA CHRISTIAN AC; (JR); Hnr Roll; Yth Ldrshp Prog; Comm Volntr; Peer Tut/Med; Chrch Yth Grp; Photog; Sci Clb; Dnce; Tennis (V); Lit Mag (E, P); Middles and Mentours Club; Joy Christian Fellowship Youth Group; Marine Biology; Photography; U of North Carolina Wilmington; Eckerd College

BOONE, WHITNEY; MARION, NC; MC DOWELL HS; (MS); Hnr Roll; Perf Att; DARE; Drma Clb; FCA; Pep Squd; Scr Kpr (L); Vllyball (L); Stu Cncl (R); Award for Most Improved in Volleyball; Forensics Detective; Model; UNC at Wilmington; U of Eastern Carolina

BOOTH, LYNDSAY; FAYETTEVILLE, NC; MASSEY HILL CLASSICAL HS; (SO); Duke TS; Hi Hnr Roll; Nat Hon Sy; Sci/Math Olympn; WWAHSS; Chrch Yth Grp; Mod UN; NtlFrnscLg; SP/M/VS; International Relation; Near and Middle Eastern Studies; Harvard U; Emory U

BOOTH, WHITNEY M; HORSE SHOE, NC; CAROLINA DAY SCH; (JR); Hnr Roll; Hab For Humty Volntr; Spec Olymp Vol; Chrch Yth Grp; NtlFrnscLg; Prom Com; Spch Team; Fld Hky (V); Sccr (J); Young Womanhood Recognition Award - Church; International Relations; International Tourism; U North Carolina Chapel Hill; Brigham Young U

BOSEMAN, CURTISHA; GOLDSBORO, NC; SPRING CREEK HS; (SO); Hnr Roll; Comm Volntr; Bnd; Chr; Clr Grd; Mch Bnd; Registered Nurse; Pre-Medicine; UNC-Charlotte; East Carolina U

BOSS, JERMESIA; WINSTON SULBRU, NC; EAST FORSYTH; (SO); Sci Fairs; St of Mnth; Yth Ldrshp Prog; Comm Volntr; Hab For Humty Volntr; Peer Tut/Med; DARE; DECA; Drma Clb; Chr; Ch Chr

BOSTIAN, TRAVIS B; MORGANTON, NC; FREEDOM HS; (FR); Ctznshp Aw; Hnr Roll; Otst Ac Ach Awd; DARE; Computers; Health Science; Appalachian State U; Western North Carolina

BOSTICK, NICHOLE; LEXINGTON, NC; NORTH DAVIDSON HS; (SO); Hnr Roll; Chr; Nurse Practitioner; Bachelor's Degree

BOUCHE, BRANDON M; APEX, NC; MIDDLE CREEK HS; (FR); Duke TS; Hnr Roll; Comm Volntr; Chrch Yth Grp; Cl Off (R); Church Mission Trips to NC & GA; Computer Engineering; Civil Engineering; North Carolina State U

BOUDREAU, CAMERON; CHAPEL HILL, NC; CEDAR RIDGE HS; (SR); Duke TS; Hnr Roll; Sci/Math Olympn; Comm Volntr; Chess; Emplmnt; Latin Clb; Cr Ctry (V L); Ninjutsu - Yellow/Black Belt; Novelist; Eckerd College

BOWDEN, PATRICE C; WILMINGTON, NC; JOHN T HOGGARD HS; (JR); Ctznshp Aw; Hi Hnr Roll; Hnr Roll; Jr Mshl; Nat Hon Sy; Nat Mrt Sch Recip; WWAHSS; Chrch Yth Grp; DECA; Emplmnt; Ntl Beta Clb; Ch Chr; Dnce; National Technical Honor Society; National Honor Society; Major in Computer Engineering; Minor in Accounting; U of North Carolina At Charlotte; North Carolina State U

BOWDEN III, MARSHALL B; CHAPEL HILL, NC; CHAPEL HILL HS; (FR); Hi Hnr Roll; Hnr Roll; MVP; Pres Ac Ftns Aw; Comm Volntr; Hosp Aide; Lcrsse (J); 2004 - Cougar Award / Student of the Year; MVP- Lacrosse / 2005 / Walk for Hope - Walker

BOWEN, ASHLEY; HENDERSON, NC; NORTHERN VANCE HS; (FR); Hnr Roll; SP/M/VS; Cosmetology; Cape Fear

BOWEN, ASHLEY R; CONCORD, NC; NORTHWEST CABARRUS HS; (FR); Hi Hnr Roll; Hnr Roll; Yth Ldrshp Prog; Hosp Aide; Red Cr Aide; Chrch Yth Grp; Mch Bnd; SP/M/VS; Nursing; Cabarrus College of Health Sciences; Rowan Cabarrus Community College

BOWEN, EMMANUELLE R A; CHARLOTTE, NC; ADVENTIST CHRISTIAN AC; (FR); Hnr Roll; Pres Sch; Sci Fairs; Comm Volntr; Emplmnt; Bnd; SP/M/VS; Swmg; Law; Car Design / Engineer; Harvard U; Stanford U

BOWEN, VALERI P; LUMBERTON, NC; WEST BLADEN HS; (JR); Ctznshp Aw; Hnr Roll; Nat Mrt LOC; Otst Ac Ach Awd; Pres Sch; St of Mnth; Chrch Yth Grp; Chr; Ch Chr; Dnce; SP/M/VS; Performing Arts; Archaeology; U of Wilmington; East Carolina U

BOWES, JOSH; HAW RIVER, NC; GRAHAM HS; (SR); Hnr Roll; MVP; Otst Ac Ach Awd; Pres Ac Ftns Aw; Hab For Humty Volntr; Chrch Yth Grp; FCA; Mth Clb/Tm; Outdrs Clb; Wdwrkg Clb; Cr Ctry (V); Tennis (V C); Wrstlg (V CL); Mathematics; U of North Carolina At Chapel Hill; North Carolina State U

BOWLIN, KAYLA A; PURLEAR, NC; WEST WILKES HS; (SR); Hi Hnr Roll; WWAHSS; Peer Tut/Med; FCA; Key Club; Ntl Beta Clb; Prom Com; French Clb; Chr; Dnce; Chrldg (V); Captain of Dance Team 2 Years; Nursing/ Ob/Gyn; UNC-Greensboro; East Carolina U

BOWMAN, EMMA; HICKORY, NC; HICKORY HS; (SO); Hnr Roll; Perf Att; Key Club; Forensic Science; Crime Scene Investigation; East Carolina; Lenoir Rhyne

BOWMAN, SUSAN; ASHEBORO, NC; ASHEBORO HS; (JR); Hi Hnr Roll; Nat Hon Sy; WWAHSS; Yth Ldrshp Prog; Comm Volntr; Key Club; Latin Clb; Chrldg (VJCL); Physical Therapy; Appalachian State U

BOWMAN, SUSAN R; ASHEBORO, NC; ASHEBORO HS; (JR); Hi Hnr Roll; Nat Hon Sy; WWAHSS; Yth Ldrshp Prog; Comm Volntr; Key Club; Chrldg (VJCL); Student LIFT; Physical Therapy; Appalachian State U; U of North Carolina

BOYCE, VIRGINIA; BELMONT, NC; SOUTH POINT HS; (JR); Gov Hnr Prg; Hi Hnr Roll; Jr Mshl; MVP; WWAHSS; Yth Ldrshp Prog; Comm Volntr; Peer Tut/Med; Chrch Yth Grp; Dbte Team; HO'Br Yth Ldrshp; Mod UN; Ntl Beta Clb; Scouts; Ch Chr; SP/M/VS; Cr Ctry (V L); Sccr (V); Adv Cncl (R); Stu Cncl (R); Senate Page; Presbyterian Youth Council; English/Journalism; Law; Davidson College; Georgetown U

BOYD, SHELISHA R; CHARLOTTE, NC; WEST MECKLENBURG HS; (FR); Hnr Roll; Perf Att; Sci Fairs; Peer Tut/Med; Chrch Yth Grp; Ch Chr; Sftball (J); Vllyball (J); Wrstlg (J); Law (Criminal) Masters; Pediatrics-Doctor; Tennessee State U; U of Miami

BRACKETT, ADRIANE J; SHELBY, NC; BURNS HS; (JR); Hnr Roll; Jr Mshl; Nat Hon Sy; Comm Volntr; Chrch Yth Grp; Emplmnt; FCA; Key Club; Ntl Beta Clb; Prom Com; Latin Clb; Adv Cncl (P); Cl Off (P); Stu Cncl (P); CR (P); Over 500 Volunteer Hours in Community and School; Pharmacy; Wingate U; U of North Carolina Chapel Hill

BRACY, SHANNON; JACKSONVILLE, NC; NORTHSIDE HS; (FR); Hnr Roll; Perf Att; Comm Volntr; Red Cr Aide; Chrch Yth Grp; Bnd; Dnce; 2005 State Team Bowling Championship; Social Worker; Pro Bowler; East Carolina U; U of North Carolina-Wilmington

BRADDY, RENAE; BELHAVEN, NC; NORTHSIDE HS; (JR); Duke TS; Jr Mshl; Kwnis Aw; Nat Hon Sy; Otst Ac Ach Awd; Perf Att; Sci/Math Olympn; Valdctrian; WWAHSS; Yth Ldrshp Prog; Peer Tut/Med; Red Cr Aide; Spec Olymp Vol; ArtClub; Emplmnt; FCA; FBLA; Key Club; Mth Clb/Tm; Ntl Beta Clb; Prom Com; SP/M/VS; Cr Ctry (V); Track (V); Secretary FBLA and Key Club; Dentistry/Orthodontics; Interior Design; UNC-Chapel Hill; North Carolina State U

BRADEN, LISA; NASHVILLE, NC; NASH CTRL HS; (JR); Hnr Roll; Nat Mrt Sch Recip; Comm Volntr; Hosp Aide; Red Cr Aide; 4-H; Chrch Yth Grp; Emplmnt; Vsity Clb; Chr; Dnce; Sftball (V); Qualify for National Scholars; Lawyer/Attorney; Public Service; UNC Wilmington; NC State

BRADFORD, BRITANNI; HUNTERSVILLE, NC; HARDING U HS; (FR); Yth Ldrshp Prog; Comm Volntr; Chrch Yth Grp; Ntl Beta Clb; Ch Chr; Volunteer At the Discovery Place & Nature Museum; Physician of Pediatrics; Biology Major; Spelman College (Atlanta, GA); Duke U (NC)

BRADLEY, CASSIE M; SHELBY, NC; BURNS HS; (JR); Ctznshp Aw; F Lan Hn Soc; Hnr Roll; Nat Hon Sy; Otst Ac Ach Awd; Pres Ac Ftns Aw; WWAHSS; Comm Volntr; Hosp Aide; Peer Tut/Med; 4-H; Chrch Yth Grp; Dbte Team; Emplmnt; FCA; Ntl Beta Clb; FFA; Off Aide; Bnd; Ch Chr; Dnce; Mch Bnd; Chrldg (V L); Gmnstcs (V); Sccr (V); Vllyball (V); CR (R); Youth in Government Member; Coca-Cola Scholar Athlete / Fashion Modeling; Pediatric Nurse Practitioner; Cosmetology; East Carolina U; U of North Carolina Wilmington

Bowen, Emmanuelle R A, Adventist Christian AC, Charlotte, NC | Bowden III, Marshall B, Chapel Hill HS, Chapel Hill, NC | Bogue Jr, Alvin C, Northeastern HS, Elizabeth City, NC | Boone, Rachel A, Metrolina Christian AC, Indian Trail, NC | Bradley, Cassie M, Burns HS, Shelby, NC

BRADLEY, KATY; KANNAPOLIS, NC; NORTHWEST CABARRUS HS; (SR); Hi Hnr Roll; Hnr Roll; Jr Mshl; Nat Hon Sy; Nat Sci Aw; Sci Fairs; WWAHSS; Peer Tut/Med; Emplmnt; Ntl Beta Clb; Ntl FFA; Off Aide; SADD; French Clb; Hsbk Rdg (V); National Agriscience Fair Winner; Chapter FFA Vice President; Veterinary Medicine; Animal Science; Virginia Tech

BRADSHAW III, JAMES A; SHELBY, NC; BURNS HS; (JR); Hnr Roll; MVP; Vsity Clb; Spanish Clb; Ftball (V L); Track (V L); Wt Lftg (V C); Defensive Most Improved Player - Football; All-Conference 3A - Southwestern Football; Business Administration; Network Technology; U of North Carolina Chapel Hill; Eastern Carolina U

BRAGMAN, KARYN; CLAYTON, NC; CLAYTON HS; (JR); Hnr Roll; MVP; Nat Hon Sy; Otst Ac Ach Awd; Pres Ac Ftns Aw; WWAHSS; Comm Volntr; Peer Tut/Med; Chrch Yth Grp; DARE; Emplmnt; FCA; FTA; Key Club; Photog; Quill & Scroll; Ch Chr; Dnce; Cr Ctry (V CL); Track (V CL); CR (R); Yrbk (E, R, P); Most Outstanding Field Events Performer-Track; Cross Country Achievement Award; Business Management/Small Entrepreneurship; Physical Therapy; North Carolina State U; U of North Carolina At Charlotte

BRAKE, NAKIA D; ROCKY MOUNT, NC; NASH CTRL HS; (FR); Perf Att; St of Mnth; Comm Volntr; Chrch Yth Grp; Scouts; Ch Chr; Lawyer; Doctor; North Carolina Central U

BRANDON, TONIKA S; HICKORY, NC; HICKORY HS; (FR); Hnr Roll; Kwnis Aw; Perf Att; DARE; Ntl Beta Clb; Teacher; Nurse; Catawba Valley Community College; Mitchell Community College

BRANDON, TRICINA; OXFORD, NC; J F WEBB HS; (JR); Otst Ac Ach Awd; Chrch Yth Grp; Prom Com; Scouts; Ch Chr; Dnce; PP Ftbl (L); Scr Kpr (L); Track (L); Vance Granville Community College

BRANDYS, COURTNEY; HIGH POINT, NC; TRINITY HS; (FR); Hnr Roll; Perf Att; Comm Volntr; DARE; ROTC; Scouts; Clb; Bnd; Mch Bnd; Pep Bnd; Zoology; Vet; North Carolina State; Auburn U

BRANNON, JANAE N; CHARLOTTE, NC; WEST MECKLENBURG HS; (FR); Hnr Roll; Nat Ldrshp Svc; Otst Ac Ach Awd; Yth Ldrshp Prog; Comm Volntr; Peer Tut/Med; Chrch Yth Grp; Emplmnt; Fr of Library; FTA; Lib Aide; Mod UN; Chr; Dnce; Drl Tm; SP/M/VS; CR (P); Received School's Leadership Award; Community Service; An Attorney; A Pediatrician; NC State; Georgia U

BRANTLEY, PAIGE; RALEIGH, NC; WAKE-FOREST-ROLESVILLE HS; (JR); Hnr Roll; MVP; Nat Hon Sy; Otst Ac Ach Awd; Yth Ldrshp Prog; Comm Volntr; Peer Tut/Med; Emplmnt; Key Club; Ntl Beta Clb; Sci Clb; PP Ftbl (V C); Sftball (V L); Vllyball (J); Academic Letter; NCHSAA 4-A all-State Honorable Mention/CAP 6 All Conference/Softball; Orthodontics; Marketing; U of North Carolina At Wilmington; Appalachian State U

BRASWELL, ALLISON; ASHEBORO, NC; ASHEBORO HS; (SO); Hi Hnr Roll; Hnr Roll; Perf Att; WWAHSS; Chrch Yth Grp; DARE; Key Club; Ntl Beta Clb; Scouts; Vsity Clb; Bskball (V); Cr Ctry (V); Sftball (V L)

BRASWELL, MEGAN N; NORWOOD, NC; SOUTH STANLY HS; (FR); Hnr Roll; Sci Fairs; St of Mnth; WWAHSS; Chrch Yth Grp; DARE; FCA; Scouts; Sftball (J); Lit Mag (R); Youth At Church; Dixie Softball; Bachelor's in Nursing; Appalachian State U; Stanly Tech

BRASWELL, TABITHA C; TODD, NC; WATAUGA HS; (FR); Hnr Roll; Perf Att; Comm Volntr; Red Cr Aide; Chrch Yth Grp; Chr; Ch Chr; Chrldg (J); Plays the Piano; Music Teacher; Appalachian State

BRATCHER, ASHLEY; RAEFORD, NC; HOKE CTY HS; (JR); Hnr Roll; Comm Volntr; Spec Olymp Vol; Emplmnt; CR (R); Talent Search Program; Degree in Business; Licensed Cosmetologist; U of Greensboro; East Carolina

BRAXTON, TRAVIS W; WILMINGTON, NC; E A LANEY HS; (SO); All Am Sch; Hi Hnr Roll; Hnr Roll; USAA; WWAHSS; Comm Volntr; Chrch Yth Grp; Scouts; Mission Trips to Ukraine Orphanages & Dominican Republic; Church Drama Team; Architecture; Chef; North Carolina State U; U of North Carolina At Wilmington

BREAZEALE, JORDAN N; MARSHVILLE, NC; PIEDMONT HS; (FR); 4H Awd; Duke TS; Hi Hnr Roll; Kwnis Aw; Yth Ldrshp Prog; Comm Volntr; Spec Olymp Vol; 4-H; Chrch Yth Grp; DARE; FCA; FBLA; Ntl Beta Clb; Quiz Bowl; Chrldg (V); Hsbk Rdg; Sccr; Beta Club; International Affairs; Duke U; UNC Chapel Hill

BREITENFELD, ROXANNE; MARSHVILLE, NC; FOREST HILLS HS; (SR); Hnr Roll; Otst Ac Ach Awd; Pres Sch; Comm Volntr; Spec Olymp Vol; DARE; Emplmnt; FCA; FBLA; Ntl Beta Clb; Pep Squd; Photog; Quill & Scroll; Bnd; Chrldg (VJ L); PP Ftbl (VJ); Scr Kpr (V); Cl Off (P, T); Stu Cncl (T, R); Yrbk (E); Varsity Cheerleading Jacket Award; Master's in English; U of NC at Wilmington

BREWER, EZRA J; POLKTON, NC; ANSON HS; (SO); Bnd

BRICE, ISAIAH D; GASTONIA, NC; BESSEMER CITY HS; (SO); Hnr Roll; Perf Att; Fr of Library; Wdwrkg Clb; Ch Chr; Ftball (V); Auburn U; Notre Dame U

BRICKHOUSE, VICTORIA; EDENTON, NC; JOHN A HOLMES HS; (MS); CRNA; UNC Chapel Hill

BRIDGEFORD, ERICA M; MIDWAY PARK, NC; WHITE OAK HS; MS; Ctznshp Aw; Hnr Roll; Nat Stu Ath Day Aw; Perf Att; Pres Ac Ftns Aw; Sci Fairs; St of Mnth; Comm Volntr; DARE; Mth Clb/Tm; Chr; CR (T); Business Marketing; Physicist; Fayetteville State; Howard U

BRIDGERS, ROBERT KYLE; RALEIGH, NC; GARNER MAGNET HS; (JR); Hnr Roll; Nat Hon Sy; Nat Mrt LOC; WWAHSS; Yth Ldrshp Prog; Comm Volntr; Peer Tut/Med; Chrch Yth Grp; Emplmnt; FCA; Ntl Beta Clb; Bsball (VJ); Wt Lftg (V); CR (R); American Legion Baseball; Architectural Design; NCSU North Carolina State U; UNCW U North Carolina @ Wilm.

BRIDGES, KATHERINE L; MATTHEWS, NC; WEDDINGTON HS; (SR); F Lan Hn Soc; Hi Hnr Roll; Hnr Roll; Nat Hon Sy; WWAHSS; Comm Volntr; Peer Tut/Med; Spec Olymp Vol; FCA; Key Club; Off Aide; French Clb; Dnce; Charlotte City Ballet Co. (Full Company Member); Pre-Med; Biology; North Carolina State U

BRIDGES, TIFFANY N; FRISCO, NC; CAPE HATTERAS SEC SCH; (SO); Ctznshp Aw; Hnr Roll; Sci Fairs; St of Mnth; Peer Tut/Med; Chrch Yth Grp; Sftball (V); Art Award; Oceanography; Marine Biology; U of North Carolina; U of Hawaii

BRIGGS, BRITTANY; WEAVERVILLE, NC; NORTH BUNCOMBE HS; (SR); Hnr Roll; Jr Mshl; WWAHSS; Hosp Aide; Chrch Yth Grp; Ntl Beta Clb; Yrbk (P); Church Drama Team; Nursing-Pediatric; UNCA U North Carolina-Asheville; AB Tech

BRIGGS, KELLY B; BURNSVILLE, NC; MTN HERITAGE HS; (FR); Ctznshp Aw; Hnr Roll; Comm Volntr; Ntl Beta Clb; Chr; Students Warning Against Tobacco; Advertising / Public Relations; Journalism; East Tennessee State U; Western Carolina U

BRIGGS, NICKEY L; MAXTON, NC; PURNELL SWEET HS; (SO); Hi Hnr Roll; Otst Ac Ach Awd; Sci Fairs; WWAHSS; Yth Ldrshp Prog; Chrch Yth Grp; Drma Clb; Ch Chr; Dnce; Sftball (J); NASA / Aises Club; Medical Degree / Doctor; U of Chapel Hill; Pembroke State U

BRIGMAN, BOBBY; GARNER, NC; GARNER HS; (FR); Hnr Roll; Sci Fairs; Sci/Math Olympn; ArtClub; Ntl Beta Clb; Rlr Hky (V); #1 in Class Rank for 1st Semester of Freshman Year; Rec. Ice Hockey Champs; Computer Engineer; NC State U; Duke U

BRINKLEY, THOMAS J; HILLSBOROUGH, NC; CEDAR RIDGE HS; (SR); DAR; F Lan Hn Soc; Hnr Roll; Jr Mshl; Otst Ac Ach Awd; Pres Ac Ftns Aw; Sci Fairs; WWAHSS; Comm Volntr; Chrch Yth Grp; Emplmnt; Ntl Beta Clb; SP/M/VS; Cr Ctry (V L); Wrstlg (V CL); Adv Cncl (R); Stu Cncl (R); Duke Comprehensive Cancer Center Intern; Male Scholar Athlete for Cedar Ridge - 2003; Graduate UNC Chapel Hill; Doctor; U of North Carolina Chapel Hill

BRINSON, MELANIE M; DUDLEY, NC; SPRING CREEK HS; (SO); Hnr Roll; Nat Hon Sy; Comm Volntr; FBLA; Quiz Bowl; Spanish Clb; Clr Grd; Track (V); Finance and Accounting; Cosmetology; U of North Carolina At Chapel Hill; Duke

BRISCOE, SHANNON; AUTRYVILLE, NC; LAKEWOOD HS; (JR); DAR; Hi Hnr Roll; Nat Hon Sy; Otst Ac Ach Awd; WWAHSS; DARE; Ntl Beta Clb; ROTC; Spanish Clb; National ServSafe Restaurant Association Exam; Physical Therapy Associate's Degree; Fayetteville Technical College; Sampson Community College

BRISLEY, DREW; ASHEBORO, NC; ASHEBORO HS; (FR); Duke TS; Hi Hnr Roll; MVP; Sci Fairs; Comm Volntr; Spec Olymp Vol; Chrch Yth Grp; FCA; Ntl Beta Clb; Sccr (J); Tennis (V L); UNC Chapel Hill; North Carolina State U

BRISSON, SPENCER T; SALISBURY, NC; EAST ROWAN HS; (FR); Duke TS; Hi Hnr Roll; Hnr Roll; Chrch Yth Grp; Appalachian State U; North Carolina State U

BRITT, JEREMY G; LUMBERTON, NC; LUMBERTON HS; (FR); Hnr Roll; ROTC; Member of Teen Summit; Computer Programmer / Computer Tech; North Carolina State; Eastern Carolina U

BRKIC, AMAR; WINSTON-SALEM, NC; REYNOLDS HS; (JR); Hi Hnr Roll; Hnr Roll; MVP; Nat Hon Sy; Nat Ldrshp Svc; Otst Ac Ach Awd; Perf Att; Pres Ac Ftns Aw; Yth Ldrshp Prog; Comm Volntr; Hab For Humty Volntr; Fr of Library; NYLC; P to P St Amb Prg; German Clb; Sccr (V L); National Junior Honors Society; Global Young Leaders Conference; International Business; Language Communication Management; U of North Carolina Charlotte; Wake Forest U

BROADHURST, LARRY D; GOLDSBORO, NC; GOLDSBORO HS; (SO); Hnr Roll; FBLA; Ntl Beta Clb; Bskball (J); CR (R); Honor Athlete; Accountant; Business Management; North Carolina A & T U

BROCK, KIMBERLY H; CHARLOTTE, NC; WEST MECKLENBURG HS; (JR); All Am Sch; Duke TS; Hi Hnr Roll; Jr Mshl; Nat Hon Sy; Otst Ac Ach Awd; Pres Sch; WWAHSS; Comm Volntr; Peer Tut/Med; Chrch Yth Grp; DARE; Drma Clb; FCA; Key Club; Lib Aide; Photog; Svce Clb; Chr; Ch Chr; SP/M/VS; Stg Cre; Cl Off (S); Yrbk (R); Bible Quizzing Honors; Missionary; Trevecca Nazarene U

BROOK, CAMILLE; DURHAM, NC; HILLSIDE HS; (SO); Hnr Roll; WWAHSS; Yth Ldrshp Prog; Comm Volntr; Peer Tut/Med; FBLA; MuAlphaTh; Bnd; Dnce; Mch Bnd; Pep Bnd; Sccr (V); Stu Cncl (V); Clarinet Captain in Marching Band; Model in HHS Fashion Society - Eminence; Neurobiology; Marine Biology; University of Miami; Stanford U

BROOKS, COURTNEY A C; GASTONIA, NC; ASHBROOK HS; (SR); Duke TS; Hnr Roll; WWAHSS; Comm Volntr; Chrch Yth Grp; Emplmnt; Tchrs Aide; Dnce; Chrldg (V); Tennis (V); Yrbk; 2002 District Doubles Champions - Tennis; 2002 Varsity Small Coed National Champions; Communications; U of North Carolina Greensboro

BROOKS, KEVIN; DAS, NC; ASHBROOK HS; (SR); St of Mnth; Bnd; Mch Bnd; Pep Bnd; SP/M/VS; Forensic Anthropology; Instrumental Music; Western Carolina U

BROOKS, SHANNON D; OAK ISLAND, NC; SOUTH BRUNSWICK HS; (SO); Hnr Roll; Sci Fairs; Scouts; Chr; Ch Chr; Dnce; SP/M/VS; Karate/ Jujitsu Out of School; 4 Year College Degree-Forensics/Dance; U of Greensboro North Carolina; U of Raleigh North Carolina

BROOKSHIRE, AMY E; HIGH POINT, NC; TRINITY HS; (JR); Hnr Roll; WWAHSS; Comm Volntr; Chrch Yth Grp; Drma Clb; FCA; FBLA; Prom Com; Chr; Dnce; SP/M/VS; International Thespian Society; Music; Christian Family / Martial Counseling; Liberty U; U of North Carolina Greensboro

BROTHERS, MEGAN; BARCO, NC; CURRITUCK CTY HS; (SO); Duke TS; Hi Hnr Roll; Hnr Roll; Jr Mshl; MVP; Otst Ac Ach Awd; Perf Att; Comm Volntr; DECA; Mth Clb/Tm; Ntl Beta Clb; Dnce; Chrldg (V CL); Track (V L); Cl Off (V); DECA; Beta Club, SGO; Dance; Psychology; Duke U; U of North Carolina At Chapel Hill

BROWER JR, LEONARD J; EFLAND, NC; ORANGE HS; (JR); Hnr Roll; MVP; WWAHSS; AL Aux Boys; Chrch Yth Grp; Emplmnt; FCA; Key Club; Ntl FFA; Spanish Clb; Lcrsse (V L); Sccr (V CL); Varsity Girls Soccer Goalkeeping Coach; 5 Years of Piano; Master's in Architecture; Business Management Degree; NC State U; UNC-Greensboro

BROWN, ALEXIS L; LAURINBURG, NC; SCOTLAND HS; (JR); 4H Awd; Hi Hnr Roll; Hnr Roll; MVP; St of Mnth; Yth Ldrshp Prog; Comm Volntr; Hab For Humty Volntr; 4-H; Chrch Yth Grp; Jr Ach; Scouts; Chr; Ch Chr; Bskball (J); Sftball (J); Track (V); Vllyball (J); Wt Lftg (J); Computer Science; Winston Salem State U

BROWN, ASHLIE E; CHARLOTTE, NC; ZEBULON VANCE HS; (JR); Hi Hnr Roll; Hnr Roll; MVP; Otst Ac Ach Awd; Pres Ac Ftns Aw; Comm Volntr; Red Cr Aide; Key Club; Prom Com; SADD; Sccr (V L); Swmg (V L); Cl Off (R); Stu Cncl (R); CR (R); Yrbk (P); Most Improved Student-Junior Year; Math Honors; Medical-Nursing; U of North Carolina-Charlotte; U of North Carolina-Wilmington

BROWN, AUTUMN; FAYETTEVILLE, NC; SEVENTY-FIRST HS; (SR); F Lan Hn Soc; Hnr Roll; MVP; Otst Ac Ach Awd; Pres Ac Ftns Aw; St of Mnth; Comm Volntr; Peer Tut/Med; Red Cr Aide; Chrch Yth Grp; DARE; Emplmnt; Mod UN; Pep Squd; Chr; Dnce; Chrldg (V C); Sccr (V); Track (V); Physician's Assistant; BSN; East Carolina U

BROWN, BRITTANY; HOLLY SPRINGS, NC; FUQUAY VARINA HS; (SR); F Lan Hn Soc; Hnr Roll; Nat Hon Sy; WWAHSS; Comm Volntr; Chrch Yth Grp; Drma Clb; Emplmnt; FCA; Ntl Beta Clb; Prom Com; Spanish Clb; SP/M/VS; Cr Ctry (V L); Dvng (C); Fncg (V); Lcrsse (J); Swmg (V CL); Track (L); Stu Cncl (R); English and Obtaining a Doctorate; U of North Carolina At Chapel Hill

BROWN, CAVONDRA S; KERNERSVILLE, NC; EAST FORSYTH HS; (JR); Hnr Roll; Nat Hon Sy; Perf Att; Comm Volntr; Chrch Yth Grp; Emplmnt; Chr; Stu Cncl (R); CR (R); Vocational Honor Society; National Junior Honor Society; Psychology; Pharmacy; U North Carolina Greensboro; U North Carolina Charlotte

BROWN, CHAD; MONROE, NC; SUN VALLEY MS; (MS); Hnr Roll; MVP; St of Mnth; Pep Squd; Photog; Chr; Bskball; Ftball; Sccr; Yrbk (E, P); Beta Club; Pep Club

BROWN, DEVIN C; SALISBURY, NC; WEST ROWAN HS; (SO); Hnr Roll; Chrch Yth Grp; Ftball (J); Computer Engineer; Geography; North Carolina State U; Florida State U

BROWN, EMILY A; BELMONT, NC; SOUTH POINT HS; (JR); Duke TS; Hnr Roll; Nat Hon Sy; WWAHSS; Comm Volntr; Drma Clb; Emplmnt; FTA; Ntl Beta Clb; Scouts; Dnce; SP/M/VS; Stg Cre; Yrbk (R, P); Girl Scout Gold Award; English Education; Theatre; Western Carolina U; U of North Carolina

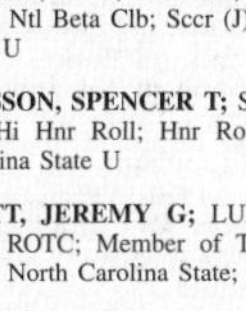
Brown, Cavondra S
East Forsyth HS
Kernersville, NC

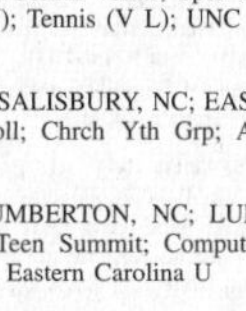
Brook, Camille
Hillside HS
Durham, NC

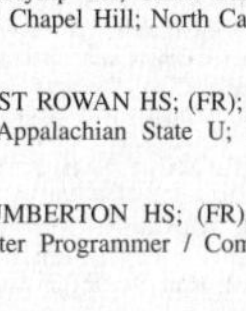
Brown, Devin C
West Rowan HS
Salisbury, NC

Broadhurst, Larry D
Goldsboro HS
Goldsboro, NC

Bridges, Tiffany N
Cape Hatteras Sec Sch
Frisco, NC

Bridgeford, Erica M
White Oak HS
Midway Park, NC

Brannon, Janae N
West Mecklenburg HS
Charlotte, NC

Brandon, Tricina
J F Webb HS
Oxford, NC

National
Honor Roll
Spring 2005

Bradshaw III, James A
Burns HS
Shelby, NC

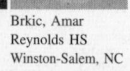

Braswell, Tabitha C
Watauga HS
Todd, NC

Bridgers, Robert Kyle
Garner Magnet HS
Raleigh, NC

Brigman, Bobby
Garner HS
Garner, NC

Brkic, Amar
Reynolds HS
Winston-Salem, NC

BROWN, JANARIA; CONOVER, NC; ST STEPHENS HS; (SO); Hnr Roll; Otst Ac Ach Awd; Perf Att; St of Mnth; Hab For Humty Volntr; DARE; Quiz Bowl; Dnce; Chrldg (V); Major in Health Sciences; U of Chapel Hill; North Carolina State

BROWN, JOSHUA J; ELIZABETH CITY, NC; PASQUOTANK CTY HS; (JR); Hnr Roll; Otst Ac Ach Awd; FBLA; Track (V); Business Administration; Environmental Science; Virginia Union U; North Carolina Central U

BROWN, KATELYN B; STATESVILLE, NC; WEST IREDELL HS; (SR); Hnr Roll; Comm Volntr; Dnce; SP/M/VS; Cheerleader in Middle/Ele.; Gymnastics Middle /Etc.; Nurse/Day Care Center; Dance/Singing; Mitchell Community College; Rowan Community College

BROWN, KATHERINE; RALEIGH, NC; LEESVILLE ROAD HS; (SO); Ctznshp Aw; Hi Hnr Roll; Hnr Roll; WWAHSS; Comm Volntr; Key Club; Scouts; Latin Clb; Bnd; Dnce; Responsibility Award in Character Education; Who's Who Among American High School Students; UNC-Chapel Hill; UNC-Wilmington

BROWN, KATHERINE L; WAKE FOREST, NC; WAKE FOREST-ROLESVILLE HS; (JR); Duke TS; Hi Hnr Roll; Jr Mshl; Nat Hon Sy; WWAHSS; Emplmnt; Key Club; Mus Clb; Sci Clb; Scouts; Bnd; Dnce; Pep Bnd; SP/M/VS; National Honor Society; Girl Scouts; Psychology; Dance; North Carolina State U; U of North Carolina-Chapel Hill

BROWN, KRISTIE; ROANOKE RAPIDS, NC; HALIFAX AC CHRISTIAN SCH; (JR); Hnr Roll; MVP; Chrch Yth Grp; Ntl Beta Clb; Prom Com; Bskball (V); PP Ftbl (V); Sftball (V); Vllyball (V); Senior Beta; Junior Beta; Interior Design; Business; East Carolina U; U North Carolina At Wilmington

BROWN, LAURA L; GREENSBORO, NC; W H PAGE; Hnr Roll; St Schl; WWAHSS; Peer Tut/Med; Jr Ach; National Technical Honors Society; Coroner; Spanish; East Carolina U; U of North Carolina Wilmington

BROWN, MARTINA L; DURHAM, NC; SOUTHERN HS; (FR); Duke TS; Hnr Roll; Comm Volntr; FBLA; Scouts; SP/M/VS; Cr Ctry; FBLA; HOSA; Physician; Howard U; Duke U

BROWN, MICHAEL P; MOORESVILLE, NC; LAKE NORMAN HS; (JR); All Am Sch; Duke TS; Gov Hnr Prg; Hi Hnr Roll; Hnr Roll; Perf Att; Pres Sch; WWAHSS; Hab For Humty Volntr; Chrch Yth Grp; FCA; FBLA; Spanish Clb; Cr Ctry (V L); Track (V L); Drummer Youth Band Church; Architecture; NC State

BROWN, MORGAN M; WINSTON-SALEM, NC; MT TABOR HS; (JR); Hnr Roll; Nat Hon Sy; Sci Fairs; WWAHSS; Comm Volntr; Peer Tut/Med; Chrch Yth Grp; Emplmnt; FCA; Key Club; Wdwrkg Clb; Spanish Clb; Dnce; Drl Tm; Flg Crps; SP/M/VS; Sch Ppr (E); Master's Degree / Education, Spanish; International Relations; U of North Carolina Chapel Hill; Wake Forest

BROWN, QUINETTE; JACKSONVILLE, NC; SOUTHWEST HS; (SR); Ctznshp Aw; Hnr Roll; Nat Ldrshp Svc; Perf Att; Comm Volntr; Emplmnt; Fr of Library; FTA; Lib Aide; Off Aide; Prom Com; SADD; Chr; PP Ftbl (V); Track (V); CR (P); Massage Therapist; High-Tech Institute; Fayetteville Tech

BROWN, ROSS J; FAIRMONT, NC; FAIRMONT HS; (FR); Ctznshp Aw; Gov Hnr Prg; Hi Hnr Roll; Hnr Roll; Otst Ac Ach Awd; Perf Att; Pres Sch; St of Mnth; Comm Volntr; Peer Tut/Med; Chrch Yth Grp; ROTC; Ch Chr; Clr Grd; Drl Tm; Pre-Law Degree; Harvard U; U of North Carolina At Chapel Hill

BROWN, SARAH W; MOUNT ULLA, NC; WEST ROWAN HS; (FR); Chrch Yth Grp; Emplmnt; Ntl FFA; Pep Squd; Ch Chr; Sccr (J); Veterinary Medicine; NC State

BROWN, TABITHA; NEW BERN, NC; WEST CRAVEN MS; (MS); Hi Hnr Roll; Hnr Roll; Perf Att; Pres Ac Ftns Aw; Sci/Math Olympn; ArtClub; Dbte Team; Lib Aide; Ntl Beta Clb; Quiz Bowl; Bnd; Sch Ppr (R); History Bowl; CSI; Appalachian State U; Duke U

BROWN, THOMAS; CHINQUAPIN, NC; EAST DUPLIN HS; (FR); Duke TS; Hi Hnr Roll; Hnr Roll; Otst Ac Ach Awd; Perf Att; Pres Sch; Salutrn; Chr; Bskball; Golf; Sccr; On Yearbook Staff; Maintain High Academic Level; Marine Biology; Electrical Engineering; Duke; U of North Carolina Wilmington

BROWN, TIFFANY B; SALEMBURG, NC; LAKEWOOD HS; (JR); Hnr Roll; Nat Hon Sy; Pres Sch; FBLA; FCCLA; Ntl FFA; Foreign Clb; Forensic Scientist; Lawyer; U of North Carolina Wilmington; East Carolina

BROWN, TRAVIS W; OAK ISLAND, NC; SOUTH BRUNSWICK HS; (SO); Hnr Roll; Perf Att; Comm Volntr; Chrch Yth Grp; DARE; Emplmnt; Scouts; Bsball (J); Ftball (J); Computer Engineer; Chemical Engineer; North Carolina State U; U of North Carolina At Charlotte

BROWN, TYLER; CHARLOTTE, NC; CHARLOTTE CHRISTIAN SCH; (SO); Duke TS; Hi Hnr Roll; Hnr Roll; Perf Att; Pres Ac Ftns Aw; Pres Sch; Comm Volntr; Schol Bwl; Scouts; SADD; Bnd; SP/M/VS; Bsball (L); Bskball (J L); Ftball (VJ L); Track (V L); Cl Off (R); Stu Cncl (R); CR (R); To Succeed; U of North Carolina; U of Florida

BROWN, VICTORIA L; COFIELD, NC; RIDGECROFT SCH; Hi Hnr Roll; Hnr Roll; Nat Hon Sy; St of Mnth; WWAHSS; Hosp Aide; Key Club; Ntl Beta Clb; Bskball (J); Vllyball (J); Basketball Sportsmen of the Year Award; Teaching; East Carolina U; U of North Carolina

BROWN HINTON, CHRISTINA C J; PELHAM, NC; ROCKINGHAM CTY HS; (FR); Gov Hnr Prg; Hi Hnr Roll; Sci/Math Olympn; Yth Ldrshp Prog; Comm Volntr; Hosp Aide; Peer Tut/Med; FCA; Mth Clb/Tm; Mus Clb; Ntl Beta Clb; Chr; Bskball; Tri-M national Music Honor Society; Legislator's School for Youth Leadership; Psychology with Emphasis in MPD; Voice/Music; U of North Carolina Chapel Hill; Harvard U

BROWN JR, PHILIP; SCOTLAND NECK, NC; SOUTHEAST HALIFAX HS; (SO); Duke TS; Hi Hnr Roll; Hnr Roll; Chrch Yth Grp; DARE; Ntl Beta Clb; ROTC; Ch Chr; Drl Tm; Ftball (J); Achieved Medal for DARE Essay; Medical; Engineering; East Carolina U; Chapel Hill NC

BRUNER, KIMBERLY N; MT AIRY, NC; MT AIRY HS; (SR); Hnr Roll; WWAHSS; DARE; Emplmnt; Key Club; Pep Squd; Spanish Clb; Chr; Business; UNC Charlotte; UNC Wilmington

BRUNO, ANGEL; FAYETTEVILLE, NC; CAPE FEAR HS; (SR); Hab For Humty Volntr; DECA; ROTC; Drl Tm; DECA; Film Making; Business Management; Digital Circles; Johnson & Wales U

BRUNSTON, SHAUNDRIA; KINSTON, NC; KINSTON HS; (SR); Comm Volntr; Drma Clb; Emplmnt; Spanish Clb; Graduate John Casabbines Modeling and Acting School; Nursing; East Carolina; Pitt Community College

BRUTON, SADE; KERNERSVILLE, NC; EAST FORSYTH HS; (FR); CARE; Comm Volntr; Chrch Yth Grp; Ch Chr; Dnce; Crosby Scholars; Veterinarian; Model; U of North Carolina; Howard U

BRYANT, CHYNA; FAYETTEVILLE, NC; E E SMITH SR HS; (FR); Hnr Roll; Perf Att; St of Mnth; Yth Ldrshp Prog; Comm Volntr; Peer Tut/Med; Dbte Team; Emplmnt; Scouts; Dnce; Dance Choreographer; Singer; North Carolina Agricultural & Technical U; Queens U of Charlotte

BRYANT, SHONTISTA; ELM CITY, NC; FIKE HS; (FR); Hnr Roll; Perf Att; St of Mnth; Chrch Yth Grp; Ch Chr

BRYANT, VERONICA; ENGELHARD, NC; MATTAMUSKEET HS; (JR); Hnr Roll; St of Mnth; WWAHSS; Red Cr Aide; Prom Com; SADD; Cl Off (V); Accounting; U of North Carolina Greensboro; North Carolina A & T State U

BUCHANAN, SHAWN; MARION, NC; MC DOWELL HS; (SR); Hnr Roll; Jr Mshl; Nat Hon Sy; Otst Ac Ach Awd; St of Mnth; WWAHSS; DECA; French Clb; Computer Science; Appalachian State U

BUCKLES, CHRISTY; SALISBURY, NC; SOUTH ROWAN HS; (SO); Ctznshp Aw; Hnr Roll; Nat Hon Sy; Otst Ac Ach Awd; Comm Volntr; DARE; ROTC; Scouts; Clr Grd; Drl Tm; Mar Art; SCUBA Diving Lessons; JROTC Raider Team-Exec Officer; Vet School-Animal Science; Cornell; NC State

BUCKNER, MELISSA; FAISON, NC; (JR); Hi Hnr Roll; Nat Hon Sy; St of Mnth; WWAHSS; CARE; Comm Volntr; Emplmnt; FCA; FBLA; Jr Cls League; Key Club; Ntl Beta Clb; Prom Com; Svce Clb; Clr Grd; Dnce; CR (R); Captain of Color Guard; Medical Degree; U of N Carolina At Chapel Hill; East Carolina U

BUEKER, DEVIN M; KILL DEVIL HILLS, NC; FIRST FLIGHT HS; (SO); Hi Hnr Roll; Otst Ac Ach Awd; St of Mnth; Peer Tut/Med; 4-H; DARE; FBLA; Key Club; Photog; Bnd; Vllyball (JC); Wt Lftg; National Junior Honor Society; Published Poetry, Math Achievement; Interior Design; Graphic Arts; UNC Wilmington and Chapel Hill; NC State

BUELTO, DESTINEY; RALEIGH, NC; WILLIAM G ENLOE HS; (JR); Hnr Roll; Comm Volntr; Peer Tut/Med; Drma Clb; Emplmnt; Key Club; Svce Clb; Japanese Clb; Orch; Bskball (J); PP Ftbl (J); Track (J); Random Acts of Kindness Club; Students Against Violence Everywhere; Biology; U of North Carolina-Chapel Hill; North Carolina State U

BUGIELSKI, LEAH B; SPARTA, NC; ALLEGHANY HS; (FR); Ctznshp Aw; Duke TS; Hnr Roll; MVP; Pres Ac Ftns Aw; Sci Fairs; Yth Ldrshp Prog; Chrch Yth Grp; DARE; FCA; Mod UN; Quiz Bowl; Ch Chr; Bskball (V); Sftball (V); Vllyball (J); Academic-Athletic Award; Biology Major; Doctorate Degree; U of North Carolina; Louisiana State U

BUIS, MANDY; MATTHEWS, NC; SUN VALLEY MS; (MS); Comm Volntr; Chr; Veterinarian

BULLARD, MICHAEL; STEDMAN, NC; CAPE FEAR HS; (SR); MVP; WWAHSS; FBLA; Ntl FFA; Bsball (V CL); Ftball (V CL); Wt Lftg (V); FFA; Business / Sports Management; Mount Olive College; Methodist College

BULLINGTON, PAMELA; LAWNDALE, NC; BURNS HS; (JR); Hi Hnr Roll; Yth Ldrshp Prog; Comm Volntr; Foreign Clb; Bnd; Clr Grd; Mch Bnd; Orch; Youth in Government Press Team; Graphic Design; Psychology; Appalachian State U; Gardner Webb U

BULLOCK, EBONY M; MACON, NC; WARREN CTY HS; (FR); 4H Awd; Ctznshp Aw; Fut Prb Slvr; Hnr Roll; Nat Hon Sy; Nat Ldrshp Svc; Otst Ac Ach Awd; Perf Att; Sci Fairs; St of Mnth; CARE; Comm Volntr; Peer Tut/Med; 4-H; ArtClub; DARE; Drma Clb; FBLA; Mus Clb; ROTC; SADD; Agricultural Technology U; North Carolina

BULLOCK, JESSICA; COATS, NC; HILLTOP CHRISTIAN SCH; (SO); Ctznshp Aw; Hi Hnr Roll; Hnr Roll; Otst Ac Ach Awd; Perf Att; Sci Fairs; St of Mnth; WWAHSS; Comm Volntr; Hosp Aide; Chrch Yth Grp; DARE; Drma Clb; Emplmnt; Prom Com; Scouts; Chr; Ch Chr; Bskball (V); Chrldg (V); Vllyball (V); Most Encouraging Person; Most Organized, Most Friendly; Veterinary; Radiology; North Carolina State U; Campbell College

BULLOCK, PHYLICIA; HENDERSON, NC; NORTHERN VANCE HS; (SO); Hnr Roll; Nat Hon Sy; Perf Att; WWAHSS; Comm Volntr; 4-H; Chrch Yth Grp; Tmpl Yth Grp; Ch Chr; Early Childhood; Cartoon Artist; Elon U; U of North Carolina-Greensboro

BULLOCK, SADE; HENDERSON, NC; SOUTHERN VANCE HS; (JR); Hnr Roll; Nat Hon Sy; St of Mnth; WWAHSS; Chess; Lit Mag (E); National Society for High School Scholars; Nursing; Western Carolina U; U of North Carolina Greensboro

BUMGARNER, BRYAN A; CONOVER, NC; BUNKER HILL HS; (JR); Hnr Roll; Perf Att; St of Mnth; Ftball (V); Medicine; Attorney; Duke U; Appalachian State U

BUMGARNER, KRISTEN; NORTH WILKESBORO, NC; WEST WILKES HS; (JR); Hnr Roll; Jr Mshl; Peer Tut/Med; Chrch Yth Grp; FCA; Key Club; Ntl Beta Clb; Prom Com; Dnce; Sccr (V); Cl Off (P); Dance Team-Varsity-Captain-Letter; Elementary Education; Elon U; U of North Carolina-Chapel Hill

BUMPAS, ALISHIA; GREENSBORO, NC; DUDLEY HS; (SO); Hnr Roll; Perf Att; DARE; ROTC; Bnd; Ch Chr; Drm Mjr; Bskball (VJ); Sftball (V); Six Year of Cheerleading Until Middle School; Math Expert; Artist & Basketball Player; Wake Forest; Duke U, GTCC, UNCG

BUNCE, SAVANNAH D; WEST END, NC; PINECREST HS; (SR); Hnr Roll; Comm Volntr; Red Cr Aide; Tchrs Aide; Sccr (V L); Track (J L); Sports Medicine; Physical Therapy; U of Texas At San Antonio; San Antonio Community College

BUNCH, MONTREA; WINDSOR, NC; BERTIE HS; (SO); Hi Hnr Roll; DARE; Financial Management & Business; Law; North Carolina State U; UNC Chapel Hill

BUNCH III, JOSEPH W; GREENVILLE, NC; NORTH PITT HS; (SR); 4H Awd; Hnr Roll; Perf Att; Sci Fairs; Peer Tut/Med; Spec Olymp Vol; 4-H; DARE; Ntl Beta Clb; Scouts; Bnd; Jzz Bnd; SP/M/VS; Bsball (L); Stu Cncl (T); Clean Up City Award; PhD in Business; Master's in Web Page Design; ECU East Carolina U

BUNTING, JO ANN; ASHEBORO, NC; ASHEBORO HS; (FR); Hnr Roll; Key Club; ROTC; Physical Therapy; Duke U; Wake Forest

BURCH, SHONDALE; MONROE, NC; PORTER RIDGE HS; (MS); Ctznshp Aw; Hnr Roll; MVP; Nat Sci Aw; Nat Stu Ath Day Aw; Otst Ac Ach Awd; Perf Att; Pres Ac Ftns Aw; Sci Fairs; St of Mnth; Comm Volntr; Hab For Humty Volntr; Peer Tut/Med; ArtClub; Cmptr Clb; Drma Clb; Fr of Library; Lib Aide; Mus Clb; Pep Squd; Tech Clb; Bnd; Chr; Dnce; SP/M/VS; Bskball (V); Chrldg (V); Cr Ctry (J); GAA (V); Mar Art; Scr Kpr; Track (J); Wt Lftg (J); Adv Cncl (R); Sch Ppr (E); Organized Own Dance Group / South Piedmont Community College; Private Investigator; Lawyer; Harvard U; U of North Carolina

BURGESS, CHAD C; IVANHOE, NC; UNION HS; (JR); Hnr Roll; Nat Hon Sy; Perf Att; Sci Fairs; WWAHSS; DARE; Ntl Beta Clb; Ntl FFA; Scouts; Vsity Clb; Track (V); Vsy Clb (V); NCHSAA Scholar Athlete; NSHSS Member

BURGESS, JUSTIN; HENDERSON, NC; SOUTHERN VANCE HS; (JR); Duke TS; Hi Hnr Roll; Nat Hon Sy; Perf Att; Chrch Yth Grp; FCA; HO'Br Yth Ldrshp; Key Club; Ntl Beta Clb; Bsball (V L); Bskball (V L); Sccr (V L); Yrbk (E, R, P); Treasurer of Key Club; Treasurer of Leo Club; Business; Education; U of North Carolina At Chapel Hill; U of North Carolina At Wilmington

BURGESS, TRAVIS K; OAKBORO, NC; WEST STANLY HS; (SO); Ctznshp Aw; Hnr Roll; Comm Volntr; Peer Tut/Med; Chrch Yth Grp; Ch Chr; Stu Cncl (T); Business Law; Medical Examiner; North Carolina State U; U of Ohio

BURKETT, KELSEY; CLEMMONS, NC; WEST FORSYTH HS; (FR); Hnr Roll; Perf Att; Mus Clb; Chr; Sftball (J); Yrbk (E, R, P); Medical; Dental; U of North Carolina Chapel Hill

BURKLEW, CAITLIN; WILLIAMSTON, NC; WILLIAMSTON HS; (JR); Duke TS; Jr Mshl; Nat Hon Sy; WWAHSS; Red Cr Aide; Chrch Yth Grp; Key Club; Ntl Beta Clb; Prom Com; Quiz Bowl; Spanish Clb; Bnd; Jzz Bnd; Mch Bnd; Adv Cncl (T); Elementary Education

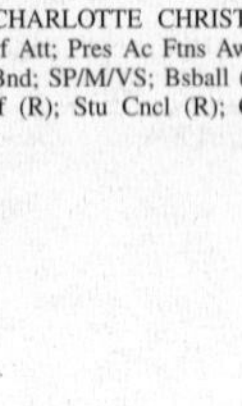

Bullington, Pamela
Burns HS
Lawndale, NC

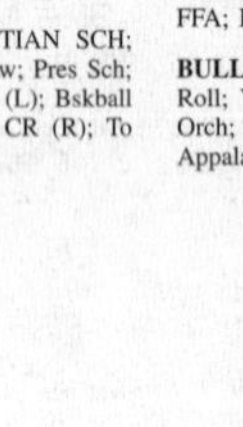

Bruton, Sade
East Forsyth HS
Kernersville, NC

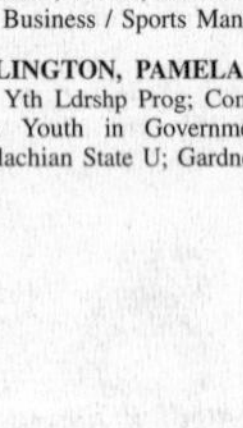

Brown Hinton, Christina C J
Rockingham Cty HS
Pelham, NC

National
Honor Roll
Spring 2005

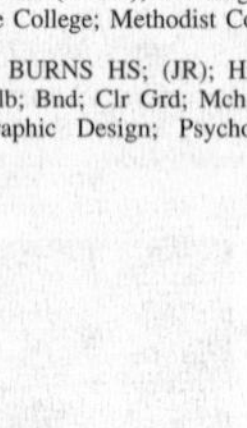

Brown, Michael P
Lake Norman HS
Mooresville, NC

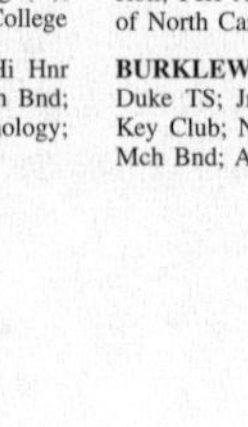

Bryant, Chyna
E E Smith SR HS
Fayetteville, NC

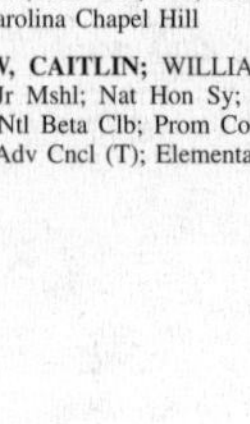

Burch, Shondale
Porter Ridge HS
Monroe, NC

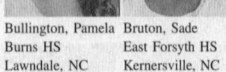

BURLESON, BRITTANY N; BANNER ELK, NC; AVERY CTY HS; (FR); Duke TS; Hi Hnr Roll; Pres Sch; Comm Volntr; Hab For Humty Volntr; FCA; Chr; Bskball (J); Vllyball (J); Sportsmanship Award For 8th Grade Basketball; BA / BS In Early Childhood or Elementary Education; Lees-Mc Rae College; Appalachian State U

BURLESON, TRAVIS W; VALDESE, NC; EAST BURKE HS; (SR); Ctznshp Aw; Hnr Roll; MVP; Nat Sci Aw; Otst Ac Ach Awd; Perf Att; Pres Ac Ftns Aw; St of Mnth; Comm Volntr; Peer Tut/Med; Spec Olymp Vol; DARE; Emplmnt; Mth Clb/Tm; Off Aide; P to P St Amb Prg; SADD; Tchrs Aide; Bnd; Chr; SP/M/VS; Ftball (VJ); Skiing (V); Track (J); Cl Off (R); Stu Cncl (R); CR (R); Social Studies; Automotive; Auto Body Repair; NASCAR Tech Institute; Catawba Valley Community College

BURLEY, LA'QUANDRA; GRIMESLAND, NC; D H CONLEY HS; (FR); Hnr Roll; WWAHSS; Comm Volntr; Chrch Yth Grp; Pediatrician; Respiratory Nurse; UNC Chapel Hill; Duke U

BURNETTE, CHRISTOPHER; ROANOKE RAPIDS, NC; NORTHWEST HS; (FR); Hi Hnr Roll; Hnr Roll; Otst Ac Ach Awd; Perf Att; St of Mnth; USAA; Red Cr Aide; FBLA; Ntl Beta Clb; Quiz Bowl; Ch Chr; Computer Technology; UNC-Chapel Hill; NC State U

BURNETTE, JOSHUA; WENDELL, NC; EAST WAKE HS; (SO); DECA; Ftball (V); Track (V); North Carolina U; North Carolina State U

BURNWORTH, COURTNEY; SANFORD, NC; WESTERN HARNETT HS; (FR); Hnr Roll; Drma Clb; Track (J); Dermatology; East Carolina U

BURR, TIFFANY; WINGATE, NC; FOREST HILLS HS; (FR); Hnr Roll; Nat Hon Sy

BURRELL, NATHAN L; CHARLOTTE, NC; NORTHSIDE CHRISTIAN AC; (JR); Ctznshp Aw; Hnr Roll; MVP; Nat Hon Sy; Perf Att; Pres Ac Ftns Aw; St of Mnth; WWAHSS; Yth Ldrshp Prog; Comm Volntr; Peer Tut/Med; Chess; Chrch Yth Grp; Cmptr Clb; Dbte Team; Drma Clb; Emplmnt; Mth Clb/Tm; NYLC; SP/M/VS; Stg Cre; Bsball (J); Bskball (VJ L); Golf (J); Mar Art (J); Sccr (J); Wt Lftg (J); Sch Ppr (R); Master's Degree in Architecture; U of North Carolina At Charlotte

BURRESS, HANNAH E; PINETOPS, NC; SOUTHWEST EDGECOMBE HS; (SO); Hnr Roll; Comm Volntr; Hosp Aide; Chrch Yth Grp; FCA; FCCLA; Chr; Ch Chr; Sccr (V); Music Therapy; U of North Carolina At Wilmington; East Carolina U

BURRIS, TASHA D; GASTONIA, NC; HUNTER HUSS HS; (FR); Hnr Roll; Otst Ac Ach Awd; Perf Att; Comm Volntr; Chrch Yth Grp; DARE; Scouts; Ch Chr; Dnce; Stu Cncl (S); School Counseling; Psychologist; Winston Salem State; Shaw U

BURROUGHS, ANTHONY; TARBORO, NC; TARBORO HS; (JR); Hnr Roll; Emplmnt; Ntl Beta Clb; Sccr (V); Physics; Computer Engineering; East Carolina U; North Carolina U

BURROUGHS, NICHOLAS V; CARY, NC; MIDDLE CREEK HS; (SO); Hi Hnr Roll; Nat Hon Sy; Chrch Yth Grp; Key Club; Key Club; Business; U of North Carolina Chapel Hill

BURROW, CASEY; SOPHIA, NC; (SR); Hi Hnr Roll; Hnr Roll; Otst Ac Ach Awd; WWAHSS; Emplmnt; Ntl Beta Clb; Off Aide; Bsball (V L); Ftball (V L); Engineering; NC State U

BURRUS, DINAH M; FAYETTEVILLE, NC; 71ST HS; (SR)

BURT, BRANDEN M; GREENVILLE, NC; D H CONLEY HS; (FR); All Am Sch; Duke TS; Hnr Roll; MVP; Perf Att; Comm Volntr; Chrch Yth Grp; FCA; FBLA; Ntl Beta Clb; Pep Squd; Bnd; Ftball (V); Business MBA or Doctorate; U of North Carolina; Duke U

BURTON, MELISSA; SOUTHPORT, NC; SOUTH BRUNSWICK HS; (JR); DAR; Hnr Roll; Sci Fairs; St of Mnth; Hab For Humty Volntr; Spec Olymp Vol; Key Club; Pep Squd; Prom Com; Ch Chr; Sccr (V); Yrbk (E, R, P); Governor's Page Program; Key Club Secretary; Multimedia Arts; Design; U of North Carolina At Greensboro; North Carolina State U

BURWELL, KATELYN; CARTHAGE, NC; PINECREST HS; (JR); Hnr Roll; Nat Hon Sy; WWAHSS; Key Club; Bskball (V L); Cr Ctry (L); PP Ftbl (V); Sccr (V L); Soccer-All-Conference; Soccer-All-Region; Psychology; Furman U; College of Charleston

BUSKE, BRADLEY J; ANGIER, NC; HARNETT CTRL HS; (FR); Duke TS; Hnr Roll; MVP; Comm Volntr; Ntl Beta Clb; Bsball (J); Bskball (J); Sccr (J); Most Valuable Player on JV Soccer; Best Defensive Player/JV Basketball; Architecture; Engineering; UNC U of NC; Duke U

BUTLER, ABBY E; CHARLOTTE, NC; WEST MECKLENBURG HS; (JR); Duke TS; Hi Hnr Roll; Hnr Roll; WWAHSS; ArtClub; Chrch Yth Grp; Emplmnt; Key Club; Ntl Beta Clb; Quiz Bowl; International Clb; Chrldg (J); Interior Design

BUTLER, CEDRICK J; HAW RIVER, NC; HUGH M CUMMINGS HS; (SO); Ctznshp Aw; Hi Hnr Roll; Hnr Roll; MVP; Otst Ac Ach Awd; Perf Att; Pres Sch; Yth Ldrshp Prog; FCA; Ntl Beta Clb; Bnd; Ch Chr; Jzz Bnd; Bsball (J L); Ftball (VJ); Track (V); Wt Lftg; Engineering; Biomedcial Engineering; NC State U

BUXTON, JASMINE C; THOMASVILLE, NC; THOMASVILLE HS; (SO); Hnr Roll; St of Mnth; Comm Volntr; Red Cr Aide; Chrch Yth Grp; Bnd; Ch Chr; Drm Mjr; Mch Bnd; Chrldg (V); Stu Cncl (R); Engineer; Business; North Carolina State U; A & T

BYNUM, MEAGAN L; APEX, NC; APEX HS; (SR); Hnr Roll; MVP; Pres Ac Ftns Aw; ArtClub; DECA; Emplmnt; Spanish Clb; Sccr (V); All-Conference - 2004, 2005; Journalism

BYRD, BRITTANY L; FRANKLINTON, NC; SOUTH GRANVILLE HS; (JR); Hnr Roll; Nat Mrt LOC; Otst Ac Ach Awd; Chrch Yth Grp; Drma Clb; Emplmnt; FBLA; Mth Clb/Tm; Mod UN; Ntl Beta Clb; Ntl FFA; SP/M/VS; Scr Kpr (V); Sftball (J); President of National FFA; Pre-Law; Charleston Southern U; U of North Carolina Wilmington

BYRD, CANDICE N; ELKIN, NC; EAST WILKES MS; (MS); Duke TS; Hi Hnr Roll; Perf Att; Sci/Math Olympn; DARE; Mth Clb/Tm; SADD; Chr; Nursing; Cosmetology; Appalachian State U; U of North Carolina

BYRD, ERIN C; THOMASVILLE, NC; THOMASVILLE HS; (SO); Hi Hnr Roll; Hnr Roll; MVP; Nat Hon Sy; Perf Att; WWAHSS; Comm Volntr; Hosp Aide; Peer Tut/Med; DARE; Mus Clb; Off Aide; Pep Squd; Tchrs Aide; Spanish Clb; Chr; Ch Chr; Dnce; Chrldg (V); Cr Ctry (V); Cl Off (P); Stu Cncl (P); Sophomore Homecoming Princess; Ob/Gyn; Physician Assistant; U of North Carolina of Chapel Hill; Florida A & M

BYRD, ZEB; BENSON, NC; JOHNSTON CHRISTIAN AC; (FR); Hi Hnr Roll; Jr Mshl; Otst Ac Ach Awd; Valdctrian; Comm Volntr; Peer Tut/Med; Chrch Yth Grp; Emplmnt; Ntl Beta Clb; Award for Highest Academic Average in Science Award for Highest Academic Average in Health/PE; Award for Highest Academic Average in History; Pharmaceutical; Child Advocate Lawyer; Campbell U Buies Creek, North Carolina; U of North Carolina in Chapel Hill, North Carolina

CABLE, R D; MURPHY, NC; MURPHY HS; (JR); Hnr Roll; Perf Att; Pres Ac Ftns Aw; Emplmnt; FCA; Ntl Beta Clb; Vsity Clb; Ftball (V L); Wrstlg (V CL)

CABOON, MEAGAN N; SMITHFIELD, NC; SMITHFIELD-SELMA SR HS; Ctznshp Aw; F Lan Hn Soc; Hnr Roll; Nat Hon Sy; Perf Att; Sci Fairs; Sci/Math Olympn; St of Mnth; WWAHSS; Yth Ldrshp Prog; Comm Volntr; Peer Tut/Med; Red Cr Aide; Chrch Yth Grp; Cmptr Clb; Fr of Library; Mth Clb/Tm; Mus Clb; Prom Com; Sci Clb; Scouts; Bnd; Ch Chr; Dnce; Jzz Bnd; Arch (J); Bskball (J); Chrldg (J); Gmnstcs (J); Hsbk Rdg (J); Scr Kpr (J); Sccr (J); Sftball (J); CR (R); Cotillion; Beauty Pageant; Teacher's Degree; Nursing Degree; U of North Carolina; Johnston Community College

CACACE, VINCENT T; CONCORD, NC; NORTHWEST CABARRUS MS; (MS); Ctznshp Aw; Hi Hnr Roll; MVP; Nat Hon Sy; Pres Ac Ftns Aw; St of Mnth; Comm Volntr; Dbte Team; Emplmnt; Quiz Bowl; Bsball (J); Ftball (J L); Hsbk Rdg (J); Ice Hky (J); National Spelling Bee- Second Place; MBA / Entrepreneur; U of Florida Miami; Boston U

CAIN, ANTHONY S; DUNN, NC; HOBBTON HS; (FR); Duke TS; Hi Hnr Roll; WWAHSS; Chrch Yth Grp; Key Club; Quiz Bowl; Sci Clb; Scouts; Bnd; Mch Bnd; Stg Cre; Cl Off (P); Sch Ppr (R); Eagle Scout Award (BSA); Forensic Serology

CALDWELL, ASHLEY; KINGS MTN, NC; BESSEMAR CITY HS; (FR); Chrch Yth Grp; Emplmnt; FCCLA; Mus Clb; SADD; Chr; Ch Chr; SP/M/VS; CR (T); Yrbk (P); Fundraisers / Nursery Worker in Church; Youth Rallies with Church; Digital Communications; Interior Design; U of North Carolina Wilmington; Western Carolina U

CALDWELL, CHRIS; CARY, NC; CARY SR HS; (JR); Hi Hnr Roll; Hnr Roll; Otst Ac Ach Awd; Perf Att; WWAHSS; Peer Tut/Med; ROTC; Scouts; Stg Cre; Aerodynamic Engineering; Nuclear Engineering; North Carolina State U; U of North Carolina Chapel Hill

CALDWELL, HARRISON C; CHARLOTTE, NC; INDEPENDENCE HS; (JR); Nat Ldrshp Svc; ROTC; Tech Clb; Ch Chr; Bio Technology; Computer Games; U of North Carolina-Chapel Hill; North Carolina State U

CALDWELL, JARVIS T; MORGANTON, NC; FREEDOM HS; (SR); Hnr Roll; MVP; Nat Hon Sy; Otst Ac Ach Awd; Perf Att; Comm Volntr; Peer Tut/Med; Spec Olymp Vol; Chrch Yth Grp; Emplmnt; Acpl Chr; Chr; Ch Chr; Bskball (C); Ftball (C); Stu Cncl (P); NW4A Two Time All-Conference Player; Superior Rating with Chamber Singers; Pharmacy; PhD; U of North Carolina, Chapel Hill; East Carolina U

CALDWELL, REVA; CHARLOTTE, NC; INDEPENDENCE HS; (JR); Hnr Roll; FCCLA; Track (V); Yrbk (P); Culinary Arts; Johnson and Wales U

CALHOUN, DARRIEL; SPRING LAKE, NC; PINE FOREST HS; (SR); ROTC; Bnd; Mch Bnd; Ftball (V C); Track (V); Senior Steering Committee; HOSA; Sports Medicine; Physical Therapy; UNC-@ Charlotte; Greensboro College

CALLEJA, VICTOR; KANNAPOLIS, NC; AL BROWN HS; (SO); Ctznshp Aw; Hnr Roll; DARE; Wdwrkg Clb; Music (Drums); Architecture; Rowan Cabarrus Community College; U of North Carolina

CALLOWAY, LINDSAY; INDIAN TRAIL, NC; METROLINA CHRISTIAN AC; (JR); Hi Hnr Roll; Jr Mshl; Otst Ac Ach Awd; Pres Sch; St of Mnth; WWAHSS; Yth Ldrshp Prog; Comm Volntr; Chrch Yth Grp; Emplmnt; Ntl Beta Clb; Prom Com; Tchrs Aide; Bskball (V); Yrbk (E); Leader in CYC (Carolina Youth Commission); Nursing (BSN); Nursing Administration (Master's Degree); Western Carolina U; U of North Carolina At Charlotte

CAMPBELL, CRISTAL T; GREENSBORO, NC; WALTER HINES PAGE HS; (SR); Ctznshp Aw; Hnr Roll; MVP; Otst Ac Ach Awd; Sci Fairs; St of Mnth; Comm Volntr; Peer Tut/Med; Red Cr Aide; ArtClub; Emplmnt; Pep Squd; Photog; Prom Com; Quill & Scroll; Tchrs Aide; Vsity Clb; Chrldg (V C); Vsy Clb (V); Cl Off (R); Stu Cncl (R); CR (R); Yrbk (E, P); Bi-Lingual (Spanish/English); Journalism; English; U of North Carolina At Pembroke; U of North Carolina At Chapel Hill

CAMPBELL, KADIJAH; ENFIELD, NC; SOUTHEAST HALIFAX HS; (SO); Hnr Roll; Perf Att; Peer Tut/Med; Spec Olymp Vol; Ntl FFA; Prom Com; Sci Clb; SADD; Jzz Bnd; Mch Bnd; Pep Bnd; Chrldg (V); Nursing; U of North Carolina; North Carolina Central U

CAMPBELL, KASEY L; COLUMBUS, NC; POLK CTY HS; (SR); Hnr Roll; St Schl; WWAHSS; Comm Volntr; Hosp Aide; Red Cr Aide; 4-H; Chrch Yth Grp; Key Club; P to P St Amb Prg; Prom Com; Sccr (J); Prom Committee; Radiologic Technology; Mary Washington Hospital School of Radiologic

CAMPBELL, SHAKIRA; CHINA GROVE, NC; SOUTH ROWAN HS; (FR); Hnr Roll; Ntl Beta Clb

CAMPBELL, SHAYLA; GREENVILLE, NC; D H CONLEY HS; (JR); Otst Ac Ach Awd; Perf Att; Comm Volntr; Chrch Yth Grp; Emplmnt; Ch Chr; Dnce; Track; East Carolina U; Winston Salem State

CAMPBELL III, JAMES E; CONCORD, NC; JAY M ROBINSON HS; (SO); Hi Hnr Roll; Hnr Roll; Mas Aw; Perf Att; Pres Ac Ftns Aw; Peer Tut/Med; Spec Olymp Vol; Emplmnt; P to P St Amb Prg; Bskball (J); Ftball (V L); World View Academy Student Ambassador Program; Business & Marketing; Broadcasting; Michigan U; U of North Carolina At Chapel Hill

CAMPBELL JR, NELSON J; MAXTON, NC; PURNELL SWETT HS; (SO); Hnr Roll; Nat Hon Sy; Comm Volntr; Peer Tut/Med; 4-H; Ntl Beta Clb; Bskball (J); Ftball (J); International Business; Business Administration; North Carolina A & T State U; North Carolina Central U

CAMPBELL JR, RICHARD; EDEN, NC; JOHN M MOREHEAD HS; (SO); Hnr Roll; Spec Olymp Vol; Chrch Yth Grp; DARE; ROTC; Clr Grd; Drl Tm; Flg Crps; Wt Lftg (J); Navy

CAMPEN, MORGAN L; ROUGEMONT, NC; NORTHERN DURHAM HS; (SO); Hnr Roll; MVP; WWAHSS; Comm Volntr; Spec Olymp Vol; Key Club; Sftball (V L); National Junior Honors Society; Forensic Sciences

CANADY, WILLIAM J; NEWPORT, NC; CROATAN HS; (FR); Ctznshp Aw; Comm Volntr; Chrch Yth Grp; DARE; Emplmnt; Ntl FFA; Wdwrkg Clb; Respiratory Therapy; Law Enforcement; Carteret Community College

CANIPE, BRITTANY N; LUMBERTON, NC; PURNELL SWETT HS; (SO); Hnr Roll; St of Mnth; Chrch Yth Grp; Mus Clb; ROTC; Acpl Chr; Chr; Ch Chr; 9th Grade Sports; JROTC Awards; Computer Technician; Master's Degree; Air Force Academy

CANNADY-HARRIS, TACARA B; RALEIGH, NC; KNIGHTDALE HS; (SO); Hnr Roll; WWAHSS; Hosp Aide; Drma Clb; FCA; SP/M/VS; Stg Cre; Chrldg (JC); Sftball (V); Athletic Trainer Student; Pre-Medicine; Duke U; UNC U

CANNON, CHELSEA; WINTERVILLE, NC; SOUTH CTRL HS; (SO); Duke TS; F Lan Hn Soc; Hi Hnr Roll; Nat Hon Sy; Perf Att; WWAHSS; Comm Volntr; Hosp Aide; Chrch Yth Grp; Ntl Beta Clb; Japanese Clb; Sccr (V CL); Physical Therapy; Radiologist; East Carolina U; U of North Carolina At Chapel Hill

CANNON, CLAIRE; GOLDSBORO, NC; SPRING CREEK HS; (MS); Hnr Roll; Chrch Yth Grp; SADD; Veterinary; North Carolina State

CANNON, LATARA; CHARLOTTE, NC; MYERS PARK HS; (JR); Hnr Roll; Perf Att; ROTC; Clr Grd; Drl Tm; Obstetrics & Gynecology; Lenoir-Rhyne College

CAO, KENNY; CHARLOTTE, NC; HARDING U HS; (SO); Marine Biology; Pediatrics; Duke U; U of North Carolina At Chapel Hill

CAPLE, CHARDAY; CHARLOTTE, NC; HARDING UNIVERSITY HS; (SO); Hi Hnr Roll; Hnr Roll; Chrch Yth Grp; Chrldg (VJC); Track (V L); Excellence in Youth Award; Excellence Award; Business Administration; Psychology; UNC-Greensboro; UNC-Chapel Hill

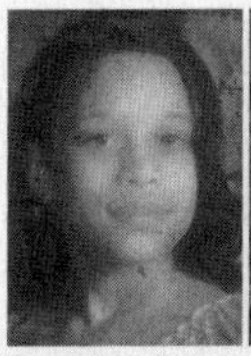
Cannady-Harris, Tacara B
Knightdale HS
Raleigh, NC

Campbell, Cristal T
Walter Hines Page HS
Greensboro, NC

Buske, Bradley J
Harnett Ctrl HS
Angier, NC

Burress, Hannah E
Southwest Edgecombe HS
Pinetops, NC

Burleson, Travis W
East Burke HS
Valdese, NC

Burnette, Christopher
Northwest HS
Roanoke Rapids, NC

Byrd, Zeb
Johnston Christian AC
Benson, NC

Campbell, Shakira
South Rowan HS
China Grove, NC

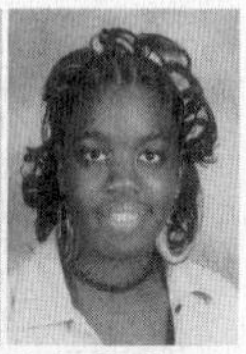
Caple, Charday
Harding University HS
Charlotte, NC

CAPRA, MARIA; WILMINGTON, NC; EUGENE ASHLEY HS; (JR); Hnr Roll; Comm Volntr; Chrch Yth Grp; Dbte Team; Drma Clb; FBLA; Photog; Chr; Ch Chr; SP/M/VS; Culinary Arts; Theatre; Cape Fear Community College; U of the Performing Arts

CARBAJAL, MARIA L; BAILEY, NC; SOUTHERN NASH HS; (FR); Hnr Roll; Otst Ac Ach Awd; St of Mnth; Comm Volntr; DARE; Ntl FFA; Dnce; Dvng (V); GAA (V); Gmnstcs (J); Ice Sktg (J); Sccr (V); Swmg (J); Vllyball (V); Wt Lftg (J); Veterinarian; Doctor

CARBOCCI, KATE; KITTY HAWK, NC; FIRST FLIGHT HS; (JR); Duke TS; Hnr Roll; St of Mnth; Comm Volntr; Key Club; Tech Clb; Psychology; Art; U of North Carolina At Chapel Hill; North Carolina State U

CARDONA, DIEGO F; STATESVILLE, NC; STATESVILLE SR; (SR); SADD; Cr Ctry; JETS Club (Junior Engineering Tech Society); SADD; Computer Engineering; U North Carolina Charlotte; U North Carolina Greensboro

CARLETON, OPAL; CARY, NC; CARY SR HS; (FR); Duke TS; Hnr Roll; Comm Volntr; Chrch Yth Grp; Emplmnt; ROTC; Clr Grd; Drl Tm; SP/M/VS; Vllyball (J); Leader in Children's Program at Church

CARLTON, JOHN C; ROCKY POINT, NC; HEIDE TRASK HS; (SR); Hnr Roll; Jr Mshl; Pres Ac Ftns Aw; Sci/Math Olympn; St of Mnth; WWAHSS; Comm Volntr; Spec Olymp Vol; ArtClub; Chess; Chrch Yth Grp; Mth Clb/Tm; Ntl Beta Clb; Scouts; Sccr (V CL); Adv Cncl (R); Honor Graduate; Junior Marshall; Chemical & Textile Engineering; NC State U

CARLYLE, JESSICA A; WILSON, NC; CMTY CHRISTIAN SCH; (SO); Hnr Roll; Perf Att; Sci Fairs; St of Mnth; WWAHSS; Red Cr Aide; Chrch Yth Grp; Emplmnt; FCA; Tchrs Aide; Dnce; Sccr (V); Vllyball (J); Most Outstanding Camper 2003; Flashing Twirrlettes - Baton; Radiology; Physical Therapy; UNCW; UNC

CARMON, RENARDO; AYDEN, NC; AYDEN GRIFTON HS; (SO); Hnr Roll; Perf Att; Comm Volntr; DARE; 8th Grade Math Achievement Award; Engineering; Accounting; U North Carolina Charlotte; Duke U

CARMONA, ANAHI; KANNAPOLIS, NC; A L BROWN HS; (SO); Hnr Roll; Bnd; Clr Grd; Mch Bnd; International Club; Psychology; Sociology; U of North Carolina Charlotte

CARPENTER, ASHLEY B; FAYETTEVILLE, NC; MASSEY HILL CLASSICAL HS; (JR); Hi Hnr Roll; Nat Hon Sy; Otst Ac Ach Awd; Perf Att; Sci/Math Olympn; WWAHSS; Comm Volntr; Lib Aide; Prom Com; Sftball (V CL); Yrbk (P); Regional Science Olympiad Gold & Bronze; Biological Scientist; Geneticist; North Carolina State U; U of North Carolina Greensboro

CARPENTER, CRYSTAL; WINSTON SALEM, NC; MOUNT TABOR HS; (SO); Hnr Roll; WWAHSS; Peer Tut/Med; Spec Olymp Vol; Chrch Yth Grp; Drma Clb; P to P St Amb Prg; Dnce; SP/M/VS; Stg Cre; Sch Ppr (R); In a Filmmaker Club; Wrote a One-Act Play in Drama Class; Cinematography; Journalism; U of North Carolina At Wilmington; U of Southern California

CARPENTER, NICHOLAS R; NEW BERN, NC; HAVELOCK HS; (SR); Hi Hnr Roll; Hnr Roll; Nat Hon Sy; Emplmnt; Pep Squd; Bnd; Jzz Bnd; Mch Bnd; Orch; Swmg (V L); Allied Health II; Veterinarian; Zoologist; North Carolina State U; U of North Carolina Chapel Hill

CARR, CHRISTOPHER; GREENVILLE, NC; D H CONLEY HS; (FR); Hnr Roll; Otst Ac Ach Awd; Perf Att; Sci/Math Olympn; Yth Ldrshp Prog; Comm Volntr; Hosp Aide; Chess; FBLA; Mth Clb/Tm; Ntl Beta Clb; Sci Clb; SP/M/VS; CR (R); Teen Court Mediator; Physician; Computer Sciences; Duke U; NC State U

CARR, DERRICK; LA GRANGE, NC; EASTERN WAYNE HS; (FR); Perf Att; Chrch Yth Grp; Psychiatrist; Child Care

CARR, KAITLIN M; CLINTON, NC; CLINTON HS; (JR); Duke TS; Jr Mshl; St of Mnth; Comm Volntr; Peer Tut/Med; Spec Olymp Vol; Chrch Yth Grp; Emplmnt; Jr Cls League; Key Club; Ntl Beta Clb; Prom Com; Scouts; Tech Clb; Bnd; Ch Chr; Mch Bnd; Sccr; Tennis; President - Pines of Carolina Planning Board; National Girl Scouts USA Delegate; Science / Genetics; U of North Carolina Chapel Hill; Davidson College

CARRINGTON, JUSTIN; RALEIGH, NC; WAKEFIELD HS; (FR); Hi Hnr Roll; WWAHSS; Key Club; Svce Clb; Chr; Cl Off (P); Stu Cncl (P); I was a section editor of my middle school's yearbook.; Student of the Year - 8th Grade; I would possibly like to major in Middle Grades Science Education; U of North Carolina-Chapel Hill; North Carolina State Univesity

CARROLL, CHRISTIN; HICKORY, NC; HICKORY HS; (FR); Ch Chr; Sccr (J); Swmg (V); Vllyball (J); Yrbk (P); Nursing; UNC

CARTER, BRANDON; BURLINGTON, NC; GRAHAM HS; (JR); Hnr Roll; Nat Hon Sy; Otst Ac Ach Awd; Perf Att; Comm Volntr; Chrch Yth Grp; Emplmnt; FCA; Bsball (V); Ftball (V); Wt Lftg (V); Computer Engineering; North Carolina State U; U of North Carolina-Chapel Hill

CARTER, BROCK; KERNERSVILLE, NC; GLENN HS; (FR); Hnr Roll; Scouts; Ftball (J); Track (V); Wrstlg (J); Stu Cncl (R); Boy Scouts; Sports Medicine; Forensic Science; U of North Carolina (Chapel Hill); Pennsylvania State U

CARTER, CHRISTINA M; HOLLISTER, NC; NORTHWEST HALIFAX HS; (JR); Hi Hnr Roll; Hnr Roll; WWAHSS; Yth Ldrshp Prog; Comm Volntr; Red Cr Aide; Emplmnt; FBLA; Ntl Beta Clb; Prom Com; Schol Bwl; SP/M/VS; Cl Off (R); CR (R); Upward Bound Praise and Gear Up; Featured on Local Radio and TV Station; Finance International Business; Accounting; Duke U; North Carolina State U

CARTER, EMILY D; GARNER, NC; SOUTH JOHNSTON HS; (JR); Ctznshp Aw; Duke TS; Jr Mshl; Nat Hon Sy; Perf Att; WWAHSS; Peer Tut/Med; AL Aux Girls; ArtClub; FCA; Pep Squd; Prom Com; Voc Ind Clb Am; Bskball (VJC); Sftball (JC); Cl Off (P); Stu Cncl (R); Art Show; Pediatric Medicine; U of North Carolina At Chapel Hill

CARTER, EVAN J; CHARLOTTE, NC; GARINGER HS; (SO); Hnr Roll; Otst Ac Ach Awd; Pres Ac Ftns Aw; WWAHSS; Pre-Medicine; PhD; Duke U; Howard U

CARTER, JASMINE; HENDERSON, NC; SOUTHERN VANCE HS; (SR); F Lan Hn Soc; Hi Hnr Roll; Hnr Roll; Nat Hon Sy; St of Mnth; WWAHSS; FBLA; Ntl Beta Clb; Spanish Clb; National Vocational Technical Honor Society; Business; NC A & T U

CARTER, LA REESHA L; PLYMOUTH, NC; PLYMOUTH HS; (JR); Hnr Roll; Jr Mshl; Nat Hon Sy; Otst Ac Ach Awd; WWAHSS; Chrch Yth Grp; Cmptr Clb; Emplmnt; FBLA; Jr Ach; Lib Aide; Mth Clb/Tm; Prom Com; Business Management; Psychology; Winston-Salem State U; North Carolina A & T

CARTER, MAURICE A; DURHAM, NC; C E JORDAN HS; (SR); Hnr Roll; Nat Hon Sy; Comm Volntr; Chrch Yth Grp; Ch Chr; Wt Lftg (C); Cl Off (R); CR (R); National Dean's List Award; Automotive Engineering; East Carolina U; North Carolina State U

CARTER, MICHELLE; CHARLOTTE, NC; HARDING U HS; (FR); Ctznshp Aw; Duke TS; Hnr Roll; Valdctrian; Comm Volntr; Chrch Yth Grp; P to P St Amb Prg; Scouts; Ch Chr; Stu Cncl (R); Captain of Battle of the Book; Co-President of National Junior Honor Society; Pre-Medicine; Business; Duke U; U of North Carolina-Chapel Hill

CARTER, SHANEKA; WILMINGTON, NC; E A LANEY HS; (JR); Hnr Roll; Otst Ac Ach Awd; Perf Att; St of Mnth; Yth Ldrshp Prog; Chrch Yth Grp; FBLA; Ch Chr; Vacation Bible School Certificate of Achievement; Outstanding Achievement for Music - Vacation Bible School; Medicine Art / Nurse Technician; Lab Technician / Business / Culinary Arts; Appalachian State U; Columbia U

CARTER, SYDNEY R; WILSON, NC; HUNT HS; (JR); Hsbk Rdg; Sftball (V CL); Vllyball (V CL); Stu Cncl (R); CR (R); President of National Honor Society; Pre-Law; International Studies; U of North Carolina-Chapel Hill; American U

CARTNER, ALLISON V; HARRELLS, NC; HARRELLS CHRISTIAN AC; (SO); Hi Hnr Roll; Sci Fairs; St of Mnth; Comm Volntr; Chrch Yth Grp; FCA; Ntl Beta Clb; Quiz Bowl; Chr; Dnce; SP/M/VS; Bskball (V); Chrldg (V); Sccr (J); Vllyball (V L); Sampson Little Players Talent Show, 3rd Place; Award from American Meteorological Society; Pre-Med; M.D.; U of North Carolina At Wilmington; U of North Carolina At Chapel Hill

CARTWRIGHT, ALECIA; FAYETTEVILLE, NC; JACK BRITT HS; (JR); Hnr Roll; Jr Mshl; Nat Hon Sy; WWAHSS; Comm Volntr; Hosp Aide; Emplmnt; Key Club; Chrldg (VJ L); Yrbk (E, R, P); Pre Medicine; U of North Carolina-Chapel Hill; East Carolina U

CARTWRIGHT, CALEB; ASHEBORO, NC; ASHEBORO HS; (SO); Chess; Chrch Yth Grp; Dbte Team; FCA; Key Club; Ntl Beta Clb; Spanish Clb; Sccr (J); Tennis (V L)

CASILLAS, ISIAH D; WILSON, NC; FIKE HS; (FR); Hi Hnr Roll; Hnr Roll; Perf Att; Ftball; Attorney; Engineer; U of North Carolina; Duke U

CASPER, MICHELLE L; ROCKY MOUNT, NC; ROCKY MOUNT SR HS; (SR); Hi Hnr Roll; Hnr Roll; Kwnis Aw; Nat Hon Sy; St Optmst of Yr; WWAHSS; Comm Volntr; Hab For Humty Volntr; AL Aux Girls; Chrch Yth Grp; Emplmnt; FBLA; Key Club; Vsity Clb; Cr Ctry (V); Sccr (V); Swmg (V); Track (V); 2004 Student Trooper Program; Vice President of Debu-ette Club; Criminology; Sociology; North Carolina State U

CASS, LAKEN; RONDA, NC; EAST WILKES MS; (MS); Hnr Roll; Pres Ac Ftns Aw; Comm Volntr; Red Cr Aide; Chrch Yth Grp; Photog; Chr; Dnce; Chrldg (V C); PP Ftbl; Sccr; Track; Stu Cncl (T)

CASSELL, KRISTIN A; EDEN, NC; MOREHEAD HS; (SO); 4H Awd; Hi Hnr Roll; Hnr Roll; Nat Hon Sy; Perf Att; WWAHSS; Comm Volntr; 4-H; Chrch Yth Grp; DARE; Key Club; Bnd; Ch Chr; NC Horse Judging Team; Butler Girl Power Club; Elementary School Teacher; Social Service Workers; North Carolina State U; U of North Carolina Chapel Hill

CASTILLO, LEIDY; CHARLOTTE, NC; INDEPENDENCE SR HS; (SO); Hi Hnr Roll; Hnr Roll; DECA; Spanish Clb; Fashion Designing; Atlanta A & T; The Art Institute of Charlotte

CASTILLO, LILIANA; CLAYTON, NC; CLAYTON HS; (JR); Hnr Roll; Comm Volntr; Hosp Aide; Spec Olymp Vol; French Clb; SP/M/VS; Secretary of French Club; Award for Best Student in Teen Living; Interior Design; Teacher; Johnston Community College; North Carolina State U

CASTLE, WILL; FLINT, NC; CARMAN-AINSWORTH HS; (SR); Hnr Roll; Perf Att; Chrch Yth Grp; DARE; Wrstlg (J); Drafting; High Performance Mechanic; Lincoln Technical Institute; Mott Community College

CAUDILL, KAYLA; LENOIR, NC; WEST CALDWELL HS; (FR); Ctznshp Aw; Hi Hnr Roll; Hnr Roll; Otst Ac Ach Awd; Sci Fairs; St of Mnth; WWAHSS; Comm Volntr; Hosp Aide; Peer Tut/Med; Chrch Yth Grp; Emplmnt; Ntl Beta Clb; Bnd; Chr; Ch Chr; Dnce; Skiing (V); Cheerleader for Power Cats; Academic Excellence Award; Law; U.S. Senator; Duke U; Ohio State U

CAVE, ELLIOT P; SALISBURY, NC; SALISBURY HS; (FR); Hi Hnr Roll; Hnr Roll; Key Club; Scouts; Golf (V); Sccr (V); Boy Scouts-Life Scout; Pre-Med Courses; Classics Major; U of North Carolina-Chapel Hill; U of Chicago

CAVER, WILLIAM E; PIKEVILLE, NC; CHARLES B AYCOCK HS; (FR); Hnr Roll; Perf Att; St of Mnth; Chrch Yth Grp; Teaches Children's Church; Plays on Church Softball Team; Architecture; Computer Programming; NC State U; Virginia Tech U

CAYTON, KRISTEN; AHOSKIE, NC; RIDGECROFT SCH; (SO); Hi Hnr Roll; Hnr Roll; WWAHSS; Comm Volntr; Chrch Yth Grp; FCA; Key Club; Ntl Beta Clb; Vsity Clb; Bnd; Bskball (V); Sccr (V); Tennis (V); Biology; North Carolina State U; Meredith College

CEARLEY, WESLEY; LINCOLNTON, NC; WEST FORSYTH HS; (JR); Cr Ctry (J); Lcrsse (J); Lived in France from 1996-2004 1 Year in Chad, Africa 1997-1998; Bilingual French/English; Physicians Assistant (PA); Anesthetist Assistant (AA); U of North Carolina At Chapel Hill; North Carolina State U

CECIL, AMY; GREENSBORO, NC; BEN L SMITH HS; (SO); Ctznshp Aw; Hnr Roll; Nat Ldrshp Svc; Perf Att; Sci Fairs; St of Mnth; Comm Volntr; DARE; Jr Ach; Ntl Beta Clb; NYLC; Scouts; Bnd; Mch Bnd; Pep Bnd; Presidential Student Service Award; Veterinary Medicine; Pre-Med; North Carolina State U; North Carolina Chapel Hill

CEPEDA, SUGEYRIS; FREMONT, NC; CHARLES B AYCOCK HS; (SR); Hnr Roll; Comm Volntr; Chrch Yth Grp; Spanish Clb; Chrldg (VJ); Cr Ctry (V); PP Ftbl (V); Sftball (J); Swmg (V); Track (V); President of Spanish Club; FCCLA / HOSA / Octagon Clubs; Professional Model; Study to Design Clothes; Eastern Carolina U; UNC Chapel Hill

CERVERA, JENNIFER E; RALEIGH, NC; MILLBROOK HS; (JR); Hnr Roll; Nat Hon Sy; St of Mnth; Comm Volntr; AL Aux Girls; Chrch Yth Grp; French Clb; Presidency of the ESL Club; National Achievers Society; Medical School / Pediatrics; Medical School / Dentistry; U of North Carolina Chapel Hill; North Carolina State U

CHAMBERS, HUNTER A; ROCKINGHAM, NC; RICHMOND SR HS; (SR); Duke TS; Hnr Roll; WWAHSS; Chrch Yth Grp; DARE; Emplmnt; Ntl Beta Clb; Scouts; Ch Chr; Stg Cre; Engineering; North Carolina State U

CHAMBERS, JANICE; SALISBURY, NC; SALISBURY HS; (JR); Hnr Roll; Nat Hon Sy; Comm Volntr; Hab For Humty Volntr; Chrch Yth Grp; Emplmnt; Key Club; Prom Com; Chrldg (V); Sccr (J); Tennis (J); Vllyball (J); Key Club; Psychology; Neurobiology; Appalachian State U; U of North Carolina At Asheville

CHAMBLEE, ALVIN S; WALNUT COVE, NC; SOUTH STOKES HS; (SR); Hnr Roll; MVP; St of Mnth; Comm Volntr; Chrch Yth Grp; Emplmnt; Bnd; Ch Chr; SP/M/VS; Bskball (VJC); Ftball (VJC); Track (V); Selected Student By the Renaissance Club; Church Choir President; Computer Engineer; Forsyth Technical Community College; North Carolina A & T State U

CHAMBLEE, CAITLYN; DURHAM, NC; NORTHERN HS; (SO); Hnr Roll; Emplmnt; FCA; Key Club; SP/M/VS; Cr Ctry (J); Swmg (J); Track (V L); Scholar Athlete; Business Administration; Marketing; U of North Carolina At Chapel Hill; North Carolina State U

CHAMBLEE JR, TONY C; AHOSKIE, NC; HERTFORD CTY HS; (FR); Hnr Roll; Perf Att; Mch Bnd; Pep Bnd; Business Technology; North Carolina A & T State U; Norfolk State U

CHAMBLISS, EMMANUEL J; CHARLOTTE, NC; INDEPENDENCE HS; (JR); Duke TS; Hnr Roll; Nat Hon Sy; Comm Volntr; Chess; Chrch Yth Grp; Mth Clb/Tm; ROTC; Scouts; Svce Clb; Tech Clb; Bnd; Ch Chr; Drl Tm; Orch; Sftball; Vllyball; Stu Cncl; North Carolina State U; U of North Carolina Chapel Hill

CHAMBLISS, JANELLE; DURHAM, NC; SOUTHERN HS; (SO); Ctznshp Aw; Hnr Roll; Perf Att; St of Mnth; WWAHSS; Chrch Yth Grp; DARE; Bnd; GAA (V); Sftball (V); CR (R); Medical; Howard U; Bennett U

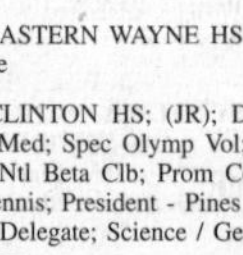
Chamblee, Alvin S
South Stokes HS
Walnut Cove, NC

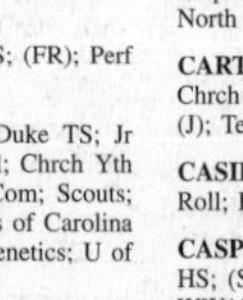
Caver, William E
Charles B Aycock HS
Pikeville, NC

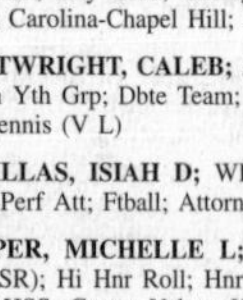
Carter, Maurice A
C E Jordan HS
Durham, NC

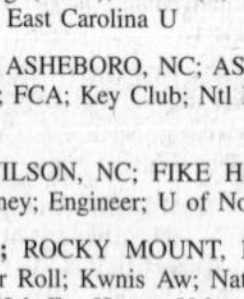
Carpenter, Crystal
Mount Tabor HS
Winston Salem, NC

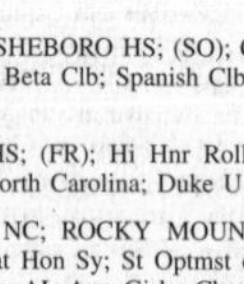
Carr, Christopher
D H Conley HS
Greenville, NC

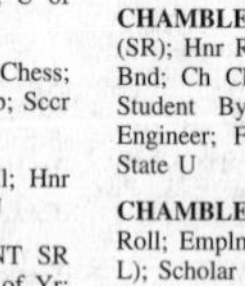
Cervera, Jennifer E
Millbrook HS
Raleigh, NC

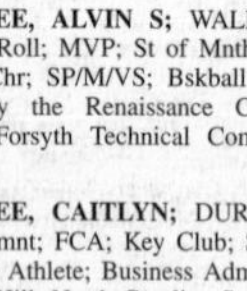
Chamblee Jr, Tony C
Hertford Cty HS
Ahoskie, NC

CHAMI, HILAL J; CHARLOTTE, NC; HARDING U HS; (SO); Hnr Roll; WWAHSS; Dbte Team; Mod UN; Sci Clb; French Clb; Sccr (J); Swmg (V); Fluent in French; Psychology-Master's; Physics; UNC Chapel Hill, NC; UNC Charlotte, NC

CHAN, COREY M; CHARLOTTE, NC; MYZAS PARK HS; (FR); Hnr Roll; Comm Volntr; Bnd; Ftball (J); Tennis (V L)

CHANDLER, JESSICA; FAYETTEVILLE, NC; CAPE FEAR HS; (SR); Hnr Roll; Medical School; East Carolina U

CHANDLER, KELLIE; ALEXANDER, NC; (MS); Duke TS; Hnr Roll; Nat Mrt LOC; Otst Ac Ach Awd; Perf Att; Pres Sch; Lib Aide; Bnd; Ch Chr; Computer Programming; U of North Carolina At Asheville

CHANG, TOU; CONOVER, NC; ST STEPHENS HS; (JR); Hnr Roll; Kwnis Aw; French Clb; Vice President for International Club; Automotive Mechanics; Automotive Technician; Clemson U; Georgia Tech U

CHAPPELL, BRANDON; HURDLE MILLS, NC; PERSON HS; (SO); Ctznshp Aw; Hnr Roll; MVP; Perf Att; Sci Fairs; St of Mnth; Comm Volntr; Chrch Yth Grp; DARE; Chr; Ch Chr; SP/M/VS; Stg Cre; Bsball; Bskball (J); Ftball (V C); Gmnstcs; Skt Tgt Sh; Swmg; Track; Wt Lftg (C); Acting/Drama; Mechanical Engineering

CHAPPELL, RANDY E; CANDOR, NC; EAST MONTGOMERY HS; (SO); Ctznshp Aw; Hnr Roll; Perf Att; St of Mnth; DARE; Ntl Beta Clb; Ntl FFA; Scouts; Cr Ctry (V L); Track (V L); 21st Century Scholars Certificate; Presidential Education Awards Program; Forestry Conservation; Wildlife Management; North Carolina State U; Montgomery Community College

CHARLES II, CHARLES D; TIMBERLAKE, NC; PERSON HS; (SO); Hnr Roll; Chrch Yth Grp; Emplmnt; Scouts; Bnd; Mch Bnd; Stg Cre; Stu Cncl (R); Eagle Scout; Order of the Arrow; Mechanical Engineering; Professional Welder; North Carolina State U; U North Carolina At Charlotte

CHAUVIN, JULIA; HILLSBOROUGH, NC; ORANGE HS; (JR); Hnr Roll; Jr Mshl; Emplmnt; HO'Br Yth Ldrshp; Key Club; Ntl Beta Clb; Photog; Bskball (J); Cr Ctry (J); PP Ftbl; Sftball (V); Tennis (V CL); CR (R); Sch Ppr (E); Athena's Train-All Girls Acting Troup-Tech Director; Fall and Summer Softball; Psychology; Women's Studies; Dickinson U; U of North Carolina At Greensboro

CHAVIS, KANEISHA S; WEST END, NC; PINECREST HS; (SO); Hnr Roll; Nat Hon Sy; Otst Ac Ach Awd; Perf Att; Pres Sch; Comm Volntr; Chrch Yth Grp; Drma Clb; Key Club; Mus Clb; Svce Clb; Chr; Ch Chr; CR (R); Key Club Member; Church Youth Group; Communications; Registered Nurse; U of North Carolina @ Chapel Hill; North Carolina State U

CHAVIS, KERWIN; MAXTON, NC; SOUTH ROBESON HS; (FR); Hnr Roll; St of Mnth; Comm Volntr; Chrch Yth Grp; ROTC; Ftball (V); Skt Tgt Sh; Wt Lftg (V); Stu Cncl (V); Law; Engineering; U North Carolina; U of Miami (FL)

CHAVIS, TRAVIS; MAXTON, NC; SWETT HS; (JR); Hnr Roll; Ntl FFA; Chr; Teaching the Neighborhood Kids Sports; I Intend To Give Blood Next Semester; Marine Biology; Physical Education Teacher for Special Ed. Kids; UNC At Chapel Hill; Coastal Carolina U

CHEEK, KELLY D; DURHAM, NC; SOUTHERN DURHAM HS; (SR); Duke TS; Hnr Roll; Nat Hon Sy; Otst Ac Ach Awd; Perf Att; Pres Ac Ftns Aw; Sci Fairs; Comm Volntr; Red Cr Aide; Chrch Yth Grp; DARE; FBLA; P to P St Amb Prg; Scouts; SADD; Tchrs Aide; Sign Clb; Chr; Chrldg (VJ L); Gmnstcs; Wt Lftg; Ruritan Club Member; Surgical Nursing; Operating Room Nurse; Liberty College in Virginia; Durham Technical Institute

CHELGREN, JOSHUA; MOORESVILLE, NC; MOORESVILLE HS; (SO); SP/M/VS; Member of LYNC - Lutheran Youth of NC; Veterinary Medicine; U of Illinois; North Carolina State U

CHELLIS, EMILY; ARDEN, NC; TC ROBERSON HS; (SO); Ctznshp Aw; Hnr Roll; Otst Ac Ach Awd; Comm Volntr; Peer Tut/Med; Chrch Yth Grp; Jr Cls League; Key Club; Scouts; Svce Clb; Chr; Ch Chr; Clr Grd; Flg Crps; Girl Scout Gold Award; Governor's School Nominee; Christian Music; History; North Greenville College; Northern Arizona College

CHEN, TAO; RICHFIELD, NC; MINERVA DELAND; (FR); F Lan Hn Soc; Hnr Roll; St of Mnth; Yth Ldrshp Prog; Comm Volntr; Hosp Aide; Red Cr Aide; ArtClub; Chess; Dbte Team; Drma Clb; Fr of Library; Mus Clb; Photog; Sci Clb; Jzz Bnd; Bsball; Bskball; Ftball; Skiing; Sccr; Sftball; Swmg; Tennis

CHENG, KATIE T; RALEIGH, NC; THE NC SCH OF SCIENCE & MATH; (JR); Duke TS; Hi Hnr Roll; Hnr Roll; Pres Ac Ftns Aw; WWAHSS; Hab For Humty Volntr; Peer Tut/Med; Dbte Team; NtlFrnscLg; Prom Com; Orch; Cr Ctry (VJ); Dvng (V L); Swmg (V L); Tennis (J); Track (V L); Stu Cncl (R); Established the Raleigh Patrol; Neuroscience; Biology; UNC-Chapel Hill; Harvard U

CHENLO, CRISTINA; RALEIGH, NC; MILLBROOK HS; (JR); Fut Prb Slvr; Nat Hon Sy; Sch Ppr (R); Character Award; International Relations; U of North Carolina Chapel Hill

CHERRY, BRANDON A; CHARLOTTE, NC; GARINGER SR HS; (JR); Ctznshp Aw; Bnd; Ch Chr; Mch Bnd; Track; Member of Usher Board @ New Saint John Baptist; Member of Drills of Hope Community Band; Florida A & M U

CHERRY, MICHAEL; CLEMMONS, NC; (JR); Hnr Roll; St of Mnth; Comm Volntr; Chrch Yth Grp; Emplmnt; Spanish Clb; Bnd; Mch Bnd; Pep Bnd; Swmg (V); Volunteer Ronald MC Donald House 2 Yrs; Crosby Scholars-6 Yrs; Engineering; Child Development Therapy; U of North Carolina-Charlotte; North Carolina State U

CHESSON, MERRITT B; EDENTON, NC; JOHN A HOLMES HS; (JR); All Am Sch; Ctznshp Aw; Duke TS; Hnr Roll; Jr Mshl; Nat Hon Sy; Nat Ldrshp Svc; USAA; Comm Volntr; Peer Tut/Med; AL Aux Girls; ArtClub; Chrch Yth Grp; Emplmnt; Key Club; Mus Clb; Spanish Clb; Chr; Ch Chr; Dnce; PP Ftbl; Sccr (V L); Tennis (V L); Track (V L); Michener Freshman Cup; DAR Good Citizen Award; Foreign Relations; William and Mary; Wake Forest U

CHEW, SHANNON M; ELIZABETH CITY, NC; PASQUOTANK CTY HS; (FR); Ctznshp Aw; Hnr Roll; Nat Hon Sy; Sci Fairs; Peer Tut/Med; Mus Clb; Scouts; Jzz Bnd; Bskball (J); Sch Ppr (R, P); Dermatology; Arabic Language; Duke U; NC State U

CHI, STEPHANIE; ASHEBORO, NC; ASHEBORO HS; (JR); Hnr Roll; WWAHSS; DARE; Emplmnt; Key Club; Sccr (V); Yrbk; Health Occupations Club - Volunteer At Nursing Homes; Doctorate Degree; U of North Carolina Chapel Hill; Eastern Carolina U

CHICO, CHARLEEN; FAYETTEVILLE, NC; WESTOVER HS; (SR); Sci Fairs; DARE; Dnce; Volunteer Work @ Daycare; A Degree in Medicine; A Degree in Nursing; U of Utah; U of Miami

CHISHOLM, CAMERON; CHARLOTTE, NC;; Ctznshp Aw; Duke TS; Hnr Roll; MVP; Nat Sci Aw; Nat Stu Ath Day Aw; Otst Ac Ach Awd; Perf Att; Sci Fairs; St of Mnth; Comm Volntr; Hab For Humty Volntr; Spec Olymp Vol; ArtClub; Chrch Yth Grp; DARE; Drma Clb; Jr Ach; Mus Clb; Outdrs Clb; Scouts; Bnd; Ch Chr; Drm Mjr; SP/M/VS; Drumming.; Engineer; Carpenter; NC A & T; UNCC

CHIULLI, MICHAEL; RALEIGH, NC; MILLBROOK HS; (SO); Duke TS; Hnr Roll; Otst Ac Ach Awd; Comm Volntr; FCA; Clb; Bnd; Sccr (J); Tennis (V L); Track (V); Stu Cncl (R); CR (R); Academic Letter; Engineering; Doctor; UNC; NC State

CHO, REBECCA S; CARY, NC; GREEN HOPE HS; (SR); Hi Hnr Roll; Hnr Roll; Jr Mshl; Nat Hon Sy; WWAHSS; Comm Volntr; Hab For Humty Volntr; Chrch Yth Grp; Key Club; Lib Aide; Ntl Beta Clb; Orch; Track (J); Church Youth Group President; Volunteer At Public Library; Finance; Business; Duke U; U of Pennsylvania

CHOE, ELIZABETH; FAYETTEVILLE, NC; SOUTHVIEW HS; (SO); Hnr Roll; Nat Hon Sy; Otst Ac Ach Awd; Perf Att; WWAHSS; Chrch Yth Grp; Orch; AIG Program; National Jr Beta Club; Designer; U of North Carolina At Chapel Hill; Duke U

CHOKSHI, YERA V; CARY, NC; WILLIAM A ENLOE HS; (FR); Hi Hnr Roll; Hnr Roll; Comm Volntr; Key Club; Ntl Beta Clb; Sci Clb; Tmpl Yth Grp; Dnce; Swmg (V L); Tennis (J); Adv Cncl (R); Vice-President of Temple Youth Group; Can Speak 4 Languages; Practices Yoga; Medical Doctor

CHOW, ERIC; DURHAM, NC; L E JORDAN HS; (JR); Duke TS; Hi Hnr Roll; Nat Hon Sy; WWAHSS; Chrch Yth Grp; Key Club; Ntl Beta Clb; Bnd; Mch Bnd; Track (V); Piano Guild; Duke U; UNC Chapel Hill

CHRISTENSEN, LAYNE C; DURHAM, NC; CHARLES E JORDAN HS; (SO); Duke TS; Hi Hnr Roll; Hnr Roll; Comm Volntr; Hab For Humty Volntr; Peer Tut/Med; Emplmnt; Key Club; Mth Clb/Tm; Dnce; Chrldg (V L); Stu Cncl; National Spanish Honor Society; Who's Who Among American HS Athletes; Harvard U; Vanderbilt U

CHUNG, ZURI; CHARLOTTE, NC; NORTH CAROLINA SCH OF THE ARTS; (JR); Hnr Roll; Otst Ac Ach Awd; Comm Volntr; ArtClub; Chrch Yth Grp; Key Club; Ntl Beta Clb; Spanish Clb; Dnce; Stg Cre; Yrbk (R); National Art Honor Society; Scholastic Art Award; Graphic Design; Illustration; Maryland Institute of Art; Cooper Union

CHUNN, KATIE; RURAL HALL, NC; NORTH FORSYTH HS; (FR); Hi Hnr Roll; Chrch Yth Grp; Bskball (V L); Sftball (V L); Vllyball (V L)

CIPOLLONI, AUBREY L; DENVER, NC; NORTHSIDE CHRISTIAN AC; (SR); Hnr Roll; Nat Hon Sy; Comm Volntr; Hab For Humty Volntr; Hosp Aide; Chrch Yth Grp; Drma Clb; Emplmnt; Spanish Clb; Chr; SP/M/VS; Chrldg (V L); Sue Myrick Youth Advisory Council; National Honor Society; Nursing; Vocal Performance; Liberty U; Palm Beach Atlantic College

CISSEL, COURTNEY; RALEIGH, NC; HILLTOP CHRISTIAN SCH; (JR); Hi Hnr Roll; Nat Hon Sy; Pres Sch; WWAHSS; Chrch Yth Grp; Quiz Bowl; Chr; Ch Chr; Chrldg (V L); Cl Off; CR (S); Yrbk (E)

CISSEL, TIFFANY; GOLDSBORO, NC; HILLTOP CHRISTIAN SCH; (SR); Hnr Roll; Valdctrian; WWAHSS; Chrch Yth Grp; Photog; Chr; Bskball (V CL); Cl Off (V, S); Yrbk; National Christian Honor Society; North Carolina Governor's Page Program; Medicine; Politics; Liberty U

CITTY, WILLS; RALEIGH, NC; WAKEFIELD HS; (JR); Hi Hnr Roll; Hnr Roll; Perf Att; WWAHSS; Comm Volntr; Chrch Yth Grp; Jr Cls League; Key Club; Pep Squd; Prom Com; Golf (V L); Stu Cncl (V); Individual Qualifier for 4-A Golf Regionals; Lamp of Knowledge Award Winner; Broadcast Journalism; Pre-Law; UNC-Chapel Hill; Stanford

CLAIBORNE, TERRELL; ROXBORO, NC; PERSON HS; (FR); Ctznshp Aw; Hnr Roll; Kwnis Aw; Perf Att; Pres Ac Ftns Aw; St of Mnth; Spec Olymp Vol

CLAMPETT, KATELYN; CARY, NC; SAINT DAVIDS SCH; (JR); Hnr Roll; Comm Volntr; Peer Tut/Med; Chrch Yth Grp; Drma Clb; FCA; Acpl Chr; Bnd; Ch Chr; SP/M/VS; Excellence In Acting; Best Comedienne; Musical Theatre; Performance; Berklee School of Music; UNC Chapel Hill

CLARK, BRITTNEY; CANTON, NC; PISGAH HS; (FR); Hnr Roll; Nat Hon Sy; Chrch Yth Grp; FCA; Chr; SP/M/VS; Bskball (J); Sftball (J); Vllyball (J); Stu Cncl (R); CR (R)

CLARK, CAITLIN M; REIDSVILLE, NC; CLOVER GARDEN SCH; (FR); Ctznshp Aw; Hnr Roll; Perf Att; Pres Ac Ftns Aw; Sci Fairs; Comm Volntr; Drma Clb; Pep Squd; Dnce; SP/M/VS; Bskball (V); Chrldg (J); CR (R); Odyssey of the Mind; Fashion Design; Fashion Photography; North Carolina State U; U of North Carolina Greensboro

CLARK, CATHRYNE B; SALISBURY, NC; SALISBURY HS; (JR); Comm Volntr; Emplmnt; Key Club; Pep Squd; Prom Com; Svce Clb; Spanish Clb; Chrldg (VJ); PP Ftbl (V); Stu Cncl (R); CR (R); Education K-5; Psychology / Working with Troubled Teens; Elon U; UNC Charlotte

CLARK, CHALONDRA; FAYETTEVILLE, NC; SOUTHVIEW HS; (SO); Hnr Roll; Perf Att; DARE; Chr; Ch Chr; Business and Administration (Master's); Sociology (Master's); North Carolina Central U

CLARK, KATIE; LENOIR, NC; HIBRITEN HS; (FR); Hnr Roll; Perf Att; Chrch Yth Grp; Drma Clb; Ntl Beta Clb; Bnd; Mch Bnd; Pep Bnd; Caldwell Community College; Appalachian State U

CLARK, LAURA R; GROVER, NC; KINGS MTN HS; (SR); Hi Hnr Roll; MVP; Otst Ac Ach Awd; Pres Ac Ftns Aw; Comm Volntr; Emplmnt; Dvng (V); Sftball (V); Swmg (V); Architecture & Drafting; U of North Carolina At Charlotte; Gaston College

CLARK, MEGAN H; SHELBY, NC; CREST HS; (SR); Hi Hnr Roll; Hnr Roll; Nat Hon Sy; WWAHSS; Comm Volntr; Peer Tut/Med; Chrch Yth Grp; FCA; FTA; Ntl Beta Clb; Chr; Ch Chr; Mars Hill Honors Chorus; Beta Club / National Honors Society; Education; U of North Carolina Charlotte

CLARK, RACHEL A; WAYNESVILLE, NC; TUSCOLA HS; (SO); Ctznshp Aw; Hi Hnr Roll; Hnr Roll; Nat Hon Sy; Otst Ac Ach Awd; St of Mnth; USAA; WWAHSS; Chrch Yth Grp; Cmptr Clb; DARE; SADD; Spanish Clb; Chr; Health Occupation; NC Chapel Hill; U of Tenn.

CLARK, REBECCA; CHARLOTTE, NC; HARDING U HS; (SO); Hnr Roll; Pep Squd; Photog; Latin Clb; Forensic Scientist

CLARK, TAYLOR; CHARLOTTE, NC; COVENANT DAY; (FR); Duke TS; Hnr Roll; Peer Tut/Med; Chrch Yth Grp; Jr Cls League; Vsity Clb; Bsball (V); Bskball (V); Business; Law; Duke; Carolina

CLARK, TEQUIA; HENDERSONVILLE, NC; EAST HENDERSON HS; (SO); Ctznshp Aw; Hi Hnr Roll; MVP; St of Mnth; WWAHSS; Comm Volntr; Peer Tut/Med; Chrch Yth Grp; Emplmnt; FCA; Scouts; Svce Clb; Chr; Ch Chr; Dnce; SP/M/VS; Bskball (JC); Track (V L); Youth of the Month/Year Nominee; Psychiatry; Acting/Singing-Performing Arts; Duke U, NC Harvard U; Spelman U, GA Howard U

CLARKE, MADONTRENIQUE' Q; FAYETTEVILLE, NC; SEVENTY-FIRST HS; (SO); WWAHSS; Peer Tut/Med; Chrch Yth Grp; Ch Chr; Dnce; Drl Tm; Yrbk (R, P); Business Administration; North Carolina A & T U; North Carolina Central U

CLAY, BROOKE; WILLOW SPRING, NC; WEST JOHNSTON HS; (JR); Hi Hnr Roll; Hnr Roll; Comm Volntr; Chrch Yth Grp; FCA; Sftball (J); Lit Mag (E, R); (HOSA) Health Occupations Students of America; DNA & Investigation; Computer Forensics; U of North Carolina Chapel Hill; Mount Olive

CLAY, COREY; CHAPEL HILL, NC; EAST CHAPEL HILL HS; (JR); Duke TS; Comm Volntr; Hab For Humty Volntr; Dnce; Master of the Sigma Beta Club; Business Administration; Business Management; Hampton U; U of North Carolina

CLAY, MORGAN; FALLSTON, NC; BURNS HS; (JR); Duke TS; Hi Hnr Roll; Hnr Roll; Jr Mshl; Jr Rot; Nat Hon Sy; Otst Ac Ach Awd; Perf Att; St of Mnth; Yth Ldrshp Prog; Comm Volntr; Peer Tut/Med; Chrch Yth Grp; Emplmnt; Ntl Beta Clb; Ntl FFA; Prom Com; Dnce; Orch; Chrldg (J); Ext Public Speaking-3rd Place; Junior Year History Award; Pre-Med. Biology, Chemistry; Emory; Wake Forest

Clark, Tequia
East Henderson HS
Hendersonville, NC

Cheek, Kelly D
Southern Durham HS
Durham, NC

Claiborne, Terrell
Person HS
Roxboro, NC

CLAYTON, WILLIAM M; RALEIGH, NC; NEEDHAM BROUGHTON HS; (SO); Duke TS; F Lan Hn Soc; Hi Hnr Roll; Hnr Roll; Perf Att; Comm Volntr; Hab For Humty Volntr; Chrch Yth Grp; Dbte Team; Emplmnt; FCA; JSA; Outdrs Clb; Scouts; Spanish Clb; Cr Ctry (J L); Track (J L); Cl Off (R); Stu Cncl (S, T); CR (R); Treasurer of Teenage Republicans; Division II Choir, District Student Council; Military (Army, Marines); Parks and Recreation; Wake Forest U; U of North Carolina in Chapel Hill

CLEGG JR, GUY; WINTERVILLE, NC; SOUTH CTRL HS; (SO); MVP; Chrch Yth Grp; DARE; Emplmnt; SADD; Bskball; Ftball (V); Automotive Technology; Zoology; North Carolina State; U of North Carolina Charlotte

CLELLAND, PARKER; HAMPSTEAD, NC; TOP SAIL HS; (FR); Hnr Roll; Chrch Yth Grp; Bnd

CLONINGER, MIRANDA K; ROCKY POINT, NC; HEDIE TRASK SR HS; (SO); Ctznshp Aw; Hnr Roll; Nat Hon Sy; Comm Volntr; Spec Olymp Vol; FCA; FBLA; Key Club; NYLC; Quiz Bowl; Adv Cncl (S); 3rd Place in the National Bar Association Essay Contest; Honors English 10 Highest Average; Law; Teaching; U of North Carolina At Chapel Hill; Harvard U

CLONTZ, JE'TANA M; CLAYTON, NC; WEST JOHNSTON HS; (SR); Hnr Roll; FTA; Ntl FFA; SADD; Clr Grd; Dnce; Mch Bnd; President of FTA; Accounting; Business; East Carolina U

CLOWNEY, JASMINE; SALISBURY, NC; SALISBURY HS; (SO); Ctznshp Aw; F Lan Hn Soc; Hi Hnr Roll; Hnr Roll; Kwnis Aw; Perf Att; Pres Sch; WWAHSS; Comm Volntr; Peer Tut/Med; Red Cr Aide; ArtClub; Chrch Yth Grp; FBLA; Key Club; Spanish Clb; Bnd; Mch Bnd; Bskball (J); PP Ftbl; Scr Kpr; Tennis; Vllyball (J); Cl Off (P); Law; Business; Harvard U; Yale U

CLOYED, CASSIDY C; ASHEVILLE, NC; A C REYNOLDS HS; (JR); WWAHSS; Peer Tut/Med; Chrch Yth Grp; SADD; SP/M/VS; Sccr (J); Law; Accountant

COATES, EMILY G; CLAYTON, NC; CLAYTON HS; (FR); Hnr Roll; Otst Ac Ach Awd; Pres Ac Ftns Aw; St of Mnth; Comm Volntr; Drma Clb; FCA; Ntl Beta Clb; Ch Chr; Sccr; Track (J); Vllyball (J); Yrbk (P); CMS Eagle Award; 1st and 3rd Place - NC State Fair / Crochet; Fashion Design; Music; Appalachian State; NC State

COBLE, AMBER; ASHEBORO, NC; ASHEBORO HS; (JR); Hnr Roll; Nat Mrt LOC; WWAHSS; Chrch Yth Grp; FCA; Key Club; Bnd; Mch Bnd; Chrldg (V); PP Ftbl; Track (V); Pre-Med; Dentistry; U of North Carolina @ Chapel Hill; Appalachian State U

COBLE, ANDREA; MOREHEAD CITY, NC; WEST CARTERET HS; (FR); 4-H member of Year; Marine Biologist; Psychologist; UNCW; UNC

COCKERELL, STEVEN R; MT AIRY, NC; MT AIRY HS; (JR); Hnr Roll; Nat Hon Sy; WWAHSS; Comm Volntr; Spec Olymp Vol; Chrch Yth Grp; Emplmnt; Key Club; Scouts; Svce Clb; Bnd; Ch Chr; Mch Bnd; Swmg (V); Biochemistry; Pre-Med; Mars Hill College; East Carolina U

COFER, MARY V; PFAFFTOWN, NC; NORTH FORSYTH HS; (FR); Ctznshp Aw; Hi Hnr Roll; Hnr Roll; MVP; St of Mnth; Comm Volntr; Hab For Humty Volntr; Chrch Yth Grp; Civil Air Pat; DARE; Key Club; ROTC; Scouts; Bnd; GAA; Sccr (V); Engineering; NCSU North Carolina State U; Wake Forest U

COFFEY, ALEX; DENVER, NC; EAST LINCOLN HS; (SO); Duke TS; WWAHSS; Comm Volntr; Chrch Yth Grp; Bnd; Mch Bnd; Pep Bnd; Golf (V)

COGDELL, MINDY; SHELBY, NC; CREST SR HS; (JR); Hnr Roll; Hosp Aide; Chrch Yth Grp; Emplmnt; FTA; Tchrs Aide; French Clb; Math; Appalachian State U; U of North Carolina Greensboro

COLE, JEREMY; GRAHAM, NC; GRAHAM HS; (JR); Duke TS; Hnr Roll; Perf Att; Bnd; Jzz Bnd; Mch Bnd; Computer Science; Duke U; North Carolina State U

COLE, JESSICA; FRANKLINVILLE, NC; EASTERN RANDOLPH HS; (FR); Hi Hnr Roll; Hnr Roll; Perf Att; DARE; Emplmnt; Ntl Beta Clb; Ntl FFA; Sci Clb; Ch Chr; Sftball (J); Vllyball (J); Business; Medical

COLEMAN, BIANCA; WILMINGTON, NC; E A LANEY HS; (JR); Hnr Roll; Otst Ac Ach Awd; WWAHSS; Comm Volntr; Peer Tut/Med; ArtClub; Chrch Yth Grp; Emplmnt; Key Club; Prom Com; Spanish Clb; Stg Cre; Stu Cncl (R); Health Occupations Students of America Member; Church Volleyball League; Pediatrics; Veterinary Medicine; North Carolina State U; East Carolina U

COLEMAN, ERIN L; GOLDSBORO, NC; GOLDSBORO HS; (SO); Hnr Roll; Nat Mrt LOC; Perf Att; St of Mnth; Comm Volntr; FBLA; Ntl Beta Clb; ROTC; Vsity Clb; Cr Ctry (V); Tennis (V); Track (V); Stu Cncl (R); Doctoral & Professional Degree; Psychology; UNC-Chapel Hill; NC State

COLEMAN, TIERAH; CHARLOTTE, NC; PHILLIP O BERRY AC OF TECH; (FR); Hnr Roll; Sci/Math Olympn; St of Mnth; Peer Tut/Med; DARE; ROTC; Scouts; Spanish Clb; Drl Tm; Bskball (V); Vllyball (V); Engineering; Chemistry; Duke U; Michigan State U

COLEMAN II, DERRICK A; CHARLOTTE, NC; GARRINGER SR HS; (SO); Ctznshp Aw; Hnr Roll; St of Mnth; Comm Volntr; ArtClub; Chrch Yth Grp; DARE; Emplmnt; Jr Ach; Ch Chr; Bskball (V); CR (V); AAU Basketball; Cartoonist; Johnson C Smith U; U of North Carolina-Charlotte

COLEY, LANIKKA T; FRANKLINTON, NC; FRANKLINTON HS; (FR); Hnr Roll; Otst Ac Ach Awd; Pres Sch; Comm Volntr; Peer Tut/Med; Chrch Yth Grp; DARE; FBLA; JSA; Prom Com; Bnd; Mch Bnd; Pep Bnd; Tennis (V); Citizenship; National Achiever, Junior Beta; Corporate Law; North Carolina Central U; Stanford U

COLLADO, MICHAEL; CREEDMOOR, NC; SOUTH GRANVILLE HS; (FR); Hnr Roll; St of Mnth; Ch Chr; Wrstlg (V C); Doctor; X-Ray Technician; North Carolina State

COLLINS, AINSLEY; FAYETTEVILLE, NC; READ ROSS CLASSICAL SCH; (FR); Duke TS; Hi Hnr Roll; Hnr Roll; MVP; Sci/Math Olympn; Comm Volntr; Peer Tut/Med; Chrch Yth Grp; Dbte Team; Drma Clb; Jr Cls League; Key Club; Ntl Beta Clb; NtlFrnscLg; Sci Clb; SP/M/VS; Placed 2nd & 3rd At Science Olympiad Regionals; Played Softball Travel for 1 Year & Recreation Softball for 2 Years; Forensic Science; Homicide Detective; U of North Carolina At Wilmington

COLLINS, ASHLEY B; HALIFAX, NC; HALIFAX AC CHRISTIAN SCH; (SO); 4H Awd; Hnr Roll; Perf Att; Hosp Aide; Chrch Yth Grp; Ntl Beta Clb; Tchrs Aide; Bskball (V); Sch Ppr (R); Yrbk (R); Private Investigator; Radiologist/Nurse; U of North Carolina; Halifax Community College

COLLINS, BRITTANY; ROXBORO, NC; PERSON HS; (SO); Ctznshp Aw; Hi Hnr Roll; Hnr Roll; Kwnis Aw; Nat Hon Sy; Otst Ac Ach Awd; Perf Att; WWAHSS; Comm Volntr; Chrch Yth Grp; Ch Chr; Cl Off (P); CR (P); Outstanding African-American Student; FCCLA; Obstetrics/Gynecology; U of Maryland; U of North Carolina

COLLINS, CHRISTOPHER C; TOBACCOVILLE, NC; WEST STOKES HS; (SR); Hnr Roll; Comm Volntr; Red Cr Aide; Spec Olymp Vol; Emplmnt; Fire Safety Engineering Technology; U of North Carolina At Charlotte

COLLINS, JACQUELINE; HOPE MILLS, NC; SOUTH VIEW HS; (JR); Nat Hon Sy; WWAHSS; Key Club; Mus Clb; Bnd; Jzz Bnd; Mch Bnd; Trumpet Section Leader; Law; U of North Carolina At Chapel Hill; Wake Forest U

COLLINS, JUSTIN R; WINGATE, NC; FOREST HILLS HS; (SO); Hnr Roll; Nat Hon Sy; Perf Att; Pres Ac Ftns Aw; St of Mnth; Comm Volntr; Chrch Yth Grp; Emplmnt; Ch Chr; Golf (V); Law; Business; Duke U; North Carolina State U

COLLINS, KENZEE; MILLERS CREEK, NC; WEST WILKES HS; (JR); Hnr Roll; Nat Hon Sy; Otst Ac Ach Awd; Comm Volntr; Peer Tut/Med; Emplmnt; FCA; Key Club; Ntl Beta Clb; Photog; Prom Com; Chrldg (VJ L); PP Ftbl (J); Cl Off (T); CR (T); Yrbk (R, P); Peer Helper Member; Student Council Member, Freshman Homecoming Queen; Nursing; Teaching; U of North Carolina At Charlotte; Appalachian State U

COLLINS, MAYAH S; ROCKY MOUNT, NC; ROCKY MOUNT HS; (SO); Hnr Roll; WWAHSS; Spanish Clb; SP/M/VS; Cr Ctry (J); Business Administration; Fashion Merchandising; Drexel U; Shaw U

COLLINS, ZACH; SALISBURY, NC; SALISBURY HS; (SO); Ftball (V); Sccr (J); Tennis (V); Track (V); Stu Cncl (R); CR (R); All-Conference Football; All-County Football; Medicine; U of North Carolina; Wake Forest

COLSON, ALEXANDER T; MAPLE HILL, NC; NORTHSIDE HS; (SO); Ctznshp Aw; Hnr Roll; Perf Att; Comm Volntr; Red Cr Aide; DARE; Drma Clb; Mus Clb; Spch Team; Chr; Dnce; SP/M/VS; Stg Cre; Ftball (J); Mar Art (V); Sccr (V); Cl Off (V); Mechanical Engineering; U of North Carolina, Chapel Hill; U of North Carolina, Wilmington

COLTRAIN, JOSHUA; WILLIAMSTON, NC; WILLIAMSTON HS; (JR); Duke TS; Hi Hnr Roll; Jr Mshl; Nat Hon Sy; Otst Ac Ach Awd; USAA; WWAHSS; Comm Volntr; Peer Tut/Med; Spec Olymp Vol; Chrch Yth Grp; Emplmnt; Key Club; Ntl Beta Clb; Spanish Clb; Treasurer and Vice P. of Key Club; Pre-Med and Medical School; Minor in Spanish; East Carolina U; U of North Carolina @ Chapel Hill

COLVIN, MONIQUE; HENDERSON, NC; SOUTHERN VANCE HS; (SR); All Am Sch; Duke TS; F Lan Hn Soc; Hi Hnr Roll; Hnr Roll; St of Mnth; USAA; WWAHSS; Hab For Humty Volntr; Ntl Beta Clb; Spanish Clb; Bnd; Mch Bnd; Sccr (V CL); Tennis (V L); Stu Cncl (R); CR (R); Major in Political Science; Law; U of North Carolina At Greensboro

CONLEY, CATHERINE; ASHEBORO, NC; ASHEBORO HS; (JR); Hi Hnr Roll; Hnr Roll; Nat Hon Sy; WWAHSS; Comm Volntr; Hab For Humty Volntr; Chrch Yth Grp; Key Club; Quiz Bowl; Sci Clb; Dnce; SP/M/VS; Sch Ppr (E); Fashion Design; Journalism; North Carolina State U

CONLEY, MICHAEL C; LINVILLE FALLS, NC; AVERY CTY HS; (SR); Hi Hnr Roll; Hnr Roll; WWAHSS; Red Cr Aide; Chrch Yth Grp; Emplmnt; Play Guitar-Self Taught; Snowboard; Business; Accounting; Maryland Community College; Appalachian State U

CONNER, SHANOYA; GASTONIA, NC; (JR); Hnr Roll; Otst Ac Ach Awd; WWAHSS; Hosp Aide; Peer Tut/Med; Chrch Yth Grp; Drma Clb; FTA; Quiz Bowl; Scouts; Svce Clb; Bnd; Ch Chr; Clr Grd; Dnce; PP Ftbl (V); Cl Off (R); Stu Cncl (R); CR (R); Sch Ppr (R); Yrbk (R, P); Black Educators Association Service Award; Biology; Mass Communications; Winston Salem State U; UNC-Chapel Hill (U of N Carolina)

CONNERS, AUSTIN; WILMINGTON, NC; E A LANEY HS; (JR); Ctznshp Aw; Hi Hnr Roll; MVP; Nat Hon Sy; Otst Ac Ach Awd; Perf Att; Pres Ac Ftns Aw; AL Aux Boys; DARE; Emplmnt; Bsball (VJ L); Ftball (J); Wade Edwards Mock Trial 2004; Law; Engineering; Duke; Wake Forest

CONNOLLY, ERIN; TAYLORSVILLE, NC; ALEXANDER CTRL HS; (JR); Hnr Roll; WWAHSS; Chrch Yth Grp; Scouts; Graphic Design; Sports Medicine; Kings College; Mars Hill College

CONNOR, CRYSTAL D; JAMESTOWN, NC; SOUTHWEST GUILFORD HS; (JR); Hnr Roll; Jr Mshl; Nat Hon Sy; WWAHSS; Peer Tut/Med; Emplmnt; Ntl Beta Clb; Photog; Quiz Bowl; Svce Clb; Spanish Clb; Ch Chr; Research Apprenticeship Program At UNC-Chapel Hill; NASA Summer High School Apprentice Research Program; Physician; Medical Researcher; U of North Carolina At Chapel Hill; Hampton U

CONOVER, JENNIFER R; SHARPSBURG, NC; SOUTHERN NASH HS; (SR); Hnr Roll; Comm Volntr; Hosp Aide; Drma Clb; Key Club; ROTC; French Clb; Yrbk (P); 4 Years in ROTC Program (Officer); Psychology; Fayetteville State U; Lynchburg College

CONROY, RYAN M; CHARLOTTE, NC; PHILLIP O BERRY AC OF TECH; (SO); Hnr Roll; St of Mnth; ROTC; Scouts; Clr Grd

CONTE, DANIELLE; CARY, NC; GREEN HOPE HS; (JR); All Am Sch; Hnr Roll; Nat Mrt LOC; Otst Ac Ach Awd; USAA; WWAHSS; Chrldg (V L); All Star Cheerleader; Honor Roll-Rotary Club; Education; Physical Therapy; NC State; UNC Charlotte

CONWAY, DAMIAN; DURHAM, NC; JORDAN HS; (JR); F Lan Hn Soc; Hnr Roll; Jr Rot; Yth Ldrshp Prog; Peer Tut/Med; Chrch Yth Grp; Emplmnt; Key Club; Sccr (V L); Stu Cncl (R); CR (R); Sch Ppr (R); I Play on a Club Soccer Team; Law; Statistics; Georgetown U; U of North Carolina At Chapel Hill

COOK, GENESIS; GREENSBORO, NC; DUDLEY HS; (FR); Hnr Roll; Comm Volntr; Chrch Yth Grp; A TIAG Girl; Lawyer

COOK, KAYLEIGH; FAYETTEVILLE, NC; TERRY SANFORD HS; (JR); Hi Hnr Roll; Hnr Roll; Nat Hon Sy; Chrch Yth Grp; Svce Clb; French Clb; Ch Chr; SP/M/VS; Stg Cre; Academic Letter-9, 10, 11; Pre-Law; North Carolina State U; East Carolina U

COOK, SAPHFIRE; HAVELOCK, NC; HAVELOCK HS; (FR); Hnr Roll; Chr; Ch Chr; SP/M/VS; A Member of Freshman & Student Council; Commercial Advertisement; Fashion Design; Duke U; New York U

COOKE, JEFFREY B; FAYETTEVILLE, NC; SOUTH VIEW HS; (JR); Duke TS; Hnr Roll; Jr Mshl; Nat Hon Sy; Perf Att; WWAHSS; Emplmnt; Scouts; Bnd; Jzz Bnd; Mch Bnd; SP/M/VS; Eagle Scout; Drum Major of SVHS Band; Architectural Engineer; North Carolina State U

COOLEY, BRITTNEY A; JACKSONVILLE, NC; NORTHSIDE HS; (FR); Ctznshp Aw; DAR; Chrch Yth Grp; ROTC; Ch Chr; Clr Grd; Drl Tm; Chrldg (V); Track (V); Cl Off (P); Stu Cncl (R); CR (P); Sch Ppr (R); Computer Engineering; Law; North Carolina Agricultural & Technical U; U of North Carolina At Chapel Hill

COOMER, DANIEL; BARCO, NC; CURRITUCK CTY HS; (FR); Ctznshp Aw; Hi Hnr Roll; Hnr Roll; St Optmst of Yr; Hosp Aide; Mth Clb/Tm; Sci Clb; Math Education; Law; Greenville U; Duke U

COON, KRYSTLE; MT AIRY, NC; MT AIRY HS; (FR); Hnr Roll; St of Mnth; WWAHSS; Comm Volntr; Chrch Yth Grp; Emplmnt; Key Club; Sftball (V); Junior National Honor Society; All American at Large; Business Management; Appalachian State; Georgia Tech

COONE, CECILY; NORWOOD, NC; SOUTH STANLY HS; (FR); Hnr Roll; Hab For Humty Volntr; Chrch Yth Grp; FCA; SP/M/VS; Sftball (J); Tennis (V); Science-Outstanding Student Award; Massage Therapy; U of Tennessee; NC State

COOPER, CHANEL; CHARLOTTE, NC; GARINGER SR HS; (JR); Hi Hnr Roll; Pres Sch; St of Mnth; WWAHSS; Peer Tut/Med; Tchrs Aide; Cl Off (V); Sch Ppr (E); NAACP Member; Attorney (Criminal Law); Biochemist; Rochester U; U of Richmond

COOPER, CHANEL N; CHARLOTTE, NC; GARINGER HS; (JR); Hi Hnr Roll; Pres Sch; Peer Tut/Med; Bnd; Cl Off (V); Sch Ppr (E); Presidential Classroom Alumnus; NAACP Member; Attorney (Criminal Law); Biochemist; U of Richmond; Rochester College

COOPER, COURTNEY S; CLINTON, NC; CLINTON HS; (SO); Hi Hnr Roll; Hnr Roll; WWAHSS; Comm Volntr; FBLA; Ch Chr; Adv Cncl (R); Computer Engineering; U of North Carolina Chapel Hill; East Carolina U

Coone, Cecily
South Stanly HS
Norwood, NC

Colson, Alexander T
Northside HS
Maple Hill, NC

Conley, Michael C
Avery Cty HS
Linville Falls, NC

COOPER, DEMONDRA; WINDSOR, NC; BERTIE HS; (SO); 4H Awd; Duke TS; Hnr Roll; Nat Hon Sy; Nat Ldrshp Svc; Otst Ac Ach Awd; Perf Att; Sci Fairs; WWAHSS; Comm Volntr; Spec Olymp Vol; DARE; Fr of Library; Mus Clb; NYLC; Bnd; Jzz Bnd; Mch Bnd; SP/M/VS; Track (V); Criminal Justice; Business Administration; North Carolina State U; North Carolina A & T State U

COOPER, JAMAL L; LUMBERTON, NC; LUMBERTON HS; (FR); Hnr Roll; Comm Volntr; Chrch Yth Grp; Chr; Business Administration; Fine Arts; U of North Carolina; Duke U

COOPER, LEANN; JACKSONVILLE, NC; JACKSONVILLE HS; (JR); Ctznshp Aw; Hnr Roll; Otst Ac Ach Awd; Peer Tut/Med; ArtClub; Scr Kpr; Business Management; Culinary Arts

COOPER, ROCHELLE A; RALEIGH, NC; MILLBROOK HS; (SO); Hnr Roll; Nat Hon Sy; Comm Volntr; Peer Tut/Med; SADD; Chr; Dnce; National Achievers Society; SAVE Club; Accounting; Psychology; Florida State U; U of North Carolina Greensboro

COPELAND, BRANDON H; CLINTON, NC; CLINTON HS; (FR); Hnr Roll; Sci Fairs; Chrch Yth Grp; Bnd; Cl Off (P); Engineering; Business; U of North Carolina Chapel Hill; Duke U

COPELAND, CAROLINE; KILL DEVIL HILLS, NC; FIRST FLIGHT HS; (JR); Hnr Roll; St of Mnth; WWAHSS; Comm Volntr; Chrch Yth Grp; Key Club; Quiz Bowl; Spanish Clb; Ch Chr; Certified Pool Operator (CPO); Non-School Related Martial Arts; Business Degree; Teaching; East Carolina U; U of North Carolina

COPELAND, JOSHUA; WILLIAMSTON, NC; WILLIAMSTON HS; (SO); Hi Hnr Roll; Hnr Roll; Comm Volntr; DARE; Ntl Beta Clb; Tech Clb; Voc Ind Clb Am; Bnd; Mch Bnd; Cr Ctry (J); NC State Leader Award; VP Skills USA, Beta Club Member; Computer Engineering; Art-Graphic Design; North Carolina State U; U of North Carolina-Greensboro

COPELAND, LAUREN N; WADE, NC; CAPE FEAR HS; (SR); Hnr Roll; Chrch Yth Grp; DARE; Ntl FFA; Scouts; Dnce; PP Ftbl (V); Dance Teacher; Radiologist; Fayetteville Technical Community College

COPES, ZACHARY; FRISCO, NC; CAPE HATTERAS SECONDARY SCH; (SO); Hnr Roll; Nat Hon Sy; Otst Ac Ach Awd; Comm Volntr; Chrch Yth Grp; FCA; Key Club; SADD; Sccr (V); Tennis (V); Stu Cncl (S); Outstanding Achievement in Eng 9 & 10 Hon, Alg 1 & 2 Hon & Geom Hon; Applied Mathematics; Physics; U of North Carolina At Chapel Hill; Wake Forest

CORBETT, CARL; HUNTERSVILLE, NC; HOPEWELL HS; (JR); Hnr Roll; MVP; Perf Att; Comm Volntr; Red Cr Aide; Mus Clb; Vsity Clb; Bnd; Bskball (J, L); Cr Ctry (V); Gmnstcs (L); Scr Kpr (J, L); Sccr (V, J); Swmg (L); Track (V, C); Vsy Clb (J); Wt Lftg (L); Assistant Coach for U13 Boy's Soccer League; Academic Internship - Physical Therapist; Physical Therapist; Occupational Therapist; Eastern Carolina; Western Carolina

CORDIN, SABRINA; MURPHY, NC; MURPHY HS; (JR); F Lan Hn Soc; Hi Hnr Roll; Nat Hon Sy; WWAHSS; Comm Volntr; Peer Tut/Med; Drma Clb; Ntl Beta Clb; Spanish Clb; Dnce; SP/M/VS; Massage Therapy; Center for Massage and Natural Health

CORNEJO, SAMUEL; CLINTON, NC; UNION HS; (SR); Hnr Roll; WWAHSS; FBLA; Mth Clb/Tm; ROTC; Tech Clb; Clr Grd; Drl Tm; Track (V); Rifle Team; IAM Club; Air Force; State Trooper; West Point (VA)

CORNELISON, STEPHANIE; ASHEBORO, NC; EASTERN RANDOLPH HS; (SO); Hi Hnr Roll; USAA; WWAHSS; Bnd; History; Medieval/Renaissance Studies; UNC-Chapel Hill; Duke U

COSTA, THIAGO; CARY, NC; CARY SR HS; (JR); Hnr Roll; Perf Att; Sci Fairs; Comm Volntr; Hosp Aide; Chrch Yth Grp; Scouts; Ch Chr; Sccr (J); Track (V); Church Basketball Team / Piano Player; Volunteer Work at Rex Hospital; Pre-Med; U of North Carolina Chapel Hill; Johns Hopkins U

COTHRAN, MOLLY; WILMINGTON, NC; E A LANEY HS; (SO); Hnr Roll; Sci/Math Olympn; Comm Volntr; Emplmnt; Off Aide; SP/M/VS; Biology; North Carolina State U; U of North Carolina At Wilmington

COTTER, KEVIN; RALEIGH, NC; CARY AC; (FR); Duke TS; F Lan Hn Soc; Hnr Roll; WWAHSS; Comm Volntr; Peer Tut/Med; Red Cr Aide; Dbte Team; Key Club; Lib Aide; Ntl Beta Clb; NtlFrnscLg; Scouts; Spch Team; Tennis (J); Stu Cncl (V, R); Eagle Scout 2005, Page for NC House of Representatives; Jr VP Beta Club for 2005-2006; International Business Management; French; U of Pennsylvania; Duke U

COUCH, EMMALEA D; DURHAM, NC; C E JORDAN HS; (SO); Ctznshp Aw; Duke TS; F Lan Hn Soc; Gov Hnr Prg; Hi Hnr Roll; Nat Hon Sy; Otst Ac Ach Awd; WWAHSS; Comm Volntr; Peer Tut/Med; Red Cr Aide; Chrch Yth Grp; DARE; Emplmnt; FTA; Key Club; SADD; Spanish Clb; Ch Chr; Sch Ppr (E); Spanish Honor Society; Master's Degree in Education; U of North Carolina; North Carolina State U

COUGHTREY, DYLAN; EDENTON, NC; JOHN A HOLMES HS; (SO); Duke TS; Hi Hnr Roll; Chrch Yth Grp; Scouts; Sccr (V); Swmg (V); Track (V); Biology; Medical Degree; Duke U; Wake Forest U

COURTS, KYLE J; RALEIGH, NC; MIDDLE CREEK HS; (JR); Hnr Roll; WWAHSS; Chrch Yth Grp; Lcrsse (V L); Sccr (V L); Architect; North Carolina State

COVEY, ASHLEY L; MEBANE, NC; EASTERN ALAMANCE HS; (FR); Hnr Roll; Comm Volntr; Chrch Yth Grp; DARE; Drma Clb; Scouts; Svce Clb; SADD; Bnd; Ch Chr; Clr Grd; Mch Bnd; Sftball (V); Community Softball; Honor Camper (Summer Camp); Nursing; Acting-Theatre Arts or Others; UNC Greensboro-North Carolina; Lee U-Tennessee

COVIL, JUSTIN B; LYNN, NC; POLK CTY HS; (SR); Ctznshp Aw; Hnr Roll; Jr Mshl; MVP; Nat Hon Sy; WWAHSS; Spec Olymp Vol; Chrch Yth Grp; FCA; Key Club; Lttrmn Clb; Ntl Beta Clb; Vsity Clb; Spanish Clb; Bsball (V CL); Bskball (V CL); Ftball (V L); Business; Engineering; U of North Carolina Chapel Hill; United States Naval Academy

COVINGTON, PAUL; RALEIGH, NC; SOUTHEAST RALEIGH HS; (SR); Nat Mrt Semif; Sci Fairs; Sci/Math Olympn; St of Mnth; Emplmnt; Key Club; Schol Bwl; Sci Clb; National Merit Special Scholarship Award; Math; UC Berkeley

COX, AMANDA; ASHEBORO, NC; ASHEBORO HS; (JR); Nat Hon Sy; Emplmnt; Key Club; Bnd; Mch Bnd; PP Ftbl; Swmg (V CL); All-Conference Swimming; History; Education; U of North Carolina Chapel Hill

COX, APRIL; LUMBERTON, NC; LUMBERTON SR HS; (SO); Hnr Roll; Nat Hon Sy; WWAHSS; Chrch Yth Grp; Early Childhood Degree; Teaching Degree; U of North Carolina At Pembroke; U of North Carolina At Wilmington

COX, BRANDON; ASHEBORO, NC; ASHEBORO HS; (FR); Duke TS; Hnr Roll; WWAHSS; Comm Volntr; Chrch Yth Grp; FCA; Key Club; Design; Business

COX, CALEB; IRON STATION, NC; EAST LINCOLN HS; (SO); Chr; Music; Business

COX, CAROLINE E; ASHEBORO, NC; ASHEBORO HS; (FR); Hnr Roll; Otst Ac Ach Awd; Perf Att; Comm Volntr; Chrch Yth Grp; FCA; Key Club; Ntl Beta Clb; Vllyball (VJCL); Class Rank #1 of 381; Perfect Attendance K-9 / 10 Years; UNC Chapel Hill

COX, CASSANDRA M; ROCKY POINT, NC; HEIDE TRASK SR HS; (JR); Hi Hnr Roll; Hnr Roll; Jr Mshl; Nat Hon Sy; Salutrn; Comm Volntr; Peer Tut/Med; Chrch Yth Grp; Emplmnt; Key Club; Prom Com; Bnd; Ch Chr; Stg Cre; Governor's Page; Nomination for Governor's School; Medical; Law; U of North Carolina At Chapel Hill; Wake Forest U

COX, DAVID N; THOMASVILLE, NC; LEDFORD SR HS; (SR); WWAHSS; Yth Ldrshp Prog; Comm Volntr; Chrch Yth Grp; FCA; Bnd; Jzz Bnd; Mch Bnd; Orch; Genetic Engineering; Biochemistry; U of North Carolina At Charlotte; Wake Forest

COX, ELECIA; HUDSON, NC; WEST CALDWELL HS; (SR); Hnr Roll; St Schl; Red Cr Aide; Cmptr Clb; Emplmnt; FCCLA; Tchrs Aide; Computers; Poetry; Child Care; Caldwell Community College

COX, PAULA W; MOUNT OLIVE, NC; HOBBTON HS; (SO); Hnr Roll; Pres Ac Ftns Aw; Comm Volntr; Chrch Yth Grp; FBLA; FCCLA; Chr; Ch Chr; Dnce; SP/M/VS; Nursing Home Volunteer; Babysitting Certificate; Registered Nurse; Teacher; North Carolina State U.; U of North Carolina At Pembroke

COX, SEAN L; GOLDSBORO, NC; GOLDSBORO HS; (SO); Hnr Roll; Bnd; Mch Bnd; Bskball (J); Ftball (V); CR (R); Pharmacy; Drafting; North Carolina State U; East Carolina U

COZART, JUSTIN; ROXBORO, NC; PERSON HS; (FR); Hnr Roll; Perf Att; Bnd; Jzz Bnd; Mch Bnd; Cr Ctry (J); Track (J); Aviation Pilot; Computer Engineering

CRADDOCK, BRANDI; ROPER, NC; WILLIAMSTON HS; (SO); Duke TS; Hi Hnr Roll; Hnr Roll; WWAHSS; Comm Volntr; Red Cr Aide; Spec Olymp Vol; Key Clb; Ntl Beta Clb; SADD; Spanish Clb; Bnd; Clr Grd; Flg Crps; Mch Bnd; U of North Carolina in Wilmington

CRADDOCK, JONATHAN D; LAKE LURE, NC; POLK CTY HS; (SR); Hnr Roll; MVP; Nat Hon Sy; USAA; WWAHSS; AL Aux Boys; Chrch Yth Grp; FCA; Ntl FFA; Bsball (V L); Ftball (V L); Coaches Award Varsity Baseball; Most Outstanding Lifter - Weightlifting

CRAIG, SAMANTHA L D; NEWTON, NC; FRED T FOARD HS; (MS); DAR; Duke TS; Hnr Roll; Kwnis Aw; Sci/Math Olympn; Chrch Yth Grp; DARE; Lib Aide; Ntl Beta Clb; Bnd; Ch Chr; Drm Mjr; Bskball (J); Golf (J); Vllyball (C); Wt Lftg (C); Yrbk (R); Jr. Beta; Duke U; North Carolina State U

CRANFORD, AMY E; ASHEBORO, NC; ASHEBORO HS; (JR); Duke TS; Hi Hnr Roll; Hnr Roll; Otst Ac Ach Awd; Perf Att; Sci Fairs; WWAHSS; Comm Volntr; Peer Tut/Med; Spec Olymp Vol; DARE; Emplmnt; FCA; Key Club; Ntl Beta Clb; Svce Clb; Vsity Clb; Bnd; Mch Bnd; Pep Bnd; SP/M/VS; Golf (V L); President of Junior Beta Club; Outstanding Young Musician; Psychology; Philosophy; U of North Carolina Chapel Hill; Duke U

CRANFORD, JENNA; SALISBURY, NC; SALISBURY HS; (JR); Hnr Roll; Nat Hon Sy; Otst Ac Ach Awd; WWAHSS; Hab For Humty Volntr; Chrch Yth Grp; DARE; Key Club; Prom Com; Spanish Clb; Chrldg (V L); Golf (J); Stu Cncl (R); Appalachian State U; U of North Carolina Wilmington

CRAVEN, TAYLOR; PINEHURST, NC; PINECREST HS; (SO); Hi Hnr Roll; Hnr Roll; Nat Hon Sy; Spec Olymp Vol; Key Club; Spanish Clb; SP/M/VS; Chrldg (VJ L); PP Ftbl (J); Sccr (J); Track (V); Coach's Award for Cheerleading; Top Sophomore Cheerleader; Interior Design; Communications; U of North Carolina At Chapel Hill; U of North Carolina At Wilmington

CRAWFORD, MORGAN T; ASHEVILLE, NC; A C REYNOLDS HS; (FR); Comm Volntr; Chrch Yth Grp; Bnd; Ch Chr; Bsball (J); Business; Accounting; Appalachian; UNC Charlotte

CRAWFORD JR, KENT D; HIGH POINT, NC; HIGH POINT CTRL HS; (SO); Hnr Roll; WWAHSS; Comm Volntr; Chrch Yth Grp; Emplmnt; HO'Br Yth Ldrshp; Key Club; Scouts; Bnd; Jzz Bnd; Eagle Scout; Handbell Choir

CRAYCROFT, CAROLINE; APEX, NC; APEX HS; (SO); Duke TS; Hnr Roll; Chrch Yth Grp; Play the Harp; Bachelor's Degree / Master's Degree in Architecture; Cornell U; Rhode Island School of Design

CREASON, ADAM; LEWISVILLE, NC; WEST FORSYTH HS; (FR); Hnr Roll; Chrch Yth Grp; Scouts; Ch Chr; Working on Eagle Award for Scouts; Computer Technology; Business

CREECH, AMBER; ZEBULON, NC; CLAYTON HS; (FR); Hi Hnr Roll; Perf Att; St of Mnth; Yth Ldrshp Prog; Comm Volntr; Chrch Yth Grp; FTA; Mth Clb/Tm; Ch Chr; Clr Grd; Dnce; College Quest Club; Theater Appreciation Club; Education; Law; North Carolina State U; Meredith College

CRICHTON, ANDREW; CARY, NC; CARY AC; (SO); Golf (VJC); Lcrsse (VJC); Leadership in Various Clubs; Business; Law or Medicine; U of North Carolina Chapel Hill; Dartmouth College

CROCKER, HALEY; FAIRVIEW, NC; AC REYNOLDS HS; (FR); Hnr Roll; Nat Hon Sy; Comm Volntr; Peer Tut/Med; Spec Olymp Vol; Drma Clb; Bnd; Mch Bnd; Stg Cre; Yrbk (P); Medical Profession; Technical Profession; Western Carolina U; U of North Carolina Asheville

CROCKER, TARA; KENLY, NC; WEST JOHNSTON HS; (JR); Hi Hnr Roll; Jr Mshl; Nat Hon Sy; Hab For Humty Volntr; Red Cr Aide; Spec Olymp Vol; Chrch Yth Grp; DARE; Emplmnt; FCA; Ntl Beta Clb; Vsity Clb; Sccr (V CL); Vllyball (V L); Stu Cncl (V); Nursing; Degree in Oncology; East Carolina U; U of North Carolina

CROMARTIE, HARRISON J; CLINTON, NC; CLINTON HS; (FR); Duke TS; Nat Sci Aw; Sci Fairs; FTA; Orch; Bsball (J); Bskball (J); Science & Math Major; Duke U; East Carolina U

CROMWELL, KATI E; HOPE MILLS, NC; SOUTH VIEW HS; (SR); Hnr Roll; St Schl; Peer Tut/Med; FTA; Lttrmn Clb; Mus Clb; Tchrs Aide; Bnd; Clr Grd; Mch Bnd; SP/M/VS; PPSqd (L); Stu Cncl (R); Top Ten Musician; Music Pedagogy; Meredith College; U of North Carolina At Greensboro

CROOK, KELLIE M; SALISBURY, NC; NORTH ROWAN HS; (SO); Hnr Roll; Perf Att; Sci Fairs; ArtClub; Bnd; Mch Bnd; Acceptance Into NCSSM (North Carolina School of Science & Math); Neonatology; Music Education; UNC Greensboro; Catawba

CROSBY, IVEY C; GREENSBORO, NC; SMITH HS; (SO); Hnr Roll; Comm Volntr; DARE; ROTC; SP/M/VS; Nursing; Computer Graphics; Duke U; A & T State U

CROSS, AUDREY A; NEW HILL, NC; NORTHWOOD HS; (SO); 4H Awd; Ctznshp Aw; Hnr Roll; MVP; Nat Sci Aw; Sci Fairs; Hab For Humty Volntr; 4-H; Chess; Chrch Yth Grp; Quiz Bowl; Chr; Sftball (V L); Psychology; U of North Carolina (Chapel Hill); Florida State

CROSS, ELIZABETH; OXFORD, NC; JF WEBB HS; (SR); Duke TS; Hnr Roll; Pres Ac Ftns Aw; WWAHSS; Yth Ldrshp Prog; Comm Volntr; Hab For Humty Volntr; Red Cr Aide; Chrch Yth Grp; Photog; Prom Com; Svce Clb; Tchrs Aide; Ch Chr; Stg Cre; Sccr (V L); Adv Cncl (R); Stu Cncl (R); CR (R); President of Service Club; Speech Pathology; Wake Forest U; Elon U

CROSS, LINDSAY; ASHEBORO, NC; ASHEBORO HS; (JR); Hnr Roll; MVP; Nat Hon Sy; Perf Att; WWAHSS; Yth Ldrshp Prog; Comm Volntr; Chrch Yth Grp; FCA; Key Club; Bskball (V L); Cr Ctry (V L); Sftball (V L); Cl Off (V); All Conference-Basketball / Team MVP; All Conference-Softball / Leading Letter Award; Business Administration; Furman U; Gardner-Webb U

CROWDER, AMANDA L; WINTERVILLE, NC; D H CONLEY HS; (JR); Nat Hon Sy; Comm Volntr; Peer Tut/Med; Ntl Beta Clb; P to P St Amb Prg; French Clb; Pre-Law; Psychology; East Carolina U; U of North Carolina At Chapel Hill

CRUDUP, RONISHA D; RALEIGH, NC; GARNER HS; (FR); Hnr Roll; St of Mnth; Yth Ldrshp Prog; Peer Tut/Med; Chrch Yth Grp; DARE; SADD; Dnce; Gmnstcs (J); Track (J); I Am on the Step Team.; Used to Be the President of S.A.V.E.; Law; Modern Dance; North Carolina State U; Duke U

Cromartie, Harrison J
Clinton HS
Clinton, NC

Creech, Amber
Clayton HS
Zebulon, NC

Craven, Taylor
Pinecrest HS
Pinehurst, NC

Crocker, Tara
West Johnston HS
Kenly, NC

Crook, Kellie M
North Rowan HS
Salisbury, NC

Cranford, Jenna
Salisbury HS
Salisbury, NC

Cozart, Justin
Person HS
Roxboro, NC

Cox, Cassandra M
Heide Trask SR HS
Rocky Point, NC

Covey, Ashley L
Eastern Alamance HS
Mebane, NC

Courts, Kyle J
Middle Creek HS
Raleigh, NC

Copeland, Brandon H
Clinton HS
Clinton, NC

Cornejo, Samuel
Union HS
Clinton, NC

Cox, Brandon
Asheboro HS
Asheboro, NC

Cox, Paula W
Hobbton HS
Mount Olive, NC

Craddock, Jonathan D
Polk Cty HS
Lake Lure, NC

Cranford, Amy E
Asheboro HS
Asheboro, NC

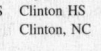

CRUMPTON, BRIAN L; REIDSVILLE, NC; CLOVER GARDEN SCH; (SO); Hi Hnr Roll; Hnr Roll; Otst Ac Ach Awd; Perf Att; Yth Ldrshp Prog; Comm Volntr; Peer Tut/Med; Ntl Beta Clb; Bsball (J); Cl Off (R); Stu Cncl (R); CR (R); Terrific Kid Award; Business / Marketing; Computer Science; U of North Carolina; Duke U

CRUMPTON, HUNTER; ABERDEEN, NC; PINECREST HS; (JR); Duke TS; F Lan Hn Soc; Gov Hnr Prg; Hnr Roll; Perf Att; WWAHSS; Yth Ldrshp Prog; Comm Volntr; Hab For Humty Volntr; Spec Olymp Vol; Chrch Yth Grp; FCA; Key Club; Lttrmn Clb; Ntl Beta Clb; NYLC; Photog; Scouts; Cr Ctry (J L); PP Ftbl (VJ); Sccr (J L); Track (VJ L); CR (R); Spanish Club-Reporter; Active Key Club Member; Anesthesiologist; Pharmacist; U of North Carolina-Chapel Hill; U of North Carolina-Wilmington

CUFFEE II, VINCENT C; RAEFORD, NC; HOKE CTY HS; (SO); Hnr Roll; SP/M/VS; Biochemistry; Physics; UNC-U of North Carolina-Pembroke; U of North Carolina-Chapel Hill

CULBRETH, CASEY; TRYON, NC; POLK CTY HS; (SO); Hi Hnr Roll; WWAHSS; Spec Olymp Vol; Key Club; Spanish Clb; Dnce; Chrldg (VJ); CR (R); 2003 Teen Miss Columbus NC; Early Childhood Education

CULBRETH, MATTHEW; ROSEBORO, NC; LAKEWOOD HS; (FR); Hi Hnr Roll; Perf Att; Sci Fairs; Sci/Math Olympn; Chrch Yth Grp; DARE; Ntl FFA; Chr; Marine Biology; Zoology; Florida State; UNCW

CUMMINGS, AMBER N; HIGH POINT, NC; TRINITY HS; (SO); Hi Hnr Roll; MVP; Chrch Yth Grp; Emplmnt; FCA; Key Club; Prom Com; Svce Clb; Vllyball (V); Stu Cncl; National Society of High School Scholars; Graphic Design; Fashion Design; New York U; Parsons School of Design

CUMMINGS, SALENA K; LUMBERTON, NC; LUMBERTON HS; (JR); Hnr Roll; Chrch Yth Grp; Ntl Beta Clb; Scr Kpr (J); Vllyball (V); NASA; ATSES; Biology Major; Business Management; U of NC Chapel Hill; North Carolina State

CUMMINGS JR, SHAUN L; HAMLET, NC; RICHMOND SR HS; (SO); Hi Hnr Roll; Hnr Roll; Perf Att; Bnd; SP/M/VS; Bsball (L); Scr Kpr (L); Sccr (L); Sftball (L); Wt Lftg (L); U of North Carolina

CUNNINGHAM, MICHAEL; CLINTON, NC; CLINTON HS; (SO); Hi Hnr Roll; Hnr Roll; Otst Ac Ach Awd; Pres Ac Ftns Aw; WWAHSS; Chrch Yth Grp; DARE; Ch Chr; Ftball (V); A-Team or Honor Roll Every Six Weeks; Technology; Accounting; Campbell U; U of Chapel Hill

CUPERO, JENNY B; CARY, NC; GREEN HOPE HS; (JR); DAR; F Lan Hn Soc; Hi Hnr Roll; MVP; Nat Hon Sy; Yth Ldrshp Prog; Comm Volntr; Hab For Humty Volntr; Chrch Yth Grp; DARE; Drma Clb; Emplmnt; FCA; FBLA; P to P St Amb Prg; Prom Com; Chr; Dnce; SP/M/VS; Swmg (V L); Stu Cncl (R); Jan Williamson Valuable Swimmer; First Place Winner of Public Speaking FVLA-State Conference; Communications; Media and Broadcasting; U of North Carolina-Chapel Hill; Elon U

CURETON, ANTONIO A; CHARLOTTE, NC; VANCE HS; (FR); Perf Att; DARE; Chr; Perfect Attendance in 8th Grade; Playing NFL Football; Being a Doctor MD; UCLA; UNC Charlotte

CURRENCE, CHELSEA A; GASTONIA, NC; HUNTER HUSS HS; (SR); Hnr Roll; Comm Volntr; Chr; Track (V); Stu Cncl (P); Gaston County Choral Assemble (A Member); Step Team (I'm Captain & Been on the Team 4 Years); UNC Charlotte; Appalachian State U

CURRIE, BRUNDON; GREENSBORO, NC; DUDLEY HS; (JR); Hnr Roll; Nat Hon Sy; ROTC; Ftball (V); Wrstlg (V)

CURRIE, JACQULYN B; ROWLAND, NC; SOUTH ROBESON HS; (SO); Perf Att; WWAHSS; Ch Chr; Chrldg (V); Architecture; Master's Degree; North Carolina A & T State U

CURRIE, LAMARRA M; APEX, NC; APEX HS; (SR); All Am Sch; F Lan Hn Soc; Hnr Roll; MVP; Nat Hon Sy; Peer Tut/Med; Spec Olymp Vol; Chrch Yth Grp; DARE; Ntl Beta Clb; P to P St Amb Prg; Chrldg (VJ L); PP Ftbl (VJ); Tennis (VJCL); Track (VJCL); Adv Cncl (R); Cl Off (R); Stu Cncl (R); CR (R); Psychology; Communications; UNC Charlotte; UNC Chapel Hill

CURTIS, CATIE; JACKSONVILLE, NC; JACKSONVILLE HS; (SO); Ctznshp Aw; Hnr Roll; St of Mnth; Comm Volntr; SADD; Track (L); Principal's List; Japanese Language Award; Disney Theme Park Manager; Photographer; NC State (North Carolina State); U of North Carolina

CUTHBERTSON, KRISTEN; SALISBURY, NC; WEST ROWAN HS; (FR); Ctznshp Aw; Hnr Roll; Nat Hon Sy; Otst Ac Ach Awd; Pres Ac Ftns Aw; St of Mnth; Peer Tut/Med; Red Cr Aide; DARE; Dbte Team; Pep Squd; SADD; Chr; Stu Cncl (R); HOSA (Health Occupation Students of America); Veterinary Medicine; Medical Assisting; North Carolina State

CZERW, LEE; CLEMMONS, NC; WEST FORSYTH HS; (SO); Duke TS; Hnr Roll; Chrch Yth Grp; Quiz Bowl; German Clb; Ace Academic English Team; German Club; Classics; Biblical Studies

DAGENHART, JORDAN; SALISBURY, NC; SALISBURY HS; (JR); Duke TS; Hi Hnr Roll; Hnr Roll; Nat Hon Sy; WWAHSS; Comm Volntr; Chrch Yth Grp; Emplmnt; Key Club; Scouts; Races National Level ATV; Motocross; Pre-Med; UNC Chapel Hill; Wake Forest U

DAHLGREN, ELIZABETH; CHARLOTTE, NC; SOUTH MECKLENBURG HS; (JR); F Lan Hn Soc; Hnr Roll; Nat Hon Sy; Perf Att; Comm Volntr; French Clb; Dnce; Chrldg; Coaching Cheerleading (Volunteer); Teaching Dance; Psychology; Dance; U of North Carolina At Chapel Hill; Appalachian State U

DALRYMPLE, MICHELLE E; HENDERSONVILLE, NC; EAST HENDERSON HS; (SO); Hi Hnr Roll; Hnr Roll; Comm Volntr; Emplmnt; Orch; Golf (J); Track (V C); Physical Therapy; Environmental; UNC Asheville; UNC Wilmington

DALTON, ELIZABETH; OXFORD, NC; J F WEBB HS; (SO); Hnr Roll; Perf Att; Hosp Aide; Spec Olymp Vol; Chrch Yth Grp; Emplmnt; Nurse Practitioner; Doctor; North Carolina State U

DAMA, CHINU; WINSTON-SALEM, NC; REYNOLDS HS; (JR); F Lan Hn Soc; Hnr Roll; Nat Hon Sy; Perf Att; WWAHSS; Comm Volntr; Hab For Humty Volntr; Peer Tut/Med; Off Aide; Sci Clb; Svce Clb; French Clb; 2 Magna Cum Laude & 1 Maxima Cum Laude Awards on the National Latin Exam; National French Honor Society & National Art Honor Society; Pre-Med; Duke U

DAMERON, JENNIFER J; SILER CITY, NC; JORDAN MATTHEWS HS; (SO); Hnr Roll; MVP; St of Mnth; WWAHSS; Peer Tut/Med; Red Cr Aide; 4-H; DECA; Emplmnt; FCA; Vsity Clb; Bskball (V L); Sftball (V L); Tennis (V L); 4-H/President; All Conference Tennis/All County Basketball; Cert. Athletic Trainer; Sports Medicine; U of South Carolina; U of North Carolina

DAMOIN, KOMLA; LAURINBURG, NC; SCOTLAND HS; (SO); F Lan Hn Soc; Hnr Roll; MVP; Otst Ac Ach Awd; Perf Att; St of Mnth; Mth Clb/Tm; Sccr (V); Math Team; Duke U; NC State

DAMON, TORY T; CLINTON, NC; CLINTON HS; (SO); Hnr Roll; Peer Tut/Med; Chrch Yth Grp; DARE; Pep Squd; Chrldg (JC); PP Ftbl (J); Medical Major; Degree of Medicine

DANG, CRYSTAL; FAYETTEVILLE, NC; DOUGLAS BYRD HS; (JR); Hi Hnr Roll; Hnr Roll; WWAHSS; Peer Tut/Med; Key Club; Key Club; Finance Academy; Business; UNC Wilmington; East Carolina U

DANG, HEATHER A; FAYETTEVILLE, NC; DOUGLAS BYRD HS; (JR); Hi Hnr Roll; Hnr Roll; Comm Volntr; Peer Tut/Med; DARE; Emplmnt; Key Club; Key Club; Finance Academy; Business; Arts; UNC Wilmington; East Carolina U

DANIEL, BRITTANY L; WAKE FOREST, NC; WAKE FOREST-ROLESVILLE HS; (JR); Hnr Roll; Jr Mshl; Nat Hon Sy; Pres Ac Ftns Aw; WWAHSS; 4-H; FCA; FBLA; Key Club; Ntl Beta Clb; Ntl FFA; ROTC; Bskball (J); Chrldg (J); Vllyball (VJ); Jr. Marshall Class Rank-20th; Early Childhood Education; North Carolina State U; U of North Carolina @ Chapel Hill

DANIEL, BROOKE L; WAKE FOREST, NC; WAKE FOREST-ROLESVILLE HS; (JR); Jr Mshl; Nat Hon Sy; Pres Ac Ftns Aw; WWAHSS; 4-H; FCA; FBLA; Key Club; Ntl FFA; Latin Clb; FFA Federation President; North Carolina State U

DANIEL, JONATHAN; SILER CITY, NC; JORDAN MATTHEWS HS; (FR); Duke TS; Hi Hnr Roll; Chrch Yth Grp; Golf (V); U of North Carolina At Chapel Hill; North Carolina State U

DANIELS, BRIAN L; FAYETTEVILLE, NC; WESTOVER HS; (FR); Pres Ac Ftns Aw; St of Mnth; Ftball (J); Terrific Kid of the Year; Lawyer; U of North Carolina At Chapel Hill

DANIELS, CAITLIN R; APEX, NC; CARY AC; (SO); Hi Hnr Roll; Nat Hon Sy; Otst Ac Ach Awd; WWAHSS; Comm Volntr; Chrch Yth Grp; Drma Clb; Key Club; Ntl Beta Clb; Chr; SP/M/VS; Fld Hky (VJ L); PP Ftbl; Sccr (J); Sftball (V); Stu Cncl (S); Key Club Vice President; Cognitive Neuroscience; Performing Arts

DANIELS, DANA M; BENSON, NC; SOUTH JOHNSTON HS; (SO); Ctznshp Aw; Hi Hnr Roll; Hnr Roll; Perf Att; Chrch Yth Grp; Ntl Beta Clb; Ntl FFA; Dnce; Star Greenhand Award (FFA); Lawyer; Doctor; Campbell U; UNC-Wilmington

DANIELS, ERIC; ELIZABETH CITY, NC; PASQUOTANK CTY HS; (JR); Nat Hon Sy; Comm Volntr; Cr Ctry; Sccr (V); Computer Programming; Computer Engineering; North Carolina State U; East Carolina U

DANIELS, JESSICA; JACKSONVILLE, NC; NORTHSIDE HS; (JR); Hnr Roll; Otst Ac Ach Awd; Perf Att; Sci Fairs; St of Mnth; WWAHSS; Red Cr Aide; Mod UN; Mus Clb; ROTC; Chr; Ch Chr; Track (V); Stu Cncl (R); Bachelor's Degree; Associate's Degree; VCU (Virginia Commonwealth U); U Arts (The U of the Arts)

DANIELS, KATHRYN; GOLDSBORO, NC; WAYNE CHRISTIAN SCH; (MS); Hi Hnr Roll; Hnr Roll; Sci/Math Olympn; Chrch Yth Grp; Ntl Beta Clb; Scouts; Bskball (V L); Sftball (V L); Vllyball (V L); Stu Cncl (R)

DANIELS, LAURIN N; ARCHDALE, NC; TRINITY HS; (SO); Hi Hnr Roll; Nat Hon Sy; Otst Ac Ach Awd; Pres Sch; USAA; WWAHSS; Yth Ldrshp Prog; Drma Clb; HO'Br Yth Ldrshp; Bnd; Clr Grd; Mch Bnd; SP/M/VS; Carolina Honor Band (UNCG); Music Direction; Christian Ministry; Brevard College; Meredith College

DANIELS, PRISHONDA; GOLDSBORO, NC; EASTERN WAYNE HS; (JR); All Am Sch; Ctznshp Aw; Hnr Roll; WWAHSS; ArtClub; Acpl Chr; Chr; Ch Chr; Art/English Education; East Carolina U; Elizabeth City State U

DAUGHTRIDGE, GIFFIN; AHOSKIE, NC; RIDGECROFT SCH; (SO); Bnd; Bsball (V L); Bskball (JC); Sccr (V L); Cl Off (S, T); Stu Cncl (S, T); Key Club Treasurer; VFW Essay Contest Winner; UNC; Princeton U

DAVENPORT, TIERRA; WILLIAMSTON, NC; WILLIAMSTON HS; (FR); Duke TS; Hnr Roll; Otst Ac Ach Awd; Perf Att; St of Mnth; Chrch Yth Grp; FCA; FBLA; Key Club; SADD; Ch Chr; Cr Ctry (V); Sftball (J); Track (V); Law; Medical; UNC Chapel Hill; NC State

DAVIS, AMANDA B; INDIAN TRAIL, NC; CHARLOTTE CHRISTIAN SCH; (SO); Duke TS; F Lan Hn Soc; Hi Hnr Roll; Yth Ldrshp Prog; Comm Volntr; Hosp Aide; Peer Tut/Med; Dbte Team; P to P St Amb Prg; Svce Clb; Spch Team; SADD; Adv Cncl (R); Stu Cncl (P); CR (P, R); Lit Mag (E); Sch Ppr (R, P); Yrbk (R, P); Piano Study for 9 Years; Medical Club; Pre-Med; Pre-Law; Duke U; Johns Hopkins U

DAVIS, CHARLESTON M; WINSTON SALEM, NC; REYNOLDS HS; (JR); Hnr Roll; Nat Mrt LOC; WWAHSS; Comm Volntr; Chess; Ftball (VJ); Wt Lftg (VJ); Computer; Science; Virginia Tech; Tennessee State

DAVIS, ERIN A; PINETOWN, NC; NORTHSIDE HS; (FR); Hi Hnr Roll; WWAHSS; Yth Ldrshp Prog; Comm Volntr; Emplmnt; Key Club; Become a Lawyer; East Carolina U; U of North Carolina

DAVIS, FELICIA; CAMERON, NC; PINECREST HS; (SR); Hnr Roll; WWAHSS; Emplmnt; FBLA; P to P St Amb Prg; Criminal Psychologist; Pre-Med Dentist; U of NC At Greensboro (UNCG); Texas Southern U (TSU)

DAVIS, HEATHER; MOUNT AIRY, NC; NORTH SURRY HS; (SR); Hi Hnr Roll; Nat Hon Sy; WWAHSS; Comm Volntr; Peer Tut/Med; Spec Olymp Vol; Chrch Yth Grp; Emplmnt; FCA; Key Club; Ch Chr; Yrbk (E); Communications/Broadcasting; Spanish; Queens U of Charlotte; Western Carolina U

DAVIS, IMOGENE; HILLSBOROUGH, NC; CEDAR RIDGE HS; (SR); 4H Awd; Hnr Roll; Nat Hon Sy; Comm Volntr; 4-H; ArtClub; Ntl FFA; Scouts; Wdwrkg Clb; French Clb; Orch; PP Ftbl (VJ); Swmg (J); Stu Cncl (R); Lit Mag (E); Art Student - Level III; Play the Violin - Currently Not in Ensemble; Animal Science / Writing; Veterinary Medicine; North Carolina State U; Texas A & M U

DAVIS, JONQUEZ L; CHARLOTTE, NC; PHILLIP O BERRY AC TECH; (JR); Perf Att; St of Mnth; WWAHSS; Comm Volntr; Hab For Humty Volntr; Chrch Yth Grp; Emplmnt; Ftball (VJ); Wrstlg (J); Male Role Model of the Year; NAACP Legal Defense Student Achievement Award; Elec. Engineering; Computer Engineering

DAVIS, JOSEPH A; GASTONIA, NC; VICTORY CHRISTIAN AC; (SO); Ctznshp Aw; DARE; Cr Ctry; Journalism; Theatre

DAVIS, LAUREN M; EAST BEND, NC; FORBUSH HS; (FR); Hi Hnr Roll; Perf Att; Pres Ac Ftns Aw; Pep Squd; Bnd; Chrldg (J); Health Science; Medical; East Carolina U; U of NC At Chapel Hill

DAVIS, MEG; INDIAN TRAIL, NC; HOMESCHOOL; (JR); 4-H; Chrch Yth Grp; Drma Clb; Emplmnt; SP/M/VS; Stg Cre; English Literature; Theater Arts; Southeastern College

DAVIS, SHANNON R; GOLDSBORO, NC; CHARLES B AYCOCK HS; (JR); All Am Sch; Ctznshp Aw; Hnr Roll; Nat Hon Sy; Nat Ldrshp Svc; Otst Ac Ach Awd; St of Mnth; USAA; WWAHSS; Yth Ldrshp Prog; Comm Volntr; Chrch Yth Grp; Jr Ach; Ntl Beta Clb; Pep Squd; P to P St Amb Prg; Photog; Tchrs Aide; French Clb; Stg Cre; Yrbk (P); Theatre Arts; Editor's Choice Award-Poetry; Bachelor's Degree; PhD; Oral Roberts U; Meredith College

DAVIS, TANESHA; TARBORO, NC; SOUTHWEST EDGECOMBE HS; (SR); Hi Hnr Roll; Hnr Roll; WWAHSS; Cmptr Clb; Emplmnt; FBLA; Prom Com; FCCLA (Club); Nursing; Accounting; East Carolina U; Fayetteville State U

DAWKINS, DORETHA; CONCORD, NC; NORTHWEST CABARRUS MS; (MS); Ctznshp Aw; Hi Hnr Roll; Hnr Roll; Otst Ac Ach Awd; Perf Att; Yth Ldrshp Prog; Comm Volntr; Peer Tut/Med; ArtClub; Chrch Yth Grp; DARE; Jr Ach; Mth Clb/Tm; Mus Clb; Pep Squd; Clb; Bnd; Ch Chr; Dnce; Pep Bnd; CR (S, R); All-County Band Of Cabarrus County; Accepted to Western Carolina U For Youth Legislators For Youth Leadership; Law Degree; Arts Degree; Harvard Law; U Of North Carolina Chapel Hill

DAWSON, BRITTANY; WINTERVILLE, NC; D H CONLEY HS; (FR); Hnr Roll; Chrch Yth Grp; Dnce; Law School; Lawyer; Georgia State U

Davis, Tanesha
Southwest Edgecombe HS
Tarboro, NC

Davis, Charleston M
Reynolds HS
Winston Salem, NC

Cuthbertson, Kristen
West Rowan HS
Salisbury, NC

Cupero, Jenny B
Green Hope HS
Cary, NC

Cummings Jr, Shaun L
Richmond SR HS
Hamlet, NC

National
Honor Roll
Spring 2005

Cummings, Amber N
Trinity HS
High Point, NC

Currence, Chelsea A
Hunter Huss HS
Gastonia, NC

Dahlgren, Elizabeth
South Mecklenburg HS
Charlotte, NC

Davis, Jonquez L
Phillip O Berry AC Tech
Charlotte, NC

Davis, Joseph A
Victory Christian AC
Gastonia, NC

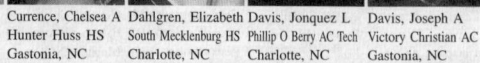

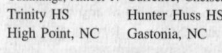

DAWSON, PHYLENCIA; AUTRYVILLE, NC; MIDWAY HS; (FR); Hnr Roll; Perf Att; Chrch Yth Grp; FBLA; Chr; Ch Chr; FCCLA - Family Career & Community Leaders of America; Legal Degree; NC State Fayetteville State U; Mt Olive College

DAWSON JR, TONY R; GATES, NC; GATES CTY HS; (SO); Ctznshp Aw; Hnr Roll; MVP; Perf Att; Comm Volntr; 4-H; Bskball (J); Cr Ctry (V); Tennis (V); Cross Country: Best Male (2004); Elizabeth City State U: Summer Transportation; Math; Science; UNC Chapel Hill; NC State U

DEAN, TRAVIS; REIDSVILLE, NC; REIDSVILLE HS; (FR); Hnr Roll; Bskball; Ftball; Track; Business; Auto Body

DEANS, CHRISTOPHER A; BATTLEBORO, NC; NORTH EDGECOMBE HS; (SO); Ctznshp Aw; Hnr Roll; Otst Ac Ach Awd; Perf Att; Comm Volntr; Chrch Yth Grp; Ntl FFA; Voc Ind Clb Am; Ftball (VJ); Wt Lftg (V); Engineering; North Carolina Agriculture & Technical State U; Elizabeth City State

DEASON, CAROL J; MATTHEWS, NC; COVENANT DAY SCH; (SO); Hnr Roll; WWAHSS; Chrch Yth Grp; Key Club; French Clb; Chr; SP/M/VS; Stg Cre; Sccr (V); Sftball (J); Tennis (J); Piano; Pre-Med; Nursing

DEBRO, CANDY; ROANOKE RAPIDS, NC; ROANOKE RAPIDS HS; (SO); Ctznshp Aw; Hi Hnr Roll; Hnr Roll; Nat Hon Sy; St of Mnth; WWAHSS; Peer Tut/Med; Chrch Yth Grp; Jr Ach; Lib Aide; Scouts; Chr; Ch Chr; Dnce; SP/M/VS; Cl Off (S); Stu Cncl (V); Attended NC School of Arts; Ballet & Contemporary Dance; Psychology; Dental Hygienist; U of Georgia; Morgan State U

DE BRUN, CAMERON; CHARLOTTE, NC; COVENANT DAY SCH; (FR); Duke TS; Dbte Team; Off Aide; Bsball (J); Tennis (V L); French Club; Engineering (Nuclear), Law; U of California; Chapel Hill

DEDMON, AMANDA L; VALE, NC; LINCOLN SCH OF TECH; (JR); Comm Volntr; Chrch Yth Grp; DARE; DECA; Emplmnt; FTA; Prom Com; Ch Chr; Sftball (L); Won 2nd Place in DECA Competition; Volunteered 104 Hours at Health Dept; Advertising & Marketing; Mathematic Teacher; Winthrop U

DEESE, STEPHANIE A; MARSHVILLE, NC; ANSON HS; (JR); MVP; Otst Ac Ach Awd; Pres Ac Ftns Aw; St of Mnth; Comm Volntr; Peer Tut/Med; ArtClub; BPA; Emplmnt; FTA; Mus Clb; Off Aide; Prom Com; Tchrs Aide; Chr; Ch Chr; Dnce; GAA (J); PP Ftbl (V); Sftball (V); Cl Off (V); Stu Cncl (V); CR (P); Yrbk (P); Leadership; Appreciation; Cosmetology; Dance; Wingate U; Duke U

DEGRAFFENREIDT, ADRIAN R; SILER CITY, NC; JORDAN MATTHEWS HS; (FR); All Am Sch; Ctznshp Aw; Hi Hnr Roll; Nat Hon Sy; Otst Ac Ach Awd; Perf Att; Sci/Math Olympn; Comm Volntr; Peer Tut/Med; DARE; Quiz Bowl; Sci Clb; President's Award for Educational Excellence; Gear Up; Marketing; Business; U of North Carolina; Wake Forest

DEITZ, BRITTANY; HICKORY, NC; ST STEPHENS HS; Ctznshp Aw; Hi Hnr Roll; Hnr Roll; Pres Ac Ftns Aw; Sci Fairs; St of Mnth; Chrch Yth Grp; Spanish Clb; Chr; Chrldg (VJ); GAA (J); Gmnstcs (J); Tennis (L); Track (J); Vllyball (J); Junior Beta Club; Juniorettes-Secretary; UNC-Medicine; Wake Forest-Medicine; UN Chapel Hill; Wake Forest

DEJAK, JESSICA; SOUTHERN PINES, NC; (SO); Hnr Roll; Chrch Yth Grp; Dbte Team; Key Club; Ch Chr; Cr Ctry (J); Scr Kpr (J); Track (J); 4 Years Piano; Journalism; Campbell U; Wingate U

DE LA PENA, AXEL; MAIDEN, NC; LINCOLN CHARTER SCH; (SO); Hnr Roll; Sci Fairs; Chess; Chrch Yth Grp; SP/M/VS; Bsball (V); Sccr (V); Med School; Business; Technologico De Monterrey; U of Texas

DELGADO CRUZ, JOSHUA; FAYETTEVILLE, NC; E E SMITH SR HS; (SR); Nat Hon Sy; WWAHSS; Bnd; Mch Bnd; Wrstlg (V L); National Honor Society; Mechanical Engineers; North Carolina Agricultural & Technical State U

DE LOATCH, EUGENIA R; GRAHAM, NC; GRAHAM HS; (JR); Hnr Roll; Nat Hon Sy; Otst Ac Ach Awd; WWAHSS; Yth Ldrshp Prog; Comm Volntr; Chrch Yth Grp; Emplmnt; FTA; Key Club; P to P St Amb Prg; Prom Com; SADD; French Clb; Chr; SP/M/VS; Adv Cncl (R); Cl Off (P); Stu Cncl (R); CR (R); Communications (Media, Etc.)

DE LOS SANTOS, ANDREW C; RALEIGH, NC; WAKEFIELD HS; (JR); Hnr Roll; WWAHSS; Chrch Yth Grp; Emplmnt; FCA; Key Club; Pep Squd; Lcrsse (V L); National Achievers Society; Who's Who of American HS Students; U of North Carolina, Chapel Hill; North Carolina State

DEMPSEY, SARAH; MT AIRY, NC; NORTH SURRY HS; (SO); Hnr Roll; WWAHSS; Comm Volntr; Chrch Yth Grp; Pharmacy; Anesthesiologist; UNC Chapel Hill; East Carolina

DENG, HUIYING; CHAPEL HILL, NC; CHAPEL HILL HS; (SO); Duke TS; Kwnis Aw; Comm Volntr; Hab For Humty Volntr; Peer Tut/Med; 4-H; Key Club; Chr; Stu Cncl (R); National Piano / Playing Auditions - District; Veterinary Medicine; Computer Sciences; North Carolina State U; U of North Carolina Chapel Hill

DENTON, JONATHAN F; BROADWAY, NC; WESTERN HARNETT HS; (SO); Hi Hnr Roll; Hnr Roll; Kwnis Aw; Otst Ac Ach Awd; Perf Att; Sci Fairs; Spec Olymp Vol; Chrch Yth Grp; DARE; Chr; Ch Chr; School Awards; Computer Engineer; Computer Technician; Fayetteville State U; CCCC

DENTON, KASEY; LOUISBURG, NC; FRANKLINTON HS; (FR); Hnr Roll; Nat Mrt LOC; Perf Att; St of Mnth; Yth Ldrshp Prog; Comm Volntr; Chrch Yth Grp; Civil Air Pat; DARE; FCA; FTA; SADD; Ch Chr; Bskball (J); Law Enforcement; Criminology; North Carolina State U; Shaw U

DESANDRE, RICHARD M; LAURINBURG, NC; SCOTLAND HS; (SO); Ctznshp Aw; Hnr Roll; Perf Att; Pres Ac Ftns Aw; St of Mnth; WWAHSS; Emplmnt; Key Club; Scouts; Pre-Med; North Carolina State U; U of North Carolina Chapel Hill

DESPAIN, AINSLEY M; CARY, NC; ATHENS DRIVE HS; (SO); Hnr Roll; Nat Sci Aw; Otst Ac Ach Awd; Chrch Yth Grp; DARE; Key Club; Mth Clb/Tm; SADD; Spanish Clb; Ch Chr; Young Womanhood Recognition (LDS Church); Aeronautics; Psychology; North Carolina State U; Brigham Young U

DEUTSCH, STEPHEN; GREENSBORO, NC; GRIMSLEY HS; (SR); Duke TS; Hi Hnr Roll; Nat Hon Sy; Perf Att; Comm Volntr; Hab For Humty Volntr; Chess; Sci Clb; Svce Clb; Bnd; Mch Bnd; Tennis (V); Cl Off (S, T); Drumline; Governor's Page; Business Management; Communications

DEVAULT, GREG; MOCKSVILLE, NC; (FR); Hnr Roll; Nat Hon Sy; Otst Ac Ach Awd; Perf Att; Pres Ac Ftns Aw; Comm Volntr; Chrch Yth Grp; DARE; FCA; Mus Clb; Bnd; Jzz Bnd; Mch Bnd; Pep Bnd; Engineer; Drafting; Duke U

DE WALD, LEIA; WASHINGTON, NC; NORTHSIDE HS; (SO); Hi Hnr Roll; Hnr Roll; Nat Hon Sy; Nat Ldrshp Svc; Otst Ac Ach Awd; Perf Att; WWAHSS; Yth Ldrshp Prog; Comm Volntr; Hosp Aide; Red Cr Aide; Chrch Yth Grp; Drma Clb; Emplmnt; FCA; HO'Br Yth Ldrshp; Key Club; Ntl Beta Clb; SADD; Chr; Ch Chr; SP/M/VS; Stg Cre; Vllyball (V); Cl Off (S); Stu Cncl (R); CR (S); Job Shadow Day Participant; Principal's Award; Music/ Drama Major; Education Major; U of North Carolina-Chapel Hill; Roanoke Bible College

DIAL, LSA-ANA; PEMBROKE, NC; PURNELL SWETT HS; (FR); Perf Att; Yth Ldrshp Prog; Chrch Yth Grp; DARE; Bnd; Mch Bnd; Band Member; Physical Therapist; Heart Surgeon; Duke U; U of North Carolina Pembroke

DICKERSON, SHARMEKA; ROCKY MOUNT, NC; NASH CTRL HS; (JR); Hnr Roll; Peer Tut/Med; Emplmnt; Bskball (V CL); Accounting; Business Management; U of North Carolina Chapel Hill; North Carolina A & T State U

DIGGS, MATTHEW A; MATTHEWS, NC; DAVID W BUTLER HS; (JR); Hnr Roll; WWAHSS; Yth Ldrshp Prog; Chrch Yth Grp; DARE; Emplmnt; Key Club; Svce Clb; French Clb; Bnd; Jzz Bnd; Yrbk (R, P); Business; Appalachian State U; UNC Charlotte

DISHAROON, KAYLA M; MOORESVILLE, NC; LAKE NORMAN HS; MS; Hnr Roll; Nat Hon Sy; Pres Sch; Comm Volntr; Chrch Yth Grp; Ntl Beta Clb; Clr Grd; Swim Team-YMCA; School News Broadcasting Club; Registered Nurse At St. Jude Hospital; Nurse Anesthetist At St Jude; Wake Forest U; U of North Carolina Wilmington

DIXON, JENNIFER; MONROE, NC; COVENANT DAY SCH; (JR); F Lan Hn Soc; Hi Hnr Roll; Nat Hon Sy; Nat Mrt LOC; Otst Ac Ach Awd; Pres Sch; Sci/Math Olympn; WWAHSS; Comm Volntr; Chrch Yth Grp; Jr Ach; Jr Cls League; Photog; Prom Com; Svce Clb; Latin Clb; Stu Cncl (T); Yrbk (E, P); 10 Years of Gymnastics; 11 Years of Piano; Physics; Astronomy; Davidson College; UNC Chapel Hill

DIXON, KRISTEN; JACKSONVILLE, NC; JACKSONVILLE HS; (FR); Hnr Roll; Otst Ac Ach Awd; Perf Att; St of Mnth; Phd; U of North Carolina Wilm.

DIXON, THOMAS K; SANFORD, NC; PROVISIONS AC; (SO); Hnr Roll; Sci Fairs; Sci/Math Olympn; WWAHSS; Chess; DARE; Chess Club; Science Club; Physical Therapy; Occupational Therapy; East Carolina U

DOBBIN, JASMINE; PIKEVILLE, NC; CHARLES B AYCOCK HS; (SO); Hnr Roll; Yth Ldrshp Prog; Comm Volntr; Chrch Yth Grp; ROTC; Ch Chr; Bskball (V); Cr Ctry (V); Sftball (V); Science; Child Care; U North Carolina Chapel Hill; Florida State U

DOBSON, LANINA; GOLDSBORO, NC; SPRING CREEK HS; (SO); Hnr Roll; Hab For Humty Volntr; Quiz Bowl; Track; Vllyball (JC); Yrbk (E); Prospective Member of National Young Leaders Conf; Journalism; Communication; Hollins U; Northwestern U

DOEBLER, KAYLA M; HENDERSONVILLE, NC; EAST HENDERSON HS; (SO); 4H Awd; Ctznshp Aw; Hnr Roll; Otst Ac Ach Awd; Perf Att; Comm Volntr; 4-H; DARE; Wt Lftg; Botany; Business; U of North Carolina-Chapel Hill; Clemson U, South Carolina

DOING, DUSTIN L; RALEIGH, NC; WAKEFIELD HS; (FR); Duke TS; Hi Hnr Roll; Drma Clb; Key Club; P to P St Amb Prg; SP/M/VS

DOLD, NICHOLAS; RALEIGH, NC; CARDINAL GIBBONS HS; (SO); Duke TS; Hnr Roll; Otst Ac Ach Awd; Sci Fairs; Sci/Math Olympn; WWAHSS; Comm Volntr; Chrch Yth Grp; Dbte Team; Emplmnt; HO'Br Yth Ldrshp; JSA; Mus Clb; NYLC; Chr; Orch; Stu Cncl (V); Lit Mag (E); Accompanist Extraordinaire - Award; 2nd Place Winner - Rotary Essay Contest; Music - Pedagogy / Performance; Liberal Arts / Literature; Oberlin Conservatory; St John's College

DOLLBERRY, ANTONIO; HAMILTON, NC; ROANOKE HS; (FR); 4H Awd; WWAHSS; Yth Ldrshp Prog; Peer Tut/Med; 4-H; FBLA; Ch Chr; CR (R); Best Dressed; Best Singer; Criminal Justice; Clothing Designer; Howard U; St Augustine

DONATHAN, JENNY L; WADESBORO, NC; ANSON HS; (FR); Hi Hnr Roll; Hnr Roll; Nat Hon Sy; Comm Volntr; Hosp Aide; Chrch Yth Grp; Emplmnt; Clb; Bnd; Sftball (V L); Vllyball (J); Yrbk (R, P); Career Club - Public Speaking 1st Place Regional / 3rd Place State; Economics; Teaching; Campbell U; UNC Chapel Hill

DONG, MEI Q; YANCEYVILLE, NC; BARTLETT YANCEY HS; (JR); Hi Hnr Roll; Hnr Roll; Jr Mshl; Otst Ac Ach Awd; Perf Att; St Schl; St of Mnth; Comm Volntr; Peer Tut/Med; Emplmnt; Key Club; Ntl Beta Clb; ROTC; Drl Tm; Sch Ppr (R); Chemical Engineering; Biomedical Engineering

DORAN, KELLY; SALISBURY, NC; SALISBURY HS; (JR); Sccr (J); Tennis (VJ L); Cl Off (V, S); Stu Cncl (S); CR (R); NHS - President; Key Club VP; Teacher; Youth Leader; UNC Chapel Hill; Wake Forest U

DOSS, MAGAN; MOCKSVILLE, NC; DAVIE CTY HS; (FR); Ctznshp Aw; Duke TS; Hnr Roll; MVP; Otst Ac Ach Awd; Sci Fairs; Sci/Math Olympn; St of Mnth; Comm Volntr; Peer Tut/Med; 4-H; Chrch Yth Grp; Emplmnt; Ntl Beta Clb, Sci Clb; Bnd; SP/M/VS; Gmnstcs (J); Sccr (VJ); Sftball (VJ); Cultural Dance; Designing; Math; Wake Forest U; U of New York

DOTSON, ALYSSA; FOREST CITY, NC; CHASE HS; (JR); Ctznshp Aw; F Lan Hn Soc; Hnr Roll; MVP; Nat Hon Sy; Nat Ldrshp Svc; WWAHSS; Comm Volntr; Peer Tut/Med; Chrch Yth Grp; FCA; Pep Squd; SADD; Vsity Clb; Clb; Ch Chr; Chrldg (J); Swmg (V L); Stu Cncl (R); Health Occupations Students of America; Pre-Med; Biology; UNC Chapel Hill; USC Columbia

DOTY, LINDSEY E; LA GRANGE, NC; EASTERN WAYNE HS; (JR); Hi Hnr Roll; Nat Hon Sy; Otst Ac Ach Awd; Perf Att; Sci Fairs; WWAHSS; Comm Volntr; Emplmnt; Key Club; Mth Clb/Tm; Ntl Beta Clb; Prom Com; Sci Clb; Foreign Clb; Horseback Riding-Outside of School; Registered Nurse; East Carolina U; U of North Carolina at Chapel Hill

DOUGLAS, RENALDO; FAYETTEVILLE, NC; DOUGLAS BYRD HS; (JR); Hi Hnr Roll; Hnr Roll; Perf Att; WWAHSS; Peer Tut/Med; ArtClub; Chrch Yth Grp; Key Club; Voc Ind Clb Am; Ftball (V); Golf (V); Wrstlg (V); Outstanding Junior - Key Club; Key Club President - Douglas Byrd HS; Architectural Engineering; Civil Engineering; North Carolina State; U of Georgia Tech

DOVE, JENNIFER N; KINSTON, NC; SOUTH LENOIR HS; (JR); Hnr Roll; Nat Hon Sy; Perf Att; WWAHSS; Comm Volntr; Chrch Yth Grp; Emplmnt; Business; Meredith College; North Carolina State U

DOWDA JR, TRAVIS; PLEASANT GARDEN, NC; SOUTHEAST GUILFORD HS; (SR); Hnr Roll; MVP; Nat Stu Ath Day Aw; WWAHSS; Comm Volntr; Key Club; Bsball (V L); Ftball (V CL); Track (V); Wt Lftg (V); All County Football Player of the Year; All Conference-Football & Baseball, Most Athletic Senior; Appalachian State

DOWNEY, AMANDA; BROADWAY, NC; LEE CTY HS; (SO); Hnr Roll; Otst Ac Ach Awd; Key Club; Chrldg (V); Juris Doctor Degree (J.D.); Master of Laws, Doctor of Judicial Science; Harvard, Yale, Georgetown, Cornell, Duke, Emory

DOWNEY, TIFFANY C; BUTNER, NC; SOUTH-GRANVILLE HS; (FR); Hnr Roll; Ch Chr; Bskball (J); Cr Ctry; Sftball (J); South-Granville School of Health & Life Science; Computer Engineer; Interior Designer; U of North Carolina; North Carolina of Agriculture & Technology

DOZIER, WESLEY E; CORNELIUS, NC; HOPEWELL HS; (JR); Hnr Roll; Pres Ac Ftns Aw; Sci Fairs; WWAHSS; Comm Volntr; Chrch Yth Grp; DECA; Emplmnt; FCA; Bsball (V); Camp Counselor for Baseball; Pre-Law; Business Administration; U of North Carolina-Chapel Hill; Elon U

DOZIER N'KOZI, JASMINE K; CHARLOTTE, NC; HARDING UNIVERSITY HS; (SO); Hi Hnr Roll; Hnr Roll; Perf Att; Comm Volntr; Hosp Aide; Peer Tut/Med; DARE; Emplmnt; Jr Ach; Photog; SADD; Ch Chr; Dnce; SP/M/VS; Golf; Sftball (V L); Yrbk (P); Fighting Back; Poetry & Arts; Pediatrician; Forensic Science; Florida A & M U; U of North Carolina At Chapel Hill

DRAYTON, CLARENCE; CLINTON, NC; CLINTON HS; (JR); Hi Hnr Roll; Otst Ac Ach Awd; St of Mnth; Military; Business; North Carolina State U; Duke U

Donathan, Jenny L
Anson HS
Wadesboro, NC

De Wald, Leia
Northside HS
Washington, NC

Deutsch, Stephen
Grimsley HS
Greensboro, NC

National
Honor Roll
Spring 2005

Deng, Huiying
Chapel Hill HS
Chapel Hill, NC

Disharoon, Kayla M
Lake Norman HS
Mooresville, NC

Dozier N'Kozi, Jasmine K
Harding University HS
Charlotte, NC

DREW, ERIN; MOORESVILLE, NC; LAKE NORMAN HS; (JR); Gov Hnr Prg; Hi Hnr Roll; Hnr Roll; Jr Mshl; Nat Hon Sy; Perf Att; Hab For Humty Volntr; Dbte Team; Emplmnt; Ntl Beta Clb; Prom Com; PP Ftbl (J); Vllyball (J); Sch Ppr (R); Nomination to National Young Leaders Conference; Invitation to National Student Leadership Conference; Secondary Education; English; Appalachian State U; U of North Carolina Chapel Hill

DREW, MARY M; MAGNOLIA, NC; JAMES KENAN HS; (SO); Hnr Roll; Nat Hon Sy; WWAHSS; Key Club; Arch (J); Skt Tgt Sh (J); Registered Nurse; Agricultural Science; East Carolina U; North Carolina State U

DUBOIS, TIFFANY N; MURPHY, NC; HIWASSEE DAM HS; (SO); All Am Sch; Hnr Roll; WWAHSS; Comm Volntr; ArtClub; Chrch Yth Grp; Pep Squd; Prom Com; Bnd; Chr; Pep Bnd; PP Ftbl (C); Track (V); Wrstlg (V); Stu Cncl (R); Highest Grade in Biology Award; Student Government Association; Forensic Anthropology; Psychology/Sociology; U of Florida; Washington U in St. Louis

DUBOSE, EMMA; CHARLOTTE, NC; SOUTH MECKLENBURG; (SO); Duke TS; Hnr Roll; Nat Hon Sy; WWAHSS; Comm Volntr; Emplmnt; SADD; Dnce; Stg Cre; Yrbk (R); Communications; College of Charleston; North Carolina State

DUBSON, TAMARA L; KERNERSVILLE, NC; CARVER HS; (SR); Hi Hnr Roll; WWAHSS; Comm Volntr; FBLA; Chr; Chrldg (VJCL); Outstanding Student; Community Service Award; Pre-Med; Doctorate Degree; East Carolina U; Forsyth Tech

DUFF, KATHERINE E; FAYETTEVILLE, NC; TERRY SANFORD HS; SP/M/VS; Bskball (J); Sccr (J); Vllyball (J); A-B Honor Roll; Academic Letter; Teaching; UNC-Wilmington (U of N Carolina); Elon College

DULUC, WENDY; CHARLOTTE, NC; VANCE; (JR); Hi Hnr Roll; Peer Tut/Med; DARE; Emplmnt; Key Club

DUNBAR, HEATHER; RALEIGH, NC; RALEIGH SR HS; (JR); Hi Hnr Roll; WWAHSS; Comm Volntr; Key Club; HOSA Member; Forensic Pathologist; Chapel Hill

DUNCAN, SHAINA M; CHARLOTTE, NC; CRAMERTON CHRISTIAN AC; (JR); Hi Hnr Roll; Hnr Roll; Chrch Yth Grp; Emplmnt; FCA; Ch Chr; Bskball (V); PP Ftbl (J); Completed POW Mentorship Program; BA in Biblical Studies; Master of Arts in Intercultural Studies; Southeastern College At Wake Forest

DUNHAM, SHAKERA C; SAINT PAULS, NC; ST PAUL'S HS; (JR); Hi Hnr Roll; Hnr Roll; MVP; Perf Att; WWAHSS; Chrch Yth Grp; Ch Chr; Bskball (V); Sftball (V); Vllyball (V); MVP-Volleyball; Childcare; Nursing; East Carolina U; U North Carolina Chapel Hill

DUNLOW, GINGER; KANNAPOLIS, NC; NORTHWEST CABARRUS MS; (MS); Ctznshp Aw; DARE; Chr; Sftball

DUNN, ALI; GLENBURN, NC; JOHN BAPST MEMORIAL HS; (JR); Hnr Roll; WWAHSS; Key Club; Chr; Fld Hky (VJ L); Tennis (V); Chemistry Award (School Year 2004-2005); Business; U of Maine (Orono)

DUNN, DEIDRA L; CHARLOTTE, NC; HARDING U HS; (SO); Duke TS; Hnr Roll; MVP; Comm Volntr; Chrch Yth Grp; Bnd; Ch Chr; Mch Bnd; Pep Bnd; Sftball (J); Cl Off; Major in Pre-Medicine; Major or Minor in Music; Duke U; Chapel Hill-U of North Carolina

DUPREE, ALLISON; FAYETTEVILLE, NC; DOUGLAS BYRD HS; (JR); Chrch Yth Grp; Elementary Education; Pediatric Nursing; Howard U; U of South Carolina

DURBIN, ASHLEY D; ASHEVILLE, NC; C A ERWIN HS; (SR); DAR; Hi Hnr Roll; Hnr Roll; Jr Mshl; Otst Ac Ach Awd; St Schl; WWAHSS; Hab For Humty Volntr; Chrch Yth Grp; Emplmnt; Ntl Beta Clb; Chr; Ch Chr; Dnce; Cr Ctry (V L); Beta Club Vice President; Most Improved in Cross Country; Psychology; UNC Chapel Hill

DYE, CHARLIE; LINCOLNTON, NC; LINCOLNTON HS; (JR); Emplmnt; Key Club; Ntl Beta Clb; Photog; Quill & Scroll; Yrbk (E, P); Vice President of HOSA; Physician; Psychologist; Elon U; U of North Carolina Wilmington

EAKES, SAMANTHA D; ROXBORO, NC; PERSON HS; (FR); Hnr Roll; Chrch Yth Grp; DARE; Emplmnt; FBLA

EARLS, JESSICA; MACCLESFIELD, NC; SOUTHWEST EDGECOMBE HS; (JR); All Am Sch; Hnr Roll; Comm Volntr; Chrch Yth Grp; Pep Squd; Photog; Sftball (J); Vllyball (VJ); Cl Off (P, V); Sch Ppr (R); Graduation Marshall Sophomore Year; Medical Field; Chemistry Major; U of North Carolina; East Carolina U

EASON, KRYSTIN L; WILMINGTON, NC; E A LANEY HS; (JR); Ctznshp Aw; Hnr Roll; MVP; WWAHSS; Comm Volntr; Peer Tut/Med; Chrch Yth Grp; Emplmnt; FCA; FBLA; FTA; Prom Com; Ch Chr; Dnce; Bskball (V); Golf (V); Sftball (V); Yrbk (P); Medical Schools; Orthopedic Surgeon; Duke U; The U of North Carolina At Chapel Hill

EASON, MORGAN; BENSON, NC; WEST JOHNSTON HS; (JR); Hnr Roll; Pres Sch; Hab For Humty Volntr; Chrch Yth Grp; FCCLA; Ntl Beta Clb; Ntl FFA; Scouts; Scr Kpr (L); Vllyball (V); Qualifying State HOSA Member; (Health Occupation Students of America); Nursing Degree; Obstetrics; U of Chapel Hill At Wilmington; East Carolina U

EASTER, CHASITY N; MOUNT AIRY, NC; WHITE PLAINS CHRISTIAN SC; (FR); Hnr Roll; Chrch Yth Grp; Chr; Ch Chr; Dvng (V); Ice Hky (V); Vllyball (J L); President Award in Reading; Dental Hygienist; Photography; Wake Forest U; U of North Carolina

EAVES, MARIEL F; DURHAM, NC; SOUTHERN HS; (SR); Hnr Roll; Perf Att; WWAHSS; ArtClub; Emplmnt; Stg Cre; Designer in Youth Art Studio (Seesaw Studio); Fashion Design; Graphic Design; The Savannah College of Art and Design; The Atlanta College of Art

EDGE, MITCHELL C; HOPE MILLS, NC; GRAY'S CREEK HS; (SR); MVP; Hab For Humty Volntr; Key Club; Ntl FFA; Sci Clb; Sccr (V CL); Tennis (V L); Outstanding Senior; Business; Marketing; I Will Be Attending East Carolina U.

EDMONDS, CYNTHIA; HENDERSON, NC; SOUTHERN VANCE HS; (SR); Hnr Roll; Jr Mshl; Nat Hon Sy; St of Mnth; WWAHSS; Hab For Humty Volntr; Lib Aide; Ntl Beta Clb; Svce Clb; Pre-Law; Law Degree; Appalachian State U

EDMONDS, RACHAEL; FRANKLIN, NC; FRANKLIN HS; (SR); Hnr Roll; Nat Hon Sy; St Schl; 4-H; Chess; Chrch Yth Grp; Emplmnt; Lib Aide; Chr; Clr Grd; Drm Mjr; Mch Bnd; Track (J); Church Youth Leadership; Music Director for Worship Services; Brigham Young U; Western Carolina U

EDMUNDSON, ANDREA M; WILSON, NC; HUNT HS; (JR); Hnr Roll; Perf Att; St of Mnth; 4-H; Chrch Yth Grp; DARE; Emplmnt; Off Aide; Tchrs Aide; Chr; Ch Chr; Pharmacist; Operations Research Analysis

EDWARDS, ANDREW C; ASHEBORO, NC; ASHEBORO HS; (SR); Hi Hnr Roll; Jr Mshl; Nat Hon Sy; WWAHSS; Yth Ldrshp Prog; Peer Tut/Med; Chrch Yth Grp; Drma Clb; FCA; Key Club; MuAlphaTh; Ch Chr; SP/M/VS; Cr Ctry (V L); Swmg (V L); Tennis (V L); Attending Campbell U

EDWARDS, EMILIE G; MORGANTON, NC; EAST BURKE HS; (SR); Hnr Roll; Nat Hon Sy; WWAHSS; Comm Volntr; Hab For Humty Volntr; Chrch Yth Grp; Drma Clb; FCA; FBLA; Key Club; Mus Clb; Svce Clb; Tchrs Aide; Acpl Chr; Chr; Ch Chr; Dnce; I Was Voted "Most Outstanding Choral Senior"; I Was 1st Runner-Up At Our School Pageant; I Will Major in Music (Voice) & Possibly Minor in English; Covenant College

EDWARDS, HEATHER; WAXHAW, NC; WEDDINGTON HS; (FR); Duke TS; Hi Hnr Roll; Otst Ac Ach Awd; Perf Att; St of Mnth; WWAHSS; Peer Tut/Med; Emplmnt; Key Club; Ntl Beta Clb; Dnce; Rotary Scholar; Doctor

EDWARDS, MARIANNE E; POLKTON, NC; WEST STANLY HS; (SO); Ctznshp Aw; Duke TS; Hi Hnr Roll; Perf Att; Pres Ac Ftns Aw; Sci Fairs; WWAHSS; Yth Ldrshp Prog; Chrch Yth Grp; DARE; FBLA; Ntl Beta Clb; NYLC; Photog; Prom Com; Scouts; Chrldg (JCL); Stu Cncl (S); Who's Who of America's High School Students (3 Times); Spec Youth Stanly; Business Degree; North Carolina State U

EDWARDS, MICHAEL S; MURFREESBORO, NC; RIDGECROFT SCH; (JR); Hi Hnr Roll; Hnr Roll; Jr Mshl; Nat Hon Sy; St of Mnth; WWAHSS; Chrch Yth Grp; Emplmnt; Key Club; Ntl Beta Clb; Prom Com; SADD; Bnd; Pep Bnd; Bskball (VJ L); Golf (V L); Sccr (J); Yrbk (R, P); Page to NC Majority Leader of House of Representatives - James Black; Accountant; U of North Carolina Chapel Hill; Chowan College

EDWARDS, NOAH; SPRUCE PINE, NC; AVERY CTY HS; (FR); Duke TS; Hnr Roll; Otst Ac Ach Awd; Pres Ac Ftns Aw; Sci Fairs; Yth Ldrshp Prog; Comm Volntr; Hab For Humty Volntr; Peer Tut/Med; Chrch Yth Grp; DARE; Drma Clb; Emplmnt; FCA; SADD; Ch Chr; SP/M/VS; Short Term Missions; Samaritan's Purse Volunteer; Culinary Arts; Photographic Arts; Johnson & Wales U; University of Georgia

EFIRD, CAROLYN; CONCORD, NC; MT PLEASANT HS; (JR); Hnr Roll; Nat Hon Sy; Perf Att; WWAHSS; 4-H; ArtClub; Drma Clb; Ntl Beta Clb; Ntl FFA; Spanish Clb; Ch Chr; Botany; Molecular Biology; Indiana U; Appalachian State U

EGGERT, COTE; MONROE, NC; SUN VALLEY MS; (MS); Hnr Roll; Pres Ac Ftns Aw; Spec Olymp Vol; ROTC; Bnd; Bskball (J); Vllyball (J); Sch Ppr (E); Pre-Med; Medicine; U of Virginia; U of South California

ELLERBE, TRISTAN L; WINSTON SALEM, NC; GLENN HS; (FR); Ctznshp Aw; Hnr Roll; Otst Ac Ach Awd; Perf Att; St of Mnth; CARE; Chess; Chrch Yth Grp; DARE; Tchrs Aide; Ch Chr; Bskball (J); Track (J); Business Administration; Sports Management; U of NC @ Chapel Hill; Howard U

ELLIOTT, ASHLEY L; BUNNLEVEL, NC; TRITON HS; (FR); Hnr Roll; Perf Att; Comm Volntr; Key Club; ROTC; Ch Chr; Drl Tm; Lawyer; Law Enforcement; North Carolina A & T; Duke

ELLIOTT, JARRELL A; WINSTON SALEM, NC; PARK LAND HS; (FR); Hnr Roll; Nat Hon Sy; Perf Att; Peer Tut/Med; Track (J); Duke, UNC; Wake Forest U

ELLIOTT, KAMERON; LOUISBURG, NC; FRANKLINTON HS; (FR); Ctznshp Aw; Duke TS; Hnr Roll; Perf Att; St of Mnth; Comm Volntr; Chess; Civil Air Pat; Drma Clb; FCA; FBLA; Ch Chr; Cl Off (P); Stu Cncl (R); Ministry; Architecture; World Harvest Bible College

ELLIOTT, MATTHEW A; CHARLOTTE, NC; NORTH MECKLENBURG HS; (JR); Hnr Roll; MVP; WWAHSS; Yth Ldrshp Prog; Hab For Humty Volntr; DECA; Ftball (V L); Sccr (V L); All-Conference, All-Region, All-State High School Soccer 2004; All-Conference Football 2004, Captain Club Soccer; Sports Marketing; U of North Carolina @ Wilmington; U of North Carolina @ Charlotte

ELLIOTT, STEVEN D; WINTERVILLE, NC; D H CONLEY HS; (FR); Duke TS; Otst Ac Ach Awd; Emplmnt; Ntl Beta Clb; Scouts; Sccr (J); Eagle Scout Award; SASI Sportsmanship Award; Computer Engineering; North Carolina State U

ELLIS, CHAKEISTA; ROBERSONVILLE, NC; ROANOKE HS; (FR); Hi Hnr Roll; Hnr Roll; DARE; Ntl Beta Clb; Pediatrics; Obstetrics; George U; East Carolina U

ELLIS, JAKE; CONCORD, NC; CONCORD HS; (JR); WWAHSS; Chrch Yth Grp; Presidential Classroom 2004 - Defense Week; Presidential Classroom 2005 - Inauguration Week; International Relations / Political Science-Government; Analytical Analgesics at the CIA; Georgetown U; American U

ELLIS, JENNIFER; LOWELL, NC; ASHBROOK HS; (FR); Hnr Roll; St of Mnth; DARE; Navy Pilot; Architect; US Naval Academy; NC State U

ELLISON, AMANDA; ASHEVILLE, NC; CLYDE A ERWIN HS; (SR); Red Cr Aide; Mus Clb; Tchrs Aide; Chr; Massage Therapist; Radiology; AB Tech Community College; UNCA

ELMORE, BRANDI; LAWNDALE, NC; BURNS HS; (JR); MVP; Ntl Beta Clb; Ntl FFA; Prom Com; Spanish Clb; Dnce; Orch; Chrldg (J); Cr Ctry (V); Teaching; Military; UNC Wilmington; UNC Chapel Hill

ELTARABOULSI, RAMI; APEX, NC; APEX HS; (JR); Hnr Roll; Kwnis Aw; Nat Hon Sy; Comm Volntr; Key Club; Spanish Clb; Track (J); Yrbk (R, P); Biomedical Engineering; Pre-Optometry; UNC Chapel Hill; NC State

EMERSON, ELLEN; SALISBURY, NC; SALISBURY HS; (SO); Hi Hnr Roll; WWAHSS; Key Club; Pep Squd; Tennis (V L); Junior Civitan; Pediatrics; UNC Chapel Hill; Duke U

EMOND, MICHELLE; GREENSBORO, NC; SOUTHEAST HS; (JR); Yth Ldrshp Prog; Chrldg (JC); Swmg (V L); Track (V); Registered Nurse; Doctor; Join the Army

ENLOE, GLENN C; HOPE MILLS, NC; SOUTHVIEW HS; (JR); Hnr Roll; Jr Mshl; Nat Hon Sy; Bnd; Mch Bnd; Academy of Scholars; IB Academy; Computer Engineering; Electronic Engineering; UNC-Chapel Hill; NC State

ESPANTO, MARTIN B S; RALEIGH, NC; WILLIAM G ENLOE HS; (SO); Hnr Roll; Perf Att; Peer Tut/Med; Red Cr Aide; Emplmnt; Sci Clb; Tchrs Aide; Medical Bioscience Academy Student; Red Cross Club (Member); Nurse Practitioner (Nursing); U of North Carolina-Chapel Hill; Duke U

ESPIN, TIFFANY; MATTHEWS, NC; BUTLER HS; (SO); Hnr Roll; WWAHSS; DECA; Key Club; Spanish Clb; Major in Psychology or Criminal Law

ESQUIVEL, LIZBETH; WELCOME, NC; NORTH DAVIDSON HS; (SO); Hi Hnr Roll; Hnr Roll; Otst Ac Ach Awd; St of Mnth; WWAHSS; CARE; Comm Volntr; DARE; Emplmnt; I Like to Volunteer Working in Any Activity.; Specialist Doctor in ENT; Lawyer; Wake Forest U; Harvard U

ETHERIDGE, WILLIAM; POWELLS POINT, NC; CURRITUCK CTY HS; Hi Hnr Roll; Otst Ac Ach Awd; Perf Att; St of Mnth; Peer Tut/Med; Emplmnt; SP/M/VS; Bskball (J); Ftball (J); Track (V); Wt Lftg (J); CR (P); Own My Own Business; Be a Doctor; Florida State U; U of North Carolina

EUDY, ANNE; CHARLOTTE, NC; SOUTH MECKLENBURG HS; (JR); F Lan Hn Soc; Jr Mshl; Nat Hon Sy; ArtClub; Chrch Yth Grp; DECA; Emplmnt; FCA; Ntl Beta Clb; P to P St Amb Prg; Quill & Scroll; Sccr (V L); Yrbk (E); Junior Marshall; Economics Award; Pre-Dental; Orthodontics; Unc-Chapel Hill; U of South Carolina

EVANS, ASHLEY; EDEN, NC; MOREHEAD HS; (SO); Hnr Roll; WWAHSS; Chrch Yth Grp; DECA; Key Club; Chr; Dental Hygiene; Guilford Technical Community College

EVANS, DAVID S; GREENSBORO, NC; DUDLEY HS; (FR); 4H Awd; Ctznshp Aw; Fut Prb Slvr; Hnr Roll; Nat Ldrshp Svc; Perf Att; Pres Ac Ftns Aw; St of Mnth; Yth Ldrshp Prog; Peer Tut/Med; Ntl Beta Clb; SADD; Ftball (J); Communications/Speech; Business; Florida U; Wake Forest

EVANS, NICHOLAS R; KITTY HAWK, NC; (SO); Duke TS; Hnr Roll; Pres Ac Ftns Aw; Peer Tut/Med; Key Club; Bnd; Cr Ctry (V); Track (V); Ambassador for UNICEF; Culinary Institute of America; Johnson and Wales

Ellison, Amanda — Clyde A Erwin HS — Asheville, NC
Duncan, Shaina M — Cramerton Christian AC — Charlotte, NC
Edmonds, Rachael — Franklin HS — Franklin, NC

EVANS SMALLWOOD, MICHAEL D; GREENSBORO, NC; NORTHWEST HS; (SR); Duke TS; Sci Fairs; WWAHSS; Red Cr Aide; ArtClub; Chess; Chrch Yth Grp; DARE; Emplmnt; FCA; Jr Cls League; French Clb; Bnd; Mch Bnd; Cr Ctry (V CL); Cyclg; PP Ftbl; Track (V L); Yrbk (E); Undergraduate in Biology or Psychology; Hawaii Pacific U

EVERETTE, JOSEPH B; TARBORO, NC; TARBORO HS; (JR); Yth Ldrshp Prog; Comm Volntr; Spec Olymp Vol; ROTC; Clr Grd; Bsball (V); North Carolina Wesleyan; Louisburg College

EVERETTE, TABITHA L; TARBORO, NC; SOUTHWEST EDGECOMBE HS; (JR); WWAHSS; Chrch Yth Grp; FBLA; Pep Squd; Tchrs Aide; Clr Grd; Elementary Education; East Carolina U; UNC Wilmington

EVERHART, ASHLEY R; RURAL HALL, NC; NORTH FORSYTH HS; (SO); Hnr Roll; Key Club; SADD; Chrldg (J); Vllyball (J); SADD; Key Club; Registered Nurse; Nurse Practitioner; Winston-Salem State U; UNC Charlotte

EVERHART, MATT; HENDERSON, NC; NORTHERN VANCE HS; (SO); Hnr Roll; Pres Ac Ftns Aw; Comm Volntr; I Play the Electric and Acoustic Guitar.; Architectural Engineering; North Carolina State U; East Carolina U

EVERIDGE, BENJAMIN; SALISBURY, NC; SALISBURY HS; (JR); Hnr Roll; Comm Volntr; Chrch Yth Grp; Key Club; Off Aide; Quiz Bowl; Jzz Bnd; Mch Bnd; Stu Cncl (R); President of the Publicity Committee; Lawyer; UNC Chapel Hill; Appalachian U

EWING, ERICA; HENDERSON, NC; NORTHERN VANCE HS; (FR); Ctznshp Aw; Hnr Roll; Otst Ac Ach Awd; Sci Fairs; St of Mnth; WWAHSS; Comm Volntr; ArtClub; Chrch Yth Grp; DARE; Drma Clb; FCA; Lib Aide; Mus Clb; Off Aide; Bnd; Ch Chr; SP/M/VS; Track (J); Yrbk (P); Veterinarian; Nursing/Surgeon's; U of North Carolina; North Carolina State

EY, TAYLOR N; WAXHAW, NC; WEDDINGTON HS; (SO); Duke TS; Jr Rot; Nat Hon Sy; Otst Ac Ach Awd; WWAHSS; Spec Olymp Vol; Chrch Yth Grp; Key Club; Ntl Beta Clb; Bnd; Mch Bnd; Black Belt in Karate; Congressional Student Lead America Leadership Conference.; Pre Medicine; Engineering; The Ohio State U; Duke U

EZEKIEL, CRYSTAL S; GREENSBORO, NC; PAGE HS; (SO); Ctznshp Aw; Fut Prb Slvr; Hi Hnr Roll; Hnr Roll; Nat Ldrshp Svc; Nat Mrt Sch Recip; Nat Sci Aw; Pres Ac Ftns Aw; St of Mnth; Yth Ldrshp Prog; Comm Volntr; Peer Tut/Med; Chrch Yth Grp; DARE; Emplmnt; Spch Team; Spanish Clb; Ch Chr; Dnce; Terry McClure Award; President's Education Award; Science Major; Anesthesiologist; Gardner Webb U; Georgia Tech

EZELL, MORGAN; WENDELL, NC; EAST WAKE HS; (SO); Hi Hnr Roll; Hnr Roll; WWAHSS; Comm Volntr; Key Club; Mus Clb; SADD; Bnd; Mch Bnd; SP/M/VS; Sccr (J); Swmg (V); Green Club; Key Club; NCSU, ECU, UNCW East Carolina; UNC North Carolina State U Raleigh, Wilmington

FABO, KARYN R; HOPE MILLS, NC; SOUTH VIEW HS; (JR); Ctznshp Aw; F Lan Hn Soc; Hi Hnr Roll; Hnr Roll; Jr Mshl; MVP; Nat Hon Sy; Otst Ac Ach Awd; Sci/Math Olympn; Yth Ldrshp Prog; Hosp Aide; Drma Clb; Key Club; Mth Clb/Tm; Ntl Beta Clb; Scouts; Foreign Clb; SP/M/VS; Stg Cre; President National Honor Spanish Society; Silver Award: Girl Scouts; Pharmacy; Campbell U; U of North Carolina-Chapel Hill

FAHRBACH, CLAIRE W; CHAPEL HILL, NC; NORTHWOOD HS; (JR); F Lan Hn Soc; Hnr Roll; Nat Hon Sy; Pres Ac Ftns Aw; ArtClub; DARE; Emplmnt; Key Club; Scouts; Svce Clb; Spanish Clb; Dnce; SP/M/VS; Cr Ctry (V L); Coach's Award-Cross Country; Graphic Design; Interior Design; NC State U; UNC Charlotte

FAIR, AMBER D; WINSTON SALEM, NC; NORTH FORSYTH HS; (SR); Hnr Roll; WWAHSS; Peer Tut/Med; Red Cr Aide; Chrch Yth Grp; FBLA; Key Club; Mth Clb/Tm; Spanish Clb; Dnce; Stu Cncl (S); Crosby Scholars (President); Big Buddy Program; Dentistry; Accounting; U of North Carolina in Greensboro; U of North Carolina in Charlotte

FAISON, CHASITY M; WENDELL, NC; SOUTHEAST RALEIGH HS; (SO); Hnr Roll; Perf Att; St of Mnth; WWAHSS; Comm Volntr; Chrch Yth Grp; DARE; Spanish Clb; Bnd; Drm Mjr; Mch Bnd; Bskball; Certified for CPR; Pediatrician; Veterinarian; Queens College; Elizabeth City State U

FAISON, DESTINY; POWELLSVILLE, NC; BERTIE HS; (SR); All Am Sch; Hnr Roll; Nat Hon Sy; Nat Sci Aw; USAA; WWAHSS; Peer Tut/Med; 4-H; Chrch Yth Grp; Emplmnt; FTA; NYLC; Tchrs Aide; Chr; Ch Chr; SP/M/VS; Cl Off (V); Early Childhood Education; Child Psychology; Winston Salem State U

FAISON, JANNASHA; GOLDSBORO, NC; GOLDSBORO HS; (SO); Hnr Roll; Cadet of the Month; Computer Science; Music; Tallahassee State U; Florida State U

FALATOVICH, JUSTIN G; CLINTON, NC; CLINTON HS; (SR); Hnr Roll; Pres Ac Ftns Aw; Comm Volntr; Spec Olymp Vol; 4-H; ArtClub; Chrch Yth Grp; Key Club; Ntl FFA; Golf; Sccr (V CL); Agricultural Business; Wake Tech; North Carolina State U

FANN, CRYSTAL B; WHITTIER, NC; SWAIN CTY HS; (FR); Hi Hnr Roll; Otst Ac Ach Awd; Comm Volntr; Peer Tut/Med; Chrch Yth Grp; FCA; Pep Squd; SADD; Ch Chr; Dnce; Bskball (V); Chrldg (V L); Cr Ctry (V L); Sftball (J); Track (V L); CR (R); Yrbk; Crowned Freshman Queen; Physical Therapy; North Carolina State; Florida State

FARGIS, RACHEL; CHARLOTTE, NC; HARDING U HS; (FR); Duke TS; Hnr Roll; Sci/Math Olympn; Scouts; Bskball; Sccr; Vllyball; Yrbk (E, P); National Junior Honor Society; National Academic League

FARRAR, JOSHUA D; MATTHEWS, NC; PIEDMONT HS; (JR); Hi Hnr Roll; Hnr Roll; Nat Hon Sy; Perf Att; Sci/Math Olympn; Peer Tut/Med; Emplmnt; FBLA; Ntl Beta Clb; Sci Clb; Scouts; Rotary Scholar 2002-2003; Multicultural Achievement Club; Pharmacy; Chemistry; Chapel Hill-U of North Carolina; Campbell U

FAULCON, JASMINE R; LITTLETON, NC; NORTHWEST HS; (JR); Hi Hnr Roll; Nat Hon Sy; WWAHSS; Peer Tut/Med; Emplmnt; Beta Club; Rotary Club Nominee; North Carolina State U; U of North Carolina in Greensboro

FAULK, SEAN; CLEMMONS, NC; WEST FORSYTH HS; (FR); Hnr Roll; Nat Hon Sy; Sci Fairs; St of Mnth; WWAHSS; Chrch Yth Grp; Emplmnt; National Geography Bee Winner; Marketing/Advertising; Providence U; Point Loma Nazarene U

FAULKENBERRY, DANIEL L; LAURINBURG, NC; SCOTLAND HS; (SO); Ctznshp Aw; Hnr Roll; Kwnis Aw; Otst Ac Ach Awd; St of Mnth; Chrch Yth Grp; Key Club; Vsity Clb; German Clb; Bnd; Cr Ctry (V L); Tennis (V L); Wt Lftg (V); Sch Ppr (R); Yrbk (E); Criminal Justice Major; Political Science / Lawyer; Coastal Carolina; East Carolina U

FEDUR, PETRONELA T; DENVER, NC; NORTH LINCOLN HS; (JR); Ctznshp Aw; F Lan Hn Soc; Otst Ac Ach Awd; Sci Fairs; St of Mnth; Comm Volntr; Chrch Yth Grp; Off Aide; Spanish Clb; Bnd; Ch Chr; Mch Bnd; Orch; JV Women's Waterpolo; Vice-President of Youth Alive; Pre-Medicine; East Carolina U; Duke U

FEEHLEY, KELSEY; MOORESVILLE, NC; LAKE NORMAN HS; (JR); Duke TS; Hi Hnr Roll; Hnr Roll; Jr Mshl; Nat Hon Sy; Otst Ac Ach Awd; Pres Sch; St Schl; St of Mnth; Yth Ldrshp Prog; Comm Volntr; Peer Tut/Med; Mth Clb/Tm; Mus Clb; Ntl Beta Clb; Sci Clb; Svce Clb; Spanish Clb; Bnd; Mch Bnd; Pep Bnd; Sccr (J); Lit Mag (R); Parliamentarian of National Honor Society; Vice President of Interact Community Service Club; Technical Writing/Professional Writing; English; Elon U; U of North Carolina At Chapel Hill

FELTON, SHANIA I; FAYETTEVILLE, NC; WESTOVER HS; (FR); Hnr Roll; Otst Ac Ach Awd; Perf Att; St of Mnth; ArtClub; Drma Clb; FBLA; Dnce; SP/M/VS; Chrldg (J); Swmg (J); Sch Ppr (R); Future Business Leaders of America; Scrabble Club; Allied Health Sciences; Journalism; Stanford U; Princeton U

FENNELL, VANISHA; GREENSBORO, NC; JAMES B DUDLEY SR HS; (JR); Peer Tut/Med; Emplmnt; Interior Designer; Winston Salem State University; UNC Chapel Hill

FERGUSON, ASHLEY C; CHAPEL HILL, NC; NORTHWOOD HS; (MS); Hnr Roll; Perf Att; Hosp Aide; ArtClub; Chrch Yth Grp; FCA; FCCLA; Key Club; Tchrs Aide; Vllyball (J)

FESLER, COLLEEN; MATTHEWS, NC; BUTLER HS; (JR); Ctznshp Aw; Hi Hnr Roll; Nat Hon Sy; Sci Fairs; WWAHSS; Comm Volntr; Hab For Humty Volntr; Chrch Yth Grp; Emplmnt; Key Club; Bnd; Chrldg (VJ); Sccr (J); Stu Cncl (R); USSF Soccer Referee; Engineering; Medicine; North Carolina State; Duke

FIELDS, NIKKI; TAR HEEL, NC; WEST BLADEN HS; (JR); Jr Mshl; MVP; Yth Ldrshp Prog; Comm Volntr; Spec Olymp Vol; Chrch Yth Grp; Ntl Beta Clb; Ntl FFA; Cr Ctry (V L); Sftball (V L); Vsy Clb (V); Vllyball (V)

FINCHER, MARSHALL D; KANNAPOLIS, NC; NORTHWEST CABARRUS MS; MS; Hnr Roll; Perf Att; Chrch Yth Grp; DARE; FCA; Scouts; Bskball; Track; Presidential Physical Fitness Past 4 Yrs.; Electrical Engineering; Mechanical Engineering; North Carolina State U; U of North Carolina Chapel Hill

FINESTONE, ANNA C; GREENVILLE, NC; D H CONLEY HS; (JR); F Lan Hn Soc; Hi Hnr Roll; Hnr Roll; Jr Mshl; Nat Hon Sy; WWAHSS; DECA; MuAlphaTh; Ntl Beta Clb; Svce Clb; Tmpl Yth Grp; French Clb; Chrldg (VJ); ELP (Economic Legal & Political Systems) Student Award; Doctor; Lawyer; U of North Carolina Chapel Hill; Duke U

FINGER, MEGAN L; RALEIGH, NC; NORTH RALEIGH CHRISTIAN AC; (SR); Hnr Roll; Jr Mshl; Nat Hon Sy; Pres Sch; WWAHSS; Comm Volntr; Drma Clb; Mus Clb; Photog; Chr; Ch Chr; Dnce; SP/M/VS; Chrldg (V); Sftball (V); NCMEA Honors Chorus 2003; Counseling Psychology; Music; U of North Carolina Chapel Hill; North Carolina State U

FINGER III, PAUL E; LINCOLNTON, NC; WEST LINCOLN HS; (JR); Hnr Roll; MVP; Pres Ac Ftns Aw; Peer Tut/Med; AL Aux Boys; Emplmnt; Bsball (V L)

FISHER, ALEXANDRA J; IRON STATION, NC; EAST LINCOLN HS; (SO); Hnr Roll; Otst Ac Ach Awd; St of Mnth; Comm Volntr; Spec Olymp Vol; ArtClub; Ntl Beta Clb; Svce Clb; Vsity Clb; Spanish Clb; Sccr (V); Vllyball (V); Yrbk (E); All-Conference Varsity Soccer; Coach's Award (V Soccer); Medical Physician; Physical Therapy; U of North Carolina; Appalachian State U

FISHER, BRITTNEY R; HOPE MILLS, NC; GRAYS CREEK HS; (SO); Hi Hnr Roll; Kwnis Aw; Nat Hon Sy; WWAHSS; Yth Ldrshp Prog; Comm Volntr; Chrch Yth Grp; Key Club; Prom Com; Bnd; Mch Bnd; Chrldg (VJ); Sftball (J); Cl Off (T); Interior Design; Broadcasting Journalism; North Carolina State; East Carolina U

FISHER, CAMERON C; ROSEBORO, NC; LAKEWOOD HS; (JR); Hi Hnr Roll; MVP; Pres Ac Ftns Aw; Sci Fairs; St of Mnth; Peer Tut/Med; Cmptr Clb; DARE; Emplmnt; FBLA; Ntl Beta Clb; Ntl FFA; Quiz Bowl; Scouts; Dnce; Sftball (VJCL); Vllyball (VJCL); Accounting; Real Estate Agent; U of North Carolina At Wilmington; U of North Carolina Chapel Hill

FISHER, CURTIS; SPRING LAKE, NC; PINE FOREST SR HS; (FR); DARE; Bsball (J); Ftball (J); Computers; Technology; North Carolina State U; Hawaii U

FISHER, DEANNA; GRIMESLAND, NC; D H CONLEY HS; (FR); Hnr Roll; Perf Att; Comm Volntr; Spec Olymp Vol; ROTC; Clr Grd; Registered Nurse; Pediatric Nurse Practitioner; U of North Carolina Chapel Hill; East Carolina U

FISHER, HEATHER; WINSTON-SALEM, NC; MT TABOR HS; (JR); Hnr Roll; MVP; Nat Hon Sy; Comm Volntr; Key Club; Sftball (V L); Elementary Education; Childhood Development; Campbell; Wingate

FISHER, KAYLAN E; WAKE FOREST, NC; WAKE FOREST-ROLESVILLE HS; (JR); Hi Hnr Roll; Jr Mshl; Nat Hon Sy; Otst Ac Ach Awd; Yth Ldrshp Prog; Comm Volntr; Hab For Humty Volntr; Peer Tut/Med; Chrch Yth Grp; DARE; FBLA; Key Club; Ntl Beta Clb; Prom Com; Quill & Scroll; Sci Clb; Ch Chr; Dnce; PP Ftbl (V C); Cl Off (P); Stu Cncl (R); CR (R); Yrbk (E, P); National Honor Society President; YMCA Leaders' Club President; Major in Chemistry; PhD in Dental Medicine; U of North Carolina At Chapel Hill; Duke U

FISHER, SCOTT; CARY, NC; RALEIGH CHARTER HS; (JR); Nat Hon Sy; Sci/Math Olympn; Comm Volntr; Emplmnt; Sci Clb; Bnd; Stu Cncl (R); CR (R); Crew - Rowing / Varsity & Letter Winner; Student Legislative Assembly - SLA; Aerospace Engineering; Mechanical Engineering; North Carolina State U; Georgia Tech U

FISHER, TOM; SALISBURY, NC; SALISBURY HS; (FR); Duke TS; Hi Hnr Roll; Perf Att; Yth Ldrshp Prog; Chrch Yth Grp; DARE; Tennis (V); CR (R); Yrbk (P); Eagle Scout; School of Design; Law School / Political Science Major

FISTER, TERESA M; SUMMERFIELD, NC; NORTHWEST HS; (SR); Hnr Roll; MVP; Nat Hon Sy; Pres Ac Ftns Aw; Comm Volntr; Peer Tut/Med; Chrch Yth Grp; Emplmnt; Svce Clb; Chr; Sftball (V CL); Track (V); Vllyball (V CL); National Honor Society; Junior Olympics Volleyball; Education; Music; Appalachian State U

FITZPATRICK, JESSICA; MT AIRY, NC; MT AIRY HS; (SR); Hnr Roll; St Schl; Hosp Aide; Red Cr Aide; Spec Olymp Vol; Key Club; Prom Com; Pharmacy; Nursing; East Carolina U

FLAMENCO, VERONICA; HENDERSONVILLE, NC; EAST HENDERSON HS; (SO); Hnr Roll; Bnd; Ch Chr; Sccr (V); Tennis; Wt Lftg; Aircraft Pilot; Anthropology; Harvard; Brevard

FLANAGAN, PATRICK; GARNER, NC; WEST JOHNSTON HS; (JR); Duke TS; Hnr Roll; WWAHSS; Yth Ldrshp Prog; Comm Volntr; Peer Tut/Med; Spec Olymp Vol; Emplmnt; Scouts; Sccr (V); PTSA Student Board Member; Engineering; North Carolina State U

FLANAGAN, SUMMER; KINSTON, NC; SOUTH LENOIR HS; (MS); Hnr Roll; Sci Fairs; DARE; Scouts; Dnce; Students Against Violence Everywhere; Pharmaceutical Degree; Psychology Degree; U of North Carolina of Wilmington; North Carolina State U

FLECK, J B; CHARLOTTE, NC; CHARLOTTE CATHOLIC HS; (JR); Comm Volntr; Peer Tut/Med; Chrch Yth Grp; Ftball (V); Ice Hky (C); Stu Cncl (R); Camp Counselor; Book Drive for Charlotte - Mecklenberg Library; Restaurant / Hotel Management; Culinary School; Appalachian State; Virginia Polytechnic Institute

FLEMINGS, DEANNA; CURRITUCK, NC; CURRITUCK CTY HS; (MS); 4H Awd; Duke TS; Hnr Roll; Otst Ac Ach Awd; 4-H; Chrch Yth Grp; Ntl Beta Clb; Chr; Clr Grd; SP/M/VS; Chrldg; Tennis; Track; Stu Cncl (R); Veterinarian; Psychologist; North Carolina State Veterinarian School; U of North Carolina

FLETCHER, CALIN L; HIGH POINT, NC; RAGSDALE HS; (FR); Chrch Yth Grp; Key Club; Golf; Active in Church Youth Group; Chef; Business Owner; Johnson and Wales U

Fincher, Marshall D
Northwest Cabarrus MS
Kannapolis, NC

Felton, Shania I
Westover HS
Fayetteville, NC

Falatovich, Justin G
Clinton HS
Clinton, NC

Fedur, Petronela T
North Lincoln HS
Denver, NC

Fisher, Cameron C
Lakewood HS
Roseboro, NC

FLETCHER, TIFFANY M; PANTEGO, NC; NORTHSIDE HS; (SR); Hnr Roll; Jr Mshl; Kwnis Aw; Perf Att; Pres Sch; Salutrn; WWAHSS; Peer Tut/Med; Red Cr Aide; Spec Olymp Vol; Chrch Yth Grp; Emplmnt; Key Club; Mth Clb/Tm; Ntl Beta Clb; Ntl FFA; Sftball (V CL); Vllyball (V CL); Yrbk (R, P); Outstanding Senior (At Northside); Panther PALS (Club); Physical Therapy; East Carolina U

FLINT, BECKY; WAXHAW, NC; WEDDINGTON HS; (FR); Hi Hnr Roll; Hnr Roll; Pres Ac Ftns Aw; WWAHSS; Comm Volntr; Hab For Humty Volntr; Key Club; Ntl Beta Clb; Chr; Sccr (J); Teaching; Business; U of North Carolina At Chapel Hill; U of Virginia

FLORES, SAUL; CHARLOTTE, NC; HARDING U HS; (SO); Ctznshp Aw; Hi Hnr Roll; Hnr Roll; MVP; Perf Att; Comm Volntr; Cmptr Clb; Key Club; Sccr (V C); President's Award; Lawyer; Computer Programmer; New York U; Pace U

FLOWERS, KENDRA; GOLDSBORO, NC; EASTERN WAYNE HS; (SO); All Am Sch; Hnr Roll; Nat Ldrshp Svc; Otst Ac Ach Awd; USAA; WWAHSS; Comm Volntr; Chrch Yth Grp; Sci Clb; Foreign Clb; Ch Chr; Pre-Medical; Forensic Science; Elon U; Duke U

FLYE III, PAUL W; ROXBORO, NC; PERSON HS; (SO); Hi Hnr Roll; Hnr Roll; East Carolina U

FLYNN, CHEVETTE; PLYMOUTH, NC; PLYMOUTH HS; (JR); Drma Clb; SP/M/VS; Stg Cre; Theater / Drama; Medical / Obstetrician; UCLA; North Carolina A & T State U

FLYNN, ELYSSIA; BURGAW, NC; HEIDE TRASK SR HS; (SO); Ctznshp Aw; Hnr Roll; WWAHSS; Comm Volntr; Spec Olymp Vol; Chrch Yth Grp; Emplmnt; Key Club; Chrldg (V CL); Sch Ppr (R); Yrbk (R, P); Future Medical Leaders of America; Pharmacy; Psychology; East Carolina U; Campbell U

FONKE, EMILY A; FAYETTEVILLE, NC; TERRY SANFORD HS; (SR); Hnr Roll; MVP; Nat Hon Sy; Pres Ac Ftns Aw; Hab For Humty Volntr; Chrch Yth Grp; Key Club; Prom Com; Vsity Clb; Spanish Clb; Ch Chr; Sccr (V); Vllyball (V); East Carolina U; U of Georgia

FONTENOT, PRINCE C; WAKE FOREST, NC; WAKE FOREST-ROLESVILLE; (JR); Hnr Roll; Perf Att; WWAHSS; Key Club; Lib Aide; Off Aide; Photog; Tchrs Aide; Wdwrkg Clb; Culinary Arts; Wake Tech

FOOTE, ALAN R; WILSON, NC; FIKE HS; (SO); Duke TS; Hnr Roll; Sci/Math Olympn; Comm Volntr; Chrch Yth Grp; Emplmnt; ROTC; Scouts; Spanish Clb; Drl Tm; Cr Ctry (V L); Swmg (V L); Eagle Scout; Spanish Club (9-Treasurer, 10-President); Aeronautical Engineering; Electrical Engineering; United States Naval Academy; United States Coast Guard Academy

FORD, HAZEL; DURHAM, NC; NORTHERN HS; (SR); Comm Volntr; DECA; Emplmnt; Key Club; Scouts; Svce Clb; SADD; Dnce; Mar Art; PP Ftbl; Scr Kpr; Stu Cncl (R); CR (R); Teens Against Consuming Tobacco; North Carolina A & T State U, Psychology

FORD, IAN H; GREENSBORO, NC; NORTHWEST GUILFORD HS; (SO); Comm Volntr; Hab For Humty Volntr; Rlr Hky (V); Southeast Roller Hockey Program; Psychology; Business; N.C. State U; UNCG

FORDHAM, DANIEL; MONROE, NC; FOREST HILLS HS; (FR); Hi Hnr Roll; Hnr Roll; Otst Ac Ach Awd; Comm Volntr; Ntl FFA; Arch (V); Ftball (V); Skt Tgt Sh (V); Track (V); Wt Lftg (V); Large Animal Veterinary; North Carolina State U

FOREMAN, LEANNA; WAXHAW, NC; WEDDINGTON HS; (SO); Hnr Roll; Sci Fairs; Comm Volntr; Chrch Yth Grp; FCCLA; Key Club; Lib Aide; Scouts; Ch Chr; Dnce; Cr Ctry; Track (L); Girl Scout Silver Award completed and Gold Award in progress (summer 2006); New York Mission Trip with My Church; Math/Accounting; U of Washington, Seattle, Washington; Gardner-Webb, Boiling Springs, North Carolina

FORESTER, ROSLYN L; POLKTON, NC; ANSON HS; (FR); Hi Hnr Roll; WWAHSS; Comm Volntr; Chrch Yth Grp; Sccr (V); Sftball (J); Certified Public Accountant; U of North Carolina Chapel Hill; Florida State U

FORMAN, CHANCELOR J; CHARLOTTE, NC; (FR); Hnr Roll; Nat Hon Sy; WWAHSS; ROTC; Computer Animation; Culinary Arts; Full Sail; Johnson & Wales

FORMAN, JENNIFER; ROCKY POINT, NC; HEIDE TRASK SR HS; (SR); Hnr Roll; Jr Mshl; Nat Hon Sy; WWAHSS; Key Club; Mth Clb/Tm; Quiz Bowl; Bskball (V L); Cr Ctry (V L); Sftball (V L); Sch Ppr (E, R); National Society of High School Scholars; Honor Graduate; Journalism/Communication Studies; U of North Carolina @ Wilmington

FORTESCUE, ELIZABETH C; WASHINGTON, NC; PUNGO CHRISTIAN AC; (JR); Hnr Roll; Otst Ac Ach Awd; Sci Fairs; WWAHSS; Chrch Yth Grp; Drma Clb; Ntl Beta Clb; Ntl FFA; Prom Com; Bskball (VJCL); Sftball (V); Vllyball (VJCL); Cl Off (S); Yrbk (E); FFA Reporter; Elementary Education; Appalachian State U; North Carolina State U

FORTNEY, JONATHAN E; WILSON, NC; FIKE HS; (SO); Hnr Roll; Peer Tut/Med; Mus Clb; Bnd; Mch Bnd; Orch; Black Belt-Martial Arts; Bilingual; Asian Studies; Music; North Carolina State; UNC-Chapel Hill

FORTUNE, LATRIVIA; WINSTON SALEM, NC; CARTER G WOODSON SCH; (FR); Hi Hnr Roll; Hnr Roll; Perf Att; Sci/Math Olympn; St of Mnth; Comm Volntr; Peer Tut/Med; DARE; DECA; Mth Clb/Tm; Off Aide; SADD; Tchrs Aide; Bskball (C); Cl Off (T); CR (R); Sch Ppr (R); Mathematics; MIT

FOSKEY, MORGAN T; FARMVILLE, NC; FARMVILLE CTRL HS; (SO); Comm Volntr; Spec Olymp Vol; Dnce; Bskball (J); Keystone Club At Boys & Girls Club (Pres.); S.A.V.E (Student Against Violence Everywhere); Pharmacy; Cosmetology; U of North Carolina At Greensboro; East Carolina U

FOSTER, ASHLEY L; CONCORD, NC; J M ROBINSON; (JR); Hnr Roll; Comm Volntr; FBLA; Ch Chr; Dnce; SP/M/VS; Track (V); Business; Psychology; Hofstra U; U of Carolina At Charl.

FOSTER, JULIAN C; GREENSBORO, NC; TRI-CITY JR AC; (FR); Hi Hnr Roll; Sci Fairs; Valdctrian; Peer Tut/Med; Drma Clb; SP/M/VS; Stg Cre; Bskball (V C); Stu Cncl (P); Sch Ppr (R); Dentistry, Business; Optometry; Southern Adventist U; North Carolina

FOSTER, LA QUASHA; WINSTON-SALEM, NC; REYNOLDS HS; (JR); F Lan Hn Soc; Hi Hnr Roll; Jr Mshl; Comm Volntr; Emplmnt; Prom Com; Svce Clb; Spanish Clb; Track (V L); Vllyball (J); Pharmacy; U of North Carolina Chapel Hill; Howard U

FOSTER, SAMANTHA; CONCORD, NC; (SO); Duke TS; Nat Hon Sy; WWAHSS; Comm Volntr; Hab For Humty Volntr; 4-H; DARE; Jr Ach; Ntl Beta Clb; Scouts; Bnd; Mch Bnd; Private Flute Lesson; Private Piano Lessons; Music Performance; Criminal Justice; U of North Carolina At Chapel Hill; Ithaca U

FOSTER II, JAMES A; PROVIDENCE, NC; BARTLETT YANCEY HS; (JR); Hnr Roll; MVP; Nat Hon Sy; Otst Ac Ach Awd; Perf Att; St of Mnth; Chrch Yth Grp; Emplmnt; Key Club; Lttrmn Clb; Ntl Beta Clb; Off Aide; Scouts; Tchrs Aide; Bsball (V); Sccr (V C); Wrstlg (V C); Eagle Scout; Veterinary Medicine; Medical Doctor; North Carolina State; U of North Carolina

FOUST, KEOSHA; BURLINGTON, NC; GRAHAM HS; (SO); Hi Hnr Roll; Chr; Principal's List; Minority Academic Achievement; Probation Officer; Alamance County Colleges

FOX, MYJA; GREENSBORO, NC; DUDLEY HS; (JR); Nat Hon Sy; Peer Tut/Med; Bsball (V CL); Made Honorable Mention Baseball 9th Grade; Sports Medicine; Elizabeth City College

FOY, JUSTIN; FAYETTEVILLE, NC; GRAYS CREEK HS; (SO); Ctznshp Aw; Hnr Roll; MVP; Nat Ldrshp Svc; Nat Stu Ath Day Aw; Otst Ac Ach Awd; Perf Att; Sci Fairs; St of Mnth; Comm Volntr; Chrch Yth Grp; DARE; Emplmnt; Mus Clb; Outdrs Clb; Scouts; Vsity Clb; Bnd; Ch Chr; Mch Bnd; SP/M/VS; Ftball (V L); Track (V L); Wt Lftg (V L); Wrstlg (V L); CR; Architecture; Construction; NC State; Virginia Tech

FRAGOSO, JORGE; KANNAPOLIS, NC; A L BROWN HS; (MS); Ctznshp Aw; Hnr Roll; St of Mnth; Peer Tut/Med; Chrch Yth Grp; Mod UN; Scouts; Ch Chr; Teacher; Photographer

FRANCIS, CHASE; CHARLOTTE, NC; DAVID W BUTLER HS; (SO); Duke TS; Hi Hnr Roll; Hnr Roll; Perf Att; Sci/Math Olympn; Comm Volntr; DARE; Emplmnt; Key Club; Svce Clb; Bnd; Jzz Bnd; Mch Bnd; Pep Bnd; Boy Scouts-Current Rank (Life Scout); History Day Competition; Music; Engineering; North Carolina State U; U of North Carolina (Charlotte)

FRANK, KIMBERLY C; WAXHAW, NC; PARKWOOD HS; (SR); All Am Sch; Hnr Roll; Nat Hon Sy; WWAHSS; Comm Volntr; Red Cr Aide; Spec Olymp Vol; Chrch Yth Grp; Emplmnt; FCA; Key Club; Ntl Beta Clb; Off Aide; French Clb; Chr; Ch Chr; Orch; SP/M/VS; Swmg (V); Track (V); Vllyball (V L); Yrbk (E); Political Science; International Relations; UNC-Chapel Hill (U of North Carolina); Davidson U

FRANKLIN, BRITTANY; HUNTERSVILLE, NC; NORTH MECK HS; (JR); Duke TS; Hnr Roll; MVP; Perf Att; Pres Ac Ftns Aw; St of Mnth; Chrch Yth Grp; DARE; DECA; FCCLA; SADD; Tchrs Aide; Chr; Chrldg (V); Gmnstcs (J); Tennis (V); State Finalist in National American Miss; Paralegal Studies; Office Administration Assistant; Kings College; Appalachian State U

FRANKLIN, SARAH J; GOLDSBORO, NC; SPRING CREEK HS; (SR); Ctznshp Aw; Hnr Roll; Nat Hon Sy; Perf Att; WWAHSS; Hosp Aide; Chrch Yth Grp; DARE; FCA; FCCLA; Prom Com; SADD; Tchrs Aide; Bnd; Chr; Mch Bnd; CAN; Nursing; Wayne Community College; East Carolina U

FRAZIER II, CLAYTON G; HENDERSON, NC; NORTHERN VANCE HS; (SO); Ctznshp Aw; Duke TS; Hi Hnr Roll; Nat Hon Sy; WWAHSS; Comm Volntr; Chrch Yth Grp; DARE; FCA; Quiz Bowl; Sci Clb; Bsball (V); Sccr (V); Stu Cncl (R)

FREITAG, SARAH E; SALISBURY, NC; SALISBURY HS; (SO); Hi Hnr Roll; Hnr Roll; MVP; Perf Att; Pres Ac Ftns Aw; WWAHSS; Comm Volntr; Hab For Humty Volntr; Chrch Yth Grp; DARE; Key Club; Ch Chr; Cr Ctry (V); Fld Hky (VJ L); Lcrsse (J); Sccr (J); Swmg (V L); CR (R); Science; U of North Carolina Raleigh Durham

FRENCH, BRITTANI; GREENVILLE, NC; D H CONLEY HS; (FR); Ctznshp Aw; Duke TS; Hnr Roll; Jr Mshl; Sci Fairs; Comm Volntr; ArtClub; DARE; Dbte Team; FCA; FBLA; Ntl Beta Clb; Prom Com; Chrldg (J); ECCATS Christmas Classic Grand Champion; Plastic Surgeon; Emergency Room Doctor; Duke U; East Carolina U

FRITTS, DALISA; LEXINGTON, NC; NORTH DAVIDSON HS; (SO); Duke TS; Hnr Roll; Perf Att; St of Mnth; Chrch Yth Grp; DARE; Ntl FFA; Scouts; Chr; Ch Chr; Dnce; Chrldg (JC); Varsity Dance Team; Commercial/Print Modeling; Major in Pediatrics; Minor in Spanish; Wake Forest U; U of North Carolina Wilmington

FRITZ, RAE; HICKORY, NC; ST STEPHENS HS; (JR); Hnr Roll; Comm Volntr; Hosp Aide; Chrch Yth Grp; Drma Clb; Emplmnt; Bnd; Dnce; SP/M/VS; Chrldg (V); Volunteer Work; Governor School Nominee (Dance); Dance Major; Theatre Major; North Carolina School of the Arts; U of North Carolina in Greensboro

FROELICH, CODY; SALISBURY, NC; NORTH ROWAN HS; (SO); All Am Sch; Hnr Roll; Nat Hon Sy; Otst Ac Ach Awd; St of Mnth; WWAHSS; Comm Volntr; ROTC; Clr Grd; Drl Tm; Urban Development; Urban Resources; Appalachian State U; U of North Carolina (Charlotte)

FRONEBERGER, DEAUNA; CHARLOTTE, NC; HARDING U HS; (FR); Hnr Roll; MVP; Comm Volntr; Peer Tut/Med; Dnce; Track; National Junior Honor Society (in Middle School); Criminal Justice; Associate's Degree; North Carolina A & T State U; Central Piedmont Community College

FROST, TANISHA; LEXINGTON, NC; LEXINGTON SR HS; (JR); Hnr Roll; WWAHSS; DECA; Prom Com; SP/M/VS; Top 25 - National DECA Competition; Marketing Career; Accounting; Barnard College; North Carolina State U

FRYE, APRIL L; LINCOLNTON, NC; LINCOLN CHARTER SCH; (SO); Sci Fairs; Peer Tut/Med; Pep Squd; Prom Com; Tchrs Aide; Ch Chr; Scr Kpr (J); Mars Hill College; North Carolina State

FRYE, CHRISTINA E; MOORESVILLE, NC; LAKE NORMAN; (JR); Hi Hnr Roll; Hnr Roll; Nat Hon Sy; Pres Sch; WWAHSS; Comm Volntr; Drma Clb; FBLA; Ntl Beta Clb; French Clb; SP/M/VS; Stg Cre; Sccr (V L); Cl Off (P); High School Focus Group; Governors School Nominee; History; Language Arts; U of North Carolina Charlotte

FULLER, ANDREA; ASHEVILLE, NC; AC REYNOLDS HS; (SR); Nat Hon Sy; Nat Mrt Fin; Valdctrian; WWAHSS; Comm Volntr; Dbte Team; NtlFrnscLg; Quill & Scroll; Ch Chr; CR (R); Yrbk (E); National History Day Finalist; Debate District Placement; History Professor; Stanford U; Duke U

FULLER, SAVANNAH S; SANFORD, NC; LEE CTY HS; (JR); Hi Hnr Roll; Hnr Roll; Nat Hon Sy; Comm Volntr; Emplmnt; Mod UN; Scouts; Cr Ctry (V); Scr Kpr (V); Track (V); Girl Scout Silver Award; Registered Nurse; Pediatrics; Appalachian U; U of North Carolina in Chapel Hill

FULP, AMANDA; PINNACLE, NC; NORTH STOKES HS; (JR); Hnr Roll; Perf Att; DARE; Scouts; Social Worker; Wilmington; Rockingham Community College

FULP, MYISHA R; CLAYTON, NC; WEST JOHNSTON HS; (JR); Hnr Roll; Comm Volntr; DARE; FCA; Bskball (V); Law; ECU-East Carolina; NC State-North Carolina

FUNDERBURK, ANGELA A; JAMESTOWN, NC; RAGSDALE HS; (JR); Hnr Roll; Jr Mshl; WWAHSS; Ch Chr; Track; Stu Cncl (R); Nursing; U of Greensboro; Winston-Salem U

FUNKHOUSER, DONALD; JACKSONVILLE, NC; NORTHSIDE HS; (SO); Duke TS; Hi Hnr Roll; Nat Hon Sy; Otst Ac Ach Awd; Perf Att; Comm Volntr; ArtClub; Chrch Yth Grp; Drma Clb; Orch; SP/M/VS; Stg Cre; All-County Orchestra Certificate; Culinary Arts; Journalism; Chapel Hill U

FUTRELL, MARTIN L; KELFORD, NC; HARTFORD CTY HS; (SO); Ftball (J)

GAIL, KENNY D; WACO, NC; BURNS HS; (FR); St of Mnth; Chrch Yth Grp; Emplmnt; Ntl FFA; ROTC; Ch Chr; Ftball (J); Wt Lftg (J); Aerospace; UIU; UNC State

GALLEMORE, MICHAEL W; HIGH POINT, NC; HIGH POINT CTRL HS; (SO); Hnr Roll; WWAHSS; Comm Volntr; Chrch Yth Grp; DARE; Emplmnt; Jr Ach; Key Club; NYLC; Prom Com; Quiz Bowl; Mch Bnd; Cl Off (S); National Leadership Conference

GAMBLE, JULIA L; FAYETTEVILLE, NC; E E SMITH SR HS; (SO); Ctznshp Aw; Hnr Roll; Comm Volntr; Chrch Yth Grp; FBLA; Ch Chr; 2003-2004 Citizenship Award; Business Administration & Economics; Pre Law (Corporate Attorney); Winston-Salem State U; U of North Carolina At Greensboro

GANDHI, ISHITA Y; WINTERVILLE, NC; D H CONLEY HS; (SO); DAR; Duke TS; Hi Hnr Roll; Hnr Roll; Otst Ac Ach Awd; Perf Att; St of Mnth; WWAHSS; Comm Volntr; Hosp Aide; Peer Tut/Med; Mth Clb/Tm; Ntl Beta Clb; P to P St Amb Prg; Dnce; Sccr (V); Vllyball (J); Stu Cncl (P); Various Dance Awards; Physician (MD); Pharmacist; U of North Carolina (Chapel Hill); Duke U

Fragoso, Jorge
A L Brown HS
Kannapolis, NC

Foster, La Quasha
Reynolds HS
Winston-Salem, NC

Fortune, Latrivia
Carter G Woodson Sch
Winston Salem, NC

Flowers, Kendra
Eastern Wayne HS
Goldsboro, NC

Fordham, Daniel
Forest Hills HS
Monroe, NC

Foy, Justin
Grays Creek HS
Fayetteville, NC

Gamble, Julia L
E E Smith SR HS
Fayetteville, NC

GANOE, KIMBERLY A; GREENSBORO, NC; PAGE HS; (JR); Hi Hnr Roll; Nat Hon Sy; WWAHSS; Comm Volntr; ArtClub; Spanish Clb; Vllyball (V L); Selected for Metro 4A Volleyball Conference Team 2004; Invited to Play in the King Kamehameha Volleyball Tournament in Hawaii; Business Management; Graphic Artist; Elon U; U of North Carolina At Chapel Hill

GANONG, JACI; OAK RIDGE, NC; NORTHWEST HS; (SR); Duke TS; Hnr Roll; Nat Hon Sy; WWAHSS; Red Cr Aide; NYLC; Play Piano, Guitar, Flute, Basketball, Soccer; Nursing; U of North Carolina At Greensboro; U of North Carolina At Chapel Hill

GANSON, TAMARA E; KING, NC; WEST STOKES HS; (JR); Ctznshp Aw; Hnr Roll; Red Cr Aide; Spec Olymp Vol; Chrch Yth Grp; Emplmnt; FCA; Pep Squd; Prom Com; Scouts; SADD; Vsity Clb; Ch Chr; Dnce; Mch Bnd; Chrldg (L); Hsbk Rdg (L); Swmg (V); Mascot, Varsity; HOSA; Large Animal Veterinarian; Public Relations Tourism; Clemson U; North Carolina State U

GARCIA, KARLA M; CARY, NC; CARDINAL GIBBONS HS; (SO); Duke TS; Hi Hnr Roll; Hnr Roll; Nat Hon Sy; Comm Volntr; Svce Clb; French Clb; Dnce; PPSqd (J); Sccr (J); Stu Cncl (T, R); CR; Highest Scholastic Average - 8th Grade; Scholar Athlete - 10th Grade; U of North Carolina Chapel Hill; Columbia U

GARCIA, MARIANA S; STATESVILLE, NC; STATESVILLE HS; (FR); Ctznshp Aw; F Lan Hn Soc; Kwnis Aw; Otst Ac Ach Awd; Perf Att; Sci Fairs; St of Mnth; Hab For Humty Volntr; Peer Tut/Med; Be a Teacher; My Own Business in Child Care; Mitchell Community College

GARCIA, RAUL; WINSTON SALEM, NC; REYNOLDS HS; (JR); Hnr Roll; Perf Att; CARE; Comm Volntr; Hab For Humty Volntr; ArtClub; Chrch Yth Grp; Fr of Library; Lib Aide; Mus Clb; Svce Clb; SADD; Tech Clb; Bnd; Ch Chr; Scr Kpr (V); Sccr (V); Most Improved; Perfect Attendance; Engineering; Commercial Architecture; North Carolina State U (Raleigh); U of North Carolina (At Charlotte)

GARDNER, HANNAH; PENLAND, NC; MITCHELL HS; (SR); Hnr Roll; Nat Hon Sy; WWAHSS; Lib Aide; Tchrs Aide; Chrldg (V); Business; Real Estate; UNC Charlotte; Johnson & Wales U Charlotte

GARDNER JR, EVERETT J; EFLAND, NC; ORANGE HS; (FR); Ctznshp Aw; Kwnis Aw; Nat Hon Sy; Otst Ac Ach Awd; Perf Att; Sci Fairs; Sci/Math Olympn; St of Mnth; WWAHSS; Comm Volntr; Peer Tut/Med; Red Cr Aide; 4-H; Chess; Chrch Yth Grp; DARE; Dbte Team; Drma Clb; Key Club; Mth Clb/Tm; Chr; SP/M/VS; Mar Art (V); Sccr; Swmg (V); Yrbk (E); Member of Robotics Team 587; Went to National Robotics Competitions; Civil Engineer V; Duke U; Campbell College or U of Chapel Hill

GARDUNO, JOSEFINA; HOLLISTER, NC; NORTHWEST HS; (FR); Hi Hnr Roll; Hnr Roll; Nat Hon Sy; Otst Ac Ach Awd; Perf Att; Sci Fairs; St of Mnth; Scouts; Secretary; Halifax Community College

GARNER, CHRISTOPHER; NEWPORT, NC; CAPE LOOKOUT MARINE SCIENCE HS; Hnr Roll; MVP; Comm Volntr; ArtClub; Quiz Bowl; Ftball (V); Wt Lftg (V); Stu Cncl (R); Participated in Writing Student Constitution; Langston Hughes Poetry Award; Architectural Design; Eastern Carolina U; U of North Carolina Wilmington

GARNER JR, WILLIAM; ASHEBORO, NC; EASTERN RANDOLPH HS; (JR); Hnr Roll; MVP; Spec Olymp Vol; Chrch Yth Grp; Emplmnt; Ntl Beta Clb; ROTC; Cr Ctry (V); Sccr (V CL); Track (V); Wrstlg (VJ L); Coaches' Award for Soccer; Sports Medicine; Physical Therapy; Wake Forest U; U of North Carolina-Greensboro

GARREN, CRYSTAL M; ABERDEEN, NC; PINECREST HS; (SR); Hi Hnr Roll; Nat Hon Sy; Nat Mrt Fin; Sci Fairs; WWAHSS; Spec Olymp Vol; Chrch Yth Grp; DARE; Dbte Team; Emplmnt; NtlFrnscLg; Quill & Scroll; Scouts; Tchrs Aide; Bnd; Mch Bnd; Sch Ppr (R); Interact Club; Girl Scout Gold Award; English Teacher; U of NC Greensboro

GARRETT, JOSEPH T; PLYMOUTH, NC; PLYMOUTH HS; (SO); Hnr Roll; Emplmnt; FBLA; Ntl Beta Clb; Scouts; Dnce; Volunteer Work with Boy Scouts; Architecture; North Carolina State U

GARRISON, MIRANDA A; BLACK MOUNTAIN, NC; OWEN HS; (SO); Duke TS; Hi Hnr Roll; Otst Ac Ach Awd; WWAHSS; Yth Ldrshp Prog; Comm Volntr; Peer Tut/Med; Chrch Yth Grp; Emplmnt; FCA; Key Club; Mth Clb/Tm; P to P St Amb Prg; SADD; French Clb; Ch Chr; Dnce; Golf (V); CR (R); Yrbk; International Business; Criminal Justice

GARTMAN, BEN; WEST END, NC; PINECREST HS; (SO); Hi Hnr Roll; Hnr Roll; WWAHSS; Chrch Yth Grp; Key Club; Sccr (J)

GARTNER, JONATHON R; HUNTERSVILLE, NC; NORTH MECKLENBURG HS; (JR); Peer Tut/Med; Emplmnt; Tech Clb; Ftball (J); 6 Years Piano, Architectural Design Club; Nat'l Tech Honor Society, Baseball/Basketball Teacher; Architecture; Public Relations; U of North Carolina; North Carolina State U

GARZA, ALEXANDRA A; ROXBORO, NC; PERSON HS; (FR); Duke TS; Hnr Roll; Otst Ac Ach Awd; Perf Att; St Schl; Key Club; NYLC; Spanish Clb; Dnce; Chemistry; Molecular Genetics; Davidson College; Princeton U

GATES JR, WILLIAM E; FAYETTEVILLE, NC; SOUTHVIEW HS; (SO); Ctznshp Aw; Hi Hnr Roll; Hnr Roll; Nat Hon Sy; Nat Sci Aw; Otst Ac Ach Awd; Perf Att; Pres Ac Ftns Aw; Sci Fairs; St of Mnth; Comm Volntr; Chrch Yth Grp; DARE; Prom Com; Wdwrkg Clb; BMX Racer; Computers

GATLING, TERRELL Q; AHOSKIE, NC; HERTFORD CTY HS; 4H Awd; Hnr Roll; DARE; FBLA; Scouts; Ch Chr; Sch Ppr (R, P); Yrbk (R); Future Business Leader of America Awards; North Carolina Central U

GAY, BRIANCA; CHARLOTTE, NC; HARDING U HS; (FR); Ctznshp Aw; Hnr Roll; Perf Att; Peer Tut/Med; DARE; Drma Clb; Jr Ach; Dnce; Drl Tm; SP/M/VS; Choreographer; Dancer; Any School of Arts

GAYDON, DENVER; JACKSONVILLE, NC; WHITE OAK HS; (MS); Ctznshp Aw; Hnr Roll; Nat Hon Sy; Sci Fairs; St of Mnth; Chess; Chrch Yth Grp; DARE; Chr; Ch Chr; SP/M/VS; Stu Cncl (R); National Junior Honor Society; Computer Specialist; Youth Minister

GEGENHEIMER, LAUREN; HIGH POINT, NC; T W ANDREWS HS; (JR); Chrch Yth Grp; Drma Clb; Emplmnt; Ntl Beta Clb; SP/M/VS; Stg Cre; Sch Ppr (R); Appalachian State U; Western Carolina U

GEIBEL III, CONRAD J; CARY, NC; GREEN HOPE HS; (SO); Hi Hnr Roll; Hnr Roll; Sci Clb; Bnd; Mch Bnd; Engineering; North Carolina State U

GEIER, BRITTNEY; MATTHEWS, NC; SUN VALLEY HS; (MS); Hnr Roll; Nat Hon Sy; Comm Volntr; Peer Tut/Med; Chrch Yth Grp; Emplmnt; Scouts; Bnd; Softball for a Recreation Team; Lawyer Criminal; Carolina (UNC); Penn State

GENDRON, DANIELLE N; CHARLOTTE, NC; CHARLOTTE CHRISTIAN SCH; (FR); Duke TS; Hi Hnr Roll; Sci/Math Olympn; Comm Volntr; Drma Clb; Chr; SP/M/VS; Sftball (L); Lit Mag (R); Advanced Brown Belt- Tae Kwon Do; Fox Hunting Member of MHI; Writing; Spanish

GENTRY, DEVIN; MORGANTON, NC; FREEDOM HS; (SR); F Lan Hn Soc; Hnr Roll; Sci Fairs; Cmptr Clb; Tchrs Aide; German Clb; Pres.-Gaming Club VP-Computer Club, Founding Mem.-Cartooning Club; Journalism; UNC-Chapel Hill-NC

GETTYS, KRISTEN E; LINCOLNTON, NC; LINCOLNTON HS; (SR); Hnr Roll; Jr Mshl; Nat Hon Sy; WWAHSS; Comm Volntr; Chrch Yth Grp; Emplmnt; Key Club; Ntl Beta Clb; Scouts; Tchrs Aide; Ch Chr; Mch Bnd; Occupational Therapy; U of North Carolina Chapel Hill

GIBBONS, CHELSEA E; HIGH POINT, NC; LEDFORD HS; (JR); Hnr Roll; MVP; Pres Ac Ftns Aw; WWAHSS; Comm Volntr; Chrch Yth Grp; DARE; FCA; Lttrmn Clb; Sci Clb; Spanish Clb; Chrldg (V L); PP Ftbl; Sftball (J); Wt Lftg; National Champion Female Senior; Nat'l Champ. Sr Coed Partner Stunt Division/All Star Cheerleader; Chemistry Major; Pre-Med; NC State; Clemson

GIBBS, BRIANNA; MORGANTON, NC; FREEDOM HS; (SR); Hnr Roll; Perf Att; WWAHSS; Mus Clb; Pep Squd; Tchrs Aide; German Clb; Acpl Chr; Chr; Bskball (J L); Track (V CL); Management Info Systems; Sports Management; Brevard College; High Point U

GIBBS, TAMMIE; DUDLEY, NC; SOUTHERN WAYNE HS; (SR); Ctznshp Aw; Duke TS; F Lan Hn Soc; Gov Hnr Prg; Hi Hnr Roll; Jr Mshl; Nat Hon Sy; Otst Ac Ach Awd; St of Mnth; WWAHSS; Comm Volntr; Hab For Humty Volntr; ArtClub; Chrch Yth Grp; FBLA; FCCLA; Prom Com; Quiz Bowl; Spanish Clb; Ch Chr; Cl Off (S); Stu Cncl (P); Scholastic Art Awards; Next Step Magazine Super Teen; Architecture; Graphic Design; North Carolina State U; East Carolina U

GIBSON, ADAM; SHARPSBURG, NC; SOUTHERN NASH HS; (FR); Hnr Roll; Scouts; Bnd; Cr Ctry (J); Track (J); Order of the Arrow (BSA); Major in Business; Major in Criminal Justice; North Carolina State U; U of North Carolina

GIBSON, BETHANY; MONROE, NC; SUN VALLEY HS; (FR); Ctznshp Aw; Hnr Roll; Hosp Aide; Chrch Yth Grp; DARE; Scouts; Bnd; Mch Bnd; Writing; Music; Wingate U

GIBSON, BRITTANY N; MURPHY, NC; MURPHY HS; (SO); Duke TS; Hi Hnr Roll; Pres Sch; WWAHSS; FCA; FBLA; Ntl Beta Clb; Spanish Clb; Chrldg (VJ); Cl Off (T); CR (T); Sch Ppr (R, P); Yrbk (R, P); Major - Political Science / Pre-Law; Minor - Spanish; U of North Carolina Chapel Hill; Tulane U

GIBSON, CANDACE; PLYMOUTH, NC; PLYMOUTH HS; (FR); Hi Hnr Roll; FBLA; Mth Clb/Tm; Nursing; PhD; North Carolina Central U; East Carolina U

GIBSON, CHARLEY; STANLEY, NC; EAST GASTON HS; (SO); WWAHSS; ROTC; Dnce; Vllyball (J); Bowling on a League; Villa Julie

GILBERT, SAXAN R; ELIZABETH CITY, NC; NORTHEASTERN HS; (SO); Hnr Roll; Chrch Yth Grp; DARE; Drma Clb; Chr; SP/M/VS; Swmg (V); Tennis (V); Yrbk (E, R, P); Superintendent's Academic Team; Drama/Theatre Arts; Marine Biology; San Diego State U; U of North Florida

GILLESPIE, JENELL L; LUMBERTON, NC; LUMBERTON HS; (SO); Hi Hnr Roll; WWAHSS; Comm Volntr; Chrch Yth Grp; Ntl Beta Clb; Bnd; Ch Chr; Mch Bnd; Law; Psychology; Howard U; North Carolina Central U

GILLESPIE JR, DAVID B; RALEIGH, NC; WAKEFIELD HS; (JR); F Lan Hn Soc; Hi Hnr Roll; Jr Mshl; Nat Hon Sy; Otst Ac Ach Awd; WWAHSS; Yth Ldrshp Prog; Comm Volntr; Emplmnt; Jr Cls League; Key Club; Prom Com; Sci Clb; Ftball (VJCL); CR; Key Club President; Perfect Score on National Latin I Exam; Psychology; Biology; U of North Carolina Chapel Hill; Wake Forest U

GILLIAM, DAVION A; WINDSOR, NC; BERTIE HS; (JR); Ctznshp Aw; Hnr Roll; Otst Ac Ach Awd; WWAHSS; Red Cr Aide; DARE; Acpl Chr; Chr; Ch Chr; SP/M/VS; Psychology; Fayetteville State U; U of NC Greensboro

GILLIS, ANDREW D; FAYETTEVILLE, NC; JACK BRITT HS; (SR); Hnr Roll; Jr Mshl; Nat Hon Sy; Pres Sch; St Schl; WWAHSS; Yth Ldrshp Prog; Comm Volntr; Peer Tut/Med; Spec Olymp Vol; Chrch Yth Grp; Emplmnt; Key Club; Lib Aide; Off Aide; Prom Com; Svce Clb; Tchrs Aide; Bnd; Ch Chr; Mch Bnd; Lit Mag (R); Sch Ppr (R); Key Club Lt. Governor; President of Navigators; Textile Engineer; Aerospace Engineer; North Carolina State U

GLADDEN, MORGAN; MEBANE, NC; EASTERN HS; (SR); Nat Hon Sy; Spec Olymp Vol; Key Club; Cr Ctry (J); Track (J); Wrstlg (J); Stu Cncl (R); Computer Programming; NC State

GLASPIE, LAKEISHA; TURKEY, NC; JAMES KENAN HS; (JR); Hi Hnr Roll; Hnr Roll; Nat Hon Sy; Perf Att; WWAHSS; Yth Ldrshp Prog; Comm Volntr; Peer Tut/Med; Emplmnt; FTA; HO'Br Yth Ldrshp; Key Club; Stu Cncl (R); CR (R); Project Uplift 2003; Pharmacy; Nutrition; Campbell; U of North Carolina & Chapel Hill

GLENN, LAUREN E; HICKORY, NC; HICKORY HS; (SO); Duke TS; Fut Prb Slvr; Hnr Roll; Pres Ac Ftns Aw; Sci Fairs; St of Mnth; Yth Ldrshp Prog; Comm Volntr; Chrch Yth Grp; Emplmnt; French Clb; Law; U of North Carolina @ Chapel Hill; U of North Carolina @ Wilmington

GLOER, MARY; APEX, NC; MIDDLE CREEK HS; (JR); Hi Hnr Roll; Hnr Roll; ArtClub; Cr Ctry (V L); First Premium Computer Art Award; Medical Science; Liberal Arts; Duke U; North Carolina State

GLOVER, ASHLEY B; JACKSONVILLE, NC; NORTHSIDE HS; (JR); Hnr Roll; Nat Hon Sy; Nat Mrt LOC; Otst Ac Ach Awd; Perf Att; USAA; WWAHSS; Peer Tut/Med; FBLA; Key Club; Ch Chr; Chrldg (C); CR (R); Attended Free Enterprise Leadership; Conference/USNMLA; Journalism; Teaching; Howard U; Duke U

GLOVER, ASHLEY L; RALEIGH, NC; NB BRIGHTON HS; (JR); Hnr Roll; Comm Volntr; Peer Tut/Med; Spec Olymp Vol; Drma Clb; ROTC; Clr Grd; Drl Tm; Mch Bnd; SP/M/VS; Philosophy; Political Science; New York U; Duke U

GLOVER, JAMES; FAYETTEVILLE, NC; E E SMITH SR HS; (SO); Ftball (VJ); Nursing; Surgery; U of North Carolina Chapel Hill; U of Miami

GLOVER, REGINA; ROCKY MOUNT, NC; NASH CTRL HS; (FR); Hnr Roll; Nat Hon Sy; Nat Stu Ath Day Aw; Otst Ac Ach Awd; Drma Clb; Spanish Clb; Dnce; Chrldg (J); Cr Ctry (J); Business Law; Florida State U; California State U

GLOVER, TANEISHA; FAYETTEVILLE, NC; E E SMITH SR HS; (SO); Peer Tut/Med; Bskball (JC); Cr Ctry (V); Track (V); Vsy Clb (V); Vllyball (J); Student Athlete Organization, Gear Up, AVID; Physical Therapy; Psychology; Louisiana State U; Chapel Hill U North Carolina

GODWIN, AMANDA; ERWIN, NC; TRITON HS; (JR); Hnr Roll; ROTC; In JROTC, My Rank Is Now Cadet Sergeant First Class; I Am On The JROTC Drill Team; Accounting; Nursing; Catawba College, Salisbury, NC; High Point U, High Point, NC

GODWIN JR, TONY R; ROXBORO, NC; PERSON HS; (FR); Hnr Roll; Peer Tut/Med; 4-H; DARE; Mus Clb; ROTC; Bnd; Ch Chr; Mch Bnd; Marching Band; JROTC; Master's Degree in Biology; Bachelor's Degree in Chemistry; U of North Carolina in Chapel Hill; North Carolina A & T in Greensboro

GOFORTH, MICHAEL D; HAMPTONVILLE, NC; STARMOUNT HS; (SO); Hnr Roll; Scouts; Bnd; Chr; Jzz Bnd; Mch Bnd; Life Scout for Boy Scouts of Am Will Be Eagle Scout Soon; Degree in Music Production; Western Carolina

GOLDEN, BRIANNA; CARY, NC; GREEN HOPE HS; (FR); Hi Hnr Roll; Hnr Roll; Nat Sci Aw; St of Mnth; Comm Volntr; Chrch Yth Grp; Ntl Beta Clb; Clb; Cr Ct Ski (VJCL); Ice Hky (VJCL); PP Ftbl; Skiing (JCL); Sftball (J); National Charity League-Secretary & President; Dupont Challenge Finalist; Public Relations; Marketing; Appalachian State U; U of Georgia

GOLDSTEIN, MACY C; ASHEVILLE, NC; CAROLINA DAY SCH; (JR); Pres Ac Ftns Aw; Pres Sch; Comm Volntr; Hab For Humty Volntr; Spec Olymp Vol; ArtClub; Dbte Team; Photog; Prom Com; SADD; Hsbk Rdg (V); Cl Off (R); International Relations; Tufts U; UNC Chapel Hill

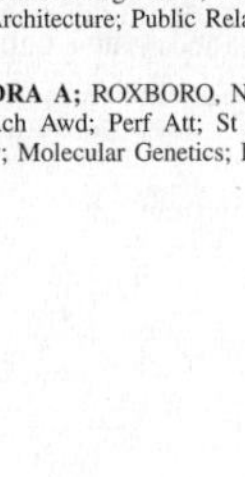

Glover, Regina
Nash Ctrl HS
Rocky Mount, NC

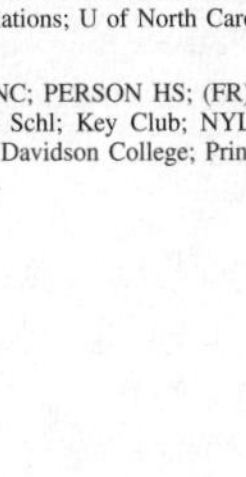

Gibbons, Chelsea E
Ledford HS
High Point, NC

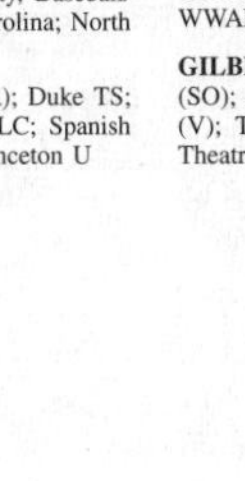

Gegenheimer, Lauren
T W Andrews HS
High Point, NC

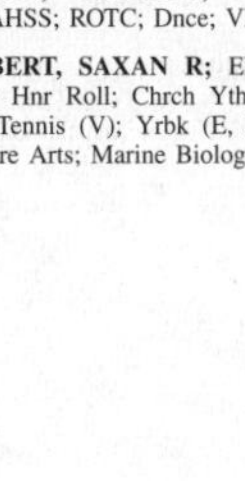

Gardner Jr, Everett J
Orange HS
Efland, NC

National
Honor Roll
Spring 2005

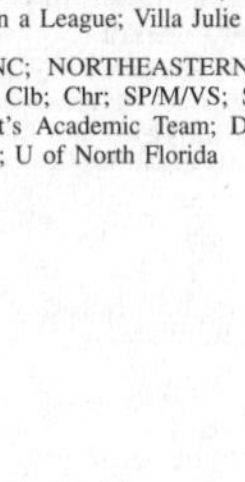

Garcia, Raul
Reynolds HS
Winston Salem, NC

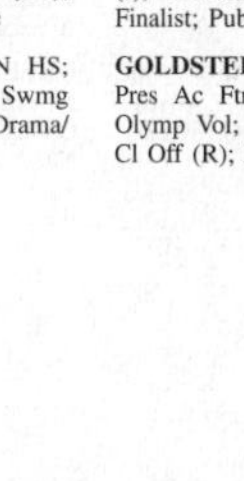

Geier, Brittney
Sun Valley HS
Matthews, NC

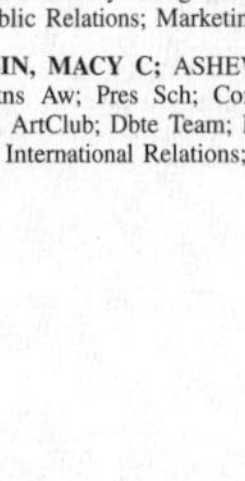

Gibson, Brittany N
Murphy HS
Murphy, NC

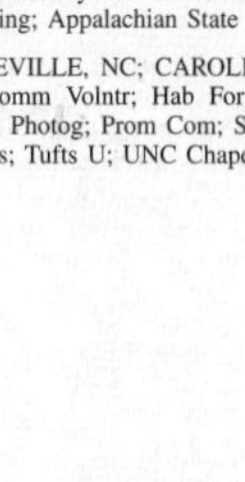

Glover, Taneisha
E E Smith SR HS
Fayetteville, NC

GOMEZ, ABRAHAM R; DOVER, NC; WCHS; (SR); Perf Att; St of Mnth; Comm Volntr; Peer Tut/Med; Chrch Yth Grp; Track (L); Outstanding Student; Bachelors Degree; Master Degree; East Carolina U; Craven Community College

GONSALVES, LIANNE; CARY, NC; CARY AC; (JR); Duke TS; F Lan Hn Soc; Hi Hnr Roll; Nat Hon Sy; Otst Ac Ach Awd; WWAHSS; Hosp Aide; Peer Tut/Med; Dbte Team; Ntl Beta Clb; Quiz Bowl; Chr; SP/M/VS; Cr Ctry (V L); Track (V L); Teen Court Attorney; Pre-Med; Biology; U of North Carolina Chapel Hill; Davidson College

GONZALEZ, ALEXIS; INDIAN TRAIL, NC; SUN VALLEY HS; (FR); Hnr Roll; Comm Volntr; ArtClub; DARE; Ntl Beta Clb; Scouts; Vsity Clb; SP/M/VS; Stg Cre; Chrldg (V); Vsy Clb (V); Siskey YMCA, Mind Body Spirit Award; Law; Communications; U of North Carolina Chapel Hill; Spelman U

GONZALEZ-GRAY, GABRIELLE; CHARLOTTE, NC; CHARLOTTE CTRY DAY SCH; MS; MVP; Nat Hon Sy; Comm Volntr; Peer Tut/Med; Prom Com; Bnd; Cr Ctry (J); Scr Kpr (VJ); Track (J); Adv Cncl (R); NJHS; Peer Counselor; Physical Therapy/Sports Medicine; Neurology; Princeton; Harvard

GOOD, ASHLEY; LENOIR, NC; WEST CALDWELL HS; (JR); Gov Hnr Prg; Hi Hnr Roll; Jr Mshl; WWAHSS; Drma Clb; Emplmnt; MuAlphaTh; Ntl Beta Clb; SP/M/VS; Tennis (V L); Cl Off (P); NC Baptist Assn Speakers Tournament Winner; U of North Carolina At Chapel Hill; Wake Forest U

GOODEN, CANDACE A; BLADENBORO, NC; WEST BLADEN HS; (JR); Hi Hnr Roll; Hnr Roll; Pres Sch; DARE; Emplmnt; Key Club; Ntl Beta Clb; SADD; Spanish Clb; Bnd; Mch Bnd; Bladen County Academic Achievement Certificate; National Jr. Beta Club; Physical Therapist; Physician Assistant; East Carolina U; U of North Carolina At Chapel Hill

GOODSON, AARON T; FAYETTEVILLE, NC; HEAD-ROYCE SCH; (SO); Duke TS; MVP; Nat Hon Sy; Sci/Math Olympn; WWAHSS; Comm Volntr; Ch Chr; Bskball (J L); Tennis (V L); Cl Off (S); CR (S); Most Valuable Player-Varsity Tennis; Computer Science; Computer Engineering; U of California-Berkeley; Stanford U

GOODSON, HANNAH; NEW HILL, NC; APEX HS; (JR); Duke TS; Hnr Roll; Nat Hon Sy; WWAHSS; Chrch Yth Grp; FCA; Bnd; Chr; Cr Ctry (VJ); Swmg (V L); Stu Cncl; Academic & Talent (Piano) Scholarship in Jr Miss Program; Nursing; Environmental Science; U of North Carolina at Chapel Hill; East Carolina U of North Carolina

GOODSON, LAURA M; FAYETTEVILLE, NC; F E SMITH SR HS; Emplmnt; Photog; Chr; Sang with Local Teen Band "Phayze 4"; Business, Esthetics or Music

GOODSON, MORGAN L; WINSTON SALEM, NC; CALVARY BAPTIST HS; (SR); Hnr Roll; Jr Mshl; Nat Hon Sy; WWAHSS; Spec Olymp Vol; Chrch Yth Grp; MuAlphaTh; Prom Com; Svce Clb; SADD; Chrldg (V CL); Sccr (V); Stu Cncl (S, T); Homecoming Court; Christian Leadership Award; Health and Exercise Science / Fitness; Liberty U

GOODWIN, BRANDON T; RALEIGH, NC; EAST WAKE HS; (SR); Hnr Roll; Perf Att; Emplmnt; Ftball (V L); Wt Lftg (V); NC State Educational Talent Search; Music Production; Computer Graphics; Elizabeth City State U; UNCA

GOOSELIN, ELIZABETH; BURGAW, NC; PENDER HS; (FR); Hnr Roll; MVP; Chrch Yth Grp; DARE; Drma Clb; Scouts; SP/M/VS; Sftball (J); Cosmetology; Cape Fear Community College; Miller-Motte Technical College - U of North Carolina

GORDON, JELISA; CHARLOTTE, NC; BRISBANE ACAD MATH & SCIENCE PREP SCH; (FR); Hnr Roll; Sci Fairs; St of Mnth; Yth Ldrshp Prog; Peer Tut/Med; Dbte Team; Drma Clb; Lib Aide; Off Aide; Pep Squd; Ch Chr; Dnce; Chrldg (J); Track; CR (R); Sch Ppr (E, R); Yrbk (E); 1st Place In Public Speaking Contest; BA Criminal Justice; Law JD / Concentration in Real Estate Law; UNC Charlotte; Tuskegee U

GORHAM, SHAKINA; FARMVILLE, NC; FARMVILLE CTRL HS; (SO); Perf Att; Pres Ac Ftns Aw; Hosp Aide; Bskball (VJ); Sftball (V); Nursing; North Carolina Agricultural & Tech State U; North Carolina School of Arts

GORIS, KRYSTAL; KILL DEVIL HILLS, NC; FIRST FLIGHT HS; (JR); Hnr Roll; Nat Hon Sy; WWAHSS; Comm Volntr; Key Club; Spanish Clb; SP/M/VS; History; Law; Columbia U; U of North Carolina Chapel Hill

GOSS, CHRISTINA S; RALEIGH, NC; FRIENDSHIP CHRISTIAN SCH; (SR); Hnr Roll; Nat Hon Sy; Sci/Math Olympn; Chrch Yth Grp; Biochemistry; Genetics; U of North Carolina Greensboro; North Carolina State U

GOUGE, PHILLIP; THURMOND, NC; EAST WILKES MS; (MS); Hnr Roll; Perf Att; Sci Fairs; Sci/Math Olympn; Chess; DARE; Chr; Sccr; Wrstlg; Scorpion Pride Award; Civil Engineering; Computer Technology; Wilkes Community College; Appalachian State University

GOULD, SAMANTHA; BISCOE, NC; EAST MONTGOMERY HS; (SO); Chrch Yth Grp; Ch Chr; Manager-Varsity Girls; Cosmo; Fashion Design; UNC Chapel Hill (Carolina)

GOULD, SYLVIA J; ARCHDALE, NC; TRINITY HS; (FR); Hnr Roll; St of Mnth; Comm Volntr; Chrch Yth Grp; ROTC; French Clb; Drl Tm; Cadet of the Week in AFJROTC; Various AFJROTC Awards; Air Force; Teaching; U of North Carolina Charlotte; U of North Carolina Greensboro

GRACE, LATOYA; LOUISBURG, NC; LOUISBURG HS; (FR); Sci Fairs; Comm Volntr; Ch Chr; Track; Associate's Degree; Lafayetteville U; Georgia Tech

GRADY III, HENRY C; MOUNT OLIVE, NC; NORTH DUPLIN JR/SR HS; (SO); Hnr Roll; Chrch Yth Grp; Ntl FFA; Bsball (J); Ftball (V)

GRAGG, KERRIE; MORGANTON, NC; WEST CALDWELL HS; (SO); Hnr Roll; Otst Ac Ach Awd; Perf Att; Sci Fairs; St of Mnth; Comm Volntr; Hab For Humty Volntr; Chrch Yth Grp; Emplmnt; FTA; Ntl Beta Clb; SADD; Spanish Clb; Ch Chr; Ice Sktg (J); Scr Kpr (J); Wt Lftg (J); Teacher; Writer; Caldwell Community Tech.; Western Piedmont

GRAHAM, CHARLES; SPRING LANE, NC; OVERHILLS HS; (JR); Hi Hnr Roll; Hnr Roll; Otst Ac Ach Awd; Perf Att; Pres Sch; 4-H; Chrch Yth Grp; Mth Clb/Tm; ROTC; Schol Bwl; Sci Clb; Clr Grd; Drl Tm; Daedalian Medal; Computer Programming/Engineering; Military Science; U of Advancing Technology; Johnson & Wales U

GRAHAM, CHRISTOPHER F; FAISON, NC; NORTH DUPLIN JR/SR HS; (FR); Hnr Roll; MVP; Otst Ac Ach Awd; Perf Att; Pres Ac Ftns Aw; DARE; SADD; Bsball (J); Bskball (J); Ftball (J); Wt Lftg (J); Upward Bound; Engineer, Lawyer, Judge; Doctor; Duke U, N.C. State U; North Carolina U

GRANT, CAMERON; FAYETTEVILLE, NC; SEVENTY-FIRST HS; (FR); Ctznshp Aw; Hnr Roll; MVP; Perf Att; Yth Ldrshp Prog; DARE; Emplmnt; P to P St Amb Prg; Bskball (J L); Dvng (V); Ftball (V); GAA (V); Gmnstcs (V); Hsbk Rdg (V); Picked to Play on Elite Basketball Team; Sociology; African American Studies; U of North Carolina; Villanova U

GRANT, VALARIE; APEX, NC; APEX HS; (SO); Duke TS; Hnr Roll; Nat Hon Sy; Pres Sch; Comm Volntr; DECA; Key Club; Chrldg (JC); PP Ftbl; Business; Pre-Law; U of North Carolina Chapel Hill; North Carolina State U

GRANTHAM, MATTHEW R; JACKSONVILLE, NC; WHITE OAK HS; (MS); Duke TS; Perf Att; Bnd; Mch Bnd; SP/M/VS; Bsball (J); Bskball (J); Sccr (J); Wrstlg (J)

GRANTHAM, TIFFANY B; GOLDSBORO, NC; GOLDSBORO HS; (SR); Hnr Roll; Otst Ac Ach Awd; WWAHSS; Drma Clb; FTA; Prom Com; Dnce; SP/M/VS; Stg Cre; Chrldg (VJ); Sftball (V); President of a Step Team; Radio/Television Production; English; North Carolina Agriculture and Technical U

GRATES, NICKI; FAYETTEVILLE, NC; TERRY SANFORD HS; (SR); Duke TS; Hnr Roll; Jr Mshl; Nat Hon Sy; Nat Sci Aw; WWAHSS; Yth Ldrshp Prog; Comm Volntr; AL Aux Girls; FCA; Key Club; Spanish Clb; Dnce; Bskball (J); Sftball (V CL); Vllyball (V CL); Stu Cncl (R); Health and Exercise Science; Sports Medicine; Furman U

GRAVELY, TIERA; WINSTON SALEM, NC; ATKINS HS; (MS); Scouts; Chr; SP/M/VS; Bskball; Most Improved Science; Meteorology; Theatre Arts; U of North Carolina

GRAVES, MORGAN; GREENSBORO, NC; DUDLEY HS; (FR); Hnr Roll; Otst Ac Ach Awd; Pres Ac Ftns Aw; St of Mnth; WWAHSS; Comm Volntr; Peer Tut/Med; Chrch Yth Grp; Emplmnt; Jr Ach; Ntl Beta Clb; Bnd; Chr; Ch Chr; Sftball (JV/V); Vllyball (V); Cl Off (V); Miss Freshman; Genetics / Biology

GRAY, CHRISTOPHER R; RALEIGH, NC; SOUTHEAST RALEIGH HS; (SR); FCA; Self-Employed Web Designer; Young American Bowlers Assn-10 Years; Computer Science; North Carolina State U

GRAY, LESLIE; ARCHCALE, NC; TRINITY HS; (JR); Hnr Roll; Jr Mshl; Nat Hon Sy; Pres Ac Ftns Aw; USAA; WWAHSS; Comm Volntr; Emplmnt; NYLC; Prom Com; Bskball (V L); Cr Ctry (V L); Swmg (V L); Tennis (L); Cl Off (V); Stu Cncl (R)

GRAY, NICHOLAS P; CHARLOTTE, NC; ZEBULON B VANCE HS; (JR); Hnr Roll; Jr Mshl; Nat Hon Sy; Perf Att; WWAHSS; ArtClub; Chrch Yth Grp; Emplmnt; Track; National Technical Honor Society Member; National Society of High School Scholars Member; Mechanical Engineering; Computer Engineering; North Carolina State U; Michigan State U

GRAY, WESTLEIGH A; ROLESVILLE, NC; WAKE FOREST-ROLESVILLE HS; (JR); Peer Tut/Med; Dbte Team; SP/M/VS; Stg Cre; Lead Roles in Musicals & Plays; Robert Winston Award in SLA Debate; UNC Wilmington, Theatre Arts, History, Psychology; UNC Wilmington; U of Appalachian State

GREEN, BRIANNA M; SPINDALE, NC; RUTHERFORDTON SPINDALE MS; MS; Hnr Roll; Peer Tut/Med; DARE; Emplmnt; Ntl Beta Clb; Chr; Dnce; Chrldg (C); Competition Cheerleading; Competition Dance; Anesthesiologist; Nurse Anesthesis; U of North Carolina; Wake Forest

GREEN, JESSICA N; MURPHY, NC; HIWASSEE DAM HS; (JR); Hi Hnr Roll; Hnr Roll; Perf Att; Comm Volntr; Hosp Aide; Emplmnt; Off Aide; SP/M/VS; Office Systems Technology; Business Administration; Tri-County Community College

GREEN, NIKKI; DALLAS, NC; NORTH GASTON HS; (SO); Hnr Roll; Perf Att; St of Mnth; ArtClub; Vllyball (J); Beta Club; Art/Photography; Business; Gaston College; U of North Carolina of Charlotte

GREEN, PRINCESS; ENFIELD, NC; N W HALIFAX HS; (SR); Hi Hnr Roll; Hnr Roll; Nat Hon Sy; Nat Sci Aw; Otst Ac Ach Awd; Perf Att; Sci Fairs; St of Mnth; USAA; Yth Ldrshp Prog; CARE; Peer Tut/Med; Red Cr Aide; ArtClub; Biology Clb; DARE; Drma Clb; Mus Clb; Pep Squd; ROTC; Sci Clb; Bnd; Chr; Dnce; Drm Mjr; Bskball (J); Chrldg (V); Gmnstcs (V); Sccr (C); Sftball (V); Swmg (V); Track (C); Wt Lftg (J); Adv Cncl (R); Cl Off (T); Stu Cncl (V); CR (P); Lit Mag (R); Sch Ppr (P); Yrbk (P); A & T; Shaw U

GREEN, TAMEEKA T; NEW BERN, NC; PAMLICA CTY HS; (SR); Hnr Roll; Perf Att; St Schl; Emplmnt; SADD; Spanish Clb; Chr; Wt Lftg; Stu Cncl (V); CR (R); Principal's Award; NC Scholar; Business Administration; Psychology; Elizabeth City State U; Fayetteville State U

GREENE, ASHLEY D; TAYLORSVILLE, NC; ALEXANDER CTRL HS; (SR); Ctznshp Aw; Nat Hon Sy; Perf Att; Pres Ac Ftns Aw; Sci Fairs; WWAHSS; Drma Clb; Tchrs Aide; President of Creative Writing; English Education; Creative Writing; U of North Carolina Asheville; Appalachian State U

GREENE, BRITTANY; BOSTIC, NC; EAST RUTHERFORD HS; (FR); Nat Hon Sy; Comm Volntr; Red Cr Aide; Chrch Yth Grp; Scouts; Clr Grd; CR (R); Western Carolina State U; Eastern Carolina State U

GREENE, CAITLIN S; HICKORY, NC; HICKORY HS; (SO); Duke TS; Hi Hnr Roll; Hnr Roll; Perf Att; Sci Fairs; Comm Volntr; Emplmnt; Off Aide; Svce Clb; Sccr (J); 2-Yr. Hickory High Academic Boosters Club; English Department European Trip; Fashion Design

GREENE, CRYSTAL R; BOSTIC, NC; EAST RUTHERFORD HS; (JR); Hnr Roll; WWAHSS; Comm Volntr; Hosp Aide; Red Cr Aide; Chrch Yth Grp; Emplmnt; FBLA; Key Club; Scouts; Tchrs Aide; Sccr (V L); Yrbk (E, R); Bachelor in Nursing-BSN; Western Carolina U

GREENE, MEREDITH A; BUIES CREEK, NC; HARNETT CTRL HS; (JR); F Lan Hn Soc; Gov Hnr Prg; Hi Hnr Roll; Jr Mshl; Sci/Math Olympn; WWAHSS; Chrch Yth Grp; FCA; HO'Br Yth Ldrshp; Key Club; Ntl Beta Clb; Sci Clb; SADD; Ch Chr; Stg Cre; Rotary Youth Leadership Award; Summer Ventures in Science and Math; Biochemistry Major; Campbell U

GREENE, PATRICIA H; BUIES CREEK, NC; HARNETT CTRL HS; (SR); F Lan Hn Soc; Fut Prb Slvr; Gov Hnr Prg; Hi Hnr Roll; Jr Mshl; Perf Att; Pres Sch; Sci/Math Olympn; WWAHSS; Chrch Yth Grp; FCA; Key Club; Ntl Beta Clb; Sci Clb; Ch Chr; Stg Cre; Sftball (JC); Woodman of the World for US History; Religion; English; Campbell U

GREENE II, VINCENT K; MEBANE, NC; DURHAM SCH OF THE ARTS; (SO); Hnr Roll; Pres Sch; Comm Volntr; Mus Clb; Bnd; Jzz Bnd; Pep Bnd; Major in Biology and Other Medical Sciences; U of North Carolina; Duke U

GREGORY, MICHELLE; GARNER, NC; WEST JOHNSTON HS; (JR); Hnr Roll; Nat Hon Sy; WWAHSS; DECA; Emplmnt; Business Administration; Management; East Carolina U; Campbell U

GRIER, JOSHUA M; RALEIGH, NC; WAKEFIELD HS; (SO); Ctznshp Aw; Hi Hnr Roll; Hnr Roll; Otst Ac Ach Awd; Chrch Yth Grp; Key Club; Engineering; North Carolina State U

GRIER, SHANEKA; CHARLOTTE, NC; GARINGER SR HS; (JR); Ctznshp Aw; Hi Hnr Roll; Hnr Roll; MVP; Otst Ac Ach Awd; Perf Att; St of Mnth; WWAHSS; Hosp Aide; Peer Tut/Med; Red Cr Aide; Civil Air Pat; DARE; Emplmnt; FBLA; Mth Clb/Tm; Pep Squd; ROTC; SADD; Bnd; Chr; Drl Tm; Mch Bnd; GAA (J); Sccr (V); Vllyball (J); CR (V); Pre-Med; Nursing; Winston Salem State U; NC State U

GRIFFIN, DANIEL; OXFORD, NC; SOUTH GRANVILLE HS; (FR); Hnr Roll; Kwnis Aw; Nat Mrt LOC; Otst Ac Ach Awd; Perf Att; Peer Tut/Med; Chrch Yth Grp; DARE; Bsball (J); National Junior Honor Society 7th-9th Grade; A/B Honor Roll Student Every School Year; Master's Degree; Business Degree; U of North Carolina

GRIFFIN, DYLAN; KERNERSVILLE, NC; EAST FORSYTH HS; (SO); Hnr Roll; Sci Fairs; Comm Volntr; Chrch Yth Grp; DARE; Key Club; Sftball (J); Blue Ridge Quarter Horse Youth Team; Auburn U; UNCG

GRIFFIN, JAQUAN; GREENSBORO, NC; DUDLEY HS; (FR); Hi Hnr Roll; Hnr Roll; Otst Ac Ach Awd; Health Science (Pediatrician); Medical School; Howard U; Duke U

Grant, Valarie
Apex HS
Apex, NC

Goodson, Laura M
F E Smith SR HS
Fayetteville, NC

Gooden, Candace A
West Bladen HS
Bladenboro, NC

National
Honor Roll
Spring 2005

Gonzalez, Alexis
Sun Valley HS
Indian Trail, NC

Grant, Cameron
Seventy-First HS
Fayetteville, NC

Gregory, Michelle
West Johnston HS
Garner, NC

GRIFFIN, KATHLEEN L; MONTREAT, NC; CHARLES D OWEN HS; (SO); Duke TS; Hnr Roll; MVP; Nat Hon Sy; WWAHSS; Yth Ldrshp Prog; Comm Volntr; Peer Tut/Med; Spec Olymp Vol; Key Club; SADD; Voc Ind Clb Am; French Clb; Swmg (V); Stu Cncl (R); Swimming - Most Improved Freshman; State MVP for Swimming - Sophomore year

GRIFFIN, TIFFANY N; MONROE, NC; FOREST HILLS HS; (JR); Hnr Roll; Peer Tut/Med; Chrch Yth Grp; Dbte Team; Voc Ind Clb Am; Vllyball (JC); I Won At Skills USA in Debate.; To Be a Cosmetologist

GRIFFIS JR, RAY; GRAHAM, NC; HUGH M CUMMINGS HS; (SO); Ctznshp Aw; Hi Hnr Roll; Hnr Roll; Comm Volntr; Chrch Yth Grp; FCA; Ftball (V); Cl Off (V); Engineering; Morehouse College; North Carolina State U

GRIFFITH, MEGHAN E; CHARLOTTE, NC; CHARLOTTE CATHOLIC HS; (FR); Hi Hnr Roll; Hnr Roll; Comm Volntr; Jr Ach; Chr; Bskball; Piano for 6 Years; Creative Advertising; Communications; Florida State U; College of Charleston

GRIGG, MATTHEW S; KINGS MTN, NC; KINGS MOUNTAIN HS; (SR); Hnr Roll; Perf Att; St of Mnth; Chess; Chrch Yth Grp; DARE; Ntl Beta Clb; NTHS Member; Architecture; U of North Carolina Charlotte

GRIGGS, MORGAN; SALISBURY, NC; SALISBURY HS; (FR); Hi Hnr Roll; MVP; Perf Att; WWAHSS; Comm Volntr; Chrch Yth Grp; Key Club; Mus Clb; Bnd; Ch Chr; Mch Bnd; Chrldg (J); Scr Kpr (V); Library Science; Appalachian State U

GRIMSLEY, PAUL; FAIRMONT, NC; FAIRMONT HS; (SO); Ctznshp Aw; Hnr Roll; Otst Ac Ach Awd; Pres Ac Ftns Aw; Sci Fairs; St of Mnth; Yth Ldrshp Prog; Chrch Yth Grp; DECA; Ntl Beta Clb; Ntl FFA; Prom Com; Svce Clb; Ch Chr; Cl Off (P); Stu Cncl (R); Yrbk (R); Teen Summit; Battle of the Books; Forensic Science; Biology; UNC-Wilmington; ECU: East Carolina U

GROGAN, HOLLY N; ELON, NC; WESTERN ALAMANCE HS; (JR); Hnr Roll; Nat Hon Sy; WWAHSS; Yth Ldrshp Prog; Comm Volntr; Chrch Yth Grp; FCA; HO'Br Yth Ldrshp; Key Club; Chrldg (VJ); Track (V); Stu Cncl (R); Sch Ppr (R); National Honor Society Member; Lieutenant Governor District 14 of Key Club; Marine Zoology (Ocean Animal Trainer); High School Teacher; U of North Carolina At Wilmington; U of North Carolina At Charlotte

GROOVER, DANIELLE; ASHEBORO, NC; ASHEBORO HS; (SO); Perf Att; WWAHSS; Comm Volntr; ArtClub; Dbte Team; Key Club; Ntl Beta Clb; Tennis (V); First In Class- School Has No Valedictorian; Latin Club; Interior Design; Graphic Design; U of Florida

GUDGER, TIFFANY J; ASHEVILLE, NC; NORTH BUNCOMBE HS; (SO); Ctznshp Aw; Duke TS; Hnr Roll; Otst Ac Ach Awd; Perf Att; Pres Ac Ftns Aw; Comm Volntr; Spec Olymp Vol; Chrch Yth Grp; DARE; FCA; Key Club; Mth Clb/Tm; Ntl Beta Clb; Svce Clb; Tchrs Aide; Chr; Dnce; SP/M/VS; Chrldg (JC); PP Ftbl; Track (L); U of North Carolina Wilmington; Clemson U

GUMAN, ASHLEY V; ANGIER, NC; CAPE FEAR CHRISTIAN AC; (SO); Hnr Roll; MVP; Sci Fairs; 4-H; ArtClub; Drma Clb; Off Aide; Chr; Bskball (V); Sccr (V); Sftball (V); Vllyball (V C); Stu Cncl; CR (S); All Conference for Basketball; Sports Medicine; Auburn U; NC State U

GUO, ROSE; WAXHAW, NC; WEDDINGTON HS; (SO); Duke TS; F Lan Hn Soc; Fut Prb Slvr; Gov Hnr Prg; Hi Hnr Roll; Hnr Roll; MVP; Nat Sci Aw; Otst Ac Ach Awd; Pres Ac Ftns Aw; Comm Volntr; Spec Olymp Vol; Chrch Yth Grp; DARE; Key Club; Lib Aide; Off Aide; Tchrs Aide; French Clb; Chr; Ch Chr; SP/M/VS; Track (J); Vllyball (J); Christopher Columbus Awards; NCSSM; Pediatrician; U of North Carolina Chapel Hill; Duke U

GURGANUS, STACIE N; GRIMESLAND, NC; D H CONLEY HS; (JR); WWAHSS; Comm Volntr; Hosp Aide; Peer Tut/Med; Chrch Yth Grp; MuAlphaTh; Latin Clb; Health Science Ambassador; Family Nurse Practitioner; Nurse; East Carolina U; U of North Carolina of Wilmington

GUTTERY, DEREK A; KITTY HAWK, NC; FIRST FLIGHT HS; (SO); Hnr Roll; Emplmnt; Key Club; Bnd; SAVE; Chain Reaction; Architect; Engineer; North Carolina State U; U of Florida

GUY, HEATHER E; HENDERSONVILLE, NC; EAST HENDERSON HS; (SR); Hnr Roll; Jr Mshl; Nat Hon Sy; WWAHSS; Peer Tut/Med; DARE; Emplmnt; FCA; Key Club; Tchrs Aide; SP/M/VS; Stg Cre; Bskball (J); Scr Kpr (V); Sftball (V L); Vllyball (VJ L); Cl Off (S, T); Finance; Business; Clemson U

GWISHIRI, NATALIE M; HAMLET, NC; RICHMOND SR HS; (SR); Hnr Roll; Comm Volntr; Emplmnt; FBLA; Ntl Beta Clb; Svce Clb; Chrldg (V); Sftball (V); Track (V); Stu Cncl; Radio / TV III; Broadcast Journalism; Hampton U

GWYN, TAYLOR M; MOUNT AIRY, NC; MOUNT AIRY HS; (FR); Duke TS; Hi Hnr Roll; Hnr Roll; St of Mnth; WWAHSS; Comm Volntr; Chrch Yth Grp; DARE; Scouts; SP/M/VS; Bskball (JC); Tennis (V); Track (V); Who's Who of American High School Students; Interior Design; Communications; Elon College; UNC-Wilmington

GYLFADOTTIR, GUDRUN B; GOLDSBORO, NC; C B AYCOCK HS; (SO); Duke TS; Hi Hnr Roll; Sci/Math Olympn; St of Mnth; WWAHSS; Comm Volntr; Peer Tut/Med; Mth Clb/Tm; Mod UN; Sci Clb; Cr Ctry (V); Swmg (V)

HADAD, CASANDRA; WHISPERING PINES, NC; UNION PINES HS; (FR); Duke TS; Hi Hnr Roll; Comm Volntr; Chrch Yth Grp; DARE; Ntl Beta Clb; Scouts; Bnd; Mch Bnd; Pep Bnd; Skiing; Girl Scout Silver and Bronze Award; Science; Math

HADDOCK, JENNA L; CANDLER, NC; ENKA HS; (SO); Hnr Roll; Otst Ac Ach Awd; Perf Att; DARE; Ntl FFA; Spanish Clb; Chrldg (J); Fashion Design; Interior Design; North Carolina State; U of North Carolina

HAGANS, BRITTANY; LA GRANGE, NC; EASTERN WAYNE HS; (SO); 4H Awd; Comm Volntr; Hab For Humty Volntr; Spec Olymp Vol; 4-H; DARE; ROTC; Chr; Dnce; Scr Kpr (J); Dancing; Fashion Designing; A & T U

HAHN, DAVID; SHARPSBURG, NC; SOUTHWEST EDGECOMBE HS; (SO); Perf Att; St of Mnth; Sci Clb; Bskball (J); Ftball (J); Woodmen of the World; Pharmacist; Beta Club; UNC Chapel Hill; Campbell

HAIRSTON, KEITH; EDEN, NC; MOREHEAD HS; (SR); Hnr Roll; MVP; French Clb; Bskball ((V)); Ftball ((V)); Track ((V)); Physical Education; Sports Medicine; Ferrum College; Western Carolina U

HALL, AMBER; SPARKS, NC; SPARKS HS; (JR); Hnr Roll; Peer Tut/Med; Key Club; Chr; Lit Mag (E); In School/Out of School Writing Contests; Biology; US History; American U-Washington DC; Christopher Newport U

HALL, ANDREW S; MARION, NC; MC DOWELL HS; (SO); Duke TS; Hi Hnr Roll; Hnr Roll; Nat Hon Sy; Otst Ac Ach Awd; Perf Att; Pres Sch; WWAHSS; Yth Ldrshp Prog; Comm Volntr; Chrch Yth Grp; NYLC; Bnd; Mch Bnd; Pep Bnd; Pharmacy; Dentistry; Campbell U; Western Carolina U

HALL, DENISE M; UNION GROVE, NC; NORTH IREDELL HS; (SO); Vet; Lawyer; UNC Chapel Hill

HALL, ROBERT; JAMESTOWN, NC; RAGSDALE HS; (JR); Hnr Roll; WWAHSS; Emplmnt; Chr; Ftball (V); Track (V); Corp Law; Harvard U; New York U

HALL, SEAN; CLYDE, NC; PISGAH HS; (JR); MVP; St of Mnth; WWAHSS; Comm Volntr; FTA; Key Club; Pep Squd; Chr; SP/M/VS; Ftball (J); Wt Lftg (J); Wrstlg (V); Business Management; Teaching; U of Georgia; Gardner-Webb U

HALL-HAYES, DEJAVON A; JACKSONVILLE, NC; JACKSONVILLE HS; (FR); Ctznshp Aw; Hi Hnr Roll; Hnr Roll; MVP; Perf Att; St of Mnth; Comm Volntr; Peer Tut/Med; DARE; Ch Chr; SP/M/VS; Ftball (J); Wt Lftg (V); Lawyer; Pro Athlete; Duke U; U of North Carolina

HALVERSTADT, BRITTANY; KERNERSVILLE, NC; EAST FORSYTH HS; (SR); Duke TS; Hi Hnr Roll; Hnr Roll; Jr Mshl; Nat Mrt Sch Recip; St of Mnth; WWAHSS; Comm Volntr; Drma Clb; Jr Cls League; Key Club; Latin Clb; Dnce; SP/M/VS; Stg Cre; Nation Junior Classical League; International Thespian Society; Chemical Engineering; Life Sciences; North Carolina State U

HAMBY, CHANNING; MURPHY, NC; MURPHY HS; (JR); Hnr Roll; WWAHSS; Yth Ldrshp Prog; Spec Olymp Vol; Chrch Yth Grp; Emplmnt; FCA; Vsity Clb; Ch Chr; Bskball (J); Chrldg (J); Sftball (J); Track (V); Vllyball (VJ L); RYLA Youth Leadership Camp; Business; Investment; Clemson U; Western Carolina State U

HAMBY, LEA-ANN; CHARLOTTE, NC; ZEBULON VANCE HS; (JR); Hnr Roll; Comm Volntr; Drma Clb; FBLA; Scouts; CR (R); Girl Scout Silver Award/Cadettes; NADA Certified Archery Instructor; Business Degree (Business Admin.); Business Degree (Human Resources); U of North Carolina-Charlotte; U of North Carolina-Greenville

HAMILTON, BRIAN; ROCKY MOUNT, NC; NASH CTRL HS; (SO); All Am Sch; Hnr Roll; Chess; Chrch Yth Grp; Chess Club; Karate; Computer Science; Psychiatry; VA Tech./Virginia Polytechnic; NC State/North Carolina State U

HAMILTON, WARREN R; WASHINGTON, NC; NORTHSIDE HS; (SO); Hnr Roll; Nat Hon Sy; WWAHSS; Comm Volntr; Spec Olymp Vol; Chrch Yth Grp; Emplmnt; FCA; FBLA; Key Club; Ntl Beta Clb; Ntl FFA; Bsball (VJ); Cr Ctry (VJ L); Beta Club; NC State U; North Carolina U

HAMLETT, JOSHUA; FRANKLINTON, NC; SOUTH GRANVILLE HS; (FR); Hnr Roll; DARE; Bnd; Ch Chr; Accounting; Technology; UNC Wilmington; Duke U

HAMLETTE, QUINCY; ROXBORO, NC; PERSON HS; (FR); St of Mnth; Yth Ldrshp Prog; ArtClub; Chrch Yth Grp; Ntl FFA; Scouts; Chr; Ch Chr; Dnce; Track; Cl Off (V); Stu Cncl (R); CR (R); Master's Degree in Science (Biotechnology); PhD in Science (Biotechnology); Shaw U; A & T U

HAMMETT, AUDREY; FAYETTEVILLE, NC; DOUGLAS BYRD HS; (FR); Hnr Roll; Perf Att; USAA; Chrch Yth Grp; Mus Clb; Foreign Clb; Chr; Ch Chr; Swg Chr; Law Degree; Arts Degree; Appalachian Mountain U; Harvard U

HAMMETT, SUZANNE; WAKE FOREST, NC; FRANKLIN AC; (SO); Hnr Roll; Chrch Yth Grp; FCA; French Clb; SP/M/VS; Stg Cre; Bskball (J); Sccr (J); Vice President of French Club; Philosophy; Education; Duke U; U of North Carolina At Chapel Hill

HAMMONDS, COURTNEY L; RED SPRINGS, NC; PURNELL SWETT HS; (FR); Hi Hnr Roll; Hnr Roll; Perf Att; St of Mnth; Chrch Yth Grp; Ntl Beta Clb; Bnd; Mch Bnd

HAMMONDS, JAMES; LUMBERTON, NC; LUMBERTON HS; (FR); Hnr Roll; Perf Att; ROTC; Ftball (J); JROTC; NASA; Lawyer; Army/Marines; Chapel Hill

HAMMONDS, STEPHANIE A; LUMBERTON, NC; LUMBERTON HS; (SO); Hi Hnr Roll; Hnr Roll; Perf Att; Sci Fairs; St of Mnth; Peer Tut/Med; FCA; Ntl Beta Clb; Chr; Dnce; Chrldg (V); Superintendent's Honor Roll; ATSES Club (Students with High GPA'S); Nursing; Cardiology; U of NC Chapel Hill; Duke U

HAMZA, BOULOUDENE; GREENSBORO, NC; B N SMITH SCH; (SR); Hnr Roll; Clr Grd; Flg Crps; SP/M/VS; Swmg (V)

HANCOCK, BETH; EFLAND, NC; ORANGE HS; (SR); F Lan Hn Soc; Hnr Roll; WWAHSS; Comm Volntr; Emplmnt; Key Club; Ntl Beta Clb; Spanish Clb; Sch Ppr (R); Yrbk (E); Key Club; Beta Club; Accounting; Pre-Law; U of North Carolina At Charlotte

HANES, NICHOLAS M; LEXINGTON, NC; EAST DAVIDSON HS; (SR); Duke TS; Hi Hnr Roll; Jr Mshl; Pres Sch; St Schl; Comm Volntr; Hab For Humty Volntr; Red Cr Aide; Emplmnt; Ntl Beta Clb; Ntl FFA; Civil Engineering; North Carolina State U

HANG, CHEUNOU; MORGANTON, NC; FREEDOM HS; (SO); Game Design; Animation; Westwood College

HANNIGAN, JESSICA; SWANNANOA, NC; CHARLES D OWEN HS; (SO); Hi Hnr Roll; Hnr Roll; USAA; WWAHSS; Peer Tut/Med; Spec Olymp Vol; Chrch Yth Grp; DARE; Key Club; Mth Clb/Tm; P to P St Amb Prg; Prom Com; PP Ftbl (V); Swmg (V); Vllyball (J); Stu Cncl (R); Yrbk (E); Trauma Surgeon; Chemistry; UNC Chapel Hill

HARDIN, CARRIE; BOSTIC, NC; EAST RUTHERFORD HS; (SO); Comm Volntr; Chrch Yth Grp; DARE; FCA; FCCLA; Mus Clb; Chr; Ch Chr; Special Education Teacher; Musical Education Teacher; UNC Charlotte

HARDIN, HAYLEY; SPINDALE, NC; CHASE HS; (JR); Hnr Roll; Peer Tut/Med; Chrch Yth Grp; Emplmnt; Lib Aide; Ntl FFA; SADD; Tchrs Aide; Dnce; Chrldg (JC); FFA Reporter; Received Greenhand and Chapter Degrees (FFA); Psychology; Veterinary; U of North Carolina of Charlotte; U of North Carolina At Chapel Hill

HARDIN, MEAGAN D; LUMBERTON, NC; PURNELL SWETT HS; (SO); Hi Hnr Roll; Hnr Roll; Perf Att; St of Mnth; Comm Volntr; Spec Olymp Vol; Chrch Yth Grp; Ntl Beta Clb; Bnd; Mch Bnd; Cl Off (R); Stu Cncl (R); CR (R); NASA Club / Aises Club; Young Christian Association - YCA; Pharmacist; Physical Therapist; U of North Carolina; U of North Carolina Pembroke

HARDIN JR, GEORGE; FOREST CITY, NC; CHASE HS; (JR); Hnr Roll; DARE; Ntl FFA; Bsball (V L); Bskball (V L); Ftball (J); Business; Physical Education; Coastal Carolina; U of North Carolina Charlotte

HARDISON, JOLANDA; GASTONIA, NC; HUNTER HUSS HS; (FR); Hnr Roll; Comm Volntr; Chrch Yth Grp; Emplmnt; Bnd; Ch Chr; Mch Bnd; Pep Bnd; Lawyer (Law Degree); Bachelor's Degree; U of North Carolina (Chapel Hill); Fayetteville State U

HARDMAN, RANDALL; CHARLOTTE, NC; METROLINA CHRISTIAN AC; (JR); Sccr (L); School Praise Band; Music Industry; U of North Carolina

HARDY, JAMEIR J; ROCKY MOUNT, NC; SOUTHWEST HS; (SO); Hnr Roll; Bskball (J); Ftball (J); Wt Lftg (J); A & T Greensboro; Duke U

HARDY, SI'YEATTA; LUMBER BRIDGE, NC; WESTOVER HS; (JR); Hi Hnr Roll; Hnr Roll; Sci Fairs; Hosp Aide; ArtClub; Chrch Yth Grp; DARE; Emplmnt; FBLA; Mus Clb; SP/M/VS; Track (V); Doctor of Pharmacy (Pharm.); Chemistry/Biochemistry; Campbell U; Shaw U

HARDY JR, LAMAR; ROCKY MOUNT, NC; NASH CTRL HS; (FR); Hnr Roll; Comm Volntr

HARE, SHELLEY A; WILSON, NC; FIKE HS; (SO); Hi Hnr Roll; Hnr Roll; 4-H; Chrch Yth Grp; Mod UN; SADD; Spanish Clb; 4-H Treasurer

HARE, TIFFANY; NEW BERN, NC; WEST CRAVEN HS; (JR); Gov Hnr Prg; Nat Hon Sy; WWAHSS; Comm Volntr; Hab For Humty Volntr; Spec Olymp Vol; 4-H; Chrch Yth Grp; FCA; Ntl FFA; Clr Grd; Dnce; Cr Ctry (V C); Track (V); Criminal Law; North Carolina State U

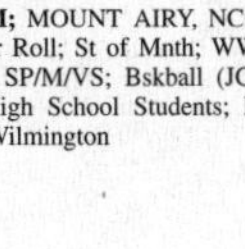
Hannigan, Jessica
Charles D Owen HS
Swannanoa, NC

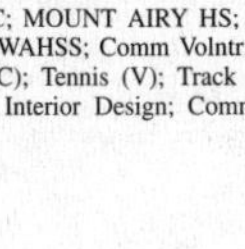
Hamby, Lea-Ann
Zebulon Vance HS
Charlotte, NC

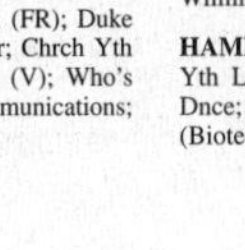
Guman, Ashley V
Cape Fear Christian AC
Angier, NC

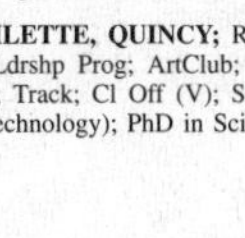
Grigg, Matthew S
Kings Mountain HS
Kings Mtn, NC

National
Honor Roll
Spring 2005

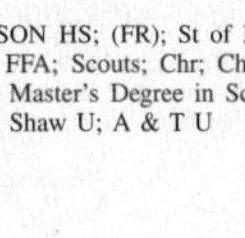
Griffith, Meghan E
Charlotte Catholic HS
Charlotte, NC

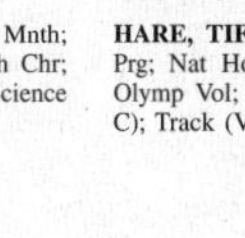
Gwyn, Taylor M
Mount Airy HS
Mount Airy, NC

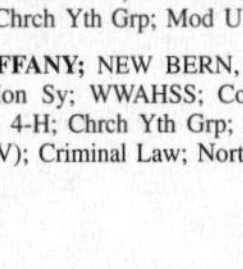
Hanes, Nicholas M
East Davidson HS
Lexington, NC

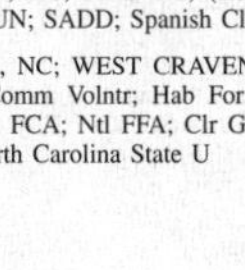
Hardy, Jameir J
Southwest HS
Rocky Mount, NC

HARGRAVES, ELIZABETH J; EAST BEND, NC; FORBUSH HS; (JR); Hnr Roll; Nat Hon Sy; Comm Volntr; Chr; Stu Cncl (R); CR (R); HOSA Reporter-03-04; HOSA President 04-05; Physical Therapy; Winston-Salem State; Western Carolina U

HARKEY, JUSTIN L; IRON STATION, NC; EAST LINCOLN HS; (JR); Duke TS; Hnr Roll; Nat Hon Sy; Otst Ac Ach Awd; Perf Att; St of Mnth; Yth Ldrshp Prog; Comm Volntr; Spec Olymp Vol; Chrch Yth Grp; Ntl Beta Clb; NYLC; Prom Com; Svce Clb; Sccr (V); Track (V); Adv Cncl; Attended Summer Ventures in Area of Chemistry; Biology; Appalachian State U

HARKEY, MATTHEW S; CHINA GROVE, NC; SOUTH ROWAN HS; (JR); MVP; DARE; Drma Clb; Emplmnt; Ntl FFA; Swmg (V L); Track (J); 2004-Broke School Record in Back Stroke in Swimming; 2005 Broke School Record in Back Stroke Again; Degree in Business; Rowan Cabarrus Community College; Wilmington State U SC

HARLEY, DERRICK D; WINSTON-SALEM, NC; CARTER G WOODSON; (FR); Hi Hnr Roll; Hnr Roll; Otst Ac Ach Awd; WWAHSS; Comm Volntr; Chr; Dnce; SP/M/VS; Voice Major; Performing Arts Major; Winston-Salem State U; NC School of the Arts

HARMON, GRAHAM; MOCKSVILLE, NC; DAVIE HS; (FR); DARE; Chr; SP/M/VS; Ftball (J); Wrstlg (J); East Carolina U; Johnson & Wales

HARPER, ALESHA V; ENFIELD, NC; NORTHWEST HS; (FR); Hi Hnr Roll; Hnr Roll; Perf Att; Comm Volntr; Chrch Yth Grp; Mus Clb; Pep Squd; Bnd; Ch Chr; Mch Bnd; Chrldg (J); Pediatrician; East Carolina U; U of North Carolina @ Chapel Hill

HARPER, BRADLEY; LUMBERTON, NC; LUMBERTON HS; (FR); Duke TS; Hi Hnr Roll; WWAHSS; Comm Volntr; ArtClub; Chrch Yth Grp; Ntl Beta Clb; Scouts; Bnd; Swmg (V); National Jr Beta Club; Architecture; North Carolina State U; Virginia Tech

HARPER, BRITTANY P; ROBBINS, NC; NORTH MOORE HS; (SO); Hnr Roll; Comm Volntr; Spec Olymp Vol; Emplmnt; FCA; Key Club; Ntl Beta Clb; Bskball (V); Sftball (V); Vllyball (V); Cl Off (P); Medical; U of North Carolina; East Carolina U

HARPER, DAVID; WAKE FOREST, NC; WAKE FOREST HS; (JR); Hnr Roll; Nat Hon Sy; WWAHSS; Chrch Yth Grp; Sci Clb; Latin Clb; Bnd; National Honor Society; Computer Science; Chemistry; Southern Wesylean U

HARRELL, CASEY A; WILMINGTON, NC; E A LANEY HS; (JR); Hnr Roll; Chrch Yth Grp; DARE; Latin Clb; Computer Sciences; Electrical Engineering; North Carolina State U; U of North Carolina At Wilmington

HARRELL, JAMES; EDENTON, NC; JOHN A HOLMES HS; (SO); Ctznshp Aw; DAR; Hi Hnr Roll; Pres Ac Ftns Aw; Comm Volntr; Chrch Yth Grp; Drma Clb; Emplmnt; Scouts; Ch Chr; Sccr (VJ L); Tennis (V L); Wrstlg (V L); Scouts; Camp Counselor; U of North Carolina At Chapel Hill

HARRELL, JARED J; MORVEN, NC; ANSON HS; (FR); Hnr Roll; Kwnis Aw; MVP; Otst Ac Ach Awd; St of Mnth; Yth Ldrshp Prog; Comm Volntr; Peer Tut/Med; DARE; Fr of Library; Lib Aide; ROTC; Ch Chr; Clr Grd; Bsball (J); Ftball (J); Medical Degree; Cardiovascular Surgeon; U of Miami; North Carolina State U

HARRELL, NICK; WILLOW SPRING, NC; FUQUAY VARINA HS; (JR); Hnr Roll; Nat Hon Sy; WWAHSS; Comm Volntr; Chrch Yth Grp; FCA; Key Club; Ntl Beta Clb; Spanish Clb; Sccr (J); Track; Wt Lftg; National; Law; NC State; UNC Chapel Hill

HARRINGTON, CANDICE D; LAURINBURG, NC; SCOTLAND HS; (JR); Hnr Roll; Perf Att; St of Mnth; Comm Volntr; ArtClub; Prom Com; Bskball (J); Nursing Degree; Miami U; U Greensboro

HARRIS, AKEYAH; STATESVILLE, NC; STATESVILLE HS; (FR); DARE; RN Nurse; Cosmetologist

HARRIS, APRIL S; OXFORD, NC; J. F. WEBB HS; (FR); 4H Awd; Hnr Roll; Perf Att; 4-H; Scouts; Ch Chr; Dnce; Stu Cncl (S); Mathematics Award; Doctor; Nurse; Duke U; A & T

HARRIS, ASHEENA; CHARLOTTE, NC; ZEBULON VANCE HS; (FR); Hi Hnr Roll; Otst Ac Ach Awd; Perf Att; Comm Volntr; Off Aide; ROTC; Dnce; SP/M/VS; Track; Church Dance; Psychologist; Actress; Johnson C. Smith; Savannah State

HARRIS, BRITTANY D; STAR, NC; EAST MONTGOMERY HS; (JR); St of Mnth; Chr; Elementary School Education; Master's Degree; U of North Carolina At Chapel Hill; Averett U

HARRIS, CALEM; MORGANTON, NC; FREEDOM HS; (SR); DAR; Hnr Roll; MVP; Nat Hon Sy; Nat Sci Aw; Otst Ac Ach Awd; Perf Att; Pres Ac Ftns Aw; Sci Fairs; St Schl; Comm Volntr; Hab For Humty Volntr; Red Cr Aide; Lttrmn Clb; P to P St Amb Prg; Svce Clb; Bskball (J L); Ftball (V L); Track (V CL); Adv Cncl (R); Cl Off (R); CR (R); Pilot for US Navy; Aeronautical Engineer; United States Naval Academy

HARRIS, CHAWANDA; YOUNGSVILLE, NC; FRANKLINTON HS; (SO); Hnr Roll; Nat Hon Sy; Perf Att; Chrch Yth Grp; DARE; Ntl Beta Clb; Bnd; Ch Chr; Bskball (V); Sftball (V); Tennis (V); Track (V); National Honor Society; National Achievers Society; Criminal Justice; Early Childhood Education; U of Miami Florida; North Carolina Central U

HARRIS, CHRISTINA M; FAYETTEVILLE, NC; SOUTHVIEW HS; (SO); Hi Hnr Roll; Hnr Roll; MVP; Perf Att; Comm Volntr; Hab For Humty Volntr; Dnce; SP/M/VS; Chrldg (V); Actress; U of Southern California; U of Miami

HARRIS, DAISHA L; CHARLOTTE, NC; VANCE HS; Hnr Roll; MVP; Perf Att; Sci Fairs; St of Mnth; Comm Volntr; Red Cr Aide; Chrch Yth Grp; DARE; Scouts; Svce Clb; Bskball (J); Track (J); AVID; Dental Hygienist; Model; U of North Carolina-Charlotte; Central Piedmont Community College

HARRIS, DANIELLE N; RALEIGH, NC; SOUTHEAST RALEIGH HS; (JR); Hnr Roll; WWAHSS; Comm Volntr; Hab For Humty Volntr; Peer Tut/Med; Chrch Yth Grp; Emplmnt; Prom Com; Sci Clb; Chrldg (J); Cl Off (S); Stu Cncl (V); Chemistry Major; Premed; U of North Carolina Chapel Hill; North Carolina State

HARRIS, JAQUAR; FORT BRAGG, NC; MASSEY HILL CLASSICAL HS; (JR); Hnr Roll; WWAHSS; Comm Volntr; ArtClub; Key Club; P to P St Amb Prg; SP/M/VS; Bskball (V); Lit Mag (R, P); Sch Ppr (R, P); Mr Congeniality - Mr Massey Hill Pageant; Business Administration; Culinary Arts; Drexel U Philadelphia

HARRIS, JESSICA; NEWPORT, NC; WEST CARTERET HS; (SO); Duke TS; Hnr Roll; Otst Ac Ach Awd; WWAHSS; Comm Volntr; Hab For Humty Volntr; Key Club; Scouts; Chr; Pre-Law; Psychology; U of North Carolina-Chapel Hill; Meredith College of North Carolina

HARRIS, JOSH; GREENSBORO, NC; WALTER HINES PAGE HS; (SR); Duke TS; Hi Hnr Roll; Nat Hon Sy; Nat Mrt Fin; Nat Mrt Sch Recip; Otst Ac Ach Awd; Pres Sch; St Schl; WWAHSS; Comm Volntr; Lit Mag (E); Engineering/Creative Writing; North Carolina State U

HARRIS, LEON; CHARLOTTE, NC; (SR); Bnd; Jzz Bnd; Ftball (V); Track; Wt Lftg; Sports Management; Livingstone College; Winston-Salem State U

HARRIS, MALLORY E; MARSHVILLE, NC; FOREST HILLS HS; (SR); Hnr Roll; St Schl; Spec Olymp Vol; Chrch Yth Grp; Drma Clb; Emplmnt; FCA; Quill & Scroll; Chrldg (V); PP Ftbl (V); Scr Kpr (V); Adv Cncl (R); Stu Cncl (R); CR (R); Yrbk (E); Nursing; Physical Therapy; Western Carolina U

HARRIS, MARY E; CHERRYVILLE, NC; BURNS HS; (JR); Hnr Roll; Jr Mshl; Nat Hon Sy; WWAHSS; Chrch Yth Grp; DARE; Emplmnt; FCA; Mus Clb; Ntl Beta Clb; Ntl FFA; Pep Squd; Chr; Chrldg; Hsbk Rdg; Nursing; U of North Carolina Chapel Hill

HARRIS, SARA; WINSTON-SALEM, NC; MT TABOR HS; (JR); Duke TS; F Lan Hn Soc; Hi Hnr Roll; Hnr Roll; Nat Mrt Semif; WWAHSS; Yth Ldrshp Prog; Peer Tut/Med; Chrch Yth Grp; Key Club; Pep Squd; Photog; Svce Clb; Vsity Clb; Latin Clb; Dnce; Chrldg (V); Stu Cncl (R); Yrbk (P); International Relations; Political Science; Duke U; Georgetown U

HARRIS, SHAREE; CHARLOTTE, NC; EAST MECKLENBURG HS; (SO); Hnr Roll; WWAHSS; Comm Volntr; Peer Tut/Med; Pep Squd; Bnd; Pep Bnd; Vllyball (JC); Architecture; Computer Science; Hampton U; U of North Carolina-Charlotte

HARRISON, BRITTAINY; CONOVER, NC; TRI-CITY CHRISTIAN SCH; (SO); Tchrs Aide; Graphic Design; Creative Writing

HARRISON III JR, LUTHER P; LUMBERTON, NC; LUMBERTON HS; (FR); Duke TS; Hi Hnr Roll; Hnr Roll; Nat Hon Sy; Perf Att; Pres Ac Ftns Aw; WWAHSS; Ntl Beta Clb; Ntl FFA; Ftball (J); Golf (J); Wt Lftg (V); Veterinarian; Marine Biologist; North Carolina State U; U North Carolina-Wilmington

HART, BRANDI; HICKORY, NC; ST STEPHENS HS; (JR); Hnr Roll; Pres Ac Ftns Aw; Peer Tut/Med; Emplmnt; Prom Com; ROTC; Clr Grd; Drl Tm; Scr Kpr (V); Early Childhood development; Veterinary medicine; North Carolina State U; Air Force Academy

HARTMAN, ELISABETH G; DAVIDSON, NC; NORTH MECKLENBURG HS; (SO); Hnr Roll; Sci Fairs; Sci/Math Olympn; St of Mnth; St Optmst of Yr; Yth Ldrshp Prog; Comm Volntr; Chrch Yth Grp; Drma Clb; Ch Chr; Orch; SP/M/VS; Stg Cre; Track; Community Lacrosse Team; Community Theatre; U North Carolina Youth Orchestra; Theater; Business; New York U; Savannah College of Arts and Design

HARVEY, RICQUETTA; GASTON, NC; NORTHAMPTON WEST HS; (FR); Hi Hnr Roll; Hnr Roll; DARE; Bnd; Mch Bnd; Business Management; U of North Carolina

HATCHER, PAGE L; LAURINBURG, NC; SCOTLAND HS; (FR); St of Mnth; Peer Tut/Med; Chrch Yth Grp; ROTC; Clr Grd; National Guard; Navy

HATHCOCK, BRITTANI; ALBEMARLE, NC; WEST STANLY HS; (SO); 4H Awd; Hi Hnr Roll; 4-H; Ntl FFA; Greenhand Degree; Green Clover Award; Forensic Scientist; Animal Scientist

HAWKINS, ERICA; ROANOKE RAPIDS, NC; NORTHWEST HS; (FR); Hi Hnr Roll; Otst Ac Ach Awd; Perf Att; St of Mnth; Red Cr Aide; Chrch Yth Grp; FBLA; Ntl Beta Clb; Dnce; Chrldg (V); Track (J); Homecoming Queen; Principal's List Award; Business Administration; Social Services; U of North Carolina-Chapel Hill; East Carolina U

HAWKINS, PAUL; COVE CITY, NC; BETHEL CHRISTIAN AC; (SR); Hi Hnr Roll; Jr Mshl; Nat Hon Sy; Otst Ac Ach Awd; Perf Att; Salutrn; Sci Fairs; St of Mnth; WWAHSS; Comm Volntr; Emplmnt; Prom Com; Quiz Bowl; Schol Bwl; Scouts; Tchrs Aide; Chr; Ch Chr; Bsball (V); Bskball (L); Golf (L); Cl Off (P, V); Eagle Scout; Championship Quiz Bowl Team; Officer / US Navy; Lawyer; US Naval Academy; Duke U

HAYDEN JR, JEFFERY A; CHARLOTTE, NC; HARDING U HS; (SO); Bnd; Drl Tm; Mch Bnd; Pep Bnd; Highest EOG Scores in My Class in 8th Grade; Mechanical Engineer; Structural Engineer; North Carolina Agricultural and Technical State U

HAYES, ALLISON; ROCKY MOUNT, NC; NASH CTRL HS; (FR); Hnr Roll; Nat Hon Sy; Otst Ac Ach Awd; Peer Tut/Med; Chrch Yth Grp; Ntl Beta Clb; Sci Clb; Scouts; Cr Ctry (J); Outstanding Student; Medical Field; Science

HAYES, BRENDAN K; WILMINGTON, NC; E A LANEY HS; (JR); Hnr Roll; Photog; Spanish Clb; Sccr; Sch Ppr (P); Yrbk (P); Play Ice Hockey and Roller Hockey; Marine Biology; U of North Carolina in Chapel Hill; UNCW

HAYES, ELIZABETH L A; DALLAS, NC; NORTH GASTON HS; (SR); WWAHSS; Hosp Aide; Chrch Yth Grp; Emplmnt; Lib Aide; Chr; Dnce; Chrldg (V); Stu Cncl (R); Yrbk (R); Who's Who Award; Nursing; Gaston College

HAYES, MAGGIE A; STATESVILLE, NC; STATESVILLE HS; (FR); DAR; Duke TS; Hi Hnr Roll; Hnr Roll; MVP; Nat Sci Aw; Pres Sch; Chrch Yth Grp; Ntl Beta Clb; Ch Chr; Mch Bnd; Sftball (V L); Duke Tip Program; Gold Renaissance at Statesville High - All-A's; BA in Business; PhD in Dermatology; U of North Carolina; North Carolina State

HAYES JR, HORACE; ORRUM, NC; FAIRMONT HS; (FR); 4H Awd; Hnr Roll; Peer Tut/Med; 4-H; Chrch Yth Grp; FCA; Pep Squd; Bnd; Ch Chr; Mch Bnd; Pep Bnd; Ftball (J); Track (J); Wt Lftg (J); Student of Excellence; Business and Office; Law; Chapel Hill U; Duke U

HAYNES, DENZEL; SHELBY, NC; CREST HS; (JR); Hnr Roll; Nat Hon Sy; Pep Bnd; Bskball (J); Wrstlg (V); Marketing; Business; Howard U; Morehouse College

HAYS, ASHLEY; WAXHAW, NC; PARKWOOD HS; (SR); Hnr Roll; Nat Hon Sy; St of Mnth; WWAHSS; Emplmnt; Tchrs Aide; French Clb; Orch; SP/M/VS; Stu Cncl; English (Education); USC Lancaster U of South Carolina-Lancaster

HEADEN, WILLIAM B; GREENSBORO, NC; SMITH HS; (FR); Ctznshp Aw; Hnr Roll; Nat Hon Sy; Otst Ac Ach Awd; Perf Att; St of Mnth; Law School; Psychology; Harvard U; Duke U

HEADY, MARY M; CHAPEL HILL, NC; CEDAR RIDGE HS; (SR); 4H Awd; F Lan Hn Soc; Hi Hnr Roll; Jr Mshl; Perf Att; WWAHSS; Comm Volntr; Peer Tut/Med; 4-H; FTA; Ntl Beta Clb; Ntl FFA; Tchrs Aide; Orch; SP/M/VS; Stg Cre; Lit Mag; Duke U Strings School; Music Exchange Program to Bolivia; History; Education; U of North Carolina At Asheville

HEALY, SHANNON E; FLAT ROCK, NC; EAST HENDERSON HS; (SO); 4H Awd; Perf Att; 4-H; Chess; Chrch Yth Grp; German Clb; Chr; Ch Chr; Stg Cre; Veterinary Assistant; Fashion Design; Blue Ridge Community College; U of North Carolina At Asheville

HEATH, S E; WINDSOR, NC; BERTIE HS; (FR); Comm Volntr; Peer Tut/Med; 4-H; DARE; Ch Chr; Bskball (J); Chrldg (V); Sftball (V); Equine Activities; Equine Business Management; Therapeutic Horsemanship; Andrew College; Saint Martin Community College

HEATH, WILLIAM B; CLINTON, NC; CLINTON HS; (SR); Ctznshp Aw; Duke TS; Hi Hnr Roll; Jr Mshl; Perf Att; Pres Ac Ftns Aw; Pres Sch; St Schl; St of Mnth; Comm Volntr; Hab For Humty Volntr; Peer Tut/Med; Chrch Yth Grp; Emplmnt; Jr Cls League; Ntl Beta Clb; Ntl FFA; Prom Com; Scouts; Svce Clb; Bnd; Mch Bnd; Stg Cre; Ftball (V L); CR (R); Eagle Scout; Biomedical Engineering; Chemical Engineering; North Carolina State U; Wake Forest U

HEAVNER, ANNA; GASTONIA, NC; HIGHLAND SCH OF TECH; (MS); Hnr Roll; MVP; St of Mnth; Chrch Yth Grp; DARE; Chr; Ch Chr; Sftball (J); Eagle Award 8th Grade; Marine Biology; UNC Wilmington; NC State Raleigh

HEDRICK, DONELLA; LUMBERTON, NC; LUMBERTON HS; (SR); Hnr Roll; RN; Nurse Practitioner; RCC; BCC

HEDRICK, WILL; JAMESTOWN, NC; SOUTHWEST GUILFORD HS; (JR); Hnr Roll; Pres Ac Ftns Aw; Sci Fairs; Chrch Yth Grp; Ntl Beta Clb; Spanish Clb; Ftball (V L); National Technical Honor Society; Computer Science; Computer Programming; U of North Carolina; NC State U

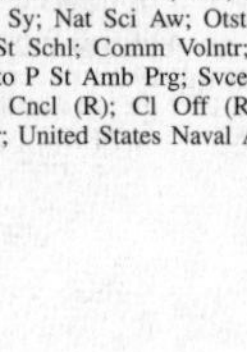
Heath, S E
Bertie HS
Windsor, NC

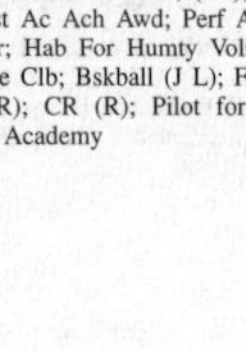
Hatcher, Page L
Scotland HS
Laurinburg, NC

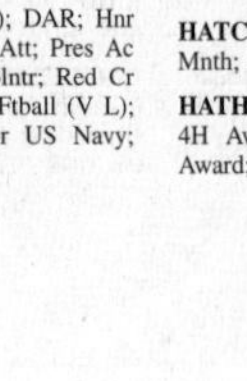
Harris, Asheena
Zebulon Vance HS
Charlotte, NC

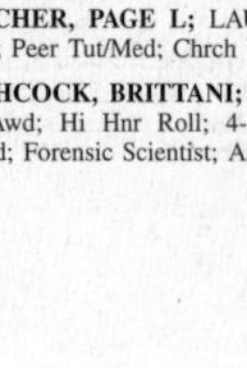
Harrell, Casey A
E A Laney HS
Wilmington, NC

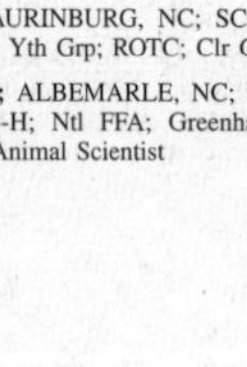
Harkey, Justin L
East Lincoln HS
Iron Station, NC

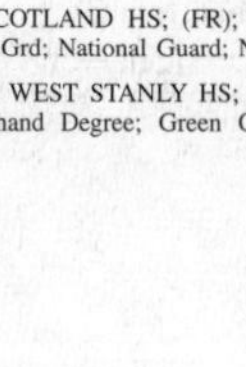
Harper, Bradley
Lumberton HS
Lumberton, NC

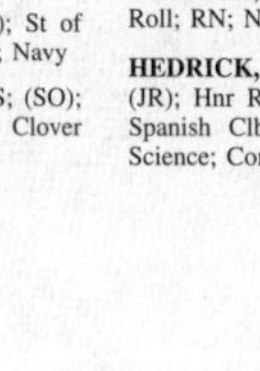
Harris, Jaquar
Massey Hill Classical HS
Fort Bragg, NC

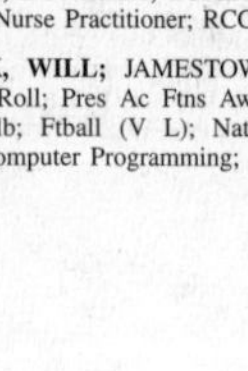
Hayden Jr, Jeffery A
Harding U HS
Charlotte, NC

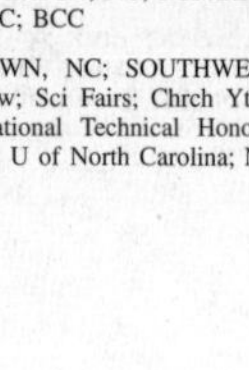
Hedrick, Will
Southwest Guilford HS
Jamestown, NC

HEDSPETH, ASHLEY L; COMO, NC; RIDGECROFT SCH; (SR); 4H Awd; Hi Hnr Roll; Hnr Roll; Jr Mshl; Otst Ac Ach Awd; Sci Fairs; St of Mnth; WWAHSS; Comm Volntr; Red Cr Aide; Spec Olymp Vol; 4-H; Chrch Yth Grp; DARE; Emplmnt; Key Club; Lttrmn Clb; Ntl Beta Clb; SADD; Ch Chr; Chrldg (V CL); Sftball (V L); Stu Cncl (P, V, R); Governors Page; Graduation Marshall; Biology; Chemistry; East Carolina U; U of North Carolina

HEEKE, LAUREN N; HICKORY, NC; ST STEPHENS HS; (SO); Duke TS; MVP; Chr; SP/M/VS; PP Ftbl; Sftball (V L); Vllyball (JC); Medical Degree-Dermatology; U of North Carolina Chapel Hill; North Carolina State U

HEGE, SAMANTHA; WINSTON-SALEM, NC; REYNOLDS HS; (JR); F Lan Hn Soc; Hi Hnr Roll; Nat Hon Sy; Mus Clb; Bnd; Dnce; Jzz Bnd; Mch Bnd; Swmg (V L); Marching Band Section Leader - 2004; Veterinarian; Marine Biology; Wake Forrest U; East Carolina U

HEHNER, CODY; SALUDA, NC; EAST HENDERSON HS; (SO); WWAHSS; Yth Ldrshp Prog; Chrch Yth Grp; Ftball (J); Wrstlg (V CL); Boys and Girls Club Youth of the Month; Computers; Robotics; U of North Carolina; Appalachian State

HEIGHINGTON, KATHERINE I; CARY, NC; CARY AC; (JR); Hnr Roll; Nat Hon Sy; Key Club; Bnd; Fld Hky (V L); Golf (J); Ice Hky (V); Ice Hockey Coach; Doctor; McMaster U; Queen's U

HELMS, DANIEL; FAYETTEVILLE, NC; SEVENTY-FIRST HS; (FR); Hnr Roll; Comm Volntr; Red Cr Aide; ROTC; Sci Clb; Drl Tm; Black Belt; Played Soccer Half of Life; Military / Pilot; Doctor; Air Force Academy; West Point

HELMS, SARAH K; MATTHEWS, NC; SUN VALLEY HS; (FR); Hi Hnr Roll; Hnr Roll; Otst Ac Ach Awd; Yth Ldrshp Prog; Chrch Yth Grp; Ntl Beta Clb; Bnd; Jzz Bnd; Mch Bnd; Pep Bnd; Drum Captain for Sun Valley Band; Rotary Scholar Award; Master's Degree in Music; Minor in Computer Animation; Appalachian State U; Duke U

HELPINGSTINE, CHASE; CHAPEL HILL, NC; CHAPEL HILL HS; (SO); Hnr Roll; MVP; Comm Volntr; Peer Tut/Med; Chess; Chrch Yth Grp; Outdrs Clb; Vsity Clb; Tennis (V L); PAC-6 Player of the Year 2004-2005 - Tennis; Jr Davis / Jr Fed Cap Team -Tennis; Chemistry; Engineering; U of North Carolina Chapel Hill; Virginia Technical College

HELTON, DANIEL; MURPHY, NC; HIWASSEE DAM HS; (FR); Duke TS; Hi Hnr Roll; Jr Mshl; MVP; Nat Hon Sy; Otst Ac Ach Awd; Pres Ac Ftns Aw; Valdctrian; WWAHSS; Chrch Yth Grp; Ntl Beta Clb; Ch Chr; Bsball (VJ); Bskball (J); Who's Who Among American High School Students; 8th Grade Valedictorian; Engineering; U of North Carolina At Chapel Hill; Georgia Technical College

HEMPHILL, JESSICA C; JULIAN, NC; SOUTHEAST GUILFORD HS; (JR); 4H Awd; Ctznshp Aw; Hnr Roll; Perf Att; Hosp Aide; 4-H; Chrch Yth Grp; Mus Clb; Ntl FFA; Spanish Clb; Ch Chr; Math Award-Merit-Most Dedicated; Team Award for Most Improvement; Bachelor of Science in Nursing; Radiologist; U of North Carolina At Greensboro; U of North Carolina At Chapel Hill

HENDERSON, ALEX; GRIMESLAND, NC; D H CONLEY HS; (SO); Hnr Roll; WWAHSS; Comm Volntr; FBLA; Ntl Beta Clb; Golf (V); Sccr (V); Mechanical Engineering; Computer Engineering; NC State U; Lenoir Community College

HENDERSON, JOCELYN Q; WILMINGTON, NC; JOHN T HOGGARD HS; (SR); F Lan Hn Soc; Hi Hnr Roll; Hnr Roll; Nat Hon Sy; Nat Ldrshp Svc; Otst Ac Ach Awd; Sci Fairs; St of Mnth; Yth Ldrshp Prog; Comm Volntr; Hab For Humty Volntr; Peer Tut/Med; Chrch Yth Grp; Emplmnt; Key Club; Mus Clb; Ntl Beta Clb; SADD; Tchrs Aide; Spanish Clb; Chr; Ch Chr; Dnce; SP/M/VS; Cr Ctry (J L); PP Ftbl (V); Sccr (JC); Track (V); Vllyball (J); National Assoc of Performing Arts & Educator Olympic Performer; National Competition Dancer and Scholarship Winner: Jazz, Tap, Hip-Hop.; Biology Major (Pre-Med/Pediatrics); Performing Arts-Dance/Vocal/Drama; North Carolina State U; U of North Carolina At Chapel Hill

HENDERSON, MARIA J; ROSMAN, NC; BREVARD HS; (SO); 4H Awd; Hnr Roll; Sci/Math Olympn; WWAHSS; Red Cr Aide; 4-H; Sci Clb; Bnd; Chr; Mch Bnd; Pep Bnd; New Century Scholars; Youth Speak; Degree in Music; Major in Music; Western Carolina U; NC School of the Arts

HENDERSON, SHARI; OXFORD, NC; CFC AC; (SO); Hnr Roll; MVP; Nat Hon Sy; WWAHSS; Ntl Beta Clb; Quiz Bowl; Chr; Ch Chr; Bskball (V C); Vllyball (VJC); Food Science / Nutrition; Business Administration; U of North Carolina Greensboro; North Carolina State U

HENDRICK, STEPHEN; INDIAN TRAIL, NC; METROLINA CHRISTIAN AC; (JR); Hi Hnr Roll; Hnr Roll; Nat Hon Sy; Perf Att; WWAHSS; Hab For Humty Volntr; Dbte Team; Mus Clb; Ntl Beta Clb; Off Aide; Tchrs Aide; Chr; SP/M/VS; Stg Cre; Bsball (V); Sccr (V); Coaching Intramural Soccer; Participate in Sports Management; Mechanical Engineering; Culinary Arts; North Carolina State; Geneva College

HENDRICKS, BERNICE K; ENFIELD, NC; SOUTHEAST HALIFAX HS; (SO); Hi Hnr Roll; Hnr Roll; Sci Fairs; St of Mnth; Quiz Bowl; ROTC; Sci Clb; Drl Tm; Beta Club, Girl Power; Science Club; Doctor's Degree; Master's Degree; Elizabeth City State U; Fayetteville State U

HENDRICKS, REGINA R; ROANOKE RAPIDS, NC; NORTHWEST HS; (SO); Ctznshp Aw; Hi Hnr Roll; Hnr Roll; Perf Att; St of Mnth; Comm Volntr; Peer Tut/Med; Chrch Yth Grp; Ntl Beta Clb; Bnd; Chr; Ch Chr; North Carolina Central; North Carolina A & T State U

HENRIQUEZ, IRIS D; BURLINGTON, NC; GRAHAM HS; (SO); Ctznshp Aw; Hnr Roll; Otst Ac Ach Awd; St of Mnth; WWAHSS; Comm Volntr; Emplmnt; Key Club; Clb; Stu Cncl (R); CR (R); Minority Achievement Award; Principal's List; Law; Political Science; UNC Chapel Hill; NC State

HENRY, TIFFANY L; MORVEN, NC; ANSON HS; (FR); Hnr Roll; Perf Att; Comm Volntr; Peer Tut/Med; DARE; Pep Squd; Scouts; SP/M/VS; Sftball; Track; Vllyball; Cl Off (V); Silver Awards-Girl Scouts; Anthology of Poetry By Young Americans; Physical Therapist / Registered Nurse; Pediatrician; U of North Carolina Charlotte; U of North Carolina Chapel Hill

HENSLEY, CASEY N; BURLINGTON, NC; WALTER WILLIAMS HS; (JR); Hnr Roll; Comm Volntr; Peer Tut/Med; Chrch Yth Grp; Emplmnt; FCA; MuAlphaTh; Swmg (L); Accountant; Financial Analyst; UNC Charlotte; Appalachian

HENSLEY, CRYSTAL; RURAL HALL, NC; WEST STOKES HS; (SR); Hnr Roll; Nat Hon Sy; WWAHSS; Red Cr Aide; Spec Olymp Vol; Emplmnt; FBLA; Sch Ppr (R); HOSA Club; Pre-Med; Pre-Pharmacy; U of North Carolina At Charlotte

HENSON, ASHLEY N; CANTON, NC; PISGAH HS; (SR); All Am Sch; Hnr Roll; Nat Hon Sy; WWAHSS; Comm Volntr; Chrch Yth Grp; FCA; FTA; Off Aide; Pep Squd; SADD; Chr; Dnce; Homecoming Court 1st Runner-Up; Secondary Education; Western Carolina U

HERNANDEZ, BELINDA; HICKORY, NC; EAST BURKE HS; (SO); Spanish Education; Art; Appalachian State U

HERNANDEZ, MARIA P; SANDY RIDGE, NC; NORTH STOKES HS; (SR); Hi Hnr Roll; Hnr Roll; MVP; Otst Ac Ach Awd; St Schl; Comm Volntr; Emplmnt; Ntl Beta Clb; SADD; Flg Crps; Chrldg (V); Scr Kpr (V); Sccr (V); Cl Off (T); CR (S); Yrbk (P); Business; Education; Rockingham Community College

HERNANDEZ, YAZMIN; SALISBURY, NC; WEST ROWAN HS; (FR); Hnr Roll; Perf Att; Sci Fairs; St of Mnth; DARE; Mus Clb; Chr; Orch; Sccr (J); Cosmetology; Design; U of California (Los Angeles); U of North Carolina

HERRERA, MARIO; SILER CITY, NC; JORDAN MATTHEWS HS; (FR); Hnr Roll; Perf Att; DARE; Tech Clb; Bnd; Ftball (J); Tennis (J); Wt Lftg (J); Surfing; Architect; Professional Sports; Cal State Fullerton; UNC Chapel Hill

HERRING, DENIECE N; PLYMOUTH, NC; PLYMOUTH HS; (JR); Hnr Roll; WWAHSS; Comm Volntr; Emplmnt; Scouts; Bnd; Mch Bnd; Information Technology; Business Management; Central U; Duke U

HERRING, KRISTIN; SEVEN SPRINGS, NC; SPRING CREEK HS; (SO); FBLA; FCCLA; Scouts; Teacher In Arts Education; Graduate & Finish At Least 4 Years Of college; Eastern Carolina U

HERRON, KIMBERLY; DURHAM, NC; BURHAM SCH OF THE ARTS; (SR); Hnr Roll; WWAHSS; Comm Volntr; Peer Tut/Med; Emplmnt; FBLA; Svce Clb; Vsity Clb; Dnce; Bskball (V L); Track (V); Vice President of the Quest! Club; Treasurer of the Quest! Club and MSEN; Political Science; Attorney; U of North Carolina Charlotte

HERUSKA, ELIZABETH; WINSTON SALEM, NC; REYNOLDS HS; (JR); Ctznshp Aw; Duke TS; F Lan Hn Soc; Hnr Roll; Nat Hon Sy; Comm Volntr; Hab For Humty Volntr; Peer Tut/Med; ArtClub; Chrch Yth Grp; Emplmnt; Outdrs Clb; Prom Com; Svce Clb; Spanish Clb; Cr Ctry (J); Tennis (V L); Track (J); Cl Off (V); National Art Honor Society; National Honor Society; Fashion Design; Landscape Architecture; North Carolina State; Fashion Institute of Technology

HESS, ADRIENNE N; MATTHEWS, NC; COVENANT DAY HS; (FR); Duke TS; Jr Cls League; Latin Clb; Sch Ppr (R)

HESTER, FAISON D; ASHEVILLE, NC; CAROLINA DAY SCH; (JR); Hnr Roll; Comm Volntr; Spec Olymp Vol; Emplmnt; Outdrs Clb; Prom Com; Scouts; Tennis (V L); Stu Cncl (R); Completion of Eagle's Scout Rank - Spring 2005; Sports Medicine; Business; Davidson College; U North Carolina Chapel Hill

HETRICK, DAVID J; MOUNT AIRY, NC; NORTH SURRY HS; (JR); Hnr Roll; Jr Mshl; MVP; Nat Hon Sy; USAA; WWAHSS; Yth Ldrshp Prog; Comm Volntr; Hosp Aide; Spec Olymp Vol; Chrch Yth Grp; DARE; Emplmnt; FCA; HO'Br Yth Ldrshp; Key Club; Chr; Bskball (VJCL); Cr Ctry (V L); Track (V L); All-State, All-Region, and All-Conference Cross Country; National Honor Society; Pre-Law, Law Degree; U of North Carolina, U of NC-Chapel Hill; Liberty U

HEWITT, CARMEN O; GREENSBORO, NC; WALTER HINES PAGE HS; (JR); Hnr Roll; WWAHSS; Comm Volntr; ArtClub; Chrch Yth Grp; FCA; Mus Clb; Off Aide; Pep Squd; Prom Com; Sci Clb; Bnd; Clr Grd; Drm Mjr; Flg Crps; Cl Off (R); Stu Cncl (R); CR (R); Business & Marketing Award; Marine Biologist; Meteorologist & Culinary Arts; U of Connecticut; U of North Carolina At Wilmington

HEWITT, CHRISTOPHER; FUQUAY VARINA, NC; HARNETT CTRL HS; (SO); Hi Hnr Roll; Nat Hon Sy; Otst Ac Ach Awd; USAA; WWAHSS; FBLA; Key Club; Ntl Beta Clb; Foreign Clb; Bnd; Mch Bnd; Pep Bnd; Political Science; Law; U of North Carolina-Chapel Hill; Campbell U

HEWITT, MEG E P; PITTSBORO, NC; CARY AC; (SO); Hnr Roll; Sci Fairs; Comm Volntr; Red Cr Aide; Emplmnt; Key Club; Acpl Chr; Chr; SP/M/VS; Bskball (V L); Cr Ctry; Golf (VJ L); Track (VJ); Vllyball (V L); Beta Club; Investment Club; Interior Design; Business; UNC Chapel Hill

HEZEL, DANNI; WINTERVILLE, NC; SOUTH CTRL HS; (SO); Ctznshp Aw; Hnr Roll; Perf Att; Spec Olymp Vol; Chrch Yth Grp; DARE; FBLA; FTA; Ntl Beta Clb; Scr Kpr (VJ); Sccr (V L); Special Education Teacher; East Carolina U; Pitt Community College

HIBBARD, JORDAN; WAXHAW, NC; METROLINA CHRISTIAN AC; (JR); Hi Hnr Roll; Hnr Roll; Jr Mshl; MVP; Nat Hon Sy; Nat Ldrshp Svc; Otst Ac Ach Awd; Perf Att; Pres Ac Ftns Aw; Pres Sch; Comm Volntr; Hab For Humty Volntr; Peer Tut/Med; Chrch Yth Grp; DARE; Emplmnt; FTA; Lttrmn Clb; Lib Aide; Ntl Beta Clb; Off Aide; Ch Chr; SP/M/VS; Stg Cre; Bsball (V L); Bskball (V CL); Mar Art (J); Wt Lftg (V); Adv Cncl (R); ACSI Leadership Conference President; Timothy Character Award; Business Management; Wingate U; Gardner Webb U

HICKERNELL, TYLER; TRINITY, NC; TRINITY HS; (FR); Hnr Roll; Pres Ac Ftns Aw; Bsball (V); Bskball (J); All Conference Honorable Mention-Baseball, USAA National Mathematics Award; All Area Honorable Mention-Baseball; Architecture; U of North Carolina Greensboro; U of Florida

HICKMAN, LAUREN; OAK RIDGE, NC; GREENSBORO DAY SCH; (FR); Duke TS; Hi Hnr Roll; Comm Volntr; Peer Tut/Med; Chrch Yth Grp; DARE; P to P St Amb Prg; Chr; Stg Cre; Chrldg; Track; Vllyball; Wt Lftg; Duke TIP Program; Poem Published W/Poetry.Com; Radiologist; Veterinarian; U North Carolina-Chapel Hill; U of Georgia

HICKOK, KORY N; LENOIR, NC; HIBRITEN HS; (FR); Hnr Roll; Perf Att; Chrch Yth Grp; Key Club; Bsball (J); Journalism; Meteorology; UNC Chapel Hill; Gardner Webb U

HICKS, ANDREW S; RAEFORD, NC; HOKE CTY HS; (JR); All Am Sch; Ctznshp Aw; Hnr Roll; Jr Mshl; Nat Hon Sy; Pres Ac Ftns Aw; Sci Fairs; USAA; Comm Volntr; Peer Tut/Med; Spec Olymp Vol; Chrch Yth Grp; DECA; Ntl Beta Clb; Prom Com; Bnd; Sccr (VJCL); Tennis (V L); Stu Cncl (R); North Carolina Beta Club State President; VFW Voice of Democracy State Finalist (Essay); North Carolina State U-Raleigh; U of North Carolina-Chapel Hill

HICKS, JUSTIN J; WINSTON SALEM, NC; REYNOLDS HS; (JR); Hnr Roll; MVP; Otst Ac Ach Awd; WWAHSS; Peer Tut/Med; Chrch Yth Grp; Vsity Clb; Spanish Clb; Ch Chr; Bskball (VJCL); Vsy Clb (V); Wt Lftg (V)

HICKS, REGINALD; KITTRELL, NC; SOUTHERN VANCE HS; (SR); Hnr Roll; Nat Hon Sy; St of Mnth; WWAHSS; FCA; Bnd; Ftball (V C); Track (V C); Stu Cncl (R); CR (R); Kodak Young Leader's Award; National Society of High School Scholars; Integrated Science & Technology; James Madison U

HICKS, SHERRY; RAMSEUR, NC; EASTERN RANDOLPH HS; (FR); St of Mnth; FBLA; Scouts; Accountant; Education; Johnson and Wales U; East Carolina U

HIGGINBOTHAM, SARAH; KNOTTS ISLAND, NC; CURRITUCK CTY HS; (SO); Hnr Roll; Nat Hon Sy; Pres Ac Ftns Aw; St of Mnth; WWAHSS; Yth Ldrshp Prog; Peer Tut/Med; DECA; Ntl Beta Clb; NYLC; SADD; Scr Kpr (V); Sftball (VJ); Vllyball (J); CR (V); Yrbk (R); SASI Camp; Dream Team; Sports Medicine; Physical Therapy; U of North Carolina at Wilmington; North Carolina State U

HIGHSMITH, DOUGLAS A; OAK CITY, NC; ROANOKE HS; (SO); Hnr Roll; Hosp Aide; Chrch Yth Grp; Ch Chr; Wt Lftg; College Tech Prep; Military Degree; East Carolina U

HIGHSMITH, JASMINE; GREENVILLE, NC; SOUTH CTRL HS; (JR); Hi Hnr Roll; Hnr Roll; Perf Att; Pres Sch; St of Mnth; WWAHSS; Comm Volntr; Drma Clb; Emplmnt; FBLA; Dnce; Poem Published in the International. Book of Poetry; Attorney-Family or Civil Law; Masters Degree; Harvard U; Georgetown U

HILL, BRITTNEY; CLEMMONS, NC; WEST FORSYTH HS; (SO); Ctznshp Aw; F Lan Hn Soc; Hnr Roll; Otst Ac Ach Awd; Pres Ac Ftns Aw; St of Mnth; WWAHSS; Red Cr Aide; Spec Olymp Vol; Chrch Yth Grp; DARE; Jr Ach; Prom Com; Ch Chr; Dnce; Drl Tm; Bskball (J); Track (V); Stu Cncl (R); Yrbk (P); African American Culture Club; Apex Club; Criminal Justice; Psychology; U of North Carolina-Charlotte; Duke U

Hicks, Andrew S
Hoke Cty HS
Raeford, NC

Hernandez, Belinda
East Burke HS
Hickory, NC

Hendricks, Regina R
Northwest HS
Roanoke Rapids, NC

Hendricks, Bernice K
Southeast Halifax HS
Enfield, NC

Helton, Daniel
Hiwassee Dam HS
Murphy, NC

Henderson, Jocelyn Q
John T Hoggard HS
Wilmington, NC

Henry, Tiffany L
Anson HS
Morven, NC

Herring, Deniece N
Plymouth HS
Plymouth, NC

Hicks, Justin J
Reynolds HS
Winston Salem, NC

HILL, HANNAH; MIDWAY PARK, NC; WHITE OAK HS; (MS); Hnr Roll; Perf Att; Pres Sch; St of Mnth; Comm Volntr; Chrch Yth Grp; DARE; Bnd; Ch Chr; Jzz Bnd; Pep Bnd; National Junior Honor Society; National Junior Art Honor Society; Law; History; Spelman; U of North Carolina Chapel Hill

HILL, HEATHER; PELHAM, NC; ROCKINGHAM CTY HS; (SR); Hnr Roll; Emplmnt; Sccr (V CL); Swmg (V L); Biology / Allied Health; Radiology; Rockingham Community College; Greensboro College

HILL, JOSHUA; GOLDSBORO, NC; EASTERN WAYNE HS; (SO); Hi Hnr Roll; WWAHSS; Chrch Yth Grp; Mth Clb/Tm; ROTC; Ch Chr; Dnce; Highest Algebra I Average Freshman Year; All A's in Math Courses; Doctorate Degree in Law; Doctorate Degree in Math (General); North Carolina State U; U of North Carolina At Chapel Hill

HILL, KRISTIN E; CHAPEL HILL, NC; EAST CHAPEL HILL HS; (FR); Ctznshp Aw; Hi Hnr Roll; Bnd; Dnce; Stu Cncl (R); French Honor Society; Marine Biology; Engineering; Duke U

HILL, LAUREN; WAKE FOREST, NC; WAKE FOREST-ROLESVILLE HS; (SO); Hi Hnr Roll; Hnr Roll; Nat Hon Sy; Otst Ac Ach Awd; Pres Ac Ftns Aw; WWAHSS; Chrch Yth Grp; Drma Clb; Emplmnt; Quill & Scroll; Latin Clb; Ch Chr; SP/M/VS; Stg Cre; Sccr (J); Yrbk (R, P); 3rd Place State Finalist for Copy Writing (Yearbook); International Fringe Festival; Creative Writing; Philosophy; Antioch U; U of North Carolina

HILL, MARYDITH A; WHITAKERS, NC; ROCKY MOUNT CHARTER; (SO); Hnr Roll; Peer Tut/Med; Chrch Yth Grp; Chr; Ch Chr; Chrldg (V); Stu Cncl (P, V); Ob/Gyn Doctor; Maternity Ward Nurse; Duke U; U of North Carolina

HILL, NATHAN D; GREENSBORO, NC; WOODBERRY FOREST SCH; (SO); Ctznshp Aw; Duke TS; Hi Hnr Roll; Perf Att; Yth Ldrshp Prog; Comm Volntr; Hab For Humty Volntr; Chrch Yth Grp; DARE; Jr Cls League; Mth Clb/Tm; NYLC; Outdrs Clb; Quiz Bowl; Spanish Clb; Bnd; Bsball (J); Sccr (JC); Lit Mag (R); Sch Ppr (R); Yrbk (R); Squash, JV; Fellowship of Christians in U and School; Davidson; Swarthmore

HILL, RAVEN S; LUMBERTON, NC; LUMBERTON JHS; (MS); Hnr Roll; Comm Volntr; Peer Tut/Med; DARE; Ntl Beta Clb; Bnd; Chrldg; Business Administration; Engineering; U of NC Chapel Hill; U North Carolina Wilmington

HILLA, SARAH; RALEIGH, NC; WAKEFIELD HS; (SO); Hi Hnr Roll; Comm Volntr; Key Club; Drl Tm; Dvng (V); PP Ftbl; Swmg (V); Track; Stu Cncl (R); Sch Ppr (R); Citadel-Top Cadet At Officer Leadership School; Top Freshman Cadet At Sanderson HS; Mass Communications; Journalism; U of North Carolina: Chapel Hill; Elon U

HILLIS, AUSTIN B; BLADENBORO, NC; BLADENBORO HS; (FR); Ctznshp Aw; Hnr Roll; MVP; St of Mnth; Chrch Yth Grp; Bsball; Bskball (V); Ftball (V); Track; Sports Medicine; U of North Carolina; U of North Carolina State

HILTON, ERICA; FAYETTEVILLE, NC; REID ROSS YR ROUND CLASSICAL HS; (SO); Hnr Roll; Chrch Yth Grp; FBLA; Jr Cls League; Dnce; Cl Off (V); Forensics; Food & Ag Sciences Institute At Penn State U; Psychology; Sociology; North Carolina Central U; Johnson C Smith U

HIMES, BRITTANY D; SALISBURY, NC; WEST ROWAN HS; (FR); Ctznshp Aw; Hnr Roll; Nat Hon Sy; Otst Ac Ach Awd; Perf Att; Sci Fairs; Comm Volntr; Peer Tut/Med; Chrch Yth Grp; Jr Cls League; Pep Squd; Ch Chr; I Play Piano; Clothing Designer; Interior Designer; North Carolina School of Art; Winston Salem U

HINSON, COURTNEY M; MINT HILL, NC; PIEDMONT CHRISTIAN SCH; (SR); Ctznshp Aw; Hnr Roll; Otst Ac Ach Awd; Pres Sch; St of Mnth; WWAHSS; Comm Volntr; Peer Tut/Med; Chrch Yth Grp; DARE; Emplmnt; Jr Ach; Key Club; Pep Squd; Photog; Scouts; Dnce; PP Ftbl (J); Sftball (J); Stu Cncl (R); CR (R); Silver Award in Girl Scouts; Dental Hygiene; Coastal Carolina Community College Jacksonville N.C.

HINSON, MATTHEW; TOBACCOVILLE, NC; NORTH FORSYTH SR HS; (JR); Duke TS; Hi Hnr Roll; Hnr Roll; Jr Mshl; Nat Hon Sy; Otst Ac Ach Awd; Perf Att; Pres Ac Ftns Aw; Comm Volntr; Hab For Humty Volntr; Peer Tut/Med; Chrch Yth Grp; Emplmnt; FCA; HO'Br Yth Ldrshp; Key Club; Prom Com; Scouts; Stg Cre; Scr Kpr (V L); Sccr (VJCL); Adv Cncl (P, R); Cl Off (P, R); Stu Cncl (P, V, R); CR (R); Wake Forest Mortor Board Representative; Corporate Law; Political Science; U of North Carolina Chapel Hill; Wake Forest U

HINSON, SPENCER H; ALBEMARLE, NC; SOUTH STANLY HS; (MS); Duke TS; Hi Hnr Roll; Chess; Emplmnt; Scouts; Bnd; Mch Bnd; Track; Biology; Herpetology; North Carolina State U

HINTON, DARRELL; RALEIGH, NC; ENLOE HS; (JR); Yth Ldrshp Prog; CARE; ArtClub; Chrch Yth Grp; Drm Mjr; Stu Cncl (V); Boxing; Football; East Carolina U; Penn State

HIX, TYLER S; GARNER, NC; GARNER HS; (FR); Hnr Roll; MVP; Otst Ac Ach Awd; Perf Att; Chrch Yth Grp; Automotive Technology; Motorcycle Repair; NC State U

HIXSON, KATIE; PFAFFTOWN, NC; MT TABOR HS; (JR); Duke TS; F Lan Hn Soc; Hi Hnr Roll; Hnr Roll; Jr Mshl; MVP; Nat Hon Sy; Pres Ac Ftns Aw; Comm Volntr; Chrch Yth Grp; Key Club; Latin Clb; Bskball (J); Sccr (J); Sch Ppr (E); Editor-In-Chief of Newspaper; Psychology; Forensics; Davidson College

HOANG, SON; CHARLOTTE, NC; WEST MECKLENBURG HS; (FR); Hnr Roll; Perf Att; WWAHSS; Chess; Chrch Yth Grp; DARE; Chr; Aerospace engineer; Architect; U of North Carolina at Charlotte; North Carolina State

HOBBS, DALTON W; CLINTON, NC; HOBBTON HS; (SO); Hnr Roll; Chrch Yth Grp; FBLA; Ch Chr; Ftball (J); Wt Lftg (J); Algebra IA; Algebra IB Tutored Students in Algebra; Engineering; Computer Technology; North Carolina State U; Sampson Community College

HOBBS, EMILY L; GREENSBORO, NC; WESTERN GUILFORD HS; (JR); Duke TS; Hi Hnr Roll; Hnr Roll; Sci Fairs; Comm Volntr; Chrch Yth Grp; Emplmnt; FCA; Key Club; Ntl Beta Clb; Spanish Clb; PP Ftbl (V); Sccr (V L); Swmg (V L); Vllyball (V L); Fellowship of Christian Athletes-Leader; U of North Carolina; North Carolina State U

HOCK, PHILIP J; CHAPEL HILL, NC; WOODS CHARTER SCH; (SO); Duke TS; F Lan Hn Soc; Hnr Roll; Sci Fairs; Comm Volntr; Chrch Yth Grp; Cmptr Clb; DARE; Emplmnt; Outdrs Clb; Sci Clb; Scouts; Youth Partner Museum of Life and Science-N.C.; Biology; Botany; North Carolina State; U of North Carolina

HODGE, RONALD P; BURLINGTON, NC; EASTERN ALAMANCE HS; (JR); Hnr Roll; Otst Ac Ach Awd; Lib Aide; Chr; Dnce; It's Showtime At the Apollo Webs Talent Search Regional Winner; Kindergarten Teacher; Assistant Nurse; Elon U; Florida State U

HODGES, AMBER K; CHARLOTTE, NC; ZEBULON VANCE HS; (JR); Hnr Roll; Nat Hon Sy; St of Mnth; WWAHSS; Yth Ldrshp Prog; Comm Volntr; Peer Tut/Med; Chrch Yth Grp; Cmptr Clb; Drma Clb; Emplmnt; Lib Aide; Tchrs Aide; Ch Chr; Stu Cncl (R); Yrbk (P); Secondary Education; U of North Carolina of Wilmington; U of North Carolina of Charlotte

HODGES, KIMBERLY M; SHOLLOTTE, NC; MIDWAY HS; (SR); Hi Hnr Roll; Hnr Roll; Nat Hon Sy; WWAHSS; Comm Volntr; Emplmnt; FBLA; Ntl Beta Clb; Photog; Spanish Clb; Clr Grd; Dnce; Yrbk (P); Associate's in Business Administration; Bartending License; Brunswick Community College

HODGES, KRISTEN M; ASHEBORO, NC; ASHEBORO HS; (SR); Duke TS; Hnr Roll; MVP; Comm Volntr; Peer Tut/Med; Red Cr Aide; Chrch Yth Grp; Cmptr Clb; Dbte Team; FCA; Key Club; Quiz Bowl; Sci Clb; Spanish Clb; Bnd; Ch Chr; Mch Bnd; Orch; Golf (V L); Sccr (V CL); Vllyball (V L); High School Webmaster - President; Wade Edward High School Mock Trial Competition; Medicine - Pre-Med / Gen Med; Missions / Ministry; Southern Wesleyan U

HOFFERT, NATALIE M; HUNTERSVILLE, NC; HOPEWELL HS; (JR); Hnr Roll; MVP; Spec Olymp Vol; DECA; Emplmnt; FCA; Lib Aide; P to P St Amb Prg; Svce Clb; Bnd; PP Ftbl; Sftball (V L); National Technical Honor Society; Fashion Marketing; Social Work; U of North Carolina Charlotte; Western Carolina U

HOFFLER PINKSTON, RACHEL N; WINSTON-SALEM, NC; REYNOLDS HS; (JR); Hnr Roll; Perf Att; WWAHSS; Hab For Humty Volntr; Peer Tut/Med; Red Cr Aide; DECA; Emplmnt; FCA; Prom Com; ROTC; Sci Clb; SADD; Spanish Clb; Bskball; Scr Kpr; Sftball; Track; International Business; Culinary Arts; U of South Carolina; U of Miami

HOFFMAN, DEBORHA; GASTONIA, NC; VICTORY CHRISTIAN AC; (SO); Hnr Roll; Nat Hon Sy; Otst Ac Ach Awd; WWAHSS; Peer Tut/Med; Ntl Beta Clb; Off Aide; Tchrs Aide; Fashion Marketing & Design; Oceanographer; Art Institute of Charlotte

HOFFMANN, ROBERT C; KITTRELL, NC; FRANKLINTON HS; (FR); All Am Sch; Ctznshp Aw; Hi Hnr Roll; Hnr Roll; Nat Hon Sy; Otst Ac Ach Awd; Pres Sch; Sci Fairs; St of Mnth; Comm Volntr; Peer Tut/Med; ArtClub; Chess; Chrch Yth Grp; DARE; Emplmnt; Mth Clb/Tm; Ntl Beta Clb; Ch Chr; Bsball (J); Yrbk (R); Bowhunter-Horse Riding; Weight Lifter-Swimming; Engineering; Military; North Carolina State U; Western Carolina U

HOGAN, TIMOTHY B; SOUTHPORT, NC; SOUTH BRUNSWICK HS; (SO); Ctznshp Aw; Hnr Roll; Otst Ac Ach Awd; Comm Volntr; Chrch Yth Grp; French Clb; Bnd; Mch Bnd; Numerous Best Junior Handler in AKC Dog Shows; Veterinarian; Real Estate Broker; North Carolina State U; U of North Carolina At Chapel Hill

HOGGARD, WILSON M; MERRY HILL, NC; LAWRENCE AC; (SO); Hi Hnr Roll; Hnr Roll; Perf Att; WWAHSS; Chrch Yth Grp; Emplmnt; Ntl Beta Clb; Ch Chr; Bsball (J); Ftball (VJ); Wt Lftg (VJ); Cl Off (S); Student Ambassador; Wild Life Management; National Parks Service; North Carolina State

HOLBROOK, KRISTINA; NEWTON, NC; NEWTON CONOVER HS; (SO); Ctznshp Aw; Hi Hnr Roll; Hnr Roll; Perf Att; Sci Fairs; Chrch Yth Grp; DARE; Lib Aide; Tchrs Aide; Bnd; Chr

HOLDEN, TYTEASHA; ROCKY MOUNT, NC; ROCKYMOUNT SR HS; (SR); WWAHSS; Chr; Ch Chr; Business; Fayetteville State U

HOLEMAN, JACQLYN M; DURHAM, NC; CE JORDAN HS; (JR); Hnr Roll; Comm Volntr; Textiles; Forensic Studies; North Carolina State U

HOLLAND, ALLISON M; LUCAMA, NC; HUNT HS; (JR); Hi Hnr Roll; Hnr Roll; Kwnis Aw; MVP; Otst Ac Ach Awd; Perf Att; Pres Ac Ftns Aw; St of Mnth; WWAHSS; Chrch Yth Grp; DARE; FCA; Key Club; Prom Com; SADD; Chr; SP/M/VS; Sftball (V L); Vllyball (V L); CR (R); Scholar Athlete for 3 Years Both Sports; Academic Excellence Champion 2 Years; Radiology; Pharmacy; North Carolina U At Wilmington; East Carolina U

HOLLAND, AMESHIA; GATES, NC; GATES CTY SR HS; (JR); Hnr Roll; Perf Att; Sci Fairs; WWAHSS; Chrch Yth Grp; Emplmnt; Prom Com; Ch Chr; Dnce; Chrldg (J); Cl Off (R); CR (R); Reporter of Club HOSA; Business; Nursing; North Carolina Agricultural & Technical U; Chowan College

HOLLAND, ISAIAH; ELM CITY, NC; RALPH L FIKE HS; (FR); Duke TS; Hnr Roll; Sci/Math Olympn; Sci Clb; Chr; Bskball (J); Ftball (V); Track (V); Wt Lftg (V); CR; Physician; Pediatrician; Duke Medical; Drexel U

HOLLIDAY, BRITTANY; FAYETTEVILLE, NC; E E SMITH SR HS; (FR); Emplmnt; P to P St Amb Prg; Orch; Math (Teaching); NC A & T State U; Fayetteville State U

HOLLIDAY, ZACHARY; MEBANE, NC; EASTERN ALAMANCE HS; (JR); Duke TS; F Lan Hn Soc; Hnr Roll; Jr Mshl; Kwnis Aw; MVP; Nat Hon Sy; Pres Sch; St Schl; WWAHSS; Comm Volntr; Peer Tut/Med; Chrch Yth Grp; FCA; Key Club; Spanish Clb; Bsball (V L); Bskball (V CL); Cr Ctry (V CL); VP National Honor Society; Foreign Language Society; Education; Accounting; U North Carolina Chapel Hill; North Carolina State U

HOLLINGSWORTH, DAVID W; FAYETTEVILLE, NC; E E SMITH SR HS; (FR); Hnr Roll; Comm Volntr; Ntl Beta Clb; Tennis (V); Math & Science Academy; Pediatrician; East Carolina U; U of North Carolina At Chapel Hill

HOLLINGSWORTH, JOSH; BURGAW, NC; PENDER HS; (SO); Hnr Roll; Perf Att; Chrch Yth Grp; DARE; Bsball (J); Bskball (J); Ftball (J); Volunteer Firefighter; Professional Firefighter; Auto Mechanic; Wilson Tech; NADC

HOLLIS, MORGAN; MARSHVILLE, NC; FOREST HILLS HS; (JR); Hnr Roll; Nat Hon Sy; WWAHSS; Spec Olymp Vol; Chrch Yth Grp; DARE; FCA; FBLA; Ntl Beta Clb; Vsity Clb; Bskball (J); PP Ftbl (J); Sftball (V L); Engineering; Pharmacy; North Carolina State U; U of North Carolina At Charlotte

HOLLOWAY, ALICIA; BURLINGTON, NC; GRAHAM HS; (SO); Ctznshp Aw; Hnr Roll; Kwnis Aw; Otst Ac Ach Awd; Perf Att; Sci Fairs; WWAHSS; Yth Ldrshp Prog; Peer Tut/Med; French Clb; Participate in Tech-Fest Annually; Criminal Psychology; Business; Duke U; Wake Forest U

HOLLOWELL, JOEL C; ELIZABETH CITY, NC; ALBEMARLE SCH; (FR); Duke TS; Hnr Roll; Perf Att; Sci/Math Olympn; Yth Ldrshp Prog; Comm Volntr; Chess; Chrch Yth Grp; Drma Clb; Quiz Bowl; Sci Clb; SP/M/VS; International Student Leadership Conference - Duke U; Criminal Justice; Veterinarian Science; North Carolina State U

HOLMAN JR, DEVORE D; MOCKSVILLE, NC; DAVIE CTY HS; (FR); Ctznshp Aw; Hnr Roll; Nat Hon Sy; Perf Att; Comm Volntr; FCA; Bnd; Ftball (J); Track; CR (P, R); Architect; Teacher / Coach; North Carolina A & T State U; North Carolina State U

HOLMES, ELIZABETH K; DUNN, NC; CAPE FEAR CHRISTIAN AC; (FR); Hi Hnr Roll; MVP; Nat Hon Sy; Sci Fairs; Sci/Math Olympn; St of Mnth; Chrch Yth Grp; Ntl Beta Clb; Quiz Bowl; Chr; Dnce; Bskball (VJC); Cl Off (R); Physical Therapy; East Carolina U; North Carolina State U

HOLT, EDWARD L; WINSTON-SALEM, NC; MT TABOR HS; (JR); Duke TS; Hi Hnr Roll; Jr Mshl; Nat Hon Sy; WWAHSS; Comm Volntr; Emplmnt; Key Club; Schol Bwl; Scouts; Bnd; Mch Bnd; Eagle Scout; Church Wind Ensemble; History; Law; U of North Carolina; Duke U

HOLT, GABRIELLE L; LILLINGTON, NC; OVERHILLS HS; (JR); Hnr Roll; Nat Hon Sy; WWAHSS; Key Club; Tennis (V); Pre-Law; Gardner-Webb U; U of North Carolina in Wilmington

HONAKER, ASHLEY M; TRINITY, NC; TRINITY HS; (FR); Hi Hnr Roll; Nat Hon Sy; FBLA; Cl Off (V); Stu Cncl (R); Presidential Award of Excellence; Doctoral Degree in History; Doctoral Degree in Teaching; U of North Carolina At Chapel Hill; U of North Carolina State

HONEA, VICTORIA L; NEW BERN, NC; HAVELOCK HS; MS

HOOD II, TONY L; CHARLOTTE, NC; HARDING U HS; (FR); Hnr Roll; Pres Sch; Comm Volntr; Veterinarian; Electrical Engineer; North Carolina State U; North Carolina A & T State U

HOOKER, BRITTANY; SNOW HILL, NC; GREEN CTRL HS; (MS); Ctznshp Aw; Hi Hnr Roll; Hnr Roll; MVP; Nat Hon Sy; Nat Mrt LOC; Nat Mrt Sch Recip; Otst Ac Ach Awd; Perf Att; Pres Ac Ftns Aw; Peer Tut/Med; DARE; Lib Aide; Pep Squd; Photog; Scouts; SADD; Tchrs Aide; Ch Chr; Dnce; Chrldg (J); PPSqd (J); Stu Cncl (S, T); Yrbk (P); Girl Scouts; Medical Field; Administration; East Carolina U; Greensboro North Carolina A & T

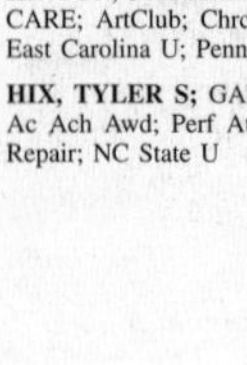
Honaker, Ashley M
Trinity HS
Trinity, NC

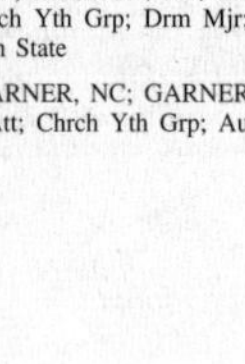
Hoffmann, Robert C
Franklinton HS
Kittrell, NC

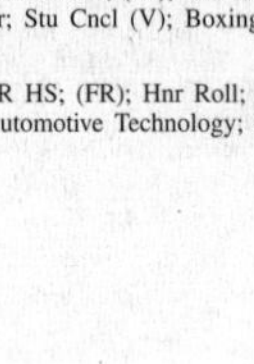
Hobbs, Dalton W
Hobbton HS
Clinton, NC

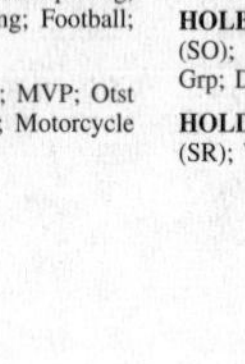
Hinson, Courtney M
Piedmont Christian Sch
Mint Hill, NC

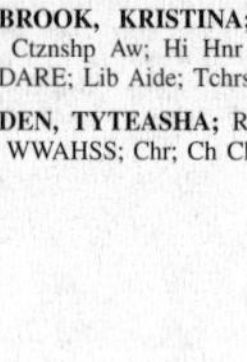
Himes, Brittany D
West Rowan HS
Salisbury, NC

National
Honor Roll
Spring 2005

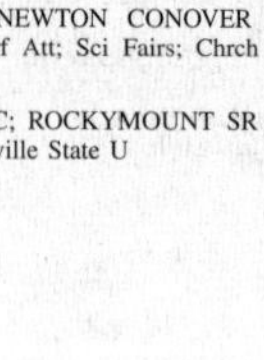
Hill, Nathan D
Woodberry Forest Sch
Greensboro, NC

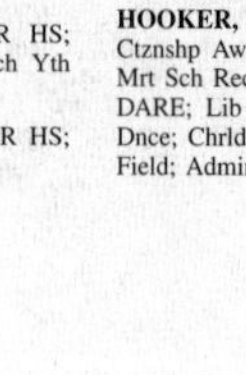
Hinson, Matthew
North Forsyth SR HS
Tobaccoville, NC

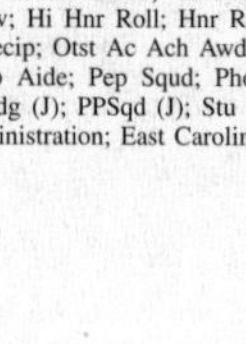
Hoffert, Natalie M
Hopewell HS
Huntersville, NC

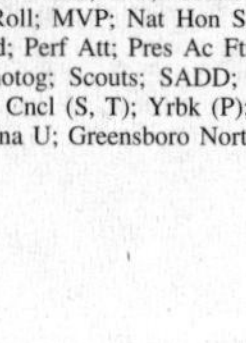
Holbrook, Kristina
Newton Conover HS
Newton, NC

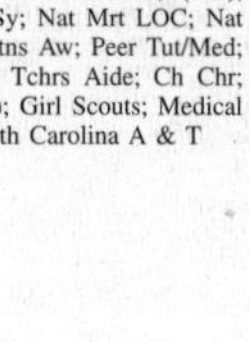
Hollis, Morgan
Forest Hills HS
Marshville, NC

HOOVER, MONICA; CLAYTON, NC; SMITHFIELD-SELMA; (JR); Hi Hnr Roll; Hnr Roll; Nat Hon Sy; Nat Stu Ath Day Aw; WWAHSS; Spec Olymp Vol; FTA; Key Club; Prom Com; Tennis (V L)

HOPKINS, ERICA; HENDERSON, NC; SOUTHERN VANCE HS; (JR); Hi Hnr Roll; Hnr Roll; Jr Mshl; Nat Hon Sy; Otst Ac Ach Awd; St of Mnth; WWAHSS; Yth Ldrshp Prog; Comm Volntr; Hab For Humty Volntr; Chrch Yth Grp; Emplmnt; FCA; Key Club; NYLC; Scouts; Sccr (V); Swmg (V); Anesthesiology; UNC At Charlotte; ECU

HOPPER, DE SHANDA I Q; LAWNDALE, NC; BURNS HS; (SR); Hnr Roll; Otst Ac Ach Awd; Peer Tut/Med; Chrch Yth Grp; Quill & Scroll; Sch Ppr (E, R, P); Distinguished Image Award; ServSafe Certification; Pre-Med; Emergency Medical Technician; Campbell U; Peace College

HOPSON, JESSICA L; GREEN MOUNTAIN, NC; MTN HERITAGE HS; (SR); Ctznshp Aw; Hnr Roll; Otst Ac Ach Awd; St of Mnth; Comm Volntr; Hosp Aide; Peer Tut/Med; Chrch Yth Grp; Emplmnt; Outdrs Clb; Pep Squd; Tchrs Aide; Chr; Ch Chr; SP/M/VS; Swg Chr; Chrldg (C); 2003 Mathematics Award; Health Occupations Students of America; Nursing; Early Childhood Education; Maryland Community College

HORD, SARAH M; SHELBY, NC; BURNS HS; (SR); Duke TS; Gov Hnr Prg; Hi Hnr Roll; Jr Mshl; Nat Hon Sy; Otst Ac Ach Awd; Sci/Math Olympn; Comm Volntr; Chrch Yth Grp; DARE; Dbte Team; Emplmnt; Ntl Beta Clb; Prom Com; Quill & Scroll; Latin Clb; Bnd; Ch Chr; Drm Mjr; Mch Bnd; Bskball (J); Sch Ppr (R); Political Science; American U Washington DC

HORNE, BYRON; CHARLOTTE, NC; HARDING U HS; (FR); Hnr Roll; Perf Att; Sci Fairs; Comm Volntr; Chrch Yth Grp; Bskball (J); Lawyer; Basketball; U of North Carolina Chapel Hill

HORNE, D GREGORY; LUMBERTON, NC; LUMBERTON HS; (FR); Chrch Yth Grp; ROTC; Chr; SP/M/VS; Bsball (J); Superintendent's Honor Roll; Computers; Engineering; NC State North Carolina State; UNCP U of North Carolina @ Pembroke

HORTON, BEN; MT AIRY, NC; NORTH SURRY HS; (SO); Hnr Roll; Perf Att; Chess; FCA; ROTC; Tech Clb; Electronics Engineer; Robotics Engineer; Surry Community College; North Carolina State U

HORTON, BROCK; DURHAM, NC; NORTHWOOD HS; (JR); Hnr Roll; Otst Ac Ach Awd; Yth Ldrshp Prog; Chrch Yth Grp; Emplmnt; FCA; Ntl FFA; Bskball (V); Vocational Honor Society; Teaching; Physical Therapy; North Carolina State U; East Carolina U

HORTON, MASON R; MT AIRY, NC; NORTH SURRY HS; (SO); Sci Fairs; St of Mnth; Red Cr Aide; Chrch Yth Grp; DARE; Sci Clb; Bnd; Jzz Bnd; Mch Bnd; Pep Bnd; Adv Cncl (S); Cl Off (T); Stu Cncl (T); CR (R); Citizenship Award; Math Teacher in Middle School; Surry Community College; North Carolina State U

HORVAT, ARIANA A; LINCOLNTON, NC; WEST LINCOLN HS; (JR); Duke TS; Hnr Roll; Jr Mshl; Nat Hon Sy; Comm Volntr; Spec Olymp Vol; Chrch Yth Grp; FCA; Ntl Beta Clb; Prom Com; Quiz Bowl; Sci Clb; Scouts; SADD; Cr Ctry (V); Sccr (V); Sftball (J); Stu Cncl (R); Girl Scout Silver Award; 1st Place in County Literary Competition; Pre-Med & Spanish; Pediatrician; UNC Chapel Hill; Furman U

HOUSER, DANA M; VALDESE, NC; FREEDOM HS; (SR); Hnr Roll; Yrbk (E); North Carolina At Wilmington; North Carolina At Chapel Hill

HOUSER, SARAH G; WAXHAW, NC; WEDDINGTON HS; (FR); Hnr Roll; St of Mnth; Comm Volntr; Peer Tut/Med; Spec Olymp Vol; Chrch Yth Grp; Key Club; Ntl Beta Clb; French Clb; Dnce; Miller Street Dance Academy Competition Team; Bachelor Degree; U of North Carolina; U of Charlotte

HOUSER, SHANA E; VALDESE, NC; FREEDOM HS; (SO); Hnr Roll; North Carolina At Wilmington; North Carolina At Greensboro

HOUSTON, CHRISTINE; FAYETTEVILLE, NC; JACK BRITT HS; (JR); Hnr Roll; Peer Tut/Med; Pep Squd; Chr; Chrldg (V); Computer Science; U of North Carolina Wilmington; North Carolina State U

HOUSTON, JUSTIN T; MAIDEN, NC; BANDYS HS; (SR); Hnr Roll; MVP; St of Mnth; Comm Volntr; Red Cr Aide; Spec Olymp Vol; Chrch Yth Grp; DARE; FCA; Pep Squd; Sci Clb; Spanish Clb; Bnd; Ch Chr; Bsball (J); Ftball (VJ L); Scr Kpr (V); Swmg (V); Track (V L); Wrstlg (V CL); Most Outstanding Wrestler - State Dual Final; Athlete of the Week (Drums & Winis-Reynolds Funeral Home); Anesthesiologist; Nursing; U of North Carolina Greensboro; U of North Carolina Pembroke

HOWARD, JONATHAN; GARNER, NC; WEST JOHNSTON HS; (JR); Hi Hnr Roll; Hnr Roll; WWAHSS; Hab For Humty Volntr; Chess; FCA; FBLA; Prom Com; French Clb; Cr Ctry (V L); Track (V L); Cl Off (T); Indoor Track-Varsity & Letter Winner; Archaeology; Athletic Training; Eastern Carolina U

HOWARD JR, KENNETH A; GARNER, NC; MIDDLE CREEK HS; (SO); Hnr Roll; Chrch Yth Grp; Ch Chr; Wt Lftg (J); Computer Science; Education; U of North Carolina Chapel Hill; North Carolina State U

HOWELL, CALEB L; ALBEMARLE, NC; NORTH STANLY HS; (SO); Ctznshp Aw; Hnr Roll; WWAHSS; Chrch Yth Grp; Civil Air Pat; FCA; Cr Ctry (V); Tennis (V); Track (V); Computer Engineering; Virginia Military Institute; U of North Carolina-Charlotte

HOWELL, KIMBERLY K; SUPPLY, NC; WEST BRUNSWICK HS; (SO); DAR; Duke TS; Hnr Roll; Nat Hon Sy; Sci Fairs; Sci/Math Olympn; WWAHSS; Comm Volntr; Peer Tut/Med; Red Cr Aide; Chrch Yth Grp; DARE; Drma Clb; Emplmnt; FTA; Photog; Prom Com; Sci Clb; SP/M/VS; Cl Off (S); Stu Cncl (S); CR (S); Sch Ppr (R, P); Yrbk (R, P); Science Olympiad; Future Teachers of America; Archaeology; Middle Eastern History; Harvard; New York U

HOWELL, TAKILIA Q; HAMILTON, NC; WAVERLY JR/SR HS; (FR); Ctznshp Aw; Duke TS; Hi Hnr Roll; Hnr Roll; Nat Hon Sy; Perf Att; Sci Fairs; St of Mnth; WWAHSS; Yth Ldrshp Prog; CARE; Peer Tut/Med; Chrch Yth Grp; DARE; Dbte Team; Drma Clb; Key Club; Lib Aide; Mth Clb/Tm; Off Aide; Ch Chr; Dnce; Flg Crps; Bsball (V); Bskball (V); Chrldg (C); Sftball (V); Adv Cncl (S); Cl Off (S); Stu Cncl (R); CR (V); Highest Average; Pediatrician Doctor; Registered Nurse; Eastern Carolina U; Duke U

HOWIE, SAMANTHA; WEAVERVILLE, NC; NORTH BUNCOMBE HS; (SO); Ctznshp Aw; DECA; Chr; Chrldg (V); Best All Around JV Cheerleading 03-04; Business; Law; NC State; Mars Hill U

HOYLE, ERIKA; CHERRYVILLE, NC; BURNS HS; (FR); DARE; SADD; Dnce; Flg Crps; SP/M/VS; Stg Cre; Journalism; Flight Attendant

HOYLE, TYLER; DUNN, NC; CAPE FEAR CHRISTIAN AC; (FR); Hi Hnr Roll; Hnr Roll; MVP; Sci Fairs; Sci/Math Olympn; Ntl Beta Clb; Bskball (J L); Golf (V CL); PGM Professional Golf Management; Law; North Carolina State U; Campbell U

HUBBARD, JESSICA; EDEN, NC; MOREHEAD HS; (SR); Nat Hon Sy; Hab For Humty Volntr; Hosp Aide; SADD; Latin Clb; Bnd; Clr Grd; Pep Bnd; Sccr (J); Swmg (V); Clinical Lab Science; Physical Therapy; Western Carolina U

HUBERT, AMANDA; FAYETTEVILLE, NC; DOUGLAS BYRD HS; (JR); Hnr Roll; Comm Volntr; DARE; Drma Clb; Ntl Beta Clb; Prom Com; Chr; Ch Chr; SP/M/VS; All-Star Softball Team for West Fayetteville Rec; Theater; U of North Carolina At Wilmington; North Carolina School of the Arts

HUDGINS, KAITLYN M; KITTY HAWK, NC; FIRST FLIGHT HS; (FR); Duke TS; Otst Ac Ach Awd; Pres Ac Ftns Aw; St of Mnth; Comm Volntr; FBLA; Key Club; Bnd; Track (V); CR (R)

HUDSON, DAVID B; FAYETTEVILLE, NC; DOUGLAS BYRD HS; (SO); Hnr Roll; Pres Ac Ftns Aw; Bsball (VJ); Cr Ctry (VJ); Track (VJ); Athletic-Major; U of North Carolina Chapel Hill; U of North Carolina Wilmington

HUFF, HERLIE; LAKE TOXAWAY, NC; BREVARD HS; (FR); Duke TS; Hnr Roll; Otst Ac Ach Awd; Perf Att; St of Mnth; Hosp Aide; DARE; Drma Clb; FBLA; Mus Clb; Ntl Beta Clb; NYLC; Chr; Dnce; SP/M/VS; Bsball (J); Bskball (J); Chrldg; Gmnstcs; Scr Kpr; Swmg; Vllyball (J); Cl Off (S); Dance, Chorus, 4th Runner Up; American Coed Sweetheart Pageant; Doctorate In Music; Law; Duke U; Harvard U

HUFF, JASON A; WILLOW SPRING, NC; HILLTOP CHRISTIAN SCH; (SO); Hnr Roll; WWAHSS; Chrch Yth Grp; Chr; Ch Chr; Bskball (VJCL); Cl Off (V); Southeastern Free Will Baptist College

HUFFMAN, MARSHA S; FORT BRAGG, NC; PINE FOREST HS; (SR); Hnr Roll; Perf Att; Red Cr Aide; Chrch Yth Grp; Bnd; Ch Chr; Dnce; Jzz Bnd; Bskball (J L); Chrldg (V); Track (J L); Vllyball (V L); Music; Art/Architectural Design; Fayetteville State U

HUGHES, AMANDA; FAYETTEVILLE, NC; DOUGLAS BYRD HS; (SR); Hnr Roll; Nat Hon Sy; Chrch Yth Grp; FBLA; FTA; Key Club; Key Clubber of the Month; Renaissance; Bachelor's Degree; Master's Degree; Fayetteville State U

HUGHES, ASHLEY J; SALISBURY, NC; EAST ROWAN HS; (FR); Ctznshp Aw; St of Mnth; Comm Volntr; Bnd; Mch Bnd; North Carolina State U

HUGHES, CANDACE K; GREEN MOUNTAIN, NC; MOUNTAIN HERITAGE HS; Ctznshp Aw; Hi Hnr Roll; Hnr Roll; Otst Ac Ach Awd; Perf Att; Pres Ac Ftns Aw; St of Mnth; Chrch Yth Grp; DARE; Chr; Chrldg; Track; Stu Cncl (P); CR (P); Lawyer Degree; Teacher Degree; Harvard U; Stanford U

HUGHES, DARYL L; COATS, NC; HILLTOP CHRISTIAN SCH; (SO); Duke TS; Hi Hnr Roll; USAA; WWAHSS; Chrch Yth Grp; Emplmnt; Chr; Bskball (V L); Chrldg (VJ L); Yrbk; Forensics; Drafting/Architecture; Appalachian State U; U of North Carolina

HUMPHREY, JOSHUA A; FAYETTEVILLE, NC; BEREAN BAPTIST AC; (SR); Hnr Roll; Perf Att; Pres Ac Ftns Aw; WWAHSS; Tchrs Aide; Bskball (V); Orthodontist; Coach; Oakwood College AL; Southern U TN

HUMPHRIES, HOLLY L; MOORESBORO, NC; CREST HS; (SO); WWAHSS; Chrch Yth Grp; FBLA; Spanish Clb; Ch Chr; Newspaper Staff; FBLA; Engineering; Minor Drafting; NC State; Clemson

HUNEYCUTT, STEPHANIE; MATTHEWS, NC; WEDDINGTON HS; (JR); Hnr Roll; Nat Ldrshp Svc; WWAHSS; Comm Volntr; Peer Tut/Med; Emplmnt; FBLA; Key Club; Prom Com; Scouts; Dnce; Stg Cre; PP Ftbl (J); Cl Off (P); 3 Time Letter Winner in Academics; Stage Manager; Teaching; Psychology; Stanford U; Duke U

HUNICHEN, KELLY A; CLAYTON, NC; WEST JOHNSTON HS; (SR); Hnr Roll; Comm Volntr; Chrch Yth Grp; Emplmnt; FCA; Ntl FFA; SADD; Chrldg (J); PP Ftbl (V); CR (R); Radiology; Cosmetology; East Carolina U; Johnston Community College

HUNSUCKER, TOSHIA; LINCOLNTON, NC; LINCOLNTON HS; (FR); DARE; Interior Designer

HUNT, BRITTANY D; LUMBERTON, NC; LUMBERTON HS; (FR); Hnr Roll; St of Mnth; WWAHSS; Yth Ldrshp Prog; Comm Volntr; Chrch Yth Grp; Ch Chr; NASA Club; Teen Uplift; Medicine; Pediatrics; U of NC Chapel Hill; Duke U

HUNT, JANNA; PEMBROKE, NC; PURNELL SWETT HS; (SO); Hnr Roll; St of Mnth; WWAHSS; Ntl Beta Clb; ROTC; Bnd; Jzz Bnd; Mch Bnd; Sftball (J); Vllyball (J); Veterinarian; Cosmetology; Purdue U; Washington State U

HUNT, KRYSTLE K; CLAYTON, NC; CLAYTON HS; (SO); Hnr Roll; Perf Att; St of Mnth; Comm Volntr; Chrch Yth Grp; Emplmnt; Ntl Beta Clb; Bnd; Ch Chr; Dnce; Membership in Health Occupations Students of America Club - 2 Years; Registered Nurse / Pediatrics; U of North Carolina Wilmington; U of North Carolina

HUNT, LAUREN L; BATH, NC; NORTHSIDE HS; (JR); Hnr Roll; MVP; WWAHSS; Spec Olymp Vol; ArtClub; Drma Clb; Key Club; Bnd; Dnce; Mch Bnd; SP/M/VS; Chrldg (V L); Cl Off (T); Co. Capt Cheerleading Squad; Honors Band; Physical Therapy; U of Florida; East Carolina U

HUNT, SHANNON A; GASTONIA, NC; VICTORY CHRISTIAN AC; (JR); Hnr Roll; Nat Stu Ath Day Aw; Perf Att; WWAHSS; 4-H; Chrch Yth Grp; DARE; Drma Clb; Emplmnt; Ntl Beta Clb; Tchrs Aide; SP/M/VS; Stg Cre; Bskball (V); Sftball (V); Sch Ppr (R); Animal Law Enforcement; Veterinarian

HUNTER, CALEB; MARSHALL, NC; MADISON HS; (SR); Hnr Roll; Jr Mshl; Nat Hon Sy; St Schl; WWAHSS; Comm Volntr; Peer Tut/Med; Red Cr Aide; Chrch Yth Grp; Emplmnt; FCA; Ntl FFA; Quiz Bowl; Tchrs Aide; Spanish Clb; Criminal Justice; Western Carolina U

HUNTER, HEATHER; KNIGHTDALE, NC; EWA; (SR); F Lan Hn Soc; Hnr Roll; Nat Hon Sy; Perf Att; Sci Fairs; St of Mnth; Peer Tut/Med; Chrch Yth Grp; Emplmnt; Photog; Prom Com; Spanish Clb; Chr; Dnce; SP/M/VS; Chrldg; PP Ftbl; Sch Ppr (E, R); Yrbk (P); Psychology; Communications; East Carolina U

HUNTER, KYLE B; HOT SPRINGS, NC; MADISON HS; (SR); Ctznshp Aw; Hi Hnr Roll; Hnr Roll; Jr Mshl; Nat Hon Sy; Otst Ac Ach Awd; Perf Att; Valdctrian; WWAHSS; Comm Volntr; Chrch Yth Grp; FCA; Ntl FFA; Stu Cncl (P); North Carolina Teaching Fellow; Biology; Secondary Education; U of North Carolina-Asheville

HUNTER, LA SHONA S; BELVIDERE, NC; PERQUIMANS CTY HS; (SO); Hnr Roll; Nat Hon Sy; Otst Ac Ach Awd; Perf Att; WWAHSS; Comm Volntr; Chrch Yth Grp; Emplmnt; Jr Ach; Prom Com; SADD; Ch Chr; Cl Off (S, T); Pre-Med; Pediatrics; Elizabeth City State U; U of North Carolina Chapel Hill

HUNTER, PHYLICIA; CHARLOTTE, NC; HARDING UNIVERSITY HS; (FR); Hnr Roll; Nat Hon Sy; Perf Att; Peer Tut/Med; Chrch Yth Grp; DARE; Bnd; Ch Chr; Drl Tm; SP/M/VS; Chrldg (VJ); Track (V); Wt Lftg (J); Pediatric Care; Medicine; Chapel Hill; U of North Carolina

HUNTER, VERONICA L; GASTONIA, NC; ASHBROOK HS; (JR); Hnr Roll; St of Mnth; Red Cr Aide; DARE; Gmnstcs (V); Cheerleading; Gymnastics; Gaston College; Prep College

HUNTER-ASHWORTH, ANNE; CARY, NC; ST DAVID'S SCH; (JR); Duke TS; Hi Hnr Roll; Nat Hon Sy; WWAHSS; Hab For Humty Volntr; Chrch Yth Grp; Prom Com; Stg Cre; Tennis (V L); Gold Key; Friday Morning Fellowship (Leader); Math; English; U of North Carolina At Chapel Hill; U of Georgia

HURD, JENNIFER C; WESTFIELD, NC; NORTH STOKES HS; (SR); Hnr Roll; Jr Mshl; DARE; Ntl Beta Clb; Spanish Clb; Cr Ctry (V); Track (V L); Biotechnology; Forsyth Tech Community College; Winston Salem State

HURD, MEGAN; STONEVILLE, NC; DALTON L MC MICHAEL HS; (SO); Hnr Roll; Otst Ac Ach Awd; Pres Ac Ftns Aw; WWAHSS; ArtClub; Ntl Beta Clb; Scouts; Swmg (V); Nursing; U of North Carolina Greensboro; Appalachian State U

HURD RODRIGUEZ, ROBERT A; FAYETTEVILLE, NC; PINE FOREST HS; (SO); Hnr Roll; Otst Ac Ach Awd; Peer Tut/Med; Vsity Clb; Bnd; Sccr (V CL); Most Outstanding Freshman and Sophomore Scholar (Highest GPA); Fayetteville Force Travel Soccer; Computer Science/Programming; History/Government; U of North Carolina-Chapel Hill; North Carolina State

HURLEY, JAMES C; CHARLOTTE, NC; VANCE HS; (SO); Hnr Roll; Drma Clb; SP/M/VS; Movie Director

Hunichen, Kelly A
West Johnston HS
Clayton, NC

Hoyle, Tyler
Cape Fear Christian AC
Dunn, NC

Howie, Samantha
North Buncombe HS
Weaverville, NC

Horton, Mason R
North Surry HS
Mt Airy, NC

Howell, Caleb L
North Stanly HS
Albemarle, NC

Hudson, David B
Douglas Byrd HS
Fayetteville, NC

Hunter, Kyle B
Madison HS
Hot Springs, NC

HUSSEY, SARAH K; CHAPEL HILL, NC; CARY AC; (FR); Hi Hnr Roll; WWAHSS; Comm Volntr; Key Club; Ntl Beta Clb; P to P St Amb Prg; Scouts; Dnce; SP/M/VS; Chrldg (V L); PP Ftbl; Tennis (J); Silver Award - Girl Scouts; Advertising; Communication; U of North Carolina Chapel Hill

HUSSEY, WILL; CHAPEL HILL, NC; CARY AC; (JR); Duke TS; Hi Hnr Roll; MVP; Nat Hon Sy; WWAHSS; Hosp Aide; Key Club; Mth Clb/Tm; Ntl Beta Clb; Scouts; Chr; Bsball (VJCL); Bskball (VJCL); Golf (V L); Cl Off (T); Stu Cncl (R); Eagle Scout; Business / Dentistry; Entrepreneur; U of North Carolina Chapel Hill; UVA

HUTCHENS, CARRIE E; DOBSON, NC; SURRY CTRL HS; (SR); Hnr Roll; Chrch Yth Grp; Hsbk Rdg; Sftball (VJ L); Vllyball (VJ); Veterinary Technician Assistant; Veterinarian; NC State

HUTCHINS, ALISA S; ELLENBORO, NC; EAST RUTHERFORD HS; (JR); Duke TS; Hi Hnr Roll; Hnr Roll; Jr Mshl; Nat Hon Sy; WWAHSS; FBLA; FCCLA; Key Club; Lib Aide; Chrldg (VJC); Cl Off (T); Part-Time Job As Waitress; Radiology; Business; Chapel Hill; Gardner Webb

HUTCHINS, ASHLIE; WINSTON SALEM, NC; LEDFORD HS; (FR); Ctznshp Aw; Hnr Roll; Otst Ac Ach Awd; Pres Sch; St of Mnth; Comm Volntr; Peer Tut/Med; Chrch Yth Grp; DARE; Drma Clb; Emplmnt; Mus Clb; Quiz Bowl; Spch Team; Chr; Ch Chr; Clr Grd; SP/M/VS; Scr Kpr (V); Sftball (J); Track (V); Yrbk (P); Talent Show-3 years (Singing); Poetry Is Published in 3 Countries; Lawyer-Domestic and Criminal; Adolescent Psychologist; Wake Forest U; U of North Carolina Chapel Hill

HUTCHINS, SAM; CHARLOTTE, NC; E E WADDELL HS; (SO); Hnr Roll; Comm Volntr; Chrch Yth Grp; FTA; Photog; Bnd; Mch Bnd; Pep Bnd; In the Conservation Group; Congressman; College Professor; Duke; UNC Chapel Hill

HUTCHINSON, REBEKAH; CREEDMOOR, NC; CJC AC; (FR); All Am Sch; Hnr Roll; Valdctrian; WWAHSS; Chrch Yth Grp; Drma Clb; Ntl Beta Clb; Quiz Bowl; SP/M/VS; Bskball (VJ); Vllyball (VJ); North Carolina House Page Program; Doctorate in Psychology; U of North Carolina Greensboro

HUX, KRISTIN B; LITTLETON, NC; HALIFAX AC CHRISTIAN SCH; (JR); Duke TS; Gov Hnr Prg; Hi Hnr Roll; Hnr Roll; Jr Mshl; Nat Hon Sy; Otst Ac Ach Awd; USAA; WWAHSS; Yth Ldrshp Prog; Chrch Yth Grp; Ntl Beta Clb; NYLC; Prom Com; Quiz Bowl; Vsity Clb; Bskball (VJ); PP Ftbl (V); Scr Kpr (J); Wt Lftg (V); Cl Off (R); Stu Cncl (R); CR (R); Yrbk (R); Pharmacy; Chemistry; U of North Carolina At Chapel Hill; North Carolina State U

HUX, TRAVIS R; LITTLETON, NC; HALIFAX AC CHRISTIAN SCH; (JR); Duke TS; Gov Hnr Prg; Hi Hnr Roll; Hnr Roll; Jr Mshl; MVP; Nat Hon Sy; Otst Ac Ach Awd; USAA; WWAHSS; Peer Tut/Med; Chrch Yth Grp; Emplmnt; Ntl Beta Clb; NYLC; Prom Com; Ftball (V); Golf (V C); PP Ftbl (V); Wt Lftg (V); Stu Cncl (V); Engineering; Business; North Carolina State U; U of North Carolina Charlotte

HUYNH, JEREMY; MEBANE, NC; EASTERN ALAMANCE HS; (SR); Nat Hon Sy; Pres Sch; Comm Volntr; Peer Tut/Med; Spec Olymp Vol; Biology Clb; Emplmnt; Key Club; Prom Com; Cr Ctry (VJ L); Track (J); Wrstlg (VJCL); Yrbk (R, P); NCHSAA Scholar Athlete; 2005 Superintendent's Award; Medicine; Government; U of North Carolina At Chapel Hill

HUYNH, TUYET-NHUNG T; FAYETTEVILLE, NC; WESTOVER HS; (FR); Hi Hnr Roll; Hnr Roll; Perf Att; Hosp Aide; Dnce; Sccr (J); Vllyball (J); CR (S); Yrbk (P); Service Award; Presidential Award; Respiratory Therapist; Duke U; UNC Chapel Hill

HWANG, JACOB; APEX, NC; ENLOE HS; (FR); Duke TS; Hnr Roll; Sci/Math Olympn; Comm Volntr; Chrch Yth Grp; Key Club; Orch; Tennis (V L); North Carolina High School Eastern Regional Orchestra; Second Place in Elizabeth Bullard Piano Competition; Medical; Engineering; Duke U; UNC

HYATT, WILLIAM V; CANDLER, NC; ERIKA HS; (SR); Hnr Roll; Nat Hon Sy; Pres Ac Ftns Aw; St Schl; Hab For Humty Volntr; Chrch Yth Grp; DARE; Scouts; Tchrs Aide; Vsity Clb; Bnd; Sccr (V CL); Stu Cncl (R); Journalism/Mass Communications; Advertising; U of North Carolina At Chapel Hill; U of Georgia At Athens

IANNUCCI, ANDREW P; RALEIGH, NC; MILLBROOK HS; (JR); Hnr Roll; Pres Ac Ftns Aw; Spec Olymp Vol; Rlr Hky (C); Tennis (V); Film; U of North Carolina Wilmington; Western Carolina U

IBARRA, EMMANUEL; YOUNGSVILLE, NC; FRANKLINTON HS; (SO); Hnr Roll; ArtClub; DARE; Wdwrkg Clb; Swg Chr; Cyclg; Drivers Ed; Architect; Engineering; NC State U; UNC

IBARRA, GLORIA; LENOIR, NC; WEST CALDWELL HS; (JR); Ctznshp Aw; Otst Ac Ach Awd; WWAHSS; Comm Volntr; Peer Tut/Med; ArtClub; Key Club; Spanish Clb; Tourism; Clothing Design; Caldwell Community College; Kings College

INGERSOLL, PATRICIA; FAYETTEVILLE, NC; GRAY'S CREEK HS; (FR); Hnr Roll; Perf Att; Hosp Aide; Chrch Yth Grp; DARE; Jr Ach; ROTC; Chr; Drl Tm; ROTC Promotion; Lawyer; Chef; Harvard U; U of North Carolina

INGERSOLL, SETH A; RALEIGH, NC; FRIENDSHIP CHRISTIAN SCH; (SR); Ctznshp Aw; Hi Hnr Roll; Jr Mshl; Nat Hon Sy; Nat Mrt Semif; Otst Ac Ach Awd; Valdctrian; WWAHSS; Yth Ldrshp Prog; Comm Volntr; Chrch Yth Grp; Drma Clb; Emplmnt; Lttrmn Clb; Mus Clb; Quiz Bowl; Schol Bwl; Svce Clb; Acpl Chr; Bnd; Chr; Ch Chr; Bsball (VJ L); Bskball (VJ L); Cl Off (P, V); Lit Mag; National Youth Leadership in Medicine; Medical Missions

IOVINO, ANGELO V; MORRISVILLE, NC; GREEN HOPE HS; (SR); Hnr Roll; Yth Ldrshp Prog; Peer Tut/Med; Mth Clb/Tm; Bnd; Chr; Mch Bnd; Teaching; Music; East Carolina U

ISENHOUR, JOHN; HICKORY, NC; HICKORY HS; (SO); Hi Hnr Roll; Hnr Roll; Ntl Beta Clb; Golf (V L); All Conference in Golf; Business; History; North Carolina State; U of South Carolina

ITTERLY, BETHANY J; KERNERSVILLE, NC; EAST FORSYTH HS; (SO); Hnr Roll; Comm Volntr; Chrch Yth Grp; Svce Clb; Latin Clb; Dnce; Cr Ctry (V L); Sccr (JC); Clothing Design; Journalism; North Carolina State; U of North Carolina At Wilmington

IVANOV, GEORGE; SUMMERFIELD, NC; NORTHWEST GUILFORD HS; (JR); Hnr Roll; Nat Hon Sy; Nat Mrt LOC; WWAHSS; Yth Ldrshp Prog; Comm Volntr; NYLC; Sci Clb; Spanish Clb; Chr; Sch Ppr; Political Science; U of North Carolina At Chapel Hill; George Washington U, Washington DC

IVERSON, JUSTIN T; CLINTON, NC; LAKEWOOD HS; (SO); Hnr Roll; MVP; Nat Hon Sy; Otst Ac Ach Awd; Perf Att; Salutrn; St of Mnth; Comm Volntr; Chess; DARE; Emplmnt; Ntl Beta Clb; Ntl FFA; Scouts; Fundamental of Technology Award; Agricultural Engineer; Landscape Architect; U of North Carolina; North Carolina State U

JACINTO, LUIS; LOUISBURG, NC; LOUISBURG HS; (FR); Hnr Roll; English Clb; Sccr (V); Bachelor's Degree; Master's Degree

JACKSON, BRITTANY; WILMINGTON, NC; E A LANEY HS; (FR); Hnr Roll; Comm Volntr; Chrch Yth Grp; DARE; Emplmnt; P to P St Amb Prg; Chr; Ch Chr; SP/M/VS; Pediatric Nursing; Paramedic; North Carolina State U; U of North Carolina

JACKSON, BRITTANY M; MARSHVILLE, NC; FOREST HILLS HS; (JR); Hnr Roll; Jr Mshl; Mas Aw; WWAHSS; Hosp Aide; Peer Tut/Med; Chrch Yth Grp; DARE; Emplmnt; Lib Aide; Ch Chr; National Rotary Scholar; Nursing

JACKSON, ERICA; PIKEVILLE, NC; CHARLES B AYCOCK HS; (FR); Hnr Roll; Perf Att; Bnd; Mch Bnd; North Carolina A & T U; NC State U

JACKSON, JAMES N; NASHVILLE, NC; SOUTHERN NASH SR HS; (SR); Hnr Roll; WWAHSS; Ntl FFA; National FFA Organization; National Technical Honor Society; Teach High School Science; Teach High School History; East Carolina U

JACKSON, JOSEPH T; TIMBERLAKE, NC; PERSON HS; (SR); Hnr Roll; MVP; Perf Att; Spec Olymp Vol; Chrch Yth Grp; FCA; FCCLA; Voc Ind Clb Am; Cr Ctry (V CL); Track (V L); Wrstlg (V); Gardner-Webb U; Guilford College

JACKSON, LATOYA; SPRING LAKE, NC; PINE FOREST HS; (FR); Hnr Roll; MVP; Perf Att; St of Mnth; Chrch Yth Grp; DARE; Drma Clb; SADD; Chr; Dnce; SP/M/VS; Stg Cre; Sccr (J); Sftball (J); Tennis (J); Track (J); Vllyball (J); Degree

JACKSON, MEAGAN H; CLINTON, NC; LAKEWOOD HS; (JR); Hnr Roll; Otst Ac Ach Awd; St Schl; St of Mnth; WWAHSS; Hosp Aide; Peer Tut/Med; Chrch Yth Grp; DARE; Emplmnt; FBLA; Foreign Clb; Stu Cncl (T); Nursing; Pre-Medicine; U of North Carolina-Wilmington; East Carolina U

JACKSON, NICHOLAS; ORRUM, NC; FAIRMONT HS; (SO); ROTC; Scouts; Clr Grd; Drl Tm; Bsball (J); Cr Ctry (J); Ftball (J); Skt Tgt Sh (J); Track (J); Military Law; Military Law Enforcement; West Point; Texas A & M

JACKSON, SACHA M; SALUDA, NC; EAST HENDERSON HS; (JR); Hnr Roll; ArtClub; Emplmnt; Sign Clb; Scholastic Art Finalist (2 Years); Interpreting for the Deaf; Gardner Webb U; Gallaudet U

JACKSON, SHANEKA R; ROPER, NC; PLYMOUTH HS; (FR); Hi Hnr Roll; Hnr Roll; Nat Hon Sy; Perf Att; Comm Volntr; Chrch Yth Grp; FBLA; Mth Clb/Tm; Scouts; SADD; Chr; Ch Chr; SP/M/VS; Published Poem; Junior National Honor Society Parliamentarian; Business Management; Nursing; Winston-Salem State U; NC State U

JACKSON, SONNIE; FAIRVIEW, NC; AC REYNOLDS HS; (SR); Hnr Roll; Nat Hon Sy; WWAHSS; Comm Volntr; Peer Tut/Med; Cr Ctry (V L); Sccr (J); National High School Scholar; Teacher; U of North Carolina Asheville; Mass Hill College

JACKSON JR, JOSEPH W; WINSTON SALEM, NC; PARKLAND HS; (JR); Hi Hnr Roll; Hnr Roll; WWAHSS; CARE; Spec Olymp Vol; Orch; Bskball; Ftball (VJ); Mar Art; Track (V); Wt Lftg; Step Team; Donate/Volunteer; Engineer; Lawyer; Virginia Commonwealth U; U of North Carolina At Chapel Hill

JAKED, JORDAN; HOLLY SPRINGS, NC; MIDDLE CREEK HS; (SO); Hi Hnr Roll; Hnr Roll; Otst Ac Ach Awd; Sci Fairs; Sci/Math Olympn; Comm Volntr; Chrch Yth Grp; FCA; Photog; Sci Clb; Chr; SP/M/VS; PP Ftbl (J); CR (R); All-County Chorus, 9th & 10th Grade; Social Event Director - Sunrise UMC Youth Group; Youth Ministry; English / English Education; U of North Carolina Greensboro; Roanoke Bible College

JALICIA, HASSELL N; PLYMOUTH, NC; PLYMOUTH HS; (JR); Nat Hon Sy; WWAHSS; DECA; Drma Clb; FBLA; PP Ftbl; Yrbk; Teacher; Dancer; Martin Community College; Fayetteville State U

JAMES, CANDIS L; ERWIN, NC; TRITON HS; (FR); WWAHSS; Chrch Yth Grp; Chr; Ch Chr; SP/M/VS

JAMES, ELVIN; ROPER, NC; PLYMOUTH HS; (SO); Hnr Roll; WWAHSS; Ntl Beta Clb; Bskball (V); Ftball (V); Computer Engineering; Computer Science; U of North Carolina Chapel Hill; Duke U

JAMES, KATHERINE; MOUNTAIN HOME, NC; WEST HENDERSON HS; (FR); Hnr Roll; Pres Ac Ftns Aw; Chrch Yth Grp; DARE; P to P St Amb Prg; Dnce; Sftball (J); Swmg (V); Teaching; Medical/Science; North Carolina State; Chapel Hill

JAMES, KRISTIN; BURGAW, NC; HARRELLS CHRISTIAN AC; (JR); Ctznshp Aw; Hnr Roll; Sci Fairs; WWAHSS; Comm Volntr; Hosp Aide; Chrch Yth Grp; Emplmnt; FCA; Ntl Beta Clb; Photog; Prom Com; Ch Chr; Dnce; Chrldg (J); Vllyball (J); Yrbk (P); Praise Team/Dance; X-Ray Technician; Teacher (Elementary); Cape Fear Community College; U of North Carolina At Wilmington

JAMES, MATTHEW; TERRELL, NC; LAKE NORMAN HS; (JR); Duke TS; Pres Sch; Peer Tut/Med; Emplmnt; Mth Clb/Tm; Quiz Bowl; SP/M/VS; Math Counts; Drama; U of Charlotte; Duke U

JAMES, REGINALD; PLYMOUTH, NC; PLYMOUTH HS; (FR); Hi Hnr Roll; MVP; Otst Ac Ach Awd; St of Mnth; Comm Volntr; Peer Tut/Med; FBLA; Mth Clb/Tm; Bsball (J); Bskball (J); Ftball (JC); Cl Off (V); Business Management; North Carolina State U; Duke U

JAMES, ZEBEDEE K; FAYETTEVILLE, NC; CAPE FEAR HS; (FR); Hi Hnr Roll; Hnr Roll; Otst Ac Ach Awd; Perf Att; Hab For Humty Volntr; Chess; DARE; Fr of Library; Lib Aide; Quiz Bowl; Tchrs Aide; Bnd; Mch Bnd; Pep Bnd; SP/M/VS; Mar Art; Chemistry; Physics

JAMMER, KRISTOPHER M; JACKSONVILLE, NC; SOUTHWEST ONSLOW HS; MS; Ctznshp Aw; Hnr Roll; Perf Att; Sci Fairs; St of Mnth; ArtClub; DARE; Sci Clb; Bnd; Chr; Ch Chr; Bsball (L); Bskball (L); Ftball (L); CR (V); Science Explorers; To Graduate At the Top of My Class; To Do the Best I Can; A & T; Duke U

JANOFSKI, ASHLEY E; WAXHAW, NC; COVENANT DAY SCH; (FR); Hi Hnr Roll; Otst Ac Ach Awd; WWAHSS; Peer Tut/Med; Chrch Yth Grp; Emplmnt; Svce Clb; Tchrs Aide; Spanish Clb; Bnd; Bskball (J); Top Biology Student-9th Grade; Top Band Student; Pediatrician

JARMAN, KRISTEN; FUQUAY VARINA, NC; SOUTHEAST RALEIGH HS; (JR); Duke TS; Hnr Roll; Sci/Math Olympn; WWAHSS; Drma Clb; Emplmnt; Key Club; Sci Clb; Scouts; Ch Chr; Orch; SP/M/VS; Sccr (J); Swmg (V L); The National Society of High School Scholars; Secondary Education; Environmental Science; North Carolina State U; U of North Carolina At Chapel Hill

JARMON, SHANICE D; GARNER, NC; GARNER SR HS; (SR); Hi Hnr Roll; Hnr Roll; Nat Hon Sy; Sci Fairs; CARE; Chrldg; PP Ftbl; Sch Ppr (R); State Rep.-Gleaners; Mass Communications; Journalism; Southern U, LA; Bethune Cookman College, Fla.

JEFFERSON, MELISSA A; GREENSBORO, NC; WALTER HINES PAGE HS; (JR); Hi Hnr Roll; Nat Hon Sy; WWAHSS; Comm Volntr; Hab For Humty Volntr; Hosp Aide; Chrch Yth Grp; Drma Clb; Emplmnt; FCA; Quill & Scroll; Scouts; Svce Clb; Chr; SP/M/VS; Nursing; U of North Carolina Greensboro

JEHOICH, CASSANDRA L; ELIZABETH CTY, NC; PASQUOTANK CTY HS; (SO); Hnr Roll; Otst Ac Ach Awd; Perf Att; Pres Sch; Sci Fairs; St of Mnth; Chrch Yth Grp; Emplmnt; Sci Clb; Scouts; Sccr (V); Wrstlg (J); SAT Awards; Forensic Science; Public Relations; UNC Pembroke; East Carolina

JETER, GABRIELLE; WINSTON SALEM, NC; MOUNT TABOR HS; (JR); Hnr Roll; Peer Tut/Med; Mus Clb; Bnd; Mch Bnd; Reflections Writing Contest Winner; Physical Therapy; Radiology; U of North Carolina At Greensboro; UNCATT

JIMENEZ, ADA E G; SALISBURY, NC; WEST ROWAN HS; (JR); Hi Hnr Roll; Hnr Roll; Nat Hon Sy; St of Mnth; Comm Volntr; CR (R); Student of the Year (Dominican Rep); Business; Technology-(computers); U of North Carolina At Chapel Hill; U of North Carolina At Charlotte

JOHN JR, JOSEPH R; RALEIGH, NC; LEESVILLE ROAD HS; (SR); SP/M/VS; Bsball (V CL); Ftball (JC); Stu Cncl (R); National Honor Society; Ass't Football Coach-Ellsville Middle School; Coach-Powder-Puff Football; Forensic Science; Law; Guilford College

Jehoich, Cassandra L
Pasquotank Cty HS
Elizabeth Cty, NC

James, Elvin
Plymouth HS
Roper, NC

Itterly, Bethany J
East Forsyth HS
Kernersville, NC

Jackson Jr, Joseph W
Parkland HS
Winston Salem, NC

Jimenez, Ada E G
West Rowan HS
Salisbury, NC

JOHNS, DAVID; WILMINGTON, NC; E A LANEY HS; (SO); Hi Hnr Roll; Hnr Roll; Nat Hon Sy; Pres Ac Ftns Aw; Comm Volntr; Chrch Yth Grp; Emplmnt; Scouts; Ftball (J L); Track (V L); Engineering; Mechanical; Clemson U

JOHNS, JASON B; ROSMAN, NC; ROSMAN HS; (FR); Duke TS; Hi Hnr Roll; Nat Stu Ath Day Aw; Otst Ac Ach Awd; Sci Fairs; WWAHSS; Peer Tut/Med; Chrch Yth Grp; DARE; Bsball (J); Bskball (J); Ftball (V); Beta Club; Sports Medicine; Sports Coach; U of Florida; U of Miami

JOHNSON, AMANDA N; BENSON, NC; SOUTH JOHNSTON HS; (JR); Hi Hnr Roll; Hnr Roll; Jr Mshl; Nat Hon Sy; WWAHSS; Yth Ldrshp Prog; Comm Volntr; Peer Tut/Med; AL Aux Girls; Chrch Yth Grp; Emplmnt; FTA; Pep Squd; Prom Com; Ch Chr; Dnce; Sch Ppr (E, R); Yrbk (E, R); Cape Fear Youth Conference Treasurer; Numerous Journalism and Dance Awards; Communications; Education; Campbell U; U of North Carolina At Chapel Hill

JOHNSON, ANTHONY L; HENDERSONVILLE, NC; EAST HENDERSON HS; (SO); Hnr Roll; MVP; WWAHSS; Comm Volntr; FCA; Mth Clb/Tm; Voc Ind Clb Am; Bskball (JC); Ftball (J); Member of FCA Club; Engineering-Mechanical; Mathematics; Duke; Texas

JOHNSON, ASHLEY; HOPE MILLS, NC; SOUTHVIEW HS; (SO); Hnr Roll; Nat Hon Sy; WWAHSS; FBLA; Key Club; Culinary Arts; Accounting; Johnson and Wales U

JOHNSON, BRITTANY; LUMBERTON, NC; LUMBERTON HS; (SO); Hnr Roll; Nat Mrt LOC; Perf Att; St Optmst of Yr; CARE; Hosp Aide; Peer Tut/Med; Chrch Yth Grp; Mus Clb; SADD; Ch Chr; Orch; Tutor Elementary Student; Usher for School Play & Church; Psychologist; Psychiatrist; Campbell U; Boone

JOHNSON, BURGUNDY; CHARLOTTE, NC; INDEPENDENCE HS; (JR); Hi Hnr Roll; Hnr Roll; WWAHSS; Peer Tut/Med; DECA; Clr Grd; Forensic Science; Veterinarian Science; Tennessee State; North Carolina Agriculture & Technology

JOHNSON, CALESHA M; GOLDSBORO, NC; EASTERN WAYNE HS; (JR); Hnr Roll; WWAHSS; Prom Com; Chr; HOSA; Pre-Medicine; Childhood Education; East Carolina U; U of Georgia

JOHNSON, CANDICE; FAYETTEVILLE, NC; WESTOVER HS; (FR); Chrch Yth Grp; FCA; ROTC; WNBA Player; Army; Duke U; UNC U

JOHNSON, CAROLINE M; KERNERSVILLE, NC; EAST FORSYTH HS; (JR); Hnr Roll; WWAHSS; Emplmnt; Key Club; Tchrs Aide; Stu Cncl (R); CR (R); Youth and Government; Criminal Justice; U of N. Florida; U of Tampa

JOHNSON, CASSANDRA D; RALEIGH, NC; SOUTHEAST RALEIGH MAGNET HS; (SO); Hnr Roll; WWAHSS; ArtClub; Key Club; Photog; Spanish Clb; CR (R); School Photography Contest Winner; North Carolina State U

JOHNSON, COMFORT; WINSTON SALEM, NC; WILEY MS; (MS); Hnr Roll; Yth Ldrshp Prog; Comm Volntr; Red Cr Aide; Chrch Yth Grp; Chr; Ch Chr; Dnce; Mch Bnd; Chrldg (J); Arts (To Sing& Dance) or to Be a Pediatrician; I Would Like to Go to Wake Forest; North Carolina School of the Arts; Juilliard in New York

JOHNSON, DONOVAN R; DURHAM, NC; CEDAR RIDGE HS; (FR); Ctznshp Aw; Hnr Roll; Perf Att; French Clb; Certificate of Excellence in Academics, Citizenship & Leadership; Meteorology; Elizabeth City State U

JOHNSON, FRANKLYN; BROWNS SUMMIT, NC; JAMES B DUDLEY SR HS; (FR); Bsball (V); Bskball (VJ); U of North Carolina at Chapel Hill; Miami U

JOHNSON, JAMIE N; JACKSONVILLE, NC; JACKSONVILLE HS; (FR); Ctznshp Aw; Hi Hnr Roll; Nat Hon Sy; Comm Volntr; FCA; Mus Clb; Chr; Dnce; SP/M/VS; Swg Chr; Bskball (J); Track (V); Wt Lftg (J); Stu Cncl (S); Fashion Design; Music; U of Central Los Angeles

JOHNSON, JESSICA B; JONESVILLE, NC; STARMOUNT HS; (SO); Chrch Yth Grp; Chr; Ch Chr; Dnce; SP/M/VS; Chrldg (V); Cosmetologist; Drama/Sing; Appalachian State U; Winston School of the Arts

JOHNSON, JOSHUA R; SILER CITY, NC; JORDAN MATTHEWS HS; (SO); Hnr Roll; WWAHSS; Chrch Yth Grp; DECA; Emplmnt

JOHNSON, KESHIA; JACKSONVILLE, NC; JACKSONVILLE HS; (JR); Hi Hnr Roll; WWAHSS; ArtClub; French Clb; Stg Cre; Nominated for Governor's School; Sequential Art; Creative Writing; School of Visual Arts; Savannah College of Art and Design

JOHNSON, LAWRENCE K; REIDSVILLE, NC; REIDSVILLE SR HS; (SO); Hnr Roll; Perf Att; ROTC; Ftball (V); Track (V); Accounting; Business Management; Marshall U; NC State

JOHNSON, MATTHEW; NORTH WILKESBORO, NC; NORTH WILKES HS; (FR); Perf Att; Comm Volntr; Ch Chr; Ftball (J)

JOHNSON, ROSA; FAYETTEVILLE, NC; SEVENTY-FIRST HS; (FR); Hnr Roll; Chrch Yth Grp; Ch Chr; Dnce; Bskball (J); CR (R); Yrbk (E); Fayetteville State U; Duke U

JOHNSON, SHENEE; FAYETTEVILLE, NC; MASSEY HILL CLASSICAL HS; (JR); Hi Hnr Roll; Nat Hon Sy; Otst Ac Ach Awd; Perf Att; St of Mnth; WWAHSS; Comm Volntr; Peer Tut/Med; Chrch Yth Grp; DARE; Dbte Team; Ntl Beta Clb; NtlFrnscLg; Prom Com; Ch Chr; Cl Off (S)

JOHNSON, SHERDENA; GREENSBORO, NC; JAMES B DUDLEY HS; (FR); Duke TS; Hnr Roll; Perf Att; Sci Fairs; WWAHSS; Comm Volntr; Peer Tut/Med; Chrch Yth Grp; DARE; Jr Ach; Mth Clb/Tm; Scouts; Ch Chr; Chrldg (J); Wt Lftg (J); Stu Cncl (P); Yrbk; National Mathematics Awards (USAA); National Art Award USNAA, USAA; Engineering; Computer Science; Duke U; NC A & T State U

JOHNSON, TAELOR M; CHARLOTTE, NC; NORTHWEST SCH OF THE ARTS; (JR); Duke TS; Hnr Roll; ArtClub; Key Club; Stg Cre; Charlotte All-Star Cheerleading-Competitive Cheerleading; National Arts Honor Society; Fashion Merchandising; Metals and Jewelry; Savannah College of Art and Design; U of South Carolina

JOHNSON, TRACI L; MT AIRY, NC; NORTH SURRY HS; (SO); Hnr Roll; Bnd; Clr Grd; Mch Bnd; Nursing; UNC Wilmington; Wake Forest U

JOHNSTON, CHRISTOPHER D; SALISBURY, NC; NORTH ROWAN HS; (SO); Duke TS; Hi Hnr Roll; MVP; Comm Volntr; Hab For Humty Volntr; Chrch Yth Grp; DARE; Bsball (J); Ftball (VJ L); Wrstlg (V); Cl Off (V); CR (R); Junior Civitan Club, Bridge to the World; Cars for Christ, Relay for Life; Math; Architecture; UNC Chapel Hill

JOLLEY, DEBRA A; FOREST CITY, NC; R S CTRL HS; (JR); Hnr Roll; Comm Volntr; Chrch Yth Grp; Emplmnt; Photog; SP/M/VS; Stg Cre; Chrldg (VJ); Gmnstcs (V); Wt Lftg (J); Cl Off (S); Stu Cncl (S); Gymnastics; Junior Miss - 3rd Runner Up / Fitness Talent Award; Magazine Editor / Journalist; Fashion Merchandising; Chapel Hill; U of Georgia

JONES, AMANDA L; WILLIAMSTON, NC; WILLIAMSTON HS; (JR); Duke TS; Hi Hnr Roll; Hnr Roll; Jr Mshl; Nat Hon Sy; Sci Fairs; Comm Volntr; Peer Tut/Med; Chrch Yth Grp; DARE; Emplmnt; Fr of Library; Key Club; Mth Clb/Tm; Prom Com; Spanish Clb; Bnd; Clr Grd; Drl Tm; Flg Crps; PP Ftbl (VJ); Tennis (VJ L); Cl Off (S); National Honor Society Geometry; Assistant Manager At Morningstar Nature Refuge; Secondary Education; Veterinary Medicine; North Carolina State U; Meredith College

JONES, BRITTANY S; FUQUAY VARINA, NC; HARNETT CTRL HS; (FR); MVP; Perf Att; Comm Volntr; Chrch Yth Grp; Key Club; Chr; Bskball (J); Sport Communication; UNC; Maryland

JONES, CANDY; LUMBERTON, NC; PURNELL SWETT HS; (SR); Hnr Roll; Nat Hon Sy; St of Mnth; Comm Volntr; Red Cr Aide; ROTC; Nursing; Dental Hygiene; Sandhills Community College; Fayetteville Tech Community College

JONES, CHARLAMY M; RALEIGH, NC; SOUTHEAST RALEIGH MAGNET HS; (JR); Hnr Roll; Nat Sci Aw; Otst Ac Ach Awd; Yth Ldrshp Prog; Comm Volntr; Hab For Humty Volntr; Peer Tut/Med; Chrch Yth Grp; Emplmnt; Key Club; Prom Com; Scouts; Ch Chr; Dnce; SP/M/VS; Stg Cre; Chrldg (V L); Gmnstcs; Track; CR (R); National Achievement Society; Forensic Medicine; Performing Arts: Dance; U of North Carolina At Greensboro; U of North Carolina At Chapel Hill

JONES, CISSLE; AHOSKIE, NC; RIDGECROFT SCH; (FR); 4H Awd; Hi Hnr Roll; Hnr Roll; Nat Hon Sy; St of Mnth; Comm Volntr; Hosp Aide; Red Cr Aide; 4-H; Chrch Yth Grp; DARE; Key Club; Ntl Beta Clb; Scouts; SADD; Vsity Clb; Bnd; Ch Chr; Hsbk Rdg; Sccr (V L); Tennis (V L); Horseback Rider; Lawyer; Veterinarian; Meredith College; North Carolina State

JONES, DE SHEA; HENDERSON, NC; SOUTHERN VANCE HS; (SR); F Lan Hn Soc; Hnr Roll; Nat Hon Sy; Otst Ac Ach Awd; St of Mnth; WWAHSS; Comm Volntr; FCA; Ntl Beta Clb; Ch Chr; Bskball (V L); Sftball (V L); Vllyball (V L); Cl Off (T); Wendy's Heisman Nominee; Who's Who Among High School Student; Accounting; Business Administration; U of North Carolina At Greensboro

JONES, DESIREE; COLERAIN, NC; BERTIE HS; (JR); Hnr Roll; Nat Mrt Sch Recip; Perf Att; St of Mnth; Peer Tut/Med; Red Cr Aide; Spec Olymp Vol; DARE; Drma Clb; Off Aide; SADD; Tchrs Aide; SP/M/VS; Member of HOSA; Pre-Med; Culinary Arts; U of North Carolina; East Carolina U

JONES, GREGORY T; WINSTON-SALEM, NC; MT TABOR HS; (JR); Ctznshp Aw; Duke TS; F Lan Hn Soc; Hi Hnr Roll; Jr Mshl; Kwnis Aw; Nat Hon Sy; Perf Att; WWAHSS; Hosp Aide; Peer Tut/Med; Chrch Yth Grp; Key Club; Spanish Clb; Cr Ctry (J); Sch Ppr (E); Governor of the Carolinas District Key Club; Past Lt Governor Div 16 / President Mt Tabor Key Club; Medicine; UNC Chapel Hill; UGA

JONES, ISAAC D; FAYETTEVILLE, NC; SEVENTY-FIRST HS; (FR); Ctznshp Aw; Hnr Roll; Otst Ac Ach Awd; Perf Att; Comm Volntr; Chrch Yth Grp; Emplmnt; Ntl Beta Clb; Chr; Ch Chr; Dnce; CR (R); Recreational Baseball MVP; Computer Engineering; U of North Carolina Chapel Hill; North Carolina State U

JONES, JAMES R; MOUNT OLIVE, NC; SOUTHERN WAYNE HS; (SR); All Am Sch; DAR; Hnr Roll; MVP; Nat Hon Sy; Perf Att; USAA; Comm Volntr; Peer Tut/Med; 4-H; DARE; Mth Clb/Tm; Ntl Beta Clb; Quiz Bowl; ROTC; Vsity Clb; Clr Grd; Drl Tm; Bskball (V); Ftball (V C); Track (V L); Vsy Clb (V); Wt Lftg (V); JROTC Outstanding Cadet Award; USAA Academic Scholar; Radiology; Physical Education; North Carolina A & T U; UNC Chapel Hill

JONES, JOANNA E; TARBORO, NC; TARBORO HS; (SR); Ctznshp Aw; Hnr Roll; Otst Ac Ach Awd; Perf Att; St of Mnth; WWAHSS; Comm Volntr; Peer Tut/Med; Chrch Yth Grp; Lib Aide; Ch Chr; Vice President of Mentor Club; Basketball Statistician for 4 Years (V & JV) Boys; Marketing; Music/Vocal Performance; Liberty U (Accepted); U of North Carolina At Greensboro

JONES, KIMBERLY; LILLINGTON, NC; HARNETT CTRL HS; (JR); Duke TS; Hnr Roll; Hab For Humty Volntr; Chrch Yth Grp; DARE; Ntl FFA; Prom Com; Scouts; Clr Grd; Orch; Stg Cre; Bskball; CR (R); Sch Ppr (R, P); Odyssey of the Mind; Education; Western Carolina; Eastern Carolina

JONES, LASHAY; GATES, NC; GATES CTY HS; (SO); Hnr Roll; St of Mnth; WWAHSS; Chrch Yth Grp; Chr; Stg Cre; Pediatrics/Nursing; Medicine/Pharmacy; Elizabeth City State U; East Carolina U

JONES, MARIO D; WARSAW, NC; JAMES KENAN HS; (SO); Hnr Roll; Nat Hon Sy; Scouts; Ftball (V); Track (V); Wt Lftg (V); Degree in Business; Major in Construction; Virginia Tech; U of North Carolina

JONES, MONICA; WAKE FOREST, NC; RALEIGH CHARTER HS; (JR); Hnr Roll; Yth Ldrshp Prog; Comm Volntr; Drma Clb; Key Club; Prom Com; Svce Clb; SP/M/VS; Tennis (J); Cl Off (R); Stu Cncl (R); CR; Sch Ppr (E, R, P); Journalism/Communications; Psychology; U of North Carolina-Chapel Hill; Howard U

JONES, NICHOLAS J; DURHAM, NC; HILLSIDE HS; (SR); Hnr Roll; Perf Att; ArtClub; Photog; Ftball (J); Track (VJ); Construction Management; Business Administration; North Carolina Agricultural & Technical State U; Grambling State U

JONES, RHONDA; FUQUAY VARINA, NC; HARNETT CTRL HS; (FR); Hi Hnr Roll; Hnr Roll; Nat Hon Sy; Otst Ac Ach Awd; Perf Att; WWAHSS; Peer Tut/Med; Chrch Yth Grp; Emplmnt; Key Club; P to P St Amb Prg; Bskball (J); 9th Grade Homecoming Candidate; Child Development; U of North Carolina; U of North Carolina Greensboro

JONES, SAMANTHA M; INDIAN TRAIL, NC; COVENANT DAY SCH; (FR); Hi Hnr Roll; Hnr Roll; Comm Volntr; Svce Clb; Stg Cre; Bskball (V L); Sftball (V L); Yrbk (E, R, P); National Junior Beta Club President (2003-2004); Athletic Training/Sports Medicine; Sport Administration; U of North Carolina At Chapel Hill; Elon U

JONES, SHANITRA N; NEW BERN, NC; NEW BERN HS; (JR); Hnr Roll; Hab For Humty Volntr; Emplmnt; Mus Clb; Bnd; Drm Mjr; Jzz Bnd; Mch Bnd; Pharmacy; Music; North Carolina A & T U; Winston Salem State U

JONES, SHEARINA R; HENRICO, NC; NCHS-WEST; (FR); 4H Awd; Duke TS; Hnr Roll; Nat Hon Sy; Perf Att; WWAHSS; Comm Volntr; Hosp Aide; 4-H; Chrch Yth Grp; DARE; Scouts; Bnd; Mch Bnd; Chrldg (J); Pediatrician; Speech Pathology; North Carolina Central U; Howard U

JONES, STEPHANIE C; GREENSBORO, NC; RAGSDALE HS; (SR); Hnr Roll; Perf Att; St of Mnth; WWAHSS; Comm Volntr; Emplmnt; Lib Aide; Ntl Beta Clb; Prom Com; Tchrs Aide; Foreign Clb; Chr; TRU - Tobacco Reality Unfiltered; FCCLA President; Elementary Education; Psychology; Elizabeth City State U; Mars Hill College

JONES, STEPHANIE L; HOPE MILLS, NC; SOUTH VIEW HS; (SR); All Am Sch; Hi Hnr Roll; Hnr Roll; Jr Mshl; Kwnis Aw; Nat Hon Sy; Perf Att; WWAHSS; Comm Volntr; Key Club; Lib Aide; Off Aide; SADD; Chr; Sch Ppr (R); President of Key Club 2004-2005; Animal Science-Vet; North Carolina State U

JONES, STEPHEN S; MAYSVILLE, NC; WHITE OAK HS; (MS); Hi Hnr Roll; Nat Hon Sy; Comm Volntr; ArtClub; Chrch Yth Grp; Bnd; Pep Bnd; Pharmacist-UNC Chapel Hill, NC; U of North Carolina, Chapel Hill

JONES, SWALANDA; LUMBERTON, NC; LUMBERTON HS; (SR); Ctznshp Aw; Hnr Roll; Comm Volntr; Emplmnt; Ntl Beta Clb; Prom Com; ROTC; Bskball (J); JROTC - Purple Heart Award; RN; NCSU; UNCP

JONES, WHITNEY S; PEMBROKE, NC; PURNELL SWETT HS; (SO); Gov Hnr Prg; Hi Hnr Roll; Hnr Roll; Otst Ac Ach Awd; WWAHSS; Comm Volntr; Peer Tut/Med; Chrch Yth Grp; Ntl Beta Clb; P to P St Amb Prg; Chrldg (JC); Dvng (L); PPSqd (J); Tennis (V); Cl Off (P); Stu Cncl (P); Yrbk (R); People to People Student Ambassador; Nursing; Pediatrics; UNC-Chapel Hill; UNC-Pembroke

JONES JR, ANTHONY; ALBEMARLE, NC; NORTH STANLY HS; (FR); Hnr Roll; Chrch Yth Grp; DARE; Scouts; Ch Chr; Ftball (J); Graphic Design; DeVry U

JONES JR, CHRISTOPHER A; MOORESVILLE, NC; MOORESVILLE HS; (SR); Hnr Roll; Spec Olymp Vol; DARE; Voc Ind Clb Am; Music Producer

Jones, James R
Southern Wayne HS
Mount Olive, NC

Johnson, Traci L
North Surry HS
Mt Airy, NC

Johnson, Donovan R
Cedar Ridge HS
Durham, NC

Johnson, Burgundy
Independence HS
Charlotte, NC

Johnson, Comfort
Wiley MS
Winston Salem, NC

Jones, Charlamy M
Southeast Raleigh Magnet HS
Raleigh, NC

Jones Jr, Anthony
North Stanly HS
Albemarle, NC

JORDAN, LESLIE; PFAFFTOWN, NC; REYNOLDS HS; (JR); Hnr Roll; Nat Hon Sy; Bnd; Jzz Bnd; Mch Bnd; Appalachian State U; U of North Carolina Greensboro

JORDAN, NICOLE L; MOUNT AIRY, NC; MOUNT AIRY HS; (JR); Hnr Roll; Nat Hon Sy; WWAHSS; Comm Volntr; Hab For Humty Volntr; Spec Olymp Vol; Chrch Yth Grp; FCA; Key Club; SADD; Voc Ind Clb Am; Flg Crps; Bskball (J); Sccr (V L); Cl Off (V); Elementary Education; Appalachian State U; U of North Carolina-Charlotte

JORDAN, RENEE N; MEBANE, NC; EASTERN ALAMANCE HS; (SO); Hnr Roll; MVP; Perf Att; Red Cr Aide; Chrch Yth Grp; DARE; Bnd; Chr; Dnce; Chrldg (V); Sftball (J); Track (V); Vllyball (J); Pediatrics; Duke U

JOYNER, ANGELICA D; TARBORO, NC; TARBORO HS; (SO); Hnr Roll; St of Mnth; Yth Ldrshp Prog; Peer Tut/Med; Chrch Yth Grp; Svce Clb; Chr; Member of MENTOR Club (ETS); Most Improved (Language Arts); Human Behavioral Science; Business & Marketing; Elizabeth City State U; Fayetteville State U

JOYNER, NICOLAS D; MOUNT AIRY, NC; NORTH SURRY HS; (SO)

JOYNER, TYLER; PLEASANT GARDEN, NC; RANDLEMAN HS; (FR); 4H Awd; Hnr Roll; Pres Sch; CARE; Comm Volntr; 4-H; DARE; FCA; SP/M/VS; Golf; Swmg; Yrbk; Youth Pastor; Crime Scene Investigator; Lee U; Appalachian College

JOYNER III, WINGATE G; AHOSKIE, NC; RIDGECROFT SCH; (SO); Duke TS; Hi Hnr Roll; Hnr Roll; MVP; Perf Att; Sci/Math Olympn; St of Mnth; Comm Volntr; DARE; FCA; Key Club; Lttrmn Clb; Ntl Beta Clb; SADD; Bsball (J); Bskball (J); Golf (V CL); Sccr (J); Yrbk (R, P); MBA; Architecture; Wake Forest; Georgia Tech

JUSTICE, JOSEPH; KINSTON, NC; BETHEL CHRISTIAN AC; (SR); Hnr Roll; Comm Volntr; Chrch Yth Grp; Emplmnt; Wdwrkg Clb; Bnd; Chr; Ch Chr; SP/M/VS; Bskball (VLJ); Golf (V); Sccr (VLJ); Cl Off (R); Criminal Justice; Liberty University

KAM, WAYNEKID; CARY, NC; SOUTHEAST RALEIGH MAGNET HS; (SO); Hi Hnr Roll; Hnr Roll; Perf Att; Lib Aide; Ntl Beta Clb; Quiz Bowl; Sci Clb; Certificate of Achievement (Duke Cancer Research Internship); The National Society of High School Scholars; Medicine; Biomedical Engineering; Duke U; Johns Hopkins U

KAN, GRACE; CHAPEL HILL, NC; CHAPEL HILL HS; (SO); Published 3 Poems; Criminal Justice; Accounting; U of North Carolina; East Carolina U

KANANOWICZ, CATHERINE M; FAYETTEVILLE, NC; DOUGLAS BYRD HS; (FR); Hnr Roll; WWAHSS; Peer Tut/Med; Drma Clb; Key Club; Orch; SP/M/VS; Chrldg (VJ); Sccr (V L); Track; CR; FSU Pre-College Math & Science Program; Green Belt Tae Kwon Do; Doctor in Pharmacy; RN; Chapel Hill U of North Carolina; Campbell U

KANG, ANITA; CHARLOTTE, NC; HARDING UNIVERSITY HS; (FR); Hnr Roll; Orch; Computer Engineer; North Carolina State College; U North Carolina

KANG, JI YOON; GOLDSBORO, NC; EASTERN WAYNE HS; (JR); Comm Volntr; Sccr (J); CR (R); Accompanist in Korean Baptist Church; Prize in the Match Competition in Korea; Medical Doctor; Scientist; UNC Chapel Hill; Duke U

KANGKOLO, MICHELLE L; RALEIGH, NC; ATHENS HS; (SR); WWAHSS; Comm Volntr; Hosp Aide; Peer Tut/Med; Chrch Yth Grp; DARE; Scouts; Chr; Clr Grd; Track (J); Stu Cncl (R); EMS Certification; HOSA; Pharmacy / BS Degree; Campbell U

KAPP, JONATHAN; WINSTON SALEM, NC; NORTH FORSYTH HS; (SO); Duke TS; Hi Hnr Roll; Nat Hon Sy; WWAHSS; Comm Volntr; Chrch Yth Grp; Key Club; Scouts; Bnd; Jzz Bnd; Mch Bnd; Boy Scouts-Order of the Arrow; Moravian Brass Band; Engineering, Computers; History; U of North Carolina-Chapel Hill; North Carolina State U

KAWECKI, CHANTAL; CHARLOTTE, NC; OLYMPIC HS; (JR); F Lan Hn Soc; Hi Hnr Roll; Jr Mshl; Nat Hon Sy; Sci/Math Olympn; WWAHSS; Peer Tut/Med; Red Cr Aide; ArtClub; Chess; DARE; Emplmnt; Sci Clb; Scouts; Svce Clb; Spanish Clb; Orch; Swmg (V L); Stu Cncl; Lifeguard; Elementary Teacher; U of NC At Charlotte; Appalachian State U-(NC)

KAY, TIFFANY; KNIGHTDALE, NC; EAST WAKE HS; (FR); Hnr Roll; Nat Hon Sy; Otst Ac Ach Awd; Sci Fairs; Comm Volntr; Chrch Yth Grp; DARE; Drma Clb; Ch Chr; Dnce; SP/M/VS; Stg Cre; Chrldg (J); PP Ftbl (J); Track (J); Medicine (Want to Be an Neonatologist); In the Arts (Dance Etc); Duke U

KEARNEY, AMANDA; HENDERSON, NC; LOUISBURG HS; (FR); Duke TS; Hi Hnr Roll; Chrch Yth Grp; Ntl Beta Clb; Bnd; Jzz Bnd; Mch Bnd; Vllyball (J); First Chair-Band; Pediatric Doctor / Physician's Assistant; Duke U; East Carolina U

KEARNEY, BRYAN A; GOLDSBORO, NC; CHARLES B AYCOCK HS; (FR); Pres Ac Ftns Aw; WWAHSS; ArtClub; Bskball (J); Renaissance Club; Architecture; Duke U; East Carolina U

KEARNEY, JASMINE; NORLINA, NC; WARREN CTY HS; (FR); Hnr Roll; Bskball (J); Track; Vllyball; Coaches' Award; Computer Tech-Major; Business-Minor; North Carolina

KEEL, DEVONA M; GREENSBORO, NC; DUDLEY HS; (SO); Hnr Roll; Nat Hon Sy; Perf Att; Pres Ac Ftns Aw; Comm Volntr; Chrch Yth Grp; DARE; FBLA; Ntl Beta Clb; ROTC; Clr Grd; Drl Tm; Scr Kpr (VJ); Track (V); CR (R); Business; Law; Johnson C Smith; The U of North Carolina

KEEL, LAKETA; WHITEVILLE, NC; WHITEVILLE HS; (SR); Hnr Roll; Perf Att; WWAHSS; Comm Volntr; Peer Tut/Med; Red Cr Aide; Chrch Yth Grp; Dbte Team; Emplmnt; FBLA; NtlFrnscLg; Bnd; Mch Bnd; FBLA; Forensics; Communications (Mass); Marketing; Winston Salem State U; Spelman College

KEENE, JEREMY; APEX, NC; MIDDLE CREEK HS; (SR); Duke TS; Hi Hnr Roll; Nat Hon Sy; WWAHSS; Comm Volntr; Hab For Humty Volntr; Peer Tut/Med; Emplmnt; Key Club; Bsball (VJ L); Engineering; North Carolina State U

KEESLER, SHANON; GREENVILLE, NC; D H CONLEY HS; (FR); St of Mnth; Peer Tut/Med; DARE; Ntl Beta Clb; Scouts; National Beta Club; National Junior Honor Society; Computer Engineering; Construction Contractor; ITT Technical Institute; ECU-East Carolina U

KEITH, JOSEPH H; OXFORD, NC; J F WEBB HS; (SO); Ctznshp Aw; Hnr Roll; Sci Fairs; St of Mnth; WWAHSS; Hab For Humty Volntr; Hosp Aide; Peer Tut/Med; Chrch Yth Grp; Emplmnt; FTA; Off Aide; Ch Chr; SP/M/VS; Sch Ppr (R); Who's Who Among High School Students; Nursing; Medical Science; N.C. Central U (North Carolina); NC Agricultural & Technical U

KELLEY, BRITTANY; HOLLY SPRINGS, NC; CARDINAL GIBBONS HS; (JR); Hi Hnr Roll; Kwnis Aw; Nat Mrt Fin; Pres Ac Ftns Aw; WWAHSS; Comm Volntr; Hosp Aide; Dnce; Chrldg (J); PP Ftbl (V); Lancer Club / Dance Club; Scholar Athlete; Pediatrician; U of North Carolina Chapel Hill; New York U

KELLY, AARON S; SNOW CAMP, NC; SOUTHERN ALAMANCE HS; (JR); Hnr Roll; Nat Hon Sy; Comm Volntr; Chrch Yth Grp; Ftball (J); Medicine; Pharmacy; U of Kentucky-Lexington; East Carolina U

KELLY, JOY V; GOLDSBORO, NC; EASTERN WAYNE HS; (JR); Ctznshp Aw; Hi Hnr Roll; Nat Hon Sy; St of Mnth; WWAHSS; Yth Ldrshp Prog; Comm Volntr; Hosp Aide; Key Club; SADD; Ch Chr; Dnce; President of FCCLA & Key Club for 2005-06; Secretary of National Vocational Honor Society; Degree in English/History to Be a Lawyer; Minor in Dance; U of North Carolina-Chapel Hill; Campbell U

KELLY, MICHELLE; ERWIN, NC; CAPE FEAR CHRISTIAN AC; (JR); Hnr Roll; Jr Mshl; Chrch Yth Grp; DARE; Ntl Beta Clb; Prom Com; Chrldg (V); Sftball (V); Vllyball (J); Veterinarian; Child Development

KENDALL, JORDAN; WAXHAW, NC; PARKWOOD HS; (FR); Hnr Roll; Perf Att; Pres Ac Ftns Aw; Bnd; Jzz Bnd; Mch Bnd; Pep Bnd; Become a Professional Athlete; U of North Carolina; Wingate U

KENDRICK, TIEARA C; DALLAS, NC; NORTH GASTON HS; (SR); Hnr Roll; MVP; Otst Ac Ach Awd; Yth Ldrshp Prog; DARE; Prom Com; Chr; Bskball (J); Chrldg (V); Track (V); Cl Off (V); Stu Cncl (V); CR (V); Commissioner's School; Legislator's School; Medical Office Assistant; Kings College-Charlotte, NC

KENNEDY, BRITTANY; LEXINGTON, NC; LEXINGTON SR HS; (SR); Ctznshp Aw; Hi Hnr Roll; Hnr Roll; MVP; Nat Mrt LOC; Otst Ac Ach Awd; Perf Att; St of Mnth; Yth Ldrshp Prog; Comm Volntr; Peer Tut/Med; Red Cr Aide; 4-H; Chrch Yth Grp; Cmptr Clb; DARE; DECA; Emplmnt; FCA; FBLA; Ch Chr; Dnce; Chrldg (J); Track (J); Vllyball (J); Cl Off (V); CR (R); Delta Sigma Theta Sorority, Inc Levin, NC; NC House of Rep. Cert. of Recognition Congr.; Physical Therapy; Human Relations (Registered Nurse); U of Nc-Greensboro, UNC-Charlotte; Winston Salem State

KENNEDY, MATTHEW S; NORTH WILKESBORO, NC; NORTH WILKES HS; (FR); Ctznshp Aw; Hnr Roll; Pres Sch; Sci Fairs; Comm Volntr; Chrch Yth Grp; Ntl Beta Clb; Scouts; Ftball (J); Received Unsung Hero Award 4th Gr.; Received Unsung Hero Award 8th Gr.; Sports Management

KENNEDY, SEAN; WILMINGTON, NC; E A LANEY HS; (SO); Duke TS; Hnr Roll; Perf Att; WWAHSS; Chrch Yth Grp; FBLA; Photog; Sci Clb; First Place Regionals in FBLA Business Calculation; Chemical Engineering; U of North Carolina State; U of North Carolina Chapel Hill

KENNER, CRYSTAL; BRYSON CITY, NC; SWAIN CTY HS; (SO); Nat Hon Sy; Yth Ldrshp Prog; Chrch Yth Grp; Drma Clb; FCA; FBLA; Mus Clb; Pep Squd; Chr; SP/M/VS; Chrldg (V); Freshman Representative Home Coming; Performing Arts; Forensic Science; Chapel Hill; Duke

KEYES, DA SHANDA N; PLYMOUTH, NC; PLYMOUTH HS; (FR); All Am Sch; Hnr Roll; Drma Clb; Ch Chr; Poems Recognized for Young Poets of NC; HOSA (Health Occupation); Law Political Science; Business Administration; Central U; UNC of Chapel Hill

KHAN, MARIAM; SHELBY, NC; BURNS HS; (JR); Hnr Roll; Drma Clb; Emplmnt; Lttrmn Clb; Ntl Beta Clb; Spanish Clb; Chr; SP/M/VS; Track (V L); Sch Ppr; National Spanish Honors Society; Gardner Webb Choral Clinic; Political Science; Law School; U of North Carolina Chapel Hill; Appalachian State U

KIDD, TYLER; RALEIGH, NC; MILLBROOK HS; (FR); Hnr Roll; Comm Volntr; DARE; Emplmnt; FCA; Ntl FFA; Sccr (J); Track (J)

KIEWERT, RYAN; DUDLEY, NC; SPRING CREEK HS; (MS); Hnr Roll; Nat Hon Sy; Perf Att; Comm Volntr; Mechanics; Duke U

KILBORN, CHRISTY; RALEIGH, NC; MIDDLE CREEK HS; (SR); Hnr Roll; MVP; WWAHSS; Comm Volntr; Peer Tut/Med; Chrch Yth Grp; FCA; Key Club; Tchrs Aide; Golf (V CL); Lcrsse (J); Yrbk (E, P); Page for North Carolina Legislature; FCU Legislative Camp for Youth Leadership; Elementary Education; U of North Carolina Wilmington

KIM, AMANDA; DURHAM, NC; C E JORDAN HS; (MS); Otst Ac Ach Awd; Perf Att; St of Mnth; Comm Volntr; ArtClub; Chrch Yth Grp; DARE; P to P St Amb Prg; Dnce; Cl Off (R); Stu Cncl (R); CR (R); Sch Ppr (R); Math & Science Education Network; Medical; Interior Designer; U of North Carolina Chapel Hill

KIM, YUKON; CLINTON, NC; CLINTON HS; (FR); Hnr Roll; Otst Ac Ach Awd; Perf Att; Comm Volntr; Jr Cls League; Key Club; Scouts; Latin Clb; Bnd; Mch Bnd; Tennis (VJ); Pharmacy; Teacher; U of North Carolina; Wake Forest

KIMBALL II, WM R; SMITHFIELD, NC; WEST JOHNSTON HS; (JR); Duke TS; Hnr Roll; MVP; Nat Hon Sy; Pres Sch; USAA; WWAHSS; Comm Volntr; Scouts; Cr Ctry (V L); Track (V L); All-State Scholar Athlete @ Season; Honorable Mention All-American USA Triathlon; Health Science; Physiology

KING, AMBER L; NEWLAND, NC; AVERY CTY HS; (SR); Ntl Beta Clb; Ch Chr; History; Mars Hill College; Lees McRae College

KING, CIARA M; RALEIGH, NC; WAKEFIELD HS; (SR); Hnr Roll; MVP; Nat Hon Sy; Otst Ac Ach Awd; Perf Att; St of Mnth; WWAHSS; Comm Volntr; Hab For Humty Volntr; ArtClub; FCA; Key Club; Ntl FFA; Svce Clb; Vsity Clb; Bskball (J); PP Ftbl (V); Track (V); Wt Lftg (V); Computer Engineering; U of North Carolina At Wilmington

KING, JESSICA; MACON, NC; HALIFAX AC CHRISTIAN SCH; (JR); Ctznshp Aw; Duke TS; Hnr Roll; Jr Mshl; WWAHSS; Comm Volntr; Emplmnt; Ntl Beta Clb; Prom Com; Bskball (J); Vllyball (J); Cl Off (P, V, T, R); Stu Cncl (T); CR (R); Yrbk (R, P); Beta Club President; Roanoke Valley Junior Miss Participant; Pharmacy; U of North Carolina At Chapel Hill; U of North Carolina At Wilmington

KING, KEYAHNA S; RAEFORD, NC; HOKE CTY HS; (JR); Hnr Roll; Perf Att; Spec Olymp Vol; DARE; Emplmnt; Ntl Beta Clb; P to P St Amb Prg; Quiz Bowl; Bnd; Clr Grd; Mch Bnd; Bskball (VJ); Chrldg; Sftball (J); Vllyball; Obstetricians; Radiology; Duke U; North Carolina State U

KING, MARIA E; GREENSBORO, NC; GRIMSLEY SR HS; (JR); Hab For Humty Volntr; Drma Clb; French Clb; Orch; SP/M/VS; Selected for All-County Orchestra; 9th Place Winner-Nat'l French Contest-French I; French Major; Drama Major; Eastern Carolina U; North Carolina State U

KING, NOAH H; RALEIGH, NC; LEESVILLE ROAD HS; (FR); Wrstlg (J)

KING, STEPHEN; BUXTON, NC; CAPE HATTERAS SEC SCH; (JR); Duke TS; Hnr Roll; Kwnis Aw; Otst Ac Ach Awd; Perf Att; St of Mnth; Yth Ldrshp Prog; Comm Volntr; Peer Tut/Med; Chrch Yth Grp; DARE; Emplmnt; SADD; Bnd; Bsball (V L); Ftball (V L); Business; Recording Engineering; East Carolina U; UNC Wilmington

KING, TRAVIS; CARTHAGE, NC; UNION PINES HS; (JR); Hnr Roll; Perf Att; Pres Ac Ftns Aw; WWAHSS; Ch Chr; Track (V); Currently in Two AP Classes; Mars Hill; Appalachian State U

KING III, ROBERT R; HAMLET, NC; RICHMOND SR HS; (SO); Hnr Roll

KING JR, TIMOTHY W; MONROE, NC; PIEDMONT HS; (JR); Hnr Roll; MVP; Bsball (V L); Computer Sciences; Law; U of South Carolina; North Carolina State U

KINNEY, ANNIE; WEST END, NC; PINECREST HS; (SO); Ctznshp Aw; Duke TS; Hi Hnr Roll; Jr Mshl; Sci Fairs; WWAHSS; Peer Tut/Med; Chrch Yth Grp; Key Club; Ntl Beta Clb; Bnd; Bskball (J); Religion; Duke U; Davidson College

KIRK, AKRISHON; GREENSBORO, NC; DUDLEY; (FR); WWAHSS; Chrch Yth Grp; Mch Bnd; Pep Bnd; PP Ftbl; Track

KIRKLAND, KRYSTAL O; FAYETTEVILLE, NC; E E SMITH SR HS; (FR); Hnr Roll; Perf Att; Chrch Yth Grp; DARE; JSA; Kwanza Clb; Scouts; Ch Chr; Orch; Youth of the Year for Sigma Gamma Phi Sorority; Piano Player for Tot for Christ Church; Medicine-Pediatrician; Psychology; UNC Chapel Hill; Elizabeth City U

Kirkland, Krystal O
E E Smith SR HS
Fayetteville, NC

King, Ciara M
Wakefield HS
Raleigh, NC

Kendrick, Tieara C
North Gaston HS
Dallas, NC

Kearney, Jasmine
Warren Cty HS
Norlina, NC

Kay, Tiffany
East Wake HS
Knightdale, NC

National
Honor Roll
Spring 2005

Kananowicz, Catherine M
Douglas Byrd HS
Fayetteville, NC

Keith, Joseph H
J F Webb HS
Oxford, NC

Kennedy, Matthew S
North Wilkes HS
North Wilkesboro, NC

King, Jessica
Halifax AC Christian Sch
Macon, NC

King, Maria E
Grimsley SR HS
Greensboro, NC

KIRKLEY, SARAH; RALEIGH, NC; NEEDHAM BROUGHTON HS; (JR); Hi Hnr Roll; Hnr Roll; Nat Hon Sy; Comm Volntr; Key Club; Off Aide; Svce Clb; Tchrs Aide; Latin Clb; Bskball (JC); Sccr (V L)

KIRLAUSKI, JOSEPH R; DURHAM, NC; C E JORDAN HS; (FR); Hi Hnr Roll; Hnr Roll; Comm Volntr; Chrch Yth Grp; Chr; Ch Chr; SP/M/VS; Bsball (J); All-State Chorus; Young American / Extracurricular an Auditioned Chorus Group / Coaches Award - Baseball; Music; Musical Theatre; East Carolina U

KIRTS, JENNIFER; YOUNGSVILLE, NC; FRANKLIN AC; (SO); Ctznshp Aw; Hi Hnr Roll; Hnr Roll; MVP; Nat Hon Sy; Otst Ac Ach Awd; Pres Ac Ftns Aw; Comm Volntr; Peer Tut/Med; Emplmnt; Bskball (JC); Cr Ctry (J); Stu Cncl (S); CR (R); Yrbk (E, P); National Honor Society; "A" Honor Roll; Business; Journalism; Duke U; U of North Carolina

KLECHA, STEVEN T; HICKORY, NC; ST STEPHENS HS; (SO); Duke TS; Hi Hnr Roll; Pres Ac Ftns Aw; Pres Sch; Sci/Math Olympn; Comm Volntr; Chrch Yth Grp; FCA; P to P St Amb Prg; Sci Clb; Scouts; Ftball (J); Track (V L); Criminal Justice; Theology

KLUEH, BRIGITTE; MATTHEWS, NC; DAVID W BUTLER HS; (JR); Hnr Roll; WWAHSS; Comm Volntr; Peer Tut/Med; Chrch Yth Grp; Key Club; Svce Clb; Dnce; Nursing

KNAUTH, WILLIAM W; CHARLOTTE, NC; (SO); Hnr Roll; Comm Volntr; Peer Tut/Med; ArtClub; Chess; History Classical; U North Carolina Chapel Hill; N.C. State U

KNIGHT, CARA; CORNELIUS, NC; NORTH MECKLENBURG HS; (JR); Hnr Roll; Nat Hon Sy; WWAHSS; Comm Volntr; FCCLA; Key Club; Mus Clb; Chr; Cr Ctry (V CL); Swmg (V L); National Technical Honor Society; Elementary Education; U of North Carolina; Elon U

KNIGHT, MELISSA L; HOPE MILLS, NC; SOUTH VIEW HS; (SR); Hnr Roll; Nat Hon Sy; St Schl; Yth Ldrshp Prog; Comm Volntr; Hosp Aide; DARE; Emplmnt; Key Club; Scouts; Cr Ctry (V L); IB; Honor Senior; Government (Undergrad); Law (Grad); Campbell U

KNOELKE, GRETCHEN K; MORGANTON, NC; FREEDOM HS; (JR); Hi Hnr Roll; Nat Hon Sy; WWAHSS; ArtClub; Tchrs Aide; Had an Original Poem Published in a National Anthology; Music; Comedy Writing; Columbia U; Duke U

KNOTTS, CANDACE; BEAR CREEK, NC; WOODS CHARTER SCH; (SO); Hnr Roll; Hab For Humty Volntr; Bskball (V); Yrbk (P); Botany; Medicine; NC State; Arizona State

KNOX, ANTHONY; KANNAPOLIS, NC; A L BROWN HS; (JR); Hi Hnr Roll; Jr Mshl; Nat Hon Sy; Perf Att; Chess; Bnd; Jzz Bnd; Mch Bnd; Pep Bnd; Bskball (V L); Wt Lftg (V); CR (R); National Honor Society; Junior Marshall - 12th; Criminal Justice; Psychology; U of North Carolina Chapel Hill; Western Carolina U

KOLATH, RICHARD A; ERWIN, NC; TRITON HS; (JR); Hnr Roll; Perf Att; Pres Ac Ftns Aw; Chrch Yth Grp; DARE; Emplmnt; ROTC; Scouts; Tchrs Aide; Clr Grd; Drl Tm; Ftball (J); Lcrsse (J); Wt Lftg (J); CR (R); JROTC-Captain in 2 Years; Join Army

KOLENOVIC, LORENA; KNIGHTDALE, NC; EAST WAKE HS; (SR); Ctznshp Aw; Hi Hnr Roll; Hnr Roll; Jr Mshl; Otst Ac Ach Awd; WWAHSS; Comm Volntr; Hosp Aide; Red Cr Aide; Emplmnt; Tchrs Aide; Wdwrkg Clb; Dnce; SP/M/VS; Stg Cre; Gmnstcs (V); Scr Kpr (V); Sftball (V); Vllyball (J); CR (P); Junior Marshall; Principal's List; RN-Nursing; Biology; U of Wilmington; Cape Fear Com College

KOLOKOLOV, EUGENE; SWANQUARTER, NC; MATTAMUSKEET JR/SR HS; (FR); Hnr Roll; Ntl FFA; FFA; Art; Architect; Computer Technician; East Carolina U; Wake Forest

KONG, JENNIFER H; RALEIGH, NC; LEESVILLE HS; (SR); F Lan Hn Soc; Hi Hnr Roll; Hnr Roll; Nat Hon Sy; Otst Ac Ach Awd; Perf Att; Pres Sch; St Schl; St of Mnth; Comm Volntr; Peer Tut/Med; Chrch Yth Grp; Emplmnt; Key Club; SADD; Tchrs Aide; Spanish Clb; Stu Cncl (R); Historian and President of Multi-Cultural Club; 3 Character Education Awards; Spanish; Graphic Design; U of North Carolina At Chapel Hill; North Carolina State U

KORNAHRENS JR, WILLIAM J; HAVELOCK, NC; HAVELOCK HS; (FR); Hi Hnr Roll; Chrch Yth Grp; Tennis (V); Cl Off (T); Altar Server (5 Years); Ham Radio Operator; Computer Software Engineer; Math Teacher; Duke U; North Carolina State U

KORNEGAY, ANTWOINE M; GOLDSBORO, NC; SOUTHERN WAYNE HS; (SO); Hnr Roll; St of Mnth; Yth Ldrshp Prog; ArtClub; Chrch Yth Grp; Ntl Beta Clb; Dentist; Lawyer; U of North Carolina-Chapel Hill; U of North Carolina-Wilmington

KOT, JESSICA; RALEIGH, NC; WAKEFIELD HS; (JR); Duke TS; Hnr Roll; Comm Volntr; Hab For Humty Volntr; Chrch Yth Grp; Emplmnt; Key Club; Pep Squd; Prom Com; SADD; Orch; Cl Off (R); Stu Cncl (R); CR (R); Piano; Nursing; Marine Biology; U of North Carolina At Wilmington; Florida U

KOTECKI, CHRISTOPHER; RALEIGH, NC; WAKEFIELD HS; (JR); Duke TS; Hnr Roll; Jr Mshl; Nat Hon Sy; Hab For Humty Volntr; Peer Tut/Med; Chrch Yth Grp; FCA; Key Club; Prom Com; Sci Clb; Spanish Clb; Sccr (J); Cl Off (R); Stu Cncl (R); CR (R); NHS; Junior Marshall; Law; U of North Carolina At Chapel Hill

KOTECKI, KARA F; RALEIGH, NC; WAKEFIELD HS; (FR); Hnr Roll; St of Mnth; Comm Volntr; Chrch Yth Grp; FCA; Key Club; Sccr (JC); Law; Physical Therapy; U of North Carolina At Chapel Hill

KRAVCHUK, ALEXANDRA; MONROE, NC; (MS); Hnr Roll; Otst Ac Ach Awd; Perf Att; St of Mnth; Comm Volntr; Chrch Yth Grp; Ntl Beta Clb; Vllyball (L); UNC Chapel Hill

KRIDER, COURTNEI; WINSTON-SALEM, NC; REYNOLDS HS; Ctznshp Aw; Hi Hnr Roll; Hnr Roll; Nat Hon Sy; Otst Ac Ach Awd; Sci Fairs; Yth Ldrshp Prog; Comm Volntr; Hab For Humty Volntr; Chrch Yth Grp; Drma Clb; Emplmnt; Mus Clb; Pep Squd; Svce Clb; Chr; Ch Chr; Dnce; SP/M/VS; PPSqd (C); Crosby Scholars; English; Political Science; Hampton U; Spelman College

KROPP, LINDSAY; PINEHURST, NC; PINECREST HS; (JR); Hi Hnr Roll; Hnr Roll; Nat Hon Sy; Pres Sch; St of Mnth; WWAHSS; Hosp Aide; Peer Tut/Med; Chrch Yth Grp; Emplmnt; Key Club; NYLC; Quill & Scroll; Schol Bwl; Spanish Clb; Bnd; Dnce; Mch Bnd; SP/M/VS; PP Ftbl (J); Sch Ppr (R); Journalism; Forensic Science; U of North Carolina At Chapel Hill; Elon U

KUCHAR, LAUREN; RUTHERFORDTON, NC; R S CTRL HS; (JR); Hi Hnr Roll; Hnr Roll; Pres Ac Ftns Aw; St of Mnth; WWAHSS; Comm Volntr; Peer Tut/Med; Chrch Yth Grp; Emplmnt; Tchrs Aide; Ch Chr; Clr Grd; Business Administration (MA.); Spanish (MA); U of North Carolina At Wilmington

KUMAR, KARAN; TARBORA, NC; L.I.C; (JR); F Lan Hn Soc; Hi Hnr Roll; Hnr Roll; Nat Hon Sy; Otst Ac Ach Awd; Perf Att; Pres Sch; Sci Fairs; CARE; Comm Volntr; 4-H; DARE; Emplmnt; Jr Ach; Spanish Clb; Chr; Bskball (J); Ftball (J); Mar Art (J); Sftball (J); Lit Mag (R); Study Medicine; Become a Doctor; New York U; Hunter College

KUSPER, MEGHAN; KANNAPOLIS, NC; NORTHWEST CABARRUS MS; (MS); Ctznshp Aw; Hi Hnr Roll; Hnr Roll; Otst Ac Ach Awd; Chrch Yth Grp; Mth Clb/Tm; Scouts; Bnd; Ch Chr; Pep Bnd; Track; Vllyball; Odyssey of the Mind; Student Council; Pre-Medical; U of NC At Chapel Hill; Duke U

LABRA, MARISOL; WARRENTON, NC; WARREN CTY HS; (FR); Bskball (J); Duke U; Vance -Granville College

LACHICHI, LEILA; RALEIGH, NC; WAKEFIELD HS; (JR); F Lan Hn Soc; Hi Hnr Roll; WWAHSS; Amnsty Intl; Emplmnt; Key Club; Pep Squd; Prom Com; Svce Clb; Tchrs Aide; PP Ftbl; Stu Cncl (R); CR (R); Science Honor Society, Academic Letterman; Freedom's Choice (Nonpartisan Political Organize); Major in History; Law Degree; North Carolina State U; U of North Carolina

LACKEY, BRANDY; CLAREMONT, NC; BUNKER HILL HS; (SO); Perf Att; ArtClub; Chr; Writing Club-Secretary; National Poet Society; Culinary Arts; Cosmetology; Johnson & Wales U

LACKEY, MICHAEL; HICKORY, NC; HICKORY HS; (SO); Hnr Roll; Nat Hon Sy; WWAHSS; Chrch Yth Grp; DARE; Ntl Beta Clb; Scouts; Bnd; Mch Bnd; Drafting; Architecture; U of North Carolina Charlotte

LACOTA-HURTADO, ALEXANDRA; SANFORD, NC; LEE CTY SR HS; (JR); Ctznshp Aw; Hnr Roll; Otst Ac Ach Awd; Minority Awards; Pediatrician; Elon College

LADD, REBECCA; WILSON, NC; HUNT HS; (SO); Hi Hnr Roll; WWAHSS; Comm Volntr; Chrch Yth Grp; FBLA; Key Club; Dnce; Chrldg (V); Cl Off (S); Stu Cncl (R); CR (R); NC Scholar Athlete; NC General Assembly Page; Physical Therapy; Pediatrics; U of North Carolina-Chapel Hill; U of North Carolina-Wilmington

LADZINSKI, ELIZABETH; MONROE, NC; MONROE HS; (JR); Duke TS; Hnr Roll; Pres Ac Ftns Aw; Yth Ldrshp Prog; Hosp Aide; Red Cr Aide; ArtClub; Emplmnt; Ntl Beta Clb; Photog; Bnd; Chr; Mch Bnd; Bskball (V L); Sccr (V L); Swmg (V L); CR (R); Co-Founder of the Romania Club - Trip to a Romanian Hospital to Aide Sick and Abandoned Children; International Business; Duke U; USC of Columbia

LAKHANI, DHARA; CHARLOTTE, NC; HARDING UNIVERSITY HS; (SO); Hnr Roll; Perf Att; St of Mnth; Comm Volntr; Hosp Aide; Key Club; Scouts; Swmg (J); Yrbk (P); Dentist; Veterinary; U North Carolina-Chapel Hill; NC State U

LAMB, ASHLEY; HAYESVILLE, NC; TOWNS CTY HS; (FR); Hi Hnr Roll; Hnr Roll; Otst Ac Ach Awd; Perf Att; Chrch Yth Grp; FCA; FBLA; Ntl Beta Clb; P to P St Amb Prg; SADD; Ch Chr; Bskball (VJ); Scr Kpr (J); Sftball (VJ L); Pianist; Interior Design/Decorating; Marine Biology; U of North Carolina; New York U

LAMB, KALI; KILL DEVIL HILLS, NC; FIRST FLIGHT HS; (SR); Duke TS; Hnr Roll; St Schl; St of Mnth; WWAHSS; Comm Volntr; Chrch Yth Grp; DARE; Emplmnt; Spanish Clb; Dnce; Chrldg (VJ); CR (R); Sch Ppr (E); UNC Wilmington

LAMB, WILL; ASHEBORO, NC; ASHEBORO HS; (SO); Hnr Roll; WWAHSS; Comm Volntr; Hosp Aide; Peer Tut/Med; Chrch Yth Grp; Dbte Team; FCA; Key Club; Mus Clb; Spanish Clb; Chr; Stu Cncl (R); CR (R); NC Governor's School - 2005; Medicine; Biology / Chemistry; UNC Chapel Hill; Elon U

LAMBERT, DANIEL R; LOCUST, NC; WEST STANLY HS; (SO); Duke TS; Hi Hnr Roll; Nat Hon Sy; Perf Att; Pres Ac Ftns Aw; Sci Fairs; WWAHSS; Hab For Humty Volntr; Sci Clb; Scouts; Ftball (V); Track (V); Wt Lftg; Eagle Scout; Citadel Military Academy; West Point Military Academy

LAMONDS, CHRISTINA V; CANDOR, NC; EAST MONTGOMERY HS; (SO); Hnr Roll; St of Mnth; Comm Volntr; Hosp Aide; DARE; HOSA (Health Occupation Students of America); Hospital Volunteer (First Health); Chemistry-Pre-Med; Forensic Science; Duke U; U of Miami

LANCASTER, KATHERINE; CHAPEL HILL, NC; CEDAR RIDGE HS; (SO); Hnr Roll; WWAHSS; Comm Volntr; Drma Clb; Dnce; SP/M/VS; Stg Cre; International Thespian Society-Member; Dance/Theatre Arts; Business Management; Point Park U; Carnegie Mellon U

LANCASTER, TAYLOR A; FUQUAY VARINA, NC; FUQUAY-VARINA HS; (JR); Gov Hnr Prg; Hi Hnr Roll; Jr Mshl; WWAHSS; Comm Volntr; ArtClub; Key Club; Ntl Beta Clb; North Carolina Governor's School; Numerous Visual Art Awards; Visual Arts; Literature

LANCE, DONAVAN; BREVARD, NC; ROSMAN HS; (SO); Hnr Roll; Nat Ldrshp Svc; Comm Volntr; Chrch Yth Grp; Ntl Beta Clb; National Honor Roll 2004; Nominated to Represent NC in National Youth Leadership Forum on Technology - 2005; Computer Science

LANDING, KELLI; JAMESTOWN, NC; SOUTHWEST GUILFORD HS; (JR); Duke TS; Hnr Roll; Nat Hon Sy; WWAHSS; Comm Volntr; Peer Tut/Med; Emplmnt; Ntl Beta Clb; Sci Clb; Dnce; Stu Cncl (R); Lit Mag (E); Journalism; Education; U of North Carolina At Chapel Hill; Duke U

LANE, KRYSTAL A; SEVEN SPRINGS, NC; SPRING CREEK HS; (SO); Hi Hnr Roll; Hnr Roll; Nat Hon Sy; Otst Ac Ach Awd; Pres Sch; St of Mnth; WWAHSS; DARE; Emplmnt; Photog; Bnd; Clr Grd; Mch Bnd; Pep Bnd; Bskball (J); Sftball (V); Vllyball (V); Yrbk (E, R, P); UNC Honor Band Clinics 2004, 2005; Virginia Tech Honor Band Clinics 2004, 2005; Future Band/Music Director; Journalism Major; U of NC/Pembroke; U of NC/Chapel Hill

LANE, MIRANDA; MORGANTON, NC; FREEDOM HS; (FR); 4H Awd; Ctznshp Aw; Hnr Roll; Otst Ac Ach Awd; ROTC; Chr; Early Childhood Development; Nurses Asst; Appalachian State U

LANGDON, AMANDA N; ANGIER, NC; TRITON HS; (SR); Duke TS; F Lan Hn Soc; Gov Hnr Prg; Hi Hnr Roll; Jr Mshl; Nat Hon Sy; Nat Mrt LOC; Otst Ac Ach Awd; Perf Att; St of Mnth; Peer Tut/Med; Spec Olymp Vol; 4-H; Chrch Yth Grp; FCA; Ntl Beta Clb; Ntl FFA; Prom Com; SADD; Vsity Clb; Bskball (VJ L); PP Ftbl (V); Sftball (VJ L); Tennis (V L); Vllyball (J); Major-Biology; Professional School-Veterinary School; North Carolina State U; Campbell U

LANKFORD, ALICIA; ELLENBORO, NC; CHASE HS; (MS); Perf Att; Comm Volntr; Mus Clb; Chr; Dnce; Crime Scene Investigation; Doctor; U North Carolina; Duke U

LAPAGE, TABBATHA; HICKORY, NC; EAST BURKE HS; (FR); Hnr Roll; St of Mnth; Comm Volntr; DARE; FCA; Sci Clb; Lees-McRae

LAPP, ROBERT G; ROCKY MOUNT, NC; NASH CTRL HS; (FR); Duke TS; Hi Hnr Roll; Nat Hon Sy; Otst Ac Ach Awd; WWAHSS; Comm Volntr; Peer Tut/Med; Red Cr Aide; Ntl Beta Clb; Quiz Bowl; Sccr (J); Tennis (J); U of North Carolina; Duke U

LARDO, TERESA F; RICHLANDS, NC; RICHLANDS HS; (JR); Hnr Roll; Mus Clb; Svce Clb; Foreign Clb; Chr; SP/M/VS; Poetry Club; Creative Writing; Psychology; Brown U; Sarah Lawrence College

LARSON, BRANDY; MOYOCK, NC; CURRITUCK CTY HS; (FR); Hnr Roll; Perf Att; St of Mnth; Spec Olymp Vol; Lib Aide; Sftball (J)

LA RUE, SUZANNE M; EMERALD ISLE, NC; CROATAN HS; (JR); Hnr Roll; ArtClub; Chrch Yth Grp; Drma Clb; Spch Team; Chr; SP/M/VS; Stg Cre; Track (V L); Lit Mag (R); Sch Ppr (P); Official in Schools Improv Club; Member of the Speech & Debate Team; Oberlin College; U of California Berkeley

LASHLEY, CHRYSTAL D; BESSEMER CITY, NC; BESSEMAR CITY HS; (SO); Duke TS; Hi Hnr Roll; Nat Hon Sy; Otst Ac Ach Awd; Pres Sch; WWAHSS; Peer Tut/Med; Red Cr Aide; Spec Olymp Vol; Chrch Yth Grp; FCA; Ntl Beta Clb; Spanish Clb; Bnd; Jzz Bnd; Mch Bnd; Pep Bnd; Sftball (JC); Health Occupational Club; Moot Court - Mock Trial Competition; Pharmacy; Forensic Science; Duke U; Gardner-Webb U

Lapage, Tabbatha
East Burke HS
Hickory, NC

Kravchuk, Alexandra
Monroe, NC

Kornegay, Antwoine M
Southern Wayne HS
Goldsboro, NC

Knight, Melissa L
South View HS
Hope Mills, NC

Kolokolov, Eugene
Mattamuskeet JR/SR HS
Swanquarter, NC

Ladzinski, Elizabeth
Monroe HS
Monroe, NC

La Rue, Suzanne M
Croatan HS
Emerald Isle, NC

LASKODY JR, GEORGE A; WILMINGTON, NC; E A LANEY HS; (JR); Duke TS; Gov Hnr Prg; Hi Hnr Roll; Hnr Roll; MVP; Nat Hon Sy; Nat Ldrshp Svc; Otst Ac Ach Awd; Perf Att; Pres Ac Ftns Aw; Comm Volntr; ArtClub; DARE; Emplmnt; Fr of Library; Outdrs Clb; Pep Squd; Scouts; Vsity Clb; Ftball (V); Sccr (V); MVP - Varsity Soccer Team; Several Championships in Soccer; Sports Medicine; Occupational Therapy; East Carolina U; West Virginia U

LASSITER, HANNAH M; SWANNANOA, NC; OWEN HS; (JR); Duke TS; Hi Hnr Roll; Jr Mshl; Comm Volntr; Chrch Yth Grp; Drma Clb; Emplmnt; Key Club; Lib Aide; Ntl Beta Clb; SADD; Clb; Bnd; Stg Cre; Sch Ppr (R); Yrbk (R); International Relations

LASSITER, JENNIFER; SWANSBORO, NC; WEST CARTERET HS; (SO); Hnr Roll; Otst Ac Ach Awd; Comm Volntr; Spec Olymp Vol; DARE; Drma Clb; Emplmnt; Key Club; Mus Clb; ROTC; Drl Tm; Flg Crps; Golf (V L); 2nd Place Knockout NJROTC; Military (Air Force); Ob/Gyn; U of North Carolina in Chapel Hill; Vanderbilt U School of Medicine

LASSITER, MATTHEW; GOLDSBORO, NC; ROSEWOOD HS; (SO); Duke TS; Hnr Roll; Lttrmn Clb; ROTC; Ftball (V L); ROTC; Computer and Game Design; Full Sail U; Duke U

LASSITER, TONI E; AHOSKIE, NC; HERITAGE HS; (MS); Otst Ac Ach Awd; Yth Ldrshp Prog; Chrch Yth Grp; Emplmnt; FBLA; Scouts; Homeroom Class President - 6th; Homeroom Security - 8th Grade; Computer Technicians; Home Decorating; New York U

LATHOM, AMBER; KANNAPOLIS, NC; A L BROWN HS; (JR); Hi Hnr Roll; Jr Mshl; Nat Hon Sy; WWAHSS; Comm Volntr; Chess; Chrch Yth Grp; Emplmnt; Mod UN; Quiz Bowl; Svce Clb; Bnd; Chr; Jzz Bnd; Mch Bnd; Swmg (V L); Doctor; Biology; Western Carolina

LATTIMORE, C J; SHELBY, NC; BURNS HS; (JR); Hnr Roll; Otst Ac Ach Awd; WWAHSS; Yth Ldrshp Prog; Comm Volntr; FCA; Ntl Beta Clb; Ntl FFA; Bsball (VJ); Bskball (J); Wt Lftg (VJ); Played JV Basketball 9th & 10th Grades; National Technical Honor Society; Engineering; Business Management; East Carolina U; NC State U

LAUFFENBURGER, MARK; HICKORY, NC; ST STEPHENS HS; (SO); Hnr Roll; MVP; Perf Att; St of Mnth; Hab For Humty Volntr; Chrch Yth Grp; Emplmnt; Spanish Clb; Ch Chr; Bskball (J); Golf (C); Wt Lftg (V); Adv Cncl (R); Cl Off (R); CR (T); Psychology; Allied Sciences; Pfeiffer U; Davidson U

LA VALLEY, JESSELYN; HAVELOCK, NC; HAVELOCK HS; (JR); Hnr Roll; MVP; WWAHSS; Comm Volntr; Peer Tut/Med; Chrch Yth Grp; FCA; Quill & Scroll; Bskball (V CL); Sftball (V CL); Vllyball (VJCL); CR (R); Lit Mag (E); Yrbk (E, P); Honor Roll (All A's); Marine Biology; Aviation; North Carolina State; Monmouth College

LAWLOR, DAN; RALEIGH, NC; (SR); Hi Hnr Roll; Hnr Roll; WWAHSS; Comm Volntr; Chrch Yth Grp; Emplmnt; Key Club; Lttrmn Clb; Svce Clb; Tchrs Aide; Vsity Clb; Bsball; Vsy Clb; Wt Lftg; American Legion Baseball Jr. & Sr.; Dental School; Coastal Carolina U

LAWRENCE, BRITTANY; LUMBERTON, NC; LUMBERTON HS; (FR); Duke TS; Hi Hnr Roll; WWAHSS; ROTC; Scouts; Orch; Chrldg (J); Sch Ppr (R); Law; Psychology; Duke U; UNC At Chapel Hill

LAWS, CAMERON E; ANGIER, NC; HARNETT CTRL HS; (SO); Hnr Roll; Kwnis Aw; Perf Att; Hab For Humty Volntr; Chrch Yth Grp; FCA; FCCLA; Key Club; Lttrmn Clb; Latin Clb; Chr; Ch Chr; SP/M/VS; Sccr (V); Graphic Design; Art History; East Carolina U; UNC Chapel Hill

LAWSON, ASHLEE; KING, NC; WEST STOKES HS; (JR); Hnr Roll; Nat Hon Sy; WWAHSS; Comm Volntr; Spec Olymp Vol; FCA; Prom Com; Bnd; Jzz Bnd; Mch Bnd; Pep Bnd; Bskball (J); Swmg (V); Tennis (V); Sports Broadcasting; Nursing; Appalachian State U; Liberty U

LAWSON, DAVID R; MATTHEWS, NC; DAVID W BUTLER HS; (JR); Hnr Roll; Nat Hon Sy; St Schl; Comm Volntr; Hab For Humty Volntr; Spec Olymp Vol; Chess; Chrch Yth Grp; DARE; Emplmnt; Jr Ach; Scouts; Lcrsse (V); Sccr (V L); U of North Carolina-Wilmington; U of North Carolina-Appalachian

LAWSON, PAIGE R; RALEIGH, NC; SOUTHEAST RALEIGH HS; (FR); Comm Volntr; Chr; SP/M/VS; Chrldg (J); CR (R); Forensic Medicine/Science; Fashion/Design; U of New York; U of Miami

LAWSON, WHITLEY; LAWSONVILLE, NC; NORTH STOKES HS; (FR); Ctznshp Aw; Hi Hnr Roll; Nat Hon Sy; Sci Fairs; Chrch Yth Grp; DARE; Bskball (V); Track (V); DARE Essay Winner; Veterinarian Degree; Marine Biology; NC State U; Virginia Tech

LAYELL, MITCHELL; THURMOND, NC; EAST WILKES MS; (MS); Hnr Roll; Pres Ac Ftns Aw; Sci Fairs; Red Cr Aide; Chess; Chrch Yth Grp; Ntl Beta Clb; SADD; Bnd; Ftball; Scr Kpr; Wt Lftg; Wrstlg; CR; Yrbk (P); Engineer; North Carolina State U

LAYTON, KRISTY; KITTY HAWK, NC; FIRST FLIGHT HS; (SO); Duke TS; Hi Hnr Roll; WWAHSS; Yth Ldrshp Prog; Comm Volntr; Peer Tut/Med; Key Club; Mth Clb/Tm; Vsity Clb; Chrldg (V L); Cr Ctry (J L); Track (V); Chemical Engineering; North Carolina State

LEACH, JONATHAN M; ASHEBORO, NC; ASHEBORO HS; (SO); Hi Hnr Roll; Perf Att; Chrch Yth Grp; FCA; Scouts; Spanish Clb; Ftball (J); Track (V); Boy Scout Order of the Arrow; U of North Carolina; Wake Forest U

LEARY, TIMOTHY W; BEAUFORT, NC; EAST CARTERET HS; (JR); Bnd; Jzz Bnd; Mch Bnd; Pep Bnd; Sophomore Brass Section Leader; Psychology; Chiropractic Medicine; U of North Carolina at Greensboro

LEATHERMAN, ADRIAN; CATAWBA, NC; BANDYS HS; (JR); Hnr Roll; Jr Mshl; Pres Sch; St of Mnth; WWAHSS; Yth Ldrshp Prog; Hosp Aide; Chrch Yth Grp; Emplmnt; Ntl Beta Clb; NYLC; Sci Clb; Ch Chr; Bskball (J); AAU Basketball 2002, 2003 & 2005; Pre-Medicine; Forensics; Pfeiffer U; U of North Carolina-Greensboro

LEATHERS, KAILEY B; CARY, NC; CMTY PARTNERS; (FR); Hi Hnr Roll; Comm Volntr; Chrch Yth Grp; Key Club; Tchrs Aide; Ch Chr; Chrldg (J); Stu Cncl (R); Sch Ppr (E, R, P); Yrbk (P); Guitar & Piano; Lawyer; Psychologist; Harvard U

LEDBETTER, A BROOKE; FOREST CITY, NC; EAST RUTHERFORD HS; (SO); Hnr Roll; Nat Hon Sy; WWAHSS; Comm Volntr; Key Club; Clr Grd; Elementary School Teacher

LEDERMANN, STEVIE; LUMBERTON, NC; LUMBERTON HS; (FR); Chrch Yth Grp; Ntl FFA; ROTC; Ch Chr; Bskball (C); National Technical Honor Society; Veterinarian; North Carolina State U; U of California Davis

LEDOUX, MICHAEL C; JACKSONVILLE, NC; JACKSONVILLE HS; (FR); Ctznshp Aw; Hi Hnr Roll; Chrch Yth Grp; FCA; Ftball (J); Wrstlg (V); Marine Corps Officer; Naval Academy

LEE, ANTHONY C; CARY, NC; CARY AC; (JR); Hnr Roll; Peer Tut/Med; Chess; Key Club; Lib Aide; Mth Clb/Tm; Mus Clb; Sci Clb; Orch; SP/M/VS; Stg Cre; Lcrsse (J); Sccr (J); Track (J); Piano- 8 Years; Concert Musician / Performing Artist; Rice U; Oberlin College

LEE, CHARLIE; ALBEMARLE, NC; NORTH STANLY HS; (JR); ArtClub; Cmptr Clb; Quiz Bowl; Sccr (V); Dental Hygienist; Engineer; East Carolina U; King's College of Charlotte

LEE, ERIKA D; CHARLOTTE, NC; GARINGER SR HS; (FR); Hnr Roll; Otst Ac Ach Awd; Perf Att; Comm Volntr; Chrch Yth Grp; Tchrs Aide; French Clb; Bnd; Forensics; Chemistry; Appalachian U

LEE, JANASIA; SNOW HILL, NC; GREENE CTRL HS; (FR); Hnr Roll; Perf Att; Comm Volntr; ROTC; Bnd; Chr; Ch Chr; Clr Grd; Chrldg (J); PP Ftbl (J); Winterguard; Lawyer; Central U; Howard U

LEE, JIN; GOLDSBORO, NC; EASTERN WAYNE HS; (JR); Ctznshp Aw; Duke TS; Gov Hnr Prg; Hi Hnr Roll; Hnr Roll; Jr Mshl; Nat Hon Sy; Pres Ac Ftns Aw; St of Mnth; WWAHSS; Comm Volntr; Peer Tut/Med; Spec Olymp Vol; Chrch Yth Grp; DARE; FCA; Ntl Beta Clb; Vsity Clb; Bnd; Dnce; SP/M/VS; Sccr (V); Computer Science; Massachusetts Institute of Technology; U of North Carolina

LEE, LAMAR; GREENSBORO, NC; RAGSDALE HS; (FR); Hnr Roll; Perf Att; Sci Fairs; St of Mnth; Comm Volntr; Chrch Yth Grp; DARE; Quiz Bowl; Scouts; Ch Chr; Bskball; Youth of Year & Usher of the Year '03; Accountant for Youth Council at Church; Accounting; Marketing; Wake Forest State U; High Point U

LEE, MARCUS; GREENVILLE, NC; D H CONLEY HS; (SO); Chess; East Carolina U; Greensboro A & T

LEE, MIKE; NEWTON, NC; NEWTON-CONOVER HS; (JR); Hnr Roll; Perf Att; Comm Volntr; Clb; International Club; Math; English; NC States in Raleigh; UNC Charlotte

LEE, SHEWAHN D; LITTLETON, NC; NORTHWEST HS; (FR); Hi Hnr Roll; Hnr Roll; Perf Att; Drma Clb; ROTC; Bnd; SP/M/VS; Cosmetology; Nursing; Elizabeth City U

LEFORT, MICHELLE P; CARY, NC; CARY AC; (SO); Hnr Roll; Sci Fairs; Yth Ldrshp Prog; Hab For Humty Volntr; Peer Tut/Med; Key Club; NYLC; Prom Com; Chr; SP/M/VS; Vllyball (V); Bio Chemistry; Diagnostic Medicine; Boston College; Duke U

LE GRAND, KAREESHA; JACKSONVILLE, NC; NORTHSIDE HS; (SR); Hnr Roll; Medical, Pre-Med; Biology; UNC-Wilmington; Coastal Carolina Community College

LEHMAN, OLIVIA; MATTHEWS, NC; WEDDINGTON HS; (SO); Hnr Roll; Comm Volntr; Chrch Yth Grp; Key Club; Spanish Clb; Track (J); Stu Cncl (R); Design; UNC Charlotte

LEINBAUGH, IAN H F; CARRBORO, NC; CHAPEL HILL HS; (SR); Duke TS; Hi Hnr Roll; Nat Hon Sy; WWAHSS; Red Cr Aide; 4-H; Chrch Yth Grp; DARE; Emplmnt; Mus Clb; Off Aide; SP/M/VS; Stu Cncl; Music; Psychology; U of North Carolina Chapel Hill

LEIPOLD, JAMES; FAYETTEVILLE, NC; REID ROSS YR ROUND CLASSICAL; (FR); DAR; Hi Hnr Roll; Perf Att; Pres Sch; Sci Fairs; Comm Volntr; Chrch Yth Grp; DARE; FCA; Orch; Church Sports; Church Music; Teaching; Colorado U

LEIS, KAITLIN; WINTERVILLE, NC; D H CONLEY HS; (SO); Hnr Roll; Comm Volntr; Chrch Yth Grp; Mus Clb; Chr; Ch Chr; Journalism; Psychiatrist/Counseling; East Carolina U

LENG, JAMES; CHARLOTTE, NC; HARDING UNIVERSITY HS; (FR); Ftball (J); Business Administration; Mechanic; Carolina Chapel Hill; North Carolina State

LEONARD, HEATHER; KILL DEVIL HILLS, NC; FIRST FLIGHT HS; (JR); Hi Hnr Roll; Jr Mshl; WWAHSS; Comm Volntr; Emplmnt; Key Club; Second Place Publication in American Library of Poetry National Contest; Key Clubber of the Month; International Relations; English; New York U; Amherst College

LE QUIRE, BRANDON; SALISBURY, NC; WEST ROWAN HS; (FR); Hnr Roll; ROTC; Scouts; Bsball; Sccr; ROTC; Computer APPS; Medical; Computers; U of North Carolina; Georgia Tech

LESLIE, LAUREN M; PINEHURST, NC; PINECREST HS; (SO); Hnr Roll; Nat Hon Sy; Pres Ac Ftns Aw; St of Mnth; Yth Ldrshp Prog; Peer Tut/Med; Spec Olymp Vol; Chrch Yth Grp; DARE; Drma Clb; Emplmnt; FCA; Key Club; Ntl Beta Clb; Chr; Ch Chr; SP/M/VS; Chrldg (VJ L); Cr Ctry (VJ); PP Ftbl (VJ); Sccr (J); Stu Cncl (S); Yrbk (R); UNC Chapel Hill, NC; UNC Wilmington, NC

LEVINSON, ELIZABETH A; RUTHERFORDTON, NC; R S CTRL HS; (JR); Hi Hnr Roll; Hnr Roll; Perf Att; Chrch Yth Grp; FCA; Ch Chr; Chrldg; Allied Health Club and Award; Volunteer: 80 Hours; Surgical; Other Medical Professions; North Carolina State U; U of North Carolina

LEWIS, ANNA; THOMASVILLE, NC; NORTH DAVIDSON HS; (MS); Hnr Roll; Otst Ac Ach Awd; Hab For Humty Volntr; Chrch Yth Grp; Chr; Ch Chr; Dnce; SP/M/VS; Teaching-Math; Defense Law; Appalachian State U; Harvard

LEWIS, ASHLEE K; HICKORY, NC; HICKORY HS; (FR); Perf Att; Spec Olymp Vol; Chrch Yth Grp; DARE; FCA; Chr; Ch Chr; Accounting; Business; Appalachian State U; U of Charlotte

LEWIS, CANDIS D L; HENDERSON, NC; NORTHERN VANCE HS; (FR); Hnr Roll; Nat Hon Sy; Clr Grd; Mch Bnd; Bskball; Sftball; Track; Harvard U; Duke U

LEWIS, CASEY N; BATH, NC; NORTHSIDE HS; (SO); Hnr Roll; Nat Hon Sy; Otst Ac Ach Awd; Perf Att; Sci/Math Olympn; Comm Volntr; Peer Tut/Med; FCA; FBLA; FCCLA; Key Club; Ntl Beta Clb; Ntl FFA; ROTC; Sci Clb; Ch Chr; Drl Tm; SP/M/VS; Bskball (V); Cr Ctry (V CL); Sftball; Track (V L); CR (R); Varsity Science Olympiad Team; FCCLA Representative; Orthopedic Surgeon; Veterinarian; U of North Carolina; North Carolina State U

LEWIS, JASMINE; CHARLOTTE, NC; INDEPENDENCE HS; (JR); Hi Hnr Roll; Nat Hon Sy; WWAHSS; Comm Volntr; Orch; Chrldg (J); Pre-Med; Law; Yale U; Harvard U

LEWIS, KEQUAWANA; TARAWA TERRACE, NC; LEJEUNE HS; (JR); Hi Hnr Roll; Hnr Roll; MVP; Otst Ac Ach Awd; Perf Att; St of Mnth; Comm Volntr; Red Cr Aide; Drma Clb; Chrldg (V); Cl Off (P); Student Of The Semester; Certificate Of Recognition For Nursing School; Pre-Medicine/ Ob-Gyn; Fashion Designer; Xavier U Of Louisiana, New Orleans; Tulane U, New Orleans

LEWIS, KYLE E; ELIZABETHTOWN, NC; EAST BLADEN HS; (JR); All Am Sch; Hnr Roll; Nat Hon Sy; Otst Ac Ach Awd; Perf Att; Sci Fairs; WWAHSS; Comm Volntr; Peer Tut/Med; Chrch Yth Grp; DARE; P to P St Amb Prg; Spanish Clb; Bnd; Ch Chr; Mch Bnd; Ftball (V); Youth Dept - Association President; State Youth Officer - Oratorical Winner; Vet-Medicine / Culinary Arts / Electrical Engineer; U of North Carolina; Clark Atlanta U

LEWIS, MEGAN L; LOUISBURG, NC; LOUISBURG HS; (SR); Hnr Roll; Jr Mshl; Nat Hon Sy; WWAHSS; Comm Volntr; Chrch Yth Grp; Emplmnt; FCCLA; Ch Chr; Stu Cncl (T); HOSA Member; National Technical Honor Society; Neonatal Nurse; Medical Examiner; Vance Granville Community College

LEWIS, MICHAEL K; CHAPEL HILL, NC; CHAPEL HILL HS; (SR); St of Mnth; Comm Volntr; Chrch Yth Grp; Ftball (L); Stu Cncl; CR (R); Outstanding Youth in Philanthropy; Medicine; Politics; Catholic U

LEWIS, RAMEL; ELIZABETHTOWN, NC; (SR); 4H Awd; Spec Olymp Vol; 4-H; Ch Chr; Bskball; Cr Ctry; Wt Lftg (V); Yrbk (E); Electrician; Winston Salem State

LEWIS, SARAH; MATTHEWS, NC; BUTLER HS; (SO); F Lan Hn Soc; Hnr Roll; WWAHSS; Comm Volntr; Chrch Yth Grp; DECA; Emplmnt; Spanish Clb; Ch Chr; Dnce

LEWIS, TIFFANY; FAYETTEVILLE, NC; (SO); Yth Ldrshp Prog; Comm Volntr; Chrch Yth Grp; FCA; Quiz Bowl; Bnd; Chr; Ch Chr; Mch Bnd; Christian Youth Fellowship President; Sports Medicine/Therapy; Sports Management; U of North Carolina-Chapel Hill; Fayetteville State U

Lewis, Jasmine
Independence HS
Charlotte, NC

Leis, Kaitlin
D H Conley HS
Winterville, NC

Lee, Charlie
North Stanly HS
Albemarle, NC

Layell, Mitchell
East Wilkes MS
Thurmond, NC

National
Honor Roll
Spring 2005

Lassiter, Jennifer
West Carteret HS
Swansboro, NC

Lee, Janasia
Greene Ctrl HS
Snow Hill, NC

Lewis, Candis D L
Northern Vance HS
Henderson, NC

Lewis, Michael K
Chapel Hill HS
Chapel Hill, NC

LICHNIAK, TABATHA; MATTHEWS, NC; (MS); All Am Sch; Duke TS; Gov Hnr Prg; Hi Hnr Roll; Hnr Roll; Nat Hon Sy; Perf Att; USAA; WWAHSS; Comm Volntr; ArtClub; DARE; Pep Squd; Scouts; Dnce; Chrldg; USA & Achievement Academy Award; Duke U. Talent/Gifted Program; Veterinarian; Duke U

LIDGARD, ELIZABETH A; KANNAPOLIS, NC; AL BROWN HS; (FR); Hi Hnr Roll; MVP; Perf Att; Drma Clb; Chr; SP/M/VS; Stg Cre; HOSA Club; Pediatrics; Forensic Scientology; East Carolina U

LIEBERS, KRISTEN; WILLOW SPRING, NC; WEST JOHNSTON HS; (JR); Hi Hnr Roll; Jr Mshl; WWAHSS; FCA; P to P St Amb Prg; Spanish Clb; Chrldg (V L); Stu Cncl (S)

LIGHT, JARED; KERNERSVILLE, NC; EAST FORSYTH HS; (JR); Hnr Roll; MVP; USAA; Yth Ldrshp Prog; Comm Volntr; Chrch Yth Grp; DARE; Prom Com; Bsball (V L); Bskball (V CL); Ftball (V L); Wt Lftg (V); CR (R); Psychology; Auburn U; North Carolina State

LIGHT, JENNIFER C; PARKTON, NC; SOUTH VIEW HS; (JR); Hnr Roll; Nat Hon Sy; WWAHSS; Hab For Humty Volntr; Chrch Yth Grp; Key Club; HOSA; National Honor Society; Master's; Bachelor's; Duke; UNC

LILLEY, NICOLAS N; HIGH POINT, NC; SOUTHWEST GUILFORD HS; (SO); Ctznshp Aw; Hnr Roll; Pres Sch; Sci Fairs; St of Mnth; Comm Volntr; Peer Tut/Med; Chess; Chrch Yth Grp; Emplmnt; Scouts; Chr; Ch Chr; Ftball (VJ); Track (V L); Wrstlg (V L); Armor Bearer; Deacon Board; MBA; U of Miami; U of Iowa

LIM, ANTHONY T; HIGH POINT, NC; TRINITY HS; (SO); Hi Hnr Roll; Nat Hon Sy; Otst Ac Ach Awd; WWAHSS; ArtClub; Chrch Yth Grp; DARE; Ntl Beta Clb; Sccr (J); Swmg (V); Track (J); Sch Ppr (R); Duke U; Stanford

LINAK, SCOTT; RALEIGH, NC; MIDDLE CREEK HS; (SO); Hi Hnr Roll; Perf Att; WWAHSS; Comm Volntr; DARE; Emplmnt; Key Club; Scouts; Svce Clb; Boy Scouts-Eagle Scout Award; Honor Roll; Computer Programmer; Languages; North Carolina State U; Appalachian State U

LINDLEY, JILL; SNOW CAMP, NC; JORDAN MATTHEWS HS; (SR); Hi Hnr Roll; WWAHSS; Yth Ldrshp Prog; Chrch Yth Grp; DECA; Emplmnt; FCA; Ntl Beta Clb; Off Aide; Prom Com; Vsity Clb; Bskball (J); Sftball (VJCL); Vllyball (VJCL); Cl Off (T); Yrbk (E, P); Hospitality; Journalism; U of North Carolina At Wilmington; East Carolina U

LING, MARSHALL; EFLAND, NC; CEDAR RIDGE HS; (SR); Hnr Roll; WWAHSS; Ntl FFA; Sccr (VJ); Active Member in Young Patriots Club; Architecture; U of North Carolina Charlotte; U of Cincinnati

LINK, EMILY M; CARY, NC; SOUTHEAST RALEIGH HS; (JR); Hnr Roll; Comm Volntr; Hab For Humty Volntr; Peer Tut/Med; Chrch Yth Grp; Emplmnt; Key Club; Scouts; Key Club Secretary; A Honor Roll; CSI, Anthropology; Radiology; UNC-Chapel Hill; East Carolina U

LIPSCOMB, MA'TIKA; GASTONIA, NC; BESSEMER CITY HS; (SO); Nat Hon Sy; WWAHSS; Comm Volntr; Peer Tut/Med; Bnd; Chr; Dnce; Chrldg (VJ); Sch Ppr (R); Academic Excellence Award; National Society of High School Scholar; Psychology; Fashion Design

LISANE, VALARIE A; GARNER, NC; GARNER MAGNET HS; (SO); All Am Sch; Hi Hnr Roll; Hnr Roll; Nat Hon Sy; Otst Ac Ach Awd; Valdctrian; WWAHSS; Chrch Yth Grp; Drma Clb; Ntl Beta Clb; Chr; Ch Chr; SP/M/VS; Wt Lftg (J); Adv Cncl (R); CR (R); Student Against Violence Everywhere - SAVE Club / Students Against Destructive Decisions - SADD Club; Fashion Design; Interior Design; Miami International U of Art & Design; The Art Institution of Fort Lauderdale

LITTLE, MARQUITA R; CHARLOTTE, NC; GARINGER SR HS; (SO); Hnr Roll; Otst Ac Ach Awd; Perf Att; 4-H; Emplmnt; ROTC; Track (V)

LITTLEJOHN, BRITANY; CHARLOTTE, NC; RESURRECTION CHRISTIAN SCH; (SO); F Lan Hn Soc; Comm Volntr; Bskball (V); Chrldg (V); Foreign Language; Veterinary; Queens College; UNC

LIU, PAM; CHAPEL HILL, NC; EAST CHAPEL HILL HS; (SO); Duke TS; F Lan Hn Soc; Hi Hnr Roll; Otst Ac Ach Awd; Sci/Math Olympn; Yth Ldrshp Prog; Hosp Aide; Peer Tut/Med; Chess; Mth Clb/Tm; Sci Clb; Bnd; Mch Bnd; Fncg (J); Lcrsse (J); Stu Cncl (R); Transferring to North Carolina School of Science & Math; Food Science; Restaurant Management/Business; Cornell U; Yale U

LIVENGOOD, CALLIE J; ROCKWELL, NC; EAST ROWAN HS; (FR); Ctznshp Aw; Hnr Roll; St of Mnth; Comm Volntr; Chrch Yth Grp; DARE; ROTC; Clr Grd; Drl Tm; JROTC Rifle Team; Military Science; Virginia Military Institute; West Point

LIVINGSTON, AUTUMN; CONCORD, NC; J.M. ROBINSON HS; (SO); Gov Hnr Prg; Hnr Roll; Otst Ac Ach Awd; St of Mnth; Chrch Yth Grp; Ch Chr; Bskball (J); Pediatrician; Modeling; A & T

LIVINGSTON, ELIZABETH; FAYETTEVILLE, NC; SOUTH VIEW HS; (SO); Hnr Roll; Pres Sch; WWAHSS; Comm Volntr; Chrch Yth Grp; DARE; FBLA; Key Club; Ntl Beta Clb; Ch Chr; Marine Biologist; Veterinarian; North Carolina State U; U of North Carolina

LOBO, KIMBERLY; LINCOLNTON, NC; LINCOLNTON HS; (SO); Kwnis Aw; Perf Att; Spec Olymp Vol; French Clb; Bnd; Taking Honors Classes; Pediatrician; Cosmetologist; Duke U; U of North Carolina Chapel Hill

LOCKAMY, EVELYN N; CLINTON, NC; CLINTON HS; (SO); Hnr Roll; DARE; SP/M/VS; 100 -Yard Dash & AIM Club; President Achievement Award & NASD; Nursing; Psychology; U of Pembroke; Sampson Community College

LOCKHART, STEPHANIE N; BURGAW, NC; (JR); Hnr Roll; DARE; Emplmnt; Lit Mag (E); Sch Ppr (R); Junior Beta Club; Art (Drawing, Painting); Forensic Science (Anthropology); Appalachian State U; U of Tennessee

LOCKLEAR, ALEXANDRA G; LAURINBURG, NC; SCOTLAND HS; (SO); Hi Hnr Roll; Hnr Roll; Otst Ac Ach Awd; Perf Att; Sci Fairs; St of Mnth; Comm Volntr; Peer Tut/Med; Chrch Yth Grp; FBLA; Key Club; Photog; Ch Chr; Dnce; Sccr (J); President's Award - 4th Grade; Making 2-4's on EOG; Pre-Med; Pediatrician; North Carolina U Chapel Hill; Duke U

LOCKLEAR, ANNISSA D; RED SPRINGS, NC; PURNELL SWETT HS; (FR); Duke TS; Hnr Roll; MVP; Nat Hon Sy; Nat Sci Aw; Otst Ac Ach Awd; Perf Att; Sci Fairs; Sci/Math Olympn; St of Mnth; Comm Volntr; Red Cr Aide; Spec Olymp Vol; Chrch Yth Grp; JSA; Mod UN; MuAlphaTh; Ntl Beta Clb; Ntl FFA; Prom Com; Sci Clb; Bnd; Drm Mjr; Jzz Bnd; Mch Bnd; GAA; Golf; Hsbk Rdg; PP Ftbl; Sftball; Swmg; Vsy Clb; Vllyball; Stu Cncl (R); Culinary Arts; Veterinarian / Equine; Duke Medical U; Dartmouth U

LOCKLEAR, ASHLEY D; PEMBROKE, NC; PURNELL SWETT HS; (FR); Hnr Roll; Kwnis Aw; Otst Ac Ach Awd; Perf Att; Sci Fairs; St of Mnth; St Optmst of Yr; Comm Volntr; Red Cr Aide; 4-H; Chrch Yth Grp; Kwanza Clb; Mus Clb; Pep Squd; Prom Com; Scouts; Bnd; Jzz Bnd; Mch Bnd; Pep Bnd; Bskball (L); Chrldg (L); PPSqd (L); Sftball (L); Concert Band; Orthopedic Surgeon; Anesthesiologist; Duke U; U of North Carolina Chapel Hill

LOCKLEAR, BONNIE; MOORESVILLE, NC; LAKE NORMAN HS; (SO); Hi Hnr Roll; Pres Ac Ftns Aw; St of Mnth; Comm Volntr; ArtClub; FCA; FBLA; Prom Com; Spanish Clb; Bnd; Dnce; Cr Ctry (V); PP Ftbl (J); Track (V, L); Stu Cncl (R); Nurse Anesthetist; Dentist; U North Carolina at Charlotte; U North Carolina at Chapel Hill

LOCKLEAR, COURTNEY; LUMBERTON, NC; PURNELL SWETT HS; (FR); Hnr Roll; Chrch Yth Grp; Math Award & Reading Award; Supervisor Award & Most Improved in Computer Skills; Nurse Practionier; Doctor / Pediatrician; UNC Pembroke; UNC Chapel Hill

LOCKLEAR, JOSHUA B; PEMBROKE, NC; PURNELL SWETT HS; (FR); Hnr Roll; Sci Fairs; Comm Volntr; DARE; Scouts; Bnd; Mch Bnd; Wt Lftg (J); Cl Off (S)

LOCKLEAR, NIKKI L; PEMBROKE, NC; PURNELL SWETT HS; (SO); 4H Awd; Hnr Roll; MVP; Sci Fairs; St of Mnth; Comm Volntr; Spec Olymp Vol; 4-H; Chrch Yth Grp; DARE; Drma Clb; Mus Clb; Ntl Beta Clb; Sci Clb; SADD; Chr; Ch Chr; Dnce; SP/M/VS; PP Ftbl (J); Sftball (V); Vllyball (V); Wt Lftg (J); Cl Off (R); Stu Cncl (R); Sch Ppr (E); Doctor / MD; Midwife; UNC Chapel Hill; UNC Pembroke

LOCKLEAR, RUTH; MAXTON, NC; PURNELL SWETT HS; (SO); Hi Hnr Roll; Hnr Roll; Otst Ac Ach Awd; St of Mnth; WWAHSS; Comm Volntr; Chrch Yth Grp; Mus Clb; Ntl Beta Clb; SADD; Bnd; Ch Chr; Mch Bnd; Pep Bnd; UNC @ Pembroke-Physical Therapist; Radiologist; UNC @ Pembroke; Slandhills Community College

LOCKLEAR, SHOMMA; SAINT PAULS, NC; ST PAULS HS; (JR); Ctznshp Aw; Hnr Roll; Comm Volntr; DARE; Ntl FFA; Prom Com; Yrbk (P); UNC Pembroke; Chapel Hill

LOCKLEAR, STACY E; MAXTON, NC; RED STRINGS; (SR); Wt Lftg; Auto Mechanics; Sand Hill Community College; Fayetteville Technology College

LOCKLENE, JOSHUA S; RED SPRINGS, NC; HOKE CTY HS; (SR); Ctznshp Aw; Sci Fairs; St Schl; Yth Ldrshp Prog; Comm Volntr; Peer Tut/Med; Chrch Yth Grp; DARE; FBLA; NYLC; Voc Ind Clb Am; Bsball (J); Ftball (J); Wt Lftg; President: Skills USA; Sec: NASA, Treas: NCNAYO; Medical Field; Engineer Tech; Pembroke State U; Sandhills Community College

LOEHMAN, JESSICA; RALEIGH, NC; SOUTHEAST RALEIGH; (SR); Hi Hnr Roll; Otst Ac Ach Awd; WWAHSS; Comm Volntr; Ntl Beta Clb; Tchrs Aide; Spanish Clb; Senior Mentor; Psychology; Meredith College

LOFTIN, SHENETTA; DURHAM, NC; SOUTHERN HS; (MS); Hnr Roll; Otst Ac Ach Awd; Perf Att; Sci Fairs; St of Mnth; WWAHSS; Comm Volntr; Peer Tut/Med; Spec Olymp Vol; DARE; Drma Clb; Off Aide; Tchrs Aide; Chr; Dnce; Bskball (V); Cr Ctry (V); Sccr (V C); Track (V); Vllyball (V C); Yrbk (E); Veterinarian; Business Administration; North Carolina A & T College; U of North Carolina-Chapel Hill

LOFTIS, AMANDA M; FRANKLINVILLE, NC; EASTERN RANDOLPH HS; (SR); Hnr Roll; WWAHSS; Yth Ldrshp Prog; CARE; Comm Volntr; Peer Tut/Med; Chrch Yth Grp; DARE; Emplmnt; Jr Ach; P to P St Amb Prg; Tchrs Aide; Dnce; Health/Medical; Business/Marketing; Greensboro College

LOFTIS, JOSHUA C; TIMBERLAKE, NC; PERSON HS; (JR); Ctznshp Aw; Gov Hnr Prg; Hnr Roll; Jr Mshl; Nat Hon Sy; St Schl; Yth Ldrshp Prog; Comm Volntr; Hab For Humty Volntr; Peer Tut/Med; Chrch Yth Grp; DECA; Emplmnt; NYLC; Prom Com; Voc Ind Clb Am; Wdwrkg Clb; Spanish Clb; SP/M/VS; Cr Ctry (V); Track (V); Aerospace Engineering; Chemical Engineering; North Carolina State U; U of North Carolina

LOFTON, ROBIN; GOLDSBORO, NC; GOLDSBORO HS; (SO); Hnr Roll; Chrch Yth Grp; FBLA; Golf; Student Government Association; Social Work; Fayetteville State U; A&T U

LOGAN, AASHA; RALEIGH, NC; WAKEFIELD HS; Hnr Roll; St of Mnth; WWAHSS; Comm Volntr; Chrch Yth Grp; Key Club; Lib Aide; Chr; Ch Chr; Dnce; Chrldg (J); Psychology; North Carolina Agriculture & Technical College

LOGAN, AMBER; RALEIGH, NC; WAKEFIELD HS; (SO); Duke TS; Hnr Roll; WWAHSS; Comm Volntr; Chrch Yth Grp; Key Club; Chr; Ch Chr; Chrldg (J); Pediatrics; Ob/Gyn; North Carolina State U; North Carolina At Chapel Hill

LONG, CAITLIN J; WILMINGTON, NC; E A LANEY HS; (JR); Hnr Roll; Nat Hon Sy; Comm Volntr; Chrch Yth Grp; Emplmnt; Stg Cre; Sftball (J); Missions Trip to Jamaica; HOSA; Biology; Pre Medicine; U of North Carolina At Chapel Hill; East Carolina U

LONG, CHELSAE; CHARLOTTE, NC; BERRY AC OF TECH; (JR); Hnr Roll; DARE; Sch Ppr (R); Dentistry; Ophthalmology; Wake Forest U; U of North Carolina Chapel Hill

LONG, KATHERINE A; GREENSBORO, NC; NORTHWEST HS; (SR); Hi Hnr Roll; Jr Mshl; Pres Ac Ftns Aw; WWAHSS; Chrldg (V); Yrbk (E); Competitive Cheerleading-6 Yrs.; Medicine; U of North Carolina

LONG, KRISTOPHER; WINSTON-SALEM, NC; MT TABOR HS; (JR); Hnr Roll; ArtClub; Emplmnt; Scouts; Ftball (V L); Wt Lftg; Business Administration; Criminal Justice; Wake Forest U; U of North Carolina

LONG, MARY M; HENDERSON, NC; NORTHERN VANCE HS; (JR); Duke TS; Hi Hnr Roll; Hnr Roll; Jr Mshl; Nat Hon Sy; Nat Stu Ath Day Aw; Pres Sch; WWAHSS; Comm Volntr; Chrch Yth Grp; FCA; Key Club; Photog; Quill & Scroll; Spanish Clb; Chr; Sccr (V L); Tennis (V CL); Cl Off (R); CR (R); Lit Mag (E, R, P); Yrbk (R); Red Cross Lifeguard & Teach Swim Lessons; Referee Rec. Department Soccer; U of North Carolina At Chapel Hill; College of Charleston

LONG, MICHAEL; SALISBURY, NC; EAST ROWAN HS; (JR); Hnr Roll; Otst Ac Ach Awd; DARE; ROTC; Scouts; FBI; CIA; U of North Carolina Chapel Hill; Duke U

LONG, STEPHEN G; ROXBORO, NC; THE NORTH CAROLINA SCH OF SCIENCE & MATH; (SO); Hi Hnr Roll; St Schl; WWAHSS; Emplmnt; Mth Clb/Tm; Quiz Bowl; Sci Clb; Bnd; Jzz Bnd; Mch Bnd; Pep Bnd; Music-Composition; To Compose For & Conduct The NC Symphony; U of North Carolina At Greensboro; Juilliard School of Music

LOPEZ, ARELI H; MONROE, NC; SUN VALLEY MS; Hnr Roll; Otst Ac Ach Awd; Sci Fairs; Chrch Yth Grp; Chr; Once a Member of Gardeners Club; Medical School; Law School; Chapel Hill College

LOR, JEANA; MORGANTON, NC; FREEDOM HS; (JR); Ctznshp Aw; Hnr Roll; Nat Stu Ath Day Aw; Otst Ac Ach Awd; Perf Att; St of Mnth; Comm Volntr; Hosp Aide; Peer Tut/Med; DARE; Outdrs Clb; Prom Com; Tchrs Aide; Sccr (J); Tennis (V); Explorer Post #226 MDPS; Pharmacist; Law Enforcement; High Point U; Greensboro College

LOR, LIA K; HICKORY, NC; HICKORY HS; (FR); Hnr Roll; Teacher; Nurse; UNC Chapel Hill; Appalachian State U

LOR, SHEENA; SALISBURY, NC; WEST ROWAN HS; (FR); Hosp Aide; Bdmtn (J); GAA (J); PP Ftbl (J); Tennis (J); Register Nurse; School Teacher; Duke U; Catawba Community College

LOVELACE, HALEY M; BOSTIC, NC; EAST RUTHERFORD HS; (FR); Ctznshp Aw; Hnr Roll; Comm Volntr; Chrch Yth Grp; Bnd; Jzz Bnd; Mch Bnd; Pep Bnd; Lawyer; Western Carolina U; North Carolina State U

LOWERY, ASHLEY S; YOUNGSVILLE, NC; WAKE FOREST-ROLESVILLE HS; (JR); Duke TS; Hnr Roll; Nat Hon Sy; Otst Ac Ach Awd; WWAHSS; Comm Volntr; Hosp Aide; Peer Tut/Med; Chrch Yth Grp; Drma Clb; Emplmnt; Ntl Beta Clb; Ntl FFA; Sci Clb; Tech Clb; Latin Clb; Ch Chr; Clr Grd; SP/M/VS; 1st Place Robotics Competition (TSA); Accepted to Summer Ventures in Science & Math; Pre Medicine; Aerospace Engineering; Illinois Institute of Technology; U of North Carolina At Chapel Hill

LOWRY, AMANDA S; PEMBROKE, NC; PURNELL SWETT HS; (SO); Hi Hnr Roll; WWAHSS; Comm Volntr; Chrch Yth Grp; FBLA; Ntl Beta Clb; Teacher; U of North Carolina Pembroke; U of North Carolina Chapel Hill

Locklear, Stacy E
Red Strings
Maxton, NC

Lilley, Nicolas N
Southwest Guilford HS
High Point, NC

National
Honor Roll
Spring 2005

Lichniak, Tabatha
Matthews, NC

Loftis, Joshua C
Person HS
Timberlake, NC

LOY, AMANDA; GIBSONVILLE, NC; EASTERN GUILFORD HS; (JR); Duke TS; Jr Mshl; Nat Hon Sy; Perf Att; WWAHSS; Ntl Beta Clb; Prom Com; Spanish Clb; Cl Off (P); Stu Cncl (P, V); Yrbk (R); Presidential Volunteer Service Award; Ranked #1 in My Class

LUCAS, ANTHONY L; RALEIGH, NC; MIDDLE CREEK HS; (FR); Hnr Roll; WWAHSS; Bnd; Mch Bnd

LUCAS, BRANDON J; WINDSOR, NC; BERTIE HS; (SO); Ctznshp Aw; Hnr Roll; Sci Fairs; Yth Ldrshp Prog; Peer Tut/Med; Chrch Yth Grp; DARE; Mus Clb; Scouts; Bnd; Jzz Bnd; Mch Bnd; Bskball (J); Sch Ppr (R); Business Administration; Criminal Justice; NC State; Hampton U

LUCAS, CARMEN M; LUCAMA, NC; JAMES B HUNT JR HS; (SO); Hnr Roll; Otst Ac Ach Awd; WWAHSS; Chrch Yth Grp; FCA; Key Club; Sign Clb; Bnd; Ch Chr; Mch Bnd; Pep Bnd; Golf (V); Swmg (V L); Fluent in Reading/Writing Braille; Play Piano, Violin, and Parjo and Flute; Photo Journalism; Social Work; North Carolina State U; U of North Carolina At Wilmington

LUCAS, ZACHARY; ROANOKE RAPIDS, NC; HALIFAX AC CHRISTIAN SCH; (SO); Duke TS; USAA; WWAHSS; Chrch Yth Grp; Ntl Beta Clb; Scouts; Svce Clb; Wt Lftg (J); Cl Off (T); Yrbk (P); History; Film and Television; Duke U; United States Naval Academy

LUCKADOO, JORDAN; RUTHERFORDTON, NC; RUTHERFORDTON-SPINDALE MS; MS; Ctznshp Aw; Hnr Roll; Perf Att; Sci/Math Olympn; St of Mnth; Comm Volntr; Peer Tut/Med; Chrch Yth Grp; DARE; Drma Clb; FCA; Ntl Beta Clb; Sci Clb; Bnd; Ch Chr; Jzz Bnd; Pep Bnd; Stu Cncl (R); CR (R); Sch Ppr (E); Yrbk (E); Doctorate in Education; Gardner-Webb U

LUNDY, DE ANDRE; FAYETTEVILLE, NC; RRCS; (FR); Hnr Roll; Perf Att; Comm Volntr; Peer Tut/Med; Ntl Beta Clb; Orch; All State Orchestra Symphonic; All County Orchestra 1st Choir Cellists; Pre-Med; Music; U of North Carolina Greensboro; Elon U

LUNDY, SARA; HAW RIVER, NC; CEDAR RIDGE HS; (JR); Hnr Roll; Nat Hon Sy; Comm Volntr; Peer Tut/Med; Chrch Yth Grp; Chr; Sftball (V L); Tennis (V L); Wrstlg (V L); Zoology; Marine Biology; NC State; UNC Wilmington

LUNSFORD, BRIAN; DURHAM, NC; NORTHERN HS; (JR); St of Mnth; Comm Volntr; Peer Tut/Med; Chrch Yth Grp; Tchrs Aide; Ch Chr; Something in the Medical Field; North Carolina Chapel Hill, North Carolina State U; North Carolina Greensboro

LUTETE, CLAIRETTE; RALEIGH, NC; (JR); Hnr Roll; Perf Att; Comm Volntr; Hosp Aide; Chrch Yth Grp; Emplmnt; Doctorate; Nursing; East Carolina U; Western Carolina U

LUZUM, JENNIFER; MATTHEWS, NC; WEDDINGTON HS; (SR); F Lan Hn Soc; Hi Hnr Roll; Jr Mshl; Jr Rot; Nat Hon Sy; WWAHSS; Comm Volntr; Hosp Aide; Peer Tut/Med; Emplmnt; Key Club; MuAlphaTh; Ntl Beta Clb; French Clb; Virginia Tech U

LYNCH, JAMIE; RALEIGH, NC; SOUTHEAST RALEIGH MAGNET HS; (SO); Hnr Roll; Comm Volntr; Key Club; Dnce; Major in Psychology; Major in Business; North Carolina State U; U of North Carolina-Chapel Hill

LYONS, D'JUAN; RURAL HALL, NC; NORTH FORSYTH HS; (SR); Hnr Roll; WWAHSS; Chrch Yth Grp; Ch Chr; Computer Engineering; Electrical Engineering; NC A & T State U; Winston-Salem State U

MAAS, JOHN; CHARLOTTE, NC; RESURRECTION CHRISTIAN SCH; (JR); Hi Hnr Roll; Otst Ac Ach Awd; Pres Sch; WWAHSS; Chrch Yth Grp; Scouts; Cr Ctry (V); Golf (V); Sccr (V); Track (V); Stu Cncl (T); Yrbk (P); Chemistry; Physics; Duke U; UNC Greensboro

MABE, JESSIE D; LAWSONVILLE, NC; NORTH STOKES HS; (FR); Ctznshp Aw; Hnr Roll; Perf Att; St of Mnth; Hosp Aide; Chrch Yth Grp; DARE; FTA; Ch Chr; Bskball (J); Sftball (V); CR (R); Yrbk (P); Lawyer; Hold Government Office (To Hold); Salem College; Western Carolina U

MACALUSO III, PETER J; MURPHY, NC; HIWASSEE DAM HS; (JR); Hi Hnr Roll; Hnr Roll; Jr Mshl; Nat Hon Sy; WWAHSS; ArtClub; FCA; Ntl Beta Clb; Quiz Bowl; Engineering; Graphic Design

MACK, KELLI A; WINSTON-SALEM, NC; REYNOLDS HS; (JR); Hnr Roll; Nat Hon Sy; Comm Volntr; Emplmnt; Svce Clb; French Clb; Dnce; SP/M/VS; CR (R); Dance Team- Varsity / Letterman; Nurse Anesthetist; Registered Nurse; U of North Carolina Wilmington; U of North Carolina Greensboro

MACK, LA'TRISH C; THOMASVILLE, NC; THOMASVILLE HS; (FR); Hi Hnr Roll; Nat Hon Sy; St of Mnth; Chrch Yth Grp; Kwanza Clb; Bnd; Chr; Ch Chr; Clr Grd; Attorney, Judge; Paralegal, Actor/Singer; Hampton U; Chapel Hill

MACK, MARGARET R; CHAPEL HILL, NC; CEDAR RIDGE HS; (JR); Duke TS; Fut Prb Slvr; Hnr Roll; Perf Att; WWAHSS; DARE; Dbte Team; FBLA; Prom Com; Bskball (V); Cr Ctry (V); Track (V); Yrbk (P); Business; Corporate Law; U of Georgia; North Carolina State U

MACK, SYDELL; FAYETTEVILLE, NC; DOUGLAS BYRD SR HS; (FR); MVP; Perf Att; Chrch Yth Grp; DARE; Mus Clb; Ch Chr; Orch; Track (V); CR (V); FAMS Club; TV Broadcasting; Fashion Designer; Singer; East Carolina U; UNC Charlotte

MACON, BRYAN; WINSTON-SALEM, NC; REYNOLDS HS; (JR); Duke TS; Hi Hnr Roll; Hnr Roll; MVP; Nat Hon Sy; Outdrs Clb; Spanish Clb; Bskball (V L); Spanish Club Officer; Business; Medicine; Duke U; U of North Carolina Chapel Hill

MAGEE, PAULA M; JACKSONVILLE, NC; NORTHSIDE HS; (JR); Hi Hnr Roll; Hnr Roll; Nat Hon Sy; Otst Ac Ach Awd; Comm Volntr; Chrch Yth Grp; Pep Squd; Chr; Ch Chr; Chrldg (V); Cheerleading Coach's Award; Computer Engineering; Orthodontist; Chapel Hill

MAHARAJH, PATTERSON A; WAXHAW, NC; CHARLOTTE CHRISTIAN SCH; (JR); Hnr Roll; Yth Ldrshp Prog; Comm Volntr; Vsity Clb; French Clb; Wt Lftg (VJ); Wrstlg (VJCL); Conference & State Champion in Wrestling; Private Pilot License; Pre-Med; Continue Pilot Training; Washington U; Lee U

MAIDON, ASHLEY L; ANGIER, NC; HARNETT CTRL HS; (SR); Cmptr Clb; FBLA; Key Club; Prom Com; Sci Clb; SADD; Foreign Clb; Bnd; Orch; Web Development; Band President; Arts Degree Major; Wake Tech Community College

MAJANO, JOSE G; FAYETTEVILLE, NC; PINE FOREST HS; (FR); Mar Art (V); Sccr (J); Wrstlg (V); Science Fair Award; Business; Military Officer; North Carolina; West Point

MAJURE, JENNY L; MOORESVILLE, NC; MOORESVILLE HS; (JR); DAR; Hi Hnr Roll; Hnr Roll; WWAHSS; Peer Tut/Med; ROTC; Academic Team Officer for NJROTC; Advertising; Acting; UNC Charlotte; Stanford U

MAKI, ANDREW J; CHARLOTTE, NC; CHARLOTTE CHRISTIAN SCH; (JR); Hnr Roll; Comm Volntr; Chrch Yth Grp; Dbte Team; Emplmnt; Outdrs Clb; Spch Team; SP/M/VS; Ftball (V); Scr Kpr (V); Track (V); Wt Lftg (V); Wrstlg (V); Cl Off (R); Engineering; North Carolina State U

MAKLIGH, MARINA; CHAPEL HILL, NC; CARY AC; (JR); Hi Hnr Roll; Hnr Roll; ArtClub; Emplmnt; Outdrs Clb; Photog; Dnce; SP/M/VS; Bskball (J); Sftball (J); Vllyball (J); MBA; U of North Carolina Chapel Hill; Boston U

MALONEY, KAITLYN; GREENVILLE, NC; D H CONLEY HS; (FR); Hnr Roll; St of Mnth; Comm Volntr; Chrch Yth Grp; Sftball (J); Vllyball (J); 1st Under World Series Champions (Softball); Traveling Softball Team (Softball), Horseback Riding; Vet or Midwife; Large and Small Animals; North Carolina State; Pitt Community College

MALTER, MALLORY L; WILMINGTON, NC; JOHN T HOGGARD HS; (JR); Ctznshp Aw; Gov Hnr Prg; Hnr Roll; Otst Ac Ach Awd; WWAHSS; Comm Volntr; Drma Clb; Ntl Beta Clb; Prom Com; Chr; Dnce; SP/M/VS; Chrldg (VJC); PP Ftbl (J); Track (V); Dance Team-Varsity; North Carolina Honors Chorus; Music Education; Elementary Teaching; East Carolina U; U of North Carolina

MANDJINY, SATHYAPRYA; HOPE MILLS, NC; SOUTH VIEW HS; (FR); DAR; Duke TS; Hnr Roll; Kwnis Aw; Otst Ac Ach Awd; St of Mnth; WWAHSS; Comm Volntr; ArtClub; Key Club; Foreign Clb; Stg Cre; Sch Ppr (R); Yrbk (R, P); Medical (Major); Biology (Major); Duke U; Johns Hopkins Medical School

MANESS, KEVIN W; ASHEBORO, NC; (JR); Hnr Roll; Comm Volntr; Peer Tut/Med; Chrch Yth Grp; Emplmnt; Ntl FFA; Outdrs Clb; Wdwrkg Clb; Spanish Clb; Arch (V); Skt Tgt Sh (V); Track (V); FFA Greenhand Degree; FFA Chapter Degree; Spanish Education; Masters or Doctors Degree; UNCG; RCC

MANLEY, JALESA; LITTLETON, NC; NORTHWEST HS; Hnr Roll; Perf Att; Comm Volntr; Chrch Yth Grp; Drma Clb; FBLA; ROTC; Ch Chr; SP/M/VS; Stg Cre; Computer Info Systems (Major); Physical Therapist (Major); A & T State U; Fayetteville State U

MANNING, AMANDA; GREENSBORO, NC; PAGE HS; (SO); Hnr Roll; WWAHSS; Hab For Humty Volntr; Chrch Yth Grp; Jr Cls League; Scouts; Ch Chr; Mch Bnd; Yrbk (P); Wind Ensemble; Junior Classical League State Medalist; Biology; Astronomy; U of North Carolina-Chapel Hill; U of Maryland-College Park

MANNING, LAURIE; GREENSBORO, NC; PAGE HS; (SR); Hnr Roll; Nat Hon Sy; Perf Att; WWAHSS; Peer Tut/Med; Chrch Yth Grp; Emplmnt; Jr Cls League; Vllyball (V); Advertising; Public Relations; U of North Carolina At Chapel Hill; U of Georgia

MANNING, NIKKI; GREENVILLE, NC; NORTH PITT HS; (MS); Ctznshp Aw; Hnr Roll; Perf Att; Hosp Aide; ArtClub; DARE; Dnce; Pitt Community College; East Carolina U

MANYIKA, DANIELLE; CHARLOTTE, NC; CHARLOTTE CHRISTIAN SCH; (JR); Ctznshp Aw; F Lan Hn Soc; Hi Hnr Roll; Perf Att; Comm Volntr; Hab For Humty Volntr; Peer Tut/Med; Chrch Yth Grp; Dbte Team; Photog; Spch Team; Ch Chr; Bskball (J); Sftball (V); Tennis (V); Church Publication: Hope Junction; Social Work; Culinary Arts; Wake Forest; Davidson U

MANZELMANN, BRIAN J; INDIAN TRAIL, NC; SUN VALLEY MS/ PORTER RIDGE HS; MS; Hnr Roll; Comm Volntr; Hab For Humty Volntr; Peer Tut/Med; Pep Bnd; SP/M/VS; Sch Ppr (R); Guitar; Physics; Engineering; U of South Florida

MARCHISON, TYLER G; LILLINGTON, NC; (JR); F Lan Hn Soc; Hnr Roll; Nat Hon Sy; WWAHSS; Hab For Humty Volntr; ArtClub; Chrch Yth Grp; Emplmnt; Key Club; Ntl Beta Clb; Prom Com; Quiz Bowl; Spanish Clb; Tennis (V L); Stu Cncl (R); CR (R); Graphic Arts; History; Appalachian State U; U of North Carolina At Wilmington

MARINELLO, JENI; CHARLOTTE, NC; CHARLOTTE CATHOLIC HS; (FR); Hi Hnr Roll; Hnr Roll; St of Mnth; Comm Volntr; Peer Tut/Med; DARE; Jr Ach; Ntl Beta Clb; SADD; Dnce; Cr Ctry (V); Track (V); Stu Cncl (V); Top Three in Shot Put; Teaching / Counseling Degree; Nursing Degree; UNC Chapel Hill; North Carolina State U

MARKUM, JENNIFER; FAYETTEVILLE, NC; BEREAN BAPTIST AC; (JR); Hi Hnr Roll; Nat Hon Sy; Sci Fairs; WWAHSS; Comm Volntr; Chrch Yth Grp; Emplmnt; Ntl Beta Clb; Tchrs Aide; Chr; Scr Kpr (V); Sccr (L); Vllyball (L); Mock Trial Competition; English; Secondary Education; Wake Forest; Appalachian

MARLOWE, ARIEL A; FAYETTEVILLE, NC; MASSEY HILL CLASSICAL HS; (FR); Duke TS; Hnr Roll; Perf Att; Pres Sch; Comm Volntr; Chrch Yth Grp; Ntl Beta Clb; Foreign Clb; Ch Chr; Orch; Sccr (V); Middle School Youth Orchestra; Highest Volunteer Hours for Freshmen Class; Aeronautical Engineer; Air Force Pilot; North Carolina State U; Embry Riddle U in Florida

MARONEY, ERIN E; ASHEBORO, NC; ASHEBORO HS; (JR); Nat Hon Sy; Comm Volntr; Chrch Yth Grp; Emplmnt; FCA; Key Club; Ntl Beta Clb; Svce Clb; Spanish Clb; Swmg (V C); Tennis (V C); Who's Who Sports 2003-04; Coach's Award for Tennis '05; Nursing; U of NC Wilmington; East Carolina U

MAROSOK, GABRIELLE; BELMONT, NC; SOUTH POINT HS; (JR); Hnr Roll; Comm Volntr; FBLA; Bskball (V CL); Sccr (J); Vllyball (V L); Nursing; Pharmaceutical; U of North Carolina At Chapel Hill

MARSH, KIERRA; GREENSBORO, NC; RAGSDALE HS; (SO); Duke TS; Hnr Roll; WWAHSS; Emplmnt; Pediatrics; UNC-Chapel Hill

MARSHALL, ALLAN; RALEIGH, NC; FRANKLIN AC; (JR); Hnr Roll; Comm Volntr; Chrch Yth Grp; Svce Clb; Jr. Curator for the Museum of Natural Sciences; Teen Servants (Volunteer Work); North Carolina State U; Wake Technical Community College

MARSHBURN, JUSTIN P; GOLDSBORO, NC; BETHEL CHRISTIAN AC; (SR); Hi Hnr Roll; Jr Mshl; Nat Hon Sy; Perf Att; Sci Fairs; Valdctrian; WWAHSS; Comm Volntr; Peer Tut/Med; ArtClub; Chrch Yth Grp; Drma Clb; Emplmnt; Vsity Clb; Bsball (V L); Bskball (VJ L); Sccr (V CL); Cl Off (V); Scholastic Award in 9th - 12th Grades; Christian Testimony in 9th Grade; Education; Ministry; Cedarville U

MARTIN, ANDREW; WILSON, NC; FIKE HS; (SO); Hi Hnr Roll; Sci/Math Olympn; WWAHSS; Yth Ldrshp Prog; Chrch Yth Grp; Mth Clb/Tm; Sci Clb; SADD; Spanish Clb; Golf (V L); Sccr (JC); Track (V L); Business; Economics; U of North Carolina At Chapel Hill; Wake Forest U

MARTIN, ANNA; PURLEAR, NC; WEST WILKES HS; (SR); Hnr Roll; Nat Hon Sy; Perf Att; WWAHSS; Comm Volntr; Peer Tut/Med; Chrch Yth Grp; DARE; Emplmnt; FCA; Key Club; Lib Aide; Ntl Beta Clb; Ch Chr; Vllyball (J); Stu Cncl (R); Senior ACTeen, Assistant Teacher At Christian Sch.; Cover of ACTeen National Magazine; Radiology; Wilkes Community College; Forsyth Tech Community College

MARTIN, LA TOYA; RURAL HALL, NC; NORTH FORSYTH HS; (SR); MVP; Comm Volntr; Hosp Aide; Red Cr Aide; Chrch Yth Grp; DARE; Emplmnt; FBLA; Bskball (V C); Track (V); Completed Allied Health 1 & 2; Major in Pediatrics; Minor in Neonatal; Winston Salem State U; North Carolina Central U

MARTINEZ, JOHNNY A; CHARLOTTE, NC; HARDING UNIVERSITY HS; (SO); Hnr Roll; St of Mnth; WWAHSS; Chess; Dbte Team; FTA; Bnd; Chr; Ch Chr; Ftball (V CL); Track (L); Wt Lftg; Wrstlg (L); President of Poetry Club; Math Education (Secondary & Higher); Furman U; Davidson College

MARTINEZ, JOSE D; MATTHEWS, NC; SUN VALLEY MS; (MS); Hnr Roll; DARE; Ftball (J); Playing College Football; UNC U of North Carolina; NC State North Carolina State

MARTINEZ, LAUREN A; ZEBULON, NC; SOUTHERN NASH HS; (FR); Otst Ac Ach Awd; St of Mnth; Comm Volntr; Peer Tut/Med; Chrch Yth Grp; DARE; Emplmnt; Ntl FFA; ROTC; Ch Chr; Track (J); Science (Bachelor's); Cosmetology; New York U; U of Southern California

MARTINEZ, VALORIE; GRANITE FALLS, NC; SOUTH CALDWELL HS; (JR); FCA; Sftball (V L)

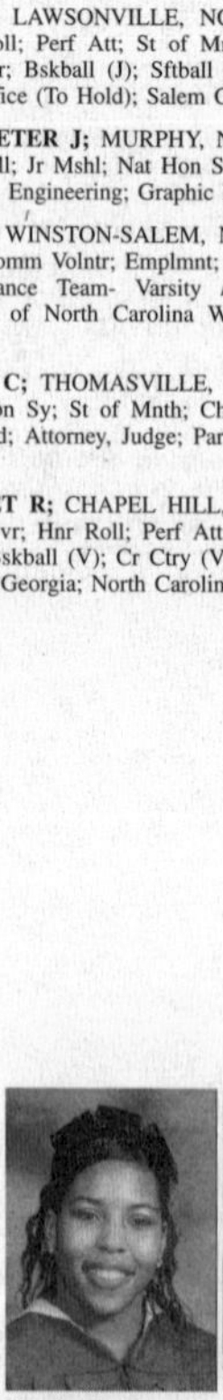

Martin, La Toya
North Forsyth HS
Rural Hall, NC

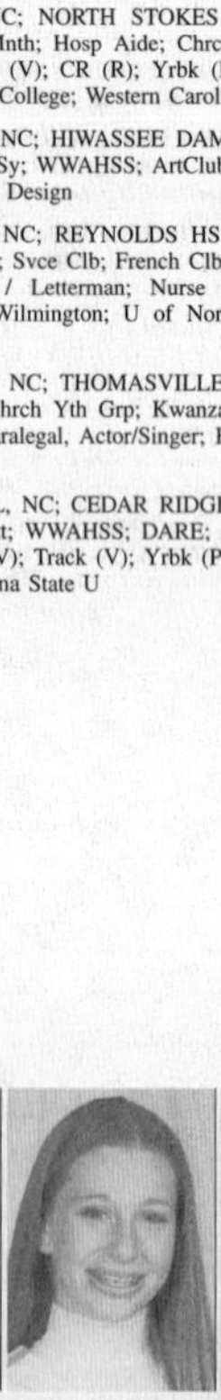

Malter, Mallory L
John T Hoggard HS
Wilmington, NC

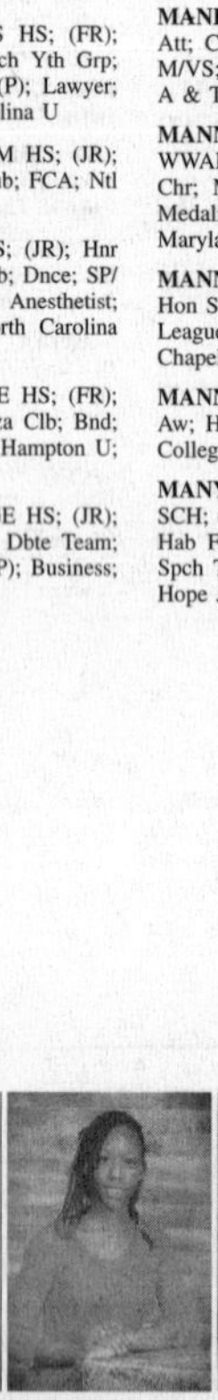

Mack, Sydell
Douglas Byrd SR HS
Fayetteville, NC

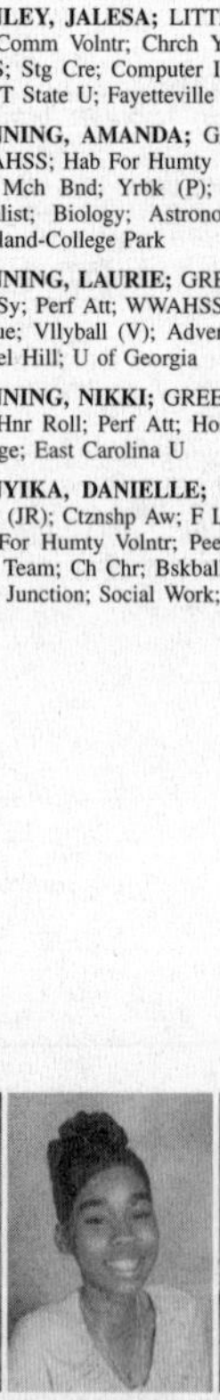

Mack, La'Trish C
Thomasville HS
Thomasville, NC

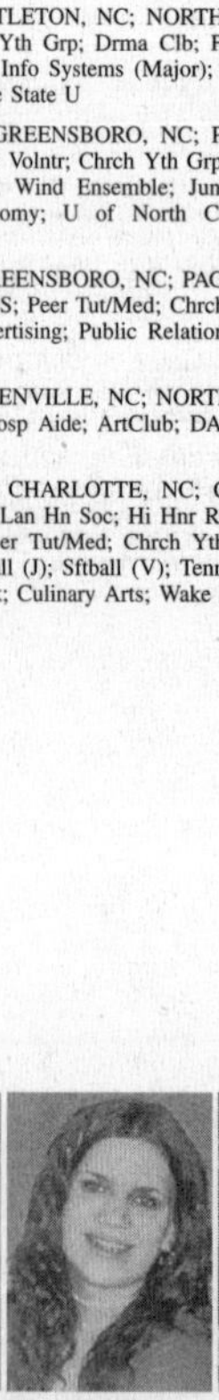

Luckadoo, Jordan
Rutherfordton-Spindale MS
Rutherfordton, NC

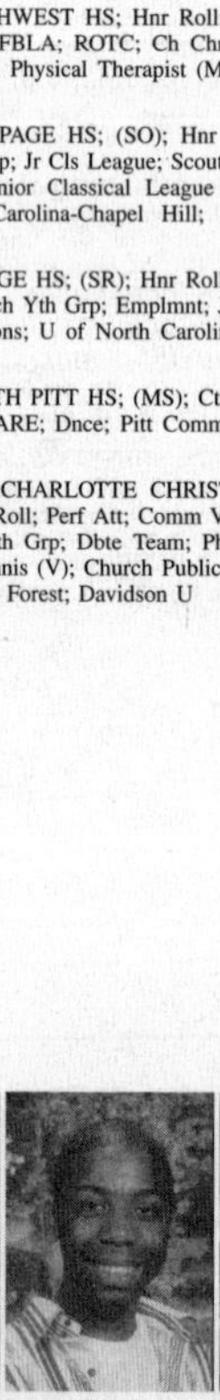

Lundy, De Andre
RRCS
Fayetteville, NC

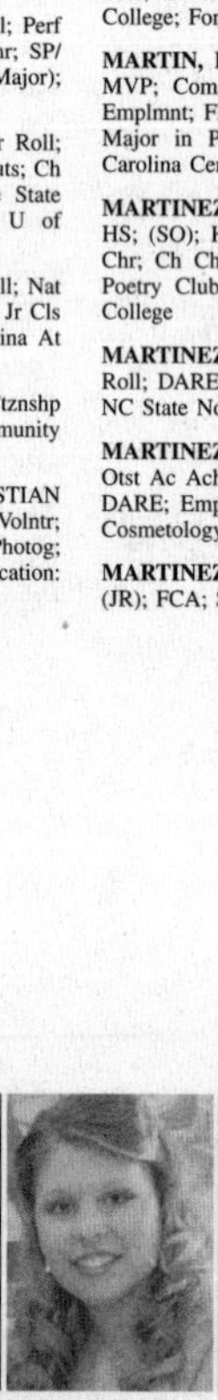

Maloney, Kaitlyn
D H Conley HS
Greenville, NC

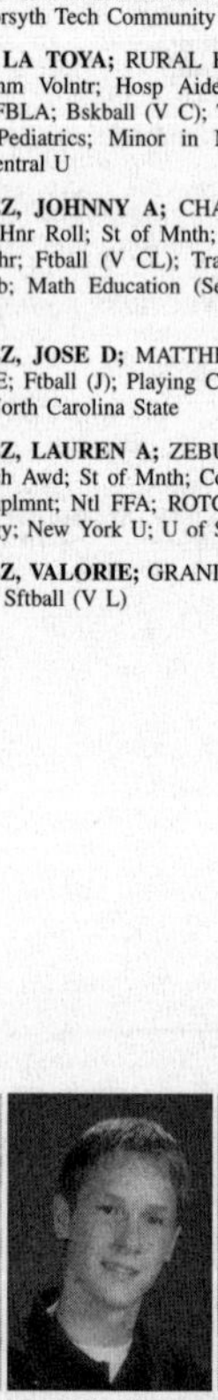

Marshall, Allan
Franklin AC
Raleigh, NC

Martinez, Jose D
Sun Valley MS
Matthews, NC

MARTINEZ, ZULEYMA; NORWOOD, NC; SOUTH STANLY HS; (FR); Hnr Roll; Otst Ac Ach Awd; Honor Society; Nursing; Biomedical Technician; Stanly Community College

MARTIN JR, ROY E; WESTFIELD, NC; NORTH STOKES HS; (SR); Hnr Roll; Otst Ac Ach Awd; Perf Att; Sci Fairs; WWAHSS; Comm Volntr; Chrch Yth Grp; DARE; Emplmnt; Prom Com; SADD; Vsity Clb; Ch Chr; Pep Bnd; Bsball (J); Ftball (VJC); PP Ftbl (J); Track (J); Wrstlg (J); Varsity & JV Football Quarterback; Automotive Tech Race Cars; Teaching Auto Technology; Forsyth Technical College Winston-Salem, NC; Nascar Technical Institute, Mooresville, NC

MASON, BREANNA; BREVARD, NC; BREVARD HS; (SO); Ctznshp Aw; Hnr Roll; Chrch Yth Grp; DARE; FCA; Ntl FFA; Bnd; Mch Bnd; Pep Bnd; Scr Kpr (V); Manager of Varsity Wrestling Team; Section Leader of Marching Band; Veterinary Medicine; Animal Science; Mars Hill College; NC State College

MASON, KEIRIEA C; CONCORD, NC; NORTHWEST CABARRUS MS; (MS); Ctznshp Aw; Duke TS; Hnr Roll; Otst Ac Ach Awd; Perf Att; Yth Ldrshp Prog; Comm Volntr; ArtClub; Chrch Yth Grp; DARE; Ch Chr; Dnce; SP/M/VS; Bskball; Yrbk (E, P); Meet the President; Received President's Education Award; Become a Professional Model/Dancer; Accounting, Dancing, Cosmetology, Nursing; Juilliard School of Dancing; UNC Chapel Hill

MASON, RACHEL M; SALISBURY, NC; NORTH ROWAN HS; (SO); Hnr Roll; St of Mnth; Comm Volntr; Chrch Yth Grp; Vllyball (J); Veterinarian; North Carolina State U

MASSEY, ADRIENNE; KANNAPOLIS, NC; A L BROWN HS; (SR); Hi Hnr Roll; Hnr Roll; Perf Att; WWAHSS; Spec Olymp Vol; Chrch Yth Grp; DARE; ROTC; Scouts; Chr; Ch Chr; Drl Tm; Track; Nursing NA I; Licensed Practical Nurse Associate Degree; Rowan Cabarrus Community College; Georgia Tech U

MASSEY, BRANDON J; EDEN, NC; MOREHEAD HS; (FR); MVP; 4-H; DARE; Emplmnt; ROTC; Law Degree; Military; NC State; UNC

MASSEY, BRITTANY S; BURLINGTON, NC; WESTERN ALAMANCE HS; (SR); Hnr Roll; Kwnis Aw; Sci Fairs; St of Mnth; WWAHSS; Comm Volntr; Peer Tut/Med; Spec Olymp Vol; ArtClub; Drma Clb; Key Club; Pep Squd; Dnce; Sccr (V); Dance Team Varsity All 4 Years Captain Jr & Sr; B in Dance; The American Musical and Dramatic Academy

MATA, ELSA E; ALBEMARLE, NC; NORTH CAROLINA SCH OF SCIENCE & MATH; (JR); Duke TS; St of Mnth; WWAHSS; Comm Volntr; Peer Tut/Med; Chrch Yth Grp; FBLA; Mth Clb/Tm; Ntl Beta Clb; Photog; Spanish Clb; Cr Ctry (J); Track (V L); Stu Cncl (S, R); CR (R); Yrbk (E); Church Activities; Church Plays; Biomedical Engineering; Genetic Engineering; Chapel Hill-U of North Carolina; Duke U

MATHESON, KANDACE; ROBBINSVILLE, NC; ROBBINSVILLE HS; (SO); Hi Hnr Roll; Nat Hon Sy; Chrch Yth Grp; Pep Squd; Ch Chr; Chrldg (V); Office Systems Technology; Tri-County Community College

MATHLIN, LEON; LINDEN, NC; PINE FOREST HS; (SO); Hnr Roll; Perf Att; Sccr (J); Computer Engineer; Software Developer; ITT Technical Institute; North Carolina State U

MATTHEWS, ARIEL J; HENDERSONVILLE, NC; EAST HENDERSON HS; (SO); Duke TS; Hnr Roll; Nat Hon Sy; Sci Fairs; Yth Ldrshp Prog; Peer Tut/Med; Chrch Yth Grp; Dnce; Chrldg (V); Sftball (V); Track (L); Psychologist; Social Worker; Chapel Hill/Duke; U of North Carolina Wilmington

MATTHEWS, ASHLEY; WENDELL, NC; EAST WAKE HS; (SO); Hi Hnr Roll; Peer Tut/Med; Chrch Yth Grp; Ntl Beta Clb; Chr; Ch Chr; Dnce; Chrldg (VJ); Travel with Youth Outreach Ministry; Represented My School for the PBS News; Pre Law; Business/Management; Spelman U; Howard U

MATTHEWS, ISAIAH W; DENVER, NC; NORTH LINCOLN HS; (SO); Ctznshp Aw; Hi Hnr Roll; Hnr Roll; MVP; Otst Ac Ach Awd; St of Mnth; Chrch Yth Grp; FCA; Ftball (J); Most Valuable Defensive Player 2004; Engineering; Pharmacy; Appalachian U in Boone, NC; Western Carolina

MAULDIN, WESLEY S; NORWOOD, NC; SOUTH STANLY HS; (FR); Ctznshp Aw; Hi Hnr Roll; Hnr Roll; Nat Hon Sy; Otst Ac Ach Awd; DARE; Scouts; Voc Ind Clb Am; Bnd; Mch Bnd; Track (J); Career in Music; Berklee School of Music; Durham School of the Arts

MAXEY, SARAH; WINSTON-SALEM, NC; MT TABOR HS; (SO); Hnr Roll; Sci Fairs; Comm Volntr; ArtClub; Chrch Yth Grp; Emplmnt; Svce Clb; Spanish Clb; Cr Ctry (J); Track (J); Scholastic Art Gold Key; Graphic Design; Interior Design; North Carolina State U; Savannah College of Art and Design

MAXWELL, ANNA; CHARLOTTE, NC; EAST MECKLENBURG HS; (JR); Hnr Roll; Yth Ldrshp Prog; Comm Volntr; Emplmnt; Off Aide; SADD; Tennis (V CL); Stu Cncl; All-Conference Tennis Player; State Qualifier (Tennis); Psychology; Counseling; U of North Carolina At Wilmington

MAXWELL, DANIELLE; CHARLOTTE, NC; NORTH MECKLENBURG SR HS; (SR); Hnr Roll; Perf Att; Comm Volntr; Dbte Team; Drma Clb; Emplmnt; Quiz Bowl; Spch Team; Chr; SP/M/VS; Stg Cre; Cl Off (R); Stu Cncl (R); CR (R); FCCLA-Director of Annual Fashion Show; Touring Teen Theatre Troupe; Fashion Merchandising; International Business; The U of North Carolina Greensboro; The U of Georgia

MAY, JASMINE; FORT BRAGG, NC; E E SMITH SR HS; (SO); Hnr Roll; Hosp Aide; Peer Tut/Med; Red Cr Aide; DARE; FTA; Dnce; Chrldg (V); Sftball (V); Business Administration; Physical Therapy; U of Miami; Florida State U

MAYES, KENDRICK T; FAYETTEVILLE, NC; E E SMITH SR HS; (SO); Hnr Roll; MVP; Yth Ldrshp Prog; Comm Volntr; Peer Tut/Med; Chrch Yth Grp; Emplmnt; Lttrmn Clb; Mth Clb/Tm; P to P St Amb Prg; Sci Clb; Spanish Clb; SP/M/VS; Bskball (J); Cr Ctry (J); Ftball (V L); Track (J); Wt Lftg (V); CR (R); Yrbk (R); Math and Science Academy; Mr E E Smith Freshman Runner-Up; Engineering; Internal Medicine; Duke U; U of North Carolina

MAYFIELD, MARDRIEKUS; LINCOLNTON, NC; LINCOLNTON HS; (FR); Ftball (VJC); Track; Wt Lftg; Lawyer; Accountant; NC State; Duke U

MAYO, JESSICA J; ROCKY MOUNT, NC; ROCKY MOUNT HS; (SO); Hnr Roll; Otst Ac Ach Awd; WWAHSS; Peer Tut/Med; FBLA; Clr Grd; Mch Bnd; Color Guard Captain; Management; Bachelor's Degree; North Carolina A & T State U; North Carolina Central U

MAYS, RAVEN; SPRING LAKE, NC; PINE FOREST HS; (FR)

MC ALISTER, CHRISTY J; BLOWING ROCK, NC; WATAUGA HS; (FR); Duke TS; Hnr Roll; Bnd; Dnce; Orch; English; History; Appalachian State U; U of Glasgow

MC ALLISTER, AMANDA; HENDERSON, NC; NORTHERN VANCE HS; (SO); Hi Hnr Roll; Nat Hon Sy; USAA; WWAHSS; Chrch Yth Grp; Dnce; Swmg; Yrbk (E, R); National Honor Society; Dentistry; Medicine; U of North Carolina; Boston College

MC AULEY, DANIEL; VASS, NC; GRACE CHRISTIAN SCH; (JR); SP/M/VS; Bskball (V L); Sccr (V CL); Yrbk (R, P); 4-H State Fair Reserve Grand Champion; Business; UNC Wilmington; Cedarville U, Westmont College

MC BEATH, NATHANIEL L; CHARLOTTE, NC; WEST MECKLENBURG HS; (JR); Hnr Roll; Jr Mshl; MVP; Nat Hon Sy; WWAHSS; Comm Volntr; Chess; Emplmnt; FCA; Key Club; Cr Ctry (V); Track (V); Coaches' Award; Most Outstanding Running Award; Game Design; Computer Science; DeVry; MIT

MC BRIDE, MACKENZIE A; RALEIGH, NC; NEEDHAM BROUGHTON HS; (SO); F Lan Hn Soc; Hi Hnr Roll; St of Mnth; Comm Volntr; Spanish Clb; Sccr (J); Completed IBMYP; Biology; Chemistry; North Carolina State U; U of North Carolina

MC CAIN, LAFAYETTE; MOORESVILLE, NC; LAKE NORMAN HS; (SO); Hnr Roll; WWAHSS; Comm Volntr; Chrch Yth Grp; Vsity Clb; Ch Chr; Bskball; Ftball (V); Wt Lftg (V); Computer Engineering; Georgia Tech; U of North Carolina

MC CALL, KAYLEY; LAKE TOXAWAY, NC; ROSMAN HS; (SO); Hi Hnr Roll; WWAHSS; Spanish Clb; Excellence Awards; Honors Courses; Nursing; Physician's Assistant

MC CALL, PRESTIGIOUS B U; CHARLOTTE, NC; WEST MECKLENBURG HS; (JR); Tech Clb; Track (V); Computer Engineer; Auto Mechanic; UNC Charlotte; NC A&T U

MC CANN, CAITLIN; GREENSBORO, NC; PAGE HS; (JR); Hnr Roll; Yth Ldrshp Prog; Comm Volntr; Drma Clb; Quill & Scroll; Vsity Clb; SP/M/VS; Stg Cre; Sftball (V L); Lit Mag (E); Creative Writing Club; Scholastic Gold & Silver Writing Awards 05; Creative Writing; Journalism; Sarah Lawrence College; Warren-Wilson College

MC CANTS, TROYCE; ASHEVILLE, NC; ASHEVILLE HS; (SO); Hnr Roll; Perf Att; St of Mnth; Chrch Yth Grp; Chr; Ftball (J); Wt Lftg (J); Finish College; Computer Degree; U of North Carolina Chapel Hill; Miami U

MC CARTER, WESLEY; LENOIR, NC; HIBRITEN HS; (JR); Ctznshp Aw; Hi Hnr Roll; Hnr Roll; MVP; Pres Ac Ftns Aw; Sci Fairs; St of Mnth; Yth Ldrshp Prog; Comm Volntr; Peer Tut/Med; Chrch Yth Grp; DARE; Emplmnt; FCA; Ntl Beta Clb; Bnd; Ch Chr; Bskball; Sccr (JC); Wt Lftg (VJ); Stu Cncl; CR; Youth in Ministry Milligan College; The Big Picture; Ministry; Preaching, Missionary; Milligan College; Lees McRae

MC CASKILL, JOSHUA; STAR, NC; EAST MONTGOMERY HS; (FR); Ch Chr; Art Achievement; Ministerial Degree At Piedmont Bible College

MC CASLIN, JACLYN S; LINCOLNTON, NC; EAST LINCOLN HS; (SO); Hi Hnr Roll; MVP; Perf Att; Comm Volntr; Spec Olymp Vol; ArtClub; Emplmnt; Ntl Beta Clb; Spanish Clb; Hsbk Rdg (L); Sccr (J); Vllyball (V); Yrbk (E); Beta Club; Law; Communications; North Carolina State

MC CLAIN, ANDRE'; FAYETTEVILLE, NC; WESTOVER HS; (JR); MVP; DARE; Orch; Bskball (V); U of North Carolina-Chapel Hill

MC CLAIN, JAMES; POLKTON, NC; AKSON HS; (JR); Ctznshp Aw; Hnr Roll; Comm Volntr; Ch Chr; Graphic Designer; Interior Designer; The Arts of Institute of Charlotte

MC CLAMY, TUNORA S; ROPER, NC; PLYMOUTH HS; (SR); Hnr Roll; Otst Ac Ach Awd; Sci Fairs; WWAHSS; Comm Volntr; Chrch Yth Grp; Emplmnt; FBLA; Prom Com; Ch Chr; Drl Tm; Chrldg (V); PP Ftbl (VJ); Cl Off (V); HOSA; Students Against Tobacco; Early Childhood Teacher / Associate's Degree; Cosmetologist; Pitt Community College; Elizabeth City State U

MC CLARNON, ALEX; CHAPEL HILL, NC; NORTHWOOD HS; (FR); Hnr Roll; Nat Hon Sy; Perf Att; Comm Volntr; Chrch Yth Grp; DARE; Key Club; Bnd; Ch Chr; Mch Bnd; Cr Ctry (J); Golf (J); Computer Engineering; U of North Carolina; Indiana U

MC CLARNON, TYLER; CHAPEL HILL, NC; NORTHWOOD HS; (JR); Hnr Roll; Nat Hon Sy; Chrch Yth Grp; Key Club; Pep Squd; Acpl Chr; Chr; Ch Chr; SP/M/VS; Ftball (V); Golf (V); Wt Lftg (V); Cl Off (S); Optometry; Dentistry; U of North Carolina Chapel Hill; Indiana U

MC CLELLAN, JOSH; RUTHERFORDTON, NC; R S CTRL HS; (SO); Hnr Roll; Kwnis Aw; St of Mnth; Comm Volntr; Hosp Aide; Peer Tut/Med; ArtClub; Chrch Yth Grp; Ntl FFA; SP/M/VS; Stu Cncl (T); Student Council - 8th Grade; Drama Plays; Teaching; Doctoring; U of North Carolina; Duke U

MC CLENDON, JENNIFER L; GREENSBORO, NC; JAMES BENSON DUDLEY SR HS; (FR); Ctznshp Aw; Hnr Roll; WWAHSS; Comm Volntr; Peer Tut/Med; Chrch Yth Grp; Ch Chr; Dnce; Chrldg (C); Sftball (J); Yrbk (R); Automotive Engineering; North Carolina Agricultural & Technical State U

MC CORD, TIFFANY; MILL SPRING, NC; POLK CTY HS; (JR); Hi Hnr Roll; Hnr Roll; Jr Mshl; MVP; Nat Hon Sy; Otst Ac Ach Awd; WWAHSS; Comm Volntr; Peer Tut/Med; FCA; Key Club; Ntl Beta Clb; Bskball (VJCL); PP Ftbl (VJ); Sftball (V CL); Vllyball (VJ L); Physical Therapy; Sports Medicine; Louisiana State U; North Carolina State U

MC CORMICK, SHAMONIQUE; LUMBERTON, NC; LUMBERTON HS; (FR); Hnr Roll; Comm Volntr; Chr; Bskball (V); Track (V); Career Development; Community Technology; UNC Pembroke; A & T U

MC CORMICK, TYLER; BOONVILLE, NC; FARBUSH HS; (FR); Hnr Roll; Chrch Yth Grp; Arch (V); Cr Ctry (V); Skt Tgt Sh (V); Overall 1st Place in State Hunter Safety Comp; 2nd in Nationals Hunter Safety Competition; Electronic Engineering; Law Enforcement; NC State; ASU

MC COY, YUSUF; AHOSKIE, NC; HERTFORD CTY HS; (SO); 4H Awd; Ctznshp Aw; Hi Hnr Roll; Hnr Roll; Nat Hon Sy; Otst Ac Ach Awd; WWAHSS; Comm Volntr; Peer Tut/Med; Drma Clb; Ntl Beta Clb; NYLC; Quiz Bowl; SP/M/VS; Stg Cre; Ftball (V); Wrstlg; Yrbk (P); Highest Grade Average in Drafting 2; Varsity Football Semifinalists At State; Graphics Design; Architectural Design; New York U; Yale U

MC CRAY, KENDERA; WINSTON-SALEM, NC; MT TABOR HS; (SO); Hnr Roll; St of Mnth; Comm Volntr; Chrch Yth Grp; Ch Chr; Dnce; Scr Kpr; English Teacher; Business Owner; Howard U; Spelman College

MC DONALD, RENEE; RALEIGH, NC; WAKEFIELD HS; (FR); Hnr Roll; WWAHSS; Drma Clb; Key Club; Dnce; SP/M/VS; Won Over 7 Dance Awards; Work with Kids Over the Summer; Actress; Psychologist; Yale; New York U

MC DUFFIE, CATHERINE; BENSON, NC; WEST JOHNSTON HS; (JR); Ctznshp Aw; Duke TS; Hi Hnr Roll; Hnr Roll; Nat Hon Sy; WWAHSS; Comm Volntr; Hab For Humty Volntr; Chrch Yth Grp; Drma Clb; Emplmnt; FCA; Ntl Beta Clb; Pep Squd; Photog; Prom Com; SP/M/VS; Stg Cre; Cr Ctry (V); Cl Off (P); Sch Ppr (R, P); Yrbk (R, P); Marketing; U of North Carolina-Greensboro; Appalachian State U

MC DUFFIE, SHANEKA L; LEXINGTON, NC; CARTER G WOODSON SCH; (FR); Hnr Roll; Chrch Yth Grp; DECA; P to P St Amb Prg; Ch Chr; Dnce; CR (V); Law; North Carolina Central; Florida State U

MC ELHANEY, MONIQUE; GASTONIA, NC; ASHBROOK HS; (FR); Nat Stu Ath Day Aw; Otst Ac Ach Awd; Perf Att; Comm Volntr; Peer Tut/Med; Chrch Yth Grp; Civil Air Pat; Cmptr Clb; DARE; Mth Clb/Tm; Mus Clb; Outdrs Clb; Pep Squd; Chr; Ch Chr; Drl Tm; Flg Crps; Hair License; Entering the Air Force

MC ELRATH, JARED A; CLYDE, NC; TUSCOLA HS; (JR); USAA; WWAHSS; Chrch Yth Grp; Emplmnt; Who's Who Among American High School Students; Haywood Community College

MC FEE, ANDREA; NEWLAND, NC; AVERY CTY HS; (FR); Ctznshp Aw; Hi Hnr Roll; Hnr Roll; MVP; Sci Fairs; St of Mnth; Comm Volntr; Chrch Yth Grp; FCA; Ch Chr; Bskball (J); Sftball (V L); Stu Cncl (R); CR (R); Architecture; Art / Math; U of North Carolina; Appalachian State U

Mc Cann, Caitlin
Page HS
Greensboro, NC

Mc Beath, Nathaniel L
West Mecklenburg HS
Charlotte, NC

Mayes, Kendrick T
E E Smith SR HS
Fayetteville, NC

Matthews, Ashley
East Wake HS
Wendell, NC

Mauldin, Wesley S
South Stanly HS
Norwood, NC

Mc Call, Prestigious B U
West Mecklenburg HS
Charlotte, NC

Mc Cray, Kendera
Mt Tabor HS
Winston-Salem, NC

MC GILL, CURTIS D; LINCOLNTON, NC; LINCOLNTON HS; (FR); Hi Hnr Roll; Hnr Roll; Perf Att; Chrch Yth Grp; Scouts; Ch Chr; Bskball (J); Ftball (J); Track (J); Wt Lftg (J); Sports Medicine; Western Carolina U; Eastern Carolina U

MC GRUDER, PRATEA L; PINEVILLE, NC; E E WADDELL HS; (SO); Hnr Roll; Comm Volntr; ROTC; Chr; Orch; Educational Talent Search Member; Tri-M-Honor Society; Pre-Veterinary Medicine; Psychology; North Carolina State U; Virginia Commonwealth U

MC HONE, BRITTANY R; ARARAT, NC; SURRY CTRL HS; (SR); Hnr Roll; Perf Att; St of Mnth; WWAHSS; Comm Volntr; Peer Tut/Med; Red Cr Aide; Chrch Yth Grp; DARE; Prom Com; Ch Chr; Dnce; SP/M/VS; Sftball; Stu Cncl (R); Nursing; Psychology; Surry Community; Meredith College

MC ILWAIN, REGINALD M; DURHAM, NC; MT ZION CHRISTIAN AC; (SO); Hi Hnr Roll; Chess; SP/M/VS; Bskball (V C); Cr Ctry (V); Track (V)

MC KEE, CHRISTOPHER; BREVARD, NC; BREVARD HS; (SO); Hnr Roll; WWAHSS; ArtClub; Chrch Yth Grp; Drma Clb; SP/M/VS; Sccr; Tennis; Teach Soccer to Kids in Comm Soccer Camp; Referee in Youth Soccer League

MC KEE, THOMAS; BREVARD, NC; BREVARD HS; (SO); Hnr Roll; WWAHSS; ArtClub; Chrch Yth Grp; Drma Clb; SP/M/VS; Sccr; Teach Soccer to Kids in Comm Soccer Camp; Referee in Youth Soccer League

MC KENZIE, ANIECE L; ROCKY POINT, NC; HEIDE TRASK HS; (JR); 4H Awd; Hnr Roll; WWAHSS; Chrch Yth Grp; Drma Clb; FCA; ROTC; Ch Chr; Bskball (V L); Cr Ctry (V); Wt Lftg; People to People Sports Ambassador; Business Mgt.; Medicine; North Carolina State U; Duke U

MC KINNON, TANGELA; TABOR CITY, NC; SOUTH COLUMBUS HS; (SR); Hnr Roll; Hosp Aide; Red Cr Aide; Spec Olymp Vol; ROTC; Bnd; Chr; Dnce; Track (V); Sch Ppr (E); Computer Programmer; Cosmetology; Southeastern Community College

MC KNIGHT, RYAN; GREENVILLE, NC; D H CONLEY HS; (SO); Hnr Roll; Comm Volntr; Peer Tut/Med; FBLA; Ntl Beta Clb; Svce Clb; Cr Ctry (V); Track (V); Rookie of the Year Cross Country (Freshman); Future Business Leaders of America Parliamentarian; Film Directing; U of Southern California; Florida State U

MC KNIGHT, SYRENTHIA; SPRING LAKE, NC; PINE FOREST HS; (SO); Hnr Roll; Perf Att; Pep Squd; Psychology; Lawyer; Fayetteville State U; Duke U

MC KOY, JANQUETTEE; LUMBERTON, NC; LUMBERTON HS; (JR); Hnr Roll; Otst Ac Ach Awd; Perf Att; WWAHSS; ROTC; Drl Tm; Cheerleading - Middle School; Basketball - Middle School; Cosmetology; Air Force; Fayetteville State U; Pembroke U

MC LAMB, AMBER M; FAYETTEVILLE, NC; REID ROSS YR ROUND CLASSICAL SCH; (SO); Hnr Roll; Comm Volntr; Peer Tut/Med; ArtClub; Key Club; Lib Aide; Ntl Beta Clb; Ntl FFA; French Clb; Sftball (J); Vllyball (J); Future Farmers of America; Criminal Psychology; Criminal Justice; U of NC At Chapel-Hill; NC State

MC LAMB, TAYLOR P; FAYETTEVILLE, NC; PINE FOREST HS; (MS); Ctznshp Aw; DAR; Hnr Roll; MVP; Nat Hon Sy; Otst Ac Ach Awd; Perf Att; Hosp Aide; Chrch Yth Grp; Ntl Beta Clb; Scouts; Bnd; Ch Chr; Jzz Bnd; Orch; Sftball; Track; Civic Oration Winner 1st Place; Civic Oration; Business Major; Major in Music; East Carolina U; North Carolina State U

MC LAURIN, ALEXANDRIA S; FAYETTEVILLE, NC; E E SMITH SR HS; (FR); Hnr Roll; Sci Fairs; Yth Ldrshp Prog; Comm Volntr; Peer Tut/Med; Chrch Yth Grp; NtlFrnscLg; Ch Chr; Stu Cncl (P); Class Rank #20/350; Doctor of Forensic Science; U of North Carolina at Chapel Hill; Spelman College

MC LAURIN, JASMINE J; FAYETTEVILLE, NC; TERRY SANFORD HS; (JR); Hnr Roll; WWAHSS; Red Cr Aide; DARE; Emplmnt; Chr; HOSA; Nursing; Criminal Justice; Pembroke State U; Fayetteville State U

MC LEAN, ANNE S; MURFREESBORO, NC; RIDGECROFT SCH; (SR); Gov Hnr Prg; Hi Hnr Roll; MVP; St of Mnth; Comm Volntr; Hab For Humty Volntr; Spec Olymp Vol; Chrch Yth Grp; Emplmnt; Key Club; Lttrmn Clb; Ntl Beta Clb; Sci Clb; SADD; Spanish Clb; Bnd; Chrldg (V C); Sccr (V C); Tennis (V); Cl Off (S); Stu Cncl (R); All Conference - Varsity Cheerleading; Pre-Med Major; North Carolina State U

MC LEOD, HANNAH; WAKE FOREST, NC; WAKEFIELD HS; (JR); Duke TS; F Lan Hn Soc; Hi Hnr Roll; Hnr Roll; Nat Hon Sy; Comm Volntr; Peer Tut/Med; Chrch Yth Grp; FCCLA; Key Club; Pep Squd; Prom Com; Clb; Ch Chr; Orch; PP Ftbl; Swmg (V); Stu Cncl; International Politics; Wake Forest U; UNC Chapel Hill

MC LINKO, KRISTEN E; WAXHAW, NC; WEDDINGTON HS; (FR); Hi Hnr Roll; Jr Rot; Otst Ac Ach Awd; Comm Volntr; Ntl Beta Clb; Vsity Clb; Spanish Clb; Orch; SP/M/VS; Tennis (V L); Yrbk (P); Charlotte Jr. Youth Symphony; 2nd Highest Grade GPA Out of 476 9th Grade; Pediatrician or Ophthalmologist; Architect; U of North Carolina At Chapel Hill

MC MANUS, PATRICK M; LENOIR, NC; WEST CALDWELL HS; (JR); Duke TS; Hnr Roll; Otst Ac Ach Awd; Peer Tut/Med; Bnd; Bsball (J); Skiing; Sccr (VJ L); Placed 5th State Drafting Camp; 8th Grade State Test-Perfect Score 100%; Engineering; N.C. State-North Carolina State

MC MILLAN, LETORIA; LUMBERTON, NC; LUMBERTON HS; (FR); Hnr Roll; Kwnis Aw; Comm Volntr; Chrch Yth Grp; ROTC; Ch Chr; Scr Kpr (J); Vllyball (J); Criminal Justice; Cosmetology; NC State U; U of NC Charlotte

MC MILLAN, TASHA N; SAINT PAULS, NC; SAINT PAUL'S HS; (JR); Ctznshp Aw; Hnr Roll; WWAHSS; Comm Volntr; Peer Tut/Med; Emplmnt; Bnd; Mch Bnd; Business Management; Early Childhood Development; U of North Carolina-Chapel Hill; U of North Carolina-Asheville

MC MILLIAN, YOLANDA; FAYETTEVILLE, NC; CARE FEAR HS; (JR); Hnr Roll; Perf Att; WWAHSS; Comm Volntr; Dbte Team; NtlFrnscLg; Spch Team; Bskball (J); Law; Psychology; Howard U; U of North Carolina Chapel Hill

MC MORRIS JR, MICHAEL; KNIGHTDALE, NC; EAST WAKE HS; (SR); Hi Hnr Roll; Nat Hon Sy; Peer Tut/Med; Spec Olymp Vol; Emplmnt; Ntl Beta Clb; Photog; Prom Com; Wt Lftg (C); Cl Off (V); Yrbk (R, P); Principal's List Award; Physical Therapist/Sports Med; U of North Carolina Greensboro; East Carolina U

MC MULLAN, EMILY; LEWISVILLE, NC; WEST FORSYTH HS; (SO); F Lan Hn Soc; Hi Hnr Roll; Hnr Roll; Nat Hon Sy; Sci Fairs; DARE; Svce Clb; Dnce; Lcrsse (J); Drama Theater; Cosmetology/Fashion Design; U of Southern California; U of Nevada, Las Vegas

MC NAIR, KIMBERLY C; WHITAKERS, NC; NORTHERN NASH HS; (SO); Hi Hnr Roll; Hnr Roll; WWAHSS; Chrch Yth Grp; Voc Ind Clb Am; Ch Chr; Architecture; North Carolina State U; North Carolina A & T State U

MC NEAL, CHERITA R; HUNTERSVILLE, NC; NORTH MECKLENBURG SR HS; (JR); Hnr Roll; WWAHSS; Comm Volntr; Peer Tut/Med; ArtClub; Chrch Yth Grp; Dbte Team; Key Club; P to P St Amb Prg; Photog; Prom Com; Scouts; Dnce; Track; Stu Cncl; Psychology; Counseling; Eastern Carolina U; Howard U

MC NEILL, DEMARIOUS; LUMBER BRIDGE, NC; HOKE CTY HS; (JR); Hnr Roll; Perf Att; WWAHSS; Yth Ldrshp Prog; Comm Volntr; Chrch Yth Grp; ROTC; Scouts; Bskball (V); National Youth Leadership Forum; Medical; ROTC

MC NEILL, JAMES E; LAURINBURG, NC; SCOTLAND HS; (FR); Hi Hnr Roll; Hnr Roll; MVP; Perf Att; St of Mnth; Comm Volntr; ROTC; Tech Clb; Bnd; Clr Grd; Drl Tm; Ftball (C)

MC PHATTER, BRYAN A; LUMBERTON, NC; LUMBERTON HS; (FR); Hnr Roll; St of Mnth; Yth Ldrshp Prog; Comm Volntr; Hab For Humty Volntr; Ntl Beta Clb; NYLC; Superintendent's Award; Master's Degree / Math & Science; Medicine Degree; Duke U; U of North Carolina

MC QUEEN, LATOYA M; MAXTON, NC; PURNELL SWETT HS; (FR); Ctznshp Aw; Fut Prb Slvr; Hnr Roll; Nat Ldrshp Svc; Otst Ac Ach Awd; Perf Att; Sci Fairs; St of Mnth; St Optmst of Yr; Yth Ldrshp Prog; CARE; Comm Volntr; Peer Tut/Med; Chrch Yth Grp; Cmptr Clb; DARE; Mus Clb; Prom Com; Quiz Bowl; Scouts; Tmpl Yth Grp; Bnd; Chr; Ch Chr; Mch Bnd; Stu Cncl (P); Sch Ppr (R); Most Likely to Succeed; Mid-Wife; East Carolina U; Harvard U

MC TURNER, TAIRA D; SHALLOTTE, NC; WEST BRUNSWICK HS; (SO); Hnr Roll; Comm Volntr; Red Cr Aide; Emplmnt; Orch; Sccr (J); Member of HOSA; Completion of Barbizon Modeling School; Pre-Med; Pennsylvania State U; U of Pennsylvania

MC WILLIAMS, JEREMY; MOORESVILLE, NC; LAKE NORMAN HS; (JR); Duke TS; Hnr Roll; Emplmnt; FBLA; Travel Roller Hockey MVP

MEADOR, LOREN T; MORAVIAN FS, NC; WILKES CTRL HS; (JR); Hnr Roll; Sci Fairs; Comm Volntr; Ftball (V L); Track (V L); Stu Cncl (R); CR (R); Pre-Med; Sports Medicine; U of North Carolina Chapel Hill; High Point U

MEADOWS, AMBER N; RALEIGH, NC; WAKEFIELD; (SO); Hi Hnr Roll; Hnr Roll; Comm Volntr; Chrch Yth Grp; Emplmnt; Tchrs Aide; Track (J)

MEBANE, TABRIKA; WILLIAMSTON, NC; WILLIAMSTON HS; (FR); Hi Hnr Roll; Hnr Roll; Perf Att; Comm Volntr; DARE; Ntl Beta Clb; SADD; Interior Design; Hilton Community College; Edgecombe Community College; Edgecombe Community College

MEDRANO, ANA L; BELHAVEN, NC; NORTHSIDE HS; (SO); Hnr Roll; Nat Hon Sy; Otst Ac Ach Awd; Perf Att; Sci/Math Olympn; WWAHSS; Hosp Aide; Chrch Yth Grp; DARE; Key Club; Lib Aide; Ntl Beta Clb; Ch Chr; Sccr (J); Stu Cncl (R); Sch Ppr (R, P); Library Club, FCCLA, Key Club, SGA & Beta Club; Forensic Science; Lawyer

MEEHAN, CHRISTINE; RALEIGH, NC; LEESVILLE ROAD HS; (FR); Hnr Roll; Comm Volntr; Chrch Yth Grp; Drma Clb; Dnce; SP/M/VS; Stg Cre; Stu Cncl (R); TV Communications; News Reporter; New York U; Long Island U: CW Post Campus

MEEKS, DAPHNE C; EDEN, NC; MOREHEAD HS; (JR); Duke TS; Hi Hnr Roll; Jr Mshl; Nat Hon Sy; WWAHSS; Chrch Yth Grp; DECA; Emplmnt; Scr Kpr (V L); Pre-Med; Medicine; U of North Carolina Chapel Hill; Duke U

MEHDI, MONA; CHARLOTTE, NC; HARDING HS; (JR); Hnr Roll; Perf Att; WWAHSS; Pep Squd; Tchrs Aide; Sccr (V); International Club; Earth and Environmental Club; Cosmetology; Fine Arts; Chaminade U of Honolulu; Central Piedmont Community College

MEJIA, ALEJANDRA; THOMASVILLE, NC; THOMASVILLE HS; (FR); Perf Att; SP/M/VS; Marines (Pilot); High Point U

MELTON, BRODRIC S L; FOUNTAIN, NC; FARMVILLE CTRL HS; (SO); Hnr Roll; Ftball (VJ); U of North Carolina; East Carolina U

MELVIN, ASHLEY D; WALNUT COVE, NC; INTRINSIC REVELATION SCH; (JR); Ctznshp Aw; Hi Hnr Roll; MVP; Perf Att; St of Mnth; Comm Volntr; Peer Tut/Med; Chrch Yth Grp; Emplmnt; Tchrs Aide; Mar Art (J); Scr Kpr (L); Sccr (C); Volunteer At Urban Ministry; EMS; Crime Scene Investigator; Forsyth Tech Community College; Greensboro College

MENDEZ, ANTONIO; FAYETTEVILLE, NC; REID ROSS YR ROUND CLASSICAL; (FR); Duke TS; Otst Ac Ach Awd; Perf Att; Comm Volntr; Chrch Yth Grp; Ch Chr; Pre-Med; Biotechnology; U of North Carolina; Duke U

MENDEZ, MARIA L; SNOW HILL, NC; GREENE CTRL HS; (FR); Ctznshp Aw; Hnr Roll; MD-Medical Doctor; East Carolina U

MENDOZA, BARBARA; WAXHAW, NC; SUN VALLEY MS; (MS); Hnr Roll; Kwnis Aw; Perf Att; Comm Volntr; Pep Squd; Chr; Dnce; Vllyball (C); Angels in Action Club; Day Care Volunteer; Teaching Degree; Entertainment Degree; Columbia U; Duke U

MENDOZA, JESTHER S D V; WINDSOR, NC; BERTIE HS; (JR); Hnr Roll; Otst Ac Ach Awd; Comm Volntr; Peer Tut/Med; Chess; Chrch Yth Grp; Quiz Bowl; Scouts; Ch Chr; SP/M/VS; Swmg; Tennis; Track (V); Cl Off; Computer Engineering; NC State U; Frostburg State U

MENIUS, MARIANNE; ASHEBORO, NC; ASHEBORO HS; (JR); Hi Hnr Roll; Nat Hon Sy; WWAHSS; Hosp Aide; Peer Tut/Med; Chrch Yth Grp; Dbte Team; Emplmnt; Key Club; Scouts; Vsity Clb; Track (V); Vllyball (V); Sch Ppr (R); Serve On Youth Council At Church; Pharmacy; International Studies; Wake Forest U; Georgetown U

MERCER, JOLEE; ABERDEEN, NC; PINECREST HS; (SR); Hnr Roll; Comm Volntr; Tchrs Aide; Massage Therapy; Sandhills Community College

MERCER, MICHAEL; WILSON, NC; FIKE HS; (FR); Hi Hnr Roll; Hnr Roll; Biology Clb; Bnd; Mch Bnd; Ftball (J); Track; Track; Football; ECU; A & T, Carolina

MERCER-PICKENS, BRITTNEY; ROCKY MOUNT, NC; ROCKY MOUNT SR HS; (JR); Ctznshp Aw; Hnr Roll; Sci Fairs; St of Mnth; WWAHSS; Comm Volntr; Chrch Yth Grp; Jr Ach; Photog; Ch Chr; Dnce; SP/M/VS; Bskball (VJ); Medical; Education; Spelman College; U of California Riverside

MEREDITH, MORGAN K; KERNERSVILLE, NC; EAST FORSYTH HS; (SO); Duke TS; Hnr Roll; Nat Hon Sy; Sci Fairs; St of Mnth; WWAHSS; Comm Volntr; Peer Tut/Med; Spec Olymp Vol; Chrch Yth Grp; Emplmnt; FCCLA; Key Club; Svce Clb; Spanish Clb; Vllyball (J); Sec of Key Club; Textiles; Fashion Design; Appalachian State U

MESSER, NATHAN D; MARS HILL, NC; MADISON HS; (SO); Hnr Roll; Chrch Yth Grp; DARE; Ntl FFA; Bsball (JC); Wild Life Resource Officer; Walters State Tennessee

METCALF, BRITTANY; LEXINGTON, NC; LEXINGTON SR HS; (FR); 4H Awd; 4-H; Chrch Yth Grp; Clr Grd; Wt Lftg (J); Lawyer; U North Carolina

METCALF, CHRISTINA; CHARLOTTE, NC; CHARLOTTE CHRISTIAN SCH; (JR); MVP; Comm Volntr; Chrch Yth Grp; Emplmnt; Stg Cre; Chrldg (JCL); Cr Ctry (V L); Cr Ct Ski; Scr Kpr (V); Track (VJ L); Interior Design; U of North Carolina Greensboro; North Carolina State U

MIANO, MARISSA; RALEIGH, NC; WAKEFIELD HS; (JR); Ctznshp Aw; Duke TS; F Lan Hn Soc; Hi Hnr Roll; Jr Mshl; Nat Hon Sy; St of Mnth; USAA; WWAHSS; Comm Volntr; Emplmnt; Key Club; Prom Com; Dnce; SP/M/VS; Stu Cncl (P, V, R); Clothing Design; North Carolina State U; U of North Carolina Chapel Hill

MIDDLETON, CHESNA A; CHARLOTTE, NC; HARDING UNIVERSITY HS; (SR); Hnr Roll; DARE; Jr Ach; Pep Squd; ROTC; JROTC Drill Team / Art; SAVE Club / Pep Club / SADD Club; Fashion Designer; Bauder College; American InterContinental U

MIDKIFF, DANIEL C; ARARAT, NC; CARROLL CTY HS; (SR); 4H Awd; Ctznshp Aw; Hi Hnr Roll; Hnr Roll; Perf Att; St of Mnth; Peer Tut/Med; Red Cr Aide; 4-H; ArtClub; Chrch Yth Grp; DARE; Emplmnt; Photog; Scouts; Bnd; Bskball; Ftball; Sccr; Duke U; Wake Forest U

Mercer-Pickens, Brittney
Rocky Mount SR HS
Rocky Mount, NC

Meehan, Christine
Leesville Road HS
Raleigh, NC

Meadows, Amber N
Wakefield
Raleigh, NC

Mc Nair, Kimberly C
Northern Nash HS
Whitakers, NC

Mc Turner, Taira D
West Brunswick HS
Shallotte, NC

Mendoza, Jesther S D V
Bertie HS
Windsor, NC

Messer, Nathan D
Madison HS
Mars Hill, NC

MILAZZO, STEPHANIE; RALEIGH, NC; FRANKLIN AC; (JR); Hnr Roll; Comm Volntr; Peer Tut/Med; Dnce; Sch Ppr (R, P); Yrbk (R, P); Dental Hygienist

MILES, JENNIFER M; HICKORY, NC; ST STEPHEN'S HS; (SR); Hi Hnr Roll; Hnr Roll; Jr Mshl; Sci Fairs; St of Mnth; WWAHSS; Comm Volntr; Hab For Humty Volntr; Peer Tut/Med; 4-H; Ntl Beta Clb; Scouts; Svce Clb; Bnd; Clr Grd; Drm Mjr; Beta Club; Math, Pre-Med; Lenoir-Rhyne College

MILLARD, DREW; COLUMBUS, NC; POLK CTY HS; (SO); Duke TS; Hnr Roll; Comm Volntr; HO'Br Yth Ldrshp; Key Club; Golf (V L); Sccr (V L); Cl Off (P, T); Hugh O'Brian Youth Leadership Award; Creative Writing; Journalism; U of North Carolina Chapel Hill; Presbyterian College

MILLER, ANGELA M; FOREST CITY, NC; EAST RUTHERFORD HS; (SR); WWAHSS; Comm Volntr; FBLA; FTA; Ntl FFA; Spanish; Business Administration; North Carolina Central U; U of North Carolina Greensboro

MILLER, CHANELLE; CHARLOTTE, NC; HARDING U HS; (FR); Duke TS; Hnr Roll; Nat Sci Aw; USAA; Chrch Yth Grp; SADD; Mch Bnd; Psychology; Law; Winston-Salem State U; Howard U

MILLER, COURTNEY Y; KENANSVILLE, NC; JAMES KENAN HS; (JR); Hi Hnr Roll; Nat Hon Sy; Chrch Yth Grp; Prom Com; SADD; Ch Chr; Track (V); Vllyball (V); Biology; Chemistry; U of North Carolina Chapel Hill; East Carolina U

MILLER, ELIZABETH R; RUFFIN, NC; CLOVER GARDEN SCH; (SO); Ctznshp Aw; Hi Hnr Roll; Hnr Roll; Kwnis Aw; Comm Volntr; Peer Tut/Med; Drma Clb; Ntl Beta Clb; Off Aide; Scouts; Tchrs Aide; SP/M/VS; Stg Cre; Stu Cncl (T); CR (R); Yrbk (P); Political Campaign Volunteer; Education; Mathematics; Liberty U; U of North Carolina Greensboro

MILLER, JASMINE D; GOLDSBORO, NC; GOLDSBORO HS; (SO); Hnr Roll; ArtClub; Drma Clb; SP/M/VS; Stg Cre; Wt Lftg (J); Theatre Arts; Dance; A & T State U; Winston-Salem State U

MILLER, JEFFREY A; RALEIGH, NC; MILLBROOK HS; (JR); Duke TS; Hi Hnr Roll; Hnr Roll; WWAHSS; Comm Volntr; Spec Olymp Vol; Chrch Yth Grp; FCA; Key Club; Stu Cncl (R); CR (R); Children of the American Revolution Society- 2004-2005 VP; 10th Grade Council Parliamentarian / 11th Grade-Historian; US History; US Government; U of North Carolina Chapel Hill; Elon U

MILLER, JENNIFER; WINSTON-SALEM, NC; MT TABOR HS; (JR); Hnr Roll; Nat Hon Sy; ArtClub; Chrch Yth Grp; Svce Clb; Latin Clb; Art Awards; Physical Therapy; Respiratory Therapy; U of North Carolina Wilmington; East Carolina U

MILLER, JESSICA M; MOORESVILLE, NC; LAKE NORMAN HS; (SR); Hi Hnr Roll; Hnr Roll; WWAHSS; Comm Volntr; Peer Tut/Med; FCA; FBLA; Key Club; Ntl Beta Clb; Latin Clb; Chrldg (V CL); Sccr (J); Tennis (VJCL); Biomedical Engineer; North Carolina State U

MILLER, JOSEPH; RALEIGH, NC; WAKEFIELD HS; (JR); Hnr Roll; Pres Ac Ftns Aw; WWAHSS; Yth Ldrshp Prog; Comm Volntr; Peer Tut/Med; Chrch Yth Grp; DARE; Emplmnt; Bnd; Drm Mjr; Jzz Bnd; Mch Bnd; Kappa Alpha Psi Scholar; Inducted Into the National Achievers Society; Video Production and Design; Digital Artist; U of North Carolina Chapel Hill; Massachusetts Institute of Technology

MILLER, JOSEPH; ROCKWELL, NC; EAST ROWAN HS; (JR); Hi Hnr Roll; Hnr Roll; Jr Mshl; Nat Hon Sy; Pres Ac Ftns Aw; Chrch Yth Grp; DARE; Emplmnt; ROTC; SADD; Bnd; Mch Bnd; Engineering; North Carolina State U

MILLER, JOSHUA A; BREVARD, NC; BREVARD HS; (FR); Ctznshp Aw; Hi Hnr Roll; Hnr Sy; Chrch Yth Grp; DARE; Emplmnt; FCA; Mth Clb/Tm; Chr; Ftball (J); Track (J); Church League Softball; Church Band; Culinary Arts; Johnson and Wales U

MILLER, JOSHUA T; LAUREL SPRINGS, NC; ALLEGHANY HS; (FR); Hnr Roll; MVP; Nat Hon Sy; Pres Ac Ftns Aw; Chrch Yth Grp; Emplmnt; FCA; Scouts; Ch Chr; Bsball (J); Ftball (JC); Wrstlg (V); Adv Cncl (R); Cl Off (T); Stu Cncl (R); Overall Male Coaches Award; Young Flyer Award - Chuck Yeager; BS in Physical Education / Health; North Carolina State U; Lenoir Rhyne U

MILLER, LINDSAY M; CHARLOTTE, NC; (MS); Duke TS; Nat Hon Sy; Pres Ac Ftns Aw; Peer Tut/Med; Chrch Yth Grp; Key Club; Track (J); Vllyball (J); Peer Counselor; Sportsmanship Award; Business Degree; Duke U

MILLER, LOGAN A; PITTSBORO, NC; NORTHWOOD HS; (SR); Hi Hnr Roll; Hnr Roll; Nat Hon Sy; Perf Att; Peer Tut/Med; Emplmnt; Bnd; Mch Bnd; Sccr; History Club; Math-Computers; Engineering; East Carolina U; North Carolina State U

MILLER, MICHAEL C; TRINITY, NC; ARCHDALE TRINITY MS; (MS); Hnr Roll; DARE; Emplmnt; ROTC; Scouts; Swg Chr; Bskball (V); Ftball (V); Skiing (L); Wrstlg (V); Yrbk (R, P); Engineering; UNCG; Chapel Hill

MILLER, MORGAN K; HIGH POINT, NC; HIGH POINT CTRL HS; (FR); Hnr Roll; Hab For Humty Volntr; Chrch Yth Grp; FCA; Key Club; Lttrmn Clb; Mth Clb/Tm; Ntl Beta Clb; Spanish Clb; Bskball (V); Tennis (V); Adv Cncl (R)

MILLER, RACHEL; ROCKWELL, NC; EAST ROWAN HS; (JR); Hi Hnr Roll; Hnr Roll; Jr Mshl; Nat Hon Sy; Nat Mrt LOC; Chrch Yth Grp; DARE; Acpl Chr; Chrldg (V L); Gmnstcs; Stu Cncl (R); UNC-Chapel Hill-Healthcare; Radiologist; U of North Carolina At Chapel Hill

MILLIKAN, KENDYL; ASHEBORO, NC; ASHEBORO HS; (JR); Duke TS; Hnr Roll; Comm Volntr; Chrch Yth Grp; FCA; Svce Clb; Acpl Chr; Chr; Ch Chr; Chrldg (J); Tennis (J); Sch Ppr (R); NG Governors School West for Choral Music; Music Therapy; Ministry; App State U; Salem College

MILLS, ALYSSA A; OXFORD, NC; JFK WEBB HS; (SO); Hnr Roll; Perf Att; Sci Fairs; St of Mnth; DARE; Ntl FFA; Clb; Zoology; Pre-Veterinary Studies; Montana State Missoula; Weber State U

MILLS, ASHLEY; RALEIGH, NC; WAKEHELD HS; (JR); Hi Hnr Roll; Hnr Roll; Nat Mrt LOC; Peer Tut/Med; Chrch Yth Grp; Ch Chr; Dnce; Bskball (J); Kappa Alpha Scholar; National Achievers Society; Career in Performing Arts; Duke U; U of North Carolina-Chapel Hill

MILLSAPS, BRETT X; HICKORY, NC; BUNKER HILL HS; (JR); Hnr Roll; MVP; Otst Ac Ach Awd; Perf Att; Pres Ac Ftns Aw; WWAHSS; Comm Volntr; Emplmnt; Lttrmn Clb; Ntl Beta Clb; Pep Squd; Bskball (JC); Ftball (V L); Selected to Attend Global Young Leadership Conference; Foreign Language; Education; U of North Carolina Chapel Hill; Western Carolina U

MILTON, JARID D H; CHARLOTTE, NC; PHILLIP O BERRY AC OF TECH; (SO); Ch Chr; Clr Grd; Drl Tm; Track (J); CR (V); Excellence in Youth Award-Delta Sigma Theta; Veteran's Outreach to Youth Assoc.-Conduct Award; Network Administration; Architecture; U of North Carolina At Chapel Hill; Virginia Military Institute

MITCHELL, DEVON; DURHAM, NC; C E JORDAN HS; (SO); Hnr Roll; Perf Att; Chrch Yth Grp; FBLA; Ch Chr; Accounting; Math Education; U of North Carolina Chapel Hill; Duke U

MITCHELL, JOEY R; SELMA, NC; NORTH JOHNSTON HS; (SR); DECA; Emplmnt; Ntl FFA; Boy Scout Eagle, Teacher's Assistant; Star Greenhand (FFA); Heavy Equipment Operator; Wetlands Expert; Wilson Community College; NC State U

MITCHELL, ROBERT G; HIGH POINT, NC; BISHOP MC GUINNESS CATHOLIC HS; (JR); Duke TS; Hi Hnr Roll; Hnr Roll; WWAHSS; Spec Olymp Vol; Bskball (J); Ftball (VJ); Golf (V); Lcrsse (V); Coaches' Award-JV Basketball

MITCHELL, SONJA T; CHARLOTTE, NC; HARDING U HS; (SO); Hnr Roll; Nat Hon Sy; WWAHSS; Comm Volntr; Peer Tut/Med; ArtClub; Chrch Yth Grp; Drma Clb; Jr Ach; Photog; Tchrs Aide; Bnd; Chr; Orch; Educational Talent Search; National Society of High School Scholars; Medical Field, Bachelor's Degree, Master's Degree, Family Therapist; Princeton U, Harvard U, Howard U, U of NC @ Chapel Hill

MITCHELL, WHITNEY K; EDEN, NC; MOREHEAD HS; (SO); Hnr Roll; Perf Att; Bskball (V); Nursing; North Carolina; Wake Forest U

MIYAZAKI, GOTA; HICKORY, NC; ST STEPHENS HS; (SO); MVP; Comm Volntr; Hab For Humty Volntr; Swmg (V); Art Contest Winner; Art; Architectural Design; North Carolina State

MLO, YZANG; GREENSBORO, NC; SMITH HS; (SO); Hnr Roll; Otst Ac Ach Awd; Perf Att; DARE; Art; Engineer; Comedian; Harvard U; Duke U

MOBOLADE, OLUREMI; CHARLOTTE, NC; CHARLOTTE CHRISTIAN SCH; (JR); F Lan Hn Soc; Hi Hnr Roll; Hnr Roll; MVP; Perf Att; Chrch Yth Grp; Dbte Team; Emplmnt; Spch Team; Bnd; Ch Chr; Jzz Bnd; Bskball (J); Track (V); Vllyball (V); Northeastern U; U of North Carolina Chapel Hill

MONTEITH, BROOKE; RUTHERFORDTON, NC; RUTHERFORDTON SPINDALE MS; MS; Hnr Roll; St of Mnth; Comm Volntr; Hosp Aide; Chrch Yth Grp; DARE; FCA; Ntl Beta Clb; Chr; Ch Chr; Stu Cncl (R); CR (R); Yrbk (E); Social Worker for the Department of Social Services; Ob/Gyn - Obstetrician; University of North Carolina Chapel Hill; University of North Carolina Asheville

MONTES, HECTOR; SILER CITY, NC; JORDAN MATTHEWS HS; (FR); Hnr Roll; Chrch Yth Grp; Ntl Beta Clb; Sccr (V); Bachelor's Degree; Master's Degree; U of North Carolina At Chapel Hill; UNC At Greensboro

MONTGOMERY, AMBER; ANGIER, NC; HILLTOP CHRISTIAN SCH; (FR); Hnr Roll; Chrch Yth Grp; Quiz Bowl; Chr; Chrldg; CR (R); Yrbk (P); Foreign Missions; Teaching; Free Will Baptist Bible Concert

MOODY, DARRELL; GARYSBURG, NC; NORTHAMPTON CTY-WEST HS; (FR); Hi Hnr Roll; Perf Att; Mch Bnd; Bskball (J); Computer Engineering; Business; U of North Carolina-Chapel Hill; Wake Forest U

MOODY, STEVEN; MORGANTON, NC; CORNERSTONE CLASSICAL AC; (JR); Hnr Roll; MVP; Perf Att; Pres Ac Ftns Aw; Comm Volntr; Red Cr Aide; Chrch Yth Grp; Emplmnt; Quiz Bowl; Tchrs Aide; Stg Cre; Sccr (VJ); Political Science; Law; U of North Carolina Chapel Hill

MOONEYHAN, SAMUEL O; CHARLOTTE, NC; INDEPENDENCE HS; (JR); Hi Hnr Roll; Nat Hon Sy; Peer Tut/Med; Chess; ROTC; Tech Clb; Clr Grd; Drl Tm; SP/M/VS; Physiotherapy; Chiropractic; U of North Carolina Charlotte; U of North Carolina State

MOORE, ALYSSA H; WAKE FOREST, NC; WAKE FOREST-ROLESVILLE HS; (JR); Duke TS; Hi Hnr Roll; MVP; Nat Hon Sy; Comm Volntr; Hab For Humty Volntr; ArtClub; Chrch Yth Grp; FCA; Ntl Beta Clb; Ntl FFA; Sci Clb; Spanish Clb; Ch Chr; PP Ftbl (V); Tennis (V); Vllyball (J); New Hope Presbytery Youth Council Member; Attendee of Summer Ventures in Science & Math; Environmental Science (BS & MS); Furman U; Duke U

MOORE, ASHLEY T; GREENSBORO, NC; DUDLEY SR HS; (SO); Hnr Roll; Comm Volntr; Nurse Practitioner; Registered Nurse; U of North Carolina @ Greensboro

MOORE, CHARMETRA; CLAREMONT, NC; BUNKER HILL HS; (JR); Hnr Roll; Perf Att; St of Mnth; DARE; FCCLA; Lib Aide; Miss FCCLA; FCCLA Club; Graphic Design; Art; Art Institute of Charlotte; U of Pennsylvania

MOORE, EBONEE A; FAYETTEVILLE, NC; WESTOVER HS; (FR); Hnr Roll; Perf Att; Off Aide; Tchrs Aide; PP Ftbl (VJ); Scr Kpr (VJ); Sftball (VJ); Vllyball (J); CR (P); Computer Technology; Georgetown U; U of North Carolina At Chapel Hill

MOORE, HOLLY; CLIFFSIDE, NC; CHASE HS; (MS); Hnr Roll; Perf Att; WWAHSS; Hosp Aide; 4-H; Chrch Yth Grp; DARE; FCA; FBLA; Scouts; Bnd; Jzz Bnd; Mch Bnd; Bskball (J); Cr Ctry (J); Sccr (J); Sftball (J); Tennis (J); Vllyball (J); Band Director; Doctor; U of North Carolina

MOORE, KATHRYN M; FUQUAY VARINA, NC; FAITH ASSEMBLY CHRISTIAN AC; (JR); Hnr Roll; Otst Ac Ach Awd; Perf Att; Sci Fairs; St Optmst of Yr; Comm Volntr; Chrch Yth Grp; Off Aide; Tchrs Aide; Ch Chr; Dnce; Drl Tm; Stg Cre; Most Valuable Dancer; Pre-Law; Performing Arts (Dance); Harvard U; Oral Roberts U

MOORE, KEARA R; AHOSKIE, NC; HERTFORD CTY HS; (SO); Hi Hnr Roll; Hnr Roll; Perf Att; Sci Fairs; St of Mnth; Yth Ldrshp Prog; Comm Volntr; Peer Tut/Med; Spec Olymp Vol; Chrch Yth Grp; Lib Aide; Mth Clb/Tm; Ntl Beta Clb; ROTC; Svce Clb; SADD; Spanish Clb; Ch Chr; Clr Grd; Drl Tm; Scr Kpr (VJ); CR (R); Top 10 of My Class-#7 Out of 300; NC-MSEN Participant; Forensic Science; U of North Carolina At Chapel Hill; Duke U

MOORE, KERI B; KINGS MOUNTAIN, NC; (FR); Hnr Roll; Nat Hon Sy; Chrch Yth Grp; Ntl Beta Clb; Ch Chr; Sftball (V); Vllyball (V); Cl Off (R); CR (R); Homecoming Class Rep

MOORE, LAUREN M; HOOKERTON, NC; MT CALVARY CHRISTIAN AC; (FR); Hnr Roll; Chrch Yth Grp; Ch Chr; Bskball (J); Chrldg (J); Sftball (V); Vllyball (V); Cl Off (V); Most Spirited Cheerleader; U North Carolina Chapel Hill; North Carolina State

MOORE, LAUREN R; SALISBURY, NC; SALISBURY HS; (JR); Duke TS; Hi Hnr Roll; Jr Mshl; Nat Hon Sy; WWAHSS; Comm Volntr; Chrch Yth Grp; Key Club; Mth Clb/Tm; Mus Clb; Spanish Clb; Bnd; Ch Chr; Mch Bnd; Woodwind Captain in Marching Band; Pre-Med / Nursing; Music Minor; UNC Chapel Hill; North Carolina State U

MOORE, NATALIE D; MOORESBORO, NC; CREST HS; (SR); Chr; Cr Ctry (V L); Track (V); Regional FFA Vice President; Chapter FFA Secretary; Secondary Education, Agriculture Ed; Minor-Horticulture; Western Carolina U; North Carolina State U

MOORE, NATALIE J; WAXHAW, NC; METROLINA CHRISTIAN AC; (JR); Hi Hnr Roll; Hnr Roll; St of Mnth; Comm Volntr; Chrch Yth Grp; Ntl Beta Clb; NYLC; Prom Com; Quiz Bowl; Tchrs Aide; SP/M/VS; Swg Chr; Bskball (V C); Scr Kpr (V); Sccr (V C); Stu Cncl (R); CR (R); Sch Ppr (R); Christian Character Award; English Literature

MOORE, TIFFANY; STATESVILLE, NC; STATESVILLE HS; (FR); Hnr Roll; Nat Stu Ath Day Aw; Pres Ac Ftns Aw; Comm Volntr; DARE; Mus Clb; ROTC; Chr; Ch Chr; SP/M/VS; Chrldg (J); Scr Kpr (J); Skiing; Sccr (J); Vllyball (J); Stu Cncl (S); Physical Fitness Awards; Singing Awards; Physical Therapy; Singer; Duke U; NC State U, A & T

MOORE, TYSHEENA L; SEDALIA, NC; EASTERN GUILFORD HS; (SR); Hnr Roll; Nat Hon Sy; Comm Volntr; Chrch Yth Grp; DARE; Emplmnt; Dnce; Drl Tm; Chrldg (J); Track; Liberal Arts; Dance; Winston Salem State; William Patterson

MOORE, WILLIAM K; CHARLOTTE, NC; COVENANT DAY SCH; (FR); MVP; Pres Ac Ftns Aw; Comm Volntr; Hab For Humty Volntr; Chrch Yth Grp; Jr Cls League; Svce Clb; Spanish Clb; Bnd; Ch Chr; Stg Cre; Bsball (J); Bskball (J); Cr Ctry (V); Golf (V); Scr Kpr (V); Vsy Clb (V); Stu Cncl (R); CR (P); Most Improved on Cross Country Team; Presidential Physical Fitness; Play College Golf; Business Degree; U of Georgia; U of North Carolina

Moore, Keara R
Hertford Cty HS
Ahoskie, NC

Miyazaki, Gota
St Stephens HS
Hickory, NC

Mitchell, Whitney K
Morehead HS
Eden, NC

Mitchell, Joey R
North Johnston HS
Selma, NC

Mitchell, Sonja T
Harding U HS
Charlotte, NC

Moore, Holly
Chase HS
Cliffside, NC

Moore, Keri B
Kings Mountain, NC

MOOREFIELD, ANA; CHARLOTTE, NC; COVENANT BAY SCH; (JR); Otst Ac Ach Awd; Comm Volntr; Chrch Yth Grp; Jr Ach; Lib Aide; Prom Com; French Clb; Ch Chr; Tennis (VJ); CR (R); Sch Ppr (E); Created the Newspaper Club; President of the French Club; Journalism; English; Elon U; College of Charleston

MOORE III, JAMES E; MOUNT OLIVE, NC; SOUTHERN WAYNE HS; (JR); Hnr Roll; Chrch Yth Grp; DECA; NYLC; Ftball (J); Accounting; International Business; Fayetteville State U; Western Carolina U

MORALES, LUISA F; KINSTON, NC; KINSTON HS; (JR); Sccr (J); Speak Two Languages (English-Spanish); Marine Biology; U of North Carolina Wilmington

MORALES, MARIA R; BURLINGTON, NC; HUGH M CUMMINGS HS; (SO); Ctznshp Aw; Hnr Roll; Perf Att; Pres Ac Ftns Aw; Presidential Award; Business Administrator; Accountant; U of North Carolina/Greensboro; North Carolina U

MORASCO, JESSICA; MOCKSVILLE, NC; DAVIE HS; (JR); Hnr Roll; Perf Att; Pres Ac Ftns Aw; Peer Tut/Med; Red Cr Aide; Chrch Yth Grp; DARE; FCA; FTA; Lib Aide; Pep Squd; Chr; Ch Chr; Dnce; SP/M/VS; Chrldg (V CL); Scr Kpr (J); Regional Cheerleading Champs; State Cheerleading Champs; Nursing; U of North Carolina; Winston Salem State U

MORENO, JULIO; STATESVILLE, NC; STATESVILLE HS; (SO); Sccr

MORGAN, ANTOINE; GREENSBORO, NC; SMITH HS; (SO); Hnr Roll; MVP; Perf Att; St of Mnth; Mth Clb/Tm; Scouts; Ch Chr; Bskball (VJ); Engineering; U of North Carolina; Wake Forest

MORGAN, ASHLEY K; JACKSONVILLE, NC; JACKSONVILLE HS; (SO); Hnr Roll; ArtClub; SADD; Swmg (J); Yrbk (R); Health, Law; Psychologist; UNC Chapel Hill; North Carolina A & T

MORGAN, ERICA; SMITHFIELD, NC; WEST JOHNSTON HS; (JR); Hnr Roll; Nat Hon Sy; Otst Ac Ach Awd; Pres Ac Ftns Aw; Pres Sch; WWAHSS; Hab For Humty Volntr; Red Cr Aide; Chrch Yth Grp; FCA; Lib Aide; Pep Squd; Prom Com; Chr; Dnce; Sccr (V); Vllyball (V); Stu Cncl (R); Church Missions; Employee At Tommy Hilfiger; Nursing; Foreign Language; East Carolina U; U of North Carolina: Wilmington

MORGAN, JOSEY; LINCOLNTON, NC; WEST LINCOLN HS; (FR); Hnr Roll; Otst Ac Ach Awd; St of Mnth; Comm Volntr; Chrch Yth Grp; Scouts; Chr; Reading Counts Award; Interior Design; Photography; The Art Institute of Charlotte; Belmont Abby

MORGAN, MICHAEL; ROCKY MOUNT, NC; TARBORO HS; (JR)

MORGAN, SUNNI; ALBEMARLE, NC; SOUTH STANLY HS; (FR); Hnr Roll; Comm Volntr; Chrch Yth Grp; DARE; FCA; Mus Clb; Quiz Bowl; Chr; Swmg (L); Wt Lftg (J); Dixie Youth Softball (5 Years); Certified As Babysitter; Marine Biologist; Obstetrician; Wilmington; NC State

MORRIS, ANNA C; FUQUAY VARINA, NC; CARY AC; (FR); Hi Hnr Roll; Valdctrian; Peer Tut/Med; Ntl Beta Clb; Svce Clb; Spch Team; PP Ftbl (J); Sccr (V L); Vllyball (J); Cl Off (S, T); Highest Science GPA in 7th & 8th Grade; Superior Rating in YAA for 3 Years; Medicine; Physical Therapist / Athletic Trainer; U of North Carolina Chapel Hill; Duke U

MORRIS, EMILY J; GERMANTON, NC; EAST FORSYTH HS; (SO); Duke TS; Hnr Roll; Nat Hon Sy; Otst Ac Ach Awd; Comm Volntr; Hosp Aide; Chrch Yth Grp; Key Club; Spanish Clb; Bnd; Chemical Engineering; Veterinarian; North Carolina State U; U of North Carolina

MORRIS, JAMES; GREENSBORO, NC; GREENSBORO DAY SCH; (FR); Duke TS; Hi Hnr Roll; MVP; Otst Ac Ach Awd; Chrch Yth Grp; Scouts; Sccr (J); Swmg (L); Order of the Arrow (Boy Scouts); Silver Maxima Cum Laude Award (Nat. Lat. Exam); North Carolina-Chapel Hill; Davidson College

MORRIS, KATHRYN; RUTHERFORDTON, NC; R S CTRL HS; (JR); Duke TS; Hi Hnr Roll; Jr Mshl; Nat Hon Sy; Nat Mrt LOC; Perf Att; Yth Ldrshp Prog; Comm Volntr; Hosp Aide; Peer Tut/Med; Chrch Yth Grp; Ntl Beta Clb; NYLC; Ch Chr; Cr Ctry (V L); Track (V L); Republican Club; Education; Law; UNC Chapel Hill

MORRIS, SHAVELLE; JACKSONVILLE, NC; NORTHSIDE HS; (JR); Hnr Roll; Perf Att; Pres Ac Ftns Aw; Comm Volntr; Hosp Aide; ArtClub; DARE; Emplmnt; FBLA; Bskball (V L); Track (V L); Vllyball (V CL); National Art Honor Society; FBLA; Major in Medicine; Become an Anesthesiologist; South Carolina State (Columbia)

MORRISON, MELISSA; POLKVILLE, NC; BURNS HS; (JR); Duke TS; Hi Hnr Roll; Hnr Roll; Nat Hon Sy; St of Mnth; WWAHSS; Yth Ldrshp Prog; Comm Volntr; Hosp Aide; Chrch Yth Grp; Emplmnt; FCA; Ntl Beta Clb; Scouts; Tmpl Yth Grp; Latin Clb; Medicine; Duke U; Western Carolina

MORROW, BRANDI; ASHEVILLE, NC; ENKA HS; (SO); Duke TS; Nat Hon Sy; Sci/Math Olympn; Yth Ldrshp Prog; Comm Volntr; Peer Tut/Med; Drma Clb; FCCLA; Key Club; Mth Clb/Tm; Ntl Beta Clb; Photog; SADD; Tchrs Aide; SP/M/VS; Stg Cre; Sch Ppr (P); Yrbk (E, P); President of FCCLA; 2nd Place Winner @ FCCLA State Competition; Advertising; Marketing; Campbell; UNC Pembroke

MORSE, BRYAN; TROY, NC; WEST MONTGOMERY HS; (FR); Hnr Roll; Perf Att; St of Mnth; Yth Ldrshp Prog; Comm Volntr; Chrch Yth Grp; NYLC; ROTC; Scouts; Bnd; Ch Chr; Jzz Bnd; Mch Bnd; Presidential Academic Excellence Award; Biology; Chemistry; North Carolina State; Appalachian State

MOSKE, KATIE L; HUNTERSVILLE, NC; NORTH MECKLENBURG HS; (JR); Hnr Roll; Nat Hon Sy; USAA; WWAHSS; Comm Volntr; Peer Tut/Med; Dbte Team; NtlFrnscLg; Sci Clb; Svce Clb; Spch Team; Vllyball (J); Cl Off (P); Stu Cncl (P); CR; IB CAS Council; Debate & Speech State Finalist; English-PhD; Foreign Language Minor

MOSLEY, CRISTY R; AULANDER, NC; BERTIE HS; (JR); All Am Sch; Hnr Roll; WWAHSS; FCCLA; Ntl Beta Clb; SADD; Chrldg (V); Certified Nursing; Mid Wife; North Carolina State U; U of North Carolina Greensboro

MOSLEY, KASSANDRA; RICHLANDS, NC; RICHLANDS HS; (MS); Hi Hnr Roll; Hnr Roll; Perf Att; Pres Ac Ftns Aw; USAA; Ntl Beta Clb; P to P St Amb Prg; Chr; Sccr; Track; Photography; Fashion Design; New York U; U of California Los Angeles

MOSS, CHRISTINA M; SANFORD, NC; WESTERN HARNETT HS; (SR); Hnr Roll; Comm Volntr; Chrch Yth Grp; Civil Air Pat; Emplmnt; Photog; ROTC; Arch; Gmnstcs; Mar Art; Swmg; Sch Ppr (E, R, P); Scuba Diving; Letter F- Are Not School Sports, Train @ Other Areas.; Bachelor's Degree in Arts and Theater Arts; Fayetteville State U; Methodist College

MOSS, ELLIOTT L; GASTONIA, NC; ASHBROOK HS; (FR); Duke TS; Hi Hnr Roll; Chr; Ftball (J); Wt Lftg; Medical Field; UNC Chapel Hill

MOSS, TIMOTHY; JACKSONVILLE, NC; JACKSONVILLE HS; (FR); Hnr Roll; Nat Hon Sy; Cr Ctry (J); Marine Biologist; Veterinarian; U of North Carolina-Wilmington; Macquarie U-Australia

MOTON, KE'ANDREA; JACKSONVILLE, NC; SOUTHWEST HS; (SO); Hnr Roll; Nat Hon Sy; Perf Att; WWAHSS; Comm Volntr; Chrch Yth Grp; FTA; SADD; Spanish Clb; Ch Chr; Dnce; Chrldg (J); PP Ftbl (J); Scr Kpr (V); Track (V); Vllyball (J); Cl Off (S); Stu Cncl (R); CR (R); Step Team; Number I in Sophomore Class; Doctorate Degree; Medicine; Duke U; U of North Carolina-Chapel Hill

MOTUZ, DANICA L; CHARLOTTE, NC; CHARLOTTE CATHOLIC HS; (FR); Duke TS; Hi Hnr Roll; Hnr Roll; MVP; Otst Ac Ach Awd; Pres Ac Ftns Aw; St of Mnth; Comm Volntr; Spec Olymp Vol; ArtClub; DARE; Ntl Beta Clb; Outdrs Clb; Photog; Fld Hky (V); Best All-Around / Basketball - Church League; Best Daughter Award; Dermatology; Geology; UNC Chapel Hill; North Carolina State U

MOUA, JAMES Y; ALBEMARLE, NC; NORTH STANLY HS; (SO); WWAHSS; Hab For Humty Volntr; Peer Tut/Med; Cmptr Clb; Sci Clb; Chr; Adv Cncl (P); Cl Off (R); Stu Cncl (P); Lab Technician; East Carolina; UNC Chapel Hills

MOYERS, DREW P; BURLINGTON, NC; GRAHAM HS; (JR); Hnr Roll; Perf Att; Vsity Clb; Bskball (V); Track (V); U of North Carolina; State U

MOZINGO, KAYLA M; SEVEN SPRINGS, NC; SPRING CREEK HS; (MS); Fut Prb Slvr; Hi Hnr Roll; Hnr Roll; Otst Ac Ach Awd; Perf Att; Pres Ac Ftns Aw; Sci/Math Olympn; Chrch Yth Grp; DARE; Emplmnt; Scouts; Chr; Dnce; SP/M/VS; Stu Cncl (V); Horseback Riding/Showing; Teacher; Horse Trainer; Duke; NC state

MUELLER, JACOB; WINSTON SALEM, NC; WEST FORSYTH HS; (SO); Hnr Roll; St of Mnth; FCA; Orch; Ftball (V); Track (V); Wt Lftg; Club Mix; All-Conference Football; Engineering; Medical; Duquesne; Wake Forest

MUHAMMAD, KHALID R; WINSTON SALEM, NC; REYNOLDS HS; (JR); Fut Prb Slvr; Hnr Roll; Perf Att; Pres Ac Ftns Aw; Comm Volntr; Peer Tut/Med; Chrch Yth Grp; Emplmnt; Ntl FFA; Voc Ind Clb Am; Stg Cre; Bskball (J); Business; Medicine; Howard; North Carolina State

MUKENDI, TEDDY; RALEIGH, NC; LEESVILLE ROAD HS; (JR); Perf Att; Comm Volntr; Clb; Chr; Sccr (V)

MULLINIX, MARISSA D; ALBEMARLE, NC; WEST STANLY HS; (SO); Duke TS; Hi Hnr Roll; Otst Ac Ach Awd; Perf Att; Comm Volntr; FTA; Svce Clb; Letter Winner in Sports Medicine; Prezell R. Robinson Teaching Scholarship; Secondary Education (Math); Genetics/DNA; UNC At Chapel Hill; Appalachian State U

MULLINS, SHARITA; WILMINGTON, NC; E A LANEY HS; (JR); Hnr Roll; Nat Hon Sy; WWAHSS; Chr; Dnce; Drl Tm; Dance Team; Gospel Choir; Chemistry Major; Pharmacy School; Georgia State; U of Georgia

MULLIS, BRITTNEY; MONROE, NC; METROLINA CHRISTIAN AC; (JR); Hi Hnr Roll; Hnr Roll; MVP; Otst Ac Ach Awd; Chrch Yth Grp; Emplmnt; Ntl Beta Clb; Prom Com; Chrldg (V CL); Sccr (V L); Certificate for Excellent Christian Character; Distinguished Christian High School Award; Neo-Natal Nursing; Carolinas College of Health Sciences; UNC-Charlotte

MULLIS, JAMES F C; SALISBURY, NC; WEST ROWAN HS; (JR); Hi Hnr Roll; WWAHSS; Bnd; Jzz Bnd; Mch Bnd; Orch; All District Band; All State Band; Music; U of North Carolina-Charlotte

MUNRO, ALEXANDER W; CHAPEL HILL, NC; WOODS CHARTER SCH; (JR); Hnr Roll; Yth Ldrshp Prog; Yrbk (R); Working 2 or 3 Jobs; Certified Pool Operator; Law School; U of North Carolina; North Carolina State

MURPHY, COLLEEN; CHAPEL HILL, NC; CHAPEL HILL HS; (SO); Hi Hnr Roll; Pres Sch; Spec Olymp Vol; Emplmnt; Fld Hky (V L); Lcrsse (J); Field Hockey All-Region Honorable Mention; Junior Link Club; Math / Business Major; Law Degree; U of Virginia; College of William and Mary

MURPHY, ERINN; REIDSVILLE, NC; REIDSVILLE HS; (FR); Duke TS; Hnr Roll; Perf Att; Comm Volntr; Drma Clb; Scouts; Bnd; Ch Chr; SP/M/VS; Stg Cre; First Place WordMaster's Challenge; First Place Centennial Study Club Creative Writing Award; English; Theatre Arts; U of North Carolina Greensboro; Wake Forest U

MURPHY, JAZMINE; DUNN, NC; TRITON HS; (FR); Hi Hnr Roll; Hnr Roll; 4-H; Bnd; Clr Grd; Chrldg (L); Sftball (L); Yrbk (P); Architecture; Child Care

MURPHY, JUSTIN D; CHINQUAPIN, NC; EAST DUPLIN HS; (JR); All Am Sch; Duke TS; Jr Mshl; Nat Hon Sy; USAA; Valdctrian; Comm Volntr; Hosp Aide; Chrch Yth Grp; FCA; Ntl Beta Clb; NYLC; Quiz Bowl; Tech Clb; Sccr (J); U of North Carolina At Chapel Hill; Appalachian State U

MURPHY, VALLYN C; RALEIGH, NC; SOUTHEAST RALEIGH MAGNET HS; (SO); Gov Hnr Prg; Hnr Roll; Kwnis Aw; Nat Hon Sy; USAA; WWAHSS; Comm Volntr; ArtClub; Emplmnt; JSA; Key Club; Chr; Junior Statesmen of America (Officer); Key Club

MURRAY, ASHLEY; HILLSBOROUGH, NC; CEDAR RIDGE HS; (FR); Hnr Roll; Perf Att; SADD; Bnd; Dnce; Mch Bnd; Pep Bnd; Sftball (J); Vllyball; Model - Barbizon Modeling; Walk for Diabetes / Walk for Health Heart; NC State; U of North Carolina Chapel Hill

MURRAY, JO REVELLE; MURFREESBORO, NC; RIDGECROFT SCH; (SO); Ctznshp Aw; Duke TS; Hi Hnr Roll; MVP; Otst Ac Ach Awd; Perf Att; St of Mnth; USAA; WWAHSS; Comm Volntr; Chrch Yth Grp; FCA; Key Club; Ntl Beta Clb; SADD; Vsity Clb; Bnd; Bskball (V L); GAA (V); Sccr (V L); Vllyball (V L); Adv Cncl (R); CR (R); Sophomore Class President; Physical / Occupational Therapy; Elementary Education Teacher; Duke U; U of North Carolina Wilmington

MURRAY, SEAN; FAYETTEVILLE, NC; (JR); Bnd; Drl Tm; Mch Bnd; Architect

MURRAY, TAYLOR; GREENSBORO, NC; WESTERN GUILFORD HS; (JR); Hnr Roll; WWAHSS; Comm Volntr; Chrch Yth Grp; FCA; Ntl Beta Clb; Bnd; Dnce; Greensboro Ballet Company-Trainee; Church Dance Worship Ministry-Leadership/Choreography Team; Dance Education

MURRIELL, QUANESHA D; GOLDSBORO, NC; GOLDSBORO HS; (SO); Hnr Roll; Nat Mrt LOC; Comm Volntr; DARE; Pep Squd; Bnd; Mch Bnd; Pep Bnd; FCCLA; Nursing (RN); Pediatrician

MUSSELWHITE, ALEX P; LUMBERTON, NC; LUMBERTON HS; (FR); Duke TS; Hi Hnr Roll; Hnr Roll; Nat Hon Sy; St of Mnth; Comm Volntr; Chrch Yth Grp; Lib Aide; Ntl Beta Clb; Scouts; Ftball (J); Wt Lftg (V); Sea Fishing Champion; President of the USA; Law / Judge; Harvard U; U of NC

MYERS, ALAN W; AHOSKIE, NC; RIDGECROFT SCH; (JR); Hnr Roll; Sci Fairs; WWAHSS; Comm Volntr; Chrch Yth Grp; Key Club; Vsity Clb; Golf (V L); Sccr (V L); Church Youth Group; Fire Department; Engineering; East Carolina U; North Carolina State U

MYRICK, BRITTNEY; COMO, NC; HERTFORD CTY HS; (JR); Hnr Roll; Jr Mshl; Nat Hon Sy; Otst Ac Ach Awd; Chrch Yth Grp; FBLA; Ntl Beta Clb; Bnd; 3rd Place in Math Fair; Excellence in Business Law; Psychology; Winston-Salem U; Johnson C. Smith U

NANCE, CHRISTOPHER; TARBORO, NC; TARBORO HS; (SR); Hnr Roll; Nat Hon Sy; Chrch Yth Grp; Ch Chr; Stg Cre; Ftball; Wt Lftg; Molecular Biology, BS Degree; Graphic Arts; North Carolina A & T State U (Accepted)

NANCE, KELLY; SILER CITY, NC; JORDAN MATTHEWS HS; (SR); Hi Hnr Roll; Hnr Roll; Otst Ac Ach Awd; Perf Att; WWAHSS; Chrch Yth Grp; DECA; Drma Clb; Lib Aide; Mus Clb; Chr; SP/M/VS; Yrbk (P); Veterinary Medicine; Business Administration; Gardner-Webb U; Liberty U

NANNEY, NICHOLE A; BREVARD, NC; BREVARD HS; (SO); Hnr Roll; WWAHSS; Comm Volntr; Chrch Yth Grp; FCA; Chrldg (V); Sftball (JC); Vllyball (J); Elementary School Teacher; Clemson U; Furman U

NARDHAUGEN, JENNIFER; FAYETTEVILLE, NC; MASSEY HILL CLASSICAL HS; (JR); Hnr Roll; Emplmnt; Bnd; Chr; Bachelor's Degree in Science; Nursing Degree; East Carolina U; U of North Carolina Wilmington

NASHER, ALI; CHARLOTTE, NC; VANCE HS; (JR); Hnr Roll; Ntl Beta Clb; Sccr (C); Doctor; UNCC Charlotte

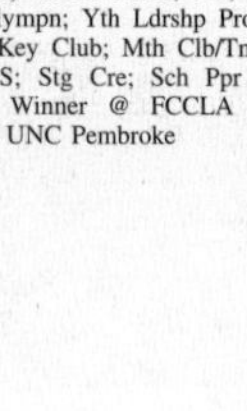
Murray, Ashley
Cedar Ridge HS
Hillsborough, NC

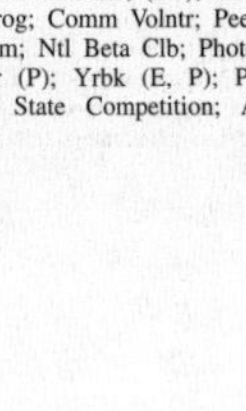
Mullinix, Marissa D
West Stanly HS
Albemarle, NC

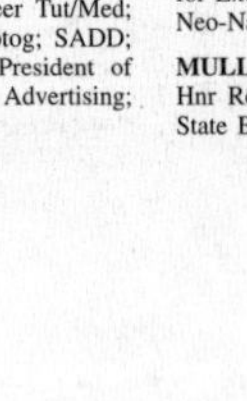
Moua, James Y
North Stanly HS
Albemarle, NC

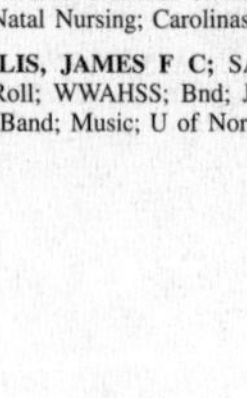
Morse, Bryan
West Montgomery HS
Troy, NC

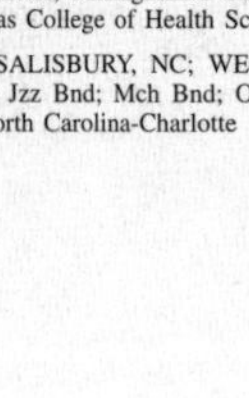
Morgan, Sunni
South Stanly HS
Albemarle, NC

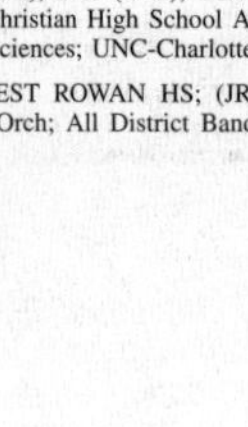
Morris, Anna C
Cary AC
Fuquay Varina, NC

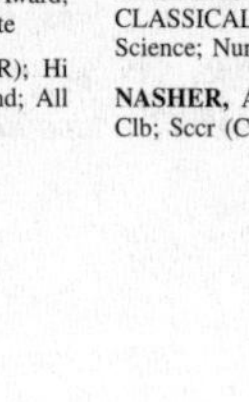
Muhammad, Khalid R
Reynolds HS
Winston Salem, NC

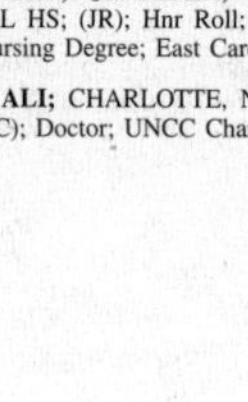
Mullis, Brittney
Metrolina Christian AC
Monroe, NC

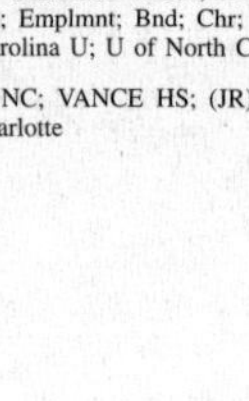
Nasher, Ali
Vance HS
Charlotte, NC

NAVARRO-WELCH, KIMBERLY; FAYETTEVILLE, NC; DOUGLAS BYRD HS; (SR); Hnr Roll; Perf Att; DARE; A and AB Honor Roll; Perfect Attendance; Associate's Degree in Nursing; Fayetteville Technical Community College

NAVAS, MARIA J; CHARLOTTE, NC; PROVIDENCE HS; (SR); Hnr Roll; Nat Hon Sy; Comm Volntr; Peer Tut/Med; ArtClub; Dnce; Veterinary Medicine; Queens U

NAY, H'BLAIH; RALEIGH, NC; SOUTHEAST RALEIGH HS; (FR); Ctznshp Aw; Hnr Roll; Hab For Humty Volntr; Chrch Yth Grp; Dnce; Tae Kwon Do; Principal's Award for Citizenship; Medicine; Engineering; NC State U; Duke U

NAZAL, MARK; HIGH POINT, NC; SOUTHWEST GUILFORD HS; (JR); Hi Hnr Roll; Jr Mshl; Nat Hon Sy; St of Mnth; Valdctrian; Comm Volntr; Chess; Emplmnt; Ntl Beta Clb; Spanish Clb; Bskball (J); Fncg (V); Ftball (V L); Track (V L); Wt Lftg (V); Wrstlg (J); Stu Cncl (R); USAA National Mathematics Award; Top 5 in Class - 1st with a 4.0 Unweighted / 5.22 Weighted; Business; Law; Harvard U; Princeton U

NEAL, BENJAMIN E; KINGS MTN, NC; BESSEMER CITY HS; Hnr Roll; Chrch Yth Grp; Emplmnt; Wdwrkg Clb; Diesel Mechanic; Gaston College

NEELY, ELIZABETH M; CHARLOTTE, NC; SOUTH MECKLENBURG HS; (JR); Duke TS; F Lan Hn Soc; Hi Hnr Roll; Hnr Roll; Jr Mshl; MVP; Nat Hon Sy; WWAHSS; Comm Volntr; Ntl Beta Clb; Photog; Quill & Scroll; Scouts; Bsball (J); Cr Ctry (V CL); Sccr (V CL); Yrbk (E, P); Girl Scout Silver Award; President-South Mecklenburg Chapter of NHS; Communications; Foreign Languages; U of Pennsylvania; U of North Carolina

NEFF, TANNER; HENDERSONVILLE, NC; EAST HENDERSON HS; (FR); Duke TS; Hnr Roll; Mth Clb/Tm; Quiz Bowl; Mch Bnd; Orch; Computer Science; Instrument Performance; U of North Carolina; U of North Carolina At Charlotte

NELSON, AMANDA; JACKSONVILLE, NC; NORTHSIDE HS; (SO); Hnr Roll; Comm Volntr; Bnd; Mch Bnd; Pep Bnd; SP/M/VS; Yrbk (R, P); Bio Chemist; RN Nurse; Harvard Medical; Costal Carolina Community

NELSON, CHANIQUA D; DURHAM, NC; C E JORDAN HS; (SO); Hosp Aide; Spec Olymp Vol; Chess; Mth Clb/Tm; Sccr (R); Stu Cncl (S); Mayor's Youth Award; Social Work; Politics; North Carolina Central U; North Carolina State U

NELSON IV, JOHN; GRIMESLAND, NC; D H CONLEY HS; (SO); Duke TS; Hi Hnr Roll; Hnr Roll; WWAHSS; Comm Volntr; Chess; Scouts; Cr Ctry (J); Political Science; English; UNC Chapel Hill; ECU

NETZER, JENNIFER D; BOLIVIA, NC; SOUTH BRUNSWICK HS; (JR); Ctznshp Aw; Hnr Roll; WWAHSS; Comm Volntr; Red Cr Aide; ArtClub; Emplmnt; Fr of Library; Prom Com; ROTC; Dnce; Drl Tm; Regular Blood Donor; Registered Nursing; Brunswick Community College; U of North Carolina of Wilmington

NEWBAUER, JAKE; RALEIGH, NC; (SO); Ctznshp Aw; Hi Hnr Roll; Hnr Roll; Comm Volntr; Comm Volntr; DECA; FCA; Key Club; Prom Com; Spanish Clb; Stu Cncl (R); CR (R); Law; Business; UNC-CH; UNCW

NEWKIRK, TRICIA; CHARLOTTE, NC; VANCE HS; (SO); Hnr Roll; Perf Att; Chrch Yth Grp; DARE; Chr; Ch Chr; Yrbk (E); Stepping; Fashion Designing; Childcare Services; Winston Salem State U; U of Chapel Hill

NEWLIN, MEGAN; MATTHEWS, NC; BUTLER HS; (SO); Hnr Roll; WWAHSS; Comm Volntr; DARE; Chrldg (J); Interior Designer; East Carolina U; U of Georgia

NEWTON, JESSICA; CLINTON, NC; CLINTON HS; (JR); Hnr Roll; WWAHSS; Comm Volntr; Red Cr Aide; 4-H; Chrch Yth Grp; DARE; Emplmnt; Scouts; Ch Chr; Bskball (V); Vllyball (V); North Carolina Native American Youth Organization; Elementary Education; Mount Olive College

NEWTON, KEALEY S; KILL DEVIL HILLS, NC; FIRST FLIGHT HS; (JR); Hnr Roll; Perf Att; St of Mnth; WWAHSS; Comm Volntr; Peer Tut/Med; Biology Clb; Chrch Yth Grp; Emplmnt; Key Club; Prom Com; Ch Chr; Sch Ppr (P); Yrbk (P); Youth Group President; Class Representative of Key Club-11th; Atmospheric Sciences-Meteorology; U of North Carolina At Asheville; North Carolina State

NGUYEN, BAO-TRAN; HARRISBURG, NC; JAY M ROBINSON HS; (FR); Hnr Roll; Otst Ac Ach Awd; Mth Clb/Tm; Mus Clb; Bnd; Mch Bnd; Track (L); All-County Band Participant; Psychology; Athletic Trainer; U of North Carolina At Chapel Hill; U of North Carolina At Charlotte

NGUYEN, LAI; FAYETTEVILLE, NC; DOUGLAS BYRD HS; (SO); Hnr Roll; WWAHSS; Comm Volntr; Chrch Yth Grp; DARE; Key Club; Sch Ppr (R, P); Honor Roll; World Geography Award; Orthodontist; Teacher; UNC Charlotte; UNC Chapel Hill

NGUYEN, LAM; FAYETTEVILLE, NC; FREEDOM HS; (SO); Hi Hnr Roll; WWAHSS; Comm Volntr; ArtClub; Chrch Yth Grp; Clb; Ch Chr; Wt Lftg

NGUYEN, LY; FAYETTEVILLE, NC; DOUGLAS BYRD HS; (JR); Hnr Roll; Jr Mshl; Kwnis Aw; Nat Hon Sy; Perf Att; Pres Ac Ftns Aw; WWAHSS; Comm Volntr; Hab For Humty Volntr; Peer Tut/Med; Chrch Yth Grp; Key Club; Quiz Bowl; Sccr (VJC); Sch Ppr (R, P); HOSA; National Honor Society; Mathematics; Oncology; UNC Chapel Hill, UNC Charlotte

NGUYEN, NICOLE; WILSON, NC; HUNT HS; (FR); Hi Hnr Roll; Sci/Math Olympn; St of Mnth; Comm Volntr; FCA; Scouts; French Clb; Bnd; Dnce; SP/M/VS; Chrldg (JC); Dance; Psychology; Duke, Penn State; U North Carolina-Chapel Hill

NGUYEN, TUAN B; CHARLOTTE, NC; HARDIN U; (FR); Perf Att; Comm Volntr; Sccr (J); Perfect Attendance; Honor Roll; Electrical Engineering; Mechanical Engineering; North Carolina State U

NICHOLS, WILLIAM C; GARNER, NC; WEST JOHNSTON HS; (SO); Hi Hnr Roll; Hnr Roll; Chrch Yth Grp; Scouts; Mch Bnd; Orch; Golf (VJ L); Most Improved Player for Golf Tours in; Was Given a Letter in Academics; Political Science; Pre-Law; UNC-U of North Carolina; Campbell U

NICKELSON, SAMANTHA; WILKESBORO, NC; EAST WILKES MS; (MS); Hnr Roll; Otst Ac Ach Awd; Pres Ac Ftns Aw; Red Cr Aide; Chrch Yth Grp; DARE; Ntl Beta Clb; SADD; Chr; Dnce; PP Ftbl (J); Swmg (J); DARE Essay Winner; Dental Hygienist

NIEMAN, JESSICA M; DUNN, NC; TRITON HS; (JR); Hnr Roll; Sci/Math Olympn; DARE; Mth Clb/Tm; Scouts; Chr; Architecture; Landscaping; UNC Wilmington (U of North Carolina)

NOBLES, PAULA L; HILLSBOROUGH, NC; DURHAM SCH OF THE ARTS/PALMAS AC; (JR); Hnr Roll; Nat Hon Sy; Otst Ac Ach Awd; Perf Att; Comm Volntr; Peer Tut/Med; Drma Clb; Emplmnt; Photog; Tchrs Aide; SP/M/VS; Psychology; Coker College; Duke U

NOLES, SAMANTHA A; RALEIGH, NC; HILLTOP CHRISTIAN SCH; (SO); Hi Hnr Roll; Nat Hon Sy; WWAHSS; Pres Sch; Sci Fairs; WWAHSS; Spec Olymp Vol; Chrch Yth Grp; Pep Squd; Chr; Ch Chr; Bskball (V); Chrldg (V CL); Stu Cncl (P); Yrbk (R); National Christian Honor Society; HCS High School Student of the Year; Teaching; Campbell U; Meredith College

NORBURG, JESSICA; WILMINGTON, NC; ASHLEY HS; (SR); Ctznshp Aw; Hi Hnr Roll; Nat Hon Sy; WWAHSS; Comm Volntr; Peer Tut/Med; Chrch Yth Grp; Drma Clb; Mus Clb; Ntl Beta Clb; Chr; Ch Chr; Dnce; Orch; International Thespian Society; North Carolina State Honor's Chorus; Music Business; Vocal Performance; Belmont U; Southern Illinois U Carbondale

NOREEN, BRADLEY D; APEX, NC; APEX HS; (JR); Duke TS; Hnr Roll; Nat Hon Sy; WWAHSS; Emplmnt; Cr Ctry (V CL); Swmg (V L); Track (V L); Cl Off (V); Stu Cncl (R); Co-Choir Young Republicans Club; All Conference XC, Track & Swimming; Dentistry; Davidson College; UNC Chapel Hill

NORMAN, MANDY; JACKSONVILLE, NC; NORTHSIDE HS; (SO); Hnr Roll; Perf Att; St of Mnth; FBLA; Chr; Ch Chr; CR (R); Principal's List; Honor Roll; Pre-Medicine; Psychology; U of North Carolina At Chapel Hill; Duke U

NORMENT, AMANDA L; CHOCOWINITY, NC; SOUTHSIDE HS; (SO); All Am Sch; Ctznshp Aw; Hi Hnr Roll; Hnr Roll; Nat Hon Sy; Otst Ac Ach Awd; WWAHSS; DARE; Ntl Beta Clb; Yrbk (E, R, P); Forensic Science; Civil Engineering; U of North Carolina-Chapel Hill; North Carolina State U

NORRIS, COY; MONROE, NC; FOREST HILLS HS; (SO); Ctznshp Aw; Duke TS; Hi Hnr Roll; Hnr Roll; Nat Hon Sy; Chrch Yth Grp; Ntl Beta Clb; Ntl FFA; Skt Tgt Sh; Wt Lftg (V); FFA Officer; 2 Year Rotary Scholar; Military Officer; Virginia Military Institute; The Citadel

NORRIS, KIRK; ELIZABETH CITY, NC; NORTHEASTERN HS; (SR); Hi Hnr Roll; Jr Mshl; MVP; Nat Hon Sy; Nat Mrt LOC; St of Mnth; Valdctrian; WWAHSS; Comm Volntr; Peer Tut/Med; Spec Olymp Vol; Chrch Yth Grp; Drma Clb; FCA; Lib Aide; Quill & Scroll; SP/M/VS; Bsball (VJ L); Cr Ctry (VJC); Yrbk (E, R); National Honor Society President; Religion; Christian Education/Ministry; Campbell U

NORRIS, NICOLE L; FAYETTEVILLE, NC; E E SMITH SR HS; (SO); Chrch Yth Grp; Dbte Team; Emplmnt; Spch Team; Sccr (V L); Manager for Men's Soccer; Volunteer for Nursery At Church; Pediatrics; Nursing; Duke U; UNC At Chapel Hill

NORTON, HOLLY D; GASTON, NC; HALIFAX AC CHRISTIAN SCH; (SO); Hnr Roll; Ntl Beta Clb; Sftball (V); Octagon Club; Nursing; Teaching; Appalachian State U

NORTON, KENNETH M; HOT SPRINGS, NC; MADISON HS; (FR); Mars Hill College; U of North Carolina

NORWOOD, SCHAEFFER D; LENOIR, NC; WEST CALDWELL HS; (FR); Hnr Roll; Perf Att; St of Mnth; DARE; Lib Aide; Chef; Pediatrician; U of North Carolina Greensboro

NORWOOD, TIERRA A; NASHVILLE, NC; NASH CTRL HS; (FR); Ctznshp Aw; Hnr Roll; Perf Att; Yth Ldrshp Prog; Comm Volntr; Peer Tut/Med; Chrch Yth Grp; DARE; Drma Clb; Emplmnt; Chr; Ch Chr; SP/M/VS; Chrldg (J); Track (V); Stu Cncl (R); Sch Ppr (E, R, P); Yrbk (P); Martin Luther King Oratorical Contest Winner 2 Yrs; Odyssey of the Mind 3 Years; Journalism; Drama; U of North Carolina Chapel Hill; Howard U

NUGENT, MICHELLE L; TROY, NC; WEST MONTGOMERY HS; (JR); Ctznshp Aw; Hi Hnr Roll; Jr Mshl; Perf Att; Pres Ac Ftns Aw; Sci Fairs; St of Mnth; WWAHSS; Yth Ldrshp Prog; Comm Volntr; Peer Tut/Med; Chrch Yth Grp; DARE; Drma Clb; Emplmnt; FCA; HO'Br Yth Ldrshp; Mth Clb/Tm; Ntl Beta Clb; Dnce; Drl Tm; SP/M/VS; Stg Cre; Chrldg (J); Cr Ctry (V L); PP Ftbl (V C); Scr Kpr (V); Sftball (V); Tennis (V L); Track (V L); Cl Off (T); Stu Cncl (T); CR (R); Sch Ppr (R, P); Yrbk (P); Students Against Drunk Driving President; JROTC Flight Commander and Drill Team Com.; Engineering; Architecture; U of North Carolina At Charlotte; North Carolina State U

NWANKWO, EZINNE; GREENSBORO, NC; DUDLEY HS; (FR); WWAHSS; Comm Volntr; Chrch Yth Grp; Ch Chr; Dnce; Stu Cncl (R); Modeling Team; Pre-Medicine; Biology; U of North Carolina At Chapel-Hill; U of North Carolina At Charlotte

O'BRIEN, JOHN J; HICKORY, NC; HICKORY HS; (FR); Hnr Roll; Comm Volntr; Chrch Yth Grp; Ftball (J); Clemson U; Wake Forest U

O'BRIEN, MICHELLE; DURHAM, NC; CE JORDAN HS; (JR); F Lan Hn Soc; Hi Hnr Roll; Hnr Roll; MVP; Nat Hon Sy; Otst Ac Ach Awd; Perf Att; Peer Tut/Med; Chrch Yth Grp; Emplmnt; Key Club; Prom Com; Chrldg (J L); Sccr (V L); Swmg (V L); Cl Off (R); CR (V, R); Yrbk (R, P); Homecoming Court; Year Round Soccer Team; Sports Medicine; Teaching; U of North Carolina Chapel Hill; Emory U

O'CONNELL, ALLISON; PITTSBORO, NC; NORTHWOOD HS; (JR); F Lan Hn Soc; Hnr Roll; Jr Mshl; Nat Hon Sy; WWAHSS; ArtClub; Drma Clb; Key Club; Sci Clb; Scouts; Voc Ind Clb Am; Spanish Clb; SP/M/VS; Stg Cre; Sccr (V); Cl Off (V); Stu Cncl (P, S); Skills USA Secretary; English or Humanities; U North Carolina Chapel Hill; U North Carolina Asheville

ODOM, MORGAN C; FAYETTEVILLE, NC; SOUTHVIEW HS; (JR); Ctznshp Aw; Hnr Roll; MVP; Sci Fairs; Sci/Math Olympn; Yth Ldrshp Prog; Comm Volntr; Hab For Humty Volntr; Peer Tut/Med; Chrch Yth Grp; Key Club; NYLC; Prom Com; Tchrs Aide; Spanish Clb; Golf (V); Sccr (V L); Tennis (V L); CR (P); Cricket Club; Architectural Engineering; Political Science; U of North Carolina At Chapel Hill; U of North Carolina At Wilmington

ODREZIN, MATT; RALEIGH, NC; NEEDHAM BROUGHTON HS; (JR); Hi Hnr Roll; Hnr Roll; Otst Ac Ach Awd; Comm Volntr; Peer Tut/Med; Chrch Yth Grp; Clb; Sch Ppr (R); Journalism; Sports Marketing; U of Georgia, Athens, Georgia; U of North Carolina- Chapel Hill, Chapel Hill, North Carolina

OGILVIE, PATRICK S; FRANKLINTON, NC; FRANKLINTON HS; (JR); Nat Hon Sy; Pres Sch; WWAHSS; Comm Volntr; Peer Tut/Med; Bsball (VJ); Guitar Club; Forensic Science; Vet Medicine; North Carolina State U; U of NC

OGULKE, LYNDA; RALEIGH, NC; SOUTH MECKLENBURG HS; (SR); 4H Awd; Ctznshp Aw; Fut Prb Slvr; Hnr Roll; MVP; Nat Mrt Fin; Nat Sci Aw; Perf Att; Sci/Math Olympn; St of Mnth; CARE; Comm Volntr; Peer Tut/Med; Chess; Chrch Yth Grp; Emplmnt; Key Club; Prom Com; Chrldg (J L); Prom Com; Vsity Clb; Clb; Bnd; Chr; Ch Chr; Dnce; Bdmtn (J); Chrldg (c); GAA (l); Golf (l); PPSqd (l); Rqtball (l); Scr Kpr (V); Sccr (c); Tennis (c); Vllyball; Stu Cncl (R); Lit Mag (R); Dentistry; Surgeon; Queens U Charlotte NC; North Carolina state U

OGUNSEMOWO, FOLAKE S; GREENSBORO, NC; JAMES B DUDLEY HS; (FR); Hi Hnr Roll; Perf Att; WWAHSS; Peer Tut/Med; Obstetrician Gynecologist; Pre-Medicine; Duke U; Wake Forest U

OLIVER, LINDSAY; SHELBY, NC; BURNS HS; (JR); Hnr Roll; Jr Mshl; Nat Hon Sy; Otst Ac Ach Awd; Comm Volntr; Ntl Beta Clb; Prom Com; Quill & Scroll; Spanish Clb; Orch; Cl Off (T); Yrbk (E); Pharmacy; Music; U of North Carolina Chapel Hill

OLIVER, TIFFANY; WILMINGTON, NC; LANEY HS; (FR); 4H Awd; Hnr Roll; Otst Ac Ach Awd; Perf Att; Pres Ac Ftns Aw; Sci Fairs; 4-H; Biology Clb; Mth Clb/Tm; Scouts; Dnce; SP/M/VS; Chrldg (VJC); Stu Cncl (S); CR (R); On School Morning Show, TBBN; PhD; Buyer; U of North Carolina Wilmington; U of North Carolina Chapel Hill

OLIVER, WHITNEY E; MORGANTON, NC; EAST BURKE HS; (SR); Hnr Roll; Nat Hon Sy; St Schl; Chrch Yth Grp; DARE; Sci Clb; Svce Clb; SADD; Tchrs Aide; Spanish Clb; Bskball (J); PP Ftbl (V C); Vllyball (VJCL); Cl Off (V); CR (R); National Honor Society; Anchor Club-Officer; Political Science; Law Degree; East Carolina U

OLSEN, JANE R; PURLEAR, NC; WEST WILKES HS; (FR); Duke TS; Hi Hnr Roll; Nat Hon Sy; Yth Ldrshp Prog; Chrch Yth Grp; Key Club; Mod UN; Ntl Beta Clb; Scouts; SP/M/VS; Sccr (V); Tennis (V); Play Piano; Duke U, TIP Program; Appalachian State U; Wake Forest U

Odom, Morgan C — Southview HS — Fayetteville, NC
Norment, Amanda L — Southside HS — Chocowinity, NC
Nobles, Paula L — Durham Sch Of The Arts/Palmas AC — Hillsborough, NC
Nichols, William C — West Johnston HS — Garner, NC
National Honor Roll Spring 2005
Newton, Jessica — Clinton HS — Clinton, NC
Noles, Samantha A — Hilltop Christian Sch — Raleigh, NC
Norton, Kenneth M — Madison HS — Hot Springs, NC
Oliver, Whitney E — East Burke HS — Morganton, NC

ONUMA, BRITNEY; WINSTON-SALEM, NC; NORTH FORSYTH HS; (FR); Hnr Roll; Perf Att; Comm Volntr; Chr; Dnce; HOSA - Health Occupation Students of America; Crosby Scholar Community Service Program; Doctor; Registered Nurse; Duke U; Wake Forest U

ORELOJA, GBOLABO; DURHAM, NC; RIVERSIDE HS; (SR); MVP; St of Mnth; WWAHSS; Yth Ldrshp Prog; Cmptr Clb; FCA; Sci Clb; SADD; Vsity Clb; SP/M/VS; Stg Cre; Sccr (V CL); Business; Pharmacy; East Carolina U

ORTIZ, MELISSA P; JACKSONVILLE, NC; WHITE OAK HS; (MS); Hnr Roll; Spanish Clb; Bnd; Pep Bnd; Track (J); Yrbk (E); Architecture; Texas A & M U Kingsville

ORTIZ, RYAN; THOMASVILLE, NC; THOMASVILLE HS; (SR); Hnr Roll; ROTC; Wdwrkg Clb; Mechanical Engineering; Construction; Cornell U; Guilford Tech Community College

O'SHAUGHNESSY, LYNN M; WAKE FOREST, NC; WAKE FOREST ROLESVILLE HS; (JR); Hi Hnr Roll; Jr Mshl; Nat Hon Sy; Perf Att; Comm Volntr; Chrch Yth Grp; Drma Clb; FCA; SP/M/VS; Stg Cre; National Honor Society; Fringe Festival 2005; Theater Arts; Science; U of North Carolina; North Carolina State

OWEN, CODY; ETOWAH, NC; WEST HENDERSON HS; (JR); DAR; Gov Hnr Prg; Hi Hnr Roll; Hnr Roll; Jr Mshl; Kwnis Aw; Nat Hon Sy; Pres Sch; Sci/Math Olympn; Comm Volntr; Peer Tut/Med; Chrch Yth Grp; DARE; Emplmnt; FCA; FTA; Key Club; Quill & Scroll; Quiz Bowl; Bsball (V); Sch Ppr (E); Youth Ministry; High School Education (History); Columbia International U; North Greenville College

OWENBY, MEGAN M; LAURINBURG, NC; SCOTLAND HS; (SO); Duke TS; Hi Hnr Roll; Chrch Yth Grp; Bnd; Ch Chr; Tennis (V L); Candidate for NC Governor's School; Traveling Soloist; High School Math Education; Music; North Greenville College; Liberty U

OWENS, ALFRED K; CHARLOTTE, NC; CHARLOTTE CHRISTIAN SCH; (SO); Duke TS; Hnr Roll; Perf Att; Pres Sch; Comm Volntr; Dbte Team; Emplmnt; Spch Team; Bnd; Bsball (J); Bskball (J); Sccr (V); Track (V); Best Defense Lawyer in Wade Edwards Mock Trial; Dentistry; Accounting; Georgetown U; U of North Carolina Charlotte

OWENS, ASHLEY; RALEIGH, NC; MILLBROOK HS; (SO); Otst Ac Ach Awd; Comm Volntr; Emplmnt; Kwanza Clb; Ntl FFA; Ch Chr; Nursing; Agriculture; North Carolina State U; North Carolina A & T

OWENS, DANNIELE; FAISON, NC; HOBBTON HS; (FR); Hnr Roll; Medicine; Psychology; U of North Carolina Chapel Hill; Duke U

OWENS, RASHAD; LUMBERTON, NC; LUMBERTON HS; (FR); Hnr Roll; Perf Att; Pres Sch; St of Mnth; Ntl Beta Clb; Sports Analyst; Computer Engineering; Math; Science; U of North Carolina

OWINGS, KARA A; SPRUCE PINE, NC; MITCHELL HS; (SO); All Am Sch; Ctznshp Aw; Hi Hnr Roll; Otst Ac Ach Awd; Perf Att; Pres Ac Ftns Aw; Sci/Math Olympn; WWAHSS; Chrch Yth Grp; FCA; FBLA; Prom Com; Vsity Clb; Ch Chr; Chrldg (V); Track (V); Wt Lftg (V); Local Award - Doug Greene Courtesy Award; Physical Therapy; Pediatrics; Appalachian State U; Duke U

OWNBY, ANDREW C; ANDREWS, NC; HIWASSEE DAM HS; (SR); Hnr Roll; Nat Mrt Sch Recip; Sci/Math Olympn; ArtClub; Emplmnt; Mus Clb; NYLC; Bnd; Ch Chr; SP/M/VS; Ftball (J); Sccr (VJ); Guitar-Piano-Drums; I Would Like to Learn More Music; I Would Like to Continue with Music of All Kinds.; Florida-For Music or Drafting; Minnesota-For Music or Drafting

OWNLEY, WALLACE M; HERTFORD, NC; ALBEMARLE SCH; (MS); Hi Hnr Roll; Hnr Roll; Nat Hon Sy; Comm Volntr; Ntl Beta Clb; Sci Clb; Bsball (V); Bskball (J); Forestry Service; North Carolina State U; Wayne Community College

OXENDINE, SAMANTHA D; LUMBERTON, NC; LUMBERTON HS; (FR); Ctznshp Aw; Hnr Roll; St of Mnth; ROTC; NASA; Doctor

OXENDINE, VICTORIA N; BATTLEBORO, NC; NASH CTRL HS; (JR); Hnr Roll; WWAHSS; Spec Olymp Vol; Drma Clb; Emplmnt; FCA; FBLA; Mus Clb; Prom Com; Chr; SP/M/VS; Chrldg (V L); PP Ftbl (V); Track (V L); CR (R); Nursing (BSN-MSN); Winston-Salem State U; U of North Carolina-Greensboro

OYELOWO, OLUTONI; WAKE FOREST, NC; WAKEFIELD HS; (JR); Hnr Roll; WWAHSS; Comm Volntr; Peer Tut/Med; Spec Olymp Vol; Chrch Yth Grp; DARE; FCCLA; Ntl FFA; P to P St Amb Prg; Ch Chr; Executive Council Parliamentarian; Youth Group Secretary; Business Administration; Interior Design; UNC Chapel Hill; East Carolina U

PACE, JAMES; HENDERSONVILLE, NC; EAST HENDERSON HS; (JR); Hnr Roll; Emplmnt; Ftball (VJ); Track (V); Wt Lftg (VJ)

PACINELLI, AMANDA; APEX, NC; APEX HS; (SO); Hnr Roll; Perf Att; Sci Fairs; Yth Ldrshp Prog; Comm Volntr; 4-H; Chrch Yth Grp; DARE; FCA; Chr; Ch Chr; Dnce; SP/M/VS; Sccr (J); Track (J); Certified Scuba Diver; Civil Engineering; Coastal Engineering; NC State; U of North Carolina

PACKER, BRANDI N; DUBLIN, NC; WEST BLADEN HS; All Am Sch; Duke TS; Hi Hnr Roll; Hnr Roll; Nat Hon Sy; Sci Fairs; St of Mnth; WWAHSS; Comm Volntr; Peer Tut/Med; Spec Olymp Vol; Chrch Yth Grp; Emplmnt; FCA; Jr Ach; Key Club; Ntl Beta Clb; Sci Clb; SADD; Ch Chr; Dnce; SP/M/VS; Sftball (J); Tennis (V); Wt Lftg; Sch Ppr (R); Yrbk; FCCLA (Future Career and Community Leaders of America); Masonic Lodge Guest Speaker; Virology; Anesthesiology; Duke U; North Carolina State U

PAGE, JENNIFER; ASHEBORO, NC; ASHEBORO HS; (SO); Hi Hnr Roll; WWAHSS; Comm Volntr; Chrch Yth Grp; FCA; Key Club; Chr; Bskball (J); Cr Ctry (V); Sftball (V); Stu Cncl (T); CR (T); Political Science; Law; Georgetown U; U of North Carolina Chapel Hill

PAIGE, TO'NETRIA; CHARLOTTE, NC; HARDING U HS; (SO); Hnr Roll; Nat Hon Sy; Perf Att; Hosp Aide; Sci Clb; Bskball (J); Member of HOSA Club; Biology; Pre-Medicine; U of North Carolina At Chapel Hill; Duke U

PAINTER, JOSHUA K; SANFORD, NC; WESTERN HARNETT HS; (FR); Hi Hnr Roll; Perf Att; Ntl Beta Clb; Sccr (V L); Travel Soccer Team, 5 Years for Fayetteville; Lawyer; Princeton; Boston U

PAINTER, STEPHANIE L; RUTHERFORDTON, NC; POLK CTY HS; (SO); Hnr Roll; Perf Att; Pres Ac Ftns Aw; Pres Sch; St of Mnth; Chrch Yth Grp; FCA; French Clb; Clr Grd; Dnce; Mch Bnd; Sftball (J); Yrbk (R); Nursing; Forensic Science; U of Alabama; U of North Carolina

PALMER, SHAMYIA; FAYETTEVILLE, NC; E E SMITH SR HS; (FR); Nat Hon Sy; Comm Volntr; ROTC; AVID Program (Honors Organization); 2nd Lieutenant (Air Force); Fayetteville State U

PALMIERI, LAURA E; GREENSBORO, NC; NORTHWEST HS; (SR); Hi Hnr Roll; Hnr Roll; Sci Fairs; St Schl; WWAHSS; Yth Ldrshp Prog; Comm Volntr; Chrch Yth Grp; DECA; Emplmnt; Mus Clb; Pep Squd; Photog; Svce Clb; Chr; Swmg (L); Yrbk (E, P); Young Life-Senior Leader; All-County Chorus; Graphic Technology; Communications, Advertising; Appalachian State U

PAMARTHI, BINDHU; CARY, NC; GREEN HOPE HS; (FR); Ctznshp Aw; Hnr Roll; St of Mnth; Yth Ldrshp Prog; Comm Volntr; Emplmnt; Svce Clb; Tmpl Yth Grp; Chr; Dnce; Stg Cre; Sch Ppr (R); Miss North Carolina Jr National Teenager; 2nd Runner-Up America's National Teenager; International News Anchor; Pediatrician; UNC Chapel Hill

PANDURO, LAURA; HOPE MILLS, NC; SOUTHVIEW HS; (JR); Hnr Roll; Comm Volntr; Peer Tut/Med; DECA; FBLA; Key Club; Foreign Clb

PARDUE, AIMEE J; HAMPTONVILLE, NC; STARMOUNT HS; (SO); Hi Hnr Roll; Otst Ac Ach Awd; Pep Squd; Chrldg (J); Stu Cncl (R); Yrbk (R); Attorney At Law; Paralegal; Duke U; U of North Carolina

PARDUE, KATHERINE R; JONESVILLE, NC; STARMOUNT HS; (SO); Hi Hnr Roll; MVP; Nat Sci Aw; USAA; Comm Volntr; Chrch Yth Grp; FCA; FTA; Mth Clb/Tm; Chr; Ch Chr; Bskball (J); Scr Kpr (V); Sftball (J); Tennis (V L); Cl Off (T); Stu Cncl (R); Education; Appalachian State U; Elon U

PARDUE, LAUREN; ZEBULON, NC; SOUTHERN NASH HS; (FR); Hnr Roll; Nat Hon Sy; St of Mnth; Bnd; Architecture; North Carolina State; Barton College

PARK, STEVE; CARY, NC; ATHENS DRIVE HS; (JR); Hnr Roll; Yth Ldrshp Prog; Hab For Humty Volntr; Chrch Yth Grp; Key Club; Mth Clb/Tm; Spanish Clb; Rlr Hky (V); Sccr (J)

PARKER, ADAM; WINSTON-SALEM, NC; REYNOLDS HS; (JR); Ctznshp Aw; Hnr Roll; MVP; Nat Hon Sy; Pres Ac Ftns Aw; Sci Fairs; WWAHSS; Yth Ldrshp Prog; Comm Volntr; Dbte Team; Outdrs Clb; Prom Com; Spanish Clb; Bnd; Bsball (VJC); Gmnstcs (V); Human Relations Award Winner; History Student of the Year - 2004; History; Politics; Wake Forest U; George Washington U

PARKER, AMY; CLAYTON, NC; CLAYTON HS; (SO); Cosmetology; Johnston Community College

PARKER, BRITTANY; ROCKY MOUNT, NC; ROCKY MOUNT SR HS; (SO); Ctznshp Aw; Hi Hnr Roll; Hnr Roll; Perf Att; Comm Volntr; Peer Tut/Med; DARE; Drma Clb; Jr Ach; Mth Clb/Tm; Scouts; Bskball (V); Cl Off (V); Stu Cncl (S); Yrbk (P); Psychology; Justice; Duke U; North Carolina A & T U

PARKER, CASEY; CARY, NC; APEX HS; (SR); Hi Hnr Roll; Hnr Roll; Nat Hon Sy; Otst Ac Ach Awd; Pres Sch; WWAHSS; Comm Volntr; Peer Tut/Med; ArtClub; Chrch Yth Grp; Emplmnt; Svce Clb; Spanish Clb; Ch Chr; PP Ftbl (J); Swmg (L); Academic Letter; Spanish Education; ESL; North Carolina State U; UNC Chapel Hill

PARKER, CLAIRE E K; GARNER, NC; CLAYTON HS; (JR); Duke TS; Hi Hnr Roll; Nat Hon Sy; WWAHSS; Comm Volntr; Emplmnt; FTA; Key Club; Quill & Scroll; Svce Clb; Sch Ppr (R); President of HOSA; Secretary of FTA; Physician's Assistant; Nurse Practitioner; UNC Chapel Hill; U of Minnesota

PARKER, GERTIE; RED SPRINGS, NC; PURNELL SWETT HS; (SO); WWAHSS; Chrch Yth Grp; Ntl Beta Clb; Chrldg; Track (V); Piano Performance; Medical Sciences; U of North Carolina At Greensboro; U of North Carolina At Charlotte

PARKER, JAZZMAN; ROCKY MOUNT, NC; NASH CTRL HS; (SO); Hnr Roll; Otst Ac Ach Awd; Emplmnt; FBLA; Bskball (JC); Business Administration; Business Management; Duke U; U of Connecticut

PARKER, JOSHUA; HENDERSON, NC; NORTHERN VANCE HS; (SO); Hnr Roll; Comm Volntr; Chrch Yth Grp; Bnd; Jzz Bnd; Mch Bnd; Bskball (J); Ftball (J); Track (V); Wrstlg (V); North Carolina State U; East Carolina U

PARKER, KELLIE L; ELLENBORO, NC; CHASE HS; (JR); Hnr Roll; Otst Ac Ach Awd; Chrch Yth Grp; Emplmnt; Pep Squd; SADD; Academics Award; HOSA Club; Registered Nurse; Isothermal Community College; U of North Carolina Charlotte

PARKER, MACK; GASTON, NC; NCHS-WEST; (JR); Hi Hnr Roll; Hnr Roll; MVP; Perf Att; WWAHSS; Ntl Beta Clb; SADD; Bnd; Mch Bnd; Bsball (V); Ftball (V C); Track (V C); Business Management; North Carolina State U

PARKER, RHONECIA; NASHVILLE, NC; NASH CTRL HS; (SO); 4H Awd; Ctznshp Aw; Hi Hnr Roll; Hnr Roll; Nat Hon Sy; Otst Ac Ach Awd; Perf Att; Sci Fairs; St of Mnth; Yth Ldrshp Prog; Comm Volntr; Hab For Humty Volntr; Peer Tut/Med; 4-H; Chrch Yth Grp; DARE; Dbte Team; Emplmnt; Jr Ach; Outdrs Clb; Scouts; Bnd; Chr; Ch Chr; Drl Tm; Cl Off (S); CR (V); 4 Years College, Law; Law School

PARKER, SARAH; FAYETTEVILLE, NC; TERRY SANFORD HS; (SO); Perf Att; Sccr; Spelling Bee Contest; Won Soccer Awards; Criminology; Law; Atlanta At & T U; East Carolina U

PARKER-MINCEY, JORDAN; RALEIGH, NC; MILLBROOK HS; (FR); Hnr Roll; MVP; DARE; Emplmnt; Bskball (J); Law School; Law Enforcement; North Carolina State; North Carolina

PARKS, BRITTANY; GOLDSBORO, NC; PATHWAY CHRISTIAN AC; (JR); Ctznshp Aw; Hi Hnr Roll; Hnr Roll; MVP; Nat Stu Ath Day Aw; Perf Att; Sci Fairs; St of Mnth; WWAHSS; Yth Ldrshp Prog; CARE; Comm Volntr; Peer Tut/Med; Chrch Yth Grp; DARE; Drma Clb; FCA; FCCLA; Mus Clb; Photog; Sci Clb; Chr; Ch Chr; Drl Tm; Swg Chr; Chrldg (J); Cr Ct Ski (L); Fld Hky (L); PPSqd (C); PP Ftbl (J); Scr Kpr (J); Sccr (L); Sftball (L); Stu Cncl (R); CR (R); Yrbk (E, R, P); Nurse, Doctor; Lawyer; Duke U

PARKS, OLIVIA A; JACKSON, NC; NORTHEAST AC; (JR); Hnr Roll; Otst Ac Ach Awd; Perf Att; WWAHSS; Red Cr Aide; Chrch Yth Grp; DARE; Ntl Beta Clb; Prom Com; French Clb; Ch Chr; Bskball (JCL); Stu Cncl (V, S); Youth Group President; Agricultural Day Camp Leader; Business Administration; Accounting; Chowan College; Halifax Community College

PARKS, SHANNON; STATESVILLE, NC; STATESVILLE HS; (FR); Hnr Roll; Otst Ac Ach Awd; USAA; Comm Volntr; Spec Olymp Vol; Chrch Yth Grp; ROTC; Clr Grd; Ftball (J); Chapel Hill UNC; UNC Appalachian State

PARRISH, TYLER; CLAYTON, NC; CLAYTON HS; (SO); Hi Hnr Roll; Nat Hon Sy; Perf Att; St of Mnth; Chrch Yth Grp; Emplmnt; Scouts; Svce Clb; Cl Off (P); Boy Scouts Life Rank; Lead America National Junior Leadership Conference - NJLC; Biology; Music; North Carolina State University; University of North Carolina

PARROTT, ASHLEY; JACKSONVILLE, NC; JACKSONVILLE HS; (JR); Hi Hnr Roll; Hnr Roll; Nat Hon Sy; Perf Att; St of Mnth; Comm Volntr; Chrch Yth Grp; Ntl FFA; Stu Cncl (R); CAPS; Onslow County Park & Recreating; Bold of Jacksonville, Inc; Speech Pathology; Pschology; North Carolina State U; Wake Forest

PARROTT, BRIANNA R; GREENSBORO, NC; PAGE HS; (FR); Hnr Roll; ROTC; Drl Tm; Orch; Track (V); Honor Roll; Physician; U of North Carolina-Greensboro

PARSON, ASHLEY N; GASTONIA, NC; GASTON DAY SCH; (SR); All Am Sch; Ctznshp Aw; Hnr Roll; Jr Mshl; Nat Hon Sy; Otst Ac Ach Awd; USAA; WWAHSS; Spec Olymp Vol; ArtClub; Chess; Chrch Yth Grp; Emplmnt; Lib Aide; Mth Clb/Tm; MuAlphaTh; Ntl Beta Clb; Stg Cre; Golf (C); Scr Kpr (V); Sftball (V); Lit Mag; Sch Ppr (E, R); Yrbk (E, P); V-Pres. National Honor Society; Sue Myrick Youth Advisory Council; Pre-Pharmacy; Forensic Science; Erskine U; St Andrews Presbyterian College

PARSONAGE, BEN; WINSTON-SALEM, NC; REYNOLDS HS; (JR); Swmg (V L); Political Science; World History; UNC of Greensboro; Wake Forest U

PARSONS, KENT; BISCOE, NC; NORTH MOORE HS; (JR); All Am Sch; Ctznshp Aw; Hi Hnr Roll; Hnr Roll; Nat Hon Sy; Otst Ac Ach Awd; Perf Att; Sci Fairs; WWAHSS; Comm Volntr; Peer Tut/Med; Chrch Yth Grp; Key Club; Ntl Beta Clb; Tchrs Aide; Bnd; Ch Chr; Mch Bnd; Cr Ctry (V); English Major-High School Education; U of North Carolina At Greensboro; U of North Carolina At Pembroke

Palmer, Shamyia
E E Smith SR HS
Fayetteville, NC

Ownby, Andrew C
Hiwassee Dam HS
Andrews, NC

Owens, Rashad
Lumberton HS
Lumberton, NC

Onuma, Britney
North Forsyth HS
Winston-Salem, NC

Oreloja, Gbolabo
Riverside HS
Durham, NC

Packer, Brandi N
West Bladen HS
Dublin, NC

Parker, Jazzman
Nash Ctrl HS
Rocky Mount, NC

PARSONS, NIKKI; WINSTON-SALEM, NC; REYNOLDS HS; (JR); All Am Sch; F Lan Hn Soc; Hi Hnr Roll; Hnr Roll; Otst Ac Ach Awd; Pres Sch; WWAHSS; Comm Volntr; Hosp Aide; Peer Tut/Med; Scouts; Svce Clb; Latin Clb; Chr; Dnce; Education; Wake Forest U; North Carolina State U

PARSONS, WHITNEY; PURLEAR, NC; WEST WILKES HS; (JR); Hnr Roll; WWAHSS; Comm Volntr; FCA; Key Club; Ntl Beta Clb; Dnce; Sccr (J); Track (J); Business Degree; U of North Carolina At Charlotte

PASPA, ALEXANDER W; HICKORY, NC; HICKORY HS; (FR); Hi Hnr Roll; Hnr Roll; Perf Att; Pres Sch; Sci Fairs; Chrch Yth Grp; Key Club; Spanish Clb; Lcrsse (J); Key Club Member; Carolina; Davidson College

PATE, KRISTEN M; CLINTON, NC; CLINTON HS; (JR); Hnr Roll; St of Mnth; WWAHSS; Comm Volntr; Chrch Yth Grp; Dbte Team; Key Club; Prom Com; Latin Clb; Clr Grd; Adv Cncl (R); Yrbk (E); 1st Runner Up in Miss CHS; Journalism Major; UNC W; NC State

PATEL, DEVANG; APEX, NC; APEX HS; (JR); Hnr Roll; Comm Volntr; Hosp Aide; DECA; Emplmnt; Ch Chr; Academic Emphasis Award; Scholarship Award; MD; Pre-Med; U of North Carolina Chapel Hill; East Carolina U

PATEL, HARSHALKUMAR M; SALISBURY, NC; SALISBURY HS; (SR); Hnr Roll; Nat Hon Sy; Nat Sci Aw; Perf Att; USAA; WWAHSS; Comm Volntr; Key Club; Mth Clb/Tm; French Clb; Bsball (V); Exercise and Sports Science; East Carolina U

PATEL, KETU D; CHARLOTTE, NC; OLYMPIC HS; (JR); F Lan Hn Soc; Hi Hnr Roll; Hnr Roll; Jr Mshl; Nat Hon Sy; Nat Sci Aw; Sci/Math Olympn; USAA; WWAHSS; Comm Volntr; Peer Tut/Med; Red Cr Aide; Key Club; MuAlphaTh; Ntl Beta Clb; Sci Clb; Spanish Clb; Dnce; Sccr (V); Tennis (V); Medicine; Pharmacy; UNC-Chapel Hill; Duke U

PATEL, NISHA A; DUNN, NC; TRITON HS; (FR); Ctznshp Aw; Hnr Roll; Otst Ac Ach Awd; Perf Att; St of Mnth; Comm Volntr; Hosp Aide; Red Cr Aide; DARE; FBLA; Key Club; Ntl Beta Clb; Sci Clb; Dnce; PPSqd (J); Sccr (J); Yrbk; Sec of the Future Bus Leaders; Surgeon; Botanical Garden; North Carolina State U

PATEL, SHAMIRKUMAR H; CHARLOTTE, NC; HARDING U HS; (FR); Sci Clb; Ice Hky (V); Biology; Pre-Med; U of North Carolina-Chapel Hill; Wake Forest U

PATEL, YOGI A; DENVER, NC; EAST LINCOLN HS; (SO); Hnr Roll; Perf Att; Pres Ac Ftns Aw; Sci Fairs; Sci/Math Olympn; Hab For Humty Volntr; Red Cr Aide; Spec Olymp Vol; ArtClub; Biology Clb; Chess; DARE; Dbte Team; Key Club; Mth Clb/Tm; Mod UN; Dnce; Lcrsse (V L); Cl Off (R); Stu Cncl (S); CR (R); Neuro Science; Biology; Emory U; Duke U

PATLIFF, CHRISTOPHER; MORVEN, NC; ANSON HS; (SO); Hi Hnr Roll; Jr Rot; Nat Hon Sy; WWAHSS; Comm Volntr; Spec Olymp Vol; ArtClub; Emplmnt; Scouts; Svce Clb; Golf (V); Sccr (V); National Society of High School Scholars; Outstanding Anson High Arts Student 2004; Forestry; Engineering; North Carolina State U; U of North Carolina Wilmington

PATTERSON, LILLIA D; GARNER, NC; SOUTHEAST RALEIGH HS; (JR); Hi Hnr Roll; Hnr Roll; Jr Mshl; WWAHSS; Comm Volntr; Hosp Aide; Key Club; Ntl Beta Clb; Prom Com; Svce Clb; CR (R); Medical Club; National Achiever's Society; Nursing; Nurse Practitioner; U of North Carolina At Chapel-Hill; Emory U

PATTISON, STARRETT G; APEX, NC; APEX HS; (SR); Hi Hnr Roll; Hnr Roll; Chess; Emplmnt; Academic Excellence Award; CPR & Lifesaving / Lifeguard Certification; Counselor / Psychology / Sociology; Business / Foreign Languages; UNC Wilmington

PATTON, BRANDON J; WINSTON SALEM, NC; NORTH FORSYTH HS; (JR); Hnr Roll; Nat Hon Sy; WWAHSS; Comm Volntr; FBLA; Key Club; Mth Clb/Tm; Spanish Clb; Ftball (J); Crosby Scholar; Big Brother/Big Sister Program; Marketing; Economics; U of North Carolina At Chapel Hill; U of North Carolina At Greensboro

PAXTON, JACQUELYN; YADKINVILLE, NC; FORBUSH HS; (MS); Hnr Roll; Lib Aide; Chr; Clr Grd; West Virginia U; Appalachian State U

PAYNE, RACHEL E; SANFORD, NC; LEE CTY HS; (JR); All Am Sch; Hnr Roll; Otst Ac Ach Awd; Pres Ac Ftns Aw; Pres Sch; USAA; Chrch Yth Grp; Emplmnt; Kwanza Clb; Mod UN; Scouts; Swmg (VJ L); Stu Cncl (R); Sch Ppr (R, P); God and Country Award; Episcopal Youth Group Officer; Episcopal Acolyte Team; Early Childhood; East Carolina; North Carolina State; U of North Carolina At Greensboro

PAYTON, KRYSTAL; LA GRANGE, NC; KINSTON HS; (JR); WWAHSS; Comm Volntr; Prom Com; Chr; Vllyball (VJ); Delta Academy Graduate; Architecture Engineering; New Jersey Institute of Technology; North Carolina State U

PEARCE, KELSEY; ROXBORO, NC; PERSON HS; (MS); Hi Hnr Roll; Hnr Roll; Nat Hon Sy; Comm Volntr; 4-H; Chrch Yth Grp; Chrldg (J L); Yrbk (R); Principal's List; Honor Roll

PEARL, ANDREW S; CLEMMONS, NC; CALVARY BAPTIST DAY SCH; (SR); Comm Volntr; Spec Olymp Vol; Bskball (J); Sccr (V); Business; Economics; U of North Carolina Charlotte

PEARSON, BRIAN C; CLINTON, NC; CLINTON HS; (JR); Hi Hnr Roll; Nat Hon Sy; Otst Ac Ach Awd; Perf Att; Pres Ac Ftns Aw; USAA; WWAHSS; Comm Volntr; Chrch Yth Grp; Key Club; Ntl Beta Clb; Quiz Bowl; Bnd; Mch Bnd; Ftball (VJ L); Wt Lftg (VJ); Pharmacy; East Carolina U; U of North Carolina Wilmington

PEARSON, RAE ANN; WINSTON SALEM, NC; REYNOLDS HS; (JR); Hnr Roll; MVP; WWAHSS; Comm Volntr; FCA; Sci Clb; Spanish Clb; Bnd; Bskball (V CL); Track (V L); CR (R); The National of High School Scholars Award; Student of the Year Award - 9th Grade; Physical Therapy; Biological / Biomedical Sciences; Winston-Salem State U; U of North Carolina Central

PEDRO, ALFREDO; WINSTON SALEM, NC; GLENN HS; (JR); Hnr Roll; WWAHSS; Comm Volntr; Chrch Yth Grp; Orch; Wrstlg (J); National Latin Honor Society; Architectural Engineering; NC State U; A & T U

PEDRO, DIEGO; LENOIR, NC; WEST CALDWELL HS; (FR); Perf Att; WWAHSS; Educational Talent Search; Vet; Meteorology; Appalachian State; U of North Carolina

PEEK, ALANA; LAKEVIEW, NC; (JR); Duke TS; Hnr Roll; WWAHSS; Chrch Yth Grp; Bnd; Ch Chr; Clr Grd; Mch Bnd; Major in Architecture; Degree As an Architect; Agricultural Technical (NC); NC State

PEELE, BRIAN A; LEWISTON, NC; BERTIE HS; (SO); All Am Sch; Hi Hnr Roll; Otst Ac Ach Awd; Sci Fairs; Peer Tut/Med; FBLA; Member of the AIG Program; Member of the MSEN Program; Software Computer Engineering; North Carolina Agricultural & Technical State U; NC State U

PEMBERTON, ASHLEE N; WILLOW SPRING, NC; FUQUAY-VARINA HS; (FR); Hi Hnr Roll; Hnr Roll; MVP; Otst Ac Ach Awd; Comm Volntr; Peer Tut/Med; Ntl Beta Clb; Orch; Stu Cncl (R); Principal's Award; Physical Therapy; Music; U of North Carolina-Wilmington; Florida State U

PENA, SINDY; DURHAM, NC; CARDINAL GIBBONS HS; (SO); Hnr Roll; Nat Hon Sy; Salutrn; Comm Volntr; Peer Tut/Med; Chrch Yth Grp; French Clb; Sccr (V); Medicine; Neonatology; U of North Carolina

PENA, YESENIA P; RALEIGH, NC; MILLBROOK HS; (SR); Hnr Roll; WWAHSS; Comm Volntr; Hab For Humty Volntr; SP/M/VS; Character Trait; Honor Roll; Business Management; Spanish Teacher; NC State

PENALOZA, CHARITY; RALEIGH, NC; LEESVILLE ROAD HS; (SR); Duke TS; Hi Hnr Roll; Hnr Roll; Jr Mshl; Nat Hon Sy; Otst Ac Ach Awd; USAA; WWAHSS; Yth Ldrshp Prog; Comm Volntr; Hosp Aide; Peer Tut/Med; Chrch Yth Grp; DARE; FBLA; Key Club; Prom Com; Sci Clb; Svce Clb; Spanish Clb; Ch Chr; Tennis (J); Adv Cncl (R); Cl Off (V); Stu Cncl (P, V); Yrbk (E); Medicine-Doctor; U of North Carolina At Chapel Hill; Southern Adventist U

PENDLETON, HALEY; MONROE, NC; FOREST HILLS HS; (FR); Hnr Roll; Perf Att; WWAHSS; Comm Volntr; DARE; Emplmnt; Ntl Beta Clb; Bnd; Dnce; Sccr (V); Swmg (V); Tennis (V); Wt Lftg (V); Junior Beta Club; Who's Who; Math & Science; Professional Sports; U of North Carolina Chapel Hill; Wingate U

PENN, DAVITA; WINGATE, NC; FOREST HILLS HS; (FR); Hnr Roll; Otst Ac Ach Awd; Comm Volntr; Chrch Yth Grp; Pep Squd; Tchrs Aide; Bnd; Chr; Ch Chr; Stu Cncl (R); Manager Varsity Basketball; Chef; Cosmetology; Johnson & Wales U; Kings College

PENNINGTON, BRITTANY; LINCOLNTON, NC; WEST LINCOLN HS; (FR); Hnr Roll; St of Mnth; CARE; Comm Volntr; Peer Tut/Med; Chrch Yth Grp; DARE; Scouts; Ch Chr; Culinary Arts; Accounting; Johnson and Wales U

PENTZ, STEFANIE; ASHEVILLE, NC; ASHEVILLE HS; (SO); Duke TS; Hnr Roll; WWAHSS; Comm Volntr; Emplmnt; Lib Aide; Bnd; Mch Bnd; Chrldg (V); Track (V); Academically Intellectually Gifted Program; Art / Painting; Psychology; Western Carolina U; Appalachian State U

PEOPLES, SHATOYA E; MOUNT GILEAD, NC; WEST MONTGOMERY HS; (JR); Hnr Roll; Nat Mrt LOC; Perf Att; Pres Sch; Yth Ldrshp Prog; Comm Volntr; Peer Tut/Med; Chrch Yth Grp; Mth Clb/Tm; Ntl Beta Clb; Prom Com; Spanish Clb; Dnce; Anesthesiology; Radiology; U of North Carolina-Chapel Hill

PEREZ DE LA OLIVA, ALEJANDRO; INDIAN TRAIL, NC; PIEDMONT HS; (JR); Ctznshp Aw; Hi Hnr Roll; Hnr Roll; Nat Hon Sy; Pres Sch; St of Mnth; Comm Volntr; Peer Tut/Med; Red Cr Aide; ArtClub; FBLA; Ntl Beta Clb; Clb; Academic Letter & Bars; National Honor Society 03-05; Clinical Laboratory Science; Psychology; U of North Carolina Charlotte; U of North Carolina Wilmington

PERFETTO, JOSEPH E; WILLOW SPRING, NC; WEST JOHNSTON HS; (SR); All Am Sch; Ctznshp Aw; Hi Hnr Roll; Hnr Roll; Nat Hon Sy; Nat Sci Aw; Nat Stu Ath Day Aw; Otst Ac Ach Awd; Pres Ac Ftns Aw; WWAHSS; Comm Volntr; 4-H; Emplmnt; FCA; P to P St Amb Prg; Tchrs Aide; Vsity Clb; Spanish Clb; Bskball; Sccr; Track; Pediatrician

PERKINSON, ASHLEE P; HENDERSON, NC; NORTHERN VANCE HS; (FR); All Am Sch; Duke TS; USAA; WWAHSS; Comm Volntr; Chrch Yth Grp; FCA; Key Club; Chr; Cr Ctry (V L); Track (V L); CR (R); Sch Ppr (R); 2005 Young Miss North Carolina; Vance County School of Excellence; Political Science; Piano Performance; Duke U

PERRY, JESSICA M; SOUTHPORT, NC; SOUTH BRUNSWICK HS; (SO); Hnr Roll; Perf Att; Sci Fairs; Chrch Yth Grp; Ntl Beta Clb; Tchrs Aide; Dnce; Marine Biology; U of NC At Wilmington

PERRY, JHORDAN; CHARLOTTE, NC; HARDING UNIVERSITY HS; (JR); F Lan Hn Soc; Hnr Roll; Comm Volntr; Peer Tut/Med; Chrch Yth Grp; DARE; Photog; Japanese Clb; SP/M/VS; Track (V); Wrstlg (V); Sch Ppr (R, P); President/Founder Poetry Club; CNN Student; Graphic Animation; Cinematography/Film Production; New York U; Florida A & M U

PERRY, JUSTIN; HOPE MILLS, NC; GRAY'S CREEK HS; (SO); Hnr Roll; WWAHSS; Comm Volntr; Emplmnt; Key Club; Pep Squd; SADD; Ftball (V); Wrstlg (V); Computer Programming/Technology; North Carolina State U

PERSON, ASHLEY; LOUISBURG, NC; LOUISBURG HS; (SR); 4H Awd; Hi Hnr Roll; Jr Mshl; Nat Hon Sy; Otst Ac Ach Awd; Perf Att; St of Mnth; WWAHSS; Yth Ldrshp Prog; Comm Volntr; 4-H; Chrch Yth Grp; Prom Com; Dnce; Nutrition; Exercise Physiology; East Carolina U

PETERS, MATTHEW P; MATTHEWS, NC; DAVID W BUTLER HS; (JR); Duke TS; Hi Hnr Roll; Nat Hon Sy; Nat Mrt Semif; Otst Ac Ach Awd; WWAHSS; Comm Volntr; Civil Air Pat; Emplmnt; Key Club; P to P St Amb Prg; Spanish Clb; Drl Tm; SP/M/VS; Stg Cre; National Student Leadership Conference; Student Pilot; Aerospace/Astronomy; Theatre; U of North Carolina At Chapel Hill; U of Southern California

PETTAWAY, ANTHONY D; CHARLOTTE, NC; WEST MECKLENBURG HS; (JR); Hnr Roll; Otst Ac Ach Awd; DARE; Bnd; Ftball (V); Track (V); Wrstlg (V); Bachelor Degree; Master Degree; Maryland U; Miami Florida U

PEYTON, TILON; ROCKY MOUNT, NC; ROCKY MOUNT SR HS; (JR); Ctznshp Aw; Hnr Roll; MVP; Otst Ac Ach Awd; Perf Att; CARE; Red Cr Aide; Chess; Chrch Yth Grp; DARE; Dbte Team; Key Club; Photog; Quiz Bowl; Bsball (V); Bskball (V); Ftball (V); Scr Kpr (V); Track (V); Stu Cncl (T); Yrbk (P); Doctor/Science; Virginia U; Georgetown U/Maryland

PFEFFERLE, LAUREN E; MATTHEWS, NC; CHARLOTTE CATHOLIC HS; (JR); Hnr Roll; WWAHSS; Comm Volntr; Hab For Humty Volntr; Chrch Yth Grp; DARE; Emplmnt; SADD; Chr; Hsbk Rdg (V); Compete in Horse Shows; Volunteer in Community; Physical Therapy; Nursing; U of South Carolina Columbia; Ohio State U

PHAN, LUY T; GREENSBORO, NC; W H PAGE; (JR); Ctznshp Aw; Hnr Roll; Perf Att; St of Mnth; Comm Volntr; Peer Tut/Med; ArtClub; Clr Grd; Drl Tm; American Legion Scholastic Excellence Medal; Graduate of Leadership Academy 2005; Psychology; Medicine; UNC Chapel Hill; Duke U

PHAN, NAM T; KERNERSVILLE, NC; EAST FORSYTH HS; (JR); Ctznshp Aw; Gov Hnr Prg; Hnr Roll; Nat Hon Sy; Nat Ldrshp Svc; Otst Ac Ach Awd; St of Mnth; Yth Ldrshp Prog; Comm Volntr; Hab For Humty Volntr; Hosp Aide; Key Club; Mus Clb; Photog; Acpl Chr; Chr; Ch Chr; Track (V); Yrbk (P); National Youth Leadership Forum on Medicine; Governor's School of NC; Dentistry; Medicine; U of North Carolina At Chapel Hill; North Carolina State U

PHELPS, KATHERYN L; COLUMBUS, NC; POLK CTY HS; (SO); Duke TS; Hnr Roll; WWAHSS; Comm Volntr; Spec Olymp Vol; Key Club; Bskball (V L); Track (V L); Vllyball (V L); Sch Ppr (R); Psychology; Interior Design; U of North Carolina Charlotte; U of North Carolina

PHILEMON, REBECCA J; INDIAN TRAIL, NC; PIEDMONT HS; (JR); Hnr Roll; St of Mnth; Comm Volntr; Chrch Yth Grp; DARE; Emplmnt; Ntl FFA; Ch Chr; Stu Cncl (R); CR (R); Health Occupations Students of America (Club); Multicultural Achievement Club; Nursing-BSN; Health Science; Queen's College; U of North Carolina

PHILLIPS, ALESHIA; CHARLOTTE, NC; PHILLIP O BERRY AC OF TECH; (SO); Hnr Roll; WWAHSS; ROTC; Sftball ((V)); National Youth Leadership Forum On Medicine; Berry Cardinal Step Team; Nursing; U of North Carolina at Chapel Hill; Florida State U

PHILLIPS, CHELSEA; HUNTERSVILLE, NC; HOPEWELL HS; (SO); Duke TS; F Lan Hn Soc; Hi Hnr Roll; Hnr Roll; Otst Ac Ach Awd; Comm Volntr; Chrch Yth Grp; DECA; Emplmnt; Spanish Clb; Chrldg (VJCL); Sccr (J); Cl Off (P, S); Yrbk (R); Principal's Award: Student of the Year; Jr Nat'l Honor Society, Odyssey of the Mind; Teaching; Law; Duke U; U of North Carolina-Chapel Hill

PHILLIPS, REBECCA; RALEIGH, NC; LEESVILLE ROAD HS; (SR); Hi Hnr Roll; Otst Ac Ach Awd; Chrldg (V L); Pharmacy; Radiology; U of North Carolina At Wilmington

Pfefferle, Lauren E
Charlotte Catholic HS
Matthews, NC

Perez De La Oliva, Alejandro
Piedmont HS
Indian Trail, NC

Pentz, Stefanie
Asheville HS
Asheville, NC

Payton, Krystal
Kinston HS
La Grange, NC

Parsons, Nikki
Reynolds HS
Winston-Salem, NC

Paspa, Alexander W
Hickory HS
Hickory, NC

Peoples, Shatoya E
West Montgomery HS
Mount Gilead, NC

Peters, Matthew P
David W Butler HS
Matthews, NC

Philemon, Rebecca J
Piedmont HS
Indian Trail, NC

PHILLIPS, REVA G; MOORESVILLE, NC; MOORESVILLE HS; (SO); Duke TS; Hnr Roll; WWAHSS; Yth Ldrshp Prog; Comm Volntr; Peer Tut/Med; Chess; Dbte Team; HO'Br Yth Ldrshp; ROTC; Drl Tm; Golf (V L); Lcrsse; Track (V L); Stu Cncl (R); Hugh O'Brian Youth Leadership Representative; Mooresville South Youth Leadership Program; BA / International Relations; Law Degree; UNC Chapel Hill; Georgetown U

PHILLIPS, RYAN; WILMINGTON, NC; JOHN T HOGGARD HS; (JR); Hnr Roll; Sci Fairs; Sci/Math Olympn; WWAHSS; Comm Volntr; Chrch Yth Grp; FCA; Ntl Beta Clb; Sci Clb; Tech Clb; Vsity Clb; Bsball (J); Cr Ctry (J); Ftball (J); Golf (V); Swmg (V); Beta Club; National Honor Society; Engineering; Oceanography; North Carolina State; Virginia Tech

PICKARD, CHASE; RALEIGH, NC; WAKEFIELD HS; (SO); Duke TS; Hnr Roll; WWAHSS; Comm Volntr; Spec Olymp Vol; DARE; Key Club; Ftball (VJ); Wt Lftg (VJ); MBA; Duke U; U of North Carolina Chapel Hill

PICKETT, DEJA; JACKSONVILLE, NC; SOUTHWEST HS; (FR); Hi Hnr Roll; Nat Hon Sy; Otst Ac Ach Awd; Perf Att; St of Mnth; Comm Volntr; P to P St Amb Prg; Chr; Dnce; Drl Tm; Stg Cre; PP Ftbl (J); Track (J); AVID; Teen Court; Criminal Law; International Studies; U of Columbia; Harvard

PIERCE, ASHLEY W; GRANITE FALLS, NC; HIBRITEN HS; (JR); Ctznshp Aw; Hnr Roll; WWAHSS; Comm Volntr; Drma Clb; Emplmnt; Key Club; Won I Dream... Scholarship; Maintain After-School Job; Computer Science; Pharmaceuticals; Appalachian State U; Gardner-Webb U

PIERCE, KRYSTY; GREENSBORO, NC; SOUTHERN GUILFORD HS; (SR); St of Mnth; WWAHSS; Comm Volntr; Peer Tut/Med; Chrch Yth Grp; Emplmnt; Lib Aide; Ntl Beta Clb; Ntl FFA; Prom Com; SADD; French Clb; Ch Chr; Cr Ctry (V L); Track (V L); National Vocational-Technical Honor Society; Meteorology; U of North Carolina At Charlotte

PILLARS, HALEY; MINERAL SPRINGS, NC; PARKWOOD HS; (JR); Hi Hnr Roll; Hnr Roll; Nat Hon Sy; Comm Volntr; Chrch Yth Grp; FTA; Key Club; Chr; Ch Chr; Dnce; SP/M/VS; All State Choir; Ballroom Dancing Showcase; Biology; Dance/Physical Therapy; Wingate U; U of North Carolina At Chapel Hill

PINCHBACK, ALEXONDRIA; FAYETTEVILLE, NC; E E SMITH SR HS; (FR); Ctznshp Aw; Hnr Roll; Comm Volntr; Peer Tut/Med; DARE; Pre-Law; Business Administration; UNC-Chapel Hill; UNC-Greensboro

PINCKNEY, CARISSA L; HIGH POINT, NC; HIGH POINT CTRL HS; (FR); Duke TS; Hi Hnr Roll; Hnr Roll; WWAHSS; Hosp Aide; Drma Clb; Key Club; Ch Chr; Orch; SP/M/VS; Swmg (V); Stu Cncl (V); Pre-Med; Yale U

PINION, JESSICA; NORWOOD, NC; SOUTH STANLY HS; (FR); Hnr Roll; Perf Att; St of Mnth; WWAHSS; Fine Crafts; Computer Apps.; Registered Nurse; Bachelors, Science; U of North Carolina-Charlotte; Stanly Community, Rowan Technical

PIPER JR, JOHN C; ADVANCE, NC; DAVIE HS; (FR); Hnr Roll; DARE; ROTC; Bnd; Wrstlg (J)

PITMAN, COTY A; BURNSVILLE, NC; MTN HERITAGE HS; (FR); Hi Hnr Roll; Hnr Roll; Kwnis Aw; MVP; Peer Tut/Med; DARE; ROTC; Wdwrkg Clb; Air Force / ROTC; Mathematics; U of North Carolina; Duke U

PITT, PRISCILLA; RALEIGH, NC; ENLOE HS; (JR); Hi Hnr Roll; Hnr Roll; Otst Ac Ach Awd; WWAHSS; Comm Volntr; Key Club; Japanese Clb; PP Ftbl (V); Spotlight on Students; Pediatrics, Biology; Nursing; UNC-Chapel Hill; Duke U

PITTMAN, ANDREW B; FAYETTEVILLE, NC; TERRY SANFORD HS; (SO); Hnr Roll; Nat Hon Sy; Otst Ac Ach Awd; Comm Volntr; Key Club; Bsball (J); Sports Medicine; Athletic Training; U North Carolina-Chapel Hill; NC State U

PITTMAN, THOMAS K; NEWLAND, NC; AVERY CTY HS; (SO); Duke TS; Hi Hnr Roll; Otst Ac Ach Awd; Perf Att; Valdctrian; Chess; Chrch Yth Grp; Emplmnt; Quiz Bowl; First in Category At Local Art Show; Work 10+ Hours A Week / Full Time In Summer; Civil Engineering; Architecture; Duke U; North Carolina State U

PITTS, ASHLEY R; ENFIELD, NC; NORTHWEST HS; (JR); Hnr Roll; Nat Hon Sy; WWAHSS; Peer Tut/Med; FBLA; Bnd; Mch Bnd; Pediatric Nurse; A & T State U; NC State U

PLACKE, JESSICA; MOCKSVILLE, NC; DAVIE HS; (JR); Hi Hnr Roll; Hnr Roll; WWAHSS; Comm Volntr; Chrch Yth Grp; Emplmnt; FCA; Ntl Beta Clb; Prom Com; Tchrs Aide; Spanish Clb; Bnd; Ch Chr; Clr Grd; Drm Mjr; Sccr (J); Sch Ppr (R); Flute Student Excellence Award; Education-K-8 Teacher; Appalachian State U; U of North Carolina

PLASTER, BRIAN; FAYETTEVILLE, NC; E E SMITH SR HS; (FR); Comm Volntr; Peer Tut/Med; U of Wisconsin-Madison; East Carolina U

PLEASANT, THOMAS E; RALEIGH, NC; MIDDLE CREEK HS; (JR); Duke TS; Hnr Roll; WWAHSS; DARE; French Clb; Swmg (V L); Produce School TV News; Forensic Science; Psychology; Appalachian State U; U of North Carolina Wilmington

PLESS, JAMI A; LOCUST, NC; WEST STANLY HS; (SO); Ctznshp Aw; Duke TS; Hi Hnr Roll; Hnr Roll; Perf Att; Sci Fairs; St of Mnth; Comm Volntr; DARE; Ntl Beta Clb; Yrbk (R, P); Safe Kids Volunteer Club; News Team; UFE-Fire-Safety Educator; Elementary Education; U of North Carolina-Charlotte; Pfeiffer

PLUMMER, ANDREW; MIDDLEBURG, NC; SOUTHERN VANCE HS; (JR); Hi Hnr Roll; Hnr Roll; Chrch Yth Grp; Bnd; Ch Chr; Jzz Bnd; Mch Bnd; Ftball (V); Track (V); Wt Lftg (V); Wrstlg (V); Architecture Major; North Carolina State U; Wake Forest

PLUMMER, JENNIFER; CAMP LEJEUNE, NC; LEJEUNE HS; (SR); Hnr Roll; Nat Hon Sy; Otst Ac Ach Awd; Comm Volntr; Spec Olymp Vol; Emplmnt; Key Club; ROTC; Scouts; SADD; 4 Medals, 16 Ribbons in JROTC; Commanding Officer in JROTC; Business Administration; Elementary Level Teaching; U of North Carolina Pembroke; U of North Carolina At Wilmington

POINDEXTER, JEFFREY K; PITTSBORO, NC; NORTHWOOD HS; (SO)

POLIKS, EDMUND; JACKSONVILLE, NC; NORTHSIDE HS; (FR); Duke TS; Hi Hnr Roll; Hnr Roll; Nat Hon Sy; Otst Ac Ach Awd; Perf Att; Sci Fairs; Sci/Math Olympn; Yth Ldrshp Prog; Comm Volntr; Peer Tut/Med; Chess; Drma Clb; Lib Aide; Mth Clb/Tm; Off Aide; Scouts; Chr; SP/M/VS; Stu Cncl (S); Math Counts Competition, Academic Derby; Science Fair 1st Place in Category; Computer Programming; Forensics; UNC Chapel Hill; Duke

POLLITT, SAMANTHA D; FAYETTEVILLE, NC; (FR); Hi Hnr Roll; WWAHSS; FBLA; Key Club; Quiz Bowl; Chr; SP/M/VS; Color Guard for 2005-2006 School Year; Psychology; Neurology; North Carolina State U; Duke U

POOLE, JASON; DALLAS, NC; NORTH GASTON HS; (SR); Hnr Roll; MVP; WWAHSS; Comm Volntr; Chrch Yth Grp; SP/M/VS; Golf (V C); Won Gaston County Acting Competition; Best Actor and Won Best Scene; Golf Course Management; Catawba Valley Community College; NC State U

POOLE, STEWART H; RALEIGH, NC; WAKEFIELD HS; (SO); Hi Hnr Roll; Perf Att; WWAHSS; Yth Ldrshp Prog; Comm Volntr; Emplmnt; Key Club; Ntl Beta Clb; Scouts; AAU Baseball; Life Scout; Business Management; NC State U (North Carolina); Appalachin State U

POPE, BRADLEY C; CANTON, NC; PISGAH HS; (JR); Hnr Roll; Chrch Yth Grp; Emplmnt; FCA; FTA; Key Club; Pep Squd; Chr; SP/M/VS; Bsball (V); Ftball (J); Wt Lftg; Elementary Education; Elementary Physical Education; Western Carolina; Clemson U

POPE, SPENCER C; RALEIGH, NC; MILLBROOK HS; (SR); Hnr Roll; Chrch Yth Grp; FCA; Mus Clb; Ch Chr; SP/M/VS; Environmental Business; Chemistry; U of North Carolina Chapel Hill; North Carolina State U

PORTER, AMY M; MURFREESBORO, NC; HERTFORD CTY HS; (FR); Hnr Roll; Perf Att; St of Mnth; Comm Volntr; Peer Tut/Med; 4-H; Chrch Yth Grp; DARE; ROTC; Spch Team; Ch Chr; Drl Tm; Active Member of Speech Team; Read and Mentor to Church Children; Fashion Design; Music; Harvard U; Hampton U

PORTER, BRANDY L; SHELBY, NC; BURNS HS; (JR); Hi Hnr Roll; Jr Mshl; Nat Hon Sy; Pres Sch; St of Mnth; Comm Volntr; Peer Tut/Med; Chrch Yth Grp; Emplmnt; FBLA; Key Club; Lib Aide; Ntl Beta Clb; Off Aide; SADD; SP/M/VS; Sch Ppr (E, R, P); Young Women's Medallion; ABA Tutor; Biology; Optometry; UNC Charlotte; Wake Forest U

PORTER, RYAN L; CHARLOTTE, NC; PHILLIP O BERRY AC OF TECH; (JR); Ctznshp Aw; Hi Hnr Roll; Hnr Roll; MVP; Nat Ldrshp Svc; Otst Ac Ach Awd; Perf Att; Pres Ac Ftns Aw; St of Mnth; St Optmst of Yr; Comm Volntr; Peer Tut/Med; Spec Olymp Vol; Chrch Yth Grp; DARE; Jr Ach; Outdrs Clb; Photog; ROTC; Scouts; Tech Clb; Clr Grd; Drl Tm; Bsball (V); Stu Cncl (R); CR (P); Teen Role Model; Superior Cadet; Civil Engineering; Architecture; U of North Carolina; North Carolina State U

POSTLE, MONIQUE K; FAYETTEVILLE, NC; WESTOVER HS; (SR); Comm Volntr; Peer Tut/Med; Chrch Yth Grp; Emplmnt; FBLA; Off Aide; Spanish Clb; Accounting, CPA; Campbell U

POTEAT, MONICA; KANNAPOLIS, NC; A L BROWN HS; (JR); Gov Hnr Prg; Hi Hnr Roll; Hnr Roll; Jr Mshl; Nat Hon Sy; Pres Sch; St Schl; WWAHSS; Yth Ldrshp Prog; Comm Volntr; Hosp Aide; Red Cr Aide; Quiz Bowl; Bnd; Dnce; Jzz Bnd; Mch Bnd; Bskball (V CL); Vllyball (V L); Harvard Book Award; Elon U Junior Scholar; Biology; Medicine (Emergency Doctor); Elon U (Already Accepted)

POTTER, KRISTEN N; WINNABOW, NC; NORTH BRUNSWICK HS; (FR); Hnr Roll; MVP; Chrch Yth Grp; Pep Squd; Dnce; Chrldg (V); Registered Nursing; UNCW

POULIMENOS, DIANA K; MATTHEWS, NC; WEDDINGTON HS; (FR); Duke TS; Hnr Roll; Perf Att; WWAHSS; Chrch Yth Grp; Fr of Library; Key Club; Ntl Beta Clb; Cr Ctry (J L); Track (J); Cl Off (R); Stu Cncl (R); Yrbk (R); Rotary Scholar; Medicine; Duke U; U of North Carolina At Chapel Hill

POWELL, ANDREW C; MATTHEWS, NC; WEDDINGTON HS; (FR); Duke TS; Pres Ac Ftns Aw; Chrch Yth Grp; Tennis (L); Vocation Bible School for Inner City Children

POWELL, CLAYTON; BELEWS CREEK, NC; EAST FORSYTH HS; (SO); Ctznshp Aw; Hnr Roll; Comm Volntr; Chrch Yth Grp; Student of the Year; U of North Charolina Charlotte; Appalachian State U

POWELL, DESIRAE A; ROXBORO, NC; PERSON HS; (SO); Hnr Roll; Nat Hon Sy; Perf Att; Chrch Yth Grp; DARE; Scouts; Bnd; Chr; Ch Chr; Duke U; U of North Carolina of Greensboro

POWELL, JESSICA A; GRANITE FALLS, NC; SOUTH CALDWELL HS; (SO); Duke TS; Hi Hnr Roll; Hnr Roll; Otst Ac Ach Awd; Perf Att; Sci Fairs; St of Mnth; WWAHSS; Comm Volntr; Chrch Yth Grp; DARE; Ntl Beta Clb; Scouts; Chr; Ch Chr; PP Ftbl (J); Pediatric Nurse; Physical Therapist; UNC Chapel Hill; UNC Charlotte

POWELL, MEGAN E; REIDSVILLE, NC; REIDSVILLE HS; (JR); Hi Hnr Roll; Jr Mshl; Perf Att; Comm Volntr; Peer Tut/Med; Chrch Yth Grp; Emplmnt; FCA; SADD; Bnd; Dnce; Drm Mjr; Mch Bnd; Chrldg (VJCL); Junior Marshall; IB Certificate Candidate; Medical Doctor; Wake Forest U; U of North Carolina Chapel Hill

POWELL, ROBERT; SALISBURY, NC; NORTH HILLS CHRISTIAN SCH; (SO); Hnr Roll; Pres Ac Ftns Aw; Sci Fairs; WWAHSS; Chrch Yth Grp; Bskball (V); Cr Ctry (V); Cl Off (V, S); Design; Marketing; Wake Forest U; U of NC At Greensboro

PRATT, BRENDA; JACKSONVILLE, NC; WHITE OAK HS; (MS); Ctznshp Aw; Hnr Roll; Bnd; Ch Chr; Pep Bnd; Graduating Young Marines

PRATT-KOLLORE, CHIAKA; GREENSBORO, NC; DUDLEY HS; (SO); Hnr Roll; Perf Att; Comm Volntr; ROTC; Drl Tm; Sftball (VJ); Vllyball (V C); Sports and Medicine; Business and Management; Spelman

PRESTON, BRYANT; REIDSVILLE, NC; REIDSVILLE HS; (FR); Ctznshp Aw; Fut Prb Slvr; Hi Hnr Roll; Hnr Roll; MVP; Nat Hon Sy; Otst Ac Ach Awd; Perf Att; Sci Fairs; Sci/Math Olympn; Peer Tut/Med; ArtClub; Chrch Yth Grp; DARE; Drma Clb; FBLA; Lib Aide; Mth Clb/Tm; Mus Clb; Bnd; SP/M/VS; Bsball (J); Wt Lftg (J); Stu Cncl (V); CR (P); Business Management; Engineering; U of North Carolina; Duke U

PREWETT, ROY; GREENSBORO, NC; PAGE HS; (SO); Hnr Roll; Comm Volntr; Drma Clb; Mus Clb; Bnd; Jzz Bnd; Mch Bnd; SP/M/VS; Most Improved Wind Ensemble Player; Biology; Music; U of North Carolina Greensboro; Appalachian State U

PRICE, ASHLEY M; INDIAN TRAIL, NC; METROLINA CHRISTIAN AC; (JR); Hnr Roll; Perf Att; St of Mnth; WWAHSS; Comm Volntr; Hosp Aide; Drma Clb; Ntl Beta Clb; SP/M/VS; School Choir; Zoology; Wildlife Biology; Wingate U; Elon U

PRICE, DAVID; LUMBERTON, NC; LUMBERTON HS; (FR); Duke TS; Hnr Roll; ROTC; Scouts; Skt Tgt Sh (J); Troop 33 Senior Patrol Leader for One Year; Gunsmithing; Montgomery Community College

PRICE, EMILY; EAST FLAT ROCK, NC; EAST HENDERSON HS; (JR); Ctznshp Aw; Hnr Roll; Nat Hon Sy; WWAHSS; Hosp Aide; Chrch Yth Grp; Emplmnt; Mus Clb; Acpl Chr; Chr; Ch Chr; History; Music; U of North Carolina At Charlotte; College of Charleston

PRICE, JOSHANE; GRIMESLAND, NC; D H CONLEY HS; (SO); Hosp Aide; Ntl Beta Clb; Dnce; North Carolina State U; Georgia Tech

PRICE, PAIGE; FAYETTEVILLE, NC; CAPE FEAR HS; (SR); Ctznshp Aw; Hi Hnr Roll; Nat Hon Sy; St of Mnth; WWAHSS; Comm Volntr; Hab For Humty Volntr; Chrch Yth Grp; Drma Clb; Key Club; Lib Aide; Ntl Beta Clb; SADD; Bnd; Mch Bnd; SP/M/VS; Sccr (J); Orthodontics; U of North Carolina Wilmington

PRIDGEN, AARON; BURGAW, NC; PENDER HS; (FR); Hnr Roll; Scouts; Woodman of the World (Social Studies); Computer Engineer; U of North Carolina At Wilmington; North Carolina State U

PRUITT, KASEY; HAYS, NC; NORTH WILKES HS; (FR); Ctznshp Aw; Hi Hnr Roll; Hnr Roll; Otst Ac Ach Awd; Sci Fairs; Comm Volntr; Chrch Yth Grp; Ntl Beta Clb; Yrbk (P); National Beta Club; UNC Charlotte; App U

PRUNTY, VELDA; CLAREMONT, NC; BANDYS HS; (JR); Hnr Roll; St of Mnth; Chrch Yth Grp; DARE; Mod UN; ROTC; Chr; Ch Chr; Wt Lftg; Pediatric Nurse; North Carolina State

PUGH, BRANDI; WINDSOR, NC; BERTIE HS; (JR); Hnr Roll; Nat Hon Sy; WWAHSS; Comm Volntr; Peer Tut/Med; Emplmnt; Bnd; Mch Bnd; Cl Off (R); Accounting/Business Mgt; Pharmacy; Elizabeth City State U; East Carolina U

PULLEN, RACHEL; RALEIGH, NC; WILLIAM G ENLOE HS; (SR); Hnr Roll; St Schl; Comm Volntr; Chrch Yth Grp; Emplmnt; Mus Clb; Tchrs Aide; Bnd; Orch; Pep Bnd; CR (R); African American Female Enrichment Organization; Youth Empowering Youth Project (Founder); Bachelor of Arts; Political Science; U of North Carolina at Greensboro

Powell, Jessica A
South Caldwell HS
Granite Falls, NC

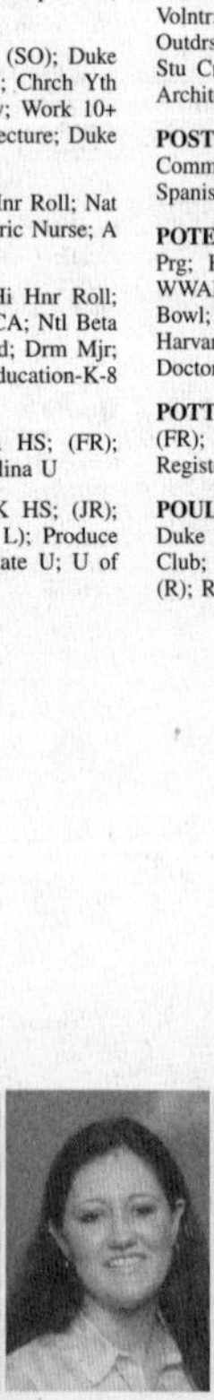
Plummer, Jennifer
Lejeune HS
Camp Lejeune, NC

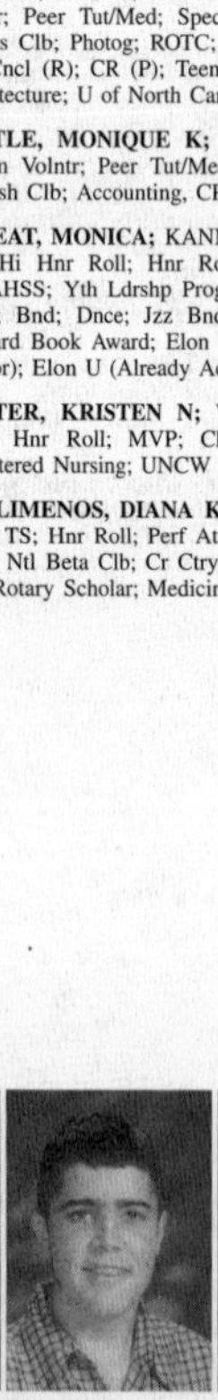
Pittman, Thomas K
Avery Cty HS
Newland, NC

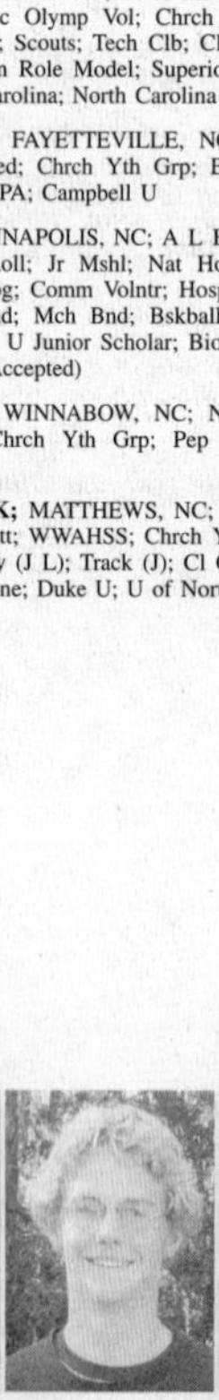
Phillips, Ryan
John T Hoggard HS
Wilmington, NC

Pinckney, Carissa L
High Point Ctrl HS
High Point, NC

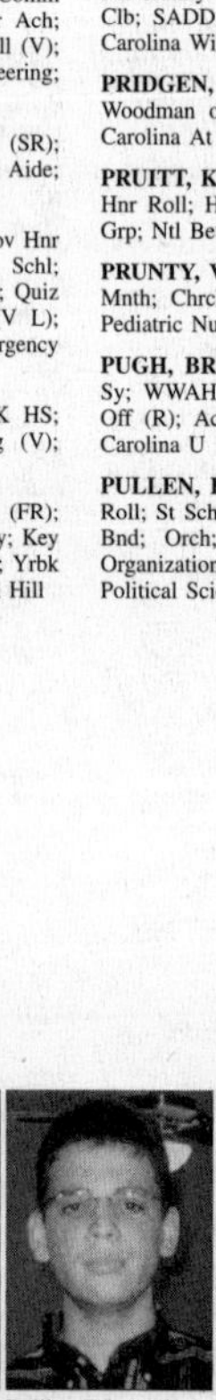
Poliks, Edmund
Northside HS
Jacksonville, NC

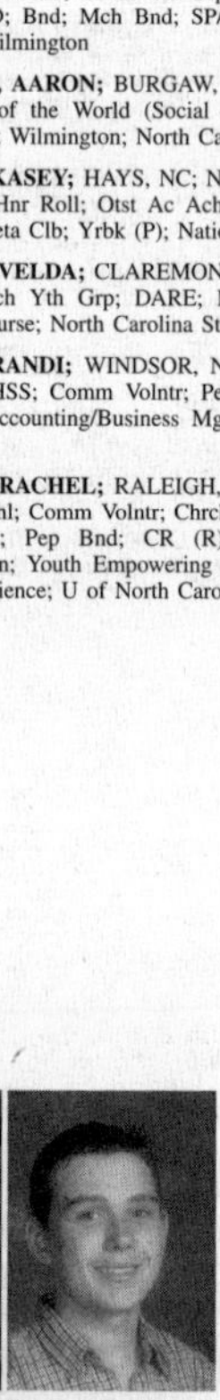
Preston, Bryant
Reidsville HS
Reidsville, NC

PULLEY, QUINTON J; SPRING HOPE, NC; SOUTHERN NASH HS; (FR); Hnr Roll; St of Mnth; Ch Chr; Ftball (J); Business Management; Mechanical Engineering; U of North Carolina; U of Miami (Florida)

PUNCH, SARAH A; LAWNDALE, NC; BURNS HS; (JR); Perf Att; Comm Volntr; DARE; Drma Clb; Ntl FFA; Chr; Ch Chr; SP/M/VS; Playing Piano; Marine Biologist; Filming /Producing /Directing; Cleveland Community College

PUNJALA, ADVAITA; CARY, NC; GREEN HOPE HS; (MS); Hnr Roll; Perf Att; Pres Sch; Sci/Math Olympn; Chess; DARE; Mus Clb; Sci Clb; Orch; Bskball (L); Stu Cncl (T); CR (T); Yrbk (P); Bachelor's Degree from a College; Doctor of Medicine Degree (MD); Duke U; Yale U

PURCELL, CASEY L; JACKSONVILLE, NC; NORTHSIDE HS; (SO); Hnr Roll; Nat Hon Sy; Perf Att; Pres Ac Ftns Aw; Comm Volntr; Hosp Aide; Spec Olymp Vol; Mus Clb; Clr Grd; Mch Bnd; Stu Cncl (P); Pre-Medicine; Biology Major (Specialize in Genetics); U of North Carolina-Chapel Hill

PURCELL, JERIKA; RAEFORD, NC; HOKE CTY HS; (JR); Ctznshp Aw; Comm Volntr; Spec Olymp Vol; Chrch Yth Grp; Emplmnt; Ch Chr; CR (R); Early Childhood Education; Medical Science (Nursing); U of North Carolina At Pembroke; Fayetteville State U

PURRINGTON, KAMILAH; RALEIGH, NC; ATHENS DRIVE HS; (JR); WWAHSS; SADD; Chr; Computer Science; Electrical Engineering; NC A & T State; NC State

PUTNAM, ERIN; JACKSONVILLE, NC; JACKSONVILLE HS; (FR); MVP; Nat Hon Sy; Comm Volntr; FCA; Schol Bwl; Bnd; Jzz Bnd; Bskball (J); Cr Ctry (L); Track (L); Battle of the Books; International Relations; Psychology; Georgetown U; Davidson College

PYATTE, JANELL M J; BANNER ELK, NC; WATAUGA HS; (SO); Hnr Roll; Perf Att; Comm Volntr; Outdrs Clb; French Clb; Presidents Education Awards Program (Outstanding Academic Achievement); Culinary Arts; Social Services; Johnson & Wales U

QUILLEN, MICHAEL; HENDERSONVILLE, NC; WEST HENDERSON HS; (FR); Hnr Roll; MVP; Nat Hon Sy; Perf Att; DARE; Emplmnt; ROTC; SADD; Drl Tm; Flg Crps; Bsball (J); Ftball (J); Golf (J); Pilot/Army; Heavy Equipment; U of Tennessee; U of Michigan

QUIMBY, NICK; WILSON, NC; FIKE HS; (SO); Ctznshp Aw; Duke TS; Nat Ldrshp Svc; Otst Ac Ach Awd; Perf Att; Pres Sch; Sci Fairs; Sci/Math Olympn; WWAHSS; DARE; Mth Clb/Tm; Quiz Bowl; Sci Clb; SADD; Spanish Clb; Bnd; Ftball (J); Aerospace Engineering; Electrical Engineering; North Carolina State U

QUINLAN, MEGAN B; FAYETTEVILLE, NC; SOUTHVIEW HS; (SR); Nat Hon Sy; St of Mnth; WWAHSS; Comm Volntr; Peer Tut/Med; DARE; Drma Clb; FBLA; Key Club; Off Aide; Photog; Foreign Clb; SP/M/VS; Sch Ppr (R); Secretary of Foreign Language Club; FBLA Member, Key Club Member; Journalism, English; U of North Carolina Pembroke

QUINN, AMANDA M; ZEBULON, NC; SMITHFIELD-SELMA HS; (SR); Hi Hnr Roll; Hnr Roll; Jr Mshl; Nat Hon Sy; Otst Ac Ach Awd; Pres Sch; WWAHSS; Comm Volntr; Peer Tut/Med; Spec Olymp Vol; Chrch Yth Grp; FCA; Key Club; MuAlphaTh; Prom Com; Tchrs Aide; Ch Chr; Chrldg (VJ L); Cl Off (S, T); CR (R); Governor's School of North Carolina; Nursing; U of North Carolina Chapel Hill

RACHELS, KYLE; SAINT PAULS, NC; WEST BLADEN HS; (JR); Duke TS; Hnr Roll; Pres Sch; Sci Fairs; Comm Volntr; Spec Olymp Vol; FCA; Ntl Beta Clb; Ntl FFA; Bsball (V); Ftball (V); Wt Lftg; Biology; Fish and Wildlife Management; North Carolina State U; U of North Carolina

RACKLEY, SEPH; CHARLOTTE, NC; E E WADDELL HS; (FR); Chr; Fncg (J); Computer Pgm, math; Art, Literature; U of North Carolina

RACZKOWSKI, HEATHER; GOLDSBORO, NC; EASTERN WAYNE HS; (JR); Hi Hnr Roll; Hnr Roll; Perf Att; Peer Tut/Med; DECA; Emplmnt; Mth Clb/Tm; Ntl FFA; Golf (V L); 3-A All-Conference for Women's Golf; Nursing; East Carolina U; U of North Carolina At Wilmington

RADFORD, LEIGHANN; PRINCETON, NC; PRINCETON SCH; (SO); Hnr Roll; Nat Hon Sy; Chrch Yth Grp; Ch Chr; Clr Grd; Member of Youth Board; Radiologist, Radiology Tech; Medicine; North Carolina State U; Barton College

RAGLAND, BIANCA; HENDERSON, NC; NORTHERN VANCE HS; (FR); Nat Stu Ath Day Aw; Perf Att; Pres Ac Ftns Aw; Sci Fairs; St of Mnth; Yth Ldrshp Prog; CARE; Comm Volntr; Peer Tut/Med; Chrch Yth Grp; Sci Clb; Ch Chr; Dnce; Drl Tm; Bskball (V); Stu Cncl (R); CR (R); MVP of the Year; Coach's Reward; Computer Engineering; Accounts; Duke U; North Carolina State U

RAHN, MEGAN; RALEIGH, NC; NEEDHAM BROUGHTON HS; (SO); Ctznshp Aw; Hi Hnr Roll; MVP; Comm Volntr; Peer Tut/Med; FCA; Bskball (V); Sccr (J); Scholar Athlete Award; State Basketball Champion 2005 4A; Sports Medicine; Athlete Trainer; UNCW-U of North Carolina Wilmington; College of Charleston

RAINES, HANNAH; TRYON, NC; POLK CTY HS; (JR); Hnr Roll; Nat Hon Sy; WWAHSS; FBLA; Key Club; Clr Grd; SP/M/VS; Stg Cre; Cl Off (S); Stu Cncl (V, S); Architecture; Clemson U; U of North Carolina Charlotte

RAINES, SHARONE J; GREENSBORO, NC; DUDLEY HS; (FR); Hnr Roll; Comm Volntr; Peer Tut/Med; Pep Squd; Bnd; Performing Arts; Engineer; Virgina Tech; Carolina

RAKITA, OGNJEN; WINSTON-SALEM, NC; REYNOLDS HS; (JR); Hosp Aide; Mth Clb/Tm; Social Studies Academic Team; International Club Officer; Electrical Engineering; Political Science; North Carolina State U; U of North Carolina Chapel Hill

RAMASUBRAMANIAN, ANUSUYA; CARY, NC; WILLIAM G ENLOE HS; (SO); Duke TS; Fut Prb Slvr; Hi Hnr Roll; Hnr Roll; Nat Hon Sy; Sci/Math Olympn; Yth Ldrshp Prog; Comm Volntr; Peer Tut/Med; Red Cr Aide; HO'Br Yth Ldrshp; Lib Aide; Mod UN; Tmpl Yth Grp; Mar Art; CR (R); Tae Kwon Do (Done Outside of Sch)-Black Belt 1st Deg Sr. Work for NC State U & The State of NC Through GIS (Geor. Inter. Systems); Chemistry/Mathematics (Graduate); Business Management/Finance/Economics; Duke U (North Carolina); Princeton U (New Jersey)

RAMIREZ, CARLOS A; CHARLOTTE, NC; CHARLOTTE CATHOLIC HS; (JR); Sccr; Track; Coach Elementary School-Aged Basketball; Teaching; Appalachian

RAMOUTAR, KALISA; CHARLOTTE, NC; ZEBULON VANCE HS; (JR); Hnr Roll; Peer Tut/Med; FBLA; Key Club; Internship; Major in Psychology; Duke, Wake Forest; Mc State, Appalachian State

RAMSEY, CHARLES L; MAPLE HILL, NC; SOUTHWEST ONSLOW HS; (SO); Hi Hnr Roll; Nat Hon Sy; Chrch Yth Grp; Spanish Clb; Bnd; Mch Bnd; Bsball (V); Lawyer, Law Degree; Engineering Degree; U of North Carolina At Chapel Hill; North Carolina State U

RAMSEY, JESSICA R; RALEIGH, NC; WAKEFIELD HS; (SR); Hnr Roll; Comm Volntr; Emplmnt; Key Club; Pep Squd; Prom Com; Sci Clb; Tech Clb; Dnce; Chrldg (J); PP Ftbl (V); Sccr (J); Stu Cncl (R); Psychology; ECU-East Carolina U

RAMSEY, MATTHEW; FRANKLIN, NC; FRANKLIN HS; (SO); Hi Hnr Roll; Nat Hon Sy; Sci Fairs; Comm Volntr; Chrch Yth Grp; FCA; Lttrmn Clb; Ntl Beta Clb; Scouts; Svce Clb; Chr; Ch Chr; Jzz Bnd; Mch Bnd; Swmg (V L); Tennis (V); Cl Off (V); Stu Cncl (R); WNC All-District Band 04/05; Outward Bound; Music Performance; Engineering

RANDSON, JACQUIA A; CHARLOTTE, NC; PHILLIP O BERRY AC OF TECH; (FR); Hnr Roll; Otst Ac Ach Awd; Comm Volntr; Chrch Yth Grp; Jr Ach; ROTC; Svce Clb; Chr; Ch Chr; Drl Tm; Delta Sigma Theta "Excellence in Youth"; Completion of Let-One Service; Pre-Medicine; Electrical Engineering; North Carolina A & T State U; North Carolina Central State U

RANKIN, JUSTIN; MATTHEWS, NC; SUN VALLEY HS; (SO); Bnd; Chr; Clr Grd; Jzz Bnd; Mu Alpha Theta (For 2 Years); French Club; Psychology; Law

RANNELS, JACLYN; WAKE FOREST, NC; WAKE FOREST-ROLESVILLE HS; (JR); F Lan Hn Soc; Hi Hnr Roll; Jr Mshl; Nat Hon Sy; Pres Ac Ftns Aw; WWAHSS; ArtClub; Mth Clb/Tm; Ntl Beta Clb; Sci Clb; French Clb; Vllyball (VJ); Architecture; North Carolina State U; U of Florida State

RATLIFF, CANDACE; CHARLOTTE, NC; HARDING U HS; (FR); Hnr Roll; Perf Att; Comm Volntr; DARE; Dbte Team; Emplmnt; Jr Ach; Scouts; Bnd; Published in a Poetry Book; Taken French for 10 Years; Marine Biology; Corporate Law; U of North Carolina Chapel Hill; Harvard U

RAU, JAIME; SOUTHPORT, NC; SOUTH BRUNSWICK HS; (JR); Hi Hnr Roll; Jr Mshl; Nat Hon Sy; Comm Volntr; Spec Olymp Vol; Emplmnt; FCA; Key Club; Prom Com; Chr; SP/M/VS; Bskball (J); Tennis (V L); Vllyball (JC); CR (R); Yrbk; Notable Service Award-Key Club; Lt. Gov. Div 4 Carolinas District; Medicine; Business; U North Carolina Chapel Hill; Appalachian State U

RAVISHANKAR, SINDHU; CARY, NC; WILLIAM G ENLOE HS; (SO); Duke TS; Hnr Roll; Perf Att; Amnsty Intl; Comm Volntr; Red Cr Aide; Emplmnt; Scouts; Tmpl Yth Grp; Bnd; Ch Chr; Dnce; Orch; Adv Cncl (V); 1st Runner-Up Miss India North Carolina Pageant 2005-Title Holder-Miss Teen America 2004 Original; Raleigh Area Flute Association Board Member (03-05) Student Rep; Major in Preventive Medicine; Minor in Music/Flute; Duke U; UNC Chapel Hill

RAY, BETHANY; WINGATE, NC; METROLINA CHRISTIAN AC; (JR); Hi Hnr Roll; Otst Ac Ach Awd; Perf Att; St of Mnth; WWAHSS; Comm Volntr; Red Cr Aide; Chrch Yth Grp; FTA; Ntl Beta Clb; Prom Com; Bnd; Chr; Ch Chr; Pep Bnd; Committed Young Christian (CYC) VP; Varsity Basketball & Baseball Manager

RAY, WILLIAM B; LUMBERTON, NC; PURNELL SWETT HS; (SO); Hnr Roll; Perf Att; WWAHSS; Spec Olymp Vol; Chrch Yth Grp; Ntl Beta Clb; Chr; Ch Chr; Bsball (J); Tennis (V); Stu Cncl (P); Yrbk (P); Psychology; Anesthesia; UNC Pembroke; UNC Chapel Hill

RAYNOR, RHONDA S; CLINTON, NC; CLINTON HS; (SO); Hnr Roll; Otst Ac Ach Awd; Comm Volntr; Emplmnt; SADD; Chr; Chrldg (V); PPSqd (V); Major in Nursing; East Carolina U; Fayetteville State U

READING, RACHEL; CHARLOTTE, NC; CHARLOTTE CHRISTIAN SCH; (JR); F Lan Hn Soc; Hi Hnr Roll; Hnr Roll; Yth Ldrshp Prog; Peer Tut/Med; Drma Clb; SADD; Chr; SP/M/VS; PP Ftbl (L); Sch Ppr (E); Won School Spelling Bee / Competed in Local Spelling Bee; Accomplished Pianist; Music; Singer / Song Writer; Belmont U; Vanderbilt U

REARDON, JAMES P; APEX, NC; APEX HS; (JR); Hnr Roll; Emplmnt; Latin Clb; SP/M/VS; VP of School GSA (Gay-Straight Alliance); Member of Japanese and Latin Clubs; Forensic Scientist At A Crime Lab; High School Teacher; U of North Carolina; North Carolina State U

REAVES, EBONY L; TARBORO, NC; TARBORO HS; (JR); Hnr Roll; Comm Volntr; Hosp Aide; Peer Tut/Med; Chrch Yth Grp; DARE; Emplmnt; Off Aide; French Clb; Ch Chr; NC Senate Page; National Teen Pageant; Legal Studies; Marketing; Harvard U; U of Maryland

REAVES, MONTRICE; WINSTON-SALEM, NC; MT TABOR HS; (JR); Hnr Roll; Sci Fairs; St of Mnth; Comm Volntr; Peer Tut/Med; Red Cr Aide; DECA; Emplmnt; Jr Ach; Scouts; Clb; SP/M/VS; Sccr (JV); Creative Director of a Fashion Label; Fashion Merchandising Coordinator; UNC Greensboro; UNC Charlotte

REDDING, STEPHEN G; PITTSBORO, NC; JORDAN MATTHEWS HS; (FR); Ftball (J); Wt Lftg (J); Science Club; Quiz Bowl; Veterinary Medicine

REDMON, ROCHELLE; WINSTON SALEM, NC; CARVER HS; (SO); Hnr Roll; Hosp Aide; Scouts; Bnd; Bskball (J); Girl Scouts; Medical; Arts

REED, JENNIFER; CHARLOTTE, NC; INDEPENDENCE HS; (JR); Hi Hnr Roll; Hnr Roll; Nat Hon Sy; WWAHSS; Comm Volntr; Drma Clb; Key Club; Clb; SP/M/VS; Stg Cre; Tennis (V); Kim Fiola Award for Leadership, Children's Theater of Charlotte, North Carolina; Theater, Psychology, Art History

REED, SHANNON; SILOAM, NC; EAST SURRY HS; (SO); Hnr Roll; WWAHSS; Chess; Chrch Yth Grp; Drma Clb; SP/M/VS; Actress; Writer-Author

REEP, ANDREW M; LINCOLNTON, NC; NORTH LINCOLN HS; (SR); Jr Mshl; Nat Hon Sy; Comm Volntr; Peer Tut/Med; Spec Olymp Vol; Chrch Yth Grp; Mus Clb; Ntl Beta Clb; Bnd; Jzz Bnd; Mch Bnd; Pep Bnd; Adv Cncl (P); President Anchor Club; NC Super Teen Award; Chemical Engineer; Paper and Pulp Sciences Degree; North Carolina State U

REEVES, ROBIN L; HAYS, NC; NORTH WILKES HS; (SO); Hnr Roll; Comm Volntr; 4-H; Chrch Yth Grp; Key Club; Ntl Beta Clb; Latin Clb; Acpl Chr; Chr; Ch Chr; Dnce; Bskball (VJC); Sftball (J); Vllyball (VJ); Key Club / Latin Club; Beta Club; Professional Sports Trainer; Sports Management; Virginia Tech U; Lenoir Rhyme U

REEVES, VANESSA L; FAYETTEVILLE, NC; WESTOVER HS; (SR); Hnr Roll; Perf Att; ROTC; Drl Tm; Track (V); Wt Lftg (J); A-B Honor Roll Was Announced in the Fayetteville Observer 2005; Military; Law Enforcement

REGALADO, DANIEL; WINSTON SALEM, NC; GLENN HS; (JR); Hnr Roll; Chrch Yth Grp; Chr; Major in Math; Wake Forest U

REGANS, DAVID E; KINGS MOUNTAIN, NC; KINGS MOUNTAIN HS; (SR); Hnr Roll; Otst Ac Ach Awd; Perf Att; WWAHSS; Yth Ldrshp Prog; Comm Volntr; Peer Tut/Med; Chrch Yth Grp; Cmptr Clb; FBLA; Lib Aide; Mus Clb; Tchrs Aide; Ch Chr; Arch (C); CR (R); Teach Youth Sunday School Class; Associate in Science Degree in Internet Technologies; Cleveland Community College

REGISTER, GREY W; STATESVILLE, NC; STATESVILLE HS; (SO); Duke TS; Hi Hnr Roll; Jr Eng Tech; Ntl Beta Clb; Bskball (J); Sccr (J); Junior Engineering Technology Society; 1st Priority; Pre Law; U of South Carolina; Appalachian State U

REID, ALLISON; MONROE, NC; WEDDINGTON HS; (SO); Duke TS; Hnr Roll; Jr Rot; Nat Hon Sy; WWAHSS; Comm Volntr; Chrch Yth Grp; Key Club; Pep Squd; Spanish Clb; Cr Ctry (J L); Track (V L); Stu Cncl (R); Coaches Award in Cross Country

REID, RAMEISHA D; GOLDSBORO, NC; EASTERN WAYNE HS; (JR); 4H Awd; Hnr Roll; WWAHSS; Comm Volntr; 4-H; Chrch Yth Grp; DARE; Mth Clb/Tm; Prom Com; SADD; Foreign Clb; Dnce; Chrldg (J); Health Occupation Students of America; Pre-Med; Biochemistry; North Carolina State U; East Carolina U

REID WILSON, SUMMER; GRIMESLAND, NC; D H CONLEY HS; (FR); Hnr Roll; Otst Ac Ach Awd; Perf Att; Peer Tut/Med; Spec Olymp Vol; 4-H; ArtClub; DARE; FCA; Lib Aide; Ntl Beta Clb; Prom Com; Dnce; SP/M/VS; Cr Ctry (V); Track (V); Stu Cncl (V); Yrbk; All Star Cheerleading (ECCATS); Model and in Numerous Pageants; Acting; Modeling

Reeves, Vanessa L
Westover HS
Fayetteville, NC

Ray, Bethany
Metrolina Christian AC
Wingate, NC

Ramsey, Jessica R
Wakefield HS
Raleigh, NC

Ramasubramanian, Anusuya
William G Enloe HS
Cary, NC

Quimby, Nick
Fike HS
Wilson, NC

Quinlan, Megan B
Southview HS
Fayetteville, NC

Ravishankar, Sindhu
William G Enloe HS
Cary, NC

Reeves, Robin L
North Wilkes HS
Hays, NC

Regans, David E
Kings Mountain HS
Kings Mountain, NC

REILLY, JENNIFER L; KNIGHTDALE, NC; NEUSE BAPTIST CHRISTIAN SCH; (SO); All Am Sch; Hnr Roll; Nat Hon Sy; Nat Ldrshp Svc; Nat Sci Aw; Perf Att; USAA; Peer Tut/Med; Chrch Yth Grp; Chr; Sccr (V); American Christian Honor Society; Earth Sciences; Photography/Other Visual Arts

REILLY, NICOLE M; BOONE, NC; WATAYGA HS; (FR); Ctznshp Aw; Hnr Roll; Perf Att; Chrch Yth Grp; FCA; Bnd; Sftball (J); U of California Los Angeles

REINHEARDT, STACY; CLAREMONT, NC; BUNKER HILL HS; (JR); Hnr Roll; St of Mnth; Comm Volntr; Sci Clb; Spanish Clb; Bnd; Clr Grd; Dnce; Mch Bnd; Bear Paw Awards; Fashion Marketing; Fashion Merchandising; Art Institute of Charlotte; CUCC Community College

REVERE, MALCOLM; CHARLOTTE, NC; RESURRECTION CHRISTIAN SCH; (FR); Pres Sch; Comm Volntr; Chrch Yth Grp; Prom Com; Ch Chr; Bsball (J); Bskball (VJ); Sccr (J); Stu Cncl (T); Sports Broadcasting; Mythology; Duke U; Miami U

REYES, ALONDRA C; LA GRANGE, NC; SPRING CREEK HS; (SO); Nat Hon Sy; WWAHSS; Emplmnt; Chr; Clr Grd; Oncology; Duke U; U of California, Los Angeles

REYES, ANTONIO J; WILMINGTON, NC; NEW HANOVER HS; (JR); Hnr Roll; Comm Volntr; Chrch Yth Grp; SP/M/VS; Stu Cncl (R); Master's in Teaching (History); BS Culinary Arts; Chowan College; Johnson and Wales U

REYES, ANTONIO R; SILER CITY, NC; JORDAN MATTHEWS HS; (SO); Duke TS; Hnr Roll; Jr Mshl; Perf Att; Comm Volntr; Chrch Yth Grp; DECA; Emplmnt; Quiz Bowl; Chr; Cr Ctry (V); 1st Place in State DECA in Sports Entertainment; 1st Place in District DECA Retail Merchandising Management; Music Industry; Guitar; Appalachian State; Oberlin Conservatory

REYES, MARIA; SEVEN SPRINGS, NC; SPRING CREEK HS; (SO); Duke TS; Hnr Roll; Nat Hon Sy; Pres Sch; St of Mnth; Nurse; Doctor; North Carolina Chapel Hill; U Of North Carolina At Greensboro

REYNOLDS, JERRY A; ROCKY MOUNT, NC; NASH CTRL HS; (FR); Chrch Yth Grp; Ch Chr; Computer Tech; Duke U

REYNOLDS, LAKEISHA; GREENSBORO, NC; DUDLEY HS; Hnr Roll; Bnd; Drl Tm; Mch Bnd; Pep Bnd; PP Ftbl; Sccr; Track; Photography; Computer Graphics; Atlanta Art Institute

REYNOLDS, MICHAEL J; THOMASVILLE, NC; LEDFORD SR HS; (JR); Hnr Roll; Spec Olymp Vol; Chrch Yth Grp; DARE; Wdwrkg Clb; Special Olympics; Roofing

REYNOLDS, SAMUEL V; DURHAM, NC; JORDAN HS; (JR); Hi Hnr Roll; MVP; WWAHSS; Yth Ldrshp Prog; Hab For Humty Volntr; Spec Olymp Vol; Chrch Yth Grp; Dbte Team; Drma Clb; Emplmnt; FCA; Key Club; Mth Clb/Tm; Scouts; SP/M/VS; Stg Cre; Ftball (J L); Lcrsse (V L); Swmg (V CL); Track (J); Eagle Scout; Community Citizenship; Business, Law; Theater Arts/Production; U of North Carolina; U of North Carolina Wilmington

REYNOLDS, WALTER; CANDOR, NC; EAST MONTGOMERY HS; (SO); Hnr Roll; Perf Att; Sci Fairs; St of Mnth; Comm Volntr; Chrch Yth Grp; DARE; Ntl FFA; Scouts; Automotive Technician; Restore Old Cars; NASCAR Technical Institute; Sandhills Community College

RHODES, ANNA; EDEN, NC; MOREHEAD HS; (JR); Hi Hnr Roll; Nat Hon Sy; Perf Att; DECA; Bnd; Cr Ctry (L); State Finalist - DECA Competition; First Chair in Band; Radiology; Marketing; U of North Carolina Charlotte; North Carolina State U

RHODES, EDWARD; STOKESDALE, NC; NORTHWEST HS; (SR); Duke TS; Hnr Roll; MVP; WWAHSS; Comm Volntr; Hab For Humty Volntr; Chrch Yth Grp; DARE; FCA; Jr Cls League; NYLC; Golf (V); Wt Lftg (V); Pre-Med / Medicine; Biology; UNC Chapel Hill; UNC Wilmington

RICE, HANLEY; MATTHEWS, NC; COVENANT DAY SCH; (JR); Duke TS; Hnr Roll; Nat Hon Sy; WWAHSS; Comm Volntr; Chrch Yth Grp; Emplmnt; Jr Ach; Jr Cls League; French Clb; Chrldg (V CL); Sch Ppr (R); Yrbk (E); Top French Student; 6th Place National French Exam; International Studies; Journalism; U of North Carolina; Gordon College

RICE, KELSEY; MATTHEWS, NC; COVENANT DAY SCH; (FR); Duke TS; Hi Hnr Roll; Nat Hon Sy; Otst Ac Ach Awd; Pres Ac Ftns Aw; WWAHSS; Chrch Yth Grp; Jr Cls League; Svce Clb; Tchrs Aide; Chrldg (V L); Track (V L); American Mathematics Competition-First Place; Top World History Student; Interior Design, Business; U of North Carolina

RICH, SHANNON C; ROCKY MOUNT, NC; NASH CTRL HS; (SO); Hi Hnr Roll; Tchrs Aide; Bsball (VJ); Bskball (VJ); Cr Ctry (VJ); Track (VJ); Psychology; UNCG of Greensboro

RICHARDS, HEIDI E; ROXBORO, NC; PERSON HS; (JR); Hi Hnr Roll; Hnr Roll; Nat Hon Sy; St Schl; Chrch Yth Grp; Drma Clb; French Clb; Bnd; Ch Chr; Mch Bnd; SP/M/VS; Section Leader of Pit Percussion; Second Place in Rotary Speech Contest; Archaeology Doctorate; Music Major; Wake Forest U; Mars Hill College

RICHARDSON, CASEY L; JEFFERSON, NC; ASHE CTY HS; (SR); 4H Awd; Hi Hnr Roll; Hnr Roll; Nat Hon Sy; Otst Ac Ach Awd; Pres Sch; WWAHSS; Comm Volntr; Hosp Aide; 4-H; Emplmnt; FTA; Mus Clb; Ntl Beta Clb; Ntl FFA; Photog; Tchrs Aide; National FFA Delegate; FFA Chapter Vice President; Agriculture Education; Vet Medicine; North Carolina State U

RICHARDSON, COLIN; CARY, NC; GREEN HOPE HS; (JR); Duke TS; Hnr Roll; Sci/Math Olympn; Comm Volntr; Hab For Humty Volntr; Chrch Yth Grp; Drma Clb; Emplmnt; Sci Clb; Scouts; Latin Clb; Bnd; Ch Chr; Mch Bnd; SP/M/VS; Boy Scouting; Three Years, Appalachian Service Project; Law; Business; Davidson College; U of North Carolina, Chapel Hill

RICHESON, RICHIE; CONCORD, NC; MT PLEASANT HS; (JR); Hnr Roll; WWAHSS; Auto Mechanics; Wyoming Tech

RICHEY, EDEN; LENOIR, NC; HIBRITEN; (FR); 4H Awd; Hnr Roll; Yth Ldrshp Prog; Comm Volntr; Peer Tut/Med; 4-H; DARE; Key Club; Scouts; SADD; Chr; Ch Chr

RICO, MIRIAM; KINSTON, NC; SOUTH LENOIR HS; (SR); Hnr Roll; St of Mnth; Yth Ldrshp Prog; Comm Volntr; Chrch Yth Grp; ROTC; Ch Chr; Vllyball (V); AIM Club; Church Volunteer; Tourism Administration; Sociology; Wayne Community College, NC State U; Lenoir Community College, Duke U

RIDINGS, CALEB J; POLKVILLE, NC; BURNS HS; (JR); Duke TS; Hnr Roll; Jr Mshl; Nat Hon Sy; WWAHSS; Chrch Yth Grp; DARE; Ntl Beta Clb; Prom Com; Scouts; Spanish Clb; Golf (V CL); Eagle Scout; National Honors Society; PGA Teaching Pro; Landscape Design; Tulane U; Clemson U

RIGGINS, KATERRA; CHARLOTTE, NC; INDEPENDENCE SR HS; (JR); Hi Hnr Roll; Hnr Roll; Nat Hon Sy; Chrch Yth Grp; DECA; Emplmnt; Chr; Ch Chr; Chrldg (VJ); Scr Kpr (V); Yrbk (E); DECA State Finalist; National Technical Honor Society; Fashion Designer; Fashion Stylist; North Carolina Agricultural and Technical State U; Savannah College of Art and Design

RIGGS, ANDY; MOUNT AIRY, NC; MOUNT AIRY HS; (SO); Hnr Roll; Otst Ac Ach Awd; Perf Att; WWAHSS; Hab For Humty Volntr; Spec Olymp Vol; Chess; Emplmnt; Key Club; SADD; Voc Ind Clb Am; Career-Technical Honor Society; Computer Science; Economics

RIGGSBEE, CANDI; POLKTON, NC; ANSON HS; (SO); DAR; Hnr Roll; Hab For Humty Volntr; Peer Tut/Med; 4-H; ArtClub; Chrch Yth Grp; DARE; Pep Squd; Photog; Ch Chr; SP/M/VS; Yrbk (P); Pep Club; Art Major; History Major; Art Institute of Charlotte

RIGHTMEYER, WHITNEY; LITTLETON, NC; HALIFAX AC CHRISTIAN SCH; (SO); Duke TS; Hnr Roll; MVP; Nat Hon Sy; Perf Att; WWAHSS; Pep Squd; Dnce; Bskball (VJ); Chrldg (J); PP Ftbl (V); Sftball (VJ); Cl Off (S); Stu Cncl (R); CR (R); Interior Design; Photography; N.C. State U (North Carolina State U); UNC Wilmington U of North Carolina Wilmington

RILEY, DEANNA A; RALEIGH, NC; WAKEFIELD HS; (JR); Hnr Roll; Peer Tut/Med; ArtClub; Chrch Yth Grp; Tchrs Aide; Mentoring and Math Tutor; Wakefield Middle School; Math Instructor; NC State; Unc-Carolina

RILEY, LAUREN N; FRANKLINTON, NC; FRANKLINTON HS; (FR); Hnr Roll; Sci Fairs; St of Mnth; Chrch Yth Grp; DARE; FCA; Dnce; Sccr (V); Vllyball (JC); Medical Field; Eastern Carolina U (ECU); U of North Carolina (UNC)

RINCON, MICHAEL A; HUNTERSVILLE, NC; NORTH MECKLENBURG HS; (JR); Hnr Roll; Comm Volntr; DARE; Dbte Team; Drma Clb; Emplmnt; Ntl Beta Clb; Scouts; SP/M/VS; Stg Cre; Beta Club; Acting; Playwright; Princeton U; Yale U

RISDON, TYLER G; HIGH POINT, NC; LEDFORD HS; (SR); Hnr Roll; MVP; Pres Ac Ftns Aw; Yth Ldrshp Prog; Comm Volntr; Chess; FCA; Ntl Beta Clb; P to P St Amb Prg; Scouts; Clb; Sccr (V L); Swmg (V L); Track (V L); National Society of High School Scholars; BSA Eagle 5/05; Civil & Structural Engineering; North Carolina State U (Accepted)

RITCH, ERIC B; RALEIGH, NC; LEESVILLE ROAD HS; (FR); Hnr Roll; Executive Chef; Business Education; Culinary Institute of America; Johnson and Wales U

RITTER, TAYLOR W; ROBBINS, NC; NORTH MOORE HS; (SR); DAR; Hi Hnr Roll; Jr Mshl; Nat Hon Sy; St of Mnth; WWAHSS; Comm Volntr; Chrch Yth Grp; Emplmnt; FCA; FBLA; Key Club; Ntl Beta Clb; Scouts; Bnd; Mch Bnd; Golf (V); Tennis (V); Mechanical Eng.; NC State U; UNC Charlotte

RIVENBARK, HANNAH; WILMINGTON, NC; E A LANEY HS; (SO); Hnr Roll; Perf Att; President's Education Award; Architecture; Art; Drexel U; North Carolina State U

RIVERA, CLARISSA; CARY, NC; ATHENS DRIVE HS; (MS); 4H Awd; Ctznshp Aw; Pres Ac Ftns Aw; Sci Fairs; St of Mnth; 4-H; ArtClub; Chrch Yth Grp; Drma Clb; Sci Clb; Tech Clb; Clr Grd; Dnce; SP/M/VS; Stu Cncl (S); CR (R); Sch Ppr (R); Dancer / Performing Arts; Actress / Theater Arts; New York U

RIVERA, KARL K; CHARLOTTE, NC; EAST MECKLENBURG HS; (FR); All Am Sch; Comm Volntr; Chess; Junior Honor Society; Computer Programmer; Business Manager; UNCC; Chapel Hill At NC

RIVERO, ELIZABETH; LENOIR, NC; HIBRITEN HS; (SO); Hnr Roll; Nat Hon Sy; Emplmnt; FCA; Ntl Beta Clb; Scr Kpr (J); Tennis (VJ); U of North Carolina; Louisiana State U

RIVERS JR, TERRY L; RALEIGH, NC; GARNER HS; (FR); Hnr Roll; Yth Ldrshp Prog; Comm Volntr; Chrch Yth Grp; Engineering; Architect; North Carolina State U; North Carolina Agricultural & Technical U

ROA, ABRAHAM; LOUISBURG, NC; LOUISBURG HS; (FR); MVP; Perf Att; English Clb; SP/M/VS; Cr Ctry (V); Sccr (V); Track (V)

ROACH, SARAH; CHARLOTTE, NC; CHARLOTTE CATHOLIC HS; (FR); Duke TS; Hi Hnr Roll; Hnr Roll; Comm Volntr; Dnce; Sftball (V); Dance Classes - Not with School; Other Softball Teams; UNC Chapel Hill; North Carolina State U

ROBERSON, GENAE; HASSELL, NC; WAVERLY JR/SR HS; (FR); Ctznshp Aw; Fut Prb Slvr; Hnr Roll; MVP; Nat Stu Ath Day Aw; Otst Ac Ach Awd; Perf Att; St of Mnth; Yth Ldrshp Prog; CARE; Comm Volntr; Hab For Humty Volntr; ArtClub; Chrch Yth Grp; Cmptr Clb; DARE; FCA; Fr of Library; Jr Ach; SADD; Bnd; Chr; Ch Chr; Dnce; Bskball (V); GAA (J); Sftball (J); Vllyball (V); Adv Cncl (R); Cl Off (R); Stu Cncl (R); CR (R); Sch Ppr (E); Yrbk (E); Many Art Awards Throughout the Years; Artist; Nurse / Physician's Assistant; NC State U; UNC Chapel Hill

ROBERSON, KYLE; HALIFAX, NC; HALIFAX AC CHRISTIAN SCH; (SO); Ctznshp Aw; Hi Hnr Roll; Hnr Roll; Perf Att; Chrch Yth Grp; Emplmnt; Ntl Beta Clb; Swmg (V); Wt Lftg (V); Weight Lifting As a Class, Not a Sport; Engineering; North Carolina State U

ROBERTS, AMANDA K; HENDERSONVILLE, NC; WEST HENDERSON HS; (JR); Hnr Roll; WWAHSS; ArtClub; Emplmnt; FCA; Pep Squd; Quill & Scroll; Dnce; Swmg (V); Yrbk (E); Interior Designer; Elementary School Teacher; Blue Ridge Community College; Western North Carolina

ROBERTS, COREY B; ZIRCONIA, NC; EAST HENDERSON HS; (SO); Hnr Roll; Sci Fairs; Small Business; Orthodontist; Western Carolina U; Furman U

ROBERTS, CORRINE E; MOORESVILLE, NC; CANNON SCH; (MS); Duke TS; Hnr Roll; Peer Tut/Med; Ntl Beta Clb; Sccr (V); Vllyball (V); Battle of the Books Quiz Bowl; Odyssey of the Mind; Veterinary Medicine; Zoology; U of Tennessee; Auburn U

ROBERTS, SHANA A; GREENSBORO, NC; SMITH HS; (SO); Hnr Roll; Sci Fairs; Svce Clb; Chr; Ch Chr; Dnce; SP/M/VS; Chrldg (V); Church Dance Team; Praise Team; Ob/Gyn; Lawyer; A & T U; UN Chapel Hill

ROBERTS, SHONALIE C; CHARLOTTE, NC; WEST MECKLENBURG HS; (JR); Hi Hnr Roll; Hnr Roll; Otst Ac Ach Awd; Perf Att; St of Mnth; WWAHSS; Comm Volntr; Peer Tut/Med; ROTC; French Clb; Sftball (J); General Legion Scholastics Award; Pre-Med Pediatrics; Business Management and Administration; High Point U; U of North Carolina At Chapel Hill

ROBINSON, BRITTANY N; AUTRYVILLE, NC; MIDWAY HS; (SO); Hi Hnr Roll; Hnr Roll; WWAHSS; Comm Volntr; FBLA; Bnd; Jzz Bnd; Mch Bnd; Dental Hygienist; Pharmacist; U of North Carolina Pembroke; Campbell U

ROBINSON, LISA M; RALEIGH, NC; WAKEFIELD HS; (FR); Comm Volntr; Peer Tut/Med; Key Club; Key Club; Fashion Design; Cosmetology; Gibbs College-Pittsburgh, PA; International Academy of Design-Chicago, IL

ROBINSON, TRAVES A; CHARLOTTE, NC; E E WADDELL HS; (SR); Hnr Roll; Chrch Yth Grp; DARE; Emplmnt; Bskball (V CL); Track (V L); Cl Off (R); National English Award Winner; Business Administration; U of North Carolina At Wilmington

ROBINSON JR, JAMES; RALEIGH, NC; WAKEFIELD HS; (FR); Hnr Roll; WWAHSS; Comm Volntr; Key Club; Track (V); Technology Enhanced Approach Learning (Teal); Accountant; Early Education; North Carolina State U; U of North Carolina

ROBLES, BRITTANY; TRINITY, NC; TRINITY HS; (JR); Hnr Roll; St of Mnth; Comm Volntr; Chrch Yth Grp; Prom Com; Bnd; Mch Bnd; Pep Bnd; Cl Off (P); Stu Cncl (V, S); National Beta Club; Youth Summer Mission Trips; Hospitality & Tourism Management; Business Administration; Western Carolina U; Gardner-Webb U

ROBNETT, KYLE A; CHARLOTTE, NC; WEST MECKLENBURG HS; (FR); Hnr Roll; Perf Att; Chrch Yth Grp; DARE; Church Mission Trips

ROCHA, MARTHA; WINSTON SALEM, NC; REYNOLDS HS; (JR); Hnr Roll; Comm Volntr; Chrch Yth Grp; Tmpl Yth Grp; Chr; Ch Chr; Piano Recital Award; Pre-Med; Physical Therapy; East Carolina U; Winston-Salem State U

Roberts, Corrine E
Cannon Sch
Mooresville, NC

Risdon, Tyler G
Ledford HS
High Point, NC

Riley, Lauren N
Franklinton HS
Franklinton, NC

Rhodes, Edward
Northwest HS
Stokesdale, NC

Reynolds, Walter
East Montgomery HS
Candor, NC

National
Honor Roll
Spring 2005

Revere, Malcolm
Resurrection Christian Sch
Charlotte, NC

Rico, Miriam
South Lenoir HS
Kinston, NC

Rincon, Michael A
North Mecklenburg HS
Huntersville, NC

Ritch, Eric B
Leesville Road HS
Raleigh, NC

Rivera, Karl K
East Mecklenburg HS
Charlotte, NC

RODRIGUEZ, BIANCA A; INDIAN TRAIL, NC; SUN VALLEY HS; MS; All Am Sch; Hnr Roll; St of Mnth; Comm Volntr; DARE; Emplmnt; Bnd; Chr; GAA; Sftball; Stu Cncl (R); In A Scholar Program; Master Degree or PhD; Medicine-Cardiology; U of North Carolina; U of Pembroke North Carolina

RODRIGUEZ, JULIO C; WINSTON SALEM, NC; NORTH FORSYTH HS; (FR); Hnr Roll

RODRIGUEZ, MARIA F; GASTONIA, NC; HUNTER HS; (JR); Nat Hon Sy; Otst Ac Ach Awd; Comm Volntr; Emplmnt; Ntl Beta Clb; Svce Clb; SP/M/VS; Tennis (V); Secretary of Interact Club; Nurse Practitioner; Performing Arts; North Carolina State U; U of North Carolina At Wilmington

RODRIGUEZ, PABLO R; MOCKSVILLE, NC; DAVIE CTY HS; (FR); Hnr Roll; Teaching; Spanish Teacher; UCLA; U of Greensboro

ROE, KRISTEN; BREVARD, NC; BREVARD HS; (SO); Hi Hnr Roll; Hnr Roll; Otst Ac Ach Awd; Sci Fairs; WWAHSS; Comm Volntr; Chrch Yth Grp; Emplmnt; Bskball (J); Chrldg (V); Stu Cncl (R); Youth Council (Volunteer Work), FCCLA Member; Missions Work W/FBC Brevard, Gatorade-Will to Win Award & Coach's Award; Pediatric Physician's Assistant; UNC Wilmington (U of North Carolina)

ROGERS, BRIDGETT R; GOLDSBORO, NC; EASTERN WAYNE HS; (SO); Ctznshp Aw; DAR; Hi Hnr Roll; Hnr Roll; MVP; St of Mnth; Yth Ldrshp Prog; Comm Volntr; Hosp Aide; Peer Tut/Med; Chrch Yth Grp; Drma Clb; Mth Clb/Tm; Mus Clb; Off Aide; P to P St Amb Prg; Svce Clb; Tchrs Aide; Chr; Ch Chr; Clr Grd; Stg Cre; Bskball (J); Gmnstcs (J); Hsbk Rdg (J); Scr Kpr (J); Track (J); Vllyball (J); Wt Lftg (J); Wrstlg (J); CR (R); Music; Parent & Childhood Development; North Carolina Central U; Shaw U

ROGERS, CHRISTINE E; GASTONIA, NC; ASHBROOK HS; (FR); Hnr Roll; Comm Volntr; ArtClub; Chrch Yth Grp; DARE; Mus Clb; Scouts; Chr; Ch Chr; Singing and Acting; Crime Investigation; U of North Carolina Greensboro; U of North Carolina Charlotte

ROGERS, HANNAH; SALISBURY, NC; WEST ROWAN HS; Ctznshp Aw; Hnr Roll; Perf Att; Peer Tut/Med; Drma Clb; SADD; Chr; SP/M/VS; Nursing; Cosmetology; Meredith; Gardner-Webb U

ROGERS, JUSTIN L; FAYETTEVILLE, NC; SEVENTY-FIRST HS; (SO); Hnr Roll; Perf Att; Sci Fairs; CARE; Peer Tut/Med; Ntl FFA; CR (R); Accountant; Architecture

ROGERS, LA SHERA; JACKSONVILLE, NC; SOUTHWEST HS; (JR); 4H Awd; Hnr Roll; Law; Psychology; UNC-Chapel Hill; NC State

ROGERS, WILLIAM B; MOORESVILLE, NC; LAKE NORMAN HS; (JR); Hnr Roll; MVP; Comm Volntr; Chrch Yth Grp; Emplmnt; Bnd; Golf (V CL); Placed 4th in '05 Regional Golf Tournament; Marketing / Business; Gardener Webb U NC; Elon U NC

ROGERSON, NICOLE; TARBORO, NC; NORTH EDGECOMBE HS; (MS); Hnr Roll; Otst Ac Ach Awd; Valdctrian; DARE; Scouts; Presidential Citation Award; DVM

ROJAS GONZALES, DOROTEO E; WINSTON SALEM, NC; REYNOLDS HS; (JR); 4H Awd; Perf Att; Comm Volntr; Spanish Clb; Chr; Sccr (J); CR (P)

ROLLINS, AMBER; SHELBY, NC; CREST SR HS; (JR); Hnr Roll; Nat Hon Sy; Otst Ac Ach Awd; WWAHSS; Peer Tut/Med; Chrch Yth Grp; FTA; Ntl Beta Clb; Vsity Clb; Chr; Sftball (V); Nurse Practitioner; Registered Nurse; U of North Carolina Charlotte; Gardner Webb U

ROLOFF, MARK; HENDERSONVILLE, NC; WEST HENDERSON HS; (JR); Duke TS; Hnr Roll; Jr Mshl; Comm Volntr; Chrch Yth Grp; Emplmnt; Quill & Scroll; Tchrs Aide; SP/M/VS; Stg Cre; Cr Ctry (V); Sch Ppr (R); Attained Scores of "5" in AP Biology & History; Community Volunteer with "Y.O.U" Church Grp.; Possibly Sciences/Psychology; Oglethorpe U; U of North Carolina

ROLON, NAZARY; FORT BRAGG, NC; E E SMITH SR HS; (JR); Dnce; PP Ftbl; Vllyball (V); Fashion Merchandising; Fashion Consulting

ROMERO, MAYRA N G; CHEROKEE, NC; SMOKY MTN HS; (SR); Hnr Roll; Sccr (V); Southwestern Community College

ROOME, MEGAN; HOLLY SPRINGS, NC; MIDDLE CREEK HS; (JR); Ctznshp Aw; Hnr Roll; Pres Ac Ftns Aw; WWAHSS; Chrch Yth Grp; FCA; Key Club; SADD; Sccr (V CL); Vllyball (V L); Lit Mag (E, R, P); Sch Ppr (E, R, P); Yrbk (E, R, P); Business; Marketing; U of North Carolina Wilmington; U of Florida

ROOPCHAN, KELLY; WINSTON SALEM, NC; NORTH FORSYTH SR HS; (FR); Duke TS; Hnr Roll; Comm Volntr; Hab For Humty Volntr; ArtClub; Drma Clb; Key Club; P to P St Amb Prg; Spanish Clb; Dnce; SP/M/VS; Stg Cre; Stu Cncl (R); Psychology; Computer Technology; North Carolina-State U

ROPER, BRITTANY L; LAKE TOXAWAY, NC; HIS SHADOW CHRISTIAN; (JR); Hnr Roll; Valdctrian; WWAHSS; Yth Ldrshp Prog; CARE; Comm Volntr; Chrch Yth Grp; Drma Clb; Emplmnt; FCA; Ch Chr; SP/M/VS; Mar Art (V L); Sftball (VJ); Wt Lftg (C); Cl Off (T); CR (P); Yrbk (P); Missions; North Greenville College; Blue Ridge Community College

ROPER, JOSHUA; CHARLOTTE, NC; GARINGER SR HS; (JR); Hnr Roll; MVP; Bsball (V); Bskball (V C); Ftball (V); Accounting; Mathematics; North Carolina State U; Virginia Tech

RORIE, DE MARVIOUS; CHARLOTTE, NC; GARINGER HS; (SO); Hnr Roll; Perf Att; Comm Volntr; Chrch Yth Grp; DARE; Kwanza Clb; Bskball (J); Ftball (VJ); Track (V); Computer Technology; Communication; U of Michigan; Winston-Salem State

ROSALES, ERICA; CHARLOTTE, NC; INDEPENDENCE HS; (JR); Hi Hnr Roll; Hnr Roll; Nat Hon Sy; Comm Volntr; Peer Tut/Med; Spanish Clb; Chr; Social Work; Teaching; U of North Carolina in Charlotte; U of North Carolina Pembroke

ROSALES, WENDY; FLAT ROCK, NC; EAST HENDERSON HS; (SR); Hnr Roll; Perf Att; St of Mnth; Comm Volntr; Peer Tut/Med; Emplmnt; Ntl Beta Clb; Ch Chr; Coordinator of Youth Group; Registered Nurse; Pediatrician; U of North Carolina

ROSAS, MANDIIE; SMITHFIELD, NC; PRINCETON SCH; (FR); Hnr Roll; Chrch Yth Grp; DARE; Ch Chr; Neurology; Duke U; U of North Carolina

ROSATO, JENNA; ROLESVILLE, NC; WAKE FOREST-ROLESVILLE HS; (JR); Duke TS; Hnr Roll; Nat Hon Sy; Otst Ac Ach Awd; WWAHSS; Comm Volntr; Chrch Yth Grp; FCA; Ntl FFA; Sci Clb; Marine Biology; Sociology; U of North Carolina At Wilmington; U of North Carolina At Chapel Hill

ROSCOE, ZACHARY M; WEST END, NC; PINECREST HS; (SR); Hnr Roll; Spec Olymp Vol; Key Club; Stg Cre; Bsball (J); Cr Ctry (V); Tennis (V); Business; Sports Science & Exercise; Appalachian State U; U of North Carolina At Wilmington

ROSE, LEE; CHARLOTTE, NC; CHARLOTTE CHRISTIAN HS; (FR); Duke TS; MVP; Ftball (V L); Track (V L); Wt Lftg (V L); Wrstlg (V L); 35 Service Hours; Business; U of North Carolina; Wake Forest U

ROSEBORO, NELSON; LINCOLNTON, NC; (SR); SADD; Chr

ROSENQUIST, ASHLEY; RURAL HALL, NC; WEST STOKES HS; (JR); Nat Hon Sy; WWAHSS; Emplmnt; Ntl Beta Clb; Yrbk (R); Medical Sonographer; Nuclear Medicine Technologist; Forsyth Technical Community College

ROSMAN, RAQUEL; LAURINBURG, NC; SCOTLAND HS; (SO); MVP; Comm Volntr; Hosp Aide; Key Club; Bnd; Sccr (VJC); Vllyball (VJC); Wt Lftg (V); Psychology; Biology; UNC Wilmington

ROSS, ALEXANDRA; RALEIGH, NC; WAKEFIELD HS; (FR); Duke TS; Hnr Roll; WWAHSS; Key Club; Sftball (J); Snowboard Team-62nd in Nation in All Division of USASA; U of North Carolina-Chapel Hill; U of North Carolina-Wilmington

ROSS, DEBORAH; OAK CITY, NC; WAVERLY JR/SR HS; (FR); Hi Hnr Roll; Hnr Roll; Ntl Beta Clb; Pediatric Care; Business Management; UNC Chapel Hill; North Carolina State

ROSS, KATHRYN; HIGH POINT, NC; HIGH POINT CTRL HS; (JR); Hi Hnr Roll; Jr Mshl; Nat Hon Sy; Chrch Yth Grp; HO'Br Yth Ldrshp; Key Club; Ntl Beta Clb; Prom Com; Sccr (V); Tennis (V); National Honor Society; Beta Club

ROSS, LAUREN; CHARLOTTE, NC; MYERS PARK HS; (JR); Duke TS; F Lan Hn Soc; Hi Hnr Roll; Jr Mshl; Jr Rot; Nat Hon Sy; WWAHSS; Yth Ldrshp Prog; Chrch Yth Grp; Emplmnt; Sci Clb; Scouts; Svce Clb; SP/M/VS; Mar Art; Adv Cncl (R)

ROSS, SHAUNNA R; REIDSVILLE, NC; REIDSVILLE HS; (SR); Hi Hnr Roll; Hnr Roll; Jr Mshl; Nat Hon Sy; Perf Att; Peer Tut/Med; Chr; BS/Biology; Medicine; Winston-Salem State; North Carolina Central U

ROWE, AKIA Y; WILSON, NC; FIKE HS; (SR); Hnr Roll; Nat Ldrshp Svc; Otst Ac Ach Awd; Perf Att; ROTC; French Clb; Wt Lftg (V); JROTC-11th-Commander; JROTC-12th-Special Assistant I'm; Accountant-Associates Degree; Wilson Technical Community College

ROWE, ERIC; PIKEVILLE, NC; CHARLES B AYCOCK HS; (SR); Hi Hnr Roll; Hnr Roll; Nat Hon Sy; St of Mnth; USAA; WWAHSS; Comm Volntr; Hosp Aide; Peer Tut/Med; Track (V); Law; Psychology; U of North Carolina Wilmington

ROYAL, NATHAN; FAYETTEVILLE, NC; TERRY SANFORD HS; (SO); Duke TS; F Lan Hn Soc; Hi Hnr Roll; Nat Hon Sy; Pres Sch; Yth Ldrshp Prog; Comm Volntr; Emplmnt; FCA; Key Club; Spanish Clb; Bsball (V L); Ftball (JC); Stu Cncl (V); Scholar Athlete; Orthopedic Surgeon; Engineer; Duke U; Georgia Tech

ROYALL, JANE; SMITHFIELD, NC; SMITHFIELD-SELMA HS; (JR); Hi Hnr Roll; Jr Mshl; Nat Hon Sy; Perf Att; Comm Volntr; Hab For Humty Volntr; Spec Olymp Vol; Chrch Yth Grp; DARE; FCA; Key Club; MuAlphaTh; Off Aide; Prom Com; Dnce; Bskball (J); PP Ftbl (V); Sccr (V L); Swmg (V CL); Cl Off (V); Stu Cncl (T); Scholar - Athlete; NC Methodist Youth Council Rep; Sports Marketing; Parks and Recreation Management; U of North Carolina Chapel Hill; North Carolina State U

RUBIO, J E Z; CANTON, NC; PISGAH HS; (FR)

RUDD, NATASHA; RALEIGH, NC; GARNER HS; (JR); Hi Hnr Roll; Hnr Roll; Hosp Aide; DARE; Emplmnt; Bnd; Nomination to Leadership Forum of Nursing National Association in Boston; Major: Nursing; Major: Medicine; Columbia U; State U of NY Upstate Medical U

RUFF, CARNELL S; HICKORY, NC; HICKORY HS; (JR); Yth Ldrshp Prog; Comm Volntr; Peer Tut/Med; Chrch Yth Grp; DARE; Emplmnt; Mus Clb; Quiz Bowl; Scouts; Acpl Chr; Chr; Ch Chr; Stg Cre; Ftball (J); Track (V); Wrstlg (J); Best Role Model-Support Our Students (Organ.); Project Potential Scholarship; Criminal Law; Psychology; North Carolina Central U; North Carolina A & T U

RUFFIN, LAURA E; JACKSONVILLE, NC; NORTHSIDE HS; (SO); Hnr Roll; WWAHSS; Comm Volntr; Chrch Yth Grp; FBLA; Lib Aide; Ch Chr; Sturgeon City; Secondary Education; Government Sciences; North Carolina State U; Winthrop U

RUIZ, DAVITH; FARMVILLE, NC; FARMVILLE CTRL HS; (SO); Hnr Roll; Perf Att; St of Mnth; Architecture; Professional Mechanic

RUIZ, LIZBETH; WINSTON SALEM, NC; REYNOLDS HS; (JR); Hnr Roll; Perf Att; St Optmst of Yr; Clb; Chr; Marine Biologist; Veterinarian

RUSCOE, LAURA; ASHEVILLE, NC; A C REYNOLDS HS; (FR); Hi Hnr Roll; MVP; Nat Hon Sy; Otst Ac Ach Awd; Comm Volntr; Hosp Aide; Chrch Yth Grp; FCA; Swmg (V L); Sch Ppr (R, P); I Swim Year-Round Competitively; Participated in Southeastern Sectional Meet; Education; Medical Field; U of North Carolina; U of Georgia

RUSSELL, EVAN A; GREENSBORO, NC; J B DUDLEY HS; (FR); Hnr Roll; Comm Volntr; Hab For Humty Volntr; Ntl Beta Clb; Scouts; Architecture; History; North Carolina State U

RUSSELL, JESSICA J; ALBEMARLE, NC; WEST STANLY HS; (JR); Hnr Roll; WWAHSS; Comm Volntr; Chrch Yth Grp; DARE; Mus Clb; Sci Clb; Bnd; Clr Grd; Mch Bnd; 3 Yrs of Who's Who; National Music Honor Society-C Guard Capt; Respiratory Therapy; Pharmacy; Wingate U; UNCC

RUTH, TIFFANY D; MOORESBORO, NC; AMBASSADOR BAPTIST AC; (SO); Hnr Roll; Otst Ac Ach Awd; Chrch Yth Grp; Chr; Ch Chr; Vllyball; Fashion Photography; Zoology; U of North Carolina Charlotte; U of North Carolina Chapel Hill

RYALS, KENDRA; DUDLEY, NC; GOLDSBORO HS; (SO); 4H Awd; Ctznshp Aw; Hi Hnr Roll; Hnr Roll; Perf Att; Pres Sch; St of Mnth; WWAHSS; Peer Tut/Med; 4-H; Drma Clb; Chr; Stg Cre; Chrldg (V); Stu Cncl (S); Varsity Cheerleader Since Freshmen Year; Nursing; Lawyer; North Carolina Central U; East Carolina U

RYALS, TONY; GOLDSBORO, NC; EASTERN WAYNE HS; (SR); Hnr Roll; Otst Ac Ach Awd; St Schl; St of Mnth; WWAHSS; Yth Ldrshp Prog; Comm Volntr; Peer Tut/Med; BPA; Chrch Yth Grp; Emplmnt; Mth Clb/Tm; Ch Chr; CR (R); Renaissance Academic Achievement; Pillar of Character Award; Pre-Dentistry; Communications; East Carolina U, Greenville

RYAN, ASHTON B; MOORESVILLE, NC; MOORESVILLE HS; (SO); Ctznshp Aw; Duke TS; Hnr Roll; St of Mnth; WWAHSS; Comm Volntr; Chrch Yth Grp; DARE; P to P St Amb Prg; Scouts; Dnce; SP/M/VS; Chrldg (V L); Pre-Med; Dentistry / Orthodontics; UNC Chapel Hill; U of North Carolina

RYAN, TAYLOR; PINEHURST, NC; PINECREST HS; (SO); Hi Hnr Roll; Hnr Roll; Comm Volntr; Chrch Yth Grp; Key Club; Scouts; Ch Chr; U of North Carolina; North Carolina State U

RYSER, CALEB P; SANFORD, NC; GRACE CHRISTIAN SCH; (SO); Hnr Roll; Nat Hon Sy; WWAHSS; Chrch Yth Grp; Photog; Bsball (V); Bskball (J); Yrbk (R, P)

SADE, LUKAS; RALEIGH, NC; WAKEFIELD HS; (FR); Hnr Roll; MVP; Comm Volntr; Key Club; Sccr (J); Classic Club Soccer; MBA; PhD; (UNC-Chapel Hill) U of North Carolina

SAINE, WILLIAM E; VALE, NC; WEST LINCOLN HS; (FR); Hi Hnr Roll; Hnr Roll; Perf Att; Comm Volntr; Spec Olymp Vol; Chrch Yth Grp; Computer Engineer

SAINTSING, JESSICA A; LEXINGTON, NC; NORTH DAVIDSON HS; (SR); Hnr Roll; Nat Mrt Sch Recip; St of Mnth; Comm Volntr; Hosp Aide; Red Cr Aide; ArtClub; DARE; Key Club; Sftball (JC); Vllyball (V C); Active Member of HOSA; Completion of CNA Program; BSN (Nursing); Physical Therapy (Bachelor's); Lenoir Rhyne; UNC Greensboro

Rowe, Akia Y
Fike HS
Wilson, NC

Rorie, De Marvious
Garinger HS
Charlotte, NC

Rodriguez, Bianca A
Sun Valley HS
Indian Trail, NC

Roopchan, Kelly
North Forsyth SR HS
Winston Salem, NC

Russell, Jessica J
West Stanly HS
Albemarle, NC

SALAZAR, GIOVANNI; CONCORD, NC; JAY M ROBINSON HS; (JR); Hi Hnr Roll; MVP; St Schl; Emplmnt; Ntl Beta Clb; Off Aide; Quiz Bowl; Sccr (V CL); 2 Time All-Conference Player (Soccer); German II Award; Engineering; Computer Science; NC State; U of Jacksonville (Fl)

SALAZAR, ONISSE; CONCORD, NC; CONCORD HS; (SR); 4H Awd; Hnr Roll; Nat Sci Aw; Perf Att; St of Mnth; St Optmst of Yr; WWAHSS; Comm Volntr; Hosp Aide; Peer Tut/Med; 4-H; ArtClub; Chess; DARE; FTA; Lib Aide; Ntl Beta Clb; SADD; Dnce; Jzz Bnd; SP/M/VS; Bsball; Sccr; Swmg; Vllyball; CR; Sch Ppr (P); Yrbk (P); A / B Honor Roll - 2 Times in One Semester; Chapel Hill; Northeast Medical Center College

SALIGA, LAUREN; HAW RIVER, NC; EASTERN ALAMANCE HS; (SO); Hi Hnr Roll; Hnr Roll; Key Club; Dnce; Bskball (J); Nursing; UNC-Wilmington; UNC-Chapel Hill

SAMS, CHRISTINA; MARSHALL, NC; MADISON HS; (SR); Spec Olymp Vol; DARE; FCA; Ntl FFA; Ch Chr; Ftball (C); Teacher's Assistant Certificate; Asheville-Buncombe Technical

SAMUELS, DEION; THOMASVILLE, NC; THOMASVILLE HS; (FR); Hnr Roll; Otst Ac Ach Awd; Comm Volntr; Red Cr Aide; Chrch Yth Grp; DARE; Emplmnt; Scouts; Ch Chr; Dnce; Bskball (L); Ftball (L); Stu Cncl (R); Pro in Basketball; Be a Barber; U of North Carolina; Texas State U

SANCHEZ, MARIANA; SALISBURY, NC; SALISBURY HS; (JR); Hi Hnr Roll; Hnr Roll; Jr Mshl; Comm Volntr; Chrch Yth Grp; Emplmnt; Key Club; Scr Kpr; Swmg (V); Vllyball (J); Junior Civitan / Spanish Club / Honor Society; Teens With A Mission Member / Key Club; Pre-Med / Children / Psychiatric; Elementary Education / Teaching; Davidson College; UNC Chapel Hill

SANCHEZ, NOE D; BEUALAVILLE, NC; EAST DUPLIN HS; (SO); Hnr Roll; MVP; Nat Hon Sy; Nat Stu Ath Day Aw; Otst Ac Ach Awd; Perf Att; St of Mnth; St Optmst of Yr; US Army Sch Ath Aw; USMC Stu Ath Aw; Amnsty Intl; Comm Volntr; Peer Tut/Med; AL Aux Boys; ArtClub; Cmptr Clb; FCA; FBLA; Ntl Beta Clb; Tech Clb; Spanish Clb; Chr; Ch Chr; SP/M/VS; Stg Cre; Bsball (V); Bskball (V); Cr Ctry (C); Ftball (V C); Track (V C); Vsy Clb (L); Wt Lftg (V L); Wrstlg (V); Cl Off (P); Yrbk (P); Set Records in East Duplin High School Playing DE, Great Football Stats; Professional Football Player-Sports; Engineering or Architecture; U of North Carolina; U of Southern California

SANCHEZ PERELDA, FABIOLA A; LEXINGTON, NC; LEXINGTON SR HS; (FR); Hnr Roll; Perf Att; St of Mnth; Spec Olymp Vol; ROTC; Chr; Drl Tm; Nursing; Photographer; Wake Forest U; North Carolina State U

SANDERS, CORDYKIA C; HOBGOOD, NC; SOUTHEAST HALIFAX HS; (JR); Hnr Roll; Otst Ac Ach Awd; Perf Att; Sci Fairs; St of Mnth; WWAHSS; Yth Ldrshp Prog; Chrch Yth Grp; DARE; Pep Squd; Bnd; Clr Grd; Mch Bnd; Pep Bnd; Bskball (J); Track (J); Doctor; Physical Therapy; North Carolina A & T; ECSU

SANDERS, DONALD; RALEIGH, NC; ENLOE HS; (JR); WWAHSS; FBLA; Ftball (V L); Track (V L); Who's Who Among American Students; Engineering; Medical

SANDERS, ERIC D; CLINTON, NC; HOBBTON HS; (SR); Hnr Roll; Nat Hon Sy; Perf Att; Sci Fairs; Red Cr Aide; DARE; Drma Clb; Ntl FFA; Tchrs Aide; SP/M/VS; Ftball (VJ L); Track (V L); Teacher/Student Volleyball; Engineering; Business; Wayne Community College; East Carolina U

SANDERS, JADARIEN L; STANLEY, NC; EAST LINCOLN HS; (SO); Nat Hon Sy; WWAHSS; Spec Olymp Vol; Chrch Yth Grp; FCA; FBLA; Ch Chr; Scr Kpr (V); Cl Off (P); Minister; Nominated to Legislator's School; Computer Technology; Business; NC State U; Hampton U

SANDERS, VINCENT M; JACKSONVILLE, NC; NORTHSIDE HS; (FR); Hi Hnr Roll; Hnr Roll; MVP; Pres Ac Ftns Aw; Pres Sch; Sci Fairs; Comm Volntr; FCA; Bsball (J); Bskball (J); Engineering; Mathematician; Duke U; U of North Carolina @ Chapel Hill

SANDERSON, CARRIE G; HARRELLS, NC; HARRELLS CHRISTIAN AC; (FR); Hi Hnr Roll; Hnr Roll; MVP; Nat Hon Sy; Nat Sci Aw; Otst Ac Ach Awd; Pres Ac Ftns Aw; Sci Fairs; Comm Volntr; Chrch Yth Grp; FCA; Ntl Beta Clb; Dnce; Bskball (J); PP Ftbl (J); Sftball (V); Vllyball (C); Wt Lftg (J); Adv Cncl (R); Cl Off (P); Stu Cncl (R); Class President 9th Grade; Homecoming Court 9th Grade; Broadcasting; Pharmacy; Wake Forest U; Meredith College

SANTOLI, MATTHEW; DAVIDSON, NC; NORTH MECKLENBURG HS; (SO); All Am Sch; Duke TS; Hi Hnr Roll; WWAHSS; Comm Volntr; Hab For Humty Volntr; Vsity Clb; Swmg (V); Engineering; Duke U; U of Virginia

SANTOS, WALESSA; CHARLOTTE, NC; NORTH MECKLENBURG HS; (JR); Hi Hnr Roll; Hnr Roll; Comm Volntr; Chrch Yth Grp; FBLA; Prom Com; Latino Clb; Chr; Ch Chr; Dnce; Wt Lftg (V); Stu Cncl (R); Participated in NCCJ Peace Journeys Conference, NCCJ Youth Council; Criminal Justice; Political Science; Pace U (NY); John Jay College of Criminal Justice

SARABIA ESTRADA, GLADYS M; CONNELLYS SPRINGS, NC; EAST BURKE HS; (FR); Hnr Roll; Otst Ac Ach Awd; St of Mnth; DARE; FCA; Bnd; Mch Bnd; Pep Bnd; Sccr (J); Music; U of North Carolina

SASSER, DYMENN E; HOOKERTON, NC; GREENE CTRL HS; (SO); Hi Hnr Roll; Hnr Roll; Otst Ac Ach Awd; Comm Volntr; Peer Tut/Med; Spec Olymp Vol; Ntl Beta Clb; A Member of HOSA; A Member of Question It; Pediatrics Major; Major in Health Sciences; Duke U; UCLA

SAULS, CARMEN E; GOLDSBORO, NC; EASTERN WAYNE HS; (JR); Ctznshp Aw; Hi Hnr Roll; Hnr Roll; Jr Mshl; Nat Hon Sy; Pres Sch; St of Mnth; WWAHSS; Comm Volntr; ArtClub; Key Club; Mth Clb/Tm; French Clb; Chr; Golf (V); National Society of High School Scholars; History; Art History; U of North Carolina at Chapel Hill; Salem College

SAUNDERS, CARRIE R; CANDOR, NC; EAST MONTGOMERY HS; (FR); All Am Sch; Ctznshp Aw; Hnr Roll; Perf Att; Sci Fairs; St of Mnth; USAA; WWAHSS; Peer Tut/Med; Ch Chr; Playing Piano; Nursing; Master's Degree; Duke U; North Carolina State

SAUNDERS, DAWN M; KELFORD, NC; BERTIE HS; (JR); Ctznshp Aw; Hi Hnr Roll; Hnr Roll; Otst Ac Ach Awd; St of Mnth; WWAHSS; Peer Tut/Med; Chrch Yth Grp; DARE; Mus Clb; Ntl Beta Clb; Pep Squd; Prom Com; Tchrs Aide; Bnd; Ch Chr; Dnce; Jzz Bnd; Chrldg (C); Cl Off (V); CR (P); Child Psychology; Social Worker; North Carolina Central U; North Carolina Agricultural and Technical State U

SAUNDERS, GWEN; KILL DEVIL HILLS, NC; FIRST FLIGHT HS; (JR); Hi Hnr Roll; Jr Mshl; Kwnis Aw; Nat Hon Sy; WWAHSS; Comm Volntr; ArtClub; Chrch Yth Grp; Key Club; Spanish Clb; Bnd; Centennial Band; Mission Trip to Africa; Arts and Humanities

SAUNDERS, SARAH; TROY, NC; WEST MONTGOMERY HS; (FR); 4H Awd; Hnr Roll; 4-H; DARE; Vice President of "Creative Hands" 4-H group; Fashion Design; Merchandising; U of North Carolina Greensboro; International Academy of Merchandising & Design (Florida)

SAUNDERS, SARA T; MATTHEWS, NC; WEDDINGTON HS; (JR); DAR; Yth Ldrshp Prog; Spec Olymp Vol; Chrch Yth Grp; Dbte Team; Drma Clb; Emplmnt; Key Club; Pep Squd; Spch Team; French Clb; SP/M/VS; Black Belt in Karate; Communications

SAVAGE, JENNIE M; WINSTON-SALEM, NC; REYNOLDS HS; (JR); Gov Hnr Prg; Hnr Roll; Sci Fairs; Comm Volntr; ArtClub; Ntl FFA; Excelling in Visual Arts; FFA - VP; Visual Arts; Biology; U of North Carolina Asheville

SAVANNAH, DESTINY; FAIRMONT, NC; LUMBERTON HS; (FR); Hnr Roll; Hosp Aide; 4-H; ROTC; Chrldg (J); Medicine; Pediatrics; U of NC Chapel Hill; North Carolina State U

SAWYER, CAROLINE; HERTFORD, NC; PERQUIMANS CTY HS; (SR); Duke TS; Hnr Roll; Chrch Yth Grp; SADD; Bnd; Mch Bnd; Vllyball (VJCL); Animal Science/Pre-Vet; North Carolina State U

SCHACH, SARAH; GREENSBORO, NC; NORTHWEST GUILFORD HS; (SO); Duke TS; Hnr Roll; Sci/Math Olympn; Sci Clb; Spanish Clb; Golf (V L); Scr Kpr (V); Business Management; Microbiology; North Carolina State U

SCHERMERHORN, DEMETRA V; BURLINGTON, NC; GREENSBORO DAY SCH; (FR); Duke TS; Hi Hnr Roll; WWAHSS; Comm Volntr; Chrch Yth Grp; Drma Clb; Mod UN; Scouts; Stg Cre; Fld Hky (V); Sftball (V); Swmg (V); Medicine; Dentistry; Stamford, UCSD

SCHLEY, COREY; GOLDSBORO, NC; EASTERN WAYNE HS; (SO); Ctznshp Aw; Hnr Roll; Perf Att; Pres Ac Ftns Aw; Yth Ldrshp Prog; Comm Volntr; Peer Tut/Med; Mth Clb/Tm; Ftball (V); Track (V); Engineering; Mathematics; North Carolina State U; U of North Carolina

SCHRADER, DOROTHY; CONCORD, NC; JAY M ROBINSON HS; (FR); Duke TS; Hnr Roll; Pres Ac Ftns Aw; FCA; P to P St Amb Prg; Dnce; Many High Awards in Dance; 2005 All-Star Kar Kid

SCHRANTZ, EVAN N; MURPHY, NC; MURPHY HS; (FR); Duke TS; Hi Hnr Roll; Yth Ldrshp Prog; Chrch Yth Grp; Bnd; Jzz Bnd; Mch Bnd; World Changers with Local Church Youth; Active in Church; Business/Finance; Science; Western Carolina U; Lee U

SCHRONCE, ANDREA J; MAIDEN, NC; MAIDEN HS; (SO); Ctznshp Aw; Duke TS; Hi Hnr Roll; Nat Ldrshp Svc; Otst Ac Ach Awd; Perf Att; Yth Ldrshp Prog; Comm Volntr; Spec Olymp Vol; ArtClub; Chrch Yth Grp; Emplmnt; FCA; Lib Aide; Ntl Beta Clb; Tchrs Aide; Chrldg (J); Adv Cncl (R); Stu Cncl (S, T); CR (R); Catawba Co. Schools Criminal Justice Internship; Catawba Co. Schools Student Leadership Conference; Corporate Lawyer; Politician; Duke U; U of N.C at Chapel Hill

SCHULTZ, KATIE; HILLSBOROUGH, NC; CEDAR RIDGE HS; (SO); Hnr Roll; WWAHSS; FBLA; Key Club; Bskball (J); Sccr (V); Sftball (J); Track (V); Vllyball (V); Stu Cncl (S); Marine Biology; Journalism; Seattle U; Duke U

SCHUTRUM JR, MICHAEL; HUNTERSVILLE, NC; NORTH MECKLENBURG HS; (JR); Hi Hnr Roll; Hnr Roll; Nat Hon Sy; Otst Ac Ach Awd; WWAHSS; Hab For Humty Volntr; DECA; Key Club; Svce Clb; SADD; Tech Clb; Stg Cre; DECA Event Finalist State Level; National Honor Society Member; Broadcast Journalism; Law; UNC Chapel Hill; Fordham U

SCIUVA, JAMES S; TRYON, NC; POLK CTY HS; (SO); WWAHSS; Comm Volntr; Key Club; Svce Clb; Sccr (V); Key Club; AYSO Soccer Referee; Pre-Med; Engineering; Virginia Poly Technical Institute; U of Notre Dame

SCOBLIC, SHAWNA; JACKSONVILLE, NC; NORTHSIDE HS; (FR); Hnr Roll; Comm Volntr; Red Cr Aide; Chrch Yth Grp; Lib Aide; ROTC; Latin Clb; SP/M/VS; Stg Cre; Arch; PP Ftbl; Tennis (V); CR (S); Jacksonville Youth Council; Child/Adolescent Psychiatrist; Psychology; U of North Carolina Wilmington; East Carolina U

SCOGGINS, BRITTANY; MC LEANSVILLE, NC; NORTHEAST HS; (JR); Hnr Roll; Perf Att; St of Mnth; WWAHSS; Prom Com; Swmg (V L); HOSA Club; Nursing; UNCG- U of North Carolina At Greensboro

SCOTT, DAVID M; MATTHEWS, NC; PIEDMONT HS; (JR); Duke TS; Hi Hnr Roll; Hnr Roll; Nat Hon Sy; Comm Volntr; Emplmnt; Ntl Beta Clb; P to P St Amb Prg; Tennis (V); National Honor Society; Rotary Scholar; Engineering; Computer Science; North Carolina State U; Appalachian State U

SCOTT, KANYSHA F; ROANOKE RAPIDS, NC; NORTHWEST HS; (FR); Ctznshp Aw; Hi Hnr Roll; Hnr Roll; Nat Hon Sy; St of Mnth; WWAHSS; Chrch Yth Grp; FBLA; Ntl Beta Clb; ROTC; SADD; Chr; Ch Chr; High Honor Roll, Honor Roll; Principal's List, Sergeant of JROTC; Pre-Med, Sociology; Pre-Law, Psychology; U of North Carolina At Chapel Hill; Elizabeth City State U

SCOTT, MEREDITH C; FAIRVIEW, NC; T C ROBERSON HS; (SR); Hnr Roll; Key Club; Off Aide; Scouts; Tchrs Aide; Ch Chr; Dnce; Lettered in Academics; Dance Award; Marketing; English; Meredith College

SCOTT, NATALIE; KITTY HAWK, NC; FIRST FLIGHT HS; (SO); Hi Hnr Roll; Hnr Roll; WWAHSS; Yth Ldrshp Prog; Comm Volntr; Chrch Yth Grp; FBLA; Key Club; Photog; Vsity Clb; Ch Chr; SP/M/VS; Chrldg (J); Cr Ctry (J); Sftball (VJ); Track (V L); Vsy Clb (V); Cl Off (S); Sch Ppr (E, R, P); 5 Yrs of Community Service At Relay for Life; Social Services; Journalism; UNC U of North Carolina; Duke

SCOTT, PRETORIA L; GARYSBURG, NC; NORTHAMPTON WEST HS; (FR); Hnr Roll; Otst Ac Ach Awd; Perf Att; WWAHSS; 4-H; Chrch Yth Grp; DARE; Bnd; Ch Chr; Vllyball (J); Yrbk (R); Cosmetologist; Business Degree; Fayetteville State U; Dudley's Cosmetology U

SCOTT, TARA S; CANTON, NC; PISGAH HS; (SO); Hnr Roll; Nat Hon Sy; Comm Volntr; Peer Tut/Med; Dnce; CR (T); Optometry; Pediatrics; Appalachian State U; Wake Forest U

SCOTT, THOMAS I; JACKSONVILLE, NC; JACKSONVILLE HS; (JR); Duke TS; Hi Hnr Roll; Hnr Roll; Mas Aw; Otst Ac Ach Awd; Sci Fairs; St of Mnth; WWAHSS; Chrch Yth Grp; Emplmnt; FCA; Eagle Scout, BSA; Past Master Councilor, Order of Dermatology; Criminal Justice; NC State; UNC Pembroke

SCOTT, TIFFANY; TOWNSVILLE, NC; NORTHERN VANCE HS; (SO); Hnr Roll; Comm Volntr; Chrch Yth Grp; Bnd; Ch Chr; Mch Bnd; Psychology (Child); Music; A & T U; Western Carolina U

SCRUGGS, SARAH C; PFAFFTOWN, NC; MT TABOR HS; (JR); Hnr Roll; MVP; Nat Hon Sy; Comm Volntr; Chrch Yth Grp; Emplmnt; FCA; FTA; Key Club; Svce Clb; Spanish Clb; Bskball (VJCL); Sftball (JC); Vllyball (VJCL); Middle School Teacher / Secondary Education; U of North Carolina Chapel Hill; East Carolina

SEABORN, CATHERINE; CHARLOTTE, NC; CHARLOTTE CHRISTIAN SCH; (SO); Duke TS; Hi Hnr Roll; USAA; WWAHSS; Bnd; Ch Chr; Cr Ctry (V); Track (V); Cl Off (S); Church Mission Trip to Costa Rica; Clemson U; Wake Forest U

SEAMAN, JESSICA M; KING, NC; WEST STOKES HS; (FR); Hi Hnr Roll; Hnr Roll; MVP; Sci Fairs; St of Mnth; Comm Volntr; Drma Clb; Bnd; SP/M/VS; Sftball (J); Vllyball (J); NCRA State Young Author Judges' Choice Award; MVP During Varsity High School Softball Tournament; Journalism; Law; U of California Los Angeles; U of North Carolina

SEAY, HALLIE E; CLYDE, NC; TUSCOLA HS; (JR); Nat Hon Sy; St of Mnth; WWAHSS; Emplmnt; FTA; Key Club; SADD; Spanish Clb; Dnce; Foreign Language Major; U of North Carolina, Wilmington

SEGUR, BRITTANY; JACKSONVILLE, NC; WHITE OAK HS; (MS); Ctznshp Aw; Hi Hnr Roll; Nat Hon Sy; Otst Ac Ach Awd; Comm Volntr; Chrldg (J); National Junior Honor Society; National Art Junior Honor Society; Teacher; Law; U of North Carolina Chapel Hill; North Carolina State

SEIFERT, KAYLEE M; SOUTHERN PINES, NC; PINECREST HS; (JR); Nat Hon Sy; WWAHSS; Comm Volntr; Spec Olymp Vol; Key Club; Pep Squd; Spanish Clb; Chrldg (VJCL); National Society of High School Scholars; Interact; Architecture; Interior Design; U of California in Irvine; U of North Carolina Chapel Hill

SELLERS, MAGGIE; SUPPLY, NC; WEST BRUNSWICK HS; (SR); Hnr Roll; Perf Att; Peer Tut/Med; DARE; Off Aide; Bnd; Chr; Fashion Buyer; Brunswick Community College

Seay, Hallie E
Tuscola HS
Clyde, NC

Schrantz, Evan N
Murphy HS
Murphy, NC

Santos, Walessa
North Mecklenburg HS
Charlotte, NC

Sanders, Vincent M
Northside HS
Jacksonville, NC

Salazar, Onisse
Concord HS
Concord, NC

Sams, Christina
Madison HS
Marshall, NC

Schley, Corey
Eastern Wayne HS
Goldsboro, NC

Scott, Tiffany
Northern Vance HS
Townsville, NC

Sellers, Maggie
West Brunswick HS
Supply, NC

SELLERS, TEKARI R; GREENSBORO, NC; DUDLEY HS; (FR); Hnr Roll; St of Mnth; Track (J); Female Mentoring Program; Marketing; Accounting; Duke U; Howard U

SEMERSKY, CHELSEA; CONCORD, NC; JAY M ROBINSON HS; (JR); Hnr Roll; Sci Fairs; Comm Volntr; Chrch Yth Grp; DARE; Emplmnt; Sftball (V); Cruise Motor Cycle Ministry; Executive Chef; Forensic Science; U of North Carolina At Charlotte; Johnson and Wales U

SEMONES, SARAH J; POLKTON, NC; ANSON HS; (FR); Ctznshp Aw; Hi Hnr Roll; Nat Hon Sy; USAA; Peer Tut/Med; Chrch Yth Grp; DARE; Tchrs Aide; Bnd; Clr Grd; Flg Crps; Mch Bnd; Peer Tutor; Community Service Work; Registered Nurse; Radiologist; Wingate U NC; Radford U VA

SESSOMS, MILLICENT N; AHOSKIE, NC; BERTIE HS; (SO); Ctznshp Aw; Gov Hnr Prg; Hi Hnr Roll; Hnr Roll; Comm Volntr; Peer Tut/Med; ArtClub; Chrch Yth Grp; DARE; Ntl Beta Clb; ROTC; Stu Cncl (R); Member of Students Against Destructive Decisions; Psychology; Criminal Justice; U of NC Chapel Hill; Duke U

SETZER, JANAIA; CHARLOTTE, NC; NORTH MECKLENBURG HS; (JR); Ctznshp Aw; Hnr Roll; MVP; Nat Hon Sy; Perf Att; St of Mnth; Comm Volntr; Peer Tut/Med; Red Cr Aide; Chrch Yth Grp; DARE; DECA; Emplmnt; Key Club; P to P St Amb Prg; Bnd; Bskball (J); Track (V); 2nd Place Winner in Delta Sigma Theta Jabber Walk; Hope Award; Nursing (RN); Administration; U of North Carolina At Chapel Hill; Georgia State U

SETZER, JESSICA; CONNELLYS SPRINGS, NC; EAST BURKE HS; (FR); Duke TS; Hnr Roll; Chrch Yth Grp; Bnd; Ch Chr; Mch Bnd; Cr Ctry (V); Lawyer; Physical Therapist; U of North Carolina-Chapel Hill

SEXTON, HOLLY; SALISBURY, NC; SALISBURY HS; (SO); Key Club; Sccr (J); Swmg (V); Tennis (V)

SHAD, MOHAMMAD; CARY, NC; CARY SR HS; (JR); Nat Hon Sy; Comm Volntr; French Clb; Cary High School Academic Achievement Award 2002-2003; Cary High School Academic Achievement Award 2003-2004; Biology; Economics; U of North Carolina Chapel Hill; U of North Carolina Greensboro

SHAFFER, NICHOLAS; LELAND, NC; NORTH BRUNSWICK HS; (SR); Peer Tut/Med; ROTC; Drl Tm; Automobile Mechanic; Bartending

SHAH, NIRAJ; GREENSBORO, NC; SOUTHWEST GUILFORD HS; (SO); Hnr Roll; Perf Att; WWAHSS; Red Cr Aide; DECA; Spanish Clb; Track (VJ); Big Brothers Big Sisters Volunteer; Environmental Club; Business Administration; Entrepreneurship; U of Pennsylvania; Babson College

SHANNON, MEGAN M; GREENSBORO, NC; SOUTHEAST GUILFORD HS; (JR); Hnr Roll; WWAHSS; Comm Volntr; Red Cr Aide; Chrch Yth Grp; Emplmnt; Key Club; Kwanza Clb; Svce Clb; Spanish Clb; Bskball (V L); Lit Mag (E, R); Key Club Secretary; English/Pre Law; Physical Therapy; U of North Carolina-Chapel Hill; North Carolina State U

SHARP, STEPHANIE D; LEXINGTON, NC; LEXINGTON SR HS; (JR); Hnr Roll; Otst Ac Ach Awd; WWAHSS; Comm Volntr; 4-H; Chrch Yth Grp; DECA; Key Club; Prom Com; Chr; Ch Chr; Dnce; Chrldg (V); Bachelor's Degree; U of North Carolina-Charlotte; Appalachian State U

SHARPE, JASMINE; HICKORY, NC; HICKORY HS; (FR); Hnr Roll; Perf Att; Comm Volntr; Peer Tut/Med; Chrch Yth Grp; Emplmnt; Ntl Beta Clb; Stu Cncl; North & South Carolina Salvation Army Youth of the Year; Project Potential Scholarship Recipient; Teaching; Pediatrician; Appalachian U; North Carolina A & T U

SHARPE, RYAN G; RALEIGH, NC; WAKEFIELD HS; (FR); Duke TS; Hnr Roll; Sci/Math Olympn; WWAHSS; Comm Volntr; Chrch Yth Grp; DARE; Jr Ach; Key Club; Ntl Beta Clb; Sci Clb; Science/Math; Computer/Technology; Harvard; Yale

SHAW, DELLA M; RALEIGH, NC; WAKEFIELD HS; (SO); Hnr Roll; Comm Volntr; Peer Tut/Med; Chrch Yth Grp; Key Club; Bnd; Mch Bnd; Pep Bnd; RAFA Level IV Winner - Fall 2004; Veterinary Medicine; Music Education; UNC Chapel Hill; UNC Wilmington

SHAW, EMILY; HENDERSON, NC; SOUTHERN VANCE HS; (SR); Duke TS; F Lan Hn Soc; Hi Hnr Roll; Jr Mshl; Nat Hon Sy; St of Mnth; WWAHSS; Comm Volntr; Chrch Yth Grp; Emplmnt; Ntl Beta Clb; Quiz Bowl; Sci Clb; Spanish Clb; Tennis (V); Cl Off (P); Yrbk (E); Biology; Spanish; U of North Carolina At Chapel Hill

SHAW, JELENA S; HOPE MILLS, NC; SOUTHVIEW HS; (JR); Hnr Roll; Nat Hon Sy; Otst Ac Ach Awd; St of Mnth; Peer Tut/Med; Lib Aide; Bskball (V); PP Ftbl (V); Sftball (V); Vllyball (V); CR; Yrbk; Student of the Year; Physical Therapy; Early Childhood Education; U of North Carolina At Chapel Hill; U of North Carolina At Charlotte

SHAW, SHENESSA; FAYETTEVILLE, NC; E E SMITH SR HS; (FR); Hnr Roll; WWAHSS; Peer Tut/Med; DARE; AVID and Who's Who Among American High School Student 2004-2005; Gear Up; Interior Design; Architect; Michigan State U; Fayetteville State U

SHAW, TIFFANY; FAIRVIEW, NC; A C REYNOLDS HS; (SO); Ctznshp Aw; Hi Hnr Roll; Hnr Roll; St of Mnth; WWAHSS; Comm Volntr; DARE; Emplmnt; Tchrs Aide; Chr; Dnce; SP/M/VS; Veterinary Assistant; Child Care; U of North Carolina Asheville; North Carolina State

SHAW, TOMEKA; TARBORO, NC; (SR); Hnr Roll; Spec Olymp Vol; DARE; Lib Aide; Ch Chr; Dnce; Swmg (V); I Love Dancing; Bike Riding; Edgecombe Comm. College

SHAYKA, MICHELE A; GASTONIA, NC; BESSEMER CITY HS; (SO); Hnr Roll; USAA; Spec Olymp Vol; Chrch Yth Grp; Ntl Beta Clb; Chr; Dnce; Radiologist; Dental Hygienist; Appalachian State; U of North Carolina Charlotte

SHEK, EVAN; MOORESVILLE, NC; LAKE NORMAN HS; (SO); Hnr Roll; Perf Att; Chemistry and Mathematics; Medicine; State U of New York Stony Brook; U of North Carolina Chapel Hill

SHELLEY, BRAXTON D; ROCKY MOUNT, NC; NORTHERN NASH SR HS; (FR); Duke TS; Hi Hnr Roll; Hnr Roll; Sci/Math Olympn; St of Mnth; Yth Ldrshp Prog; Comm Volntr; Chrch Yth Grp; Mth Clb/Tm; Quiz Bowl; Bnd; Ch Chr; Adv Cncl (R); 9 Out of 272 Eastern NC Math Competition; National Junior Beta Club; Political Science; Government; U of North Carolina-Chapel Hill; Harvard U

SHELTON, MARESSA N; CHARLOTTE, NC; HARDING UNIVERSITY HS; (FR); All Am Sch; Hnr Roll; Chrch Yth Grp; Dbte Team; Bnd; Mch Bnd; Winston Salem

SHEPHERD, FOREST T; SILER CITY, NC; JORDAN MATTHEWS HS; (SO); Hnr Roll; Voc Ind Clb Am; Cr Ctry (V); Ftball (V); Tennis (V); Masters in Small Business Management; North Carolina State U; U of North Carolina

SHERRER, VALERIE; NEWPORT, NC; WEST CARTERET HS; (SO); Duke TS; Hnr Roll; Pres Ac Ftns Aw; St of Mnth; Comm Volntr; Key Club; Sftball (V L); Vllyball (V L); Professor of Literature; Appalachian; UNC-Chapel Hill

SHIELDS, AMBER M; DURHAM, NC; SOUTHERN HS; (SO); Hnr Roll; Kwnis Aw; Otst Ac Ach Awd; Perf Att; Pres Ac Ftns Aw; St of Mnth; Comm Volntr; DARE; Tchrs Aide; Ch Chr; Dnce; SP/M/VS; Chrldg (V CL); CR (R); Miss Freshman; Miss Sophomore; Ped Nurse; U of North Carolina; North Carolina State U

SHIELDS, JAMIE; LA GRANGE, NC; NORTH LENLOR HS; (SR); Hnr Roll; Ftball (V); Wt Lftg (V)

SHIFLETT, CANDIS; ROCKWELL, NC; EAST ROWAN HS; (FR); Hi Hnr Roll; Pres Ac Ftns Aw; Yth Ldrshp Prog; Chrch Yth Grp; DARE; Ntl FFA; SADD; Chr; SP/M/VS; Stu Cncl (R); Architecture-Residential/Commercial; Engineering; North Carolina State U; Auburn U, Alabama

SHIPP, J HUNTER; RALEIGH, NC; GARNER HS; (FR); Hnr Roll; St of Mnth; Comm Volntr; Chrch Yth Grp; Ftball (J); Business Management

SHIPP, OLIVIA M; CLINTON, NC; CLINTON HS; (FR); Duke TS; Pres Ac Ftns Aw; WWAHSS; Comm Volntr; Spec Olymp Vol; 4-H; Chrch Yth Grp; Jr Cls League; Key Club; Latin Clb; Bnd; Ch Chr; Dnce; Mch Bnd; Tennis (J); CR (R); All-District Band; Latin I - Academic Award; Health Sciences; Duke U; U of North Carolina Chapel Hill

SHIREY, CASEY; KINGS MOUNTAIN, NC; KINGS MOUNTAIN HS; (JR); Ctznshp Aw; Hnr Roll; MVP; WWAHSS; Comm Volntr; Peer Tut/Med; Spec Olymp Vol; FBLA; FTA; Mod UN; Ntl Beta Clb; P to P St Amb Prg; Photog; Svce Clb; Sccr (C); Ambassador; National Society of High School Scholars; Physical Therapy; Athletic Training; Western Carolina U; U of North Carolina Wilmington

SHIVER, THOMAS I; HILLSBOROUGH, NC; CEDAR RIDGE HS; (SO); Duke TS; Hi Hnr Roll; Hnr Roll; Perf Att; WWAHSS; Chrch Yth Grp; DARE; Jr Cls League; Key Club; Mus Clb; Latin Clb; Bnd; Orch; Participant-NC Junior Classical / League State Convention UNC-Chapel Hill; Invitation to 2005 National Student Leadership Conference; Computer Graphics; NC State U

SHOEMAKER, JESSIE; CLEVELAND, NC; WEST ROWAN HS; (JR); Hnr Roll; Nat Hon Sy; WWAHSS; Red Cr Aide; ArtClub; Chrch Yth Grp; DARE; Emplmnt; Track (V); Lit Mag (R, P); Participated in Jujitsu; Art; English-(writer); Appalachian State U; Pfeiffer U

SHUFORD, JOSHUA; HICKORY, NC; HICKORY HS; (FR); Ctznshp Aw; Duke TS; Hnr Roll; MVP; Otst Ac Ach Awd; Sci Fairs; Comm Volntr; Peer Tut/Med; Chrch Yth Grp; DARE; Dbte Team; Drma Clb; FCA; Key Club; Mus Clb; Prom Com; Dnce; SP/M/VS; Stg Cre; Ftball (VJ); Lcrsse (V); Track (V); Wt Lftg (L); CR (R); Business Management; International Business; Wake Forest U; Florida State U

SHUKLA, ADIT; RALEIGH, NC; WAKEFIELD HS; (FR); Hi Hnr Roll; Kwnis Aw; Perf Att; Sci Fairs; Sci/Math Olympn; Comm Volntr; Key Club; Ntl Beta Clb; Science Olympiad; Web Team; Graphic Design; Business Management; UPenn; Cornell

SHULER, ELAINA; CLYDE, NC; TUSCOLA HS; (FR); All Am Sch; USAA; Comm Volntr; Svce Clb; Golf (V L); Broadcast Journalism; Magazine Editor; East Carolina U; UNC-Wilmington

SIDDIGI, REBEKAH; ASHEBORO, NC; ASHEBORO HS; (FR); Hi Hnr Roll; Otst Ac Ach Awd; Perf Att; USAA; WWAHSS; Comm Volntr; Key Club; Track (J); Stu Cncl (R); Volunteer At Teen Court Every Month; Art; Archaeology

SIDER, ARAFAT; RALEIGH, NC; MILLBROOK HS; (JR); Hnr Roll; WWAHSS; Dbte Team; Bnd; Stg Cre; Bskball (J); Dvng (J); Ftball (J); Swmg (J); Track (V); Wt Lftg (VJ); Automotive Industry; Engineering; North Carolina State U; U of North Carolina in Wilmington

SIDERS, G C; GRIMESLAND, NC; D.H. CONLEY; (SO); MVP; Chrch Yth Grp; Bsball (J)

SIDERS, SAMANTHA R; GRIMESLAND, NC; D H CONLEY HS; (JR); F Lan Hn Soc; Hnr Roll; WWAHSS; Hosp Aide; Chrch Yth Grp; Emplmnt; Spanish Clb; Ch Chr; Chrldg (VJ); PP Ftbl (J); Track (V); Letter in Academics; 2004 Princess of Pitt County; Biology Teacher; Bob Jones U

SIERRA, MARIBEL J; BISCOE, NC; EAST MONTGOMERY HS; (SO); Ctznshp Aw; Hi Hnr Roll; St of Mnth; WWAHSS; Comm Volntr; ArtClub; FBLA; Visual Arts Achievement; Biology Major; Master's Degree or PhD; U of NC At Chapel Hill; North Carolina School of the Arts

SIFERS, TIFFANY L; YOUNGSVILLE, NC; NEUSE BAPTIST CHRISTIAN SCH; (SO); Nat Sci Aw; Yth Ldrshp Prog; Comm Volntr; Chrch Yth Grp; Drma Clb; NYLC; Pep Squd; Spch Team; Bnd; Chr; Ch Chr; Mch Bnd; Bskball (VJ); Sccr (V); Sftball (V); Vllyball (VJC); Sch Ppr (R); 3 Mission Trips to the Dominican Republic; Pre-Med; Veterinary Med; Oklahoma State U; Liberty U

SIFFORD, YLONDA N; FAYETTEVILLE, NC; SEVENTY-FIRST HS; (FR); Ctznshp Aw; Hnr Roll; Nat Hon Sy; Otst Ac Ach Awd; Comm Volntr; DARE; Bnd; Clr Grd; Mch Bnd; Sftball (J); CR (R); Sch Ppr (R); Yrbk (E, P); Major in Medicine; PhD; Harvard U; Spelman College

SILER, CHANTELL; SILER CITY, NC; JORDAN MATTHEWS HS; (FR); Hnr Roll; St of Mnth; Chrch Yth Grp; Drma Clb; Dnce; SP/M/VS; I'm Eligible for NCSSM; Won Savings Bond for Honor Roll; Performing Arts; Business Management; North Carolina School of the Arts; Long Island U-Brooklyn Campus

SIMMONS, AMBER N; SCOTLAND NECK, NC; HOBGOOD AC; (JR); Hnr Roll; Chrldg (VJ); Respiratory Therapist; Accounting; East Carolina U; North Carolina State U

SIMMONS, ASHLEY A; LUMBERTON, NC; LUMBERTON HS; (SO); Hosp Aide; Fr of Library; Nursing Aide; Gynecologist; U of Pembroke; UNC

SIMMONS, JUSTIN A; WESTFIELD, NC; NORTH STOKES MS; (SO); Hnr Roll; Ntl Beta Clb; Bskball (J); Ftball (J); Track (V); Scholar Athlete; Computer Software Engineering; Barber; Guilford College; Emory U

SIMPSON, CHRISTINA; FUQUAY VARINA, NC; FUQUAY-VARINA HS; (SR); Hnr Roll; Otst Ac Ach Awd; Chrch Yth Grp; DECA; Emplmnt; Prom Com; Scouts; Business Administration; Wake Technical Community College

SIMPSON, JULIUS A; WINTERVILLE, NC; D H CONLEY HS; (SO); Duke TS; F Lan Hn Soc; Hnr Roll; WWAHSS; Yth Ldrshp Prog; Comm Volntr; Peer Tut/Med; Emplmnt; Ntl Beta Clb; NYLC; Chr; Ch Chr; Cl Off (V); Peer Mediator of the Year 1999-2000; Pre-Law Major; Criminal Prosecution Lawyer; Duke U; North Carolina Central U

SIMPSON, LAKEISHA; RALEIGH, NC; SOUTHEAST RALEIGH MAGNET HS; (SO); Hnr Roll; Comm Volntr; Emplmnt; Key Club; Photog; Clr Grd; Dnce; Bachelor's in Art; Master's in Business; Spelman College; Georgia Institute of Technology

SIMPSON, RYAN A; CHARLOTTE, NC; HARDING UNIVERSITY HS; (JR); Hnr Roll; Jr Eng Tech; Comm Volntr; Chrch Yth Grp; DARE; Mus Clb; Bnd; Ch Chr; Mch Bnd; Pep Bnd; Bskball (VJ)

SINESE, SARAH M; JACKSONVILLE, NC; WHITE OAK HS; (MS); Hi Hnr Roll; Hnr Roll; Otst Ac Ach Awd; Perf Att; Sci Fairs; Valdctrian; Comm Volntr; Off Aide; Tchrs Aide; Chr; Pep Bnd; Chrldg (J); National Junior Honor Society; President's Education Award

SISK, BRITTANY N; BESSEMER CITY, NC; BESSEMER CITY HS; (SO); Hnr Roll; WWAHSS; Comm Volntr; Peer Tut/Med; Chrch Yth Grp; DARE; FCA; Fr of Library; Lib Aide; Tchrs Aide; Bnd; Clr Grd; Dnce; Mch Bnd; Track (V); Stu Cncl; Yrbk (R, P); Miss BCHS Pageant 1st Runner-Up; Talent Show-Winner; Teaching / Special Education; UNC Chapel Hill; Appalachian State

SITTHIDETH, JOHN; HIGH POINT, NC; RAGSDALE HS; (FR); Bskball (J); Ftball (J); Track (J); Wt Lftg (J); Mass Communication; Music Production; U of Miami; Ohio State

SIZEMORE, CHAD M; ASHEBORO, NC; (FR); Hnr Roll; Comm Volntr; Hab For Humty Volntr; Key Club; Wt Lftg (V); Computer Engineer; Randolph Community College

Simpson, Lakeisha
Southeast Raleigh Magnet HS
Raleigh, NC

Shelton, Maressa N
Harding University HS
Charlotte, NC

Sharpe, Jasmine
Hickory HS
Hickory, NC

Setzer, Jessica
East Burke HS
Connellys Springs, NC

Sellers, Tekari R
Dudley HS
Greensboro, NC

Sessoms, Millicent N
Bertie HS
Ahoskie, NC

Shaw, Della M
Wakefield HS
Raleigh, NC

Simpson, Christina
Fuquay-Varina HS
Fuquay Varina, NC

Sisk, Brittany N
Bessemer City HS
Bessemer City, NC

SLADE, TURNER M; SCOTLAND NECK, NC; HOBGOOD AC; (FR); Hnr Roll; Comm Volntr; Chrch Yth Grp; Emplmnt; FCA; Ch Chr; Ftball (J); Golf (J); Architect; North Carolina State U

SLEDGE, BRIA S; RALEIGH, NC; WAKEFIELD HS; (JR); Comm Volntr; ArtClub; Chrch Yth Grp; Key Club; Ch Chr; Senate Page; National Art Honor Socity (NAHS); Psychology; Central North Carolina; A & T

SLOAN JR, MICHAEL A; DURHAM, NC; HILLSIDE HS; (FR); Hnr Roll; Otst Ac Ach Awd; Perf Att; Pres Ac Ftns Aw; Comm Volntr; Pep Squd; Scouts; Bnd; Jzz Bnd; Mch Bnd; Pep Bnd; Teen Court Participant; Biography Club; Law Degree; Howard U

SMALL, MARKUS; FORT BRAGG, NC; E E SMITH SR HS; (FR); 4H Awd; Hnr Roll; Otst Ac Ach Awd; Perf Att; St of Mnth; Comm Volntr; 4-H; DARE; Chr; Ch Chr; Bskball (J); Ftball (J); Track (J); Wt Lftg (J); Mathematical; Engineering/Mechanic; Oklahoma U; Miami U (FL)

SMATHERS, JOSHUA; CANDLER, NC; ENKA HS; (JR); Hnr Roll; Nat Hon Sy; Perf Att; WWAHSS; Chrch Yth Grp; FCA; Ntl FFA; Wdwrkg Clb; Ftball (V); Criminal Justice; Culinary; Western Carolina U; U of North Carolina At Charlotte

SMITH, ADRIENNE; ASHEVILLE, NC; A C REYNOLDS HS; (FR); Hnr Roll; Perf Att; DARE; Bskball (J); Vllyball; Wt Lftg (J)

SMITH, ALEXANDER M; PARKTON, NC; ST PAUL'S HS; (FR); 4-H; Drma Clb; Ntl FFA; Mar Art; Michigan State U

SMITH, ALICIA; HAVELOCK, NC; HAVELOCK HS; (SO); Hi Hnr Roll; Hnr Roll; St of Mnth; Ntl Beta Clb; Bnd; Mch Bnd; Stu Cncl (R); Botany; Visual Arts; U of North Carolina-Charlotte.; U of Maryland Eastern Shore

SMITH, AMANDA R; STATESVILLE, NC; NORTH IREDELL HS; (JR); Hnr Roll; Perf Att; WWAHSS; Emplmnt; Bnd; Chr; Flg Crps; Mch Bnd; Flag Corps Captain; Health Occupations Students of America (HOSA); Nursing or Other Medical Related Major; North Carolina State U; Johnson C Smith U

SMITH, ANNA M; WINSTON SALEM, NC; CAREER CTR HS; (SR); Hnr Roll; Otst Ac Ach Awd; Perf Att; Sci Fairs; St of Mnth; Comm Volntr; Red Cr Aide; Spec Olymp Vol; Chrch Yth Grp; Drma Clb; Mus Clb; Svce Clb; SADD; Chr; Ch Chr; Dnce; Bskball (V); GAA (J); PP Ftbl (J); Wt Lftg (J); Cl Off (P); CR (P); Lit Mag (E); Certificate of Adult CPR; Internship Baptist Hospital; Nursing; Doctorate; Winston-Salem State U; Forsyth Tech

SMITH, ASHLEY M; HICKORY, NC; HICKORY HS; (SO); DAR; Hnr Roll; Nat Hon Sy; Perf Att; Hab For Humty Volntr; Chrch Yth Grp; Sftball (V); Leadership 2000; Juniorettes; Nursing; Psychology; North Carolina State U; U of NC At Chapel Hill

SMITH, ASHLEY R; TROY, NC; WEST MONTGOMERY HS; (SR); Hi Hnr Roll; Jr Mshl; St Schl; Chrch Yth Grp; Emplmnt; FBLA; Ntl Beta Clb; Pep Squd; Photog; Prom Com; Latin Clb; Chrldg (V CL); Sccr (V L); Yrbk (R, P); Pharmacy; U of North Carolina At Chapel Hill

SMITH, ASHTON; SAINT PAULS, NC; GRAY'S CREEK HS; (SO); Hnr Roll; Otst Ac Ach Awd; Sci Fairs; Sci Clb; Vsity Clb; Orch; Vsy Clb (V L); Athletic Trainer, Football, Wrestling, Baseball; Registered Nursing; East Carolina U; U of North Carolina

SMITH, BRITTANIE S; RALEIGH, NC; SOUTHEAST RALEIGH HS; (JR); Hnr Roll; MVP; St of Mnth; Yth Ldrshp Prog; Comm Volntr; Chrch Yth Grp; Emplmnt; Key Club; Scouts; SP/M/VS; Bskball; Sports Medicine; Criminal Justice; Winston Salem State U; North Carolina Central U

SMITH, CASSANDRA C; FAYETTEVILLE, NC; E E SMITH SR HS; (JR); WWAHSS; Chrch Yth Grp; Chr; Ch Chr; SP/M/VS; I Attend Night School; Early Graduation; Child Psychology; Music; Methodist College

SMITH, CHAUNCEY T; WINSTON SALEM, NC; WEST FORSYTH HS; (FR); Ctznshp Aw; Hnr Roll; St of Mnth; Peer Tut/Med; DARE; Ftball (J); Track; Wt Lftg; Student of the Year Award; Physical Education; Sport/Fitness Administration; U of Georgia

SMITH, DAVINA A; ELIZABETH CTY, NC; PASQUOTANK CTY HS; (JR); Hi Hnr Roll; Hnr Roll; Perf Att; St of Mnth; USAA; WWAHSS; Red Cr Aide; Mus Clb; Sci Clb; Latin Clb; Bnd; Mch Bnd; Orch; Pep Bnd; National Youth Leadership Forum in Medicine; Superintendent's Academic Team Award-SAT; Medical Degree; Internship in Pediatrics; Hampton U; North Carolina A & T State U

SMITH, DELISHA H; RALEIGH, NC; SOUTHEAST RALEIGH MAGNET HS; (SO); Hnr Roll; Comm Volntr; Hab For Humty Volntr; Key Club; Sccr (J); President-Haven House Youth Involvement Board; Play Soccer for CASL; Master's Degree in Architectural Design; Law Degree; North Carolina State U; Hampton U

SMITH, DENEKA R; OXFORD, NC; S F WEBB HS; (SO); Ctznshp Aw; Hnr Roll; Perf Att; Sftball (J); Vllyball (J); Registered Nurse; North Carolina Agriculture and Technical

SMITH, ELIZABETH; EFLAND, NC; CEDAR RIDGE HS; (SO); Hnr Roll; Chrch Yth Grp; Emplmnt; Key Club; Swmg; Who's Who; National Society of High School Scholars; Elementary Education

SMITH, GWENDOLYN C; CHARLOTTE, NC; WEST MECKLENBURG HS; (JR); WWAHSS; Emplmnt; Mathematics Education; Education-Administration; Fayetteville State U; Queens College

SMITH, JACQUELYN; HOPE MILLS, NC; SOUTHVIEW HS; (FR); Ctznshp Aw; Duke TS; Hi Hnr Roll; Hnr Roll; Comm Volntr; Hab For Humty Volntr; Chrch Yth Grp; DARE; Key Club; Pep Squd; Scouts; Bnd; CR (R); Sch Ppr (R); Yrbk (R, P); Key Club; English Major; North Carolina State; Wilmington

SMITH, JAMES T; MT AIRY, NC; NORTH SURRY HS; (SO); Peer Tut/Med; Chess; ROTC; Computer Programmer; Historian; Florida State U; UNC Chapel Hill

SMITH, JASMINE; STATESVILLE, NC; STATESVILLE HS; (FR); Hnr Roll; Otst Ac Ach Awd; Sci Fairs; Comm Volntr; Peer Tut/Med; Ntl Beta Clb; Scouts; SADD; Bskball; Stu Cncl (S); Business; Medical; U of Tennessee; U of North Carolina

SMITH, JENNIFER L; CARY, NC; CARY HS; (JR); Hnr Roll; Kwnis Aw; Comm Volntr; Key Club; Svce Clb; Business Management; North Carolina State U; U of Carolina Wilmington

SMITH, JOEL; FAYETTEVILLE, NC; SOUTH VIEW HS; (JR); Hi Hnr Roll; Jr Mshl; Nat Hon Sy; WWAHSS; Key Club; Scouts; Sccr (VJCL); National Honor Society Treasurer; Key Club National Spanish Honor Society; U of North Carolina; North Carolina State U

SMITH, JONATHAN D; COLFAX, NC; SOUTHWEST GUILFORD HS; (JR); Hnr Roll; Perf Att; WWAHSS; Ntl Beta Clb; Bnd; Mch Bnd; Pep Bnd; Bsball (V); Play Professional Baseball; Major in Communications; U of North Carolina At Greensboro; Wake Forest U

SMITH, KOURTNEY M; FRANKLINTON, NC; SOUTH GRANVILLE HS; (JR); F Lan Hn Soc; Hnr Roll; Nat Hon Sy; WWAHSS; Chrch Yth Grp; FCA; Ch Chr; International Foreign Language Award; HOSA Award-1st Place B Regional; Teaching (Elementary); Journalism/Writing; Southeast Seminary; UNC-Chapel Hill

SMITH, KRYSTLE; FAYETTEVILLE, NC; DOUGLAS BYRD HS; (JR); Hnr Roll; WWAHSS; Comm Volntr; Drma Clb; Stg Cre; International Thespian Society; Accounting; Criminal Justice; U of North Carolina At Charlotte

SMITH, LACHON T; GREENSBORO, NC; PAGE HS; (JR); WWAHSS; Comm Volntr; Chrch Yth Grp; Scouts; French Clb; Bnd; Chr; Ch Chr; Track (V); Modeling; Acting; North Carolina Art State U; Winston Salem State U

SMITH, MATTHEW D; WILMINGTON, NC; E A LANEY HS; (JR); Hnr Roll; Nat Hon Sy; Perf Att; Yth Ldrshp Prog; Comm Volntr; AL Aux Boys; Chrch Yth Grp; DARE; Emplmnt; Scouts, N.C. Boys State Order of the Arrow; Free Enterprise Youth Leadership; Computer Engineering; Cooking; North Carolina State; U of Maryland

SMITH, MELISSA A; APEX, NC; APEX HS; (SR); Hnr Roll; WWAHSS; Comm Volntr; Chrch Yth Grp; Emplmnt; FCA; Key Club; Prom Com; Tchrs Aide; French Clb; Ch Chr; PP Ftbl (V); Stu Cncl (R); CR (R); Church Youth Council; BS Nursing; MS Nursing; Western Carolina U

SMITH, RACHEL E; WILSON, NC; JAMES B HUNT; (JR); Duke TS; F Lan Hn Soc; Gov Hnr Prg; Hi Hnr Roll; Nat Hon Sy; Otst Ac Ach Awd; WWAHSS; Comm Volntr; Hosp Aide; Red Cr Aide; Chrch Yth Grp; Emplmnt; FCA; Key Club; Lttrmn Clb; Prom Com; Svce Clb; Vsity Clb; Ch Chr; Dnce; Stg Cre; Cr Ctry; Sccr; Cl Off (S)

SMITH, SADONNA; ASHEVILLE, NC; AC REYNOLDS HS; (SO); Hnr Roll; ArtClub; Pep Squd; Chrldg (J); Radiology; Nursing; U of Charlotte; U of Asheville

SMITH, SHARLETTA; GARNER, NC; GARNER HS; (SO); 4H Awd; Comm Volntr; 4-H; Chrch Yth Grp; DARE; Emplmnt; Ch Chr; Basketball, Pres. of Choir, Pres. Sunday School All of the Church; Lawyer; Doctor; North Carolina State U; Duke U

SMITH, SHAVONTAE C; RAEFORD, NC; HOKE CTY HS; (SR); Otst Ac Ach Awd; Perf Att; St of Mnth; Yth Ldrshp Prog; Comm Volntr; Chrch Yth Grp; DARE; Tmpl Yth Grp; Ch Chr; Registered Nurse; Cosmetology; Fayetteville State U; Sandhills Community College

SMITH, TYLER S; VALDESE, NC; EAST BURKE HS; (FR); Ctznshp Aw; Hnr Roll; Sci Fairs; St of Mnth

SMITH, WALKER; KANNAPOLIS, NC; NORTHWEST CABARRUS MS; (MS); Hnr Roll; Perf Att; St of Mnth; Comm Volntr; Chrch Yth Grp; DARE; Photog; Bsball; Ftball; Wt Lftg; Law Enforcement; Sports Medicine; U of North Carolina; U of Georgia

SMITH, WILLIAM; GOLDSBORO, NC; SOUTHERN WAYNE HS; (SO); Duke TS; Hi Hnr Roll; Nat Hon Sy; WWAHSS; Yth Ldrshp Prog; FBLA; FTA; Ntl Beta Clb; Bsball (J); Ftball (V); Tennis (V); Track (V); Wt Lftg (V); Free Enterprise Leadership Conference; Student Athlete Summer Institute; Business-Sports Marketing; Law; U of North Carolina-Chapel Hill; East Carolina U-Greenville

SMITHER, MATTHEW R; MOUNT PLEASANT, NC; MT PLEASANT HS; (JR); Ctznshp Aw; Hi Hnr Roll; Jr Mshl; Hab For Humty Volntr; Peer Tut/Med; Spec Olymp Vol; ArtClub; Chrch Yth Grp; Emplmnt; Ntl Beta Clb; Nominated for Governor's School-3V; History; Youth Pastor; Columbia International U; Campbell U

SMITH III, JUNIOUS; FAYETTEVILLE, NC; MASSEY HILL CLASSICAL HS; (JR); Perf Att; WWAHSS; Comm Volntr; Drma Clb; Key Club; NtlFrnscLg; Quiz Bowl; Foreign Clb; SP/M/VS; Bskball; Mar Art; Secretary, Sunday School 5 Years; Sports Broadcaster/Analyst; Statistician; Hampton U; U of North Carolina At Chapel Hill

SNEED, CHRISTOPHER T; MT AIRY, NC; MT AIRY HS; (JR); Hi Hnr Roll; Nat Hon Sy; WWAHSS; Comm Volntr; Spec Olymp Vol; Chrch Yth Grp; Key Club; Pep Squd; Quiz Bowl; Voc Ind Clb Am; Stu Cncl (R); Career Technical Educational Honors Society; Engineer; Teacher; North Carolina State U; U of North Carolina Charlotte

SNEED, TASHA L; HENDERSON, NC; NORTHERN VANCE HS; (JR); Chrch Yth Grp; Bnd; Ch Chr; Mch Bnd; Track (V); CR (R); AMP Club-11th Grade; Working @ Bojangle's; Lawyer/Criminal Justice; Sociology; U of North Carolina Pembroke; North Carolina Central U

SNIPES, TIERRA S; SILER CITY, NC; JORDAN MATTHEWS HS; (SO); 4H Awd; Hnr Roll; Kwnis Aw; MVP; St of Mnth; St Optmst of Yr; Comm Volntr; Hab For Humty Volntr; Hosp Aide; 4-H; Chrch Yth Grp; DARE; Emplmnt; Prom Com; SADD; Ch Chr; Dnce; SP/M/VS; Bskball (J); Chrldg (J); PP Ftbl; Sftball; Track (V); Stu Cncl (T); Pediatric Nurse; Business Management; UNC; East Carolina U

SNOW, GRETA; DUNN, NC; TRITON HS; (SO); Duke TS; F Lan Hn Soc; Hi Hnr Roll; MVP; Nat Hon Sy; Otst Ac Ach Awd; Sci Fairs; USAA; WWAHSS; Comm Volntr; Hosp Aide; Peer Tut/Med; Emplmnt; Ntl Beta Clb; Quiz Bowl; Orch; Bskball (V L); Sftball (V L); Tennis (V L); Vllyball (V L); Stu Cncl (T); CR (R); 1st Place ACSI Piano Competition - 2003 & 2003; Organist 2001-2005; Dermatology; Psychology; Wake Forest U; UNC Chapel Hill

SNYDER, SPENCER A; WINSTON SALEM, NC; LEDFORD HS; (JR); Duke TS; Hnr Roll; Pres Sch; Comm Volntr; Chrch Yth Grp; DARE; Drma Clb; Emplmnt; Ntl Beta Clb; Latin Clb; SP/M/VS; Wrstlg (J); Lead Guitarist in Local Band; Engineering; Law; NC State

SOMASUNDARAM, ARAVIND; LEWISVILLE, NC; WEST FORSYTH HS; (FR); Hnr Roll; FBLA; Bskball; Track (V); Medicine; Law; U of North Carolina

SOTELO, ISAEL; GREENSBORO, NC; BEN L SMITH HS; (JR); Hnr Roll; WWAHSS; Comm Volntr; French Clb; Wrstlg (VCL); Computer Science; Computer Engineering; North Carolina State U Greensboro; NC A & T State U

SOTO, BRIAN; FAYETTEVILLE, NC; SEVENTY-FIRST HS; (FR); Hnr Roll; St of Mnth; Chrch Yth Grp; ROTC; Bskball (J); Ftball (J); Track (J); Engineer; Air Force Fighter Pilot; U of North Carolina Pembroke

SOTO, EDDY J; JACKSONVILLE, NC; NORTHSIDE HS; (SO); MVP; DARE; Ftball (VJ L); Track (V L); Stu Cncl (R); Sports Medicine; U of Miami (FL); Bowling Green State U

SOUTHAM, EMILEE; ANGIER, NC; CAPE FEAR CHRISTIAN AC; (FR); Hi Hnr Roll; WWAHSS; Comm Volntr; Chrch Yth Grp; Ntl Beta Clb; Scouts; Bnd; Chr; Ch Chr; Bskball (VJ); Sccr (V L); Vllyball (J); Heaven Sent - CD Published; History Major; North Carolina State U; U of Hawaii

SPARKS, AARON B; SANDY RIDGE, NC; NORTH STOKES HS; (SO); 4H Awd; Hi Hnr Roll; Hnr Roll; Nat Hon Sy; Perf Att; Sci Fairs; St of Mnth; 4-H; Chrch Yth Grp; FCA; FBLA; Ntl Beta Clb; Ntl FFA; Scouts; Vsity Clb; Bsball (V L); Ftball (V L); NC State North Carolina State

SPARKS, BRANDY; BENSON, NC; WEST JOHNSTON HS; (JR); Hi Hnr Roll; Nat Hon Sy; WWAHSS; Peer Tut/Med; Emplmnt; FCA; FBLA; Svce Clb; Tennis (V L); Elementary Education; North Carolina State U

SPARKS, LYNZEE; MOORESVILLE, NC; (SR); DAR; Hnr Roll; Pres Sch; St of Mnth; WWAHSS; Comm Volntr; Chrch Yth Grp; DARE; Dbte Team; FBLA; Scouts; SADD; Tchrs Aide; Chr; Drl Tm; SP/M/VS; Track (V); President Award for Academics; All American High School Student; Psychology

SPARKS, SHERRI; FALCON, NC; CAPE FEAR HS; (SR); Emplmnt; Emmanuel College

SPEAGLE, JOSHUA H M; VALE, NC; FRED T FOARD HS; (SO); Hnr Roll; Comm Volntr; Chrch Yth Grp; Voc Ind Clb Am; Ftball (V L); Track (V L); History Teacher; High School Football Coach; Tennessee U; Memphis U

SPEARS, JUSTIN R; PURLEAR, NC; WEST WILKES HS; (SO); Hnr Roll; St of Mnth; Comm Volntr; Peer Tut/Med; Chrch Yth Grp; DARE; FCA; Bsball (VJ L); Ftball (J); Stu Cncl (R); CR (P); Lettered in Academics; Computer Related; Basketball; North Carolina State U; Eastern Carolina U

SPEARS, OCTAVIA S; CHARLOTTE, NC; ZEBULON VANCE HS; (JR); Hnr Roll; DARE; Business Degree; Law

Sneed, Tasha L
Northern Vance HS
Henderson, NC

Smith, Gwendolyn C
West Mecklenburg HS
Charlotte, NC

Smith, Ashton
Gray's Creek HS
Saint Pauls, NC

Smith, Anna M
Career Ctr HS
Winston Salem, NC

Slade, Turner M
Hobgood AC
Scotland Neck, NC

Small, Markus
E E Smith SR HS
Fort Bragg, NC

Smith, Davina A
Pasquotank Cty HS
Elizabeth Cty, NC

Smith, Melissa A
Apex HS
Apex, NC

Sparks, Lynzee
Mooresville, NC

SPEED, CHRISTOPHER; WINTERVILLE, NC; D H CONLEY HS; (FR); Hnr Roll; Perf Att; Sci Fairs; Sci/Math Olympn; Ntl Beta Clb; Sci Clb; Scouts; Cinematography; Journalism; East Carolina U; North Carolina State

SPEIGHT, CHARLES T; PINETOWN, NC; NORTHSIDE HS; (FR); Hi Hnr Roll; Hnr Roll; Perf Att; WWAHSS; Key Club; Ftball (J); Track (V); Art; Science; Dartmouth College; U Of Notre Dame

SPENA, GREGORY; TABOR CITY, NC; SOUTH COLUMBUS HS; (SO); Duke TS; Nat Hon Sy; Sci Fairs; Chrch Yth Grp; FCA; Mus Clb; Quiz Bowl; Schol Bwl; Sci Clb; Bnd; Ch Chr; Jzz Bnd; Mch Bnd; Tennis (J); Track (J); High School Band Director

SPENCE, CHENA; ELIZABETH CITY, NC; PASQUOTANK CTY HS; (JR); Hnr Roll; MVP; Perf Att; Bskball (JC); SAT Award; Doctorate; Medical Field; East Carolina U; Campbell U

SPENCER, AMANDA V; FAIRFIELD, NC; MAHAMUSKEET HS; (SO); Perf Att; St of Mnth; Chrch Yth Grp; DARE; Bnd; Ch Chr; Mch Bnd; SP/M/VS; Bskball (J); Chrldg (J); Sftball (J); Stu Cncl (R); Band Merit / Perfect Attendance; Junior Beta / Educational Talent Search Program; Associate's Degree / Criminal Law; Bachelor's Degree / Business Administration; UNC Chapel Hill; Duke U

SPENCER, AMARYLLIS; FAYETTEVILLE, NC; SEVENTY-FIRST HS; (SO); F Lan Hn Soc; Hnr Roll; Otst Ac Ach Awd; Perf Att; St of Mnth; Peer Tut/Med; Chess; Chrch Yth Grp; DARE; Chr

SPENCER-MATTOX, CIERA; CHARLOTTE, NC; HARDING U HS; (SO); Hi Hnr Roll; Hnr Roll; Nat Hon Sy; Perf Att; WWAHSS; Yth Ldrshp Prog; Comm Volntr; Peer Tut/Med; Chrch Yth Grp; Off Aide; Sci Clb; Tchrs Aide; Ch Chr; Dnce; Medicine; U of North Carolina At Chapel Hill; Wake Forest U

SPILLARS, CHELSEA; FLETCHER, NC; A C REYNOLDS HS; (FR); Hnr Roll; Perf Att; Spanish Clb; SP/M/VS; Stg Cre; Sccr (C); CR (R); Yrbk (R, P); Computer Sciences; U of Wilmington; U of North Carolina

SPINELLA, KYLE; MORRISVILLE, NC; CARY HS; (SR); Hnr Roll; 3 Academic Achievement Awards - GPA 3.5+; Biology; U of North Carolina Greensboro

SPIVEY, CHUVCILO; LOUISBURG, NC; LOUISBURG HS; (FR); FBLA; Track (V); Fashion Designer; Psychologist; Howard U; North Carolina A & T State

SPIVEY, MATTHEW G; RALEIGH, NC; MILLBROOK HS; (JR); Duke TS; Hi Hnr Roll; Hnr Roll; Jr Mshl; Nat Hon Sy; Nat Mrt Fin; Comm Volntr; Chrch Yth Grp; Emplmnt; FCA; Lttrmn Clb; Svce Clb; Vsity Clb; Sccr (V L); Tennis (V L); Stu Cncl (R); I Have Found the Lord Jesus and Know That I Live Only By His Grace; U of North Carolina; U of Virginia

SPIVEY, ROBIN A; COATS, NC; CAPE FEAR CHRISTIAN AC; (JR); Hi Hnr Roll; Jr Mshl; Otst Ac Ach Awd; WWAHSS; ArtClub; Ntl Beta Clb; Off Aide; Prom Com; Tchrs Aide; Cl Off (P, S, T); Stu Cncl (R); Sch Ppr; Yrbk; Art Awards; Published Poet; Graphic Art & Design; Business Administration; Wake Technical Community College; Campbell U

SPRAGUE, KAYLA; KERNERSVILLE, NC; ROBERT B GLENN HS; (SO); Hnr Roll; Nat Hon Sy; Perf Att; Chrch Yth Grp; Emplmnt; Svce Clb; Vsity Clb; Scr Kpr (V); Swmg (V); Vsy Clb (V); Medicine; Sports; Eastern Carolina U; Appalachian State

SPRINGER, KERIANNE; CHINA GROVE, NC; SOUTH ROWAN HS; (SR); 4H Awd; Duke TS; Hi Hnr Roll; Jr Mshl; Nat Hon Sy; Nat Mrt LOC; St Schl; St of Mnth; USAA; Valdctrian; Comm Volntr; Hosp Aide; Peer Tut/Med; 4-H; ArtClub; Chrch Yth Grp; Cmptr Clb; Prom Com; Quiz Bowl; Svce Clb; Tech Clb; Orch; Cr Ctry (V L); Swmg (V L); Track (V L); Cl Off (T, R); Stu Cncl (T); Violin-Salisbury Youth Symphony; Governor's School; Pediatrician; Furman U

SPRINGFIELD-COBB, EVAN L; DURHAM, NC; SOUTHERN HS; (FR); Hnr Roll; MVP; Perf Att; Sci Fairs; Comm Volntr; Chrch Yth Grp; DARE; Mth Clb/Tm; Sci Clb; Scouts; Bskball (J); Georgia Technical Institute

SPRUILL, DEMARIUS; WILLIAMSTON, NC; WILLIAMSTON HS; (FR); Chr; Bskball (C); Ftball (J); Track; Yrbk (E); Honor Roll; Computer Engineer; Masters Degree; North Carolina Agriculture & Technology; Georgia Agriculture & Technology

SPRUILL, LATISHA Q; PLYMOUTH, NC; PLYMOUTH HS; (SO); WWAHSS; Criminal Law; Business; John Jay College

SPRUILL, RESHONDA M; LEWISTON, NC; BERTIE HS; (SR); Comm Volntr; Spec Olymp Vol; SADD; Cl Off (S); CR (S); Social Work; Criminal Justice; North Carolina Agricultural & Technical State

SPRUILL, SHIRLEY L; COMO, NC; RIDGECROFT SCH; (SO); 4H Awd; Hnr Roll; MVP; Perf Att; St of Mnth; 4-H; Key Club; Lttrmn Clb; Ntl Beta Clb; Vsity Clb; Bnd; Ch Chr; Arch (V L); Vsy Clb (V); Vllyball (V L); Cl Off (V); Stu Cncl (R); 4-H; Veterinary Medicine; Virginia Tech; North Carolina State U

STACKHOUSE, SASHA R; ROWLAND, NC; (JR); Nat Hon Sy; Chrch Yth Grp; Emplmnt; Mus Clb; ROTC; SADD; Chr; Ch Chr; Dnce; Drl Tm; Bskball (V); GAA (V); PP Ftbl (V); Vllyball (V); Wt Lftg (V); Finalist in National American Miss Pageant; Pre-Med, Business and Management; Law; Fayetteville State U; U of North Carolina Greensboro

STALLINGS, JASMINE; FORT BRAGG, NC; E E SMITH SR HS; (FR); Hnr Roll; Perf Att; Chrch Yth Grp; DARE; Drma Clb; ROTC; Drl Tm; Track (V L); EE Smith Track Team's Outstanding Female New Comer; Health Science; Aerospace Science; East Carolina U

STANBERY, BRANDON J; MILLERS CREEK, NC; WEST WILKES; (FR); Hnr Roll; St of Mnth; Emplmnt; Key Club; Ftball (J); Scr Kpr (J); Wt Lftg (J); Stu Cncl (R)

STANFORD, BRITNEY N; GREENVILLE, NC; FARMVILLE CTRL HS; (SO); Hnr Roll; Otst Ac Ach Awd; Perf Att; Pres Ac Ftns Aw; PP Ftbl; Track; National Junior Honor Society; Strings; Massachusetts Institute of Technology

STANFORD, RYAN; GREENSBORO, NC; PAGE HS; (JR); DAR; Duke TS; Hi Hnr Roll; MVP; Nat Hon Sy; Otst Ac Ach Awd; Comm Volntr; Chrch Yth Grp; Emplmnt; Bnd; Jzz Bnd; Bsball (J); Swmg (V L); Summer Swim Coach; Play in Semi-Professional Bluegrass Band (Beaconwood); Engineering; Biomedical; North Carolina State U; Duke U

STANKAVAGE, SARAH E; DURHAM, NC; CE JORDAN HS; (JR); Duke TS; Hi Hnr Roll; MVP; WWAHSS; Comm Volntr; Chrch Yth Grp; Emplmnt; Key Club; Prom Com; Vsity Clb; SP/M/VS; Bskball (J); Swmg (V L); State Swimming Finalist; All-Conference Swimming; U of North Carolina Chapel Hill; U of North Carolina Wilmington

STANLEY, SONYA; RALEIGH, NC; MIDDLE CREEK HS; (SO); Hnr Roll; Peer Tut/Med; Spanish Clb; Track; National Achievers Society; Communications; Information Systems; U of North Carolina Chapel Hill; University of Elon

STANLEY JR, JAMES J; SALISBURY, NC; WEST ROWAN HS; (FR); Hi Hnr Roll; Hnr Roll; Peer Tut/Med; ROTC; Engineering; Law; NASCAR Technical Institute; U of North Carolina

STAPLES II, JERRY Q; GREENSBORO, NC; GRIMSLEY HS; (SO); Hnr Roll; Yth Ldrshp Prog; Comm Volntr; Chrch Yth Grp; Acpl Chr; Ch Chr; Stu Cncl (R); GYC Santa's Workshop Chair; Major in Law (Supreme Court Justice); Minor Computer Technician; Hillman; Morris Brown College

STARKEY, ERIC; CARY, NC; APEX HS; (JR); Hi Hnr Roll; Hnr Roll; Otst Ac Ach Awd; St Schl; Peer Tut/Med; Golf (V); Political Science; English; U of North Carolina; U of Florida

STARKS, AMECIA; FAYETTEVILLE, NC; 71ST HS; (FR); Hnr Roll; Otst Ac Ach Awd; Comm Volntr; Dnce; Arts Academy for Dance; Miss Freshman 71st; Computer Programming; U of North Carolina

STECHER, ANDREA; MURPHY, NC; HIWASSEE DAM HS; (SO); Ctznshp Aw; Hnr Roll; Jr Mshl; Nat Hon Sy; WWAHSS; Comm Volntr; Spec Olymp Vol; 4-H; ArtClub; DARE; Emplmnt; FCA; Mod UN; Scouts; SADD; Dnce; Chrldg (V CL); Gmnstcs; Cl Off (V); Stu Cncl (R)

STEEPLES, TIFFANY; GREENSBORO, NC; WALTER HINES PAGE HS; (FR); Ctznshp Aw; Hnr Roll; St of Mnth; Chrch Yth Grp; DARE; Dnce; Chrldg (C); CR (R); Received a $500 Scholarship Award; Elementary School Teacher; Business Woman; Chapel Hill of North Carolina

STEINBACHER, SARINA; CLEMMONS, NC; WEST FORSYTH HS; (SO); Hnr Roll; Otst Ac Ach Awd; Pres Ac Ftns Aw; Comm Volntr; Mus Clb; Orch; Lcrsse (J); 2004 NBL BMX National #7; 2005 NC State Games Gold BMX; Doctor; Accountant; U of North Carolina Chapel Hill; U of Wilmington North Carolina

STEINMAN, MELISSA; HIGH POINT, NC; ANDREWS HS; (SR); Hnr Roll; Nat Hon Sy; Comm Volntr; ArtClub; Emplmnt; Key Club; Ntl Beta Clb; Photog; Prom Com; Scouts; SP/M/VS; College Tech Prep Completer; Forensic Science; Archaeology; Guilford Technical Community College; U of North Carolina At Greensboro

STEPHENS, ADAM; CLINTON, NC; CLINTON HS; (SO); 4H Awd; Hi Hnr Roll; Otst Ac Ach Awd; Pres Sch; WWAHSS; Yth Ldrshp Prog; Chrch Yth Grp; Jr Cls League; Ntl FFA; Quiz Bowl; Spch Team; Ftball (J); Brain Game Participant; FFA Extemporaneous Speaking; Orthopedic Surgeon; Vet; U of Florida; U of North Carolina

STEPHENSON, LAUREN; CLAYTON, NC; WEST JOHNSTON HS; (JR); Hi Hnr Roll; Otst Ac Ach Awd; Pres Sch; WWAHSS; Chrch Yth Grp; Emplmnt; FCA; Bskball (J); Sftball (J); Tennis (V L); Track (V); Sch Ppr (E); North Carolina State U; U of North Carolina At Chapel Hill

STEPHENSON, SEAN; FOUR OAKS, NC; WEST JOHNSTON HS; (SO); Hnr Roll; Nat Hon Sy; ROTC; Voc Ind Clb Am; Ftball (J); Engineering; Marine Science; North Carolina State U; Barton College

STEPP, S E; LINCOLNTON, NC; LINCOLNTON HS; (SR); Hnr Roll; St of Mnth; Comm Volntr; Hab For Humty Volntr; Red Cr Aide; Chrch Yth Grp; DARE; DECA; Emplmnt; FBLA; Ntl Beta Clb; P to P St Amb Prg; Prom Com; Bnd; Bskball (J); Chrldg (V C); Sftball (V); Vllyball (VJ); Cl Off (P); Stu Cncl (R); CR (R); Advertising; Marketing; U of North Carolina Charlotte

STEVENS, ASHLEY; CLINTON, NC; CLINTON HS; (FR); Hi Hnr Roll; Hnr Roll; Mch Bnd; Lawyer; Accountant; U of North Carolina; East Carolina U

STEVENSON, DOMINIQUE; CHARLOTTE, NC; OLYMPIC HS; (SO); Hnr Roll; Otst Ac Ach Awd; Medical Science; Software Design; U of North Carolina At Chapel Hill; U of North Carolina At Greensboro

STEVENSON, KELLY D; REIDSVILLE, NC; REIDSVILLE HS; (SR); Hi Hnr Roll; Hnr Roll; Nat Hon Sy; Nat Stu Ath Day Aw; Otst Ac Ach Awd; Perf Att; Pres Sch; WWAHSS; Yth Ldrshp Prog; Comm Volntr; Peer Tut/Med; Chrch Yth Grp; NYLC; Bskball (V); Yrbk (E); Scholar-Athlete - '01-'02; Burlington Cup Athletic Award; Mathematics; Art; Averett U; Greensboro College

STEVENSON, MICHAEL G; GREENVILLE, NC; SOUTH CTRL HS; (FR); Perf Att; Comm Volntr; Chess; Chrch Yth Grp; Bskball (J); Finance; Business

STEWART, BRANDON; STATESVILLE, NC; STATESVILLE HS; (FR); Hnr Roll; Chrch Yth Grp; Ntl FFA; Ch Chr; Ftball (J); Committee Chairman of FFA Club; HOSA Club; Family Physician; Dental Hygienist; Wake Forest U; East Carolina U

STEWART, JESSICA C; MORGANTON, NC; FREEDOM HS; (JR); Hnr Roll; Perf Att; Pres Ac Ftns Aw; Comm Volntr; Chrch Yth Grp; DARE; Key Club; Scouts; Svce Clb; SADD; Chrldg (VJ); Sch Ppr (R); Yrbk (R); Journalism; North Carolina State U; U of North Carolina Wilmington

STEWART, KENAN L; PIKEVILLE, NC; CHARLES B AYCOCK HS; (FR); Duke TS; Hi Hnr Roll; Perf Att; St of Mnth; WWAHSS; Comm Volntr; Chrch Yth Grp; DARE; FCA; Ntl Beta Clb; Scouts; Vsity Clb; Ch Chr; Ftball (J); Swmg (V L); Vsy Clb; Wt Lftg; Stu Cncl (R); CR (R); Sch Ppr (R); Piano- 8 Years / Boy Scouts; National Guild of Piano Auditions; U of North Carolina Chapel Hill

STEWART JR, WILLIE; LUMBERTON, NC; PURNELL SWETT HS; (SR); Hnr Roll; MVP; Perf Att; Sci Fairs; Red Cr Aide; Bnd; Mch Bnd; SP/M/VS; Bsball (VJ); Bskball (J); Ftball (J); PP Ftbl (V); Wt Lftg (V); Business Management; U of North Carolina Pembroke

STIMSON JR, SCOTT R; DAVIDSON, NC; NORTH MECKLENBURG HS; (JR); Hnr Roll; Comm Volntr; Red Cr Aide; Spec Olymp Vol; Chrch Yth Grp; DECA; Key Club; Prom Com; Lcrsse (V); Sccr (V); Stu Cncl (R); Vice President of DECA; 3 School Clubs; Business; Finance; U Of North Carolina; U of Georgia

STINSON, KATELYN; MEBANE, NC; EASTERN ALAMANCE HS; (JR); Ctznshp Aw; DAR; Hi Hnr Roll; Hnr Roll; Jr Mshl; Nat Hon Sy; Otst Ac Ach Awd; WWAHSS; Peer Tut/Med; Chrch Yth Grp; Emplmnt; Key Club; Dnce; Cr Ctry (V CL); Track (V L); Architecture; Mathematics; North Carolina State U; U of North Carolina-Chapel Hill

STOCKS, ANDREA; TARBORO, NC; TARBORO HS; (FR); 4H Awd; Hi Hnr Roll; Hnr Roll; MVP; Sci/Math Olympn; Yth Ldrshp Prog; Comm Volntr; Hab For Humty Volntr; 4-H; Chrch Yth Grp; Ntl Beta Clb; NYLC; Sccr (V CL); Swmg (V CL); Medical Science Club; Forensics; Medical Field; North Carolina State U; Appalachian State U

STOKES, CHRISTOPHER; GREENVILLE, NC; D H CONLEY HS; (SO); Duke TS; Hnr Roll; USAA; ArtClub; Chrch Yth Grp; FBLA; Ntl Beta Clb; Sccr (J); Writing; Computer Graphics; U of North Carolina-Chapel Hill; U of North Carolina-Wilmington

STOLLENMAIER, JESSICA; CANDLER, NC; MT PISGAH AC; (JR); Emplmnt; Prom Com; Bskball; Gmnstcs; Sftball; CR (R); Girls Club Religious VP; Speaker; Southern Adventist U; Coastal Carolina U

STONE, AMBER; INDIAN TRAIL, NC; SUN VALLEY MS; (MS); Ctznshp Aw; Hnr Roll; Otst Ac Ach Awd; Perf Att; St of Mnth; Yth Ldrshp Prog; Comm Volntr; DARE; Kwanza Clb; Pep Squd; Scouts; Chr; Dnce; Orch; Stu Cncl (R); Master's Degree in Law; Inclusive Childhood Development; Harvard Law School

STONE, JESSE; SALISBURY, NC; NORTH ROWAN HS; (SO); Hnr Roll; St of Mnth; Peer Tut/Med; Chrch Yth Grp; Clr Grd; Medical Degree; U of North Carolina-Chapel Hill; U of North Carolina-Greensboro

STONE, REBECCA A; ROBBINS, NC; NORTH MOORE HS; (SO); Hi Hnr Roll; St of Mnth; WWAHSS; Yth Ldrshp Prog; Comm Volntr; Peer Tut/Med; Spec Olymp Vol; Chrch Yth Grp; Emplmnt; FBLA; Key Club; Mus Clb; Ntl Beta Clb; Svce Clb; Vsity Clb; Bnd; Ch Chr; Dnce; SP/M/VS; Chrldg (V); Teacher; Elon U

STONEBRAKER JR, MATTHEW V; JACKSONVILLE, NC; JACKSONVILLE HS; (FR); Chess

Stevenson, Kelly D
Reidsville HS
Reidsville, NC

Stallings, Jasmine
E E Smith SR HS
Fort Bragg, NC

Springfield-Cobb, Evan L
Southern HS
Durham, NC

Spinella, Kyle
Cary HS
Morrisville, NC

Spencer, Amaryllis
Seventy-First HS
Fayetteville, NC

Spencer-Mattox, Ciera
Harding U HS
Charlotte, NC

Stackhouse, Sasha R
Rowland, NC

Starks, Amecia
71st HS
Fayetteville, NC

Stokes, Christopher
D H Conley HS
Greenville, NC

STONEROAD, KATI E; NEWPORT, NC; WEST CARTERET HS; (JR); Hnr Roll; WWAHSS; Comm Volntr; Chrch Yth Grp; FCA; Prom Com; Acpl Chr; Ch Chr; SP/M/VS; Swg Chr; Track (V); Adv Cncl (R); Stu Cncl (R); CR (R); Yrbk (R, P); Religion; Performing Arts; East Cardinal U; South Eastern Theological Seminary

STOTTS, CATHERINE; PITTSBORO, NC; WOODS CHARTER SCH; (SO); Hi Hnr Roll; Hnr Roll; Otst Ac Ach Awd; Comm Volntr; Peer Tut/Med; Drma Clb; Emplmnt; SP/M/VS; Bskball (V); Stu Cncl (R); CR (R); Yrbk (R); School Spirit Award; Highest Humanities Award; Physical Therapy; Marine Biology; U of Virginia; U of North Carolina-Chapel Hill

STOUDT, WILLIAM; HOPE MILLS, NC; SOUTH VIEW HS; (JR); Hnr Roll; WWAHSS; Comm Volntr; Hab For Humty Volntr; Peer Tut/Med; Key Club; Orch; Bowling; Biology; Chemistry; UNC-Chapel Hill; ECU

STOUT, ASHLEY M; ROLESVILLE, NC; WAKE FOREST-ROLESVILLE HS; (FR); Hnr Roll; Pres Ac Ftns Aw; Comm Volntr; Hab For Humty Volntr; Peer Tut/Med; Chrch Yth Grp; DARE; Drma Clb; Emplmnt; Key Club; Ntl Beta Clb; Vsity Clb; SP/M/VS; Cr Ctry (V); Swmg (V); Business; New York U Stern; U of North Carolina Wilmington

STOUT, BEVERLY; HICKORY, NC; HICKORY HS; (FR); Hnr Roll; Clr Grd; Drl Tm; Raider Team; U of North Carolina, Chapel Hill; Florida State U

STOWE, BRITTANY L; CHARLOTTE, NC; INDEPENDENCE SR HS; (JR); Hnr Roll; Nat Hon Sy; Perf Att; Emplmnt; Psychology; Social Worker; North Carolina Agriculture & Technical State U; Virginia Union U

STRADER, KARIE A; STANFIELD, NC; WEST STANLY HS; (JR); F Lan Hn Soc; Hi Hnr Roll; Hnr Roll; Nat Hon Sy; Bnd; Mch Bnd; Track (V); Woodwind Captain; Psychology; U of North Carolina Chapel Hill; Elon U

STRAUSS, JEMMA M S; CHAPEL HILL, NC; CEDAR RIDGE HS; (SO); Duke TS; F Lan Hn Soc; Hnr Roll; Nat Hon Sy; Nat Ldrshp Svc; Yth Ldrshp Prog; Comm Volntr; Peer Tut/Med; Drma Clb; Mod UN; NYLC; Photog; Tchrs Aide; French Clb; SP/M/VS; Sccr (V L); Lit Mag (R); Yrbk (E, R, P); Psychiatry; U of North Carolina Chapel Hill

STRAWN, KATHERINE N; MARSHVILLE, NC; FOREST HILLS HS; (SR); Hnr Roll; St of Mnth; Comm Volntr; Chrch Yth Grp; FCA; Ntl Beta Clb; Ntl FFA; SADD; Work At Union County Court House for Union County Public Schools; Nursing Degree

STRICKLAND, CINDY L; ROANOKE RAPIDS, NC; ROANOKE RAPIDS HS; (SO); Hnr Roll; Comm Volntr; Chrch Yth Grp; SADD; Bnd; Mch Bnd; Pediatrician; Band Director; Appalachian State U; UNC Chapel Hill

STRICKLAND, COREY; HOPE MILLS, NC; GRAY'S CREEK HS; (JR); Hnr Roll; WWAHSS; Comm Volntr; Chrch Yth Grp; P to P St Amb Prg; Sch Ppr (E, R); National Society of High School Scholars; Journalism; International Studies; U of Chapel Hill; Appalachian State

STRICKLAND, KIMBERLY; ROWLAND, NC; SOUTH ROBESON HS; (FR); Hnr Roll; Dnce; Editor's Choice Award (4 of the Most); PhD; Master's Degree; Chapel Hill U; Duke U

STRICKLAND, ZACKARY A; WILSON, NC; HUNT HS; (JR); Duke TS; Hi Hnr Roll; Hnr Roll; Nat Hon Sy; Otst Ac Ach Awd; Pres Ac Ftns Aw; WWAHSS; Comm Volntr; Peer Tut/Med; Red Cr Aide; ArtClub; Key Club; Vsity Clb; Bsball (VJCL); Ftball (VJCL); Wt Lftg (V); WDT All-Area Defensive Unit for Football Eastern State Champions; Member of 3-A; Pre-Med; Doctor; U of North Carolina At Chapel Hill; U of North Carolina At Wilmington

STRONG, NICK; JACKSONVILLE, NC; RICHLANDS HS; (JR); Hnr Roll; Chrch Yth Grp; FCA; Ch Chr; Ftball (V); Track (V); Wt Lftg (V); Firefighter; EMS; Coastal Carolina Community College; North Carolina State

STROUD, JALYSIA; KENANSVILLE, NC; JAMES KENAN HS; (SO); Hnr Roll; Comm Volntr; 4-H; DARE; Ntl Beta Clb; Quiz Bowl; ROTC; Clr Grd; Drl Tm; Track (V); Leaders of Tomorrow /Delta Sigma Theta; Journalism

STROUD, RACHEL N; AHOSKIE, NC; HERTFORD CTY HS; (SO); Hi Hnr Roll; Hnr Roll; Perf Att; Spec Olymp Vol; Emplmnt; ROTC; Clr Grd; Sftball (V); Bachelor's Degree; Astronomy; North Carolina State U; East Carolina U

STUBBS, CHERYL L; FAYETTEVILLE, NC; TERRY SANFORD HS; (SO); Duke TS; F Lan Hn Soc; Hnr Roll; Nat Hon Sy; Comm Volntr; Hab For Humty Volntr; ArtClub; Chrch Yth Grp; Spanish Clb; Cr Ctry (V L); Sccr (V L); North Carolina Scholar Athlete; Church Youth Council; Applied Visual Arts

STUBBS, LAUREN; GREENSBORO, NC; GRIMSLEY HS; (SO); Duke TS; Hi Hnr Roll; Otst Ac Ach Awd; Sci/Math Olympn; Comm Volntr; Chrch Yth Grp; DARE; FCA; Photog; Svce Clb; French Clb; Ch Chr; Chrldg (V L); Physical Therapy; Cinematography and Film Arts

STYLES, TIFFANY R; SPRUCE PINE, NC; MTN HERITAGE HS; (SR); WWAHSS; Peer Tut/Med; DECA; Emplmnt; Lib Aide; Prom Com; Vllyball (J); Psychology; Business; U of Colorado Boulder

STYRON, CRYSTAL A; MURFREESBORO, NC; RIDGECROFT SCH; (FR); Duke TS; Hnr Roll; Nat Hon Sy; Otst Ac Ach Awd; St of Mnth; Comm Volntr; Hab For Humty Volntr; 4-H; Key Club; Ntl Beta Clb; Scouts; SADD; Vsity Clb; Bnd; Dnce; Tennis (V); Cl Off (V); CR; Science Olympiad State Finalist (4th Place); Rotary Club Writing Contest Winner - 1st Place; Doctor / Medicine; Actress; Duke U

SUGGS, NICOLE E; WEST JEFFERSON, NC; ASHE CTY HS; (SR); DAR; Hi Hnr Roll; Jr Mshl; WWAHSS; Spec Olymp Vol; Mth Clb/Tm; Ntl Beta Clb; ROTC; JROTC Raider Team Commander; Pre-Med; Duke U

SUITS, ASHLEY; GASTONIA, NC; NORTH GASTON HS; (FR); WWAHSS; Ntl Beta Clb; Bnd; Mch Bnd

SUITT, CRYSTAL N; DURHAM, NC; (JR); Hnr Roll; WWAHSS; Peer Tut/Med; DARE; Bskball (J); Fashion; Business; Clark Atlanta U; U of North Carolina Chapel Hill

SULLIVAN, SHARYN D; SUPPLY, NC; WEST BRUNSWICK HS; (JR); Hnr Roll; ArtClub; Chrch Yth Grp; Drma Clb; Sci Clb; SADD; Dnce; A4 Teacher

SUMMERLIN, CHAELIE; MOUNT AIRY, NC; MOUNT AIRY HS; (FR); Hi Hnr Roll; Pres Ac Ftns Aw; Pres Sch; Sci Fairs; St of Mnth; Comm Volntr; 4-H; DARE; Emplmnt; Key Club; Yrbk (R, P); Maintaining a High GPA While Being Successful in a Part-Time Job; Winning Essay Contests; Complete Juris Doctorate Degree; Duke U; Wake Forest U

SUMMERS, ISHMAEL D; FAYETTEVILLE, NC; E E SMITH SR HS; (SR); Hnr Roll; FBLA; Ch Chr; Ftball (V L); Accounting; Business Administration; East Carolina U; Fayetteville State U

SUTHERLAND, COREY; ROCKY POINT, NC; HEIDE TRASK HS; (SR); WWAHSS; Spec Olymp Vol; Chrch Yth Grp; Emplmnt; Key Club; Ch Chr; Special Education Teacher; Cape Fear Community College; East Carolina U

SUTTLES, CRYSTAL; RANDLEMAN, NC; RANDLEMAN HS; (FR); Hnr Roll; Otst Ac Ach Awd; Pres Ac Ftns Aw; St of Mnth; Lib Aide; Ntl Beta Clb; Chr; Dnce; Step Team; Dance Team; Law; Doctor; U of North Carolina Greensboro; U of Tennessee Knoxville

SUTTLES, KACIE; CHAPEL HILL, NC; NORTHWOOD HS; (FR); Hi Hnr Roll; MVP; Perf Att; Pres Ac Ftns Aw; WWAHSS; Comm Volntr; Chrch Yth Grp; Key Club; Dnce; Sftball (J); Vllyball (V L); MVP- JV Volleyball/ Competed in Dance Competition; MVP- JV Softball; Dance; Recreation & Sports; UNC-Chapel Hill; UNC-Wilmington

SWEET, NICOLE; APEX, NC; APEX HS; (SO); Hnr Roll; Kwnis Aw; Pres Ac Ftns Aw; Chrch Yth Grp; Vllyball (V); Engineering; Math Major; North Carolina State U; Ohio State U

SWEEZY, AMY L; HENDERSONVILLE, NC; NORTH HENDERSON HS; (JR); Hnr Roll; Perf Att; WWAHSS; Comm Volntr; Key Club; Dnce; Chrldg (VJCL); Swmg (V); Track (V L); Stu Cncl (R); Who's Who Among American High School Students; Assoc. in Science Degree; AB Technical Comm. College; Central Piedmont Community College

SWEPSON, BRIANNA; GREENSBORO, NC; WESTERN GUILFORD HS; (SR); Hnr Roll; St of Mnth; Comm Volntr; Emplmnt; Quiz Bowl; Schol Bwl; Ch Chr; Fashion Design; Marketing; Clark Atlanta U; Virginia State U

SWICEGOOD, KATIE; CHARLOTTE, NC; CHARLOTTE CHRISTIAN SCH; (JR); Hi Hnr Roll; USAA; WWAHSS; Comm Volntr; Chrch Yth Grp; Photog; Chrldg (V CL); PP Ftbl (V); Track (V L); Cl Off (V); Bible Study; Communications; Broadcasting; North Carolina State U; U of South Carolina

SWICEGOOD, MAXWELL; SALISBURY, NC; SALISBURY HS; (JR); All Am Sch; Ctznshp Aw; Duke TS; Hi Hnr Roll; Jr Mshl; Kwnis Aw; Nat Hon Sy; Otst Ac Ach Awd; Pres Sch; St Schl; Comm Volntr; Hab For Humty Volntr; AL Aux Boys; Chrch Yth Grp; Cmptr Clb; HO'Br Yth Ldrshp; Jr Ach; Key Club; Mth Clb/Tm; Mus Clb; Jzz Bnd; Golf (V L); Sccr (V L); Track (V L); Cl Off (P); Stu Cncl (R); CR (P, R); Junior Chief Marshal / Biology Award; Spanish II & III Awards / Chemistry Award; Law; Business; UNC Chapel Hill; Vanderbilt U

SWINSON, ALISHA; GOLDSBORO, NC; EASTERN WAYNE HS; (FR); Hnr Roll; Comm Volntr; Won Oratorical Competition in Church; Awards from Church; Registered Nurse; Mostly in Labor and Delivery/Nursery Award; Winston Salem State U

SYMONE, MONIE; GREENVILLE, NC; (MS); MVP; Nat Stu Ath Day Aw; Sci Fairs; Comm Volntr; Spec Olymp Vol; ArtClub; Chess; DARE; FBLA; Scouts; Bnd; Chr; Ch Chr; Bskball; Sccr; Sftball; Stu Cncl (V); CR (P); Winner of a Journalism (Essay) Contest; Winner of an Expressive Poetry Contest; Fashion Designer; Entrepreneur; U of South Florida; U of Illinois

SZYMCZYK, MACIE J; RALEIGH, NC; OUTHEAST RALEIGH; (JR); Hnr Roll; Otst Ac Ach Awd; Sci Fairs; Sci/Math Olympn; Yth Ldrshp Prog; Dbte Team; JSA; Key Club; Quiz Bowl; Sci Clb; Cr Ctry (V L); Fncg (V); Track (V L)

TABARES, JUAN G; GASTONIA, NC; ASHBROOK HS; (SR); ROTC; Drl Tm; Sccr (V); National Technical Honor Society; Multimedia Web Design; Graphic Design; ITT Technical Institute -Accepted

TABON, JOY; MIDDLEBURG, NC; NORTHERN VANCE HS; (SR); WWAHSS; Hosp Aide; Chr; Dnce; Cr Ctry (V L); Dvng (V); Fld Hky (J); Ftball (V); Gmnstcs (V); Hsbk Rdg (V); Ice Hky (V); Lcrsse (C); Athlete's Foot Award; Nursing; North Carolina Central U

TABOR, LAURA; CARY, NC; CARY SR HS; (SO); Duke TS; Hi Hnr Roll; St of Mnth; WWAHSS; Red Cr Aide; Chrch Yth Grp; Dbte Team; Jr Ach; Lib Aide; ROTC; Stu Cncl (R); CR (R); Lit Mag (R); Sch Ppr (R); 8 Years of Bible Quiz with Church; Journalism; English; U of North Carolina At Chapel Hill; Elon U

TABRON, REBECCA; APEX, NC; MIDDLE CREEK HS; (SO); Hi Hnr Roll; Hnr Roll; Otst Ac Ach Awd; Chrch Yth Grp; Emplmnt; Key Club; Svce Clb; Chr; Ch Chr; Dnce; Sftball (J); Pharmacy; Nursing; U of North Carolina Wilmington; Winston-Salem State U

TAFT, HEIDI; POLKTON, NC; ANSON SR HS; (FR); Hnr Roll; Perf Att; St of Mnth; Comm Volntr; Cmptr Clb; DARE; Mth Clb/Tm; Photog; Clb; Hsbk Rdg; Swmg; Yrbk (P); Homecoming Queen; Pharmacist; Bachelor's Degree; U of North Carolina Chapel Hill; East Carolina

TALLENTS, ANDREA; OAKBORO, NC; SOUTH ROWAN HS; (JR); Hnr Roll; Nat Hon Sy; Perf Att; Yth Ldrshp Prog; Chrch Yth Grp; Drma Clb; FCA; Off Aide; Pep Squd; French Clb; Bskball (J); Tennis (L); CR (R); Pre-Vet; Biology/Teacher; Gardner Webb U; U of Central Oklahoma

TALLEY, TREY; RALEIGH, NC; FRANKLIN AC; (SO); Duke TS; Yth Ldrshp Prog; Chrch Yth Grp; FCA; Bsball (J); Ftball (J); SAVE Club; Law; Business/Economics; Duke U, Durham, North Carolina; U of Chicago, Chicago, Illinois

TANNER, JACQUELYN; APEX, NC; MIDDLE CREEK HS; (FR); Hi Hnr Roll; Otst Ac Ach Awd; Juris Doctorate; Education; North Carolina State U; U of North Carolina Chapel Hill

TANNER, KEDRICO B; WADESBORO, NC; ANSON HS; (FR); MVP; Nat Hon Sy; Peer Tut/Med; Chrch Yth Grp; Bsball; Bskball; Ftball (J); Scr Kpr (L); Track (V); Wt Lftg (L); Chemistry; Technology / Art; U Southern California; Memphis

TART, SARAH B; DUNN, NC; CAPE FEAR CHRISTIAN AC; (FR); Ctznshp Aw; Hi Hnr Roll; Hnr Roll; MVP; Otst Ac Ach Awd; Sci Fairs; St of Mnth; WWAHSS; Comm Volntr; Chrch Yth Grp; DARE; Mth Clb/Tm; Mus Clb; Ntl Beta Clb; Quiz Bowl; Bnd; Chr; Ch Chr; Bskball (VJC); Vllyball (VJ); Major in Occupational Therapy

TARVER, CHERILYN; CHARLOTTE, NC; HARDING U HS; (SO); Hnr Roll; Comm Volntr; Chrch Yth Grp; DARE; Jr Ach; Chrldg (J); Computer Engineer; Computer Programmer; U Of North Carolina at Chapel Hill; North Carolina State U

TATE, MICHAEL R; HIGH POINT, NC; RAGSDALE HS; (SO); Hnr Roll; Perf Att; ROTC; Clr Grd; Drl Tm; Track (V); Business and Economics; Arts and Sciences; North Carolina Central U; North Carolina Agriculture and Technology U

TATE, SOLOMON; GREENSBORO, NC; SMITH HS; (SO); Ctznshp Aw; Hi Hnr Roll; Hnr Roll; Perf Att; St of Mnth; Comm Volntr; Peer Tut/Med; Chess; Chrch Yth Grp; Cmptr Clb; DARE; Emplmnt; SADD; Bnd; Chr; Ch Chr; SP/M/VS; Bskball; Ftball; Wt Lftg; Yrbk (E, P); Law; Forensic Science; North Carolina Central U Durham

TAYLOR, BRITT A; WILSON, NC; HUNT HS; (SO); Duke TS; Hi Hnr Roll; Otst Ac Ach Awd; Perf Att; Sci/Math Olympn; WWAHSS; Comm Volntr; Peer Tut/Med; FCA; Key Club; Sci Clb; Bnd; Ch Chr; Mch Bnd; Pep Bnd; Cr Ctry (J); Sccr (V L); Swmg (V L); Track (V L); Medical Doctor; Veterinary Medicine; Duke U; Wake Forest

TAYLOR, BRITTANY M; SALISBURY, NC; SALISBURY HS; (SO); Ctznshp Aw; Hi Hnr Roll; Hnr Roll; MVP; WWAHSS; Comm Volntr; Key Club; Dnce; Chrldg (VJCL); PP Ftbl (V); Cl Off (S); CR (R); Miss Jr. North Carolina Teen; Sunburst City Winner; Radiology; Lawyer; UNC Chapel Hill; U of Virginia

TAYLOR, CHRISTA; MURFREESBORO, NC; HERTFORD CTY HS; (JR); Hnr Roll; Otst Ac Ach Awd; Chrch Yth Grp; FCA; Mth Clb/Tm; Prom Com; Ch Chr; Bskball (J); Track (V); Vllyball (V); Joined the Club of HOSA; Pre-Med Biology; Psychology; Winston-Salem State U; North Carolina Central U

TAYLOR, GARRETT; BRYSON CITY, NC; SWAIN CTY HS; (FR); Hi Hnr Roll; Perf Att; Comm Volntr; Spec Olymp Vol; FCA; Bsball (J); Ftball (V L); Wrstlg (V L); Stu Cncl (R); 2004 State 1-A football Championship; Healthcare-Sports Medicine; East Carolina U; Western Carolina U

TAYLOR, GERENEICIA D; JACKSONVILLE, NC; NORTHSIDE HS; (JR); Hnr Roll; Otst Ac Ach Awd; Perf Att; St of Mnth; Peer Tut/Med; Chrch Yth Grp; DARE; Emplmnt; Ch Chr; Church Step Team; Student of the Week; Psychology Major; Journalism Major; Florida State U; Fayetteville State U

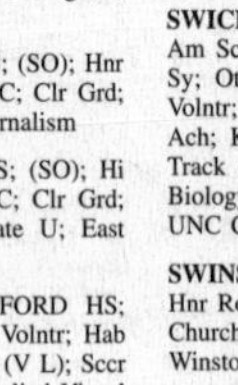
Tabron, Rebecca
Middle Creek HS
Apex, NC

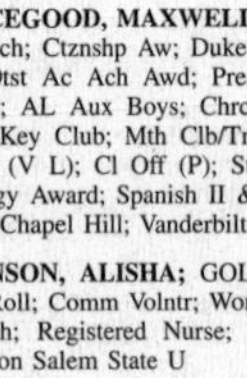
Tabares, Juan G
Ashbrook HS
Gastonia, NC

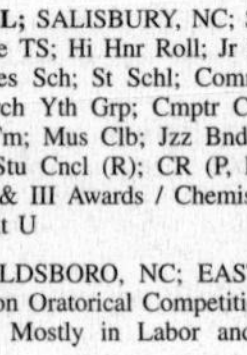
Stroud, Rachel N
Hertford Cty HS
Ahoskie, NC

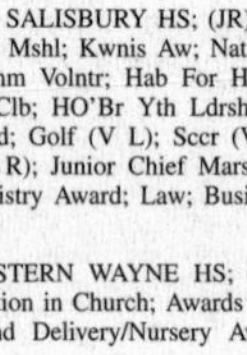
Sutherland, Corey
Heide Trask HS
Rocky Point, NC

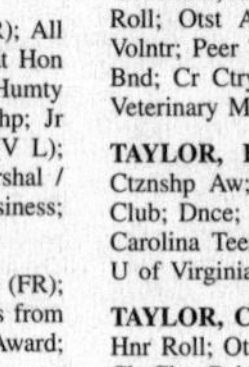
Taft, Heidi
Anson SR HS
Polkton, NC

TAYLOR, KAITLYN R; CONWAY, NC; RIDGECROFT SCH; (FR); Hi Hnr Roll; Otst Ac Ach Awd; Perf Att; Sci/Math Olympn; St of Mnth; WWAHSS; Comm Volntr; Chrch Yth Grp; Key Club; Ntl Beta Clb; SADD; Bnd; Chrldg (JC); Cl Off (P); Stu Cncl (R); Algebra I Award - 8th Grade; Pharmacy; Education; U of North Carolina Chapel Hill; NC State U

TAYLOR, MATTHEW D; HAVELOCK, NC; HAVELOCK HS; (FR); Duke TS; Hnr Roll; Sci Fairs; Sci/Math Olympn; Yth Ldrshp Prog; Comm Volntr; Chess; Drma Clb; Mth Clb/Tm; Mus Clb; Quiz Bowl; Scouts; Bnd; Mch Bnd; Pep Bnd; SP/M/VS; Music Theory; Aerospace Engineering; United State Air Force Academy At Colorado Springs; Oxford U

TAYLOR, MATTHEW E; ROBERSONVILLE, NC; ROANOKE HS; (SR); Hnr Roll; US Army Sch Ath Aw; USMC Stu Ath Aw; WWAHSS; Comm Volntr; Chrch Yth Grp; DARE; Emplmnt; Bsball (V L); Ftball (V L); Wt Lftg (V); All-Conference - Football; Wendy's Heisman Award Nominee; Pre-Med; East Carolina U; Appalachian State U

TAYLOR, SHANNON E; CARY, NC; CARY SR HS; (SO); Duke TS; Hi Hnr Roll; Otst Ac Ach Awd; WWAHSS; Comm Volntr; Dbte Team; NYLC; ROTC; Clr Grd; Drl Tm; Skt Tgt Sh (J); Sons of the American Revolution Award; Aerospace Engineering; Spanish

TAYLOR, VICTORIA I; GREENSBORO, NC; NORTH WEST GUILFORD HS; (FR); Ctznshp Aw; Duke TS; Hnr Roll; Pres Ac Ftns Aw; Sci Fairs; Comm Volntr; Hab For Humty Volntr; Spec Olymp Vol; Dbte Team; Orch; Sccr (J); Duke U; Bryn Mawr College

TEAGUE, JORDAN L; SALISBURY, NC; NORTH ROWAN HS; (SO); Ctznshp Aw; Duke TS; Hnr Roll; Perf Att; Sci Fairs; St of Mnth; Chrch Yth Grp; DARE; Bnd; Clr Grd; Dnce; Jzz Bnd; PP Ftbl (V); Scr Kpr (V); Sccr (V L); CR (R); Psychologist; Nurse; U of North Carolina At Chapel Hill; North Carolina State U

TEER, JOSHUA R; ELON, NC; CLOVER GARDEN CHARTER SCH; (SO); Hnr Roll; Otst Ac Ach Awd; Perf Att; St of Mnth; Comm Volntr; Spec Olymp Vol; Emplmnt; Ntl Beta Clb; Sci Clb; Bsball (V); Bskball (V); Scr Kpr (J); Stu Cncl (R); Marine Biology; Veterinarian; North Carolina State U; U of North Carolina Wilmington

TEETER, CHRISTOPHER; JACKSONVILLE, NC; JACKSONVILLE HS; (FR); Duke TS; Hi Hnr Roll; Perf Att; Chrch Yth Grp; FCA; Bnd; Wrstlg (V); State Qualifier in Wrestling; Mission Trips to Inner Cities (Church Group); Medical Research; Politics; Duke U; Campbell U

TEETER, KAYLA B; OAKBORO, NC; WEST STANLY HS; (SO); Ctznshp Aw; Hi Hnr Roll; Otst Ac Ach Awd; Sci Fairs; Ntl Beta Clb; Sci Clb; Bnd; Chrldg (J L); Beta Club; Student of the Year; Accounting/Business; Medical Field/Pharmacy; Wingate U; North Carolina State U

TEETERS, JUSTIN; LENOIR, NC; WEST CALDWELL HS; (SO); 4H Awd; Ctznshp Aw; Hi Hnr Roll; Hnr Roll; Nat Hon Sy; Perf Att; Pres Ac Ftns Aw; St of Mnth; Comm Volntr; Hosp Aide; 4-H; Chrch Yth Grp; DARE; FCA; Ntl Beta Clb; Quiz Bowl; Svce Clb; Bnd; 1st Chair; Pre-Medicine; BS; U of Pittsburgh; U of Minnesota

TEJADA, VANESSA I; SALISBURY, NC; WEST ROWAN HS; (SO); Ctznshp Aw; F Lan Hn Soc; Hi Hnr Roll; Nat Hon Sy; Otst Ac Ach Awd; Pres Ac Ftns Aw; Yth Ldrshp Prog; Comm Volntr; Emplmnt; Svce Clb; Vsity Clb; Ch Chr; West Rowan High School

TEMONEY, THERESA; WILMINGTON, NC; EUGENE ASHLEY HS; (SO); Hnr Roll; Otst Ac Ach Awd; Yth Ldrshp Prog; Comm Volntr; DARE; Emplmnt; Ntl Beta Clb; ROTC; Acpl Chr; Chr; Dnce; Drl Tm; Track (J); Sch Ppr (E); Outstanding Achievement in Poetry; Psychology/Sociology; English/Creative Writing; Barton College; Campbell U

TEMPLE, LAURA; SEVEN SPRINGS, NC; NORTH CAROLINA SCH OF SCIENCE AND MATH; (JR); Hi Hnr Roll; Perf Att; WWAHSS; Comm Volntr; Chess; DARE; FTA; Lttrmn Clb; Lib Aide; Mth Clb/Tm; Prom Com; Vsity Clb; Chrldg (V); PP Ftbl (V); Vsy Clb (V)

TEMPLES, AMY; INDIAN TRAIL, NC; METROLINA CHRISTIAN AC; (JR); Hi Hnr Roll; Hnr Roll; Nat Hon Sy; St of Mnth; Yth Ldrshp Prog; Comm Volntr; Peer Tut/Med; Chrch Yth Grp; Emplmnt; Ntl Beta Clb; Pep Squd; Tchrs Aide; Chr; Chrldg (V); Extracurricular-Guitar; Leader with the Carolina Youth Commission; Criminology; Sociology; Appalachian State U

TENESACA, DIANA; MONROE, NC; SUN VALLEY HS; (MS); St of Mnth; Comm Volntr; Chrch Yth Grp; Chr; Peacemaker Award

TENNYSON, ANDREW; CHAPEL HILL, NC; CE JORDAN HS; (JR); Duke TS; F Lan Hn Soc; Hi Hnr Roll; Hnr Roll; Jr Mshl; Nat Hon Sy; Nat Mrt Semif; WWAHSS; Comm Volntr; Chess; Emplmnt; Key Club; Mth Clb/Tm; Quiz Bowl; Spanish Clb; Bsball (J); Sch Ppr (E, R, P); President Key Club; Captain Brain & Quiz Teams; President National Honors Society; Political Science; Public Policy; Duke U; Stanford U

TERRY, TEWANDA; ERWIN, NC; (FR); Hnr Roll; Perf Att; WWAHSS; Chrch Yth Grp; Key Club; Mus Clb; Chr; Ch Chr; Cl Off (T); Registered Nurse; Midwife; East Carolina U

TESNOW, A B; ROSMAN, NC; ROSMAN HS; (SO); Hi Hnr Roll; Hnr Roll; MVP; Nat Hon Sy; Pres Sch; WWAHSS; ArtClub; Chrch Yth Grp; Emplmnt; FCA; FBLA; Ntl Beta Clb; Ntl FFA; Bskball (VJ); Ftball (J); Golf (V); Computer Engineering; North Carolina State

THACKER III, PAUL D; DURHAM, NC; CEDAR RIDGE HS; (SO); 4H Awd; Hnr Roll; Nat Hon Sy; Otst Ac Ach Awd; Pres Sch; USAA; WWAHSS; Comm Volntr; 4-H; Chrch Yth Grp; DARE; FCA; Bnd; Chr; Ch Chr; Jzz Bnd; Lcrsse (V); Track (V); Video Production Club; Neurology; Engineering; U of North Carolina Chapel Hill; Duke U

THAO, GAO; ALBEMARLE, NC; WEST STANLY HS; (JR); Hnr Roll; Perf Att; Track; Math Award; Registered Nurse

THAO, LENA; MORGANTON, NC; FREEDOM HS; (SR)

THAO, SANDY; WAXHAW, NC; PARKWOOD HS; (FR); Hnr Roll; Visual Arts/Graphics; Medical/Doctor; U of North Carolina Chapel Hill; U of North Carolina Asheville

THAO, YER; LAUREL HILL, NC; SCOTLAND HS; (SO); 4H Awd; Hnr Roll; Sci Fairs; St of Mnth; Comm Volntr; Peer Tut/Med; 4-H; ArtClub; DARE; Mus Clb; Chr; Dnce; Bskball (L); Vllyball (L); CR (R); Yrbk (P); Architecting and Computer Engineering; Joining the Marines

THAXTON, JOSH; STAR, NC; EAST MONTGOMERY HS; (FR); Hnr Roll; Perf Att; Emplmnt; Ntl FFA; Future Farmers of America; Business Management; Wake Forest; Marshall U

THAYER, BAILEY; EDEN, NC; MOREHEAD HS; (SR); Hi Hnr Roll; Nat Hon Sy; DECA; Latin Clb; Sccr (V); Vet Science; Veterinary Medicine; NC State U

THOMAS, ASHLEY B; WILLOW SPRING, NC; WEST JOHNSTON HS; (JR); 4H Awd; Hnr Roll; Perf Att; WWAHSS; Yth Ldrshp Prog; Hab For Humty Volntr; Peer Tut/Med; Spec Olymp Vol; 4-H; Chrch Yth Grp; DARE; Emplmnt; FCA; FCCLA; Pep Squd; Spanish Clb; Tennis (V); Track (V); HOSA; Doctor/Medical; Appalachian State U; East Carolina U

THOMAS, JACOB; GARNER, NC; WEST JOHNSTON HS; (JR); DAR; Hnr Roll; Pres Ac Ftns Aw; St of Mnth; Comm Volntr; Hab For Humty Volntr; ROTC; Bnd; Clr Grd; Mch Bnd; SP/M/VS; Swmg; Tennis (V); Track (V); PhD in Dentistry; Citadel Military Institute; Virginia Military Institute

THOMAS, KHA'ISHA A; ROCKY MOUNT, NC; NASH CTRL HS; (JR); Hnr Roll; Comm Volntr; Bskball (VJCL); Cr Ctry (VJ); PP Ftbl (VJ); Track (V L); Wt Lftg (VJ); Business Marketing; Accounting; Campbell U; Wake Forest U

THOMAS, LA TASHA; MAXTON, NC; HOKE CTY HS; (JR); Hnr Roll; Nat Hon Sy; WWAHSS; Comm Volntr; Spec Olymp Vol; Chrch Yth Grp; Ntl Beta Clb; Prom Com; Bnd; Ch Chr; Dnce; Stu Cncl; Yrbk; Gear Up Ambassador; FAU; Sport Management; Sport Administration; U of North Carolina-Raleigh; East Carolina U

THOMAS, MICHAEL T; WINGATE, NC; FOREST HILLS HS; (FR); Duke TS; Hi Hnr Roll; Hnr Roll; Nat Hon Sy; Pres Ac Ftns Aw; Peer Tut/Med; Chrch Yth Grp; DARE; Mus Clb; Bnd; Mch Bnd; Pep Bnd; 1st Alternate-NC State Honor Band '05; 1st Choir District Band '05; Pharmacist; Professional Musician; U of North Carolina At Chapel Hill; Wingate U

THOMAS, NIGEEYAH A; LUMBERTON, NC; LUMBERTON HS; (FR); Ctznshp Aw; Hi Hnr Roll; Hnr Roll; MVP; Nat Sci Aw; Otst Ac Ach Awd; Pres Ac Ftns Aw; Sci Fairs; Comm Volntr; Peer Tut/Med; Chrch Yth Grp; DARE; Drma Clb; FCA; Ntl Beta Clb; Quiz Bowl; ROTC; Ch Chr; Drl Tm; Mch Bnd; Bskball (J); Computer Science; PhD; Harvard U; Princeton U

THOMAS, REGINALD W; ROXBORO, NC; PERSON HS; (JR); Hnr Roll; Otst Ac Ach Awd; Perf Att; Ntl FFA; Bnd; Ch Chr; Mch Bnd; Aeronautics and Aerospace Engineering; Bachelor's Degree; North Carolina State U; U of Virginia

THOMAS, SARA; CLEMMONS, NC; NORTH DAVIDSON HS; (SO); Ctznshp Aw; Hnr Roll; Nat Hon Sy; Nat Ldrshp Svc; Nat Mrt LOC; USAA; DARE; FCA; Lib Aide; Ntl FFA; Svce Clb; Chr; Registered Nurse

THOMAS, SHANA; BUNNLEVEL, NC; HAMETT CTRL HS; (SO); Hnr Roll; Pres Ac Ftns Aw; WWAHSS; Comm Volntr; Key Club; Ntl Beta Clb; Latin Clb; Chr; Culinary Arts; Business; Johnson & Wales U; East Carolina U

THOMPSON, AMBER L; CHARLOTTE, NC; HARDING U HS; (SO); Perf Att; WWAHSS; Comm Volntr; Chrch Yth Grp; Jr Ach; Key Club; Scouts; Bnd; Ch Chr; Clr Grd; Dnce; Sftball (J); Track (J); Homecoming Court; Fashion Merchandising, Accounting; Clark Atlanta U; U of Georgia, A & T U NC

THOMPSON, COURTNEY E; NORWOOD, NC; SOUTH STANLY HS; (FR); Ctznshp Aw; Hnr Roll; Sci Fairs; Voc Ind Clb Am; Bnd; Mch Bnd; Most Respectful-Given By Principal; OR Nurse; Cabarrus College of Health Science

THOMPSON, DAVID; CHARLOTTE, NC; HOPEWELL HS; (JR); Hnr Roll; Perf Att; WWAHSS; DARE; Spch Team; Bskball (J); Award for Outstanding Academic Achievements in Math; Finance & Accounting; Sports Fitness; Brevard College; Central Carolina U

THOMPSON, DEENASHA; FAYETTEVILLE, NC; WESTOVER HS; (FR); Hnr Roll; Perf Att; Mod UN; Scouts; Chr; Ch Chr; Bskball (J); Medical Doctor; Modeling; Virginia State College; York College

THOMPSON, JOSHUA T; LEXINGTON, NC; NORTH DAVIDSON HS; (JR); Nat Hon Sy; Chrch Yth Grp; Dbte Team; Emplmnt; ROTC; Scouts; Bnd; Chr; Drl Tm; Eagle Scout; Pre-Law; Pre-Optometry; Wake Forest U; North Carolina State U

THOMPSON, MEREDITH N; HENDERSON, NC; NORTHERN VANCE HS; (FR); Duke TS; Hi Hnr Roll; Nat Ldrshp Svc; Otst Ac Ach Awd; USAA; Comm Volntr; Emplmnt; Chr; Ch Chr; SP/M/VS; Sftball (V L); Swmg (V L); Vllyball (V L); Young Scholars Award; School of Excellence/Academic Athletic Award; Orthodontics/Major; Photography/Minor; Davidson/Appalachian State U; Wake Forest U

THOMPSON, NATALIE S; MONROE, NC; PIEDMONT HS; (JR); Ctznshp Aw; Hi Hnr Roll; Hnr Roll; Nat Hon Sy; Nat Ldrshp Svc; Otst Ac Ach Awd; St of Mnth; WWAHSS; Comm Volntr; Peer Tut/Med; Chrch Yth Grp; Emplmnt; Mus Clb; Ntl Beta Clb; Svce Clb; SADD; Acpl Chr; Chr; Ch Chr; SP/M/VS; Sch Ppr (E); Yrbk (E); Nursing; Pharmacy; Wingate; UNC

THOMPSON, NATHAN; ELLENBORO, NC; CHASE HS; (JR); Hi Hnr Roll; Hnr Roll; Perf Att; St Schl; WWAHSS; Emplmnt; Ntl FFA; Yrbk (P); FFA Chapter Officer; Sport Broadcasting; Sport Management; North Carolina State U

THOMPSON, SIERRA; FAYETTEVILLE, NC; E E SMITH SR HS; (SO); WWAHSS; Emplmnt; FBLA; ROTC; Mass Communications (Radio Broadcast); Small Business/Marketing; Winston-Salem State U; Campbell U

THOMPSON, THERESA; HOPE MILLS, NC; SOUTHVIEW HS; (SR); Chrch Yth Grp; Emplmnt; Cr Ctry (V C); Track (V C); CR (R); Received Merit Scholarship ($2500) from Mt Olive; Received Honors Scholarship ($1500) from Mt Olive; Political Science; Psychology; Mount Olive College

THOMPSON, WHITNEY N; GASTONIA, NC; VICTORY CHRISTIAN AC; (JR); Hnr Roll; MVP; Comm Volntr; Chrch Yth Grp; DARE; Ntl Beta Clb; Prom Com; Ch Chr; Bskball (V); Chrldg (V); Sftball (V); Vllyball (V); Cl Off (P, V)

THORNTON, CHRISTIE; CHARLOTTE, NC; INDEPENDENCE HS; (JR); Hi Hnr Roll; Jr Mshl; WWAHSS; Comm Volntr; Chrch Yth Grp; Key Club; National Art Honor Society; Business Management; Graphic Design; Davidson College; North Carolina State U

THREADGILL, KIMBERLY R; THOMASVILLE, NC; THOMASVILLE HS; (JR); Hi Hnr Roll; Hnr Roll; MVP; Nat Hon Sy; Perf Att; WWAHSS; Peer Tut/Med; Chrch Yth Grp; Emplmnt; NYLC; Spanish Clb; Ch Chr; Dnce; Vllyball (V); Stu Cncl (R); CR (R); Nursing; Winston-Salem State U; UNC-Greensboro/UNC-Chapel Hill

THRIVENI, THOMAS; SALISBURY, NC; SALISBURY HS; (JR); Duke TS; Hnr Roll; Jr Mshl; Nat Hon Sy; Valdctrian; WWAHSS; Chrch Yth Grp; Key Club; Mth Clb/Tm; Quiz Bowl; Scouts; Sccr (J); Tennis (V L); Key Club Lt Governor; Boy Scout; MD; U of North Carolina At Chapel Hill; Duke U

TIDWELL, SHAVON; CHARLOTTE, NC; NORTHWEST SCH OF THE ARTS; (JR); Ctznshp Aw; Hi Hnr Roll; Hnr Roll; Perf Att; St of Mnth; Comm Volntr; ArtClub; Chrch Yth Grp; DARE; Mus Clb; NYLC; Bnd; Chr; Ch Chr; Drl Tm; Chrldg; Stu Cncl (R); Yrbk (R); Volunteer At Goodwill; Organize Step Team; Singing/Chorus Major; Band/Web Designing; Greensboro School of the Arts; U School of the Arts in New York

TILDSLEY JR, MICHAEL S.; FAYETTEVILLE, NC; JACK BRITT HS; (SR); All Am Sch; F Lan Hn Soc; Nat Hon Sy; Pres Sch; WWAHSS; Comm Volntr; Peer Tut/Med; Quiz Bowl; Tchrs Aide; Spanish Clb; Jzz Bnd; All-American Scholar; Who's Who Among American HS Students; Pharmacy; Campbell U; U of UNC (Chapel Hill)

TILLETT, JESSICA; KITTY HAWK, NC; FIRST FLIGHT HS; (SO); Hnr Roll; WWAHSS; Comm Volntr; Chrch Yth Grp; Key Club; Vsity Clb; Spanish Clb; Chrldg (V L); Biology (Major); NC State U

TILLMAN, TARA K; MOUNT OLIVE, NC; SOUTHERN WAYNE HS; (SO); Hi Hnr Roll; Nat Hon Sy; Otst Ac Ach Awd; WWAHSS; Comm Volntr; ArtClub; Chrch Yth Grp; Emplmnt; FTA; Ntl Beta Clb; Sci Clb; Spanish Clb; Tennis (V); Percell-Robinson Scholar; Teacher; Math Major; U of North Carolina At Wilmington; Duke

TILSON, JESSICA M; BELVILLE, NC; N BRUNSWICK HS; (FR); Drma Clb; SP/M/VS; Theatre Arts; Clemson U; Florida State U

TINSLEY, AUSTIN R; SUMMERFIELD, NC; NORTHWEST HS; (SO); Hnr Roll; MVP; Comm Volntr; DARE; Ftball (J); Sccr (JC); North Carolina State U; North Carolina @ Chapel Hill

Tilson, Jessica M
N Brunswick HS
Belville, NC

Thompson, Amber L
Harding U HS
Charlotte, NC

Thomas, Nigeeyah A
Lumberton HS
Lumberton, NC

Terry, Tewanda
Erwin, NC

Teeter, Kayla B
West Stanly HS
Oakboro, NC

National
Honor Roll
Spring 2005

Teeter, Christopher
Jacksonville HS
Jacksonville, NC

Thomas, Kha'Isha A
Nash Ctrl HS
Rocky Mount, NC

Thomas, Sara
North Davidson HS
Clemmons, NC

Thompson, Joshua T
North Davidson HS
Lexington, NC

Thompson, Whitney N
Victory Christian AC
Gastonia, NC

TIPTON, JOCELYN N; ASHEVILLE, NC; ENKA HS; (SO); Hi Hnr Roll; Hnr Roll; Hosp Aide; Chrch Yth Grp; Emplmnt; Ntl Beta Clb; Dnce; Scr Kpr (V); Stats for Varsity Soccer; AIG; Health Sciences; Bachelor and Medical Degree; U of Florida; U of Tennessee

TOMPKINS, JOSEPH; MOORESVILLE, NC; LAKE NORMAN HS; (JR); Hi Hnr Roll; Hnr Roll; Comm Volntr; Chess; Chrch Yth Grp; DARE; Ntl Beta Clb; Ftball (VJ L); Lit Mag (E); M-Fuge-Mission Work; Played Hockey for About 6 Years with YMCA; IT Major; History Major; U of North Carolina Charlotte UNCC; Western Carolina U-WCU

TOMS, CHARLOTTE D; RUTHERFORDTON, NC; RUTHERFORDTON-SPINDALE MS; MS; Ctznshp Aw; Hi Hnr Roll; Hnr Roll; Kwnis Aw; Comm Volntr; Peer Tut/Med; Chrch Yth Grp; DARE; FCA; Ntl Beta Clb; Scouts; Chr; Sftball (J); New Century Scholars; National Honor Society; Law; Orthodontics; U of Tennessee Knoxville; Yale U

TONEY, JEREMIAH S; FLAT ROCK, NC; EAST HENDERSON HS; (SO); Ctznshp Aw; Hi Hnr Roll; Hnr Roll; Otst Ac Ach Awd; Perf Att; Pres Sch; St of Mnth; Comm Volntr; Chrch Yth Grp; DARE; DECA; Emplmnt; FCA; ROTC; Wdwrkg Clb; Bnd; Ch Chr; Plays Drum in Church Band; Played Drums At Recording Studio for CCD; Mechanical Engineering; NC State; Chapel Hill

TONNEMACHER, NATHANIEL; CARY, NC; GREEN HOPE HS; (FR); St of Mnth; Comm Volntr; Rlr Hky (C); Business Mgmt.; U of Texas; Auburn U

TONON, LAUREN; CHARLOTTE, NC; PROVIDENCE HS; (SO); Duke TS; Hnr Roll; WWAHSS; Comm Volntr; Peer Tut/Med; Chrch Yth Grp; Key Club; MuAlphaTh; Bskball (V); Sccr (J); Tennis; Wt Lftg; Georgetown U

TORRENCE, JOSIE; FAYETTEVILLE, NC; REID ROSS YR ROUND CLASSICAL; (SO); Ctznshp Aw; Hnr Roll; Perf Att; Comm Volntr; Hosp Aide; Chrch Yth Grp; Jr Cls League; Ntl Beta Clb; Scouts; SADD; Ch Chr; Orch; Criminal Justice/ Master's Degree; Medical / PhD; UNC Pembroke

TOWNSEND, ANGELIQUE D; GREENSBORO, NC; SMITH HS; (FR); Hnr Roll; Perf Att; Yth Ldrshp Prog; DARE; Drma Clb; Tchrs Aide; Bnd; Dnce; SP/M/VS; Stg Cre; Astronomy; Engineering; Wake Forest U; Mercer U

TOWNSEND, MEGAN B; JACKSONVILLE, NC; JACKSONVILLE HS; (FR); Hnr Roll; Perf Att; WWAHSS; Chr; Chrldg (V); Whos Who Among American HS Students; USAA National Cheerleader Arch. Award; UNC-Wilmington; UNC-State

TOWNSEND, SARAI; HICKORY, NC; HICKORY HS; (FR); Hnr Roll; WWAHSS; Chr; SP/M/VS; Songwriting; Performance; Berklee College Of Music- Boston, Massachusetts; Savannah College of Art and Design-Savannah, Georgia

TOWNSEND, TALISHA; FAYETTEVILLE, NC; 71ST HS; (SO); Hnr Roll; Nat Sci Aw; Perf Att; Ch Chr; Marching Elites; Psychology; Cosmetology; Hampton U; Fayetteville State U

TRAMMELL, AMANDA L; HARRELLS, NC; HARRELLS CHRISTIAN AC; (FR); Hnr Roll; Chrch Yth Grp; FCA; Ntl Beta Clb; Chrldg (V L); Sftball (V); FCA; Shout to the Lord-Puppet Team; Pediatrics; Appalachian State; North Carolina State U

TRAN, KAILYN; MC LEANSVILLE, NC; GRIMSLEY HS; (JR); Comm Volntr; Hab For Humty Volntr; Scouts; French Clb; Cr Ctry (V L); Lcrsse (V L); Girl Scout Silver Award; Lacrosse Coach's Award; Architectural Engineering; Interior Design; North Carolina State U; Virginia Technical Institute

TRAN, PHILIP; FAYETTEVILLE, NC; E E SMITH SR HS; (FR); Hnr Roll; Nat Hon Sy; Otst Ac Ach Awd; Pres Sch; Red Cr Aide; Quiz Bowl

TRAN, TAN; RALEIGH, NC; MILLBROOK HS; (SO); Hnr Roll; SADD; Cameraman for School Talent Show; Worked / Reported on School News Show; Computer Science / Programming / Engineering; Programming & Broadcasting / TV Production; North Carolina State U; U of North Carolina Chapel Hill

TREMAIN, CAMERON B; HICKORY, NC; HICKORY HS; (FR); Hi Hnr Roll; Hnr Roll; Sci Fairs; Sci/Math Olympn; Peer Tut/Med; Emplmnt; Quiz Bowl; Ftball (J); I Have Been in an Honor Band.; Chemical Engineering; BS; North Carolina State U; Georgia Tech

TRENT, AUSTIN A; LEWISTON WOODVILLE, NC; RIDGECROFT SCH; (FR); Hnr Roll; Otst Ac Ach Awd; St of Mnth; Key Club; Ntl Beta Clb; SADD; Ride Horses Competitively - Not with School; Equine Vet; Small Animal Vet; North Carolina State U; College of Charleston

TRETHAWAY, CHRISTINE E; WINSTON-SALEM, NC; REYNOLDS HS; (JR); Duke TS; Gov Hnr Prg; Hi Hnr Roll; Hnr Roll; Jr Mshl; Nat Hon Sy; WWAHSS; Comm Volntr; ArtClub; FCA; Spanish Clb; Golf (V L); Lcrsse (V); Scr Kpr (V); National Art Honor Society; North Carolina Award for Outstanding Volunteer Service; Communications / Mass Media; Meteorology; Eckerd College; U of Miami

TREVINO, JUANITA; RAEFORD, NC; HOKE CTY HS; (SR); Hnr Roll; WWAHSS; DECA; FCA; FBLA; Chr; SP/M/VS; Sccr (J); Early Graduating; Business Administration; U of North Carolina Pembroke

TREXLER JR, STEVEN B; SALISBURY, NC; EAST ROWAN HS; (JR); Hi Hnr Roll; Jr Mshl; Nat Hon Sy; Junior Civitan Scholar; Mechanical Engineering; Architecture; U of North Carolina At Raleigh; North Carolina State U

TRIMBLE, JAY S; MOORESVILLE, NC; MOORESVILLE HS; (SO); Hi Hnr Roll; Nat Hon Sy; Perf Att; WWAHSS; Comm Volntr; Chrch Yth Grp; FCA; Scouts; Bnd; Ch Chr; Jzz Bnd; Mch Bnd; Tennis (V L); Engineering; North Carolina State U; UNC Charlotte

TRIPLIN, MORGAN; WINSTON SALEM, NC; GLENN HS; (FR); Hnr Roll; Perf Att; Sci Fairs; CARE; Comm Volntr; Hab For Humty Volntr; Chrch Yth Grp; DARE; ROTC; Bnd; Ch Chr; Drl Tm; Stu Cncl (R); Church Missionary Worker; Volunteer Tutoring; Business Law; Graphic Design; Wake Forest U; North Carolina State U

TRIPP, ERVING I; MOREHEAD CITY, NC; WEST CARTERET HS; (SO); Ctznshp Aw; Hnr Roll; WWAHSS; Chrch Yth Grp; Emplmnt; FCA; Ch Chr; Bsball (J); Bskball (J); Ftball (V); Stu Cncl; Fellowship Christian Athletes; Who's Who; Computer Engineer; North Carolina State U; Wake Forest U

TRIVETTE JR, TONY L; NORTH WILKESBORO, NC; WEST WILKES HS; (SO); Hnr Roll; St of Mnth; Comm Volntr; Peer Tut/Med; Chrch Yth Grp; Emplmnt; FCA; Key Club; Mod UN; P to P St Amb Prg; Bsball (JC); Bskball (JC); Ftball (J); Stu Cncl (T); Teaching; Appalachian State U; U of North Carolina At Chapel Hill

TROTTER, ANDREW; YOUNGSVILLE, NC; FRANKLINTON HS; (FR); Hi Hnr Roll; Hnr Roll; MVP; Perf Att; Sci Fairs; St of Mnth; Comm Volntr; Chrch Yth Grp; FCA; Bsball (JC); Bskball (JC); Ftball (V L); Scholar Athlete of the Year 8th Grade; 2nd Highest Average 8th Grade; High School Education; Engineering; North Carolina State U; Duke U

TSENG, PAMELA; RALEIGH, NC; RAVENSCROFT SCH; (SO); Hnr Roll; Otst Ac Ach Awd; Red Cr Aide; Spec Olymp Vol; Emplmnt; Key Club; Quill & Scroll; Sftball (V); Vllyball (J); CR (R); Sch Ppr (R); Sportsmanship Award for JV Softball; Service Award for Book Club; Dentistry; Psychology; U of North Carolina At Chapel Hill; Duke U

TSUI, HEI LAM; GOLDSBORO, NC; EASTERN WAYNE HS; (SR); Nat Hon Sy; Perf Att; WWAHSS; Yth Ldrshp Prog; Comm Volntr; Peer Tut/Med; ArtClub; Emplmnt; Mth Clb/Tm; Mus Clb; Sci Clb; Scouts; Foreign Clb; Acpl Chr; Mar Art; Physical Therapy; U of North Carolina At Chapel Hill; Eastern Carolina U

TUCKER, ASHLEY E; CHARLOTTE, NC; INDEPENDENCE SR HS; (JR); Duke TS; Hnr Roll; MVP; Nat Hon Sy; Comm Volntr; Peer Tut/Med; Emplmnt; Jr Ach; Lttrmn Clb; Scouts; Vsity Clb; French Clb; Bnd; Chr; Pep Bnd; Bskball (V); Scr Kpr (V); Sccr (VJ L); Vllyball (VJ L); Stu Cncl (V); Clothing and Textiles; Fashion Merchandising; North Carolina State U; Parsons School of Design

TUCKER, ASHLEY E; CLAYTON, NC; CLAYTON HS; (SO); Hi Hnr Roll; Otst Ac Ach Awd; Yth Ldrshp Prog; Comm Volntr; Chrch Yth Grp; Quill & Scroll; Bnd; Yrbk (E); Advantage Hospice and Home Care Volunteer; Interact Club; Pharmacy / Medicine; Journalism; UNC Chapel Hill; Campbell U

TUCKER, JORDAN P; DOBSON, NC; SURRY CTRL HS; (SR); Hi Hnr Roll; Hnr Roll; MVP; Pres Ac Ftns Aw; WWAHSS; Comm Volntr; Chrch Yth Grp; DARE; Emplmnt; FCA; Lttrmn Clb; SADD; Vsity Clb; Bsball (J); Bskball (VJ); Ftball (VJCL); Vsy Clb (V); Wt Lftg (VJ); Vocational Honor Society; Scholar Athlete; Civil Engineering; U of North Carolina Charlotte

TUCKER, LASHAYE; HICKORY, NC; HICKORY HS; (JR); Ctznshp Aw; Hnr Roll; DARE; Mth Clb/Tm; Citizenship; Howard U

TUFT JR, ULYSSES; SHELBY, NC; BURNS HS; (JR); Ch Chr; Ftball (VJCL); Track (VJCL); Wt Lftg (VJC); National Technical Honor Society; 2004-05 Who's Who; Business Administration; Computer Technology; Duke U; U of North Carolina Chapel Hill

TUNSTALL, ASHLEY; CHARLOTTE, NC; (JR); Ctznshp Aw; Hnr Roll; Drma Clb; Mus Clb; Chr; Stg Cre; Major-Performing Arts; Minor-History; NYU Spelman; U of Charlotte NC

TURMAN, TRAVIS; GREENSBORO, NC; GRIMSLEY HS; (SO); Otst Ac Ach Awd; Perf Att

TURNER, CHELSEA C; ZEBULON, NC; FRANKLIN AC; (SO); 4H Awd; Hnr Roll; Nat Hon Sy; Comm Volntr; Peer Tut/Med; 4-H; Chrch Yth Grp; Drma Clb; Ch Chr; SP/M/VS; Chrldg (J); Hsbk Rdg; Vllyball (JC); 2003 State Champion (4-H); AQHA Competitor; Animal Science; Design; North Carolina State U

TURNER, JONATHAN; GREENSBORO, NC; DUDLEY HS; (FR); Ctznshp Aw; Hnr Roll; Perf Att; Comm Volntr; Peer Tut/Med; Jr Ach; Mus Clb; Schol Bwl; Scouts; Bnd; Mch Bnd

TURNER, LATISHA R; ROBERSONVILLE, NC; WAVERLY JR/SR HS; (FR); Sci/Math Olympn; Comm Volntr; Bnd; Flg Crps; Mch Bnd; Chrldg (J); Sftball (V); Cosmetology; Law; Harvard Law School; Martin Community College

TURNER, PATRICIA J; MOUNT GILEAD, NC; WEST MONTGOMERY HS; (JR); Hnr Roll; Chrch Yth Grp; Ntl Beta Clb; Ch Chr; Dnce; Chrldg (V); CR (R); Law Degree; Livingston U; North Carolina Central

TUSET, JUAN E; RALEIGH, NC; CJC AC; (SO); Nat Hon Sy; Nat Sci Aw; Otst Ac Ach Awd; USAA; WWAHSS; Comm Volntr; Peer Tut/Med; Chrch Yth Grp; Ntl Beta Clb; Quiz Bowl; Bskball (V C); Cr Ctry; CR (R); Mime Group; Summer Internship; Electrical Engineering; Industrial Design; North Carolina State U; Hampton U

TUTTLE, CHASE; WINSTON SALEM, NC; NORTH FORSYTH HS; (SO); Duke TS; Hi Hnr Roll; Hnr Roll; WWAHSS; Comm Volntr; Chrch Yth Grp; FCA; Key Club; Mth Clb/Tm; Svce Clb; Bnd; Ch Chr; Mch Bnd; Yrbk (R); National Honor Society; Mathematics Education; Spanish; Furman U; Elon U

TWISDALE, ANNA; HENDERSON, NC; SOUTHERN VANCE HS; (JR); Duke TS; F Lan Hn Soc; Hnr Roll; Jr Mshl; Nat Hon Sy; St of Mnth; Hosp Aide; Chrch Yth Grp; Emplmnt; FCA; Key Club; Ntl Beta Clb; Spanish Clb; Ch Chr; Sftball (V); Vllyball (J); Summer Ventures in Science & Math (2004); NC Governor's School (2005); Nursing; U of North Carolina-Chapel Hill; East Carolina U

TYSON, NATALIE V; WINTERVILLE, NC; D H CONLEY HS; (SO); Hnr Roll; Otst Ac Ach Awd; Hab For Humty Volntr; Hosp Aide; Mth Clb/Tm; Ntl Beta Clb; Dnce; Chrldg (V); Radiologist; Marine Biologist; Duke U; U of North Carolina

UMANZOR, BRENDA; KERNERSVILLE, NC; GLENN HS; (SR); Hnr Roll; Jr Mshl; Perf Att; Comm Volntr; Emplmnt; Fr of Library; Spanish Clb; Ch Chr; Basketball; Soccer; Pediatrician; Lawyer; U of North Carolina At Chapel Hill; Liberty U

UMPHLETT, LINDSEY M; ELIZABETH CITY, NC; NORTHEASTERN HS; (FR); Hnr Roll; Sci Fairs; Chrch Yth Grp; Bnd; Dnce; Mch Bnd; Pep Bnd; Nursing; Teaching; U of North Carolina; East Carolina U

UNDERDUE, JARVIS; KENLY, NC; NORTH JOHNSTON HS; (JR); Hnr Roll; ROTC

UNDERWOOD, ALLISON; ROSEBORO, NC; CAPE FEAR HS; (FR); Hi Hnr Roll; Otst Ac Ach Awd; WWAHSS; Comm Volntr; Hosp Aide; Chrch Yth Grp; Drma Clb; SP/M/VS; Sftball (J); Nurse Anesthetist; Pediatrician; East Carolina U; Chapel Hill, U of North Carolina

UNDERWOOD, KATHRYN; REIDSVILLE, NC; REIDSVILLE HS; (FR); Hnr Roll; Vllyball (J); Business / Marketing; U of North Carolina

UNDERWOOD, SARAH; CARRBORO, NC; CHAPEL HILL HS; (JR); Ctznshp Aw; Duke TS; F Lan Hn Soc; Comm Volntr; Chrch Yth Grp; Key Club; Outdrs Clb; Tchrs Aide; Chr; Dnce; Stu Cncl (R); Summer Ventures in Science & Mathematics; Biological Sciences; Environmental Science; U of Virginia; U of North Carolina Chapel Hill

UPCHURCH, AMBER L; ROBBINS, NC; NORTH MOORE HS; (JR); Hi Hnr Roll; Hnr Roll; Jr Mshl; WWAHSS; Comm Volntr; Emplmnt; FCA; FBLA; Key Club; Ntl Beta Clb; Prom Com; French Clb; Sftball (J); Vllyball (J); Cl Off (P, V); Stu Cncl (V); CR (R); Yrbk (R, P); Civil War Essay 1st Place State Award; Social Work; Psychology; U of North Carolina Greensboro; East Carolina U

UPCHURCH, JENNIFER B; HILLSBOROUGH, NC; NORTHERN HS; (JR); Ctznshp Aw; Gov Hnr Prg; Hnr Roll; Jr Mshl; Nat Hon Sy; Perf Att; Comm Volntr; Peer Tut/Med; Chrch Yth Grp; Emplmnt; Key Club; Prom Com; Svce Clb; Dnce; Chrldg (V L); PP Ftbl (J); Junior Counselor At YMCA Camp Kanata; Elected Key Club President (2005-2006); Social Work; Special Education; U of North Carolina Chapel Hill; Wake Forest U

UPTON, BRITTANY L; BOSTIC, NC; EAST RUTHERFORD HS; (FR); Hnr Roll; WWAHSS; Comm Volntr; Hosp Aide; Chrch Yth Grp; Dbte Team; Key Club; Ch Chr; Sccr (L); Swmg (L); Academic Team

URICK, HEATHER; PLYMOUTH, NC; LAWRENCE AC; (SO); Hnr Roll; WWAHSS; Yth Ldrshp Prog; Comm Volntr; Drma Clb; Ntl Beta Clb; SADD; Vsity Clb; Chr; Dnce; Chrldg (V); Vsy Clb (V); Geography Award, World History Award; Writing Seminar Award; Cardiologist; Ob/Gyn; ECU; Peace

VACCARI, CAROLINA; DURHAM, NC; (SR); Key Club; Bskball (V); Cr Ctry (V); Exchange Student to USA; Brazilian Colleges

VALDOVINOS, FANNY; BISCOE, NC; EAST MONTGOMERY HS; (FR); Hnr Roll; Nat Hon Sy; Otst Ac Ach Awd; Perf Att; Sci Fairs; St of Mnth; WWAHSS; Peer Tut/Med; 4-H; DARE; Business

VANCE, AMBER D; LENOIR, NC; HIBRITEN HS; (FR); Hnr Roll; Key Club; Ch Chr; I Have a Dream Scholarship; Educational Talent Search (ETS); Radiology; Nursing; Caldwell Community College and Technical Institute

VANCE, PAIGE; HICKORY, NC; ST STEPHENS HS; (SO); Ctznshp Aw; Hi Hnr Roll; Hnr Roll; Otst Ac Ach Awd; Pres Ac Ftns Aw; Sci Fairs; St of Mnth; CARE; Comm Volntr; Hab For Humty Volntr; ArtClub; Chrch Yth Grp; Emplmnt; FCA; Ntl Beta Clb; Svce Clb; Dnce; SP/M/VS; Stg Cre; Chrldg (VJ); PPSqd (J); Wt Lftg (J); Chaplain of Juniorettes Club; Graphic or Interior Design; Plastic Surgeon; U of Chapel Hill Charlotte; Eastern Carolina U

Turner, Chelsea C
Franklin AC
Zebulon, NC

Tucker, Ashley E
Independence SR HS
Charlotte, NC

Triplin, Morgan
Glenn HS
Winston Salem, NC

National
Honor Roll
Spring 2005

Tonon, Lauren
Providence HS
Charlotte, NC

Tucker, Ashley E
Clayton HS
Clayton, NC

Upchurch, Jennifer B
Northern HS
Hillsborough, NC

VAN DER KAMP, KATHERINE; DUNN, NC; TRITON HS; (FR); Sci Clb; Louisiana State U

VAN DRIESEN, ASHLEIGH; CURRITUCK, NC; CURRITUCK CTY HS; (JR); Duke TS; Hnr Roll; Peer Tut/Med; Chrch Yth Grp; Emplmnt; Bskball (V); Sftball (V); Vllyball (V); Education; Architecture; East Carolina; NC State

VANEGAS, MARGARITA; HURDLE MILLS, NC; PERSON HS; (SR); Peer Tut/Med; Chrch Yth Grp; ROTC; Chr; Ch Chr; Drl Tm

VANG, VENDY; HICKORY, NC; ST. STEPHENS HS; (FR)

VANN, JOANNA E; CLINTON, NC; CLINTON HS; (SR); All Am Sch; Hi Hnr Roll; Nat Hon Sy; WWAHSS; Comm Volntr; Spec Olymp Vol; Chrch Yth Grp; Emplmnt; Key Club; Ntl Beta Clb; Ntl FFA; Prom Com; Tech Clb; Clr Grd; Dnce; Chrldg (J); Sccr (V); Yrbk (R); East Carolina U

VAN POWELL JR, RANDOLPH; CHARLOTTE, NC; CROSSROADS CHARTER HS; (SO); Vsity Clb; Bskball (V); To Own My Own Business; CPCC Charlotte

VARGAS, ADRIANA C B; RURAL HALL, NC; NORTH FORSYTH HS; (SO); Ctznshp Aw; Peer Tut/Med; Stu Cncl (P); Designer; Graphic Designer; New York U; Wake Forest U

VASQUEZ, JESSICA; MONROE, NC; MONROE HS; (FR); Hnr Roll; Otst Ac Ach Awd; Chapel Hill U; Duke U

VAUGHN, ASHLEY L; MONROE, NC; PIEDMONT HS; (JR); Hnr Roll; Jr Rot; MVP; Nat Hon Sy; Pres Ac Ftns Aw; WWAHSS; Comm Volntr; Hosp Aide; Chrch Yth Grp; FCA; Ntl Beta Clb; Prom Com; Dnce; Chrldg; Cr Ctry; Track; Stu Cncl; Yrbk; 3-A Conference Runner of the Year; 3rd Place in State Track 800 Meter; Physical Therapy; N.C. State U; U of North Carolina

VAUGHN, ASHLEY R; WINSTON SALEM, NC; REYNOLDS HS; (JR); Hi Hnr Roll; Hnr Roll; WWAHSS; Comm Volntr; Peer Tut/Med; Red Cr Aide; Chrch Yth Grp; Prom Com; Spanish Clb; Ch Chr; Law; Social Work; UNC-Chapel Hill; Howard U

VAUGHN, HILLARY; LAWNDALE, NC; BURNS HS; (JR); WWAHSS; Chrch Yth Grp; Ntl FFA; Degree in Nursing; RN or LPN; Cleveland Community College

VAUGHN JR, JERRY L; LA GRANGE, NC; KINSTON HS; (JR); Hnr Roll; Nat Hon Sy; WWAHSS; Comm Volntr; Peer Tut/Med; Cmptr Clb; DECA; Ftball (V CL); Track (V L); Wt Lftg (V L); Computer Programming; Master's; North Carolina State U; Carnegie Mellon U

VAUGHT, AUDESSA; CHAPEL HILL, NC; CHAPEL HILL HS; (FR); Hnr Roll; Comm Volntr; Peer Tut/Med; Emplmnt; Scouts; Tmpl Yth Grp; Chr; Swmg (J); Criminal Justice

VAZQUEZ ROMERO, MONSERRAT; PLEASANT GARDEN, NC; RANDLEMAN HS; (FR); Hnr Roll; Comm Volntr; FCA; Good Attendance; Veterinary; Dentist; Harvard U; UN State

VEGA, LEHA; MONROE, NC; FOREST HILLS HS; (JR); Hnr Roll; FBLA; Biology Award 2004; Lawyer; Super Model; UNC; SPCC

VEGERANO, JOEY; WINSTON SALEM, NC; WEST FORSYTH HS; (FR); Hi Hnr Roll; Hnr Roll; Chess; Chrch Yth Grp; DARE; Off Aide; Pop-Warner Football-4 years; Biotechnology; Architect; U of North Carolina; Wake Forest U

VELAZQUEZ, NANCY; HENDERSON, NC; SOUTHERN VANCE HS; (JR); Hnr Roll; Otst Ac Ach Awd; St of Mnth; Comm Volntr; Fashion Designer; Have My Own Spa; Vance Granville Community College

VENNING, JALESA; WINSTON SALEM, NC; MT TABOR HS; (JR); Duke TS; Hnr Roll; Nat Hon Sy; Perf Att; Pres Sch; WWAHSS; Comm Volntr; Chrch Yth Grp; DECA; Key Club; Prom Com; Latin Clb; Track (V L); CR; DECA Vice President; Crosby Scholar President; Biochemistry; Pediatric Cardiology; Hampton U

VERA, JAMIE L; HIGH POINT, NC; T W ANDREWS HS; (SR); Hnr Roll; Jr Mshl; MVP; Nat Hon Sy; St of Mnth; Comm Volntr; Chrch Yth Grp; FCA; Key Club; Ntl Beta Clb; GAA; Sftball (V CL); Vllyball (V CL); Accounting; U of NC At Charlotte

VERALDI, MEGAN N; RALEIGH, NC; WAKEFIELD HS; (SO); Hnr Roll; MVP; WWAHSS; Yth Ldrshp Prog; Spec Olymp Vol; Chrch Yth Grp; FCA; Key Club; Pep Squd; Sccr (V L); Swmg (V L); Stu Cncl (R); Yrbk (E); Pep Club/Key Club; Wake Boarding; Architecture; Marine Biology; North Carolina State

VERBAL, EBONY; SPRING LAKE, NC; PINE FOREST HS; (JR); Hnr Roll; FCCLA; Prom Com; Ob/Gyn; RN; U of North Carolina At Chapel Hill; East Carolina U

VESS, CAROLYN J; OAK ISLAND, NC; SOUTH BRUNSWICK HS; (JR); 4H Awd; Hnr Roll; St of Mnth; Comm Volntr; Peer Tut/Med; 4-H; Chrch Yth Grp; DARE; Chr; Elementary Teacher; Doctor; U of Florida; Johnson & Wales U

VETIL, AURELIEN; CARY, NC; GREEN HOPE HS; (JR); Duke TS; Hi Hnr Roll; Hnr Roll; Jr Mshl; Comm Volntr; Chess; Drma Clb; FTA; Ntl Beta Clb; French Clb; SP/M/VS; Played Ice Hockey, Soccer; Trilingual (English/French/Spanish); Doctor; Biochemical Engineer; UNC Chapel Hill; Duke U

VICK, HEATHER; ROANOKE RAPIDS, NC; ROANOKE RAPIDS HS; (SO); Duke TS; Hnr Roll; WWAHSS; Peer Tut/Med; Chrch Yth Grp; Chr; Ch Chr; Dnce; Tennis (V); Myrick School of Dance - Dance Team; Peer Helper; Music / Dance; East Carolina U

VIET, TRAN T; HIGH POINT, NC; HIGH POINT CTRL HS; (SR); Hnr Roll; Nat Hon Sy; Otst Ac Ach Awd; WWAHSS; Comm Volntr; Hab For Humty Volntr; ArtClub; Chess; Key Club; Mth Clb/Tm; Ntl Beta Clb; NYLC; Prom Com; Cr Ctry (V C); Sccr (J); Tennis (V); Track (V C); National Technical Honor Society; Political Science; Law; UNC Charlotte

VILAKUANH, LARRY; MOUNT GILEAD, NC; WEST MONTGOMERY HS; (FR); 4H Awd; Ctznshp Aw; Hnr Roll; Otst Ac Ach Awd; Perf Att; Pres Ac Ftns Aw; Pres Sch; Sci Fairs; St of Mnth; St Optmst of Yr; CARE; Comm Volntr; Peer Tut/Med; 4-H; DARE; Drma Clb; ROTC; Svce Clb; SADD; Dnce; Drl Tm; Flg Crps; SP/M/VS; Cl Off (R); CR (R); Business Administration; Banking and Finance; Stanly Community College

VILLAGOMEZ, AMY; ASHEBORO, NC; ASHEBORO HS; (JR); Duke TS; Hnr Roll; Nat Hon Sy; Hab For Humty Volntr; Drma Clb; Emplmnt; Key Club; Ntl Beta Clb; P to P St Amb Prg; Quiz Bowl; Sci Clb; French Clb; Chr; Ch Chr; SP/M/VS; Lit Mag (E); Sch Ppr (R); Political Science / International Diplomacy; Journalism; New York U; U of North Carolina Chapel Hill

VILLEGAS, ELIZABETH; CHARLOTTE, NC; HARDING U HS; (SO); Hnr Roll; Chess; ROTC; Tennis (V); Environmental Club; Rifle Team

VINCENT, MARK L; FORT BRAGG, NC; E E SMITH SR HS; (JR); Hnr Roll; WWAHSS; Key Club; ROTC; Stu Cncl (R); Business; Military Science; West Point; North Carolina A & T State U

VINES, CONDELVIAN R; NASHVILLE, NC; NASH CTRL HS; (FR); Hnr Roll; Lawyer; Nurse; NC State U (NC State); U of North Carolina (UNC)

VINKLER, JOHN J; WAXHAW, NC; CHARLOTTE CATHOLIC HS; (FR); Hnr Roll; Perf Att; Pres Ac Ftns Aw; Comm Volntr; Peer Tut/Med; DARE; Sccr (JC); Architectural Engineering / Design; Marine Biology; Duke U; U of South Carolina

VIOLETTE, THOMAS; GOLDSBORO, NC; SPRING CREEK HS; (MS); Hnr Roll; Perf Att; Scouts; Bnd; Community Service with Boy Scouts; Work for NASA; Archeologist, Architect; Phoenix College in MA; Massachusetts Institute of Technology

VIVAS, LISETTE; MONROE, NC; MONROE HS; (FR); St of Mnth; ArtClub; DECA; French Clb; Yrbk (P); Science Award; Outstanding Achievement Award; Computer Graphics; Designer; Appalachian State U

VOLK, JESSICA M; GREENVILLE, NC; D H CONLEY HS; (SO); Ctznshp Aw; MVP; Yth Ldrshp Prog; Comm Volntr; Spec Olymp Vol; Chrch Yth Grp; DARE; DECA; Ntl Beta Clb; Scouts; Vllyball (V); Sassy Award Sportsmanship; Marketing; Elon; Peace

VOLPE, NICKI G; JACKSONVILLE, NC; JACKSONVILLE HS; (SO); Comm Volntr; Peer Tut/Med; Chrch Yth Grp; FCA; Dnce; English Exam Award; Math Exam Award; Psychology; Criminal Justice; U of North Carolina @ Chapel Hill; U of Wilmington in North Carolina

VORONTSOVA, LENA; HILLSBOROUGH, NC; CEDAR RIDGE HS; (JR); Comm Volntr; Peer Tut/Med; Dnce; International Studies / Diplomacy; Slovanic Languages; UNC Chapel Hill; Florida State U

VU, DIANA; PINEHURST, NC; PINECREST HS; (SO); Hnr Roll; Comm Volntr; Emplmnt; Leo Club; UNC or Duke U; UNC of Chapel Hill

WADDELL, BRIAN L; WINNABOW, NC; NORTH BRUNSWICK HS; (SR); Hnr Roll; ROTC; Ch Chr; Clr Grd; Drl Tm; Degree in Architecture; UNC Charlotte

WADE, LELA; CONNELLYS SPRINGS, NC; EAST BURKE HS; (SO); Ctznshp Aw; Hnr Roll; Perf Att; Sci Fairs; St of Mnth; Peer Tut/Med; Neonatal Nursing; 4 Years; UNC Chapel Hill; Kings College

WADSWORTH, JENNIFER A; SELMA, NC; SMITHFIELD-SELMA SR HS; (SO); Hi Hnr Roll; Nat Stu Ath Day Aw; WWAHSS; Comm Volntr; Spec Olymp Vol; FCA; Key Club; MuAlphaTh; Sci Clb; International Clb; Bnd; Orch; SP/M/VS; Swmg (V L); Tennis (V L); Cl Off (T); CR (R); Sch Ppr (E); Acceptance to the SVSM Program; Acceptance to the NC School of Science & Mathematics; Biomedical Engineering; Duke U; Worcester Polytechnic Institute

WAGGLE, MELANIE L; ELIZABETH CTY, NC; PASQUOTANK CTY HS; (FR); Ctznshp Aw; Hnr Roll; Otst Ac Ach Awd; Sci Fairs; Chrch Yth Grp; Off Aide; Tchrs Aide; Chrldg (J); Sftball (J); Obstetrics/Pediatrics; Doctorate Degree; Florida State U; U of North Carolina Chapel Hill

WAGONER, ERIN M; ARCHDALE, NC; TRINITY HS; (JR); All Am Sch; Hi Hnr Roll; Jr Mshl; MVP; WWAHSS; Comm Volntr; Chrch Yth Grp; Drma Clb; Emplmnt; HO'Br Yth Ldrshp; MuAlphaTh; Ntl Beta Clb; French Clb; Chr; SP/M/VS; Tennis (V); Cl Off (S); 2004 HOBY Ambassador; Broadcast Communications; International Studies; Elon U

WAGSTAFF, CHRIS; DURHAM, NC; RIVERSIDE HS; (SO); Hnr Roll; Kwnis Aw; Comm Volntr; Speak Spanish and German; Junior Civitan Club; Architectural Degree; Criminal Justice; Virginia Commonwealth U; North Carolina State U

WAHAB, EMMA; BATH, NC; NORTHSIDE HS; (JR); Hnr Roll; Jr Mshl; Sci/Math Olympn; WWAHSS; Comm Volntr; Spec Olymp Vol; Chrch Yth Grp; Key Club; Ntl Beta Clb; Sci Clb; SADD; Bnd; Jzz Bnd; Mch Bnd; Orch; Cr Ctry (J); Sftball (J); Track (J); Cl Off (T); Volunteering; Re-Enacting; Military Officer; Foreign Affairs Major; NC State U; West Point Military Academy

WALKER, CHRISTOPHER J; GASTONIA, NC; NORTH GASTON HS; (SO); Hnr Roll; USAA; Ftball (V); Wt Lftg (V); Athletic Trainer; Physical Therapy Sports Medicine; UNC-Chapel Hill; UNC-Charlotte

WALKER, KAYLA J; RALEIGH, NC; MILLBROOK HS; (MS); Hnr Roll; Otst Ac Ach Awd; Bnd; Orch; Pediatric Doctor; Nursing; New York U; U of North Carolina Chapel Hill

WALKER, KRYSTINA M; GOLDSBORO, NC; SPRING CREEK HS; (SO); Hi Hnr Roll; Kwnis Aw; Nat Hon Sy; Otst Ac Ach Awd; Comm Volntr; Peer Tut/Med; ArtClub; Chrch Yth Grp; Quiz Bowl; Chr; Ch Chr; Swg Chr; Adv Cncl (R); Yrbk (E, R, P); Published in 2004 Wayne Collection; A Prudential Spirit of Community Honoree; Pre-Med; Pre Law; U of North Carolina At Chapel Hill; Elon College

WALKER, MARTHA A; WILMINGTON, NC; E A LANEY HS; (SO); Hi Hnr Roll; Otst Ac Ach Awd; Perf Att; Pres Ac Ftns Aw; WWAHSS; Comm Volntr; Peer Tut/Med; Red Cr Aide; Chrch Yth Grp; DARE; Key Club; Ntl Beta Clb; Off Aide; Tchrs Aide; Ch Chr; Dnce; Chrldg (J); HOSA; Bible Club - Vice President; Pediatrician; Pathologist; UNC Wilmington; UNC Chapel Hill

WALKER-WHITE, MICANDRA; FAYETTEVILLE, NC; DOUGLAS BYRD HS; (SO); Drma Clb; SP/M/VS; French Team; Graphic Designer; Cosmetologist; UNC-Chapel Hill; UNC-Pembroke

WALL, KALEB; GREENSBORO, NC; GRIMSLEY HS; (FR); Hnr Roll; Perf Att; Bskball; Ftball (J); Track (V); Wt Lftg (J); Law School Juris Doctorate; Master's in English; U of North Carolina Chapel Hill; U of Miami Florida

WALL, KENDRA D; WADESBORO, NC; ANSON HS; (FR); Hnr Roll; St of Mnth; Peer Tut/Med; Chrch Yth Grp; Chr; Ch Chr; SP/M/VS; Best Student Award; 2 Parliamentary Procedure Trophies; Pediatrician; Duke U; Shaw U

WALL, LACIE J; NEW LONDON, NC; NORTH STANLY HS; (FR); Hnr Roll; Perf Att; Sci Fairs; DARE; Dbte Team; Emplmnt; Spch Team; Bnd; Ch Chr; Mch Bnd; Pep Bnd; Swmg (V); Tennis (V); Stu Cncl (S); First Place Grand Supreme in the Miss Stanly County Pageant; First Place American Royalty; Court Justice; Duke U; North Carolina State U

WALLACE, ALYSEN; CHARLOTTE, NC; HARDING UNIVERSITY HS; (JR); Duke TS; F Lan Hn Soc; Hi Hnr Roll; Jr Mshl; Nat Hon Sy; WWAHSS; Comm Volntr; Chrch Yth Grp; Drma Clb; Photog; Sci Clb; German Clb; Ch Chr; SP/M/VS; Stg Cre; Track; Cl Off (R); Yrbk (P); National Honor Society President; Junior Marshal; Dentistry (Orthodontist); Psychology; Davidson College; North Carolina State U

WALLACE, BRADLEY S; KANNAPOLIS, NC; AL BROWN HS; (JR); All Am Sch; Ctznshp Aw; Hi Hnr Roll; Hnr Roll; Perf Att; St of Mnth; Comm Volntr; Chess; Chrch Yth Grp; DARE; Bnd; Jzz Bnd; Mch Bnd; Pep Bnd; Tennis; Wrstlg; Band Section Leader; Honor Roll; Mechanical Engineering; North Carolina State U

WALSH, MOLLY ELIZABETH; HIGH POINT, NC; HIGH POINT CTRL HS; (SO); Hi Hnr Roll; Comm Volntr; Peer Tut/Med; ArtClub; Key Club; Prom Com; Scouts; Spanish Clb; Dnce; SP/M/VS; Vllyball (V L); Cl Off (T, R); CR (R); Sch Ppr (R); Red Cross Club; Marine Biology

WALTERS, ELIZABETH; FAIRMONT, NC; LUMBERTON HS; (FR); FCA; Ntl Beta Clb; Cr Ctry; Superintendent's Academic Award; Broadcast Journalism; Interior Design; North Carolina State U; U of NC Chapel Hill

WALTERS, JOSHUA; DENVER, NC; EAST LINCOLN HS; (SR); Perf Att; Comm Volntr; Emplmnt; Ntl FFA; Scouts; Completed EMT Training State Certified; Fire Fighter; Paramedic; Gaston College

WALTON, CCIERA; MIDWAY PARK, NC; WHITE OAK HS; (MS); Hnr Roll; Perf Att; St of Mnth; Bnd; Mch Bnd; Pep Bnd; Accelerated Reader

WALTON, SHAUNTIA; LUMBERTON, NC; LUMBERTON HS; (FR); Hnr Roll; Comm Volntr; Ch Chr; Upward Bound Highest Points Award; Design Arts; Health Sciences; U of North Carolina At Chapel Hill; East Carolina U

Walker, Martha A
E A Laney HS
Wilmington, NC

Vinkler, John J
Charlotte Catholic HS
Waxhaw, NC

Villagomez, Amy
Asheboro HS
Asheboro, NC

National
Honor Roll
Spring 2005

Vegerano, Joey
West Forsyth HS
Winston Salem, NC

Waggle, Melanie L
Pasquotank Cty HS
Elizabeth Cty, NC

Wall, Lacie J
North Stanly HS
New London, NC

WALTON, TANEISHA; LUMBERTON, NC; LUMBERTON HS; (SR); Hnr Roll; St Schl; WWAHSS; Yth Ldrshp Prog; Emplmnt; Dnce; Mch Bnd; Performed in Dance Concerts; Section Leader in Marching Band - 2 Years; Fayetteville State U

WAND, LAUREN; HUNTERSVILLE, NC; HOPEWELL HS; (JR); Hnr Roll; Nat Hon Sy; WWAHSS; Comm Volntr; Jr Cls League; Ntl Beta Clb; Svce Clb; Spanish Clb; Swmg (V); In Top 10% of Class; Nutritionist; Clemson U; U of North Carolina At Chapel Hill

WANG, HENGYUN; CHARLOTTE, NC; MYERS PARK HS; (SO); Duke TS; Hi Hnr Roll; Hnr Roll; MVP; Nat Hon Sy; Otst Ac Ach Awd; WWAHSS; Comm Volntr; Chess; DARE; Dbte Team; Mth Clb/Tm; Sci Clb; Ftball (J L); Swmg (VJCL); Winner of Honorable Mention At State Math Contest; International Baccalaureate Program Candidate; Medical; Business; Duke U; U of Pennsylvania

WANI, NILESH B; RALEIGH, NC; CARY AC; (SO); Duke TS; Hnr Roll; Otst Ac Ach Awd; WWAHSS; Comm Volntr; Key Club; Lib Aide; Tennis (JC); JV Tennis 2005 Sportsmanship Award; Chemistry; Duke U; U of North Carolina Chapel Hill

WANSKER, ROB; CHARLOTTE, NC; CHARLOTTE CHRISTIAN SCH; (FR); Duke TS; Hnr Roll; Perf Att; Sci/Math Olympn; Comm Volntr; Chess; Chrch Yth Grp; Bnd; Pep Bnd; Ftball (J); Golf (J); Wt Lftg; Gold Standard for Volunteer Hours; Astronomy; History; Wake Forest U; Bowling Green State U

WARD, DARREN T; GOLDSBORO, NC; EASTERN WAYNE HS; (SR); Hnr Roll; MVP; St of Mnth; Comm Volntr; DECA; Prom Com; Vsity Clb; Foreign Clb; Ch Chr; Bskball (V); Vsy Clb (V); Occupational Therapy; Criminal Justice; East Carolina U (Accepted)

WARD, DAVIDA; RAEFORD, NC; HOKE CTY HS; (JR); Hi Hnr Roll; Hnr Roll; Jr Mshl; Nat Mrt Fin; Otst Ac Ach Awd; Pres Sch; St Schl; Peer Tut/Med; Chrch Yth Grp; Drma Clb; FBLA; SADD; Dnce; SP/M/VS; Competed in Various Talent Shows; 3rd Place National Step Team Champions; Accounting; Theatre Arts; Catawba College; U of North Carolina At Greensboro

WARD, NICHOLAS; SHALLOTTE, NC; WEST BRUNSWICK HS; (SO); 4H Awd; Duke TS; Hi Hnr Roll; Nat Hon Sy; Sci/Math Olympn; USAA; WWAHSS; Comm Volntr; 4-H; Chess; Chrch Yth Grp; Dbte Team; Emplmnt; Sci Clb; SADD; Tennis (V L); CR (R); Sch Ppr (R); Yrbk (E); Regional & State Science Olympiad Winner; Optometry; Engineering

WARF, LINDLEY R; WALKERTOWN, NC; EAST FORSYTH HS; (SO); Hi Hnr Roll; Hnr Roll; Comm Volntr; Chrch Yth Grp; Emplmnt; Chrldg (J); June 05-Will Go on Romania Mission Trip; International Relations; Political Science; NC State College; U of Kentucky

WARFIELD, CAITLAND; CANDLER, NC; ERIKA HS; (JR); Hi Hnr Roll; Nat Hon Sy; Otst Ac Ach Awd; WWAHSS; Peer Tut/Med; Emplmnt; FCA; Ntl Beta Clb; ROTC; Spanish Clb; Chrldg (V); Sccr (V); Wt Lftg (V); State Champions-Cheerleading Squad; Law; Dental Hygiene/Dentistry; U, Tennessee-Knoxville; AB Tech

WARING, MATTHEW D; WADESBORO, NC; ANSON HS; (SR); Hnr Roll; Perf Att; WWAHSS; Quiz Bowl; Architecture; Interior Design; U of Virginia; North Carolina State U

WARNER, CHANDLER; REIDSVILLE, NC; ROCKINGHAM CTY HS; (SO); Duke TS; Hi Hnr Roll; Hnr Roll; Otst Ac Ach Awd; Perf Att; Chrch Yth Grp; Emplmnt; FCA; Key Club; Mus Clb; Ntl Beta Clb; Scouts; Bnd; Mch Bnd; Pep Bnd; Bsball (J); Environmental Engineering; Natural Resources; Duke U; North Carolina State U

WARREN, ANDREA; OXFORD, NC; J F WEBB HS; (JR); 4H Awd; Perf Att; WWAHSS; Hosp Aide; 4-H; Chrch Yth Grp; DARE; Ntl FFA; Scouts; SADD; Orch; SP/M/VS; Hsbk Rdg; Perfect Attendance; Veterinarian; Pharmacist; North Carolina State U; Vance Granville Community College

WARREN, CHELSEA; RALEIGH, NC; ATHENS DRIVE HS; (SO); Hnr Roll; St of Mnth; Emplmnt; Key Club; Ntl Beta Clb; P to P St Amb Prg; Spanish Clb; Lcrsse (V); Stu Cncl (R); U of North Carolina-Chapel Hill; North Carolina State U

WARREN, DARRYL; MERRY HILL, NC; BERTIE HS; (JR); Perf Att; WWAHSS; Emplmnt; Prom Com; Bnd; Ch Chr; Mch Bnd; Computer Science; Mass Communication; North Carolina A & T State U; Shaw University

WARREN, JENNIFER; KINSTON, NC; KINSTON HS; (SO); Duke TS; Hnr Roll; WWAHSS; Yth Ldrshp Prog; Comm Volntr; Hosp Aide; ArtClub; Drma Clb; Quiz Bowl; Svce Clb; French Clb; Dnce; Sccr (V); Anchor Club-Vice President; French Club-Historian; Elementary Education; Photography; U of North Carolina; Duke U

WARSHAW, BRITTANY L; LINCOLNTON, NC; NI LINCOLN HS; (JR); Hi Hnr Roll; Hnr Roll; Perf Att; St of Mnth; Comm Volntr; Hosp Aide; Peer Tut/Med; ArtClub; Chrch Yth Grp; DARE; Dbte Team; Drma Clb; Photog; Prom Com; Ch Chr; Dnce; SP/M/VS; Gmnstcs (V); CR (R); Sch Ppr (R, P); Education; Psychology; North Carolina State U; U of North Carolina-Charlotte

WASHINGTON, CASSANDRA R; DUNN, NC; TRITON HS; (SO); Hnr Roll; Perf Att; WWAHSS; Yth Ldrshp Prog; Comm Volntr; Spec Olymp Vol; Chrch Yth Grp; DARE; Drma Clb; FBLA; ROTC; Scouts; Chr; Ch Chr; Drl Tm; SP/M/VS; Big Brother, Big Sister; Law; A & T U; East Carolina U

WASHINGTON, JESSICA L; RALEIGH, NC; WILLIAM G ENLOE HS; (JR); Hnr Roll; Pres Ac Ftns Aw; Clr Grd; Dnce; Sccr (V CL); CR; Girl Scout Silver Award; Journalism; Pre-Law

WASHINGTON, TREY A; NEW LONDON, NC; NORTH STANLY HS; (JR); Ctznshp Aw; Hi Hnr Roll; Hnr Roll; Jr Mshl; Nat Hon Sy; Otst Ac Ach Awd; Comm Volntr; Bskball (VJC); Ftball (VJ); Wt Lftg (VJ); Engineering; Business/Management; U of North Carolina-Chapel Hill; North Carolina State U

WATKINS, DOMINIQUE; GREENSBORO, NC; DUDLEY HS; (JR); Hnr Roll; Nat Hon Sy; Sci Fairs; St of Mnth; WWAHSS; Chrch Yth Grp; Stu Cncl (R); Yrbk (P); Biology; Nursing; U of North Carolina (Chapel Hill); NC A & T State U

WATKINS, LAMAR R; FOREST CITY, NC; EAST RUTHERFORD HS; (FR); Hnr Roll; Pres Ac Ftns Aw; WWAHSS; Yth Ldrshp Prog; Comm Volntr; Hab For Humty Volntr; Peer Tut/Med; FBLA; Key Club; Tchrs Aide; Bskball (VJ); Track (V); Wt Lftg (V); Adv Cncl (R); Cl Off (P); Stu Cncl (R); CR (P); Yrbk (R, P); House of Representatives Page; Business; Engineering; Duke U; U of North Carolina

WATKINS, WILLIAM; BREVARD, NC; BREVARD HS; (FR); Hnr Roll; Computer Technology; Business; Duke U; Clemson U

WATLINGTON, ASHLEY L; GREENSBORO, NC; DUDLEY HS; (SO); Hnr Roll; Otst Ac Ach Awd; Perf Att; St of Mnth; Yth Ldrshp Prog; Comm Volntr; Peer Tut/Med; DECA; Mth Clb/Tm; ROTC; Mch Bnd; Pep Bnd; Sftball (V); Cl Off; MS Sophomore; Corporate Law; International Business

WATSON, CAMERON; SALISBURY, NC; NORTH ROWAN HS; (SO); Ctznshp Aw; Duke TS; Hnr Roll; MVP; Perf Att; Yth Ldrshp Prog; Comm Volntr; Peer Tut/Med; Chrch Yth Grp; DARE; Emplmnt; Wdwrkg Clb; Bnd; Ch Chr; Pep Bnd; Bsball (V); Ftball (V); Skt Tgt Sh (V); Wt Lftg (V); Wrstlg (V); Stu Cncl (R); Leadership Rowan; Service Above Self Award; Business Degree; Computer Systems Manager; Duke U; U of North Carolina, Chapel Hill

WATSON, JAMES H; RALEIGH, NC; WAKEFIELD HS; (JR); Hnr Roll; Tchrs Aide; Bskball (V CL); Lamp of Knowledge; Business; U of North Carolina; U of North Carolina At Wilmington

WATSON, JESSICA; LENOIR, NC; HIBRITEN HS; (FR); Duke TS; Hnr Roll; Nat Hon Sy; Comm Volntr; Chrch Yth Grp; Key Club; Bnd; Ch Chr; Flg Crps; Pep Bnd; Missions Work

WATSON, MARCUS; WILMINGTON, NC; NEW HANOVER HS; (SO); Hnr Roll; Perf Att; ROTC; Drl Tm; Track; Entrepreneur; North Carolina State U

WATSON, MATTHEW C; BAILEY, NC; SOUTHERN NASH HS; (FR); Hnr Roll; Chrch Yth Grp; Bsball (J); Ftball (J); Wrstlg (V); Sports Medicine; East Carolina U

WATSON, MICHELE; MT AIRY, NC; MT AIRY HS; (SO); Hi Hnr Roll; Hnr Roll; Otst Ac Ach Awd; Perf Att; St of Mnth; Peer Tut/Med; Red Cr Aide; Spec Olymp Vol; DARE; Key Club; SADD; Ch Chr; Nurse; Therapist; U of North Carolina; North Carolina State U

WATSON, STEPHEN; JACKSONVILLE, NC; JACKSONVILLE HS; (SO); Hi Hnr Roll; St of Mnth; Comm Volntr; Peer Tut/Med; Pep Squd; Vsity Clb; Bskball (J); Business; Communications; UNC; UNCC

WATTERSON, MARY C; WILSON, NC; JAMES B HUNT HS; (SO); Hi Hnr Roll; Hnr Roll; WWAHSS; FCA; Key Club; Golf (V); Optimist Oratorical Contest Winner; Political Science; American History; North Carolina State U; U of North Carolina At Greenboro

WATTS, JESSICA; HICKORY, NC; HICKORY HS; (SO); Hnr Roll; Hosp Aide; Chrch Yth Grp; Key Club; Ntl Beta Clb; Prom Com; PhD in Psychology

WATTS, J T; ASHEVILLE, NC; ASHEVILLE HS; (SR); Ctznshp Aw; F Lan Hn Soc; Hnr Roll; Nat Hon Sy; Nat Mrt LOC; Otst Ac Ach Awd; WWAHSS; Comm Volntr; Chrch Yth Grp; Drma Clb; Jr Cls League; Acpl Chr; Chr; SP/M/VS; Stg Cre; Outstanding Graphic Design; Top 5 Percentile - National Latin Exam; Technical Theatre; Classical Languages; U of North Carolina Asheville; Brevard College

WAYMAN, LOVANNA A; STANFIELD, NC; WEST STANLY HS; (SR); Ctznshp Aw; Hnr Roll; St of Mnth; WWAHSS; DARE; Drma Clb; Kwanza Clb; Ntl FFA; SP/M/VS; Stg Cre; CR (P); Yrbk

WEAR, SUSIE E; SALISBURY, NC; SALISBURY HS; (FR); Hi Hnr Roll; Pres Ac Ftns Aw; Yth Ldrshp Prog; Comm Volntr; Chrch Yth Grp; Key Club; Pep Squd; Sccr (V); Swmg (V); Tennis (V); Representative to Youth Legislative Assembly in Raleigh; All Central Carolina Conference Swimmer; Law; Medicine; UNC Chapel Hill; Duke U

WEATHERLY, AMANDA; KITTY HAWK, NC; FIRST FLIGHT HS; (SO); Hi Hnr Roll; St of Mnth; FTA; Key Club; Spanish Clb; Teen Court; Teen Talk Hotline; Teaching; Wake Forest

WEATHERS, JESSICA H; GASTONIA, NC; ASHBROOK HS; (SR); Hnr Roll; Comm Volntr; Chrch Yth Grp; Emplmnt; Mus Clb; Pep Squd; Chr; Dnce; Chrldg (VJ); Dance Team; Civinettes; Nursing; U of North Carolina Charlotte

WEAVER, LAUREN; OAK RIDGE, NC; NORTHWEST HS; (SR); Hnr Roll; Nat Hon Sy; Sci/Math Olympn; WWAHSS; Yth Ldrshp Prog; Hab For Humty Volntr; Peer Tut/Med; Chrch Yth Grp; DARE; FCA; Jr Ach; Svce Clb; Ch Chr; National Honor Society (2 Years); 3 1st Place Medals in Science Olympiad; Chemistry; Physics; U of North Carolina At Greensboro

WEAVER, RACHEL MARIE; RUTHERFORDTON, NC; R S CTRL HS; (FR); Hnr Roll; Comm Volntr; DARE; FBLA; Ch Chr; Business Law; Doctor; Harvard Law School; UNC

WEAVER, SARA; CHINA GROVE, NC; SOUTH ROWAN HS; (JR); Hnr Roll; Nat Hon Sy; St of Mnth; WWAHSS; Comm Volntr; Peer Tut/Med; Red Cr Aide; ArtClub; Emplmnt; FCA; Lib Aide; Off Aide; Prom Com; Svce Clb; Spanish Clb; Cl Off (T); Stu Cncl (V); Journalism; Political Science; U of NC At Chapel Hill; College of Charleston

WEBB, BARRY J; CHARLOTTE, NC; GARINGER SR HS; (JR); Hnr Roll; MVP; Otst Ac Ach Awd; Perf Att; St of Mnth; WWAHSS; Comm Volntr; Emplmnt; Bsball (V); Bskball (V); Ftball (V); Bacteriology; Environmental Science; North Carolina State U; U of North Carolina At Wilmington

WEBB, DIESHIA L; GASTON, NC; NORTHAMPTON CTY HS WEST; (FR); Hnr Roll; Nat Hon Sy; St of Mnth; Comm Volntr; Peer Tut/Med; Chrch Yth Grp; DARE; Photog; Chr; Ch Chr; Sch Ppr (P); Yrbk (P); Miss Teen Bee Pageant Winner; Child Psychology; English Teacher; Miami U; Penn State U

WEBB, RACHEL; WILSON, NC; HUNT HS; (SO); Hi Hnr Roll; Hnr Roll; MVP; Sci Fairs; Comm Volntr; Hab For Humty Volntr; Spec Olymp Vol; Chrch Yth Grp; Emplmnt; FCA; Key Club; Mod UN; Pep Squd; Sci Clb; Ch Chr; Chrldg (V L); CR (R); Physical Therapy; Interior Design; NC State U; Barton College

WEBER, ZEBULON C; STATESVILLE, NC; STATESVILLE HS; (JR); Comm Volntr; Law Enforcement; Military

WEEKLY, ASHLEY; MONROE, NC; SUN VALLEY MS; (MS); Hnr Roll; Otst Ac Ach Awd; Comm Volntr; Ntl Beta Clb; Pep Squd; West Virginia U; UNC Chapel Hill

WEEKS, BRITTANY; CLINTON, NC; CLINTON HS; (JR); Duke TS; Hi Hnr Roll; Jr Mshl; WWAHSS; Yth Ldrshp Prog; Hosp Aide; Spec Olymp Vol; Chrch Yth Grp; Jr Cls League; Key Club; Ntl Beta Clb; Prom Com; Scouts; Bnd; Clr Grd; Dnce; Mch Bnd; Sccr (V L); Cl Off (R); Sch Ppr (E); Church Youth Handbell Choir; Governor's School Nominee in Academics & Dance; Biology; Pre-Med; U of North Carolina Chapel Hill; Wake Forest U

WEEKS, JUSTINE; BRYSON CITY, NC; SWAIN CTY HS; (FR); Hnr Roll; Comm Volntr; Peer Tut/Med; Chrch Yth Grp; Yrbk (P); New Century Scholar; RN; Southwestern Co College; Western North Carolina U

WEEKS, MICHAEL F; RALEIGH, NC; CARY AC; (JR); Hnr Roll; Dbte Team; Key Club; Bnd; Wrstlg (V)

WEEKS, NICK; DUNN, NC; TRITON HS; (FR); Duke TS; Hi Hnr Roll; MVP; Otst Ac Ach Awd; Perf Att; Sci/Math Olympn; Comm Volntr; DARE; Mus Clb; Vsity Clb; Chr; Swg Chr; Ftball (J); Lcrsse (V); Wt Lftg (J); Architecture; Teaching; U of North Carolina; U of Miami

WEEKS, TAYLOR L; HOPE MILLS, NC; MASSEY HILL CLASSICAL HS; (SO); Perf Att; WWAHSS; Chrch Yth Grp; Chr; Ch Chr; Dnce; Fayetteville State U

WEEKS, WHITNEY S; RALEIGH, NC; CARY AC; (FR); Hnr Roll; Key Club; Bnd

WEINER, RACHEL E; CHARLOTTE, NC; ZEBULON VANCE HS; (SR); Duke TS; Hi Hnr Roll; Jr Mshl; Nat Hon Sy; Nat Mrt Sch Recip; Perf Att; Salutrn; WWAHSS; Hab For Humty Volntr; ArtClub; Emplmnt; Key Club; Cr Ctry (V L); Swmg (V CL); Track (V L); Swimming-Cougar Award; Physics; Environmental Science; UNC-Chapel Hill

WELCH, ABBY D; GASTONIA, NC; FORESTVIEW HS; (FR); Ctznshp Aw; Hnr Roll; Nat Hon Sy; Peer Tut/Med; Chrch Yth Grp; DARE; Chr; Ch Chr; Dnce; Stu Cncl (R); CR (R); Teacher; Teacher's Assistant; Western Carolina U; UNC Charlotte

WELCH, KATHLEEN T; GREENSBORO, NC; NORTHWEST HS; (SR); Ctznshp Aw; Duke TS; Hi Hnr Roll; Nat Hon Sy; WWAHSS; ArtClub; Cmptr Clb; Emplmnt; Svce Clb; Ch Chr; 3rd State Skills USA 3-D Animation and Computer Visualization; 1st in State-We the People Competition; Early Childhood Teacher; Graphic Arts; East Carolina U; Appalachian State U

WELKER, BRANDI; CANTON, NC; PISGAH HS; (FR); Hnr Roll; DARE; Dnce; Teacher; Doctor; Western Carolina U

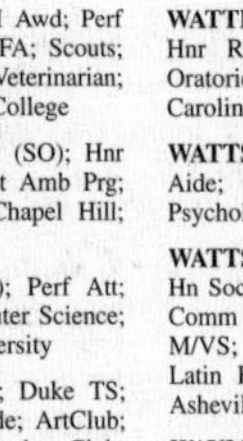

Watkins, Lamar R
East Rutherford HS
Forest City, NC

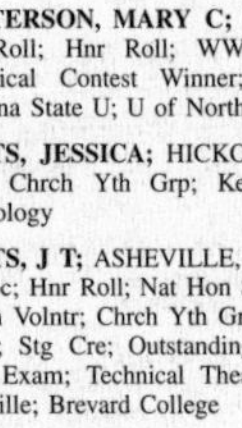

Washington, Cassandra R
Triton HS
Dunn, NC

National
Honor Roll
Spring 2005

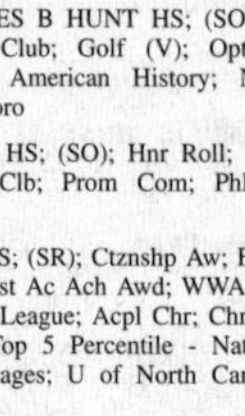

Waring, Matthew D
Anson HS
Wadesboro, NC

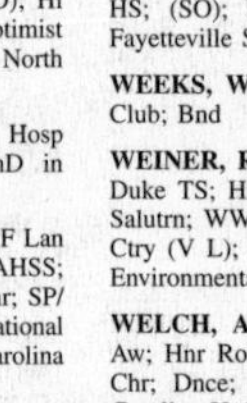

Weaver, Rachel Marie
R S Ctrl HS
Rutherfordton, NC

WELLER, PATRICE; WASHINGTON, NC; NORTHSIDE HS; (FR); Hi Hnr Roll; Otst Ac Ach Awd; Perf Att; Salutrn; WWAHSS; Chrch Yth Grp; Drma Clb; Key Club; Mth Clb/Tm; Ntl Beta Clb; Scouts; Ch Chr; SP/M/VS; Chrldg (V); Prezell R. Robinson Scholar; Mathematics State Finals; Latin American Studies; Education; North Carolina State U; U of North Carolina

WELLINGTON, DOMINIQUE S; GOLDSBORO, NC; GOLDSBORO HS; (SO); 4H Awd; Hnr Roll; Nat Hon Sy; Otst Ac Ach Awd; Perf Att; Comm Volntr; Peer Tut/Med; 4-H; Chrch Yth Grp; Drma Clb; Prom Com; Bnd; Clr Grd; Dnce; SP/M/VS; Chrldg (V); Track (V); Cl Off (T); Nursing; Business; U of North Carolina Greensboro; North Carolina Central U

WENGER, SAMANTHA; HOPE MILLS, NC; GRAYS CREEK HS; (FR); Chrch Yth Grp; Bnd; Ch Chr; Mch Bnd; Chrldg (JC); Cheer Dynamics Competitive Team; Doctorate in Neuroscience; Baylor U; Rice U

WERLINE, MADISON; GREENSBORO, NC; WESTERN GUILFORD HS; (JR); Hnr Roll; Nat Hon Sy; Otst Ac Ach Awd; Comm Volntr; Hab For Humty Volntr; Spec Olymp Vol; ArtClub; Chrch Yth Grp; Ntl Beta Clb; Bnd; Mch Bnd; Tennis (V L); All-County Band, Outstanding Band Member; National Honor Society, Beta Club Art Honor Society; Music Therapy; Psychology; Appalachian State U; Transylvania U

WERTH, GEOFFREY; SPRUCE PINE, NC; AVERY CTY HS; (SR); Ftball (VJCL); Track (V); United In Christ - Club Leader; North Carolina State

WEST, DWAN; AHOSKIE, NC; BERTIE HS; (JR); Ctznshp Aw; Hnr Roll; Otst Ac Ach Awd; Perf Att; WWAHSS; Chrch Yth Grp; Jr Ach; Mth Clb/Tm; Tech Clb; Chr; Ch Chr; Bskball (V); Cl Off (P); Yrbk (E); Highest Average in Math, US History, English, Science; Most Improved; Become an Engineer; Become a Basketball Player; Elizabeth City Stay U; Old Dominion U

WEST, KELLY; ASHEVILLE, NC; CAROLINA DAY SCH; (JR); Hnr Roll; Otst Ac Ach Awd; Yth Ldrshp Prog; Comm Volntr; Spec Olymp Vol; Chess; Chrch Yth Grp; Emplmnt; FCA; Prom Com; Svce Clb; Chr; SP/M/VS; Chrldg (V); Scr Kpr; Sccr (J); Vllyball (VJ); Yrbk (P); Roots & Shoots Club; Volunteer at the Y for Y Leaders; Restaurant / Food Services Management; Interior Design; North Carolina State U; College of Charleston

WEST, TERRICA V; NEW BERN, NC; WEST CRAVEN HS; (SO); Chrch Yth Grp; DARE; Drma Clb; Mus Clb; Dnce; Vllyball (J); I'm About to Win Track Next Week; Acting/Modeling; Interior Designer/Lawyer; Join Navy/ Agriculture & Technology; Fayetteville State, State U

WESTBROOK, VICTOR; CASTLE HAYNE, NC; E A LANEY HS; (FR); Ctznshp Aw; Duke TS; Hi Hnr Roll; Nat Hon Sy; Otst Ac Ach Awd; Perf Att; Pres Sch; Comm Volntr; Civil Air Pat; Civil Air Patrol; Computer Engineering

WHAREY, KELLY; RALEIGH, NC; SOUTHEAST RALEIGH MAGNET HS; (JR); Hnr Roll; Comm Volntr; Peer Tut/Med; Emplmnt; Key Club; Chr; Key Club; Biologist; Physicist; North Carolina State U; U of North Carolina Chapel Hill

WHEATLEY, REBECCA; EDEN, NC; MOREHEAD HS; (SR); Hnr Roll; WWAHSS; DARE; DECA; Emplmnt; Nursing Degree; Rockingham Community College; Guilford Technical College

WHISENANT, ANDREW K; SALISBURY, NC; SALISBURY HS; (JR); Ctznshp Aw; Hnr Roll; Nat Hon Sy; WWAHSS; Comm Volntr; AL Aux Boys; Chrch Yth Grp; Emplmnt; Key Club; Mus Clb; Quiz Bowl; Scouts; Bnd; Ch Chr; Jzz Bnd; Mch Bnd; CR (R); Eagle Scout; County Spelling Bee Champion; History / Political Science; UNC Chapel Hill; Wingate U

WHISENANT, MEGAN R; HORSE SHOE, NC; ROSMAN HS; (FR); Hnr Roll; MVP; Pres Sch; Sci Fairs; WWAHSS; Chr; Chrldg (J); Pediatric Medical Doctor; Specialist Nurse; Duke U; UNC Chapel Hill

WHISNANT, BRANDON; LENOIR, NC; WEST CALDWELL HS; (FR); Hnr Roll; St of Mnth; Architecture; Engineering; Georgia Tech; U of North Carolina Charlotte

WHISNANT, NICHOLAS R; LEXINGTON, NC; LEXINGTON SR HS; Chr; Neurosurgeon; U of Miami; Florida State U

WHISNANT, ROBIN A; SOUTHPORT, NC; SOUTH BRUNSWICK HS; (FR); Hnr Roll; Comm Volntr; DARE; ROTC; Bnd; Chr; Clr Grd; Dnce; Movie Director; UNCW; UNC

WHITAKER, TERRY; ROCKY MOUNT, NC; NASH CTRL HS; St of Mnth; Bnd

WHITE, ASHLAND H T; FAYETTEVILLE, NC; GRAY'S CREEK HS; (SO); Chrch Yth Grp; DARE; Key Club; Ntl FFA; Vsity Clb; Dnce; Chrldg (VJ L); Vsy Clb (J); Vllyball (J); Best All Around (Cheer Ltd. Summer Camp); Veterinarian; Marine Biologist; North Carolina State U; East Carolina U

WHITE, BRITTANY; CHARLOTTE, NC; WEST CHARLOTTE HS; (JR); Hnr Roll; WWAHSS; Peer Tut/Med; DARE; Ch Chr; Scr Kpr (V); Who's Who Among American High School Students; Criminal Law; Psychology; Duke U; UNCC

WHITE, JAMIE L; CHARLOTTE, NC; WEST MECKLENBURG HS; (FR); Ctznshp Aw; Hi Hnr Roll; Hnr Roll; MVP; Otst Ac Ach Awd; Perf Att; St of Mnth; Peer Tut/Med; Chrch Yth Grp; FBLA; Chrldg (J); Track (J); Pediatrician; Lawyer; Howard U

WHITE, KATHRYN E; CHAPEL HILL, NC; WOODS CHARTER SCH; (SO); Hnr Roll; Sci Fairs; Comm Volntr; Peer Tut/Med; Photog; Scouts; Tchrs Aide; Adv Cncl; Mathematics; Computer; Appalachian State U; UNC-Asheville

WHITE, KIMBERLY M; AULANDER, NC; BERTIE HS; (JR); Hnr Roll; WWAHSS; Comm Volntr; Spec Olymp Vol; FBLA; Bnd; Mch Bnd; Chrldg; Master's Degree in Business; Start Own Business; North Carolina State U; U of North Carolina Greensboro

WHITE, MARCUS R; CLINTON, NC; CLINTON HS; (JR); 4H Awd; Hi Hnr Roll; Jr Mshl; Otst Ac Ach Awd; Perf Att; Sci Fairs; WWAHSS; Yth Ldrshp Prog; Comm Volntr; Peer Tut/Med; Spec Olymp Vol; 4-H; Chess; Chrch Yth Grp; Emplmnt; FCA; FBLA; FTA; JSA; Bnd; Ch Chr; Dnce; Drl Tm; Chrldg (V); Cr Ctry (V L); PPSqd (V); Track (V); Adv Cncl; Cl Off (R); Teen Court; Rotary Conference; Law / History; Fine Arts / Business; U of North Carolina Chapel Hill; U of Georgia

WHITE, MELISSA M; JACKSONVILLE, NC; SOUTHWEST HS; (SO); Hnr Roll; Comm Volntr; Track (J); Medical Major; Modeling/Fashion; North Carolina A & T U; U of North Carolina At Chapel Hill

WHITE, SARAH E; GREENSBORO, NC; PAGE HS; (JR); Hi Hnr Roll; Hnr Roll; Otst Ac Ach Awd; Sci/Math Olympn; Chrch Yth Grp; DARE; FCA; High School Teacher; Psychologist; Guilford College

WHITE, TYESHA M; TARBORO, NC; TARBORO HS; (FR); 4H Awd; Hnr Roll; USAA; Comm Volntr; Hosp Aide; 4-H; Chrch Yth Grp; Ntl Beta Clb; Japanese Clb; Ch Chr; International Studies; North Carolina State U; East Carolina U

WHITEHEAD, KYLA; SCOTLAND NECK, NC; SOUTHEAST HALIFAX HS; (FR); Hnr Roll; Michigan State; Florida State

WHITEHURST, BRITTANY N; ROCKY MOUNT, NC; NASH CTRL HS; (JR); Hnr Roll; Perf Att; Yth Ldrshp Prog; Hab For Humty Volntr; Chess; Chrch Yth Grp; Drma Clb; FCA; FTA; Prom Com; Ch Chr; SP/M/VS; Swmg (V); High School English Teacher; Drama; U of North Carolina Chapel Hill; North Carolina State U

WHITE JR, MARK E; GREENVILLE, NC; SOUTH CTRL HS; (SR); Nat Mrt Semif; WWAHSS; Comm Volntr; Emplmnt; FBLA; Ftball (J); Choices (Minority Club); Pre-Law; PhD; San Jose State U; East Carolina U

WHITLEY, JUSTIN; WILSON, NC; JAMES B. HUNT HS; (SR); 4H Awd; Duke TS; Hi Hnr Roll; Otst Ac Ach Awd; Pres Sch; Sci/Math Olympn; Comm Volntr; 4-H; Chrch Yth Grp; FCA; FBLA; Key Club; Ntl FFA; Prom Com; Sci Clb; Skt Tgt Sh; Graduation Marshal; Member of Academic Excellence Society; To Be a Veterinarian; North Carolina State U

WHITMORE, JORY; DENVER, NC; EAST LINCOLN HS; (SO); Hnr Roll; Chess; Chrch Yth Grp; Mth Clb/Tm; Quiz Bowl; Scouts; Bnd; Mch Bnd; Pep Bnd; Lcrsse (V); Swmg (V); Music; Science; U of North Carolina Chapel Hill

WHITSETT, CHELISA; GREENSBORO, NC; DUDLEY HS; (FR); Hnr Roll; Comm Volntr; ROTC; Ch Chr; Clr Grd; Jr ROTC; Doctor Pediatric/ Dentist Pediatric; Cosmetologist; Greensboro College; Guilford College

WHITT, JULIA N; POWELLSVILLE, NC; BERTIE HS; (SO); Hnr Roll; WWAHSS; Comm Volntr; Chrch Yth Grp; Dbte Team; Voc Ind Clb Am; The National Society of High School Scholars; Business Management; Art; U of NC Chapel Hill; U of North Carolina Wilmington

WHYTE, LEON T; CANDLER, NC; ENKA HS; (SR); WWAHSS; Yth Ldrshp Prog; Comm Volntr; Chrch Yth Grp; Drma Clb; Emplmnt; Mus Clb; Off Aide; Quiz Bowl; Svce Clb; Jzz Bnd; SP/M/VS; Film Production; Music; Appalachian State U

WICKER, ELIZABETH; SANFORD, NC; LEE SR; (SR); Hi Hnr Roll; Hnr Roll; Jr Mshl; Kwnis Aw; Nat Hon Sy; Nat Ldrshp Svc; Pres Ac Ftns Aw; St of Mnth; USAA; WWAHSS; Comm Volntr; Hab For Humty Volntr; Peer Tut/ Med; AL Aux Girls; BPA; Chrch Yth Grp; Drma Clb; Emplmnt; FCA; FBLA; Key Club; Chr; SP/M/VS; Chrldg (V); Gmnstcs; Wt Lftg (V); Secretary & Treasurer of FBLA / Morehead Nominee; Business Administration; UNC Chapel Hill

WICKER, FRANCHESCA N; CAMERON, NC; WESTERN HARNETT HS; (SR); All Am Sch; Ctznshp Aw; Hi Hnr Roll; Hnr Roll; Nat Hon Sy; Nat Ldrshp Svc; Nat Mrt Sch Recip; Nat Mrt Semif; Otst Ac Ach Awd; Perf Att; Comm Volntr; Hosp Aide; Peer Tut/Med; Chrch Yth Grp; Emplmnt; FBLA; Lttrmn Clb; Ntl Beta Clb; ROTC; Svce Clb; Tchrs Aide; National Society of High School Scholars; Who's Who Among American High School Student; Science; Ophthalmology PhD; Sandhills Community College; U of North Carolina At Chapel Hill

WIGGS, CHRISTEN; RALEIGH, NC; SOUTHEAST RALEIGH HS; (SR); Hnr Roll; Nat Mrt LOC; Otst Ac Ach Awd; St of Mnth; WWAHSS; Peer Tut/ Med; DARE; DECA; Outstanding Student in Accounting; Best Attitude in DECA; Psychology; Law; Wake Tech Community College; Bennett College

WILDER, K'QVONTAY; DUDLEY, NC; SOUTHERN WAYNE HS; (SO); Nat Hon Sy; DARE; Voc Ind Clb Am; Bskball (J); Track (V); Math; Electrical Engineering; UNC Wilmington; UNC Chapel Hill

WILHOIT, LINDSAY R; ASHEBORO, NC; ASHEBORO HS; (JR); Ctznshp Aw; Duke TS; Hi Hnr Roll; Hnr Roll; Nat Sci Aw; Otst Ac Ach Awd; Comm Volntr; Hab For Humty Volntr; Peer Tut/Med; Chrch Yth Grp; FCA; Key Club; Scouts; Svce Clb; Spanish Clb; Bnd; Chr; Ch Chr; Mch Bnd; Tennis (J); Track (J); Play Piano, Guitar & Flute - 1st Chair AHS Ensemble; Member of Health Occupations Club; Dentist; Orthodontist; U of North Carolina Chapel-Hill; Wake Forest U

WILKE, ANNALEIGHA; JACKSONVILLE, NC; JACKSONVILLE HS; (SO); Hi Hnr Roll; Hnr Roll; Perf Att; Emplmnt; ROTC; Mar Art; Drawing; Graphic Design; U of North Carolina At Wilmington; East Carolina U

WILKERSON, ERICA J; FAYETTEVILLE, NC; E E SMITH SR HS; (FR); Ctznshp Aw; Hnr Roll; Kwnis Aw; Nat Hon Sy; Otst Ac Ach Awd; Comm Volntr; Peer Tut/Med; Chrch Yth Grp; DARE; NtlFrnscLg; Quiz Bowl; Scouts; Vsity Clb; Bskball (V); Track (V); Vllyball (VJ); Wt Lftg (V); Adv Cncl (R); CR (P); Presidents Award (Merit); Principal's Advisory Council; Sports Medicine; Children's Doctor; UNC-Chapel Hill; Tennessee U

WILKINS, BRITTANY S; ROPER, NC; PLYMOUTH HS; (FR); Hi Hnr Roll; Perf Att; St of Mnth; Comm Volntr; Chrch Yth Grp; Drma Clb; Mth Clb/Tm; Chr; Ch Chr; Stu Cncl (R); CR (R); U of North Carolina Greensboro; Johnson C Smith U

WILKINS, DARIUS L; DURHAM, NC; SOUTHERN HS; (SO); Hnr Roll; Perf Att; Chr; English Major

WILKISON, SARAH E; PINEHURST, NC; PINECREST HS; (SO); Duke TS; Hi Hnr Roll; Nat Hon Sy; Otst Ac Ach Awd; WWAHSS; Yth Ldrshp Prog; Comm Volntr; Peer Tut/Med; Chrch Yth Grp; Jr Ach; Key Club; French Clb; Chr; Tennis (V L); Politics; French; Princeton U; Duke U

WILLIAMS, ADRIANNA; LEWISTON, NC; BERTIE HS; (FR); 4H Awd; Hi Hnr Roll; Hnr Roll; Perf Att; St of Mnth; 4-H; Ntl Beta Clb; Orch; Principal's List on Last Report Card of 9th Grade; Graphic Design-Art; Animation; The Art Institute of Atlanta Georgia

WILLIAMS, ANDREA D; REIDSVILLE, NC; REIDSVILLE HS; (FR); Hnr Roll; Sci Fairs; Chrch Yth Grp; ROTC; Drl Tm; Volleyball with Church Youth; Computer Tech; Volleyball Coach; ECPI; U of North Carolina

WILLIAMS, ANGEL R; LOCUST, NC; WEST STANLY HS; (SR); Hnr Roll; Sci Fairs; WWAHSS; Yth Ldrshp Prog; Comm Volntr; Chrch Yth Grp; FTA; Jr Ach; Mth Clb/Tm; Sci Clb; Bskball (V); Math Club Science Club; Junior Civitan; Pharmacy; Wingate U

WILLIAMS, ASHLEY; COMO, NC; BERTFORD CO HS; (FR); Did well on Report Card; Received 2 Most Improved Awards - Grade 8; English Education; Music Performance; U of North Carolina Chapel Hill; Winston Salem State U

WILLIAMS, ASHLEY M; LILLINGTON, NC; CONTINENTAL AC; Perf Att; Comm Volntr; Peer Tut/Med; 4-H; Chrch Yth Grp; DARE; Emplmnt; Mus Clb; Off Aide; SP/M/VS; Graduated at 16 Years Old in 2004; Nurse / CNA / RN; Arizona State; North Carolina State

WILLIAMS, BRITTANY N; FAYETTEVILLE, NC; REID ROSS YR ROUND CLASSICAL; (SO); 4H Awd; Ctznshp Aw; Comm Volntr; 4-H; Chrch Yth Grp; Drma Clb; Bnd; Ch Chr; Dnce; SP/M/VS; Fayetteville Spikers Volleyball Team; All-County Band 2003; Criminal Justice; Criminal Psychology; Winston-Salem U; U of Pennsylvania

WILLIAMS, CAITLIN; CLYDE, NC; TUSCOLA HS; (FR); Ctznshp Aw; Duke TS; Hi Hnr Roll; Hnr Roll; Otst Ac Ach Awd; Perf Att; Pres Ac Ftns Aw; Sci Fairs; St of Mnth; Comm Volntr; Chrch Yth Grp; DARE; Dbte Team; Drma Clb; FCA; Mth Clb/Tm; Spanish Clb; SP/M/VS; Sccr (JC); CR (R); On Youth Council for Western North Carolina Diocese; Psychology (Therapist); Law (Attorney); U of North Carolina At Chapel Hill; Harvard U

WILLIAMS, COLE R; WAYNESVILLE, NC; TUSCOLA HS; (FR); Comm Volntr; Chrch Yth Grp; DARE; Emplmnt; Skiing; Medical Doctor; Paleontologist

WILLIAMS, CORRINE D; GOLDSBORO, NC; GOLDSBORO HS; (SO); Hi Hnr Roll; Hnr Roll; Perf Att; Pres Ac Ftns Aw; St of Mnth; Comm Volntr; Peer Tut/Med; Chess; Chrch Yth Grp; Mth Clb/Tm; Mus Clb; Quiz Bowl; Scouts; Chr; Ch Chr; Dnce; Cl Off (S); Stu Cncl (R); Yrbk (E); President of an Independent Youth Organization; Lawyer; Pediatrician; Spelman College; Emory U

Williams, Brittany N
Reid Ross Yr Round Classical
Fayetteville, NC

Williams, Adrianna
Bertie HS
Lewiston, NC

Wilhoit, Lindsay R
Asheboro HS
Asheboro, NC

White, Ashland H T
Gray's Creek HS
Fayetteville, NC

National
Honor Roll
Spring 2005

West, Kelly
Carolina Day Sch
Asheville, NC

Wilkins, Brittany S
Plymouth HS
Roper, NC

Williams, Andrea D
Reidsville HS
Reidsville, NC

Williams, Cole R
Tuscola HS
Waynesville, NC

WILLIAMS, DANIELLE; RURAL HALL, NC; NORTH FORSYTH HS; (JR); F Lan Hn Soc; Hi Hnr Roll; Hnr Roll; Jr Mshl; Nat Hon Sy; Otst Ac Ach Awd; Perf Att; WWAHSS; Comm Volntr; Chrch Yth Grp; FCA; Key Club; SADD; French Clb; Bnd; Dnce; Sch Ppr (R); National Society of High School Scholars; Mortarboard Student Leadership Conference; Journalism; U of North Carolina-Chapel Hill

WILLIAMS, DAVID L; FAYETTEVILLE, NC; REID ROSS YR ROUND CLASSICAL SCH; (SO); Hi Hnr Roll; Hnr Roll; Perf Att; Comm Volntr; Peer Tut/Med; ArtClub; Chrch Yth Grp; Psychology; Science Teacher (Biology, Environmental Science Etc); U of North Carolina; North Carolina State

WILLIAMS, DEIDRE; ROCKY MOUNT, NC; NASH CTRL HS; (JR); Hnr Roll; Perf Att; St of Mnth; Comm Volntr; Chrch Yth Grp; FCCLA; Scouts; Scr Kpr (J); Silver Medal Out State Competition for FCCLA; Nursing; East Carolina U; U of North Carolina-Wilmington

WILLIAMS, DONNA M; CONOVER, NC; WEST LINCOLN HS; (FR); Hnr Roll; Amnsty Intl; Chrch Yth Grp; Chr; Ch Chr; Clr Grd; Mch Bnd; Music; Teaching; East Carolina U; Western Carolina U

WILLIAMS, ELIZABETH M; DEEP RUN, NC; BETHEL CHRISTIAN AC; (SR); Hnr Roll; Jr Rot; Nat Hon Sy; Perf Att; WWAHSS; Comm Volntr; Chrch Yth Grp; Drma Clb; Emplmnt; Prom Com; Tchrs Aide; SP/M/VS; Chrldg (VJ L); Cl Off (S, T); Organized A School-Wide Environmental Clean-Up Day; Junior Miss Participant; Social Studies / Secondary Education; Science / Secondary Education; Meredith College NC; Campbell U NC

WILLIAMS, HARRISON; AUTRYVILLE, NC; MIDWAY HS; (SO); Hnr Roll; Hosp Aide; FBLA; Ch Chr; Engineering

WILLIAMS, JEFFREY; WESTFIELD, NC; NORTH STOKES HS; (SR); Duke TS; F Lan Hn Soc; Jr Mshl; MVP; Nat Hon Sy; Otst Ac Ach Awd; Pres Ac Ftns Aw; Valdctrian; WWAHSS; Comm Volntr; Hab For Humty Volntr; Peer Tut/Med; FCA; HO'Br Yth Ldrshp; Ntl Beta Clb; Ntl FFA; Prom Com; Vsity Clb; Ch Chr; Bsball (VJCL); Bskball (VJCL); Cr Ctry (V CL); Ftball (J); Cl Off (P); All-Conference (Basketball); Multiple Highest Class Average Awards; Major in Mathematics; Master's in Secondary Education; U of North Carolina At Chapel Hill

WILLIAMS, JIMMY L; CHARLOTTE, NC; WEST MECKLENBURG HS; (JR); Hnr Roll; Perf Att; WWAHSS; Comm Volntr; Peer Tut/Med; Chess; Chrch Yth Grp; DARE; Emplmnt; FCA; ROTC; Scouts; Wdwrkg Clb; Ch Chr; Bsball (J); Cr Ctry (L); Scr Kpr (L); Swmg (L); Accepted Jesus As My Savior; Nominated for the National Society of HS Scholars; Religion; Construction; Gardner-Webb U; Central Piedmont Community College

WILLIAMS, KLADE'; CHARLOTTE, NC; WEST MECKLENBURG HS; (SO); Ctznshp Aw; Hi Hnr Roll; Nat Hon Sy; Otst Ac Ach Awd; Perf Att; St of Mnth; Comm Volntr; Peer Tut/Med; Chrch Yth Grp; DARE; Dbte Team; Emplmnt; SADD; Chr; Ch Chr; Chrldg (J); Gmnstcs (J); Scr Kpr (J); Swmg (J); Track (J); Stu Cncl (S); Sch Ppr (E); Christian Character Award; Participation; Industrial Engineering; Fashion Design; New York U; Fashion Institute of Technology

WILLIAMS, MOXIE; RALEIGH, NC; BROUGHTON; (SR); Hi Hnr Roll; Hnr Roll; Comm Volntr; Peer Tut/Med; Chess; Civil Air Pat; DECA; Emplmnt; Scouts; Japanese Clb; Boy Scouts Leadership Position; DECA State - 2nd Place in E-Commerce; Major Computer Science; East Carolina U

WILLIAMS, ROBIN; WINSTON SALEM, NC; NORTH FORSYTH HS; (FR); Otst Ac Ach Awd; St of Mnth; Chrch Yth Grp; Dnce; Mch Bnd; Volunteer Orderly; Modeling, Own Business; Lawyer, Professional Singer; Winston-Salem State U; A & T State

WILLIAMS, STEPHANIE; CARY, NC; CARY HS; (SO); MVP; St of Mnth; Comm Volntr; Chrch Yth Grp; Svce Clb; Chrldg (V); Member of Alpha Beta Club; Medical Doctor; Lawyer; Duke U; North Carolina State U

WILLIAMS, STEPHANIE N; MOORESVILLE, NC; LAKE NORMAN HS; (SR); Duke TS; Hnr Roll; St Schl; Emplmnt; Mus Clb; Bnd; Chr; Clr Grd; Dnce; Chrldg (V); Cl Off (P); Stu Cncl (R); CR (P); Silver and Bronze Renaissance Winner; DARE - Outstanding Essay Award Winner - 5th Grade; Psychology; Computer Programming; U of North Carolina Charlotte

WILLIAMS, TAQUONIA N; FAYETTEVILLE, NC; REID ROSS YR ROUND CLASSICAL; (SO); Ctznshp Aw; Hnr Roll; Perf Att; Yth Ldrshp Prog; Comm Volntr; DARE; Emplmnt; FBLA; Ntl Beta Clb; Off Aide; Quiz Bowl; Scouts; Chr; Sftball (J); Girl Scout Silver Award; MSEN / Pre-College; U of Miami; U of North Carolina Chapel Hill; U of North Carolina Pembroke; U of North Carolina Chapel Hill

WILLIAMS, TAYLOR L; CARY, NC; CARY SR HS; (FR); Hnr Roll; Otst Ac Ach Awd; St of Mnth; St Optmst of Yr; Comm Volntr; Peer Tut/Med; ArtClub; Emplmnt; Outdrs Clb; Photog; ROTC; Bnd; Chr; Drl Tm; Flg Crps; Sftball (J); Tutoring; Guitar Playing; Reporter / Journalist; Music; North Carolina State U; U of North Carolina

WILLIAMS, WHITNY J; JACKSONVILLE, NC; JACKSONVILLE HS; (FR); Hnr Roll; Elizabeth City U; Hampton U

WILLIAMS, ZACHARY M; WAYNESVILLE, NC; PISGAH HS; (FR); Ctznshp Aw; Hnr Roll; MVP; Nat Hon Sy; Otst Ac Ach Awd; St of Mnth; Comm Volntr; Chrch Yth Grp; DARE; FCA; Ftball (J); Wt Lftg (J); Pre-Med; U of North Carolina; Wake Forest U

WILLIAMS JR, M ANTHONY; CONCORD, NC; NORTHWEST CABARRUS HS; (JR); Ctznshp Aw; Hnr Roll; Nat Ldrshp Svc; Otst Ac Ach Awd; Perf Att; Sci/Math Olympn; St of Mnth; WWAHSS; Yth Ldrshp Prog; Comm Volntr; Peer Tut/Med; Spec Olymp Vol; Chrch Yth Grp; DARE; Dbte Team; Emplmnt; Jr Ach; NYLC; Quiz Bowl; Tchrs Aide; Bsball; Bskball (V CL); Ftball (V L); Wt Lftg (V); Sailors Athletic Honors Award; Who's Who Honor Student Award; Engineering Program; Math Program; North Carolina State U; Wake Forest U

WILLIAMSON, LILLIE D; WILMINGTON, NC; E A LANEY HS; (SO); Ctznshp Aw; Duke TS; Hi Hnr Roll; Otst Ac Ach Awd; Perf Att; Sci/Math Olympn; Comm Volntr; Mth Clb/Tm; Mus Clb; Sci Clb; Ch Chr; Dnce; Yrbk (E); Accepted Into / Participated in the 2005 North Carolina Summer Ventures in Science & Math; Outstanding Leadership Award; Molecular Biology / Emphasis on Forensics; Forensic Anthropology; UNC Chapel Hill; U of Tennessee Knoxville

WILLIAMSON, MELISSA T; FAYETTEVILLE, NC; SEVENTY-FIRST HS; (SR); Hnr Roll; Jr Mshl; Nat Hon Sy; Otst Ac Ach Awd; WWAHSS; Comm Volntr; Peer Tut/Med; Chrch Yth Grp; Emplmnt; Quiz Bowl; Spanish Clb; Chr; Ch Chr; SP/M/VS; Tennis (V); Track (J); Sch Ppr (R); Spanish National Honors Society; Pediatric Doctor / Major in Pre-Med; Singing; Fayetteville State U; Fayetteville Tech Community College

WILLIAMSON, NICOLE A; WINSTON SALEM, NC; WESTCHESTER AC; (JR); Hnr Roll; Jr Mshl; Nat Hon Sy; Otst Ac Ach Awd; Yth Ldrshp Prog; Comm Volntr; Chrch Yth Grp; Emplmnt; Prom Com; Quill & Scroll; Scouts; Svce Clb; SADD; French Clb; Swmg (V); Tennis (V); Stu Cncl (R); Yrbk (R); Academic All-Conference (9th, 10th Grade); Wildcat Award for Swimming; Business Management; Pharmaceuticals; U of North Carolina At Chapel Hill; College of Charleston

WILLIAMSON, RASHARD; REIDSVILLE, NC; REIDSVILLE HS; (FR); Hnr Roll; Chrch Yth Grp; Mth Clb/Tm; Bnd; Mch Bnd; Ftball (J); Computer Programming; Music Producer; U of North Carolina Chapel Hill; U of North Carolina Greensboro

WILLIAMSON II, DANNY J; POLKTON, NC; ANSON HS; (FR); Hnr Roll; Otst Ac Ach Awd; Perf Att; Pres Ac Ftns Aw; Sci Fairs; Yth Ldrshp Prog; Comm Volntr; Peer Tut/Med; Chrch Yth Grp; DARE; ROTC; Ch Chr; Drl Tm; SP/M/VS; Bskball (J); Assistant Church Pianist, Excellence in Exploration Award, Promoted to Corporal Cadet; Outstanding Cadet of the Year Jr ROTC; Meteorology; Air Force Non-Commissioned Officer; Duke U; U of Miami

WILLIS, ALLISON; ASHEVILLE, NC; CAROLINA DAY SCH; (SO); Hi Hnr Roll; Hnr Roll; Otst Ac Ach Awd; Comm Volntr; Red Cr Aide; Spec Olymp Vol; Emplmnt; Pep Squd; Prom Com; SADD; Fld Hky (V L); Adv Cncl (R); Placed 11th in National French Contest (Nationally); Highlander's Society; Medical Degree; Law Degree; Vanderbilt U; William and Mary College

WILLOUGHBY, SKYE; CANTON, NC; PISGAH HS; (FR); Hnr Roll; Nat Hon Sy; Comm Volntr; 4-H; Chrch Yth Grp; Pep Squd; Bnd; Skateboarding; Snowboarding; Doctorate in Psychology; Government Intelligence; U of Tennessee; U of North Carolina

WILMOT, CYNTHIA J; GREENVILLE, NC; FARMVILLE CTRL HS; (SO); 4H Awd; Comm Volntr; 4-H; Sci Clb; Bnd; Chr; Orch; Sccr (V L); Award for Maintaining a 3.0 / GPA; Science Club; Aerospace Engineer; Doctor; NC State U; Air Force Academy

WILSON, ALISON; BESSEMER CITY, NC; BESSEMER CITY HS; (SO); Hi Hnr Roll; Nat Hon Sy; Perf Att; Spec Olymp Vol; Chrch Yth Grp; Ch Chr; Track (V)

WILSON, ASHLEY M; REIDSVILLE, NC; REIDSVILLE HS; (JR); Hnr Roll; Nat Hon Sy; WWAHSS; Comm Volntr; Hosp Aide; FCA; Svce Clb; SADD; Bnd; Mch Bnd; Pep Bnd; Vllyball (V); Phi Belta Pi (Service Sorority); Fellowship Christian Athletics; Medical Doctor (Ob-Gyn); U of North Carolina; Wave Forest U

WILSON, ASHLEY R; HICKORY, NC; HICKORY HS; (FR); Homecoming Court; Fashion Design; Business and Marketing; Duke U; Johnson & Wales U

WILSON, BETSY; CHAPEL HILL, NC; CEDAR RIDGE HS; (FR); Duke TS; Hi Hnr Roll; Hnr Roll; MVP; Pres Ac Ftns Aw; Pres Sch; Sci Fairs; Chrch Yth Grp; Bskball (V); Lcrsse (J); Sccr (J); Vllyball (V); Yrbk (R); VP - Lacrosse Club; Physical Therapy; Sports Medicine; U of North Carolina Chapel Hill; U of North Carolina Charlotte

WILSON, BRITTANY; MATTHEWS, NC; WEDDINGTON HS; (FR); Hi Hnr Roll; Perf Att; St of Mnth; WWAHSS; Peer Tut/Med; Drma Clb; Key Club; Ntl Beta Clb; Spanish Clb; Bskball (J); Rotary Scholar; The U of NC At Chapel Hill

WILSON, CHASITY B; SMITHFIELD, NC; SMITHFIELD-SELMA HS; (JR); Hi Hnr Roll; Hnr Roll; Nat Hon Sy; Sci Fairs; Comm Volntr; Spec Olymp Vol; Drma Clb; Emplmnt; Jr Ach; Off Aide; Photog; Chr; SP/M/VS; Yrbk (E, P); Science Fair 1st Place; HOSA Club; Bachelor of Science; DVM-Doctor of Veterinary Medicine; U of North Carolina; North Carolina State U

WILSON, DEREK R; CHARLOTTE, NC; OLYMPIC HS; (SO); Duke TS; Hi Hnr Roll; Comm Volntr; Peer Tut/Med; DARE; Bsball; Mar Art; Yrbk (P); Played Challenge Little League Baseball; Video Game Design Engineer; Computer Programming; U of North Carolina Chapel Hill; U of Duke At NC

WILSON, GREGORY A; GREENSBORO, NC; SOUTHERN GUILFORD HS; (JR); Duke TS; Hi Hnr Roll; Hnr Roll; Jr Mshl; Jr Rot; Nat Hon Sy; Otst Ac Ach Awd; Pres Sch; WWAHSS; Comm Volntr; Ntl FFA; Svce Clb; Tchrs Aide; French Clb; Stg Cre; Sccr (V L); Cl Off (V); National Honor Society; Interact Club President; Textile Engineering; Viticulture and Enology; North Carolina State U; U of North Carolina Chapel Hill

WILSON, JABREL; FAYETTEVILLE, NC; SEVENTY-FIRST HS; (FR)

WILSON, JEFFREY J; KANNAPOLIS, NC; A L BROWN HS; (FR); Hnr Roll; St of Mnth; Peer Tut/Med; Chess; DARE; Quiz Bowl; ROTC; Stu Cncl (R); UNC Charlotte; Duke U

WILSON, JESSE M; KANNAPOLIS, NC; SOUTH ROWAN HS; (SO); Hnr Roll; Nat Hon Sy; Otst Ac Ach Awd; St of Mnth; Comm Volntr; Chrch Yth Grp; Emplmnt; Ntl FFA; Scouts; Ftball (V); Wt Lftg (V); Eagle Scout At Age 13 for Troop 206 St Enoch Lutheran Church; Engineering Degree; North Carolina State U

WILSON, KADEN E; RALEIGH, NC; WAKEFIELD HS; (JR); Hi Hnr Roll; Hnr Roll; Otst Ac Ach Awd; Pres Ac Ftns Aw; Emplmnt; FCA; Key Club; Sccr (J L); Track (V); Lamp of Knowledge; NTHS; Industrial Design; Engineering; NCSU; UNC Charlotte

WILSON, KELLY P; THOMASVILLE, NC; TRINITY HS; (JR); Duke TS; Hnr Roll; Comm Volntr; Chrch Yth Grp; FCA; MuAlphaTh; Ntl Beta Clb; Photog; Quill & Scroll; Spanish Clb; Bskball (V L); Cr Ctry (V); PP Ftbl (V); Sftball (J); Tennis (V); Yrbk (E, P); Political Science; Psychology; American U; College of William and Mary

WILSON, KIMBER L; GREENSBORO, NC; BEN L SMITH HS; (SR); Ctznshp Aw; Hi Hnr Roll; Hnr Roll; Nat Hon Sy; St of Mnth; Comm Volntr; Hab For Humty Volntr; Hosp Aide; Chrch Yth Grp; DARE; Emplmnt; Ntl Beta Clb; Off Aide; Prom Com; Tchrs Aide; Bnd; Ch Chr; Clr Grd; Dnce; Track (V L); CR (R); All Conference Track & Field (Discus) 2003-04 & 2004-05; Captain of BIS Marching Band Auxiliary Squad; Nursing; Early Childhood Education; NC A & T State U; East Carolina U

WILSON, MARKUS D; JACKSONVILLE, NC; JACKSONVILLE SR; (FR); Ctznshp Aw; Hnr Roll; MVP; Otst Ac Ach Awd; Perf Att; St of Mnth; Lib Aide; Mus Clb; Clb; Bnd; Mch Bnd; Ftball; Wrstlg; County Basketball; Church Choir Drummer, Church Usher; Mathematics Engineer; Science; UNC Chapel Hill; Wake Forest

WILSON, MATTHEW; FAYETTEVILLE, NC; MASSEY HILL CLASSICAL HS; (JR); Hnr Roll; Nat Hon Sy; Perf Att; WWAHSS; ArtClub; Orch; Venture Scholars Program; Computer Animation; Graphics Design; St Augustine College; UNC Greensboro

WILSON, ROSHIEKA; PLYMOUTH, NC; PLYMOUTH HS; (SO); All Am Sch; Duke TS; Hi Hnr Roll; Hnr Roll; MVP; Nat Hon Sy; Otst Ac Ach Awd; USAA; WWAHSS; Yth Ldrshp Prog; Comm Volntr; Peer Tut/Med; Red Cr Aide; Chrch Yth Grp; DECA; Drma Clb; Emplmnt; Jr Ach; Mth Clb/Tm; Mus Clb; Ntl Beta Clb; Chr; Clr Grd; Dnce; Mch Bnd; Chrldg (C); PPSqd (J); Cl Off (T); Stu Cncl (T); CR (T); Pediatrician / Doctor; Obstetrician / Doctor; Duke U North Carolina; East Carolina U NC

WILSON, SAMANTHA; OAK ISLAND, NC; SOUTH BRUNSWICK HS; (SO); Hnr Roll; Sci Fairs; WWAHSS; Chrch Yth Grp; Chr; First Place in Science Fair; Survived Cancer; Photography Major; Cosmetology; North Carolina State U; U of North Carolina in Wilmington

WILSON, SARA N; ABERDEEN, NC; PINECREST HS; (JR); Hab For Humty Volntr; Bnd; Mch Bnd; Vllyball (J); Sandhills Community College

WILSON, TERRELL A; MOCKSVILLE, NC; DAVIE CTY HS; (SR); Hi Hnr Roll; Hnr Roll; WWAHSS; Emplmnt; FCA; Mus Clb; Chr; Bskball (L); Ftball (L); Mathematics, Secondary Education; Appalachian State U

WILSON II, VIC; SHELBY, NC; VICTORY CHRISTIAN AC; (SO); Hnr Roll; Nat Hon Sy; WWAHSS; Peer Tut/Med; Emplmnt; FCA; Tchrs Aide; Bsball (V); Bskball (V); Wt Lftg (J); Miami U; Florida State U

WINDLEY, JUSTIN G; CHOCOWINITY, NC; SOUTHSIDE HS; (SO); Duke TS; Hi Hnr Roll; Nat Hon Sy; Otst Ac Ach Awd; Bnd; Mch Bnd; Bsball (V); Cr Ctry (V); Ftball (J); Track (V); North Carolina Scholar Athlete; Marine Biology; UNC Wilmington; UNC Chapel Hill

Wilson, Jesse M
South Rowan HS
Kannapolis, NC

Wilson, Derek R
Olympic HS
Charlotte, NC

Willis, Allison
Carolina Day Sch
Asheville, NC

Williamson II, Danny J
Anson HS
Polkton, NC

Williams, Elizabeth M
Bethel Christian AC
Deep Run, NC

Williamson, Lillie D
E A Laney HS
Wilmington, NC

Wilson, Ashley R
Hickory HS
Hickory, NC

Wilson, Jeffrey J
A L Brown HS
Kannapolis, NC

Wilson II, Vic
Victory Christian AC
Shelby, NC

WINECOFF, DANA; CHARLOTTE, NC; PIEDMONT HS; (SR); Perf Att; Comm Volntr; Spec Olymp Vol; DARE; Emplmnt; FBLA; Photog; Scouts; Tchrs Aide; Clb; Very Special Art-VSA-4 Yrs.; Off. Teacher's Ass't.; Girl Scout 7 Years; Attend a Four Year College and Receive My Master's In Psychology; U North Carolina Charlotte; U of Wilmington

WINFIELD, DARRYL L; ROCKY MOUNT, NC; ROCKY MOUNT HS; (FR); ArtClub; Mus Clb; Outdrs Clb; Photog; ROTC; Svce Clb; Tech Clb; Wdwrkg Clb; Bnd; Chr; Drm Mjr; Bskball (J); Ftball (J); Skt Tgt Sh; Track; Wt Lftg (J); Wrstlg (J); Engineering; Mechanic

WINN JR, LARRY D; GOLDSBORO, NC; EASTERN WAYNE HS; (JR); Hnr Roll; Nat Hon Sy; Otst Ac Ach Awd; Perf Att; Comm Volntr; Foreign Clb; Academic Excellence Award; Christian Character Award; Electrical Engineering; Graphic Arts and Industrial Design; Duke U; U of North Carolina State

WINSLOW, JAMIE; BELVIDERE, NC; JOHN A HOLMES HS; (SO); Hi Hnr Roll; MVP; Perf Att; Comm Volntr; 4-H; Chrch Yth Grp; Emplmnt; Quiz Bowl; Sci Clb; Sftball (V L); Class Rank-#1-All Albemaric Team (Softball); Acceptance Into NC School of Science & Math; Biology; Chemistry; Duke; UNC-Chapel Hill

WINSTEAD, DALE S; NASHVILLE, NC; SOUTHERN NASH SR HS; (SR); 4H Awd; Hnr Roll; Comm Volntr; 4-H; BPA; FBLA; Ntl FFA; Sccr (V L); 4-H Sandy Cross-President; 4-H Nash County Council-President; Agricultural Business Management; Mount Olive College

WINTER, HILLARY M; BURGAW, NC; HEIDE TRASK SR HS; (JR); Ctznshp Aw; Hi Hnr Roll; Jr Mshl; Nat Hon Sy; Yth Ldrshp Prog; Hab For Humty Volntr; Peer Tut/Med; Spec Olymp Vol; AL Aux Girls; Chrch Yth Grp; Emplmnt; FCA; Key Club; Mth Clb/Tm; Quiz Bowl; Scouts; Bnd; Drm Mjr; Jzz Bnd; SP/M/VS; Sccr (C); Vllyball (J); President of FCA (Fellowship of Christian Athletes); Acceptance Into Rap Program At UNC-Chapel Hill (RAP-Research Apprenticeship Program); Medicine/Research; Political Science; Meredith College; U of North Carolina At Chapel Hill

WITALISON, ERIN E; GOLD HILL, NC; GRAY STONE DAY SCH; (SO); Duke TS; MVP; WWAHSS; Chrch Yth Grp; Quiz Bowl; Bskball (V L); Sftball (V CL); Vllyball (V L)

WITHERS, JUSTIN R; CHARLOTTE, NC; E E WADDELL HS; (FR); Otst Ac Ach Awd; Perf Att; ArtClub; Chess; Chrch Yth Grp; Cmptr Clb; DARE; ROTC; Scouts; Vsity Clb; Bnd; Ch Chr; Dnce; Drl Tm; Ftball (J); Wt Lftg (J); Football, Basketball; Criminal Justice; UNC-Charlotte

WITTENAUER, ASHLEY; GARNER, NC; WEST JOHNSTON HS; (SO); Hi Hnr Roll; Hnr Roll; Otst Ac Ach Awd; FCA; Ntl Beta Clb; Spanish Clb; Acpl Chr; Chr; Dnce; SP/M/VS; Chrldg (V L); 1st Place Trophy in 2005 Chorus Festival for WJHS Show Choir; Medical Careers; Degree in Pharmacy; U of North Carolina-Chapel Hill; Duke U

WOLF, AMANDA D; DUNN, NC; TRITON HS; (JR); Hnr Roll; Nat Hon Sy; Sci Fairs; WWAHSS; Comm Volntr; ArtClub; Chrch Yth Grp; DARE; Ntl Beta Clb; Scouts; SADD; Sccr (V); Swmg (V); Adv Cncl; 2nd Place in Gen. William C Lee Essay; Most Improved Varsity Swim Team; Marine Biology; U of North Carolina in Wilmington; North Carolina State U

WOMACK, JAMEY G; MARION, NC; MC DOWELL HS; (SO); Hnr Roll; Nat Hon Sy; Otst Ac Ach Awd; Chrch Yth Grp; FCA; Lib Aide; Ntl Beta Clb; Ch Chr; Sftball (L); Yrbk (R, P); Genetic Counselor; Journalism; NC State; East Carolina U

WOMACK, WHITNEY; WINSTON SALEM, NC; NORTH FORSYTH HS; (JR); Hnr Roll; WWAHSS; Comm Volntr; Chrch Yth Grp; Emplmnt; Key Club; Ch Chr; Nursing-Major (Bachelors and Masters); Childhood Education Minor; U of North Carolina Charlotte; U of North Carolina Greensboro

WOMBLE, CHRIS T; CARY, NC; GREEN HOPE HS; (JR); F Lan Hn Soc; Hi Hnr Roll; Nat Hon Sy; Otst Ac Ach Awd; Comm Volntr; Chrch Yth Grp; Emplmnt; FCA; Key Club; Ntl Beta Clb; Prom Com; Cr Ctry (V L); Lcrsse (V L); Track (V L); Stu Cncl (R); Pre-Med; Pharmacy/Physical Therapy; UNC; Wake Forest U

WOMBLE, JESSICA N; TARBORO, NC; TARBORO HS; (SR); Hnr Roll; Comm Volntr; Red Cr Aide; Spec Olymp Vol; ArtClub; Prom Com; ROTC; Tchrs Aide; French Clb; SP/M/VS; JROTC Color Guard; French Club & Book Club; Associate Degree/Art; Master's Degree/Art; Edgecombe Community College; East Carolina U

WONG, CHUNG Y; GREENSBORO, NC; GREENSBORO DAY SCH; (SO); Hi Hnr Roll; Nat Hon Sy; Nat Stu Ath Day Aw; Otst Ac Ach Awd; Yth Ldrshp Prog; HO'Br Yth Ldrshp; Mth Clb/Tm; Sccr (V); Vllyball (V); Operation Service; Admission Ambassadors; Art & Design; International Business; Wake Forest U; UNC-Chapel Hill

WOOD, CHIMENE; MORRISVILLE, NC; GREEN HOPE HS; Hnr Roll; Nat Hon Sy; WWAHSS; ArtClub; Japanese Clb; Creative Writing; Drawing; Meredith College

WOOD, DANIEL P; ADVANCE, NC; DAVIE CTY HS; (JR); Duke TS; Hnr Roll; Jr Rot; Perf Att; Comm Volntr; Emplmnt; Svce Clb; NCHSAA and NWBOA; Junior Civitan; Computer Science; Information Systems; U of N Carolina At Wilmington; U of N Carolina At Charlotte

WOOD, JOHN L; ELIZABETH CITY, NC; NORTHEASTERN HS; (SO); Duke TS; Hi Hnr Roll; Nat Hon Sy; Sci Fairs; Comm Volntr; Chrch Yth Grp; Drma Clb; Pep Squd; Quiz Bowl; Scouts; Bnd; Jzz Bnd; Mch Bnd; Pep Bnd; Swmg (V L); International Business; UNC Chapel Hill (U of North Carolina); Duke U

WOOD, JORDAN; HILLSBOROUGH, NC; CEDAR RIDGE HS; (SO); F Lan Hn Soc; WWAHSS; 4-H; Outdrs Clb; Hsbk Rdg; Veterinary Medicine; NC State U; Duke U

WOOD, RYAN W; PINEHURST, NC; PINECREST HS; (FR); Duke TS; Hi Hnr Roll; Jr Mshl; St of Mnth; Comm Volntr; Hab For Humty Volntr; ArtClub; Chrch Yth Grp; DARE; Sci Clb; Scouts; Stu Cncl (R); Art Olympian; Yearbook Cover; Computer Science; Architect; North Carolina State U

WOOD, SUSAN; MATTHEWS, NC; PIEDMONT HS; (JR); Perf Att; WWAHSS; FCA; FBLA; Prom Com; Bskball (J); Chrldg (V L); PP Ftbl (V); Stu Cncl (R); 1st Runner-Up in Miss Piedmont Pageant; Nursing; U of North Carolina At Charlotte; Carolina Medical Center

WOOD, ZACH; PITTSBORO, NC; NORTHWOOD HS; (SO); Hi Hnr Roll; Hnr Roll; Pres Sch; Chrch Yth Grp; Dbte Team; Drma Clb; Quiz Bowl; French Clb; Bnd; Mch Bnd; Sccr (J); Medical Doctor; Computer Programmer; U of North Carolina; North Carolina State U

WOODALL, CHARLES D; PEACHLAND, NC; ANSON HS; (FR); 4H Awd; Ctznshp Aw; Hnr Roll; Comm Volntr; 4-H; Chrch Yth Grp; DARE; Ftball (VJ)

WOODARD, EMILY S; HENDERSON, NC; NORTHERN VANCE HS; (SO); Duke TS; Hnr Roll; Perf Att; Yth Ldrshp Prog; Peer Tut/Med; FCCLA; Ch Chr; Yrbk (R, P); Junior Honor Society; Forensic Science; Special Victims Investigation Criminal Justice; U of North Carolina in Chapel Hill; East Carolina U

WOODLE, SCOTT; ROARING RIVER, NC; EAST WILKES MS; (MS); Hnr Roll; Perf Att; Chess; Electrician; Computer Programmer; U of North Carolina

WOODS, COLTON W; FRANKLIN, NC; FRANKLIN HS; (JR); Hi Hnr Roll; Nat Hon Sy; Perf Att; Pres Sch; Comm Volntr; Peer Tut/Med; Chrch Yth Grp; Emplmnt; FCA; Lttrmn Clb; Ntl Beta Clb; Chr; Sccr (V L); Nominated for Governor's School; Nominated for Boy's State; Business Management; Marketing; NC State U; Western Carolina U

WOOLARD, CHRISTOPHER D; WASHINGTON, NC; NORTHSIDE HS; (JR); Hnr Roll; Nat Hon Sy; Perf Att; WWAHSS; Red Cr Aide; FBLA; Key Club; Ntl Beta Clb; Tech Clb; Spanish Clb; Ftball (V); FBLA-President; Mechanical Engineering; North Carolina State U; Wake Forest U

WOOTEN, ASHLEY; KINSTON, NC; KINSTON HS; (JR); Hnr Roll; Nat Hon Sy; WWAHSS; Bnd; Mch Bnd; Track (V); Anchor Club; AKA Debutante; Premedicine; Engineering; Duke U; Winston Salem U

WORMALD, JONATHAN; APEX, NC; APEX HS; (SO); Hi Hnr Roll; WWAHSS; Scouts; Bnd; Mch Bnd; Track (V); Aerospace Engineering; Physics; Massachusetts Institute of Technology; Georgia Tech

WORRIAX, LILLIAN C; PEMBROKE, NC; PURNELL SWETT HS; (SO); Hnr Roll; Otst Ac Ach Awd; Comm Volntr; Chrch Yth Grp; DARE; Ntl Beta Clb; Sch Ppr (R); National Society of Beta Club; Marine Biology; Physical Therapy; UNC Chapel Hill; East Carolina U

WORSLEY, LA SHAYE; CHARLOTTE, NC; HARDING U HS; (FR); Hnr Roll; Otst Ac Ach Awd; Pres Sch; St of Mnth; Chrch Yth Grp; Ch Chr; Mch Bnd; St. Lady Madison Achievement Award; Recognition By Bill Cosby; Medical Doctor; Cosmetology; Clark Atlanta U; Temple U

WRIGHT, BRANDON; RALEIGH, NC; MILLBROOK HS; (JR); Hnr Roll; Perf Att; AL Aux Boys; Chrch Yth Grp; Ch Chr; Ftball (V L); Stu Cncl (R); 1st Team All-Conference Center - Football; National Achievers Society; Law; Architecture; Georgetown U; U of North Carolina

WRIGHT, DERRIKA; WILSON, NC; E T BEDDINGFIELD HS; (JR); Hi Hnr Roll; Hnr Roll; Jr Mshl; Sci/Math Olympn; WWAHSS; Comm Volntr; Peer Tut/Med; Spec Olymp Vol; AL Aux Girls; Emplmnt; Key Club; Prom Com; Quiz Bowl; French Clb; Bnd; Mch Bnd; Orch; Pep Bnd; CR (S); Attended Girl State; Medical; U of Chapel Hill North Carolina

WRIGHT, DESIMAN; FAYETTEVILLE, NC; DOUGLAS BYRD HS; (FR); Hnr Roll; Perf Att; Ch Chr; Bskball (J); Electric Engineering; Business; Howard U; Georgetown U

WRIGHT, DESIREE; JACKSONVILLE, NC; JACKSONVILLE HS; (SO); Hi Hnr Roll; Hnr Roll; Otst Ac Ach Awd; Comm Volntr; Lib Aide; Ntl FFA; Chr; PP Ftbl (V); Track (V L); Chemistry; Biological Sciences; U of North Carolina At Chapel Hill; U of North Carolina At Charlotte

WRIGHT, KIMBERLEE E L; CHARLOTTE, NC; NORTHWEST SCH OF ARTS; (JR); Otst Ac Ach Awd; WWAHSS; Comm Volntr; Drma Clb; Key Club; Chr; Ch Chr; SP/M/VS; Theatre; Spelman College

WRIGHT, MATT; SALISBURY, NC; SOUTH ROWAN HS; (SR); All Am Sch; Hi Hnr Roll; Nat Hon Sy; St Schl; WWAHSS; Comm Volntr; Peer Tut/Med; Chrch Yth Grp; FCA; Quiz Bowl; Vsity Clb; Bskball (VJ L); Track (V L); NC Scholar; Scholar Athlete; Biology-(Pre-Med); Biochemistry-(Pre-Med); Campbell U

WRIGHT, STACY L; HIGHLANDS, NC; HIGHLANDS HS; (JR); Duke TS; Hnr Roll; Perf Att; Comm Volntr; Chess; Chrch Yth Grp; Emplmnt; Ntl Beta Clb; Bnd; Sccr (V); Nursing; Western Carolina U

WUBBE, EMMA; CHARLOTTE, NC; HOME SCH; (JR); Comm Volntr; Emplmnt; 5 Poems Published; 1 Short Story Published; Writing; Education; Wingate U; U of North Carolina

WUJCIK, AMANDA M; RALEIGH, NC; WAKEFIELD HS; (JR); Hnr Roll; Otst Ac Ach Awd; Yth Ldrshp Prog; Comm Volntr; Hab For Humty Volntr; Peer Tut/Med; Emplmnt; Key Club; Pep Squd; Prom Com; Tchrs Aide; Ftball; PP Ftbl (VJ); Stu Cncl; Government Page; Key Club-Kids Voting Coordinator; Teaching/Psychology; Sports Management; North Carolina State; U of North Carolina At Wilmington

WURL, ADELE; RALEIGH, NC; WAKEFIELD HS; (SO); Hnr Roll; Perf Att; Comm Volntr; Peer Tut/Med; ArtClub; Svce Clb; Dnce; Sftball (J); Leaders Club Member (YMCA); Vet.; Forensic Scientist; Appalachian State U; North Carolina State U

WYNGAARDEN, JESSICA; DURHAM, NC; CHARLES E JORDAN HS; (JR); Comm Volntr; Key Club; Chrldg (V L); Psychology; Meredith College; Duke U

WYRICK, KALYN; BURLINGTON, NC; WESTERN ALAMANCE HS; (JR); Hnr Roll; Sci Fairs; Comm Volntr; Red Cr Aide; Spec Olymp Vol; DARE; Drma Clb; FTA; Key Club; Pep Squd; Svce Clb; SADD; Clr Grd; Dnce; SP/M/VS; PPSqd (V); Cl Off (V); CR (V); Elementary/Special/Secondary Education; Business Major; Elon U; Wake Forest U

XIONG, JOHN; ALBEMARLE, NC; ALBEMARLE HS; (JR); Hi Hnr Roll; Hnr Roll; Pres Ac Fns Aw; Peer Tut/Med; ArtClub; DARE; FBLA; Spanish Clb; Cr Ctry (V C); Sccr (V); Track (V C); Stu Cncl (T); Civil Engineering; Agricultural Engineering; U of Wilmington; U of Charlotte

YANCEY, RYAN; ROXBORO, NC; PERSON HS; (SO); Ctznshp Aw; Hnr Roll; Nat Hon Sy; St Schl; Comm Volntr; Peer Tut/Med; Chrch Yth Grp; Scouts; Spanish Clb; Bnd; Jzz Bnd; Mch Bnd; Pep Bnd; Chemistry; U of North Carolina-Chapel Hill; Duke U

YANG, LIYUAN; RALEIGH, NC; W.G. ENLAE HS; (SO); Hnr Roll; Nat Hon Sy; Perf Att; WWAHSS; Comm Volntr; Key Club; Mth Clb/Tm; Tchrs Aide; Orch; United States Academic Decathlon; Science Olympiad; Premedicine; Harvard U; Yale U

YARA, JENNIFER; HOPE MILLS, NC; SOUTHVIEW HS; (FR); Hnr Roll; Sccr; Sch Ppr (E, R, P); Yrbk (R, P); International Baccalaureate Academy; Architect; Doctor; North Carolina State U; Duke U

YARBORO, SAMANTHA N; OAK ISLAND, NC; SOUTH BRUNSWICK HS; (JR); Hi Hnr Roll; Jr Mshl; Nat Hon Sy; WWAHSS; Comm Volntr; Chrch Yth Grp; Emplmnt; FCA; Key Club; Ntl Beta Clb; Prom Com; Clr Grd; Flg Crps; Cl Off (P); Stu Cncl (V); Yrbk (E, R, P); Business Management; Orthodontistry; U of NC At Chapel Hill; Appalachian

YARBOROUGH, ROCKELLE; FARMVILLE, NC; FARMVILLE CTRL HS; (SO); Duke TS; Hnr Roll; Otst Ac Ach Awd; Yth Ldrshp Prog; Comm Volntr; Chrch Yth Grp; FTA; Prom Com; Svce Clb; Chr; Ch Chr; Dnce; SP/M/VS; Chrldg (V); PP Ftbl (V); Cl Off (S, T); Stu Cncl (R); CR (S); Cheerleader Coach's Award; Psychology; Education; North Carolina State U; East Carolina U

YARMOLENKO, IRINA; CHAPEL HILL, NC; CHAPEL HILL HS; (JR); Hnr Roll; Hab For Humty Volntr; Red Cr Aide; ArtClub; SP/M/VS; Tennis (J); Lit Mag (E); Piano; Poetry Club / Spoken Word; Neuroscience; Music; U of North Carolina Chapel Hill; U of North Carolina Wilmington

YATES, NICOLE G; MILLERS CREEK, NC; WEST WILKES HS; (SR); Duke TS; Hnr Roll; MVP; Nat Hon Sy; WWAHSS; Peer Tut/Med; Chrch Yth Grp; Emplmnt; FCA; Key Club; Ntl Beta Clb; Prom Com; Chr; Chrldg (VJC); Yrbk (E, R); 11 Years Piano; Health Education; Teaching, Social Worker; Application State

YATES, TERRELL; EDWARD, NC; SOUTHSIDE HS; (SO); WWAHSS; Bnd; Mch Bnd; Track; Dermatologist; U of North Carolina Wilmington; Emerald U

YAWN, JORDAN; FREMONT, NC; CHARLES B AYCOCK HS; (FR); Hnr Roll; WWAHSS; Peer Tut/Med; Chrch Yth Grp; Vsity Clb; Bskball (J); Ftball (J); Wt Lfg (J); Master's Degree; UNC Chapel Hill; UNC Wilmington

Wujcik, Amanda M
Wakefield HS
Raleigh, NC

Woodard, Emily S
Northern Vance HS
Henderson, NC

Wood, Jordan
Cedar Ridge HS
Hillsborough, NC

Wittenauer, Ashley
West Johnston HS
Garner, NC

Winecoff, Dana
Piedmont HS
Charlotte, NC

Winn Jr, Larry D
Eastern Wayne HS
Goldsboro, NC

Woodall, Charles D
Anson HS
Peachland, NC

Wright, Brandon
Millbrook HS
Raleigh, NC

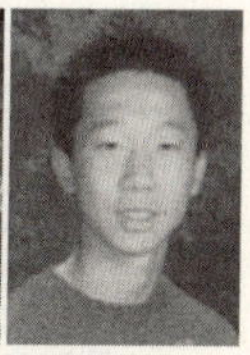
Xiong, John
Albemarle HS
Albemarle, NC

YEE, LIBBY; MATTHEWS, NC; DAVID W BUTLER HS; (SR); F Lan Hn Soc; Hnr Roll; Jr Mshl; Nat Hon Sy; Sci/Math Olympn; Valdctrian; WWAHSS; Comm Volntr; Peer Tut/Med; Key Club; Mth Clb/Tm; MuAlphaTh; Prom Com; French Clb; Chr; Clr Grd; Orch; Tennis (J); CR (R); Tri-Music Honor Society; Chemistry; Pre-Med; East Carolina U

YORK, JOHN C; WINSTON SALEM, NC; WEST FORSYTH HS; (JR); Hnr Roll; Nat Hon Sy; Nat Mrt LOC; WWAHSS; Comm Volntr; Peer Tut/Med; Red Cr Aide; ArtClub; Chrch Yth Grp; Emplmnt; FCA; FBLA; Key Club; Prom Com; SADD; CR (T); Secca Art Show; National Art Honor Society; Electrical Engineering; Pastoral Ministries; North Carolina State U; Southeastern U

YOST, BRENT D; CHINA GROVE, NC; SOUTH ROWAN HS; (JR); Hnr Roll; Nat Hon Sy; St of Mnth; WWAHSS; Comm Volntr; Chrch Yth Grp; Ntl FFA; National Honor Society; FFA Officer; Architecture-Drafting; U of North Carolina-Charlotte; Appalachian State

YOUNG, AMANDA C; MONROE, NC; ROSE PARK SCH; (JR); Duke TS; Hi Hnr Roll; Nat Hon Sy; Yth Ldrshp Prog; Comm Volntr; Peer Tut/Med; Chrch Yth Grp; Dbte Team; Emplmnt; Lib Aide; Mus Clb; Tchrs Aide; Vsity Clb; Orch; SP/M/VS; Chrldg (J); Vllyball (J); Stu Cncl (R); Yrbk (R, P); Accomplished Pianist; Music; English; Columbia Women's College

YOUNG, BRANDON; CANTON, NC; PISGAH HS; (FR); Hnr Roll; Nat Stu Ath Day Aw; Perf Att; Comm Volntr; Spec Olymp Vol; Acpl Chr; Wrstlg (V)

YOUNG, DONALD J; CORNELIUS, NC; HOPEWELL HS; (JR); Ctznshp Aw; Hnr Roll; Pres Ac Ftns Aw; Yth Ldrshp Prog; Comm Volntr; Spec Olymp Vol; Biology Clb; DARE; DECA; Emplmnt; FCA; Mth Clb/Tm; Svce Clb; Latin Clb; Stg Cre; Bskball (V L); Ftball (V L); Wt Lftg (V); Cl Off; Stu Cncl; Pharmacist; UNC Chapel Hill; Campbell College

YOUNG, DYLAN V; PISGAH FOREST, NC; BREVARD HS; (FR); Ctznshp Aw; Duke TS; Hnr Roll; Chrch Yth Grp; Emplmnt; FCA; Ftball (J); Golf (V); Architecture; Drafting; NC State; UNC

YOUNG, KHADIJA R; ROPER, NC; PLYMOUTH HS; (FR); Hi Hnr Roll; Hnr Roll; MVP; Nat Hon Sy; 4-H; Chr; Ch Chr; Arch (V); Bskball (V); Sftball (V); Vllyball (V); Duke U; Michigan State U

YOUNG, MEGAN; MATTHEWS, NC; WEDDINGTON HS; (FR); Hnr Roll; Pres Ac Ftns Aw; WWAHSS; Comm Volntr; Biology Clb; Chrch Yth Grp; DARE; FBLA; Key Club; Chr; SP/M/VS; Tennis Academy of North Carolina Participant; Marine Biology; Forensics; UNC At Wilmington

YOUNG, WALTER; CHARLOTTE, NC; HARDING U HS; (FR); Ctznshp Aw; Hi Hnr Roll; Hnr Roll; MVP; Nat Hon Sy; Otst Ac Ach Awd; Perf Att; St of Mnth; St Optmst of Yr; Comm Volntr; Peer Tut/Med; Chrch Yth Grp; DARE; FCA; Jr Ach; Ch Chr; Bskball (J); Ftball (J); Golf (L); Track (L); Top 10 Scholar Award; Homecoming King; Telecommunication or Broadcasting; Business Management; U of North Carolina; North Carolina State U

YOUNGBLOOD, FELICIA K; RURAL HALL, NC; NORTH FORSYTH HS; (SO); Ctznshp Aw; Hnr Roll; Nat Hon Sy; Perf Att; St of Mnth; WWAHSS; CARE; Comm Volntr; Chrch Yth Grp; Drma Clb; FCA; Key Club; SADD; Chr; Ch Chr; Dnce; SP/M/VS; PPSqd (V L); Upward Cheerleading Coach-Volunteer; All-State Choir-2005; Drama/Theatre Arts; Medical Field/Surgery; North Carolina School of the Arts; New York U

ZAKRZEWSKI, DECEMBER; HOLLY SPRINGS, NC; MIDDLE CREEK HS; (JR); Hnr Roll; Kwnis Aw; MVP; Otst Ac Ach Awd; Comm Volntr; Hab For Humty Volntr; Peer Tut/Med; ArtClub; Chrch Yth Grp; Emplmnt; Key Club; Prom Com; Spanish Clb; Bnd; Mch Bnd; Pep Bnd; SP/M/VS; Lcrsse (V); Vllyball (J); Spanish; Marine Biology; Florida State U; Michigan State U

ZARWOLO, BILL S; GREENSBORO, NC; PAGE HS; (JR); Fut Prb Slvr; Hi Hnr Roll; Hnr Roll; Nat Hon Sy; Nat Ldrshp Svc; Otst Ac Ach Awd; Perf Att; Pres Sch; Sci Fairs; Yth Ldrshp Prog; Comm Volntr; Hosp Aide; Red Cr Aide; Chrch Yth Grp; Drma Clb; Outdrs Clb; Pep Squd; P to P St Amb Prg; Photog; Sci Clb; SADD; Chr; Ch Chr; Drl Tm; Mch Bnd; Bskball (V); Scr Kpr (V); Sccr (V); Tennis (V); Track (V); Vllyball (V); Wt Lftg (V); Wrstlg (V); Cl Off (R); Sch Ppr (P); Royal Ambassador (Church Program); Most Behaved Student; 4 Year College Degree; Civil Engineering; North Carolina A & T U; North Carolina U Raleigh

ZDANOWSKI, BRIANNA; SUMMERFIELD, NC; BISHOP MC GUINNESS CATHOLIC HS; (JR); Hnr Roll; Comm Volntr; Peer Tut/Med; Spec Olymp Vol; Lib Aide; Chr; Dnce; Multiple Science Classes; In Art II Freshman Year & Spanish II; Hospital Pathologist Major; Art Minor; Guilford College U; Medical School At Wake Forest

ZEHNTNER, ERIN G; FRANKLIN, NC; FRANKLIN HS; (SR); Yth Ldrshp Prog; Comm Volntr; Chess; Emplmnt; Mus Clb; Pep Squd; Bnd; Drm Mjr; Jzz Bnd; Mch Bnd; Community Swimming; Music Education; English Major; Western Carolina U; Appalachian State U

ZELIN, ALEXANDRA; CHARLOTTE, NC; SOUTH MECKLENBURG HS; (SO); F Lan Hn Soc; Hi Hnr Roll; Hnr Roll; Nat Hon Sy; WWAHSS; Comm Volntr; Spec Olymp Vol; Quill & Scroll; SADD; Tmpl Yth Grp; Spanish Clb; Swmg (V L); Yrbk (E)

ZOLZER, CAITLYNNE; MOORESVILLE, NC; LAKE NORMAN HS; (JR); Duke TS; Hnr Roll; Jr Mshl; Nat Hon Sy; Comm Volntr; Hosp Aide; Emplmnt; Lib Aide; Ntl Beta Clb; Outdrs Clb; Prom Com; SADD; Spanish Clb; Cr Ctry (V L); Sftball (J); Pre-Med; Nursing; U of North Carolina Chapel Hill; Wake Forest U

Zdanowski, Brianna
Bishop Mc Guinness Catholic HS
Summerfield, NC

Young, Brandon
Pisgah HS
Canton, NC

Young, Donald J
Hopewell HS
Cornelius, NC

Ohio

ABOOD, NICHOLAS G; STOW, OH; CUYAHOGA FALLS HS; (JR); Hi Hnr Roll; WWAHSS; Comm Volntr; Chrch Yth Grp; Drma Clb; Scouts; Chr; Dnce; SP/M/VS; Stg Cre; Sccr (J); Eagle Scout; Who's Who America HS Students/Rotary Scholar; Media Productions; Acting; Kent State; Toledo

ABRAMS, JASLYN T; YOUNGSTOWN, OH; CHANEY HS; (SO); WWAHSS; Comm Volntr; SADD; Chr; Ch Chr; Vllyball (V); Criminal Prosecutor; Pharmaceutical Consultant; Bowling Green State U; Hampton U

ACKROYD, LAKEN; ASHTABULA, OH; WEST JHS; (MS); Hnr Roll; Nat Hon Sy; Otst Ac Ach Awd; Perf Att; Pres Ac Ftns Aw; St of Mnth; Comm Volntr; DARE; Mod UN; Quiz Bowl; Bnd; Flg Crps; Mch Bnd; Chrldg (J); Track (J); CR (R); Sch Ppr (R); Political Science Degree; Lawyer; Indiana Wesleyan U; Harvard U

ADAMS, DANIELLE R; MENTOR, OH; MENTOR HS; (SR); Hnr Roll; St of Mnth; WWAHSS; Off Aide; Sci Clb; Tchrs Aide; Renaissance List; PSEO; Business Management; Hiram College

ADAMS, ELISHA; WOODSFIELD, OH; SWISS HILLS VO TECH SCH; (JR); 4H Awd; Hi Hnr Roll; Perf Att; Pres Ac Ftns Aw; St of Mnth; 4-H; Chess; Voc Ind Clb Am; Chr; Hsbk Rdg; Auto Tech

ADAMS, KRYSTAL A; ASHTABULA, OH; (SR); Hnr Roll; Perf Att; Red Cr Aide; Emplmnt; Off Aide; Chrldg (VJ L); Cr Ctry (J); PP Ftbl (J); Scr Kpr (J); Track (J); Cl Off (T); Stu Cncl (R); Business Club, Perseverance Award Nov. 2004; Homecoming Court/Committee; Nursing; Resp.Therapy; Mercyhurst; Edinboro

ADAMS, SHANNON M; CINCINNATI, OH; SETON HS; (FR); Hnr Roll; Pres Sch; Red Cr Aide; Chrch Yth Grp; DARE; Dbte Team; Scouts; Latin Clb; Orch; Swmg (V); Law

ADAMS, STEPHANIE M; NORTH ROYALTON, OH; PADUA FRANCISCAN HS; (JR); Hnr Roll; Perf Att; St of Mnth; Emplmnt; Key Club; Spanish Clb; Swmg (J); Tennis; Coach Cheerleading Team; Work Two Jobs; Health Care; Education; Kent State; Akron State

ADAMS, TAMMY; COLUMBUS, OH; GROVEPORT MADISON HS; (JR); Hnr Roll; Perf Att; St of Mnth; WWAHSS; Chrch Yth Grp; DARE; Vacation Bible School; Works Blood Drives; Dental Hygiene; Columbus State U; Ohio State U

ADAMS, TAMMY K; COLUMBUS, OH; EASTLAND CAREER CTR; (JR); Ctznshp Aw; Hnr Roll; Nat Hon Sy; Perf Att; WWAHSS; Chrch Yth Grp; Church Youth Group; Dental Hygiene; Ohio State; Columbus State

ADDAIR, AMBER; HOWARD, OH; DANVILLE JR/SR HS; (JR); Hi Hnr Roll; Nat Hon Sy; WWAHSS; ArtClub; Biology Clb; DARE; Emplmnt; Prom Com; Tchrs Aide; Spanish Clb; Bnd; Jzz Bnd; Mch Bnd; Pep Bnd; Bskball (J); Sftball (V); Vllyball (V); Cl Off (T); Sch Ppr (E, R); Ohio State U-Newark Branch; Ohio State U-Main Campus

ADKINS, CHRISTY; DAYTON, OH; BELMONT HS; (JR); Hnr Roll; Nat Hon Sy; Perf Att; Nursing; Kettering College of Medical Arts; Sinclair Community College

ADKINS, KRISTIE; NILES, OH; MC KINLEY HS; (FR); Hnr Roll; Perf Att; St of Mnth; FTA; Spanish Clb; Chr; School Teacher; Lawyer; Ohio State U

AGIN, A MACKENZIE; CINCINNATI, OH; NORTHWEST HS; (JR); F Lan Hn Soc; Hnr Roll; Nat Hon Sy; Perf Att; WWAHSS; Comm Volntr; ArtClub; Chrch Yth Grp; Emplmnt; Key Club; Wdwrkg Clb; SP/M/VS; Bskball (J L); Sccr (VJCL); Track (V L); Stu Cncl (S); CR (R); Yrbk (E, R, P); Young Life; Interior Design; U of Cincinnati; Kent State U

ALBERTS, CORTNEY; SOUTH POINT, OH; SOUTH POINT HS; (JR); Hnr Roll; Pres Sch; Sci Fairs; WWAHSS; Comm Volntr; ArtClub; Drma Clb; MuAlphaTh; Off Aide; Photog; Spanish Clb; Chrldg (V CL); PP Ftbl; Yrbk (E); Psychiatry; Pediatrics; Ohio State U; Marshall U

ALBRECHTA, LEIGH A; FREMONT, OH; FREMONT ROSS HS; (SO); Hi Hnr Roll; Pres Sch; USAA; WWAHSS; Chrch Yth Grp; Key Club; Off Aide; Dnce; Gmnstcs (V); Stu Cncl (R); CR (P); Jack Jones Scholarship; Lead Female Role in Toledo Ballet-"Coppelia"; Professional Ballet Dancer

ALBRIGHT, BRYAN M; AKRON, OH; ELLET HS; (SO); Ctznshp Aw; Perf Att; Comm Volntr; DARE; Drma Clb; Key Club; Mus Clb; Acpl Chr; Chr; SP/M/VS; Skiing; Madrigals in School; Veterinary Technician; Chef/Culinary Arts; U of Akron; Kent State U

ALDERMAN-TUTTLE, ZOEY; VIENNA, OH; MATHEWS HS; (JR); Hnr Roll; Nat Hon Sy; WWAHSS; Drma Clb; HO'Br Yth Ldrshp; Key Club; Prom Com; Spanish Clb; Chr; SP/M/VS; CR (R); Sch Ppr (E, R); Yrbk (R); Fashion Merchandising; Kent State U

ALESHIRE, KRISTIN; ZANESVILLE, OH; BISHOP ROSECRANS HS; (JR); 4H Awd; Hi Hnr Roll; MVP; Nat Hon Sy; Otst Ac Ach Awd; St Optmst of Yr; WWAHSS; Yth Ldrshp Prog; Comm Volntr; 4-H; AL Aux Girls; Key Club; Prom Com; Chrldg (V CL); Gmnstcs; Tennis (V L); Cl Off (S, T); Stu Cncl (P); Pre-Med / Optometry; Biology; Ohio State; Ohio U Athens

ALEXANDER, BILLY; SPRINGFIELD, OH; TECUMSEH HS; (SO); 4H Awd; Hi Hnr Roll; Otst Ac Ach Awd; Pres Ac Ftns Aw; Sci/Math Olympn; WWAHSS; 4-H; Chrch Yth Grp; DARE; Off Aide; Ftball (V L); Track (V L); Wt Lftg (V); Aerospace Engineering; Purdue U; Princeton U

ALI, AMANDA O; LAGRANGE, OH; KEYSTONE HS; (FR); Yth Ldrshp Prog; Sftball (J)

ALICEA, KENITH J; CINCINNATI, OH; FINNEYTOWN MS; (FR); Hnr Roll; Comm Volntr; Chrch Yth Grp; Wdwrkg Clb; Chr; Ch Chr; Wrstlg (V); Cincinnati U; Ohio State

ALI SABUR, ABBAS; CLEVELAND, OH; LUTHERAN HS EAST; (SO); Hnr Roll; P to P St Amb Prg; Tchrs Aide; SP/M/VS; Sftball (L); History Award; Honors English Award; Architecture; Writer; Case Western U; Oberlin College

ALKIRE, ZACHARY T; BELPRE, OH; BELPRE HS; (JR); Hi Hnr Roll; Jr Eng Tech; Nat Hon Sy; Pres Ac Ftns Aw; WWAHSS; Yth Ldrshp Prog; Comm Volntr; Prom Com; Sci Clb; French Clb; Chr; Bsball (V L); Bskball (V L); Golf (V); Cl Off (P); Ohio Association of Student Councils Staff Member; Two-Time Tri-Valley Conference All-Academic Team; Business; Finance; Ohio State U; Coastal Carolina

ALLEN, AMBER L; YOUNGSTOWN, OH; AUSTINTOWN FITCH HS; (SR); Hnr Roll; Emplmnt; Jr Ach; Off Aide; Tchrs Aide; National English Merit Award; Fitch High School Honorary Scholastic Achievement Club; Nursing; U of South Florida

ALLEN, COURTNEY; CANTON, OH; (FR); Ctznshp Aw; Hnr Roll; St of Mnth; Hab For Humty Volntr; Peer Tut/Med; Pep Squd; Chrldg (J); Sftball (J); Registered Nurse; Doctor; Ohio State U; Malone U

ALLEN, LINDSEY M; DAYTON, OH; CHAMINADE-JULIENNE HS; (SR); Nat Hon Sy; Valdctrian; WWAHSS; Comm Volntr; Emplmnt; Pep Squd; Photog; Chrldg (V); Psychology; U of Dayton

ALLEN, TRISTAN; SOUTH POINT, OH; SOUTH POINT HS; (JR); Hnr Roll; Sci Fairs; Spec Olymp Vol; ArtClub; Chrch Yth Grp; DARE; Dbte Team; Emplmnt; Mod UN; NtlFrnscLg; Photog; Bnd; Clr Grd; Flg Crps; Mch Bnd; Yrbk (E); Upward Bound; Forensic Psychology; Ohio State U; Marshall U

ALLMAN, CHARLES T; NEW MARSHFIELD, OH; (SO); Ctznshp Aw; Hi Hnr Roll; Hnr Roll; Otst Ac Ach Awd; 4-H; DARE; Sccr (V L); Vice President of 4-H Group; Forestry; Archaeology; Hocking College; Ohio U

AMBELIOTIS, NICOLE; MIDDLETOWN, OH; LAKOTA EAST HS; (SO); Hi Hnr Roll; Hnr Roll; Comm Volntr; Chrch Yth Grp; DARE; Emplmnt; Key Club; Outdrs Clb; Pep Squd; SADD; Latin Clb; Chrldg (V L); Track (V L); Fitness Competitor; Dance Winner; Physician; Therapist; Ohio State U; U of Pittsburgh

AMERINE, JENNA; VIENNA, OH; MATHEWS HS; (SO); F Lan Hn Soc; Hi Hnr Roll; Hnr Roll; WWAHSS; Drma Clb; Key Club; Mus Clb; Pep Squd; French Clb; Bnd; Mch Bnd; Pep Bnd; SP/M/VS

AMES, KETURAH C; URBANA, OH; TRIAD HS; (JR); 4H Awd; Perf Att; Sci Fairs; 4-H; Prom Com; SADD; Spanish Clb; Chr; Chrldg (V L); Yrbk (P)

AMRINE, BRIAN; LEWIS CTR, OH; OLENTANGY HS; (JR); Hnr Roll; Nat Hon Sy; Perf Att; St of Mnth; WWAHSS; Yth Ldrshp Prog; Chrch Yth Grp; DECA; Emplmnt; FCA; Jr Ach; Svce Clb; Chr; Bskball; Cr Ctry (V L); Skiing; Sccr (J); Track (J); Wrstlg (J); Cl Off (R); Stu Cncl (V, R); Economics; Law; Duke U; Georgetown U

ANACKER, MICHAEL W; DAYTON, OH; ALTER HS; (JR); Hi Hnr Roll; Nat Hon Sy; Comm Volntr; Spec Olymp Vol; Key Club; Spanish Clb; Chr; Bsball (V L); Cr Ctry (V L); Ftball (J); Wrstlg (V CL); Academic All-Other Ran At State in Cross Country 2004; John Sullivan Award-Wrestling; Pre-Med; Engineering; U of Dayton; Case Western

ANANDAPPA, CASSANDRA; COLUMBUS, OH; BISHOP WATTERSON HS; (FR); Hi Hnr Roll; Comm Volntr; Chrch Yth Grp; P to P St Amb Prg; Bnd; Ch Chr; Pep Bnd; Sch Ppr (E); Medical Degree; Music / Literary Arts Major; Northwestern U; Loyola U

ANDERS, KARYN J; ELMORE, OH; WOODMORE HS; (JR); Hnr Roll; WWAHSS; Drma Clb; FTA; Key Club; Tchrs Aide; French Clb; Chr; SP/M/VS; Yrbk (R); Education; English; Heidelberg; Bowling Green

ANDERSON, CHELSEE J; SALINEVILLE, OH; SOUTHERN LOCAL JR/SR HS; (SO); Hi Hnr Roll; Hnr Roll; WWAHSS; 4-H; Chrch Yth Grp; DARE; Scouts; Sftball (V); Vllyball (L); Holds School Record for Best Batting Average in Softball; Veterinarian Medicine Nursing, Teacher; Ohio State U; Youngstown State U

ANDERSON, JOSH; OREGONIA, OH; LEBANON HS; (JR); Hnr Roll; Sci/Math Olympn; WWAHSS; Peer Tut/Med; AL Aux Boys; Dbte Team; Sci Clb; Scouts; Spanish Clb; Electrical Engineering; International Studies; Kettering U

ANDERSON, JUSTIN B; STREETSBORO, OH; STREETSBORO HS; (FR); Hnr Roll; Otst Ac Ach Awd; St of Mnth; Electrician-Maplewood Vocational School

ANDERSON, NICHOLAS A; GREENVILLE, OH; GREENVILLE SR HS; (JR); Hnr Roll; Nat Ldrshp Svc; Perf Att; WWAHSS; ArtClub; Chess; Chrch Yth Grp; Emplmnt; Off Aide; SADD; Tchrs Aide; Stg Cre; Bsball (VJ); Bskball (J); Track (J); Stu Cncl

ANDOH, ADJOA; COLUMBUS, OH; ST FRANCIS DE SALES HS; (JR); Hi Hnr Roll; Hnr Roll; Nat Hon Sy; St Schl; WWAHSS; Peer Tut/Med; AL Aux Girls; DARE; Drma Clb; Mth Clb/Tm; Pep Squd; Latin Clb; Chr; Ch Chr; SP/M/VS; Stg Cre; Chrldg (J); PP Ftbl (J); International Thespian Society; Pre-Medicine; Xavier U; Case Western Reserve U

ANDREWS, MEAGAN S; CANTON, OH; PERRY HS; (JR); St of Mnth; DARE; Key Club; Pep Squd; Tchrs Aide; Bnd; Chr; Mch Bnd; Orch; Track (V L)

ANDREWS, RYAN M; WEST LAFAYETTE, OH; RIDGEWOOD HS; (SR); F Lan Hn Soc; Hnr Roll; WWAHSS; Comm Volntr; Chess; Emplmnt; Lib Aide; Mod UN; Pep Squd; Tchrs Aide; Foreign Clb; Bsball (V); Bskball (J); Cr Ctry (V); Golf (V); Sccr (V); Track (V); Stu Cncl; Yrbk (R); Bass Guitar - Band; Chemistry-Bio / Engineering; Music Technician; Ohio State U - Accepted

ANGEL, SAMANTHA; GROVE CITY, OH; WEST HS; (FR); Hi Hnr Roll; Hnr Roll; Otst Ac Ach Awd; Perf Att; Pres Ac Ftns Aw; Pres Sch; St of Mnth; 4-H; Chrch Yth Grp; Mod UN; Scouts; Bnd; Sftball (V); Nursing; Psychology; The Ohio State U; Ohio U

ANGEL, WILLIAM; TOLEDO, OH; WHITMER HS; (SO); Hnr Roll; St of Mnth; Chrch Yth Grp; DARE; FCA; Ftball (J); Wt Lftg (J); Math Major; Biology Major; U of Toledo; Bowling Green State U

ANGELOTTI, ASHLEY; WARREN, OH; HOWLAND HS; (SO); Hi Hnr Roll; USAA; Comm Volntr; Peer Tut/Med; Dbte Team; Key Club; Mth Clb/Tm; Mod UN; Spch Team; Spanish Clb; Bnd; Mch Bnd; Lit Mag (E); Yrbk (R); Yale Summer School 2004; Future Leaders of America Award; Attorney; Engineer; Yale; U of Chicago

ANTANAITIS, LAURA-KATHLEEN; CUYAHOGA FALLS, OH; CUYAHOGA VALLEY CHRISTIAN AC; (JR); Hi Hnr Roll; Nat Hon Sy; USAA; WWAHSS; Yth Ldrshp Prog; Comm Volntr; Hab For Humty Volntr; Peer Tut/Med; Chrch Yth Grp; Drma Clb; Emplmnt; FBLA; NYLC; Spanish Clb; Dnce; Stg Cre; Cl Off (V); Stu Cncl (V); Yrbk (P); Concerned About Teen Sexuality Speaker - CATS; Pre-School Teacher's Aide; Communication Major / Master's Degree; Spanish Minor; Grove City College; St Mary's of Maryland

ANTES, CALLIHAN; LANCASTER, OH; BLOOM-CARROLL HS; (SR); 4H Awd; Hi Hnr Roll; Hnr Roll; Nat Hon Sy; Otst Ac Ach Awd; Perf Att; Sci Fairs; WWAHSS; Comm Volntr; Red Cr Aide; 4-H; FBLA; FCCLA; Off Aide; Sci Clb; Spanish Clb; Stu Cncl (V); Yrbk (P); Pharmacy / PharmD D; Ohio State U; Ohio State U Newark

ANTES, RACHEL; LANCASTER, OH; BLOOM-CARROLL HS; (SR); 4H Awd; All Am Sch; Hnr Roll; Kwnis Aw; Nat Hon Sy; Nat Ldrshp Svc; Otst Ac Ach Awd; Perf Att; Pres Sch; Sci Fairs; Comm Volntr; FBLA; FCCLA; Key Club; Off Aide; Quiz Bowl; Sci Clb; Spanish Clb; Stu Cncl (T); CR (R); OSU-N Scholar Scholarship; LeFevre Foundation Scholarship; Psychology / Bachelor's & Master's Degrees; Education / Bachelor's & Master's Degrees; Ohio State U

ANTHONY, GALEN L; LYONS, OH; EVERGREEN HS; (SO); Hnr Roll; Otst Ac Ach Awd; Chrch Yth Grp; Bnd; Mch Bnd; Pep Bnd; Wrstlg (V L); Academic Letter Award; Engineering; Lourdes

APEL JR, JOHN P; WHEELERSBURG, OH; WHEELERSBURG HS; Hnr Roll; USAA; WWAHSS; Yth Ldrshp Prog; Comm Volntr; Chrch Yth Grp; HO'Br Yth Ldrshp; Key Club; NYLC; Prom Com; Spanish Clb; Ch Chr; SP/M/VS; Bsball; Ftball; Cl Off (P); HOBY; Boys' State Delegate, Freshman & Sophomore Years; Music; Spanish; Middle Tennessee State U; Miami of Ohio

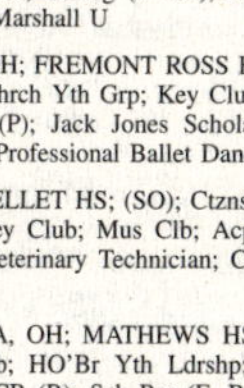
Allman, Charles T
New Marshfield, OH

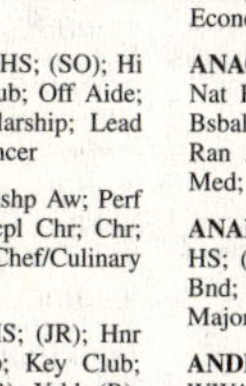
Alexander, Billy
Tecumseh HS
Springfield, OH

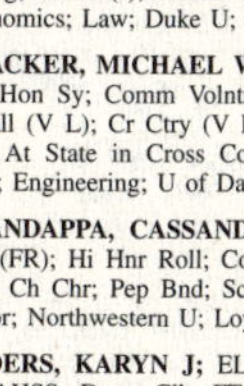
Adkins, Kristie
Mc Kinley HS
Niles, OH

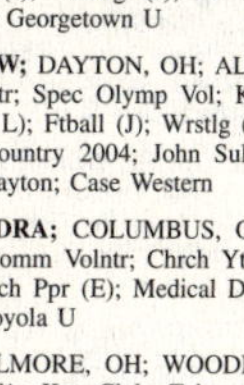
Adams, Krystal A
Ashtabula, OH

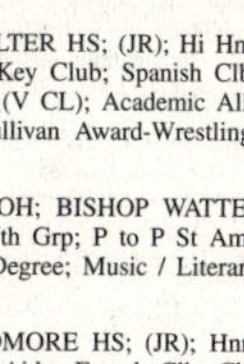
Adams, Tammy
Groveport Madison HS
Columbus, OH

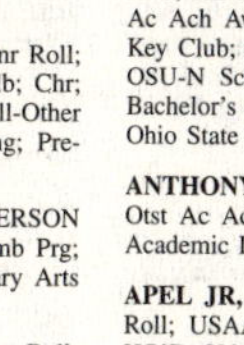
Allen, Courtney
Canton, OH

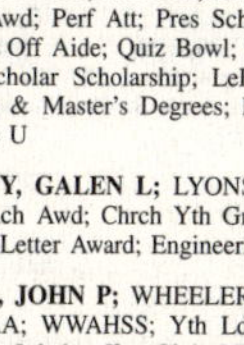
Angel, Samantha
West HS
Grove City, OH

APONTE, SHEENA; CLEVELAND, OH; JOHN MARSHALL HS; (SO); Hnr Roll; MVP; Red Cr Aide; FCA; Sccr (V L); Track (V CL); Ninth Grade Academic Honorary; Peer Mediator; Radiology; Music Producer; Cleveland State U; Clark U

APPEL, MAGGIE; PLEASANT PLN, OH; LITTLE MIAMI HS; (SR); Hnr Roll; WWAHSS; Comm Volntr; Peer Tut/Med; Emplmnt; Tchrs Aide; Spanish Clb; Chr; Sch Ppr (E, R, P); Contest Choir; Internship; Psychology; Wright State

AQUINO JR, CONRAD B; CINCINNATI, OH; NORTHWEST HS; (SR); Hi Hnr Roll; Hnr Roll; Perf Att; Hosp Aide; Emplmnt; Key Club; Off Aide; Scouts; Wdwrkg Clb; Bnd; Jzz Bnd; Mch Bnd; Eagle Scout Rank; Pre-Pharmacy; U of Cincinnati

ARBUCKLE, ANNIE; BYESVILLE, OH; MEADOWBROOK HS; (JR); Hnr Roll; Otst Ac Ach Awd; Pres Ac Ftns Aw; Sci Fairs; Bskball (J); Sftball (V); Nursing/Aide; Professional Athlete; Zanesville; Ohio State

ARGENTI, SANTINO R; LORAIN, OH; LORAIN ADMIRAL KING HS; (SR); Ctznshp Aw; Hnr Roll; Otst Ac Ach Awd; Comm Volntr; Chess; DARE; Scouts; Golf (VJ L); Chess Club President; Eagle Scout - April 2005; Golf Course Management; Architecture; Penn State U; California State Polytechnic U

ARIZMENDI, ASHLEY N; ELYRIA, OH; ELYRIA HS; (SO); Hnr Roll; St of Mnth; Spec Olymp Vol; Off Aide; Tchrs Aide; Pediatrician

ARMOCIDA, STEPHANIE; VALLEY CITY, OH; MIDVIEW HS; (FR); Hnr Roll; Perf Att; St of Mnth; Off Aide; Sccr (J); Business Field

ARMSTRONG, ELIZABETH R; MEDINA, OH; MEDINA HS; (JR); Hi Hnr Roll; Hnr Roll; Comm Volntr; Peer Tut/Med; Chrch Yth Grp; FCA; Off Aide; Tech Clb; French Clb; Acpl Chr; Chr; Ch Chr; Stg Cre; Sccr (J); Track (J); Soccer - Sportsmanship Award; Physics; Education / Young Adults; U of Akron; Ohio State U

ARNOLD, JOHNATHAN B; CINCINNATI, OH; ANDERSON CTY HS; (JR); F Lan Hn Soc; Hi Hnr Roll; Hnr Roll; Nat Hon Sy; Otst Ac Ach Awd; Perf Att; St of Mnth; Comm Volntr; Spec Olymp Vol; DECA; Emplmnt; Chr; SP/M/VS; CR (R); Athletic Trainer

ARTHUR, CASSIE N; JACKSON, OH; WELLSTON HS; (SO); All Am Sch; Hi Hnr Roll; Otst Ac Ach Awd; Pres Ac Ftns Aw; Pres Sch; St of Mnth; USAA; WWAHSS; Lib Aide; Pep Squd; P to P St Amb Prg; Sftball (J); Vllyball (JC); Zoology; Neuropsychology; Cornell U; Murdoch U

ARTHUR, MELISSA L; WEST CHESTER, OH; (JR); Hnr Roll; Yth Ldrshp Prog; Comm Volntr; Spec Olymp Vol; DECA; Emplmnt; Key Club; NYLC; Chrldg (V); Gmnstcs (V); CR (R); Law; Miami Oxford

ARTHUR, STEVEN; COLUMBUS, OH; SOUTH HS URBAN AC; (SO); Hnr Roll; Perf Att; Comm Volntr; Hab For Humty Volntr; Chrch Yth Grp; DARE; ROTC; Chr; Ch Chr; Clr Grd; Drl Tm; Engineering/Customizing; Blue Printing; Michigan U

ARTHUR-MENSAH, AWURAFUA; AMHERST, OH; LAKE RIDGE AC; MS; Hi Hnr Roll; Hnr Roll; Chrch Yth Grp; Pep Squd; Chr; Dnce; Orch; SP/M/VS; Chrldg (JV); Track; Stu Cncl (R); CR (R); Gymnastics - Level 8 (Private Gym); JV- Competitive Cheerleader (Private Gym); Pediatric Medicine; Duke U; U of California Los Angeles

ASH, CHRISTIAN A; BRISTOLVILLE, OH; LAKEVIEW HS; (FR); Hnr Roll; Comm Volntr; Tchrs Aide; Track; To Become Head Chef.; To Own Ownership of Restaurant; Pittsburg Institute of Fine Arts

ASHLEY, LAURA J; CINCINNATI, OH; CONNER HS; (SR); Hnr Roll; Nat Hon Sy; St of Mnth; Comm Volntr; Chrch Yth Grp; Emplmnt; FBLA; Prom Com; Clr Grd; Adv Cncl (R); Cl Off (P); Stu Cncl (P, V); CR (R); Candidate for School Board; Superintendent's Student Advisory Council; Business; Law; Moorhead State U - Accepted with Commonwealth Scholarship

ATALA, SARAH R; HILLIARD, OH; DARBY HS; (FR); Hnr Roll; Otst Ac Ach Awd; Perf Att; St of Mnth; WWAHSS; Yth Ldrshp Prog; Comm Volntr; Chrch Yth Grp; DARE; Key Club; SADD; Chr; Ch Chr; Lawyer; OSU

ATHANAS, MICHELLE; LORAIN, OH; LORAIN SOUTHVIEW HS; (SO); Hi Hnr Roll; Otst Ac Ach Awd; Perf Att; WWAHSS; Comm Volntr; Chrch Yth Grp; Drma Clb; Key Club; Mod UN; Scouts; Dnce; SP/M/VS; Track (V); Vllyball (J); Unity Club - Church's Basketball Team & Dance Group; Sunday School Teacher

ATKINSON, TIFFANY; WEST SALEM, OH; NORTHWESTERN HS; (SO); Hi Hnr Roll; Emplmnt; Tchrs Aide; PP Ftbl; Scr Kpr (V); Track (V); Stu Cncl (R); Sch Ppr (E); Teachers Awards - English 9 / 10 / Geometry / French I / II / Physical Science / Biology Accelerated; Volunteered for the Salvation Army; Master's Degree in Law; New York U

ATROZSKIN, ALI; GARFIELD HTS, OH; GARFIELD HTS HS; (JR); Hnr Roll; ArtClub; Physician's Assistant; Physical Therapist; Ursuline College; John Carroll College

ATTAR, STEPHEN; CANTON, OH; EDISON JHS; (FR); SP/M/VS; Stu Cncl (P); CR (V); Sch Ppr (E); Power of the Pen; Art Prizes; Doctor; Business Man; Kent State U; Youngstown U

AVERY, DESIRAE M; GENOA, OH; GENOA HS; (SR); Hi Hnr Roll; Nat Hon Sy; WWAHSS; AL Aux Girls; Chrch Yth Grp; Emplmnt; Key Club; Prom Com; Tchrs Aide; Bskball (V CL); Chrldg (V CL); PP Ftbl (V C); Sftball (V CL); Cl Off (R); Stu Cncl (P); Yrbk (E, P); Business; Accounting; Ohio Northern U

AVKSHTOL, VERA; STRONGSVILLE, OH; STRONGSVILLE HS; (SR); Hi Hnr Roll; Hnr Roll; MVP; Otst Ac Ach Awd; ArtClub; Key Club; Mth Clb/Tm; MuAlphaTh; Latin Clb; Tennis (V L); Track (L); Received Senior Athletic Award; Received Ohio Tennis Coaches' Association Golden Racquet Award; Pre-Medicine; Biomedical Engineering; Boston U; Case Western Reserve U

AYARKWAH, BELINDA; CINCINNATI, OH; WINTON WOODS HS; (JR); Hi Hnr Roll; Hnr Roll; Otst Ac Ach Awd; Perf Att; St of Mnth; WWAHSS; Comm Volntr; ArtClub; Chrch Yth Grp; Keeping Honor Roll Status; Community Service Award; Midwifery; Nurse; U of Cincinnati; Miami U

AYERS, ABBY M; NEW PHILADELPHIA, OH; NEW PHILADELPHIA HS; (JR); Hnr Roll; Pres Ac Ftns Aw; Comm Volntr; Peer Tut/Med; Chrch Yth Grp; Emplmnt; Key Club; Pep Squd; Prom Com; Sci Clb; Chr; Chrldg (V L); Superior Rating State Choir Final-04/05; Leadership & All Star Award (Large Group) Cheer Camp-04; Veterinary Medicine; Ohio State U; Muskingum

AYERS, JEREMY; BELPRE, OH; BELPRE HS; (JR); Hi Hnr Roll; Hnr Roll; Pres Ac Ftns Aw; WWAHSS; Yth Ldrshp Prog; Comm Volntr; DARE; French Clb; Computer Engineering; Georgia Institute of Technology; Case Western Reserve

AZAR, RACHAEL; ROOTSTOWN, OH; SOUTHEAST HS; (SR); Hnr Roll; Nat Hon Sy; WWAHSS; Comm Volntr; Hosp Aide; Peer Tut/Med; ArtClub; Chrch Yth Grp; Emplmnt; FCA; Tchrs Aide; French Clb; Classics; Literature; U of North Carolina; Kent State U

BAEHRENS, AIMEE; OAK HARBOR, OH; OAK HARBOR HS; (SO); Hi Hnr Roll; Otst Ac Ach Awd; Perf Att; St of Mnth; WWAHSS; DARE; Emplmnt; Key Club; Sci Clb; Vsity Clb; French Clb; Bnd; Mch Bnd; Pep Bnd; Cr Ctry (V L); Track (V L)

BAI, BEIBEI; DAYTON, OH; BEAVER CREEK HS; (SO); Hnr Roll; Sci Fairs; St of Mnth; Peer Tut/Med; DARE; Dbte Team; Drma Clb; Mth Clb/Tm; MuAlphaTh; NtlFrnscLg; Scouts; Spch Team; Bnd; SP/M/VS; Stg Cre; Speech and Debate; Math Club; Pre-Med; Anthropology; Columbia U; Harvard U

BAILEY, KERI L; FAIRFIELD, OH; FAIRFIELD HS; (JR); Hnr Roll; Otst Ac Ach Awd; Pres Ac Ftns Aw; WWAHSS; Comm Volntr; Peer Tut/Med; DARE; Emplmnt; Prom Com; Tchrs Aide; French Clb; Orch; Chrldg (VJ L); PP Ftbl; Track (V L); Adv Cncl; CR; 2 Year Gmc All-Academic Achievement; 2002-2003 All-American Cheerleader; Elementary Education; Marine Biology; U of Tennessee; Miami U-Ohio

BAIRD, SCOTT F; SHELBY, OH; SHELBY SR HS; (FR); 4H Awd; Hi Hnr Roll; Hnr Roll; Otst Ac Ach Awd; Pres Sch; Sci Fairs; WWAHSS; Comm Volntr; 4-H; Chrch Yth Grp; DARE; Emplmnt; Bnd; Mch Bnd; Bskball (J); Ftball (J); Wt Lftg (J); Cl Off (V); Stu Cncl (R); Superintendent's Honors List; Scholar Athlete Award; Medical; Education; Ohio State U; Kentucky U

BAJAJ, DEVANSH; ORRVILLE, OH; ORRVILLE HS; (SO); Hnr Roll; Perf Att; St of Mnth; CARE; Comm Volntr; Peer Tut/Med; Chess; Cmptr Clb; DARE; Mth Clb/Tm; Outdrs Clb; SADD; Bskball; Ice Sktg; Mar Art; Sccr; CR (R); Lit Mag; To Serve Mankind by Providing Health Care; Become a Doctor

BAKA, MARIE; WARREN, OH; CHAMPION HS; (JR); Stg Cre; Track (V); Stu Cncl (T); Yrbk (P); Attended Dolan Learning Centers; Chemistry; Anthropology

BAKER, ALICIA M; HAMILTON, OH; ST JOHN'S INTERNATIONAL SCH; (SR); Hi Hnr Roll; Nat Hon Sy; Otst Ac Ach Awd; Salutrn; Comm Volntr; Red Cr Aide; ArtClub; Chrch Yth Grp; Orch; Lit Mag (E); American Women's Club Community Service Award; Student of the Year in French & Math; Veterinary Medicine; French; Ohio State U

BAKER, CASEY; POWELL, OH; HOWE MILITARY SCH; (FR); Ctznshp Aw; Hi Hnr Roll; Otst Ac Ach Awd; Comm Volntr; DARE; Scouts; Bnd; Mch Bnd; Bsball (V L); Outstanding Musician (Gold); Most Trustworthy Medal; Musical Composition/Education/Performance; Criminal Justice; Wake Forest U; Notre Dame U

BAKER, CHELSEA; CANFIELD, OH; AUSTINTOWN FITCH HS; (FR); Ctznshp Aw; Hnr Roll; St of Mnth; DARE; Bskball (V); Mar Art; Stu Cncl (S); Second Degree Black Belt - Tae Kwon Do Karate; Digital Imagining; Cosmetology; U of Las Vegas; UCLA

BAKER, ERIN; GREEN SPRINGS, OH; CLYDE HS; (FR); Hi Hnr Roll; Hnr Roll; Pres Sch; St of Mnth; Key Club; Off Aide; Bskball (J); Vllyball (C); Sports Academic Awards; Camp Med at MCO Hospital Toledo; Pediatrician; Ohio State U

BAKER, KAYLA M; NEWARK, OH; WILSON MS; (MS); Ctznshp Aw; Hnr Roll; Nat Hon Sy; Otst Ac Ach Awd; Perf Att; St of Mnth; Yth Ldrshp Prog; Comm Volntr; Peer Tut/Med; Spec Olymp Vol; DARE; Lib Aide; Mus Clb; Off Aide; SADD; Tchrs Aide; Spanish Clb; Bnd; Gmnstcs (V); Track (L); Vllyball (L); Stu Cncl (S, T); Gymnastic Awards; Corporate Law; Pennsylvania State U (Penn State)

BAKER, RICHARD F; JACKSON, OH; JACKSON HS; (FR); Fut Prb Slvr; Hnr Roll; Sci Fairs; Comm Volntr; ArtClub; Dbte Team; FBLA; Lib Aide; Off Aide; Wdwrkg Clb; Dnce; Cr Ctry; Golf; Stu Cncl (V); Yrbk (R); History Major; Ohio State

BAKO, BRITTANY R; WARREN, OH; CHAMPION HS; (JR); Hnr Roll; MVP; WWAHSS; Comm Volntr; Emplmnt; Key Club; Off Aide; Photog; Prom Com; SP/M/VS; Stg Cre; Chrldg (V); Sccr (V); Track (V); Cl Off (V, R); Yrbk (E, P)

BALDINGER, NINA K; GALENA, OH; DELAWARE AREA CAREER CTR; (SR); Hnr Roll; Comm Volntr; Peer Tut/Med; Chrch Yth Grp; Emplmnt; P to P St Amb Prg; Merit Roll, Grads JOG; Excellent Attendance; Criminology; Law Enforcement; Baldwin-Wallace College

BALDINGER JR, JAMES; DELAWARE, OH; RB HAYES HS; (JR); Hnr Roll; Otst Ac Ach Awd; Pres Sch; WWAHSS; Emplmnt; SADD; Wdwrkg Clb; Wild Life / Forestry

BALL, ALEX; GALLIPOLIS, OH; GALLIA AC HS; (SO); Chr; Physical Therapy; Ohio U

BALLARD, BEN; NEW PHILADELPHIA, OH; NEW PHILADELPHIA HS; (JR); Hnr Roll; Nat Hon Sy; WWAHSS; Comm Volntr; Hosp Aide; FTA; Key Club; Sci Clb; Scouts; French Clb; Bnd; Jzz Bnd; Mch Bnd; Pep Bnd; Band Historian; Pit Section Leader; Engineer; Case Western Reserve U; The Ohio State U

BALLON, DANIELLE N; COLUMBUS, OH; FASTMOOR AC; (SR); Hi Hnr Roll; Hnr Roll; MVP; Nat Hon Sy; Otst Ac Ach Awd; Perf Att; WWAHSS; Peer Tut/Med; Emplmnt; Off Aide; Vsity Clb; Stg Cre; Sccr (V CL); Sftball (V L); Accounting; U of Akron

BALMER, CARYN; PANDORA, OH; PANDORA-GILBOA HS; (SR); Hnr Roll; Emplmnt; Photog; Sci Clb; Tchrs Aide; German Clb; SP/M/VS; Chrldg (VJ L); Nursing; Ohio Northern U

BALMERT, STEPHANIE L; LORAIN, OH; LORAIN ADMIRAL KING HS; (FR); Hnr Roll; Drma Clb; ROTC; Clr Grd; Drl Tm; Naval Career; Child Therapist; Ohio State; Michigan State

BANDELOW, KYLENE; CLEVELAND, OH; MAYFIELD HS; (JR); Hnr Roll; Sci Fairs; St of Mnth; Comm Volntr; Chrch Yth Grp; DARE; Emplmnt; Off Aide; Scouts; Tchrs Aide; Acpl Chr; Bnd; Chr; Drl Tm; Swmg; Yrbk (R, P); AVIS Award; Community Softball Summer League; Early Childhood Education; Lakeland Community College; Baldwin-Wallace College

BARANSKI, TRINA; WARREN, OH; HOWLAND HS; (SR); Ctznshp Aw; Hnr Roll; Nat Hon Sy; Pres Ac Ftns Aw; Sci Fairs; WWAHSS; Comm Volntr; Peer Tut/Med; DARE; Drma Clb; Key Club; Off Aide; Tchrs Aide; Spanish Clb; Acpl Chr; Dnce; Drm Mjr; SP/M/VS; Sch Ppr; Who's Who Among American High School Students; Business Administration; Bowling Green State U

BARANYK, BETHANY; ALLIANCE, OH; ALLIANCE HS; (FR); Hi Hnr Roll; Sci Fairs; Chrch Yth Grp; Key Club; Mod UN; Chr; Orch; SP/M/VS; Teen Court; Destination Imagination

BARANYK, MATTHEW; ALLIANCE, OH; ALLIANCE HS; (JR); Hi Hnr Roll; Nat Hon Sy; Otst Ac Ach Awd; AL Aux Boys; Chrch Yth Grp; Emplmnt; Key Club; Chr; Orch; SP/M/VS; Swg Chr; Architect; Akron U

BARAZ, EUGENE; CLEVELAND, OH; MAYFIELD HS; (JR); Hnr Roll; Dnce; Track (V); Physical Therapy; Cleveland State U

BARGER, MATTHEW; PICKERINGTON, OH; PICKERINGTON HS NORTH; (JR); Hi Hnr Roll; Sci/Math Olympn; St of Mnth; Comm Volntr; Peer Tut/Med; Emplmnt; FBLA; Key Club; Sci Clb; Scouts; German Clb; SP/M/VS; Stg Cre; Stu Cncl (R); Bowling, Eagle Scout; Pharmacy; Ohio Northern U; U Of Toledo

BARKER, KELSEY; WEST CHESTER, OH; LAKOTA EAST HS; (SO); Hi Hnr Roll; Hnr Roll; St of Mnth; Peer Tut/Med; 4-H; Chrch Yth Grp; FTA; Bnd; Hsbk Rdg (V); Education; Psychology; Miami U; Ohio State U

BARKOCY, CARLY; CINCINNATI, OH; FINNEYTOWN HS; (JR); Duke TS; Hi Hnr Roll; Nat Hon Sy; Sci/Math Olympn; WWAHSS; Comm Volntr; Chrch Yth Grp; DARE; FCA; Key Club; Pep Squd; Quiz Bowl; Bnd; Mch Bnd; Pep Bnd; SP/M/VS; National Honor Society; Mercantile Library Award; Belmont U; Eastern Kentucky U

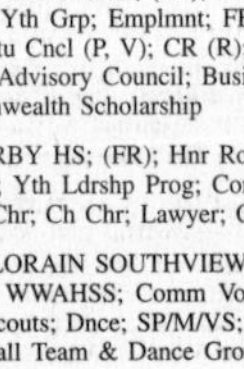

Bandelow, Kylene
Mayfield HS
Cleveland, OH

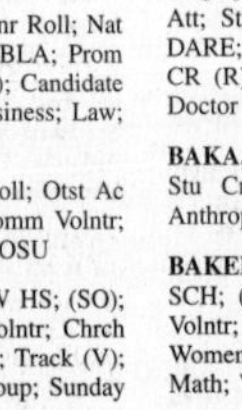

Atkinson, Tiffany
Northwestern HS
West Salem, OH

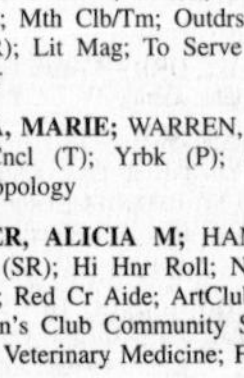

Athanas, Michelle
Lorain Southview HS
Lorain, OH

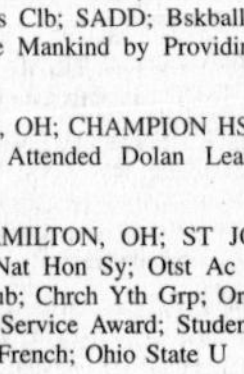

Argenti, Santino R
Lorain Admiral King HS
Lorain, OH

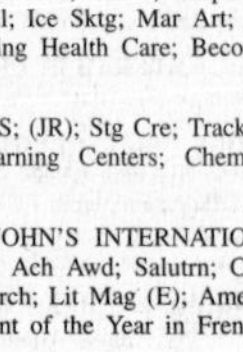

Arthur, Steven
South HS Urban AC
Columbus, OH

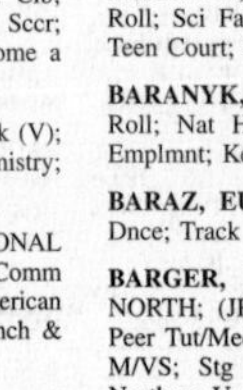

Ball, Alex
Gallia AC HS
Gallipolis, OH

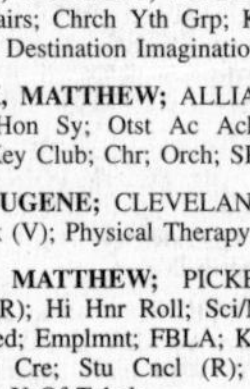

Baranski, Trina
Howland HS
Warren, OH

BARNES, JOSHUA; SYLVANIA, OH; NORTHVIEW HS; (FR); Ctznshp Aw; Hnr Roll; Comm Volntr; Chr; Architecture; U of Cincinnati

BARNES, KALA; DAYTON, OH; FAIRMONT HS; (MS); Perf Att; St of Mnth; Peer Tut/Med; ArtClub; Chrch Yth Grp; Lib Aide; Off Aide; Scouts; SADD; Bnd; Ch Chr; Chrldg (L); Mar Art; CR (R); Barbizon Modeling & Acting School; Criminology; Photography; Texas U; Sinclair Community College

BARNES, KRYSTAL A; MARYSVILLE, OH; MARYSVILLE HS; (JR); Hnr Roll; Otst Ac Ach Awd; Sci Fairs; St of Mnth; Yth Ldrshp Prog; Comm Volntr; Chrch Yth Grp; DARE; Emplmnt; Scouts; Tchrs Aide; Chr; Track (J); U of South Carolina; Columbus State

BARNETT, STEPHANIE; SPRINGFIELD, OH; SHAWNEE HS; (SO); 4H Awd; Hi Hnr Roll; Hnr Roll; MVP; Sci Fairs; Comm Volntr; 4-H; Key Club; Scouts; SADD; Bnd; Chr; Clr Grd; Flg Crps; Golf (J); Sftball (C); Vllyball (L); On the Shawnee Bowling Team; 4-H / K-9 Princess 2003; Early Childhood Education; Spanish Teacher; Wright State U; Wittenberg U

BARR, JEREMY; YOUNGSTOWN, OH; AUSTINTOWN FITCH HS; (FR); Perf Att; Yth Ldrshp Prog; Ch Chr; Cr Ctry (L); Track (V); Sports Massage

BARR, SARA M; CANTON, OH; HOOVER HS; Ctznshp Aw; DAR; Hnr Roll; MVP; Nat Hon Sy; Otst Ac Ach Awd; Pres Ac Ftns Aw; Pres Sch; Comm Volntr; Peer Tut/Med; Spec Olymp Vol; Emplmnt; Key Club; Quill & Scroll; Svce Clb; Spanish Clb; Bskball (VJC); Cr Ctry (V); Track (V CL); Sch Ppr (E, R); USATF Junior Olympic National Qualifier; Journalism; Case Western Reserve U

BARRINGER, JOSH; NORTH JACKSON, OH; JACKSON-MILTON HS; (JR); Hnr Roll; MVP; Sci/Math Olympn; USAA; WWAHSS; Peer Tut/Med; DARE; FCA; Key Club; Prom Com; SADD; Tchrs Aide; Bskball (V L); Ftball (V L); Wt Lftg (V); Stu Cncl (R); CR (R); Gatorade Will to Win Award; Pharmacist; Sports Medicine; Toledo U; Youngstown State

BARSTOW, NATHAN K; ALBANY, OH; ALEXANDER HS; (SO); Hnr Roll; Otst Ac Ach Awd; Sci Fairs; Peer Tut/Med; Spec Olymp Vol; DARE; Mod UN; Scouts; Tchrs Aide; French Clb; Bnd; Model United Nations; Mechanical Engineering; Computer Programming; Ohio U; Shawnee State U

BARTH, JESSICA S; CANTON, OH; JACKSON HS; (SR); Ctznshp Aw; Hi Hnr Roll; Pres Sch; St of Mnth; Hab For Humty Volntr; Emplmnt; Key Club; Pep Squd; French Clb; Bnd; Mch Bnd; Pep Bnd; Swmg (V); Girl Scout Gold Award; President's Award; Teacher-Biology; The U of Akron

BARTHOLOW, HEATHER M; LONDON, OH; LONDON HS; (JR); Hi Hnr Roll; Kwnis Aw; Nat Hon Sy; Perf Att; WWAHSS; Comm Volntr; Emplmnt; Jr Ach; Prom Com; SADD; SP/M/VS; Stg Cre; Chrldg (V); Track (V); Cl Off (V); Stu Cncl (R); Forensic Science; Defiance College; Ohio State U

BARTOW, KARINA A; COLLINS, OH; WESTERN RESERVE HS; (FR); Hi Hnr Roll; Hnr Roll; Drma Clb; French Clb; Stg Cre; French Club; Bridal Consultant; Author

BASFORD, MICHELLE; MASSILLON, OH; JACKSON HS; (JR); Hnr Roll; St of Mnth; WWAHSS; Comm Volntr; DARE; Key Club; Off Aide; Tchrs Aide; Spanish Clb; I Was Accepted Into the Aultman Hosp Career Ac; I Want to Enter Either the Medical Field or Education; Akron U; Walsh U

BASS, SHAWN A; WASHINGTON COURT HOUSE, OH; MIAMI TRACE HS; (JR); Hi Hnr Roll; Otst Ac Ach Awd; Perf Att; Pres Ac Ftns Aw; Pres Sch; Sci Fairs; Yth Ldrshp Prog; Comm Volntr; Peer Tut/Med; Chrch Yth Grp; DARE; FCA; Ntl FFA; P to P St Amb Prg; Quiz Bowl; ROTC; Voc Ind Clb Am; Ch Chr; Clr Grd; Drl Tm; Wrstlg (VJ); CR (R); Church Representative of Church Board; FIF Organization; Business; Wood Working; Circleville Bible College

BATCHMAN, AARON N; MEDINA, OH; MEDINA SR HS; (SR); F Lan Hn Soc; Hnr Roll; MVP; Nat Hon Sy; Peer Tut/Med; Red Cr Aide; Chrch Yth Grp; Emplmnt; Key Club; Orch; Cr Ctry (V C); Lcrsse (V); Swmg (V); Track (V); Mechanical Engineering; U of Dayton

BATES, ASHLEY M; LORAIN, OH; CLEARVIEW HS; (JR); Hi Hnr Roll; Hnr Roll; Nat Hon Sy; Otst Ac Ach Awd; Perf Att; WWAHSS; Peer Tut/Med; Chrch Yth Grp; Emplmnt; Off Aide; Tchrs Aide; Ch Chr; SP/M/VS; Sch Ppr (E, R); Children's Services; Social Work; Case Western Reserve; Ohio State U

BATESOLE, BRIANA; AVON LAKE, OH; AVON LAKE HS; (JR); Ctznshp Aw; Hi Hnr Roll; Nat Hon Sy; Nat Ldrshp Svc; Otst Ac Ach Awd; Pres Ac Ftns Aw; USAA; WWAHSS; Comm Volntr; Chrch Yth Grp; Emplmnt; Key Club; Scouts; Tchrs Aide; Vsity Clb; Ch Chr; Cr Ctry (VJ L); Dvng (V L); Gmnstcs; Hsbk Rdg; PP Ftbl; Skiing; Swmg (V CL); Track (V L); Elementary Education; Otterbein College; Wittenberg U

BATTLE, KYLE E; CINCINNATI, OH; SYCAMORE HS; (SO); Ctznshp Aw; Hnr Roll; Pres Ac Ftns Aw; Yth Ldrshp Prog; Comm Volntr; Chrch Yth Grp; DARE; Jr Ach; Pep Squd; Bskball (V L); Ftball (V L); Track (V L); Adv Cncl; Cl Off (P); Stu Cncl (P); Professional Sports; Sports Journalism; Brown U; U of North Carolina-Chapel Hill

BAUER, JOSHUA; WARREN, OH; HOWLAND HS; (JR); Hnr Roll; St of Mnth; Scouts; Eagle Scout; Own My Own Business; Business Major; Ohio State U; Pittsburgh Art Institute

BAUMANN, LIESL; WESTERVILLE, OH; WESTERVILLE NORTH HS; (SR); All Am Sch; Hi Hnr Roll; Nat Hon Sy; Otst Ac Ach Awd; Perf Att; Salutrn; St of Mnth; USAA; WWAHSS; Comm Volntr; Peer Tut/Med; Emplmnt; Key Club; Scouts; Svce Clb; Bnd; Mch Bnd; Orch; Pep Bnd; National Council of Teachers of English Award Winner in Writing; Ohio U, American History; Chemistry; Biology; Miami U; U of Dayton

BEAL, MICHELLE; MIDDLEFIELD, OH; CARDINAL HS; (SO); Ctznshp Aw; Hnr Roll; St of Mnth; Hab For Humty Volntr; Chrch Yth Grp; Key Club; Pep Squd; Spanish Clb; Bnd; Mch Bnd; Pep Bnd; Bskball (J); Cr Ctry (V); Sftball (V); Journalism; Sports; Ohio State U

BEAM, AUTUMN; PEMBERVILLE, OH; EASTWOOD HS; (SO); Hnr Roll; Kwnis Aw; Otst Ac Ach Awd; Yth Ldrshp Prog; Comm Volntr; Chrch Yth Grp; Drma Clb; HO'Br Yth Ldrshp; Mus Clb; International Clb; Bnd; Jzz Bnd; Mch Bnd; SP/M/VS; Band Librarian and Section Leader; OMEA District 1 Honors Band (1st Choir); Music Education; Photography; VanderCook College of Music; Roosevelt U

BEAM, BRANDY; ZANESVILLE, OH; WEST MUSKINGUM HS; (SO); Dnce; Architecture; Interior Design

BEAMER, ROBBIE; KENTON, OH; KENTON SR HS; (FR); Ctznshp Aw; Hnr Roll; Otst Ac Ach Awd; Chrch Yth Grp; Bnd; Mch Bnd; Ftball (J); Mar Art; Wt Lftg; Computer Programmer; ITT Tech

BECK, JORDAN; WAUSEON, OH; PETTISVILLE HS; (SR); 4H Awd; Hnr Roll; Perf Att; Sci Fairs; WWAHSS; Comm Volntr; Peer Tut/Med; 4-H; Chrch Yth Grp; Ntl FFA; Prom Com; Spanish Clb; Chr; Bskball (J L); Cr Ctry (V CL); Track (V L); Cl Off (T); FFA Chapter President; Attended Washington Leadership Conference; Animal Sciences; Animal Nutrition; The Ohio State U

BECKEMEIER, MEGAN; BECKEMEIER, OH; TALAWANDA HS; (FR); Perf Att; Peer Tut/Med; Chrch Yth Grp; Key Club; Scouts; Bnd; Mch Bnd; Teaching; Ohio State; Miami

BEDNAR, SHELLEY; MANTUA, OH; (SR); Hnr Roll; Nat Hon Sy; WWAHSS; Drma Clb; Tchrs Aide; Bnd; Drm Mjr; Jzz Bnd; SP/M/VS; Vllyball (V); Band Council President; Vice President of National Honor Society; Dual Major in Business Management & Marketing; Ohio Northern U

BEERY, DAVID T; AKRON, OH; BARBERTON HS; (FR); Hnr Roll; WWAHSS; Comm Volntr; Tchrs Aide; Acpl Chr; Chr; Ch Chr; SP/M/VS; Sccr (J); International Poetry Contest Winner; Marine Corps - Auto Mechanics

BEIL, BRITT; CORTLAND, OH; LAKEVIEW HS; (FR); Hnr Roll; Otst Ac Ach Awd; WWAHSS; Drma Clb; Acpl Chr; Chr; SP/M/VS; Youngstown State U; Ohio State U

BEINLICH, COURTNEY; DAYTON, OH; ALTER HS; (FR); Hnr Roll; WWAHSS; Comm Volntr; Key Club; Latin Clb; Bskball; Sccr (J); Business Degree; Miami U

BEISWENGER, APRIL; NEY, OH; FAIRVIEW; (JR); Hi Hnr Roll; Hnr Roll; MVP; Nat Hon Sy; Otst Ac Ach Awd; WWAHSS; Emplmnt; Mth Clb/Tm; Prom Com; SADD; Vsity Clb; Bskball (JC); Sftball (V L); Vsy Clb (V L); Vllyball (V CL); Cl Off (S, T); Stu Cncl (S); Yrbk (E, P); National Honors Society; Student Council; Radiology; Ultra Sounds; Owens Community College; Saint Francis College

BELKOFER, DANIELE; FAIRFIELD, OH; FAIRFIELD HS; (JR); Hnr Roll; WWAHSS; Comm Volntr; Hab For Humty Volntr; Chrch Yth Grp; Emplmnt; FCA; Latin Clb; Dnce; PP Ftbl; Track (J); Medical Research; Architect; Massachusetts Institute of Technology; Harvard

BELL, KAITLIN E; SALEM, OH; WEST BRANCH HS; (JR); Hnr Roll; Pres Ac Ftns Aw; St of Mnth; Emplmnt; Off Aide; SADD; Sftball (V); Vllyball (J); Physical Therapy Assistant; Stark Tech; Kent State

BELL, LARONYA N; AKRON, OH; ARCHBISHOP HOBAN HS; (JR); Hi Hnr Roll; WWAHSS; Hosp Aide; Peer Tut/Med; Chrch Yth Grp; Emplmnt; Jr Ach; French Clb; Ch Chr; Dnce; Drl Tm; PP Ftbl; Tennis; Lit Mag (R); Scholastic Honors Award - 2 Times; Law; Business; Xavier U; Howard U

BELL, LESLIANN M; WARREN, OH; WARREN CHRISTIAN SCH; (SR); Hi Hnr Roll; Hnr Roll; Nat Hon Sy; WWAHSS; Drma Clb; Emplmnt; Chrldg (V); Who's Who Among American High School Students; Cheerleading/ Drama Team; Zoo Biology; Pre-Vet; Malone College

BELLE, ANDRE; COLUMBUS, OH; EASTLAND CAREER CTR HS; (JR); Hnr Roll; Yth Ldrshp Prog; Comm Volntr; Peer Tut/Med; Chrch Yth Grp; DARE; Emplmnt; Spanish Clb; Bnd; Ch Chr; Jzz Bnd; Pep Bnd; Cl Off (P); CR (P); Dental; Cooking; Ohio State U; U of North Carolina

BELLROSE, HEATHER; MASSILLON, OH; JACKSON HS; (SO); Hi Hnr Roll; WWAHSS; Comm Volntr; Hosp Aide; ArtClub; Emplmnt; Key Club; Pep Squd; Photog; Spanish Clb; Chrldg (J); Sch Ppr (E, R, P); Photographer; Own a Business; Party Planning; Otterbein College; Marietta College

BELTRAN JR, RICARDO; NILES, OH; MC KINLEY HS; (FR); Hi Hnr Roll; Hnr Roll; MVP; Perf Att; USAA; WWAHSS; Mth Clb/Tm; Off Aide; Spanish Clb; Ftball (C); Track (V L); Wt Lftg (VJ); Accounting; Architecture; Ohio State U; Michigan U

BELU, GEORGE A; LORAIN, OH; LORAIN SOUTHVIEW HS; (SO); Hnr Roll; WWAHSS; Comm Volntr; Spec Olymp Vol; Key Club; Golf (J); Secretary of Key Club; Engineering; U of Akron; U of Toledo

BENANZER, JODI; SIDNEY, OH; HOUSTON HS; (FR); Hnr Roll; Nat Hon Sy; Chrch Yth Grp; Spanish Clb; Bnd; Chr; Mch Bnd; Pep Bnd; Bskball (V); Sftball (V); Vllyball (V); Physical Education Teacher; Cedarville U; Wright State U

BENDEN, BOB; CLEVELAND, OH; FAIRVIEW HS; (SO); Hnr Roll; Bsball (J); Bskball (J); Education; Sports Management; Miami of Ohio; U of Notre Dame

BENEDICT, MICHELLE; STEUBENVILLE, OH; STEUBENVILLE HS; (MS); Hnr Roll; Nat Hon Sy; Sci Fairs; Comm Volntr; Red Cr Aide; Chrch Yth Grp; Drma Clb; Key Club; Ntl Beta Clb; Scouts; Bnd; Ch Chr; Drm Mjr; Mch Bnd; Dvng (L); Sccr (L); Swmg (L); Track (L); Yrbk (P); Crime Scene Investigating; Astronomy; Ohio State U; Mc Gill U

BENHAM, WILL; SYLVANIA, OH; NORTHVIEW HS; (SO); Photog; Architectural Engineering; Video Game Development; Bowling Green State U; University of Toledo

BENNETT, ANDREW A; CANTON, OH; GLEN OAK HS; (JR); Hi Hnr Roll; Chrch Yth Grp; DARE; Emplmnt; Key Club; Wdwrkg Clb; Bnd; Mch Bnd; Pep Bnd; Wrstlg (V); Law Enforcement; Forensic Science; Stark State Technical College; Kent Stark Technical College

BENNETT, JEFF; NORWALK, OH; WESTERN RESERVE HS; (FR); Hnr Roll; Nat Mrt Fin; Otst Ac Ach Awd; Perf Att; Pres Sch; Comm Volntr; DARE; SADD; Vsity Clb; Foreign Clb; Bskball (J); Cr Ctry (V CL); Track (V L); Wt Lftg (V); Cl Off (T); Honor Roll all four grading periods; Help others who are struggling in other classes to understand it; Business Law; Athletic Trainer, Teacher; Texas U (Longhorns); Ohio State U

BENNETT, SAMUEL; COLUMBUS, OH; GRANDVIEW HEIGHTS HS; Ctznshp Aw; Hi Hnr Roll; Hnr Roll; St of Mnth; WWAHSS; ArtClub; Chrch Yth Grp; Emplmnt; Bnd; Jzz Bnd; Mch Bnd; Pep Bnd; Tours with Jazz Band (NYC, Nassau); 4 Years-Who's Who High School Students; Chemistry; Health Sciences; OSU-Ohio State U

BENSON, EVAN; WARREN, OH; WGHS; (SO); Ctznshp Aw; Fut Prb Slvr; Hi Hnr Roll; Hnr Roll; Jr Eng Tech; Nat Stu Ath Day Aw; Perf Att; Sci Fairs; St of Mnth; Yth Ldrshp Prog; Comm Volntr; Peer Tut/Med; Red Cr Aide; Chrch Yth Grp; DARE; Drma Clb; Kwanza Clb; Mus Clb; Schol Bwl; Sci Clb; Tech Clb; Acpl Chr; Ch Chr; Flg Crps; Stg Cre; Bsball (V); Bskball (J); Cyclg (J); Ftball (J); Gmnstcs (V); Scr Kpr (J); Vllyball (J); Wt Lftg (J); Automotive Mechanic; Carpenter; Ohio State U; Marquette

BENSON, JOHANNA; AKRON, OH; COPLEY HS; (JR); Hnr Roll; Nat Hon Sy; Perf Att; Pres Ac Ftns Aw; Sci Fairs; St of Mnth; WWAHSS; Comm Volntr; Key Club; Lttrmn Clb; NtlFrnscLg; Spch Team; Vsity Clb; French Clb; Bnd; Mch Bnd; Gmnstcs (V L); Track (V L); Vllyball (V L); Cl Off (S); Stu Cncl (R); Early Childhood Education; Baldwin Wallace College

BENTLEY, EVAN; PICKERINGTON, OH; PICKERINGTON HS NORTH; (SO); Hi Hnr Roll; Pres Sch; Comm Volntr; Chrch Yth Grp; Emplmnt; Tech Clb; German Clb; Chr; Swg Chr; Golf (V L); Meteorology

BENTLEY, PAIGE; SYLVANIA, OH; NORTHVIEW HS; (FR); ArtClub; Chrch Yth Grp; DARE; Chr; Chrldg (J); Physical Therapist; Pediatrician

BENTON, ANESIA M; LIMA, OH; LIMA SR HS; (FR); Hi Hnr Roll; Hnr Roll; Nat Mrt Fin; Otst Ac Ach Awd; Perf Att; Comm Volntr; Peer Tut/Med; DARE; DECA; Emplmnt; Jr Ach; Mus Clb; SADD; Vsity Clb; Bnd; Chr; Chrldg (V); GAA (V); Vllyball (V); Adv Cncl (P); Stu Cncl (V); Captain of Freshman Cheerleading; Teaching / Education; Master's Degree; Ohio State U

BENTZ, CARLYN; CANTON, OH; GLEN OAK HS; (JR); Hnr Roll; Nat Hon Sy; WWAHSS; Comm Volntr; Chrch Yth Grp; DARE; DECA; Emplmnt; Key Club; Pep Squd; Prom Com; Spanish Clb; Chr; Dnce; SP/M/VS; Cl Off (S, T); Stu Cncl (S, T, R); Freshman Volleyball; International Business; Spanish; Ohio U; Ohio State U

BENZ, AMY; TIFFIN, OH; OLD FORT HS; (SO); Ctznshp Aw; Hnr Roll; Nat Hon Sy; Sci Fairs; FCCLA; Pep Squd; Tchrs Aide; Bnd; Mch Bnd; Pep Bnd; SP/M/VS; Track (V L); Vllyball (V L); Stu Cncl (R); Pharmacy; Physical Therapy; U of Toledo; U of Cincinnati

BERASTROM, IAN R; SPENCER, OH; CLOVERLEAF HS; (SO); Hnr Roll; Peer Tut/Med; Key Club; Lib Aide; Off Aide; Outdrs Clb; Scouts; Tchrs Aide; Foreign Clb; Cr Ctry; Mar Art; Skiing; Track; Meteorology; Aerospace Engineering; Florida Institute of Technology

Bennett, Andrew A
Glen Oak HS
Canton, OH

Bauer, Joshua
Howland HS
Warren, OH

Bartow, Karina A
Western Reserve HS
Collins, OH

National
Honor Roll
Spring 2005

Barth, Jessica S
Jackson HS
Canton, OH

Bell, Lesliann M
Warren Christian Sch
Warren, OH

Benton, Anesia M
Lima SR HS
Lima, OH

BERDINE III, JOSEPH V; HUDSON, OH; HUDSON HS; (JR); Hnr Roll; WWAHSS; Yth Ldrshp Prog; Comm Volntr; Hab For Humty Volntr; Emplmnt; FCA; Key Club; Lttrmn Clb; Svce Clb; Vsity Clb; Sign Clb; Bsball (V L); Ftball (V L); Wt Lftg (V); Wrstlg (V); Life Teen, Key Club; Habitat Humanity; Engineering

BEREKSI, ANISSA; PERRYSBURG, OH; ST URSULA AC; (FR); Hnr Roll; Jr Eng Tech; Pres Ac Ftns Aw; Comm Volntr; DARE; Sci Clb; Spanish Clb; Bskball (J); Varsity Crew; Engineering; Astronomy; Ohio State U

BERETICH, MEGAN; BALTIMORE, OH; PICKERINGTON HS NORTH; (SO); Hi Hnr Roll; Hnr Roll; Chrch Yth Grp; Drma Clb; Photog; French Clb; Bnd; Chr; Swg Chr; Yrbk (R, P); Chorale; Youth Connections Club; Journalism; Music; Miami U Ohio; Denison U

BERMAN, CAITLIN; SYLVANIA, OH; NORTHVIEW HS; (FR); Hi Hnr Roll; Pres Sch; St of Mnth; Comm Volntr; Peer Tut/Med; Drma Clb; French Clb; Chr; Dnce; Stg Cre; Business; Interior Design; U of Connecticut; Miami of Ohio U

BERNARD, CAITLIN; NORTH ROYALTON, OH; NORTH ROYALTON HS; (SO); Hnr Roll; WWAHSS; Chrch Yth Grp; Key Club; Off Aide; French Clb; Bnd; Flg Crps; Skiing (C); Ohio U; College of Wooster

BERNARD, KEITH C; TIFFIN, OH; TIFFIN COLUMBIAN HS; (FR); Hnr Roll; St of Mnth; Mod UN; Off Aide; Bsball (J); Bskball; Golf (J); Teacher; Landscape/Architecture; Ohio State U; U of Arizona

BERNATH, JESSICA; PIONEER, OH; NORTH CTRL SCH; (FR); Hnr Roll; Peer Tut/Med; DARE; SADD; Spanish Clb; Bnd; Mch Bnd; Pep Bnd; Chrldg (J); Vllyball (J)

BERRY, ABBY J; ALEXANDRIA, OH; NORTHRIDGE HS; (SO); 4H Awd; Ctznshp Aw; Hnr Roll; Otst Ac Ach Awd; Sci Fairs; St of Mnth; Peer Tut/Med; 4-H; Chrch Yth Grp; SADD; Tchrs Aide; Track (V L); Vllyball (J); Ohio State U

BERRY, CHRISTOPHER J; UNIONTOWN, OH; GREEN HS; (SR); WWAHSS; Comm Volntr; Hosp Aide; Chrch Yth Grp; Emplmnt; FCA; Lib Aide; Spanish Clb; Chr; Stg Cre; Bsball (J); Weightlifting; Business; Political Science; The Ohio State U; Miami U (Ohio)

BESSETTE, JESSICA; SYLVANIA, OH; NORTHVIEW HS; (FR); Hnr Roll; Nat Hon Sy; Comm Volntr; Peer Tut/Med; Chrch Yth Grp; DARE; Lib Aide; Chr; Sccr (J); Journalism; Berkeley; MSU-Michigan State U

BEZEAU, JUSTIN D; SWANTON, OH; SWANTON HS; (FR); All Am Sch; Hnr Roll; Otst Ac Ach Awd; Comm Volntr; Peer Tut/Med; Off Aide; Tchrs Aide; Chr; Swg Chr; Cr Ctry (V); Ftball (V); Track (V); Wrstlg (V); Scholar Athlete All 4 Sports Freshman Year; Electrical Engineer; U of Michigan

BIANCHI, LYDIA; DAYTON, OH; BELLBROOK HS; (SO); Hi Hnr Roll; Hnr Roll; Otst Ac Ach Awd; Chrch Yth Grp; DARE; Drma Clb; Emplmnt; Off Aide; Scouts; Chr; Dnce; SP/M/VS; Annual Youth in Ministry Award; Acting / Dance; Photography; Wright State U; New York U

BIAS, JENNIFER R; RAVENNA, OH; CRESTWOOD HS; (JR); Hnr Roll; Nat Hon Sy; Pres Sch; St of Mnth; Yth Ldrshp Prog; Comm Volntr; Emplmnt; NtlFrnscLg; Prom Com; Sci Clb; Spch Team; Tchrs Aide; French Clb; PP Ftbl (C); Swmg (V CL); Tennis (J); Cl Off; Stu Cncl; FCCLA (Family, Career, Community, Leaders of America); Engineering; Pre-Law; U of Akron; Miami U (Oxford, Ohio)

BIHUN, LEANNA; CLEVELAND, OH; PARMA SR HS; Ctznshp Aw; Hi Hnr Roll; Hnr Roll; Nat Hon Sy; Otst Ac Ach Awd; Perf Att; St of Mnth; Comm Volntr; Peer Tut/Med; DARE; Off Aide; Quiz Bowl; SADD; Cl Off (R); Stu Cncl (V); CR (P); Best in Science House 8 Times; Major in Performing Arts; Business Degree; U of Los Angeles; Baldwin Wallace

BILLINGS, HOPE J; TOLEDO, OH; BOWSHER HS; (MS); Ctznshp Aw; Hnr Roll; Perf Att; St of Mnth; Comm Volntr; Chrch Yth Grp; Jr Ach; Pep Squd; Scouts; Bnd; Ch Chr; Dnce; Orch; Bskball; Sftball; Stu Cncl (R); Accountant; Owens Tech; U of Toledo

BILLITER, MEGAN; CINCINNATI, OH; PRINCETON HS; (JR); Hnr Roll; Comm Volntr; 4-H; DARE; ROTC; Ch Chr; Stg Cre; Swmg; JROTC; 4-H

BILLOTTE, CHINA; MANSFIELD, OH; MADISON COMP HS; (FR); Ctznshp Aw; Hnr Roll; Otst Ac Ach Awd; Pres Ac Ftns Aw; St of Mnth; Comm Volntr; Off Aide; Tchrs Aide; Track (V L); Master's Degree; Ashland U; Michigan U

BILTZ, SARA E; KENT, OH; FIELD HS; (JR); 4H Awd; Hi Hnr Roll; Hnr Roll; Nat Hon Sy; St of Mnth; Comm Volntr; 4-H; Prom Com; French Clb; Scr Kpr; Tennis (J); Stu Cncl (R); Yrbk (E, R, P)

BING, RYAN E; BELLVILLE, OH; CLEAR FORK HS; (SO); Hnr Roll; St of Mnth; WWAHSS; Comm Volntr; Chrch Yth Grp; Emplmnt; Fr of Library; Quiz Bowl; SADD; Golf (V L); Tennis (V L); Business Degree of Some Kind; Ohio State U; Kent State U

BING, SCOTT M; BELLVILLE, OH; CLEAR FORK HS; (SR); Hi Hnr Roll; MVP; Nat Hon Sy; Pres Ac Ftns Aw; St of Mnth; WWAHSS; Comm Volntr; Spec Olymp Vol; Emplmnt; Lttrmn Clb; Sci Clb; SADD; Tchrs Aide; Vsity Clb; Bsball (VJ L); Golf (VJCL); CR (T); Sch Ppr (E, P); Yrbk (E, P); Franklin B Walter Award; Professional Golf Management; Coastal Carolina U

BINKLEY, RACHAEL; BRADFORD, OH; UPPER VALLEY JVS; (JR); Hnr Roll; Perf Att; St of Mnth; Chrch Yth Grp; Bnd; Mch Bnd; Pep Bnd; Culinary Institute of America; Johnson & Wales

BIRD, FELICIA D; WELLSTON, OH; WELLSTON HS; (SR); Hnr Roll; St of Mnth; Emplmnt; Prom Com; Stu Cncl; Physical Therapist; Hocking College

BIRD, MARY; LOVELAND, OH; GOSHEN HS; (FR); Ctznshp Aw; Hi Hnr Roll; Hnr Roll; Perf Att; St of Mnth; DARE; Tchrs Aide; I Am on the Bowling Team.; School Teacher; UC of Cincinnati; Miami U of Ohio

BISCHOFF, EMILY; MONROEVILLE, OH; MONROEVILLE HS; (SO); 4H Awd; Hi Hnr Roll; Hnr Roll; Nat Hon Sy; Perf Att; Yth Ldrshp Prog; 4-H; Chrch Yth Grp; Emplmnt; Key Club; Ntl FFA; Quiz Bowl; Spanish Clb; Bskball (VJC); Scr Kpr (V); Sftball (V L); Vllyball (JC); Renaissance Club; Medical Field

BISHOP, DANIELLE A; TOLEDO, OH; ROGERS HS; (SR); Hnr Roll; Sci Fairs; WWAHSS; Comm Volntr; Hosp Aide; Emplmnt; Tchrs Aide; French Clb; CR (V); Community Service Group; Teen Institute; Occupational Therapy; Eastern Michigan U; Cleveland State U

BISHOP, KIARA N; MT GILEAD, OH; CARDINGTON-LINCOLN HS; (SR); 4H Awd; Ctznshp Aw; Hi Hnr Roll; Nat Hon Sy; Pres Ac Ftns Aw; Yth Ldrshp Prog; Comm Volntr; Peer Tut/Med; 4-H; Emplmnt; Ntl FFA; Prom Com; Sci Clb; Spanish Clb; Chr; Animal Science; Psychology; Ohio State U; Otterbein College

BLACK, JENNIFER; HILLIARD, OH; HILLIARD DARBY HS; (JR); Hi Hnr Roll; Hnr Roll; Nat Hon Sy; St of Mnth; WWAHSS; Comm Volntr; Peer Tut/Med; Red Cr Aide; Emplmnt; Key Club; Yrbk (R, P); Medicine; Fashion; Miami U (OH); Ohio State U

BLACK, RYAN D; WILLOUGHBY, OH; WILLOUGHBY SOUTH HS; (SO); Hnr Roll; DARE; Key Club; Bnd; Tennis (J); Student Advisor for DARE Program; Broadcasting; Writer, News Paper Columnist; Ohio U; Penn State

BLACKLIDGE, SARA R; NEW CARLISLE, OH; CEDARVILLE HS; (SO); Hnr Roll; St of Mnth; Chrch Yth Grp; Emplmnt; Key Club; Prom Com; Chr; Sch Ppr (R); Yrbk (R); Ministry; Cedarville U

BLAIR, MC KENZIE; CAREY, OH; CAREY HS; (JR); 4H Awd; Hnr Roll; Nat Hon Sy; St of Mnth; WWAHSS; Yth Ldrshp Prog; Comm Volntr; 4-H; Chrch Yth Grp; DECA; Drma Clb; Emplmnt; Prom Com; SADD; Tchrs Aide; Bnd; Mch Bnd; Pep Bnd; SP/M/VS; Sftball (V L); Vllyball (JC); Basketball Star; Speech Therapy; Occupational Therapy; Miami U of Ohio; U of Toledo

BLAKE, KIARA; CLEVELAND, OH; HEALTH CAREERS CTR; (FR); Ctznshp Aw; Hnr Roll; Mas Aw; MVP; Nat Hon Sy; Perf Att; WWAHSS; Comm Volntr; Chrch Yth Grp; Ch Chr; Bskball (V L); Tennis (V); I Would Like to Go Into Pre-Med.; I Would Like to Become a Journalist, Also a Doctor.; North Carolina Central U; Michigan State U

BLAKE, NICOLLE; RAVENNA, OH; SOUTHEAST HS; (SR); Hi Hnr Roll; MVP; Nat Hon Sy; WWAHSS; Comm Volntr; Drma Clb; Emplmnt; FCA; NtlFrnscLg; Off Aide; Bnd; Dnce; Mch Bnd; Pep Bnd; Skiing; Sccr (V CL); Track (V CL); Yrbk (P); Business; U of Toledo; Allegheny

BLAKELY, CHRISTINA; DAYTON, OH; FAIRBORN HS; (FR); Hnr Roll; Sci Fairs; Chrch Yth Grp; Acpl Chr; Lawyer; Fine Arts in Acting; Wright State U; Shenandoah U

BLAKLEY, DEAN; HAMILTON, OH; TALAWANDA HS; (SR); Bnd; Mch Bnd; Pep Bnd; Talawanda FFA Vice President; Carpentry/Construction Management; Hocking College

BLUST, AMBERLEE; CINCINNATI, OH; (MS); Hi Hnr Roll; Hnr Roll; Nat Hon Sy; Perf Att; Sci Fairs; Comm Volntr; Scouts; Chr; SP/M/VS; Stg Cre; Chrldg (C); Vllyball (J)

BOAKYE, PAULA; COLUMBUS, OH; WALNUT RIDGE HS; (FR); Hi Hnr Roll; Chrch Yth Grp; Ch Chr; Medical Doctor-Masters Degree; Nursing-Bachelors Degree; New York U; Columbia U

BOATNER, DREW; WOOSTER, OH; NORTHWESTERN HS; (SO); Hnr Roll; WWAHSS; 4-H; Chrch Yth Grp; Film / Television; Business

BOCK, TABATHA; COLUMBUS, OH; BEECHCROFT HS; (SO); Hi Hnr Roll; Hnr Roll; Drma Clb; SP/M/VS; Sftball (J); Swmg (L); Vllyball (VJ); Teacher; Lawyer; Bowling Green U

BODLEY, AMBER; LOVELAND, OH; GOSHEN HS; (FR); Hnr Roll; Chrch Yth Grp; Stu Cncl (R); Early Childhood Education; English; Wright State U; Ohio State

BODRICK, FATIMA; FAIRFIELD TWP, OH; FAIRFIELD SR HS; (SO); Hnr Roll; Nat Hon Sy; Perf Att; Pres Sch; WWAHSS; Yth Ldrshp Prog; Comm Volntr; Chrch Yth Grp; Dbte Team; Ch Chr; Dnce; Orch; Scr Kpr (J); Track (J); Vllyball (L); Who's Who Among High School Students; National Honor Society; Lawyer; Veterinarian; Hampton U; Tennessee State U, Ohio State U

BOHRER, CHELSEA; OTTAWA, OH; OTTAWA GLANDORF HS; (SR); Hi Hnr Roll; Hnr Roll; Nat Hon Sy; WWAHSS; Comm Volntr; Hosp Aide; Chrch Yth Grp; Emplmnt; Key Club; Spanish Clb; Bnd; Chr; Dnce; Mch Bnd; Tennis (J L); Pre-Medicine; Nursing; Wright State U

BOICE, CARI; BRADNER, OH; LAKOTA HS; (JR); 4H Awd; Hi Hnr Roll; Hnr Roll; Nat Hon Sy; WWAHSS; Peer Tut/Med; 4-H; AL Aux Girls; Chrch Yth Grp; Key Club; Lttrmn Clb; Ntl FFA; Quiz Bowl; Schol Bwl; Bnd; Mch Bnd; Pep Bnd; Hsbk Rdg (V C); Track (V); Vsy Clb (V); Yrbk (R); OIHA-Ohio Inter Scholastic Horseman's Assoc-Sportsmanship Winner; Veterinarian; Equine Science

BOLDEN, RENEE; LIMA, OH; LIMA SR HS; (FR); Hi Hnr Roll; Hnr Roll; Perf Att; Hosp Aide; Chrch Yth Grp; DARE; Law; Spelman College; Ohio State U

BOLENDER, KENNA; CIRCLEVILLE, OH; CIRCLEVILLE HS; (SO); Hi Hnr Roll; Hnr Roll; Perf Att; Pres Sch; St of Mnth; WWAHSS; Comm Volntr; Peer Tut/Med; 4-H; DARE; Key Club; Off Aide; Svce Clb; Sccr (VJ); Stu Cncl (R); Yrbk (R, P); Homecoming Representative for Sophomore Class; Hotel Management; Hospitality Management; Niagara U; Sullivan U

BOND, KESHIA D; BRUNSWICK, OH; BRUNSWICK HS; (JR); Otst Ac Ach Awd; Comm Volntr; Jr Ach; Off Aide; Tchrs Aide; Jogs; Tri-C

BONETTI, AMANDA; TALLMADGE, OH; TALLMADGE HS; (SO); 4H Awd; Hnr Roll; Otst Ac Ach Awd; Pres Ac Ftns Aw; Pres Sch; Sci Fairs; St of Mnth; Comm Volntr; Peer Tut/Med; 4-H; Biology Clb; Chrch Yth Grp; Emplmnt; Off Aide; Pep Squd; Schol Bwl; CR (R); FCCLA; Architecture; Interior Design (Minor); Kent State U

BONNER, BRIANNA; CLEVELAND, OH; LUTHERAN HS EAST; (FR); Hnr Roll; St of Mnth; Chr; Vllyball (V); Coaches' Award - Volleyball; Law; Psychology; Clark Atlanta U; Duke U

BONNIN, PABLO; DAYTON, OH; ALTER HS; (SR); Hnr Roll; Comm Volntr; ArtClub; DARE; Emplmnt; Key Club; Spanish Clb; Mar Art; Sccr; Swmg; Tennis; Dan Second Degree Tae Kwon Do; Architecture; U of Cincinnati; Miami U

BONVISSUTO, THERESA; CLEVELAND, OH; PADUA FRANCISCAN HS; (JR); Hi Hnr Roll; Nat Hon Sy; WWAHSS; Comm Volntr; Peer Tut/Med; Red Cr Aide; Key Club; Scouts; French Clb; Dnce; Orch; SP/M/VS; Lit Mag (R); Royal Youth Ballet Company; Ballet Dancer-Professional; U of Cincinnati; Butler U-Indiana

BOOKER, CANAIA M; TOLEDO, OH; SCOTT HS; (SO); Ctznshp Aw; Hnr Roll; Nat Ldrshp Svc; Perf Att; St of Mnth; Yth Ldrshp Prog; Hosp Aide; Peer Tut/Med; Chrch Yth Grp; Dbte Team; Emplmnt; Mod UN; Pep Squd; P to P St Amb Prg; Chr; Dnce; Orch; SP/M/VS; Chrldg (V); Track (J); Vllyball (J); Cl Off (P); Stu Cncl (R); Sch Ppr (R, P); Pre-Med; Child Development; Spelman College; Morgan State U

BORCHERT, JESSICA; BRECKSVILLE, OH; BRECKSVILLE-BROADVIEW HEIGHTS HS; (SR); Hnr Roll; DECA; Tchrs Aide; Sftball (J); Cl Off (T); National Technical Honors Society; Outstanding Student of the Year; Business Management; Finance; Cuyahoga Community College; Cleveland State U

BORGERT, BREANNA; WAPAKONETA, OH; WAPAKONETA HS; (SO); Hi Hnr Roll; Hnr Roll; Otst Ac Ach Awd; St of Mnth; Comm Volntr; Emplmnt; Off Aide; Tchrs Aide; Spanish Clb; Swmg (V L); Vllyball (J); Cl Off (T); Scholar Athlete Award; Academic Letter; Optometry; Accounting; Ohio State U; Miami U (Ohio)

BOSELA, RAY; MANTUA, OH; CRESTWOOD HS; (JR); Hnr Roll; Emplmnt; Bnd; Jzz Bnd; Mch Bnd; Medical Research; Music; Medical Colleges

BOSKOVITCH, NICHOLE; OLMSTED FALLS, OH; OLMSTED FALLS HS; (FR); Hnr Roll; Otst Ac Ach Awd; St of Mnth; Comm Volntr; Photog; Scouts; Chr; Dnce; Chrldg (J); Sccr (J); Sftball (J); CR (R); Ob/Gyn Physics; Surgeon; Case Western; Florida U

BOSLEY, JASON; NEW ALBANY, OH; NEW ALBANY HS; (JR); Hnr Roll; Hab For Humty Volntr; Wrstlg; Volunteer Ohio Wildlife Center; Volunteer Habitat Humanity; Computer Science; Environmental Science

BOSWELL, TIERRA; COLUMBUS, OH; EAST HS; (SO); Ctznshp Aw; Hi Hnr Roll; Otst Ac Ach Awd; Perf Att; Sci Fairs; Comm Volntr; Peer Tut/Med; Drma Clb; Emplmnt; Flg Crps; Chrldg; Sccr; Columbus Science Fair Winner; Columbus School Writing Contest; Book Writer; Professor, Elementary Teacher; Harvard, Georgetown; Yale, Princeton

Boskovitch, Nichole
Olmsted Falls HS
Olmsted Falls, OH

Boakye, Paula
Walnut Ridge HS
Columbus, OH

Bird, Felicia D
Wellston HS
Wellston, OH

Biltz, Sara E
Field HS
Kent, OH

National
Honor Roll
Spring 2005

Billings, Hope J
Bowsher HS
Toledo, OH

Blakely, Christina
Fairborn HS
Dayton, OH

Bodrick, Fatima
Fairfield SR HS
Fairfield Twp, OH

Boswell, Tierra
East HS
Columbus, OH

BOWENS, SHANNON; WILLOUGHBY, OH; WILLOUGHBY SOUTH HS; (SO); Hi Hnr Roll; WWAHSS; Comm Volntr; Chrch Yth Grp; Emplmnt; Key Club; Bnd; Jzz Bnd; Mch Bnd; Pep Bnd; American Cancer Society Relay for Life Team Captain; Music; Film

BOWERSOCK, JILL; NEW MATAMORAS, OH; FRONTIER HS; (JR); F Lan Hn Soc; Hi Hnr Roll; MVP; Nat Hon Sy; WWAHSS; Chrch Yth Grp; Drma Clb; FCA; Key Club; Off Aide; Prom Com; Spanish Clb; SP/M/VS; Bskball (V L); Chrldg (V CL); Vllyball (V L); 1st Team District 12 Volleyball; Honorable Mention Basketball; Dental Hygienist; West Liberty State College; Marietta College

BOWLES, AARON C; THORNVILLE, OH; SHERIDAN HS; (SR); Hi Hnr Roll; Hnr Roll; Nat Hon Sy; Perf Att; Pres Ac Ftns Aw; WWAHSS; Chrch Yth Grp; Emplmnt; Track (V); Principal's List / Honor Roll; Engineering / Master's Degree; Miami U; Ohio State U

BOWMAN, DAVID; SAINT CLAIRSVILLE, OH; ST JOHN CTRL HS; (JR); Hi Hnr Roll; Nat Hon Sy; WWAHSS; Comm Volntr; Prom Com; SP/M/VS; Cr Ctry (V L); Ftball (J); Track (V L); Cl Off (T); Academic All-Ohio; Athletic-All-Ohio; Physical Therapy

BOWSER, ASHLEY R; NORTH ROYALTON, OH; PADUA FRANCISCAN HS; (JR); Hnr Roll; Sci Fairs; DARE; Emplmnt; Key Club; Latin Clb; Bnd; Dnce; Mch Bnd; SP/M/VS; Cl Off (S); Princess North Royalton; Nursing; Kent State U; Toledo U

BOYCE, ASHLEY N; WINGETT RUN, OH; FRONTIER HS; (SR); Hnr Roll; Nat Hon Sy; WWAHSS; Peer Tut/Med; 4-H; BPA; Chrch Yth Grp; FCA; Key Club; Chr; Ch Chr; Stu Cncl (S); Key Club President; Upward Bound; Equine Facility Management; Equine Health Technology; Otterbein College

BOYCE, J J; COLLINS, OH; WESTERN RESERVE HS; (FR); Hnr Roll; Otst Ac Ach Awd; French Clb; Ftball (V L); Track (V L); Wt Lftg; Wrstlg (VJ L); Cl Off (P); Youth for Youth; Held Job for Four Years; Professional Football; Coach; Ohio State U; Mount Union

BOYLE, BRIANNE R; CANTON, OH; GLEN OAK HS; (JR); Hnr Roll; Nat Hon Sy; Perf Att; WWAHSS; Comm Volntr; DECA; Emplmnt; Pep Squd; Chrldg (V L); Stu Cncl (R); Marketing; Psychology; Ohio U; Akron U

BRABHAM, SAMANTHA D; VINTON, OH; RIVER VALLEY HS; (JR); 4H Awd; Hnr Roll; MVP; Nat Hon Sy; Perf Att; WWAHSS; Comm Volntr; Peer Tut/Med; 4-H; ArtClub; Emplmnt; Key Club; Ntl Beta Clb; Off Aide; Prom Com; French Clb; Dnce; Chrldg (V L); Cr Ctry (J L); PP Ftbl; Sftball (J); Track (L); Cl Off (V); Fashion Merchandising / Design; Business Administration; U of Rio Grande; Kent State U

BRACEY, TYRONE; TOLEDO, OH; SOUTHVIEW HS; (JR); Hnr Roll; Video Game Designer, Artist; Boxer; Lourdes College; U of Toledo

BRACKMANN, AMANDA R; CINCINNATI, OH; SETON HS; (SR); Hnr Roll; WWAHSS; Comm Volntr; Chrch Yth Grp; Emplmnt; Mus Clb; Bnd; Chr; Ch Chr; Mch Bnd; Steel Drum Band; Psychology; Bellarmine U; Otterbein U

BRADDOCK, PAUL; MILFORD, OH; MILFORD HS; (JR); Hi Hnr Roll; Hnr Roll; Yth Ldrshp Prog; Comm Volntr; Chess; DECA; Sccr (VJ); Wrstlg (J); Adv Cncl; Engineering; Business; Ohio State U

BRADEN, BRETT R; HOMEWORTH, OH; WEST BRANCH HS; (SR); Perf Att; St of Mnth; WWAHSS; Drma Clb; Emplmnt; Fr of Library; Pep Squd; Scouts; SADD; German Clb; Chr; SP/M/VS; Stg Cre; Bsball (V L); Ftball (J); Yrbk (P); Perfect Attendance; Human Resource Management; Business Administration; Youngstown State U; U of Akron

BRADLEY, BIANCA L; DAYTON, OH; COLONEL WHITE HS FOR THE ARTS; (SO); Ctznshp Aw; Hi Hnr Roll; Hnr Roll; Nat Hon Sy; St of Mnth; WWAHSS; Comm Volntr; SP/M/VS; Sch Ppr (R); Journalism; Theater

BRADLEY, NIKITA M; ASHVILLE, OH; TEAYS VALLEY HS; (SO); Sci Fairs; DARE; Drma Clb; Bnd; Mch Bnd; SP/M/VS; Stg Cre; Honors Math and English Courses; German 1 and 2; Psychology; Dramatic Arts; Otterbein; U of Massachusetts

BRADLEY, TIFFANY E; FAIRFIELD, OH; WARREN CTY CAREER CTR; (SR); Hi Hnr Roll; Hnr Roll; Nat Hon Sy; Otst Ac Ach Awd; Perf Att; Hosp Aide; Emplmnt; Quiz Bowl; SADD; Voc Ind Clb Am; Chr; Cl Off (R); CR (R); Sch Ppr (P); Psychology; Social Worker; Wright State U; U of Cincinnati

BRADNER, BRITTNEY; TOLEDO, OH; CARDINAL STRITCH HS; (SO); Hnr Roll; Otst Ac Ach Awd; Hab For Humty Volntr; Chrch Yth Grp; Scouts; Spanish Clb; Bskball (V); Track (V); Vllyball (V); Cl Off (P); Stu Cncl (R); CR (P); Sch Ppr (R, P); Yrbk (R, P); Club Volleyball JO 5 Yrs; Active in CYO; Journalism; Writing; Ohio U/Delaware College; Bowling Green U/Ashland U

BRANCH, TYLER K; IRONTON, OH; DAWSON-BRYANT HS; (SO); Ctznshp Aw; Hnr Roll; MVP; Nat Ldrshp Svc; St of Mnth; USAA; Yth Ldrshp Prog; Comm Volntr; Peer Tut/Med; Chrch Yth Grp; FCA; FBLA; Jr Ach; Key Club; NYLC; Outdrs Clb; SADD; Bsball (V); Bskball (V); Ftball (V); Track (V L); Wt Lftg (V); USAA National Leadership, Presidential Award; Lead America; Chemistry/Biology/Doctor of Medicine; Anesthesiologist; Marshall U-Huntington WV

BRANDENBURG, JESSICA L; ELYRIA, OH; MIDVIEW HS; (SR); Hi Hnr Roll; Hnr Roll; Perf Att; WWAHSS; Comm Volntr; Emplmnt; Off Aide; Scouts; Tchrs Aide; Vllyball (V); All County Academic VB Team; District Academic VB Team; Early Childhood Education; Forensic Science; Miami U Ohio - Accepted

BRANDOW, KAYLA M N; TOLEDO, OH; WAITE HS; (JR); Ctznshp Aw; Hnr Roll; WWAHSS; Comm Volntr; Peer Tut/Med; ArtClub; Chr; Art (Visual Arts); Forensics

BRAUN, ERIC; CELINA, OH; CELINA HS; (JR); Hnr Roll; Nat Hon Sy; St of Mnth; Comm Volntr; FCA; Lttrmn Clb; Photog; Vsity Clb; Bsball (V L); Sccr (V CL); Wrstlg (V CL); First Team All-WBL; Baseball-Junior; Special Mention; Soccer-Sophomore; Mechanical Engineer; Education; Wright State U; U of Toledo

BRAUN, ERIC; CLEVELAND, OH; BRUSH HS; (SR); Hnr Roll; Peer Tut/Med; Drma Clb; Emplmnt; FBLA; Key Club; Mus Clb; Acpl Chr; Chr; Dnce; SP/M/VS; Most Improved - Bass; Recognition for Algebra II; Computer Science; Computer Information System; Kent State U

BRAVO, RAFAEL; DOVER, OH; DOVER HS; (FR); Hnr Roll; Comm Volntr; Sccr (J); Law-Judge; Kent State U; Duke U

BRAY, CHELSEA M; HUNTSVILLE, OH; INDIAN LAKE HS; (FR); Hnr Roll; WWAHSS; 4-H; DARE; Drma Clb; Key Club; Chr; SP/M/VS; Stg Cre; Bskball (J); Vllyball (J); Teaching/Education; Engineering; Ohio State U; Bowling Green U

BREECE, CHELSSIE; MARION, OH; ELGIN HS; (SR); Hnr Roll; Nat Hon Sy; Otst Ac Ach Awd; Sci Fairs; St of Mnth; USAA; WWAHSS; Comm Volntr; Ntl FFA; Stu Cncl (R); Ohio Star State Taxonomy; Ohio Star Horticulture; Biology; The Ohio State U-Marion Campus

BREMENOUR, CHELSEA; CLEVELAND, OH; CHARLES F BRUSH HS; (SO); Hnr Roll; WWAHSS; Yth Ldrshp Prog; Comm Volntr; Peer Tut/Med; Key Club; Orch; Scr Kpr (VJ); Sccr (V L); Environmental Club; Knitting Club; Law; Education; New York U; Brown U

BRENNER, TIFFANY; NAVARRE, OH; FAIRLESS HS; (SO); Hi Hnr Roll; Hnr Roll; MVP; St of Mnth; Cr Ctry (V L); Track (V L); Teaching

BREWER, CASSANDRA R; MOGADORE, OH; MOGADORE JR/SR HS; (SR); Hnr Roll; Nat Hon Sy; Salutrn; WWAHSS; Chrch Yth Grp; Off Aide; Prom Com; Tchrs Aide; French Clb; Bskball (V); Cr Ctry (V L); PP Ftbl (V); Track (V L); Adv Cncl (S); Cl Off (S); Math Education; U of Akron

BREWER, SAMANTHA J; LUCASVILLE, OH; VALLEY HS; (FR); Hnr Roll; Comm Volntr; Chrch Yth Grp; DARE; Mus Clb; Bnd; Chr; Mch Bnd; Pep Bnd; Bskball; Sftball; Vllyball; Web Staff; Shawnee; Ohio State

BRICKNER, AARON; FOSTORIA, OH; HOPEWELL LOUDON LOCAL SCH; (SR); Hi Hnr Roll; Nat Hon Sy; 4-H; Ftball (V); National Honor Society; Mechanical Engineering; U of Cincinnati

BRINCEFIELD, LEAH; MIDDLE POINT, OH; LINCOLNVIEW SCH; (SR); Hnr Roll; Jr Rot; Nat Hon Sy; St of Mnth; Comm Volntr; Drma Clb; Sci Clb; Spanish Clb; SP/M/VS; Chrldg (V L); Stu Cncl (V); Sch Ppr; Yrbk (E); Gold Honor Roll; Nursing; Wright State U

BRINDLE, STEPHANIE; PICKERINGTON, OH; PICKERINGTON NORTH HS; (JR); Hi Hnr Roll; Nat Hon Sy; Perf Att; St of Mnth; WWAHSS; DARE; French Clb; Bskball (V L); Sccr (V L); CR; Nursing; Sports Medicine; Ohio State U; Miami U

BRINKMAN, RYAN; CINCINNATI, OH; LITTLE MIAMI HS; (JR); Hi Hnr Roll; Nat Hon Sy; Otst Ac Ach Awd; WWAHSS; Comm Volntr; Peer Tut/Med; ArtClub; Dbte Team; Drma Clb; Emplmnt; Key Club; Schol Bwl; French Clb; Bnd; Jzz Bnd; Mch Bnd; Pep Bnd; Ftball (VJ L); Sccr (V L); Tennis (J); Track (V L); Wrstlg (V); Future Family Community Leaders of America; Psychology; Case Western U; Ohio State U

BRISLEN, MARY; CAMBRIDGE, OH; CAMBRIDGE HS; (SO); Hi Hnr Roll; Hnr Roll; Nat Hon Sy; Otst Ac Ach Awd; Pres Sch; Sci Fairs; Yth Ldrshp Prog; Comm Volntr; Hosp Aide; Peer Tut/Med; Chrch Yth Grp; Emplmnt; HO'Br Yth Ldrshp; Key Club; Pep Squd; Bnd; Mch Bnd; Pep Bnd; CR (R); Neurology; Psychology; Notre Dame U; Ohio State U

BRISTOW, BRITTANEY E; FAIRFIELD, OH; WARREN CTY CAREER CTR; (JR); Hi Hnr Roll; Hnr Roll; Perf Att; Sci Fairs; St of Mnth; Comm Volntr; Hosp Aide; Red Cr Aide; DARE; Emplmnt; Key Club; Photog; SADD; Ch Chr; Volunteer Zoo, Children's Center Church, Nursing Home; Volunteer Hospital, Skills USA; Bachelors in Nursing; Miami U Hamilton; Miami U Oxford

BRITANOVA, JULIA; WADSWORTH, OH; WADSWORTH HS; (JR); Hnr Roll; Perf Att; Peer Tut/Med; DARE; Emplmnt; SADD; Bdmtn (J); Bskball (J); Swmg (J); Vllyball (J); Computer Accounting; Business Manager; Akron U; Kent State

BRITE, CHANTE'; COLUMBUS, OH; WESTERVILLE NORTH HS; (SR); Hnr Roll; Otst Ac Ach Awd; Perf Att; St of Mnth; Yth Ldrshp Prog; Comm Volntr; Peer Tut/Med; Red Cr Aide; Chrch Yth Grp; Emplmnt; P to P St Amb Prg; Prom Com; SP/M/VS; PP Ftbl (V); Stu Cncl (R); CR (R); Indoor Soccer League; Won Awards in New York for Acting; Theatre (Acting); Journalism; The Ohio State U; Cincinnati U

BRITTON, AMBER; KILLBUCK, OH; (SO); 4H Awd; Hnr Roll; 4-H; Chrch Yth Grp; Sci Clb; 4-H President; Lawyer; Vet

BRITZ, MADDIE; GAMBIER, OH; MT VERNON HS; (JR); Kwnis Aw; Comm Volntr; Key Club; Sccr (J); National Youth Leadership Forum on Medicine; Medicine / Pediatrician; U of Redlands

BROCKLESBY, VALERIE; CRESTLINE, OH; CRESTLINE HS; (SO); Hnr Roll; Nat Hon Sy; Perf Att; Sci Fairs; St of Mnth; Comm Volntr; Peer Tut/Med; ArtClub; DARE; Emplmnt; Jr Ach; Key Club; Tchrs Aide; Bskball (J); Chrldg (V CL); Tennis (VJCL); Track (V L); Cl Off (P); Sch Ppr (R); Business Major; Medical or Literature; The Ohio State U

BRODMAN, STEPHEN; UPPER SANDUSKY, OH; ST MICHAEL'S AC; (SR); Hnr Roll; Nat Hon Sy; St of Mnth; Yth Ldrshp Prog; Comm Volntr; Jr Cls League; Acpl Chr; Ch Chr; Bsball (V L); Bskball (V); Adv Cncl (R); Yrbk (P); Presidential Award for Academic Excellence; National Latin Exam; Nursing-RN; Marion Technical College

BRODNIK, JORDAN; COLUMBUS, OH; BEXLEY HS; (SR); Hi Hnr Roll; Hnr Roll; DARE; Emplmnt; Quill & Scroll; Spanish Clb; Bskball (J); Ftball (V L); Sccr (VJCL); Stu Cncl (R); CR (R); Sch Ppr (R); Coca-Cola Sportsmanship Award; Outstanding Leader Award; Pre-Med; Business; Miami U; Ohio State U

BRONAUGH, JESSICA; DAYTON, OH; MEADOWDALE HS; (FR); Ctznshp Aw; Hnr Roll; Perf Att; Sci Fairs; St of Mnth; Comm Volntr; Peer Tut/Med; Chrch Yth Grp; DARE; Scouts; Bnd; Chr; Dnce; Sch Ppr (R); Yrbk (R); New York U; Spelman College

BROOKER, ABBIE L; BEVERLY, OH; FORT FRYE HS; (SR); F Lan Hn Soc; Hi Hnr Roll; Nat Hon Sy; WWAHSS; Comm Volntr; Chrch Yth Grp; Prom Com; SADD; Chr; SP/M/VS; Cl Off (V); Stu Cncl (R)

BROTHERS, ADRIENANA; CLEVELAND, OH; MARTIN LUTHER KING HS; MS; Hnr Roll; St of Mnth; Comm Volntr; Peer Tut/Med; ArtClub; Chr; Ch Chr; Orch; Stg Cre; Chrldg (J); Mar Art (J); Track (J); Sch Ppr; Lady Legacy; Youth Group - Atia-Fi-Batia; Law; MBA / Professional Degree Program; Harvard U; Yale U

BROWN, ANTHONY K; TIFFIN, OH; TIFFIN COLUMBIAN HS; (FR); Hnr Roll; Pres Ac Ftns Aw; St of Mnth; Mod UN; Acpl Chr; Bnd; Jzz Bnd; SP/M/VS; Bskball (J); Ftball (J); Track (V L); Student Mentor

BROWN, ASHLEY; BARBERTON, OH; BARBERTON HS; (FR); Hi Hnr Roll; Perf Att; Comm Volntr; Key Club; Chr; Bskball; Sccr (V L); Sftball; Stu Cncl (R); Architect; Teacher; U of North Carolina; Kent State

BROWN, CONSTANCE; SANDUSKY, OH; SANDUSKY HS; (JR); St of Mnth; Emplmnt; Bnd; Mch Bnd; International Club; Social Work; Psychology; Toledo U; Bowling Green State U Fireland

BROWN, DEREK; LANCASTER, OH; LANCASTER HS; (JR); Hnr Roll; Chrch Yth Grp; Key Club; Spanish Clb; Chr; Ch Chr; SP/M/VS; Swg Chr; Sccr (V CL); Engineering; Architecture

BROWN, DONALD A; CINCINNATI, OH; ROBERTA TAFT INFO TECH HS; (FR); Ctznshp Aw; Hnr Roll; MVP; ArtClub; DARE; Emplmnt; Ftball (VJ); Winner in Citywide Art Competition '04/ '05; Master's Degree in Art; MBA; UCLA; U of Cincinnati

BROWN, EMILY B; WHEELERSBURG, OH; WHEELERSBURG HS; (SO); Hi Hnr Roll; Comm Volntr; Peer Tut/Med; Chrch Yth Grp; DARE; Emplmnt; Key Club; Chr; SP/M/VS; Cl Off (P); Stu Cncl (R); Yrbk (E); Foreign Language; Medical Field; The Ohio State U

BROWN, JASMINE; CLEVELAND, OH; GARFIELD HEIGHTS HS; (JR); Hnr Roll; Nat Hon Sy; WWAHSS; Comm Volntr; DARE; Drma Clb; Emplmnt; Svce Clb; Acpl Chr; Bnd; Mch Bnd; SP/M/VS; Tennis (JV); Cl Off (V); Member of the International Thespian Society; Honor Bar Thespian; Double Major in Performing Arts and Journalism; Vassar College; Ohio University Athens

BROWN, JASON; LANCASTER, OH; BERNE UNION; (SO); MVP; Perf Att; Red Cr Aide; DECA; Emplmnt; Pep Squd; Quiz Bowl; Tchrs Aide; Vsity Clb; Wdwrkg Clb; Spanish Clb; Ftball (V L); Track (V L); Wt Lftg (V L); MBA; Engineering; Ohio State U; Purdue U

Brewer, Samantha J
Valley HS
Lucasville, OH

Brandow, Kayla M N
Waite HS
Toledo, OH

Bradley, Nikita M
Teays Valley HS
Ashville, OH

Bradley, Bianca L
Colonel White HS For The Arts
Dayton, OH

National
Honor Roll
Spring 2005

Bowser, Ashley R
Padua Franciscan HS
North Royalton, OH

Branch, Tyler K
Dawson-Bryant HS
Ironton, OH

Bremenour, Chelsea
Charles F Brush HS
Cleveland, OH

Britanova, Julia
Wadsworth HS
Wadsworth, OH

BROWN, JUSTIN A; LANCASTER, OH; (JR); Hi Hnr Roll; Hnr Roll; Nat Hon Sy; Perf Att; WWAHSS; Peer Tut/Med; Red Cr Aide; AL Aux Boys; DECA; Emplmnt; Lttrmn Clb; Pep Squd; Tchrs Aide; Vsity Clb; French Clb; Ftball (V L); Vsy Clb (V L); Wt Lftg (V CL); Stu Cncl (T); Sch Ppr (E); Powder Puff Football Coach; McDonalds Ohio High School Football Scholar Athlete; Pharmacy (Pharm.D); Business Administration (MBA); U of Toledo; Ohio Northern U

BROWN, KATIE; CANTON, OH; JACKSON HS; (FR); Hi Hnr Roll; Hnr Roll; Otst Ac Ach Awd; Perf Att; St of Mnth; WWAHSS; Peer Tut/Med; Chrch Yth Grp; Dbte Team; Emplmnt; Key Club; NtlFrnscLg; Spanish Clb; Bnd; Mch Bnd; Cr Ctry; Lcrsse; Three I Ratings in OMEA District Solo & Ensemble in Class A; Medical Science; Engineering; U of Pennsylvania; Princeton U

BROWN, LINDSEY; DAYTON, OH; ARCHBISHOP ALTER HS; (JR); Hi Hnr Roll; Hnr Roll; Nat Hon Sy; Pres Sch; Sci Fairs; Yth Ldrshp Prog; Comm Volntr; Peer Tut/Med; Chrch Yth Grp; Emplmnt; Key Club; NYLC; P to P St Amb Prg; Svce Clb; Tchrs Aide; Spanish Clb; Clr Grd; Dnce; Drl Tm; Flg Crps; PPSqd (V C); Yrbk (P); Middle Childhood Eudcation; School Counseling; U of Dayton; Xavier U

BROWN, MARKEYTA; DAYTON, OH; MEADOWDALE HS; (FR); WWAHSS; Yth Ldrshp Prog; Mus Clb; Bnd; Drl Tm; Wright-Stepp; Business / Management; Central State U

BROWN, MICHAEL; CLEVELAND, OH; JOHN F KENNEDY HS; (JR); Hi Hnr Roll; Hnr Roll; Nat Hon Sy; Perf Att; Comm Volntr; DARE; Emplmnt; Bnd; Mch Bnd; Ftball (VJ); Wt Lftg (J); Stu Cncl (R); Bachelor's Degree in Criminal Justice; Business Management / Culinary; Cleveland State U / Tri-C

BROWN, REANTE; CLEVELAND, OH; VILLA ANGELA ST JOSEPH HS; MS; Ctznshp Aw; Hnr Roll; Otst Ac Ach Awd; Perf Att; Sci Fairs; Comm Volntr; Peer Tut/Med; Cmptr Clb; Lib Aide; Mod UN; Mus Clb; Off Aide; Svce Clb; Tchrs Aide; Chr; Ch Chr; SP/M/VS; Bskball; Adv Cncl (R); Cl Off (V); Stu Cncl (V); CR (R); Sch Ppr (R, P); I Won 2nd Place in Spelling Bee; I Say the Pledge of Allegiance; Lawyer; Teacher; Harvard U; Yale U

BROWN, SARAH L; DOVER, OH; DOVER HS; (FR); Hnr Roll; Nat Hon Sy

BROWN, TIPHANIE; CLEVELAND, OH; LUTHERAN HS EAST; (JR); Hnr Roll; St of Mnth; Chrch Yth Grp; Bnd; Ch Chr; Dnce; Chrldg (V L); Sftball (L); Vllyball (V L); Bright Futures Award; Student Athlete Award; Chemistry; Journalism; Case Western Reserve U; Miami U

BROWNFIELD, T'RIA; CAMBRIDGE, OH; CAMBRIDGE HS; (SR); Hnr Roll; WWAHSS; Comm Volntr; Emplmnt; Spanish Clb; PP Ftbl (J); Vllyball (J); Sociology; Business; U of Akron

BROWN JR, JACKY C; RICHMOND HTS, OH; RICHMOND HTS HS; (SR); MVP; Perf Att; Sci Fairs; Comm Volntr; Peer Tut/Med; Chrch Yth Grp; DARE; Emplmnt; FCA; Key Club; Sci Clb; Bnd; Drm Mjr; Jzz Bnd; Mch Bnd; Bskball (V L); Cr Ctry (V L); Track (V L); Stu Cncl (R); Most Outstanding & Most Improved Athlete; Breaking 2 School Track & Field Records; Music Major; Performing Arts Major; Notre Dame Ohio; U of Cincinnati

BROWNSWORD, RACHEL; CANTON, OH; CANTON SOUTH HS; (FR); Hnr Roll; Perf Att; Merit Roll; Law; Business; Stark State College; Walsh U

BRUEGGEMAN, SAHRA; MADISON, OH; MADISON HS; (FR); Hnr Roll; Tchrs Aide; Bnd; Mch Bnd; Pep Bnd; Criminology; Criminal Justice; Pitt U; Penn State

BRUGLER, MAX; WARREN, OH; CHAMPION HS; (JR); Hi Hnr Roll; Hnr Roll; MVP; Nat Stu Ath Day Aw; St of Mnth; WWAHSS; Chrch Yth Grp; Key Club; Off Aide; Tchrs Aide; Bsball (VJ L); Bskball (VJ L); Ftball (J); Sccr (VJ L); State Record Holder / Soccer-Highest # of Assists in a Season; Education; Francis Marion U; Capital U

BRUNER, LAURA; WAUSEON, OH; PETTISVILLE HS; (SR); 4H Awd; Ctznshp Aw; Hi Hnr Roll; Nat Hon Sy; Sci Fairs; Valdctrian; WWAHSS; Comm Volntr; Peer Tut/Med; 4-H; Chrch Yth Grp; Emplmnt; Ntl FFA; Prom Com; Tchrs Aide; Spanish Clb; Chr; Dnce; SP/M/VS; Bskball (J); Chrldg (J); Cr Ctry (V L); Track (V L); Cl Off (S); Attended Intel International Science & Engineering Fair; Student Director of "The Nerd"; Plant Pathology; Plant Genetics; The Ohio State U

BRUNS, MEGAN; MARIA STEIN, OH; MARION LOCAL HS; (SO); 4H Awd; Hnr Roll; Pres Ac Ftns Aw; Peer Tut/Med; 4-H; ArtClub; DARE; Emplmnt; Mth Clb/Tm; Pep Squd; Sci Clb; Tchrs Aide; Cr Ctry (V); Track (V); Yrbk (E, R, P); Scholar Athlete Award; All Mac -Track; Architecture; Miami U Ohio; U of Dayton

BRUST, RACHEL; NEW HOLLAND, OH; WESTFALL MS; 4H Awd; DAR; Fut Prb Slvr; Hnr Roll; 4-H; Chrch Yth Grp; DARE; Photog; SP/M/VS; Chrldg; Stu Cncl; 7th Grade Talent Search - SAT Test; Art and Design; Fashion Merchandising

BRYAN, ANNA; DAYTON, OH; ARCHBISHOP ALTER HS; (SO); Hnr Roll; Pres Ac Ftns Aw; Yth Ldrshp Prog; Hab For Humty Volntr; Emplmnt; Key Club; NYLC; SADD; French Clb; Sccr (J); Knights For Life - Pro-Life Group; Sports Medicine; Graphic Design; U of Dayton

BRYAN, MATTHEW D; KENSINGTON, OH; CARROLLTON HS; (SO); Bskball (J); Ftball (J); Track (J); Aeronautics; Surgery & Meteorology

BRYAN, NICK; ZANESVILLE, OH; BISHOP ROSECRANS HS; (JR); Hi Hnr Roll; Hnr Roll; MVP; Otst Ac Ach Awd; WWAHSS; Emplmnt; Key Club; Golf (V CL); Tennis (V L); Biology Student of the Year; (Bio Ii) of the Year; Biology

BUCHENROTH, BRITTA L; HUNTSVILLE, OH; INDIAN LAKE HS; (SR); Hnr Roll; Nat Hon Sy; Otst Ac Ach Awd; Perf Att; Sci Fairs; St of Mnth; Valdctrian; WWAHSS; Comm Volntr; Peer Tut/Med; ArtClub; Drma Clb; Key Club; Mus Clb; Prom Com; Sci Clb; Tchrs Aide; Spanish Clb; Chr; SP/M/VS; Swg Chr; Vllyball (J); Cl Off (S); Biology/Pre-Med; Ohio Wesleyan U

BUCKINGHAM, STACI; WOOSTER, OH; WOOSTER HS; (JR); Hnr Roll; Otst Ac Ach Awd; Perf Att; WWAHSS; Comm Volntr; Peer Tut/Med; Key Club; Chr; Sccr (C); Swmg (V); Scholar Athlete Award; NEAC All Star (Swimming); Physical Therapy; Pre-Med; Hiram U; Ohio Northern U

BUCKLER, CHRISTOPHER B; IRONTON, OH; ROCK HILL HS; (FR); Hi Hnr Roll; Hnr Roll; St of Mnth; Spec Olymp Vol; Chrch Yth Grp; DARE; Ftball (J L); Computer Technology; Ohio State; Marshall U

BUDDE, DANIELLE; LANCASTER, OH; WILLIAM V FISHER CATHOLIC HS; (JR); Hnr Roll; WWAHSS; Chrch Yth Grp; Drma Clb; Emplmnt; Key Club; SADD; Bnd; Dnce; Mch Bnd; SP/M/VS; International Studies; Xavier U; Kenyon College

BUDZIAK, KELLY; NORTH ROYALTON, OH; NORTH ROYALTON HS; (FR); Hnr Roll; Peer Tut/Med; Chrch Yth Grp; DARE; Drma Clb; Emplmnt; Key Club; Off Aide; Scouts; Spanish Clb; Stg Cre; Skiing (V); Track (V); Math; Teaching Degree; Ohio State U

BUECHTER, MARIKYLE; PIQUA, OH; LEHMAN CATHOLIC HS; (SR); Hnr Roll; Nat Hon Sy; Sci Fairs; USAA; WWAHSS; Comm Volntr; Red Cr Aide; Emplmnt; NYLC; Prom Com; SADD; PP Ftbl; Sccr (V CL); Sftball (VJ L); Sch Ppr (R); Yrbk (E, P); Top 100 in Pigua Academics; Kairos-21 Rector; Sport Management; U of Dayton

BUELTERMAN, KELSEY; CINCINNATI, OH; SETON HS; (FR); Hnr Roll; Chr; Lcrsse (J); Sccr (J)

BUESCHER, ASHLEY; NORTH OLMSTED, OH; LUTHERAN HS WEST; (FR); Hnr Roll; Chrch Yth Grp; Chr; Vllyball

BUESCHER, JACLYN N; LEBANON, OH; WARREN CTY CAREER CTR; (SR); Hnr Roll; Nat Hon Sy; Comm Volntr; Hosp Aide; Chrch Yth Grp; Emplmnt; Tchrs Aide; Voc Ind Clb Am; Cl Off (S); Citizenship Award At Pre-Teen America; Radiology; Social Work; Sinclair Community College; U of Cincinnati

BULLOCK, LYDIA M; DAYTON, OH; MOUND STREET AC; (JR); Comm Volntr; Peer Tut/Med; Chrch Yth Grp; Emplmnt; ROTC; Bnd; Chr; Dnce; Certified Nursing Assistant; Obstetrician; Master's Degree / Medicine; U of Dayton; Clark Atlanta U

BUMGARDNER, BRIAN; BELLAIRE, OH; BELLAIRE HS; (SO); Hnr Roll; Ftball (VJ); Wt Lftg (J)

BUNGER, ASHLEY; CINCINNATI, OH; MC AULEY HS; (JR); Hnr Roll; Nat Hon Sy; Pres Ac Ftns Aw; WWAHSS; Comm Volntr; Hosp Aide; Spec Olymp Vol; Key Club; P to P St Amb Prg; Sci Clb; Spanish Clb; Chrldg (J); Cr Ctry (V); Gmnstcs (V); Track (V); Key Club President; Pharmacy; Chemical Engineering; Purdue U; Ohio Northern

BURCHFIELD, JESSIE; GARFIELD HTS, OH; GARFIELD HEIGHTS HS; (JR); Ctznshp Aw; Hi Hnr Roll; Hnr Roll; Nat Hon Sy; Perf Att; St of Mnth; WWAHSS; Comm Volntr; Peer Tut/Med; ArtClub; Scouts; Svce Clb; Tchrs Aide; Sftball (JC); Chemistry / Education - Master's Degree; Bachelor's Degree in Art; Allegheny College; Ohio U

BURGER, BRYAN J; SUNBURY, OH; DELAWARE AREA CAREER CTR; (SR); 4H Awd; Hnr Roll; Otst Ac Ach Awd; Perf Att; St of Mnth; Comm Volntr; 4-H; Emplmnt; Acpl Chr; Ch Chr; Cl Off (P); Captain of Police Explorer Post (Top Position); Pianist/Composer; Criminal Justice Degree; Music Degree; Hocking College; Columbus State Community College

BURGER, STEPHANIE R; NORTH ROYALTON, OH; NORTH ROYALTON HS; (SO); Comm Volntr; Hab For Humty Volntr; Spec Olymp Vol; Key Club; Pep Squd; Bnd; Mch Bnd; Zoology; Kent State U; Bowling Green U

BURKE, ABBIGAIL K; EAST PALESTINE, OH; COLUMBIANA HS; (SO); Ctznshp Aw; Hi Hnr Roll; Hnr Roll; Nat Hon Sy; Nat Sci Aw; Otst Ac Ach Awd; Sci Fairs; St of Mnth; Comm Volntr; ArtClub; Chrch Yth Grp; DARE; Lib Aide; Off Aide; Pep Squd; P to P St Amb Prg; Tchrs Aide; Chr; Dnce; Bskball (J); Chrldg (VJ); Scr Kpr (J); Stu Cncl (V); Outstanding Citizen Award; Blue Ribbon 1st Place Art Awards; Master's Degree in Art; Interior Designer; Art Institute of Pittsburgh; Ohio State U

BURKE, KARI B; MIDDLETOWN, OH; WARREN CTY CAREER CTR; (SR); Hi Hnr Roll; Hnr Roll; Nat Hon Sy; Pres Sch; St of Mnth; WWAHSS; Comm Volntr; Hosp Aide; Red Cr Aide; Chrch Yth Grp; Emplmnt; Quiz Bowl; SADD; Tchrs Aide; Voc Ind Clb Am; Bnd; Mch Bnd; Pep Bnd; Cl Off (V); Stu Cncl (S); CR (R); National Technical Honor Society Historian; Quiz Bowl Team Member; Radiologic Technology; Raymond Walters College

BURKE, MOLLY; PAINESVILLE, OH; RIVERSIDE HS; (SO); Hi Hnr Roll; Hnr Roll; Otst Ac Ach Awd; Yth Ldrshp Prog; Comm Volntr; Hosp Aide; DARE; Emplmnt; Key Club; Prom Com; Tchrs Aide; Hsbk Rdg; PP Ftbl; Sftball; Track; Adv Cncl (R); Leader's Club - YMCA; Optometry

BURKHART, CIERA L; BEALLSVILLE, OH; BEALLSVILLE HS; (SR); All Am Sch; Hnr Roll; Kwnis Aw; Nat Hon Sy; Otst Ac Ach Awd; Pres Sch; Salutrn; St of Mnth; USAA; WWAHSS; Comm Volntr; AL Aux Girls; Chrch Yth Grp; FCA; Mod UN; Off Aide; Prom Com; Sci Clb; Spanish Clb; Chr; Sftball (V L); Track (V L); Vllyball (V L); Cl Off (S); Yrbk (E, R, P); Nursing; U of Akron

BURKHART, NICK; CLYDE, OH; CLYDE HS; (FR); Hnr Roll; Chr; Ftball (JC); Track (V); Wt Lftg (J); Ohio State Columbus

BURKS, SHARKITTA L; TOLEDO, OH; SPRINGFIELD HS; (JR); Hnr Roll; St Schl; Comm Volntr; Peer Tut/Med; Chrch Yth Grp; Emplmnt; Ch Chr; SP/M/VS; Stg Cre; PP Ftbl; Pre-Med; Optometry; Ohio State U; Yale U

BURNETT, SHAMEKA A; YOUNGSTOWN, OH; AUSTINTOWN FITCH HS; (FR); Hnr Roll; Otst Ac Ach Awd; ArtClub; Chrch Yth Grp; Bnd; Ch Chr; Dnce; Jzz Bnd; Bskball (J); Track (J); Church Mime Ministry; Dance Group; Journalism; Business Administration / Cartoonist; LSU; Howard U

BURR, KRISTIE; GENEVA, OH; MADISON HS; (FR); Ctznshp Aw; Hnr Roll; Chrch Yth Grp; Wdwrkg Clb; Lawyer

BURROUGHS, MARISSA; CINCINNATI, OH; ANDERSON HS; (JR); F Lan Hn Soc; Hi Hnr Roll; Nat Hon Sy; Otst Ac Ach Awd; Perf Att; WWAHSS; Comm Volntr; Key Club; Lib Aide; Spanish Clb; Chr; Lcrsse (J); PP Ftbl (V); Intramural Basketball and Softball; Just Say No Leader; Architecture/Interior Design; Graphic Design; Savannah College of Art and Design; U of Cincinnati

BUSCH, BILLIE; CLEVELAND, OH; JOHN MARSHALL HS; (SO); Nat Hon Sy; Nat Sci Aw; Peer Tut/Med; Chrch Yth Grp; DARE; Jr Ach; SADD; Tchrs Aide; Bnd; Ch Chr; Jzz Bnd; Mch Bnd; Cl Off (R); Pediatrician; Professional Musician; Baldwin Wallace; Case Western Reserve

BUTLER, ASHLEY; ASHLAND, OH; ASHLAND HS; (JR); Hi Hnr Roll; Nat Hon Sy; WWAHSS; Comm Volntr; Chrch Yth Grp; Emplmnt; Key Club; Off Aide; Photog; Prom Com; Svce Clb; Vsity Clb; Tennis (J); National Society of High School Scholars; Medicine; Psychology; Case Western Reserve U; Duke U

BUTLER, JENIESA; LIMA, OH; LIMA SR HS; (JR); Hnr Roll; Red Cr Aide; Bskball (L); Nursing Home Volunteer; Nursing; Studies in Communications; U of Cincinnati; Ohio State

BUTVIN, RACHEL; CLEVELAND, OH; GARFIELD HTS HS; (JR); Hi Hnr Roll; Hnr Roll; Nat Hon Sy; Comm Volntr; Peer Tut/Med; Red Cr Aide; DARE; Dbte Team; Emplmnt; Mus Clb; Svce Clb; Bnd; Dnce; Mch Bnd; Orch; PP Ftbl (J); Tennis (V C); President of National Honor Society; Vice President of Students of Service; Forensic Science; Early Childhood Education; Ohio Northern U; Defiance College

BUZZARD, ASHLEY; EAST LIVERPOOL, OH; EAST LIVERPOOL HS; (JR); Hnr Roll; WWAHSS; DARE; Voc Ind Clb Am; Radiology; Jefferson Community College

BYRD, DELILAH L; CLEVELAND, OH; SOUTH HS; Nat Hon Sy; Perf Att; Chrch Yth Grp; DARE; Emplmnt; Fr of Library; ROTC; Bnd; Dnce; Chrldg (J); Swmg (J); Cl Off (P); Stu Cncl (P); CR (R); Mechanical Engineer; Horticulture; West Point Military Academy; Virginia Marti

BYROM, ASHLEY R; NILES, OH; NILES MC KINLEY HS; (SR); Hnr Roll; Kwnis Aw; MVP; Sci Fairs; St of Mnth; WWAHSS; Comm Volntr; Red Cr Aide; Jr Ach; Key Club; Lib Aide; Off Aide; Pep Squd; Svce Clb; SADD; Tchrs Aide; Sftball (V CL); Vllyball (V CL); Stu Cncl (R); Softball-All Conference, All-Academic Team; Volleyball-All Conference, All-Academic Team; Biomedical Sciences; Biology; Thiel College; Hiram College

CADWALLADER, EVAN; WILMINGTON, OH; CLINTON-MASSIE SCH; (FR); 4H Awd; Hi Hnr Roll; Hnr Roll; Yth Ldrshp Prog; Comm Volntr; 4-H; Emplmnt; Quiz Bowl; Wdwrkg Clb; Bskball (J); Skt Tgt Sh (V); President of 4-H Club; Scholastic Clay Target Program Team; Pilot; Orthodontist; Ohio State U

Butvin, Rachel
Garfield Hts HS
Cleveland, OH

Brown Jr, Jacky C
Richmond Hts HS
Richmond Hts, OH

Brown, Justin A
Lancaster, OH

Brown, Reante
Villa Angela St Joseph HS
Cleveland, OH

Byrd, Delilah L
South HS
Cleveland, OH

CAFFEY, ADRIANE; DAYTON, OH; MEADOWDALE HS; (FR); 4H Awd; Ctznshp Aw; Fut Prb Slvr; Hi Hnr Roll; Hnr Roll; Nat Hon Sy; Otst Ac Ach Awd; Perf Att; Sci Fairs; St of Mnth; Comm Volntr; Hab For Humty Volntr; Peer Tut/Med; Chess; Chrch Yth Grp; DARE; Drma Clb; Mus Clb; Photog; SADD; Spanish Clb; Bnd; Chr; Ch Chr; Dnce; Bdmtn (J); Bskball (J); Chrldg (J); Cr Ctry (J); Sccr (J); Tennis (J); Track; Vllyball (J); CR (S); Medicine / Doctorate; Ob/Gyn; Wright State U; Ohio State U

CAGE, T J; WARREN, OH; CHAMPION HS; (SO); Hnr Roll; Perf Att; St of Mnth; WWAHSS; Yth Ldrshp Prog; Comm Volntr; Peer Tut/Med; Chrch Yth Grp; Emplmnt; HO'Br Yth Ldrshp; Key Club; Lttrmn Clb; Pep Squd; Tchrs Aide; Bskball (J); Ftball (V L); Skiing (V); Track (V L); Wt Lftg (V); Teaching; Physical Therapy; Kent State U; Mercyhurst College

CAI, WENDY; HILLIARD, OH; HILLIARD DAVIDSON HS; (JR); F Lan Hn Soc; Hi Hnr Roll; Nat Hon Sy; WWAHSS; Comm Volntr; Hosp Aide; Spec Olymp Vol; Emplmnt; Key Club; SADD; French Clb; Orch; Yrbk (E); Pediatrician; Psychologist/Psychiatrist; Duke U; Northwestern U

CAIN, JANELLE; PERRY, OH; PERRY HS; (JR); Hnr Roll; Nat Hon Sy; Red Cr Aide; ArtClub; Key Club; Prom Com; Vsity Clb; Swmg (V); States for Swimming; Interior Design; Business; East Carolina U; U of North Carolina At Wilmington

CALCEI, CASEY; CANAL FULTON, OH; NORTHWEST HS; (SO); Chr; Chrldg (V); Track (V); Stu Cncl (R); All Star Cheerleader & Dancer for 6 Yrs.; Good Student Past 2 Yrs.; Elementary Education; Akron U; Kent State U

CALDWELL, BERNARD; COLUMBUS, OH; BROOKHAVEN HS; (JR); Hi Hnr Roll; Hnr Roll; Emplmnt

CALDWELL, JESSICA; COLUMBUS, OH; GROVEPORT MADISON HS; (FR); All Am Sch; Hnr Roll; Nat Hon Sy; Nat Ldrshp Svc; St of Mnth; DARE; Quiz Bowl; Chr; Wrstlg; CR (R); National Junior Honor Society; All-American Scholar; Cosmetology; Pediatrician; U of Kentucky

CALENDINE, KIRSTIE; MONTVILLE, OH; LEDGEMONT HS; (FR); Hi Hnr Roll; Hnr Roll; Otst Ac Ach Awd; Perf Att; St of Mnth; Emplmnt; Track (J); Yrbk (E, P); Participation in Art Shows; Solo Photography; Art; English Lit; Virginia-Marti School of Art and Design; Ohio State U

CALLIHAN, ERICA; CIRCLEVILLE, OH; CIRCLEVILLE HS; (FR); Fut Prb Slvr; Hi Hnr Roll; MVP; Perf Att; Pres Ac Ftns Aw; Sci Fairs; St of Mnth; St Optmst of Yr; Comm Volntr; Peer Tut/Med; ArtClub; DARE; FBLA; Key Club; Off Aide; Spanish Clb; Sccr (J); Stu Cncl (R); CR (R); Psychologist; Interior Design; Ohio State U; Wright State U

CALVELAGE, ELIZABETH; MIDDLE POINT, OH; LINCOLNVIEW SCH; (JR); Hnr Roll; Nat Hon Sy; Comm Volntr; Emplmnt; Sci Clb; French Clb; Bnd; Clr Grd; Dnce; Flg Crps; Cl Off (S); Stu Cncl; Interior Design; Architecture; Miami U; Ball State U

CAMPBELL, CODY A; FAIRFIELD, OH; FAIRFIELD FRESHMAN HS; (FR); 4H Awd; Pres Sch; St of Mnth; Comm Volntr; 4-H; DARE; Scouts; Wdwrkg Clb; Spanish Clb; Butler Cty Sheriff Explorers; Bowling League; Crime Scene Investigations; Eastern Kentucky U

CAMPBELL, DUSTIN C; BURTON, OH; NEWBURY HS; (FR); 4H Awd; 4-H; Bskball (J); Ftball (J); Wt Lftg (J); Military Academy; Ohio State U; Virginia Military Institute

CAMPBELL, STACEY; DAYTON, OH; BEAVERCREEK HS; (FR); Ctznshp Aw; Hnr Roll; Otst Ac Ach Awd; DARE; Tchrs Aide; Nursing; Master's Degree; Wright State U; Sinclair Community College

CAMPBELL, WHITNEY; HAMILTON, OH; HAMILTON HS; (JR); Hi Hnr Roll; Hnr Roll; Nat Hon Sy; Pres Sch; St of Mnth; WWAHSS; Chr; JV Bowling; Top Twenty Award; Biology (Major); Miami U (Oxford)

CAMPBELL, WHITNEY R; HAMILTON, OH; BADIN HS; (SR); Hi Hnr Roll; Hnr Roll; Nat Hon Sy; WWAHSS; DARE; DECA; Key Club; SADD; PP Ftbl; National Honor Society Treasurer; BHS Ambassador; Pharmacy; U of Cincinnati

CANTER, JENNIFER; RAY, OH; JACKSON HS; (JR); Hnr Roll; Sci Fairs; DECA; Drma Clb; Emplmnt; Quill & Scroll; Spch Team; Chr; Stg Cre; Yrbk (R, P); Egyptology; Rio Grand U

CAPOTA, TODD; BRUNSWICK, OH; BRUNSWICK HS; (JR); Hnr Roll; Comm Volntr; Business; Financial Advisor; Ohio State; Ohio U

CAPUANO, CARA; MASSILLON, OH; PERRY HS; (JR); Hi Hnr Roll; Kwnis Aw; Nat Hon Sy; Perf Att; WWAHSS; Chrch Yth Grp; Key Club; Off Aide; Scouts; Clb; Tennis (V); Mass Communications; Journalism

CARDENAS, AMANDA M; PICKERINGTON, OH; PICKERINGTON HS NORTH; (SO); Hi Hnr Roll; Otst Ac Ach Awd; Comm Volntr; Drma Clb; Emplmnt; Spanish Clb; Chr; Dnce; SP/M/VS; Equine Studies; Performing Arts; Otterbein College; U of Kentucky

CARPER, CHRISTINA M; SUGAR GROVE, OH; (SR); 4-H; SP/M/VS; Mock Trial Winning Team 2005; Mock Trial 2004/Save the Children Art Winner 2001; Theater Arts/Ancient World Drama; Advanced Art; Ohio State, Ohio U; School in Art & Design or Theatre

CARPER, COLLEEN; LOUISVILLE, OH; LOUISVILLE HS; (SR); Hi Hnr Roll; Nat Hon Sy; Nat Ldrshp Svc; Pres Sch; Sci Fairs; USAA; WWAHSS; Comm Volntr; Peer Tut/Med; Spec Olymp Vol; HO'Br Yth Ldrshp; Key Club; Mus Clb; NtlFrnscLg; Off Aide; Spch Team; French Clb; Bnd; Jzz Bnd; Mch Bnd; State Qualifier in International Extemp; Books For Africa; Journalism; Political Science; Ashland U; Mt Union College

CARPMAIL, STEPHEN J; AMHERST, OH; LORAIN ADMIRAL KING HS; (FR); Ctznshp Aw; Hi Hnr Roll; Hnr Roll; Otst Ac Ach Awd; Perf Att; Sci Fairs; St of Mnth; WWAHSS; Emplmnt; FTA; Jr Ach; SP/M/VS; Purple Belt in Martial Arts; Straight A's - 7th & 8th Grade; Medicine / MD; Medicine / Psychology PhD; Harvard Medical; U of Michigan

CARR, CORY; TOLEDO, OH; WHITMER CAREER & TECH CTR; (JR); Ctznshp Aw; Hnr Roll; Otst Ac Ach Awd; Emplmnt; MuAlphaTh; Bsball (J); Construction Technology/Club; Architecture; Landscape Architecture; U of Philadelphia; Drexel U

CARR, JUSTIN W; OREGON, OH; CLAY HS; (FR); Hi Hnr Roll; Hnr Roll; Perf Att; Pres Sch; DARE; Ftball; Wt Lftg; President's Education Award; Architecture; Law Enforcement; Ohio State; Toledo U

CARR, SARAH; CINCINNATI, OH; SETON HS; (FR); Biology Clb; Spanish Clb

CARROLL, BRANDON; BLOOMINGDALE, OH; STEUBENVILLE HS; (MS); Hnr Roll; MVP; Perf Att; Sci Fairs; Sci/Math Olympn; St of Mnth; Comm Volntr; Spec Olymp Vol; Chrch Yth Grp; SP/M/VS; Bsball; Bskball; Ftball (C); Sccr; Track; Wt Lftg; Engineering; Architecture; Ohio State

CARSON, KATELYN A; EAST ROCHESTER, OH; UNITED LOCAL HS; (JR); Hi Hnr Roll; Nat Hon Sy; Nat Mrt LOC; WWAHSS; Peer Tut/Med; AL Aux Girls; Chrch Yth Grp; Emplmnt; Key Club; Off Aide; Schol Bwl; Svce Clb; French Clb; Chr; Ch Chr; SP/M/VS; Stg Cre; Track (V L); Cl Off (T); Stu Cncl (R); Sch Ppr (E, R); 3-Year Academic Letter Recipient; International Relations; Political Science; Georgetown U; Duke U

CARTER, D'ANGELO; CINCINNATI, OH; AIKEN UNIVERSITY HS; (JR); Hnr Roll; Sci Fairs; Sci/Math Olympn; St of Mnth; Comm Volntr; Bnd; Mch Bnd; Pep Bnd; Computer Technician; Music; Northern Kentucky U; Kentucky State U

CARTER, JASMINE; LIMA, OH; LIMA SR HS; (SO); Hi Hnr Roll; Hnr Roll; Perf Att; St of Mnth; WWAHSS; Comm Volntr; Ch Chr; Cl Off (S); English (Lawyer); Math (Architect); Ohio State; Tuskegee State U

CARTER, TARA; PICKERINGTON, OH; PICKERINGTON HS NORTH; (SO); Hi Hnr Roll; Hnr Roll; Pres Ac Ftns Aw; Pres Sch; St of Mnth; Yth Ldrshp Prog; Peer Tut/Med; ArtClub; DARE; Emplmnt; Key Club; Photog; Chr; Sccr (V); Stu Cncl (P); Sunnyside Up Leadership Camp; Mediator / Mediation Trainer; Education; Coaching; Ohio State U; U of Kentucky

CARTER, TAYLOR A; PICKERINGTON, OH; PICKERINGTON HS NORTH; (JR); Hi Hnr Roll; Hnr Roll; Perf Att; WWAHSS; Comm Volntr; Spec Olymp Vol; Chrch Yth Grp; Emplmnt; Key Club; Orch; Student Athletic Trainer Asst.-All Sports; Pharmacy; Miami U-Ohio; Emory U-Georgia

CARTWRIGHT, SARAH J; CANTON, OH; EAST CANTON HS; (SO); Hnr Roll; MVP; Chrch Yth Grp; Lttrmn Clb; Tchrs Aide; Vsity Clb; Chr; SP/M/VS; Sftball (V L); Vllyball (V L); Stu Cncl; Hit a Softball Over the Fence; Be Happy; Find Job Perfect for Me; Malone; Walsh

CARTY, KAELA; ELYRIA, OH; ELYRIA HS; (FR); Hi Hnr Roll; Perf Att; St of Mnth; WWAHSS; Peer Tut/Med; Spec Olymp Vol; Drma Clb; Key Club; P to P St Amb Prg; Bnd; Chr; Mch Bnd; SP/M/VS; Thespians; Student Ambassador; Zoology; Veterinary Medicine; Ohio State U; Miami U (In Ohio)

CASADA, AMANDA M; CINCINNATI, OH; MC AULEY HS; (SR); F Lan Hn Soc; Hi Hnr Roll; Nat Hon Sy; Otst Ac Ach Awd; Perf Att; Sci/Math Olympn; St of Mnth; WWAHSS; Comm Volntr; Hab For Humty Volntr; Hosp Aide; Emplmnt; Key Club; Svce Clb; Spanish Clb; Track (V); CR (R); Leadership Council; Ranked 3rd in Class; Nursing; U of Cincinnati

CASEY JR, STEPHEN L; SPRING VALLEY, OH; BELLBROOK HS; (SO); Hnr Roll; Perf Att; WWAHSS; Chrch Yth Grp; DARE; Chr; Placed 4th in the Nation in Recipe Contest; Bellbrook Volunteer Police Association; Culinary Arts; Culinary Institute of America; Johnson and Wales U

CASSIN, BRIAN; CINCINNATI, OH; ANDERSON HS; (JR); Hnr Roll; Bskball; Lcrsse (V L); Ohio U; U of Dayton

CASTLE, LINDSAY N; MARYSVILLE, OH; MARYSVILLE HS; (SO); Hi Hnr Roll; Hnr Roll; Perf Att; Pres Ac Ftns Aw; Pres Sch; Sci Fairs; Sci/Math Olympn; St of Mnth; Chrch Yth Grp; DARE; Emplmnt; FCA; Scouts; Bskball (J); Sftball; Sch Ppr (R, P); Yrbk (R, P); Business Management; Middle Tennessee State U; Belmont U

CATANIA, BRITTANY; OXFORD, OH; TALAWANDA HS; (SO); Hi Hnr Roll; Hnr Roll; MVP; Perf Att; Key Club; Scouts; Chr; Dvng (V); Swmg (V); Cl Off (T); Girl Scout Silver Award; Medicine, Pre-Med; Miami U; Wright State U

CATANZARO, CATHERINE; LIBERTY TWSP, OH; LAKOTA EAST HS; (JR); F Lan Hn Soc; Hi Hnr Roll; Otst Ac Ach Awd; Pres Ac Ftns Aw; WWAHSS; Comm Volntr; Peer Tut/Med; Emplmnt; Spanish Clb; Sftball (J); Vllyball (J L); Interpreter; Kent State U-Ohio; Wright State U-Ohio

CELESTINO, ERIKA L; TROY, OH; TROY HS; (JR); All Am Sch; Hi Hnr Roll; Nat Ldrshp Svc; USAA; WWAHSS; French Clb; Bnd; USAA International Foreign Language Award; Architecture; Pre-Med; Ohio State U; Carnegie Mellon U

CEPHAS, CHERRALLE M; CANTON, OH; TIMKEN SR HS; (FR); Hnr Roll; Comm Volntr; Chrch Yth Grp; ROTC; Ch Chr; Drl Tm; Lawyer; Doctor; UCLA; U of Portland

CHADWELL, ERIN; MILFORD, OH; CLERMONT NORTHEASTERN HS; (FR); Hnr Roll; Nat Hon Sy; Perf Att; Chrch Yth Grp; Ntl FFA; French Clb; Bnd; Chr; Dnce; Sch Ppr (R); Super Student; Career Club; Business; U of Cincinnati

CHAMPA, JACQUELYN; WILLOUGHBY, OH; WILLOUGHBY SOUTH HS; (SO); Hnr Roll; Perf Att; Comm Volntr; Chrch Yth Grp; Key Club; Sci Clb; Scouts; Bnd; Mch Bnd; Pep Bnd; Stg Cre; Principal's List; Biochemistry; Forensics; Fordham U; Eastern Michigan U

CHANEY, EMILY; TORONTO, OH; EDISON HS; (JR); Hnr Roll; Nat Hon Sy; WWAHSS; Red Cr Aide; ArtClub; Chrch Yth Grp; P to P St Amb Prg; Prom Com; Spanish Clb; Sccr (V L); Swmg (V L); Justice Studies; Kent State U

CHANG, APRIL; WEST CHESTER, OH; THE SUMMIT CTRY DAY SCH; (JR); Hi Hnr Roll; Otst Ac Ach Awd; Pres Ac Ftns Aw; Sci Fairs; Yth Ldrshp Prog; Comm Volntr; ArtClub; Chrch Yth Grp; Key Club; Prom Com; Spanish Clb; Bnd; Dnce; Orch; SP/M/VS; Bskball; Chrldg; Track (V); Cl Off (P); Stu Cncl (V); CR (P); Yrbk (E, P); Babel Tower (Multicultural Club)-Founder & Pres.; Spanish Club (Language Club)-President; International Business/ Economics/Marketing; International Diplomacy; George Washington U; Brown U

CHAPMAN, AMANDA; SWANTON, OH; (SR); Ctznshp Aw; Hnr Roll; ArtClub; Drma Clb; Prom Com; SADD; Bnd; Pep Bnd; SP/M/VS; Track (J); Nursing; Teaching; Lourdes College

CHAPMAN, JESSICA; MASSILLON, OH; (FR); Chrch Yth Grp; Tchrs Aide; Foreign Clb; Bnd; Flg Crps; Mch Bnd

CHAPMAN, KIMBERLY A; PATRIOT, OH; SOUTH GALLIA HS; (JR); Hnr Roll; Sci Fairs; Early Childhood; Nurse's Aide; Ohio State U; Shawnee State U

CHAPMAN, MEGAN E; SWANTON, OH; SWANTON HS; (JR); Hnr Roll; MVP; Perf Att; WWAHSS; French Clb; Bnd; Jzz Bnd; Mch Bnd; Orch; Sftball (V); Education/Physical Education; Sports Trainer; Ohio State U; Wooster College

CHECK, STEPHEN; WILLOUGHBY, OH; (JR); Otst Ac Ach Awd; Pres Sch; Comm Volntr; Bskball; Nursing; Kent State U; Walsh U

CHEEMA, JAWAD M; COLUMBUS, OH; HAMILTON TWP HS; (JR); Hnr Roll; Otst Ac Ach Awd; Perf Att; St of Mnth; Comm Volntr; Peer Tut/Med; AL Aux Boys; DECA; DECA National Competitor; Boys State Delegate; Electrical Engineer / Ohio State; Pre-Med / NYU

CHEN, ASHLEY; NEWARK, OH; NEWARK CATHOLIC HS; (SR); Hnr Roll; Key Club; Ashland U

CHEN, JENNY; LANCASTER, OH; LANCASTER HS; (JR); Hi Hnr Roll; Nat Hon Sy; Otst Ac Ach Awd; St of Mnth; Comm Volntr; Peer Tut/Med; Key Club; Latin Clb; Chr; Swg Chr; Tennis (V); Track (V); Cl Off (P); Stu Cncl (R)

CHEVALIER, JESSICA; AKRON, OH; GREEN HS; (SR); Hnr Roll; Nat Hon Sy; Otst Ac Ach Awd; WWAHSS; Red Cr Aide; Chrch Yth Grp; Bskball (J); Sccr (V CL); Track (V CL); Cl Off (T); Stu Cncl (R); CR (R); Academic Team; Major Aerospace Engineering; Minor Business; The Ohio State U; U of Akron

CHILDERS, KATEY; DAYTON, OH; CARROLL HS; (SO); Hnr Roll; Pres Ac Ftns Aw; Sci/Math Olympn; Hosp Aide; Chrch Yth Grp; Emplmnt; Mth Clb/Tm; Pep Squd; Scouts; SADD; Spanish Clb; Chrldg (J); Sccr (J); State Championship - Soccer; Pre-Med; Pharmaceutical; Wright State U; Ohio State U

CHILLCOTT, RACHAEL; ASHTABULA, OH; LAKESIDE HS; (FR); Hi Hnr Roll; Hnr Roll; Comm Volntr; Biology Clb; Emplmnt; Chrldg (J); Sftball (V); Vllyball (J); Advertising; Graphic Design; Ottawa U Ont Canada

CHOI, DONGHOON; AKRON, OH; COPLEY HS; (FR); Ctznshp Aw; Hnr Roll; Nat Hon Sy; Chrch Yth Grp; DARE; Bnd; Mch Bnd; Pep Bnd; Bskball; Mar Art; Church Pianist; Dentist; Michigan State U; Virginia State U

Carr, Sarah
Seton HS
Cincinnati, OH

Campbell, Stacey
Beavercreek HS
Dayton, OH

Callihan, Erica
Circleville HS
Circleville, OH

National
Honor Roll
Spring 2005

Cain, Janelle
Perry HS
Perry, OH

Capota, Todd
Brunswick HS
Brunswick, OH

Carter, Jasmine
Lima SR HS
Lima, OH

CHOUDHARY, VIKAS; REYNOLDSBURG, OH; ST CHARLES PREP; (SO); Hnr Roll; Sci Fairs; Comm Volntr; Hab For Humty Volntr; Chess; Stu Cncl (R); Local, State, and National Chess Awards; Silver Medalist in the National Latin Exam; Doctorate in Mathematics; Doctorate in Engineering; Ohio State U; Case Western Reserve U

CHOUJAA, NESRENE F; STOW, OH; OUR LADY OF THE ELMS; (SR); Ctznshp Aw; F Lan Hn Soc; Hi Hnr Roll; Nat Hon Sy; Nat Ldrshp Svc; Pres Ac Ftns Aw; St Optmst of Yr; WWAHSS; Yth Ldrshp Prog; Comm Volntr; French Clb; Dnce; SP/M/VS; Adv Cncl (V); Stu Cncl (P); CR (P); Yrbk (E); Medicine; Journalism; Case Western Reserve U

CHRISTMAN, ASHLEY; LORAIN, OH; LORAIN ADMIRAL KING/ LORAIN MS; MS; Hi Hnr Roll; Hnr Roll; Nat Hon Sy; Perf Att; St of Mnth; Peer Tut/Med; DARE; Chr; Stu Cncl (R); Yrbk (E, P); National Junior Honor Society; Academic Challenge; Law; Government; Harvard U; Brown U

CHUPP, AMBER; BEACH CITY, OH; FAIRLESS HS; (SO); Ctznshp Aw; St of Mnth; DARE; Chr; Zoology; Early Childhood; Kent State U Stark; Stark State College

CICCARELLO, MICHELLE; NORTH ROYALTON, OH; NORTH ROYALTON HS; (SO); Hnr Roll; St of Mnth; WWAHSS; ArtClub; Emplmnt; Key Club; Spanish Clb; Dnce; Drl Tm; SP/M/VS; Track (J); Pride in Academics; Captain of Jr. Elite Dance Team; Criminology; Forensic Science; U of Cincinnati

CIERA, ANDERSON; AKRON, OH; (JR); Ctznshp Aw; Hnr Roll; Perf Att; Chrch Yth Grp; Track (J L); Malone Christian College; Central School of Practical Nursing

CIRIACO, CHRISTINE; CINCINNATI, OH; MOTHER OF MERCY HS; (JR); Hnr Roll; Perf Att; St of Mnth; WWAHSS; Comm Volntr; ArtClub; Key Club; SADD; French Clb; Stu Cncl (R); Family, Career, & Community Leaders of America Representative; Scholastics Art Award; Pre-Med / Pediatrician; Interior Design

CITAK, MARCIN A; LORAIN, OH; LORAIN SOUTHVIEW HS; (SO); Hnr Roll; St of Mnth; Comm Volntr; Key Club; Mod UN; Skiing; Tennis (V); Mechanical Engineering; Case Western Reserve U

CLAMPITT, JENNA C; CLEVELAND, OH; RICHMOND HTS HS; (JR); Hnr Roll; Nat Hon Sy; Red Cr Aide; Emplmnt; Key Club; Prom Com; Scouts; Bnd; Jzz Bnd; Pep Bnd; PP Ftbl (VJ); Skiing (V); Sftball (V L); Vllyball (V L); Cl Off (P, V); Stu Cncl (V); Junior Class Attendant - Princess; Matt Stats; Sports Medicine; Radiology; Ohio State U; Capital U

CLARK, ALISON; SPRING VALLEY, OH; BELLBROOK HS; (JR); Ctznshp Aw; Hi Hnr Roll; Hnr Roll; Nat Hon Sy; Otst Ac Ach Awd; Pres Ac Ftns Aw; WWAHSS; Comm Volntr; Peer Tut/Med; Emplmnt; Key Club; Prom Com; Sftball (V, C); Swmg (V, C); Track (V); Vllyball (V); Adv Cncl (T); Cl Off (V); Heisman Scholar Athlete Nominee; Business; Journalism; Stanford University; Yale University

CLARK, ASHLEY A; TORONTO, OH; TORONTO HS; (FR); Hi Hnr Roll; Perf Att; Chr; Chrldg (V)

CLARK, CHASE; LANCASTER, OH; LANCASTER HS; (JR); Hi Hnr Roll; Hnr Roll; Comm Volntr; Key Club; Sccr (V L); Volunteered for Charity News; Volunteered to Run a Kids Soccer Camp; Business/Marketing Degree; Engineering Degree; Miami U Ohio; U of South Carolina-Columbia

CLARK, HANNAH R; SPRINGFIELD, OH; KENTON RIDGE HS; (FR); All Am Sch; Hi Hnr Roll; Perf Att; WWAHSS; Chrch Yth Grp; FCA; Bskball (J); Sccr (J); Sftball (J)

CLARK, MINDY S; MONTPELIER, OH; NORTH CTRL SCH; (FR); Ctznshp Aw; Hnr Roll; St of Mnth; DARE; Spanish Clb; Medical Doctor; Veterinarian; Bowling Green U; Medical College of Toledo

CLARK, MONICA; RAVENNA, OH; SOUTHEAST HS; (SO); 4H Awd; Ctznshp Aw; Hnr Roll; Otst Ac Ach Awd; Pres Ac Ftns Aw; St of Mnth; Comm Volntr; Emplmnt; Off Aide; Tchrs Aide; Chr; Dnce; Chrldg (V L); Cr Ctry (V L); Track (V L); Cl Off (R); Business, Sales; Radiologist; Ohio State U; Kent State U

CLARK, SARAH; GENOA, OH; GENOA HS; (FR); Hi Hnr Roll; Perf Att; St of Mnth; WWAHSS; Peer Tut/Med; Emplmnt; Key Club; Off Aide; Pep Squd; P to P St Amb Prg; Prom Com; Tchrs Aide; Vsity Clb; Dnce; SP/ M/VS; Chrldg (V L); Gmnstcs; Cl Off (V); Stu Cncl; Dental Hygienist; Education; Bowling Green U; Owens Tech College

CLARKE, KELSEY; NORTH ROYALTON, OH; NORTH ROYALTON HS; (FR); Hi Hnr Roll; St of Mnth; WWAHSS; Key Club; Spanish Clb; Sftball (J); Vllyball (C)

CLARKE, MATTHEW; GALLIPOLIS, OH; GALLIA AC HS; (SR); Hnr Roll; Nat Hon Sy; WWAHSS; Chrch Yth Grp; Emplmnt; Key Club; Off Aide; Bsball (J L); Medical Doctor; Ohio State U

CLARKE, SHANNON R; MEDINA, OH; MEDINA HS; (SO); Hi Hnr Roll; Hnr Roll; Hab For Humty Volntr; Peer Tut/Med; Chrch Yth Grp; JSA; Key Club; French Clb; Chr; Huddle Organization - Teaching Youth About Drinking Drugs, Peer Pressure; Psychology / PhD Psychiatry; Ohio State U; Columbia U

CLAWSON III, JOSEPH R; DAYTON, OH; WALTER E. STEBBINS HS; Hi Hnr Roll; Hnr Roll; Pres Ac Ftns Aw; Comm Volntr; Spec Olymp Vol; DARE; ROTC; Wdwrkg Clb; Bskball (VJ L); Ftball (J L); Sccr (V L); Swmg (J L); Track (J L); Engineering; Architecture; West Virginia U; Florida State U

CLAY, D'MYA; COLUMBUS, OH; EAST HS; (SO); Hi Hnr Roll; Hnr Roll; MVP; St of Mnth; Peer Tut/Med; Chrch Yth Grp; DARE; FCA; Off Aide; Bskball (V C); Track (V); Vllyball (V C); Student Athletic Leadership Council; Banking/Accounting; Merchandize Distributing; U of North Carolina; Virginia State U

CLAY, JOHANNA M; NEWARK, OH; OHDELA AC; (SR); 4H Awd; Yth Ldrshp Prog; Comm Volntr; Red Cr Aide; 4-H; ArtClub; Chrch Yth Grp; Drma Clb; Emplmnt; Off Aide; Photog; Chr; Ch Chr; SP/M/VS; Stg Cre; Bachelor Of Science In Nursing (BSN); Mount Vernon Nazarene U; Central Ohio Technical College

CLAY, TIMOTHY O; PIQUA, OH; PIQUA HS; (FR); Hnr Roll; Nat Ldrshp Svc; Otst Ac Ach Awd; Perf Att; DARE; Tchrs Aide; Bskball (J); Ftball (J); Wt Lftg (J); Getting a Career in Architecture; A Degree in Criminal Justice; Ohio State U; U of Southern California (USC)

CLAYBAUGH, JESSICA L; CELINA, OH; CELINA HS; (SR); Hi Hnr Roll; Nat Hon Sy; Otst Ac Ach Awd; Perf Att; Quill & Scroll; ROTC; Sci Clb; Svce Clb; Interior Design; Fashion Design; Sinclair Community College; Art Institute of Chicago

CLAYTON, CANDACE; SPRINGFIELD, OH; NORTHWESTERN HS; (JR); Ctznshp Aw; Hnr Roll; MVP; Nat Hon Sy; St of Mnth; WWAHSS; Peer Tut/ Med; DARE; FCCLA; Off Aide; Chr; Chrldg (L); Tennis (V CL); National Federation of Music Clubs; USTA Member; Criminal Defense Lawyer; Senator; Vanderbilt U

CLAYTON, EMILY S; COLUMBUS, OH; GRANDVIEW HEIGHTS HS; (SO); Ctznshp Aw; Hnr Roll; St of Mnth; Hosp Aide; Chrch Yth Grp; DARE; FCA; Key Club; Off Aide; Sci Clb; Tchrs Aide; French Clb; Bnd; Mch Bnd; Pep Bnd; Track; Adv Cncl (R); Stu Cncl (R); CR (R); Yrbk (R, P); Key Club-Officer-Secretary, Science Club,; Youth to Youth, French Club; Biology, Vet Medicine; Music; Ohio State U; Ohio Dominican

CLEMENT, ALYSSA A; NEW ALBANY, OH; NEW ALBANY HS; (SO); Red Cr Aide; Emplmnt; Chrch Yth Grp; Tchrs Aide; Bnd; Ch Chr; Mch Bnd; Swmg (J); Track (V); Stu Cncl (R); Student Council (Two Years); Criminology; Princeton U

CLEMENTS, MICHAEL D; WILLOUGHBY, OH; WILLOUGHBY SOUTH HS; (SR); Hi Hnr Roll; Nat Hon Sy; Perf Att; Pres Ac Ftns Aw; Valdctrian; WWAHSS; Comm Volntr; Chrch Yth Grp; Emplmnt; Schol Bwl; Ch Chr; Bsball (VJ L); Sccr (V CL); Scholar Athlete Award; Best Offensive Player Award; Civil Engineering; U of Akron; Case Western Reserve U

CLIFTON, BRITTANY; LEBANON, OH; KINGS HS; (MS); Otst Ac Ach Awd; ArtClub; Drma Clb; Acpl Chr; SP/M/VS; Stu Cncl (T); Law; Xavier; U of Cincinnati

CLINE, DESTINY; WASHINGTON COURT HOUSE, OH; WASHINGTON HS; (FR); Ctznshp Aw; Hnr Roll; Otst Ac Ach Awd; Chrch Yth Grp; DARE; Criminal Justice (Forensic); Correctional Officer; Southern State Community College; Wilmington College

CLINE, SHAWNTAE; BELPRE, OH; BELPRE HS; (JR); Hnr Roll; MVP; Nat Hon Sy; Pres Ac Ftns Aw; Comm Volntr; Chrch Yth Grp; Mod UN; Chr; Bskball (V L); Cr Ctry (V L); Track (V L); Vllyball (V L); Stu Cncl (V); TVC All-Academic; 1st Team All TVC; Business Administration

COEN, EMILIE; COLUMBUS, OH; WHETSTONE HS; (JR); Hi Hnr Roll; Hnr Roll; Nat Hon Sy; Perf Att; WWAHSS; Yth Ldrshp Prog; Comm Volntr; Peer Tut/Med; ArtClub; Chrch Yth Grp; DECA; Emplmnt; Pep Squd; Photog; Prom Com; Chrldg (V L); Scr Kpr (V); Sccr (J); Track (J); Wt Lftg (V); Cl Off (P); Stu Cncl (T); Sch Ppr (E, R, P); Youth Representative to the Board of Trustees at Church; Public Relations; Psychology; Tufts U; Brown U

COFFEY, SAMUEL; MIDDLETOWN, OH; LAKOTA EAST HS; (SO); Hi Hnr Roll; WWAHSS; Comm Volntr; Chrch Yth Grp; Emplmnt; Scouts; Bnd; Jzz Bnd; Sccr (V L); Track (J L); Captain-Cincinnati United Premier Soccer Club; Business; U of Dayton; U of Cincinnati

COFFMAN, CHRIS; CANTON, OH; CANTON SOUTH HS; (JR); Hnr Roll; Perf Att; Student of the Marking Period; DeVry U; Stark State College

COFFMAN, MEGAN; COSHOCTON, OH; COSHOCTON CTY CAREER CTR; (JR); Ctznshp Aw; Hi Hnr Roll; Hnr Roll; Otst Ac Ach Awd; Pres Ac Ftns Aw; Sci Fairs; St of Mnth; DARE; Stu Cncl (P, V); 1st Place DARE Award Essay; Citizenship Award; Pediatrician; Ohio State U

COGAN, MAGGIE; CHESTERLAND, OH; WEST GEAUGA HS; (SO); Hnr Roll; St of Mnth; WWAHSS; Key Club; Dnce; Skiing; Stu Cncl (R); HUGS (Helping Us Grow Stronger); Snow Boarding; Fashion Design, Business; Dance; Indiana U; U of Cincinnati

COGAN, MICHELLE; MINERVA, OH; MINERVA HS; (JR); 4H Awd; Hi Hnr Roll; Hnr Roll; Otst Ac Ach Awd; Perf Att; St of Mnth; WWAHSS; 4-H; Chrch Yth Grp; Key Club; Prom Com; Quiz Bowl; SADD; International Clb; Sch Ppr (E)

COHEN, BRIAN; HILLIARD, OH; HILLIARD DARBY HS; (JR); FCA; Ftball (VJ); Skiing; Vllyball (J); Wt Lftg (VJ); Scholar Athlete Award; Engineering; Architect; Ohio State U; West Virginia

COLANT, KRISTINA; STRONGSVILLE, OH; PADUA HS; (FR); Hnr Roll; Perf Att; WWAHSS; Comm Volntr; Red Cr Aide; Key Club; Italian Clb; SP/ M/VS; Cl Off (R); Dance (Ballet, Pointe, Jazz); Italian Club; Fashion; Education

COLE, CHELSEA; AKRON, OH; NORTH HS; (FR); Hnr Roll; Perf Att; DARE; Drma Clb; Off Aide; Chr; SP/M/VS; Sftball (V); Vllyball (J); Drama Club; Registered Nurse; Forensic Scientist; Kent State U; Akron U

COLE, CHRIS; DIAMOND, OH; SOUTHEAST HS; (SR); Hnr Roll

COLE, JOHNNY; BRIDGEPORT, OH; BRIDGEPORT HS; (SO); Hi Hnr Roll; Hnr Roll; WWAHSS; P to P St Amb Prg; Quiz Bowl; Spanish Clb; Bskball (J); Ftball (V); Wt Lftg (V); Winner in Al Scheid Writing Contest; Ohio State U; Kent State U

COLEMAN, ADAM; LANCASTER, OH; BLOOM-CARROLL HS; (FR); Hnr Roll; WWAHSS; Chrch Yth Grp; Key Club; French Clb; Bskball; Key Club Class Representative

COLEMAN, BRITNEY; CINCINNATI, OH; WITHROW UNIVERSITY HS; (JR); Ctznshp Aw; Hi Hnr Roll; Hnr Roll; St of Mnth; Comm Volntr; Peer Tut/Med; DARE; Emplmnt; Clb; SP/M/VS; Bskball (J); Chrldg (J); Cr Ctry (V); Vllyball (J); Wt Lftg; Sch Ppr (E, R, P); Yrbk (E, R, P); A Honors Club; Poetry Club; Nursing; Drama; Tennessee State; Spelman U

COLEMAN, TERA N; SOUTH POINT, OH; SOUTH POINT HS; (JR); Hi Hnr Roll; Sci Fairs; Sci/Math Olympn; WWAHSS; Chrch Yth Grp; Drma Clb; Emplmnt; Mth Clb/Tm; MuAlphaTh; Pep Squd; Spanish Clb; Chrldg (V); PP Ftbl; Track (V); Cl Off (P, V); Yrbk; Honors English II Class Award; Freshman Homecoming Attendant; Pre-Law; Political Science; Ohio State U; Marshall U

COLLIER, STEVEN; DAYTON, OH; BELMONT HS; (JR); Hi Hnr Roll; Hnr Roll; Nat Hon Sy; Perf Att; Sci/Math Olympn; Comm Volntr; Peer Tut/ Med; Emplmnt; Wright Stepp Scholarship $26,00 Full Four Year Scholarship; Chemical Engineering; Computer Science; Wright State U; Miami U Ohio

COLLINS, DOMINIQUE M; DAYTON, OH; MOUND ST AC; (JR); Hi Hnr Roll; Otst Ac Ach Awd; Comm Volntr; Business Degree; Computer Tech; Wright St U; U of Dayton

COLLINS, VANESSA; TOLEDO, OH; LIBBEY HS; (JR); Hnr Roll; Perf Att; Peer Tut/Med; Drma Clb; HO'Br Yth Ldrshp; Mth Clb/Tm; Quiz Bowl; Ch Chr; SP/M/VS; Swg Chr; Sftball (V); Stu Cncl; Accounting; Banking/ Finance; Owens Community College; Bowling Green U

COMPTON, VALAINA; CONNEAUT, OH; EDGEWOOD HS; (SO); Ctznshp Aw; Chrch Yth Grp; French Clb; Bnd; Jzz Bnd; Mch Bnd; Pep Bnd; Track (V); Solo & Ensemble; Music; Abilene Christian U

CONEAL, TIMOTHY; CINCINNATI, OH; WITHROW UNIVERSITY HS; (SO); Hi Hnr Roll; Hnr Roll; Nat Hon Sy; St of Mnth; Yth Ldrshp Prog; Comm Volntr; Peer Tut/Med; ArtClub; Chess; Chrch Yth Grp; FCA; Fr of Library; Mth Clb/Tm; Mus Clb; Chr; SP/M/VS; Stg Cre; Bsball; Bskball; Cr Ctry; Sccr; Tennis; Track; Wt Lftg; Have Most Hr. with 307 Hrs; 3.0 Honor Roll; Law; Design; Syracuse; Miami U

CONLEY, KAITLYN; WESTERVILLE, OH; WESTERVILLE NORTH HS; (JR); St of Mnth; Comm Volntr; Chrch Yth Grp; Key Club; Mod UN; Off Aide; Sftball (J); PRIDE, ASTRA; Student Council

CONLEY, LEAH S; LITHOPOLIS, OH; BLOOM-CARROLL HS; (SO); Hi Hnr Roll; Hnr Roll; Pres Ac Ftns Aw; Sci Fairs; WWAHSS; Peer Tut/Med; Chrch Yth Grp; DARE; FCA; FBLA; FCCLA; Key Club; Sci Clb; Tchrs Aide; Tennis (J); CR; Yrbk (P); Interior Design; Law; Georgetown U; Princeton U

CONNORS, KAELIE; PAINESVILLE, OH; RIVERSIDE HS; (SO); Hi Hnr Roll; Hnr Roll; WWAHSS; ArtClub; Dbte Team; DECA; Drma Clb; FCA; JSA; Key Club; Mus Clb; Bnd; Mch Bnd; Orch; Pep Bnd; Cr Ctry (J); Mar Art (V); Sftball (J); Swmg (V); Track (V); Stu Cncl (R); CR (R); US Naval Sea Cadet Corps; Internship At NASA; Aerospace Engineering; Aviation; United States Naval Academy; United States Merchant Marine Academy

CONRAD, HEATHER L; CANTON, OH; GLEN OAK HS; (JR); Hnr Roll; 4-H; DARE; DECA; Jr Ach; Scouts; Chr; Second Degree Orange Belt in Martial Arts; Major in Accounting; Minor in Business Marketing; The U of Akron; Baldwin Wallace College

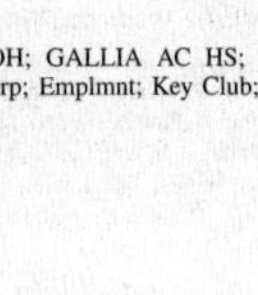
Collins, Dominique M
Mound St AC
Dayton, OH

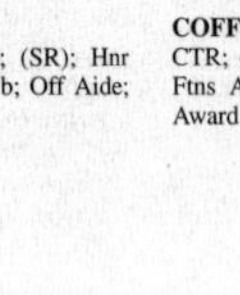
Coffman, Megan
Coshocton Cty Career Ctr
Coshocton, OH

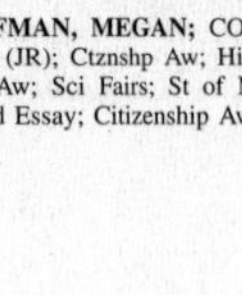
Clay, D'Mya
East HS
Columbus, OH

National
Honor Roll
Spring 2005

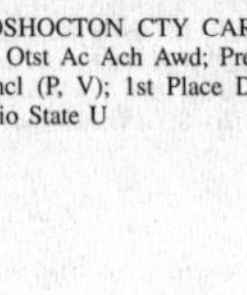
Clawson III, Joseph R
Walter E. Stebbins HS
Dayton, OH

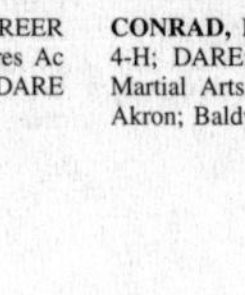
Collier, Steven
Belmont HS
Dayton, OH

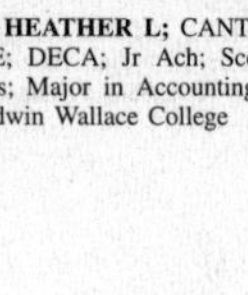
Compton, Valaina
Edgewood HS
Conneaut, OH

COOK, HALEY; CIRCLEVILLE, OH; CIRCLEVILLE HS; (JR); Hnr Roll; Pres Ac Ftns Aw; WWAHSS; Key Club; SP/M/VS; Chrldg (V L); Sccr (L); Cl Off (T); Nursing; Ohio State U

COOK, JORDAN R; PAINESVILLE, OH; RIVERSIDE HS; (SO); Hnr Roll; WWAHSS; Chrch Yth Grp; Key Club; Lib Aide; Tchrs Aide; Ch Chr; SP/M/VS; Elementary Education

COOK, MORGAN; MAGNOLIA, OH; SANDY VALLEY JR/SR HS; (JR); Hi Hnr Roll; Nat Hon Sy; Pres Sch; Sci Fairs; WWAHSS; Comm Volntr; Peer Tut/Med; AL Aux Girls; Chrch Yth Grp; Emplmnt; Lttrmn Clb; Off Aide; P to P St Amb Prg; Prom Com; Sci Clb; Ch Chr; Jzz Bnd; SP/M/VS; Bskball (V L); Golf (V L); Sftball (V L); Track; Vsy Clb (V L); Vllyball; Wt Lftg; Adv Cncl (R); Cl Off (P); Stu Cncl (R); CR (P); Sch Ppr; Yrbk (R, P); Chemistry Student of the Year; Geometry Student of the Year; Broadcasting; Business; New York U; Northwestern U

COOK, WYNTER N; LOGAN, OH; LOGAN HS; (JR); 4H Awd; Hnr Roll; Perf Att; Pres Ac Ftns Aw; St of Mnth; 4-H; Chrch Yth Grp; Emplmnt; Off Aide; Tchrs Aide; Bnd; Mch Bnd; Pep Bnd; Track (L); Public Service / Foreign Missions; Lee U; Circleville Bible College

COOLEY, LAUREN; CLYDE, OH; CLYDE HS; (FR); Hi Hnr Roll; Hnr Roll; Otst Ac Ach Awd; Perf Att; Lib Aide; Mth Clb/Tm; French Clb; Sccr (J); Cl Off (P)

COON, JULIE; LIMA, OH; LIMA SR HS; (JR); Hi Hnr Roll; Nat Hon Sy; Comm Volntr; Chrch Yth Grp; Emplmnt; Bnd; Mch Bnd; Early Childhood Teacher; Ohio State Lima; Bluffton Community College

COONEY, LINDSAY N; WARREN, OH; (JR); Hi Hnr Roll; Hnr Roll; Nat Hon Sy; Nat Stu Ath Day Aw; Otst Ac Ach Awd; St of Mnth; WWAHSS; DARE; Key Club; Tchrs Aide; Bnd; Chr; Ch Chr; Clr Grd; Track (J); Vllyball (VJCL)

COPELAND JR, SILAS V; NILES, OH; MC KINLEY HS; (FR); Ctznshp Aw; Hi Hnr Roll; Hnr Roll; MVP; Nat Hon Sy; Otst Ac Ach Awd; Perf Att; Sci Fairs; St of Mnth; Comm Volntr; Peer Tut/Med; DARE; Emplmnt; FBLA; FTA; NtlFrnscLg; Off Aide; Tchrs Aide; Stg Cre; Bskball (J); Cr Ctry (VJ); Ftball (VJ); Track (VJ); Wt Lftg (J); Cl Off (R); Stu Cncl (V); Sch Ppr (R); Accepted to Ohio Business Week; Silver Medalist for Jr Olympics 4x400 / 400M; Criminology; Criminal Justice; North Carolina U; Southern California U

COPLEY, TABITHA; CRESTON, OH; NORWAYNE HS; (SR); Hnr Roll; Nat Hon Sy; Otst Ac Ach Awd; St of Mnth; Yth Ldrshp Prog; Comm Volntr; Red Cr Aide; Chrch Yth Grp; DARE; Emplmnt; Photog; Prom Com; GAA (C); Hsbk Rdg (C); Mar Art (C); Skiing (C); Yrbk (P); Veterinary Assisting; Medical Assisting; Akron U

CORBETT, CHAS; GREENVILLE, OH; GREENVILLE HS; (FR); Hnr Roll; Nat Hon Sy; Chess; Key Club; Sci Clb; Orch; Tennis (J); CR (R); Yrbk (E); Law Degree; Harvard Law; Yale U

CORDER, STEPHANIE L; COLUMBUS, OH; WALNUT RIDGE HS; (FR); Hi Hnr Roll; Hnr Roll; Nat Hon Sy; Nat Sci Aw; Perf Att; Sci Fairs; Chrch Yth Grp; Off Aide; Bnd; Jzz Bnd; Mch Bnd; Orch; Bskball (L); Sftball (J); Swmg (V); Tennis (J); Track (L); Special Olympics Basketball (March, 2005)

CORVIN, COURTNEY E; WELLSTON, OH; WELLSTON HS; (JR); Hnr Roll; St of Mnth; WWAHSS; Comm Volntr; AL Aux Girls; Chrch Yth Grp; DARE; Drma Clb; Fr of Library; Off Aide; Bnd; Ch Chr; Mch Bnd; Pep Bnd; National Honor Student

COSBY, SETH M; SPRINGFIELD, OH; KENTON RIDGE HS; (JR); F Lan Hn Soc; Hnr Roll; Nat Hon Sy; Pres Ac Ftns Aw; USAA; WWAHSS; Comm Volntr; Peer Tut/Med; Chrch Yth Grp; DARE; FCA; Svce Clb; SADD; Tchrs Aide; Bsball (V CL); Bskball (J); Ftball (V L); Leo Club; Protective Services; Firefighter; Wright State U; Ohio State U

COSTANTINO, ELIZABETH A; WARREN, OH; CHAMPION HS; (JR); Hnr Roll; Pres Ac Ftns Aw; WWAHSS; Key Club; Off Aide; Tchrs Aide; Bnd; Dnce; Mch Bnd; Pep Bnd; Advertising; Photography; Slippery Rock U; Kent State U

COSTELLO, CHELSEY; CANTON, OH; EAST CANTON HS; (FR); Hnr Roll; Chrch Yth Grp; Mth Clb/Tm; Pep Squd; Scouts; Tchrs Aide; Chrldg (J); Sftball (J); Track (J); Science; Forensic Science; Notre Dame College; Ohio State U

COTTON, SHONTA; LIMA, OH; LIMA SR HS; (JR); Hosp Aide; Emplmnt; SADD; Stu Cncl; CR; Student Council; Worked At McDonalds At Age 15 Till 17 Still Work for Shawnee Manor

COTTRELL, JACOB W; DEERFIELD, OH; SOUTHEAST HS; (SR); Hi Hnr Roll; Nat Hon Sy; Salutrn; Comm Volntr; Chrch Yth Grp; P to P St Amb Prg; Quiz Bowl; Orch; Golf (L); National Honor Society; Computer Science; Kent State U

COTTRELL, LAURA A; LUCASVILLE, OH; VALLEY HS; (JR); Hnr Roll; Perf Att; Comm Volntr; Chrch Yth Grp; Bnd; Ch Chr; Mch Bnd; Pep Bnd; Cosmetology; Dog Grooming

COUCH, MELINDA D; NEW CARLISLE, OH; TECUMSEH HS; (FR); Hnr Roll; Chrldg (J); Stu Cncl (R); Sch Ppr; Teaching; Ohio State U

COUGHLIN, ALEX; GALLOWAY, OH; WESTLAND HS; (SO); Hnr Roll; Nat Hon Sy; Perf Att; St of Mnth; Peer Tut/Med; DARE; Bsball (J); WISE (Westland Instills Scholastic Excellence); Law; Teaching; The Ohio State U; Ohio U

COURTNEY, KYLE; PICKERINGTON, OH; PICKERINGTON HS NORTH; (SO); Hi Hnr Roll; Hnr Roll; Emplmnt; National Youth Leadership Forum on Technology; Computer Science; Business; Massachusetts Institute of Technology; DeVry U

COX, MC KENZIE; SYLVANIA, OH; ST URSULA AC; (FR); Hi Hnr Roll; Hnr Roll; Pres Ac Ftns Aw; USAA; Comm Volntr; Chrch Yth Grp; DARE; French Clb; Vllyball (C); Stu Cncl (R); Crew Team; Medical Degree in Dermatology; Heart Surgeon; The U of North Carolina At Chapel Hill; Duke U

COXON, RACHEL L; ASHTABULA, OH; EDGEWOOD HS; (SR); Hnr Roll; St of Mnth; WWAHSS; DARE; Off Aide; SADD; Tchrs Aide; Bskball (VJ L); Sccr (V L); Sftball (VJ L); SADD; Service Club; Early Childhood Education; Lakeland Community College

COYNE, HEATHER; CHAGRIN FALLS, OH; GILMOUR AC; (SO); Hi Hnr Roll; Nat Hon Sy; WWAHSS; Comm Volntr; Hosp Aide; SADD; Bskball (VJ L); Sccr (V CL); Sftball (J); Yrbk (R); Most Improved Player in Basketball; English; Northwestern U; U of Notre Dame

COYNE, MICHELLE; PARMA, OH; PADUA FRANCISCAN HS; (SO); Hi Hnr Roll; Nat Hon Sy; WWAHSS; Hab For Humty Volntr; Peer Tut/Med; Red Cr Aide; Chrch Yth Grp; Dbte Team; Drma Clb; HO'Br Yth Ldrshp; Key Club; Spanish Clb; Chr; Ch Chr; SP/M/VS; Chrldg (JC); Sftball (J); Vllyball (J); Cl Off (P); CR (P); Habitat for Humanity; Teen Institute, Peer Ministry, Retreat Leader; Psychology; Education (Secondary)

CRAIG, CHRISTINA; CINCINNATI, OH; WITHROW UNIVERSITY HS; (FR); Hnr Roll; Comm Volntr; DARE; Pediatrician; Surgeon; Clark U; Harvard

CRANK, MARISSA; CANTON, OH; CANTON SOUTH HS; (FR); Hnr Roll; Hosp Aide; Pep Squd; Foreign Clb; Dnce; Chrldg (J); Cl Off (T); Yrbk (P)

CRAWFORD, CIERA E; CLEVELAND, OH; JOHN MARSHALL HS; (SO); Ctznshp Aw; Hnr Roll; MVP; Perf Att; Sci Fairs; St Optmst of Yr; Comm Volntr; DARE; Tchrs Aide; French Clb; Dnce; PPSqd; Stu Cncl (R); French Club; OSU Young Scholars Program; Majors: Advertising and Engineering; The Ohio State U; Pennsylvania State U

CRAWFORD, MONTANA; CLYDE, OH; CLYDE HS; (FR); Hnr Roll; Dbte Team; Spanish Clb; Law; Criminal Justice

CRESTON, ABBY; SANDUSKY, OH; SANDUSKY HS; (FR); Ctznshp Aw; Hnr Roll; Perf Att; Pres Sch; ArtClub; Emplmnt; Bnd; Mch Bnd; Orch; Chrldg (J); Stu Cncl (R); CR (R); Sandusky Swan Club (Synchronized Swimming); Political Science; Ohio State; Lehigh U

CRISP, ELIZABETH H; NILES, OH; NILES MC KINLEY HS; (FR); Hi Hnr Roll; Hnr Roll; Perf Att; Pres Sch; Sci Fairs; St of Mnth; WWAHSS; Drma Clb; Key Club; Spch Team; Spanish Clb; Bnd; Dnce; Mch Bnd; SP/M/VS; Sccr (J); Education; Psychiatry

CROCK, CHRISTOPHER A; CALDWELL, OH; SHENANDOAH HS; (JR); Hi Hnr Roll; Hnr Roll; Perf Att; Pres Ac Ftns Aw; Sci/Math Olympn; Ftball (V L); Wt Lftg (V L); Wrstlg (V L); Business Management; Engineering; Ashland U

CROFTCHECK, ANDREW; GRAFTON, OH; MIDVIEW HS; (FR); Hnr Roll; Perf Att; Comm Volntr; Chess; Chrch Yth Grp; FCA; Scouts; Ftball (VJ); Wt Lftg (VJ); Journalism

CROOKS, STEPHANIE; BERKEY, OH; EVERGREEN HS; (SO); Ctznshp Aw; Comm Volntr; Peer Tut/Med; 4-H; Chrch Yth Grp; Drma Clb; Chr; SP/M/VS; Early Childhood Education; Bowling Green U; Toledo U

CROUT, LEAH J; PICKERINGTON, OH; HARVEST PREP SCH; (SR); Hi Hnr Roll; Nat Hon Sy; Pres Sch; St of Mnth; Valdctrian; Comm Volntr; Peer Tut/Med; Chrch Yth Grp; FCA; Ch Chr; SP/M/VS; Adv Cncl (R); Fellowship of Christian Athletes President; Praise and Worship Team Captain; Early Childhood Education; Political/Social Work; Ohio Dominican U; Capital U

CROWDER, AERIA; DAYTON, OH; ARCHBISHOP ALTER HS; (FR); Hnr Roll; WWAHSS; Key Club; Dnce; Flg Crps; Law; Dance; New York U; Howard U

CROZIER, OLIVIA; CARROLL, OH; BLOOM CARROLL HS; (JR); 4H Awd; Hi Hnr Roll; Hnr Roll; Nat Hon Sy; Perf Att; WWAHSS; 4-H; Chrch Yth Grp; FCA; Key Club; Prom Com; Tchrs Aide; Chr; SP/M/VS; Cr Ctry (V L); Sftball (J); Track (V L); Stu Cncl (R); Physical Therapy; Ohio State U; Mount Vernon Nazarene U

CUDAL, JEREANNE F L; FAIRBORN, OH; CARROLL HS; (SO); Hnr Roll; Sci Fairs; WWAHSS; Comm Volntr; Jr Cls League; Key Club; Mth Clb/Tm; Latin Clb; National High School Scholars Society; Cum Laude on National Latin Exam; Pre-Med; U of California San Francisco; U of California Berkeley

CULWELL, THERESA; JACKSON, OH; JACKSON HS; (JR); Hnr Roll; Perf Att; Sci Fairs; St of Mnth; ArtClub; Lib Aide; Off Aide; Prom Com; Art Rewards; Poem Rewards; Major in Photography; Physical Therapy; Shawnee U-Portsmouth; Ohio U-Athens

CUMMINS, SARA; CINCINNATI, OH; WESTERN HILLS DESIGN TECH SCH; (SO); Ctznshp Aw; Hi Hnr Roll; Hnr Roll; Nat Hon Sy; Perf Att; St of Mnth; USMC Stu Ath Aw; ArtClub; DARE; Jr Ach; Sci Clb; Scouts; Photograph; Design; U of Cincinnati; Ohio State U

CUNNINGHAM, CARMAN; KENT, OH; FIELD HS; (JR); Ctznshp Aw; Hi Hnr Roll; Hnr Roll; Nat Hon Sy; Otst Ac Ach Awd; St of Mnth; USAA; WWAHSS; Comm Volntr; Hab For Humty Volntr; Peer Tut/Med; DARE; Drma Clb; Emplmnt; Pep Squd; Photog; Vsity Clb; Chr; Bskball (J); Chrldg (C); PP Ftbl (V); Tennis (L); Vllyball (L); Stu Cncl (R); CR (R); Sch Ppr (P); Yrbk (P); Pre-Medicine; Pre-Veterinarian; Mount Union College; Hiram College

CUNNINGHAM, KEVIN J; LANCASTER, OH; BLOOM-CARROLL HS; (SR); Hi Hnr Roll; MVP; Pres Ac Ftns Aw; Emplmnt; Lttrmn Clb; Ftball (V CL); Track (V L); All-League Football; All-County Football; Otterbein College

CUNNINGHAM, RYAN; WARREN, OH; HOWLAND HS; (JR); Peer Tut/Med; German Clb; Bnd; Ch Chr; Jzz Bnd; Mch Bnd; Bowling League; Music Education; Social Sciences Education; Kent State U; Youngstown State U

CURRIE, BRIANNA; ELYRIA, OH; ELYRIA HS; (JR); Hi Hnr Roll; Hnr Roll; Nat Hon Sy; Otst Ac Ach Awd; Pres Sch; WWAHSS; Comm Volntr; Chrch Yth Grp; Emplmnt; Key Club; Chr; Ch Chr; Drl Tm; Orch; Scr Kpr (J); Doctor's Degree in Medicine

CURRY, VERONICA; LIMA, OH; LIMA SR HS; (FR); Ctznshp Aw; Hnr Roll; Comm Volntr; Chrch Yth Grp; DARE; Off Aide; SADD; Tchrs Aide; Ch Chr; SP/M/VS; Nursing; Ohio State U; Texas State U

CUSTER, CHRISTINE; LINDSEY, OH; WOODMORE HS; (FR); Hi Hnr Roll; Hnr Roll; Perf Att; Pres Ac Ftns Aw; St of Mnth; 4-H; Chrch Yth Grp; DARE; Key Club; Scouts; Spanish Clb; Chr; Sch Ppr (R); Elementary Education; Secondary Education; Bowling Green State U; Cedarville U

CUTLER, YVETTE J; CLEVELAND, OH; WARRENSVILLE HS; (SO); Perf Att; St of Mnth; CARE; Hab For Humty Volntr; Hosp Aide; DARE; Dnce; Drl Tm; Lit Mag (E); Sch Ppr (E); Yrbk (E); Strive For 5 At 75 Award; Fast Toward Award; Law School; Music/Dancing/Singing; Clark Atlanta; Miami State

CUTRIGHT JR, STEPHEN; RAVENNA, OH; SOUTHEAST HS; (SR); Hi Hnr Roll; Hnr Roll; Perf Att; Pres Ac Ftns Aw; ArtClub; Cmptr Clb; DARE; Wdwrkg Clb; Sccr (C); Building Computers, Programming, High Power Car Audio; Computer Science; Electrical Engineering; Stark

CUTSHAW, KRISTIN L; EATON, OH; EATON HS; (SO); Perf Att; WWAHSS; Chrch Yth Grp; Drma Clb; Chr; Ch Chr; SP/M/VS; X-Ray Technician; East Tennessee State U-Johnson City; Tusculum College-Greenville, TN

CYRUS, AMBER D R; WAVERLY, OH; WAVERLY HS; (JR); Nat Hon Sy; Comm Volntr; Vsity Clb; French Clb; Golf (V); Cl Off (R); Yrbk (P); I'm Number Two on the Boys Golf Team.; I Won Girls Sectionals, Taking 1st Place.; Nursing; Pre-Med; Ohio State U; Shawnee State

CZACHERSKI, NICOLE; PARKMAN, OH; CARDINAL HS; (FR); Ctznshp Aw; Hnr Roll; St of Mnth; WWAHSS; Comm Volntr; Chrch Yth Grp; Scouts; Spanish Clb; Bnd; Clr Grd; Jzz Bnd; Pep Bnd; Vllyball (J); Cl Off (T); Freshman Spanish Excellence Award; Education; Spanish; Boston U; Ohio State U

DAHLHOFER, HALLIE; OAK HARBOR, OH; OAK HARBOR HS; (SO); Hnr Roll; Pres Ac Ftns Aw; Sci Fairs; Key Club; Sci Clb; Cr Ctry (J); Swmg (V L); Track (J); Key Club Bulletin Editor; Thespians; Nursing/Doctor; Fine Arts; Ohio State U; Michigan State U

DAILEY, CHANEL; COLUMBUS, OH; BROOKHAVEN HS; (FR); Hnr Roll; Perf Att; DARE; Acpl Chr; Chr; Chrldg (C); Nursing; Doctor; Columbus State U

DAILEY, JAMIE A; LORAIN, OH; LORAIN SOUTHVIEW HS; (SO); Hnr Roll; WWAHSS; Comm Volntr; Spec Olymp Vol; Drma Clb; Photog; French Clb; SP/M/VS; Stg Cre; Chrldg (V CL); Tennis (J); Vllyball (J); Fashion Design; Business Management; Kent State

DAINES, KEVIN; PATRIOT, OH; RIVER VALLEY HS; (JR); Hnr Roll; Nat Hon Sy; WWAHSS; 4-H; ArtClub; Chrch Yth Grp; Key Club; Ntl Beta Clb; Youth Minister; Missionary; Kentucky Christian U; Johnson Bible College

Cyrus, Amber D R
Waverly HS
Waverly, OH

Crawford, Ciera E
John Marshall HS
Cleveland, OH

Cotton, Shonta
Lima SR HS
Lima, OH

Corbett, Chas
Greenville HS
Greenville, OH

National
Honor Roll
Spring 2005

Cook, Wynter N
Logan HS
Logan, OH

Crank, Marissa
Canton South HS
Canton, OH

Cutright Jr, Stephen
Southeast HS
Ravenna, OH

Dailey, Jamie A
Lorain Southview HS
Lorain, OH

DALE, SHALAY; CLEVELAND, OH; HEALTH CAREERS CTR; (SO); Ctznshp Aw; Hi Hnr Roll; Hnr Roll; Otst Ac Ach Awd; Sci Fairs; Comm Volntr; Peer Tut/Med; Chrch Yth Grp; Drma Clb; Ch Chr; Dnce; Pediatrician; Writer; Case Western Reserve U; Cleveland State U

DALTON, TERI; CLEVELAND, OH; GARFIELD HEIGHTS HS; (SO); Perf Att; WWAHSS; Chr

D'AMORE, PAUL; BROOK PARK, OH; BEREA HS; (JR); Hnr Roll; Perf Att; Comm Volntr; Emplmnt; Bnd; Mch Bnd; Golf (J); Track (V L); Community Service Letter; Teaching; Math; Ohio State U; Ohio U

DAMRON, CHELSEA S; SOUTH POINT, OH; SOUTH POINT HS; (SO); Hnr Roll; Spec Olymp Vol; ArtClub; Chrch Yth Grp; Drma Clb; Off Aide; Pep Squd; Prom Com; Tchrs Aide; Bskball (V L); Chrldg (J); Cr Ctry (V L); GAA (V); PP Ftbl (J); Track (V L); Physical Therapy; Ohio U

DAMRON, JENNA M; CANAL WINCHESTER, OH; HAMILTON TOWNSHIP HS; (SR); Hnr Roll; Nat Hon Sy; WWAHSS; Comm Volntr; Peer Tut/Med; Red Cr Aide; Chrch Yth Grp; DECA; Emplmnt; FCA; Off Aide; Pep Squd; Tchrs Aide; Bnd; Ch Chr; Mch Bnd; Pep Bnd; Chrldg (VJCL); PP Ftbl; The Zonta Club of Columbus Nominee; Obetz Zucchini Court, and Phi Delta Kappa; Early Childhood Development; Middle Childhood Development; Otterbein College (Accepted)

DANCY, KATIE; CANTON, OH; PERRY HS; (JR); Hnr Roll; Nat Hon Sy; Otst Ac Ach Awd; Comm Volntr; Spec Olymp Vol; Chrch Yth Grp; FTA; Key Club; SADD; Yrbk (E, R, P); Bowling Team (Varsity); Secondary Education; History; Walsh College; Malone College

DANIELS, BRIAN; WARREN, OH; CHAMPION HS; (SO); Hi Hnr Roll; Sci/Math Olympn; St of Mnth; WWAHSS; Comm Volntr; Chrch Yth Grp; Key Club; Mth Clb/Tm; Golf (J); Track (V); Church Youth Council; Electrical Engineer; Computers; Ohio State U; Youngstown State U

DANIELS, CATHARINE A; LONDON, OH; LONDON HS; (SR); 4H Awd; Ctznshp Aw; Hi Hnr Roll; Hnr Roll; Kwnis Aw; MVP; Nat Hon Sy; Otst Ac Ach Awd; Perf Att; Pres Ac Ftns Aw; Comm Volntr; Peer Tut/Med; 4-H; Chrch Yth Grp; DARE; Drma Clb; Fr of Library; Jr Ach; Off Aide; Prom Com; Bskball (V L); Chrldg (V); PP Ftbl; Sccr (V L); Sftball (V CL); Tennis (V); Track (V L); Adv Cncl; Cl Off (P); Stu Cncl; Sportsman & Integrity Award - 5 Times; School Psychology; Miami U Ohio

DANIELS, DANIELLE A; CLEVELAND, OH; JAMES FORD RHODES HS; (SO); Ctznshp Aw; Hi Hnr Roll; Hnr Roll; Otst Ac Ach Awd; CR (P); Early Childhood Education (Prek-3); Culinary Arts; The Art Institute of Pittsburg; Ursuline College

DANIELS, MARY; CARROLL, OH; BLOOM-CARROLL; (SR); Hnr Roll; Otst Ac Ach Awd; WWAHSS; Red Cr Aide; Photog; Sci Clb; Spanish Clb

DANIELS, MIKE; LORAIN, OH; LORAIN ADMIRAL KING HS; (FR); Ctznshp Aw; Fut Prb Slvr; Hi Hnr Roll; Hnr Roll; Otst Ac Ach Awd; Perf Att; Bnd; Ftball; Wrstlg (J); Member of National Junior Honor Society; 1st Place - Lake Erie JV Tournament 7th / 8th - Upward Bound Program; Sports Medicine / Athletic Trainer; Morehouse College; Miami U

DANNEMILLER, ABIGAIL M; PICKERINGTON, OH; LIBERTY UNION HS; (JR); 4H Awd; Hi Hnr Roll; Hnr Roll; Nat Hon Sy; Nat Stu Ath Day Aw; Otst Ac Ach Awd; Perf Att; WWAHSS; Comm Volntr; Red Cr Aide; 4-H; Chrch Yth Grp; FCA; Key Club; Svce Clb; Foreign Clb; Chr; Golf (V L); Track (V L); State 4-H Ambassador, Reserve Ch. Rabbit-OSF; Clock Trophy-Ohio State Fair-Junior Demonstration; Registered Nurse; Ohio State U; Ohio U

DARAH, MICHAEL; SYLVANIA, OH; NORTHVIEW HS; (JR); Hnr Roll; MVP; Perf Att; Pres Ac Ftns Aw; Yth Ldrshp Prog; Comm Volntr; DARE; Emplmnt; HO'Br Yth Ldrshp; Off Aide; Sccr (J); Track (J); Physical Therapy; Physician's Assistant

DARRAH, TIMOTHY S; HANOVERTON, OH; SOUTHERN LOCAL HS; (JR); Ctznshp Aw; Duke TS; Fut Prb Slvr; Kwnis Aw; Otst Ac Ach Awd; Sci/Math Olympn; ArtClub; Chess; Chrch Yth Grp; Dbte Team; Mth Clb/Tm; Off Aide; P to P St Amb Prg; Quiz Bowl; Bsball (J); Wt Lftg (V); 2 Yr. Varsity Debater; Mathematics; Astrophysics; Duke U; Michigan State U

DARROW, BLAKE A; STREETSBORO, OH; STREETSBORO HS; (JR); Hi Hnr Roll; Hnr Roll; MVP; Otst Ac Ach Awd; Pres Ac Ftns Aw; WWAHSS; Comm Volntr; Chess; DARE; Emplmnt; Jr Ach; Ftball (V L); Skiing; Track (V L); Wt Lftg (V); Mid West Talent Search, NU Participant; Identified As "Talented & Gifted" Program, MI; Mechanical Engineer; Kent State U; Oberlin College

DARST, KRIS A; ALBANY, OH; ALEXANDER HS; (SO); Hnr Roll; Comm Volntr; Spec Olymp Vol; Chrch Yth Grp; Emplmnt; Off Aide; Tchrs Aide; Bnd; Mch Bnd; Pep Bnd; Nursing; Hocking Technical College

DAUGHERTY, JACOB M; CINCINNATI, OH; COLERAIN HS; (JR); Hnr Roll; Otst Ac Ach Awd; WWAHSS; Bsball (V); Physics; Sports Management; Coastal Carolina; Ohio State

DAUGHERTY, KRISTA; MIDDLEFIELD, OH; CARDINAL HS; (SO); Hnr Roll; Perf Att; St of Mnth; DARE; Emplmnt; Mth Clb/Tm; French Clb; Chr; Stg Cre; Teen Institute; Poetry; Photography; Hiram College

DAVE, BRINDA; GALLOWAY, OH; HILLIARD DARBY HS; (SO); Hnr Roll; Otst Ac Ach Awd; St of Mnth; Yth Ldrshp Prog; Comm Volntr; Hab For Humty Volntr; Peer Tut/Med; Chrch Yth Grp; Fr of Library; Key Club; Lttrmn Clb; Off Aide; Pep Squd; P to P St Amb Prg; Spch Team; Bnd; Dnce; Mch Bnd; Pep Bnd; Renaissance Club and Church: Divine Brain Trust Group; Citywide Youth Council and Youth to Youth (National); Medicine; Engineering

DAVENPORT, JACQUELINE M; AVON, OH; AVON HS; (SR); Hi Hnr Roll; Nat Hon Sy; WWAHSS; Comm Volntr; Hab For Humty Volntr; Peer Tut/Med; Key Club; Off Aide; Vsity Clb; Bskball (VJCL); Cr Ctry (V L); Track (V L); Vsy Clb (V); Ohio State U Columbus; Ashland U

DAVIS, BRANDON; WARREN, OH; WARREN G HARDING HS; (SO); Hnr Roll; St of Mnth; WWAHSS; Chrch Yth Grp; DARE; FCA; Ftball (V); Track (L); Wt Lftg (V); Sports Medicine; Business; Ohio State U, Bowling Green; Penn State U

DAVIS, JOCHELLE R; TOLEDO, OH; SCOTT HS; (SO); Hnr Roll; St of Mnth; Chr; Adv Cncl (R); Social Studies Award - 2005; Nursing; Child Care; U of Cincinnati; Wright State U

DAVIS, KAITLIN; SOUTHINGTON, OH; SOUTHINGTON LOCAL SCH; (FR); Ctznshp Aw; Hi Hnr Roll; Hnr Roll; MVP; St of Mnth; Yth Ldrshp Prog; Chrch Yth Grp; Pep Squd; Schol Bwl; Ch Chr; Pep Bnd; Bskball; Chrldg (J); Sftball (J); Track (VJ); Cl Off (T); Church Worship Band; Church Discipleship Program; PhD in Psychology; Mathematics; Ohio State U; Youngstown State U

DAVIS, KASHEENA; CLEVELAND, OH; MAYFIELD HS; (JR); Perf Att; St of Mnth; Comm Volntr; Peer Tut/Med; Emplmnt; Scouts; SADD; Chr; Drl Tm; Bskball (J); Early Childhood Education; Music Producer; Clark Atlanta U; Miami U

DAVIS, KIA; SPRINGFIELD, OH; SPRINGFIELD NORTH HS; (JR); Ctznshp Aw; Hnr Roll; Otst Ac Ach Awd; Perf Att; Pres Sch; Sci Fairs; WWAHSS; Comm Volntr; Emplmnt; Key Club; Prom Com; Svce Clb; Tchrs Aide; Spanish Clb; PP Ftbl (V); Stu Cncl (R); CR (R); Yrbk; Dentist; Flagler U; U of Miami

DAVIS, KRISTEN; DAYTON, OH; ARCHBISHOP ALTER HS; (JR); Hnr Roll; WWAHSS; Key Club; French Clb; Student Ambassador; Peer Ministry; Pharmacy; Purdue U; Ohio Northern U

DAVIS, LUCAS M; ELMORE, OH; WOODMORE HS; (FR); Ctznshp Aw; Hnr Roll; Jr Ach; Key Club; Bsball (J); Ftball (J); Wt Lftg (J); School Teacher and Coach; Bowling Green State U, Defiance Colleges; Heidelberg

DAVIS, MAEDRIANN; CINCINNATI, OH; AIKEN UNIVERSITY HS; (JR); Perf Att; Chrch Yth Grp; Bnd; Ch Chr; Mch Bnd; Cincinnati State; UC

DAVIS, REBECCA M; LANCASTER, OH; EASTLAND CAREER CTR; (SR); Ctznshp Aw; Hnr Roll; P to P St Amb Prg; Prom Com; Cl Off (T); Stu Cncl; CR (R); Dental Hygienist; Nursing; Columbus State; Hocking

DAVIS, VIRGINIA N; MT PERRY, OH; MAYSVILLE 6-12 HS; (FR); 4H Awd; Hi Hnr Roll; Otst Ac Ach Awd; Perf Att; WWAHSS; Comm Volntr; 4-H; Chrch Yth Grp; Drma Clb; Key Club; P to P St Amb Prg; Quiz Bowl; Spanish Clb; Chr; SP/M/VS; Vllyball (J); Stu Cncl (R); Mission Trip to Mexico August 2004; Bible Club and Leo Club; Acting / Musical Theatre; Criminal Law; Ohio State U

DAVIS, WHITNIE P; XENIA, OH; XENIA HS; (SO); Hi Hnr Roll; Hnr Roll; Kwnis Aw; Nat Hon Sy; WWAHSS; Comm Volntr; Emplmnt; Key Club; Tchrs Aide; Sftball (VJCL); Pediatrician; Child Psychologist; Wittenburg U; Wright State U

DAWSON, ANDREA; DAYTON, OH; MEADOWDALE HS; (FR); Hi Hnr Roll; Hnr Roll; St of Mnth; WWAHSS; Chrch Yth Grp; Pep Squd; Ch Chr; Dnce; Chrldg (C); Track (L); Stu Cncl (P); Singer/Music; Cosmetologist/Or English; A U in Florida; Harvard U

DAWSON, CAITLIN; MONROE, OH; LAKOTA EAST HS; (SO); Hi Hnr Roll; Hnr Roll; Pres Sch; St of Mnth; WWAHSS; Chrch Yth Grp; Jr Cls League; Bnd; Mch Bnd; Pep Bnd; Biomedical Engineering; Doctorate Degree; Yale U; Case Western Reserve U

DAWSON JR, ALVIN L; TOLEDO, OH; ROGERS HS; (FR); Ctznshp Aw; Fut Prb Slvr; Hi Hnr Roll; Perf Att; St of Mnth; Chess; Chrch Yth Grp; DARE; Jr Ach; Mus Clb; Tchrs Aide; Bnd; Drl Tm; Mch Bnd; Orch; Stu Cncl (R); Won $300 Music Scholarship Last Year from TYO Remembrance Fund; 1 Rating in the Solo / Ensemble Contest; Degree in Marine Biology or Music Education; Musician; Florida A & M U; Central State U

DEAKINS, DANIEL J; NORTON, OH; NORTON HS; (SO); MVP; Nat Mrt Sch Recip; St of Mnth; Comm Volntr; Chrch Yth Grp; DARE; Drma Clb; FCA; Off Aide; Tchrs Aide; SP/M/VS; Bsball (C); Bskball (J); Ice Hky (CL); Scr Kpr (VJ); Track (V L); Stu Cncl (R); Youth Basketball Coach; Actor / Film Maker; Police Officer; UCLA; Ohio State U

DEAN, AUSTIN S; WOODVILLE, OH; WOODMORE HS; (SO); Acpl Chr; Chr; Ch Chr; SP/M/VS; Bskball (VJ); Golf (VJ); Track (V); Cl Off (P); HOBY Leadership Recipient; Key Club President; Political Science

DE GIRALAMO, GREGORY J; CLEVELAND, OH; PADUA FRANCISCAN HS; (JR); Hnr Roll; WWAHSS; Dbte Team; HO'Br Yth Ldrshp; Key Club; Quiz Bowl; Latin Clb; Stu Cncl; CR; NASA Intern Semi-Finalist; Nearly 100 Service Hours-Key Club-'04 '05; Physics; Aerospace; Case Western Reserve, Baldwin-Wallace College; John Carroll U

DEHNER, STEPHEN; DAYTON, OH; (SR); Emplmnt; Key Club; Scouts; Latin Clb; Sccr (JC); Swmg (L); Track (L); Eagle Scout; Business (Majoring History): Maybe Law; The Citadel Military College

DELANEY, VYASIA C; MACEDONIA, OH; JOHN F KENNEDY HS; (FR); Chrch Yth Grp; Ch Chr; Certificate for Young Authors Program; Attorney, Law; Cleveland State U; Akron U

DELONG, SAMANTHA M; MT STERLING, OH; MADISON PLAINS HS; (SR); Hi Hnr Roll; Hnr Roll; Otst Ac Ach Awd; WWAHSS; Comm Volntr; Peer Tut/Med; ArtClub; DARE; Emplmnt; Photog; Prom Com; Tchrs Aide; French Clb; Chrldg (J); Stu Cncl (S); CR (R); 4 Crowns & Titles in Local Beauty Pageants; Teen Reporter for WBNS 10 TV Local News; Broadcasting; Teacher; Manatee Community College Florida; Florida Gulf Coast U

DE MANGE, JESSICA; YORKSHIRE, OH; VERSAILLES HS; (SR); Comm Volntr; Chrch Yth Grp; Emplmnt; FTA; Lttrmn Clb; SADD; Chr; Early Childhood Education; Bachelor Degree; Wright State U-Lake Campus

DE MARCO, ASHLEY; GENEVA, OH; GENEVA SECONDARY SCH; (FR); Hnr Roll; Perf Att; Sci Fairs; St of Mnth; Comm Volntr; DARE; Lib Aide; Mus Clb; Bnd; Drl Tm; Chrldg; Track; Musician of the Year; Ohio Reads (Mentoring); Meteorology; Music; Miami U; Ohio State U

DEMARCO III, MICHAEL A; YOUNGSTOWN, OH; CARDINAL MOONEY HS; (JR); Hi Hnr Roll; Hnr Roll; Nat Hon Sy; Comm Volntr; Peer Tut/Med; Biology Clb; DARE; Emplmnt; Ntl Beta Clb; Sci Clb; Svce Clb; SADD; Spanish Clb; Golf; Congressional Student Leadership Conference; Pre-Med; Biology; The U of Notre Dame; U of Southern California

DE MARTINI, NICCOLE M; WARREN, OH; CHAMPION HS; (SO); Hi Hnr Roll; Hnr Roll; WWAHSS; Emplmnt; Key Club; Lib Aide; Tchrs Aide; Dnce; Chrldg (J); Sftball (J); Snowboarding; Law; Business; New York U; Yale U

DEMBKOWSKI, ROBIN M; CLEVELAND, OH; PADUA FRANCISCAN HS; (SR); Hi Hnr Roll; Hnr Roll; Nat Hon Sy; WWAHSS; Yth Ldrshp Prog; Peer Tut/Med; Chrch Yth Grp; Dbte Team; Emplmnt; HO'Br Yth Ldrshp; Key Club; Mus Clb; Scouts; Spanish Clb; Acpl Chr; Chr; Ch Chr; Orch; Skiing; Yrbk; Concert Mistress; Physical Therapy; Ohio U

DEMLER, JENNIFER; YOUNGSTOWN, OH; AUSTINTOWN FITCH HS; (FR); Hnr Roll; St of Mnth; Dnce; Gmnstcs (L); Jubelle; Veterinarian; Ohio State

DENDINGER, SONYA; MT GILEAD, OH; MT GILEAD HS; (SO); 4H Awd; Hnr Roll; Perf Att; St of Mnth; Comm Volntr; 4-H; DARE; Off Aide; Tchrs Aide; Art Awards; Professional Degree / Child Education; Ohio State U

DENMEADE, ALEESHA; CANTON, OH; HOOVER HS; (SR); Hnr Roll; Nat Hon Sy; Peer Tut/Med; Chess; Chrch Yth Grp; Tchrs Aide; Clb; Sccr (V C); Track (V); Forensic Chemistry; American Sign Language; Malone College

DENNIS, JALESSA; CINCINNATI, OH; WITHROW UNIVERSITY HS; (FR); Ctznshp Aw; Hnr Roll; Perf Att; Sci Fairs; Comm Volntr; Peer Tut/Med; DARE; Medical; Law Studies; Clark Atlanta U; Georgetown U

DENNISON, AMANDA B; PERRY, OH; PERRY HS; (SO); Hnr Roll; Otst Ac Ach Awd; WWAHSS; Drma Clb; Key Club; SP/M/VS; Stg Cre; Editor's Choice Award in Poetry; Poet of the Year (2003); Biomedical Engineering; Orthopedic Surgery; Columbia U; Duke U

DERMER, JONATHAN; BEACHWOOD, OH; BEACHWOOD HS; (SR); Hi Hnr Roll; Hnr Roll; Nat Hon Sy; Comm Volntr; Jr Ach; Mod UN; Tmpl Yth Grp; Vsity Clb; Bnd; Sccr (V L); Tennis (V L); Wrstlg (V L); Top 20% of Graduating Class; Member-Saltzman Youth Panel; Financial Planner / Finance; Wealth Management Services; Boston U

DERY, DANIEL J; TOLEDO, OH; ST FRANCIS DE SALES HS; (SR); F Lan Hn Soc; Hi Hnr Roll; Nat Mrt LOC; Perf Att; Salutrn; WWAHSS; Yth Ldrshp Prog; Comm Volntr; Peer Tut/Med; Emplmnt; Mth Clb/Tm; Mus Clb; NYLC; Quiz Bowl; Orch; SP/M/VS; Cr Ctry (V); Sccr (J); Lit Mag (R); Mu Phi Epsilon Music Scholarship; AP Scholar; Music; Education; Xavier U

DESKIN, TODD E; GREENVILLE, OH; GREENVILLE SR HS; (JR); Hi Hnr Roll; Hnr Roll; Otst Ac Ach Awd; Perf Att; Pres Sch; St of Mnth; WWAHSS; Peer Tut/Med; AL Aux Boys; Chess; Key Club; Mth Clb/Tm; Quiz Bowl; Sci Clb; SADD; Spanish Clb; Ftball (V); Track (V); Wrstlg (V); Engineering and Technology; Science/Mathematics; Massachusetts Institute of Technology; U of Miami

Dendinger, Sonya
Mt Gilead HS
Mt Gilead, OH

Davis, Maedriann
Aiken University HS
Cincinnati, OH

Davis, Kaitlin
Southington Local Sch
Southington, OH

Dalton, Teri
Garfield Heights HS
Cleveland, OH

Davis, Brandon
Warren G Harding HS
Warren, OH

De Marco, Ashley
Geneva Secondary Sch
Geneva, OH

Deskin, Todd E
Greenville SR HS
Greenville, OH

DESLANDES, JINNA; PICKERINGTON, OH; PICKERINGTON HS NORTH; (SO); Hi Hnr Roll; Nat Hon Sy; Perf Att; St of Mnth; Hosp Aide; DARE; Emplmnt; Photog; Chr; Track (V); Scoring High on the PLAN Test; Obstetrician / Gynecologist; Criminology; Ohio State U; Clark Atlanta U

DESMOND, SHANNON; SYLVANIA, OH; NOTRE DAME AC; (FR); Hi Hnr Roll; WWAHSS; Comm Volntr; Dnce; Orch; Golf (V); CR (R)

DE VAUGHN II, KEITH; DAYTON, OH; MEADOWDALE HS; (JR); Hnr Roll; Perf Att; Sci/Math Olympn; WWAHSS; Yth Ldrshp Prog; Comm Volntr; Chrch Yth Grp; Emplmnt; Math Olympics Winner Twice; Northern Hills Youth Connection NHYC Community Officer; Video Game Designer; U of Advanced Technology

DE VAULT, MELISSA; COLUMBUS, OH; WALNUT RIDGE HS; (FR); Hnr Roll; Nat Hon Sy; Perf Att; Comm Volntr; Jr Ach; Clr Grd; Orch; Sftball (J); Veterinarian; Crime Scene Investigator; Ohio State U; Art Institute of Pittsburg

DEVORE, NATHAN; WILLOUGHBY, OH; WILLOUGHBY SOUTH HS; (SO); Hi Hnr Roll; Hnr Roll; St of Mnth; WWAHSS; Chrch Yth Grp; Drma Clb; Emplmnt; Key Club; SP/M/VS; Stg Cre; Ftball (J); Cl Off (P); Rebel of the Semester; Computer Science; Premed; Case Western Reserve U

DEXTER, DANIEL R; CANTON, OH; HOOVER HS; Hnr Roll; WWAHSS; Emplmnt; Varsity Bowling; Fine Arts; Drafting and Industrial Design; Stark State College of Technology

DIEHL, KATIE; ELMORE, OH; WOODMORE; (FR); 4H Awd; Hi Hnr Roll; Hnr Roll; Perf Att; 4-H; Chrch Yth Grp; DARE; Key Club; Scouts; Spanish Clb; Chr; Sccr

DIERSING, AMANDA; CINCINNATI, OH; NORTHWEST HS; (SR); Hi Hnr Roll; Nat Mrt Fin; Otst Ac Ach Awd; WWAHSS; Comm Volntr; Peer Tut/Med; Emplmnt; Key Club; Off Aide; Pep Squd; Svce Clb; Dnce; Pep Bnd; SP/M/VS; Chrldg (V); PPSqd (V); Sftball (J); Cl Off (R); Stu Cncl (R); CR (R); Yrbk (R, P); Uknighted Knights (Athletic Club); U of Cincinnati

DILLON, ANNA K; PHILO, OH; PHILO HS; (SR); Hnr Roll; WWAHSS; Comm Volntr; Hosp Aide; Chrch Yth Grp; Scouts; Chr; Sch Ppr (R); Participated in Girl Scout Government As Alternate Delegate, Delegate and Troop Secretary; Business Management; Literature; Zane State College; Ohio U of Zanesville

DILTZ, CASSIE; CIRCLEVILLE, OH; CIRCLEVILLE HS; (FR); Hi Hnr Roll; Kwnis Aw; Otst Ac Ach Awd; Perf Att; Pres Ac Ftns Aw; St of Mnth; Comm Volntr; Red Cr Aide; Key Club; Chr; SP/M/VS; Sccr (J); Yrbk (R, P); Symphonic Chair

DI MATTEO, STEPHEN M; PAINESVILLE, OH; RIVERSIDE HS; (JR); Hi Hnr Roll; Perf Att; WWAHSS; Emplmnt; Key Club; German Clb; Ice Hky (C); Sch Ppr (R); Yrbk (R); Sports Management; Journalism; Bowling Green State; Ohio State

DINH, JOSIE T; HAMILTON, OH; STEPHEN T BADIN HS; (JR); Hi Hnr Roll; Jr Eng Tech; WWAHSS; Comm Volntr; Hosp Aide; ArtClub; Chrch Yth Grp; Key Club; SADD; Bdmtn (J); Cr Ctry (J); Mar Art (V); Tennis (J); Vllyball (J); AAYAT Intern; Big Brother Big Sister Mentor; Medical; Miami U (Oxford); Case Western Reserve U

DINIGER, DAVID A; NEW WASHINGTON, OH; SENECA EAST HS; (FR); 4H Awd; Hnr Roll; Perf Att; Comm Volntr; 4-H; Chess; Chrch Yth Grp; DARE; Ntl FFA; Ohio State U

DISHMAN, LEAH; PERRYSBURG, OH; PERRYSBURG HS; (JR); Hi Hnr Roll; Hnr Roll; MVP; Otst Ac Ach Awd; Perf Att; Pres Ac Ftns Aw; Pres Sch; Comm Volntr; Chrch Yth Grp; Drma Clb; Bnd; Ch Chr; Mch Bnd; Orch; Bskball (VJCL); Vllyball (C); Stu Cncl (R)

DISMUKE, ROMEL; ASHTABULA, OH; WEST JHS; (MS); MVP; Otst Ac Ach Awd; Perf Att; Sci Fairs; Chrch Yth Grp; Fr of Library; Mus Clb; SADD; SP/M/VS; Bsball; Bskball; Ftball; Track; Sports Medicine; Professional Athlete; U of North Carolina; Wake Forest U

DOBBS, LAUREN; AVON LAKE, OH; AVON LAKE HS; (SO); Hi Hnr Roll; WWAHSS; Spec Olymp Vol; Drma Clb; Key Club; Mod UN; Spanish Clb; Chr; SP/M/VS; President of Drama Club; Received Excellence Award for Model UN; Major in International Relations & Political Science; Georgetown U; New York U

DODDI, MITHRA; DUBLIN, OH; DUBLIN SCIOTO HS; (FR); Hi Hnr Roll; Hnr Roll; Otst Ac Ach Awd; Pres Sch; Sci/Math Olympn; St of Mnth; Comm Volntr; ArtClub; DARE; Mth Clb/Tm; P to P St Amb Prg; Japanese Clb; Orch; Track (J); Academic Distinction Award

DOLAN, RYAN C; NEWARK, OH; NEWARK CATHOLIC HS; (JR); Ctznshp Aw; Hnr Roll; MVP; Perf Att; Sci Fairs; Fr of Library; Lib Aide; Chr; Ftball (V); Wrstlg (V); Library Assistant; Mechanical Engineering; Electrical Engineering; U.S. Naval Academy; Ohio State U

DONNELLY, BRIDGETTE; CINCINNATI, OH; SUMMIT CTRY DAY SCH; (SR); Hnr Roll; WWAHSS; Yth Ldrshp Prog; Comm Volntr; Pep Squd; SADD; Spanish Clb; Bskball (V L); Fld Hky (V L); Sftball (V L); CR (R); Mock Trial Team; Outstanding Attorney Award; Attorney; Northern Kentucky U

DONNENWIRTH, ERIC J; WESTERVILLE, OH; WESTERVILLE NORTH HS; (JR); Hi Hnr Roll; MVP; Comm Volntr; Chess; Emplmnt; Pep Squd; Scouts; Bnd; Jzz Bnd; Mch Bnd; Pep Bnd

DORE, DOMINIC A; COLLINS, OH; WESTERN RESERVE HS; (FR); Hnr Roll; Otst Ac Ach Awd; St of Mnth; Yth Ldrshp Prog; French Clb; Bnd; Jzz Bnd; Track (J); Stu Cncl (R); Presidential Academic Achievement; Law - Lawyer / Judge; Harvard Law School; Oberlin College

DORRICOTT, ALEXA; COLUMBIA STATION, OH; COLUMBIA HS; (FR); Ctznshp Aw; Hi Hnr Roll; MVP; Pres Ac Ftns Aw; Pres Sch; Sci Fairs; Comm Volntr; Quiz Bowl; Chr; Dnce; Bskball; Skiing; Track (V L); Vllyball (V L); Cl Off (P); Stu Cncl (P); CR (R); State Science Fair; 6 New School Records for Track; Career in Medicine / Possibly Physical Therapy; Major in Sports Medicine / Spanish

DOUGHTY, RACHEL; NEWARK, OH; NEWARK HS; (SR); Hnr Roll; Nat Hon Sy; Nat Stu Ath Day Aw; St of Mnth; WWAHSS; Yth Ldrshp Prog; Chrch Yth Grp; Emplmnt; FCA; French Clb; Bskball (J); Sftball (V L); Vllyball (V CL); Stu Cncl (R); CR (R); Sch Ppr (R); Leo Club (Volunteer Group); Journalism; Ohio U

DOUGHTY JR, BRIAN; DAYTON, OH; PATTERSON CAREER TECH CTR; (SR); Hi Hnr Roll; Hnr Roll; WWAHSS; DECA; Photog; Tchrs Aide; Bskball (V); Cr Ctry (V); Swmg (V); Stu Cncl (R); Machine Troops; Pharmacist; Business and Management; U of Cincinnati; U of Maryland Eastern Shore

DOUGLAS, ANDREA G; CLEVELAND, OH; EUCLID HS; (SO); Ctznshp Aw; Hi Hnr Roll; Hnr Roll; Otst Ac Ach Awd; Perf Att; WWAHSS; Mth Clb/Tm; Mus Clb; Bnd; Mch Bnd; Pep Bnd; Chrldg (V); Tennis (V); Business Administration; Medical Technology

DOWNARD, WHITNEY G; MC ARTHUR, OH; VINTON CTY HS; (SR); Hnr Roll; Perf Att; WWAHSS; Comm Volntr; Red Cr Aide; DECA; Emplmnt; Prom Com; Spanish Clb; Obstetrician; Ohio U; Ohio U of Athens

DOWNEY, APRIL L; COLUMBUS, OH; EASTMOOR MS; (MS); DARE; Drma Clb; Clb; Chr; SP/M/VS; Music; Modeling

DOWNEY, SHANNON; MEDINA, OH; MEDINA SR HS; (JR); Hnr Roll; Nat Hon Sy; WWAHSS; Comm Volntr; Chrch Yth Grp; Emplmnt; Key Club; Quill & Scroll; Svce Clb; Bnd; Dnce; Mch Bnd; Sch Ppr (E); Yrbk (E); Key Club- VP; Journalism; English / Education; Ohio State U; Akron U

DOZIER, JEFF R; WARREN, OH; CHAMPION HS; (FR); 4H Awd; Hnr Roll; Kwnis Aw; Sci Fairs; Peer Tut/Med; 4-H; Drma Clb; Key Club; Mus Clb; Sci Clb; Bnd; Jzz Bnd; Mch Bnd; Pep Bnd; Cr Ctry (V L); Track (V L); CR (R); Bowling Vl; Forensic Science; Teacher; Youngstown State U; Akron U

DRESKIN, ALENA; CLEVELAND, OH; (SR); Comm Volntr; Drma Clb; Chr; SP/M/VS; Hero Behind the Scene; Broadcasting; Kent State U

DROHMAN, JESSIE; NEWARK, OH; NEWARK HS; (JR)

DRUMM, HILARY; FARMERSVILLE, OH; VALLEY VIEW; (SO); Hnr Roll; St of Mnth; Comm Volntr; Chrch Yth Grp; DARE; Emplmnt; Mus Clb; Scouts; Spanish Clb; Ch Chr; Clr Grd; Drl Tm; Teacher; Wright State

DUCK, RYAN; CANTON, OH; TIMHIN; (MS); Hnr Roll; Nat Hon Sy; Perf Att; Peer Tut/Med; DARE; Mus Clb; Bnd; Jzz Bnd; Mch Bnd

DUFFEY, JANAE; WESTERVILLE, OH; NORTHSIDE CHRISTIAN SCH; (JR); Ctznshp Aw; Hi Hnr Roll; Hnr Roll; Otst Ac Ach Awd; St of Mnth; Comm Volntr; Emplmnt; Pep Squd; Prom Com; Quiz Bowl; Vsity Clb; Chr; SP/M/VS; Chrldg (V CL); Vllyball (VJCL); Cl Off (P); Yrbk (E, R); Ohio Music Education Association Award for Ensemble; Psychology; Elementary Education; Ohio State U; Franklin U

DUFFIELD, SAMANTHA G; BARBERTON, OH; BARBERTON HS; (FR); Hnr Roll; St of Mnth; WWAHSS; Yth Ldrshp Prog; 4-H; Chrch Yth Grp; DARE; Drma Clb; Tchrs Aide; Teacher; Own a Day Care Center

DUGAN, ROB; MASSILLON, OH; EDISON JHS; (FR); Hi Hnr Roll; St of Mnth; Peer Tut/Med; Spch Team; Wdwrkg Clb; Clb; Bsball (J); Ftball (J); Track (V); Wt Lftg (J); Cl Off (V); Stu Cncl (V); Won Most Outstanding Freshman Award; Engineering; Architecture; Ohio State U; Kent State U

DUKES, BRITTANY; CLEVELAND, OH; JAMES FORD RHODES; (SO); Hnr Roll; Otst Ac Ach Awd; Perf Att; Sci Fairs; St of Mnth; Comm Volntr; ArtClub; DARE; Drma Clb; Mth Clb/Tm; Mus Clb; ROTC; Scouts; Clb; Chr; Dnce; Bskball (J); Chrldg (J); Track (J); Sch Ppr (E)

DULANEY, TINA M; JACKSON, OH; JACKSON HS; (JR); Hnr Roll; ArtClub; Sci Clb; Art Club; Science Club; Art; Accounting; Stanford

DUNLAP, BRIDGET; LIMA, OH; LIMA SR HS; (SO); Hnr Roll; Sftball (J); Ohio State; FSU

DUNSING, MARIAH; NILES, OH; NILES MC KINLEY HS; (FR); Ctznshp Aw; Hnr Roll; Kwnis Aw; Pres Ac Ftns Aw; Pres Sch; Sci Fairs; St of Mnth; WWAHSS; Comm Volntr; Dbte Team; Drma Clb; Key Club; NtlFrnscLg; Spch Team; SADD; Spanish Clb; Bnd; Mch Bnd; SP/M/VS; Stg Cre; Placing Third in Public Forum Debate Once; Attending the Junior-Statesman Summer School Soph Year; Political Science Major with an Economics Minor; Joint Political Science and Economics Major, with Literature; Columbia U; New York U

DUNWOODY, KATIE J; MILLERSPORT, OH; MILLERSPORT JR SR HS; MS; Hnr Roll; Nat Hon Sy; Perf Att; Comm Volntr; Peer Tut/Med; 4-H; DARE; Scouts; Tchrs Aide; Chrldg (L); Lettered in Academics; Horticulture; Education; Harvard U; Ohio State

DURAINE, ROBERT; CONNEAUT, OH; EDGEWOOD HS; (SO); Ctznshp Aw; Hnr Roll; Chess; Chrch Yth Grp; Mod UN; Stg Cre; Ftball (VL); Track (V); Wrstlg (VL); Wrestling/Heavyweight-All County, Northeastern Conference Champion and Sectional Champion; 3 Time Letter Winner in Football and Wrestling; Biology/Medical Field; Ohio State U, Temple U, Penn State U; U of Minnesota, Edinboro U

DURBAK, JOSEPH; RAVENNA, OH; WARD DAVIS HS; (SO); Hi Hnr Roll; Perf Att; Scouts; Sccr (L); Track (V); Knights of Columbus Youth of the Year Award; Perfect Attendance; Electronic Engineering; Mechanics; Baldwin Wallace U; Massachusetts Institute of Technology

DURBIN, COURTNEY L; PERRYSBURG, OH; ST URSULA AC; (FR); Hi Hnr Roll; Comm Volntr; DARE; Sci Clb; Bskball (V); Sccr (L); Track (L); Cl Off (T); Pre-Med; Pre-Law; U of North Carolina; U of Notre Dame

DURGALA, AMBER; CUYAHOGA FALLS, OH; CUYAHOGA FALLS HS; (SR); Hi Hnr Roll; Hnr Roll; WWAHSS; Comm Volntr; Hosp Aide; Sch Ppr (R); National Merit Award; Who's Who Among American HS Students; Criminology; Law; Ohio U; Ohio State

DURINA, LINDSEY R; HUBBARD, OH; URSULINE AC; (MS); Hi Hnr Roll; St of Mnth; DARE; Tchrs Aide; Dnce; Bskball; Sftball; Track; Stu Cncl; Lawyer

DURIS, TOM; WALBRIDGE, OH; LAKE HS; (SO); Hi Hnr Roll; Hnr Roll; WWAHSS; Emplmnt; Ice Hky (V L); Accounting; Ohio State U; U of Toledo

DURO, CAROLYN A; ALLIANCE, OH; ALLIANCE HS; (SR); Hnr Roll; Nat Hon Sy; WWAHSS; Chrch Yth Grp; Drma Clb; Emplmnt; Key Club; Bnd; Chr; Ch Chr; Jzz Bnd; Tennis (V); Music Performance; Capital U

DURO, RACHAEL E; ALLIANCE, OH; ALLIANCE HS; (SO); Hnr Roll; Sci Fairs; WWAHSS; Chrch Yth Grp; Key Club; Bnd; Chr; Ch Chr; Jzz Bnd

DUSZKIEWICZ, ANNA; MOGADORE, OH; FIELD HS; (JR); All Am Sch; Hi Hnr Roll; Hnr Roll; WWAHSS; Yth Ldrshp Prog; Comm Volntr; 4-H; Chrch Yth Grp; Emplmnt; FCA; Lib Aide; Mus Clb; French Clb; Chr; Ch Chr; Cr Ctry (J); Tennis (V); Track (V); Early Childhood Education; Journalism; Kent State U; Ohio State U

DUTRIDGE, ASHLEY; TOLEDO, OH; WHITMER HS; (SR); All Am Sch; F Lan Hn Soc; Nat Hon Sy; Comm Volntr; Drma Clb; Prom Com; Stg Cre; Cl Off (S); Sch Ppr (E); President's Award for Outstanding Academic Excellence; Political Science; Psychology; The U of Findlay

DUTY, DERREK K; PATRIOT, OH; SOUTH GALLIA HS; (SR); 4H Awd; Hi Hnr Roll; Hnr Roll; 4-H; Chrch Yth Grp

DWORKIN, KELSEY; DAYTON, OH; ALTER HS; (FR); Hnr Roll; Nat Hon Sy; Otst Ac Ach Awd; Sci Fairs; WWAHSS; Comm Volntr; Key Club; Spanish Clb; Cr Ctry (J); Track (J); Psychology; Miami U; U of Kentucky

DWYER, SARAH; CINCINNATI, OH; NORTHWEST HS; (SR); Hnr Roll; St of Mnth; WWAHSS; Comm Volntr; Drma Clb; Emplmnt; Key Club; Tchrs Aide; Bnd; Mch Bnd; Orch; Pep Bnd; Stu Cncl (R); Sch Ppr (E); Award of Knighthood (Band); Journalism Scholarship; Bachelor's in Journalism; Bachelor's in Political Science; Muskingum College

DYE, DEVIN J; CANTON, OH; JACKSON HS; (SO); Hnr Roll; Spanish Clb; Bnd; Mch Bnd; Pep Bnd; Bsball (V L); Aeronautical Engineering; U of Cincinnati; West Virginia U

EALOM, ANTONIO; CLEVELAND, OH; COLLINWOOD HS; (FR); Ctznshp Aw; Hi Hnr Roll; Hnr Roll; Nat Mrt LOC; Otst Ac Ach Awd; Perf Att; Sci Fairs; St of Mnth; US Army Sch Ath Aw; Comm Volntr; Peer Tut/Med; Red Cr Aide; Chess; DARE; Drma Clb; Mus Clb; ROTC; Acpl Chr; Clr Grd; Dnce; SP/M/VS; Bsball (V); Golf (V); Sccr (V); Track (V); Stu Cncl (R); Doctor / Medical Degree; Police / Law Degree; Kent State U

EARHART, BRANDAE; CINCINNATI, OH; FINNEYTOWN HS; (JR); F Lan Hn Soc; Hnr Roll; Nat Hon Sy; Chrch Yth Grp; Drma Clb; FCA; Key Club; Mus Clb; Tchrs Aide; Chr; Clr Grd; SP/M/VS; Stg Cre; Vllyball; Received "Big Heart Award" in 8th Grade; Early Childhood Education; Spanish Education; Miami U-Oxford, OH; U of Dayton-Dayton, OH

EARLEY, SHANE; NEW MATAMORAS, OH; FRONTIER HS; (JR); Hnr Roll; Nat Hon Sy; WWAHSS; BPA; Chrch Yth Grp; DARE; Ftball (VJ); Developer of School Website; Publisher of Sports Programs; Website Development; Computer Graphics; Ohio State U; DeVry U

Duffield, Samantha G
Barberton HS
Barberton, OH

Dore, Dominic A
Western Reserve HS
Collins, OH

Dismuke, Romel
West JHS
Ashtabula, OH

Donnenwirth, Eric J
Westerville North HS
Westerville, OH

Durbin, Courtney L
St Ursula AC
Perrysburg, OH

EARLY, RYAN; TOLEDO, OH; WHITMER HS; (JR); Hnr Roll; Emplmnt; Law Degree; U of Michigan in Ann Arbor; U of Pennsylvania

EASTER, LITISHA M; TOLEDO, OH; SCOTT HS; (SO); Hnr Roll; Otst Ac Ach Awd; Perf Att; St of Mnth; Comm Volntr; Peer Tut/Med; Chrch Yth Grp; Pep Squd; P to P St Amb Prg; Pep Bnd; Bskball (J); Sftball (JC); Vllyball (JC); Adv Cncl (R); Cl Off (P); Stu Cncl (S); CR (P, R); Homecoming Court; Jefferson Madison Leadership Camp; Business Admin.; Business Management; Central State; Northern Kentucky State

EBBRECHT, STEPHANIE M; PIKETON, OH; PIKETON HS; (SO); Hi Hnr Roll; Hnr Roll; Nat Hon Sy; Otst Ac Ach Awd; Perf Att; WWAHSS; Comm Volntr; 4-H; Chess; Chrch Yth Grp; Drma Clb; Bnd; Dnce; SP/M/VS; Wt Lftg (V); Police Officer or a Doctor; Yale; Harvard

EBERHART, JUDD M; LANCASTER, OH; LANCASTER HS; (JR); Hi Hnr Roll; Nat Hon Sy; WWAHSS; Comm Volntr; DARE; Key Club; Lttrmn Clb; Spanish Clb; Bskball (V L); Wt Lftg (V); Stu Cncl (R); CR (R); Renaissance Committee; Teen Institute; Miami (Ohio) U; Xavier U

EBERTS, KRISTIN; THE PLAINS, OH; ATHENS HS; (SR); F Lan Hn Soc; Hi Hnr Roll; Nat Hon Sy; Nat Mrt LOC; Pres Sch; Chrch Yth Grp; Drma Clb; Mod UN; Photog; Quill & Scroll; Scouts; Tchrs Aide; Spanish Clb; SP/M/VS; Bskball (V L); Sftball (V L); Yrbk (E, P); Photo Journalism; Ohio U

EBY, JASON R; NORTH ROYALTON, OH; NORTH ROYALTON HS; (SR); Hi Hnr Roll; Kwnis Aw; Nat Hon Sy; Otst Ac Ach Awd; Pres Sch; St of Mnth; Valdctrian; WWAHSS; Yth Ldrshp Prog; Comm Volntr; Peer Tut/Med; Red Cr Aide; Chrch Yth Grp; Drma Clb; Emplmnt; Key Club; Mod UN; Off Aide; Prom Com; SADD; SP/M/VS; Stg Cre; Cl Off (P); CR (P); Phi Kappa Beta Student Recognition; Outstanding Senior Award; Business; Law; Northwestern U

ECKLE, TRENT H; WASHINGTON COURT HOUSE, OH; WASHINGTON HS; (FR); Hnr Roll; Otst Ac Ach Awd; Perf Att; St of Mnth; Yth Ldrshp Prog; DARE; Emplmnt; Off Aide; Outdrs Clb; SP/M/VS; Bsball (J); Bskball (J); Ftball (J); Freshman Leadership; Academy of Scholars; Veterinary Science; Zoology; Ohio State U

EDDY, JOSHUA; BIDWELL, OH; RIVER VALLEY HS; (SR); 4H Awd; Hi Hnr Roll; Nat Hon Sy; WWAHSS; 4-H; Chrch Yth Grp; Drma Clb; Key Club; Ntl Beta Clb; Ntl FFA; Off Aide; SP/M/VS; Bsball (V); Ftball; Wrstlg (V); Sch Ppr (R)

EDEBURN, EMILY E; CINCINNATI, OH; ST URSULA AC; (JR); Hnr Roll; Comm Volntr; Chess; DARE; Drma Clb; Emplmnt; Latin Clb; SP/M/VS; Stg Cre; Bskball (J); GAA (J); Won 2004 Kids Voting Speech Contest; Produced Fall Play & Spring Musical Sophomore-Senior Year; Film Production; Business I.E. Marketing & Sales; Florida State U; Indiana U

EDWARDS, ALEXIS; ZANESVILLE, OH; MAYSVILLE HS; (FR); Hnr Roll; Otst Ac Ach Awd; Comm Volntr; Drma Clb; Key Club; Mus Clb; Pep Squd; Spanish Clb; Chr; SP/M/VS; Chrldg (JC); Cr Ctry; Track (V); Cl Off (P); All Star Cheerleading - Outside of School; Psychology; Ohio State U

EDWARDS, APRIL; CINCINNATI, OH; NORTHWEST HS; (SR); F Lan Hn Soc; Hnr Roll; Nat Hon Sy; WWAHSS; Comm Volntr; Drma Clb; Emplmnt; Key Club; Prom Com; Tchrs Aide; Bnd; Mch Bnd; SP/M/VS; Bskball; Cr Ctry (V L); Sccr (V CL); Track (V CL); Cl Off (P, T); Stu Cncl (R); Yrbk (P); Second Team, All League-Soccer; Uknighted Knights; Engineering; Photography; Valparaiso U

EDWARDS III, JOHNNIE C; SHELBY, OH; SHELBY HS; (FR); Hnr Roll

EDWARDS JR, MARK S; WESTERVILLE, OH; DELAWARE AREA CAREER CTR; (SR); Hnr Roll; Sci Fairs; Peer Tut/Med; 4-H; Emplmnt; Vsity Clb; Wdwrkg Clb; Cr Ctry (J); Sccr (V); Wrstlg (J); Police Science Degree; Hocking Technical College

EFFLER, MAGGIE; CINCINNATI, OH; MOTHER OF MERCY HS; (SR); Hnr Roll; Perf Att; St of Mnth; Comm Volntr; ArtClub; Drma Clb; Tchrs Aide; SP/M/VS; Stg Cre; Lit Mag (E); Lead Capple Critic; English; Education; U of Dayton; Miami U

EIBEL, ALANNA; CANTON, OH; GLEN OAK HS; (SR); Hi Hnr Roll; Hnr Roll; Nat Hon Sy; WWAHSS; Spec Olymp Vol; BPA; Off Aide; Spch Team; Tennis (J); Diploma with Honors; Award of Merit; Sales; Marketing; U of Akron

EIDSON, TYLER J; KENT, OH; KENT ROOSEVELT HS; (FR); Hi Hnr Roll; Hnr Roll; Spec Olymp Vol; Chrch Yth Grp; DARE; Emplmnt; P to P St Amb Prg; Wdwrkg Clb; Latin Clb; Lcrsse (J); Scr Kpr (V); Sccr (J); Student Ambassador People to People; Power of the Pen; CYO Athlete of Character Award; Panda; Engineering; Law Enforcement; The Ohio State U; Syracuse U

EISEL, JAMES M; WEST UNITY, OH; MILLCREEK-WEST UNITY; (SR); Hi Hnr Roll; Otst Ac Ach Awd; Sci Fairs; WWAHSS; Yth Ldrshp Prog; Comm Volntr; AL Aux Boys; Chrch Yth Grp; Emplmnt; Ntl FFA; SP/M/VS; Bskball; Ftball; Track; Wt Lftg; 1st Team All League Football; 2nd Team All State Nose Guard Football; Engineer

ELARDO, AMBER; CLEVELAND, OH; PARMA SR HS; (JR); Ctznshp Aw; Hi Hnr Roll; Otst Ac Ach Awd; St of Mnth; Yth Ldrshp Prog; Emplmnt; Stu Cncl (R); Lit Mag (E); Yrbk (E); Pre-Med; Radiology; Ohio State U; U of Akron

ELCHERT, JESSICA R; DELAWARE, OH; RUTHERFORD B HAYES HS; (SO); Hi Hnr Roll; Hnr Roll; Pres Sch; Sci Fairs; ArtClub; Emplmnt; Lib Aide; Scouts; Spanish Clb; Sftball (J); Stu Cncl (R); Girl Scouts for 8 Years; Multiple Honor Rolls and Merit Rolls; Education; Mathematics; Ohio State U; Winthrop U

ELDRIDGE, ASHLEY; BRYAN, OH; BRYAN HS; (JR); Hi Hnr Roll; Hnr Roll; Nat Hon Sy; WWAHSS; Emplmnt; Prom Com; Latin Clb; Acpl Chr; Chr; SP/M/VS; Academic Varsity B; National Latin Award of Merit; Business; Northwest State Community College

ELESWARPU, SARADA; WEST CHESTER, OH; LAKOTA EAST HS; (SO); Hi Hnr Roll; Nat Hon Sy; HO'Br Yth Ldrshp; MuAlphaTh; Tmpl Yth Grp; Ch Chr; Dnce; SP/M/VS; Cl Off (V); Stu Cncl (V); Sch Ppr (E); President-Elect of Mu Alpha Theta; Bharata Natyam Arangetram; Biology; Journalism; Case Western Reserve; Northwestern

ELKING, HEIDI; MARIA STEIN, OH; MARION LOCAL HS; (SO); Hi Hnr Roll; WWAHSS; Comm Volntr; Chrch Yth Grp; FTA; Mth Clb/Tm; Pep Squd; Sci Clb; SADD; Bnd; Clr Grd; Sftball (J); Vllyball (JC); Cl Off (S, R); Stu Cncl (R); Yrbk; Muse Machine; Vets Team; Finance; Accounting; U of Dayton; U of Notre Dame

ELLENBURG, KATHRYN; MONROE, OH; MONROE HS; (JR); Hnr Roll; Nat Hon Sy; Perf Att; St of Mnth; WWAHSS; Peer Tut/Med; Emplmnt; Tchrs Aide; Chrldg (VJ); Sccr (V); Cl Off (P); Stu Cncl (R); Yrbk (E, R, P); Jesse Mayabb Scholarship; Elementary Education; Ohio State U; Bowling Green U

ELLIOTT, TA'LISHA L; DAYTON, OH; MEADOWDALE HS; (JR); Hnr Roll; WWAHSS; Comm Volntr; Hosp Aide; Chrch Yth Grp; Emplmnt; FCA; ROTC; Ch Chr; SP/M/VS; Sch Ppr (R); Honor Roll, Perfect Attendance; Real Estate; Early Childhood Education; TN State U; U of Cincinnati

ELLIS, BRITTANY; MORROW, OH; LITTLE MIAMI; (JR); Hi Hnr Roll; Hnr Roll; Perf Att; DARE; Voc Ind Clb Am; Yrbk (E, P)

ELLIS, JESSICA; LEWISBURG, OH; TRI-COUNTY NORTH HS; (SR); Hnr Roll; MVP; Nat Hon Sy; Perf Att; Sci Fairs; WWAHSS; Comm Volntr; Ntl FFA; Prom Com; Tchrs Aide; Bskball (J L); PP Ftbl (V L); Sccr (V CL); Sftball (J); Track (V L); Stu Cncl (S); Yrbk (R, P); Business Management; Urbana U

ELLYSON, BRITTANY; EAST ROCHESTER, OH; UNITED LOCAL HS; (JR); Hi Hnr Roll; Nat Hon Sy; WWAHSS; Chrch Yth Grp; Key Club; French Clb; Track (V L); Yrbk; Elementary Teacher

ELMERICK, MICHAEL; SULLIVAN, OH; ASHLAND HS; (JR); Hnr Roll; Business Management/Marketing; Computer Sciences; Bowling Green State U; Ohio State U

ELMI, SUFI; COLUMBUS, OH; BROOKHAVEN HS; (FR); Hi Hnr Roll; Hnr Roll; Nat Hon Sy; Nat Ldrshp Svc; Comm Volntr; Chess; DARE; Doctor; Wright State U; Ohio State U

ELMORE, DANIELLE; WEST FARMINGTON, OH; CHAMPION HS; (SR); Hi Hnr Roll; Hnr Roll; Kwnis Aw; St of Mnth; WWAHSS; Emplmnt; Key Club; Pep Squd; Tchrs Aide; Track (V); Yrbk (E); Bowling Green State U; Hiram

ELY, CAMERON D; SYLVANIA, OH; NORTHVIEW HS; (SO); Hnr Roll; Chrch Yth Grp; Svce Clb; Orch; Bsball (J)

ELY, GABRIELLE; EUCLID, OH; LAKE CATHOLIC HS; (MS); Hi Hnr Roll; Hnr Roll; Sci Fairs; Sci/Math Olympn; St Schl; St of Mnth; Comm Volntr; Peer Tut/Med; DARE; Drma Clb; Jr Ach; Tchrs Aide; Ch Chr; Dnce; SP/M/VS; Stg Cre; Chrldg (J); Cr Ctry (J); Sch Ppr (R); Yrbk (R); Great Lakes Scholar-2004; Started Up Class News Letter in Jr; Reconstructive Plastic Surgeon; Lawyer; Case Western Reserve U; Harvard Law School

ELY, JACLEINE; GALLOWAY, OH; HILLIARD DARBY HS; (JR); Hnr Roll; Otst Ac Ach Awd; Pres Sch; Hab For Humty Volntr; Peer Tut/Med; ArtClub; Chrch Yth Grp; Pep Squd; Bskball (J); Cr Ctry (J); Track (V L); MLK Junior Scholar Award; Ohio Governor's Regional Art Show Award; Architecture-Major; Fashion and Merchandise-Minor; Ohio State U; U of Cincinnati

EMEAGHARA, ADA; COLUMBUS, OH; (SR); MVP; WWAHSS; Peer Tut/Med; Bskball (V); Bright Future Honoree; MVP of Basketball Team (Westville North); Law; Medicine; The Ohio State U; U of Cincinnati

ENDICOTT, AMANDA G; LIMA, OH; LIMA SR HS; (JR); Hi Hnr Roll; Hnr Roll; Nat Hon Sy; Otst Ac Ach Awd; Comm Volntr; Peer Tut/Med; Chrch Yth Grp; Bnd; Dnce; Mch Bnd; Pep Bnd; Stu Cncl (R); Big Brothers / Big Sisters; Articles Published in the Newspaper; Early Childhood Education; English; Ohio State U; Bluffton Community College

ENDRES, PAULINE; DAYTON, OH; CTRVILLE HS; (JR); F Lan Hn Soc; Perf Att; WWAHSS; Comm Volntr; Peer Tut/Med; Emplmnt; Tchrs Aide; French Clb; Sftball (V); French Club; Pre-Med

ENFLO, KRISTEL; KENT, OH; KENT ROOSEVELT HS; (JR); Fut Prb Slvr; Hnr Roll; MVP; Nat Hon Sy; Biology Clb; Chrch Yth Grp; Key Club; Photog; Prom Com; Quill & Scroll; German Clb; Fld Hky (L); Lcrsse (J); Lit Mag (P); Community Problem Solving; Awards for Photography; Photography; Art History; Boston U; Art Institute of Pittsburgh

ENGELHART, JOHN O; BRUNSWICK, OH; BRUNSWICK HS; (JR); Hnr Roll; Perf Att; St of Mnth; Comm Volntr; Hab For Humty Volntr; ArtClub; BPA; Chrch Yth Grp; Cmptr Clb; Emplmnt; Jr Ach; Key Club; Tchrs Aide; Acpl Chr; Chr; Swmg (V); Tennis (J); Track (J); Snowboarding / Ski Club; All Men's Choir; Human Resource Management; Electrical Engineering; U of Toledo; Bryant & Stratton College

ENGLISH, DEIDRA; GNADENHUTTEN, OH; INDIAN VALLEY HS; (JR); Hi Hnr Roll; St of Mnth; WWAHSS; Comm Volntr; Chrch Yth Grp; Emplmnt; FCA; Pep Squd; Prom Com; Sftball (JC); Vllyball (V CL); Academic Letter Winner, Pep Club Co-President; Member of Students with a Testimony (SWAT); Pre-Med; Social Worker; Wright State; The Ohio State

EPPERLY, RACHEL N; COLUMBUS, OH; GAHANNA CHRISTIAN AC; (SO); Hnr Roll; WWAHSS; Comm Volntr; Chrch Yth Grp; Emplmnt; FCA; Ch Chr; Chrldg (V); Medicine-Dermatology; Ohio State U

ERICKSON, LESLIE A; NEW CARLISLE, OH; TECUMSEH HS; (FR); Hnr Roll; Perf Att; Peer Tut/Med; 4-H; Chrch Yth Grp; DARE; Ntl FFA; P to P St Amb Prg; Scouts; Chr; Sccr (J); Track (V); Earning Girl Scout Silver Award; Veterinarian; Agricultural Education Career; Ohio State U; Colorado State U

ERNY, BRETT; CLEVELAND, OH; LINCOLN-WEST HS; (FR); Ctznshp Aw; Hi Hnr Roll; Hnr Roll; Perf Att; Sci/Math Olympn; Comm Volntr; Chess; Mth Clb/Tm; Computers / Electronic Graphic Design; Lawyer; Cleveland State

ESCH, LANCE A; HUNTSVILLE, OH; INDIAN LAKE HS; (SR); Hnr Roll; MVP; Perf Att; St of Mnth; Yth Ldrshp Prog; Cmptr Clb; Key Club; Lttrmn Clb; Off Aide; Tchrs Aide; Vsity Clb; Spanish Clb; Sccr (V CL); Track (V CL); Wrstlg (V CL); Wrestling State Runner-Up 2005 152 Pound; Web Design; Networking; Rio Grande U

ESCHBAUGH, JARED J; MILLERSPORT, OH; NEWARK CATHOLIC HS; (JR); Nat Hon Sy; Sci Fairs; St of Mnth; Yth Ldrshp Prog; Comm Volntr; DARE; Scouts; Bskball (J); Ftball (V); Golf (J); Track (V); Biology; M.D.; Ohio U; Ohio State U

ESTOCK, MARY; BELOIT, OH; WEST BRANCH HS; (SR); 4H Awd; Ctznshp Aw; Fut Prb Slvr; Hnr Roll; Jr Mshl; Nat Hon Sy; St of Mnth; Comm Volntr; Peer Tut/Med; 4-H; AL Aux Girls; Chrch Yth Grp; Dbte Team; Emplmnt; FCCLA; NYLC; Scouts; Chr; SP/M/VS; Skiing; Stu Cncl (R); CR (R); Strategic Communications; Political Science; The Ohio State U

EUBANKS, JESSICA N; GREENFIELD, OH; GREENFIELD (MC CLAIN) HS; (FR); Ctznshp Aw; Hnr Roll; Comm Volntr; Peer Tut/Med; Chrch Yth Grp; Drma Clb; Ntl FFA; Pep Squd; Tchrs Aide; Chr; SP/M/VS; Chrldg (J L); Track (L); Stu Cncl (R); First Year Member of FFA (McClain); First Year Member of Highland Co. Stand Team; Youth Ministry/Missionary Work; Kentucky Christian College; Asbury College

EUSEY, MATTHEW L; CRESTLINE, OH; CRESTLINE HS/PIONEER CTC; (JR); Ctznshp Aw; Hi Hnr Roll; Hnr Roll; Perf Att; Sci Fairs; Peer Tut/Med; ArtClub; FCCLA; Key Club; Ntl FFA; SADD; Spanish Clb; Bnd; Jzz Bnd; Mch Bnd; Pep Bnd; Cr Ctry (V L); Tennis (V L); Cl Off (V); Stu Cncl (R); Music Education; Music Theory; Bowling Green State U

EVANS, BRITTNEY; LIMA, OH; ALLEN CTY CHRISTIAN HOME SCHERS; (FR); Hi Hnr Roll; Hnr Roll; Otst Ac Ach Awd; Pres Ac Ftns Aw; Sci Fairs; Comm Volntr; Hosp Aide; Peer Tut/Med; 4-H; Chrch Yth Grp; Drma Clb; Mus Clb; Off Aide; Scouts; Bnd; Chr; Drm Mjr; Flg Crps; Sch Ppr (R); Head Majorette; 4-H Club Secretary; Physician; Ohio State U

EVANS, NICOLETTE M; LIMA, OH; BATH HS; (FR); Hi Hnr Roll; Peer Tut/Med; DARE; Flg Crps; Swmg (V)

EVERLY, SARAH H; CRESTLINE, OH; CRESTLINE HS; (JR); Hnr Roll; St of Mnth; Yth Ldrshp Prog; Comm Volntr; Drma Clb; FCCLA; Key Club; Off Aide; Pep Squd; Prom Com; Bnd; Jzz Bnd; Mch Bnd; Pep Bnd; Cl Off (S, T); Intramural Bowling League Top Female Score; Candidate for National Honor Society; Criminal Justice; Criminology

EYRE, ALEXANDER W; PATASKALA, OH; WATKINS MEMORIAL HS; (FR); Hnr Roll; Sci Fairs; St of Mnth; Quiz Bowl; Scouts; Bnd; Jzz Bnd; Swmg (V); Eagle Scout; Engineering; Environmental Engineering; Massachusetts Institute of Technology

FABIANI, BRIANNA L; CAREY, OH; CAREY SCH; (SO); Hnr Roll; Otst Ac Ach Awd; Perf Att; St of Mnth; WWAHSS; Comm Volntr; ArtClub; Chrch Yth Grp; DARE; Drma Clb; Emplmnt; Pep Squd; Quiz Bowl; Scouts; Bnd; Chr; Jzz Bnd; Mch Bnd; Cr Ctry (V); Track (V); Cl Off (S); Medical; Law; Ohio State U; U of Southern California

FAGAN, LINDSAY J; MANSFIELD, OH; TEMPLE CHRISTIAN SCH; (FR); Hi Hnr Roll; Nat Sci Aw; Sci Fairs; Comm Volntr; Chrch Yth Grp; Quiz Bowl; Bnd; Orch; Sccr (V); Cl Off (T); CSO; Elementary Teacher; Missionary; Pensacola; Cedarville U

Enflo, Kristel
Kent Roosevelt HS
Kent, OH

Ely, Jacleine
Hilliard Darby HS
Galloway, OH

National
Honor Roll
Spring 2005

Ely, Gabrielle
Lake Catholic HS
Euclid, OH

Eusey, Matthew L
Crestline HS/Pioneer Ctc
Crestline, OH

FAHEY, KASEY; ASHTABULA, OH; STS JOHN AND PAUL CATHOLIC HS; (FR); Hi Hnr Roll; Pres Ac Ftns Aw; Biology Clb; Key Club; Bskball; Chrldg (V C); Member of Key Club; High Honors; Communications; Accounting; Walsh U; Ohio State U

FAHMY, CAROL; BIDWELL, OH; GALLIA AC HS; (SO); Hnr Roll; MVP; WWAHSS; 4-H; Chrch Yth Grp; Key Club; Mod UN; Bnd; Chr; Mch Bnd; SP/M/VS; Cr Ctry (V); Track (V); Marketing; Communication Arts; Ohio State U; Cedarville U

FAIRBANKS, ANDREW J; WEST CHESTER, OH; LAKOTA EAST HS; (FR); Hi Hnr Roll; Nat Hon Sy; Sci Fairs; WWAHSS; Peer Tut/Med; Emplmnt; P to P St Amb Prg; Wdwrkg Clb; Bnd; Jzz Bnd; Playing AAA Ice Hockey; Made Mid-American Select Ice Hockey Team; Engineering; Start a Successful Business; U of Cincinnati; Purdue U

FAIRBANKS, IEISHA; CINCINNATI, OH; HUGHES CTR HS; (SO); Ctznshp Aw; MVP; Perf Att; Yth Ldrshp Prog; Comm Volntr; Peer Tut/Med; Emplmnt; Off Aide; Dnce; Drl Tm; SP/M/VS; Stg Cre; Mar Art (V); Sftball (V); CR (R); Sch Ppr (R); Business Management; Law; Bellarmine U; U of Cincinnati

FALK, DEANNA; TOLEDO, OH; ST URSULA AC; (SO); Hi Hnr Roll; Hnr Roll; Perf Att; Salutrn; Sci Fairs; St of Mnth; Comm Volntr; ArtClub; Chr; SP/M/VS; Chrldg (V); Art/Design; Education

FALK, EMILY; COLUMBUS, OH; GRANDVIEW HEIGHTS HS; (JR); Hi Hnr Roll; WWAHSS; Comm Volntr; ArtClub; Emplmnt; HO'Br Yth Ldrshp; Photog; Sci Clb; Spanish Clb; Sftball (V L); Horseback Riding; Science; Art; Ohio State U; Miami U

FANTIDIS, ELENI; WARREN, OH; HOWLAND HS; (JR); Ctznshp Aw; Hnr Roll; Perf Att; St of Mnth; Chrch Yth Grp; Off Aide; Scouts; Tchrs Aide; Dnce; One Year in Attendance Office

FARABAUGH, ELISSE C; WILLOUGHBY, OH; WILLOUGHBY SOUTH HS; (SO); Hi Hnr Roll; Hnr Roll; Perf Att; St of Mnth; WWAHSS; Jr Ach; Key Club; Scouts; Bnd; Mch Bnd; Swmg (J); Education; French; Miami U (UNC); Bowling Green State U

FARIA, REBECCA; COLUMBUS, OH; BEXLEY HS; (JR); Hi Hnr Roll; Nat Hon Sy; Red Cr Aide; Chrch Yth Grp; DARE; Off Aide; Sci Clb; Tchrs Aide; Spanish Clb; Chr; Dnce; Lcrsse (J); Sch Ppr (R); Journalism; Dance; Northwestern U; New York U

FARKAS, CATHERINE E; BRUNSWICK, OH; BRUNSWICK HS; (JR); Hnr Roll; WWAHSS; Comm Volntr; 4-H; Emplmnt; Scouts; French Clb; Chr; Cr Ctry (V L); Swmg (V CL); Track (V L); Competitive Equestrian; Confirmation; Biology; Pre-Dentistry; Miami U; Ohio State U

FARKAS-MORALES, JULIANNA; ASHTABULA, OH; LAKESIDE HS; (SO); Hnr Roll; Perf Att; Spanish Clb; Track (V L); Vllyball (J); Artwork Displayed At Local Arts Center; Business; Psychology; Baldwin Wallace U; Kent State U

FARLEY, ADAM; PERRYSBURG, OH; PERRYSBURG HS; (JR); Hnr Roll; Perf Att; French Clb; Bsball (J); Golf (J); Tennis (J); Business Management; Accounting; Bowling Green State U; U of Michigan

FARLEY, JESSICA; GRAFTON, OH; MIDVIEW HS; (FR); 4H Awd; Hnr Roll; Comm Volntr; Peer Tut/Med; 4-H; Emplmnt; Scouts; Bnd; Jzz Bnd; Mch Bnd; CR (R); Yrbk (R); Bachelor of Science and Nursing; Law Degree; Case-Western Reserve U; Ohio State U

FAULKNER, ASHLEY M; PORTSMOUTH, OH; WHEELERSBURG HS; (SR); Hnr Roll; Nat Hon Sy; USAA; WWAHSS; Hosp Aide; Key Club; Prom Com; Stg Cre; Tennis (V); Yrbk (E); Early Childhood Education; Shawnee State U

FAVA, QUILLEN; NORTH ROYALTON, OH; NORTH ROYALTON HS; (JR); Hi Hnr Roll; Hnr Roll; Nat Hon Sy; Otst Ac Ach Awd; Pres Ac Ftns Aw; Sci Fairs; St of Mnth; WWAHSS; Comm Volntr; Red Cr Aide; Chrch Yth Grp; DARE; Drma Clb; Emplmnt; Key Club; Mus Clb; Svce Clb; Latin Clb; Bnd; Ch Chr; Dnce; Mch Bnd; Psychology; Religious Studies; Denison U; Holy Cross

FAWCETT, ERIN; CEDARVILLE, OH; CEDARVILLE HS; (SO); 4H Awd; Ctznshp Aw; Hnr Roll; Otst Ac Ach Awd; St of Mnth; WWAHSS; Comm Volntr; 4-H; Chrch Yth Grp; Drma Clb; Key Club; Quiz Bowl; Tchrs Aide; Bnd; Ch Chr; Mch Bnd; SP/M/VS; Chrldg (V L); Sccr (V); Tennis (J); Cl Off (S); Freshman of the Year; Ranked # 1 in Class; Mathematics; Cedarville U; United States Naval Academy

FAWCETT, MATTHEW; CEDARVILLE, OH; CEDARVILLE HS; (SO); 4H Awd; St of Mnth; 4-H; Chrch Yth Grp; Bnd; Jzz Bnd; Mch Bnd; Pep Bnd; Sccr (V); Tennis (V L); Cl Off; Engineering; Music Education; Cedarville U; US Naval Academy

FAY, JENNA; BELLEFONTAINE, OH; BELLEFONTAINE HS; (JR); Hnr Roll; Kwnis Aw; Nat Hon Sy; Pres Ac Ftns Aw; Yth Ldrshp Prog; Comm Volntr; 4-H; DARE; Drma Clb; Emplmnt; HO'Br Yth Ldrshp; Key Club; Mod UN; Photog; Chr; SP/M/VS; Chrldg (V L); Sftball (V L); Cl Off (S); Yrbk (E); HOBY; 4-H Camp Counselor; International Business; Social Work; Ohio State U; U of Kentucky

FEEMAN, LINDSEY; BELLVILLE, OH; CLEAR FORK HS; (FR); Hnr Roll; Comm Volntr; Chrch Yth Grp; Chr; Ch Chr; Student of the Quarter; Student of the Week; Mount Vernon Nazarene U

FELLURE, RICHARD; BALTIMORE, OH; LIBERTY UNION HS; (SO); 4H Awd; Hnr Roll; Perf Att; WWAHSS; 4-H; FCA; Wdwrkg Clb; Foreign Clb; Ftball (V L); Track (V L); Wt Lftg; Wrstlg (V L); Stu Cncl (R); Medical Science; Law; Ohio Wesleyan U; Wittenburg U

FELTZ, ERIN; MARIA STEIN, OH; MARION LOCAL HS; (SO); Hnr Roll; Comm Volntr; Chrch Yth Grp; Bnd; Mch Bnd; Pep Bnd; Sftball (J); Swmg (V); Education; State Colleges

FERGUSON, COURTNEY; FINDLAY, OH; VAN BUREN HS; (FR); 4H Awd; Ctznshp Aw; Hi Hnr Roll; MVP; Nat Hon Sy; 4-H; Emplmnt; Bskball (V); Track (V); Vllyball (J); Stu Cncl (R); Physical Therapy; Ohio State U; U of Findlay

FERGUSON, SCOTT; MILFORD, OH; MILFORD HS; (JR); Hnr Roll; Comm Volntr; DECA; Emplmnt; Tchrs Aide; Ftball (J L); Stu Cncl (R); Yrbk (R); 1st Place @ DECA Competition Against 64 Other Teams.; Pursue a 4 Year Degree in Business Management; Ohio State U; Ohio U

FERGUSON, SEAN; WESTERVILLE, OH; WESTERVILLE NORTH HS; (JR); Hnr Roll; Otst Ac Ach Awd; Comm Volntr; Emplmnt; Bsball (V); Engineering; Ohio State U; Toledo U

FERRALL, SARAH E; HILLIARD, OH; HILLIARD DARBY HS; (SO); Hi Hnr Roll; Hnr Roll; Perf Att; St of Mnth; Comm Volntr; Key Club; Photog; French Clb; Chr; Yrbk (R, P); Elementary Education; Princeton U; American U

FERRALL, WILLIAM A; HILLIARD, OH; HILLIARD DARBY HS; (JR); Hnr Roll; Nat Hon Sy; St of Mnth; Hab For Humty Volntr; Chrch Yth Grp; Emplmnt; Key Club; Prom Com; Tchrs Aide; German Clb; Bnd; Mch Bnd; SP/M/VS; Cl Off (T); Political Science; Creative Writing; Brown U; Harvard U

FERRARA, ALLISON; SPRINGBORO, OH; SPRINGBORO HS; (SO); Hi Hnr Roll; Perf Att; WWAHSS; Yth Ldrshp Prog; ArtClub; Chrch Yth Grp; Key Club; NYLC; Foreign Clb; SP/M/VS; Track (V); Stu Cncl (R); Secondary Education; Stanford U; U of Virginia

FERREE, KATHERINE; YOUNGSTOWN, OH; AUSTINTOWN FITCH HS; (FR); Hnr Roll; Drma Clb; Bnd; Mch Bnd; SP/M/VS; Sftball (VL); Vllyball; Rifle Line; Dentist; Forensic Science; U of Florida; Ohio State

FERRER, BRYAN; CANTON, OH; CANTON SOUTH HS; (FR); MVP; Comm Volntr; Chrch Yth Grp; FCA; Cr Ctry (V L); Sccr (V L); Track (J); CR (R); Broadcasting; Professional Player; Ohio State U; Akron U

FETTY, ART; TORONTO, OH; EDISON HS; (JR); All Am Sch; Hi Hnr Roll; Hnr Roll; Nat Hon Sy; Perf Att; WWAHSS; Comm Volntr; AL Aux Boys; Ntl Beta Clb; Bsball (L); Bskball (L); Ftball (L); American Legion Baseball; Dental School; West Virginia U; Ashland U

FIELDS, MONICA A; RICHMOND HTS, OH; BEAUMONT SCH; (SO); Ctznshp Aw; Hnr Roll; Perf Att; St of Mnth; Comm Volntr; Hosp Aide; Peer Tut/Med; Civil Air Pat; Track (J); Graphic Designer; Junior High Teacher; John Carroll U

FIFER, JENNIFER L; MEDINA, OH; MEDINA SR HS; (SR); Hnr Roll; Key Club; Off Aide; Latin Clb; Track (V); United States Naval Sea Cadets; Nursing; Cleveland State U

FILO, PAIGE M; DAYTON, OH; ALTER HS; (FR); Hi Hnr Roll; Hnr Roll; Comm Volntr; Key Club; Spanish Clb; Dnce; Computer Science; U of Dayton

FINCH, CAITLIN; FARMDALE, OH; BLOOMFIELD HS; (FR); 4H Awd; Hnr Roll; WWAHSS; Comm Volntr; 4-H; Chrch Yth Grp; Mth Clb/Tm; Spanish Clb; Bnd; Chr; SP/M/VS; Stg Cre; Scr Kpr (VJ); Vllyball (J); Yrbk (P); 4-H Vice President of Swine Club; National Honor Student - United States Achievement; Accounting; Music Business

FINELLI, TARYN; PICKERINGTON, OH; PICKERINGTON HS NORTH; (JR); Hi Hnr Roll; Nat Hon Sy; Perf Att; Comm Volntr; DARE; Drma Clb; SADD; Spanish Clb; Chr; SP/M/VS; Chrldg (VJ L); Gmnstcs (V); Track (V); Talent Show Director; Volunteer Work; Journalism; Psychology; Miami U; Xavier

FINK, HEATHER; KENTON, OH; KENTON SR HS; (FR); Hnr Roll; Chr; Flg Crps; Bowling Green; OSU (Ohio State U)

FINKE, ALEX; DAYTON, OH; ARCHBISHOP ALTER HS; (FR); Otst Ac Ach Awd; Sci Fairs; Key Club; Spanish Clb; Ch Chr; Dnce; SP/M/VS; Stg Cre; Sch Ppr (E); Performing Arts

FINKEN, CLAYTON; OAK HARBOR, OH; OAK HARBOR HS; (SO); Hnr Roll; Perf Att; Sci Fairs; St of Mnth; Comm Volntr; Peer Tut/Med; Red Cr Aide; Chrch Yth Grp; DARE; Emplmnt; Lib Aide; Mus Clb; Photog; Quiz Bowl; Scouts; Bnd; Ch Chr; Jzz Bnd; Mch Bnd; Dvng (V L); Skt Tgt Sh; Swmg (V L); Vsy Clb (V L); Civil War and WWII Reenactor; Member of All-Ohio State Fair Band; History/History Teacher; Criminal Justice/Police Officer; Ohio State U; U of Toledo

FIORENTINO JR, BRIAN; NILES, OH; MC KINLEY HS; (FR); Mus Clb; Chr; SP/M/VS; Ftball (J); Track (J); Wt Lftg (J); Bells and Bows; Architecture; Business Management; Michigan; Illinois

FISCHBACH, SARAH; ELYRIA, OH; MIDVIEW HS; (FR); Hi Hnr Roll; Hnr Roll; St of Mnth; ROTC; Archeology; Science; Princeton U; San Diego U

FISCHER, ADRIENNE; CLEVELAND, OH; JOHN MARSHALL HS; (SO); Ctznshp Aw; F Lan Hn Soc; Hnr Roll; Nat Hon Sy; Perf Att; Sci Fairs; Hosp Aide; Drma Clb; Mth Clb/Tm; French Clb; Stg Cre; Yrbk (P); Science Honorary; English; Fashion Design; New York U

FISHER, CLYDE M I; CLEVELAND, OH; BENEDICTINE HS; (JR); Fut Prb Slvr; Yth Ldrshp Prog; Comm Volntr; Hosp Aide; Chrch Yth Grp; Emplmnt; Fr of Library; Ntl Beta Clb; Bnd; Chr; SP/M/VS; Bskball (J); Cr Ctry (J); Ftball (J); Lcrsse (J); Track; Fraternity Beta; Forensic Science; Engineer; U Michigan, Washington State U; U Florida, U IL, NYU

FISHER, DEBORAH; CINCINNATI, OH; READING JR/SR HS; (JR); Hi Hnr Roll; Nat Hon Sy; Otst Ac Ach Awd; Perf Att; WWAHSS; Comm Volntr; ArtClub; Emplmnt; Key Club; Photog; Scouts; Spanish Clb; SP/M/VS; Stg Cre; Track (V L); Vllyball (JCL); Varsity Bowling - 2 Years; Special Education; Social Work; Bowling Green State U; San Diego State U

FISHER, SARA; WELLSTON, OH; WELLSTON HS; (JR); Ctznshp Aw; Hi Hnr Roll; Hnr Roll; Nat Hon Sy; Otst Ac Ach Awd; Perf Att; St of Mnth; USAA; WWAHSS; Yth Ldrshp Prog; Comm Volntr; Chrch Yth Grp; DARE; Jr Ach; Pep Squd; Pep Bnd; Forensic Science; Physical Therapy; Ohio U; Shawnee State U

FISHER III, THEODORE C; BOWERSTON, OH; CONOTTON VALLEY JR/SR HS; (JR); 4H Awd; Sci Fairs; Comm Volntr; 4-H; Scouts; Bskball (J); Yrbk (R); Dental Field; Nursing; Kent State

FITHEN, KRISHELE L; TORONTO, OH; EDISON HS; (JR); Hnr Roll; Ntl Beta Clb; Prom Com; Skiing (V); Track (V); Wt Lftg (J); Jefferson Community College; Kent State

FITZPATRICK, KELLY; HUDSON, OH; HUDSON HS; (JR); Hnr Roll; MVP; Nat Hon Sy; Comm Volntr; Peer Tut/Med; Emplmnt; Key Club; Sign Clb; Chr; Fld Hky (VJCL); Lcrsse (J); Sftball (J); Sch Ppr (R); Key Club Junior Representative; Miami U; Ohio U

FLAD, RACHEL; GROVEPORT, OH; BISHOP HARTLEY HS; (JR); Hnr Roll; Nat Hon Sy; St of Mnth; WWAHSS; Comm Volntr; Peer Tut/Med; Chrch Yth Grp; Svce Clb; Bskball (V CL); Lcrsse (V L); Diocesan Youth Council; Youth to Youth; Forensic Science; West Virginia U; George Washington U

FLAHERTY, ELLEN; CINCINNATI, OH; NORTHWEST HS; (JR); F Lan Hn Soc; Hi Hnr Roll; Hnr Roll; Nat Hon Sy; WWAHSS; Comm Volntr; Peer Tut/Med; ArtClub; Key Club; Dnce; Sccr (J); Irish Dancer for 9 Years; Zoology; Marine Biology; U of North Carolina At Wilming.; Thomas More College

FLAMM, LAURA; HILLIARD, OH; HILLIARD DAVIDSON HS; (JR); F Lan Hn Soc; Hi Hnr Roll; Hnr Roll; Nat Hon Sy; WWAHSS; Yth Ldrshp Prog; Comm Volntr; Spec Olymp Vol; Chrch Yth Grp; Emplmnt; Key Club; Svce Clb; SADD; French Clb; Bnd; Lcrsse (V L); Sccr (JC); Stu Cncl (R); Yrbk (R); College of William & Mary Chancellor Academy; Key Club Class Rep; PR Next Year; Neuroscience; College of William and Mary

FLEMING, TASHA N; RUSSELLS POINT, OH; INDIAN LAKE HS; (FR); Hnr Roll; Perf Att; Peer Tut/Med; Drma Clb; Key Club; Chr; SP/M/VS; Scr Kpr (J); Sftball (J); Wt Lftg (J); Business Major; Psychology; Bowling Green State U; Ohio State U

FLETCHER, ARSENIO; DAYTON, OH; MEADOWDALE HS; (JR); Hnr Roll; Nat Hon Sy; Perf Att; Chrch Yth Grp; Bnd

FLETCHER, SARAH K; MANSFIELD, OH; TEMPLE CHRISTIAN SCH; (JR); Sci Fairs; Chrldg (V); Vllyball (V); Nursing; Capital U; Ashland U

FLETCHER III, JAMES; DAYTON, OH; DAYTON EARLY COLLEGE AC; (SO); Hi Hnr Roll; Hnr Roll; Perf Att; St Schl; St of Mnth; Peer Tut/Med; Chrch Yth Grp; Emplmnt; Mus Clb; Outdrs Clb; ROTC; Bnd; Ch Chr; SP/M/VS; Ftball (J); Lcrsse (J); Wt Lftg (J); Stu Cncl (P); Yrbk (P); Student of the Year; Sinclair Community College Young Scholar; Medical Technology, Pre-Med; Sinclair Community College, Wright State U; Penn State U

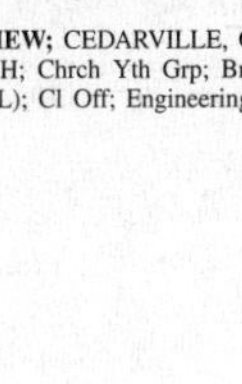
Fisher, Clyde M I
Benedictine HS
Cleveland, OH

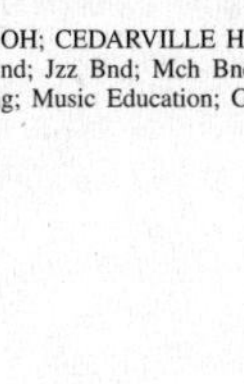
Fetty, Art
Edison HS
Toronto, OH

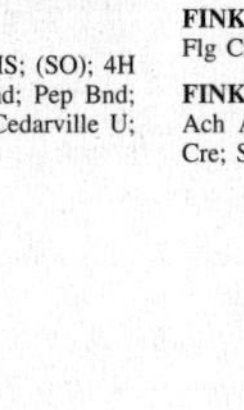
Fava, Quillen
North Royalton HS
North Royalton, OH

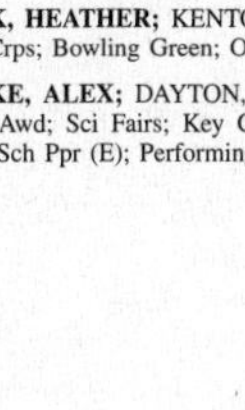
Farley, Jessica
Midview HS
Grafton, OH

National
Honor Roll
Spring 2005

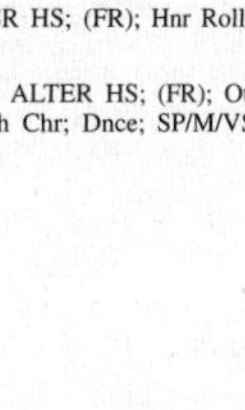
Farkas, Catherine E
Brunswick HS
Brunswick, OH

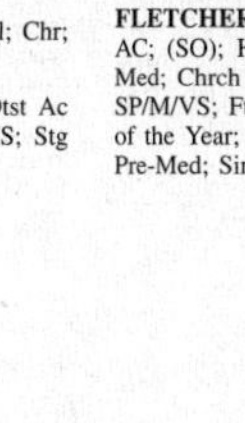
Ferguson, Scott
Milford HS
Milford, OH

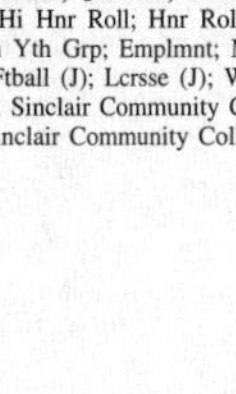
Fiorentino Jr, Brian
Mc Kinley HS
Niles, OH

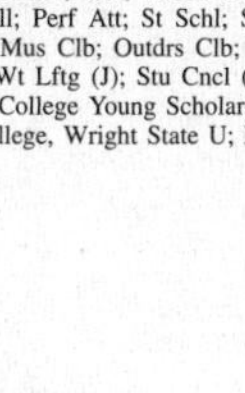
Fisher, Deborah
Reading JR/SR HS
Cincinnati, OH

FLORES, JESSICA L; CLEVELAND, OH; HEALTH CAREERS CTR; (SO); Ctznshp Aw; Hi Hnr Roll; Hnr Roll; Nat Mrt Fin; Otst Ac Ach Awd; Sci Fairs; St of Mnth; Yth Ldrshp Prog; Comm Volntr; Peer Tut/Med; Red Cr Aide; Drma Clb; Emplmnt; Mth Clb/Tm; Off Aide; Photog; Spch Team; SADD; Tchrs Aide; Stu Cncl (R); Yrbk (E); Physical Education Leader; Emergency Room Nurse; Labor and Delivery Nurse; Kent State U; Cuyahoga Community College

FLOWERS, DONOVAN; DAYTON, OH; CTRVILLE HS; (SR); Pres Sch; Salutrn; Peer Tut/Med; DARE; DECA; Emplmnt; Key Club; Pep Squd; Prom Com; Spanish Clb; Chr; Dnce; Tennis (V L); 1st in the State for Ad Campaign; Junior Leadership Academy (DECA); Marketing; Bachelor's; U of Kentucky; U of Tennessee

FLOYD, LLORALYN; AKRON, OH; BUCHTEL HS; (FR); Perf Att; WWAHSS; Comm Volntr; Peer Tut/Med; Chrch Yth Grp; Emplmnt; Off Aide; ROTC; Ch Chr; Bskball (J); Business Administration; U of Akron

FOOTE, KYLE D; GENEVA, OH; GENEVA SECONDARY SCH; (SO); Hnr Roll; Perf Att; WWAHSS; Comm Volntr; Chrch Yth Grp; Drma Clb; Bnd; Chr; Ch Chr; Mch Bnd; Skiing (V); Highest Praise (US Choral Traveling Christian Group); Malone College

FORBES, ASHLEY; AVON LAKE, OH; AVON LAKE HS; (FR); Hnr Roll; Pres Ac Ftns Aw; Chrch Yth Grp; Key Club; Bnd; Bskball (L); Sccr (J); Sftball (J); Cl Off (S); Stu Cncl (R); Middle School Education; Marine Biology

FORSTEIN, SABRINA; GENEVA, OH; MADISON HS; (JR); Hnr Roll; Perf Att; Pres Ac Ftns Aw; WWAHSS; Tchrs Aide; Chr; Cr Ctry (V); Track (V); Physical Therapy; Athletic Training; Ashland U

FORSTEIN, SAMANTHA; GENEVA, OH; MADISON HS; (JR); Hnr Roll; Perf Att; St of Mnth; WWAHSS; Key Club; Lib Aide; Chr; Graphic Design; The Art Institute of Pittsburgh; Ohio Institute of Photography and Technology

FOULKS, BRITTANY; DOYLESTOWN, OH; CHIPPEWA HS; (FR); Ctznshp Aw; Hnr Roll; Pres Sch; Sci Fairs; Comm Volntr; DARE; Scouts; Svce Clb; SADD; Bnd; Chr; Mch Bnd; SP/M/VS; Sftball (J); DARE Award; 2 Gold Presidential Academic Awards; Teacher; Computer Engineering; Ohio State U; Akron U

FOUREMAN, RACHEL E; GREENVILLE, OH; GREENVILLE HS; (FR); 4H Awd; Hi Hnr Roll; WWAHSS; 4-H; Chrch Yth Grp; DARE; Key Club; Off Aide; Spanish Clb; Ch Chr; Stg Cre; Who's Who of American High School Students

FOUSS, ASHLEY L; LOWELL, OH; MARIETTA HS; (JR); Hi Hnr Roll; Hnr Roll; Kwnis Aw; WWAHSS; Comm Volntr; Key Club; Off Aide; Prom Com; SADD; Sccr (V); Otterbein College; Marietta College

FRANCIS, SAMANTHA M; GROVE CITY, OH; GROVE CITY HS; MS; Hnr Roll; Otst Ac Ach Awd; Comm Volntr; Chrch Yth Grp; Drma Clb; Bnd; Chr; Dnce; Mch Bnd; Skiing; Stu Cncl (R); CR (R); Zoology; Drama/Acting; The Arts Institute

FRANK, REBECCA S; WESTLAKE, OH; HOME SCH; (SR); Perf Att; Sci Fairs; Yth Ldrshp Prog; Comm Volntr; Chrch Yth Grp; Emplmnt; Fr of Library; Photog; Tchrs Aide; SP/M/VS; Sftball; Swmg; Sch Ppr (E); English Major; Malone College

FRANKART, BENJAMIN R; TIFFIN, OH; SENTINEL VOC SCH; (SR); U of Dayton

FRANKLIN, TAYONA L; COLUMBUS, OH; SOUTH HIGH URBAN AC; (SR); Hnr Roll; Perf Att; Chrch Yth Grp; Emplmnt; Tchrs Aide; Ch Chr; Drl Tm; Scr Kpr; CAIR Ohio Award; Early Childhood Development; Columbus State Community College; Ohio Dominican U

FRANTZ, JAIMIE; NILES, OH; MC KINLEY HS; (FR); Ctznshp Aw; Hi Hnr Roll; Hnr Roll; MVP; Nat Mrt LOC; Otst Ac Ach Awd; Perf Att; Pres Sch; Sci Fairs; St of Mnth; Comm Volntr; FTA; Svce Clb; Italian Clb; Bnd; Bskball (JC); Track (V L); Engineering; Physical Therapist; Stanford U; Texas Tech U

FRANTZ, NOELLE B; PAINESVILLE, OH; RIVERSIDE HS; (JR); 4H Awd; Hi Hnr Roll; Hnr Roll; Nat Hon Sy; Otst Ac Ach Awd; WWAHSS; Yth Ldrshp Prog; Comm Volntr; Peer Tut/Med; 4-H; AL Aux Girls; Chrch Yth Grp; DARE; Drma Clb; Emplmnt; Tmpl Yth Grp; German Clb; Bnd; SP/M/VS; Chrldg (V C); Yrbk (E, R); Academic Letter Winner; National Honors Society Member; Biomedical Engineering

FRANZ, RYAN E; PAINESVILLE, OH; RIVERSIDE HS; (JR); Hnr Roll; Otst Ac Ach Awd; WWAHSS; Chrch Yth Grp; Key Club; Prom Com; Tchrs Aide; Bnd; Ch Chr; Psychology; Sociology; Ohio U; Ohio Northern U

FREED, BENJAMIN L; LIMA, OH; BATH HS; (FR); Ctznshp Aw; Hnr Roll; MVP; Otst Ac Ach Awd; St of Mnth; Chrch Yth Grp; DARE; Quiz Bowl; Bsball; Bskball; Ftball (J); Track (V); Engineering; Lawyer; Ohio State; Michigan State

FREEMAN, JACOB; LANCASTER, OH; (JR); Hnr Roll; St of Mnth; WWAHSS; DARE; Key Club; Off Aide; Svce Clb; Latin Clb; Cr Ctry (C); Track (V); Wrstlg (V); Yrbk; Nursing; Mortuary Science; Hocking Technical College; Cincinnati School of Mortuary Science

FREEMAN, MELISSA; LANCASTER, OH; LANCASTER HS; (JR); Hi Hnr Roll; Hnr Roll; St of Mnth; WWAHSS; Peer Tut/Med; Lib Aide; Tchrs Aide; Latin Clb; Modern/Classical Languages; English; Ohio State U; The U of Findley

FREEMAN, TORRANCE; DAYTON, OH; MEADOWDALE HS; (SO); Hi Hnr Roll; Hnr Roll; Nat Mrt LOC; Otst Ac Ach Awd; WWAHSS; Peer Tut/Med; Emplmnt; Bsball (V); Ftball (J); National Merit Finalist; Computer Engineering; Business Administration; Purdue; Wright State U

FREER, ALEXANDER S; WARREN, OH; CHAMPION HS; (JR); Ctznshp Aw; Hi Hnr Roll; St of Mnth; WWAHSS; Key Club; Bnd; Jzz Bnd; Mch Bnd; Bsball (V); Cr Ctry (V L); U of Notre Dame; United States Military Academy-West Point

FREEZE, ELIZABETH A; DAYTON, OH; ARCHBISHOP ALTER HS; (JR); Hi Hnr Roll; Otst Ac Ach Awd; WWAHSS; Comm Volntr; Chrch Yth Grp; Drma Clb; Jr Cls League; Key Club; P to P St Amb Prg; SADD; Latin Clb; SP/M/VS; Stg Cre; Sftball (V L); Vllyball; Secretary / Latin Club; History / International Studies

FREY, ALYSSA; TERRACE PARK, OH; MARIEMONT HS; (SO); Hnr Roll; St of Mnth; Comm Volntr; Key Club; Bnd; Clr Grd; Mch Bnd; Pep Bnd; Golf (V); Lcrsse (V); Spirit Club; Vet; Culinary Arts; Ohio U; Tennessee

FRIESEN, JUSTIN; DALTON, OH; CTRL CHRISTIAN SCH; (SO); Chr; Orch; SP/M/VS; Sccr (JC); Anesthesiology; Medical Research; U of British Columbia; Mc Gill U

FROMAN, KRISTEN M; CINCINNATI, OH; NORTHWEST HS; (JR); Hnr Roll; WWAHSS; Comm Volntr; Hab For Humty Volntr; Chrch Yth Grp; Key Club; P to P St Amb Prg; Tchrs Aide; Chrldg (V); Stu Cncl (R); CR (R); Pediatrician; U of Cincinnati; U of Kentucky

FROST, CHRISTIAN; CINCINNATI, OH; NORTHWEST HS; (JR); Hnr Roll; WWAHSS; ArtClub; DARE; Key Club; Sccr (V CL); Stu Cncl (R); CR (R); 1st Team All League FAUC-Soccer; All City-Honorable Mention; Business; Rice U; Howard U

FRUSTOS, ALLY; ALLIANCE, OH; ALLIANCE HS; (SO); Hnr Roll; Sci Fairs; WWAHSS; Peer Tut/Med; Spec Olymp Vol; Chrch Yth Grp; Key Club; Off Aide; Tchrs Aide; Chr; SP/M/VS; PP Ftbl; Vllyball (V); Stu Cncl (T); Yrbk (P); Key Club; Student Senate; Education; Special Education; Kent State U; Ohio U

FUHRMAN, SUZANNE; HAMILTON, OH; STEPHEN T BADIN HS; (SR); Hnr Roll; WWAHSS; Comm Volntr; Peer Tut/Med; ArtClub; Drma Clb; Emplmnt; Key Club; Foreign Clb; SP/M/VS; Tennis (V L); Key Club Treasurer; Bowling Team; Wittenberg U

FULLER, KATHRYN R; WILLARD, OH; WILLARD HS; (MS); Hnr Roll; Nat Hon Sy; Sci Fairs; St of Mnth; Comm Volntr; AL Aux Girls; Bnd; Mch Bnd; Chrldg (J); Midwest Talent Search-SAT Taker in 7th Gr; Emergency Medicine; Physician Specializing in Trauma; Ohio State U; U North Carolina (Tarheels)

FURER, JOSEPH; RIDGEWAY, OH; RIDGEMONT HS; (JR); Hi Hnr Roll; Hnr Roll; WWAHSS; Yth Ldrshp Prog; Emplmnt; Prom Com; Spanish Clb; Bsball (V); Sch Ppr (R); Yrbk (R); Physical Therapy; Education; U of Findlay; Ohio State U

FURR, BRANDON W; PLYMOUTH, OH; PLYMOUTH HS; (SR); Hnr Roll; Nat Hon Sy; Otst Ac Ach Awd; St of Mnth; Comm Volntr; ArtClub; Chrch Yth Grp; FCA; Prom Com; Foreign Clb; Bsball (V L); Bskball (V L); Golf (V L); History Club; Computer Engineering; Computer Science; Ashland U; Akron U

FURROW, DANIELLE; TROY, OH; TROY HS; (JR); Ctznshp Aw; Hi Hnr Roll; Hnr Roll; Perf Att; Pres Ac Ftns Aw; Sci Fairs; Comm Volntr; DARE; Emplmnt; Off Aide; Prom Com; Vsity Clb; Cr Ctry (V C); Track (V); CR (R); Principal's List; Pre-Med; Boston U; Duke U

FURY, ROBERT; CHAGRIN FALLS, OH; CHAGRIN FALLS HS; Hi Hnr Roll; Nat Hon Sy; Nat Stu Ath Day Aw; Otst Ac Ach Awd; BPA; Chrch Yth Grp; Bnd; Mch Bnd; Ftball; GAA (J); Lawyer; Cleveland State U; Case Western U

FURZ, BROOKE; NORTH ROYALTON, OH; NORTH ROYALTON HS; (FR); WWAHSS; Peer Tut/Med; DARE; Key Club; Snowboard & Dance; Lifeguard; Pilot; Business; Ohio State U; Ohio U

GABOR, JASZMIN; CLEVELAND, OH; GARFIELD HEIGHTS HS; (SO); Hnr Roll; Comm Volntr; Chr; Renaissance Award Winner; Public Communications; Business/Law

GADBERRY, KRISTI; TIFFIN, OH; OLD FORT HS; (FR); Hnr Roll; St of Mnth; 4-H; Quiz Bowl; Bnd; Chr; Vllyball (J); Teaching; Accounting

GAGLIARDI, MARISSA; PAINESVILLE, OH; PERRY HS; (FR); Hi Hnr Roll; Otst Ac Ach Awd; WWAHSS; Comm Volntr; Hab For Humty Volntr; Peer Tut/Med; Key Club; Mar Art (V); Sftball (JV); Swmg (JV); Vllyball (JV); Wt Lftg (V); Stu Cncl (R); CR (R); Silver Medal at CSU Karate Tournament; Pediatrician, Photojournalism; Education; Miami of Ohio; New York U

GAINES, SANDRA; LORAIN, OH; SOUTHVIEW HS; (SR); Hnr Roll; Nat Mrt Sch Recip; Chrch Yth Grp; Tchrs Aide; Medical; LCCC; Youngstown U

GAINEY JR, DEREK; YOUNGSTOWN, OH; UNITED LOCAL HS; (JR); Hi Hnr Roll; Hnr Roll; MVP; Otst Ac Ach Awd; Perf Att; Sci/Math Olympn; St of Mnth; Yth Ldrshp Prog; Comm Volntr; Chrch Yth Grp; Key Club; Mth Clb/Tm; Wdwrkg Clb; Spanish Clb; Bsball (V); Bskball (V L); Ftball (V); Wt Lftg (V); Stu Cncl (R); Law; Ohio State U; Penn State U, Youngstown State U

GALBRAITH, TIMOTHY; STREETSBORO, OH; CRESTWOOD HS; (JR); Hnr Roll; St of Mnth; WWAHSS; DARE; Scouts; Tchrs Aide; Wdwrkg Clb; Sch Ppr (R, P); Mental Health Counselor; Psychology; U of Akron; Baldwin Wallace College

GALLAGHER, AMBER; YOUNGSTOWN, OH; AUSTINTOWN FITCH HS; (SR); Nat Hon Sy; WWAHSS; Yth Ldrshp Prog; Comm Volntr; Peer Tut/Med; Dbte Team; Drma Clb; NtlFrnscLg; Spch Team; SADD; SP/M/VS; Stg Cre; Cr Ctry (V CL); Track (V CL); Cl Off (P); Speech & Debate Team President; National Honor Society; Bachelor's Degree Marketing; Bachelor's Degree Sales; Youngstown State U; U of Akron

GALLAUGHER, DANIELLE R; JACKSON, OH; JACKSON HS; (JR); 4H Awd; Hi Hnr Roll; Hnr Roll; MVP; Otst Ac Ach Awd; St of Mnth; Comm Volntr; Peer Tut/Med; 4-H; BPA; Emplmnt; Jr Ach; Lib Aide; Off Aide; Prom Com; Quill & Scroll; Bskball (J); Sftball (V CL); Adv Cncl (R); Member of Student Health; Dental Hygienist; Radiology; U of Rio Grande; Shawnee State U

GALLO, RACHELE C F; AKRON, OH; COPLEY HS; (FR); Hi Hnr Roll; Hnr Roll; Chrch Yth Grp; DARE; Spanish Clb; Bnd; Mch Bnd; Sftball (J); Member of Young Life; Math; Education; Baldwin Wallace College; Case Western Reserve U

GALLOWAY, HEATHER M; MC DERMOTT, OH; NORTHWEST HS; (SO); Hnr Roll; WWAHSS; DARE; Pep Squd; Chr; I've Been on the P.R.I. D.E. Team; Nursing; Dental; Shawnee State U; Ohio State U

GALLOWAY, JENNIFER; WOOSTER, OH; WOOSTER HS; (SO); Hi Hnr Roll; Hnr Roll; DARE; Police Officer; Police Academy

GANGER, NATASHA; TROY, OH; TROY HS; (SO); Hi Hnr Roll; Hnr Roll; Nat Hon Sy; Pres Ac Ftns Aw; Chrch Yth Grp; DARE; Key Club; Bnd; Chr; Dnce; Mch Bnd

GARCIA, ARRIKA C; DAYTON, OH; BEAVERCREEK HS; (JR); Hnr Roll; MVP; Perf Att; WWAHSS; Peer Tut/Med; P to P St Amb Prg; Tchrs Aide; Sccr (J); Ambassador for Peter's Photography; Fashion Merchandising; Fashion Marketing; Virginia Marti College of Art & Design

GARDNER, KIMBERLY; SHELBY, OH; SHELBY SR HS; (SR); 4H Awd; Hnr Roll; Perf Att; WWAHSS; 4-H; Lttrmn Clb; Ntl FFA; Prom Com; Track (V L); Vllyball (J); FFA - Reporter; Agricultural Communications; Ohio State U Mansfield

GARDNER, MELINA M; FAYETTE, OH; GORHAM FAYETTE SCH; (JR); 4H Awd; Hnr Roll; Perf Att; Sci Fairs; Comm Volntr; 4-H; ArtClub; Chrch Yth Grp; Cmptr Clb; DARE; Emplmnt; Prom Com; Sci Clb; Bnd; Pep Bnd; Sftball (V); Track (V); Vllyball (J); Stu Cncl (S); Yrbk (P); Boxing; Physical Therapy; Entertainment Law; Defiance; U of Toledo

GARGANO, MARISSA C; NILES, OH; MC KINLEY HS; (FR); Hi Hnr Roll; WWAHSS; Key Club; Off Aide; Sccr (V)

GARGASZ, ALEXIS; YOUNGSTOWN, OH; POLAND MS; (MS); Hnr Roll; Comm Volntr; Chrch Yth Grp; DARE; Pep Squd; Scouts; SADD; Bskball; Swmg; Other Cultures; Art; Michigan State; New York U

GARRETT, ALLISON R; CAMDEN, OH; PREBEL SHAWNEE; (SR); Hi Hnr Roll; Hnr Roll; Perf Att; Sci Fairs; St of Mnth; WWAHSS; Comm Volntr; Peer Tut/Med; Emplmnt; Lib Aide; Off Aide; Tchrs Aide; Chr; Chrldg (J); PP Ftbl (J); Scr Kpr (J); Sftball (VJ); Vllyball (J); Student of the Month; National Honor Society Nominee; Elementary Education; Accounting; Miami U

GARTRELL, MELISSA; LEESVILLE, OH; CONOTTON VALLEY JR/SR HS; (JR); WWAHSS; Prom Com; Bnd; Mch Bnd; Pep Bnd; Bskball (J); Chrldg (VJ L); Track (V); Cl Off (T); 3 Years High School Honor's Band; Radiology; Hospitality; Kent; Akron

GARVIN, RAISA J; LEWIS CTR, OH; WESTERVILLE CTRL HS; (JR); Hnr Roll; Nat Hon Sy; Otst Ac Ach Awd; WWAHSS; Comm Volntr; Chrch Yth Grp; DARE; Emplmnt; Key Club; Prom Com; Drl Tm; Track (V L); Cl Off (P); Stu Cncl (R); Sch Ppr (R); Vice President of National Sorority of Phi Delta Kappa, Inc Xinos Club; Pre-Law; Business Management; Hampton U; Cornell U

Gargasz, Alexis
Poland MS
Youngstown, OH

Francis, Samantha M
Grove City HS
Grove City, OH

Frustos, Ally
Alliance HS
Alliance, OH

GASE, ALLISON H; TIFFIN, OH; TIFFIN COLUMBIAN HS; (FR); Hi Hnr Roll; Hnr Roll; MVP; Nat Mrt LOC; Perf Att; Pres Sch; St of Mnth; Yth Ldrshp Prog; Comm Volntr; Chrch Yth Grp; DARE; Jr Ach; Mod UN; Off Aide; Chr; Dnce; Chrldg (C); Track (V L); Vllyball (C); State Qualifier in Choir; 47th in GTCTM (Math Award); Medical Field; Dennison U (Ohio)

GASTON, VALQUISA; COLUMBUS, OH; LINDEN-MC KINLEY HS; (FR); Hi Hnr Roll; Hnr Roll; Otst Ac Ach Awd; St of Mnth; Chrch Yth Grp; DARE; Off Aide; Pep Squd; Ch Chr; Chrldg (J); Track (J); Stu Cncl (R); Accountant; Lawyer; Florida State U; Miami State U

GATES, FELICIA; CLEVELAND, OH; HEALTH CAREERS CTR; (SO); Ctznshp Aw; Hnr Roll; St of Mnth; CARE; Comm Volntr; Red Cr Aide; DARE; Dbte Team; Drma Clb; Mth Clb/Tm; Dnce; Mch Bnd; SP/M/VS; Stg Cre; Track (J); Obstetrician

GATES, MEGAN A; MONROEVILLE, OH; MONROEVILLE HS; (JR); 4H Awd; Hi Hnr Roll; Hnr Roll; WWAHSS; Comm Volntr; 4-H; Drma Clb; Emplmnt; Key Club; Ntl FFA; French Clb; SP/M/VS; Bskball (VJ); Landscape Design; Floral Design; Ohio State U

GATRELL, ANDREA; BEACH CITY, OH; FAIRLESS HS; (JR); Hnr Roll; Nat Hon Sy; WWAHSS; Comm Volntr; Spec Olymp Vol; Chrch Yth Grp; Key Club; Lib Aide; Prom Com; Bnd; Bskball (V L); Sftball (V L); Medical Field

GAU, PHILIA; HUDSON, OH; HUDSON HS; (JR); Hi Hnr Roll; Nat Hon Sy; St of Mnth; Peer Tut/Med; Emplmnt; Key Club; German Clb; Bnd; Biology; Swarthmore College; Cornell U

GAY, MELODY; HAMILTON, OH; LAKOTA WEST HS; (FR); Hi Hnr Roll; Nat Hon Sy; Chrch Yth Grp; Drma Clb; MuAlphaTh; Chr; SP/M/VS; Lcrsse (J); Voted for Nazarene Youth Council; Voice Competitions; Teaching Major; Lawyer; Ohio State U; Mount Vernon Nazarene U

GAZZO, MARIA; CLEVELAND, OH; PADUA FRANCISCAN HS; (JR); Hnr Roll; WWAHSS; Key Club; Scouts; German Clb; Teen Institute; Peer Ministry; German; Education

GEALSHA, AUBREY; MINERAL CITY, OH; BUCKEYE CAREER CTR HS; (JR); 4H Awd; Hi Hnr Roll; Hnr Roll; Nat Hon Sy; Perf Att; Yth Ldrshp Prog; 4-H; Lttrmn Clb; P to P St Amb Prg; CR (R); Yrbk (E, R, P); 4-H - 3 Time County Winner; 4-H-Top 3 State Superior Award Winner; Bachelor of Fine Arts; Media Arts and Animation; Pittsburg Art Institute; Bradley Art Institute

GEARHEART, MARY; WARREN, OH; CHAMPION HS; (SR); Hnr Roll; WWAHSS; Yth Ldrshp Prog; Comm Volntr; Chrch Yth Grp; Emplmnt; Key Club; Pep Squd; Prom Com; SADD; Tchrs Aide; SP/M/VS; Stg Cre; Mar Art (J); Skiing (V); Sccr (J); Track (V); Stu Cncl (R); Yrbk (R, P); Champion Teens Care; Disciples of Christ; Psychology; Education; Kent State Trumbull

GEDDAM, LAKSHMI M; MASON, OH; WILLIAM MASON HS; (JR); Hi Hnr Roll; Nat Hon Sy; Sci Fairs; Comm Volntr; Hosp Aide; Peer Tut/Med; ArtClub; FTA; Dnce; National Art Honor Society; Pre-Medicine; MD; U of Akron; Drexel U

GEE, BRANDY; MANSFIELD, OH; MANSFIELD SR HS; (FR); Hnr Roll; Otst Ac Ach Awd; Sci Fairs; St of Mnth; Comm Volntr; Chrch Yth Grp; Emplmnt; Flg Crps; Vllyball; Cl Off (S); Stu Cncl (R); Tyger Ambassadors; Power of the Pen; Business / Corporate Law; Criminal Justice; Roanoke College; U of North Carolina Charlotte

GENTRY, HANNAH; COLUMBUS, OH; BEECHCROFT HS; (SR); All Am Sch; Hi Hnr Roll; Hnr Roll; Nat Hon Sy; Nat Ldrshp Svc; Perf Att; St of Mnth; Comm Volntr; DARE; Drma Clb; Emplmnt; Fr of Library; NYLC; Off Aide; Tchrs Aide; Pre-Law; Business Management; Kent State; Akron U

GEORGE, AUSTIN-MICHAEL; HUNTSVILLE, OH; INDIAN LAKE HS; (JR); Hi Hnr Roll; Hnr Roll; Kwnis Aw; MVP; Perf Att; Sci Fairs; WWAHSS; Yth Ldrshp Prog; Comm Volntr; Chrch Yth Grp; Drma Clb; Key Club; Lttrmn Clb; Prom Com; Sci Clb; Tchrs Aide; Vsity Clb; SP/M/VS; Bsball (V L); Bskball (V L); Ftball (V L); Vsy Clb (V L); Wt Lftg (V); Cl Off (R); NHS; Boys State; Criminal Justice; Psychology; U of Toledo; Wright State U

GEORGE, BRYANNA; BARBERTON, OH; BARBERTON HS; (FR); Hnr Roll; MVP; Nat Hon Sy; Otst Ac Ach Awd; Perf Att; St of Mnth; WWAHSS; Comm Volntr; Red Cr Aide; Chrch Yth Grp; DARE; Emplmnt; Jr Ach; Lib Aide; Off Aide; SADD; Tchrs Aide; Dnce; Drl Tm; Bskball (C); Track (V L); Maintained an Honor Roll Status Since Grade School; MVP for Basketball; College Basketball; Business or Medical Studies; Tennessee; Connecticut U

GEORGE, CATHERINE P; DELAWARE, OH; RUTHERFORD B HAYES HS; (JR); Hnr Roll; Perf Att; Comm Volntr; Key Club; French Clb; Bnd; Jzz Bnd; Mch Bnd; Pep Bnd; Music Education; Math Education; Capital U; Marietta College

GERBER, DARREN L; APPLE CREEK, OH; CTRL CHRISTIAN SCH; (JR); Ctznshp Aw; Hnr Roll; Perf Att; Pres Ac Ftns Aw; Comm Volntr; Chess; Chrch Yth Grp; DARE; FCA; Bskball (V); Sccr (V); Tennis (V); Cl Off (R); CR (R)

GERBER, JESSICA; MARYSVILLE, OH; MARYSVILLE HS; (SO); 4H Awd; Hnr Roll; Otst Ac Ach Awd; Perf Att; Comm Volntr; 4-H; Bnd; Mch Bnd; Pep Bnd; National Latin Examination-Outstanding; 1st Clarinet Chair-Symphonic Board; Classics (Greek and Latin); Mathematics; Northwestern U, Evanston, Illinois; Miami U, Oxford, Ohio

GERBICK, LINDSEY S; LAGRANGE, OH; KEYSTONE HS; (JR); Ctznshp Aw; Hi Hnr Roll; Hnr Roll; Nat Hon Sy; Pres Sch; Sci Fairs; 4-H; Chrch Yth Grp; DARE; Emplmnt; FCCLA; Lib Aide; Off Aide; Tchrs Aide; Vllyball (V L); AWANAS-Church Youth Group (Six Years); Sports Medicine; Magazine Editing/Marketing; Ohio State U; Kent State U

GERMAK, STEVE; CANTON, OH; GLEN OAK HS; (JR); Hi Hnr Roll; Hnr Roll; Nat Hon Sy; WWAHSS; Comm Volntr; Peer Tut/Med; Chrch Yth Grp; Key Club; Scouts; Tchrs Aide; International Clb; Chr; Ch Chr; Cr Ctry (J); Boy Scouts; Altar Server; Engineering; U of Dayton; Ohio State U

GERTZ, CODY J B; CINCINNATI, OH; READING HS; (SO); Hi Hnr Roll; Hnr Roll; Nat Hon Sy; Yth Ldrshp Prog; Comm Volntr; Peer Tut/Med; Emplmnt; Key Club; Outdrs Clb; SADD; Stg Cre; Stu Cncl (R); CR (P); Sch Ppr (E); A Member of FCCLA; A Former Member of National Jr. Honor Society; Business/Law; Miami Oxford U; U of Cincinnati

GESLAK, PAUL; CANTON, OH; EARLY COLLEGE TIMKEN HS; (MS); Ctznshp Aw; Perf Att; St of Mnth; Chess; Jr Ach; Early College High School; Associate's Degree By 2009; Stark State College

GIANDOMENICO, MICHAEL; STEUBENVILLE, OH; STEUBENVILLE HS; MS; Bsball (VJ); Bskball (VJ); Ftball (VJ); Golf (VJ); Track (VJ)

GIBB, COURTNEY; SALEM, OH; SALEM HS; (SO); Hnr Roll; Peer Tut/Med; Chr; Dnce

GIBBONS, CAITLIN; TOLEDO, OH; ST URSULA AC; (SO); Hnr Roll; Comm Volntr; Chrch Yth Grp; Drma Clb; Dnce; Bskball (J); Physical Therapist; Athletic Trainer; Valparaiso U; U of Toledo

GIBNEY, ARDEN M; WESTERVILLE, OH; WESTERVILLE NORTH HS; (SR); Gov Hnr Prg; Hi Hnr Roll; Nat Hon Sy; Pres Ac Ftns Aw; Pres Sch; St Schl; St of Mnth; WWAHSS; Emplmnt; Key Club; Quill & Scroll; Svce Clb; Adv Cncl (R); Sch Ppr (E, R, P); Yrbk (E, R, P); State Board Award of Merit; President's Award of Academic Excellence, Ohio U Gateway Scholarship; Will Attend: Ohio U E W Scripps School of Journalism

GIBSON, JESSICA L; COLUMBUS, OH; COLUMBUS ALT HS; (JR); Ctznshp Aw; Hi Hnr Roll; Nat Hon Sy; Pres Sch; WWAHSS; Yth Ldrshp Prog; Comm Volntr; Spec Olymp Vol; Chess; Emplmnt; Key Club; SP/M/VS; Sftball (J); Track (L); In the Know / Enjoy Theatre; Anime Club / Published Writer; Forensic Science; Engineering

GIBSON, KELSIE; FINDLAY, OH; FINDLAY HS; (FR); Hnr Roll; Otst Ac Ach Awd; St of Mnth; Yth Ldrshp Prog; Bnd; Mch Bnd; Orch; Pep Bnd; Stu Cncl (T); TI; STAND; Law; Medicine; Bowling Green State U; U of Findlay

GIBSON, MEGAN; TIFFIN, OH; TIFFIN COLUMBIAN; (FR); Hnr Roll; MVP; Perf Att; St of Mnth; USAA; Peer Tut/Med; Sftball (J); Vllyball (J); Wt Lftg

GIBSON, ROSS; MARIETTA, OH; MARIETTA HS; (SR); Hnr Roll; WWAHSS; Comm Volntr; Chrch Yth Grp; Emplmnt; Key Club; Golf (J); Track (J); Aerospace Engineer; Embry-Riddle Aeronautical U

GIFFORD, BEN; COLUMBUS, OH; THOMAS WORTHINGTON HS; (FR); Hi Hnr Roll; MVP; St of Mnth; Yth Ldrshp Prog; Emplmnt; Mth Clb/Tm; Ftball; Lcrsse (V L); Wt Lftg; Wrstlg; Stu Cncl (R); CR (R); Completed Leadership Plus Clinic; Leadership Award MS Wrestling; Pre-Law; Business; Duke U; U of Virginia

GILBERT, CHANTEL; ELYRIA, OH; ELYRIA HS; (SR); Ctznshp Aw; Hi Hnr Roll; Hnr Roll; Nat Hon Sy; Otst Ac Ach Awd; WWAHSS; ArtClub; Emplmnt; Key Club; Tchrs Aide; Spanish Clb; Sccr (J); Yrbk; Ultimate Frisbee Club; Psychology; Ithaca College

GILCHRIST, MICHAEL; ELYRIA, OH; ELYRIA HS; (SO); Ctznshp Aw; Hnr Roll; Perf Att; St of Mnth; Cartoon Artist; Chef; Lorain County Community College; Oberlin College

GILCREST, STEPHANIE; ROOTSTOWN, OH; SOUTHEAST HS; (SR); Hnr Roll; 4-H; Emplmnt; Mus Clb; Off Aide; Bnd; Mch Bnd; Pep Bnd; Skiing; Business Management; Dental Hygienist; Kent State U

GILKERSON, DONALD; THOMPSON, OH; LEDGEMONT HS; (SO); 4H Awd; Otst Ac Ach Awd; Comm Volntr; 4-H; DARE; Scouts; Bsball (V L); Bskball (J L); Ftball (V L); Culinary Arts; Pennsylvania Culinary Institute

GILL, ALEXIS; CORTLAND, OH; MATHEWS HS; (SO); Hi Hnr Roll; Hnr Roll; Comm Volntr; Red Cr Aide; Key Club; Lttrmn Clb; Prom Com; Spanish Clb; Bskball (J); Vllyball (V); Play Club Volleyball- 2 Seasons; Penn State U; New York U

GILLESPIE, CRISSY; MONROEVILLE, OH; MONROEVILLE HS; (SR); Hi Hnr Roll; Hnr Roll; Nat Hon Sy; Perf Att; Sci Fairs; WWAHSS; Comm Volntr; Aqrium Clb; ArtClub; Emplmnt; Key Club; Kwanza Clb; Lib Aide; Ntl FFA; NYLC; Chrldg (J); Gmnstcs; Track (V L); Cl Off (P); Stu Cncl (R); Play Guitar - Outside of School; FFA Committee Chairman - 3 Yrs; Pharmacy; Veterinarian; U of Toledo

GILLESPIE, LISA; JACKSON, OH; WELLSTON HS; (JR); Hi Hnr Roll; Nat Hon Sy; St of Mnth; WWAHSS; 4-H; Civil Air Pat; Drma Clb; Bnd; Ch Chr; Stg Cre; Sftball (J); Pastoral Ministries; Music; World Harvest Bible College; The Ohio State U

GILLOGLY, W NICHOLAS; ALBANY, OH; ALEXANDER HS; (FR); 4H Awd; Hnr Roll; Sci/Math Olympn; Comm Volntr; 4-H; Chrch Yth Grp; Spanish Clb; Bsball (J); Hsbk Rdg (V); Sccr (J); Civil War Reenacting; Mechanical Engineering; Civil Engineering; West Point

GILMER, SHAQUITA; TOLEDO, OH; WOODWARD HS; (SO); Hi Hnr Roll; WWAHSS; Peer Tut/Med; Sch Ppr (R); Outstanding News Reporter Award; Nursing; Law; Toledo U; Ohio State

GILRONAN, ELISSA N; WARREN, OH; CHAMPION HS; Hi Hnr Roll; Perf Att; Comm Volntr; Chrch Yth Grp; Emplmnt; Key Club; Scouts; Bnd; Dnce; Mch Bnd; Bskball; Track (J); Majorette; Doctor; Kent State U; Ohio State U

GILSON, MARY C; NORTH OLMSTED, OH; MAGNIFICAT HS; (JR); Hi Hnr Roll; Pres Sch; St of Mnth; WWAHSS; Drma Clb; Mus Clb; Chr; Dnce; SP/M/VS; Skiing; Stu Cncl (R); CR (R); Musical Theater; New York U; Ithaca College

GINN, TANA S; MANSFIELD, OH; MANSFIELD SR HS; (SR); Hnr Roll; MVP; Otst Ac Ach Awd; WWAHSS; DARE; Emplmnt; Chr; Bskball (V); Track (V); Vllyball (V); Girls Basketball-Final Four; Nursing; Physical Education; U of Louisville; Clark Atlanta U

GIPSON, KAREN; BARBERTON, OH; BARBERTON HS; (SO); CARE; Chrch Yth Grp; Chr; SP/M/VS; Writer; Singer; North Carolina Central U; U of North Carolina

GISSINGER JR, CHRIS; CANAL FULTON, OH; NORTHWEST HS; (FR); Hnr Roll; Chess; Bnd; Jzz Bnd; Mch Bnd; Pep Bnd; Bsball; CR (R); Academic Challenge; Music; History; Ohio State U; Kent State U

GIVENS, SUMMER R; CLEVELAND, OH; THE INTERNATIONAL PREP HS; (SR); Hnr Roll; Valdctrian; Yth Ldrshp Prog; Comm Volntr; Chrch Yth Grp; Emplmnt; Bnd; Ch Chr; Drm Mjr; Chrldg (J); Stu Cncl (S); Early Childhood Education; Alabama A & M U; The Ohio State U

GLENN, ASHLEY N; BREMEN, OH; FAIRFIELD UNION HS/FAIRFIELD CAREER CTR; (JR); Hnr Roll; MVP; Comm Volntr; Red Cr Aide; DARE; Latin Clb; Chr; Sftball (J); Yrbk (P); 2 Years Latin Club; Anything in Medical Field

GLENN, JASMINE; LIMA, OH; SOUTH MS; (MS); Hnr Roll; MVP; Nat Stu Ath Day Aw; Perf Att; St of Mnth; Comm Volntr; Peer Tut/Med; ArtClub; Chrch Yth Grp; DARE; Drma Clb; Emplmnt; Kwanzia Clb; Mus Clb; SADD; Ch Chr; Drl Tm; SP/M/VS; Bskball; Sftball; Vllyball; Master's Degree; The U of California; Columbus U

GOEHRING, AMANDA J; FREMONT, OH; FREMONT ROSS HS; (JR); Hnr Roll; Comm Volntr; DARE; Beauty Pageant State Winner; Auto-Collision; Cosmetology; Owens Tech

GOHEEN, STACEY L; CINCINNATI, OH; NORTHWEST HS; (SO); Hnr Roll; DARE; Emplmnt; Key Club; Sccr (V); NWHS Page Award 2003-2004 for JV Soccer-Outstanding Player; Interior Design; Ohio State, Miami U; U of Cinti, U of Bay

GOINS, CHRISTOPHER C; TROY, OH; TROY HS; (SR); WWAHSS; Hab For Humty Volntr; Emplmnt; Key Club; Tchrs Aide; French Clb; Stg Cre; Sccr (J); International Business & Marketing; Ohio State U

GOINS, JOSHUA; REYNOLDSBURG, OH; HARVEST PREPARATORY SCH; (SR); Ctznshp Aw; Hi Hnr Roll; Nat Hon Sy; St of Mnth; WWAHSS; Comm Volntr; ArtClub; Chrch Yth Grp; Emplmnt; Chr; Bskball (VJ); Ftball (V L); Cl Off (V); Digital Design Major; U of Cincinnati

GOISER, JENAVIONE; CLEVELAND, OH; COLLINWOOD HS; (JR); Ctznshp Aw; Hnr Roll; Nat Hon Sy; Perf Att; St of Mnth; Comm Volntr; Peer Tut/Med; Emplmnt; NYLC; Outdrs Clb; Pep Squd; Chrldg (J); Stu Cncl (R); Citizen Organization; Music Performance - Vocal; Theatre Arts; Central State U; Hampton U

GOLDBERG, JACQUELYNE; CINCINNATI, OH; INDIAN HILL HS; (JR); Hnr Roll; Nat Hon Sy; Yth Ldrshp Prog; Comm Volntr; Peer Tut/Med; DECA; Emplmnt; Prom Com; Svce Clb; Fld Hky (V L); Track (V); Cl Off (P); Ohio Girls Buckeye State; Mayerson Foundation Leadership; International Business; Spanish; U of Miami; Boston U/Tulane U

GOLEY, WHEELER S; VANDALIA, OH; WAYNN HS; (SO); Bnd; Cl Off (T); Sch Ppr (E); Bowling Awards; Engineering (Mechanical); Ohio State

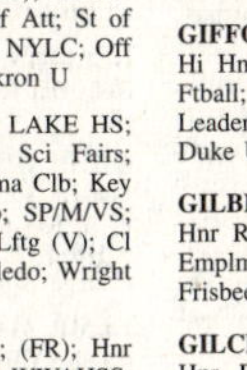

Gill, Alexis
Mathews HS
Cortland, OH

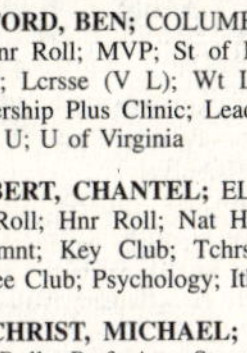

Gaston, Valquisa
Linden-Mc Kinley HS
Columbus, OH

National
Honor Roll
Spring 2005

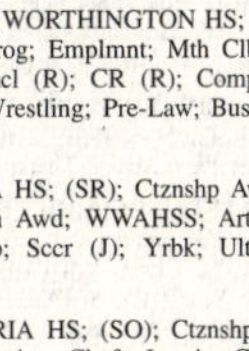

Gase, Allison H
Tiffin Columbian HS
Tiffin, OH

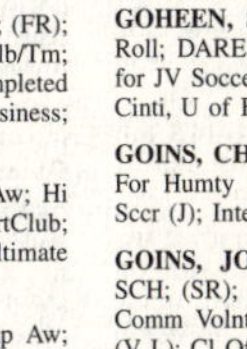

Glenn, Ashley N
Fairfield Union HS/Fairfield Career Ctr
Bremen, OH

GOMES, GABRIEL I S; RICHMOND HTS, OH; RICHMOND HEIGHTS HS; (FR); Ctznshp Aw; Hi Hnr Roll; Otst Ac Ach Awd; WWAHSS; Peer Tut/Med; Emplmnt; Key Club; P to P St Amb Prg; Bnd; Jzz Bnd; Mch Bnd; Pep Bnd; Track (V L); Named Outstanding Freshman Reader; People to People Delegate; Engineer; Medical Research; Johns Hopkins; Case Western Reserve U

GOMEZ, JAMIE; MARIETTA, OH; MARIETTA HS; (JR); F Lan Hn Soc; Hi Hnr Roll; Kwnis Aw; WWAHSS; Key Club; Spanish Clb; Spanish Interpreter / Teacher; Interpreter for the Deaf - Taking Classes; Marietta College; Ohio U

GONZALES, TIONNA; COLUMBUS, OH; EASTLAND CAREER CTR; (SR); Nat Hon Sy; Perf Att; Peer Tut/Med; Red Cr Aide; Chrch Yth Grp; Drl Tm; Eastland Diversity Group (Vice President); Eastland Step Team; Early Childhood Development; Dental; Wright State U

GONZALEZ, KATLIN; YOUNGSTOWN, OH; JACKSON MILTON HS; (FR); Hi Hnr Roll; WWAHSS; Key Club; Chrldg (V); Dentistry; Nursing; Ohio State; Youngstown State U

GONZALEZ, MOLLY S; HAMMONDSVILLE, OH; BEAVER LOCAL HS; (SR); Hi Hnr Roll; Hnr Roll; Nat Hon Sy; WWAHSS; Drma Clb; Ntl Beta Clb; Prom Com; SADD; Acpl Chr; Chr; SP/M/VS; Chrldg (J); Stu Cncl (R); CR (R); Sch Ppr (R); Volunteer for American Cancer Society; Volunteer for St. Jude's Children's Hospital; Forensic Science

GOOD, BRIAN; URBANA, OH; URBANA HS; (FR); DARE; Bsball (L); Urbana Baseball League Champion Two Years in a Row ('02, '03) Asst. Coach Little League; Engine Building/Rebuilding; Auto Body Development/Repair; Nascar Technical Institute; Universal Technical Institute

GOOD, LEVI; STRYKER, OH; STRYKER HS; (JR); Hnr Roll; Nat Hon Sy; Emplmnt; Prom Com; Bnd; Jzz Bnd; Mch Bnd; Pep Bnd; Cl Off (P); Business Management

GORDON, RICARDO; CINCINNATI, OH; HARMONY HS; (JR); Ctznshp Aw; Hnr Roll; MVP; Perf Att; St of Mnth; Comm Volntr; ArtClub; Cmptr Clb; DARE; Drma Clb; Prom Com; SADD; Tchrs Aide; Vsity Clb; SP/M/VS; Stg Cre; Bsball (V); Bskball (J); Ftball (V); Wt Lftg (V); CR (V); Yrbk (P); Computer Tech; Graphic Design; Georgia Tech; Cincinnati

GORNIAK, KELLEY; DAYTON, OH; BEAVERCREEK HS; (JR); Hnr Roll; Nat Hon Sy; Comm Volntr; Hosp Aide; ArtClub; Drma Clb; Emplmnt; French Clb; Bnd; Mch Bnd; Orch; SP/M/VS; Ice Sktg (V); Yrbk (E, P); Being Identified as Gifted in Art; Ice Skating Awards; Fashion Design / BS Degree; Fine Arts Print Making / BFA Degree; U of Cincinnati- DAAP; Rhode Island School of Design

GOSHDIGIAN, DEANNA; CINCINNATI, OH; NORTHWEST HS; (JR); WWAHSS; Comm Volntr; Chrch Yth Grp; Key Club; International Clb; Sccr (VL); Yrbk (R, P); Junior Soccer League; Top 10% of Class; Broadcast Journalism; Education

GOSTICH, MARTIN; WILLOUGHBY, OH; WILLOUGHBY SOUTH HS; (JR); Ctznshp Aw; Hnr Roll; Nat Stu Ath Day Aw; Key Club; Golf (V); Willoughby South Summer; Baseball League; Science; Pre-Medical; Ohio State U

GOTTHARDT, DANIEL; CARROLL, OH; BCHS; (SR); Hnr Roll; WWAHSS; Quiz Bowl; Sci Clb; French Clb; Sch Ppr (R); PR For French Club; BA Creative Writing; U of Evansville

GOUGH, LADENA; MADISON, OH; MADISON HS; (FR); Hnr Roll; St of Mnth; DARE; Emplmnt; Off Aide; Tchrs Aide; Vllyball (J); Business; Cooking

GRABLE, ERIKA; CUYAHOGA FALLS, OH; CUYAHOGA FALLS HS; Hnr Roll; Comm Volntr; DARE; Chr; Vllyball; CR (R); 2005 II - Summit Soap Box Derby; Bolich Middle School Peer Tutoring; U of Akron

GRABSKI, ASHLEY M; SEVEN HILLS, OH; PADUA FRANCISCAN HS; (JR); Hi Hnr Roll; Hnr Roll; Nat Hon Sy; Hab For Humty Volntr; Chrch Yth Grp; Key Club; SADD; Spanish Clb; Chr; Ch Chr; SP/M/VS; Sftball (J); CR (R); Junior Retreat Leader, Renewal Retreat Leader; CYO Varsity Basketball, Reachout; Pre-Med; Nursing; John Carroll U; Xavier U

GRACE, BETH; LISBON, OH; LISBON DAVID ANDERSON HS; (JR); WWAHSS; DARE; Tchrs Aide; Spanish Clb; Pediatrics; Nursing; Kent State; Hannah Mullins College

GRACE, BRYSTLE; WOOSTER, OH; WAYNE CTY SCH CAREER CTR; (JR); Hi Hnr Roll; Medical Assisting; Surgical Technician; High Tech Institute

GRADERT, AMANDA; BROADVIEW HTS, OH; NORTH ROYALTON HS; (SO); Perf Att; Pres Ac Ftns Aw; St of Mnth; WWAHSS; Key Club; Dnce; Chrldg (V); Master's; PhD; Ohio State U; Loyola U

GRADY, AMANDA N; WASHINGTON COURT HOUSE, OH; WASHINGTON HS; (FR); Hnr Roll; St of Mnth; Lib Aide; Bnd; Mch Bnd; Pep Bnd; Stg Cre; Chrldg (J); Tennis (J); Track (V)

GRADY, DANIELLE K; HILLIARD, OH; HILLIARD DARBY HS; (JR); Hnr Roll; Nat Hon Sy; Key Club; Spanish Clb; Orch; Key Club Vice President 05-06; Accounting; Finance; Ohio Northern U; Miami U

GRAFTON, MARJORIE M; TORONTO, OH; EDISON HS; (JR); Hi Hnr Roll; Nat Hon Sy; WWAHSS; Peer Tut/Med; Drma Clb; Emplmnt; Ntl Beta Clb; Prom Com; Spanish Clb; Bnd; Chr; Dnce; SP/M/VS; Track (V); Stu Cncl; Psychology; Criminology

GRAHAM, DANIEL E; PIQUA, OH; PIQUA HS; (SR); Hnr Roll; St of Mnth; Emplmnt

GRAHAM, EMILIE K; DEFIANCE, OH; DEFIANCE SR HS; (SR); Hnr Roll; Nat Hon Sy; DECA; Drma Clb; Prom Com; Acpl Chr; Bnd; Dnce; Mch Bnd; Swmg (V L); Vllyball (JC); Marketing; Miami U

GRAHAM, LAUREN D; NEW CARLISLE, OH; TECUMSEH HS; (SO); Hi Hnr Roll; WWAHSS; Chrch Yth Grp; Bnd; Chr; Ch Chr; Stg Cre; Bskball (J); Sftball (V); Vllyball (V)

GRAHAM, TANESHA; DAYTON, OH; MEADOWDALE HS; (SO); Hi Hnr Roll; Peer Tut/Med; Chrldg (V); Track (V); Stu Cncl (R); CR (R); Pharmacy Technician; Physician's Assistant; Kentucky State U; Michigan State U

GRAVES, KAITLYN B; CANTON, OH; TIMKEN/EARLY COLLEGE HS; (FR); Ctznshp Aw; Hnr Roll; St of Mnth; Degree in Game Design; Major in Animation & Gaming; Westwood College Online

GRAY, JAKE; NAPOLEON, OH; NAPOLEON HS; (JR); Hnr Roll; Chess

GRAY, KIRBIE; STEUBENVILLE, OH; HARDING MS; (MS); Hnr Roll; Perf Att; Comm Volntr; Hosp Aide; Peer Tut/Med; Drma Clb; Key Club; Mus Clb; SADD; Tchrs Aide; Vsity Clb; Bnd; Mch Bnd; Pep Bnd; SP/M/VS; Tennis (J); Vsy Clb (J); SADD; Helps; Judge; Lawyer; Ohio U; Harvard U

GRAY, STACIE M; COLUMBUS, OH; (SR); Hnr Roll; Peer Tut/Med; Prom Com; Freshman Mentor; Terrific Teen; Nursing; Mt. Carmel College of Nursing; Capital U

GREEN, ANESHA; CLEVELAND, OH; MARTIN LUTHER KING HS; (MS); Hi Hnr Roll; Hnr Roll; Nat Hon Sy; St of Mnth; Comm Volntr; DARE; Bnd; Drl Tm; Lady Legacy; Pediatrician; Ohio State

GREEN, STEFAN B; ST CLAIRSVILLE, OH; ST CLAIRSVILLE HS; (SO); Ctznshp Aw; Hi Hnr Roll; Otst Ac Ach Awd; Pres Sch; Comm Volntr; Chrch Yth Grp; Tchrs Aide; Bsball (J); Bskball (J); Ftball (J); Wt Lftg (J); Cl Off (V); Engineering; Accounting; The Ohio State U; Youngstown State U

GREEN, STEPHANIE O; LORAIN, OH; LORAIN ADMIRAL KING HS; (FR); Drma Clb; Orch; SP/M/VS; Writing; Journalist / Writer; Oberlin College

GREENE, ADAM; COLUMBUS, OH; GRANDVIEW HEIGHTS HS; (JR); Hnr Roll; MVP; Perf Att; Pres Ac Ftns Aw; St of Mnth; Comm Volntr; Peer Tut/Med; Spanish Clb; Bnd; Mch Bnd; Pep Bnd; Sccr (V CL); Architecture; Sociology; U of Maryland; Catholic U

GREENE, LAURA; PICKERINGTON, OH; PICKERINGTON HS NORTH; (JR); Hi Hnr Roll; Nat Hon Sy; WWAHSS; Chrch Yth Grp; Drma Clb; FCA; Spanish Clb; Chr; Ch Chr; Orch; SP/M/VS; Track (J L); Sport & Wellness Management; Nutrition/Health; Otterbein College; Miami U of Ohio

GREENLEE, JESSICA A; BARNESVILLE, OH; BARNESVILLE HS; (JR); F Lan Hn Soc; Hnr Roll; Otst Ac Ach Awd; WWAHSS; Drma Clb; FTA; Key Club; Forest Ranger; Game Warden; Hocking Technical College

GREGORY, ALEXANDRA C; COLUMBUS, OH; BISHOP HARTLEY HS; (FR); Hnr Roll; Pres Sch; Sci Fairs; St of Mnth; WWAHSS; Comm Volntr; Chrch Yth Grp; DARE; Scouts; Ch Chr; Dnce; SP/M/VS; Ballet Dancer; Architect / Physical Therapist; Ohio State U; Loyola U

GREGORY, VICTORIA L; BROOK PARK, OH; MIDPARK HS; (JR); Hi Hnr Roll; Hnr Roll; Nat Hon Sy; Perf Att; Polan's Career Center-Cosmetology; Masso Therapy; Ohio State U; Cleveland State

GRENFELL, ELIZABETH; MEDINA, OH; MEDINA HS; (JR); Hi Hnr Roll; MVP; Nat Hon Sy; Otst Ac Ach Awd; St of Mnth; Comm Volntr; AL Aux Girls; Chrch Yth Grp; Emplmnt; Key Club; SADD; Spanish Clb; SP/M/VS; Sccr (JC); Stu Cncl (R); CR (R); Sch Ppr (E); Huddle; Journalism; Advertising; Ohio State U; Miami U

GREVE, MELISSA A; CINCINNATI, OH; MOTHER OF MERCY HS; (SO); Hnr Roll; Drma Clb; Key Club; Chr; SP/M/VS; Stg Cre; Guitar Lessons; SADD Member; Xavier U; Mount St Joe

GRIFFIN, ELLIOT; DAYTON, OH; NORTHMONT HS; (FR); Hnr Roll; Pres Sch; WWAHSS; Peer Tut/Med; Tchrs Aide; Dnce; Bskball (J L); Sccr (J L); Stu Cncl (R); Yrbk (P); Student Athletic Training Aide; Teen Summit; Athletic Training; Psychology; U of North Carolina At Chapel Hill; Florida A & M U

GRIFFIN, JESSICA; SHERRODSVILLE, OH; CONOTTON VALLEY JR SR HS; (JR); Hi Hnr Roll; Hnr Roll; Nat Hon Sy; WWAHSS; Peer Tut/Med; Off Aide; Photog; Prom Com; Ch Chr; Stu Cncl (R); Sch Ppr (E, R, P); National Honor Society; United States Achievement Academy; Education; Biology; Malone College; Walsh U

GRIFFITH, ASHLEY; MAUMEE, OH; MAUMEE HS; (SR); Hnr Roll; MVP; Nat Hon Sy; Hosp Aide; Chrch Yth Grp; DECA; Emplmnt; Sci Clb; Tchrs Aide; Vsity Clb; Spanish Clb; Chrldg (J); Gmnstcs (V); Sftball (L); 2nd Place at Nationals for DECA; Business; Education; U of Toledo; Bowling Green State U

GRIFFITH, KRISTEN; CLEVELAND, OH; EUCLID HS; (SO); Ctznshp Aw; Hi Hnr Roll; Hnr Roll; Otst Ac Ach Awd; Pres Sch; WWAHSS; Chrch Yth Grp; Emplmnt; Key Club; Chr; Dnce; SP/M/VS; Stg Cre; Swmg (V)

GRIFFITH, TIM W; COLUMBUS, OH; GRANDVIEW HEIGHTS HS; (JR); Ctznshp Aw; Hnr Roll; Nat Ldrshp Svc; Otst Ac Ach Awd; St of Mnth; WWAHSS; Peer Tut/Med; Emplmnt; Off Aide; Tchrs Aide; Golf (V L); Sch Ppr (R, P); Martial Arts; 1st Degree Brown Belt; Journalism; Broadcast Journalism; Ohio U; Ohio State U

GRIGGER, MELISSA; HAMILTON, OH; LAKOTA EAST HS; (SO); Hi Hnr Roll; WWAHSS; Comm Volntr; Chrch Yth Grp; MuAlphaTh; Scouts; Cr Ctry (V)

GRIGOLI, JESSICA; STREETSBORO, OH; STREETSBORO HS; (FR); Hnr Roll; St of Mnth; Comm Volntr; DARE; Ntl Beta Clb; Dnce; BETA club

GRILLOT, COLLEEN E; VERSAILLES, OH; VERSAILLES HS; (JR); Hnr Roll; WWAHSS; Track (V)

GRIMM, LAUREN; GENOA, OH; GENOA AREA HS; (SO); Hnr Roll; Chrch Yth Grp; DARE; Prom Com; Quiz Bowl; Scouts; Spanish Clb; Bnd; Chr; Ch Chr; Flg Crps; Cl Off (R); Stu Cncl (R); CR (R); Editor's Choice Award/Poetry.Com; Psychology; Criminal Justice; Wright State U; Bowling Green State U

GRIZZARD, BRANDYN; MASSILLON, OH; WASHINGTON HS; (FR); Hnr Roll; Nat Hon Sy; WWAHSS; Chrch Yth Grp; FCA; Off Aide; Bnd; Ch Chr; Jzz Bnd; Ftball (J); Wt Lftg (J); Adv Cncl (S); Business

GROSS, GENEVA K; JACKSON, OH; OAK HILL HS; (SR); Hi Hnr Roll; Nat Hon Sy; Salutrn; WWAHSS; Comm Volntr; Red Cr Aide; 4-H; ArtClub; Chrch Yth Grp; DARE; Emplmnt; FCCLA; Off Aide; Sci Clb; Cl Off (V); Sch Ppr (R); Yrbk (E, R, P); Ohio First Scholarship Winner; Bachelor's of Science in Nursing; U of Rio Grande

GRUBER, SCOTT D; EDISON, OH; MT GILEAD HS; (SO); Hnr Roll; Comm Volntr; 4-H; Emplmnt; FCA; Bskball (J); Ftball (J); Track (V); Physical Therapy; Athletic Training

GRUEY, STEWART; KINGSVILLE, OH; (FR); 4-H; Fr of Library; Ftball (J); Tennis (J); Altar Server; Vacation Bible School Helper; History; Walsh U; Kent U Ashtabula Campus

GRUHN, MATTHEW; STRONGSVILLE, OH; PADUA FRANCISCAN HS; (SR); Hi Hnr Roll; Nat Hon Sy; Nat Mrt Fin; Pres Ac Ftns Aw; WWAHSS; Yth Ldrshp Prog; AL Aux Boys; Dbte Team; Mod UN; Off Aide; Quiz Bowl; German Clb; Sch Ppr (R); National Society of High School Scholars; Intramural Football; Law; Princeton U, Princeton, NJ; Yale U, New Haven, CT

GULLETT, JESSICA R; BETHEL, OH; BETHEL-TATE HS; (JR); Hnr Roll; Perf Att; Comm Volntr; Chrch Yth Grp; Quiz Bowl; Sci Clb; Bnd; SHOCK - Students Helping Our Community's Kinship; Skills USA; Advanced Medical Imaging; Hocking College

GULLEY, J MICHAEL; SHADYSIDE, OH; ST JOHN CTRL HS; (JR); Hnr Roll; Jr Rot; Hosp Aide; Emplmnt; Sci Clb; Svce Clb; Spanish Clb; SP/M/VS; Cl Off (V); Stu Cncl (T); CR (R); Pharmacy; Ohio Northern U; Duquesne U

GULLION, BILLY; WAVERLY, OH; WAVERLY HS; (SO); 4H Awd; Hi Hnr Roll; Hnr Roll; WWAHSS; 4-H; Wdwrkg Clb; Bskball (J); Golf (V); Stu Cncl (R)

GUMP, HEATHER L; NEW MATAMORAS, OH; FRONTIER HS; (JR); F Lan Hn Soc; Hnr Roll; Nat Hon Sy; USAA; WWAHSS; Comm Volntr; BPA; FCA; Key Club; Off Aide; Prom Com; Tchrs Aide; Spanish Clb; Bskball (V); Vllyball (J); Physical Education Major; Day Care Minor; Shawnee Baptist College

GUMP, MATTHEW; TOLEDO, OH; WHITMER HS; (FR); Peer Tut/Med; Chrch Yth Grp; FCA; Scouts; Bnd; Jzz Bnd; Mch Bnd; Pep Bnd; Construction; Architecture

GUNASEKERA, NICOLE S; DAYTON, OH; MIAMI VALLEY SCH; (SO); Hi Hnr Roll; MVP; Nat Hon Sy; Sci Fairs; WWAHSS; Yth Ldrshp Prog; Comm Volntr; Hab For Humty Volntr; Hosp Aide; Chrch Yth Grp; DARE; Emplmnt; Mod UN; Off Aide; Tchrs Aide; Dnce; Mar Art; Swmg (V); Stu Cncl (R); Lit Mag (R); Sch Ppr (R); Yrbk (E, R, P); Multiple School Record Holder in Swimming; Physician; Northwestern U; Yale U

GUPTA, ANSHULI; ZANESVILLE, OH; BISHOP ROSECRANS HS; (SO); Hi Hnr Roll; Hnr Roll; MVP; Nat Hon Sy; Pres Sch; WWAHSS; Comm Volntr; DARE; Key Club; Lttrmn Clb; Quiz Bowl; Tmpl Yth Grp; Vsity Clb; Bnd; Sftball (V); Tennis (V L); Stu Cncl (R); Muskingum County Community Youth Foundation; Mock Trial; Medicine; Law; Johns Hopkins U; Ohio State U

Graham, Tanesha
Meadowdale HS
Dayton, OH

Gomez, Jamie
Marietta HS
Marietta, OH

Grafton, Marjorie M
Edison HS
Toronto, OH

GURKA, MATTHEW J; GREENWICH, OH; SOUTH CTRL HS; (JR); Hnr Roll; 4-H; Chrch Yth Grp; Emplmnt; Bnd; Mch Bnd; Pep Bnd; Northern Ohio SERC Outstanding Student Achievement Award; Computer Engineering; National Technical Institute for the Deaf; Rochester Institute of Technology

GURM, CARLY V; MORROW, OH; LITTLE MIAMI HS; (SR); Hnr Roll; Nat Hon Sy; Perf Att; Yth Ldrshp Prog; Comm Volntr; ArtClub; Sci Clb; Clb; Bnd; Jzz Bnd; Mch Bnd; Pep Bnd; Hsbk Rdg; Nursing; Otterbein College

GUSEILA, CRISTIANA; CLEVELAND, OH; NORMANDY HS; (MS); All Am Sch; Ctznshp Aw; Otst Ac Ach Awd; Perf Att; St of Mnth; Comm Volntr; Chess; Chrch Yth Grp; DARE; Drma Clb; Off Aide; Tchrs Aide; Bnd; Ch Chr; Dnce; Bsball (J); Bskball (J); Scr Kpr (J); Sccr (J); Sftball (J); Swmg (J); Tennis (J); Track (J); Stu Cncl (V); CR (S); Law School; College Partnership; Cuyahoga Community College

GUTTNER, MYRA P; CANAL WINCHESTER, OH; BLOOM-CARROLL HS; (SR); 4H Awd; Hi Hnr Roll; MVP; Nat Hon Sy; Pres Ac Ftns Aw; Sci Fairs; WWAHSS; 4-H; Emplmnt; FBLA; P to P St Amb Prg; Sci Clb; Tchrs Aide; Spanish Clb; Track (V); Vllyball (VJC); Yrbk (R, P); School Clubs- Science, Spanish, Business; Business; Pharmacy; Ohio Northern U; Butler U

GUY, JUSTIN; OREGON, OH; CLAY HS; (JR); Hnr Roll; MVP; Perf Att; St of Mnth; BPA; FCA; Vsity Clb; French Clb; Bskball (J); Ftball (V); Sccr (V CL); 1st Team All-League - Soccer; Business Management; Sports Management; Ohio State U; Ohio U

HAAS, NIKI; BYESVILLE, OH; MEADOWBROOK HS; (SO); Hnr Roll; Otst Ac Ach Awd; Perf Att; Sci Fairs; St of Mnth; Peer Tut/Med; 4-H; Chrch Yth Grp; DARE; Tchrs Aide; Bnd; PP Ftbl (J); Sccr (V); Dental Assistant; Dental Hygienist; Ohio State U; Ohio U

HADDAD, NICOLE; NORTHWOOD, OH; NORTHWOOD HS; (JR); Ctznshp Aw; Hi Hnr Roll; Hnr Roll; Nat Hon Sy; Perf Att; St of Mnth; WWAHSS; Yth Ldrshp Prog; Red Cr Aide; DARE; Emplmnt; Key Club; Prom Com; French Clb; SP/M/VS; PP Ftbl (J); Sftball (V); Vllyball (V); Stu Cncl (R); Yrbk (R, P); Buckeye Girls State; National Junior Leadership Conference; U of Toledo; Bowling Green State U

HADI, KEVIN; WARREN, OH; WARREN JFK HS; (JR); Hi Hnr Roll; Nat Hon Sy; Otst Ac Ach Awd; Pres Sch; Yth Ldrshp Prog; Comm Volntr; Mth Clb/Tm; MuAlphaTh; Sci Clb; Ch Chr; SP/M/VS; Academic Awards; Music Achievements; Medicine; Science; Northwestern U; Washington U in St. Louis

HAFER, JOHN; CINCINNATI, OH; COLERAIN HS; (SR); F Lan Hn Soc; Hnr Roll; MVP; Nat Hon Sy; Perf Att; WWAHSS; Comm Volntr; Peer Tut/Med; Key Club; Off Aide; Tchrs Aide; French Clb; Ftball (V L); Swmg (V L); Adv Cncl (R); CR (R); Business Degree; MBA; Centenary College of Louisiana

HAFFNER, EMILY J; CINCINNATI, OH; MC AULEY HS; (SO); Hi Hnr Roll; Nat Hon Sy; Perf Att; Comm Volntr; Peer Tut/Med; Spec Olymp Vol; Key Club; Scouts; French Clb; Dnce; Orch; Stg Cre; Superior Award - U of Cincinnati Math Bowl; Service Award 2 Years; Prosthetics / Orthotics; Occupational Therapist; U of Cincinnati; Xavier U

HAGANS, DESHAY M; DAYTON, OH; COLONEL WHITE HS FOR THE ARTS; (SO); Hi Hnr Roll; Hnr Roll; Otst Ac Ach Awd; Sci Fairs; Valdctrian; WWAHSS; Peer Tut/Med; Emplmnt; Key Club; P to P St Amb Prg; Tchrs Aide; Sftball (J); Cl Off (S); President of Key Club; Ohio State Young Scholar; Medical; Business; Harvard U; Princeton U

HAHN, ALYCIA; CINCINNATI, OH; WESTERN HILL HS; (FR); Hnr Roll; MVP; DARE; Drma Clb; P to P St Amb Prg; Vllyball (J); Stu Cncl (S); Journalism; Communications; New York U; Ohio State U

HAHN, JEANETTE; CRIDERSVILLE, OH; WAPAKONETA HS; (JR); Hi Hnr Roll; Hnr Roll; Chrch Yth Grp; French Clb; Academic Letter & Pin; 3-D Award; Restaurant Management; Hotel Management; U of Akron

HAIGH, ELIZABETH T; CARROLL, OH; WILLIAM V FISHER CATHOLIC HS; (SO); 4H Awd; Hi Hnr Roll; MVP; WWAHSS; Comm Volntr; Hab For Humty Volntr; 4-H; Chrch Yth Grp; Emplmnt; Key Club; Bskball (VJ L); PP Ftbl (J); Sccr (V L); Track (V L); Peer Advocates, Pro-Life Club; Volunteer for Therapeutic Horseback Riding, 8 Years; U of Dayton

HAINES, BRITTANY; URBANA, OH; GRAHAM HS; (SO); Hi Hnr Roll; Hnr Roll; Sci Fairs; Hab For Humty Volntr; Chrch Yth Grp; Emplmnt; Sccr (J); Graham Manatee Snorkel Trip; S.T.A.R.S. Abstinence Group; Forensic Science; Criminal Justice; Sinclair Community College; Clark State Community College

HALE, CHAD; ENON, OH; GREENON HS; (SR); Hnr Roll; Perf Att; Sci Fairs; Chrch Yth Grp; DARE; Emplmnt; Lttrmn Clb; Ntl FFA; Bsball (V); Bskball (V); Ftball (V); Stu Cncl (R); 4 Yrs. Perfect Attendance; Education; Shawnee State U

HALEY, ANDREA; BELLEFONTAINE, OH; INDIAN LAKE HS; (SR); Hnr Roll; Nat Hon Sy; Otst Ac Ach Awd; Pres Sch; Valdctrian; WWAHSS; Peer Tut/Med; Drma Clb; Emplmnt; Key Club; Off Aide; Prom Com; Sci Clb; Tchrs Aide; Spanish Clb; Chr; SP/M/VS; Vllyball (J); Yrbk (E); Honda/OSU Math Merit Medalist; Franklin B Walter Scholarship Nominee; Pharmacy; U of Toledo

HALEY, TONYA M; BELLEFONTAINE, OH; INDIAN LAKE HS; (FR); Hi Hnr Roll; Hnr Roll; Perf Att; Pres Ac Ftns Aw; WWAHSS; 4-H; Drma Clb; Emplmnt; Key Club; Sci Clb; Tech Clb; Spanish Clb; Chr; SP/M/VS; Vllyball (J); Cl Off (P)

HALL, JASON M; COLUMBIANA, OH; COLUMBIANA HS; (SR); Hnr Roll; MVP; WWAHSS; Comm Volntr; Emplmnt; Golf (V CL); Honors and AP Classes; PSEO Student at Kent State U; Business / Finance; Slippery Rock U

HALL, JOSH; BARNESVILLE, OH; BARNESVILLE HS; (SO); Hnr Roll; Pres Ac Ftns Aw; Comm Volntr; Chrch Yth Grp; Wdwrkg Clb; An Active Member - Sons Of The American Legion; Ohio State U; Ohio U

HALL, MEGAN; CAREY, OH; CAREY SCH; (SO); Hi Hnr Roll; Hnr Roll; Nat Hon Sy; DECA; Emplmnt; SADD; Spanish Clb; Yrbk (R, P); DECA; Business Law; U of Findlay

HALL, MICHAEL; ELYRIA, OH; MIDVIEW HS; (JR); Hi Hnr Roll; Nat Hon Sy; Nat Sci Aw; St of Mnth; USAA; WWAHSS; Hab For Humty Volntr; Peer Tut/Med; Civil Air Pat; Emplmnt; FCA; ROTC; Scouts; Tchrs Aide; Bnd; Mch Bnd; Pep Bnd; Cr Ctry (J); Ftball (J); Track (L); Wt Lftg (J); AM Vets National Merit Award; Military Order of World Wars National Merit Award; Meteorology / Atmosphere Science; Civil Engineering; United States Air Force Academy; Ohio State U

HALL, RASHAD; DUBLIN, OH; DUBLIN JEROME HS; (JR); Hnr Roll; Yth Ldrshp Prog; Comm Volntr; ArtClub; Selected for Celebration of Excellence; Pre-Med / Biology; Mathematics; Colorado U Denver; Ohio State U

HALLER, THOMAS R; XENIA, OH; CARROLL AC; (SR); Ctznshp Aw; F Lan Hn Soc; Hnr Roll; Kwnis Aw; Nat Hon Sy; Sci Fairs; WWAHSS; Comm Volntr; Peer Tut/Med; Chess; Chrch Yth Grp; Emplmnt; Key Club; Scouts; Spanish Clb; Ch Chr; Ftball (VJ L); Wt Lftg (V); Wrstlg (J); Secretary of Key Club / Eagle Scout; VP of National Honors Society; Biomedical Engineering; Spanish; Wright State U; Ohio State U

HALLETT, KAYCEE; OAK HARBOR, OH; OAK HARBOR HS; (SO); Hnr Roll; MVP; Pres Ac Ftns Aw; Sci Fairs; St of Mnth; Chrch Yth Grp; Drma Clb; FCA; Key Club; Lttrmn Clb; Lib Aide; Vsity Clb; Foreign Clb; Chr; SP/M/VS; Cr Ctry (V L); Swmg (V L); Track (V L); Entered in Poetry Contest; High School Teacher; Author; Bowling Green State U; U of Toledo

HALTER, EDEN; SYLVANIA, OH; NORTHVIEW HS; (SO); Hnr Roll; Pep Squd; French Clb; Bnd; Mch Bnd; Pep Bnd; Chrldg (J); Early Childhood Development; Massage Therapy; Ohio State U; Bowling Green State U

HAMAD, MOHAMMAD; CLEVELAND, OH; JOHN MARSHALL HS; (JR); Ctznshp Aw; F Lan Hn Soc; Hi Hnr Roll; Hnr Roll; Nat Hon Sy; Perf Att; Sci Fairs; WWAHSS; Yth Ldrshp Prog; Hosp Aide; Peer Tut/Med; ArtClub; Chrch Yth Grp; DARE; Lib Aide; Mth Clb/Tm; NYLC; Sci Clb; Tchrs Aide; Bnd; Stu Cncl (R); Grads Net 1000 Award Winner; Math Honorary; Pharmacy; Masters Degree in Science/Math Fields; John Carroll U; Case Western Reserve U

HAMAYEL, MOHANAD A; SPRINGFIELD, OH; SPRINGFIELD NORTH HS; (SR); Hi Hnr Roll; Hnr Roll; Nat Hon Sy; Otst Ac Ach Awd; Pres Ac Ftns Aw; Comm Volntr; Peer Tut/Med; Emplmnt; Tchrs Aide; Clb; Bnd; Ch Chr; Rqtball (J); Sccr (J); Tennis (J); Vllyball (J); CR (R); Award of Academic Excellence; National Honors, High GPA; Engineer; Surgeon; Wright State U; Clark State College

HAMILTON, COURTNEY; COLUMBUS, OH; HILLIARD DAVIDSON HS; (JR); F Lan Hn Soc; Hi Hnr Roll; Nat Hon Sy; Valdctrian; WWAHSS; Comm Volntr; Spec Olymp Vol; Emplmnt; Key Club; Prom Com; Scouts; SADD; French Clb; Ch Chr; Lcrsse (VJ L); Sccr (JC); Sftball; Stu Cncl (R); First Cut of National Merit, But Still Don't Know If I'm a Semifinalist or Not

HAMILTON, STEPHEN; COLUMBUS, OH; BEECHCROFT HS; (SO); Hi Hnr Roll; Hnr Roll; Otst Ac Ach Awd; WWAHSS; Comm Volntr; Red Cr Aide; Chrch Yth Grp; DARE; Emplmnt; Jr Ach; Ch Chr; Scr Kpr (V); Sccr (V); Swmg (V); Sch Ppr (E); 2 Year Varsity Soccer Award; Veterinarian; Chef / Culinary Arts; Ohio State U

HAMMETT, SHANTEL L M; AKRON, OH; FIRESTONE HS; (JR); Hnr Roll; Otst Ac Ach Awd; WWAHSS; Comm Volntr; Chrch Yth Grp; Emplmnt; Off Aide; Pep Squd; Ch Chr; Stu Cncl (R); Member of Firestone Gospel Choir; Fashion Merchandising; U of Akron

HAMMOND, BENJAMIN; CINCINNATI, OH; CINCINNATI HILLS CHRISTIAN AC; (JR); Hi Hnr Roll; Hnr Roll; Nat Hon Sy; Chrch Yth Grp; Emplmnt; Bnd; Pep Bnd; Bsball (J); Bskball (VJ); Chemistry; Biomedical Engineering

HAMMOND, BRITTANY; LANCASTER, OH; LANCASTER HS; (SR); Hi Hnr Roll; Hnr Roll; WWAHSS; 4-H; Key Club; Mus Clb; Off Aide; Tchrs Aide; Latin Clb; Bnd; Jzz Bnd; Mch Bnd; Pep Bnd; Yrbk (R, P); Early Childhood Education; U of Dayton

HAMMONS, JONATHON E; LIMA, OH; LIMA SR HS; (FR); Hnr Roll; Perf Att; Chrch Yth Grp; DARE; Emplmnt; Bsball (JCL); Bskball (J); Sccr (J L); Notre Dame

HAMRICK, BRITTANY; COLUMBUS, OH; GAHANNA LINCOLN HS; (SR); Hnr Roll; Nat Hon Sy; DARE; Emplmnt; Off Aide; P to P St Amb Prg; Scouts; Voc Ind Clb Am; Skills USA Health Occupation Knowledge Bowl Winner At Local Level; Teaching; Neonatal Intensive Care; Ohio State U; Columbus State Community College

HANBY, LAURA; COLUMBUS, OH; WESTERVILLE NORTH HS; (SR); All Am Sch; Hnr Roll; Nat Hon Sy; Otst Ac Ach Awd; WWAHSS; Hosp Aide; Peer Tut/Med; Key Club; Ch Chr; English; Ohio State U; U of Notre Dame

HANDERMANN, SARA; CINCINNATI, OH; NORTHWEST HS; (SR); Hnr Roll; Nat Hon Sy; St of Mnth; WWAHSS; Comm Volntr; Peer Tut/Med; Spec Olymp Vol; Chrch Yth Grp; Emplmnt; Key Club; Off Aide; Prom Com; Ch Chr; Stu Cncl (R); Lit Mag (E); U of Rochester's Humanities & Social Science Award; Ambassador of Goodwill At Northwest; Nursing; Physical Therapy; Belmont U

HANDY, TIFFANY L; PARMA, OH; PARMA SR HS; (SR); Hi Hnr Roll; Hnr Roll; Pres Sch; Sci Fairs; WWAHSS; Yth Ldrshp Prog; Emplmnt; Off Aide; Completed 2 Yrs. of Post Secondary Educ.; Forensic Science Degree; Criminal Investigations W/Forensics; Mercyhurst College

HANKINS, KAYLA; LIMA, OH; APOLLO CAREER CTR; (SR); Hi Hnr Roll; Hnr Roll; St of Mnth; Comm Volntr; Hosp Aide; Drma Clb; Emplmnt; Tchrs Aide; Acpl Chr; Chr; SP/M/VS; Cl Off (P); Early Childhood; Law Major; Toledo U

HANUSCHAK, KAYLA; CANFIELD, OH; AUSTINTOWN FITCH HS; (FR); Hnr Roll; Spec Olymp Vol; Bnd; Mch Bnd; Bskball (JC); Vllyball (JC); 3rd Degree Black Belt Instructor-Karate; Jr. Olympic Volleyball, AAU Basketball

HARDING, DANE; YELLOW SPRINGS, OH; CEDARVILLE MHS; (SO); Hnr Roll; Perf Att; Comm Volntr; Chrch Yth Grp; Ntl FFA; Bskball (J); Cr Ctry (V L); Track (V L); Stu Cncl (R); Actor; Meteorologist

HARDING, HILLARY J; PORTSMOUTH, OH; PORTSMOUTH HS; (SO); Hnr Roll; Juvenile Diabetic with Insulin Pump; College for Health Care; College for Midwife; Shawnee State U; Ohio State U

HARDVAL, JORDAN; FOWLER, OH; MATHEWS HS; (JR); Hnr Roll; Nat Hon Sy; Perf Att; WWAHSS; Yth Ldrshp Prog; AL Aux Girls; Drma Clb; Key Club; Prom Com; Spanish Clb; Stg Cre; Vllyball (V CL); Cl Off (S); Sch Ppr (R); Yrbk (R); Literature; Psychology

HARDY, ASHLEY; LIMA, OH; LIMA SR HS; (JR); Hnr Roll; Peer Tut/Med; Prom Com; Drl Tm; Lima-UMADAOP; Nursing; Art; U of Toledo; Alabama A & M U

HARMER, TROY A; ZANESVILLE, OH; MAYSVILLE HS; (SO); Hnr Roll; Nat Hon Sy; USAA; WWAHSS; DARE; Key Club; Off Aide; P to P St Amb Prg; SADD; French Clb; Ftball (J); Mar Art (VJ); Track (VJ); Wt Lftg (J); Key Club; French Club; College; Ohio U

HARNER, ANDREW; NEW LONDON, OH; NEW LONDON HS; (JR); Hi Hnr Roll; Nat Hon Sy; St of Mnth; WWAHSS; Yth Ldrshp Prog; Peer Tut/Med; AL Aux Boys; Chess; Emplmnt; Key Club; Mod UN; French Clb; Bnd; Jzz Bnd; Mch Bnd; Pep Bnd; Cr Ctry (V L); Track (J L); Creative Writing; Music Theory/Composition; Bowling Green State U; Ohio Northern

HARP, NATOSHA; NORWALK, OH; WESTERN RESERVE HS; (FR); Hi Hnr Roll; Hnr Roll; Comm Volntr; ArtClub; Chrch Yth Grp; Lib Aide; Spanish Clb; Has Had Two Poems Published; Student of the Quarter; Veterinary; Criminal Justice; Vet Tech Institute

HARPER, JILLIAN P; CINCINNATI, OH; NORTHWEST HS; (JR); F Lan Hn Soc; Hnr Roll; Comm Volntr; ArtClub; Drma Clb; Key Club; International Clb; SP/M/VS; Stu Cncl (R); Spanish Honor Society; Forensic Science; Art; Youngstown State U; U of Cincinnati

HARPER, TIARRA M; CLEVELAND, OH; SOLON HS; (MS); Chrch Yth Grp; DARE; Dbte Team; Lib Aide; Off Aide; SADD; Tchrs Aide; Ch Chr; Dnce; Chrldg (V C); Stu Cncl (P); Yrbk (E); Broadcast Journalism; College Professor; Hampton U; Howard U

HARRELL JR, ERIC; DAYTON, OH; PATTERSON CAREER CTR; (SO); Ctznshp Aw; Hnr Roll; Perf Att; Sci Fairs; St of Mnth; Chrch Yth Grp; Ch Chr; Drl Tm; Drm Mjr; Boxing, Drums; Business Tech. Prep; Sinclair Community College

HARRIS, CLARISSA; WARREN, OH; HOWLAND HS; (JR); Hnr Roll; Perf Att; St of Mnth; Comm Volntr; Peer Tut/Med; Chrch Yth Grp; Tchrs Aide; Italian Clb; Cr Ctry (V L); Track (V); Italian Speaking Competition-3rd Place; Fundraising 5k Run-Top Finisher; Medical Field; Kent State U; Bowling Green U

HARRIS, JOHN; ASHTABULA, OH; WEST JHS; (MS); Hnr Roll; Chess; Chrch Yth Grp; Scouts; Bnd; Sccr (J); Archeology; History; Harvard U

HARRIS, MYCHAELA D; SWANTON, OH; ECOT; (SO); Hnr Roll; Otst Ac Ach Awd; WWAHSS; Tchrs Aide; Vllyball (V); Hugh O'Brian Outstanding Soph Nomination; ECOT Eagle Pride Program Nomination; Psychology; Writing-Poetry; U of Findlay; U of Bowling Green

Harris, Mychaela D
ECOT
Swanton, OH

Harmer, Troy A
Maysville HS
Zanesville, OH

Hamayel, Mohanad A
Springfield North HS
Springfield, OH

Haines, Brittany
Graham HS
Urbana, OH

Hagans, Deshay M
Colonel White HS For The Arts
Dayton, OH

National
Honor Roll
Spring 2005

Guseila, Cristiana
Normandy HS
Cleveland, OH

Hale, Chad
Greenon HS
Enon, OH

Hamrick, Brittany
Gahanna Lincoln HS
Columbus, OH

Harper, Tiarra M
Solon HS
Cleveland, OH

Harris, Clarissa
Howland HS
Warren, OH

HARRIS, NICOLE M; AKRON, OH; ELLET HS; (SO); Ctznshp Aw; F Lan Hn Soc; Hnr Roll; MVP; Perf Att; St of Mnth; Peer Tut/Med; DARE; Emplmnt; Mus Clb; Outdrs Clb; Scouts; Vsity Clb; GAA (V); Scr Kpr (V); Sftball (V); Vllyball (V)

HARRIS, QUINNDALIN M; LIMA, OH; LIMA SR HS; (SR); Hnr Roll; MVP; Otst Ac Ach Awd; Peer Tut/Med; Chrch Yth Grp; Emplmnt; Prom Com; Vllyball (J); Honors Convocation 01-02; Honors Convocation 02-03; Physical Therapy; Athletic Training; U of Toledo; Wright State U

HARRISON, BRITTANY N; IRONTON, OH; DAWSON-BRYANT HS; (FR); Comm Volntr; 4-H; Chrch Yth Grp; FCA; Ch Chr; Bskball (VJ); Sftball (V); Track (V); Vllyball (J); Teaching; Marshall U; Ohio U

HARRISON, DIONNA; STEUBENVILLE, OH; STEUBENVILLE HS; (MS); Ctznshp Aw; Hnr Roll; Nat Sci Aw; Otst Ac Ach Awd; Perf Att; Sci Fairs; Peer Tut/Med; SADD; SP/M/VS; Bskball (V L); Sftball (VJ); Track (V); Cl Off (V, S, T); Law; Technology; Ohio State U; U of Georgia

HARROLD, SCOTT M; CAREY, OH; CAREY SCH; (SO); Hnr Roll; Nat Hon Sy; Off Aide; Vsity Clb; Bsball (V L); Ftball (J); U of Findlay; Ohio State U

HARTFORD, KELSEY; MONROE, OH; MONROE JR/SR HS; (JR); Hi Hnr Roll; Hnr Roll; MVP; Nat Hon Sy; Perf Att; Pres Ac Ftns Aw; WWAHSS; Comm Volntr; Emplmnt; Off Aide; Prom Com; Tchrs Aide; Vsity Clb; Bskball (L); Chrldg (VJ L); PP Ftbl; Sftball (V CL); Vsy Clb (V); Cl Off (S); Stu Cncl (S); CR (R); Yrbk (E, R, P); Nursing; Psychology; Miami U Oxford; Bowling Green State U

HARTMAN, KRISTEN M; NORTH JACKSON, OH; JACKSON-MILTON HS; (FR); Hnr Roll; Perf Att; WWAHSS; Key Club; Yrbk (P); Perfect Attendance; Vet; Nurse; Kent State U

HARTONG, TRACY; CLEVELAND, OH; PADUA HS; (SR); Hnr Roll; Nat Hon Sy; WWAHSS; Yth Ldrshp Prog; Red Cr Aide; ArtClub; Chrch Yth Grp; Drma Clb; Key Club; French Clb; Dnce; Mch Bnd; SP/M/VS; Stg Cre; Skiing (J); Track (V); Architecture; The Ohio State U

HARTUNG, APRIL; CINCINNATI, OH; OAK HILLS HS; (FR); Ctznshp Aw; Hi Hnr Roll; Nat Hon Sy; Otst Ac Ach Awd; Pres Ac Ftns Aw; Peer Tut/Med; DARE; Chr; Chrldg (J); Gmnstcs (J); Bachelor's, Master's; Miami Oxford U

HASSAN, NADIA; COLUMBUS, OH; WESTLAND HS; (JR); Hnr Roll; Perf Att; St of Mnth; WWAHSS; Comm Volntr; Peer Tut/Med; ArtClub; Key Club; Pep Squd; Prom Com; French Clb; Stu Cncl (R); Lit Mag (R); Yrbk (R); President of 05-06 Key Club; President of Somali Council of Girls; Pre-Med (PhD); Pre-Law (PhD); Cornell U; UCLA

HASSETT, CHRISTOPHER; BRUNSWICK, OH; PADUA HS; (SR); Nat Hon Sy; Perf Att; WWAHSS; Comm Volntr; Chrch Yth Grp; Emplmnt; Key Club; Tchrs Aide; Ice Hky (J); Sccr (V); Tennis (V); National Honor Society; Pharmacy; U of Kentucky

HASSON, CYNTHIA R; CAREY, OH; CAREY SCH; (JR); Hnr Roll; ArtClub; Drma Clb

HASTINGS, SAMANTHA; LIMA, OH; OPT/BATH; (JR); Ctznshp Aw; Hnr Roll; MVP; Nat Hon Sy; Comm Volntr; DARE; Emplmnt; Scouts; Chr; SP/M/VS; Lit Mag (E); Sch Ppr (E); Yrbk (E); Full Time Mother at 16; Played Basketball / Football / Track / Weight Lifting Before Having Child; Nursing / RN; Phlebotomy.; Ohio State; Rhodes

HATEM, CHERINE K; ROCKY RIVER, OH; ROCKY RIVER HS; (SR); Hi Hnr Roll; Nat Hon Sy; Pres Sch; WWAHSS; Comm Volntr; Red Cr Aide; Chrch Yth Grp; Scouts; Hsbk Rdg (J); Swmg (J); Track (V)

HAUGHT, BRITTANY N; MINGO JUNCTION, OH; BUCKEYE LOCAL HS; (FR); Hi Hnr Roll; FCA; Bnd; Dnce; Mch Bnd; Chrldg; Cl Off (T)

HAULER, RENEE; MONROEVILLE, OH; MONROEVILLE HS; (JR); Hi Hnr Roll; MVP; Nat Hon Sy; WWAHSS; Peer Tut/Med; Key Club; Prom Com; Chrldg (V CL); Stu Cncl (R)

HAVERLICK, BRITTANY H; BARBERTON, OH; BARBERTON HS; (SO); Hi Hnr Roll; Kwnis Aw; Otst Ac Ach Awd; Pres Ac Ftns Aw; St of Mnth; Comm Volntr; Key Club; Off Aide; Prom Com; Tchrs Aide; Chr; Vllyball (V L); Stu Cncl (R); Yrbk (R); Christian Leadership Award; Psychology / Counselor; Teacher; Kent State U; Ohio U

HAWK, KADEY A; CANTON, OH; GLEN OAK HS; (SO); Sci Fairs; Red Cr Aide; DARE; Key Club; Lib Aide; Off Aide; Scouts; Girl Scouts 8 Years; Medical; Tucson U; Kent State U

HAWKINS, FARAREIA; DAYTON, OH; MEADOWDALE HS; (JR); Hnr Roll; MVP; Nat Hon Sy; Perf Att; WWAHSS; Comm Volntr; FCA; Key Club; Bnd; Bskball (VJC); PP Ftbl (V CL); Sftball (V); Vllyball (V); Law; Business; U of Connecticut; U of Tennessee

HAWORTH, JOANNA; CIRCLEVILLE, OH; CIRCLEVILLE HS; (SO); 4H Awd; Ctznshp Aw; Hnr Roll; Kwnis Aw; Perf Att; Sci Fairs; St of Mnth; Yth Ldrshp Prog; Comm Volntr; 4-H; Chrch Yth Grp; Emplmnt; FCA; Key Club; Off Aide; Prom Com; SADD; Chr; Dnce; SP/M/VS; Swg Chr; Chrldg; Cr Ctry; Tennis (J); Track (V L); Cl Off (S); Stu Cncl (R); Yrbk (R, P); Teen Health Coalition & STAND Mentor; FCA Leader; Psychology; Acting; Ohio State U

HAWTHORNE, JOSEPH T; CANAL WINCHESTER, OH; HARVEST PREP SCH; (JR); Hi Hnr Roll; MVP; Nat Hon Sy; St of Mnth; WWAHSS; Chrch Yth Grp; FCA; P to P St Amb Prg; Prom Com; SP/M/VS; Bsball (V L); Ftball (V L); Sccr (V CL); Adv Cncl (R); National Honor Society

HAYDEN, EMILY; EAST LIVERPOOL, OH; EAST LIVERPOOL HS; (JR); Hnr Roll; Peer Tut/Med; Red Cr Aide; DARE; Drma Clb; Mus Clb; P to P St Amb Prg; Bnd; Jzz Bnd; Mch Bnd; Orch; Chrldg (V L); Gmnstcs (J); Sftball (J); Stu Cncl (R); Band President 2005-2006 Secretary 04-05; Thespian Secretary '05-06; Health Careers '04-05'; Pediatrician; Doctor; Bethany College; Kent State Downtown E. Liverpool

HAYS, KRYSTAL; TOLEDO, OH; START HS; (SO); Ctznshp Aw; Hi Hnr Roll; Hnr Roll; Otst Ac Ach Awd; St of Mnth; DARE; Emplmnt; Post Secondary - PSEOP; Red Cross Babysitting Club; Physical Therapy; Bachelor's Degree; U of Toledo; Owens Community College

HAYWOOD, BRITTNEY; COLUMBUS, OH; (SO); Chrch Yth Grp; DARE; Fr of Library; Ch Chr; SP/M/VS; Stg Cre; Social Worker; Columbus State Community College

HAZIMIHALIS, MARIA G; CAMPBELL, OH; CAMPBELL MEMORIAL HS; (JR); Hi Hnr Roll; Yth Ldrshp Prog; Comm Volntr; Hosp Aide; Peer Tut/Med; Chrch Yth Grp; Drma Clb; Mth Clb/Tm; Off Aide; Prom Com; Spch Team; Tchrs Aide; French Clb; Dnce; Cl Off (T); Youth Leadership Mahoning Valley Alumni; St. John Chrysostom Oratorical Festival Winner; Pharmacy; Duquesne U; Ohio Northern U

HEADWORTH, CATHRINE; AKRON, OH; COPLEY HS; (FR); Hnr Roll; Otst Ac Ach Awd; Sci/Math Olympn; Comm Volntr; DARE; Dbte Team; Key Club; NtlFrnscLg; Tchrs Aide; German Clb; Bnd; Mch Bnd; Pep Bnd; Stg Cre; Track (J); Engineering; Teacher; Akron U; Bowling Green College

HEATH, KRISTAL N; LORAIN, OH; LORAIN ADMIRAL KING HS; (FR); Hnr Roll; Drma Clb; Bnd; SP/M/VS; Stg Cre; Track; Summer Theatre; Theatre; Photography; Oberlin College; Mount Union

HECK, KELLY M; TOLEDO, OH; WOODWARD HS; (SR); Peer Tut/Med; DECA; Tchrs Aide; German Clb; National Honor Society; Computer Science/Technology; U of Toledo

HEDGES, CHAD; LANCASTER, OH; BERNE UNION HS; (JR); Ctznshp Aw; MVP; WWAHSS; Comm Volntr; BPA; DECA; Lttrmn Clb; Outdrs Clb; Vsity Clb; Chr; Ftball (C); Track (V); Vsy Clb (C); Wt Lftg (V); Stu Cncl (R); Physical Education; Ohio U

HEDGES, ROXY; WESTERVILLE, OH; DELAWARE AREA CAREER CTR; (JR); Ctznshp Aw; Hnr Roll; Otst Ac Ach Awd; Perf Att; St of Mnth; Yth Ldrshp Prog; Comm Volntr; Hab For Humty Volntr; Red Cr Aide; Chess; DARE; Drma Clb; Lib Aide; Prom Com; Tchrs Aide; Chr; SP/M/VS; Cr Ctry; Tennis; Vllyball; Cl Off (S); Stu Cncl (V); CR (R); Yrbk (P); Joined Law Enforcement Lab; Volunteer Work (Battle of Bands); Become a Homicide Investigator; Work for the FBI; Michigan State U

HEDMOND, SHANE; WESTERVILLE, OH; ST CHARLES PREP HS; (JR); Hnr Roll; WWAHSS; Hab For Humty Volntr; Emplmnt; Bsball (V); Sch Ppr (R); AMC Intramural Pin Award (Math); Architecture; Business; U of Kentucky; U of Cincinnati

HEFFNER, SAMANTHA P; LIMA, OH; LIMA SR HS; (FR); Hnr Roll; Comm Volntr; Peer Tut/Med; Chrch Yth Grp; DARE; Spanish Clb; Orch; Wt Lftg (C); Stu Cncl (R); CR (R); President of Church Youth Group; SNL Praise Team - Bass / Violin; Law; Psychology; Ohio Northern U; Bluffton U

HEILMAN, JESSICA R; COLUMBUS, OH; GRANDVIEW HEIGHTS HS; (JR); Hnr Roll; Nat Hon Sy; Pres Sch; St Schl; WWAHSS; Comm Volntr; Peer Tut/Med; ArtClub; Chrch Yth Grp; Emplmnt; FCA; JSA; Off Aide; Prom Com; Sci Clb; Acpl Chr; Dnce; SP/M/VS; Swg Chr; Chrldg (JC); Adv Cncl (R); Stu Cncl (R); Lit Mag (E, P); Lead Character in Fall Play; Leader Fellowship of Christian Athletes; Education; Teaching; Miami U of Ohio

HEINEY, CODY A; NEW MATAMORAS, OH; FRONTIER HS; (JR); Ctznshp Aw; Fut Prb Slvr; Hnr Roll; MVP; Nat Hon Sy; Perf Att; Pres Ac Ftns Aw; Sci Fairs; WWAHSS; Yth Ldrshp Prog; Comm Volntr; Peer Tut/Med; Biology Clb; BPA; Chrch Yth Grp; Emplmnt; FBLA; Ntl FFA; Off Aide; Prom Com; Chr; Clr Grd; SP/M/VS; Stg Cre; Arch (L); Bsball (J); Bskball (V C); Ftball (V C); Scr Kpr; Swmg (L); Vsy Clb (V); Stu Cncl (R); CR (R); Yrbk (R); Boy Scouts of America-Eagle Scout Rank; Motorcycle Mechanics Institute

HELLWIG, KRISTA A; ELMORE, OH; WOODMORE HS; (FR); 4H Awd; Hnr Roll; Otst Ac Ach Awd; Yth Ldrshp Prog; Comm Volntr; Hab For Humty Volntr; 4-H; Chrch Yth Grp; Drma Clb; Emplmnt; Key Club; Ntl FFA; Scouts; Bnd; Ch Chr; Mch Bnd; Pep Bnd; Sccr; Track; Vllyball; Girl Scouts 8 Yrs; 4-H Awards, Red Cross Baby Sitting Course; Veterinarian; Physical Education; Ohio State U; Bowling Green State U

HEMPEL, ANDREA; CINCINNATI, OH; NORTHWEST HS; (SO); F Lan Hn Soc; Hnr Roll; Comm Volntr; Chrch Yth Grp; Drma Clb; Key Club; Mus Clb; Chr; SP/M/VS; Stu Cncl (R); Key Club; Interior Design; Med School; U of Cincinnati

HEMSTREET, JESSICA L; AVON LAKE, OH; AVON LAKE HS; (SR); Hnr Roll; Pres Sch; WWAHSS; Chrch Yth Grp; Emplmnt; Key Club; Scouts; SADD; Tchrs Aide; French Clb; Bnd; Mch Bnd; Pep Bnd; SP/M/VS; Girl Scout Silver Award; Girl Scout Gold Award; Speech Pathology and Audiology; U of Akron; U of Iowa

HENDERSON, KELLY R; HUNTSBURG, OH; CHARDON HS; (SR); Hnr Roll; Nat Hon Sy; Otst Ac Ach Awd; St of Mnth; Yth Ldrshp Prog; Comm Volntr; Hab For Humty Volntr; Peer Tut/Med; 4-H; Chrch Yth Grp; Drma Clb; FCA; Off Aide; Prom Com; Tchrs Aide; Ch Chr; SP/M/VS; Stg Cre; Chrldg (JC); Cl Off (P, V); Stu Cncl (R); Representative of the National Honor Society; Representative of Prom Committee; Journalism / Communications; Education; Columbus State Community College; Baldwin Wallace College

HENDERSON, MEGAN M; WHEELERSBURG, OH; WHEELERSBURG HS; (SO); Key Club; Bnd; Chr; Clr Grd; Flg Crps

HENFLING, MICHAEL; CLEVELAND, OH; RICHMOND HEIGHTS HS; (SR); Ctznshp Aw; Hnr Roll; MVP; Nat Hon Sy; USAA; Comm Volntr; Bnd; Jzz Bnd; Mch Bnd; Pep Bnd; Bsball (V CL); Ftball (V L); Skiing (L); Cl Off (P, V, T); Stu Cncl (T, R); Team MVP - Baseball 2004; Defensive MVP Football 2004; Meteorology; Engineering; Ohio Northern U

HENKIN, MICHAEL; CLEVELAND, OH; CHARLES F BRUSH HS; (SO); Hi Hnr Roll; Hnr Roll; Nat Hon Sy; Otst Ac Ach Awd; St of Mnth; Comm Volntr; Peer Tut/Med; Spec Olymp Vol; Key Club; Photog; Skiing (J); Yrbk (R, P); AVID Environmentalist; Lifeguard; Graphic Artist; National Geographic Photographer; Miami U of Ohio; Northwestern U

HENNES, LA TEIA; HILLIARD, OH; HILLIARD DARBY HS; (SR); Hnr Roll; Pres Sch; Comm Volntr; Chrldg (VJ L); Athletic Scholar Award; Student Athlete of the Month; Business; Meteorology; Ohio State U

HENNESSY, AMANDA; CLEVELAND, OH; PADUA; (SO); Hnr Roll; Comm Volntr; Peer Tut/Med; Chrch Yth Grp; Key Club; SADD; Skiing; Track (J); Economics/Finance; Marketing; Miami of Ohio; U of DA

HENRY, BRETT; WEST SALEM, OH; NORTHWESTERN HS; (SO); 4H Awd; Hnr Roll; 4-H; Ntl FFA; Biology

HENRY, BRYN; LOVELAND, OH; MT NOTRE DAME; (SR); Comm Volntr; Golf (V); President's Award for Educational Achievement; Communications / TV; Broadcasting; Ohio U

HENRY, DANIELLE; CINCINNATI, OH; NORTHWEST HS; (JR); F Lan Hn Soc; Hi Hnr Roll; Nat Hon Sy; Otst Ac Ach Awd; St of Mnth; WWAHSS; Chrch Yth Grp; Key Club; SP/M/VS; Chrldg (V); Stu Cncl (S); Architecture

HENRY, GRACE; PERRYSBURG, OH; PERRYSBURG HS; (JR); Gov Hnr Prg; Hi Hnr Roll; Hnr Roll; Nat Hon Sy; Perf Att; Sci Fairs; Sci/Math Olympn; Comm Volntr; Peer Tut/Med; ArtClub; DARE; Emplmnt; Sci Clb; Scouts; SADD; Tchrs Aide; Spanish Clb; Chr; PP Ftbl (J); Sccr (L); Stu Cncl (R); CR (R); Spanish Clb; Bachelor's in Marketing; Bachelor's in Design; Bowling Green U; U of Toledo

HENRY, JIMMY; TIPPECANOE, OH; CONOTTON VALLEY JR/SR HS; (JR); Hnr Roll; Chrch Yth Grp; SP/M/VS; Jr High and High School Choir; Pharmacology

HENRY, TONISHA; GROVEPORT, OH; GROVEPORT MADISON HS; (FR); Hnr Roll; Nat Hon Sy; St of Mnth; Comm Volntr; Peer Tut/Med; Chrch Yth Grp; P to P St Amb Prg; Spanish Clb; Work At Donatoes; Dental Surgeon; Ohio State U

HENRY IV, ROBERT L; CLEVELAND, OH; LIGHTHOUSE AC; (SO); Ctznshp Aw; Nat Stu Ath Day Aw; Pres Ac Ftns Aw; WWAHSS; Yth Ldrshp Prog; Comm Volntr; Peer Tut/Med; Chrch Yth Grp; Emplmnt; FCA; Scouts; Bnd; Ch Chr; SP/M/VS; Bsball (L); Ftball (J); Ice Sktg; Mar Art; Swmg (L); Wt Lftg (L); Cl Off (R); Sch Ppr (R); Presidential Award for Volunteerism; Pro-Football Player; Culinary Arts; Tenessee State; Michigan State, Miami of Ohio

HENSLEY, CARLY; DAYTON, OH; CARROLL HS; (SO); Hnr Roll; Sci Fairs; WWAHSS; Comm Volntr; ArtClub; Chrch Yth Grp; Drma Clb; Emplmnt; HO'Br Yth Ldrshp; Key Club; Scouts; French Clb; SP/M/VS; Stg Cre; Yrbk (E); Key Club Officer; Consumer Science Club; Fashion Design; Graphic Design

HERNANDEZ, ANITA; COLUMBUS, OH; BROOKHAVEN HS; (SO); Hnr Roll; Nat Hon Sy; St of Mnth; Cosmetology

Hellwig, Krista A
Woodmore HS
Elmore, OH

Heilman, Jessica R
Grandview Heights HS
Columbus, OH

Hatem, Cherine K
Rocky River HS
Rocky River, OH

Haworth, Joanna
Circleville HS
Circleville, OH

Henderson, Megan M
Wheelersburg HS
Wheelersburg, OH

HERNANDEZ, CALI L; CORTLAND, OH; LAKEVIEW HS; (FR); Hnr Roll; Peer Tut/Med; Lib Aide; Ntl Beta Clb; Tchrs Aide; Cr Ctry (V); Golf (V); Track (V); Bachelor or Master in Education; Youngstown State

HERNANDEZ, RICHARD L; DAYTON, OH; BEAVERCREEK HS; (SO); Ctznshp Aw; Hi Hnr Roll; Otst Ac Ach Awd; Comm Volntr; Hab For Humty Volntr; Red Cr Aide; Chrch Yth Grp; Emplmnt; FCA; Tchrs Aide; Wdwrkg Clb; Bsball (J); Cr Ctry (V); Track; Wrstlg (J); Selected to Represent Wright Patterson AFBA & Advanced Space Academy; Active Participant - Congressional Awards Program; Outdoor Exploration; Public Services; Oklahoma State; Hocking College

HERNDON, MICAIAH A; GROVEPORT, OH; HARVEST PREP SCH; (SR); Hi Hnr Roll; MVP; Nat Hon Sy; St of Mnth; WWAHSS; Comm Volntr; Peer Tut/Med; Chrch Yth Grp; FCA; Tchrs Aide; Spanish Clb; Ch Chr; Bskball (V CL); Chrldg (J); Cr Ctry (V CL); Sccr (V CL); Track (V CL); Cl Off (R); Sch Ppr (R); Yrbk (P); Chemistry; Biology; The Ohio State U; Kenyon College

HERRE, ANDREW H; MAINEVILLE, OH; KINGS HS; (JR); Hi Hnr Roll; Nat Hon Sy; Mth Clb/Tm; Off Aide; French Clb; Golf (V); Tennis (V); Medicine; Wake Forest U; Miami U

HERRMANN, ANNA; CINCINNATI, OH; MC AULEY HS; (SO); Hnr Roll; Nat Hon Sy; Yth Ldrshp Prog; Comm Volntr; Peer Tut/Med; Spec Olymp Vol; Drma Clb; Emplmnt; HO'Br Yth Ldrshp; Key Club; Scouts; Svce Clb; Latin Clb; Sftball (J); Mock Trial; Law; Psychology; Ohio State U; Miami U

HERSHEY, BENJAMIN G; MILFORD, OH; MILFORD HS; (FR); Ctznshp Aw; Hi Hnr Roll; Hnr Roll; Nat Hon Sy; Otst Ac Ach Awd; St of Mnth; DARE; Off Aide; Ftball (V); Skiing (V); National Junior Honor Society; Art Award of the Year / President's Education Award Program; Law; Business; Harvard U; Stanford U

HERVEY, MARK; MAINEVILLE, OH; ST XAVIER HS; (SR); Hnr Roll; WWAHSS; Prom Com; Stu Cncl (V); Business; Indiana U

HESLEP, MELISSA K; ASHLAND, OH; ASHLAND HS; (JR); Ctznshp Aw; Hi Hnr Roll; Hnr Roll; Comm Volntr; Chrch Yth Grp; DARE; Emplmnt; Prom Com; Dnce; SP/M/VS; Stg Cre; CR (R); Sch Ppr (R, P); Yrbk (P); International Studies; George Washington U; Michigan

HESS, ERICA; BELLEFONTAINE, OH; BENJAMIN LOGAN HS; (JR); Hnr Roll; Nat Hon Sy; WWAHSS; Chrch Yth Grp; Drma Clb; Key Club; Off Aide; Tchrs Aide; Spanish Clb; Mch Bnd; Orch; Pep Bnd; SP/M/VS; Chrldg (V L); Golf (V L); Dental Hygiene; Ohio State U; College of Wooster

HESSEL, MICHAEL; SCOTT, OH; LINCOLNVIEW HS; (SR); 4H Awd; Hi Hnr Roll; Jr Rot; Nat Hon Sy; St of Mnth; WWAHSS; 4-H; Emplmnt; Ntl FFA; Sci Clb; FFA - President; Mechanical Engineering; Rhodes College

HESSON, ALEXANDRIA; MONROE, OH; MONROE HS; (JR); Hnr Roll; MVP; Perf Att; St of Mnth; Chrch Yth Grp; DARE; Emplmnt; Photog; Prom Com; Vsity Clb; Chr; SP/M/VS; Stg Cre; PP Ftbl; Sccr (V CL); Track (V L); Soccer-League Player of the Year - 2004; Education / Teaching; Ohio Northern U; Wittenberg U

HEWITT, PATRICK; WARREN, OH; JOHN F KENNEDY HS; (SO); Hnr Roll; Nat Hon Sy; WWAHSS; Yth Ldrshp Prog; Comm Volntr; AL Aux Boys; Chrch Yth Grp; HO'Br Yth Ldrshp; Key Club; MuAlphaTh; NtlFrnscLg; Scouts; Spch Team; Cr Ctry (V L); Sccr (J); Swmg (V L); Eagle Scout; Piano; Architecture; American History; Notre Dame

HIANS, BRITTANY; YOUNGSTOWN, OH; AUSTINTOWN FITCH HS; (SR); Hnr Roll; Nat Hon Sy; WWAHSS; Comm Volntr; Emplmnt; Off Aide; Pep Squd; Photog; Prom Com; SP/M/VS; Chrldg (V L); Sftball (J); Track (V L); Cl Off (R); Yrbk (R, P); NHS -2 Yrs; Who's Who Among HS Students - 4 Yrs; U of Akron

HICKMAN, MONICA; BREMEN, OH; WM V FISHER CATHOLIC HS; (JR); Hi Hnr Roll; Hnr Roll; Nat Hon Sy; WWAHSS; Comm Volntr; Drma Clb; Emplmnt; HO'Br Yth Ldrshp; Key Club; Prom Com; SP/M/VS; Cl Off (P, V); Film Studies Club; Secretary of Key Club; Psychology; Fashion Merchandising; Kent State U; U of Pittsburgh

HICKS, DIONNA; WESTERVILLE, OH; THOMAS WORTHINGTON HS; (JR); Ctznshp Aw; Perf Att; St of Mnth; Comm Volntr; ArtClub; Chrch Yth Grp; DARE; Emplmnt; Off Aide; Prom Com; Scouts; Spch Team; Chr; Dnce; Drl Tm; SP/M/VS; Lcrsse (J); Stu Cncl (R); CR (R); Mass Communication with a Focus on Radio/TV & Film; Clark - Atlanta; Ohio U

HIGGINS, NATASHA; DAYTON, OH; COLONEL WHITE HS FOR THE ARTS; (FR); Hi Hnr Roll; Hnr Roll; Otst Ac Ach Awd; Perf Att; Sci Fairs; St of Mnth; Comm Volntr; ROTC; Bnd; Drl Tm; Mch Bnd

HIGGINS V, JOHN; CINCINNATI, OH; NORTHWEST HS; (FR); Hnr Roll; Chrch Yth Grp; Drma Clb; Key Club; French Clb; SP/M/VS; Stg Cre; Acting; Law; New York U

HILDEBRAND, CARRIE; MOUNT GILEAD, OH; (JR); 4H Awd; Hnr Roll; 4-H; Emplmnt; Chrldg (V); Sftball (J); Cl Off (S); Yrbk (R); Dental Hygienist; Physical Therapy; The Ohio State U

HILL, JASMINE; CLEVELAND, OH; LUTHERAN HS EAST; (FR); Ctznshp Aw; Hnr Roll; Perf Att; St of Mnth; Chrldg (J); Co-Manager - Softball Team; Interior Design; Fashion Merchandising

HILL, JONATHAN A; AKRON, OH; COPLEY HS; (FR); Hnr Roll; Otst Ac Ach Awd; Chrch Yth Grp; Medicine; Education; U of Miami; Clemson U

HILL, JORDAN A; CARROLLTON, OH; CARROLLTON HS; (SR); Hnr Roll; MVP; Nat Hon Sy; WWAHSS; Chrch Yth Grp; Emplmnt; FCA; Off Aide; Tchrs Aide; Bnd; Dnce; Mch Bnd; Track (V); Sch Ppr (R); Yrbk (E); Baldwin Wallace College

HILL, MALEA; COLUMBUS, OH; EASTLAND CAREER CTR HS; (JR); Hnr Roll; Dental Hygiene; Ohio State U; Columbus State U

HILL, REBECCA C; MC DERMOTT, OH; NORTHWEST HS; (SR); Hi Hnr Roll; WWAHSS; Comm Volntr; Red Cr Aide; Chrch Yth Grp; Drma Clb; Off Aide; P to P St Amb Prg; Prom Com; Tchrs Aide; Bnd; Drm Mjr; Mch Bnd; Pep Bnd; Swmg (V); P.R.I.D.E. Team; Education; Ohio State U; Wright State U

HIMES, JAMES D; YOUNGSTOWN, OH; FITCH HS; Join Air Force; USF

HINDERS, CAROLYN R; BELLBROOK, OH; BELLBROOK HS; (SO); Hi Hnr Roll; Sci Fairs; WWAHSS; Comm Volntr; Peer Tut/Med; Chrch Yth Grp; Key Club; Lib Aide; Off Aide; Bnd; Mch Bnd; Pep Bnd; Secretary of Key Club; Elementary Education; Bowling Green State U; Ohio State U

HINKLE, ALLISON; JEFFERSON, OH; JEFFERSON AREA HS; (SR); Hnr Roll; Nat Hon Sy; WWAHSS; Comm Volntr; Chrch Yth Grp; Emplmnt; FCA; Acpl Chr; Chr; SP/M/VS; Sftball (J); Tennis (V CL); Vllyball; Update My School's Website; Physical Education; Malone College

HINKLE, RYAN M; DUBLIN, OH; BISHOP WATTERSON HS; (JR); Hnr Roll; Nat Hon Sy; Otst Ac Ach Awd; WWAHSS; Comm Volntr; Ftball (V CL); Rugby Club Co-Captain; Career in Medicine; Wake Forest U; U of Notre Dame

HIPP, RACHEL A; SEVEN HILLS, OH; PADUA FRANCISCAN HS; (JR); Hi Hnr Roll; Nat Hon Sy; Nat Stu Ath Day Aw; WWAHSS; Comm Volntr; AL Aux Girls; Chrch Yth Grp; Drma Clb; Emplmnt; Key Club; Off Aide; Scouts; Latin Clb; Acpl Chr; Chr; Orch; SP/M/VS; Vllyball (VJ L); Peer Ministry, Junior Olympic Volleyball; Music Ministry; Pre-Vet, Pre-Pharmacy; Pre-Med; Ohio State U

HITCHCOCK, JORDAN L; AKRON, OH; COPLEY HS; (SO); Hnr Roll; MVP; WWAHSS; Chrch Yth Grp; Photog; Sccr (J); Sch Ppr (P); Teacher; Flagler College / St Augustine FL; Hollins College

HIXENBAUGH, JOSHUA; YOUNGSTOWN, OH; AUSTINTOWN FITCH HS; (FR); Hnr Roll; Comm Volntr; Chrch Yth Grp; Cmptr Clb; Emplmnt; Scouts; Tchrs Aide; Yrbk (P); TV Production; Engineering; Computer Programming; U of Southern California; Ohio State U

HLAVAC, DIANE; WILLOUGHBY, OH; SOUTH HS; (FR); Hnr Roll; Perf Att; Comm Volntr; Key Club

HLAVAC, TIM; WILLOUGHBY, OH; WILLOUGHBY SOUTH HS; (SR); Hi Hnr Roll; Nat Hon Sy; Nat Mrt Fin; Perf Att; St of Mnth; USAA; Valdctrian; WWAHSS; Comm Volntr; Emplmnt; Key Club; Ftball (V CL); Wt Lftg; Stu Cncl; Student Athlete of the Year; Business-Finance; Insurance; Bowling Green State U

HOBGOOD, JOSHUA C; LIMA, OH; LIMA SR HS; (FR); Hnr Roll; Comm Volntr; Chrch Yth Grp; Emplmnt; Acpl Chr; Ftball (V L); Wt Lftg; Wrstlg (V L); Only Freshman Varsity Football Player; Business; Law; Notre Dame; Ohio State

HOBSON, SHAREA E; SYLVANIA, OH; NORTHVIEW HS; (SR); Hnr Roll; WWAHSS; Red Cr Aide; Chrch Yth Grp; Dbte Team; Bnd; Ch Chr; Pep Bnd; Business Management; Music; Owens Community College Toledo; West Virginia U

HODGES, LAKARI C; CLEVELAND, OH; HEALTH CAREERS CTR; (SO); Ctznshp Aw; Hnr Roll; Otst Ac Ach Awd; WWAHSS; Upward Bound Program; Pediatrician; Forensic Specialist

HODGES, MATTHEW D; COLUMBUS, OH; BISHOP WATTERSON HS; (JR); Hnr Roll; Nat Hon Sy; Sci Fairs; WWAHSS; Comm Volntr; Peer Tut/Med; Emplmnt; Chr; Ftball (V L); Wrstlg (V L); Adv Cncl (R); English as a Second Language Tutor; Sports Medicine; Ohio State; Miami U Ohio

HOERRLE, ANGELIA; AUSTINBURG, OH; GENEVA SECONDARY SCH; (FR); Hnr Roll; Otst Ac Ach Awd; Pres Sch; Sci Fairs; Sci/Math Olympn; Sci Clb; Svce Clb; Bnd; Mch Bnd; Stu Cncl (R); Sch Ppr (E); Majorette; Pediatrician; Medical Field; Johns Hopkins U

HOFACRE, ANGI; DALTON, OH; WAYNE CTY SCH CAREER CTR; (SR); Hi Hnr Roll; Hnr Roll; MVP; Nat Hon Sy; St of Mnth; Comm Volntr; Spec Olymp Vol; Chrch Yth Grp; Emplmnt; FCA; Tchrs Aide; Bnd; Mch Bnd; Sccr (VJCL); Track (V L); Stu Cncl; Teacher of Excellence Award; FCCLA State Competition Gold Star Winner; Early Childhood Education; Wayne College

HOFFMAN, BRENDAN; CAREY, OH; CAREY SCH; (FR); Perf Att; DARE; Bsball (J); Ftball (J); Wt Lftg (J); Paperboy for Six Years - March '98 - Present; Computer Technology; Real-Estate Salesman; Findlay U; Toledo U

HOFFMAN, EMILY; AKRON, OH; COPLEY HS; (SO); Hi Hnr Roll; Nat Hon Sy; Chess; Emplmnt; Key Club; NtlFrnscLg; Sci Clb; Spch Team; Spanish Clb; Dnce; Stg Cre; Sftball (J); Tennis (J); Sch Ppr (R); Biomedical Engineering

HOGAN, ERIKA; BYESVILLE, OH; MEADOWBROOK HS; (JR); Hnr Roll; Nat Hon Sy; Tchrs Aide; Dnce; SP/M/VS; Chrldg (V L); Registered Nurse; Teacher; Muskingum College; Malone College

HOGUE, JESSICA; PHILO, OH; PHILO HS; (SR); MVP; Salutrn; St of Mnth; WWAHSS; Yth Ldrshp Prog; Comm Volntr; Hosp Aide; Peer Tut/Med; Emplmnt; FCCLA; NYLC; Prom Com; Quiz Bowl; SADD; Tchrs Aide; Vsity Clb; Bskball (J); Skiing; Sccr (V CL); Sftball (V CL); Track (J); Cl Off (V); Academic Athletic Award-4 Years; 1st Team-All Eastern District Soccer Player; Pediatric Nurse Practitioner; Ohio State U

HOLBROOK, JARED; WARREN, OH; WARREN G HARDING HS; (FR); Hnr Roll; Emplmnt; Graphic Art; Ohio State; Kent State

HOLBROOK, RICHELE L; PLYMOUTH, OH; PLYMOUTH HS; (SR); Hnr Roll; Otst Ac Ach Awd; Yth Ldrshp Prog; Peer Tut/Med; Chrch Yth Grp; Drma Clb; Emplmnt; FCA; Scouts; SADD; Bnd; Ch Chr; Jzz Bnd; Mch Bnd; Chrldg (V L); Track (V L); Master's Degree / Nursing; Med Central School of Nursing; North Central State College

HOLDEN, BRIAN S; LOVELAND, OH; MILFORD HS; (FR); Ctznshp Aw; Hnr Roll; Yth Ldrshp Prog; Vsity Clb; Bsball (J); Ftball (J); Wrstlg (V); Yrbk (R); Business Major; Associate's Degree; Wake Forest U; Florida State U

HOLDEN, MARY E; LEESBURG, OH; FAIRFIELD LOCAL HS; (JR); Hi Hnr Roll; Hnr Roll; MVP; Otst Ac Ach Awd; Perf Att; Comm Volntr; Hab For Humty Volntr; Peer Tut/Med; Chrch Yth Grp; Prom Com; SADD; Tchrs Aide; Vsity Clb; Spanish Clb; Bskball (J L); Sccr (V CL); Sftball (V CL); Vllyball (V CL); Stu Cncl (R); Pre-Med-Going to Be an Orthopedic Surgeon; Ohio Wesleyan U; Ohio Dominican U

HOLDREN, KAYLA J; NEWPORT, OH; FRONTIER HS; (JR); Hi Hnr Roll; Hnr Roll; Nat Hon Sy; Otst Ac Ach Awd; WWAHSS; Comm Volntr; Hab For Humty Volntr; BPA; Key Club; Svce Clb; Spanish Clb; Yrbk (E, P); Spanish National Honor Society; Americanism and Government Winner; Psychology; Education (High School); U of North Carolina; U of Cincinnati

HOLLEY, JILL; WILLIAMSBURG, OH; WESTERN BROWN HS; (SR); Hnr Roll; WWAHSS; FCCLA; Power of One; Psychology; Forensics; Wilmington College of Ohio

HOLLEY, JUSTIN M; POMEROY, OH; MEIGS HS; (JR); 4H Awd; 4-H; Ntl FFA; Outdrs Clb; Wdwrkg Clb; Skiing; Wt Lftg; Wrstlg

HOLMAN, CHELSEA; ARCADIA, OH; ARCADIA SCH; (SO)

HOLMES, THOMAS; HUNTSBURG, OH; STONE ARCH CHRISTIAN HOMESCHOOL; (JR); 4H Awd; 4-H; Chess; 4-H Gold Medals for Dog Care & Achievement; Computers; Grove City College; College of the Ozarks

HOLSINGER, ERIN; CANTON, OH; EAST CANTON HS; (SO); Hnr Roll; Otst Ac Ach Awd; Perf Att; Chrch Yth Grp; Off Aide; Tchrs Aide; Acpl Chr; Bnd; Chr; SP/M/VS; Vllyball (J); Soccer Club; Competitive Swim; Marine Biologist; Major in Natural Sciences; Ohio State; U of Southern California

HOLSTEIN, SARA; SPRINGBORO, OH; SPRINGBORO HS; (SO); Ctznshp Aw; Hi Hnr Roll; Peer Tut/Med; Chrch Yth Grp; Key Club; Lib Aide; Off Aide; Tchrs Aide; Yrbk (P); National Junior Honor Society; Student of the Year; Veterinarian; Marine Biologist; U of Miami; U of Central Florida

HOLTGRIFE, GRETCHEN M; OXFORD, OH; TALAWANDA HS; (SO); WWAHSS; Key Club; Coastal Carolina U; San Francisco State U

HOLTON JR, BYRON J; LIMA, OH; LIMA SR HS; Hnr Roll; Chrch Yth Grp; DARE; Ftball (J); Track (J); Masters Degree; Marketing; Indiana U; Miami U

HOLZAPFEL, ZANE; WELLSTON, OH; WELLSTON HS; (SO); Hnr Roll; Comm Volntr; Emplmnt; NYLC; Bskball (V L); Ftball (V CL); Track (J); Wt Lftg (V); 2004 State Play Off's Football; Precinct Leader for President Bush 04'; Broadcast Journalism/Communication; Education/Coaching; Bowling Green State U; Ohio U

HOMAN, KURT; MARIA STEIN, OH; MARION LOCAL HS; (SO); Hi Hnr Roll; Hnr Roll; Otst Ac Ach Awd; Chrch Yth Grp; Mth Clb/Tm; Sci Clb; Vsity Clb; Bsball (VJ); Bskball (J); Golf (VJ); Pharmacy; Athletic Training; Ohio State; U of Findlay

HOMEROSKY, EMILY K; OAK HILL, OH; SOUTH WEBSTER; (SO); 4H Awd; Hi Hnr Roll; Perf Att; WWAHSS; Yth Ldrshp Prog; Comm Volntr; 4-H; Chrch Yth Grp; Drma Clb; HO'Br Yth Ldrshp; Key Club; Mus Clb; Pep Squd; Spanish Clb; Bnd; Chr; Clr Grd; Pep Bnd; Chrldg (V L); Gmnstcs; Skiing; Sftball (V L); Vllyball (V L); Adv Cncl (R); Cl Off (S); Yrbk (R)

Holbrook, Richele L
Plymouth HS
Plymouth, OH

Hill, Rebecca C
Northwest HS
Mc Dermott, OH

Hill, Jasmine
Lutheran HS East
Cleveland, OH

Hill, Jonathan A
Copley HS
Akron, OH

Holzapfel, Zane
Wellston HS
Wellston, OH

HOOD, ERIN; CINCINNATI, OH; MC AULEY HS; (SR); DAR; Hi Hnr Roll; Hnr Roll; Nat Hon Sy; Otst Ac Ach Awd; St of Mnth; Comm Volntr; Hosp Aide; Peer Tut/Med; Key Club; Svce Clb; Golf (V C); Yrbk (R, P); Graphic Design; U of Cincinnati

HOOKS, JOSHUA; LIMA, OH; LIMA SR HS; (FR); Hnr Roll; Chrch Yth Grp; Ch Chr; Wrstlg (V); Architect; Harvard

HOPKINS, JADE; COLUMBUS, OH; GROVEPORT MADISON HS; (FR); Hnr Roll; Mus Clb; Ch Chr; SP/M/VS; Chrldg; Teaching; Master's Degree; Ohio State U; New York U

HOPKINS, RANDI; CARDINGTON, OH; HIGHLAND HS; (SR); 4H Awd; Hi Hnr Roll; Hnr Roll; Nat Hon Sy; Pres Sch; Comm Volntr; 4-H; AL Aux Girls; Chrch Yth Grp; Drma Clb; Lib Aide; Ntl FFA; Spch Team; Vsity Clb; Chr; SP/M/VS; Stg Cre; Bskball (V L); Hsbk Rdg; Vllyball (JC); Ohio FFA Gold Rated Treasurer; Ohio 4-H Teen Council Member; History Education; Otterbein College

HORN, ALEX; DAYTON, OH; CTRVILLE HS; (JR); Ctznshp Aw; MVP; Yth Ldrshp Prog; Peer Tut/Med; Emplmnt; Lib Aide; NYLC; Prom Com; Svce Clb; Tchrs Aide; Spanish Clb; Bnd; Bsball (V); Ftball (J); Work-Bob Evans

HORNSBY, CATIE; CINCINNATI, OH; MOTHER OF MERCY HS; (SO); Hi Hnr Roll; WWAHSS; Comm Volntr; Chrch Yth Grp; Drma Clb; Key Club; Spanish Clb; Chr; Ch Chr; SP/M/VS; Lcrsse (V); President PALS Assoc - Pals with the Elderly; Thespian

HORTON, ATTACHE; CLEVELAND, OH; MARTIN LUTHER KING HS; (MS); Ctznshp Aw; Hnr Roll; Otst Ac Ach Awd; Perf Att; ArtClub; Chess; DARE; Mus Clb; SP/M/VS; Bskball (J); Chrldg (J); Drill Team; Art Club; Lawyer; Master's Degree; Akron U

HORTON, BRITTANY; WELLINGTON, OH; KEYSTONE HS; (FR); 4-H; Ntl FFA; Scouts; Tech Clb; Bnd; Veterinarian Medicine; Ohio State U

HORTON, MEAGAN; LIMA, OH; (JR); Hnr Roll; Yth Ldrshp Prog; Chrch Yth Grp; Scouts; Bskball (J); Stu Cncl (P); Early Childhood Education; Columbus State; Owens Community College

HORTON, SAMANTHA; CASSTOWN, OH; MIAMI EAST HS; (FR); WWAHSS; 4-H; Key Club; Sccr (J); Cl Off (V)

HOSFELD, DANI; GREENVILLE, OH; GREENVILLE HS; (SO); Hnr Roll; WWAHSS; Hab For Humty Volntr; Chrch Yth Grp; Key Club; Pep Squd; Tchrs Aide; Spanish Clb; Jzz Bnd; Orch; Cr Ctry (J); Golf (VJ L); Swmg (VJ L); Landscape Architecture; Ohio State U

HOTTEL, BRADLEY D; WOOSTER, OH; NORTHWESTERN HS; (SO); Hnr Roll; Perf Att; Peer Tut/Med; 4-H; Chrch Yth Grp; DARE; Emplmnt; Ntl FFA; Bnd; Ch Chr; Mch Bnd; Pep Bnd; Bsball (V); Bskball (V); Ftball (V L); FFA Chapter Degree; 3 Sport Athlete; Forensic Scientist; Pastoral Ministry; The Ohio State U; U of Akron

HOTZE, JOSH; MIDDLETOWN, OH; MONROE HS; (JR); Hnr Roll; MVP; Emplmnt; Bsball (VJ); Golf (VJ L); Mechanical Engineering; Ohio State U; U of Cincinnati

HOUSE, DAREN; CLEVELAND, OH; M L KING LAW & PUB SERV; (SR); Hnr Roll; Bskball (V)

HOVAN, PAUL A; CANTON, OH; TIMKEN SR HS; (MS); Hnr Roll; St of Mnth; Comm Volntr; Accepted Into the Early College High School, Will Graduate High School W/A 2 Yrs Assoc. Degree; Computer Sciences; U of Toledo

HOWARD, ASHLEY; LIMA, OH; LIMA SR HS; (SO); Hnr Roll; Comm Volntr; Hab For Humty Volntr; Chrch Yth Grp; DARE; Chr; Ch Chr; SP/M/VS; Stg Cre; Communication, Media; Music; Asbury College; ONU

HOWARD-GRAY, RAVIN S; CINCINNATI, OH; WITHROW UNIVERSITY HS; (FR); Hnr Roll; Comm Volntr; Chrch Yth Grp; Jr Ach; Contestant on Apollo; Sang At the Mayors Address; Music/Vocals; Business; Juilliard; Clark Atlanta U

HOWE III, ROBERT H; ASHTABULA, OH; ST JOHN & PAUL HS; (FR); Hnr Roll; Comm Volntr; Bsball (J); Ftball (V L); Police Officer

HOWELL III, WILLIAM R A; STEUBENVILLE, OH; STEUBENVILLE HS; (JR); Ctznshp Aw; Hnr Roll; Sci Fairs; Comm Volntr; Chess; Chrch Yth Grp; SADD; French Clb; Yrbk; Law Day; Mock Trial; Forensic Science; Law; Ohio Northern U; Arizona State U

HOWES, DENNIELLE; CLEVELAND, OH; JANE ADDAMS BCC; (JR); Hnr Roll; MVP; DARE; Basketball All-Star for Recreation Center; Accounting; NBA Coach; Clark Atlanta U; Morehouse U

HOWETT, LINDSEY; BROOKVILLE, OH; BROOKVILLE HS; (FR); Hi Hnr Roll; Nat Sci Aw; Comm Volntr; Clb; Bnd; Clr Grd; Pep Bnd; Sccr (V); Stu Cncl (R); CR (R); American History (Teacher); Physical Science (Teacher); Bowling Green U; Eastern Kentucky U

HRIC, EMILY C; NEWBURY, OH; NEWBURY HS; (FR); 4H Awd; Hnr Roll; Nat Mrt LOC; Otst Ac Ach Awd; Perf Att; WWAHSS; 4-H; Off Aide; Scouts; Hsbk Rdg (J); Junior Counselor-YMCA; Who's Who for Middle School-National; Equestrian; Medical; Kent State U-Ohio; U of Toledo-Ohio

HU, ANGELA; CLEVELAND, OH; CHARLES F BRUSH HS; (SO); Hnr Roll; WWAHSS; Comm Volntr; Chrch Yth Grp; Key Club; Dnce; Psychology; Engineering; Case Western Reserve U; Cornell U

HUANG, MELISSA; NORTH ROYALTON, OH; NORTH ROYALTON HS; (SR); Hi Hnr Roll; Hnr Roll; Nat Hon Sy; Perf Att; WWAHSS; Comm Volntr; Peer Tut/Med; ArtClub; Drma Clb; Emplmnt; Key Club; Mth Clb/Tm; Mod UN; Off Aide; Sci Clb; Stg Cre; President of Multi-Culture Club; Pre-Medicine; Northeastern U College of Medicine

HUDEC, MINDY A; ATWATER, OH; WATERLOO HS; (SO); St of Mnth; Comm Volntr; Emplmnt; FTA; Lib Aide; SADD; Tchrs Aide; Cl Off (R); CR (R); Sch Ppr (R, P); Yrbk (P); Maplewood Career Center/Careers with Young Children; Class Historian; Education; Special Needs Education; Kent State U; Walsh U

HUFFAKER, BLAKE L; TROY, OH; TROY HS; (SO); Hi Hnr Roll; Nat Hon Sy; Otst Ac Ach Awd; Perf Att; Pres Ac Ftns Aw; WWAHSS; Spec Olymp Vol; Chrch Yth Grp; Emplmnt; Key Club; Scouts; Svce Clb; Spanish Clb; Bnd; Mch Bnd; Pep Bnd; Skiing; Tennis (V L); Eagle Scout; Architecture; Engineering

HUGHES, ASHLEY E; CARROLL, OH; BLOOM-CARROLL HS; (JR); Hi Hnr Roll; MVP; Nat Hon Sy; Pres Ac Ftns Aw; Sci Fairs; WWAHSS; Key Club; Lttrmn Clb; NYLC; Off Aide; Sci Clb; Svce Clb; Tchrs Aide; Vsity Clb; Bskball (V); Vllyball (V); First Frosh. Ever to Be 1st Team All-League Volleyball; AAU - All-American - 2 Yrs; Nutrition; Athletic Training; Ohio State U

HUGHES, JAIME A; NORTH LIMA, OH; CARDINAL MOONEY HS; (SO); Hnr Roll; WWAHSS; Comm Volntr; Peer Tut/Med; DARE; Photog; Svce Clb; SADD; Spanish Clb; Lit Mag (E); Sch Ppr (E); Yrbk (P); Publication - Our 100 Most Famous Poets; Publication - The Best Poems & Poets of 2004; Journalism / Writer; Public Relations / Creative Writing Teacher; Bellarmine U; East Michigan U

HUGHES, KEITH; CARDINGTON, OH; MT GILEAD HS; (FR); Otst Ac Ach Awd; ArtClub; Ftball (J); Track (V); Wt Lftg (V); Wrstlg (V); Business Management; Acting; Miami Florida; Ohio State U

HUGHES III, EDWARD; MC DONALD, OH; MC DONALD HS; (FR); Hnr Roll; Otst Ac Ach Awd; Comm Volntr; Lit Mag (P); Sch Ppr (P); Police Officer; Lawyer; Youngstown State U; Ohio State U

HUGHETT, ZACH; MARYSVILLE, OH; MARYSVILLE HS; (JR); Ctznshp Aw; Hnr Roll; Sci Fairs; Hosp Aide; Chrch Yth Grp; DARE; Dbte Team; Drma Clb; Lib Aide; SADD; Stg Cre; Had to Overcome ADHD / Tourette's Syndrome

HUMAN II, RICHARD A; HAMILTON, OH; CINCINNATI HILLS CHRISTIAN AC; (SO); Hi Hnr Roll; Hnr Roll; Perf Att; St of Mnth; Comm Volntr; Chrch Yth Grp; Scouts; Bnd; Jzz Bnd; Pep Bnd; SP/M/VS; Golf (V); Track (V); Medical / Radiology; Belmont U; U of Dayton

HUMBERT, NICOLE; MIDDLETOWN, OH; LAKOTA EAST HS; (SO); Ctznshp Aw; Hi Hnr Roll; Nat Hon Sy; St of Mnth; WWAHSS; Chrch Yth Grp; Emplmnt; Dnce; Cr Ctry (J L); Golf (V L); Lcrsse (JC); Medicine-Anesthesiologist; Princeton; Michigan

HUML, LAUREN; STRONGSVILLE, OH; PADUA FRANCISCAN HS; (JR); Hi Hnr Roll; Nat Mrt LOC; WWAHSS; Hab For Humty Volntr; Peer Tut/Med; Chrch Yth Grp; DARE; Emplmnt; Jr Cls League; Key Club; Sccr (VJCL); Track (V L); Pro-Life Organization; Eucharistic Minister; Business; Education; U of Dayton; John Carroll U

HUMPHREY, SHAUNA; MADISON, OH; MADISON HS; (FR); Hnr Roll; Nat Sci Aw; Sci Fairs; St of Mnth; WWAHSS; FBLA; Chr; Sccr (J); Track (V L); Honors English

HUNTER JR, PATRICK L; CANTON, OH; MC KINLEY SR HS; (MS); Hnr Roll; Lttrmn Clb; Lib Aide; Quill & Scroll; Quiz Bowl; Clb; Bskball; Ftball; Track; Social Studies- Student of the Year- 2004 7th Grade; Pre-Med; Cardio-Thorasic Surgery; UCLA; Oberlin College

HURLEY, CHRISTINA; TIFFIN, OH; CALVERT HS; (SO); Hi Hnr Roll; Hnr Roll; Pres Sch; Sci Fairs; 4-H; Chrch Yth Grp; SADD; French Clb; SP/M/VS; Bskball; Cr Ctry (V L); Sccr (V L); Track (V L); Yrbk; Vet; Medical; Ohio State U

HURST, LUCAS; FAIRBORN, OH; FAIRBORN HS; (FR); Hnr Roll; Perf Att; Sci Fairs; ArtClub; Bnd; Jzz Bnd; Mch Bnd; Golf; Stu Cncl; Computer Engineering; Ohio State U; Wright State U

HURST, TAYLOR; DAYTON, OH; ARCHBISHOP ALTER HS; (FR); Hi Hnr Roll; Perf Att; Sci Fairs; St of Mnth; Comm Volntr; Peer Tut/Med; Red Cr Aide; Emplmnt; Key Club; Scouts; French Clb; Vllyball; French Club; Lifeguarding; Teaching; Business; Miami Oxford; U of Kentucky

HURTUBISE, JENNIFER; DAYTON, OH; ALTER HS; (FR); Hnr Roll; Sci Fairs; WWAHSS; Yth Ldrshp Prog; Comm Volntr; Emplmnt; Key Club; Scouts; Spanish Clb; Chrldg (J); Sccr (VJCL)

HUTCHINSON, EMMALIESE N; XENIA, OH; XENIA HS; (SR); Hnr Roll; Nat Hon Sy; Emplmnt; Off Aide; P to P St Amb Prg; Sci Clb; Tchrs Aide; Spanish Clb; Yrbk (E, P)

HUTCHISON, SHELBY L; NEWARK, OH; NEWARK HS; (SO); Ctznshp Aw; Hi Hnr Roll; Hnr Roll; Nat Stu Ath Day Aw; Otst Ac Ach Awd; St of Mnth; WWAHSS; Emplmnt; Orch; Chrldg (JC); CR (R); Elementary Education

HUTCHISON, TOMMY; CEDARVILLE, OH; CEDARVILLE MIDDLE HS; (SO); Ctznshp Aw; Hnr Roll; Pres Ac Ftns Aw; St of Mnth; WWAHSS; Comm Volntr; Chrch Yth Grp; Emplmnt; Key Club; Mus Clb; Quiz Bowl; Tchrs Aide; Vsity Clb; Bnd; Ch Chr; Jzz Bnd; Mch Bnd; Bskball (V L); Sccr; Tennis (V L); Cedarville Soccer Club; Sports Management; Teaching of Music; Cedarville U; Ohio State U

HUTTON, ASHLEY L; CINCINNATI, OH; KINGS HS; (JR); St of Mnth; WWAHSS; Comm Volntr; Emplmnt; Pep Squd; Prom Com; German Clb; Chr; PP Ftbl (J); Sftball (JC); Cl Off (R); Stu Cncl (R); CR (P); Law; Psychology; Miami U; Northern Kentucky U

HYME, ASHLEY S; WESTERVILLE, OH; WESTERVILLE SOUTH HS; (SR); Hi Hnr Roll; Hnr Roll; Otst Ac Ach Awd; Perf Att; St of Mnth; Chrch Yth Grp; DARE; Bnd; Clr Grd; Dnce; Mch Bnd; Pharmacy; Otterbein College

ICSMAN, DEVAN; MEDINA, OH; HIGHLAND HS; (SR); Ctznshp Aw; Kwnis Aw; Nat Ldrshp Svc; St of Mnth; WWAHSS; Yth Ldrshp Prog; Comm Volntr; Peer Tut/Med; Red Cr Aide; Chrch Yth Grp; Emplmnt; Jr Cls League; Key Club; Svce Clb; SADD; Tchrs Aide; Vsity Clb; Chr; Ch Chr; SP/M/VS; Chrldg (V L); Cr Ctry (J); Track (J); Vsy Clb (V); Adv Cncl (R); Stu Cncl (R); Music Merchandising; Travel/Tourism Management; Eastern Kentucky U

INDERHEES, MOLLY A; CINCINNATI, OH; MC AULEY HS; (SO); Hi Hnr Roll; Perf Att; WWAHSS; Comm Volntr; Spec Olymp Vol; Key Club; P to P St Amb Prg; Spanish Clb; Bskball (V L); Sccr (JCL); Stu Cncl (R); CR (R); Physical Therapist; Doctor

INGRAM, JOHN; CLEVELAND, OH; JOHN F KENNEDY HS; (JR); Hnr Roll; Sci Fairs; Comm Volntr; Peer Tut/Med; DARE; Emplmnt; Mus Clb; Sci Clb; Scouts; Tchrs Aide; Dnce; Ohio State U; Berkeley College of Music

INSCHO, AMANDA; CTRBURG, OH; BIG WALNUT HS; (SR); Hnr Roll; Comm Volntr; Emplmnt; Dnce; Drl Tm; Teen Advisors; Captain of Dance Team - Senior Year; Elementary Education; Ashland University OH; Ohio State University

IRELAND, ROSS; UNIONTOWN, OH; HOOVER HS; (SR); Hnr Roll; Nat Hon Sy; WWAHSS; Yth Ldrshp Prog; Comm Volntr; Drma Clb; Emplmnt; Jr Ach; Lib Aide; Off Aide; French Clb; SP/M/VS; Cr Ctry (J); Certified Open Water Diver; Ultimate Frisbee Captain; Hospitality Management; Banking/Finance; Pennsylvania Culinary Institute; Ohio State U

IRICK, REBECCA N; GOSHEN, OH; GOSHEN HS; (FR); Hi Hnr Roll; Hnr Roll; Otst Ac Ach Awd; Perf Att; St of Mnth; USMC Stu Ath Aw; Chess; Chrch Yth Grp; DARE; Ch Chr; Medicine; Bachelor's; Miami U; Drexel U

ISABEL, KRISTIN M; LEROY, OH; RIVERSIDE HS; (SO); 4H Awd; Yth Ldrshp Prog; 4-H; Key Club; Cr Ctry (L); Hsbk Rdg; Lcrsse; Track (L); Snowboarding; Non-Performance Arts; PhD / Veterinary; Business; Ohio State; Miami of Ohio

ISOM, MICHAEL; LORAIN, OH; LAK LORAIN ADMIRAL KING HS; (FR); Bsball (V); Bskball (V); Ftball (J); Track (V); Wrstlg (J); Design; Art; Florida State; Ohio State

ITTU, ALYSSA; CLEVELAND, OH; FAIRVIEW HS; (SR); Hnr Roll; MVP; Comm Volntr; Chrch Yth Grp; Key Club; Lib Aide; Prom Com; Tchrs Aide; Chr; Golf (V CL); Sftball (V CL); Adv Cncl (R); Education; Sports Medicine

JACKS, AMANDA P; COLUMBUS, OH; HARVEST PREP SCH; (SR); Hi Hnr Roll; Hnr Roll; Nat Hon Sy; WWAHSS; Comm Volntr; Chrch Yth Grp; Emplmnt; Off Aide; Tchrs Aide; Vllyball (V L); Yrbk (P); Physical Therapy; Photography; Ohio Dominican U; Ohio U

JACKSON, AMANDA N; COLUMBUS, OH; WALNUT RIDGE HS; (FR); Hi Hnr Roll; Hnr Roll; Nat Hon Sy; Otst Ac Ach Awd; Sci Fairs; St of Mnth; Comm Volntr; Peer Tut/Med; DARE; Lib Aide; Mth Clb/Tm; Off Aide; Pep Squd; Tchrs Aide; Chr; Dnce; Drl Tm; Ability to Do Sign Language; Law; Psychology; Stanford U; Georgetown U

JACKSON, BRYAN; CINCINNATI, OH; WITHROW UNIVERSITY HS; (FR); Ctznshp Aw; Hnr Roll; Otst Ac Ach Awd; Perf Att; St of Mnth; DARE

JACKSON, CHELSAY; CRESTLINE, OH; CRESTLINE HS; (SO); Hnr Roll; Perf Att; WWAHSS; Comm Volntr; Drma Clb; Key Club; Chr; SP/M/VS; Tennis (J); Vllyball (J); Stu Cncl (R); Vice-President of FCCLA; Law; The Ohio State U; Miami U

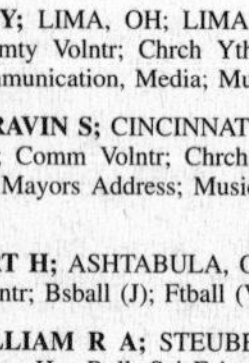
Inscho, Amanda
Big Walnut HS
Centerburg, OH

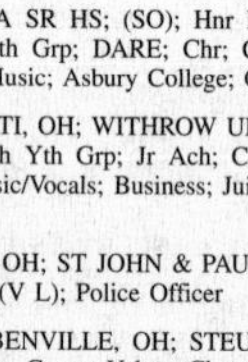
Hughes, Keith
Mt Gilead HS
Cardington, OH

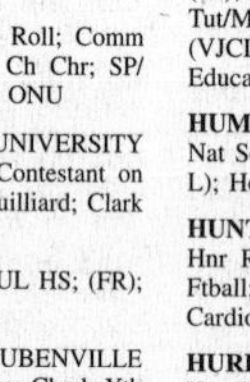
Howell III, William R A
Steubenville HS
Steubenville, OH

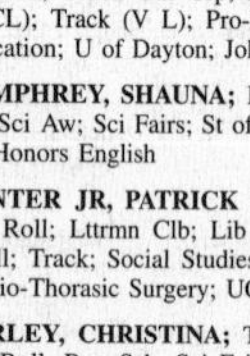
Horton, Meagan
Lima, OH

National
Honor Roll
Spring 2005

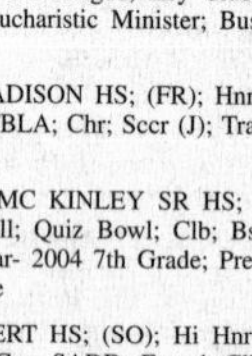
Hopkins, Jade
Groveport Madison HS
Columbus, OH

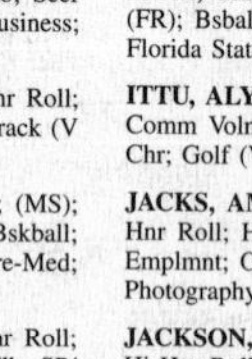
Hric, Emily C
Newbury HS
Newbury, OH

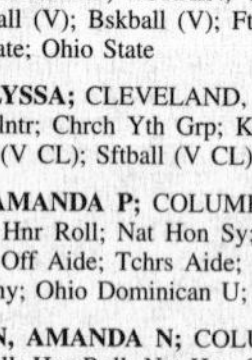
Hughes III, Edward
Mc Donald HS
Mc Donald, OH

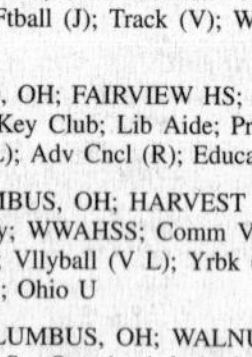
Jackson, Amanda N
Walnut Ridge HS
Columbus, OH

JACKSON, DAMION; COLUMBUS, OH; WALNUT RIDGE HS; (FR); Bnd; Brought My Grades Up; Computers; Graphic Design; Harvard; Ohio State U

JACKSON, ERIN B; WILLOUGHBY, OH; WILLOUGHBY SOUTH HS; (FR); Hnr Roll; Otst Ac Ach Awd; Chrch Yth Grp; DARE; Emplmnt; Key Club; Spanish Clb; Chr; Lawyer; Doctor; Notre Dame; UCLA

JACKSON, JASMINE S; CINCINNATI, OH; WITHROW UNIVERSITY HS; (FR); Ctznshp Aw; Hnr Roll; Otst Ac Ach Awd; Sci Fairs; St of Mnth; Comm Volntr; Chrch Yth Grp; Emplmnt; Mus Clb; Off Aide; Tchrs Aide; Ch Chr; U of Cincinnati Upward Bound; Sign Language; Juvenile Lawyer/ Counselor; U of Cincinnati; Georgia Tech U

JACKSON, TYLER D; N LEWISBURG, OH; TRIAD HS; (JR); Hnr Roll; Perf Att; Emplmnt; Bsball (VJ L); Bskball (VJ L); Ftball (V L); FCCLA-Outstanding Sophomore; Business Management; Physical Therapy; Muskingum College; Wright State U

JACOB, BRITTANY; ELYRIA, OH; ELYRIA HS; (FR); Ctznshp Aw; Hnr Roll; Perf Att; St of Mnth; Spec Olymp Vol; Chrch Yth Grp; DARE; Drma Clb; Scouts; Bnd; Mch Bnd; SP/M/VS; Bskball (J); Mar Art (J); Sccr (J); Tennis (J); Girl Scout Silver Award; Acting, Firefighting; Forensics, Author; Lorain County Community College; Ohio State U

JACOB, JO ELLEN; NILES, OH; NILES MC KINLEY HS; (JR); All Am Sch; Hi Hnr Roll; Hnr Roll; Nat Hon Sy; WWAHSS; Comm Volntr; Peer Tut/ Med; Drma Clb; Emplmnt; FTA; JSA; Key Club; Mus Clb; SADD; French Clb; Chr; SP/M/VS; Yrbk (E, R, P); 2 Year Attendee of Summer Honors Institute; Master's in Integrated Social Studies W/ Minor in Theater Arts

JACOB, TRAVIS; CINCINNATI, OH; LA SALLE HS; (SO); Hi Hnr Roll; Hnr Roll; Comm Volntr; DARE; Emplmnt; Ftball (J); Track (J); Wt Lftg (V); Pharmacy; Mechanical Engineer; U of Cincinnati

JACOBS, COURTNEY J; REYNOLDSBURG, OH; REYNOLDSBURG HS; (SR); Ctznshp Aw; Hnr Roll; Perf Att; St of Mnth; Comm Volntr; Peer Tut/ Med; Chrch Yth Grp; Emplmnt; Photog; Tchrs Aide; Oncology Nursing; Chiropractic Work; U of South Florida; Ohio State U

JACOBS, DANIELA L; BELLVILLE, OH; CLEAR FORK HS; (FR); Hnr Roll; WWAHSS; Chrch Yth Grp; Mount Vernon Nazarene U

JACOBS, MICHELLE L; PERRYSBURG, OH; PERRYSBURG HS; (SR); Hi Hnr Roll; Nat Hon Sy; Peer Tut/Med; Drma Clb; Spanish Clb; PP Ftbl; Yrbk (R); Spanish Club Representative; Nursing; Spanish; Bowling Green State U

JAEGER, BRANDI C; ASHTABULA, OH; WEST JHS; (MS); Ctznshp Aw; Hnr Roll; Nat Hon Sy; Otst Ac Ach Awd; Perf Att; St of Mnth; Yth Ldrshp Prog; Comm Volntr; Chrch Yth Grp; DARE; Fr of Library; Lib Aide; Mus Clb; Off Aide; Scouts; SADD; Chr; Ch Chr; Dnce; SP/M/VS; Ice Sktg (L); Sccr (C); Vllyball (C); Adv Cncl (S); CR (R); Sch Ppr (E); Yrbk (P); English Festival Winner; National Junior Honor Society; Surgeon / Chef; Lawyer / Teacher; Yale U; Harvard U

JAFFAL, RAWAN; CLEVELAND, OH; JOHN MARSHALL HS; (SO); Ctznshp Aw; Hnr Roll; Otst Ac Ach Awd; Perf Att; WWAHSS; Emplmnt; Fr of Library; Lib Aide; CR (P); Meditation; Art Field; Wedding Consultant; Xavier U; Kent State

JAGRU, RYAN; MAPLE HTS, OH; (SR); Hi Hnr Roll; Hnr Roll; Nat Hon Sy; Nat Ldrshp Svc; Yth Ldrshp Prog; Drma Clb; NtlFrnscLg; NYLC; Spch Team; Ch Chr; SP/M/VS; Ftball (J); Sccr (V CL); Ohio State Forensic Champions-Dramatic Interp. 2005; 2 Time Forensics National Qualifier 2004-2005; Theatre Arts; Communications/International Studies; Baldwin Wallace College

JAMES, TIM; SALEM, OH; LEETONIA; (JR); Hnr Roll; MVP; Nat Hon Sy; Perf Att; Sci Fairs; WWAHSS; Chrch Yth Grp; Chr; Bsball; Cr Ctry (V C); Track (C)

JANSON, CLAY; BREWSTER, OH; FAIRLESS HS; (FR); Ctznshp Aw; Hi Hnr Roll; Otst Ac Ach Awd; Perf Att; St of Mnth; Comm Volntr; Key Club; Tchrs Aide; Bnd; Mch Bnd; Pep Bnd; Political Science/Attorney; College History Teacher; Mount Union College; Akron U

JANSON, KENNETH J; NORTH BLOOMFIELD, OH; BLOOMFIELD HS; (SO); Ctznshp Aw; Hnr Roll; Otst Ac Ach Awd; Perf Att; St of Mnth; USAA; Valdctrian; WWAHSS; Comm Volntr; Peer Tut/Med; Chrch Yth Grp; DARE; Off Aide; Prom Com; SADD; Tchrs Aide; Sccr; Cl Off (V); CR (R); Yrbk (E, R, P); Relay for Life-President; Poetry Achievement Award; Accounting / Business Management; Computer Programming

JAQUSZTYN, AGATA; LOWELLVILLE, OH; POLAND MS; (MS); Ctznshp Aw; Hnr Roll; Nat Hon Sy; Perf Att; Salutrn; Sci/Math Olympn; St of Mnth; Comm Volntr; Peer Tut/Med; Mod UN; Off Aide; National Junior Honor Society; Mathematics; Youngstown State U; Ohio State U

JAROS, LINDSEY; PAINESVILLE, OH; RIVERSIDE HS; (SO); Hi Hnr Roll; Chrch Yth Grp; Key Club; Swmg (V L); District Qualifier in Swimming; Medical; Miami U Ohio

JAROUCHE, SEREEN; TOLEDO, OH; TOLEDO ISLAMIC AC; (FR); Hi Hnr Roll; Hnr Roll; Sci Fairs; St of Mnth; St Optmst of Yr; Comm Volntr; Dnce; Jzz Bnd; SP/M/VS; Stg Cre; Bskball; Vllyball; Stu Cncl (R); Pharmacy; Business; U of Toledo

JARVI, ERIK; MANTUA, OH; CRESTWOOD HS; (JR); Hi Hnr Roll; Hnr Roll; Perf Att; WWAHSS; Chrch Yth Grp; Quiz Bowl; Bnd; Mch Bnd; Quiz Team; Engineering; The U of Akron

JASPER, SARAH B; SANDUSKY, OH; ST MARYS CTRL CATHOLIC HS; (JR); Hnr Roll; WWAHSS; Comm Volntr; Key Club; Mod UN; Prom Com; Chrldg (V L); Tennis (V L); Tennis-Co Captain, Coaches' Award MVP; Varsity Runners-Up At Nationals Comp Team Cheer; Dennison; Capital

JAVA, AMANDA; W FARMINGTON, OH; CHAMPION HS; (JR); Hnr Roll; Key Club; P to P St Amb Prg; Sccr (J); Track (V); Business; Kent State U; Youngstown State U

JEFFRIES III, JAMES V; CANTON, OH; GLENOAK HS; (JR); Hnr Roll; Nat Hon Sy; Pres Sch; USAA; WWAHSS; Comm Volntr; Spec Olymp Vol; Chrch Yth Grp; Dbte Team; DECA; Key Club; NtlFrnscLg; Off Aide; P to P St Amb Prg; Cr Ctry (J); Sccr (J); Tennis (V CL); 2nd Team Federal League Tennis 2004 & 2005; 2 Time National DECA Qualifier; Business / Marketing; Sports Marketing; Ferris State U

JENKINS, CASIE; SAINT PARIS, OH; GRAHAM HS; (SR); Hnr Roll; Sci Fairs; WWAHSS; Comm Volntr; 4-H; Emplmnt; Ntl FFA; Prom Com; Chr; Chrldg (V CL); Stu Cncl (S); Yrbk (P); Mascot-Varsity/Letter Winner; Agricultural Education; Ohio State U Agricultural Technical Institute

JENKINS, ISHA B; CINCINNATI, OH; ST BERNARD-ELMWOOD PLACE HS; (JR); St of Mnth; Bskball (J); Health Technology

JENKINS, STEPHANIE L; MEDWAY, OH; TECUMSEH HS; (FR); 4H Awd; Hnr Roll; Otst Ac Ach Awd; St of Mnth; Yth Ldrshp Prog; Comm Volntr; 4-H; Chrch Yth Grp; DARE; Drma Clb; Pep Squd; SADD; Spanish Clb; Ch Chr; SP/M/VS; Chrldg (J); Sccr (J); Sftball (J); Awards in Horse Back Riding; Nurse or Ob/Gyn; Wright State U; Miami U

JENKINS, TOMY; AKRON, OH; FIRESTONE HS; (JR); Hnr Roll; Photog; Cr Ctry (J); Sea Cadets (2004 Cadet of the Year); Magnet Arts Program; United States Naval Academy

JENKINS, ZACHARY T; IRONTON, OH; IRONTON HS; (FR); Hnr Roll; Nat Hon Sy; Ctznshp Aw; Chrch Yth Grp; Scouts; Spanish Clb; Bnd; Mch Bnd; Pep Bnd; SP/M/VS; Golf (J); Doctorate Degree; Pharmacy; Ohio State U; Wittenberg U

JENNINGS, CHRISTOPHER J; HAMILTON, OH; NEW MIAMI JR/SR HS; (SR); Ctznshp Aw; Hnr Roll; Perf Att; WWAHSS; Bsball (VJ); Positive Student Award; Who's Who Among American H.S. Students-Sports Edition

JENNINGS, MEGAN; LIMA, OH; LIMA SR HS; (JR); Ctznshp Aw; Hnr Roll; St of Mnth; WWAHSS; Comm Volntr; Spanish Clb; Yrbk (E); Participated in Choir; Graphic Design; Web Designer

JESSE, KIRK A; NEY, OH; FAIRVIEW HS; (JR); Hnr Roll; Perf Att; Chrch Yth Grp; Vsity Clb; Bsball (V); Bskball (V); Ftball (V); Vsy Clb (V); Law Enforcement; Criminal Justice; Defiance College; North West State Community College

JIANG, DIANA; MASON, OH; WM MASON HS; (JR); Hi Hnr Roll; Nat Hon Sy; Otst Ac Ach Awd; Sci/Math Olympn; WWAHSS; Comm Volntr; Peer Tut/Med; ArtClub; Dbte Team; Emplmnt; NtlFrnscLg; Quiz Bowl; Spch Team; Bnd; Mch Bnd; Pep Bnd; National Chemistry Olympiad; Ohio Buckeye Girls State; Biomedical Engineering; International Business

JIANG, YANG; SYLVANIA, OH; NORTHVIEW HS; (FR); Duke TS; Hi Hnr Roll; Comm Volntr; DARE; FCA; Quiz Bowl; Scouts; Adv Cncl (R); Accounting; Masters of Business Administration; U of Michigan; U of Chicago

JIMENEZ, MADELINE; STEUBENVILLE, OH; (MS); Ctznshp Aw; Hnr Roll; Perf Att; Comm Volntr; Peer Tut/Med; Red Cr Aide; DARE; Key Club; Track (V); Lawyer; Technician & Automatics; Michigan State U; Harvard U

JIMENEZ, MONICA; DEFIANCE, OH; DEFIANCE HS; (MS); Ctznshp Aw; Hnr Roll; Otst Ac Ach Awd; Perf Att; Chrch Yth Grp; DARE; Jr Ach; Acpl Chr; Dnce; Swg Chr; Stu Cncl (T); Participant-National American Miss; Corporate Law; Accounting; Berkeley College; Harvard U

JOHNS, TARYN R; WASHINGTON COURT HOUSE, OH; WASHINGTON HS; (FR); Hnr Roll; Perf Att; DARE; Off Aide; Tchrs Aide; Dnce; Sftball (J); Track (L); Nail Tech; Head Start Teacher; Ohio State U

JOHNSON, ALEISHA; TOLEDO, OH; ROY C START HS; (SO); Hnr Roll; Drma Clb; Track (V); Nominated Poet of the Year By International Society of Poets; Fashion Design; Chemical Engineer

JOHNSON, ALEX; WESTERVILLE, OH; ST FRANCIS DE SALES HS; (JR); Hi Hnr Roll; Hnr Roll; Nat Hon Sy; Peer Tut/Med; DARE; Mth Clb/Tm; Off Aide; P to P St Amb Prg; Latin Clb; Skiing (V); Sccr (J); Stu Cncl (R); CR (R); Ambassador Drug Free Program; Patent Law; Indiana; Harvard

JOHNSON, ALISON; CINCINNATI, OH; MC AULEY HS; (JR); Hi Hnr Roll; WWAHSS; Yth Ldrshp Prog; Spec Olymp Vol; Emplmnt; Key Club; NYLC; P to P St Amb Prg; Swmg (V L); Tennis (JC); Sch Ppr (R); Ambassador for New Students; Marketing; Communications; Butler U; Miami U

JOHNSON, ALLIE; COLUMBIA STATION, OH; COLUMBIA HS; (FR); Hnr Roll; Chess; DARE; Drma Clb; Jr Ach; Dnce; Chrldg (V); Scr Kpr (V); Track (V); Journalism; Fashion; Ohio State U; Kent State U

JOHNSON, ALYSE M; MAUMEE, OH; NOTRE DAME AC; (SO); Hi Hnr Roll; Perf Att; WWAHSS; Comm Volntr; Peer Tut/Med; Chrch Yth Grp; Pep Squd; Bnd; Jzz Bnd; Mch Bnd; Orch; Forensics; Criminal Psychology

JOHNSON, ANGELICA; WARREN, OH; WARREN G HARDING HS; (JR); Ctznshp Aw; Hnr Roll; Nat Hon Sy; Perf Att; WWAHSS; Yth Ldrshp Prog; Comm Volntr; Peer Tut/Med; Chrch Yth Grp; Emplmnt; Lib Aide; Photog; SADD; Chr; Ch Chr; Drl Tm; Vllyball; Sch Ppr (R); Yrbk (R, P); Law; Edward Waters; Penn State

JOHNSON, BRITTANY D; CINCINNATI, OH; WITHROW UNIVERSITY HS; (JR); Comm Volntr; Chrch Yth Grp; Stu Cncl (S); Yrbk; Nursing; Accounting; U of Cincinnati; Cincinnati State

JOHNSON, JAQUIS; COLUMBUS, OH; WALNUT RIDGE HS; (FR); Hnr Roll; Otst Ac Ach Awd; Perf Att; Yth Ldrshp Prog; Comm Volntr; Chess; DARE; Dnce; Drl Tm; Orch; Bsball; Chrldg; Vllyball (J); Dentist; Veterinarian; Central State U

JOHNSON, JASMINE L; PARMA, OH; VALLEY FORGE HS; (JR); WWAHSS; Track (V); I Am in My School's Boxing Club; Physical Therapy/ Sports Medicine; Art/Design; Atlanta A & T

JOHNSON, KAILEY A; ASHTABULA, OH; LAKESIDE HS; (SO); Cr Ctry (V L); Track (V L); Nursing; Business; Brigham Young U (Utah); Malone College (Ohio)

JOHNSON, LUKE; NORTHWOOD, OH; LAKE HS; (SO); Hi Hnr Roll; Nat Hon Sy; Otst Ac Ach Awd; Quiz Bowl; Tchrs Aide; Spanish Clb; National Honor Society; Spanish Club; Computer Technology; Ohio State U; Michigan U

JOHNSON, MARIE; COLUMBUS, OH; WHETSTONE HS; (FR); 4H Awd; Hi Hnr Roll; Hnr Roll; DARE; Tchrs Aide; Orch; Sftball (L); Swmg (L); Made Honor Roll All 4-Times; Teacher; Veterinarian; Ohio State U; Shawnee State U

JOHNSON, T'AIRRA S; CLEVELAND, OH; LINCOLN WEST HS; (JR); Ctznshp Aw; Hnr Roll; Perf Att; Sci Fairs; Sci/Math Olympn; Peer Tut/Med; DARE; Fr of Library; POETRY CLU Clb; Dnce; Swmg; Track; Vllyball

JOHNSON I, PEREZ; CINCINNATI, OH; WITHROW UNIVERSITY HS; (FR); Ctznshp Aw; Hnr Roll; Drma Clb; Sccr (V); Voice Acting; Electronic Engineer; Dalton Acting College; Juilliard Acting College

JOHNSON III, WILLIE; CLEVELAND, OH; COLLINWOOD HS; (FR); Ctznshp Aw; MVP; Nat Sci Aw; Sci Fairs; Sci/Math Olympn; Red Cr Aide; ArtClub; DARE; Mth Clb/Tm; Mus Clb; Sci Clb; SADD; Ch Chr; Bskball (C); Ftball (C); Tennis (C); FSU; Ohio

JOHNSTON, ALLYSON; GALLIPOLIS, OH; GALLIA AC; (FR); Hi Hnr Roll; WWAHSS; Chrch Yth Grp; Key Club; Bnd; Ch Chr; Jzz Bnd; Mch Bnd; History Day; Teacher; Music Education; Ohio State U; Princeton U

JOHNSTON, LAUREN; COLUMBUS, OH; WORTHINGTON CHRISTIAN HS; (FR); Hnr Roll; Comm Volntr; Chrch Yth Grp; Emplmnt; Lib Aide; Tchrs Aide; SP/M/VS; Stg Cre; Stu Cncl (R); High School Math Teacher

JONES, ADRIANA; CINCINNATI, OH; NORWOOD HS; (SO); Ctznshp Aw; Hnr Roll; Otst Ac Ach Awd; Pres Ac Ftns Aw; Comm Volntr; Chr; Chrldg (J); PP Ftbl (J); Swmg (V); Track (V); Cl Off (T); Community Service "The Anthony Munoz Project"; To Become a Pharmacist; U of Cincinnati

JONES, DANIELLE; DAYTON, OH; MEADOWDALE HS; (FR); Hnr Roll; St of Mnth; DARE; Emplmnt; Perfect Attendance the Entire School Year; RETS Technical Institution; Sinclair Community College

JONES, ERICA; TOLEDO, OH; ALLIANCE AC OF TOLEDO; (FR); Ctznshp Aw; Hi Hnr Roll; Hnr Roll; Otst Ac Ach Awd; Perf Att; St of Mnth; Peer Tut/Med; Drma Clb; Off Aide; Tchrs Aide; Dnce; Chrldg; Stu Cncl (P); Yrbk (P); Most Creative Writer; Top Student; Doctor; Bachelor's Degree; Spelman College; U of Toledo

JONES, JESSICA; CLEVELAND, OH; HEALTH CAREERS CTR; (SO); Ctznshp Aw; Hi Hnr Roll; Hnr Roll; Perf Att; Sci Fairs; St of Mnth; DARE; Drma Clb; Scouts; Dnce; Drl Tm; SP/M/VS; Chrldg (C); RN; Dentist; Stanford U, Brown U; Ohio State U

JONES, KIANA C; CLEVELAND, OH; SHAW HS; (SO); Chrch Yth Grp; Dnce; Bskball (J); Chrldg (V); Track (J); Sch Ppr (R); Culinary Arts; Health Field / Nurse; Cleveland State U; Ohio State U

JONES, KIASHA L; CLEVELAND, OH; COLLINWOOD HS; (SO); All Am Sch; Hnr Roll; WWAHSS; Chrch Yth Grp; Ch Chr; Sftball (V); National Jr Honor Society; Nursing; Lawyer / Law Enforcement

Johnson, Angelica
Warren G Harding HS
Warren, OH

Jennings, Christopher J
New Miami JR/SR HS
Hamilton, OH

Jenkins, Casie
Graham HS
Saint Paris, OH

Jaqusztyn, Agata
Poland MS
Lowellville, OH

Jacob, Brittany
Elyria HS
Elyria, OH

Jagru, Ryan
Maple Hts, OH

Jenkins, Tomy
Firestone HS
Akron, OH

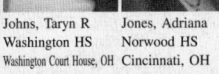

Johns, Taryn R
Washington HS
Washington Court House, OH

Jones, Adriana
Norwood HS
Cincinnati, OH

JONES, MARIA A; WASHINGTON COURT HOUSE, OH; MIAMI TRACE HS; (SO); Hi Hnr Roll; Hnr Roll; Perf Att; Sci Fairs; Comm Volntr; Peer Tut/Med; Chrch Yth Grp; DARE; Emplmnt; Fr of Library; Jr Ach; Lib Aide; Ntl Beta Clb; Sci Clb; Sch Ppr (R, P); Psychology; Modeling & Fashion Design; Bluffton U; Ohio U

JONES, MELVIN L; CLEVELAND, OH; EAST TECH HS; (SO); Nat Sci Aw; Perf Att; Sci Fairs; Red Cr Aide; Cmptr Clb; ROTC; Tech Clb; Wdwrkg Clb; Bnd; Computer Tech; Automotive; DeVry; Tri C-Cuyhoga Community College

JONES, RANA; CINCINNATI, OH; HUGHES CTR; (SR); St of Mnth; Comm Volntr; Chrch Yth Grp; Wrstlg (V); Teaching, Master's Degree; Hawaii Community College; Hawaii Pacific

JONES, ROBERT; COLUMBUS, OH; (MS); Ctznshp Aw; Hnr Roll; Otst Ac Ach Awd; Perf Att; St of Mnth; Chrch Yth Grp; Bnd; Ch Chr; Bskball; Ftball; Vllyball; Angel Mime At Come As You Are; Won Denominational Church Usher; Ohio State U

JONES JR, HERMAN; CINCINNATI, OH; WITHROW UNIVERSITY HS; (FR); Ctznshp Aw; Hi Hnr Roll; Perf Att; Chrch Yth Grp; Ch Chr; Dnce; Ftball; Lawyer

JORDAN, KATIE J; MC DERMOTT, OH; NORTHWEST HS; (JR); 4H Awd; Hi Hnr Roll; Hnr Roll; WWAHSS; Comm Volntr; 4-H; Chrch Yth Grp; Pep Squd; Vsity Clb; Bskball (V C); Vllyball (V C); Cl Off (V); Sch Ppr (R); Yrbk (E); Horseback Riding Showmanship; Horse Training; Medical Diagnosis & Treatment; Medical Technologies; Marshall U; Ohio U

JORDAN, LAURIE C; WESTERVILLE, OH; WESTERVILLE CTRL HS; (FR); Ctznshp Aw; Hnr Roll; St of Mnth; Peer Tut/Med; DARE; Pep Squd; Chr; Dnce; Medicine-Brain Surgeon; Xavier U; Johns Hopkins

JORDAN, MICHAEL; BRADNER, OH; ELMWOOD HS; (JR); Hnr Roll; Perf Att; Sci Fairs; DARE; Emplmnt; Chr; SP/M/VS; Magic Club; Own and Operate Restaurant Chain; Bowling Green State U

JORDAN, RA'SHAWN; COLUMBUS, OH; BROOKHAVEN HS; (SO); Hi Hnr Roll; Hnr Roll; Comm Volntr

JORDAN, SARAH N; TOLEDO, OH; ST URSULA AC; (FR); Hi Hnr Roll; Hnr Roll; Perf Att; Pres Ac Ftns Aw; Comm Volntr; DARE; Tchrs Aide; French Clb; Chr; Vllyball; Stu Cncl (R); Fashion Designer; Wedding Planner

JOSEPH, BROOKE; NILES, OH; MC KINLEY HS; (FR); Hnr Roll; Italian Clb; Chrldg (J); Ftball (V); Hsbk Rdg (V); Lcrsse (C); Sftball (J)

JOYCE, MICHAEL D; AVON LAKE, OH; (FR); Hi Hnr Roll; Sci/Math Olympn; Chrch Yth Grp; Emplmnt; Bnd; Chr; Stg Cre; Sccr (J); Stu Cncl (R); Ecology Club; Diversity Awareness Club; Veterinarian; Cornell U (New York); Ohio State U

JUDSON, ELIZABETH; CLEVELAND, OH; GARFIELD HTS HS; (JR); Comm Volntr; Peer Tut/Med; Emplmnt; Bskball (V); Pre-Dentistry; Orthodontist

JUERGENS, ANDREA; SPRINGFIELD, OH; SHAWNEE HS; (FR); Hi Hnr Roll; Sci Fairs; Peer Tut/Med; Chrch Yth Grp; Drma Clb; Emplmnt; Key Club; Off Aide; SADD; Bnd; Mch Bnd; Orch; Pep Bnd; Wt Lftg (J); Stu Cncl; Doctor; Pharmacist; Ohio U; U of Cincinnati

JUSTICE, DANIELLE; MILFORD, OH; MILFORD HS; (JR); Hnr Roll; Nat Hon Sy; Peer Tut/Med; Drma Clb; Mod UN; Svce Clb; Lcrsse (V); Track (J); Government Club President; History/Law; Political Science; Ohio State U; U of Pennsylvania

JUTTE, PAUL; MIDDLETOWN, OH; LEMON MONROE LOCAL HS; (SO); Hi Hnr Roll; Otst Ac Ach Awd; Perf Att; Pres Sch; St of Mnth; WWAHSS; Acpl Chr; Chr; Dnce; SP/M/VS; Tennis (V L); Cl Off (T); Stu Cncl (T); CR (R); Leads in Musicals & Summer Theatre; Full Time Employment in Summer; Architect; Computer Engineer

KABACK, JOSHUA M; YOUNGSTOWN, OH; LIBERTY HS; (SR); Hi Hnr Roll; Hnr Roll; Nat Hon Sy; Yth Ldrshp Prog; Comm Volntr; Emplmnt; HO'Br Yth Ldrshp; Mod UN; Prom Com; Quiz Bowl; Tmpl Yth Grp; Sccr (V CL); Tennis (V CL); Stu Cncl (S); CR (R); Internship for US Congressman; Law/Political Science; Business; Miami U (Attending)

KAHLE, WM D; CANTON, OH; TIMKEN SR HS; (MS); Hnr Roll; Nat Mrt LOC; Comm Volntr; Civil Engineering; Forensic; Florida State U; Ohio State U

KAISER, ASHLEY; CINCINNATI, OH; NORTHWEST HS; (SR); Hnr Roll; Otst Ac Ach Awd; Comm Volntr; Biology Clb; Off Aide; Sci Clb; Svce Clb; Tchrs Aide; Ftball (L); Wrstlg (L); Key Club; Unknighted Knights; Nursing; Phoenix College

KALABON, MICHELLE E; CLEVELAND, OH; GARFIELD HEIGHTS HS; (SO); Hnr Roll; Nat Hon Sy; Emplmnt; Acpl Chr; SP/M/VS; Swg Chr; Vllyball (J); Cl Off (P); Project Love; Criminal Justice

KALINOSKI, LAUREN L; TOLEDO, OH; ST URSULA AC; (FR); Hi Hnr Roll; Comm Volntr; ArtClub; Chrch Yth Grp; Quiz Bowl; Stg Cre; Sftball; Best of Show in 2005 School Art Show; School Art 1 Award; Architecture; Art; U of Notre Dame; U of Cincinnati

KAMMAN, LISA M; NORTH ROYALTON, OH; NORTH ROYALTON HS; (SR); Otst Ac Ach Awd; Perf Att; St of Mnth; Comm Volntr; Peer Tut/Med; Chrch Yth Grp; Key Club; Svce Clb; Spanish Clb; Bnd; Mch Bnd; Poem Published in Literary Magazine; PTA Reflections Outstanding Achievement; Early Childhood Education; Intervention Specialist (Special Education); Walsh U

KANE, MEGAN; NEWARK, OH; NEWARK CATHOLIC HS; (JR); Hnr Roll; Nat Hon Sy; WWAHSS; Hab For Humty Volntr; Key Club; Prom Com; Sftball (V); Vllyball (V L); Cl Off (T); Communications; Journalism; U of Akron; U of Kentucky

KANU, JOHN; COLUMBUS, OH; WHETSTONE HS; (FR); Hnr Roll; Perf Att; DARE; SP/M/VS; Sccr (J); Track (J); Mechanical Engineering; Electrical Engineering; Ohio State U; Maryland U

KAPUSINSKI, NICK; AKRON, OH; COPLEY HS; (SO); Hnr Roll; WWAHSS; Comm Volntr; Key Club; French Clb; Bnd; Mch Bnd; Letter Winner in Band and Academics; Marine Biology; U of Toledo

KARALIC, SEJLA; AKRON, OH; GARFIELD HS; (SR); Ctznshp Aw; Hi Hnr Roll; Nat Hon Sy; Perf Att; WWAHSS; Comm Volntr; Dbte Team; Drma Clb; Emplmnt; Key Club; NtlFrnscLg; Prom Com; Spch Team; SP/M/VS; Stg Cre; Sccr (V C); Stu Cncl (R); Sch Ppr (E); Mock Trial Outstanding Attorney Award; Scholastics Silver Key Art Award; Political Science; Business Finance; U of Akron

KARASH, RACHEL; LAKE MILTON, OH; JACKSON-MILTON; (JR); Hi Hnr Roll; Hnr Roll; Kwnis Aw; MVP; Nat Hon Sy; Otst Ac Ach Awd; WWAHSS; Peer Tut/Med; AL Aux Girls; ArtClub; Drma Clb; Key Club; Off Aide; Prom Com; SADD; SP/M/VS; Bskball (V CL); PP Ftbl (V); Track (V L); Vllyball (V CL); Cl Off (V); Stu Cncl (R)

KARDASZ, KAYLEE; LEBANON, OH; LEBANON HS; (FR); Perf Att; Comm Volntr; Aerospace; Advanced Art; Animal Biology; Marine Biology; Florida State; U of Cincinnati

KARL, COLLEEN; DAYTON, OH; BEAVERCREEK HS; (SO); Comm Volntr; Peer Tut/Med; Chrch Yth Grp; DARE; Drma Clb; Lib Aide; Photog; Ch Chr; Sccr (J L); Track (V); U of Dayton; Ohio U

KARR, KASEY; WARREN, OH; CHAMPION HS; (JR); Hi Hnr Roll; Hnr Roll; St of Mnth; WWAHSS; Key Club; Pep Squd; Prom Com; Tchrs Aide; Cr Ctry (V); Sftball (V C); Adv Cncl; Stu Cncl (R); CR (R); Yrbk; Biochemical Engineering; Dartmouth College; Purdue U

KASALES, CRYSTAL; EDISON, OH; MT GILEAD HS; (SO); Ctznshp Aw; Hi Hnr Roll; Nat Hon Sy; WWAHSS; Comm Volntr; DARE; Jr Ach; Ntl FFA; Chr; SP/M/VS; Major in Psychology

KASIOR, DAVID A; OREGON, OH; CLAY HS; (SR); 4H Awd; Hnr Roll; Otst Ac Ach Awd; Perf Att; St of Mnth; Comm Volntr; 4-H; DARE; Lib Aide; Mth Clb/Tm; Mus Clb; Ntl FFA; Off Aide; Tchrs Aide; Bnd; Jzz Bnd; Mch Bnd; Pep Bnd; Ftball (V); FFA - Greenhand - Chapter / State / Degrees; Band Awards- Squad Leader / Marcher of the Week; Construction / Engineering; Computer / Technology Related; Owens Community College

KASSIMER, ASHLEY; ROOTSTOWN, OH; WARD DAVIS HS; (SO); Hnr Roll; Drma Clb; Chr; SP/M/VS; Sccr (J); Entertainment; Dance; Ohio U; Kent State U

KATTERHENRY, STACEY; WAPAKONETA, OH; WAPAKONETA HS; (JR); 4H Awd; Hnr Roll; Sci Fairs; WWAHSS; 4-H; Chrch Yth Grp; Prom Com; Tchrs Aide; Spanish Clb; Dnce; Chrldg (L); Vllyball (J L); Cl Off (S); Stu Cncl (R); Sch Ppr (E, R); Academic Letter; Early Childhood Education; Wright State Lake Campus

KAUFMAN, KAITLIN; PROSPECT, OH; ELGIN HS; (SR); All Am Sch; Hi Hnr Roll; Nat Hon Sy; Perf Att; Pres Sch; WWAHSS; Peer Tut/Med; Lttrmn Clb; Off Aide; Pep Squd; Acpl Chr; Chr; SP/M/VS; Swg Chr; All Ohio State Fair Choir; Physician Assistant; U of Findlay

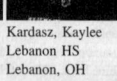

KAUFMAN, WHITNEY; CINCINNATI, OH; COLERAIN HS; (JR); Hnr Roll; Nat Hon Sy; Comm Volntr; Chr; Dnce; Sccr (J L); Track (J); Certified Lifeguard Including CPR / First Aid; A / B Honor Roll / Academic Excellence; Law; Astronomy; U of Louisville; U of Kentucky

KAY, AMANDA; CINCINNATI, OH; MOTHER OF MERCY HS; (JR); Hi Hnr Roll; Hnr Roll; Perf Att; St of Mnth; Comm Volntr; Chrch Yth Grp; Key Club; Outdrs Clb; Sci Clb; Svce Clb; Smart Team Member; Medicine; Occupational Therapy; Northern Kentucky U

KAYLOR, TODD; THORNVILLE, OH; MILLERSPORT JR SR HS; (MS); Hnr Roll; Red Cr Aide; 4-H; Chrch Yth Grp; DARE; Scouts; Bnd; Mch Bnd; Pep Bnd; Sccr; Mathematics; Math Professor; Ohio U; Ohio U Lancaster

KEARNEY, HOLLY D; LUCASVILLE, OH; VALLEY HS; (FR); Hi Hnr Roll; Otst Ac Ach Awd; Perf Att; Sci Fairs; Peer Tut/Med; Chrch Yth Grp; DARE; Lib Aide; Scouts; Chr; Ch Chr; Bskball (J); Scr Kpr (VJ); Sccr (J); Cl Off (P); Master's Degree in Medical School; Doctorate Degree in Medical School

KEEFER, CASEY; WEST CHESTER, OH; LAKOTA EAST HS; (JR); Ctznshp Aw; Hi Hnr Roll; MVP; Otst Ac Ach Awd; WWAHSS; Spec Olymp Vol; Bskball (V C); Cr Ctry (V); Sccr (J); Track (V); All Academic Ohioan (F04); All Ohioan XC (3x) Track (X2); Kinesiology; Sports Science

KEETON, KARA; DAYTON, OH; BEAVER CREEK HS; (JR); Hnr Roll; MVP; Sci Fairs; Comm Volntr; Peer Tut/Med; Chrch Yth Grp; Emplmnt; FCA; Photog; SADD; Tchrs Aide; Drl Tm; Hsbk Rdg; Bryerfest Drill Team Comp. Champions; Equine Management; Ohio State U; Ohio U

KELLER, KENDRA; HUDSON, OH; HUDSON HS; (JR); Ctznshp Aw; DAR; Hi Hnr Roll; MVP; Nat Hon Sy; Comm Volntr; Hosp Aide; Peer Tut/Med; Chrch Yth Grp; FCA; Key Club; Photog; Svce Clb; Vsity Clb; Clb; Yrbk (P); National Honor Society; Academic Achievement Award; Occupational Therapy-Masters; U of Findlay; Ohio Northern U

KELLER, KYLE; BARBERTON, OH; BARBERTON HS; (FR); Hi Hnr Roll; Perf Att; Key Club; Tennis (J); Marine Biologist; Ohio State; Bowling Green

KELLEY, DAMIAN L; CINCINNATI, OH; WYOMING HS; (SR); All Am Sch; Ctznshp Aw; Hi Hnr Roll; Hnr Roll; MVP; Nat Hon Sy; Perf Att; St Schl; St of Mnth; WWAHSS; Comm Volntr; Peer Tut/Med; Cmptr Clb; DARE; Emplmnt; Jr Ach; NYLC; Prom Com; Stg Cre; Ftball (V); Track (V); Wt Lftg (V); Cl Off (R); CR (R); Tutor-Elem; Summer Employ.; Civil Eng./Sch. Accepted 1-05 for Villanova U; Villanova U

KELLY, CIERRA M; CLEVELAND, OH; MARTIN LUTHER KING HS; (FR); Ctznshp Aw; Hnr Roll; MVP; Nat Hon Sy; Perf Att; St of Mnth; WWAHSS; Comm Volntr; Hosp Aide; Peer Tut/Med; ArtClub; Chess; Chrch Yth Grp; DARE; Drma Clb; Kwanza Clb; Mus Clb; Off Aide; Bnd; Chr; Ch Chr; Dnce; Bskball (J); Golf (J); Sftball (J); Vllyball (J); CR (V); Received Award for Top Mock Trial Attorney; Received Honor & Merit Roll; Law / Attorney; Law Degree / Criminal; Baldwin Wallace; Akron U

KELLY, SHASTA; AKRON, OH; KENMORE HS; (SR); Otst Ac Ach Awd; Yth Ldrshp Prog; Comm Volntr; Peer Tut/Med; Chrch Yth Grp; P to P St Amb Prg; Scouts; Ch Chr; SP/M/VS; Track (V); Sch Ppr (E); Criminal Justice Tech. Secretary Admin; Actress; Akron U.; Wooster U, OH

KEMEN, JENNIFER; CINCINNATI, OH; COLERAIN HS; (SR); F Lan Hn Soc; Hnr Roll; Nat Hon Sy; WWAHSS; Emplmnt; Key Club; Off Aide; Chr; Dnce; PP Ftbl; Vllyball (VJCL); Competition Show Choir; Animal Science; Clemson U

KEMERLEY, JANA M; CAREY, OH; CAREY SCH; (FR); 4H Awd; Hi Hnr Roll; Hnr Roll; Nat Hon Sy; Perf Att; St of Mnth; Comm Volntr; Peer Tut/Med; Red Cr Aide; 4-H; Chrch Yth Grp; DARE; SADD; Spanish Clb; Bnd; Chr; Ch Chr; Jzz Bnd; Sftball (VJ); Teen Leadership Team Member; 4-H Club Officer; Social Worker; Sports Medicine; Bowling Green State U; The Ohio State U

KEMPF, JOSHUA; GALION, OH; GALION HS; (FR); Hi Hnr Roll; Hnr Roll; Perf Att; Chess; Chrch Yth Grp; DARE; Drma Clb; SADD; Bnd; Mch Bnd; SP/M/VS; Swg Chr; Tennis

KENLEY, SARA; SPRINGFIELD, OH; SHAWNEE HS; (SO); Chrch Yth Grp; Key Club; Lttrmn Clb; SADD; Vsity Clb; Bnd; Mch Bnd; Pep Bnd; Sccr (JC); Wt Lftg (L); Music Education, Spanish Education; Early Childhood Education

KENNEDY, DESHAWN; COLUMBUS, OH; WALNUT RIDGE HS; (FR); Hnr Roll; Comm Volntr; Chess; DARE; Wrstlg (V); Recreational Flag Football; Recreational Hockey; Professional Football; Computer Tech; Ohio State U; Wilber Force U

KENNEDY, TIFFANY; BOLIVAR, OH; TUSKY VALLEY HS; (SR); Hnr Roll; Chr; Bskball (J); Nursing; Doctor; Cleveland State U

KENTNER, LINDSEY; WAPAKONETA, OH; WAPAKONETA HS; (SO); Hi Hnr Roll; MVP; Perf Att; Comm Volntr; FCA; HO'Br Yth Ldrshp; Lib Aide; Svce Clb; Spanish Clb; Chr; Bskball (V); Cr Ctry (V); Sccr (V); Track (V); Cl Off (P); Sch Ppr (R); Kodak Young Leaders Award; Laws of Life Essay Winner; Pre-Med; Bellarmine U; Cedarville U

KERMAN, MONICA A; PAINESVILLE, OH; RIVERSIDE HS; (SO); Hi Hnr Roll; Hnr Roll; Otst Ac Ach Awd; Perf Att; St of Mnth; Comm Volntr; Peer Tut/Med; ArtClub; Chrch Yth Grp; DARE; Emplmnt; Off Aide; Ch Chr; Orch; Yrbk (E); Works Closely with MD Children in All Study Halls; Anesthesiology RN; Kent State; Ohio State

KERSCHER, MARK A; CINCINNATI, OH; TURPIN HS; (SO); Hnr Roll; Perf Att; Sci Fairs; Sci/Math Olympn; St of Mnth; WWAHSS; DARE; Emplmnt; Photog; Prom Com; Skiing (V); Sccr (VJ L); Track (VJ L); Spanish Student of the Quarter; Mechanical or Civil Engineering; Virginia Tech; Georgia Tech

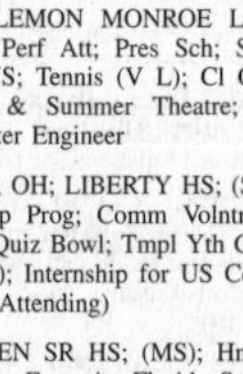

Kasior, David A
Clay HS
Oregon, OH

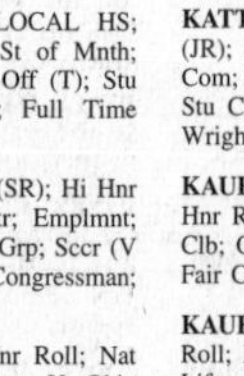

Juergens, Andrea
Shawnee HS
Springfield, OH

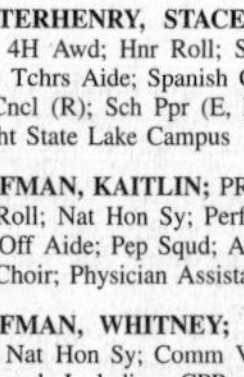

Joyce, Michael D
Avon Lake, OH

National
Honor Roll
Spring 2005

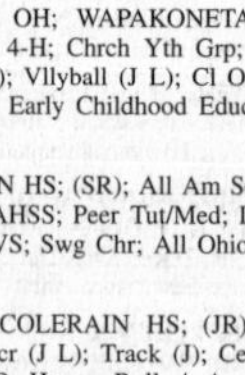

Jones, Rana
Hughes Ctr
Cincinnati, OH

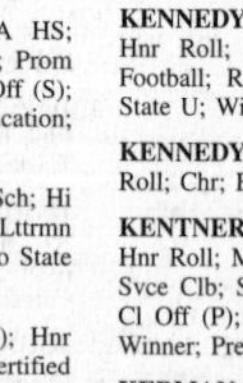

Kardasz, Kaylee
Lebanon HS
Lebanon, OH

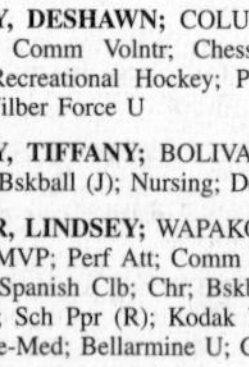

Kaufman, Whitney
Colerain HS
Cincinnati, OH

KERSHNER, LEAH J; DAYTON, OH; MIDDLETOWN CHRISTIAN; (SR); Hnr Roll; Nat Hon Sy; WWAHSS; Chrch Yth Grp; Mth Clb/Tm; Prom Com; Spch Team; Spanish Clb; SP/M/VS; Bskball (J); Psychology; Wright State U

KEYSOR, JESSICA; LIMA, OH; LIMA SR HS; (JR); Ctznshp Aw; Hnr Roll; Nat Hon Sy; Nat Ldrshp Svc; Otst Ac Ach Awd; Perf Att; Comm Volntr; Chrch Yth Grp; DARE; Chr; Ch Chr; Adv Cncl (R); CR (R); Youth Teacher; Child Development; I Want a Master's Degree; Ohio State; Rhodes

KHAIR, TIBA; COLUMBUS, OH; LINDEN-MC KINLEY HS; (FR); Hi Hnr Roll; Hnr Roll; Chrldg (J); Business Management; Chef; Ohio State U; Columbus State

KHAN, AZKA; KENT, OH; THEODORE ROOSEVELT HS; (SR); Hnr Roll; DECA; Drma Clb; Quill & Scroll; DECA Club Secretary; Magazine Journalism; Public Relations; Kent State University

KHAN, FARAZ; NEW ALBANY, OH; GAHANNA LINCOLN HS; (SR); Hi Hnr Roll; Perf Att; Pres Ac Ftns Aw; St of Mnth; Valdctrian; WWAHSS; Comm Volntr; Red Cr Aide; DECA; Emplmnt; Off Aide; Quiz Bowl; SP/M/VS; Ohio DECA President 2004-2005; 1st in the Nation / Hospitality Marketing Research Event - DECA; Business Administration; Marketing; Ohio State U

KHAN, MARIAM; HILLIARD, OH; HILLIARD DARBY HS; (JR); Hnr Roll; Nat Ldrshp Svc; Otst Ac Ach Awd; Perf Att; St of Mnth; Hosp Aide; DARE; Drma Clb; Mus Clb; Off Aide; P to P St Amb Prg; Acpl Chr; Chr; Dnce; SP/M/VS; Sch Ppr (E); Choir Awards/Recognition; Broadcasting Journalism; English Literature; The Ohio State U; Ohio U

KIDNER, KYLEY L; ASHTABULA, OH; LAKESIDE HS; (SO); All Am Sch; Hnr Roll; Nat Ldrshp Svc; Sci Fairs; St of Mnth; USAA; WWAHSS; Off Aide; Spanish Clb; Bskball (J); Tennis (V L); Interior Design; U of Miami; Ohio State

KIEP, MEREDITH; HAMILTON, OH; BADIN HS; (JR); Hi Hnr Roll; MVP; Otst Ac Ach Awd; Pres Ac Ftns Aw; WWAHSS; Comm Volntr; DARE; DECA; Emplmnt; Jr Ach; Key Club; SADD; Vllyball (V C); Captain - Freshman Volleyball Team; Rotary Club Award of Merit; Psychology; Business; College of Mount St Joseph; Xavier U

KIESEL, TIFFANY C; TIFFIN, OH; TIFFIN COLUMBIAN HS; (SO); Hnr Roll; Kwnis Aw; Perf Att; St of Mnth; DARE; Jr Ach; Scouts; Massage Therapy; Cosmetology; Bowling Green State U; Oklahoma State U

KIGER, AUSTIN T; LANCASTER, OH; LANCASTER HS; (JR); Ctznshp Aw; F Lan Hn Soc; Hi Hnr Roll; Hnr Roll; Nat Hon Sy; Nat Ldrshp Svc; Perf Att; Pres Sch; WWAHSS; Yth Ldrshp Prog; Comm Volntr; Chrch Yth Grp; FCA; Key Club; NYLC; Off Aide; French Clb; Skt Tgt Sh; Tennis (V L); Adv Cncl (R); Cl Off (V); Stu Cncl (R); CR (R); Yrbk (E, R); Ohio Business Week; Congressional Student Leadership Conference; Political Science Major; International Law Major; The American U; George Washington U

KILBANE, KEVIN; COLUMBUS, OH; WHETSTONE HS; (SR); Hi Hnr Roll; Hnr Roll; Nat Hon Sy; Otst Ac Ach Awd; Perf Att; Comm Volntr; AL Aux Boys; Chrch Yth Grp; DECA; Off Aide; Bnd; Mch Bnd; Student Ambassador to the Superintendent; Kidspeak - Kids in Government; Political Science; Law; Ohio State U

KILBANE, RYAN D; MEDINA, OH; MEDINA SR HS; (JR); Hnr Roll; Nat Hon Sy; Sci/Math Olympn; Comm Volntr; Peer Tut/Med; Emplmnt; Key Club; Tech Clb; Tennis (J); Currently Enrolled in Aviation Ground School; Airplane Pilot; Aeronautical Engineer; Ohio U; United States Air Force Academy

KIMBLE, BOBBI T; CINCINNATI, OH; TAFT INFORMATION TECH HS; (JR); Ctznshp Aw; Hnr Roll; Nat Hon Sy; Otst Ac Ach Awd; Perf Att; WWAHSS; Drl Tm; Chrldg (J); Registered Nurse

KING, JORDAN; COLUMBUS, OH; UPPER ARLINGTON HS; (JR); Ctznshp Aw; Hnr Roll; WWAHSS; Comm Volntr; Outdrs Clb; Svce Clb; Jzz Bnd; Orch; SP/M/VS; Cr Ctry (J L); Track (J); Columbus Symphony Youth Orchestra; Environmental Club President's Volunteer Service Award; Education; Music

KINGREY, NATALIE; BELLEFONTAINE, OH; BELLEFONTAINE HS; (JR); Hnr Roll; Comm Volntr; DARE; Key Club; Photog; SADD; Spanish Clb; Chr; Psychology; Education; Ohio U; U of Cincinnati

KINTER, COURTNEY; HAMILTON, OH; (JR); Hnr Roll; WWAHSS; Yth Ldrshp Prog; Comm Volntr; Peer Tut/Med; Chrch Yth Grp; SADD; Spanish Clb; Peer Counseling; Mentoring; Physical Therapy (Trainer); Teaching; Miami U; Ohio State U

KIRK, TACY; ST CLAIRSVILLE, OH; ST CLAIRSVILLE HS; (SO); 4H Awd; Ctznshp Aw; Hi Hnr Roll; Hnr Roll; Otst Ac Ach Awd; Sci Fairs; St of Mnth; USAA; Comm Volntr; Peer Tut/Med; 4-H; Chrch Yth Grp; Emplmnt; Mod UN; Off Aide; Svce Clb; Tchrs Aide; French Clb; 4-H Camp Counselor; Law; Journalism; New York U; Ohio State U

KIRKLAND, BRITTANY A; TWINSBURG, OH; TWINSBURG HS; (SR); Hnr Roll; WWAHSS; Comm Volntr; Red Cr Aide; Emplmnt; Mus Clb; Pep Squd; Prom Com; Tchrs Aide; Acpl Chr; Dnce; Mch Bnd; Swg Chr; Bskball (VJ); Cr Ctry (J); PP Ftbl (C); Track (J); Stu Cncl (T); Engineering; The U of Toledo

KIRKPATRICK, SEAN; MOGADORE, OH; MOGADORE JR/SR HS; (SO); Hnr Roll; Cr Ctry (V L); Track (V L); Architect; Akron U; Kent State U

KISKIS, KRYSTAL; CROWN CITY, OH; GALLIA AC HS; (SR); 4H Awd; Hnr Roll; Nat Hon Sy; WWAHSS; Yth Ldrshp Prog; 4-H; Chrch Yth Grp; DARE; Key Club; Prom Com; Wdwrkg Clb; Dnce; SP/M/VS; Sftball (VJ); National Honor Society; Early Education Major; Minor in Visual Arts; Rio Grande College

KLINE, ASHLEY; LEWISTOWN, OH; INDIAN LAKE HS; (FR); Hnr Roll; WWAHSS; Comm Volntr; Chrch Yth Grp; Drma Clb; Key Club; Lib Aide; Scouts; Tchrs Aide; Tech Clb; Spanish Clb; Bnd; Chr; Ch Chr; Pep Bnd; Sch Ppr (P); Yrbk (P); Girl Scouts Bronze and Silver Award; Pharmacist; Public Relations; Otterbein College; Bowling Green State U

KLOSTERMAN, ERIC L; CELINA, OH; CELINA HS; (SR); Hnr Roll; Jr Eng Tech; Nat Hon Sy; Nat Mrt LOC; Otst Ac Ach Awd; St of Mnth; WWAHSS; Comm Volntr; Spanish Clb; Bskball (V CL); Sccr (V CL); Vsy Clb (V); Junior Scholars; Junior Engineering Technical Society - JETS; Sports Administration; Ball State U

KLOSTERMAN, TRAVIS; CELINA, OH; MARION LOCAL HS; (SO); Hnr Roll; Comm Volntr; Chrch Yth Grp; Mth Clb/Tm; Sci Clb; Voc Ind Clb Am; Ftball (J L); Wt Lftg (J); Jr Firefighter; Architecture; Firefighter

KNAPIK, KATIE; ELYRIA, OH; MIDVIEW HS; (FR); Hnr Roll; Pres Ac Ftns Aw; St of Mnth; Veterinarian; Ohio State U

KNIGHT, KIANA; CLEVELAND, OH; LINCOLN-WEST HS; (FR); Hnr Roll; Otst Ac Ach Awd; DARE; Ch Chr; Dnce; SP/M/VS; Bskball; Judge; Lawyer; Clark Atlanta U; Ohio State

KNOTTS, ANNIE M; NEWARK, OH; NEWARK HS; (FR); Hnr Roll; Otst Ac Ach Awd; Perf Att; St of Mnth; Chrch Yth Grp; DARE; Spanish Clb; Played Soccer for 7 Yrs (Got People to People Sports Ambassador Letter); Pro-Soccer Player; (OSU) Ohio State U

KOEHLER, NOAH J; HAMILTON, OH; STEPHEN T BADIN HS; (SR); Hnr Roll; Kwnis Aw; MVP; Sci/Math Olympn; USAA; Yth Ldrshp Prog; Comm Volntr; Chess; Mth Clb/Tm; NYLC; 4 Yr. Letter Varsity Bowling; Captain Senior Yr.; Ohio State Summer Robotics; LeadAmeria CSI; Computer Science; Aviation & Astronomy; Miami U At Oxford OH; The Ohio State U

KOEHNEKE, LIZ; SPRINGBORO, OH; SPRINGBORO HS; (JR); Hnr Roll; Otst Ac Ach Awd; Perf Att; Pres Ac Ftns Aw; Comm Volntr; Peer Tut/Med; Chrch Yth Grp; DARE; Emplmnt; FCA; Key Club; Mus Clb; Off Aide; Photog; Chr; SP/M/VS; Bskball (VJ L); PP Ftbl (J); Scr Kpr (J); Track (VJ L); Stu Cncl (R); Yrbk (P); Teacher-Education; Michigan State U; U of Michigan

KOEPPE, LEAH K; CINCINNATI, OH; FINNEYTOWN; (FR); Hnr Roll; Comm Volntr; Chrch Yth Grp; Emplmnt; FCA; Key Club; Prom Com; Scouts; Chr; Sccr (VJ L)

KOHLHEPP, ERIN; XENIA, OH; CARROLL HS; (SR); F Lan Hn Soc; Hnr Roll; Nat Hon Sy; Perf Att; WWAHSS; Hab For Humty Volntr; Peer Tut/Med; Chrch Yth Grp; Drma Clb; Key Club; Spanish Clb; Ch Chr; SP/M/VS; Bskball (J); Lit Mag (R); Pre-Physical Therapy; Miami U

KOHLRIESER, LUCAS J; WAPAKONETA, OH; WOPAK HS; (SO); Hi Hnr Roll; Hnr Roll; Perf Att; Emplmnt; Lttrmn Clb; Off Aide; Spanish Clb; Ftball (V L); Psychology; Medical; Ohio State; North Carolina State

KOHNEN, AARON J; WAPAKONETA, OH; WAPAKONETA HS; (FR); Hnr Roll; Nat Stu Ath Day Aw; Emplmnt; Bnd; Mch Bnd; Pep Bnd; Tennis (J L); Member of District 3 Ohio Honors Band - French Horn; Music Education - Instrumental; Math Education; U of North Carolina; Bowling Green U

KOHUT, MISSY; YOUNGSTOWN, OH; AUSTINTOWN FITCH; (SR); Nat Mrt Sch Recip; WWAHSS; Comm Volntr; Drma Clb; NtlFrnscLg; Off Aide; Pep Squd; Spch Team; SADD; Chr; Dnce; SP/M/VS; Stg Cre; 2004 Miss Congeniality in Miss Teen Ohio; 2005 3rd in State Speech Tournament; Communications; U of Akron

KOLB, EMILY; HARRISON, OH; MC AULEY HS; (SO); 4H Awd; Hnr Roll; Nat Hon Sy; Perf Att; Pres Ac Ftns Aw; Comm Volntr; 4-H; ArtClub; Key Club; Hsbk Rdg (V); Sftball (J); Pediatrics; Ohio State U

KOLUDROVICH, RACHEL; NORTH ROYALTON, OH; NORTH ROYALTON HS; (SO); Hnr Roll; St of Mnth; WWAHSS; ArtClub; Key Club; Spanish Clb; Dnce; Gmnstcs (V); Key Club I Art Club; Spanish Club; Nursing; Eastern Michigan U; Kent State U

KONCSICS, DAVID; CANTON, OH; GLEN OAK HS; (JR); Ctznshp Aw; Hnr Roll; Nat Hon Sy; Otst Ac Ach Awd; Sci Fairs; WWAHSS; Comm Volntr; DECA; Drma Clb; Mod UN; Off Aide; SP/M/VS; Ftball (J); Wrstlg (V); 2000 Ohio Karate State Champion; Who's Who Among American H.S. Students; Marketing; Business Administration; U of Pennsylvania; Ohio State U

KONOFF, ALICIA M; TOLEDO, OH; WAITE R MORRISON HS; (JR); Red Cr Aide; Jr Ach; Tchrs Aide; Sftball (V); Vllyball (V); Carpentry I; Owens Technical College

KORDES, MORGAN; CORTLAND, OH; LAKEVIEW HS; (FR); Hi Hnr Roll; Hnr Roll; Perf Att; Bnd; Orch; Track; Perfect Attendance

KOREN, AMANDA; NILES, OH; NILES MC KINLEY HS; (FR); Hnr Roll; Comm Volntr; Hosp Aide; Key Club; Bnd; Mch Bnd; Pep Bnd; 5th Grade Band Mentor Solo & Ensemble; Volunteer Every Thursday @ St. Joseph Hospital

KORMAN, ROSALYNNE; CINCINNATI, OH; FINNEYTOWN HS; (FR); F Lan Hn Soc; Hi Hnr Roll; WWAHSS; Comm Volntr; Key Club; Tmpl Yth Grp; Orch; Scr Kpr (V); Sccr (J); Swmg (V); Track (V); Sch Ppr (R); Academic Team JV Captain; MD/BA Program; Biology Major

KOROSEC, AMANDA L; COSHOCTON, OH; COSHOCTON HS; (SR); Ctznshp Aw; Hi Hnr Roll; Hnr Roll; MVP; Otst Ac Ach Awd; Perf Att; St of Mnth; Comm Volntr; Hab For Humty Volntr; Spec Olymp Vol; Chrch Yth Grp; DARE; Drma Clb; FCA; Key Club; Off Aide; SADD; Tchrs Aide; Dnce; Chrldg (VJCL); PP Ftbl (V); Scr Kpr (V); Track (V L); Wt Lftg (V); Pole Vaulting Silver Medal at District; Pole Vaulting Bronze Medal at Regionals; College Major-Nursing; Bachelor's Degree/Pre-Medicine; Ohio State U; Kent State U

KORPITA, ADAM M; ROOTSTOWN, OH; SOUTHEAST HS; (SR); Ctznshp Aw; Hnr Roll; Nat Hon Sy; Perf Att; WWAHSS; Drma Clb; Emplmnt; Mus Clb; Quiz Bowl; Scouts; Bnd; Mch Bnd; Pep Bnd; Stg Cre; Golf (V L); Boy Scouts; Venture Crew; Meteorology; Ohio State U

KOSANOVICH, LAUREN M; BARBERTON, OH; COPLEY HS; (JR); Hnr Roll; Nat Hon Sy; Otst Ac Ach Awd; St of Mnth; WWAHSS; Comm Volntr; Hosp Aide; Biology Clb; Drma Clb; Key Club; French Clb; Bnd; Mch Bnd; Stg Cre; CR (R); Sch Ppr (R, P); History Education; College of William & Mary

KOSELA, KATIE; YOUNGSTOWN, OH; POLAND MS; (MS); Hnr Roll; Otst Ac Ach Awd; Chess; Mod UN; Tech Clb; Track; World War II Historian; Forensic Scientist; Akron State U; Youngstown State U

KOSHIO, YURI; NEW ALBANY, OH; NEW ALBANY HS; (JR); Hi Hnr Roll; Hnr Roll; Kwnis Aw; Otst Ac Ach Awd; Sci/Math Olympn; Comm Volntr; Red Cr Aide; Sci Clb; German Clb; Bnd; Mch Bnd; Academy of Scholars; Summa Cum Laude; Chemical Engineering; Mechanical Engineering; Massachusetts Institute of Technology; Case Western Reserve U

KOSIR, SUSIE; WOOSTER, OH; WOOSTER HS; (JR); Hi Hnr Roll; Nat Hon Sy; Yth Ldrshp Prog; Peer Tut/Med; Chrch Yth Grp; Lcrsse (J); Sftball (JC); Tennis (JC)

KOSTO, VICTORIA E; GARFIELD HTS, OH; GARFIELD HEIGHTS HS; (SO); Ctznshp Aw; Hnr Roll; Otst Ac Ach Awd; Sci Fairs; St of Mnth; DARE; Off Aide; Scouts; Tchrs Aide; Bnd; Chrldg (J); Christianity Award; Tutor-English & Math; Medical; Arts; Savannah College of Art and Design; UCLA

KOTECKI, BRITTANI I; MEDINA, OH; MEDINA HS; (SR); F Lan Hn Soc; Hnr Roll; Otst Ac Ach Awd; Sci Fairs; WWAHSS; Comm Volntr; Peer Tut/Med; Chrch Yth Grp; Drma Clb; Key Club; Prom Com; German Clb; SP/M/VS; Lcrsse (J); Tennis (V L); Stu Cncl (R); 2005 Debutante Medina County Young Women's Leadership Ball; 2005 Contestant in International Model / Talent Competition in LA; Majoring in Television / Radio; Ithaca College; Roy H Park School of Communications

KOTNIK, MOLLIE I; CLEVELAND, OH; GARFIELD HTS HS; (JR); Hnr Roll; Nat Hon Sy; Sci Fairs; Yth Ldrshp Prog; Comm Volntr; Spec Olymp Vol; Chrch Yth Grp; DARE; Emplmnt; Scouts; Svce Clb; Acpl Chr; Chr; Ch Chr; Dnce; Chrldg (V L); PP Ftbl; 10-Year Figure Skater with USFSA; 10-Year City Softball Player; Chemistry / Forensics; Spanish; Bowling Green State U; Baldwin-Wallace College

KOTOWSKI, KYLIE L; MEDINA, OH; MEDINA HS; (SR); Hnr Roll; Nat Hon Sy; WWAHSS; Comm Volntr; Peer Tut/Med; AL Aux Girls; Chrch Yth Grp; Emplmnt; Key Club; Mth Clb/Tm; Quill & Scroll; Scouts; Svce Clb; Dnce; Scr Kpr (VJ); Skiing (C); Sccr (J); Sch Ppr (E); Rolie Platz Award; Girls Leaders Club; Business / Corporate Lawyer; Law Degree / Corporate Lawyer; Furman U

KOVALAK, NICOLE; MESOPOTAMIA, OH; BLOOMFIELD HS; (SO); Hnr Roll; Perf Att; St of Mnth; ArtClub; Off Aide; Prom Com; Bskball (V); Chrldg (V); Sftball (V); Vllyball (V); Yrbk (P); Office Aide; Student of the Month; Photography; Business Management; Kent State U; Ohio State U

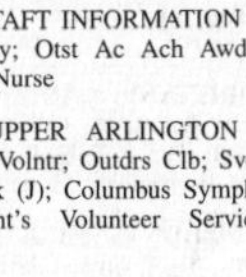
Kosela, Katie
Poland MS
Youngstown, OH

Koehler, Noah J
Stephen T Badin HS
Hamilton, OH

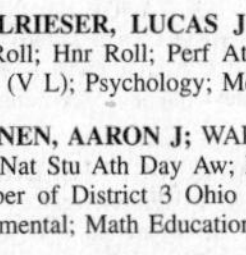
Knight, Kiana
Lincoln-West HS
Cleveland, OH

National
Honor Roll
Spring 2005

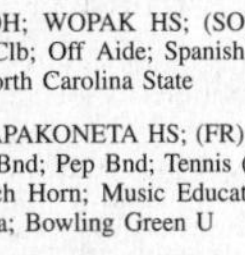
Kiep, Meredith
Badin HS
Hamilton, OH

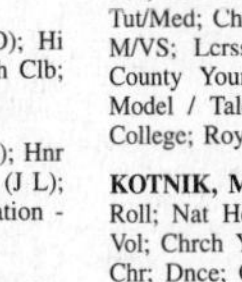
Kolb, Emily
Mc Auley HS
Harrison, OH

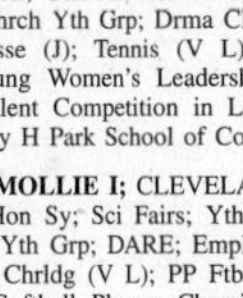
Kosto, Victoria E
Garfield Heights HS
Garfield Hts, OH

KRAMER, JUSTIN D; MECHANICSTOWN, OH; CARROLLTON HS; (SO); Hnr Roll; Nat Sci Aw; WWAHSS; Comm Volntr; Ntl FFA; Off Aide; Outdrs Clb; ROTC; Tchrs Aide; Wdwrkg Clb; Drl Tm; Scr (V); Heating and Cooling

KRANSTUBER, ALLYSON; MEDINA, OH; MEDINA HS; (SR); F Lan Hn Soc; Hi Hnr Roll; Hnr Roll; Nat Hon Sy; Pres Sch; WWAHSS; Comm Volntr; Peer Tut/Med; Spec Olymp Vol; Chrch Yth Grp; Drma Clb; Mth Clb/Tm; Quill & Scroll; Svce Clb; SADD; Spanish Clb; Bnd; Dnce; Mch Bnd; Bskball (J); Yrbk (E); Participant in Spring Leadership Ball; Pre-Veterinarian Medicine; The Ohio State U

KRASZY, DAMIAN; CLEVELAND, OH; GARFIELD HEIGHTS HS; (JR); Perf Att; Comm Volntr; BPA; Chrch Yth Grp; Emplmnt; Bskball (J); Website Development Team; Business Professionals of America; Computer Engineer; Computer Programmer; DeVry U

KRAUSE, JODI; MALTA, OH; MORGAN HS; (JR); 4H Awd; Sci Fairs; WWAHSS; 4-H; Chrch Yth Grp; DARE; Bskball (J); Vllyball (L); Server / Defense Award Volleyball; Exercise; Nutrition; Ohio U Zanesville; Ohio U Athens

KRETZMANN, JUSTIN; MANSFIELD, OH; ASHLAND HS; (JR); 4H Awd; Hnr Roll; Nat Hon Sy; Otst Ac Ach Awd; Pres Ac Ftns Aw; St of Mnth; WWAHSS; Comm Volntr; Peer Tut/Med; 4-H; Chrch Yth Grp; Emplmnt; Quiz Bowl; Sci Clb; Scouts; Svce Clb; Chr; Skiing; Engineering; Rochester Institute of Technology; U of Cincinnati

KRIEGER, NIKOLAS I; NORTH ROYALTON, OH; NORTH ROYALTON HS; MS; Hnr Roll; St of Mnth; DARE; Mth Clb/Tm; Tech Clb; Bnd; Aerospace Engineering; U of Michigan Ann Arbor.; U of Cincinnati

KRISHER, ALYSSA; WAPAKONETA, OH; WAPAKONETA HS; (SO); 4H Awd; Hnr Roll; Perf Att; USAA; 4-H; Emplmnt; 4-H Club President; High School Bowling Team (Varsity); Business; Ohio State U

KRISTOFF, KELLI N; PICKERINGTON, OH; PICKERINGTON HS CTRL; (JR); Hi Hnr Roll; Perf Att; Comm Volntr; Chrch Yth Grp; Drma Clb; Mus Clb; Pep Squd; Svce Clb; Tmpl Yth Grp; Bnd; Dnce; Jzz Bnd; Mch Bnd; Puppet Ministry; Elementary Education; Miami U of Ohio; Ohio U

KROMER, LUKAS; CAREY, OH; CAREY SCH; (JR); Hnr Roll; Nat Hon Sy; Nat Sci Aw; Perf Att; St of Mnth; WWAHSS; Comm Volntr; Chrch Yth Grp; DARE; Drma Clb; Lttrmn Clb; Lib Aide; Prom Com; Quiz Bowl; Scouts; Bnd; Jzz Bnd; Mch Bnd; Stg Cre; Cr Ctry (V CL); Track (V L); Cl Off (R); Stu Cncl (R); CR; MAL Leadership; All A's Award; Aerospace Engineer; Chemical Engineer; Embry Riddle Aeronautical U; The Ohio State U

KRUEGER, BENJAMIN W; WEST SALEM, OH; NORTHWESTERN HS; (SO); 4H Awd; Hnr Roll; Nat Hon Sy; Otst Ac Ach Awd; Yth Ldrshp Prog; 4-H; Emplmnt; Outdrs Clb; Wdwrkg Clb; Arch; Skt Tgt Sh; Vllyball; Wt Lftg; Snow Boarding / Paint Ball / Ice Hockey; Hunting / Unofficial Volleyball; History; Business; Ohio State U

KRUMREIG, TIM; OBERLIN, OH; FIRELANDS HS; (FR); Hnr Roll; Comm Volntr; Drma Clb; Stg Cre; Youth Fund Advisory Committee; Counselor in Training At Common Ground; Meteorology; Music

KRUPP, JENNA; TIFFIN, OH; TIFFIN COLUMBIAN; (FR); Hnr Roll; St of Mnth; Chrch Yth Grp; Mod UN; Chr; Ch Chr; SP/M/VS; Vllyball (J); Cl Off (P); Stu Cncl (R); CR (R)

KRUSEL, ASHLEY; MASSILLON, OH; JACKSON HS; (SO); Hi Hnr Roll; St of Mnth; Comm Volntr; Key Club; German Clb; Chr; Church Volunteer; Medicine; Northeastern Ohio U; Gannon U College of Medicine

KUEHL, MARIA; WAPAKONETA, OH; WAPAKONETA HS; (SO); WWAHSS; Emplmnt; Sccr (V L); Track (V L); Cl Off (T); Pharmacy; Law; Ohio State U; Ohio U

KUFCHAK, HEATHER J; WESTERVILLE, OH; WESTERVILLE SOUTH HS; (SR); Hi Hnr Roll; Hnr Roll; Otst Ac Ach Awd; St of Mnth; Mus Clb; Ch Chr; Orch; SP/M/VS; Winner of 2004 Columbus Symphony Young Musician's Competition; Quarter Finalist in Fischoff National Chamber Music Competition; Violin Performance; Colburn School of Performing Arts; Manhattan School of Music

KUHN, HANNAH M; CINCINNATI, OH; MC AULEY HS; (FR); Hi Hnr Roll; Perf Att; WWAHSS; Comm Volntr; Key Club; Spanish Clb; Pharmacology; Education; Miami U; Ohio U

KUMPF, JOSHUA W; CANTON, OH; JACKSON HS; (SR); Hi Hnr Roll; Nat Hon Sy; Nat Mrt Sch Recip; Otst Ac Ach Awd; St of Mnth; WWAHSS; Comm Volntr; Hab For Humty Volntr; AL Aux Boys; Chrch Yth Grp; Emplmnt; German Clb; Cr Ctry (V CL); Track (V L); Stu Cncl (R); Sch Ppr (R); Yrbk (R); Academic All-Ohio; President's Award for Education Excellence; Political Science; International Relations; Kenyon College

KUNSTAR, TOM; AKRON, OH; COPLEY HS; (FR); Master's Degree in Physics; Master's Degree in Math

KURUC, AMANDA B; RICHMOND, OH; EDISON HS; (JR); Hi Hnr Roll; Hnr Roll; Nat Hon Sy; Comm Volntr; Red Cr Aide; Spec Olymp Vol; Chrch Yth Grp; Emplmnt; Lib Aide; Ntl Beta Clb; Scouts; Spanish Clb; Skiing (V); Swmg (V L); Stu Cncl (R); Sch Ppr (E); Close Up Participant; Business Administration; Legal Studies; Franciscan U of Steubenville; Kent State U

KYER, IAN; CUYAHOGA FALLS, OH; CUYAHOGA FALLS HS; (JR); Chess; Chess Club

KYER, TIM; CUYAHOGA FALLS, OH; CUYAHOGA FALLS HS; (MS); Bnd; Bskball; Cr Ctry; Physical Education Teacher; Business

KYSILKA, CHRIS; HAMILTON, OH; LAKOTA EAST HS; (JR); Hi Hnr Roll; Nat Hon Sy; Otst Ac Ach Awd; Perf Att; Sci/Math Olympn; St of Mnth; WWAHSS; Yth Ldrshp Prog; Comm Volntr; Chrch Yth Grp; Cmptr Clb; Emplmnt; Mth Clb/Tm; Outdrs Clb; Schol Bwl; Sci Clb; Svce Clb; High Honor Roll; Mission Work-Church; Chemical Engineering; Rose-Hulman Institute of Technology; Case-Western

LA CROIX, LEANNE; CINCINNATI, OH; WINTON WOODS HS; (JR); Hnr Roll; Otst Ac Ach Awd; WWAHSS; Comm Volntr; Chrch Yth Grp; Mod UN; Orch; Sccr (JC); Bowling Team Junior Varsity; Knitting Club; Medicine; State U of New York Buffalo; Dayton U

LADD, BRITTANY M; DAYTON, OH; WEST CARROLLTON SR HS; (SR); Chrch Yth Grp; Ch Chr; Church Youth Leader; Praise and Worship Leader; Music Major; Journalism; Sinclair

LADD, CYNTHIA M; FORT JENNINGS, OH; FORT JENNINGS HS; (SR); Hnr Roll; St of Mnth; Comm Volntr; Peer Tut/Med; DARE; FCCLA; Off Aide; Prom Com; Scouts; Tchrs Aide; Bnd; Mch Bnd; SP/M/VS; Poems Published; Two Different Times/Publishers; 1st & 2nd Place Ribbons on Hand Made Quilts; Paralegal; International Business College

LAFERTY, TRIANA; ASHTABULA, OH; LAKESIDE HS; (SO); Hi Hnr Roll; Hnr Roll; WWAHSS; Comm Volntr; Peer Tut/Med; Chrch Yth Grp; Spanish Clb; Bnd; Mch Bnd; Pep Bnd; Chrldg (V); Stu Cncl (R); CR (R); Psychology; Law; Case Western Reserved; Xavier

LAKOSH, STEVE; CANTON, OH; CANTON SOUTH HS; (JR); Perf Att; Chrch Yth Grp; FCA; Aviation; Design; Pittsburgh College of Aviation; Stark State College

LAMADE, MATTHEW J; MEDINA, OH; MEDINA SR HS; (JR); Hab For Humty Volntr; Scouts; Spanish Clb; Orch; Lcrsse (J); Sccr (J); Boy Scout World Conservation Award; Criminal Justice; USA Coast Guard; Lycoming College; U of Pittsburgh Bradford

LAMB, ELISHA; WILMINGTON, OH; CLINTON-MASSIE SCH; (JR); All Am Sch; Hnr Roll; Nat Hon Sy; Otst Ac Ach Awd; WWAHSS; Comm Volntr; Chrch Yth Grp; Key Club; Off Aide; SADD; Chr; Dnce; SP/M/VS; Physician; Physician's Assistant; Sinclair Community College; Kettering Medical School of Arts

LAMPKIN, TIFANEE; TOLEDO, OH; ROGERS HS; (SO); Hi Hnr Roll; Nat Stu Ath Day Aw; Yth Ldrshp Prog; Comm Volntr; Peer Tut/Med; Tchrs Aide; Bskball (jv, v); Play JV / Varsity Basketball; One of the Team's Mentors; Basketball for Texas A & M U; Law School; Texas A & M U; Owens Community College

LANDES, CARRIE; HILLIARD, OH; HILLIARD DARBY HS; (SR); DAR; Hnr Roll; Nat Hon Sy; Perf Att; WWAHSS; Chrch Yth Grp; Emplmnt; Key Club; Sci Clb; Tchrs Aide; Chr; SP/M/VS; President-Hilliard Darby Key Club; Nursing; Pre-Medicine; Mount Carmel College of Nursing

LANDES, JENNA; TIPP CITY, OH; BETHEL HS; (SO); 4H Awd; Hnr Roll; Otst Ac Ach Awd; Perf Att; St of Mnth; 4-H; Emplmnt; Mod UN; Tchrs Aide; Spanish Clb; Vllyball (J); Theology/Religion; Med Sec; Cedarville U

LANDIS, LINDSAY M; NORTH LIMA, OH; SOUTH RANGE HS; (SR); Hi Hnr Roll; Jr Mshl; Nat Hon Sy; Valdctrian; WWAHSS; Comm Volntr; Chrch Yth Grp; Emplmnt; FCA; FTA; Key Club; Quill & Scroll; Quiz Bowl; PP Ftbl; Stu Cncl (V); Yrbk; Medical Field; Malone College - Attending Fall 2005

LANE, ANNA; COLUMBUS, OH; GRANDVIEW HEIGHTS HS; (JR); Hnr Roll; St of Mnth; WWAHSS; Peer Tut/Med; ArtClub; Emplmnt; Key Club; Sci Clb; French Clb; Sftball (V L); Tennis (J); Most Improved-Tennis 2004; Forensic Science; Chemistry; U of Miami, FL; U of Michigan

LANGE, NICOLE; XENIA, OH; CARROLL HS; (SO); Hnr Roll; Key Club; SADD; Spanish Clb; Cr Ctry (V); Track (V); Yrbk (E); Ohio State U; U of Dayton

LANGLOIS, BRITTANY; OREGON, OH; CLAY HS; (SR); Hi Hnr Roll; Hnr Roll; St of Mnth; WWAHSS; ArtClub; BPA; International Clb; Bskball (J); Sccr (V); Track; Vllyball; Cl Off (P); CR (R); Sch Ppr (E); Ohio Association / BPA State Officer; Business Administration - Major; Graphic Design - Minor; U of San Francisco

LANGMAN, JULIA; CANTON, OH; GLEN OAK HS; (JR); Hi Hnr Roll; Nat Hon Sy; Hosp Aide; Key Club; Mod UN; Tchrs Aide; International Clb; Bnd; Mch Bnd; Lit Mag (E, P); Yrbk (R, P); Journalism; English-Creative Writing; Bowling Green State U; Kent State U

LANNERT, AMANDA L; URBANA, OH; WEST LIBERTY SALEM JR/SR HS; (SO); Hnr Roll; Perf Att; WWAHSS; 4-H; Spanish Clb; Chr; SP/M/VS; Hsbk Rdg (C); Sftball (J); Vllyball (J); Freshman Justice Award; Vet; Acting

LAPOINT, MICHELLE L; TOLEDO, OH; ROGERS HS; (FR); Ctznshp Aw; Hnr Roll; St of Mnth; Peer Tut/Med; DARE; Outdrs Clb; Writing Poems; Bowling; Police Officer; Pediatrician; U of Toledo

LARSON, CHRISTOPHER; CLEVELAND, OH; VALLEY FORGE HS; (SO); Hnr Roll; Perf Att; Chrch Yth Grp; Skiing; Computer Animator; Ohio State U; U of Cincinnati

LARSON, NATALIE; OXFORD, OH; TALAWANDA HS; (JR); Hi Hnr Roll; Nat Hon Sy; WWAHSS; Comm Volntr; Hosp Aide; 4-H; FCCLA; Key Club; Tchrs Aide; French Clb; Swmg (V); Tennis (V); Helped Raise $580 to Send to a Shelter for Abused Horses; Physical Therapy; Occupational Therapy; Vanderbilt U; Tulane U

LARTZ, AMANDA; CAREY, OH; CAREY SCH; (JR); Hnr Roll; WWAHSS; Drma Clb; Prom Com; Chr; SP/M/VS; Stg Cre; Track (V L); Anthology of Eleventh Grade Poetry; Record Producer; Writer; Capital U; Catawba College

LASURE, STEPHANIE; ZANESVILLE, OH; BISHOP ROSECRANS HS; (JR); Hi Hnr Roll; Hnr Roll; Key Club; Pep Squd; Prom Com; SADD; Chrldg (V L); Vllyball (V); Elementary Education; Pharmacy; Ohio State U; Ohio Northern

LAURICIA, ANDREA; LORAIN, OH; SOUTHVIEW HS; (JR); Hnr Roll; Pres Sch; WWAHSS; Mod UN; Scouts; Bnd; Mch Bnd; Pep Bnd; SP/M/VS; Sccr (V L); International Studies; Pre-Law; Ohio Wesleyan U; Otterbein College

LAVALLO, CHRISTOPHER; CLEVELAND, OH; MARTIN LUTHER KING HS; MS; Nat Hon Sy; Golf; Wrstlg; Doctor; Michigan State; Florida State

LAVEY, ALYSHA; BRADFORD, OH; BRADFORD HS; (JR); Hnr Roll; Perf Att; WWAHSS; Peer Tut/Med; FTA; Lib Aide; Prom Com; Tchrs Aide; Vsity Clb; Chrldg (V); PP Ftbl (V); Sftball (V); Vsy Clb (V); Vllyball (V); Cl Off (T); Physical Therapist; Job with Younger Kids; Ohio U; Toledo

LAVIN, KIMBERLY; AKRON, OH; FIRESTONE HS; (JR); Hi Hnr Roll; Nat Hon Sy; Sci Fairs; Comm Volntr; Red Cr Aide; Emplmnt; Stg Cre; Mar Art; Skiing; Tennis (V CL); State Science Fair-Superior; Coming Together Teen Board-Volunteer Award; Medicine; Psychology / Education

LAWRENCE, KALI A; ELYRIA, OH; ELYRIA HS; (FR); Hi Hnr Roll; Otst Ac Ach Awd; St of Mnth; WWAHSS; Peer Tut/Med; Spec Olymp Vol; Chrch Yth Grp; Key Club; Tchrs Aide; Bnd; Ch Chr; Team-Up Mentoring Program; Accepted Into Who's Who Among American High School Students; Teaching; Library Science; Oberlin College; Denison U

LAWRENCE, ZACHARY; AKRON, OH; REVERE HS; (SR); Hnr Roll; Jr Eng Tech; Nat Hon Sy; Sci/Math Olympn; Comm Volntr; Spec Olymp Vol; Emplmnt; Photog; Scouts; Tchrs Aide; Bskball (J); Ftball (J); Golf (V L); Yrbk (R); Chemistry; Medicine; Ohio State U

LAWSON, BRYAN; AKRON, OH; EAST HS; (SO); Hnr Roll; Perf Att; Sci Fairs; WWAHSS; Comm Volntr; Red Cr Aide; Chrch Yth Grp; Emplmnt; Off Aide; P to P St Amb Prg; ROTC; Tchrs Aide; Ch Chr; Clr Grd; Drl Tm; Cr Ctry (J L); Sccr; Track (L); Stu Cncl (R); Architecture; Engineering; Kent State U; Ohio State U

LAWSON, DASHAUN; LORAIN, OH; LORAIN SOUTHVIEW HS; (FR); Hnr Roll; Perf Att; Bskball; Ftball; Medical; U of North Carolina; U of Cincinnati

LEACH, BRITTANY; CANTON, OH; GLEN OAK HS; (JR); Perf Att; Comm Volntr; Key Club; Off Aide; Pep Squd; Scouts; INTERNATIL Clb; Bnd; Mch Bnd; Pep Bnd; OMEA Superior Rating for Ensemble; Girl Scouts Silver Award; Psychology; Music; Ohio State U; U of Akron

LEAK, SYMPHONY N; COLUMBUS, OH; HOKE CTY HS; (FR); Hnr Roll; Perf Att; St of Mnth; CARE; DARE; Chr; Sociology; Fayetteville State U; Pembroke State U

LEAR, KRISTEN M; CINCINNATI, OH; FINNEYTOWN HS; (SO); Hnr Roll; Nat Sci Aw; Otst Ac Ach Awd; USAA; WWAHSS; Comm Volntr; Key Club; Scouts; Orch; Stu Cncl (S); Girl Scout Gold Award Recipient; Key Club President 2005-2006; Veterinary Medicine; Zoology

LEBLANC, PAULINE L; LANCASTER, OH; LANCASTER SR HS; (JR); Hnr Roll; Chrch Yth Grp; DARE; Scouts; German Clb; Chr; Secondary High School Teacher (Math); Ohio U of Lancaster; Ohio U of Athens

LEBOVITZ, EMMA; CHESTERLAND, OH; WEST GEAUGA SR HS; (JR); Hnr Roll; Nat Ldrshp Svc; WWAHSS; DARE; Key Club; NYLC; Tchrs Aide; Vsity Clb; Bskball (J); Sccr (V L); Track (V); Stu Cncl (R); CR (R); Hugs Member Team Leader; Orthodontist; DePaul, George Washington

Larson, Christopher
Valley Forge HS
Cleveland, OH

Lamb, Elisha
Clinton-Massie Sch
Wilmington, OH

National
Honor Roll
Spring 2005

Krupp, Jenna
Tiffin Columbian
Tiffin, OH

Leblanc, Pauline L
Lancaster SR HS
Lancaster, OH

LECHLEITER, SARAH; DAYTON, OH; ARCHBISHOP ALTER HS; (FR); Hi Hnr Roll; Pres Ac Ftns Aw; Pres Sch; Sci Fairs; WWAHSS; Comm Volntr; Chrch Yth Grp; Key Club; P to P St Amb Prg; Svce Clb; Spanish Clb; Chrldg (JC); Stu Cncl (R); CR (R); Outstanding Jr. Optimist; Jr. Optimist Club President; Architecture; U of Virginia; Miami U

LEDFORD, TYLER; WEST LIBERTY, OH; (JR); Hnr Roll; MVP; Prom Com; Chr; SP/M/VS; Stg Cre; Bsball (V); Bskball (V C); Stu Cncl (R); 2nd Team All District Basketball; District 9 1st Team OHC 1st Team; Physical Education; Sports Training

LEE, BRITTANY; MIDDLEFIELD, OH; CARDINAL HS; (FR); Hi Hnr Roll; Hnr Roll; St of Mnth; WWAHSS; Comm Volntr; 4-H; Chrch Yth Grp; DARE; Key Club; Scouts; Bnd; Jzz Bnd; Mch Bnd; Stg Cre; Vllyball (J); Sch Ppr (E, R); Famous Poets Competition - Finals; Power of the Pen - District Winner / Best of Round; Veterinarian; Veterinarian Technician; Becker College; U of Massachusetts

LEE, JAMES; TOLEDO, OH; (MS); Hi Hnr Roll; Perf Att; Yth Ldrshp Prog; Comm Volntr; Chess; Mth Clb/Tm; Quiz Bowl; French Clb; Ftball (J); U of Michigan

LEE, JESSICA; TOLEDO, OH; WHITMER CAREER & TECH CTR; (JR); Hnr Roll; Nat Hon Sy; WWAHSS; Hosp Aide; ArtClub; Mth Clb/Tm; MuAlphaTh; Sccr (J); Stu Cncl (R); Neurosurgeon; Neurologist; Miami U Oxford OH; U of Toledo

LEE, SHAREESE; CINCINNATI, OH; AIKEN UNIVERSITY HS; (SR); Hnr Roll; Kwnis Aw; Valdctrian; Comm Volntr; ArtClub; Drma Clb; Honor in Chemistry; Honor in History; Animation; Savannah College of Art and Design

LEESER, KRISTA L; CANAL FULTON, OH; NORTHWEST HS; (JR); Hnr Roll; Comm Volntr; Chrch Yth Grp; Drma Clb; Emplmnt; FCA; Chr; Dnce; SP/M/VS; Mar Art; Church Youth Group; Tap Dance-10 Years; Early Childhood Education; Kindergarten Teacher; U of North Carolina At Chapel Hill; U of North Carolina At Wilmington

LEESMAN, MEGHAN R; CINCINNATI, OH; MOTHER OF MERCY HS; (SO); Hi Hnr Roll; Hnr Roll; Perf Att; St of Mnth; WWAHSS; Peer Tut/Med; Chrch Yth Grp; Drma Clb; Key Club; Spanish Clb; Chr; Ch Chr; SP/M/VS; Cincinnati Young People's Theatre; Flute Ensemble; Speech Pathology; U of Cincinnati; Eastern Kentucky U

LEGGETT, JESSICA; CINCINNATI, OH; NORTHWEST HS; (JR); F Lan Hn Soc; Hi Hnr Roll; Hnr Roll; MVP; Nat Hon Sy; WWAHSS; Yth Ldrshp Prog; Peer Tut/Med; Emplmnt; Key Club; Chr; Sftball (JCL); Vllyball (JCL); Cl Off (T); Stu Cncl (T); CR (T); National Youth Leadership Forum; Varsity Bowling (Other Gov't. Programs); Pre-Law; Psychology; Harvard U; Stanford U

LE GRAIR, CHRISTOPHER; AKRON, OH; GARFIELD HS; (JR); Hnr Roll; Perf Att; WWAHSS; Chrch Yth Grp; Track (V); 3.0 Club; Junior Leadership; Elementary Education; Elementary Administration; Central State U; Youngstown State U

LEHANE, REBECCA; COLUMBIA STATION, OH; COLUMBIA HS; (FR); Hi Hnr Roll; Hnr Roll; Sci Fairs; 4-H; Chrch Yth Grp; DARE; Drma Clb; Chr; SP/M/VS; Stg Cre; Cr Ctry (V L); Hsbk Rdg (V); Skiing (V); Track (V L); Stu Cncl (R); Cut a Children's Music CD; Play Piano Guitar and Recorder; Equestrian & Livestock Vet; Ohio State U

LEIMGRUBER, MELISSA; CYGNET, OH; NORTH BALTIMORE JR/SR HS; (FR); 4H Awd; Hnr Roll; Otst Ac Ach Awd; St of Mnth; Comm Volntr; 4-H; Chrch Yth Grp; Pep Squd; Tchrs Aide; Spanish Clb; Bnd; Mch Bnd; Pep Bnd; Cl Off (T); Bowling Green State U

LE MASTER, KYLE; LODI, OH; NORTHWESTERN HS; (SO); Hnr Roll; Nat Hon Sy; WWAHSS; Bnd; Ftball (J); Astronomy; Business Management

LEMMERT, KURT A; SPRINGFIELD, OH; SPRINGFIELD NORTH HS; (FR); Ctznshp Aw; Hi Hnr Roll; MVP; Pres Sch; St of Mnth; Chrch Yth Grp; Bsball (V); Bskball (J); Teaching Degree; Fireman; Ohio State; Wright State

LEMON, KALA; JACKSON, OH; JACKSON HS; (SR); Hnr Roll; St of Mnth; Emplmnt; Off Aide; Prom Com; Quill & Scroll; Scouts; Clb; Bskball (VJ); Sftball (VJCL); Vllyball (VJ); All-Academic Seal; Psychiatry; Ohio U

LENNON, CHUCK; CANTON, OH; MC KINLEY HS; (MS); Hnr Roll; Ftball (J); Wrstlg (J); Spelling Bee; Ohio State U

LENT, ANDREW; RENO, OH; FRONTIER HS; (SR); 4H Awd; Kwnis Aw; USAA; WWAHSS; Yth Ldrshp Prog; Comm Volntr; Peer Tut/Med; 4-H; BPA; Chrch Yth Grp; Drma Clb; FCA; Key Club; Prom Com; Spanish Clb; Bnd; Chr; Mch Bnd; Pep Bnd; Sch Ppr (R); Culinary Arts; Marine Biology; Hocking College

LENTZ, DEANNA; CHARDON, OH; CHARDON HS; (SO); Hi Hnr Roll; Pres Ac Ftns Aw; Sci/Math Olympn; St of Mnth; Chrch Yth Grp; Mth Clb/Tm; Tchrs Aide; French Clb; Bnd; Mch Bnd; Pep Bnd; Cr Ctry (J); Envirothon Team Member; Foreign Affairs; Biochemistry

LEON, SARAH; LORAIN, OH; LORAIN SOUTHVIEW HS; (FR); Hi Hnr Roll; Hnr Roll; Svce Clb; Bnd; Mch Bnd; Sftball (L); Stay Tobacco-Free Athletes Mentor Program; Project Grad; Belgian/Cultures Courses; Psychology; UCLA; Lorain County Community College

LEONARD, MEGAN R; CAREY, OH; CAREY SCH; (JR); Hnr Roll; Nat Hon Sy; ArtClub; Drma Clb; Emplmnt; FCCLA; Off Aide; Prom Com; SADD; Tchrs Aide; Bnd; Jzz Bnd; Mch Bnd; Orch; Yrbk (R); Early Childhood Ecucation; Heidelberg College; Findlay U

LEONE, TALIA; COLUMBUS, OH; HILLIARD DARBY HS; (JR); Hnr Roll; Red Cr Aide; Cr Ctry (V L); Track (V L); Biomedical Engineering; Medical or Engineering Field; Toledo U; Akron U

LEUNG, KATRINA; COLUMBUS, OH; NEW ALBANY HS; (JR); Comm Volntr; ArtClub; Mus Clb; Ch Chr; Bdmtn (V); Swmg (V); Track (V); Cl Off (T); Lit Mag (E); Club Treasurer; Best Prefect; Nutrition; Music

LEUTZ, JULIANNA; COLUMBUS, OH; GRANDVIEW HEIGHTS HS; (JR); Ctznshp Aw; Hnr Roll; MVP; St of Mnth; WWAHSS; Sci Clb; Spanish Clb; Mch Bnd; Sccr (J); Sftball (V CL); Swmg (V CL); Cl Off (T); Stu Cncl (R); Becoming a Pilot; Computer Advertising; Embry-Riddle Aeronautical U (AZ); Embry-Riddle Aeronautical U (FL)

LEVY, HALLI M; SOLON, OH; SOLON HS; (SR); Hnr Roll; Otst Ac Ach Awd; WWAHSS; Comm Volntr; Key Club; Prom Com; SADD; Tchrs Aide; Tmpl Yth Grp; Chrldg (J); Stu Cncl (R); CR (R); Sch Ppr (E, R); News Program Reporter; Flag Football Participant; Advertising & Public Relations; Broadcast Journalism; U of Missouri

LEWIS, BREDIA A; CINCINNATI, OH; WITHROW UNIVERSITY HS; (FR); Ctznshp Aw; Fut Prb Slvr; Hnr Roll; Nat Hon Sy; Otst Ac Ach Awd; Perf Att; Yth Ldrshp Prog; Comm Volntr; Peer Tut/Med; Chrch Yth Grp; Cmptr Clb; DARE; Drma Clb; Emplmnt; FCA; Jr Ach; Pep Squd; Ch Chr; Dnce; Drl Tm; Pep Bnd; Bsball (J); Bskball (J); Sftball (J); Yrbk (R); Soccer, Computer; Assist Sunday School Teacher.; Lawyer (Criminal Justice); Business Marketing; Clark Atlanta U; Spelman

LEWIS, KAITLYN; SAINT CLAIRSVILLE, OH; ST JOHN'S CTRL HS; (JR); Hnr Roll; Sci Fairs; WWAHSS; Comm Volntr; Chrch Yth Grp; Emplmnt; JSA; Scouts; SADD; Spanish Clb; Silver Award in Girl Scouts; Physical Therapy; Wheeling Jesuit U; Robert Morris U

LEWIS, LATISHA; CLEVELAND, OH; HEALTH CAREERS CTR; (SO); Ctznshp Aw; Hab For Humty Volntr; Chrch Yth Grp; DARE; Chr; Ch Chr; Chrldg (V); Stu Cncl (V); Yrbk (R); High Stepping Varsity; Medical-Pediatrician or Nurse; Pharmacist; Ohio State U

LI, IRIS; TWINSBURG, OH; TWINSBURG HS; (MS); 4H Awd; Ctznshp Aw; Gov Hnr Prg; Hi Hnr Roll; Hnr Roll; Nat Hon Sy; Nat Ldrshp Svc; Otst Ac Ach Awd; Perf Att; St of Mnth; Peer Tut/Med; 4-H; DARE; FTA; Jr Ach; Lib Aide; Mth Clb/Tm; Off Aide; Tchrs Aide; Pediatrician; Harvard College; Yale U

LI, JASON; WEST CHESTER, OH; LAKOTA EAST HS; (SO); Hi Hnr Roll; Otst Ac Ach Awd; Jr Cls League; Quiz Bowl; Bnd; Mch Bnd; Orch; Sch Ppr (R); Medicine; Music; Case Western Revue U; Rice U

LI, KEVIN; SYLVANIA, OH; SYLVANIA NORTHVIEW HS; (SO); F Lan Hn Soc; Hi Hnr Roll; Hnr Roll; Otst Ac Ach Awd; Pres Ac Ftns Aw; Pres Sch; Comm Volntr; Drma Clb; Mth Clb/Tm; French, Spanish Clb; Chr; SP/M/VS; Stg Cre; Northview Winter Table Tennis Tournament- Second Place; Selected for the National Youth Leadership Forum on Medicine; Medical-Pediatrician; Media-Graphics; Duke U; U of Michigan

LI, LINDA; MASSILLON, OH; JACKSON HS; (FR); 4H Awd; Hnr Roll; WWAHSS; Comm Volntr; Dbte Team; Key Club; NtlFrnscLg; Spch Team; Spanish Clb; Bnd; Mch Bnd; Lcrsse (J); Skiing (V); Medical; Business; Case Western; U of Pennsylvania

LI, MICHAEL; ASHLAND, OH; ASHLAND HS; (JR); Hnr Roll; Nat Hon Sy; Nat Mrt LOC; Perf Att; WWAHSS; Yth Ldrshp Prog; Comm Volntr; Red Cr Aide; Chrch Yth Grp; DARE; Emplmnt; Mth Clb/Tm; Vsity Clb; Spanish Clb; Orch; Golf (J); Skiing; Tennis (V L); Engineering; Business; Carnegie Mellon; Massachusetts Institute of Technology

LIANOPOULOS, CHRISTINA; CLEVELAND, OH; RICHMOND HEIGHTS HS; (SO); Hnr Roll; WWAHSS; Comm Volntr; Drma Clb; Emplmnt; Key Club; SP/M/VS; Scr Kpr; Cl Off (S, T); CR (R); Key Club Member; REAL Member; Bio-Medical Engineering; Biochemistry Researching; Case Western Reserve U

LIEDEL, KAYLA; SWANTON, OH; EVERGREEN HS; (JR); Ctznshp Aw; Hi Hnr Roll; Nat Hon Sy; Perf Att; Comm Volntr; Peer Tut/Med; Drma Clb; Prom Com; Quiz Bowl; SADD; Bnd; Mch Bnd; Pep Bnd; SP/M/VS; Biology; Veterinary; Kent State U; Bowling Green State U

LIGHTFOOT, VICTORIA Y; YOUNGSTOWN, OH; RAYEN HS; (JR); Ctznshp Aw; Hnr Roll; Nat Hon Sy; Nat Sci Aw; Otst Ac Ach Awd; Perf Att; St of Mnth; USAA; WWAHSS; Comm Volntr; Dbte Team; Svce Clb; Chr; Track (V); Adv Cncl (R); Sch Ppr (E, R); Rayer Honor Roll Society; Business; Performing Arts; Hampton State U; Clark Atlanta State U

LIGUORI, KRISTEN A; CLARKSVILLE, OH; CLINTON-MASSIE HS; (SR); DAR; Hi Hnr Roll; Hnr Roll; Nat Hon Sy; Otst Ac Ach Awd; Perf Att; St of Mnth; USAA; Valdctrian; WWAHSS; Comm Volntr; Peer Tut/Med; DARE; Drma Clb; Emplmnt; Key Club; Svce Clb; Tchrs Aide; Chr; Drl Tm; SP/M/VS; Chrldg (V CL); PP Ftbl (V); Sftball (J L); Vllyball (J L); Cl Off (V); Stu Cncl (R); Yrbk (P); Show Choir; Electronic Media; Public Relations; U of Cincinnati

LILLY, TIFFINY E; NEWBURY, OH; KENSTON HS; (SR); Hnr Roll; Perf Att; St of Mnth; Off Aide; SADD; Tchrs Aide; Cl Off (V); Community Service Award 2001-2006; Child Care; Teacher; Lakeland

LIMBACHER, LAUREN M; HILLIARD, OH; HILLIARD DARBY HS; (FR); Hi Hnr Roll; Hnr Roll; Otst Ac Ach Awd; Key Club; Bnd; Dnce; Mch Bnd; Pep Bnd; Skiing (C); Crayola Crayons Contest Winner; School Psychologist; English Teacher-Secondary; U of Dayton; Miami of Ohio

LIMBERT, JESSE M; WAPAKONETA, OH; WAPAKONETA HS; (SO); 4H Awd; Hi Hnr Roll; Hnr Roll; Perf Att; Peer Tut/Med; 4-H; Chrch Yth Grp; DARE; Emplmnt; Photog; Quiz Bowl; Spanish Clb; Bnd; Mch Bnd; Pep Bnd; Engineering; Environmental Sciences; U of Cincinnati; Xavier U

LINABARGER, MAX; WILLOUGHBY, OH; WILLOUGHBY SOUTH HS; (SO); Chr; Swg Chr; Bsball (V L); Varsity Letter for Baseball As a Sophomore; Ashland U; Ohio U

LINDAMOOD, KAYLA; MILFORD CTR, OH; FAIRBANKS HS; (SO); Hnr Roll; St of Mnth; Comm Volntr; Chrch Yth Grp; Personal Piano Lessons; Mission Trip to Mexico; Music Composition & Art; Serving God; Mount Vernon Nazarene College-Ohio; Cedarville U-Ohio

LINDENBERGER, SABRINA; GREENWICH, OH; SOUTH CTRL HS; (MS); Hnr Roll; Freshman Cheerleader; Cosmetologist; Auto Mechanic; Ohio State; Toledo

LINDER, BECKIE; WAKEMAN, OH; WESTERN RESERVE HS; (FR); 4H Awd; Hi Hnr Roll; Hnr Roll; Otst Ac Ach Awd; Perf Att; St of Mnth; Yth Ldrshp Prog; 4-H; Acpl Chr; Chr; SP/M/VS; Bskball; Sftball (J C); Cl Off (V); Youth 4 Youth; American History; Archeology; Bowling Green State U; Pennsylvania Culinary Institute

LINDER, SAMANTHA K; LOUISVILLE, OH; LOUISVILLE HS; (JR); Hi Hnr Roll; Hnr Roll; WWAHSS; ArtClub; Chrch Yth Grp; Emplmnt; Spanish Clb; Made Top 5% - Who's Who Among American HS Students; Early Childhood Education; Education; Ohio State U; Malone College

LINDSEY, JACOB; DUBLIN, OH; DUBLIN COFFMAN HS; (JR); Ctznshp Aw; Hnr Roll; Nat Hon Sy; Sci Fairs; Chrch Yth Grp; Drma Clb; SP/M/VS; Stg Cre; Stu Cncl (R); Citizenship Award; Member of the International Thespian Society; English; Creative Writing; Rice U; Duke U

LINDSEY, REBECCA V; CLEVELAND, OH; COLLINWOOD HS; (SR); MVP; Bskball (V); Cr Ctry (L); Swmg (V); Track (L); Vllyball (V); Sch Ppr; Business Marketing; Shawnee State; Cleveland State

LING, LISA M; FRANKLIN, OH; BISHOP FENWICK HS; (SO); Hi Hnr Roll; MVP; Key Club; Spanish Clb; Bskball (V L); Tennis (V CL); Cl Off (S); Pediatrics; Nursing; Wright State U; U of Dayton

LINGROSS, AMACA; CINCINNATI, OH; WESTERN HILLS UNIV HS; (SO); Ctznshp Aw; Hnr Roll; Nat Sci Aw; Otst Ac Ach Awd; Perf Att; Sci Fairs; St of Mnth; Comm Volntr; Peer Tut/Med; ArtClub; Biology Clb; Chess; Drma Clb; Mth Clb/Tm; ROTC; Sci Clb; Bnd; SP/M/VS; Vllyball (J); Art; Photography; Berea College; U of Cincinnati

LINK, LAURA; CELINA, OH; CELINA HS; (JR); Hi Hnr Roll; Jr Eng Tech; Nat Hon Sy; Otst Ac Ach Awd; St of Mnth; WWAHSS; Peer Tut/Med; 4-H; Chrch Yth Grp; DARE; Emplmnt; FCA; Lttrmn Clb; Prom Com; Vsity Clb; Bskball (V CL); Sccr (V CL); National Honor Society Vice President; Pharmacy; Ohio Northern U

LINKHART, MARIAH; XENIA, OH; XENIA HS; 4H Awd; Hi Hnr Roll; Nat Hon Sy; Perf Att; Pres Sch; WWAHSS; Comm Volntr; 4-H; Drma Clb; Ntl FFA; Tchrs Aide; Chr; SP/M/VS; Sccr (J); Drama Club; Agriculture Communications; The Ohio State U

LINTON, SHANNON; BARBERTON, OH; BARBERTON HS; (JR); Hi Hnr Roll; Hnr Roll; Nat Hon Sy; Perf Att; WWAHSS; Comm Volntr; Hosp Aide; Chrch Yth Grp; Emplmnt; Key Club; Photog; Scouts; Tchrs Aide; French Clb; Stg Cre; Stu Cncl (S); CR (R); Sch Ppr (E); Education; Ohio State U; Kent State U

LIPSCOMB, JENNA M; DAYTON, OH; WAYNE HS; (SR); Hnr Roll; Nat Hon Sy; WWAHSS; Comm Volntr; Hab For Humty Volntr; Peer Tut/Med; Emplmnt; HO'Br Yth Ldrshp; Off Aide; Prom Com; Svce Clb; Tchrs Aide; Cr Ctry (J); PP Ftbl; Sftball (VJ L); Cl Off (P); Stu Cncl (P, R); Miami U; The Ohio State U

LIST, JENNIFER; CINCINNATI, OH; MC NICHOLAS HS; (SR); Hnr Roll; St of Mnth; Comm Volntr; Pep Squd; SP/M/VS; Chrldg (VJ L); U of Cincinnati

Lewis, Bredia A
Withrow University HS
Cincinnati, OH

National
Honor Roll
Spring 2005

Lehane, Rebecca
Columbia HS
Columbia Station, OH

LITTLE, BRITTANY; CINCINNATI, OH; TURPIN HS; (JR); Hnr Roll; Sci Fairs; Comm Volntr; Chrch Yth Grp; Chrldg (J L); Gmnstcs (V L); PP Ftbl (J); Track (V L); Coaches' Award for Gymnastics; Scholar Athlete for Gymnastics; Advertising/Journalism; Business; Ohio U Athens; Miami U, Ohio

LITTLE, SARAH; JAMESTOWN, OH; GREENEVIEW HS; (JR); Ctznshp Aw; Hnr Roll; Nat Hon Sy; Perf Att; WWAHSS; Comm Volntr; AL Aux Girls; Chrch Yth Grp; Emplmnt; FTA; Key Club; Chr; SP/M/VS; Stg Cre; Swg Chr; PP Ftbl; Sftball (V L); Vllyball (VJ); Stu Cncl (R); Yrbk (P); Buckeye Girls State; Secondary Education/History; Cincinnati Christian U

LITTLEJOHN, JAMES; WELLSTON, OH; WELLSTON HS; (SO); WWAHSS; Ntl FFA; Bsball (J); Ftball (VJ); Track (V L); Stu Cncl (R); Anesthesiology; Plastic Surgeon; Ohio State U; U of Southern California

LITWINICK, VALERIE; EASTLAKE, OH; WILLOUGHBY SOUTH HS; (FR); WWAHSS; Key Club; Spanish Clb; Chr

LIZARRIBAR, ADRIANA; CLYDE, OH; CLYDE HS; (FR); Tennis (J); Track (V); Nutritionist; Science Teacher; Florida State U

LOCKEMER, SCOTT M; NEWBURY, OH; NEWBURY HS; (FR); Hnr Roll; Nat Hon Sy; Pres Sch; St of Mnth; USAA; DARE; Emplmnt; Scouts; Bsball (V)

LOCKWOOD, CHRISTIAN T; MIAMISBURG, OH; MIAMISBURG HS; (SO); Hnr Roll; Hab For Humty Volntr; Graphic Design

LOCY, CHELSEA; ASHTABULA, OH; WEST JHS; (MS); Hnr Roll; MVP; Nat Hon Sy; Perf Att; Pres Ac Ftns Aw; St of Mnth; Comm Volntr; Peer Tut/Med; Chrch Yth Grp; Mus Clb; Quiz Bowl; Bnd; Ch Chr; Mch Bnd; Chrldg; Scr Kpr; Swmg; Stu Cncl (R); Sch Ppr (R); Yrbk

LOGAN, RALAINA L; YOUNGSTOWN, OH; WOODROW WILSON HS; (FR); Yth Ldrshp Prog; FBLA; Ch Chr; Dnce; Chrldg (J); Psychology; Dance; Ohio State U

LOGSDON, ASHLEY; PICKERINGTON, OH; PICKERINGTON HS NORTH; (FR); Hi Hnr Roll; WWAHSS; Chrch Yth Grp; Key Club; Mth Clb/Tm; Off Aide; Spanish Clb; Chr; Ch Chr; Dnce

LOHBECK, KYLE; CINCINNATI, OH; (SO); Hnr Roll; Comm Volntr; Emplmnt; Bsball (J); Ftball (J); Skiing (J); Wt Lftg (J); Wrstlg (VJ); Server At Sunday Mass; Service to Community; Ohio State U

LONG, AMBER L; CRESTON, OH; CLOVERLEAF HS; (SR); 4H Awd; Hi Hnr Roll; Hnr Roll; Kwnis Aw; Nat Hon Sy; Perf Att; WWAHSS; Comm Volntr; Hosp Aide; 4-H; DARE; Emplmnt; Jr Ach; Key Club; Scouts; SADD; Tchrs Aide; Chr; United Way Youth Volunteer Award; Student of the Month / 12-2004; Nursing; Akron U

LONG, ROBBIE; SAINT PARIS, OH; GRAHAM HS; (FR); Hi Hnr Roll; Hnr Roll; Otst Ac Ach Awd; Pres Sch; Comm Volntr; Emplmnt; Scouts; Ftball (J); Track (V); Wt Lftg (V); Boy Scouts-Star Scout/Senior Patrol Leader; Athletic Trainer; Emergency Medical Technician; Ohio State U; Bowling Green State U

LOOMIS, BRITTNEY; CLEVELAND, OH; NORMANDY HS; (JR); Hnr Roll; Peer Tut/Med; DARE; Emplmnt; Lib Aide; Off Aide; SADD; Plays Rugby for Parma Rugby Football Club; A Computer Lab Assistant; Marine Biology; Doctor of Veterinary Medicine (DVM); Ohio State U; Ohio U

LOPEZ, ANDREW; LOUISVILLE, OH; EAST CANTON HS; (SO); Hnr Roll; Perf Att; Chrch Yth Grp; Lttrmn Clb; Cr Ctry (J); Track (L); Wt Lftg (J); Sch Ppr (R); I Attended MEDCAMP; Orthopedic Surgery; Medicine; Mount Union U; Ohio Northern U

LOPRESTE, AARON; BELPRE, OH; BELPRE HS; (FR); Hi Hnr Roll; Emplmnt; Mod UN; Off Aide; Scouts; Chr; Bskball (J L); Cr Ctry (V L); Track (V L)

LOPRESTI, MICHAEL J; WESTERVILLE, OH; THE COLUMBUS AC; (FR); Hnr Roll; Golf (V L); Swmg (V L); Volunteer At Columbus Colony Nursing Home; USA Swimming & Member NAAC Swim Team; Pre-Med; Miami U (Oxford, Ohio); Duke U

LORENZANA, DESIREE; LORAIN, OH; LORAIN SOUTHVIEW HS; (FR); Hnr Roll; Perf Att; Dnce; Tennis (J); Track (J); Stu Cncl (P); CR (V); Nursing; Medical / Doctor; Clark Atlanta U; Ohio State U

LORITTS, SHANNON; DAYTON, OH; (JR); Hnr Roll; St of Mnth; WWAHSS; Comm Volntr; Chrch Yth Grp; Chr; Track; Business Management; Fisk U

LOTT, JEANNA; MOGADORE, OH; FIELD HS; (JR); Perf Att; USAA; WWAHSS; Comm Volntr; Scouts; Girl Scouts Silver Award; Member of National Society of High School Scholars; Writer; Chef; U of Akron; Harvard

LOUDERMILK, AMANDA; CINCINNATI, OH; NORTHWEST HS; (JR); F Lan Hn Soc; Hnr Roll; WWAHSS; Comm Volntr; Hosp Aide; Peer Tut/Med; Chrch Yth Grp; Emplmnt; Key Club; Pep Squd; German Clb; Bnd; Chr; Ch Chr; Clr Grd; Successfully Completed Nurse's Aide Training Program; Occupational Therapy; Cincinnati State

LOVE, ABBEY; CINCINNATI, OH; MC AULEY HS; (JR); F Lan Hn Soc; Hi Hnr Roll; Hnr Roll; MVP; Nat Hon Sy; Otst Ac Ach Awd; Pres Ac Ftns Aw; St of Mnth; WWAHSS; Comm Volntr; Peer Tut/Med; Spec Olymp Vol; Chrch Yth Grp; Emplmnt; Key Club; Off Aide; P to P St Amb Prg; Svce Clb; SADD; Spanish Clb; Bnd; Orch; SP/M/VS; Scer (JC); Swmg (J); Track (V L); Cl Off (T); Yrbk (P); Social Work; Occupational Therapy

LOVE, TIFFANY; CINCINNATI, OH; WINTON WOODS HS; (SR); Ctznshp Aw; Hi Hnr Roll; Hnr Roll; Nat Hon Sy; Sci Fairs; St of Mnth; Comm Volntr; Chrch Yth Grp; DARE; Jr Ach; ROTC; Acpl Chr; Ch Chr; Chrldg (V C); Cl Off (S); Sch Ppr (R); NJROTC; Use to Be in Band and Choir At School; Major in Physical Therapy; Music; Tennessee State U; U of Cincinnati

LOVICK, JESSICA L; MANTUA, OH; CRESTWOOD HS; (JR); Ctznshp Aw; Hnr Roll; Nat Hon Sy; Pres Sch; WWAHSS; Chrch Yth Grp; Emplmnt; Sci Clb; Scouts; Tchrs Aide; French Clb; Bnd; Drm Mjr; Jzz Bnd; Mch Bnd; Contemporary Youth Orchestra; Secondary Education-English; Secondary Education-History; Baldwin Wallace; Miami U (OH)

LOWE, KELSEY; HAMILTON, OH; FAIRFIELD FRESHMAN HS; (FR); Ctznshp Aw; Hi Hnr Roll; Perf Att; Sci Fairs; St of Mnth; Comm Volntr; Chrch Yth Grp; DARE; Tchrs Aide; Dnce; Chrldg (J); Track (L); Competitive Cheerleading (Ace); Asst Coach for 5th Grade Cheer; Computer Programming; Accounting; Miami U; Ohio State

LOWE, LEMARQUNITA; BEDFORD, OH; BEDFORD HS; (SR); Hnr Roll; Nat Hon Sy; St of Mnth; WWAHSS; Red Cr Aide; DECA; Emplmnt; Lib Aide; Off Aide; Prom Com; Tchrs Aide; Spanish Clb; Adv Cncl (P); Cl Off (P); Stu Cncl (R); CR (P); Bedford Rotarian; YWCA Recipient; Political Science; English; Bowling Green State U

LOWE, OCTAVEYA L; CLEVELAND, OH; GLENVILLE HS; (SR); Hi Hnr Roll; Hnr Roll; WWAHSS; Comm Volntr; Peer Tut/Med; ArtClub; Off Aide; Tchrs Aide; Dnce; Adv Cncl (R); CR (R); Psychology; Acting; Bowling Green State U

LOWE, ROBERT M; LOVELAND, OH; GOSHEN HS; (JR); Hi Hnr Roll; Nat Hon Sy; Otst Ac Ach Awd; Perf Att; Pres Ac Ftns Aw; St of Mnth; WWAHSS; Scouts; Tchrs Aide; Ftball (VJ); Eagle Scout in Boy Scouts Troop 237; Vet; Ohio State U; Wilmington College

LOWRY, BOBBIE L; TRENTON, OH; MONROE HS; (JR); Hnr Roll; Nat Hon Sy; Perf Att; Comm Volntr; BPA; Emplmnt; Acpl Chr; Sch Ppr (E); Teaching; Business Management

LUCAS, BRANDON; DELLROY, OH; CARROLLTON HS; (SO); Hnr Roll; Otst Ac Ach Awd; St of Mnth; WWAHSS; Comm Volntr; Chrch Yth Grp; Emplmnt; Off Aide; Tchrs Aide; Wdwrkg Clb; Bskball (J); Cr Ctry (V L); Track (V L); STAMP - Stay Tobacco-Free Athlete Mentor Program; Mechanical Engineering; Fire Fighting

LUCAS, CHAD R; SHERWOOD, OH; FAIRVIEW HS; (SO); Hnr Roll; Comm Volntr; Peer Tut/Med; Chrch Yth Grp; DARE; FBLA; FCCLA; Mus Clb; Off Aide; SADD; Bnd; Ch Chr; Mch Bnd; Pep Bnd; Chrldg (J); Track (V); FCCLA-Sec and Treas; SAE; Family Medicine; Plastic Surgeon; Ohio State U; U of Tennessee

LUCAS, KARA; DOYLESTOWN, OH; CHIPPEWA HS; (FR); Hi Hnr Roll; Hnr Roll; Perf Att; Pres Sch; St of Mnth; Bnd; Mch Bnd; Stg Cre; Business; Education; College of Wooster; Youngstown State U

LUEHRING, ANDREW; LAKEWOOD, OH; LAKEWOOD HS; (JR); Hi Hnr Roll; Nat Hon Sy; WWAHSS; Yth Ldrshp Prog; Comm Volntr; Drma Clb; Emplmnt; Key Club; Lib Aide; Mod UN; Quill & Scroll; Quiz Bowl; Wdwrkg Clb; Bnd; Mch Bnd; Orch; Skiing; Tennis (J)

LUKAS, SERAH; CYGNET, OH; NORTH BALTIMORE JR/SR HS; (FR); Hi Hnr Roll; St of Mnth; WWAHSS; Peer Tut/Med; ArtClub; Ntl FFA; Bskball (J); Vllyball (J)

LUMP II, MICHAEL B; CHILLICOTHE, OH; PAINT VALLEY JR/SR HS; (SR); Hnr Roll; Nat Hon Sy; Otst Ac Ach Awd; Sci/Math Olympn; WWAHSS; Red Cr Aide; Spec Olymp Vol; BPA; Sci Clb; Ftball (J L); Business Professionals of America National Contest Qualifier; DeVry Institute of Technology

LUPP, ELIZABETH; CINCINNATI, OH; MC AULEY HS; (SO); Hi Hnr Roll; WWAHSS; Comm Volntr; Key Club; Svce Clb; Sccr (J); Coach Assistant - Youth Volleyball; Math; Sciences

LUTE, ASHLEY M; PORTSMOUTH, OH; NORTHWEST HS; (SO); 4H Awd; Hnr Roll; Nat Hon Sy; Sci Fairs; WWAHSS; Hosp Aide; 4-H; DARE; Pep Squd; Pep Club; Who's Who Among American H.S. Kids; Nurse; Physical Therapist; OSU; Penn State

LY, ANTHONY; CINCINNATI, OH; WESTERN HILLS DESIGN TECH SCH; (SO); Hnr Roll; Nat Hon Sy; Perf Att; Accounting; Mathematics; Miami U Ohio; U of Cincinnati

LYKINS, KRISTI M; WHEELERSBURG, OH; WHEELERSBURG HS; (FR); Hnr Roll; WWAHSS; Chrch Yth Grp; DARE; Key Club; Chr; Clr Grd; GAA (J); Sccr (V); Swmg (J); Tennis (JC); Track (L); Wt Lftg (VJ); Mock Trial; Youth Employed Services (YES); Music Major; Marshal U; Ohio State U

LYNN, KRISTEN N; GALLIPOLIS, OH; GALLIA AC HS; (FR); Hnr Roll; WWAHSS; Comm Volntr; Chrch Yth Grp; Key Club; Mod UN; P to P St Amb Prg; Quiz Bowl; Chr; Ch Chr; SP/M/VS; Stg Cre; Cr Ctry (J); Sccr (J L); English/Journalism; Kentucky Christian U

LYONS, KAYLA; CROOKSVILLE, OH; MORGAN HS; (JR); Hnr Roll; Nat Hon Sy; Comm Volntr; Key Club; Lttrmn Clb; Off Aide; Prom Com; Quill & Scroll; Tchrs Aide; Vsity Clb; French Clb; Chrldg (V CL); Sftball (V L); Vsy Clb (L); Stu Cncl; Yrbk (E); Homecoming Attendant; Nursing; Ohio State U; Ohio U

LYONS, MICHAEL; CAMBRIDGE, OH; CAMBRIDGE HS; (SO); 4H Awd; Hnr Roll; Nat Hon Sy; WWAHSS; Comm Volntr; Peer Tut/Med; Chess; Emplmnt; Key Club; Mod UN; Ftball (VJ L); Wt Lftg (VJ); Cl Off (P, V); Stu Cncl (R)

MAAG, JONATHAN W; CUYAHOGA FALLS, OH; WALSH JESUIT HS; (JR); Hnr Roll; Comm Volntr; Chess; Bnd; Stg Cre; Business Management; Theatre Management; Miami U (Ohio); Ohio U

MACDOWELL, JULIA L; WINCHESTER, OH; (SO); Hnr Roll; Otst Ac Ach Awd; Sci Fairs; Comm Volntr; Chrch Yth Grp; Acpl Chr; Chr; Vllyball (VJ); Associate's Degree in Psychology; U of Cincinnati-Clermont College

MACKEY, LAUREN; MADISON, OH; MADISON HS; (SR); 4H Awd; Hnr Roll; MVP; Nat Hon Sy; Pres Ac Ftns Aw; Sci Fairs; Comm Volntr; 4-H; Biology Clb; Chrch Yth Grp; Emplmnt; Photog; Sci Clb; Bnd; Ch Chr; SP/M/VS; Sftball; Swmg; Tennis; President and VP / 4-H Club; Youth Group Leadership Team; Communications; Music / Theater / Acting; Cedarville U; Grace College

MADDOX, GABRIELLE; COLUMBUS, OH; ST FRANCIS DE SALES HS; (FR); Hnr Roll; Otst Ac Ach Awd; St of Mnth; Comm Volntr; Peer Tut/Med; Chrch Yth Grp; DARE; Ch Chr; Ohio Interscholastic Writing League Certificate of Merit; President's Award for Educational Excellence; PhD to Become a Veterinarian; Ohio State U; Indiana U

MADEWELL, LEE; TOLEDO, OH; WHITMER HS; (JR); Hnr Roll; Yth Ldrshp Prog; CR (R); ATF Agent; Law Graduate; Western Michigan U; Kalamazoo U

MADISON, BREEANCA; COLUMBUS, OH; AFRICENTRIC SEC HS; (SO); Hnr Roll; Fr of Library; P to P St Amb Prg; Ch Chr; Dnce; Mch Bnd; SP/M/VS; Bskball (V); Cr Ctry (V); Track (V); Stu Cncl (R); Accepted To Ohio U Upward Bound; Psychologist; Music; Ohio State U; Ohio U

MADISON, CHELSEA; CLEVELAND, OH; SOUTH HS; (JR); Hnr Roll; Perf Att; Sci Fairs; Yth Ldrshp Prog; Chrch Yth Grp; DARE; Emplmnt; Key Club; Off Aide; Nursing; Lawyer; Cleveland State U; Ashland College

MAGNUSON, MATT; PICKERINGTON, OH; PICKERINGTON HS NORTH; (SO); Hi Hnr Roll; Perf Att; Chrch Yth Grp; Emplmnt; P to P St Amb Prg; National Latin Exam Cum Laude; People to People Ambassador to Australia; Aeronautical Engineering; Engineering

MAGOTO, JESSICA; VERSAILLES, OH; VERSAILLES HS; (SO); Hnr Roll; ArtClub; FTA; SADD; French Clb; Vllyball (J); Trainer; High School Level Mathematics Teacher; Sports Medicine; The U of North Carolina; Wright State U

MAGYAR, MATTHEW; AVON LAKE, OH; AVON LAKE HS; (JR); Hi Hnr Roll; Nat Hon Sy; Hab For Humty Volntr; Key Club; Mod UN; Quill & Scroll; Sci Clb; Spanish Clb; Chr; Skiing; Sftball (L); Track; Stu Cncl (R); Sch Ppr (R); Pre-Med; U of Notre Dame; Miami U

MAHOUSKI, NICOLE; SALEM, OH; SALEM HS; (JR); Hi Hnr Roll; Hnr Roll; Nat Hon Sy; WWAHSS; Comm Volntr; Emplmnt; Key Club; Spanish Clb; Bnd; Mch Bnd; SP/M/VS; Vllyball (J); Pre-Med; Ohio U; Kent State U

MAINES, TRISHA; LISBON, OH; SOUTHERN LOCAL HS; (JR); Hnr Roll; Nat Hon Sy; WWAHSS; ArtClub; Drma Clb; Pep Squd; Prom Com; Sci Clb; Tchrs Aide; Spanish Clb; Bnd; Dnce; Mch Bnd; Pep Bnd; Chrldg (VJ); Teaching; Veterinarian; Kent State (Salem)

MAIONE, JOSIE; SPRINGBORO, OH; SPRINGBORO HS; (SO); Hi Hnr Roll; St of Mnth; WWAHSS; Hosp Aide; ArtClub; Chrch Yth Grp; DARE; Emplmnt; Key Club; Off Aide; Photog; SADD; Vllyball (V); Stu Cncl (R); Yrbk (R, P); Who's Who Among High School Students; Black Belt (TKD Karate); Pediatric Medicine; Journalism; Miami U of Oxford; Ohio State U

MALICOAT, RYAN; BATAVIA, OH; BATAVIA HS; (SO); Hnr Roll; Sci Fairs; Off Aide; Bsball; Renaissance Club; Computer Specialist

MALKIMAN, OLGA E; COLUMBUS, OH; BEXLEY HS; (JR); Hi Hnr Roll; Hnr Roll; Nat Hon Sy; Nat Mrt LOC; WWAHSS; Yth Ldrshp Prog; Peer Tut/Med; P to P St Amb Prg; Tmpl Yth Grp; Vllyball (J); Sch Ppr (E, R); Youth Group President; Business Major; Law School; U of Michigan Ann Arbor; Columbia U

Mackey, Lauren
Madison HS
Madison, OH

Maag, Jonathan W
Walsh Jesuit HS
Cuyahoga Falls, OH

Long, Robbie
Graham HS
Saint Paris, OH

Lott, Jeanna
Field HS
Mogadore, OH

Maione, Josie
Springboro HS
Springboro, OH

MALLOREY, CHRISTINE; TORONTO, OH; EDISON HS; (JR); Hi Hnr Roll; Hnr Roll; Nat Mrt LOC; Otst Ac Ach Awd; WWAHSS; Comm Volntr; Peer Tut/Med; Chrch Yth Grp; Ntl Beta Clb; Bnd; Jzz Bnd; Mch Bnd; Pep Bnd; Sccr (V L); Swmg (V L); Track (J)

MALONE, MALLORY; SOUTH VIENNA, OH; NORTHEASTERN HS; (SO); Perf Att; St of Mnth; Quiz Bowl; Spanish Clb; Bnd; Mch Bnd; Pep Bnd; Spanish Club Secretary; Major in Forensic Science; Minor in Art; Ohio State U

MALORNI, ANGELA; CUYAHOGA FALLS, OH; CUYAHOGA FALLS HS; (SO); Hi Hnr Roll; Jr Rot; WWAHSS; DECA; Drma Clb; Key Club; Spanish Clb; Art Was Chosen to Be Entered in Scholastics Competition

MANFRONI, MICHAEL; WILLOUGHBY, OH; WILLOUGHBY SOUTH HS; (JR); Hi Hnr Roll; Nat Hon Sy; WWAHSS; Comm Volntr; Drma Clb; Emplmnt; Key Club; NYLC; Scouts; Spanish Clb; SP/M/VS; Stg Cre; Yrbk (R, P); Interior Design; U of Cincinnati

MANGAN, JACOB; TIPP CITY, OH; BETHEL HS; (SO); Hi Hnr Roll; St of Mnth; Comm Volntr; Hab For Humty Volntr; DARE; Lib Aide; Wdwrkg Clb; Bnd; Pep Bnd; Bsball (J); Bskball (J); Medicine; Business Management; U of Michigan; Oklahoma Baptist U

MANGUM, CRAIG; COLUMBUS, OH; UPPER ARLINGTON HS; (SO); Hnr Roll; Peer Tut/Med; Chrch Yth Grp; Off Aide; Quill & Scroll; Scouts; Cr Ctry (J); Sccr (J); Track (J); Adv Cncl (R); Stu Cncl (R); Lit Mag (R); Yrbk (E); Co-Leader of Career Development Student Council; Member of Character Enrichment Team; Brigham Young U; Northwestern U

MANN, BRIAN R; SWANTON, OH; PIKE-DELTA-YORK HS; (JR); 4H Awd; Ctznshp Aw; Hi Hnr Roll; Nat Hon Sy; USAA; WWAHSS; 4-H; AL Aux Boys; Chrch Yth Grp; Quiz Bowl; Spanish Clb; Bnd; Drm Mjr; Mch Bnd; Pep Bnd; Top Male Student of Class for Past 3 Years, Ranking 1 Out of 117; Biochemistry Major; Clinical Laboratory Studies; Wittenberg U; Ohio Northern U

MANSFIELD, KRISTINA; SYLVANIA, OH; NORTHVIEW HS; (SR); Hnr Roll; Comm Volntr; Flg Crps; Early Childhood Education; Indian River Community College; Owens Community College

MANSFIELD, ROBIN; NAPOLEON, OH; NAPOLEON HS; (SR); 4H Awd; Hnr Roll; WWAHSS; Comm Volntr; Peer Tut/Med; Spec Olymp Vol; 4-H; Chrch Yth Grp; Svce Clb; SADD; French Clb; Chr; Tennis (J); Public Relations; Bowling Green State U

MANSFIELD, SARA; SOUTHINGTON, OH; SOUTHINGTON LOCAL SCH; (SO); 4H Awd; Hnr Roll; St of Mnth; Comm Volntr; 4-H; Chrch Yth Grp; Emplmnt; Mus Clb; Ntl Beta Clb; Ntl FFA; Off Aide; Tchrs Aide; Bnd; Mch Bnd; Pep Bnd; Hsbk Rdg; Band; Baton; Vet; The U of Findlay

MARCH, RICKIESHA A; CLEVELAND, OH; LUTHERAN HS EAST; (SR); Hnr Roll; Nat Hon Sy; St of Mnth; Valdctrian; WWAHSS; Comm Volntr; Peer Tut/Med; Cmptr Clb; Emplmnt; Photog; Spanish Clb; Ch Chr; Bskball (VJ L); Cl Off (P); Stu Cncl (P); CR (R); Sch Ppr (P); Yrbk (E, P); President National Honor Society; Pre-Med; Psychology; U of Rochester; Hofstra U

MARCIN, JOSH; AKRON, OH; FIRESTONE HS; (SR); Hi Hnr Roll; Hnr Roll; MVP; Nat Hon Sy; Otst Ac Ach Awd; St Schl; USAA; Yth Ldrshp Prog; Comm Volntr; Chrch Yth Grp; Dbte Team; Emplmnt; NtlFrnscLg; Spch Team; Bsball (V L); Cr Ctry (V L); State Champion Lincoln-Douglas Debate; 4-Time NFL National Qualifier Debate; Political Science; Journalism; U of Maryland; John Carroll

MARCINKOWSKI, NATHAN F; MEDINA, OH; MEDINA HS; (FR); Hnr Roll; Comm Volntr; Cr Ctry; Swmg; Track

MARGELOWSKY, TANYA; MADISON, OH; PERRY HS; (SO); Hnr Roll; Comm Volntr; Emplmnt; Sccr (V); Track (J); Won Volunteer of the Year Award At VFW Ladies Auxiliary; Law; Seton Hall U South Orange, New Jersey; U of Colorado at Boulder - Boulder, Colorado

MARKHAM, KYLE E; GROVE CITY, OH; GROVE CITY HS; (JR); Hnr Roll; Nat Hon Sy; Comm Volntr; Key Club; Spanish Clb; Bnd; Mch Bnd; President of Spanish Club; Secretary of Key Club; International Business; Foreign Language; American U; U of Michigan

MARLING, KELLEY; CHILLICOTHE, OH; CHILLICOTHE HS; (SR); F Lan Hn Soc; Hnr Roll; Nat Hon Sy; Perf Att; WWAHSS; Chrch Yth Grp; Emplmnt; FCA; Key Club; Mus Clb; Ntl Beta Clb; Prom Com; Spanish Clb; Bnd; Jzz Bnd; Mch Bnd; Pep Bnd; Young Democrats of America; Early Childhood Education; The Ohio State U; Ohio U

MARRS, ASHLEY; GOSHEN, OH; GOSHEN HS; (SO); Hnr Roll; St of Mnth; Design; U of Cincinnati; Miami Ohio

MARSH, NATHAN; MASSILLON, OH; EDISON JHS; (FR); Hnr Roll; Scouts; Spanish Clb; Bnd; Mch Bnd; Pep Bnd; Yrbk (R, P); Teaching; Accounting; Ohio State U; U of Texas

MARSHALL, SARAH; LIMA, OH; LIMA SR HS; (SO); Hnr Roll; Orch; Sftball (V L); Swmg (V CL); Vllyball (V CL); Teaching (Elementary); Bowling Green State U; Ohio State U

MARTEL, MELISSA J; BEACHWOOD, OH; BEACHWOOD HS; (FR); Hi Hnr Roll; Hnr Roll; Hosp Aide; Drma Clb; Chr; Stg Cre; Tennis (J); Yrbk (R); Medicine; New York U

MARTIN, AMANDA J; WILLOUGHBY, OH; WILLOUGHBY SOUTH HS; (JR); Hnr Roll; WWAHSS; Comm Volntr; Chrch Yth Grp; Emplmnt; FBLA; Key Club; Off Aide; Tchrs Aide; Spanish Clb; Chrldg (V L); Cl Off (V); Member of Neo All Star Cheerleading; Fashion Merchandising; Interior Design; Coastal Carolina U; U of North Carolina-Wilmington

MARTIN, AMY J; SALESVILLE, OH; CAMBRIDGE HS; (JR); Hi Hnr Roll; Hnr Roll; Perf Att; 4-H; Off Aide; Yrbk (E); Nurse; Kent State U; Ohio State U

MARTIN, JEREMY D; LIMA, OH; LIMA SR HS; (SO); Ctznshp Aw; Hi Hnr Roll; Nat Hon Sy; Otst Ac Ach Awd; Pres Sch; Emplmnt; Quiz Bowl; Cr Ctry; Environmental Studies; Political Science; Antioch College-Yellow Springs OH

MARTIN, JULIE; NORTH ROYALTON, OH; PADUA FRANCISCAN HS; (JR); Hnr Roll; WWAHSS; Comm Volntr; Red Cr Aide; Key Club; Tennis (J); Volunteering As a Cheerleading Coach for a Grade School; Engineering; Business; Bowling Green State U; Ohio State U

MARTIN, KATRICE; CLEVELAND, OH; (JR); Hnr Roll; Kwnis Aw; WWAHSS; Hosp Aide; Peer Tut/Med; DARE; Drma Clb; Key Club; Scouts; Bnd; Mch Bnd; Pep Bnd; Chrldg (J); CR (R); Sch Ppr (P); Yrbk (P); Volunteer At TOUCH; C-Town Performing Arts; BA-In Business Management; California State U of Los Angeles; New York U

MARTIN, NICHOLAS B; SOUTH BLOOMINGVILLE, OH; VINTON CTY HS BUCKEYE HILL VOC SCH; (SR); Hnr Roll; Comm Volntr; DARE; Scouts; Voc Ind Clb Am; Auto Body Fabrication; Nashville Auto Diesel College

MARTIN, SKYLER K; NEW ALBANY, OH; NEW ALBANY HS; (SO); 4H Awd; Hnr Roll; Nat Hon Sy; Perf Att; Sci Fairs; Sci/Math Olympn; WWAHSS; Comm Volntr; 4-H; Chrch Yth Grp; Emplmnt; Lttrmn Clb; Mod UN; Sci Clb; Bnd; Jzz Bnd; Mch Bnd; Pep Bnd; Information System Computer Science; Mass Institute of Technology; Ohio State U

MARTIN, TAJA; DAYTON, OH; MEADOWDALE HS; (JR); Hnr Roll; Perf Att; St of Mnth; WWAHSS; Comm Volntr; Hosp Aide; Chrch Yth Grp; Ohio State Young Scholars Program; Pediatrician; Ohio State U; U of South Florida

MARVIN, LYNDSAY M; ELYRIA, OH; ELYRIA HS; (JR); Hi Hnr Roll; Nat Hon Sy; WWAHSS; Comm Volntr; Peer Tut/Med; Spec Olymp Vol; Emplmnt; Key Club; Tchrs Aide; French Clb; PP Ftbl (J); CR (R); Eco Team; Kent State U; Oberlin College

MARZELLA, THOMAS J; NORTH ROYALTON, OH; NORTH ROYALTON HS; (SO); Hi Hnr Roll; Hnr Roll; Perf Att; WWAHSS; Drma Clb; Emplmnt; Key Club; Lttrmn Clb; Mus Clb; P to P St Amb Prg; SADD; Spanish Clb; Chr; SP/M/VS; Swg Chr; Swmg (V); Stu Cncl (R); Lead Part in the Crucible; Online Counselor; Psychology; Mathematics; Miami U; Ohio U

MASON, MATTHEW; DAYTON, OH; WEST CARROLLTON HS; (JR); DARE; ROTC; Navy; Computers or Mechanics

MAST, KATY; BRISTOLVILLE, OH; BLOOMFIELD HS; (SO); Hnr Roll; Perf Att; Chrch Yth Grp; Prom Com; Bnd; Chr; Chrldg (VJCL); Vllyball (J); Yrbk (P); Cheerleading MVP; Library Club / Bible Club / Relay for Life; Elementary Teaching; Interior Decorating; Malone College; Youngstown State U

MASTROIANNI, EMILY; MONROEVILLE, OH; MONROEVILLE; (JR); All Am Sch; Hi Hnr Roll; Nat Hon Sy; WWAHSS; Peer Tut/Med; Key Club; Mod UN; Chr; Dnce; Track (V); Vllyball (V)

MATASH, KRISTIN; NILES, OH; JOHN F KENNEDY HS; (JR); Hnr Roll; Comm Volntr; Emplmnt; Key Club; Svce Clb; Chrldg (V); Sch Ppr (R); Ohio U

MATHERS, ROBIN A N; CAMBRIDGE, OH; CAMBRIDGE HS; (JR); Hnr Roll; Clr Grd; Zane State College

MATHEWS, EMILY R; WALBRIDGE, OH; LAKE HS; (SO); Hnr Roll; Peer Tut/Med; Chrch Yth Grp; DARE; Quiz Bowl; Scouts; Vsity Clb; French Clb; Bskball (JC); Sccr (V CL); Sftball (V L); Medicine; Physical Therapy; Muskingum College; The Ohio State U

MATHIAS, KARIE J; DOVER, OH; DOVER HS; (SO); Hnr Roll; ArtClub; Drma Clb; Emplmnt; Key Club; Wrstlg (L); Chemistry; Pre-Dentistry

MATNEY, KEVIN K; BARBERTON, OH; BARBERTON HS; (SO); Hnr Roll; Hab For Humty Volntr; Chess; Chrch Yth Grp; Drma Clb; Scouts; Bnd; Dnce; Mch Bnd; Pep Bnd; Sccr (J); DI Team-2004 Globals; Top Dance-Disney 2003; Computer Science / Technology; Electronic Engineer; Brigham Young U; Brown U

MATTHEWS, JEAUBAER C; CINCINNATI, OH; ROBERT A TAFT INFO TECH HS; (JR); Ctznshp Aw; Hi Hnr Roll; Hnr Roll; Otst Ac Ach Awd; Perf Att; Sci Fairs; WWAHSS; Comm Volntr; Chrch Yth Grp; DARE; Emplmnt; Jr Ach; Ftball (V); Wt Lftg; Wrstlg (V); Stu Cncl (R); Ronald McDonald House Volunteer; Outstanding African-American Scholar; Anesthesiologist; Chemical Engineer; Auburn U; Miami U FL

MATTHEWS, JORDAN; NEWBURY, OH; NEWBURY HS; (FR); Nat Hon Sy; St of Mnth; Chrch Yth Grp; Ch Chr; Bskball (J); PP Ftbl (J); Track (J); National Honor Society; Partnership for Success; Health Career; Educational Career; U of Central Arkansas; Kent State U

MATTHEWS, TIFFANY; DELAWARE, OH; RUTHERFORD B HAYES HS; (FR); Hnr Roll; Clr Grd; Psychology; Law; U of Notre Dame; U of Boston

MAXWELL, ASHLEY; LIMA, OH; LIMA SR HS; (FR); Ctznshp Aw; Hnr Roll; St of Mnth; DARE; Sch Ppr (E, R, P); Fashion Designer; Ohio State U

MAXWELL, CASSONDRA; ELYRIA, OH; MIDVIEW HS; (FR); Hi Hnr Roll; Hnr Roll; Perf Att; Peer Tut/Med; Chrch Yth Grp; Key Club; Scouts; Tennis (J); Pediatrician; RN; Duke; Yale U

MAXWELL, MELANIE; NEW LONDON, OH; WESTERN RESERVE HS; (SO); Hnr Roll; Comm Volntr; Drma Clb; Pep Squd; Tchrs Aide; Stg Cre; Chrldg (JCL); Scr Kpr (V L); Stu Cncl (R); Poetry/Literature; Business; Firelands Bowling Green U; Ashland U

MAXWELL, SAMANTHA; MC CONNELSVILLE, OH; MORGAN HS; (SR); Hi Hnr Roll; Nat Hon Sy; WWAHSS; Comm Volntr; Red Cr Aide; Drma Clb; Emplmnt; Key Club; Off Aide; Prom Com; Quill & Scroll; French Clb; Chr; SP/M/VS; Cl Off (P); Stu Cncl; Lit Mag (R); Vocalist for Fairs, Pageants & Special Events; Senior Editor for Media Productions-School News Broadcast; Commercial Music-Voice Performance; I Will Attend Belmont U

MAY, ASHLEY N; LIMA, OH; LIMA SR HS; (JR); Hi Hnr Roll; Nat Hon Sy; Comm Volntr; Emplmnt; Early Childhood Volunteer; Honors Student; Early Childhood Education; Cosmetology; Ohio State Branch; Ohio State

MAY, DAVID C; MAGNOLIA, OH; SANDY VALLEY JR/SR HS; (JR); Hnr Roll; Nat Hon Sy; Perf Att; Chrch Yth Grp; Emplmnt; Prom Com; Jzz Bnd; Bsball (V CL); Bskball (V L); Cr Ctry (J L); Yrbk (R, P); History Teacher; Sports Medicine; U of Cincinnati

MAY, SONEQUA; CLEVELAND, OH; MARTIN LUTHER KING HS; Ctznshp Aw; Hnr Roll; Nat Mrt Semif; Perf Att; St of Mnth; Cmptr Clb; DARE; SADD; Bnd; SP/M/VS; Chrldg (J); Track (J); Nurse RN; Teacher; Kent State U; Harvard U

MAYER, KRISTEN M; ROCK CREEK, OH; GENEVA SECONDARY SCH; (JR); Hnr Roll; Comm Volntr; Lttrmn Clb; Bnd; Mch Bnd; International Club; Biology; Zoology/Marine Biology; U of Hawaii At Manoa; Cleveland State U

MAYS, SAMANTHA B; WAVERLY, OH; WAVERLY HS; (SO); Hi Hnr Roll; MVP; Otst Ac Ach Awd; Pres Ac Ftns Aw; Pres Sch; Comm Volntr; Chrch Yth Grp; DARE; Vsity Clb; Spanish Clb; Bskball (V L); Vllyball (V L); Pharmacy; Nutrition; Northern Kentucky U; Ohio Northern U

MC ADAMS, JESSICA; COLUMBUS, OH; BISHOP WATTERSON HS; (JR); Hnr Roll; WWAHSS; Scouts; Clr Grd; Art 101 Winter Guard - Most Improved; Kismet Winter Guard - Most Dedicated; International Business; Ohio State U; U of Toledo

MC AFEE, SAMANTHA; JEWETT, OH; HARRISON CTRL HS; (SR); Hi Hnr Roll; Hnr Roll; Jr Rot; Perf Att; 4-H; Chrch Yth Grp; DARE; Drma Clb; Emplmnt; SP/M/VS; Stg Cre; Bskball (J); Yrbk (P); Nursing; Religion (Pastor); J.C.C.; Trinity School of Nursing

MC CABE, PATRICK H; OXFORD, OH; TALAWANDA HS; (SR); Hnr Roll; Perf Att; WWAHSS; Chess; Key Club; Prom Com; Tchrs Aide; Orch; Ice Hky (V L); Lt. Governor, Div S, Key Club; Criminal Justice; Miami U

MC CAIN, JESSICA; CINCINNATI, OH; WINTON WOODS HS; (SR); Hnr Roll; Pres Sch; WWAHSS; Comm Volntr; Chrch Yth Grp; DECA; Emplmnt; Pep Squd; Scouts; Chrldg (V); Physical Therapy; Chiropractor; U of Cincinnati

MC CALL, BREANA; LORAIN, OH; LORAIN ADMIRAL KING HS; (FR); Hnr Roll; Perf Att; Sci Fairs; Comm Volntr; ArtClub; Outdrs Clb; Wdwrkg Clb; Central State U; Clark Atlanta U

MC CANN, LACURYA; DAYTON, OH; MEADOWDALE HS FOR INTERNATIONAL STUDIES; (JR); Perf Att; Prom Com; Sch Ppr (E, R); Yrbk (P); Nursing; Business Management; Sinclair Community College

MC CARTNEY, MEGAN; SALEM, OH; UNITED LOCAL HS; (JR); Hi Hnr Roll; Hnr Roll; Otst Ac Ach Awd; Key Club; Mth Clb/Tm; Off Aide; Svce Clb; Sftball (L); Tennis (L); Medicine; Math; Northeastern Ohio College of Medicine; Youngstown State U

Maxwell, Ashley
Lima SR HS
Lima, OH

Marvin, Lyndsay M
Elyria HS
Elyria, OH

March, Rickiesha A
Lutheran HS East
Cleveland, OH

Mansfield, Kristina
Northview HS
Sylvania, OH

Mansfield, Robin
Napoleon HS
Napoleon, OH

Matney, Kevin K
Barberton HS
Barberton, OH

Mays, Samantha B
Waverly HS
Waverly, OH

MC CAVISH, TIFFANY L; MUNROE FALLS, OH; STOW-MUNROE FALLS HS; (SR); Comm Volntr; Chrch Yth Grp; Drma Clb; Emplmnt; FTA; Off Aide; Photog; Tchrs Aide; Wdwrkg Clb; SP/M/VS; Chrldg (J); Child Care Club; FEA-Ohio Future Educators of America; Psychology; Education; Bowling Green State U

MC CLAIN, MATTHEW; LUCASVILLE, OH; VALLEY HS; (FR); Hnr Roll; Wdwrkg Clb; Bskball (J); Ftball (J); Track (V); Electrician; Ohio U

MC CLELLAN, ELIZABETH; DAYTON, OH; CTRVILLE HS; (JR); F Lan Hn Soc; Hnr Roll; WWAHSS; DECA; French Clb; Dnce; Placed Fifith at DECA - ICDC in E-Commerce; Dance; Business / Marketing Management; Miami U Oxford; U of Pittsburgh

MC CLINTOCK, EVAN; PAINESVILLE, OH; RIVERSIDE; (SO); Hnr Roll; WWAHSS; Emplmnt; FCA; Key Club; Off Aide; Tchrs Aide; Cr Ctry (V L); Track (V)

MC CLINTOCK, KYLE; PAINESVILLE, OH; RIVERSIDE HS; (SR); Hnr Roll; WWAHSS; Emplmnt; Key Club; Off Aide; Ftball (V L); Wt Lftg (V); Sports Medicine Pre Physical Therapy; Otterbein College

MC CLOUD, DAN; YOUNGSTOWN, OH; CARDINAL MOONEY HS; (JR); Hnr Roll; Nat Hon Sy; Nat Ldrshp Svc; Pres Ac Ftns Aw; Peer Tut/Med; Emplmnt; FBLA; Photog; Svce Clb; Spanish Clb; Bsball (V L); Bskball (V); Ftball (V); Wt Lftg (V); Sch Ppr (R, P); Altar Server; Knights of Columbus Free Throw Runner Up; Sports Marketing; Real Estate; Duquesne U; Miami of Ohio

MC CLOUD, RAFFIEL; TOLEDO, OH; WAITE HS; (SO); MVP; Otst Ac Ach Awd; Perf Att; St of Mnth; WWAHSS; Tchrs Aide; Bskball (V L); Cr Ctry (V L); Track (V L); I Want to Earn a Degree in Business; I Also Want to Earn a Master's Degree; The U of Cincinnati; Drexel U

MC CLURE, ERIN; WOOSTER, OH; NORTHWESTERN HS; (SO); Ctznshp Aw; Hnr Roll; Yth Ldrshp Prog; Pep Squd; Prom Com; Tchrs Aide; Spanish Clb; Stg Cre; Bskball (J); PP Ftbl (V); Scr Kpr (V); Track (V); Vllyball (V); Cl Off (T); Stu Cncl (R); CR (R); Sch Ppr (E); Wrestling Statistician; Office Teacher Aide; Psychiatry; Business; New York U; Syracuse U

MC COLLUM, ERRICK; CANTON, OH; GLEN OAK HS; (JR); Ctznshp Aw; Hi Hnr Roll; Hnr Roll; MVP; Nat Hon Sy; Perf Att; WWAHSS; Comm Volntr; Peer Tut/Med; Chrch Yth Grp; DECA; Drma Clb; Tchrs Aide; SP/M/VS; Bskball (V CL); Starting Point Guard on Varsity and Was All Federal League, District 4, County, NEID; Want to Major in Broadcasting/ Communications; Bachelor's Degree; U of North Carolina; Wake Forest U

MC CONNELL, JOHN L; RICHMOND, OH; JEFFERSON CTY JOINT VOC SCH; (JR); 4H Awd; Perf Att; 4-H; Chrch Yth Grp; Cmptr Clb; Emplmnt; Acpl Chr; Chr; SP/M/VS; Ftball (J); PC Repair; IT; Jefferson Community College; DeVry

MC CONNELL, MORGAN; BLOOMVILLE, OH; SENECA EAST HS; (FR); 4H Awd; Ctznshp Aw; Hnr Roll; Yth Ldrshp Prog; Comm Volntr; 4-H; Ntl FFA; Bskball (J); Cr Ctry (V L); Track (V); Psychology

MC COURT, CHEYANNA; DEERFIELD, OH; SOUTHEAST HS; (JR); 4H Awd; Nat Mrt Sch Recip; WWAHSS; Yth Ldrshp Prog; Comm Volntr; Peer Tut/Med; 4-H; Chrch Yth Grp; Emplmnt; Pep Squd; Prom Com; Ch Chr; Stu Cncl (V); Pep Club; FCCLA; Physical Therapy (Children); Massage Therapy (Children)

MC COURT, KEVIN; BRUNSWICK, OH; BRUNSWICK HS; (JR); Hi Hnr Roll; Hnr Roll; Nat Hon Sy; Otst Ac Ach Awd; Pres Sch; Comm Volntr; Hosp Aide; Peer Tut/Med; Chess; Drma Clb; Emplmnt; Key Club; Tchrs Aide; Spanish Clb; Chr; SP/M/VS; Stg Cre; Skiing (V); Business Marketing; Law; Ohio State U; Kent State U

MC COY, RICKY; LUCASVILLE, OH; VALLEY HS; (SR); 4H Awd; Hnr Roll; WWAHSS; 4-H; FBLA; Wdwrkg Clb; Pharmacist; Shawnee State U

MC DANIEL, KRAMER G; CLEVELAND, OH; LUTHERAN HS EAST; (SO); Hnr Roll; Mas Aw; Nat Hon Sy; Nat Stu Ath Day Aw; St of Mnth; WWAHSS; Comm Volntr; Hosp Aide; Red Cr Aide; AL Aux Girls; Chrch Yth Grp; DARE; Emplmnt; Lttrmn Clb; Off Aide; Prom Com; Svce Clb; Chr; Ch Chr; Bskball (VJ); Chrldg (V); Sftball (V L); Vllyball (VJ); Sch Ppr (E); National Honor Society; Student Athlete Award; Psychologist; Engineering; Oberlin College; Ursuline College

MC DEVITT, JONATHAN; SALEM, OH; UNITED LOCAL HS; (JR); Hnr Roll; WWAHSS; Emplmnt; Key Club; Tchrs Aide; French Clb; Scr Kpr (J); Ruriteens; Key Club; Medicine; Communications; Ohio State U; Youngstown State U

MC DONOUGH, LAURA; OXFORD, OH; TALAWANDA HS; (JR); Hi Hnr Roll; Nat Hon Sy; Perf Att; WWAHSS; Comm Volntr; Emplmnt; Key Club; Spanish Clb; Tennis (J); Pre-Calculus Award; Spanish III Award; Engineering; Rose-Hulman Institute of Technology; Ohio State U

MC DOUGLE, IAN; CAREY, OH; CAREY SCH; (SO); 4H Awd; Hnr Roll; Nat Hon Sy; Yth Ldrshp Prog; 4-H; Chrch Yth Grp; DECA; Drma Clb; Emplmnt; Quiz Bowl; Bnd; Chr; Mch Bnd; SP/M/VS; Bskball (J); Cr Ctry (V L); Track (V L); Juris Doctor; Ohio Northern U; U of Toledo

MC EWAN, KAYLN; DAYTON, OH; ARCHBISHOP ALTER HS; (FR); Hi Hnr Roll; Hnr Roll; Sci Fairs; Yth Ldrshp Prog; Comm Volntr; Key Club; Spanish Clb; Chrldg (C); Club Soccer

MC FADDEN, DANA; CLEVELAND, OH; JAMES FORD RHODES HS; (JR); Hi Hnr Roll; Hnr Roll; Nat Hon Sy; Perf Att; Sci Fairs; WWAHSS; Comm Volntr; Peer Tut/Med; DARE; FTA; Jr Ach; Masters Degree; Elementary Education; Notre Dame; Baldwin Wallace

MC GEACHY, COURTNEY T; REYNOLDSBURG, OH; REYNOLDSBURG HS; (JR); Hi Hnr Roll; Nat Hon Sy; WWAHSS; Comm Volntr; Peer Tut/Med; DARE; DECA; Emplmnt; Svce Clb; Tchrs Aide; Chr; Tennis (J); Ohio State U Medical School MD Camp; DECA Rising Star 1st Place State Competition; Medical Degree; PhD in Research; Xavier U of LA; North Carolina A & T U

MC GEEHEN, SARAH; NORTH RIDGEVILLE, OH; NORTH RIDGEVILLE HS; MS; Hi Hnr Roll; Hnr Roll; Perf Att; DARE; Lib Aide; Tchrs Aide; Chrldg; Sftball; Forensic Science; Psychologist; Xavier U of Louisiana; Mount Union College

MC GILL, NAJA; COLUMBUS, OH; EAST HS; (JR); Hi Hnr Roll; Hnr Roll; Nat Hon Sy; Otst Ac Ach Awd; St of Mnth; Comm Volntr; ArtClub; Ohio State MD Camp; I Would Like to Be a Doctor; U of North Carolina; Princeton

MC GINNIS, KELLY; GENOA, OH; GENOA AREA HS; (SO); Hi Hnr Roll; Hnr Roll; Chrch Yth Grp; Key Club; Bnd; Ch Chr; Mch Bnd; Pep Bnd; Cr Ctry (V)

MC GLOWN, BRIAN; TOLEDO, OH; SCOTT HS; (SO); Hnr Roll; Comm Volntr; Peer Tut/Med; Emplmnt; Doctorate Degree in Physical Science; Physiologist

MC GOWAN, MIRACLE; COLUMBUS, OH; EAST HS; (SO); Hnr Roll; Otst Ac Ach Awd; WWAHSS; Comm Volntr; Chrch Yth Grp; DARE; FCA; P to P St Amb Prg; Ch Chr; Bskball (J L); Scr Kpr (J); Law; Yale U; Harvard U/U of North Carolina (Chapel Hill)

MC GOWAN, SARAH; CLEVELAND, OH; GARFIELD HEIGHTS HS; (SO); Hnr Roll; MVP; Nat Hon Sy; Perf Att; WWAHSS; Comm Volntr; Peer Tut/Med; Emplmnt; Acpl Chr; Cr Ctry (V L); Track (L); Students of Service (Volunteer Group); Show Choir; Accountant; Veterinarian; Kent U; Bowling Green U

MC GUIRE, RYAN A; HILLIARD, OH; HILLIARD DAVIDSON SR HS; (JR); Hi Hnr Roll; Hnr Roll; Kwnis Aw; MVP; St of Mnth; Yth Ldrshp Prog; Comm Volntr; Peer Tut/Med; Key Club; Kwanza Clb; Lttrmn Clb; SADD; Vsity Clb; Spanish Clb; Bskball (V L); Ftball (J); Vllyball (V L); Business; OSU-Ohio State U; U of Cincinnati

MC HUGH, HEATHER; TILTONSVILLE, OH; BUCKEYE LOCAL HS; (SO); Hi Hnr Roll; WWAHSS; Emplmnt; FCA; SADD; Vsity Clb; Bnd; Mch Bnd; Scr Kpr (V); Sftball (V L); Merit Scholar; National Spanish Exam Participant; Athletic Training / Exercise Science; Spanish Translations; Waynesburg; Slippery Rock State College

MC HUGH, SAMUEL; WEST FARMINGTON, OH; CROSSROADS AC; (SR); Hnr Roll; Perf Att; Valdctrian; Yth Ldrshp Prog; Comm Volntr; Emplmnt; Tchrs Aide; SP/M/VS; Yrbk (R, P); Presidential Campaign Volunteer; Broadcasting; Religious Studies; Allegheny Wesleyan College

MC INTURFF, ANGELA-NICOLE E; CANTON, OH; HOOVER HS; (SR); Hnr Roll; WWAHSS; Comm Volntr; Peer Tut/Med; Chrch Yth Grp; Emplmnt; Off Aide; Scouts; Spanish Clb; Scr Kpr (V); Sch Ppr (R, P); Business Administration; The Ohio State U

MC INTYRE, JORDAN M; STEUBENVILLE, OH; STEUBENVILLE HS; MS; All Am Sch; Ctznshp Aw; Hi Hnr Roll; Perf Att; Sci/Math Olympn; Comm Volntr; Chrch Yth Grp; Key Club; Bsball; Bskball (L); Ftball (L); Track (L); NAACP Youth Council; Law-Attorney

MC KEE, AMANDA; CANTON, OH; GLEN OAK HS; (JR); Hnr Roll; Sci Fairs; Sci/Math Olympn; Chrch Yth Grp; Emplmnt; Key Club; Swmg (V L); 2005 District Qualifier; 2nd Team All Federal League; Forensic Science; Akron U; Stark State College

MC KEE, AMBER L; CINCINNATI, OH; NORTHWEST HS; (FR); Hnr Roll; WWAHSS; DARE; Key Club; Scouts; Dnce; Key Club; Elementary Teacher; Fashion Designer; U of Cincinnati

MC KOWN, SARAH E; AKRON, OH; ELLET HS; (SO); Hnr Roll; Perf Att; Sci Fairs; St of Mnth; WWAHSS; Yth Ldrshp Prog; Hosp Aide; Peer Tut/Med; Red Cr Aide; DARE; Fr of Library; Lib Aide; Mth Clb/Tm; Mus Clb; Off Aide; Tchrs Aide; Spanish Clb; Chr; Clr Grd; Mch Bnd; Stg Cre; Bskball (J); Sftball (L); Swmg (J); Tennis (L); Track; Vllyball (V); Stu Cncl (S); Sch Ppr (R); Yrbk (R)

MC LAUGHLIN, ANGELINA; DAYTON, OH; STIVERS SCH FOR THE ARTS; (FR); Hi Hnr Roll; Otst Ac Ach Awd; Jzz Bnd; Chrldg (J L); Swmg (J L); Astronaut; Aerospace Engineer; Ohio State U

MC LAUGHLIN, BREE; CONNEAUT, OH; EDGEWOOD HS; (SR); WWAHSS; Mod UN; Off Aide; Pep Squd; Sci Clb; Svce Clb; SADD; Tchrs Aide; Tech Clb; Chr; Dnce; Bskball (V); Chrldg (VJCL); Vllyball (J); Wildlife Dance Team Captain; Public Relations; Ohio U

MC MAHAN, HOLLY J; ROOTSTOWN, OH; SOUTHEAST HS; (SR); Hi Hnr Roll; Hnr Roll; Nat Hon Sy; WWAHSS; Comm Volntr; Chrch Yth Grp; FCA; Bnd; Mch Bnd; Pep Bnd; Venture Crew 2558; Medical Pre-Professional Academy; Bachelor's Degree in Chemistry; Kent State U

MC MAHON, ABBEY; LIBERTY TOWNSHIP, OH; LAKOTA EAST HS; (JR); Hi Hnr Roll; Nat Hon Sy; Otst Ac Ach Awd; St of Mnth; WWAHSS; Comm Volntr; Peer Tut/Med; Chrch Yth Grp; Drma Clb; Emplmnt; FTA; Quill & Scroll; Tchrs Aide; Spanish Clb; Bnd; SP/M/VS; Stu Cncl (R); Sch Ppr (E); Chief Editor of Our School's News Magazine the Spark; Communications; Business Marketing; U of Dayton; Indiana U

MC MULLEN, MELISSA; RAVENNA, OH; CRESTWOOD HS; (JR); Hnr Roll; Perf Att; Pres Sch; St of Mnth; Chrch Yth Grp; DARE; Photog; Tchrs Aide; Bnd; Chr; Dnce; Sccr (J); Business Degree; Hiram College

MC NICHOLS, TAMELA; CHILLICOTHE, OH; ZANE TRACE HS; (SO); Hi Hnr Roll; Hnr Roll; St of Mnth; WWAHSS; Chrch Yth Grp; DARE; FCA; Tchrs Aide; Who's Who Among American High School Students; Golden Presidential Award; Business Management; Shawnee State U

MC NULTY, NEIL; CINCINNATI, OH; CLARK MONTESSORI SCH; (FR); Otst Ac Ach Awd; Bnd; Bskball (J); Sccr (V); Track (V); Scholar Athlete / Academic Honors; Law; Therapy - Mental Health; Ohio State U; U of Cincinnati

MC PHERSON, MICHELLE; CLEVELAND, OH; IMANI INST LEADERSHIP; (SO); Sci Fairs; Comm Volntr; Peer Tut/Med; Dbte Team; Prom Com; Dnce; Drl Tm; Stu Cncl (R); Medical Assisting; Forensic Specialist; Remington College; CSU

MC QUILLIN, AMY; PICKERINGTON, OH; PICKERINGTON HS NORTH; (SO); Hi Hnr Roll; P to P St Amb Prg; Photog; Scouts; Basketball Rec League; Poetry Has Been Published Nationally; Advertising or Marketing; Graphic Design

MC SWANE-WILLIAMS, NISHA; PICKERINGTON, OH; PICKERINGTON HS NORTH; (SO); Hi Hnr Roll; Hnr Roll; Pres Sch; Sci Fairs; St of Mnth; Red Cr Aide; Chr; Golf (V L); Cl Off (P); Stu Cncl (S); Sch Ppr (E, R); Psychology; Journalism; Stanford U; Harvard

MC WILLIAMS, MIKE; CANTON, OH; CANTON SOUTH HS; (JR); 4H Awd; 4-H; BPA; Bnd; Placed in Top 10 - Tech Prep Showcase; Student of the Marking Period; Computer Game Programmer; Make a Good Amount of Money; Stark State College; Kent State

MEADOWS, SHEA; WHEELERSBURG, OH; WHEELERSBURG HS; (FR); Hi Hnr Roll; Comm Volntr; Peer Tut/Med; 4-H; Chrch Yth Grp; DARE; Key Club; Ftball (VJ); Swmg (V); Track (V); Wt Lftg (V); Certificate of Educational Development National; Medical Field-Premed; Sports Medicine; Ohio State U; Graceland U

MEAGHER, CORTNEY; NEWBURY, OH; NEWBURY HS; (FR); Ctznshp Aw; Hi Hnr Roll; Hnr Roll; Otst Ac Ach Awd; St of Mnth; 4-H; Chrch Yth Grp; DARE; Pep Squd; Bnd; Dnce; Chrldg (J); Hsbk Rdg; PP Ftbl; Scr Kpr (V); Vllyball (J); Stu Cncl; Forensic Science

MEARS, ALLISON K; BERKEY, OH; EVERGREEN HS; (SR); 4H Awd; Ctznshp Aw; Hnr Roll; Nat Hon Sy; Otst Ac Ach Awd; WWAHSS; Comm Volntr; 4-H; AL Aux Girls; ArtClub; Chrch Yth Grp; Drma Clb; Emplmnt; Prom Com; SADD; Bnd; Drm Mjr; SP/M/VS; Sftball (J); Cl Off (S); Stu Cncl (R); Majorette Line Captain; Middle Childhood Education; Bowling Green State U

MEDVED, KAYLA; LISBON, OH; COLUMBIANA EXEMPTED VILLAGE HS; (SO); Hi Hnr Roll; Hnr Roll; Otst Ac Ach Awd; WWAHSS; Comm Volntr; Emplmnt; Hsbk Rdg; Scr Kpr; Psychology; Law Enforcement; Wooster College; Case Western U

MEHOK, ALEX; CLEVELAND, OH; SOUTH HS; (SO); Nat Stu Ath Day Aw; Otst Ac Ach Awd; Perf Att; Comm Volntr; Red Cr Aide; Chess; Emplmnt; Fr of Library; Mus Clb; Quiz Bowl; Wdwrkg Clb; Latin Clb; Chr; Mch Bnd; Stg Cre; Bsball; Bskball; Ftball; Scr Kpr; Sccr; Wt Lftg; Manager-Football, Basketball, Baseball; Bowling-On the Team

MEIGHEN, ERIC A; CANTON, OH; TIMKEN SR HS; (FR); Hnr Roll; St of Mnth; Scouts; Bnd; Jzz Bnd; Mch Bnd; Pep Bnd

MEISTER, HOLLY; SALINEVILLE, OH; CARROLLTON HS; (SO); Hnr Roll; Perf Att; Peer Tut/Med; 4-H; Off Aide; Tchrs Aide; French Clb; Sftball (J); Vllyball (J); Education; Medical Fields; Youngstown State U; Kent State U

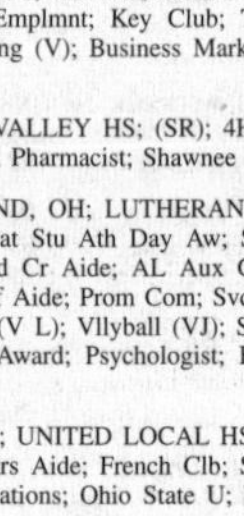
Mc Kee, Amber L
Northwest HS
Cincinnati, OH

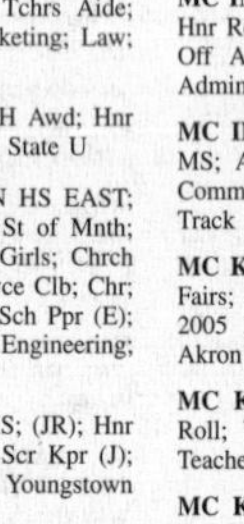
Mc Court, Kevin
Brunswick HS
Brunswick, OH

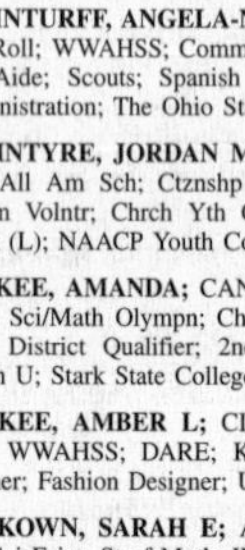
Mc Clintock, Kyle
Riverside HS
Painesville, OH

National
Honor Roll
Spring 2005

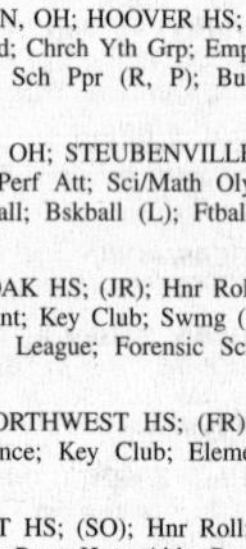
Mc Clintock, Evan
Riverside
Painesville, OH

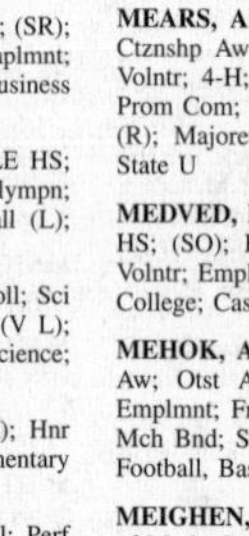
Mc Daniel, Kramer G
Lutheran HS East
Cleveland, OH

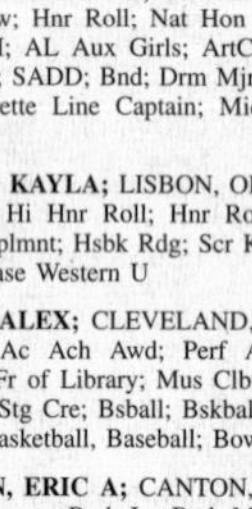
Mc Swane-Williams, Nisha
Pickerington HS North
Pickerington, OH

MEISTER, NIKKI; CINCINNATI, OH; NORTHWEST HS; (JR); F Lan Hn Soc; Hnr Roll; Nat Hon Sy; St of Mnth; Comm Volntr; Peer Tut/Med; Chrch Yth Grp; Drma Clb; Emplmnt; Key Club; Prom Com; Vsity Clb; Spanish Clb; SP/M/VS; Stg Cre; Bskball (V); Sccr (V); Sftball (V); Cl Off (V); Stu Cncl (V); CR (V); Yrbk (P); Spanish Honor Society; National Honor Society; Education; Theatre; Ohio State U; Miami Oxford U

MELEGARI, SARAH; CANTON, OH; EAST CANTON HS; (SO); Hnr Roll; Comm Volntr; Chrch Yth Grp; Off Aide; Tchrs Aide; Cr Ctry (J); Sccr (J); Track (J); Louisville Soccer Club Division Champions (2004); Criminal Justice; Forensics (Crime Scene Investigator); Allegheny College; Northern Kentucky U

MELLINGER, CHRISTOPHER L; AKRON, OH; GREEN HS; (JR); Nat Hon Sy; Perf Att; Chrch Yth Grp; Jr Cls League; Latin Clb; Bnd; Jzz Bnd; Mch Bnd; Engineering; Music Performance; The U of Akron; Case Western Reserve U

MELONE, ANTHONY M; COLUMBIANA, OH; COLUMBIANA HS; (SO); Hnr Roll; USMC Stu Ath Aw; DARE; Drma Clb; Scouts; Tchrs Aide; SP/M/VS; Ftball (VJ L); Scr Kpr (J); Track (VJ L); CR (R); National Junior Honor Society; Telecommunications; Journalism; Youngstown State U; Kent State U

MENDENHALL, AMBER N; ALBANY, OH; ALEXANDER LOCAL SCH; (FR); Hnr Roll; Chrch Yth Grp; Drma Clb; French Clb; Acpl Chr; Ch Chr; SP/M/VS; Track (J); 9 Years of Piano; Sing & Play Piano for Church Band; Major in Piano Pedagogy; Master's Degree in Classical Piano; Juilliard School of Performing Arts; Ohio U

MENDEZ, NOELIA; MIDDLETOWN, OH; MIDDLETOWN HS; (SR); Hnr Roll; WWAHSS; Comm Volntr; Hab For Humty Volntr; Tchrs Aide; Bnd; CR (T); Volunteer for Blood Drive; Volunteer for Miami Valley Hospital; Registered Nurse; Lawyer; Sinclair Community College; Raymond Walters / U of Cincinnati

MENDICINO, SAMANTHA E; WILLOUGHBY, OH; WILLOUGHBY SOUTH HS; (SO); Ctznshp Aw; Hnr Roll; St of Mnth; Key Club; Spanish Clb; Dnce; Honor Roll; Lawyer; Social Worker; Bowling Green State U; NYU

MERCER, AMBER R; ZANESVILLE, OH; MAYSVILLE HS; (JR); Hnr Roll; Perf Att; WWAHSS; Dbte Team; Drma Clb; Lttrmn Clb; Lib Aide; Prom Com; SADD; Vsity Clb; Spanish Clb; Chr; SP/M/VS; Stg Cre; Sccr (V); American Cancer Society Volunteer; Youth Softball; English; Drama; Kenyon College; Marietta College

MEREDITH, MATT; WESTERVILLE, OH; WESTERVILLE CTRL HS; (SO); St of Mnth; Key Club; Golf (J); Tennis (V L); Student Athlete of the Month (April 2004); Student of the Month (April 2005); Medical; U of Virginia; U of Notre Dame

MERRILL, J D; FREMONT, OH; CLYDE HS; (FR); Ctznshp Aw; Hi Hnr Roll; Hnr Roll; Chrch Yth Grp; Drma Clb; FCA; Key Club; Chr; Ch Chr; SP/M/VS; Swg Chr; Wrstlg (J); Ex Band Member; Bachelor's Degree; Ohio State U

MERRIT, PHILLIP; CINCINNATI, OH; WITHROW UNIVERSITY HS; (SO); Ctznshp Aw; Hnr Roll; Comm Volntr; Chrch Yth Grp; Spanish Clb; Veterinarian; Computer Programmer

MERRITT, BRITTANY N C; HAMLER, OH; PATRICK HENRY HS; (FR); Hi Hnr Roll; Hnr Roll; MVP; Nat Hon Sy; St of Mnth; Comm Volntr; DARE; Emplmnt; Pep Squd; SADD; Chr; Drm Mjr; Chrldg (J); Gmnstcs (V); Track (L); Wt Lftg; Forensic Science; Law; U of Toledo; U of Michigan

MERRITT, KELLY R; ASHTABULA, OH; GENEVA HS; (SR); DARE; Emplmnt; Chrldg (J); Employment with U Hospital Health System Memorial Hospital of Geneva; Degree in Radiology; Lakeland Community College

MERRITTS, TAYLOR R; CINCINNATI, OH; CLARK MONTESSORI SCH; (SO); Hnr Roll; Comm Volntr; Ch Chr; SP/M/VS; Music Theory; FBI Investigator

MERRY, CALLIE R; STRASBURG, OH; STRASBURG FRANKLIN HS; (SR); Hi Hnr Roll; Nat Hon Sy; Perf Att; Valdctrian; WWAHSS; Hosp Aide; Emplmnt; Lib Aide; Off Aide; Pep Squd; Prom Com; Quiz Bowl; Schol Bwl; Chr; Chrldg (VJCL); Vllyball (VJ); Cl Off (V); Stu Cncl; Biology; Denison U

MESSENGER, ALLYSON; BOWLING GREEN, OH; PENTA BOWLING GREEN HS; (SR); Hnr Roll; Nat Hon Sy; St of Mnth; Peer Tut/Med; Red Cr Aide; ArtClub; Chrch Yth Grp; DECA; Emplmnt; Pep Squd; Prom Com; Tchrs Aide; Vllyball (JC); Cl Off (V); Spanish National Honor Society; Marketing; The Ohio State U

MESSMER, ANTHONY; ZANESVILLE, OH; WEST MUSKINGUM HS; (SO); Ctznshp Aw; Hi Hnr Roll; Otst Ac Ach Awd; St of Mnth; WWAHSS; Comm Volntr; Peer Tut/Med; Key Club; Key Club; Honor Roll; Student Tutor; Principal's List; Teams-Engineering Club; Engineering (Aeronautical or Mechanical); Case Western Reserve; Massachusetts Institute of Technology (MIT)

MESTICHELLI, KATI; NILES, OH; MC KINLEY HS; (FR); Hi Hnr Roll; Otst Ac Ach Awd; USAA; WWAHSS; Hab For Humty Volntr; Chrch Yth Grp; Drma Clb; Emplmnt; NtlFrnscLg; Spch Team; French Clb; Bnd; Ch Chr; Mch Bnd; SP/M/VS; Tennis (J); Journalism; Theater; Yale U; Houghton U

METERA, CHELSEA; ELYRIA, OH; ELYRIA HS; (FR); Hi Hnr Roll; Hnr Roll; Otst Ac Ach Awd; Perf Att; Sci/Math Olympn; St of Mnth; Spec Olymp Vol; DARE; Vllyball (J); Stu Cncl (R); Psychology; Forensics; Ohio State U; Bowling Green

METTE, AMANDA; CINCINNATI, OH; ANDERSON HS; (JR); Hnr Roll; Emplmnt; Lib Aide; Prom Com; Cr Ctry (J); PP Ftbl (J); Sch Ppr (E, R); Yrbk (E, R); Play Softball Outside of School; Business; Interior Design; U of Dayton; Ohio State U

METZ, AMANDA M; CINCINNATI, OH; MOTHER OF MERCY HS; (FR); Hnr Roll; St of Mnth; WWAHSS; Comm Volntr; Drma Clb; Key Club; SP/M/VS; Tennis (J); Law

MEYER, BECCA; AKRON, OH; COPLEY HS; (SO); Hnr Roll; Key Club; Bnd; Mch Bnd; Plays Oboe, Sax, Flute, Trumpet; Marine Biology; U of Miami; North Carolina

MEYERS, ASHLEY; CHILLICOTHE, OH; CHILLICOTHE HS; (JR); Hnr Roll; Perf Att; Chrch Yth Grp; DARE; Off Aide; Quiz Bowl; Chr; Ch Chr; Stu Cncl (R); FCCLA; Teacher; Ohio U Chillicothe; Ohio State U

MICHLING, ROB; TORONTO, OH; JEFFERSON CTY JOINT VOC SCH; (JR); Hnr Roll; Cl Off (T); Cisco Certification; United States Air Force; ITT Tech; Penn State

MICKEL, CHRISTINA; NILES, OH; NILES MC KINLEY HS; (JR); Hnr Roll; Nat Hon Sy; Sci Fairs; WWAHSS; Comm Volntr; Hosp Aide; Red Cr Aide; AL Aux Girls; Chrch Yth Grp; Emplmnt; Key Club; SADD; French Clb; Bnd; Drl Tm; PP Ftbl; Vllyball (V L); Stu Cncl (R); Sch Ppr (R, P); Yrbk (R, P); National Honors Society; Girls State; Physical Therapy; Akron U; U of Toledo

MILEY, JASON C; WEST SALEM, OH; NORTHWESTERN HS; (SO); Hnr Roll; 4-H; Chrch Yth Grp; Emplmnt; Ntl FFA; Quiz Bowl; Bsball (J); Bskball (J); Jr Holstein Club-Director; 4-H club President

MILLER, ALYSSA J; GENOA, OH; GENOA AREA HS; (SR); F Lan Hn Soc; Hi Hnr Roll; Nat Hon Sy; Perf Att; WWAHSS; Comm Volntr; Red Cr Aide; Chrch Yth Grp; Emplmnt; Key Club; Lib Aide; Off Aide; Spanish Clb; Chr; SP/M/VS; Sftball (J); Athletic Trainer's Aide (Football, Basketball); Pre-Medicine; Physician's Assistant; Heidelberg College

MILLER, ALYSSA J; ZANESVILLE, OH; MAYSVILLE HS; (FR); Hi Hnr Roll; Hnr Roll; WWAHSS; Comm Volntr; Peer Tut/Med; 4-H; Chrch Yth Grp; Key Club; Tchrs Aide; Spanish Clb; Chr; Scr Kpr (V); Stu Cncl; Law; Architecture

MILLER, AMANDA; GENOA, OH; (JR); Hnr Roll; Perf Att; WWAHSS; Comm Volntr; Chrch Yth Grp; Emplmnt; Key Club; Tchrs Aide; Chr; Sftball (J); Law; U of Toledo

MILLER, ASHLEY; CHILLICOTHE, OH; CHILLICOTHE HS; (JR); Hnr Roll; Sci Fairs; St of Mnth; WWAHSS; ArtClub; DARE; Off Aide; Prom Com; Latin Clb; Sccr (J); Business; Ohio State U

MILLER, CHELSEA; PAINESVILLE, OH; RIVERSIDE HS; (SO); 4H Awd; Hi Hnr Roll; Pres Sch; WWAHSS; Comm Volntr; 4-H; HO'Br Yth Ldrshp; Key Club; Lib Aide; Prom Com; Tchrs Aide; SP/M/VS; Swg Chr; Chrldg (V L); Sftball (J); Stu Cncl (R); Yrbk (P); Junior Council - Secretary; Leadership Student Council; Pediatrician; Case Western Reserve

MILLER, EMILY J; SPRINGFIELD, OH; SPRINGFIELD NORTH HS; (JR); Ctznshp Aw; Hnr Roll; St of Mnth; Comm Volntr; Drma Clb; Emplmnt; Key Club; Bnd; Mch Bnd; Pep Bnd; SP/M/VS; PP Ftbl (V); Section Leader for Marching Band/Flutes 2 Yrs; Music Education; Performance Flute (Woodwinds); Wright State U; Wittenberg U

MILLER, ERICA; CAMBRIDGE, OH; CAMBRIDGE HS; (JR); Hi Hnr Roll; Nat Hon Sy; WWAHSS; Chrch Yth Grp; Key Club; Mod UN; Acpl Chr; Bnd; Mch Bnd; Pep Bnd; Psychology; Music; Ohio Valley College; York College

MILLER, EVAN M; NEWARK, OH; LICKING VALLEY; (SO); DAR; Hnr Roll; Otst Ac Ach Awd; Comm Volntr; Hab For Humty Volntr; Peer Tut/Med; Chrch Yth Grp; Emplmnt; FCA; Off Aide; Ftball (J); Track (V); Air Force Academy-Law Degree; Forensic Psychology; United States Air Force Academy; Ohio State U

MILLER, GREG; CLARKSVILLE, OH; CLINTON-MASSIE SCH; (FR); All Am Sch; Hnr Roll; Yth Ldrshp Prog; Off Aide; Bsball (J); Bskball (J); Ftball (V)

MILLER, JESSIE; NASHPORT, OH; TRI-VALLEY HS; (JR); Hi Hnr Roll; Nat Hon Sy; USAA; WWAHSS; Comm Volntr; Drma Clb; Emplmnt; Quiz Bowl; French Clb; Stg Cre; Sch Ppr (R); Yrbk (P); French Club Vice President; Astronomy/Astrophysics; Chemistry

MILLER, KATY; ASHLAND, OH; ASHLAND HS; (SR); 4H Awd; Hnr Roll; St Schl; Comm Volntr; Peer Tut/Med; 4-H; Chrch Yth Grp; DARE; Emplmnt; Ntl FFA; Sci Clb; FFA Officer-President, Vice-President, Secretary; 4-H Officers-President, Secretary, Photographer; Horse Production and Management; Ohio State U Agricultural Technical Institution

MILLER, KAYLA N; NORWALK, OH; WESTERN RESERVE HS; (FR); Hnr Roll; Comm Volntr; Peer Tut/Med; Chrch Yth Grp; Drma Clb; SP/M/VS; Stg Cre; Bskball (J); Sftball (VJ); Worked for HOSTS as a Volunteer; Detective; Air Force or Army Reserve; Bowling Green U; Harvard U

MILLER, LINDSAY; CELINA, OH; CELINA HS; (SR); Hnr Roll; Otst Ac Ach Awd; Yth Ldrshp Prog; 4-H; Chrch Yth Grp; Dbte Team; Vsity Clb; Spanish Clb; Bnd; Chr; Mch Bnd; SP/M/VS; Tennis (V); Athletic Scholar - 4 Years; Psychology; Walsh U

MILLER, MERIDITH L; BELPRE, OH; BELPRE HS; (JR); Hi Hnr Roll; Nat Hon Sy; Perf Att; Pres Sch; Yth Ldrshp Prog; Comm Volntr; Peer Tut/Med; Red Cr Aide; Chrch Yth Grp; Drma Clb; Prom Com; Quiz Bowl; Chr; SP/M/VS; Bskball (VJC); Cl Off (S); Regional Scholar; Top Ten; Education; Counseling; Ohio Valley College; Harding U

MILLER, MICHELE; DAYTON, OH; FAIRMONT HS; (SR); F Lan Hn Soc; Hi Hnr Roll; Nat Hon Sy; Perf Att; USAA; WWAHSS; Hosp Aide; ArtClub; Chess; Scouts; Spanish Clb; Stu Cncl (R); CR (R)

MILLER, MIRANDA L; WILLOUGHBY, OH; WILLOUGHBY SOUTH HS; (SO); Nat Hon Sy; Perf Att; Pres Sch; Comm Volntr; Emplmnt; Key Club; Chr; Clr Grd; Dnce; Flg Crps; History; French; Mount Union College; Yale U

MILLER, MONICA; TIFFIN, OH; CALVERT HS; (SO); Hnr Roll; Sci Fairs; French Clb; Chrldg (V); Psychology; Photography

MILLER, NATHAN E; MAGNOLIA, OH; SANDY VALLEY JR/SR HS; (JR); Hnr Roll; Nat Hon Sy; Sci Fairs; WWAHSS; Peer Tut/Med; Spec Olymp Vol; Chess; Emplmnt; Lib Aide; Sci Clb; Bnd; Jzz Bnd; Mch Bnd; Pep Bnd; Teaching; Mathematics; Kent State; Akron U

MILLER, SAMUEL A; DAYTON, OH; ALTER HS; (FR); Emplmnt; Key Club; Spanish Clb; Golf (J); Vllyball (J); Key Club; Spanish Club; Dentistry; Engineering; Notre Dame; The Ohio State U

MILLER, SARAH A; DAYTON, OH; WAYNE HS; (MS); Ctznshp Aw; Hnr Roll; Perf Att; St of Mnth; Chr; PP Ftbl; Veterinary Medicine; Art; College of Veterinary Medicine-Ohio State U; College of Veterinary Medicine-Michigan State U

MILLER, TIFFANY; OSGOOD, OH; MARION LOCAL HS; (SO); 4H Awd; Hnr Roll; 4-H; Chrch Yth Grp; Off Aide; Bnd; Ch Chr; Mch Bnd; Orch; Bskball (J L); Multiple 4-H Achievements

MILLER, WILLIAM H; BARBERTON, OH; BARBERTON HS; (SR); Hnr Roll; Nat Hon Sy; Chrch Yth Grp; Scouts; Ch Chr; National Technical Honor Society; Computer Science; U of Akron

MILLIGAN, MEGAN; CLEVELAND, OH; HEALTH CAREERS CTR; (SO); Ctznshp Aw; Hi Hnr Roll; Hnr Roll; Perf Att; WWAHSS; Peer Tut/Med; Chrch Yth Grp; Mth Clb/Tm; Drl Tm; SP/M/VS; Stu Cncl (R); CR (R); Was Chosen to Attend Classes At Cleveland State; Pre-Med; Journalism; Miami U; Ohio State U

MILLIKEN, KYLIA; WELLSTON, OH; WELLSTON HS; (SO); Hi Hnr Roll; Jr Ach; Ntl FFA; P to P St Amb Prg; Tchrs Aide; German Clb; Sftball (J); Criminal Justice; Medicine; Ohio U

MINER, DARLENE D; SOUTHINGTON, OH; SOUTHINGTON LOCAL SCH; (SO); Hnr Roll; Nat Hon Sy; Perf Att; St of Mnth; Comm Volntr; Chrch Yth Grp; DARE; DECA; Scouts; Chr; Brownies-Girl Scouts; Office Aide; Marketing & Sales; Computer Tech; Kent State; Ohio State

MIRMAJLESSI, SEYED; TOLEDO, OH; WOODWARD HS; (JR); Ctznshp Aw; Hi Hnr Roll; Hnr Roll; Nat Hon Sy; Perf Att; Jr Ach; MCO Graduation Award; Criminal Law; Business; UCLA; NYU

MITCHELL, GLENN A; STEUBENVILLE, OH; STEUBENVILLE HS; MS; 4H Awd; DAR; Perf Att; Sci/Math Olympn; Comm Volntr; Sci Clb; SADD; Bskball (J); Track (V)

MITCHELL, SHANNON M; NEGLEY, OH; EAST PALESTINE HS; (SR); Hnr Roll; St of Mnth; WWAHSS; Comm Volntr; Peer Tut/Med; Emplmnt; Pep Squd; Bnd; Mch Bnd; Chrldg (JCL); Scr Kpr (VJ L); PALS; Social Concern; BSN in Nursing; Youngstown State U

MIZER, ASHLEIGH N; HOWARD, OH; MT VERNON HS; (JR); Ctznshp Aw; Kwnis Aw; Nat Hon Sy; Nat Ldrshp Svc; WWAHSS; Comm Volntr; ArtClub; Chess; Chrch Yth Grp; FCA; Key Club; Prom Com; Vllyball (J); Cl Off (V); Sch Ppr (R); National Art Award; Communications; Journalism; Denison U; Ohio U

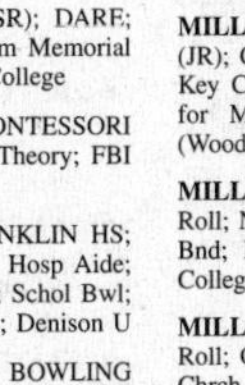
Miller, Kayla N
Western Reserve HS
Norwalk, OH

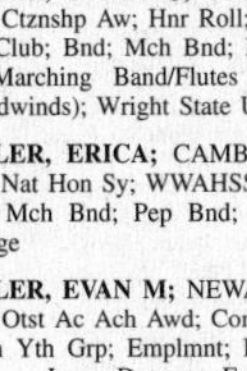
Miller, Greg
Clinton-Massie Sch
Clarksville, OH

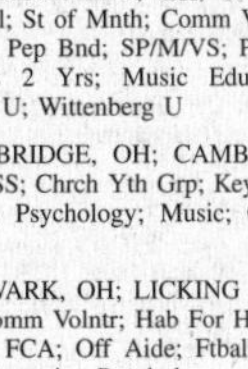
Melegari, Sarah
East Canton HS
Canton, OH

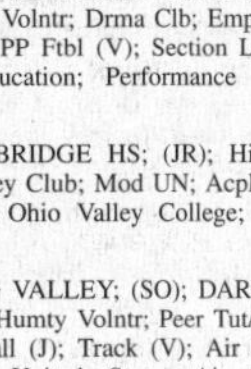
Melone, Anthony M
Columbiana HS
Columbiana, OH

Mitchell, Glenn A
Steubenville HS
Steubenville, OH

MOBLEY, SHEHAN V; CINCINNATI, OH; WITHROW UNIVERSITY HS; (JR); Hi Hnr Roll; Hnr Roll; Nat Hon Sy; Nat Ldrshp Svc; WWAHSS; CARE; Hosp Aide; Peer Tut/Med; ArtClub; DARE; Emplmnt; Jr Ach; Mth Clb/Tm; Ntl Beta Clb; Pep Squd; SADD; Drl Tm; Cl Off (R); Stu Cncl (R); Nurse Practitioner; Capital U; Pennsylvania State U

MOELLER, JEREMY; WAYNESVILLE, OH; WAYNESVILLE; (JR); Hnr Roll; Nat Ldrshp Svc; Perf Att; Creation of School Website; Boy Scouts; ITT Program; Sinclair Community College; Wright State U

MOFF, BRIAN; COLUMBIANA, OH; COLUMBIANA HS; (SR); 4H Awd; Hnr Roll; Nat Hon Sy; Perf Att; Comm Volntr; 4-H; Biology Clb; Emplmnt; P to P St Amb Prg; Quiz Bowl; Foreign Clb; Bsball (V CL); Wt Lftg (V); Environmental Resource Science; Ohio State Agriculture Technical Institute

MOHAMMAD, NASSAR; COLUMBUS, OH; THOMAS WORTHINGTON HS; (JR); Hosp Aide; Bnd; Pep Bnd; Golf (J); Biological Sciences; Pre-Med; Ohio State U; Ohio U

MOLIQUE, ELIZABETH; MONROEVILLE, OH; MONROEVILLE/EHOUE; (JR); Hnr Roll; Perf Att; St of Mnth; Key Club; Voc Ind Clb Am; Flg Crps; Toledo U; Bowling Green State U

MOLLENO, CATHERINE; LORAIN, OH; LORAIN SOUTHVIEW HS; (SO); Hnr Roll; Perf Att; WWAHSS; Comm Volntr; Chrch Yth Grp; Drma Clb; Key Club; Mod UN; Mus Clb; Ch Chr; SP/M/VS; Tennis (J); Southview Idol Winner 2005; Archaeology; Nursing; Case Western Reserve U

MOLLETT, HOLLY; WHEELERSBURG, OH; SOUTH WEBSTER JR/SR HS; (JR); Hnr Roll; Nat Hon Sy; Otst Ac Ach Awd; Perf Att; WWAHSS; Comm Volntr; Peer Tut/Med; Red Cr Aide; Key Club; Prom Com; Spanish Clb; Spanish Club Secretary 2 Consecutive Years; Pediatrics; Secondary Education; Shawnee State U; Ohio State U

MOLONEY, ALLYSON L; OXFORD, OH; TALAWANDA HS; (SO); Hnr Roll; Key Club; Fld Hky (V); Miami U; Ohio U

MONAHAN, TERI; MIDDLETOWN, OH; LAKOTA EAST HS; (SO); Hi Hnr Roll; Hnr Roll; St of Mnth; Chrch Yth Grp; Chr; Ch Chr; Liberty Jr. Honor Society

MONASTERE, CHELSEA M; SHELBY, OH; SHELBY HS; (FR); Hnr Roll; Nat Hon Sy; Otst Ac Ach Awd; Hab For Humty Volntr; Chrch Yth Grp; DARE; Drma Clb; Key Club; P to P St Amb Prg; Chr; Ch Chr; SP/M/VS; Track (J); Journalism; Law; Columbia U; Liberty U

MONNIN, CATHERINE J; SPRINGFIELD, OH; TECUMSEH HS; (SR); 4H Awd; Hi Hnr Roll; Hnr Roll; Otst Ac Ach Awd; Yth Ldrshp Prog; Comm Volntr; 4-H; Chrch Yth Grp; Emplmnt; FCA; Ntl FFA; Prom Com; French Clb; Bnd; Chr; Dnce; SP/M/VS; Bskball (J); PP Ftbl (V); Sccr (V C); FFA Reporter-2004-2005; Clark Co. Jr. Fairboard 2004-2006; Animal Science; 4-H Youth Extension; Ohio State U; Columbus State Community College

MONROE, ROSHAUNDA; CINCINNATI, OH; WESTERN HILL HS; (SO); Sci Fairs; St of Mnth; Comm Volntr; Peer Tut/Med; DARE; Clr Grd; Drl Tm; Bskball (J); Criminal Justice; R/N; Cincinnati State; U Cincinnati

MONTGOMERY, PAUL E; CLEVELAND, OH; VALLEY FORGE HS; (JR); Hnr Roll; Drma Clb; P to P St Amb Prg; Chr; SP/M/VS; Stg Cre; Vanguard of VS Film Club; Cinematography; U of Southern California

MOOK, JESSEY P; MAGNOLIA, OH; SANDY VALLEY JR/SR HS; (SR); Hnr Roll; St of Mnth; WWAHSS; Comm Volntr; Chess; Chrch Yth Grp; Emplmnt; FCA; Bnd; Jzz Bnd; Pep Bnd; SP/M/VS; Bskball (J); Cr Ctry (V CL); Track (V CL); 2 Year State Qualifier / Cross County; 1 Year State Qualifier Track; Children Ministry; Youth Ministry; Indiana Wesleyan U

MOORE, AMANDA M; MAGNOLIA, OH; SANDY VALLEY JR/SR HS; (JR); Gmnstcs (V L); Sftball (V L); Vllyball (V L); CR; Sch Ppr (R); Science Fair District Finalist 2005; Girls State Alternate; Physical Therapy / Sports Training; Stark State College; Kent State U

MOORE, AUTUMN; QUAKER CITY, OH; ROSECRANS HS; (FR); 4H Awd; Hnr Roll; 4-H; Drma Clb; Key Club; Pep Squd; Dnce; SP/M/VS; Bskball (J); Track (V L); Stu Cncl (R); Communications; Drama

MOORE, COURTNEY; ALLIANCE, OH; ALLIANCE HS; (JR); Hnr Roll; Otst Ac Ach Awd; Sci Fairs; St of Mnth; Chrch Yth Grp; Key Club; Prom Com; Voc Ind Clb Am; Bnd; Chr; Ch Chr; Jzz Bnd; Cl Off (R); Stu Cncl (R); CR (R); Show Choir; Music Education; Bowling Green U; Bluffton U

MOORE, DANIELLE; LIMA, OH; (SO); Hnr Roll; Perf Att; Comm Volntr; Peer Tut/Med; Red Cr Aide; Chess; Dbte Team; Drma Clb; Emplmnt; Mus Clb; P to P St Amb Prg; Prom Com; Wdwrkg Clb; Chr; Orch; SP/M/VS; Stg Cre; Stu Cncl (R); Lit Mag (R); Sch Ppr (P)

MOORE, JOSEPH; ELYRIA, OH; CLEARVIEW HS; (JR); Ctznshp Aw; Hnr Roll; MVP; Otst Ac Ach Awd; St of Mnth; Emplmnt; Off Aide; Bsball (J L); Bskball (J L); Ftball (V L); Track; Wt Lftg; Business Management; Computers; Business Management; Computers; Ohio State U; West Virginia U

MOORE, KELLI E; TORONTO, OH; EDISON HS; (JR); Hi Hnr Roll; Hnr Roll; WWAHSS; Chrch Yth Grp; DARE; Drma Clb; Ntl Beta Clb; Scouts; SP/M/VS; Stg Cre; Bskball (V L); Vllyball (V L); Veterinarian; Marine Biologist; Ohio State U; U of Miami, Florida

MOORE, MITCHELL A; SOMERSET, OH; FISHER CATHOLIC HS; (FR); 4H Awd; Pres Ac Ftns Aw; Sci Fairs; Comm Volntr; 4-H; DARE; Scouts; SADD; Wdwrkg Clb; Cr Ctry; Track; COSI-Columbus Volunteer; Engineering; Business; Ohio State U; Ohio U, Duke U

MORALES, EDDAIRIS M; LORAIN, OH; LORAIN SOUTHVIEW HS; (SR); Hi Hnr Roll; Hnr Roll; Nat Hon Sy; Nat Ldrshp Svc; Otst Ac Ach Awd; St of Mnth; WWAHSS; Yth Ldrshp Prog; Comm Volntr; Peer Tut/Med; Spec Olymp Vol; Key Club; Off Aide; Prom Com; Tchrs Aide; Bnd; Mch Bnd; Pep Bnd; Adv Cncl (R); US Congressional Service Award; President's U.S. Service Award; Nursing; U of Akron

MORFORD, WARREN C; SOUTH POINT, OH; SOUTH POINT HS; (JR); Hnr Roll; Nat Hon Sy; Perf Att; Comm Volntr; Chrch Yth Grp; Emplmnt; Sccr (V L)

MORGAN, AMBER N; WARREN, OH; CHAMPION HS; (JR); Hnr Roll; Pres Ac Ftns Aw; Pres Sch; WWAHSS; Key Club; Off Aide; Photog; Bnd; Dnce; Mch Bnd; SP/M/VS; Yrbk (R, P); Office / Teacher's Aide; Assisted with Potential New Teacher Interviews; Genetic Counselor; Kent State U; Case Western Reserve U

MORRIS, BROOKE; SOUTH CHARLESTON, OH; SOUTHEASTERN HS; (FR); Hnr Roll; Comm Volntr; Peer Tut/Med; DARE; Acpl Chr; FCCLA; Teaching Education; Physical Therapist; Cedarville College; Wittenberg U

MORRIS, HEATHER A; TIFFIN, OH; TIFFIN COLUMBIAN HS; (JR); Hnr Roll; Nat Hon Sy; Peer Tut/Med; FCA; Prom Com; Vllyball (V); Yrbk; Scholar Athlete; Doctor of Pharmacy; U of Findlay

MORRIS, JOHNATHON; VAN WERT, OH; LINCOLNVIEW SCH; (SR); Hnr Roll; Jr Rot; Nat Hon Sy; St of Mnth; WWAHSS; 4-H; Chrch Yth Grp; Emplmnt; Ntl FFA; Prom Com; Sci Clb; Spanish Clb; Bnd; Mch Bnd; Pep Bnd; Bskball; Golf (V L); Wt Lftg; Engineer; U of Toledo

MORRIS, KENNETH; ROCKBRIDGE, OH; LOGAN ELM HS; (JR); Hnr Roll; WWAHSS; Emplmnt; FCA; Photog; SADD; Tchrs Aide; Vsity Clb; Bskball (VJCL); Cr Ctry (V CL); Track (V L); Vsy Clb (V); Web Page - Editor / Reporter / Photographer; YMCA Youth Coordinator; Business

MORRIS, SHAUNDA M; MORROW, OH; GREENTREE HEALTH SCIENCE AC; (JR); Hnr Roll; Perf Att; Peer Tut/Med; Honor Roll; Perfect Attendance; X-Ray Tech; Therapist; Kettering College (Medical)

MORRIS, TURRELL R; COLUMBUS, OH; EAST HS; (SO); Hnr Roll; Perf Att; Comm Volntr; Peer Tut/Med; Chess; Chrch Yth Grp; DARE; Scouts; Chr; Ch Chr; Bsball (V); Bskball (V); Golf (V); Stu Cncl (R); Graphics Designer/Lawyer; Fashion Designer/Doctor; Duke U; U of Maryland

MORRISON, MICHELLE C; NORTH CANTON, OH; HOOVER HS; (SO); Perf Att; WWAHSS; Yth Ldrshp Prog; Comm Volntr; Chrch Yth Grp; Emplmnt; Key Club; Kwanza Clb; Spanish Clb; Dnce; SP/M/VS; African American Society Club; Key Club and DFY; Master's Degree in Teaching; Apply to a Beauty College; Phoenix U; Kent State

MOSCARILLO, MORGAN M; HUDSON, OH; HUDSON HS; (MS); Ctznshp Aw; Hi Hnr Roll; Peer Tut/Med; Chrch Yth Grp; Key Club; Scouts; Spanish Clb; Bnd; Dnce; Chrldg; Track; Stu Cncl (R); Yrbk; Midwest Talent Search; Medical Field

MOSER, ROBYN R; HARROD, OH; APOLLO CAREER CTR; (SR); 4H Awd; Hnr Roll; 4-H; DARE; Emplmnt; Prom Com; Quiz Bowl; Scouts; Tchrs Aide; Bnd; Flg Crps; Mch Bnd; Stg Cre; Stu Cncl (R)

MOSES, WARREN L; LIMA, OH; SOUTH MS; (MS); Hi Hnr Roll; Hnr Roll; Perf Att; DARE; Acpl Chr; Bsball; Bskball (J); Ftball (J); Wrstlg (J); School Choir; Business, Law (Pro Football Hobby); Work on Planes & Jets; Michigan U

MOSLEY, DONIVAN; CINCINNATI, OH; PRINCETON HS; (JR); Ctznshp Aw; Hnr Roll; Otst Ac Ach Awd; Perf Att; Comm Volntr; DARE; P to P St Amb Prg; SADD; Bsball (VJ); Bskball (VJ); Ftball; Spanish I-II; Sign Language "A" Student; Physical Therapy; Illinois U; Syracuse U

MOSQUERA, SHIRLEY D; AKRON, OH; CENTRAL HS; (FR); Hnr Roll; Perf Att; Sci Fairs; Orch; National Jr Honor Society; Veterinarian; Law

MOSS, LAUREN E; HAMILTON, OH; TALAWANDA HS; (SO); 4H Awd; Hi Hnr Roll; Otst Ac Ach Awd; WWAHSS; Comm Volntr; Peer Tut/Med; 4-H; Chrch Yth Grp; Emplmnt; Key Club; Ntl FFA; Orch; FFA (2 Years); 4-H (8 years); Psychology; Philosophy; Cornell U; Princeton U

MOTTS, SOPHIA; WAYNESBURG, OH; SANDY VALLEY JR/SR HS; (JR); Hnr Roll; Nat Hon Sy; Perf Att; WWAHSS; Chrch Yth Grp; Off Aide; Pep Squd; Bnd; Mch Bnd; Orch; Pep Bnd; Track (V L); Nursing; Business; Malone College; Asbury College

MOUSIE, RACHEL; CINCINNATI, OH; NORTHWEST HS; (JR); Hi Hnr Roll; Hnr Roll; MVP; Nat Hon Sy; St of Mnth; WWAHSS; Comm Volntr; ArtClub; Chrch Yth Grp; Drma Clb; Emplmnt; Key Club; Off Aide; Prom Com; Svce Clb; Bnd; Mch Bnd; Pep Bnd; SP/M/VS; Cr Ctry (V); Sccr (V); Track (V); Cl Off (V); Stu Cncl (R); Sch Ppr (R, P); Unknighted Knights; Lead in School Musical; Theatre; Journalism; Miami Oxford

MOXLEY, KRISTIAN; DELAWARE, OH; RUTHERFORD B HAYES HS; (FR); Ctznshp Aw; Hnr Roll; Perf Att; Comm Volntr; Peer Tut/Med; DARE; Drma Clb; Emplmnt; Mus Clb; Chr; Ch Chr; Dnce; Stu Cncl (R); CR (V)

MOYNIHAN, RACHAEL; MARTINS FERRY, OH; MOUNT DE CHANTAL HS; (SO); Ctznshp Aw; Hnr Roll; MVP; Otst Ac Ach Awd; Sci Fairs; WWAHSS; Comm Volntr; Chess; Key Club; Photog; SADD; Chr; Swmg (V L); Cl Off (S); CR (S); Yrbk (E); Swimming Nationals; Art; Doctor; Chatum College; Ohio U

MUFFLEY, JILL; CHRISTIANSBURG, OH; GRAHAM HS; (JR); Hi Hnr Roll; Hnr Roll; Nat Hon Sy; Otst Ac Ach Awd; Chr; Bskball (J); Sccr (VJ L); Track (V L); Registered Nurse

MUIR, JEFFREY; CLEVELAND, OH; GARFIELD HEIGHTS HS; (JR); Hnr Roll; Comm Volntr; Peer Tut/Med; Emplmnt; Mus Clb; Orch; SP/M/VS; Renaissance Award Winner; Musical Director for School Plays; Music Performance; Pharmaceutical Technologies; Baldwin Wallace U; Cleveland Institute of Music

MULLAPUDI, MANASA; DAYTON, OH; BEAVERCREEK HS; (FR); Hnr Roll; Nat Sci Aw; Pres Sch; Sci Fairs; USAA; Comm Volntr; Hosp Aide; Chess; DARE; Scouts; Bnd; Swmg; Tennis (V); Stu Cncl (R); Yrbk; Medical School; U of Cincinnati; Ohio State

MULLINS, ANDREW E; ASHTABULA, OH; WEST JHS; (MS); Ctznshp Aw; Hnr Roll; Otst Ac Ach Awd; Sci Fairs; St of Mnth; Comm Volntr; Chess; Chrch Yth Grp; DARE; Mth Clb/Tm; SP/M/VS; Stg Cre; Ftball (J); Track; Wrstlg (L); Sch Ppr (P); Culinary Arts; U of Notre Dame; Kent State U

MULLINS, SAMUEL; LEWISBURG, OH; TRI-COUNTY NORTH HS; (JR); Hi Hnr Roll; Hnr Roll; Jr Rot; Nat Hon Sy; WWAHSS; 4-H; Emplmnt; Prom Com; Quill & Scroll; Sci Clb; Spanish Clb; Bskball (VJCL); Ftball (VJCL); Hsbk Rdg; Mar Art; Wt Lftg; Cl Off (V, R); Stu Cncl (P, V, R); Yrbk (R, P); Rotarian Honory / Music Machine; 4H Member - 2 Years; Ohio State U; Miami U

MURPHY, MICHAEL E; LIMA, OH; LIMA SR HS; (FR); DARE; Bnd; Jzz Bnd; Mch Bnd; Pep Bnd; Auto Mechanics

MURPHY, RYAN; DALTON, OH; TUSLAW JR/SR HS; (FR); Hnr Roll; MVP; Perf Att; Yth Ldrshp Prog; Chrch Yth Grp; Emplmnt; FCA; NYLC; Bsball (J); Bskball (J); Ftball (V); Track (J); Wt Lftg (V); Stu Cncl (R); Deacon of My Church; Computer Analyst, Education/Coaching; Business Management/Corporate Executive; Ohio State U; Akron U

MURPHY, RYAN P; HAMILTON, OH; FAIRFIELD FRESHMAN HS; (FR); Hnr Roll; Perf Att; Pres Ac Ftns Aw; Comm Volntr; Chrch Yth Grp; DARE; Wrstlg (J); Athlete of the Week; High School Science Teacher; Master's Degree; Purdue U; Iowa State U

MURRAY, DAMON; FAYETTEVILLE, OH; FAYETTEVILLE PERRY HS; (FR); St of Mnth; WWAHSS; Yth Ldrshp Prog; Chrch Yth Grp; Drma Clb; NYLC; SP/M/VS; Bskball (J); Cl Off (P); USAA National Speech and Drama Award; Who's Who Among American HS Students; Performing Arts; Kentucky Christian U

MURRAY, KELLI; MEDINA, OH; MEDINA HS; (SO); Hnr Roll; WWAHSS; Comm Volntr; Chrch Yth Grp; Emplmnt; Key Club; French Clb; Orch; In GL C; Elementary School Teacher; Master's Degree; Brigham Young U Idaho; Brigham Young U Utah

MURRETT, COLLEEN; LAKEWOOD, OH; LAKEWOOD HS; (JR); Hi Hnr Roll; Nat Hon Sy; Sci Fairs; WWAHSS; Comm Volntr; Key Club; Mod UN; Sci Clb; Wdwrkg Clb; German Clb; Orch; Cr Ctry (J); Hsbk Rdg; Track (J); Chemistry

MURRY, EBONY; CINCINNATI, OH; COLERAIN HS; (JR); Hnr Roll; WWAHSS; Yth Ldrshp Prog; Drma Clb; Key Club; NYLC; Prom Com; Spanish Clb; Dnce; Track (L); Pediatrician Doctor; Fashion Designer; University of Cincinnati; Ohio State

MUSSELMAN, DANIELLE M; WAPAKONETA, OH; WAPAKONETA HS; (FR); 4H Awd; Hi Hnr Roll; Otst Ac Ach Awd; Perf Att; Peer Tut/Med; 4-H; Chrch Yth Grp; Spanish Clb; Chr; Flg Crps; Vllyball (L); Scholar Athlete Award; Award for - Outstanding Dedication in Freshman Choir; Interior Design; Freelance Photography; College for Creative Studies; Ohio State U

MUZZY, NICKI; DEERFIELD, OH; SOUTHEAST HS; (SR); Hnr Roll; Pres Ac Ftns Aw; Comm Volntr; Tour Guide for Maplewood Career Center; Associate's Degree in Information Tech; Associate's Degree in Dental Hygiene; Cuyahoga Community College; DeVry U

MYERS, CHRISTOPHER M W; WILLIAMSBURG, OH; CLERMONT NORTHEASTERN HS; (SO); Nat Hon Sy; Ntl FFA; Wdwrkg Clb; Bsball (J)

Mousie, Rachel
Northwest HS
Cincinnati, OH

Moore, Joseph
Clearview HS
Elyria, OH

Molique, Elizabeth
Monroeville/Ehoue
Monroeville, OH

National
Honor Roll
Spring 2005

Moeller, Jeremy
Waynesville
Waynesville, OH

Moscarillo, Morgan M
Hudson HS
Hudson, OH

Moxley, Kristian
Rutherford B Hayes HS
Delaware, OH

MYUNG, GIHYUN; AKRON, OH; COPLEY HS; (SR); 4H Awd; Hi Hnr Roll; Nat Hon Sy; Nat Mrt LOC; Otst Ac Ach Awd; Perf Att; Hosp Aide; SADD; Bnd; Mch Bnd; Adv Cncl; Cl Off (R); Stu Cncl (R); CR (R); Sch Ppr (E); National Commended Student; Honors Student in Math and Science; Biochemistry; Pediatrician; Northwestern

NAKBUTSRI, SIKARIN; CINCINNATI, OH; NORWOOD HS; (SR); Hnr Roll; Perf Att; Comm Volntr; Scouts; Tmpl Yth Grp; Foreign Clb; Dnce; Exchange Student from Thailand; Scholarship for Good Grades and Good Manners; International Affairs; Business Management; Northern Kentucky U; U of Cincinnati

NAMKA, LYVIA; COLUMBUS, OH; BEECHCROFT HS; (SR); Hnr Roll; Otst Ac Ach Awd; Perf Att; WWAHSS; Comm Volntr; Peer Tut/Med; Chrch Yth Grp; Emplmnt; French Clb; Ch Chr; Sftball (V); Academic Excellence Certificate of Participation in Writing Excellence; Full-Time University Student; Get a Bachelor's Degree in Pharmacy or Nursing; Ohio State U; New York U

NAPIER, AMBER D; WOOSTER, OH; WAYNE CTY SCHS CAREER CTR; (JR); Emplmnt; Prom Com; Scouts; PP Ftbl; Preschool Teacher; Child Psychologist

NARO, BETHANY; LORAIN, OH; CLEARVIEW HS; (SO); Ctznshp Aw; Hi Hnr Roll; Hnr Roll; Nat Hon Sy; Otst Ac Ach Awd; WWAHSS; Yth Ldrshp Prog; Comm Volntr; Chrch Yth Grp; Off Aide; Tchrs Aide; Chr; Ch Chr; Chrldg (J); Track (V); Registered Nurse; LCCC / Possibly Transfer to a U

NASH, HEATHER; YOUNGSTOWN, OH; AUSTINTOWN FITCH HS; (FR); 4H Awd; Ctznshp Aw; Hnr Roll; 4-H; ArtClub; Chrch Yth Grp; DARE; Ch Chr; Secretary of 4-H Group; Winner of DARE Essay Contest; Corporate Business; Law; Kent State U; Ohio State U

NAYFELD, LEO; CINCINNATI, OH; WYOMING HS; (SO); Hnr Roll; Pres Ac Ftns Aw; WWAHSS; Tmpl Yth Grp; Sccr (J); Sftball (J); Tennis (VJ L); Vllyball (J); Wrstlg (J); Who's Who Among American Students; National Honor Roll; Business; Law; Stanford; Brandeis

NEAL, MICHAEL; CINCINNATI, OH; NORTHWEST HS; (SR); Hi Hnr Roll; Hnr Roll; BPA; Chrch Yth Grp; Drma Clb; Key Club; Mus Clb; ROTC; Acpl Chr; Chr; Ch Chr; SP/M/VS; Outstanding Knight Award; Computer Information Systems; Pastoral Ministry; Cincinnati State Technical & Community College; Crown College of the Bible

NEEDHAM, RACHAEL; MEDINA, OH; MEDINA HS; (JR); Hnr Roll; Nat Hon Sy; WWAHSS; Comm Volntr; Hosp Aide; Dbte Team; Drma Clb; Emplmnt; Key Club; Latin Clb; Chr; Dnce; SP/M/VS; Stg Cre; Skiing (J); Sftball (J); CR (R); UNICEF Volunteer; Public Relations; Marketing; Kent U; Ohio State U

NEFF, VERONICA; ALLIANCE, OH; MALLINGTON HS; (JR); Hnr Roll; Chrldg (J); Business; Financial Analyst; Kent State U

NELSEN, GREGORY; CINCINNATI, OH; FINNEYTOWN HS; (JR); Hnr Roll; MVP; Nat Hon Sy; Comm Volntr; Chrch Yth Grp; Bnd; Ftball (V); Wrstlg (V); Cincinnati State; U of Cincinnati

NELSON, LAURA A; WESTERVILLE, OH; NEW ALBANY HS; (JR); Ctznshp Aw; Hi Hnr Roll; Hnr Roll; Otst Ac Ach Awd; Perf Att; Comm Volntr; Hab For Humty Volntr; DARE; Mod UN; Photog; Chr; Habitat for Humanity Participant; Medical Field; Business; Radford U; Duke U

NELSON, MATTHEW A; MILFORD CTR, OH; MARYSVILLE HS; (JR); Hnr Roll; DARE; Bsball (J L); Sccr (J L); Scholar Athlete; Union Post 79 American Legion Baseball; Architecture / Building Design / Engineering; Aviation

NELSON, RYAN; AKRON, OH; ELLET HS; (SO); Hi Hnr Roll; Hnr Roll; MVP; Pres Ac Ftns Aw; St of Mnth; WWAHSS; Sccr (VJ L); Wrstlg (VJ L); President's Award; Veterinary Medicine; The Ohio State U

NEMEC, MELISSA A; SPRINGFIELD, OH; CATHOLIC CTRL HS; (SR); Hi Hnr Roll; Nat Hon Sy; St of Mnth; WWAHSS; Yth Ldrshp Prog; Comm Volntr; Jr Ach; Key Club; Mth Clb/Tm; NYLC; SADD; Swmg (V CL); Track (V L); CR (T); NAS-Treasurer; Physician's Assistant; Butler U

NEMETH, JOHNEY; COSHOCTON, OH; COSHOCTON HS; (SR); MVP; WWAHSS; Comm Volntr; Red Cr Aide; Spec Olymp Vol; Key Club; Lttrmn Clb; Tchrs Aide; Vsity Clb; Ftball (V CL); Track (V L); Wrstlg (V CL); Outstanding Athlete of Class of 2005; Academic Letter; Law; Otterbein College

NERI, GINA M; TALLMADGE, OH; NORTH HS; (SR); Ctznshp Aw; Hnr Roll; DARE; Pep Squd; Scouts; Chr; Stg Cre; Sftball (VJ); I Was in 3.0 Club.; To Become a Forensic Scientist; I Would Like to Be a Lawyer.; Youngstown State U; Kent State U

NESSELROAD, OLIVIA J; MC CONNELSVILLE, OH; MORGAN HS; (JR); Hi Hnr Roll; Perf Att; Sci Fairs; WWAHSS; Comm Volntr; Peer Tut/Med; AL Aux Girls; ArtClub; Chrch Yth Grp; DARE; Emplmnt; FCCLA; Key Club; Lib Aide; Acpl Chr; SP/M/VS; Bskball (J); Chrldg (J); Yrbk (E, R, P); Prayer Group; Marketing; Franklin U; Ohio State U

NEUMAN, ADRIENNE; GENOA, OH; GENOA AREA HS; (JR); Hi Hnr Roll; Hnr Roll; Perf Att; WWAHSS; Peer Tut/Med; 4-H; ArtClub; Chrch Yth Grp; Key Club; NYLC; Prom Com; Spanish Clb; Golf; PP Ftbl (VJ); Yrbk; Business; Medicine; Ohio State U; U of Toledo

NEUMANN, AMANDA M; BUCYRUS, OH; (SO); Hnr Roll; Bskball (VJ); Social Services; Ohio State U; Miami State U

NEUMANN, ANDREA; CLEVELAND, OH; PADUA FRANCISCAN HS; (SO); Hnr Roll; Comm Volntr; Key Club; German Clb; Bnd; Peer Ministry; 2003 International Model & Talent Assoc Team Fashion Award; Early Education; Boston U; Mount Holyoke

NEWBROUGH, HANNAH; NILES, OH; MC KINLEY HS; (FR); Hnr Roll; WWAHSS; FTA; Italian Clb; Bskball (J); Chrldg (J); Track (V); Vllyball (J)

NEWELL, IESHA C; FREMONT, OH; FREMONT ROSS HS; (JR); Hnr Roll; Otst Ac Ach Awd; Pres Ac Ftns Aw; WWAHSS; DARE; Key Club; Outdrs Clb; Pep Squd; Chrldg (J); PP Ftbl (J); Track (J); Psychologist; Doctor; U of Toledo

NEWKIRK, ALLIE; FAIRFIELD, OH; FAIRFIELD FRESHMAN HS; (FR); Ctznshp Aw; Hnr Roll; Nat Hon Sy; Otst Ac Ach Awd; Perf Att; St of Mnth; ArtClub; DARE; Scouts

NEWMAN, BRANDI L; CINCINNATI, OH; NORTHWEST HS; (JR); Hi Hnr Roll; Hnr Roll; Otst Ac Ach Awd; St of Mnth; WWAHSS; Comm Volntr; Emplmnt; Off Aide; Spanish Clb; Acpl Chr; Chr; Dnce; SP/M/VS; Chrldg (VJCL); Gmnstcs (V); Sccr (V); Track (V); Stu Cncl (R); Yrbk (P); Model-New View Model Mgmt.; Interior Designer; Dance Major; Ohio State U; U of Cincinnati

NICHOLAS, ANTHONY; CANTON, OH; CONOTTON VALLEY JR/SR HS; (JR); USAA; Emplmnt; Ftball (V L); Track (V L); Wrstlg (V L)

NICKELL, HILARY; PIKETON, OH; PIKETON HS; (FR); 4H Awd; Hnr Roll; Pres Sch; Sci Fairs; Peer Tut/Med; 4-H; ArtClub; DARE; Sci Clb; Scouts; Bskball (VJ); Sftball (VJ); Vllyball (VJ); Art Awards; Physical Educator; Mathematics; U of North Carolina; U of Kentucky

NICOL, HANNAH; WAPAKONETA, OH; WAPAKONETA HS; (SR); 4H Awd; F Lan Hn Soc; Hi Hnr Roll; Hnr Roll; St of Mnth; St Optmst of Yr; WWAHSS; 4-H; Chrch Yth Grp; Drma Clb; Emplmnt; FCA; German Clb; Chr; SP/M/VS; Swg Chr; Cl Off (V); Stu Cncl (V); Miss Summer Moon of Wapakoneta; Linguistics; Bowling Green State U

NIECE, JAMES S; DAYTON, OH; CARROLL AC; (SR); Chess; Drma Clb; Emplmnt; Key Club; SP/M/VS; U of Toledo

NIECE, KATY; DAYTON, OH; CARROLL HS; (SO); Hnr Roll; Sci Fairs; WWAHSS; Drma Clb; Key Club; Kwanza Clb; P to P St Amb Prg; SP/M/VS; Tennis (J); Cl Off (R); Stu Cncl (R); Elementary Education

NIEDERHAUSEN, RACHEL; CINCINNATI, OH; MOTHER OF MERCY HS; (FR); Hi Hnr Roll; Pres Ac Ftns Aw; Sci Fairs; St of Mnth; WWAHSS; Yth Ldrshp Prog; Comm Volntr; Peer Tut/Med; DARE; Key Club; Quiz Bowl; Scouts; Svce Clb; Stg Cre; Vllyball; Pharmacy; Accounting; U of Cincinnati; Northern Kentucky U

NIESE, JACOB S; DELTA, OH; ST FRANCIS DE SALES HS; (FR); Hnr Roll; Nat Hon Sy; Otst Ac Ach Awd; Sci Fairs; Comm Volntr; Chess; Chrch Yth Grp; DARE; Emplmnt; Scouts; SP/M/VS; CR (R); Yrbk (R); Christian Service Award; Knights of Columbus Religion Award; Computer Science & Engineering; Computer Programming; Ohio State U; MIT

NIESE, JESSICA F; NORWALK, OH; EDISON HS; (FR); Ctznshp Aw; Hi Hnr Roll; Hnr Roll; St of Mnth; Drma Clb; Mus Clb; Off Aide; SADD; Tchrs Aide; Tech Clb; Acpl Chr; Bnd; Mch Bnd; SP/M/VS; Cl Off (S); Stu Cncl (R); Freshman Marcher of the Year; $200 Savings Bond Writing Contest; Nursing; Bowling Green State U; John Carroll U

NIGHSWANDER, JANELLE; BERKEY, OH; EVERGREEN HS; (JR); Ctznshp Aw; Hnr Roll; Nat Hon Sy; Perf Att; ArtClub; Prom Com; Radiology; Owens Community College

NOBLE, JAMAR; CINCINNATI, OH; KOKOMO AC; (SO); Ctznshp Aw; Hnr Roll; Perf Att; Hab For Humty Volntr; Chrch Yth Grp; Student of the Week

NOLAN, KRISTA; LONDON, OH; LONDON HS; (JR); Hnr Roll; St of Mnth; DARE; Emplmnt; Jr Ach; Lib Aide; Dnce; Sccr (V L); Pre-Med; Forensics; Ohio State U; Ohio Northern U

NOLLER, CASEY; TIFFIN, OH; OLD FORT HS; (FR); 4H Awd; Hnr Roll; 4-H; Horseback Riding (Not School); Veterinarian; Horse or Dog Trainer; U of Findlay

NORMAN JR, ZACH; CINCINNATI, OH; WESTERN HILLS DESIGN TECH SCH; (FR); Ctznshp Aw; Hnr Roll; Bsball (V L); Criminal Justice; U of Southern California; Rice U

NORRIS, JENNA; MEDINA, OH; MEDINA SR HS; (FR); Hnr Roll; Chrch Yth Grp; Key Club; Spanish Clb; Vllyball (J); CYO Basketball; Junior Olympic Volleyball; Veterinarian; Psychologist

NORTHCUTT, MEGAN M; CINCINNATI, OH; ANDERSON HS; (JR); Hi Hnr Roll; Hnr Roll; Otst Ac Ach Awd; WWAHSS; Comm Volntr; Drma Clb; Chr; Dnce; SP/M/VS; Stg Cre; Dance Team-Letter/Honors Choir/Show Choir; Academic Achievement Awards-Spanish, English Thespian Society, Spanish Honor Society, Principal's Forum

NORTHUP, SAMANTHA L; GALLIPOLIS, OH; GALLIO AC HS; (FR); Hnr Roll; 4-H; Key Club; Mod UN; Ntl FFA; Scouts; Sftball (J)

NOTESTONE, MINDY; LANCASTER, OH; LANCASTER HS; (JR); Hi Hnr Roll; Nat Hon Sy; WWAHSS; DARE; Key Club; Off Aide; Svce Clb; Vsity Clb; Spanish Clb; Bskball (J); Vllyball (V); Stu Cncl (R); Yrbk (R, P); Secondary Mathematics Education; Miami U; Ohio State U

NOVAK, LINDSEY; SHEFFIELD LAKE, OH; BROOKSIDE HS; (SR); Hi Hnr Roll; Nat Hon Sy; WWAHSS; Yth Ldrshp Prog; Comm Volntr; Chrch Yth Grp; Emplmnt; Prom Com; SADD; Bskball (V CL); PP Ftbl (V); Sftball (V CL); Vllyball (V CL); Sch Ppr (E, R, P); Yrbk (E, R, P); Junior Olympic Volleyball; Beach Volleyball; Physical Therapy; Sports Medicine; U of Toledo

NOVICKY, TONI; CLEVELAND, OH; PADUA FRANCISCAN HS; (FR); Sci Fairs; Comm Volntr; Peer Tut/Med; Chrch Yth Grp; Drma Clb; Pep Squd; Svce Clb; French Clb; SP/M/VS; Lit Mag (E); Participation Competitive Cheer Squad; Education; Culinary Arts; Ohio U; Baldwin Wallace

NOVIKS, SARAH M; NORTH ROYALTON, OH; NORTH ROYALTON HS; (JR); Hnr Roll; Nat Hon Sy; St of Mnth; Comm Volntr; Peer Tut/Med; Spec Olymp Vol; Chrch Yth Grp; DARE; Key Club; German Clb; Ch Chr; Clr Grd; Dnce; Orch; Gmnstcs; Tennis; Stu Cncl; Treasurer of Key Club International; Member of National Honors Society; Early Childhood Education; Child Development; Bowling Green U; Ohio State U

NUNN JR, TIMOTHY B; CAMBRIDGE, OH; CAMBRIDGE HS; (SR); Hi Hnr Roll; Hnr Roll; MVP; Nat Hon Sy; Perf Att; St of Mnth; WWAHSS; ArtClub; Chrch Yth Grp; Dbte Team; Drma Clb; Emplmnt; Key Club; Scouts; Spch Team; Chr; Ch Chr; SP/M/VS; Stg Cre; Sccr (V CL); Tennis (V CL); Stu Cncl (P); CR (R); Sch Ppr (R); Ohio Mock Trial - Captain; Certified Red Cross Disaster Relief Worker; Computer Engineering; Law; Ohio State U; Ohio Northern U

NUSBAUM, PAT; CAREY, OH; CAREY SCH; (SO); Hnr Roll; Perf Att; Yth Ldrshp Prog; Chrch Yth Grp; DARE; DECA; Scouts; SADD; Chr; Bskball (JC); Ftball (JC); Ohio State U-Doctor Degree; Ohio State U

NYE, SHANNON; TIFFIN, OH; OLD FORT HS; (SO); Ctznshp Aw; Hi Hnr Roll; Hnr Roll; Nat Hon Sy; Otst Ac Ach Awd; St of Mnth; WWAHSS; Comm Volntr; Emplmnt; FCCLA; Pep Squd; Prom Com; Tchrs Aide; Bskball (J); Sftball (V L); Vllyball (V L); Cl Off (R); Stu Cncl (R); CR (R); Physical Therapy; Radiology; U of Toledo; Miami U

OAKMAN, BRITTANY; WAPAKONETA, OH; WAPAKONETA HS; (SO); Hnr Roll; Perf Att; Chrch Yth Grp; DARE; Emplmnt; Scouts; Chr; Sccr (V L); Cl Off (T); 6 Years of Piano; Pharmacist; Optometrist; Ohio Northern U; Ohio State U

OBERGAS, JOSHUA J; WAKEMAN, OH; WESTERN RESERVE; (SR); Hnr Roll; WWAHSS; Yth Ldrshp Prog; Comm Volntr; Peer Tut/Med; Red Cr Aide; 4-H; Chrch Yth Grp; Key Club; Lib Aide; Spanish Clb; SP/M/VS; Sch Ppr; Top Student in Computer Class; Computer Science; Political Science; Ashland U

O'BRIEN, JULIE; STRUTHERS, OH; STRUTHERS HS; (SO); Hnr Roll; USAA; WWAHSS; Comm Volntr; ArtClub; DARE; Drma Clb; Emplmnt; FTA; Mus Clb; Pep Squd; Svce Clb; Bnd; Mch Bnd; SP/M/VS; Youngstown State U

OCAMPO, TRICIA; PARMA, OH; PADUA FRANCISCAN HS; (JR); Hi Hnr Roll; Hnr Roll; Nat Hon Sy; WWAHSS; Comm Volntr; Red Cr Aide; Dbte Team; Key Club; Svce Clb; Bnd; Jzz Bnd; Orch; Pep Bnd; Lit Mag; Yrbk (R); Clinical Laboratory Science; Medicine

O'CONNER, KELLY; CINCINNATI, OH; MOTHER OF MERCY HS; (FR); Hnr Roll; Key Club; Vllyball (J); Stu Cncl (R); Interior Design; Miami U Ohio; Ohio State U

O'CONNOR, ALEX; CINCINNATI, OH; TURPIN HS; (SO); Ctznshp Aw; Hi Hnr Roll; Hnr Roll; Kwnis Aw; Otst Ac Ach Awd; Perf Att; Pres Sch; Sci Fairs; St of Mnth; Cmptr Clb; Mth Clb/Tm; Off Aide; Spch Team; Tchrs Aide; Tech Clb; Engineering; Architecture

O'CONNOR, RACHEL; PAINESVILLE, OH; RIVERSIDE HS; (JR); Hi Hnr Roll; Hnr Roll; Nat Hon Sy; WWAHSS; Comm Volntr; Drma Clb; Emplmnt; HO'Br Yth Ldrshp; Prom Com; Bnd; Mch Bnd; Pep Bnd; Stg Cre; Stu Cncl (R); Yrbk (E, P); Mock Trial; Leadership Lake County; Psychology; Art History; Ohio State U; New York U

ODA, KELLI R; TROY, OH; TROY HS; (JR); Hi Hnr Roll; Chrch Yth Grp; Key Club; Bskball (V); Golf (V); Stu Cncl (R); CR (R); Neurology; Political Science

Nusbaum, Pat
Carey Sch
Carey, OH

Niederhausen, Rachel
Mother Of Mercy HS
Cincinnati, OH

Newman, Brandi L
Northwest HS
Cincinnati, OH

Nemeth, Johney
Coshocton HS
Coshocton, OH

Neri, Gina M
North HS
Tallmadge, OH

Northcutt, Megan M
Anderson HS
Cincinnati, OH

Obergas, Joshua J
Western Reserve
Wakeman, OH

ODA, MAGGIE L; TROY, OH; TROY HS; (FR); Hi Hnr Roll; Hnr Roll; Sci Fairs; St of Mnth; WWAHSS; Spec Olymp Vol; Chrch Yth Grp; Key Club; P to P St Amb Prg; Tchrs Aide; Bskball (L); Sccr (J L); Track (V L); Washington U in St Louis

ODOM, TAMEKA L; COLUMBUS, OH; COLUMBUS ALT HS; (SR); Hnr Roll; Sci Fairs; Comm Volntr; Peer Tut/Med; Chrch Yth Grp; DARE; Key Club; Mth Clb/Tm; Off Aide; Chr; Ch Chr; Dnce; Drl Tm; Cheerleading Coach- Linden Eagles Youth Association; Drill Team Instructor- Hamilton Elementary Alt School; Financing - Major; Accounting - Minor; U of Cincinnati - Accepted; Hampton U - Pending

OFFENBERGER, MISTY; WATERFORD, OH; WATERFORD HS; (SR); 4H Awd; Hi Hnr Roll; Hnr Roll; Perf Att; Sci/Math Olympn; St of Mnth; WWAHSS; Comm Volntr; Hosp Aide; Red Cr Aide; 4-H; AL Aux Girls; Chrch Yth Grp; Drma Clb; Ntl FFA; Prom Com; Tchrs Aide; Vsity Clb; SP/M/VS; Bskball (J); Sftball (V CL); Vllyball (V CL); Wt Lftg (V); Sch Ppr (R); Yrbk (R); Spanish Club; Upward Bound; Agricultural Education; Ag Communications; The Ohio State U-Agricultural Technical Institute

OGLESBY, ASHLEY L; DAYTON, OH; MEADOWDALE HS; (SO); Hi Hnr Roll; Hnr Roll; Works a Job After School; Law / Nursing; Engineering; Xavier U

OHMURA, JACQUELINE F; PAINESVILLE, OH; RIVERSIDE HS; (SO); Hi Hnr Roll; WWAHSS; Comm Volntr; ArtClub; DECA; Drma Clb; Key Club; Lib Aide; Tchrs Aide; French Clb; Bnd; Jzz Bnd; Mch Bnd; Pep Bnd; Sccr (V); Track (V L); Adv Cncl (V); Stu Cncl (T); First Chair Euphonium Wind Symphony Cleveland; Biomedical Engineering

OKESON, BRAD; NOVELTY, OH; WEST GEAUGA SR HS; (JR); Hi Hnr Roll; St of Mnth; WWAHSS; Comm Volntr; Peer Tut/Med; Emplmnt; Key Club; Lib Aide; P to P St Amb Prg; Photog; Bnd; Mch Bnd; SP/M/VS; Swmg (V CL); Stu Cncl (R); Yrbk (R, P); Student Athlete Award for Swimming; News Herald "Player of Week" for Swimming; Mechanical Engineering; Business; The Ohio State U; Massachusetts Institute of Technology

OKLANDER, DIANA; CLEVELAND, OH; MAYFIELD HS; (SR); Hnr Roll; St of Mnth; WWAHSS; DECA; Emplmnt; Key Club; Mod UN; Photog; Chr; SP/M/VS; Gmnstcs (V); Business Management; Public Relations; John Carroll U; Ursuline College

OLARI, NICOLE E; COLUMBUS, OH; INDEPENDENCE HS; (SO); Hnr Roll; Bskball (V); Girl Scouts; Nursing

OLAYA, JAMES J; LAURA, OH; NEWTON HS; (JR); Hnr Roll; Nat Hon Sy; WWAHSS; Comm Volntr; Chrch Yth Grp; Prom Com; Spanish Clb; Bnd; Mch Bnd; Bskball (J); Sccr (V L); President-Spanish Club; President-Church Youth Group; Computer Game/Video Game Developer; Music; Edison State CC; Wright State U

OLSZEWSKI, AMANDA; PICKERINGTON, OH; PICKERINGTON HS NORTH; (SO); Ctznshp Aw; Hi Hnr Roll; Hnr Roll; Jr Eng Tech; Peer Tut/Med; Chrch Yth Grp; Lttrmn Clb; Off Aide; Bskball (V L); Sccr (V L); Adv Cncl (R); Athletic Training; Physical

ONDECKER, JULIANN; BARBERTON, OH; BARBERTON HS; (SO); Hi Hnr Roll; Hnr Roll; Kwnis Aw; Otst Ac Ach Awd; Yth Ldrshp Prog; Comm Volntr; FCA; Key Club; Chrldg (J); Skiing; Sftball (J); Vllyball (V C); Cl Off (T); Stu Cncl (R); Gatorade Rookie of the Year; Pre-Med; MD / Pediatrician; Ohio State U; Northeastern Ohio College of Medicine

ONDO, CADY; CANTON, OH; JACKSON HS; (SO); Hnr Roll; Perf Att; WWAHSS; Comm Volntr; Key Club; Spanish Clb; Stg Cre; Chrldg (J)

ONDO, LINDSEY; CANTON, OH; JACKSON HS; (SR); Hnr Roll; Nat Hon Sy; St of Mnth; WWAHSS; Comm Volntr; Hab For Humty Volntr; Hosp Aide; Dbte Team; Key Club; Mth Clb/Tm; NtlFrnscLg; Off Aide; Spanish Clb; Gmnstcs (V L); Chemical Engineering; The U of Akron

ORAHOOD, JAMI; CORTLAND, OH; LAKEVIEW HS; (FR); Hi Hnr Roll; Hnr Roll; Peer Tut/Med; Chrch Yth Grp; Bnd; Ch Chr; Mch Bnd; Sftball (J); Youngstown State; Grove City

ORANGE, JESSICA; NEWBURY, OH; NEWBURY HS; (FR); Ctznshp Aw; Hnr Roll; MVP; Pres Ac Ftns Aw; St of Mnth; Chess; Drma Clb; Mus Clb; Bnd; Chr; SP/M/VS; Ice Hky (V C); Vllyball (J); Cl Off (T); Stu Cncl (T); Psychology; Music

OROFINO, MARCUS; ZANESVILLE, OH; (FR); Hnr Roll; Nat Sci Aw; Key Club; FBLA Future Leaders of America; Key Club; Psychiatry; Computer IT; RIT; OUZ

OROS, AMANDA; CLEVELAND, OH; GARFIELD HEIGHTS HS; (JR); Ctznshp Aw; Nat Mrt Fin; Otst Ac Ach Awd; Perf Att; Hab For Humty Volntr; ArtClub; Tchrs Aide; Skills USA Design Winner - Third Place; Best in Show for Garfield Heights Holidays Art Competition; Fashion Design; Fashion Illustration; Columbus College of Art and Design; Virginia Marti College of Art and Design

ORTMAN, STEVE; COLLINS, OH; WESTERN RESERVE HS; (FR); Perf Att; St of Mnth; Peer Tut/Med; Emplmnt; Lib Aide; Mod UN; Pep Squd; Wdwrkg Clb; Bnd; Mch Bnd; Pep Bnd; Stu Cncl (R); Intonation Award - Music; Architecture; Interior Designer; Kent State; Pittsburg Art Institute

OSAD, BRITTANIE; CLEVELAND, OH; FAIRVIEW HS; (SO); Hnr Roll; MVP; Pres Ac Ftns Aw; Sci Fairs; Comm Volntr; Emplmnt; Bnd; Chr; Mch Bnd; Orch; Bskball (J); Chrldg (L); Scr Kpr (J); Sccr (V L); Track (J); Pass, Punt, & Kick 2 Years (2nd In Ohio) 12-13 Yr); Barbizon Graduate 9-30-01; Forensic Detective/Photographer

OSBORNE, ALISSA; COLUMBIANA, OH; COLUMBIANA HS; (SO); 4H Awd; Hnr Roll; Nat Hon Sy; Sci Fairs; 4-H; Chrch Yth Grp; Lib Aide; Off Aide; Track (V); Yrbk (E, R, P); Professional Bridal Consultant; Ohio State University; Pennsylvania State University

OSBORNE, LEANNE; MILFORD, OH; GOSHEN HS; (SO); Hnr Roll; St of Mnth; Chrch Yth Grp; Tchrs Aide; Played Volleyball in 7th Grade; Was Involved in Marching Band; Photography; Cosmetology; Cincinnati State College; U of Cincinnati Clermont

OSBORNE, TAWNY B; CLYDE, OH; CLYDE HS; (SO); Ctznshp Aw; Hnr Roll; Otst Ac Ach Awd; Chrch Yth Grp; DARE; Tchrs Aide; Bnd; Mch Bnd; Pep Bnd

OSTER, YOLANDA; LEBANON, OH; LEBANON HS; (SR); Hnr Roll; WWAHSS; ArtClub; Chrch Yth Grp; Emplmnt; FBLA; SADD; Tchrs Aide; Tennis (V); Track (L); Interior Design; Kent State U

OSTRONISKY, JENNIFER; CANAL FULTON, OH; NORTHWEST HS; (FR); Hnr Roll; Comm Volntr; Chrch Yth Grp; Bskball (J); Sftball (J); Teacher

OSWALD, COREY V; MONROE, OH; LAKOTA EAST HS; (SO); Hi Hnr Roll; Hnr Roll; Otst Ac Ach Awd; St of Mnth; German Clb; Engineering

OU, GUANQING G; BEAVERCREEK, OH; BEAVERCREEK HS; (SO); Hi Hnr Roll; Hnr Roll; WWAHSS; Comm Volntr; Hosp Aide; Dbte Team; Mth Clb/Tm; MuAlphaTh; NtlFrnscLg; P to P St Amb Prg; Spch Team; Chr; Orch; Bdmtn; All-State Musician; Runner-Up Iowa High School Forensic League Competition; Astrophysics; Biochemical Engineering; Princeton U; Dartmouth U

OWENS, BRIANA; VAN WERT, OH; LINCOLNVIEW SCH; (JR); Hi Hnr Roll; MVP; St of Mnth; WWAHSS; Peer Tut/Med; Chrch Yth Grp; Pep Squd; Prom Com; Sci Clb; Tchrs Aide; French Clb; Bnd; Mch Bnd; Pep Bnd; Bskball (V C); Golf (V C); Sftball (V); Cl Off (T)

OWENS, DEANNA; CINCINNATI, OH; PRINCETON HS; (JR); Hnr Roll; MVP; Nat Hon Sy; Otst Ac Ach Awd; Perf Att; WWAHSS; Emplmnt; NYLC; Prom Com; Orch; Chrldg (V CL); Cl Off (T); Stu Cncl (T); CR (R); Pit Orchestra; Morning School Announcements Anchor; Pre-Medicine; Bio-Chemistry; Ohio U-Athens; Hampton U

OWENS, DENISE; CLEVELAND, OH; SOUTH HS; (SO); Ctznshp Aw; Nat Mrt LOC; Perf Att; WWAHSS; Comm Volntr; Chrch Yth Grp; Drma Clb; FCCLA; Mth Clb/Tm; Vsity Clb; Ch Chr; SP/M/VS; Bskball (V); Sftball (V); Track (l); Vllyball (c v); Doctor; Sports Management; Akron State U; Duke U

OYER, MALACHI; CIRCLEVILLE, OH; CIRCLEVILLE HS; (FR); Hnr Roll; Perf Att; Pres Ac Ftns Aw; Comm Volntr; Chrch Yth Grp; Key Club; Bnd; Swmg (V CL); State Geography Bee Participant

OYER, OBADIAH J; CIRCLEVILLE, OH; CIRCLEVILLE HS; (JR); Hnr Roll; Nat Hon Sy; Perf Att; Comm Volntr; Chrch Yth Grp; Emplmnt; HO'Br Yth Ldrshp; Key Club; Mth Clb/Tm; Pep Bnd; Sccr (VJCL); Track (VJ L); Stu Cncl (R); Computer Engineering; Business Management

OZANICH, LAUREN; WARREN, OH; CHAMPION HS; (JR); Hnr Roll; Nat Hon Sy; St of Mnth; Chrch Yth Grp; Key Club; Off Aide; Pep Squd; Tchrs Aide; Bnd; Mch Bnd; Pep Bnd; Chrldg (JC); Skiing (V); Track (V); Key Club Secretary; Journalism; Ohio State U

PACANOVSKY, AARON; LAKEWOOD, OH; LAKEWOOD HS; (JR); Hi Hnr Roll; Hnr Roll; Nat Hon Sy; Sci Fairs; Comm Volntr; Emplmnt; Key Club; Mod UN; German Clb; Ski Club; Biology; Business Administration; Defiance College; Heidelberg College

PACIFICO, CHRIS; BRIDGEPORT, OH; BRIDGEPORT HS; (SO); Hnr Roll; Comm Volntr; Spanish Clb; Track (V); Wt Lftg; Treasurer of Spanish Club; Lawyer; Computer Engineering; Belmont Technical College; Ohio U Eastern

PAINTER, LAUREN; MALVERN, OH; MALVERN HS; (JR); Ctznshp Aw; Hnr Roll; WWAHSS; Comm Volntr; Emplmnt; Lib Aide; Off Aide; Prom Com; Tchrs Aide; Chrldg (VJ L); Stu Cncl; CR (T); Yrbk (E, P); Nursing; Kent State U; Walsh U

PALLANTE, JESSICA K; NILES, OH; NILES MC KINLEY HS; (JR); Hnr Roll; Nat Hon Sy; Comm Volntr; ArtClub; Key Club; French Clb; Bskball (V L); Sccr (V L); District Honors in Soccer; Conference Honor's in Basketball; Ohio State U; Youngstown State

PALLANTE, KRISTINA; NILES, OH; MC KINLEY HS; (FR); Hnr Roll; Pres Sch; Sci Fairs; St of Mnth; Hosp Aide; FTA; Italian Clb; Bskball (J); Vllyball (J); Nursing; Medicine; Kent State U; Youngstown State U

PALMER, ASHLEY; MASSILLON, OH; JACKSON HS; (JR); Hnr Roll; Sci Fairs; WWAHSS; Comm Volntr; Hab For Humty Volntr; Red Cr Aide; Chrch Yth Grp; Emplmnt; FCCLA; Key Club; Off Aide; Pep Squd; Scouts; SADD; Ch Chr; CR (P); Certified in Professional Modeling; Certified in Etiquette; Pre-Med; Pre-Law; U of Manchester; Ohio State U

PANJABI, SALONI; AURORA, OH; AURORA HS; (SO); Ctznshp Aw; Hi Hnr Roll; Hnr Roll; Perf Att; St of Mnth; WWAHSS; Comm Volntr; Peer Tut/Med; DARE; Key Club; Lib Aide; Mth Clb/Tm; P to P St Amb Prg; Quiz Bowl; Tmpl Yth Grp; Spanish Clb; Bnd; Dnce; Mch Bnd; Pep Bnd; Bskball (J); Scr Kpr; Skiing (J); Sccr (J); Tennis (J L); Cl Off (S); Stu Cncl (R); CR (S); Black Belt in Tae Kwon Do; Used To Be Beauty Pageant; Neurology; Cardiology; Stanford U; Carnegie-Mellon U

PANTELIS, CASSANDRA L; VIENNA, OH; MC KINLEY HS; (FR); Hi Hnr Roll; Perf Att; Sci Fairs; St of Mnth; WWAHSS; Chrch Yth Grp; Emplmnt; Italian Clb; Bnd; Jzz Bnd; Mch Bnd; Chrldg (J); Who's Who Among Americas Middle School Students; NEOUCOM

PAPA, AMANDA; CLEVELAND, OH; MAGNIFICAT HS; (SO); Hi Hnr Roll; Hnr Roll; Comm Volntr; Chrch Yth Grp; Mth Clb/Tm; Mod UN; MuAlphaTh; Chr; Ch Chr; Dnce; SP/M/VS; CR (R); Law; Psychology; Northwestern U

PAPARIZOS, IRENE C; WILLOUGHBY, OH; WILLOUGHBY SOUTH HS; (JR); Hi Hnr Roll; Nat Hon Sy; St of Mnth; WWAHSS; Yth Ldrshp Prog; Comm Volntr; Chrch Yth Grp; Key Club; Tchrs Aide; Greek Clb; Bnd; Mch Bnd; Principal's List; Education

PAPIO, ANGELINA; DAYTON, OH; BEAVERCREEK HS; (SO); Hnr Roll; Bnd; Dedicated Individuals Rebuilding Tomorrow Today; Veterinarian; Ohio State U; Wright State

PAPPAS, JESSICA; OREGON, OH; CLAY HS; (JR); Hnr Roll; WWAHSS; ArtClub; BPA; Chrch Yth Grp; Emplmnt; Key Club; Quill & Scroll; Sftball (J); Track (V L); Vllyball (VJ); Cl Off (R); Stu Cncl (S); CR (R); Yrbk (E); Visual Communication; Graphic Interior Design; Ohio State U; Kent State

PARKER, BETHANY; SAINT PARIS, OH; TECUMSEH HS; (FR); Hnr Roll; Peer Tut/Med; Ntl FFA; CR (R); The Stars Mentoring Program

PARKER, MATTHEW L; DELAWARE, OH; RUTHERFORD B HAYES HS; (FR); Hnr Roll; MVP; Perf Att; Sci Fairs; St of Mnth; Comm Volntr; DARE; Scouts; Golf (J); Swmg (V L); Member Boy Scouts of America; Member Church Youth Group; Radiology / Medicine; Engineering; Ohio Wesleyan U; Miami U Ohio

PARKER, NOEL A; EUCLID, OH; EUCLID HS; (JR); Comm Volntr; Tchrs Aide; Medical School; Nursing; Tri C (Cuyahoga Comm College); Lakeland Community College

PARKER, TEANNA M; TOLEDO, OH; SCOTT HS; (SO); Ctznshp Aw; Hnr Roll; Perf Att; Spanish Clb; Chrldg (JC); Scr Kpr (J); Sftball (J); Management; Own A Business; U of Toledo; U of Bowling Green

PARKINSON, MELISSA; CINCINNATI, OH; MC ANLEY HS; (JR); Hi Hnr Roll; Hnr Roll; Comm Volntr; Spec Olymp Vol; ArtClub; Chrch Yth Grp; Jr Cls League; Key Club; Latin Clb; National Latin Honor Society; Interior Design; U of Cincinnati DAAP

PARKS, RYAN J; DAYTON, OH; (JR); Hnr Roll; Nat Ldrshp Svc; WWAHSS; Comm Volntr; Bnd; SP/M/VS; Wt Lftg; Bowling; Boxing; Business Entrepreneurship; Architectural Engineer; Washington State; U of Cincinnati

PARSONS, BUBBA; HAMMONDSVILLE, OH; ECOT; (SO); Hnr Roll; Perf Att; St of Mnth; Chrch Yth Grp; Scouts; Tchrs Aide; President of Farm Bureau Group; Youngstown State U; Kent State U

PARTHEMORE, ADAM; LAKEVIEW, OH; INDIAN LAKE HS; (FR); Hnr Roll; ArtClub; Chr; PhD; Michigan U

PATEL, MARGI; ASHTABULA, OH; EDGEWOOD HS; (SO); Ctznshp Aw; Hnr Roll; Perf Att; Sci Fairs; DARE; Home Arts Club (Cooking Club); Most Improved Student; Nursing; Pharmacy, Pre-Med; Case Western Reserve U; Cleveland State U

PATEL, NILAM M; GALLIPOLIS, OH; GALLIA AC; (SO); Hi Hnr Roll; Sci/Math Olympn; WWAHSS; Emplmnt; HO'Br Yth Ldrshp; Key Club; P to P St Amb Prg; Yrbk (E); Ohio State U; Marshall U

PATEL, SILKI; STRONGSVILLE, OH; STRONGSVILLE HS; (SO); Hi Hnr Roll; Hnr Roll; Otst Ac Ach Awd; Perf Att; Comm Volntr; Emplmnt; Fr of Library; Key Club; Spanish Clb; Stu Cncl (R); Asian-American Cultural Club; Law; Psychology; Northwestern U; Case Western Reserve

PATEL, SUNIL; CINCINNATI, OH; ANDERSON HS; (JR); Hnr Roll; Emplmnt; Tchrs Aide; New Student Group; Business; Pharmacy; U of Cincinnati; Eastern Michigan

Pantelis, Cassandra L
Mc Kinley HS
Vienna, OH

Osborne, Leanne
Goshen HS
Milford, OH

Osad, Brittanie
Fairview HS
Cleveland, OH

National
Honor Roll
Spring 2005

Odom, Tameka L
Columbus Alt HS
Columbus, OH

Owens, Deanna
Princeton HS
Cincinnati, OH

Patel, Sunil
Anderson HS
Cincinnati, OH

PATIL, VINEET D; HILLIARD, OH; HILLIARD DAVIDSON HS; (JR); Hi Hnr Roll; Hnr Roll; Nat Hon Sy; Nat Mrt LOC; Sci Fairs; Sci/Math Olympn; Comm Volntr; Hosp Aide; Peer Tut/Med; Chess; Cmptr Clb; Key Club; Spanish Clb; Bnd; Sccr (J); Tennis (V); National Honor Society, Piano Recitals; Coordinator At Riverside Methodist Hospital; Biology (Major); Physician; Princeton U; U of Pennsylvania

PATRICK, SHANA; SHREVE, OH; TRIWAY HS; (JR); Hi Hnr Roll; Hnr Roll; Perf Att; Comm Volntr; Peer Tut/Med; DARE; Drma Clb; Emplmnt; French Clb; SP/M/VS; Business Management; Accounting; Wake Forest U; College of Wooster

PATTERSON, SARA; TOLEDO, OH; OTTAWA HILLS HS; (SO); Hnr Roll; Nat Hon Sy; Comm Volntr; DARE; French Clb; Dnce; Dance Team; Teaching Degree; English & Mathematics Major; Tulane U; Cincinnati U

PATTILLO, BRITTANY; CINCINNATI, OH; NORWOOD HS; (JR); Hnr Roll; Otst Ac Ach Awd; Perf Att; St of Mnth; WWAHSS; Key Club; Photog; Chr; Chrldg (V); Cr Ctry (V); Track (V); Photojournalism; Northern Kentucky; Florida State U

PATTON, AMBER D; RAVENNA, OH; FIELD HS; (JR); WWAHSS; Hab For Humty Volntr; Chrch Yth Grp; Emplmnt; Off Aide; Bskball (V L); PP Ftbl (J); Sftball (V); Stu Cncl (V); CR; Yrbk; USAA National Minority Leadership Award; Magazine Journalism; Newspaper Journalism; Ohio State U; Kent State U

PAUKOVICH, CHARLEIGH; WARREN, OH; CHAMPION HS; (FR); Hnr Roll; Otst Ac Ach Awd; Pres Ac Ftns Aw; USAA; WWAHSS; Comm Volntr; Red Cr Aide; Chrch Yth Grp; Emplmnt; Key Club; Scouts; Bskball (JC); Chrldg (J); GAA (J); Track (V L); Cl Off (T); Girl Scout Bronze / STAMP; Girl Scout Silver

PAUL, TIFFANY; ZANESVILLE, OH; BISHOP ROSECRANS HS; (JR); 4H Awd; Hnr Roll; MVP; Nat Hon Sy; Comm Volntr; Peer Tut/Med; 4-H; Chrch Yth Grp; Drma Clb; Emplmnt; Key Club; Pep Squd; Stg Cre; Bskball (J); Sftball (V L); Vllyball (V L); Key Club Treasurer; Muskingum County Grange; Biomedical Engineering; Chemical Engineering; Miami U; Ohio State U

PAULETTI, GUINEVERE; TIFFIN, OH; OLD FORT HS; (JR); Ctznshp Aw; Hnr Roll; Nat Hon Sy; Chrch Yth Grp; Emplmnt; Chr; Ch Chr; SP/M/VS; Fine Arts Singing Vocal Solo Rated Superior; Musical Theater; Theater; Bowling Green; Ohio State

PAULSEN, EMILY M; SPRINGFIELD, OH; SHAWNEE HS; (SR); 4H Awd; Fut Prb Slvr; Hi Hnr Roll; Nat Hon Sy; Nat Mrt Fin; Nat Stu Ath Day Aw; Pres Sch; St of Mnth; WWAHSS; Comm Volntr; 4-H; Off Aide; Pep Squd; Prom Com; SADD; Vsity Clb; Bnd; Chr; Swg Chr; Chrldg (V); PP Ftbl (V); Stu Cncl (R); CR (R); President of Varsity "S"; Food and Fashion Board; Marketing Major; MBA; Ashland U

PEABODY, AMANDA; SWANTON, OH; SWANTON HS; (FR); Hi Hnr Roll; MVP; Sci Fairs; St of Mnth; Comm Volntr; Peer Tut/Med; Emplmnt; Fr of Library; Quiz Bowl; Bnd; Mch Bnd; Pep Bnd; Stg Cre; Cr Ctry; Sccr (J); Track (V); Stu Cncl (V); Sch Ppr (R); Most Improved Player; Creative Writing Club; Marine Biology; Astrology; Ohio U; Ball State U

PEARSON, CARLESHA; TOLEDO, OH; WHITMER CAREER & TECH CTR; (JR); Hnr Roll; Nat Hon Sy; WWAHSS; Comm Volntr; Computer Tech; 4 Year College; U of Toledo; U of Cincinnati

PEDELA, ERIN; WEST CHESTER, OH; BISHOP FENWICK HS; (SO); Hi Hnr Roll; Comm Volntr; Key Club; French Clb; Chr; Vllyball (V)

PEFFER, CHRISTY; BROADVIEW HEIGHTS, OH; NORTH ROYALTON HS, (SR); Hnr Roll; Nat Hon Sy; WWAHSS; Comm Volntr; Peer Tut/Med; ArtClub; Drma Clb; Key Club; Lttrmn Clb; Lib Aide; Pep Squd; Vsity Clb; Latin Clb; Clr Grd; Dnce; SP/M/VS; Stg Cre; Cr Ctry (V L); Track (V); Lit Mag (E, R); Sch Ppr (R); Communications; Walsh U

PEGRAM, KATY; CINCINNATI, OH; COLERAIN HS; (SR); Hi Hnr Roll; Hnr Roll; Perf Att; Comm Volntr; Peer Tut/Med; Emplmnt; Key Club; Mus Clb; Off Aide; Bnd; Mch Bnd; Orch; Pep Bnd; Section Leader in Band; Letter Winner in Band; Music Education; Equestrian Science; Findley U; Northern Kentucky U

PEIGOWSKI, SAMANTHA; CORTLAND, OH; MATHEWS HS; (SO); Hnr Roll; WWAHSS; Red Cr Aide; Key Club; French Clb; Chr; SP/M/VS; Chrldg (V); Sccr (J); CR (S); Early Childhood Education; Muskingum U

PELINO, TONY; COLUMBUS, OH; ST FRANCIS DE SALES HS; (JR); Hnr Roll; Nat Hon Sy; Amnsty Intl; Peer Tut/Med; Mth Clb/Tm; Italian Clb; Ftball (J); Track (J); Wrstlg (J); Youth to Youth Advisory Board; Chemistry; Mathematics

PENDLETON, EMILY N; LINDSEY, OH; WOODMORE HS; (SO); 4H Awd; Hi Hnr Roll; Hnr Roll; MVP; Nat Hon Sy; Pres Ac Ftns Aw; St of Mnth; WWAHSS; Comm Volntr; Peer Tut/Med; 4-H; FTA; Key Club; Pep Squd; Prom Com; Tchrs Aide; Vsity Clb; French Clb; Bnd; Flg Crps; Mch Bnd; Pep Bnd; Track (V CL); Vllyball (V L); Cl Off (S, T); CR (R); 2004 Div. III State Champion Discus 1st Place; 2004-Ranked 13th in Nation-Discus; Education; Architecture

PENNINGTON, AMY J; FAYETTE, OH; EVERGREEN HS; (SO); Ctznshp Aw; Hnr Roll; 4-H; Drma Clb; Quiz Bowl; Tchrs Aide; Bnd; Chr; Ch Chr; Jzz Bnd; Music Education; Marine Biology; U of Michigan; U of Miami

PEOPLES, NATASHA; DAYTON, OH; PATTERSON CAREER TECH CTR; (JR); Hnr Roll; Nat Hon Sy; Comm Volntr; Key Club; Sci Clb; Occupational Therapist; Dental Hygiene/Hygienist; Florida A & M U; Ohio State U

PEPPERS JR, PIETRO; COLUMBUS, OH; BROOKHAVEN HS; (SO); Ctznshp Aw; Hnr Roll; Perf Att; St of Mnth; Comm Volntr; Peer Tut/Med; Chrch Yth Grp; DARE; Lib Aide; Ice Hky (J); Altar Server; Football & Baseball; Movie Star; Lawyer; Ohio State U; Miami U

PEREZ, CHRISTIAN; CLEVELAND, OH; LINCOLN-WEST HS; (FR); Hi Hnr Roll; Hnr Roll; Bsball (V); Ftball (J); Sccr (V); Wrstlg (V); Mechanical Engineer; Automotive Engineer; Kent State U; Cleveland State U

PEREZ, CHRISTOPHER V; WESTERVILLE, OH; NEW ALBANY HS; (SO); Chrch Yth Grp; DARE; Emplmnt; P to P St Amb Prg; Chr; Ftball (V L); Track (V L); Wt Lftg; Wrstlg (J); Stu Cncl (R); CR (R); History; Physics; Purdue U; U of Notre Dame

PERKINS, CHRISTINA; MEDINA, OH; MEDINA HS; (JR); Hnr Roll; Nat Hon Sy; WWAHSS; Comm Volntr; Chrch Yth Grp; Drma Clb; Emplmnt; FCA; JSA; Key Club; Prom Com; Spanish Clb; Ch Chr; SP/M/VS; Swmg (L); Track (J); Stu Cncl (P); Girls Leaders Club; Spanish Club Treasurer; Psychology; Abilene Christian U; U of Texas

PERKINS, LESLIE R; MARYSVILLE, OH; MARYSVILLE HS; (SR); Ctznshp Aw; Hnr Roll; Perf Att; St of Mnth; Peer Tut/Med; Emplmnt; Tchrs Aide; Bnd; Mch Bnd; Pep Bnd; Elementary Education; Ohio State U Marion

PERRUCI, CAROLINE A; MARIETTA, OH; ECOT; (SO); Hi Hnr Roll; Otst Ac Ach Awd; Sci/Math Olympn; WWAHSS; Comm Volntr; Chrch Yth Grp; Civil Air Pat; Mth Clb/Tm; Bnd; Ch Chr; Mch Bnd; Pep Bnd; Track (J); Secretary of National Junior Honor Society; Presidential Physical Fitness Award; Pilot/Aviation; NASA Scientist; Embry-Riddle Aeronautical U; U of Texas in Austin

PERRY, JOSHUA; ALEXANDRIA, OH; LICKING CTY JOINT VOC SCH; (SR); ArtClub; Ftball; Skiing; Track; CR (R); 3rd Place in Architecture At the JVS; First Junior Ever to Take Engineering; Masters in Mechanical Engineering; Lincoln Tech; Hocking College

PERRY, MARK; DOYLESTOWN, OH; CHIPPEWA HS; (FR); Hnr Roll; Otst Ac Ach Awd; Sci Fairs; St of Mnth; Peer Tut/Med; Chrch Yth Grp; Bsball (V); Bskball; Ftball (V); Stu Cncl (R); CR (R); Two Sportsmanship Awards; Doctor of Sports Medicine; Orthodontist; Ohio State U; U of Texas

PERRY, STEPHANIE; SPRINGFIELD, OH; SPRINGFIELD NORTH HS; (SO); Hnr Roll; Clr Grd; Dnce; Concert Choir; Merit Roll; English; Wittenberg U; Ohio State U

PETERS, BRITNEY; WESTERVILLE, OH; WESTERVILLE NORTH HS; (SR); Hi Hnr Roll; Hnr Roll; Nat Hon Sy; Otst Ac Ach Awd; Perf Att; WWAHSS; Comm Volntr; Red Cr Aide; DARE; Emplmnt; Key Club; Tennis (VLC); Treasurer of National Honor Society; Accounting; Miami U, Oxford, Ohio

PETERS, MICHAEL; COLUMBUS, OH; WALNUT RIDGE HS; (FR); Chrch Yth Grp

PETERSON, JOVANNA A; CINCINNATI, OH; HYDE PARK SCH; MS; Ctznshp Aw; Hi Hnr Roll; Hnr Roll; Otst Ac Ach Awd; Chrch Yth Grp; Drl Tm; Chrldg (C); Sccr (J); Stu Cncl; Yrbk; Treasurer of Church Virtuous Womens-Ministry; Spelman College Atlanta, Georgia

PETIYA, ASHLEY L; WARREN, OH; CHAMPION HS; (SO); Hnr Roll; WWAHSS; Comm Volntr; Key Club; Destination Imagination; Champion Teen Care; Air Traffic Control; Photography; Ohio State U; Kent State U

PETRACCA, CHELSIE; DOVER, OH; DOVER HS; (SO); Hnr Roll; Otst Ac Ach Awd; Perf Att; Pres Sch; Emplmnt; Key Club; Chr; Stg Cre; Bowling League - 7 Years; Plays Guitar; X-Ray Tech

PETRILLI, JEFFERY; NILES, OH; MC KINLEY HS; (FR); Hi Hnr Roll; St of Mnth; Peer Tut/Med; Off Aide; SADD; Italian Clb; Ftball (C); Pharmacist; Radiologist; Ohio U; Akron U

PETTY, CHELSEA N; WEST LIBERTY, OH; WEST LIBERTY SALEM HS; (SO); Ctznshp Aw; Yth Ldrshp Prog; Off Aide; Prom Com; SADD; Tchrs Aide; SP/M/VS; Vllyball (J); Stu Cncl (R); Dental Hygienist; Advertising and Marketing; Ohio State U; Wright State U

PFEIFER, STEPHANIE; CARDINGTON, OH; MARION CATHOLIC HS; (SR); Hi Hnr Roll; Nat Hon Sy; WWAHSS; AL Aux Girls; Emplmnt; Key Club; French Clb; Bskball (V CL); Sftball (V L); Track (V L); Vllyball (V CL); 4 Yr Piano Student; Homecoming Queen; Criminal Justice; Ohio Dominican U; U of Toledo

PFISTER, JESSICA M; MENTOR, OH; MENTOR HS; (SR); Ctznshp Aw; Hi Hnr Roll; Hnr Roll; MVP; Nat Hon Sy; Comm Volntr; Peer Tut/Med; Chrch Yth Grp; Emplmnt; FBLA; Svce Clb; Tchrs Aide; Bskball (J); Sftball (V CL); Stu Cncl (P); Yrbk (E, P); Homecoming Queen of Senior Class; Speech and Language Pathology; Spanish; Butler U

PFOFF, JENNIFER; GROVE CITY, OH; GROVE CITY HS; (FR); Hi Hnr Roll; Hnr Roll; ArtClub; Chrch Yth Grp; ROTC; Dnce; Fashion Designing; Ohio State; Columbus College of Art and Design

PFUND, CHRISTOPHER; SWANTON, OH; EVERGREEN HS; (SO); Ctznshp Aw; Hi Hnr Roll; Comm Volntr; FCA; Lttrmn Clb; SADD; Vsity Clb; Bsball (V L); Bskball (V L); Ftball (V CL); Scr Kpr; Track (V L); Vsy Clb (V); Wt Lftg (V C); Yrbk (R); National Junior Honor Society; Engineering; Finance; U of Michigan; U of Florida

PHAM, DAN; CLEVELAND, OH; JOHN MARSHALL HS; (SO); Hnr Roll; Otst Ac Ach Awd; Perf Att; Peer Tut/Med; Mth Clb/Tm; Fncg (V); Stu Cncl (R); Ninth Grade Academic Honorary; Culinary Arts; Graphic Design; Ohio State U; The Art Institute of Philadelphia

PHILLIPS, ALTON; CAREY, OH; CAREY SCH; (FR); Hnr Roll; Nat Hon Sy; Pres Sch; Comm Volntr; Chrch Yth Grp; Spanish Clb; Bnd; Pep Bnd; Bskball (J); Ftball (J); Wt Lftg (J); Cl Off (P); K of C Religion Award; Orthopedic Surgeon; The Ohio State U; U of Cincinnati

PHILLIPS, ASHLEY; WHEELERSBURG, OH; SCIOTOVILLE CMTY EAST HS; (SR); Hnr Roll; WWAHSS; Yth Ldrshp Prog; Hosp Aide; Red Cr Aide; Chrch Yth Grp; Chr; Ch Chr; SP/M/VS; Stg Cre; Obstetrician / Gynecology; Master's Degree; Shawnee State U; Ohio State U Southern

PHILLIPS, BRITNEY K; TOLEDO, OH; MAUMEE HS; (JR); Hnr Roll; WWAHSS; Chrch Yth Grp; DARE; Chr; Spectrum Children's Teacher's Aide; Teacher; U of Toledo; Bowling Green State U

PHILLIPS, JORDAN A; LIMA, OH; LIMA SR HS; (FR); Hnr Roll; St of Mnth; Chrch Yth Grp; DARE; Emplmnt; Bskball (J); Religion; Oral Roberts U; Ashland U

PHILLIPS, KAELY; LEBANON, OH; LEBANON HS; (FR); 4H Awd; Hnr Roll; St of Mnth; Comm Volntr; Hab For Humty Volntr; 4-H; Chrch Yth Grp; DARE; FBLA; Tchrs Aide; Bskball (CL); Vllyball (JCL); Child Psychology; Journalism; Ohio State U; U of Southern California

PHILLIPS, MOLLY; LIMA, OH; PERRY HS; (SO); Hi Hnr Roll; Nat Hon Sy; Otst Ac Ach Awd; St of Mnth; Peer Tut/Med; 4-H; Chrch Yth Grp; Emplmnt; Vsity Clb; Bskball (V); Vsy Clb (V); Vllyball (V); Accounting; Veterinarian

PHILLIPS JR, ROBERT; LIMA, OH; LIMA SR HS; (SR); Hnr Roll; WWAHSS; Chrch Yth Grp; DARE; Emplmnt; SADD; Bsball (J); Bskball (V); Ftball (J); Computer Engineering; Indiana Institute of Technology

PHILLIS, MEGAN L; SALEM, OH; UNITED LOCAL HS; (JR); Hi Hnr Roll; Nat Hon Sy; WWAHSS; Peer Tut/Med; Chrch Yth Grp; FCCLA; Key Club; Off Aide; Prom Com; PP Ftbl (C); Sftball (J); Vllyball (V); Cl Off (P); Yrbk (E, P); Ruriteens; Elementary Education K-3; Kent State; Thiel

PHONCHONE, CHANTHONG; CAREY, OH; CAREY SCH; (SR); Hnr Roll; WWAHSS; Comm Volntr; ArtClub; Chrch Yth Grp; DECA; Drma Clb; Lib Aide; Prom Com; SADD; Spanish Clb; Chr; National Technical Honor Society; National Junior Honor Society / National Honor Award; Office Information; Medical Record Administration; Owens Community College; U of Northwestern Ohio

PIASER, RIKKI; ASHTABULA, OH; WEST JHS; (MS); Hnr Roll; Bnd; Music

PIAZZA, BRIAN M; GRAFTON, OH; KEYSTONE HS; (FR); Hnr Roll; Sci Fairs; Comm Volntr; DARE; Scouts; Bnd; Chr; Jzz Bnd; Mch Bnd; Sccr (V); Teaching; Music; Bowling Green State U; Ashland U

PICCIRILLO, ALESCIA N; CLEVELAND, OH; MAYFIELD HS; (SR); Hnr Roll; Nat Hon Sy; Sci Fairs; Peer Tut/Med; DARE; Chr; Scr Kpr; Cl Off (R); Yrbk; Athletic Trainer; Special Education; Early Childhood; Akron; Bowling Green

PICKENS, JUSTIN D; COLUMBUS, OH; AFRICENTRIC EARLY COLLEGE HS; (SO); Ctznshp Aw; Hi Hnr Roll; Hnr Roll; Perf Att; Comm Volntr; Chrch Yth Grp; P to P St Amb Prg; Bnd; Bskball (J); Ftball (V); Track (V); Wt Lftg (V); CR (R); Qualified To Bowl In The State of Ohio Family Doubles Tournament; Pediatrician; Management; Ohio State U; Michigan U

PICKRELL, ASHTON; OREGONIA, OH; CLINTON-MASSIE SCH; (FR); Hnr Roll; Comm Volntr; Chess; Mar Art; Ohio U Athens

PIECHOWSKI, JENNIFER; STRONGSVILLE, OH; STRONGSVILLE HS; (JR); Hnr Roll; Nat Hon Sy; WWAHSS; Yth Ldrshp Prog; Comm Volntr; Chrch Yth Grp; DARE; Emplmnt; Skiing; Sftball (L); Campaign Manager for Strongsville's Successful Fire/Paramedic Levy; Assisted Mayor Perciak in His 2003 Mayoral Campaign; Pre-Medicine; Ohio State U; U of Cincinnati

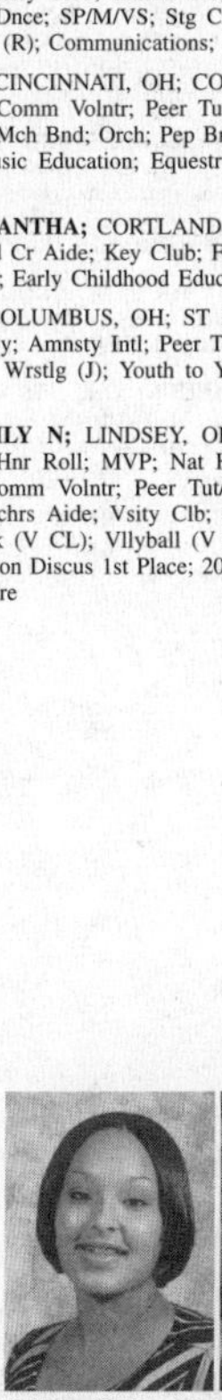
Phillips, Britney K
Maumee HS
Toledo, OH

Pfister, Jessica M
Mentor HS
Mentor, OH

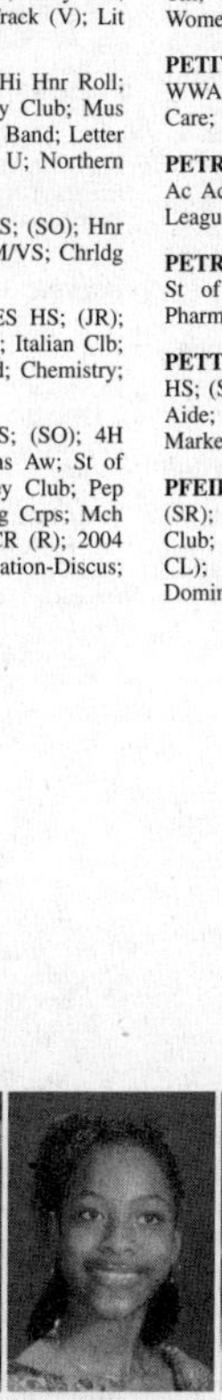
Peterson, Jovanna A
Hyde Park Sch
Cincinnati, OH

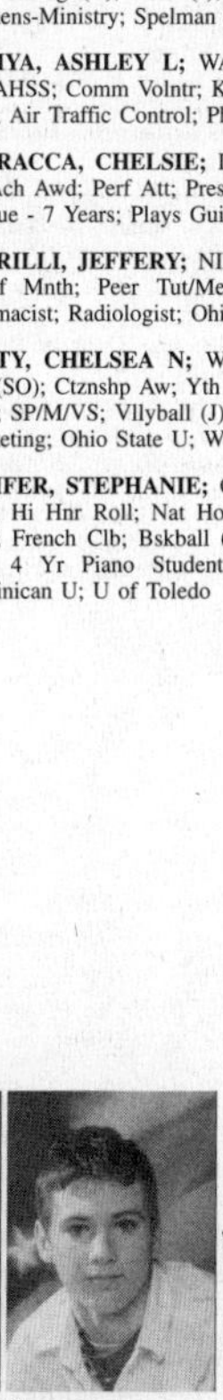
Perry, Joshua
Licking Cty Joint Voc Sch
Alexandria, OH

National
Honor Roll
Spring 2005

Pattillo, Brittany
Norwood HS
Cincinnati, OH

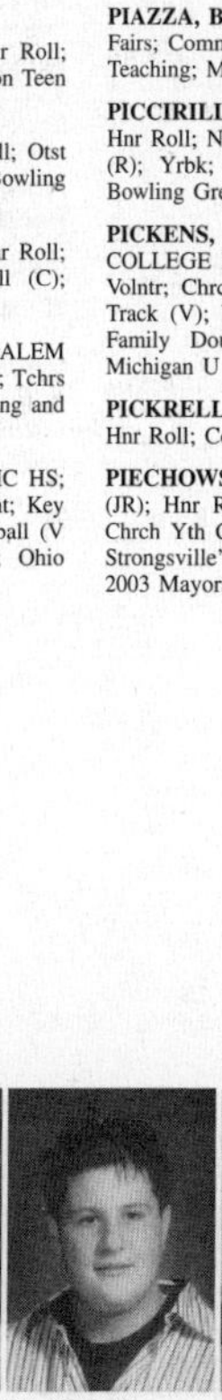
Petrilli, Jeffery
Mc Kinley HS
Niles, OH

Pfoff, Jennifer
Grove City HS
Grove City, OH

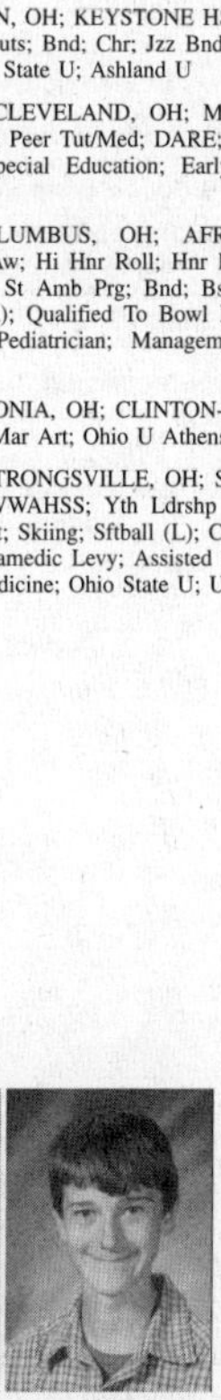
Piazza, Brian M
Keystone HS
Grafton, OH

PILLIOD, AMBER; LIBERTY CTR, OH; LIBERTY CTR HS; (JR); 4H Awd; Hi Hnr Roll; Hnr Roll; St of Mnth; WWAHSS; 4-H; Chrch Yth Grp; Emplmnt; FCA; FBLA; SADD; Spanish Clb; Yrbk (R, P); Radiology; Medical Field; Arizona State U; Ohio State U

PINNICKS, CYNTHIA A; BRUNSWICK, OH; BRUNSWICK HS; (JR); Hnr Roll; Perf Att; Comm Volntr; Chrch Yth Grp; Drma Clb; Emplmnt; SP/M/VS; Stg Cre; Thespian Society; Outstanding Achievement Award Biology; Creative Writing; Biology; Kent State U

PINTADO, CHRISTINA; ROSSFORD, OH; ROSSFORD HS; (SO); Hi Hnr Roll; Hnr Roll; Perf Att; Pres Ac Ftns Aw; St of Mnth; Art Honors; Poster Contest Awards

PIRTLE, DWIGHT; LIMA, OH; LIMA SR HS; (JR); Hnr Roll; Perf Att; Yth Ldrshp Prog; Peer Tut/Med; Chrch Yth Grp; DECA; Emplmnt; Prom Com; Spanish Clb; Track; Adv Cncl (R); Cl Off (V); Stu Cncl (V); CR (R); DECA State Quatnet; Pharmaceutical Representative; U of Cincinnati; Duke U; Boise State U

PITT, KRISTINE; PICKERINGTON, OH; PICKERINGTON HS NORTH; (SO); Hi Hnr Roll; Comm Volntr; Drma Clb; Chr; Ice Sktg; Figure Skating; Piano; HS Literature Teacher / HS Education; Figure Skating Instructor; Ohio U; Bowling Green U

PITTMAN, SETH T; NORTH LAWRENCE, OH; TUSLAW JR/SR HS; (FR); Hnr Roll; St of Mnth; WWAHSS; Chrch Yth Grp; Civil Air Pat; FCA; Spanish Clb; Acpl Chr; Swg Chr; Bskball (VJ); Ftball (VJ); Wt Lftg (VJ)

PITTS, SHARINTA L; CLEVELAND, OH; SHAW HS; (SR); Hnr Roll; Perf Att; WWAHSS; Comm Volntr; Chrch Yth Grp; Emplmnt; Prom Com; Ch Chr; Stu Cncl (S, T); Accounting; Ohio U; Hampton U

PIZZO, LUCIA G; LAKEWOOD, OH; LAKEWOOD HS; (SR); Hnr Roll; Kwnis Aw; Nat Hon Sy; Otst Ac Ach Awd; Perf Att; Pres Sch; WWAHSS; Yth Ldrshp Prog; Comm Volntr; Hosp Aide; Peer Tut/Med; Drma Clb; Emplmnt; Jr Cls League; Key Club; German Clb; Bnd; Chr; Mch Bnd; Stg Cre; Gmnstcs (V L); Swmg (J); Tennis (V CL); Stu Cncl; Major / English; Master's Degree; Kenyon College - Accepted / Attending

PLATT, AMANDA; UNIONTOWN, OH; GREEN HS; (SR); Hnr Roll; Nat Hon Sy; Comm Volntr; Chrch Yth Grp; Vsity Clb; Chrldg (VJ L); Yrbk (R); Ohio U

PLATT, BETHANY; GAHANNA, OH; EVANGEL CHRISTIAN AC; (SO); Hi Hnr Roll; Yth Ldrshp Prog; Chrch Yth Grp; Emplmnt; FCA; Bskball (V); Otterbein College; Cedarville U

POEPPELMAN, CINDY; WAPAKONETA, OH; WAPAKONETA HS; (SO); Hi Hnr Roll; Mus Clb; Svce Clb; Spanish Clb; Chr; Dnce; SP/M/VS; Swg Chr; Bskball (J); Ohio State U; Bowling Green State U

POMEROY, SARAH; WORTHINGTON, OH; BISHOP WATTERSON HS; (FR); Hnr Roll; Otst Ac Ach Awd; Sci Fairs; Sci/Math Olympn; St of Mnth; DARE; Drma Clb; Mus Clb; Scouts; Spch Team; Bnd; Jzz Bnd; Mch Bnd; Stg Cre; Skiing (VJ); Stu Cncl (R); CR (R); $1,250 of Academic and Band Scholarship; 4th Place at Regional Writing Team Competition; Education / Teaching; Law / Politics; Michigan State U; Bowling Green State U

PONTI, DOMINIQUE; PAINESVILLE, OH; RIVERSIDE; (FR); Hi Hnr Roll; Perf Att; Drma Clb; Key Club; Off Aide; French Clb; Bnd; Sccr (V L); Stu Cncl (R); SAFE Students Acting for the Environment; AFS; Architectural Degree; Doctor

PONTIOUS, EMILY; CIRCLEVILLE, OH; CIRCLEVILLE HS; (JR); Hnr Roll; St of Mnth; Key Club; Svce Clb; Chr; SP/M/VS; Bskball (V); Track (V); Vllyball (V); Stu Cncl (R); Elementary Education; Ohio U Lancaster

PONZI, CAROLYN L; SOUTHINGTON, OH; SOUTHINGTON LOCAL SCH; (FR); Ctznshp Aw; Hi Hnr Roll; Hnr Roll; Otst Ac Ach Awd; St of Mnth; WWAHSS; Comm Volntr; Hosp Aide; Peer Tut/Med; Emplmnt; Ntl Beta Clb; P to P St Amb Prg; Scouts; Svce Clb; Cr Ctry (V L); Skiing; Track (V L); Vllyball (V L); Cl Off (P); CR (P); Silver Award-Girl Scouts; Pres Award Gold; Ad Art; Medical Field; Brigham Young; Savannah Art

POON, JENNIFER S; CINCINNATI, OH; INDIAN HILL HS; (SR); F Lan Hn Soc; Hi Hnr Roll; Hnr Roll; Nat Hon Sy; Perf Att; Pres Ac Ftns Aw; WWAHSS; Comm Volntr; Chrch Yth Grp; Jr Cls League; Latin Clb; Orch; SP/M/VS; Vllyball (VJCL); Community Service-RASKALS (Random Acts of Simple Kindness Affecting Local Srs.); Exploratory Studies; U of Cincinnati

POORMAN, KRISTEN; DOVER, OH; DOVER HS; (FR); Hnr Roll; Otst Ac Ach Awd; Perf Att; Sci Fairs; St of Mnth; WWAHSS; Comm Volntr; Peer Tut/Med; ArtClub; Chrch Yth Grp; Jr Ach; Key Club; Mus Clb; Sci Clb; French Clb; Bnd; Mch Bnd; Pep Bnd; Sccr (J); Swmg (J); CR (T); Concert Band; Law; Engineering; Harvard U; Milwaukee School of Engineering

POPE, DIJANAE R; LEBANON, OH; LEBANON HS; (FR); Hnr Roll; Comm Volntr; ROTC; Tae Kwon Do - Senior-Brown Belt - YMCA; Law Enforcement; Miami U; Ohio State

POPIK, AMY F; EASTLAKE, OH; WILLOUGHBY SOUTH HS; (FR); Otst Ac Ach Awd; WWAHSS; Key Club; Mus Clb; Spanish Clb; Chr; Clr Grd; Flg Crps; Mch Bnd; Performing Chorus; Architecture/Interior Design; Music Education/Singing

PORTER, CATE; DOVER, OH; DOVER HS; (SO); Hi Hnr Roll; WWAHSS; Comm Volntr; Emplmnt; Key Club; Sch Ppr (R); Physical Therapy; Slippery Rock U

PORTER, EDWARD G; CLEVELAND, OH; COLLINWOOD HS; (FR); Hnr Roll; Otst Ac Ach Awd; Art; Cleveland State; Cuyahoga Community College

PORTIS, FRANCHERE M; CLEVELAND, OH; MARTIN LUTHER KING HS; MS; Ctznshp Aw; Hnr Roll; Otst Ac Ach Awd; Perf Att; Sci Fairs; St of Mnth; DARE; Orch; Track (J); Pediatrician; Florida State

POSADA, ANDRES; CHILLICOTHE, OH; CHILLICOTHE HS; (SR); Sccr (V); Air Force; Police Officer

POSTOER, ANASTASIA P; COLUMBUS, OH; DUBLIN COFFMAN HS; (JR); MVP; Comm Volntr; Peer Tut/Med; ArtClub; Biology Clb; Chess; Chrch Yth Grp; DARE; Key Club; Latin Clb; Dnce; Fncg (V C); Lcrsse (J)

POWELL, ASHLEY M; CLEVELAND, OH; COLLINWOOD HS; (SO); Hnr Roll; Otst Ac Ach Awd; Perf Att; St of Mnth; Stu Cncl (R); Journalism; Performing Arts; Spelman College; U of Alabama

POWELL, CARLY A; AKRON, OH; GREEN HS; (JR); Nat Hon Sy; Perf Att; Pres Sch; Chr; Dnce; Track; Pianist; Guitar Player & Artist; Medical & Business; Art; Kent State U

POWELL, DARRELL M; COLUMBUS, OH; LINDEN-MC KINLEY HS; (FR); Hnr Roll; Nat Hon Sy; Otst Ac Ach Awd; Perf Att; ArtClub; DARE; Wdwrkg Clb; Bskball (V); Ftball (V); Cl Off (V); Business; Virginia Tech U; Auburn U

POWELL, LACEY; HAMILTON, OH; FAIRFIELD FRESHMAN HS; (FR); Hnr Roll; Nat Hon Sy; Perf Att; St of Mnth; Yth Ldrshp Prog; Comm Volntr; Peer Tut/Med; Chrch Yth Grp; ASL Clb; Orch; Greater Miami Youth Symphony; Honor's Orchestra; Occupational Therapy; Speech Therapy; Miami U in Oxford, OH; Kentucky U

POWERS, AMANDA; CINCINNATI, OH; MC AULEY HS; (SR); Hnr Roll; Comm Volntr; Drma Clb; Jr Cls League; Key Club; Svce Clb; French Clb; SP/M/VS; Anthropology; Ohio U

POWERS, STEPHANIE M; FARMERSVILLE, OH; VALLEY VIEW; (SR); Ctznshp Aw; Hi Hnr Roll; Kwnis Aw; MVP; Otst Ac Ach Awd; Perf Att; Pres Ac Ftns Aw; Pres Sch; Prom Com; Scouts; Tchrs Aide; Wdwrkg Clb; Dnce; Bskball (V L); Track (V L); Vllyball (V L); CR (R); Rae Burick Women in Sports; All-Miller Publishing Team-1st Team; Forensic Science; Nursing; Defiance College; Wright-State

POYNTON, BRIANNE K; MEDINA, OH; MEDINA SR HS; (SO); Ctznshp Aw; F Lan Hn Soc; Hi Hnr Roll; Otst Ac Ach Awd; Sci Fairs; St of Mnth; Comm Volntr; Peer Tut/Med; Chrch Yth Grp; Drma Clb; Emplmnt; Key Club; Off Aide; Latin Clb; Orch; SP/M/VS; Girls Leadership Club; Drug Prevention Awareness Teacher; Doctorate Degree in Medicine; Law; Notre Dame U; Ohio State U

PRANGE, ERICA; CUYAHOGA FALLS, OH; CUYAHOGA FALLS HS; (JR); Hi Hnr Roll; Nat Hon Sy; Perf Att; WWAHSS; Comm Volntr; Key Club; Lib Aide; Off Aide; Spanish Clb; Yrbk (R, P); Archaeology; Writing; The College of Wooster; Oberlin College

PREGIBON, LEANN; NILES, OH; NILES MC KINLEY HS; (JR); Hi Hnr Roll; Hnr Roll; Kwnis Aw; Nat Hon Sy; St of Mnth; WWAHSS; Emplmnt; Key Club; Off Aide; Svce Clb; Dnce; Chrldg (VJCL); PP Ftbl (J); Industrial Engineering; Ohio State U; Youngstown State U

PRENGER, KIMBERLY; CELINA, OH; MARION LOCAL HS; (JR); 4H Awd; Hnr Roll; 4-H; DARE; Bnd; Ch Chr; Mch Bnd; Marching Band - 3 Years of Superior Ratings at State; Nursing; The Community Hospital School of Nursing; Sinclair Community College

PRESSLEY, MEGHAN; SANDUSKY, OH; PERKINS HS; (JR); Yth Ldrshp Prog; Mod UN; SADD; Vsity Clb; Voc Ind Clb Am; Spanish Clb; Track (V L); Vice President-CBBS; Business Management; Ohio State U; U of Cincinnati

PRESUTTO, ASHLEY; LORAIN, OH; LORAIN SOUTHVIEW HS; (FR); Hnr Roll; Chrch Yth Grp; Bskball; Track (J); Pediatrician; Doctorate Degree; Ohio State U; Kent State U

PRICE, ALEX M; TIFFIN, OH; OLD FORT HS; (SO); All Am Sch; Ctznshp Aw; Hi Hnr Roll; Nat Hon Sy; Otst Ac Ach Awd; Perf Att; St of Mnth; Valdctrian; WWAHSS; Yth Ldrshp Prog; Comm Volntr; Peer Tut/Med; ArtClub; Emplmnt; Lib Aide; Mus Clb; NYLC; Quiz Bowl; Tchrs Aide; Vsity Clb; Bnd; Mch Bnd; Pep Bnd; Stg Cre; Cr Ctry (J L); Track (V L); Cl Off (R); Taking College Courses As a Sophomore; Indoor Track Participant; Master's and Doctorate Degree; Major in Surgery and Minor in Medicine; Ohio State U Medical College; Miami U Ohio

PRICE, EMILY L; LEBANON, OH; LEBANON HS; (SO); Hi Hnr Roll; Hnr Roll; Nat Hon Sy; Otst Ac Ach Awd; Sci Fairs; Sci/Math Olympn; WWAHSS; Comm Volntr; ArtClub; Biology Clb; Chrch Yth Grp; SADD; Chinese Clb; Ch Chr; Sccr (J); Track (V); Stu Cncl (R); CR (R); Regional Finals in Science Olympiad, Principal's Award; Award for Most Outstanding Freshmen; Plastic Surgeon; Medical Field; Johns Hopkins U; Harvard U

PRIEBE, KATHERINE; ROCKY RIVER, OH; (JR); F Lan Hn Soc; Hi Hnr Roll; Nat Hon Sy; Otst Ac Ach Awd; St of Mnth; Comm Volntr; DARE; Drma Clb; NtlFrnscLg; Scouts; SADD; Spanish Clb; Acpl Chr; Dnce; SP/M/VS; Swg Chr; Lit Mag (R)

PRIESTER, AMANDA; CHARDON, OH; RIVERSIDE HS; (SO); 4H Awd; Hnr Roll; Nat Mrt LOC; Perf Att; St of Mnth; Yth Ldrshp Prog; Comm Volntr; 4-H; ArtClub; Chrch Yth Grp; Emplmnt; Key Club; Lib Aide; Photog; SADD; Ch Chr; PP Ftbl (J); Scr Kpr (J); Sftball; Stu Cncl (R); CR (R); Yrbk (E); Art Shows and Ribbons; Fashion Design; Teaching

PRIMAVERA, KATELYN; HILLIARD, OH; HILLIARD DARBY HS; (JR); F Lan Hn Soc; Hi Hnr Roll; Nat Hon Sy; WWAHSS; Comm Volntr; Emplmnt; Key Club; Off Aide; Pep Squd; Tchrs Aide; French Clb; Chrldg (V L); Sch Ppr (E); National Honors Society; French Honors Society; Forensic Chemistry; Magazine Editing; Ohio U; West Virginia U

PRITCHARD, DERRIK; ZANESVILLE, OH; MAYSVILLE HS; (FR); Hi Hnr Roll; Otst Ac Ach Awd; WWAHSS; Comm Volntr; Key Club; Spanish Clb; Golf (J); Skiing; Track (J)

PROKOP, DANIEL M; CORTLAND, OH; MATHEWS HS; (FR); 4H Awd; F Lan Hn Soc; Hnr Roll; Sci Fairs; WWAHSS; 4-H; Drma Clb; Key Club; French Clb; Chr; SP/M/VS; Sccr (V L); Bowling; Physics; Chemistry; Carnegie Mellon; Mercyhurst U

PROTZMAN, ASHLEY C; GORDON, OH; ARCANUM HS; (JR); Hnr Roll; Perf Att; St of Mnth; Chrch Yth Grp; Emplmnt; FCA; SADD; Chr; Ch Chr; Sftball (J); Team Works Competition For Skills USA; 4 Year Apprenticeship - Masonry Program

PROVOST, MEGAN; NAVARRE, OH; FAIRLESS HS; (SO); Hnr Roll; Comm Volntr; 4-H; Key Club; French Clb; Bnd; Dnce; Mch Bnd; Model, 4-H; Modeling; Fashion Industry; Akron U; Kent State U

PRUITT, SARAH; CLINTON, OH; NORTHWEST HS; (SO); Hnr Roll; St of Mnth; Comm Volntr; Hosp Aide; Peer Tut/Med; Emplmnt; Off Aide; Spanish Clb; Volunteer for Arthritis Foundation; Animal Rescue Club; Early Childhood Education; Pediatrician; The College of Wooster; Baldwin Wallace

PUCKETT, JOY A; OTWAY, OH; NORTHWEST HS; (SO); Hi Hnr Roll; Nat Hon Sy; Perf Att; Pres Ac Ftns Aw; WWAHSS; Peer Tut/Med; Chrch Yth Grp; Bnd; Ch Chr; Jzz Bnd; Mch Bnd; Vllyball (V); Talented and Gifted Program; Church Quizzing Team; Occupational Therapy; Shawnee State U; Marshall U

PUCKETT, TRACIE; HILLSBORO, OH; HILLSBORO HS; (SO); Hi Hnr Roll; Hnr Roll; WWAHSS; Hosp Aide; Drma Clb; Off Aide; Bnd; Chr; SP/M/VS; Stg Cre; Education; Theater; Ohio State U

PUCKETT, WHITNEY C; SALINEVILLE, OH; SOUTHERN LOCAL HS; (JR); Hnr Roll; Nat Hon Sy; WWAHSS; Lttrmn Clb; Off Aide; Pep Squd; Prom Com; Tchrs Aide; Chrldg; Vllyball; Cl Off (S); Stu Cncl (S); CR (R); Yrbk; Would Like to Become a Nurse; Go to Hanna Mullens School of Nursing

PUGH, TIMOTHY T; FAIRBORN, OH; FAIRBORN HS; (SO); Ctznshp Aw; Hnr Roll; Nat Hon Sy; Otst Ac Ach Awd; Perf Att; Pres Sch; Sci Fairs; Yth Ldrshp Prog; Comm Volntr; Chrch Yth Grp; Emplmnt; P to P St Amb Prg; ROTC; Scouts; Orch; Cr Ctry (V); Sccr (J); Swmg (V); Track (V); Military Career Office Engineering; Air Force Academy; Wright State U

PULEO, SAGAN; BRUNSWICK HILLS, OH; BRUNSWICK HS; (JR); Hi Hnr Roll; Hnr Roll; Nat Hon Sy; Perf Att; Comm Volntr; Peer Tut/Med; Emplmnt; Key Club; P to P St Amb Prg; Prom Com; Svce Clb; French Clb; Dnce; Golf (VJ); Skiing (J); Sccr (J); VOFT; Athletic Trainer-Letterman; Forensic Psychology; Criminal Justice; Kent State U; Ohio State U

PULFER, ANN M; LIMA, OH; LIMA SR HS; (JR); Hi Hnr Roll; Red Cr Aide; Chrch Yth Grp; Emplmnt; Clb; Oceanography; English/Spanish Translator; U of Miami, Coral Gables, FL; Ohio State U

PUNKAR, KEVIN A; ASHTABULA, OH; STS JOHN AND PAUL CATHOLIC HS; (FR); Hi Hnr Roll; MVP; Otst Ac Ach Awd; Bskball (J); Cr Ctry (V L); Tennis (V L); Cl Off (T); US Marine Corps Scholastic Excellence Award

PURCELL, MOLLY; CTRBURG, OH; CTRBURG HS; (SR); Ctznshp Aw; Hnr Roll; Nat Hon Sy; Nat Mrt Fin; WWAHSS; Peer Tut/Med; Emplmnt; Quiz Bowl; Tchrs Aide; Spanish Clb; Chr; Cr Ctry (J L); Track (J L); Human Dietetics; Pre-Med; Ohio State U

Pugh, Timothy T
Fairborn HS
Fairborn, OH

Powers, Stephanie M
Valley View
Farmersville, OH

Powell, Carly A
Green HS
Akron, OH

Pontious, Emily
Circleville HS
Circleville, OH

Poorman, Kristen
Dover HS
Dover, OH

Pruitt, Sarah
Northwest HS
Clinton, OH

Pulfer, Ann M
Lima SR HS
Lima, OH

PYLES, ELISABETH; CEDARVILLE, OH; CEDAR CLIFF HS; (SR); Ctznshp Aw; Hi Hnr Roll; Hnr Roll; Nat Hon Sy; Otst Ac Ach Awd; Pres Sch; St of Mnth; US Army Sch Ath Aw; Valdctrian; WWAHSS; Chrch Yth Grp; Emplmnt; Key Club; Mod UN; Tchrs Aide; Chr; Bskball (V CL); PP Ftbl (V); Track (V L); Vllyball (V CL); Cl Off (V); Education; Business Management; Cedarville U

PYLES, JOANNA R; CEDARVILLE, OH; CEDARVILLE MHS; (SO); Hnr Roll; St of Mnth; WWAHSS; Chrch Yth Grp; Key Club; Chr; Ch Chr; SP/M/VS; Track (V L); Vllyball (V L); Class Representative for the Key Club; Nursing; Communications / Public Speaking; Cedarville U

QUANCE, JAMIE C; CINCINNATI, OH; WESTERN HILLS HS; (SR); F Lan Hn Soc; Hi Hnr Roll; Nat Hon Sy; Perf Att; Valdctrian; WWAHSS; Comm Volntr; Peer Tut/Med; DARE; Drma Clb; Emplmnt; HO'Br Yth Ldrshp; Jr Ach; Tchrs Aide; Spanish Clb; Bnd; Stu Cncl (S); CR (R); Sch Ppr (E); National Society of Collegiate Scholars; VFW Certificate of Recognition; Pure Mathematics/Sec. Education; Doctorate; Miami U-Oxford; U of Cincinnati

QUEENER, ISHIA; YOUNGSTOWN, OH; WOODROW WILSON HS; (JR); Peer Tut/Med; Emplmnt; Lib Aide; Ch Chr; Dnce; Drm Mjr; Bskball (J); Chrldg (J); Clark; Texas State

QUICKSALL, KRISTIN; DUBLIN, OH; DUBLIN COFFMAN HS; (JR); Hnr Roll; Nat Hon Sy; Otst Ac Ach Awd; Comm Volntr; Hab For Humty Volntr; Peer Tut/Med; Chrch Yth Grp; Emplmnt; Prom Com; SADD; Bnd; Mch Bnd; Pep Bnd; DYA Softball; DYA Volleyball; Animal Science; Veterinarian; The Ohio State U; Tennessee U

RAAB, CANDICE; WAYNESVILLE, OH; WAYNESVILLE HS; (JR); Hnr Roll; MVP; Nat Hon Sy; Comm Volntr; Peer Tut/Med; Chrch Yth Grp; Prom Com; SADD; Tchrs Aide; Vsity Clb; Bnd; Mch Bnd; Pep Bnd; Swmg (V L); Tennis (V CL); Cl Off (V); Stu Cncl (V); CR (R); Swimming State Qualifier 2003, 2004; Rae Bunck Women in Sports Nominee 03, 04; Physical Therapy; Athletic Training; U of Kentucky; Miami U, Oxford

RABABAH, HANA M; DAYTON, OH; WAYNE HS; (JR); 4H Awd; F Lan Hn Soc; Hi Hnr Roll; Hnr Roll; Nat Hon Sy; Perf Att; USAA; WWAHSS; Yth Ldrshp Prog; Hosp Aide; Peer Tut/Med; FTA; Lib Aide; Off Aide; Scouts; Tchrs Aide; Cl Off (R); Stu Cncl (T); CR (S); Lit Mag (R); Muslim Youth Club; Ophthalmology; Ohio State U; Wright State U

RADEL, MELISSA; CARDINGTON, OH; CARDINGTON-LINCOLN HS; (SR); 4H Awd; Hnr Roll; Nat Hon Sy; Otst Ac Ach Awd; Perf Att; Comm Volntr; 4-H; Chrch Yth Grp; Drma Clb; Emplmnt; Ntl FFA; P to P St Amb Prg; Prom Com; Sci Clb; Bnd; Clr Grd; Dnce; Flg Crps; Sftball (J); Track (J); Yrbk (E, P); Forensic Science; Equestrian Studies / Western Riding; The U of Findlay

RADEMACHER, ALLISON; MORROW, OH; KINGS HS; (SR); DAR; Hi Hnr Roll; MVP; St of Mnth; WWAHSS; Comm Volntr; ArtClub; DARE; Drma Clb; NtlFrnscLg; Photog; Spch Team; Stg Cre; Sccr (J); Swmg (V L); Vllyball (J); Mock Trial-Received Best Witness Award; Published Multiple Times; Molecular Genetics; The Ohio State U

RADEMAKER, ABBY; BRYAN, OH; BRYAN HS; (SO); Hi Hnr Roll; Hnr Roll; Sci Fairs; Sci/Math Olympn; Vllyball (J); Nursing; Vet Assistant

RAFFEL, MEGAN M; GREENVILLE, OH; GREENVILLE HS; (FR); All Am Sch; Hnr Roll; WWAHSS; Yth Ldrshp Prog; Comm Volntr; Chess; Chrch Yth Grp; FCA; Key Club; Spanish Clb; Bnd; Mch Bnd; Chrldg (V); Sftball (V); Cl Off (V); Stu Cncl; Medical Field; Politics

RAGER, JESSIE L; NEW PHILADELPHIA, OH; INDIAN VALLEY HS; (SR); 4H Awd; Hnr Roll; 4-H; Ntl FFA; Bnd; Mch Bnd; Hsbk Rdg; PP Ftbl; FFA-Treasurer; Horse Science; Ag. Business; Agricultural Tech. Institute-OSU

RAGER, LUANA; NEW LONDON, OH; NEW LONDON HS; (SO); Hi Hnr Roll; Hnr Roll; WWAHSS; Comm Volntr; Hab For Humty Volntr; Peer Tut/Med; Chrch Yth Grp; Drma Clb; Emplmnt; Key Club; Mod UN; SADD; Tchrs Aide; Vsity Clb; Chr; Ch Chr; Mch Bnd; SP/M/VS; Scr Kpr (L); Chorus Officer; Special Education; Accounting; Bowling Green State U; Chicago State U

RAHE, BENJAMIN K; STOW, OH; STOW-MUNROE FALLS HS; (SO); Ctznshp Aw; Hnr Roll; Otst Ac Ach Awd; Comm Volntr; Peer Tut/Med; Chrch Yth Grp; DARE; Drma Clb; Jr Cls League; Mth Clb/Tm; Off Aide; Svce Clb; Latin Clb; Chr; Ch Chr; SP/M/VS; Dvng (V L); Ftball (J); 2 Year Scholastic Letter Winner; History Award, 4 Missions Trips; Astronaut; Worship Leader; US Air Force Academy; Kent State

RAINES, DANIELLE; PICKERINGTON, OH; PICKERINGTON HS NORTH; (SO); Hi Hnr Roll; Chrch Yth Grp; Emplmnt; Yrbk; Leo Club Secretary; Elementary Education; Miami U

RAMIREZ, RUTH A; COLUMBUS, OH; NORTHSIDE CHRISTIAN SCH; (JR); Hnr Roll; Perf Att; Chrch Yth Grp; Emplmnt; Acpl Chr; Chr; SP/M/VS; Swg Chr; Yrbk; Christian Character Award; Business; Accounting; Ohio State U

RAMSEY, KRISTIAN K; WOOSTER, OH; NORTHWESTERN HS; (SR); Hi Hnr Roll; Hnr Roll; Nat Hon Sy; Comm Volntr; Red Cr Aide; Emplmnt; Voc Ind Clb Am; Vllyball (J); Physical Therapy; Pre-Med; Akron U; Walsh U

RANDLEMAN, JAYLA L; LORAIN, OH; SOUTHVIEW HS; (JR); Hi Hnr Roll; Hnr Roll; Perf Att; Sci/Math Olympn; WWAHSS; Comm Volntr; ArtClub; Dbte Team; Emplmnt; Jr Ach; Key Club; Mod UN; Tchrs Aide; Tennis (V); Sch Ppr (R); Unity Club Vice-President; Major in Philosophy and English; Law Degree; Spelman College; Harvard U

RANGAN, PREETHY; ATHENS, OH; ATHENS HS; (JR); F Lan Hn Soc; Hnr Roll; Nat Hon Sy; Otst Ac Ach Awd; Pres Ac Ftns Aw; Pres Sch; Sci Fairs; Yth Ldrshp Prog; Comm Volntr; Hosp Aide; Peer Tut/Med; Drma Clb; Mod UN; Mus Clb; Photog; Quill & Scroll; Tchrs Aide; French Clb; Bnd; SP/M/VS; Stg Cre; CR (R); Sch Ppr (E, R); Indian Classical Dance; Pre-Med / Chemistry; Math

RANSBOTTOM, KYLE; ZANESVILLE, OH; MAYSVILLE 6-12 HS; (FR); Hi Hnr Roll; Perf Att; WWAHSS; Comm Volntr; Chrch Yth Grp; DARE; Drma Clb; Key Club; Quiz Bowl; Bnd; Mch Bnd; Orch; Pep Bnd; SP/M/VS; Vice President of the LEO club; United States Naval Academy, Annapolis

RAPP, ASHLEY; CARROLL, OH; BLOOM-CARROLL HS; (SR); Hnr Roll; Sci Fairs; Red Cr Aide; Emplmnt; Photog; Prom Com; PP Ftbl (V L); Sftball (V CL); Nursing / Bachelor's Degree; Shawnee State U; Mt Carmel College of Nursing

RASFELD, KATIE; CINCINNATI, OH; MC NICHOLAS HS; (JR); F Lan Hn Soc; Hnr Roll; Nat Hon Sy; Perf Att; Comm Volntr; ArtClub; Chrch Yth Grp; Drma Clb; Emplmnt; Svce Clb; SP/M/VS; Stg Cre; Vllyball (J L); Treasurer and Founding Member of Venture Crew 867 / International Thespian Society VP; Mock Trial; Psychology / Sociology / Theatre and Spanish; Ohio State U

RATCLIFF, NIKKI; URBANA, OH; URBANA HS; (JR); Hnr Roll; DARE; Scouts; Clb; SP/M/VS; FCCLA; Day Care; Wittenberg U; Clark State U

REAVEN, ANDREW; CANTON, OH; GLEN OAK HS; (SO); Ctznshp Aw; Hnr Roll; Nat Ldrshp Svc; Pres Ac Ftns Aw; Sci Fairs; Yth Ldrshp Prog; Hab For Humty Volntr; Emplmnt; Key Club; NYLC; Tmpl Yth Grp; Acpl Chr; Chr; Bskball (J); Cr Ctry (J); Scr Kpr (J); Skiing (J); Track (J); Wt Lftg (J); Youth Group Leadership; Youth Group Sports; M.D.; Northwestern U; Ohio State U

REBHOLZ, BRYAN D; CINCINNATI, OH; ELDER HS; (SR); Hi Hnr Roll; Hnr Roll; Nat Hon Sy; Perf Att; Comm Volntr; Emplmnt; Bskball (J); First Honors All of Junior & Senior Year; Average of 100% in Business Classes; Finance; Business; U of Cincinnati

REBOVICH, AURA E; GARRETTSVILLE, OH; JAMES GARFIELD HS; (SO); Ctznshp Aw; Hnr Roll; Kwnis Aw; Otst Ac Ach Awd; St of Mnth; WWAHSS; Yth Ldrshp Prog; Comm Volntr; Red Cr Aide; ArtClub; Chrch Yth Grp; Drma Clb; Emplmnt; HO'Br Yth Ldrshp; Key Club; Prom Com; Tchrs Aide; Chr; SP/M/VS; Stg Cre; PP Ftbl (J); Vllyball (J); Cl Off (V); Stu Cncl (P, R); CR (R); HOBY Leadership Seminar Representative; 3rd Place Kiwanis Veteran - Speech; Communications / Media Studies; Journalism; St John's U; Hofstra U

REDDY, JESSIKA; ST CLAIRSVILLE, OH; MT DE CHANTAL; (JR); Ctznshp Aw; DAR; Hnr Roll; Nat Hon Sy; Sci Fairs; St of Mnth; WWAHSS; Comm Volntr; Hosp Aide; Chess; Key Club; Quill & Scroll; Spanish Clb; Track (V); Cl Off (T); CR (T); Yrbk (E); Doctor; George Washington U; Ohio State

REDMAN, DANIELLE R; MIAMISBURG, OH; MIAMISBURG HS; (SR); Hnr Roll; Nat Hon Sy; Comm Volntr; Hab For Humty Volntr; Peer Tut/Med; Chrch Yth Grp; DARE; Emplmnt; JSA; SADD; Foreign Clb; Bnd; Jzz Bnd; Mch Bnd; Pep Bnd; Renaissance Scholar; Secondary Education; Social Studies; U of Toledo

REED, ALEXANDRA L; MIAMISBURG, OH; MIAMISBURG HS; (SR); Hi Hnr Roll; Hnr Roll; Nat Hon Sy; Peer Tut/Med; Chrch Yth Grp; Emplmnt; Off Aide; SADD; Bnd; Mch Bnd; Pep Bnd; SP/M/VS; Nursing; Wright State U

REED, CHARLY; MC CONNELSVILLE, OH; MORGAN HS; (JR); Hi Hnr Roll; Sci Fairs; WWAHSS; Comm Volntr; Chrch Yth Grp; DARE; Key Club; Off Aide; Tchrs Aide; Tech Clb; Bskball (J); Vllyball (J); Tech Prep Showcase - Superior Rating; Infant, Child, Adult CPR Certified / AED Certified; Radiologic Technologist; Respiratory Technician; Washington State Community College; Zane State College

REED, KALEB D; BURBANK, OH; NORTHWESTERN HS; (SO); Hi Hnr Roll; Jr Eng Tech; MVP; WWAHSS; Yth Ldrshp Prog; 4-H; Chrch Yth Grp; Emplmnt; Mth Clb/Tm; Tech Clb; Wdwrkg Clb; Bskball (V L); Ftball (V L); PP Ftbl (C); Wt Lftg; CR (R); Youth-4-Youth Student Council; Sports Medicine; Ohio State

REEL, DANIELLE; CLEVELAND, OH; MAX S HAYES HS; (JR); Ctznshp Aw; Hnr Roll; Perf Att; Sci Fairs; Comm Volntr; DARE; Drma Clb; Key Club; Photog; Svce Clb; Tchrs Aide; SP/M/VS; Yrbk (P); Most Improved-Bowling Team; Merit Roll; English; Visual Arts; New York U; Hunter College

REEVES, DIANA M; PICKERINGTON, OH; PICKERINGTON HS NORTH; (JR); Hnr Roll; St of Mnth; Comm Volntr; Peer Tut/Med; Chrch Yth Grp; Tchrs Aide; Bnd; Ch Chr; Dnce; SP/M/VS; Lit Mag (R); Vice President - Church Youth Group; Stick Fighting Classes Club; Journalism; Psychology; Columbus State Community College; Ohio U of Lancaster Ohio

REICHEL, ASHLEY; BRUNSWICK, OH; BRUNSWICK HS; (JR); Hnr Roll; Otst Ac Ach Awd; Comm Volntr; Off Aide; Photog; Tchrs Aide; Spanish Clb; Yrbk (R, P); Varsity Wrestling Statistician; Varsity Athletic Trainer; Baldwin-Wallace; Bowling Green

REID, JENNIFER; WESTERVILLE, OH; WESTERVILLE NORTH HS; (JR); Ctznshp Aw; Hi Hnr Roll; Otst Ac Ach Awd; Pres Sch; St of Mnth; WWAHSS; Comm Volntr; Hosp Aide; Peer Tut/Med; Chrch Yth Grp; Emplmnt; Off Aide; Svce Clb; French Clb; Chr; I CAN Program in Elementary Schools; Pre-Medicine; Forensic Science; New York U; Miami U

REIDER, CIANNA E.; NILES, OH; MC KINLEY HS; (FR); Hnr Roll; Nat Hon Sy; St of Mnth; WWAHSS; Drma Clb; Spch Team; Spanish Clb; Chr; Dnce; SP/M/VS; Golf; Tennis

REIFENBERG, MEGAN; SPRINGBORO, OH; SPRINGBORO HS; (FR); Hi Hnr Roll; St of Mnth; WWAHSS; Chrch Yth Grp; Key Club; Bnd; Hsbk Rdg; Relay for Life (American Cancer Society Fundraiser); Gold Coin Award; General Physician; Pharmacist; U of Pennsylvania; Miami U

REINCHELD, KATIE R; PICKERINGTON, OH; PICKERINGTON HS NORTH; (JR); Hi Hnr Roll; Nat Hon Sy; WWAHSS; Yth Ldrshp Prog; Comm Volntr; ArtClub; Chrch Yth Grp; Drma Clb; Emplmnt; Key Club; Photog; Chr; Nursing; Art; Ohio State U

REINHART, CORY L; CANTON, OH; EAST CANTON HS; (FR); Hnr Roll; Perf Att; Bskball; Ftball (J); Wt Lftg; Major in Education; Mount Union; Malone

REINHORN, ALEX; THORNVILLE, OH; MILLERSPORT JR/SR HS; (MS); Ctznshp Aw; Hnr Roll; MVP; Nat Hon Sy; Otst Ac Ach Awd; Perf Att; Yth Ldrshp Prog; Chrch Yth Grp; DARE; Dbte Team; Scouts; Chr; SP/M/VS; Stg Cre; Swg Chr; Bsball (L); Bskball (L); Ftball (L); GAA (L); Golf (L); Skiing; Sccr; Track (L); Drive Chip & Putt-Winner of Longest Drive on the Golf Channel - 2004; Dental; Sports; Cincinnati Ohio; Xavier U Ohio

REISS, AMANDA; FRAZEYSBURG, OH; TRI-VALLEY HS; (JR); Hi Hnr Roll; Nat Hon Sy; Pres Sch; St of Mnth; WWAHSS; Yth Ldrshp Prog; Comm Volntr; Hosp Aide; Peer Tut/Med; Chrch Yth Grp; Drma Clb; Emplmnt; FCA; HO'Br Yth Ldrshp; Pep Squd; Prom Com; Svce Clb; Dnce; Drl Tm; Chrldg (V CL); Track (J); Adv Cncl (V); Cl Off (P); Stu Cncl (V); CR (R); Pre-Law; Pre-Med

REIST, HEATHER M; CINCINNATI, OH; COLERAIN HS; (JR); Hnr Roll; Otst Ac Ach Awd; Sci Fairs; DARE; Vsity Clb; Bskball (V L); GAA (V); Sccr (V L); 3 Year Varsity Letter Winner-Soccer; 2 Year Varsity Basketball; Athletic Training Education; Photography / Multi-Media Communication; Bowling Green State U; Thomas More College

RELICK, ANSON F; SPRINGBORO, OH; SPRINGBORO HS; (JR); Hi Hnr Roll; Nat Hon Sy; WWAHSS; Chrch Yth Grp; Key Club; Mth Clb/Tm; SADD; Acpl Chr; Dnce; Modern Dance; Fordham U; Juilliard

RELIFORD, AMANDA K; LANCASTER, OH; LANCASTER HS; (JR); Hi Hnr Roll; Nat Hon Sy; WWAHSS; Comm Volntr; Peer Tut/Med; Chrch Yth Grp; Emplmnt; Key Club; Svce Clb; French Clb; Vllyball (V L); Stu Cncl (R); Secondary Education; Teaching Degree; Ohio U of Athens

REMBERT, RICARDO; CLEVELAND, OH; COLLINWOOD HS; (JR); Ctznshp Aw; Hnr Roll; FCA; Ftball (V); Track (V); Business; Sports Training; Michigan State U; Miami U Ohio

REMINGTON, NATE; ASHLAND, OH; ASHLAND HS; (JR); Hi Hnr Roll; Hnr Roll; MVP; Perf Att; Valdctrian; WWAHSS; Chrch Yth Grp; Emplmnt; Off Aide; Prom Com; Sccr (VJCL); Member of National Society of High School Scholars; 11th Grade Americanism Test Winner - Ashland County; Finance; Economics; Miami U Ohio; Bowling Green State U

RENNER, MATTHEW A; WARSAW, OH; RIVER VIEW HS; (JR); Hnr Roll; Chrch Yth Grp; Digital Electronics Competition; Electronics; Automotive; Lincoln Tech; Kent State U Tuscarawas

RENNER, WHITNEY; EATON, OH; EATON HS; (SO); All Am Sch; Hi Hnr Roll; Hnr Roll; MVP; Otst Ac Ach Awd; WWAHSS; Yth Ldrshp Prog; Comm Volntr; Chrch Yth Grp; Emplmnt; Jr Ach; Lttrmn Clb; Off Aide; Photog; Prom Com; Sci Clb; Bskball; Sccr (V L); Track (V L); Vsy Clb; Cl Off (T); Stu Cncl (R); Junior Leadership of Greater Dayton; Peer Leader; Organic Chemistry; Human Studies; Miami U in Oxford; Arizona State U

RENSCH, BRI; NORTH BALTIMORE, OH; NORTH BALTIMORE JR/SR HS; (FR); Hnr Roll; Nat Hon Sy; WWAHSS; ArtClub; Off Aide; Prom Com; Spanish Clb; Bskball (V); Sftball (V); Vllyball (V); Cl Off (V); MAL Leadership

Reliford, Amanda K
Lancaster HS
Lancaster, OH

Quance, Jamie C
Western Hills HS
Cincinnati, OH

Ramsey, Kristian K
Northwestern HS
Wooster, OH

RENZENBRINK, LENA; CINCINNATI, OH; NORTHWEST HS; (SO); Hi Hnr Roll; Nat Hon Sy; Otst Ac Ach Awd; Comm Volntr; Key Club; Bnd; Sccr (V); Adv Cncl (R); Advisory Council-U-Knight to Knights for Sport Players; Physical Therapy; Architecture; Miami U; Ohio State U

REPINE, DANIELLE; MOUNT VICTORY, OH; RIDGEMONT SR HS; (FR); Hnr Roll; St of Mnth; Comm Volntr; DARE; Drma Clb; Ntl FFA; Outdrs Clb; Chr; Swg Chr; Sftball (J); Track (J)

RETZLOFF, KYLE W; DAYTON, OH; CHAMINADE-JULIENNE HS; (SO); Ctznshp Aw; Hi Hnr Roll; Otst Ac Ach Awd; Sci Fairs; Yth Ldrshp Prog; Comm Volntr; Chess; Dbte Team; Fr of Library; Quiz Bowl; Scouts; Spch Team; Bsball (J); Scr Kpr (J); Stu Cncl (R); 2003 Youth in Ministry Award-St. Luke; Father Jansen Memorial Scholarship Recipient; History; U of Notre Dame; United States Naval Academy

REU, JUDY; SOLON, OH; SOLON HS; (MS); Hi Hnr Roll; Otst Ac Ach Awd; St of Mnth; Chrch Yth Grp; Emplmnt; Chr; Orch; SP/M/VS; Sccr (J); Track (J); Female Leadership Award; Midwest Talent Search; Law - Major; Business - Major; Stanford U; Duke U

REXROAD, BENJAMIN; AKRON, OH; COVENTRY HS; (SR); Hnr Roll; Nat Hon Sy; St of Mnth; WWAHSS; Yth Ldrshp Prog; Drma Clb; Emplmnt; Fr of Library; HO'Br Yth Ldrshp; Key Club; Lib Aide; SP/M/VS; Stg Cre; Stu Cncl (V, T); Sch Ppr (E, R); Yrbk (E, R); Humanities; The U of Akron

REYNOLDS, CHRISTINE; LORAIN, OH; CLEARVIEW HS; (JR); All Am Sch; Gov Hnr Prg; Hi Hnr Roll; Hnr Roll; MVP; Nat Mrt LOC; Pres Sch; WWAHSS; Comm Volntr; Scouts; Tchrs Aide; Vsity Clb; Bnd; Chr; SP/M/VS; Bskball (V L); Vsy Clb (J); Vllyball (J); Academic Letters; Medicine; Business

RHINE, COLLIN T; LUCASVILLE, OH; VALLEY HS; (FR); Hnr Roll; DARE; Wdwrkg Clb; Bsball (J); Bskball; Wildlife Management

RHODES, DARIUS L; COLUMBUS, OH; AFRICENTRIC SEC HS; (SO); Hi Hnr Roll; Hnr Roll; Sci Fairs; Sci/Math Olympn; St of Mnth; Yth Ldrshp Prog; Comm Volntr; Peer Tut/Med; Dbte Team; Kwanza Clb; Mth Clb/Tm; P to P St Amb Prg; Sci Clb; Bnd; Chr; Mch Bnd; SP/M/VS; Ftball (V CL); Track (V CL); Stu Cncl (P); CR (V); Scholar Athlete 2 Yrs Running - Football; Played Varsity Football Every Year; PhD in Architecture and Engineering; Graduate in Top Percent of Class; Ohio State U; Harvard U

RICE, CORY; NORTH ROYALTON, OH; NORTH ROYALTON HS; Hi Hnr Roll; Nat Hon Sy; St of Mnth; WWAHSS; Peer Tut/Med; Key Club; Spanish Clb; Sccr (V); Sports Medicine; Business; Ohio U; Miami U

RICE, MAKONNEN L; TOLEDO, OH; WOODWARD HS; (SO); Ctznshp Aw; Hi Hnr Roll; Sci Fairs; Comm Volntr; Chess; Chrch Yth Grp; Dbte Team; Emplmnt; Quiz Bowl; Scouts; Ftball (V); Tennis (V); Track (V); Wrstlg (V); Chiropractor; Environmental Science; Miami U; Stanford U

RICE, MICHAEL; ASHTABULA, OH; JEFFERSON AREA HS; (SR); Second Place in VICA Skills Test; Want to Be ASE Certified; Also Want to Be a Master Mechanic; Ohio Technical College

RICE, SEAN C; NORTH ROYALTON, OH; NORTH ROYALTON HS; (JR); Hi Hnr Roll; Nat Hon Sy; St of Mnth; WWAHSS; Peer Tut/Med; Key Club; Spanish Clb; Bskball (V); Sccr (V); Medicine; Business; Miami U; Ohio State U

RICH, CORALMARIE; MASSILLON, OH; CANTON CTRL CATHOLIC; (SO); Hi Hnr Roll; Hnr Roll; WWAHSS; Bnd; Drm Mjr; Mch Bnd; 2005 Europe Tour Ohio Ambassador of Music; 3 Time Published Poet; Interior Design; Creative Writing; Arcadia U; Pratt Institute

RICH, DANIELLE; MIDDLEBRANCH, OH; GLEN OAK HS; (JR); Hi Hnr Roll; Hnr Roll; Nat Sci Aw; Otst Ac Ach Awd; Sci Fairs; St of Mnth; USAA; Comm Volntr; ArtClub; Emplmnt; Yrbk (R); JV Bowling; Jam Skating; Graphic Design; Interactive Media Technology; Stark State College of Technology; U of Akron

RICHARDSON, NATE; CANTON, OH; JACKSON HS; (JR); Hnr Roll; WWAHSS; Comm Volntr; DECA; Key Club; Lttrmn Clb; Spanish Clb; Sccr (V L); 1st Team Mock Trial; Qualified for Nationals in DECA '05; Pre-Med; Pre Law; Ohio U

RICHTER, TAYLOR; NEW KNOXVILLE, OH; NEW KNOXVILLE LOCAL SCH; (SO); Hi Hnr Roll; Sci Fairs; St of Mnth; Yth Ldrshp Prog; Peer Tut/Med; Chrch Yth Grp; Emplmnt; HO'Br Yth Ldrshp; Pep Squd; Quiz Bowl; Schol Bwl; Spanish Clb; Chr; SP/M/VS; Chrldg; Scr Kpr (V); Track (J L); Vllyball (J L); Cl Off (S); Lit Mag (R); Yrbk (R, P); Church Drama Productions; Architecture; Engineering; U of Cincinnati; Carnegie Mellon U

RICKEY, ALEXANDER T; WAYNESVILLE, OH; CLINTON-MASSIE HS; (FR); Hnr Roll; Scouts; Bnd; Jzz Bnd; Mch Bnd; Pep Bnd; Tennis (V); Drumline; Boy Scouts; Music Teacher; Pharmacist; Wright State U; Miami U

RICO, CHRISTOPHER W; MENTOR, OH; MENTOR HS; (SR); Ctznshp Aw; Hi Hnr Roll; Hnr Roll; MVP; Otst Ac Ach Awd; St of Mnth; Comm Volntr; Chess; Chrch Yth Grp; DARE; Emplmnt; Mod UN; Off Aide; Scouts; Tchrs Aide; Chr; Ch Chr; SP/M/VS; Stu Cncl (R); Sch Ppr (R); Yrbk (P); Summa Cum Laude; Film; U of Toledo; U of Miami Florida

RIDDLE, CHERISH; ASHTABULA, OH; LAKESIDE HS; (SO); Hi Hnr Roll; Perf Att; WWAHSS; Yth Ldrshp Prog; Comm Volntr; Chrch Yth Grp; Ch Chr; Bskball (V); Track; Criminal Justice; Graphic Design; The U of Akron; Lakeland U

RIEMAN, CAROL; CRESTLINE, OH; CRESTLINE HS; (SR); 4H Awd; Hnr Roll; Nat Hon Sy; St of Mnth; 4-H; Key Club; Chr; Tennis (V CL); Cl Off (P, V, T); President of Future Career Community Leaders of America Club; Criminal Justice; Forensic Science; North Central State College

RIESE, ROBBIE; MASSILLON, OH; TUSLAW JR/SR HS; (FR); Hnr Roll; Chrch Yth Grp; FCA; Tchrs Aide; Clb; Bsball (J); Bskball (J); Ftball (J); Coaching; Ohio State U; U of Akron

RIESTENBERG, KATIE; CINCINNATI, OH; MOTHER OF MERCY HS; (JR); Hi Hnr Roll; Nat Hon Sy; St of Mnth; WWAHSS; Yth Ldrshp Prog; Comm Volntr; Hosp Aide; Peer Tut/Med; Biology Clb; Drma Clb; Emplmnt; Key Club; Sci Clb; Tchrs Aide; French Clb; Stg Cre; Vllyball (JC); U of Rochester Humanities & Social Sciences Award; Religion Award At Mother of Mercy HS; Nursing; Education; Ohio State U; U of Cincinnati

RIETSCHLIN, MATTHEW L; SHILOH, OH; PLYMOUTH HS; (SR); 4H Awd; Hnr Roll; Nat Hon Sy; Perf Att; St of Mnth; WWAHSS; 4-H; AL Aux Boys; ArtClub; Emplmnt; Ntl FFA; Bsball (V); Bskball (V L); Ftball (V CL); Landscaping Design / Build; Columbus State Community College

RIGBY, BRANDY; PAINESVILLE, OH; RIVERSIDE HS; (JR); Hi Hnr Roll; WWAHSS; Comm Volntr; Key Club; SADD; Tchrs Aide; Yrbk (E); Early Childhood Education; Ohio U; Bowling Green State U

RIGGINS, JAQUALA; YOUNGSTOWN, OH; RAYEN HS; (SO); Hnr Roll; Nat Hon Sy; Otst Ac Ach Awd; WWAHSS; Peer Tut/Med; Pep Squd; Tchrs Aide; SP/M/VS; Track (V); Vllyball (J); Computer Graphics / Technology; Theatre / Drama; Ohio State U; Penn State U

RIMMELIN, DODLE; PERRYSBURG, OH; ST URSULA AC; (SR); Hi Hnr Roll; Jr Eng Tech; Nat Hon Sy; Pres Ac Ftns Aw; Pres Sch; St of Mnth; USAA; Comm Volntr; Peer Tut/Med; Mth Clb/Tm; Pep Squd; Svce Clb; Tmpl Yth Grp; Vsity Clb; French Clb; Chrldg (VJ L); Cr Ctry (V L); Varsity / JV / Letter Winner- Crew; International Studies; Pre-Med; Boston College; Northwestern U

RINCK, TIFFANY; CLEVES, OH; MOTHER OF MERCY HS; (SO); Hnr Roll; CARE; Comm Volntr; Drma Clb; Key Club; History; Theater; U of Cincinnati; Transylvania U

RINEHART, JULIE; SPRINGFIELD, OH; SHAWNEE HS; (SR); All Am Sch; Fut Prb Slvr; Hi Hnr Roll; Jr Rot; Nat Hon Sy; Nat Sci Aw; Pres Sch; St of Mnth; Comm Volntr; Peer Tut/Med; ArtClub; Chrch Yth Grp; Drma Clb; FCA; Key Club; Off Aide; Vsity Clb; Bnd; Chr; SP/M/VS; Stg Cre; Sftball (V L); Vllyball (V CL); Stu Cncl (S); Lit Mag (E); Sch Ppr (E, R); Show Choir; Relay for Life Team; Political Science; Law; American U

RIPPY, DOUGLAS; COLUMBUS, OH; LINDEN-MC KINLEY HS; (FR); WWAHSS; Comm Volntr; Emplmnt; Vsity Clb; Bnd; SP/M/VS; Bskball (V); Ftball; 4.0 GPA; Graduate With 4.0 GPA; Temple University; Ohio State University

RISNER, OLIVIA L; CAREY, OH; CAREY HS; (JR); 4H Awd; Hi Hnr Roll; Hnr Roll; Nat Hon Sy; Perf Att; Pres Sch; WWAHSS; Red Cr Aide; 4-H; ArtClub; DARE; DECA; Drma Clb; Emplmnt; Off Aide; Prom Com; Bnd; Chr; Jzz Bnd; Mch Bnd; Cl Off (V); Stu Cncl (V); Nursing; OBGYN; Ohio State U; Mercy College of Northwest Ohio

RITCHIE, COURTNEY; MILFORD, OH; MILFORD HS; (JR); Hnr Roll; Comm Volntr; Peer Tut/Med; Chrch Yth Grp; Emplmnt; FCCLA; Scouts; Tchrs Aide; Vsity Clb; Dvng (V L); PP Ftbl (V); Swmg (J L); Vsy Clb (V); Silver Award for Girl Scouts; Psychology; Elementary Education; Baldwin-Wallace; Wittenberg

RITTER, PRESTON T; ORWELL, OH; GRAND VALLEY HS; (MS); Scouts; Ftball (J); Wt Lftg (J); Wrstlg (J); Engineering; Ohio State U; Kent State U

RITTMAN, SANDRA M; LEBANON, OH; BISHOP FENWICK HS; (SO); Hi Hnr Roll; Otst Ac Ach Awd; WWAHSS; Yth Ldrshp Prog; Comm Volntr; Chrch Yth Grp; Emplmnt; Key Club; NYLC; P to P St Amb Prg; Golf (J); Tennis (V L); Track (V L); Vllyball (J); CR (R); Pro-Merits Award Winner; Medicine / MD, PhD; English / BA, MA; Miami U Ohio; Princeton U

RIVERA, MONICA S; YOUNGSTOWN, OH; WOODROW WILSON HS; (JR); Hi Hnr Roll; Hnr Roll; Fashion Design; Fashion Merchandising; New York U; Kent State U

RIVERS, DYANA; MARTINSVILLE, OH; WILMINGTON HS; (FR); Ctznshp Aw; Hi Hnr Roll; Hnr Roll; St of Mnth; Chrch Yth Grp; DARE; Emplmnt; Scouts; Bnd; Church Band; Community Band; Pediatric; Physician; Indiana U School of Medicine; Ohio State U College of Medicine & Public Health

ROBART, MELISSA C; PIQUA, OH; PIQUA HS; (SR); Nat Hon Sy; St of Mnth; Comm Volntr; Tchrs Aide; Vllyball (V CL); Players Choice Award-Volleyball-2004; Game Ball Award-School Record for Aces in Season Career; Elementary School Teacher-Early Childhood Education; Ohio U

ROBERTS, BRITTANY; EUCLID, OH; THE EUCLID HS OF THE ARTS; (SR); Ctznshp Aw; Hi Hnr Roll; Hnr Roll; Nat Hon Sy; Otst Ac Ach Awd; St of Mnth; Comm Volntr; Peer Tut/Med; Chrch Yth Grp; DARE; Emplmnt; Key Club; Prom Com; Tchrs Aide; Ch Chr; Dnce; Drl Tm; Flg Crps; Mch Bnd; Pep Bnd; Lit Mag (R); Sch Ppr (R); Participated In My School's 2005 Fashion Show; Had Several Compositions In The Senior Art show; Journalism; Vocal and/or Performing Arts; U of Berkeley, New York City College of Technology, U of Texas; Columbia U

ROBERTS, RACHAEL; NORTH RIDGEVILLE, OH; NORTH RIDGEVILLE HS; (SO); Hnr Roll; Nat Hon Sy; ArtClub; Wdwrkg Clb; Yrbk (P); Psychology

ROBERTSON, SAMANTHA; FELICITY, OH; FELICITY-FRANKLIN HS; (FR); 4H Awd; Comm Volntr; Peer Tut/Med; 4-H; ArtClub; Chrch Yth Grp; Won Many Beauty Pageants; Grand Champion Beginner Showman; Major in Computer Design; Become an Animatronics Engineer; Cincinnati State; Northern Kentucky

ROBERTSON, TERENCE L; COLUMBUS, OH; WALNUT RIDGE HS; (FR); Hnr Roll; St of Mnth; Wrstlg (V); Technology; Business; Ohio State U; Ohio Wesleyan

ROBILOTTO, LANE; PAINESVILLE, OH; RIVERSIDE-PAINESVILLE TOWNSHIP HS; (FR); Hnr Roll; Pres Sch; Sci Fairs; St of Mnth; Peer Tut/Med; Emplmnt; Key Club; Tchrs Aide; Bsball (J); Bskball (VJC); Ftball (VJ); Academic Letter; Electrical Engineering; Robotics; Stanford U; U of Miami

ROBINSON, DAVA; CINCINNATI, OH; CLARK MONTESSORI SCH; (FR); Comm Volntr; Bnd; Swmg (jv); Photography; Fine Arts; Antioch U; University of Cincinnati

ROBINSON, JESSICA E; BOWERSTON, OH; CONOTTON VALLEY JR/SR HS; (FR); WWAHSS; Bskball (V L); Sftball (J); Vllyball (JC); Stu Cncl (R)

ROBINSON, JESSICA L; BARBERTON, OH; OHDELA AC; (SO); Hosp Aide; DARE; Drma Clb; Scouts; Chrldg; Doctor; Chemical Engineer; Akron U; Kent State U

ROBINSON, SHAREE N; TOLEDO, OH; SCOTT HS; (SO); Hnr Roll; Nat Hon Sy; Otst Ac Ach Awd; Yth Ldrshp Prog; Comm Volntr; ArtClub; Mus Clb; Pep Squd; Scouts; Tchrs Aide; Spanish Clb; Bnd; Drl Tm; Mch Bnd; Pep Bnd; Chrldg (C); Adv Cncl (R); Band Letter Winner; Choreographer / Dancer; Business Owner; Ohio State U

ROBINSON, SHAYLA N; CLEVELAND, OH; RICHMOND HTS HS; (SO); Hi Hnr Roll; Comm Volntr; Key Club; Acpl Chr; Dnce; Cl Off (R); Member of an Organization Called REAL; Interested in Majoring At John Carroll U; Wishes to Own Restaurant; John Carroll U; Notre Dame College

ROBISON, MATTHEW R; LEWIS CTR, OH; OLENTANGY HS; (FR); 4H Awd; Duke TS; MVP; Perf Att; St of Mnth; CARE; Comm Volntr; Hab For Humty Volntr; 4-H; Aqrium Clb; ArtClub; Chrch Yth Grp; Cmptr Clb; DARE; Mus Clb; Photog; SP/M/VS; Bsball; Bskball; Ftball; Sftball; Swmg; Track; Wt Lftg; Art; Fishing; Football; JUS; OSU Ohio State; College Football

ROBISON, SEAN T; CINCINNATI, OH; WITHROW UNIVERSITY HS; (FR); Hnr Roll; Nat Hon Sy; Otst Ac Ach Awd; Comm Volntr; ArtClub; DARE; Scouts; Perfect Attendance Award; Great Academics; Computer Analysis; Architect; U of Cincinnati; Ohio State U

ROCCA, KRISTEN N; ZANESVILLE, OH; WEST MUSKINGUM HS; (SR); Hnr Roll; WWAHSS; Comm Volntr; BPA; Emplmnt; FBLA; Key Club; Off Aide; Pep Squd; Prom Com; Sccr (V); Track (V); Stu Cncl (R); Fellowship of Christian Athletes & Students; Ohio U; Communication; Ohio U

ROCHE, DANNY; WEST CHESTER, OH; LAKOTA EAST HS; (SO); Hi Hnr Roll; Hnr Roll; WWAHSS; ArtClub; Cr Ctry (J); Track (J); Xavier U; UCLA

ROCHTE, KATIE; POWELL, OH; WORTHINGTON CHRISTIAN HS; (SO); Hnr Roll; Hosp Aide; Peer Tut/Med; Chrch Yth Grp; Emplmnt; Acpl Chr; Cr Ctry (V); Stu Cncl (S); Nursing; Psychology; Ohio State U; Otterbein College, New York U

ROCK, KRISTEN; NORTH ROYALTON, OH; PADUA FRANCISCAN HS; (JR); Hi Hnr Roll; Hnr Roll; MVP; Nat Hon Sy; Pres Sch; WWAHSS; Peer Tut/Med; Spec Olymp Vol; Chrch Yth Grp; Emplmnt; Key Club; Spanish Clb; Sccr (V L); Elected to Pastoral Council At Church; Hon. Mention for Conference & Greater Cleveland (Soccer); Secondary Education; Music Management; Lemoyne U; Elizabethtown U

Rivera, Monica S
Woodrow Wilson HS
Youngstown, OH

Rich, Coralmarie
Canton Ctrl Catholic
Massillon, OH

Retzloff, Kyle W
Chaminade-Julienne HS
Dayton, OH

National
Honor Roll
Spring 2005

Repine, Danielle
Ridgemont SR HS
Mount Victory, OH

Rich, Danielle
Glen Oak HS
Middlebranch, OH

Robinson, Shayla N
Richmond Hts HS
Cleveland, OH

ROCKEY, MARY L A; BETHEL, OH; SOUTHERN HILLS JVS CAREER CTR; (SR); Hnr Roll; Otst Ac Ach Awd; Perf Att; St of Mnth; WWAHSS; Comm Volntr; DARE; Emplmnt; FCCLA; SADD; Voc Ind Clb Am; Bskball (J); PP Ftbl (V); Cl Off (P); Stu Cncl (R); CR (P); CERT Member; Rising Sun Award; State Highway Patrol; Hocking College

ROCKWELL, EMILY; BARNESVILLE, OH; BARNESVILLE HS; (SO); 4H Awd; Hi Hnr Roll; Sci Fairs; WWAHSS; 4-H; Key Club; Mth Clb/Tm; Pep Squd; P to P St Amb Prg; Photog; Quiz Bowl; Vsity Clb; Bnd; Drl Tm; Drm Mjr; Swmg (V L); Vsy Clb; Yrbk; Actuarial Science; Penn State; Cornell

ROCKWELL, ZEKE; BARNESVILLE, OH; BARNESVILLE HS; (SO); Hnr Roll; ArtClub; Quiz Bowl; Bnd; Mch Bnd; Animation; Cartooning

ROCKWOOD, JOHN; PICKERINGTON, OH; PICKERINGTON HS NORTH; (SO); Hi Hnr Roll; MVP; Perf Att; St of Mnth; Yth Ldrshp Prog; ArtClub; Chrch Yth Grp; Lttrmn Clb; P to P St Amb Prg; Scouts; Vsity Clb; German Clb; Cr Ctry (J); Ftball (V); Sccr; Track; Wrstlg (V L); People to People Student Ambassador; Science; Medicine; Ohio State U; Toledo State U

RODGERS, BETHANY D; HILLSBORO, OH; WHITE OAK JR/SR HS; (JR); Hnr Roll; Equine Management & Training; Equine Massage Therapy

RODRIGUEZ, ELLIOT; NORTH RIDGEVILLE, OH; NORTH RIDGEVILLE HS; (SO); Ctznshp Aw; Hi Hnr Roll; Hnr Roll; Perf Att; Red Cr Aide; Tchrs Aide; Spanish Clb; Bnd; Jzz Bnd; Ftball (V L); Wt Lftg (V); Adelaide-Voight Award; Medical Field; Engineer; Ohio U; Bowling Green

ROE, MICHAEL; DAYTON, OH; BEAVERCREEK HS; (JR); Hnr Roll; Nat Hon Sy; Nat Mrt Semif; Sci/Math Olympn; Comm Volntr; Drma Clb; Mth Clb/Tm; MuAlphaTh; Stg Cre; Sccr (JC); Free the Children; Network-Drug & Alcohol Prevention; Biology; Biomedical Engineering; Miami U OH; Purdue U

ROEDER, JAMES C; NORTH OLMSTED, OH; NORTH OLMSTED HS; (SO); Hi Hnr Roll; Hnr Roll; Pres Ac Ftns Aw; Comm Volntr; Peer Tut/Med; Emplmnt; Cr Ctry (V L); Track (V L); Summer Science Academy for Gifted Students; Spurs Tutor (Elementary Education Reading); Ohio State U; The U of Notre Dame

ROGERS, COURINEE; PIONEER, OH; NORTH CTRL SCH; (FR); Hnr Roll; St of Mnth; Spec Olymp Vol; DARE; SADD; Spanish Clb; Bnd; Mch Bnd; Pep Bnd; Chrldg (J); Legal; Radiology

ROHALL, ADRIANA V; STRATTON, OH; EDISON HS; (JR); Hi Hnr Roll; Hnr Roll; St of Mnth; WWAHSS; Yth Ldrshp Prog; Comm Volntr; Red Cr Aide; Emplmnt; Ntl Beta Clb; Pep Squd; Prom Com; Spanish Clb; Bnd; Chr; Dnce; Chrldg (V L); PP Ftbl (V); Swmg (V L); Track (V); Wt Lftg (V); Cl Off (V); Stu Cncl; CR; Sch Ppr (R); Yrbk (E, R, P); HOBY Nominee; CANAM National Cheer & Dance Champ; Athletic Training; Occupational Therapy; West Virginia U; Mount Union College

ROHRBACHER, MISTY J; SANDUSKY, OH; EDISON HS; (SR); Hnr Roll; St of Mnth; Comm Volntr; Red Cr Aide; Quiz Bowl; Vsity Clb; Bnd; Mch Bnd; First Aid & Safety, CPR, Certified; Certified Nursing Assistant; Associate of Applied Business (Paralegal); Stautzenberger College

ROHRER, KELLY C; CANTON, OH; (SO); Hi Hnr Roll; Key Club; P to P St Amb Prg; Dnce; Drm Mjr; Vllyball (J); Participant-1996 & 2000 Macy's Parade NYC, Twirling; Team USA Participant-2003 World Twirling Corps Champions-France; Sports Marketing; Sports Journalism; U of California At Los Angeles (UCLA); New York U (NYU)

ROLFES, JENNA; CELINA, OH; CELINA HS; (SR); Hnr Roll; St of Mnth; WWAHSS; Peer Tut/Med; Emplmnt; FBLA; Lib Aide; Off Aide; Photog; Prom Com; Tchrs Aide; German Clb; Yrbk (P); Future Business Leaders of America - Historian; Teenage Republicans; Psychology; Business / Pharmaceutical Sales; U of Findlay

ROMANI, JEANNA; OKEANA, OH; ROSS SR HS; (SR); Hi Hnr Roll; Nat Hon Sy; Pres Ac Ftns Aw; St of Mnth; Comm Volntr; Peer Tut/Med; Emplmnt; FCCLA; Key Club; Prom Com; Quill & Scroll; Svce Clb; SADD; Spanish Clb; PP Ftbl (V); Sccr (V L); Stu Cncl (V); Yrbk (E); Early Childhood Education; Bellarmine U

ROMANS, AMANDA L; GROVE CITY, OH; GROVE CITY HS; (SO); Hnr Roll; Nat Hon Sy; WWAHSS; Chrch Yth Grp; Emplmnt; Key Club; Off Aide; Feets of Clay; Marketing; U of Kentucky; Ohio State U

RONAU, MEGAN; MAUMEE, OH; MAUMEE HS; (SR); Hnr Roll; WWAHSS; DECA; Emplmnt; French Clb; Chr; Cr Ctry (V L); Track (V); DECA State Award; DECA National Participant; Business; Marketing; Owens Community College

ROOD, MEGAN M; TORONTO, OH; EDISON HS; (JR); Hi Hnr Roll; Hnr Roll; Comm Volntr; Peer Tut/Med; ArtClub; DARE; Ntl Beta Clb; Journalism; Meteorology; Youngstown State College; Bethany State College

ROPP, BRITTANY; WEST LIBERTY, OH; GRAHAM HS; (SO); 4H Awd; Hi Hnr Roll; Hnr Roll; Sci Fairs; Comm Volntr; 4-H; Hsbk Rdg; Veterinary; U of Findlay

ROSEBERRY, ANNA; GALION, OH; COLONEL CRAWFORD HS; (FR); DAR; Hi Hnr Roll; Hosp Aide; Chrch Yth Grp; Svce Clb; French Clb; Chr; SP/M/VS; Cr Ctry (V L); Track (V L); Wt Lftg; Yrbk (R, P); DAR Award Recipient; Cross Country Time-Drop Award - Star Award; Pediatric Nurse; Interior Design

ROSEUM, CAITLIN C; WILLOUGHBY HILLS, OH; WILLOUGHBY SOUTH HS; (SO); Hnr Roll; St of Mnth; ArtClub; Chrch Yth Grp; HO'Br Yth Ldrshp; Key Club; Mus Clb; Off Aide; P to P St Amb Prg; Bnd; Ch Chr; Dnce; Jzz Bnd; Cr Ctry (V L); Track (V L); Stu Cncl (R); CR (S); Berklee College of Music; U of Miami (Florida)

ROSICH, ALLYSON; MANSFIELD, OH; CLEAR FORK HS; (FR); Ctznshp Aw; Hi Hnr Roll; Nat Ldrshp Svc; Otst Ac Ach Awd; Yth Ldrshp Prog; Comm Volntr; Lttrmn Clb; Pep Squd; Scouts; SADD; Vsity Clb; Chr; Dnce; SP/M/VS; Skiing (V); Sccr (V L); Vsy Clb (V L); Stu Cncl (S); Solo & Ensemble Contest / Superior Rating for Solo / Superior Rating for Ensemble; Physical Therapist; Personal Trainer; Ohio State U

ROSS, SARA A; WARREN, OH; WARREN G HARDING HS; (SO); Hnr Roll; WWAHSS; Comm Volntr; Peer Tut/Med; Chrch Yth Grp; Key Club; French Clb; Scr Kpr; Sccr (J); Tennis (V); Key Club Officer; Nursing; Psychology; Kent State; Ohio State U

ROSSELLI, ANTHONY J; YOUNGSTOWN, OH; POLAND MS; (MS); Hi Hnr Roll; Otst Ac Ach Awd; Pres Ac Ftns Aw; Comm Volntr; Bnd; Cr Ctry; Sccr; Tennis; Stu Cncl; USTA - Ranked Tennis Player; Journalism; Secondary Education; Duke U; Ohio U

ROTERT, JOSEPH P; MIAMISBURG, OH; MIAMISBURG HS; (SR); Hnr Roll; Nat Hon Sy; Comm Volntr; Chrch Yth Grp; JSA; Lttrmn Clb; French Clb; Bsball (J); Ftball (V L); Best New Caddy; All Conference - Football; Stock Broker; Engineering; Ohio State U

ROTHERMEL, LAUREN; CANTON, OH; GLEN OAK HS; (JR); Hnr Roll; Nat Hon Sy; WWAHSS; Comm Volntr; Key Club; Off Aide; Pep Squd; Scouts; French Clb; Bnd; Mch Bnd; Yrbk (E, R, P); National Honor Society; Nursing; Capital U; Wright State U

ROUCH, TIFFANIE; SPRINGFIELD, OH; (FR); Hnr Roll; St of Mnth; Comm Volntr; DARE; Kwanza Clb; Photog; Scouts; Spanish Clb; Clr Grd; Chrldg (V); Sftball (J); Track (L); Service Hours; Forensic Science; Crime Scene Investigator; Akron U

ROUSE, RICHARD M; DAYTON, OH; CTRVILLE HS; (JR); Otst Ac Ach Awd; WWAHSS; Peer Tut/Med; Prom Com; Tchrs Aide; Spanish Clb; Bnd; Mch Bnd; World Champion Winter Drumline; Honors Symphonic Band

ROUSH, CORY; ZANESVILLE, OH; MAYSVILLE HS; (FR); Hi Hnr Roll; WWAHSS; Chrch Yth Grp; FTA; Key Club; Chr; Ch Chr; SP/M/VS; Cl Off (R); Stu Cncl (R); CR (R); Leo Club; Education; Computer Science

ROUSH, PATRICK; IRONTON, OH; DAWSON-BRYANT HS; (SR); Hnr Roll; Nat Hon Sy; USAA; WWAHSS; Comm Volntr; Chrch Yth Grp; FCA; Mth Clb/Tm; MuAlphaTh; Off Aide; Prom Com; SADD; Bsball (V C); Ftball (V C); Track (V); Wt Lftg (V); Stu Cncl (R); Marketing & Sales; Marshall U; Shawnee State U

ROWE, CHRISTOPHER; CLEVELAND, OH; COLLINWOOD HS; (SR); Hnr Roll; MVP; Perf Att; Sci Fairs; St of Mnth; CARE; Hosp Aide; Red Cr Aide; ArtClub; Cmptr Clb; DARE; Emplmnt; Mth Clb/Tm; Photog; ROTC; Acpl Chr; Swg Chr; Bsball (V); Bskball (J); Stu Cncl (P); Yrbk (P); Law; Art; U of Akron; UCLA

ROWE, SHANA D; COLUMBUS, OH; LIFESKILLS CTR OF NORTHERN COLUMBUS; (SR); Comm Volntr; Peer Tut/Med; Tchrs Aide; SP/M/VS; Two Plays "Oh, God What Color Is Trouble" and "First Love"; SAVE Awards; Primary and Secondary Education, Management; Photography, Culinary Arts, Communication; Ohio State U/Buckhead U; Clark-Atlanta U/Morris Brown

ROWLAND, ASHLEY; CARROLL, OH; BLOOM-CARROLL HS; (JR); Hi Hnr Roll; Nat Hon Sy; Nat Mrt LOC; Otst Ac Ach Awd; Perf Att; Pres Ac Ftns Aw; Sci Fairs; WWAHSS; Key Club; Photog; Sci Clb; Spanish Clb; Bskball (V L); Cr Ctry (V L); Sccr (V L); Track (V L); Who's Who Among High School Athletes; Architecture; Journalism; Ohio State U; Ohio U Athens

RUBENSTEIN, NICOLE; BETHEL, OH; U S GRANT JOINT VOC SCH; (JR); Hnr Roll; Hab For Humty Volntr; DARE; Voc Ind Clb Am; Cut-A-Thon; Food Drives

RUBY, KAITLIN E; COSHOCTON, OH; COSHOCTON HS; (FR); Hnr Roll; Pres Ac Ftns Aw; Pres Sch; Sci Fairs; WWAHSS; Yth Ldrshp Prog; Red Cr Aide; Chrch Yth Grp; Emplmnt; Key Club; Chr; Ch Chr; Sccr (V L); Swmg (V L); Cl Off (P); Community Choir; Coshocton Youth Foundation; Civil Engineering; Education

RUCKER, JACKIE; DAYTON, OH; TROTWOOD MADISON HS; (SO); Hi Hnr Roll; MVP; Nat Hon Sy; Perf Att; Sci Fairs; Yth Ldrshp Prog; Biology Clb; DARE; Dbte Team; Drma Clb; Pep Squd; Sci Clb; Scouts; SP/M/VS; Bskball (J); Chrldg (J); Sccr (V L); Track (V); Stu Cncl (R); Registered Nurse; Computer and Information Service Mgr.

RUCKI, BRAD; OREGON, OH; CLAY HS; (JR); Hi Hnr Roll; FBLA; Bsball (J); Bskball (V L); Ftball (V L); All Year Honor-Roll; Sports Management; Visual Communications; Bowling Green State U; U of Toledo

RUIVIVAR, DANIELLE N; MARYSVILLE, OH; MARYSVILLE HS; (SR); Hnr Roll; Pres Ac Ftns Aw; Sci Fairs; St of Mnth; WWAHSS; Comm Volntr; Peer Tut/Med; ArtClub; DARE; Emplmnt; Off Aide; Outdrs Clb; Photog; Prom Com; Tchrs Aide; SP/M/VS; PP Ftbl (V); Sccr (V); Sch Ppr (R, P); Yrbk (R, P); MVP of Soccer Team; 2nd Team OCC- 2 Yrs Soccer; Advertising / Marketing; U of North Carolina Wilmington - Attending Fall 2005

RUIZ, TABATHA; CANTON, OH; TIMKEN SR HS; (FR); Ctznshp Aw; Hnr Roll; MVP; Nat Hon Sy; Otst Ac Ach Awd; Perf Att; St of Mnth; Peer Tut/Med; DARE; Scouts; Adv Cncl (R); Cl Off (P); Stu Cncl (R); CR (P); Kids Connection; Lawyer; Counselor; Harvard Law School; Princeton Law School

RUMMELL, TIFFANY; SHELBY, OH; SHELBY HS; (FR); Ctznshp Aw; Hnr Roll; Otst Ac Ach Awd; Perf Att; Sci Fairs; St of Mnth; ArtClub; Chrch Yth Grp; DARE; Jr Ach; Prom Com; Tmpl Yth Grp; French Clb; Bnd; Dnce; Vllyball (J); Stu Cncl (R); CR (R); Yrbk (E, P); Architect; Teacher; Stanford U; Princeton U

RUNCO, JULIANNE; STEUBENVILLE, OH; STEUBENVILLE HS; (SR); Hi Hnr Roll; Nat Hon Sy; Perf Att; Valdctrian; WWAHSS; Comm Volntr; Chrch Yth Grp; FCA; Ntl Beta Clb; French Clb; Bnd; Jzz Bnd; Mch Bnd; Pep Bnd; Swmg (V CL); Mathematics; Secondary Education; The Ohio State U; Denison U

RUNYON, WESSLY; IRONTON, OH; IRONTON HS; (FR); Ctznshp Aw; Hnr Roll; Perf Att; Peer Tut/Med; Chrch Yth Grp; Bsball (J); Bskball (J); Ftball (J); Physical Therapist; Math Teacher; Marshall U; Ohio State

RUSH, ERIKA N; KENTON, OH; KENTON SR HS; (FR); 4H Awd; Hnr Roll; Yth Ldrshp Prog; Comm Volntr; 4-H; Chrch Yth Grp; FCA; Lttrmn Clb; SADD; Bnd; Chr; Ch Chr; Mch Bnd; Cr Ctry (V L); GAA (V); Track (V L); Active Member of the UCC & Youth Group; Actor in Mission Trips; Education; Phys.; ONU; OSU Loma Branch

RUSH, SYDNEY; TOLEDO, OH; ST URSULA AC; (FR); Hnr Roll; ArtClub; Spanish Clb; Dvng (V L); Sccr (J); Track (V); Business Degree; U of San Diego

RUSSELL, REBA M; WELLSTON, OH; WELLSTON HS; (SO); 4H Awd; Hi Hnr Roll; Hnr Roll; Otst Ac Ach Awd; Perf Att; St of Mnth; USAA; Yth Ldrshp Prog; 4-H; ArtClub; Drma Clb; Jr Ach; Scouts; Bnd; Mch Bnd; Pep Bnd; SP/M/VS; Veterinarian; Pediatrician; Hocking Technical College

RUSSELL, TORI; CLEVELAND, OH; FAIRVIEW HS; (SO); Hnr Roll; Drma Clb; SP/M/VS; Swmg (V); Education; Computer Technology; Baldwin Wallace College; U of Akron

RUTHERFORD, MELISSA A; NILES, OH; MC KINLEY HS; (FR); Hnr Roll; Perf Att; Sci Fairs; Comm Volntr; Hosp Aide; Chrch Yth Grp; Lib Aide; Tchrs Aide; Bnd; Ch Chr; Clr Grd; Dnce; Cr Ctry; Sccr; Track; Future Nurses; Medical / Anything Doctor, Nurse; Legal / Lawyer; Ohio State U; Youngstown State U

RYAN, OLIVIA; MONROEVILLE, OH; MONROEVILLE HS; (JR); Hi Hnr Roll; Nat Hon Sy; Sci Fairs; St of Mnth; WWAHSS; Hosp Aide; Peer Tut/Med; Emplmnt; Key Club; Off Aide; Prom Com; Tchrs Aide; Bskball (V); Scr Kpr (V); Track (V L); Cl Off (T); Yrbk (E); National Honors Society; Nuclear Medicine Technologist; Findlay; Lorain County Community College

RYAN, RENA M; TROY, OH; TROY HS; (SR); DAR; Hi Hnr Roll; Hnr Roll; MVP; Pres Ac Ftns Aw; Comm Volntr; Hab For Humty Volntr; Peer Tut/Med; Key Club; Chr; Bskball (J); Forensic Science; Northern Kentucky U

SABO, BRITTANY; PICKERINGTON, OH; PICKERINGTON HS CTRL; (JR); Hi Hnr Roll; Comm Volntr; Peer Tut/Med; Chr; Golf (V); Stu Cncl; Distinguished Honor Roll; Psychology; Pre-Med; U of Michigan; Bowling Green U

SAGE, CORY R; CHARDON, OH; CHARDON HS; (FR); Hi Hnr Roll; Hnr Roll; Perf Att; Pres Sch; St of Mnth; Yth Ldrshp Prog; Comm Volntr; DARE; Emplmnt; NYLC; Sci Clb; Bsball; Recreation League Basketball

SAINE, JILLIAN M; LIMA, OH; LIMA SR HS; (SO); Hi Hnr Roll; Hnr Roll; Nat Hon Sy; WWAHSS; Comm Volntr; Chrldg (V); Registered Nurse; Teacher

SALTSMAN, MALLORY B; WELLSTON, OH; WELLSTON HS; (SO); 4H Awd; Hi Hnr Roll; Hnr Roll; WWAHSS; Yth Ldrshp Prog; Comm Volntr; 4-H; Chrch Yth Grp; Drma Clb; Pep Squd; Quiz Bowl; Bnd; Chr; Clr Grd; SP/M/VS; American Cancer Society/Relay for Life Volunteer; Jackson Cty Leadership Team; Medical Degree in Plastic Surgery; Performing Arts Education; Ohio U; Medical College of Georgia

SALYERS, MICHAEL A; EVANSPORT, OH; TINORA/FOUR CTY VOC HS; (SR); Hnr Roll; DARE; Emplmnt; Ntl FFA; Scouts; Wrstlg (V L); Diesel Mechanics; Ohio Technical College-Cleveland

Rucker, Jackie
Trotwood Madison HS
Dayton, OH

Rohrbacher, Misty J
Edison HS
Sandusky, OH

Rockey, Mary L A
Southern Hills Jvs Career Ctr
Bethel, OH

Roeder, James C
North Olmsted HS
North Olmsted, OH

Sage, Cory R
Chardon HS
Chardon, OH

SAMELKO, LAURYN; STRONGSVILLE, OH; STRONGSVILLE HS; (JR); Hnr Roll; Nat Ldrshp Svc; WWAHSS; Yth Ldrshp Prog; Comm Volntr; Key Club; Mth Clb/Tm; Scouts; Spanish Clb; Vllyball (JC); Stu Cncl (R); CR (R); Pre-Med; Occupational Therapy; Loyola U of Chicago; U of Miami

SANCHEZ, ALICIA F; CORTLAND, OH; JOHN F KENNEDY HS; (JR); Hi Hnr Roll; Nat Hon Sy; WWAHSS; Comm Volntr; Peer Tut/Med; Chrch Yth Grp; Sci Clb; SADD; Scr Kpr (L); Sccr (L); Track (J); Sch Ppr (R); Yrbk (E); Presidential Classroom International Leaders Summit; Ohio High School Athletic Association 2004 OHSAA Foundation: Captain/Leaders Conference; International Relations/Business; Law

SANCHEZ, MARIAH; AMSACN, OH; LAKOTA HS; (FR); Hnr Roll; Perf Att; Sci Fairs; St of Mnth; Comm Volntr; Peer Tut/Med; DARE; Quiz Bowl; Tchrs Aide; Bnd; Chr; Mch Bnd; Pep Bnd; Ohio State

SANEDA, JOSHUA; CANAL WINCHESTER, OH; HARVEST PREP SCH; (JR); Hi Hnr Roll; Nat Hon Sy; Sci Fairs; St of Mnth; WWAHSS; Comm Volntr; Chrch Yth Grp; Emplmnt; FCA; Prom Com; Spanish Clb; Chr; SP/M/VS; Bsball (V L); Ftball (V CL); Adv Cncl (R); Cl Off (P, S); Stu Cncl (R); CR; National Society of High School Scholars; 1st Place-OSU Exercise Award at State SC Fair 2003; Athletic Training; Business Management; Otterbein College; Wilmington College

SATTERFIELD, JONATHON D; GALLOWAY, OH; MADISON CHRISTIAN; (SR); Hnr Roll; Comm Volntr; Chrch Yth Grp; Emplmnt; Mus Clb; Photog; Chr; Ch Chr; Orch; Yrbk (E); Music Education Degree; Capital U

SATTLER, ANDREA C; MARYSVILLE, OH; MARYSVILLE HS; (FR); Hnr Roll; Perf Att; Pres Sch; Comm Volntr; Peer Tut/Med; Chrch Yth Grp; Jr Cls League; Lib Aide; Sccr (J L); Sftball (J L); National Member of the National Piano - Playing Auditions; Nursing; Sports Medicine; Ohio State U; U of Missouri Columbia

SAUDER, LANAE K; MANSFIELD, OH; MADISON COMP HS; (JR); Duke TS; Hnr Roll; MVP; Perf Att; Sci Fairs; St of Mnth; WWAHSS; Comm Volntr; Chrch Yth Grp; Emplmnt; Key Club; Lib Aide; Prom Com; French Clb; Bnd; Mch Bnd; Orch; Sftball (J); Tennis (V CL); Stu Cncl (R); Leadership Club; Executive Committee; Business; Pre-Law; U of Texas Austin; Ohio State U Columbus

SAULTER, LEAH J; CANTON, OH; CANTON SOUTH HS; (SO); Hnr Roll; Nat Hon Sy; Otst Ac Ach Awd; Pres Ac Ftns Aw; Chrch Yth Grp; Foreign Clb; Ch Chr; Tennis (J); Astronomy; Harvard U; U of Miami

SAVNIK, SHAE M; YOUNGSTOWN, OH; FITCH HS; (SR); Bskball (JCL); Sftball (J); Track (JCL); Yrbk (R, P); National Honor Society; MVP Basketball; Athletic Trainer; U of Akron

SAWKINS, SYDNEY; TOLEDO, OH; WHITMER HS; (FR); ArtClub; Flg Crps; Orch; Sccr (J); Book Club; Veterinarian; Masters Degree DVM (Doctor of Vet. Med.); Ohio State U

SAXON, TESSA R; GALLIPOLIS, OH; GALLIA AC HS; (FR); Hnr Roll; WWAHSS; Yth Ldrshp Prog; Chrch Yth Grp; Key Club; NYLC; SADD; Chr; SP/M/VS; Vllyball; Veterinarian; Rio Grande U; Pensacola Christian College

SAXTON, VALERIE D; ZANESVILLE, OH; ZANESVILLE HS; (JR); 4H Awd; F Lan Hn Soc; Hi Hnr Roll; Hnr Roll; Otst Ac Ach Awd; Hosp Aide; 4-H; DARE; Jr Cls League; Tchrs Aide; Latin Clb; Chr; Vllyball (J L); Volunteered At County Home for 3 Years; Women of Science Award; Nursing; Criminal Justice; Ohio U-Zanesville; Ohio State U-Columbus

SAYRE, COURTNEY M; PARIS, OH; MINERVA HS; (SR); Hnr Roll; Otst Ac Ach Awd; Sci Fairs; WWAHSS; Off Aide; Aultman Career Academy; Registered Nurse; Physician's Assistant; Aultman College of Nursing & Health Sciences

SCARBERRY, SHAYNE P; THURMAN, OH; GALLIA AC HS; (SO); 4H Awd; Hnr Roll; MVP; Perf Att; 4-H; Wdwrkg Clb; Cr Ctry (V L); Sccr (V L); Track (V L); Horses, Pigs 4-H; Pharmacy; Doctorate; Ohio State U; Rio Grande U

SCARBRO, ADAM; CLEVELAND, OH; LINCOLN-WEST HS; (SO); Ctznshp Aw; St of Mnth; Comm Volntr; Peer Tut/Med; Aqrium Clb; Emplmnt; Bnd; Master's Degree / Animal Science; Biology; Ohio State; Ohio Northern Reserve U

SCERE, NADINE; TOLEDO, OH; CTRL CATHOLIC HS; (SO); Hnr Roll; Nat Hon Sy; Perf Att; Sci Fairs; St of Mnth; Comm Volntr; Mus Clb; Spanish Clb; Dnce; Orch; SP/M/VS; OMEA District I Solo & Ensemble Contest / Rating I In Class C; Music; Pre-Medical Studies; Eastern Michigan U; Duke U

SCHAEFER, JESSICA; DAYTON, OH; ARCHBISHOP ALTER HS; (FR); Otst Ac Ach Awd; Emplmnt; Key Club; Spanish Clb; Cr Ctry (J); Key Club; Spanish Club; U of Dayton

SCHAFLE, KYLE; BRECKSVILLE, OH; PADUA FRANCISCAN HS; (SR); Hnr Roll; WWAHSS; Comm Volntr; Key Club; SADD; Skiing; Hotel Management; Pace U; U of Denver, Kent State U

SCHEERER, SARA; NORWALK, OH; WESTERN RESERVE HS; (FR); 4H Awd; USAA; WWAHSS; 4-H; Emplmnt; Spanish Clb; Bnd; Mch Bnd; Pep Bnd; Bskball (J); Sftball (V L); Vllyball (J); Criminal Justice; Lawyer

SCHIFANO, STEVEN R; CANTON, OH; JACKSON HS; (JR); Hnr Roll; St of Mnth; WWAHSS; Comm Volntr; Key Club; Voc Ind Clb Am; Spanish Clb; Bnd; Mch Bnd; Pep Bnd; Ice Hky (V); Mighty Moose Elementary Outreach; Skills USA Computer Maintenance Silver Medal Winner; Information Technologies; Stark State College of Technology; U of Akron

SCHLATHER, MAUREEN T; AVON, OH; AVON HS; (FR); Ctznshp Aw; Hi Hnr Roll; Pres Ac Ftns Aw; Sci Fairs; St of Mnth; USMC Stu Ath Aw; WWAHSS; Comm Volntr; Chrch Yth Grp; DARE; Jr Ach; JSA; Key Club; Tchrs Aide; Spanish Clb; Dnce; Drl Tm; PPSqd (V); Stu Cncl (R); CR (T); Championship Level Irish Dancer; Leo Club; Accounting; History / Political Science; John Carroll U; Dartmouth College

SCHMETZER, KALLI; CINCINNATI, OH; (SO); Hi Hnr Roll; Hnr Roll; St of Mnth; WWAHSS; Chrch Yth Grp; Emplmnt; Key Club; Mod UN; Orch; Teaching; History

SCHMIDT, JORY; COLUMBUS, OH; GAHANNA LINCOLN HS; (JR); Hnr Roll; Comm Volntr; Mus Clb; Bnd; Mch Bnd; Orch; Pep Bnd; Independent Band (Drixa); Music Performance; Recording Technology; Ohio State U; Capital U

SCHMIDT, LAUREN N; CINCINNATI, OH; NORTHWEST HS; (JR); F Lan Hn Soc; Hi Hnr Roll; Nat Hon Sy; Otst Ac Ach Awd; St of Mnth; WWAHSS; Key Club; Foreign Clb; Chr; Lit Mag (E); Sch Ppr (R); Orange Belt in Karate (Not in School); Young Life; Creative Writing; Japanese; Miami U Oxford; U of Evansville

SCHMIDT, TONYA R; TOLEDO, OH; WHITMER CAREER & TECH CTR; (JR); Hnr Roll; Perf Att; BPA; Drma Clb; Off Aide; Pep Squd; Acpl Chr; Chr; Officer in Chorale; Music; Ohio State U; U of Toledo

SCHMITTER, EMMA J; LOGAN, OH; LOGAN HS; (SO); Ctznshp Aw; Hi Hnr Roll; Hnr Roll; Otst Ac Ach Awd; Perf Att; Pres Ac Ftns Aw; St of Mnth; Peer Tut/Med; Spec Olymp Vol; Chrch Yth Grp; Emplmnt; Key Club; Off Aide; Pep Squd; Bnd; Ch Chr; Mch Bnd; SP/M/VS; Adv Cncl (R); Treasurer of Key Club; Clarinet Ensemble; Physical Therapy; Cosmetology; Ohio State U; Stanford U

SCHNEIDER, ALEX P; CINCINNATI, OH; COLERAIN HS; (JR); Hnr Roll; Nat Hon Sy; Perf Att; Hab For Humty Volntr; Emplmnt; Stu Cncl (S)

SCHNELL, MORGAN; NORWALK, OH; WESTERN RESERVE; (SO); Comm Volntr; 4-H; Chrch Yth Grp; DARE; Off Aide; Tchrs Aide; Spanish Clb; Chr; Track (V); Education; Bowling Green State U; Firelands Bowling Green

SCHOLES, MELISSA; DAYTON, OH; XENIA CHRISTIAN HS; (SO); USAA; Cr Ctry (V); Track (V); National Society of High School Scholars; Kinesiology/Sports Medicine

SCHOLES, STEPHANIE; DAYTON, OH; XENIA CHRISTIAN HS; (SR); All Am Sch; Nat Hon Sy; Nat Mrt LOC; Nat Stu Ath Day Aw; Sci Fairs; USAA; WWAHSS; Comm Volntr; Chrch Yth Grp; Off Aide; Tchrs Aide; Swmg (V CL); CR (R); Yrbk (E, P); French Education; Grace College

SCHOONOVER, DEVIN J; LANCASTER, OH; LANCASTER HS; (JR); Hi Hnr Roll; Hnr Roll; Peer Tut/Med; ArtClub; Emplmnt; Sccr (V CL); National Art Society; Teacher; Marine Biology; Ohio U

SCHOTTENSTEIN, COREY M; COLUMBUS, OH; BEXLEY HS; (JR); Hnr Roll; MVP; Emplmnt; SADD; Tmpl Yth Grp; Bskball (C); Golf (V L); Stu Cncl; Business; U of Miami; Indiana U

SCHRACK, AUTUMN; BELLVILLE, OH; CLEAR FORK HS; (JR); Hnr Roll; Nat Hon Sy; Perf Att; Comm Volntr; Chrch Yth Grp; French Clb; Bnd; Drm Mjr; Majorette Captain 2 Years; Principal's Academic Award 3 Years; Marketing; Public Relations; Bowling Green State U; Otterbein College

SCHULER, ASHLEY; WEST SALEM, OH; NORTHWESTERN RESERVE; (SO); Hnr Roll; Off Aide; Bskball (VJCL); Member of Youth 4 Youth; Master's Degree in Science / Anesthesiologist; Ohio State U; Duke U

SCHULTZ, ASHLEY M; LAKEVIEW, OH; INDIAN LAKE HS; (FR); Hnr Roll; Perf Att; WWAHSS; Comm Volntr; Emplmnt; Key Club; Pep Squd; French Clb; Bnd; Jzz Bnd; Mch Bnd; Pep Bnd; Track (V); Bowling-Varsity, Junior Varsity; Young Marines; Forensic Science; Math; Ohio State; Bowling Green

SCHULTZ, CARLY A; GENOA, OH; GENOA AREA HS; (JR); 4H Awd; Hi Hnr Roll; Otst Ac Ach Awd; Pres Sch; St of Mnth; WWAHSS; Comm Volntr; 4-H; AL Aux Girls; Chrch Yth Grp; DARE; Drma Clb; Key Club; Lttrmn Clb; Prom Com; Bnd; Chr; Ch Chr; Jzz Bnd; Bskball (V L); Track (V L); Stu Cncl (R); CR (R); Yrbk (R); Key Club President '05-'06; 4-H Club President '04-'06; To Be an Educator; To Earn a PhD; Bowling Green State U; The Ohio State U

SCHULTZ, EMILY; SEVEN MILLS, OH; PADUA HS; (SR); Hi Hnr Roll; Nat Hon Sy; WWAHSS; Hab For Humty Volntr; Peer Tut/Med; Red Cr Aide; DARE; Emplmnt; Key Club; Photog; Svce Clb; Bnd; Mch Bnd; SP/M/VS; Stg Cre; Lit Mag (R); Yrbk (R, P); Retreat Team Leader (2 Yrs.); Pro-Life Group; TRIE

SCHULTZ, JARED; PATASKALA, OH; GRANVILLE CHRISTIAN AC; (SO); Hnr Roll; Mth Clb/Tm; Wdwrkg Clb; Bskball (J); Sccr (V L); Sch Ppr (E); Yrbk (E); Mount Vernon Nazarene; Ohio State U

SCHULZE, KRISTI; MARIA STEIN, OH; MARION LOCAL HS; (JR); Hnr Roll; MVP; ArtClub; DARE; Emplmnt; FTA; Lttrmn Clb; Mth Clb/Tm; Pep Squd; Prom Com; Swmg (V CL); Track (V CL); Psychology; Counseling; Wright State U; Sinclair Community College

SCHUPP, ANTHONY J; WILLOUGHBY, OH; (JR); Hi Hnr Roll; Hnr Roll; Nat Hon Sy; Otst Ac Ach Awd; Perf Att; Comm Volntr; Key Club; Spanish Clb; Skiing (V); Tennis (J); Track (J); NHS (National Honor Society); AP Courses; Electrical Engineering; Business; Case Western Reserve; Bowling Green U

SCHWAB, EMILY; FAIRFIELD, OH; MC AULEY HS; (FR); Hnr Roll; Comm Volntr; Key Club; Svce Clb; Golf (J); Stu Cncl (R); Service Leader, First Honors All Year, & President of Scrapbook Club; Psychology; Sociology; Boston College; Loyola U Chicago

SCHWAB, EMILY C; CINCINNATI, OH; COLERAIN HS; (SR); F Lan Hn Soc; Hi Hnr Roll; Hnr Roll; Pres Sch; WWAHSS; Yth Ldrshp Prog; Comm Volntr; ArtClub; Emplmnt; Off Aide; Prom Com; French Clb; Dnce; Straight "A" Award; Cum Laude; Pharmacy; Finding Cure for Breast Cancer

SCHWARTZ, RACHEL M; TROY, OH; TROY HS; (SO); Hi Hnr Roll; Hnr Roll; Comm Volntr; Peer Tut/Med; Key Club; Scouts; Chr; Clr Grd; Dnce; Flg Crps; In Astra and Running for Treasurer; Member of FCCLA; Psychology; Teaching; Bowling Green State U; Ohio State U

SCHWITZGABLE, SARAH A; CANTON, OH; GLENOAK; (JR); Hnr Roll; Nat Hon Sy; Comm Volntr; Emplmnt; Key Club; Off Aide; Prom Com; Tchrs Aide; Clb; Bskball; Cr Ctry (V L); Track (V L); Stu Cncl (R)

SCIACCA-COX, CAYLEB C; WASHINGTON COURT HOUSE, OH; WASHINGTON HS; (FR); Ctznshp Aw; Hnr Roll; MVP; Otst Ac Ach Awd; Perf Att; St of Mnth; CARE; Peer Tut/Med; Chrch Yth Grp; DARE; Emplmnt; Lib Aide; Tchrs Aide; Stg Cre; Bsball (VJ); Bskball (VJC); Ftball (JCL); Track (JCL); Wt Lftg; Stu Cncl (T); Samuel Adams Award; Criminal Law; Coaching; Ohio State U; U of Cincinnati

SCOFIELD, DANIEL A; MEDINA, OH; MEDINA HS; (JR); F Lan Hn Soc; Hi Hnr Roll; Hnr Roll; Nat Hon Sy; WWAHSS; Comm Volntr; Peer Tut/Med; Chrch Yth Grp; Emplmnt; Key Club; German Clb; Stg Cre; Sccr (J); German National Honor Society - President / Secretary; German American Partnership Program - Exchange Student; Architecture; U of Cincinnati; Ohio State U

SCOTT, ANGELA; HARROD, OH; TEMPLE CHRISTIAN SCH; (JR); Hi Hnr Roll; Hnr Roll; WWAHSS; Yth Ldrshp Prog; Comm Volntr; Chrch Yth Grp; Drma Clb; Mth Clb/Tm; Prom Com; Chr; SP/M/VS; Vllyball (J); Cl Off (V); Sch Ppr (R); Yrbk (P); Laws of Life School Winner (2003); Laws of Life Top Sophomore Winner (2004); Music Performance; Sign Language

SCOTT, KERRI; TORONTO, OH; EDISON HS; (JR); Hi Hnr Roll; Hnr Roll; Nat Hon Sy; Chrch Yth Grp; Emplmnt; Prom Com; Scouts; Spanish Clb; Chrldg; Sccr (V L); Sftball; Swmg (V L); Wt Lftg (V); Cl Off (S); Stu Cncl (R); Close-Up; Speech Pathology; U of Akron; Ohio State U

SCOTT, MICHELLE; WARREN, OH; CHAMPION HS; (SO); Hnr Roll; USAA; Cmptr Clb; DARE; Key Club; P to P St Amb Prg; SADD; Tchrs Aide; Bnd; Clr Grd; Jzz Bnd; Mch Bnd; Track (V); Vllyball (J); Computer Engineer; Computer Science; Ohio State U; Youngstown State U

SCOTT, MICHELLE L; CANAL FULTON, OH; NORTHWEST HS; (SO); Hnr Roll; Chrch Yth Grp; French Clb; Skiing; Sccr (V L); Marine Biology

SCOTT, MORGAN; HILLIARD, OH; HILLIARD DARBY HS; (JR); Hi Hnr Roll; Hnr Roll; Sci/Math Olympn; St of Mnth; WWAHSS; Comm Volntr; German Clb; Sccr (V); Swmg (J); Psychology; Radio Broadcast

SCOTT, NATALIE M; DEFIANCE, OH; DEFIANCE SR HS; (SR); Hnr Roll; Nat Mrt Fin; WWAHSS; AL Aux Girls; Chrch Yth Grp; DECA; Emplmnt; FCA; HO'Br Yth Ldrshp; Pep Squd; Prom Com; Bskball (J); Chrldg (V CL); Track (V L); Interior Design; Bowling Green State U

SCOTT, SHARON A; ELYRIA, OH; ELYRIA HS; (JR); Ctznshp Aw; Hnr Roll; Otst Ac Ach Awd; WWAHSS; Comm Volntr; Spec Olymp Vol; Chrch Yth Grp; Key Club; Off Aide; SADD; Tchrs Aide; Spanish Clb; Stu Cncl (R); Lorain County Alliance of Black School Educators; Law; Business; Miami U (Oxford Ohio)

SEARS, JESSICA; WEST CHESTER, OH; LAKOTA WEST HS; (SO); Hi Hnr Roll; Comm Volntr; Peer Tut/Med; Chrch Yth Grp; Emplmnt; Bskball (J); Sccr (JC); J. Kyle Braid Leadership Semi Final; Mock Trial/Pride Club; Orthopedic Medicine; Physical Therapy; The U of North Carolina; Wake Forest U

Sciacca-Cox, Cayleb C
Washington HS
Washington Court House, OH

Schottenstein, Corey M
Bexley HS
Columbus, OH

Schwartz, Rachel M
Troy HS
Troy, OH

SEBALD, BECCA; HAMILTON, OH; BADIN HS; (SO); 4H Awd; DAR; Hi Hnr Roll; Pres Ac Ftns Aw; St of Mnth; WWAHSS; Yth Ldrshp Prog; 4-H; Emplmnt; Key Club; P to P St Amb Prg; SADD; Dnce; Education; Miami U Ohio

SEDIGE, SUSAN; SYLVANIA, OH; NORTHVIEW HS; (FR); Hnr Roll; Comm Volntr; DARE; French Clb; Golf (J L); Law; Medicine; Stanford U; U of Honolulu

SEGULIN, STEPHANIE; MEDINA, OH; MEDINA HS; (SO); Hnr Roll; WWAHSS; Chrch Yth Grp; Key Club; Sftball (J); Student Athletic Trainer, Letter Winner; Sports Medicine / Athletic Training

SEIFERT, KARLA; BARBERTON, OH; BARBERTON HS; (SO); Ctznshp Aw; Hnr Roll; MVP; Perf Att; St of Mnth; Drma Clb; Key Club; Tchrs Aide; Chr; SP/M/VS; Chrldg (J); Gmnstcs; PP Ftbl; Key Club; Ohio State U

SEKIGUCHI, TOMOKO; HILLIARD, OH; HILLIARD DAVIDSON HS; (JR); Hi Hnr Roll; Hnr Roll; Nat Hon Sy; Perf Att; WWAHSS; Comm Volntr; Peer Tut/Med; Spec Olymp Vol; Chrch Yth Grp; DARE; Emplmnt; FCA; Fr of Library; Key Club; SADD; Clb; Orch; SP/M/VS; Cr Ctry (L); Tennis (J); Track (J); Stu Cncl (R); Yrbk (R); Freshman Focus Leader; Cultural Mediator; International Relations; Public Relations; Ohio State U; Capital U

SELVARAJAH, RAMONA; SPRINGFIELD, OH; SPRINGFIELD NORTH HS; (JR); Ctznshp Aw; DAR; Hi Hnr Roll; Hnr Roll; Nat Hon Sy; St Optmst of Yr; Comm Volntr; Hosp Aide; Jr Ach; Photog; Prom Com; Tchrs Aide; Tennis (V); Stu Cncl (R); CR (R); Piano; Special Wish; Dentistry; Pre-Med; New York U; Ohio State U

SENNHENN, JARROD W; LORAIN, OH; LORAIN SOUTHVIEW HS; (SO); Hi Hnr Roll; Otst Ac Ach Awd; Perf Att; WWAHSS; Spec Olymp Vol; Key Club; Mod UN; Bnd; Mch Bnd; Orch; Pep Bnd; Golf (J); Sccr (J); CR (R); Key Club Vice President; Member of School's Governing Council; Veterinary Science; Plastic Surgery; Ohio State U; Case Western Reserve

SERGENT, JENNIFER; WARREN, OH; CHAMPION HS; (SR); Hnr Roll; St of Mnth; Red Cr Aide; Key Club; Off Aide; Pep Squd; Bnd; Mch Bnd; Pep Bnd; SP/M/VS; Stu Cncl (R); Student Mentor for Red Cross; Band President-Senior Year; Kent State-Trumbull

SESCO, BENJAMIN; ASHTABULA, OH; WEST JHS; (MS); Hi Hnr Roll; Hnr Roll; Nat Hon Sy; Chess; Chrch Yth Grp; Bnd; Mch Bnd; Golf (J); Stu Cncl (R); National Jr Honor Society; Engineering; Information Science; Ohio State U; Yale U

SEVERANCE, SAMANTHA; CAMBRIDGE, OH; JOHN GLENN HS; (FR); Hi Hnr Roll; Hnr Roll; Comm Volntr; Chrch Yth Grp; Key Club; Orch; Track; Psychology; Psychiatry

SEVERINI, SILVIA V P; HUDSON, OH; HUDSON HS; (JR); Hnr Roll; MVP; Comm Volntr; Photog; Svce Clb; Spanish Clb; Dnce; Gmnstcs; Sccr (J); Track (V L); BS in Nursing

SEXTON, CATHERINE; FINDLAY, OH; FINDLAY HS; (JR); Hnr Roll; Perf Att; St of Mnth; Comm Volntr; Chrch Yth Grp; Scouts; Spanish Clb; Chr; Mat Maid; Culinary Arts; Business Management; U of Findlay; Pennsylvania Culinary Art Institute

SEZGINIS, ALKAN; NORTHWOOD, OH; NORTHWOOD HS; (JR); Hi Hnr Roll; Hnr Roll; Otst Ac Ach Awd; Perf Att; St of Mnth; Hosp Aide; Bskball (J); Golf (J L); Track (VJ); Cl Off (P); Most Improved-Boys Basketball; Pre-Med; Journalism; Ohio State U; New York U

SHAFFER, AMBER; ELMORE, OH; WOODMORE HS; (SO); Hi Hnr Roll; Otst Ac Ach Awd; Pres Sch; St of Mnth; WWAHSS; Comm Volntr; Drma Clb; Key Club; Ntl FFA; Prom Com; French Clb; Bnd; Mch Bnd; Pep Bnd; SP/M/VS; Stu Cncl (R); Star Greenhand Award-FFA; Outstanding Freshman Marcher-Marching Band; Equine Management; Chemistry; U of Findlay; Bowling Green State U

SHAFFER, FREDRICK; GEORGETOWN, OH; RIPLEY UNION LEWIS HUNTINGTON HS; (JR); Hnr Roll; St of Mnth; USMC Stu Ath Aw; DARE; Emplmnt; ROTC; Voc Ind Clb Am; Wdwrkg Clb; Bnd; Drl Tm; Mch Bnd; Pep Bnd; JVS Diploma; Master Carpenter Certificate

SHAFFER, RYAN; AKRON, OH; FIRESTONE HS; (SR); Ctznshp Aw; Hnr Roll; Nat Mrt Fin; WWAHSS; Comm Volntr; DECA; Emplmnt; Scouts; Bsball (V L); Cr Ctry (J L); Sccr (V L); DECA National Competitor in Marketing Management Series Event; Gold Seal Graduate; Business Degree in Marketing; Master's Degree; Ohio U; U of Akron

SHAFFER, SARAH; WEST UNITY, OH; MILLCREEK-WEST UNITY; (JR); Hnr Roll; Nat Hon Sy; Perf Att; Pres Ac Ftns Aw; Sci Fairs; DARE; Emplmnt; Off Aide; Prom Com; Sci Clb; Tchrs Aide; Spanish Clb; Bnd; Mch Bnd; Pep Bnd; Bskball (J); Scr Kpr (V); Sftball (J); Vllyball (V); Cl Off (S); CR (S); Early Childhood Education; Bluffton U Ohio

SHAHADEH, HADEAL; CLEVELAND, OH; JOHN MARSHALL HS; (JR); Ctznshp Aw; Hnr Roll; Nat Hon Sy; Perf Att; Sci Fairs; WWAHSS; Comm Volntr; Off Aide; French Clb, Skiing; Yrbk (P); Multicultural Club; Classical Academy (College Prep-Course); Bachelor's Degree; Master's Degree; Cleveland State U

SHAHBODAGHI, DAVID; NEW ALBANY, OH; NEW ALBANY HS; (JR); Ctznshp Aw; Hi Hnr Roll; Hnr Roll; Comm Volntr; Chess; Cmptr Clb; NYLC; Quiz Bowl; Bnd; Mch Bnd; Cr Ctry (V); Track (V); Cl Off (T); Eagle Award Recipient; Pre-Med; Muskingum

SHAHEEN, NAHDIA; OREGON, OH; CLAY HS; (SR); Hnr Roll; WWAHSS; Yth Ldrshp Prog; Red Cr Aide; BPA; Chrch Yth Grp; DECA; Emplmnt; HO'Br Yth Ldrshp; Key Club; Prom Com; Quill & Scroll; Sftball (JC); Adv Cncl (R); Cl Off (R); Stu Cncl (R); CR (R); Yrbk (R, P); Ohio Association of Student Council Representative; Relay for Life Committee / Cancer Society; Small Business Management; Marketing; Owens Community College; U of Toledo

SHANKEL, BENJAMIN; CANTON, OH; EAST CANTON HS; (FR); Hi Hnr Roll; Hnr Roll; Otst Ac Ach Awd; Pres Sch; USAA; USMC Stu Ath Aw; Yth Ldrshp Prog; Chess; Chrch Yth Grp; Mth Clb/Tm; Acpl Chr; Ch Chr; SP/M/VS; Stg Cre; Bsball; Ftball (J); Skiing; Wt Lftg; Cl Off (V); Stu Cncl (R); Honors Choir; Ohio State U; Malone College

SHARMA, SURABHI; DAYTON, OH; BEAVERCREEK HS; (JR); Yth Ldrshp Prog; Comm Volntr; Hosp Aide; Peer Tut/Med; Tmpl Yth Grp; Spanish Clb; Dnce; India Club Youth Representative / Karate Yellow Belt / Classical Dance; Volunteer at Miami Valley Hospital / India Club Executive Committee Youth Rep; Medical; Health Care; Case Western U; Ohio State U

SHARP, KATELIN A; AKRON, OH; COPLEY/FAIRLAWN HS; (JR); Comm Volntr; Off Aide; French Clb; Chr; Vsy Clb (J); Vllyball; Physical Therapy; Middle Childhood Education; Ohio U; U of Toledo

SHAUCK, CHLOE; LORAIN, OH; MARION L. STEELE; (MS); Hi Hnr Roll; Perf Att; Pres Sch; Comm Volntr; Spec Olymp Vol; Drma Clb; Mus Clb; Scouts; Tchrs Aide; Chr

SHAW, AARON; STRASBURG, OH; STRASBURG FRANKLIN HS; (JR); Hnr Roll; St of Mnth; WWAHSS; Comm Volntr; Hosp Aide; AL Aux Boys; Emplmnt; HO'Br Yth Ldrshp; Tchrs Aide; Golf (J); Track (V); Stu Cncl; Doctor of Orthopedics; Bowling Green U; MCO (Medical College of Ohio)

SHAW, AARON R; WARREN, OH; CHAMPION HS; (JR); WWAHSS; Comm Volntr; Chrch Yth Grp; Key Club; Bnd; Jzz Bnd; Mch Bnd; Pep Bnd; Cr Ctry; Relay for Life Volunteer; History Teacher; Youngstown State U; Kent State U

SHAW, COURTNEY; ASHTABULA, OH; EDGEWOOD HS; (SO); Hnr Roll; WWAHSS; Pep Squd; Bnd; Drm Mjr; Mch Bnd; Pep Bnd; Chrldg (J)

SHAW, JESSICA; VAN WERT, OH; LINCOLNVIEW SCH; (JR); Hnr Roll; Otst Ac Ach Awd; Comm Volntr; 4-H; DARE; Prom Com; Sci Clb; Tchrs Aide; Spanish Clb; Bskball; Golf (V L); Sftball (V L); Sch Ppr (P); Yrbk (P); 7th Place of 50 Golfers At Tournament; Maintain 36 GPA; BS in Nursing; BS in Veterinary Medicine; International Business College; U of Findley

SHAWVER III, RICK; LORAIN, OH; LORAIN SOUTHVIEW HS; (FR); DARE; Jr Ach; Scouts; Wdwrkg Clb; Bskball (J); Ftball; Wt Lftg; Boy Scouts of America; Bowling; Law; Medicine; Ohio State U

SHEETS, HOLLY; COLUMBUS, OH; WALNUT RIDGE HS; (FR); Hi Hnr Roll; Hnr Roll; Chrch Yth Grp; DARE; Emplmnt; Lib Aide; Off Aide; Scouts; Bnd; Jzz Bnd; Mch Bnd; Sftball (V L); Tennis (V L); Stu Cncl (T); National Junior Honor Society; Veterinarian; Ohio State U; Mount Vernon Nazarene College

SHEETS, STACY D M; FAIRBORN, OH; FAIRBORN HS; (SO); DAR; Hnr Roll; Pres Sch; St of Mnth; Comm Volntr; Chrch Yth Grp; DARE; Lib Aide; ROTC; French Clb; Bnd; Manager of Basketball Team; Master Sgt in ROTC; Nurse; EMT; Wright State; Kentucky

SHEFFIELD, LAURKITA; CINCINNATI, OH; HUGHES CTR; (SO); Ctznshp Aw; Hi Hnr Roll; Hnr Roll; Perf Att; Comm Volntr; Quiz Bowl; Real Estate Agent/Developer/Investor; Business; U of Cincinnati

SHERIFF, AMANDA L; FRAZEYSBURG, OH; TRI-VALLEY HS; (JR); Ctznshp Aw; Hnr Roll; Perf Att; WWAHSS; Chrch Yth Grp; Emplmnt; Fr of Library; Lib Aide; Scouts; Accounting (CPA); Business; Zane State College; Muskingum College

SHERMAN, AMY; LONDON, OH; LONDON HS; (SR); 4H Awd; Hi Hnr Roll; Nat Hon Sy; WWAHSS; 4-H; AL Aux Girls; Jr Ach; Tchrs Aide; SP/M/VS; Bskball (J); Chrldg (V L); Quick Recall / In the Know - Member of School News Program; School News Program; Art; Communication Arts; Wilmington College

SHEROCK, NICOLE; MASSILLON, OH; JACKSON HS; (JR); Hnr Roll; Nat Hon Sy; Pres Sch; St of Mnth; Yth Ldrshp Prog; Comm Volntr; Hab For Humty Volntr; Chrch Yth Grp; Emplmnt; Key Club; Tchrs Aide; Spanish Clb; Chr; Skiing; 3 Year Member of Student Council; Business Management; Biology; Ohio U; Kent State U

SHERWOOD, SCOTT; WARREN, OH; HOWLAND HS; (JR); Hnr Roll; Comm Volntr; Spanish Clb; Cr Ctry (V); Track (V); Coach's Award for Hard Work in Cross Country; Engineering; Teaching

SHINABERRY, SARAH; WESTERVILLE, OH; WORTHINGTON CHRISTIAN HS; (FR); Hnr Roll; Chrch Yth Grp; FCA; Acpl Chr; SP/M/VS; Skiing; Student Youth Leader At Church; Worship Team At Church; Bachelor of Arts; Ohio Colleges

SHIPMAN, STEPHANIE; TOLEDO, OH; WOODWARD HS; (SO); Hi Hnr Roll; Hnr Roll; Perf Att; Sci Fairs; Yth Ldrshp Prog; Chrch Yth Grp; Emplmnt; French Clb; Bnd; Flg Crps; Jzz Bnd; Mch Bnd; Sftball (V L); CR (V); Jefferson Madison Leadership; Teen Pep; Nursing; Bowling Green State U; U of Toledo

SHIREMAN, STEPHANIE; CURTICE, OH; NOTRE DAME AC; (FR); Hi Hnr Roll; Comm Volntr; Ch Chr; Published Poet; 3rd Place Language Day at UT / Spanish; MRI Tech; Degree in Nuclear Medicine; Owens Community College; U of Findlay

SHODA, LIZ; EASTLAKE, OH; WILLOUGHBY SOUTH HS; (JR); Hi Hnr Roll; Nat Hon Sy; WWAHSS; Emplmnt; Key Club; Tchrs Aide; Spanish Clb; Sftball (V L); 5+ Years of Travel Fast Pitch Softball; 9+ Years of Piano Lessons; Psychology; Journalism; Oberlin College; Muskingum College

SHOEMAKER, SARAH-BETH; PEEBLES, OH; ADAMS CTY CHRN SCH; (SO); Hnr Roll; Nat Hon Sy; Comm Volntr; Chrch Yth Grp; Cmptr Clb; Drma Clb; Emplmnt; FCA; Fr of Library; Lib Aide; Mus Clb; Chr; Ch Chr; SP/M/VS; Stg Cre; Bskball (V); Chrldg (V); Gmnstcs (V); Cl Off (P); Early Childhood Development; Communication; Shawnee State U

SHOOK, KELLI; LANCASTER, OH; STANBERY 9TH GRADE SCH; (FR); Chr; Medical Field; Animal Science; Ohio U; Ohio State U

SHOOP, MELISSA J; MAUMEE, OH; MAUMEE HS; (JR); Hnr Roll; Perf Att; WWAHSS; Comm Volntr; Chrch Yth Grp; Emplmnt; Chr; Ch Chr; Sftball; Track; Early Childhood Education

SHORT, KENDRA; WAPAKONETA, OH; WAPAKONETA HS; (SO); Hnr Roll; Perf Att; Comm Volntr; ArtClub; Chrch Yth Grp; FCA; Key Club; Lib Aide; Quiz Bowl; Spanish Clb; Bnd; Cr Ctry (V L); Track (V L); Scholar Athlete Award; Marine Biology

SHOWERS IV, FLOYD; YOUNGSTOWN, OH; RAYEN HS; (MS); Hnr Roll; Sci Fairs; Tchrs Aide; Bskball (C); Ftball (C); Stu Cncl; CR; Neocam Program at YSU; Computer Technology; Business Management; Miami Florida U; Syracuse New York

SHUEY, SABRINA; ZANESVILLE, OH; WEST MUSKINGUM HS; (FR); 4H Awd; Hi Hnr Roll; St of Mnth; WWAHSS; Comm Volntr; 4-H; Chrch Yth Grp; Drma Clb; FCA; Key Club; Quiz Bowl; SADD; Dnce; SP/M/VS; Sccr (J); Accountant; Teacher; Muskingum; Ashland

SHUK, JOULIA; COPLEY, OH; COPLEY HS; (FR); Hi Hnr Roll; Hnr Roll; Nat Hon Sy; Sci/Math Olympn; Comm Volntr; Spch Team; German Clb; Bnd; Mch Bnd; Sch Ppr (R); Academic Challenge; Business Computer Engineer; Communications; Ohio Miami U; Ohio State U

SHULTZ, ANDREW; PERRYSBURG, OH; PERRYSBURG HS; (SO); Hnr Roll; Perf Att; WWAHSS; Comm Volntr; Spec Olymp Vol; Chrch Yth Grp; P to P St Amb Prg; SP/M/VS; Stg Cre; Lcrsse (VJ); National Ski Patrol; People to People; Architecture; Landscape Architecture; Colorado State U; Syracuse U

SHUMAKER, ALYSSA B; WESTERVILLE, OH; WESTERVILLE CTRL HS; (SO); DAR; Hi Hnr Roll; St of Mnth; Comm Volntr; Peer Tut/Med; ArtClub; Chrch Yth Grp; Drma Clb; Emplmnt; FCA; Key Club; Mus Clb; Chr; Orch; SP/M/VS; Swg Chr; PP Ftbl; Vllyball (J); Adv Cncl; Stu Cncl (P); Sch Ppr (E, R); Key Club President for Two Years; Voted "Most Likely to Succeed" Two Years in a Row; Missions; Performance Arts; Cedarville U; Baptist Bible College & Graduate School

SHUMAN, JESSICA S; COLUMBUS, OH; EAST HS; (JR); Hnr Roll; Nat Hon Sy; Emplmnt; Off Aide; Stu Cncl (R); Biology; Pre-Med; Ohio State U; Ohio Dominican U

SIDERS, SHANNON; DAYTON, OH; ALTER HS; (SO); Hnr Roll; Comm Volntr; Chrch Yth Grp; Key Club; P to P St Amb Prg; SADD; Spanish Clb; Bskball; Cr Ctry (J); Secondary Education; Politics; Miami U

SIEBENHAAR, HANNAH; CANAL FULTON, OH; NORTHWEST HS; (SO); Hi Hnr Roll; Hnr Roll; Comm Volntr; Drma Clb; P to P St Amb Prg; French Clb; Bnd; Mch Bnd; SP/M/VS; Stg Cre; President's Education Award Program; World Traveler; Marine Biology

SIEBOLD, KRISTIN A; EASTLAKE, OH; WILLOUGHBY SOUTH HS; (JR); Hi Hnr Roll; Nat Hon Sy; WWAHSS; Peer Tut/Med; DARE; Drma Clb; Key Club; Sci Clb; Tchrs Aide; Bnd; Drm Mjr; Jzz Bnd; Mch Bnd; Secondary Education (English, Chem., or Music); Early Childhood Education; Miami U OH; Baldwin Wallace College OH

SIEH, ANTHONY O; COLUMBUS, OH; WEST HS; (SO); Comm Volntr; Spanish Clb; Sccr (V); Tennis (J); Track (V); Auto Body Specialist; Medical Assistant; Columbus State Community College; Ohio State U

SIEVERS, MICHAEL; SPRINGBORO, OH; BISHOP FENWICK HS; (JR); Hi Hnr Roll; WWAHSS; Comm Volntr; Emplmnt; Key Club; Scouts; Spanish Clb; Cr Ctry (J); Eagle Scout; U of Dayton; Xavier U

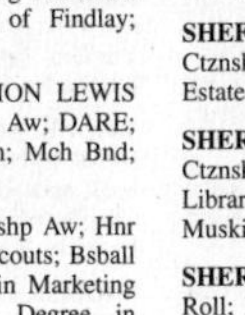

Shoop, Melissa J
Maumee HS
Maumee, OH

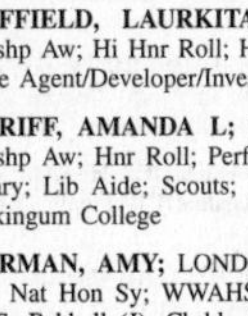

Shoemaker, Sarah-Beth
Adams Cty Chrn Sch
Peebles, OH

National
Honor Roll
Spring 2005

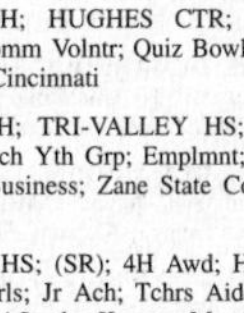

Shawver III, Rick
Lorain Southview HS
Lorain, OH

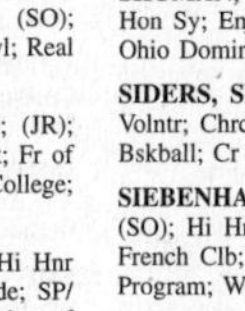

Showers IV, Floyd
Rayen HS
Youngstown, OH

SILVA, FELICIA N; FREMONT, OH; CLYDE HS; (FR); Hnr Roll; Perf Att; St of Mnth; DARE; Tchrs Aide; Spanish Clb; Took Care of Deceased Grandpa; Played Basketball in 5th & 6th Grade; Business Management; Interpreter for Spanish People; Owens Community College; Bowling Green State U

SILVERSTEIN, SYDNEY L; BEACHWOOD, OH; LAUREL SCH; (FR); Hi Hnr Roll; Otst Ac Ach Awd; Valdctrian; Yth Ldrshp Prog; Comm Volntr; Dbte Team; Mth Clb/Tm; Mus Clb; NtlFrnscLg; NYLC; Tmpl Yth Grp; Chr; Lcrsse (J); Tennis (J)

SILVIEUS, HOPE N; ASHTABULA, OH; STS JOHN AND PAUL CATHOLIC HS; (FR); Ctznshp Aw; Sci Fairs; Comm Volntr; Emplmnt; Key Club; Scr Kpr (VJ); Vllyball (J); Master's Degree in Teaching; Kent State U - Ashtabula; Youngstown State U

SIMMERMAN, ELIZABETH; CANTON, OH; HOOVER HS; (SR); Hi Hnr Roll; Hnr Roll; Nat Hon Sy; Nat Mrt LOC; Pres Ac Ftns Aw; WWAHSS; Spec Olymp Vol; Lib Aide; Prom Com; Quill & Scroll; Sccr (V CL); CR (R); Sch Ppr (E); National Merit Commended Student; U of Pittsburgh

SIMMONS, MALLORY; PAINESVILLE, OH; RIVERSIDE HS; (JR); Hnr Roll; WWAHSS; Chrch Yth Grp; DARE; Emplmnt; Key Club; Prom Com; Bnd; Mch Bnd; PP Ftbl (V); Track (V); Master's Degree; Neonatal Nurse

SIMPSON, JAVONNE; LIMA, OH; SOUTH MS; (MS); Hi Hnr Roll; Hnr Roll; Nat Hon Sy; Nat Sci Aw; Otst Ac Ach Awd; Perf Att; St of Mnth; Comm Volntr; Peer Tut/Med; ArtClub; DARE; Dbte Team; Outdrs Clb; Tchrs Aide; Bnd; Drm Mjr; SP/M/VS; Swg Chr; Stu Cncl (P); Sch Ppr (R); Yrbk (R); Go to College; Maintain a Good Career; Wright State; Atlanta A & M

SIMPSON, KELLEY; MOGADORE, OH; FIELD HS; (JR); Hnr Roll; Nat Hon Sy; Otst Ac Ach Awd; Perf Att; WWAHSS; Comm Volntr; Peer Tut/Med; AL Aux Girls; Emplmnt; Pep Squd; Prom Com; Svce Clb; Spanish Clb; Vllyball (J); Stu Cncl (R); Outstanding Student of 9 Weeks; Buckeye Girls State-Alternate; Music Business Management; U of Miami; U of Southern California

SIMS, SHAUNSE; CLEVELAND, OH; MARTIN LUTHER KING HS; (MS); Ctznshp Aw; Hnr Roll; MVP; Perf Att; St of Mnth; Yth Ldrshp Prog; Comm Volntr; DARE; Dnce; Drl Tm; Bskball (JC); Swmg (J); Track (C); Accounting; Accounting / WNBA; Duke U; North Carolina

SINGH, AMANDEEP; BROOK PARK, OH; MIDPARK; (JR); Ctznshp Aw; Hi Hnr Roll; Hnr Roll; Kwnis Aw; Nat Ldrshp Svc; Nat Mrt Fin; Otst Ac Ach Awd; Perf Att; Pres Sch; WWAHSS; CARE; Comm Volntr; Peer Tut/Med; DARE; Dbte Team; Emplmnt; Jr Ach; JSA; Key Club; NtlFrnscLg; NYLC; Dnce; Bskball (J); Cr Ctry (V CL); GAA (V L); Scr Kpr (VJ); Sftball (V); Track (V CL); Vsy Clb (V L); Adv Cncl (P); Cl Off (P, R); Stu Cncl (R); CR (P); Yrbk (R); Lt Gov Key Club International; Miss Brook Park 2nd Runner-Up; U of North Carolina; Psychology; U of North Carolina; Elon U

SINGHOFF, ANGELA G; CINCINNATI, OH; NORTHWEST HS; (JR); Key Club; Went Through Modeling Classes; Social Work; Eastern Michigan U; Cincinnati State U

SIRAK, LAUREN; CANFIELD, OH; BOARDMAN HS; (SR); F Lan Hn Soc; Hnr Roll; Nat Hon Sy; WWAHSS; Comm Volntr; Key Club; Prom Com; SADD; Bskball (V L); Sccr (V CL); Track (V L); Cl Off (R); Graduating with Honors; Integrated Health and Sciences; Physician's Assistant; Kent State U

SITO, MICHAEL; ELYRIA, OH; ELYRIA HS; (FR); Ctznshp Aw; Hi Hnr Roll; Hnr Roll; Otst Ac Ach Awd; Perf Att; Pres Ac Ftns Aw; St of Mnth; DARE; Emplmnt; Bsball (J); Golf (J); Getting a Bachelor's Degree

SITTON, DALENA; LORAIN, OH; LORAIN SOUTHVIEW HS; (FR); Hi Hnr Roll; Perf Att; Drma Clb; Pep Squd; Bnd; Drm Mjr; Mch Bnd; Pep Bnd; Registered Nurse; Respiratory Therapist

SIZEMORE, JOSHUA B; BELPRE, OH; BELPRE HS; (SO); Hnr Roll; Perf Att; Pres Ac Ftns Aw; Pres Sch; Chr; Bsball (J); Bskball (J); Ftball (VJ); Teen Institute; Physical Therapy; Ohio State U; North Carolina

SKINNER, KAYLEE M; LAGRANGE, OH; KEYSTONE HS; Hnr Roll; Sci Fairs; Yth Ldrshp Prog; Comm Volntr; DARE; Off Aide; Tchrs Aide; Bnd; SP/M/VS; Bsball; GAA; Sccr; Vllyball; Presidential Award in Education; Premier Soccer Goalie; Pediatrics / Medical Field; Ashland U; Lorain County Community College

SKINNER, TAELOR; ASHVILLE, OH; TEXAS VALLEY HS; (SO); Fut Prb Slvr; Hnr Roll; Perf Att; Sci Fairs; Sci/Math Olympn; St of Mnth; DARE; Drma Clb; Emplmnt; Mus Clb; Quiz Bowl; Spanish Clb; Chr; SP/M/VS; Sch Ppr (R); Poetry Contest 2nd Place; Published Poet; Creative Writing; English

SKIRVIN, JESSICA; HAMILTON, OH; LAKOTA WEST HS; (SR); Hi Hnr Roll; Nat Hon Sy; Comm Volntr; Peer Tut/Med; MuAlphaTh; Bnd; Mch Bnd; Qualifier for 2004 and 2005 AIME.; 2002 Ohio Mock Trial Outstanding Witness; Accounting; Mathematics; U of Pittsburgh

SLAGLE, JESSICA; PICKERINGTON, OH; PICKERINGTON HS; (JR); Hi Hnr Roll; Hnr Roll; Spec Olymp Vol; DARE; Dnce; Dance; U of Akron; North Carolina School of Arts

SLIWA, NATALIE M; EUCLID, OH; EUCLID HS; (SR); Hnr Roll; Perf Att; St of Mnth; WWAHSS; Peer Tut/Med; DARE; Emplmnt; Key Club; Mus Clb; Off Aide; Chr; Sch Ppr (E, R, P); Mayor's Team; Journalism; Bowling Green State U

SLOCUM, MARISSA W; ASHLAND, OH; MAPLETON HS; (SR); Chr; Sccr (V); Vllyball (VJ); Massage Therapy; North Central State College

SLONE, HOLLY; CANAL WINCHESTER, OH; CANAL WINCHESTER HS; (SR); Hnr Roll; Perf Att; St of Mnth; Off Aide; Medical Assisting Technology; Ohio U Lancaster

SMART, TANISHA L; LIMA, OH; LIMA SR HS; (JR); Hi Hnr Roll; Hnr Roll; Nat Hon Sy; Nat Stu Ath Day Aw; Otst Ac Ach Awd; Perf Att; St of Mnth; CARE; Comm Volntr; DARE; Mus Clb; Chr; Ch Chr; Bskball (VJ); Cr Ctry (V); Track (VJ); Cl Off (T); Sch Ppr (R); Dayton College; Toledo College

SMATHERS, BRYN; ALBANY, OH; ALEXANDER HS; (SO); Ctznshp Aw; Hnr Roll; Otst Ac Ach Awd; Perf Att; Pres Ac Ftns Aw; Peer Tut/Med; Spec Olymp Vol; Biology Clb; DARE; Ntl FFA; Pep Squd; French Clb; Bsball (V); Ftball (V CL); Wt Lftg (V); Academic Scholar Award; 2nd Place in Motocross Championship Logan OH; Mathematics Major; Succeed in Every Personal & Life Goal; Ohio U; Hocking College

SMITH, AMANDA; DOVER, OH; DOVER HS; (SO); 4H Awd; Hnr Roll; Kwnis Aw; Pres Ac Ftns Aw; St of Mnth; Peer Tut/Med; Red Cr Aide; 4-H; Chrch Yth Grp; HO'Br Yth Ldrshp; Key Club; Foreign Clb; Bnd; Mch Bnd; Stg Cre; Accounting; Law; Muskingum College

SMITH, AMANDALYN; COLUMBUS, OH; BRIGGS HS; (FR); Hnr Roll; Perf Att; St of Mnth; WWAHSS; Comm Volntr; Chrch Yth Grp; SP/M/VS; Vllyball; Sch Ppr (E); Cedarville U; Ohio U

SMITH, ASHLEE N; LAKE MILTON, OH; JMHS; (FR); Comm Volntr; Key Club; Sci Clb; Sftball (V); Vllyball; Junior Olympics Volleyball; People to People Volleyball; Criminal Justice/Law/Design; Ohio State; Penn State

SMITH, ASHLEY R; DAYTON, OH; DUNBAR HS; (JR); Hnr Roll; Nat Hon Sy; Otst Ac Ach Awd; WWAHSS; Peer Tut/Med; Vsity Clb; Drl Tm; Chrldg (V); Track (V L); Graduate of Wright Stepp Program Which Was Sponsored By Wright State U; Business Management; Astronomy; Alabama A & M; Wright State U

SMITH, BRANDI R; MARYSVILLE, OH; MARYSVILLE HS; (SO); Hnr Roll; Drma Clb; Chr; SP/M/VS; Pitched for Rec Softball Teams for 3 Years; Pre-Med; Linguistics; Ohio State U

SMITH, BRANDON; LUCASVILLE, OH; VALLEY HS; (FR); 4H Awd; Hnr Roll; Perf Att; Sci Fairs; Yth Ldrshp Prog; 4-H; Chrch Yth Grp; DARE; Wdwrkg Clb; Ch Chr; Sccr (V); 2nd Place Lucasville Kiwanis/MLS Soccer; Pass, Shoot, & Dribble Competition; 2nd Place School Art Show; Shawnee State U

SMITH, BRANDON L; CABLE, OH; TRIAD HS; (SR); Hi Hnr Roll; Hnr Roll; Comm Volntr; DARE; Wdwrkg Clb; Ftball (J); Track (V); Won 3rd Place Art Show; Won 1st Place Art Show; Police Officer

SMITH, BRITTNY; DAYTON, OH; MEADOWDALE HS; (JR); Hnr Roll; Sci Fairs; St of Mnth; Comm Volntr; Psychology; U of Missouri; Lincoln U

SMITH, CHASE; ZANESVILLE, OH; MAYSVILLE HS; (FR); Hi Hnr Roll; Hnr Roll; MVP; Nat Hon Sy; Otst Ac Ach Awd; WWAHSS; Emplmnt; Key Club; Vsity Clb; Bsball (J); Bskball (J); Golf (V L); Wrstlg (J); Key Club; Petroleum Engineer; Veterinarian; Ohio U; U of Marietta

SMITH, DAVID; RITTMAN, OH; WAYNE CTY SCHS CAREER CTR; (SR); Hi Hnr Roll; Hnr Roll; Comm Volntr; Bskball (J); Stu Cncl (R); 180 Hours As Assistant Trainer; Physical Therapy; Registered Nurse; U of Akron

SMITH, DEMARCO; CINCINNATI, OH; AIKEN UNIVERSITY HS; (JR); Ctznshp Aw; Hi Hnr Roll; Hnr Roll; Perf Att; St of Mnth; Comm Volntr; Emplmnt; Leadership; Criminal Justice; Architect; U of Cincinnati; Xavier U

SMITH, DEMARIO; MAPLE HEIGHTS, OH; MAPLE HEIGHTS HS; (JR); All Am Sch; MVP; DARE; Wdwrkg Clb; Bskball (JC); Ftball (VJCL); Business Degree; Alabama State U

SMITH, JACOB; CLINTON, OH; NORTHWEST HS; (FR); Hnr Roll; Otst Ac Ach Awd; Perf Att; Pres Sch; Comm Volntr; Fr of Library; NYLC; French Clb; Bnd; Jzz Bnd; Mch Bnd; Sch Ppr (R); Academic Challenge Team; Midwest Talent Search (27 on ACT); Political Science; Statistics

SMITH, MARI K; CINCINNATI, OH; WALNUT HILLS HS; (JR); Hi Hnr Roll; Hnr Roll; WWAHSS; ArtClub; Chrch Yth Grp; Emplmnt; Bnd; Chr; Jzz Bnd; Mch Bnd; Communication Sciences and Disorders; U of Cincinnati

SMITH, MOLLY; FINDLAY, OH; (SR); St of Mnth; Comm Volntr; Peer Tut/Med; Red Cr Aide; 4-H; Chrch Yth Grp; DARE; Drma Clb; FCA; Ntl FFA; Prom Com; Spch Team; Chr; Ch Chr; Dnce; SP/M/VS; Cr Ctry (J); Hsbk Rdg (V); Track (V C); 4-H VP and President 2001-2004; FFA Assistant Treasurer 2002-2003; Agriculture Education Teacher; Biology Teacher; U of Findlay; Ohio State Lima Campus

SMITH, MOLLY J; DAYTON, OH; ARCHBISHOP ALTER HS; (JR); Bskball (V L); Cr Ctry (J); Track (V L); National Honor Society Member; Science / Medicine; U of Dayton; Ohio State U

SMITH, MORGYN; NORWALK, OH; WESTERN RESERVE HS; (FR); Hnr Roll; Otst Ac Ach Awd; Perf Att; Sci Fairs; St of Mnth; Comm Volntr; DARE; Spanish Clb; Bnd; Stg Cre; Art-Artwork Judged / Part of the Gifted Program; Helping the School Draw Pictures for Yearbook; Graphic Arts - Drawing / Computer Arts; Actress / Marine Biologist; Bowling Green U; Ohio State U

SMITH, RANDY; AKRON, OH; TALLMADGE CHRISTIAN AC; (MS); Perf Att; Red Cr Aide; DARE

SMITH, RAYMOND E; SPRINGFIELD, OH; SPRINGFIELD NORTH HS; (SO); Ctznshp Aw; Hi Hnr Roll; Hnr Roll; Kwnis Aw; Otst Ac Ach Awd; Pres Sch; Sci Fairs; St of Mnth; WWAHSS; Comm Volntr; Emplmnt; HO'Br Yth Ldrshp; Key Club; Lib Aide; NYLC; Off Aide; Svce Clb; President, Kiwanis Key Club; Leadership Representative Distinguished Honoree; Political Science; Financial Agenting/Business Representative; U of California-Berkeley; U of California-Los Angeles

SMITH, RYAN B; BETHEL, OH; U S GRANT JOINT VOC SCH; (JR); Hnr Roll; Perf Att; Chrldg; Adv Cncl (P); Stu Cncl (R); Nail Model At Regionals for Skills USA; Business Management; Psychology; U of Cincinnati; Cincinnati State

SMITH, STEPHANIE; AKRON, OH; FIRESTONE HS; (SR); Nat Hon Sy; Valdctrian; WWAHSS; Comm Volntr; Chrch Yth Grp; Off Aide; Bnd; Mch Bnd; Pep Bnd; SP/M/VS; Lit Mag (E); Theoretical Physics; Ohio U

SMITH, TAMMY R; AKRON, OH; FIRESTONE HS; (SR); MVP; Sci Fairs; Comm Volntr; ArtClub; Emplmnt; Jr Ach; Photog; Prom Com; Scouts; Vsity Clb; Spanish Clb; Swmg (V); Visual Art Program; Fashion Design; U of Cincinnati

SMITH, TIFFANY; CINCINNATI, OH; READING HS; (JR); Hi Hnr Roll; Nat Hon Sy; Sci Fairs; Comm Volntr; Emplmnt; Key Club; Prom Com; Chr; SP/M/VS; Scr Kpr (V); Yrbk (P); Psychology; Photography; Ohio U; U of Cincinnati

SMITH, TORI A; MOGADORE, OH; FIELD HS; (SR); 4H Awd; Hi Hnr Roll; Nat Hon Sy; WWAHSS; 4-H; Physical Therapy; Kent State U; North Eastern Ohio U College of Medicine

SMITH, VERONICA; HAMILTON, OH; LAKOTA WEST HS; (JR); Hnr Roll; WWAHSS; Yth Ldrshp Prog; Comm Volntr; Emplmnt; Track (V); Focus Group, USATF & AAU Track & Field; Multi-Cultural Club

SMITH, WHITNEY; MARYSVILLE, OH; MARYSVILLE HS; (JR); Hnr Roll; Pres Sch; WWAHSS; Emplmnt; Tchrs Aide; Bnd; Mch Bnd; Pep Bnd; Stg Cre; Bskball (J); Sccr (J); Medicine; Film Production; Ohio State U; Kent State U

SMITHNOSKY, STEPHANIE M; CUYAHOGA FALLS, OH; ST VINCENT-ST MARY HS; (SO); Hnr Roll; Drma Clb; Mus Clb; Chrldg (J); Geometry Excellence; State Finalist in Teen Miss Pageant; Drama-Designing; UCLA; Juilliard

SMOLJAN, NATASA; EASTLAKE, OH; WILL SOUTH HS; (SO); Hi Hnr Roll; Hnr Roll; Comm Volntr; Key Club; Sci Clb; German Clb; John Carroll; Notre Dame College

SNADER, MICHAEL; WEST SALEM, OH; NORTHWESTERN HS; (SO); 4H Awd; Hnr Roll; WWAHSS; 4-H; Chrch Yth Grp; Photog; Scouts; Wdwrkg Clb; Track; Forensic Scientist; Ohio State U; College of Wooster

SNIDER, KASEY; NASHPORT, OH; BISHOP ROSECRANS HS; (JR); Hi Hnr Roll; Hnr Roll; Nat Hon Sy; Perf Att; WWAHSS; Comm Volntr; Chrch Yth Grp; Emplmnt; Key Club; Pep Squd; Svce Clb; Bskball (VJ); Tennis (VJ L); Track (V L); Art and Design; Ohio State U; Ohio U

SNIDER, SARAH; RICHMOND, OH; EDISON HS; (JR); All Am Sch; Hi Hnr Roll; Nat Hon Sy; Otst Ac Ach Awd; USAA; Yth Ldrshp Prog; Peer Tut/Med; Spec Olymp Vol; Chrch Yth Grp; Emplmnt; Lib Aide; Ntl Beta Clb; Sci Clb; Scouts; Svce Clb; Spanish Clb; Ch Chr; Skiing (J); Yrbk (E); Church Liturgist; Physician Assistant; Research Biologist; Duquesne U

SNODGRASS, MARIAH A; COLUMBUS, OH; HARVEST PREP SCH; (SR); Hnr Roll; Nat Hon Sy; WWAHSS; Comm Volntr; Spanish Clb; Bskball (V L); Sccr (V L); Cl Off (V); Senior Chapel Committee (SCC); Just Cause (Community Service); Pre-Law (Bachelor's Degree); Criminology; Howard U; Hampton U

SNOW, JUSTIN; MIDDLETOWN, OH; MIDDLETOWN HS; (JR); Hnr Roll; Otst Ac Ach Awd; Perf Att; Pres Ac Ftns Aw; WWAHSS; Spec Olymp Vol; Off Aide; Spanish Clb; Sccr (J); Track (VJ); Physical Therapy; Health Administration

SNYDER, LACONA A; WAVERLY, OH; WAVERLY HS; (SO); Hi Hnr Roll; Hnr Roll; Perf Att; Sci Fairs; Emplmnt; Jr Ach; Quiz Bowl; Sci Clb; French Clb; Stu Cncl (V); Forensics / Business Management; Music; Berklee School of Music; Ohio State U

Smith, Ashley R — Dunbar HS — Dayton, OH
Slagle, Jessica — Pickerington HS — Pickerington, OH
Silva, Felicia N — Clyde HS — Fremont, OH
Skinner, Kaylee M — Keystone HS — Lagrange, OH
Smith, Morgyn — Western Reserve HS — Norwalk, OH

SNYDER, WILLIAM J; COLUMBUS, OH; (SO); Chrch Yth Grp; DARE

SOKOL, JASEN; AVON LAKE, OH; AVON LAKE HS; (SO); Hi Hnr Roll; Sci/Math Olympn; Spec Olymp Vol; Emplmnt; Key Club; Quiz Bowl; Spanish Clb; Bnd; Mch Bnd; Pep Bnd; Pharmacy; Business; Ohio State U; U of Toledo

SOKOL, MEREDITH E; BRUNSWICK, OH; BRUNSWICK HS; (JR); Hnr Roll; Off Aide; French Clb; Golf (J); Yrbk (E, R, P); VOFT; Dermatology; Ohio State; Kent State

SOLANKI, KRUPA; CANFIELD, OH; CANFIELD HS; (FR); Hnr Roll; Key Club; Mth Clb/Tm; Scouts; Bnd; Mch Bnd; Pep Bnd; Tennis; JETS Club; Young Leaders; Medicine; Ohio State U

SOPKO, RYAN J; PARMA, OH; VALLEY FORGE HS; (JR); Hnr Roll; Perf Att; Comm Volntr; Chrch Yth Grp; Pep Squd; Bsball (VJ L); Bskball (J); Golf (V L); Wt Lftg; Education; Baldwin Wallace; Cleveland State U

SPANGLER, HEATHER; CIRCLEVILLE, OH; CIRCLEVILLE HS; (FR); 4H Awd; Hnr Roll; Otst Ac Ach Awd; Perf Att; Pres Ac Ftns Aw; St of Mnth; Comm Volntr; Peer Tut/Med; 4-H; Chrch Yth Grp; DARE; FCA; Key Club; Mth Clb/Tm; SADD; Vsity Clb; Chr; Ch Chr; SP/M/VS; Bskball; Sftball (V L); Vllyball (V L); Sch Ppr; Junior National Honors Society; Math Counts State Qualifier; Psychologist; Law; Miami U Ohio; Case Western U

SPANGLER, RACHAEL; CIRCLEVILLE, OH; CIRCLEVILLE HS; (FR); 4H Awd; Hnr Roll; Otst Ac Ach Awd; Perf Att; Pres Ac Ftns Aw; St of Mnth; Comm Volntr; Peer Tut/Med; 4-H; Chrch Yth Grp; DARE; FCA; Key Club; Mth Clb/Tm; SADD; Vsity Clb; Chr; Ch Chr; SP/M/VS; Bskball (VJ); Sftball (V L); Vllyball (VJ); Archie Griffen Sportsmanship Award; National Junior Honor Society; Primatologist; Large Animal Veterinarian; U of Maine; Northwestern

SPANGLER, SCOTT A; SHELBY, OH; SHELBY SR HS; (SR); Hi Hnr Roll; Hnr Roll; WWAHSS; DARE; Emplmnt; Ntl FFA; SP/M/VS; Bsball (V L); Golf (V CL); Landscape Architecture; Business; Ohio State U Mansfield; Bowling Green State U

SPEECE, BRITTANY D; WOOSTER, OH; CTRL CHRISTIAN SCH; (JR); Hi Hnr Roll; Perf Att; Yth Ldrshp Prog; Chrch Yth Grp; Pep Squd; Chr; Skiing; Tennis (V); CR (R)

SPENCE, SAMANTHA; HARRISON, OH; HARRISON HS; (SO); 4H Awd; Hi Hnr Roll; Hnr Roll; WWAHSS; Comm Volntr; Spec Olymp Vol; 4-H; Chrch Yth Grp; Jr Cls League; Key Club; Tchrs Aide; Latin Clb; 4-H Secretary; Pharmacy

SPENCE, WILLIAM; TOLEDO, OH; ROGERS HS; (SO); Ctznshp Aw; Hnr Roll; Otst Ac Ach Awd; Perf Att; St of Mnth; DARE; SADD; Bsball (V); Business; Toledo University, Ohio; Owens Ohio

SPILKER, KRISTIN M; CLEVELAND, OH; PADUA FRANCISCAN HS; (JR); Hnr Roll; Emplmnt; Key Club; U of Akron; Ohio U

SPOONER, DUSTY C; MILLFIELD, OH; ATHENS HS; (SR); 4H Awd; Ctznshp Aw; Hnr Roll; Otst Ac Ach Awd; WWAHSS; Comm Volntr; 4-H; Biology Clb; Chrch Yth Grp; Emplmnt; Lib Aide; Ntl FFA; Off Aide; Sci Clb; Hsbk Rdg; I DARE You Award 4-H; FFA 4-H Junior Fairboard; Degree in Veterinary Medicine; Degree in Farrier Science & Business; Ohio State U; Hocking College

SPRINGER, LA SHARA; LIMA, OH; LIMA SR HS; (JR); Hnr Roll; Nat Hon Sy; Perf Att; Comm Volntr; DARE; Lib Aide; CR (R); Honor Roll; Perfect Attendance; Nursing; Computer Technician; U of North Carolina At Greensboro; Catherine Gibbs College

STAHL, SAMANTHA C; TOLEDO, OH; ALLIANCE AC OF TOLEDO; (SO); Hnr Roll; Perf Att; St of Mnth; Director's List - 4 Times; Certificate of Appreciation; Teacher; Lawyer; U of Toledo; Bowling Green U

STAHL, TIFFANY; BATAVIA, OH; CNE; (SR); 4H Awd; Hnr Roll; Hosp Aide; 4-H; DECA; Emplmnt; Ntl FFA; ROTC; FFA Greenhand Degree; Certified Nursing Assistant; LPN; RN; Scarlet Oaks / LPN Program

STAKER, RYAN D; ZANESVILLE, OH; BISHOP ROSECRANS HS; (SO); Hi Hnr Roll; Hnr Roll; Sci Fairs; WWAHSS; Comm Volntr; Peer Tut/Med; Chrch Yth Grp; Emplmnt; Key Club; Bsball (V L); Freshman Basketball; Student of the Year-English I, Biology, Chemistry, French II, Religious Ed; Pharmacy; Optometry; Ohio Northern U; Ohio State U

STALDER, LESLIE N; MIAMISBURG, OH; MIAMISBURG HS; (JR); Hi Hnr Roll; Hnr Roll; St of Mnth; Yth Ldrshp Prog; Hab For Humty Volntr; Peer Tut/Med; Emplmnt; FBLA; NYLC; Off Aide; Spanish Clb; Top Two in Speech; Psychology; Pre-Vet; Ohio State; Wright State

STALLARD, STACEY K; TIFFIN, OH; OLD FORT HS; (FR); 4H Awd; Ctznshp Aw; Hnr Roll; Otst Ac Ach Awd; Perf Att; Sci Fairs; St of Mnth; Peer Tut/Med; 4-H; Bnd; Pep Bnd; Bskball (J L); Cr Ctry (V L); Track (V L); Dentistry; Medical Field; Ohio State U; Findlay College

STALLINGS, KEVIN; MANSFIELD, OH; MADISON COMP HS; (FR); Hnr Roll; Chrch Yth Grp; Tennis (J); CSI; Game Designer; Ohio State

STALLTER, BRIAN H; CELINA, OH; CELINA HS; (SR); Hi Hnr Roll; Jr Eng Tech; AL Aux Boys; FBLA; Prom Com; Quiz Bowl; Bsball (J); Ftball (J); Wrstlg (J); Cl Off (V); Yrbk (P); Aeronautical Engineering; Mechanical Engineering; Ohio State U

STANDOHAR, ELAINE; CORTLAND, OH; JOHN F KENNEDY HS; (JR); Hi Hnr Roll; Hnr Roll; Nat Hon Sy; Peer Tut/Med; DARE; Emplmnt; Key Club; Sci Clb; SADD; Cr Ctry (V L); PP Ftbl; Scr Kpr (V L); Sccr (JC); Track (J); Buckeyes Girls State Member; Forensic Scientist/Criminalist; Veterinarian; Chaminade U of Honolulu; U of Central Florida

STANTON, MICHAEL; TIMBERLAKE, OH; WILLOUGHBY SOUTH HS; (SO); Hi Hnr Roll; Perf Att; St of Mnth; WWAHSS; Comm Volntr; Chrch Yth Grp; Key Club; Spanish Clb; Pharmacy; Ohio Northern U; Toledo U

STAPLETON, JOHNNIE; IRONTON, OH; ROCK HILL HS; (SO); Hnr Roll

STARKEY, JANNA M; FRANKLIN, OH; SPRINGBORO HS; (SO); Hi Hnr Roll; USAA; WWAHSS; Comm Volntr; Peer Tut/Med; Chrch Yth Grp; Key Club; Lib Aide; Photog; SADD; Pediatrician; Georgetown College; U of Kentucky

STARKS, DOMINIQUE; CLEVELAND, OH; SOUTH HS; (SR); Hi Hnr Roll; Nat Mrt Sch Recip; Comm Volntr; Chrch Yth Grp; Tchrs Aide; Vsity Clb; Bskball (VJC); Cr Ctry (V); All City High School Basketball Game; Professional Basketball Game

STARMS, ALTA D; DAYTON, OH; COLONEL WHITE HS FOR THE ARTS; (SO); Hi Hnr Roll; Hnr Roll; MVP; Nat Hon Sy; Otst Ac Ach Awd; Perf Att; Sci Fairs; Sci/Math Olympn; St of Mnth; Comm Volntr; Hosp Aide; Peer Tut/Med; DARE; Drma Clb; JSA; Key Club; Photog; Flg Crps; SP/M/VS; Chrldg (V); Gmnstcs; Tennis (J); Track (V); Key Club; Dayton Chapter Del-Teens; Nursing; Physician's Assistant

STARR, ADAM J; TORONTO, OH; EDISON HS; (JR); MVP; Comm Volntr; Red Cr Aide; DARE; Scouts; Acpl Chr; SP/M/VS; Ftball (L); Track (L); Wt Lftg (V); CR (P); Fire Deps; Scouting; Soil Water Conservation; Forestry

ST CLAIR, SAMUEL; BELPRE, OH; BELPRE HS; (FR); Hnr Roll; St of Mnth; Yth Ldrshp Prog; DARE; Pep Squd; French Clb; Wrstlg (V); Navy Seals

STEBBINS, CHAD I; FARMERSVILLE, OH; VALLEY VIEW; (SR); 4H Awd; Hi Hnr Roll; Hnr Roll; Nat Hon Sy; WWAHSS; Comm Volntr; 4-H; ArtClub; Drma Clb; FTA; Ntl FFA; Off Aide; SADD; Tchrs Aide; SP/M/VS; Stg Cre; Agricultural Education Instructor; The Ohio State U

STECK, JUSTIN; CLEVELAND, OH; GARFIELD HTS HS; (JR); Hnr Roll; Yth Ldrshp Prog; Chrch Yth Grp; DARE; Drma Clb; Emplmnt; Off Aide; Tchrs Aide; SP/M/VS; Stg Cre; Mar Art (L); Received - Best Actor Award - 3 Yrs; Major in Theatre / Perform or Teach Theatre; Cleveland State U

STEELE, NATASHA; BYESVILLE, OH; MEADOWBROOK HS; (SO); Hnr Roll; MVP; Nat Hon Sy; Perf Att; WWAHSS; Peer Tut/Med; Mod UN; Ntl FFA; Scouts; Tchrs Aide; Bskball; Chrldg; Sftball (VJCL); Vllyball (J); Cl Off (S); CR (S, R); 2 Poems Published; National FFA Officer: Reporter for Local; Business Management; Accounting; Zane State College; Mount Vernon

STEIB, TOM; PAINESVILLE, OH; RIVERSIDE HS; (FR); Hi Hnr Roll; Hnr Roll; Perf Att; DARE; Emplmnt; Key Club; Tchrs Aide; Ftball; Wt Lftg; CR (R); Inducted to Great Lake Scholars; Biochemistry; Medical School; Cornell U; U of Pennsylvania

STEINERT, CAITLIN M; KENT, OH; KENT THEODORE ROOSEVELT HS; (SR); Nat Hon Sy; Chrch Yth Grp; Key Club; Latin Clb; Bnd; Mch Bnd; Orch; SP/M/VS; Tennis (V); Booster (School Spirit) Club; Interactive Multimedia; Education; Ohio U

STEINMETZ, MATTHEW A; BELLEVUE, OH; BELLEVUE SR HS; (SR); 4H Awd; Ctznshp Aw; Hnr Roll; Nat Hon Sy; Perf Att; WWAHSS; Yth Ldrshp Prog; Comm Volntr; Peer Tut/Med; 4-H; AL Aux Boys; Chrch Yth Grp; Emplmnt; Jr Ach; Lttrmn Clb; Ntl FFA; Svce Clb; Ch Chr; Ftball (VJ L); Wt Lftg (VJ); FFA State Farmer; Ohio State U Land Grant Scholarship; Agricultural Systems Management; Ohio State U

STENGER, DANIEL W; NEWARK, OH; NEWARK HS; (SO); Ctznshp Aw; Hi Hnr Roll; Hnr Roll; Nat Mrt Sch Recip; Otst Ac Ach Awd; St of Mnth; Yth Ldrshp Prog; Comm Volntr; Peer Tut/Med; DARE; Mth Clb/Tm; Foreign Clb; Orch; Track (J); Wt Lftg (J); CR (R); I Passed the SAT Test in the 8th Grade.; I Received the Highest Score on My Violin.; Forensic Scientist/ Criminal Justice; Engineering; The Ohio State U; Northwestern Colleges

STENNETT, TARA; LIBERTY CTR, OH; NAPOLEON HS; (SR); Hnr Roll; Otst Ac Ach Awd; Perf Att; WWAHSS; Comm Volntr; Red Cr Aide; ArtClub; BPA; Emplmnt; SADD; Spanish Clb; Chrldg (J L); Sccr (V L); Accounting/ Business; Psychology; Bowling Green State U; Northwest State Community College

STEPHANIK, DANIELLE; MARIETTA, OH; MARIETTA HS; (JR); Hi Hnr Roll; Hnr Roll; MVP; Nat Hon Sy; Otst Ac Ach Awd; USAA; WWAHSS; Spec Olymp Vol; Emplmnt; FBLA; Key Club; Off Aide; Prom Com; Tchrs Aide; Chr; Bskball (J L); Sccr (V CL); Track (V L); Cl Off (S, T); Rowing-Varsity, (L); Nutrition/Dietetics; Indiana U of Pennsylvania

STEPHENS, BEN; SHELBY, OH; SHELBY HS; (FR); 4H Awd; Hnr Roll; 4-H; Ftball; 4-H; Career in Graphic Arts; Ohio State U

STERN, BRAD; POWELL, OH; DUBLIN SCIOTO HS; (JR); Hnr Roll; Nat Hon Sy; Emplmnt; Bnd; Skiing; Yrbk; Engineer & Design Mechanical; Cal State U

STEVENS, CHRISTOPHER; SPRINGFIELD, OH; TECUMSEH HS; (FR); Ctznshp Aw; Hi Hnr Roll; Hnr Roll; Perf Att; St of Mnth; Outdrs Clb; Stu Cncl (R); Student Council; Freshman/Sophomore Class Council; Teaching Degree (For Film Studies); Architecture; Harvard U; Ohio State U

STEVENS, JEN; PERRY, OH; PERRY HS; (SO); Hnr Roll; MVP; Otst Ac Ach Awd; Perf Att; Chess; DARE; Key Club; Scouts; Vsity Clb; French Clb; Bskball (J); Scr Kpr (V); Sccr (V L); Sftball (J); Yrbk (E); Forensic Science; Equestrian Studies

STEVENS, SAMANTHA; CLYDE, OH; CLYDE HS; (FR); Hi Hnr Roll; Key Club; Spanish Clb; Chr; Tennis (J); Teacher; Photographer; Ohio State U

STEVENS, SHANIQUA V; GROVE CITY, OH; COLUMBUS ALT HS; (SO); Peer Tut/Med; DARE; Chr; Orch; Attend Ohio Dominican After School; Computer Tech; Wright State; DeVry U

STEVENS, TIFFANY M; MC DERMOTT, OH; NORTHWEST HS; (SO); Hi Hnr Roll; Hnr Roll; DARE; Drma Clb; SP/M/VS; Vllyball (VJ); Lead in Off-Broadway Performance; Continue My Acting Career; Writing & Poetry; Wright State U; Ohio State U

STEWARD, RYAN C; BLANCHESTER, OH; BLANCHESTER HS; (FR); Ctznshp Aw; Hnr Roll; Nat Hon Sy; Otst Ac Ach Awd; Perf Att; Cmptr Clb; DARE; Drma Clb; Mus Clb; Quiz Bowl; Schol Bwl; Bnd; Jzz Bnd; Mch Bnd; Orch; Bskball (J); Track (J); CR (R); Called Up to High School Band While Still in 8th Grade; Music; Science; Ohio State U; Cincinnati Performing Arts Academy

STEWART, DEBRA A; CIRCLEVILLE, OH; LOGAN ELM HS; (SR); Hi Hnr Roll; Hnr Roll; MVP; Nat Hon Sy; Perf Att; WWAHSS; ArtClub; BPA; Drma Clb; Off Aide; Prom Com; Tchrs Aide; Chr; Clr Grd; Flg Crps; Tennis (V CL); Track (J); Sch Ppr; National Art Honor Society; Bowling Team; Graphic Design; Interior Design; Wilmington College; Capital U

ST GEORGE, JOSEPH; YOUNGSTOWN, OH; CARDINAL MOONEY HS; (SO); Hnr Roll; WWAHSS; Yth Ldrshp Prog; Comm Volntr; Chrch Yth Grp; Drma Clb; FBLA; HO'Br Yth Ldrshp; NtlFrnscLg; Svce Clb; Spch Team; Spanish Clb; Chr; Ch Chr; SP/M/VS; Golf (V L); Tennis (V L); Cl Off (R); Stu Cncl (R); FBLA Officer; State and National Speech Qualifier; Political Science; Broadcast Journalism; George Washington U; Boston College

STITZLEIN, RYAN; GROVE CITY, OH; GROVE CITY HS; (JR); 4H Awd; Hi Hnr Roll; Kwnis Aw; Nat Hon Sy; WWAHSS; Comm Volntr; Peer Tut/ Med; 4-H; Key Club; SADD; Spanish Clb; Bnd; Mch Bnd; Lit Mag (R); Key Clubber of the Year; District Pride Award for Leadership; Bachelor's of Political Science:Communications; Law Degree; Miami U; Ohio U

STODDARD, ANDREW E; HUDSON, OH; CUYAHOGA VALLEY CHRISTIAN AC; (SR); Hi Hnr Roll; Nat Hon Sy; WWAHSS; Yth Ldrshp Prog; Chrch Yth Grp; Emplmnt; FCA; Jr Cls League; NtlFrnscLg; Lcrsse (V); Sccr (VJ L); Cl Off (R); National Latin Honor Society; Student-Athlete Scholarship Awards; Secondary Education; Youth Ministry; Moody Bible Institute; U of North Carolina-Chapel Hill

STOLTZ, DANIKA E C; COLUMBUS, OH; GRANDVIEW HEIGHTS HS; (SO); Hi Hnr Roll; Sci/Math Olympn; Chrch Yth Grp; Sci Clb; Bnd; Mch Bnd; Pep Bnd; Sccr (V L); Swmg (V); Track (V)

STOLTZ, JAKOB; COLUMBUS, OH; GRANDVIEW HEIGHTS HS; (JR); Ctznshp Aw; Hi Hnr Roll; St of Mnth; WWAHSS; Chess; Sci Clb; Scouts; Bnd; Jzz Bnd; Mch Bnd; Pep Bnd; Sccr (V L); Track (V); Wrstlg (V L); Knowledge Masters; Spanish Club

STOMBAUGH, ALYSSA; CAREY, OH; CAREY SCH; (SO); Hnr Roll; Nat Hon Sy; Drma Clb; Scouts; Tchrs Aide; Bnd; Chr; Mch Bnd; SP/M/VS; Bskball (J); National Honor Society; Doctor of Chiropractic

ST ONGE, BARRETT; GALLIPOLIS, OH; GALLIA AC; (FR); Chrch Yth Grp; Key Club; Chr; Track (J L); Life Guard; Doctor; OSU

ST ONGE, KARLAXNE; GALLIPOLIS, OH; GALLIA AC; Hnr Roll; Nat Hon Sy; WWAHSS; Chr; SP/M/VS; Swg Chr; Lifeguard; Fashion Designers; OSU

STOPAR, MELANIE; AKRON, OH; COPLEY HS; (FR); Key Club; Bnd; Clr Grd; Dnce; Mch Bnd; Key Club; Nuclear Medicine; Ultra Sound Technology; U of Akron; Kent State U

STORGILL, KIMBERLY; WESTERVILLE, OH; (JR); Hnr Roll; WWAHSS; Chrch Yth Grp; Bnd; Chr; Jzz Bnd; Mch Bnd

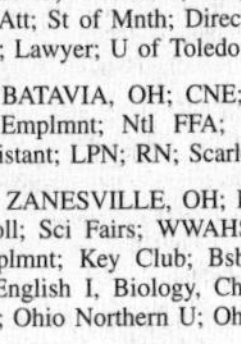
Stevens, Jen
Perry HS
Perry, OH

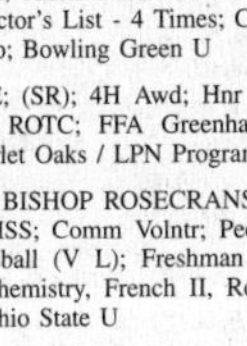
Starms, Alta D
Colonel White HS For The Arts
Dayton, OH

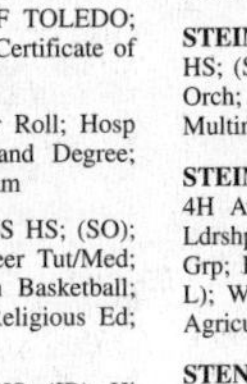
Stalder, Leslie N
Miamisburg HS
Miamisburg, OH

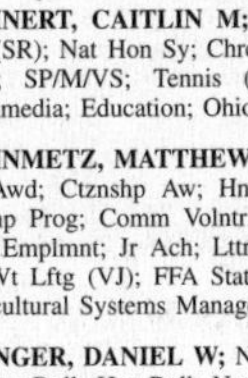
Stahl, Tiffany
CNE
Batavia, OH

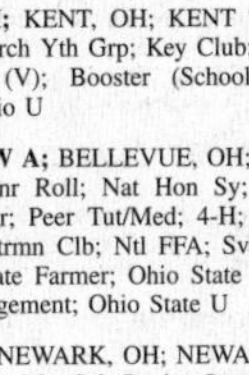
Spooner, Dusty C
Athens HS
Millfield, OH

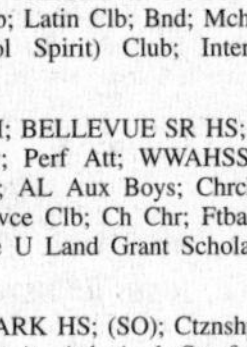
Springer, La Shara
Lima SR HS
Lima, OH

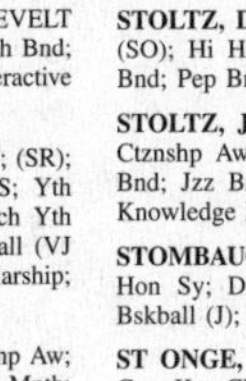
Stapleton, Johnnie
Rock Hill HS
Ironton, OH

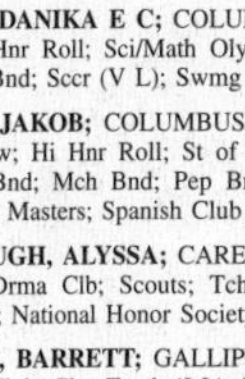
Starr, Adam J
Edison HS
Toronto, OH

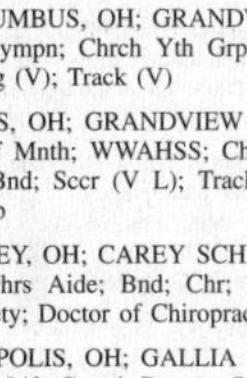
Stevens, Tiffany M
Northwest HS
Mc Dermott, OH

STORY, EVAN C; CLEVELAND, OH; FAIRVIEW HS; (SO); Hnr Roll; Perf Att; Sci Fairs; Yth Ldrshp Prog; Hab For Humty Volntr; Chrch Yth Grp; DARE; Chr; Bsball (J); Mission Trip; Broadcasting; Sports Management; Syracuse U; Otterbein College

STOTTSBERRY, ASHLEY D; ZANESVILLE, OH; WEST MUSKINGUM HS; (FR); WWAHSS; 4-H; Chrch Yth Grp; FBLA; Key Club; Dnce; Member of Stand; Teaching; Ohio State U

STOUFFER, MATTHEW; KINGSVILLE, OH; EDGEWOOD HS; (SO); Hnr Roll; St of Mnth; WWAHSS; Comm Volntr; Chrch Yth Grp; Mod UN; NRA Certified Apprentice Rifle Instructor; Fire Department Cadet First Responder

STOUT, AMBER C; NORTH ROYALTON, OH; NORTH ROYALTON HS; (FR); Hi Hnr Roll; Hnr Roll; Perf Att; Key Club; French Clb; Cr Ctry (J); Criminal Justice; Teaching

STOVER, HOLLY; ALVORDTON, OH; NORTH CTRL SCH; (FR); Hnr Roll; DARE; Drma Clb; Spanish Clb; Bnd; Mch Bnd; Pep Bnd; SP/M/VS; Vllyball (J); Ohio State U

STRADER, JULIANNE A; BUCYRUS, OH; COLONEL CRAWFORD HS; (JR); 4H Awd; Hi Hnr Roll; Comm Volntr; 4-H; Chrch Yth Grp; Emplmnt; Ch Chr; Bskball (J); Track (J); Yrbk; 4-H - 7 Yrs

STRADER, KATIE S; GRAFTON, OH; MIDVIEW HS; (FR); Hnr Roll; St of Mnth; Drma Clb; Key Club; SP/M/VS; Stg Cre; Doctor of Psychology; Writing; Ohio State; Miami U

STRAKER, BENNETT; OXFORD, OH; TALAWANDA HS; Mch Bnd; Key Club; Music; Engineering; Ohio State; Miami U

STRAND, ALEXIS A; NEWARK, OH; NEWARK CATHOLIC HS; (JR); Gov Hnr Prg; Hi Hnr Roll; Nat Hon Sy; St of Mnth; Yth Ldrshp Prog; Comm Volntr; Hosp Aide; Peer Tut/Med; Sci Clb; Latin Clb; Founder of School Science Club; Latin Co-Counsel President; Veterinary Medicine; Washington State U; Carroll College

STRASBAUGH, MAGGIE; FINDLAY, OH; LIBERTY BENTON HS; (SR); F Lan Hn Soc; Hi Hnr Roll; Nat Hon Sy; Otst Ac Ach Awd; Perf Att; St of Mnth; Valdctrian; WWAHSS; Comm Volntr; Chrch Yth Grp; Emplmnt; Lttrmn Clb; Prom Com; Svce Clb; Tchrs Aide; Vsity Clb; French Clb; Cr Ctry (V CL); Track (V CL); Marketing; Finance; Ohio U; Miami U

STRATTON, ARRON; BUCYRUS, OH; BUCYRUS HS; (SO); WWAHSS; Mus Clb; Bnd; Mch Bnd; Pep Bnd; Cr Ctry; Track; Stu Cncl

STRAUB, COREY L; OLD FORT, OH; OLD FORT HS; (SR); 4H Awd; Ctznshp Aw; Hnr Roll; Nat Hon Sy; Salutrn; USAA; WWAHSS; Bnd; Chr; Pep Bnd; SP/M/VS; Sch Ppr (R, P); Jazz Ensemble; Manager for Basketball Team; Computer Science & Engineering; U of Toledo

STREETER, KATIE; GALION, OH; COLONEL CRAWFORD HS; (FR); Hnr Roll; Perf Att; Cmptr Clb; DARE; Drma Clb; FCCLA; Mus Clb; Chr; Bskball (V L); Sftball (V L); Cl Off (V); Physical Therapy / Lawyer; Early Childhood Education; Duke U; Michigan State

STRICKLING, CARISSA; MIAMISBURG, OH; MIAMISBURG HS; (SR); Hnr Roll; Nat Hon Sy; Perf Att; Sci Fairs; St of Mnth; Comm Volntr; Chrch Yth Grp; DARE; Emplmnt; Jr Ach; SADD; Tchrs Aide; Latin Clb; Chr; Bskball (J); Sftball (L); Vllyball (J); Veterinarian; U of Findlay

STRIDSBERG, CHELSEA; SPRINGFIELD, OH; SPRINGFIELD NORTH HS; (JR); 4H Awd; Hi Hnr Roll; Otst Ac Ach Awd; Pres Ac Ftns Aw; Sci Fairs; St of Mnth; Yth Ldrshp Prog; Comm Volntr; Red Cr Aide; 4-H; Chrch Yth Grp; DARE; Emplmnt; Key Club; P to P St Amb Prg; Chrldg (JC); Lcrsse; Track (V); Physician Assistant; Kettering College of Medical Arts

STRIZHEUS, NATASHA; HILLIARD, OH; HILLIARD DARBY HS; (SO); Hi Hnr Roll; Perf Att; St of Mnth; WWAHSS; Comm Volntr; Peer Tut/Med; Chrch Yth Grp; Key Club; Outdrs Clb; Orch; Yrbk (R); Power of the Pen; National Oratorical Society; Chemical Engineering; Accounting

STROCK, ADRIAN M; RITTMAN, OH; RITTMAN HS; (SO); Hnr Roll; Otst Ac Ach Awd; St of Mnth; Chrch Yth Grp; Drma Clb; FCA; HO'Br Yth Ldrshp; Key Club; Off Aide; Pep Squd; Prom Com; Chr; SP/M/VS; Swg Chr; Bskball (J); Cl Off (P); Stu Cncl; HOBY Representative of Rittman High School; Scouting / Venture Crew President; Musical Theatre

STROCK, LATISHA; SOUTHINGTON, OH; SOUTHINGTON LOCAL SCH; (FR); Hi Hnr Roll; Hnr Roll; Drma Clb; Emplmnt; Lib Aide; Ntl Beta Clb; Bnd; Mch Bnd; Pep Bnd; Yrbk (P); Farming; Vet

STROHM, LUKE A; PLYMOUTH, OH; PLYMOUTH HS; (SR); Hnr Roll; Perf Att; St of Mnth; Emplmnt; P to P St Amb Prg; Bnd; Jzz Bnd; Mch Bnd; Pep Bnd; Golf (V); Physical Education Award; Net Working; Business Administration; North Central State College; Ohio State U Mansfield Campus

STROUD, TOREY; NORWALK, OH; NORWALK HS; (SR); Hnr Roll; Perf Att; St of Mnth; Hosp Aide; Red Cr Aide; ArtClub; Chrch Yth Grp; DARE; DECA; Emplmnt; Lttrmn Clb; Mus Clb; Tchrs Aide; Bnd; Pep Bnd; SP/M/VS; Bsball (J); Ftball (V L); Cl Off (P); Yrbk (R, P); Marketing Student of the Year; Firefighting; Marketing; Owens Community College

STROUSE, CHELSEA M; MANSFIELD, OH; MANSFIELD SR HS; MS; Ctznshp Aw; Hnr Roll; Otst Ac Ach Awd; Perf Att; Sci Fairs; St of Mnth; DARE; SADD; Bnd; Chr; Dnce; SP/M/VS; Sccr; CR (R); G.O.A.L.S; Lawyer; Fashion Designer; Ohio State U; Miami U

STULL, SARAH D; KENT, OH; THEODORE ROOSEVELT HS; (JR); Hnr Roll; Nat Hon Sy; WWAHSS; Comm Volntr; Drma Clb; Emplmnt; Key Club; Off Aide; P to P St Amb Prg; Photog; Svce Clb; Latin Clb; Chr; Stg Cre; Homecoming Choir; Lion's Club Award; Photography; Pharmacy; Cleveland Institute of Art; Kent State U

STUMP, JOSH; LAGRANGE, OH; KEYSTONE HS; (FR); Hi Hnr Roll; Hnr Roll; Sci Fairs; Yth Ldrshp Prog; 4-H; DARE; Off Aide; Scouts; Bnd; Jzz Bnd; Mch Bnd; Pep Bnd; Stu Cncl (P); Yrbk (E); Auto Mechanic; Video Game Designer

STUMPP, AUDREY; COLUMBUS, OH; GRANDVIEW HEIGHTS HS; (JR); Ctznshp Aw; Hnr Roll; Sci/Math Olympn; WWAHSS; Yth Ldrshp Prog; Emplmnt; Key Club; Sci Clb; Vsity Clb; Bnd; Mch Bnd; Pep Bnd; Tennis (J); Education

STURGEON, RICHARD A; WHEELERSBURG, OH; WHEELERSBURG HS; (JR); 4H Awd; Hi Hnr Roll; Nat Hon Sy; Comm Volntr; Peer Tut/Med; 4-H; Chrch Yth Grp; Emplmnt; Key Club; NYLC; Prom Com; Quiz Bowl; Clb; Chr; SP/M/VS; Ftball (V L); Track (L); Wt Lftg; Psychology; Spanish; Centre College

STURGILL, HOLLY R; PERRY, OH; RIVERSIDE HS; (SR); Hnr Roll; Nat Hon Sy; Pres Sch; St of Mnth; WWAHSS; Peer Tut/Med; Red Cr Aide; Chrch Yth Grp; Emplmnt; Lttrmn Clb; Mus Clb; Prom Com; Tchrs Aide; Spanish Clb; Bnd; Ch Chr; Mch Bnd; Pep Bnd; Stu Cncl (R); Sch Ppr (E); Academic Letter; Band Letter; English Education; Malone College

STURGILL, KENNETH J; PLYMOUTH, OH; PLYMOUTH HS; (SR); 4H Awd; Ctznshp Aw; Hnr Roll; Nat Hon Sy; Perf Att; Pres Ac Ftns Aw; St of Mnth; USAA; WWAHSS; Yth Ldrshp Prog; Comm Volntr; Peer Tut/Med; 4-H; Chrch Yth Grp; Emplmnt; FCA; Scouts; Clb; Bnd; Bsball (V L); Bskball (V L); Ftball (V L); Cl Off (V); Stu Cncl (R); Yrbk (E); Boy Scout Eagle Award; 4-H State Representative; Law; Ohio Northern U

STURRETT, BRITTANY; CANTON, OH; JACKSON HS; (JR); Otst Ac Ach Awd; Comm Volntr; Hab For Humty Volntr; Lib Aide; Spanish Clb; Chrldg (J); Sftball (J); Breast Cancer, Money Raised Walk; Diagnosis Research; Interior Design; NYC for Interior Design; Boston for Interior Design Suffolk

SUCHYTA, ERIC; DAYTON, OH; ARCHBISHOP ALTER HS; (JR); Hi Hnr Roll; Nat Hon Sy; Sci/Math Olympn; USAA; Peer Tut/Med; Chess; Key Club; Schol Bwl; Sci Clb; French Clb; Patterson Chemistry Essay Award; Science Olympiad Medals; Chemistry; Physics; Illinois; Wisconsin

SUCHYTA, SCOTT; DAYTON, OH; ARCHBISHOP ALTER HS; (JR); Hi Hnr Roll; Nat Hon Sy; Sci/Math Olympn; USAA; Peer Tut/Med; Chess; Key Club; Schol Bwl; Sci Clb; SADD; French Clb; Patterson Chemistry Essay Contest 2nd Place; Science Olympiad Medals; Chemistry; Physics; Illinois; Wisconsin

SULLIVAN, ALI; LAKEWOOD, OH; LAKEWOOD HS; (SR); Hnr Roll; Perf Att; Sci Fairs; WWAHSS; Peer Tut/Med; Emplmnt; Bnd; Sccr (V L); Track (V); Adv Cncl (R); Sch Ppr (R); Bachelor's in Nursing; Ohio U

SULLIVAN, JESSICA N; CINCINNATI, OH; NORTHWEST HS; (FR); Hi Hnr Roll; WWAHSS; Key Club; Prom Com; Quiz Bowl; Spanish Clb; Social Studies/History

SULLIVAN, JULIE M; CINCINNATI, OH; NORTHWEST HS; (SO); Hi Hnr Roll; Hnr Roll; Salutrn; WWAHSS; Chrch Yth Grp; Drma Clb; Key Club; Quiz Bowl; Spanish Clb; Chr; SP/M/VS; Knight Award; Section Leader in Chorus & Soloist; Music; Accounting

SULONEN, BRETT M; WARREN, OH; CHAMPION HS; (JR); Hi Hnr Roll; Hnr Roll; Nat Hon Sy; Otst Ac Ach Awd; St of Mnth; WWAHSS; Emplmnt; Key Club; Off Aide; Prom Com; Bnd; Jzz Bnd; Mch Bnd; Pep Bnd; Bsball (V L); Bskball (J); Sccr (V L); Stu Cncl (R); Band President 2005-06; Athletic Trainer

SULSER, JOSH; JOHNSTOWN, OH; JOHNSTOWN MONROE HS; (JR); Hnr Roll; Drma Clb; Emplmnt; Quiz Bowl; Wdwrkg Clb; SP/M/VS; I'm a blue-one belt in tae-Kwon-doe; I lettered in varsity quiz bowl as a junior; political science; law; Denison U, Granville, Ohio.; Oberlin U, Oberlin, Ohio

SUMMERS, KYLE; URBANA, OH; URBANA HS; (JR); Hnr Roll; Off Aide; Chr; Bskball (J); Ftball (J); Broadcasting (Sports); Sports Journalism; U Indianapolis

SUNDBERG, HANNAH M E; ANDOVER, OH; PYMATUNING VALLEY HS; (SR); 4H Awd; Ctznshp Aw; Hnr Roll; WWAHSS; 4-H; Chrch Yth Grp; FCA; Mod UN; Ntl FFA; Off Aide; Tchrs Aide; Bnd; Chr; Drm Mjr; Mch Bnd; Sftball (VJ L); 4-H For 10 Years; State FFA Degree Recipient; Master's Degree in Agricultural Education; Ohio State U

SUNDHEIMER, JEREMY A; MASSILLON, OH; PERRY HS; (SR); Hnr Roll; Perf Att; Emplmnt; Bsball; Culinary Arts (Bachelor's); Restaurant Management (Associate's); Pennsylvania Culinary Institute; Pittsburgh U

SUPANIK, NICHOLE; MT PLEASANT, OH; BRIDGEPORT HS; (SO); 4H Awd; Hnr Roll; WWAHSS; 4-H; Off Aide; Dnce; Hsbk Rdg; Mar Art (J); Sftball (VJ); Vllyball (J); Criminal Justice

SUSTAR, ANDREW; CLEVELAND, OH; CHARLES F BRUSH HS; (SO); Hnr Roll; Pres Ac Ftns Aw; WWAHSS; Scouts; Bsball (J); Ftball; Wrstlg; Ski Club; Chemistry; Ohio State U

SUSTAR, MICHELLE S; NEWBURY, OH; NEWBURY HS; (FR); Hi Hnr Roll; Nat Hon Sy; Comm Volntr; DARE; Bnd; Chrldg (J); Stu Cncl (P); On 2 Public Access Shows; Private Voice & Flute Lessons

SUTTER, SHANNA; CRESTLINE, OH; COLONEL CRAWFORD HS; (FR); F Lan Hn Soc; Hnr Roll; Jr Ach; French Clb; Chr; Bskball (J); Track (J); Teaching; Nursing; Ohio State; Toledo

SUTTLES, KAYLYN O; CINCINNATI, OH; COLERAIN HS; (JR); F Lan Hn Soc; Hi Hnr Roll; Hnr Roll; Nat Hon Sy; Perf Att; St of Mnth; Comm Volntr; Key Club; Prom Com; Bskball (JCL); Sftball (V L); Vllyball (V L); Student Council General Assembly; Math or Science Education

SUTTON, KRISSY; MARIETTA, OH; MARIETTA HS; (FR); Comm Volntr; BPA; Key Club; Sccr (J); Sftball (J)

SUTTON, STACY; CLEVELAND, OH; GARFIELD HTS HS; (JR); Hnr Roll; MVP; Nat Hon Sy; Perf Att; WWAHSS; Comm Volntr; Red Cr Aide; Chrch Yth Grp; Emplmnt; Svce Clb; Spanish Clb; Bnd; Ch Chr; Mch Bnd; SP/M/VS; Bskball (J); Cr Ctry (V L); PP Ftbl (V); Track (V L); SOS Executive Board; Psychology; Athletic Trainer; UNC Chapel Hill; Kent State U

SVOBODA, BRITTANIE N; WILLOWICK, OH; EASTLAKE NORTH HS; (SR); Hi Hnr Roll; Nat Hon Sy; Comm Volntr; DARE; Key Club; Tchrs Aide; Spanish Clb; Chr; Cr Ctry (V); Sccr (V); Track (V); Medical-RN; Lakeland Community College

SWAN, BRIAN; CANTON, OH; EAST CANTON HS; (JR); F Lan Hn Soc; Hi Hnr Roll; Hnr Roll; Otst Ac Ach Awd; Perf Att; Comm Volntr; Peer Tut/Med; FCA; Lttrmn Clb; Off Aide; Tchrs Aide; Vsity Clb; Spanish Clb; Dnce; SP/M/VS; Bsball (V L); Bskball (V L); Ftball (V L); Vsy Clb (V L); Wt Lftg (V L); Cl Off (R); Stu Cncl (R); Engineering; Education; Kent State; Akron

SWARN, ASHLEY-NOEL; MANSFIELD, OH; MANSFIELD SR HS; (SR); Hnr Roll; Sci Fairs; St of Mnth; WWAHSS; Emplmnt; Jr Ach; Chr; Orch; Bskball (V); Cr Ctry (V); Track (V); Positive Opportunities Program; Medical Degree; Ohio State U

SWARTZ, LEAH M; CELINA, OH; CELINA HS; (SR); Hnr Roll; Nat Mrt LOC; ArtClub; Chrch Yth Grp; Emplmnt; Photog; Tchrs Aide; Latin Clb; Ch Chr; Lit Mag (R); Art Awards; Dental Hygiene; Sinclair Community College

SWARTZ, RYAN; CLINTON, OH; GREEN HS; (SR); Hi Hnr Roll; Hnr Roll; Comm Volntr; Chrch Yth Grp; Cmptr Clb; Emplmnt; Swmg (V L); Tennis (V L); Scholar Athlete Award; Youth Leadership Forum Nominee; Computer Science; Engineering; Bowling Green State U; U of Akron

SWARTZ, TIFFANY L; MIDDLETOWN, OH; LAKOTA EAST HS; (JR); Hi Hnr Roll; Hnr Roll; St of Mnth; Cr Ctry (V); Track (V); Nursing; Indiana U, Coastal Carolina; Ball State

SWEARINGEN, AMY; COLUMBUS, OH; WHETSTONE HS; (SR); Sccr (J); Swmg (V CL); Stu Cncl (P); DECA / Nationals; National Honor Society; Education; Ohio U

SWIGART, LEIGH; HAMILTON, OH; BADIN HS; (SR); Hi Hnr Roll; Otst Ac Ach Awd; WWAHSS; Comm Volntr; ArtClub; Chrch Yth Grp; Drma Clb; Key Club; SP/M/VS; Sch Ppr (R); French; English; Wright State U; Miami U

SWISHER, JOHN; NILES, OH; MC KINLEY HS; (FR); Hnr Roll; Perf Att; WWAHSS; Bnd; Jzz Bnd; Mch Bnd; Pep Bnd; Ftball

SWISHER, KATHERINE M; MARTIN, OH; GENOA HS; (SR); Ctznshp Aw; Hi Hnr Roll; Comm Volntr; 4-H; DARE; Emplmnt; Lib Aide; Mus Clb; Scouts; Tchrs Aide; Bnd; Chr; Dnce; Flg Crps; Girl Scout Gold Award; Early Childhood Education-Bachelor of Science; Minor in Dance; Ohio Northern U

SZABO, MICHAEL D; PAINESVILLE, OH; RIVERSIDE HS; (JR); 4H Awd; Hnr Roll; WWAHSS; AL Aux Boys; Emplmnt; Key Club; German Clb; Bnd; Pyramid of Remembrance - Established Memorial in Arlington Cemetery; Reader of the Week in News Herald; Biology Major; History; Gannon U; Baldwin-Wallace College

SZECHY, LAUREN C; NORTH ROYALTON, OH; NORTH ROYALTON HS; (SO); Hnr Roll; Pres Ac Ftns Aw; WWAHSS; ArtClub; Chrch Yth Grp; Emplmnt; Key Club; Lttrmn Clb; Dnce; Chrldg (J); Dvng (V L); Gmnstcs (V L); Mar Art; Skiing; Track (V L); Dental; U of Dayton; Miami U (Ohio)

SZEKELY, HEATHER N; WEST SALEM, OH; VCS OHIO; (SO); Hnr Roll; Comm Volntr; Chrch Yth Grp; Chr; Track High School; Nursing; Working with Handicap Children

Sutter, Shanna
Colonel Crawford HS
Crestline, OH

Stull, Sarah D
Theodore Roosevelt HS
Kent, OH

Strouse, Chelsea M
Mansfield SR HS
Mansfield, OH

Strohm, Luke A
Plymouth HS
Plymouth, OH

Stroud, Torey
Norwalk HS
Norwalk, OH

Supanik, Nichole
Bridgeport HS
Mt Pleasant, OH

Swisher, John
Mc Kinley HS
Niles, OH

SZELTNER, ADAM D; CLEVELAND, OH; MIDPARK HS; (JR) Hnr Roll; Perf Att; Peer Tut/Med; Emplmnt; Bsball (V); Bskball (J); Ftball (V L); Sccr (J); Electroneurodiagnostics

TACKETT, LINDSAY M; BUTLER, OH; CLEAR FORK HS; (SR) Hnr Roll; Nat Hon Sy; Perf Att; WWAHSS; Yth Ldrshp Prog; Comm Volntr; Red Cr Aide; Chrch Yth Grp; Lttrmn Clb; Vsity Clb; Bnd; Mch Bnd; Pep Bnd; Bskball (V L); Vllyball (V L); Famous Poets Society; Forensic Chemistry; Eastern Kentucky U; West Virginia U

TANDON, NAVDEEP; KENT, OH; (SO) Hnr Roll; Kwnis Aw; Perf Att; WWAHSS; Hosp Aide; FBLA; Key Club; Schol Bwl; Scouts; Chr; Sccr (J); Tennis (V L); Highest Average in Geometry; Secretary of Student Council; Become a Doctor; Case Western Reserve; Duke U

TANDON, SUNPREET; KENT, OH; THEODORE ROOSEVELT HS; (SR); Nat Hon Sy; Nat Mrt LOC; WWAHSS; Comm Volntr; AL Aux Boys; FBLA; Key Club; Schol Bwl; Spch Team

TATE, DAVID; CINCINNATI, OH; FINNEYTOWN HS; (FR) Hi Hnr Roll; Hnr Roll; Sci/Math Olympn; Comm Volntr; DARE; Emplmnt; Wdwrkg Clb; Chr; Stg Cre; Video Club; Science Olympiad; Theology; Chemistry; Miami U; Ohio State U

TAULBEE, RON; WEST CHESTER, OH; LAKOTA EAST HS; (SO); Hi Hnr Roll; Ftball (J); Perfect Attend.; Ohio State U

TAYLOR, ABBY K; LYONS, OH; EVERGREEN HS; (SO); 4H Awd; Ctznshp Aw; Hi Hnr Roll; Hnr Roll; Pres Ac Ftns Aw; Hab For Humty Volntr; Peer Tut/Med; Red Cr Aide; 4-H; Chrch Yth Grp; DARE; Prom Com; SADD; Vsity Clb; Bnd; Mch Bnd; Pep Bnd; Bskball (J); Cr Ctry (V); Track (V); Vsy Clb (V); Stu Cncl (R); Representative of SADD; Do Stats for the Varsity Football Team; Physical Fitness / Personal Trainer; Biology / Science Background; Ohio State U; Kent State U

TAYLOR, ASHLEY B; CLEVELAND, OH; SOUTH HS; (SR) Ctznshp Aw; Hnr Roll; Hosp Aide; Chrch Yth Grp; DARE; Key Club; Ch Chr; Yrbk (E); Pre-Med; History; Marion College of Indiana

TAYLOR, RACHAEL; GALLOWAY, OH; WEST HS; (FR) Hi Hnr Roll; Hnr Roll; MVP; Otst Ac Ach Awd; Perf Att; Sci/Math Olympn; St of Mnth; Comm Volntr; Chrch Yth Grp; FCA; Off Aide; SADD; Vsity Clb; Bskball (J); Chr; Dnce; Sccr; Track; Battle of the Books; Social Services; Photography; Ohio State U; Miami U

TAYLOR, STEPHEN; COLUMBUS, OH; NORTHSIDE CHRISTIAN SCH; (JR); Hnr Roll; Perf Att; Chrch Yth Grp; Drma Clb; Emplmnt; Mus Clb; Prom Com; Vsity Clb; Ch Chr; SP/M/VS; Bskball (JC); Sccr (V L); BCSA Fine Arts 3rd Classical Piano; Bob Jones U Fine Arts 1st in Ceramics; Physical Therapy; Sports Medicine; Cedarville U; Ohio State U

TAYLOR, TORI; NEW MATAMORAS, OH; FRONTIER HS; (JR); F Lan Hn Soc; Hi Hnr Roll; Nat Hon Sy; WWAHSS; BPA; Key Club; Pep Squd; Prom Com; Chr; Dnce; Bskball (V L); Chrldg (V L); Sftball (V L); Vllyball (V L); Cl Off (S); National Honor Society; Who's Who Among Amer. H.S. Students & Sports Edition; Marietta College

TAYLOR, WHITNEY; TERRACE PARK, OH; MARIEMONT HS; (FR); Hnr Roll; Comm Volntr; Chrch Yth Grp; Emplmnt; Key Club; Latin Clb; Dnce; Sftball (V); Vllyball (J); Rec Basketball; Primary School Teacher; Psychiatrist; Texas A & M U; Miami U

TAYLOR, ZEBADIAH; KENTON, OH; KENTON SR HS; (FR) Hnr Roll; Perf Att; Ftball (J); Wt Lftg; Ohio State U

TEER, QUINCI; CLEVELAND, OH; LUTHERAN HS EAST; (SO); Ctznshp Aw; Hnr Roll; Nat Hon Sy; Perf Att; St of Mnth; WWAHSS; Peer Tut/Med; ArtClub; Chrch Yth Grp; Mus Clb; Scouts; Tchrs Aide; Bnd; Chr; Ch Chr; Mch Bnd; Bskball (V CL); Chrldg (V); Scr Kpr (V); Sftball (V L); Vllyball (V); Office Aide/Help; Administration Education; Interior Designer; Duke U, NC; The Ohio State, OH

TEER JR, QUINTUS; CLEVELAND, OH; LUTHERAN HS EAST; (FR); Ctznshp Aw; Hnr Roll; Nat Hon Sy; WWAHSS; Chrch Yth Grp; Mus Clb; Scouts; Chr; Ch Chr; Bsball (V); Bskball (VJC); Education Administration; John Carroll U; Ohio State U, OH

TENNANT, KYLE; CORTLAND, OH; LAKEVIEW HS; (SO) Hnr Roll; Yth Ldrshp Prog; Peer Tut/Med; Chrch Yth Grp; Drma Clb; Jr Ach; Quiz Bowl; Spanish Clb; Acpl Chr; Bnd; Jzz Bnd; SP/M/VS; Lit Mag (E); Sch Ppr (R); On Staff of Tribune Chronicle's Page One Teen Page; Bible/Theology; Music; Wheaton College; Moody Bible Institute

TERRELL, LEAH; NEW CARLISLE, OH; TECUMSEH HS; (FR) Hnr Roll; Nat Hon Sy; Peer Tut/Med; DARE; FBLA; Tchrs Aide; Bsball; Sftball; Swmg; Poetry; County Finalist; Psychology; Physical Therapy; Ohio State U; Whittenburg

TERRY, LATOYA R; GAHANNA, OH; WESTERVILLE NORTH HS; (SR) Hnr Roll; Nat Hon Sy; Emplmnt; Off Aide; Business Administration; Deaf Education; Otterbein College; Columbus State Community College

THARP, JENNIFER; MT VERNON, OH; MT VERNON HS; (JR) Hnr Roll; Nat Hon Sy; Pres Ac Ftns Aw; Sci Fairs; WWAHSS; Comm Volntr; Chrch Yth Grp; DARE; Emplmnt; FCA; Key Club; Off Aide; Scouts; Tchrs Aide; Chr; Medicine; College of Wooster; Miami of Ohio

THISTLETHWAITE, CHELSEA; CINCINNATI, OH; ANDERSON HS; (JR); F Lan Hn Soc; Hi Hnr Roll; Nat Hon Sy; WWAHSS; Comm Volntr; Peer Tut/Med; Chrch Yth Grp; Emplmnt; FCA; Key Club; Spanish Clb; Bskball (V P); PP Ftbl (VJ); Sftball (JCL); Vllyball (V C); Architecture; Interior Design; U of Illinois; Ohio State

THOBE, BETHANY; MARIA STEIN, OH; MARION LOCAL HS; (JR); 4H Awd; Hnr Roll; Comm Volntr; Peer Tut/Med; 4-H; Chrch Yth Grp; FTA; Mth Clb/Tm; Prom Com; Sci Clb; Tchrs Aide; Vsity Clb; Bnd; SP/M/VS; Bskball (J); Sftball (V); Pathology; Pediatrician; Ohio Northern U; Notre Dame

THOMAS, ASHLEY N; ADDYSTON, OH; TAYLOR HS; (SR); Ctznshp Aw; Hnr Roll; MVP; Nat Ldrshp Svc; Nat Stu Ath Day Aw; WWAHSS; Yth Ldrshp Prog; Comm Volntr; Peer Tut/Med; Chrch Yth Grp; DARE; Emplmnt; Key Club; Off Aide; Pep Squd; Tchrs Aide; Vsity Clb; Dnce; Drl Tm; SP/M/VS; Chrldg (V CL); Gmnstcs (V); Track (V CL); Yrbk (R, P); Picked to Attend Cheer Hawaii USA Camp; Most Spirited 4 Years; Communications; Minor in Business; UN; Cincinnati State

THOMAS, BRANDON; EASTLAKE, OH; EASTLAKE NORTH HS; (SO); Ctznshp Aw; Hnr Roll; St of Mnth; Yth Ldrshp Prog; Comm Volntr; Hosp Aide; Peer Tut/Med; Chrch Yth Grp; Emplmnt; Lib Aide; P to P St Amb Prg; Quill & Scroll; Svce Clb; Tchrs Aide; Chr; Scr Kpr (V); School Newspaper Advertising Manager; Ohio U

THOMAS, IMANI; RICHMOND HILLS, OH; RICHMOND HTS HS; (SO); Hnr Roll; WWAHSS; Chrch Yth Grp; Key Club; Svce Clb; Chr; Ch Chr; Dnce; SP/M/VS; Chrldg (V L); Sftball (J); Major - Business Management; Minor - Early Childhood Education; Michigan State U; Tennessee State U

THOMAS, KATIE; TRENTON, OH; EDGEWOOD HS; (JR); F Lan Hn Soc; Hnr Roll; MVP; Pres Ac Ftns Aw; WWAHSS; Comm Volntr; Chrch Yth Grp; DARE; DECA; Emplmnt; Photog; Tchrs Aide; Vsity Clb; Dnce; DARE; Chrldg (V); Dvng (V); 1st Team MML Cheerleading; German Honor Society; Nursing; Teaching; Ohio State U; U of Kentucky

THOMAS, MEGAN; GRAND RAPIDS, OH; OTSEGO HS; (SO); 4H Awd; St of Mnth; WWAHSS; 4-H; Chrch Yth Grp; Ntl FFA; Bnd; Chr; Mch Bnd; SP/M/VS; Bskball (J L); Sccr (V L); Track (V); Reporter for FFA Chapter 2005-2006; Medical Field

THOMAS, SARAH; SYLVANIA, OH; NORTHVIEW HS; (FR); Hnr Roll; Chrch Yth Grp; Vllyball

THOMAS, TODD; CAREY, OH; CAREY SCH; (JR); Hnr Roll; Nat Hon Sy; WWAHSS; AL Aux Boys; Chrch Yth Grp; Drma Clb; Emplmnt; Prom Com; Quiz Bowl; Bnd; Chr; Jzz Bnd; SP/M/VS; Cr Ctry (V L); Sccr; Sch Ppr (R); Radiology; Bowling Green State U

THOMASSON, AMBER; ELYRIA, OH; ELYRIA HS; (SR); Hnr Roll; Comm Volntr; DARE; FTA; Key Club; Scouts; Tchrs Aide; Mch Bnd; Early Childhood Education; Kent State U

THOMPSON, JON; CLEVELAND, OH; LUTHERAN HS EAST; (SO); Ctznshp Aw; Hnr Roll; WWAHSS; Yth Ldrshp Prog; Comm Volntr; Peer Tut/Med; Emplmnt; FCA; P to P St Amb Prg; SCLC Youth Membership / CS Brigade Member; Youth Tutor / Help Educate for Service; Law

THOMPSON, MICHAEL; CLEVELAND, OH; COLLINWOOD HS; (SO); Hnr Roll; Nat Hon Sy; WWAHSS; Comm Volntr; Chrch Yth Grp; Cmptr Clb; Ch Chr; Ftball (J); Track (J)

THOMPSON, RAKIA C; DAYTON, OH; COLONEL WHITE HS FOR THE ARTS; (JR); Hi Hnr Roll; Hnr Roll; Nat Hon Sy; Otst Ac Ach Awd; Perf Att; Pres Sch; ArtClub; Mus Clb; ROTC; Tchrs Aide; Chr; Stg Cre; Bskball (VJ); Track (J); Medical; Building Contractor; Hampton U; Norfolk State

THOMPSON, ROBERT L.; CLEVELAND, OH; JOHN F KENNEDY HS; (SO); Perf Att; St of Mnth; Mth Clb/Tm; ROTC; Cr Ctry (V L); Track (V L); Business and Management; Engineering; Morehouse College; Tennessee State U

THOMPSON, ZALA V; LORAIN, OH; CLEARVIEW HS; (JR); Hnr Roll; Nat Hon Sy; Otst Ac Ach Awd; Comm Volntr; Peer Tut/Med; Emplmnt; Lib Aide; Tchrs Aide; French Clb; Stu Cncl (R); Sch Ppr (E, R); Participant in Lewis Educational & Research Collaborative Internship Program - LERCIP; Nursing; Diagnostic Medical Sonography; Cincinnati U; Ohio State U

THORNBERRY, BRANDON; CANTON, OH; (MS) Hnr Roll; Nat Hon Sy; ArtClub; NtlFrnscLg; Mar Art (J)

TIGNER, STEFANIE K; BALTIMORE, OH; (SR); Hnr Roll; Perf Att; Pres Ac Ftns Aw; Sci Fairs; St of Mnth; Yth Ldrshp Prog; Comm Volntr; ArtClub; FCA; Mod UN; Vsity Clb; Bskball (J); Sccr; Track (V); Wt Lftg; Working with Our School Trainer; Helping with 6th Grade Girls Basketball Team; Sports Medicine; Athletic Training; Capital U; Ohio U

TIMMEL, AMANDA; PICKERINGTON, OH; PICKERINGTON HS NORTH; (JR); Hi Hnr Roll; Otst Ac Ach Awd; Perf Att; Sci/Math Olympn; St of Mnth; Comm Volntr; Chrch Yth Grp; Key Club; Pep Squd; Sci Clb; Bnd; Dnce; Mch Bnd; Pep Bnd; Cr Ctry (J); Track (J); Capital U Junior Winds; Physical Therapy/Pre-Med; Elementary Education; Bowling Green State U; Miami U, Ohio

TIMMONS, ASHLEY M; DAYTON, OH; KETTERING FAIRMONT HS; (SR); Nat Hon Sy; St of Mnth; Comm Volntr; Spec Olymp Vol; Dbte Team; DECA; Emplmnt; Off Aide; Prom Com; Spch Team; Tchrs Aide; Spanish Clb; Sccr; Track; Cl Off (R); Stu Cncl (R); CR (R); National Honors Society; Kettering Mayor's Award; Marketing & Public Relations; Bowling Green State U

TINKHAM, JOSHUA L; NEWARK, OH; NEWARK HS; (SO); Hnr Roll; MVP; Nat Hon Sy; Yth Ldrshp Prog; Peer Tut/Med; DARE; Orch; Bsball (J); Golf (V); Mar Art; Symphony Orchestra; History; Government; Ohio State U; U of Miami

TIPPIE, CHRISTINA; SAINT MARYS, OH; NEW KNOXVILLE LOCAL SCH; (FR); 4H Awd; Hi Hnr Roll; Hnr Roll; Otst Ac Ach Awd; St of Mnth; 4-H; DARE; German Clb; Business and Management; Wright State U; Rhodes State College

TISCHLER, RENEE; CLEVELAND, OH; PARMA SR HS; (JR); Hi Hnr Roll; Nat Hon Sy; Otst Ac Ach Awd; Perf Att; WWAHSS; Sci/Math Olympn; WWAHSS; Comm Volntr; Red Cr Aide; ArtClub; Drma Clb; HO'Br Ftbl (J); Stu Cncl (R); Yrbk (J); NASA Sharp Summer Intern; HO'Br Ftbl (J); Stu Cncl (R); Yrbk (J); NASA Sharp Summer Intern

TOBIAS, AMANDA; NEW CARLISLE, OH; TECUMSEH HS; (FR); Hi Hnr Roll; St of Mnth; Chrch Yth Grp; Jr Ach; Bnd; Jzz Bnd; Mch Bnd; Orch; Bskball; Music Education; Elementary Education; Cedarville U; Ohio State U

TOBIN, ALENA; CHAGRIN FALLS, OH; CHAGRIN FALLS HS; (SO); Hnr Roll; Quill & Scroll; Bnd; Mch Bnd; Sch Ppr (R); Have Played Piano for 11 Years; Have Played Flute for 6 Years; Creative Writing; Journalism; Miami U; Hiram College

TODD, KELLY; DRESDEN, OH; TRI-VALLEY; (JR); Hnr Roll; Nat Hon Sy; WWAHSS; Comm Volntr; Hosp Aide; Peer Tut/Med; 4-H; Chrch Yth Grp; FCA; Prom Com; Svce Clb; Tchrs Aide; Vsity Clb; Spanish Clb; Bskball (V L); Skiing; Sccr (V CL); Track (V L); Cl Off (T); Stu Cncl (T)

TOLIN, KATE; MAGNOLIA, OH; SANDY VALLEY JR/SR HS; (JR); Hi Hnr Roll; MVP; Perf Att; Sci Fairs; St of Mnth; Comm Volntr; Hab For Humty Volntr; Chrch Yth Grp; Prom Com; Sci Clb; Ch Chr; Jzz Bnd; Mch Bnd; Pep Bnd; Bskball (V L); Cr Ctry (V L); Track (V L); Cl Off (S); Sch Ppr (R); All County Cross Country -1st Team; Part of 4x800m Relay School Record; Forensic Science; Business; Baldwin-Wallace College; Kent State U

TOLLIVER, BRANDON D; CLEVELAND, OH; MARTIN LUTHER KING HS; (SO); Hnr Roll; MVP; Nat Hon Sy; Perf Att; St of Mnth; WWAHSS; Comm Volntr; Chrch Yth Grp; Lttrmn Clb; Lib Aide; Quill & Scroll; Quiz Bowl; Tchrs Aide; Chr; Ch Chr; Dnce; Cr Ctry; Sccr; Track; Ohio State Dental; PhD; Ohio State U; Kent State U

TOMASELLO, GINA E; NORTH ROYALTON, OH; NORTH ROYALTON HS; (SO); Hnr Roll; Nat Hon Sy; Otst Ac Ach Awd; Sci Fairs; WWAHSS; Comm Volntr; Spec Olymp Vol; Chrch Yth Grp; DARE; Jr Cls League; Key Club; Mod UN; Mus Clb; Prom Com; Scouts; Bnd; Ch Chr; Mch Bnd; Scr Kpr (J); Skiing (J); Aviation/Aeronautic Engineer; Music Minor-French Horn; Embry-Riddle U of Aeronautics; Ohio State U

TOMLINSON, JANELLE E; WESTERVILLE, OH; WESTERVILLE CTRL HS; (JR); 4H Awd; WWAHSS; Hab For Humty Volntr; Hosp Aide; Peer Tut/Med; 4-H; Key Club; Ntl Beta Clb; Off Aide; Prom Com; French Clb; Drl Tm; SP/M/VS; Stu Cncl (R); Superintendent's Advisory Committee; Chemistry; Forensic Science; Ohio State U; Stanford U

TONNIS, ALLISON; CINCINNATI, OH; MC AULEY HS; (JR); Perf Att; Comm Volntr; Hosp Aide; Key Club; Spanish Clb; Dnce; Tennis; Hospital Volunteer; History Club; Nursing; U of Cincinnati; College of Mount St Joseph

TORBIC, JENNIFER; AVON LAKE, OH; AVON LAKE HS; (SO); Hi Hnr Roll; MVP; Pres Ac Ftns Aw; Key Club; Off Aide; Tchrs Aide; Chr; Bskball (J L); Accounting Degree / Foreign Languages

TORRES-RUIZ, GILBERT; CLEVELAND, OH; LINCOLN-WEST HS; (FR); Ctznshp Aw; Hnr Roll; Nat Hon Sy; Peer Tut/Med; ROTC; Lincoln-West Book Club; Business Management; Performing Arts; U of California Los Angeles; Berkeley

TRAN, CATHY; WICKLIFFE, OH; SOUTH HS; (SO); Hnr Roll; Emplmnt; Key Club; Sci Clb; Spanish Clb; Yrbk (R); International Business; Foreign Service; U of Pennsylvania; U of Michigan

TRAN, LINH; CINCINNATI, OH; NORTHWEST HS; (JR); Hnr Roll; Otst Ac Ach Awd; WWAHSS; Comm Volntr; Key Club; Sci Clb; Spanish Clb; Yrbk (P); Pre-Med; U of Southern California; U of Cincinnati

TRARES, JAMES; RAVENNA, OH; CRESTWOOD HS; (JR); Hi Hnr Roll; Nat Hon Sy; Nat Sci Aw; St of Mnth; WWAHSS; Scouts; Tchrs Aide; Bnd; Ch Chr; Jzz Bnd; Mch Bnd; French; Music

TRAUX, AMBER; BARNESVILLE, OH; BARNESVILLE HS; (SR); Hnr Roll; Sci Fairs; WWAHSS; Hosp Aide; Red Cr Aide; ArtClub; DARE; Drma Clb; FCCLA; FTA; Key Club; Ntl FFA; Prom Com; Chr; SP/M/VS; Bskball; Cr Ctry; Mar Art; PP Ftbl; Track; Candy Striper; RN; Marine Biologist; Belmont Technical College

TREASURE, CANDACE; TROY, OH; TROY HS; (SR); Hi Hnr Roll; Hnr Roll; Otst Ac Ach Awd; Hab For Humty Volntr; Peer Tut/Med; Spec Olymp Vol; Chrch Yth Grp; DARE; Emplmnt; Key Club; Prom Com; Tchrs Aide; Stu Cncl; Teen Leadership Troy; Astra; Spanish; International Business; The U of Dayton; Ohio State U

TRIMBLE, ANTHONY; YOUNGSTOWN, OH; CHANEY HS; (FR); Otst Ac Ach Awd; Perf Att; Yth Ldrshp Prog; Chrch Yth Grp; DARE; Bsball (J); Bskball; Ftball (J); Wt Lftg (V); Professional Football Player; Construction Worker; Ohio State U; Penn State U

TRIMBLE, KATHERINE B; HUDSON, OH; HUDSON HS; (SR); Nat Ldrshp Svc; Comm Volntr; Red Cr Aide; Chrch Yth Grp; Emplmnt; Sign Clb; Hsbk Rdg (V); Sccr (J); Yrbk (R); Non-Profit Organization Management; Ohio U

TROJACK, HEATHER E; MEDINA, OH; MEDINA HS; (SR); F Lan Hn Soc; Hnr Roll; Nat Hon Sy; Drma Clb; Emplmnt; Jr Cls League; Quill & Scroll; Latin Clb; Orch; SP/M/VS; Stg Cre; Stu Cncl (R); CR (R); Sch Ppr (E); Yrbk (R); Latin Club Co-President; S.H.U.D.D.L.E. Teacher; Magazine Journalism; Ball State U

TRUNKO, COURTNEY; AKRON, OH; COPLEY HS; (JR); Hnr Roll; Nat Hon Sy; Perf Att; Comm Volntr; Chrch Yth Grp; Key Club; Clb; Bnd; Philosophy; Photography; Ohio State University; Kent State University

TRUSNIK, SHELLEY; CLEVELAND, OH; GARFIELD HTS HS; (JR); Nat Hon Sy; WWAHSS; Comm Volntr; AL Aux Girls; Emplmnt; Svce Clb; Tchrs Aide; Scr Kpr (VJ); Yrbk (R, P); Fashion Merchandising; Public Relations; Bowling Green; Ohio Northern

TRYKOWSKI, TIFFINY; CHARDON, OH; CHARDON HS; (FR); Hi Hnr Roll; Nat Hon Sy; Perf Att; St of Mnth; Yth Ldrshp Prog; Comm Volntr; Peer Tut/Med; Chrch Yth Grp; NYLC; P to P St Amb Prg; Scouts; French Clb; Bnd; Mch Bnd; Pep Bnd; Sftball; Stu Cncl (P, R); Midwest Talent Search; American Field Service; Applied Mathematics; Engineering; Miami U; Cornell U

TSANGEOS, ANGELO J; CANTON, OH; GLEN OAK HS; (JR); Ctznshp Aw; Hi Hnr Roll; Hnr Roll; Nat Hon Sy; Otst Ac Ach Awd; Perf Att; Sci Fairs; Sci/Math Olympn; St of Mnth; WWAHSS; Comm Volntr; Chess; DECA; Emplmnt; Mth Clb/Tm; Quiz Bowl; Tchrs Aide; Vsity Clb; Spanish Clb; Golf (V CL); District DECA Winner; DECA State Competitor (2 Events); Business/Marketing; Accounting; Duke U; Ohio State U

TUBBS, WESLEY R; LA RUE, OH; MARION CATHOLIC HS; (SR); Hnr Roll; Sci Fairs; WWAHSS; Peer Tut/Med; ArtClub; Drma Clb; Emplmnt; FCA; Off Aide; Photog; Spanish Clb; Chr; Stg Cre; Bskball (J); Scr Kpr; Sftball (V); Vllyball (VJ); Wt Lftg; Yrbk (E, R, P); Spanish Club / VIP Club; Fellowship Christian Athletes; Criminology; Ohio State U Marion; Marion Technical College

TUCKER, CASEY R; LIMA, OH; ELIDA HS; (SR); Hi Hnr Roll; Hnr Roll; Nat Hon Sy; Otst Ac Ach Awd; Sci/Math Olympn; WWAHSS; Hosp Aide; Chrch Yth Grp; Emplmnt; Off Aide; Tchrs Aide; Chr; Ch Chr; SP/M/VS; Swg Chr; Chrldg (V); Nursing (RN/BSN); U of Cincinnati

TURLEY, JOHN P; CLEVELAND, OH; VALLEY FORGE HS; (JR); Hnr Roll; St of Mnth; Emplmnt; Bnd; Jzz Bnd; Mch Bnd; Peer Mediation; Forensic Science; Special Effects & Movie Design; Ohio State U

TURNER, KERRI L; KENTON, OH; KENTON SR HS; (SR); 4H Awd; Hnr Roll; WWAHSS; Comm Volntr; 4-H; Emplmnt; Ntl FFA; Diversified Crop Production Award (FFA); Accounting Award (FFA); Accounting; Ohio Northern U; The U of Findlay

TURNER, MARJORY; TOLEDO, OH; ROGERS HS; (SR); Ctznshp Aw; Hi Hnr Roll; Hnr Roll; Nat Ldrshp Svc; Otst Ac Ach Awd; Perf Att; St of Mnth; Yth Ldrshp Prog; Peer Tut/Med; Chrch Yth Grp; Drma Clb; FCA; Mth Clb/Tm; Off Aide; Tchrs Aide; SP/M/VS; Cr Ctry (J); Track (J); Old News Boy Scholarship; Education; U of Toledo

TYLER, JESSICA; SPRINGFIELD, OH; SHAWNEE HS; (SO); Hi Hnr Roll; Hnr Roll; Otst Ac Ach Awd; Sci Fairs; Hosp Aide; Chrch Yth Grp; Drma Clb; Key Club; Off Aide; SADD; Tchrs Aide; Chr; Ch Chr; Orch; SP/M/VS; Stu Cncl (R); Highest Principal's Award; County Writing Competition Award; Ob/Gyn; Maternity Nurse; Wright State U

TYLER JR, VINCENT L; COLUMBUS, OH; COLUMBUS AFRICENTRIC; (SO); Hnr Roll; Perf Att; Comm Volntr; DARE; SADD; Bnd; Bskball (J); Ftball (VJ); Ohio State U; Miami U

TYREE, MOLLY; POWELL, OH; OLENTANGY LIBERTY HS; (JR); Hnr Roll; Comm Volntr; Svce Clb; Skiing; Tennis (J); Midwest Talent Search

TYSON, KATIE; RISINGSUN, OH; DAKOTA HS; (SO); Hnr Roll; Perf Att; St of Mnth; Comm Volntr; DARE; Emplmnt; Medical Aid/Nursing Career; Law/Probation Officer/Lawyer; Bowling Green State U; Terra Community College

UFFERMAN, MATTHEW; FREDERICKTOWN, OH; HIGHLAND HS; (SR); Hi Hnr Roll; Ntl FFA; Bsball (V L); Bskball (V L); Honorable Mention MOAC in Basketball; Advisor for the FFA; Agronomist; Ohio State Agriculture Technical Institute

ULREICH, JULIE M; OXFORD, OH; TALAWANDA HS; (SR); Hnr Roll; Otst Ac Ach Awd; St of Mnth; Comm Volntr; 4-H; FCCLA; Off Aide; Student of the Month At My Job At Miami U; FFA/Top Fruit Salesperson for the Past 3 Yrs; Early Childhood Education; Miami U

UNDERWOOD, ESTHER S; DAYTON, OH; DAYTON CHRISTIAN HS; (FR); WWAHSS; Comm Volntr; Hab For Humty Volntr; Photog; Bskball (J); Track (V); Vllyball (J); Photography

UNTENER, MARY; DAYTON, OH; ALTER HS; (FR); Hnr Roll; MVP; Key Club; Cr Ctry (V); Swmg (V); Track (V); GACL - Player Of The Year For Cross Country; Nursing

URIAS, BRENDA; TOLEDO, OH; WAITE HS; (MS); Chrch Yth Grp; Chr; Vllyball; Forensic Science; Interior Design; Ohio State U

UTENDORF, ABBIE; ELMORE, OH; WOODMORE HS; (FR); Ctznshp Aw; Hi Hnr Roll; Perf Att; St of Mnth; Chrch Yth Grp; DARE; Emplmnt; FTA; Key Club; Quiz Bowl; Scouts; Tchrs Aide; Bnd; Mch Bnd; Pep Bnd; Track (V); Vllyball (J); Physical Therapy; Pharmacy

UTENDORF, JODI L; GROVER HILL, OH; WAYNE TRACE HS; (SR); Hnr Roll; Nat Hon Sy; St of Mnth; WWAHSS; FTA; Off Aide; Schol Bwl; Stg Cre; Chrldg (J); Cr Ctry (V); Post Secondary; Radiology; U of Saint Francis, Ft. Wayne

UTTER, MAKINZIE; MAINEVILLE, OH; URSULINE AC; (JR); Hi Hnr Roll; Hnr Roll; MVP; St of Mnth; Comm Volntr; Peer Tut/Med; Red Cr Aide; DARE; Emplmnt; SADD; Vllyball (J); Participated in Big Sister Program; Teens for Life Club; Psychology; Law; Miami U; U of Dayton

VANAMAN, BRITTNEY; WESTERVILLE, OH; WESTERVILLE NORTH HS; (SR); Hi Hnr Roll; Hnr Roll; Nat Hon Sy; Otst Ac Ach Awd; St of Mnth; WWAHSS; Comm Volntr; AL Aux Girls; Emplmnt; Jr Ach; Chr; Stu Cncl (R); High School Social Studies Education (Major); Political Science-Minor; Otterbein College (Accepted)

VAN BUSKIRK, EMILY; KENTON, OH; KENTON SR HS; (FR); 4H Awd; Hnr Roll; Perf Att; Pres Ac Ftns Aw; 4-H; Scouts; Bnd; Chr; Mch Bnd; Pep Bnd; Tennis (V); Track (V); Veterinarian Assistant; Culinary School; Ohio State U; Ohio Northern U

VANCE, CIERA; COLUMBUS, OH; BROOKHAVEN HS; (SO); Hnr Roll; Nat Hon Sy; Perf Att; WWAHSS; Peer Tut/Med; DARE; Lib Aide; P to P St Amb Prg; French Clb; Bskball (V); Cr Ctry (J); Pre-Med; Psychology; U of North Carolina; Spelman

VAN DAM, ALEK; MASSILLON, OH; EDISON JHS; (FR); Hnr Roll; Perf Att; Scouts; Wdwrkg Clb; Bnd; Mch Bnd; Robotic Engineering

VANDERGRIFF, ROGER K; WARREN, OH; JOHN F KENNEDY HS; (JR); Hnr Roll; Yth Ldrshp Prog; Hosp Aide; HO'Br Yth Ldrshp; Mth Clb/Tm; Cr Ctry (J); Sccr (V); Track (J); Yrbk; Hugh O'Brian Youth Leadership; Volunteer in Hospital Pharmacy; Pharmacy or Medicine

VANDERPOOL, JUDITH; WEST UNION, OH; (MS); Hnr Roll; Sci Fairs; SP/M/VS; Bskball (VJ); Chrldg (V); Sccr (V); Stu Cncl (R); CR (R); 1st Place 7th Grade Science Fair, Superior in Regionals Fair; 1st Place 8th Grade Science Fair; Medicine; Fashion Design

VAN DOREN, EMILY; MEDINA, OH; MEDINA HS; (JR); Hnr Roll; Nat Hon Sy; Nat Mrt Semif; Chrch Yth Grp; Emplmnt; Key Club; French Clb; Bnd; Chr; Mch Bnd; Architecture; Interior Design; Cooper Union; Ohio State U

VANDYKE, TIFFINI; BELPRE, OH; BELPRE HS; (FR); Hnr Roll; Perf Att; Pres Ac Ftns Aw; Comm Volntr; Drma Clb; Scouts; Spanish Clb; Chr; Dnce; SP/M/VS; Stu Cncl (R); CR (R); Dance Ballet, Jazz, Modern; Fashion Design / Marketing; Dancer / Actress; Ohio State

VANNI, RACHEL L; CLEVELAND, OH; CHARLES F BRUSH HS; (SO); Hnr Roll; Comm Volntr; Key Club; Scouts; Orch; Yrbk (R, P); Genetics; Orthodontist

VAN VOORHIS, RYAN; WAYNESBURG, OH; EAST CANTON HS; (FR); 4H Awd; Hnr Roll; 4-H; Chrch Yth Grp; Chr; Bsball (J); Ftball (VJ); Wt Lftg; Church Youth Group; 4-H

VARGA, MELISSA; CANAL FULTON, OH; NORTHWEST HS; (JR); Hnr Roll; Nat Hon Sy; Otst Ac Ach Awd; Yth Ldrshp Prog; Comm Volntr; Chrch Yth Grp; Drma Clb; French Clb; Acpl Chr; Chr; SP/M/VS; Sccr (JC); Academic Challenge Team; Piano for 7 Years; English Major; Creative Writing; Kenyon College; Denison U

VAUGHN, CASEY; CAREY, OH; CAREY SCH; (FR); Hnr Roll; Nat Hon Sy; Otst Ac Ach Awd; Pres Sch; DECA; Emplmnt; SADD; Spanish Clb; Bnd; Mch Bnd; Pep Bnd; Bskball (J); Chrldg (V); Gmnstcs (J); Cl Off (P); Stu Cncl (R); CR (R); Business Management; Findlay U; OSU

VAUGHN, RAECHEL; CAREY, OH; CAREY SCH; (JR); Hnr Roll; Nat Hon Sy; WWAHSS; Red Cr Aide; DECA; Emplmnt; Off Aide; Prom Com; SADD; Tchrs Aide; Spanish Clb; Bnd; Chr; Jzz Bnd; Bskball (V CL); Vllyball (J); Sch Ppr (R); Yrbk (R, P); Business; Cincinnati, Ohio

VELJOVIC, ZELJKA; MIDDLETOWN, OH; LAKOTA EAST HS; (SO); Ctznshp Aw; F Lan Hn Soc; Hnr Roll; Nat Hon Sy; Sci Fairs; Yth Ldrshp Prog; Comm Volntr; Spec Olymp Vol; Chrch Yth Grp; Emplmnt; Bskball (J); Track (J)

VENCI, ANTHONY; STEUBENVILLE, OH; STEUBENVILLE HS; (MS); DAR; Hi Hnr Roll; Hnr Roll; MVP; Pres Sch; Sci/Math Olympn; WWAHSS; CARE; Peer Tut/Med; Red Cr Aide; Key Club; Bskball (L); Ftball (L); Track (L); Wt Lftg; Engineering

VERGARA, JOSEPH E; ELYRIA, OH; LORAIN ADMIRAL KING HS; (SR); Hnr Roll; Chrch Yth Grp; Drma Clb; Oberlin Choristers; Computer Science; Lorain County Community College; Yale

VERHAEGHE, HANNAH; WESTERVILLE, OH; EVANGEL CHRISTIAN AC; (SO); Comm Volntr; Red Cr Aide; Chrch Yth Grp; FCA; Off Aide; Prom Com; Tchrs Aide; Spanish Clb; Bnd; Chr; Ch Chr; Bskball (J); Yrbk (P); Worship Leader in Chapel; President's Assistant in Student Council; Major in Spanish Education; Paramedic; Belmont College (TN); Middle Tennessee

VERMILLION, CORY; BUCYRUS, OH; BUCYRUS HS; Hnr Roll; Perf Att; Chess; Scouts; Bskball (J L); Scr Kpr; Track (V L); Wt Lftg; Chess Club; Art Club; Earth & Space Science; Architecture; Ohio State U; Duke U

VERNON, KEARRA C; CINCINNATI, OH; JACOBS HS; (JR); Hi Hnr Roll; Hnr Roll; Chrch Yth Grp; DARE; Chr; Took Part in Community Youth Group; Took Karate and Won 5 Gold, Silver, and a Bronze; Pediatrics; Nursing; U of Cincinnati; Cincinnati State

VERNON, RYAN; MOUNT VERNON, OH; EAST KNOX HS; (JR); Hnr Roll; Chrch Yth Grp; Bnd; Jzz Bnd; Mch Bnd; Pep Bnd; Recording Sciences; Conservatory of Recording Arts and Sciences

VICKERS, RYAN A; MADISON, OH; MADISON HS; (JR); Hnr Roll; WWAHSS; Comm Volntr; Chrch Yth Grp; Emplmnt; Vsity Clb; Spanish Clb; Ftball (V); Track (J); Wt Lftg (V); Wrstlg (V); Karate; Weight Lifting; Military; Bachelor's Degree in Science; West Point; Annapolis

VILLANUEVA, NELSON; JAMESTOWN, OH; GREENEVIEW HS; (SO); Ctznshp Aw; St of Mnth; WWAHSS; Key Club; Student of the Month of January 2004; Student of the Month of February 2005, I Write Poetry; Lawyer; Teacher; Ohio State U; U of Cincinnati

VILLARREAL, JESSICA; PARMA, OH; VALLEY FORGE HS; (JR); Hnr Roll; Hosp Aide; Chrch Yth Grp; DARE; Chr; Girls Rugby Team; Medical; Math; U of Texas At Austin

VILLERS, ANDREA; MIDDLEFIELD, OH; CARDINAL HS; (SO); Hnr Roll; WWAHSS; Comm Volntr; Chrch Yth Grp; Spanish Clb; Chr; SP/M/VS; Swg Chr; Track (V L); Vllyball (V L); Cl Off (S); ACS - Relay for Life-Team Captain; Senior Citizen Clean-Up / Volunteer

VINCENT, BRITTANY N; COLUMBUS, OH; WEST HS; (FR); Hi Hnr Roll; Hnr Roll; Perf Att; DARE; Chr; Chrldg (VJ); Sftball; Stu Cncl (R); Mrs. Junior America Columbus; Interior Designer; Nurse; OSU; Columbus State

VINE, STEFANIE; PERRYSBURG, OH; ROSSFORD HS; (SR); Hnr Roll; St of Mnth; Journalism; Language Arts; Bowling Green State U

VIOLANTE, CASSIE; YOUNGSTOWN, OH; POLAND MS; (MS); Hi Hnr Roll; Off Aide; Chr; Dnce; Chrldg; Stu Cncl

VISALDEN, JONATHAN; LORAIN, OH; SOUTHVIEW HS; (SR); Hnr Roll; Nat Hon Sy; WWAHSS; Comm Volntr; Peer Tut/Med; Emplmnt; Key Club; Ftball (J); Office Aide; Criminal Justice; U of Bowling Green

VOGEL, MEGAN; CINCINNATI, OH; MOTHER OF MERCY HS; (JR); Hi Hnr Roll; Nat Hon Sy; Comm Volntr; Peer Tut/Med; DARE; Drma Clb; French Clb; Chr; Sccr (J); Stu Cncl (R); National Honor Society; Ohio U; Centre College

VOJTECH, ANGELA; NEWBURY, OH; NEWBURY HS; (FR); Hnr Roll; Pres Ac Ftns Aw; USAA; Drma Clb; Off Aide; Chr; SP/M/VS; Track (J); I Have a Part-Time Job.; Journalism; Political Science; Columbia U; Ohio State U

Villarreal, Jessica
Valley Forge HS
Parma, OH

Underwood, Esther S
Dayton Christian HS
Dayton, OH

Ulreich, Julie M
Talawanda HS
Oxford, OH

Trykowski, Tiffiny
Chardon HS
Chardon, OH

Turner, Kerri L
Kenton SR HS
Kenton, OH

Villanueva, Nelson
Greeneview HS
Jamestown, OH

Vincent, Brittany N
West HS
Columbus, OH

VOLLMER, MIRANDA M; WEST UNITY, OH; MILLCREEK-WEST UNITY; (SR); 4H Awd; Hi Hnr Roll; Nat Hon Sy; Otst Ac Ach Awd; Sci Fairs; WWAHSS; Comm Volntr; Peer Tut/Med; Red Cr Aide; 4-H; AL Aux Girls; Chrch Yth Grp; DARE; Dbte Team; Emplmnt; FBLA; Pep Squd; Bnd; Mch Bnd; Pep Bnd; SP/M/VS; Bskball (J); Sftball (V L); Cl Off (V, T); Stu Cncl (P); CR (V, T); Sch Ppr (R, P); Yrbk (E, R, P); National Honor Society President; Political Science; Lawyer; Eastern Michigan U

VON DEYLEN, ADAM; NAPOLEON, OH; NAPOLEON HS; (JR); Hi Hnr Roll; Nat Hon Sy; Chrch Yth Grp; Chr; Ch Chr; National Honor Society

VUKELICH, CHRISTOPHER; MORROW, OH; LITTLE MIAMI HS; (SR); All Am Sch; F Lan Hn Soc; Hi Hnr Roll; Nat Hon Sy; Perf Att; US Army Sch Ath Aw; WWAHSS; Comm Volntr; DARE; Schol Bwl; Bnd; Ftball (V L); French National Honor Society; BS Mechanical Engineering; Rose-Hulman Institute of Technology; Ohio Northern U

WADDEL, CHRISTINA M; DAYTON, OH; ARCHBISHOP ALTER HS; (SO); Hnr Roll; WWAHSS; Comm Volntr; Key Club; French Clb; Vllyball (V); Academic Honor Roll; Architecture / Interior Design; Norte Dame; U of Cincinnati

WADE, CRYSTAL; GALLIPOLIS, OH; GALLIA AC HS; (SO); Hnr Roll; Perf Att; Yth Ldrshp Prog; Comm Volntr; Chrch Yth Grp; Mod UN; Scouts; Stg Cre; Track (V L); Vllyball (J); Veterinary; Law; Ohio State U

WADE, JOSHUA; PICKERINGTON, OH; PICKERINGTON HS NORTH; (SO); WWAHSS; Chrch Yth Grp; Bskball (J); Bachelor's Degree in Electrical Engineering; Master's Degree in Computer Engineering; U of Cincinnati; Drexel U

WADE, KUONA; MAPLE HEIGHTS, OH; MAPLE HTS HS; (FR); Ctznshp Aw; Hi Hnr Roll; Hnr Roll; MVP; Otst Ac Ach Awd; Pres Sch; St of Mnth; Hosp Aide; DARE; Emplmnt; Pep Squd; Drl Tm; Bskball (J); Chrldg (J); Track; Vllyball (J); Stu Cncl (R); Pharmacist; MD; U of Toledo; Central State U

WADE, LISA; CORTLAND, OH; MAPLEWOOD HS; (SR); Hnr Roll; Pep Squd; French Clb; Bnd; Pep Bnd; Yrbk (P); Medical Coding; Youngstown College; Capital College

WAGNER, AMANDA N; BLUFFTON, OH; CORY-RAWSON HS; (SR); 4H Awd; Hnr Roll; Nat Hon Sy; St of Mnth; Valdctrian; WWAHSS; 4-H; Chrch Yth Grp; Off Aide; Bnd; Jzz Bnd; Mch Bnd; Swg Chr; Bskball (V CL); Sftball (V CL); Stu Cncl (T); Pre-Veterinary Medicine; The U of Findlay

WAGNER, ANGELA F; SPRINGFIELD, OH; KENTON RIDGE HS; (JR); Ctznshp Aw; F Lan Hn Soc; Hi Hnr Roll; Hnr Roll; Nat Hon Sy; Nat Mrt LOC; Otst Ac Ach Awd; St of Mnth; WWAHSS; Yth Ldrshp Prog; Comm Volntr; Hosp Aide; Peer Tut/Med; Chrch Yth Grp; DARE; Emplmnt; Mus Clb; Prom Com; Scouts; SADD; Tchrs Aide; Acpl Chr; Chr; Ch Chr; SP/M/VS; Leo Club; STAR; Business/Economics; Music/Drama; Wright State U; Ohio State U

WAGNER, HOLLY A M; JACKSON CTR, OH; UPPER VALLEY JOINT VOC SCH; (JR); Perf Att; St of Mnth; BPA; Emplmnt; Off Aide; P to P St Amb Prg; Chr; State for the Business Academy; Student of the Month and UVJVS; Edison Community College; U of Dayton

WAGNER, LAINE; UNION CITY, OH; GREENVILLE HS; (JR); Hnr Roll; MVP; Nat Hon Sy; St of Mnth; WWAHSS; Comm Volntr; Spec Olymp Vol; Emplmnt; Key Club; Prom Com; SADD; Vsity Clb; Spanish Clb; Acpl Chr; Chr; Stg Cre; Ftball (V); Sccr (V); Track (V); Stu Cncl; The Ohio State U

WAGNER, MARK; KENT, OH; KENT ROOSEVELT; (SR); Hi Hnr Roll; Hnr Roll; MVP; Nat Hon Sy; Otst Ac Ach Awd; Pres Ac Ftns Aw; WWAHSS; Comm Volntr; Hab For Humty Volntr; Red Cr Aide; DECA; Emplmnt; Prom Com; Latin Clb; Bsball (V L); Golf (V CL); Stu Cncl (R); Exercise Physiology; Exercise Science; Miami of Ohio; Ohio U

WAJERT, KEVIN; DEFIANCE, OH; DEFIANCE HS; (SR); Hnr Roll; MVP; Cmptr Clb; Sccr (V CL); Tennis (V CL); History Club; Golf Course Management; Tri-State U; Capital U

WAKEFIELD, ELIZABETH B; NORTH ROYALTON, OH; N ROYALTON HS; (SR); Fut Prb Slvr; Hi Hnr Roll; Hnr Roll; Nat Hon Sy; St of Mnth; WWAHSS; Yth Ldrshp Prog; Comm Volntr; Hab For Humty Volntr; Peer Tut/Med; Chrch Yth Grp; Key Club; Latin Clb; Bnd; Mch Bnd; Stu Cncl (R); Pride in Academics Award; Student of the Month - Biology II, American History, English; Biology / Chemistry / Pre-Med; College of Wooster

WALKER, ASHLEY J; VENEDOCIA, OH; SPENCERVILLE HS; (JR); Ctznshp Aw; Hi Hnr Roll; Nat Hon Sy; Otst Ac Ach Awd; St of Mnth; Comm Volntr; Chrch Yth Grp; DARE; Emplmnt; FCCLA; Photog; Prom Com; Scouts; SADD; Chr; Scr Kpr; Sftball (J L); Vllyball (VJCL); Cl Off (S); Stu Cncl (R); VFW Youth Essay Award; President's Education Award; Accounting; Actuary; Ohio State U; Liberty U

WALKER, DAVID S; MIDDLETOWN, OH; LAKOTA EAST HS; (SO); Hi Hnr Roll; Hnr Roll; Chrch Yth Grp; Emplmnt; P to P St Amb Prg; Sccr (VJCL); Nominated As a Freshman for a Leadership Award.; Played on DESA International Soccer Team in England; Professional Soccer Player; Law/ Business

WALKER, ERIN N; ABERDEEN, OH; RIPLEY HS; (SR); Hi Hnr Roll; Nat Hon Sy; St of Mnth; Valdctrian; WWAHSS; Hosp Aide; Peer Tut/Med; Emplmnt; Mus Clb; Prom Com; Tchrs Aide; Vsity Clb; Spanish Clb; Bnd; Chr; Mch Bnd; Pep Bnd; Bskball (V C); Chrldg (V); Cr Ctry (V); Sccr (V C); Sftball (V C); Track (V); Vllyball (V C); Cl Off (T); Sch Ppr (R); Yrbk (R, P); Physical Education Major; English Minor; Mount Vernon Nazarene U; Ohio U

WALLAR, MICHAEL; NAVARRE, OH; FAIRLESS HS; (SO); Hi Hnr Roll; St of Mnth; Yth Ldrshp Prog; Emplmnt; Mod UN; NYLC; Cl Off (V); Sch Ppr (R); Teacher

WALLS, MIRANDA; BAINBRIDGE, OH; PAINT VALLEY HS; (JR); 4H Awd; Hnr Roll; Perf Att; Sci Fairs; WWAHSS; Peer Tut/Med; Spec Olymp Vol; 4-H; DARE; Emplmnt; Pep Squd; Prom Com; Chrldg (V); Sftball (J); Vllyball (J); Won 1st Place in Art Contest; Veterinarian; Veterinarian Technician; Shawnee State U; Ohio State U

WALSH, JONATHAN L; HUDSON, OH; HUDSON HS; (SO); Hnr Roll; Perf Att; Chrch Yth Grp; DARE; Emplmnt; Sci Clb; Scouts; Tech Clb; Life Scout BSA; Computer Science; Graphic Arts; Full Sail Florida; Ohio State U

WALSH, VANESSA; NILES, OH; MC KINLEY HS; (FR); Hi Hnr Roll; USAA; WWAHSS; Comm Volntr; FTA; Key Club; Spanish Clb; Bnd; Mch Bnd; Pep Bnd; Sccr (J); Track (J); Education; Medicine; Ohio State U; Kent State U

WALTER, STEVEN R; CAREY, OH; CAREY SCH; (FR); ArtClub; Spanish Clb; President's Education Award; USAA National Art Award

WALTERBUSCH, STACY R; CELINA, OH; MARION LOCAL HS; (SR); Hi Hnr Roll; Hnr Roll; Nat Hon Sy; Otst Ac Ach Awd; Perf Att; Pres Ac Ftns Aw; Yth Ldrshp Prog; Comm Volntr; Peer Tut/Med; Chrch Yth Grp; DARE; Drma Clb; FTA; Mth Clb/Tm; Off Aide; Prom Com; SADD; Bnd; Ch Chr; Mch Bnd; Pep Bnd; PP Ftbl (V); Yrbk (E); Soup Kitchen Volunteer; Trimming Trees at Spiritual Center; Teacher; Social Worker; U of Toledo; U of Dayton

WALTERS, LINDSEY J; HUNTSBURG, OH; CARDINAL HS; (JR); Hnr Roll; Perf Att; WWAHSS; Comm Volntr; Emplmnt; Key Club; Lib Aide; Tchrs Aide; SP/M/VS; Stg Cre; Bskball (V CL); PP Ftbl (V); Scr Kpr (V); Sftball (V CL); Yrbk (P); 2005 Chagrin Valley Conference/Sportsmanship Award/2nd Team Cuc Softball; Occupational Therapy; Law; Ohio Northern U

WALTON, CHRIS; FRANKLIN, OH; FRANKLIN HS; (SR); Hi Hnr Roll; Hnr Roll; Mth Clb/Tm; Off Aide; Tchrs Aide; Golf (J L); Tennis (V CL); Biology; Master's Degree (Medical School); Wright State U; Saint Louis U

WALTON, NORA; UPPER SANDUSKY, OH; MOHAWK HS; (SR); Ctznshp Aw; Hi Hnr Roll; Nat Hon Sy; Nat Ldrshp Svc; St of Mnth; WWAHSS; Yth Ldrshp Prog; Comm Volntr; Emplmnt; Prom Com; SADD; Tchrs Aide; Vsity Clb; Spanish Clb; Chr; Dnce; SP/M/VS; Stg Cre; Cr Ctry (V); Cl Off (V); Stu Cncl (R); Sch Ppr (R); Yrbk (R); Medical Sciences; Marion Technical College

WARD, HEATHER T; SHELBY, OH; SHELBY HS; (FR); Hnr Roll; Comm Volntr; Bnd; Dnce; Mch Bnd; Art; Performance Art - Dancing / Acting

WARD, JAMES; CLEVELAND, OH; JANE ADDAMS HS; (SR); Ctznshp Aw; MVP; Nat Stu Ath Day Aw; St of Mnth; Spec Olymp Vol; Chrch Yth Grp; Emplmnt; Cr Ctry (V); Golf (C); Sccr (V); Tennis (C); Track (V); Bowling Championship High School 04/05; Paralegal; Physical Therapist; Arizona State; Kent State

WARE, TIERRA A; REYNOLDSBURG, OH; REYNOLDSBURG HS; (SR); Hnr Roll; Pres Sch; WWAHSS; Comm Volntr; Chrch Yth Grp; DECA; Member of the Columbus Youth Commission; Pre-Med; Ohio State U

WARNER, ARI M; CLEVELAND, OH; CLEVELAND HTS HS; (SO); Hnr Roll; Emplmnt; Mus Clb; Orch; SP/M/VS; Bsball (V L); Scholarship Winner Cleveland Inst of Music / Concert Master - Lead Violinist Heights High Symphony; Commissioned Artist / Painter / Camp Counselor / Scholarship Winner to Blue Lake Music Camp MI; Commercial Art / Design

WARNER, EBONY; LIMA, OH; LIMA SR HS; (SO); Hnr Roll; Nat Hon Sy; Perf Att; Comm Volntr; Emplmnt; Sftball (J); Editor's Choice Award Achievement in Poetry; Sports Medicine; Mansfield

WARNER, STEPHANIE; LANCASTER, OH; LANCASTER HS; (SR); Hi Hnr Roll; Nat Hon Sy; Pres Sch; WWAHSS; Comm Volntr; Chrch Yth Grp; Drma Clb; Key Club; Latin Clb; Bnd; Ch Chr; Mch Bnd; Pep Bnd; Track (VJ L); Chemistry; Criminal Justice; Miami U

WARNOCK, ALAN; TWINSBURG, OH; TWINSBURG HS; (JR); Ctznshp Aw; Hnr Roll; Otst Ac Ach Awd; Perf Att; Sci Fairs; Sci/Math Olympn; St of Mnth; Peer Tut/Med; DARE; Bsball (V L); Ftball (V L); Wt Lftg (V); USSSA Baseball Title; Coaching and Improving Kids; Computer Science; Case Western Reserve; Akron U

WARREN, CAROLINE; COLUMBUS, OH; GAHANNA LINCOLN HS; (SR); Ctznshp Aw; Hnr Roll; St of Mnth; Yth Ldrshp Prog; Comm Volntr; Chrch Yth Grp; DECA; NYLC; Prom Com; Sccr (JC); Adv Cncl (R); Stu Cncl (R); CR (R); 4yr Student Council Rep; 1st Place National DECA Winner; Business Management; Marketing Management; Ohio U

WARREN, LINDSEY; AKRON, OH; ELLET HS; (SO); Hnr Roll; Comm Volntr; Chrch Yth Grp; Emplmnt

WATKINS, KALINA; LIMA, OH; LIMA SR HS; (SO); Chrch Yth Grp; Emplmnt; Scouts; Chr; CR (R); Buyer / Open Own Clothing Store; Bluffton University; Kent State University

WATSON, ADRIENNE; FREMONT, OH; FREMONT ROSS HS; (JR); F Lan Hn Soc; Hi Hnr Roll; Hnr Roll; Nat Hon Sy; Otst Ac Ach Awd; Pres Ac Ftns Aw; St of Mnth; WWAHSS; Comm Volntr; Chrch Yth Grp; DARE; Pep Squd; Vsity Clb; Drm Mjr; Chrldg (V CL); Stu Cncl (R); Feature Twirler for the Ross High Band 2003 School Year; Pre Law; Ohio State U

WATSON, EVA M; GRANVILLE, OH; GRANVILLE HS; (JR); Hnr Roll; Comm Volntr; Drma Clb; Emplmnt; Key Club; Chr; SP/M/VS; Stg Cre; Fld Hky (V C); Sccr (J); Started Field Hockey Team @ My High School; Thespian Society; Theatre Major; College Professors-Performance Theatre; Kalamazoo College; College of Wooster

WATSON, JONATHAN M; WARREN, OH; WARREN G. HARDING HS; (JR); Hnr Roll; Otst Ac Ach Awd; Comm Volntr; Chrch Yth Grp; Tchrs Aide; Ch Chr; Ftball (V); Teaching (Teacher); Engineering; Youngstown State U; U of Maryland

WATSON, MOLLY; DOVER, OH; DOVER HS; (FR); 4H Awd; Hnr Roll; 4-H; Key Club; Dnce; SP/M/VS; Stg Cre; Vllyball (J L); 4-H/Horse Shows; Piano; Veterinarian

WATSON, RICHARD C; WILLOW WOOD, OH; SYMMES VALLEY HS; (SO); Ctznshp Aw; Hnr Roll; Perf Att; WWAHSS; Comm Volntr; Peer Tut/ Med; 4-H; Emplmnt; FCCLA; Ntl FFA; Off Aide; Stg Cre; National FFA Member; National FFA Office Holder-Sentinel; Electrical Engineer; Surveyor/ Engineer; Ohio State U

WATT, VICTORIA L; SEVILLE, OH; MEDINA HS; (SR); Hnr Roll; St of Mnth; Peer Tut/Med; Red Cr Aide; Emplmnt; Key Club; Kwanza Clb; Quiz Bowl; Tchrs Aide; Bnd; Mch Bnd; Graduating with Honors Diploma; Treasurer of Key Club; Nursing / RN License; U of Akron; U of Wayne

WATTS, KATIE; WILLOUGHBY, OH; WILLOUGHBY SOUTH HS; (SO); Hi Hnr Roll; Hnr Roll; Comm Volntr; Chrch Yth Grp; Key Club; Off Aide; Spanish Clb; Bnd; Mch Bnd; Swmg (J L); Track (V L); Key Club; Spanish Club; Psychology; Medical; Miami U; Ohio State U

WAUGH, SARAH B; JACKSON, OH; JACKSON HS; (SR); Red Cr Aide; Chrch Yth Grp; Quill & Scroll; Sftball (V CL); Vllyball (V L); Business Administration; Shawnee State U

WAYAND, MARISSA; LIBERTY TOWNSHIP, OH; LAKOTA EAST HS; (JR); Hnr Roll; MVP; Sci Fairs; St of Mnth; Comm Volntr; Peer Tut/Med; Chrch Yth Grp; Emplmnt; Lib Aide; Pep Squd; Photog; Tchrs Aide; Vsity Clb; Chr; Dnce; Chrldg (L); Sccr (L); Cl Off (P); Stu Cncl (P); Yrbk (R, P); Paralegal; Legal Assistant; Western Kentucky U; Eastern Kentucky U

WEAVER, ERIC T; SALINEVILLE, OH; SOUTHERN LOCAL HS; (SR); Hnr Roll; Nat Hon Sy; Nat Mrt LOC; USAA; WWAHSS; Comm Volntr; Red Cr Aide; Chrch Yth Grp; DARE; Drma Clb; Emplmnt; Spanish Clb; SP/ M/VS; Lit Mag; Yrbk; NP Honor Society; Who's Who Among Am-HS; Psychology; Calvin College; Malone College

WEAVER, JENNIFER; BUCYRUS, OH; COLONEL CRAWFORD HS; (FR); 4H Awd; Hi Hnr Roll; Perf Att; Comm Volntr; 4-H; DARE; Svce Clb; French Clb; Chr; SP/M/VS; Chrldg (J); Sftball (J); Swmg (V L); Vllyball (J); State Qualifier- 4-H Project - Horsemanship; Competitor in All-Ohio Youth Horse Show; Writer / Magazine Editor; Otterbein College

WEAVER, JERRI; CANTON, OH; TIMKEN SR HS; (FR); Ctznshp Aw; Hnr Roll; Nat Hon Sy; Pres Sch; St of Mnth; Chrch Yth Grp; DARE; ROTC; Ch Chr; Stu Cncl (R); Architect; Lawyer; Walsh State; Kent State

WEEDEN, OLIVIA; LAKEWOOD, OH; LAKEWOOD HS; (SR); Orch; SP/ M/VS; Vllyball (VJCL); Advertising Design; Fashion Institute of Technology

WEEDEN, QUINTIN; CLEVELAND, OH; LUTHERAN HS EAST; (SO); Nat Hon Sy; St of Mnth; Chrch Yth Grp; Ch Chr; Bskball (J); Student of the Month; Student of the Week; Graduate with 4.0 or Higher; College Basketball; Purdue U; Duke U

WEEKS, WILLA; EUCLID, OH; LUTHERAN HS EAST; (JR); Hnr Roll; St of Mnth; WWAHSS; Comm Volntr; Peer Tut/Med; Chrldg (V C); Sftball (V); Vllyball (V L); Yrbk (P); 21st Century Leadership Award; Award for Excellence; Medicine - Ob/Gyn; PhD; Harvard U; Case Western Reserve U

WEHMEYER, HOLLY; HUBBARD, OH; HUBBARD HS; (SO); Hnr Roll; Hab For Humty Volntr; Biology Clb; Lib Aide; SADD; French Clb; Bnd; Chr; Dnce; Flg Crps; Photography; Wildlife Study; Ohio State U; U of Cincinnati

Watson, Jonathan M
Warren G. Harding HS
Warren, OH

Walker, David S
Lakota East HS
Middletown, OH

Warner, Ari M
Cleveland Hts HS
Cleveland, OH

WEHRLE, ERICA L; BLAKESLEE, OH; EDON NORTHWEST SCH; (SR); Hi Hnr Roll; Nat Hon Sy; WWAHSS; Chrch Yth Grp; DARE; Emplmnt; Tchrs Aide; Spanish Clb; Bnd; Mch Bnd; Pep Bnd; Stu Cncl (R); Yrbk (P); Cross Country Manager; Hospitality Management; U of Findlay

WEILAND, CHRIS; GENOA, OH; WOODMORE HS; (FR); Hi Hnr Roll; Hnr Roll; St of Mnth; WWAHSS; DARE; Key Club; Ftball (V L); Track (V L); Wrstlg (V L); I Am a Member of Key Club, Academic All-Ohio Wrestling Team 2004; I Am a Member of Trinity Lutheran Church; Ohio State Veterinary Science; Ohio State U; U of Toledo

WEIMER, EMILY; GALION, OH; COLONEL CRAWFORD HS; (FR); Hnr Roll; Comm Volntr; Peer Tut/Med; 4-H; Lib Aide; Bnd; Chr; Mch Bnd; Pep Bnd; Grand Reserve Champion at Crawford Fair; Member of ABBA / ADRC / O5DRC; Criminal Scene Investigator; Veterinarian / Lawyer

WEIRICK, BRAD; MIDDLEFIELD, OH; CARDINAL HS; (SO); Hnr Roll; WWAHSS; Hab For Humty Volntr; Chess; Bnd; Jzz Bnd; Mch Bnd; Pep Bnd; Aeronautical Engineering; Civil Engineering; Ohio State; Air Force ROTC

WEIRICK, JAMES; MANSFIELD, OH; TEMPLE CHRISTIAN SCH; (JR); Nat Hon Sy; WWAHSS; Scouts; Journalism

WELCH, ALLISON B; MANCHESTER, OH; ADAMS CTY CHRISTIAN SCH; (SO); Bskball (V); Sccr (V); Vllyball (V); Volunteer At Nursing Home; Church Youth Group; Nursing; Physical Therapy

WELCH, JEFF; MOUNT ORAB, OH; SOUTHERN HILLS JVS CAREER CTR; (JR); Chrch Yth Grp; Mus Clb; Voc Ind Clb Am; Wdwrkg Clb; Cl Off (S); Secretary of Carpentry; Architecture; Construction Management; Gardner-Webb; Defiance

WELKER, LINDSEY K; MAPLE HEIGHTS, OH; MAPLE HEIGHTS HS; (JR); 4H Awd; Ctznshp Aw; Hnr Roll; MVP; Nat Hon Sy; Otst Ac Ach Awd; Pres Sch; Peer Tut/Med; BPA; DARE; Vsity Clb; Voc Ind Clb Am; Vllyball (V L); Cl Off (T); NHS 2004 / Junior Olympic Club Team; Lake Erie League MVP - 2004 PUC; Law; Criminal Justice; Xavier U; Ashland U

WELLS, BRISTEN; NEW CARLISLE, OH; TECUMSEH HS; (FR); 4H Awd; Hi Hnr Roll; Hnr Roll; Perf Att; St of Mnth; Comm Volntr; Peer Tut/Med; 4-H; Chrch Yth Grp; FCA; Ntl FFA; Ch Chr; SP/M/VS; Hsbk Rdg; Public Speaking Awards; Horse Judging Award; Doctorate Veterinary Medicine; Michigan State U; U of Tennessee

WELLS, KATHARINE; CLEVELAND, OH; GARFIELD HEIGHTS HS; (JR); Ctznshp Aw; Hnr Roll; Nat Hon Sy; Comm Volntr; Drma Clb; Scouts; Tchrs Aide; Ch Chr; SP/M/VS; Stg Cre; Lit Mag (R); Sch Ppr (R); Honor Bar for National Thespian Society

WELLS, MEGAN E; KENT, OH; FIELD HS; (SR); Hnr Roll; Hosp Aide; Drma Clb; French Clb; Bnd; Mch Bnd; Orch; Pep Bnd; Yrbk (R, P); French Club; Indoor Drum Line; Technical Design for the Theatre; Kent State U

WENGER, KIRSTEN C; WOOSTER, OH; CTRL CHRISTIAN SCH; (SO); Hnr Roll; Chrch Yth Grp; Chr; SP/M/VS; Bskball (J); Vllyball (J); Trip to Panama; Art; Drama

WESSLING, KIARA M; FAIRBORN, OH; FAIRBORN HS; (SO); Ctznshp Aw; DAR; Hi Hnr Roll; Key Club; French Clb; Orch; Stu Cncl (R); Law; Foreign Language

WEST, JOURDAN L; FAIRVIEW PARK, OH; FAIRVIEW HS; (SO); Hnr Roll; Sci Fairs; Chrch Yth Grp; DARE; Drma Clb; Bnd; Mch Bnd; Pep Bnd; Stg Cre; Synchronettes; Solo/Ensemble Contest; Bachelor's Degree; Major-Math &/or Education; Kent State U; Bowling Green U

WESTBROOK, ASHLEE; EMPIRE, OH; EDISON HS; (JR); Hi Hnr Roll; Hnr Roll; Nat Hon Sy; WWAHSS; Ntl Beta Clb; Acpl Chr; Bnd; Jzz Bnd; Mch Bnd; Sch Ppr; Cosmetology; Aeronautic Space Engineer; Embry-Riddle Aeronautic U; Ohio U

WESTFALL, JESSICA; CLEVELAND, OH; VALLEY FORGE HS; (JR); Hi Hnr Roll; Nat Stu Ath Day Aw; Otst Ac Ach Awd; Sci Fairs; St of Mnth; Comm Volntr; DARE; Emplmnt; Off Aide; P to P St Amb Prg; Tchrs Aide; Vsity Clb; Voc Ind Clb Am; PP Ftbl (V); Sftball (J); Track (V); Vllyball (C); Cl Off (S); Stu Cncl (R); Student Aide (To the Athletic Trainer); Vocational School Secretary; Bachelor of Nursing

WESTFALL, NAOMI J; DALTON, OH; CTRL CHRISTIAN SCH; (SO); Hnr Roll; Sci/Math Olympn; Mth Clb/Tm; Off Aide; Tchrs Aide; Acpl Chr; Scr Kpr (L); Cl Off (P); Community Service / Missions; Oncology; U of Akron; Johns Hopkins U

WESTGERDES, RAYMOND L; HIGGINSPORT, OH; SOUTHERN HILLS JVS CAREER CTR; (JR); Hnr Roll; Otst Ac Ach Awd; Perf Att; Sci Fairs; Comm Volntr; Chrch Yth Grp; DARE; FCCLA; Ntl FFA; Pep Squd; Prom Com; Tchrs Aide; Voc Ind Clb Am; Chr; Bsball (VJ); Cl Off (R); Cadet Fire Fighter; Graphic Arts; Architect; Montana State U; Ohio State U

WESTRICK, JENNIFER; OTTAWA, OH; MILLER CITY HS; (SR); Hnr Roll; Nat Hon Sy; Otst Ac Ach Awd; Sci Fairs; St of Mnth; WWAHSS; Comm Volntr; Peer Tut/Med; Chrch Yth Grp; Emplmnt; Ntl FFA; Quiz Bowl; SADD; Tchrs Aide; Bnd; Flg Crps; Cl Off (T); Junior Fair Participant; Dairy Science; Animal Science; Ohio State Agricultural Technical Institute

WHARRAM, SAMANTHA; MADISON, OH; MADISON HS; (JR); Hi Hnr Roll; Hnr Roll; Perf Att; WWAHSS; FCA; Key Club; Mth Clb/Tm; Prom Com; SADD; Tchrs Aide; Chr; Bskball (V L); Track (V L); Vllyball (V L); CR (R); Doctor; Forensic Science

WHATMAN, BETHANY; BELLVILLE, OH; CLEAR FORK HS; (FR); Hnr Roll; SADD; Bskball (J); Sccr (J); Sftball (V); Accounting; New York U; North Carolina U

WHEELER, DESTINY; COLUMBUS, OH; WEST HS; (JR); Hi Hnr Roll; Hnr Roll; Perf Att; Lib Aide; Off Aide; Chr; Drl Tm; Mch Bnd; Nurse; Fashion Designer; Columbus State Community College; Ohio State U

WHEELER, LACEY R; EAST CANTON, OH; EAST CANTON HS; (SR); 4H Awd; Hnr Roll; WWAHSS; Comm Volntr; 4-H; Chrch Yth Grp; FCA; Lttrmn Clb; Off Aide; Prom Com; Tchrs Aide; Vsity Clb; Chr; SP/M/VS; Bskball (J); Sftball (V CL); Vsy Clb; Vllyball (V L); Stu Cncl (T); Early Childhood Education; Middle Education; Ohio Dominican U; Youngstown State U

WHEELER, MATTHEW; BARBERTON, OH; COPLEY HS; (FR); Sci Fairs; Sci/Math Olympn; Comm Volntr; Peer Tut/Med; Chess; Chrch Yth Grp; DARE; Svce Clb; Bnd; Mch Bnd; Bsball; Mar Art; Sftball

WHEELER, MEGAN E; JEFFERSON, OH; LAKESIDE HS; (SR); Hnr Roll; Nat Hon Sy; WWAHSS; Peer Tut/Med; AL Aux Girls; Emplmnt; Bnd; Mch Bnd; Golf (V L); CR (T); Nursing; Kent State-Ashtabula; Toledo U

WHITAKER, CHRIS; GOSHEN, OH; GOSHEN HS; (FR); Hi Hnr Roll; Hnr Roll; Nat Hon Sy; St of Mnth; Chrch Yth Grp; DARE; Bnd; U of Kentucky

WHITE, ALEK; MOGADORE, OH; FIELD HS; (SR); Perf Att; Pres Sch; Comm Volntr; Hosp Aide; Red Cr Aide; Chess; Key Club; Spanish Clb; Mch Bnd; Sccr (V L); Track (V L); Wrstlg (V L); Ohio State; Kent State

WHITE, ANTHONY A; GRAFTON, OH; MIDVIEW HS; (JR); Ctznshp Aw; Hnr Roll; Perf Att; Sci Fairs; St of Mnth; DARE; Sch Ppr (R); Journalist; Sports Writer; Lorain County Community College; Baldwin Wallace College

WHITE, ASHLEY M; NILES, OH; WARREN CHRISTIAN SCH; (FR); Hi Hnr Roll; Hnr Roll; St of Mnth; Comm Volntr; Hosp Aide; Mth Clb/Tm; Scouts; Chr; Dnce; Certified Safe Sitter; Teacher; Work with Animals; Youngstown State U; Kent State U

WHITE, CHERELLE L; COLUMBUS, OH; MIFFLIN HS; (SO); Hi Hnr Roll; Hnr Roll; St of Mnth; Comm Volntr; Chrch Yth Grp; DARE; Drma Clb; Emplmnt; Tchrs Aide; Ch Chr; SP/M/VS; To Graduate with Honors; To Attend College of Choice; Wright State; Spelman College

WHITE, JESSICA; BELLBROOK, OH; BELLBROOK HS; (SO); Hi Hnr Roll; Hnr Roll; Comm Volntr; Chrch Yth Grp; Drma Clb; Pep Squd; Spanish Clb; Bnd; Mch Bnd; Pep Bnd; SP/M/VS; Swmg (J); Foreign Language; Miami U Oxford

WHITE, NICOLE R; NEWCOMERSTOWN, OH; NEWCOMERSTOWN HS; (FR); Comm Volntr; Drma Clb; SP/M/VS; Bskball; Track; A Doctorate in Psychology; The U of Akron; The Ohio State U

WHITT, CHRISTIAN L C; WHEELERSBURG, OH; WHEELERSBURG HS; (SO); Hnr Roll; Sci Fairs; WWAHSS; Comm Volntr; Chrch Yth Grp; DARE; Key Club; Quiz Bowl; Bnd; Chr; Ch Chr; Mch Bnd; Golf (J); Swmg (V); Key Club Vice-President; Community Theatre Award for Best New Actor; Acting; Movie & Television Production; Wright State U; UCLA

WHITT, TOMASAE; CLEVELAND, OH; LINCOLN-WEST HS; (FR); Ctznshp Aw; Hnr Roll; Otst Ac Ach Awd; Perf Att; WWAHSS; Comm Volntr; Hab For Humty Volntr; DARE; Dbte Team; Fr of Library; SP/M/VS; CR (P); Criminal Justice (Lawyer); Business Management; Ohio State U; Howard U

WIELKIEWICZ, MANDY; NASHPORT, OH; TRI-VALLEY HS; (JR); Hi Hnr Roll; Hnr Roll; Nat Hon Sy; WWAHSS; Comm Volntr; Peer Tut/Med; Drma Clb; FCA; Prom Com; French Clb; SP/M/VS; Bskball (J); Who's Who Among American High School Students; National Honor Society; Criminology; Pre-Law; Ohio State; Miami of Ohio

WILBER, NIKITA L; OREGON, OH; CLAY HS; (JR); Hi Hnr Roll; Hnr Roll; Comm Volntr; Spec Olymp Vol; Mth Clb/Tm; Special Education Teaching; U of Toledo

WILDER, MELISSA K; MIAMISBURG, OH; PREBLE SHAWNEE; (SO); Nat Hon Sy; Perf Att; Comm Volntr; Peer Tut/Med; Tchrs Aide; CR (P); Dean's List / President's List; Perfect Attendance; Teacher; Social Services; U of Phoenix on Line; Sinclair

WILDMAN, KRISTOPHER; WARREN, OH; CHAMPION HS; (FR); Hnr Roll; St of Mnth; WWAHSS; Chrch Yth Grp; Key Club; Off Aide; Bskball; Ftball (V L); Track; Wt Lftg; Cl Off (P); Stu Cncl; Engineering

WILEY, CAITLIN; CANTON, OH; EAST CANTON HS; (SO); Nat Hon Sy; Otst Ac Ach Awd; Comm Volntr; Peer Tut/Med; Chrch Yth Grp; Mth Clb/Tm; Prom Com; Scouts; Tchrs Aide; French Clb; Bnd; Dnce; Drm Mjr; Mch Bnd; Cl Off (P); Stu Cncl; CR (S); French Club Officer; Band Officer; Nursing; Physician Assistant; Aultman Hospital School of Nursing; Northern Kentucky U

WILEY, ERIN E; MEDINA, OH; MEDINA SR HS; (SO); F Lan Hn Soc; St of Mnth; WWAHSS; Comm Volntr; Hab For Humty Volntr; Peer Tut/Med; Drma Clb; Emplmnt; Fr of Library; Key Club; Lib Aide; Off Aide; SADD; Chr; Dnce; Drl Tm; SP/M/VS; Cl Off (P); CR (R); Major in Elementary Education; Minor in Dance Theatre; New York U; Bowling Green State U

WILHELM, AMANDA S; MONROEVILLE, OH; MONROEVILLE HS; (JR); 4H Awd; Hi Hnr Roll; Nat Hon Sy; Otst Ac Ach Awd; Sci Fairs; St of Mnth; WWAHSS; Peer Tut/Med; 4-H; Key Club; Mod UN; Ntl FFA; Off Aide; P to P St Amb Prg; Prom Com; Bskball (V); Sftball (V); Vllyball (V); Cl Off (V); Stu Cncl (P); Yrbk; Medical Field

WILHELM, JACQUELINE D; PUT IN BAY, OH; PUT-IN-BAY SCH; (SR); Ctznshp Aw; Hi Hnr Roll; MVP; Nat Ldrshp Svc; Nat Stu Ath Day Aw; Otst Ac Ach Awd; Pres Ac Ftns Aw; USAA; Valdctrian; WWAHSS; Comm Volntr; Peer Tut/Med; AL Aux Girls; Cmptr Clb; HO'Br Yth Ldrshp; Mod UN; Prom Com; Tchrs Aide; Bskball (V CL); Cl Off (V); Stu Cncl (V, T); National Honor Society; Physical Therapy; U of Findlay

WILHELM, KASEY; MONROEVILLE, OH; MONROEVILLE HS; (SO); Hnr Roll; Emplmnt; Lttrmn Clb; Ntl FFA; Bskball (J); Ftball (VJ L); Track (VJ L)

WILKEY, TYLER J; WADSWORTH, OH; WADSWORTH HS; (JR); Hnr Roll; Comm Volntr; Chrch Yth Grp; Key Club; Bnd; Mch Bnd; Business; Construction Management; U of Cincinnati; U of Dayton

WILLE, ADRIEN; GRAFTON, OH; HOMESCHOOLED; (SR); 4H Awd; St of Mnth; Yth Ldrshp Prog; Comm Volntr; Peer Tut/Med; Red Cr Aide; 4-H; ArtClub; Chrch Yth Grp; Cmptr Clb; Emplmnt; Mth Clb/Tm; Photog; Svce Clb; Ch Chr; Dnce; Bskball; Gmnstcs; Mar Art; Skiing; Cl Off (P); Kajukenbo Brown Belt; Community Youth Leader; Graphic Design Major; Spanish Major; Brigham Young U; Southern Virginia U

WILLIAMS, ALLISON M; LORAIN, OH; LORAIN SOUTHVIEW HS; (SR); Hi Hnr Roll; Hnr Roll; Nat Hon Sy; Perf Att; St of Mnth; Chrch Yth Grp; Key Club; Mod UN; Mus Clb; Tchrs Aide; Acpl Chr; Bnd; Ch Chr; Mch Bnd; Scr Kpr (J); Wrstlg; Presidential Volunteer Service Award; Early Childhood Education - Pre-K Thru 3rd Grade; Lorain County Community College; Marietta College

WILLIAMS, APRIL; COLUMBUS, OH; (SO); Hnr Roll; Chrch Yth Grp; DARE; Bsball (J); Bskball (VJ); Sftball (V); Vllyball (V); Yrbk (R); Lawyer; Nurse; OSU; UCLA

WILLIAMS, CHARLES T; WEST CHESTER, OH; CINCINNATI CHRISTIAN SCH; (SR); Hi Hnr Roll; Hnr Roll; Comm Volntr; Chrch Yth Grp; Emplmnt; Off Aide; Tchrs Aide; Chr; Ch Chr; Sccr (J); Mechanical Engineering; U of Cincinnati

WILLIAMS, CHIANTE; CLEVELAND, OH; MARTIN LUTHER KING HS; MS; All Am Sch; Hi Hnr Roll; Nat Hon Sy; Otst Ac Ach Awd; St of Mnth; Bskball; Vllyball; CR (R); Journalism; Communications; Ohio State U; Harvard State U

WILLIAMS, DIAMOND; CLEVELAND, OH; JOHN MARSHALL HS; Ctznshp Aw; Otst Ac Ach Awd; St of Mnth; ArtClub; DARE; Scouts; SADD; Clb; Ch Chr; Bskball; Cyclg; Hsbk Rdg; Rqtball; Vllyball; CR; Medical; Cleveland State U (Su)

WILLIAMS, GREGORY; LUCASVILLE, OH; VALLEY HS; (FR); Hnr Roll; Otst Ac Ach Awd; Comm Volntr; 4-H; Chrch Yth Grp; DARE; Emplmnt; Lib Aide; Quiz Bowl; Scouts; Chr; Scr Kpr (J); Sccr (J); Tennis (J); Yrbk; Radiologist; Anesthesiologist; Miami U of Ohio; U of Cincinnati

WILLIAMS, JASMINE; CLEVELAND, OH; MARTIN LUTHER KING HS; MS; Ctznshp Aw; Hnr Roll; MVP; Nat Hon Sy; Nat Mrt LOC; Perf Att; St of Mnth; Comm Volntr; Peer Tut/Med; Chess; Chrch Yth Grp; Cmptr Clb; DARE; FCA; Jr Ach; Chrldg (J); Track (J); Hair Stylist; Master's Degree; Akron; Community College

WILLIAMS, JEANGELA; DAYTON, OH; PATTERSON CAREER CTR; (SO); Hi Hnr Roll; Hnr Roll; Perf Att; St of Mnth; CR (R); Cosmetology; Nursing; Business; Alabama A & M U; Atlanta State U

WILLIAMS, KOURTNEY; COLUMBUS, OH; SOUTH URBAN AC; (JR); Hi Hnr Roll; Nat Hon Sy; St of Mnth; WWAHSS; Emplmnt; Tchrs Aide; Stu Cncl; National Honor Society; Who's Who Among Americas High School Students; Psychologist; Spelman College; Capital U

WILLIAMS, KYLA; URBANA, OH; GRAHAM HS; (SR); Hnr Roll; Photography; Clark State Community College

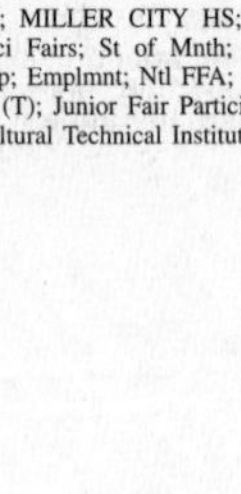

Wilkey, Tyler J
Wadsworth HS
Wadsworth, OH

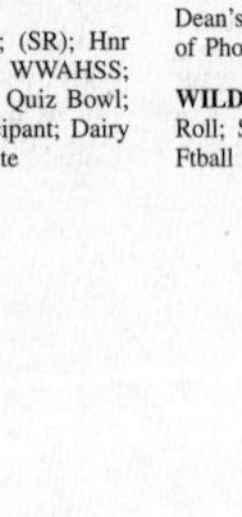

White, Ashley M
Warren Christian Sch
Niles, OH

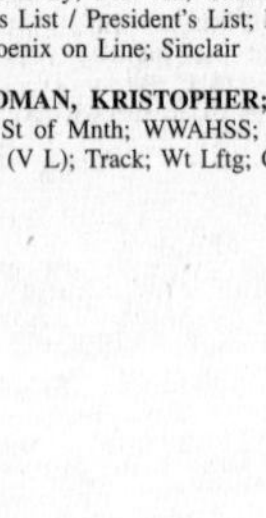

Westgerdes, Raymond L
Southern Hills JVS Career Ctr
Higginsport, OH

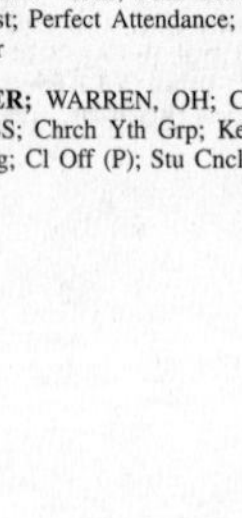

Wessling, Kiara M
Fairborn HS
Fairborn, OH

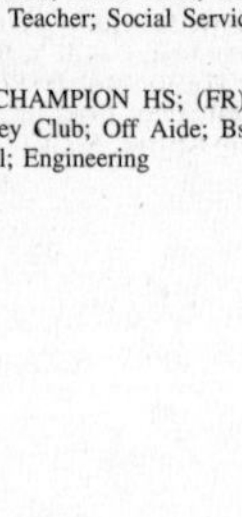

West, Jourdan L
Fairview HS
Fairview Park, OH

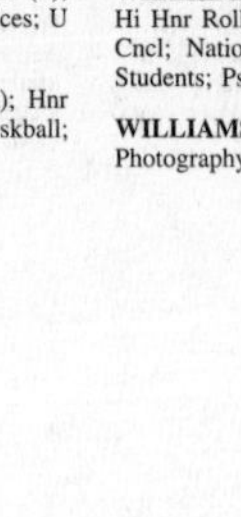

White, Jessica
Bellbrook HS
Bellbrook, OH

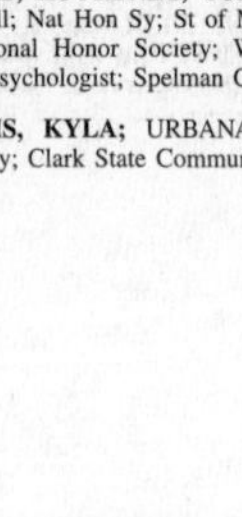

Wille, Adrien
Homeschooled
Grafton, OH

WILLIAMS, LEKEYTA; COLUMBUS, OH; BROOKHAVEN HS; (SO); Hi Hnr Roll; MVP; Perf Att; Peer Tut/Med; Chrch Yth Grp; FCA; Sci Clb; Bnd; Ch Chr; Mch Bnd; Bskball (J); Sftball (V); Vllyball (V); Stu Cncl (R); NAACP; Black Nurses Association; Nursing; Music; Spelman College; Vanderbilt U

WILLIAMS, NAJI; LORAIN, OH; CLEARVIEW HS; (SO); Hnr Roll; Nat Stu Ath Day Aw; Perf Att; Comm Volntr; Chrch Yth Grp; FCA; Off Aide; Quiz Bowl; Tchrs Aide; Ch Chr; Bskball (J); Track (V); Cl Off (P); Stu Cncl (R); Major in European History; Major in Journalism; Columbia U; Texas State U

WILLIAMS, NICOLE; POWELL, OH; WORTHINGTON KILBOURNE; (JR); F Lan Hn Soc; Hi Hnr Roll; Nat Hon Sy; WWAHSS; Comm Volntr; Chrch Yth Grp; Emplmnt; Ch Chr; Clr Grd; Orch; SP/M/VS; Physical Therapy; Engineering; Brigham Young U

WILLIAMS, TATIANNA M; CLEVELAND, OH; CLEVELAND SCH OF THE ARTS; (JR); Hnr Roll; Nat Hon Sy; WWAHSS; Bsball (V); Culinary Arts; Business Management; Johnson and Wales U; Kendall College

WILLIAMSON, JUSTIN M; MT GILEAD, OH; MT GILEAD HS; (FR); Chrch Yth Grp; DARE; Dnce; SP/M/VS; Bsball (J); Ftball (J); Archaeology; Historian

WILLIAMSON, KYERA; REYNOLDSBURG, OH; PICKERINGTON HS NORTH; (SO); Hi Hnr Roll; Hnr Roll; Perf Att; St of Mnth; Comm Volntr; Peer Tut/Med; Photog; Ch Chr; Chrldg (J); Gmnstcs (J); Swmg (J); Track (J); Journalism; Business Management; Clark Atlanta U; Norfolk U

WILLIAMSON, LINDSEY; AKRON, OH; ELLET HS; (JR); Hnr Roll; Perf Att; WWAHSS; Comm Volntr; Drma Clb; Emplmnt; Key Club; Lttrmn Clb; Mus Clb; Off Aide; Prom Com; Scouts; Acpl Chr; Orch; SP/M/VS; Bskball (J); Cr Ctry (L); Track (L); Stu Cncl (R); OSMA Youth Awareness Participant; 2004 Miss Jr Teen Akron, Ohio; Major in Architecture and Design; Kent State U; Ohio State U

WILLIS, LA TANYA; REYNOLDSBURG, OH; HARVEST PREP SCH; (JR); Hi Hnr Roll; Nat Hon Sy; St of Mnth; WWAHSS; Peer Tut/Med; Spec Olymp Vol; BPA; Chrch Yth Grp; Emplmnt; Prom Com; Chrldg (V); Adv Cncl; Physical Therapy; Forensics; Duke U; North Carolina State U

WILLIS, LESLIE S; MILLERSPORT, OH; MILLERSPORT JR SR HS; MS; Hnr Roll; Chrch Yth Grp; Lib Aide; Bnd; Chr; Mch Bnd; Pep Bnd; Sccr (L); Show Choir; Lawyer

WILSON, BRITTANY M; MEDINA, OH; (JR); Hnr Roll; Nat Hon Sy; WWAHSS; Comm Volntr; Chrch Yth Grp; Key Club; French Clb; Bnd; Chr; Mch Bnd; Elementary School Teacher; Bowling Green State U; The Ohio State U

WILSON, CHASSITY; COLUMBIANA, OH; COLUMBIANA HS; (SO); Hnr Roll; Peer Tut/Med; Chrch Yth Grp; DARE; Tchrs Aide; Spanish Clb; Ch Chr; Basketball 3 Yrs - 3rd / 4th / 6th Grade; Band 4 Yrs - 5th / 6th / 7th / 8th Grade; Medical Degree in Pediatrics; Bachelor Degree Interior Design; U of Maryland; Ohio State U

WILSON, CHRIS; LEESBURG, OH; MC CLAIN HS; (FR); Chr; Sccr (J); Swmg (V)

WILSON, DEBORAH; WICKLIFFE, OH; SOUTH HS (WILLOUGHBY); (SO); Hnr Roll; WWAHSS; Hosp Aide; Key Club; Sci Clb; Spanish Clb; Heart Surgeon; PhD; Ohio State U; Case Western Reserve

WILSON, JENNA; SPRINGFIELD, OH; CATHOLIC CTRL HS; (SR); Hnr Roll; WWAHSS; Jr Ach; Key Club; Bskball (J); Golf (V L); Sftball (V L); Business Administration; King College

WILSON, KARRAH; CRESTON, OH; NORWAYNE HS; (SR); Hi Hnr Roll; Hnr Roll; Red Cr Aide; Emplmnt; Chrldg (V CL); Sftball (J); Yrbk (E); Business Management Technology; U of Akron

WILSON, KATHERINE; LOVELAND, OH; GOSHEN HS; (SR); Hi Hnr Roll; Hnr Roll; WWAHSS; Peer Tut/Med; DARE; DECA; Emplmnt; DECA State Qualifier; Journalism; English; U of Cincinnati

WILSON, NATHAN; CANTON, OH; EAST CANTON HS; (FR); Hi Hnr Roll; Otst Ac Ach Awd; Pres Ac Ftns Aw; Off Aide; Tchrs Aide; Bsball (J); Bskball (J); Golf (J); Stu Cncl (R); Yrbk (E); Sports Management; Bowling Green State U; Kent State U

WILSON, REBEKAH; PICKERINGTON, OH; PICKERINGTON HS NORTH; (SO); Hi Hnr Roll; Comm Volntr; Chrch Yth Grp; Emplmnt; Key Club; Chr; Ch Chr; Track (V); Yrbk (R); Key Club; Business Management; Communications; Marshall U; Ohio U

WILSON, SARA; WARREN, OH; CHAMPION HS; (JR); Hi Hnr Roll; Hnr Roll; Comm Volntr; Emplmnt; Key Club; Off Aide; Pep Squd; Prom Com; Stg Cre; Skiing (V); Track (J); Stu Cncl (R); Yrbk (P); STAND; Bzz Agent; March of Dimes; Nursing; Medical Secretary; Kent State U; Ohio State U

WILSON, STACY A; CEDARVILLE, OH; CEDARVILLE MHS; (SO); Hnr Roll; WWAHSS; Bnd; Mch Bnd; Cr Ctry (V L); Track (V L); Marine Biology

WILSON, STEVE; CONCORD, OH; RIVERSIDE HS; (SO); Hnr Roll; MVP; Otst Ac Ach Awd; Perf Att; Comm Volntr; Peer Tut/Med; DARE; Scouts; Ice Hky (V); Natural Sciences; Engineering; Kettering U; Drexel U

WILT, ASHLEY E; COSHOCTON, OH; RIVER VIEW HS; (SR); All Am Sch; Hnr Roll; Nat Hon Sy; Otst Ac Ach Awd; USAA; WWAHSS; Peer Tut/Med; Spec Olymp Vol; Emplmnt; Lttrmn Clb; Mth Clb/Tm; Off Aide; SADD; Tchrs Aide; Spanish Clb; Sftball (V); Stu Cncl (R); CR (T); Yrbk (E, P); Secondary Education / Math; Special Education; Ursuline College

WINDLE, KALEIGH; NEW ALBANY, OH; NEW ALBANY HS; (JR); Hnr Roll; Chrch Yth Grp; FCA; Lttrmn Clb; Prom Com; Scouts; Vsity Clb; Bnd; Dnce; Mch Bnd; Cr Ctry (V L); Lcrsse (J); Sccr (J); Track (V L); Dance Team Capt. 2004 Sports Leadership Club; Team Member of the Year-Dance (2004); Sports Medicine/Physical Therapy; Ohio State U; Ohio U

WINEBAR, REBECCA L; BLUFFTON, OH; BLUFFTON HS; (SR); All Am Sch; Hi Hnr Roll; Nat Hon Sy; Perf Att; USAA; WWAHSS; Hab For Humty Volntr; Peer Tut/Med; Chrch Yth Grp; Emplmnt; Mth Clb/Tm; Scouts; SADD; Bnd; Mch Bnd; Pep Bnd; SP/M/VS; Girl Scout Silver Award; National Hispanic Scholar; Economics; Political Science; Duke U; Miami U Ohio

WINEBARGER, LAURA A; MONROEVILLE, OH; MONROEVILLE HS; (JR); Hnr Roll; WWAHSS; Drma Clb; FTA; Key Club; Mod UN; Acpl Chr; Chr; Clr Grd; SP/M/VS; Post Secondary Options; Musical Theatre; Music Education; Cincinnati Conservatory of Music; Wright State U

WINEBRENNER, ABBY; MAINEVILLE, OH; KINGS HS; (JR); Hnr Roll; Otst Ac Ach Awd; St of Mnth; Comm Volntr; Chrch Yth Grp; Photog; Vsity Clb; Spanish Clb; Bskball (V); Track (V); Student of the Year-Interior Design; Interior Design; Advertising

WINFREY-LEAVELLE, DONTE; DAYTON, OH; (SO); Hi Hnr Roll; Hnr Roll; Perf Att; Chrch Yth Grp; Ch Chr; Ftball (VJ)

WINTER, AMANDA; MT VERNON, OH; MT VERNON HS; (SR); 4H Awd; Hnr Roll; Kwnis Aw; Nat Hon Sy; Pres Sch; Peer Tut/Med; 4-H; Chrch Yth Grp; Drma Clb; Key Club; Sci Clb; Spanish Clb; Bnd; Mch Bnd; Orch; SP/M/VS; Yrbk (E); Kiwanis Spanish Award; Zoology Major; Keeper at Columbus Zoo; Ohio Wesleyan U

WINTER, STEPHEN; LEESVILLE, OH; CONOTTON VALLEY JR/SR HS; (JR); WWAHSS; Chrch Yth Grp; Emplmnt; Bnd; Bskball (J); Cl Off (P); Yrbk (E, P); Biology; Doctorate; Kent State

WINTERS, TIFFANY M; KILLBUCK, OH; RIVER VIEW/COSHOCTON CTY CAREER CTR; (JR); Hi Hnr Roll; Otst Ac Ach Awd; St of Mnth; WWAHSS; 4-H; Chrch Yth Grp; SADD; Voc Ind Clb Am; Chrldg (J); Sftball (J); Cl Off (P); VICA - Officer / Reporter; Student of the Month; Registered Nurse; Doctor; Lenoir-Rhyne College; Baldwin-Wallace College

WIREMAN, TRAVIS; WAPAKONETA, OH; WAPAKONETA HS; (SO); Hnr Roll; Otst Ac Ach Awd; Perf Att; Pres Ac Ftns Aw; St of Mnth; WWAHSS; Comm Volntr; Ntl FFA; French Clb; Bskball (J); Golf (V); Aviation, Aviator, Astronaut; Pro Golfer; Purdue

WITRY, BENJAMIN J; MARYSVILLE, OH; MARYSVILLE HS; (SO); Hnr Roll; Chrch Yth Grp; FCA; Tchrs Aide; Wrstlg (J L); Wrestling Spirit Award; Scholar Athlete; Business Degree; Ohio State U; Kent State

WOLF, ANDREW; MIDDLETOWN, OH; LAKOTA EAST HS; (SO); Hi Hnr Roll; Chrch Yth Grp; Bnd; Jzz Bnd; Mch Bnd; Tennis (J); Biology; Journalism

WOLF, FRED; GRANVILLE, OH; GRANVILLE HS; (SO); Hnr Roll; Otst Ac Ach Awd; Perf Att; Pres Ac Ftns Aw; WWAHSS; Chrch Yth Grp; Emplmnt; FCA; Lttrmn Clb; Scouts; Vsity Clb; Bsball (J); Ftball (J); Wrstlg (V); Cl Off (P); Stu Cncl (R); CR (P); President of Boy Scout Troop; Young Life; Pre-Law

WONDERS, JARED D; DEFIANCE, OH; TINORA HS; (JR); Hi Hnr Roll; Nat Hon Sy; WWAHSS; Comm Volntr; AL Aux Boys; Chrch Yth Grp; DARE; Emplmnt; German Clb; Chr; Ch Chr; SP/M/VS; Swg Chr; Bsball (V L); Golf (V L); I DARE You-Leadership Award; Outstanding Chem I Student; Doctor of Pharmacy; Ohio Northern U; U of Toledo

WOOD-BURGESS, STACY; BELLBROOK, OH; BELLBROOK HS; (SO); Hi Hnr Roll; Hnr Roll; Comm Volntr; Chrch Yth Grp; DARE; Dbte Team; Drma Clb; Acpl Chr; Bnd; Chr; Ch Chr; Swmg; Youth Choir Director; Debate Team; Law; Voice; Juilliard School; Ohio State U

WOODWORTH, MANDI; MARSHALLVILLE, OH; SMITHVILLE HS; (FR); Hnr Roll; ArtClub; Foreign Clb; Bskball (L); Teacher; Michigan U; Toledo U

WOOLF, BRITON P; KENT, OH; ROOSEVELT HS; (SO); DARE; Work Related Fields; Counselor; Kent State U

WORRELL, JACQUELINE; DAYTON, OH; BEAVERCREEK HS; (SO); Hnr Roll; Hosp Aide; Peer Tut/Med; SADD; French Clb; Doctor; Marketing; Miami U; Boston College

WORTHINGTON, ALI; NEY, OH; FAIRVIEW HS; (MS); Fut Prb Slvr; Hi Hnr Roll; Hnr Roll; Nat Hon Sy; Nat Ldrshp Svc; Otst Ac Ach Awd; Perf Att; Sci/Math Olympn; St of Mnth; Yth Ldrshp Prog; Comm Volntr; Hab For Humty Volntr; Peer Tut/Med; 4-H; Chrch Yth Grp; Fr of Library; Lttrmn Clb; Mus Clb; SADD; Wdwrkg Clb; Spanish Clb; Chr; Dnce; SP/M/VS; Sftball (J); Track (J); Vllyball (J); Cl Off (R); Stu Cncl (R); Sch Ppr (R); Won Softball Tournaments in 2001 / 2005 3rd Place / 2002; Performing Arts; Teaching Degree; U of Michigan; U of Indianapolis

WRIGHT, JASMINE N; CINCINNATI, OH; WITHROW UNIVERSITY HS; (SO); Ctznshp Aw; Hnr Roll; Nat Hon Sy; Otst Ac Ach Awd; Perf Att; Sci Fairs; St of Mnth; WWAHSS; Peer Tut/Med; Red Cr Aide; Chess; DARE; Scouts; Vsity Clb; Spanish Clb; Chrldg (V); Sftball (V); Vllyball (V); Wt Lftg (V)

WRIGHT, LORA; RIPLEY, OH; RIPLEY-UNION-LEWIS-HUNTINGTON HS; (SR); Hnr Roll; MVP; Sci Fairs; St of Mnth; WWAHSS; Chrch Yth Grp; DARE; Prom Com; Tchrs Aide; Chr; Chrldg (V); Cr Ctry (J); Track (V); Sch Ppr (E, R); All League - Cross Country; PSO - 2 Yrs at Chatfield College; Criminal Justice; Political Science; Morehead State U; Mount Saint Joseph College

WURM, VICTORIA J; TIFFIN, OH; OLD FORT HS; (JR); Hnr Roll; Nat Ldrshp Svc; Perf Att; Chr; Dnce; SP/M/VS; Swmg (V L); Ballet, OMEA Choral; Modern Dance; Communications; Tiffin U

WURSTER, CHELSEA; DEFIANCE, OH; MT CARMEL SCH; (JR); Hi Hnr Roll; Hnr Roll; MVP; St of Mnth; Chr; Bskball (V); Cl Off (V); Placed 10th in State - National Spanish Exam; Major in Pre-Law / Law School; Morehead State U; U of Michigan

WYANT, KARINA; COLUMBUS, OH; GAHANNA LINCOLN HS; (JR); Comm Volntr; Emplmnt; Key Club; Chr; French; Education; Ohio State U; Lake Erie College

WYATT, LATIKA C; AKRON, OH; COVENTRY HS; (SO); Hi Hnr Roll; Hnr Roll; Otst Ac Ach Awd; Perf Att; St of Mnth; Comm Volntr; Hosp Aide; Spec Olymp Vol; DARE; Emplmnt; Outdrs Clb; Dnce; Drl Tm; PPSqd (C); I March in the Summer Time; Health Care/Nursing; Child Care/Pediatrician; Akron U; Kent State U

WYMER, LARISSA; NORTH BALTIMORE, OH; NORTH BALTIMORE JR/SR HS; (JR); Hi Hnr Roll; Perf Att; WWAHSS; Yth Ldrshp Prog; Comm Volntr; ArtClub; Chrch Yth Grp; Drma Clb; HO'Br Yth Ldrshp; Mus Clb; Tchrs Aide; Spanish Clb; Bnd; Jzz Bnd; Mch Bnd; SP/M/VS; PP Ftbl (V); Sftball (V L); Vllyball (V L); Stu Cncl (R); All-Ohio State Fair Band; Tri-M Music Honor Society; Pre-Vet; Pre-Dentistry; U of Findlay; Purdue U

WYMER, TANG; CINCINNATI, OH; LAKOTA WEST HS; (SO); WWAHSS; Yth Ldrshp Prog; Bnd; Jzz Bnd; Sccr (J); Cincinnati Keyboard Club Scholarship; Lead American - Congressional Student Leadership Conference; Business Management; Political Science; U of Georgetown; U of Michigan

WYNE, JASON; CARROLL, OH; BLOOM-CARROLL HS; (SR); Hnr Roll; WWAHSS; Emplmnt; Lib Aide; Bsball (J); Bskball (V L); Sccr (V L); Ohio U; Kent State

WYSONG, KELLY; WESTERVILLE, OH; WESTERVILLE NORTH HS; (SR); Hnr Roll; Otst Ac Ach Awd; Pres Ac Ftns Aw; Emplmnt; Sftball (V L); Outstanding Scholar Athlete Awards; Academic Merit Awards; Medicine; Law; Ohio U; Ohio State U & Miami U (Ohio)

YANG, MAELEE; HOLLAND, OH; NOTRE DAME AC; (FR); Ctznshp Aw; Hi Hnr Roll; MVP; Nat Sci Aw; Otst Ac Ach Awd; Sci Fairs; Valdctrian; Comm Volntr; Peer Tut/Med; Spec Olymp Vol; ArtClub; Emplmnt; Jr Ach; Scouts; Spch Team; Vsity Clb; Lcrsse (V); Tennis (J); CR (R); Scholarship Winner; Athlete of the Week; Master in Business; Medical Doctor; U of Pennsylvania; Princeton

YARAB, JESSICA; YOUNGSTOWN, OH; URSULINE HS; (FR); Hnr Roll; St of Mnth; WWAHSS; Comm Volntr; Peer Tut/Med; Emplmnt; Bskball (J); Sftball (V L); Vllyball (JC); Stu Cncl (R); Martial Arts; Voice/Piano/Flute; Forensic Science; Law; U of California Los Angeles; U of Texas

YASMIN, NADIRA; COLUMBUS, OH; WORTHINGTON KILBOURNE HS; (JR); F Lan Hn Soc; Hnr Roll; Nat Hon Sy; Comm Volntr; DARE; Key Club; Svce Clb; Lcrsse (J); Worthington Rugby Club; Interact Club; Pre-Med; Ohio State U; Cornell Medical College

YATES, JEANNIE M; URBANA, OH; GRAHAM HS; (SR); Ctznshp Aw; MVP; Peer Tut/Med; Emplmnt; Mar Art (C); Ohio State Jr. Grand Champ. in Karate; Business Law; Athletic Education; Akron U; Clark State Community College

YEAGER, KYLE; NEWARK, OH; NEWARK CATHOLIC HS; (JR); Hnr Roll; Nat Hon Sy; Yth Ldrshp Prog; Drma Clb; Stg Cre; Cr Ctry (V CL); Track (V L); Ohio State U

YEATER, KRISTYN; ASHLAND, OH; ASHLAND HS; (JR); Hnr Roll; Nat Hon Sy; Perf Att; WWAHSS; Comm Volntr; Chrch Yth Grp; Prom Com; Vllyball (VJC); Stu Cncl (R); CR (R); Yrbk (R); Mass Communications; Journalism; Winthrop U

Wireman, Travis
Wapakoneta HS
Wapakoneta, OH

Wilson, Sara
Champion HS
Warren, OH

Wilson, Karrah
Norwayne HS
Creston, OH

Williams, Lekeyta
Brookhaven HS
Columbus, OH

Williamson, Justin M
Mt Gilead HS
Mt Gilead, OH

Windle, Kaleigh
New Albany HS
New Albany, OH

Wonders, Jared D
Tinora HS
Defiance, OH

YECHOOR, NIRUPAMA; SYLVANIA, OH; MAUMEE VALLEY CTRY DAY; (JR); Hi Hnr Roll; Comm Volntr; Hosp Aide; Mod UN; Prom Com; Bskbll (V L); Fld Hky (V L); Track (V L); Cl Off (S); Lit Mag (R); Yrbk (R)

YI, JESSICA; COLUMBUS, OH; NEW ALBANY HS; (SO); Perf Att; WWAHSS; Comm Volntr; Hosp Aide; Chrch Yth Grp; Emplmnt; Mod UN; Bnd; Mch Bnd; PP Ftbl (J); Swmg (V L); Tennis (J); Track (J); OMEA (Ohio Music Education Assoc.) 4 Yrs-Ratings 1; Swimming-(Qualifier for District Finals); Pre-Medicine; Hotel Management/International Business; U Of Notre Dame; U of Southern California

YIM, HELEN; COLUMBUS, OH; GAHANNA LINCOLN HS; (SR); Hnr Roll; Nat Mrt LOC; Comm Volntr; Peer Tut/Med; Chrch Yth Grp; DECA; Emplmnt; Ch Chr; Flg Crps; SP/M/VS; Model Arab League; 3rd in States for DECA Competition; Business Administration; Marketing; Ohio State U (Main Campus)

YOAKUM, BRANDIE R; WASHINGTON COURT HOUSE, OH; WASHINGTON HS; (SO); Hnr Roll; Nat Hon Sy; Otst Ac Ach Awd; St of Mnth; Comm Volntr; DARE; Emplmnt; Jr Ach; Lib Aide; Mus Clb; Off Aide; Tchrs Aide; German Clb; Bnd; Mch Bnd; Pep Bnd; SP/M/VS; Stu Cncl (R); Yrbk (E, R, P); Medical Field (Pediatrician); Early Childhood Education; (OSU) Ohio State U; Wright State

YOCUM, ANNALISA; URBANA, OH; GRAHAM HS; (SR); Hi Hnr Roll; Hnr Roll; 4-H; ArtClub; Had a Poem Published; Interior Design; Writing; The Illinois School of Art-Schaumburg; Columbus College of Art and Design

YOPP, STEPHANIE; CONNEAUT, OH; EDGEWOOD SR HS; (SR); 4H Awd; Hnr Roll; 4-H; DARE; Emplmnt; Off Aide; Chr; Dental Hygiene; Dental Assistant; Lakeland Community College; Lake Erie College

YOST, KAELY; MALVERN, OH; MALVERN HS; (JR); Hnr Roll; Nat Hon Sy; Sci Fairs; Sftball (V)

YOUNG, JILLIAN L; CINCINNATI, OH; COLERAIN HS; (JR); F Lan Hn Soc; Hi Hnr Roll; Hnr Roll; Otst Ac Ach Awd; Comm Volntr; Chrch Yth Grp; Photog; Bnd; Ch Chr; Stu Cncl (R); Softball Team for Church; Christmas Drama; Criminal Justice; Art / Photography-Graphic Design; Miami U; Bowling Green State U

YOUNG, SARA L; LIMA, OH; BATH HS/APOLLO CAREER CTR; (SR); Hnr Roll; Nat Hon Sy; Early Childhood Education; Rhodes State; Ohio State U Lima

YOUNG, VASHONDA; CLEVELAND, OH; JOHN F STEVENS HS; (FR); Comm Volntr; Peer Tut/Med; Chrch Yth Grp; DARE; Fr of Library; Chr; Ch Chr; SP/M/VS; Culinary Arts; Veterinarian Medicine; Cleveland State U; Drexel U

YUTZY, COURTNEY; PLAIN CITY, OH; JONATHAN ALDER HS; (SR); DAR; Hi Hnr Roll; Nat Hon Sy; Otst Ac Ach Awd; Pres Sch; St of Mnth; Valdctrian; Comm Volntr; Chrch Yth Grp; DARE; Mus Clb; Quill & Scroll; Spanish Clb; Chr; Ch Chr; SP/M/VS; Yrbk (R, P); Worship Arts; Christian Ministries; Spring Arbor U; Belmont U

ZAIKOVA, ALEXANDRA V; PERRY, OH; PERRY HS; (FR); Key Club; Bnd; Chr; Mch Bnd; Child Physician; Astronomer; Ohio State U; Harvard U

ZAKI, KAREEM S; MASON, OH; ST XAVIER HS; (SO); Hi Hnr Roll; Otst Ac Ach Awd; Perf Att; Sci Fairs; Yth Ldrshp Prog; Comm Volntr; Chess; Chrch Yth Grp; FBLA; HO'Br Yth Ldrshp; Mth Clb/Tm; Vsity Clb; Clb; Bskball (J); Vsy Clb (V); Stu Cncl; CR; Sch Ppr (R); 4th in the Nation - Crew / Rowing / 8th Grade Graduation Speaker; National Jr Honors / Academics Awards - French / English / Math; World Recognized Surgeon & Establish Hospitals in Less Fortunate Countries; Congressman; Harvard U; Johns Hopkins U

ZANGMEISTER, MIRIAM A; ZANESVILLE, OH; BISHOP ROSECRANS; (SO); Hi Hnr Roll; Nat Hon Sy; Comm Volntr; Emplmnt; Key Club; Ch Chr; Sccr (V L); Swmg (V L); Track (V L)

ZEAK, KELLY; COLUMBUS, OH; WHETSTONE HS; (FR); Hnr Roll; Perf Att; Drma Clb; SP/M/VS; Snowboarding; Acting; Chef; Columbus State; Culinary Institute of America

ZEIGER, SARA A; WEST CHESTER, OH; LAKOTA EAST HS; (JR); Hi Hnr Roll; Comm Volntr; Chrch Yth Grp; FCA; Tchrs Aide; Bnd; Dnce; Jzz Bnd; Pep Bnd; Chrldg (J); JETS Team (Junior Engineering Technical Society); Theology/Religion; Psychology

ZHENG, XIDI; CLEVELAND, OH; (SR); All Am Sch; Hi Hnr Roll; Hnr Roll; Nat Hon Sy; Perf Att; WWAHSS; Comm Volntr; Red Cr Aide; Cmptr Clb

ZICKEFOOSE, RYAN L; KENT, OH; KENT ROOSEVELT HS; (SR); DECA; Emplmnt; Bsball (VJ L); Bskball (J); U of Akron

ZIEGLER, KRISTEN M; GOSHEN, OH; CLERMONT NORTHEASTERN HS; (SR); Hi Hnr Roll; Hnr Roll; St of Mnth; Ntl FFA; French Clb; SP/M/VS; Yrbk (E, P)

ZIMMERMAN, ALISON; PERRYSVILLE, OH; LOUDONVILLE HS; (SO); Hi Hnr Roll; Sci Fairs; St of Mnth; WWAHSS; Hosp Aide; Foreign Clb; Chr; SP/M/VS; Bskball (JC); Track (V L); Vllyball (J); Cl Off (T); Pharmacy; Biomedical Engineering; Ohio Northern U

ZOELLNER, STEPHANIE L; CINCINNATI, OH; SETON HS; (FR); Hnr Roll; Perf Att; Peer Tut/Med; ArtClub; DARE; Mus Clb; Scouts; Chr; SP/M/VS; Intramural Sports; Computer Engineer; Computer Technology Coordinator; Mount St Joseph; Northern Kentucky U

Pennsylvania

AARONSON, BRITTANY; MECHANICSBURG, PA; MECHANICSBURG AREA SR HS; (JR); F Lan Hn Soc; Hnr Roll; Nat Hon Sy; Otst Ac Ach Awd; St of Mnth; Peer Tut/Med; DARE; Mus Clb; Tchrs Aide; Chr; SP/M/VS; Elementary School Teacher; Gymnastics Coach; Temple University; Shippensburg University

ABADIA, SANDRA L; BERWYN, PA; CONESTOGA HS; (SO); Hnr Roll; Comm Volntr; Key Club; Pep Sqd; P to P St Amb Prg; Spanish Clb; SP/M/VS; Chrldg (V); Service and Leadership Award; Business Management; Business Owner / Entrepreneur; Penn State U; James Madison U

ABBOTT, ALI; WEXFORD, PA; PINE-RICHLAND HS; (JR); Hi Hnr Roll; Hnr Roll; Nat Stu Ath Day Aw; WWAHSS; Hnr Roll; Otst Ac Ach Awd; Emplmnt; Jr Ach; Key Club; Pep Squd; Vsity Clb; Acpl Chr; Dnce; Chrldg (VJCL); PPSqd (VJ); John Carroll U; Duquesne U

ABDELAZIEM, FAHTIMAH; MOOSIC, PA; RIVERSIDE JR/SR HS; (FR); Hnr Roll; Peer Tut/Med; Dnce; Dvng (V); PPSqd; Spanish Club; Law / Attorney; Interior Design; Penn State U; Harvard U

ABUISO, DANIELLE; BARTONSVILLE, PA; POCONO MTN EAST HS; (SO); Hnr Roll; Dnce; Lawyer; Accountant; New York U; Princeton U

ACCRISTO, JESSICA; MECHANICSBURG, PA; CUMBERLAND VALLEY HS; (SO); Ctznshp Aw; Hnr Roll; Comm Volntr; Hab For Humty Volntr; Spec Olymp Vol; Chrch Yth Grp; Key Club; Photog; Ch Chr; Sch Ppr (P); Outstanding Newspaper (Through School/Scholastic); Journalism; Photography; HACC (Harrisburg Area Community College)

ACKERS, FRED; FREELAND, PA; HAZLETON AREA HS; (SO); Hi Hnr Roll; Hnr Roll; WWAHSS; Schol Bwl; Mch Bnd; Vic Lesco Memorial Award - Hazleton YABA; Hotel / Motel Management; Sports Broadcaster; Luzerne County Community College; Kings College

ACORD, JOLINE; OXFORD, PA; OXFORD AREA HS; (SR); Hi Hnr Roll; Hnr Roll; WWAHSS; Emplmnt; Voted Most Eccentric Female '05; Collision Repair and Refinishing Technology; Automotive Training Center

ADAIR, STACY N; PITTSBURGH, PA; TAYLOR ALLDERDICE HS; (SO); Outdrs Clb; Editor's Choice Award for Outstanding Achievement in Poetry; Translation (French); Translation (Russian); Kent State U; Duquesne U

ADAM, KATIE; MERTZTOWN, PA; BRANDYWINE HEIGHTS HS; (JR); Hi Hnr Roll; Hnr Roll; Nat Hon Sy; Key Club; Prom Com; Spanish Clb; Chrldg (V L); Cl Off (T); United States Achievement Academy; Secondary Education / Biology; Elementary Education; Kutztown U; Bloomsburg U

ADAMCHIK, DASHA; PITTSBURGH, PA; OAKLAND CATHOLIC HS; (FR); Hi Hnr Roll; Hnr Roll; Hab For Humty Volntr; Swmg (J); Tennis (V); Marine Biology; Law; Brown U; U of Pennsylvania

ADAMEK, LAUREN E; BOOTHWYN, PA; CHICHESTER SR HS; (FR); Bnd; Dnce; Mch Bnd; Tennis (V); Track (J); Elementary Education; West Chester U; U of Delaware

ADAMEROVICH, ZACHARY L; LATROBE, PA; GREATER LATROBE SR HS; (JR); F Lan Hn Soc; Gov Hnr Prg; Hi Hnr Roll; Nat Hon Sy; St of Mnth; Comm Volntr; Hab For Humty Volntr; Peer Tut/Med; Chrch Yth Grp; Emplmnt; Jr Ach; Key Club; NtlFrnscLg; Sci Clb; Tchrs Aide; German Clb; Formation of Business Club; Business Administration; Marketing; Carnegie Mellon U; Lehigh U

ADAMS, JENNIFER; WASHINGTON, PA; WASHINGTON, PA; HS; (SO); Hi Hnr Roll; Hnr Roll; Prf Att; Key Club; Scouts; Spanish Clb; Bnd; Dnce; Mch Bnd; Girl Scout Silver Award; Steel Drum Band Member; Political Science; Law Degree; Dickinson College; Bucknell U

ADAMS, LEA; OTTSVILLE, PA; PALISADES HS; (SO); Hi Hnr Roll; Hnr Roll; Nat Hon Sy; St of Mnth; Comm Volntr; Dbte Team; Spch Team; Spanish Clb; SP/M/VS; Yrbk (R, P); Camp Counselor; Architecture; English

ADU-BOAHENE, VICTOR O; DREXEL HILL, PA; UPPER DARBY HS; (JR); Hi Hnr Roll; Perf Att; Comm Volntr; Chrch Yth Grp; Mth Clb/Tm; Sci Clb; Sccr (V L); I'm Best in Playing Ping Pong.; And Better in Volleyball; Biomedical Sciences; Engineering; Princeton U (NJ); U of Pennsylvania (Philly)

AGUILERA, KRISTI L; PHILADELPHIA, PA; NORTHEAST HS; (SR); Hnr Roll; Chrch Yth Grp; Ch Chr; Sftball (J P); Lawyer; Vice-President of Youth Group in Church; Education; Interior Design; Philadelphia Biblical U; U of Pennsylvania

AHLSEEN, K INGELIS; PARADISE, PA; LANCASTER CHRISTIAN SCH; (SR); Hi Hnr Roll; Jr Mshl; Nat Hon Sy; Otst Ac Ach Awd; Comm Volntr; Peer Tut/Med; Emplmnt; NYLC; Tchrs Aide; Spanish Clb; Bskball (V C); Fld Hky (V C); Adv Cncl (R); Stu Cncl (R); Homecoming Queen; Anatomy/Psychology Club; Nursing; Lancaster Institute of Health Sciences School of Nursing

AHLUWALIA, AMIT; RIDLEY PARK, PA; RIDLEY HS; (SO); Hnr Roll; Sci Fairs; St of Mnth; Comm Volntr; Emplmnt; Scouts; Bnd; Mch Bnd; Pep Bnd; Architecture; Drexel U; U of Pennsylvania

AHMED, ASMA; UPPER DARBY, PA; UPPER DARBY HS; (SO); Gov Hnr Prg; Hi Hnr Roll; Hnr Roll; Amnsty Intl; Comm Volntr; Hosp Aide; ArtClub; Fr of Library; Tchrs Aide; Chr; Fld Hky (V); Stu Cncl (S); Doctor; Lawyer; Yale U

AHMED, SARA; UPPER DARBY, PA; UPPER DARBY HS; (JR); Hi Hnr Roll; Hnr Roll; Nat Hon Sy; Pres Sch; St of Mnth; Comm Volntr; FBLA; Sci Clb; Chr; Track (J)

AIELLO, DAN; VANDERGRIFT, PA; KISKI AREA HS; (JR); Gov Hnr Prg; Hi Hnr Roll; Hnr Roll; Nat Hon Sy; Nat Mrt LOC; Sci/Math Olympn; Comm Volntr; Peer Tut/Med; Key Club; Quiz Bowl; SADD; Spanish Clb; Cl Off (T); Stu Cncl (R); Yrbk (E); Lt. Governor of Division Co: PA District of Key Club International; Special Education; Elementary Education; Penn State U; Millersville U

AIKENS, ROBERT; PUNXSUTAWNEY, PA; PUNXSUTAWNEY AREA SR HS; Hnr Roll; Pres Ac Ftns Aw; WWAHSS; Comm Volntr; Red Cr Aide; Emplmnt; Prom Com; Sci Clb; Golf; Track; Wrstlg (C L); Most Improved Wrestler, 3rd District Wresltler 2x; JV Championship for Wrestling; Machinist; I-Tech

AINEY, ALYSON A; KINGSLEY, PA; MONTROSE AREA SD; (JR); F Lan Hn Soc; Hnr Roll; Nat Hon Sy; WWAHSS; Chrch Yth Grp; French Clb; Orch; Dvng (V); Tennis (J); CR (T); Yrbk (R); Culinary Arts

AKPOR-MENSAH, CAROL E; EASTON, PA; EASTON AREA HS; (JR); Hnr Roll; Comm Volntr; Peer Tut/Med; Chrch Yth Grp; Emplmnt; Sci Clb; French Clb; Biomedical Engineer; Pharmacy; Marquette U; Lock Haven

ALBRECHT, P J; WATERFORD, PA; FORT LEBOEUF SD; (SO); Hnr Roll; MVP; Nat Hon Sy; Perf Att; Sci Fairs; St of Mnth; Comm Volntr; Peer Tut/Med; Emplmnt; Biology Clb; Outdrs Clb; Sci Clb; Scouts; Wdwrkg Clb; Wrstlg (J); Bachelor's Degree; Edinboro U; U of Phoenix

ALBRIGHT, JORDAN; MARTINSBURG, PA; SPRING COVE SD; (JR); Bskball (V C); Golf (V L); Skiing; Vsy Clb (V V); Wt Lftg; National Honor Society; Juniata; Penn State U

ALBRIGHT, MEGAN; MECHANICSBURG, PA; EAST PENNSBORO AREA HS; (FR); Hi Hnr Roll; Hnr Roll; Otst Ac Ach Awd; Spec Olymp Vol; Chrch Yth Grp; Vsity Clb; French Clb; Bskball (J); Fld Hky (V L); Sccr (V L); Cl Off (P)

ALDHUMANI, ALI; ERIE, PA; WILSON MS; (MS); All Am Sch; Hnr Roll; Doctor; Computer Engineer

ALDRIDGE, IMANI A; BRODHEADSVILLE, PA; PLEASANT VALLEY HS; (SO); Hi Hnr Roll; Hnr Roll; Chess; Dbte Team; FBLA; Ch Chr; Dnce; Drl Tm; Debate Award; MBA; Law; Penn State; Rutgers U

ALEXANDER, LAURA A; ALIQUIPPA, PA; HOPEWELL HS; (FR); All Am Sch; Hi Hnr Roll; Otst Ac Ach Awd; Perf Att; Pres Sch; Sci Fairs; CARE; Comm Volntr; Peer Tut/Med; Chrch Yth Grp; Dbte Team; Drma Clb; Mth Clb/Tm; NtlFrnscLg; Pep Sqd; P to P St Amb Prg; French Clb; SP/M/VS; Chrldg (J L); Skiing (J); Tennis (J); Stu Cncl (R); CR (R); Amanda Duffy Scholar Award; Law; Politics; Harvard U; Oxford U

ALEXANDER, RHONDA; PHILADELPHIA, PA; NORRIS S BARRATT MS; MS; 4H Awd; Ctznshp Aw; Hnr Roll; ArtClub; Chrch Yth Grp; Drma Clb; Mth Clb/Tm; Dnce; Bskball; Chrldg (C); Yrbk (P); Law; Cosmetology; Lincoln Colleges; Temple U

ALFORD, TREVOR C; NEW CUMBERLAND, PA; TRINITY HS; (JR); Hi Hnr Roll; Hnr Roll; Nat Hon Sy; Sci Fairs; WWAHSS; Comm Volntr; Peer Tut/Med; Emplmnt; Key Club; Spch Team; Latin Clb; Bskball (L); Fbtall (VJ); CR (R); CYO Parish Basketball Team; Latin Award; Psychiatry; Investment Banking; U of Chicago; Wharton School of Business

AL-HASHIMI, OMAR; MONROEVILLE, PA; GATEWAY SD; (SO); Hnr Roll; Comm Volntr; Hab For Humty Volntr; ArtClub; German Clb; Member of Ski Club; Taught Elementary Kids German; Business; Architecture; Penn State U

ALI, AMAR; UPPER DARBY, PA; BEVERLY HILLS MS; (MS); Ctznshp Aw; Hi Hnr Roll; Hnr Roll; Perf Att; St of Mnth; Comm Volntr; Chr; Distinguished Honor Roll

ALIO, DANIELLE L; NORTH WALES, PA; KENNEDY-KENRICK CATHOLIC HS; (FR); Hnr Roll; Perf Att; Drma Clb; Mus Clb; Chr; Ch Chr; SP/M/VS

ALLEN, BENJAMIN; PORT ROYAL, PA; JUNIATA CTY SD; (JR); Ctznshp Aw; Hi Hnr Roll; MVP; Nat Hon Sy; Otst Ac Ach Awd; St of Mnth; USAA; WWAHSS; Comm Volntr; Peer Tut/Med; Chrch Yth Grp; Emplmnt; Key Club; Prom Com; Vsity Clb; Bsball (V L); Bskball (V L); Sccr (V CL)

ALLEN, COREY L; READING, PA; READING HS; (JR); Perf Att; Comm Volntr; Chrch Yth Grp; Voc Ind Clb Am; Track (V); Rocket Scientist

ALLEN, DANA; FOLCROFT, PA; AC PARK HS; (SO); Hnr Roll; Otst Ac Ach Awd; St of Mnth; DARE; Chrldg; Sftball (P); Sch Ppr (R, P); Softball & Cheerleading for Folcraft; Pediatrician; Fashion Designer; Penn State U; Temple U

ALMODOVAR, ROCIO; READING, PA; READING HS; (FR); Hnr Roll; Perf Att; French Clb; Chr; Going to Take the National French Test; Upward Bound Program; Medical; Music; Kutztown U

ALMONTE, ESTEFANIA; ALLENTOWN, PA; WILLIAM ALLEN HS; (SO); Hnr Roll; Sci Fairs; Dnce; Drl Tm; Working Hard At School; Achieving Good Grades; Law and Enforcement; Health Career (Nursing); Penn State; Muhlenberg U College

ALSHEFSKI, KEVIN; HAZLETON, PA; HAZLETON AREA SD; (JR); Hi Hnr Roll; Hnr Roll; Engineering; Computers; Penn State; Luzerne Community College

ALTEMOSE, AMANDA M; BRODHEADSVILLE, PA; PLEASANT VALLEY; (FR); Hi Hnr Roll; WWAHSS; Comm Volntr; Spec Olymp Vol; FBLA; Key Club; Clr Grd; Dnce

AMICE, RACHEL; MECHANICSBURG, PA; CUMBERLAND VALLEY HS; (SO); Comm Volntr; Chrch Yth Grp; Key Club; NtlFrnscLg; Spanish Clb; Business Management; Fashion Marketing; Penn State U

AMICUCCI, SEAN; ERIE, PA; NORTHWEST PA COLLEGIATE AC; (SR); Hi Hnr Roll; St of Mnth; Yrbk (E, R, P); King TV Student of the Month; Communication - TV/Radio; Gannon U; Ithaca College

AMMON, CHARLES; GLENMOORE, PA; BISHOP SHANAHAN HS; (FR); Hnr Roll; Emplmnt; Mth Clb/Tm; NYLC; Bsball (V); Electrical Engineering; Biochemical Engineering; U of Maryland; Johns Hopkins U

AMOUR, ELI E; PITTSBURGH, PA; PITTSBURGH SD; (SO); Ctznshp Aw; Hi Hnr Roll; Hnr Roll; Perf Att; St of Mnth; Comm Volntr; Chrch Yth Grp; Emplmnt; Photog; Work At Retirement Home; I Would Like to Become a Doctor.

ANANTHAN, VIVEK; ALLENTOWN, PA; PARKLAND HS; (SO); Hi Hnr Roll; Pres Ac Ftns Aw; Sci Fairs; St of Mnth; Comm Volntr; FBLA; Mth Clb/Tm; Mod UN; Scouts; Tmpl Yth Grp; Spanish Clb; Sccr (J); Tennis (J); Life Scout; Played Piano for 8 Years; Medicine; Business; Columbia U; U of Pennsylvania

ANDERKO, AMANDA J; MC KEESPORT, PA; MC KEESPORT AREA SD; (FR); Hnr Roll; MVP; Perf Att; Sci Fairs; St of Mnth; Comm Volntr; Hosp Aide; Peer Tut/Med; Chrch Yth Grp; DARE; Drma Clb; Pep Squd; Scouts; Svce Clb; Spch Team; Flg Crps; Chrldg (VJ); Stu Cncl (R); Color Guard - Captain; Majorette; Early Childhood Education; California U Pennsylvania

ANDERSEN, MELISSA; REVERE, PA; PALISADES HS; (SR); Hnr Roll; Comm Volntr; Biology Clb; French Clb; Chr; Clr Grd; Sccr (J); Vol. Firefighter for U.B.E.; Pre-Vet Program; Delaware Valley College

ANDERSON, ANDREW; MECHANICSBURG, PA; MECHANICSBURG AREA SR HS; (SO); Ctznshp Aw; F Lan Hn Soc; Hi Hnr Roll; MVP; Nat Hon Sy; Pres Ac Ftns Aw; WWAHSS; Yth Ldrshp Prog; Comm Volntr; Emplmnt; HO'Br Yth Ldrshp; Key Club; Svce Clb; French Clb; Sccr (J); Wrstlg (V CL); Stu Cncl (R); 3x Nat'l Qualifier; History Day-England Exchange; Journalism; Film

ANDERSON, CHRISTINA F; WEST CHESTER, PA; BISHOP SHANAHAN HS; (JR); Hi Hnr Roll; Chrch Yth Grp; Emplmnt; Jr Ach; Italian Clb; Bnd; Dnce; Pep Bnd; Church Worship Band; Youth Group Band; Criminal Justice; Forensic Science; Kings College; Franklin & Marshall College

ANDERSON, CYDNEY; PITTSBURGH, PA; PENN HILLS HS; (JR); Hnr Roll; Nat Hon Sy; WWAHSS; Comm Volntr; Peer Tut/Med; Emplmnt; Key Club; Spanish Clb; Track and Field for My Uncle's Company; Elem.; Pitt U; Kal U

ANDERSON, PAIGE E; CARLISLE, PA; CUMBERLAND VALLEY HS; (SO); Hnr Roll; WWAHSS; Key Club; Spanish Clb; Cr Ctry (V); Track (V); Sch Ppr (R); Forensic Scientist; Sports Medicine; Penn State U; Boston U

Akpor-Mensah, Carol E — Easton Area HS — Easton, PA
Ahluwalia, Amit — Ridley HS — Ridley Park, PA
Aguilera, Kristi L — Northeast HS — Philadelphia, PA
Adam, Katie — Brandywine Heights HS — Mertztown, PA
Adu-Boahene, Victor O — Upper Darby HS — Drexel Hill, PA
Aikens, Robert — Punxsutawney Area SR HS — Punxsutawney, PA
Aldhumani, Ali — Wilson MS — Erie, PA

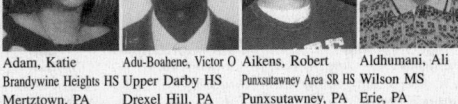

ANDERSON, RYAN; OAKMONT, PA; RIVERVIEW JR/SR HS; (JR); Hnr Roll; Nat Hon Sy; Hab For Humty Volntr; Drma Clb; Key Club; Spanish Clb; SP/M/VS; Bsball (J L); Bskball (J L); Skiing (V); Sccr (VJCL); Law; Pre-Med; U of Pittsburgh; Penn State U

ANDREWS, NATHAN; SPRING MILLS, PA; PENNS VALLEY AREA HS; (JR); Hi Hnr Roll; Nat Hon Sy; St of Mnth; Valdctrian; WWAHSS; Yth Ldrshp Prog; Comm Volntr; Peer Tut/Med; Red Cr Aide; Key Club; Mth Clb/Tm; Quiz Bowl; Svce Clb; Ftball (V L); Wrstlg (V L); Stu Cncl (R); Lit Mag (E); MENSA Society; Engineering; Pre-Med; Penn State U; Massachusetts Institute of Tech

ANGELUCCI, TORI; NORRISTOWN, PA; KENNEDY-KENRICK CATHOLIC HS; (FR); 4H Awd; Hi Hnr Roll; Hnr Roll; Sci/Math Olympn; Comm Volntr; 4-H; Lawyer; Psychologist; Penn State U; Arcadia U

ANNADATHA, APUROOPA; PITTSBURGH, PA; CHARTIERS VALLEY HS; (JR); Hi Hnr Roll; Otst Ac Ach Awd; Perf Att; St of Mnth; Comm Volntr; Hosp Aide; Svce Clb; Vsity Clb; Spanish Clb; Dnce; PP Ftbl (V); Tennis (V C); Vsy Clb (V C); Volunteer at Science Center - Carnegie; Performed for the Veterans / Dance; Pre-Med; PhD; U of Pittsburgh; U of Texas Austin

ANTONACCIO, BRI; HANOVER, PA; HANOVER PUBLIC HS; (JR); Hnr Roll; Kwnis Aw; Red Cr Aide; Emplmnt; Key Club; Prom Com; Chr; Dnce; Chrldg (V L); PP Ftbl (V); Sftball (J); Key Club-Treasurer; Art II; Graphic Design; Photography; Tyler School of Art (Temple U); Kutztown U

ANTOSHIN, YURIY; BENSALEM, PA; BENSALEM TOWNSHIP SD; (SO); Kwnis Aw; St of Mnth; Bsball (J); Swmg (V); Vllyball (J); Water Polo; Math Tutoring; Accounting; Marketing; Drexel U; Temple U

APOSTOLIS, MARINA J; BEAVER FALLS, PA; BEAVER FALLS HS; (SR); Hnr Roll; St of Mnth; Yth Ldrshp Prog; Comm Volntr; Hab For Humty Volntr; Emplmnt; FBLA; Key Club; Off Aide; Prom Com; SADD; Ch Chr; PP Ftbl (V); Cl Off (V); Stu Cncl (R); Pre-Pharmacy; Clarion U

ARANA, CLAUDIA; READING, PA; READING HS; (JR); Fld Hky (J); Sccr (J); Yrbk (P); Volunteer for Special ED; Marine Biology; Day Care Education

ARAUJO, INDIANA; READING, PA; READING HS; (SO); Hnr Roll; Perf Att; ArtClub; DARE; Chr; Bskball (J); Sftball (J); Track (J); Legal Society; Graduate of BBA; Law School; Business; Penn State U

ARBOGAST JR, JOHN; PT MARION, PA; ALBERT GALLATIN HS; (SO); Hnr Roll; Comm Volntr; SADD; French Clb; Bnd; Mch Bnd; Bsball (J); Chef; Computer Technician; Le Cordon Bleu Culinary Art School; West Virginia U

ARCHON, NICOLE; HATBORO, PA; (FR); Nat Hon Sy; Otst Ac Ach Awd; Comm Volntr; Chrch Yth Grp; Drma Clb; Ch Chr; Dnce; SP/M/VS

ARMANI, AZAD; DREXEL HILL, PA; MONSIGNOR BONNER HS; (FR); MVP; Otst Ac Ach Awd; Perf Att; Pres Ac Ftns Aw; Emplmnt; Rlr Hky (J); Sports Medicine; Meterology; Drexel U; Penn State

ARMSTRONG, CARLY; CAMP HILL, PA; CAMP HILL HS; (FR); Hnr Roll; Comm Volntr; Hab For Humty Volntr; Peer Tut/Med; 4-H; Chrch Yth Grp; Dbte Team; Pep Squd; Scouts; Sccr (JVVL); Wt Lftg; CR (R); Youth Group Officer; Law; Animal Science/ Biology; Oregon State University; Gonzaga U

ARNOLD, TYLER; KUTZTOWN, PA; KUTZTOWN AREA HS; (SR); Hnr Roll; Pres Ac Ftns Aw; USAA; WWAHSS; DARE; Emplmnt; Key Club; P to P St Amb Prg; Prom Com; Bsball; Ftball; Stu Cncl (R); Certified Scuba Diver; Communications; Theology/History/Philosophy; Kutztown U

AROCENA, TERESA; HATFIELD, PA; NORTH PENN HS; (JR); Spec Olymp Vol; Key Club; Dnce; Track; Motra Philippine Folk Dance Group; National Association of Student Councils, 2006 Conference Planning Committee; Nursing; Physical Therapy; Temple U; West Chester U

ARRUBLA, FELICIA; EASTON, PA; EASTON AREA HS; (SR); Hnr Roll; WWAHSS; Spanish Clb; Spanish Honor Society/Spanish Club; Nursing; Physical Therapy; Northampton Community College

ARTHUR, ALLISON; OAKMONT, PA; RIVERVIEW JR/SR HS; (JR); Hi Hnr Roll; Nat Hon Sy; Pres Sch; WWAHSS; Yth Ldrshp Prog; Comm Volntr; Peer Tut/Med; AL Aux Girls; Chrch Yth Grp; Key Club; Mod UN; NYLC; SADD; Vsity Clb; Sccr (V); Track (V); Vllyball (V); Stu Cncl; Elementary Education; Secondary Education; Penn State U; U of Pittsburgh

ARTHUR, DORLUS M; PHILADELPHIA, PA; OLNEY HS; (JR); 4H Awd; F Lan Hn Soc; Hi Hnr Roll; Hnr Roll; MVP; Perf Att; Ch Chr; Dnce; Mch Bnd; SP/M/VS; Bsball; Bskball; Ftball; Gmnstcs; Rqtball; Sccr; Tennis; Vllyball; Becoming Fluent in English in 2 Years; Having All A's in a Row on My Report Card; Medical Assistant; Medical Doctor; Temple U; Pennsylvania U

ARTHUR, MOLLY M; PITTSBURGH, PA; OAKLAND CATHOLIC HS; (SO); Hi Hnr Roll; WWAHSS; Comm Volntr; Hab For Humty Volntr; President - Busted Club; Law School; Hofstra U

ARTIS, CATHERINE L; EAST STROUDSBURG, PA; EAST STROUDSBURG HS SOUTH; (FR); Hi Hnr Roll; St of Mnth; Key Club; Yrbk (R, P); Step Team; To Become a Respectable Lawyer; Penn State; Columbia U

ASHMAN, VICTORIA; FREELAND, PA; HAZLETON AREA HS; (SR); Hi Hnr Roll; Hnr Roll; WWAHSS; Comm Volntr; Emplmnt; Key Club; Mus Clb; SADD; Bnd; Mch Bnd; Master's in Nursing; College Misericordia

ASHTON, EMILY; DALLAS, PA; LAKE LEHMAN JR/SR HS; (SO); Hi Hnr Roll; Hnr Roll; Nat Hon Sy; 4-H; Key Club; Spanish Clb; Swmg (V); Sch Ppr (E, R); 4-H Secretary; Mulberry Poet's Society Winner; Equine Business Management; Equine Studies; Cazenovia College; Centenary College

ASKEN, TRISTEN; CAMP HILL, PA; TRINITY HS; (JR); F Lan Hn Soc; Hi Hnr Roll; Nat Hon Sy; Sci Fairs; Hab For Humty Volntr; Peer Tut/Med; Chess; Emplmnt; Key Club; Pep Squd; Prom Com; French Clb; Sccr (V CL); Cl Off (V); Stu Cncl (R); CR (R); Scholarship Writing Silver Key; Peers Actively Listening Mentor; Physical Therapy; Villanova U; U of Pittsburgh

ASKINS, ANNIE; SLICKVILLE, PA; GREENSBURG SALEM SD HS; (JR); Nat Hon Sy; Comm Volntr; Emplmnt; Spanish Clb; President of Animal Awareness Club; Business Management; Accounting; U of Clarion; U of Pittsburgh

ASPROS, NICOLE; STROUDSBURG, PA; POCONO MOUNTAIN EAST HS; (FR); Hi Hnr Roll; St of Mnth; USAA; WWAHSS; Chrch Yth Grp; DARE; Fld Hky (J); Sccr (J); Vllyball (V); Stu Cncl (R)

ASSETTO, ABBY; ALLENTOWN, PA; EMMAUS HS; (SO); F Lan Hn Soc; Hi Hnr Roll; Nat Hon Sy; Otst Ac Ach Awd; Comm Volntr; Drma Clb; Emplmnt; Quill & Scroll; Orch; Lit Mag (E); Goalie-Intramural Soccer League; Engineering; Graphic Arts; Penn State U; U of Michigan

ASTON, REBEKAH; EAST GREENVILLE, PA; SALEM CHRISTIAN SCH; (FR); All Am Sch; Hi Hnr Roll; Hnr Roll; Nat Ldrshp Svc; Perf Att; Chrch Yth Grp; Handbells / Chimes; Classical Guitar; Math

ATTAYADMAWITTAYA, PAWEENA; MILL HALL, PA; KEYSTONE CTRL SD; (SR); Hi Hnr Roll; Otst Ac Ach Awd; Cmptr Clb; Dbte Team; Bdmtn (J); Bskball (VJ); Stu Cncl (S); Yrbk (E, P); Creative Writing Awards; Graphic Designer; Advertising; U of California, Los Angeles; The Academy of Arts

AUER, BRIANA; ERIE, PA; MC DOWELL INT HS; (FR); Hi Hnr Roll; Otst Ac Ach Awd; Chrch Yth Grp; Key Club; Mod UN; Quiz Bowl; SWEP - School Wide Enrichment Program; Law

AUGE, ERIKA; READING, PA; MUHLENBERG HS; (SR); Hi Hnr Roll; Hnr Roll; Comm Volntr; Peer Tut/Med; 4-H; DARE; Emplmnt; Jr Ach; SADD; SP/M/VS; Stg Cre; Chrldg (J); Track (J); Lit Mag (E); Yrbk (P); Invited to Volunteer Luncheon to Shake the Senator's Hand; Bachelor's / Master's Degree - Speech-Hearing Pathology / Audiology; Secondary Art Education / Minor in Art History; East Stroudsburg U

AVALOS, ALMA K; READING, PA; READING HS; (FR); Hnr Roll; Nat Hon Sy; DARE; Latin Clb; Dnce; Bsball (V); Cr Ctry (V); Sccr (J); Track (J); Vllyball (V); CR (S); PEPP; ASTRA; Graphic Design - 4 Yr Degree; Interior Design - 4 Yr Degree; Art Institute of Philadelphia; Penn State U

AVELAR, JESSICA B; CALIFRONIA, PA; CALIFORNIA AREA HS; (SR); Hnr Roll; Nat Hon Sy; Perf Att; Chrch Yth Grp; Emplmnt; Scouts; SADD; Chr; PP Ftbl; Sftball (J); Sch Ppr (R); Journalism Club; Writing; California U of Pennsylvania

AVERSA, ANTHONY; MALVERN, PA; GREAT VALLEY HS; (JR); Hi Hnr Roll; Comm Volntr; Emplmnt; Photog; Svce Clb; Sccr (J); Track (V); Pre-Med; Bio-Chemistry; Cornell U

AYRAPETOV, ASYA; ERIE, PA; NW PA COLLEGIATE AC; (SR); Hi Hnr Roll; Hnr Roll; Otst Ac Ach Awd; WWAHSS; Comm Volntr; Lib Aide; Mod UN; Prom Com; French Clb; Chr; Ch Chr; Dnce; Lit Mag (E, R); Sch Ppr (E, R, P); Russian Language Award; French Language Award; Optometry; Mathematics; Gannon U; Pennsylvania State Behrend College

AZARD, PATRICIA; PHILADELPHIA, PA; OLNEY HS; (SO); Hnr Roll; Nat Hon Sy; Pres Sch; St of Mnth; Chrch Yth Grp; Fr of Library; Mth Clb/Tm; HAITIAN Clb; Chr; Ch Chr; Dnce; SP/M/VS; Bsball; Bskball; Chrldg; Gmnstcs; PPSqd; Rqtball; Sccr; Tennis; In 2 1/2 Years, I Have Become Fluent in English.; Major: Pre-Medicine Degree: BA; Pediatrics; Temple U

AZMY, CHRISTINA; STATE COLLEGE, PA; STATE COLLEGE AREA HS; (SR); Hi Hnr Roll; Chrch Yth Grp; Key Club; Ch Chr; Drl Tm; Pennsylvania State U

AZMY, JOSEPH; STATE COLLEGE, PA; STATE COLLEGE AREA HS; (JR); Hi Hnr Roll; Chrch Yth Grp; Key Club; Ch Chr; Journalism; Law; Vanderbilt U; Pennsylvania State U

BABYOK, JESSICA; BEAVER FALLS, PA; BIG BEAVER FALLS HS; (SR); Hi Hnr Roll; Hnr Roll; St of Mnth; Drma Clb; Emplmnt; FBLA; SADD; French Clb; SP/M/VS; Sch Ppr (E, R); Video Production; Film Studies; U of Regina; Point Park U

BACA, ALLISON; NEW COLUMBIA, PA; WATSONTOWN CHRISTIAN AC; (FR); Hi Hnr Roll; Chrch Yth Grp; Photog; Chr; Ch Chr; Cl Off (P); Stu Cncl (R); Sch Ppr (R); Fencing (Outside of School); Piano; Journalism/ Creative Writing, Medicine; Foreign Language

BACKENSTOSE, AMANDA; DOWNINGTOWN, PA; DOWNINGTOWN EAST HS; (JR); DAR; Hi Hnr Roll; Nat Hon Sy; Otst Ac Ach Awd; Perf Att; Comm Volntr; Peer Tut/Med; Chrch Yth Grp; Mus Clb; Scouts; Bnd; Mch Bnd; Pep Bnd; Variety of Community Service; Girl Scout of 9 Years, Youth Group; Communications-Broadcast Journalism; U of Virginia; Penn State U

BACON, DANIELLE N; MCKEESPORT, PA; MC KEESPORT AREA SD; (FR); Hnr Roll; Comm Volntr; Chrch Yth Grp; Bnd; Sccr (J); Swmg (J)

BADAC, KRISTA; NEW KENSINGTON, PA; KISKI AREA SR HS; (JR); Hi Hnr Roll; Nat Hon Sy; Perf Att; WWAHSS; Comm Volntr; Peer Tut/Med; ArtClub; Chrch Yth Grp; Drma Clb; Emplmnt; Key Club; Off Aide; SADD; Chr; Ch Chr; Clr Grd; Dnce; Environmental Club; Pride Club; Elementary Education; Penn State U

BAER, DREW; ERIE, PA; FAIRVIEW HS; (SO); Hi Hnr Roll; Nat Hon Sy; WWAHSS; Comm Volntr; Emplmnt; Key Club; Vsity Clb; Spanish Clb; Bskball (J); Sccr (V L); Tennis (V L); Certified SCUBA Diver

BAER, MATT; FRIEDENS, PA; NORTH STAR HS; (JR); Hnr Roll; St of Mnth; WWAHSS; Comm Volntr; Scouts; Chr; SP/M/VS; English Major; Indiana U of Pennsylvania; U of Pittsburgh At Johnstown

BAGAN, SERGEY; WAPWALLOPEN, PA; BERWICK AREA SR HS; (MS); Hnr Roll; St of Mnth; Chr; Stu Cncl (R); Sch Ppr (E); Good Samaritan; Doctor; Columbia College; Penn State

BAH, NJAMEH; EASTON, PA; EASTON AREA HS; (JR); F Lan Hn Soc; Nat Hon Sy; Comm Volntr; Sci Clb; French Clb; Cr Ctry (V); Civics 101 Pilot Program; Smile Challenge Weekend; Pharmacy; Pre Medicine; Temple U; Penn State U Park

BAILEY, AMANDA; GREENOCK, PA; ELIZABETH FORWARD HS; (SO); Hi Hnr Roll; Pres Ac Ftns Aw; Peer Tut/Med; ArtClub; Emplmnt; SADD; Chrldg (V L); Swmg (V L); WPIAL Swimming Qualifier-2 yrs; NCA All-American Award, Balfour Pathway to Leadership; Chiropractor; Rollins U; U of Pittsburgh

BAILEY, ERIC; LANCASTER, PA; HEMPFIELD HS; (SO); Hi Hnr Roll; Comm Volntr; Peer Tut/Med; Spec Olymp Vol; Chrch Yth Grp; Key Club; Orch; Lcrsse (V); Stu Cncl (R); Honorable Mention Scholastic Arts Fair; Member of Cocalico Skeet Team; Medical; Law; Johns Hopkins U; Princeton U

BAILEY, JANEE; CLIFTON HEIGHTS, PA; UPPER DARBY HS; (JR); Hi Hnr Roll; Hnr Roll; Nat Ldrshp Svc; Otst Ac Ach Awd; Perf Att; Sci Fairs; Yth Ldrshp Prog; Comm Volntr; Hosp Aide; Spec Olymp Vol; Chrch Yth Grp; FBLA; Svce Clb; SADD; Ch Chr; SP/M/VS; Stg Cre; PP Ftbl (J); Vllyball (J); Stu Cncl (R); CR (R); Royal Voices Club; Ushering; Business Management; Restaurant Owner; Drexel U; Johnson & Wales U

BAILEY, JAREN P; HARRISBURG, PA; CTRL DAUPHIN HS; (SO); Hi Hnr Roll; Hnr Roll; Nat Hon Sy; Pres Ac Ftns Aw; Sci/Math Olympn; St of Mnth; FBLA; 4-Diamond Mini-Thon; CYO Basketball; Civil Engineering; Architectural Engineering; Drexel U; Lehigh Valley College

BAILEY, JEFFREY T; PITTSBURGH, PA; PLUM SR HS; (SO); Hnr Roll; Ftball (V); Wt Lftg (V); Psychology; Chemistry; U of Pittsburgh; West Virginia U

BAKER, ALEC; POTTSTOWN, PA; OWEN J ROBERTS HS; (JR); Hnr Roll; MVP; Nat Ldrshp Svc; WWAHSS; DECA; Emplmnt; Lcrsse (J); Top 16 At DECA Internationals; For Commerce 1st Place States As Fr Soph, Jr; Develop New Innovative Technology; Own a Fortune 500 Company; Babson College; Penn State U

BAKER, AMANDA; CORAOPOLIS, PA; MONTOUR HS; (SO); Hi Hnr Roll; Perf Att; WWAHSS; SADD; SP/M/VS; Track (V); Stu Cncl (R); Sch Ppr (R); Journalism; Northwestern U; U of North Carolina

BAKER, ANDREW; CORRY, PA; CORRY AREA HS; (FR); Perf Att; Sci Fairs; St of Mnth; Comm Volntr; Chrch Yth Grp; Emplmnt; Key Club; Sci Clb; Swmg (V L); Stu Cncl (R); YMCA Swim Team 4 Years; Church Youth Group; Early Childhood Education; Culinary Arts; Liberty U; Mercyhurst Northeast

BAKER, BRITTANY L; FRANKLIN, PA; FRANKLIN HS; (SO); Hnr Roll; Peer Tut/Med; Chrch Yth Grp; DARE; German Clb; Chr; Yrbk (R); Student Council Member; English Degree; Journalism; Edinboro U; Slippery Rock U

BAKER, CHRISTOPHER; COATESVILLE, PA; COATESVILLE AREA SR HS; (JR); Hnr Roll; Sci Fairs; Track (V); Pre-Law; Psychology; USC; Florida A & M U

BAKER, CODY J; GARDNERS, PA; UPPER ADAMS SD; Scouts; Bnd; Bskball (J); Ftball (J); Meteorologist; Policeman; Shippensburg U; Gettysburg College

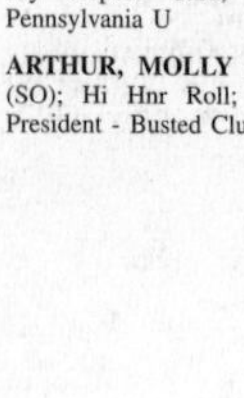
Baker, Brittany L
Franklin HS
Franklin, PA

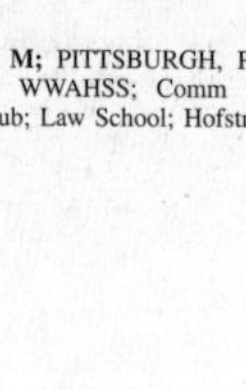
Baer, Drew
Fairview HS
Erie, PA

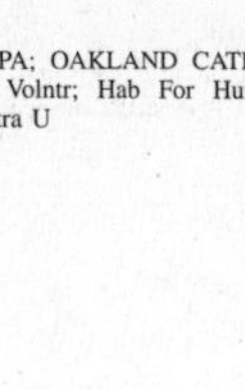
Artis, Catherine L
East Stroudsburg HS South
East Stroudsburg, PA

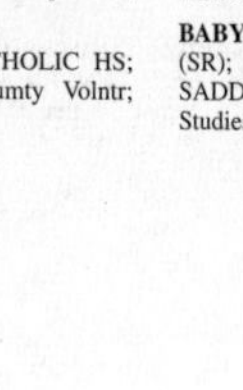
Armani, Azad
Monsignor Bonner HS
Drexel Hill, PA

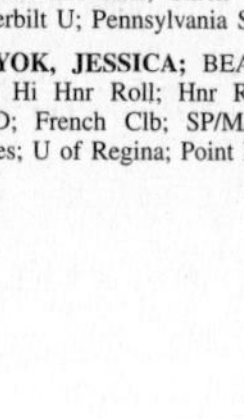
Archon, Nicole
Hatboro, PA

National
Honor Roll
Spring 2005

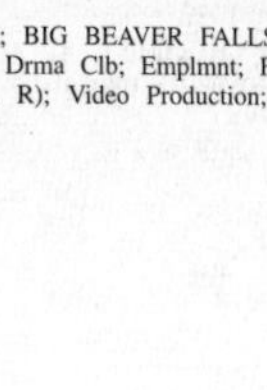
Angelucci, Tori
Kennedy-Kenrick Catholic HS
Norristown, PA

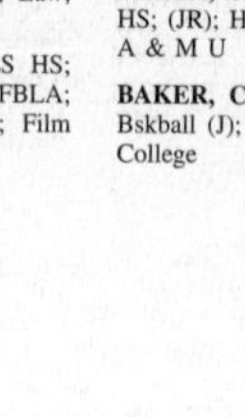
Arthur, Dorlus M
Olney HS
Philadelphia, PA

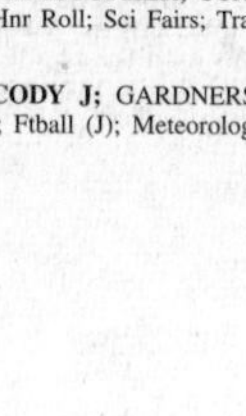
Ashton, Emily
Lake Lehman JR/SR HS
Dallas, PA

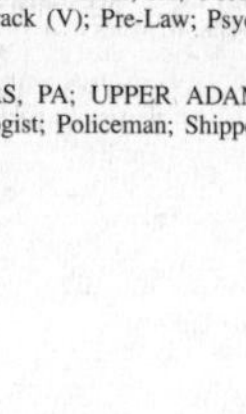
Bailey, Eric
Hempfield HS
Lancaster, PA

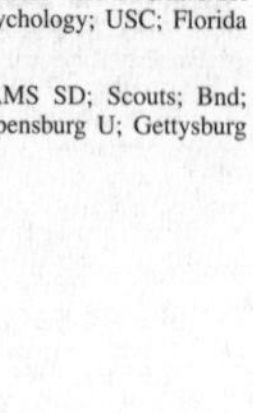
Bailey, Janee
Upper Darby HS
Clifton Heights, PA

BAKER, HUNTER S; ENOLA, PA; EAST PENNSBORO AREA HS; (JR); Hnr Roll; Pres Ac Ftns Aw; 49 Clb; Wrstlg (J); Financial Engineer

BAKER, JASON; KENNETT SQUARE, PA; UNIONVILLE HS; (JR); Hi Hnr Roll; MVP; Comm Volntr; Chrch Yth Grp; Ftball (V L); Track (V L); Indoor Track; Chemical Engineering; Business Finance; Lehigh U; Lafayette College

BAKER, LAUREN; BETHLEHEM, PA; BETHLEHEM CATHOLIC HS; (SO); Hnr Roll; WWAHSS; Comm Volntr; Chrch Yth Grp; Key Club; Dnce; SP/M/VS; Chrldg (J); Yrbk (R); Sports Management

BAKER, MEGAN M; WYOMING, PA; DALLAS HS; (JR); Hnr Roll; Sci/Math Olympn; WWAHSS; Comm Volntr; Chrch Yth Grp; FBLA; Key Club; Prom Com; Sci Clb; SADD; Sccr (C); Swmg (V); Track; Sch Ppr (E, R); Certified Lifeguard; Public Relations; DeSales U

BALDWIN, STEPHANY; DARLINGTON, PA; BLACKHAWK HS; (SO); Hi Hnr Roll; Hnr Roll; MVP; Comm Volntr; Peer Tut/Med; DARE; Emplmnt; Key Club; French Clb; Chr; Ch Chr; SP/M/VS; Swmg (L); Vllyball (J); Official Cheerleader / Catcher of Women's Softball League; Hotel Manager / Owner; Chiropractor; Michigan State; U of Arizona

BALL, KASI; BERWICK, PA; BERWICK AREA SR HS; (MS); Hi Hnr Roll; Comm Volntr; Peer Tut/Med; Chrch Yth Grp; Ch Chr; Chrldg (L); Sftball (L); CR (R); Yrbk (R); Swimming; School Teacher; Veterinarian

BALLIET, JENNIFER; NORTHAMPTON, PA; NORTHAMPTON AREA SCH; (SO); Hi Hnr Roll; Hnr Roll; Dbte Team; Drma Clb; German Clb; Bnd; Jzz Bnd; SP/M/VS; Stg Cre; Skipped Grade 8; People to People Student Ambassador; Biology; Law; Carleton College; Amherst College

BALTHASER, BENJAMIN J; HAMBURG, PA; KINGS AC; (FR); Hi Hnr Roll; Hnr Roll; Perf Att; Pres Ac Ftns Aw; Sci Fairs; Comm Volntr; Chrch Yth Grp; Lcrsse (C); Sftball (L); Stu Cncl (V); Community Service; Become a Pilot (Airplane); Kutztown U; Valley Forge

BAMBI, HARRY W; NORRISTOWN, PA; NORRISTOWN AREA HS; (SO); Hnr Roll; DECA; Mth Clb/Tm; Orch

BANECKER, ERIC J; PHILADELPHIA, PA; ROMAN CATHOLIC HS; (SO); Hnr Roll; Perf Att; Pres Sch; WWAHSS; Chrch Yth Grp; Dbte Team; Emplmnt; Spch Team; Italian Clb; Student Ambassador; President - Parish Youth Group; Political Science; Economics; Georgetown U; U of Pennsylvania

BANGURA, FUDIA; COATESVILLE, PA; COATESVILLE AREA SR HS; (JR); Hi Hnr Roll; Hnr Roll; Otst Ac Ach Awd; Perf Att; St of Mnth; Emplmnt; Track; Stu Cncl; Medical / Doctor; Theater / Actress; Penn State U; New York College

BANKS, ANGELA A; POTTSTOWN, PA; POTTSGROVE SR HS; (SO); Hi Hnr Roll; Hnr Roll; Nat Hon Sy; Perf Att; Sci Fairs; St of Mnth; WWAHSS; Comm Volntr; Peer Tut/Med; 4-H; Chrch Yth Grp; Cmptr Clb; Emplmnt; Scouts; Dnce; Drl Tm; Bskball (J); Track (L); Vllyball; Girls Track Pac-10 Championship; Educational Counselor; Psychology; Penn State U; Slippery Rock U

BANOV, DEREK M; PHILADELPHIA, PA; CHESTNUT HILL AC; (JR); Hi Hnr Roll; Hnr Roll; Comm Volntr; Chess; Emplmnt; P to P St Amb Prg; Photog; Cr Ctry (C); Mar Art; Track; Cl Off (P); Stu Cncl (V); 2005 NCTE Achievement Award in Writing Nominee; 2004 Published Opinion Piece in Community Newspaper; Psychology; Law; Duke U; U of Virginia

BAO, CHEN; MONROEVILLE, PA; GATEWAY SR HS; (JR); Hi Hnr Roll; Nat Hon Sy; Nat Mrt Semif; Amnsty Intl; Comm Volntr; Peer Tut/Med; ArtClub; Jr Cls League; P to P St Amb Prg; Spch Team; SP/M/VS; Stu Cncl (V, T, R); CR (R); Sch Ppr (R); Mock Trial Team; PA Governor's school for International Studies; Law; Political Sciences; Yale U; Duke U

BARBARETTA, CORAL; HARRISBURG, PA; CTRL DAUPHIN HS; (FR); Hnr Roll; Perf Att; St of Mnth; Chrch Yth Grp; Scouts; Spanish Clb; Girl Scouts Bronze Award & Silver Award; Visual Arts

BARBISH, MARY; PITTSBURGH, PA; TAYLOR ALLDERDICE HS; (JR); Hi Hnr Roll; Nat Hon Sy; Comm Volntr; Emplmnt; Key Club; Bnd; Dnce; Key Club Editor; Elementary Religion Teacher; Industrial Engineering; Civil Engineering

BARBOUR, CHANEL M; CHESTER, PA; CHESTER HS; (SR); Hnr Roll; Perf Att; Comm Volntr; Key Club; Surgical Technician; Lock Haven U

BARBOUR, CHELSEE; BRIDGEVILLE, PA; SOUTH FAYETTE TOWNSHIP HS; (JR); Hi Hnr Roll; Nat Hon Sy; WWAHSS; Emplmnt; Chr; History; Teacher; U of Penn Erie; Thiel College

BAREFIELD, AMANDA C; PHILADELPHIA, PA; A PHILLIP RANDOLPH HS; (SO); Hnr Roll; Perf Att; Sci Fairs; Comm Volntr; Emplmnt; Pep Squd; Tmpl Yth Grp; Drl Tm; Chrldg (V); CR (R); Nursing; Temple U

BARNES, AMY L; BELLE VERNON, PA; BELLE VERNON AREA HS; (JR); Hi Hnr Roll; Nat Hon Sy; Comm Volntr; Emplmnt; CR (R); Physician; Medical Career

BARNES, KATHLEEN A; BENSALEM, PA; NAZARETH AC; (SO); Hnr Roll; WWAHSS; Comm Volntr; DARE; Emplmnt; SADD; Lcrsse (J L); Sftball (J); Tennis (V L); Business (MBA); Archaeology; Drexel U; U of Pennsylvania

BARNETT, JACLYN; RIDLEY PARK, PA; RIDLEY SD; (JR); Hnr Roll; Bskball (VJ L); Sftball (VJ L); Millersville U; West Chester U

BAROL, JARED; BALA CYNWYD, PA; LOWER MERION HS; (SO); Hi Hnr Roll; Hnr Roll; Sci Fairs; Sci/Math Olympn; Comm Volntr; Peer Tut/Med; Chess; Cmptr Clb; Drma Clb; Emplmnt; Mth Clb/Tm; Mus Clb; NYLC; Sci Clb; Mch Bnd; Orch; SP/M/VS; Stg Cre; Stu Cncl (R); CR (R); Master's Degree / International Service; International Relations Major; George Washington U; American U

BARON, ANDREW; LITITZ, PA; LANCASTER CTRY DAY SCH; (SR); F Lan Hn Soc; Hi Hnr Roll; Otst Ac Ach Awd; Sci/Math Olympn; Comm Volntr; Peer Tut/Med; Mod UN; Photog; Golf (VJ); Lcrsse (VJ L); Skiing (VJ); Sccr (V L); Cl Off (P, V); Lit Mag (R); Summa Cum Laude on Nat'l Latin Exam 2002; Outstanding Academic Achievement-U of Richmond 2004; Biology or Chemistry Major; Medical School; Tufts U; Georgetown U

BARONE, KIMBERLY A; WOMELSDORF, PA; TULPEHOCKEN HS; (SR); Ctznshp Aw; Hnr Roll; MVP; Nat Hon Sy; Otst Ac Ach Awd; Pres Ac Ftns Aw; Pres Sch; Yth Ldrshp Prog; Comm Volntr; Peer Tut/Med; Chrch Yth Grp; Emplmnt; P to P St Amb Prg; Acpl Chr; Bnd; Chr; Jzz Bnd; Bskball (J L); Tennis (V CL); Track (V L); President of Community Service Club; Berk's Best-Foreign Language; International Business (Business Admin); The George Washington U

BARONE, NICHOLAS A; PITTSBURGH, PA; BALDWIN HS; (JR); Ctznshp Aw; Hi Hnr Roll; Nat Hon Sy; Otst Ac Ach Awd; Pres Sch; St of Mnth; WWAHSS; Comm Volntr; Peer Tut/Med; Red Cr Aide; Drma Clb; Emplmnt; Mth Clb/Tm; Mus Clb; Pep Squd; Drm Mjr; Jzz Bnd; Mch Bnd; SP/M/VS; PMEA District Band; PMEA Regional Band; Engineering; Music; U of Pittsburgh; Case Western Reserve

BARONIO, SHAINA; MC DONALD, PA; CANON MC MILLAN HS; (JR); Hnr Roll; Perf Att; Pres Ac Ftns Aw; Pres Sch; St of Mnth; Comm Volntr; ArtClub; Chrch Yth Grp; Lib Aide; Mth Clb/Tm; Tchrs Aide; Spanish Clb; Chr; Assists Disabled Mother with the House Work; Pre-Veterinary Medicine - Major; Creative Writing - Minor; California U

BARRETT, LEA D; MORTON, PA; STRATH HAVEN HS; (SO); Hi Hnr Roll; Hnr Roll; Perf Att; DARE; Scouts; SADD; Chr; Sftball (VJ L); Swmg (J L); CR (R); The International Library of Poetry Semi-Finalist-2005; Poem Published in Eternal Portraits-2005; Early Education; Law; Drew U; Arizona State U

BARTHALOW, STEVEN T; WARFORDSBURG, PA; HERITAGE AC; (FR); Hnr Roll; MVP; Chrch Yth Grp; SP/M/VS; Bsball (V L); Bskball (V L); Sccr (V L); Computer Tech; Missionary; Bible Baptist College; Cedarville U

BARTHOLOMEW, SHARON; REEDERS, PA; POCONO MTN EAST HS; (SO); F Lan Hn Soc; Hnr Roll; St of Mnth; WWAHSS; Emplmnt; Scouts; SADD; Dnce; SP/M/VS; Chrldg (VJCL); Marine Biology

BASHORE, ASHLEY; MIFFLINTOWN, PA; JUNIATA CTY SD; (JR); All Am Sch; Hnr Roll; Prom Com; Sccr (J L); Mathematics Award; Scholastic I; Penn State U; York College

BASNAK, MEGAN J; JAMESTOWN, PA; JAMESTOWN AREA SD; (SR); Hi Hnr Roll; Nat Hon Sy; Valdctrian; Emplmnt; Spch Team; Spanish Clb; Bnd; Chr; Mch Bnd; Pep Bnd; Stu Cncl; Participant in County and District Bands; Awarded Rotary Youth Leadership Award; Interior Design; Mercyhurst College

BATES, ASHLEY; LATROBE, PA; GREATER LATROBE HS; (SO); Hnr Roll; MVP; Otst Ac Ach Awd; St of Mnth; WWAHSS; Comm Volntr; ArtClub; Emplmnt; Key Club; French Clb; Skiing; Sccr (VJ L); Art Shows; Art Teacher; Graphic Design; Seton Hill U; Pittsburgh School of the Arts

BATES, KACEY T; WILLIAMSPORT, PA; WILLIAMSPORT AREA HS; (SR); Hnr Roll; Perf Att; St of Mnth; WWAHSS; Comm Volntr; Emplmnt; Key Club; Nursing; Bloomsburg U; Pennsylvania College of Technology

BATOR, BRIAN K; ERIE, PA; HARBORCREEK JR/SR HS; (SR); Hnr Roll; MVP; Nat Hon Sy; WWAHSS; Comm Volntr; ArtClub; Bsball (V CL); Ice Hky (V CL); Youth Hockey Coach for 4 Years; Art Education; Fine Arts; Franklin Pierce College (Fall 2005)

BATTAGLIA, NIKKI; SPRINGFIELD, PA; SPRINGFIELD HS; (SO); Hnr Roll; WWAHSS; ArtClub; Emplmnt; Photog; SADD; Tchrs Aide; Chr; Chrldg (V); Sftball (J); Adv Cncl (R); National Language Examination; Operation Smile; Marine Biology; Forensic Science; Millersville U; U of Miami

BAUBLITZ, KATELYN E; HANOVER, PA; HANOVER HS; (SO); Hi Hnr Roll; Nat Sci Aw; Otst Ac Ach Awd; Perf Att; USAA; WWAHSS; Comm Volntr; Key Club; Chr; Ch Chr; SP/M/VS; PP Ftbl; Who's Who Among American High School Students 2004-05; U.S.A.A. Award Winner-Science 2004-05; Teaching; Penn State U; Millersville U

BAUER, CARLISA N; DUNCANSVILLE, PA; SPRING COVE SD; (JR); Hi Hnr Roll; Hnr Roll; Nat Hon Sy; Chr; SP/M/VS; Mar Art; Track; Yrbk (P); Photography; Medical; Indiana U of Pennsylvania; Penn State U

BAUER, ERIKA E; MECHANICSBURG, PA; MECHANICSBURG AREA HS; (JR); Ctznshp Aw; Hnr Roll; Pres Ac Ftns Aw; Sci Fairs; St of Mnth; WWAHSS; ArtClub; DARE; Emplmnt; Key Club; Photog; Spch Team; SP/M/VS; Fld Hky (J); Sftball (J); Stu Cncl (R); Yrbk (E, P); Art Honor Society; Art Therapy; Art Teacher; Pittsburgh; Tyler Art School

BAUER, KELLY; LANCASTER, PA; HEMPFIELD HS; (JR); F Lan Hn Soc; Hi Hnr Roll; Nat Hon Sy; Otst Ac Ach Awd; Perf Att; St of Mnth; WWAHSS; Comm Volntr; Hab For Humty Volntr; Peer Tut/Med; Key Club; Scouts; Dnce; SP/M/VS; PP Ftbl (V); Skiing (V); Biology/Chemistry; Communications; Clemson U; Elon College

BAUGHMAN, AYLA M; JEANNETTE, PA; PENN TRAFFORD HS; (JR); Gov Hnr Prg; Hi Hnr Roll; Hnr Roll; Nat Hon Sy; Sci/Math Olympn; WWAHSS; Comm Volntr; Hosp Aide; DARE; Emplmnt; SADD; Latin Clb; Bskball (VJ L); Ftball (VJ L); Sftball (VJ); Sch Ppr (R, P); Sports Medicine, Sports Trainer; National Honor Society/Young Democrats; Physical Therapy; Medicine; Pennsylvania State U; U of Pittsburgh

BAUGHMAN, NICHOLAS; ERIE, PA; ERIE CITY SD; Hi Hnr Roll; Hnr Roll; DARE; Drma Clb; Bnd; Bsball (J); Ftball (J); Ice Hky (J); Masters in Law

BAUKNIGHT, JEREMY D; HARRISBURG, PA; CTRL DAUPHIN HS; (SO); Hi Hnr Roll; Hnr Roll; Nat Hon Sy; St of Mnth; Chrch Yth Grp; Mth Clb/Tm; Chr; Sccr (J); Vllyball (VJ); Youth & Government; Club Teams-Soccer & Volleyball; Engineering

BAUMGARDNER, CARYN; MIFFLINTOWN, PA; JUNIATA HS; (FR); Hi Hnr Roll; Hnr Roll; WWAHSS; Spec Olymp Vol; 4-H; Emplmnt; Key Club; Bnd; Mch Bnd; Fld Hky (J); Track (V L); Key Club; Keystone State Games (Field Hockey); Elementary Education; Shippensburg U

BAXTER, KATHRYN; GLENSIDE, PA; ABINGTON SR HS; (SO); All Am Sch; Hnr Roll; WWAHSS; Comm Volntr; Chrch Yth Grp; Key Club; Bnd; Ch Chr; Stu Cncl (R); Sch Ppr (R); Odyssey of the Mind; Political Communications; Education

BAYLETS, REVA; CENTRE HALL, PA; PENNS VALLEY AREA HS; (FR); Hi Hnr Roll; St of Mnth; WWAHSS; Key Club; SADD; French Clb; Lit Mag (E); High School Teacher-English Major; High School Teacher-History Major; Penn State, State College

BAYZICK, JENNIFER L; CONYNGHAM, PA; HAZLETON AREA HS; (SO); Hi Hnr Roll; MVP; WWAHSS; Chrch Yth Grp; Emplmnt; Key Club; Off Aide; Sci Clb; Scouts; Fld Hky (V CL); Sccr (V L); Stu Cncl (R); CR (R); Serento Gardens Student Board-(Drug & Alcohol Awareness); Education; Math

BEAMAN, MARIA D; PHILADELPHIA, PA; STRAWBERRY MANSION; (SR); Hi Hnr Roll; Hnr Roll; Nat Hon Sy; Otst Ac Ach Awd; St of Mnth; Yth Ldrshp Prog; Chrch Yth Grp; ROTC; Tchrs Aide; Tmpl Yth Grp; Ch Chr; Vllyball (V); Stu Cncl (V, S); School Fashion Show; Bowling; Veterinary Medicine / DVM; Degree of Veterinary Medicine; Tuskegee U

BECHTOL, CHRISTINA; UNIONTOWN, PA; ALBERT GALLATIN HS; (FR); Hosp Aide; Chrch Yth Grp; Drma Clb; SP/M/VS; Sftball; Law Degree; Yale; Harvard

BECKER, DANIEL W; SOUTHAMPTON, PA; MIDDLE BUCKS INST OF TECH HS; (JR); Hi Hnr Roll; Hnr Roll; St of Mnth; Chrch Yth Grp; Emplmnt; Vsity Clb; Sccr (V); Automotive Technology; Automotive Engineering; Bucks County Community College

BECKER, MARCIA R; NEW KENSINGTON, PA; VALLEY HS; (FR); Hi Hnr Roll; Hnr Roll; Perf Att; Chess; Chrch Yth Grp; Drma Clb; Mus Clb; French Clb; Chr; Ch Chr; SP/M/VS; Tennis (J); Vllyball (V); Rotary; Who's Who Among American Middle School Students; Music Education Major; French Major / Drama Minor; Indiana U of Pennsylvania; Duquesne U

BEECH, ALLISON; COATESVILLE, PA; BISHOP SHANAHAN HS; (JR); Ctznshp Aw; Hnr Roll; Perf Att; Hosp Aide; Peer Tut/Med; Dbte Team; Lib Aide; Scouts; Spanish Clb; Bnd; Pep Bnd; Stg Cre; Girl Scout Gold & Silver Awards; The Chapel of Four Chaplains Legion of Honor Award; Spanish; Education; Immaculata U; Dickinson College

BEGANY, JOSEPH; BETHLEHEM, PA; LIBERTY HS; (SO); Hnr Roll; Perf Att; St of Mnth; WWAHSS; Comm Volntr; Ftball (V); Wt Lftg; Student of Month 3 Times in Jr HS; Criminal Justice; Journalism; Michigan; Villanova

BEGELMAN, RACHEL; BENSALEM, PA; BENSALEM HS; (SO); Ctznshp Aw; Hi Hnr Roll; Hnr Roll; Otst Ac Ach Awd; Pres Ac Ftns Aw; Pres Sch; St of Mnth; Yth Ldrshp Prog; Comm Volntr; Peer Tut/Med; ArtClub; Dbte Team; Drma Clb; Emplmnt; Mus Clb; Pep Squd; Prom Com; Schol Bwl; Acpl Chr; Dnce; SP/M/VS; Stg Cre; Chrldg (V C); Track (L); Adv Cncl (R); Cl Off (P); Stu Cncl (P, R); CR (R); Lit Mag (R); Yrbk (E); International Thespian Award; Theater Arts / Acting; Fashion Merchandising / Graphic Design; New York U; Carnegie-Melon U

Begany, Joseph
Liberty HS
Bethlehem, PA

Banov, Derek M
Chestnut Hill AC
Philadelphia, PA

Beech, Allison
Bishop Shanahan HS
Coatesville, PA

BEHNING, MARISSA L; CRANBERRY TWP, PA; SENECA VALLEY (SO); Hi Hnr Roll; WWAHSS; Yth Ldrshp Prog; 4-H; Key Club; Vsity Clb; Chr; Cr Ctry (V L); Swmg (V L); Track (V L); Stu Cncl (R)

BELKNAP, ELIZABETH; DOWNINGTOWN, PA; DOWNINGTOWN EAST SR HS; (SO); Hi Hnr Roll; Hnr Roll; Nat Hon Sy; Perf Att; Pres Ac Ftns Aw; Yth Ldrshp Prog; Chrch Yth Grp; DARE; Outdrs Clb; SADD; Spanish Clb; Dnce; Bskball (J); Scr Kpr (VJ)

BELL, HEATHER A; HERSHEY, PA; HERSHEY HS; (FR); Hi Hnr Roll; Pres Ac Ftns Aw; Chrch Yth Grp; DARE; Chr; Ch Chr; Orch; SP/M/VS; Track (V); Vllyball (J); NHRA Jr. Drag Racing; Medicine; Education; Brigham Young U; Penn State U

BELL, MEGHAN; FREELAND, PA; BISHOP HAFEY HS; (SO); Hi Hnr Roll; WWAHSS; Chrch Yth Grp; Drma Clb; Key Club; Pep Squd; SADD; Chr; SP/M/VS; Chrldg (V); Spanish National Honor Society; Big Brothers/Big Sisters Volunteer; Elementary Education; Kings College; Scranton U

BELL, SARA; BRYN MAWR, PA; RADNOR HS; (SR); Hi Hnr Roll; Nat Hon Sy; Nat Mrt Semif; Otst Ac Ach Awd; Comm Volntr; ArtClub; Key Club; Photog; Sci Clb; Ice Hky (J); MD; Physics; Tufts U

BELL, SHEENA; POTTSGROVE SR HS; (SO); Ctznshp Aw; Hi Hnr Roll; Otst Ac Ach Awd; Pres Sch; Sci Fairs; St of Mnth; Comm Volntr; Key Club; Sftball (V); Cl Off (V); Sports Medicine; Doctorate Degree; Villanova U; Howard U

BELLAMY, AIESHA M; HARRISBURG, PA; HARRISBURG HS; (SR); Ctznshp Aw; Hnr Roll; MVP; Nat Hon Sy; WWAHSS; Comm Volntr; Peer Tut/Med; Chess; Emplmnt; Pep Squd; Vsity Clb; Bskball (V CL); Track (L); Vsy Clb (L); Sch Ppr (E, R); Yrbk (E, R); The Patriot News "Big 15 Team"; Conference "Sportsmanship Award"; Computer Science; Bachelor's Degree in Art/Science; Duquesne U; Saint Joseph's U

BELL IV, JAMES; PITTSTON, PA; PITTSTON AREA SD; (JR); WWAHSS; Comm Volntr; Bnd; Sccr (V L); School Ski Club; Physical Education; Wilkes U; East Stroudsburg U

BELLO-OGUNU, EMMANUEL; LANDISVILLE, PA; HEMPFIELD HS; (JR); Hi Hnr Roll; Nat Hon Sy; WWAHSS; Yth Ldrshp Prog; Comm Volntr; Hab For Humty Volntr; Spec Olymp Vol; Chrch Yth Grp; Key Club; Bskball; Sccr; Track (V L); Vllyball; Stu Cncl; Renaissance Club; Odyssey of the Mind; Computer Engineering; U of Pennsylvania; Carnegie-Mellon U

BELTRAN, LUIS E; READING, PA; READING HS; (SO); Hnr Roll; Comm Volntr; ArtClub; Vllyball (V); Architect; Pro Volleyball Player; Penn State; Lehigh U

BELTRAN, ZACCHAEUS; SCRANTON, PA; DUNMORE SD; (MS); Hi Hnr Roll; Nat Hon Sy; Scouts; Bnd; Chr; Mch Bnd; MD; U of Scranton

BELZ, VALERIE; SEWICKLEY, PA; NORTH ALLEGHENY INT SCH; (SO); Hnr Roll; Otst Ac Ach Awd; Pres Ac Ftns Aw; St of Mnth; WWAHSS; Yth Ldrshp Prog; Comm Volntr; Chrch Yth Grp; Emplmnt; Key Club; SP/M/VS; Chrldg (J); Stu Cncl (R); National Poetry Contest Winner; Extra Effort Award Winner; Elementary Education

BENCIVENGA, NICHOLAS A; OAKMONT, PA; RIVERVIEW HS; (JR); Hnr Roll; WWAHSS; Peer Tut/Med; Key Club; Spanish Clb; Bsball (VJ L); Wt Lftg (V); Musical Major in Guitar; Major in Business and Accounting; Duquesne U; Berklee College of Music

BENDER, MANDY J; POTTSTOWN, PA; OWEN J ROBERTS; (SR); Hnr Roll; MVP; DARE; DECA; Emplmnt; Key Club; Chrldg (V L); Fld Hky (V); Sftball (VJ L); Student Store, "Just Say No"; Key Club; Elementary Education; Special Education; Pennsylvania State U

BENDER, SAMUEL R; DILLSBURG, PA; NORTHERN YORK HS; (SR); Hnr Roll; Comm Volntr; Spec Olymp Vol; Chrch Yth Grp; Emplmnt; Key Club; SADD; Ftball (V JL); Track (VJ); Stu Cncl (J); Self Taught Guitar Player; Played Middle Linebacker; Electrical Engineering; U of South Carolina

BENES, JORDAN; HERMITAGE, PA; HICKORY HS; (SO); Hnr Roll; Pres Ac Ftns Aw; WWAHSS; Chr; Bsball (VJ); Bskball (VJ); Architecture

BENFER, ELLEN; NEW BERLIN, PA; MIFFLINBURG AREA SD; (SR); 4H Awd; Ctznshp Aw; Hi Hnr Roll; Perf Att; Pres Ac Ftns Aw; Comm Volntr; 4-H; Ntl FFA; Bnd; Mch Bnd; Pep Bnd; Stg Cre; Sccr (J); Sftball (J); Music; Pennsylvania State U

BENFER, MARK A; NEW BERLIN, PA; MIFFLINBURG AREA SD; (SR); 4H Awd; Gov Hnr Prg; Hi Hnr Roll; Hnr Roll; Nat Hon Sy; Perf Att; St of Mnth; WWAHSS; Comm Volntr; 4-H; Ntl FFA; Prom Com; Environmental Resource Management; Pennsylvania State U

BENGLE, LISA; FEASTERVILLE TREVOSE, PA; NAZARETH AC; (SO); Hnr Roll; Perf Att; WWAHSS; Svce Clb; Mathematics Honor Society; Presidential Award 2003; Medical; Art

BENJAMIN, FRANTZ; LANCASTER, PA; LAN-CHESTER CHRISTIAN SCH; Hnr Roll; Nat Ldrshp Svc; St of Mnth; USAA; SP/M/VS; Stg Cre; Medical Sciences; Law; Stanford U; Brown U

BEN NAIM, NATALIE; PHILADELPHIA, PA; CENTRAL HS; (JR) F Lan Hn Soc; Sci Fairs; Comm Volntr; DARE; Prom Com; Hebrew Clb; Dnce; Cl Off (R); CR (R); Work After School; Business; Law

BENNETT, CHRISTOPHER J; TANNERSVILLE, PA; POCONO MOUNTAIN EAST HS; (SO); F Lan Hn Soc; Hi Hnr Roll; Hnr Roll; Nat Hon Sy; Comm Volntr; Emplmnt; FBLA; Scouts; Chr; Karate-Brown Belt; Biology; Zoology; East Stroudsburg U; Virginia Polytechnic

BENNETT, HOPE; BEAVER FALLS, PA; BIG BEAVER FALLS HS; (JR); Hi Hnr Roll; Hnr Roll; Comm Volntr; DARE; Key Club; Prom Com; SADD; Spanish Clb; Bnd; Drl Tm; SP/M/VS; Track (V); Vllyball (V L); Cl Off (V); Bachelor's Degree / Education; Slippery Rock U; Clarion U

BENNETT, MICHAEL D; PITTSBURGH, PA; CAPA HS; (FR); Ctznshp Aw; Hi Hnr Roll; Hnr Roll; Pres Sch; Comm Volntr; Peer Tut/Med; Chrch Yth Grp; Mus Clb; Ntl Beta Clb; Scouts; Bnd; Orch; SP/M/VS; Think-A-Thon Team; Music; Education; UNC; CMU

BENNETT, RICKIE L; HARRISBURG, PA; CTRL DAUPHIN EAST HS; (FR); Hi Hnr Roll; Hnr Roll; Nat Hon Sy; WWAHSS; Key Club; Chr; Cr Ctry (J); Education

BENNETT, SEAN; NORRISTOWN, PA; METHACTON HS; (SO); Hi Hnr Roll; WWAHSS; Comm Volntr; FCA; HO'Br Yth Ldrshp; NYLC; Bsball (J); Cl Off (V); TV Production / Morning Announcements; Engineering; Finance; Lehigh U; Stanford U

BENNETT, TANYA; HAZLETON, PA; HAZLETON AREA HS; (SO); Hnr Roll; Nat Hon Sy; WWAHSS; DARE; FBLA; SADD; Teaching; Penn State; New York U

BENNETT JR, CHARLES T; PITTSBURGH, PA; PITTSBURGH SD; MS; Chess; Scouts; Sch Ppr (R); Culinary Arts Chef

BENSON, BEAU; JENKINTOWN, PA; JENKINTOWN HS; (JR); F Lan Hn Soc; Hi Hnr Roll; Nat Hon Sy; Sci Fairs; Comm Volntr; Drma Clb; HO'Br Yth Ldrshp; Mod UN; Prom Com; Spch Team; Tchrs Aide; French Clb; SP/M/VS; Cl Off (S); Sccr (R); CR (S); Sch Ppr (E); Yrbk (E); Performed Off-Broadway; Appeared on Television and in Movies; Drama and Performing Art; Creative Writing; Columbia U; New York U

BENSON, TIYANA S; PHILADELPHIA, PA; OVERBROOK HS; (JR); Ctznshp Aw; Hi Hnr Roll; Hnr Roll; Nat Hon Sy; Otst Ac Ach Awd; Perf Att; Sci Fairs; St of Mnth; WWAHSS; Yth Ldrshp Prog; Comm Volntr; Hab For Humty Volntr; Hosp Aide; Chrch Yth Grp; Cmptr Clb; Drma Clb; NYLC; Pep Squd; P to P St Amb Prg; Prom Com; Tchrs Aide; Ch Chr; Dnce; Drl Tm; SP/M/VS; Cr Ctry (V); Gmnstcs (V); Scr Kpr (V); Sccr (V); Sftball (V); Track (V); Vllyball (V); Cl Off (R); CR (R); Yrbk (R); 410 on SATS; Finishing Rise Rosemont College Residential Page; Pre-Med / Chemistry Science; Theater; Penn State U Park; West Chester U

BENTLEY, KENNETH; PHILADELPHIA, PA; SCH FOR CREATIVE & PERF ARTS; (JR); Emplmnt; Mar Art; Bemidji State U; Art School of Minnesota

BENTON, MATTHEW T; PHILADELPHIA, PA; MASSENA CTRL HS; (JR); Hnr Roll; Perf Att; St of Mnth; Yth Ldrshp Prog; Comm Volntr; ArtClub; Chess; Emplmnt; FCA; NYLC; Svce Clb; Bskball (V); Track (V); Stu Cncl (T); Over 100 Hours in Community Service - City Heroes / City Year; Scholarships to Susquehannock Camp for Boys; Architecture / Master's Degree; Engineering; Cornell U; Penn State U

BENZENHOEFER, KELSEY; APOLLO, PA; KISKI AREA HS; (JR); Hi Hnr Roll; Hnr Roll; Nat Hon Sy; Perf Att; WWAHSS; Comm Volntr; Peer Tut/Med; ArtClub; Chrch Yth Grp; Key Club; SADD; French Clb; Bnd; Track (V); Sch Ppr (R); Yrbk; Treasurer of National Honor Society

BEOETHY, NICHOLAS D; LANSDOWNE, PA; MONSIGNOR BONNER HS; (FR); Hnr Roll; Sccr (J)

BERARDI, LOUIS J; ALDAN, PA; MONSIGNOR BONNER HS; (FR); Hnr Roll; DARE; Ftball (J); Engineering

BEREZHNA, ZLATA; CRESCO, PA; POCONO MOUNTAIN EAST HS; (FR); Gov Hnr Prg; Hnr Roll; St of Mnth; WWAHSS; Comm Volntr; Off Aide; SADD; Russian Clb; Chr; Dnce; SP/M/VS; Track (V); Master's Degree in Social Work/Counseling; Minor in History; Penn U of Pennsylvania; U of Scranton

BERG, BRANDON M; MERCER, PA; MERCER AREA HS; (SR); Hi Hnr Roll; Hnr Roll; Pres Ac Ftns Aw; Pres Sch; Comm Volntr; Peer Tut/Med; Emplmnt; Off Aide; Photog; Quill & Scroll; Schol Bwl; SADD; Clb; Stg Cre; Bskball (J); Track (VJ L); Cl Off (J); Stu Cncl (R); Yrbk (E); Students for Charity; Journalism Technology; Journalism; Criminal Law; Thiel College

BERHE, FEVEN A; HARRISBURG, PA; CTRL DAUPHIN EAST HS; (SO)

BERKHEIMER, BRANDON; FELTON, PA; YORK CTY SCH OF TECH; (SO); Hi Hnr Roll; Hnr Roll; Perf Att; Play Baseball for Conrods; Electronics Degree; York College

BERNATOWICZ, TIFFANY L; TURTLE CREEK, PA; WOODLAND HILLS HS; MS; Hnr Roll; Pres Sch; ArtClub; Chrch Yth Grp; Scouts; Bnd; Clr Grd; Jzz Bnd; Mch Bnd; The President's Award for Academics; Instrumentalist Magazine Merit; Actress; Lawyer; U of Southern California; U of California Los Angeles

BERNSTEIN, WHITNEY; PITTSBURGH, PA; PLUM SR HS; (JR); Hnr Roll; Hosp Aide; FBLA; Scouts; Tech Clb; RN; U of Pittsburgh

BERNSTIEL, CORINNE; POTTSTOWN, PA; POTTSGROVE HS; (SO); Hi Hnr Roll; Hnr Roll; Otst Ac Ach Awd; Ntl Math Olympn; WWAHSS; St of Mnth; WWAHSS; Yth Ldrshp Prog; Drma Clb; Emplmnt; Key Club; Mth Clb/Tm; Off Aide; Quiz Bowl; Sci Clb; SADD; Chr; Orch; SP/M/VS; Sccr (J); Sftball (JC); Stu Cncl (R); CR (R); Lit Mag; Sch Ppr (R); Key Club President; National Society of High School Scholars; Pre-Law; Psychology; Ursinus College; New York U

BEROES, JULIE E; PITTSBURGH, PA; THE CREATIVE AND PERF ARTS SCH; (JR); Ctznshp Aw; Gov Hnr Prg; Hi Hnr Roll; Nat Hon Sy; Comm Volntr; Drma Clb; Chr; Dnce; SP/M/VS; Stg Cre; Adv Cncl (S); Compassionate Friends Volunteer; Altar Server St Paul Cathedral; Musical Theater; New York U; Carnegie Mellon U

BERRIER, ANASTASIA M; CARLISLE, PA; TRINITY HS; (SR); F Lan Hn Soc; Hi Hnr Roll; Nat Hon Sy; Nat Mrt Sch Recip; Otst Ac Ach Awd; Perf Att; Valdctrian; WWAHSS; Comm Volntr; Hab For Humty Volntr; Emplmnt; Key Club; Pep Squd; Quiz Bowl; Spch Team; Latin Clb; Chr; SP/M/VS; Stg Cre; Lit Mag (R); Sch Ppr (R); Handbell Choir; Forensic Science; Duquesne U

BERRIER, HEATHER; EAST WATERFORD, PA; JUNIATA CTY SD; (JR); Hi Hnr Roll; Hnr Roll; USAA; Comm Volntr; Spec Olymp Vol; Emplmnt; Prom Com; Foreign Clb; Track (V); Elementary Education; Early Childhood Education; Millersville U; Shippensburg U

BERRIER, MELISSA; MIFFLIN, PA; JUNIATA HS; (JR); Hi Hnr Roll; Perf Att; Pres Ac Ftns Aw; USAA; WWAHSS; Chrch Yth Grp; Emplmnt; Ntl FFA; Prom Com; Bnd; Jzz Bnd; Mch Bnd; Sftball (VJ L); FFA Chapter Treasurer; Modern Music Masters; Nursery/Landscape; Pennsylvania College of Technology; Pennsylvania State U

BERRIER, OLIVIA; CARLISLE, PA; TRINITY HS; (SO); Hi Hnr Roll; Hnr Roll; Perf Att; Sci Fairs; WWAHSS; Comm Volntr; Spec Olymp Vol; Emplmnt; Key Club; Latin Clb; Cr Ctry (J L); Lit Mag (R); Amateur Radio Club; Respect Life Club; Science; Engineering

BERTELE, FRANCIO; PHILADELPHIA, PA; NORTHEAST CATHOLIC BOYS HS; MS; Bskball; Ftball; Sftball; Miami U; Penn State U

BERTOCCHI, SAMANTHA; GREENVILLE, PA; REYNOLDS JR/SR HS; (FR); Hi Hnr Roll; WWAHSS; Chrch Yth Grp; Key Club; Chr; Flg Crps; Chrldg (J); Stu Cncl; CR; Key Club Lieutenant Governor; Flag Captain; Communications; Evangel U

BERTOLINA, KALEY; IRWIN, PA; CTRL WESTMORELAND CTC; (FR); Hnr Roll; Chrch Yth Grp; Computer Programming; Pittsburgh Technical Institute; West Virginia Career Institute

BETTS, LINDA; WARREN, PA; WARREN AREA HS; (FR); Hi Hnr Roll; WWAHSS; ArtClub; Acpl Chr; Ch Chr; Cr Ctry (J); Swmg (V L); Track (J); Logos Program; Art Lessons from Local Art Teacher for 10 Years; Art; Interior Design; Penn State Behrens

BETTS, TIMOTHY J; LINDEN, PA; WILLIAMSPORT AREA HS; (SO); Hnr Roll; WWAHSS; Comm Volntr; Spec Olymp Vol; Scouts; Tchrs Aide; Bnd; Chr; Ch Chr; Jzz Bnd; Odyssey of the Mind-State Level; Eagle Scout

BETZ, JENNIFER; IVYLAND, PA; COUNCIL ROCK HS NORTH; (SO); F Lan Hn Soc; Hi Hnr Roll; MVP; Pres Ac Ftns Aw; St of Mnth; Key Club; German Clb; Orch; Dvng (L); Third Place At State Diving Championships; Pharmacist; Teaching; U of Michigan; U of North Carolina

BEVERLY, ALYSSIA N; LANCASTER, PA; LANCASTER MENNONITE HS; (JR); Ctznshp Aw; Hi Hnr Roll; Hnr Roll; Yth Ldrshp Prog; Comm Volntr; DARE; Emplmnt; NYLC; Photog; Wdwrkg Clb; Bskball (J L); Member of Youth Leadership Council; Political Science; Sociology; The College of William and Mary; Franklin and Marshall College

BEZAK, MICHAEL R; PITTSBURGH, PA; PITTSBURGH SD; (SO); DAR; Hi Hnr Roll; Hnr Roll; Sci Fairs; Valdctrian; Comm Volntr; ArtClub; Chess; DECA; College Major in World History; The U of Pittsburgh; Robert Morris U

BICHER, ALLISON; MYERSTOWN, PA; EASTERN LEBANON CTY HS; (SO); Hi Hnr Roll; Hnr Roll; Pres Ac Ftns Aw; Chrch Yth Grp; Lttrmn Clb; Pep Squd; Prom Com; Vsity Clb; Bskball (V L); Fld Hky (V L); Track (V L); Vsy Clb (V); Cl Off (V); Medical Technology; Mathematics

BIDUS, MICHELE; LANCASTER, PA; MANHEIM TWP HS; (SO); Ctznshp Aw; Hnr Roll; WWAHSS; Chrch Yth Grp; Emplmnt; Key Club; Stg Cre; Bskball (J); Cr Ctry (J); Golf (J); Sftball (V); Track (J L); Stu Cncl; Students Against Starvation; Business

Bernatowicz, Tiffany L — Woodland Hills HS — Turtle Creek, PA
Bennett, Tanya — Hazleton Area HS — Hazleton, PA
Belz, Valerie — North Allegheny Int Sch — Sewickley, PA
Bello-Ogunu, Emmanuel — Hempfield HS — Landisville, PA
National Honor Roll Spring 2005
Belknap, Elizabeth — Downingtown East SR HS — Downingtown, PA
Bengle, Lisa — Nazareth AC — Feasterville Trevose, PA
Berkheimer, Brandon — York Cty Sch Of Tech — Felton, PA
Beverly, Alyssia N — Lancaster Mennonite HS — Lancaster, PA

BIEBEL, JAMES; WATERFORD, PA; FORT LEBOEUF SD HS; (SO); Hi Hnr Roll; Nat Hon Sy; Otst Ac Ach Awd; Perf Att; Pres Sch; St of Mnth; Comm Volntr; Emplmnt; Bnd; Drm Mjr; Mch Bnd; SP/M/VS; Stu Cncl (R); Duke of Snowball Dance 2005; Student of the Month March 2004; Business Major; Law Degree; Boston U; Case Western Reserve

BIERLY, AARON D; ELYSBURG, PA; SOUTHERN COLUMBIA; (SR); Hnr Roll; WWAHSS; 4-H; DARE; Photog; Scouts; Bnd; Chr; Mch Bnd; SP/M/VS; Bskball (J); Sccr (V L); Track (V L); County & State Envirothon Participant; Pennsylvania Fish & Bear Commission Conservation Award; Geology Major; Paleontology; U of Pittsburgh At Johnstown

BILGER, DONNA; WILLOW HILL, PA; FANNETT METAL; (FR); Hi Hnr Roll; Hnr Roll; ArtClub; Ntl FFA; Clr Grd; Mch Bnd

BILLUPS, JOSEPH M; PHILADELPHIA, PA; PHILADELPHIA ELECTRICAL & TECH CHARTER HS; (JR); Hnr Roll; Emplmnt; Bsball; Bskball; Sccr; MVP Awards; Best Offensive Player Awards; Pro Basketball Player; Pro Soccer Player

BILODEAU, EMMA; SAINT MARYS, PA; ST MARYS AREA HS; (SR); 4-H; DARE; Scouts; Cr Ctry (V); Swmg (V); Track (V); Vllyball (J); Legal Assistant; Dubois Business College

BINGAMAN, R CYRUS; HARRISBURG, PA; CTRL DAUPHIN HS; (SO); Ctznshp Aw; Gov Hnr Prg; Hnr Roll; Nat Hon Sy; Perf Att; French Clb; Orch; Ftball (J); Mar Art (V L); Track (V L); Vllyball (J); Pilot; Psychology; Penn State U; Lehigh Valley College

BINGHAM, STEPHANIE; POTTSTOWN, PA; POTTSGROVE HS; (SR); Hi Hnr Roll; Hnr Roll; Pres Sch; WWAHSS; Comm Volntr; Spec Olymp Vol; Chrch Yth Grp; Drma Clb; Emplmnt; Key Club; Photog; Sci Clb; Vsity Clb; Chr; Dnce; SP/M/VS; Fld Hky (V L); Vsy Clb (V); CR (R); Sports Medicine; West Chester U

BIRCH, JERRELL; LANCASTER, PA; (JR); Hnr Roll; Nat Hon Sy; St of Mnth; Emplmnt; Stu Cncl (R); CR (R); Business; Real Estate; U of Kentucky; Millersville U

BIRKBECK, JESSICA; NEWTOWN, PA; COUNCIL ROCK HS NORTH; (JR); Hi Hnr Roll; Nat Hon Sy; St of Mnth; WWAHSS; Comm Volntr; SADD; German Clb; Dnce; Chrldg (V); Marketing; Penn State U

BISHOP, JONATHAN R; TYRONE, PA; TYRONE AREA HS; (SO); Hi Hnr Roll; Hnr Roll; Nat Hon Sy; Sci Fairs; WWAHSS; Yth Ldrshp Prog; Comm Volntr; Peer Tut/Med; Red Cr Aide; Drma Clb; Emplmnt; Key Club; Scouts; Spanish Clb; SP/M/VS; Stg Cre; Cr Ctry (VJ); Ftball (J); Ice Hky (VJ L); Rlr Hky (J); Skiing (VJ); Track (VJ); Cl Off (S); Stu Cncl; CR (S); Sch Ppr (E); Key Club-Lieutenant Governor, Vice President; Leadership Blair County Youth Chamber of Commerce

BITTER, FREDERICK H; BUTLER, PA; MERCERSBURG AC; (JR); Hi Hnr Roll; Hnr Roll; St of Mnth; Yth Ldrshp Prog; Comm Volntr; Chrch Yth Grp; Emplmnt; Outdrs Clb; Scouts; Tmpl Yth Grp; Spanish Clb; Bnd; Stg Cre; Ftball (VJ); Skiing (J); Tennis (VJ); Track (VJ); Wt Lftg (J); Eagle Scout Troop #53; Bachelor's Degree / Science or Business; Master's Degree in Business Administration; St. Joseph's U Philadelphia; Northeastern U Boston

BITTING, KETRA; MIFFLINTOWN, PA; JUNIATA CTY SD; (JR); Hi Hnr Roll; Hnr Roll; Pres Ac Ftns Aw; WWAHSS; Chrch Yth Grp; Emplmnt; Lib Aide; Bnd; Flg Crps; Mch Bnd; Tennis (J); Pre-Med

BIXLER, AMANDA; TURBOTVILLE, PA; WARRIOR RUN SD HS; (JR); Hnr Roll; Nat Stu Ath Day Aw; Photog; Prom Com; Spanish Clb; Sccr (V L); Track (V L); Yrbk (E, P); Who's Who Among American High School Students; Education; Art; Bloomsburg U; Kutztown U

BIXLER, RACHEL; PIPERSVILLE, PA; CTRL BUCKS HS EAST HS; (JR); DAR; Hnr Roll; WWAHSS; Comm Volntr; Peer Tut/Med; Key Club; Mod UN; Chr; SP/M/VS; PP Ftbl (J); Stu Cncl (R); Reading Olympics President; Occupational Therapist; Elizabethtown College; Alvernia College

BIZZARI, FRANK; LANSDOWNE, PA; MONSIGNOR BONNER HS; (JR); Hnr Roll; Nat Hon Sy; Perf Att; WWAHSS; Bsball (J L); Ftball (V L); CR (R); Political Science; Pre-Law; Kings College; Albright College

BLACK, BRIAN S; HERMITAGE, PA; HERMITAGE SD; (SO); Hnr Roll; Chrch Yth Grp; Drma Clb; Scouts; Bnd; Jzz Bnd; Mch Bnd; Pep Bnd; Sccr (J); Life Scout; Assistant Patrol Leader; Architecture

BLACK, BRITTANY; BEAVER FALLS, PA; BLACKHAWK HS; (JR); Hi Hnr Roll; Hnr Roll; Kwnis Aw; WWAHSS; Key Club; Spanish Clb; Cr Ctry (V L); Sccr (VJ L); Key Club Treasurer; Pharmacy Doctorate; U of Pittsburgh; Slippery Rock U

BLACK, DYLAN T; WAYNESBORO, PA; HERITAGE AC; (SO); Hnr Roll; Chrch Yth Grp; Ch Chr; SP/M/VS; Psychology; Engineering in a Technical Field

BLACK, MARQUIS; PHILADELPHIA, PA; SAMUEL FELS HS; (SR); Emplmnt; Business Management; Community College of Philadelphia; Johnson & Wales U

BLACK, MEGAN C; WASHINGTON, PA; TRINITY AREA SD; (JR); Hi Hnr Roll; Nat Hon Sy; Otst Ac Ach Awd; Pres Ac Ftns Aw; St of Mnth; WWAHSS; Comm Volntr; FTA; Key Club; Lib Aide; Prom Com; SADD; Spanish Clb; SP/M/VS; Chrldg (V); Cl Off (V); Stu Cncl (R); Yrbk (E); Vice-President PTSA; President Spanish Club; Education; Computer Science; U of Pittsburgh-Pittsburgh; Nova Southeastern U

BLACKSTON, MARIO; HARRISBURG, PA; (JR); Hnr Roll; Mas Aw; MVP; CARE; Comm Volntr; DARE; Drma Clb; Scouts; Vsity Clb; Ch Chr; Drl Tm; Bsball (V); Ftball (V CL); Made Top 50 Lineman in Country; Law; Teaching; U of Central Florida; Delaware U

BLAIN, HOLLY; MILLERSBURG, PA; MILLERSBURG AREA HS; (JR); Hi Hnr Roll; Hnr Roll; Emplmnt; Chrldg (V); PP Ftbl (V); Accounting

BLAIR, LINDY; GREENSBURG, PA; GREENSBURG SALEM HS; (SO); DAR; Hi Hnr Roll; Pres Ac Ftns Aw; Sci/Math Olympn; USAA; Chrldg (V); Stu Cncl; Millennium Dreamer Award 2000; Physical Therapy

BLAIR, WILLIAM P; JEANNETTE, PA; PENN-TRAFFORD HS; (SR); Hi Hnr Roll; Nat Hon Sy; Comm Volntr; Emplmnt; Photog; Member of National Honor Society; Member of the Community Action Program; Management of Information Systems; U of Pittsburgh At Greensburg

BLAKER, SASHEEN N; GRAYSVILLE, PA; WEST GREENE HS; (SO); Hi Hnr Roll; Hnr Roll; WWAHSS; Quill & Scroll; Vllyball; Sch Ppr (R, P); Crime Scene Investigator; Graphic Design; Waynesburg College; International Academy of Design & Technology Pittsburgh

BLAKEY, BRANDON; DOYLESTOWN, PA; CTRL BUCKS HS EAST; (SO); Hi Hnr Roll; Hnr Roll; Pres Ac Ftns Aw; Comm Volntr; Hab For Humty Volntr; Peer Tut/Med; Drma Clb; Key Club; Spanish Clb; Chr; SP/M/VS; Track (V L); Vllyball (J); Distinguished Spanish Honors Award; Pre-Med; Biochemistry; Duke U; Stanford U

BLAKEY, BRIANNE; DOYLESTOWN, PA; CTRL BUCKS HS EAST; (JR); Hi Hnr Roll; Nat Hon Sy; Otst Ac Ach Awd; Pres Sch; Amnsty Intl; Comm Volntr; Hab For Humty Volntr; Key Club; Mod UN; P to P St Amb Prg; Sch Ppr (E); National History Day- 11th Nationally; Relay for Life; Business; Neuroscience; U of Pennsylvania; Bucknell U

BLANK, NOELLE; GREENSBURG, PA; GREENSBURG SALEM SD HS; (FR); Hi Hnr Roll; Pres Sch; Comm Volntr; ArtClub; Chrch Yth Grp; Chr; SP/M/VS; Stg Cre; Cr Ctry (V); Vllyball (J); Teacher's Award for Best Art Student; Hospice Award for Youngest Volunteer; Veterinary Medicine; Biology; U of Pittsburgh; Pennsylvania State U

BLASI, NICHOLE; PITTSTON, PA; PITTSTON AREA HS; (SO); Hi Hnr Roll; Nat Hon Sy; St of Mnth; DARE; Key Club; Dnce; Cr Ctry (V L); Sccr (V); Swmg (V); Track (V); Piano Guild 7 Year Member

BLASS, JOSHUA; GALETON, PA; GALETON AREA SD; (JR); ArtClub; Skiing; Ski Club; Art Club; Wildlife Management; Photography; Westmoreland Community College; Bucks County Community College

BLEVINS, AMY; NOTTINGHAM, PA; ELKTON CHRISTIAN SCH; (JR); Hi Hnr Roll; Hnr Roll; MVP; Nat Hon Sy; Perf Att; Chrch Yth Grp; Off Aide; Prom Com; Tchrs Aide; Ch Chr; Chrldg (V L); Sccr (V L); Vllyball (V CL); Business; Pharmaceutical Sales; Penn State U

BLISS, NICOLE; GOULDSBORO, PA; NORTH POCONO HS; (FR); Hi Hnr Roll; Hnr Roll; Nat Hon Sy; Comm Volntr; Dnce; Veterinary Assistant; U of Scranton

BLOCH, SASHA L; WYOMING, PA; DALLAS SR HS; (JR); Hnr Roll; Nat Hon Sy; WWAHSS; Yth Ldrshp Prog; Hosp Aide; Emplmnt; Key Club; P to P St Amb Prg; Tmpl Yth Grp; Dnce; Swmg (V); National History Day in PA State Participant; National Society of High School Scholars; International Studies Major; Elon U; College of William and Mary

BLOUGH, DEVIN; HOOVERSVILLE, PA; SHADE-CENTRAL CITY SD; (FR); Hi Hnr Roll; Hnr Roll; Chess; Chrch Yth Grp; Bnd; Mch Bnd; Pep Bnd; Local Archery Team; AYSO Soccer; Engineering; Video Game Design

BLUMSTEIN, MEGHAN J; BERWYN, PA; CONESTOGA HS; (SO); Ctznshp Aw; F Lan Hn Soc; Hi Hnr Roll; Hnr Roll; Emplmnt; Key Club; P to P St Amb Prg; Scouts; SP/M/VS; Cr Ctry (V); Crew Team Varsity

BOBB, JASON; DAUPHIN, PA; CTRL DAUPHIN HS; (FR); Ctznshp Aw; Hnr Roll; St of Mnth; Ftball (J); Engineering

BOBELLA, MICHAEL; MONROEVILLE, PA; GATEWAY SD; (SO); Hnr Roll; Perf Att; Comm Volntr; Red Cr Aide; ArtClub; DARE; Off Aide; Scouts; Bnd; Swmg (V); Track (V)

BOHUNICKY, STEFANIE; NORTHAMPTON, PA; NORTHAMPTON AREA SR HS; (SO); Hnr Roll; Perf Att; Hosp Aide; Drma Clb; P to P St Amb Prg; Dnce; SP/M/VS; Stg Cre; Fld Hky; Tennis; Track; Secretary of the Creative Writing Club; Theatre; Music; New York U; DeSales U

BOLAND, MATTHEW; VANDERGRIFT, PA; KISKI AREA HS; (SR); Hi Hnr Roll; Nat Hon Sy; Pres Ac Ftns Aw; St of Mnth; WWAHSS; Comm Volntr; Peer Tut/Med; Chess; Key Club; SADD; German Clb; Bskball (VJ L); Cl Off (P); Stu Cncl (R); National Honor Society President; German Club Vice President; Chemical Engineering; MBA; Pennsylvania State U-Schreyers Honors College

BOLYARD, MONICA; WATERFORD, PA; FORT LEBOEUF SD; (FR); Hnr Roll; Otst Ac Ach Awd; Pres Ac Ftns Aw; Sci Fairs; Comm Volntr; Peer Tut/Med; 4-H; Emplmnt; Ch Chr; Cr Ct Ski; Skiing; Sccr; Swmg; Yrbk; Marine Biology; Environmental Biology

BONK, DAVID; NEW KENSINGTON, PA; NEW KENSINGTON-ARNOLD SD; (FR); Hi Hnr Roll; Perf Att; Comm Volntr; Bsball (J); Bskball (J); Stu Cncl (R); Yrbk (R); Interact Club; Leo Club

BONNER, ANGELA R; PITTSBURGH, PA; SCHENLEY HS; (JR); Hi Hnr Roll; Hnr Roll; Nat Hon Sy; Perf Att; Sci Fairs; St of Mnth; Comm Volntr; Emplmnt; Ntl Beta Clb; Quiz Bowl; Svce Clb; Bnd; Mch Bnd; Tennis (V); Stu Cncl; Japan Bowl 3rd Place; Japanese Language Teacher; Japanese Translator; U of Pittsburgh; Saint Vincent College

BOOKHEIMER, TITUS; WORCESTER, PA; METHACTON HS; (SO); Hnr Roll; Perf Att; Comm Volntr; Bsball (VJ L); Ftball (VJ L); Wt Lftg; Engineer; Sports; Virginia Tech; Villanova U

BOOTERBAUGH, AARON P; POTTSTOWN, PA; POTTSGROVE SR HS; (FR); Hnr Roll; Otst Ac Ach Awd; Ftball (L); Lcrsse (J); Architecture; Engineering; Penn State U; U of California

BORDELL, RYAN; COAL TOWNSHIP, PA; NORTHUMBERLAND CTY VOC TECH SCH; MS; Emplmnt; Bskball (J); Junior Volunteer Firefighter; Welding

BORGHI, BRITTANY A; ZELIENOPLE, PA; SENECA VALLEY SHS; (JR); Hi Hnr Roll; Nat Hon Sy; Otst Ac Ach Awd; WWAHSS; Chrch Yth Grp; Dbte Team; Drma Clb; Emplmnt; Key Club; Mod UN; Prom Com; Chr; SP/M/VS; Swg Chr; Track (J); Cl Off (S); Stu Cncl (R); Mock Trial Competition; Teens 'N' Tots Club; English / Journalism; Theater; Columbia U; American U

BORISENKO, TATYANA; WATERFORD, PA; SENECA HS; (FR); Fut Prb Slvr; Hi Hnr Roll; Hnr Roll; Otst Ac Ach Awd; Perf Att; St of Mnth; Valdctrian; Yth Ldrshp Prog; Peer Tut/Med; Chrch Yth Grp; Dbte Team; Emplmnt; Tchrs Aide; French Clb; Bnd; Ch Chr; SP/M/VS; Stg Cre; Erie's Promise Future Problem Solver; Erie Junior Forensic League; Cake Decorator; Dentist; Behrend Penn State Erie; Mercyhurst College

BORLAND, JOEL; UNIONTOWN, PA; LAUREL HIGHLANDS SD; (FR); Hnr Roll; St of Mnth; Emplmnt; Spanish Clb; Ftball (J); Sccr (J); Cl Off (P); Stu Cncl (R); Physician Assistant; Film and Video Production; U of Pittsburgh; Saint Francis U

BORTSALAS, STEPHEN C; THORNDALE, PA; LAN-CHESTER CHRISTIAN SCH; (FR); All Am Sch; Ctznshp Aw; Hi Hnr Roll; Hnr Roll; MVP; Nat Hon Sy; Otst Ac Ach Awd; USAA; SP/M/VS; Bskball (V CL); Church Play Actor, Basketball Co-MVP Player of Year, Basketball Offensive Player of Year; United States Achievement Academy Award Leadership Academy, College Basketball; NBA Basketball Player; Movie Director/Producer/Writer; Temple U, Full Sail, Pensacola U; Duke U, Real World Education, Syracuse U, St. Joseph's U

BOST, CHRISTOPHER P; IRVINE, PA; YOUNGSVILLE MIDDLE SR HS; (SO); Hi Hnr Roll; Nat Hon Sy; Otst Ac Ach Awd; Sci Fairs; St of Mnth; Yth Ldrshp Prog; Comm Volntr; Spec Olymp Vol; ArtClub; Chrch Yth Grp; Mth Clb/Tm; P to P St Amb Prg; SADD; German Clb; Ftball (V); Track (V L); Cl Off (P); Eagle's Eye Communications Team; Salvation Army's Links; Teaching-History; Meteorology; Penn State U; Edinboro State U

BOTTI-LODOVICO, MARIA Y; GIBSONIA, PA; AQUINAS AC; (SR); Hi Hnr Roll; Comm Volntr; Drma Clb; Emplmnt; Mus Clb; NYLC; Acpl Chr; Chr; SP/M/VS; Stu Cncl (R); CR (R); Sch Ppr (R); Yrbk (R); Pianist-Performed Meranofest - Merano Italy; Marian Garcia Piano Competition -- Penn State; Piano Performance; Concert Pianist-Doctorate Music; Cleveland Institute Music; Oberlin Conservatory

BOVE, LAURA; BETHEL PARK, PA; BETHEL PARK SD; (SO); Nat Hon Sy; Yth Ldrshp Prog; Comm Volntr; Hosp Aide; Chrch Yth Grp; Drma Clb; SP/M/VS; Chrldg (VJC); Adv Cncl (R); Stu Cncl (R); Pharmacy; Business; Duquesne; Penn State

BOWEN, HEATHER C; LEVITTOWN, PA; HARRY S TRUMAN HS; (SR); Hi Hnr Roll; Hnr Roll; Nat Hon Sy; Perf Att; Pres Ac Ftns Aw; WWAHSS; Comm Volntr; Peer Tut/Med; Chrch Yth Grp; Emplmnt; Mus Clb; Bnd; Chr; VP & Treasurer of Choral Club; Asst. Manager @ Kantagree Farm, Wrightstown, Pa; Equine Studies; Centenary College

BOWEN, LEIGH; DRAVOSBURG, PA; MC KEESPORT AREA SD; (SO); Hi Hnr Roll; Hnr Roll; Perf Att; Sci Fairs; WWAHSS; Comm Volntr; Spch Team; Orch; SP/M/VS; Sftball (J); Junior Tombenteens of Duquesne; Attended Future Leaders of America Convention; Law; Business Management; Duquesne U

Bowen, Heather C
Harry S Truman HS
Levittown, PA

Bortsalas, Stephen C
Lan-Chester Christian Sch
Thorndale, PA

Blevins, Amy
Elkton Christian Sch
Nottingham, PA

Black, Megan C
Trinity Area SD
Washington, PA

Black, Brian S
Hermitage SD
Hermitage, PA

National
Honor Roll
Spring 2005

Billups, Joseph M
Philadelphia Electrical & Tech Charter HS
Philadelphia, PA

Blank, Noelle
Greensburg Salem SD HS
Greensburg, PA

Bonner, Angela R
Schenley HS
Pittsburgh, PA

Bost, Christopher P
Youngsville Middle SR HS
Irvine, PA

Botti-Lodovico, Maria Y
Aquinas AC
Gibsonia, PA

BOWER, KASSANDRA; NEWPORT, PA; NEWPORT JR/SR HS; (FR); Hi Hnr Roll; Otst Ac Ach Awd; Chrch Yth Grp; Sftball (J); Teaching; Photography; Penn State; Harrisburg Area Community College

BOWERS, BESSIE; PHILADELPHIA, PA; CHARLES CARROLL HS; (SR); Hi Hnr Roll; Hnr Roll; Perf Att; Comm Volntr; White Williams Scholar; Psychology; Social Work; Temple U; La Salle U

BOWERS, JIMMY; HARRISBURG, PA; CTRL DAUPHIN HS; (FR); Hnr Roll; Sccr (J); Sports Management; Penn State U; U North Carolina

BOWERSOX, ASHLEY; MIDDLEBURG, PA; MIDD-WEST SD; (JR); Hnr Roll; WWAHSS; Comm Volntr; Red Cr Aide; Chrch Yth Grp; Emplmnt; FCCLA; Key Club; Prom Com; Scouts; Drl Tm; Cl Off (V); Stu Cncl (R); CR (R); Bowling Team; Dentist

BOWERSOX, LAUREN M; TURBOTVILLE, PA; WARRIOR RUN SD; (JR); Hi Hnr Roll; Hnr Roll; MVP; Perf Att; Prom Com; Spanish Clb; Acpl Chr; Chr; SP/M/VS; Bskball (J); Sccr (VJ L); Vsy Clb (V L); US National Soccer Awards; 2nd Place-PA National Goalie War; Foreign Language (Spanish) Education; Foreign Language Business Admin.; Albright College-Reading; Penn State-Berks Campus

BOWMAN, JAMES; WILLIAMSPORT, PA; LOYALSOCK TOWNSHIP HS; (SO); Hnr Roll; Chrch Yth Grp; Key Club; Spanish Clb; Bnd; Jzz Bnd; SP/M/VS; Ftball (J)

BOWMAN, JONATHON; WILLIAMSPORT, PA; LOYALSOCK TWP HS; (SO); Hi Hnr Roll; WWAHSS; Chrch Yth Grp; Key Club; Spanish Clb; Bnd; Jzz Bnd; SP/M/VS; Ftball (J); Stu Cncl (R); AYSO Soccer Coach - Volunteer

BOWMASTER, JOHN; MARTINSBURG, PA; SPRING COVE SD; (JR); Hi Hnr Roll; Hnr Roll; Emplmnt; Business Management; Law; Penn State; Lock Haven

BOWSER, ALICIA R; WEST NEWTON, PA; YOUGH SR HS; (FR); Hnr Roll; Sci Fairs; Biology Clb; FCA; Scouts; Bnd; Chr; Jzz Bnd; SP/M/VS; County & District Band (4 Times Each); County Chorus; Biology Teacher; Forensic Science; California U; U of Pittsburgh

BOWSER, COURTNEY J; WORTHINGTON, PA; LENAPE TECH; (SR); All Am Sch; Hnr Roll; 4-H; Chrch Yth Grp; Scouts; Cl Off (S, T); Median School of Allied Health Careers

BOYD, RACHEL M; POTTSTOWN, PA; POTTSGROVE HS; (SR); St of Mnth; WWAHSS; Key Club; Dnce; Elementary Education; Millersville U

BOYD-CHISHOLM, GABRIELLA N; HARRISBURG, PA; HARRISBURG HS; (FR); Hnr Roll; Emplmnt; Track (V); Ob/Gyn; Howard; Spelman

BOYD JR, MARTIN R; PHILADELPHIA, PA; OVERBROOK HS; (SO); Ctznshp Aw; Hnr Roll; Perf Att; Business Major; Temple U; Penn State U

BOYEK, AMANDA; TOWANDA, PA; NOTRE DAME HS; (SO); Hi Hnr Roll; Kwnis Aw; Pres Sch; WWAHSS; Yth Ldrshp Prog; Comm Volntr; ArtClub; Key Club; French Clb; SP/M/VS; Stg Cre; Track (V); Biology Major; Liberal Arts Major; Georgetown U

BOYER, AARON S; LATROBE, PA; RIDGEVIEW AC CS; (JR); Hnr Roll; Pres Ac Ftns Aw; Comm Volntr; ArtClub; DARE; Sci Clb; Bskball (J); Ftball (VJ); Vllyball (J); Wrstlg (J); Chemistry

BOYER, SARA; BETHLEHEM, PA; LIBERTY HS; (SO); Orch; Chrldg (J); Lcrsse (V); Biology

BOYLAN, LIAM; SCRANTON, PA; WEST SCRANTON HS; (FR); Nat Mrt LOC; Comm Volntr; DARE; Chr; I Got an Award for a Civil War Essay in 8th Grade; I'd Like to Be Involved with the Law; Wrestler for the WWE; U of Scranton; Penn State U

BOYLE, CHRISTOPHER; WILKES BARRE, PA; HANOVER JR/SR HS; (FR); Hnr Roll; Nat Sci Aw; Sci Fairs; WWAHSS; Chess; DARE; Key Club; Drm Mjr; Mch Bnd; SP/M/VS; Stg Cre; Ftball (J); Golf (V); Lcrsse; Sccr (V); Tennis (V); Track (VJ); Vllyball (V); Wt Lftg (V); Stu Cncl; Sch Ppr (R, P); Yrbk (R, P); Reflections; Science Fair; Lawyer (Law School); Notre Dame U; Wilkes College

BRADBURN JR, MICHAEL R; PITTSBURGH, PA; BALDWIN HS; (SR); Ctznshp Aw; Hi Hnr Roll; MVP; Nat Hon Sy; Pres Sch; WWAHSS; Comm Volntr; Peer Tut/Med; Spec Olymp Vol; FBLA; Mth Clb/Tm; Tech Clb; Sch Ppr (R); Yrbk (R); Bowling, V, JV, L; Computer Science; U of Pittsburgh

BRADY, CREGEN; CLEARFIELD, PA; CLEARFIELD AREA HS; (SO); Ctznshp Aw; Perf Att; Comm Volntr; Peer Tut/Med; Chess; Lib Aide; Mus Clb; Outdrs Clb; Bnd; Chr; Mch Bnd; Orch; Bsball (J); Ftball (J); Stu Cncl (R); Architectural Drafting; Music - Teacher / Performer; James Madison U; Western Michigan U

BRADY, DANIELLE; LANSDALE, PA; NORTH PENN HS; (JR); Hi Hnr Roll; Hnr Roll; Nat Hon Sy; Pres Sch; WWAHSS; Spec Olymp Vol; Emplmnt; FTA; Key Club; Fld Hky (J); Rugby; 9th Grade Girl's Softball-Asst. Coach; Education

BRADY, GENNY L; DU BOIS, PA; DU BOIS HS; (MS); Hnr Roll; Chr; Clr Grd; Dnce; Flg Crps; Good Kid Award 2 Yrs Running- School; Performing Arts; Penn State; Boston School of Fine Arts

BRADY, JAMIE E; GIBSONIA, PA; PINE-RICHLAND HS; (JR); Hnr Roll; WWAHSS; Key Club; Chrldg (V CL); Gmnstcs (V L); PP Ftbl (V); Skiing; Who's Who Among American HS Students; Orthopedic Medicine; Physical Therapy; U of Pittsburgh; Penn State U (U Park)

BRADY, JOHN P; SHAVERTOWN, PA; WYOMING SEMINARY PREP; (JR); Hi Hnr Roll; Hnr Roll; MVP; Nat Ldrshp Svc; WWAHSS; Comm Volntr; Peer Tut/Med; Emplmnt; Mth Clb/Tm; Sci Clb; Skiing (J); Sccr (J); Tennis (J); Sch Ppr (R); State Computer 2004; Pre-Med-Physics; Engineering; Drexel U; Villanova

BRADY, MOLLY E; FALLENTIMBER, PA; MASHANNON VALLEY JR/SR HS; (FR); Hi Hnr Roll; Hnr Roll; St of Mnth; Spanish Clb; Bnd; Chr; Ch Chr; Jzz Bnd; Vllyball (J); Author; Penn State U; Juniata College

BRANDON, LINDSAY; GIBSONIA, PA; PINE RICHLAND HS; (JR); Hi Hnr Roll; Hnr Roll; Pres Sch; Chrldg (J); Elementary Education; Early Childhood Education

BRANDON, SARA B; KELTON, PA; ELKTON CHRISTIAN SCH; (SO); Hnr Roll; Nat Hon Sy; Yth Ldrshp Prog; Chrch Yth Grp; Drma Clb; Pep Squd; Ch Chr; Dnce; SP/M/VS; Bskball (V CL); Chrldg (V CL); Cl Off (P); Yrbk (E, P); Fashion Designer; Neonatalogist

BRANDON JR, ANTHONY; PHILADELPHIA, PA; OVERBROOK HS; (JR); Hnr Roll; Perf Att; Comm Volntr; Emplmnt; Mus Clb; Mch Bnd; Tennis (J); Academy Honor Roll; Chemistry; Biology; Morehouse U; Lock Haven U

BRANT, FRANCESCA; BERLIN, PA; SHANKSVILLE-STONYCREEK HS; (FR); Chr; Penn State

BRANT, JENNIFER M; DERRY, PA; DERRY AREA HS; (SR); Hi Hnr Roll; Nat Hon Sy; Perf Att; WWAHSS; Yth Ldrshp Prog; Red Cr Aide; Voc Ind Clb Am; Occupational Therapy; Psychology; Westmoreland Community College; U of Pittsburgh

BRANT, TIA R; MILLERTON, PA; NORTHERN TIOGA SD; (FR); Hi Hnr Roll; Hnr Roll; Nat Hon Sy; WWAHSS; Comm Volntr; Chrch Yth Grp; Bnd; Ch Chr; Jzz Bnd; Mch Bnd; Patchwork Puppet Ministries; Music Education; Music Performance and Composition; Houghton Bible College; Mansfield U

BRASHEAR, ADAM; MYERSTOWN, PA; EASTERN LEBANON CTY HS; (SR); F Lan Hn Soc; Hi Hnr Roll; Nat Hon Sy; St of Mnth; WWAHSS; Chrch Yth Grp; FCA; Quiz Bowl; Tchrs Aide; Bnd; Jzz Bnd; Mch Bnd; SP/M/VS; Vice President of National Honor Society; California U of Pennsylvania; Indiana U of Pennsylvania

BRAVERMAN, ERIKA J; BENSALEM, PA; BENSALEM TOWNSHIP SD; (JR); Hi Hnr Roll; Hnr Roll; Otst Ac Ach Awd; Pres Ac Ftns Aw; St of Mnth; DARE; Emplmnt; Prom Com; Bnd; Chr; Dnce; Jzz Bnd; Chrldg (V); Fld Hky (V); PP Ftbl (V); Stu Cncl (R); Medical Field / Four Year Degree; Business / Four Year Degree; Penn State

BRAXTON, BOBBIE S; BETHLEHEM, PA; LIBERTY HS; (SO); Hnr Roll; Otst Ac Ach Awd; St of Mnth; Emplmnt; Drl Tm; Business; Management; Rutgers U; Nyc

BRAYMER, BECKY; HERMITAGE, PA; HICKORY HS; (SO); 4H Awd; F Lan Hn Soc; Hnr Roll; Pres Ac Ftns Aw; WWAHSS; Comm Volntr; Peer Tut/Med; 4-H; Chrch Yth Grp; Key Club; Off Aide; French Clb; Chr; Bskball (J L); Hsbk Rdg (V); Scr Kpr (C); 4-H Awards; Accounting; Education; Gannon U; Edinboro U

BREITMAYER, DAVID J; DOWNINGTOWN, PA; DOWNINGTOWN WEST HS; (SR); Ctznshp Aw; Hi Hnr Roll; Hnr Roll; Nat Hon Sy; WWAHSS; Lttrmn Clb; Tchrs Aide; Orch; Lcrsse (V L); National Honor Society; Criminal Justice; West Chester U-Enrolled

BREMER, MARK; BRODHEADSVILLE, PA; PLEASANT VALLEY HS; (FR); Hnr Roll; Comm Volntr; Chrch Yth Grp; DARE; Emplmnt; Key Club; Scouts; Bnd; Ch Chr; Mch Bnd; Active Participant in Key Club / Church Youth Group; Machinist / Tap & Die Maker

BRENEMAN, LINZY M; TEMPLE, PA; MUHLENBERG SR HS; (JR); Hi Hnr Roll; Nat Hon Sy; Pres Ac Ftns Aw; Yth Ldrshp Prog; Comm Volntr; Emplmnt; SADD; German Clb; Ch Chr; Track (V L); Vllyball (V L); Medicine; Nutrition; Brigham Young U Idaho; U of Utah

BRENNER, CHRISTINA; HUNTINGDON VALLEY, PA; ABINGTON SR HS; (SO); Hi Hnr Roll; Pres Sch; USAA; WWAHSS; Comm Volntr; DARE; FBLA; Key Club; Scouts; Tchrs Aide; Sccr (J); Yrbk (E)

BRETZ, ELIZABETH; HARBORCREEK, PA; HARBORCREEK JR/SR HS; (SR); Hnr Roll; Nat Hon Sy; Perf Att; WWAHSS; Comm Volntr; Chrch Yth Grp; Emplmnt; International Relations; Foreign Service Officer; Houghton College; Waynesburg College

BRICE, JASMINE; PITTSBURGH, PA; PITTSBURGH SD; (MS); Hnr Roll; Quiz Bowl; Tech Clb; Orch; Stu Cncl (V); Advanced in Electronics; Theater/ Drama; Music; U of Pennsylvania; U of Pittsburgh

BROADWATER, COURTNEY M; BERLIN, PA; SHANKSVILLE-STONYCREEK HS; (FR); Bnd; Chr; Mch Bnd; Secondary Education / English; U of Pittsburgh Johnstown

BRODT, AMANDA; BETHLEHEM, PA; LIBERTY HS; (JR); Hnr Roll; Comm Volntr; Spec Olymp Vol; Emplmnt; Prom Com; Bnd; Mch Bnd; Orch; Psychology; Secondary Education; Marymount U; Lehigh U

BROGNA, JESSICA; PITTSTON, PA; PITTSTON AREA HS; (SO); Hi Hnr Roll; Nat Hon Sy; Perf Att; AL Aux Girls; Tennis (V L); Volunteer with Marine Corps; Photography/Design; Education; Marywood U; Kings College

BROOKINS, NURIDEEN; PITTSBURGH, PA; PITTSBURGH SD; (JR); Hnr Roll; Yth Ldrshp Prog; Comm Volntr; Hosp Aide; Chrch Yth Grp; Emplmnt; Chr; Medical Explorers U of Pittsburgh; Medical Careers After School Program; Medicine; Law School; U of Pittsburgh

BROOKS, LAUREN I; BLOSSBURG, PA; NORTH PENN HS; (SO); Hi Hnr Roll; Nat Hon Sy; Comm Volntr; Spec Olymp Vol; Chrch Yth Grp; Key Club; Cl Off (S); Stu Cncl (R); Key Club; Student Council; Social Work; Penn State U; Lock Haven U

BROOKS, MORGAN; PHILADELPHIA, PA; CREATIVE PERF ARTS HS; (FR); Ctznshp Aw; Hi Hnr Roll; Hnr Roll; Nat Hon Sy; Otst Ac Ach Awd; Pres Sch; St of Mnth; Comm Volntr; Chrch Yth Grp; Dnce; Alpha Kappa Alpha Sorority Mentor Pgm; Court Sketch Artist/Journalism; Novelist

BROSH, DENIER T; MT CARMEL, PA; MT CARMEL AREA; (SO); Hi Hnr Roll; Nat Hon Sy; ArtClub; Chrldg (V); Physical Therapy; Physician's Assistant; Bloomsburg U; Bucknell U

BROUSE, ASHLEY E; TURBOTVILLE, PA; WARRIOR RUN SD; (JR); Hi Hnr Roll; Hnr Roll; MVP; Nat Hon Sy; Pres Ac Ftns Aw; St of Mnth; Peer Tut/Med; Prom Com; Vsity Clb; Spanish Clb; Scr Kpr (V); Sccr (V CL); Track (V L); Cl Off (T); Stu Cncl (V); Yrbk (P); Speech Language Pathologist; Minor in Spanish; Bloomsburg U

BROWN, ANDREW; HERMITAGE, PA; HICKORY HS; (SR); All Am Sch; Hi Hnr Roll; Hnr Roll; Nat Hon Sy; Perf Att; Pres Ac Ftns Aw; Pres Sch; St of Mnth; WWAHSS; Yth Ldrshp Prog; Comm Volntr; Chrch Yth Grp; Mth Clb/Tm; Photog; Spanish Clb; Cr Ctry (V CL); Golf (V L); Track (V L); Tri-Athlete Award; Who's Who Twice; Chemistry; Mathematics; Westminster College; U of Vermont

BROWN, ASHLEY M; WAYNESBORO, PA; WAYNESBORO AREA SR HS; (JR); Hnr Roll; WWAHSS; Chrch Yth Grp; DARE; FBLA; P to P St Amb Prg; Scouts; Secretary of Local FBLA Chapter; Graphic Design; Pittsburg-Art Institute or; Bradley Academy

BROWN, BRITTNEY; BETHEL PARK, PA; BETHEL PARK SD HS; (SO); Hnr Roll; Scouts; SADD; Sccr (V); Track (V L); Sports Medicine; Pediatrician; Duquesne; Washington-Jefferson

BROWN, CHADDEA; ALLENTOWN, PA; WILLIAM ALLEN HS; (FR); Ctznshp Aw; Hi Hnr Roll; Hnr Roll; Nat Hon Sy; Otst Ac Ach Awd; Perf Att; St of Mnth; Mth Clb/Tm; Dnce; Drl Tm; Stu Cncl (S); Teaching; Doctor; Tuskegee U; Harvard U

BROWN, CORDELL; MC KEESPORT, PA; MC KEESPORT AREA SCH DIST; (FR); MVP; St of Mnth; DARE; Ftball (J); Wrstlg (J); Doctor; Law; Pittsburgh U; Cal U

BROWN, LINDSAY; PHOENIXVILLE, PA; PHOENIXVILLE AREA HS; (SO); Hnr Roll; WWAHSS; Chrch Yth Grp; Emplmnt; Key Club; Chr; Hsbk Rdg (V); Lit Mag (F); Vocal Ensemble; Key Club VP & Presidential Classroom Alumni; Law Degree (Pre-Law); International Relations; New York U; Dartmouth

BROWN, MATTHEW H; DOYLESTOWN, PA; CTRL BUCKS HS EAST; (JR); Hi Hnr Roll; Nat Hon Sy; WWAHSS; Comm Volntr; Drma Clb; Emplmnt; Key Club; Bnd; Stg Cre; History Day; Business / Stock Broker; New York U; U of Pennsylvania

BROWN, NISA L; PHILADELPHIA, PA; (MS); Hnr Roll; Nat Hon Sy; St of Mnth; Comm Volntr; Drma Clb; Svce Clb; Dnce; SP/M/VS; GAA (V); Scr Kpr (V); Sftball (V); Track (V); Stu Cncl (P); CR (P); Sch Ppr (E); Neonatologist; RN

BROWN, RANEICE; PHILA, PA; KENSINGTON HS; (SR); Hnr Roll; Perf Att; St of Mnth; Comm Volntr; Peer Tut/Med; Drma Clb; Chrldg (L); Community College

BROWN, RAQUEL; PHILADELPHIA, PA; PHILADELPHIA HS FOR GIRLS; (JR); Hnr Roll; Yth Ldrshp Prog; Chrch Yth Grp; Dnce; Drl Tm; SP/M/VS; Pre-Medicine; Nursing (Pediatrician); Howard U; Millersville U

BROWN, REBECCA; CLINTON, PA; ROBINSON TWP CHRISTIAN SCH; (JR); Hi Hnr Roll; Nat Mrt Fin; Pres Sch; 4-H; Chrch Yth Grp; Drma Clb; Mth Clb/Tm; Tchrs Aide; Drl Tm; SP/M/VS; Stg Cre; Cr Ctry; Track; Sch Ppr (E); Animal Genetics; Agricultural Animal Breeding; Cornell U; Clemson U

Brenner, Christina
Abington SR HS
Huntingdon Valley, PA

Brady, John P
Wyoming Seminary Prep
Shavertown, PA

Boyd-Chisholm, Gabriella N
Harrisburg HS
Harrisburg, PA

Bowser, Alicia R
Yough SR HS
West Newton, PA

National
Honor Roll
Spring 2005

Bowersox, Lauren M
Warrior Run SD
Turbotville, PA

Brady, Genny L
Du Bois HS
Du Bois, PA

Brant, Francesca
Shanksville-Stonycreek HS
Berlin, PA

Brosh, Denier T
Mt Carmel Area
Mt Carmel, PA

BROWN, STEVEN; BOSWELL, PA; NORTH STAR SD; (MS); Ctznshp Aw; Hi Hnr Roll; Hnr Roll; MVP; St of Mnth; Comm Volntr; Peer Tut/Med; Cmptr Clb; Outdrs Clb; Tech Clb; SP/M/VS; Arch (V); Bsball (V); Golf (V); Skt Tgt Sh (V); Wt Lftg (V); Wrstlg (V); Stu Cncl (T); Yrbk (E); Somerset County Scrabble Champion, 4 Times; Engineering; Penn State U

BRUBACHER, SARA M; DILLSBURG, PA; NORTHERN YORK HS; (FR); Hi Hnr Roll; St of Mnth; WWAHSS; Spec Olymp Vol; Chrch Yth Grp; DARE; Emplmnt; Key Club; Bnd; Chr; Mch Bnd; Orch; Swmg (L); Gold Key Writing Award; Peace Studies; International Studies

BRUCKNER, SETH; WASHINGTON, PA; TRINITY AREA SD; (JR); Hnr Roll; Pres Ac Ftns Aw; Sci Fairs; Comm Volntr; Hab For Humty Volntr; Chrch Yth Grp; Dbte Team; Lttrmn Clb; SADD; Vsity Clb; French Clb; SP/M/VS; Ftball (V CL); Lcrsse (V L); Wt Lftg (V); Stu Cncl (R); Yrbk (R); Political Science; Pennsylvania State U; Pittsburgh U

BRUDVIG, KELSEY; HOLLIDAYSBURG, PA; HOLLIDAYSBURG AREA SR HS; (JR); Hnr Roll; Nat Hon Sy; Comm Volntr; Prom Com; SADD; Spanish Clb; Chr; Stu Cncl (R); National Honor Society; Foundation for Teaching Economics; Communications; Law; New York U; U of Kentucky

BRUMBAUGH, ABBI; WILLIAMSBURG, PA; WILLIAMSBURG CMTY SD; (FR); Hi Hnr Roll; Hnr Roll; Otst Ac Ach Awd; Perf Att; Comm Volntr; Emplmnt; Mth Clb/Tm; Mus Clb; Tchrs Aide; Chr; Mount A; State College-Penn State

BRUMBERG, SARAH; SUMMERVILLE, PA; BROOKVILLE AREA SD; (SR); Nat Hon Sy; Emplmnt; Clr Grd; Mch Bnd; Stg Cre; Business Administration; Medical Coding; U of Pittsburgh- Titusville

BRUMFIELD, JESSICA N; COATESVILLE, PA; BISHOP SHANAHAN HS; (JR); F Lan Hn Soc; Hnr Roll; Nat Hon Sy; Nat Mrt LOC; Comm Volntr; Tchrs Aide; Hsbk Rdg; CR (R); C-3 Rating - United States Pony Club; Business; Equestrian Studies; West Chester U; Delaware County Community

BRUNDAGE, MEGAN; FREDONIA, PA; REYNOLDS HS; (JR); Hi Hnr Roll; Nat Hon Sy; WWAHSS; Comm Volntr; Chrch Yth Grp; Key Club; Bnd; Mch Bnd; Distinguished Editor of Key Club; State Member of Reynolds Academic Decathlon Team; Journalism; Public Relations; Kent State U; Mt Union College

BRUNGO, LINDSEY R; NEW KENSINGTON, PA; KISKI AREA HS; (SR); Hi Hnr Roll; Hnr Roll; Perf Att; Comm Volntr; Chess; Chrch Yth Grp; Drma Clb; Key Club; Mus Clb; SADD; French Clb; Chr; SP/M/VS; Swg Chr; Chrldg (V); Track (V); Lit Mag (R); Sch Ppr (R); Yrbk (R); Editor and Historian of Key Club; Varsity Winter Track; Marketing; Advertising; Cannon U

BRUNNER, RENEE; RIDGWAY, PA; RIDGWAY AREA HS; (JR); Hi Hnr Roll; Hnr Roll; WWAHSS; Peer Tut/Med; Emplmnt; Prom Com; Sccr (J L); Track (J); Elementary Education; Edinboro U; Saint Vincent College

BRUNSWICK-SIMMONS, PHILLIP; UPPER DARBY, PA; UPPER DARBY HS; (JR); Hnr Roll; Perf Att; Prom Com; Stu Cncl (R); Sch Ppr (E); Royal Registry; Culinary Arts; The Restaurant-School-Walnut Hill College

BRUSH, LYNNEA; HALLSTEAD, PA; BLUE RIDGE HS; (FR); Hi Hnr Roll; WWAHSS; Chrch Yth Grp; Bnd; Ch Chr; Mch Bnd; Pep Bnd; Big Brothers / Big Sisters; Forensics Science; Entomology; Penn State; Princeton U

BRYANT, J'RHON S E; UPPER DARBY, PA; UPPER DARBY HS; (JR); Perf Att; Chrch Yth Grp; Ch Chr; Jeffery Weatherington Award; Teaching; Cooking; Ohio State U

BRYANT-MC CALL, MELODY L; PHILADELPHIA, PA; DOBBINS VOC-TECH HS; (JR); Hnr Roll; Perf Att; Comm Volntr; Peer Tut/Med; Photog; Sccr (V); Vllyball (V); 11th Grade Perfect Attendance; First Graduating Class of Stepping Stone Award; Digital Media Production; Teaching; Community College of Philadelphia

BRYSON, KATIE; NORRISTOWN, PA; KENNEDY-KENRICK CATHOLIC HS; (FR); Hnr Roll; Perf Att; Bnd; Stg Cre; Music; English

BUCCAFURI, CORINNA P; GLENSIDE, PA; ABINGTON SR HS; (SO); Ctznshp Aw; F Lan Hn Soc; Hi Hnr Roll; Hnr Roll; Nat Hon Sy; Pres Sch; Comm Volntr; Drma Clb; Key Club; Stg Cre; Chrldg (L); Lit Mag (R); Veterinarian; Biology Degree; U of Pennsylvania; Cornell U

BUCHAN, BRIANNE; PARKHILL, PA; CONEMAUGH VALLEY JR/SR HS; (JR); Hnr Roll; Nat Hon Sy; St of Mnth; WWAHSS; Outdrs Clb; Pep Squd; Photog; Spanish Clb; Chrldg (V L); PP Ftbl (V); Vllyball (V L); Stu Cncl (R); Sch Ppr (E, R); Yrbk (P); Elementary Education; Penn State; Indiana U of Pennsylvania

BUCHKO, CHELSEA; MCKEESPORT, PA; MC KEESPORT AREA HS; (SO); DAR; Hnr Roll; Perf Att; Sci Fairs; St of Mnth; Comm Volntr; Emplmnt; Orch; SP/M/VS; Tennis (V); Stu Cncl (R); EFACC Accompanist; Skiing; Forensic Scientist; Profession Musician

BUCHMAN, JUSTINE; SAYLORSBURG, PA; PLEASANT VALLEY HS; (SR); Hi Hnr Roll; Nat Hon Sy; Otst Ac Ach Awd; WWAHSS; Comm Volntr; Spec Olymp Vol; Emplmnt; Key Club; Mth Clb/Tm; 3rd Highest Average - Sophomore Year; Engineering; U of Pittsburgh

BUCHOLZ, WILLIAM; JAMESTOWN, PA; JAMESTOWN AREA SD HS; (FR); Hi Hnr Roll; Otst Ac Ach Awd; Comm Volntr; Bsball (J); Wrstlg (J); Stu Cncl (R); Medical; Engineering; Pennsylvania State U; Pittsburgh U

BUCKLEY, ANDREW T; BENSALEM, PA; BENSALEM HS; (JR); Hnr Roll; Hab For Humty Volntr; Ftball; Medical Technology; Radiology; Temple U; Penn State U

BUCKLEY, NICOLE; FRANKLIN, PA; ROCKY GROVE JR/SR HS; (SO); Hi Hnr Roll; Hnr Roll; Nat Hon Sy; WWAHSS; Comm Volntr; Chrch Yth Grp; Chrldg (V L); Cr Ctry (J); Scr Kpr (V); Track (J); CR (R); Yrbk (P); Grove City College

BUCKLEY JR, MICHAEL J; UPPER DARBY, PA; UPPER DARBY HS; (JR); Hi Hnr Roll; Perf Att; Peer Tut/Med; Spec Olymp Vol; Emplmnt; FBLA; Mar Art; Wt Lftg; Accounting; Law Enforcement; West Chester U; Penn State U

BUESINK, MICHAEL L; NORTH EAST, PA; NORTH EAST HS; (JR); Hnr Roll; WWAHSS; Biology Clb; Chrch Yth Grp; Emplmnt; Bsball (V L); Bskball (V L); Golf (V L); Stu Cncl (R); Ecology Club; AFS; Sports Medicine; Golf Course Management; Penn State U, U Park; Purdue U, West Lafayette

BUI, VICTORIA; HARRISBURG, PA; CTRL DAUPHIN HS; (FR); Hnr Roll; St of Mnth; Comm Volntr; Chr; Stu Cncl (R); Sch Ppr (R); Yrbk (R); Legal Studies & Business Management; International Relations

BULETZA, COREY J; ST CLAIR, PA; POTTSVILLE AREA HS; (SO); Hi Hnr Roll; Perf Att; WWAHSS; Key Club; SADD; Spanish Clb; Bsball (VJ L); Bskball (VJ L); Ftball (VJ L); Physical Therapy; Pharmacology

BULLER, MELANIE B; MARCUS HOOK, PA; THE CHRISTIAN AC; (JR); Hi Hnr Roll; MVP; Pres Ac Ftns Aw; Bskball (V CL); Fld Hky (V L); Sftball (V L); Stu Cncl (R); CR (R); Varsity Basketball Team Captain; Journalism; Physical Therapy; Temple U; New York U

BURDGE, SAMANTHA; EAST WATERFORD, PA; JUNIATA CTY SD; (JR); Hnr Roll; Nat Hon Sy; WWAHSS; Comm Volntr; Drma Clb; Lib Aide; Pep Squd; Prom Com; Tech Clb; Bnd; Mch Bnd; Orch; Pep Bnd; 3 Poems Published with 2 Editor's Choice Awards; 2nd Place in Art Show At the Juniata County Fair; Psychology; Art Therapy; Marywood U; Arcadia U

BURESH, BETH L; PITTSBURGH, PA; NORTH ALLEGHENY HS; (FR); Hnr Roll; Nat Hon Sy; Chrch Yth Grp; Dbte Team; Key Club; NtlFrnscLg; Bnd; Stu Cncl (S); National Junior Honor Society

BURFORD, LAUREN; PARKESBURG, PA; COOTESVILLE AREA SR HS; (SO); Ctznshp Aw; Hnr Roll; Sci Fairs; St of Mnth; ArtClub; DARE; Lttrmn Clb; Dnce; Drm Mjr; Mch Bnd; SP/M/VS; Tennis (V); Science Award; Art Award; Psychology; Nursing; U of Delaware; Millersville U

BURGE, DAVID; MCKEESPORT, PA; MC KEESPORT AREA SD; (FR); Ctznshp Aw; Hnr Roll; Nat Hon Sy; Otst Ac Ach Awd; Sci Fairs; WWAHSS; Yth Ldrshp Prog; Comm Volntr; Chrch Yth Grp; DARE; Drma Clb; Emplmnt; Fr of Library; Lib Aide; Mus Clb; Off Aide; Acpl Chr; Chr; Ch Chr; SP/M/VS; Bskball (J); Ftball; Adv Cncl (V); Stu Cncl (R); Sch Ppr (R); Pastor/Case Masters Divinity; Masters American Government; Lancaster Bible College; Penn State U

BURGER, JENNIFER L; SEWICKLEY, PA; QUAKER VALLEY HS; (SO); Hi Hnr Roll; MVP; Pres Ac Ftns Aw; Chrch Yth Grp; Emplmnt; Key Club; French Clb; Chr; Swmg (V L); Tennis (V); Vllyball (V CL); Lifeguard; Red Cross Certification; Marine Biology; Bucknell U; Dennison U

BURGESS, ALEXANDRA; GREENCASTLE, PA; SHALOM CHRISTIAN AC; (SO); 4H Awd; Hnr Roll; Comm Volntr; 4-H; Chrch Yth Grp; Drma Clb; Emplmnt; Chr; SP/M/VS; Hsbk Rdg (L); Sccr (V); Vllyball (J); Graphic Design; Art / Physical Education; Covenant College; Barton College

BURGESS, LINDSAY M; MALVERN, PA; GREAT VALLEY HS; (JR); Hi Hnr Roll; Comm Volntr; ArtClub; Emplmnt; Photog; Chr; Lit Mag; Distinguished Honors; Journalism; Photography; Iowa College; Adelphi U

BURGOS, DANNY R; CHESTER, PA; CHESTER HS; (SO); Video Games Design; Programmer; Art Institute of Philadelphia

BURK, SARA J; BETHLEHEM, PA; LIBERTY HS; (SR); Hnr Roll; Nat Hon Sy; Comm Volntr; Spec Olymp Vol; Chrch Yth Grp; Emplmnt; SADD; Bnd; Swmg (V); Track (V L); Academic Achievement Award; Physical Education/Therapy; Business (Management); Springfield College; West Chester U

BURKHART, BRITTANY; SUNBURY, PA; SHIRELLAMY SD; (SO); ArtClub; FBLA; Fld Hky (VJ); National Art Honor Society; FBLA; Nursing School

BURNS, CARLY; CRANBERRY TWP, PA; SENECA VALLEY SHS; (SO); Hi Hnr Roll; WWAHSS; Comm Volntr; Hosp Aide; Chrch Yth Grp; Emplmnt; Key Club; SADD; Stg Cre; Tennis (J); Key Club Secretary & VP; SADD Officer; Fashion; Mathematics Related Fields; U of Pittsburgh; Kent State

BURNS, JAMES P; GLENOLDEN, PA; MONSIGNOR BONNER HS; (JR); 4H Awd; Sci Fairs; St of Mnth; Comm Volntr; Peer Tut/Med; 4-H; Biology Clb; Chrch Yth Grp; DARE; Emplmnt; Bsball (V); Bskball (V); Ftball (J); Education; Business; Penn State U; West Chester U

BURNSWORTH, KATHRINE; NEMACOLIN, PA; CARMICHAELS AREA JR/SR HS; (SO); Hi Hnr Roll; Hnr Roll; ArtClub; Fr of Library; Lib Aide; Photog; French Clb; Acpl Chr; Chr; Swg Chr; Sch Ppr (P); Yrbk (P); Photo Journalism; Commercial Photography; Art Institute of Philadelphia; Art Institute of Pittsburgh

BURNWORTH, LINDSEY L; FINLEYVILLE, PA; RINGGOLD SD; (FR); Hi Hnr Roll; Comm Volntr; Off Aide; SADD; Chrldg (V); Stu Cncl (R); Interact Club; Ski Club; Law; Psychology; Stanford U; U of Pittsburgh

BURRIS, KELSI; WERNERSVILLE, PA; CONRAD WEISER HS; (JR); Ctznshp Aw; Hi Hnr Roll; Nat Hon Sy; Sci Fairs; St of Mnth; Comm Volntr; Peer Tut/Med; ArtClub; Key Club; Prom Com; Svce Clb; Tchrs Aide; President of Algorithmic Club; President of Television Production Club; Video Production/Cinema; Photography; Temple U; U of Pittsburgh

BURROWS, BRIAN J; BLOOMSBURG, PA; CTRL COLUMBIA HS; (SR); Ctznshp Aw; Hnr Roll; Pres Sch; WWAHSS; Yth Ldrshp Prog; Comm Volntr; Peer Tut/Med; Chrch Yth Grp; Cmptr Clb; Emplmnt; FBLA; HO'Br Yth Ldrshp; German Clb; SP/M/VS; Golf (J); Skiing; Sccr (J); Track (J); Wrstlg (V); PA Governor's School for the Arts - Acting; National Miracle Child-Children's Miracle Network - 2004; Political Science; Communications & Rhetorical Studies; Syracuse U

BURYKIN, LEV; ERIE, PA; FORT LEBOEUF SD; (JR); Hnr Roll; Nat Hon Sy; Emplmnt; Bskball; Ftball; Film/Cinematography; Criminal Justice; Edinboro U; Penn State U - Behrend

BUSH, ALISHA D; ERIE, PA; EAST HS; (JR); Hnr Roll; WWAHSS; Yth Ldrshp Prog; Chrch Yth Grp; Emplmnt; Ch Chr; School of Communications; Erie Meadville Partnership Program; Criminal Psychology; Education; Gannon U; Slippery Rock College

BUSH, KRISTAL; PHILADELPHIA, PA; IMHOTEP CHARTER HS; (SO); Hnr Roll; MVP; Nat Hon Sy; Perf Att; Sci Fairs; Sci/Math Olympn; St of Mnth; Comm Volntr; Peer Tut/Med; Ch Chr; Chrldg (V); PPSqd (V); Sch Ppr (R); Social Worker; Nurse

BUSH, SABRINA; CANTON, PA; CANTON HS; (JR); Hi Hnr Roll; Hnr Roll; St of Mnth; WWAHSS; Comm Volntr; Drma Clb; Emplmnt; Lttrmn Clb; Spanish Clb; SP/M/VS; Stg Cre; Chrldg (VJ L); Writing; Occupational Therapy; Pennsylvania State U; Kutztown U

BUSH, TIERA; PHILADELPHIA, PA; (SR); Hnr Roll; Perf Att; Sci Fairs; St of Mnth; Comm Volntr; Dnce; Community Service; Part-Time Job; Social Work; U of Penn; Lincoln U

BUTKOWSKI, CASSANDRA; BETHLEHEM, PA; LIBERTY HS; (SO); Hnr Roll; WWAHSS; Comm Volntr; Chr; Pre-Med; Temple U; U of Pennsylvania

BUTLER, BEN; DREXEL HILL, PA; UPPER DARBY HS; (JR); Hi Hnr Roll; Emplmnt; Business Law & Management; Business; Drexel U; West Chester U

BUTLER, BRETT C; CATASAUQUA, PA; CATASAUQUA AREA SD; (SR); Hnr Roll; Jr Rot; MVP; WWAHSS; Comm Volntr; Emplmnt; Jr Ach; Prom Com; Vsity Clb; Bskball (J); Sccr (V CL); Track (V L); Stu Cncl (R); 1st Team Colonial League-Soccer; 1st Team Morning Call-All Area Soccer; Secondary Education / History; Wesley College

BUTLER JR, RANDY J.; ALLENTOWN, PA; WILLIAM ALLEN HS; (FR); Hnr Roll; Nat Hon Sy; Otst Ac Ach Awd; St of Mnth; Bnd; Mch Bnd; Bsball (J); Allentown Police Academy 6 Wks., Participated in the Upward Bound Program And Won Several Awards; Great Program Completion 8-15-03, Participated in the Friend Inc. Program; Baseball Player; Business Manager; Kutztown U College; Muhlenberg U College

BUTTERBAUGH, TYLER; CASSANDRA, PA; ADMIRAL PEARY AVTS; (JR); Hnr Roll; Nat Hon Sy; Perf Att; WWAHSS; Comm Volntr; Voc Ind Clb Am; Automotive Technology - Associate's Degree; Wyo Tech

BUTTERS, JILLIAN; MORRIS, PA; LIBERTY JR SR HS; (SO); 4H Awd; Hi Hnr Roll; Hnr Roll; Perf Att; Comm Volntr; Spec Olymp Vol; 4-H; Chrch Yth Grp; Key Club; Bnd; Ch Chr; Mch Bnd; SP/M/VS; Vllyball (VJC)

BUTTON, AMANDA N; HALLSTEAD, PA; BLUE RIDGE HS; (FR); Hi Hnr Roll; Chrch Yth Grp; SADD; Bnd; Mch Bnd; Bskball (J); Sftball (J); Art; Art Institute Philadelphia

BUZBY, STEVE; CAMP HILL, PA; CAMP HILL SD; (SO); Hnr Roll; Bskball (J); Golf (V L); Track (V); CR (R)

Butkowski, Cassandra
Liberty HS
Bethlehem, PA

Burk, Sara J
Liberty HS
Bethlehem, PA

Burdge, Samantha
Juniata Cty SD
East Waterford, PA

Buckley Jr, Michael J
Upper Darby HS
Upper Darby, PA

Buccafuri, Corinna P
Abington SR HS
Glenside, PA

Buchan, Brianne
Conemaugh Valley JR/SR HS
Parkhill, PA

Burgess, Alexandra
Shalom Christian AC
Greencastle, PA

Burrows, Brian J
Central Columbia HS
Bloomsburg, PA

Butler Jr, Randy J.
William Allen HS
Allentown, PA

BYE, ELEANOR T; HOLICONG, PA; CTRL BUCKS HS EAST; (SO); Ctznshp Aw; Hi Hnr Roll; Hnr Roll; Nat Hon Sy; Pres Ac Ftns Aw; Comm Volntr; DARE; Emplmnt; Photog; Spanish Clb; Bnd; Hsbk Rdg; Equestrian Dressage; Equestrian Eventing; Fine Arts; Graphic Arts; Savannah College of Arts; Penn State U

CABRERA, LIZ B; ALLENTOWN, PA; L.E. DIERUFF HS; (JR); Ctznshp Aw; F Lan Hn Soc; Hi Hnr Roll; Hnr Roll; Otst Ac Ach Awd; WWAHSS; Peer Tut/Med; Chrch Yth Grp; Key Club; Spanish Clb; Chr; Ch Chr; Cl Off (V); Spanish Honors Society

CACCO, TERESA M; APOLLO, PA; KISKI AREA HS; (SR); Hi Hnr Roll; Nat Hon Sy; St of Mnth; WWAHSS; Comm Volntr; Peer Tut/Med; Chrch Yth Grp; Key Club; Cr Ctry (V C); Track (V C); Engineer; Chemist; U of Pittsburgh; Penn State U

CAFFERY, STEPHANIE; COLLEGEVILLE, PA; KENNEDY KENRICK CHS; (FR); Hi Hnr Roll; Hnr Roll; Perf Att; Sci Fairs; St of Mnth; Comm Volntr; Hab For Humty Volntr; Svce Clb; Spanish Clb; Sch Ppr (R); UCLA; Notre Dame

CAIRNS, ANGELA; POTTSVILLE, PA; POTTSVILLE AREA HS; (SO); Hi Hnr Roll; WWAHSS; Peer Tut/Med; Key Club; SADD; Spanish Clb; Bnd; Jzz Bnd; Mch Bnd; Tennis (V L); Elementary Education

CALABRESE, MICHELLE; GIBSONIA, PA; PINE-RICHLAND HS; (FR); Ctznshp Aw; DAR; Hi Hnr Roll; Comm Volntr; Peer Tut/Med; Key Club; GAA (VJ); Sccr (VJ); Adv Cncl (R); Cl Off (V, T); Stu Cncl (R); CR (R); Science Department Award; Key Communicators; Biomedical Engineering; Genetics; Duke U; U of Notre Dame

CALAFATI, LISA M; MERTZTOWN, PA; BRANDYWINE HEIGHTS AREA HS; (SO); Hi Hnr Roll; Hnr Roll; WWAHSS; Comm Volntr; Key Club; Chr; Vllyball (J); Nursing / Psychiatrics; Cedar Crest College

CALDWELL, CECELEY; IRWIN, PA; MC KEESPORT AREA SD; (FR); Ctznshp Aw; Hnr Roll; Pres Ac Ftns Aw; Comm Volntr; Chrldg (VJ); Business; Journalism; Point Park College; Penn State U

CALFO, RYAN; PITTSBURGH, PA; PITTSBURGH SD CAREER CONNECTIONS CHARTER HS; MS; Ctznshp Aw; Hi Hnr Roll; Hnr Roll; MVP; Perf Att; St of Mnth; Peer Tut/Med; Chrch Yth Grp; Cmptr Clb; DARE; Lib Aide; Wdwrkg Clb; Bsball (J); Sccr (J); Sftball (J); Physics Degree

CALISE, LOUIS; DREXEL HILL, PA; UPPER DARBY HS; (SO); Hi Hnr Roll; Hnr Roll; Otst Ac Ach Awd; Pres Sch; St of Mnth; Comm Volntr; Peer Tut/Med; Emplmnt; Bskball (J); Lcrsse (J); Tennis (J); Track; Stu Cncl (S); Member of Young Life Youth Group; Business & Sports; Law School; Villanova U; Penn State Main Campus

CALLAHAN, RYAN P; POTTSTOWN, PA; POTTSGROVE SR HS; (SO); Ctznshp Aw; Gov Hnr Prg; Hi Hnr Roll; Hnr Roll; Otst Ac Ach Awd; St of Mnth; DARE; Emplmnt; Quiz Bowl; Scouts; Honors Programs; Medical Doctor; Plastic Surgeon; Penn State U; West Chester U

CALLENDER, JARON M; NEW KENSINGTON, PA; VALLEY HS; (FR); Ctznshp Aw; Nat Hon Sy; Nat Mrt Sch Recip; Comm Volntr; Hosp Aide; Red Cr Aide; Drma Clb; Mus Clb; Scouts; Bnd; Chr; Jzz Bnd; SP/M/VS; Bskball (V); Sccr (V); Track (V); Lit Mag (R); Sch Ppr (E, R); Yrbk (R); Computer Tech; Sports or Journalism; Penn State U; St Vincent

CAMPANA, DANIEL; GREENVILLE, PA; REYNOLDS HS; (JR); Hi Hnr Roll; Nat Hon Sy; St of Mnth; WWAHSS; Peer Tut/Med; Key Club; Off Aide; Distinguished Key Club Vice President; High Honor Roll; Pharmacy; Duquesne U

CAMPBELL, BRYAN S; BETHLEHEM, PA; BETHLEHEM CATHOLIC HS; (FR); Hnr Roll; MVP; Perf Att; Comm Volntr; Biology Clb; Chrch Yth Grp; Key Club; Quiz Bowl; Schol Bwl; Spanish Clb; SP/M/VS; Bsball (J); Bskball (J); CR (T); Sch Ppr (R); Yrbk (R); Biology; Engineering; DeSales U; Boston College

CAMPBELL, EMILY; GREENSBURG, PA; GREENSBURG SALEM HS; (SR); All Am Sch; Hi Hnr Roll; Hnr Roll; Nat Hon Sy; WWAHSS; Comm Volntr; Spec Olymp Vol; Emplmnt; NtlFrnscLg; Photog; Spch Team; Mch Bnd; Stg Cre; Swmg (V L); Sch Ppr (E, R); Mock Trial State Champions; Marketing; Journalism; Duquesne U

CAMPBELL, JESSICA L; BEAVER FALLS, PA; BEAVER FALLS HS; (FR); Hnr Roll; Peer Tut/Med; Chrch Yth Grp; DARE; Key Club; Spanish Clb; Sftball (J); Vllyball (J); Elementary Education; Child Psychology; U of Pittsburgh; Texas Tech

CAMPBELL, KHADIJAH A; PHILADELPHIA, PA; FRANKLIN LEARNING CTR; (SR); Hi Hnr Roll; Hnr Roll; MVP; WWAHSS; Comm Volntr; Red Cr Aide; SP/M/VS; Bskball (V C); Cr Ctry (V C); Sftball (V); Track (V); Sch Ppr (E); Sports Management; Sports Medicine

CAMPBELL, NICOLE; COATESVILLE, PA; COATESVILLE AREA SR HS; (JR); Hnr Roll; Nat Hon Sy; Otst Ac Ach Awd; Comm Volntr; Peer Tut/Med; Red Cr Aide; Chrch Yth Grp; Mus Clb; Svce Clb; Acpl Chr; Bnd; Chr; Ch Chr; Stu Cncl (R); Leo Club / Jr Lions Club; Flute Soloist and Section Leader; Music Education; Music Therapy; West Chester U; U of Massachusetts Amherst

CANGIALOSI, MELISSA; KUNKLETOWN, PA; PLEASANT VALLEY HS; (SO); Hi Hnr Roll; Perf Att; WWAHSS; Spec Olymp Vol; Chrch Yth Grp; Key Club; Bnd; Ch Chr; Mch Bnd; SP/M/VS; Key Club Vice President; Mathematics; Secondary Education; Marywood U; College of St Rose

CANTAMAGLIA, ANTONIO D; DOUGLASSVILLE, PA; DANIEL BOONE AREA HS; (SR); WWAHSS; Yth Ldrshp Prog; Jr Ach; Key Club; Spanish Clb; Bnd; Jzz Bnd; SP/M/VS; Stg Cre; Biology; Shippensburg U

CAPLINGER, DEREK; FOGELSVILLE, PA; NORTHWESTERN LEHIGH HS; (FR); Hi Hnr Roll; Hnr Roll; Track (J); Veterinarian

CAPPA, GREGORY M; READING, PA; EXETER TWP SR HS; (JR); Hnr Roll; Nat Hon Sy; Sci/Math Olympn; Comm Volntr; Mth Clb/Tm; Quiz Bowl; Sci Clb; Scouts; German Clb; Bnd; Jzz Bnd; Mch Bnd; Vllyball (V); Actuary; Mathematics; Villanova U; Johns Hopkins U

CAPUTA III, THOMAS J; BRISTOL, PA; BUCKS CTY TECH HS; (SR); Hnr Roll; District VICA Winner; VICA State Competitor; Network Systems Administrator; Pennsylvania College of Technology

CARABALLO, EMMANUEL; READING, PA; READING HS; (SO); Emplmnt; ROTC; Acpl Chr; Bnd; Chr; Mch Bnd; Teacher- Volunteer in School; Music Ed and Composition; Teaching Degree; West Chester U; Indiana U Pennsylvania

CARDINELLA, S ANTHONY; KUNKLETOWN, PA; PLEASANT VALLEY HS; Hi Hnr Roll; Hnr Roll; WWAHSS; Comm Volntr; Drma Clb; Emplmnt; JSA; Key Club; SP/M/VS; Mar Art; Skiing; Sccr; Junior States of America; World History Teacher; Kutztown U; Moravian U

CARDONE, KAITLYN M; SCRANTON, PA; DUNMORE SD; (MS); Hi Hnr Roll; Nat Hon Sy; Perf Att; St of Mnth; Bnd; Chr; Jzz Bnd; Mch Bnd; Chrldg (J); Music Education; Elementary Education; Mansfield U; Millersville U

CARIAS, PRISCILA; READING, PA; READING SR HS; (SR); Comm Volntr; Peer Tut/Med; Red Cr Aide; Dnce; Business; Banking / Accounting; Millersville U Pennsylvania; Reading Area Community Center

CARLSON, BRIAN J; WAYNESBORO, PA; WAYNESBORO AREA SR HS; (SR); Hi Hnr Roll; Hnr Roll; Perf Att; St of Mnth; WWAHSS; Comm Volntr; Spec Olymp Vol; Chess; Chrch Yth Grp; Emplmnt; Key Club; Ftball (J); Track (J); EMT, National Technical Honor Society; Police Officer; EMT; Hagerstown Community College

CARMASINE, ALEX; YARDLEY, PA; PENNSBURY HS EAST; (JR); Hi Hnr Roll; Hnr Roll; Otst Ac Ach Awd; Pres Sch; St of Mnth; Comm Volntr; ArtClub; Chrch Yth Grp; Emplmnt; Stg Cre; Track (VJ); Performing Arts-Classical Pianist; Volunteer Camp Counselor for Pennsbury Honor Historical Museum, Johns Hopkins Cty Talent Search, Teach Piano to 4 Young Children; Music Education and Performance

CARMICHAEL, DEJA; ERIE, PA; WILSON MS; (MS); Hnr Roll; Drma Clb; Scouts; Wdwrkg Clb; Bnd; Bskball; Vllyball; Medical Doctor; Business

CARMICHAEL, JANIECE; UPPER DARBY, PA; UPPER DARBY HS; (JR); Hnr Roll; Comm Volntr; Peer Tut/Med; Spec Olymp Vol; Emplmnt; Chr; Stu Cncl (R); CR (R); Poet of the Month (From International Society of Poets); Elementary Education; Nursing; Arcadia U; Cabrini College

CARNEY, KRISTINA; MEDIA, PA; CARDINAL O'HARA HS; (SO); Hnr Roll; Perf Att; Chess; Chrch Yth Grp; Emplmnt; Off Aide; Bnd; Mch Bnd; SP/M/VS; Stg Cre; Fld Hky (V); Lcrsse (VJ); Yrbk (E, P); Respect Life Club; Costume Club; Forensic Science; Set Design; Long Island U; Marymount U

CARNS, JADE; CHARLEROI, PA; CHARLEROI AREA HS; (SO); Hi Hnr Roll; Hnr Roll; Otst Ac Ach Awd; Peer Tut/Med; FBLA; Off Aide; Pep Squd; SADD; Spanish Clb; Bnd; Bskball (VJ); Chrldg (J); Gmnstcs (V); Scr Kpr (VJ); Stu Cncl (R); Criminal Justice / Law; Penn State U; Pittsburgh U

CARP, LINDA M; LANSDALE, PA; NORTH PENN HS; (JR); Hi Hnr Roll; Hnr Roll; Nat Hon Sy; WWAHSS; Yth Ldrshp Prog; Comm Volntr; Spec Olymp Vol; Emplmnt; Key Club; NYLC; Chrldg (V C); PP Ftbl; President of Teen Leaders Club; Penn State U

CARPENTER, KAITLYN J; ALBURTIS, PA; ALLENTOWN CTRL CATHOLIC HS; (JR); Hi Hnr Roll; Comm Volntr; Pep Squd; Tennis (V CL); Tennis District Champion - Singles 2002; PA State Doubles 3rd Place - 2004; Nurse Anesthetist - Nursing; Penn State; William & Mary College

CARR, ANGELICA; POINT MARION, PA; ALBERT GALLATIN SR HS; (FR); ROTC; Bnd; Clr Grd; Drl Tm; Drm Mjr; Mch Bnd; Won the Fire Prevention Essay Contest / Published in Creative Communication Book / 2004; Nominated / Attending Art Instruction School; Art and or Music / Teacher; Join the Military Specializing in Mortuary Services; West Virginia U

CARR, DANIELLE; BENSALEM, PA; BENSALEM HS; (JR); Hnr Roll; Sci Fairs; Comm Volntr; Peer Tut/Med; Chrch Yth Grp; Emplmnt; Off Aide; Prom Com; Scouts; Tchrs Aide; Chrldg (J); Gmnstcs (J); PP Ftbl (J); Community Service - Church; Volunteer Cheerleading Contest Summer Rec Program; RN / Nursing BA; Pharmacy; Frankford Hosp. School of Nursing; Bucks County Comm College

CARR, MARIETTA R; MECHANICSBURG, PA; BISHOP MC DEVITT HS; (SR); Hi Hnr Roll; Nat Hon Sy; Nat Mrt LOC; WWAHSS; Comm Volntr; NYLC; Svce Clb; Spanish Clb; Chr; Clr Grd; Flg Crps; Yrbk (E); History; Museum Studies; Northeastern U; St Michael's College

CARRINGTON, SAPPHIRE; ALLENTOWN, PA; WILLIAM ALLEN HS; (JR); Hnr Roll; WWAHSS; Comm Volntr; Chrch Yth Grp; Drma Clb; Emplmnt; Scouts; Acpl Chr; Chr; SP/M/VS; Sccr (J); 2 Time Regional Chorus Member; Acceptance Into Who's Who America; Elementary Education PhD; Psychology PhD; Indiana Wesleyan U; Kutztown U

CARROLL, ALYSHA N; GARDNERS, PA; ADAMS CTY CHRISTIAN AC; (SO); Hi Hnr Roll; Hnr Roll; Sci Fairs; St of Mnth; Chrch Yth Grp; Mus Clb; Bnd; Stu Cncl (R); Sch Ppr (E); Yrbk (E); Fine Arts Competition-Superior Rating in Poetry, Short Story, Sign Language, Human Video; Writing; Psychology; York College; Wilson College

CARROLL, CHRISTOPHER T; NEW EAGLE, PA; RINGGOLD SD; (FR); Hi Hnr Roll; Otst Ac Ach Awd; St of Mnth; Comm Volntr; Chrch Yth Grp; Scouts; Chr; 2nd Place - American Legion Award; Principal Role in "Beauty & the Beast"; Chiropractor; Ophthalmologist

CARROZZA, ANTHONY J; READING, PA; READING HS; (JR); Hi Hnr Roll; Nat Hon Sy; Comm Volntr; Jr Cls League; Cr Ctry (V); Track (V); RHS Chemistry Achievement Award; Teaching Math; Teaching Chemistry; Kutztown U

CARTER, CHELSEA; COLLEGEVILLE, PA; METHACTON HS; (SO); Hi Hnr Roll; WWAHSS; Comm Volntr; Key Club; Lib Aide; NYLC; Tchrs Aide; Spanish Clb; CR (R); Job at Retirement Community; Local Church Volunteer; Medical Field; Chemistry Engineering; Princeton U; Georgetown U

CARTER, KAMIA L; PHILADELPHIA, PA; CARDINAL DOUGHERTY HS; (SR); All Am Sch; Hnr Roll; Nat Hon Sy; Nat Ldrshp Svc; Nat Mrt Fin; Otst Ac Ach Awd; Perf Att; St of Mnth; Valdctrian; WWAHSS; Comm Volntr; Hab For Humty Volntr; Peer Tut/Med; Emplmnt; FTA; Off Aide; Prom Com; Stu Cncl (R); Psychology; Arcadia U; Neumann College

CARTER, MELANIE; MC KEESPORT, PA; MC KEESPORT AREA SD; (JR); Hnr Roll; St of Mnth; WWAHSS; Comm Volntr; DARE; Lib Aide; Ch Chr; Bskball (J); Top of the Shop Award; Master's Degree Psychology; Waynesburg College; U of North Carolina Chapel Hill

CARTER, THOMAS D; GLENSHAW, PA; SHALER AREA HS; (JR); Ctznshp Aw; Hnr Roll; MVP; Nat Hon Sy; Pres Ac Ftns Aw; Comm Volntr; DARE; Vsity Clb; Bsball (V L); Cr Ctry (V CL); Ice Hky (V CL); Stu Cncl (P, R); Nominee for Outstanding Young Citizens Award; Criminal Justice

CARTWRIGHT, CHRISTOPHER; HARRISBURG, PA; CTRL DAUPHIN HS; (SR); Hi Hnr Roll; Nat Hon Sy; Perf Att; WWAHSS; Comm Volntr; Peer Tut/Med; Spec Olymp Vol; Chrch Yth Grp; Dbte Team; Mth Clb/Tm; Scouts; German Clb; Sccr (VJ); Rank of First Class Boy Scout; National Honor Society Member; Business / Education; Sports Medicine; Bucknell U; Lehigh U

CARUGATI, CHRISTINE; BEAVER, PA; BEAVER AREA HS; (SO); Hi Hnr Roll; Comm Volntr; Spanish Clb; SP/M/VS; Bskball; Cl Off (P); Stu Cncl (R); International Business; U of Pittsburgh; Carnegie Mellon

CARUGATI, KATI; BEAVER, PA; BEAVER AREA HS; (SR); Hi Hnr Roll; WWAHSS; Hab For Humty Volntr; Key Club; Bskball; Sch Ppr (E, R); English & Business; U of Pittsburgh

CASIELLO, CAITLIN; GILLETT, PA; NOTRE DAME HS; (SO); Hi Hnr Roll; USAA; WWAHSS; Dbte Team; Key Club; Mth Clb/Tm; Mod UN; Sch Ppr (E, R); English-Writing; Law/Political Science; Princeton U; Bryn Mawr College

CASSELBURY, CASANDRA; MESHOPPEN, PA; ELK LAKE SCH; (FR); 4H Awd; Hnr Roll; WWAHSS; 4-H; Key Club; SADD; Cl Off (T); Ski Club Not a Team; Nursing; Education; Kentucky State U; Penn State U

CASSELLE, ASHLEY D; PHILADELPHIA, PA; (SR); Hnr Roll; Nat Hon Sy; Perf Att; WWAHSS; Peer Tut/Med; Emplmnt; Off Aide; Dnce; Stu Cncl (R); CR (R); Biochemistry; Temple U; U of the Sciences

CASSETORI, MARY ELENA; JESSUP, PA; VALLEY VIEW HS; (SO); 4H Awd; Hi Hnr Roll; Hnr Roll; 4-H; Dnce; Chrldg (V); Cr Ctry (J); Hsbk Rdg (J); Track (J); Vllyball (V); Veterinarian; U of Scranton; Penn State - Main Campus

CASTAGNERO, MATTHEW S; PITCAIRN, PA; GATEWAY SD; (SO); Hi Hnr Roll; Hnr Roll; Comm Volntr; Peer Tut/Med; SADD; Dvng (V); Ftball (J); Track (V); Volunteer Pitcairn Camp B Counselor; Church Volunteer; Sports Management; Communication; Penn State U; Duke U

Carroll, Alysha N
Adams Cty Christian AC
Gardners, PA

Carney, Kristina
Cardinal O'Hara HS
Media, PA

Calafati, Lisa M
Brandywine Heights Area HS
Mertztown, PA

Calise, Louis
Upper Darby HS
Drexel Hill, PA

Carrozza, Anthony J
Reading HS
Reading, PA

CASTILLO, RANDY D; BETHLEHEM, PA; BETHLEHEM AREA VOC TECH SCH; (FR); Hnr Roll; Art; Auto Technician

CASTON, LATOYA S; PHILADELPHIA, PA; PHILADELPHIA ELECTRICAL & TECH CHARTER HS; (JR); Hi Hnr Roll; Hnr Roll; Nat Hon Sy; Otst Ac Ach Awd; Perf Att; Comm Volntr; Chrch Yth Grp; Prom Com; SP/M/VS; Chrldg; Stu Cncl (P); Sign Language; Science; Education; Howard U; Delaware State College

CATALANO, HELENANN; ALBRIGHTSVILLE, PA; CARBON CTY AVTS; (JR); Hi Hnr Roll; Hnr Roll; Nat Mrt Fin; Nat Mrt LOC; Otst Ac Ach Awd; Sci Fairs; St of Mnth; DARE; DECA; SADD; Chr; SP/M/VS; Yrbk (E); East Stroudsburg Literary Essay Winner; 3rd Place DECA State Competition 2005; Marketing; Interior Design; Notre Dame U; East Stroudsburg U

CEBULSKI JR, GERARD L; BLAKESLEE, PA; PLEASANT VALLEY HS; (SO); Hi Hnr Roll; Hnr Roll; Comm Volntr; Chess; Chrch Yth Grp; DARE; Dbte Team; Drma Clb; Emplmnt; Mus Clb; Scouts; Bnd; Chr; SP/M/VS; Stg Cre; Ftball (J); Skiing; Tennis (V); Track (J); Wt Lftg; Volunteered - Annual County Fair; Assisted Girl Scouts Leaders; Sports Medicine; Law Enforcement; Pennsylvania State U; U of North Carolina

CEDENO, WARMARIE; READING, PA; READING HS; (JR); Hnr Roll; St of Mnth; Comm Volntr; Dnce; HOSA Member; Nursing; Forensic Science; RACC

CENISIO, MICHAEL; KENNETT SQUARE, PA; CARDINAL O'HARA HS; (JR); Hnr Roll; MVP; Comm Volntr; Emplmnt; Ice Hky (V C); International Business; Pre Law; Boston College, MA; UNH, (U of New Hampshire)

CENTAR, RYAN; DUNCANSVILLE, PA; BISHOP GUILFOYLE HS; (SO); Hi Hnr Roll; WWAHSS; Comm Volntr; Chrch Yth Grp; Tennis (V); Black Belt in Tae-Kwon-Do; U of Pittsburgh; Notre Dame U

CERRO, NICOLE; MONROEVILLE, PA; GATEWAY SD; (SO); Hi Hnr Roll; Hnr Roll; Peer Tut/Med; ArtClub; Off Aide; Art Portfolio; Art Education; Slippery Rock U

CERULLO, KATIE; POTTSVILLE, PA; POTTSVILLE AREA HS; (SO); Hi Hnr Roll; Perf Att; Peer Tut/Med; Key Club; SADD; Spanish Clb; Stu Cncl (R); Biochemistry

CHA, KYU-SUN; BENSALEM, PA; BENSALEM TOWNSHIP SD; (SO); Hnr Roll; Perf Att; St of Mnth; Comm Volntr; Chrch Yth Grp; Schol Bwl; Ch Chr; Orch; Cr Ctry (V); Track (V); Piano Accompanist; Keyboard Player At Church; Health; Writing; Princeton U; Cornell U

CHAIN, KAYLIN; MT PLEASANT, PA; MT PLEASANT AREA HS; (SO); Hi Hnr Roll; MVP; Pres Ac Ftns Aw; WWAHSS; Comm Volntr; ArtClub; Lttrmn Clb; Vsity Clb; Ftball (V L); PP Ftbl (V); Sccr (V L); Track (V); Gamma Omega; NAHS; Business / Fashion Merchandising; Graphic / Fashion Design

CHALELA, DEAN; NEWTOWN, PA; COUNCIL ROCK HS NORTH; (SO); Hi Hnr Roll; Hnr Roll; Perf Att; Pres Ac Ftns Aw; Comm Volntr; P to P St Amb Prg; German Clb; Bsball (J); President of Operation Smile Club; Electrical Engineering; Economics; Florida State; Penn State

CHAMBERS, JOSH; VANDERBILT, PA; FAYETTE CTY AVTS; (SO); Hnr Roll; Chrch Yth Grp; Pastry Chef; Culinary Chef Teacher

CHAMBERS, KRISTINA; MIFFLINTOWN, PA; JUNIATA CTY SD; (JR); Hi Hnr Roll; Hnr Roll; Nat Hon Sy; Perf Att; WWAHSS; Hosp Aide; Spanish Clb; Fld Hky (VJC); Tennis (J); Indoor Field Hockey V, J; Sports Management; Sports Broadcasting/TV & Radio; York College; Penn State U

CHANDLER, IESHA; ERIE, PA; ERIE CITY SD; (FR); Hnr Roll; Comm Volntr; DARE; Pep Squd; Stu Cncl (S); To Become a Pediatrician; Nursing; Pediatrician; Gannon U

CHARLES, SHAWNAYIAH; PHILADELPHIA, PA; NORRIS S BARRATT MS; MS; Hnr Roll; Peer Tut/Med; Drl Tm; Chrldg (L); Yrbk; Pediatrician/Doctor; Basketball Player

CHASLER, JULIA K; MECHANICSBURG, PA; TRINITY HS; (SR); Hi Hnr Roll; Hnr Roll; Kwnis Aw; Nat Hon Sy; Pres Sch; Sci Fairs; WWAHSS; Yth Ldrshp Prog; Comm Volntr; Hab For Humty Volntr; Spec Olymp Vol; Chrch Yth Grp; DARE; Emplmnt; Fr of Library; Key Club; Lib Aide; NYLC; Prom Com; Chr; Stg Cre; Sch Ppr (R); Bible School Asst., Scholastic Writing Award; Captain of Team Trinity in the MS Walk 2 Yrs; Bachelor of Science in Psychology; PsyD; U of Pittsburgh

CHATTIN, HANNAH; KUTZTOWN, PA; THE KING'S AC; (FR); Hi Hnr Roll; Hnr Roll; Chrch Yth Grp; Bskball (VJ); Track (V); Honorable Mention At County Science Fair; 3rd Place At ACSI Arts Festival; Montana Wilderness School of the Bible

CHAU, KIM L; PHILADELPHIA, PA; BARTRAM HS; (SR); Comm Volntr; Hosp Aide

CHEA, DARRA; YORK, PA; YORK CTY SCH OF TECH; (JR); Hi Hnr Roll; Hnr Roll; Nat Hon Sy; Perf Att; Peer Tut/Med; Jr Ach; Mth Clb/Tm; Regional Math 24 Champion; State Math 24 Representative; Start My Own Business; Thaddeus Stevens

CHEN, LILI; GOULDSBORO, PA; NORTH POCONO HS; (JR); Hi Hnr Roll; Nat Hon Sy; Otst Ac Ach Awd; Perf Att; WWAHSS; Yth Ldrshp Prog; Comm Volntr; Dbte Team; Emplmnt; FBLA; Schol Bwl; Sci Clb; Chr; Clr Grd; Orch; Tennis (J); Won "Editor's Choice Award" At Poetry-Com; First Place At State Science Academy; Law; Business Administration; U of Pennsylvania; U of Chicago

CHEN, LILY; WEXFORD, PA; NORTH ALLEGHENY INT HS; (SO); Hnr Roll; Perf Att; WWAHSS; Comm Volntr; Hosp Aide; Peer Tut/Med; Dbte Team; Key Club; Mth Clb/Tm; NtlFrnscLg; Spch Team; Bnd; Mch Bnd; Adv Cncl (R); Cl Off (P); Stu Cncl (R); CR (P); National Junior Honor Society-Vice-President; School Board Representative; International Business; Business Management

CHEREWKA, MATTHEW; CAMP HILL, PA; TRINITY HS; (FR); Sci Fairs; WWAHSS; Comm Volntr; Chrch Yth Grp; Key Club; P to P St Amb Prg; Svce Clb; Latin Clb; Orch; Ftball (J); Lcrsse (V)

CHIAPPETTA, KAYLA E; BEAVER FALLS, PA; BIG BEAVER FALLS HS; (FR); Hnr Roll; St of Mnth; WWAHSS; Key Club; Off Aide; Spanish Clb; Key Club; Spanish Club

CHILDS, DAVINAH S; PHILADELPHIA, PA; CENTRAL HS; (JR); Hi Hnr Roll; Hnr Roll; Otst Ac Ach Awd; Pres Sch; Comm Volntr; Peer Tut/Med; Fr of Library; Lib Aide; Off Aide; Svce Clb; Stu Cncl (R); Highest Standing in Biology; Ranked 12 Out of 546 Students; Elementary Education; Business Administration; Brown U; Duke U

CHIN, HARRY; PHILADELPHIA, PA; CENTRAL HS; (SR); Hnr Roll; Comm Volntr; Emplmnt; Information Science & Technology; Penn State U

CHMIELEWSKI, ROXANNE; KUNKLETOWN, PA; PLEASANT VALLEY HS; (JR); Hnr Roll; Comm Volntr; Hab For Humty Volntr; Spec Olymp Vol; DARE; Key Club; Sccr (J); Yrbk (E, R, P); Lieutenant Governor (Key Club); Scranton U

CHOROSER, STEPHANIE; JENKINTOWN, PA; ABINGTON SR HS; (JR); Hi Hnr Roll; Nat Hon Sy; Nat Mrt LOC; WWAHSS; Comm Volntr; Emplmnt; Key Club; Svce Clb; Spanish Clb; Swmg (V); Member of Champions of Caring; President's Silver Community Service Award; Medicine; Language; Amherst College; Brown U

CHOWDHURY, IMRAN H; UPPER DARBY, PA; UPPER DARBY HS; (JR); Ctznshp Aw; Gov Hnr Prg; Hi Hnr Roll; Hnr Roll; Nat Hon Sy; Perf Att; Pres Sch; St of Mnth; Yth Ldrshp Prog; Comm Volntr; Hosp Aide; Peer Tut/Med; Chrch Yth Grp; Cmptr Clb; NYLC; P to P St Amb Prg; Quiz Bowl; Schol Bwl; Sci Clb; Tmpl Yth Grp; Cl Off (R); Stu Cncl (R); CR (R); Sch Ppr (R); Founder & President of the Muslim Club in UDHS; Award of Excellence in Programming/Controls; Biomedical Engineering/Pre-Med; Medical School; U of Pennsylvania; Johns Hopkins U

CHRISTIANA, STEPHANIE; WEXFORD, PA; PINE-RICHLAND HS; (JR); Hi Hnr Roll; Comm Volntr; Peer Tut/Med; Key Club; Chr; Chrldg (V L); Representative of SADD (Students Against Destructive Decisions); Physical Therapy; Miami of Ohio; Penn State U

CHRISTIE, WILLIAM A; WEXFORD, PA; NORTH ALLEGHENY INT HS; (SO); Hi Hnr Roll; Nat Hon Sy; Sci/Math Olympn; Valdctrian; WWAHSS; Comm Volntr; Peer Tut/Med; Chrch Yth Grp; Key Club; Bnd; Bskball; Sccr (J); Student Council Welcome Committee; Friend Connection with Mentally Challenged Students

CHRISTINE JR, ROBERT M; BENSALEM, PA; CONWELL-EGAN CATHOLIC HS; (JR); Hnr Roll; CARE; Chrch Yth Grp; DARE; Mth Clb/Tm; Ftball (V); Wt Lftg; Sports Medicine; Psychology; King's College; Lock Haven U

CHURCH, KIRSTEN; BEAVER SPRINGS, PA; MIDD-WEST SD; (JR); Bnd; Chr; Mch Bnd; SP/M/VS; Varsity/Junior Varsity Bowling; Culinary Arts; Indiana U of Pennsylvania

CIAK, BRIAN; PITTSBURGH, PA; NORTH HILLS HS; (FR); Hnr Roll; Perf Att; Sci Fairs; Comm Volntr; DARE; Emplmnt; Scouts; German Clb; Orch; Bskball; Cr Ctry (L); Skiing; Track (L); Wt Lftg; Young Achievers Award; Penn State U

CIAK, JEFF; PITTSBURGH, PA; NORTH HILLS HS; (FR); Hnr Roll; Sci Fairs; Comm Volntr; Chess; DARE; Emplmnt; Mod UN; Scouts; German Clb; Bnd; Jzz Bnd; Mch Bnd; Pep Bnd; Cr Ctry (L); Track; Wt Lftg; Young Achievers Award; Penn State U

CICALE, CASEY F; MOOSIC, PA; RIVERSIDE JR/SR HS; (JR); Hi Hnr Roll; Nat Hon Sy; St of Mnth; Bsball (V); Bausch & Lomb Science Award; NEMA & USNMA Awards; Mathematics; Exercise Science; U of Scranton

CICCIO, RACHEL; ROYERSFORD, PA; SPRING FORD SR HS; (SO); Ctznshp Aw; Nat Ldrshp Svc; St of Mnth; Biology Clb; Emplmnt; Sci Clb; Yrbk (P); FCS Club; Marine Biologist; Sales Representative; Pennsylvania State U; Saint Joseph's U

CICERCHI, LISA R; ALIQUIPPA, PA; CTR AREA SD; (SO); Hi Hnr Roll; Hnr Roll; WWAHSS; Comm Volntr; Chrch Yth Grp; Svce Clb; Spanish Clb; Gmnstcs (V L); Sccr (V L); Track (V L); Stu Cncl (R); Teacher

CINTRON, CHASITY; READING, PA; READING HS; (JR); Fut Prb Slvr; Hnr Roll; Nat Mrt LOC; Perf Att; St of Mnth; Peer Tut/Med; DARE; Emplmnt; Jr Ach; Vllyball (J); Stu Cncl (R); Lawyer; Clarion State College; Temple U

CIRUCCI, JULIE; SCHNECKSVILLE, PA; PARKLAND HS; (SO); Criminal Justice; Forensic Science

CLAAR, JAYME C; HOLLIDAYSBURG, PA; HOLLIDAYSBURG AREA SR HS; (JR); Hnr Roll; WWAHSS; Comm Volntr; Chrch Yth Grp; Emplmnt; Jr Ach; Key Club; Off Aide; Chr; Dnce; Skiing; Vllyball; Cl Off (T); Teaching; Indiana U of PA; Penn State U

CLAPCICH, MANDI; ASTON, PA; THE CHRISTIAN AC; (JR); WWAHSS; Comm Volntr; Hab For Humty Volntr; Chrch Yth Grp; Drma Clb; Emplmnt; Quiz Bowl; Tchrs Aide; SP/M/VS; Stg Cre; Bskball (V); Linguistics; Illustration; William and Mary; Penn State

CLARK, ASHLEY N; WHITE HALL, PA; WHITEHALL HS; (SR); Hi Hnr Roll; Hnr Roll; ArtClub; Emplmnt; SADD; Art Club Vice President; Elementary Education Teacher; Kutztown U; Lehigh-Carbon Community College

CLARK, BEN; WEXFORD, PA; PINE-RICHLAND HS; (JR); Ctznshp Aw; Hi Hnr Roll; Nat Hon Sy; USAA; WWAHSS; Comm Volntr; Spec Olymp Vol; Chrch Yth Grp; Emplmnt; Key Club; Prom Com; Bnd; Jzz Bnd; Mch Bnd; Stg Cre; Skiing; Adv Cncl (R); Cl Off (P); Stu Cncl (P); CR (R); Superintendent's Key Communicators; Christian Foundations; Entertainment Engineering; Mechanical Engineering & Theatre Design; Penn State U; Purdue U

CLARK, JASMINE; PHILADELPHIA, PA; PHILADELPHIA HS; (JR); Hnr Roll; Otst Ac Ach Awd; WWAHSS; Yth Ldrshp Prog; Comm Volntr; Chrch Yth Grp; Mus Clb; Chr; Secretary of School Choir; Section Leader of Gospel Choir in School; Biology; Pre-Optometry; Temple U; Drexel U

CLARK, KRYSTYN L; SCRANTON, PA; LOURDESMONT SCH; (SR); Hnr Roll; Nat Ldrshp Svc; St of Mnth; Comm Volntr; Peer Tut/Med; DARE; Emplmnt; Social Work; Penn State

CLARK, STACEY; NORRISTOWN, PA; METHACTON HS; (SO); Hnr Roll; Perf Att; Pres Ac Ftns Aw; WWAHSS; Comm Volntr; Spec Olymp Vol; Chrch Yth Grp; FCA; Key Club; Tennis (V L); Track (V L)

CLARK, SUSAN E; MECHANICSBURG, PA; CUMBERLAND VALLEY HS; (SO); Ctznshp Aw; Hnr Roll; Nat Hon Sy; Perf Att; WWAHSS; Peer Tut/Med; Spec Olymp Vol; Key Club; Scouts; Bnd; Chr; Fld Hky (VJ); Lcrsse; Sch Ppr (P); Peer Helpers; Big Brothers/Big Sisters; Radiology; Pre-Med; U of Pittsburgh; St Joseph's U

CLARK, TASHANDA M; PHILADELPHIA, PA; GERMANTOWN HS; (SR); Hnr Roll; Nat Hon Sy; Comm Volntr; Peer Tut/Med; Red Cr Aide; Cmptr Clb; Off Aide; Prom Com; Tech Clb; Bskball (J); Cl Off (T); Stu Cncl (S); Yrbk (E); Computer Science; Business Technology; Indiana U of PA

CLEMENS, ERIN E; BERWICK, PA; BERWICK AREA SR HS; (SO); Hi Hnr Roll; Nat Hon Sy; WWAHSS; Comm Volntr; Chrch Yth Grp; Emplmnt; Key Club; Lib Aide; Chr; Ch Chr; Stu Cncl (R); Yrbk (P); Science Olympiad; Modernairas-Select Women's Choir; Elementary Education; Special Education

CLEMENS, TARA; BERWICK, PA; BERWICK AREA SR HS; (FR); Hi Hnr Roll; WWAHSS; Comm Volntr; Chrch Yth Grp; DARE; Key Club; Chr; Ch Chr; National Junior Honor Society; Elementary Education; Writing/Music; Bloomsburg U

CLINE, CATHERINE A; NEW CUMBERLAND, PA; TRINITY HS; (FR); Hnr Roll; Key Club; Ski Club

CLINE, HALEY A; NEW CUMBERLAND, PA; TRINITY HS; (JR); Hnr Roll; Key Club; Spanish Clb; Who's Who Among American High School Students; Penn State U-Harrisburg

CLOSKEY, SHANE; RUFFS DALE, PA; YOUGH HS; (FR); Hnr Roll; Ftball (J)

CLOUGH, RACHEL A; MILLMONT, PA; PENN VIEW CHRISTIAN AC; (FR); Hi Hnr Roll; Hnr Roll; Chrch Yth Grp; Chr; Ch Chr; Music; Education; Penn View Bible Institute

CLOUSER, ANDREA; STATE COLLEGE, PA; STATE COLLEGE SOUTH HS; (FR); Hi Hnr Roll; Hnr Roll; Perf Att; Hab For Humty Volntr; Peer Tut/Med; Chrch Yth Grp; DARE; Photog; Scouts; Chr; Ch Chr; Sftball (V); Track (JCL); Played Softball for 10 Years in Summer; I've Been Taking Piano for 6 Years; Penn State U; Major-Psychology Minor-Biology; Penn State U; Miami State U

Cicale, Casey F
Riverside JR/SR HS
Moosic, PA

Chalela, Dean
Council Rock HS North
Newtown, PA

National
Honor Roll
Spring 2005

Caston, Latoya S
Philadelphia Electrical & Tech Charter HS
Philadelphia, PA

Clark, Susan E
Cumberland Valley HS
Mechanicsburg, PA

COATES, KAYLYNN; GREENVILLE, PA; REYNOLDS JR/SR HS; (FR); Ctznshp Aw; Hi Hnr Roll; Comm Volntr; Chrch Yth Grp; Key Club; Clb; Bnd; Chr; Equine Vet; Ohio State U

COBB, SARAH; NORRISTOWN, PA; NORRISTOWN AREA HS; (SO); 4H Awd; Gov Hnr Prg; Hi Hnr Roll; Nat Hon Sy; Otst Ac Ach Awd; Pres Ac Ftns Aw; Sci Fairs; Comm Volntr; 4-H; Chrch Yth Grp; DECA; Emplmnt; Mth Clb/Tm; German Clb; Chr; Sftball (J); CR; Vice President 4-H Equestrian Club - Will Ride State; Honors & Tri-County Chorus Member; International Business/Sales; Law

COCCIA, LACIE L; EDINBURG, PA; MOHAWK HS; (JR); F Lan Hn Soc; Hi Hnr Roll; Nat Hon Sy; USAA; Comm Volntr; Peer Tut/Med; FBLA; NYLC; P to P St Amb Prg; Prom Com; Sci Clb; SADD; Spanish Clb; Cl Off (T); Gifted Program, Ecology Club; College in High School, Chem Club; Forensic Science; Duquesne U; West Virginia U

COCCO, TONY; ALLENTOWN, PA; LOUIS E DIERUFF HS; (JR); Hnr Roll; Nat Hon Sy; Peer Tut/Med; Chess; Cmptr Clb; Drma Clb; Tech Clb; SP/M/VS; National Honor Society; Computer Science; Brown U; Columbia U

COERVER, AUTUMN L; MERCERSBURG, PA; JAMES BUCHANAN HS; (SO); Hi Hnr Roll; Hnr Roll; Hosp Aide; Peer Tut/Med; Spec Olymp Vol; Chrch Yth Grp; Emplmnt; FCA; Spanish Clb; Stu Cncl (R); Education; Veterinary Medicine; Wilson College; Slippery Rock U

COHEN, AMY L; WYNNEWOOD, PA; LOWER MARION HS; (SO); Hi Hnr Roll; WWAHSS; Yth Ldrshp Prog; Comm Volntr; Prom Com; Tmpl Yth Grp; Orch; SP/M/VS; Track (J); Stu Cncl (R); National French Exam Award; National Latin Exam Award

COHEN, EMILY B; GLENSIDE, PA; SPRINGFIELD HS; (SR); Ctznshp Aw; Hi Hnr Roll; Nat Hon Sy; Pres Sch; WWAHSS; Yth Ldrshp Prog; Red Cr Aide; Chrch Yth Grp; Drma Clb; Emplmnt; Key Club; SADD; Tmpl Yth Grp; Acpl Chr; Bnd; Chr; SP/M/VS; Fld Hky (J); Sftball (V); Cl Off (T); Stu Cncl (T); CR (R); Yrbk (R); Political Science; Broadcast Journalism; U of Maryland; U of Wisconsin

COHN, CHRISTINA; NORRISTOWN, PA; NORRISTOWN AREA HS; (JR); Hnr Roll; Nat Hon Sy; Comm Volntr; Spec Olymp Vol; Chrch Yth Grp; Emplmnt; Key Club; Mth Clb/Tm; Vice President of Youth Group-2 Years; 4 Year CCD Teacher; Elementary Education; Religious Studies

COLAIEZZI, KEVIN D; POTTSTOWN, PA; POTTSGROVE SR HS; (FR); Ctznshp Aw; Hi Hnr Roll; Otst Ac Ach Awd; St of Mnth; Chr; Golf (J); Law; Secondary Education / Math Major; Penn State; West Chester U

COLARUSSO, TAHNEE M; YATESVILLE, PA; PITTSTON AREA HS; (SR); Ctznshp Aw; Hi Hnr Roll; Hnr Roll; Nat Hon Sy; Otst Ac Ach Awd; Emplmnt; Key Club; Pep Squd; Spanish Clb; Dnce; Bskball (J); Chrldg (J); Gmnstcs (J); Track (J); Yrbk (E); Nurse-RN; College Misericordia; Penn State U Scranton

COLEMAN, ANDY; WEXFORD, PA; NORTH ALLEGHENY INT HS; (SO); Hi Hnr Roll; Hnr Roll; WWAHSS; Comm Volntr; Chess; Chrch Yth Grp; Emplmnt; Key Club; Bnd; Jzz Bnd; Mch Bnd; Ultimate Frisbee Team Distinguished Achievement-7th Grade Johns Hopkins; Outstanding Young Citizen Award; Penn State U

COLON, JOSE; PHILADELPHIA, PA; WILLIAM PENN HS; (JR); 4H Awd; Hi Hnr Roll; Hnr Roll; Sci Fairs; Comm Volntr; 4-H; ArtClub; Photog; Vsity Clb; Drm Mjr; Ftball (J); Swmg (V); Sch Ppr (E, R, P); Law Criminal Justice; Football Professionally; Temple

COMANDY, GENA; SCRANTON, PA; SCRANTON HS; (JR); Johnson College

CONKLIN, AMANDA; SUSQUEHANNA, PA; BLUE RIDGE HS; (FR); Hi Hnr Roll

CONKLIN, KRISTY; BEACH LAKE, PA; HONESDALE HS; (SR); 4H Awd; Hnr Roll; WWAHSS; Comm Volntr; 4-H; Emplmnt; Chrldg (V L); Elementary Education; Arcadia U

CONLEY, CHRIS; TURTLE CREEK, PA; GREATER WORKS CHRISTIAN SCH; MS; Hi Hnr Roll; Hnr Roll; Comm Volntr; Emplmnt; SP/M/VS; Bskball (V); Class Nomination for Most Academically Improved; Criminal Justice; Medical School

CONNER, LAUREN K; MECHANICSBURG, PA; MECHANICSBURG AREA HS; (JR); Hi Hnr Roll; Nat Hon Sy; St of Mnth; WWAHSS; Key Club; Bskball (V); Cr Ctry (V); Sccr (V); Yrbk; Psychology

CONNOLLY, JACK; WEXFORD, PA; NORTH ALLEGHENY HS; (SO); Hi Hnr Roll; Nat Hon Sy; Perf Att; St of Mnth; WWAHSS; Comm Volntr; Key Club; Bdmtn (J); Bsball (J); Ftball (VJ L); Extra Effort Award Dec. 2005; Finance Degree; Master's Degree; Carnegie Mellon U; Duke U

CONNOLLY, MAGGIE; BUTLER, PA; BUTLER SR HS; (SR); WWAHSS; Comm Volntr; Emplmnt; ROTC; Skt Tgt Sh (V); Board of Governor's Scholarship; First Place Kneeler for Rifle Team in European Finals; Psychology; Sociology; Indiana U of Pennsylvania

CONNOLLY, TED; WEXFORD, PA; NORTH ALLEGHENY HS; (FR); Adv Cncl (R); Freshman Basketball Team Captain; AAU Basketball Team; Orthodontics; Journalism; Duke U; UNC-U of North Carolina

CONNORS, KAITLYN; PITTSTON, PA; PITTSTON AREA HS; Ctznshp Aw; Hi Hnr Roll; Hnr Roll; MVP; Nat Hon Sy; Nat Sci Aw; Sci Fairs; St of Mnth; WWAHSS; Yth Ldrshp Prog; Comm Volntr; DARE; Emplmnt; Lttrmn Clb; Mth Clb/Tm; Pep Squd; Prom Com; Sci Clb; Foreign Clb; Dnce; Fld Hky (V L); Sftball (V L); Cl Off (P); CR (P); National Honor Society; Who's Who Among American High School Students; Law; Chiropractics; U of Pittsburgh; Villanova U

CONSTANTINO, ROSS C; WEXFORD, PA; NORTH ALLEGHENY; (SO); Ctznshp Aw; Hi Hnr Roll; Hnr Roll; Nat Hon Sy; Pres Ac Ftns Aw; WWAHSS; Yth Ldrshp Prog; Comm Volntr; Chrch Yth Grp; Emplmnt; FBLA; Key Club; Bskball (J)

CONTINO, SAMANTHA; MILFORD, PA; DELAWARE VALLEY HS; (FR); Hi Hnr Roll; Hnr Roll; Perf Att; Comm Volntr; Hab For Humty Volntr; 4-H; Drma Clb; Scouts; Vsity Clb; Bnd; Dnce; Jzz Bnd; SP/M/VS; Swmg (V); Swimming/Swim Coach; Art/Band Teacher

CONVEY, JACLYN; LANSDALE, PA; NORTH PENN HS; (JR); Hnr Roll; Comm Volntr; DARE; Key Club; Prom Com

COOK, DEANNA; NEWVILLE, PA; BIG SPRING SD; (JR); Ctznshp Aw; Hi Hnr Roll; Hnr Roll; Nat Hon Sy; Otst Ac Ach Awd; Perf Att; Comm Volntr; Peer Tut/Med; Chrch Yth Grp; Key Club; Bnd; Chr; Mch Bnd; Stg Cre; Computer Science; Business

COOK, LAUREN; NEW BLOOMFIELD, PA; TRINITY HS; (JR); Hnr Roll; Nat Hon Sy; Sci Fairs; Comm Volntr; Red Cr Aide; Emplmnt; French Clb; Dnce; Sccr (J); Swmg (V); Yrbk (P); PAL (Peers Actively Listening) Leader; Lifeguard; Pre-Med; Franklin & Marshall College; Boston College

COOMBES JR, MICHAEL J; GOULDSBORO, PA; LOURDESMONT SCH; (FR); Hi Hnr Roll; Hnr Roll; St of Mnth; DARE; Key Club; Stu Cncl (V); Forensic Science; Penn State U; Kutztown U

COOPER, BRITTANY; AUBURN, PA; POTTSVILLE AREA SD; (SO); Hi Hnr Roll; Hnr Roll; St of Mnth; Peer Tut/Med; SADD; Tchrs Aide; Nursing School; Pottsville School of Nursing

COOPER, JAMES R; STROUDSBURG, PA; POCONO MTN EAST HS; (SO); F Lan Hn Soc; Hi Hnr Roll; Hnr Roll; Nat Hon Sy; St of Mnth; DARE; Emplmnt; Chr; National Jr Honor Society; USAA International Foreign Language Award; Psychiatrist; Harvard U; UNC

COOPER, JULIA; JENKINTOWN, PA; JENKINTOWN HS; (JR); DAR; F Lan Hn Soc; Hnr Roll; Nat Hon Sy; Sci Fairs; Yth Ldrshp Prog; Drma Clb; HO'Br Yth Ldrshp; Bnd; Chr; Jzz Bnd; Pep Bnd; Bskball (V L); Lcrsse (J); Tennis (V L); Cl Off (V); Stu Cncl (R); CR (R); Yrbk (R); English Major; Law School; College of William and Mary; U of Virginia

COOPER, MARCUS T; PHILADELPHIA, PA; ABRAHAM LINCOLN HS; (JR); Ctznshp Aw; Hnr Roll; Perf Att; Chrch Yth Grp; Bskball (V); Ftball (V); Track (V); Attended Arcadia U Scholarship Program- 1 Year; Opportunities OHC In Health Care Program / Currently Attending Temple U OHC Program; PhD in Cardiology; Physician's Assistant; U of Southern California; Temple U

COOPER, TERRENCE K; PHILADELPHIA, PA; NORTHEAST HS; (JR); 4H Awd; Hnr Roll; Pres Sch; St of Mnth; WWAHSS; Chess; DARE; Emplmnt; Mth Clb/Tm; Stg Cre; Ftball (V); Track (V); Wt Lftg (V); Little League Football; Middle School Basketball & Baseball; Psychology; Sports Management; Lock Haven U; Robert Morris U

COPES, DAN; LE RAYSVILLE, PA; ELK LAKE HS; (FR); Hnr Roll; Nat Hon Sy; St of Mnth; Key Club; Quiz Bowl; Spanish Clb; Bnd; Jzz Bnd; Sccr (J); Track (J); Vllyball (J); Cl Off (P); Stu Cncl (R); Physical Fitness Award; Physical Therapy; Music

CORNWALL, KEVIN E; HERMITAGE, PA; HICKORY HS; (SO); F Lan Hn Soc; Hi Hnr Roll; WWAHSS; Drma Clb; Mth Clb/Tm; French Clb; Bnd; Jzz Bnd; Mch Bnd; Pep Bnd; Tennis; Mechanical or Aerospace Engineering; Theatre

CORONA, MIA; BANGOR, PA; BANGOR AREA HS; (SO); Hi Hnr Roll; Hnr Roll; WWAHSS; Comm Volntr; Emplmnt; Dnce; SP/M/VS; Lit Mag (R); Sch Ppr (R); Yrbk (R); 2005 Miss Pennsylvania Teen USA Pageant Delegate; English Major; Writing; Moravian College; Penn State U

CORRADINO, TRISTA A; CTRL CITY, PA; SHADE-CENTRAL CITY SD; (SO); Hnr Roll; MVP; Nat Hon Sy; Pres Ac Ftns Aw; Sci Fairs; WWAHSS; ArtClub; Chrch Yth Grp; SADD; Vsity Clb; Spanish Clb; Chr; Bskball (V); Sftball (V L); Vsy Clb; Vllyball (J); Played the Piano for 11 Years; Play the Organ for Church; Nursing / Physical Therapy; Law School; IUP; Pitt

CORREIA, DIANA; BETHLEHEM, PA; LIBERTY HS; (SO); Comm Volntr; Hosp Aide; Bnd; Chr; Mch Bnd; Stg Cre; Fld Hky (J); Lcrsse (V); Church Altar Server; Plays in 8th Grade; Nursing

CORRIGAN, GABRIELLE L; SUNBURY, PA; SUNBURY CHRISTIAN AC; (SO); Hi Hnr Roll; WWAHSS; Chrch Yth Grp; Emplmnt; Envirothon; Mission Trip to Honduras in 2004; World Missions; Theological Studies; Valley Forge Christian College; Philadelphia Biblical U

CORSEY, NIKISHIA; POTTSTOWN, PA; POTTSTOWN SR HS; (SO); Hnr Roll; Perf Att; St of Mnth; Yth Ldrshp Prog; Comm Volntr; Peer Tut/Med; Drma Clb; Key Club; Mus Clb; Ntl Beta Clb; Ntl FFA; Tchrs Aide; Chr; Dnce; SP/M/VS; Stg Cre; Bskball (J); CR (R); Professional Rapper; Georgia Tech; Temple U

CORTESE, GAGE M; STOYSTOWN, PA; NORTH STAR SD; (MS); Hnr Roll; Otst Ac Ach Awd; Perf Att; St of Mnth; Biology Clb; Outdrs Clb; Scouts; Wdwrkg Clb; Ch Chr; Stg Cre; Sccr; CR (V); Star Scout; Surveying Engineer; Chiropractor; Penn St U Park Campus; U of Pittsburgh At Johnstown

COSTA, TIFFANY; EASTON, PA; EASTON HS; (FR); Hnr Roll; Perf Att; Sci Fairs; St of Mnth; CARE; DARE; Drma Clb; FTA; Spch Team; SADD; Chr; SP/M/VS; Fld Hky (V); Cl Off (R); CR (R); Law/Social Work; Education; Adelphi; Harvard U

COSTANZA, BRITTNEY; EAST STROUDSBURG, PA; STROUDSBURG HS; (SO); Hnr Roll; St of Mnth; Comm Volntr; Hosp Aide; Emplmnt; Dnce; Track (J); Physical Therapist (Sports); Massage Therapist

COSTELLO, TIMOTHY B; CORRY, PA; CORRY AREA HS; (SR); Hi Hnr Roll; Nat Hon Sy; Perf Att; USAA; WWAHSS; Comm Volntr; Chrch Yth Grp; Emplmnt; Key Club; Off Aide; Bnd; Drm Mjr; Jzz Bnd; Mch Bnd; Swmg (V CL); Cl Off (T); Stu Cncl (R); Rotary Boy of the Month; Psychology; Geneva College

COTE, AUBREE; BETHLEHEM, PA; BETHLEHEM CATHOLIC HS; (FR); Hi Hnr Roll; Comm Volntr; Key Club; SP/M/VS; CR (R); Teacher; DeSales U; Alvernia College

COULSON, CHRISTINA; PHILADELPHIA, PA; IMHOTEP CHARTER HS; (JR); Ctznshp Aw; Hi Hnr Roll; Hnr Roll; Perf Att; Comm Volntr; Chrch Yth Grp; Emplmnt; Pep Squd; Prom Com; Chr; Ch Chr; Chrldg (V); Cr Ctry (V); Stu Cncl (V); Yrbk (P); Pediatric Medicine; Sports Medicine; North Carolina A & T; U of Southern California

COULSON, ERICA M; DILLSBURG, PA; NORTHERN YORK HS; (JR); Hi Hnr Roll; Otst Ac Ach Awd; WWAHSS; Spec Olymp Vol; Emplmnt; Key Club; Prom Com; Scouts; SADD; Bnd; Chr; Mch Bnd; Nursing; Medical School

COULSON, JENNIFER S; BETHEL PARK, PA; BETHEL PARK SD; (SO); All Am Sch; Hi Hnr Roll; Nat Hon Sy; WWAHSS; Scouts; Dnce; Orch; Sccr (J)

COULSON, PHILLIP R; BETHEL PARK, PA; BETHEL PARK SR HS; (SR); All Am Sch; Fut Prb Slvr; Hnr Roll; Nat Hon Sy; WWAHSS; Peer Tut/Med; AL Aux Boys; Dbte Team; Mod UN; NtlFrnscLg; Spch Team; Cr Ctry (V L); Political Science; Pre-Law; American U

COULTER, TRICIA; PITTSBURGH, PA; PLUM SR HS; (SO); Ctznshp Aw; F Lan Hn Soc; Hi Hnr Roll; Hnr Roll; Perf Att; WWAHSS; Hab For Humty Volntr; Emplmnt; Orch; Stg Cre; Swmg (V L); Tennis (VJ); Sch Ppr (R); Yrbk (E); Pharmacy; U of Pittsburgh

COURIE, ARLEIGH; CARMICHAELS, PA; CARMICHAELS AREA JR/SR HS; (JR); Hi Hnr Roll; Nat Hon Sy; Otst Ac Ach Awd; WWAHSS; Peer Tut/Med; ArtClub; Chess; Chrch Yth Grp; Emplmnt; Lib Aide; Mus Clb; Spanish Clb; Chr; Psychology / Medical; Social Work

COURTNEY, KYLE; GREENVILLE, PA; GREENVILLE SR HS; (JR); Hi Hnr Roll; Nat Hon Sy; St of Mnth; Comm Volntr; Key Club; Vsity Clb; Spanish Clb; Cr Ctry (J L); Track (V L); Yrbk (R); Spanish National Honor Society; Civil Engineering; Chemical Engineering; U of Pittsburgh; Lehigh U

COUSLEY, KELSEY; GREENVILLE, PA; GREENVILLE HS; (FR); Hi Hnr Roll; Hnr Roll; Pres Sch; St of Mnth; USAA; WWAHSS; Comm Volntr; Chrch Yth Grp; Key Club; Spch Team; Chr; Dnce; Bskball (J); Scr Kpr (J); Track (V); Vllyball (J); Am. Legion Voice of Democracy-1st Place 2004; World Servants Missionary; Teaching; Psychiatry; Penn State U; U of Pittsburgh

COVERT, KAYLA M; MOON TWP, PA; MOON AREA HS; (JR); Hi Hnr Roll; Hnr Roll; Nat Hon Sy; Otst Ac Ach Awd; Perf Att; Pres Ac Ftns Aw; St of Mnth; DARE; Key Club; Prom Com; SADD; Spanish Clb; Chr; Dnce; SP/M/VS; Chrldg (VJ); Track (VJ L); Stu Cncl (R); Scholar Athlete at Moon High School; Physical Therapy; Sports Medicine; U of Pittsburgh; Slippery Rock U

COWAN, BENJAMIN; CARLISLE, PA; (JR); Hnr Roll; Yth Ldrshp Prog; Chrch Yth Grp; Green Belt in Judo; Psychology; Shippensburg

COX, ASHTON L; WAYNESBORO, PA; WAYNESBORO AREA SR HS; (SR); Hi Hnr Roll; Hnr Roll; Sci Fairs; St of Mnth; Comm Volntr; DARE; Key Club; Fld Hky (J); Sch Ppr (R); Member of YAC for 4 Yrs; Attended a Vocational School for 3 Yrs POCTC; Information Technology; Computer Science; HCC-Hagerstown Community College

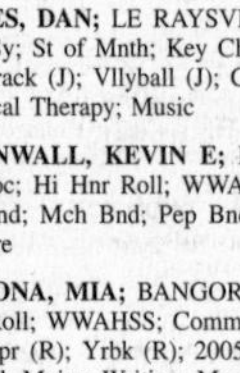

Cote, Aubree
Bethlehem Catholic HS
Bethlehem, PA

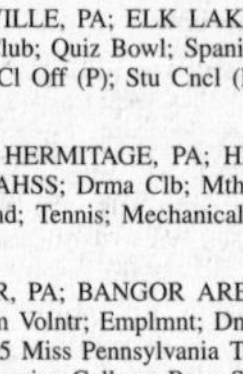

Coerver, Autumn L
James Buchanan HS
Mercersburg, PA

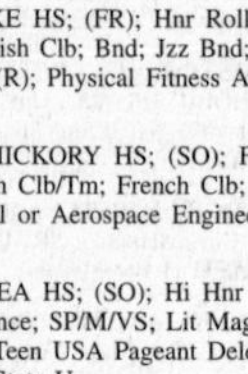

Cooper, James R
Pocono Mtn East HS
Stroudsburg, PA

CRAIG, JACK; VERONA, PA; RIVERVIEW JR/SR HS; (SO); Hi Hnr Roll; Hnr Roll; Kwnis Aw; Sci Fairs; WWAHSS; Hosp Aide; Chess; Key Club; Mod UN; P to P St Amb Prg; Quiz Bowl; Spanish Clb; Chr; Ch Chr; Stg Cre; Ftball (J); Track (J); Wrstlg (L); Zoology; Bachelor's Degree; U of Florida

CRATE, SAMANTHA; BROOKVILLE, PA; BROOKVILLE HS; Ctznshp Aw; Hnr Roll; Otst Ac Ach Awd; Perf Att; Pres Ac Ftns Aw; Sci Fairs; Comm Volntr; Peer Tut/Med; Spec Olymp Vol; Chrch Yth Grp; Lib Aide; Pep Squd; Scouts; Sign Clb; Chr; Chrldg (J); Gmnstcs (J); Sftball (J); Choreographer; Nursing; Stanford; Harvard

CRAVEN, LAMONT; PITTSBURGH, PA; SCHENLEY HS; (JR); Hi Hnr Roll; Hnr Roll; Emplmnt; Track (V); International Business; Psychology; Howard U; Morehouse College

CRAVENER, JEFFREY; YORK, PA; CTRL YORK HS; (JR); Hnr Roll; Yth Ldrshp Prog; Comm Volntr; Peer Tut/Med; ArtClub; Chrch Yth Grp; Cmptr Clb; Wt Lftg (J); Artist; Cartoonist

CRAVER, ASHLEY; PITTSBURGH, PA; PENN HILLS HS; (SO); Hnr Roll; Nat Sci Aw; Key Club

CRAWFORD, HARLEY; LEWISTOWN, PA; LEWISTOWN AREA HS; (FR); 4H Awd; Hi Hnr Roll; Hnr Roll; Nat Hon Sy; 4-H; DARE; P to P St Amb Prg; German Clb; Hsbk Rdg; Give Horseback Riding Lessons; Lift Weights At Home; Equine Vet.; Horse Trainer; Findlay U

CRAWFORD, LAUREN; MIFFLIN, PA; JUNIATA HS; (JR); Hi Hnr Roll; Hnr Roll; Nat Hon Sy; WWAHSS; 4-H; Key Club; Prom Com; Bnd; Clr Grd; Mch Bnd; Keystone Jr Rodeo Association; Pediatric Nurse; Pennsylvania State U; Bloomsburg U

CRAWFORD, LAUREN M; PHILADELPHIA, PA;; Hnr Roll; Otst Ac Ach Awd; Perf Att; St of Mnth; St Optmst of Yr; Yth Ldrshp Prog; Comm Volntr; Hosp Aide; Peer Tut/Med; ArtClub; Biology Clb; Chess; Chrch Yth Grp; Cmptr Clb; Dbte Team; Drma Clb; Mth Clb/Tm; Ch Chr; Drl Tm; SP/M/VS; Bsball (C); Bskball (C); Cr Ctry; Gmnstcs; Ice Sktg; Mar Art; Sftball; Swmg; Sch Ppr; Yrbk; Finalist for Ms. Jr Teen Pageant; Gospel Singer; Veterinarian; Electrical Engineer; Temple U; Drexel U

CRAWFORD, WILLIAM P; WAMPUM, PA; MOHAWK AREA HS; (SO); Hnr Roll; 4-H; Wdwrkg Clb; Bnd; Mch Bnd; Sccr (VJ L); Participates in Academic Game Competition; Teaching; Duquesne U

CREAN, BILL; PITTSBURGH, PA; SCHENLEY HS; (JR); Hi Hnr Roll; WWAHSS; Comm Volntr; Chrch Yth Grp; Drma Clb; French Clb; Bnd; Jzz Bnd; Mch Bnd; SP/M/VS; Skiing (V); Sccr (J); American Guild of Organists Scholarship; Biology / Genetics; Music; Fordham U; Cornell U

CREPER, LAUREN; EXPORT, PA; KISKI AREA HS; (JR); Hi Hnr Roll; Perf Att; WWAHSS; Comm Volntr; Emplmnt; Key Club; Lttrmn Clb; Bnd; Mch Bnd; Perfect Attendance; Ranked 19 Out of 356 Junior; Chemistry/ Biology; DNA; Seton Hill College-Greensburg; Saint Vincent College-Latrobe

CRESS, TRISH; PHOENIXVILLE, PA; PHOENIXVILLE HS; (FR); Hi Hnr Roll; Hnr Roll; Key Club; Mar Art (J); Martial Arts for 5 Years; Key Club; I Would Like to Become a Vet.

CREVAR, JAMIE; MC KEESPORT, PA; MC KEESPORT AREA SD; (JR); Hnr Roll; Otst Ac Ach Awd; Perf Att; Sci Fairs; St of Mnth; Comm Volntr; AL Aux Girls; Chrch Yth Grp; Emplmnt; Jr Ach; Off Aide; Tchrs Aide; PP Ftbl (J); Nursing Degree / RN; Teaching; Community College; Duquesne U

CREWS, ANDREA; BARTO, PA; BRANDYWINE HEIGHTS HS; (SR); Hi Hnr Roll; Hnr Roll; Nat Hon Sy; Comm Volntr; ArtClub; Mth Clb/Tm; Spanish Clb; Vllyball (V L); Major in Fashion Design; Philadelphia U; Albright College

CRIADO, KARLENE; GREENSBURG, PA; GREENSBURG SALEM SD; (FR); Hi Hnr Roll; Otst Ac Ach Awd; Pres Ac Ftns Aw; Yth Ldrshp Prog; Comm Volntr; Chrch Yth Grp; Scouts; Chr; Gmnstcs (V); Skiing; Vllyball (J); Cl Off; CR; Yrbk (R, P); Teaching; Accounting; U of Pittsburgh; Penn State U

CRITES, BRIA N; HANOVER, PA; SPRING GROVE AREA SR HS; (SR); Hi Hnr Roll; Nat Hon Sy; Perf Att; St of Mnth; WWAHSS; Chrch Yth Grp; Emplmnt; Bskball (J); Sccr (V); Physical Therapy; Carroll Community College

CROCKETT, RASHOD; ERIE, PA; WILSON MS; (MS); 4H Awd; Ctznshp Aw; Hnr Roll; Perf Att; St of Mnth; Peer Tut/Med; Chrch Yth Grp; Pep Squd; Ch Chr; Cr Ctry; Ftball; Runner Up in Geography; In PEPP 2 Yrs; Police Officer; Lawyer; Penn State U; Stanford

CROKE, AMANDA; AMBLER, PA; WISSAHICKON HS; (SO); Hnr Roll; Sci Fairs; Comm Volntr; ArtClub; Biology Clb; Chrch Yth Grp; Emplmnt; Key Club; Photog; Scouts; Latin Clb; Chr; Fld Hky (J); Lcrsse (J); Track (J); Silver Award (Girl Scouts); Secretary for Key Club; Biology; Psychology; Delaware Valley College; U of Maryland

CRONAUER, REBECCA; PORTAGE, PA; CTRL CAMBRIA HS; (SO); Ctznshp Aw; Hi Hnr Roll; Hnr Roll; Sci Fairs; WWAHSS; Jr Ach; NtlFrnscLg; Bskball; Swmg (L); Tennis (V); Biology; Pre-Med

CRONCE, NATALYA; COATESVILLE, PA; COATESVILLE AREA SR HS; (JR); Hi Hnr Roll; Hnr Roll; Pres Ac Ftns Aw; Mus Clb; ROTC; Acpl Chr; Chr; Level #6 Gymnast State Champion; History Idol Contest Winner; Pharmacy; Accounting

CRONIN, BRYAN; MONACA, PA; CTR AREA SD HS; (SO); Hi Hnr Roll; Perf Att; WWAHSS; Svce Clb; German Clb; Track (J); Who's Who-High School-2yrs; Engineering

CROOMS, ERICHA; NORTH WALES, PA; NORTH PENN HS; (SR); Hi Hnr Roll; Hnr Roll; Nat Hon Sy; Otst Ac Ach Awd; WWAHSS; Spec Olymp Vol; Key Club; Honor Roll; Fashion Marketing; Education; Immaculate U

CROSBY, WHITNEY A; WEST NEWTON, PA; YOUGH SD; (FR); Hnr Roll; Perf Att; St of Mnth; CARE; Comm Volntr; Peer Tut/Med; Chrch Yth Grp; Pep Squd; Ch Chr; Chrldg (J); Track (J); Law; Nursing; Duke; Clark Atlanta

CROSS, MELANIE; TIOGA, PA; NORTHERN TIOGA SD; (FR); Hnr Roll; DARE; Bskball (J); Nursing; Mansfield U

CROUCH, KRYSTAL; DU BOIS, PA; DUBOIS AREA SD HS; (FR); Hi Hnr Roll; Peer Tut/Med; DARE; Emplmnt; Chr; Nursing; Day Care

CROZIER, JUSTIN; NEWVILLE, PA; BIG SPRING SD; (SO); Otst Ac Ach Awd; Perf Att; DARE; Emplmnt; Wdwrkg Clb; Wrstlg (V); Mining Engineer

CRUZ, GABRIELA; READING, PA; READING HS; (JR); Hi Hnr Roll; FBLA; In Talent Search; Accounting; Business Management; Albright College; Penn State Berks Campus

CRUZ, MICHEL'LE; PHILADELPHIA, PA; MASTERY CHARACTER HS; (FR); Hnr Roll; Chrch Yth Grp; Ch Chr; Yrbk (E)

CUELLAR, GUIZLENA; PHILADELPHIA, PA; PHILADELPHIA MILITARY AC; (FR); Hnr Roll; Perf Att; Comm Volntr; Red Cr Aide; Chrch Yth Grp; DARE; Emplmnt; Pep Squd; ROTC; Drl Tm; Chrldg (V); Sftball (V); Cl Off; Criminal Justice Degree; Law Degree; U of Pennsylvania; Villanova U

CULUM, MARKO; WAYNESBORO, PA; WASH; (JR); Sccr (V)

CULVAHOUSE, TYLER E; BEAVER FALLS, PA; BLACKHAWK HS; (JR); Hi Hnr Roll; Hnr Roll; MVP; Nat Hon Sy; Chrch Yth Grp; Key Club; Sccr (V L); Swmg (V L); Vllyball; Engineering; Carnegie Mellon U; Penn State U

CUNNION, KYLE; MONTOURSVILLE, PA; LOYALSOCK TWP HS; (SO); Hi Hnr Roll; Comm Volntr; Emplmnt; Key Club; Golf (J); Cl Off (V); Stu Cncl (R); Finance; Business; Villanova U; U of Pennsylvania

CUPP, KURTIS L; HARRISBURG, PA; CTRL DAUPHIN HS; (FR); Hi Hnr Roll; Hnr Roll; Nat Hon Sy; Perf Att; Peer Tut/Med; Scouts; Soccer for CASA; Rausch Creek Motocross - Racing Club; Pre-Med; Electrical Engineering; Penn State U; Harrisburg Area Community College

CURILLA, BILL; HAZLETON, PA; HAZLETON AREA HS; (JR); Hi Hnr Roll; Hnr Roll; Otst Ac Ach Awd; St of Mnth; WWAHSS; Comm Volntr; Emplmnt; Vsity Clb; Ftball (VJ); Wt Lftg (VJ); Sch Ppr (R); Yrbk (R); Sports Outside of School They Include Basketball and Baseball; Education; Physical Education; Penn State U; Bloomsburg U

CURRY, CHRISTINE; MARCUS HOOK, PA; CHICHESTER SR HS; (FR); Hnr Roll; Nat Hon Sy; Biology Clb; Spanish Clb; Sccr; Sftball; Law Enforcement; Lawyer; Widener Law School; West Chester U

CURRY, JEANETTE; SAYLORSBURG, PA; PLEASANT VALLEY HS; (JR); Hnr Roll; Comm Volntr; Spec Olymp Vol; Chrldg (V); SADD Member; Business Management; Marketing; Temple U; Shippensburg U

CURSIO, CHELSEA; ALTOONA, PA; BISHOP GUILFOYLE HS; (SO); F Lan Hn Soc; Hi Hnr Roll; Pres Ac Ftns Aw; Comm Volntr; Red Cr Aide; NtlFrnscLg; Latin Clb; Chrldg (V); Catholic Daughters of America Award; Reading Team 1st Place; Pharmacy; Sports Medicine; Youngstown State U; Temple U

CURTIS, URIAH J; HARRISBURG, PA; CTRL DAUPHIN HS; (JR); Hnr Roll; Perf Att; Bskball (J); Wrstlg (J); Physical Therapy; Law Enforcement; Shippensburg U; Harrisburg Area Community College

CUSTER, COURTNEY; BERLIN, PA; SHANKSVILLE-STONYCREEK HS; (FR); Hnr Roll; Chrch Yth Grp; Scouts; Bnd; Chr; Ch Chr; Mch Bnd; Chrldg (V L); Sftball (J); Vllyball (J); Cl Off (T); Nursing; Physical Therapy / Sports Medicine; West Virginia U; Penn State U

CUSTER, JEREMY; NEW BRIGHTON, PA; NEW BRIGHTON AREA HS; (JR); Hi Hnr Roll; Nat Hon Sy; Comm Volntr; Chrch Yth Grp; Vsity Clb; Stg Cre; Bsball (V); Golf (V L); Academic Games; Aerospace Engineer; Air Force Academy; Embry-Riddle

CUSTER, WHITNEY Y; FRIEDENS, PA; SHANKSVILLE-STONYCREEK HS; (FR); Hnr Roll; WWAHSS; Drma Clb; Chr; SP/M/VS; Chrldg (V); Stu Cncl (R); Journalism; U of Pittsburgh Johnstown

CVITKUSIC, SANJA; PITTSBURGH, PA; BALDWIN HS; (JR); Hi Hnr Roll; Nat Hon Sy; Otst Ac Ach Awd; Yth Ldrshp Prog; Comm Volntr; Mod UN; NYLC; German Clb; Dnce; Mar Art (V); CR (P); Black Belt in Tae Kwon Do; Aspire Foundation; Food Science / Engineering; German Language; Penn State U; Delaware Valley College

CYBULSKI, ALYSSA; DALLAS, PA; DALLAS HS; (FR); Hi Hnr Roll; Nat Hon Sy; Comm Volntr; Key Club; Scouts; Clb; Fld Hky (J); Track (V L); Physical Therapy; Sports Medicine; U of Scranton; Brown U

CZAJKOWSKI, ANTHONY; NEW KENSINGTON, PA; NEW KENSINGTON-ARNOLD SD HS; (SO); Hi Hnr Roll; Comm Volntr; Losing Weight Joined a Gym & Lifting Weights; Ministry Work

CZARNECKI, JUSTIN; CONSHOHOCKEN, PA; KENNEDY-KENRICK CATHOLIC HS; (FR); Hnr Roll; Otst Ac Ach Awd; Perf Att; Sci Fairs; Sci/ Math Olympn; Bsball; Poem Published in Anthology of Poetry By Young Americans; President's Award for Educational Excellence; Mathematics/ Accounting; Technology; Villanova; Florida State

DAHER, IVANA; EAST STROUDSBURG, PA; EAST STROUDSBURG HS SOUTH; (SO); Hnr Roll; Nat Ldrshp Svc; Perf Att; USAA; WWAHSS; ArtClub; FBLA; Key Club; Foreign Clb; Bskball (L); Business Administration; English Language & Literature; Fordham U

DAHIR, MUNEEB; EAST STROUDSBURG, PA; E BURG (SOUTH) HS; (JR); Hi Hnr Roll; Hnr Roll; Nat Hon Sy; Comm Volntr; Spec Olymp Vol; Emplmnt; FBLA; Photog; Sccr (J); Engineering; Finance; East Stroudsburg U; Penn State U

DALEY, AMANDA; PITTSBURGH, PA; KEYSTONE OAKS HS; (FR); Ctznshp Aw; Hnr Roll; Comm Volntr; Emplmnt; Scouts; SADD; Chr; Dnce; Mch Bnd; SP/M/VS; Cr Ctry (V); PPSqd (V); Stu Cncl; 12 Years of Dancing; State Finalist for PA in National Miss American Teen Pageant; Dance/ Choreographer; Business Ownership; The Juilliard School; Texas A & M U

DALTON, BERNADETTE; OXFORD, PA; ST MARK'S HS; (JR); Hi Hnr Roll; Hnr Roll; WWAHSS; Comm Volntr; Hab For Humty Volntr; Emplmnt; Key Club; Svce Clb; Sftball (J); Vllyball (J); Stu Cncl (R); Colonial Dames National Essay Contest Winner; Entrepreneurship; Business Administration; U of Maryland; Villanova U

DANCY, DANIELLE D; ERIE, PA; ERIE CITY SD; (FR); Hnr Roll; Perf Att; Chrch Yth Grp; Cmptr Clb; Basketball; Medical

DANDRIDGE, SHAWN R; COATESVILLE, PA; COATESVILLE AREA SR HS; (JR); Hnr Roll; MVP; Pres Ac Ftns Aw; Comm Volntr; Chrch Yth Grp; Emplmnt; FCA; Ch Chr; Dnce; Bskball (V); Ftball (V); Track (V); Business Administration; St Joseph U; Duke U

DANIELS, JAMISON; FRANKLIN, PA; FRANKLIN HS; (SO); Hnr Roll; Chrch Yth Grp; DARE; Bsball (J); Ftball (J); Psychology; Artist; Virginia Tech; U of Pittsburgh

DANIELS, LYNSEY; BEAVER MEADOWS, PA; MMI PREP; (FR); Hi Hnr Roll; Hnr Roll; ArtClub; Cr Ctry

DANIELS, SAMANTHA J; MILAN, PA; ATHENS AREA HS; (SR); Hnr Roll; Nat Hon Sy; Otst Ac Ach Awd; Chrch Yth Grp; Emplmnt; Ntl FFA; Vsy Clb (VJ L); Adv Cncl (R); Medical Administrative Assistant; Elmira Business Institute

DANKANIS, TIFFANY R; PHILADELPHIA, PA; NESHAMINY HS; (JR); Hnr Roll; Otst Ac Ach Awd; Perf Att; St of Mnth; Comm Volntr; Vllyball (J); Lourdesmont Representative; Girl Scout Representative; Therapist; Psychology

DARABANT, CHRISTINA; LANGELOTH, PA; BURGETTSTOWN HS; (JR); Hi Hnr Roll; Hnr Roll; Otst Ac Ach Awd; Comm Volntr; Chr; Dnce; Swg Chr; High Honor Roll; Honor Roll; Nursing; Law Enforcement; Duquesne U; U of Pittsburgh

DARBY, STEPHEN; HERMITAGE, PA; HICKORY HS; (FR); Hnr Roll; Chrch Yth Grp; Drma Clb; Bnd; Mch Bnd; Studio Photography; Youngstown State U

DARMER, KIERSTEN M; LIMEKILN, PA; EXETER TWP SR HS; (JR); Hnr Roll; Jr Mshl; Nat Hon Sy; Perf Att; Sci Fairs; Comm Volntr; Chrch Yth Grp; Bnd; Mch Bnd; Orch; Served on Church Mission Trips; Junior Counselor for Church's AWANA Program; Medical Laboratory Technology; Forensics; Edinboro U of Pennsylvania; Lock Haven U of Pennsylvania

DARON, BETHANY; SHAVERTOWN, PA; LAKE LEHMAN SD; (JR); Hi Hnr Roll; Nat Hon Sy; St of Mnth; WWAHSS; Comm Volntr; Hosp Aide; Red Cr Aide; Chrch Yth Grp; Key Club; Stu Cncl (R); Sch Ppr (R); Yrbk (E); Youth Salute; Junior Leadership Nominee; Medical Imaging; College Misericordia

DAS, RAJARSHI; DOWNINGTOWN, PA; DOWNINGTOWN EAST HS; (SR); Hi Hnr Roll; Nat Hon Sy; Nat Mrt Fin; Peer Tut/Med; ArtClub; Quiz Bowl; Tennis (V); Lit Mag (R); Physics

DAUPHINAIS, DESIREE'; TIOGA, PA; NORTHERN TIOGA SD; (FR); Ctznshp Aw; Hnr Roll; DARE; Mus Clb; Pep Squd; Vllyball (J); Stu Cncl (S); Yrbk (P); Lock Haven

Darmer, Kiersten M
Exeter Twp SR HS
Limekiln, PA

Dandridge, Shawn R
Coatesville Area SR HS
Coatesville, PA

Czajkowski, Anthony
New Kensington-Arnold SD HS
New Kensington, PA

Cupp, Kurtis L
Central Dauphin HS
Harrisburg, PA

Cronce, Natalya
Coatesville Area SR HS
Coatesville, PA

Cress, Trish
Phoenixville HS
Phoenixville, PA

Crawford, Lauren M
Philadelphia, PA

Creper, Lauren
Kiski Area HS
Export, PA

Cuellar, Guizlena
Philadelphia Military AC
Philadelphia, PA

Cvitkusic, Sanja
Baldwin HS
Pittsburgh, PA

Czarnecki, Justin
Kennedy-Kenrick Catholic HS
Conshohocken, PA

Daher, Ivana
East Stroudsburg HS South
East Stroudsburg, PA

DAVENPORT, DANIEL; LANGHORNE, PA; CONWELL-EGAN CATHOLIC HS; (SR); Hi Hnr Roll; St of Mnth; WWAHSS; Emplmnt; Mth Clb/Tm; Svce Clb; Bnd; Jzz Bnd; Student of the Month; Engineering; Drexel U

DAVIES, ADAM; NEW BRIGHTON, PA; NEW BRIGHTON AREA HS; (JR); Hi Hnr Roll; Hnr Roll; Nat Hon Sy; Pres Ac Ftns Aw; Yth Ldrshp Prog; Comm Volntr; Peer Tut/Med; AL Aux Boys; Emplmnt; Bsball (J); Bskball (V); Yrbk (R); Took 1st Place in Nationals in Presidents for Academic Games; Business; Lawyer; Duke; UNC At Chapel Hill

DAVIN, LAURA A; BETHEL PARK, PA; BETHEL PARK SD; (SO); Hnr Roll; Nat Hon Sy; Comm Volntr; Dnce; SP/M/VS; Sftball (V L)

DAVIS, ADRIENNE-LEIGH; MILTON, PA; MEADOWBROOK CHRISTIAN SCH; (SO); Hi Hnr Roll; Hnr Roll; Pres Ac Ftns Aw; WWAHSS; Comm Volntr; Chrch Yth Grp; Emplmnt; Key Club; Chr; SP/M/VS; Bskball (J); Sccr (V); Track (V); Stu Cncl (R); Yrbk (E); Distinguished Honor Roll

DAVIS, BECKY; DILLSBURG, PA; NORTHERN YORK CTY HS; (FR); Hi Hnr Roll; WWAHSS; Comm Volntr; Peer Tut/Med; Chrch Yth Grp; Key Club; Bnd; Clr Grd; Dnce; Law; Political Science

DAVIS, BRETT; BOILING SPRINGS, PA; BOILING SPRINGS HS; (JR); Hnr Roll; Pres Ac Ftns Aw; WWAHSS; Yth Ldrshp Prog; Comm Volntr; Peer Tut/Med; Chrch Yth Grp; FCA; Bsball (V CL); Sccr (J L); Young Life; Math Teacher; Shippensburg U

DAVIS, CHRISTINA; MOUNT POCONO, PA; POCONO MOUNTAIN EAST HS; (FR); F Lan Hn Soc; Hi Hnr Roll; Hnr Roll; MVP; Comm Volntr; ArtClub; Emplmnt; Ch Chr; Howard U; Duke

DAVIS, CHRISTOPHER; PITTSBURGH, PA; PLUM SR HS; (SO); Hi Hnr Roll; Nat Sci Aw; Sci/Math Olympn; German Clb; Pre-Med; U of Pittsburgh

DAVIS, ELISABETH C; ORRSTOWN, PA; CHAMBERBURG AREA SR HS; (FR); Hi Hnr Roll; Hnr Roll; WWAHSS; Chrch Yth Grp; Drma Clb; French Clb; Chr; Orch; SP/M/VS; National American Miss State Finalist; Drama / Musical Theater; Music; Case Western U; New York U

DAVIS, JAMES B; WELLSVILLE, PA; NORTHERN YORK HS; (SR); F Lan Hn Soc; Hi Hnr Roll; Nat Hon Sy; Nat Mrt LOC; WWAHSS; Emplmnt; Key Club; Mth Clb/Tm; French Clb; SP/M/VS; Cr Ctry (V L); Track (V); Key Club (2004-2005 Vice President); Rotary Club Student of the Month 01/05; Electrical Engineering; Penn State U

DAVIS, JESSICA M; READING, PA; READING HS; (JR); Hnr Roll; St of Mnth; Spec Olymp Vol; Dnce; Nursing; Paralegal; Lehigh Valley College; Elmira

DAVIS, KRISTIN; PHILADELPHIA, PA; ST HUBERT CATHOLIC HS; (SO); Hnr Roll; DARE; Emplmnt; Nursing; Physician Assistant; Penn State; La Salle

DAVIS, MISTY J; CATAWISSA, PA; COLUMBIA-MONTOUR AVTS; (JR); Hi Hnr Roll; Hnr Roll; Nat Hon Sy; Perf Att; St of Mnth; Comm Volntr; Peer Tut/Med; Red Cr Aide; Chrch Yth Grp; DARE; Emplmnt; Jr Ach; Tchrs Aide; Straight "A" Student and Mom to Alex Jordan Davis; Artistic Abilities and Talent; Dental Assistant; Nursing; Bloomsburg U of Pennsylvania; College Misericordia

DAVIS, SAMANTHA; COATESVILLE, PA; BISHOP SHANAHAN HS; (JR); Hnr Roll; Comm Volntr; DARE; Emplmnt; Mth Clb/Tm; NYLC; SP/M/VS; Chrldg (VJ L); Camp Counselor For 5-8 yr Olds; Psychology; Psychiatry; Lehigh U; South Carolina U

DAWSON, JENNIFER A; PITTSBURGH, PA; SHADYSIDE AC SR SCH; (FR); Hi Hnr Roll; Hnr Roll; Pres Ac Ftns Aw; Comm Volntr; Spec Olymp Vol; Chrch Yth Grp; Emplmnt; French Clb; Chr; Cr Ctry (V L); Ice Sktg (J); Lcrsse (J); Stu Cncl (R)

DAY, CHRISSY; WEST FINLEY, PA; WEST GREENE HS; (JR); Hnr Roll; Nat Hon Sy; WWAHSS; Drma Clb; Lttrmn Clb; Vsity Clb; Scr Kpr (J); Track (V L); Vsy Clb (V L); Vllyball (V L); Yrbk (R, P); Winter Volleyball; International Real Estate

DAY, PATRICIA; BENSALEM, PA; BENSALEM TOWNSHIP SD HS; (FR); Ctznshp Aw; Hi Hnr Roll; Hnr Roll; Kwnis Aw; Otst Ac Ach Awd; Sci/Math Olympn; St of Mnth; Hab For Humty Volntr; Chrch Yth Grp; Track (V); Hulmeville Soccer Select Team; Peacemaking Committee; Forensic Science; Marine Biology; Cedar Crest College; U of Penn

DEAN, NAIM; PHILADELPHIA, PA; WILLIAM PENN HS; (JR); F Lan Hn Soc; Hnr Roll; Perf Att; Comm Volntr; Peer Tut/Med; Cr Ctry (V); Track (V); Game Clock Manager for JV & Varsity Basketball; Tennis Manager (But for Only Two Matches); Master's Degree; Graphic Design; The Art Institute of Philadelphia; Temple U

DEAVEN, KATALINA; PALMYRA, PA; LOWER DAUPHIN HS; (JR); F Lan Hn Soc; Hi Hnr Roll; Hnr Roll; Nat Hon Sy; WWAHSS; Drma Clb; Mus Clb; Spanish Clb; Dnce; Orch; SP/M/VS; Skiing; Volunteer Club; Journalism; Georgetown U

DEAVOR, NATASHA; HARRISBURG, PA; CTRL DAUPHIN HS; (JR); Hnr Roll; Perf Att; Outdrs Clb; Vllyball (V); Perfect Attendance; Working with Children; Harrisburg Community College 2 Years; Harrisburg Penn State 2 Years

DECIANTIS, DANIEL L; MARCUS HOOK, PA; THE CHRISTIAN AC; (JR); Ctznshp Aw; Duke TS; Hi Hnr Roll; Nat Hon Sy; Sci Fairs; Chess; Chrch Yth Grp; Quiz Bowl; Tchrs Aide; Bnd; Chr; Orch; SP/M/VS; Sccr (V L); Tennis (V L); Yrbk (R, P); Literature Degree; History Degree; Davidson U; Marietta College (Ohio)

DECKER, KERI; MARTINSBURG, PA; SPRING COVE SD; (JR); Hi Hnr Roll; Emplmnt; FBLA; Prom Com; Snowboarding; Radiology Technician; Legal Assistant; Mount Aloysius; Penn State U

DEETS, SHELBY; TITUSVILLE, PA; MAPLEWOOD JR/SR HS; (MS); 4H Awd; Hnr Roll; 4-H; Sci Clb; Bnd; Jzz Bnd; Mch Bnd; Pep Bnd; I Show Dogs; My Dog (Shanook) and I Received Our CGC (Canine Good Citizenship); Doctor of Veterinary Medicine; Major in Music; Penn State U; Edinboro U of Pennsylvania

DE FAZIO, VINCENT; PITTSBURGH, PA; (FR); Hi Hnr Roll; Nat Hon Sy; Perf Att; Ntl Beta Clb; Architecture; Syracuse U; Martin College

DEFRAIN, DEVAN J M; NESCOPECK, PA; BERWICK AREA SR HS; (MS); Hnr Roll; St of Mnth; Ftball; Video Game Designer; Michigan State; Miami

DE HOFF, ABBY L; HARRISBURG, PA; CTRL DAUPHIN HS; (MS); Hnr Roll; Emplmnt; Bskball (L); Fld Hky (L); Sccr (L); Baby Sitting Certification; YMCA Camp Counselor Jr; Phys Ed Teacher; Penn State U

DEIST, JILL; BOSWELL, PA; NORTH STAR HS; (SO); Hi Hnr Roll; Hnr Roll; Sccr (VJC); Sftball (V)

DE JESUS, ALICIA; READING, PA; READING HS; (JR); Hnr Roll; St of Mnth; Comm Volntr; Emplmnt; Lib Aide; Prom Com; Tchrs Aide; Voc Ind Clb Am; HOSA President; Nursing Degree; Kutztown U; Penn State Berks Lehigh

DELACIO, JOHN; GIBSONIA, PA; PINE-RICHLAND HS; (FR); Hi Hnr Roll; Hnr Roll; Nat Stu Ath Day Aw; Comm Volntr; Peer Tut/Med; Chess; Scr Kpr (V); Skiing; Sccr; Vllyball (J); Cl Off (V); Member "Key Communicator" with Superintendent; Aerospace Engineers; Lawyer; Massachusetts Institute of Technology; Georgetown U

DE LAURIER, MARQUERITTE; PITTSBURGH, PA; SCHENLEY HS; (JR); Hi Hnr Roll; Comm Volntr; French Clb; Dnce; Swmg (V); Vllyball (V); Mock Trial; Student Advisory Council; Psychology; Pre-Med; Penn State; U of California San Diego

DELGROS, ELIZABETH; HERMITAGE, PA; HERMITAGE SD; (SO); F Lan Hn Soc; Hi Hnr Roll; WWAHSS; Peer Tut/Med; Chrch Yth Grp; Drma Clb; Emplmnt; Mth Clb/Tm; French Clb; Bnd; Mch Bnd; SP/M/VS; Stg Cre; Psychology; Carnegie-Mellon; U of Pittsburgh

DELLIGATTI, AMANDA; GILBERTSVILLE, PA; BOYERTOWN AREA SR HS; (JR); Ctznshp Aw; Hi Hnr Roll; Nat Hon Sy; Otst Ac Ach Awd; Pres Sch; Comm Volntr; Emplmnt; Key Club; Dnce; CR (R); Communications; Marketing; Fordham U; Drexel U

DEL MASTRO, ERICA A; WEXFORD, PA; NORTH ALLEGHENY HS; (JR); Hnr Roll; Comm Volntr; Hab For Humty Volntr; Chrch Yth Grp; DARE; Emplmnt; Prom Com; SADD; SP/M/VS; Track (VJ L); Stu Cncl (V); CR; Yrbk (E, P); Religious Education Teacher; Retreat Leader; Elementary Education; Secondary Education; Pennsylvania Penn State U, PA; Elon U, NC

DE LOACH, LORRAINE; LANSDALE, PA; NORTH PENN HS; (SR); Hi Hnr Roll; Hnr Roll; WWAHSS; Amnsty Intl; Spec Olymp Vol; 4-H; DARE; Key Club; Scouts; Pharmacy Technician; Graphic Designer; Montgomery County Community College

DE LOOF, JARED; SPRING MILLS, PA; PENNS VALLEY AREA HS; (FR); Spec Olymp Vol; Emplmnt; JSA; Key Club; P to P St Amb Prg; SADD; French Clb; Track (J); Stu Cncl (R); Foreign Service; Georgetown U; George Washington U

DELP, MEGAN; HERMITAGE, PA; HERMITAGE SD; (SO); F Lan Hn Soc; Hi Hnr Roll; WWAHSS; Peer Tut/Med; Chrch Yth Grp; Drma Clb; Mod UN; French Clb; Bnd; Chr; SP/M/VS; Treasurer of French Club; Biotechnology; Genetics; Rochester Institute of Technology

DE LUCA, GINA; VANDERGRIFT, PA; KISKI AREA HS; (JR); Hnr Roll; Comm Volntr; Emplmnt; Key Club; Off Aide; Pep Squd; Prom Com; SADD; Chr; Dnce; SP/M/VS; Chrldg (V L); Gmnstcs (V); Stu Cncl (R); CR (R); Nutrition; Personal Training; Indiana U of Pittsburgh; Slippery Rock U

DE LUCA, MORGAN; DILLSBURG, PA; NORTHERN HS; (FR); Hi Hnr Roll; WWAHSS; Peer Tut/Med; Spec Olymp Vol; Chrch Yth Grp; Key Club; P to P St Amb Prg; Cr Ctry (J); Sccr (J); Envirothon; People to People Student Ambassador; Languages

DE MARCO, JOSH; WATERFORD, PA; FORT LEBOEUF SD; (JR); Peer Tut/Med; Scouts; Bnd; Jzz Bnd; Mch Bnd; Orch

DE MATTEIS, DESIREE; ALIQUIPPA, PA; HOPEWELL AREA SCH DISTRICT; (JR); Hnr Roll; Pres Ac Ftns Aw; WWAHSS; Hosp Aide; ArtClub; Off Aide; German Clb; Stg Cre; Skiing; Sccr (J); Sftball (VJ L); Swmg (V); Principal's Student Leadership Advisory; Scholar Athlete Award; Nursing; Forensics; Carlow College; Waynesburg College

DEMCHAK, MATTHEW; JOHNSTOWN, PA; CTRL CAMBRIA HS; (FR); Hi Hnr Roll; Perf Att; Chrch Yth Grp; Chr; Ftball (J); Wt Lftg (J); Stu Cncl (R); Captain Pony League Baseball Team; Teaching; Criminology; U of Pittsburgh; Indiana U of Pennsylvania

D'EMIDIO, ASHLEY L; BRISTOL, PA; BRISTOL JR/SR HS; (SR); Hi Hnr Roll; Nat Hon Sy; Comm Volntr; Dbte Team; Emplmnt; Lib Aide; Mod UN; Prom Com; Spch Team; Bskball (J); Adv Cncl (T); Cl Off (T); Stu Cncl (R); CR (R); Best Witness- Mock Trial; Dermatology; West Chester U

DEMPSEY, BEAUTINE; PHILADELPHIA, PA; NORTHEAST HS; (JR); Hnr Roll; Nat Hon Sy; WWAHSS; Pep Squd; Drl Tm; Track (V); Business Owner; Psychologist; U of Pittsburgh; Temple U

DEMPSEY, JACLYN; DUNMORE, PA; DUNMORE SD; (MS); Hi Hnr Roll; Nat Hon Sy; St of Mnth; Comm Volntr; Peer Tut/Med; DARE; Scouts; Bnd; Ch Chr; Dnce; Mch Bnd; Bskball; Skiing; Vllyball; Yrbk (E, P); Junior National Honor Society Officer; Doctor; Accountant; Duke; Colgate

DEMSEY, KRISTIN L; GLENSHAW, PA; SHALER AREA HS; (JR); Hi Hnr Roll; Hnr Roll; Otst Ac Ach Awd; Perf Att; St of Mnth; Peer Tut/Med; Drma Clb; Emplmnt; FTA; Jr Ach; Key Club; Off Aide; Chr; SP/M/VS; Swg Chr; PP Ftbl; Sftball (J); Track (V); AIU Conducting Apprenticeship / Accompanist Awards; Music Education; Duquesne U; Indiana U of Pennsylvania

DENNETT, CAITLIN E; POTTSTOWN, PA; POTTSGROVE HS; (JR); Ctznshp Aw; Gov Hnr Prg; Hi Hnr Roll; Nat Hon Sy; St of Mnth; Emplmnt; FTA; Key Club; Sci Clb; Tchrs Aide; SPANISH LA Clb; Bskball (J); Sccr (V); Sftball (J); Yrbk; Team Captain Relay for Life ACS; Washington U; Duke U

DENNIS, DEMI A; LANSDALE, PA; OKEECHOBEE JUV. JUSTICE VISION HS; (SO); Hi Hnr Roll; Hnr Roll; Nat Hon Sy; DARE; Emplmnt; Lib Aide; Chr; Dnce; Cr Ctry (V); Hsbk Rdg (V); Registered Nurse; Temple U

DENSLINGER, MICHELLE; MECHANICSBURG, PA; EAST PENNSBORO AREA HS; (FR); Hnr Roll; Peer Tut/Med; Spec Olymp Vol; Chrch Yth Grp; Scouts; Latin Clb; Fld Hky (J); Principal's Award; Academic Honors; Physical Therapist; Meteorologist; U of Pittsburgh; Penn State U

DENSLINGER, SARA; MECHANICSBURG, PA; EAST PENNSBORO AREA HS; (FR); Hnr Roll; Peer Tut/Med; Spec Olymp Vol; Chrch Yth Grp; Latin Clb; Principal's Award; Academic Honors; Physical Therapy; Lawyer; Penn State U; U of Pittsburgh

DE PAOLIS, DANIELLE L; MURRYSVILLE, PA; FRANKLIN REG HS; (JR); Hi Hnr Roll; WWAHSS; Yth Ldrshp Prog; Chrch Yth Grp; Chr; Clr Grd; Sccr (V); Track (V); Yrbk (R, P); Engineering; Carnegie Mellon U; U of Pittsburgh

DE PAUL, KRISTI; PITTSBURGH, PA; PLUM SR HS; (SO); Hi Hnr Roll; Peer Tut/Med; Emplmnt; SP/M/VS; Chrldg (J); Cl Off (V); Pre-Med

DE PRINCE, JOSEPH; COLLINGDALE, PA; AC PARK HS; (SR); Emplmnt; Play Guitar; Drexel U

DE PUY, KAYLA E; WEST MIDDLESEX, PA; HERMITAGE SD; (SO); Hnr Roll; Otst Ac Ach Awd; Pres Ac Ftns Aw; Hosp Aide; Drma Clb; Scouts; Bnd; Chr; Drm Mjr; Stg Cre; Bowling Varsity Captain; YABA Youth Leader Treasurer; Doctor; Political Science; Slippery Rock U

DERMO, RONI L; POTTSVILLE, PA; POTTSVILLE AREA HS; (JR); Hi Hnr Roll; WWAHSS; Comm Volntr; Emplmnt; Key Club; Quill & Scroll; Chrldg (V); Sccr (J); Track (V); Lit Mag (P); Sch Ppr (P); Yrbk (P); Among Highest Scoring on PSAT / NMSQT; Pre-Med; Franklin and Marshall U; St Joseph's U

DERO, JESSICA; COATESVILLE, PA; BISHOP SHANAHAN HS; (JR); Hnr Roll; Sci Fairs; Peer Tut/Med; Mth Clb/Tm; French Clb; Stg Cre; Was a Bug in BBBS program; Honorable Mention in Science Fair; Engineering; Biology; Cornell U; Manhattan College

DE SABATO, JESSICA; PHILADELPHIA, PA; GIRARD AC MUSIC PROGRAM; (SO); Hnr Roll; Perf Att; WWAHSS; Chr; Stu Cncl (R); Forensic Science; Psychology; U of Pennsylvania; Harvard U

DESAI, NESHA; MECHANICSBURG, PA; CUMBERLAND VALLEY HS; (JR); Hnr Roll; WWAHSS; ArtClub; Key Club; Spanish Clb; Key Club Historian; Recreational Softball; Speech Pathology; U of Pittsburgh

DE SANTIS, SUSANNE N; ERIE, PA; COLLEGIATE AC; (SR); Hi Hnr Roll; Nat Hon Sy; Perf Att; WWAHSS; Peer Tut/Med; Spec Olymp Vol; Chrch Yth Grp; Spanish Clb; Bskball (V CL); Golf (V CL); Sccr (V L); Stu Cncl (R); Yrbk (E); Freshman Orientation Volunteer; Student Usher Society

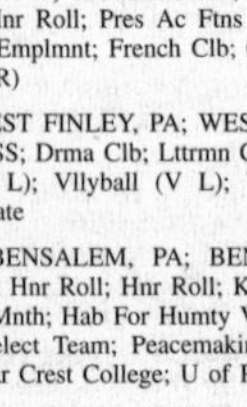
Dero, Jessica
Bishop Shanahan HS
Coatesville, PA

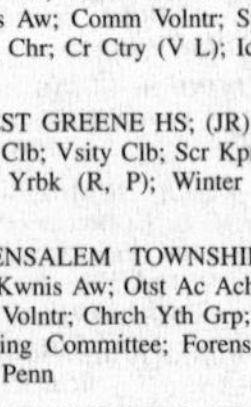
De Puy, Kayla E
Hermitage SD
West Middlesex, PA

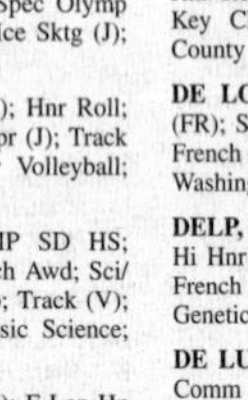
Deavor, Natasha
Central Dauphin HS
Harrisburg, PA

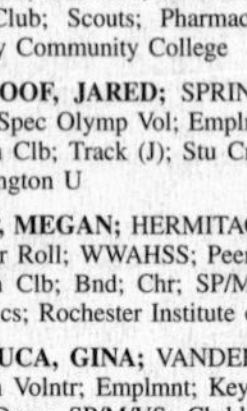
Davis, Samantha
Bishop Shanahan HS
Coatesville, PA

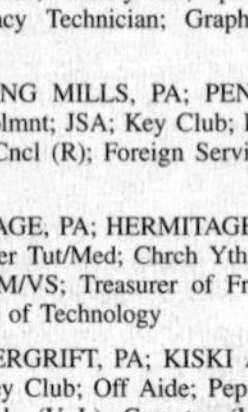
Davis, James B
Northern York HS
Wellsville, PA

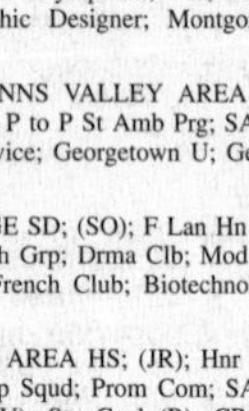
Davis, Jessica M
Reading HS
Reading, PA

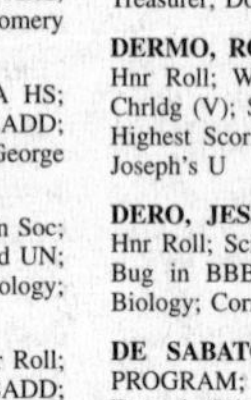
De Matteis, Desiree
Hopewell Area Sch District
Aliquippa, PA

Dermo, Roni L
Pottsville Area HS
Pottsville, PA

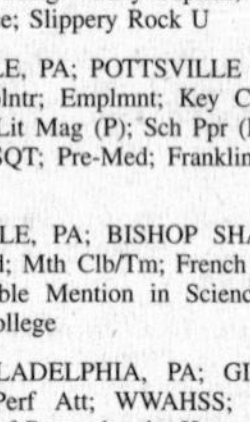
De Sabato, Jessica
Girard AC Music Program
Philadelphia, PA

DE SENSI, ROBERTO P; PITTSBURGH, PA; NORTH ALLEGHENY HS; (FR); Hnr Roll; Comm Volntr; Chrch Yth Grp; Key Club; Scouts; Chr; Bskball; Mar Art; Architecture

DETRICK, BROOKE; HOLLIDAYSBURG, PA; HOLLIDAYSBURG AREA SR HS; (SO); Hnr Roll; WWAHSS; Comm Volntr; Spec Olymp Vol; Key Club; Sftball (VJ); Nursing; U of Pittsburgh; Temple U

DEVINNEY, CRAIG; ALLISON PARK, PA; SHALER AREA INT SCH; (JR); Ctznshp Aw; Hi Hnr Roll; Hnr Roll; Comm Volntr; Emplmnt; Bskball (V); Duquesne U

DE VITO, DENISE; GREENVILLE, PA; REYNOLDS HS; (FR); Hi Hnr Roll; WWAHSS; Comm Volntr; Chrch Yth Grp; Key Club; Chr; Track; Theatre Arts / Dancing & Singing; Photography; Brigham Young U Idaho

DEVLIN, ANN M; UPPER DARBY, PA; UPPER DARBY HS; (JR); Hi Hnr Roll; Hnr Roll; Otst Ac Ach Awd; Perf Att; Comm Volntr; Peer Tut/Med; Spec Olymp Vol; ArtClub; FCA; Svce Clb; SADD; Clb; Chr; Homecoming; Science-Animal Anatomy; Veterinarian; Manor College; St. Joseph's

DEVLIN, BRIANNA M; LAFAYETTE HL, PA; PLYMOUTH WHITEMARSH HS; (FR); Hnr Roll; Otst Ac Ach Awd; SADD; Bskball; PP Ftbl; Sftball; Master's Degree / PhD - Education; Master's Degree / PhD - Medicine; Villanova U; Notre Dame U

DEVOE, SHANE W; PARKESBURG, PA; LAN-CHESTER CHRISTIAN SCH; (SO); Hi Hnr Roll; Hnr Roll; Sci Fairs; USAA; Yth Ldrshp Prog; Comm Volntr; Chrch Yth Grp; Emplmnt; Lib Aide; Off Aide; Scouts; Tchrs Aide; Wdwrkg Clb; SP/M/VS; Stg Cre; Stu Cncl; Outstanding Christian Testimony Award; Pharmacy

DHADLI, PARNEET K; MECHANICSBURG, PA; CUMBERLAND VALLEY HS; (JR); F Lan Hn Soc; Hi Hnr Roll; Hnr Roll; Nat Hon Sy; Comm Volntr; Hosp Aide; Key Club; Spanish Clb; Lcrsse (VJ); Medicine; Temple U

DIAMOND, DANIELLE; CRANBERRY TWP, PA; SENECA VALLEY SR HS; (JR); Hi Hnr Roll; Hnr Roll; MVP; Nat Hon Sy; Otst Ac Ach Awd; Pres Sch; WWAHSS; Peer Tut/Med; Chrch Yth Grp; Emplmnt; Key Club; P to P St Amb Prg; Vsity Clb; Track (V L); Vsy Clb (V); Vllyball (V L); Sch Ppr (R); Jr. Olympic Volleyball Team-Nationals 04/05 with Pittsburgh Elite Volleyball Team; Psychology; Business Communications

DIAS, TAYLOR K; ALLENTOWN, PA; SALISBURY HS; (JR); Hnr Roll; Jr Rot; WWAHSS; Yth Ldrshp Prog; Comm Volntr; Peer Tut/Med; Red Cr Aide; Key Club; SADD; Chr; Chrldg (C); Sccr (J); Adv Cncl; Stu Cncl; CR; Highly Active in Student Government; President of the Interact Club; Engineering; Civil Litigation; Lehigh; Lafayette

DIAZ, CANDY; CHESTER, PA; CHESTER HS; (JR); Hnr Roll; Dentist; Temple U; Penn State U

DIBELL, JASON M; WATERFORD, PA; FORT LEBOEUF SD; (SO); Hnr Roll; St of Mnth; Emplmnt; Wdwrkg Clb; Computer Engineering; Business; Penn State U; Behrend College

DICKEY, ALISHA M; TIDIOUTE, PA; YOUNGSVILLE MIDDLE SR HS; (SR); Hi Hnr Roll; Hnr Roll; Nat Hon Sy; WWAHSS; ArtClub; DARE; SADD; German Clb; Chr; Vllyball (J); Student Council; Indiana U of Pennsylvania

DICKISON, ALEXANDRA; EAST STROUDSBURG, PA; EAST STROUDSBURG HS SOUTH; (SO); Ctznshp Aw; Hi Hnr Roll; Otst Ac Ach Awd; Yth Ldrshp Prog; Svce Clb; Chr; Clr Grd; SP/M/VS; Swg Chr; Adv Cncl (R); Cl Off (V); Musical Theater; Business; Arizona State U; Ithaca College

DICKMANN, JULIE; LANSDALE, PA; NORTH PENN HS; (SR); Hnr Roll; Spec Olymp Vol; Tchrs Aide; Elementary Education; Millersville U

DIEFENDERFER, MICAH; ZIONSVILLE, PA; SALEM CHRISTIAN SCH; (FR); Hnr Roll; Chrch Yth Grp; Bsball (V); Bskball (VJ); Sccr (VJC); Sch Ppr (R); Air Traffic Control / Management; Geneva College

DIEMER, DANIELLE; BERWICK, PA; COLUMBIA-MONTOUR AVTS; (SO); Hnr Roll; Comm Volntr; Ntl FFA; Prom Com; Voc Ind Clb Am; Chrldg (V L); Cl Off (S); Sch Ppr (R); USA Skills - VICA; Armed Forces; Parson New York Design School

DIEROLF, GINA; READING, PA; NORTHEAST MS; (MS); Chrch Yth Grp; Journalist; English Major; Reading Area Community College; Albright College

DI LAURO, ALYCE A; DREXEL HILL, PA; UPPER DARBY HS; (JR); Hi Hnr Roll; Hnr Roll; Nat Hon Sy; Photog; Stg Cre; Swmg (V); Sch Ppr (R); Yrbk (E); Photography; Graphic Arts; Penn State U; St. Joe's U

DILLMAN, ROSEANN C; PLYMOUTH MEETING, PA; PLYMOUTH WHITEMARSH HS; (SO); Hi Hnr Roll; Hnr Roll; Nat Hon Sy; Comm Volntr; Peer Tut/Med; ArtClub; Emplmnt; Photog; SP/M/VS; PP Ftbl (J); Sftball (L); CR (R); Sch Ppr (E); Black Belt - Kempo Karate; Acoustic / Electric Guitarist; Communications Major; Medical Field; Shippensburg U; Columbia U

DIMINICK, ALYSSA; LEMOYNE, PA; TRINITY HS; (FR); Hi Hnr Roll; WWAHSS; Comm Volntr; Key Club; Lttrmn Clb; Pep Squd; P to P St Amb Prg; Spanish Clb; Chrldg (V); Vllyball (J); Pre-Med; Art/Design; Villanova U; New York U

DIMINICK, JOSEPH K; LEMOYNE, PA; TRINITY HS; (JR); Hnr Roll; Sci Fairs; WWAHSS; Yth Ldrshp Prog; Comm Volntr; Peer Tut/Med; Key Club; Lttrmn Clb; P to P St Amb Prg; Spanish Clb; Bskball (V L); Ftball (V L); Track (V L); Peers Actively Listening Leader; Student Ambassador; Dental; Medical; Boston College; New York U

DINGER, SARAH G; BROOKVILLE, PA; BROOKVILLE AREA SD; (JR); All Am Sch; Hi Hnr Roll; Hnr Roll; Nat Hon Sy; USAA; WWAHSS; Comm Volntr; Spec Olymp Vol; Chrch Yth Grp; Emplmnt; Prom Com; Scouts; Spanish Clb; Bnd; Chr; Jzz Bnd; SP/M/VS; Track (V); Stu Cncl (R); Lit Mag (R, P); Girl Scout Silver Award; Writing Club

DINGMAN, CHERYL A; LANSDALE, PA; NORTH PENN HS; (SR); Hnr Roll; MVP; Pres Ac Ftns Aw; WWAHSS; Spec Olymp Vol; Key Club; Cr Ctry (V C); Track (V C); Various Art Awards; MVP Cross Country & Trade State Qualifier; BFA in Communications Design; BS in Art Education; Will Attend Kutztown U

DI NUCCI, JILL S; GLENSHAW, PA; SHALER AREA INT SCH; Bskball (V CL); Sch Ppr (R); Speech and Debate Team; WPIAL - Basketball Freshman of Year 2003; Journalism; Psychology; Bucknell U; Duquesne U

DIPRATO, MARCO; NORTH WALES, PA; LASALLE COLLEGE HS; (SO); Hi Hnr Roll; Hnr Roll; Italian Clb; Bnd; Jzz Bnd; Bskball (J); Ftball (J); Track (J); Pianist-10 Yrs and Going; Mock Trial Lawyer-(Club); Law; Architectural Engineering; LaSalle College; Villanova

DIRADDO, ANNAMARIE V; WARMINSTER, PA; WILLIAM TENNENT HS; (JR); Hnr Roll; Otst Ac Ach Awd; Comm Volntr; Red Cr Aide; ArtClub; Emplmnt; Key Club; Photog; Dnce; Journalism; Art History

DIRKX, KAITLIN; GLENMOORE, PA; OWEN J ROBERTS HS; (SR); Hi Hnr Roll; Hnr Roll; Comm Volntr; Spec Olymp Vol; ArtClub; Emplmnt; P to P St Amb Prg; Swmg (V L); Tennis (J); Piano Player; Journalism; Law; American U; Temple U

DI SANTO, NICOLAS; HARRISBURG, PA; TRINITY HS; (JR); Hi Hnr Roll; Hnr Roll; MVP; Nat Ldrshp Svc; Otst Ac Ach Awd; Hab For Humty Volntr; Chess; Emplmnt; Spanish Clb; Golf (V C); Tennis (V); Intramural Basketball Champs/Captain; Volunteer YMCA Youth Basketball; Business Admin; Real Estate Development; Morehead State U; U of Connecticut

DITZLER, ASHLEY; NEWVILLE, PA; BIG SPRING SD; (JR); Comm Volntr; SADD; Bskball (J C); Vllyball (V); Stu Cncl (R); Team Made Play-Offs During the 2004-2005 Basketball; Medical Field / Doctor or Dentist; Graphic Design / Bachelor's Degree; Penn State; Art Institute of Pittsburgh

DITZLER, BRIAN R; WINDBER, PA; SHADE-CENTRAL CITY SD; (SO); Hi Hnr Roll; Nat Hon Sy; Emplmnt; Lttrmn Clb; Scouts; Vsity Clb; Arch; Ftball (V L); Skt Tgt Sh; Track (V L); Vsy Clb (V L); Wt Lftg (V); Stu Cncl (R); Life Scout- Soon Eagle; Attend College

DODSON IV, ALBERT E; GIBSONIA, PA; PINE-RICHLAND HS; (JR); Hi Hnr Roll; Hnr Roll; Nat Hon Sy; USAA; Comm Volntr; Emplmnt; Key Club; NtlFrnscLg; P to P St Amb Prg; SADD; Aerospace Engineering; Mechanical Engineering; Carnegie Mellon U; Georgia Tech

DOERFLER, MEGAN; SARVER, PA; FREEPORT HS; (SO); Hi Hnr Roll; Pres Ac Ftns Aw; Comm Volntr; Emplmnt; FCA; Key Club; Chr; Dnce; SP/M/VS; Chrldg (JCL); PP Ftbl (J); Scr Kpr (V); Sftball (J); Yrbk (P); MD

DOLBY, ADAM; CLARION, PA; CLARION AREA JR/SR HS; (SO); Chr; SP/M/VS; Swg Chr; Bsball; Bskball; Ftball; Skiing; Vsy Clb; Wt Lftg; Education; Business Management; Penn State U; Clarion U

DOMBROWSKI, DESIREE M; PHILADELPHIA, PA; KENSINGTON HS; (SR); Sftball; Vllyball; Young Author Award; Magnificent Student Award; Child Care

DONATELLO, ASHLEY; TAYLOR, PA; RIVERSIDE JR/SR HS; (JR); Hi Hnr Roll; Comm Volntr; Chrch Yth Grp; DARE; Dnce; Chrldg (VJ); Cl Off (S); Education; Mathematics; Penn State U; U of Scranton

DONN, ASHLEY; KULPMONT, PA; MT CARMEL AREA JR/SR HS; (SO); Hi Hnr Roll; Hnr Roll; Nat Hon Sy; Comm Volntr; Peer Tut/Med; Chrch Yth Grp; Emplmnt; Scouts; Bnd; Chr; Ch Chr; Jzz Bnd; Stu Cncl; Sch Ppr; Music Education; Mansfield U

DONNELLY, RUTHANN; PHILADELPHIA, PA; FRANKLIN LEARNING CTR; (SO); Hi Hnr Roll; Perf Att; Sci Fairs; Comm Volntr; Chrch Yth Grp; DARE; Lib Aide; Various Church Activities; Temple U; Penn State U

DONNER, DUSTIN; HERMITAGE, PA; HICKORY HS; (FR); Otst Ac Ach Awd; St of Mnth; Peer Tut/Med; Red Cr Aide; Drma Clb; Mth Clb/Tm; Pep Squd; SADD; Chr; Mch Bnd; Orch; Pep Bnd; SP/M/VS; Stg Cre; Track; Stu Cncl

DONOHUE, HALEY K; OAKMONT, PA; RIVERVIEW JR/SR HS; (SO); Hnr Roll; Kwnis Aw; Nat Hon Sy; Pres Sch; WWAHSS; Comm Volntr; Key Club; Lib Aide; SADD; French Clb; Chr; Orch; SP/M/VS; PMEA District Orchestra; PMEA District Choir; Major - Political Science; Minor - Music; U of Pittsburgh; Carnegie Mellon U

DORATT, JACQUELYN R; COATESVILLE, PA; LAN-CHESTER CHRISTIAN SCH; (SO); Hnr Roll; WWAHSS; Tchrs Aide; SP/M/VS; Scr Kpr (VJ); Vllyball (V); Cl Off (P); Stu Cncl (S); CR (R); Pediatrics; Biology; Drexel; Johns Hopkins Medical U

DORLUS, MACKENSON; PHILADELPHIA, PA; OLNEY HS; (JR); ArtClub; Bnd; Jzz Bnd; Mch Bnd; Bskball (V); Sccr (V); Vllyball (V); I Used to Be Number One Student in Class; Law Studies; Medical Studies; Temple U; Drexel U

DOROGY, ELIZABETH A; HARMONY, PA; SENECA VALLEY INT HS; (SO); Hi Hnr Roll; WWAHSS; Key Club; Lttrmn Clb; Vsity Clb; Chr; Sftball (V L); Vllyball (V L); Stu Cncl (R); English; Physical Therapy

DORSEY, MORGAN; WALNUTPORT, PA; NORTHAMPTON HS; (JR); Hi Hnr Roll; Hnr Roll; Spanish Clb; Work At a Public Library; Pre-Med; Ob/Gyn; Muhlenberg College

DOS DIAZ, GERARDO; READING, PA; READING HS; (FR); Hnr Roll; Spec Olymp Vol; ArtClub; Chrch Yth Grp; Clb; Vllyball (V C); Most Improved Volleyball Player - 9th Grade; Professional Volleyball Player / Degree in Graphic Design

DOUCETTE, SAMANTHA A; WEST NEWTON, PA; YOUGH SD; (SO); Scouts; French Clb; Mch Bnd

DOUMA, STEPHANIE; HARRISBURG, PA; CTRL DAUPHIN SD; (FR); Hi Hnr Roll; Perf Att; St of Mnth; Comm Volntr; Chrch Yth Grp; Mus Clb; Scouts; Bnd; Chr; Dnce; Mch Bnd; National Junior Honor Society; Ophthalmology

DOUTHIT, MICHAEL; SHIPPENVILLE, PA; CLARION AREA JR/SR HS; (SO); 4H Awd; Hi Hnr Roll; Hnr Roll; Sci/Math Olympn; Comm Volntr; Hab For Humty Volntr; Spec Olymp Vol; 4-H; Chrch Yth Grp; Emplmnt; Scouts; Bnd; Jzz Bnd; Mch Bnd; Pep Bnd; Track (V); PharmD; U of Pittsburgh; Duquesne U

DOWNEY, ASHLEY; RICES LANDING, PA; JEFFERSON-MORGAN HS; (JR); Hi Hnr Roll; WWAHSS; Bnd; Mch Bnd; SP/M/VS; Track (V); National Society of High School Scholars; Marine Biology; Author; Virginia Wesleyan College; College of William and Mary

DOWNEY, KARA E; LANCASTER, PA; MANHEIM TWP HS; (SO); Hi Hnr Roll; Hnr Roll; WWAHSS; Comm Volntr; Hab For Humty Volntr; Spec Olymp Vol; Chrch Yth Grp; Emplmnt; Key Club; SADD; SP/M/VS; Stg Cre; Lit Mag; Business; Law; Xavier U; U of Notre Dame

DOWNING, KYREE; PHILADELPHIA, PA; KENSINGTON HS; (MS); Peer Tut/Med; ArtClub; Bnd; Orch; SP/M/VS; Ftball (J); Sftball (J); Track (J); Police Officer (Narcotics); Doctor; Temple U

DRANE, MICHAEL R; PITTSBURGH, PA; PENN HILLS SR HS; (SR); Hi Hnr Roll; Hnr Roll; Comm Volntr; Chrch Yth Grp; DARE; Emplmnt; Bnd; Jzz Bnd; Mch Bnd; Civil War Reenactor; Teach History; Shippensburg State U

DRANKO, ERICA L; IRWIN, PA; NORWIN SD; (SR); Hi Hnr Roll; Jr Rot; Nat Hon Sy; Pres Sch; Sci Fairs; WWAHSS; Comm Volntr; Hosp Aide; Chrch Yth Grp; Drma Clb; Emplmnt; Off Aide; SADD; Spanish Clb; Chr; Ch Chr; PP Ftbl (V); Skiing (V); National Honor Society Vice President; Pharmacy; Pediatrics; West Virginia U

DREHER, NICHOLAS; WORCESTER, PA; LA SALLE COLLEGE HS; (SO); Hi Hnr Roll; Hnr Roll; Otst Ac Ach Awd; Pres Sch; Sci Fairs; Sci/Math Olympn; Amnsty Intl; Chrch Yth Grp; Emplmnt; Scouts; Bnd; Political Science; Law; U of Pennsylvania; U of Scranton

DRENNEN, RACHEL; WARREN, PA; WARREN AREA HS; (JR); Hi Hnr Roll; Perf Att; Yth Ldrshp Prog; Comm Volntr; Chrch Yth Grp; Mod UN; P to P St Amb Prg; Quiz Bowl; French Clb; Acpl Chr; SP/M/VS; Chrldg (J); Tennis (V L); Stu Cncl (R); Sch Ppr (R); Spirit Leader on Cheerleading Squad; Healthy Communities/Healthy Youth Board Member; Law; Political Science; American U; U of Pittsburgh

DREW, TYRELL S; MT HOLLY SPGS, PA; BOILING SPRINGS HS; (JR); Ctznshp Aw; Hnr Roll; WWAHSS; Yth Ldrshp Prog; Comm Volntr; Spec Olymp Vol; Chrch Yth Grp; Emplmnt; Lib Aide; Bsball (J); Secondary Education; Photography; Shippensburg; Millersville

DRISCOLL, ANTHONY J; CLARION, PA; CLARION AREA JR/SR HS; (SO); Hnr Roll; WWAHSS; Comm Volntr; Bsball (V); Ftball (V L); Wrstlg (V L); Golf Course Design; Landscape Architect; Clarion U; Penn State U

DROZD, CAMILA; STROUDSBURG, PA; POCONO MTN WEST HS; (SR); Ctznshp Aw; Hi Hnr Roll; Nat Hon Sy; Otst Ac Ach Awd; Perf Att; St of Mnth; Valdctrian; WWAHSS; Spec Olymp Vol; Mod UN; Vsity Clb; Skiing; Tennis (V L); Member of National Society of High School Scholars; District XI Tennis Scholar Athlete; Lehigh U

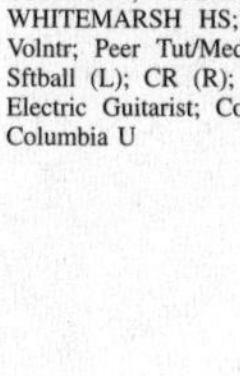
Drennen, Rachel
Warren Area HS
Warren, PA

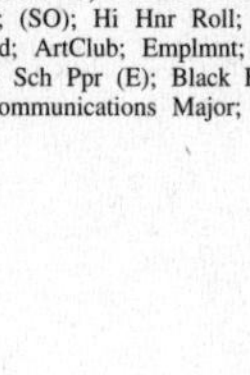
Donnelly, Ruthann
Franklin Learning Ctr
Philadelphia, PA

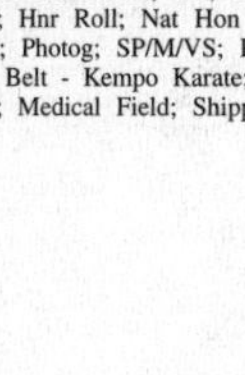
Ditzler, Brian R
Shade-Central City SD
Windber, PA

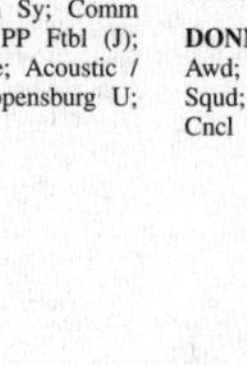
Di Nucci, Jill S
Shaler Area Int Sch
Glenshaw, PA

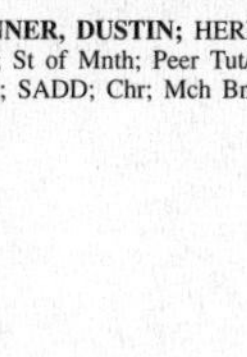
Diamond, Danielle
Seneca Valley SR HS
Cranberry Twp, PA

National
Honor Roll
Spring 2005

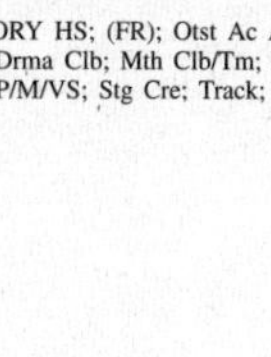
Devlin, Ann M
Upper Darby HS
Upper Darby, PA

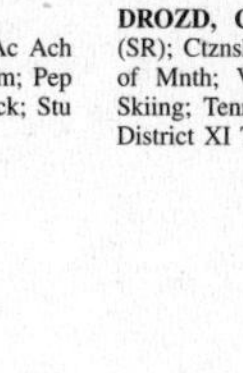
Diprato, Marco
Lasalle College HS
North Wales, PA

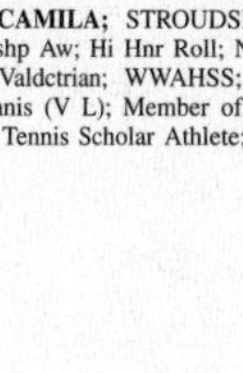
Dodson IV, Albert E
Pine-Richland HS
Gibsonia, PA

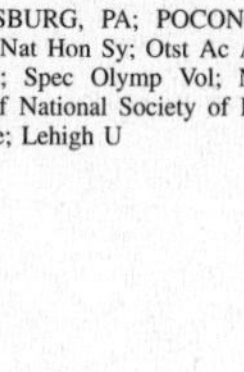
Dorlus, Mackenson
Olney HS
Philadelphia, PA

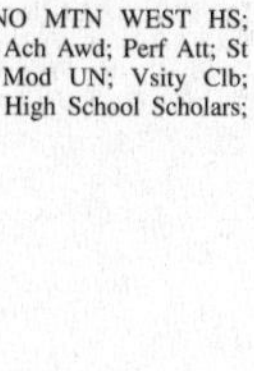
Douthit, Michael
Clarion Area JR/SR HS
Shippenville, PA

DRUMMOND POPE, RACHEL E; RUSSELL, PA; EISENHOWER HS; (SR); Hi Hnr Roll; Hnr Roll; Nat Hon Sy; WWAHSS; Comm Volntr; Emplmnt; Key Club; P to P St Amb Prg; Prom Com; German Clb; Dnce; Chrldg (V); GAA; Skiing; Track (V CL); Vllyball (V L); Sch Ppr (R, P); Fashion Designer; Kent State U

DRURY, AUTUMN; EAST STROUDSBURG, PA; EAST STROUDSBURG HS SOUTH; (JR); Hi Hnr Roll; Hnr Roll; WWAHSS; Comm Volntr; Emplmnt; Key Club; P to P St Amb Prg; Foreign Clb; Lit Mag (R); Sch Ppr (E); Yrbk (R); People to People Student Ambassador; Journalism/English; Psychology; Northampton Community College

DRURY, KIERSTEN; EAST STROUDSBURG, PA; EAST STROUDSBURG HS SOUTH; (SO); Hnr Roll; WWAHSS; Comm Volntr; Emplmnt; Fld Hky (J); Sftball (J); Registered Nurse/Obstetrics; East Stroudsburg U

DRZIK, JOHN; NEW GALILEE, PA; BIG BEAVER FALLS HS; (JR); Hi Hnr Roll; Nat Hon Sy; Perf Att; Pres Sch; WWAHSS; Biology Clb; Chrch Yth Grp; Key Club; Scouts; Spanish Clb; Bnd; Ch Chr; Jzz Bnd; Mch Bnd; Stu Cncl (R); Math Education; Geneva College; Gannon U

DUCK, BOBBY J; HUNTINGDON, PA; TUSCARORA BLENDED LEARNING CHARTER SCH; (FR); Hnr Roll; Otst Ac Ach Awd; Law Assistant; Lawyer; Ohio State U; Law School

DUDA, PATRICK J; DONORA, PA; RINGGOLD HS; (SR); Ctznshp Aw; Hi Hnr Roll; Hnr Roll; Nat Hon Sy; Nat Ldrshp Svc; Otst Ac Ach Awd; Sci/Math Olympn; St of Mnth; Valdctrian; WWAHSS; Comm Volntr; Peer Tut/Med; Red Cr Aide; Chess; Emplmnt; FBLA; Jr Ach; Mus Clb; Prom Com; Sci Clb; Wdwrkg Clb; Bnd; Chr; Ch Chr; SP/M/VS; Bsball (V); Bskball (V); Cr Ctry (V); Cyclg; Ftball (V); Track (V); Vsy Clb; Wt Lftg; Cl Off (P); Stu Cncl (P); CR (P); Yrbk (E); Academic Achievement Award in 2004; Pre-Med / Bachelor of Science Biology; California U Pennsylvania

DUDEK, RENEE M; DOWNINGTOWN, PA; UPATTINAS SCH; (JR); F Lan Hn Soc; Hnr Roll; MVP; Comm Volntr; Peer Tut/Med; 4-H; Cmptr Clb; P to P St Amb Prg; Photog; Prom Com; Quiz Bowl; Scouts; Spanish Clb; Bnd; Chr; Dnce; SP/M/VS; Bskball (V); Chrldg (V); Fncg (V); Sccr (J); Vllyball (V); Adv Cncl (V); Stu Cncl (S); CR (V); Sch Ppr (R); Yrbk (E); Vice President of School Board; Student Teaching Spanish; Literature; Philosophy; Bard College; Oberlin College

DUFFY, HANNAH C; MT PLEASANT, PA; MT PLEASANT SECONDARY SCH; (SR); Hi Hnr Roll; Nat Hon Sy; Perf Att; WWAHSS; Comm Volntr; Hosp Aide; Spec Olymp Vol; Emplmnt; SADD; President of National Art Honor Society; Nurse's Aide; Biology / 4-Year College; Medical School; Saint Vincent College - Accepted

DUFRESNE, ALBERT J; CARNEGIE, PA; CARLYNTON SD; (FR); Bskball (J); Ftball (J)

DUGGAN, JOLENE M; SCRANTON, PA; HOMESCHOOL; (JR); WWAHSS; Comm Volntr; Hosp Aide; Chrch Yth Grp; Dnce; Junior Volunteer-Captain; Nursing Home Volunteer; Pre-Med; Messiah College

DUKE, SARAH; MIFFLINBURG, PA; MIFFLINBURG AREA HS; (SO); Hi Hnr Roll; Hnr Roll; Nat Hon Sy; Otst Ac Ach Awd; St of Mnth; Comm Volntr; Emplmnt; Jr Ach; Key Club; French Clb; Sccr (V L); Track (V); Pharmacy; Physical Therapy; Penn State U; Bloomsburg U

DUMAS, ASHLEY M; UNION CITY, PA; (JR); Hi Hnr Roll; Hnr Roll; Emplmnt; Chr; Veterinarian; Doctor; Mercyhurst College; Gannon U

DUNCAN, ALEXANDER; ROYERSFORD, PA; SPRING FORD SR HS; (SO); Hnr Roll; Best Art Student Since 7th Grade; Am Stateboarder in Best of the East; Architecture/Design; Fine Arts; The New School, San Diego, CA

DUNHAM, NOAH P; STROUDSBURG, PA; POCONO MOUNTAIN EAST HS; (FR); Hnr Roll; Chrch Yth Grp; Cr Ctry (J); Track (J); Certified Scuba Diver; U.S. Army

DUNN, CHELSEA; CANONSBURG, PA; RIDGEVIEW AC CS; (FR); Hi Hnr Roll; Hnr Roll; Otst Ac Ach Awd; Comm Volntr; Chrch Yth Grp; DARE; Jr Ach; Scouts; Wdwrkg Clb; Chrldg (J); Nursing; Cosmetology; Washington and Jefferson College; Penn State U

DUNN, MATTHEW R; PARKESBURG, PA; LAN-CHESTER CHRISTIAN SCH; (JR); Hnr Roll; USAA; Chrch Yth Grp; Emplmnt; SP/M/VS; Cl Off (P); Stu Cncl (R); Yrbk (R, P); Secondary Teaching; Pastoral Ministries; Philadelphia Biblical U; Baptist Bible College

DUONG, YEN-DUYEN; BENSALEM, PA; BENSALEM TOWNSHIP SD; (SO); Hi Hnr Roll; Chrldg (V); Involved in Student Government; 10th Gr Activities Committee Association; Business; Penn State U

DUPEL, NICOLAS; CORAOPOLIS, PA; MOON AREA HS; (FR); Hnr Roll; DECA; Scouts; Cr Ctry (J); Swmg (V); Law; Air Force Pilot; Harvard U; Yale U

DUPREE, DERICK; HAMBURG, PA; HAMBURG AREA HS; (FR); Hnr Roll; Sci Fairs; Yth Ldrshp Prog; Comm Volntr; DARE; Outdrs Clb; Dnce; Ftball (C); Ice Sktg; Rlr Hky; Skiing; Track; Wt Lftg (V); Stu Cncl (R); National Physical Fitness Award; Criminal Justice; Chemistry; U of North Carolina

DURBIN, ZACHARY; CARMICHAELS, PA; CARMICHAELS AREA JR/SR HS; Hnr Roll; 4-H; Bsball (J)

DURHAM, ASHLEY; HANOVER, PA; SOUTH WESTERN HS; (JR); Hi Hnr Roll; Hnr Roll; Perf Att; Tennis (VJ); Currently Taking Guitar Lessons; Accounting; York College of Pennsylvania

DURSTINE, CHELSIE; GREENSBURG, PA; GREENSBURG SALEM SD HS; (FR); Hi Hnr Roll; Hnr Roll; Perf Att; Chr; Education; Foreign Language; St Vincent College; Duquesne U

DUSKEY, ERIN; CAMP HILL, PA; EAST PENNSBORO AREA HS; (SO); Ctznshp Aw; Hi Hnr Roll; Hnr Roll; Mas Aw; Comm Volntr; Spec Olymp Vol; Chrch Yth Grp; Mus Clb; Scouts; Latin Clb; Bnd; Chr; Ch Chr; Mch Bnd; Stu Cncl (R); Job's Daughters International Past Honor Queen; Health-Physician Assistant; St Vincent College; St Francis U

DUVALL IV, HARRY V; ELIZABETH, PA; ELIZABETH FORWARD HS; (FR); Hi Hnr Roll; Hnr Roll; Otst Ac Ach Awd; Yth Ldrshp Prog; NYLC; Scouts; Ftball (J); Wrstlg (J); National Junior Leaders; Psychology; Philosophy; Northwestern; Oxford

DZIAMNISKI, CHARLENE; CORAOPOLIS, PA; MOON AREA HS; (MS); Hi Hnr Roll; Hnr Roll; Nat Hon Sy; Nat Sci Aw; Otst Ac Ach Awd; Perf Att; Sci Fairs; Comm Volntr; Peer Tut/Med; ArtClub; Chrch Yth Grp; Drma Clb; Mus Clb; Clr Grd; Orch; SP/M/VS; Stg Cre; Bdmtn (V); Cr Ctry (V); GAA (V); Mar Art (V); Tennis (V); CR (V); Sch Ppr (P); Artist of the Week; Karate Award; Voice Actress; Pageant Director; Mellon U; Pittsburgh U

DZWONEK, JENNIFER; NEWTOWN, PA; COUNCIL ROCK HS NORTH; (JR); F Lan Hn Soc; Hi Hnr Roll; Hnr Roll; Perf Att; Comm Volntr; Spec Olymp Vol; Emplmnt; Key Club; Chrldg (V); Over 250 LINCS Hours; Special Education; Psychology; Penn State U Park; U of Maryland

EARGLE, BRADLEY; MIFFLINTOWN, PA; JUNIATA CTY SD; (JR); Hi Hnr Roll; Hnr Roll; Pres Sch; St of Mnth; WWAHSS; Comm Volntr; Emplmnt; Prom Com; Scouts; Vsity Clb; Bnd; Jzz Bnd; Mch Bnd; SP/M/VS; Golf (V L); Eagle Scout; District/Regional Band; Communications; Public Relations; Elizabethtown College; Messiah College

EARNEST, ASHLEY N; ALTOONA, PA; ALTOONA AREA HS; (SR); Ctznshp Aw; Hi Hnr Roll; Nat Hon Sy; Perf Att; Pres Ac Ftns Aw; Comm Volntr; Peer Tut/Med; Prom Com; Tchrs Aide; Bskball (V CL); Track (V CL); CR (R); PSSA Superstar-National; Altoona Mirror Track & Field All Star Team; Elementary Education; Duquesne U PA

EBERLE, MARC A; PITTSBURGH, PA; PENN HILLS SR HS; (JR); Hi Hnr Roll; Hnr Roll; WWAHSS; Chrch Yth Grp; FCA; Key Club; Spanish Clb; SP/M/VS; Ice Hky (VJCL); Vllyball (V L); Meteorology; Penn State U; Ohio State U

EBERSOLE, NICKOLAS; MOUNT JOY, PA; DONEGAL HS; (SR); Hi Hnr Roll; Nat Hon Sy; Sci Fairs; St of Mnth; USMC Stu Ath Aw; WWAHSS; Hab For Humty Volntr; Tchrs Aide; Vsity Clb; Bsball (V L); Cr Ctry (V L); Vsy Clb (V); Member of National Honor Society; Criminal Justice

ECKEL, JENNA L; EASTON, PA; EASTON AREA HS; (SO); Hnr Roll; Nat Hon Sy; Pres Ac Ftns Aw; St of Mnth; WWAHSS; Comm Volntr; Spec Olymp Vol; Key Club; Acpl Chr; Chr; SP/M/VS; Skiing (V); Choir Officer; Active Member of Key Club; Business; U of Florida; Penn State

ECKENROTH, ZACHARY J; HARRISBURG, PA; CTRL DAUPHIN HS; (SO); Hnr Roll; Nat Hon Sy; Perf Att; Yth Ldrshp Prog; Comm Volntr; Peer Tut/Med; Chrch Yth Grp; DARE; Emplmnt; FCA; Chr; Ftball (V L); Wrstlg (JC); Forensic Science; Navy Seals; Miami U Coral Gables

ECKERT, ASHLEY N; LITITZ, PA; LANCASTER CTY CTC; (JR); Hnr Roll; Perf Att; Chrch Yth Grp; DARE; Drma Clb; Emplmnt; Jr Ach; Scouts; Voc Ind Clb Am; Chr; Ch Chr; Orch; SP/M/VS; Sccr; Sftball (J); Yrbk (E, P); Massage/Physical Therapist; Harrisburg Area Community College; Lancaster General School of Nursing

ECKMAN, LIZ; MECHANICSBURG, PA; MECHANICSBURG AREA SR HS; (JR); F Lan Hn Soc; Hnr Roll; Nat Hon Sy; WWAHSS; Chrch Yth Grp; Key Club; Chr; Orch; SP/M/VS; Tennis (J); Yrbk (E); Michigan State U; Penn State U

EDEM, ARIT; PHILADELPHIA, PA; CARVER HS; (JR); Sci Fairs; Dnce; Chrldg (V); Adv Cncl (R); Yrbk (P); Pre-Med; Law; Howard U; Hampton U

EDGAR, ANDREW; DALLAS, PA; DALLAS AREA HS; (FR); Hnr Roll; FBLA; Key Club; Track (J); 4th Place Future Business Leaders of America Regional Competition; Business

EDMONDS, DIAMOND S; PHILADELPHIA, PA; PHILADELPHIA HS FOR CREATIVE & PERF ARTS; (FR); Hnr Roll; Otst Ac Ach Awd; Valdctrian; Comm Volntr; Ch Chr; Dnce; 2004 Valedictorian (8th Grade) Germantown Settlement Charter School; Computer Science; Architecture; Spelman College; New York U

EDWARDS, ASHLEY; MECHANICSBURG, PA; MECHANICSBURG AREA SR HS; (SO); Hnr Roll; Key Club; Mod UN; Bskball; Cr Ctry; Sccr; Water Polo

EDWARDS, CURTIS; READING, PA; GOVERNOR MIFFLIN SR HS; (JR); Hnr Roll; Pres Ac Ftns Aw; WWAHSS; Cr Ctry (V); Ftball (V); Track (V); Wrstlg (V); Aerospace Engineering; Chemical Engineering; The Air Force Academy; Northeastern U

EDWARDS, JAMALL; PHILADELPHIA, PA; OVERBROOK HS; (SO); Hnr Roll; Otst Ac Ach Awd; Perf Att; Peer Tut/Med; Chrch Yth Grp; Dbte Team; Tchrs Aide; Clb; Bnd; Ch Chr; Orch; Classical Pianist-Settlement Music Sch; Next Generation-Boys Singing Camp-Church; Computer & Technology; Music; U of Pennsylvania

EGAN, ALYSSA; ST CLAIR, PA; POTTSVILLE HS; (SO); Hi Hnr Roll; WWAHSS; Comm Volntr; Key Club; Spanish Clb; Chr; Chrldg (V); Track (VJCL); Zoology; Cosmetology

EGAN, PATRICK J; BRIDGEVILLE, PA; BISHOP CANVEIN HS; (SO); Hi Hnr Roll; Pres Ac Ftns Aw; Comm Volntr; FBLA; Sccr (V); Tennis (V)

EGER, JOCELYN M; CRESSON, PA; PENN CAMBRIA HS; (MS); Ctznshp Aw; Hi Hnr Roll; Hnr Roll; Perf Att; Sccr; Stu Cncl (R); Yrbk (E); Certificate of Achievement; Criminal Justice; Interior Design; Penn State; Mount Aloysius

EGIDI, ZACHARY; MONESSEN, PA; MONESSEN HS; (JR); F Lan Hn Soc; Hi Hnr Roll; Nat Hon Sy; Nat Ldrshp Svc; Otst Ac Ach Awd; Perf Att; St of Mnth; Comm Volntr; Peer Tut/Med; Red Cr Aide; ArtClub; Drma Clb; FBLA; Mus Clb; Prom Com; Svce Clb; SADD; French Clb; Bnd; Mch Bnd; SP/M/VS; Stg Cre; Golf (J); Track (C); Cl Off (P); CR (P); Yrbk (R); American Legion Award Winner; Rensselaer Medal Award Winner; Chemical Engineering; Environmental Engineering; Florida Institute of Technology; Alfred U

EHLER, ZACH; PITTSBURGH, PA; (SO); Comm Volntr; Peer Tut/Med; Chrch Yth Grp; Play Ultimate on School Team; Boy Scout/Eagle Scout; Business; Colorado College

EHRENZELLER, BRYTTANI; MIFFLINTOWN, PA; JUNIATA HS; (FR); Hi Hnr Roll; Hnr Roll; Comm Volntr; Spec Olymp Vol; Chrch Yth Grp; Key Club; Chr; Forensics/Criminalistics Scientist; U of Yuma, Arizona

EHRENZELLER, CARRIE; MIFFLINTOWN, PA; JUNIATA CTY SD; (JR); Hnr Roll; Nat Hon Sy; WWAHSS; Spec Olymp Vol; Chrch Yth Grp; Lttrmn Clb; Prom Com; Vsity Clb; Bnd; Chr; Drm Mjr; Mch Bnd; Track (V L); Vsy Clb (V); Majorette Captain; Elementary Education; Penn State U; Bloomsburg U

EICHENLAUB, ERIK; GILBERTSVILLE, PA; BOYERTOWN AREA SR HS; (SO); Hi Hnr Roll; Otst Ac Ach Awd; Pres Ac Ftns Aw; Pres Sch; Sci Fairs; WWAHSS; ArtClub; Chrch Yth Grp; DARE; Jr Ach; Outdrs Clb; Lcrsse (J); Sccr (V); Stu Cncl (R); Architecture; U of Pittsburg; Penn State U

EISENHART, STEPHEN E; MC ADOO, PA; HAZLETON AREA HS; (JR); Hnr Roll; Comm Volntr; DARE; Emplmnt; Outdrs Clb; Scouts; Ftball (VJ); Ski Club; Hunting and Fishing Club; Mechanical Engineering; Pre-Law; Penn State (Main Campus); Kings College

EISLEY, ERIKA C; WATSONTOWN, PA; WARRIOR RUN HS; (JR); 4H Awd; Hnr Roll; Comm Volntr; 4-H; Chrch Yth Grp; French Clb; Mch Bnd; Arch; Bdmtn; Hsbk Rdg; Sch Ppr (R); Co-Founder of School Equine Club; President of Local 4-H Group; Equine Business Management; Business Management; Cazenovia College; U of Findley

ELDER, MICHAEL; NORRISTOWN, PA; KENNEDY-KENRICK CATHOLIC HS; (FR); Hnr Roll; Perf Att; Sci/Math Olympn; Comm Volntr; Spch Team; Track (V); Yrbk (R); Connections; Sonoro Convocation Participant; Meteorology; Veterinary Studies; Penn State U; Villanova

ELLIOTT, LANCE M; BRACKNEY, PA; MONTROSE AREA SD; (SO); Hnr Roll; Perf Att; French Clb; Tennis (V); Japanese Minor; Forensic Science Major; Mansfield U

ELLIS, LYNDSAY; SHAVERTOWN, PA; DALLAS HS; (FR); Hnr Roll; WWAHSS; Key Club; Bskball (V); Sccr (V); Graphic Design

EL-NACCACHE, DARINE W; CLIFTON HEIGHTS, PA; UPPER DARBY HS; (JR); Hi Hnr Roll; Hnr Roll; Otst Ac Ach Awd; Art Major 1 and 2; Youth Essay Certificate of Merit; Physician; Oral Medicine; Drexel U; Penn State U

ELQORCHI, SHANNON; HARVEYS LAKE, PA; (JR); Hi Hnr Roll; Nat Hon Sy; Pres Sch; Comm Volntr; Key Club; Off Aide; Vsity Clb; Fld Hky (V); PPSqd (V); Track (J)

ELWOOD, SARA A; WORTHINGTON, PA; LENAPE TECH; (SR); Hnr Roll; WWAHSS; Chrch Yth Grp; Prom Com; Bnd; Chr; Dnce; Cl Off (R); Hospitality Management; Travel & Tourism; Butler County Community College

EMERICK, BRITTANI HOPE; BUFFALO MILLS, PA; HYNDMAN MIDDLE SR HS; (JR); Hi Hnr Roll; Nat Hon Sy; Pres Ac Ftns Aw; St of Mnth; WWAHSS; Comm Volntr; Peer Tut/Med; Red Cr Aide; Jr Ach; Off Aide; Prom Com; Quiz Bowl; Cl Off (S); Leadership I; Elementary Educations; Computers/Math

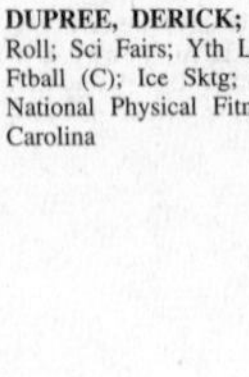
Elwood, Sara A
Lenape Tech
Worthington, PA

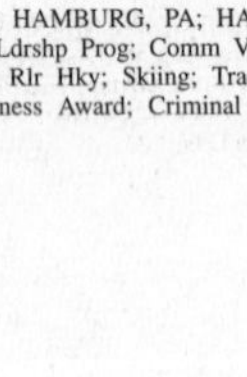
Earnest, Ashley N
Altoona Area HS
Altoona, PA

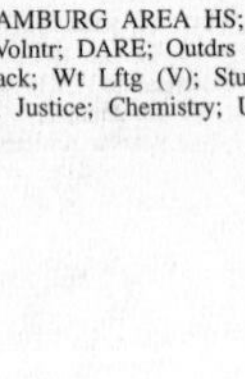
Duvall IV, Harry V
Elizabeth Forward HS
Elizabeth, PA

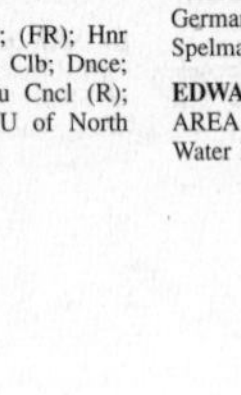
Duda, Patrick J
Ringgold HS
Donora, PA

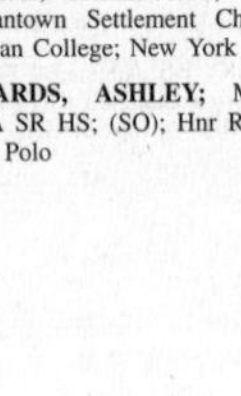
Duck, Bobby J
Tuscarora Blended Learning Charter Sch
Huntingdon, PA

National
Honor Roll
Spring 2005

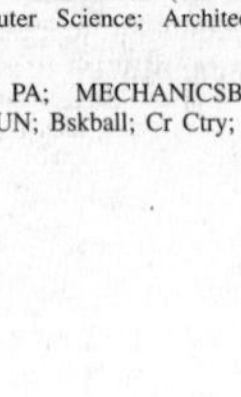
Drury, Autumn
East Stroudsburg HS South
East Stroudsburg, PA

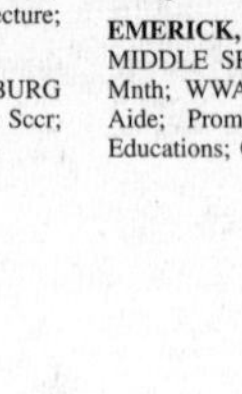
Dunn, Chelsea
Ridgeview AC CS
Canonsburg, PA

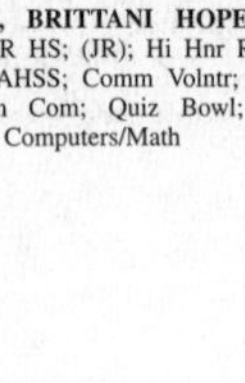
Dzwonek, Jennifer
Council Rock HS North
Newtown, PA

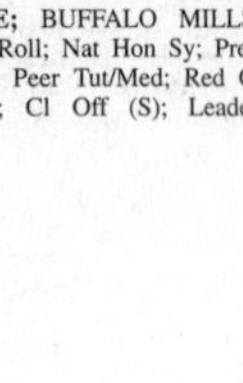
Edwards, Jamall
Overbrook HS
Philadelphia, PA

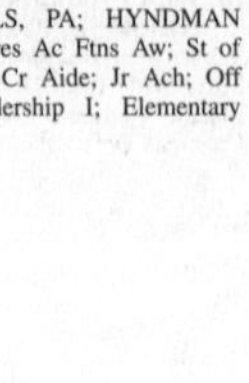
Eger, Jocelyn M
Penn Cambria HS
Cresson, PA

EMLING, MICHAEL V; CRANBERRY TWP, PA; SENECA VALLEY SHS; (SO); Ctznshp Aw; Hi Hnr Roll; Otst Ac Ach Awd; Pres Sch; St of Mnth; USAA; WWAHSS; Comm Volntr; Key Club; Off Aide; P to P St Amb Prg; Bskball (J); Vllyball (V L); Stu Cncl (P); Winner of 3 Scholarships to PASC Summer Leadership Workshops; Winner of the Robinson Family Fund Award for Academics; Business; Law; U of Virginia; U of North Carolina Chapel Hill

EMMERT, ABBY N; HALLSTEAD, PA; BLUE RIDGE HS; (FR); Hi Hnr Roll; Hnr Roll; Bnd; Bskball (VJ); Medicine; Business

ENCIU, ANTONINA; HERSHEY, PA; MILTON HERSHEY SCH; (JR); Gov Hnr Prg; Hi Hnr Roll; Hnr Roll; Perf Att; Pres Ac Ftns Aw; St of Mnth; WWAHSS; Hab For Humty Volntr; Hosp Aide; Peer Tut/Med; FCA; JSA; Mod UN; P to P St Amb Prg; Vsity Clb; Bnd; Chr; Dnce; Drm Mjr; Chrldg (V L); Dvng (V L); Gmnstcs (V); Sccr (J); Swmg (V); Track (J); Vsy Clb (V L); Adv Cncl (V); Yrbk (E, P); National Society of High School Scholars; National Youth Leadership Forum on Medicine; Pediatric Dentistry; Cosmetic Surgeon; UCLA; Claremont McKenna College

ENGLISH, JONATHAN; SHAMOKIN DAM, PA; SUNBURY CHRISTIAN AC; (JR); Hi Hnr Roll; Hnr Roll; Chrch Yth Grp; Emplmnt; Tchrs Aide; Chr; SP/M/VS; Bskball (V); Track (V); Vllyball (V); Cl Off (V); Stu Cncl (S); Grew Up As A Missionary Kid in Papua New Guinea; Physical Therapy; Youth Pastor; Messiah College; Philadelphia Biblical U

ENGLISH, RYAN J; HARMONY, PA; SENECA VALLEY SHS; (JR); Hi Hnr Roll; Hnr Roll; Nat Hon Sy; WWAHSS; Comm Volntr; Chrch Yth Grp; Emplmnt; Key Club; Scouts; Bnd; Cl Off (V); Stu Cncl; Eagle Scout; Leadership - Second Mile; Architectural Engineering; Chemical Engineering; Pennsylvania State U

ENSLOW, ERIC; PITTSBURGH, PA; SHALER AREA INT SCH; (JR); F Lan Hn Soc; Hi Hnr Roll; Nat Hon Sy; Otst Ac Ach Awd; Sci Fairs; Amnsty Intl; Peer Tut/Med; Chrch Yth Grp; Emplmnt; FTA; Key Club; Mod UN; Mus Clb; NtlFrnscLg; Japanese Clb; Bnd; Ch Chr; Mch Bnd; SP/M/VS; President of Model UN; Japanese National Honor Society; Education / History; Political Science; University of Pittsburgh; Duquesne U

ERDMAN JR, MICHAEL S; NORTHUMBERLAND, PA; SUNBURY CHRISTIAN AC; (SO); Hnr Roll; Pres Ac Ftns Aw; Hab For Humty Volntr; Chrch Yth Grp; DARE; Emplmnt; FCA; Scouts; Bskball (VJ L); Sccr (V L); Track (V L); Yrbk (R, P); Automotive Technician; Collision Repair; Pennsylvania School of Technology

ERHART, SARAH E; GLENSHAW, PA; SHALER AREA HS; (JR); Ctznshp Aw; Hi Hnr Roll; Hnr Roll; Nat Hon Sy; Perf Att; St of Mnth; Comm Volntr; Emplmnt; FBLA; Off Aide; Chr; PP Ftbl (V); Sftball (JCL); Swmg (V L); Stu Cncl (R); North Hills Outstanding Citizen - 2 Years; Junior National Honor Society; International Business; Marketing; Robert Morris U; U of Pittsburgh

ESHBACH, WES; GILBERTSVILLE, PA; BOYERTOWN AREA SR HS; (SO); Hnr Roll; Otst Ac Ach Awd; Perf Att; St of Mnth; DARE; Emplmnt; Build Homes; Penn Tech Vocational School

ESHBAUGH, SARAH; MONACA, PA; CTR AREA SD; (JR); Hi Hnr Roll; Nat Hon Sy; Otst Ac Ach Awd; WWAHSS; Yth Ldrshp Prog; CARE; Comm Volntr; Spec Olymp Vol; Lttrmn Clb; Pep Squd; Prom Com; SADD; Spanish Clb; Bnd; Clr Grd; Mch Bnd; SP/M/VS; PP Ftbl (V); Scr Kpr (V); Track (V); Stu Cncl (P); Beaver County Outstanding Young Woman; Miss Geneva Color Guard; Secondary Mathematics Education; Doctorate in Psychology; Edinboro U of Pennsylvania; Clarion U

ESHELMAN, DIANE; WOMELSDORF, PA; CONRAD WEISER HS; (SO); Kwnis Aw; WWAHSS; Comm Volntr; Chrch Yth Grp; Drma Clb; Emplmnt; Jr Cls League; Key Club; Ntl FFA; Scouts; Chr; Ch Chr; SP/M/VS; Girl Scout Silver Award; Psychology; Penn State; Pittsburgh U

ESOPI, MIA E; DALLAS, PA; DALLAS HS; (SO); Hi Hnr Roll; Hnr Roll; Nat Hon Sy; Pres Ac Ftns Aw; Comm Volntr; Chrch Yth Grp; Emplmnt; Key Club; Work with Local Veterinarian; Community Service (Volunteer, Library Auctions, Etc); Veterinary Medicine; Biology; Penn State U; U of Pennsylvania

ETLING, EMILY B; GREENSBURG, PA; GREENSBURG SALEM SD; (FR); Hi Hnr Roll; Perf Att; Pres Ac Ftns Aw; St of Mnth; Mth Clb/Tm; Mod UN; Dnce; Fld Hky; Skiing; Sftball; Track; Attorney

ETZEL, JAKE; ELIZABETH, PA; ELIZABETH FORWARD HS; (SO); Hnr Roll; WWAHSS; Drma Clb; Wdwrkg Clb; Bnd; Mch Bnd; Wrstlg (V L); Fly Fishing; Air Plane Mechanics; Teaching; PIA; Penn State

EVANS, ALICIA N; SHAVERTOWN, PA; DALLAS HS; (SO); Hi Hnr Roll; Nat Hon Sy; Otst Ac Ach Awd; WWAHSS; Comm Volntr; Emplmnt; Svce Clb; SADD; Bskball (JCL); Tennis (V L); Stu Cncl (R); NEDT Award; Times Leader Short Story Contest Winner; Psychology; Medicine; Bucknell U; U of California Los Angeles

EVANS, NIKKI M; MC CLURE, PA; INDIAN VALLEY HS; (JR); Ctznshp Aw; Hi Hnr Roll; Hnr Roll; Nat Hon Sy; Otst Ac Ach Awd; Sci Fairs; St of Mnth; Yth Ldrshp Prog; Comm Volntr; Peer Tut/Med; Chrch Yth Grp; Drma Clb; Prom Com; Sci Clb; Spanish Clb; Clr Grd; Mch Bnd; SP/M/VS; Stg Cre; Sftball (V); Stu Cncl (R); CR (R); Yrbk (E); Envirothon; Tobacco Busters; Chemistry; Forensics

EVANS JR, MARK A; SHAVERTOWN, PA; DALLAS AREA HS; (FR); Hi Hnr Roll; Hnr Roll; WWAHSS; Comm Volntr; FBLA; Key Club; Boy Scouts of America-Life Scout; Operation Honduras-Volunteer (3 Years); Medical Field

EVERETT, JEFFREY J; BLOSSBURG, PA; NORTH PENN JR/SR HS; (SR); All Am Sch; DAR; Hnr Roll; Kwnis Aw; MVP; Nat Hon Sy; Nat Ldrshp Svc; Nat Mrt LOC; St of Mnth; USAA; Comm Volntr; Peer Tut/Med; Spec Olymp Vol; Drma Clb; Key Club; Schol Bwl; Svce Clb; Tchrs Aide; Vsity Clb; Bnd; Mch Bnd; Orch; SP/M/VS; Bskball (V CL); Track (V L); Vsy Clb (V); Adv Cncl (V); Stu Cncl (R); CR (R); Engineering; Play Basketball; Penn State Behrend

FABIANI, SAMANTHA; BEAVER FALLS, PA; BLACKHAWK HS; (SO); Hi Hnr Roll; Hnr Roll; WWAHSS; Comm Volntr; Drma Clb; Key Club; Chr; SP/M/VS; Bskball (J); Track (V); Recreational Basketball Referee; District Chorus; BFA in Music; BFA in Musical Theater

FADOK, SARAH E; PITTSBURGH, PA; PITTSBURGH HS FOR THE CREATIVE AND PERF ARTS; (FR); Hi Hnr Roll; Hnr Roll; Comm Volntr; Dnce; Stg Cre; Dance Competition Award & Dance Achievements; Singing Awards; Major-Dance/Business; Goal-Dance Instructor-Own Studio; Columbia College Chicago; Point Park U

FAIR, PAMELA; JAMESTOWN, PA; JAMESTOWN AREA SD; (SO); Hnr Roll; Nat Hon Sy; Comm Volntr; Chrch Yth Grp; Emplmnt; P to P St Amb Prg; Spanish Clb; Bnd; Chr; Mch Bnd; Pep Bnd; Bskball (J); Chrldg (L); Member of Relay for Life; Participant in Academic Games; Marine Biology, Zoology; Music; U of Maryland-College Park; Westminster

FAIR, RACHEL R; MOHRSVILLE, PA; SCHUYLKILL VALLEY HS; (SR); Hi Hnr Roll; Hnr Roll; Nat Hon Sy; Pres Sch; WWAHSS; Mod UN; Quill & Scroll; Spanish Clb; Bnd; Mch Bnd; SP/M/VS; Cr Ctry (C); Track (V); Sch Ppr (R); Yrbk (E); Students Opposed to Drug and Alcohol Abuse; Psychology; Spanish; Millersville U

FAIRCHILD, LAUREN; MERTZTOWN, PA; BRANDYWINE HEIGHTS HS; (SO); Hi Hnr Roll; St of Mnth; WWAHSS; Yth Ldrshp Prog; Comm Volntr; Chrch Yth Grp; Emplmnt; HO'Br Yth Ldrshp; Key Club; Scouts; Spanish Clb; Chr; Ch Chr; Bskball; Fld Hky (J); Stu Cncl (R); Psychology; Marketing; Drexel U; Marymount Manhattan College

FAIRLEY, REBECCA; BEAVER, PA; BEAVER AREA HS; (SR); Hi Hnr Roll; Nat Hon Sy; Otst Ac Ach Awd; Sci Fairs; St of Mnth; WWAHSS; Hab For Humty Volntr; Emplmnt; Key Club; Mth Clb/Tm; Mus Clb; Photog; Bnd; Chr; Ch Chr; Jzz Bnd; Show Choir / Scuba Certified; Member of Tri-M Society; Civil Engineering; U of Akron; Arcadia U

FAJT, EMILY; WEXFORD, PA; PINE RICHLAND HS; (JR); Ctznshp Aw; Hi Hnr Roll; Nat Hon Sy; ArtClub; Scouts; Chr; SP/M/VS; Lcrsse (V); Sccr (J); Tennis (J L); CR (R); Elementary Education; Secondary Education; Penn State U

FAKE, CHRISTOPHER M; HANOVER, PA; HANOVER HS; (JR); Ctznshp Aw; Hi Hnr Roll; Hnr Roll; Nat Hon Sy; Perf Att; St of Mnth; WWAHSS; Comm Volntr; Emplmnt; Key Club; Vsity Clb; SP/M/VS; Stg Cre; Tennis (V); Vsy Clb (V); Stu Cncl (R); Key Club-Vice President; Assistant Director Drama Night; Education/Guidance; Psychology; Coastal Carolina College

FALATOVICH, ALEXANDER; SUGARLOAF, PA; HAZLETON AREA HS; (SO); Hi Hnr Roll; Nat Hon Sy; Otst Ac Ach Awd; Sci Fairs; St of Mnth; WWAHSS; Comm Volntr; Peer Tut/Med; Red Cr Aide; Emplmnt; Schol Bwl; Sci Clb; Presidential Classroom - National Security and Defense; Jr High Boys Basketball Student Coach / Little League Assistant Coach / Green Belt Kenpo Martial Arts; Math / Physics; Criminal Justice; Bucknell U; Pennsylvania State U

FANCHER, DOMINIQUE D; PITTSBURGH, PA; CAPA HS; (SR); Hnr Roll; Comm Volntr; Peer Tut/Med; DARE; Drma Clb; Dnce; SP/M/VS; Sch Ppr (R); Most Improved in Theatre; Point Park (Theatre); Bradford (Business)

FANG, CHEN; AMBLER, PA; UPPER DUBLIN HS; (JR); Duke TS; Hi Hnr Roll; Hnr Roll; Nat Hon Sy; Sci Fairs; WWAHSS; Yth Ldrshp Prog; Comm Volntr; Cmptr Clb; HO'Br Yth Ldrshp; Prom Com; Tech Clb; Swmg (V); Cl Off (P); Stu Cncl (R); State Science Fair-PJAS-1st Place; American Legion Award; Computer Science; Bio-Engineering; Massachusetts Institute of Technology; Carnegie Mellon U

FANTO, STEPHANIE; HARLEYSVILLE, PA; NORTH PENN HS; (JR); Hi Hnr Roll; Hnr Roll; MVP; Otst Ac Ach Awd; Sci Fairs; St of Mnth; WWAHSS; Yth Ldrshp Prog; Comm Volntr; Peer Tut/Med; Spec Olymp Vol; DARE; Emplmnt; FBLA; Key Club; NYLC; Bskball (V L); Fld Hky (J); PP Ftbl (V); Sftball (V L); Stu Cncl (R); Sports Management

FARBER, ROBERT; BENSALEM, PA; BENSALEM TOWNSHIP SD; (FR); Ctznshp Aw; Hi Hnr Roll; Hnr Roll; Nat Hon Sy; Nat Sci Aw; Otst Ac Ach Awd; Perf Att; St of Mnth; Comm Volntr; Emplmnt; Mth Clb/Tm; ROTC; Wdwrkg Clb; Black Belt in Tang So Do Karate; Jr ROTC Program; Computers; West Point Academy

FARINELLI, CAROLINE; MECHANICSBURG, PA; MECHANICSBURG AREA SR HS; (SO); Ctznshp Aw; Hi Hnr Roll; Nat Hon Sy; St of Mnth; Peer Tut/Med; Key Club; Sch Ppr (E); Co-Chairman of Thon - Dance Marathon to Raise Money for Leukemia

FARRA, LAUREN; CONSHOHOCKEN, PA; PLYMOUTH WHITEMARSH HS; (SO); Hnr Roll; Sociology; Physiology; West Chester U

FARRELLY, SHANNON; UPPER DARBY, PA; UPPER DARBY HS; (JR); Nat Hon Sy; Nat Ldrshp Svc; Peer Tut/Med; Spec Olymp Vol; Emplmnt; Fld Hky (JC); PP Ftbl (V); Cl Off (V)

FARREY, SARA; HARVEYS LAKE, PA; LAKE LEHMAN JR/SR HS; (SO); Hi Hnr Roll; Nat Hon Sy; Peer Tut/Med; Red Cr Aide; DARE; Key Club; Chrldg (VJC); Track (VJ L)

FARROW III, CARL E; MONACA, PA; CTR AREA SD; (SO); Hi Hnr Roll; Pres Ac Ftns Aw; WWAHSS; Comm Volntr; Hab For Humty Volntr; Hosp Aide; Chrch Yth Grp; Emplmnt; Prom Com; Bskball (J); Ftball (VJ L); Wt Lftg (J); Stu Cncl; Spanish Competition; Habitat For Humanity; Otho-Doctor; Physical Therapy; U of Pittsburgh

FASCIO-BURKE, AMY; VERONA, PA; PENN HILLS HS; (SR); Hnr Roll; Kwnis Aw; St of Mnth; WWAHSS; Comm Volntr; Hab For Humty Volntr; Spec Olymp Vol; Chrch Yth Grp; Drma Clb; Emplmnt; Key Club; P to P St Amb Prg; Photog; SP/M/VS; Sch Ppr (E, P); Senior Key Club Board Member; Veterinary Medicine; Photography; U of Pittsburgh

FATZINGER, ANTHONY; ALLENTOWN, PA; WILLIAM ALLEN HS; (JR); Hi Hnr Roll; Hnr Roll; Perf Att; WWAHSS; Emplmnt; Acpl Chr; Bnd; Chr; Jzz Bnd; Ice Hky (V); Psychology; Forensic Psychology; William and Mary

FAZZINI, C MATTHEW; WAYNE, PA; CONESTOGA HS; (JR); Hnr Roll; Key Club; Bskball (V CL)

FEDICK, JUSTIN; PHOENIXVILLE, PA; PHOENIXVILLE HS; (JR); F Lan Hn Soc; Hi Hnr Roll; Hnr Roll; Sci Fairs; Comm Volntr; Peer Tut/Med; Chrch Yth Grp; Emplmnt; Key Club; Bnd; Jzz Bnd; Mch Bnd; Orch; Bsball (J); President of Key Club; Student Tutor; Engineering; Computer Science; U of Pennsylvania; Villanova U

FEDOR, EMILY A; LATROBE, PA; GREATER LATROBE HS; (SO); F Lan Hn Soc; Hi Hnr Roll; Perf Att; WWAHSS; Chrch Yth Grp; Key Club; Lttrmn Clb; Spanish Clb; Bskball (VJ L); Cr Ctry (V L); Track (V L); Latrobe Area Interfaith Vol. Caregives-Faith in Action

FEDOR, MARRISSA; WILKES-BARRE, PA; HANOVER AREA JR/SR HS; (FR); Hi Hnr Roll; Nat Hon Sy; Perf Att; Sci Fairs; Comm Volntr; Chrch Yth Grp; Drma Clb; Acpl Chr; Bnd; Chr; Ch Chr; Chrldg (V); Cr Ctry (V); Track (V); Yrbk (E); Leo Club; Elementary Education; Kings College; Wilkes U

FEDORCZYK, KRISTIN; GREENVILLE, PA; REYNOLDS JR SR HS; (SO); Hi Hnr Roll; Otst Ac Ach Awd; St of Mnth; USAA; WWAHSS; Chrch Yth Grp; Key Club; Bnd; Sftball (V L); Vllyball (JC)

FEE, JAMES J; HAVERTOWN, PA; ST JOE'S PREP; (JR); Hnr Roll; Hab For Humty Volntr; Emplmnt; Cr Ctry (V); Tennis (V); Scranton U; Catholic U

FEENEY, MATTHEW; POTTSVILLE, PA; POTTSVILLE AREA HS; (SO); Hi Hnr Roll; Hnr Roll; DARE; Key Club; SADD; Spanish Clb; Ftball (VJ L); Track (VJ L); Stu Cncl (R)

FEGELY, JESSICA; MERTZTOWN, PA; BRANDYWINE HEIGHTS HS; (JR); Hi Hnr Roll; Nat Hon Sy; Otst Ac Ach Awd; USAA; WWAHSS; Comm Volntr; Chrch Yth Grp; Emplmnt; Key Club; Spanish Clb; Acpl Chr; Bnd; Chr; Dnce; Chrldg (V L); Gmnstcs; Sftball (V L); Yrbk (P); National Student Leadership Conference; Nominated As People to People Student Ambassador; Pre-Med / Oncology

FEGLEY, APRIL; MAHANOY CITY, PA; MAHANOY AREA; (SO); Hnr Roll; Perf Att; Spanish Clb

FENG, ANGEL; PHILADELPHIA, PA; CENTRAL HS; (FR); Hi Hnr Roll; Hnr Roll; Otst Ac Ach Awd; Perf Att; Sci Fairs; Valdctrian; Peer Tut/Med; Chess; Chrch Yth Grp; Cmptr Clb; DARE; Quiz Bowl; Schol Bwl; Tchrs Aide; Co-Webmaster Class Website for School; Teacher's Assistant for the Chinese School of Chinese Chamber of Commerce; Computer Science / Technology; Psychology; Harvard U; U of Pennsylvania

FENSTERMAKER, ADAM; WALNUTPORT, PA; NORTHAMPTON HS; (SO); Hi Hnr Roll; Hnr Roll; Peer Tut/Med; Emplmnt; FTA; Bskball (J); Vllyball (J); Elementary Education; Sports Coach; East Stroudsburg U; Kutztown U

FERDINAND, NICHOLAS; ZION GROVE, PA; HAZLETON AREA HS; (SO); Hi Hnr Roll; USAA; Kung Fu; Law Enforcement; Military Analyst; Kings College; Wilkes U

Fedorczyk, Kristin
Reynolds JR SR HS
Greenville, PA

Fedor, Emily A
Greater Latrobe HS
Latrobe, PA

Eshbach, Wes
Boyertown Area SR HS
Gilbertsville, PA

Erdman Jr, Michael S
Sunbury Christian AC
Northumberland, PA

Erhart, Sarah E
Shaler Area HS
Glenshaw, PA

Fedor, Marrissa
Hanover Area JR/SR HS
Wilkes-Barre, PA

Feng, Angel
Central HS
Philadelphia, PA

FERLAN, SARA; GIBSONIA, PA; DEER LAKES HS; (FR); Hi Hnr Roll; Hnr Roll; Bnd; Jzz Bnd; Mch Bnd; Physician; Counselor; Johns Hopkins Medical U; Pitt

FERRER, TANIA; EASTON, PA; EASTON AREA HS; (SO); Hi Hnr Roll; Hnr Roll; Nat Hon Sy; WWAHSS; Peer Tut/Med; French Clb; Chr; Ch Chr; Bachelor's Degree; Master's Degree; Columbia U; New York U

FERRI, ANDREW T; DOWNINGTOWN, PA; BISHOP SHANAHAN HS; (SO); Ctznshp Aw; Hnr Roll; Perf Att; Sci Fairs; Cmptr Clb; Tech Clb; Asian Clb; Wrstlg (V); Part Time Employee At Acme Grocery Market for the Past 1.5 years; Engineering, Chemistry; Computer Programming; Villanova; Penn State

FERRIELL, KRISTIN A; DUNCANSVILLE, PA; HOLLIDAYSBURG HS; (JR); Hi Hnr Roll; Nat Hon Sy; St of Mnth; WWAHSS; Comm Volntr; Key Club; Scouts; French Clb; Bnd; Jzz Bnd; Mch Bnd; SP/M/VS; Sch Ppr (R); Rotary Club Essay Contest Winner; Dermatology

FERRY, NICHOLE; MOUNT PLEASANT MILLS, PA; HOMESCHOOL; (SO); Hnr Roll; Sci Fairs; WWAHSS; Red Cr Aide; Chrch Yth Grp; Photog; Law; Secondary Education

FERRY, TODD J; GREAT BEND, PA; BLUE RIDGE HS; (JR); Hi Hnr Roll; Hnr Roll; Perf Att; St of Mnth; WWAHSS; Emplmnt; Bnd; Chr; Mch Bnd; Orch; Physics; Psychology; Broome Community College; Mansfield U

FETKOVICH, LUKE A; GREENSBURG, PA; GREENSBURG SALEM HS; (SO); Hi Hnr Roll; Hnr Roll; USAA; Comm Volntr; Hosp Aide; Spec Olymp Vol; Emplmnt; Spanish Clb; National English Merit Award (10th); Academic Team @ GSHS

FETSKO, VERONICA; GREENVILLE, PA; REYNOLDS JR-SR HS; (FR); Hi Hnr Roll; St of Mnth; Comm Volntr; Key Club; Chr; Dnce; Chrldg (V)

FETTERMAN, AUTUMN L; SHIPPENSBURG, PA; BIG SPRING SD; (SO); Hnr Roll; DARE; Chr; Clr Grd; Martial Arts - Not Taken in School; Law; New York U

FEYOCK, ANDREW C; OAKDALE, PA; CHARTIERS VALLEY HS; (SO); Hi Hnr Roll; Hnr Roll; Otst Ac Ach Awd; St of Mnth; Comm Volntr; Spec Olymp Vol; P to P St Amb Prg; Vsity Clb; Stg Cre; Bsball (VJ); Ftball (VJ L); Vsy Clb (VJ L); Wt Lftg (VJ); Stu Cncl (R); Arts; Sciences; Penn State U

FICKES, MICHAEL; KENNETT SQUARE, PA; UNIONVILLE HS; (JR); Hi Hnr Roll; Hnr Roll; Nat Hon Sy; WWAHSS; Yth Ldrshp Prog; Comm Volntr; Chess; FBLA; Mth Clb/Tm; Cr Ctry (J); Tennis (J); Track (J)

FIFE, MEGAN; DOYLESTOWN, PA; CTRL BUCKS EAST; (JR); F Lan Hn Soc; Hi Hnr Roll; WWAHSS; Comm Volntr; Peer Tut/Med; Drma Clb; Key Club; Prom Com; Spanish Clb; SP/M/VS; Vllyball (J)

FIKES, TARA; BOOTHWYB, PA; CHICHESTER SR HS; (FR); Hi Hnr Roll; Otst Ac Ach Awd; St of Mnth; Comm Volntr; Fld Hky (VJ); Lcrsse (V); Majorettes-Twirling; Forensics; Chemistry / Biology

FILCHNER, COURTNEE M; PALMERTON, PA; PALMERTON AREA SD; (FR); Hi Hnr Roll; Hnr Roll; Otst Ac Ach Awd; Perf Att; WWAHSS; Chrch Yth Grp; Clb; Chr; SP/M/VS; Pediatrician; Lawyer; Lycoming College; Penn State

FILER, JASON R; SHIPPENSBURG, PA; SHIPPENSBURG HS; (SR); Hnr Roll; WWAHSS; Hosp Aide; Peer Tut/Med; Spec Olymp Vol; Chrch Yth Grp; DARE; Emplmnt; Prom Com; Scouts; Tchrs Aide; Chr; Ch Chr; Ftball (J); Track (J); Stu Cncl (R); Secondary Education; Mathematics; Shippensburg U

FILLMAN, WESTON; TOPTON, PA; BRANDYWINE HEIGHTS HS; (SO); Hi Hnr Roll; Hnr Roll; Otst Ac Ach Awd; Perf Att; Pres Ac Ftns Aw; St of Mnth; WWAHSS; Yth Ldrshp Prog; Peer Tut/Med; Emplmnt; FBLA; Key Club; NYLC; Quiz Bowl; Schol Bwl; Scouts; Spanish Clb; Bnd; Chr; Jzz Bnd; Mch Bnd; Vllyball (J); Sch Ppr (R); Attended NYLF -National Youth Leadership Federation; Medicine-Psychiatry, Dermatology; Psychology / BA /MA / PhD; Boston U; Temple U

FINALLE, KARI D; DU BOIS, PA; DU BOIS AREA HS; (SR); Hnr Roll; Jr Rot; Nat Hon Sy; Perf Att; St of Mnth; WWAHSS; Comm Volntr; Hab For Humty Volntr; Hosp Aide; Chrch Yth Grp; Scouts; Svce Clb; Stg Cre; Vllyball (J); Interact Club Treasurer; Physical Therapy; Pharmaceuticals; Penn State Dubois

FINKBINER, JACOB; GLENMOORE, PA; LANCHESTER CHRISTIAN SCH; (FR); Hi Hnr Roll; Hnr Roll; MVP; Pres Ac Ftns Aw; Chrch Yth Grp; Scouts; Bnd; Bsball; Bskball (V); Ftball (V); Stu Cncl; AWANA Participation & Leadership; Missions Trip to Philadelphia; Ministry; Policeman

FINLEY, JOE; SOUDERTON, PA; SOUDERTON AREA HS; (JR); Hnr Roll; Comm Volntr; Peer Tut/Med; Emplmnt; Bsball (V); Ftball (V); Golf (J); Latin Award; Pharmacy; Meteorology; Penn State U; Temple U

FIORELLI, CHARISSA; BENSALEM, PA; BENSALEM TOWNSHIP SD; (SO); Hi Hnr Roll; Hnr Roll; Nat Hon Sy; Comm Volntr; ArtClub; Prom Com; Dnce; SP/M/VS; Modeling; PA Free Enterprise Week; Dance / Ballet; Business / Law; U of the Arts; Penn State

FIORENTINO, ANGELINA; SAINT THOMAS, PA; JAMES BUCHANAN HS; (JR); Hi Hnr Roll; Hnr Roll; Nat Hon Sy; WWAHSS; Comm Volntr; Chess; DARE; Key Club; Dnce; Cl Off (S, T); CR (R); EMT Certification; Fire Essentials A-D; Criminal Justice/Law Enforcement; Medical Examiner; Russell Sage; Pennsylvania State U

FIORENTINO, MICHELE N; BERWYN, PA; CONESTOGA HS; (JR); Key Club; SADD; Bskball (J); Lcrsse (V); Sccr (V); Track (J); President - SADD; Vice President - Key Club

FIORI, RACHAEL; GILBERTSVILLE, PA; BOYERTOWN AREA SR HS; (JR); Hi Hnr Roll; Nat Hon Sy; Otst Ac Ach Awd; WWAHSS; Peer Tut/Med; HO'Br Yth Ldrshp; Lib Aide; Svce Clb; Chr; Orch; Lcrsse (V); President of Leo Club; First Chair Cello in Orchestra and Ensemble; Journalist; Photographer

FIRDA, MATTHEW G; MCKEESPORT, PA; MC KEESPORT AREA SD; (FR); Ftball (J); Track (VJ); Business; Veterinarian; Penn State; Pittsburgh Miami

FISHER, ABIGAIL M; BERWYN, PA; AC OF NOTRE DAME DE NAMUR; (JR); Hi Hnr Roll; Yth Ldrshp Prog; Comm Volntr; Peer Tut/Med; ArtClub; Chrch Yth Grp; Mus Clb; NYLC; Quill & Scroll; Svce Clb; Chr; Ch Chr; SP/M/VS; Stg Cre; Track (J); Lit Mag (E); Sch Ppr (R); Communications; Journalism; Fordham U; Boston College

FISHER, CAITY; BOYERTOWN, PA; BOYERTOWN AREA SR HS; (JR); Ctznshp Aw; Hi Hnr Roll; Hnr Roll; MVP; Nat Hon Sy; Otst Ac Ach Awd; Pres Ac Ftns Aw; St of Mnth; Peer Tut/Med; Spec Olymp Vol; Emplmnt; FBLA; Key Club; Off Aide; Chr; Cr Ctry (V CL); Swmg (V L); Track (V L); Cl Off (R); Stu Cncl (R); CR (R); Yrbk (P); Outstanding Citizenship Award-Mike O'Pake; Coaches' Award; Secondary Education; Elementary Education; Penn State; Shippensburg U

FISHER, KYLE A; WEST MILTON, PA; LEWISBURG AREA HS; (SR); F Lan Hn Soc; Hi Hnr Roll; Nat Hon Sy; WWAHSS; Red Cr Aide; DARE; Emplmnt; Prom Com; Spanish Clb; Sccr (V L); Stu Cncl (R); State Games of America-Gold Medalist-Soccer-2000; Penn State U

FISHER, MIRANDA; NEWVILLE, PA; BIG SPRING SD; (JR); Hnr Roll; Nat Hon Sy; Comm Volntr; Peer Tut/Med; Spec Olymp Vol; Emplmnt; SADD; Cr Ctry (V); PP Ftbl; Scr Kpr; National Honors Society PR Officer; Donated Hair to Locks of Love; Athletic Training; Sports Psychology; Penn State U; U of Pittsburgh

FISHER, SHAKARAH; PHILADELPHIA, PA; BEN FRANKLIN HS; (FR); Hnr Roll; Vllyball (J); Nursing; Photography

FISHER, TODD; HUMMELSTOWN, PA; HERSHEY HS; (FR); Hi Hnr Roll; Perf Att; Pres Ac Ftns Aw; Emplmnt; Bskball (J); Golf; Vllyball (J); Architecture; Engineering; Penn State U; Cornell U

FISHER III, JOHN C; GREENCASTLE, PA; JAMES BUCHANAN HS; (SR); 4H Awd; Hnr Roll; Kwnis Aw; MVP; St of Mnth; 4-H; Ntl FFA; Bnd; Mch Bnd; Sccr (J); Swmg (V CL); Reporter and Historian Office Local FFA; National FFA Dairy Evaluation 1st Place Team; Doing Science; Virginia Tech

FITZGERALD, HOPE R; DENVER, PA; COCALICO HS; (SR); Ctznshp Aw; Hi Hnr Roll; Hnr Roll; Nat Hon Sy; Comm Volntr; Chrch Yth Grp; DARE; Drma Clb; Emplmnt; P to P St Amb Prg; Tchrs Aide; Bnd; Ch Chr; Orch; Presidential Award for Outstanding Academic Achievement; Presidential Award for Excellence in Educational Achievement; Special Education Teacher

FITZGERALD, KELSEY; WAYNE, PA; CONESTOGA HS; (SO); Hi Hnr Roll; Hnr Roll; Pres Ac Ftns Aw; Comm Volntr; Peer Tut/Med; Key Club; Mod UN; Chr; Sccr (J); REACH; Pre-Law / Law School; McGill U; New York U

FITZPATRICK, SARAH E; PITTSBURGH, PA; SHALER AREA HS; (JR); Hi Hnr Roll; Hnr Roll; Otst Ac Ach Awd; Hosp Aide; Peer Tut/Med; Emplmnt; Chr; PP Ftbl (J); Track (J); Stu Cncl (R); Outstanding Young Citizen Award; Secondary Education; Physical Therapist; U of Pittsburgh; Robert Morris U

FLACHS, ANDREW; ELVERSON, PA; OWEN J ROBERTS HS; (JR); F Lan Hn Soc; Gov Hnr Prg; Hi Hnr Roll; Nat Hon Sy; Pres Ac Ftns Aw; USAA; WWAHSS; Peer Tut/Med; Chess; Drma Clb; Emplmnt; Jr Cls League; Lttrmn Clb; Mus Clb; Quiz Bowl; Latin Clb; Acpl Chr; Bnd; Chr; Jzz Bnd; Cr Ctry (J L); Track (V L); District and Regional Band (Alto Sax); President of National Honor Society; Music; Political Science; Oberlin College; Bucknell U

FLAHERTY, JESSICA; PITTSBURGH, PA; TAYLOR ALLDERDICE HS; (FR); Hi Hnr Roll; Hnr Roll; St of Mnth; Chrch Yth Grp; DARE; Law; Nursing

FLAMER, ALISHA J; PHILADELPHIA, PA; OVERBROOK HS; (JR); Gov Hnr Prg; WWAHSS; Comm Volntr; DARE; Emplmnt; FBLA; Bdmtn (V); Stu Cncl (R); Michael J Walker Award; Second Place Portfolio Award; Pre-Med; Temple U; Drexel U

FLAMGLETTI, NIKKI; PITTSBURGH, PA; NORTH ALLEGHENY HS; (SO); Hnr Roll; Nat Hon Sy; Otst Ac Ach Awd; Perf Att; Pres Ac Ftns Aw; WWAHSS; Yth Ldrshp Prog; Chrch Yth Grp; Emplmnt; Mch Bnd; CR (R); Public Relations; U of Pittsburgh; U of North Carolina

FLANIGAN, AMY; PITTSBURGH, PA; BALDWIN HS; (JR); Ctznshp Aw; Hi Hnr Roll; Nat Hon Sy; WWAHSS; Red Cr Aide; Spec Olymp Vol; Chrch Yth Grp; Jr Cls League; Key Club; Bnd; Dnce; Mch Bnd; SP/M/VS; Yrbk; Pharmacy; U of Pittsburgh; Duquesne U

FLEMMING, KATHRYN; WEST CHESTER, PA; BISHOP SHANAHAN HS; (SO); Gov Hnr Prg; Hnr Roll; Perf Att; Pres Ac Ftns Aw; Sci Fairs; WWAHSS; Comm Volntr; Svce Clb; Bnd; Chr; SP/M/VS; Bskball (J); Sftball (V); Swmg (V); Vllyball (VJ); Stu Cncl (T); Yrbk (E); Pennsylvania Junior Academy of Science Participant; First Place In Science Fairs - 3 Years; Medicine /Criminology / Science/ Math; Journalism / Writing; Immaculate U; Neumann College

FLEMMINGS, JESSICA; PHILADELPHIA, PA; BEN FRANKLIN HS; (SO); Ctznshp Aw; Hnr Roll; Perf Att; St of Mnth; Outdrs Clb; Lcrsse (C); Business Youth, SAT Pre-Class; Registered Nurse; Penn State; Temple U

FLOOD, KATIE M; EVANS CITY, PA; SENECA VALLEY SHS; (JR); Hi Hnr Roll; Nat Hon Sy; Comm Volntr; Peer Tut/Med; Chrch Yth Grp; Dbte Team; Key Club; NtlFrnscLg; Spch Team; SADD; Chr; Ch Chr; SP/M/VS; Chrldg (V L); Sccr (J); Track (J); Debate Team; English; Psychology; Washington College; Saint Mary's College of Maryland

FLORES, ANGELA J; FREDONIA, PA; REYNOLDS JR/SR HS; (JR); Ctznshp Aw; Hi Hnr Roll; Hnr Roll; Kwnis Aw; Nat Hon Sy; Otst Ac Ach Awd; St of Mnth; Comm Volntr; Emplmnt; Key Club; Prom Com; SADD; Bnd; Stg Cre; Cl Off (S); Yrbk; 2004-2005/2005-2006-Key Club Secretary; (Kiwanis) 2004-2005 3rd Place State (394.5 Service Hours) Award; Secondary Spanish Education; Secondary English Education; Westminster College; Grove City College

FOGEL, KEITH; MIFFLINBURG, PA; MIFFLINBURG HS; (SO); Perf Att; Pres Ac Ftns Aw; St of Mnth; Comm Volntr; Chrch Yth Grp; Key Club; Vsity Clb; Bsball (V); Bskball (V); Ftball (V); CR (R); Key Club President; Physical Therapy

FOLK, ANTHONY; HALLSTEAD, PA; BLUE RIDGE HS; (SO); Hi Hnr Roll; Hnr Roll; Nat Hon Sy; Otst Ac Ach Awd; St of Mnth; WWAHSS; Comm Volntr; Bdmtn (J); Bskball (J); Skiing (J); Wt Lftg (J); Website Design; Motor Cross; Business Management; Psychology; Penn Tech; RIT

FONTAINE, KATHRYN R; GILBERTSVILLE, PA; BOYERTOWN AREA SR HS; (SO); Hi Hnr Roll; Hnr Roll; Otst Ac Ach Awd; Pres Sch; Comm Volntr; Chrch Yth Grp; DARE; Emplmnt; Pep Squd; Vsity Clb; Ch Chr; Dnce; Chrldg (VJCL); Gmnstcs (J); UCA All Star Cheerleading Award; Business Management; Psychology; James Madison U; Towson U

FORCE, BRYCE; BERWICK, PA; BERWICK AREA SR HS; (MS); Hi Hnr Roll; Hnr Roll; DARE; Chr; Bskball; Ftball; Engineering; Computer Science; Stanford U; Penn State U

FOREBACK, MORGAN D; JEROME, PA; CONEMAUGH TWP HS; (FR); Comm Volntr; AL Aux Girls; Chrch Yth Grp; Schol Bwl; Spch Team; French Clb; Bnd; Chr; SP/M/VS; High School Math Teacher; Fashion Designer / Coordinator; Robert Morris U; UCLA

FOREMAN, BEN; QUAKERTOWN, PA; BETHLEHEM CATHOLIC HS; (SO); Hi Hnr Roll; Hnr Roll; WWAHSS; Comm Volntr; Key Club; Connie Mack Baseball; Business; Computer Science; Penn State; Villanova U

FORTE, SARAH; PALMERTON, PA; PALMERTON AREA SD; (SR); Bskball (J); Sftball (J); Stu Cncl; Business Administrative; Medical; Lincoln Technical Institute; Northampton Community College

FOSTER, AMBER E; MONT CLARE, PA; SPRING-FORD SR HS; (SO); Hi Hnr Roll; Hnr Roll; Comm Volntr; Emplmnt; Clr Grd; Mch Bnd; Track (L); Medal in Discus in Track; Reached PAC-10 Level in Track; Early Childhood Education; Interior Design; The Art Institute of Philadelphia; Montgomery County Cmty College

FOSTER, DANIKA; DILLSBURG, PA; NORTHERN HS; (FR); Fut Prb Slvr; Hi Hnr Roll; Pres Sch; St of Mnth; WWAHSS; Comm Volntr; Spec Olymp Vol; Chrch Yth Grp; Key Club; Mth Clb/Tm; SADD; Bnd; Chr; Mch Bnd; SP/M/VS; York County Junior Honors Choir; Envirothon Team (Top Team); Biology/Science Related; Youth Ministry/Relations; Messiah College; U of Alaska

FOWLER, ANTOINE; PHILADELPHIA, PA; BENJAMIN RUSH MS; (MS); Hnr Roll; MVP; Perf Att; St of Mnth; ArtClub; Spch Team; Bsball (C); Bskball (V); Ftball (C); Sports Medicine; Graphic Design; Temple U; Miami U

FOWLER, DANIEL; LANSDALE, PA; NORTH PENN HS; (JR); Hi Hnr Roll; Hnr Roll; Nat Hon Sy; Perf Att; Comm Volntr; Spec Olymp Vol; Emplmnt; Key Club; SADD; CR (R); Attended National Youth Leadership Forum; Chemistry; History; U of Pennsylvania; Junior College

Foreback, Morgan D
Conemaugh Twp HS
Jerome, PA

Fontaine, Kathryn R
Boyertown Area SR HS
Gilbertsville, PA

Fiorelli, Charissa
Bensalem Township SD
Bensalem, PA

Finley, Joe
Souderton Area HS
Souderton, PA

Fikes, Tara
Chichester SR HS
Boothwyb, PA

Filer, Jason R
Shippensburg HS
Shippensburg, PA

Flood, Katie M
Seneca Valley SHS
Evans City, PA

Force, Bryce
Berwick Area SR HS
Berwick, PA

Foster, Amber E
Spring-Ford SR HS
Mont Clare, PA

NATIONAL HONOR ROLL SPRING 2005 — Pennsylvania

FOX, ALLISON B; YORK, PA; CHRISTIAN SCH OF YORK; (SR); Hnr Roll; Nat Hon Sy; Peer Tut/Med; AL Aux Girls; Chrch Yth Grp; Chr; SP/M/VS; Fld Hky (V); Scr Kpr (V); Sccr (V); Math; Houghton College

FOX, CARRIE; MOUNT MORRIS, PA; WAYNESBURG CTRL HS; (SR); Hi Hnr Roll; Nat Hon Sy; WWAHSS; Yth Ldrshp Prog; Comm Volntr; Chrch Yth Grp; Lttrmn Clb; Mus Clb; NYLC; SADD; French Clb; Bnd; Jzz Bnd; Mch Bnd; Gmnstcs (V); Skiing; Simply Do God's Will for My Life!; Valley Forge Christian College

FOX, JACLYN; ROCKTON, PA; CLEARFIELD HS; (SO); Hnr Roll; St of Mnth; WWAHSS; FCA; Key Club; Dnce; Tennis (V); Girl Scout Silver Award; Baton Twirler; Pharmacy; Computer; Temple U; Penn State U

FOX, JEFF; BERLIN, PA; SHANKSVILLE STONYCREEK SCH; (SO); Hnr Roll; Pres Ac Ftns Aw; Chrch Yth Grp; Bsball (V)

FOX, LOUIS; GLENMOORE, PA; WESTTOWN SCH; (SO); Comm Volntr; Chess; Emplmnt; Bsball (J); Bskball (V); Lcrsse (J); Wt Lftg; CR (R); Pharmacy Technician; Dorm Prefect; Sports Medicine; Pharmacy; U of North Carolina; U of Maryland

FRAELICH, JAMES A; NORRISTOWN, PA; ROOSEVELT ALT; (SO); Hnr Roll; Nat Hon Sy; Nat Stu Ath Day Aw; St of Mnth; Comm Volntr; Scouts; Wdwrkg Clb; Track (V); Student of the Month; Athletic Coordinator; Michigan; Penn State

FRAIN, SIOBHAN; SAYLORSBURG, PA; PLEASANT VALLEY HS; (JR); Hi Hnr Roll; Hnr Roll; WWAHSS; Comm Volntr; Emplmnt; Key Club; Scouts; Bnd; Chr; Clr Grd; Mch Bnd; Master's Degree in History Education; Anthropology; West Chester U; Kutztown U

FRANCE, HOLLY; PITTSTON, PA; TRIBORO CHRISTIAN AC; (SR); Hnr Roll; Valdctrian; Chrch Yth Grp; Prom Com; Psychologist; Luzerne County Community College

FRANCIS, DOMINIQUE; PHILADELPHIA, PA; OVERBROOK HS; (SO); Ctznshp Aw; Hnr Roll; Otst Ac Ach Awd; Perf Att; Sci/Math Olympn; St of Mnth; Dbte Team; Drma Clb; Ch Chr; Sccr; CR (T); Most Disciplined; Language Arts; Pre-Med; Criminal Justice; Howard U; Harvard U

FRANCIS, RUTH A; HUNTINGDON VALLEY, PA; ABINGTON HS; (SO); Kwnis Aw; Scout; Emplmnt; Key Club; Tchrs Aide; Dnce; SP/M/VS; Scr Kpr (J L); Stu Cncl (R); CR (R); Business; Dance Minor; U of Maryland; Northeastern

FRANTZ, MICHAEL C; LOGANTON, PA; CTRL MTN HS; (SR); Hi Hnr Roll; Hnr Roll; Become a Navy Dep Member 20040908; Navy Shipdate Is 20050901

FREDERICK, KAITLYN; GREENVILLE, PA; GREENVILLE HS; (JR); Hnr Roll; Key Club; Sci Clb; Vsity Clb; Spanish Clb; Bskball (V); Chrldg (V L); Tennis (V L); Track (V L); Volunteer for Children's Summer Camps; (Earth Explorers/Homemakers/Art); Forensic Science; Biology/Chemistry; Mercyhurst College; Clarion, Edinboro; Thiel

FREDERICKS, KATIE L; BETHLEHEM, PA; NAZARETH AREA SD; (JR); Hi Hnr Roll; Hnr Roll; Spec Olymp Vol; Emplmnt; Scouts; French Clb; Dnce; Cr Ctry (J); Biochemistry; Nursing; Massachusetts College of Pharmacy; Elizabethtown College

FREILER, MEGAN E; POTTSVILLE, PA; POTTSVILLE AREA HS; (SO); F Lan Hn Soc; Hi Hnr Roll; WWAHSS; Chrch Yth Grp; Key Club; German Clb; Bnd; Mch Bnd; Sccr (V); Stu Cncl (R); Schuylkill County Honors Band; Fashion Merchandising; Business; Indiana U of Pennsylvania; Susquehanna U

FRETTS, DURANNA; GROVE CITY, PA; GROVE CITY HS; (SO); Hi Hnr Roll; WWAHSS; Yth Ldrshp Prog; Hab For Humty Volntr; Chrch Yth Grp; DARE; Key Club; Quill & Scroll; Sccr (J); Sch Ppr (E); Greenville Reading & Competition Winner; Social Science / Psychology; Philosophy & Religion; Westminster College U; Ithaca College

FRETZ, BARBARA; HARRISBURG, PA; CTRL DAUPHIN HS; (FR); Hi Hnr Roll; Hnr Roll; Sci Fairs; Sci/Math Olympn; St of Mnth; Scouts; Spanish Clb; Bskball (J); Sftball (J); Vllyball (J L); Teaching; Culinary Arts; Penn State U; Indiana U of Pennsylvania

FREY, AMBER; NEWPORT, PA; NEWPORT SD; (FR); Hi Hnr Roll; Hnr Roll; Pres Ac Ftns Aw; Chrch Yth Grp; Fld Hky (V); Skiing (V); Track (V); Ski Club; Youth Ministries of Central PA Group; Physical Therapy; Teaching

FRIEDERICK, BILL; PHILADELPHIA, PA; FATHER JUDGE HS; (SR); DAR; Hi Hnr Roll; Hnr Roll; Chess; Scouts; Varsity Bowling, Letter Winner All-Catholic 2004; Business/Marketing/Management; Arcadia U; Holy Family U

FRIEDMAN, AMANDA J; CHESTER, PA; THE CHRISTIAN AC; (JR); Hi Hnr Roll; Hnr Roll; Nat Hon Sy; Otst Ac Ach Awd; Pres Sch; Comm Volntr; Chrch Yth Grp; Drma Clb; Off Aide; Tchrs Aide; Ch Chr; SP/M/VS; Stg Cre; Yrbk (R, P); Pres. of Church Youth Group; Counselor of the Week Award; Elementary Education; Children's Ministry; Maranatha Baptist Bible College; Bob Jones U

FRISK, SAMANTHA; ENON VALLEY, PA; BLACKHAWK HS; (FR); Hnr Roll; WWAHSS; Spec Olymp Vol; Chrch Yth Grp; Emplmnt; Key Club; Bnd; Mch Bnd; Orch; SP/M/VS; National Society of High School Scholars; Accounting

FRITSCH, MELISSA E; THORNTON, PA; WEST CHESTER EAST HS; (FR); Hnr Roll; Bnd; Dvng (V L); Competitive Cheerleading; Marine Biology; Secondary Education Teacher; Pennsylvania State U; U of Michigan

FRITZ III, JAMES; SOUDERTON, PA; SOUDERTON AREA HS; (SR); Hnr Roll; Bsball (V); Ftball (V L); Football Honorable Mention Offensive Line; Honor Roll, Soap Box, World Rally Champ; Business Management; Nicholls College

FROMM, ALLISON; BERWYN, PA; CONESTOGA HS; (JR); Hi Hnr Roll; Hnr Roll; Comm Volntr; DARE; Emplmnt; Mus Clb; Scouts; Chr; Mar Art; Sccr; Camp Counselor; GSA; Teacher; Temple U; West Chester U

FRY, APRIL; POTTSTOWN, PA; POTTSTOWN SR HS; (FR); ROTC

FRYMOYER, TRACI L; LAURELDALE, PA; MUHLENBERG SR HS; (JR); Hi Hnr Roll; Hnr Roll; Sci/Math Olympn; St of Mnth; Comm Volntr; Chrch Yth Grp; Emplmnt; Sci Clb; Bskball (J); Voc Ind Clb Am; Stg Cre; Tennis (J); Track (V); Yrbk (R); Congressional Recognition from Tim Holden; Certificate of Recognition of Senator O'Pate; Nurse / Work in Hospital; Home Health Aide; Reading Hospital School of Nursing; Nursing Schools

FUEHRER, JASON T; LITITZ, PA; WARWICK HS; (SR); Hi Hnr Roll; Nat Hon Sy; Otst Ac Ach Awd; Pres Sch; St of Mnth; WWAHSS; Emplmnt; Ftball (J); Sccr (J); Athletic Trainer; Lebanon Valley College - Doctorate in Physical Therapy; Minor in Athletic Training; Lebanon Valley College

FULLER, LEANNE; DU BOIS, PA; DU BOIS AREA HS; (JR); Hi Hnr Roll; Hnr Roll; MVP; Nat Hon Sy; WWAHSS; Peer Tut/Med; Emplmnt; Scouts; Vsity Clb; Swmg (V L); Vllyball (V L); Swimming MVP 2004-2005; Education; Edinboro U of PA; Pennsylvania State U

FULMER, AMANDA; NEMACOLIN, PA; CARMICHAELS AREA JR/SR HS; (JR); Hnr Roll; Nat Hon Sy; Perf Att; Hosp Aide; Chrch Yth Grp; Voc Ind Clb Am; CNA; LPN; LBI Laurel Business Institute; WVJC West Virginia Jr College

FULTON, ELIZABETH; MIDDLETOWN, PA; MIDDLETOWN AREA HS; (SO); 4H Awd; Hi Hnr Roll; Hnr Roll; Nat Hon Sy; WWAHSS; Spec Olymp Vol; 4-H; Drma Clb; Key Club; Lib Aide; Bnd; Chr; Mch Bnd; Orch; Tennis (V); Key Club Secretary; Biology; Art History; Cornell U; Lafayette

FULTZ, ALYSSA B; CARLISLE, PA; CUMBERLAND VALLEY HS; (SO); Hnr Roll; Nat Hon Sy; WWAHSS; Peer Tut/Med; Key Club; German Clb; Elementary School Teacher

FUNAHASHI, AMY; WEST CHESTER, PA; BREED HENDERSON; Hnr Roll; Comm Volntr; Chr; Lcrsse (J); Tennis (J)

FYE, WILLIAM J; TIOGA, PA; NORTHERN TIOGA SD; (SO); Hi Hnr Roll; Hnr Roll; Comm Volntr; Bsball (V); Bskball (V); Sccr (J); Electronic Engineering; Physical Education; Penn State U; Mansfield U

GABANI, PRASHANT; MC DONALD, PA; SOUTH FAYETTE TOWNSHIP HS; (FR); All Am Sch; Hi Hnr Roll; Nat Mrt LOC; Otst Ac Ach Awd; Perf Att; Pres Sch; St of Mnth; USAA; Comm Volntr; Peer Tut/Med; Mth Clb/Tm; Sci Clb; Tech Clb; Clb; Chr; PI Contest (Memorized 150 Digits Of Pi In School competition) 1st Place; TSA State Conference - Structural Engineering - National Qualifier with 3rd Place; CAD 2-D - Top Ten; Biomedical Engineering; Medical Science; U of Pittsburgh, Pennsylvania; Carnegie Mellon U, Pittsburgh, Pennsylvania

GABER, RACHEL; CORRY, PA; CORRY AREA HS; (SR); Hnr Roll; Comm Volntr; Spec Olymp Vol; Key Club; French Clb; Yrbk (R, P); Speech Pathology; Elementary Education; Edinboro U

GABRYLUK, CHRISTOPHER; BATH, PA; NORTHAMPTON AREA SR HS; (JR); Hi Hnr Roll; Hnr Roll; MVP; Nat Hon Sy; Sci/Math Olympn; WWAHSS; Yth Ldrshp Prog; Comm Volntr; Peer Tut/Med; Spec Olymp Vol; Chrch Yth Grp; DECA; Mth Clb/Tm; Mod UN; Off Aide; Prom Com; SADD; Vsity Clb; Ch Chr; Bskball (J); Ftball (VJCL); PP Ftbl; Track (V CL); Wt Lftg; Football Scholar Athlete; Track Scholar Athlete (School Record-Javelin); Biomedical Engineering; Bucknell U

GAFFNEY, TAURA A; LATROBE, PA; EASTERN WESTMORELAND CTC; (SR); Hnr Roll; Voc Ind Clb Am; Skills USA; National Technical Honor Society; Technical Support; Westmoreland County Community College

GAGE, ALAN; LAWTON, PA; ELK LAKE HS; (FR); F Lan Hn Soc; Hnr Roll; Perf Att; St of Mnth; USAA; WWAHSS; Chrch Yth Grp; Drma Clb; Key Club; Lib Aide; Scouts; French Clb; Chr; SP/M/VS; Stu Cncl (R); Musical Theatre; Performing Arts

GAGLIONE, LINDSAY; HARRISBURG, PA; CTRL DAUPHIN (FR); Hnr Roll; Perf Att; Chrch Yth Grp; Chr; Moo Duk Kwan-Blue Belt

GAINEY, SHANEAN; PHILADELPHIA, PA; EDISON; (SR); Ctznshp Aw; Hnr Roll; Sci Fairs; St of Mnth; Comm Volntr; Scouts

GALADE, GINGER L; HAZLETON, PA; BISHOP HAFEY HS; (SO); F Lan Hn Soc; Hi Hnr Roll; Nat Hon Sy; Perf Att; WWAHSS; Hosp Aide; Emplmnt; Key Club; Mth Clb/Tm; Chrldg (J); Psychology

GALANTE, JON M; STROUDSBURG, PA; PLEASANT VALLEY HS; (FR); Bnd; Jzz Bnd; Mch Bnd; Skiing; District Orchestra; Key Club / FBLA; Anesthesiologist; Medical Research

GALE, AMBER L; PITTSBURGH, PA; CORRICK HS; (SR); Hi Hnr Roll; Hnr Roll; Sci Fairs; Comm Volntr; Chrch Yth Grp; Scouts; Ch Chr; Certificate for Preventing Teen Pregnancy; Journalism; Liberal Arts; Community College of Allegheny County

GALICZNSKI, ALISHA; PHILADELPHIA, PA; BENJAMIN RUSH MS; MS; Ctznshp Aw; Hnr Roll; Perf Att; Sci Fairs; St of Mnth; DARE; Lib Aide; Spch Team; Dnce; Yrbk (E); Principal's Award; Nursing; Temple University Philadelphia; University of Pennsylvania Philadelphia

GALLAGHER, KELLYE L; MORTON, PA; RIDLEY HS; (SO); Ctznshp Aw; Hi Hnr Roll; MVP; Otst Ac Ach Awd; Sci Fairs; St of Mnth; Comm Volntr; Bskball (V); Lcrsse (V); Sccr (V); All Delco Soccer - HM; AAU Basketball All-Tournament Team; Elementary Education; Business Management; U of Delaware; Villanova U

GALVICK, MATTHEW; PITTSTON TWP, PA; PITTSTON AREA HS; (JR); Hi Hnr Roll; Nat Hon Sy; Perf Att; Sci/Math Olympn; St of Mnth; WWAHSS; Peer Tut/Med; Emplmnt; Mth Clb/Tm; Sccr (V CL); Tennis (V L); Track (J); Bowling; Penn State U

GAMBALE, NICOLE; BENSALEM, PA; BENSALEM TOWNSHIP SD HS; (SO); Hnr Roll; Kwnis Aw; Nat Hon Sy; St of Mnth; WWAHSS; Chrch Yth Grp; Mth Clb/Tm; Bskball (V); Sccr (V); Sftball (V); English; Marine Biology/Psychology

GAMBERONI, JESSICA; YOUNGWOOD, PA; GREENSBURG CTRL CATHOLIC HS; (JR); F Lan Hn Soc; Hi Hnr Roll; Nat Hon Sy; Nat Stu Ath Day Aw; Pres Sch; WWAHSS; Comm Volntr; Peer Tut/Med; Spec Olymp Vol; DARE; Emplmnt; Mth Clb/Tm; MuAlphaTh; Prom Com; SADD; Latin Clb; Bskball (V L); Cr Ctry (V L); Sftball (V L); Recipient of McKenna Foundation; Women in Engineering Award; Biomedical Engineering; Radiology; U of Delaware; Carnegie Mellon U

GAMBLE, REBEKAH; NEW EAGLE, PA; RINGGOLD HS; (FR); Hnr Roll; Comm Volntr; Chess; Lib Aide; Published Writer / Poetry; Member of PETA; English; Art; Carnegie Mellon U; California U of Pennsylvania

GANTZ, ASHLEY L; ERIE, PA; ERIE CITY SD; (SO); Hnr Roll; MVP; Perf Att; Spec Olymp Vol; Sccr (V); Track; Wt Lftg; Criminal Justice; Protective Services; Edinboro

GARBER, JANELLE; ELIZABETHTOWN, PA; ELIZABETHTOWN AREA HS; (JR); Hi Hnr Roll; Hnr Roll; MVP; Nat Hon Sy; Sci Fairs; St of Mnth; WWAHSS; Comm Volntr; Chrch Yth Grp; Emplmnt; Vsity Clb; Bskball (V CL); Fld Hky (V L); Elementary Education; Nursing; West Chester U; Shippensburg U

GARCIA, CARMEN R; READING, PA; READING HS; (SO); Hnr Roll; MVP; Otst Ac Ach Awd; Perf Att; St of Mnth; Sftball; Lawyer / Designer; Law Degree; U of Pennsylvania Law School

GARCIA, CINDY M; READING, PA; SOUTHWEST MS; (MS); Hnr Roll; Nat Hon Sy; St of Mnth; NYLC; Astronaut Degree; Doctor Degree; Kutztown U; Penn State U

GARDNER, MATTHEW R; ROBESONIA, PA; CONRAD WEISER HS; (SR); Ctznshp Aw; Gov Hnr Prg; Hi Hnr Roll; Nat Hon Sy; Otst Ac Ach Awd; Perf Att; Pres Sch; Sci Fairs; Sci/Math Olympn; St of Mnth; Peer Tut/Med; Mth Clb/Tm; Ntl FFA; Scouts; Bsball (VJ); Berks Best in Mathematics - 2005; Reserve Grand Champion Rio Berks Science Fair; Animal Science / Microbiology; Penn State U

GARGANO, LISA M; ASTON, PA; THE CHRISTIAN AC; (JR); Hnr Roll; Nat Hon Sy; St of Mnth; Drma Clb; Tchrs Aide; Bnd; Chr; SP/M/VS; Awarded from President's Excellence Awareness Program; Awarded Character Trait of Enthusiasm; Math Teacher, Secondary Education; West Chester U; Eastern U

GAROFALO, ROB; MECHANICSBURG, PA; TRINITY HS; (SR); Hnr Roll; WWAHSS; Comm Volntr; Hab For Humty Volntr; Spec Olymp Vol; Key Club; Latin Clb; Track (J); Biology; Pre-Podiatry; Shippensburg U

GARRETT, KATHY; NAZARETH, PA; NAZARETH HS; (SO); Hi Hnr Roll; Pres Ac Ftns Aw; Sci Fairs; Sci/Math Olympn; USAA; Comm Volntr; Peer Tut/Med; DARE; Photog; Sci Clb; Tchrs Aide; Dnce; Dance Competition Awards; Pharmacist; Psychologist; Moravian College; Lehigh U

GARRITY, DANIEL; WATERFORD, PA; FORT LEBOEUF SD; (JR); Hnr Roll; Perf Att; Emplmnt; Lib Aide; Ftball (VJ L); Wt Lftg (VJ); USSA Academic Achievement in Math/Science Leadership; Class Leadership Award At Erie County Tech.; Electronics Engineer; Educational Instructor for Elementary School; Edinboro U; Penn State, Boston

GASIM, AZZA A; UPPER DARBY, PA; UPPER DARBY HS; (FR); Ctznshp Aw; Hi Hnr Roll; Hnr Roll; WWAHSS; Comm Volntr; Hab For Humty Volntr; Hosp Aide; ArtClub; DARE; Dbte Team; Emplmnt; Fr of Library; FBLA; Lib Aide; P to P St Amb Prg; Chr; SP/M/VS; CR (P); Presidential Gold Award; Distinguished Honor Roll; Medical; Biology; U of Pennsylvania; Drexel U

GASPARETTO, AUTUM; PITTSBURGH, PA; NORTH ALLEGHENY INTERMIDIATE; (SO); Clr Grd; Drl Tm; Vllyball

GATANIS, SUSAN; ALLENTOWN, PA; SALISBURY HS; (JR); Hi Hnr Roll; Hnr Roll; Nat Hon Sy; WWAHSS; Key Club; Prom Com; SADD; Stu Cncl (R); Yrbk (E); Baton Twirling; Communications/Journalism; Susquehanna U; Bloomsburg U

GAUGHAN, ASHLEY; OAKMONT, PA; RIVERVIEW JR/SR HS; (SO); Hi Hnr Roll; Hnr Roll; Nat Hon Sy; Chrch Yth Grp; Emplmnt; Key Club; Lib Aide; SADD; French Clb; Orch; Sftball (J); Vllyball (J); Elementary Education

GAULT, JACINDA; JAMESTOWN, PA; JAMESTOWN AREA SD; (SO); Ctznshp Aw; Hi Hnr Roll; Nat Hon Sy; Chrch Yth Grp; Spch Team; Spanish Clb; Bnd; Flg Crps; Pep Bnd; Vllyball (J); Lawyer; Historian; Yale U

GAYE, EDWARD; DARBY, PA; PENN WOOD HS; (SO); 4H Awd; Hi Hnr Roll; Hnr Roll; USAA; Yth Ldrshp Prog; Hosp Aide; Red Cr Aide; Ftball (L); Sccr (V); Technology, Math; Sports Soccer; Community College

GEARHART, BETH; MARTINSBURG, PA; CENTRAL HS; (SR); 4H Awd; Hi Hnr Roll; St of Mnth; 4-H; Chrch Yth Grp; Emplmnt; Tchrs Aide; Vsity Clb; Cr Ctry (V CL); Skiing; Track (V CL); Penn State U Altoona; Juniata College

GEARHART, ERICA; NEW KENSINGTON, PA; BURRELL HS; (JR); Hi Hnr Roll; Nat Hon Sy; WWAHSS; Comm Volntr; Red Cr Aide; Prom Com; Scouts; Spanish Clb; Bnd; Mch Bnd; Stu Cncl (R); American Red Cross Club-Treasurer; Reading Railroad; U of Pittsburgh; Pennsylvania State U

GEBAUER, MEGAN; EIGHTY FOUR, PA; PETERS TOWNSHIP HS; (JR); Hi Hnr Roll; Pres Sch; Emplmnt; Photog; Psychology; Biology; Penn State U; U of Pittsburgh

GEEDEY, EMILEE M; LEWISTOWN, PA; LEWISTOWN AREA HS; (FR); St of Mnth; Key Club; German Clb; Bnd; Jzz Bnd; SP/M/VS; Fld Hky (VJ)

GEIBEL, KEVIN; BUTLER, PA; BUTLER SR HS; (SR); Hi Hnr Roll; Hnr Roll; Emplmnt; Vsity Clb; Rlr Hky (V C); Working at Texas Road House; Criminal Justice System; Pennsylvania State U Behrend Campus

GEIMAN, BRIAN; HANOVER, PA; SOUTHWESTERN HS; (JR); Hi Hnr Roll; Hnr Roll; Perf Att; Computer Programming

GELTMACHER, HEATHER; MOUNT JOY, PA; DONEGAL HS; (JR); Hnr Roll; Emplmnt; Counseling; Early Childhood Education; Millersville U

GENEROTTI, JACKIE; PHOENIXVILLE, PA; AC OF NOTRE DAME; (JR); Hnr Roll; Sci Fairs; ArtClub; Emplmnt; Quill & Scroll; SP/M/VS; Sftball (V); Yrbk (E); Certified Lifeguard; Landmark Organization Volunteer; Bioengineering; Forensic Science; Penn State U; Lehigh U

GENERY, KELLI; HAZLETON, PA; HAZLETON AREA HS; (FR); Hi Hnr Roll; Hnr Roll; St of Mnth; Off Aide; SADD; Foreign Clb; Chr; HAFL Cheerleading / Spirit Award; PAL Basketball - 3rd Place; Doctors Degree / PhD; Medicine; Penn State U

GENISE, SARAH M; WEXFORD, PA; NORTH ALLEGHENY INT HS; (FR); Duke TS; Hnr Roll; Hosp Aide; DARE; Svce Clb; Beta Club in Leesville Middle School in Raleigh, NC; Art; Psychology; NYU; UC Santa Cruz

GENTILE, ASHLEE M; WERNERSVILLE, PA; CONRAD WEISER HS; (JR); Hi Hnr Roll; Hnr Roll; Pres Ac Ftns Aw; St of Mnth; WWAHSS; DARE; Emplmnt; Key Club; Ntl FFA; P to P St Amb Prg; Spanish Clb; Fld Hky (V L); PP Ftbl; Sccr (VJ); Track; Big Brothers / Big Sisters / Certificate of Achievement; Certificate of Honor / Key Club VP; Pharmacist / Pharmacological Science; Archaeologist; Juniata College; Penn State U - Main Campus

GEORGE, AMANDA; HAZLETON, PA; HAZLETON AREA SD; (SO); Hi Hnr Roll; Otst Ac Ach Awd; Perf Att; St of Mnth; WWAHSS; Comm Volntr; Peer Tut/Med; Drma Clb; FBLA; Key Club; Ch Chr; SP/M/VS; Mar Art; Altar Server; Education/Administration; Business; U of North Carolina; U of California-Los Angeles

GEORGE, FELICIA R; SHENANDOAH, PA; SHENANDOAH VALLEY; (FR); Hi Hnr Roll; Hnr Roll; Nat Hon Sy; Comm Volntr; Vllyball (J); Lawyer; Harvard Law School

GEORGE, JENNIFER E; ELIZABETHTOWN, PA; ELIZABETHTOWN AREA HS; (SR); Hnr Roll; Perf Att; WWAHSS; Chrch Yth Grp; DARE; Emplmnt; Key Club; Prom Com; Bnd; Mch Bnd; PP Ftbl (C); Sccr (J); Prom Committee; Elementary Education; Lock Haven U

GEORGE, PHILIP J; FEASTERVILLE TREVOSE, PA; BENSALEM TOWNSHIP SD; (SR); Hnr Roll; USMC Stu Ath Aw; Chess; Chrch Yth Grp; ROTC; Swmg (L); Marine Corp Junior ROTC - 2 Yrs, Rank 1st Lieutenant; Film Festival Award; Already in the Army / Rank of Private; Computer or Electric Engineer; Bucks County Comm College; PA State Colleges As Per Military Contract

GEORGE, ROBERT T; VANDERGRIFT, PA; KISKI AREA HS; (SR); Hi Hnr Roll; Nat Hon Sy; Sci Fairs; WWAHSS; Peer Tut/Med; Chrch Yth Grp; Key Club; SADD; Tennis (J); Yrbk (E, P); President Youth Ministry; Relay for Life Team Leader; Computing and Information Technology; Photography; St. Vincent College

GEORGES, SAEED; ALLENTOWN, PA; LOUIS E DIERUFF HS; (SO); Hnr Roll; WWAHSS; Comm Volntr; Key Club; SADD; Vllyball (VJC); Stu Cncl (T); Key Club-Treasurer; Teen Works of Lehigh Valley-Member; Criminal Justice / Homicide; Penn State; Muhlenberg College

GERHARD, KAYLEE; GREENSBURG, PA; GREENSBURG SALEM SD; (FR); Hi Hnr Roll; Hnr Roll; MVP; Pres Ac Ftns Aw; Chr; Sftball; Vllyball (J); Nursing; Psychology; Carlow College; Duquesne U

GERHART, LYDIA; SASSAMANSVILLE, PA; BOYERTOWN AREA SR HS; (SO); Hnr Roll; Sci Fairs; Chrch Yth Grp; DARE; Mus Clb; Svce Clb; Bnd; Chr; Mch Bnd; Pep Bnd; Stu Cncl (R); Music Award; Service Award; Music; Art; Messiah College PA

GERLACH, KIM; BERWICK, PA; BERWICK AREA SR HS; (SO); Hi Hnr Roll; Nat Hon Sy; WWAHSS; Key Club; SADD; Spanish Clb; Sccr (V L); Vllyball (V L); Stu Cncl (R); Yrbk (R); Dayton H. Clewell Memorial General Science Award; Honor Award-Distinguished Honors All Year; Chemical Engineering; Carnegie Mellon U; Massachusetts Institute of Technology

GERSTENBERGER, KRISTA G; PHOENIXVILLE, PA; PHOENIXVILLE AREA HS; (JR); Hi Hnr Roll; Hnr Roll; Nat Hon Sy; Otst Ac Ach Awd; Sci Fairs; St of Mnth; WWAHSS; Chrch Yth Grp; DARE; Lttrmn Clb; Vsity Clb; German Clb; Stg Cre; Fld Hky (V); Lcrsse (V); PP Ftbl (V); Vsy Clb (V); Cl Off (T); Stu Cncl (T); Yrbk (R); Kodak Young Leader's Award; Graphic Arts; Advertising/Marketing; Drexel; Penn State

GESSNER, DAKOTA W; MIFFLINBURG, PA; MIFFLINBURG AREA SD; (SO); Ctznshp Aw; Hi Hnr Roll; Hnr Roll; Nat Hon Sy; Ntl FFA; Bsball (J); Ftball (V L); Wt Lftg; Academic Excellence Award; 6th Grade History Teacher; Bachelor's Degree in Education; Bloomsburg U; Lock Haven U

GETWAY, AMANDA; HERMITAGE, PA; HERMITAGE SD; (SO); Hi Hnr Roll; WWAHSS; Chrch Yth Grp; Drma Clb; Bnd; Chr; Ch Chr; Orch; Cr Ctry (J); Track (J); Library Sciences; Westminster College

GETZ, ALYSSA M; PITTSTON, PA; PITTSTON AREA SD; (JR); Hi Hnr Roll; Hnr Roll; Nat Hon Sy; WWAHSS; Chrch Yth Grp; Emplmnt; Key Club; Tech Clb; Chrldg (V CL); Track (V); Stu Cncl; Sch Ppr; Yrbk; National Honor Society Treasurer; Elementary Education (Major); Special Education (Minor); East Stroudsburg U

GIACOPONELLO, ANNA; WALLINGFORD, PA; STRATH HAVEN HS; (JR); Hi Hnr Roll; Hnr Roll; Comm Volntr; Hosp Aide; ArtClub; DARE; Dbte Team; Chr; Non-Academic Clubs; Business; Psychology; Sarah Lawrence College; Temple U

GIANNOTTI, AMANDA; READING, PA; EXETER TWP SR HS; (JR); Hnr Roll; Prom Com; Bnd; Chr; Jzz Bnd; Mch Bnd; Bskball (V); Athletic Training (Lettered); Dental Hygiene; West Chester U

GIBBS, BELINDA L; PITTSBURGH, PA; PEABODY HS; (SO); Hnr Roll; St of Mnth; Comm Volntr; Peer Tut/Med; Ob/Gyn; Writer; Yale U; Pittsburgh U

GIBBS, CRYSTAL; UPPER DARBY, PA; UPPER DARBY HS; (JR); Ctznshp Aw; Hi Hnr Roll; Hnr Roll; Perf Att; Peer Tut/Med; Red Cr Aide; Spec Olymp Vol; Chrch Yth Grp; Emplmnt; Mus Clb; Pep Squd; Prom Com; Ch Chr; Dnce; SP/M/VS; Track (V); Adv Cncl (R); Stu Cncl (R); CR (R); 9th Grade Orientation Guide; Church Outreach Community Program; Radiologic Technology; Nursing; U of Pennsylvania; Drexel U

GIBBS, KIMYETTE; PHILADELPHIA, PA; BEN FRANKLIN HS; (SO); Comm Volntr; ROTC; Scouts; Dnce; Chrldg; Navy JROTC; Cosmetology; Community College of Philadelphia; Harvard U

GIBBS, STEPHANIE; CHESTER, PA; CARDINAL OHARA HS; (SR); Hnr Roll; Nat Hon Sy; WWAHSS; Comm Volntr; Chrch Yth Grp; Emplmnt; Tchrs Aide; Chr; Dnce; Chrldg (C); Track (J); Stu Cncl (S); Business Administration; Accounting; Kutztown U; Newman College

GIBSON, JACKIE; JERSEY SHORE, PA; JERSEY SHORE AREA SR HS; (SO); Hi Hnr Roll; MVP; Pres Ac Ftns Aw; Pres Sch; Key Club; Bskball (V L); Sftball (V L); Stu Cncl (V); Pharmacy

GIBSON, KELLY; GREENSBURG, PA; GREATER LATROBE HS; (SR); F Lan Hn Soc; Hi Hnr Roll; Jr Rot; Nat Hon Sy; Otst Ac Ach Awd; St of Mnth; Comm Volntr; Peer Tut/Med; Dbte Team; Emplmnt; Key Club; NtlFrnscLg; Svce Clb; German Clb; Lcrsse; Busted! PA's Youth Anti-Tobacco Movement; Psychology; Juniata College

GIEDROC, ALYSSA J; HOWARD, PA; BALD EAGLE AREA JR/SR HS; (SR); Hi Hnr Roll; Hnr Roll; Nat Hon Sy; Perf Att; WWAHSS; Red Cr Aide; Spec Olymp Vol; Chrch Yth Grp; Drma Clb; Svce Clb; Vsity Clb; French Clb; Bnd; Dnce; Mch Bnd; Stg Cre; PP Ftbl; Sccr (VJCL); Sftball (J); Track (V L); Vsy Clb (L); Chef-Culinary Arts and Systems BS; Pennsylvania College of Technology

GIFFORD, AARON; WAYNESBURG, PA; WEST GREENE MIDDLE SR HS; (FR); Hi Hnr Roll; Hnr Roll; Nat Sci Aw; WWAHSS; 4-H; Bskball (VJCL); Track (V L)

GILCRIST JR, TODD C; HARRISBURG, PA; CTRL DAUPHIN SD HS; (SO); Hnr Roll; Comm Volntr; Chrch Yth Grp; Emplmnt; Bskball (J); Ftball (V); Stu Cncl (R); Business Communications; Public Relations; South Carolina U; U of Maryland

GILLIN, KARA L; MINERAL POINT, PA; CAMBRIA CTY CHRISTIAN SCH; (SO); Hnr Roll; Sci Fairs; 4-H; ArtClub; Chrch Yth Grp; Jr Ach; Mus Clb; NYLC; Chr; SP/M/VS; Horse 4-H Participant; Grandparents Club; Education; Biology; Houghton College; Penn State U

GILLIS, DAVID; MECHANICSBURG, PA; TRINITY HS; (SR); WWAHSS; Comm Volntr; Chess; Chrch Yth Grp; Key Club; Scouts; Bsball (V); Ftball (V L); Ham Radio Licensed Operator; Indiana U of Pennsylvania

GILLIS, VERNON L; UPPER DARBY, PA; UPPER DARBY HS; (JR); Hnr Roll; MVP; Perf Att; St of Mnth; Spec Olymp Vol; DECA; Bskball (V L); Ftball (V L); Track (V); Stu Cncl (R); CR (R); West Chester U; Widener U

GILLMAN, AMY; KENNETT SQUARE, PA; UNIONVILLE HS; (JR); F Lan Hn Soc; Hi Hnr Roll; Hnr Roll; Nat Hon Sy; Otst Ac Ach Awd; Yth Ldrshp Prog; Comm Volntr; Peer Tut/Med; Emplmnt; Acpl Chr; Drm Mjr; Orch; SP/M/VS; Lcrsse (J); Scr Kpr (J); Sch Ppr (R); Teen Freedom Corps International Club; LINK (Leadership Club); Film; History; New York U; Temple U

GILMARTIN, THOMAS; WEXFORD, PA; NORTH ALLEGHENY INT HS; (SO); Hnr Roll; Nat Hon Sy; WWAHSS; Comm Volntr; Chrch Yth Grp; Key Club; Bnd; Jzz Bnd; Mch Bnd; Cr Ctry (V L); Track (V L)

GINGRAS, MARISSA B; PITTSBURGH, PA; NORTH ALLEGHENY INT HS; (SO); Ctznshp Aw; Hnr Roll; St of Mnth; WWAHSS; Comm Volntr; Peer Tut/Med; Chrch Yth Grp; Emplmnt; Jr Cls League; Key Club; Chr; Ch Chr; SP/M/VS; Cl Off (R); Stu Cncl (R); Lit Mag (E); Key Club International (Publicity Chair); National Junior Honors Society; Wildlife Biology; Environmental Science

GIONTA, GINA; PITTSBURGH, PA; PENN HILLS SR HS; (JR); Hi Hnr Roll; Hnr Roll; Kwnis Aw; Perf Att; WWAHSS; Comm Volntr; Hosp Aide; Emplmnt; Key Club; Scouts; German Clb; Biology; Physical Therapy

GITLIN, SHOSHANA L; DALLAS, PA; DALLAS SR HS; (SR); Hnr Roll; WWAHSS; Comm Volntr; Emplmnt; Key Club; SADD; Lcrsse (J); Scr Kpr (J); Tennis (CL); Track (C); Treasurer of the International Club; Key Club Book Scholarship; Biology; Bio-Behavioral Health; Pennsylvania State U

GLADISH, ALLISON; PITTSBURGH, PA; NORTH HILLS HS; (SR); Hnr Roll; MVP; WWAHSS; Hosp Aide; Peer Tut/Med; Emplmnt; Off Aide; Bskball (J); Tennis (VJ); Track (VJ); Dean's Award Scholarship; French Competition Award; Chemistry; Pre-Medicine/Pediatrics; Washington & Jefferson College

GLADISH, SCOTT; MELCROFT, PA; MC KEESPORT AREA SD; (SO); Hi Hnr Roll; Hnr Roll; Perf Att; Sci/Math Olympn; Chrch Yth Grp; Pep Squd; Tech Clb; Ftball (J); Swmg (J)

GLASS, RYAN; ERIE, PA; FAIRVIEW HS; (SO); All Am Sch; Hi Hnr Roll; Hnr Roll; Nat Hon Sy; St of Mnth; WWAHSS; Comm Volntr; Key Club; Spanish Clb; Bsball (J); Golf (V L); Ice Hky (V CL); Stu Cncl (R); CR (R); City Lacrosse Team; Architecture; U of Michigan; Penn State

GLENN, BRIANNA; CLARION, PA; CLARION AREA JR/SR HS; (SO); Hnr Roll; Perf Att; Comm Volntr; Chrch Yth Grp; Scouts; Bnd; Chr; Mch Bnd; Bskball (J); Track (V); Vllyball (J); History Teacher; Elementary Education Teacher

GLENN, JOSEPH; CLIFTON HEIGHTS, PA; SPRINGFIELD HS; (JR); Hnr Roll; Perf Att; Yth Ldrshp Prog; Scouts; Acpl Chr; Bnd; Chr; Mch Bnd; Ftball; Skiing; Eagle Scout; Computer programming; Business management; Penn State

GLOVER, CASSANDRA; BRADFORD, PA; BRADFORD AREA HS; (MS); Hnr Roll; Compass Learning Achievement; Biology; Penn State; Harvard U

GLOVER, EMILY E; BRIDGEVILLE, PA; SOUTH FAYETTE TOWNSHIP HS; (FR); Hi Hnr Roll; Hnr Roll; St of Mnth; Chrch Yth Grp; Drma Clb; Emplmnt; Prom Com; German Clb; Chr; Dnce; SP/M/VS; Stg Cre; Stu Cncl (P); CR (R); PMEA District Chorus; Student of the Month; Education; Fine Arts/Performing Arts; West Virginia U; Clarion State U

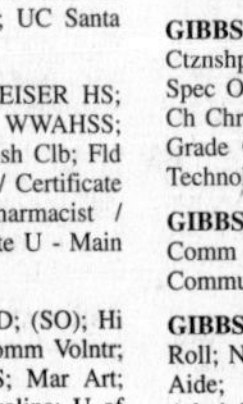
Gibbs, Kimyette
Ben Franklin HS
Philadelphia, PA

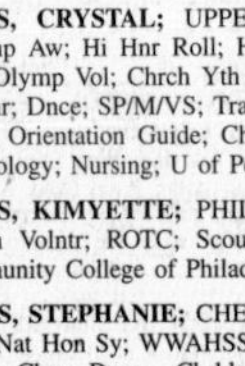
George, Philip J
Bensalem Township SD
Feasterville Trevose, PA

National
Honor Roll
Spring 2005

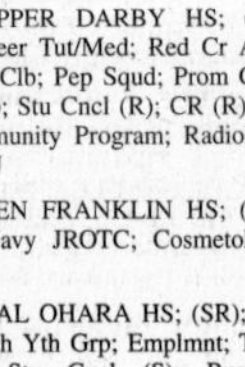
George, Felicia R
Shenandoah Valley
Shenandoah, PA

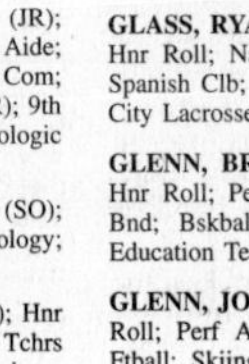
Gladish, Allison
North Hills HS
Pittsburgh, PA

GODEK, GABRIELA M; KUNKLETOWN, PA; PLEASANT VALLEY HS; (SO); Hnr Roll; Comm Volntr; Dbte Team; FBLA; Scouts; Clr Grd; Mch Bnd; Community Service At Day Care; Mathematics; Teaching; Kutztown U; East Stroudsburg U

GOEKE, ROBERT B; HERMITAGE, PA; HICKORY HS; (SO); Hi Hnr Roll; Hnr Roll; Perf Att; Pres Ac Ftns Aw; St of Mnth; Comm Volntr; Jr Ach; Off Aide; Bsball (V L); Bskball (J); Helped Out in the Community Doing Yard Work; Architecture; Athletics; Florida State U; Kansas U

GOFFART, AMY; ROARING SPRING, PA; SPRING COVE SD; (JR); Hi Hnr Roll; Hnr Roll; Perf Att; Yth Ldrshp Prog; Hosp Aide; Chrch Yth Grp; DECA; Emplmnt; FBLA; Scouts; Vsity Clb; Bskball (VJ); Sftball (VJ L); Vsy Clb (V); Pennsylvania Free Enterprise Week; Business Administration/ Marketing; South Hills School of Business (Altoona, PA)

GOGAL, KAILA; ALLENTOWN, PA; PARKLAND HS; (JR); Hnr Roll; Chr; Skiing (C); Swmg (V); Stu Cncl (R); Psychology; Sociology; Penn State U; Bloomsburg U

GOGOTSI, PAVEL; IVYLAND, PA; COUNCIL ROCK HS NORTH; (FR); F Lan Hn Soc; Sci/Math Olympn; Comm Volntr; Mth Clb/Tm; German Clb; CR (R); Black Belt in Tang Soo Do; German Honor Society; Bio Genetic Engineering; Materials Engineering; Drexel U; Massachusetts Institute of Technology

GOHEEN, DAYBA; READING, PA; ANTIETAM MIDDLE/SR HS; (FR); Ctznshp Aw; Hnr Roll; Nat Hon Sy; Comm Volntr; Chrch Yth Grp; DARE; Drma Clb; Acpl Chr; Chr; SP/M/VS; Chrldg (J); Fld Hky (J); Scr Kpr (J); Sccr (J); Stu Cncl (R); Yrbk (P); Peer Mediator; Several Art Awards; Early Childhood Education; Physical Therapist; Kutztown U; New York U

GOLDBERG, ERIKA; JENKINTOWN, PA; ABINGTON HS; (SO); Hnr Roll; Nat Hon Sy; Sci Fairs; Comm Volntr; ArtClub; Key Club; Svce Clb; Stg Cre; Key Club; Building with Books; Art; New York U

GOLDEN, HANNAH E; GLENSHAW, PA; SHALER AREA HS; (JR); Hi Hnr Roll; Hnr Roll; Nat Hon Sy; Otst Ac Ach Awd; Comm Volntr; Chrch Yth Grp; Emplmnt; Scouts; Spanish Clb; Lcrsse (VJ); Math/Science; Engineering; Marquette, Syracuse, Pitt, Penn State, Lehigh.

GOLDSMITH, TYEISHA T; PHILADELPHIA, PA; OVERBROOK HS; (SO); Nat Hon Sy; Perf Att; Comm Volntr; Peer Tut/Med; Sccr (J); Adv Cncl (R); Culinary Artist; Veterinarian; The Art Institute of New York; Argosy U

GOLDSTEIN, MATT; BENSALEM, PA; BENSALEM TOWNSHIP SD HS; (JR); Hi Hnr Roll; Hnr Roll; Information Technology; Bachelor's; ITT Tech (Bensalem, Pa); Temple U

GOLDSTINE, CHRISTIAN W; PHILA, PA; GEORGE PEPPER MS; (MS); Perf Att; St of Mnth; Sftball (V); Completed Eastwick Passage of Right Program; Automobile Mech.; Community College of Philadelphia

GOLEMBIEWSKI, DANA; NEW KENSINGTON, PA; ST JOSEPH HS; (FR); Hi Hnr Roll; Hnr Roll; Comm Volntr; Drma Clb; SP/M/VS; Chrldg (J); PA Junior Academy Science-First Award; Teaching; Marine Biologist; U of Pittsburgh

GONDER, LARISSA; POTTSTOWN, PA; POTTSGROVE HS; (JR); Hi Hnr Roll; Hnr Roll; Nat Hon Sy; Otst Ac Ach Awd; Pres Ac Ftns Aw; Pres Sch; USAA; WWAHSS; Drma Clb; Emplmnt; Key Clb; Mus Clb; French Clb; Acpl Chr; Chr; SP/M/VS; Swg Chr; Fld Hky (J); CR (R); Lit Mag (R); Winner of Local Newspaper's Design-An-Ad Contest; Advertising/Pr/ Journalism; Theatre

GONGLIK, AMY; EFFORT, PA; PLEASANT VALLEY HS; (JR); Hi Hnr Roll; Nat Hon Sy; WWAHSS; Comm Volntr; Peer Tut/Med; ArtClub; Chrch Yth Grp; Key Club; Mth Clb/Tm; Bskball (J); PP Ftbl (J); National Honor Society; National Art Honor Society-Treasurer

GONKARNUE, NEAMON; PHILADELPHIA, PA; BARTRAM HS; (JR); Ctznshp Aw; Hi Hnr Roll; Hnr Roll; Perf Att; WWAHSS; Chrch Yth Grp; Cmptr Clb; Emplmnt; Ch Chr; Nursing; Medical Technology; Lock Haven U; Moravian College

GONSALVES, NATASHA; READING, PA; READING HS; (JR); Hnr Roll; Nat Hon Sy; Otst Ac Ach Awd; Peer Tut/Med; Spec Olymp Vol; DARE; Emplmnt; Quiz Bowl; Tchrs Aide; German Clb; Sccr (V CL); Track (V); Yrbk (E); IEP - Gifted Programs; Psychology; Criminal Justice; West Chester U Pennsylvania

GONZALEZ, BRYAN O; PALMERTON, PA; PALMERTON AREA SD HS; (SO); Hnr Roll; Otst Ac Ach Awd; Sci Fairs; St of Mnth; Comm Volntr; Chess; DARE; Dbte Team; Mth Clb/Tm; Mar Art (C); Communication Club; NASA Shuttle Pilot; Commercial Airline Pilot; Penn State

GONZALEZ, CECILEY; READING, PA; NORTHEAST MS; (MS); Hi Hnr Roll; Hnr Roll; Peer Tut/Med; Chrch Yth Grp; Ch Chr; Architect; Doctor

GONZALEZ, JOSE; BETHLEHEM, PA; FREEDOM HS; (JR); Hnr Roll; Nat Hon Sy; WWAHSS; Drma Clb; Mus Clb; Acpl Chr; Chr; Ch Chr; Dnce; Business Administration; Music Engineering; Kutztown U; Penn State of the Lehigh Valley

GONZALEZ, KATHERINE; BETHLEHEM, PA; BETHLEHEM CATHOLIC; (FR); Comm Volntr; Chrch Yth Grp; Key Club; Bnd; Jzz Bnd; Mch Bnd; Pep Bnd; Fld Hky (J); Sccr (V L); Track (L)

GONZALEZ, MARIGUEL; PHILADELPHIA, PA; JOHN W. HALLAHAN; MS; 4H Awd; Hnr Roll; Perf Att; 4-H; Chrch Yth Grp; DARE; Jr Ach; Mus Clb

GONZALEZ, MONICA; STROUDSBURG, PA; STROUDSBURG HS; (JR); Hi Hnr Roll; Otst Ac Ach Awd; Yth Ldrshp Prog; Comm Volntr; Chrch Yth Grp; French Clb; Dnce; Track (J); Sch Ppr (R); Latina Queen 2004 of Northeastern Pennsylvania; Nursing; Pre-Med; New York U; Catholic U of America

GOOD, MANDY; TERRE HILL, PA; GARDEN SPOT HS; (SR); Ctznshp Aw; DAR; Hi Hnr Roll; Hnr Roll; Nat Hon Sy; Pres Sch; Sci Fairs; Comm Volntr; Peer Tut/Med; Chrch Yth Grp; Emplmnt; Ntl FFA; Off Aide; Fld Hky (JC); FFA Chapter Vice President; State Star in Agribusiness; Associate's Degree in Accounting; Junior CPA; Consolidated School of Business

GOODFELLOW, LUKE W; MOUNT PLEASANT, PA; CTRL WESTMORELAND CTC; (SO); Hi Hnr Roll; Hnr Roll; Perf Att; Pres Ac Ftns Aw; Sci/Math Olympn; Peer Tut/Med; Chrch Yth Grp; MOS Word; MOS Excel; Software Engineer; Computer Program; Carnegie Mellon U; Westmoreland County Community College

GORDNER, JONATHAN N; HUGHESVILLE, PA; HUGHESVILLE JR-SR HS; MS; Hnr Roll; Emplmnt; Chr; Bsball (J); Ftball (J); Wt Lftg (J); Wrstlg (J); State Police Academy; Veterinarian

GORDON, ASHLEY; FLEETWOOD, PA; OLEY VALLEY HS; (JR); Hnr Roll; Nat Hon Sy; WWAHSS; Comm Volntr; Peer Tut/Med; FBLA; Sch Ppr (E, R); Secondary Education; Foreign Languages

GORDON, ELIZABETH J; MIFFLINBURG, PA; MIFFLINBURG HS; (FR); Hi Hnr Roll; Hnr Roll; Pres Ac Ftns Aw; Chrch Yth Grp; Emplmnt; Spanish Clb; Chr; Mar Art; National Society of High School Scholars; First Degree Tae Kwon Do - Black Belt; Political Science; History; United States Naval Academy; Albright College

GORDON, MEGHAN E; ALTOONA, PA; BISHOP GUILFOYLE HS; (SO); Hnr Roll; Pres Ac Ftns Aw; Pres Sch; Comm Volntr; Chrldg (V); Track (V); Radiology / Medical Field; Marketing / Sales

GORENTY, MELISSA K; MIDDLEPORT, PA; POTTSVILLE AREA SD; (FR); Hi Hnr Roll; Pres Sch; St of Mnth; Yth Ldrshp Prog; Spanish Clb; Flg Crps; Stg Cre; Sch Ppr (R); Ecology Club; American Legion Award

GORETSKY, YASYA; SCRANTON, PA; SCRANTON HS; (JR); Hi Hnr Roll; Hnr Roll; Valdctrian; Comm Volntr; Peer Tut/Med; Spec Olymp Vol; ArtClub; Emplmnt; Lttrmn Clb; Vsity Clb; Spanish Clb; Swmg (V L); Track (V); National Art Honor Society; All-American Scholar Award; Architecture; Baruch College; UC Berkeley; Pennsylvania State U

GORHAM, STEVEN; LEVITTOWN, PA; BUCKS CTY TECH HS; (SR); Hnr Roll; Emplmnt; Martial Arts; Computer Electronics

GORMAN JR, KENNETH J; CRANBERRY TWP, PA; SENECA VALLEY; (SO); Hi Hnr Roll; WWAHSS; Emplmnt; Key Club; Sccr (VJ L); Stu Cncl (T)

GORMLEY, JENNIFER; MECHANICSBURG, PA; CUMBERLAND VALLEY HS; (JR); F Lan Hn Soc; Hnr Roll; Nat Hon Sy; Comm Volntr; ArtClub; Emplmnt; Key Club; Prom Com; French Clb; Chr; SP/M/VS; Golf; Skiing; Sccr; Swmg; Stu Cncl (R); Yrbk (E); National Art Honor Society; Graphic Design; Marketing; Clemson U; Virginia Tech U

GORSKI, RACHAEL; BARTONSVILLE, PA; POCONO MTN EAST HS; (FR); Hnr Roll; St of Mnth; Bnd; Fld Hky (J); Psychology; Pennsylvania State U; North Carolina U

GOSTO, MINJA; PITTSBURGH, PA; SHALER AREA INT SCH; (JR); Ctznshp Aw; F Lan Hn Soc; Hi Hnr Roll; Hnr Roll; Otst Ac Ach Awd; WWAHSS; Comm Volntr; Emplmnt; Mod UN; Spanish Clb; PP Ftbl (VJ); Skiing; Sch Ppr (R, P); Excellence in Spanish Award; National Junior Honor Society; Psychology; Spanish Language; Allegheny College; Pittsburgh U

GOTTSCHALK, JESSICA; LANCASTER, PA; MANHEIM TOWNSHIP; (FR); Hi Hnr Roll; Otst Ac Ach Awd; St of Mnth; Peer Tut/Med; Spec Olymp Vol; Drma Clb; Key Club; Dnce; Stg Cre

GOTTSCHALK, LAURA; BENSALEM, PA; BENSALEM TOWNSHIP SD HS; (JR); Hi Hnr Roll; Hnr Roll; Perf Att; Pres Ac Ftns Aw; Comm Volntr; Chrch Yth Grp; PP Ftbl (V); Alvernia College; Mansfield State U

GOULD, SADA J E; HARRISBURG, PA; HARRISBURG HS; (FR); Ctznshp Aw; Hi Hnr Roll; Hnr Roll; Perf Att; Sci Fairs; DARE; Drma Clb; Pep Squd; Chr; Dnce; SP/M/VS; Stu Cncl (V); Modeling for Barbizon; Physiology; Pennsylvania U

GOVOSTIS, CHRISTINE; ALLENTOWN, PA; WILLIAM ALLEN HS; (SO); Hnr Roll; St of Mnth; Photog; Chr; Dnce; SP/M/VS; Stg Cre; Chrldg (J); Sccr (J); Yrbk (E); Poetry Award; Dance / Highest Degree; Vet / Highest Degree

GOWEN, MICHAEL; EBENSBURG, PA; CTRL CAMBRIA; (FR); Hi Hnr Roll; WWAHSS; Comm Volntr; Bskball (V L)

GRABOWSKI, MORGAN L; PITTSBURGH, PA; SHALER AREA HS; (JR); Ctznshp Aw; F Lan Hn Soc; Hi Hnr Roll; Nat Hon Sy; Otst Ac Ach Awd; Pres Ac Ftns Aw; Sci Fairs; St of Mnth; Comm Volntr; Hosp Aide; Emplmnt; FBLA; Key Club; Dnce; PP Ftbl (V); Sccr (J); Track (V); Cl Off (R); Stu Cncl (R); MOUS Certification - Microsoft Word; Certified Public Accountant; Engineering; Penn State U; U of Pittsburgh

GRADY, AMANDA; BETHEL PARK, PA; BETHEL PARK SD HS; (JR); WWAHSS; Chr; Vllyball (JC); Member of Ways and Means; Member of FCCLA; Marine Biology; U of Tampa; Eckerd

GRAHAM, ELEANOR; BRODHEADSVILLE, PA; PLEASANT VALLEY HS; (FR); Hi Hnr Roll; Hnr Roll; Nat Hon Sy; Perf Att; WWAHSS; Chrch Yth Grp; Drma Clb; FBLA; Key Club; Mus Clb; Spanish Clb; Bnd; Dnce; Jzz Bnd; Pep Bnd; Sch Ppr (R, P); Carbon County Band; Penn State U

GRAHAM, LESLIE; POTTSTOWN, PA; (SO); Ctznshp Aw; Hi Hnr Roll; Nat Hon Sy; St of Mnth; WWAHSS; Key Club; Mth Clb/Tm; Sci Clb; Sftball (JC); Tennis (J); Stu Cncl (R); CR (R); Sch Ppr (R, P); Yrbk (R); International Relations & Affairs; Law; Villanova U; Georgetown U

GRALA, MORGAN E; MANSFIELD, PA; MANSFIELD HS; (SR); Ctznshp Aw; Hnr Roll; Kwnis Aw; Nat Hon Sy; St of Mnth; WWAHSS; Yth Ldrshp Prog; Comm Volntr; Peer Tut/Med; Red Cr Aide; Emplmnt; FBLA; Key Club; Scouts; Tchrs Aide; Acpl Chr; Bnd; Chr; Bskball (VJCL); Sccr (VJ L); Youth Leadership Class of 2004; Eagle Scout Rank / BSA; Health / Physical Education Teacher; East Stroudsburg U

GRANNETINO, STEPHANIE; GLENMOORE, PA; OWEN J ROBERTS HS; (SR); Hnr Roll; Nat Hon Sy; Comm Volntr; Emplmnt; Lttrmn Clb; Spanish Clb; Dnce; Drm Mjr; Mch Bnd; SP/M/VS; Bskball (VJCL); Teens Against Tobacco Use-Treasurer; Architecture; Philadelphia U

GRANT, KADINE; PHILADELPHIA, PA; RANDOLPH CTHS; (JR); Ctznshp Aw; Hnr Roll; Perf Att; Comm Volntr; Chrch Yth Grp; Ch Chr; Yrbk (E); Nursing; Master's Degree; Temple U

GRANTHAM-FLOWERS, JOSEF N; READING, PA; READING HS; (SO); 4H Awd; Hnr Roll; MVP; Otst Ac Ach Awd; St of Mnth; Comm Volntr; 4-H; DARE; Emplmnt; Photog; ROTC; Scouts; Clr Grd; Drl Tm; SP/ M/VS; Chrldg (V L); Track (V); Yrbk (E, R, P); Secondary Education; Astronomy (Major); West Chester U (PA.); U of Pennsylvania, U Park

GRASLEY, KALLI; BERWICK, PA; BERWICK AREA SR HS; (SR); All Am Sch; DAR; Hi Hnr Roll; Nat Hon Sy; Salutrn; St of Mnth; USAA; WWAHSS; Comm Volntr; Red Cr Aide; Emplmnt; Key Club; Acpl Chr; Chr; Track (V); Biology / Pre-Vet; Ursinus College

GRASLEY, MARINNA; BERWICK, PA; BERWICK AREA SR HS; (MS); Hnr Roll; Perf Att; Peer Tut/Med; Chrch Yth Grp; FCA; Mus Clb; Bnd; Chr; Dnce; Mch Bnd; Performing Ministries; Arts and Humanities; Human Services; Juilliard; Bloomsburg U

GRATHERS, VERNELL B; PHILLA, PA; OVERBROOK HS; (SO); Ctznshp Aw; Hnr Roll; Perf Att; Sci Fairs; ArtClub; Chrch Yth Grp; DARE; Emplmnt; Scouts; Bnd; Ch Chr; Clr Grd; SP/M/VS; Bskball (VJ); Rlr Hky (J); Scr Kpr (J); Adv Cncl (V); Stu Cncl (V); CR (V); Criminal Justice; Animal Doctor; Temple U; Drexel U

GRAVER, BRYN; PLYMOUTH MEETING, PA; PLYMOUTH WHITEMARSH HS; (SO); Hi Hnr Roll; Otst Ac Ach Awd; St of Mnth; DECA; Key Club; P to P St Amb Prg; Cl Off (T); Manager of Boys Lacrosse Team; Marketing; Business; U of Richmond; James Madison U

GRAY, ASHLEY L; MECHANICSBURG, PA; CUMBERLAND VALLEY HS; (JR); Hnr Roll; Sci Fairs; WWAHSS; Comm Volntr; Chrch Yth Grp; Emplmnt; Key Club; Scouts; Ch Chr; SP/M/VS; Vllyball (JCL); Acceptance Into CASA (Capital Area School for the Arts); Musical Performance; Political Science; Duquesne; Point Park

GRAY, E'LISHA J S; PHILADELPHIA, PA; CENTRAL HS; (SO); Otst Ac Ach Awd; Perf Att; Sci Fairs; Valdctrian; WWAHSS; Comm Volntr; Peer Tut/ Med; Outdrs Clb; Spanish Clb; SP/M/VS; Stg Cre; Track (V); Adv Cncl (R); CR (R); Mentally Gifted Program; Johns Hopkins Center for Talented Youths; PhD - Gynecology/Obstetrics; Florida A & M U; Johns Hopkins U

GRAY, LYDIA; BELLWOOD, PA; BELLWOOD-ANTIS HS; (JR); Ctznshp Aw; Hi Hnr Roll; Kwnis Aw; Nat Hon Sy; St of Mnth; WWAHSS; Comm Volntr; Peer Tut/Med; Chrch Yth Grp; Dbte Team; FCA; Key Club; NtlFrnscLg; Schol Bwl; Spch Team; SADD; Chr; Cr Ctry (V); Speech League National Qualifier; Key Club President; Major-Communications for News Broadcasting; U of Florida

GRAY, RAEMON; PITTSBURGH, PA; PERRY TRADITIONAL AC; (SO); Hnr Roll; Bskball (JC); Trinity Lutheran Church-Junior Counselor-Mentor; Juris Doctorate; MBA; U of Pittsburgh; Syracuse U

Grant, Kadine
Randolph CTHS
Philadelphia, PA

Gould, Sada J E
Harrisburg HS
Harrisburg, PA

Gordon, Elizabeth J
Mifflinburg HS
Mifflinburg, PA

Gonsalves, Natasha
Reading HS
Reading, PA

National
Honor Roll
Spring 2005

Gogotsi, Pavel
Council Rock HS North
Ivyland, PA

Gorenty, Melissa K
Pottsville Area SD
Middleport, PA

Grabowski, Morgan L
Shaler Area HS
Pittsburgh, PA

Grathers, Vernell B
Overbrook HS
Philla, PA

GRAY, SABRIYA M; PHILADELPHIA, PA; UPPER DARBY HS; (SR); Hnr Roll; Otst Ac Ach Awd; Perf Att; WWAHSS; Comm Volntr; Dnce; Drl Tm; National Society of High School Scholars; Who's Who; Sanford Brown Institute for Medical Assistants & Forensics; Sanford Brown Institute; Temple U

GRAY, STEPHANIE; EASTON, PA; EASTON AREA HS; (SO); Hi Hnr Roll; Nat Hon Sy; Sci Fairs; Comm Volntr; DECA; Sccr (V L); Stu Cncl (R); Yrbk; Medicine/Science; Education; Lehigh U; U of Delaware

GREELEY, CORTNEY; BROOKVILLE, PA; BROOKVILLE AREA SD; (SR); Hi Hnr Roll; Hnr Roll; Nat Hon Sy; Pres Ac Ftns Aw; St of Mnth; Yth Ldrshp Prog; Comm Volntr; Chrch Yth Grp; Emplmnt; Quiz Bowl; SADD; Spanish Clb; Bnd; Jzz Bnd; Mch Bnd; Pep Bnd; Bskball (JC); Golf (V L); Track (V L); Stu Cncl (R); CR (R); March of Dimes Volunteer / Student Co-Chair; Nursing; Robert Morris U; U of Pittsburgh

GREEN, AMANDA; UPPER DARBY, PA; UPPER DARBY HS; (JR); Hnr Roll; Perf Att; Emplmnt; Drl Tm; Track (VJ); Principal for the Day; Speech Pathology

GREEN, DAVID; HARRISBURG, PA; CTRL DAUPHIN EAST HS; (FR); Hi Hnr Roll; Hnr Roll; Perf Att; Valdctrian; Comm Volntr; Chess; Chrch Yth Grp; Bskball; Ftball; Sftball; Track; Cl Off (S); Stu Cncl (T)

GREEN, GWENDOLYN; NEWVILLE, PA; BIG SPRING SD; (JR); Ctznshp Aw; Hnr Roll; Otst Ac Ach Awd; Comm Volntr; Chrch Yth Grp; DARE; SADD; Chr; Ch Chr; Golf; Lcrsse; Stu Cncl (R); Yrbk (P); Medical Arts; Nursing; Thompson Institute

GREEN, KENISHIA; READING, PA; READING HS; (SO); Hnr Roll; Perf Att; St of Mnth; Jr Ach; Dnce; SP/M/VS; Club Baba Na Kaka -Dancing; Talent Search / Outside Plays; Theatre; Acting for Film

GREEN, RACHEL E; CAMP HILL, PA; CAMP HILL HS; (SO); Hi Hnr Roll; Comm Volntr; Chrch Yth Grp; Chr; SP/M/VS; Sccr; Sftball; Swmg; Tennis (V); Stu Cncl (R); Yrbk (R); Piano - 5 Years; Linguistics; Medical Math & Science; U of Virginia; Princeton U

GREEN, VIRGINIA L; SAYLORSBURG, PA; PLEASANT VALLEY HS; (SO); Hi Hnr Roll; Hnr Roll; Kwnis Aw; Nat Hon Sy; WWAHSS; Peer Tut/Med; Spec Olymp Vol; ArtClub; Drma Clb; Key Club; Photog; Acpl Chr; Chr; SP/M/VS; Stg Cre; Yrbk (E); Key Club President; Elementary Education; Psychology

GREEN, WANISHA; PITTSBURGH, PA; PITTSBURGH SD; (JR); Hi Hnr Roll; Hnr Roll; Perf Att; St of Mnth; Yth Ldrshp Prog; Comm Volntr; Sci Clb; Dnce; Stu Cncl (R); Elementary Education; California U; Indiana U of Pennsylvania

GREENAWAY, KARI; JERSEY SHORE, PA; JERSEY SHORE SR HS; (SO); Hi Hnr Roll; Hnr Roll; Emplmnt; Key Club; Prom Com; Sccr (J); Stu Cncl; Relay for Life; Physical Therapy; Occupational Therapy; Indiana U of Pennsylvania

GREENBERG, BRIAN P; JENKINTOWN, PA; JENKINTOWN HS; (JR); F Lan Hn Soc; Hnr Roll; Nat Hon Sy; Perf Att; Sci Fairs; Comm Volntr; Peer Tut/Med; Emplmnt; Off Aide; Photog; Quiz Bowl; SADD; Tchrs Aide; Chr; Bsball (J); Bskball (VJ); Ftball (V); Track (V); Accounting; Business and Finance; York College of Pennsylvania; Shippensburg U

GREENBERG, JESSE; PORT MATILDA, PA; STATE COLLEGE AREA HS; (SR); Hi Hnr Roll; Nat Mrt Fin; Comm Volntr; Hosp Aide; Emplmnt; Mus Clb; Quiz Bowl; Bnd; Mch Bnd; Tennis (VJ L); Yrbk (R); AP Scholar with Honor; AAA Award Recipient-Athletics, Academics Attitude; Chemistry; Mathematics; Williams College

GREENBLATT, HANNAH G; LANCASTER, PA; MANHEIM TWP HS; (FR); Pres Ac Ftns Aw; Sci Fairs; Comm Volntr; DARE; Jr Ach; Key Club; P to P St Amb Prg; Scouts; SADD; Tmpl Yth Grp; Fld Hky (J); Swmg (V); Track (J); Play Piano; Fashion Design; Business; New York U; UCLA

GREENWALD, JED; PITTSBURGH, PA; TAYLOR ALLDERDICE HS; (FR); Hi Hnr Roll; Hnr Roll; Tmpl Yth Grp; Swmg; Film; Law; Penn State; U of Pittsburgh

GREENWAY, CORY M; EAST STROUDSBURG, PA; EAST STROUDSBURG SR HS SOUTH; (SO); Hi Hnr Roll; Hnr Roll; WWAHSS; Emplmnt; Bnd; State Bowling Championships (1st Place); Car Body Designer; Pratt Institute; New England Institute of Technology

GREENWAY, KELLY; MECHANICSBURG, PA; TRINITY HS; (SO); WWAHSS; Hab For Humty Volntr; Spec Olymp Vol; Key Club; Pep Squd; Vllyball (J); CYO Basketball for Good Shepherd; Business; Entrepreneurship; U of Delaware

GREER, JORDAN L; BIRDSBORO, PA; EXETER TWP SR HS; (SO); Hnr Roll; Perf Att; Key Club; Skiing (C); Track (V)

GREER, SAMANTHA; WAMPUM, PA; BIG BEAVER FALLS HS; (SO); Hi Hnr Roll; Hnr Roll; Comm Volntr; Key Club; Spanish Club; Business Management / Owner; Briarwood College; Duff's Business Institute

GREER GRIFFITH, JESSICA; MEADOWBROOK, PA; ABINGTON SR HS; (SO); Ctznshp Aw; Hi Hnr Roll; Otst Ac Ach Awd; WWAHSS; Comm Volntr; Hosp Aide; Red Cr Aide; ArtClub; Key Club; Mth Clb/Tm; Mod UN; Svce Clb; Spanish Clb; Bnd; Chr; Dvng (J); Sftball (J); Tennis (V L); Black Belt in Tae Kwon Do; Champion of Caring Award, Member of Teen Youth Forum (ACT); Princeton U; Harvard U

GREGG, ABBIGAIL C; BEAVER FALLS, PA; BIG BEAVER FALLS HS; (JR); Hi Hnr Roll; Nat Hon Sy; Otst Ac Ach Awd; Pres Sch; WWAHSS; Comm Volntr; Chrch Yth Grp; Emplmnt; Key Club; Lib Aide; Bnd; Jzz Bnd; Mch Bnd; Pep Bnd; American Legion Essay Winner; English; History; Geneva College; Carnegie Mellon U

GREGG, AMBER L; LEWISTOWN, PA; LEWISTOWN AREA HS; (JR); Hi Hnr Roll; Hnr Roll; ArtClub; Emplmnt; Prom Com; Dnce; Chrldg (V L); PP Ftbl (V); Health/Medical; Shippensburg U; Lock Haven U

GREGORY, MILAYA-SHARDAE; PHILADELPHIA, PA; MERCY VOC HS; (SR); Hi Hnr Roll; Hnr Roll; WWAHSS; Emplmnt; Prom Com; Chrldg (V); Psychology; Pre-Med / Biology; Chestnut Hill College

GREINER, MICHAEL; BEAVER FALLS, PA; BLACKHAWK HS; (JR); Hnr Roll; Nat Stu Ath Day Aw; WWAHSS; Peer Tut/Med; Chrch Yth Grp; Dbte Team; Key Club; Prom Com; Scouts; German Clb; Cr Ctry (V); Sccr (VJC); Track (V L); Boy Scouts of America - Senior Patrol Leader; Venturer Crew 407, VP of Key Club; Political Science; Criminal Justice; United States Military Academy; United States Naval Academy

GRESE, MIKE; BADEN, PA; NORTH ALLEGHENY HS; (SO); Hnr Roll; Nat Hon Sy; Pres Ac Ftns Aw; Sci Fairs; WWAHSS; Comm Volntr; FBLA; Key Club; Cr Ctry (L); Track (L); Scholar Athlete Awards; Economics; Georgetown U; Syracuse U

GRGIC, CLARISSA; MONROEVILLE, PA; GATEWAY SD; (SO); Chrch Yth Grp; FBLA; Svce Clb; Accounting; Psychology; U of Pennsylvania; U of North Carolina

GRIBBIN, LANCE; PHILADELPHIA, PA; GEORGE WASHINGTON HS; (SR); Nat Sci Aw; Sci Fairs; Red Cr Aide; Ntl FFA; Vsity Clb; Ftball (V); Participate in Play It Smart Program; Community Service Red Cross; Engineering; Computer Sciences; Lock Haven U; Penn State U

GRIBIN, NIKOLAY; WAYNESBORO, PA; WAYNESBORO AREA SR HS; (JR); Peer Tut/Med; Sccr (L); Penn State U; U MD

GRIBSCHAW, ANDREW; PITTSBURGH, PA; PLUM SR HS; (SO); Hnr Roll; Sci/Math Olympn; WWAHSS; Civil Air Pat; Spanish Clb; Skt Tgt Sh (V L); Engineering

GRIFFEY, ZACHARY; SECANE, PA; RIDLEY SD; (JR); Hi Hnr Roll; Hnr Roll; Sci Fairs; St of Mnth; Peer Tut/Med; 4-H; Emplmnt; Off Aide; Scouts; SADD; CR (R); Passed CLEP Exam for Statistics; Engineering; Bio Chemistry; Drexel U; U of Pittsburgh

GRIFFIN, DEANNA; LANSDOWNE, PA; UPPER DARBY HS; (SO); Ctznshp Aw; DAR; Hi Hnr Roll; Hnr Roll; Otst Ac Ach Awd; Perf Att; Pres Sch; St of Mnth; Yth Ldrshp Prog; Comm Volntr; Peer Tut/Med; Chrch Yth Grp; Pep Squd; Prom Com; Svce Clb; Tchrs Aide; Chr; Ch Chr; Mch Bnd; SP/M/VS; Drexel Hill Middle School Challengers - (School Honor Society); Pharmacy; U of the Sciences in Philadelphia; Hampton U

GRIFFITH, SABLE; DILLSBURG, PA; NORTHERN HS; (SO); Hi Hnr Roll; Peer Tut/Med; Spec Olymp Vol; Chrch Yth Grp; Key Club; SADD; Chr; Photography; Graphic Design; Pennsylvania College of Art and Design

GRIFFITH, TIFFANY; ABINGTON, PA; ABINGTON SR HS; (JR); Key Club; Stg Cre; Nursing; Elementary Education; Temple U; Drexel U

GRIM, ASHLEY; WASHINGTON, PA; TRINITY AREA SD HS; (SO); Hi Hnr Roll; Hnr Roll; Perf Att; Pres Ac Ftns Aw; Sci Fairs; Comm Volntr; Peer Tut/Med; FTA; Lib Aide; Prom Com; SADD; German Clb; SP/M/VS; Chrldg (V); PP Ftbl (L); Cl Off (V); Stu Cncl (R); CR (R); Yrbk (R); Advertisement; Penn State U

GRIMES, RACHAEL K; WILLIAMSPORT, PA; WILLIAMSPORT AREA HS; (FR); Hi Hnr Roll; Hnr Roll; St of Mnth; ArtClub; Drma Clb; Emplmnt; Key Club; Bnd; Chr; Mch Bnd; SP/M/VS; Stu Cncl (R); Williamsport Symphony Youth Orchestra; Indoor Percussion; Music Education; Egyptology; Boston U; Berklee School of Music in Boston

GRIMM, CHELSEY A; LANSDALE, PA; NORTH PENN HS; (SR); F Lan Hn Soc; Hnr Roll; Nat Hon Sy; WWAHSS; Comm Volntr; Hab For Humty Volntr; Spec Olymp Vol; Chrch Yth Grp; DARE; Emplmnt; Prom Com; SADD; German Clb; Bskball (V L); PP Ftbl (V); Sccr (V L); Sftball (V L); Adv Cncl (R); CR (R); Exchange Student to Salzgitter, Germany for Senior Year; International Business; German Minor; Boston U; Pennsylvania State U

GROCHALSKI, R M; CARLISLE, PA; BS HS; (FR); Hnr Roll; Perf Att; Sci Fairs; Comm Volntr; Outdrs Clb; Wdwrkg Clb; Spanish Clb; Bsball (J); Ftball (V); Wt Lftg (V); Engineer; PSU; Shippensburg U

GROSS, DANIELLE M; DOUGLASSVILLE, PA; DANIEL BOONE AREA HS; (JR); F Lan Hn Soc; Hi Hnr Roll; Hnr Roll; Nat Hon Sy; WWAHSS; DARE; Emplmnt; Key Club; Chrldg (V); Sch Ppr (P); Architecture; Temple; Penn State

GROSS, KYLIE A; NORRISTOWN, PA; METHACTON HS; (SO); Hnr Roll; WWAHSS; Chrldg (JC); Track (V); Who's Who Among American Students - Sports Edition

GROSS, MATTHEW; WARRINGTON, PA; MIDDLE BUCKS INST OF TECH; (JR); Bnd; Automotive Technology; Mechanical Engineering

GROSSMAN, ALLISON N; HERSHEY, PA; HERSHEY HS; (FR); Hi Hnr Roll; Hnr Roll; St of Mnth; Drma Clb; Emplmnt; Lib Aide; French Clb; SP/M/VS; Stg Cre; Lit Mag (R); Set Design for School Musical; Psychology; Journalism; New York U; Columbia U

GROVE, JOSHUA A; NEW PARK, PA; KENNARD DALE HS; (SR); Hi Hnr Roll; Nat Hon Sy; Chrch Yth Grp; Emplmnt; Mod UN; Ntl FFA; FFA Officer-Chaplain; Environthon Team; History; Secondary Education; Shepherd U

GROVES, TIFFANY; GILBERTSVILLE, PA; BOYERTOWN AREA SR HS; (SO); Hnr Roll; Comm Volntr; Peer Tut/Med; ArtClub; DARE; Emplmnt; Scouts; Chr; Dnce; Helper - HEARTS - After School Program; Nursing; Massage Therapy; Pennsylvania School of Muscle Therapy; Reading Area Community College

GUADALUPE, SANDY; READING, PA; READING HS; (FR); Hnr Roll; MVP; Perf Att; Pres Ac Ftns Aw; St of Mnth; Comm Volntr; DARE; ROTC; Scouts; Spanish Clb; Dnce; Bskball (J); Connecticut U; Master's Degree; Connecticut U; Penn State U

GUBA, MICHAEL; NUREMBERG, PA; HAZLETON AREA HS; (SO); Hnr Roll; Comm Volntr; Chess; Chrch Yth Grp; Drma Clb; Stg Cre; Law; History; Drexel U; St John's U

GUDMUNDSEN, ERIK; UPPER DARBY, PA; UPPER DERBY HS; (JR); Comm Volntr; Peer Tut/Med; P to P St Amb Prg; German Clb; Wrstlg (J); Mechanical Engineering; Civil Engineering; Purdue U; U of Pennsylvania

GUERRA, KAYLEE N; LANCASTER, PA; MANHEIM TWP HS; (JR); Hnr Roll; WWAHSS; Peer Tut/Med; Chrch Yth Grp; Key Club; Sftball (V L); Bowling- Varsity / Captain; Psychology; U of Delaware; Lockhaven U

GUILLEN, JIMMY; ALLENTOWN, PA; WILLIAM ALLEN HS; (SO); Ctznshp Aw; Hnr Roll; Otst Ac Ach Awd; Perf Att; St of Mnth; Comm Volntr; Peer Tut/Med; Chess; DARE; Mth Clb/Tm; Clb; Bsball (J); I Played Baseball for the City; I Played Basketball for the City; Computer Engineering; Columbia U, the Fu Foundation School of Engineering & Applied; The Pennsylvania State U, High Valley Corpus of Berk of N.C. Valley College

GULA, JOSEPH V; PITTSBURGH, PA; PENN HILLS SR HS; (SO); Fut Prb Slvr; Hi Hnr Roll; Perf Att; WWAHSS; Chrch Yth Grp; Key Club; Scouts; Bnd; Jzz Bnd; Mch Bnd; Orch; German Club

GULBRANDSEN, STEPHANI; NEWTOWN, PA; COUNCIL ROCK HS NORTH; (SR); Hi Hnr Roll; Nat Hon Sy; Otst Ac Ach Awd; St of Mnth; Emplmnt; Mus Clb; Scouts; German Clb; Bnd; Mch Bnd; Girl Scout Gold Award; Girl Scout Silver Award; Doctorate in Engineering; Franklin W Olin College of Engineering

GULDBRAND, TINE L; LEWISTOWN, PA; LAHS; (FR); Hi Hnr Roll; MVP; Nat Sci Aw; Otst Ac Ach Awd; St of Mnth; Key Club; German Clb; Presidential Academic Award; Field Hockey Award; Law; Michigan State; Penn State

GULDNER, TIPHANI; ENOLA, PA; EAST PENNSBORO AREA HS; (FR); Hnr Roll; Otst Ac Ach Awd; Peer Tut/Med; Spec Olymp Vol; Drma Clb; Key Club; Spanish Clb; Chr; SP/M/VS; Sccr (J); Student Council; American Legion Writing Contest 1st Place; Theatre; Psychology; Pennsylvania State U; U of California Los Angeles

GUNSELMAN, LAUREN S; EPHRATA, PA; EPHRATA HS; (SR); F Lan Hn Soc; Hnr Roll; Nat Hon Sy; Sci Fairs; Emplmnt; Bskball (J); Fld Hky (VJ); Track (J); Pharmacy; U of Sciences in Philadelphia

GUSTAFSON, LAURA; ALBURTIS, PA; BRANDYWINE HEIGHTS HS; (SO); Ctznshp Aw; F Lan Hn Soc; Hi Hnr Roll; Hnr Roll; Comm Volntr; Chrch Yth Grp; Drma Clb; Key Club; German Clb; Acpl Chr; Chr; Ch Chr; Flg Crps; Tennis (J); Missionary; Secondary Education Teacher; Liberty U; Word of Life

GUSTAS, KELLIE; HERMITAGE, PA; HICKORY HS; (SO); F Lan Hn Soc; Hi Hnr Roll; Nat Hon Sy; Pres Ac Ftns Aw; WWAHSS; Comm Volntr; Peer Tut/Med; Chrch Yth Grp; DARE; Jr Ach; Key Club; Lttrmn Clb; Photog; Scouts; SADD; Bskball (VJ); Golf (V L); Sccr (V L); Vsy Clb (V L); Went to States in Golf; Pharmacy

GUTHRIE, MINDY S; BEAVER FALLS, PA; BEAVER FALLS HS; (SR); Hi Hnr Roll; Hnr Roll; Nat Hon Sy; Emplmnt; FBLA; Photog; Bnd; Mch Bnd; Sch Ppr (E, R); Criminal Investigation; Security; Community College of Beaver County

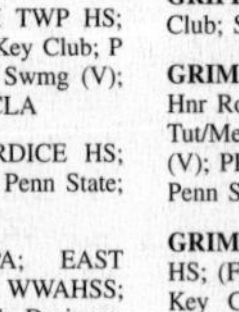
Grim, Ashley
Trinity Area SD HS
Washington, PA

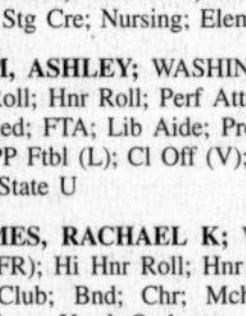
Griffin, Deanna
Upper Darby HS
Lansdowne, PA

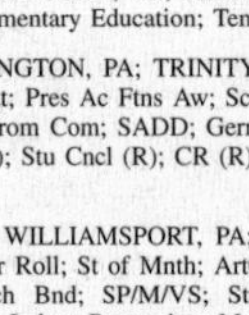
Greenblatt, Hannah G
Manheim Twp HS
Lancaster, PA

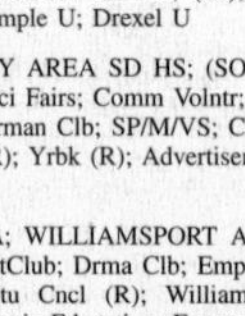
Greer Griffith, Jessica
Abington SR HS
Meadowbrook, PA

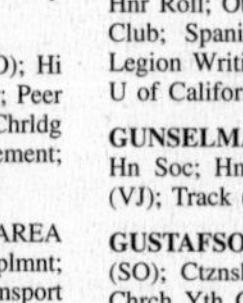
Guldbrand, Tine L
LAHS
Lewistown, PA

GUTKOWSKI, JESSICA L; WASHINGTON, PA; CHARTIERS-HOUSTON SD; (JR); SP/M/VS; Vllyball (J); People to People Ambassador; Who's Who; Graphic Artist; U of Pittsburg

GUTTSCHALL, JENNIFER; CRUM LYNNE, PA; RIDLEY SD HS; (JR); Hnr Roll; St of Mnth; Emplmnt; Off Aide; Tchrs Aide; Lcrsse (V); Sccr (V); Club Gymnastics; Gym Major; Nursing, Biology; Athletic Training Sports Medicine; Lock Haven U; U of Scranton

GYAPONG, GEOFFREY N; LANSDALE, PA; NORTH PENN HS; (JR); Hi Hnr Roll; Hnr Roll; Perf Att; Pres Sch; WWAHSS; Comm Volntr; DARE; Key Club; Chr; Tennis; Business Administration; Information Technology; New York U; U of Michigan

HABERLE, CRYSTAL; EAST STROUDSBURG, PA; SCOTLAND SCH FOR VETERANS' CHILDREN; Hnr Roll; Pres Ac Ftns Aw; Peer Tut/Med; Spec Olymp Vol; Chrch Yth Grp; Bnd; Chr; SP/M/VS; Bskball (VJ); Chrldg (V); Vllyball (VJ); Red Blazer Ambassador Club; Biology; Shippensburg U; Temple U

HAFER, LAUREN; ELVERSON, PA; OWEN J ROBERTS HS; (SR); DAR; Hnr Roll; Nat Hon Sy; Comm Volntr; DECA; Drma Clb; Emplmnt; Jr Cls League; Key Club; NYLC; P to P St Amb Prg; SP/M/VS; Sccr (V); CR (R); National Honor Society - President; People to People International Student Chapter President; International Relations / Affairs; James Madison U

HAGGE, KRISTA; WATERFORD, PA; FORT LEBOEUF SD; (FR); Hi Hnr Roll; MVP; St of Mnth; Sftball (J); Vllyball (J); Dentistry; U of North Carolina

HAGUE, SHELBY; ROBESONIA, PA; CONRAD WEISER HS; (FR); Hi Hnr Roll; Hnr Roll; Kwnis Aw; Perf Att; St of Mnth; WWAHSS; Comm Volntr; Peer Tut/Med; Aqrium Clb; Chrch Yth Grp; DARE; Drma Clb; Key Club; Mus Clb; Ntl FFA; Photog; Chr; Ch Chr; Clr Grd; Mch Bnd; Stu Cncl (R); Sch Ppr (R); Pastry Chef; Florida State U

HAINES, RACHEAL; BENSALEM, PA; BENSALEM TOWNSHIP SD HS; (JR); Hi Hnr Roll; Hnr Roll; Pres Ac Ftns Aw; Yth Ldrshp Prog; Comm Volntr; Red Cr Aide; DARE; NYLC; P to P St Amb Prg; Prom Com; Dnce; Stu Cncl (R); Yrbk (E); Vice President of Community Service Club; Radiology; Business Physical Therapy; Penn State; Drexel

HAKE, AMY; DOVER, PA; DOVER AREA HS; (SR); Hi Hnr Roll; Hnr Roll; Nat Hon Sy; Otst Ac Ach Awd; Perf Att; WWAHSS; Hab For Humty Volntr; Chrch Yth Grp; Emplmnt; Scouts; Bnd; Chr; Mch Bnd; Sccr (J); Health Sciences; Lock Haven U of Pennsylvania

HALE, KEVIN; BETHLEHEM, PA; LIBERTY HS; (SR); Hnr Roll; Nat Hon Sy; Otst Ac Ach Awd; Mus Clb; Bnd; Mch Bnd; Orch; District 10 Band (PMEA); District 10 Orchestra (PMEA); Engineering; Meteorology; The Pennsylvania State U; U of Delaware

HALE, NICOLE S; PHILADELPHIA, PA; G W CARVER HS; (SR); Hi Hnr Roll; Hnr Roll; Nat Hon Sy; Nat Mrt Semif; Pres Sch; WWAHSS; Comm Volntr; Peer Tut/Med; Red Cr Aide; Chrch Yth Grp; DARE; Emplmnt; FBLA; Ntl Beta Clb; Prom Com; Chr; Ch Chr; SP/M/VS; Bdmtn; Bskball; Rqtball; Skiing; Tennis (V CL); Vllyball (V); Adv Cncl (R); Cl Off (P, V); CR (R); Neuroscience/Psychology; Speech Pathology/Audiology; Bloomsburg U; Drexel U

HALL, STEPHEN J; AVONDALE, PA; ARCHMERE AC; (JR); Hnr Roll; Comm Volntr; Hab For Humty Volntr; Bskball (V CL); Sccr (V CL); Club Soccer State Semi Finalist 5 Years; Business; Law; U of Maryland; St Joseph's U

HALLOWELL, PAUL H; GREENVILLE, PA; GREENVILLE HS; (JR); 4H Awd; Hi Hnr Roll; Nat Hon Sy; Pres Ac Ftns Aw; St of Mnth; WWAHSS; Comm Volntr; 4-H; Chrch Yth Grp; Cmptr Clb; Key Club; Lttrmn Clb; Vsity Clb; Cr Ctry (V CL); Track (V L); Wrstlg (V CL); Stu Cncl (R); Architectural Engineering; Penn State U

HALM, HANNAH; CENTRE HALL, PA; PENNS VALLEY AREA HS; (FR); Hi Hnr Roll; Nat Sci Aw; WWAHSS; Comm Volntr; Key Club; Lit Mag (E); Who's Who of American H.S. Students; USAA National Science Merit Award; Public Relations; Architecture; Penn State U; New York U

HAMLETTE, DIAMAND N; POTTSTOWN, PA; POTTSGROVE HS; (SO); Hnr Roll; St of Mnth; WWAHSS; Comm Volntr; Key Club; French Clb; Bskball (J); Fld Hky (J); PP Ftbl (C); CR (R); Highest English Average Award; Homecoming Princess; Paralegal; Criminal Justice / Lawyer; Villanova U; New York U

HAMM, SHANNON L; ERIE, PA; FT LEBOEUF HS; (SO); Hi Hnr Roll; Hnr Roll; Otst Ac Ach Awd; Chrch Yth Grp; Drma Clb; Scouts; Chr; Clr Grd; Dnce; SP/M/VS; Achievement Team; District Chorus; Musical Theatre; Vocal; Penn State U; Kentucky State U

HAMMOND, BRIANNE; PITTSBURGH, PA; PLUM SR HS; (SO); Hnr Roll; Comm Volntr; Chrch Yth Grp; Cmptr Clb; French Clb; Bnd; Computer Science; Archeology; Temple U; Indiana U-Pennsylvania

HAMMOND, ELLEN; OAKMONT, PA; RIVERVIEW JR/SR HS; (JR); Hnr Roll; Yth Ldrshp Prog; Peer Tut/Med; Chrch Yth Grp; Emplmnt; Key Club; Ch Chr; Dnce; Chrldg (JC); Cr Ct Ski (V); Sccr; Stu Cncl (T); Psychology; Pharmacy; Duquesne U; Boston College

HAMMOND, RACHEL M; EAST EARL, PA; LANCASTER CTY CTC; (SR); Hnr Roll; Hosp Aide; Emplmnt; FBLA; Scouts; Tremendous Effort Award (Volunteer); Volunteer of the Month Nominee; Registered Nurse; Reading Hospital School of Nursing

HAN, HYE J; ATHENS, PA; NOTRE DAME HS; (JR); Hi Hnr Roll; Hnr Roll; Nat Hon Sy; Nat Mrt LOC; USAA; WWAHSS; Yth Ldrshp Prog; Amnsty Intl; Comm Volntr; Peer Tut/Med; Dbte Team; Mth Clb/Tm; Mod UN; NYLC; Bnd; Chr; SP/M/VS; Bdmtn; Alfred U Math Competition (11th/363); Michigan Music Festival (Division One); Diplomat; Ambassador; George Washington U; Georgetown U

HANELY, MELISSA A; PLEASANTVILLE, PA; VENANGO CATHOLIC HS; (SR); Gov Hnr Prg; Hi Hnr Roll; Nat Hon Sy; Valdctrian; WWAHSS; Cl Off (P, S, T); Sch Ppr (E); Yrbk (E); Business; Foreign Language; Gannon U

HANG, ANTHONY; DREXEL HILL, PA; (JR); Hi Hnr Roll; Hnr Roll; WWAHSS; Comm Volntr; Part of Building with Books; Muslim Society of Upper Darby; Sociology; History; U of California; New York U

HANIFIN, JEFFREY; JENKINTOWN, PA; ABINGTON HS; (SR); Ctznshp Aw; Hnr Roll; Nat Hon Sy; WWAHSS; AL Aux Boys; Emplmnt; Key Club; NYLC; Svce Clb; Vsity Clb; Bsball (V L); Vsy Clb (V); Stu Cncl (R); Yrbk (E); Congressional Award for Service; Presidential Service Award; Engineering Major; Systems Engineer; George Mason U

HANKINSON, SHANE C; NEW BALTIMORE, PA; BERLIN BROTHERS VALLEY SD; (SR); All Am Sch; Hi Hnr Roll; Hnr Roll; MVP; Nat Sci Aw; St of Mnth; WWAHSS; Comm Volntr; Emplmnt; Jr Ach; Ntl FFA; SP/M/VS; Bsball (V); Bskball (J); Ftball (V CL); Wt Lftg; Cl Off (V); Stu Cncl (R); Keystone Boys State Award; Civil Engineering; Bucknell U

HANNON, MEGAN; EDWARDSVILLE, PA; WYOMING VALLEY WEST HS; (SO); Hi Hnr Roll; Hnr Roll; Perf Att; WWAHSS; Yth Ldrshp Prog; Comm Volntr; Peer Tut/Med; Drma Clb; Lib Aide; Mus Clb; NYLC; Prom Com; Quill & Scroll; Spanish Clb; Chr; Dnce; SP/M/VS; Vllyball (J); Stu Cncl (R); Lit Mag (R); Sch Ppr (R); Yrbk (E); Education; Bloomsburg U; College Misericordia

HANSEN, CAMILLA; CHADDS FORD, PA; UNIONVILLE; (SO); Hi Hnr Roll; Nat Hon Sy; Sci Fairs; Fld Hky (J); Lcrsse (J)

HANSON, CHRISTOPHER; ALIQUIPPA, PA; CTR AREA SD HS; (SO); Hnr Roll; Peer Tut/Med; DARE; Emplmnt; German Clb; SP/M/VS; Arch (C); Cr Ctry (V); Fncg (C); Mar Art (C); Wrstlg (V); Cl Off (R); Chemical Engineering; Master's Degree; Penn State U; Robert Morris U

HANSON JR, SCOTT D; WINDSOR, PA; YORK CO SCH OF TECH; (JR); Hi Hnr Roll; Hnr Roll; Perf Att; St of Mnth; Hab For Humty Volntr; Ftball

HAQ, SAMI; SCHWENKSVILLE, PA; SPRING FORD SR HS; (SO); Ctznshp Aw; Hnr Roll; Perf Att; Chrch Yth Grp; DARE; Computers; Math

HARDY, ASHLEY C; PHILADELPHIA, PA; SIMON GRATZ HS; (MS); Ctznshp Aw; Hnr Roll; Perf Att; St of Mnth; Comm Volntr; DARE; Drma Clb; Mus Clb; Off Aide; Outdrs Clb; Tmpl Yth Grp; Dnce; Drl Tm; SP/M/VS; Stg Cre; Bskball (J); Dancer; Writer; Penn State

HARDY, JENNA E; UNIONTOWN, PA; LAUREL HIGHLANDS SD; (FR); Hi Hnr Roll; Hnr Roll; Otst Ac Ach Awd; Pres Ac Ftns Aw; Hab For Humty Volntr; Hosp Aide; Spec Olymp Vol; Chrch Yth Grp; Emplmnt; Jr Ach; Mth Clb/Tm; Off Aide; Quiz Bowl; Scouts; SADD; Bskball (V L); Skiing (V CL); Sccr (V L); Track (V); Life Science Student of the Year; Travel/Tourism/Hospitality; Microbiologist/Chemist; West Virginia U; Carnegie Mellon U

HARDY, NAOMI; HUNTINGDON VALLEY, PA; ABINGTON HS; (SO); All Am Sch; Ctznshp Aw; F Lan Hn Soc; Hnr Roll; Nat Hon Sy; Nat Ldrshp Svc; WWAHSS; Comm Volntr; Hab For Humty Volntr; ArtClub; Key Club; Svce Clb; Dnce; Orch; SP/M/VS; Pre-Med; University of Pennsylvania

HARNISH, KAYLA; LEECHBURG, PA; KISKI AREA HS; (JR); Hi Hnr Roll; Hnr Roll; Nat Hon Sy; Perf Att; WWAHSS; Comm Volntr; Peer Tut/Med; Chrch Yth Grp; Emplmnt; Key Club; SADD; Chr; SP/M/VS; Nursing

HARRINGTON, KATE; DOYLESTOWN, PA; CTRL BUCKS HS EAST; (JR); F Lan Hn Soc; Hi Hnr Roll; Kwnis Aw; Nat Hon Sy; Pres Ac Ftns Aw; WWAHSS; Comm Volntr; Red Cr Aide; Chrch Yth Grp; Emplmnt; Key Club; Spanish Clb; Dnce; Scr Kpr (V); Sftball (J); Adv Cncl (P); Secretary of National Honors Society; Nursing; Physical Therapy; Boston College; Stonehill College

HARRIS, JASMINE R; PHILADELPHIA, PA; SIMON GRATZ HS; (SO); Ctznshp Aw; Hnr Roll; MVP; Perf Att; Sci Fairs; St of Mnth; Comm Volntr; Chrch Yth Grp; Ch Chr; Bskball (V C); Scr Kpr (J); Sftball (V); Vllyball (J); All Public-City Wide Basketball; Medicine / Doctor - General Practice; U of Pennsylvania; Temple U

HARRIS, MYCHELLA; PITTSBURGH, PA; OLIVER HS; (SR); Ctznshp Aw; Hnr Roll; Nat Hon Sy; Otst Ac Ach Awd; Perf Att; St of Mnth; Prom Com; Voc Ind Clb Am; Dnce; Stu Cncl (R); Book Club; Fashion Merchandising; Interior Design

HARRISON, BRANDON; COATESVILLE, PA; COATESVILLE AREA SR HS; (JR); Hnr Roll; Perf Att; Comm Volntr; Chrch Yth Grp; Drma Clb; Emplmnt; Chr; Ch Chr; Cr Ctry (J); Track (J); Perfect Attendance; Biomedical Engineer; Industrial Engineering

HARSHBARGER, ASHLEY; MIFFLINTOWN, PA; JUNIATA CTY SD; (JR); 4H Awd; Hi Hnr Roll; Hnr Roll; Otst Ac Ach Awd; Pres Ac Ftns Aw; St of Mnth; 4-H; Mus Clb; Ntl FFA; Prom Com; Quiz Bowl; Bnd; Mch Bnd; Fld Hky (VJ); FFA-Officer (Numerous Awards); 4-H Dairy Club; Agriculture and Extension Education; Dairy Science; Pennsylvania State U; Delaware Valley College

HARSHBERGER, ALEX; HOLLIDAYSBURG, PA; (FR); Hnr Roll; Nat Hon Sy; Chrch Yth Grp; Bnd; Jzz Bnd; Mch Bnd; Orch; Secretary of National Junior Honor Society; Math/Science; Music; Carnegie Mellon U; Georgetown U

HARSHBERGER, JEREMY A; CAIRNBROOK, PA; SHADE-CENTRAL CITY SD; (SO); Hi Hnr Roll; Nat Hon Sy; WWAHSS; Peer Tut/Med; Vsity Clb; Chr; Ftball (V L); Track (V); Wt Lftg (V); Wrstlg (V L); Stu Cncl (R); Seton Hill U

HART, CORY; HOOVERSVILLE, PA; SHADE-CENTRAL CITY SD; (FR); Hi Hnr Roll; Hnr Roll; MVP; Sci/Math Olympn; WWAHSS; Peer Tut/Med; Quiz Bowl; Schol Bwl; Scouts; SADD; Bnd; Mch Bnd; Pep Bnd; Bskball (J); Track (V L); Cl Off (P); Stu Cncl (R); CR (R); Lake Erie Regiment Drum and Bugle Corps; Percussion Performance; Music Education; Indiana U of Pennsylvania; U of Massachusetts

HART, TRAVIS; READING, PA; EXETER TWP SR HS; (SO); Hi Hnr Roll; WWAHSS; Comm Volntr; Key Club; Latin Clb; Bnd; Bsball (J); Golf (J); Intramural Basketball; Sports Communications; Sports Medicine; Syracuse U; Quinnipiac U

HARTFORD, MATT; NEW KENSINGTON, PA; KISKI AREA HS; (JR); Hi Hnr Roll; Kwnis Aw; MVP; Nat Hon Sy; Pres Ac Ftns Aw; WWAHSS; Comm Volntr; Peer Tut/Med; Emplmnt; FBLA; Key Club; Mth Clb/Tm; MuAlphaTh; SADD; Vsity Clb; Spanish Clb; Ftball (VJ L); Swmg (V CL); Tennis (V CL); Track (V); Adv Cncl (R); Stu Cncl (P, R); Mathematics; Business; U of North Carolina (Chapel Hill); Duke U

HARTLAUB, LIZ; YORK, PA; CHRISTIAN SCH OF YORK; (JR); Hnr Roll; Comm Volntr; Hosp Aide; Chrch Yth Grp; Drma Clb; Emplmnt; Photog; Ch Chr; Yrbk (P); Registered Nurse / Nurse Practitioner; York College; Harrisburg Area Community College

HARTMAN, AMANDA; DALLAS, PA; LAKE LEHMAN HS; (SO); Hi Hnr Roll; Hnr Roll; Nat Hon Sy; WWAHSS; Comm Volntr; Hosp Aide; Red Cr Aide; Emplmnt; Fr of Library; Key Club; Dnce; Chrldg; Elementary Education; Business; Penn State U (State College)

HARTMAN, AMANDA M; QUINCY, PA; WAYNESBORO AREA SR HS; (JR); Hnr Roll; Nat Hon Sy; WWAHSS; Comm Volntr; Chrch Yth Grp; Key Club; Nursing; Child Care; Penn State Mont Alto

HARTMAN, LORRAINE M; DILLSBURG, PA; NORTHERN HS; (SR); Hnr Roll; WWAHSS; Spec Olymp Vol; Key Club; Bnd; Chr; Clr Grd; Dnce; Tennis (J L); Track (V); Captain-Indoor Color Guard; Band Treasurer; Secondary Education; Millersville U

HARTMANN, ALLISON; E STROUDSBURG, PA; EAST STROUDSBURG HS SOUTH; (FR); Ch Chr; Girls/Boys Soccer Manager; Cosmetology

HARTMANN, SAMANTHA E; E STROUDSBURG, PA; EAST STROUDSBURG HS SOUTH; (JR); Hi Hnr Roll; Nat Hon Sy; Perf Att; WWAHSS; Comm Volntr; Spec Olymp Vol; Chrch Yth Grp; DARE; Emplmnt; Jr Ach; Key Club; Bnd; Bskball (J); Sftball (V); Tennis (V)

HARTNEY, JULIA; CLIFTON HEIGHTS, PA; UPPER DARBY HS; (JR); Hi Hnr Roll; Hnr Roll; Perf Att; WWAHSS; Yrbk; Dancing for 9 Years; Elementary Education; Interior Design; West Chester; York College

HARTWIG, MEGAN K; WEXFORD, PA; NORTH ALLEGHENY HS; (SO); Perf Att; Comm Volntr; Chrch Yth Grp; Key Club; Bskball (J); Track (V); Honors World Cultures; Special Education; Physical Education; U Of Notre Dame; Purdue U

HARTZ, ASHLEY S; CRANBERRY TWP, PA; SENECA VALLEY SHS; (JR); Hnr Roll; WWAHSS; Comm Volntr; Peer Tut/Med; Chrch Yth Grp; Key Club; Off Aide; SADD; Stg Cre; Stu Cncl (S, T, R); Teens For Tots; Mexico Mission Trips; Physical Therapy; Miami U Ohio; Penn State

Hartman, Amanda
Lake Lehman HS
Dallas, PA

Harris, Jasmine R
Simon Gratz HS
Philadelphia, PA

National
Honor Roll
Spring 2005

Haines, Racheal
Bensalem Township SD HS
Bensalem, PA

Hartwig, Megan K
North Allegheny HS
Wexford, PA

HASKELL, BONNIE; PHOENIXVILLE, PA; GREAT VALLEY HS; (JR); Hi Hnr Roll; Kwnis Aw; Nat Ldrshp Svc; St of Mnth; WWAHSS; Comm Volntr; Hosp Aide; Emplmnt; HO'Br Yth Ldrshp; Key Club; NYLC; Schol Bwl; Sci Clb; Svce Clb; Spanish Clb; Bnd; Bskball; Tennis (V L); Track (J); Stu Cncl (R); CR (R); Creating Service Club At Middle School; President of Ecology Club; Psychology; Advertising; The College of William and Mary; Brown U

HASSETT, SHEA A; ETTERS, PA; TRINITY HS; (JR); Hnr Roll; WWAHSS; Comm Volntr; Key Club; Spanish Clb; Bskball; Elementary Education; Art History; Juniata College; Lycoming College

HATFIELD, LINDSEY; LANSDALE, PA; NORTH PENN HS; (JR); Hnr Roll; Red Cr Aide; Spec Olymp Vol; Chrch Yth Grp; Key Club; Prom Com; Acpl Chr; Chr; Ch Chr; PP Ftbl; Skiing; Stu Cncl; Public Relations; Music; New York U; Pace U

HAUCK, ASHLEY; BOYERTOWN, PA; BRANDYWINE HEIGHTS HS; (SO); Hi Hnr Roll; Hnr Roll; Otst Ac Ach Awd; St of Mnth; WWAHSS; Yth Ldrshp Prog; ArtClub; Emplmnt; Key Club; Vllyball (V L); Nomination for the National Youth Leaders Conference

HAULMAN, ZACHARY; ALTOONA, PA; ALTOONA AREA HS; (SR); Hnr Roll; Nat Hon Sy; Comm Volntr; Peer Tut/Med; Ftball (V CL); Track (V L); Physical Therapy; Attending U of Pittsburgh

HAUPT, AARON; MCADOO, PA; HAZLETON AREA HS; (JR); Hi Hnr Roll; Hnr Roll; Information Technology; PC Technician

HAUSER, KAYLA C; GREENVILLE, PA; GREENVILLE HS; (JR); Hi Hnr Roll; Nat Hon Sy; St of Mnth; USAA; WWAHSS; Comm Volntr; Key Club; Prom Com; Vsity Clb; Chr; Chrldg (V L); Tennis (V L); Vsy Clb (V); Education; Nursing

HAWKINS, NICHOLAS D; ERIE, PA; ERIE CITY SD; (FR); Hi Hnr Roll; Hnr Roll; Emplmnt; Ftball (V L); Wt Lftg (V); Protective Services; Criminal Justice

HAWN, WENDY; HUNTINGDON, PA; JUNIATA VALLEY HS; (JR); Hnr Roll; Perf Att; Sci Fairs; St of Mnth; DARE; Emplmnt; Vsity Clb; Track (V); Physical Therapy; Ultra Sounding; Mount Aloysius College; Slippery Rock U

HAYES, ATALIE T; NEW KENSINGTON, PA; KISKI AREA HS; (SO); Hi Hnr Roll; Perf Att; Sci Fairs; WWAHSS; Comm Volntr; Chrch Yth Grp; DARE; Key Club; SADD; Bnd; Flg Crps; Jzz Bnd; Mch Bnd; Bskball (J); Church Youth Group; Music Education; Pharmacy; Grove City College; Duquesne U

HAYES, ELLISSA L; BENSALEM, PA; BENSALEM TOWNSHIP SD; (JR); Hi Hnr Roll; Hnr Roll; MVP; Pres Ac Ftns Aw; St of Mnth; Emplmnt; P to P St Amb Prg; Prom Com; Scouts; Stg Cre; Swmg; Track; Stu Cncl (R); CR (R); AV-Audio Video-Taping / Interviewing; Waterpolo Club/Safe-Sitter Club; Plastic Surgery / Pre-Med; Veterinary Surgery; Shippensburg U; Penn State

HAYES, WHITNEY; BETHEL PARK, PA; BETHEL PARK SD; (SO); Hnr Roll; Comm Volntr; Spec Olymp Vol; Chrch Yth Grp; Drma Clb; Mus Clb; Outdrs Clb; Prom Com; Bnd; Chr; Ch Chr; Jzz Bnd; Sftball (J); Wt Lftg (J); Cl Off (P); CR (R); Junior School Board Rep; River City Youth Choral Participant; Music Education; Vocal Performance; California U; West Chester U

HAYNES, MATTHEW; VERONA, PA; PENN HILLS HS; (SO); SP/M/VS; High School Bowling Team (Varsity); Orthopedics; U of Pittsburgh

HAYNIE JR, KENNETH L; TROUT RUN, PA; LIBERTY JR SR HS; (SO); Hi Hnr Roll; Hnr Roll; Comm Volntr; Spec Olymp Vol; Key Club; Scouts; Bnd; Chr; Mch Bnd; SP/M/VS; Ftball (V); Criminal Justice; Pennsylvania State U; Temple U

HAZLETT, DAVID; OAKMONT, PA; RIVERVIEW JR/SR HS; (FR); Hnr Roll; WWAHSS; Yth Ldrshp Prog; Peer Tut/Med; Spec Olymp Vol; Drma Clb; Key Club; Tchrs Aide; SP/M/VS; Cr Ctry (J); Track (J); Stu Cncl (R); CR (R); Outside of School Art Classes; Teaching Degree; Secondary Education; Penn State Main Campus

HEALY, THOMAS J; HARRISBURG, PA; CTRL DAUPHIN HS; (FR); Hnr Roll; Otst Ac Ach Awd; Pres Ac Ftns Aw; Sci Fairs; Sci/Math Olympn; St of Mnth; Comm Volntr; Orch; Stg Cre; Bsball (J); Ftball; Travel Baseball Club; Professional Baseball Player; Engineering; U of Notre Dame; U of Miami

HEARTH, KAILEE M; STOYSTOWN, PA; SHANKSVILLE-STONYCREEK HS; (FR); Hnr Roll; Pres Ac Ftns Aw; Chr; Scr Kpr (VJ); Massage Therapy; Indiana U of Pennsylvania; U of Pittsburgh Johnstown

HEARY, LAUREN N; SOUDERTON, PA; SOUDERTON AREA HS; (SR); Hi Hnr Roll; Hnr Roll; Comm Volntr; Emplmnt; Chr; Pennsylvania Free Enterprise Week (PFEW); Volunteer W/Multiple Disabilities Students; Medical Administrative Assistant Technology; The Cittone Institute

HEBEN, ASHLEY L; HERMITAGE, PA; HICKORY HS; (SO); Hi Hnr Roll; Hnr Roll; Chr; Chrldg (J); National Society of High School Scholars; Physical Therapy

HECK, MEGHAN; COVINGTON, PA; NORTH PENN JR/SR HS; (SR); Hi Hnr Roll; Hnr Roll; Nat Hon Sy; St of Mnth; USAA; WWAHSS; Yth Ldrshp Prog; Peer Tut/Med; Red Cr Aide; Spec Olymp Vol; Emplmnt; HO'Br Yth Ldrshp; Key Club; Off Aide; Prom Com; Scouts; Tchrs Aide; Bskball (VJCL); Vllyball (VJ L); Relay for Life Volunteer; Social Work; Mansfield U

HEDRICK, STEVE; SCHWENKSVILLE, PA; SPRING FORD SR HS; (SO); Hnr Roll; Hab For Humty Volntr; Chrch Yth Grp; Sci Clb; Scouts; Spanish Clb; Star Scout in Boy Scouts; Youth Leader in Church

HEEMAN, KYLIE; STATE COLLEGE, PA; STATE COLLEGE SOUTH HS; (FR); Hi Hnr Roll; Hnr Roll; WWAHSS; Hosp Aide; DARE; Mth Clb/Tm; Photog; Scouts; SADD; Reading Team Placed First in Competition; 12 Maroon and Gray Awards; Language-Foreign; Writing/Journalism; New York U; Penn State

HEFFLINE, VALERIE; POTTSTOWN, PA; POTTSTOWN HS; (SO); Hnr Roll; Pres Ac Ftns Aw; Yth Ldrshp Prog; ArtClub; Chrch Yth Grp; DECA; Sftball (V); Education; Mount Vernon U

HEINTZ, ELIZABETH M; DALLAS, PA; DALLAS HS; (JR); Hi Hnr Roll; Hnr Roll; Nat Hon Sy; WWAHSS; Comm Volntr; Key Club; Prom Com; Fld Hky (V L); Nursing; York College; Westchester U

HEINTZ, THERESA M; DALLAS, PA; DALLAS HS; (SO); WWAHSS; Comm Volntr; Key Club; Vllyball (V L); Stu Cncl (R); Nursing; Physical Therapy; Bloomsburg; Westchester

HEISEY, LAUREN E; MECHANICSBURG, PA; MECHANICSBURG AREA SR HS; (SO); Hi Hnr Roll; Hnr Roll; Perf Att; St of Mnth; WWAHSS; Comm Volntr; Spec Olymp Vol; ArtClub; Chrch Yth Grp; Key Club; Tech Clb; Track (V L); Technology Students Association "TSA" 4 Yrs National Finalist; Engineering; Accounting

HELBLING, MALLORY P; PITTSBURGH, PA; SHALER AREA HS; (JR); Hi Hnr Roll; Hnr Roll; Kwnis Aw; Nat Hon Sy; Otst Ac Ach Awd; Pres Sch; WWAHSS; Yth Ldrshp Prog; Comm Volntr; Peer Tut/Med; Spec Olymp Vol; FBLA; FTA; Jr Ach; Key Club; Off Aide; SADD; Chr; SP/M/VS; Yrbk; Peer Mentoring / Big Brother Big Sister; Outstanding Young Citizen; Pre-Law; U of Pittsburgh

HELEM, NADIA; PHILADELPHIA, PA; OVERBROOK HS; (SR); Hnr Roll; Otst Ac Ach Awd; Comm Volntr; Hab For Humty Volntr; Chess; Dbte Team; Emplmnt; Mus Clb; Tchrs Aide; Dnce; Stg Cre; Sccr (J); Adv Cncl (P); Stu Cncl (R); CR (P); Lead Attorney of Overbrook's Mock Trial Team; Veterinary Care; Law; Chestnut Hill; West Chester

HELLER, MIKE; RICES LANDING, PA; CARMICHAELS AREA JR/SR HS; (JR); Hi Hnr Roll; Nat Hon Sy; Dbte Team; Quiz Bowl; Gifted Program; Web Page Design; Graphic Arts; Penn State U; ITT Technical Institute

HEMMING, TONY; NEWTOWN, PA; COUNCIL ROCK HS NORTH; (JR); Hi Hnr Roll; Nat Hon Sy; Comm Volntr; Chrch Yth Grp; Emplmnt; Bnd; Jzz Bnd; Mch Bnd; Stu Cncl (R); National Merit Selection, Not Yet Placed; Teach ESL Classes for Latino Adults; Mechanical Engineering; Business/ Management; Cornell U; U of California-Berkeley

HEMPHILL, STEPHANIE; NOTTINGHAM, PA; WEST NOTTINGHAM AC (9TH); (SO); Hi Hnr Roll; St of Mnth; Peer Tut/Med; Emplmnt; Hsbk Rdg (V); Vllyball (V); Swimming (7 Yrs) Out of School; Odyssey of the Mind (9th Grade); Architecture; Marine Biology; U of Pennsylvania; Brown U

HENDERSON, BRITTANY; PITTSBURGH, PA; PERRY TRADITIONAL AC; (SO); Ctznshp Aw; Hi Hnr Roll; Hnr Roll; Perf Att; St of Mnth; Comm Volntr; DARE; Mch Bnd; Girl Scouts of Southwestern PA; Volunteer Work; Bachelor's Degree in Medical; MD; U of Pittsburgh

HENDERSON, JACLYN; WEXFORD, PA; NORTH ALLEGHENY INT HS; (JR); Hnr Roll; Perf Att; Ch Chr; Stu Cncl (R); Computer Science; E-Commerce

HENDERSON, JAZMINE M; PITTSBURGH, PA; PITTSBURGH SD; (FR); Ctznshp Aw; Hi Hnr Roll; Hnr Roll; Nat Sci Aw; Cmptr Clb; Jr Ach; Lib Aide; Mth Clb/Tm; Quiz Bowl; SADD; French Clb; Drl Tm; Chrldg (J); PPSqd (J); Cl Off (V); Stu Cncl (V); CR (S); Black College

HENDERSON, JOE-LEA; CANONSBURG, PA; RIDGEVIEW AC CS; (JR); Hi Hnr Roll; Perf Att; Business Management; Florida State U

HENDRICKSON, JENNIFER; PITTSBURGH, PA; NORTH ALLEGHENY INT HS; (FR); All Am Sch; Hnr Roll; Perf Att; WWAHSS; Yth Ldrshp Prog; Comm Volntr; Chrch Yth Grp; Emplmnt; Key Club; Prom Com; Chrldg (V); Stu Cncl; Sport Committee Scholar Athlete Award; Semi Publicity Rep; Middle School Teacher; Guidance Counselor; Virginia Tech; Pittsburgh

HENEGAN, AMY K; JAMESTOWN, PA; JAMESTOWN AREA SD; (SO); Hi Hnr Roll; Nat Hon Sy; Otst Ac Ach Awd; Pres Ac Ftns Aw; WWAHSS; Comm Volntr; Chrch Yth Grp; Emplmnt; Spanish Clb; Bnd; Mch Bnd; Chrldg (V L); Cr Ctry (V L); Gmnstcs; Track (V L); Cl Off (P); Stu Cncl (R); Usage Level 9 Gymnast/State & Region & Medal Winner; Voice of District Democracy Essay/Speech 3rd Place

HENG, SCOTT; UPPER DARBY, PA; UPPER DARBY HS; (JR); Hi Hnr Roll; Hnr Roll; Comm Volntr; Spec Olymp Vol; Tchrs Aide; Tennis (L); CR (R); Table Tennis Club; Pharmacy; U of the Sciences in Philadelphia; Temple U

HENITZ, KELLY E; CATASAUQUA, PA; CATASAUQUA AREA SD; (SR); Hi Hnr Roll; WWAHSS; Hosp Aide; Spec Olymp Vol; Child Psychology; Kutztown U

HENRY, ASHLEY; LEWISTOWN, PA; LEWISTOWN AREA HS; (JR); Hnr Roll; WWAHSS; Spec Olymp Vol; Chrch Yth Grp; Key Club; Off Aide; Prom Com; SADD; Spanish Clb; SP/M/VS; Fld Hky (J); Communications; Graphic Design; Juniata College

HENSON, TYREE; PHILADELPHIA, PA; MURRELL DOBBINS HS; (JR); Hnr Roll; Perf Att; Comm Volntr; Hab For Humty Volntr; Chrch Yth Grp; Outdrs Clb; Ftball (VJ); Phi Beta Osi Mathematics; Accounting; Penn State U; Moore House U

HEPLER, RACHEL J; ERIE, PA; ERIE CITY SD; (SR); Hnr Roll; Comm Volntr; Chrch Yth Grp; Emplmnt; Prom Com; Tchrs Aide; Medals in Academic Sports League; Amelia Earhart Leadership Award; Pre-Medicine; Gannon U

HERB, NIKKI; HALIFAX, PA; HALIFAX AREA HS; (SO); Ctznshp Aw; Hnr Roll; Nat Hon Sy; Nat Stu Ath Day Aw; Perf Att; USAA; Comm Volntr; Spec Olymp Vol; Chrch Yth Grp; FTA; Mth Clb/Tm; Scouts; Chr; Chrldg (VJC); Sftball (J); Vllyball (J); Stu Cncl (R); Yrbk (R); Region E Representative in PA Assoc. of Student Councils; FIA, Stand Tall, Youth Group Treasurer; Mathematics Secondary Education; Millersville U

HERDT, COURTNEY N; BEAVER FALLS, PA; BEAVER FALLS HS; (SO); All Am Sch; Hi Hnr Roll; Kwnis Aw; Otst Ac Ach Awd; Perf Att; USAA; WWAHSS; Comm Volntr; Drma Clb; Key Club; SADD; Vsity Clb; Spanish Clb; Bnd; Chr; Jzz Bnd; Mch Bnd; Chrldg (V L); Cr Ctry (J); Swmg (V L); Track (V L); Secondary Mathematics; Massachusetts Institute of Technology; Carnegie Mellon

HERILLA, TEKLA J; EAST MILLSBORO, PA; BROWNSVILLE AREA HS; (JR); Hnr Roll; Comm Volntr; Chrch Yth Grp; Emplmnt; Cr Ctry (VJ); Track (VJ); People to People Student Ambassador; National Spanish Honor Society; Veterinarian; Education Special Children; Gannon U; Penn State U

HERMAN, JASON; UNION CITY, PA; UNION CITY HS; (JR); Hi Hnr Roll; Hnr Roll; Comm Volntr; Ftball (J); Wrstlg (J); Stu Cncl (R)

HERNANDEZ, CRISTINA; EASTON, PA; EASTON AREA SR HS; (JR); Hnr Roll; Comm Volntr; DARE; Drma Clb; Off Aide; SADD; Chr; Skiing (V); Snowboarding, Ski Club; Students Against Violating the Earth; Doctor of Vet Medicine; Master's; Forensics; Texas A & M U in College Station; Boston U

HERNANDEZ, OLIVERIO; NORTHAMPTON, PA; NORTHAMPTON SR HS; (JR); Hi Hnr Roll; Hnr Roll; Comm Volntr; Peer Tut/Med; DECA; Drma Clb; Emplmnt; Tchrs Aide; Writing; Architecture; Drexel U; New York U

HERNANDEZ, SAMANTHA; LANCASTER, PA; MANHEIM TWP HS; (SR); Hi Hnr Roll; Hnr Roll; Nat Hon Sy; St of Mnth; Peer Tut/Med; Bnd; PP Ftbl (V); Operation Smile Vice President; Pre-Med / Biology; Neuroscience; St Joseph's U; Columbia U

HERNANDEZ-CRUZ, MARIA; BENSALEM, PA; BENSALEM TOWNSHIP SD; (FR); All Am Sch; F Lan Hn Soc; Fut Prb Slvr; Nat Hon Sy; St of Mnth; CARE; Comm Volntr; Hosp Aide; AL Aux Girls; Aqrium Clb; Cmptr Clb; FTA; Lib Aide; Mth Clb/Tm; Scouts; Spanish Clb; Ch Chr; Dnce; SP/M/VS; Swg Chr; Bsball (V); Bskball (V); Gmnstcs (V); Ice Hky (V); Ice Sktg (V); Mar Art (V); Swmg (V); Tennis (V); Cl Off (V); CR (R); Yrbk (E); Bensalem High School

HERSHBERGER, SHAWNA; SCHWENKSVILLE, PA; ST PIUS X HS; (SR); Hi Hnr Roll; Hnr Roll; Nat Hon Sy; WWAHSS; Chrch Yth Grp; Drma Clb; Photog; Svce Clb; Spch Team; Chr; Ch Chr; SP/M/VS; Stg Cre; Lit Mag (R); Ministry President; Drama Club President; Secondary Education/English; Theatre; King's College

HERZING, EMILY; SAINT MARYS, PA; ST MARYS AREA HS; (SR); Hnr Roll; Nat Hon Sy; WWAHSS; Yth Ldrshp Prog; Comm Volntr; Peer Tut/ Med; Spec Olymp Vol; Chrch Yth Grp; Drma Clb; Lttrmn Clb; Lib Aide; Mod UN; NYLC; Prom Com; Spch Team; SP/M/VS; Stg Cre; Bskball (J L); Scr Kpr (V L); Sccr (VJCL); Track (J L); Cl Off (P); Stu Cncl (P); Member of Leaders in Training; Member of Toastmasters; Political Science; International Relations; Westminster College; Thiel College

HESS, DANIELA; BUCKINGHAM, PA; CTRL BUCKS HS EAST; (SO); F Lan Hn Soc; Hi Hnr Roll; Chrch Yth Grp; Key Club; P to P St Amb Prg; Chr; Stg Cre; Sccr (J); National Junior Honor Society; Participation in National History Day; Pre-Med; University of Pennsylvania

HESS, LAURA A; DREXEL HILL, PA; CARDINAL O'HARA HS; (JR); Hi Hnr Roll; Nat Hon Sy; Comm Volntr; Hab For Humty Volntr; Peer Tut/Med; Emplmnt; Off Aide; Prom Com; Svce Clb; French Clb; Lcrsse (VJ); Sccr (JC); Students Against Destructive Decisions; Nursing; Villanova U; U of Delaware

Hayes, Whitney
Bethel Park SD
Bethel Park, PA

Hayes, Ellissa L
Bensalem Township SD
Bensalem, PA

National
Honor Roll
Spring 2005

Hassett, Shea A
Trinity HS
Etters, PA

Herdt, Courtney N
Beaver Falls HS
Beaver Falls, PA

HESS, MEGAN E; NEW BRIGHTON, PA; NEW BRIGHTON AREA HS; (SO); Hi Hnr Roll; Hnr Roll; Nat Hon Sy; Pres Sch; Sci Fairs; WWAHSS; Spec Olymp Vol; ArtClub; SADD; Spanish Clb; Chr; Clr Grd; Drl Tm; Flg Crps; Track (J); Stu Cncl (R); Sch Ppr (R); Yrbk (E, R, P); Ushers Club; Lioness Club; Business; Marketing/Advertising; Carnegie Mellon U; U of Pittsburgh

HESS, MICHAEL; PITTSBURGH, PA; BISHOP CANEVIN HS; (SO); Hi Hnr Roll; Jr Rot; Otst Ac Ach Awd; Comm Volntr; Emplmnt; SP/M/VS; Sccr (VJ); CR (R); Inaugural Member of Bishop Canevin HS; Junior AOH (Ancient Order of the Liberals; Business (MBA), Film; Law School; Villanova, U Penn Law School; Carnegie Mellon

HESSIAN, CAITIE; DALLAS, PA; DALLAS HS; (JR); Hnr Roll; Red Cr Aide; Key Club; Prom Com; SADD; Bskball (J); Golf (J); PP Ftbl (V); Skiing (L); Stu Cncl (R); CR (R); Teaching-Elementary

HETHERINGTON, MEGAN; WHITEHALL, PA; WHITEHALL HS; (MS); Hi Hnr Roll; Hnr Roll; Perf Att; Pres Ac Ftns Aw; Pres Sch; St of Mnth; Hab For Humty Volntr; Peer Tut/Med; Red Cr Aide; Drma Clb; Key Club; Tchrs Aide; Spanish Clb; Clr Grd; Bskball (J); Swmg; Vllyball (J); Stu Cncl (R); Principal's Award; Various Subject Achievement Certificates; Law Major; Performing Arts; Harvard Law School; Princeton U

HETRICK, JEREMY; JOHNSTOWN, PA; CTRL CAMBRIA HS; (FR); Hi Hnr Roll; Hnr Roll; Bnd; Chr; Bskball (J); President Award; Musicianship Award; Teacher / Social Studies; Penn State U; U Pittsburgh

HETRO, NICHOLAS J; WYOMING, PA; DALLAS HS; (SO); Hi Hnr Roll; Nat Hon Sy; Emplmnt; Key Club; Cr Ctry (V); Track (V); Atmospheric Sciences; Naval Academy; Penn State

HIBBS, JACLYN A; POTTSTOWN, PA; POTTSGROVE HS; (JR); Ctznshp Aw; Hi Hnr Roll; Hnr Roll; Nat Hon Sy; Otst Ac Ach Awd; Key Club; Sci Clb; Dnce; Bskball (J); Fld Hky (J); Track (V L); Cl Off (R); Stu Cncl (V, R); CR (R); Yrbk (R, P); Film and Cinematography; Clarion U

HICKOK, ELONNAI; MORTON, PA; STRATH HAVEN HS; (JR); Hnr Roll; Comm Volntr; ArtClub; Chrch Yth Grp; Sci Clb; French Clb; Bnd; Flg Crps; Mch Bnd; Cr Ctry (V); Track (V); Sch Ppr (R); Danced with Rock School of PA Ballet; Indoor Track-Varsity, Varsity Arts Letter; International Social Service; Language Major; Texas Christian U, Indiana U; Illinois U, Vermont U

HICKS, TIERRA N; PHILADELPHIA, PA; OVERBROOK HS; (JR); Hi Hnr Roll; Hnr Roll; Nat Hon Sy; WWAHSS; Peer Tut/Med; Tchrs Aide; Dnce; CR; Criminal Justice; Howard U; Delaware State U

HICKS, TIM; PHILADELPHIA, PA; SIMON GRATZ HS; (FR); St of Mnth; Chess; SP/M/VS; Bsball (V); Physical Fitness Award; Peacemaker of the Month; Culinary Arts; Communication Technology; Hampton U; North Carolina

HICKS, TRAVIS; HARRISBURG, PA; CTRL DAUPHIN HS; (FR); Hnr Roll; Comm Volntr; Bnd; Chr; Jzz Bnd; Chemistry; Bucknell University

HIGGINS, MAURA; SEWICKLEY, PA; NORTH ALLEGHENY INT; (SO); Ctznshp Aw; Hi Hnr Roll; MVP; Nat Hon Sy; Otst Ac Ach Awd; Perf Att; WWAHSS; Comm Volntr; Chrch Yth Grp; DARE; Key Club; Prom Com; Spanish Clb; Dnce; Track (V L); Cl Off (S)

HIGH, JESSICA; HOPELAND, PA; EPHRATA HS; (SR); F Lan Hn Soc; Hi Hnr Roll; Nat Hon Sy; Sci Fairs; St of Mnth; WWAHSS; Comm Volntr; Chrch Yth Grp; Emplmnt; Mus Clb; German Clb; Orch; SP/M/VS; Yrbk (E); Tri-M-Secretary; German NHS; Major in Business Administration; Minor in Music; Harrisburg Area Community College; Eastern U

HIGHFIELD, CHARLENE; PITTSBURGH, PA; CHARTER HIGH CAREER CONNECTIONS; MS; Ctznshp Aw; Hnr Roll; Nat Hon Sy; Otst Ac Ach Awd; Comm Volntr; DARE; SADD; Bskball (V); Cr Ctry (V); Sccr (V); Sftball (V); Car Designer

HILBERT II, GARY A; PHILADELPHIA, PA; BENJAMIN RUSH MS; MS; Hnr Roll; Otst Ac Ach Awd; St of Mnth; DARE; Bskball; Medical Field; Computer Technology; Harvard U; Penn State

HILDABRANT, COLE A; BANGOR, PA; PIUS X HS; (SO); SP/M/VS; Stg Cre; Bsball (V L); Bskball (V L); Ftball (V L); Vsy Clb (V); National Honor Society; Real Estate; Education; Rutgers U; Va. Tech

HILDEBRAND, ALLISON; JOHNSTOWN, PA; CTRL CAMBRIA HS; (JR); Hi Hnr Roll; Hnr Roll; MVP; Nat Hon Sy; Otst Ac Ach Awd; WWAHSS; ArtClub; Chrch Yth Grp; Prom Com; Bnd; Chr; Chrldg (J); Pharmacy; U of Pittsburgh Johnstown; U Pittsburgh

HILDENBRAND, JULIE; RUFFS DALE, PA; YOUGH SD; (FR); Hi Hnr Roll; WWAHSS; Chrch Yth Grp; Dnce

HILL, ALYSSA; SCRANTON, PA; DUNMORE SD; (MS); Hi Hnr Roll; Hnr Roll; Nat Hon Sy; Comm Volntr; Chrch Yth Grp; Svce Clb; SADD; Chr; Ch Chr; Political Science

HILL, COLIN; PORT MATILDA, PA; STATE HS; (SO); Hi Hnr Roll; Hnr Roll; Pres Sch; Key Club; Business; Hotel and Restaurant Management; Temple U; West Chester U

HILL, COURTNEY E; WILLIAMSPORT, PA; LOYALSOCK TOWNSHIP HS; (SO); Comm Volntr; Peer Tut/Med; Chrch Yth Grp; Drma Clb; Emplmnt; Key Club; SADD; Spanish Clb; Ch Chr; Sftball (V); Stu Cncl (R); Forensics; Nursing; Mansfield U; Penn State U

HILL, JACQUELYN; PHILADELPHIA, PA; FRANKLIN LEARNING CTR; (SO); Hnr Roll; Comm Volntr; White Williams Scholarship Program; Web Designer; Photographer; Temple U; DeVry U

HILL, JUSTIN S; READING, PA; MUHLENBERG SR HS; (JR); Hi Hnr Roll; Hnr Roll; Emplmnt; Bnd; Brown Belt in Karate; Business Management; Sports Promotion; Bloomsburg U of Pennsylvania; Shippensburg U Pennsylvania

HILL, LESONDRA; READING, PA; READING HS; (SO); Ch Chr; Albright College

HILL, MEGAN C; VERONA, PA; PENN HILLS HS; (JR); Ctznshp Aw; Hi Hnr Roll; Nat Hon Sy; Sci Fairs; Sci/Math Olympn; WWAHSS; Chrch Yth Grp; FCA; Key Club; SADD; Spanish Clb; Sccr (V CL); Track (V L); Cl Off (P); Stu Cncl (R); Chemistry Award from Seton Hill U; All-WPIAL, All-Section in Soccer; Engineering; Political Science

HILLARD, BRITTNEY; DALLAS, PA; LAKE LEHMAN HS; (JR); Hnr Roll; Nat Hon Sy; Pres Ac Ftns Aw; WWAHSS; Comm Volntr; Emplmnt; Key Club; Off Aide; Sccr (V CL); Key Club Secretary; Elementary Education; Sports Medicine; Penn State; Bloomsburg U

HILLENBRAND, BRENT A; DEVON, PA; CONESTOGA HS; (SO); Hi Hnr Roll; WWAHSS; Peer Tut/Med; Key Club; German Clb; Distinguished Honor Roll; Hussian School of Art - Poster Design Award; Architecture; 3D Modeling and Animation

HILLMAN, KEVIN R; NEW PHILADELPHIA, PA; POTTSVILLE AREA HS; (SO); Hi Hnr Roll; Perf Att; Comm Volntr; Quill & Scroll; Scouts; Bnd; Mch Bnd; Sch Ppr (E); Yrbk (R); Martial Arts Black Belt & Teacher; American Legion Award for Highest Academic Scores in 8th Gr; Penn State U

HINCHLIFFE, JOSEPH; WOODLAND, PA; CLEARFIELD AREA HS; (SO); WWAHSS; Ftball (J); Track (V); Criminal Justice

HINES, MATTEUW; UPPER DARBY, PA; UPPER DARBY HS; (JR); Hi Hnr Roll; Hnr Roll; Comm Volntr; Peer Tut/Med; Ftball (V); School Orientator; Computer Engineering; Virginia Tech; Temple U

HINTERBERGER, MEGAN; ALTOONA, PA; BELLWOOD-ANTIS HS; (FR); Hi Hnr Roll; Hnr Roll; WWAHSS; Comm Volntr; Chrch Yth Grp; Key Club; Vllyball (J); Architecture; Dentistry; Pennsylvania State U

HITE, AMANDA; NORTHERN CAMBRIA, PA; CAMBRIA CTY CHRISTIAN SCH; (JR); Hnr Roll; Chrch Yth Grp; Jr Ach; Mus Clb; Prom Com; Svce Clb; Chr; Flg Crps; Bskball (V L); Youth Ministries; Music; Penn State U; Geneva College

HITESHUE, LAUREN R; GREENSBURG, PA; HEMPFIELD HS; (JR); Hi Hnr Roll; Hnr Roll; ArtClub; Emplmnt; Chrldg (J); Member of S.A.D.D.; Manager of Boys Baseball Team; Math Major; Pitt; Westmoreland Community C.

HOANG, CATHERINE T; LEMOYNE, PA; TRINITY HS; (JR); Hi Hnr Roll; Hnr Roll; Nat Hon Sy; Sci Fairs; Peer Tut/Med; Chess; Key Club; Pep Squd; Prom Com; Vsity Clb; Bskball (J L); Track (V L); Vllyball (V L); Cl Off (S); Stu Cncl (S); Business; Accounting; Villanova; St Joseph

HODGE, KEISHA; FEASTERVILLE TREVOSE, PA; BENSALEM TOWNSHIP SD; (SO); Hi Hnr Roll; Hnr Roll; Kwnis Aw; Perf Att; Pres Ac Ftns Aw; St of Mnth; Peer Tut/Med; DARE; Emplmnt; Kwanza Clb; Scouts; SADD; Bnd; Chr; Dnce; Drl Tm; Track (V); Business Management; Accounting / Finance; Drexel U; Temple U

HODGES, PATRICK B; PITTSBURGH, PA; BETHEL PARK SD; (SO); Hnr Roll; Bnd; Mch Bnd; Tennis (J); Engineering; Math; U of Pittsburgh; U of Dayton

HOEY, MEGHAN; DOYLESTOWN, PA; CTRL BUCKS HS EAST HS; (JR); F Lan Hn Soc; Hi Hnr Roll; Comm Volntr; Emplmnt; Key Club; Football Manager (Varsity Letter Winner); Key Club Vice President; Biology; Education; Penn State; U of North Carolina

HOFF, LINDSEY; PORT MATILDA, PA; STATE COLLEGE SOUTH HS; (SO); Hi Hnr Roll; Nat Sci Aw; DARE; Photog; German Clb; Bnd; Chr; Sftball (V); Club Sports (Basketball & Softball); 2nd Mile Program-Workout Program; Culinary Arts; Business; Penn State U; Lock Haven U

HOFFER, NOELLE; HARRISBURG, PA; TRINITY HS; (FR); Hi Hnr Roll; Hnr Roll; WWAHSS; Comm Volntr; Chrch Yth Grp; Key Club; Spanish Clb; Dnce; Chrldg (V); Swmg (V L); Lit Mag (E); Pennsylvania High School Swimming Coaches' Association All-State Honorable Mention; A Bachelor's Degree to Become a Pediatrician; Penn State U; Franklin & Marshall U

HOFFMAN, ASHLEY N; LEWISTOWN, PA; LEWISTOWN HS; (JR); Hnr Roll; Comm Volntr; Voc Ind Clb Am; SP/M/VS; CR (V); Nursing; Lawyer; Indiana U of Pennsylvania

HOFFMAN, RACHAEL; GREENVILLE, PA; REYNOLDS JR SR HS; (SO); 4H Awd; Hi Hnr Roll; Hnr Roll; St of Mnth; WWAHSS; 4-H; Emplmnt; Key Club; Chr; Ch Chr; SP/M/VS; Swg Chr; Vllyball (J); Stu Cncl (R); Piano Achievement; English; Music; Grove City College; Westminster College

HOFFMAN, SAMANTHA; DRUMS, PA; HAZLETON AREA HS; (SO); Hnr Roll; Drma Clb; Acpl Chr; Chr; SP/M/VS; Chamber Choir; Fashion Merchandising; Make-Up Artistry

HOFFMAN, SHANNON; BOYERTOWN, PA; BOYERTOWN AREA SR HS; (SO); Hi Hnr Roll; Hnr Roll; Otst Ac Ach Awd; Comm Volntr; ArtClub; Chrch Yth Grp; DARE; Key Club; Svce Clb; Chr; Ch Chr; PP Ftbl (V); Track (J); Stu Cncl (R); CR (R); Select Crafts / Ceramics; Mission Trips; Doctor / Nurse; Biologist

HOFFMAN, TYLER J; POTTSTOWN, PA; POTTSGROVE SR HS; (FR); Hi Hnr Roll; Hnr Roll; St of Mnth; DARE; Emplmnt; Sci Clb; Scouts; Wdwrkg Clb; Lcrsse (V); Rlr Hky (J); Skiing (V)

HOFFMASTER, MICHELLE; WINDSOR, PA; RED LION AREA SR HS; (JR); Hnr Roll; USAA; Nursing; York College PA; Bloomsburg U PA

HOFMANN, COLLEEN; ROBESONIA, PA; CONRAD WEISER HS; (SR); Hi Hnr Roll; Hnr Roll; St of Mnth; WWAHSS; Comm Volntr; Emplmnt; Key Club; P to P St Amb Prg; Prom Com; Tchrs Aide; Tech Clb; Stu Cncl (R); People to People Student Ambassador to Australia; Elementary Education / Special Education; Millersville U

HOGUE, ASHLEY; MEADVILLE, PA; SAEGERTOWN JR/SR HS; (JR); Hnr Roll; Spanish Clb; Vllyball (V L); A Bachelor's Degree; Indiana U of Pennsylvania; Bloomsburg U

HOHMAN, LORA M; HERMITAGE, PA; HICKORY HS; (SO); F Lan Hn Soc; Hi Hnr Roll; St of Mnth; WWAHSS; Chrch Yth Grp; Emplmnt; Scouts; Spch Team; French Clb; Bnd; Chr; Mch Bnd; Orch; Track; French Tutor; Church Altar Server and Religious Ed. Volunteer; Math

HOLDER, MARY K; CAMP HILL, PA; TRINITY HS; (SO); Hnr Roll; Pres Sch; WWAHSS; Comm Volntr; Peer Tut/Med; Emplmnt; Key Club; Spanish Clb; Bskball (VJCL); PP Ftbl (VJ); Vllyball (VJ L); Shamrock Ambassador-School Rep; Marine Biology; U of Notre Dame; Mount St Mary's U

HOLDORF, AMANDA N; YORK, PA; YORK CATHOLIC; (JR); Hi Hnr Roll; Nat Hon Sy; Sci Fairs; Comm Volntr; Peer Tut/Med; Spec Olymp Vol; Chrch Yth Grp; P to P St Amb Prg; Vsity Clb; Spanish Clb; Dnce; SP/M/VS; Tennis (V L); Vsy Clb (L); Stu Cncl (R); York County Junior Miss Participant; Secretary/Treasurer of National Honor Society; Math; Immaculata U; Franciscan U of Steubenville

HOLLAND, CRYSTAL; WATERFORD, PA; FORT LEBOEUF SD; (JR); Hnr Roll; Perf Att; Comm Volntr; DARE; Emplmnt; Mod UN; Scouts; Chr; Own My Own Business; Edinboro U; Michigan State U

HOLLAND, HEATHER; WATERFORD, PA; FORT LEBOEUF SD; (JR); Hnr Roll; WWAHSS; Emplmnt; Pep Squd; Chrldg (V L); Track (V); Business Degree; Accounting-Bachelor's Degree; Penn State of Pennsylvania; Clarion U

HOLLERAN, JOE; GREENVILLE, PA; GREENVILLE HS; (JR); Hi Hnr Roll; Hnr Roll; Nat Hon Sy; WWAHSS; Cmptr Clb; Key Club; Prom Com; Sci Clb; Bskball (V L); Tennis (V L); Track (J); Yrbk (E); Junior Icon; Grove City College; Washington & Jefferson College

HOLLERAN, KEVIN; HOLLAND, PA; COUNCIL ROCK HS SOUTH; (SR); Hnr Roll; Nat Hon Sy; Comm Volntr; Hosp Aide; Dbte Team; Emplmnt; Fr of Library; NYLC; Spanish Clb; Sch Ppr (R); Political Science; Rutgers U

HOLLEY, AMANDA E Z; SAINT CLAIR, PA; POTTSVILLE AREA HS; (SO); Ctznshp Aw; Hi Hnr Roll; Hnr Roll; Sci Fairs; St of Mnth; WWAHSS; Comm Volntr; Key Club; Lttrmn Clb; SADD; Spanish Clb; Drm Mjr; Mch Bnd; Sftball (J); Cl Off (S); Stu Cncl (R); CR (R); Majorette; Sophomore Homecoming Winner; Mechanical Engineering; Architectural Engineering; U of Delaware; Pennsylvania State U

HOLLIDAY, ABREE; PHILADELPHIA, PA; BENJAMIN RUSH MS; (MS); Hnr Roll; Pres Sch; St of Mnth; Comm Volntr; Hab For Humty Volntr; Peer Tut/Med; DARE; Lib Aide; Mth Clb/Tm; Scouts; Spch Team; Dnce; Drl Tm; SP/M/VS; Gmnstcs; Track; Philadelphia AIDS Walk; National Academic League; Psychology; Medical Doctor; Temple U; Drexel U

HOLLIS, HAVEN; ASTON, PA; CHICHESTER SR HS; (FR); Hnr Roll; Psychology / Literature; Temple University; Arcadia U

HOLLOMAN, STACIE; HAZLETON, PA; HAZLETON AREA HS; (JR); Ctznshp Aw; Hi Hnr Roll; Hnr Roll; Nat Ldrshp Svc; WWAHSS; Comm Volntr; FBLA; Key Club; SADD; Foreign Clb; Tennis; Stu Cncl; National English Merit Award; Outstanding Citizen Award; Law; Secondary Education-History; Bloomsburg U; Penn State U

Hoffer, Noelle
Trinity HS
Harrisburg, PA

Hillard, Brittney
Lake Lehman HS
Dallas, PA

Hilbert II, Gary A
Benjamin Rush MS
Philadelphia, PA

Hess, Megan E
New Brighton Area HS
New Brighton, PA

Hicks, Tim
Simon Gratz HS
Philadelphia, PA

Hillman, Kevin R
Pottsville Area HS
New Philadelphia, PA

Holland, Crystal
Fort Leboeuf SD
Waterford, PA

HOLLOWAY, TELIA; PHILADELPHIA, PA; FRANKFORD HS; (SR); Ctznshp Aw; Hnr Roll; Pres Ac Ftns Aw; Yth Ldrshp Prog; Comm Volntr; Peer Tut/Med; Chrch Yth Grp; Ch Chr; Dnce; SP/M/VS; Fld Hky (VJ); Ftball (J); Scr Kpr (J); Track (J)

HOLMES, DANNI L; HUNTINGDON, PA; HUNTINGDON AREA HS; (SO); Ctznshp Aw; Hi Hnr Roll; Hnr Roll; Kwnis Aw; WWAHSS; Yth Ldrshp Prog; Comm Volntr; Hab For Humty Volntr; Spec Olymp Vol; DARE; Key Club; Ntl FFA; Tchrs Aide; Voc Ind Clb Am; Wdwrkg Clb; Teacher for Special Education; Animal Sciences (Vet); Penn State U; Shippensburg U

HOLODNIK, CHRISTINE L; PITTSBURGH, PA; OAKLAND CATHOLIC HS; (FR); Hi Hnr Roll; WWAHSS; Comm Volntr; Chrch Yth Grp; Emplmnt; Chr; Bskball; Rowing; Spanish (4 Yrs.) Swimming; Pediatric Physical Therapy

HOLTER, ANDREW; BERWICK, PA; BERWICK AREA SR HS; (JR); Hnr Roll; WWAHSS; Chrch Yth Grp; Key Club; Lib Aide; Ftball (J); Sccr (V); Vllyball (V, J); Stu Cncl (R); Awarded Distinguished Vice President of Key Club International at PA Key Club Convention; Participated - Sister City Exchange Program from Berwick PA, to Berwick-upon-Tweed UK; History Teacher; Indiana University of Pennsylvania

HOLTMAN, STEPHANIE R; NEW KENSINGTON, PA; NEW KENSINGTON-ARNOLD SD; (FR); 4H Awd; Hnr Roll; 4-H; DARE; Mod UN; ROTC; Scouts; Wdwrkg Clb; Honor Guard; Cosmetology; Pittsburgh Beauty Academy

HOLZER, KAYLA; LATROBE, PA; GREATER LATROBE SR HS; (JR); Hnr Roll; Hosp Aide; Key Club; Lttrmn Clb; Pep Squd; Spanish Clb; Chrldg (V L); Lcrsse (J); Sch Ppr (R); Dance, Out of School for 9 Years; All-Star Cheerleading Competition Squad; Pediatrician; Nutritionist; Hofstra U; Penn State U

HOOVER, ANDREW P; ALTOONA, PA; BISHOP GUILFOYLE HS; (SR); Hi Hnr Roll; Hnr Roll; USAA; WWAHSS; Emplmnt; Voc Ind Clb Am; Wdwrkg Clb; CR (P, S, T); High Honors in Cabinet Making / Finished Carpentry and Building Construction Technology and Math; Cabinet Making/ Mill Working; Carpentry, Own Business; Pennsylvania College of Technology

HOOVER, RODNEY; LITITZ, PA; WARWICK HS; (SR); Hi Hnr Roll; Sci Fairs; Peer Tut/Med; DARE; Emplmnt; P to P St Amb Prg; Tchrs Aide; Sccr; Microsoft Certified; People to People Student Ambassador; Judge (Pre-Law); Computer Science; Lebanon Valley College

HOPSON, TARA M; UPPER DARBY, PA; UPPER DARBY HS; (SR); Hi Hnr Roll; Hnr Roll; Perf Att; WWAHSS; Hosp Aide; Chrch Yth Grp; Emplmnt; Scouts; Ch Chr; Drl Tm; Track (J); Pre-Law/Government; Political Science; Eastern U

HORN, DANIEL C; PHILADELPHIA, PA; MAPLE SHADE HS; (JR); Hi Hnr Roll; Hnr Roll; DECA; Bsball (V L); Bskball (V L); Computer Sciences; Stockton U; Penn State

HORST, BRADLEY T; LANCASTER, PA; MANHEIM TWP HS; (SR); Hi Hnr Roll; Hnr Roll; Kwnis Aw; WWAHSS; Yth Ldrshp Prog; Comm Volntr; Spec Olymp Vol; Chrch Yth Grp; Drma Clb; Emplmnt; Key Club; Acpl Chr; Bnd; Chr; Ch Chr; County Band; County Chorus; Political Science; Russian; Temple U

HORST, ERIC; LITITZ, PA; WARWICK HS; (FR); Hi Hnr Roll; Pres Ac Ftns Aw; St of Mnth; Chrch Yth Grp; Drma Clb; SP/M/VS; Cr Ctry (J); Track (J); Sch Ppr (R); Mock Trial Team; Political Science; Law

HORVATH, SHEREE; HUNLOCK CREEK, PA; LAKE LEHMAN JR/SR HS; (JR); Hi Hnr Roll; Hnr Roll; MVP; Nat Hon Sy; WWAHSS; Yth Ldrshp Prog; Comm Volntr; Peer Tut/Med; Chrch Yth Grp; HO'Br Yth Ldrshp; Key Club; Prom Com; Bskball (V L); Ftball (V L); Sftball (V L); Vllyball (V L); National Honor Society; Key Club Member, Peer Helpers; Anesthesiology; Chemical Engineering; Villanova U; Bucknell U

HOSEY, NYTARA C; FARRELL, PA; FARRELL HS; (JR); Hnr Roll; WWAHSS; Comm Volntr; Chr; Chrldg (J); Track (V); Sch Ppr (E)

HOUSEWEART, TREVOR; BENTON, PA; COLUMBIA-MONTOUR AVTS; (FR); Hi Hnr Roll; Hnr Roll; Nat Hon Sy

HOUSLER, ELAINE; BRADFORD, PA; BRADFORD AREA SD; (MS); Hi Hnr Roll; Dnce; Chrldg (J); Vllyball; Stu Cncl

HOUSTON, AISHA; UPPER DARBY, PA; UPPER DARBY HS; (JR); Hi Hnr Roll; Hnr Roll; Otst Ac Ach Awd; Perf Att; Comm Volntr; Tchrs Aide; Dnce; Jump Rope for Heart the American Heart Association; Psychology; Bachelor's Degree in Nursing; Saint Joseph U; Temple U

HOVANEC, SHELLEY R; DRUMS, PA; HAZLETON AREA HS; (SR); Hnr Roll; WWAHSS; Red Cr Aide; Spec Olymp Vol; Chrch Yth Grp; Emplmnt; Key Club; Off Aide; SADD; Key Club President; Guidance Office Assistant; Elementary Ed; Early Childhood Dev.; Millersville U

HOWARD, JASMINE L; CLAIRTON, PA; CLAIRTON CITY SD; (SO); Hnr Roll; Sci Fairs; St of Mnth; Comm Volntr; Peer Tut/Med; Chrch Yth Grp; Drma Clb; P to P St Amb Prg; ROTC; Clr Grd; Flg Crps; Bskball (VJ L); PP Ftbl; Sftball (V); Assistant Coach of 7th & 8th Grade Basketball Teams; Participated in HIV / AID Awareness Walk; Pediatric Nursing; Child Psychologist; U of Pittsburgh; Duquesne U

HOWARD-FOLEY, CHELSEA; CAMP HILL, PA; CAMP HILL HS; (FR); Hi Hnr Roll; Peer Tut/Med; Scouts; Bnd; Jzz Bnd; Mch Bnd; Girl Scout Silver Award; Cum Laude National Latin Exam Award; English Literature; Writing; Stanford U; U of California Berkeley

HOWE, GEOFFREY; HARLEYSVILLE, PA; SOUDERTON AREA HS; (JR); Hnr Roll; Nat Hon Sy; Comm Volntr; Emplmnt; FBLA; Bsball (J); Ftball (V L); Wrstlg (V L); Engineering; Architecture

HOWELL, LAURA; NORRISTOWN, PA; METHACTON HS; (SO); Ctznshp Aw; Hnr Roll; Pres Ac Ftns Aw; WWAHSS; Comm Volntr; Chrldg (V); College; Ursinus College

HOWELL, MISHA; CLARKS SUMMIT, PA; ABINGTON HEIGHTS HS; (JR); Hnr Roll; WWAHSS; Chess; P to P St Amb Prg; Tech Clb; 2003 National Russian Essay - Contest Silver Medal Winner; 2004 National Russian Essay Contest - Bronze Medal Winner; German Major; Education Minor; New York U; East Stroudsburg U of Pennsylvania

HOWELL, MORGAN S; HARRISBURG, PA; CTRL DAUPHIN EAST HS; (FR); Hnr Roll; Comm Volntr; FBLA; Runway Modeling; Psychology; Fashion Design

HOWLEY, MARYBETH; HONEY BROOK, PA; TWIN VALLEY HS; (MS); Ctznshp Aw; Hnr Roll; MVP; Pres Ac Ftns Aw; ArtClub; Chrch Yth Grp; DARE; Chrldg (V); Track (V); Principal's Advisory Club; To Do Something in PR; Arizona State College; Washington State College

HOYT, TRISHA C; ERIE, PA; FAIRVIEW HS; (SR); Hi Hnr Roll; Hnr Roll; Nat Hon Sy; WWAHSS; Chrch Yth Grp; Emplmnt; Tchrs Aide; Bnd; Ch Chr; Cr Ctry (JCL); Track (J L); Elementary Education; U of Pittsburgh At Johnstown

HUANG, YING-HSIEN; STATE COLLEGE, PA; STATE COLLEGE AREA HS; (SR); Hnr Roll; St of Mnth; Yth Ldrshp Prog; Comm Volntr; ArtClub; Key Club; Flg Crps; Member of the Fine Art Club; Historian of the YMCA Teen Leader's Club; Molecular Biology; Arts; Penn State U

HUBBARD, NINA; PINE GROVE, PA; PINE GROVE AREA SD; (FR); Hi Hnr Roll; Hnr Roll; Otst Ac Ach Awd; ArtClub; Cmptr Clb; French Clb; 1st Place Winner in the PP&L Art Contest / Student of the Week; 1st Place Winner in the "Peace Poster" Art Contest

HUDGINS, ASHLEY; DALLAS, PA; LAKE LEHMAN SD; (SR); Hnr Roll; Mus Clb; Chr; Yrbk (R); Pharmacy; Alvernia

HUDOCK, ALLISON L; DRUMS, PA; HAZLETON AREA HS; (SR); F Lan Hn Soc; Nat Hon Sy; USAA; WWAHSS; Comm Volntr; Hosp Aide; Chrch Yth Grp; Emplmnt; Key Club; SADD; Nursing; Spanish; Bloomsburg U; College Misericordia

HUET, ALISON; NEW KENSINGTON, PA; KISKI AREA HS; (JR); Hi Hnr Roll; Nat Hon Sy; Sci Fairs; Sci/Math Olympn; WWAHSS; Comm Volntr; Peer Tut/Med; Key Club; Off Aide; SADD; Spanish Clb; Acpl Chr; Vice President of National Honor Society; Treasurer of Key Club; Pharmacy

HUFF, RACHEL; DILLSBURG, PA; NORTHERN YORK CTY HS; (JR); F Lan Hn Soc; Hi Hnr Roll; MVP; Nat Hon Sy; WWAHSS; Comm Volntr; Hab For Humty Volntr; Spec Olymp Vol; DARE; Key Club; Mod UN; Prom Com; SADD; Sccr (V); Swmg (V); Tennis (V); Cl Off (S); Yrbk (E, R); Key Club-President; Liberal Arts; Business

HUGHES, CHRISTINA; PITTSTON, PA; PITTSON AREA SD; (FR); Hnr Roll; Veterinarian; Cardiologist-Radiologist; King's College

HUGHES, ROBIN; TRANSFER, PA; REYNOLDS JR/SR HS; (FR); Hi Hnr Roll; Otst Ac Ach Awd; St of Mnth; WWAHSS; Comm Volntr; Peer Tut/Med; Chess; Chrch Yth Grp; DARE; Key Club; Scouts; SADD; Bnd; Jzz Bnd; Mch Bnd; Cyclg; Boy Scout & Order of Arrow; Youth Group & Bible Study Leader; Design Engineer; Pilot; Air Force Academy; Florida State U

HUGO, SAMANTHA L; WALNUTPORT, PA; NORTHAMPTON AREA SR HS; (SO); 4H Awd; Hi Hnr Roll; Hnr Roll; Comm Volntr; Peer Tut/Med; 4-H; Chrch Yth Grp; Dbte Team; FBLA; Outdrs Clb; Spanish Clb; Ski Club

HUILKER, SHAWN; LOCK HAVEN, PA; KEYSTONE CTRL AVTS; (SO); Hnr Roll; Perf Att; Scouts; Bskball (J); Honor Cadet; Tender Foot in Boy Scouts; Computer Programming; Computer Graphics/Web Design; Pennsylvania School of Technology in Williamsport; Penn State U

HULL, MICHAEL E; WATERFORD, PA; FT LEBOEUF HS; (SO); Hi Hnr Roll; Otst Ac Ach Awd; Pres Ac Ftns Aw; Comm Volntr; Chrch Yth Grp; Jzz Bnd; Bsball (J); Ftball (V); Wrstlg (V); Engineer

HUMMEL, LINDSEY K; ROBESONIA, PA; CONRAD WEISER HS; (JR); 4H Awd; Ctznshp Aw; Hi Hnr Roll; St of Mnth; Peer Tut/Med; 4-H; ArtClub; Jr Cls League; Key Club; Prom Com; Chr; SP/M/VS; Chrldg (V L); Arts-Fashion Merchandising / Design; Communications; Albright College

HUMPHREYS, ROBERT M; HARRISBURG, PA; CTRL DAUPHIN SD HS; (JR); Hi Hnr Roll; Hnr Roll; Nat Hon Sy; WWAHSS; Comm Volntr; Chrch Yth Grp; Emplmnt; Scouts; Bsball (J); Ftball (V L); Wrstlg (J L); Accounting; Sports Management; IND

HUNCHUCK, MICHELLE; UNIONTOWN, PA; LAUREL HIGHLANDS SD; (FR); Hi Hnr Roll; WWAHSS; Chrch Yth Grp; Mus Clb; Photog; SADD; Spanish Clb; Bnd; Chr; Mch Bnd; Skiing; Vllyball (VJ); Yrbk (P); Medicine; Sports Medicine; California U of PA

HUNDLEY, TYISHA; PHILADELPHIA, PA; MASTERY CHARTER HS; (FR); Ctznshp Aw; Hnr Roll; Otst Ac Ach Awd; Perf Att; St of Mnth; Comm Volntr; Chrch Yth Grp; Ch Chr; Drl Tm; Volunteer Work; Pediatrician; Lawyer; Temple U; Rutgers U

HUNSBERGER, CHRISTEN; HATBORO, PA; UPPER MORELAND HS; (JR); Hnr Roll; Perf Att; Pres Ac Ftns Aw; Comm Volntr; Voc Ind Clb Am; Chrldg (V L); Cl Off (V); Sch Ppr (R); Project 540; Volunteer At Community Summer Camp; Business

HUNT, LAUREN M; WASHINGTON, PA; WASHINGTON HS; (JR); All Am Sch; Hi Hnr Roll; Nat Hon Sy; Sci Fairs; USAA; WWAHSS; Yth Ldrshp Prog; Hosp Aide; Key Club; Lttrmn Clb; SADD; Dnce; Tennis (V L); Yrbk (R); Member of Senior Company of the Pittsburgh Youth Ballet Co.; Pharmacy; Business; Davidson College; Wake Forest

HUNTER, CALE; WARREN, PA; WARREN AREA HS; (SO); Hnr Roll; DARE; Bskball (J); Tennis (L); Stu Cncl (R); Likes to Dance; Altar Server At Church; Architecture; Theology; United States Coast Guard Academy; U of Pittsburgh

HUSEMAN, REBECCA M; WOMELSDORF, PA; CONRAD WEISER HS; (FR); Hi Hnr Roll; Otst Ac Ach Awd; St of Mnth; WWAHSS; Comm Volntr; Chrch Yth Grp; Emplmnt; Jr Cls League; Key Club; Track (V); Stu Cncl (R); Pharmacologist; Psychologist

HUSTED, MORGAN; LANCASTER, PA; MANHEIM TWP HS; (FR); Hnr Roll; Chrch Yth Grp; Drma Clb; Key Club; Stg Cre; Track (J); Nutritionist / Dietician; Actress; New York U

HUTCHISON, AMY; NEW CASTLE, PA; NESHANNOCK HS; (SR); Hnr Roll; WWAHSS; Lib Aide; Photog; Prom Com; Bnd; Chr; Mch Bnd; Pep Bnd; Vllyball (VJ L); Lt. in Marching Band; Music Education; Secondary Education; Geneva College

HUTH, ASHLEY; DAUPHIN, PA; CTRL DAUPHIN HS; (FR); Hnr Roll; Nat Hon Sy; St of Mnth; Comm Volntr; Peer Tut/Med; Spec Olymp Vol; Mth Clb/Tm; P to P St Amb Prg; Scouts; Spanish Clb; Mch Bnd; Vllyball (J); Stu Cncl (R); National Junior Honor Society / Girl Scouts; Junior Olympic Volleyball / Bronze & Silver; Doctor- Work with Pre-Mature Babies; Dentistry; UCLA; Penn State U

HUYNH, RICKY; PHILADELPHIA, PA; CENTRAL HS; (JR); Hnr Roll; Chrch Yth Grp; Piano; Student Environmental Action Society; Psychology; Astronomy; U of Pennsylvania; Penn State U

HWANG, JESSIE; NORRISTOWN, PA; MERION MERCY AC; (JR); Duke TS; F Lan Hn Soc; Hnr Roll; Nat Hon Sy; Perf Att; Comm Volntr; Peer Tut/ Med; Biology Clb; Emplmnt; Fr of Library; Mth Clb/Tm; Sci Clb; Orch; Cr Ctry (J); Swmg (J); Yrbk (R); Johns Hopkins Talent Search; Business; Harvard U; Yale U

IGOU, BROOKE; NEW PARIS, PA; CHESTNUT RIDGE HS; (FR); Hnr Roll; MVP; Otst Ac Ach Awd; WWAHSS; Comm Volntr; Chrch Yth Grp; Emplmnt; FBLA; SADD; Tchrs Aide; Chr; Skiing (J); Vllyball (V L); MVP - Volleyball; Registered Nurse; Medical Field; Arizona State; Fairmont U

IHNAT, GARY; YATESVILLE, PA; PITTSTON AREA; (JR); Hi Hnr Roll; Nat Hon Sy; Otst Ac Ach Awd; Sci/Math Olympn; WWAHSS; Peer Tut/Med; Chess; Mth Clb/Tm; Bskball (V L); Tennis (V CL)

IKELER, KATHRYN S; BERWYN, PA; CONESTOGA HS; (SO); Hi Hnr Roll; WWAHSS; Chrch Yth Grp; Key Club; Human Rights Club / 31st Annual Chesty County Art Exhibition for HS Students - Work Selected; Art and Piano Classes / Recreational Soccer; Studio Art; English; U of Pennsylvania; Pennsylvania Academy of the Fine Arts

IM, JESSICA; COLLEGEVILLE, PA; METHACTON HS; (SO); Hnr Roll; Comm Volntr; Peer Tut/Med; Biology Clb; Emplmnt; Key Club; SADD; Clr Grd; Golf (J); Sccr (J); Cl Off (S); Stu Cncl (R); Peer Connection; Dermatologist; United Nations Representative; Stanford U; Johns Hopkins U

IMADOJEMU, TOHAN P; HARRISBURG, PA; CTRL DAUPHIN HS; (SO); Hnr Roll; Perf Att; Emplmnt; FCCLA; Real Estate; Advertising; Harvard U; Penn State U

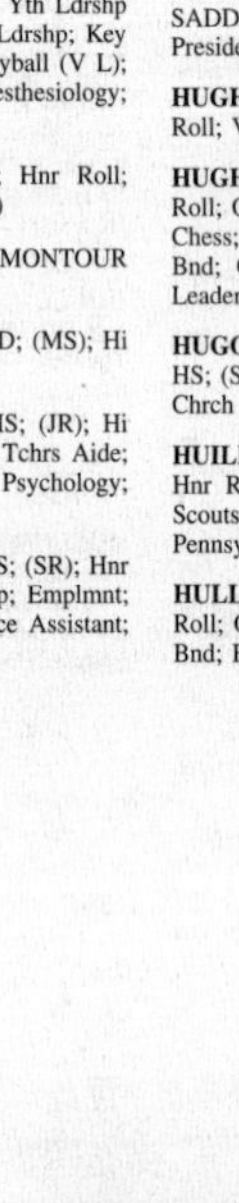

Horn, Daniel C
Maple Shade HS
Philadelphia, PA

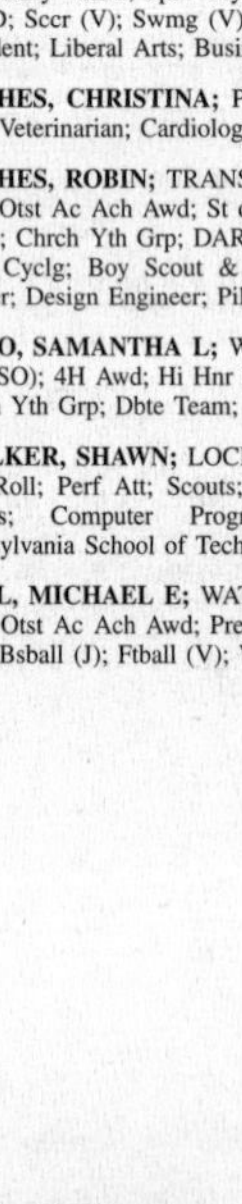

Hoover, Andrew P
Bishop Guilfoyle HS
Altoona, PA

National
Honor Roll
Spring 2005

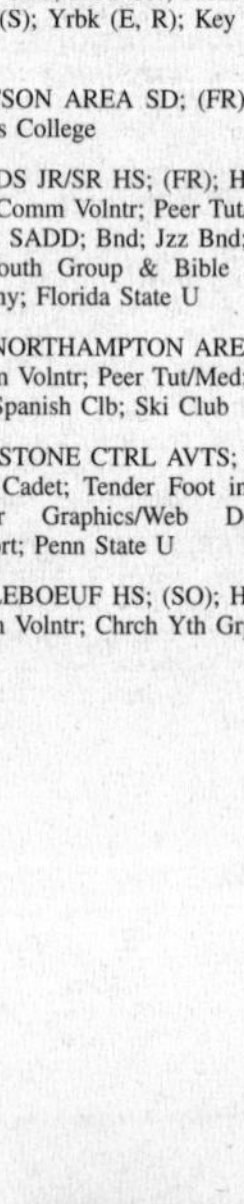

Holmes, Danni L
Huntingdon Area HS
Huntingdon, PA

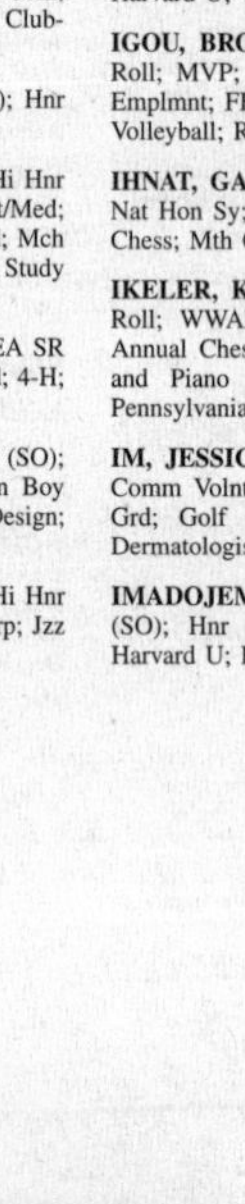

Howell, Laura
Methacton HS
Norristown, PA

IMPINK, GREG; GREENSBURG, PA; GREATER LATROBE HS; (JR); F Lan Hn Soc; Hi Hnr Roll; Jr Rot; Nat Hon Sy; Perf Att; St of Mnth; Hosp Aide; Chrch Yth Grp; Mus Clb; Scouts; French Clb; Bnd; Jzz Bnd; Mch Bnd; Orch; Tri-M Music Honor Society; Eagle Scout

INDERBITZEN, SEAN; MECHANICSBURG, PA; MECHANICSBURG AREA SR HS; (FR); Hnr Roll; Nat Hon Sy; WWAHSS; Chrch Yth Grp; Emplmnt; Key Club; Bnd; Chr; Ch Chr; Wt Lftg (J); Wrstlg (J); Ministry / Youth Pastor; Messiah College

INGRAM, ASHLEY N; DENVER, PA; COCALICO HS; (SR); Hnr Roll; Emplmnt; FBLA; Mus Clb; Photog; Bnd; Chr; Mch Bnd; Track Manager; Psychology; Penn State U

INMAN, JESSICA D; NEW BRIGHTON, PA; FREEDOM AREA HS; (JR); Hi Hnr Roll; Nat Hon Sy; Perf Att; St of Mnth; WWAHSS; Yth Ldrshp Prog; Comm Volntr; Chrch Yth Grp; Drma Clb; Lttrmn Clb; Off Aide; Prom Com; SADD; Vsity Clb; Spanish Clb; Dnce; Drl Tm; SP/M/VS; Bskball (J L); PP Ftbl (V); Vllyball (V L); High Scores for Volleyball; Rookie of the Year (Drill Team); Secondary Teaching; Math; Slippery Rock U; Westminster College

IWASKIW, JOANNA; NEWTOWN, PA; COUNCIL ROCK HS NORTH; (FR); F Lan Hn Soc; Hnr Roll; Comm Volntr; Spec Olymp Vol; Chrch Yth Grp; German Clb; Bnd; Mch Bnd; Sftball (J); Member of Symphonic Band Flutist; In Bucks County PA HS Music Festival 2005; Teaching/Education; Architecture; Boston U; Duke U

JACKOWSKI, AMANDA; SPRING CITY, PA; OWEN J ROBERTS HS; (JR); Hi Hnr Roll; Hnr Roll; Sci Fairs; Comm Volntr; Peer Tut/Med; Spec Olymp Vol; Chrch Yth Grp; DECA; Drma Clb; Key Club; Photog; Prom Com; Scouts; French Clb; SP/M/VS; Fld Hky (J); Lcrsse (J); PP Ftbl (J); Cl Off (T); Stu Cncl (R); Yrbk (P); Pre Law; Business Management; Ursinus College; Gettysburg College

JACKSON, AMANDA L; HARRISBURG, PA; CTRL DAUPHIN HS; (MS); Hnr Roll; Nat Hon Sy; Comm Volntr; Peer Tut/Med; Chrch Yth Grp; Scouts; Bnd; Chr; Bskball; Sch Ppr (E, R); County Choir; Honors Choir; Journalism; Bachelor's Degree; Penn State U; Ithaca College

JACKSON, BRADLEY S; WARRINGTON, PA; MIDDLE BUCKS INST TECH; (JR); Sci Fairs; Yth Ldrshp Prog; Peer Tut/Med; Chrch Yth Grp; Emplmnt; Stg Cre; Paper Route - for 5 Years; Played Township Basketball - 6 Yrs / Ministry Leadership Team for Church Youth Group; Information Technology; Computer Science; Penn College of Technology

JACKSON, CRYSTAL; PHILADELPHIA, PA; BODINE HS; (JR); Nat Hon Sy; WWAHSS; Hosp Aide; Chess; Vsity Clb; Dnce; Chrldg (V); Adv Cncl (R); Stu Cncl (R); Yrbk (R); Business; Psychology; Penn State; Duke U

JACKSON, JASMINE; MOUNT PLEASANT, PA; MT PLEASANT AREA JR/SR HS; (FR); Hi Hnr Roll; Hnr Roll; WWAHSS; Bnd; Jzz Bnd; Chrldg (V); Track (V)

JACOBS, BRETT; DOUGLASSVILLE, PA; DANIEL BOONE HS; (JR); Hi Hnr Roll; Hnr Roll; Nat Hon Sy; Perf Att; Pres Ac Ftns Aw; Pres Sch; WWAHSS; Hab For Humty Volntr; Hosp Aide; Peer Tut/Med; FBLA; Key Club; Prom Com; Sccr (V L); Track (V L); Treasurer of National Honor Society; Treasurer of FBLA / Editor of Key Club; Sport Management; Accounting; York College of Pennsylvania

JACOBS, BRITTANY; COLVER, PA; CTRL CAMBRIA HS; (JR); Hi Hnr Roll; Hnr Roll; Nat Hon Sy; Otst Ac Ach Awd; Perf Att; WWAHSS; Comm Volntr; Chrch Yth Grp; Prom Com; PP Ftbl; Sccr (J); Track (V); Vice President of Church Youth Group; Involved in Colver Sportsman's Club BB-Gun League; Nursing

JACOBS, CHRIS; DILLSBURG, PA; NORTHERN HS; (FR); Hi Hnr Roll; Otst Ac Ach Awd; St of Mnth; WWAHSS; Comm Volntr; Chrch Yth Grp; Key Club; Bnd; Jzz Bnd; Mch Bnd; Pep Bnd; Envirothon; Pennsylvania & Appalachian Audubon Societies; Ornithology; Botany, Biology; Messiah College; Cornell U

JACOBS, MARISSA; DILLSBURG, PA; NORTHERN YORK HS; (FR); Ctznshp Aw; Hi Hnr Roll; Hnr Roll; Comm Volntr; Spec Olymp Vol; Chrch Yth Grp; DARE; Key Club; Dnce; Teaching; Messiah College

JACOBY, ANN; HUMMELSTOWN, PA; HERSHEY HS; (FR); Hi Hnr Roll; Hnr Roll; Otst Ac Ach Awd; Perf Att; Pres Ac Ftns Aw; Comm Volntr; Chrch Yth Grp; Emplmnt; SADD; French Clb; Dnce; SP/M/VS; Stg Cre; Fld Hky (J); GAA (J); Piano Instruction X 7 Years; American Studies; The Arts; The College of William and Mary; Columbia U in the City of New York

JACOBY, JONATHAN; DRUMS, PA; HAZLETON AREA HS; (JR); Hnr Roll; Otst Ac Ach Awd; Pres Ac Ftns Aw; Comm Volntr; Sccr (L); Stu Cncl (V); Outstanding Achievement in School; Marine Biology; Zoology; Kutztown U; Millersville U

JACOBY, TAMMY J; APOLLO, PA; APOLLO-RIDGE SD; (JR); Hnr Roll; Nat Hon Sy; Bnd; Mch Bnd; Zoology

JAFRI, SYEDA S; DOWNINGTOWN, PA; COATESVILLE AREA SR HS; (JR); Red Cr Aide; Key Club; Skiing (V); Medicine; Surgery

JAGOTA, MEHAR; MALVERN, PA; GREAT VALLEY HS; (JR); Hi Hnr Roll; Nat Hon Sy; Nat Mrt Semif; Otst Ac Ach Awd; Pres Ac Ftns Aw; Pres Sch; Sci/Math Olympn; St of Mnth; WWAHSS; Comm Volntr; Jr Cls League; Key Club; Prom Com; Quiz Bowl; Schol Bwl; Sci Clb; Svce Clb; Latin Clb; Cr Ctry (J); Tennis (V L); Cl Off (S); Stu Cncl (S); Sch Ppr (E); Ecology Club Vice-President; Indoor Soccer & Dodge Ball Club; Business; Law; Stanford U; Princeton U

JAMES, ALBERTA J; PHILADELPHIA, PA; OVERBROOK HS; (SO); Hi Hnr Roll; Hnr Roll; WWAHSS; Comm Volntr; Peer Tut/Med; Drma Clb; Stu Cncl (R); Acting Classes at Walnut Theatre; Tutoring / Sisterhood; Actress / Writer / Songstress; Director / Song Writer; U of Penn; Drexel U

JAMES, GEMISE C; HARRISBURG, PA; CTRL DAUPHIN EAST HS; (SR); WWAHSS; FBLA; Key Club; Tennis (J); Lead Singer of Junior National Parang Competition; Business Administration-Management; Film-Directing; Pennsylvania State U-Harrisburg; Atlanta State U

JAMES, IVORY; CLAIRTON, PA; CLAIRTON CITY SD; (SO); Hi Hnr Roll; Ch Chr; Dnce; Bskball (V); Degree in Medicine; Entertainment Marketing; U of Southern California

JAMISON, LACEY; FRANKLIN, PA; VENANGO CATHOLIC HS; (JR); Hi Hnr Roll; Hnr Roll; WWAHSS; Yth Ldrshp Prog; Comm Volntr; Hosp Aide; Chrch Yth Grp; DARE; Emplmnt; Prom Com; Scouts; Chrldg (V); Cl Off (T); Yrbk (P); Vol. Firefighter Jr.; Emergency Medical Tech.; Nursing; Gannon

JANCUK, VERONICA; MECHANICSBURG, PA; CUMBERLAND VALLEY; (JR); Hnr Roll; Otst Ac Ach Awd; Hosp Aide; Emplmnt; Key Club; Nursing (RN); BSN; Penn State Hamsburg; Hamsburg Area Community College

JANFLONE, JILLIAN; WASHINGTON, PA; WASHINGTON HS; (SO); Ctznshp Aw; DAR; Hi Hnr Roll; USAA; WWAHSS; Comm Volntr; Drma Clb; FTA; Key Club; Mod UN; Bnd; SP/M/VS; Stg Cre; Cr Ctry (V); Track (V); Lit Mag (E); Sch Ppr (E); English; Writing/Journalism; Mercyhurst; Wittenberg

JANICKI, ROBIN; MONACA, PA; CTR AREA SD; (SO); Hnr Roll; WWAHSS; CARE; Spec Olymp Vol; Chrch Yth Grp; Scouts; Clb; Clr Grd; Drl Tm; Gmnstcs (V L); PPSqd (V L); Track (J); Ski Club; Junior Tamburitzans; Meteorology; Teaching

JANSSON, KARI L; DOYLESTOWN, PA; CTRL BACKS EAST HS; (JR); Ctznshp Aw; Hi Hnr Roll; Hnr Roll; Pres Ac Ftns Aw; Pres Sch; WWAHSS; Emplmnt; Key Club; PP Ftbl (V); Sccr (V L); Employee Achievement Award; BA / MBA Business / Management; Penn State U; U of Virginia

JANUSZ, GEORGE A; PITTSBURGH, PA; BRASHEAR HS; (SO); Ctznshp Aw; Hi Hnr Roll; Nat Hon Sy; Otst Ac Ach Awd; Perf Att; Pres Sch; WWAHSS; Architect; Engineer; Duquesne U; U of Pittsburgh

JAPHET, DANIELLE; ASTON, PA; SUN VALLEY HS; (FR); Hi Hnr Roll; Hnr Roll; Yth Ldrshp Prog; Comm Volntr; Peer Tut/Med; ArtClub; Chess; Drma Clb; Mth Clb/Tm; Off Aide; Svce Clb; Bnd; Chr; SP/M/VS; Swg Chr; Chrldg (V); Dvng (V); National Jr. Honor Society; American Music Abroad Participant; Forensic Sciences; Teaching; U of Phoenix; U of Central Florida

JAWORSKI, EMILY ANN; PITTSBURGH, PA; PENN HILLS SR HS; (JR); Hi Hnr Roll; Hnr Roll; Nat Hon Sy; Otst Ac Ach Awd; USAA; WWAHSS; Comm Volntr; ArtClub; Emplmnt; Key Club; French Clb; Chrldg (VJCL); Stu Cncl; Girl Scouts-Silver Award; Just Say No Club; Art Education; Elementary Education; Pennsylvania State U; U of Pittsburgh

JEAN-LOUIS, JULIE; PHILADELPHIA, PA; CENTRAL HS; (FR); 4H Awd; Ctznshp Aw; Hi Hnr Roll; Hnr Roll; Nat Hon Sy; Otst Ac Ach Awd; Perf Att; Sci Fairs; St of Mnth; Valdctrian; Peer Tut/Med; 4-H; Chrch Yth Grp; DARE; Chr; Ch Chr; Student of the Year; Principal's Award; Social Worker; Physician; U of Pennsylvania; Howard U

JEMETZ, SARAH; EDINBORO, PA; (JR); Hnr Roll; Nat Hon Sy; Prom Com; Chrldg (V); Sccr (V); Yrbk (R, P); Business Education (Secondary Level); Health Education (Secondary Level)

JENKINS, BETH A; WAYNESBURG, PA; WEST GREENE MIDDLE SR HS; (FR); Hi Hnr Roll; USAA; WWAHSS; Chrch Yth Grp; Ntl FFA; Track (V); Biological; Agricultural; Penn State; West Virginia U

JESIKIEWICZ, JANELLE; PITTSTON, PA; PITTSTON AREA; (JR); Ctznshp Aw; Hi Hnr Roll; Nat Hon Sy; Pres Sch; Sci/Math Olympn; St of Mnth; WWAHSS; Comm Volntr; Peer Tut/Med; DARE; Key Club; Pep Squd; Prom Com; Sci Clb; Tech Clb; Foreign Clb; Cr Ctry (V CL); Sccr (V L); Track (V CL); Cl Off (S)

JOHN, MARYAM; BENSALEM, PA; BENSALEM TOWNSHIP SD; (SO); Hi Hnr Roll; Hnr Roll; St of Mnth; Comm Volntr; FBLA; Ch Chr

JOHNS, ASHLEY; FORD CITY, PA; LENAPE TECH; (JR); Hi Hnr Roll; Hnr Roll; Comm Volntr; Peer Tut/Med; Chr; Clr Grd; Stg Cre; PP Ftbl (J); Yrbk (R); Physical Therapist Assistant; Hospitality; Penn State Shenango; Penn State Dubois

JOHNS, ERIN M; MCKEESPORT, PA; SERRA CATHOLIC HS; (JR); Hi Hnr Roll; Hnr Roll; Nat Hon Sy; Sci Fairs; WWAHSS; Hosp Aide; Chrch Yth Grp; FBLA; Prom Com; Dnce; Chrldg (V); Pharmacy; Duquesne U; U of Pittsburgh

JOHNSON, AMBER; UNION CITY, PA; UNION CITY HS; (JR); Hnr Roll; Nat Hon Sy; Lttrmn Clb; Prom Com; Vsity Clb; Bskball (V L); Sftball (V L); Stu Cncl (R); National Honor Society; Business; Photography

JOHNSON, ARCHITA; PHILADELPHIA, PA; STRAWBERRY MANSION MIDDLE SR HS; (JR); Ctznshp Aw; Hnr Roll; Otst Ac Ach Awd; Perf Att; Sci Fairs; St of Mnth; Bskball (V); Sftball (V); Vllyball (V C); Bachelor's Degree; Temple U; Penn State U

JOHNSON, ASHLEY M; COATESVILLE, PA; COATESVILLE AREA SR HS; (JR); Hnr Roll; Perf Att; WWAHSS; Comm Volntr; Chrch Yth Grp; DARE; DECA; Scouts; Chr; Ch Chr; Elementary Teacher; Lawyer; Virginia State U; Lincoln U

JOHNSON, AULDWIN M; PINE FORGE, PA; PINE FORGE AC; (JR); Comm Volntr; Chrch Yth Grp; Cmptr Clb; DARE; Emplmnt; Photog; Prom Com; Quiz Bowl; Chr; Drm Mjr; Scr Kpr (V); Sch Ppr (P); Yrbk (P); Soloist Performer; Psychology; Music; Oakwood College; Andrews U

JOHNSON, BRITTENY P; CLAIRTON, PA; WILSON CHRISTIAN AC; (SO); Hnr Roll; Chrch Yth Grp; Quiz Bowl; Vllyball (J); Bible Quizzing; Science; Duquesne; Penn State

JOHNSON, CHAD; SPRINGBORO, PA; CONNEAUT VALLEY HS; (JR); Hi Hnr Roll; Ntl FFA; Physical Science; Biology; Penn State; Pittsburgh U

JOHNSON, DEREK; STOCKDALE, PA; CHARLEROI AREA HS; (SR); Hnr Roll; Sci Fairs; USAA; ArtClub; Lttrmn Clb; Track (V L); Wrstlg (V CL); Aeronautical Engineering; Shippensburg U; Penn State U

JOHNSON, HARRISON T; WARREN, PA; WARREN AREA HS; (JR); 4H Awd; Hi Hnr Roll; Jr Eng Tech; Sci/Math Olympn; Comm Volntr; 4-H; Mod UN; Quiz Bowl; Schol Bwl; Sci Clb; French Clb; Sccr (V L); Track (V L); 7th Place, State Envirothan; Bio Chemical Engineering; Mechanical Engineering

JOHNSON, JANELL N; CHESTER, PA; CHESTER HS; (SR); Ctznshp Aw; Hnr Roll; WWAHSS; Key Club; Elementary Education; Temple U

JOHNSON, JOHN M; PHILADELPHIA, PA; NORRIS S BARRATT MS; MS; Hnr Roll; MVP; Comm Volntr; Spec Olymp Vol; Chrch Yth Grp; DARE; Tchrs Aide; Bskball (V); Cl Off (R); Syracuse U; Villanova U

JOHNSON, KATELYN A; SAYLORSBURG, PA; PLEASANT VALLEY HS; (SO); Hi Hnr Roll; WWAHSS; Comm Volntr; Spec Olymp Vol; Chrch Yth Grp; Key Club; Scouts; Bnd; Dnce; Mch Bnd; SP/M/VS; Leo Club President; Tap Dancer; Meteorology; Biotechnology; Pennsylvania State U; Cornell U, Princeton U

JOHNSON, KELLIE; WATERFORD, PA; FORT LEBOEUF SD; (FR); Hnr Roll; Comm Volntr; Chess; DARE; Certified in First Aid/CPR; Babysitting Certification; Accounting; Psychiatry; Gannon U; Mercyhurst College

JOHNSON, KYLLE; WARREN, PA; WARREN AREA HS; (JR); Hi Hnr Roll; Hnr Roll; Perf Att; WWAHSS; AL Aux Boys; Prom Com; Spanish Clb; Bsball (VJ); Ftball (J); Stu Cncl (R); Ski Club; History Club; Medical Scientist; Biologist; West Chester U of Pennsylvania; U of West Virginia

JOHNSON, LAURA J; WEST CHESTER, PA; BISHOP SHANAHAN HS; (FR); Hnr Roll; Comm Volntr; ArtClub; Mus Clb; Bnd; Chr; Dnce; SP/M/VS; Archdiocesan Piano Competition-2nd Place; Fine Arts Award-8th Grade; Music-Art / Spanish; Architect; Villanova U; U of Pennsylvania

JOHNSON, MONICA; BRADFORD, PA; BRADFORD AREA HS; (SO); Hnr Roll; Hosp Aide; Ice Sktg (J); Vllyball (J); Wt Lftg (J); Meteorologist; U of Minnesota

JOHNSON, ROBIN; WEST CHESTER, PA; UNIONVILLE HS; (SR); F Lan Hn Soc; Hi Hnr Roll; Nat Hon Sy; WWAHSS; Comm Volntr; Peer Tut/Med; P to P St Amb Prg; Scouts; Dnce; Engineering; International Business

JOHNSON, ZARA B; COVINGTON, PA; NORTH PENN HS; (SO); Hnr Roll; Yth Ldrshp Prog; Spec Olymp Vol; Key Club; Photog; Chrldg (V); All Star Cheerleading; Had an Article About Me in Newspaper for Special Olympics; Criminal Justice; Health; Penn State U; Texas A & M

JONES, BRENDA N; LATROBE, PA; EASTERN WESTMORELAND CTC; (JR); All Am Sch; Hi Hnr Roll; Nat Ldrshp Svc; Otst Ac Ach Awd; USAA; Scouts; National Technical Honor Society; General Business Management; Multimedia Technology; Westmoreland County Community College; Pitt At Greensburg

JONES, CARLY R; NAZARETH, PA; NAZARETH HS; (SR); Hi Hnr Roll; Hnr Roll; MVP; Perf Att; WWAHSS; Chrch Yth Grp; Pep Squd; Photog; SADD; Chrldg (V CL); Track (V); Sch Ppr (P); Had Photography in Galleries in Town; Photography; Graphic Design; Temple U

Johnson, Derek
Charleroi Area HS
Stockdale, PA

Johnson, Britteny P
Wilson Christian AC
Clairton, PA

Japhet, Danielle
Sun Valley HS
Aston, PA

Johnson, Ashley M
Coatesville Area SR HS
Coatesville, PA

Johnson, John M
Norris S Barratt MS
Philadelphia, PA

JONES, JOSHUA; AVONDALE, PA; AVON GROVE HS; (JR) Hi Hnr Roll; Hnr Roll; MVP; Nat Mrt LOC; Yth Ldrshp Prog; Comm Volntr; Peer Tut/Med; Chrch Yth Grp; Key Club; Off Aide; Vsity Clb; Wdwrkg Clb; Bsball (J); Bskball (V, L); Scr Kpr; Wt Lftg; Commentator / Lector For Four Years At Assumption Of The Blessed Virgin Mary Church; Altar Server For Five Years At Assumption Of The Blessed Virgin Mary Church; Master's in Business Administration; Master's in Engineering; University of Delaware; University of Pennsylvania

JONES, KYLE; PITTSFIELD, PA; YOUNGSVILLE MIDDLE SR HS; (JR); Hnr Roll; Perf Att; Pres Ac Ftns Aw; Sci Fairs; 4-H; DARE; Emplmnt; Scouts; Clb; Bnd; Jzz Bnd; Stg Cre; Cr Ctry (VCL); Track (VL); 4th in State Cross Country, 2004; Mechanical Engineering; Sports Medicine; U of Louisville, Kentucky; Otterbein College

JONES, LATASHA; PHOENIXVILLE, PA; RENAISSANCE AC; (JR); Hnr Roll; Perf Att; WWAHSS; Hosp Aide; Key Club; Chr; Ch Chr; Clr Grd; Bskball (VJ); Vllyball (V); Registered Nurse; Nurse; U of North Carolina; Cabrini College

JONES, PAMELA J; CLARKSBURG, PA; APOLLO-RIDGE SD; (SO); Hnr Roll; Chrch Yth Grp; French Clb; Bnd; Mch Bnd; Stg Cre; Web Designer; Indiana U of Pennsylvania

JONES, SAKURA R; BENSALEM, PA; BENSALEM HS; (JR); Hnr Roll; Chrch Yth Grp; Emplmnt; Marine Biology; Zoology; St Joseph's U; Lycoming College

JONES, SETH M; CLARION, PA; CLARION AREA JR/SR HS; (SO); Hi Hnr Roll; Hnr Roll; Otst Ac Ach Awd; Perf Att; Pres Ac Ftns Aw; ArtClub; Chess; FBLA; Chr; Bskball (J); Ftball (J); Golf (V); Wt Lftg (J); Placed in Multiple Professional Art Shows; Won Chess Tournament Among Schools; Business / Accounting; U of North Carolina; U of Pittsburgh

JONES, ZACH; FRIENDSVILLE, PA; ELK LAKE HS; (SO); 4H Awd; Hi Hnr Roll; Hnr Roll; Nat Hon Sy; Pres Ac Ftns aw; WWAHSS; Comm Volntr; 4-H; Emplmnt; Key Club; Bnd; Skiing (V); Sccr (L); Stu Cncl (V); Yrbk (R); National Honor Society; Honor Roll; Syracuse U; Penn State U

JOSTAD, DANIELLE R; CARMICHAELS, PA; CARMICHAELS AREA JR/SR HS; (FR); DAR; Hnr Roll; Nat Hon Sy; WWAHSS; Comm Volntr; AL Aux Girls; Chrch Yth Grp; DARE; Dbte Team; Emplmnt; Scouts; Bnd; Chr; Dnce; Mch Bnd; Bskball (J); Skiing (J); Sftball (J); Stu Cncl (V); Upward Bound; Zoology; Alabama State

JOYCE, CHRISTOPHER; EAST STROUDSBURG, PA; EAST STROUDSBURG HS SOUTH; (SO); Hi Hnr Roll; Hnr Roll; Perf Att; St of Mnth; WWAHSS; Comm Volntr; Hab For Humty Volntr; ArtClub; Photog; Chr; Ch Chr; Stg Cre; Lit Mag (R); Artwork Appeared in 360 Degrees Art Show; Member of Wooddale UM Church Youth Group; Bachelor of Fine Arts; Forensic Psychology; Waynesburg College; Philadelphia U of Fine Arts

JOYCE, DANIEL A; PHOENIXVILLE, PA; ARCHBISHOP CARROLL HS; (SO); Hnr Roll; Pres Ac Ftns Aw; Sci Fairs; Yth Ldrshp Prog; Comm Volntr; DARE; Scouts; Foreign Clb; Bskball (V); Lcrsse (V); Best Buddies; School Student Ambassador; Sports; Engineering; Drexel U; U of Notre Dame

JULIANO, KELSEY L; SCHWENKSVILLE, PA; PERKIOMEN VALLEY HS; (SO); Ctznshp Aw; Hi Hnr Roll; Hnr Roll; Nat Hon Sy; Otst Ac Ach Awd; Sci Fairs; Comm Volntr; Peer Tut/Med; DARE; Emplmnt; Photog; Spanish Clb; Dnce; Bskball (J); Yrbk (P); Outstanding Achievement in Science / Social Studies; Nursing; Photography; U of Pittsburgh; Temple U

JUNDA, ANASTASIA; DANIELSVILLE, PA; BETHLEHEM CATHOLIC HS; (FR); Hnr Roll; Drma Clb; Key Club; NtlFrnscLg; P to P St Amb Prg; SP/M/VS; CR; Quilting; Raising Dairy and Fiber Goats; International Law; Theatre / Design; Georgetown University; Fashion Institute of Technology NY

JUYA, MORSALA; STROUDSBURG, PA; STROUDSBURG HS; (JR); Hnr Roll; Nat Hon Sy; Otst Ac Ach Awd; St of Mnth; WWAHSS; Comm Volntr; Hosp Aide; Peer Tut/Med; Jr Ach; Key Club; Sci Clb; Vsity Clb; Russian Clb; Swmg (V); Vllyball (V); Volunteer At the Hospital; Volunteer At the Elementary School; Pediatrician; East Stroudsburg U

KACH, JEN; BETHLEHEM, PA; BETHLEHEM CATHOLIC HS; (FR); Hi Hnr Roll; Perf Att; WWAHSS; Comm Volntr; Chrch Yth Grp; Key Club; Spanish Clb; Chr; SP/M/VS; Ranked First in Class; Journalism; Disney Imaginer; Penn State; College of William & Mary

KACH, SARAH; BETHLEHEM, PA; BETHLEHEM CATHOLIC HS; (JR); Hi Hnr Roll; Perf Att; WWAHSS; Comm Volntr; Chrch Yth Grp; Drma Clb; Key Club; Spanish Clb; Chr; SP/M/VS; Ranked 4th in Class; Biology Master's Degree; Journalism; Penn State U

KADEL, JENN; DOYLESTOWN, PA; (JR); F Lan Hn Soc; Hi Hnr Roll; Hnr Roll; Otst Ac Ach Awd; Sci Fairs; Comm Volntr; Emplmnt; Key Club; Cr Ctry (V CL); Track (V CL); Stu Cncl; High & Distinguished Honor Roll; Volunteer At Lakeview Retirement Home; Sports Medicine; Law; Haverford College; U of Delaware

KADUKE, TODD; PITTSBURGH, PA; TAYLOR ALLDERDICE HS; (SO); Ctznshp Aw; Hi Hnr Roll; Hnr Roll; Nat Hon Sy; Nat Sci Aw; Otst Ac Ach Awd; Perf Att; Comm Volntr; Chrch Yth Grp; DARE; Emplmnt; Bnd; Ftball (V); Sccr (V, L); Sftball (V L); Presidential Award of Excellence; Engineering; Law; Stanford; Carnegie Mellon U

KAING, JENNY; PHOENIXVILLE, PA; SPRING FORD SR HS; (SR); Hnr Roll; Pres Ac Ftns Aw; Peer Tut/Med; DECA; Emplmnt; Key Club; Lib Aide; Asian Clb; Interior Design; Philadelphia U

KAISER, JULIA; ELKINS PARK, PA; ABINGTON SR HS; (JR); Hnr Roll; Nat Hon Sy; Comm Volntr; ArtClub; Key Club; CR (R); Sch Ppr (R); Yrbk (P); Congressional Award Recipient; National Old Navy T-Shirt Design Contest Winner; Commercial/Advertising Art; Design/Visual Communications; U of Delaware; U of Maryland, Baltimore County

KALINA, JACQUELYN L; BRIDGEVILLE, PA; SOUTH FAYETTE TOWNSHIP HS; (JR); Hi Hnr Roll; MVP; Nat Hon Sy; Nat Mrt LOC; Otst Ac Ach Awd; Perf Att; Pres Sch; St of Mnth; WWAHSS; Comm Volntr; Chrch Yth Grp; Lttrmn Clb; Bskball (V CL); Skiing (V); Vllyball (V CL); Sch Ppr (R); Yrbk (R); Medicine; Pharmacy; Penn State; John Carroll

KALMBACH, KATELYN E; BELLEFONTE, PA; GRACE PREP HS; (JR); 4H Awd; DAR; Hi Hnr Roll; MVP; Nat Hon Sy; Nat Ldrshp Svc; Nat Mrt LOC; Otst Ac Ach Awd; Pres Ac Ftns Aw; Sci Fairs; USAA; WWAHSS; Yth Ldrshp Prog; Peer Tut/Med; Spec Olymp Vol; 4-H; Chrch Yth Grp; Emplmnt; Prom Com; Tchrs Aide; Chr; SP/M/VS; Stg Cre; Bskball (VJL); Sccr (VJL); Track (V J); Cl Off (P, V); Stu Cncl (V, S); Yrbk; Participant in Miss Teen of PA Pageant, Christmas Banquet Queen; Profiler with the FBI, Asked to Participate in Outstanding Young Women; Psychology; Spanish; Lock Haven U

KALTENBAUGH, CORY A; BOSWELL, PA; NORTH STAR SD; (MS); Ctznshp Aw; Hnr Roll; Comm Volntr; Peer Tut/Med; Bsball; Ftball; Wrstlg

KAMANU II, DANIEL I; READING, PA; READING HS; (SR); Hnr Roll; Nat Hon Sy; Otst Ac Ach Awd; Perf Att; St of Mnth; Yth Ldrshp Prog; Peer Tut/Med; Kwanza Clb; Mus Clb; Prom Com; Spanish Clb; Acpl Chr; Chr; Swg Chr; CR (R); Peer Mediator; Gospel Choir; Pre-Med; Nursing; Albright College; Alvernia College

KAMBAJA, JOANN; UPPER DARBY, PA; UPPER DARBY HS; (SR); Hi Hnr Roll; Perf Att; Sci Clb; Track (V CL); Pre-Medical; Biology; Temple U; West Chester U of Pennsylvania

KAMPS, TYLER; RICHBORO, PA; COUNCIL ROCK HS NORTH; (SO); Hi Hnr Roll; Hnr Roll; Pres Ac Ftns Aw; St of Mnth; Comm Volntr; Stu Cncl (R); Business Degree; Villanova; U of North Carolina-Chapel Hill

KANE, ANTHONY; PITTSBURGH, PA; PITTSBURGH SD; (SO); Ctznshp Aw; Hi Hnr Roll; Hnr Roll; Bnd; Attorney; Biology Teacher; Temple U; U of Pittsburgh

KANE, KATERI L; CARLISLE, PA; TRINITY HS; (JR); Hi Hnr Roll; Nat Hon Sy; Comm Volntr; Peer Tut/Med; Spec Olymp Vol; DARE; Drma Clb; Key Club; Scouts; Chr; SP/M/VS; Sftball (VJ L); I Have Been a Girl Scout for 13 Yrs; I Am Working on My Gold Award for Scouts; I Would Like to Become a Physical Therapist; I Would Also Like to Continue in Drama; Saint Francis U

KANE, KATIE; GIBSONIA, PA; PINE-RICHLAND HS; (JR); Hi Hnr Roll; Nat Hon Sy; Otst Ac Ach Awd; Spec Olymp Vol; Cr Ctry (V L); Swmg (V CL); Stu Cncl (V); Architecture; Interior Design

KAO, DEBRA; MECHANICSBURG, PA; CUMBERLAND VALLEY HS; (JR); Ctznshp Aw; F Lan Hn Soc; Gov Hnr Prg; Hnr Roll; Kwnis Aw; Nat Hon Sy; Valdctrian; WWAHSS; Yth Ldrshp Prog; Comm Volntr; Hosp Aide; Peer Tut/Med; ArtClub; Chrch Yth Grp; Emplmnt; HO'Br Yth Ldrshp; Key Club; Mth Clb/Tm; Mod UN; Quiz Bowl; Jzz Bnd; Tennis (J L); Yrbk (R); Scholastics Gold Key-Personal Essay; Odyssey of the Mind-First Place; Medicine; Visual Arts; Swarthmore College; Brown U

KAPPELER, LINDSAY N; VERONA, PA; PENN HILLS HS; (JR); Hnr Roll; Nat Hon Sy; WWAHSS; Comm Volntr; Chrch Yth Grp; DARE; Emplmnt; Fr of Library; Key Club; Off Aide; French Clb; Clr Grd; Dnce; SP/M/VS; Scr Kpr (J); Student Athletic Trainer; Medical Careers Club-President; Nursing; Sports Medicine

KARELIA, DEEPKAMAL; HARRISBURG, PA; CTRL DAUPHIN EAST HS; (SR); Healthcare Professional; Pharmacy Graduate; Harrisburg Area Community College; Penn State U

KARNAUKH, VIKTOR; ERIE, PA; CENTRAL HS; (SO); Bskball; Sccr; Vllyball; Penn State U

KARPINSKI, JESSICA; POTTSTOWN, PA; POTTSGROVE HS; (SR); Hnr Roll; Kwnis Aw; MVP; Otst Ac Ach Awd; Perf Att; WWAHSS; Comm Volntr; Emplmnt; Key Club; Photog; Sci Clb; Scouts; Latin Clb; Tennis (J); Stu Cncl (R); Girl Scouts Gold Award; Art History; Archaeology; Pennsylvania State U

KARUNANIDHI, PRAVEEN; SEWICKLEY, PA; NORTH ALLEGHENY SR HS; (JR); Hi Hnr Roll; Otst Ac Ach Awd; Perf Att; Pres Ac Ftns Aw; St of Mnth; WWAHSS; Comm Volntr; Key Club

KASARDA, KAITLIN A; CAMP HILL, PA; TRINITY HS; (JR); Hi Hnr Roll; Nat Hon Sy; Sci Fairs; WWAHSS; Comm Volntr; Hab For Humty Volntr; Spec Olymp Vol; ArtClub; Emplmnt; Key Club; Sci Clb; Spanish Clb; Bnd; Chr; Jzz Bnd; Mch Bnd; Skiing; Sccr (V L); Sftball (V); Capital Area School for the Arts; Penn Summer Arts Studio; Film/Media; Ancient Studies; U of Maryland Baltimore County; Ithaca

KASMARI, ALLISON; MINERSVILLE, PA; NATIVITY BVM HS; (SR); DAR; Hi Hnr Roll; Nat Hon Sy; Salutrn; Sci Fairs; St of Mnth; WWAHSS; Comm Volntr; Peer Tut/Med; Mth Clb/Tm; Svce Clb; Vsity Clb; French Clb; Chr; Ch Chr; Bskball (VJC); Cr Ctry (J); Sftball (VJC); Vllyball (VJC); Cl Off (V, R); Stu Cncl (R); Yrbk (E); Biology/Pre-Medical; U of Delaware; Ursinus College

KASTOUN, RANA; WHITEHALL, PA; WHITEHALL COPLAY HS; (JR); Hnr Roll; Peer Tut/Med; Pep Squd; Cl Off (P); Stu Cncl (R); Been a Peer Mediator for Three Years; Nursing; Pre-Med; U of Pennsylvania; Drexel

KATZ, CHANCE N; TROUT RUN, PA; LIBERTY JR/SR HS; (SO); Hi Hnr Roll; Hnr Roll; MVP; Otst Ac Ach Awd; Perf Att; Sci Fairs; Ftball (J); Scr Kpr (V); Tennis (L); Business Management Degree; Pennsylvania State U; Pittsburgh U

KATZMAN, DAVID; HUMMELSTOWN, PA; HERSHEY HS; (JR); Hi Hnr Roll; Nat Hon Sy; Otst Ac Ach Awd; Emplmnt; Mth Clb/Tm; Quill & Scroll; Quiz Bowl; French Clb; Bnd; Jzz Bnd; Mch Bnd; Pep Bnd; Cl Off (P, T); Stu Cncl (R); Sch Ppr (E); Regional Band; District Band; Mathematics; Political Science; Yale; Columbia

KAUFER, AARON; KINGSTON, PA; WYOMING VALLEY WEST; (SO); Ctznshp Aw; Hi Hnr Roll; Nat Hon Sy; Otst Ac Ach Awd; Pres Ac Ftns Aw; Salutrn; Sci/Math Olympn; USAA; WWAHSS; Comm Volntr; Peer Tut/Med; Emplmnt; Lib Aide; Mth Clb/Tm; Prom Com; Quill & Scroll; Sci Clb; Svce Clb; Tmpl Yth Grp; Orch; Tennis (V L); Cl Off (P); Stu Cncl (R); Lit Mag (R); Yrbk (E); Latin Achievement Exam-Medalist; JCC Award-Most Valuable Youth; Law-Business; Politics; Princeton U; U of North Carolina (UNC)

KAUFFMAN, AMANDA; FRIEDENS, PA; NORTH STAR SD; (MS); Hnr Roll; Otst Ac Ach Awd; Sci/Math Olympn; Comm Volntr; Mth Clb/Tm; Sccr (L); Math 24 Challenge; Vet; Lawyer; UPJ; Penn State U

KAUFFMAN, NOLAN; MECHANICSBURG, PA; (FR); Hnr Roll; Pres Sch; Comm Volntr; Key Club; Mth Clb/Tm; Quiz Bowl; Spanish Clb; Ftball (J); Volleyball (Junior Olympic Club); Lawyer and Politics; Villanova U; Notre Dame U

KAUFMAN, JAMES; GREENSBURG, PA; GREENSBURG SALEM SD; (FR); 4H Awd; Hi Hnr Roll; 4-H; Chrch Yth Grp; Wdwrkg Clb; Chr; Stu Cncl (R); Deacon At My Church; UKC Dog Show Participant; Veterinarian; Biologist; U of Pennsylvania School of Veterinary Medicine; College of Veterinary Medicine At Ohio State U

KAUFOLD, MELISSA; MUNHALL, PA; STEEL VALLEY HS; (SO); Hi Hnr Roll; WWAHSS; Comm Volntr; Key Club; Swmg (V L); Elementary Education; Secondary Education

KAVANAGH, KATHERINE B; GLENMOORE, PA; BISHOP SHANAHAN HS; (FR); Hnr Roll; St of Mnth; SP/M/VS

KAY, JENNIFER E; LITITZ, PA; MANHEIM TWP HS; (SO); Hi Hnr Roll; Hnr Roll; Kwnis Aw; Key Club; Quiz Bowl; Jzz Bnd; Orch; Stg Cre; Key Club Board Member; Quiz Bowl

KAZI, LAILA; PHILADELPHIA, PA; HS FOR THE CREATIVE AND PERF ARTS; (JR); Ctznshp Aw; Hnr Roll; Nat Hon Sy; Otst Ac Ach Awd; Peer Tut/Med; Pep Squd; Vsity Clb; Orch; Tennis (V); Yrbk; HS Major - Visual Arts and Minor in Music / Violin; Doctor's Degree / Plastic Surgeon; Arizona State U; U of Phoenix

KEARNEY, ELIZABETH; FOLSOM, PA; RIDLEY HS; (SO); 4H Awd; Hi Hnr Roll; Hnr Roll; Pres Ac Ftns Aw; Hosp Aide; Prom Com; Clb; Sccr (V); Sftball (V); Nurse; Guidance Counselor; East Stroudsburg U; Penn State Main Campus

KEELER, SHARI L; MIFFLINBURG, PA; MIFFLINBURG AREA SD; (JR); Hnr Roll; St of Mnth; Emplmnt; Scouts; Fld Hky; Participate In School Blood Drives; Aced Welding and Electrical Classes; Architectural Drafting; Business Management; Pennsylvania College of Technology Williamsport

KEELEY, LAURA I; GIBSONIA, PA; PINE-RICHLAND HS; (SO); Hi Hnr Roll; Otst Ac Ach Awd; Sci Fairs; WWAHSS; Yth Ldrshp Prog; Comm Volntr; Hosp Aide; Emplmnt; Key Club; Lttrmn Clb; SADD; Bnd; SP/M/VS; Sftball (V L); Vllyball (V L); Cl Off (T); Yrbk (R); Law; Journalism; Harvard U; U Of Notre Dame

KEEN, KYLE C; BOYERTOWN, PA; BOYERTOWN AREA SR HS; (JR); Hi Hnr Roll; Hnr Roll; MVP; Perf Att; Pres Ac Ftns Aw; WWAHSS; Comm Volntr; Spec Olymp Vol; ArtClub; Chrch Yth Grp; Emplmnt; Key Club; Photog; Prom Com; Svce Clb; Wdwrkg Clb; Chr; Ch Chr; SP/M/VS; Sccr (V CL); Tennis (V CL); Stu Cncl (R); CR (R); Yrbk (R); Who's Who Among American Athletes; Nominee Berks County Best; Doctor; Architectural Engineer; Messiah College; Liberty U

KEESEMAN, AMBER; SHIPPENSBURG, PA; SHIPPENSBURG AREA HS; (SO); Ctznshp Aw; Hi Hnr Roll; Kwnis Aw; Perf Att; Sci Fairs; WWAHSS; Fld Hky (J L); Sftball (JCL); Stu Cncl (R); Computer Science; Psychology

KEHLER, KONRAD J; SHAMOKIN, PA; SHAMOKIN AREA HS; (FR); Hnr Roll; Vsity Clb; Ftball (J); Wrstlg (V L); Meteorology; Penn State

KELCHNER, KIMBERLY; FOLSOM, PA; RIDLEY SD; (JR); Hi Hnr Roll; Hnr Roll; St of Mnth; WWAHSS; Chrldg (JC); Student Senate / Homeroom Rep; Interact Club; Elementary Education; Special Education

KELLER, ALAN; MONACA, PA; CTR AREA SD HS; (SO); Hi Hnr Roll; WWAHSS; Hab For Humty Volntr; Chrch Yth Grp; Lttrmn Clb; Vsity Clb; German Clb; Bnd; Mch Bnd; Stg Cre; Ftball (J); Track (V L); Cl Off (T); Pre-Med; Engineering; U of Pittsburgh; U of North Carolina

KELLER, CHRISTIE; DOVER, PA; NORTHERN HS; (SO); F Lan Hn Soc; Hnr Roll; Pres Ac Ftns Aw; St of Mnth; Spec Olymp Vol; Chrch Yth Grp; Key Club; P to P St Amb Prg; Photog; SADD; French Clb; Hsbk Rdg; Skiing; Swmg (L); Track (VJ); Scuba Diving; French Teacher; Psychologist; U of Pittsburgh; Franklin and Marshall College

KELLER, MICHELLE; DALLAS, PA; DALLAS HS; (FR); Hnr Roll; Comm Volntr; DARE; Key Club; Chr; Clr Grd; Photography

KELLY, HEATHER L; CARNEGIE, PA; KEYSTONE OAKS HS; (JR); Hi Hnr Roll; Hnr Roll; Perf Att; Pres Sch; St of Mnth; WWAHSS; DARE; Scouts; SADD; Vllyball (VJ L); English Teacher; Lawyer; Wingate U; South Carolina U

KELLY, SARAH; EASTON, PA; EASTON AREA SR HS; (SO); Hnr Roll; WWAHSS; Chrch Yth Grp; Acpl Chr; Ch Chr

KELLY, SHANNA; TARENTUM, PA; HIGHLANDS SD; (MS); Ctznshp Aw; Hi Hnr Roll; Hnr Roll; Pres Ac Ftns Aw; Pres Sch; Sci Fairs; St of Mnth; Comm Volntr; Hosp Aide; Chrch Yth Grp; DARE; Wdwrkg Clb; Chr; Stg Cre; Law; Harvard U; Stanford U

KELLY, TASHEIKA S; EAST STROUDSBURG, PA; STROUDSBURG HS; (JR); Hnr Roll; Dnce; Drl Tm; Dance Hip Hop, Ballet, Tap Jazz; Theater; School of Performing Arts (Bronx) NY; Visual and Performing Arts (PA)

KEMP, MEGAN M; CAMP HILL, PA; CAMP HILL HS; (SO); F Lan Hn Soc; Hi Hnr Roll; Hnr Roll; P to P St Amb Prg; Bnd; Mch Bnd; Orch; SP/M/VS; Stu Cncl; Yrbk (E, P); Magna Cum Laude - National Latin Exam

KENDLE, KATELYN; APOLLO, PA; KISKI AREA HS; (SO); Hi Hnr Roll; Perf Att; Pres Ac Ftns Aw; WWAHSS; Comm Volntr; Chrch Yth Grp; Emplmnt; Key Club; SADD; Bnd; Jzz Bnd; Cr Ctry (V L); Track (V L); Secondary Education-Math; Pennsylvania State U

KENNEDY, ASHLEY N; WAYMART, PA; WESTERN WAYNE; (SO); Hi Hnr Roll; Hnr Roll; Otst Ac Ach Awd; Pres Ac Ftns Aw; Sci Fairs; WWAHSS; Comm Volntr; Hosp Aide; Peer Tut/Med; DARE; Drma Clb; Emplmnt; Vsity Clb; French Clb; Chr; Dnce; SP/M/VS; Chrldg (V); Cr Ctry (V); Track (V); Sch Ppr (R); Coach Jr, Cheerleading; Criminal Law; Pre-Med; Penn State Main Campus; Bloomsburg U

KENNEDY, BRITTANY; PITTSBURGH, PA; SCHENLEY HS; (FR); Ctznshp Aw; Hnr Roll; Hab For Humty Volntr; Chrch Yth Grp; Photog; Scouts; Spanish Clb; Chr; Ch Chr; Drl Tm; Orch; Cr Ctry (V); Track (V); Scholarship Pittsburgh Filmmakers; Black History Art Essay Winner; Production; Writing / Poetry; Carnegie Mellon; Pitt College

KENNEDY, DANIEL B; NEW WILMINGTON, PA; WILMINGTON AREA HS; (JR); Hi Hnr Roll; USMC Stu Ath Aw; Spec Olymp Vol; Chrch Yth Grp; Emplmnt; Mod UN; ROTC; Bnd; Golf (VJ L); Sch Ppr (E, R); Eagle Boy Scout; Congressional Leadership Participant; Architecture; Engineering

KENNINGER, ALLISON M; PALMERTON, PA; PALMERTON AREA SD; (FR); Hi Hnr Roll; Hnr Roll; Perf Att; Pres Ac Ftns Aw; Comm Volntr; ArtClub; Chrch Yth Grp; Lib Aide; Scouts; Veterinary Science; Astronomy

KENSTOWICZ, ANDRE; PITTSBURGH, PA; CTRL CATHOLIC HS; (SO); Hi Hnr Roll; Hosp Aide; Emplmnt; Spanish Clb; Bsball; Bskball; Ftball; Sch Ppr (R); AFS High School Student Scholarship- Year in Costa Rica; Marine Biology / Oceanography; Environmental Science; U of Washington; UC Berkeley

KEPHART, KAYLAN; PUNXSUTAWNEY, PA; PUNXSUTAWNEY CHRISTIAN SCH; (SO); Hi Hnr Roll; St of Mnth; WWAHSS; Chrch Yth Grp; Chr; Sccr (V L); Stu Cncl (S)

KEPHART, STEPHANIE E; DREXEL HILL, PA; UPPER DARBY HS; (SO); Hnr Roll; ArtClub; Chr; Clr Grd; Dnce; Gmnstcs; Sftball; Girl Scouts; Drexel Hill Softball League; Teaching; DCCC; Penn State U

KEPPEN, HEIDI; STOYSTOWN, PA; SHANKSVILLE-STONYCREEK HS; (SO); Hi Hnr Roll; Hnr Roll; Nat Hon Sy; WWAHSS; Yth Ldrshp Prog; Comm Volntr; 4-H; Chrch Yth Grp; Drma Clb; Emplmnt; Lib Aide; Mus Clb; Schol Bwl; Bnd; Chr; Jzz Bnd; SP/M/VS; Honors Band; Recreational Therapy; Youth / Music Ministry; Houghton College; Lancaster Bible College

KERMALLI, FATEMA; WHITEHALL, PA; WHITEHALL HS; (SO); Hi Hnr Roll; USAA; WWAHSS; Amnsty Intl; Comm Volntr; Spec Olymp Vol; Biology Clb; Dbte Team; Key Club; Svce Clb; USAA National Science Merit Award; Ranked 4th in Class Last Year (9th Grade); Pre-Med

KERN, BETHANIE; AVELLA, PA; AVELLA AREA JR/SR HS; (FR); Hi Hnr Roll; WWAHSS; Bnd; Dnce; Jzz Bnd; Mch Bnd; Sftball; Vllyball; Architecture / Drafting

KERSTETTER, ALYCIA; HALIFAX, PA; HALIFAX AREA HS; (SR); Hi Hnr Roll; Hnr Roll; St of Mnth; Emplmnt; Prom Com; Vsity Clb; Chrldg (V L); PP Ftbl; Sccr (V CL); Track (V L); Cl Off (P); Stu Cncl (V); Yrbk (E); Tri-Valley League Scholar Athlete; Bachelor of Science in Nursing; U of North Carolina At Wilmington; Duquesne U of PA

KEYSER, JAKE; WALNUTPORT, PA; NORTHAMPTON AREA SR HS; (SO); Hi Hnr Roll; Hnr Roll; Perf Att; St of Mnth; Vsity Clb; Ftball (V); Wt Lftg (V); Captain of High School F-Ball Team 2 Years; First Investor in My School; Athletic Trainer/Training; Physical Therapist; U of East Stroudsburg; Western U

KHRISTOV, VLADIMIR; STATE COLLEGE, PA; STATE COLLEGE SOUTH HS; Hnr Roll; Perf Att; Pres Sch; Mth Clb/Tm; Sci Clb; Swmg (J); Water Polo, Junior Varsity; Aviation Engineer

KIDWELL, CORIN; AKRON, PA; EPHRATA HS; (SR); F Lan Hn Soc; Hi Hnr Roll; MVP; Nat Hon Sy; WWAHSS; Peer Tut/Med; Chrch Yth Grp; Emplmnt; FCA; Mus Clb; Photog; Chr; Orch; Sccr (V CL); Vllyball (V CL); Mathematics; Business/Finance; Elizabethtown College

KIEHL, KATHLEEN; DOUGLASSVILLE, PA; DANIEL BOONE AREA HS; (SR); Hi Hnr Roll; Kwnis Aw; Nat Hon Sy; Drma Clb; Jr Ach; Key Club; Prom Com; French Clb; Chrldg (V); Sch Ppr (R); Yrbk (E); Berk's Best Nominee; Top Ten; Advertising & Marketing Communications; Fashion Institute of Technology

KIGHT, HANNAH; CORRY, PA; CORRY AREA HS; (SO); Hi Hnr Roll; Nat Hon Sy; Perf Att; Key Club; Tchrs Aide; Bnd; Jzz Bnd; Mch Bnd; Secretary of Key Club; Participant of Pennsylvania Regional 2 Band; English; Music; Grove City College

KILBERT, LAUREN; HERMITAGE, PA; HERMITAGE SD; (SO); F Lan Hn Soc; Hi Hnr Roll; Nat Stu Ath Day Aw; Perf Att; WWAHSS; Hosp Aide; ArtClub; Drma Clb; Key Club; Lttrmn Clb; Mth Clb/Tm; SADD; French Clb; Bnd; Mch Bnd; Pep Bnd; Cr Ctry (V L); Track (V L); Scholar Athlete; State Cross Country Team; Nursing; Robert Morris U; Penn State

KILE, JENA; READING, PA; EXETER TWP SR HS; (JR); Hi Hnr Roll; Comm Volntr; Chrch Yth Grp; DARE; Prom Com; Bnd; Chr; Mch Bnd; Special Education; Kutztown U; Penn State U

KILGORE, CASEY; BROAD RUN, PA; FAUQUIER HS; (JR); Hi Hnr Roll; Hnr Roll; Track (V L); Business; Major Business; Penn State; George Mason

KILIANY, CAROLYN; PITTSBURGH, PA; NORTH ALLEGHENY HS; (SO); Hnr Roll; Nat Hon Sy; WWAHSS; Comm Volntr; Chrch Yth Grp; Jr Cls League; Key Club; Scouts; Ch Chr; Orch; Stu Cncl (R); Lit Mag (R); Outstanding Young Citizen; Extra Effort Award; Biology

KILLOSKY, JESSE; MC KEESPORT, PA; SOUTH ALLEGHENY HS; (SR); Hi Hnr Roll; WWAHSS; Bskball (V CL); PP Ftbl (V L); Yrbk (E); Animal Science; U of Pennsylvania

KIM, CHRISTINE; MEADOWBROOK, PA; ABINGTON SR HS; (JR); Hi Hnr Roll; Nat Hon Sy; WWAHSS; Comm Volntr; Peer Tut/Med; Chrch Yth Grp; Key Club; Orch; SP/M/VS; Yrbk (E); Presidential Award; Congressional Award; U of Pennsylvania

KIM, DENNIS; PLYMOUTH MEETING, PA; PLYMOUTH WHITEMARSH HS; (SO); Hi Hnr Roll; Hnr Roll; Perf Att; Pres Sch; Hab For Humty Volntr; Peer Tut/Med; FBLA; Svce Clb; Involved in Steering Committee; Student Council; Pre-Med; Cosmetic Surgery / Plastic Surgery; Harvard U; George Washington U

KIM, JOYCE; MIFFLIN, PA; JUNIATA HS; (JR); Gov Hnr Prg; Hi Hnr Roll; Hnr Roll; Perf Att; Pres Sch; St of Mnth; Peer Tut/Med; Spec Olymp Vol; Chrch Yth Grp; Key Club; P to P St Amb Prg; Vsity Clb; Bskball (V); Track (V); Yrbk (P); Pediatrician/Pre-Med; Pennsylvania State U; Pittsburgh U

KIM, MYUNG K; MECHANICSBURG, PA; CUMBERLAND VALLEY HS; (JR); Hnr Roll; Chrch Yth Grp; Key Club; Mod UN; French Clb; Business Finance; International Business; Penn State U; U of Maryland

KIM, SOO-YEON; MIFFLIN, PA; JUNIATA CTY SD; (JR); Hi Hnr Roll; Hnr Roll; Perf Att; St of Mnth; WWAHSS; Spec Olymp Vol; Key Club; Prom Com; Chr; Bskball (V); Track (V); Pre-Med; Pennsylvania State U; U of Pittsburg

KIMMY, MELISSA R; CORRY, PA; CORRY AREA HS; (SO); Hi Hnr Roll; Nat Hon Sy; Perf Att; USAA; WWAHSS; Chrch Yth Grp; Key Club; Acpl Chr; Bnd; Mch Bnd; SP/M/VS; Track (V L); Stu Cncl (S); Mathematics; Music

KINBACK, RYAN T; WILMORE, PA; FOREST HILLS SD; (SO); Hi Hnr Roll; Nat Hon Sy; Spanish Clb; Ftball (J); Track (J); Wt Lftg (V); U of Pittsburgh

KINDT, CHRISTINA; TEMPLE, PA; MUHLENBERG SR HS; (JR); Hosp Aide; Broadcasting; Journalism; Point Park U; Cedar Crest College

KING, ALISON M; DREXEL HILL, PA; UPPER DARBY HS; (JR); Hi Hnr Roll; Nat Hon Sy; Peer Tut/Med; Emplmnt; Scouts; French Clb; Bnd; Chr; Ch Chr; Dnce; 6th Place in National French Contest; English Student of the Year; English; Secondary Education; U of Maryland; The College of New Jersey

KING, JANELL A; PHILADELPHIA, PA; PARKWAY CTR CITY HS; (SR); Ctznshp Aw; Hi Hnr Roll; Hnr Roll; Otst Ac Ach Awd; Perf Att; Pres Sch; Yth Ldrshp Prog; Comm Volntr; Peer Tut/Med; Red Cr Aide; Emplmnt; NYLC; Pep Squd; Photog; Prom Com; Schol Bwl; Tchrs Aide; Chr; Dnce; SP/M/VS; Stg Cre; Chrldg (C); Cl Off (R); Stu Cncl (R); CR (P); Lit Mag (R); Yrbk (E); National Merit Scholar; Most Likely to Be a Defense Attorney; Business Management; Fashion Merchandising; Howard U

KING, JOANNA L; MECHANICSBURG, PA; CUMBERLAND VALLEY HS; (SO); WWAHSS; Comm Volntr; Chrch Yth Grp; Key Club; Orch; Lcrsse (J); Key Club, Historian; Young Life, Youth Group; Photography; Sports Management; Elon U, U of Mary Washington, Belmont U

KING, MELISSA; BERWYN, PA; CONESTOGA HS; (JR); Hnr Roll; Peer Tut/Med; Key Club; Chr; Track (J); Peer Mediator - Public Relations Committee; Pre-Med; Boston College; James Madison U

KING, REUBEN; TARENTUM, PA; HIGHLANDS SD; (MS); Hnr Roll; Perf Att; Chrch Yth Grp; Chr; Swg Chr; Bskball (L); Ftball (L); Chosen for Jr. National Youth Leadership Conference; A Major in History; A Major in Biology; U of Pittsburgh; U of Texas-El Paso

KING, TIFFANY; SEVEN VALLEYS, PA; DALLASTOWN AREA HS; (SR); Hnr Roll; WWAHSS; Bnd; Mch Bnd; Honor Roll; Forensic Chemistry; York College of Pennsylvania

KINNAMON, ALEX M; LEECHBURG, PA; LENAPE TECH; (JR); MVP; Drma Clb; Quiz Bowl; Voc Ind Clb Am; SP/M/VS; Quiz Bowl Varsity MVP; Culinary Arts (BS); General Education (BS); Art Institute; Point Park

KINNE, CATELYN; LANCASTER, PA; LANCASTER CTY CTC; (JR); Hnr Roll; Bachelors in Health and Science; Lancaster General College of Nursing; Harrisburg Community College

KIRCH, SAMANTHA; HUMMELSTOWN, PA; (SO); Ch Chr; SP/M/VS; Lcrsse (JC); Stu Cncl (R); CR (R); Key Club V.P., Distinguished Honor Roll; Production Crew Manager; Elem. Ed; Journalism; Penn State U Schreyer Honors College; U of VA

KIRKMAN, SHADOW; COUDERSPORT, PA; COUDERSPORT AREA SD; (FR); Hi Hnr Roll; Hnr Roll; Pres Ac Ftns Aw; Comm Volntr; DARE; Emplmnt; Sci Clb; Svce Clb

KIRSCH, STEPHEN J; PITTSBURGH, PA; NORTH ALLEGHENY INT HS; (FR); All Am Sch; Hi Hnr Roll; Nat Hon Sy; St of Mnth; WWAHSS; Comm Volntr; Hab For Humty Volntr; Peer Tut/Med; AL Aux Boys; Chrch Yth Grp; Key Club; Bskball; Adv Cncl (R); CR (R); Key Club-Vice President; Joan Spicher Student Award (2004); International Affairs

KISAK, SCOTT; NORTH VERSAILLES, PA; EAST ALLEGHENY HS; (JR); Hnr Roll; Emplmnt; Orch; Apprenticeship for Forest Trail Tech

KISENWETHER, AMANDA A; BERWICK, PA; BERWICK AREA SR HS; (JR); Hi Hnr Roll; Nat Hon Sy; Pres Ac Ftns Aw; Comm Volntr; Emplmnt; FBLA; Prom Com; Spanish Clb; Chrldg (V); PP Ftbl (V); Track (V); Yrbk (P); Early Childhood Education; Bloomsburg U; Kings College

KLAAS, BRITTANY; GIBSONIA, PA; PINE-RICHLAND HS; (JR); Hi Hnr Roll; Comm Volntr; Chrch Yth Grp; Emplmnt; Key Club; Prom Com; Acpl Chr; Ch Chr; SP/M/VS; Tennis (V); Stu Cncl (R); Honors Choir; Choir Officer; Music Business; Elementary Education; Grove City College; Belmont U

KLEE, MARGARET J; MECHANICSBURG, PA; CUMBERLAND VALLEY; (JR); Hnr Roll; Comm Volntr; Spec Olymp Vol; Emplmnt; Key Club; French Clb; SP/M/VS

KLEES, ALICIA M; HARRISBURG, PA; CTRL DAUPHIN HS; (FR); Hi Hnr Roll; Pres Sch; Sci/Math Olympn; St of Mnth; Comm Volntr; Biology Clb; Mus Clb; Sci Clb; Scouts; Latin Clb; Dnce; Jzz Bnd; Orch; SP/M/VS; Sch Ppr (E); Yrbk (E); Astrophysics; Aeronautical Engineering; Harvard U; Florida Institute of Technology

King, Janell A
Parkway Ctr City HS
Philadelphia, PA

Keller, Christie
Northern HS
Dover, PA

Kiehl, Kathleen
Daniel Boone Area HS
Douglassville, PA

KLICK, DEANNA; VANDERGRIFT, PA; KISKI AREA HS; (SO); Hi Hnr Roll; Sci Fairs; Chrch Yth Grp; Drma Clb; Emplmnt; SADD; Chr; SP/M/VS; Track (V); Stu Cncl (R); Political Science; Business Management; U of Pittsburg; St Vincent's College

KLINE, JONATHAN D; POTTSTOWN, PA; POTTSTOWN SR HS; (FR); Hnr Roll; St of Mnth; DARE; DECA; Key Club; Prom Com; Bskball (L); Sccr (L); Stu Cncl (R)

KLINE, KEVIN T; NORRISTOWN, PA; NORRISTOWN ARPA HS; (SO); DAR; Hi Hnr Roll; Hnr Roll; Nat Hon Sy; Pres Sch; Chess; Chrch Yth Grp; Key Club; Mth Clb/Tm; German Clb; SP/M/VS; Sccr (J); Bowling (JV for 2 Years); Computer Engineering; Forensic Sciences; Penn State U; Harvard U

KLINE, PATTY; PHILADELPHIA, PA; GEORGE WASHINGTON HS; (SO); Hnr Roll; DARE; Scouts; Teaching in Elementary School

KLINGENSMITH, JAMIE; EPHRATA, PA; EPHRATA HS; (SR); Nat Hon Sy; WWAHSS; Emplmnt; Orch; Yrbk (E); Ski Club; Bachelor of Science in Clinical Dietetics & Nutrition; Master of Science-Emphasis in Clinical Dietetics

KLINGER, KEVIN F; NORTHUMBERLAND, PA; SUNBURY CHRISTIAN AC; (SO); Hnr Roll; Perf Att; Chrch Yth Grp; Forestry; Wildlife Photography

KLOHONATZ, KRISTIN; GREENSBURG, PA; GREATER LATROBE SR HS; (SO); F Lan Hn Soc; Hi Hnr Roll; Perf Att; WWAHSS; Key Club; French Clb; Sccr (J L); Veterinarian; Marine Biologist; Penn State U; U of Pennsylvania

KLOTZ, JESSICA; PEN ARGYL, PA; PEN ARGYL HS; (SO); Hnr Roll; Emplmnt; Svce Clb; Voc Ind Clb Am; Acpl Chr; Chr; Mch Bnd; Autobody Refinishing and Collision; Pennsylvania College of Technology; Ohio Technical College

KNOPP, JOHN E; GREENSBURG, PA; RIDGEVIEW AC CHARTER SCH; (SO); Hnr Roll; Chr; Preacher; Oral Roberts U

KNORR, AMANDA; CRANBERRY TWP, PA; SENECA VALLEY SHS; (SO); Hi Hnr Roll; Perf Att; WWAHSS; Key Club; French Clb; Chr; Cl Off (S); Law; Marketing and Advertising; U of Pittsburgh; New York U

KNORR, REBECCA; COLLEGEVILLE, PA; METHACTON HS; (SO); Hi Hnr Roll; Hnr Roll; St of Mnth; WWAHSS; Amnsty Intl; Comm Volntr; Drma Clb; Key Club; Mus Clb; Svce Clb; Tmpl Yth Grp; Chr; SP/M/VS; CR (R); Veterans Day Essay Winner 1st Place; Tri-M Honor Society; Working W/ Children; Music; U of Delaware; Penn State

KNOUSE, LINDSEY; MECHANICSBURG, PA; CUMBERLAND VALLEY HS; (SO); Hnr Roll; Perf Att; WWAHSS; Comm Volntr; Hab For Humty Volntr; Emplmnt; Key Club; German Clb; Cumberland Valley Area Softball (CVAGSA); Physical Therapy; Science; U of Pittsburgh; U of Pennsylvania

KNOX, RACHEL; GIBSONIA, PA; HAMPTON HS; (SR); DAR; Hi Hnr Roll; MVP; WWAHSS; Comm Volntr; Mod UN; SADD; Lcrsse (V CL); CR (T); Neuroscience; FBI; U of Pittsburgh

KOCIOLA, DANIEL J; HOLLIDAYSBURG, PA; HOLLIDAYSBURG AREA SR HS; (JR); Hnr Roll; Perf Att; Hab For Humty Volntr; Peer Tut/Med; Chrch Yth Grp; Emplmnt; Fr of Library; Key Club; Scouts; French Clb; Key Club, French Club; Boy Scouts; Engineer; Penn State U; Lehigh U

KODISH, BROOKE; LEWISTOWN, PA; LEWISTOWN AREA HS; (JR); Hi Hnr Roll; Nat Hon Sy; Pres Ac Ftns Aw; Peer Tut/Med; Emplmnt; Key Club; Prom Com; Bskball (V L); Chrldg (J); PP Ftbl (V); Sccr (V L); Wt Lftg; Cl Off (T); Tobacco Busters (Club); Character Traits Committee; Bloomsburg U; Shippensburg U

KOEHLER, RACHEL L; PHILADELPHIA, PA; ARCHBISHOP CARROLL HS; (SR); Hnr Roll; Comm Volntr; Chrch Yth Grp; Off Aide; Tchrs Aide; Early Childhood Education; Special Education; East Stroudsburg U; West Chester U

KOENIG, KATRINA; LANDENBERG, PA; ST MARY'S HS; (SO); Hnr Roll; St of Mnth; Comm Volntr; DARE; NYLC; Scouts; Bnd; Dnce; Black Belt in Tang Soo Do; 13 Year Cancer Survivor; Dancing

KOETTERITZ, MICHELLE A; POTTSTOWN, PA; POTTSGROVE HS; (JR); All Am Sch; Ctznshp Aw; Gov Hnr Prg; Hi Hnr Roll; Nat Hon Sy; Otst Ac Ach Awd; Perf Att; Pres Ac Ftns Aw; Pres Sch; Salutrn; Comm Volntr; Hosp Aide; Peer Tut/Med; Chrch Yth Grp; Emplmnt; Key Club; Mth Clb/Tm; Off Aide; Prom Com; Quiz Bowl; Sci Clb; Ch Chr; SP/M/VS; Fld Hky (V L); PP Ftbl (C); Scr Kpr (V); Skiing; Track (V L); Vsy Clb (V); Cl Off (P); Stu Cncl (R); CR (R); Perfect Attendance; Ranked 2nd in Class Standings; Biology; Pre-Med; Penn State U; U of Delaware

KOHLER, JACQUELYNN G; BETHEL PARK, PA; BETHEL PARK SD; (SO); Hnr Roll; WWAHSS; Comm Volntr; Dbte Team; NtlFrnscLg; Scouts; Dnce; Medicine; Law; Georgetown U; Stanford U

KOHLER, KRISTEN; POTTSTOWN, PA; POTTSGROVE HS; (SO); Ctznshp Aw; Hi Hnr Roll; Hnr Roll; Nat Hon Sy; Otst Ac Ach Awd; Pres Sch; WWAHSS; Comm Volntr; Chrch Yth Grp; DARE; Drma Clb; JSA; Key Club; Mth Clb/Tm; Mus Clb; Vsity Clb; Chr; SP/M/VS; Swg Chr; Tennis (V); CR (V); Lit Mag (R, P); History Club; PRIDE Award; Business Law; Forensic Pathology; Pennsylvania State U; New York U

KOHR, AMBER; HARRISBURG, PA; CTRL DAUPHIN HS; (SO); Hi Hnr Roll; Hnr Roll; Bskball (J); Fld Hky (J); Veterinarian

KOHSER, STEPHANIE; PITTSBURGH, PA; PITTSBURGH SD; (JR); Ctznshp Aw; Hi Hnr Roll; Nat Hon Sy; Otst Ac Ach Awd; Pres Sch; Sci Fairs; Comm Volntr; Lttrmn Clb; Lib Aide; Quill & Scroll; Quiz Bowl; Clb; Bnd; Clr Grd; Dnce; SP/M/VS; Sons of American Revolution; GSA Volunteer of the Year Award; Science; Carnegie Mellon U; U of Pittsburgh

KOKALES, JOHN; OAKMONT, PA; RIVERVIEW JR/SR HS; (FR); Hi Hnr Roll; Hnr Roll; Pres Sch; Chrch Yth Grp; Key Club; Schol Bwl; French Clb; Bsball (J); Runner-Up, Commonwealth Freedom Award Essay; Greek Orthodox Youth Association Basketball; International Affairs; Graphic Design; Notre Dame; U of Pittsburgh

KOLLER, GABRIELLE; WERNERSVILLE, PA; CONRAD WEISER HS; (FR); Hi Hnr Roll; Perf Att; Pres Ac Ftns Aw; St of Mnth; Comm Volntr; Chrch Yth Grp; Drma Clb; Emplmnt; Ntl FFA; Chr; Ch Chr; Dnce; SP/M/VS; Swmg (V); Track (V); County Chorus; FFA County Creed; Music/Arts; Nutrition; Pennsylvania State U; Muhlenberg State U

KOLMUS, ROSEMARY; POTTSTOWN, PA; OWEN J ROBERTS HS; (JR); DAR; Hi Hnr Roll; Hnr Roll; Nat Hon Sy; Otst Ac Ach Awd; Pres Ac Ftns Aw; Sci Fairs; Comm Volntr; Peer Tut/Med; Chrch Yth Grp; Drma Clb; Emplmnt; Mus Clb; Svce Clb; Vsity Clb; Chr; Ch Chr; SP/M/VS; Sccr (V); Track (V); CR (R); Sch Ppr (R); Teens Against Tobacco Use; Anchor Club-Community Service; Elementary Education; Psychology; Cedarville U; Houghton College

KOLOS, KYLE H; LANGHORNE, PA; CONWELL-EGAN CATHOLIC HS; (SR); Hi Hnr Roll; Hnr Roll; Otst Ac Ach Awd; St of Mnth; WWAHSS; Spec Olymp Vol; Emplmnt; Key Club; Off Aide; Lcrsse (J); Sccr (V CL); CR (R); 4 Yr - Participant in Schools Annual Spirit Night; Business; Penn State U - Attending; U of Pittsburgh

KONECKE, STEPHANIE M; WYOMING, PA; DALLAS SR HS; (SO); Hi Hnr Roll; Nat Hon Sy; WWAHSS; Peer Tut/Med; Key Club; Bnd; Bskball (V L); Sccr (V); Sportsmanship Award; Student of the Quarter; Forensics; Criminology

KOON, AMBER N; COATESVILLE, PA; COATESVILLE AREA SR HS; (JR); Hi Hnr Roll; Hnr Roll; Nat Hon Sy; Perf Att; WWAHSS; Bnd; Chr; Mch Bnd; Track (V); 5th in District Track Meet; Medical Doctor

KOPANIA, KRISTIN; HOLLAND, PA; COUNCIL ROCK HS SOUTH; (FR); Hi Hnr Roll; Hnr Roll; Otst Ac Ach Awd; Perf Att; Red Cr Aide; French Clb; Ice Hky (V); Lcrsse (J); Lit Mag (R); Sch Ppr (R); Published Poem; Forensic Science; Nursing School; Princeton U; Florida Metropolitan U

KOPEE JR, JOHN A; WILKES BARRE, PA; JAMES M COUGHLIN HS; (JR); Ctznshp Aw; Hi Hnr Roll; Nat Hon Sy; WWAHSS; Emplmnt; FBLA; Key Club; Mus Clb; Scouts; Spch Team; Spanish Clb; Bnd; Chr; Jzz Bnd; Mch Bnd; Tennis (V); Track (V); Eagle Scout; Church Organist; Law School; Business; U of Pennsylvania; U of Scranton

KOPEN, VICTOR; HERMITAGE, PA; HICKORY HS; (SO); Hnr Roll; Sci Fairs; Yth Ldrshp Prog; Comm Volntr; Spanish Clb; Bsball; Golf; Skiing; Sccr (L); Track (V); Doctor of Medicine; Chemical Engineer; U of Michigan; U of Southern California

KOREN, MATTHEW; WHITEHALL, PA; WHITEHALL HS; (FR); MVP; Perf Att; WWAHSS; Yth Ldrshp Prog; Key Club; Cr Ctry (V L); Skiing (V); Sccr (V L); Track (V L); Cl Off (S); Stu Cncl (R); Community Service Church; Penn State; Lehigh U

KORNSEY, ALLISON; POTTSTOWN, PA; POTTSGROVE SR HS; (SO); Ctznshp Aw; St of Mnth; Comm Volntr; Key Club; Sci Clb; Svce Clb; Latin Clb; Chr; Fld Hky (J L); Tri-Alpha Winner; Science Major

KOSARAJU, SIDDHARTHA; WAYNE, PA; RADNOR HS; (FR); Nat Hon Sy; Otst Ac Ach Awd; Comm Volntr; Mth Clb/Tm; Scouts; Bnd; Mch Bnd; Pep Bnd; Tennis (J)

KOSASIN, JULIUS; UPPER DARBY, PA; UPPER DARBY HS; (JR); Hi Hnr Roll; Hnr Roll; Otst Ac Ach Awd; Perf Att; Comm Volntr; Emplmnt; Quiz Bowl; Business; Computer; Penn State U; Drexel U

KOSER, ERICA; MOUNT JOY, PA; ELIZABETHTOWN AREA HS; (JR); Hi Hnr Roll; Nat Hon Sy; Pres Ac Ftns Aw; St of Mnth; WWAHSS; Yth Ldrshp Prog; Hab For Humty Volntr; Chrch Yth Grp; Emplmnt; Key Club; Lttrmn Clb; Prom Com; Vsity Clb; Track; Vsy Clb; Vllyball; Yrbk (E); Major in Elem Education; Juniata

KOSKIE, DREW T; WILLIAMSPORT, PA; WILLIAMSPORT HS; (SO); Ctznshp Aw; Hi Hnr Roll; Otst Ac Ach Awd; Pres Sch; USAA; WWAHSS; Peer Tut/Med; Emplmnt; Key Club; Mch Bnd; Yrbk (P); Architectural Engineering; Penn State U; Bucknell U

KOSTICH, ASHLEY A; THOMPSONTOWN, PA; JUNIATA CTY SD; (SO); All Am Sch; Hnr Roll; USAA; WWAHSS; Comm Volntr; Spec Olymp Vol; Chrch Yth Grp; Key Club; Lttrmn Clb; Vsity Clb; Ch Chr; Dnce; Bskball (V); Chrldg (V L); Track (V L); Vsy Clb (V); Psychology; Sociology; Penn State U

KOVACS, JOE; NAZARETH, PA; BETHLEHEM CATHOLIC HS; (SO); Hnr Roll; Jr Eng Tech; Jr Rot; Nat Sci Aw; Pres Ac Ftns Aw; Sci Fairs; Sci/Math Olympn; WWAHSS; Comm Volntr; Red Cr Aide; Biology Clb; Chrch Yth Grp; Key Club; Sci Clb; Svce Clb; SP/M/VS; Ftball (V); Track (V); Wt Lftg (V); State Notary - Knights of Columbus; PJAS 1st Place; Aeronautical Research; Education

KOWAL, KIMBERLY; STROUDSBURG, PA; STROUDSBURG HS; (JR); Hnr Roll; FBLA; Photog; Orch; Sccr (V CL); Yrbk (R); Rookie of the Year (2004); Bio Chemistry; Chemistry; Temple U; Philadelphia U

KPODI, NYENE; BRISTOL, PA; TRUMAN SR HS; (SO); Hnr Roll; Perf Att; St of Mnth; Chrch Yth Grp; Emplmnt; Bnd; Ch Chr; Drm Mjr; Sccr (V); Track (V); Engineering; Architecture; Messiah U; Kutztown U

KRAHNKE, BRYAN; ERIE, PA; ERIE CITY SD; (SR); Hnr Roll; Perf Att; Comm Volntr; Chrch Yth Grp; Emplmnt; Cr Ctry (V L); Mar Art; Swmg (V L); Track (VJ L); Volunteer Fireman; Culinary Arts

KRAHNKE, DEBRA; ERIE, PA; ERIE CITY SD; (FR); Hnr Roll; Pres Ac Ftns Aw; Comm Volntr; Spec Olymp Vol; Chrch Yth Grp; Cr Ctry (J); Ice Sktg; Track (J); Cosmetology

KRAMER, MONICA C; UPPER DARBY, PA; UPPER DARBY HS; (JR); F Lan Hn Soc; Hi Hnr Roll; Hnr Roll; Nat Hon Sy; Perf Att; Peer Tut/Med; Emplmnt; French Clb; Bnd; Chr; Jzz Bnd; Mch Bnd; Treasurer of National Honor Society; French/Linguistics; Education; U of Pennsylvania; Middlebury College

KRASINSKI, PAUL; ERIE, PA; FORT LEBOEUF SD; (FR); Ctznshp Aw; Hnr Roll; MVP; Perf Att; Sci Fairs; Yth Ldrshp Prog; Peer Tut/Med; Bsball (J); Golf (J); Ice Hky (VJC); Stu Cncl (R); Good Citizen Award-8th Grade; Penn State U

KRATZ, CHRISTINE M; NORRISTOWN, PA; NORRISTOWN HS; (SO); Hnr Roll; Comm Volntr; Chrch Yth Grp; Key Club; Mth Clb/Tm; Mus Clb; Outdrs Clb; German Clb; Bnd; Clr Grd; Mch Bnd; Lcrsse (V); Asian-American Club; NAFAD (Norristown Area Fight Against Drugs); Psychology Major (Music Therapy); Music Major

KRAUS, ELIZABETH R; APOLLO, PA; KISKI AREA HS; (JR); WWAHSS; Yth Ldrshp Prog; Comm Volntr; Hosp Aide; Emplmnt; Key Club; French Clb; Stg Cre; Bskball (J); Tennis (J); Track (V); Stu Cncl (R); Sch Ppr (R); Yrbk (E); National Youth Leadership Forum on Law; Pre-Law; Philosophy; Duquesne; Washington & Jefferson

KRAUSE, JOSHUA; BRISBIN, PA; MOSHANNON VALLEY JR/SR HS; (SO); Hi Hnr Roll; Hnr Roll; Nat Hon Sy; St of Mnth; Drma Clb; Emplmnt; Mus Clb; Spanish Clb; Bnd; Jzz Bnd; Mch Bnd; Orch; Sccr; Stu Cncl (R); Yrbk (E, P); Tri-M Music Honor Society; Class Rank-14th Out of 115; Education-History, Computer; Business; Penn State-Main Campus; Indiana U of Pennsylvania

KRAUTH, MEGHAN; VANDERGRIFT, PA; KISKI AREA HS; (SO); St Optmst of Yr; Drma Clb; Chr; Vllyball (L); Stu Cncl (V); Most Improved Student 02-03; Teacher; Beautician

KRAVETS, DIANA; HARRISBURG, PA; CTRL DAUPHIN EAST HS; (FR); Hi Hnr Roll; Nat Hon Sy; Comm Volntr; Chrch Yth Grp; FBLA; Key Club; Stg Cre; Yrbk

KREBS, KRISTINA; PITTSBURGH, PA; NORTH ALLEGHENY HS; (FR); Hi Hnr Roll; Nat Hon Sy; St of Mnth; Bnd; Vllyball; Stu Cncl (R); National Junior Honor Society; National Latin Exam Gold Medal, North Allegheny Student of the Month-Oct. 2004; Doctoral Degree; Psychoneuro Immunology; Ivy League

KRECKMAN, CASSANDRA; CRESCO, PA; POCONO MOUNTAIN EAST HS; MS; Hi Hnr Roll; Hnr Roll; Nat Hon Sy; Otst Ac Ach Awd; Pres Ac Ftns Aw; Sci Fairs; St of Mnth; Comm Volntr; Chrch Yth Grp; DARE; Jr Ach; SADD; Spanish Clb; SP/M/VS; Stg Cre; Skiing; Sftball; Cl Off (R); Stu Cncl (R); CR (R); National Junior Honor Society; Pennsylvania Junior Academy of Sciences; Forensic Scientist; Veterinary; Harvard Law School

KREGER, ZACHARY; MORRIS, PA; LIBERTY JR SR HS; (SO); Hi Hnr Roll; Nat Hon Sy; Perf Att; Comm Volntr; Chrch Yth Grp; Emplmnt; Ntl FFA; Scouts; Bnd; Mch Bnd; Bskball (JC); Ftball (J); Eagle Scout; Animal Science

Kopania, Kristin
Council Rock HS South
Holland, PA

Koenig, Katrina
St Mary's HS
Landenberg, PA

National
Honor Roll
Spring 2005

Knopp, John E
Ridgeview AC Charter Sch
Greensburg, PA

Kreckman, Cassandra
Pocono Mountain East HS
Cresco, PA

KRESCANKO, TINA M; CROYDON, PA; HARRY S TRUMAN HS; (SO); Hnr Roll; Perf Att; Comm Volntr; Dbte Team; Acpl Chr; Chr; Swg Chr; Cr Ctry (J); Sccr (J); Track (J); Sch Ppr (R); Newspaper, SADD; Medical; Nursing; Temple U; Penn State U

KRUEGER, ELYSE; LANSDALE, PA; NORTH PENN HS; (FR); Ctznshp Aw; Hi Hnr Roll; Nat Hon Sy; Yth Ldrshp Prog; Comm Volntr; Peer Tut/Med; Spec Olymp Vol; Mth Clb/Tm; Mus Clb; Sci Clb; Bnd; Clr Grd; Dnce; Mch Bnd; Stu Cncl (R); CR (R); Lit Mag (E); Sch Ppr (E); Law Degree; Medical Degree

KRUG, MATTHEW B; SUSQUEHANNA, PA; BLUE RIDGE HS; (FR); Hi Hnr Roll; WWAHSS; Chrch Yth Grp; Bnd; Mch Bnd

KUEHNER JR, RAYMOND G; GOULDSBORO, PA; NORTH POCONO HS; (FR); Hnr Roll; Perf Att; Pres Ac Ftns Aw; St of Mnth; Comm Volntr; Baseball 7 Yrs. All-Stars; Jr. Volunteer, Firefighter; Criminal Justice, Law Enforcement; Penn State (U Park)

KUHLMAN, BRAD; BIRDSBORO, PA; DANIEL BOONE AREA HS; (SR); Hi Hnr Roll; Hnr Roll; Nat Hon Sy; WWAHSS; Comm Volntr; Emplmnt; FBLA; Jr Ach; Key Club; German Clb; Sccr (V); Information Systems Technology

KUHNS, BRANDON; NEW BERLIN, PA; MEADOWBROOK CHRISTIAN SCH; (JR); Hnr Roll; Pres Ac Ftns Aw; WWAHSS; Chrch Yth Grp; Key Club; Chr; SP/M/VS; Bsball (V); Sccr (J); Cl Off (P); Stu Cncl (T); President of My Youth Group; Religion; Houghton College; Lancaster Bible College

KUHNS, RYAN; NEW BERLIN, PA; MEADOWBROOK CHRISTIAN SCH; (FR); Hnr Roll; Chrch Yth Grp; Key Club; Chr; SP/M/VS; Sccr (J); Track (VJ); Cl Off (S); Stu Cncl; Science; Medical / Engineering

KUKUCKA, NATALIE; EBENSBURG, PA; CTRL CAMBRIA HS; (SO); Hi Hnr Roll; Perf Att; WWAHSS; Chrch Yth Grp; Drma Clb; Emplmnt; NtlFrnscLg; Bnd; Chr; Mch Bnd; SP/M/VS; Tennis (V); Stu Cncl (R); Black Belt in Karate; Pre-Med; Ob/Gyn

KULIK, ROBERT J; NORTH HUNTINGDON, PA; NORWIN SD; (SR); Hi Hnr Roll; Hnr Roll; MVP; Nat Hon Sy; Pres Ac Ftns Aw; Comm Volntr; DARE; Emplmnt; Lttrmn Clb; Vsity Clb; Chr; Sccr (VJ L); Tennis (V); MVP-Freshman Soccer-2001; Unsung Hero Award Soccer-2002; Business; Computer; U of Pittsburgh-Greensburg; Robert Morris College

KULP, ANDREW; LANCASTER, PA; MANHEIM TWP; (JR); Hi Hnr Roll; Yth Ldrshp Prog; Chess; Emplmnt; Architecture; Drexel U; Penn State

KULP, KARLI; FOGELSVILLE, PA; 21ST CENTURY CYBER CHARTER SCH; (SR); Hi Hnr Roll; Hnr Roll; Emplmnt; America's Second Harvest Volunteer; Pastry Arts; The Restaurant School At Walnut Hill College

KUNERT, CHELSEA R; NEW KENSINGTON, PA; PLUM SR HS; (JR); Hi Hnr Roll; Nat Hon Sy; Comm Volntr; Hosp Aide; Peer Tut/Med; French Clb; Chr; Secondary Education / Math; Finance / Law; Penn State U; U of Pittsburgh

KUNKEL, AMANDA L; TAMAQUA, PA; TAMAQUA AREA HS; (SR); Ctznshp Aw; F Lan Hn Soc; Hi Hnr Roll; Hnr Roll; Nat Hon Sy; Otst Ac Ach Awd; Perf Att; Sci Fairs; WWAHSS; Yth Ldrshp Prog; Comm Volntr; Peer Tut/Med; Chrch Yth Grp; DARE; Emplmnt; HO'Br Yth Ldrshp; Lib Aide; Pep Squd; Photog; Svce Clb; Bnd; Clr Grd; Flg Crps; Mch Bnd; Track (V); Stu Cncl; Poetry Club-President; Big Brothers-Big Sisters; Education; Wilkes U; Kutztown U

KUNKLE, STEPHANIE D; FORD CITY, PA; LENAPE TECH; (JR); Hnr Roll; Comm Volntr; Peer Tut/Med; Scouts; Clr Grd; Mch Bnd; Silver Award Girl Scouts; Pastry Chef; Photographer; Indiana U of PA

KURELJA, COURTNEY M; MIFFLINBURG, PA; MUFFLINBURG AREA; (SO); Hi Hnr Roll; MVP; Nat Hon Sy; Perf Att; Yth Ldrshp Prog; Comm Volntr; DARE; Key Club; Svce Clb; Vsity Clb; French Clb; Chr; Bskball (V L); Fld Hky (V L); Skiing (J); Sftball (V); Vsy Clb (V); Education; Writing; Boston U; Syracuse U

KUSNYER, DANIEL S; WEXFORD, PA; NORTH ALLEGHENY HS; (FR); Key Club; Bskball; Scholar Athlete Award 2004-2005

KUZO, AMY; HARRISBURG, PA; CTRL DAUPHIN HS; (SO); Hi Hnr Roll; Hnr Roll; Nat Hon Sy; Otst Ac Ach Awd; St of Mnth; Chrch Yth Grp; Students of the Month - January 2005; Nutritionist; Psychologist; Penn State U; U of Delaware

KWAKU, DANIEL F; READING, PA; READING HS; (SR); Comm Volntr; Ch Chr; Bskball (J); Ftball (VJ); Track (VJ); Wt Lftg (VJ); Pre-Med; Albright College; Kutztown U

KWASNIEWSKI, LAUREN; ELIZABETH, PA; ELIZABETH FORWARD HS; (SO); Hi Hnr Roll; WWAHSS; Drma Clb; Bnd; Jzz Bnd; Mch Bnd; SP/M/VS; The National Society of High School Scholars; Mock Trials

KWITOSKI, CHELSI; MECHANICSBURG, PA; CUMBERLAND VALLEY HS; (FR); Hnr Roll; Key Club; Orch; Lcrsse (J); Key Club; Teacher-History Major; Lawyer-Law & Criminal Major; Elizabethtown College; Stanford

KWON, DANNY; PITTSBURGH, PA; SETON LA SALLE HS; (SO); Hi Hnr Roll; Hnr Roll; Comm Volntr; Peer Tut/Med; Spec Olymp Vol; Chess; Cmptr Clb; Mth Clb/Tm; Mus Clb; Svce Clb; SADD; Bnd; Jzz Bnd; Mch Bnd; Orch; Bsball (J); Golf (V); Skiing (V); Altar Service; Environmental Club; Medical Doctor; Business; Washington U St. Louis; Duke U

KWON, TOMMY; PITTSBURGH, PA; SETON LA SALLE HS; (JR); Hi Hnr Roll; Nat Hon Sy; St of Mnth; WWAHSS; Comm Volntr; Peer Tut/Med; Spec Olymp Vol; Chrch Yth Grp; Mth Clb/Tm; SADD; Tech Clb; Bnd; Mch Bnd; Orch; Skiing; Stu Cncl (P); Pre-Med; Medical Degree; Harvard U; Northwestern U

LA BROZZI, KAITLYN M; ERIE, PA; MC DOWELL HS; (SO); Hnr Roll; DARE; Chr; Violinist; Pianist; Pianist (Professional); Juilliard; Mercyhurst College

LACEK, ANDREW J; NEW TRIPOLI, PA; NORTHWESTERN LEHIGH HS; (FR); Hi Hnr Roll; Otst Ac Ach Awd; Sci Fairs; St of Mnth; Valdctrian; Mar Art; Wt Lftg; Student of the Month Award; Anesthesiologist; Pharmacist or Surgeon; William & Mary; Muhlenburg

LACEY III, JAMES C; EASTON, PA; EASTON AREA HS; (SO); Hnr Roll; St of Mnth; Bsball (J); Ftball (J); Forensic Accountant; Kutztown U; Penn State

LA DUCA, ADAM; ALLENTOWN, PA; ALLENTOWN CTRL CATHOLIC HS; (SR); Hnr Roll; WWAHSS; Comm Volntr; Emplmnt; SADD; Ftball (VJ); Wt Lftg (V); Sch Ppr (R); Write For School Sports Magazine; Accounting; Business; Kutztown U of Pennsylvania; Moravian College

LAIRD, LEILA; COGAN STATION, PA; WILLIAMSPORT AREA HS; (JR); Hnr Roll; Perf Att; Pres Sch; St of Mnth; Comm Volntr; Chrch Yth Grp; Key Club; Svce Clb; SADD; Chr; Ch Chr; SP/M/VS; CR (R); Newberry Lioness Service Award; Elementary Education; Penn College; Houghton College

LAM, LILY; CAMP HILL, PA; CUMBERLAND VALLEY HS; (JR); Hnr Roll; Perf Att; WWAHSS; Key Club; Family Physician

LAMBERT, KATELIN M; CHAMBERSBURG, PA; CHAMBERSBURG AREA SR HS; (SO); Hnr Roll; Chrch Yth Grp; Emplmnt; Jr Cls League; Pep Squd; Prom Com; Vsity Clb; Latin Clb; Chr; Scr Kpr (VJ); Swmg (V L); Vsy Clb (V); Cl Off (S); Stu Cncl (R); CR (R); Pre-Law; Political Science; American U

LAMBERTI, RACHAEL; PITTSBURGH, PA; PLUM SR HS; (JR); Hnr Roll; MVP; Nat Hon Sy; Nat Mrt Sch Recip; Perf Att; Pres Ac Ftns Aw; USAA; USMC Stu Ath Aw; Comm Volntr; Peer Tut/Med; Emplmnt; Jr Ach; Off Aide; Photog; Prom Com; SADD; Hsbk Rdg; PP Ftbl (C); Scr Kpr (V); Track (J); Stu Cncl (S, R); Softball - Outside of School / 3 Teams; IUP

LAMOUREUX, ALEXANDER; MECHANICSBURG, PA; CUMBERLAND VALLEY HS; (JR); WWAHSS; Hab For Humty Volntr; Key Club; French Clb; Who's Who Among American High School Students; Criminal Justice; Computer Sciences; Shippensburg U; West Virginia U

LANCASTER, ASHLEY A; LEWISBURG, PA; MONTGOMERY AREA HS; (SR); Hi Hnr Roll; Hnr Roll; Nat Hon Sy; WWAHSS; Peer Tut/Med; Red Cr Aide; Chrch Yth Grp; Emplmnt; FBLA; Chr; Ch Chr; Bskball (J); Sftball (J); Stu Cncl (R); CR (R); National Fine Arts Participant; District Bible Quiz Participant; Youth Pastor; Valley Forge Christian College

LANCASTER, JAIME L; TELFORD, PA; SOUDERTON AREA HS; (SR); Hi Hnr Roll; Hnr Roll; Pres Ac Ftns Aw; Sci/Math Olympn; Comm Volntr; Chrch Yth Grp; DARE; Emplmnt; Tchrs Aide; Bskball (V CL); Sccr (V L); Secondary Education; Millersville U

LANCIOTTI, TYLER; JAMESTOWN, PA; JAMESTOWN AREA SD; (FR); Hi Hnr Roll; Hnr Roll; WWAHSS; Comm Volntr; Peer Tut/Med; Chrch Yth Grp; Emplmnt; Outdrs Clb; Photog; Tchrs Aide; Ftball; Track (V); Wrstlg (J L); Cl Off (V); Stu Cncl (R); CR (R); #12 Played Football At Kennedy Christian Catholic School (Firebirds) Summer Before 2004; Law; Computer Engineer; U of Pennsylvania; Notre Dame U

LAND, WILLIAM; APOLLO, PA; (SO); Hi Hnr Roll; Otst Ac Ach Awd; Perf Att; Sci/Math Olympn; WWAHSS; Comm Volntr; Key Club; Mth Clb/Tm; MuAlphaTh; Spanish Clb; Bnd; Chr; Bskball (J); Ftball; Tennis (V); V.P. of Math Team; Freshman Math Student of the Year; Mechanical Engineering; Chemical Engineering; Stanford U; Vanderbilt U

LANDES, STEFANIE; SAYLORSBURG, PA; PLEASANT VALLEY HS; (SO); Hi Hnr Roll; WWAHSS; Spec Olymp Vol; ArtClub; Chrch Yth Grp; Key Club; Ch Chr; Editor for Schools Key Club '05-'06 / Play Guitar - Takes Lessons; National Art Honor Society Secretary; High School Art Teacher; Interior Designer; Maryland Institute College of Art; The Art Institute of New York City

LANE, DEREK; LANCASTER, PA; MC CASKEY HS; (FR); Hnr Roll; Perf Att; Sci Fairs; Computer Animator; Graphic Designer; Brown College

LANG, DEREK J; CATASAUGUA, PA; ALLENTOWN CTRL CATHOLIC HS; (JR); Hi Hnr Roll; Nat Mrt Semif; Comm Volntr; Chrch Yth Grp; Emplmnt; Mth Clb/Tm; Mod UN; NYLC; Sch Ppr (R); U of Pittsburgh; Cornell

LANG, MARISSA; BEAVER, PA; BEAVER AREA HS; (JR); Ctznshp Aw; Hnr Roll; Kwnis Aw; WWAHSS; Comm Volntr; Hab For Humty Volntr; Red Cr Aide; DARE; Drma Clb; Emplmnt; Key Club; Prom Com; SADD; Spanish Clb; Chr; Dnce; SP/M/VS; Chrldg (VJ L); Stu Cncl (R); Distinguished Officer for Key Club; Dance Scholarship to Las Vegas; Musical Theater / Dance; Business; Point Park U; Kent State U

LANG, NICHOLAS T; WEXFORD, PA; NORTH ALLEGHENY INT; (FR); Hnr Roll; WWAHSS; Comm Volntr; Chrch Yth Grp; Key Club; Bskball (J)

LANGAN, ALEX; HERSHEY, PA; HERSHEY HS; (JR); Hi Hnr Roll; Hnr Roll; Nat Hon Sy; Comm Volntr; Emplmnt; NYLC; German Clb; Ftball (J); Lcrsse (J); Criminology; Business Management; U of Maryland; Johns Hopkins U

LANGE, REBECCA; HARRISBURG, PA; CTRL DAUPHIN EAST HS; (SO); Hi Hnr Roll; Jr Rot; Nat Hon Sy; Otst Ac Ach Awd; St of Mnth; WWAHSS; Yth Ldrshp Prog; Comm Volntr; Hosp Aide; Peer Tut/Med; ArtClub; Chrch Yth Grp; Drma Clb; Emplmnt; Scouts; Bnd; Chr; Dnce; SP/M/VS; Fld Hky (J); Medicine; Journalism; Penn State U; Stanford U

LANGELL, ANNA D; PITTSBURGH, PA; SHALER AREA INT SCH; (JR); F Lan Hn Soc; Hi Hnr Roll; Kwnis Aw; Nat Hon Sy; Otst Ac Ach Awd; Pres Ac Ftns Aw; St of Mnth; WWAHSS; Comm Volntr; Spec Olymp Vol; BPA; FBLA; Key Club; Mod UN; SADD; French Clb; Skiing; Sccr (V L); Track (J); Pittsburgh Strikers Soccer; Taught French Elementary Lessons; Major in Journalism; Editor of a Magazine; New York U; Penn State U

LANGFORD, LAURA; GIBSONIA, PA; PINE RICHLAND HS; (SO); Ctznshp Aw; Hi Hnr Roll; Otst Ac Ach Awd; Pres Sch; Sci Fairs; Peer Tut/Med; DARE; Emplmnt; NtlFrnscLg; Chrldg; Hsbk Rdg (V); Outstanding Young Citizen Award; Foreign Exchange Student Host; Biology; Medicine; Grove City College; Carnegie Mellon U

LANGMANN, GABRIELLE A; CARNEGIE, PA; BISHOP CANEVIN HS; (SO); Hi Hnr Roll; Pres Sch; Yth Ldrshp Prog; Comm Volntr; Peer Tut/Med; Chrch Yth Grp; FBLA; Pep Squd; Svce Clb; Bnd; Jzz Bnd; Mch Bnd; Stg Cre; Sccr (V L); Stu Cncl (R); Lit Mag (R); Sch Ppr (R); Johns Hopkins U Talent Search; American Legion Award; Pre-Med; Biochemistry & Biophysics; Yale U; Johns Hopkins U

LANK, BRANDON; AMITY, PA; TRINITY HS; (SO); MVP; St of Mnth; DARE; Wdwrkg Clb; Lit Mag (E); Pitt U; Florida U

LA PLANTE, SAIDAH; PHOENIXVILLE, PA; CTR FOR ART TECH-PICKERING; (JR); Nat Hon Sy; Emplmnt; Restaurant Management; Culinary Arts; Walnut Hill College Restaurant School of Phila

LA ROSA, MELISSA; EASTON, PA; EASTON AREA HS; (JR); Hi Hnr Roll; Pres Ac Ftns Aw; Sci Fairs; WWAHSS; Comm Volntr; Key Club; Chrldg; All American NCA Cheerleader Honor Society; Nat'l Honor Society/Spanish; Sports Medicine; Athletic Personal Training; U of Georgia; NC State or U of Miami

LARSEN, LEANDRA; SAYLORSBURG, PA; PLEASANT VALLEY HS; (SR); Hnr Roll; Perf Att; Comm Volntr; Hosp Aide; Key Club; Bnd; Mch Bnd; Pep Bnd; Astronomy; Earth Science; West Chester U

LARSEN, STEPHEN; WAYNESBORO, PA; WAYNESBORO AREA SR HS; (SO); Hnr Roll; Pres Ac Ftns Aw; St of Mnth; Emplmnt; Key Club; Scouts; Ftball (J); Boy Scouts; Volunteer Firefighter; Criminology; Shippensburg U; Penn State

LARSON, RYAN M; POTTSTOWN, PA; POTTSGROVE HS; (JR); Ctznshp Aw; Hi Hnr Roll; Hnr Roll; Nat Hon Sy; Otst Ac Ach Awd; WWAHSS; Hosp Aide; Emplmnt; Key Club; NYLC; Sci Clb; French Clb; Bsball (V L); Golf (V L); Aeronautical Science; Military Tactics; United States Air Force Academy; Embry Riddle Aeronautical U

LASINSKI, STEPHANIE; GIBSONIA, PA; PINE RICHLAND HS; (SR); Ctznshp Aw; Hi Hnr Roll; Nat Hon Sy; Otst Ac Ach Awd; WWAHSS; Comm Volntr; Spec Olymp Vol; Key Club; Prom Com; SADD; Bskball (V L); PP Ftbl; Sftball (V L); Vllyball (J); Cl Off (S); Stu Cncl; Coached At BB & SB Clinics; Scholar Athlete; Biology; Pre-Med; Allegheny College

LASKEY, MORGAN; PITTSBURGH, PA; PITTSBURGH SD HS; (JR); Hi Hnr Roll; Hnr Roll; WWAHSS; Chrch Yth Grp; Emplmnt; Dnce; Chrldg (JC); Stu Cncl (R); Creative and Performing Arts High Schools Most Outstanding Junior Dancer; BFA in Dance; Dance in a Professional Dance Company; Ohio State U, Ohio; Fordham U, Nyc, NY

LATTA JR, HARRY L; WATERFORD, PA; FT LEBOEUF HS; (SO); Hi Hnr Roll; MVP; Nat Hon Sy; St of Mnth; WWAHSS; Comm Volntr; Peer Tut/Med; Bsball (V L); Bskball (V L); National Honor Society; Sports-Communications, Coaching; Duke; Notre Dame

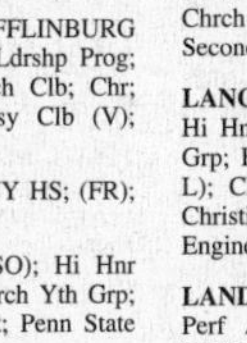
Lanciotti, Tyler
Jamestown Area SD
Jamestown, PA

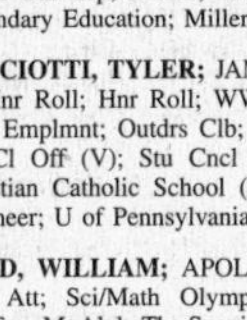
La Brozzi, Kaitlyn M
Mc Dowell HS
Erie, PA

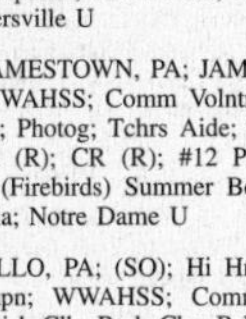
Kuehner Jr, Raymond G
North Pocono HS
Gouldsboro, PA

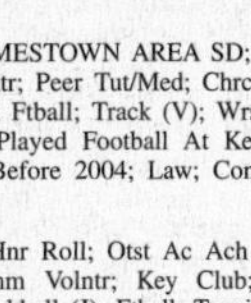
Kwaku, Daniel F
Reading HS
Reading, PA

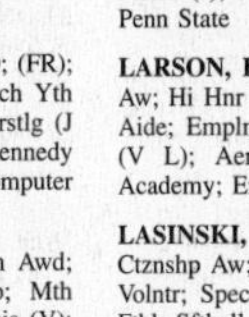
Larson, Ryan M
Pottsgrove HS
Pottstown, PA

LAU, THUY-DUONG; UPPER DARBY, PA; UPPER DARBY HS; (JR); Hi Hnr Roll; Hnr Roll; Nat Hon Sy; Comm Volntr; Prom Com; Svce Clb; Lcrsse (J); Vllyball (V C); CR (R); Business Award for Superwrite; Education; Business/Accounting; West Chester U; Temple U

LAUBHAM, KAITLIN A; EXPORT, PA; FRANKLIN REG HS; (SR); Hi Hnr Roll; Nat Hon Sy; Chrch Yth Grp; Drma Clb; Emplmnt; Bnd; Chr; Mch Bnd; SP/M/VS; Sch Ppr (E, R); Clarion U Poetry Contest Winner (2 Years); Bagpipes-Competitive; English; Theater; Asbury College; Grove City College

LAUFFER, ALEXANDRA; NARVON, PA; GARDEN SPOT HS; (SR); Hi Hnr Roll; Nat Hon Sy; Nat Mrt LOC; Pres Sch; WWAHSS; Chrch Yth Grp; Drma Clb; Ntl FFA; Vsity Clb; Bnd; Chr; Mch Bnd; SP/M/VS; Chrldg (V CL); Cr Ctry (J); Vsy Clb (V); Cl Off (P, S); CR (R); Academic Hall of Fame for Agriculture; PA Governor's School for the Ag Sciences-2004; Ag & Extension Education; Poultry Science (Minor); Pennsylvania State U

LAUR, CATHERINE V; MONROEVILLE, PA; GATEWAY SD; (SO); Hnr Roll; Hab For Humty Volntr; Chrch Yth Grp; Emplmnt; Scouts; PP Ftbl (J); Sftball (J); Student Athletic Training; Physical Therapy; Athletic Training; Pennsylvania State U

LA VALVA, CRYSTAL; EASTON, PA; EASTON AREA HS; (FR); Hnr Roll; Perf Att; Clb; Chr; Sftball (J); Vllyball (J); Medical; Washington U; U of Phoenix

LAWMAN, JENNIFER; BROOKVILLE, PA; BROOKVILLE AREA SD; (JR); Hi Hnr Roll; Hnr Roll; Perf Att; St of Mnth; WWAHSS; Yth Ldrshp Prog; Prom Com; Spanish Clb; Chr; SP/M/VS; Sccr (V L); Swmg (V L); Track (V); Stu Cncl (R); CR (R); Nation Junior Honor Society-Historian; Optometry; Pharmacy; Pennsylvania State U

LAWRENCE, AMY L; HANOVER, PA; HANOVER HS; (FR); Hnr Roll; Otst Ac Ach Awd; Comm Volntr; Key Club; Tchrs Aide; Chr; Sftball (J); Tennis (J); Horseback Riding-Not School Related; Equestrian Science

LAWRENCE, RASHEENA J; PHILADELPHIA, PA; JOHN BARTRAM HS; (SR); Hi Hnr Roll; Hnr Roll; Nat Hon Sy; WWAHSS; Yth Ldrshp Prog; Comm Volntr; Chrch Yth Grp; Cmptr Clb; Drma Clb; Emplmnt; Dnce; SP/M/VS; Stu Cncl (R); Lit Mag (E); Law & Justice; Psychology; Temple Beasley School of Law; West Chester U

LAWSON, KATI; MECHANICSBURG, PA; MECHANICSBURG AREA SR HS; (SO); Hnr Roll; Key Club; Mod UN; NtlFrnscLg; P to P St Amb Prg; French Clb; Track (V L); Stu Cncl (R); Sch Ppr (E); Varsity Water Polo; Journalism; Ancient History; New York U; UC Berkeley

LAYMAN, MEAGAN; BELLE VERNON, PA; CTRL WESTMORELAND CTC; (SO); Comm Volntr; Dbte Team; Bnd; Chr; Jzz Bnd; Mch Bnd; Bookworm - Reading Club; Forensics Bible Club; Computer Animation; Penn State U; U of Pittsburgh

LAZAR, ALLISON; HERMITAGE, PA; HICKORY HS; (SO); F Lan Hn Soc; Hi Hnr Roll; WWAHSS; Peer Tut/Med; Drma Clb; Mth Clb/Tm; SADD; Tmpl Yth Grp; French Clb; Bnd; Dnce; Flg Crps; Mch Bnd; Golf (V); Cl Off (S); CR (S); Who's Who In Math; Who's Who Science; Business; Foreign Language-French

LE, HUONG; UPPER DARBY, PA; UPPER DARBY HS; (JR); Hi Hnr Roll; Hnr Roll; Perf Att; ArtClub; Prom Com; Track (J); Graphic Design; Drexel U; Temple (Tyler School of Art)

LE, NICOLE; EPHRATA, PA; EPHRATA HS; (MS); Hi Hnr Roll; Hnr Roll; Pres Ac Ftns Aw; Dnce; Chrldg (J); Cl Off (P); Stu Cncl (P); Medical/ Veterinary; Law; Princeton; Yale

LE, TUYET; BETHLEHEM, PA; BETHLEHEM CATHOLIC HS; (FR); Hnr Roll; Comm Volntr; Chrch Yth Grp; Key Club; Medical Fields; Lehigh U

LEACH, HAZEL; DUNCANNON, PA; SUSQUENITA HS; (SR); Hnr Roll; Sci Fairs; St of Mnth; WWAHSS; Emplmnt; FCA; FBLA; Prom Com; Scouts; SADD; French Clb; Chr; Cr Ct Ski (V C); Track (J); Horizons; CROSS; Nursing; HACC

LEAMAN, AMANDA; PHOENIXVILLE, PA; CTR FOR ART TECH-PICKERING; (JR); Hnr Roll; Red Cr Aide; Spec Olymp Vol; Prom Com; SADD; Voc Ind Clb Am; HOSA Clb; HOSA; Registered Nurse-BSN; Alvernia; West Chester U

LEASHER, VINCENT; BENSALEM, PA; BENSALEM TOWNSHIP SD; (SO); Hi Hnr Roll; Hnr Roll; Perf Att; Sci Fairs; St of Mnth; Bnd; Jzz Bnd; Mch Bnd; Pep Bnd; Black Belt in Tae Kwon Do

LEATHERBURY, TADREYA; PHILADELPHIA, PA; OVERBROOK HS; (SO); Ctznshp Aw; Hnr Roll; St of Mnth; Peer Tut/Med; DARE; Bnd; Mch Bnd

LEBEL, BENJAMIN; STROUDSBURG, PA; PIUS X HS; (SO); Hnr Roll; Otst Ac Ach Awd; Comm Volntr; ArtClub; Mus Clb; Off Aide; P to P St Amb Prg; Ftball; Wt Lftg; Awards Monroe County Arts Student; Piano 8 Years; Architecture; Drexel, U of Pa, U of Boston; Penn State U

LEE, BRIAN E; GREENSBURG, PA; CHRISTIAN FELLOWSHIP AC; (SO); Hnr Roll; Sci/Math Olympn; WWAHSS; Chrch Yth Grp; Tchrs Aide; Bskball; Sccr; Sftball; Flag Football; Missions Trip to Guatemala; Criminal Justice

LEE, DEBORAH M; LANSDALE, PA; NORTH PENN HS; (JR); F Lan Hn Soc; Hi Hnr Roll; Nat Hon Sy; Otst Ac Ach Awd; Perf Att; WWAHSS; Yth Ldrshp Prog; Comm Volntr; Peer Tut/Med; Spec Olymp Vol; Chess; Key Club; Mth Clb/Tm; NYLC; Outdrs Clb; P to P St Amb Prg; German Clb; Lcrsse (J); PP Ftbl (J); Sccr (C); Model Student; Straight A's Award; Biology Major; Medical Degree (Doctor); Dartmouth College; Brown U

LEE, HANSEOK; MIFFLIN, PA; JUNIATA HS; (JR); 4H Awd; Hnr Roll; Nat Hon Sy; Perf Att; WWAHSS; Comm Volntr; Spec Olymp Vol; 4-H; Chrch Yth Grp; Key Club; Mth Clb/Tm; Mus Clb; Ntl Beta Clb; Prom Com; Scouts; Chr; Golf (J); Mar Art (V); Sccr (V); Track (V); Biology; DSD; UCLA: U of California, Los Angeles; UGA: U of Georgia

LEE, JUAH; NORTH WALES, PA; NORTH PENN HS; (JR); Hnr Roll; Perf Att; WWAHSS; Yth Ldrshp Prog; Comm Volntr; Spec Olymp Vol; Chrch Yth Grp; FBLA; Key Club; Bnd; Tennis (J); Stu Cncl (R); Business; Accounting; Northeastern U; Clark U

LEEMHUIS, DOROTHY; ERIE, PA; MC DOWELL HS; (JR); Hi Hnr Roll; Jr Eng Tech; Nat Hon Sy; WWAHSS; Chrch Yth Grp; FCA; Key Club; Ch Chr; Orch; Track (V)

LEES, KIRA A; MONROEVILLE, PA; GATEWAY HS; (JR); Hi Hnr Roll; Nat Hon Sy; Sci Fairs; St of Mnth; Amnsty Intl; Comm Volntr; Peer Tut/Med; ArtClub; Chrch Yth Grp; Jr Cls League; Key Club; Lib Aide; NtlFrnscLg; Scouts; Chr; Dnce; SP/M/VS; Stg Cre; Project Area Leadership; Writing Center; English; Psychology; Tufts U; Oberlin College

LEFKOWITZ, CATHERINE; SEWICKLEY, PA; NORTH ALLEGHENY INT HS; (SO); Hnr Roll; Nat Hon Sy; Sci Fairs; St of Mnth; WWAHSS; Amnsty Intl; Hosp Aide; Peer Tut/Med; Emplmnt; Key Club; Lttrmn Clb; Prom Com; SADD; Vsity Clb; French Clb; Chr; Dvng (V L); Tennis (V); Adv Cncl (R); Stu Cncl (R); Secretary of Key Club (Distinguished Officer); Vice President of Zonta International; Dermatology; U of Pennsylvania; Emory U

LEHMAN, JUSTINE; BERLIN, PA; BERLIN BROTHERS VALLEY SD; (SO); Hi Hnr Roll; Hnr Roll; Comm Volntr; 4-H; Track (V); Sch Ppr (R, P); Dairy Showmanship Award; Jr. 4-H leader; Large Animal Veterinarian; Cornell U; Penn State

LEHMAN, RYAN D; MT PLEASANT, PA; MT PLEASANT AREA; (SO); Hi Hnr Roll; MVP; Comm Volntr; Emplmnt; Quiz Bowl; Sccr (V L); Track (V L); Gamma Omega / Gifted Program; Youth Soccer Referee; Bio Technology

LEMOI, JOSHUA A; WILLIAMSPORT, PA; LOYALSOCK TWP HS; (SO); Hnr Roll; Jr Rot; WWAHSS; Comm Volntr; Chrch Yth Grp; DARE; Key Club; SADD; Spanish Clb; Bskball (J); Sccr (V L)

LENTZ, LEESHA; POTTSTOWN, PA; POTTSGROVE SR HS; (FR); Ctznshp Aw; Gov Hnr Prg; Hi Hnr Roll; Hnr Roll; Nat Hon Sy; Otst Ac Ach Awd; St of Mnth; Comm Volntr; Hosp Aide; Peer Tut/Med; ArtClub; DARE; Emplmnt; French Clb; Lcrsse (V); Lit Mag (R); Sch Ppr (R); Award for 4.0 Avg for 3 Yrs; English Award for Three Years, History Award; Journalism; Psychology; Oxford U; Duke U

LEO, JESSICA; DOYLESTOWN, PA; CTRL BUCKS HS EAST; (SO); F Lan Hn Soc; Hi Hnr Roll; WWAHSS; Comm Volntr; Key Club; French Clb; Chr; Mch Bnd; SP/M/VS; Select Choir; Hotel / Restaurant Management; Music; Penn State U

LEON, INGRID A; LEBANON, PA; LEBANON HS; (JR); Hi Hnr Roll; Hnr Roll; Perf Att; St of Mnth; Comm Volntr; Peer Tut/Med; ArtClub; DARE; Emplmnt; Lib Aide; Dnce; Stg Cre; Track (J); Sch Ppr (R); Human Resource Manager; Medical Secretary; Bronx Community College (NYC); Manhattan Borough Community College

LEON, MELISSA M; HUNTINGDON VALLEY, PA; ABINGTON SR HS; (SO); Hi Hnr Roll; Nat Hon Sy; WWAHSS; Comm Volntr; Peer Tut/Med; Drma Clb; Key Club; SP/M/VS; Stu Cncl (R); Sch Ppr (R); Yrbk (R, P); Actor / Communications / Journalism / Business

LE PERE, DARREN B; WEXFORD, PA; NORTH ALLEGHENY HS; (SO); Hi Hnr Roll; Nat Hon Sy; Pres Ac Ftns Aw; WWAHSS; Emplmnt; Key Club; Mth Clb/Tm; Tchrs Aide; Ftball (J); Lcrsse (V L); Wt Lftg; Volunteers 2-3 Hrs./Wk. with Mentally Challenged in Gym Class; Pre-Med; Stanford U; U of California Los Angeles

LERCH, STACI S; LEWISTOWN, PA; LEWISTOWN AREA HS; (JR); Hi Hnr Roll; Nat Hon Sy; WWAHSS; Comm Volntr; Peer Tut/Med; Spec Olymp Vol; Chrch Yth Grp; Emplmnt; Key Club; Spanish Clb; Chrldg (V L); Stu Cncl (R); Tri-Valley Scholar Athlete; Key Club Lt. Governor; Marketing

LESONIK, SHERAH; ERIE, PA; FORT LEBOEUF SD HS; (FR); Arch (J); Archaeology; Zoology; Mercyhurst

LESUER, DOMINICK; PHILADELPHIA, PA; CAMELOT FEL AC; Hnr Roll; Otst Ac Ach Awd; Perf Att; Bskball; Mar Art (L); Rlr Hky (L); Computer Tech; Computer Analysis; Temple U

LEUENBERGER, LAURA; HERSHEY, PA; HERSHEY HS; (JR); 4H Awd; Hi Hnr Roll; Nat Hon Sy; Otst Ac Ach Awd; WWAHSS; Comm Volntr; Hab For Humty Volntr; 4-H; Chrch Yth Grp; Emplmnt; Key Club; Mth Clb/Tm; Photog; Prom Com; Quill & Scroll; Chr; Ch Chr; SP/M/VS; Stg Cre; Lcrsse (J); Sftball (J); Vllyball; Cl Off (V); Stu Cncl (R); Sch Ppr (E, R, P); 2006 National Merit Program- In Process; Government and Law Program - School Representative; Political Science; U of Virginia; Penn State U

LEWIS, ANTONIA; FOLCROFT, PA; AC PARK HS; (JR); Ctznshp Aw; Hnr Roll; Nat Hon Sy; Perf Att; WWAHSS; ArtClub; Chrch Yth Grp; SP/M/VS; Track (J); Stu Cncl (R); Highest Academic Achievement in Foreign Language; President's Education Award Jan. 2003; Psychology; Forensic Science; West Chester U; Fordham U

LEWIS, DAVID C; WILKES BARRE, PA; E L MEYERS HS; (JR); Hi Hnr Roll; Hnr Roll; MVP; WWAHSS; AL Aux Boys; Dbte Team; Key Club; Bsball (V L); Ftball (V L); Adv Cncl (P); Cl Off (P); Stu Cncl (P); CR (P); Elementary Education; Criminal Justice; King's College Wilkes-Barre; Wilkes U

LEWIS, JACLYN C; NORRISTOWN, PA; NORRISTOWN AREA HS; (JR); Hnr Roll; Comm Volntr; Key Club; French Clb; Cr Ctry (V); Elementary Education; Early Childhood Education; Salisbury U (MD); Shippensburg (PA)

LEWIS, MATTHEW J; ERIE, PA; STRONG VINCENT HS; (JR); Ctznshp Aw; Nat Hon Sy; Perf Att; Sci Fairs; US Army Sch Ath Aw; WWAHSS; Peer Tut/Med; ROTC; French Clb; Bnd; Jzz Bnd; Chrldg (V CL); Ftball (V L); Wt Lftg (V); Wrstlg (V); Cl Off (T); CR; A Few Other Leadership Awards; In A Production WQLN; Engineering; Yale U; Pennsylvania State U

LEWIS, MELISSA; PITTSBURGH, PA; SCHENLEY HS; (SO); Hnr Roll; Nat Hon Sy; Yth Ldrshp Prog; Comm Volntr; Peer Tut/Med; Cmptr Clb; Emplmnt; Fr of Library; Chr; Criminal Justice; Howard U

LEWIS, THOMAS; PITTSBURGH, PA; CARLYNTON JR/SR HS; (FR); Hnr Roll; Chr; Evangelism; Toccoa Falls College

LI, ANDREW K; MECHANICSBURG, PA; CUMBERLAND VALLEY HS; (JR); Hnr Roll; WWAHSS; Comm Volntr; Red Cr Aide; Emplmnt; Key Club; Spanish Clb; Bnd; Mch Bnd; Tennis (V); 2nd Degree Black Belt in Karate; Pharmacy; Accounting; Pennsylvania State U; U of Pittsburgh

LIACOURAS, MICHAEL; WEST CHESTER, PA; HENDERSON HS; (JR); Ctznshp Aw; F Lan Hn Soc; Hi Hnr Roll; Nat Hon Sy; WWAHSS; Lcrsse (V L); Sccr (V L); National Honor Society; Spanish National Honor Society; Finance; Accounting; Villa Nova U

LIEB, MICHELE; EBENSBURG, PA; CTRL CAMBRIA HS; (SR); Hi Hnr Roll; Nat Hon Sy; Otst Ac Ach Awd; WWAHSS; Comm Volntr; Drma Clb; Bnd; Chr; SP/M/VS; Stg Cre; Chrldg (V L); Vllyball (J); Pre-Veterinary Medicine; Biology; Edinboro U of PA

LIEBLING, BENJAMIN A; GROVE CITY, PA; GROVE CITY SR HS; (SO); Hi Hnr Roll; Nat Stu Ath Day Aw; WWAHSS; Comm Volntr; Chrch Yth Grp; FCA; Mod UN; NYLC; Bskball (V L); Business Law; Personal Law; Duke U; U of Virginia

LIED, KRISTEN; WEXFORD, PA; NORTH ALLEGHENY INT HS; (FR); Hi Hnr Roll; Hnr Roll; Nat Hon Sy; Otst Ac Ach Awd; Salutrn; Yth Ldrshp Prog; Comm Volntr; Chrch Yth Grp; Key Club; Chr; SP/M/VS; Stu Cncl (R); Fine Art-Numerous; Honors English-Highest GPA

LIKAJ, LORENA; PHILADELPHIA, PA; NAZARETH AC HS; (SO); Hnr Roll; WWAHSS; Mod UN; Italian Clb; World Affairs Club; Pediatrician; Harvard U; Princeton U

LIKEN, JOSHUA R; PHILADELPHIA, PA; CENTRAL HS; (SR); Comm Volntr; Chrch Yth Grp; Cr Ctry (J L); Gmnstcs (V L); Track (V L); Silver Service Award of PA / Area Sunday School Association; Graphic Arts; Kinesiology; Temple U; Drexel U

LILLIE, REBEKAH; GREENVILLE, PA; GREENVILLE HS; (JR); Hnr Roll; WWAHSS; Chrch Yth Grp; Key Club; Vsity Clb; Bnd; Chr; Ch Chr; Jzz Bnd; Varsity Band Letter; Elementary Education; Geneva College; Eastern Nazarene College

LILLY, RENEE M; HERMITAGE, PA; HICKORY HS; (SO); 4H Awd; Hi Hnr Roll; WWAHSS; 4-H; Chrch Yth Grp; Spanish Clb; Bnd; Mch Bnd; Orch; Swmg (V); Equestrian/4-H; YMCA Swim Team; Pre-Veterinary Medicine/Equine Veterinary; Equine Chiropractics

LINDSEY, DENISE M; SEWICKLEY, PA; QUAKER VALLEY HS; (JR); Hi Hnr Roll; Hnr Roll; WWAHSS; Comm Volntr; Hosp Aide; Emplmnt; Key Club; Bskball (V L); Vllyball (J); Vice President of Key Club; Head of Women's Group for Minorities; Early Child Education; Spelman College; U of Alabama

Lentz, Leesha
Pottsgrove SR HS
Pottstown, PA

Lebel, Benjamin
Pius X HS
Stroudsburg, PA

National
Honor Roll
Spring 2005

Leaman, Amanda
Ctr For Art Tech-Pickering
Phoenixville, PA

Lewis, David C
E L Meyers HS
Wilkes Barre, PA

LING, YAN; LATROBE, PA; GREATER LATROBE SR HS; (JR); F Lan Hn Soc; Hi Hnr Roll; Nat Hon Sy; Pres Ac Ftns Aw; Sci/Math Olympn; St of Mnth; WWAHSS; Comm Volntr; Peer Tut/Med; ArtClub; Chess; Emplmnt; Key Club; Lib Aide; NtlFrnscLg; Sci Clb; Clb; Engineering; Mathematics; Stanford U

LINTELMAN, CHARLIE; WATERFORD, PA; FORT LEBOEUF SD; (SO); Hnr Roll; Perf Att; Comm Volntr; Peer Tut/Med; Chrch Yth Grp; Emplmnt; Off Aide; Landscape Architecture; Penn State U; Gannon U

LIPPY, NATE; HANOVER, PA; HANOVER HS; (SR); Hnr Roll; Pres Ac Ftns Aw; St of Mnth; Key Club; Bsball (V CL); Bskball (V CL); Sch Ppr (R); Yrbk (P); Student of the Month 1998; Bachelors in Accounting; Minor in Business Management; Shippensburg U; Slippery Rock U

LIPSKI, JAIME; DALLAS, PA; LAKE-LEHMAN HS; (SO); Hi Hnr Roll; Nat Hon Sy; St of Mnth; WWAHSS; Yth Ldrshp Prog; Chrch Yth Grp; Key Club; SADD; Fld Hky (V L); Swmg (V); Track (V L); National Honor Society; 2nd Team All-State Field Hockey; Sports Psychology; Boston College; Villa Nova U

LISBON JR, RANDY L; JENNERSTOWN, PA; NORTH STAR HS; (JR); Bnd; Jzz Bnd; Mch Bnd; Music; Art

LISZEWSKI, APRIL M; MOOSIC, PA; RIVERSIDE JR/SR HS; (JR); Hi Hnr Roll; Hnr Roll; Nat Hon Sy; WWAHSS; Emplmnt; Spanish Clb; Nursing; Massage Therapy; College Misericordia; Mansfield U

LISZKA, BRIAN R; JAMESTOWN, PA; JAMESTOWN AREA SD; (SR); Hi Hnr Roll; Nat Hon Sy; Pres Ac Ftns Aw; USAA; Prom Com; Spanish Clb; Cr Ctry (V L); Wrstlg (V L); Cl Off (P); President Student Outreach; Vice President Spanish Club; Master's in Mechanical Engineering; Gannon U; U of Pittsburgh

LITTLE, JAMAR C; PITTSBURGH, PA; PITTSBURGH SD; (SO); Hi Hnr Roll; CARE; Bnd; Jzz Bnd; Orch; SP/M/VS; Bsball (V); Ftball (V); Track (V); Wt Lftg; Computer and Information Science Major; Electronics Major; U of Miami; West Virginia U

LITTLE, JASMIN; PITTSBURGH, PA; BRASHEAR HS; (SO); Ctznshp Aw; Hi Hnr Roll; Hnr Roll; Perf Att; Comm Volntr; Mus Clb; Drl Tm; Bskball; Track (L); U of Pittsburgh

LIU, GEORGE; PITTSBURGH, PA; MT LEBANON HS; (JR); Hi Hnr Roll; Nat Hon Sy; Perf Att; Sci Fairs; Yth Ldrshp Prog; Comm Volntr; NYLC; Sci Clb; Spanish Clb; Mch Bnd; Skt Tgt Sh (J); Tennis (V); Medicine; Biology

LIVINGSTON, CORRINE F; JAMESTOWN, PA; JAMESTOWN AREA SD; (FR); Hi Hnr Roll; Hnr Roll; Otst Ac Ach Awd; Comm Volntr; Peer Tut/Med; 4-H; Chrch Yth Grp; Lttrmn Clb; Vsity Clb; Bnd; Mch Bnd; Pep Bnd; Bskball (VJCL); Sftball (J L); Vllyball (JCL); Stu Cncl (R); Animal Sciences; Pennsylvania State U; Duke U

LIZZIO, MATTHEW M; BRODHEADSVILLE, PA; PALMERTON AREA HS; (SR); Hnr Roll; Emplmnt; Wdwrkg Clb; Skiing; Machine Tool Technology; Plastics & Polymer Technology; BS Degree; Williamson Free School of Mechanical Trades; Pennsylvania, Technical College

LLANEZA, ANDREW J; NEW KENSINGTON, PA; VALLEY HS; (JR); Hi Hnr Roll; MVP; WWAHSS; Peer Tut/Med; Chrch Yth Grp; Emplmnt; Tchrs Aide; Bsball (VJ L); Bskball (J); Golf (VJ L); Law Psychology; History, Literature; U of Pittsburgh

LLANTIN, RICARDO; MECHANICSBURG, PA; (JR); 4H Awd; Hi Hnr Roll; Hnr Roll; Nat Hon Sy; Perf Att; St of Mnth; WWAHSS; Hab For Humty Volntr; Peer Tut/Med; 4-H; FTA; Mus Clb; NYLC; Tchrs Aide; Acpl Chr; Chr; Ch Chr; Swg Chr; Stu Cncl (V); CR (S); Music Education; Culinary Arts; Hartwick U; U of Santa Rosa

LLOYD, GEORGE L N; LEWISBURG, PA; MIFFLINBURG AREA HS; (SR); Emplmnt; Key Club; Prom Com; Bsball (VJ L); Wt Lftg (V); Cl Off (V); Stu Cncl (R); CR (R); Yrbk (R); Drafting; PA College of Technology

LO, JONATHAN; ALLENTOWN, PA; LEHIGH VALLEY CHRISTIAN HS; (SO); Ctznshp Aw; Hi Hnr Roll; Hnr Roll; Nat Hon Sy; Perf Att; Pres Sch; Sci Fairs; Sci/Math Olympn; WWAHSS; Chrch Yth Grp; Law; Science; U of Pennsylvania; Temple U

LOCKE, AMANDA; MECHANICSBURG, PA; CUMBERLAND VALLEY HS; (SO); Nat Hon Sy; German Clb; United States Pony Club (C-2 rating); Biology Major; Secondary Education & Administration; Shippensburg U; Millersville U & Kutztown U

LOCKHART, MEGAN R; EAST STROUDSBURG, PA; STROUDSBURG HS; (JR); Hi Hnr Roll; Hnr Roll; Emplmnt; SADD; Vsity Clb; Chr; Fld Hky (VJ L); Track (V L); Physical Education Teacher; Elementary Education Teacher; Shippensburg; Penn State (Leigh Valley)

LOFTUS, MEGAN; MOOSIC, PA; RIVERSIDE JR/SR HS; (MS); Hi Hnr Roll; Hnr Roll; DARE; SADD; Bskball (J); Sftball (J); Youth Group / Moosic Youth Center; Advertising; Art Institute / New York City

LOGAN, ALAINA; PHILADELPHIA, PA; GERMANTOWN-LANKENAU HS; (SO); Hi Hnr Roll; Hnr Roll; Drma Clb; Vllyball (J); Upward Bound Math & Science

LOMBARDO, DANA; GIBSONIA, PA; PINE-RICHLAND HS; (JR); Hi Hnr Roll; Nat Hon Sy; WWAHSS; Comm Volntr; ArtClub; Emplmnt; Key Club; NtlFrnscLg; Photog; Svce Clb; Chr; Published Author; Completed Vet-Science Apprenticeship Program; Veterinary Sciences; DA Education; Westminster College; Ohio State U

LONG, AMBER M; SLICKVILLE, PA; GREENSBURG - SALEM HS; (SO); Hnr Roll; Comm Volntr; Emplmnt; Chr; PP Ftbl (J); Biology; Pittsburgh U, PA; Saint Vincent

LONG, CHRISTOPHER; HAZLETON, PA; HAZLETON AREA SD; (SO); Hi Hnr Roll; Hnr Roll; FCA; Scouts; Spanish Clb; Ftball (V); Fellowship of Christian Athletes; Medicine; Vanderbilt U; U Of Notre Dame

LONG, JAMES E; NORTH HUNTINGTON, PA; NORWIN SD; (SR); Hnr Roll; Perf Att; Drma Clb; Emplmnt; Chr; Dnce; SP/M/VS; Swg Chr; Musical Theatre; Clarion U (Already Accepted)

LONG, KENNY; FAYETTE CITY, PA; WILSON CHRISTIAN AC; (JR); Hi Hnr Roll; Hnr Roll; Nat Hon Sy; Comm Volntr; Peer Tut/Med; Scouts; Marketing; Business Administration; Harvard U; Babson College

LONGENBACH, SARAH; BATH, PA; NORTHAMPTON SR HS; (SO); SP/M/VS; Stg Cre

LONGOBARDI, NINA M; NORRISTOWN, PA; NORRISTOWN AREA HS; (JR); Hi Hnr Roll; Hnr Roll; Nat Hon Sy; St of Mnth; Comm Volntr; Emplmnt; Key Club; Mth Clb/Tm; Outdrs Clb; Svce Clb; French Clb; Stu Cncl (R); Key Club President 03-04 and 04-05; Key Club Division 21 Lieutenant Governor 05-06; Sociology; Social Work; Elizabethtown-PA; Lycoming-PA

LOOKABAUGH, BRAD; NEW KENSINGTON, PA; KISKI AREA HS; (SO); Hi Hnr Roll; Nat Hon Sy; Perf Att; Pres Ac Ftns Aw; Sci Fairs; Sci/Math Olympn; Comm Volntr; Peer Tut/Med; Chrch Yth Grp; Key Club; Mth Clb/Tm; MuAlphaTh; Mus Clb; Spanish Clb; Chr; SP/M/VS; Swg Chr; Bskball (V L); Golf (V); Tennis (V L); MBA; Medical Degree; Duke U; Notre Dame U

LORENT, LACEY M; TRANSFER, PA; REYNOLDS JR/SR HS; (FR); Hi Hnr Roll; Hnr Roll; Kwnis Aw; WWAHSS; Peer Tut/Med; Key Club; Bnd; Chr; Mch Bnd; Key Club; Pastry Chef; Slippery Rock U; West Virginia U

LORIGAN, SHAWN; JAMESTOWN, PA; JAMESTOWN AREA SD; (SO); Hi Hnr Roll; Hnr Roll; Nat Hon Sy; Perf Att; Sci Fairs; Sci/Math Olympn; Comm Volntr; Chess; Chrch Yth Grp; Emplmnt; Bnd; Mch Bnd; Pep Bnd; SP/M/VS; Bskball (J); Cl Off (T); Stu Cncl (R)

LOSITO, JOSEPH; EAST STROUDSBURG, PA; EAST STROUDSBURG HS; (FR); History; Army; Princeton; Rutgers

LOUGHMAN, GARRETT W; WASHINGTON, PA; TRINITY AREA SD; (SO); Hnr Roll; Peer Tut/Med; FTA; German Clb; Math Tutoring and Mentoring; Accounting Major; Master's in Business & Accounting; U of Pittsburgh; Robert Morris College

LOUTITT, MELISSA; MONONGAHELA, PA; RINGGOLD SD; (FR); Hi Hnr Roll; Hnr Roll; SADD; Bnd; Mch Bnd; Vllyball (J); President's Award for Educational Excellence; Psychologist / Psychiatrist; Book Publisher; Arizona State U; Emerson College

LOWE, ALICIA; LANCASTER, PA; MANHEIM TWP HS; (JR); Hnr Roll; Kwnis Aw; St of Mnth; Comm Volntr; Emplmnt; Key Club; Stg Cre; Students Against Starvation; Sunday School Aide at Church; Elementary Education; U of Delaware; Messiah

LOWER, LISA; PALMERTON, PA; PALMERTON AREA SD; (FR); Hi Hnr Roll; Perf Att; Pres Ac Ftns Aw; WWAHSS; ArtClub; Chrch Yth Grp

LOWRY, BRENNAN; HERMITAGE, PA; HICKORY HS; (SR); F Lan Hn Soc; Hi Hnr Roll; Hnr Roll; Nat Hon Sy; WWAHSS; Mth Clb/Tm; Quiz Bowl; Schol Bwl; Sci Clb; French Clb; Ftball (J); Rlr Hky (V); Cl Off (S); Stu Cncl (R); Nanotechnology; Cornell U; Case Western Reserve

LOZORAK, CAITLIN; POTTSTOWN, PA; POTTSGROVE HS; (JR); Ctznshp Aw; Gov Hnr Prg; Hi Hnr Roll; Hnr Roll; Nat Hon Sy; Otst Ac Ach Awd; WWAHSS; FTA; Key Club; Vsity Clb; French Clb; Chr; Bskball (J); Fld Hky (J); Sftball (V L); Vsy Clb (V); Stu Cncl (R); Yrbk (R); Mathematics; Education; Penn State U; Kutztown U

LU, BETTY; UPPER DARBY, PA; UPPER DARBY HS; (SO); Hnr Roll; Comm Volntr; Peer Tut/Med; Spec Olymp Vol; Orch; Vllyball (L); CR (R); Yrbk (P)

LUCAS, MACY M; PITTSBURGH, PA; CITY HS; (SO); Nat Hon Sy; Comm Volntr; Peer Tut/Med; Red Cr Aide; ArtClub; Dbte Team; Drma Clb; Mth Clb/Tm; Mus Clb; Photog; Tchrs Aide; Spanish Clb; Chr; Dnce; Swmg (V); Vllyball (V); Lit Mag (E); Sch Ppr (R); Yrbk (P); Microsoft Office Excel Certified / 80 Wpm; Spanish Honors; English / Nursing / Physics; Foreign Language / Music / Communication; Florida U

LUCAS, STEVE; LEECHBURG, PA; KISKI AREA HS; (JR); Hi Hnr Roll; Nat Hon Sy; Pres Sch; Sci/Math Olympn; WWAHSS; Yth Ldrshp Prog; DARE; Drma Clb; Key Club; Spch Team; French Clb; Chr; SP/M/VS; Stg Cre; Swg Chr; Tennis (J L); Stu Cncl (R); Sch Ppr (E); Yrbk (E); Mock Trial; Starting a Political Club on My Own; Public Relations; Film Studies; Ohio U; U of Pittsburgh

LUCE, ASHLEY; NEW MILFORD, PA; BLUE RIDGE HS; (FR); Hi Hnr Roll; Hnr Roll; WWAHSS; Comm Volntr; Chrch Yth Grp; Wdwrkg Clb; Acpl Chr; Bnd; Chr; Mch Bnd; Scr Kpr (V); Sftball (VJ); Vllyball (J); Teaching; Crime Scene Investigation

LUCE, GREGORY; ERIE, PA; MC DOWELL INT HS; (FR); Hnr Roll; St of Mnth; Comm Volntr; ROTC; Environmental Science; Forestry; Penn State U

LUCIANI, TERESA; GREENVILLE, PA; GREENVILLE HS; (JR); Hnr Roll; WWAHSS; Comm Volntr; Chrch Yth Grp; Emplmnt; Key Club; Sci Clb; Spanish Clb; Chrldg (V L)

LUIZZI, JOE; NEWTOWN, PA; COUNCIL ROCK HS NORTH; (FR); F Lan Hn Soc; Pres Ac Ftns Aw; St of Mnth; Comm Volntr; Scouts; Ftball (J); Track (J); Wrstlg (J); Pre-Med; Biochemistry

LUKETIC, DANIEL; MC KEESPORT, PA; MCK AREA HS; (FR); Ctznshp Aw; Hnr Roll; Sci Fairs; St of Mnth; Bnd; Bsball; Guitars; Graphic Occupations; Computers

LUSANE-WEAVER, TENISHA; READING, PA; READING HS; (FR); Hnr Roll; Perf Att; Sci Fairs; DARE; Drma Clb; Chr; Dnce; SP/M/VS; Chrldg (V); Sch Ppr (R); General Arts Achievement Award; Varsity Athletic Award; Psychology; Performing Arts; Cheney U; Howard U

LUTJENS, BRITTANY; STROUDSBURG, PA; STROUDSBURG HS; (JR); Hnr Roll; Comm Volntr; Red Cr Aide; Chrch Yth Grp; DARE; Emplmnt; Key Club; Chr; Nursing Associate's Degree in RN; Nursing BSN; Pittsburgh U; Moravian College

LUTTERMAN, AMBER; LATROBE, PA; GREATER LATROBE SR HS; (JR); Hi Hnr Roll; WWAHSS; Emplmnt; Key Club; Lttrmn Clb; Pep Squd; French Clb; Chrldg (V); Yrbk (E); Physician's Assistant PA; CRNA Nurse Anesthetist; Duquesne U

LUTZ, SHAWN; SHIPPENVILLE, PA; KEYSTONE HS; (SR); Nat Hon Sy; Otst Ac Ach Awd; St of Mnth; Chess; DECA; Emplmnt; Cl Off (P); Business Achievement Award-2004; Marketing-Bachelor's; Clarion U

LUV, YEE; PHILADELPHIA, PA; CAPA HS; (FR); Hnr Roll; Sci Fairs; St of Mnth; Drma Clb; Sci Clb; SP/M/VS; Track (V); Vllyball (V); Pharmacist; Theatre; New York U; Columbia College Chicago

LY, CYNTHIA; UPPER DARBY, PA; UPPER DARBY HS; (SO); Hi Hnr Roll; Hnr Roll; Otst Ac Ach Awd; Perf Att; Comm Volntr; ArtClub; SADD; Sch Ppr (R); Building with Books; Hero Club; Fashion Design; Pharmacy; Art Institute of Philadelphia; U of the Sciences in Philadelphia

LY, DANIEL; HERSHEY, PA; HERSHEY HS; (FR); Hi Hnr Roll; Sci/Math Olympn; Quiz Bowl; Sci Clb; Stg Cre; Sccr (J); Track (V); Biomedical Engineering; Molecular Biology; U of Pennsylvania; Duke U

LYONS, EMILY; PITTSBURGH, PA; NORTH HILLS HS; (JR); Hi Hnr Roll; Nat Hon Sy; Perf Att; WWAHSS; Comm Volntr; Chrch Yth Grp; Emplmnt; NtlFrnscLg; Spch Team; Spanish Clb; Chr; Lit Mag (E); Yrbk (E, P); Karate; English; Education; U of Notre Dame; Pennsylvania State U

MABREY, MONAE; UPPER DARBY, PA; UPPER DARBY HS; (FR); Hi Hnr Roll; Hnr Roll; Otst Ac Ach Awd; Perf Att; Pres Sch; St of Mnth; Yth Ldrshp Prog; Comm Volntr; Peer Tut/Med; Chrch Yth Grp; Mus Clb; P to P St Amb Prg; Sci Clb; Scouts; Acpl Chr; Bnd; Ch Chr; Mch Bnd; CR (V); National Junior Honor Society; Completed: Girl Scout Silver Award; Architecture; Engineering; U of Pennsylvania; Cornell U

MACAS, SHAWN; STEWARTSTOWN, PA; YORK CTY SCH OF TECH; (JR); Hi Hnr Roll; Hnr Roll; Nat Hon Sy; Chess; Sci Clb; Ftball (VJ); Electrical; Business

MACIO, MARIA; ALIQUIPPA, PA; CTR AREA SD; (SO); Hi Hnr Roll; Perf Att; Comm Volntr; Hab For Humty Volntr; Peer Tut/Med; Emplmnt; Pep Squd; Vsity Clb; Spanish Clb; Chr; Dnce; Chrldg (V); PP Ftbl (J); Vsy Clb (V); Stu Cncl (R); Academic Highest Honors; Health Field; Pittsburgh U; Pennsylvania State U

MACIORKOSKI, JACOB; DUNCANNON, PA; TRINITY HS; (JR); Hnr Roll; Comm Volntr; Hab For Humty Volntr; Chess; Key Club; Bsball (V); Sccr (V L); Middle School Gifted Program; Aeronautical Engineering; Political/Military Science; United States Air Force Academy; Boston U

MACK, JEANNA M; GILBERT, PA; PLEASANT VALLEY HS; (JR); Hi Hnr Roll; Hnr Roll; WWAHSS; Comm Volntr; Spec Olymp Vol; Chrch Yth Grp; Drma Clb; Scouts; Bnd; Chr; Ch Chr; Mch Bnd; Lutheran Summer Music Academy; Pharmacy; Lincoln Tech; Shippensburg U

Luce, Gregory
Mc Dowell Int HS
Erie, PA

Loftus, Megan
Riverside JR/SR HS
Moosic, PA

Lo, Jonathan
Lehigh Valley Christian HS
Allentown, PA

National
Honor Roll
Spring 2005

Llaneza, Andrew J
Valley HS
New Kensington, PA

Loutitt, Melissa
Ringgold SD
Monongahela, PA

Luciani, Teresa
Greenville HS
Greenville, PA

MACK, KAYLA A; CTRL CITY, PA; SHADE-CENTRAL CITY SD; (SO); All Am Sch; Hi Hnr Roll; Nat Hon Sy; Nat Ldrshp Svc; USAA; WWAHSS; Peer Tut/Med; Emplmnt; SADD; SADD President; The American Legion Certificate of School Award; Forensic Science / CSI or Criminal Justice; Social Worker or Pediatrics; Drexel U; Carlow U

MACK, RACHEL; LITITZ, PA; MANHEIM TWP HS; (JR); Hi Hnr Roll; Nat Hon Sy; WWAHSS; Drma Clb; Key Club; Chr; SP/M/VS; Swmg (V L); Sch Ppr (E); Performing Arts Club Secretary; BFA in Acting / Theatre

MACKIEWICZ, ANNA; MONROEVILLE, PA; GATEWAY HS; (SO); Hi Hnr Roll; Otst Ac Ach Awd; Pres Sch; St of Mnth; WWAHSS; Comm Volntr; Dbte Team; Drma Clb; Key Club; Mus Clb; Chr; Duquesne City Music Center Student; Mock Trial Participant/Video Club and SCA Member; Pre Law; Political Science; U of Virginia

MAC LUCKIE, CORRIN L; POTTSTOWN, PA; POTTSGROVE HS; (JR); Hi Hnr Roll; Nat Hon Sy; Otst Ac Ach Awd; WWAHSS; Comm Volntr; Chrch Yth Grp; Emplmnt; Key Club; Sci Clb; Ch Chr; Dnce; EMT; Golden Falcon Award; Biological Anthropology; Forensic Science; Penn State U; U of Pittsburgh

MADDOX, TERRICA; NEW KENSINGTON, PA; NEW KENSINGTON-ARNOLD SD; (FR); Ctznshp Aw; Hnr Roll; Otst Ac Ach Awd; Chrch Yth Grp; SADD; Vllyball (J); Stu Cncl; I'm on My Church Mime Team.; I'm Also in Interact.; I Want to Major in the Medical Field.; Howard U

MADENSKY, KEVIN P; CLARKS SUMMIT, PA; ABINGTON HEIGHTS HS; (SO); Hi Hnr Roll; Sci Fairs; Comm Volntr; Emplmnt; Stu Cncl (R); Robotics Team; Lector At Church; Business Management; Architecture; Michigan State U; U of Arizona

MAGAZINE, JENNA M; LANSDALE, PA; NORTH PENN HS; (JR); Hi Hnr Roll; Nat Hon Sy; Otst Ac Ach Awd; WWAHSS; Comm Volntr; Spec Olymp Vol; Emplmnt; Key Club; PP Ftbl (V); Sccr (V); Track (V); CR (R); Premier Soccer Club; Business; Law; Penn State U; U of Tampa

MAGLIOZZI, DAN; DOYLESTOWN, PA; CTRL BUCKS HS EAST; (JR); F Lan Hn Soc; Hi Hnr Roll; WWAHSS; Emplmnt; Key Club; Spanish Clb; SP/M/VS; Bskball (VJ); Stu Cncl; Pre-Med; U of North Carolina Chapel Hill; Pennsylvania State U

MAGUIRE, NICOLE; HARRISBURG, PA; CTRL DAUPHIN EAST HS; (SO); Hnr Roll; WWAHSS; Emplmnt; Chrldg (V L); Stu Cncl (R); CR (R); Physical Therapy; Fashion Magazine Editor; U of Delaware

MAIORINO, KELLY L; PITTSBURGH, PA; OAKLAND CATHOLIC HS; (JR); Hi Hnr Roll; WWAHSS; Yth Ldrshp Prog; Hosp Aide; Sftball (V L); Pre-Medicine

MAIURO, MELISSA; COUDERSPORT, PA; COUDERSPORT AREA SD HS; (JR); Hi Hnr Roll; Nat Hon Sy; Pres Sch; Comm Volntr; Peer Tut/Med; Red Cr Aide; Emplmnt; Mth Clb/Tm; Ntl FFA; Prom Com; Vsity Clb; Chrldg (V L); Golf (V L); PP Ftbl (V); Vsy Clb (V L); Stu Cncl (S); CR; Sch Ppr (E); Attended National Student Leadership Conference; Board Member-Drug & Alcohol Committee; Pre-Law; International Business; American U

MAJKOWSKI, SARAH; CLAIRTON, PA; SETON LA SALLE HS; (JR); Hi Hnr Roll; Hnr Roll; Nat Hon Sy; Perf Att; Sci Fairs; Yth Ldrshp Prog; Comm Volntr; Peer Tut/Med; ArtClub; Chrch Yth Grp; DARE; Drma Clb; Jr Ach; Mth Clb/Tm; Pep Squd; Scouts; Chr; Dnce; SP/M/VS; Stg Cre; Chrldg (V); Hsbk Rdg; PP Ftbl (V); Skiing; Member of School Volunteer Club; Member of Varsity Bowling Team; Architecture; Business; Carnegie Mellon U

MAKEEVER, SHELLEY A; BENTLEYVILLE, PA; BENTWORTH HS; (SR); Hnr Roll; Nat Mrt LOC; USAA; Psychology; Social Work; California U of PA

MALCOTTI, MARIANA; NANTY GLO, PA; CTRL CAMBRIA HS; (FR); Hi Hnr Roll; Otst Ac Ach Awd; Pres Ac Ftns Aw; Pres Sch; Sci Fairs; WWAHSS; Peer Tut/Med; DARE; Emplmnt; Jr Ach; Bnd; Chr; Dnce; SP/M/VS; Scr Kpr; Sftball; Swmg; Vllyball; Stu Cncl (R); Psychology; Nursing; U of Pittsburgh

MALESICH, MORGAN M; MOUNT JOY, PA; DONEGAL HS; (JR); Hi Hnr Roll; Hnr Roll; Sci Fairs; Comm Volntr; Chrch Yth Grp; Drma Clb; Emplmnt; Pep Squd; Chr; SP/M/VS; Yrbk (E, R, P); Booster Club; Fashion Merch; Drexel; Berkeley

MALIK, LAUREN; WEXFORD, PA; NORTH ALLEGHENY HS; (SO); F Lan Hn Soc; Hnr Roll; Kwnis Aw; Nat Hon Sy; Pres Ac Ftns Aw; Peer Tut/Med; Chrch Yth Grp; Key Club; Bnd; Mch Bnd; Orch; Pep Bnd; Adv Cncl (R); Pittsburgh Youth Pops Orchestra; Volunteering at Nursing Homes; Art Education; Bachelor's of Fine Arts; Ohio Northern U; Swarthmore

MALINAK, ERIC J; CAMP HILL, PA; EAST PENNSBORO AREA HS; (FR); Hi Hnr Roll; Nat Hon Sy; Otst Ac Ach Awd; Emplmnt; Lib Aide; Ftball (J); Track (V); Wt Lftg; Engineering; Law Enforcement

MALIS, DEANNA R; DONORA, PA; RINGGOLD SD; (FR); Hi Hnr Roll; Hnr Roll; Comm Volntr; Hab For Humty Volntr; Spec Olymp Vol; Chrch Yth Grp; DARE; Drma Clb; SADD; SP/M/VS; Chrldg (L); Scr Kpr (J); Lawyer; Dentist; Pittsburgh U; New York U

MALLIK, SAMANTHA J; PLUMVILLE, PA; MARION CTR; (SR); Hi Hnr Roll; USAA; WWAHSS; Red Cr Aide; Chrch Yth Grp; Dbte Team; Emplmnt; FBLA; Sci Clb; Acpl Chr; SP/M/VS; Chrldg (V L); PP Ftbl; Sccr (V L); Swmg (V L); Track (V L); Stu Cncl (R); Psychology; Political Science; Duquesne U

MALONE, CONNOR J; HARRISBURG, PA; CTRL DAUPHIN HS; (SO); Hnr Roll; Nat Hon Sy; Comm Volntr; Emplmnt; Prom Com; Skiing; Sccr (V L); Cl Off (V); 4 Diamonds; Criminal Justice; Penn State U; UNC

MANENTO, NICHOLAS A; EASTON, PA; EASTON AREA SR HS; (SO); St of Mnth; WWAHSS; FTA; Stu Cncl (R); Secondary Education / History; Kutztown U

MANFREDI, LAUREN; HAZLETON, PA; HAZLETON AREA HS; (SO); Hi Hnr Roll; Hnr Roll; WWAHSS; Comm Volntr; Emplmnt; FBLA; Key Club; Bskball (J); Business Major; Penn State U

MANIERI, CHRISTINA A; DOWNINGTOWN, PA; BISHOP SHANAHAN HS; (JR); Hi Hnr Roll; Hnr Roll; Nat Hon Sy; Comm Volntr; Peer Tut/Med; Red Cr Aide; Emplmnt; Off Aide; Svce Clb; SADD; French Clb; Sch Ppr (R); Yrbk (R); Media Arts Club; Law; Medicine; Georgetown U; Villanova U

MANN, KIMBERLY J; DREXEL HILL, PA; UPPER DARBY HS; (SO); Hi Hnr Roll; Hnr Roll; Comm Volntr; Emplmnt; Chr; Dnce; SP/M/VS; Sccr (JC); Swmg (V); Adv Cncl (R); Coach Youth Basketball; Umpire Little League Softball; Elementary Education; Architecture; U of Notre Dame; Wake Forest U

MANN, TABITHA R; JERSEY SHORE, PA; JERSEY SHORE AREA SR HS; (FR); Hi Hnr Roll; MVP; Emplmnt; Key Club; Sccr (V); Autism Psychology; Villanova; Penn State U

MANOLUKAS, GEORGE; BEAVER FALLS, PA; BLACKHAWK HS; (JR); Hi Hnr Roll; Hnr Roll; Kwnis Aw; Nat Hon Sy; Nat Stu Ath Day Aw; Otst Ac Ach Awd; WWAHSS; Comm Volntr; Peer Tut/Med; Chrch Yth Grp; Key Club; Lttrmn Clb; Ftball (V, L); Track; Wt Lftg; Wrstlg (VLC); Adv Cncl (R); CR (R); Wrestling Leadership Award - Joe Burkhead Award; Altar Boy; Engineering; Architecture; Virginia Tech; Pennsylvania State University

MANTILLA, ADAM J; READING, PA; READING HS; (FR); MVP; Perf Att; DARE; Bskball (C); FBI Agent; District Attorney; North Carolina; Penn State

MANTUSH, AMY; DRUMS, PA; HAZLETON AREA HS; (JR); Hi Hnr Roll; MVP; Nat Hon Sy; WWAHSS; Comm Volntr; Emplmnt; FBLA; Key Club; Scouts; SADD; Bskball (V L); Track (V L); Vllyball (V); Stu Cncl (R); CR (R); District Champion (3 Events) in Track 2004

MAPP, KYLE L; LANSDOWNE, PA; PENN WOOD EAST JHS; (FR); Ctznshp Aw; Hnr Roll; Yth Ldrshp Prog; Comm Volntr; Chrch Yth Grp; Cmptr Clb; Mus Clb; Off Aide; Ch Chr; Ftball (J); Wt Lftg; Part of Music and Arts Ministry At Church; Computer Technician; Computer Engineering; Business; Spelman College; Texas Tech

MARCELLI, NICHOLAS; HERMITAGE, PA; HICKORY HS; (SO); Hi Hnr Roll; Pres Ac Ftns Aw; USAA; WWAHSS; Yth Ldrshp Prog; Sccr (VJCL); Tennis (V L)

MARCH, MANDY; DOUGLASSVILLE, PA; DANIEL BOONE HS; (SO); Ctznshp Aw; Hi Hnr Roll; Otst Ac Ach Awd; St of Mnth; WWAHSS; Comm Volntr; Drma Clb; Emplmnt; Key Club; Prom Com; French Clb; Dnce; SP/M/VS; Cl Off (V); Psychology; Education; Pennsylvania State U; Yale U

MARGEVICH, KENNA; WAPWALLOPEN, PA; BISHOP HAFEY HS; (SO); F Lan Hn Soc; Hi Hnr Roll; Hnr Roll; WWAHSS; Comm Volntr; Hosp Aide; Drma Clb; Emplmnt; Key Club; Chr; SP/M/VS; Stg Cre; 11th Place in National Spanish Contest; Major in Marine Biology; Minor in Spanish; Stony Brook U; Penn State U

MARHEVKA, RACHEL J; READING, PA; EXETER TWP SR HS; (JR); Hi Hnr Roll; Nat Hon Sy; Otst Ac Ach Awd; Pres Sch; USAA; WWAHSS; Peer Tut/Med; Chrch Yth Grp; Emplmnt; FBLA; Key Club; Spanish Clb; Yrbk; Key Club; Monitoring Underprivileged Children; Communications/Journalism; Sales and Advertisement; U of North Carolina; Bucknell U

MARIANACCI, SARAH; DALLAS, PA; DALLAS HS; (SO); Hi Hnr Roll; Nat Hon Sy; Otst Ac Ach Awd; WWAHSS; Yth Ldrshp Prog; Comm Volntr; ArtClub; HO'Br Yth Ldrshp; Key Club; Svce Clb; Dnce; SP/M/VS; NEDT Award; Straight A Award

MARINOS, JORDAN; LEWISTOWN, PA; LEWISTOWN HS; (FR); Hnr Roll; MVP; Chrch Yth Grp; DARE; Key Club; SP/M/VS; Fld Hky (V L); Stu Cncl (R); Penn State U

MARION, RACHAEL; GREENSBURG, PA; GREENSBURG SALEM SD; (FR); Hi Hnr Roll; Hnr Roll; Perf Att; Pres Ac Ftns Aw; St of Mnth; Chr; Vllyball (V); Adv Cncl (R); Stu Cncl (R); Teacher; Medical/Science Field; California U of Pennsylvania; Seton Hill U

MARIOTTI, ADAM; HERMITAGE, PA; HICKORY HS; (SO); Hi Hnr Roll; Perf Att; WWAHSS; President's Award for Educational Excellence

MARLES, FRANK; PHILADELPHIA, PA; EDISON-FAREIRA HS; (JR); Fut Prb Slvr; Hnr Roll; Nat Hon Sy; Perf Att; St of Mnth; WWAHSS; Comm Volntr; BPA; Chrch Yth Grp; Dbte Team; DECA; Emplmnt; Fr of Library; FBLA; Jr Ach; Ch Chr; Wrstlg (J); CR (P); Sch Ppr (R); Award for Public Speaking; Award for Business Communications; Accounting; Law and Government; U of Penn; Penn State-U Park

MARONE, JACQUELINE M; DUNMORE, PA; CAREER TECH CTR-LACKAWANNA; (SR); Hnr Roll; Nat Hon Sy; Comm Volntr; Red Cr Aide; SADD; Skiing (J); Work; Volunteer at a Veterans Home; Owning My Own Salon; Keystone College; Empire College

MARONE, KASSAUNDRA; COATESVILLE, PA; COATESVILLE AREA SR HS; (JR); Hi Hnr Roll; Hnr Roll; Nat Hon Sy; St of Mnth; WWAHSS; Comm Volntr; Chrch Yth Grp; Emplmnt; Bnd; Drm Mjr; Jzz Bnd; Mch Bnd; Yrbk (R); Band President; Band Section Leader; Elementary Education; Secondary Education; Millersville U; West Chester U

MARRANCA, PAUL J; PITTSTON, PA; WYOMING SEMINARY; (JR); Hi Hnr Roll; Nat Hon Sy; Yth Ldrshp Prog; Comm Volntr; Emplmnt; Jr Ach; Tennis (V CL); Sch Ppr (R); Elected to BLUE KEY; Member Jr Leadership Class of '05; Business; Sports Management; New York U; Haverford

MARSCH, JOANNA; LANCASTER, PA; MANHEIM TOWNSHIP HS; (JR); Hi Hnr Roll; Nat Hon Sy; WWAHSS; Comm Volntr; Chrch Yth Grp; Drma Clb; Emplmnt; Key Club; Mus Clb; Tech Clb; Acpl Chr; Bnd; Chr; Mch Bnd; LLMEA County Band, Orchestra, Chorus; PMEA; Music Education; Piano Pedagogy; Westminster Choir College; Ithaca College

MARSH, JACLYN D; CLEARFIELD, PA; CLEARFIELD AREA HS; (SO); WWAHSS; Comm Volntr; Chrch Yth Grp; Key Club; Bnd; Orch; Swmg (V L); Forensic Science

MARSH, MICHELLE; BUSHKILL, PA; (MS); Hnr Roll; St of Mnth; Comm Volntr; Scouts; Chr; Bskball (V); Fld Hky (V); Sftball (V); Stu Cncl (R); Yrbk (R); Elementary Teacher

MARSH, ZACHARY; HARWICK, PA; SPRINGDALE HS; (SR); Nat Hon Sy; St of Mnth; WWAHSS; Comm Volntr; Hab For Humty Volntr; ArtClub; Biology Clb; Drma Clb; Emplmnt; FBLA; Key Club; SADD; Spanish Clb; SP/M/VS; Track; Adv Cncl (V); Political Science; Theatre; Westminster College; U of Pittsburgh-Johnstown

MARSHALEK, GEORGE; WEXFORD, PA; NORTH ALLEGHENY SR HS; (SO); Nat Hon Sy; Pres Ac Ftns Aw; WWAHSS; Comm Volntr; Peer Tut/Med; Chrch Yth Grp; Emplmnt; Key Club; Stu Cncl (R); NJHS - National Junior Honor Society; Who's Who Among Students. H.S.; Broadcast Communications; Pennsylvania State U; Syracuse U

MARSICANO, NICOLE; VANDLING, PA; FOREST CITY REG SCH; (SR); Hi Hnr Roll; Nat Hon Sy; USAA; WWAHSS; Peer Tut/Med; Red Cr Aide; Emplmnt; FBLA; Vsity Clb; Chr; Bskball (C); Sccr (V CL); Cl Off (V); Governor's School Participant for Information Technology @ Drexel U; Engineering; Penn State U; Drexel U

MARSILI, KRISTI; VANDERGRIFT, PA; KISKI AREA HS; (SO); Hi Hnr Roll; Hnr Roll; MVP; Perf Att; WWAHSS; DARE; Emplmnt; Key Club; Chr; Sftball (V L); Vllyball (V L); Who's Who-Voted Most Popular Honors; Top 10% of Class (Middle School) Highest Batting English Avg.; Film Maker; Penn State, Clarion; Indiana U of PA

MARTELL, LAUREN; CLEARFIELD, PA; CLEARFIELD AREA HS; (SO); Hi Hnr Roll; Hnr Roll; Perf Att; WWAHSS; Comm Volntr; Chess; Chrch Yth Grp; Drma Clb; FCA; Key Club; Mus Clb; Scouts; Spanish Clb; Bnd; Chr; Ch Chr; Dnce; Tennis (J); Key Club; Teen Court; Cosmetologist; Makeup Artist

MARTHENS, ADAM F; PITTSBURGH, PA; PITTSBURGH SD; (SR); Ch Chr; Fncg (CL); Psychiatrist; Johns Hopkins U; Penn State U

MARTIN, ANDRE L; PHILADELPHIA, PA; BEN FRANKLIN HS; (FR); All Am Sch; Ctznshp Aw; Fut Prb Slvr; Hi Hnr Roll; Hnr Roll; Jr Mshl; MVP; Nat Hon Sy; Nat Mrt LOC; Nat Stu Ath Day Aw; Comm Volntr; Peer Tut/Med; AL Aux Boys; Chess; Cmptr Clb; DARE; Dbte Team; Emplmnt; FBLA; Lib Aide; Bnd; Dnce; Bskball (VJ); Ftball (VJ); Swmg (V); Track (V); Wt Lftg (V); Stu Cncl (V, R); Yrbk (E, R); Computer Tech Master; PhD / Business; Pittsburgh; Michigan

MARTIN, BENJAMIN G; WASHINGTON, PA; TRINITY HS; (JR); Ctznshp Aw; Hi Hnr Roll; Kwnis Aw; ArtClub; Key Club; SADD; Sch Ppr (R, P)

MARTIN, DUSTIN A; WILLIAMSBURG, PA; WILLIAMSBURG CMTY SD; (JR); Ctznshp Aw; Perf Att; WWAHSS; Comm Volntr; Red Cr Aide; Chrch Yth Grp; FCA; Tchrs Aide; Bsball (V); Bskball (VJ L); Ftball (J); Yrbk (E, R, P); Coaching Basketball; Scouting Basketball

MARTIN, EMMANUEL; ERIE, PA; ERIE CITY SD; (JR); Hi Hnr Roll; Hnr Roll; Nat Hon Sy; Pres Sch; WWAHSS; Chrch Yth Grp; Emplmnt; FBLA; Jr Ach; JSA; Mus Clb; Tmpl Yth Grp; Vsity Clb; SP/M/VS; Bskball (V); Ftball (V); Track (V); Vsy Clb (V); Cl Off (R); Stu Cncl (S); CR (V); Music Production; Children Doctor; Maryland; LSU

Malone, Connor J
Central Dauphin HS
Harrisburg, PA

Malis, Deanna R
Ringgold SD
Donora, PA

National
Honor Roll
Spring 2005

Mackiewicz, Anna
Gateway HS
Monroeville, PA

Mapp, Kyle L
Penn Wood East JHS
Lansdowne, PA

MARTIN, KARLI A; EAST STROUDSBURG, PA; STROUDSBURG HS; (JR); Hnr Roll; Comm Volntr; Photog; SADD; Chr; SP/M/VS; Swg Chr; Fld Hky (V CL); Sccr (V L); Mountain Valley Conference 1st Team Goalie Field; Pocono Record All Area Team Goalie Hockey; Graphic Art and Design/ Advertising Art; Guidance Counselor; Kutztown U; Shippensburg U

MARTIN, KELLY; HANOVER TWP, PA; HANOVER AREA JR/SR HS; (JR); Hi Hnr Roll; Nat Hon Sy; WWAHSS; Key Club; Pre-Medicine

MARTIN, LATASHA A; GRANTVILLE, PA; LEBANON CTY CAREER AND TECH HS; (SR); Hi Hnr Roll; Hnr Roll; Perf Att; Voc Ind Clb Am; Ch Chr; Dnce; Bskball (J L); Track (V L); Adv Cncl (P); Cl Off (P); Sch Ppr (R); Lebanon's Rotary Student of the Month; Skills USA State Bronze Medalist; Attend Valley Forge for Gen. Ed. Courses; Further My Pastry Education At the CIA; Valley Forge Christian College; The Culinary Institute of America

MARTIN, LEXI; BETHLEHEM, PA; LEHIGH VALLEY CHR PERF ARTS HS; (JR); Hi Hnr Roll; Hnr Roll; Nat Hon Sy; Pres Ac Ftns Aw; WWAHSS; Comm Volntr; Spec Olymp Vol; Chrch Yth Grp; Drma Clb; Mth Clb/Tm; Prom Com; Scouts; Vsity Clb; Chr; Ch Chr; Dnce; SP/M/VS; Cr Ctry (V L); Lcrsse (V L); Swmg (V); Stu Cncl (V); CR (R); National Honors Society; Dance; Theater; New York U-Tisch School of the Arts; U of California, San Diego

MARTIN, MARGARET; POTTSVILLE, PA; POTTSVILLE AREA SD; (FR); Clr Grd

MARTIN, PHILIP W; ABINGTON, PA; ABINGTON SR HS; (SO); Hi Hnr Roll; Hnr Roll; Nat Hon Sy; WWAHSS; Chrch Yth Grp; DARE; Emplmnt; Key Club; Lcrsse (V); Swmg (V); Stu Cncl (R); 150 + Service Hours

MARTIN, SEAN; NEW KENSINGTN, PA; VALLEY HS; (FR); Hnr Roll; DARE; Bnd; Mch Bnd; Tae Kwon Do; State Police Camp Cadet Program; Customizing Car Specialist; Penn State

MARTIN, SHAINA E; MERCERSBURG, PA; JAMES BUCHANAN HS; (SR); 4H Awd; All Am Sch; Hi Hnr Roll; Nat Hon Sy; USAA; Comm Volntr; 4-H; Chrch Yth Grp; Emplmnt; FCA; Ntl FFA; Bnd; Mch Bnd; Orch; Bskball (V CL); Track (V CL); National Winning FFA Dairy Judging Team; Dairy Manager; Penn State U

MARTIN, TRAYONA; PHILADELPHIA, PA; BEN FRANKLIN HS; (FR); Hnr Roll; Comm Volntr; DARE; Tmpl Yth Grp; Ch Chr; Dnce; Major in Psychology or Law; Professional Degree - PhD or Masters; Florida State College; Howard U

MARTINO, KIM; NEW CASTLE, PA; SHENANGO AREA SD; (JR); Hnr Roll; WWAHSS; Vsity Clb; Bskball (V L); Cr Ctry (V L); Sftball (V L); Vsy Clb (V L); Education; Mathematics; Slippery Rock U; Geneva College

MARTS, NICHOLAS D; MC KEESPORT, PA; EAST ALLEGHENY HS; (JR); Hi Hnr Roll; Hnr Roll; Nat Hon Sy; Comm Volntr; Emplmnt; Mth Clb/Tm; Orch; Ftball (VJCL); Track (VJC); Wt Lftg (VJ); Nominee in the National Society of High School Scholars; Business / Nutrition / Personal Trainer; Penn State - Main Campus; Bucknell U

MARUCA, ANGELO; UNIONTOWN, PA; LAUREL HIGHLANDS SD HS; (FR); Ctznshp Aw; Hi Hnr Roll; Hnr Roll; Perf Att; St of Mnth; Comm Volntr; Chrch Yth Grp; Emplmnt; Mus Clb; SADD; Spanish Clb; Chr; SP/ M/VS; Track (J); Elementary School Teacher

MARVIN, ERIK; HALLSTEAD, PA; BLUE RIDGE HS; (FR); Hi Hnr Roll; Hnr Roll; Bnd; Mch Bnd; Auto Mechanic; Diesel Mechanic; Johnson's College; ITT Tech

MARZOLF, GERALD M; GALLITZIN, PA; PENN CAMBRIA HS; (JR); Hi Hnr Roll; Hnr Roll; Nat Hon Sy; Otst Ac Ach Awd; WWAHSS; Yth Ldrshp Prog; Comm Volntr; Chrch Yth Grp; German Clb; Cyclg; Wrstlg (VJ); Scholastic Scrimmage-Scholastic Quiz; German Club-National Honor Society; Foreign Affairs; Diplomacy; U of Pennsylvania; Georgetown U

MASCARO, MELANIE; MONROEVILLE, PA; GATEWAY SR HS; (JR); Hi Hnr Roll; St of Mnth; Comm Volntr; Key Club; Chr; PP Ftbl (J); Track; Yrbk; French; Chatham College; U of Pittsburgh-Johnston

MASON, LINDSEY J; SCOTTDALE, PA; YOUGH SD; (JR); Hi Hnr Roll; Hnr Roll; Nat Hon Sy; WWAHSS; Comm Volntr; Peer Tut/Med; SADD; French Clb; Historian of CAP/SADD; Aerospace Engineering; Mathematics; Florida Institute of Technology; Purdue U

MASTALSKI, ALISON; BEAVER FALLS, PA; BIG BEAVER FALLS AREA HS; (JR); Hi Hnr Roll; Hnr Roll; Nat Hon Sy; Pres Ac Ftns Aw; WWAHSS; Chrch Yth Grp; DARE; Emplmnt; Key Club; Prom Com; Vsity Clb; Spanish Clb; Chrldg (VJ L); GAA (J); PP Ftbl (J); Vsy Clb (VJ); CR (S); Yrbk (R, P); Elementary Ed; Home Economics/Cooking Teacher; U of Pittsburgh Main Campus; Slippery Rock U

MASTBAUM, ANDREW T; BOILING SPRINGS, PA; CUMBERLAND VALLEY HS; (SR); F Lan Hn Soc; Nat Hon Sy; Nat Mrt LOC; Sci/Math Olympn; St of Mnth; WWAHSS; Yth Ldrshp Prog; Comm Volntr; Peer Tut/ Med; Cmptr Clb; Drma Clb; Jr Cls League; Mth Clb/Tm; NYLC; Sci Clb; Scouts; Latin Clb; Eagle Scout; PA Governor's School; Physics; Lehigh U

MATHEW, ANNA; LANGHORNE, PA; NESHAMINY HS; (SO); Hi Hnr Roll; Hnr Roll; Pres Sch; WWAHSS; Comm Volntr; Hosp Aide; Peer Tut/ Med; ArtClub; Chrch Yth Grp; Svce Clb; SADD; Ch Chr; Published in - Anthology of Young Americans - '04; Top 5% in Class; Pre-Med; MD; Drexel U

MATHEWS, JULIE; E GREENVILLE, PA; UPPER PERKIOMEN HS; (JR); Hi Hnr Roll; Hnr Roll; St of Mnth; Apprenticeship Program for Electrical

MATHIEU, SARA; ALIQUIPPA, PA; CTR AREA SD; (SO); Hi Hnr Roll; Yth Ldrshp Prog; Peer Tut/Med; French Clb; Chr; SP/M/VS; Stu Cncl (R); Journalism; Communications; New York U; Columbia U

MATHIS, KENISHA M; PHILADELPHIA, PA; GERMANTOWN-LANKENAU HS; (SO); Comm Volntr; Chrch Yth Grp; Scouts; Ch Chr; Dnce; Drl Tm; SP/M/VS; Pediatrician; Social Worker; Howard U; Spelman U

MATHIS III, THEODORE J; CANONSBURG, PA; CANON MC MILLAN HS; (FR); Hnr Roll; Chrch Yth Grp; Bskball (VJ); Ftball (J); Track (VJ L); Wt Lftg (VJ); Nominated 2 Times - People's Ambassador to Travel Overseas; Engineering; NFL; Ohio State U; West Virginia U

MATKAN, LAUREN; BEAVER FALLS, PA; BLACKHAWK HS; (SO); Hi Hnr Roll; Hnr Roll; Kwnis Aw; Otst Ac Ach Awd; Perf Att; Pres Sch; St of Mnth; WWAHSS; Spec Olymp Vol; Drma Clb; Key Club; Spanish Clb; Swmg (V L); Cl Off (R); Pharmacy

MATOS, NICOLE; STROUDSBURG, PA; POCONO MTN EAST HS; (JR); Hi Hnr Roll; Hnr Roll; WWAHSS; Peer Tut/Med; SADD; Sftball (J); Forensic Psychologist

MATSUMURA, MIO C; NEWFOUNDLAND, PA; NORTH POCONO HS; (JR); Hi Hnr Roll; Nat Hon Sy; WWAHSS; Hosp Aide; Red Cr Aide; Clr Grd; Mch Bnd; Orch; Cty Summer Program

MATTA, ANGELICA; NEW KENSINGTON, PA; ST JOSEPH HS; (FR); Hnr Roll; Sci Fairs; Peer Tut/Med; Drma Clb; Emplmnt; Jr Ach; Pep Squd; P to P St Amb Prg; Stg Cre; Chrldg (J); Tennis (J); Pennsylvania Junior Perfect Score Science Achievement; National History Day; Political Science, Corporate Law; Law; Duquesne U; The U of Pittsburgh

MATTERN, ZACHARY; WARREN, PA; WARREN AREA HS; (JR); Hnr Roll; Comm Volntr; Red Cr Aide; Emplmnt; Lttrmn Clb; Prom Com; Ftball (V L); Track (V); Wt Lftg (V); Major in Physical Therapy; Doctorate Degree; Gannon U; Mercyhurst U

MATTERS, MARTINA; CLARKS MILLS, PA; LAKEVIEW SD HS; (JR); Hnr Roll; Otst Ac Ach Awd; DARE; Emplmnt; SADD; Chr; Track (V); Accounting; Bachelor's Degree; Clarion U

MATTHEWS, DEAN; PITTSBURGH, PA; PLUM SR HS; (SO); Hnr Roll; Sci Fairs; Comm Volntr; Gifted & Talented Education Program; "Golf" Published In - Anthology of Poetry By Young Americans - 1997; Music Degree; New York U; U of Pittsburgh

MATTOCKS, JODI; HERMITAGE, PA; HICKORY HS; (JR); F Lan Hn Soc; Hnr Roll; Comm Volntr; Chrch Yth Grp; Drma Clb; Key Club; Mus Clb; Spanish Clb; Chr; Ch Chr; Memorization Awards-Bible Quiz; Upwards Soccer Coach; Journalism; Degree in Law; Gettysburg U; Thiel College

MATTOCKS, RACHEL F; BEAVER FALLS, PA; BEAVER FALLS HS; (SR); Hi Hnr Roll; Hnr Roll; St of Mnth; WWAHSS; Chrch Yth Grp; Drma Clb; Emplmnt; FBLA; Key Club; Photog; Spanish Clb; Sch Ppr (R); Yrbk (R, P); Entrepreneurship; Interior Design; Central Pennsylvania College

MATTSON, BETHANY J; ERIE, PA; NORTHWEST PA COLLEGIATE AC; (SR); Hi Hnr Roll; Nat Hon Sy; Comm Volntr; Chr; Bskball (V L); Sftball (V CL); Vllyball (V L); Wendy's Heisman Scholar Athlete Nominee; Elementary Education; Grove City College

MATTSON, JAMI; ERIE, PA; FT LEBOEUF HS; (SO); Gov Hnr Prg; Hi Hnr Roll; Chrch Yth Grp; Wdwrkg Clb; French Clb; Chrldg (VJ L); Gmnstcs (J); Spelling Bee Champ 7 & 8th Grade; Lawyer; Psychologist; Penn State U; Gannon U

MATTSON, TARRAH L; DRUMS, PA; HAZLETON AREA HS; (SR); Nat Hon Sy; WWAHSS; FBLA; Key Club; Mth Clb/Tm; Ntl FFA; Sci Clb; Ecology Club; S.A.D.D/S.A.D.A.; Elem. Ed.; Millersville U

MATYAS, RACHEL; DOYLESTOWN, PA; CTRL BUCKS HS EAST; (SO); Hi Hnr Roll; WWAHSS; Chrch Yth Grp; Key Club; Swmg (V); Track (V); Science; Medicine

MAUK, REBECCA H; POTTSTOWN, PA; POTTSGROVE SR HS; (FR); Hnr Roll; Otst Ac Ach Awd; Comm Volntr; ArtClub; Dbte Team; Scouts; Bnd; Clr Grd; Stg Cre; Project-Reach-Out; Art; Teacher (Special-Ed. or Art); Kutztown U; Penn State U

MAUN, BRANDON; GREENVILLE, PA; REYNOLDS SD; (FR); Hi Hnr Roll; St of Mnth; Golf (L); Wrstlg (L); Physical Education Award

MAXEY, STEPHANIE A; REINHOLDS, PA; LANCASTER CTY CTC; (SR); Hnr Roll; Comm Volntr; Mus Clb; SP/M/VS; Chrldg (J); Fld Hky (J); Track (V); Miss Denver Fair Candidate 2004; Radiology; Health Career; LGH School of Allied Health Careers; Reading School of Radiology

MAXSHURE, TARELLE; PITTSBURGH, PA; PITTSBURGH SD; (SR); Hnr Roll; Nat Hon Sy; Fine Arts (Music); Business

MAXWELL, MARISA; NEWPORT, PA; NEWPORT SD; (SO); Hi Hnr Roll; Nat Hon Sy; Otst Ac Ach Awd; Pres Ac Ftns Aw; St of Mnth; Yth Ldrshp Prog; Comm Volntr; Peer Tut/Med; Spec Olymp Vol; Chrch Yth Grp; Prom Com; Bskball (V L); Fld Hky (V L); Track (V L); Cl Off (P); Stu Cncl (V); Physical Therapy; FBI

MAZON, CINDY; SANDY LAKE, PA; LAKEVIEW SD; (SR); Hnr Roll; Nat Hon Sy; Perf Att; Culinary Arts; Associates; Pennsylvania Culinary Institute; Teal College

MAZUREK, CARRIE A; EAST VANDERGRIFT, PA; KISKI AREA HS; (JR); Hi Hnr Roll; Hnr Roll; Nat Hon Sy; WWAHSS; Comm Volntr; Peer Tut/Med; Chrch Yth Grp; Emplmnt; Key Club; Spanish Clb; Chr; Ch Chr; Stg Cre; Swmg (V L); Track (J L); National Honor Society; Student Athletic Training; Physical Therapy; Teaching; U of Pittsburgh; Slippery Rock U

MC AFEE, CASSIE E; LEECHBURG, PA; LEECHBURG AREA HS; (JR); Hnr Roll; Comm Volntr; ArtClub; Emplmnt; Prom Com; Chr; Stg Cre; PP Ftbl (J); Stu Cncl (R); Sch Ppr (R); Member of (STAT) Students Taking Action Today; Degree in Elementary Education; Slippery Rock U; Westminster College

MC ALEER, LAUREN; ERIE, PA; FAIR VIEW HS; (SO); Perf Att; Key Club; P to P St Amb Prg; Spanish Clb; Sftball (J); Vllyball (JC); Stu Cncl (R); CR (R)

MC ALMAN, NICHOLAS A; BLAKESLEE, PA; POCONO MTN WEST HS; (SR); Hi Hnr Roll; Hnr Roll; Chess; Penn State

MC ARDLE, ANNA; BRACKENRIDGE, PA; HIGHLANDS SD; (MS); Hnr Roll; Nat Hon Sy; Otst Ac Ach Awd; St of Mnth; Comm Volntr; Chrch Yth Grp; Scouts; Bnd; Mch Bnd; Mar Art (V); Mathematics; Education; Notre Dame U; Brown U

MC BETH, COREY L; YOUNGWOOD, PA; CTRL WESTMORELAND CTC; (SO); Hi Hnr Roll; Hnr Roll; MVP; Comm Volntr; Web Design; Graphic Design; Seton Hill U; Penn State U

MC BURNEY, KELLY A; SPRINGFIELD, PA; MARPLE NEWTOWN HS; (SR); Hnr Roll; MVP; Nat Hon Sy; Comm Volntr; Spec Olymp Vol; Chrch Yth Grp; Emplmnt; Chr; Lcrsse (V); PP Ftbl (V); Sccr (V); Sch Ppr (E); Nursing / BSN / Pharmaceutical Sales; Marketing; East Stroudsburg U - Accepted; Temple U

MC CABE, CAYSI; NAZARETH, PA; NAZARETH HS; (JR); Hnr Roll; Perf Att; Pres Ac Ftns Aw; WWAHSS; DARE; Dnce; Computer Programming; Hofstra U

MC CABE, KELLY; MIFFLINBURG, PA; MIFFLINBURG AREA HS; (JR); Hi Hnr Roll; Nat Hon Sy; Comm Volntr; Key Club; Prom Com; German Clb; Sccr (V); Track (V); Cl Off (V); United Christian Teens; National Honor Society President; Psychology; Social Sciences; Susquehanna U; Messiah College

MC CABE, KELLY; WYOMING, PA; WYOMING AREA HS; (JR); Hi Hnr Roll; Nat Hon Sy; Perf Att; St of Mnth; WWAHSS; Yth Ldrshp Prog; Comm Volntr; Peer Tut/Med; Chrch Yth Grp; Emplmnt; FBLA; SADD; Spanish Clb; Bskball (V); Vllyball (J); Sch Ppr (E, R); Secretary of Journalism Club; Writer; English Teacher; U of Maryland; U of Notre Dame

MC CAIN, MACKENZIE L; NEW MILFORD, PA; BLUE RIDGE HS; (FR); Ctznshp Aw; Hi Hnr Roll; Jr Rot; MVP; Nat Hon Sy; Nat Stu Ath Day Aw; Otst Ac Ach Awd; St of Mnth; Chr; SP/M/VS; Bskball (J); Sftball (J); Cl Off (P); Stu Cncl (R); CR (R); National Junior Honor Society; USAA National History & Govt. Award; History Teacher; Sports Medicine; Mansfield U; Penn State

MC CALL, SARAH I; WATERFORD, PA; FORT LEBOEUF SD; Hnr Roll; Perf Att; Comm Volntr; ArtClub; Chrch Yth Grp; Emplmnt; Chrldg (V CL); Mathematics; Teaching; Mercyhurst College; North Carolina State U

MC CALMONT, TIFFANI; ROXBURY, PA; CHAMBERSBURG AREA SR HS; (JR); Hnr Roll; WWAHSS; Key Club; Voc Ind Clb Am; VP of Key Club; VICA; Bradley Art Institute

MC CANN, SHAWNA; BEAVER FALLS, PA; BLACKHAWK HS; (SO); Hi Hnr Roll; Otst Ac Ach Awd; WWAHSS; Comm Volntr; Peer Tut/Med; Spec Olymp Vol; Drma Clb; Key Club; Off Aide; Svce Clb; Spanish Clb; Track (V); President of Key Club, Top 15% of Class; President's Award for Educational Excellence

MC CANN, STEPHANIE; BEAVER FALLS, PA; BLACKHAWK HS; (MS); Hi Hnr Roll; Perf Att; Comm Volntr; Spec Olymp Vol; Key Club; Spanish Clb; Track (J); Presidential Academic Awards

Mc Beth, Corey L
Central Westmoreland CTC
Youngwood, PA

Mathis, Kenisha M
Germantown-Lankenau HS
Philadelphia, PA

Marts, Nicholas D
East Allegheny HS
Mc Keesport, PA

Martin, Lexi
Lehigh Valley Chr. Perf Arts HS
Bethlehem, PA

Martin, Margaret
Pottsville Area SD
Pottsville, PA

Mathis III, Theodore J
Canon Mc Millan HS
Canonsburg, PA

Mc Burney, Kelly A
Marple Newtown HS
Springfield, PA

MC CARTHY, ANNA L; WELLSBORO, PA; WELLSBORO HS; (SR); Hi Hnr Roll; Hnr Roll; Nat Hon Sy; Otst Ac Ach Awd; Pres Ac Ftns Aw; St of Mnth; WWAHSS; Hab For Humty Volntr; Peer Tut/Med; 4-H; ArtClub; Emplmnt; Outdrs Clb; Photog; Prom Com; Tchrs Aide; Chr; Cr Ctry (J L); Sftball (V L); Cl Off (P); Wellsboro High School Laurel Festival Queen Pageant; Internship with Chesapeake Bay Foundation; Environmental Studies; Political Science; Pittsburgh U; Allegheny College

MC CARTHY, CAROLINE; BRADFORDWOODS, PA; NORTH ALLEGHENY INT HS; (FR); Ctznshp Aw; St of Mnth; WWAHSS; Comm Volntr; Chrch Yth Grp; FBLA; Key Club; Scouts; Dnce; Stu Cncl (P, V); Letter for Bowling Team; Who's Who American High Schools; Business; Pennsylvania State U; James Madison U

MC CARTHY, EILEEN; AUDUBON, PA; METHACTON HS; (SO); Hi Hnr Roll; Yth Ldrshp Prog; Key Club; Track (V); Competed at Penn Relays

MC CAUSLIN, JASON R; VERONA, PA; PENN HILLS SR HS; (JR); Hi Hnr Roll; Hnr Roll; Nat Hon Sy; Perf Att; Sci Fairs; WWAHSS; Comm Volntr; Hab For Humty Volntr; Chrch Yth Grp; Emplmnt; Key Club; SADD; German Clb; Ice Hky (V L); Tennis (V L); Vllyball (J); All-Star Dek Hockey; Math; Computer Science; Westminster College

MC CLARREN, AMANDA; HOLLSOPPLE, PA; CONEMAUGH TOWNSHIP JR/SR HS; (JR); Hnr Roll; WWAHSS; Comm Volntr; Chrch Yth Grp; Emplmnt; Svce Clb; SADD; Bnd; Clr Grd; Mch Bnd; Orch; PP Ftbl (VJ); Track (VJCL); Academic Awards Banquette for Culinary; Hotel Management; Master's Degree in Business; Virginia College; South Carolina U

MC CLARY, BRANDON; PHILADELPHIA, PA; CENTRAL HS; (JR); Ctznshp Aw; Hnr Roll; St of Mnth; Comm Volntr; Chess; DARE; Gmnstcs (V); Two Years of Space Camp; Aerospace & Aeronautical Engineer; U of Alabama in Huntsville; Embry-Riddle Aeronautical U

MC COMBIE, TARA; EBENSBURG, PA; CTRL CAMBRIA HS; (SO); Hi Hnr Roll; Hnr Roll; Pres Sch; USAA; Chess; Mus Clb; Chr; Dnce; SP/M/VS; Stg Cre; Sccr (J); AV/Tech Crew; Newsroom Worker; Technical Theatre; Forensic Pathologist; Mount Aloysius College; Art Institute in Pittsburgh

MC CONNELL, ASHLEY; STONEBORO, PA; LAKEVIEW SD; (SO); 4H Awd; Hnr Roll; Pres Ac Ftns Aw; Peer Tut/Med; 4-H; DARE; Off Aide; Cr Ctry (V L); Track (V); Winner of Short Story Contests; Physical Therapy; Pennsylvania State U; Slippery Rock U

MC CORMICK, ERIN; GREENVILLE, PA; GREENVILLE HS; (JR); Hnr Roll; Nat Hon Sy; WWAHSS; Peer Tut/Med; ArtClub; Key Club; Prom Com; Sci Clb; Vsity Clb; Chr; Bskball (V L); Sftball; Track (V L); Vsy Clb; Cl Off (R); Stu Cncl (R); Sports Medicine; Slippery Rock U

MC COY, KELLI; BOYERTOWN, PA; BOYERTOWN AREA SR HS; (SO); Ctznshp Aw; Hi Hnr Roll; Hnr Roll; Perf Att; Pres Ac Ftns Aw; DARE; Drma Clb; Emplmnt; Chr; SP/M/VS; Chrldg (V); Gmnstcs; PP Ftbl (L); Sftball (J); Music / Drama / Theatre Major; Fashion Design Major; U of the Arts Philadelphia; U of New York

MC COY, MIRIAH; LEWISTOWN, PA; LEWISTOWN HS; (SO); 4H Awd; Hi Hnr Roll; Nat Hon Sy; WWAHSS; Comm Volntr; Hosp Aide; 4-H; Key Club; Chrldg (V); Panther Pride Award; Early Childhood Development

MC COY, TYLISHA; ERIE, PA; WILSON MS; (MS); Ctznshp Aw; Fut Prb Slvr; Hnr Roll; Peer Tut/Med; Cosmetologist; Business; Mercyhurst; Penn State

MC CRACKEN, MALLORY; BETHEL PARK, PA; BETHEL PARK SD; (JR); Hnr Roll; Perf Att; WWAHSS; Comm Volntr; Chrch Yth Grp; Emplmnt; Chr; Dnce; Chrldg (V); Scholarships for Dance to International Dance Programs; Numerous High Awards at Dance Competitions; Arts and Communication; Education

MC CURDY, ELIZABETH; GREENVILLE, PA; GREENVILLE HS; (JR); Hi Hnr Roll; Nat Hon Sy; Pres Sch; St of Mnth; WWAHSS; Comm Volntr; Emplmnt; Key Club; Lttrmn Clb; Prom Com; Sci Clb; Vsity Clb; Spanish Clb; Bskball (V L); Sftball; Track (V L); National Honor Society Inductee; Physician Assistant; Education; Gannon U; Duquesne U

MC CURDY, KIMBERLY; OAKMONT, PA; RIVERVIEW HS; (FR); Hi Hnr Roll; Otst Ac Ach Awd; Pres Sch; Yth Ldrshp Prog; Comm Volntr; Peer Tut/Med; Chrch Yth Grp; Emplmnt; Key Club; NYLC; Tchrs Aide; Spanish Clb; Dnce; Stg Cre; Bskball (VJ); GAA (V); Sftball (VJ); Vllyball (J); Stu Cncl (R); Physician; Law; U of Pittsburgh

MC CUSKER, LIAM; WARRINGTON, PA; MIDDLE BUCKS INST OF TECH; (JR); Hi Hnr Roll; Hnr Roll; Pres Ac Ftns Aw; Comm Volntr; Vsity Clb; Wdwrkg Clb; Chr; Lcrsse (J); Track (VJ); Piano for Eight Years; Engineering; Business; Drexel U; Penn State

MC DERMOTT, PATRICK T; VANDERGRIFT, PA; (SR); Hi Hnr Roll; Nat Hon Sy; St of Mnth; WWAHSS; Comm Volntr; Peer Tut/Med; Chrch Yth Grp; Emplmnt; Key Club; Prom Com; SADD; German Clb; Acpl Chr; Chr; SP/M/VS; Swg Chr; Bskball (VJ L); Cl Off (S, T); Stu Cncl (R); Biology; Political Science; John Carroll U

MC DILDA, BRIDGET; MECHANICSBURG, PA; CUMBERLAND VALLEY HS; (JR); Hnr Roll; Spec Olymp Vol; ArtClub; Key Club; Rugby Player in School; Horseback Rider Outside of School; Major in Equine Studies, Specific Training; Averett U; Lake Erie College

MC DONALD, HEATHER L; WYOMING, PA; DALLAS HS; (JR); Hnr Roll; Perf Att; WWAHSS; Yth Ldrshp Prog; Comm Volntr; DARE; Drma Clb; Key Club; P to P St Amb Prg; Scouts; Dnce; SP/M/VS; Sch Ppr (E, R, P); Shakespeare Club Charter Member & Secretary; Herizons (Women's Issues Club) Charter Member

MC DONALD, KATIE; ERIE, PA; MC DOWELL INT HS; (SR); Hnr Roll; Sci Fairs; WWAHSS; Red Cr Aide; Vsity Clb; GAA (V); PP Ftbl; Sccr (V CL); Cl Off (S); Physical Therapy; Saint Francis U

MC DONNELL, MADDALENA; VANDERGRIFT, PA; KISKI AREA HS; (JR); Hi Hnr Roll; Nat Hon Sy; Comm Volntr; Peer Tut/Med; Emplmnt; Key Club; Mth Clb/Tm; Cr Ctry (V L); Track (J); Westinghouse Science Honors Institute; Women in Science Chemistry Award from Seton Hill U; Psychology; Philosophy; U of Pittsburgh; Carnegie Mellon U

MC ELHANEY, KEVIN S; JAMESTOWN, PA; JAMESTOWN AREA SD; (SR); 4H Awd; All Am Sch; Hi Hnr Roll; Nat Hon Sy; Pres Ac Ftns Aw; WWAHSS; 4-H; Chrch Yth Grp; Emplmnt; Spanish Clb; Bsball; Wrstlg; Stu Cncl; Chemical Engineering; Gannon U; Penn State U

MC ELROY, SETH D; UNIONTOWN, PA; LAUREL HIGHLANDS SR HS; (JR); Hi Hnr Roll; Nat Hon Sy; Nat Mrt Semif; Otst Ac Ach Awd; Sci/Math Olympn; St of Mnth; USAA; WWAHSS; Comm Volntr; Chrch Yth Grp; Emplmnt; Jr Ach; Mth Clb/Tm; NYLC; Outdrs Clb; Quiz Bowl; Ch Chr; Yrbk (P); Envirothon Team; Quiz Team Captain; International Relations; Linguistics; George Washington U; American U

MC ELWEE, SEAN P; UPPER DARBY, PA; UPPER DARBY HS; (JR); Hi Hnr Roll; Hnr Roll; Otst Ac Ach Awd; Perf Att; St of Mnth; Comm Volntr; Peer Tut/Med; Chrch Yth Grp; Drma Clb; Emplmnt; Mus Clb; Off Aide; Tchrs Aide; French Clb; Acpl Chr; Chr; Ch Chr; SP/M/VS; Stu Cncl (R); CR (R); Sch Ppr (R); Sang At St. Patrick's Cathedral and Cathedral of St. John the Divine.; Selected for PMEA District Chorus; Music Education-Choral; High School Choral Director; West Chester U of Pennsylvania; Eastern U

MC FADDEN, KIM; FLEETWOOD, PA; BRANDYWINE HEIGHTS HS; (FR); Hi Hnr Roll; Hnr Roll; Nat Hon Sy; Perf Att; WWAHSS; 4-H; Chrch Yth Grp; Key Club; Svce Clb; Bnd; Chr; Mch Bnd; Orch; NYSSMA Solo Competition 27/28 - Violin; Mathematics / Sciences; Animals; Kutztown U

MC GINN, DALLAS; SHAMOKIN, PA; SHAMOKIN AREA HS; (JR); Bsball (J); Bskball (J); Police Officer; EMT

MC GINNIS, BRETT E; REYNOLDSVILLE, PA; DUBOIS AREA HS; (SO); Hnr Roll; Sci Fairs; Sci/Math Olympn; Yth Ldrshp Prog; Comm Volntr; Peer Tut/Med; Chrch Yth Grp; Drma Clb; Emplmnt; HO'Br Yth Ldrshp; Sci Clb; Scouts; Bnd; Mch Bnd; SP/M/VS; Stu Cncl (R); HOBY Attendee; Boy Scouts; Major in Biochemistry; Go to Med School-Anesthesiology; U of Pennsylvania; Princeton U

MC GRADY, THOMAS J; PLYMOUTH, PA; GREATER NANTICOKE AREA SD; (JR); Hi Hnr Roll; Nat Hon Sy; Pres Sch; WWAHSS; Yth Ldrshp Prog; Comm Volntr; Chrch Yth Grp; Drma Clb; Emplmnt; Mus Clb; French Clb; Chr; Ch Chr; Mch Bnd; Orch; Ftball (VJ L); Track (VJC); Stu Cncl (R); Sch Ppr (R)

MC GRANOR, NICKI; PENFIELD, PA; DUBOIS AREA HS; (SO); Hnr Roll; St of Mnth; WWAHSS; Clr Grd; Elementary Teacher; Day Care Business; Indiana U of Pennsylvania; Penn State Dubois Campus

MC GRATH, KELLY; BOYERTOWN, PA; BOYERTOWN SR HS; (JR); Hi Hnr Roll; Nat Hon Sy; Sci/Math Olympn; WWAHSS; Comm Volntr; Peer Tut/Med; Chrch Yth Grp; DARE; Emplmnt; Key Club; Mth Clb/Tm; Sci Clb; Cl Off (R); Youth Group; Key Club; International Business; Finance; U of Richmond; Georgetown U

MC GRATH, KEVIN; BOYERTOWN, PA; BOYERTOWN AREA SR HS; (JR); Hi Hnr Roll; Nat Hon Sy; Pres Ac Ftns Aw; WWAHSS; Emplmnt; Key Club; Lcrsse (V L); Stu Cncl (R); CR (R); Journalist of the Year 2003; Keystone Award for Journalism (2); English; U of Pittsburgh; Penn State U

MC GRAW, MEGAN; CAMP HILL, PA; CEDAR CLIFF HS; (SR); Hnr Roll; Nat Hon Sy; Photog; Quill & Scroll; Chr; Yrbk (E, R); Accounting Club - 2 Years; Business Administration; Accounting; Harrisburg Area Community College; Elizabethtown College

MC GRAW, TAWNI; BRACKNEY, PA; MONTROSE AREA SD HS; (SO); 4H Awd; Hnr Roll; Peer Tut/Med; 4-H; Emplmnt; French Clb; Fld Hky (J); Skiing (J); Kickboxing; Dental; Florida State; Buffalo

MC GREGOR, SHANE; EBENSBURG, PA; CTRL CAMBRIA; (FR); Hi Hnr Roll; MVP; Sci Fairs; Chess; Chrch Yth Grp; Mth Clb/Tm; Bnd; Chr; Bsball (V); Bskball (J); Ftball (J); Wt Lftg; Stu Cncl (P)

MC KAY, ROBBIE; BETHLEHEM, PA; NORTHAMPTON AREA SCH; (SO); Hi Hnr Roll; Hnr Roll; Nat Sci Aw; Sci/Math Olympn; Emplmnt; Golf (VCL); Scr Kpr; Medical Profession; Golf-Related Profession; Lehigh U, Bethlehem, PA; Penn State, State College, PA

MC KAY, SHANA; HOLMES, PA; RIDLEY HS; (FR); Hnr Roll; St of Mnth; Emplmnt; Mod UN; Mus Clb; Chr; Track (J); CR (R); Lit Mag (P); Medical / Nurse; Photography; Penn State; Widener College

MC KNIGHT, KIESHIA D; HUNTINGDON, PA; HUNTINGDON AREA HS; (JR); Hi Hnr Roll; Hnr Roll; WWAHSS; Comm Volntr; Peer Tut/Med; Spec Olymp Vol; 4-H; Chrch Yth Grp; Key Club; SADD; Tchrs Aide; Chr; Fld Hky (J); Track (V); National Society of High School Scholars; Participate in Goju Karate; Criminal Justice; Childhood Psychology; Juniata College

MC LANE, KAT; SCRANTON, PA; SCRANTON HS; (JR); Hnr Roll; Nat Hon Sy; WWAHSS; Comm Volntr; ArtClub; Emplmnt; Photog; Dnce; SP/M/VS; Photographs in Art Exhibitions; Photo Journalism

MC LEAN, JENNIFER; BIRDSBORO, PA; DANIEL BOONE AREA HS; (JR); Hi Hnr Roll; Nat Hon Sy; Hab For Humty Volntr; FCA; FBLA; Key Club; Prom Com; Vsity Clb; Cr Ctry (V); Sccr (V C); Track (V); Prom Com; Varsity Club; Business; Psychology; Shippensburg U; Bloomsburg U

MC MILLEN, DANIELLE; GREENVILLE, PA; GREENVILLE HS; (JR); F Lan Hn Soc; Hi Hnr Roll; Nat Hon Sy; Otst Ac Ach Awd; Perf Att; St of Mnth; WWAHSS; Comm Volntr; Cmptr Clb; Key Club; Prom Com; Sci Clb; Vsity Clb; Spanish Clb; Acpl Chr; Chr; Dnce; Drl Tm; Chrldg (V L); PPSqd (V CL); Scr Kpr; Vsy Clb; Cl Off (T); Stu Cncl; Yrbk (E)

MC MILLEN, GABRIELLE S; FORD CITY, PA; LENAPE TECH; (JR); Hi Hnr Roll; Hnr Roll; Perf Att; WWAHSS; FBLA; Voc Ind Clb Am; Nominated for Who's Who Among High School Students; Culinary Arts; Winner Institute; Pennsylvania Culinary Institute of Pittsburgh

MC MILLEN, TONY; CLARION, PA; CLARION AREA JR/SR HS; (SO); Hi Hnr Roll; Hnr Roll; Pres Ac Ftns Aw; Sci/Math Olympn; Chess; Chrch Yth Grp; Sci Clb; Chr; Swg Chr; Bskball; Ftball (V L); Swmg (V C); Archaeology; Miami of Florida

MC MULLIN, BRANDON; ASTON, PA; SUN VALLEY HS; (SR); Ctznshp Aw; Hnr Roll; WWAHSS; Comm Volntr; Red Cr Aide; Drma Clb; Emplmnt; Pep Squd; Photog; Prom Com; SP/M/VS; Sccr (V); Stu Cncl (R); CR (R); Sun Valley School Mascot; TV Studio Anchor; Theater; Performing Arts; Hofstra U

MC NAMARA, JACQUELYN J; EASTON, PA; EASTON AREA HS; (SO); Hi Hnr Roll; Hnr Roll; Perf Att; Pres Ac Ftns Aw; Sci Fairs; St of Mnth; Peer Tut/Med; Chrch Yth Grp; DARE; Key Club; Off Aide; Sci Clb; Bskball (J); Vllyball (J); Teacher; Child Care Director

MC NAMARA, KATHLEEN; PITTSBURGH, PA; CARLYNTON SD; (FR); Hi Hnr Roll; Nat Hon Sy; Comm Volntr; Chrch Yth Grp; Scouts; Chr; Girl Scout Silver Award; Pediatrician; Pastry Chef; U of Pittsburgh; Pittsburgh School of Culinary Arts

MC NAMEE, JESSICA; SWARTHMORE, PA; RIDLEY SD; (SO); Hnr Roll; Nat Hon Sy; Drma Clb; Dnce; Cl Off (T); Dance Team - Captain; Award for Commendation; Elementary Education; Dance Minor / Bachelor's Degree; New York

MC NEIL, RACHEL; BIG RUN, PA; PUNXSUTAWNEY AREA HS; (JR); All Am Sch; Hi Hnr Roll; Nat Hon Sy; St of Mnth; USAA; WWAHSS; Chrch Yth Grp; Sci Clb; Ch Chr; Chrldg (V CL); PP Ftbl (J); Stu Cncl (R); Pediatric Medicine

MC RAE, CAITLIN; POTTSTOWN, PA; POTTSGROVE SR HS; (FR); Hnr Roll; Nat Hon Sy; Comm Volntr; Quiz Bowl; Sci Clb; Scouts; Bnd; Clr Grd; Mch Bnd; Orch; Sccr (J); Bronze Award for Girl Scouts; Silver Award for Girl Scouts; Psychology; Medicine; Notre Dame; U of Pennsylvania

MC TAGUE, STEPHANIE L; PHILADELPHIA, PA; GEORGE WASHINGTON HS; (JR); Hi Hnr Roll; Hnr Roll; Nat Hon Sy; Peer Tut/Med; ArtClub; Chrch Yth Grp; Drma Clb; Emplmnt; HO'Br Yth Ldrshp; Dnce; SP/M/VS; Chrldg (V C); Nursing RN, BSN; Penn State U; Abington School of Nursing

MC TISH, KATHERINE; MOHNTON, PA; TWIN VALLEY HS; (SO); Fut Prb Slvr; Hi Hnr Roll; Comm Volntr; Chrch Yth Grp; Scouts; German Clb; Bnd; Jzz Bnd; Mch Bnd; Bskball (J); German Award; Future Problem Solvers-State Bowl; Psychology; English; The Pennsylvania State U; New York U

MC VAY, KELLY L; COUDERSPORT, PA; COUDERSPORT AREA SD; (FR); Hi Hnr Roll; Hnr Roll; Chr; Bskball (VJ); Sftball (V); Vllyball (J); Marine Biologist; Pennsylvania State U

MEANS, ARIANNE; VERONA, PA; PENN HILLS HS; (JR); Hi Hnr Roll; Nat Hon Sy; WWAHSS; Yth Ldrshp Prog; Comm Volntr; Peer Tut/Med; Chrch Yth Grp; Emplmnt; Key Club; Scouts; Spanish Clb; Physical Therapy; Environmental Studies; U of Pittsburgh; York College

Mc Knight, Kieshia D
Huntingdon Area HS
Huntingdon, PA

Mc Coy, Kelli
Boyertown Area SR HS
Boyertown, PA

Mc Combie, Tara
Central Cambria HS
Ebensburg, PA

National
Honor Roll
Spring 2005

Mc Causlin, Jason R
Penn Hills SR HS
Verona, PA

Mc Cracken, Mallory
Bethel Park SD
Bethel Park, PA

Mc Millen, Tony
Clarion Area JR/SR HS
Clarion, PA

MECK, CRISTY LYNN; CTRL CITY, PA; SHADE-CENTRAL CITY SD; (FR); Hi Hnr Roll; Hnr Roll; Nat Ldrshp Svc; USAA; Chrch Yth Grp; SADD; Chrldg (V); Sftball (J); Vllyball (J); Literature; Forensic Science; Princeton U; Washington U St. Louis

MEDVITZ, MELANIE C; UNIONTOWN, PA; LAUREL HIGHLANDS SR HS; (SO); Hi Hnr Roll; Hnr Roll; Pres Sch; WWAHSS; Comm Volntr; Sccr (V L); Track (V L); US Soccer Fed Ref PA West, Natl Society of HS Scholars, WPIAL Qualifier 2004 & 2005 Long Jump & Triple Jump; Engineering; Psychology; Pennsylvania State U; U of Pittsburgh

MEEHAN, MEREDITH M; GLENSHAW, PA; SHALER AREA HS; (JR); DAR; F Lan Hn Soc; Hi Hnr Roll; Nat Hon Sy; Otst Ac Ach Awd; St of Mnth; Comm Volntr; Dbte Team; Emplmnt; Mod UN; Spch Team; PP Ftbl (J); Skiing; Stu Cncl (R); CR (R); Sch Ppr (R); Member of Steel City Rowing Team; Won 3 Silver Medals at Nationals / Teach Blind Youth How to Row; International Relations; Linguistics; United States Naval Academy; Yale U

MEHELICH, TASHA; BUTLER, PA; BUTLER SR HS; (JR); Hnr Roll; Comm Volntr; ROTC; Spanish Clb; Chr; Clr Grd; Vllyball (J); LET I and III Superior Cadet Award; Military Officers Association of America; Law Enforcement; Education; Slippery Rock; Virginia Tech

MEHTA, BHAKTI; PITTSBURGH, PA; CHARTIERS VALLEY HS; (JR); Hnr Roll; Nat Hon Sy; St of Mnth; Comm Volntr; Peer Tut/Med; Lib Aide; Tchrs Aide; Tmpl Yth Grp; Spanish Clb; Dnce; Orch; SP/M/VS; Lit Mag; Interact Club; Medicine; U of Pittsburgh

MEISING, JESSICA; OAKMONT, PA; RIVERVIEW JR/SR HS; (FR); Hnr Roll; Pres Sch; Comm Volntr; Key Club; Chr; Stg Cre; Sftball (J); Vllyball (J); Stu Cncl; SADD Club; President's Achievement Award; History Major; History Teacher; U of Pittsburgh; Slippery Rock U

MEITZLER, ADREA; ALBURTIS, PA; BRANDYWINE HEIGHTS AREA HS; (SO); Hi Hnr Roll; Hnr Roll; Kwnis Aw; WWAHSS; ArtClub; Drma Clb; Emplmnt; Key Club; Scouts; Vllyball (VJ L); Forensic Science; Marine Biology; Kutztown U; Penn State U

MEKHAIL, JOHN P; CAMP HILL, PA; CAMP HILL HS; (SO); Hnr Roll; Perf Att; Yth Ldrshp Prog; Comm Volntr; DARE; Mus Clb; Bnd; Chr; Tennis (V); Nominated for Global Young Leaders Conference; 2004 Champion WSR Tennis Tournament; World History and Cultures; Journalism; USC; Cal State

MELENDEZ, ANGEL R; PHILADELPHIA, PA; NORTHEAST CATHOLIC BOYS HS; (FR); Hnr Roll; Comm Volntr; Chrch Yth Grp; Bskball (J); Coaching; Accounting & Finance, Mathematics & Statistics; Business Administration; Saint Joseph's U; Temple U

MELETICHE, NINA M; EASTON, PA; EASTON AREA HS; (SR); Hi Hnr Roll; Nat Hon Sy; Nat Mrt LOC; Sci Fairs; St of Mnth; Yth Ldrshp Prog; Comm Volntr; Spec Olymp Vol; Drma Clb; NYLC; Outdrs Clb; Prom Com; Latin Clb; Chr; Mch Bnd; Orch; SP/M/VS; Cr Ctry (V L); Track (V L); Cl Off (P, V); Major in Criminology and Criminal Justice; Minor in Science; U of South Carolina; U of Maryland

MEMO, MARYBETH E; NEW CASTLE, PA; NESHANNOCK HS; (JR); Hnr Roll; WWAHSS; ArtClub; Chrch Yth Grp; FBLA; Prom Com; Spanish Clb; Bnd; Ch Chr; Mch Bnd; Bskball (V); Students Helping Students; Teaching; Westminster College

MENK, LINDSAY; LOWER BURRELL, PA; ST JOSEPH HS; (FR); Hi Hnr Roll; Hab For Humty Volntr; Peer Tut/Med; Chrch Yth Grp; DARE; NtlFrnscLg; P to P St Amb Prg; Svce Clb; Chr; SP/M/VS; Tennis (J); CR (R); Yrbk; Service Scholarship to St Joseph High School; National History Day Competition; Journalism

MERCURIO, ELAINA R; PIPERSVILLE, PA; CTRL BUCKS HS EAST; (SO); Hi Hnr Roll; Nat Hon Sy; Otst Ac Ach Awd; WWAHSS; Drma Clb; Key Club; Chr; SP/M/VS; CR (R); Ski Club; Soup Kitchen; Business; Communications

MERRILL, JENNA L; BEACH HAVEN, PA; BERWICK AREA SR HS; (SR); All Am Sch; Hi Hnr Roll; Nat Hon Sy; Pres Ac Ftns Aw; St of Mnth; WWAHSS; Comm Volntr; Emplmnt; Key Club; Fld Hky (V L); PP Ftbl (V); Swmg (V CL); 1000 Career Points / Swimming; Pre-Med; Language Arts; U of Pittsburgh

MERRITT, MARIKA N; SUSQUEHANNA, PA; BLUE RIDGE HS; (FR); Hi Hnr Roll; St of Mnth; WWAHSS; Comm Volntr; Chrch Yth Grp; Drma Clb; FBLA; P to P St Amb Prg; Quiz Bowl; Scouts; SADD; Bnd; Mch Bnd; SP/M/VS; Stg Cre; Leo Club / Girl Scout Silver Award; Pride Club / American Legion Jr Auxiliary; Law; Penn State

MERRYMAN, MELANIE D; HARRISBURG, PA; CTRL DAUPHIN HS; (FR); Hnr Roll; Nat Hon Sy; Perf Att; Pres Sch; Sci Fairs; St of Mnth; Comm Volntr; Peer Tut/Med; Chrch Yth Grp; Emplmnt; Mus Clb; Scouts; Chr; Jzz Bnd; Mch Bnd; SP/M/VS; Teens Against Tobacco Use; Young Democrats; Nursing

MERTZ, BRETT A; POTTSTOWN, PA; POTTSTOWN SR HS; (FR); DARE; ROTC; Chr; Ftball (J)

METZ, COURTNEY E; SHIPPENSBURG, PA; SHIPPENSBURG AREA HS; (SR); Hi Hnr Roll; Hnr Roll; Nat Hon Sy; Nat Mrt Fin; Pres Ac Ftns Aw; St of Mnth; Peer Tut/Med; Spec Olymp Vol; Chrch Yth Grp; Drma Clb; Emplmnt; Mth Clb/Tm; Prom Com; Quill & Scroll; Scouts; Bnd; Mch Bnd; Orch; Pep Bnd; Fld Hky (V L); Sccr (J L); Stu Cncl (R); Lit Mag (R, P); Sch Ppr (E, R); Mass Communications; U of North Carolina At Asheville

MEZA, DARYL C; EAST STROUDSBURG, PA; ABEKA AC; (SO); Comm Volntr; Chrch Yth Grp; Tchrs Aide; Ch Chr; Fncg; Active Supporter of the Republican Party; Political Science; Law; East Stroudsburg U; New York School of Law

MICHA, MILAGROSA N; ALLISON PARK, PA; HAMPTON HS; (SR); Hnr Roll; Perf Att; Comm Volntr; SP/M/VS; Founder of S.T.O.P. Club in School (Students Together Organizing Prevention); Want to Be a Civil Rights Attorney and Activist; Majoring in Secretarial and Political Science; U of Houston-Downtown; Rice U

MICHENER, RACHEL F; PHOENIXVILLE, PA; PHOENIXVILLE AREA HS; (SR); Hnr Roll; Sci Fairs; WWAHSS; Peer Tut/Med; Emplmnt; Key Club; Prom Com; Scouts; SADD; Tchrs Aide; Hsbk Rdg; Track; Committee to Assist and Educate Kids Against Smoking; Business Affairs; Social Welfare & Assistance; West Chester U

MICHKOFSKY, GINA; EBENSBURG, PA; CTRL CAMBRIA HS; (SR); Hi Hnr Roll; Otst Ac Ach Awd; Pres Ac Ftns Aw; WWAHSS; Comm Volntr; Chrch Yth Grp; DARE; Jr Ach; Off Aide; Chr; Bskball (J); Scr Kpr (V); School Office Worker; Interact Club; Psychology; U of Pittsburgh

MICHTCHAK, VITALIA; EASTON, PA; EASTON AREA HS; (SO); Hi Hnr Roll; Hnr Roll; Otst Ac Ach Awd; Sci Fairs; Peer Tut/Med; Peer Assistance; PJAS 2nd Place; Lawyer; Journalist; Stanford U; U of Maryland-Baltimore

MICK, COURTNEY C; EASTON, PA; EASTON AREA SR HS; (FR); Hnr Roll; Emplmnt; Off Aide; Dnce; Play the Piano; Ballet Dancer; Business; Accounting; New York U; Rutgers U New Brunswick Campus

MICKLES, ROBERT L; FAIRLESS HILLS, PA; BUCKS CTY TECH HS; (SR); Hi Hnr Roll; Hnr Roll; Perf Att; St of Mnth; DARE; Emplmnt; SP/M/VS; Skills USA VICA; Visual Effects & Motion Graphics; Film/Video Production; The Art Institute of Philadelphia; New York Film Academy

MIDDLETON, KENNY; BROOKHAVEN, PA; CHASTER HS; (SO); Ctznshp Aw; Hi Hnr Roll; Hnr Roll; Perf Att; Chrch Yth Grp; Cmptr Clb; Emplmnt; Bsball (J); Bskball; Ftball (J); Distinguished Honor Roll; Math; Accountant; U of Texas; Stanford U

MIDDLETON, SARA; FINLEYVILLE, PA; RINGGOLD-SD; (FR); Peer Tut/Med; SADD; PP Ftbl (J); Sccr (J); Track (J)

MIGLIOZZI, JOHN; PITTSBURGH, PA; NORTH ALLEGHENY INT HS; (FR); Ctznshp Aw; Hi Hnr Roll; Nat Hon Sy; Otst Ac Ach Awd; Pres Sch; WWAHSS; Yth Ldrshp Prog; Comm Volntr; Chrch Yth Grp; Emplmnt; Key Club; Outdrs Clb; Scouts; Bnd; Jzz Bnd; Stg Cre; Cr Ctry; Extra Effort Award, Goal (Gifted Program); Piano 10 Year National Guild, Assistant Basketball Coach (YMCA); Architecture; Civil Engineering; Carnegie Mellon U; U Of Notre Dame

MIKELL, LARAYIA; PHILADELPHIA, PA; OVERBROOK HS; (SO); Hnr Roll; St of Mnth; Chrch Yth Grp; SADD; Bnd; Drl Tm; Track (V); Vllyball (V); Drexel U Summer Camp; Physical Therapy/Sports Medicine; Howard U; Temple U

MIKULA, BRITTANY; ALIQUIPPA, PA; CTR AREA SD; (SO); Hi Hnr Roll; Chrch Yth Grp; French Clb; Bnd; Clr Grd; Dnce; Mch Bnd; Track (V); Baton Twirler

MILLER, ALEXIS K; POTTSTOWN, PA; POTTSGROVE HS; (SR); Hi Hnr Roll; Nat Hon Sy; Otst Ac Ach Awd; Pres Ac Ftns Aw; USAA; WWAHSS; ArtClub; Key Club; Mth Clb/Tm; Photog; French Clb; Bnd; Graphic Design; Pratt Institute

MILLER, ALYSSA; SHAVERTOWN, PA; DALLAS AREA HS; (SO); Hi Hnr Roll; Hnr Roll; Nat Hon Sy; Perf Att; USAA; WWAHSS; Comm Volntr; Chrch Yth Grp; Emplmnt; FBLA; Key Club; Scouts; Sccr (VJ); Sch Ppr (R); Yrbk (R); Law; U of Pittsburgh; Pennsylvania State U

MILLER, AMANDA M; EAST STROUDSBURG, PA; EAST STROUDSBURG HS SOUTH; (SR); Hi Hnr Roll; Hnr Roll; Nat Hon Sy; Comm Volntr; Hab For Humty Volntr; Hosp Aide; ArtClub; DARE; Key Club; P to P St Amb Prg; Scouts; Voc Ind Clb Am; Foreign Clb; Lit Mag (R); Yrbk (E, P); Leader in Training for Girl Scouts of America; Elementary Education; East Stroudsburg U (Have Been Accepted)

MILLER, ANTHONY; EFFORT, PA; PLEASANT VALLEY HS; (FR); Hi Hnr Roll; Otst Ac Ach Awd; Comm Volntr; Spec Olymp Vol; DARE; FBLA; JSA; Key Club; SADD; Sch Ppr (E); Director of Fundraising - JSA; Volunteer Assistant Coach of Youth Baseball; Law; Political Science; Georgetown U; Columbia U

MILLER, AUTUMN D; ALUM BANK, PA; CHESTNUT RIDGE HS; (SR); 4H Awd; Hi Hnr Roll; Hnr Roll; Nat Hon Sy; Comm Volntr; 4-H; FBLA; Key Club; Off Aide; Prom Com; SADD; Bnd; Drm Mjr; Jzz Bnd; Mch Bnd; Hsbk Rdg; Cl Off (P); Stu Cncl (S); CR (S); Criminal Justice; Lock Haven U

MILLER, BAILEE M; BEAVER FALLS, PA; BEAVER CTY CHRISTIAN SCH; (SR); Hi Hnr Roll; MVP; Otst Ac Ach Awd; St of Mnth; Comm Volntr; Hab For Humty Volntr; Peer Tut/Med; Chrch Yth Grp; Emplmnt; NYLC; Vsity Clb; Chr; SP/M/VS; Bskball (VJCL); Sccr (V L); Sftball (VJ); Vllyball (VJ L); Sports Medicine; Physical Therapy; U of Pittsburgh

MILLER, CASEY L; HARRISBURG, PA; CTRL DAUPHIN EAST HS; (JR); Ctznshp Aw; Hi Hnr Roll; Nat Hon Sy; St of Mnth; WWAHSS; Comm Volntr; Peer Tut/Med; Chrch Yth Grp; Emplmnt; Prom Com; Bnd; Chr; Fld Hky (J); Skiing (J); CR (R); Citizenship Award; Psychiatrist; Child Psychology; U of Pennsylvania; U of Pittsburgh

MILLER, DANA L; QUARRYVILLE, PA; SOLANCO HS; (SR); Hi Hnr Roll; Hnr Roll; Perf Att; Sci Fairs; Comm Volntr; Peer Tut/Med; Red Cr Aide; Chrch Yth Grp; Emplmnt; Pep Squd; Photog; Prom Com; Chrldg (J); Tennis (VJ); Sch Ppr (R); Hospitality/Business Management; Nursing; York Technical Institute

MILLER, DANIEL; CAMP HILL, PA; CAMP HILL HS; (SO); Hi Hnr Roll; Otst Ac Ach Awd; Perf Att; Sci/Math Olympn; WWAHSS; Comm Volntr; Drma Clb; Svce Clb; Bnd; Chr; Ch Chr; Jzz Bnd; Scr Kpr (V); Sccr (V L); Wrstlg (J); CR (R); Scholastic Writing Award

MILLER, DEANNA N; BETHEL PARK, PA; BETHEL PARK HS; (SR); Hi Hnr Roll; Nat Hon Sy; WWAHSS; Comm Volntr; Chrch Yth Grp; Emplmnt; Svce Clb; Bnd; Dnce; Drl Tm; SP/M/VS; PPSqd (CL); 1st Chair Flutist; Pre-Med; Biochemistry; Washington & Jefferson College; Allegheny College

MILLER, JASHINA N; CHESTER, PA; CHESTER HS; (SO); Hi Hnr Roll; Hnr Roll; Yth Ldrshp Prog; Comm Volntr; BPA; Dbte Team; Key Club; Sci Clb; Secretary of the National Association of Negro Business & Professional Women; Writers Workshop Achiever at Widener U; Registered Nurse; Marketing; Morgan State U; Temple U

MILLER, JESSICA; CHAMBERSBURG, PA; CHAMBERSBURG AREA SR HS; (SO); Hi Hnr Roll; Hnr Roll; Nat Hon Sy; Comm Volntr; Peer Tut/Med; Spec Olymp Vol; Chrch Yth Grp; FCA; FBLA; P to P St Amb Prg; Tennis (V L); Accepted to the Presidential Classroom Scholars Program; Law; Duke U; U of Maryland

MILLER, JESSICA; POTTSTOWN, PA; OWEN J ROBERTS HS; (SO); Hnr Roll; Comm Volntr; Chrch Yth Grp; DECA; Key Club; Spanish Clb; Fld Hky (V); Lcrsse (J); Stu Cncl (R); CR (R); Yrbk (E); DECA-State Winner Pa 2005; DECA-National Finalist '05 Award of Excellence; Business Adm/Marketing

MILLER, JILL; LAFAYETTE HILL, PA; PLYMOUTH WHITEMARSH HS; (JR); Hnr Roll; Stu Cncl (R); Bowling Club; Nutrition; Social Work; Towson U; Penn State

MILLER, JOHN P; LOCK HAVEN, PA; KEYSTONE CTRL SD; (SR); Hnr Roll; Perf Att; Chess; FBLA; Bnd; Computer Science; Pennsylvania College of Technology

MILLER, JORDAN; SOUTH PARK, PA; SOUTH PARK HS; (SO); Hi Hnr Roll; WWAHSS; Chr; Law; Medical; U of Pittsburgh; Penn State

MILLER, KAHLA M; REYNOLDSVILLE, PA; DUBOIS AREA HS; (SR); Hnr Roll; WWAHSS; Red Cr Aide; Lib Aide; Chr; Administrative Medical Assisting; Nursing (RN); Dubois Business College

MILLER, KATELYN L; BLANDON, PA; FLEETWOOD AREA HS; (SO); Ctznshp Aw; Hi Hnr Roll; Nat Hon Sy; Sci/Math Olympn; St of Mnth; WWAHSS; Yth Ldrshp Prog; Comm Volntr; Peer Tut/Med; Spec Olymp Vol; Chrch Yth Grp; Emplmnt; FCA; HO'Br Yth Ldrshp; Jr Ach; Photog; Bnd; Chr; Ch Chr; Mch Bnd; Track (J); Stu Cncl (R); Lit Mag (R); HOBY Ambassador; Special Education; Missions; Wheaton College; Gordon College

MILLER, KIMBERLY; BETHEL PARK, PA; BETHEL PARK SR HS; (SO); Ctznshp Aw; Hi Hnr Roll; Nat Hon Sy; Otst Ac Ach Awd; Pres Sch; Sci Fairs; WWAHSS; Chrch Yth Grp; Drma Clb; Jr Ach; Sci Clb; Spch Team; SP/M/VS; Bskball; Vllyball; Cl Off (S); Stu Cncl; Sch Ppr (E); Pre-Med / Medicine; Teaching; Miami of Ohio U

MILLER, KIMBERLY; LEOLA, PA; CONESTOGA VALLEY HS; (JR); Hi Hnr Roll; Hnr Roll; Nat Hon Sy; Sci Fairs; Sci/Math Olympn; Yth Ldrshp Prog; Comm Volntr; Peer Tut/Med; Chrch Yth Grp; NYLC; P to P St Amb Prg; Quiz Bowl; Adv Cncl (R); Yrbk (E); Mock Trial; Pre-Veterinary Medicine; Political Science

MILLER, LA'TUNDRA; MC KEESPORT, PA; MC KEESPORT AREA SD; (SO); Hi Hnr Roll; Hnr Roll; WWAHSS; Peer Tut/Med; Bskball (J); Law / Lawyer; Defense Lawyer; Hampton U; Yale U

Miller, Kimberly
Bethel Park SR HS
Bethel Park, PA

Miller, Jessica
Chambersburg Area SR HS
Chambersburg, PA

Miller, La'Tundra
Mc Keesport Area SD
Mc Keesport, PA

Miller, Anthony
Pleasant Valley HS
Effort, PA

Michtchak, Vitalia
Easton Area HS
Easton, PA

Merritt, Marika N
Blue Ridge HS
Susquehanna, PA

Memo, Marybeth E
Neshannock HS
New Castle, PA

Meletiche, Nina M
Easton Area HS
Easton, PA

National
Honor Roll
Spring 2005

Mehelich, Tasha
Butler SR HS
Butler, PA

Menk, Lindsay
St Joseph HS
Lower Burrell, PA

Metz, Courtney E
Shippensburg Area HS
Shippensburg, PA

Mickles, Robert L
Bucks Cty Tech HS
Fairless Hills, PA

Miller, Amanda M
East Stroudsburg HS South
East Stroudsburg, PA

MILLER, LEWIS J; DREXEL HILL, PA; UPPER DARBY HS; (SO); Hi Hnr Roll; Hnr Roll; MVP; Nat Hon Sy; Otst Ac Ach Awd; Perf Att; Pres Ac Ftns Aw; Sci Fairs; St of Mnth; Comm Volntr; Emplmnt; Vsity Clb; Ftball (V L); Earned College Credits At HS Technical Career Path Program; Law; Engineering; Penn State U; Villanova U

MILLER, LINDSEY; MALVERN, PA; DELAWARE CTY CHRISTIAN SCH; (SR); Hi Hnr Roll; Nat Hon Sy; WWAHSS; Chrch Yth Grp; Emplmnt; Tchrs Aide; Chrldg (V CL); CR (R); Yrbk (E); Mathematics; Virginia Polytechnic Inst & State U; Pennsylvania State U

MILLER, MATTHEW P; BECHTELSVILLE, PA; BOYERTOWN SR HS; (JR); Ctznshp Aw; Hi Hnr Roll; Otst Ac Ach Awd; Perf Att; Comm Volntr; Chess; Chrch Yth Grp; DARE; Emplmnt; Photog; Spanish Clb; Tennis (J); Sch Ppr (R, P); School Teacher; Business; Penn State Main Campus; Pittsburg U

MILLER, SARAH; NEW FREEDOM, PA; SUSQUEHANNOCK HS; (SO); F Lan Hn Soc; Hi Hnr Roll; Otst Ac Ach Awd; Pres Ac Ftns Aw; Yth Ldrshp Prog; Comm Volntr; Emplmnt; Fld Hky (V L); Lcrsse (V); Adv Cncl (R); Cl Off (P); Stu Cncl (R); American Legion Award-8th Grade; National Latin Award-Gold Summa Cum Laude; Biological Sciences; Graphic Design; Ohio State U, Columbus Campus; U of Pennsylvania

MILLER, STEPHANIE; POTTSTOWN, PA; POTTSGROVE HS; (SO); Hi Hnr Roll; Nat Hon Sy; WWAHSS; Comm Volntr; Chrch Yth Grp; Key Club; Mth Clb/Tm; Sci Clb; Sftball (J); Tennis (J); Yrbk (R); History Club; Graphic Design; Graphic Arts

MILLER, TONI L; ALBURTIS, PA; BRANDYWINE HEIGHTS HS; (SR); Hnr Roll; MVP; Nat Hon Sy; Perf Att; WWAHSS; DARE; Emplmnt; Photog; Voc Ind Clb Am; Sftball (V L); Tennis (V L); 2nd Place at Districts for Photography; Student of The Quarter; Sports Administration; Coaching; Lockhaven U of PA

MILLIGAN, KEVIN; NEWTOWN, PA; COUNCIL ROCK HS NORTH; (SO); Hnr Roll; Emplmnt; Tech Clb; Magazine Journalist; Computer Programmer; Penn State (Abington); Princeton

MILLIKAN, KATE W; MECHANICSBURG, PA; MECHANICSBURG AREA SR HS; (SO); Hnr Roll; Pres Ac Ftns Aw; WWAHSS; Yth Ldrshp Prog; Comm Volntr; ArtClub; DARE; Emplmnt; Jr Cls League; Key Club; NYLC; Chr; SP/M/VS; Fld Hky (VJ); Sccr (VJ); Swmg (J); Cl Off (V, T); Environmental Club; Industrial Design / Law; U of North Carolina; Notre Dame

MILLIRON, BRENT; ALTOONA, PA; BISHOP GUILFOYLE HS; (SO); Hi Hnr Roll; Hnr Roll; Pres Ac Ftns Aw; Comm Volntr; Bsball (V); Bskball (V); Ftball (J); Dentistry; U of Pittsburgh

MILLS, ALLISON; MIFFLINTOWN, PA; JUNIATA CTY SD; (JR); Hi Hnr Roll; Nat Hon Sy; Pres Sch; St of Mnth; WWAHSS; Comm Volntr; Chrch Yth Grp; Emplmnt; Lttrmn Clb; Prom Com; SADD; Vsity Clb; Dnce; SP/M/VS; Chrldg (V CL); Vsy Clb; Stu Cncl (R); Student of Marking Period 2 Years; Sweetheart Court-Sophomore; Architectural Engineering; Drexel; Penn State

MILLS, VANICE; PHILADELPHIA, PA; TOMSON EDUCATION DIRECT; (JR)

MILROY, KATIE; MOSCOW, PA; NORTH POCONO HS; (FR); Red Cr Aide; DARE; Skiing; Red Cross Club; Registered Nurse; Neo-Natal Nursing; Penn State U; Marywood U

MILUNOVIC, NIKOLINA R; PHILADELPHIA, PA; PHILADELPHIA HS FOR CREATIVE & PERF ARTS; (JR); Comm Volntr; Peer Tut/Med; Outdrs Clb; Dnce; Exchange Year in USA 2004-2005; Languages; Psychology; Cambridge U; Princeton U

MINGIONE, KASEY; BIRDSBORO, PA; DANIEL BOONE AREA HS; (SO); All Am Sch; Hi Hnr Roll; WWAHSS; Key Club; French Clb; Fld Hky (J); Medical Field; Kutztown U; Millersville U

MINGORA, CHRISTINA; BETHLEHEM, PA; BETHLEHEM CATHOLIC; (SO); Hnr Roll; Perf Att; USAA; WWAHSS; Comm Volntr; Key Club; SADD; Spanish Clb; Bskball (J); Fld Hky (V L); Track (V L)

MIN LWIN, SU; PHOENIXVILLE, PA; PHOENIXVILLE AREA HS; (SO); Hnr Roll; Comm Volntr; Hosp Aide; Chrch Yth Grp; DARE; Key Club; Photog; SP/M/VS; Fld Hky (V); Tennis (J); CR (P); Yrbk (E); Business; Law; Penn State (U of Penn); New York U

MINNOCK, BRIANNA K; MARS, PA; PINE-RICHLAND HS; (SO); Hnr Roll; Nat Ldrshp Svc; Otst Ac Ach Awd; Yth Ldrshp Prog; Comm Volntr; Hosp Aide; Spec Olymp Vol; Chrch Yth Grp; Dbte Team; Emplmnt; Fr of Library; Mod UN; NtlFrnscLg; Scouts; Spch Team; Swmg (J); Track (J); Vllyball (V L); Stu Cncl (T); CR (R); Girl Scout Silver Award; Guidance Humanitarian Award; Nurse; Gov't Work (FBI, CIA); Juniata; CMU

MINOSKI, RYAN; PITTSBURGH, PA; BALDWIN HS; (JR); Hnr Roll; Perf Att; Sci Fairs; Comm Volntr; Photog; Scouts; Lit Mag (E); Photography Club; Da Vincian Society; English; Journalism; U of Pittsburgh; Duquesne U

MINTZER, MARY R; BETHLEHEM, PA; BETHLEHEM CATHOLIC HS; (FR); Hi Hnr Roll; WWAHSS; Comm Volntr; Key Club; Spanish Clb; Dnce; Fld Hky (J)

MISHRA, IPSA; MECHANICSBURG, PA; CUMBERLAND VALLEY HS; (JR); Duke TS; Hi Hnr Roll; Pres Sch; Hab For Humty Volntr; ArtClub; Dbte Team; Key Club; Mod UN; Tmpl Yth Grp; CR (R); Sch Ppr (R); Finalist for PA Governor's School for the Arts; National Silver Key for Drawing (Scholastics); International Studies; Economics; U of Chicago; Brown U

MITCHELL, JESSE; PATTON, PA; CAMBRIA HEIGHTS HS; (JR); Hi Hnr Roll; Nat Hon Sy; Sci Fairs; WWAHSS; Chrch Yth Grp; Emplmnt; FCA; Quill & Scroll; Sci Clb; Bnd; English Major; Political Science Major; Penn State U

MITCHELL JR, ROBERT M; PITTSBURGH, PA; PLUM SR HS; (SO); Hi Hnr Roll; Otst Ac Ach Awd; Perf Att; Sci Fairs; St of Mnth; Comm Volntr; Peer Tut/Med; ArtClub; DARE; Sci Clb; Stu Cncl (R); Architectural Engineer; Lawyer; U of Pittsburgh; Duquesne U

MITRA, RAJIB; HUNTINGDON VALLEY, PA; ABINGTON SR HS; (SO); Hi Hnr Roll; Hnr Roll; Nat Hon Sy; Sci Fairs; Sci/Math Olympn; Comm Volntr; Drma Clb; Key Club; Sci Clb; Svce Clb; French Clb; Orch; SP/M/VS; Engineering; Biology; Cornell U; Carnegie Mellon

MKRTYCHEV, DMITRIY A; HARRISBURG, PA; CTRL DAUPHIN EAST HS; (JR); Hnr Roll; WWAHSS; Key Club; Mod UN; Sch Ppr (E); Model UN; Key Club; Law / Criminal Justice; Philosophy / Religion; Dickinson U; U of Pittsburg

MLADENOVA, VESSELINA; EAST STROUDSBURG, PA; STROUDSBURG HS; (JR); Hi Hnr Roll; Otst Ac Ach Awd; Perf Att; Comm Volntr; Peer Tut/Med; Emplmnt; FBLA; Key Club; Tchrs Aide; 1st Place Java FBLA Regionals; Dentist; Doctor; Penn State U; East Stroudsburg U

MOHLER, HANNAH E; MILLERSTOWN, PA; GREENWOOD HS; (SO); Hi Hnr Roll; Hnr Roll; Otst Ac Ach Awd; St of Mnth; WWAHSS; Peer Tut/Med; Chrch Yth Grp; Emplmnt; Prom Com; Chr; Fld Hky (J); Cl Off (S); Stu Cncl (R); CR (R); S.O.S. Member (Students Offering Support), Received Presidential Award; Certified Lifeguard; Architecture; Photography

MOLENDINI, LISA M; HAZLETON, PA; HAZLETON AREA HS; (SR); F Lan Hn Soc; Hi Hnr Roll; Nat Hon Sy; Nat Ldrshp Svc; USAA; WWAHSS; Yth Ldrshp Prog; Comm Volntr; ArtClub; Emplmnt; FBLA; Key Club; Off Aide; SADD; Foreign Clb; Clr Grd; Orch; Stu Cncl (R); Sch Ppr (E, R); Edgar L. Dessen Community Service Award; James S. Keiper Youth Volunteer Award; Communications Major W/Emphasis in Public Relations; Susquehanna U

MONDA, ANTHONY; NORTH HAMPTON, PA; NORWIN SD; (SR); Hnr Roll; Nat Hon Sy; Otst Ac Ach Awd; WWAHSS; Emplmnt; Pharmacy; Chemical Engineer; Carnegie Mellon U; U of Pittsburgh

MONIER, PHILLIP; WEST NEWTON, PA; YOUGH SR HS; (FR); Hi Hnr Roll; St of Mnth; USAA; Yth Ldrshp Prog; Comm Volntr; Peer Tut/Med; Chrch Yth Grp; Drma Clb; Bnd; Chr; Jzz Bnd; Mch Bnd; Percussion Ensemble; Pep Band; Major-Psychology; Minor-Music Theory; Penn State

MONIGHAN, LOGAN J; ROBESONIA, PA; CONRAD WEISER HS; (JR); Hi Hnr Roll; Hnr Roll; Kwnis Aw; Nat Hon Sy; St of Mnth; Comm Volntr; ArtClub; Chrch Yth Grp; FCA; Key Club; Prom Com; Svce Clb; Spanish Clb; Chr; Dnce; SP/M/VS; Cl Off (S); Key Club President 2005-2006; NHS President 2005-2006; English; Cinematography; New York U; Temple U

MONKS, DANIELLE; ALLENTOWN, PA; SALISBURY HS; (SR); Hnr Roll; Nat Hon Sy; Peer Tut/Med; Chr; Dnce; SP/M/VS; Dance; U of North Texas

MONTALBANO, CHELSEA; NORRISTOWN, PA; METHACTON HS; (SO); Hi Hnr Roll; Hnr Roll; Otst Ac Ach Awd; Pres Sch; WWAHSS; Comm Volntr; Key Club; Clb; Fld Hky (J); Art; English; Westchester U; Ursinus College

MONYAK, MELISSA; CORAOPOLIS, PA; MONTOUR HS; (JR); Hnr Roll; WWAHSS; Yth Ldrshp Prog; Comm Volntr; Hab For Humty Volntr; Chrch Yth Grp; DARE; Drma Clb; Emplmnt; Scouts; SADD; Tchrs Aide; Bnd; Mch Bnd; SP/M/VS; Girl Scout Gold Award; Elementary Education; Robert Morris U PA

MOON, ALICIA R; BERLIN, PA; SHANKSVILLE-STONYCREEK HS; (SO); Hi Hnr Roll; Hnr Roll; Nat Hon Sy; WWAHSS; Lib Aide; Scouts; Bnd; Math Teacher; Ohio Valley College; U of Pittsburgh Johnstown

MOORE, BROOKE T; NEW KENSINGTON, PA; BURRELL HS; (SR); Hnr Roll; Hab For Humty Volntr; ArtClub; Sftball (V); Track (V); Medical Assisting; Massage Therapy; Pittsburgh Technical Institute

MOORE, CRAIG O H; PHILADELPHIA, PA; JOHN BARTRAM HS; (SR); Hnr Roll; Perf Att; St of Mnth; English; History; Temple; Penn State

MOORE, DESMOND; EASTON, PA; EASTON AREA SR HS; (SO); Hnr Roll; MVP; Pres Ac Ftns Aw; St of Mnth; Comm Volntr; Chrch Yth Grp; DARE; Ch Chr; Drl Tm; Bskball (J); Ftball (VJC); Track (V L); Stu Cncl (V); Sports Marketing; Sports Broadcasting; Florida State U; U of Florida

MOORE, DEYLAN; LANSDOWNE, PA; MONSIGNOR BONNER HS; (FR); Ctznshp Aw; Hnr Roll; Perf Att; St of Mnth; Chrch Yth Grp; Scouts; Bnd; Law; Chemical Engineer; Harvard U; Temple U

MOORE, ELISE; APOLLO, PA; KISKI AREA HS; (JR); Hi Hnr Roll; Nat Hon Sy; Perf Att; WWAHSS; Comm Volntr; Peer Tut/Med; Emplmnt; Key Club; Pep Squd; SADD; Bnd; Jzz Bnd; Mch Bnd; Sftball (V L); Meals on Wheels Volunteer; YMCA Volunteer; Secondary Education; Sports Medicine; Slippery Rock U of Pennsylvania; Robert Morris U

MOORE, FRANKLIN L; GLENMOORE, PA; COATESVILLE AREA SR HS; (JR); Hnr Roll; Nat Hon Sy; Ftball (J); Tennis (J); Track (V); Architectural Engineering; Juris Doctorate of Law; U of Delaware; Penn State U

MOORE, MICHAEL W; CRESCO, PA; EAST STROUDSBURG HS SOUTH; (FR); Hi Hnr Roll; Pres Ac Ftns Aw; Sci Fairs; Sci/Math Olympn; Comm Volntr; Peer Tut/Med; Chrch Yth Grp; DARE; Emplmnt; Scouts; Cr Ctry (J); Skt Tgt Sh (V); Track (V); Eagle Boy Scout; Aeronautical Engineering; Aircraft Pilot; Air Force Academy, Denver, CO; Embry-Riddle, Daytona, FL

MOORE, STEVEN A; TEMPLETON, PA; LENAPE TECH; (SR); Hnr Roll; Perf Att; Comm Volntr; Lib Aide; Mus Clb; Off Aide; Tchrs Aide; Wdwrkg Clb; Bnd; Chr; Mch Bnd; Sccr (V CL); Culinary Arts-Associates and Batchelor; Art Institute of Pittsburgh

MOORE, TASHA J; HOLLIDAYSBURG, PA; HOLLIDAYSBURG AREA SR HS; (JR); Hnr Roll; Nat Hon Sy; Otst Ac Ach Awd; WWAHSS; Emplmnt; Jr Ach; Key Club; Bskball (J L); Track (V L); Outstanding Junior in Vocational Elective; President's Award for Educational Excellence; Civil Engineer; Pennsylvania State U

MORACK, LUCAS; BEAVER FALLS, PA; BLACKHAWK HS; (SO); Hnr Roll; Perf Att; WWAHSS; Comm Volntr; Spanish Clb; Chr; Expressions Chorus Group; Music; Radio Broadcasting

MORALES, DEBORAH N; BETHLEHEM, PA; BETHLEHEM AREA VOC TECH SCH; (FR); Hnr Roll; Comm Volntr; ArtClub; DARE; Emplmnt; Scouts; Wdwrkg Clb; Wt Lftg; Art Programs; Nurse

MORAN, ZANE M; PORT CARBON, PA; NATIVITY BVM HS; (SR); Hi Hnr Roll; Hnr Roll; MVP; Pres Ac Ftns Aw; Comm Volntr; Red Cr Aide; Spanish Clb; Bskball (V); Sccr (V CL); Cl Off (R); Sports Medicine/Athletes; Lock Haven U

MORANTZ, CHARLES; LANGHORNE, PA; NESHAMINY HS; (SR); Hi Hnr Roll; Nat Hon Sy; Pres Ac Ftns Aw; St of Mnth; Comm Volntr; Peer Tut/Med; Emplmnt; FBLA; Off Aide; P to P St Amb Prg; Sci Clb; Scouts; Bnd; Scr Kpr (V); Stu Cncl (R); Second Degree Black Belt in Tae Kwon Do; Eagle Scout, Science Bowl; Biomedical Engineering; Pennsylvania State U

MORELLI, JESSICA N; IMPERIAL, PA; WEST ALLEGHENY HS; (SR); Hi Hnr Roll; MVP; Nat Hon Sy; Perf Att; WWAHSS; Comm Volntr; Spec Olymp Vol; DARE; Key Club; Lttrmn Clb; Off Aide; Quiz Bowl; SADD; Spanish Clb; Chr; Bskball (V CL); PP Ftbl (V C); Sftball (V CL); Cl Off (V); American Legion Award; Who's Who Among High School-Sports Edition; Pharmacy; Physical Therapy; Allegheny College

MORGALIS, DEANNA; POTTSVILLE, PA; POTTSVILLE AREA HS; (JR); Hnr Roll; WWAHSS; Key Club; SADD; German Clb; Cr Ctry (V L); Sftball (J)

MORGAN, ALLY; MIFFLINBURG, PA; MIFFLINBURG AREA HS; (JR); Hi Hnr Roll; Hnr Roll; Nat Hon Sy; WWAHSS; Yth Ldrshp Prog; Comm Volntr; Hosp Aide; Chrch Yth Grp; Drma Clb; Jr Ach; Key Club; Mus Clb; P to P St Amb Prg; Prom Com; Spanish Clb; Bnd; Chr; Jzz Bnd; Mch Bnd; Sch Ppr (R); Secretary/Treasurer of Band; Youth Leadership Award Recipient; Human Resources Management; Public Relations; Villanova U; Grove City College

MORGAN, CAITIE M; WASHINGTON, PA; TRINITY HS; (JR); Hnr Roll; Nat Hon Sy; WWAHSS; Chrch Yth Grp; SADD; German Clb; PP Ftbl (V); Sftball; Vllyball (V CL); Hustle Award At State Champs V-Ball; 9 Years of TWIST, Softball Camp; Filming Arts/Director; Communications & Marketing; Ohio U; Waynesburg College

MORGAN, CASSANDRA M; LEETSDALE, PA; QUAKER VALLEY HS; (SO); Hnr Roll; WWAHSS; Comm Volntr; Peer Tut/Med; Chrch Yth Grp; Key Club; Lib Aide; Mus Clb; Orch; Honors Orchestra at WVU; Honors Orchestra at North Hills PA; Law; Medical

MORGAN, CODY A; CANADENSIS, PA; POCONO MOUNTAIN EAST HS; (FR); Hi Hnr Roll; St of Mnth; USAA; Emplmnt; International Foreign Language Award; Photo Journalist; Foreign Language (Interpreter)

MORGAN, LAURA M; DALLAS, PA; DALLAS HS; (JR); Sci/Math Olympn; Chrch Yth Grp; Emplmnt; Key Club; Mth Clb/Tm; NtlFrnscLg; Scouts; Bnd; Chr; SP/M/VS; Fld Hky (J); Track; Key Club Charter Member; Math Award; Engineering; Computer Science; Penn State U Park; Lehigh U

Morgan, Laura M
Dallas HS
Dallas, PA

Morantz, Charles
Neshaminy HS
Langhorne, PA

Moore, Craig O H
John Bartram HS
Philadelphia, PA

Monier, Phillip
Yough SR HS
West Newton, PA

Mitchell Jr, Robert M
Plum SR HS
Pittsburgh, PA

Mingora, Christina
Bethlehem Catholic
Bethlehem, PA

Miller, Lewis J
Upper Darby HS
Drexel Hill, PA

Milunovic, Nikolina R
Philadelphia HS For Creative & Perf Arts
Philadelphia, PA

Molendini, Lisa M
Hazleton Area HS
Hazleton, PA

Monighan, Logan J
Conrad Weiser HS
Robesonia, PA

Moore, Franklin L
Coatesville Area SR HS
Glenmoore, PA

Morack, Lucas
Blackhawk HS
Beaver Falls, PA

MORGAN, LAUREN; JOHNSTOWN, PA; FERNDALE AREA HS; (FR); Hi Hnr Roll; Otst Ac Ach Awd; Comm Volntr; Drma Clb; Emplmnt; Mus Clb; Scouts; Spch Team; French Clb; Bnd; Clr Grd; Dnce; Mch Bnd; Chrldg (J); Vllyball (J); Forensics; Law; Journalism; Stanford U, Palo Alto, California; New York U, New York City, New York

MORGAN, NATHANIEL T; WEST CHESTER, PA; BISHOP SHANAHAN HS; (JR); Hnr Roll; Nat Hon Sy; Peer Tut/Med; Emplmnt; Scouts; Stg Cre; Ftball (V); Track (V); Eagle Scout; Sound Crew; Aeronautical / Aerospace Engineering; Sound Engineering; United States Naval Academy; Arizona State U

MORGAN, TROY; GOULDSBORO, PA; NORTH POCONO HS; (FR); Hi Hnr Roll; Hnr Roll; Comm Volntr; Peer Tut/Med; Sci Clb; Spanish Clb; Stu Cncl (R); CR (R); To Become An Architect; To Get a Bachelor's Degree; Penn State U; Texas

MORNINGSTAR, LACEY L; DOVER, PA; DOVER AREA HS; (MS); Ctznshp Aw; Hi Hnr Roll; Hnr Roll; Nat Stu Ath Day Aw; Perf Att; Comm Volntr; Fr of Library; Lib Aide; Mus Clb; Chr; Dnce; Chrldg (J); PPSqd (J); Stu Cncl (R); CR (R); Athletic Award; Owning a Business; Marine Biology; U of North Carolina; Gettysburg College

MORRISON, MARY; HAZLETON, PA; HAZLETON AREA HS; (FR); Hi Hnr Roll; Hnr Roll; Emplmnt; Scouts; Stg Cre; Bronze Award in Girl Scouts; Teaching; Bloomsburg U

MORRISSEY, JILL C; MECHANICSBURG, PA; MECHANICSBURG AREA SR HS; (SR); F Lan Hn Soc; Hi Hnr Roll; Nat Hon Sy; Otst Ac Ach Awd; St of Mnth; WWAHSS; Yth Ldrshp Prog; Comm Volntr; Peer Tut/Med; Red Cr Aide; Chrch Yth Grp; Key Club; Photog; Scouts; Spch Team; Tech Clb; German Clb; Bnd; Jzz Bnd; Mch Bnd; Stg Cre; Yrbk (R); International Relations; Tufts U

MOSER, JANELLE N; ALLENTOWN, PA; SALISBURY HS; (JR); Hi Hnr Roll; Hnr Roll; Nat Hon Sy; Pres Sch; WWAHSS; Comm Volntr; Dbte Team; FBLA; Key Club; Prom Com; SADD; Chr; SP/M/VS; Chrldg (V); Sccr (V); Stu Cncl (R); Sch Ppr (R, P); Member of Debate Semi-Finals and Finals Team; Key Club Service Organization; Political Science; International Relations; American U; U of Virginia

MOSES, JENNIFER M; JEFFERSONVILLE, PA; NORRISTOWN AREA HS; (SO); Hi Hnr Roll; Nat Hon Sy; Comm Volntr; Peer Tut/Med; Chrch Yth Grp; Drma Clb; Key Club; Mth Clb/Tm; SP/M/VS; Stu Cncl (R); Ninth Grade Science Award; Horticulture Club; Astronomy

MOSKAL, RACHEL; CARMICHAELS, PA; CARMICHAELS AREA JR/SR HS; (FR); Hi Hnr Roll; Hnr Roll; FBLA; Spanish Clb; Chr; Ch Chr; Chrldg (J); Sccr (V L); Sftball (V L); Upward Bound; Fashion Styling; Psychology; Fashion Institute of Design & Merchandising

MOSQUEA, CLARIVEL; HAZLETON, PA; HAZLETON AREA HS; (SO); Hnr Roll; Perf Att; St of Mnth; Comm Volntr; DARE; Emplmnt; Mus Clb; Scouts; Chr; Ch Chr; Dnce; Scr Kpr (VJ); Sccr (J); Vllyball (J); Real Estate Agent, Accounting; Music, Dance; Penn State; St John's

MOSSBURG, JASON; QUAKERTOWN, PA; PALISADES HS; (SR); Hnr Roll; Otst Ac Ach Awd; St of Mnth; Comm Volntr; Peer Tut/Med; Chrch Yth Grp; Drma Clb; Emplmnt; Lib Aide; SP/M/VS; Tennis (C); Major in Education; Social Studies Teacher; Bucks County Community College; Kutztown U

MOUA, COUA; EPHRATA, PA; EPHRATA HS; (JR); Hi Hnr Roll; Hnr Roll; Nat Hon Sy; Chrch Yth Grp; Emplmnt; Spanish Clb; Chr; Ch Chr; Track (J); I'm in Spanish NHS & NHS; Business, Economics; Journalism; Scranton, Sienna, Temple; Marywood, Penn State

MOYER, CARA; DUNCANSVILLE, PA; SPRING COVE SD; (JR); Hi Hnr Roll; Hnr Roll; Comm Volntr; Yrbk (E)

MOYNIHAN, MOLLY; WEXFORD, PA; NORTH ALLEGHENY HS; (SO); Ctznshp Aw; F Lan Hn Soc; Hi Hnr Roll; Hnr Roll; Nat Hon Sy; Pres Ac Ftns Aw; St of Mnth; WWAHSS; Comm Volntr; Hosp Aide; Chrch Yth Grp; Jr Cls League; Key Club; Bnd; Tennis (V); Class Council; Scholar Athlete Award; Biology; Engineering

MRAKOVICH, KRYSTIE; MARIETTA, PA; DONEGAL HS; (SO); Hnr Roll; AL Aux Girls; Emplmnt; FBLA; Photog; Stu Cncl (V); Child Psychologist; Defense Attorney; Millersville U; Franklin and Marshall

MUCHNICK, MATTHEW; BENSALEM, PA; BENSALEM TOWNSHIP SD; (SO); Ctznshp Aw; Hi Hnr Roll; MVP; Pres Ac Ftns Aw; Sci Fairs; FBLA; Sccr (J); Tennis (V); Baseball for Valley AA; Athletes in Service; Medicine-Sports or Pediatrics; Chemistry; U of Pennsylvania; Drexel U

MUELLER, ASHLEY M; ALTOONA, PA; BELLWOOD-ANTIS HS; (JR); Ctznshp Aw; Hi Hnr Roll; Hnr Roll; Nat Hon Sy; Otst Ac Ach Awd; Pres Ac Ftns Aw; St of Mnth; WWAHSS; Yth Ldrshp Prog; Comm Volntr; Peer Tut/Med; Chrch Yth Grp; Drma Clb; FCA; Jr Ach; Key Club; Lttrmn Clb; NtlFrnscLg; SADD; Acpl Chr; Chr; SP/M/VS; Scr Kpr (V); Track (V L); Vllyball (J); Stu Cncl (R); Alumni of Leadership Blair County Youth; Received Citizen of the Year Award 3 Times; Registered Nurse; Pennsylvania State U

MUELLER, NATHANIEL E; BETHEL PARK, PA; BETHEL PARK SD; (SO); Hi Hnr Roll; WWAHSS; Comm Volntr; Chrch Yth Grp; Civil Air Pat; Jr Ach; Skt Tgt Sh (V); Engineer; Air Force Academy

MUENCH, WALTER K; RIDLEY PARK, PA; HOMESCHOOL; (JR); Duke TS; Hi Hnr Roll; Nat Mrt LOC; Nat Mrt Semif; Perf Att; St Schl; Comm Volntr; Chrch Yth Grp; Dbte Team; Drma Clb; Mth Clb/Tm; NYLC; Tchrs Aide; Chr; Dnce; SP/M/VS; Stg Cre; Fncg; Sch Ppr (E); Advanced Pianist; Debate Captain; Science; Engineering; Duke U; U of Chicago

MUHA, JONATHAN; BOILING SPRINGS, PA; BOILING SPRINGS HS; (JR); Hnr Roll; WWAHSS; Sccr (V, L); Track (V); Architecture; Math; Penn State Main Campus; Pennsylvania College of Technology Williamsport

MUKHOTI, ANISH; BENSALEM, PA; BENSALEM TOWNSHIP SD; (SO); Ctznshp Aw; F Lan Hn Soc; Hnr Roll; MVP; Sci Fairs; St of Mnth; Comm Volntr; Drma Clb; Lib Aide; Mus Clb; BENGALI Clb; Chr; Bskball (J); Sccr (L); Tennis (L); Engineer; Architect; St. Joseph's U; Villanova U

MUKHTARZADA, LILA J; DOUGLASSVILLE, PA; DANIEL BOONE AREA HS; (SR); Hi Hnr Roll; Nat Hon Sy; WWAHSS; Comm Volntr; Peer Tut/Med; Emplmnt; Jr Ach; Key Club; SADD; French Clb; Yrbk (E); NSHSS, Berk's Best; Distinguished Honors; Want to Become a Pediatric Surgeon; Albright College

MULARSKI, ROSS T; GREENSBURG, PA; GREENSBURG SALEM SD; (FR); Hi Hnr Roll; Hnr Roll; Nat Hon Sy; Pres Ac Ftns Aw; Bsball (J); Bskball (J); Ftball (J); Golf (J); American Legion Baseball; Bat Boy Westmoreland County Comm. Coll.; U of Pittsburgh

MULHOLLAND, LAUREN; BOILING SPRINGS, PA; BOILING SPRINGS HS; (FR); Hi Hnr Roll; Hnr Roll; Chrch Yth Grp; Drma Clb; Foreign Clb; Bnd; Chr; Ch Chr; Mch Bnd; Scholastic Writing Certificate of Merit Award; Education; Theatre; Elizabethtown College; Eastern U

MULKERN, CHRISTINE; PITTSBURGH, PA; NORTH ALLEGHENY HS; (SO); Ctznshp Aw; Hi Hnr Roll; Nat Hon Sy; Nat Stu Ath Day Aw; Otst Ac Ach Awd; Pres Ac Ftns Aw; Pres Sch; WWAHSS; Comm Volntr; Hab For Humty Volntr; Hosp Aide; Chrch Yth Grp; Emplmnt; Key Club; Mus Clb; Chr; Skiing (J); Swmg (V L); CR (R); Most Improved Swimmer Award; Law; Medicine; U of Pittsburgh; U of Virginia

MULL, AMY; EPHRATA, PA; LANCASTER CTY CTC; (SR); Hi Hnr Roll; Nat Hon Sy; Perf Att; Track (J); Physical Therapy; Harrisburg Area Community College; Harcum College

MULLEN, JENNA K; BEAVER FALLS, PA; BIG BEAVER FALLS HS; (JR); Hi Hnr Roll; Nat Hon Sy; Perf Att; Yth Ldrshp Prog; Emplmnt; Key Club; NYLC; Prom Com; SADD; Vsity Clb; Chr; Flg Crps; Cr Ctry (V L); Swmg (V CL); Track (V L); Pre-Med; Biology; Johns Hopkins U; Washington Jefferson College

MULLEN JR, ROBERT W; PHILADELPHIA, PA; NORTHEAST CATHOLIC BOYS HS; (FR); Hi Hnr Roll; Hnr Roll; Perf Att; Emplmnt; Off Aide; Ftball (JCL); Track (J); Wrstlg (J); Altar Server; Knights of Columbus; Lawyer; Doctor; Penn State U; U Of Notre Dame

MULLER, GRACE; PITTSBURGH, PA; OAKLAND CATHOLIC HS; (SO); Hi Hnr Roll; WWAHSS; Hosp Aide; Scouts; Bnd; Mch Bnd; Fncg (V L); Cl Off (V); Bucknell

MUNOZ, IRINA A A; NEW CASTLE, PA; SHENANGO AREA SD; (SR); Hi Hnr Roll; Otst Ac Ach Awd; Perf Att; Sci Fairs; Sci/Math Olympn; Valdctrian; Comm Volntr; Hab For Humty Volntr; Chrch Yth Grp; Drma Clb; Spanish Clb; Chr; Dnce; SP/M/VS; Swg Chr; Bskball (V); Track (V); Vllyball (J); Cl Off (T); Yrbk (E, P); Honor Strip - For Being Selected as the Student Example of the School; Several Diplomas as the Best Student in Different Subjects; Industrial Engineering / Master's Degree; Architecture / Bachelor's Degree; Stanford U; Tenn State U

MURAWSKI, VANESSA; HOUTZDALE, PA; MOSHANNON VALLEY JSHS; (JR); Nat Hon Sy; St of Mnth; Comm Volntr; Chrch Yth Grp; Drma Clb; Mus Clb; Prom Com; Tchrs Aide; Vsity Clb; French Clb; Bnd; Chr; Drm Mjr; Jzz Bnd; Sccr (V L); American Legion Certificate of Appreciation; Music Performance; Music Education; Messiah; Slippery Rock U

MURNIN, KATIE; BETHLEHEM, PA; BETHLEHEM CATHOLIC HS; (JR); Hi Hnr Roll; Comm Volntr; Peer Tut/Med; Key Club; Chrldg; Yrbk; Captain Cheer Squad; Penn State U; Catholic U

MURPHY, EMILY K; WEXFORD, PA; NORTH ALLEGHENY INT HS; (SO); Hi Hnr Roll; Nat Hon Sy; WWAHSS; Chrch Yth Grp; Key Club; Bnd; Mch Bnd; Lcrsse (J); Church Youth Group; Athletic Training; Physical Therapy

MURPHY, MELANIE; NORRISTOWN, PA; METHACTON HS; (SO); Hi Hnr Roll; St of Mnth; WWAHSS; Chrch Yth Grp; FCA; Key Club; SP/M/VS

MURPHY, SARA; PHOENIXVILLE, PA; CTR FOR ARTS AND TECH HS; (SO); 4H Awd; Hnr Roll; Kwnis Aw; 4-H; Chrch Yth Grp; Drma Clb; Key Club; Scouts; SADD; Voc Ind Clb Am; Chr; Cl Off (V); Sch Ppr (E, R, P); Zoo Science; Animal Behavior; Delaware Valley College; University of Pennsylvania

MURRAY, ELIZABETH; PHILADELPHIA, PA; PHILA HS FOR GIRLS; (SO); All Am Sch; Ctznshp Aw; Hnr Roll; Otst Ac Ach Awd; Perf Att; Sci Fairs; St of Mnth; WWAHSS; Comm Volntr; Peer Tut/Med; DARE; Dbte Team; NYLC; Scouts; Italian Clb; Dnce; Chrldg (V); Gmnstcs (V); Cl Off (R); Sch Ppr (E); Animal Science; Veterinary Medicine; U of Pennsylvania; Drew U

MURRAY, MEGAN; SUGARLOAF, PA; BISHOP HAFEY HS; (SO); F Lan Hn Soc; Hi Hnr Roll; WWAHSS; Comm Volntr; Key Club; Mus Clb; Orch; SP/M/VS; CR (R); Business Management; Corporate Law

MURTHA, JOE; MOUNT PLEASANT, PA; CTRL WESTMORELAND CTC; (SO); Hnr Roll; Nat Hon Sy; Tech Clb; Spanish Clb; Skiing (V); Electronics Engineer; Penn State U; ITT Technical

MUSER, KIRSTEN J; LAURYS STATION, PA; PARKLAND HS; (JR); F Lan Hn Soc; Hi Hnr Roll; Nat Hon Sy; Sci Fairs; Emplmnt; Mus Clb; Bnd; Mch Bnd; Indoor Percussion/Drumline; Concert Band Officer (Treasurer); Dentistry; Lehigh U; U of Rochester

MUSSER, AMANDA L; E PETERSBURG, PA; HEMPFIELD HS; (JR); Hab For Humty Volntr; Chrch Yth Grp; DARE; Jr Ach; Key Club; Lcrsse (J); Sftball (J); Social Worker; Elementary Education; Millersville U; Bloomsburg U

MUSSER, CARLA S; STEVENS, PA; EPHRATA HS; (SR); Nat Hon Sy; Comm Volntr; Chrch Yth Grp; Emplmnt; Registered Nurse; Lancaster Institute for Health Education

MUSTO, KEVIN; PITTSTON, PA; PITTSTON AREA HS; (JR); Ctznshp Aw; Hi Hnr Roll; Nat Hon Sy; Sci/Math Olympn; St of Mnth; St Optmst of Yr; USAA; WWAHSS; Yth Ldrshp Prog; Comm Volntr; Peer Tut/Med; Mth Clb/Tm; Pep Squd; Quiz Bowl; Schol Bwl; Sci Clb; Foreign Clb; Bskball (V); Golf (V L); Stu Cncl (P); Winner Wilkes U Chemistry Contest; Rensselaer Science Medal; Medicine; Penn State U; U of Scranton

MUTHLER, BRITTNEY H; JERSEY SHORE, PA; JERSEY SHORE AREA SR HS; (SR); Hi Hnr Roll; Hnr Roll; Nat Hon Sy; WWAHSS; Peer Tut/Med; Chrch Yth Grp; FBLA; Key Club; Lib Aide; Prom Com; Bnd; Chr; PP Ftbl (VJ); Tennis (J L); Stu Cncl (T); Relay for Life Participant; Radiology; Radiation Therapy; Pennsylvania College of Technology; Allegheny Community College

MUTZ, JACQUELINE; WHITEHALL, PA; WHITEHALL HS; (JR); F Lan Hn Soc; Hi Hnr Roll; Nat Hon Sy; Salutrn; USAA; Valdctrian; Yth Ldrshp Prog; Comm Volntr; Peer Tut/Med; Spec Olymp Vol; Chrch Yth Grp; HO'Br Yth Ldrshp; Key Club; SADD; Stu Cncl (R); Respect Club; Education; Psychology; Duquesne U; Villanova U

MVULA, NATASHA Z; PHILADELPHIA, PA; FRANKLIN LEARNING CTR; (SO); Hnr Roll; Otst Ac Ach Awd; Perf Att; Comm Volntr; ArtClub; Mod UN; Sccr (V); Sftball (V); Tennis; Biochemistry; Medicine; U of Pennsylvania; Penn State U

MYERS, JAY D; MEDIA, PA; PENNCREST HS; (SR); Hi Hnr Roll; Hnr Roll; Eagle Scout; Engineering; Penn State U

MYERS, SAMANTHA K; MIDDLETOWN, PA; MIDDLETOWN AREA HS; (JR); Hnr Roll; Peer Tut/Med; Prom Com; Chr; Bskball (V); Fld Hky (V); Sftball (V); Elementary Education; Secondary Education; Millersville U; Lock Haven U

MYERS, TAHIRA; YORK, PA; CTRL YORK HS; (FR); Hi Hnr Roll; Fr of Library; Lib Aide; Clr Grd; Sch Ppr (R); Student of the Week; School Book Club; Hotel and Restaurant Management; Culinary Arts; Cornell U; U of Pennsylvania

MYERS, TYLER; OAKMONT, PA; RIVERVIEW HS; (JR); Hi Hnr Roll; Nat Hon Sy; Otst Ac Ach Awd; Sci/Math Olympn; Yth Ldrshp Prog; Key Club; Mod UN; NYLC; Prom Com; SADD; Spanish Clb; Chr; Cr Ctry (V CL); Track (V CL); Cl Off (P); Chemistry; Biology

MYRAKLO, AMANDA; INKERMAN, PA; PITTSTON AREA HS; (JR); Hi Hnr Roll; Nat Hon Sy; Sci/Math Olympn; USAA; WWAHSS; ArtClub; Biology Clb; Chrch Yth Grp; Emplmnt; Key Club; Sci Clb; Orch; Sftball (VJ); Swmg (V L); Sch Ppr (R, P), Upward Bound; Sunday Dispatch Correspondent; Publishing/English; Design

NAGEL, JONATHAN E; DOYLESTOWN, PA; CTRL BUCKS HS EAST; (SO); Hi Hnr Roll; Hnr Roll; Pres Ac Ftns Aw; Chess; Chrch Yth Grp; NYLC; Scouts; Acpl Chr; Chr; Ftball (VJ); Doylestown Rugby Club; Japanese Culture Club / Ski Club; Business; Engineering; Drexel U; Villanova U

NAGEL, ROBERT C; LANSDALE, PA; NORTH PENN HS; (JR); Hnr Roll; Nat Hon Sy; WWAHSS; Comm Volntr; Peer Tut/Med; Spec Olymp Vol; DARE; Emplmnt; Key Club; Scouts; Mentorship-Architecture

NAGI, MARIAM; DANVILLE, PA; DANVILLE HS; (SO); Hi Hnr Roll; Nat Hon Sy; St of Mnth; Prom Com; Chr; Sccr (J); Tennis (V); Track (J); Piano; Bilingual-Arabic; Pre-Law/Law; Corporate Law

Mukhoti, Anish
Bensalem Township SD
Bensalem, PA

Muench, Walter K
Homeschool
Ridley Park, PA

National
Honor Roll
Spring 2005

Muchnick, Matthew
Bensalem Township SD
Bensalem, PA

Murray, Elizabeth
Phila HS For Girls
Philadelphia, PA

NAGLE, MEGAN; ALTOONA, PA; BISHOP GUILFOYLE HS; (SO); Hi Hnr Roll; Perf Att; Comm Volntr; Red Cr Aide; SADD; Vsity Clb; Bskball (J); PP Ftbl (V); Vllyball (JC); Cl Off (V); Stu Cncl (R); Medicine; Duke U; U of Virginia

NAIK, RICHA; LITITZ, PA; MANHEIM TWP HS; (SO); SP/M/VS; Sch Ppr (E); Debate Club; Journalism

NAIR, ABHINAV; LAFAYETTE HILL, PA; PLYMOUTH WHITEMARSH HS; (SO); Hi Hnr Roll; Sci Fairs; WWAHSS; Yth Ldrshp Prog; Comm Volntr; FBLA; Spanish Clb; Lcrsse (J); Cl Off (S); National Junior Leadership Conference; Congressional Student Leadership Conference; Biomedical Engineering; Biotechnology; U of Pennsylvania; Princeton

NAMA, SIRISH; EXPORT, PA; FRANKLIN REG HS; (SO); Comm Volntr; Hab For Humty Volntr; Tmpl Yth Grp; Cr Ctry; Track; Wrstlg; Black Belt Tae Kwon Do; M.D.; Case Western Reserve U; George Washington U

NAPERKOWSKI, ALEX; WYOMING, PA; DALLAS HS; (FR); Hnr Roll; WWAHSS; Comm Volntr; Peer Tut/Med; Chrch Yth Grp; DARE; Key Club; Lib Aide; Scouts; Clb; Chr; Girl Scout Cadette Silver Award; Social Worker (Welfare, Child Dev); Journalism

NAPOLITAN, BIANCA; HERMITAGE, PA; HICKORY HS; (SO); Ctznshp Aw; Hi Hnr Roll; Nat Hon Sy; Otst Ac Ach Awd; St of Mnth; WWAHSS; Comm Volntr; Peer Tut/Med; Key Club; Off Aide; Tchrs Aide; Vsity Clb; Spanish Clb; Bnd; Bskball (J); Vllyball (VJCL); The Teacher's Selection Anthology of Poetry 2003; Quest Bowls; Pharmacist; Doctor; Pitt; Duquesne U

NARASIMHAN, SNEHA; WALLINGFORD, PA; STRATH HAVEN HS; (SO); Ctznshp Aw; Hnr Roll; Perf Att; Pres Sch; Sci Fairs; Comm Volntr; ArtClub; Tmpl Yth Grp; Bnd; Chr; Mch Bnd; Cr Ctry (J); Track (J); Hi-Q Academic Team; Aeronautical Engineering-Doctorate; Biochemical Engineering; Massachusetts Institute of Technology; U of Pennsylvania

NAREHOOD, JESSICA; MEXICO, PA; JUNIATA HS; (SO); WWAHSS; Comm Volntr; Spec Olymp Vol; Key Club; Mus Clb; Pep Squd; Spanish Clb; Bnd; Clr Grd; Mch Bnd; SP/M/VS; Chrldg (VJ); Fld Hky (J); Track (J); Registered Nursing; Elementary School Teacher; Juniata College; Edinboro College

NARETTO, DANIELLE; SEWICKLEY, PA; QUAKER VALLEY HS; (SO); Hi Hnr Roll; St of Mnth; Comm Volntr; Key Club; Spanish Clb; Vllyball (V L); Business Management/Marketing; Fashion Merchandising; Georgetown; U of Virginia

NASH, IAN; SEWICKLEY, PA; QUAKER VALLEY HS; (JR); Hi Hnr Roll; Comm Volntr; Hab For Humty Volntr; Peer Tut/Med; Key Club

NATALE, ANTHONY; POTTSTOWN, PA; POTTSGROVE HS; (SO); Hi Hnr Roll; Hnr Roll; Mth Clb/Tm; Mus Clb; Bnd; Jzz Bnd; Mch Bnd; Musician of the Year - 8th Grade; Junior National Honor League; Music Education; West Chester State U; Indiana U Pennsylvania

NATALE, MOLLY; EASTON, PA; EASTON AREA HS; (FR); Hnr Roll; Drma Clb; SP/M/VS; Play Basketball (For Community); Play Softball (For Community); Interior Decorator; Teacher; New York U; Duke U

NATARAJAN, NAVIN; MOUNTAIN TOP, PA; (FR); F Lan Hn Soc; Hi Hnr Roll; Nat Hon Sy; Sci Fairs; Peer Tut/Med; ArtClub; Orch; Tennis (V); Pennsylvania Junior Academy of Science-Winner; Medical School; Business School

NATHAN, ASHWIN; BRYN MAWR, PA; RADNOR HS; Nat Hon Sy; Hab For Humty Volntr; Chess; Cmptr Clb; Key Club; Quiz Bowl; Tech Clb; Bnd; Jzz Bnd; Pep Bnd; SP/M/VS; Cr Ctry (J); Tennis (J); Bausch and Lomb Science Award; Persistence Award in Cross Country; Bioengineering; Electrical Engineering

NAWARYNSKI, ADAM R; PHILADELPHIA, PA; NORTHEAST CATHOLIC BOYS HS; (FR); 4H Awd; Ctznshp Aw; Hi Hnr Roll; Hnr Roll; Nat Hon Sy; Nat Sci Aw; Otst Ac Ach Awd; Perf Att; Sci Fairs; St of Mnth; Comm Volntr; Hosp Aide; Peer Tut/Med; ArtClub; Chess; Mus Clb; Off Aide; Outdrs Clb; Tchrs Aide; Tech Clb; Wdwrkg Clb; Business; Temple U

NEDLEY, MARIE E; WHITE, PA; CONNELLSVILLE AREA HS; (SO); Hi Hnr Roll; Nat Hon Sy; Chrch Yth Grp; Drma Clb; Emplmnt; Swmg (V L); Swim Record Holder; Art & Design; Sports Education; Penn State U; U of Pittsburgh

NEFF, AARON T; GARDNERS, PA; ADAMS CTY CHRISTIAN AC; (JR); Hi Hnr Roll; Otst Ac Ach Awd; WWAHSS; Chrch Yth Grp; Drma Clb; Emplmnt; Prom Com; Bnd; Jzz Bnd; Bskball (VJC); Stu Cncl (P); Mexico Mission Trips Summer 2003 and 2004; Full Time Ministry; Valley Forge Christian College; Messiah College

NEFF, ASHLEY; MC KEESPORT, PA; MC KEESPORT AREA HS; (SO); Hi Hnr Roll; Hnr Roll; Perf Att; Sci Fairs; St of Mnth; Emplmnt; Photog; Scouts; Bnd; Mch Bnd; Sch Ppr (R, P); Psychology; Washington and Jefferson College; University of Pittsburgh

NEIL, ZACHARY; CHARLEROI, PA; CHARLEROI AREA HS; (JR); Hnr Roll; SADD; Vsity Clb; Bsball (V L); Bskball (VJ L); Ftball; Skiing; Wt Lftg; Business; Sports Management; U of Pittsburgh; Waynesburg College

NEILL, CRYSTAL; SIGEL, PA; BROOKVILLE AREA SD; (JR); Hnr Roll; Emplmnt; Mth Clb/Tm; Mod UN; Spanish Clb; Chr; Orch; Sccr (VJ L); Stu Cncl (S); CR (R); Mock Trial Team; March of Dimes Volunteer; Business; Culinary Arts; Penn State U; Calvin College

NELSON, ALYSSA K; HARRISBURG, PA; CTRL DAUPHIN EAST HS; (FR); Hnr Roll; MVP; Pres Ac Ftns Aw; St of Mnth; WWAHSS; Comm Volntr; Key Club; Lib Aide; Chr; Dnce; Sccr (V L); Stu Cncl (T); Library Volunteer; Journalism; Physical Therapy; Penn State U; Lebanon Valley College

NELSON, KAITLYN; BENSALEM, PA; ARCHBISHOP RYAN HS; (JR); Hi Hnr Roll; Nat Hon Sy; Otst Ac Ach Awd; Pres Sch; WWAHSS; Comm Volntr; Off Aide; SADD; Dnce; CR (R); Yrbk; Diocesan Scholar; Academic High School Scholarship; Pre-Med; Business; Lehigh U; Villanova U

NELSON, KRYSTAL L; NORVELT, PA; MT PLEASANT AREA HS; (SR); Hi Hnr Roll; Hnr Roll; Perf Att; WWAHSS; Chrch Yth Grp; Tennis (V L); Dental Hygiene; Paralegal; Western School of Health and Business; Westmoreland County Community College

NEMETH, BETHANY; HOMESTEAD, PA; STEEL VALLEY HS; (JR); Hi Hnr Roll; Hnr Roll; Nat Hon Sy; Otst Ac Ach Awd; WWAHSS; DARE; Key Club; Bnd; Jzz Bnd; Mch Bnd; Pep Bnd; PP Ftbl (J); Becoming a Teacher; Slippery Rock U; Chatham College

NEMETH, JEFFREY W; DINGMANS FERRY, PA; DELAWARE VALLEY HS; (SR); 4H Awd; Hi Hnr Roll; St of Mnth; WWAHSS; Bsball (V CL); 4-H seeing Eye Puppy Raiser; Business; Kings U; U of Scranton

NEUMANN, ERIC D; MILFORD, PA; DELAWARE VALLEY HS; (SO); Ctznshp Aw; Hi Hnr Roll; Pres Ac Ftns Aw; Pres Sch; Sci Fairs; St of Mnth; USAA; Comm Volntr; Chrch Yth Grp; Emplmnt; Mod UN; Bnd; Chr; Ch Chr; Sccr (V L); Cl Off (V); Sch Ppr (R); Odyssey of the Mind; Foreign Film Club, Philosophy Club; Architecture; History: Minor

NEWKIRK, SIERA; PHILADELPHIA, PA; FRANKLIN LEARNING CTR; (SO); Hi Hnr Roll; Hnr Roll; Perf Att; St of Mnth; Comm Volntr; DARE; Emplmnt; Tchrs Aide; Track (J); Temple LEAP Teen Court Summer Program; In Thomas Jefferson Future Docs Program; Nursing Degree; Temple U; West Chester U

NGO, ARTHUR; UPPER DARBY, PA; UPPER DARBY HS; (SO); Gov Hnr Prg; Hi Hnr Roll; Hnr Roll; MVP; Nat Hon Sy; Otst Ac Ach Awd; Perf Att; USMC Stu Ath Aw; ArtClub; Wt Lftg (C); Marine Corps Push Ups Champion Award; Art Award; Pharmacy; Landscape Architecture; U of Sciences in Philadelphia; Temple Ambler

NGUYEN, DINH; PHILADELPHIA, PA; PHILADELPHIA HS; (JR); F Lan Hn Soc; Hnr Roll; WWAHSS; Chess; Asian Clb; Bdmtn (V); Vllyball (V); Elementary Education; Master's Degree; Temple U; Penn State Abington

NGUYEN, HIEN; BETHLEHEM, PA; BETHLEHEM CATHOLIC HS; (FR); Hi Hnr Roll; WWAHSS; Comm Volntr; Key Club; Track (V L); Fact Club; Accounting /Marketing; Computer Engineering; U of Pennsylvania; Lehigh U

NGUYEN, KATHERINE; UPPER DARBY, PA; UPPER DARBY HS; (JR); Hi Hnr Roll; Hnr Roll; Perf Att; St of Mnth; Comm Volntr; ArtClub; Prom Com; Acpl Chr; Chr; Clr Grd; Dnce; PP Ftbl (J); CR (R); Upper Darby Royal Music Instrumental Program Achievements; Community Service Award; Fine Arts; Art History; U of the Arts; Temple, Tyler School of Art

NGUYEN, LISA; PHOENIXVILLE, PA; PHOENIXVILLE AREA HS; (SO); Hi Hnr Roll; WWAHSS; Comm Volntr; Key Club; Vsity Clb; Tennis (V CL); CR (R); New York U

NGUYEN, TAM; PHILADELPHIA, PA; PREP CHARTER HS; (FR); Chrch Yth Grp; Drm Mjr; Stu Cncl (R); CR (R); Business; Technology; Temple U; Penn State

NGUYEN, THANH-LAN; UPPER DARBY, PA; UPPER DARBY HS; (JR); Hi Hnr Roll; Nat Hon Sy; Perf Att; St of Mnth; Comm Volntr; Peer Tut/Med; Spec Olymp Vol; ArtClub; Chrch Yth Grp; Lib Aide; Prom Com; Svce Clb; Tchrs Aide; Ch Chr; Dnce; SP/M/VS; Stu Cncl (R); CR (P); Geometry Award; Pharmacy; MD; U of Penn; U of Science of Philadelphia

NICHOLS, LISA K; GLENSIDE, PA; ABINGTON SR HS; (SO); Hi Hnr Roll; Hnr Roll; Kwnis Aw; Nat Hon Sy; St of Mnth; WWAHSS; Emplmnt; Key Club; Off Aide; Svce Clb; Dnce; Stg Cre; Therapeutic Horseback Riding Leader & Volunteer; Attorney; Animal Science; Arcadia U; Bloomsburg U

NICKLOW, ANDREW J; BOSWELL, PA; NORTH STAR HS; (SO); Hnr Roll; St of Mnth; Chess; Emplmnt; Bsball (V); Ftball (V L); Wt Lftg (V); Law Enforcement; Conservation Officer; Pittsburgh U; Indiana U of Pennsylvania

NICOLELLA, ABBI J; WASHINGTON, PA; WASHINGTON HS; (SO); All Am Sch; Hi Hnr Roll; Hnr Roll; Otst Ac Ach Awd; Perf Att; Pres Sch; WWAHSS; Yth Ldrshp Prog; Comm Volntr; Hab For Humty Volntr; Peer Tut/Med; Chrch Yth Grp; DARE; Drma Clb; Emplmnt; Key Club; Lib Aide; Mod UN; Prom Com; Bnd; Mch Bnd; SP/M/VS; Stg Cre; Cr Ctry (V); Swmg (V); Adv Cncl (R); Cl Off (T); CR (R); Lit Mag (R); Sch Ppr (R); Youth Group & Community Service; Presidential Scholar; Law; Journalism; Brown U; Columbia U

NICOLETTI, RACHEL F; PHILADELPHIA, PA; CAPA HS; (FR); Comm Volntr; Drma Clb; Acpl Chr; Ch Chr; Dnce; Stg Cre; Sccr (J); Leading Roles in Many Musicals

NICONOVICH, SANDY; GILBERTSVILLE, PA; BOYERTOWN AREA SR HS; (SO); Hi Hnr Roll; Pres Ac Ftns Aw; Pres Sch; St of Mnth; Peer Tut/Med; DARE; Emplmnt; Chrldg (V); Gmnstcs; Track; Director - Leo Club; Model; Communications; Marketing; Penn State; Villanova U

NIEDOMYS, AMBER N; WARREN, PA; WARREN CTY CAREER CTR; (SO); SP/M/VS; Cr Ctry (J); PP Ftbl (V); Track (V); Vsy Clb (V); Adv Cncl (R); Fashion Design; Teacher; Penn State; Slippery Rock

NIGH, MICHAEL; WAYNE, PA; CONESTOGA HS; (SO); Hnr Roll; Pres Ac Ftns Aw; Sci Fairs; WWAHSS; Hab For Humty Volntr; Peer Tut/Med; Emplmnt; FBLA; Key Club; P to P St Amb Prg; Bsball (J); Ftball (J); Skiing (V); Work Part Time Throughout Soph Year; Accounting; Penn State U

NIKLEWICZ, RENEE; BEAVER FALLS, PA; BLACKHAWK HS; (JR); Hi Hnr Roll; Nat Hon Sy; Nat Stu Ath Day Aw; Otst Ac Ach Awd; Perf Att; Pres Sch; WWAHSS; Yth Ldrshp Prog; Comm Volntr; Peer Tut/Med; FCA; Key Club; Prom Com; Bnd; Chr; Dvng (V); Tennis (V L); Track (VJ L); Cl Off (P, V); Stu Cncl (R); CR (R); Sch Ppr (R); Yrbk (E, P); 3 Years in a Row, Pittsburgh Soap Box Derby Champion; Seton Hill, Women in Science Award for Chemistry; Pharmacy; U of Pittsburgh; Northeastern U

NIKOLOVA, AIFER; STROUDSBURG, PA; STROUDSBURG HS; (JR); Comm Volntr; FBLA; Key Club; FBLA Member Since Freshman Year; Went to State Competition for FBLA; Medical; Business; Saint Jude's U; Penn State

NIVER, SHIMALIEN; BRADFORD, PA; BRADFORD AREA HS; Hnr Roll; Microbiologist

NIZNIK, JENNA; MECHANICSBURG, PA; CUMBERLAND VALLEY HS; (SO); Hi Hnr Roll; Hnr Roll; Nat Hon Sy; Otst Ac Ach Awd; Perf Att; WWAHSS; Comm Volntr; Spec Olymp Vol; Chrch Yth Grp; Emplmnt; Key Club; Svce Clb; SADD; Vsity Clb; Spanish Clb; Bskball (J); Sccr (V L); Biology; Mathematics; U of Pennsylvania; Johns Hopkins

NOEL, AMANDA; PORT MATILDA, PA; BALD EAGLE AREA JR/SR HS; (SR); Hi Hnr Roll; Hnr Roll; Perf Att; Comm Volntr; Hosp Aide; Spec Olymp Vol; Emplmnt; HO'Br Yth Ldrshp; SADD; Dnce; Chrldg (J); PP Ftbl (V); Sccr (VJ L); Stu Cncl (R); Pre-Pharmacy; Pre-Med; Juniata College; Franklin & Marshall College

NOH, ADA; BADEN, PA; NORTH ALLEGHENY INT HS; (SO); Hnr Roll; Nat Hon Sy; Perf Att; St of Mnth; Yth Ldrshp Prog; Comm Volntr; Peer Tut/Med; Chrch Yth Grp; Dbte Team; Key Club; NtlFrnscLg; Prom Com; Svce Clb; Spch Team; Bnd; Dnce; Mch Bnd; Stu Cncl (R); CR (R); Bowling Team; Dentistry; Fashion; Case Western Reserve

NOKES, DOMINIC; PHILADELPHIA, PA; DELAWARE VALLEY CHART HS; (SO); Ctznshp Aw; Hnr Roll; Comm Volntr; Chrch Yth Grp; Emplmnt; Scouts; Ch Chr; Stg Cre; Bsball (VJ); Ftball (J); Cl Off (T); Eagle Scout; Concerned Blackmen Merit Award; Sports Management; Psychology; Howard U; Tennessee State

NOLDY, CASSANDRA M; JESSUP, PA; VALLEY VIEW HS; (SR); Hnr Roll; Comm Volntr; FBLA; Prom Com; SADD; Sch Ppr (E); Volunteerism in the Nurses Office Award; Nursing (Pediatrics); Radiology; Horry-Georgetown Technical College

NORRIS, HOLLY; POTTSTOWN, PA; POTTSGROVE HS; (JR); Hi Hnr Roll; Nat Hon Sy; Perf Att; WWAHSS; Key Club; French Clb; Chr; Fld Hky (J); CR (R); Early Childhood Education; Retail and Marketing; Penn State U; Kutztown U

NOTARANGELO, EMILY; TURBOTVILLE, PA; WARRIOR RUN SD; (JR); Drma Clb; French Clb; Chr; SP/M/VS; Fld Hky (V L); Biology (Genetics); Psychology; U of Pittsburgh; Penn State U

NOVAK, ANDREW P; ALLISON PARK, PA; (SO); Hnr Roll; St of Mnth; Yth Ldrshp Prog; Comm Volntr; Hosp Aide; Peer Tut/Med; DARE; Key Club; P to P St Amb Prg; Photog; SADD; Spanish Clb; Stu Cncl (R); Lit Mag; Tri-Athlete; Psychologist; U of Pittsburgh; U of California

NUBER, MARK F; ERIE, PA; MERCYHURST PREPARATORY SCH; (SR); Hnr Roll; Comm Volntr; Ice Hky (V C); Rookie of the Year - Hockey; Mercyhurst College

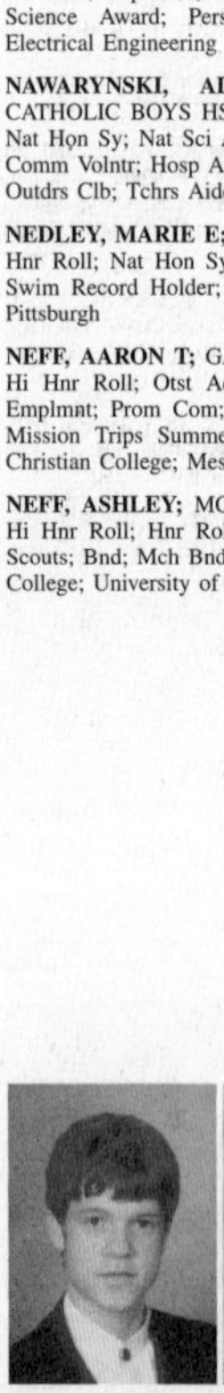

Nuber, Mark F
Mercyhurst Preparatory Sch
Erie, PA

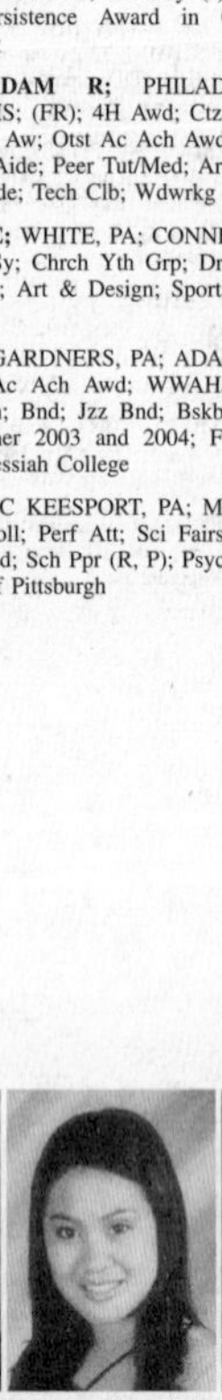

Nguyen, Katherine
Upper Darby HS
Upper Darby, PA

Neumann, Eric D
Delaware Valley HS
Milford, PA

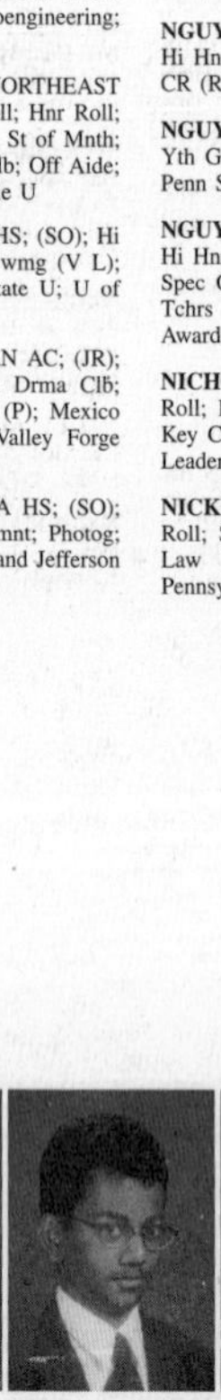

Natarajan, Navin
Mountain Top, PA

Natale, Anthony
Pottsgrove HS
Pottstown, PA

Naik, Richa
Manheim Twp HS
Lititz, PA

Narasimhan, Sneha
Strath Haven HS
Wallingford, PA

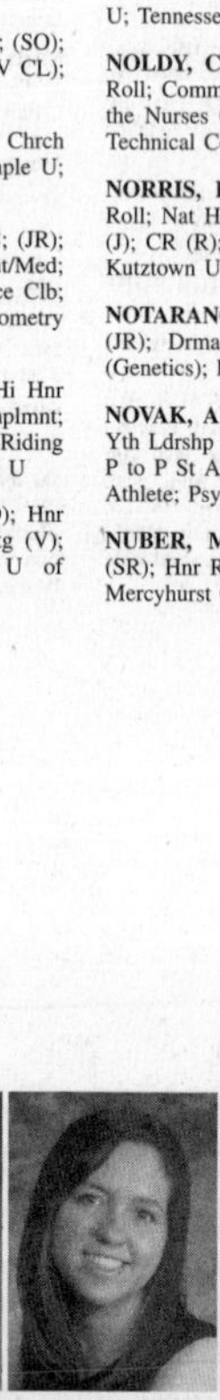

Nelson, Krystal L
Mt Pleasant Area HS
Norvelt, PA

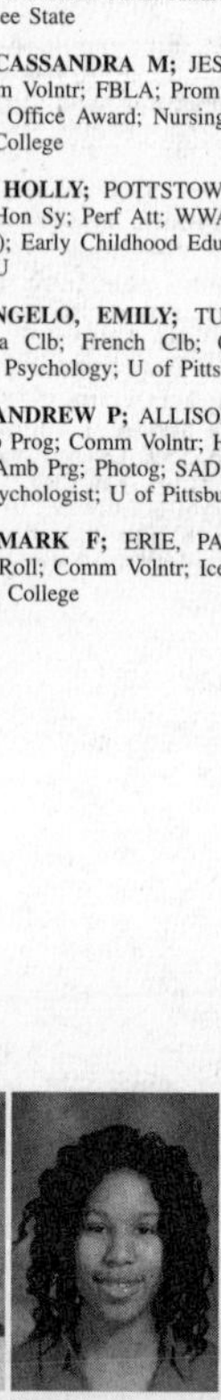

Newkirk, Siera
Franklin Learning Ctr
Philadelphia, PA

Niconovich, Sandy
Boyertown Area SR HS
Gilbertsville, PA

Noldy, Cassandra M
Valley View HS
Jessup, PA

NULL, BRANDON L; LITTLESTOWN, PA; LITTLESTOWN HS; (JR); Ctznshp Aw; Hnr Roll; Otst Ac Ach Awd; WWAHSS; Yth Ldrshp Prog; Comm Volntr; Red Cr Aide; Spec Olymp Vol; DECA; Emplmnt; FBLA; HO'Br Yth Ldrshp; Ntl FFA; Off Aide; Pep Squd; Svce Clb; Acpl Chr; Chr; SP/M/VS; Swg Chr; Adv Cncl (R); Stu Cncl (T, R); CR (R); Yrbk (R, P); PA FBLA State Officer Central Vice President; DECA State Champion, 1st Place Award Winner; Political Science/Pre-Law; Broadcasting; Gettysburg College; Flagler College

NUNEZ, ANNA N; HAZLETON, PA; HAZLETON AREA SD; (JR); Hnr Roll; Perf Att; Comm Volntr; Columbia U; Penn State U

NUNEZ, YANIBELLE; PHILADELPHIA, PA; HUNTINGDON VALLEY CHRN AC; (FR); Hi Hnr Roll; Hnr Roll; Perf Att; Comm Volntr; Chrch Yth Grp; DARE; Drma Clb; SP/M/VS; Bskball (J); Cr Ctry (J); Sccr (J); Stu Cncl (T); Yrbk; Bus-Monitor; Safety Monitor; Nurse; Doctor; Temple U; Philadelphia Community College

NYAH, YAH S; PHILADELPHIA, PA; JOHN BARTRAM HS; (FR); Hnr Roll; Otst Ac Ach Awd; St of Mnth; Comm Volntr; Peer Tut/Med; ArtClub; Emplmnt; P to P St Amb Prg; SP/M/VS; Track (J); Penn Relay; (MD) Medical Doctor; Penn State/State College; Yale

O'AGOSTINO, TERILYNN; SCRANTON, PA; SCRANTON HS; (SR); Hnr Roll; Nat Hon Sy; ArtClub; Photog; Art Honor Society; Kutztown U

OBER, KRISTINE; MOUNT JOY, PA; DONEGAL HS; (SO); Hi Hnr Roll; Hnr Roll; WWAHSS; Comm Volntr; Key Club; Chr; Ch Chr; Stg Cre; Early Childhood Education; Photography; Elizabethtown College; Kutztown U

O'BRIEN, KEELEY; MONONGAHELA, PA; RINGGOLD SD; (FR); Hi Hnr Roll; St of Mnth; Chrch Yth Grp; Ch Chr; SP/M/VS; Sccr (J); Track (V); Cl Off (S); CR (R); Ninth Grade Chorus / Vice-President; Physical Therapy; Nutritionist / Dietitian

O'CONNELL, ASHLEY; DOUGLASSVILLE, PA; DANIEL BOONE AREA HS; (JR); Hi Hnr Roll; Hnr Roll; Nat Hon Sy; Sci/Math Olympn; Comm Volntr; Hosp Aide; ArtClub; FBLA; Key Club; Mus Clb; Prom Com; Sci Clb; Svce Clb; French Clb; Chr; Dnce; Swg Chr; Bskball (J); Sch Ppr (E, R); President of Chorus/President French Club; Select Choir; Pre-Medical; Biology; U of Pennsylvania; Princeton U

O'CONNOR, CAITLIN; UNIONTOWN, PA; UNIONTOWN AREA HS; (SO); Hi Hnr Roll; St of Mnth; WWAHSS; Comm Volntr; HO'Br Yth Ldrshp; Mth Clb/Tm; Photog; SADD; French Clb; Dnce; SP/M/VS; Chrldg (V); Stu Cncl (R); Sch Ppr (R); Yrbk (R); Miss Teen Pennsylvania USA Delegate; Ranked # 1 in Class / Member of the National Society of High School Scholars; Pre-Law; Performing Arts / Drama; Princeton U; Stanford U

O'DONNELL, MICHAEL; RIDLEY PARK, PA; RIDLEY SD; (JR); Hi Hnr Roll; Nat Ldrshp Svc; Sci Fairs; St of Mnth; Comm Volntr; Chess; FBLA; P to P St Amb Prg; Tech Clb; Chr; Sch Ppr (R); Yrbk (R); Computer Engineering; Computer Science; Drexel U; St Joseph's U

O'DONOVAN, KYLE R; ALLISON PARK, PA; SHADY SIDE AC; (SO); Bsball (V CL); Golf (J); Cl Off (P); Science Olympiad Team Captain - 3rd in Nation; Philanthropic Society Benefiting ALS; MD / MBA; Yale U; Princeton U

OGBURN, APRIL N; OXFORD, PA; OXFORD AREA HS; (SR); Ctznshp Aw; Hnr Roll; Otst Ac Ach Awd; Perf Att; Peer Tut/Med; Emplmnt; FBLA; Stu Cncl (R); CR (R); Psychology; U of Pittsburgh

O'HARE, MERIT E; PITTSBURGH, PA; NORTH ALLEGHENY INT HS; (FR); Hi Hnr Roll; MVP; Nat Hon Sy; Sci Fairs; Yth Ldrshp Prog; Amnsty Intl; Comm Volntr; Peer Tut/Med; Chrch Yth Grp; Key Club; Lib Aide; Scouts; Svce Clb; Cr Ctry (J L); Track (J); CR (R); Lit Mag (R); Wildlife Rehab; Foreign Affairs; U Of Notre Dame; UVA & Duke U

OLAFSEN, SARAH; NORRISTOWN, PA; KENNEDY-KENRICK CATHOLIC HS; (FR); Hi Hnr Roll; Hnr Roll; Comm Volntr; Chrch Yth Grp; Lib Aide; Bskball (V); Fld Hky (V); Sftball (V); BS in Secondary Education; Minor in Biology or Social Studies; Pennsylvania State U; Villanova U

O'LEAR, LAUREN; BETHLEHEM, PA; FREEDOM HS; (SR); All Am Sch; Hi Hnr Roll; Nat Hon Sy; WWAHSS; Comm Volntr; DECA; Emplmnt; FBLA; Scouts; SADD; Tchrs Aide; Acpl Chr; Bnd; Chr; Dnce; Cr Ctry (J); National Society of High School Scholars; USAA National History & Government; Actress; Photojournalism; Temple U

O'LEARY-CHIDESTER, EVA; STATE COLLEGE, PA; STATE COLLEGE SOUTH HS; (FR); Hi Hnr Roll; Completed Suzuki Violin Up to Books; Published a Children's Book Locally; Advertising-Graphic Design; Photography-Journalism; Schreyer Honors College-Penn State U

OLEKSA, LINDSEY M; MUNHALL, PA; STEEL VALLEY HS; (JR); Hi Hnr Roll; Hnr Roll; Nat Hon Sy; WWAHSS; Comm Volntr; Emplmnt; Key Club; Off Aide; Scouts; SADD; Bnd; Mch Bnd; SP/M/VS; Stg Cre; PP Ftbl (J); Stu Cncl

OLIVER, CATHERINE E M; PITTSTON, PA; PITTSTON AREA HS; (JR); Nat Hon Sy; ArtClub; Bnd; Chr; Jzz Bnd; Mch Bnd; Music Education; Geneva College; Wilkes U

OLIVER, CRAIG M; LANSDALE, PA; NORTH PENN HS; (JR); Hnr Roll; MVP; Emplmnt; Key Club; Bnd; Mar Art; Wrstlg (V L); Business Management Admin.; MBA; U of Pittsburgh; U of Delaware

OLIVER, JULIANNE; PITTSTON, PA; PITTSTON AREA HS; (SR); Hnr Roll; WWAHSS; Emplmnt; Bnd; Chr; Clr Grd; Mch Bnd; Swmg (V L); Track (VJ L); Sch Ppr (E, R, P); Yrbk (E); English/Pre-Law; College Misericordia

OLIVER, REBECCA; WELLSBORO, PA; HOMESCHOOL; (SR); Hi Hnr Roll; Hnr Roll; Perf Att; WWAHSS; Chrch Yth Grp; Emplmnt; Ch Chr; Chrldg (L); Sccr (L); Travel and Tourism; Business; Millersville U; Mansfield U

OLIVER, SARAH; BEAVER FALLS, PA; BEAVER FALLS SR HS; (FR); Hi Hnr Roll; Otst Ac Ach Awd; Perf Att; WWAHSS; ArtClub; Key Club; P to P St Amb Prg; Chr; Dnce; SP/M/VS; Vllyball (J); Algebra Achievement Award; Academic Achievement Honor; Artist; Child Development

OLSHAVSKY, JESSICA N; SHARPSVILLE, PA; SHARPSVILLE HS; (SR); Hi Hnr Roll; Hnr Roll; Pres Ac Ftns Aw; WWAHSS; Comm Volntr; Hosp Aide; ArtClub; Chrch Yth Grp; Emplmnt; Mus Clb; Prom Com; Scouts; Tech Clb; Chr; Bskball (V L); Sftball (J); Graduating Youngest in My Class - 17 Yrs Old); Graduating in the Top 20% of the Class; PhD in Radiology / Starting Own Clinic; Gannon U

OLSON, ASHLEY; BETHLEHEM, PA; LIBERTY HS; (SO); Hnr Roll; Comm Volntr; Chrch Yth Grp; Emplmnt; Scr Kpr (J); Sftball (J); Nursing; Education; Penn State; Temple

OLSON, ELIZABETH J; MECHANICSBURG, PA; CUMBERLAND VALLEY HS; (SO); Hi Hnr Roll; Hnr Roll; Nat Hon Sy; WWAHSS; Comm Volntr; Spec Olymp Vol; Chrch Yth Grp; Key Club; Spanish Clb; Orch; Honored By Elks Lodge #2257; SADD Club; Chemical Science

OLSZOWKA, ALLISON; OIL CITY, PA; OIL CITY HS; (JR); Hnr Roll; MVP; Otst Ac Ach Awd; Perf Att; Comm Volntr; Spec Olymp Vol; Off Aide; Prom Com; Vsity Clb; Chrldg (JCL); Sftball (V L); Vsy Clb; Stu Cncl; Junior Exec; Stand Tall; Psychology; Special Education; Penn State Behrend; Gannon U

OMAR, BASSAM; COLLEGEVILLE, PA; SPRING-FORD SR HS; (SO); Hnr Roll; Pres Ac Ftns Aw; Emplmnt; Bskball (L); Mar Art (L); Wt Lftg (L); Part Time Job As Waiter; Own My Own Restaurant; Business Management; Ursinus College

ONADERU, DEBORAH T; UPPER DARBY, PA; UPPER DARBY HS; (JR); Ctznshp Aw; Hi Hnr Roll; Hnr Roll; Nat Ldrshp Svc; Otst Ac Ach Awd; Perf Att; St of Mnth; Comm Volntr; Hab For Humty Volntr; Peer Tut/Med; ArtClub; Dbte Team; Svce Clb; Dnce; Cl Off (V); Building with Books; HERO Club; Law/JD; Psychology/PhD; New York U; Columbia U

ONDER, KRISTEN; HAZLETON, PA; HAZLETON AREA HS; (SR); F Lan Hn Soc; Hi Hnr Roll; Nat Hon Sy; Pres Ac Ftns Aw; WWAHSS; Comm Volntr; Hosp Aide; Emplmnt; Key Club; Off Aide; Fld Hky (V L); Stu Cncl (R); CR (R); Ethnicity Advisory Board; Education; Business; Pennsylvania State U

ONDIK, TRACI; HOMESTEAD, PA; STEEL VALLEY; (JR); Nat Hon Sy; Perf Att; WWAHSS; Key Club; French Clb; Chr; Yrbk (E)

ONDRIEZEK, CHRISTINE; LATROBE, PA; DERRY AREA HS; (JR); All Am Sch; F Lan Hn Soc; Hi Hnr Roll; Perf Att; St of Mnth; USAA; WWAHSS; Comm Volntr; Drma Clb; Lttrmn Clb; NtlFrnscLg; Quiz Bowl; Spanish Clb; Chr; Dnce; SP/M/VS; Track (V); Vllyball (V L); Cl Off (S); Stu Cncl (R); Academic Excellence Society; Nat'l Leadership: Service Award; Pre-Dental; Pre-Med; Duquesne U; U of Pittsburgh

ONEILL, COLLEEN; ORWIGSBURG, PA; BLUE MOUNTAIN HS; (JR); Ctznshp Aw; F Lan Hn Soc; Hi Hnr Roll; Hnr Roll; Nat Hon Sy; Perf Att; Comm Volntr; Dbte Team; Drma Clb; Emplmnt; International Clb; Ch Chr; Dnce; SP/M/VS; Altar Server at St Ambrose RC Church; 10 Year Piano Student; Forensic Pathologist; Biology; DeSales U; Cedar Crest College

O'NEILL, MAUREEN T; ABINGTON, PA; ABINGTON HS; (SO); Perf Att; Sci/Math Olympn; Comm Volntr; Drma Clb; Emplmnt; Key Club; Mus Clb; Vsity Clb; Bnd; Dnce; Pep Bnd; Cr Ctry (V L); Dvng (L); Swmg (L); Track (V L); Stu Cncl (V, R); Yrbk (P); Medical Field

ONGARI, ALBINA; PHILADELPHIA, PA; FRANKLIN LEARNING CTR; (JR); F Lan Hn Soc; Hi Hnr Roll; Perf Att; Sci Fairs; WWAHSS; Comm Volntr; Fr of Library; Sci Clb; Tchrs Aide; Sftball (V); Tennis (V); Vllyball (J); 2nd Place on Delaware Science Fair; Biology; Pharmacist; U of Pennsylvania; Penn State U

OPAZO, JENNIFER; UPPER DARBY, PA; UPPER DARBY HS; (JR); Hnr Roll; WWAHSS; Peer Tut/Med; ArtClub; Mod UN; P to P St Amb Prg; Prom Com; Dnce; PP Ftbl (J); Bowling Club; Modeling; Elementary Education; West Chester U; Temple U

OPRISU, JENNIFER A; BEAVER FALLS, PA; BLACKHAWK HS; (SR); Hi Hnr Roll; Nat Hon Sy; Otst Ac Ach Awd; WWAHSS; Emplmnt; Key Club; Chr; PP Ftbl (VJ); Magnum Cum Laude on National Latin Exam; Honor Graduate; Biology; Pre-Veterinary Medicine; Thiel College; Washington & Jefferson College

ORELLANA, PAOLA; EAST STROUDSBURG, PA; STROUDSBURG HS; (JR); Hi Hnr Roll; Hnr Roll; Perf Att; St of Mnth; WWAHSS; Comm Volntr; FBLA; Key Club; French Clb; Track (L); National Student Leadership Conference; Bryant U Accounting Institute; Finance; International Business; New York U; Columbia U

ORLOWSKI, ANNE; MALVERN, PA; BISHOP SHANAHAN HS; (FR); Hnr Roll; St of Mnth; WWAHSS; Comm Volntr; Chrch Yth Grp; DARE; Emplmnt; Jr Ach; Scouts; Cr Ctry (V L); Track (V L); Two Time Penn Relay Medalist; Nutritionist; Sports Psychologist; Columbia U; U of Pennsylvania

ORLOWSKI, KELLIE; WATTSBURG, PA; SENECA HS; (FR); Hnr Roll; Sci Fairs; Sci/Math Olympn; Voc Ind Clb Am; Bskball (J); Stu Cncl (R); Teacher; Edinboro; Thiel

ORR, CHRISTOPHER; HONEY BROOK, PA; BISHOP SHANAHAN HS; (FR); Hi Hnr Roll; Hnr Roll; Sci Fairs; Emplmnt; Bskball (club); Rlr Hky (club); Sccr (JL); Serve as a Sexton and Sacristan at St. Peter's in Honey Brook; Formed an Alt-Rock Band; Music; Architectural Engineering

ORTIZ, BIANCA L; READING, PA; READING HS; (FR); Hi Hnr Roll; Hnr Roll; Otst Ac Ach Awd; Sci Fairs; St of Mnth; Comm Volntr; DARE; French Clb; Chr; Talent Search / Club College; French Club; Marine Biology; Photography; Brigham Young U Hawaii; Penn State U

ORTIZ, STEPHANIE M; EASTON, PA; EASTON AREA HS; (JR); Spec Olymp Vol; Emplmnt; Scouts; Cosmetology At Career Institute of Tech; Cosmetology; Business Management; Jean Madeline Aveda Institute; Cedar Crest College

ORTIZ, STEVEN; BETHLEHEM, PA; BETHLEHEM AREA VOC TECH SCH; (FR); Tattoo Artist

OSBORNE, JAMES A; PHILADELPHIA, PA; HUNTINGDON VALLEY CHRN AC; (SO); Hnr Roll; Comm Volntr; Chrch Yth Grp; DARE; Ch Chr; Clr Grd; SP/M/VS; Bskball (V); Pathfinder of the Year; Business Administration; Computer Technology; North Carolina U; St Joseph's U

OSCAR, BERNICE; PHILADELPHIA, PA; PHILADELPHIA HS FOR GIRLS; (SO); Hi Hnr Roll; Otst Ac Ach Awd; Perf Att; Sci Fairs; St of Mnth; Comm Volntr; Chrch Yth Grp; Ch Chr; Drl Tm; Orch; SP/M/VS; Stu Cncl (R); Yrbk (E); Outstanding Achievement in French I; Psychology; Pre-Medicine; Temple U; Drexel U

OSCAR, JEAN; PHILADELPHIA, PA; LANKENAU HS; (JR); Ctznshp Aw; Hi Hnr Roll; Otst Ac Ach Awd; Perf Att; Sci Fairs; St of Mnth; Yth Ldrshp Prog; Comm Volntr; Peer Tut/Med; Chrch Yth Grp; Cmptr Clb; Emplmnt; Mus Clb; Off Aide; Acpl Chr; Ch Chr; Drl Tm; Flg Crps; President of Beacon Program (Central East Math School); Medical Physician; Biology; Temple U; Drexel U

OSTERHOUT, CAITLIN M; LEESPORT, PA; SCHUYLKILL VALLEY HS; (JR); Hi Hnr Roll; Hnr Roll; Nat Hon Sy; Otst Ac Ach Awd; Pres Ac Ftns Aw; Pres Sch; Comm Volntr; Peer Tut/Med; Chrch Yth Grp; Emplmnt; Quill & Scroll; SADD; Tchrs Aide; Chr; Ch Chr; Dnce; Gmnstcs (VJC); Sch Ppr (E, R); Attended 5 National Championships; Nominated Athlete of the Year - 2005; Speech Pathology; Spanish; Bloomsburg U; West Chester U

OSTROM, CAT; LIBERTY, PA; LIBERTY JR/SR HS; (SO); Hi Hnr Roll; Hnr Roll; Nat Hon Sy; Spec Olymp Vol; Chrch Yth Grp; FBLA; Key Club; Spanish Clb; Bnd; Clr Grd; SP/M/VS; Bskball (V); Sccr (V); Track (V); Cl Off (P); Stu Cncl (R); Interior Design; Ministry

OSTROSKY, AILENE; MC KEESPORT, PA; MC KEESPORT AREA SD; (JR); Hnr Roll; Voc Ind Clb Am; Worked on Make-Up For School Plays; Business / Management; Robert Morris College; Bradford College

OSWALD, BRITTNEY; WHITEHALL, PA; WHITEHALL-COPLAY HS; (FR); Hnr Roll; Perf Att; Key Club; Spanish Clb; Degree in Law

OWEN, ALLISON; CAMP HILL, PA; EAST PENNSBORO AREA HS; (FR); Hi Hnr Roll; Hnr Roll; Sci Fairs; Comm Volntr; Spec Olymp Vol; Drma Clb; Key Club; P to P St Amb Prg; Tchrs Aide; Latin Clb; Chr; SP/M/VS; Skiing; Tennis (J); Whitikar Science Center Volunteer; Community Theatre; Education (K-8); Business; U of North Carolina; Massachusetts Institute of Technology

OWENS, DEVIN R; WATERFORD, PA; FORT LEBOEUF SD; (JR); Hnr Roll; Comm Volntr; Emplmnt; Scouts; Bskball (JC); Sccr (VJCL); Track (J); Landscape Arch

OWENS, JUSTIN M; DU BOIS, PA; DUBOIS AREA HS; (FR); Hi Hnr Roll; Pres Ac Ftns Aw; Pres Sch; St of Mnth; WWAHSS; Peer Tut/Med; Red Cr Aide; Chrch Yth Grp; Emplmnt; Wdwrkg Clb; Bskball (J); Medical Doctor; Lawyer; Auburn U; Penn State U

Ostrosky, Ailene
Mc Keesport Area SD
Mc Keesport, PA

Osborne, James A
Huntingdon Valley Chrn AC
Philadelphia, PA

Owens, Justin M
Dubois Area HS
Du Bois, PA

Ortiz, Stephanie M
Easton Area HS
Easton, PA

Ondriezek, Christine
Derry Area HS
Latrobe, PA

Oliver, Craig M
North Penn HS
Lansdale, PA

O'Connor, Caitlin
Uniontown Area HS
Uniontown, PA

O'Connell, Ashley
Daniel Boone Area HS
Douglassville, PA

Null, Brandon L
Littlestown HS
Littlestown, PA

Nunez, Anna N
Hazleton Area SD
Hazleton, PA

Olafsen, Sarah
Kennedy-Kenrick Catholic HS
Norristown, PA

Olson, Ashley
Liberty HS
Bethlehem, PA

Opazo, Jennifer
Upper Darby HS
Upper Darby, PA

Ortiz, Bianca L
Reading HS
Reading, PA

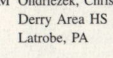

OYANA, MERCY; PHILADELPHIA, PA; CENTRAL HS; (SR); Hi Hnr Roll; Hnr Roll; WWAHSS; Comm Volntr; Peer Tut/Med; Chrch Yth Grp; Emplmnt; Tchrs Aide; Yrbk (E); Psychology; Sign Language; Goshen College

PACCIO, AISLYNN S; HALLSTEAD, PA; BLUE RIDGE HS; (FR); Hi Hnr Roll; Hnr Roll; ArtClub; Photog; Arts Alive Award of $300 for Best Painting of Surrounding Counties; Arts; Photography

PACEK, BECKY; NATRONA HTS, PA; (SO); DAR; Hi Hnr Roll; Pres Ac Ftns Aw; WWAHSS; Comm Volntr; Hosp Aide; DARE; Drma Clb; Emplmnt; Bnd; Chr; Dnce; SP/M/VS; Sccr (V L); Stu Cncl (P); Everyday Hero Award; Journalism; Drama; Point Park College; Duquesne U

PACILLA, MATTHEW; WASHINGTON, PA; WASHINGTON HS; (JR); Hnr Roll; Vsity Clb; Spanish Clb; Bsball (V); Ftball (V L); Lead America/ CSLC; Political Science/Am. Government; ROTC

PADAKI, AJAY; ALLENTOWN, PA; EMMAUS HS; (SO); F Lan Hn Soc; Hi Hnr Roll; Nat Hon Sy; Otst Ac Ach Awd; Sci Fairs; Sci/Math Olympn; St of Mnth; Yth Ldrshp Prog; Hosp Aide; Peer Tut/Med; Chrch Yth Grp; FBLA; Mth Clb/Tm; Quill & Scroll; Spanish Clb; Chr; Cr Ctry (J); Track (J); Adv Cncl (R); Sch Ppr (E); Kid to Kid; Medicine; Business; Harvard U; U of Pennsylvania

PAGAN, CINDY; PHILADELPHIA, PA; FRANKLIN LEARNING CTR; (SO); Hnr Roll; Red Cr Aide; Vllyball (V); Red Cross Club; Aspira; Health Science; Medical Field; Cornell U; Temple U

PAGE, TAIYA L; PITTSBURGH, PA; PENN HILLS SR HS; (SO); Hi Hnr Roll; Hnr Roll; Sci Fairs; Drma Clb; French Clb; Plastic Surgeon; Penn State U; Spelman College

PAGLIARA, ANDREW J; ALTOONA, PA; BISHOP GUILFOYLE HS; (SO); Hi Hnr Roll; Hnr Roll; Sci Fairs; Comm Volntr; Chess; Drma Clb; SADD; Clb; Ch Chr; SP/M/VS; Bskball (J); Ftball (V); Wt Lftg (V); Spanish Club, Father Leo Award Full Scholarship to Penn Free Enterprise Week; Criminal Justice; Business; Stanford U; UC Berkeley

PAGLIONE, CHRISTINA; BRISTOL, PA; BRISTOL JR/SR HS; (SR); Hi Hnr Roll; Nat Hon Sy; Pres Sch; St of Mnth; WWAHSS; Yth Ldrshp Prog; Comm Volntr; Peer Tut/Med; Dbte Team; Lib Aide; Mod UN; P to P St Amb Prg; Prom Com; Italian Clb; Fld Hky (J); Track (J); Cl Off (S); Stu Cncl (S); CR (S); Yrbk (E); Communications / TV, News, Broadcasting; Elementary Education; Temple U; Cabrini College

PAILIN, LINDSEY; ABINGTON, PA; ABINGTON SR HS; (SO); Hnr Roll; MVP; WWAHSS; Comm Volntr; Hosp Aide; FCA; FBLA; Key Club; Sccr (V); Rookie of the Year - Soccer; Health and Physical Education; Physical Therapy; Sports Medicine; U of Maryland; U of Virginia

PALISIN, KELSEY M; HERMITAGE, PA; HICKORY HS; (SR); Hnr Roll; Nat Hon Sy; WWAHSS; Comm Volntr; Peer Tut/Med; Chrch Yth Grp; Emplmnt; Latin Clb; Chr; Scr Kpr (J); Track (J); Vice President of Latin Honor Society; Forensic Science; Youngstown State U

PALOCAREN, ANTONY J; WEST MIFFLIN, PA; WEST MIFFLIN HS; (JR); Hi Hnr Roll; Chrch Yth Grp; ROTC; Sccr (V); Track (V); AFJROTC Financing Officer; Cricket School Captain-India; Aerospace Engineering; Aeronautical Engineering; Pennsylvania State U, U Park; Case Western Reserve U

PALUMBO, ANGELA D; PITTSBURGH, PA; PENN HILLS HS; (SO); Hi Hnr Roll; USAA; WWAHSS; Drma Clb; FCA; Key Club; P to P St Amb Prg; Scouts; SADD; Spanish Clb; SP/M/VS; Sccr (V L)

PALUMBO, ED; CARLISLE, PA; CUMBERLAND VALLEY HS; (JR); All Am Sch; Hnr Roll; Otst Ac Ach Awd; Comm Volntr; Emplmnt; Key Club; Spanish Clb; Ice Hky (VJ); Sch Ppr (E, R); School Newspaper Won 1st Place W/Special Merit in ASPA (American Scholastic Press Assn); Sports Management/Administration; Journalism; U of Massachusetts-Amherst; Ithaca College

PANAGIOTOU, VERONIKA; WEXFORD, PA; NORTH ALLEGHENY INT; (SO); Hnr Roll; Kwnis Aw; St of Mnth; WWAHSS; Yth Ldrshp Prog; Comm Volntr; Chrch Yth Grp; Key Club; Lib Aide; Svce Clb; Chr; Stg Cre; Lit Mag (E)

PANG, CRYSTAL; PHILADELPHIA, PA; NORTHEAST HS; (JR); Hi Hnr Roll; Nat Hon Sy; WWAHSS; Peer Tut/Med; FBLA; Mod UN; Flg Crps; Orch; SP/M/VS; Bskball (VJC); MBA; Marketing; U of Pennsylvania; Harvard U

PANIC, SANJA; PHILADELPHIA, PA; NORTHEAST HS; (JR); Hnr Roll; Sci Fairs; St of Mnth; Comm Volntr; Hosp Aide; Peer Tut/Med; ArtClub; Chrch Yth Grp; DARE; Emplmnt; FBLA; Mod UN; Chr; Dnce; SP/M/VS; Adv Cncl (V); CR (R); State Finalist 2005 Miss Pennsylvania; 3rd Place in FBLA; Business

PARASHAC, PAUL; WILKES BARRE, PA; BISHOP HOBAN; (JR); Hi Hnr Roll; MVP; Nat Hon Sy; Nat Mrt LOC; WWAHSS; Comm Volntr; Emplmnt; Spanish Clb; Bsball (V L); Bskball (J); Ftball (V L); Stu Cncl (R); CR (R); Keystone State Games-Baseball 3 Yrs; American Legion Baseball; Business Management / Pre Law; Engineering; Villanova U; U of Delaware

PARCHER, JUSTINE; JAMESTOWN, PA; JAMESTOWN AREA SD HS; (SO); Ctznshp Aw; Hi Hnr Roll; Nat Hon Sy; Otst Ac Ach Awd; Perf Att; Pres Ac Ftns Aw; Comm Volntr; Peer Tut/Med; Chrch Yth Grp; Emplmnt; P to P St Amb Prg; Spanish Clb; Chrldg (V); Cr Ctry (V); Track (V); Stu Cncl (R); Yrbk (P); Art and Design; Psychology; Cazenovia College; Penn State

PARFITT, SHEA L; N CAMBRIA, PA; PENNS MANOR HS; (JR); 4H Awd; Hi Hnr Roll; 4-H; FBLA; Prom Com; SADD; Wdwrkg Clb; Bnd; Clr Grd; Mch Bnd; Track (V); Accounting; Indiana U of Pennsylvania; California U of Pennsylvania

PARISE, CHRISTINA; PITTSBURGH, PA; PENN HILLS SR HS; (SO); Ctznshp Aw; Hi Hnr Roll; Hnr Roll; Perf Att; Comm Volntr; Hosp Aide; Chrch Yth Grp; Jr Ach; Key Club; French Clb; Scr Kpr (J); Stu Cncl (P); U of Pittsburgh

PARISI, MARY JO; COLLEGEVILLE, PA; (FR); Drma Clb; Clr Grd; Dnce; Mch Bnd; SP/M/VS; History Education; Theater Major

PARK, HYUN W; LANSDALE, PA; NORTH PENN HS; (SR); Hi Hnr Roll; Hnr Roll; Nat Hon Sy; Nat Mrt Fin; Nat Mrt Sch Recip; Nat Mrt Semif; WWAHSS; Peer Tut/Med; Spec Olymp Vol; Chrch Yth Grp; FBLA; Key Club; Mth Clb/Tm; Prom Com; Ch Chr; Stg Cre; PP Ftbl (VJC); Cl Off (T, R); Stu Cncl (R); CR (R); Distinction in American Mathematics Competition; Renaissance Award; Medical Doctor; Biology; New York U

PARK, JENNIFER; GLENSIDE, PA; CHETTENHAM HS; (JR); Hnr Roll; Chrch Yth Grp; Key Club; Ch Chr; Orch; Chrldg (V); Education

PARK, KYLE; FAIRLESS HILLS, PA; PENNSBURG HS EAST; (JR); Hi Hnr Roll; Hnr Roll; St of Mnth; ArtClub; DARE; Prom Com; SP/M/VS; Stg Cre; Sch Ppr (R); Video Production; Film Director; Screenwriter; LaSalle U; Temple U

PARKER, ROXANNE; PHILADELPHIA, PA; (JR); Hnr Roll; Drma Clb; SP/M/VS; CR (R); Scholarship to Stanford U; Discover Program (2003); Secondary Education; Stanford U; Duke

PARKER, TIARA; CARBONDALE, PA; CARBONDALE AREA JR/SR HS; (JR); Hnr Roll; Nat Hon Sy; Otst Ac Ach Awd; WWAHSS; ArtClub; Bskball; Track; Top Newcomer Award for Track and Field; State Finalist in the 2005 Miss Pennsylvaina Teen Pageant; Business Administration; Entrepreneurship; Hampton University; Central Penn College

PARKS, CARLEY; WOMELSDORF, PA; CONRAD WEISER HS; (FR); Hnr Roll; St of Mnth; Comm Volntr; Chrch Yth Grp; Key Club; Chr; Voices Correspondent - Reading Eagle; Early Childhood Education; Journalism; Kutztown U; Alvernia College

PARKS, DEVON; GREENVILLE, PA; GREENVILLE HS; (JR); F Lan Hn Soc; Hi Hnr Roll; Nat Hon Sy; St of Mnth; WWAHSS; Comm Volntr; Emplmnt; Key Club; Prom Com; Sci Clb; Scouts; Vsity Clb; Spanish Clb; Track (V L); Vsy Clb (V); Vllyball (V); Stu Cncl; Girl Scout Silver & Gold Awards; Head of Junior Class Float Committee; Elementary Education; Interior Design & Fashion Merchandising; Kent State U; Penn State U

PARKS, REBECCA; STROUDSBURG, PA; HOMESCHOOL; (JR); Hnr Roll; Otst Ac Ach Awd; St of Mnth; Comm Volntr; Hosp Aide; Peer Tut/Med; ArtClub; Chrch Yth Grp; DARE; Drma Clb; Emplmnt; Mus Clb; Photog; Scouts; SP/M/VS; Performed in Schools "Battle of the Boats"; Lead Role in "Charlotte's Web"; Acting; Performing Arts; Florida School of the Arts

PARR, THOMAS; DOWNINGTOWN, PA; COATESVILLE AREA SR HS; (JR); Hi Hnr Roll; Nat Hon Sy; USAA; WWAHSS; Hosp Aide; Mch Bnd; Orch; Swmg (V); Lifeguard; Swimming Instructor; Chemical Engineering; Drexel U; Rowan U

PARRISH, THERESA A; BROOMALL, PA; CARDINAL O'HARA HS; (SR); Hi Hnr Roll; Hnr Roll; Otst Ac Ach Awd; Perf Att; Pres Sch; Comm Volntr; Chrch Yth Grp; Svce Clb; Sftball; Grand Prize Winner of Seacamp Scholarship Essay Contest; Girl Scout Silver Award; Animal Science (Veterinary); Biology; Albright College; Delaware Valley College

PARRY, SAMANTHA; TRAINER, PA; CHICHESTER SR HS; (FR); Hnr Roll; Pres Sch; Vllyball (J); Nurse; Lawyer; Harvard U; Penn State U

PARSONS, SHENANDOAH; BEAVER FALLS, PA; BIG BEAVER FALLS HS; (SO); Chrch Yth Grp; Key Club; Chr; Clr Grd; Flag Line Co-Captain; Elementary Education; Special Education; Slippery Rock U

PASCOE, ALICIA; EFFORT, PA; PLEASANT VALLEY; (SO); Hi Hnr Roll; Perf Att; WWAHSS; Spec Olymp Vol; Key Club; Bnd; Mch Bnd; Pep Bnd

PASCUZZI, BRIAN; WARREN, PA; WARREN AREA HS; (SR); Hi Hnr Roll; Nat Hon Sy; Nat Mrt LOC; WWAHSS; Comm Volntr; Prom Com; Sci Clb; Vsity Clb; Cr Ctry (V L); Sccr (V L); Wrstlg (V CL); U.S. Military Academy; U of Pittsburgh

PASCUZZI, DANIEL; WARREN, PA; WARREN AREA HS; (SO); Hi Hnr Roll; Chrldg (J); Cr Ctry (J); Sccr (J); Wrstlg (V L)

PASKEL, TERELLE L; PHILADELPHIA, PA; NORTHEAST CATHOLIC BOYS HS; (FR); Hnr Roll; Ftball (J); BA or MA in Engineering; FBI, Federal Government; Miami U, Syracuse U; Villanova U

PASKY JR, R J; ERIE, PA; ERIE CITY SD; (SR); Hnr Roll; Otst Ac Ach Awd; Perf Att; St of Mnth; Comm Volntr; Peer Tut/Med; Chrch Yth Grp; Off Aide; ROTC; Wdwrkg Clb; Bnd; Drl Tm; Bsball (J); Ftball (J); Track (J L); Medical; Medical; Gannon U; Edinboro U

PASQUINELLI, SARA; GIBSONIA, PA; PINE-RICHLAND HS; (JR); Ctznshp Aw; Hi Hnr Roll; MVP; Nat Hon Sy; Otst Ac Ach Awd; WWAHSS; Comm Volntr; Hosp Aide; AL Aux Girls; Chrch Yth Grp; Emplmnt; Key Club; Mod UN; Off Aide; Prom Com; Bnd; Mch Bnd; Orch; PP Ftbl (V); Scr Kpr (V); Sftball (VJCL); Adv Cncl (R); Stu Cncl (R); Sch Ppr (E); American Legion Community Service Award; American History Achievement Award; History Teacher or Researcher; Communications, Broadcast Journalism, Sportscaster; Wake Forest U; Elon U

PASTULA, JENNIFER; NEWPORT, PA; NEWPORT SD; (SO); Hi Hnr Roll; Hnr Roll; Nat Hon Sy; Otst Ac Ach Awd; Perf Att; Comm Volntr; Chrch Yth Grp; Emplmnt; Mar Art; Sch Ppr (R); 9 Belts in Tong Soo Do; Red & Black on the Way; English-Creative Writing; Communications-Filming; Lycoming College; Harrisburg Area Community College

PATEL, DIPAL; BRIDGEVILLE, PA; SOUTH FAYETTE TOWNSHIP HS; (SO); Hi Hnr Roll; Hnr Roll; St of Mnth; ArtClub; FBLA; Sci Clb; Pediatrician; Pharmacist; Pennsylvania State U; U of Pittsburgh

PATEL, JALPA; SOUDERTON, PA; NORTH PENN HS; Hnr Roll; WWAHSS; Comm Volntr; Key Club; Honor Roll 2001-2003; Who's Who Among High School Student 2003; Nursing College

PATEL, KRUPA; NORRISTOWN, PA; METHACTON HS; (SO); Nat Hon Sy; WWAHSS; Key Club; Tennis (J); WRA Basketball League; Whitpain Tennis; Medical / Pediatrician; Architect; Boston U; Penn State Main Campus

PATEL, MITAL; HATFIELD, PA; NORTH PENN HS; (JR); Hi Hnr Roll; Perf Att; WWAHSS; Spec Olymp Vol; Key Club; National Junior Honor Society; Vice President of ICA; Chemistry; Penn State U; Lehigh U

PATIENCE, TURQUOISE; POTTSTOWN, PA; POTTSTOWN SR HS; (FR); Ctznshp Aw; Hnr Roll

PATRISS, CLIFFORD T; MILLERTON, PA; NORTHERN TIOGA SD; (FR); Ctznshp Aw; Hi Hnr Roll; Hnr Roll; Otst Ac Ach Awd; Perf Att; Comm Volntr; DARE; Emplmnt; Outdrs Clb; Scouts; Wdwrkg Clb; Bskball (J); Honor English 9; Magic Club; Teaching (Education-High School Level); Sports Medicine; Harvard U; Princeton U

PATTERSON, LISA; UPPER DARBY, PA; UPPER DARBY HS; (JR); Hi Hnr Roll; Hnr Roll; Peer Tut/Med; Chrch Yth Grp; Drma Clb; Ch Chr; Dnce; Drl Tm; Golf; Training for Culinary Chef; Drama Play As a Child; Business; Education; Penn State U; Howard U

PATTERSON, SHIRLEE; SCOTLAND, PA; SCOTLAND SCH FOR VETERANS CHILDREN; (SR); Hnr Roll; Pres Ac Ftns Aw; WWAHSS; Spec Olymp Vol; Emplmnt; Bnd; Ch Chr; Drl Tm; SP/M/VS; Bskball (V); Track (V); Vllyball (V CL); Nursing / RN

PATTOCK, ALEXIS M; NEW KENSINGTON, PA; PLUM SR HS; (SO); Hnr Roll; Orch; Girls' Leadership Association Member; National Merit Science Award; Biology Major; Pennsylvania State U

PATTON, CORTEZ E; PHILADELPHIA, PA; WILLIAM W BODINE HS; (JR); Ctznshp Aw; Hnr Roll; Otst Ac Ach Awd; Perf Att; St of Mnth; WWAHSS; Comm Volntr; Peer Tut/Med; Mod UN; Member: National Society of HS Scholars; Political Science

PAUNOVIC, KATIE R; BEAVER FALLS, PA; BLACKHAWK HS; (JR); Hi Hnr Roll; Nat Hon Sy; Otst Ac Ach Awd; WWAHSS; Drma Clb; Key Club; Spanish Clb; Chr; Dnce; SP/M/VS; Governor's School for the Arts - Semifinalist; Elementary Education; Duquesne U

PAVLICK, JONATHAN; POTTSTOWN, PA; POTTSGROVE HS; (JR); Ctznshp Aw; Hi Hnr Roll; Hnr Roll; Nat Hon Sy; Otst Ac Ach Awd; St of Mnth; WWAHSS; Comm Volntr; ArtClub; Emplmnt; Key Club; Sci Clb; French Clb; Adv Cncl (R); Yrbk (R, P); Ray Kroc Award; Golden Falcon Award; Fine Arts; Advertising /Business; Penn State U Main Campus; U of Pennsylvania

PAVLIK, PHILIP; NEW KENSINGTON, PA; PLUM SR HS; (SO); Hi Hnr Roll; Hnr Roll; Nat Hon Sy; ArtClub; Mus Clb; Spanish Clb; Award Winning Bowler; Engineering; Actuary; U of Pittsburgh; Rutgers U

PAYNE, CHRISTINA; PHILADELPHIA, PA; ROXBOROUGH HS; (JR); Ctznshp Aw; MVP; Otst Ac Ach Awd; Perf Att; Sci Fairs; St of Mnth; Yth Ldrshp Prog; Comm Volntr; Hosp Aide; Drma Clb; Emplmnt; FBLA; Mus Clb; Prom Com; Tchrs Aide; Bnd; Chr; Drl Tm; Orch; Chrldg (V); Stu Cncl (R); CR (P); Yrbk (P); Girl of the Year; Schoolman's Club Award; Business Administration; Accounting; Temple U; Drexel U

PAYNE, DONNITA; PHILADELPHIA, PA; BEN FRANKLIN HS; (FR); Hnr Roll; Comm Volntr; Outdrs Clb; White William Scholar; Beautician; Poetic

Park, Hyun W
North Penn HS
Lansdale, PA

Palocaren, Antony J
West Mifflin HS
West Mifflin, PA

Pagliara, Andrew J
Bishop Guilfoyle HS
Altoona, PA

National
Honor Roll
Spring 2005

Paccio, Aislynn S
Blue Ridge HS
Hallstead, PA

Palumbo, Ed
Cumberland Valley HS
Carlisle, PA

Pasquinelli, Sara
Pine-Richland HS
Gibsonia, PA

PAYNE, JESSICA M; GETTYSBURG, PA; GETTYSBURG HS; (SR); Hi Hnr Roll; Nat Hon Sy; Otst Ac Ach Awd; Perf Att; Pres Ac Ftns Aw; St of Mnth; Yth Ldrshp Prog; Comm Volntr; Red Cr Aide; Drma Clb; Emplmnt; Lttrmn Clb; Mus Clb; Pep Squd; Photog; Prom Com; SADD; Bnd; Mch Bnd; Pep Bnd; SP/M/VS; Chrldg (V L); Fld Hky (V); Swmg (V L); Tennis (V CL); Cl Off (R); Stu Cncl (R); Criminal Justice; Drexel U; Fordham U

PEACHEY, FRANK G; MIFFLINBURG, PA; MIFFLINBURG AREA HS; (SR); Hnr Roll; Nat Hon Sy; Pres Ac Ftns Aw; WWAHSS; Peer Tut/Med; Key Club; Sci Clb; French Clb; Ftball (J); Wrstlg (V CL); CR (R); Treasurer of Key Club; PIAA State Qualifier; History; Secondary Education; Millersville U

PEARLMAN, ASHLEY L; PHILADELPHIA, PA; ARCHBISHOP RYAN HS; (SO); Hi Hnr Roll; Hnr Roll; Perf Att; Sci Fairs; St of Mnth; WWAHSS; Comm Volntr; Peer Tut/Med; ArtClub; DARE; P to P St Amb Prg; Dnce; Math Award-9th Grade; Veterinary Medicine; Forensics Science; U of Pennsylvania; Penn State U

PEARSON, KELSEY; WASHINGTON, PA; TRINITY HS; (SO); Hi Hnr Roll; Scouts; Bnd; Mch Bnd; Photography; Film Making; Art Institute of Pittsburgh

PECK, DANIELLE L; WILLIAMSBURG, PA; WILLIAMSBURG CMTY SD; (FR); Ctznshp Aw; Hnr Roll; ArtClub; Bskball (J); Sftball (V); Stu Cncl (P); Doctors Nurse, RN or LPN; Penn State U

PEDERSEN, SARAH; STATE COLLEGE, PA; STATE COLLEGE AREA HS; (JR); Hi Hnr Roll; Spec Olymp Vol; Key Club; Fld Hky (V L); Mar Art

PEDRIANI, AMBER; SUGARLOAF, PA; HAZLETON AREA HS; (JR); Hi Hnr Roll; Hnr Roll; Nat Hon Sy; WWAHSS; Comm Volntr; Chrch Yth Grp; DARE; Emplmnt; Key Club; Scouts; Ch Chr; Ftball (V L); Swmg (V); Track (V); Vllyball (J); Adv Cncl (R); Stu Cncl (R); Students Against Drug Abuse-Club; Health Occupations Students of America-Club; Physical Therapy; Arcadia U; Temple U

PELKEY, DEANN A; EASTON, PA; EASTON HS; (JR); Hi Hnr Roll; Nat Hon Sy; WWAHSS; Comm Volntr; Peer Tut/Med; Chrch Yth Grp; Drma Clb; Emplmnt; FBLA; FTA; Key Club; Off Aide; Scouts; Chr; Dnce; SP/M/VS; CR (R); 10 Year Dancing Award; Outstanding Leadership; Elementary Education; Kutztown U; West Chester U

PELLEGRINO, TIM M; PHOENIXVILLE, PA; PHOENIXVILLE AREA HS; (SR); Hi Hnr Roll; Hnr Roll; WWAHSS; Comm Volntr; Peer Tut/Med; Chrch Yth Grp; Dbte Team; Scouts; Spanish Clb; Sccr (J); Tennis (J); Eagle Scout; Firefighter; Engineering; Medical Doctor; United States Naval Academy; Boston College

PELLETIER, ANGELINA M; WILLIAMSPORT, PA; JERSEY SHORE AREA SR HS; (SR); Hi Hnr Roll; Hnr Roll; Nat Hon Sy; St of Mnth; WWAHSS; Peer Tut/Med; FBLA; Key Club; Lib Aide; Mod UN; Prom Com; Stg Cre; Stu Cncl (S); Big Brother/Big Sister; Chamber of Commerce Student of the Year; Psychology; Lycoming College

PELLICCIARO JR, RICHARD; BOOTHWYN, PA; CONCORDVILLE PREP HS; (SO); Hi Hnr Roll; Hnr Roll; Otst Ac Ach Awd; Pres Ac Ftns Aw; Sci Fairs; Comm Volntr; Peer Tut/Med; Chrch Yth Grp; Cmptr Clb; Emplmnt; Lib Aide; Mth Clb/Tm; Photog; Tchrs Aide; Tech Clb; SP/M/VS; Stg Cre; Bskball (V); Stu Cncl (T); CR (T); Yrbk (P); Attended Global Young Leaders Conference; American Mathematics Competition School Winner; MS Ed-Mathematics; BS-Computer and Information Sciences; Temple U; West Chester U

PELLISH, JACQUELINE C; POTTSVILLE, PA; POTTSVILLE AREA HS; (SR); Hi Hnr Roll; Kwnis Aw; WWAHSS; Comm Volntr; DARE; Emplmnt; Key Club; SADD; French Clb; Chrldg (V CL); Sccr (J); Kiwanis Community Service Award; Government / Political Affairs; Millersville U; Muhlenberg College

PELOQUIN, JEREMY; PORT ROYAL, PA; JUNIATA CTY SD; (JR); Hi Hnr Roll; Hnr Roll; WWAHSS; Comm Volntr; Chrch Yth Grp; Drma Clb; Emplmnt; P to P St Amb Prg; Prom Com; Scouts; SP/M/VS; Stg Cre; Bsball (VJ); Ftball (VJ L)

PENNESI, JENNA; LATROBE, PA; GREATER LATROBE HS; (JR); F Lan Hn Soc; Hi Hnr Roll; Pres Ac Ftns Aw; St of Mnth; WWAHSS; Comm Volntr; Peer Tut/Med; Spec Olymp Vol; Key Club; Lttrmn Clb; Pep Squd; Vsity Clb; Spanish Clb; Bskball (VJ); Sftball (V CL); Vsy Clb (V); Yrbk (E); All-Section Player in Softball; Yearbook Manager; Physical Therapy; Education (K-12); Robert Morris College; U of Pittsburgh

PENROD, BRIANNA E; BETHLEHEM, PA; BETHLEHEM CATHOLIC HS; (FR); Hi Hnr Roll; Hnr Roll; Pres Sch; WWAHSS; Yth Ldrshp Prog; Comm Volntr; Red Cr Aide; Chess; DARE; Drma Clb; Emplmnt; Key Club; Mth Clb/Tm; Spanish Clb; Chr; Ch Chr; SP/M/VS; Track (J); Cl Off (R); Lit Mag (E); Published Poet-Fall & Spring "Young Poets" of PA; Diocesan Choir of All Catholic HS; Pediatrician; Physician; Barry U; Arizona State U

PENTZ, JUSTIN D; ROCKTON, PA; DUBOIS AREA HS; (FR); Hi Hnr Roll; Comm Volntr; Outdrs Clb; Skt Tgt Sh (V L); National Champion in Competitive Shooting; National Rifle Association Youth Advisory Board Member 2005; Forestry; Medical Degree; U of West Virginia; U of Pennsylvania

PERCHAK, NOELLE M; TRESCKOW, PA; HAZLETON AREA HS; (SR); Hi Hnr Roll; Hnr Roll; Nat Hon Sy; Perf Att; WWAHSS; FBLA; Key Club; Off Aide; SADD; Stu Cncl (R); Yrbk (P); Homecoming Court; Elementary Education; Photography; Bloomsburg U

PEREZ, BILLY; PHILADELPHIA, PA; CARDINAL DOUGHERTY HS; (JR); Hnr Roll; Nat Hon Sy; Otst Ac Ach Awd; Perf Att; WWAHSS; Peer Tut/Med; DARE; HOSA / MCHA; Family Physician; Orthopedic Doctor; Temple U; Penn State U

PERKINS, KAYLA; SEWICKLEY, PA; QUAKER VALLEY HS; (JR); Hi Hnr Roll; Hnr Roll; Comm Volntr; ArtClub; Key Club; Prom Com; Chrldg (C); Sftball; Bowling; Quaker Valley Summer Softball; Psychology; Business Management; Penn State; U of Pittsburgh

PERL, CASSANDRA; CTRL CITY, PA; SHANKSVILLE-STONYCREEK HS; (SO); Hnr Roll; Nat Hon Sy; WWAHSS; Comm Volntr; Hosp Aide; 4-H; Drma Clb; Lib Aide; Mus Clb; NtlFrnscLg; Schol Bwl; Bnd; Chr; Pep Bnd; SP/M/VS; Tennis; Elementary Education; Music Education; Indiana U of Pennsylvania; Providence College

PERRY, ASHLEY; JAMESTOWN, PA; JAMESTOWN AREA SD; (SO); Hnr Roll; WWAHSS; Bskball (J L); Relay for Life (Cancer Support Program); Thiel College; Slippery Rock

PERRY, JESSICA; FEASTERVILLE TREVOSE, PA; BENSALEM TOWNSHIP SD; (JR); Hnr Roll; Comm Volntr; Emplmnt; Prom Com

PERSON, TRAVIS; READING, PA; READING SR HS; (SR); MVP; Chrch Yth Grp; Accounting

PESSA, AMBER; ERIE, PA; ERIE CITY SD; (FR)

PETERS, JONATHAN M; NORTHAMPTON, PA; NORTHAMPTON AREA SCH; (SR); Hi Hnr Roll; Hnr Roll; Pres Sch; Emplmnt; Won Award for Art Picture; Won Award for Music Writing; Automotive License; Machinist License Degree; UTI

PETERS, LYNSEY; TAYLOR, PA; RIVERSIDE JR/SR HS; (JR); Hi Hnr Roll; Hnr Roll; Nat Hon Sy; WWAHSS; Bnd; Mch Bnd; National Honors Society; Psychology; Wilkes U

PETERSEN, MICHELLE L; DUSHORE, PA; SULLIVAN CTY HS; (JR); Hnr Roll; WWAHSS; 4-H; Chrch Yth Grp; DARE; Emplmnt; Prom Com; Dnce; Chrldg (JC); USAA National Mathematics Award; Accounting; Business; Pennsylvania College of Technology; Mansfield U

PETERSON, JOSHUA N; SHIPPENSBURG, PA; CUMBERLAND VALLEY CHRISTIAN SCH; (FR); All Am Sch; Hi Hnr Roll; WWAHSS; Chrch Yth Grp; Bskball (VJ); Golf; Ice Hky

PETRAGLIA III, FRANK W; CRANBERRY TWP, PA; SENECA VALLEY HS; (JR); Hi Hnr Roll; Nat Hon Sy; Otst Ac Ach Awd; Pres Sch; Sci/Math Olympn; WWAHSS; Comm Volntr; Key Club; Mth Clb/Tm; Vsity Clb; Bskball (J); Lcrsse (VJCL); N.H.S. National Honor Society; Presidential Scholar; Electrical Engineering; Premed; Cornell U; Northwestern U

PETRAKIS, NICOLE; MONROEVILLE, PA; GATEWAY SD; (SO); Hi Hnr Roll; FBLA; Key Club; Off Aide; Chr; Wrstlg (L); Yrbk (E, P); First Degree Black-Belt Decided; Tae Kwon Do Instructor; Dermatologist; Duquesne U; U of Pittsburgh At Johnstown

PETROLE, JONATHAN; TRESCKOW, PA; HAZLETON AREA SD HS; (SO); Hnr Roll; Bsball (J); Bskball (J); Aau Basketball; Temple; Harvard

PETTINE, NATHANIEL S; POTTSTOWN, PA; POTTSGROVE HS; (SO); Hi Hnr Roll; Hnr Roll; Nat Hon Sy; Sci/Math Olympn; WWAHSS; Comm Volntr; Key Club; Mth Clb/Tm; Vsity Clb; Latin Clb; Ftball (V); Lcrsse (V L); Golden Falcon Club; History; Engineering; U of Pennsylvania

PETTIT, LARRY M; SYCAMORE, PA; WEST GREENE MIDDLE SR HS; (FR); 4H Awd; Comm Volntr; Peer Tut/Med; 4-H; Emplmnt; Ntl FFA; Wdwrkg Clb; Wrstlg (V); Stu Cncl

PETTNER, MATTHEW; MONACA, PA; CTR AREA SD; (SO); Hi Hnr Roll; Hnr Roll; Perf Att; WWAHSS; Comm Volntr; Scouts; German Clb; Bskball (J); Captain-Jr Volunteer Fire Dept (Center Township); Secretary-Jr Fireman (Center Township #1); Teaching

PETTUS, TAMIA R; PHILADELPHIA, PA; LINCOLN HS; (SR); Ctznshp Aw; WWAHSS; Comm Volntr; Chrch Yth Grp; Chr; SP/M/VS; Class Treasure; Nursing; Music Performing; La Salle U; Community College

PEZICH, ERIKA; ALLISON PARK, PA; HAMPTON HS; (SO); Fut Prb Slvr; Hi Hnr Roll; MVP; Otst Ac Ach Awd; Pres Ac Ftns Aw; Sci Fairs; Sci/Math Olympn; WWAHSS; Chrch Yth Grp; DARE; Dbte Team; Mth Clb/Tm; Mod UN; Sccr (V L); Track (V L); Olympic Development-PA West Soccer; Who's Who Among High School Students-Sports Edition; Law; Education; Duquesne U; Miami of Ohio

PFEIL, ASHLEY; ASTON, PA; SUN VALLEY HS; (JR); Hnr Roll; Comm Volntr; Emplmnt; SADD; Chr; National Art Honor Society Member; Rookie of the Year for Concord Flames Women's Ice Hockey; Art Education; U of Toronto; York U

PFISTER, KATIA D; HARLEYSVILLE, PA; NORTH PENN HS; (JR); Hnr Roll; Comm Volntr; Chrch Yth Grp; Emplmnt; Key Club; Dnce; Bskball (V); Cr Ctry (V); Sccr (V); Track (V); National Technical Honor Society; Emergency Management Services; Drexel U; Montgomery County Community College

PHAM, MYKIM H; HOMESTEAD, PA; STEEL VALLEY HS; (JR); Hi Hnr Roll; Hnr Roll; Nat Hon Sy; Otst Ac Ach Awd; Perf Att; Pres Sch; WWAHSS; Comm Volntr; Hosp Aide; DARE; Drma Clb; Key Club; Lib Aide; Prom Com; SADD; Tchrs Aide; Spanish Clb; Bnd; Chr; Dnce; Mch Bnd; Tennis (V); Vllyball (V); Stu Cncl (R); CR (R); Yrbk (E, P); Going on 3 Yrs of Chemistry Olympics; Participated in the Pennsylvania Junior Academy of Sciences; Biology; Chemistry; U of Pittsburgh; Duquesne U

PHAM, VINH; PHILADELPHIA, PA; NORRIS S BARRATT MS; (MS); Hnr Roll; Perf Att; Gmnstcs; Technology; Temple U

PHAN, PHUONG T T; READING, PA; READING HS; (SR); Hnr Roll; Nat Hon Sy; Comm Volntr; Peer Tut/Med; Chrch Yth Grp; Cmptr Clb; Spanish Clb; Ch Chr; Dnce; Pharmacist; Biochemistry; Franklin & Marshall College; Alvernia College

PHEASANT, BETH M; FORT LOUDON, PA; FANNETT-METAL JR/SR HS; (JR); Hi Hnr Roll; Nat Hon Sy; Nat Ldrshp Svc; Perf Att; Pres Sch; Sci Fairs; WWAHSS; Hosp Aide; Red Cr Aide; Spec Olymp Vol; Mus Clb; Sci Clb; Tchrs Aide; Chr; Vice President of Chorus; Robotics Club Treasurer; Nursing; Certified Nurse Practitioner; Penn State U

PHELPS, AMANDA; JULIAN, PA; CTRL PA INST OF SCI HS; (SR); Hnr Roll; Perf Att; Emplmnt; Pep Squd; Dnce; Yrbk; Piano Lessons; Business Management; South Hills

PHILBERT, ANDY; STROUDSBURG, PA; STROUDSBURG HS; (SO); Hnr Roll; DARE; Chr; Bskball (VJ)

PHILLIPS, CHRISSY; PITTSBURGH, PA; PENN HILLS HS; (SR); Hi Hnr Roll; Nat Hon Sy; Pres Sch; WWAHSS; Peer Tut/Med; FTA; Key Club; Scouts; Vllyball (V L); Elementary Education; Pitt Johnstown

PHILLIPS, JOVIANN S; PHILADELPHIA, PA; OVERBROOK HS; F Lan Hn Soc; Hi Hnr Roll; Hnr Roll; Otst Ac Ach Awd; Perf Att; Comm Volntr; Peer Tut/Med; Medical Degree; Law Degree; U of Pennsylvania; Harvard U

PHILLIPSON, RACHEL; DOYLESTOWN, PA; CTRL BUCKS EAST; (SO); Hi Hnr Roll; WWAHSS; Peer Tut/Med; Key Club; Dvng (V); Tennis (V)

PHUNG, JENNIFER; UPPER DARBY, PA; UPPER DARBY HS; (JR); Hi Hnr Roll; Hnr Roll; Nat Hon Sy; Comm Volntr; Hosp Aide; Peer Tut/Med; Orch; Tennis (V L); Yrbk (E)

PIATT, JESSICA; WASHINGTON, PA; TRINITY HS; (JR); Hnr Roll; Otst Ac Ach Awd; Perf Att; Comm Volntr; Chrch Yth Grp; Emplmnt; Ch Chr; Dnce; Marriage Counseling; Neurology Major; Pittsburgh U; Allegheny College

PICARD, JESSICA; SCOTRUN, PA; POCONO MTN EAST HS; (FR); Hnr Roll; Otst Ac Ach Awd; Perf Att; St of Mnth; Comm Volntr; Chrch Yth Grp; DARE; Drma Clb; Chr; Dnce; Track (J); Lawyer

PICCIRILLI, JEFFREY M; ALIQUIPPA, PA; CTR AREA SD; (SO); Hi Hnr Roll; Peer Tut/Med; DARE; Lttrmn Clb; Sccr (V L); Stu Cncl; Intramural Basketball & Volleyball; Pharmacy; Pitt College; Duquesne U

PIEKARSKI, ROBERT; SHENANDOAH, PA; SHENANDOAH VALLEY JR/SR HS; (SR); All Am Sch; Hi Hnr Roll; Hnr Roll; Nat Hon Sy; Nat Ldrshp Svc; Otst Ac Ach Awd; USAA; WWAHSS; Yth Ldrshp Prog; Comm Volntr; Emplmnt; Svce Clb; Bskball (J); Sch Ppr (R); Bloomsburg U

PIERCE, JESSICA; SYCAMORE, PA; WEST GREEN MIDDLE SR HS; (FR); Hi Hnr Roll; WWAHSS; Ntl FFA; SADD; Track (V); Leo Club; National High School Rodeo Association; Veterinary Medicine; Ohio State U; Kansas State U

PIETROWSKI, ASHLEY; OLD FORGE, PA; OLD FORGE HS; (JR); Hi Hnr Roll; Nat Hon Sy; Otst Ac Ach Awd; WWAHSS; Peer Tut/Med; Red Cr Aide; Chrldg (VJC); Gmnstcs; Skiing; Sftball (JC); Cl Off (V); Sch Ppr (R); Pharmacy; Temple U; Pitt

PIFER, ERIC; FAIRVIEW, PA; FAIRVIEW HS; (SR); Hi Hnr Roll; Hnr Roll; St of Mnth; WWAHSS; Comm Volntr; Chrch Yth Grp; Drma Clb; Emplmnt; FCA; Lib Aide; Bnd; Drl Tm; Mch Bnd; SP/M/VS; Culinary Arts; Pennsylvania Culinary Institute

PIHS, THERESA; JOHNSTOWN, PA; GREATER JOHNSTOWN HS; (SR); Hnr Roll; Otst Ac Ach Awd; St of Mnth; USAA; Yth Ldrshp Prog; Chrch Yth Grp; FCA; Sccr (J); Medical Laboratory Assisting; Forensics; Mount Aloysius College; Allegany College of Maryland

Pham, Vinh
Norris S Barratt MS
Philadelphia, PA

Pessa, Amber
Erie City SD
Erie, PA

Pearson, Kelsey
Trinity HS
Washington, PA

Pentz, Justin D
Dubois Area HS
Rockton, PA

Philbert, Andy
Stroudsburg HS
Stroudsburg, PA

PINGILI, MIKHILA R; DEVON, PA; CONESTOGA HS; (SO); Hnr Roll; Comm Volntr; Peer Tut/Med; Key Club; Orch; Medicine; U of Pennsylvania; Drexel U

PINTOF, ERICA; MARCUS HOOK, PA; CHICHESTER SR HS; (FR); Hi Hnr Roll; Hnr Roll; St of Mnth; Peer Tut/Med; 4-H; DARE; FBLA; Mod UN; SADD; Chr; Clr Grd; SP/M/VS; Sccr (J L); Law; Villanova U; Harvard U

PINTOR, SANDRA; BETHLEHEM, PA; BETHLEHEM CATHOLIC HS; (FR); Hnr Roll; Key Club; FACT Club; History Professor; Pennsylvania State; Moravian College

PIPER, NICHOLLE; CTRL CITY, PA; SHANKSVILLE STONYCREEK SCH; (SO); Hnr Roll; Nat Hon Sy; WWAHSS; Drma Clb; Schol Bwl; Bnd; Chr; Jzz Bnd; Mch Bnd; Tennis (V); Track (V)

PITMAN, COURTNEY; MECHANICSBURG, PA; MECHANICSBURG AREA SR HS; (JR); Hi Hnr Roll; Hnr Roll; Nat Hon Sy; Sci Fairs; Key Club; Photog; Prom Com; Cr Ctry (J); Sccr (V L); Cl Off (T); Yrbk (R, P); Social Sciences; Education; U of South Carolina; Northeastern U

PLUMMER, ANTHONY J; SOUTH FORK, PA; GREATER JOHNSTOWN AVTS; (SO); Hnr Roll; Medical Degree; Mt. Aloysius College; U of California

PLUMMER, ELIZABETH T; FOREST GROVE, PA; CTRL BUCKS HS EAST; (JR); Hi Hnr Roll; Hnr Roll; Comm Volntr; Spec Olymp Vol; 4-H; Emplmnt; Key Club; Lttrmn Clb; Lib Aide; Mod UN; Photog; Quill & Scroll; Sftball (J); Cl Off (V); Stu Cncl (V, S, R); CR (R); Yrbk (E); Horseback Riding; Key Club-Community Service; Liberal Arts

PLUMMER, JESSICA V V; PHILADELPHIA, PA; MASTERY CHARTER HS; (FR); Ctznshp Aw; Hnr Roll; Nat Hon Sy; Otst Ac Ach Awd; Sci Fairs; Sci/Math Olympn; St of Mnth; Valdctrian; Yth Ldrshp Prog; Hab For Humty Volntr; ArtClub; Chess; Chrch Yth Grp; Dbte Team; Drma Clb; Jr Ach; Mth Clb/Tm; Mus Clb; Dnce; Drl Tm; SP/M/VS; Chrldg (V); Track; Wt Lftg; Stu Cncl (T); Sch Ppr (E, R); Yrbk (E, P); Valedictorian; MVP for Cheerleading Squad; Pharmacy; Forensic Science; Temple U; Pennsylvania State U

PODLEYON, KRISTA M; HERMITAGE, PA; HICKORY HS; (SO); Hnr Roll; Pres Sch; WWAHSS; Comm Volntr; SADD; Latin Clb; Chr; Drm Mjr; Yrbk (R); Penn State; Youngstown State

POLACHEK, EMILY C; DALLAS, PA; DALLAS SR HS; (FR); Hi Hnr Roll; Key Club; Scouts; Chrldg (V); CR (R); Secondary English Teacher; Beautician; North Carolina State; Pittsburgh U

POLINSKY, ALEXANDRA; MONROEVILLE, PA; GATEWAY HS; (JR); Hi Hnr Roll; Jr Rot; MVP; Nat Hon Sy; Amnsty Intl; Comm Volntr; Hosp Aide; ArtClub; Chrch Yth Grp; Drma Clb; Emplmnt; Jr Cls League; P to P St Amb Prg; Ch Chr; SP/M/VS; Vllyball (V L); Cl Off (T)

POLLARD, DARREL; PITTSBURGH, PA; PERRY TRADITIONAL AC; (SO); Hi Hnr Roll; Hnr Roll; Comm Volntr; Jujitsu (Martial Arts); Criminal Justice; Howard U

POLLITT, LATOYA; PHILADELPHIA, PA; CENTRAL HS; (SR); Ctznshp Aw; Hnr Roll; Nat Hon Sy; WWAHSS; Comm Volntr; Peer Tut/Med; Chrch Yth Grp; Emplmnt; Off Aide; Pep Squd; Dnce; Pep Bnd; Adv Cncl (T, R); CR (R); Morgan State U; West Chester U

POLLOCK, COLBY M; POTTSTOWN, PA; POTTSTOWN SR HS; (MS); Ctznshp Aw; Hnr Roll; MVP; Sci/Math Olympn; St of Mnth; ArtClub; Chrch Yth Grp; Clr Grd; Lcrsse (J); Sftball (J); Yrbk (R); Dek Hockey - J; Law and Legal Studies; Forensic Science; Virginia Tech; Pittsburgh U

POMAIBO, NICOLE; MC KEESPORT, PA; MC KEESPORT AREA SD; (JR); Hnr Roll; Perf Att; Scouts; Business / Management; Community College of Allegheny County

POMPEY, EDDIE; SPRINGVILLE, PA; ELK LAKE SCH; (FR); Hi Hnr Roll; Hnr Roll; Nat Hon Sy; St of Mnth; Comm Volntr; Hab For Humty Volntr; Key Club; Quiz Bowl; Skiing; Johns Hopkins Search for Talented Youth; Rosetti Art Exhibit-Won Ribbons 3 Yrs; Electronic Engineering; Massachusetts Institute of Technology

PONDER, FREDRICA P; UPPER DARBY, PA; UPPER DARBY HS; (JR); Hnr Roll; Perf Att; St of Mnth; Yth Ldrshp Prog; Hosp Aide; Peer Tut/Med; Chrch Yth Grp; Emplmnt; FCA; Mus Clb; Chr; Ch Chr; Bskball (J); Sftball (L); I Volunteered At Lankenau Hospital; I Volunteered At Parham Chapel; Science; PhD in Medicine; Temple U; Penn State U

POORMAN, ALYSSA; DOYLESTOWN, PA; CTRL BUCKS SOUTH HS; (JR); 4H Awd; Ctznshp Aw; Hi Hnr Roll; MVP; Nat Hon Sy; Nat Stu Ath Day Aw; Otst Ac Ach Awd; Pres Ac Ftns Aw; WWAHSS; Comm Volntr; 4-H; Emplmnt; Key Club; P to P St Amb Prg; Svce Clb; Fld Hky (V CL); Lcrsse (V L); Adv Cncl (R); Stu Cncl (R); Political Science

POPA, MICHELLE; MIDDLETOWN, PA; MIDDLETOWN AREA HS; (FR); Hnr Roll; Perf Att; Pres Ac Ftns Aw; Emplmnt; Key Club; Bnd; Chr; Fld Hky (J); National History Day Award-District; Cosmetology & Business

POPE, STEVE; ERIE, PA; ERIE CITY SD; (SO); Hi Hnr Roll; Hnr Roll; Otst Ac Ach Awd; Sci Fairs; St of Mnth; Comm Volntr; Emplmnt; Mth Clb/Tm; Pep Squd; Sccr (VJ); Wrstlg (J); Electricity; Math; Penn State; Pitt

POPLASKI, JANEL; SHAMOKIN, PA; SHAMOKIN AREA SD; (JR); Hi Hnr Roll; Nat Hon Sy; Chrch Yth Grp; Chr; Orch; SP/M/VS

POPOWICH, ALYSSA; DOYLESTOWN, PA; CTRL BUCKS HS EAST; (SO); F Lan Hn Soc; Hi Hnr Roll; MVP; WWAHSS; Peer Tut/Med; Key Club; Fld Hky (J); PP Ftbl; Sccr (V L); Stu Cncl (R); West Point Alumni Leadership Award; Leadership Camp - Norwich U; Marine Biology; American Literature; Princeton U; College of William and Mary

PORATH, BRYAN M; BOSWELL, PA; NORTH STAR HS; (SO); Hnr Roll; Pres Ac Ftns Aw; Emplmnt; Arch (V); Several Student Awards in Many Classes; I Lift But Not on a Team.; Criminology; Bachelor's Degree; Ohio State U; Penn State U

PORCELLI, JOHN; NORRISTOWN, PA; NORRISTOWN AREA HS; (JR); Ctznshp Aw; DAR; Hnr Roll; Nat Hon Sy; Nat Ldrshp Svc; Chrch Yth Grp; DECA; Mth Clb/Tm; P to P St Amb Prg; Sccr (VJCL); DECA-District Winner

PORIS, ERIC M; SOUTHAMPTON, PA; COUNCIL ROCK HS SOUTH; (SR); Hi Hnr Roll; Hnr Roll; Nat Hon Sy; Perf Att; Comm Volntr; Hosp Aide; Emplmnt; Spanish Clb; SP/M/VS; Sccr (VJCL); Cl Off (V); Brian Eastburn Award (Dedication & Leadership); Homecoming King; Special Education; Business Management; Pennsylvania State U; Virginia Polytechnic Institute of Technology

PORTER, A A; BENSALEM, PA; BENSALEM TOWNSHIP SD; (SO); Hi Hnr Roll; Hnr Roll; WWAHSS; Comm Volntr; ArtClub; Civil Air Pat; Drma Clb; Mod UN; ROTC; French Clb; Stg Cre; Intelligence / Criminal Justice; Military

PORTER, BRENT W; GREENVILLE, PA; GREENVILLE HS; (JR); Hi Hnr Roll; Hnr Roll; Ftball (V L); Golf (V); Rlr Hky (V); Tennis (V L); Wt Lftg (V); Yrbk (E); Honor Roll-High Honors; Clubs; Physical Therapy; Phys Ed.; Pitt U; Mercyhurst College

PORTER, DAMON T; TARENTUM, PA; HIGHLANDS SD; (MS); Ctznshp Aw; Hi Hnr Roll; Hnr Roll; MVP; Otst Ac Ach Awd; Perf Att; St of Mnth; St Optmst of Yr; Bskball (V); CR (R); Won Sections in Basketball in 7th Grade; Won Gateway Tournament 2 Times in a Row; Business; Teaching (School); Michigan State U; Duke U, Good Academic School

PORTER, KELLY E; MECHANICSBURG, PA; CUMBERLAND VALLEY HS; (JR); Hnr Roll; Perf Att; Sci Fairs; Emplmnt; Key Club; Bnd; Vllyball (VJ L); Elementary Education; Psychology; Millersville U; Elizabethtown

POTASH, AUBREY; MIFFLINBURG, PA; MIFFLINBURG AREA HS; (SO); DAR; Hi Hnr Roll; Kwnis Aw; Nat Hon Sy; Pres Ac Ftns Aw; St of Mnth; Comm Volntr; Drma Clb; Key Club; Svce Clb; French Clb; Acpl Chr; Bnd; Chr; Dnce; Stu Cncl (R); Ray H Kroc Youth Achievement Award; Presidential Physical Fitness Award (For 4 Years); Education-(Music or Secondary); Journalism (Theater); Bucknell U; Susquehanna U

POTTS, LAREINA; MC KEESPORT, PA; MC KEESPORT AREA SD; (FR); Perf Att; St of Mnth; Peer Tut/Med; Bskball (VJ); Degree in Business

POTTS, RASHEED; CHESTER, PA; CHESTER HS; (FR); Chrch Yth Grp; Photog

POWERS, GWEN; BETHEL, PA; TULPEHOCKEN HS; (SR); 4H Awd; Hnr Roll; Nat Hon Sy; Otst Ac Ach Awd; Comm Volntr; Peer Tut/Med; 4-H; Emplmnt; Ntl FFA; Quiz Bowl; FFA-President; 4-H President; Animal Science & Production; Butler County Community College, El Dorado, KS

PRATCHENKO, JOEY; ALIQUIPPA, PA; CTR AREA SD; (SO); Hi Hnr Roll; Perf Att; Pres Ac Ftns Aw; Pres Sch; Comm Volntr; Hab For Humty Volntr; Peer Tut/Med; Chrch Yth Grp; Vsity Clb; Spanish Clb; Bnd; Chr; Jzz Bnd; Mch Bnd; Cr Ctry (V); Swmg (V L); Track (V); Cl Off (V); Stu Cncl; CR (R); Spanish Club; Josten's Leadership Conference; Architecture; Culinary Arts; Massachusetts Institute of Technology; Virginia Tech

PRATER, BRITTANY; DALLAS, PA; DALLAS HS; (JR); Ctznshp Aw; Hi Hnr Roll; Hnr Roll; Nat Hon Sy; Comm Volntr; Peer Tut/Med; Key Club; Prom Com; SADD; Golf (V L); PP Ftbl; Stu Cncl; CR; Junior Leadership Wilkes-Barre; Life Smarts; Sports Management; U of Pittsburgh At Bradford; State U of New York At Cortland

PRESCOTT, HEATHER; COATESVILLE, PA; CTR FOR ART TECH HS-PICKERING; (JR); Hnr Roll; Peer Tut/Med; Red Cr Aide; Emplmnt; SADD; CR (S); Accountant; Job Corps; Delaware Community College

PREZIUSO, NICOLE; MARCUS HOOK, PA; CHICHESTER SR HS; (FR); Hi Hnr Roll; Pres Ac Ftns Aw; Sftball (V); Vllyball (V); First Place National Gymnastics; Competitive Gymnastic for 9 Years; Psychiatrist; Cosmetology; U of Pennsylvania; Florida State U

PRIBELSKY, KATLYN C; BERLIN, PA; (FR); 4H Awd; Hnr Roll; Comm Volntr; 4-H; Chrch Yth Grp; SADD; Bnd; Mch Bnd; Pep Bnd; Track (V); Vllyball (J); Physical Therapist; IUP

PRICE, TYSHAE; PHILADELPHIA, PA; BENJAMIN RUSH MS; (MS); Hnr Roll; St of Mnth; Comm Volntr; Peer Tut/Med; ArtClub; Dbte Team; Emplmnt; Pep Squd; Spch Team; Tchrs Aide; Drl Tm; SP/M/VS; Cl Off (P); Stu Cncl (P); CR (P); Captain of Drill Team; Perform in Yearly Fashion Show (Shades); Master's Degree in Fashion Design; Career in the Arts; U of PA; NYU

PRIMAK, EMILY R; MIFFLINTOWN, PA; JUNIATA HS; (SO); Hnr Roll; MVP; Nat Hon Sy; Nat Mrt Fin; Pres Ac Ftns Aw; St of Mnth; WWAHSS; Spec Olymp Vol; Key Club; Vsity Clb; Bnd; Jzz Bnd; Mch Bnd; Sccr (VJ); Track (V L); Vsy Clb (V L); Editor of Key Club Chapter; Who's Who Among High School Students; Veterinary Science; Zoology; Penn State U; Shippensburg U

PRIOLEAU, ASHLIE; MONROEVILLE, PA; GATEWAY HS; (SO); Hi Hnr Roll; MVP; Perf Att; WWAHSS; Yth Ldrshp Prog; Comm Volntr; Peer Tut/Med; Chrch Yth Grp; DARE; Drma Clb; FBLA; Tchrs Aide; Bskball (V L); Sports Medicine (Major); Science Mathematics (Minor); Carnegie Mellon U

PROCTOR, NIKIA N; PHILADELPHIA, PA; WEST CATHOLIC HS; (JR); Hnr Roll; Perf Att; Pres Sch; WWAHSS; Yth Ldrshp Prog; Comm Volntr; Peer Tut/Med; Emplmnt; SADD; Psychology; Sociology; Millersville U of Pennsylvania; Drexel U

PROPES, ASHLEY; MECHANICSBURG, PA; MECHANICSBURG AREA SR HS; (SO); Hnr Roll; WWAHSS; Spec Olymp Vol; Chrch Yth Grp; Emplmnt; Key Club; Stg Cre; Skiing; Track; Vllyball (V); Cl Off (P); National Art Honor Society; Marine Biology; Psychology; U of Georgia; Messiah College

PRUGH, HANNAH; SAYRE, PA; NOTRE DAME HS; (SO); Hi Hnr Roll; WWAHSS; Hosp Aide; Key Club; Spanish Clb; Chr; Bskball (J); Adopt-A-Highway; SPCA Volunteer

PRUSAK, PETER D; ROULETTE, PA; HEBRON CTR CHRISTIAN SCH; (JR); F Lan Hn Soc; Hi Hnr Roll; Nat Hon Sy; USAA; Valdctrian; WWAHSS; Peer Tut/Med; Chrch Yth Grp; Dbte Team; Drma Clb; Emplmnt; FCA; Quiz Bowl; Wdwrkg Clb; French Clb; Bnd; SP/M/VS; Arch; Bsball; Bskball (V L); Golf; Mar Art; Scr Kpr; Skt Tgt Sh; Skiing (V); Sch Ppr (E); Who's Who Among High School Students; Regional and International Medals for Academics; Religion; Engineering; Liberty U; Virginia Military Academy

PRUTZMAN, KATIE; NEW TRIPOLI, PA; NORTHWESTERN LEHIGH HS; (FR); Hi Hnr Roll; St of Mnth; 4-H; Chrch Yth Grp; Scouts; Vllyball (J); 2002 PMEA District 10 Band Festival; German; Teaching; Middle Berry College in Vermont; Penn State U

PSHAR, JUSTIN M; FREELAND, PA; HAZLETON AREA SD; (SO); Hi Hnr Roll; Perf Att; WWAHSS; American Legion Award; Education (High School) Math or French; Bloomsburg U; Penn State U (Hazleton Campus)

PUGH, JESSICA; CTRL CITY, PA; SHANKSVILLE STONY CREEK S; (FR); Hnr Roll; USAA; Red Cr Aide; Chrch Yth Grp; Chr; Bskball (J); Vllyball (VJ L)

PYROS, ALYSSA G; SHAVERTOWN, PA; DALLAS HS; (FR); Hi Hnr Roll; MVP; Nat Hon Sy; Otst Ac Ach Awd; WWAHSS; Comm Volntr; Chrch Yth Grp; Fld Hky (V L); Sccr (V L); Adv Cncl (R); International Club

QUARTARARO, VINCENT; BATH, PA; BETHLEHEM CATHOLIC HS; (JR); Hnr Roll; Perf Att; Sci Fairs; WWAHSS; Comm Volntr; 4-H; ArtClub; Chess; Key Club; Photog; Ch Chr; Arch; Skt Tgt Sh; Track (V L); Sch Ppr (P); Yrbk (P); Amateur Billiards Player of Pool Hall; Initiative Award at Elementary School; Journalism; Photography; Northampton Community College; Kutztown U

QUATRANI, STEVE; E GREENVILLE, PA; UPPER PERKIOMEN HS; (JR); Hi Hnr Roll; Hnr Roll; Comm Volntr; DARE; Emplmnt; Ftball (V L); Swmg (V L); Military

QUIGG, JARED E C; READING, PA; MUHLENBERG HS; (SR); Ctznshp Aw; Hi Hnr Roll; Hnr Roll; Perf Att; Dbte Team; Mod UN; Quiz Bowl; Golf (V); President of Model UN Club; Academic Challenge; Social Studies Education; Comedian; Mansfield U

QUIGLEY, ALAN G; NEW CASTLE, PA; NESHANNOCK TOWNSHIP SD; (JR); Hnr Roll; Spanish Clb; Bsball (V L); Merit Award-Spanish; Honor Award-Academic; Business Degree; Physical Education; Slippery Rock U; Westminster College-New Wilmington, PA

QUILL JR, RAYMOND C; POTTSTOWN, PA; POTTSTOWN SR HS; (FR); Ctznshp Aw; St of Mnth; Chrch Yth Grp; DARE; Fr of Library; Bnd; Chr; SP/M/VS; Ftball (VJ); Sccr (J); Track (J); Wt Lftg (J); 5th Grade Graduation Award / DARE Award; Bio-Medical Engineer; Study Forensic Science; U of Miami; Florida Metropolitan U

QUINN, AMANDA; MORRISVILLE, PA; PENNSBURY HS EAST; (SR); All Am Sch; Hi Hnr Roll; Hnr Roll; Nat Hon Sy; USAA; WWAHSS; Comm Volntr; Hab For Humty Volntr; Red Cr Aide; ArtClub; Mus Clb; Orch; SP/M/VS; Drawing Hanging on Wall in My School; USAA Award for Art; East Asian Studies; Ursinus College

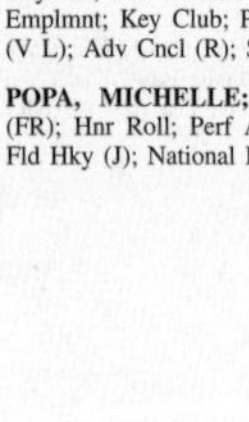

Quinn, Amanda
Pennsbury HS East
Morrisville, PA

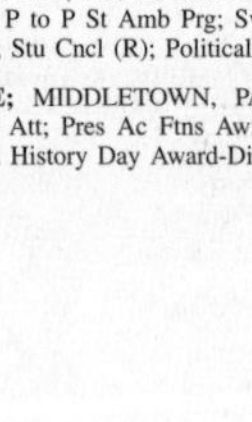

Price, Tyshae
Benjamin Rush MS
Philadelphia, PA

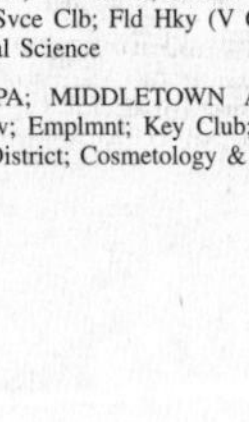

Ponder, Fredrica P
Upper Darby HS
Upper Darby, PA

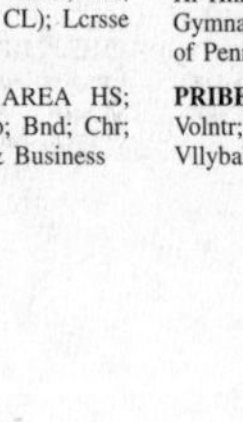

Pollock, Colby M
Pottstown SR HS
Pottstown, PA

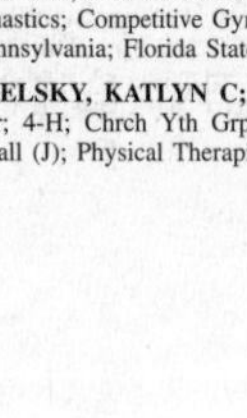

Pollard, Darrel
Perry Traditional AC
Pittsburgh, PA

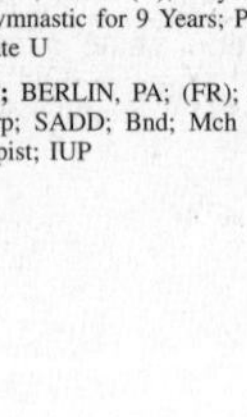

Plummer, Jessica V V
Mastery Charter HS
Philadelphia, PA

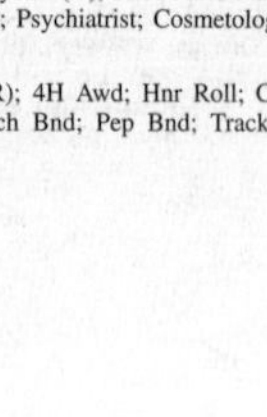

Polachek, Emily C
Dallas SR HS
Dallas, PA

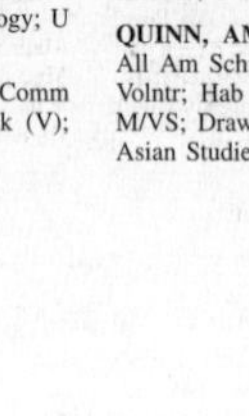

Pomaibo, Nicole
Mc Keesport Area SD
Mc Keesport, PA

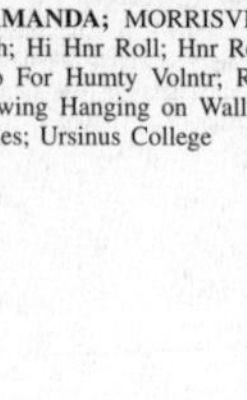

Prater, Brittany
Dallas HS
Dallas, PA

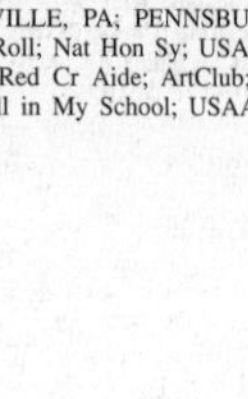

Proctor, Nikia N
West Catholic HS
Philadelphia, PA

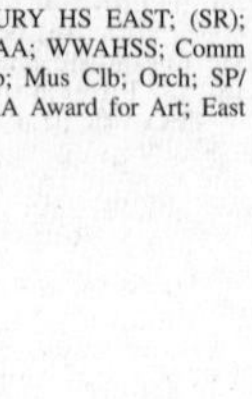

Propes, Ashley
Mechanicsburg Area SR HS
Mechanicsburg, PA

QUIST, J LAUREN; MECHANICSBURG, PA; MECHANICSBURG AREA SR HS; (SO); F Lan Hn Soc; Hnr Roll; Nat Hon Sy; WWAHSS; Hosp Aide; Chrch Yth Grp; Key Club; Orch; Cr Ctry (V); Swmg (J); Track (V); Stu Cncl (R); Pre-Med

RACHKOWSKI, LAUREN; PITTSTON, PA; WYOMING AREA HS; (SR); Hi Hnr Roll; Hnr Roll; Nat Hon Sy; USAA; WWAHSS; Chrch Yth Grp; Emplmnt; FBLA; Scouts; French Clb; Girl Scouts: Gold Award and Silver Award; FBLA-Competition Winner 4th Place At States; Pharmacy; Wilkes U; U of the Sciences

RADACHY, JOSEPH W; HERMITAGE, PA; HICKORY HS; (SO); Hnr Roll; WWAHSS; Comm Volntr; Chrch Yth Grp; Emplmnt; Bnd; Chr; Mch Bnd; Stg Cre; Criminal Justice; Mercyhurst College; Youngstown State, Slippery Rock U

RADOS, KELLIE A; WEST CHESTER, PA; VILLA MARIA AC; (SR); F Lan Hn Soc; Hi Hnr Roll; Nat Hon Sy; Nat Mrt LOC; Sci/Math Olympn; WWAHSS; Comm Volntr; ArtClub; Mth Clb/Tm; MuAlphaTh; Mus Clb; Photog; Orch; Lit Mag (E); Business Leadership Academy; International Business; Saint Joseph's U

RADZAVICH, NATHAN; REYNOLDSVILLE, PA; DUBOIS AREA SD HS; (JR); Hnr Roll; Nat Hon Sy; Comm Volntr; Vsity Clb; Ftball (V L); Wt Lftg (V); USAF

RAEZER, HEATHER; ULSTER, PA; ATHENS AREA HS; (JR); Hi Hnr Roll; Hnr Roll; Emplmnt; Big Brothers/Sisters Program; Youth Apprentice; Elementary Education; Special Education; Mansfield U; Lock Haven U

RAGIN, ANDRIA N; UPPER DARBY, PA; UPPER DARBY HS; (JR); Hi Hnr Roll; Hnr Roll; Nat Hon Sy; St of Mnth; Peer Tut/Med; Dnce; Track (VJ); CR (R); Yrbk (E); Biology Major; Master's Degree; Kutztown U; Drexel U

RAK, EMILY R; ALLENTOWN, PA; WILLIAM ALLEN HS; (JR); Hnr Roll; WWAHSS; Emplmnt; Key Club; ROTC; Dnce; Veterans of Foreign Wars Award-For Outstanding Achievement & Leadership Ability; Interior Design; Rosemont College; Bay Path College

RAKOWSKY, SHANA; PERKASIE, PA; PENNRIDGE HS; (SO); F Lan Hn Soc; Hi Hnr Roll; Hnr Roll; Nat Hon Sy; Pres Ac Ftns Aw; Yth Ldrshp Prog; Comm Volntr; Peer Tut/Med; Emplmnt; Prom Com; Svce Clb; Vsity Clb; Dnce; Bskball (VJC); PP Ftbl (V); Skiing; Sccr (J); Adv Cncl; CR

RALLS, MALLORIE A; MECHANICSBURG, PA; CUMBERLAND VALLEY HS; (JR); Hnr Roll; Nat Hon Sy; WWAHSS; Comm Volntr; Hab For Humty Volntr; Key Club; Bnd; SP/M/VS; HMMS Soccer League; Art Major; Kutztown U; Penn State U

RAMASAMY, DEEPA; MANSFIELD, PA; MANSFIELD JR/SR HS; (JR); Hi Hnr Roll; Kwnis Aw; Nat Hon Sy; Otst Ac Ach Awd; WWAHSS; Yth Ldrshp Prog; Tennis (V); Stu Cncl (T); 2004 & 2005 - Odyssey of the Mind World Finalist; Accepted to PA Governor's School for Health Care; Pre-Med; Susquehanna U; Lycoming College

RAMOS, MICHAEL; EASTON, PA; EASTON AREA HS; (JR); Hnr Roll; Comm Volntr; Computer-Programming; Master's Degree; East Stroudsburg U of Pennsylvania; Kutztown U of Pennsylvania

RAMSER, KRISTEN; GIBSONIA, PA; PINE RICHLAND HS; (JR); Hi Hnr Roll; Hnr Roll; Comm Volntr; ArtClub; Emplmnt; Bskball (L); Track; Art Club; AFS; History; Classics; Allegheny; Duquesne

RANCK, COURTNEY L; MILLERTON, PA; NORTHERN TIOGA SD; (FR); Ctznshp Aw; Hi Hnr Roll; Hnr Roll; Vllyball; Help Mrs. Alexander and Students; Interior Design; Florida U

RANDOLPH, MILDRED; LANSDOWNE, PA; PENN WOOD HS; (SO); Ctznshp Aw; Hi Hnr Roll; Hnr Roll; Nat Mrt Fin; Perf Att; Pres Sch; St of Mnth; Chrch Yth Grp; Dnce; Fld Hky (J L); Del Val Athletic League Athletic Directors Sportsmanship Award; Business (General or Management); Communications; Howard U; U of Pennsylvania

RANERI, SAMUEL; GREENSBURG, PA; HEMPFIELD AREA SR HS; (JR); Hnr Roll; Pres Ac Ftns Aw; WWAHSS; Chrch Yth Grp; Lttrmn Clb; Sccr (V L); Dentist; Kent State U; Duquesne U

RANSOM, ZAKIYA N; EASTON, PA; EASTON AREA HS; (JR); F Lan Hn Soc; Hi Hnr Roll; Hnr Roll; DECA; Emplmnt; FBLA; Chrldg (JC); CR (R); Finance; Business Administration; Pennsylvania State U; Bloomsburg U

RAPACH, FELICIA K; ZION GROVE, PA; HAZLETON AREA HS; (SR); Hnr Roll; Perf Att; St of Mnth; WWAHSS; Comm Volntr; ArtClub; Emplmnt; Key Club; Off Aide; Chr; Who's Who Among High School Students; Key Club Advisory Board; Elementary Education; Alvernia College; Bloomsburg U

RAUB, SARAH E; NEW MILFORD, PA; BLUE RIDGE HS; (JR); Hi Hnr Roll; Hnr Roll; Otst Ac Ach Awd; Pres Sch; Drma Clb; FBLA; Bnd; Chr; Clr Grd; Dnce; Sccr (V L); Stu Cncl; Sch Ppr (R); Dedication Award for Dance; Psychology; Musical Theatre; Mansfield U

RAUCH, ANGIE; GREENSBURG, PA; GREENSBURG SALEM SD; (FR); Gov Hnr Prg; Hi Hnr Roll; Hnr Roll; Nat Hon Sy; Otst Ac Ach Awd; Pres Ac Ftns Aw; Sci Fairs; Comm Volntr; Cmptr Clb; Dbte Team; Emplmnt; Fr of Library; Lib Aide; Mth Clb/Tm; Sci Clb; Tchrs Aide; Chr; Gmnstcs (V); Scr Kpr (V); Swmg (L); Vllyball (V); Stu Cncl (P); CR (P); Sch Ppr (R); Psychology; Homicide Detective; Pittsburgh (U) in Oakland; Harvard U

RAZAWICH, ROBIN; DALLAS, PA; DALLAS HS; (JR); Hi Hnr Roll; Hnr Roll; Nat Hon Sy; WWAHSS; Comm Volntr; Key Club; Prom Com; SADD; Bskball (VJ L); Cr Ctry (V L); Tennis (V L); Track (V L); Stu Cncl (R); All A's in 9th Grade; XC State Champions 2002; Sports Medicine; Education

REA, CHELSEA; BEAVER FALLS, PA; BIG BEAVER FALLS HS; (FR); Hi Hnr Roll; Nat Hon Sy; St of Mnth; WWAHSS; Key Club; SADD; Bnd; Mch Bnd; Scr Kpr (J); Education; Westminster College; Geneva College

READ, REBECCA M; CLEARFIELD, PA; CLEARFIELD AREA HS; (SO); F Lan Hn Soc; Hi Hnr Roll; WWAHSS; Chrch Yth Grp; Key Club; German Clb; Bnd; Chr; Mch Bnd; Orch; Tennis (V); Ytbk (R); Law

REAGLE, JESSICA N; BETHLEHEM, PA; FREEDOM HS; (SR); Hnr Roll; WWAHSS; Chrch Yth Grp; Emplmnt; Scouts; Chr; Paralegal / Psychology; Northampton Community College; Kutztown U

REBARCHAK, ADRIENNE; HAZLETON, PA; HAZLETON AREA HS; (SR); F Lan Hn Soc; Hi Hnr Roll; Nat Hon Sy; WWAHSS; Comm Volntr; Peer Tut/Med; Chrch Yth Grp; Emplmnt; FBLA; Key Club; Cr Ctry (V); Sftball (V CL); Swmg (V L); Adv Cncl; Stu Cncl; Students Against Drug Abuse President; Religious Education Teacher; Secondary Education; Mathematics; Bloomsburg U

REDENSKY, EHCO; SCRANTON, PA; SCRANTON HS; (FR); Hnr Roll; Comm Volntr; Chrch Yth Grp; DARE; Chrldg (J); Criminal Justice; Forensic Scientist; U of Scranton; Keystone U

REED, AMANDA; REYNOLDSVILLE, PA; DUBOIS AREA SD; (FR); 4H Awd; Hab For Humty Volntr; 4-H; Clr Grd

REED, DANA; OAKDALE, PA; WEST ALLEGHENY HS; (JR); Hi Hnr Roll; Kwnis Aw; WWAHSS; Comm Volntr; FTA; Key Club; Prom Com; SADD; Spanish Clb; Bnd; Bskball (V); PP Ftbl (J); Track (V); Wt Lftg (V); Adv Cncl (R); Elementary Education; Edinboro U of Pennsylvania; Slippery Rock U

REED, DANIELLE M; BRADFORD, PA; (JR); Hnr Roll; Nat Hon Sy; St of Mnth; WWAHSS; Comm Volntr; Red Cr Aide; Outdrs Clb; Prom Com; Skiing; CR (V); Volunteer for Salvation Army; Elementary Education; Criminal Justice; Saint Bonaventure U; Edinboro U

REED, STEFANI; JERSEY SHORE, PA; JERSEY SHORE AREA SR HS; (FR); Ctznshp Aw; Hi Hnr Roll; Hnr Roll; Perf Att; DARE; Key Club; Tennis (J); Wrstlg; CR (R); Primatology; Interior Design; Ball State U; Penn State

REEDER, KEVIN M; POTTSTOWN, PA; POTTSGROVE SR HS; (FR); Golf (J); Engineering; Business; U of Pennsylvania; Penn State

REESE, JESSICA; CAMP HILL, PA; CUMBERLAND VALLEY HS; (JR); Duke TS; F Lan Hn Soc; Hi Hnr Roll; Kwnis Aw; Nat Hon Sy; Nat Mrt LOC; Sci/Math Olympn; WWAHSS; Yth Ldrshp Prog; Comm Volntr; Peer Tut/Med; Emplmnt; Key Club; Mod UN; Schol Bwl; Svce Clb; Chr; Orch; Stg Cre; Bskball (L); Tennis (J L); Odyssey of the Mind; Drug & Alcohol Youth Advisory Board; Bio Chemistry; Chemistry; Swarthmore; U of Pennsylvania

REGER, ERIC; MANOR, PA; HEMPFIELD AREA HS; (SR); Ctznshp Aw; F Lan Hn Soc; Hi Hnr Roll; Hnr Roll; Pres Ac Ftns Aw; USAA; WWAHSS; Comm Volntr; Chrch Yth Grp; Emplmnt; Scouts; French Clb; Bsball (J); Cr Ctry (V CL); Track (V L); Designated As "Scholar Athlete"; Hershey Track & Field National Finisher; Environmental Engineering; California U of Pennsylvania; U of Pittsburgh

REGNOSKY, HEATHER; DALLAS, PA; DALLAS HS; (JR); Hi Hnr Roll; Hnr Roll; Nat Hon Sy; Chrch Yth Grp; Drma Clb; Emplmnt; Key Club; Mus Clb; Foreign Clb; Chr; SP/M/VS; District Chorus; German Award; Elementary Education; Music

REICHARD, HEATHER; TRANSFER, PA; REYNOLDS HS; (SR); Ctznshp Aw; Hnr Roll; Kwnis Aw; WWAHSS; Comm Volntr; Hab For Humty Volntr; Peer Tut/Med; ArtClub; Chrch Yth Grp; Emplmnt; Key Club; Prom Com; Chr; Ch Chr; Flg Crps; Mch Bnd; Adv Cncl (R); Criminal Justice; Communications; Youngstown State U

REICHARD, MARY ANN; GREENSBURG, PA; GREENSBURG SALEM SD HS; (JR); Hnr Roll; MVP; Chrch Yth Grp; Emplmnt; Chr; Ch Chr; Bskball (V); CR (S); NSDUH (United States Public Health Survey); MVP At Work Twice (West Penn Foods); Medical Field (Paramedic); Business Administrations; Slippery Rock (PA); Seton Hill (Greensburg, PA)

REID, MEAGHAN L; PIPERSVILLE, PA; C.B. EAST HS; (JR); F Lan Hn Soc; Hi Hnr Roll; Kwnis Aw; Nat Hon Sy; Sci Fairs; WWAHSS; Yth Ldrshp Prog; Comm Volntr; Hosp Aide; Drma Clb; Emplmnt; Key Club; Chr; SP/M/VS; Stg Cre; Bskball (J); Cr Ctry (J); Adv Cncl (T); Stu Cncl (S); Yrbk (E); Treasurer for NHS; Treasurer for Key Club; Pre-Med; Biology

REID, TIFFANY F L; PHILADELPHIA, PA; (SR); Hi Hnr Roll; Peer Tut/Med; Chess; SP/M/VS; Bskball (V); Dean's List; Accountant; U of Maryland Eastern Shore; East Carolina

REIGHARD, NICHOLAS J; JOHNSTOWN, PA; CONEMAUGH VALLEY JR/SR HS; (JR); Ctznshp Aw; Hi Hnr Roll; Nat Hon Sy; Perf Att; St of Mnth; Comm Volntr; Quiz Bowl; Schol Bwl; Spanish Clb; Ch Chr; Sch Ppr (R, P); Yrbk (R, P); Newspapers in Education Banquet; Member of the Challenge Program; Secondary Education; Foreign Language; Penn State U; St Francis U

REILLY, THOMAS W; SPRINGFIELD, PA; MONSIGNOR BONNER HS; (JR); Hnr Roll; Cr Ctry (J); Cr Ct Ski (J); Track (V CL); Elementary Education; Occupational Therapy; Lehigh U; LaSalle U

REILLY JR, PATRICK F J; MOSCOW, PA; NORTH POCONO HS; (FR); Hi Hnr Roll; Hnr Roll; Sci Fairs; St of Mnth; Comm Volntr; Peer Tut/Med; FBLA; Mus Clb; Sci Clb; SADD; Bnd; Jzz Bnd; Mch Bnd; Orch; Track (J); Junior Academy of Science; History Club; Architectural Engineering; Engineering; U of Notre Dame; Duke U

REIMEL, ERIN N; EPHRATA, PA; EPHRATA HS; (SR); Hi Hnr Roll; Hnr Roll; MVP; Nat Hon Sy; WWAHSS; Yth Ldrshp Prog; Comm Volntr; Peer Tut/Med; Chrch Yth Grp; Emplmnt; Lib Aide; Tchrs Aide; Vsity Clb; Fld Hky (J); Lcrsse (V CL); Spanish Education; Eastern U

REINERT, VIRGINIA G; DALLAS, PA; DALLAS HS; (FR); Hi Hnr Roll; Otst Ac Ach Awd; Pres Ac Ftns Aw; Sci Fairs; Comm Volntr; Chrch Yth Grp; Key Club; Mus Clb; Bnd; Chr; Ch Chr; Dnce; Cr Ctry (J); Track (J); Stu Cncl (R); Lit Mag (R); Company 1 Member of Ballet Northeast; SC Member of the Choral Society of Northeast PA; Secondary Education Ph.D; Archaeology

REINHARDT, DAVID; ALTOONA, PA; BISHOP GUILFOYLE HS; (SO); Hi Hnr Roll; Hnr Roll; Comm Volntr; Emplmnt; SADD; Vsity Clb; Clb; Cr Ctry (V); Ice Hky (V L); Vsy Clb (V L); Stu Cncl (R); Military Officer; Doctor; West Point Military Academy; Naval Academy

REINHART, CRYSTAL; HAMBURG, PA; HAMBURG HS; (FR); Hi Hnr Roll; Hnr Roll; MVP; Comm Volntr; Peer Tut/Med; Chrch Yth Grp; DARE; Outdrs Clb; GAA (J); Sftball (J); Wildlife Management; Pennsylvania State U; Michigan State U

REISIG, NICK; RICHBORO, PA; COUNCIL ROCK HS NORTH; (FR); Ctznshp Aw; Hi Hnr Roll; Hnr Roll; MVP; Otst Ac Ach Awd; Perf Att; Pres Ac Ftns Aw; St of Mnth; Comm Volntr; Bskball (J); Ftball (J); Vllyball (J); Wt Lftg (J); Scholar Athlete Award (8th Grade); Broadcasting; Teaching German or History; Villanova U; Saint Joseph's U

REITENBACH, SARA; HARRISBURG, PA; CTRL DAUPHIN SD; (FR); Hnr Roll; Nat Hon Sy; Sci Fairs; Peer Tut/Med; ArtClub; Chrch Yth Grp; Emplmnt; Spanish Clb; Stg Cre; Bskball; Graphic Arts/Design

REITH, KENDRA L; GALETON, PA; GALETON AREA SD; (SR); Hi Hnr Roll; Hnr Roll; Nat Hon Sy; St of Mnth; WWAHSS; ArtClub; Emplmnt; Prom Com; Schol Bwl; Dnce; Chrldg (VJC); Cl Off (P); Stu Cncl (T); National Honor Society; Communications Media; Indiana U of Pennsylvania

RENALDI, CHRISTOPHER A; PITTSBURGH, PA; PLUM SR HS; (JR); Hnr Roll; Nat Hon Sy; Perf Att; Emplmnt; Scouts; Acpl Chr; Chr; Stu Cncl (R); Lead Singer for a Band; Music Teacher; U of Pittsburgh; Pennsylvania State U

RENNICK, HEIDI L; APOLLO, PA; GREATER WORKS AC; (SR); Hi Hnr Roll; Hnr Roll; Sci Fairs; WWAHSS; Comm Volntr; Chrch Yth Grp; Drma Clb; Emplmnt; Prom Com; Tchrs Aide; Stg Cre; Yrbk (E); Creative Writing; Early Childhood Education; Journalism; Oral Roberts U

RENSHAW, JEFFREY; MECHANICSBURG, PA; MECHANICSBURG AREA SR HS; (SR); F Lan Hn Soc; Hnr Roll; Kwnis Aw; Nat Hon Sy; Sci/Math Olympn; St of Mnth; WWAHSS; Peer Tut/Med; Chess; Emplmnt; HO'Br Yth Ldrshp; Key Club; Mth Clb/Tm; Scouts; Bnd; Mch Bnd; Orch; Stg Cre; Eagle Scout; Economics; Boston College

RENTSCHLER, LAURA; HAMBURG, PA; KINGS AC; (SO); Hi Hnr Roll; Hnr Roll; Perf Att; Comm Volntr; Emplmnt; Orch; Bskball (V); Scr Kpr (VJ); Track (V); Class Chaplain; Music/Music Therapy; English; Messiah, Slippery Rock; York

REPASH, KATELYN; HELLERTOWN, PA; SAUCON VALLEY HS; (SO); All Am Sch; Hi Hnr Roll; Nat Hon Sy; Nat Ldrshp Svc; Otst Ac Ach Awd; Pres Sch; USAA; WWAHSS; Yth Ldrshp Prog; Comm Volntr; ArtClub; Mus Clb; NYLC; Outdrs Clb; P to P St Amb Prg; Bnd; Fld Hky (J); Johns Hopkins Youth Scholar; National Society of High School Scholars; Environmental Law; Yale U; Boston U

RESTO, JESSICA; NEW HOLLAND, PA; GARDEN SPOT HS; (MS); Hosp Aide; DARE; Acpl Chr; Chr; Dnce; Chrldg (J); President's Education Awards Program; NYU

Reinhart, Crystal
Hamburg HS
Hamburg, PA

Reichard, Mary Ann
Greensburg Salem SD HS
Greensburg, PA

Reger, Eric
Hempfield Area HS
Manor, PA

National
Honor Roll
Spring 2005

Rapach, Felicia K
Hazleton Area HS
Zion Grove, PA

Reid, Tiffany F L
Philadelphia, PA

Repash, Katelyn
Saucon Valley HS
Hellertown, PA

RETTER, JASON A; APOLLO, PA; KISKI AROA HS; (JR); Hi Hnr Roll; Hnr Roll; Kwnis Aw; Perf Att; Pres Ac Ftns Aw; Sci Fairs; WWAHSS; Comm Volntr; Spec Olymp Vol; Emplmnt; Key Club; Lttrmn Clb; Mus Clb; Pep Squd; SADD; Vsity Clb; Bnd; Bsball (VJCL); Ftball (VJCL); Track (J); Vsy Clb (VJ); Wt Lftg (VJ); Stu Cncl; CR; Sch Ppr (R); Pittsburgh Tigers AAU Baseball; American Legion Baseball Team; Education-Coaching; Administration; United States Military Academy; United States Naval Academy

RETZENA, ALYSSA M; SHAVERTOWN, PA; DALLAS HS; (JR); Hi Hnr Roll; Hnr Roll; Nat Hon Sy; Comm Volntr; Red Cr Aide; FBLA; Key Club; Prom Com; Fld Hky (J); Swmg (V L); Track (V L); Stu Cncl (R); Charter Member of Mini-Thon; Architecture; Interior Architecture; Penn State Main Campus; St Leo U

REX, ALYSSA; COPLAY, PA; WHITEHALL HS; (SO); Hi Hnr Roll; MVP; Perf Att; Yth Ldrshp Prog; Comm Volntr; Fld Hky (V); Cl Off (S); Yrbk (E); Genetics

REYNOLDS, LINDSEY; WATSONTOWN, PA; WARRIOR RUN SD HS; (JR); Hi Hnr Roll; Nat Hon Sy; St of Mnth; WWAHSS; Emplmnt; Prom Com; Vsity Clb; Spanish Clb; Bskball (V L); Stu Cncl (R); Who's Who Among American High School Students; Pre Law; PSU

RHOADS, RACHEL M; CARLISLE, PA; CUMBERLAND VALLEY HS; (JR); Hi Hnr Roll; WWAHSS; Comm Volntr; Red Cr Aide; ArtClub; Chrch Yth Grp; Key Club; Sci Clb; Spanish Clb; Bskball (L); Stu Cncl (R); CR (R); National AA Honor Society Secretary; Clay Club Treasurer; Business; Teaching; Penn State Main Campus; U of Maryland

RHODES, BIANCA D; POTTSTOWN, PA; POTTSTOWN SR HS; (FR); Hnr Roll; I Intend to Go to Work and Be Successful.; I Want to Major in Modeling; To Be a Model; Nursing; U of Virginia; U of Southern California

RHODES, CRYSTAL D; GREENSBURG, PA; GREENSBURG SALEM HS; (SO); Hnr Roll; Nat Hon Sy; Perf Att; Scouts; Chr; CR (P); Seton Hill U; Robert Morris U

RHODES, KHALIA P; NORRISTOWN, PA; NORRISTOWN AREA HS; (SR); Gov Hnr Prg; Hnr Roll; Nat Mrt Semif; WWAHSS; Comm Volntr; Chrch Yth Grp; Emplmnt; Chr; Ch Chr; Orch; Track (V); Stu Cncl (R); Who's Who Among American High School Students; Pennsylvania Governor's School of Excellence; Forensic Science; Cedar Crest College; U of Pittsburgh

RHYMER, CHRISTOPHER S; POTTSTOWN, PA; OWEN J ROBERTS HS; (SR); Hi Hnr Roll; Hnr Roll; Chess; Chess Club; Engineering Sciences; Kutztown U; Montgomery County Community College

RICHARD, HILLARY A; WEXFORD, PA; NORTH ALLEGHENY HS; (FR); Ctznshp Aw; Hnr Roll; Nat Hon Sy; Otst Ac Ach Awd; WWAHSS; Comm Volntr; Key Club; Prom Com; Chr; Fld Hky (J); Ecology; Psychology; Brown U

RICHARDS, HANNAH; MIFFLINBURG, PA; MIFFLINBURG AREA HS; (JR); Hnr Roll; Nat Hon Sy; Pres Ac Ftns Aw; WWAHSS; Comm Volntr; Red Cr Aide; Chrch Yth Grp; Key Club; Prom Com; Svce Clb; Spanish Clb; Chr; SP/M/VS; Fld Hky (V L); Gmnstcs (V); Skiing (V); United Christian Teens Member; BSN; Missionary

RICHARDS, KATIE J; SHAMOKIN, PA; SUNBURY CHRISTIAN AC; (SO); MVP; Comm Volntr; Chrch Yth Grp; Tchrs Aide; Bskball (V L); Sccr (V L); Track (V); Yrbk (R, P); Student Leader for Church Youth Group; History; Politics; Messiah College; Bloomsburg U

RICHARDSON, CEPHUS; CHESTER, PA; CHESTER HS; (JR); Hnr Roll; Kwnis Aw; WWAHSS; Yth Ldrshp Prog; Comm Volntr; Peer Tut/Med; Dbte Team; Key Club; Mus Clb; Sci Clb; Bnd; Chr; SP/M/VS; Cl Off (P); Stu Cncl (P, V); CR (R); Sch Ppr (R, P); Yrbk (P); Key Club - Sergeant at Arms / 11th Grade; Treasurer of the Science Academy -11th Grade; Music; Political Science; Cheyney University

RICHARDSON, MATTHEW J; KINGSTON, PA; WYOMING VALLEY WEST HS; (JR); F Lan Hn Soc; Hi Hnr Roll; Nat Sci Aw; Sci Fairs; Emplmnt; Mus Clb; Latin Clb; Bnd; Computer Programming; Computer Engineering; Dickinson College; Pennsylvania State U

RICHMOND, MONIKE; HARRISBURG, PA; CTRL DAUPHIN EAST HS; (JR); Hi Hnr Roll; Yth Ldrshp Prog; Comm Volntr; Chrch Yth Grp; Emplmnt; Jr Ach; Ch Chr; Meteorologist; Elementary School Teacher; Oakwood Union College; Columbia Union College

RICKARDS, ZACHARY; EAST STROUDSBURG, PA; EAST STROUDSBURG HS SOUTH; (FR); Ctznshp Aw; Hi Hnr Roll; MVP; Sci/Math Olympn; St of Mnth; Yth Ldrshp Prog; Comm Volntr; Peer Tut/Med; Spec Olymp Vol; Chrch Yth Grp; FCA; Mth Clb/Tm; Tchrs Aide; Chr; SP/M/VS; Stg Cre; Bskball (J); Ftball (J); American Legion Leadership Award; Chris Taylor Award; Math Teacher; Basketball Coach

RIGLIN, JACOB; CLEARFIELD, PA; CLEARFIELD AREA SD; (SO); Hi Hnr Roll; Hnr Roll; Nat Hon Sy; WWAHSS; Comm Volntr; Chrch Yth Grp; Lttrmn Clb; Scouts; Vsity Clb; Ftball (VJ); Wrstlg (V)

RILEY, AMANDA; BEAVER FALLS, PA; BIG BEAVER FALLS SR HS; (JR); Hi Hnr Roll; Hnr Roll; Nat Hon Sy; Otst Ac Ach Awd; Perf Att; St of Mnth; WWAHSS; ArtClub; FBLA; Key Club; SADD; Spanish Clb; Dnce; Drl Tm; Bskball (VJ); PP Ftbl (VJ); High Honor Roll; Perfect Attendance; Journalism; Fashion Merchandising

RILEY, JENNIFER; NEW FREEPORT, PA; WEST GREENE SR HS; (JR); Hi Hnr Roll; Hnr Roll; WWAHSS; Chrch Yth Grp; Ntl FFA; Quill & Scroll; SADD; Spanish Clb; Bskball (J); Chrldg (V); Scr Kpr (2 yr); Vllyball (2 yr); Cl Off (P, V); Stu Cncl (R); Lit Mag (E, P); Sch Ppr (E, P); Leo / Pulse Club / Miss Jacktown Fair Contestant for 2 Years; An -A- Art Student; Psychology; Lawyer or Teacher; Waynesburg College; West Virginia U

RILEY, REBECCA; GREENVILLE, PA; GREENVILLE SR HS; (SR); Jr Rot; Yth Ldrshp Prog; Comm Volntr; Peer Tut/Med; Chrch Yth Grp; Lttrmn Clb; Photog; Vsity Clb; Chr; Stg Cre; Chrldg (V L); Track (V L); Vsy Clb (V L); Sch Ppr (R); RYLA Leadership Program; W.I.N.G. Women Inspiring the Next Generation; Thiel (Accepted) Psychology; Religion; Thiel College (Accepted); Geneva College (Accepted)

RINEHIMER, LAURA; WILKES BARRE, PA; HANOVER AREA JR/SR HS; (FR); Hi Hnr Roll; Nat Hon Sy; Otst Ac Ach Awd; Peer Tut/Med; Key Club; Bnd; Chr; Ch Chr; Mch Bnd; Fld Hky (V L); Scr Kpr (VJ); Sccr (V L); Swmg (V L); Pennsylvania Junior Academy of Science Regional First Place Award; Pennsylvania Junior Academy of Science 2nd Place States Award; Elementary Education; Psychology; Misericordia College; Wesleyan U

RIOS, MARTIN; STROUDSBURG, PA; STROUDSBURG HS; (JR); Hi Hnr Roll; Hnr Roll; Nat Hon Sy; Peer Tut/Med; Chess; Key Club; Mod UN; Spanish Clb; Track (J); Treasurer of Bowling Club; Quest Scholar Semi-Finalist; Political Science and Government; JD in Law; Dickinson College; Vassar College

RISH, JIM; CAMP HILL, PA; CAMP HILL SD HS; (FR); Hnr Roll; Perf Att; Sci Fairs; Sci/Math Olympn; Bnd; Bsball (V); Ice Hky (V); Sccr (J); Architecture; Civil Engineering; U of Wisconsin; Pennsylvania State U

RITCHIE, DAN; UPPER DARBY, PA; UPPER DARBY HS; (JR); Hi Hnr Roll; Hnr Roll; Nat Hon Sy; Otst Ac Ach Awd; Comm Volntr; Hab For Humty Volntr; Red Cr Aide; ArtClub; DARE; Emplmnt; FTA; Prom Com; Scouts; SADD; Jzz Bnd; Lcrsse (J); CR (R); National Art Honor Society/ Student Achievement Award/1st Prize Drawing 7th Congressional District Art Competition By Curt Weldon; Art Major-BA, Teaching Degree (Art); Computer Graphics, Cartoon, Drawing; Art Institute of Philadelphia; Ringling School of Art and Design

RITENOUR, CASEY; LATROBE, PA; GREATER LATROBE HS; (SR); Hi Hnr Roll; Hnr Roll; WWAHSS; Comm Volntr; Spec Olymp Vol; Emplmnt; Key Club; Lttrmn Clb; Photog; Spanish Clb; Vllyball (V L); Presidential Volunteer Service Award; Outdoor Odyssey Leadership Academy Graduate; Physical Therapy; U of Pittsburgh At Johnstown

RIVERA, ALEXEI M; HAZLETON, PA; HAZLETON AREA HS; (SO); Hnr Roll; Otst Ac Ach Awd; Comm Volntr; Foreign Clb; Ftball (J); Criminal Law; Psychology; Pennsylvania State; Bloomsburg U

RIVERA, MARA; PHILADELPHIA, PA; EDISON HS; (JR); Hnr Roll; Emplmnt; Bachelor's Degree; Community College; Temple

RIVERS, DANIELLE M; PHILADELPHIA, PA; MURRELL DOBBINS AVTS; (SO); Ctznshp Aw; Hnr Roll; St of Mnth; Comm Volntr; FBLA; Medical Administration; Business Administration; Penn State U

RIZVI, AFSHAN; MECHANICSBURG, PA; CUMBERLAND VALLEY HS; (SR); F Lan Hn Soc; Hnr Roll; Nat Hon Sy; Sci/Math Olympn; WWAHSS; ArtClub; Key Club; Quiz Bowl; Sci Clb; Svce Clb; Spanish Clb; National Art Honor Society; Biochemistry Major; Pediatrician-Profession (Pre-Med); Carnegie Mellon U (Attending in Fall 2005)

ROACH, KYLIE; DUNCANSVILLE, PA; HOLLIDAYSBURG SR HS; (SR); Hi Hnr Roll; Hnr Roll; Nat Hon Sy; WWAHSS; Emplmnt; Jr Ach; Off Aide; Dnce; National Honor Society; Nursing/Nurse Anesthetist; Anesthesiology; Mount Aloysius College

ROACH, TIMOTHY; DOYLESTOWN, PA; CTRL BUCKS HS EAST; (JR); Hi Hnr Roll; Hnr Roll; Nat Hon Sy; Nat Mrt LOC; Otst Ac Ach Awd; Perf Att; Dbte Team; Emplmnt; Key Club; Photog; Bskball (VJ L); Ftball (V); Club Basketball / Crew / Lacrosse; Biology / Biochemistry; Pre-Med; U of Pittsburgh

ROBERTS, DEARDISS S; POTTSTOWN, PA; PINE FORGE AC; Comm Volntr; Chrch Yth Grp; Tchrs Aide; U of Maryland Eastern Shore; LaSierra U

ROBERTS, JOCELYN; ERIE, PA; WILSON MS; (MS); Hnr Roll; CARE; Sch Ppr (R); Yrbk (R); 1st Place in Brain Bowl Competition; Law Degree; Harvard Law

ROBINETT, KATHERINE; STATE COLLEGE, PA; STATE COLLEGE SOUTH HS; (SO); Yrbk (E, P); Psychology; Psychiatry; Penn State U; Cornell U

ROBINSON, BRITTANY; PITTSBURGH, PA; PITTSBURGH SD; (JR); Hi Hnr Roll; Hnr Roll; Perf Att; St of Mnth; Stg Cre; Sftball (L); Forensics (Chemistry); Slippery Rock U

ROBINSON, JASON B; NEWVILLE, PA; BIG SPRING SD; (SR); Ctznshp Aw; Hnr Roll; Chrch Yth Grp; DARE; SADD; Sccr (L); Le Cordon Bleu Culinary Program

ROBINSON, MARCUS; CARMICHAELS, PA; CARMICHAELS AREA JR/SR HS; (FR); Hi Hnr Roll; Hnr Roll; Comm Volntr; Bsball (VJ); Bskball (J); Wt Lftg; Physical Therapy; Sports Medicine; Penn State U; West Virginia U

ROBINSON, SAMANTHA G; COLLEGEVILLE, PA; KOINONIA AC; (SO); F Lan Hn Soc; Hi Hnr Roll; Hnr Roll; Nat Sci Aw; Otst Ac Ach Awd; Yth Ldrshp Prog; Hab For Humty Volntr; Chrch Yth Grp; Emplmnt; Key Club; Svce Clb; Chr; Dnce; SP/M/VS; Swmg (VJ); Stu Cncl (R); Sch Ppr (R); History; Finance; Boston College; Washington College (MD)

ROBINSON, TIARA; READING, PA; READING HS; (JR); Perf Att; St of Mnth; Comm Volntr; Spec Olymp Vol; Chrch Yth Grp; Emplmnt; Key Club; Ch Chr; Drl Tm; Business Management; Morris Brown College; Georgia State U

ROBSON, BRIAN; ERIE, PA; MC DOWELL INT HS; (SO); Nat Hon Sy; WWAHSS; Bsball (J L); Computer Technology; North Carolina U; U of Nevada Las Vegas

ROCCA, VANESSA; WEXFORD, PA; NORTH ALLEGHENY HS; (SR); Hnr Roll; MVP; Otst Ac Ach Awd; Pres Ac Ftns Aw; Spec Olymp Vol; DECA; Vsity Clb; Gmnstcs (V); CR (R); Scholar Athlete, Guardian, Life Girls Going Places National Finalist; Architecture; Arizona State College

ROCKWELL, TIFFANY A; EAST FREEDOM, PA; CTRL; (JR); Hnr Roll; Hosp Aide; Chr

RODGERS, EMILY G; PALMERTON, PA; CARBON CTY AVTS; (JR); Hi Hnr Roll; Comm Volntr; ArtClub; DECA; Massage Therapist; Pastry Chef; Lehigh Valley College; Northampton Community College

RODKEY, ADAM; JOHNSTOWN, PA; FOREST HILLS SD; (SO); Hi Hnr Roll; Hnr Roll; Otst Ac Ach Awd; Chrch Yth Grp; Emplmnt; Wdwrkg Clb; Ftball (J); Vllyball (J); Pharmacy; Chemistry; U of Pittsburgh; Johns Hopkins U

RODRIGUEZ, DESIREE M; WERNERSVILLE, PA; CONRAD WEISER HS; (JR); Ctznshp Aw; Hnr Roll; St of Mnth; WWAHSS; Comm Volntr; Peer Tut/Med; Emplmnt; Ntl FFA; Dnce; Track (V L); Cosmetology; Fashion Design; Empire Beauty School; Reading Area Community College

RODRIGUEZ, JESSICA A; HARRISBURG, PA; CTRL DAUPHIN HS; (SR); Hi Hnr Roll; Hnr Roll; Nat Hon Sy; Peer Tut/Med; Chrch Yth Grp; Emplmnt; Key Club; Tchrs Aide; Spanish Clb; Chr; SP/M/VS; Sch Ppr (R); Yrbk (E); Mock Trial; Christians in Action; Education-Elementary; Religious Studies; Elizabethtown College; Messiah College

RODRIGUEZ, LUIGI; PHILADELPHIA, PA; KENSINGTON HS; (SR); Hnr Roll; Otst Ac Ach Awd; Comm Volntr; Peer Tut/Med; Chrch Yth Grp; Drm Mjr; Business Education; Penn State; LaSalle U

RODRIGUEZ, MARIAH E; PHILADELPHIA, PA; (MS); Ctznshp Aw; Hnr Roll; St of Mnth; DARE; Jr Ach; Mus Clb; Scouts; Chr; Dnce; Bsball; Chrldg; Sftball; Yrbk (P); Community Sports-Soccer, Basketball; Volunteer Community Events; Paralegal; Cosmetologist; Temple U

RODRIGUEZ, MELISSA M; HARRISBURG, PA; CTRL DAUPHIN EAST HS; (FR); Ctznshp Aw; Hnr Roll; Otst Ac Ach Awd; Perf Att; Sci Fairs; St of Mnth; DARE; FTA; P to P St Amb Prg; Dnce; Stu Cncl (P); Law (Criminal); Education; Harrisburg Area Community College; Penn State U

RODRIGUEZ, NORA; PHILADELPHIA, PA; CENTRAL HS; (SR); Hnr Roll; Perf Att; St of Mnth; Comm Volntr; Hab For Humty Volntr; Red Cr Aide; Chrch Yth Grp; Off Aide; Bskball (J); Culinary Arts; Culinary Institute of America; Johnson & Wales U

RODRIGUEZ, YESSENIA; EASTON, PA; EASTON AREA SR HS; (FR); Ctznshp Aw; Hnr Roll; MVP; Otst Ac Ach Awd; Perf Att; St of Mnth; WWAHSS; ArtClub; Chrch Yth Grp; Cmptr Clb; Key Club; Mus Clb; Pep Squd; Photog; Scouts; Acpl Chr; Clr Grd; Dnce; Drl Tm; Bskball (V); Started Own Dance Team; Singer; Dancer; Performing Art Colleges

RODRIGUEZ, YOLANDA; READING, PA; READING HS; (FR); Ctznshp Aw; Hnr Roll; Otst Ac Ach Awd; Perf Att; St of Mnth; Talent Search / Club College; RHS Honors Pass; Pediatrician; Medical Degree; Philadelphia U; North Carolina U

ROGATO, CHRISTINA; MOSCOW, PA; NORTH POCONO HS; (FR); Hi Hnr Roll; Hnr Roll; Bnd; Mch Bnd; Pep Bnd; Track (J); Vllyball (J)

ROLLINS, RYAN; PHILADELPHIA, PA; ROXBOROUGH HS; (FR); WWAHSS; Ntl Beta Clb; Mentally Gifted Program; Graphic Designer; Drexel U

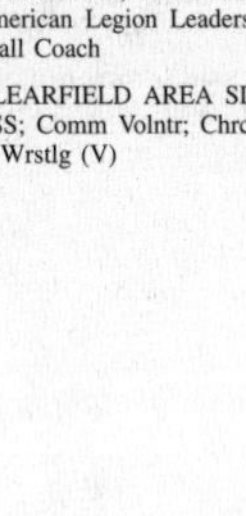

Rodriguez, Luigi
Kensington HS
Philadelphia, PA

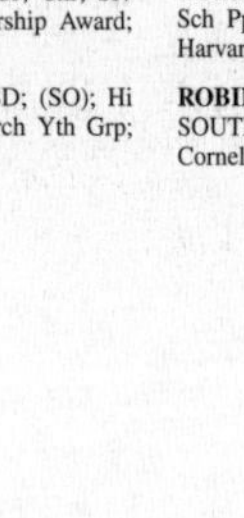

Robinson, Jason B
Big Spring SD
Newville, PA

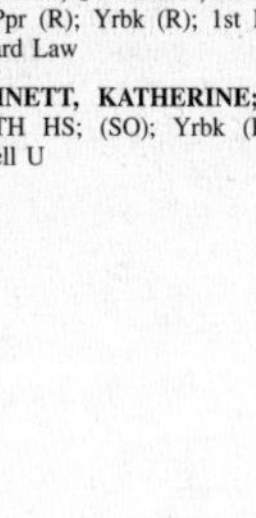

Ritchie, Dan
Upper Darby HS
Upper Darby, PA

National
Honor Roll
Spring 2005

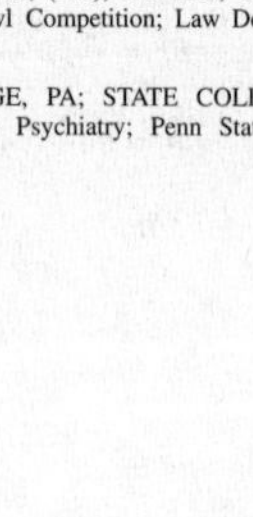

Richmond, Monike
Central Dauphin East HS
Harrisburg, PA

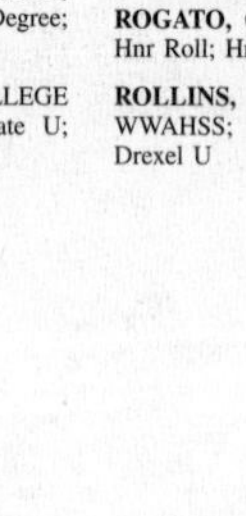

Rodgers, Emily G
Carbon Cty AVTS
Palmerton, PA

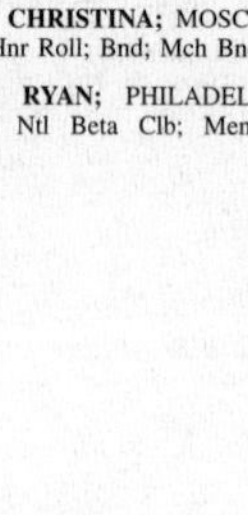

Rodriguez, Yolanda
Reading HS
Reading, PA

ROLON, JACOB G; COLMAR, PA; NORTH PENN HS; (JR); Hnr Roll; WWAHSS; Spec Olymp Vol; Key Club; Stu Cncl (T, R); Family Medicine; Temple U

ROMAN, STEPH M; CAIRNBROOK, PA; SHADE-CENTRAL CITY SD; (SO); Ctznshp Aw; Hi Hnr Roll; Hnr Roll; Nat Hon Sy; WWAHSS; Chrch Yth Grp; Drma Clb; Lttrmn Clb; Vsity Clb; Spanish Clb; SP/M/VS; Bskball (V); Sftball (V); Vllyball (VJ L); CR; Fashion Designing; Teaching; Shippensburg U; West Virginia U

ROMOLINI, FAITH; WARRINGTON, PA; CTRL BUCKS HS SOUTH; (JR); Hi Hnr Roll; Nat Hon Sy; WWAHSS; Comm Volntr; Peer Tut/Med; Spec Olymp Vol; Key Club; Stu Cncl (R); Community Service; Marketing; Villanova U; St. Joseph's U

ROONEY, AMANDA M; BEAVER FALLS, PA; BLACKHAWK HS; (FR); Hi Hnr Roll; Otst Ac Ach Awd; WWAHSS; Chrch Yth Grp; Key Club; Spanish Clb; Bskball (V); Chrldg (L); Sch Ppr; Yrbk (E, R, P); Veterinary Medicine; Notre Dame

ROOS, AUBREY; ALLENTOWN, PA; SALISBURY HS; (JR); Hi Hnr Roll; Hnr Roll; Nat Hon Sy; Key Club; Sccr; National Honor Society; Health Care; Temple; Penn State U

ROSARIO, ANTHONY; UPPER DARBY, PA; UPPER DARBY HS; (JR); Hi Hnr Roll; Hnr Roll; Pre-Medicine; Biology; U of the Sciences Philadelphia; West Chester U

ROSATI, BENJAMIN A; OAKDALE, PA; SOUTH FAYETTE TOWNSHIP HS; (FR); Hi Hnr Roll; Hnr Roll; Nat Hon Sy; Perf Att; Pres Sch; Emplmnt; FBLA; Scouts; Bnd; Jzz Bnd; Bskball (J); Sccr (J); Track (J); U S American Legion Award; Electrical Engineering; Research and Development; Carnegie Mellon; U of Pittsburgh

ROSATI, CHRISTINA; MC DONALD, PA; BISHOP CANEVIN HS; (SO); Ctznshp Aw; Hi Hnr Roll; Otst Ac Ach Awd; Sci Fairs; Peer Tut/Med; Chrch Yth Grp; FBLA; P to P St Amb Prg; Quiz Bowl; Svce Clb; Dnce; Sftball (V); Adv Cncl; Sch Ppr (R); Regional Treasurer - FBLA; Alternate Quiz Bowl Team; Chemistry; Chemical Engineering; Duke; Villanova U

ROSATO, HEATHER; HAZLETON, PA; BISHOP HAFEY HS; (SO); F Lan Hn Soc; Hi Hnr Roll; Hnr Roll; Perf Att; WWAHSS; Comm Volntr; Hosp Aide; Chrch Yth Grp; Drma Clb; Mus Clb; Chr; Stg Cre; Bskball (VJ); Stu Cncl (R); Elementary / Special Education; Real Estate; Penn State U

ROSE, ANTHONY R; ERIE, PA; ERIE CITY SD; (SR); Hnr Roll; Ftball (V C); Wrstlg (V C); Probation Officer; State Trooper; Indiana U of Pennsylvania; Edinboro U

ROSE, KARISSA A; YOUNGSVILLE, PA; YOUNGSVILLE MIDDLE SR HS; (FR); Hnr Roll; Nat Sci Aw; Sci Fairs; Comm Volntr; Chrch Yth Grp; DARE; Scouts; Svce Clb; Spanish Clb; Dnce; Chrldg (V L); Cl Off (S); Stu Cncl (R); Linda Dies Dance Express Co.; Zoology; Mammalogy; Penn State

ROSE, MEGAN; PITTSBURGH, PA; BETHEL PARK SR HS; (JR); Hi Hnr Roll; MVP; Nat Hon Sy; Yth Ldrshp Prog; Comm Volntr; Peer Tut/Med; Prom Com; Quiz Bowl; Scouts; Orch; SP/M/VS; Sftball (J); Tennis (V L); Track (V); Member of Pride; Pre-Med; Grove City College; Baldwin-Wallace College

ROSEMAS, KAYLA; EBENSBURG, PA; CTRL CAMBRIA HS; (JR); Hi Hnr Roll; Hnr Roll; Nat Hon Sy; WWAHSS; Prom Com; Chrldg (V L); PP Ftbl; Track (V); Physical Therapy; Occupational Therapy

ROSENBERRY, D A; CHAMBERSBURG, PA; CHAMBERSBURG AREA SR HS; (JR); Nat Hon Sy; Nat Mrt Semif; Sci/Math Olympn; St of Mnth; WWAHSS; Peer Tut/Med; Drma Clb; Emplmnt; MuAlphaTh; Sci Clb; Orch; Stg Cre; Mechanical - Automotive Engineering; Drexel U; Carnegie Mellon U

ROSNOV, JESSICA; PLYMOUTH MEETING, PA; PLYMOUTH WHITEMARSH HS; (JR); Hnr Roll; St of Mnth; Comm Volntr; Fld Hky (J); Stu Cncl (R); Early Education; Syracuse U

ROSS, KATHERINE; SALTSBURG, PA; KISKI AREA HS; (JR); Hi Hnr Roll; Nat Hon Sy; WWAHSS; Comm Volntr; Peer Tut/Med; Dbte Team; Emplmnt; Key Club; SADD; Spanish Clb; Chr; SP/M/VS; Swg Chr; Vice President-Key Club; President-Mock Trial; Medicine

ROSS, LAUREN; FEASTERVILLE TREVOSE, PA; BENSALEM TOWNSHIP SD; (FR); Hnr Roll; Comm Volntr; Off Aide; Broad Street Run; Sesame Place Classic; Elementary School Teacher; Gym Teacher / Education; Bucks County Community College; Arcadia U

ROSS, MARGARET; PITTSBURGH, PA; PITTSBURGH SD; (SO); Ctznshp Aw; Hnr Roll; Comm Volntr; Peer Tut/Med; ArtClub; Chrch Yth Grp; Emplmnt; Photog; Tchrs Aide; Student Dress Designer-School & Outside Fashion Shows; Fashion Institute of Technology, NY

ROSS, NICOLE C; TYRONE, PA; BELLWOOD-ANTIS HS; (JR); Hi Hnr Roll; Hnr Roll; MVP; Nat Hon Sy; Pres Ac Ftns Aw; St of Mnth; WWAHSS; Comm Volntr; FCA; Key Club; Off Aide; Spch Team; SADD; Spanish Clb; Vllyball (V L); Stu Cncl (V); Yrbk (E); Citizen of the Year - 2003-2005; Elementary Education; Special Education; Pennsylvania State U; Mount Aloysius College

ROSSI, ANGELA M; MONROEVILLE, PA; VINCENTIAN AC/ DUQUESNE U; (JR); Hi Hnr Roll; Nat Hon Sy; St of Mnth; Comm Volntr; Hab For Humty Volntr; Peer Tut/Med; Chrch Yth Grp; SADD; Fld Hky (V L); Lcrsse (V L); Stu Cncl (T); Sch Ppr (E); Yrbk (R); Woman of Science Award from Seton Hall U; Wells College 21st Century Leadership Award; Pre Pharmacy or Optometry; Journalism

ROSSI, KAYLYN; POTTSTOWN, PA; POTTSGROVE SR HS; (FR); Ctznshp Aw; DAR; Gov Hnr Prg; Hnr Roll; Otst Ac Ach Awd; Perf Att; St of Mnth; Comm Volntr; ArtClub; DARE; Dbte Team; Scouts; Fld Hky; Ftball (J); Lcrsse (J); Editor; Writer

ROSSI, LIZ; BETHLEHEM, PA; BETHLEHEM CATHOLIC HS; (JR); Hi Hnr Roll; Nat Hon Sy; Perf Att; WWAHSS; Comm Volntr; Chrch Yth Grp; Key Club; NtlFrnscLg; Spanish Clb; Chr; Sftball (J); Parish Advisory Council-Youth Member; Teen Advisory Board - Bethlehem Area Public Library; Secondary Education / History; Theology; Marywood U; DeSales U

ROSTEN, LAURA L; HARRISBURG, PA; CTRL DAUPHIN SD; (FR); Hi Hnr Roll; St of Mnth; Peer Tut/Med; Emplmnt; Spanish Clb; Dnce; Chrldg (VJ); Takes Dance - Hip Hop; Marketing

ROSTOCKI, JANA; HAZLETON, PA; HAZLETON AREA HS; (SR); F Lan Hn Soc; Hi Hnr Roll; Nat Hon Sy; Perf Att; WWAHSS; Comm Volntr; Emplmnt; FBLA; Key Club; Off Aide; SADD; Cr Ctry (V); Track (V); Lehigh U

ROTH, BRITTANY; MC KEESPORT, PA; SOUTH ALLEGHENY HS; (SR); Hnr Roll; WWAHSS; Comm Volntr; Bnd; Drl Tm; PP Ftbl; Track; Vllyball; Cl Off (S); Yrbk (R); Downtown McKeesport Association Queen 2003; Senior Majorette Co-Captain; Dental Hygiene; U of Pittsburgh

ROTONDARO, VINCE A; PITTSTON, PA; SETON CATHOLIC; (SR); Hnr Roll; Sci Fairs; Comm Volntr; Drma Clb; Emplmnt; Key Club; Stg Cre; Bsball (VJ); Golf (VJ); Yrbk; History; Political Science; Shippensburg U; Albright College

ROVINSKI, MICHAEL J; SPRINGFIELD, PA; MONSIGNOR BONNER HS; (JR); Hnr Roll; Perf Att; Sci Fairs; Comm Volntr; Chrch Yth Grp; Cmptr Clb; Sci Clb; Scouts; Tech Clb; Stg Cre; Cr Ctry (J); CR (R); Nominated For Congressional Student Leadership Conference & Attend NSLC July '05; Computer Science; Math; U of Maryland; Drexel U

ROWAN, KYLE S; EAST STROUDSBURG, PA; POCONO MOUNTAIN EAST HS; (FR); Sccr (V)

ROWE, LINDA; BENSALEM, PA; BENSALEM TOWNSHIP SD; (SO); Hnr Roll; WWAHSS; Comm Volntr; Peer Tut/Med; Dbte Team; Tchrs Aide; Lit Mag (R); Professor of English Literature; ESL Teacher; U of Pennsylvania; Penn State U

ROWELL, ALEXANDRA N; BERWYN, PA; CONESTOGA HS; (JR); Duke TS; Hi Hnr Roll; Hnr Roll; Nat Hon Sy; Nat Ldrshp Svc; Comm Volntr; Peer Tut/Med; Chrch Yth Grp; DARE; Dbte Team; Emplmnt; Key Club; P to P St Amb Prg; Sftball (J); Student Ambassador for People to People - Summer 2005; Political Science / Lawyer; History; Georgetown U; George Washington U

ROWRY, JAVON; ERIE, PA; WILSON MS; (MS); Hnr Roll; Nat Hon Sy; Perf Att; ArtClub; Lttrmn Clb; Chr; Ran and Running Track; A Part of PEPP and CHAMPS; Culinary Arts; Track and Field; Penn State Behrens

RUANE, THERESE C; SCRANTON, PA; SCRANTON HS; (JR); Hi Hnr Roll; Hnr Roll; Nat Hon Sy; Pres Ac Ftns Aw; St of Mnth; Comm Volntr; Peer Tut/Med; ArtClub; Emplmnt; Fr of Library; Mus Clb; Svce Clb; Vsity Clb; French Clb; Orch; Sccr (VJ); Track (J); Stu Cncl (R); CR (R); Treasurer of National Honor Society; Political Science Club Member; Veterinary Medicine; French; U of Pennsylvania; Drexel U

RUBIN, ADAM; WILLIAMSPORT, PA; LOYALSOCK TWP HS; (JR); Hi Hnr Roll; Hnr Roll; Perf Att; WWAHSS; Chess; Key Club; Spanish Clb; Information Sciences / Technology; Penn State U; U of Pittsburgh

RUBY, SARA; OIL CITY, PA; OIL CITY SR HS; (SR); Hnr Roll; WWAHSS; Comm Volntr; Peer Tut/Med; Cmptr Clb; DARE; Emplmnt; Acpl Chr; Chr; Stg Cre; Swmg (L); Psychiatry; Secondary Education; Edinboro U of Pennsylvania

RUDA, RYAN; DALLAS, PA; (SR); Hi Hnr Roll; Sci Fairs; St of Mnth; Key Club; Cr Ctry (V CL); Swmg (V CL); Track (V CL); President National Honor Society; Pre-Med; Lehigh U

RUDAKEWIZ, ASHLEY M; BETHLEHEM, PA; BETHLEHEM CATHOLIC HS; (FR); Hi Hnr Roll; Hnr Roll; Comm Volntr; Key Club; Chr; Ch Chr; Dnce; Theater Arts Program Outside School Dance - Act, Sing, Piano; Drama Major; Teaching Minor; Carnegie Melon; DeSales U

RUDESKI, JACLYN; WILKES BARRE, PA; HANOVER AREA JR/SR HS; (SO); Hnr Roll; Nat Hon Sy; Perf Att; WWAHSS; Comm Volntr; Chrch Yth Grp; Key Club; P to P St Amb Prg; Scouts; Chr; Clr Grd; Stu Cncl; Yrbk; People to People Student Ambassador; Elementary Education; Bloomsburg U

RUDOLPH, SADE M; LANCASTER, PA; J.P. MC CASKEY HS; (JR); Hi Hnr Roll; Hnr Roll; Otst Ac Ach Awd; Perf Att; WWAHSS; Comm Volntr; Peer Tut/Med; Chrch Yth Grp; Emplmnt; Jr Ach; Tchrs Aide; Chrldg (V); Accounting; Business; Millersville U; Consolidated School of Business

RUDZINSKAS, SARAH; PITTSBURGH, PA; NORTH ALLEGHENY HS; (SO); F Lan Hn Soc; Hi Hnr Roll; Hnr Roll; Nat Hon Sy; Perf Att; Pres Ac Ftns Aw; St of Mnth; Yth Ldrshp Prog; Comm Volntr; Chrch Yth Grp; Jr Cls League; Key Club; Mus Clb; Ch Chr; Orch; SP/M/VS; CR (R); Lit Mag (E); 2 Year Member of the Diocesan Youth Council of Pittsburgh; Big Brothers Big Sisters of America; Medical Technologies; Genetics

RUFF, BETH; SOMERSET, PA; ROCKWOOD AREA JR/SR HS; (JR); Ctznshp Aw; Hi Hnr Roll; WWAHSS; Chrldg (V); Sch Ppr (R); Law; Education; California U; Slippery Rock U

RUGGERI, SHERRIE; APOLLO, PA; KISKI AREA SCH DISTRICT; (JR); Hi Hnr Roll; Hnr Roll; Perf Att; WWAHSS; Key Club; Mus Clb; Chr; Swg Chr; Scr Kpr (J); Elementary Education; Day Care; Slippery Rock U; Clarion U

RUHL, JOHN A; MIFFLINBURG, PA; MIFFLINBURG AREA HS; (SO); Hnr Roll; Nat Hon Sy; Perf Att; WWAHSS; Key Club; Bskball (J); Ftball (J); Wt Lftg (J); Key Club; Entrepreneurship Club; Criminology; Biology

RULLAN, ANDREW J; WEXFORD, PA; (SO); Hnr Roll; Pres Ac Ftns Aw; Yth Ldrshp Prog; Key Club; Bnd; Jzz Bnd; Mch Bnd; Ftball (V); Lcrsse (V L); National Junior Honor Society & Philanthropic Chair; Pre-Med/Medicine; Biomedical Engineering; Johns Hopkins U; Georgetown

RUMLEY, MELISSA N; SPRING CITY, PA; OWEN J. ROBERTS HS; (SO); Hi Hnr Roll; Hnr Roll; WWAHSS; Comm Volntr; Emplmnt; Photog; Scouts; Dnce; Tennis (J); Track (L); Sch Ppr (R); Anchor Club Participant; 2nd Place in Friends of the Arts Narrative Competition; Communications; Business; New York U; Howard U

RUSK, CALI A; KUNKLETOWN, PA; PLEASANT VALLEY HS; (FR); Hi Hnr Roll; Nat Hon Sy; Comm Volntr; Spec Olymp Vol; Chrch Yth Grp; JSA; Key Club; Mus Clb; Tennis (V L); Track; Playing Piano 10 Years; Ski Race Team - Shawnee Mountain / Church Youth Group; Law / Architect; Journalism; Moravian College; Cornell U

RUSSELL, IVORY; PHILADELPHIA, PA; SOUTH PHILADELPHIA HS; (JR); Ctznshp Aw; Hi Hnr Roll; Hnr Roll; Nat Hon Sy; WWAHSS; Peer Tut/ Med; Dbte Team; Wdwrkg Clb; Tutor Other Students; Participate in Mock Trials At Temple U; Lawyer; Temple U

RUSSELL, JESSICA; FINLEYVILLE, PA; RINGGOLD SD; (FR); 4H Awd; Hi Hnr Roll; St of Mnth; 4-H; Outdrs Clb; Bskball (CL); Reserve Grand Champion - Saddle Up Open Show; Mountain Rams Club / Ski Club; Veterinarian; Science Majors; Ohio State U; Wilmington College

RUSSIKOFF, NICOLE; BENSALEM, PA; BENSALEM TOWNSHIP SD; (FR); Hnr Roll; St of Mnth; DARE; Scouts

RUUD, LAUREN; ALIQUIPPA, PA; CTR AREA SD; (SO); Hi Hnr Roll; MVP; Perf Att; Pres Ac Ftns Aw; Sci Fairs; Comm Volntr; Red Cr Aide; Spec Olymp Vol; Chrch Yth Grp; DARE; Emplmnt; Outdrs Clb; Spanish Clb; PP Ftbl (V); Skiing (V); Tennis (V L); Track (V); Stu Cncl (R); Teen Leadership; World Language Competition; Biological Science; Medicine; U of Pittsburgh; Penn State U

RYAN, ALEXA K; UNIONTOWN, PA; LAUREL HIGHLANDS HS; (MS); Ctznshp Aw; Hi Hnr Roll; Hnr Roll; Otst Ac Ach Awd; St of Mnth; Comm Volntr; ArtClub; Drma Clb; Lib Aide; Mus Clb; Off Aide; Acpl Chr; Chr; Dnce; SP/M/VS; Gmnstcs; Mar Art; Swmg; Track; Stu Cncl (P, V); Sch Ppr (E, R); 2nd Runner-Up 2005 Miss Pennsylvania Jr. Teen; Art Award Featured in Local Art Show; To Obtain a Masters Degree of Performing Arts W/ Emphasis in Theatrics/Dancing/Acting; Juilliard School; Berkeley U (California)

RYAN, NADIA C; BEAVER FALLS, PA; BEAVER FALLS; (SR); All Am Sch; Hi Hnr Roll; Hnr Roll; USAA; WWAHSS; Emplmnt; FBLA; Key Club; Pep Squd; Svce Clb; Spanish Clb; Drl Tm; Ice Sktg; USFSA Figure Skating Gold Test Medalist; Performer for Wheeling Symphony on Ice / Liz Bragle Ice Dance Trophy; Athletic Training; Physical Education; Slippery Rock U

RYAN, OLIVIA M; BEAVER FALLS, PA; BEAVER FALLS HS; (FR); Hi Hnr Roll; Kwnis Aw; USAA; WWAHSS; Comm Volntr; Svce Clb; Spanish Clb; Bnd; Mch Bnd; Orch; SP/M/VS; High School Stomp Team; Fashion Design

RYAN, THOMAS; EASTON, PA; EASTON AREA HS; (SO); Hi Hnr Roll; MVP; Nat Hon Sy; Sci Fairs; Comm Volntr; Peer Tut/Med; Biology Clb; Key Club; French Clb; Bsball (J); Bskball (V L); Cr Ctry (V L); Cl Off (R); CR (R); Mechanical or Architectural Engineer; Sports Agent; U of Central Florida; U of North Carolina

RYPCZYK III, FRANK D; CTRL CITY, PA; SHADE-CENTRAL CITY SD; (SO); Hnr Roll; Nat Hon Sy; Pres Ac Ftns Aw; USAA; WWAHSS; Comm Volntr; Chrch Yth Grp; Scouts; Chr; Ftball (V L); Wrstlg (V L); Envirothon; Small Engine Mechanic; Professional Wrestling

Ryan, Nadia C
Beaver Falls
Beaver Falls, PA

Russell, Jessica
Ringgold SD
Finleyville, PA

Rosnov, Jessica
Plymouth Whitemarsh HS
Plymouth Meeting, PA

Rosati, Benjamin A
South Fayette Township HS
Oakdale, PA

Rose, Anthony R
Erie City SD
Erie, PA

Ryan, Alexa K
Laurel Highlands HS
Uniontown, PA

Ryan, Olivia M
Beaver Falls HS
Beaver Falls, PA

RZEPNICKI, ABBY; POTTSTOWN, PA; POTTSGROVE HS; (JR); Hi Hnr Roll; Hnr Roll; Nat Hon Sy; St of Mnth; Comm Volntr; Hosp Aide; Emplmnt; Key Club; NYLC; Prom Com; Sci Clb; Vsity Clb; Fld Hky (VJ L); Lcrsse (VJ L); PP Ftbl (VJ); Adv Cncl (R); Stu Cncl (R); CR (R); Key Club; History Club; Nursing; Political Science; Penn State U; James Madison U

RZUCIDLO, MATTHEW; COATESVILLE, PA; OCTORARA HS; (SR); Hi Hnr Roll; Hnr Roll; Perf Att; Comm Volntr; Peer Tut/Med; Ntl FFA; Tchrs Aide; Bnd; Mch Bnd; Pep Bnd; FFA Keystone Degree; Agriculture Business; Dairy Science; Pennsylvania State U

SABA, ANTHONY; HARRISBURG, PA; CTRL DAUPHIN HS; (FR); Ctznshp Aw; Hi Hnr Roll; Nat Hon Sy; St of Mnth; Emplmnt; Lib Aide; Track (J); Student Council; Forensic Science; Computer Technology; Virginia Tech; Boston College

SABIA, JIM; WAYMART, PA; NORTH POCONO HS; (FR); Hi Hnr Roll; Hnr Roll; MVP; Sci Fairs; WWAHSS; Comm Volntr; Peer Tut/Med; Spec Olymp Vol; Chess; Chrch Yth Grp; Sci Clb; Acpl Chr; SP/M/VS; Bskball (V); Ftball; Track (V); Wt Lftg; Children's Choir of Marywood U; Pediatrician, Physical Therapist; Science Major; N. Carolina (UNC); Penn State U Pitt

SABON, DANIEL; SWIFTWATER, PA; POCONO MTN EAST HS; (FR); Comm Volntr; Scouts; Bnd; Ftball (C); Wrstlg; Professional Sports; Design Cars; Notre Dame U; Penn State

SACCHETTI, ALEXANDRA; EXTON, PA; BISHOP SHANAHAN HS; (JR); Hi Hnr Roll; Hnr Roll; Comm Volntr; Emplmnt; Prom Com; Svce Clb; Dnce; Yrbk (E); Pharmacy; U of Delaware, James Madison; Penn State

SAELER, JESSICA; BUTLER, PA; BUTLER AREA HS; (SR); Hnr Roll; Comm Volntr; Chrch Yth Grp; Emplmnt; SADD; Spanish Clb; Swmg (V); Track (V); CR (T); Sch Ppr (E); Yrbk (P); Academic Achievement Awards; Religious Studies; Communications; Westminster College

SAGLIOCOLO, TIA; DEXTER, PA; WYOMING AREA SECONDARY CTR; (SO); Hi Hnr Roll; Hnr Roll; Nat Hon Sy; Hosp Aide; Drma Clb; SADD; French Clb; SP/M/VS; Stg Cre; Candy Striping; Psychology; Physical Therapy

SAINOVICH, COURTNEY; BEAVER FALLS, PA; BLACK HAWK HS; (SR); Hi Hnr Roll; Hnr Roll; Nat Hon Sy; Pres Sch; WWAHSS; Hab For Humty Volntr; Hosp Aide; Peer Tut/Med; Chrch Yth Grp; Drma Clb; Emplmnt; Key Club; P to P St Amb Prg; Prom Com; Chr; SP/M/VS; Golf (V L); Outstanding Young Woman Finalist; Key Club President; Past District Editor; Furman U SC

SAKALOUSKY, KELLI; FRANKLIN, PA; ROCKY GROVE JR SR HS; (SO); Hi Hnr Roll; St of Mnth; USAA; Chrch Yth Grp; Bnd; Dnce; Chrldg (V L); Tennis

SALAHEDIN, AMY; KINGSTON, PA; WYOMING VALLEY WEST HS; (FR); Hi Hnr Roll; Hnr Roll; St of Mnth; St Optmst of Yr; Peer Tut/Med; Orch; Lit Mag (E); 4th Place in National Spanish Exam; Participant in National History Day; Degree in Education or Child Psychology; Seton Hall U; Yale U

SALAZAR, KASAUNDRA; BENSALEM, PA; BENSALEM TOWNSHIP SD; (FR); Hi Hnr Roll; Pres Ac Ftns Aw; Comm Volntr; DARE; Photog; ROTC; Vllyball (V); Skipped 1st Grade; Won All-School Spelling Bee - 5th Grade; Accounting; Interior Design; Temple U; Kansas State U

SALGADO, CYNTHIA; PHILA, PA; THOMAS A EDISON HS; (SR); Hnr Roll; Nat Hon Sy; Chrch Yth Grp; Sftball (V); Cl Off (T); White Williams Scholarship; Robotics; Business Major; Chef; Community College of Philadelphia; Temple U

SALLA, ARIANNE; DALLAS, PA; LAKE LEHMAN HS; (SO); Hi Hnr Roll; Nat Hon Sy; WWAHSS; Comm Volntr; Drma Clb; Key Club; SADD; Tchrs Aide; Foreign Clb; Dnce; SP/M/VS; Stg Cre; Chrldg (V); Stu Cncl (R); Sch Ppr (R, P); Yrbk (P); Johns Hopkins Talent Search; Communications; Theater Arts; Vassar College; Florida State U

SALLOM, DAVID H; CONSHOHOCKEN, PA; PLYMOUTH WHITEMARSH HS; (SO); Hi Hnr Roll; Hnr Roll; Salutrn; Good Citizenship Award from Senator Allyson Schwartz; Principal's Award / Salutatorian Award - 8th Grade; Computer Programming; Philosophy; Rider College NJ; Stevens Institute of Technology NJ

SALVADOR, GABRIELLE; ENOLA, PA; CUMBERLAND VALLEY HS; (SO); Hnr Roll; Comm Volntr; Chrch Yth Grp; Emplmnt; Key Club; Scouts; Spanish Clb; Dnce; Bskball (J); Sftball (J); Young Life Christian Group; Dance Scholarship At Wevodau Dance Center; Business; Child Psychology; Penn State U; The Wharton School of the U of PA

SALVANO, JULIE K; NORRISTOWN, PA; NORRISTOWN AREA HS; (SR); Hnr Roll; Perf Att; DECA; Emplmnt; Acpl Chr; Chr; Took Six Years of Private Singing Lessons; Belonged to West Chester U Honors Choir; Music Industry Studies; Millersville U

SALVO, CHARLES; PITTSTON TWP, PA; PITTSTON AREA HS; (JR); Ctznshp Aw; Hi Hnr Roll; Nat Hon Sy; Pres Ac Ftns Aw; WWAHSS; Yth Ldrshp Prog; Peer Tut/Med; Emplmnt; Lttrmn Clb; Mth Clb/Tm; Pep Squd; Sci Clb; Scouts; Vsity Clb; Spanish Clb; Bsball (J); Bskball (V L); Ftball (V L); Skiing (V); Tennis (V); Wt Lftg (V); Eagle Scout; National Honor Society Historian; Dentistry; School Teacher

SANCHEZ, REINALDO; MT POCONO, PA; POCONO MTN EAST HS; (SO); Hnr Roll; Peer Tut/Med; DARE; Outdrs Clb; Scouts; Bskball (L); Track (L); Wt Lftg (L); Sports; Math

SANDERS, CRISTIN M; STROUDSBURG, PA; STROUDSBURG HS; (SR); Hnr Roll; WWAHSS; Spec Olymp Vol; Emplmnt; FBLA; P to P St Amb Prg; Photog; Track (V CL); Vllyball (V L); Region 21 Pres. FBLA 2004-2005; Marketing; Morgan State U

SANDOVAL, YARELI R; READING, PA; MUHLENBERG SR HS; (JR); Hi Hnr Roll; Hnr Roll; Perf Att; Comm Volntr; Hab For Humty Volntr; Spanish Clb; Track (J); Accounting / Bachelor's Degree; Pre-Pharmacy; Pennsylvania State U; Temple U

SANGER, JONATHAN; HERSHEY, PA; HERSHEY HS; (FR); Hi Hnr Roll; Otst Ac Ach Awd; Chrch Yth Grp; Lib Aide; Photog; Track; Outstanding Character Award in 8th Grade; Aeronautical Engineering

SANNER, KARLYE; APOLLO, PA; ST JOSEPH HS; (FR); Hi Hnr Roll; Hnr Roll; Chrch Yth Grp; Drma Clb; P to P St Amb Prg; Chr; Dnce; SP/M/VS; Chrldg (V); Tennis (J); Student Ambassador; Dance Major/Acting; Chiropractor; New York U; Point Park College

SANSAET, JESSICA; BARTONSVILLE, PA; POCONO MTN EAST HS; (FR); Hi Hnr Roll; Hnr Roll; Nat Hon Sy; St of Mnth; SADD; Chr; Dnce; SP/M/VS; Chrldg (V); Law; Performing Arts / Dance

SANTIAGO, CRYSTAL; MONT CLARE, PA; SPRING-FORD SR HS; (JR); Hnr Roll; Sci Clb; Spanish Clb; Marine Biology

SANTIAGO, JULIO; PHILADELPHIA, PA; (FR); CARE; Comm Volntr; Mth Clb/Tm; Flg Crps; SP/M/VS; Bsball (V); Sccr (J)

SANTORO, CHRISTOPHER; NORRISTOWN, PA; KENNEDY-KENRICK CATHOLIC HS; (FR); Hnr Roll; MVP; St of Mnth; DARE; Ftball (V L); Lcrsse (V); Cl Off (P); Stu Cncl (R); Lit Mag (R); Criminal Justice; Military Science; Notre Dame; Air Force Academy

SANTORO, HAYLIE; CHARLEROI, PA; CHARLEROI AREA HS; (SO); Hi Hnr Roll; Hnr Roll; MVP; Otst Ac Ach Awd; Perf Att; Off Aide; Clr Grd; Dnce; Drl Tm; Mch Bnd; Vllyball; Yrbk (R, P); Make-A-Wish Foundation of Western PA; Family Career and Community Leaders of America; Pastry Arts; Culinary Arts; Pennsylvania Culinary Institute

SANZI, LAUREN C; LATTIMER MINES, PA; (FR); Hi Hnr Roll; FBLA; Bskball (J); Teaching; Penn State; Bloomsburg U

SARANG, ROHAN; BENSALEM, PA; BENSALEM TOWNSHIP SD; (SO); Hnr Roll; Comm Volntr; Valley Basketball; Accounting; Temple U

SARGENT, MARGUERITE E; WASHINGTON, PA; WASHINGTON HS; (FR); Hi Hnr Roll; MVP; Sci Fairs; WWAHSS; Comm Volntr; Chrch Yth Grp; DARE; Dbte Team; Key Club; Lttrmn Clb; SADD; Vsity Clb; Foreign Clb; Stg Cre; Bskball (V L); Cr Ctry (V); GAA (V); Track (V L); Vsy Clb (V L); Vllyball (V L); Stu Cncl (R); CR (R); Student Rep At Sports Conferences; Student Guide At High School; Social Work

SARGENT, RYAN; WASHINGTON, PA; TRINITY AREA SD HS; (JR); Hi Hnr Roll; Hnr Roll; Pres Sch; ArtClub; Illustration, Sequential Art

SARTORETTO, JESSICA; BATH, PA; BETHLEHEM CATHOLIC HS; (SO); Hi Hnr Roll; Pres Ac Ftns Aw; Sci Fairs; Sci/Math Olympn; St of Mnth; Hosp Aide; Chrch Yth Grp; Key Club; Pep Squd; Spanish Clb; Bskball (J); Fld Hky (V); Sccr (V); English Major; College of William and Mary; U of Delaware

SARVEY, TIFFANIE F; ALIQUIPPA, PA; HOPEWELL HS; (SO); Hi Hnr Roll; Hnr Roll; Otst Ac Ach Awd; WWAHSS; Comm Volntr; ArtClub; Chrch Yth Grp; Emplmnt; Prom Com; Spanish Clb; Clr Grd; Mch Bnd; National Art Honor Society; Computer Arts; Graphic Design; Academy of the Arts U; Alfred U

SASSAMAN, EMILY; POTTSTOWN, PA; POTTSTOWN HS; (JR); Ctznshp Aw; Gov Hnr Prg; Hi Hnr Roll; MVP; Nat Hon Sy; Nat Mrt Sch Recip; Nat Sci Aw; Otst Ac Ach Awd; Perf Att; Pres Ac Ftns Aw; Comm Volntr; Hosp Aide; Spec Olymp Vol; Chrch Yth Grp; DARE; Emplmnt; Key Club; Ntl Beta Clb; NYLC; Prom Com; Sci Clb; Ch Chr; Fld Hky (V); Sftball (V); Vsy Clb (V); Cl Off (S); Stu Cncl (R); CR (R); Yrbk (E); Homecoming Court; Key Club President; Dental Hygiene; Radiology

SATH, SOL A; MIFFLINTOWN, PA; JUNIATA CTY SD; (JR); Ctznshp Aw; Hnr Roll; Nat Hon Sy; Perf Att; Pres Ac Ftns Aw; Comm Volntr; Spec Olymp Vol; Chrch Yth Grp; Emplmnt; Bnd; Mch Bnd; SP/M/VS; Track; Veterinary; Medicine; Delaware Valley College; U of Pennsylvania

SATTERLEE, ASHLEY; CARLISLE, PA; TRINITY HS; (FR); Hi Hnr Roll; Key Club; French Clb; Bskball (J); Track (V L)

SAUERS, ALICIA; MIFFLINBURG, PA; MIFFLINBURG AREA SD; (JR); Hi Hnr Roll; Nat Hon Sy; WWAHSS; Hosp Aide; Chrch Yth Grp; Ntl FFA; German Clb; Sccr (J); Horseback Riding; Equestrian Studies; U of Findlay

SAUERS, KATIE; MIFFLINBURG, PA; MIFFLINBURG AREA HS; (SR); Hi Hnr Roll; Hnr Roll; Nat Hon Sy; WWAHSS; Drma Clb; Emplmnt; Mth Clb/Tm; Prom Com; Scouts; Svce Clb; French Clb; Chr; SP/M/VS; Stg Cre; Chrldg (V C); Girl Scout Silver Award; Certified Lifeguard; Elementary Education; Special Education; Millersville U

SAUNDERS, AMIN; PHILADELPHIA, PA; OVERBROOK HS; (SO); Otst Ac Ach Awd; St of Mnth; Comm Volntr; Business Management; U of Delaware; U of Maryland U

SAUNDERS, MONIQUE; ALLENTOWN, PA; WILLIAM ALLEN HS; (SR); Hnr Roll; Nat Hon Sy; WWAHSS; Chrch Yth Grp; SADD; Dnce; Drl Tm; Chrldg (VJCL); Gmnstcs; Sch Ppr (R); USAA National History & Government Award; History; Kean College; Rutgers U

SAVILLE, TYLER; PITTSTON, PA; WYOMING AREA; (JR); Hi Hnr Roll; Nat Hon Sy; St of Mnth; WWAHSS; Yth Ldrshp Prog; Hab For Humty Volntr; Red Cr Aide; Emplmnt; FBLA; Jr Ach; Key Club; Spanish Clb; Bsball (C); Bskball (V); Ftball (C); Wt Lftg (V); Stu Cncl (R); CR (R)

SAVVIDES, MILTO; EASTON, PA; EASTON AREA HS; (SO); Hi Hnr Roll; Sccr (J); Acceptance/Participation in Lehigh U Science Fair; Aerospace Engineer; Physics; Massachusetts Institute of Technology; Cooper Union

SAWLA, ROBIN; NORRISTOWN, PA; RENAISSANCE AC; (FR); Hnr Roll; Nat Hon Sy; Perf Att; WWAHSS; Comm Volntr; DARE; Fr of Library; Key Club; Chr; Fld Hky; Swmg; Vllyball; Psychology; Performing Arts; New York U; West Chester U

SAYED, HESHAM; UPPER DARBY, PA; UPPER DARBY HS; (JR); Hi Hnr Roll; Hnr Roll; Sccr (J); Accounting; Business Administration; Temple U; Drexel U

SAYERS, JOHN A; COATESVILLE, PA; COATESVILLE AREA SR HS; (JR); Hnr Roll; St of Mnth; WWAHSS; Peer Tut/Med; Spec Olymp Vol; Biology Clb; Chrch Yth Grp; Sci Clb; German Clb; Bnd; Mch Bnd; Pep Bnd; CR (R); Sch Ppr (E); Computer Software Engineering; Information Technology; DeVry U; U of Pittsburgh

SAYRE, BRITTANY; DALLAS, PA; DALLAS HS; (JR); WWAHSS; Red Cr Aide; ArtClub; Key Club; Stg Cre; Skiing; Track; Sch Ppr (P); Yrbk (P); 3rd Place Rosetti Art Show Photography Winner; Shakespeare Club Chair Member; Film and Television; Photography; Columbia College Chicago

SCAFELLA, AMY; DALLAS, PA; DALLAS HS; (SO); Hnr Roll; WWAHSS; Key Club; Clr Grd; Pep Bnd; Chrldg (V); Stu Cncl (R); Shakespeare Club; Word Games; Interior Design; Fashion Design and Merchandising; Cazenovia College; Rhode Island School of Design

SCANLAN, KRISTINA; EBENSBURG, PA; CTRL CAMBRIA HS; (FR); Hi Hnr Roll; Sci Fairs; WWAHSS; Comm Volntr; ArtClub; Chrch Yth Grp; Dbte Team; Scouts; Tchrs Aide; Sccr (J); Track (V); President's Education Awards Program; Home Economics Award & Mural Art Award; Dermatology; Duquesne U; Villanova U

SCANLON, JENNIFER; CLIFTON HEIGHTS, PA; UPPER DARBY HS; (JR); Hi Hnr Roll; Perf Att; WWAHSS; Vsity Clb; Cr Ctry (V); Track (V); International Business; Accounting; Drexel U; Ursinus College

SCANLON, RYAN D.; PENN RUN, PA; PENNS MANOR AREA JR/SR HS; (JR); Hi Hnr Roll; Sci/Math Olympn; WWAHSS; Scouts; Bnd; Jzz Bnd; Mch Bnd; Pep Bnd; Cr Ctry (V L); Track (V); Electrical Engineering

SCARCIA, KASSANDRA; CATASAUQUA, PA; CATASAUQUA HS; (FR); Hi Hnr Roll; Otst Ac Ach Awd; Pres Sch; Yth Ldrshp Prog; Peer Tut/Med; Chrch Yth Grp; Dbte Team; Quiz Bowl; SADD; Clr Grd; Sccr; Cl Off (T); Lit Mag (R); Sch Ppr (E); National History Day State Camp Participant; Student Council / Ace Team / Gifted Program; Journalism; Law; Boston U; Oxford U

SCARTON, KATIE; HERMITAGE, PA; HERMITAGE SD; (SO); Hi Hnr Roll; Perf Att; Pres Ac Ftns Aw; St of Mnth; Chrch Yth Grp; Pep Squd; Spanish Clb; Bnd; Chr; Flg Crps; Jzz Bnd; Chrldg (JC); Gmnstcs; Hsbk Rdg; PPSqd (J); Track (V); I Took Dance for 3 Yrs.; I Took Competitive Gymnastics for 8 Yrs. (Not with School).; Sports Medicine; Equine Studies

SCATENA, ELIZABETH; PITTSTON TWP, PA; PITTSTON AREA HS; (JR); Ctznshp Aw; Hi Hnr Roll; Nat Hon Sy; Perf Att; Pres Sch; Sci/Math Olympn; WWAHSS; Comm Volntr; Chrch Yth Grp; Emplmnt; Mth Clb/Tm; Pep Squd; Prom Com; Sci Clb; International Clb; Dnce; Chrldg (VJCL); Cr Ctry (J); Track (J); Cl Off (T); Stu Cncl (R); National Honor Society Vice-President; Who's Who Among American High School Students; Business, Pre-Law; Psychology; Penn State, U Park Campus; DeSales U

SCATENA, LINDSAY A; OAKMONT, PA; RIVERVIEW JR/SR HS; (SO); Hi Hnr Roll; Nat Hon Sy; Sci/Math Olympn; WWAHSS; Comm Volntr; Hab For Humty Volntr; Chrch Yth Grp; Key Club; Mod UN; Spanish Clb; Bnd; Chr; Dnce; SP/M/VS; Chrldg (VJCL); Cr Ctry (V L); Skiing; Track (VJ L); National History Day; Pennsylvania Junior Academy of Science

Sath, Sol A
Juniata Cty SD
Mifflintown, PA

Sarang, Rohan
Bensalem Township SD
Bensalem, PA

National
Honor Roll
Spring 2005

Sainovich, Courtney
Black Hawk HS
Beaver Falls, PA

Sauers, Katie
Mifflinburg Area HS
Mifflinburg, PA

SCAVONE, ALYSA; DALLAS, PA; LAKE LEHMAN HS; (JR); Hi Hnr Roll; Hnr Roll; Nat Hon Sy; WWAHSS; Comm Volntr; Red Cr Aide; Chrch Yth Grp; Emplmnt; Key Club; Off Aide; Prom Com; SADD; Cr Ctry (V L); Fld Hky (J); Track (VJ); Key Club Secretary; Physical Therapy; Occupational Therapy; Bloomsburg U; Penn State Hazelton

SCELSI, NICOLE M; GREENVILLE, PA; REYNOLDS SD; (FR); USAA; Chr; Mch Bnd

SCHADLER, TYLER J; POTTSTOWN, PA; POTTSTOWN SR HS; (FR); Bsball (J); Bskball (J); Temple U; Ohio State U

SCHALLER, ANNA; PITTSBURGH, PA; SHALER AREA INT SCH; (JR); Ctznshp Aw; F Lan Hn Soc; Hi Hnr Roll; Hnr Roll; Nat Hon Sy; Otst Ac Ach Awd; St of Mnth; Comm Volntr; Peer Tut/Med; BPA; FBLA; Skiing (V); Tennis (V L); Peer Mediation; Business Major; U of Pittsburgh; Duquesne U

SCHAU, MACKENZI; STATE COLLEGE, PA; STATE COLLEGE SOUTH HS; (FR); Hi Hnr Roll; Hnr Roll; St Schl; Red Cr Aide; DARE; Key Club; Photog; Chrldg (J L); Stu Cncl (R); Mathematics Achievements/Honors; Accounting/Business; Computer Graphics/Programming; Columbia U; Harvard U

SCHECHTMAN, ASHLEY; BENSALEM, PA; BENSALEM TOWNSHIP SD; (SO); Ctznshp Aw; Hnr Roll; DARE; ROTC; Nursing; Temple U

SCHELLMAN, SARAH B; SLIPPERY ROCK, PA; SLIPPERY ROCK; (FR); Hnr Roll; Nat Hon Sy; Perf Att; Pres Sch; WWAHSS; Bnd; Mch Bnd; Stg Cre; Zoology; Marine Biology

SCHEUERMANN, CARISSA; FINLEYVILLE, PA; RINGGOLD SD; (FR); Ctznshp Aw; Hi Hnr Roll; Pres Ac Ftns Aw; Sci Fairs; Chrch Yth Grp; DARE; Drma Clb; NtlFrnscLg; Off Aide; SADD; SP/M/VS; Chrldg (V); Gmnstcs (V); Scr Kpr (J); CR (R); Gymnastics Level 8 / Regional 3rd Place; Communications; Education; Pittsburgh U; Penn State U

SCHIBLI, KAITLIN M; HERMITAGE, PA; HICKORY HS; (SO); Hnr Roll; Otst Ac Ach Awd; Comm Volntr; Chess; Chrch Yth Grp; Emplmnt; Lttrmn Clb; SADD; Vsity Clb; Spanish Clb; Chr; Drm Mjr; Mch Bnd; Vllyball (V L); Cl Off (T); Speech Development; Journalism; Clarion U; Penn State U

SCHILDT, NADIA J; EAST BERLIN, PA; ADAMS CTY CHRISTIAN AC; (SO); Hi Hnr Roll; USAA; WWAHSS; Chrch Yth Grp; Ch Chr; Sch Ppr (E); Yrbk (E); Law; Special Education

SCHIMP, WILLIAM; MARIETTA, PA; DONEGAL HS; (SO); Ftball (VJ); Wt Lftg; Engineering; Penn State U

SCHMIDT, KARA; HOLLIDAYSBURG, PA; HOLLIDAYSBURG AREA SR HS; (JR); Hi Hnr Roll; Nat Hon Sy; WWAHSS; Yth Ldrshp Prog; Hosp Aide; Peer Tut/Med; Key Club; Mth Clb/Tm; French Clb; Sch Ppr (R); 2 2nd Places in APPLE Foreign Language French Competition; Pre-Medicine; Washington U in St. Louis; Princeton U

SCHMIEG, NATHANIEL D; DEVON, PA; CONESTOGA HS; (JR); Hnr Roll; Nat Mrt LOC; Nat Sci Aw; Sci/Math Olympn; WWAHSS; Comm Volntr; Emplmnt; Key Club; Mth Clb/Tm; Bnd; Track (V); Stu Cncl; CR; National Junior Honors Society; National Science Award; Cornell U; U of Pennsylvania

SCHMITTLEIN, MICHAEL; DEVON, PA; CONESTOGA HS; (SO); Hnr Roll; Chess; Key Club; Sccr (J); Track (J); Chess Club; Key Club

SCHNEEBERGER, KATHERINE E; MECHANICSBURG, PA; CUMBERLAND VALLEY HS; (FR); Hnr Roll; WWAHSS; Comm Volntr; Chrch Yth Grp; Key Club; Cr Ctry (JCL); Track (V L); Math; Engineering

SCHNEIDER, MICKY; CLAIRTON, PA; CLAIRTON CITY SD HS; (JR); Hnr Roll; ROTC; Clr Grd; Drl Tm; Ftball (V); Wt Lftg (V); California U of Pennsylvania; West Virginia U

SCHNEIDER, NICHOLE; JAMESTOWN, PA; JAMESTOWN AREA SD; (FR); Hnr Roll; Perf Att; Pres Ac Ftns Aw; Sci Fairs; Chrch Yth Grp; Emplmnt; Scouts; Dnce

SCHOENING, RYAN; DRUMORE, PA; SOLANCO HS; (FR); Hi Hnr Roll; Hnr Roll; Nat Hon Sy; Chrch Yth Grp; Drma Clb; NYLC; Bnd; Mch Bnd; SP/M/VS; Lawyer; Teacher of Law; Harvard U; New York U

SCHOFIELD, LAURA; WEST CHESTER, PA; WEST CHESTER EAST HS; (SO); F Lan Hn Soc; Hi Hnr Roll; Jr Rot; Yth Ldrshp Prog; CARE; DECA; Fld Hky (J); Swmg (J); Fugett Science Award; Fugett Scholar-3 Years of Academic Excellence; International Business; Foreign Language (French); George Washington U; Georgetown U

SCHRODING, KAIA; NEW PHILA, PA; POTTSVILLE AREA HS; (SO); Ctznshp Aw; Hi Hnr Roll; Hnr Roll; Pres Ac Ftns Aw; Sci Fairs; Sci/Math Olympn; Comm Volntr; ArtClub; Chrch Yth Grp; Drma Clb; Quiz Bowl; Schol Bwl; Chr; Ch Chr; SP/M/VS; Stg Cre; Swmg (V L); Vllyball (JC); National Art Honor Society; Short Story Writing Award; Architecture; Linguistics; Penn State U; Temple U

SCHULMAN, BRITTANY N; DOYLESTOWN, PA; CTRL BUCKS HS EAST; (JR); F Lan Hn Soc; Hi Hnr Roll; Hnr Roll; Amnsty Intl; Comm Volntr; Peer Tut/Med; Mod UN; Prom Com; Spanish Clb; SP/M/VS; Adv Cncl (R); Cl Off (S); Stu Cncl (R); Sch Ppr (R); Created an Exhibit for the PA Mercer Museum; Given the - Honor of Addressing the Assembly - Award - End of 9th Grade; Political Science; Pre-Law; Brown U; Harvard U

SCHULTZ, MELISSA L; BEAVER, PA; BEAVER HS; (JR); Ctznshp Aw; Hi Hnr Roll; Nat Hon Sy; Nat Mrt LOC; US Army Sch Ath Aw; WWAHSS; Comm Volntr; Chrch Yth Grp; Emplmnt; FCA; Key Club; ROTC; German Clb; Chr; Cr Ctry (VJ L); Dvng (V); Track (V L); Vllyball (J); German Club Treasurer; Architectural Engineering; Penn State; Drexel

SCHWAB, EDWARD; COATESVILLE, PA; HIGH POINT BAPTIST AC; (JR); Hi Hnr Roll; Hnr Roll; Pres Sch; Stg Cre; Yrbk (E); History (Medieval); Theology; Messiah College; Nyack College

SCHWARTZ JR, JOHN; DOYLESTOWN, PA; CTRL BUCKS HS EAST; (SO); F Lan Hn Soc; Hi Hnr Roll; Comm Volntr; Peer Tut/Med; Drma Clb; Key Club; P to P St Amb Prg; Chr; SP/M/VS; Cr Ctry (J); Track (V); Bucks County Music Educator's Association; Harvard U; Yale U

SCIANDRA, ANTHONY F; UPPER DARBY, PA; UPPER DARBY HS; (JR); Hi Hnr Roll; Hnr Roll; Nat Hon Sy; Perf Att; DECA; FBLA; Bnd; Chr; Mch Bnd; Cr Ctry (V); Swmg (V); Track (V); Stu Cncl (R); CR (R); Citizenship Award; Business; Villanova U, U of Pennsylvania; Penn State U

SCIULLI, VERONICA; PITTSBURGH, PA; TAYLOR ALLDERDICE HS; (SR); Ctznshp Aw; Hi Hnr Roll; Hnr Roll; Comm Volntr; Peer Tut/Med; Emplmnt; Pep Squd; Tchrs Aide; Tech Clb; Dnce; Chrldg (V CL); Cl Off (S); Stu Cncl (R); Yrbk (E, R, P); Robotics, FIRST; Athletic Training, Exercise, Science; Slippery Rock U

SCOTT, ALEXANDRA; MONROEVILLE, PA; GATEWAY SD HS; (SO); Hi Hnr Roll; WWAHSS; Peer Tut/Med; FBLA; Dnce; Chrldg (V); Stu Cncl (R); Gateway's Gifted Program (A&M); Sales & Marketing/Hr/Finance; Forensics; Penn State U; U of Michigan

SCOTT, CASEY; POTTSTOWN, PA; POTTSGROVE SR HS; (SO); Chrch Yth Grp; Chrldg (J); Track (V); Nursing; ER Doctor; U of Pennsylvania; Temple U

SCOTT, ERIN L; WEST CHESTER, PA; BISHOP SHANAHAN HS; (JR); Hi Hnr Roll; Pres Ac Ftns Aw; Sci Fairs; Comm Volntr; Peer Tut/Med; Emplmnt; Lttrmn Clb; Prom Com; Svce Clb; Vsity Clb; Lcrsse (J); Sccr (V L); CR (T, R); Sch Ppr (R); Yrbk (R); Community Service Club-Class; Representative; Biology; Pre-Med; Lehigh U; Washington College

SCOTT, JASMINE L P; PITTSBURGH, PA; PITTSBURGH SD; (SR); Ctznshp Aw; Hnr Roll; Dnce; SP/M/VS; Spanish Speaking Proficiency Award; African-American Competition Awards; Criminal Justice & Law; Carlow U; Point Park College, Duquesne U

SCOTT, JASON J; EAST STROUDSBURG, PA; STROUDSBURG HS; (JR); Hnr Roll; Yth Ldrshp Prog; Peer Tut/Med; ArtClub; DARE; Emplmnt; FBLA; Key Club; NYLC; P to P St Amb Prg; Vsity Clb; Bskball (VJCL); National Youth Leadership Alumni (Law); College Board's: One of the Most Prospective Juniors; Law; Political Science; Stanford U; Boston U

SCOTT, MICHAEL; NEW KENSINGTON, PA; PLUM SR HS; (JR); Hnr Roll; Ftball (V L); Vllyball (V L); Engineering

SCOTT, WYATT; CAMP HILL, PA; CAMP HILL HS; (SO); Hi Hnr Roll; Hnr Roll; MVP; Emplmnt; Ftball (V L); Track (V); Wrstlg (J L); Scholastic Writing 1st Place-Short Story - 10th Grade; Scholastic Writing Honorable Mention / Short Story - 8th Grade; Architecture; Art; Virginia Tech; James Madison U

SCOTTO, MARIA; ALLENTOWN, PA; LEHIGH VALLEY CHRISTIAN HS; (SO); Sci Fairs; St of Mnth; Chrch Yth Grp; DARE; Emplmnt; Fld Hky (V); Mar Art (L); Sccr (V); 2nd Degree Black Belt; Accounting; Military; Villanova; Air Force Academy

SCOZA, STEPHEN J; NEWTOWN, PA; COUNCIL ROCK HS NORTH; (SO); F Lan Hn Soc; Hi Hnr Roll; Hosp Aide; DARE; Emplmnt; French Clb; Computer Science; History; Stanford; Princeton

SCULL, ALEX; DU BOIS, PA; DUBOIS AREA SD; (FR); Hnr Roll; Perf Att; St of Mnth; Golf (J); Track (J); Cl Off (T); Stu Cncl (R)

SEAMANS, HEATHER; NEW MILFORD, PA; BLUE RIDGE HS; (FR); Hi Hnr Roll; WWAHSS; SADD; Bnd; Mch Bnd; Track (J); Cl Off (T); Stu Cncl (R); Political Science; Columbia U; Harvard U

SEBZDA, KELLY N; ELIZABETHTOWN, PA; ELIZABETHTOWN AREA HS; MS; Hi Hnr Roll; Hnr Roll; Otst Ac Ach Awd; Sci Fairs; Chrch Yth Grp; DARE; Lib Aide; Chr; Dnce; Chrldg (J); Hsbk Rdg (J); Track (J); CR (R); Lit Mag (E); Early Childhood Education; Law; Penn State U; Lancaster Bible College

SEDGWICK, ANNA; HOUTZDALE, PA; MOSHANNON VALLEY JSHS; (SO); Hi Hnr Roll; Hnr Roll; Perf Att; Chrch Yth Grp; Bnd; Mch Bnd; Tri-M Music Honor Society; Lock Haven U; Penn State U

SEEL, MOLLY; POTTSTOWN, PA; OWEN J ROBERTS HS; (SR); Hi Hnr Roll; Hnr Roll; Nat Hon Sy; Lttrmn Clb; Mus Clb; Spanish Clb; Acpl Chr; Chr; Ch Chr; Jzz Bnd; Fld Hky (J); Tennis (J); Track; Homecoming Court; Communications (Broadcasting); Music; Fordham U

SEGAL, HEATHER M; JESSUP, PA; VALLEY VIEW HS; (JR); Hnr Roll; WWAHSS; Spanish Clb; Spanish Club; Red Cross Certified Baby Sitter; Graphic Designer; Art Psychologist; Pennsylvania Worthington; U of Scranton

SEIDEL, MEGAN; HERSHEY, PA; HERSHEY HS; (FR); Hi Hnr Roll; St of Mnth; Emplmnt; Key Club; Lib Aide; Off Aide; Svce Clb; SADD; Tchrs Aide; Spanish Clb; Stu Cncl (R); Travel and Tourism Major

SEIDERS, NATHAN M; NEWVILLE, PA; BIG SPRING SD; (FR); Hi Hnr Roll; Hnr Roll; Nat Hon Sy; St of Mnth; DARE; Emplmnt; P to P St Amb Prg; Marines / Navy Service; Further Education in the Military; Shippensburg College ROTC

SELL, ASHLEIGH; POTTSTOWN, PA; POTTSGROVE HS; (SO); Ctznshp Aw; Hi Hnr Roll; MVP; Nat Hon Sy; Pres Sch; St of Mnth; WWAHSS; Comm Volntr; Peer Tut/Med; Chrch Yth Grp; Drma Clb; Emplmnt; Key Club; Mus Clb; Off Aide; Sci Clb; French Clb; Chr; Ch Chr; SP/M/VS; Swg Chr; Stu Cncl (R); CR (R); Scholarship; Pharmacist; Optometrist; Penn State

SELLERS, BARYONA L; COATESVILLE, PA; (SR); Hnr Roll; Chr; Cosmetology License; Business Management Degree; Lehigh Valley College

SELWAY, TIM; YORK, PA; (SR); Gov Hnr Prg; Hi Hnr Roll; Hnr Roll; Nat Hon Sy; Pres Ac Ftns Aw; Vsity Clb; Bsball (V); Sccr (J); Swmg (V); Yrbk (E); U of Maryland College Park

SENAY, GEORGE; SHARON, PA; SHARON HS; (JR); Comm Volntr; Ftball (V); Track (V)

SESTOK, MARC; PITTSBURGH, PA; PLUM SR HS; (SO); Hi Hnr Roll; Hnr Roll; Nat Hon Sy; ArtClub; DARE; Emplmnt; German Clb; Golf (V); Ski-Club Member / Tea Club Member; Law; Criminology; U of Pittsburgh; Columbia U

SETTLE, KAITLIN M; ELVERSON, PA; OWEN J ROBERTS HS; (JR); Hnr Roll; Nat Hon Sy; Comm Volntr; Peer Tut/Med; Spec Olymp Vol; Chrch Yth Grp; Emplmnt; Key Club; Prom Com; French Clb; SP/M/VS; Bskball (VJCL); Fld Hky (J); Sccr (V L); Track (J); Stu Cncl; CR; Key Club Secretary; International Relations; French Language; U of Virginia; College of William and Mary

SETZER, CASSANDRA; LAWRENCEVILLE, PA; NORTHERN TIOGA SD; (FR); Ctznshp Aw; Hi Hnr Roll; Hnr Roll; Otst Ac Ach Awd; Comm Volntr; Peer Tut/Med; DARE; Drma Clb; Dnce; SP/M/VS; Bskball (J); Track (L); Vllyball (J); Stu Cncl (R); Performing Arts; Ultrasound Tech

SETZKORN, ANDREW; FRANKLIN, PA; VALLEY GROVE SD; (FR); Hnr Roll; Nat Hon Sy; Comm Volntr; Chrch Yth Grp; DARE; Bnd; Bskball (VJ); Cr Ctry (J); Tennis (J); Academic Honors

SEVIN, ALEXA; SEWICKLEY, PA; QUAKER VALLEY HS; (JR); Hi Hnr Roll; Nat Hon Sy; Nat Mrt Semif; Peer Tut/Med; Chrch Yth Grp; DARE; Emplmnt; Jr Ach; Prom Com; Chr; Dnce; Chrldg (V); Sftball (V); Vllyball (V); Youth and Government-Treasurer; Mock Trial; PharmD; Duquesne U; Ohio Northern U

SEWELL, COLLIN A; LANSDALE, PA; METHACTON HS; (SO); F Lan Hn Soc; Hi Hnr Roll; Hnr Roll; Nat Mrt LOC; Otst Ac Ach Awd; Pres Ac Ftns Aw; Sci Fairs; Comm Volntr; Emplmnt; Key Club; Mod UN; NYLC; Spanish Clb; Bsball (J); M-Award for Academic Excellence; Model UN-Outstanding Top Delegate; Political Science; Foreign/International Affairs; U of Virginia; College of William and Mary

SGARLATA, TRAVIS; PITTSBURGH, PA; BRASHEAR HS; (SO); Ctznshp Aw; Hi Hnr Roll; Hnr Roll; Comm Volntr; FCA; High Honor Roll; I Would Like to Be a Head Chef.; I Would Like to Get a Bachelor's.; The Art Institute of Pittsburgh; Pennsylvania Culinary Arts

SHABLESKY JR, MITCHELL; BEAVER FALLS, PA; BIG BEAVER FALLS AREA HS; (SO); Hi Hnr Roll; Nat Hon Sy; Otst Ac Ach Awd; St of Mnth; Comm Volntr; Chrch Yth Grp; Emplmnt; FBLA; Key Club; Outdrs Clb; Bnd; Mch Bnd; Orch; SP/M/VS; Cr Ctry (V L); Pre 1840 Re-Enactor; Target Shooting Gold & Silver Medals; Military; West Point; West Virginia U

SHADLE, CHRISTOPHER J; MECHANICSBURG, PA; TRINITY HS; (JR); F Lan Hn Soc; Hi Hnr Roll; Nat Hon Sy; Sci Fairs; WWAHSS; Yth Ldrshp Prog; Comm Volntr; Hab For Humty Volntr; Peer Tut/Med; Emplmnt; Key Club; NYLC; Quiz Bowl; Vsity Clb; Latin Clb; SP/M/VS; Sccr (V L); Cl Off (P); Stu Cncl (P, R); Youth Leadership Forum on Medicine At G'town; Medicine-Surgeon/MD; U of Notre Dame; Duke U

SHAFFER, BENJAMIN L; SHANKSVILLE, PA; SHANKSVILLE-STONYCREEK HS; (FR); Hnr Roll; Comm Volntr; 4-H; Chrch Yth Grp; Drma Clb; Bnd; Mch Bnd; Pep Bnd; SP/M/VS; Track (V); Praise Band / Reading Competition; Teens Against Tobacco Use - TATU; Auto Restoration / Auto Mechanics; PA College of Technology; Wyo Tech

Sewell, Collin A
Methacton HS
Lansdale, PA

Scott, Erin L
Bishop Shanahan HS
West Chester, PA

Schoening, Ryan
Solanco HS
Drumore, PA

Schmittlein, Michael
Conestoga HS
Devon, PA

Schmieg, Nathaniel D
Conestoga HS
Devon, PA

National
Honor Roll
Spring 2005

Schau, Mackenzi
State College South HS
State College, PA

Schneider, Nichole
Jamestown Area SD
Jamestown, PA

Sciulli, Veronica
Taylor Allderdice HS
Pittsburgh, PA

Scott, Jasmine L P
Pittsburgh SD
Pittsburgh, PA

Scott, Jason J
Stroudsburg HS
East Stroudsburg, PA

SHAFFER, BETHANY; LITTLESTOWN, PA; CARROLL CHRISTIAN HS; (SR); Hi Hnr Roll; Hnr Roll; MVP; Pres Ac Ftns Aw; Peer Tut/Med; Chrch Yth Grp; Emplmnt; Off Aide; Photog; Prom Com; Tchrs Aide; Bnd; Chr; Chrldg (V C); Sccr (J); Vllyball (J); Yrbk (R, P); Pediatric Nursing; Elementary Education; Kentucky Christian U; Liberty U

SHAFFER, COURTNEY M; JENNERSTOWN, PA; NORTH STAR HS; (SO); CR (R); S.A.D.D.; Who's Who of American Students; Art Education; Millersville U; Indiana U of Pennsylvania

SHAFFER, DANIELLE; STOYSTOWN, PA; SHANKSVILLE STONY CREEKS; (FR); 4H Awd; Ctznshp Aw; Hnr Roll; Pres Ac Ftns Aw; Pres Sch; Comm Volntr; 4-H; Scouts; Bnd; Chr; Mch Bnd; Bskball (J); Vllyball (J)

SHAFFER, ZACHARY J; SOUTH WILLIAMSPORT, PA; SOUTH WILLIAMSPORT JR/SR HS; (SR); Hi Hnr Roll; Hnr Roll; St of Mnth; WWAHSS; Hab For Humty Volntr; Key Club; Mth Clb/Tm; Outdrs Clb; Tennis (V L); State Finalist, Gold Medal, US Academic Decathlon; US Achievement Academy International Foreign Lang. Award; Pre-Med; Medical Research; Moravian College; Indiana U of Pennsylvania

SHAH, AMRUTA; BENSALEM, PA; BENSALEM TOWNSHIP SD; (JR); Hi Hnr Roll; Hnr Roll; Otst Ac Ach Awd; Perf Att; WWAHSS; Comm Volntr; Hosp Aide; Red Cr Aide; Lib Aide; Mth Clb/Tm; GUJARATI Clb; Bdmtn; Lit Mag (R); Student Government Association / SGA; PA Clean Up Day; Chemist; Pharmacist; Temple U; U of the Science in Philadelphia

SHAH, ASHKA; MORRISVILLE, PA; PENNSBURY HS; (SO); Ctznshp Aw; Hnr Roll; Otst Ac Ach Awd; Perf Att; Pres Sch; St of Mnth; Yth Ldrshp Prog; Comm Volntr; Hosp Aide; Dbte Team; Emplmnt; NtlFrnscLg; Scouts; Svce Clb; Tmpl Yth Grp; Dnce; SP/M/VS; Stg Cre; Yrbk (E); Silver Award (From Girl Scouts); Principal's Award for Math (And Academic) Excellence; Major-Medical; Degree-Doctor; U of Pennsylvania (Penn State); Johns Hopkins U School of Medicine

SHAH, KAVITA J; BETHLEHEM, PA; BETHLEHEM CATHOLIC HS; (FR); Hi Hnr Roll; Otst Ac Ach Awd; Perf Att; Sci Fairs; WWAHSS; Hosp Aide; Key Club; Kwanza Clb; Mth Clb/Tm; NtlFrnscLg; Schol Bwl; Scouts; Chr; Dnce; Mar Art (V); Sccr (J); Marine Biology; Journalism; U of Delaware; Pennsylvania State College

SHAH, RUJUTA; BENSALEM, PA; BENSALEM TOWNSHIP SD; (SO); Ctznshp Aw; F Lan Hn Soc; Fut Prb Slvr; Hi Hnr Roll; Hnr Roll; Nat Hon Sy; Nat Mrt LOC; Otst Ac Ach Awd; Perf Att; St of Mnth; Amnsty Intl; Comm Volntr; Red Cr Aide; Biology Clb; Chrch Yth Grp; DARE; Emplmnt; Jr Ach; Lib Aide; Off Aide; Tchrs Aide; Chrldg (J); Cyclg (J); Gmnstcs (J); Rqtball (J); Scr Kpr (J); Skt Tgt Sh (J); Tennis (J); Track (J); Indian Cooking Club; House Aide; Medical Science; Bio Medical Science; Princeton U; University of Penn

SHAL, SAMANTHA; CONNELLSVILLE, PA; CONNELLSVILLE HS; (SR); F Lan Hn Soc; Hi Hnr Roll; Nat Hon Sy; Otst Ac Ach Awd; Drma Clb; Photog; Prom Com; SADD; French Clb; Bnd; Jzz Bnd; SP/M/VS; Stg Cre; Sccr (V); Cl Off (P); Stu Cncl (R); Yrbk (E); Photography; Penn State- U Park

SHANK, KAITLYN; HUMMELSTOWN, PA; HERSHEY HS; (FR); Hi Hnr Roll; Chrch Yth Grp; Chr; Ch Chr; Cr Ctry (V L); Track (V); Chosen to Speak to Panel of Doctors About Her Insulin Pump; English Teacher; Nutritionist

SHANKAR, REKHA; BERWYN, PA; CONESTOGA HS; (SO); Hnr Roll; Otst Ac Ach Awd; St of Mnth; WWAHSS; Comm Volntr; Peer Tut/Med; Stg Cre; Yrbk; 4th Place in National Spanish Exam in 2003; Participated in 3 Dances for South Asian Culture Club; Medicine; Film; Princeton U; U of Pennsylvania

SHAREK, MELISA; APOLLO, PA; KISKI AREA HS; (JR); Hi Hnr Roll; Hnr Roll; MVP; Perf Att; Pres Ac Ftns Aw; Sci Fairs; Comm Volntr; Hosp Aide; Key Club; Lttrmn Clb; Vsity Clb; Bnd; Sccr (V CL); Track (V L); SADD Club, Red Ribbon Committee, Ski Club; Assisted Special Ed Students; Physical Education; Exercise Science; Slippery Rock U

SHARPE, DANIA; HARRISBURG, PA; CTRL DAUPHIN EAST HS; (FR); Comm Volntr; FBLA; Key Club; Mch Bnd; Stg Cre; Bskball; Sftball; Yrbk; Journalism; Business; Messiah College; Penn State U

SHARPE, NATALIE; PHILADELPHIA, PA; GEORGE WASHINGTON HS; (SO); Bnd; Mch Bnd; Orch; Veterinary Sciences

SHAW, HEATHER A; READING, PA; READING HS; (FR); Hnr Roll; Nat Hon Sy; Perf Att; St of Mnth; Bnd; Chr; Dnce; SP/M/VS; Talent Search; Berks Pride; Pediatric Nurse; Temple U

SHAW, JAIMEE; JAMESTOWN, PA; JAMESTOWN AREA SD; (FR); Hnr Roll; MVP; Perf Att; Pres Ac Ftns Aw; Sci Fairs; St of Mnth; Comm Volntr; ArtClub; DARE; Lib Aide; Off Aide; Svce Clb; Spch Team; SADD; Spanish Clb; Bnd; Mch Bnd; Pep Bnd; SP/M/VS; Bskball (VJCL); Golf (V); Scr Kpr (J); Track (VJ); Cl Off (P); Relay for Life Member; Organized Class Float for Fair Parade; Forensic Science; Teaching-Physical Education; Duke; Pepperdine

SHAYTER, ASHLEY; HARRISBURG, PA; CTRL DAUPHIN EAST HS; (JR); Ctznshp Aw; Hnr Roll; Nat Hon Sy; Perf Att; Comm Volntr; Spec Olymp Vol; Drma Clb; Key Club; Sign Clb; SP/M/VS; Stg Cre; American Legion Essay Contest; Taught CCD Classes on Sundays; Veterinary Medicine / DVM; Art / Design; U of Pennsylvania; Cornell U

SHEA, KELSEY A; PITTSBURGH, PA; CARLYNTON JR/SR HS; (SO); Chr; Sccr (V); Girls Ensemble Member; Business; Music Composition; Drexel U; Robert Morris U

SHEA, MELANIE; TIONESTA, PA; WEST FOREST HS; (JR); 4H Awd; Hi Hnr Roll; Hnr Roll; Pres Ac Ftns Aw; 4-H; Chrch Yth Grp; Emplmnt; FCCLA; Prom Com; SADD; Vsity Clb; Scr Kpr (L); Vllyball (L); Stu Cncl (R); Yrbk (E); PA State Police Tobacco Awareness Award; English Major; English Literature; U of Pittsburgh; U of North Carolina

SHEARER, ASHLEY; BENSALEM, PA; HOMESCHOOLED; (MS); Comm Volntr; ArtClub; Chrch Yth Grp; Drma Clb; Emplmnt; Tchrs Aide; Spanish Clb; Dnce; SP/M/VS; Sccr (J); Marine Biology; Theatre; Philadelphia Bible U; North Carolina State U

SHEDLOSKY, SARA; MECHANICSBURG, PA; CUMBERLAND VALLEY HS; (JR); F Lan Hn Soc; Hnr Roll; WWAHSS; Hab For Humty Volntr; FBLA; Key Club; Spanish Clb; Fld Hky; Scr Kpr (V); Track; Stu Cncl; Competed At FBLA State Competition; National Foreign Language Honor Society; Marketing; Communications; James Madison U; Villanova U

SHELMAN, COREY; COVINGTON, PA; NORTH PENN JR/SR HS; (SO); Hnr Roll; WWAHSS; Comm Volntr; Chrch Yth Grp; Key Club; Law Enforcement; Marine Biology; Mansfield U

SHEMA, LEAH K; HARRISBURG, PA; CTRL DAUPHIN HS; (SO); Hnr Roll; Perf Att; Comm Volntr; Emplmnt; Fld Hky (J L); Sftball (V L); Travel Softball Team Placed 9th at Nationals; 4-Diamonds Volunteer; Sport Medicine; Physical Therapy; U of Pittsburgh; UCLA

SHEPHERD, ABIGAIL; POTTSTOWN, PA; POTTSGROVE HS; (SO); Ctznshp Aw; Hi Hnr Roll; Nat Hon Sy; Otst Ac Ach Awd; Perf Att; St of Mnth; WWAHSS; Comm Volntr; Peer Tut/Med; Key Club; Off Aide; Sci Clb; Tchrs Aide; Spanish Clb; Fld Hky (J); Track (J); Lit Mag (E); Yrbk (R, P); History Club; PRIDE Member; Political Science Major; Villanova U; College of William & Mary

SHERBIN, MATTHEW; WEXFORD, PA; NORTH ALLEGHENY HS; (SO); Hi Hnr Roll; Nat Hon Sy; Pres Ac Ftns Aw; WWAHSS; Yth Ldrshp Prog; Comm Volntr; Emplmnt; Key Club; NYLC; Prom Com; Ftball (J); Lcrsse (J); National Youth Leadership Forum on Medicine; Member S.C. Principal's Advisory Committee; Business Management; Pre-Med; Duke U; Johns Hopkins U

SHERBONDY, MACKENZIE; GREENVILLE, PA; REYNOLDS JR/SR HS; (FR); Hi Hnr Roll; Comm Volntr; Chrch Yth Grp; Key Club; Scouts; Chr; Ch Chr; Chrldg (J); Sftball; Vllyball (J); Cl Off (V); Girl Scout Silver Award; Penn State U

SHERMAN II, STEPHEN J; HERMITAGE, PA; HICKORY HS; (SO); Hi Hnr Roll; Hnr Roll; MVP; St of Mnth; WWAHSS; Comm Volntr; Chrch Yth Grp; DARE; Emplmnt; Fr of Library; Jr Ach; Lttrmn Clb; Outdrs Clb; Vsity Clb; Chr; Ftball (V); Skiing; Vsy Clb (V L); Wrstlg (V CL); Yrbk (R); Mortuary Science; MBA; Ohio State U; Naval Academy

SHEVITZ, QUENTIN; FRANKLIN, PA; ROCKY GROVE JR/SR HS; (FR); Hnr Roll; St of Mnth; WWAHSS; Emplmnt; Vllyball (J); Stu Cncl; Jr Bowling League; State Police Officer

SHICKORA, NADINE; MCADOO, PA; HAZLETON AREA SD; (SO); Hi Hnr Roll; Nat Hon Sy; St of Mnth; WWAHSS; FBLA; Adv Cncl (R); Optometry

SHIEL, KATHLEEN; PHILADELPHIA, PA; FRANKLIN LEARNING CTR; (SO); Ctznshp Aw; Hi Hnr Roll; Hnr Roll; Otst Ac Ach Awd; St of Mnth; Lib Aide; Photog; SP/M/VS; Stg Cre; Sch Ppr (P); Yrbk (E, R, P); Communications/Performing Arts; Photography

SHIM, SARAH; ELKINS PARK, PA; ABINGTON HS; (SO); Hi Hnr Roll; Comm Volntr; Chrch Yth Grp; Key Club; Orch; U of Pennsylvania; Princeton U

SHIMKO, KRISTINE; WILKES BARRE, PA; HANOVER AREA JR/SR HS; (JR); Ctznshp Aw; Hi Hnr Roll; Hnr Roll; WWAHSS; DARE; Drma Clb; Emplmnt; Key Club; Fld Hky (V CL); Sccr (V); Swmg (V L); Yrbk; Criminal Law; Citadel ROTC college; Air Force

SHIMKO, OLIVIA; BURGETTSTOWN, PA; BURGETTSTOWN HS; (SO); Hnr Roll; MVP; Nat Sci Aw; Otst Ac Ach Awd; Perf Att; Pres Ac Ftns Aw; Sci Fairs; WWAHSS; Comm Volntr; Hosp Aide; Lttrmn Clb; Sci Clb; Vsity Clb; SP/M/VS; Bskball (V CL); PP Ftbl; Track (V L); Vllyball (V L); Adv Cncl (R); Stu Cncl (S); Yrbk; PJAS; Leo Club; Anatomy; Anesthesiologist; West Virginia U; Mercyhurst College

SHIN, ESTHER; LANSDALE, PA; METHACTON HS; (JR); Hi Hnr Roll; Hnr Roll; WWAHSS; Comm Volntr; Hab For Humty Volntr; Peer Tut/Med; Chrch Yth Grp; FBLA; Key Club; Mod UN; Ch Chr; Lcrsse (J); Adv Cncl (R); Cl Off (V); Stu Cncl (R); CR (R); Treasurer, Secretary, and Project Coordinator in Church Youth Group; Dentist; Pediatrician; Penn State U; Boston U

SHIPMAN, NORAH; WATSONTOWN, PA; WARRIOR RUN SD; (JR); Hnr Roll; Nat Hon Sy; Nat Mrt Fin; Nat Mrt LOC; Perf Att; Sci/Math Olympn; Chrch Yth Grp; FBLA; Key Club; Mth Clb/Tm; Prom Com; Vsity Clb; Ch Chr; Orch; Bskball (JC); Cr Ctry (V L); Sftball (V L); Lit Mag (E); Sch Ppr (E, R, P); Journalism; History; Lehigh U; Northeastern U

SHIRER, DAVID F; PITTSBURGH, PA; PENN HILLS HS; (JR); Hi Hnr Roll; Nat Hon Sy; WWAHSS; Comm Volntr; Chrch Yth Grp; FCA; Key Club; Swmg (V); Vllyball (J)

SHIREY, JAY; HANOVER, PA; HANOVER HS; (JR); Hi Hnr Roll; Nat Hon Sy; USAA; WWAHSS; Comm Volntr; Chrch Yth Grp; Emplmnt; Key Club; SP/M/VS; Bskball (V); Ftball (V); Track (V); Vsy Clb (V); National Honor Society; Key Club, Academic Honor Roll; Mechanical Engineering; Physical Therapy; US Coast Guard Academy; Grove City College

SHIRLEY, CAIT; HARLEYSVILLE, PA; NORTH PENN HS; (JR); Hi Hnr Roll; Hnr Roll; Pres Sch; WWAHSS; Comm Volntr; Spec Olymp Vol; Emplmnt; Key Club; Prom Com; Fld Hky (VJ); PP Ftbl; Track (V); Adv Cncl (R); The National Society of High School Scholars; Elementary Education; St. Joseph's U; Cabrini College

SHIVELY, HAZEL; EAST STROUDSBURG, PA; EAST STROUDSBURG HS; (JR); Ctznshp Aw; Hnr Roll; Nat Hon Sy; WWAHSS; Comm Volntr; Spec Olymp Vol; Chrch Yth Grp; Jr Ach; Key Club; Cr Ctry (V); Sccr (V); Cl Off (P); Sch Ppr (R); Secondary Education; Nursing; Penn State U

SHOTSBERGER, ASHLYN; NEWPORT, PA; NEWPORT SD; (SO); Hi Hnr Roll; Hnr Roll; Nat Hon Sy; Otst Ac Ach Awd; Student of the Quarter; Sophomore of the Year Nominee; Graphic Design; Bradley Academy of the Visual Arts

SHOW, ELIZABETH; BLAKESLEE, PA; POCONO MOUNTAIN WEST HS; (JR); Hnr Roll; Comm Volntr; Chr; Swg Chr; Tennis (J); Psychology; Law; College Misericordia; Drexel U

SHOW, JESSICA A; UNIONTOWN, PA; LAUREL HIGHLANDS SD HS; (FR); Hi Hnr Roll; Hnr Roll; St of Mnth; Jr Ach; Scouts; Bnd; Chr; Ch Chr; Mch Bnd; Bskball; Skiing; Music Teacher; Business; Penn State U; West Virginia U

SHOWALTER, CHAD; DENVER, PA; COCALICO HS; (SR); Hnr Roll; Pres Ac Ftns Aw; St of Mnth; Comm Volntr; Emplmnt; P to P St Amb Prg; Wdwrkg Clb; Teaching; Millersville U

SHOWERS-LEWIS, MELINDA; GETTYSBURG, PA; LITTLESTOWN HS; (JR); Hnr Roll; WWAHSS; Comm Volntr; Chrch Yth Grp; DECA; Emplmnt; FBLA; Pep Squd; Prom Com; Scouts; Chrldg (JC); PP Ftbl (V); Vllyball (V L); Yrbk (E); Pennsylvania Apple Princess 2005; Who's Who Among American H.S. Students; Elementary Education; Psychology; Shippensburg U; Millersville U

SHRADER, BRANDON; WILKES BARRE, PA; HANOVER AREA JR/SR HS; (SR); Hi Hnr Roll; Hnr Roll; Nat Hon Sy; WWAHSS; Drma Clb; Emplmnt; Key Club; Mus Clb; Bnd; Chr; Mch Bnd; SP/M/VS; Golf (V); Aerospace Engineering; Penn State U Main Campus

SHUBA, DEANNA; WASHINGTON, PA; TRINITY AREA SD; (SR); Hnr Roll; Vo Tech Health Assistant; Become a Police Officer; Pittsburgh Technical Institute

SHUCKHART, ASHLEY M; CARMICHAELS, PA; CARMICHAELS AREA JR/SR HS; (JR); Hi Hnr Roll; Hnr Roll; ArtClub; Spanish Clb; Sccr (V CL); Physical Therapy; Penn State U; Slippery Rock U

SHUKER, ADAM; READING, PA; NORTHEAST MS; (MS); Ctznshp Aw; Hnr Roll; Nat Hon Sy; Comm Volntr; Chrch Yth Grp; Emplmnt; Ftball (C)

SHULTZ, BRYNN; TEMPLE, PA; MUHLENBERG SR HS; (JR); Sci Clb; SADD; Yrbk (E); Leo Club; Student Volunteers; Elementary Education; Millersville U; California U Pennsylvania

SHULTZ, MARA C; CAMP HILL, PA; CAMP HILL HS; (SO); Hnr Roll; Pres Ac Ftns Aw; Comm Volntr; Hosp Aide; Peer Tut/Med; Dbte Team; Mus Clb; Vsity Clb; Spanish Clb; Chr; SP/M/VS; Bskball (J); Sftball (V L); Mixed Ensemble; Business; Music Technology; New York U; U of Arizona

SHUMAKER, CODY; ENOLA, PA; EAST PENNSBORO AREA HS; (FR); Hi Hnr Roll; Hnr Roll; Nat Hon Sy; Otst Ac Ach Awd; Chess; Dbte Team; Law; Harvard Law School; Dickinson U

SHUSTERMAN, LINDSAY; LAFAYETTE HILL, PA; WOODLYNDE HS; (JR); 4H Awd; Hi Hnr Roll; Hnr Roll; Nat Hon Sy; Otst Ac Ach Awd; Perf Att; Pres Ac Ftns Aw; Comm Volntr; Peer Tut/Med; Emplmnt; Fld Hky (V); Tennis (V); Yrbk (E); High Honors; Restaurant and Hospitality Management; Drexel; Johnson & Wales

Shusterman, Lindsay
Woodlynde HS
Lafayette Hill, PA

Shaw, Heather A
Reading HS
Reading, PA

Shepherd, Abigail
Pottsgrove HS
Pottstown, PA

SHUTTER, LINDSAY A; MYERSTOWN, PA; ELCO HS; (SR); Hi Hnr Roll; Nat Hon Sy; St of Mnth; WWAHSS; Pep Squd; Prom Com; Tchrs Aide; Chrldg (V L); Track (V L); Penn State U

SHUTTS, LAURA M; WILLIAMSPORT, PA; JERSEY SHORE AREA SR HS; (JR); Hi Hnr Roll; Nat Hon Sy; St of Mnth; WWAHSS; Red Cr Aide; Chrch Yth Grp; Emplmnt; FBLA; Key Club; Mod UN; Prom Com; Bskball (V L); Tennis (J L); Track (V L); Cl Off (T); CR (T); Lycoming County Dairy Royalty; Constitutional Convention Delegate; Bachelors Degree in Nursing; Mansfield U of Pennsylvania; Bloomsburg U of Pennsylvania

SICIGNANO, MICHAEL; POTTSTOWN, PA; POTTSGROVE SR HS; (FR); U of South Florida; Florida State U

SICKELS, KATHRYN L; MONONGAHELA, PA; RINGGOLD HS; (MS); Hi Hnr Roll; Hnr Roll; USAA; Comm Volntr; Chr; SP/M/VS; Stu Cncl (R); Sch Ppr (E); Johns Hopkins Talent Search 2004-05; National American Miss PA State Finalist 2005; Veterinarian; Teacher; Washington & Jefferson College; Penn State U

SICKLE, DANIELLE; BUTLER, PA; BUTLER HS; (FR); Ctznshp Aw; Hi Hnr Roll; Otst Ac Ach Awd; Comm Volntr; Chrch Yth Grp; Drma Clb; Outdrs Clb; Latin Clb; Acpl Chr; Chr; Ch Chr; SP/M/VS; CR (R); Girls Ensemble Chorus; Teacher / Secondary Education; Occupational Therapist; Grove City College; Penn State U

SIDOR, SARAH; NAZARETH, PA; NAZARETH AREA SD; (JR); Ctznshp Aw; Hi Hnr Roll; Hnr Roll; Perf Att; Pres Sch; ArtClub; French Clb; Science Olympiad; Scholastic Scrimmage; Education; Kutztown U; Bloomsburg U

SIEGER, MATTHEW D; LITITZ, PA; MANHEIM TWP HS; (SR); Hi Hnr Roll; Nat Hon Sy; St of Mnth; Comm Volntr; Peer Tut/Med; Chrch Yth Grp; Tennis (V); Engineering; Bucknell U

SIEGFRIED, BRIELLE A; WHITEHALL, PA; WHITEHALL HS; (JR); Hi Hnr Roll; Hnr Roll; WWAHSS; Spec Olymp Vol; Key Club; Pep Squd; Bnd; Dnce; Sftball (V); Key Club, Pep Club, Respect Club; Elementary Edu.; Lehigh; Moravian

SIKORA, KIMBERLY; GIBSONIA, PA; PINE-RICHLAND HS; (JR); Hi Hnr Roll; Hnr Roll; WWAHSS; Comm Volntr; Chrch Yth Grp; Emplmnt; Key Club; Pep Squd; Prom Com; SADD; Chrldg (VJCL); PP Ftbl (J); Sftball (J); Stu Cncl; CR; Penn State U; U of Pittsburgh

SILVA, SAMUEL P; LEMONT FURNACE, PA; LAUREL HIGHLANDS SD; (JR); St of Mnth; Acpl Chr; Bnd; Jzz Bnd; Mch Bnd; Bachelor of Music Performance; Bachelor of Music Education; Furman U; West Virginia U

SILVIS, JUSTIN L; SOUTH FORK, PA; FOREST HILLS SD; (SO); Hi Hnr Roll; Hnr Roll; Perf Att; Comm Volntr; Scouts; Bskball (J); History Teacher; Electrician; U of Pittsburgh At Johnstown; U of Pittsburgh

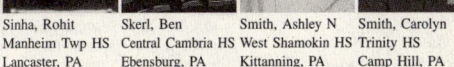

SILVIS, SARAH R; APOLLO, PA; APOLLO-RIDGE SD; (JR); Hnr Roll; Nat Hon Sy; Chr; Chemist; PhD / Professor; Penn State U; California U of Pennsylvania

SIMEON, RUTH M; PHILADELPHIA, PA; CENTRAL HS; (SO); Hnr Roll; Sci Fairs; Sci/Math Olympn; Comm Volntr; Chrch Yth Grp; Mus Clb; Off Aide; Clb; Chr; Ch Chr; Dnce; Track (J); CR (P); Treasurer of S.A.L.S.A/ Aspira Club; Dental Hygienist; U of New York; Penn State

SIMISI, ALLISON; ALTOONA, PA; BELLWOOD-ANTIS HS; (SR); Ctznshp Aw; Hnr Roll; Nat Hon Sy; WWAHSS; AL Aux Girls; Key Club; Spanish Clb; Bskball (V L); Cr Ctry (V L); Sftball (J L); Track (V L); Stu Cncl (R); Yrbk (E); National Honor Society Vice President; Art Therapy; Art Education; Seton Hill U

SIMMONS, MICHAEL L; HANOVER, PA; SOUTH WESTERN HS; (SR); Hi Hnr Roll; Nat Hon Sy; Sci Fairs; St of Mnth; WWAHSS; Chess; Dbte Team; Scouts; Ftball (VJ L); Hsbk Rdg (V); Track (VJCL); Eagle Scout Award; Accepted to United States Military Academy-West Point

SIMMONS, TANEESHA; PHILADELPHIA, PA; STRAWBERRY MANSION MIDDLE SR HS; (JR); Comm Volntr; DARE; Bskball (V); Sftball (V); Stu Cncl (T); Scholarship; Engineer (Chemical); Cheney U; Temple U

SIMMS, KRYSTAL; PHILADELPHIA, PA; PINE FORGE AC; (JR); Hnr Roll; WWAHSS; Comm Volntr; Chrch Yth Grp; Drma Clb; Emplmnt; SP/M/VS; Bsball (V); Psychiatry, High School Counselor; Temple U Philadelphia, PA; Oakwood College Huntsville, AL

SIMMS, SHALA; ARDMORE, PA; UPPER DARBY HS; (SR); Hi Hnr Roll; Hnr Roll; Nat Hon Sy; Chr; Swg Chr; Bskball (J); Cr Ctry (V CL); Ice Hky; Skiing (J); Track (V CL); Wrstlg (J); Yrbk (R, P); Sports Administration; Lock Haven U

SIMPSON, BEV; WEST SUNBURY, PA; MONITEAU JR/SR HS; (SO); Sci Fairs; Peer Tut/Med; Lib Aide; Mus Clb; Spanish Clb; Chr; Drl Tm; Mch Bnd; SP/M/VS; PPSqd (V); PP Ftbl (V); Track (VJ); Nutritionist / Food Science; Forensic Science; Slippery Rock U

SIMPSON, NATHAN; MOUNTAIN TOP, PA; CRESTWOOD HS; (MS); Hnr Roll; Perf Att; Comm Volntr; Peer Tut/Med; Drma Clb; SP/M/VS; Stu Cncl (R); CR (R); Sch Ppr (R); 3rd in School Geography Bee; 1st in Patriot Essay Competition; Lawyer (Law); Performing Arts; Villanova; Harvard

SIMS, LANITA C L; PHILADELPHIA, PA; HS FOR THE CREATIVE AND PERF ARTS; (JR); Ctznshp Aw; Hnr Roll; Perf Att; WWAHSS; Chrch Yth Grp; Ch Chr; Drl Tm; Orch; Perfect Attendance Award; Art Education; Fine Arts; U of the Arts; Millersville U

SINGH, PUNIT; EASTON, PA; EASTON AREA HS; (JR); Hi Hnr Roll; Hnr Roll; Nat Hon Sy; Sci Fairs; WWAHSS; Comm Volntr; DARE; DECA; Key Club; Mod UN; Outdrs Clb; Photog; Scouts; Spanish Clb; Tennis (V); Cl Off (R); Stu Cncl (R); DeMolay; Finance; U of Pennsylvania; New York U

SINGH, RANJODH; UPPER DARBY, PA; UPPER DARBY HS; (JR); F Lan Hn Soc; Hi Hnr Roll; MVP; Nat Hon Sy; Pres Sch; Yth Ldrshp Prog; Peer Tut/Med; Spec Olymp Vol; Biology Clb; DARE; Mod UN; Sci Clb; Vsity Clb; Spanish Clb; Bsball (VJ); Mar Art (V); Cl Off (R); Stu Cncl (R); CR (R); Cardiologist; Dermatologist; U of Philadelphia; Columbia U

SINHA, ROHIT; LANCASTER, PA; MANHEIM TWP HS; (JR); Hi Hnr Roll; Nat Hon Sy; Otst Ac Ach Awd; Peer Tut/Med; Red Cr Aide; Chess; Cmptr Clb; Key Club; Ontario Association of Physics Teachers Award; Canadian Math Competition-131 Rank; Computer Engineering; Aeronautical Engineering; Cornell U; Georgia Institute of Technology

SINKEVICH, JAMES; PITTSBURGH, PA; CHARTIERS VALLEY HS; (JR); Track (V); Wrstlg (L); German Club; Pharmacy; Education; Washington and Jefferson; U of Pittsburgh

SIRAJ, WAHEEDAH; HARRISBURG, PA; CTRL DAUPHIN HS; (MS); Hi Hnr Roll; Hnr Roll; Nat Hon Sy; St of Mnth; Comm Volntr; Hosp Aide; Peer Tut/Med; Drma Clb; Emplmnt; Lib Aide; Off Aide; Scouts; Spch Team; Dnce; SP/M/VS; Stg Cre; Mar Art (J); Scr Kpr (J); Tennis (J); Honors Society; Recycling Committee; Psychology; Harvard U; Yale U

SISCO, TASHANA D; PHILADELPHIA, PA; CARVER HS; (JR); Ctznshp Aw; Hnr Roll; Nat Hon Sy; WWAHSS; Comm Volntr; Hosp Aide; Chess; Swmg (V); Lit Mag (R); Sch Ppr (R); Obstetrician; Cosmetologist; Temple University School of Medicine; U of Pennsylvania

SISSOKO, KEMA; UPPER DARBY, PA; UPPER DARBY HS; (JR); Comm Volntr; Peer Tut/Med; Spec Olymp Vol; Chr; Track (V); Pediatrician; Temple U

SITES, NICHOLAS C; GLENVILLE, PA; SOUTH WESTERN HS; (SR); Hi Hnr Roll; Otst Ac Ach Awd; WWAHSS; Chrch Yth Grp; DARE; Emplmnt; Ftball (V L); Skiing (V); Wt Lftg (V); Aviation; U of North Dakota

SIVAKUMAR, CHANDRASEKAR; BLUE BELL, PA; WISSAHICKON HS; (SO); Hi Hnr Roll; Hnr Roll; Otst Ac Ach Awd; Perf Att; St of Mnth; Tennis (J); 50 Hours Community Volunteering At U Penn; Engineering; Business

SIX, ERIKA; HANOVER, PA; LITTLESTOWN HS; (SR); Hnr Roll; MVP; Perf Att; St of Mnth; WWAHSS; Spec Olymp Vol; DECA; Emplmnt; Pep Squd; Prom Com; Vsity Clb; Bskball (JV); Fld Hky (VCL); PP Ftbl; Scr Kpr (V); Sftball (VCL); Vsy Clb (CL); Yrbk (E); USAA National Business Education Award; 2nd place at DECA Conference in Hotel Management; Business Administration; Lebanon Valley College, Annville, PA

SKENA, ROSSILYNNE; TRAFFORD, PA; PENN-TRAFFORD HS; (JR); Hi Hnr Roll; Nat Hon Sy; Otst Ac Ach Awd; USAA; WWAHSS; Comm Volntr; Peer Tut/Med; Chrch Yth Grp; Prom Com; Scouts; Svce Clb; SADD; Spanish Clb; Stg Cre; Skiing; Cl Off (S); Stu Cncl (R); CR (R); Lit Mag (R); Sch Ppr (E); Yrbk (R); Outstanding High School Journalist Award; Presidential Classroom Participant; Journalism; English Writing; Northwestern U; Penn State U

SKERDA, JESSICA R; MILTON, PA; MEADOWBROOK CHRISTIAN SCH; (FR); Hnr Roll; USAA; WWAHSS; Comm Volntr; ArtClub; Key Club; French Clb; Chr; SP/M/VS; Bskball (V); Sccr (V); Track (V); Air Force; Pharmaceutical; Boston U; U of Science in Philadelphia

SKERL, BEN; EBENSBURG, PA; CTRL CAMBRIA HS; (SR); Hi Hnr Roll; Nat Hon Sy; Valdctrian; Peer Tut/Med; Drma Clb; Mth Clb/Tm; Bnd; SP/M/VS; Bsball (J); Track (V); Relay for Life; Chemistry; Music; U of Pittsburgh

SKINNER, BRITTANY L; WEXFORD, PA; NORTH ALLEGHENY INT HS; (SO); Hnr Roll; MVP; St of Mnth; WWAHSS; Key Club; Chrldg (V); Sftball; Track (V); CR (P); Yrbk (E, R, P); Advertising; Fashion Merchandising; Penn State U; Pittsburgh U

SKRZYPEK, MICHELLE; KERSEY, PA; SAINT MARYS AREA HS; (FR); Hnr Roll; Spec Olymp Vol; Lib Aide; Off Aide; Dnce; Vllyball (J)

SLANE, MYLISSA; WARMINSTER, PA; NAZARETH AC HS; (SO); Hi Hnr Roll; Hnr Roll; Otst Ac Ach Awd; Perf Att; St of Mnth; Comm Volntr; Peer Tut/Med; Svce Clb; Drm Mjr; Lit Mag (E); Received Sullivan Scholarships in Elem. School; The American Legion Certificate; Pediatrician/ Psychologist; Early Childhood Education

SLICKER, KAYLA; VANDERGRIFT, PA; KISKI AREA HS; (SO); Hi Hnr Roll; Hnr Roll; Otst Ac Ach Awd; Perf Att; WWAHSS; Comm Volntr; ArtClub; Drma Clb; Key Club; Photog; SADD; Stg Cre; Golf; Skiing; Track (J); Politics Committee; Ski Club; Art - Teacher / Therapy; Nursing / Veterinary; Duquesne U; Pittsburgh State U

SLIFER, KRISTINA; VERONA, PA; PLUM SR HS; (SO); Hi Hnr Roll; Hnr Roll; Perf Att; WWAHSS; Comm Volntr; Chr; Bskball (V); Winning 2nd Place Literature in Reflections; Public Relations; Seton Hill U; U of Pittsburgh

SLIVKA, CHRISTOPHER R; LEVITTOWN, PA; NOTRE DAME HS; (JR); F Lan Hn Soc; Hi Hnr Roll; Nat Hon Sy; Otst Ac Ach Awd; Perf Att; Pres Sch; WWAHSS; Comm Volntr; Emplmnt; Mth Clb/Tm; NYLC; P to P St Amb Prg; Spanish Clb; Lcrsse (J); Marine Sciences & Biology; U of Miami; U of N Carolina

SLIWINSKI, MATT; REYNOLDSVILLE, PA; DU BOIS AREA HS; (FR); 300 Game-Bowling; Psychology

SLOSAR, ASHLEY; OAKMONT, PA; RIVERVIEW JR/SR HS; (SO); DAR; Hi Hnr Roll; WWAHSS; Comm Volntr; Drma Clb; Key Club; Mod UN; French Clb; Chr; Dnce; Orch; SP/M/VS; Skiing (V); Track (V); Cl Off (P); 2nd Place Oratorical Contest Key Club Convention

SLOYER, TIM; EASTON, PA; EASTON AREA HS; (JR); Hnr Roll; Emplmnt; Ftball (V); Wt Lftg (V); Culinary Arts; Northampton County Community College

SMAIL, VANESSA; FORD CITY, PA; LENAPE TECH; (JR); Hi Hnr Roll; Chrch Yth Grp; Ch Chr; Sftball (VJ); Stu Cncl (S); District and Sectional Fine Arts

SMALLS, BRITTANY M; PITTSBURGH, PA; PENN HILLS SR HS; (SO); Hi Hnr Roll; Hnr Roll; Otst Ac Ach Awd; ArtClub; Drma Clb; French Clb; Dnce; Distinguished Cadet (ROTC); 2 Special Commendations (ROTC); Law; Fashion and Design; Columbia U; Marymount Manhattan

SMALLS, EDDIE; PHILADELPHIA, PA; WILLIAM PENN SR HS; (SR); Hi Hnr Roll; Hnr Roll; Bskball (VJ L); Tennis (V L); Sch Ppr (R); African American History; Bachelors Degree; Temple U; Bethune Cookman

SMALLS, KALIAH; PHILADELPHIA, PA; CREATIVE AND PERF ARTS; (FR); Hnr Roll; Perf Att; Sci Fairs; St of Mnth; Comm Volntr; Spec Olymp Vol; DARE; Drma Clb; Jr Ach; Mus Clb; Tchrs Aide; SP/M/VS; Stu Cncl (P); Broadcast Journalism; Communications; Temple U; U of Pennsylvania

SMEDDY, BRIAN; DREXEL HILL, PA; MONSIGNOR BONNER HS; (JR); Hnr Roll; Nat Hon Sy; Pres Sch; St of Mnth; WWAHSS; Emplmnt; SADD; Pro-Life; Economics Degree; Accounting Degree; St Joseph's U; Drexel U

SMIACH, KRISTIN; SOUTH FORK, PA; FOREST HILLS SD; (SR); Hi Hnr Roll; Nat Hon Sy; Perf Att; WWAHSS; Prom Com; SADD; Spanish Clb; Sftball (V); Track (V); Adv Cncl (R); U of Pittsburgh At Johnstown; Saint Francis U

SMIGEL, SEAN; LANCASTER, PA; MANHEIM TWP HS; (SR); Ctznshp Aw; Hnr Roll; WWAHSS; Emplmnt; Key Club; Cr Ctry (V L); Tennis (V); Optimist Club Citizen Award; International Business; U of Pittsburgh

SMITH, AARON; FALLS, PA; TUNKHANNOCK AREA HS; (SO); Hnr Roll; WWAHSS; Comm Volntr; Hab For Humty Volntr; Spec Olymp Vol; Emplmnt; Key Club; Ftball (V); Track (V); Volunteer Firefighter; Relay for Life, Habitat for Humanity

SMITH, ASHLEY N; KITTANNING, PA; WEST SHAMOKIN HS; (SO); 4H Awd; Hi Hnr Roll; Hnr Roll; Spec Olymp Vol; 4-H; Chr; Mar Art; Leo Club; Photographer

SMITH, BRANDON; FRANKLIN, PA; VALLEY GROVE SD; (JR); 4H Awd; Hi Hnr Roll; Nat Hon Sy; St of Mnth; Comm Volntr; 4-H; Chrch Yth Grp; DARE; Prom Com; Schol Bwl; French Clb; Foreign Exchange Student to Japan-Summer 2003; Japanese Language and Culture; East Asian Studies; U of Pittsburgh

SMITH, BRITNEY; LEHIGHTON, PA; LEHIGHTON HS; (FR); Hnr Roll; Physical Therapy; Medical Doctor MD.; Daemen College

SMITH, CAROLYN; CAMP HILL, PA; TRINITY HS; (SO); Hi Hnr Roll; Sci Fairs; Spec Olymp Vol; Chrch Yth Grp; Dbte Team; Spch Team; French Clb; Lit Mag (R); Lincoln Douglas Debate District Champion; Two Gold Key Scholastic Writing Awards; English; History; U of Richmond; College of William & Mary

SMITH, CATHERINE; MC GRANN, PA; FORD CITY HS; (FR); Hi Hnr Roll; Hnr Roll; Comm Volntr; Chrch Yth Grp; Scouts; SADD; Bnd; Chr; Mch Bnd; Pep Bnd; Bskball (J); Sftball (J); Track; Pre-Law; Forensic Science; Indiana U of Pennsylvania; Duquesne U

SMITH, CHASITY; VANDERGRIFT, PA; RIDGEVIEW AC CS; (JR); Hnr Roll; Swmg (J); Basketball; Medical Field; Penn State

SMITH, COREY; CAMP HILL, PA; CEDAR CLIFF HS; (JR); Hi Hnr Roll; Nat Hon Sy; WWAHSS; DARE; Quiz Bowl; Schol Bwl; German Clb; Drafting Award; Architecture; Lehigh U; Drexel U

Smith, Chasity
Ridgeview AC CS
Vandergrift, PA

Smalls, Brittany M
Penn Hills SR HS
Pittsburgh, PA

Sivakumar, Chandrasekar
Wissahickon HS
Blue Bell, PA

Simpson, Nathan
Crestwood HS
Mountain Top, PA

Silvis, Justin L
Forest Hills SD
South Fork, PA

National
Honor Roll
Spring 2005

Sickle, Danielle
Butler HS
Butler, PA

Sinha, Rohit
Manheim Twp HS
Lancaster, PA

Skerl, Ben
Central Cambria HS
Ebensburg, PA

Smith, Ashley N
West Shamokin HS
Kittanning, PA

Smith, Carolyn
Trinity HS
Camp Hill, PA

SMITH, DERRICK A; EXPORT, PA; KISKI AREA HS; (SR); Hi Hnr Roll; Hnr Roll; Perf Att; WWAHSS; Dbte Team; Key Club; Tennis (J); Yrbk (R); Westinghouse Science Honors Institute Student; Olympian Status At Indoor Archery; U of Mary Washington

SMITH, DIANA; SHAVERTOWN, PA; DALLAS HS; (FR); Hi Hnr Roll; Nat Hon Sy; Amnsty Intl; Comm Volntr; Peer Tut/Med; Key Club; Dnce; Fld Hky (J); Sftball (V); Lit Mag (R); Sch Ppr (R); Diversity / Amnesty Club Officer; Take Guitar Lessons Privately; Business; English; U of Michigan

SMITH, ELIZABETH; BLOOMSBURG, PA; COLUMBIA-MONTOUR AVTS; (FR); Ctznshp Aw; Hi Hnr Roll; Hnr Roll; Pres Ac Ftns Aw; St of Mnth; Drma Clb; Ntl FFA; Scouts; Chr; SP/M/VS; Stg Cre; Bskball (J); Cosmetologist; Actress / Singer; Bloomsburg U; Penn Tech

SMITH, HALIMA; NEW BLOOMFIELD, PA; WEST PERRY HS; (JR); Hi Hnr Roll; Hnr Roll; MVP; Nat Hon Sy; St of Mnth; WWAHSS; Comm Volntr; Hosp Aide; Emplmnt; Lib Aide; Photog; Vsity Clb; Foreign Clb; Bskball (V L); Sftball (J); Track (V L); Vsy Clb (V L); Stu Cncl (R); Sch Ppr (E, R, P); National Honor Society President; PIAA State Tournament in Basketball & Track; Pre Medical Studies; Psychology; U of Pittsburgh; U of Maryland

SMITH, JACQUELINE A; KUNKLETOWN, PA; PLEASANT VALLEY HS; (FR); Hi Hnr Roll; Perf Att; WWAHSS; JSA; Key Club; Tennis (V); Track (V); Sch Ppr (R); Political Science; Law; New York U; Brown U

SMITH, JESSICA; LEBANON, PA; CEDAR CREST HS; (FR); Acpl Chr; Chr; Orch; SP/M/VS; Medical Science

SMITH, KATIE L; DARLINGTON, PA; BLACKHAWK HS; (SR); Hi Hnr Roll; Hnr Roll; Nat Hon Sy; Perf Att; WWAHSS; Comm Volntr; Hab For Humty Volntr; Peer Tut/Med; Key Club; English Clb; Chr; SP/M/VS; Stg Cre; PP Ftbl (V); Leo Club; Psychology; Penn State Beaver

SMITH, KELLY; DEVON, PA; CONESTOGA HS; (SO); Hi Hnr Roll; Pres Ac Ftns Aw; St of Mnth; Comm Volntr; Hab For Humty Volntr; Peer Tut/Med; Emplmnt; Key Club; Photog; Chr; Dnce; Tennis (V); Yrbk

SMITH, KRYSTIN; SCRANTON, PA; SCRANTON HS; (SO); Hnr Roll; MVP; 4-H; DARE; Jr Ach; Scouts; SADD; SP/M/VS; Sccr (J); Sftball (J); Girl Scout Silver Award; Teens Against Tobacco Use; Lawyer; Senator; Duquesne U; Dickinson U

SMITH, LESLIE E; STROUDSBURG, PA; POCONO MTN EAST HS; (SO); Hi Hnr Roll; Hnr Roll; Otst Ac Ach Awd; Perf Att; St of Mnth; Comm Volntr; Dnce; Bskball (V); CR (R); Morning Announcements; Temple U; NYU

SMITH, LYNN; ELTON, PA; FOREST HILLS SD; (SO); Hnr Roll; MVP; Perf Att; Sftball (J); Vllyball (L); Yrbk (E); Psychology; Early Childhood Development; U Of Notre Dame; Indiana U South Bend

SMITH, MARTY D; PITTSBURGH, PA; GEORGE WESTINGHOUSE HS; (JR); Hnr Roll; St of Mnth; Comm Volntr; Emplmnt; Tchrs Aide; Pharmacist; PharmD; Duquesne U; Pitt

SMITH, MATTHEW; BENSALEM, PA; BENSALEM TOWNSHIP SD; (SR); Hnr Roll; Perf Att; Pres Ac Ftns Aw; Comm Volntr; ROTC; Bskball (J); Ftball (J); Wt Lftg (J); Executive Officer in Marine Corps JROTC; Sports Administration; ROTC; Temple U; Lock Haven U of Pennsylvania

SMITH, MICHELLE A; YORK, PA; CTRL YORK HS; (SR); Hi Hnr Roll; Nat Hon Sy; St of Mnth; WWAHSS; Comm Volntr; Chrch Yth Grp; SADD; Vsity Clb; Chr; Skiing (V); Sftball (VJ L); Vsy Clb (V L); Vllyball (VJCL); Top 5% of Class; Springettsbury Lions Club Award; Biological Sciences; U of Delaware

SMITH, NAOMI; WHITE HAVEN, PA; CRESTWOOD HS; (SO); Hnr Roll; Chrch Yth Grp

SMITH, PHILIP B; NANTICOKE, PA; TRIBORO CHRISTIAN AC; (JR); Hi Hnr Roll; Hnr Roll; Otst Ac Ach Awd; Chrch Yth Grp; SP/M/VS; Sccr (V); Gatorade Will to Win Athlete in Soccer; Geology; Luzerne County Community College; West Chester U

SMITH, REBECCA; PITTSBURGH, PA; JHS-CMTY DAY SCH; Hi Hnr Roll; Hnr Roll; Pres Ac Ftns Aw; Sci Fairs; St of Mnth; Comm Volntr; Hosp Aide; Peer Tut/Med; Tmpl Yth Grp; SP/M/VS; Bskball (J); Cr Ctry (V); Sccr (V); Sftball (V); Forensic Science; Political Sciences; Johns Hopkins U; George Washington U

SMITH, RIANN N; MCKEESPORT, PA; MC KEESPORT AREA SD; (FR); Sci Fairs; Comm Volntr; Chrch Yth Grp; Chr; Bskball

SMITH, SARAH; EFFORT, PA; PLEASANT VALLEY; (SO); Hi Hnr Roll; Perf Att; WWAHSS; Spec Olymp Vol; Chrch Yth Grp; Key Club; Bnd; Ch Chr; Mch Bnd

SMITH, SHANE; CORRY, PA; CORRY AREA HS; (JR); Hi Hnr Roll; Hnr Roll; Nat Hon Sy; Nat Mrt LOC; WWAHSS; Comm Volntr; Chrch Yth Grp; Key Club; Prom Com; SP/M/VS; Cr Ctry (V); Track (V)

SMITH, SHANNON; ACME, PA; RIDGEVIEW AC CS; (JR); Hi Hnr Roll; Hnr Roll; Nat Hon Sy; Perf Att; Comm Volntr; Peer Tut/Med; Emplmnt; Stu Cncl (R); Addiction Counselor; Psychologist; Duquesne U; Bradford

SMITH, STACEY; WEXFORD, PA; PINE RICHLAND HS; (SO); Hi Hnr Roll; Comm Volntr; Peer Tut/Med; Key Club; Dnce; Mch Bnd; SP/M/VS; CR (R); Elementary Education; Medical Profession; Wake Forest U; Mercyhurst College

SMITH, STEPHANIE L; TAYLOR, PA; RIVERSIDE JR/SR HS; (FR); Hi Hnr Roll; Hnr Roll; MVP; Peer Tut/Med; Track (V); Stu Cncl (R); Rookie of the Year - Softball; Mayor's Award - Softball; Teacher; Fashion Illustrator / Designer; Penn State; UCLA

SMITH, TWYLANDA; PITTSBURGH, PA; WESTINGHOUSE HS; (SO); Hi Hnr Roll; Hnr Roll; After School Job; Fashion/Design; Virginia U; Pennsylvania U

SMITH, WESTLEY A; MIFFLINBURG, PA; MIFFLINBURG AREA HS; (JR); Hi Hnr Roll; Hnr Roll; Nat Hon Sy; Ntl FFA; Bsball; Ftball; FFA Awards; Motorcycle Mechanic; Motorcycle Mechanics Institute

SMYTH, ALISON; UPPER DARBY, PA; UPPER DARBY HS; (SO); Hi Hnr Roll; Chrch Yth Grp; P to P St Amb Prg; Chr; Sch Ppr (E, R); Veterinary Medicine; Journalism

SNELL, NA-KEYDA R; PITTSBURGH, PA; PENN HILLS SR HS; (JR); Hi Hnr Roll; Hnr Roll; WWAHSS; Comm Volntr; Key Club; Scouts; Drl Tm; Track (J); Veterinarian; Art; Delaware; Ohio State

SNISCAK, ANNE; CAMP HILL, PA; TRINITY HS; (FR); Hi Hnr Roll; Comm Volntr; Key Club; Spanish Clb; SP/M/VS; Swmg; Tennis (V); Track (V L); Medicine; Law; College of William & Mary; Duke

SNODDY, BETH A; ALLENWOOD, PA; WARRIOR RUN SD; (JR); Hi Hnr Roll; Nat Hon Sy; Chrch Yth Grp; Mth Clb/Tm; Prom Com; Vsity Clb; Spanish Clb; Ch Chr; Bskball (VJ L); Cr Ctry; Fld Hky; Sccr (J); Track (V L); Vsy Clb; Wt Lftg; Cl Off (V); Stu Cncl (R); CR (R); Who's Who Among American HS Students; Physical Education and Health

SNODGRASS, RYAN J; PITTSBURGH, PA; PENN HILLS HS; (SR); Hi Hnr Roll; Hnr Roll; MVP; St of Mnth; WWAHSS; Yth Ldrshp Prog; Comm Volntr; DARE; FCA; Key Club; Spanish Clb; Sccr (V); Adv Cncl (P); Honor Student, Who's Who Athlete; All-Section/All WPIAL; Financing; Business; Gardner Webb U

SNYDER, AMANDA M; ERIE, PA; WILSON MS; (MS); Hnr Roll; Peer Tut/Med; Red Cr Aide; Lib Aide; Off Aide; Scouts; Tchrs Aide; Clr Grd; Flg Crps; Sccr (C); CR (R); Sch Ppr (E, R); Yrbk (E, R, P); PEPP; TLC; Medical; Pediatrician; Penn State

SNYDER, ANDREW; FRIEDENS, PA; SHANKSVILLE-STONYCREEK HS; (SO); Hnr Roll; Drma Clb; Chr; SP/M/VS; Stu Cncl (R); Accounting; Computer Sciences

SNYDER, JARED R; EPHRATA, PA; LANCASTER CTY CTC; (SR); 4H Awd; Hnr Roll; Nat Hon Sy; 4-H; Voc Ind Clb Am; Chr; Architectural Computer Aided Drafting; York Technical Institute

SNYDER, KRISTEN; WEXFORD, PA; NORTH ALLEGHENY HS; (SO); Hnr Roll; Pres Ac Ftns Aw; WWAHSS; Comm Volntr; Emplmnt; Key Club; SADD; Chr; Adv Cncl (R); Stu Cncl (R); Medicine (Pediatrics)

SNYDER, LEAH; BENSALEM, PA; BENSALEM HS; (SR); Hi Hnr Roll; Nat Hon Sy; St of Mnth; Comm Volntr; Peer Tut/Med; Chrch Yth Grp; Emplmnt; Prom Com; Svce Clb; Tmpl Yth Grp; Community Service Club President; Student of the Month; Secondary Education; Spanish; U of Pittsburgh

SNYDER, MELISSA; CARLISLE, PA; CUMBERLAND VALLEY HS; (JR); Hnr Roll; Chrch Yth Grp; Key Club; Orch; Swmg (V); Won Scholastic Certificate of Merit for Short Story; Participate in USA Swim Team and Club Swim Team; English Teacher; Novelist

SODEN, SARAH E; LANCASTER, PA; MANHEIM TWP HS; (JR); Hi Hnr Roll; Nat Mrt Fin; Sci Fairs; WWAHSS; Chrch Yth Grp; Emplmnt; Key Club; Chr; Stg Cre; Cr Ctry (J); PP Ftbl (V); Fellowship of Christian Students; Medical Missions; Taylor U; Bryan College

SOFF, MAGGIE; CHESWICK, PA; SPRINGDALE JR/SR HS; (SO); Hi Hnr Roll; Hnr Roll; Nat Hon Sy; Pres Sch; WWAHSS; Comm Volntr; Chrch Yth Grp; Drma Clb; Emplmnt; FBLA; Key Club; Mus Clb; Spanish Clb; Acpl Chr; Chr; SP/M/VS; Track (V); Stu Cncl (T); Academic Games; GATE Program; Pre-Law/Law; Advertising/Public Relations; William & Mary; Pennsylvania State U

SOLEYE, NINIOLA; WALLINGFORD, PA; STRATH HAVEN HS; (JR); All Am Sch; Ctznshp Aw; Hi Hnr Roll; Hnr Roll; Comm Volntr; Svce Clb; I Play the Flute and Piano (Private Lessons); Published Poetry; Business; Law; U of Pennsylvania; Rutgers U

SOLORZANO, VERONICA; PHILADELPHIA, PA; BENSALEM TOWNSHIP SD; (JR); Hnr Roll; Dnce; Air Force / Interior Design; Physical Therapy / Teacher; Temple U; Lincoln U

SOLOSKI, JOE; CHALFONT, PA; CTRL BUCKS SOUTH; (SO); Hnr Roll; MVP; Nat Stu Ath Day Aw; Pres Ac Ftns Aw; Emplmnt; Bsball (J); Bskball (V); AAU Basketball & AAU Baseball; Summer Counselor at Boys Basketball Camp; Sports Management; U North Carolina; Penn State

SOLT, JESSICA M; KUNKLETOWN, PA; PLEASANT VALLEY HS; (FR); Ctznshp Aw; Hi Hnr Roll; Nat Hon Sy; Comm Volntr; Spec Olymp Vol; Chess; Chrch Yth Grp; FBLA; JSA; Key Club; Sch Ppr (R); 4th Place - Regional Competition in Business Math for FBLA; Teaching Career / Math Master's Degree

SOMERS, ALAINA M; CRANBERRY TWP, PA; SENECA VALLEY SHS; (JR); Hi Hnr Roll; Hnr Roll; Nat Hon Sy; Otst Ac Ach Awd; Perf Att; Pres Sch; Comm Volntr; Peer Tut/Med; Biology Clb; Chrch Yth Grp; Lib Aide; Mth Clb/Tm; Mod UN; P to P St Amb Prg; Quiz Bowl; Schol Bwl; Stg Cre; Mar Art; Track (VJ); Sch Ppr (E, R); Second Place Nationally in Academic Games Propaganda Game; 1st Place - Regional History Day Exhibit Category; American History / Studies; English; Yale U; Columbia U

SONI, NIKET; BENSALEM, PA; BENSALEM TOWNSHIP SD; (FR); Hnr Roll; Perf Att; FBLA; Biology; Pre-Med; NYU; U of Boston

SOPKO, HEATHER; CLAIRTON, PA; CLAIRTON CITY SD HS; (FR); Hi Hnr Roll; ROTC; Bnd; Mch Bnd; Orch; SP/M/VS; Ftball (V); Yrbk (E, P); District Band; Jr Superior Cadet JROTC; Surgical Nurse; Physician's Assistant; U of Pittsburgh; Penn State U

SOTTOLANO, NICOLE; EASTON, PA; EASTON AREA HS; (JR); 4H Awd; Hnr Roll; Nat Hon Sy; Yth Ldrshp Prog; Comm Volntr; Peer Tut/Med; 4-H; Chess; Emplmnt; Sci Clb; Chr; CR (T); SAVE Club Member; Medical School; Villanova U

SOWERS, STEVEN; MERCERSBURG, PA; JAMES BUCHANAN HS/ FRANKLIN CTY; (SO); Hnr Roll; Otst Ac Ach Awd; Pres Ac Ftns Aw; Sci Fairs; Comm Volntr; Peer Tut/Med; ArtClub; Emplmnt; Key Club; Photog; Cr Ctry (V); Track (V); Stu Cncl (R); Yrbk (P); Associate's in Graphic Design; Hagerstown Business College; Art Institute of Miami

SPANGLER, GINGER; MIFFLINBURG, PA; MIFFLINBURG AREA HS; (JR); Hnr Roll; Perf Att; St of Mnth; WWAHSS; Comm Volntr; 4-H; Chrch Yth Grp; Emplmnt; Key Club; Ntl FFA; Prom Com; Stg Cre; Sccr (V); Track (J); Cl Off; Pennsylvania Governor's School for Ag Sciences; Agriculture Education; Penn State U; U of Wyoming

SPAYD, JONATHAN; READING, PA; WILSON HS; (SR); F Lan Hn Soc; Hi Hnr Roll; WWAHSS; Comm Volntr; Chrch Yth Grp; Emplmnt; P to P St Amb Prg; German Clb; Skiing; Studied & Perform on the Violin, Fiddle, Guitar; Built to Last Work Camp Missions Trip: 40 Hrs Volunteer

SPECTOR, SHERRI S; MORRISVILLE, PA; THE HUN SCH OF PRINCETON; (SR); Hi Hnr Roll; Nat Hon Sy; Nat Mrt Fin; Nat Mrt Sch Recip; Pres Sch; WWAHSS; Yth Ldrshp Prog; Comm Volntr; Peer Tut/Med; Drma Clb; Key Club; Tmpl Yth Grp; SP/M/VS; Stg Cre; President of Key Club 2 Years; Cum Laude; Become a Doctor Specializing in Surgery; Muhlenberg College

SPEDALE, MARISSA; DOYLESTOWN, PA; CTRL BUCKS HS EAST; (SO); Hi Hnr Roll; Otst Ac Ach Awd; Pres Sch; WWAHSS; Comm Volntr; Emplmnt; Key Club; Photog; Chr; Bskball (L); PP Ftbl; Stu Cncl (R); Lit Mag (R); National Junior Honor Society; Elementary Education; Communications; Boston College; U of Maryland

SPEICHER, STEPHANIE M; GREENSBURG, PA; GREENSBURG SALEM SD; (FR); Hi Hnr Roll; Pres Sch; Sci Fairs; Hosp Aide; Peer Tut/Med; Scouts; Dnce; Chrldg (V); Psychology; Criminal Justice; Indiana U of Pennsylvania; West Virginia U

SPELLMAN, COLLEEN D; PINE FORGE, PA; PINE FORGE AC; (JR); Hnr Roll; Perf Att; Yth Ldrshp Prog; Comm Volntr; Chrch Yth Grp; Dbte Team; Tchrs Aide; Chr; Ch Chr; Bskball (V); Ftball (V); Gmnstcs (V); Debate Team; 500+ Community Service Hours; Optometry; Nursing; Oakwood College; Andrews U

SPENCE, ASHLEY; MECHANICSBURG, PA; CUMBERLAND VALLEY HS; (SO); Hnr Roll; WWAHSS; Chrch Yth Grp; Key Club; Spanish Clb; Dnce; Youth Group/Missions; Biology Major; Pediatric Doctor

SPENCE, TANA; CLAIRTON, PA; CLAIRTON CITY SD; (SO); All Am Sch; Hi Hnr Roll; Hnr Roll; Nat Hon Sy; Otst Ac Ach Awd; Perf Att; Yth Ldrshp Prog; Comm Volntr; Peer Tut/Med; Chrch Yth Grp; Cmptr Clb; Emplmnt; Off Aide; Pep Squd; Vsity Clb; Ch Chr; Dnce; Drl Tm; Chrldg (V); GAA (V); PPSqd (V); CR (R); Computer; Psychology; Morehouse School of Medicine; Alabama State U

SPERRY, NICHOLAS J; MIFFLINTOWN, PA; JUNIATA CTY SD; (JR); Hnr Roll; MVP; Nat Hon Sy; St of Mnth; WWAHSS; Comm Volntr; Spec Olymp Vol; Chrch Yth Grp; Lttrmn Clb; Prom Com; Vsity Clb; Bskball (J); Ftball (V L); Track (V L); 300 H League Champion; 4 Year College

SPINA, PHILLIP; ELIZABETHTOWN, PA; LANCASTER CATHOLIC HS; MS; P to P St Amb Prg; Skiing (J); Swmg (J); Track (J); Destination Imagination Global Competition

Snoddy, Beth A
Warrior Run SD
Allenwood, PA

Smith, Krystin
Scranton HS
Scranton, PA

Smith, Halima
West Perry HS
New Bloomfield, PA

National
Honor Roll
Spring 2005

Smith, Elizabeth
Columbia-Montour AVTS
Bloomsburg, PA

Smith, Philip B
Triboro Christian AC
Nanticoke, PA

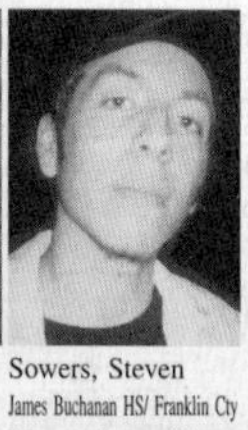
Sowers, Steven
James Buchanan HS/ Franklin Cty
Mercersburg, PA

SPROAT, WILLIAM; PHILADELPHIA, PA; NORTHEAST CATHOLIC BOYS HS; (SO); Hnr Roll; Comm Volntr; Chess; Cmptr Clb; DARE; Drma Clb; Mth Clb/Tm; Mus Clb; Scouts; Bnd; Stg Cre; Education/Teaching; Mathematics; Gettysburg College; West Chester

SPROULE, KEELEY; CRANBERRY TWP, PA; SENECA VALLEY SHS; (SR); Ctznshp Aw; Hi Hnr Roll; Nat Hon Sy; Nat Mrt Sch Recip; Otst Ac Ach Awd; Pres Sch; WWAHSS; Comm Volntr; Chrch Yth Grp; Drma Clb; Emplmnt; Key Club; Mus Clb; Acpl Chr; Chr; Dnce; SP/M/VS; Stu Cncl (T); CR (R); PMEA Honors / Regional & District Chorus; Thespian Society; Music Education; Kent State U

SRINIVASA, SAVITA; MONROEVILLE, PA; GATEWAY SR HS; (JR); Hi Hnr Roll; Nat Hon Sy; Sci Fairs; Mus Clb; German Clb; Dnce; Orch; German Teacher in an Elementary School; 3 Years-Multicultural Fest. (Fund Raiser); Chemistry; Music Teacher; Carnegie Mellon U; U of Pittsburgh

SRIVASTAVA, SHIKCHHA; BERWYN, PA; CONESTOGA HS; (FR); Hnr Roll; WWAHSS; Key Club; Scouts; Sch Ppr (R, P); Silver Award in Girl Scouts; Lawyer; NYU

STABLEY, LINDSEY A; DALLASTOWN, PA; DALLASTOWN AREA HS; (SR); Hnr Roll; Perf Att; DARE; Emplmnt; Stu Cncl (R); Scholastic Art Awards Competition; Microbiology; Human Biology; York College of Pennsylvania

STAHL, GABRIEL L; HARRISBURG, PA; CTRL DAUPHIN EAST HS; (JR); Comm Volntr; Key Club; Bnd; Chr; Stg Cre; Bskball (J); Fld Hky (J); Lcrsse (J); Community Service; Elementary Education; Business; Shippensburg U; Lebanon Valley College

STAHL, STEPHEN A; MONTROSE, PA; MONTROSE AREA SD; (SO); Hi Hnr Roll; WWAHSS; Chrch Yth Grp; Emplmnt; French Clb; Bnd; Jzz Bnd; Bsball (J); Cr Ctry (V L); Aeronautical Engineering

STAHLMAN, BRANDON; VANDERGRIFT, PA; LENAPE TECH; (JR); Ctznshp Aw; Nat Hon Sy; Nat Mrt Sch Recip; Perf Att; St of Mnth; St Optmst of Yr; Yth Ldrshp Prog; Comm Volntr; Hosp Aide; Peer Tut/Med; Chrch Yth Grp; Cmptr Clb; Drma Clb; Jr Ach; Mus Clb; Photog; SADD; Voc Ind Clb Am; CR (R); Culinary Arts; IUP (Indiana U of PA)

STALH, MEGAN; SUMMERHILL, PA; CTRL CAMBRIA HS; (FR); Hi Hnr Roll; Hnr Roll; MVP; Otst Ac Ach Awd; Perf Att; Comm Volntr; 4-H; Chrch Yth Grp; DARE; Jr Ach; Chr; Vllyball (JC); Nutritionist; Physical Therapist

STALLINGS, CHARDA; MARCUS HOOK, PA; CHICHESTER SR HS; (FR); Hnr Roll; Otst Ac Ach Awd; St of Mnth; ArtClub; Stg Cre; Consistent Homework Award; Massage Therapy; Art School

STANTON, AMANDA L; IRWIN, PA; YOUGH SD; (SO); Yth Ldrshp Prog; Comm Volntr; AL Aux Girls; French Clb; Chr; Lcrsse (V); North Huntingdon Township Junior Police; Venture Crew Unit #222; Neurology; Attorney; Louisiana State U; Penn State U

STARANKO, SHAUNA L; NORMALVILLE, PA; CONNELLSVILLE AREA; (JR); Hi Hnr Roll; Nat Hon Sy; Comm Volntr; Red Cr Aide; 4-H; Chrch Yth Grp; Quill & Scroll; Quiz Bowl; SADD; Bnd; Chr; Ch Chr; SP/M/VS; Chrldg (V); Track (V L); Stu Cncl (T); Sch Ppr (R); Broadcast Journalism

STARK, ABIGAIL; CLARKS SUMMIT, PA; TRIBORO CHRISTIAN AC; (SO); Chrldg; Sccr; Track; Soccer - Most Dedicated; Pre-Med

STARR, DEARBHAIL M; WAYNE, PA; CONESTOGA HS; (JR); Hnr Roll; Otst Ac Ach Awd; Comm Volntr; Chrch Yth Grp; Drma Clb; Key Club; Mus Clb; Chr; Dnce; SP/M/VS; Bskball (J); Fld Hky (V); Qualified Sailing Instructor / ISA Standard; Classical Vocal Training; Journalist; Law / Politics; Trinity College of Dublin Ireland; Cambridge U - UK

STAS, JULIE; WEXFORD, PA; NORTH ALLEGHENY HS; (SO); Ctznshp Aw; Hi Hnr Roll; MVP; Nat Hon Sy; Otst Ac Ach Awd; WWAHSS; Yth Ldrshp Prog; Comm Volntr; Chrch Yth Grp; Key Club; Pep Squd; French Clb; PP Ftbl (C); Scr Kpr (C); Vllyball (J); CR (R); Spirit Committee; Junior Olympics Volleyball; Communication; Fashion Design; UCLA-U of California Los Angeles

STAUFFER, JUSTIN L; AKRON, PA; LANCASTER CTY CTC; (SR); Perf Att; Sci Fairs; Comm Volntr; Peer Tut/Med; Emplmnt; Bskball (J); Devotional Leader in Homeroom; Most Improved Basketball Player 02-03; Respiratory Therapist; Stevens Trade School

STAWASZ, RYAN; HATFIELD, PA; NORTH PENN HS; (JR); Hi Hnr Roll; Hnr Roll; Nat Hon Sy; Otst Ac Ach Awd; Comm Volntr; Spec Olymp Vol; BPA; Chrch Yth Grp; FBLA; Key Club; Golf (V); Skiing (V); Black Belt in Karate; Entrepreneurship; Accounting; Pittsburgh U; Villanova U

STEEL, MICHAEL R; FREEDOM, PA; FREEDOM HS; (SO); Ctznshp Aw; Hi Hnr Roll; Nat Ldrshp Svc; Otst Ac Ach Awd; St of Mnth; Comm Volntr; ArtClub; Drma Clb; Mth Clb/Tm; Mod UN; NtlFrnscLg; Off Aide; Pep Squd; Svce Clb; Bnd; Chr; Mch Bnd; SP/M/VS; Golf (J); Skiing; Track (J); Sch Ppr (R); Yrbk (R); American Legion School Award; Member of Teen Leadership Care (TLC); Law or Political Sciences; Minor in Drama or the Romance Languages; U of Pennsylvania in Philadelphia; Princeton U

STEELE, ERICA E; PHOENIXVILLE, PA; PHOENIXVILLE AREA HS; (JR); Hnr Roll; Comm Volntr; Emplmnt; Key Club; Book Club Member; Involved in Community Service; International Business; Accounting; U of Pennsylvania; Fairleigh Dickinson U

STEFANYSZYN, ERICA J; TIMBLIN, PA; PUNXSUTAWNEY AREA HS; (JR); All Am Sch; Hi Hnr Roll; Nat Hon Sy; WWAHSS; Peer Tut/Med; Emplmnt; Photog; Sci Clb; Spanish Clb; PPSqd (J); PP Ftbl; Skiing; Sftball (VJ); Student Athletic Trainer; Chorus - Treasurer; Pre-Dentistry; U of Pittsburgh; Pennsylvania State U

STEHLE, SARAH M; PITTSBURGH, PA; CAREER CONNECTIONS CHARTER HS; (SR); Ch Chr; Bskball (J); Business Career; Writer/Short Stories; Community College of Allegheny County; La Roche College

STEIN, JUSTIN; NEW HOPE, PA; COUNCIL ROCK HS NORTH; (SO); Hi Hnr Roll; Hnr Roll; Perf Att; Sci Fairs; Sci/Math Olympn; ArtClub; Chrch Yth Grp; Scouts; Vllyball (J); Guitar Outside of School; Artist Outside and Inside School; Chemistry; Art; Penn State; U of Michigan

STEINHART, AARON; POTTSVILLE, PA; POTTSVILLE AREA HS; (FR); Hi Hnr Roll; Hnr Roll; Perf Att; WWAHSS; Comm Volntr; Key Club; German Clb; Swmg (V); Martial Arts - Brown Belt; Accountant / CPA; College Math Professor; Princeton U; Villanova U

STEPP, NICOLE; PHOENIXVILLE, PA; (SO); Hnr Roll; Peer Tut/Med; 4-H

STERNER, CHRISTOPHER R; ROCKWOOD, PA; ROCKWOOD HS; (SO); Hi Hnr Roll; Hnr Roll; St of Mnth; Comm Volntr; Bnd; Chr; Bsball (J); Bskball (J); Sccr (VJ); Track (V); Business Management

STERNGOLD, DAVID; MUNCY, PA; MUNCY HS; (FR); Hi Hnr Roll; Pres Ac Ftns Aw; St of Mnth; Yth Ldrshp Prog; ArtClub; Emplmnt; Bskball (J L); Sccr (V L); Tennis (V L); Adv Cncl (R); Cl Off (P); Stu Cncl (R); Lit Mag (E); Diplomatic Service / Foreign Service; Princeton U; U of Michigan

STEVENS, MARISSA A; MASONTOWN, PA; ALBERT GALLATIN HS; (JR); All Am Sch; Ctznshp Aw; DAR; F Lan Hn Soc; Gov Hnr Prg; Hi Hnr Roll; Nat Hon Sy; Nat Ldrshp Svc; Otst Ac Ach Awd; Sci/Math Olympn; Comm Volntr; Hosp Aide; Dbte Team; Jr Ach; Mth Clb/Tm; Mod UN; NYLC; P to P St Amb Prg; Quiz Bowl; Schol Bwl; Bnd; Dnce; Mch Bnd; Orch; Competitive Dance Team Member-Clarinet Section Leader; Student Dance Instructor-Academic League; Archaeology; History / Music; Harvard; Carnegie-Mellon

STEVENSON, KERI A; WILKES BARRE, PA; HANOVER AREA JR/SR HS; (JR); F Lan Hn Soc; Hi Hnr Roll; Jr Eng Tech; Nat Hon Sy; Perf Att; Sci Fairs; WWAHSS; Yth Ldrshp Prog; Peer Tut/Med; Drma Clb; Emplmnt; Key Club; Mod UN; Svce Clb; SP/M/VS; Chrldg (V CL); Sftball (J); Stu Cncl (R); Yrbk (E); National History Day-State Award; PA Junior Academy of Science-State Award; Mathematics/Engineering; Neuroscience; Harvard U; Princeton U

STEWARD, REBECCA; WATERFORD, PA; FT LEBOEUF HS; (SO); Hnr Roll; Chrch Yth Grp; Mod UN; Chr; SP/M/VS; Chrldg (VJ L); Cr Ctry (J); Gmnstcs (V); Yrbk; Varsity Cheerleader-Football & Basketball; Biology; Edinboro College

STEWART, MONTEL; PITTSBURGH, PA; PITTSBURGH SD; (SO); Hnr Roll; St of Mnth; Comm Volntr; Chess; DARE; Tech Clb; Vllyball (J); U of California; U of Pittsburgh

STILSON, COREY A; ULYSSES, PA; NORTHERN POTTER SD; (JR); Hi Hnr Roll; Hnr Roll; Nat Hon Sy; St of Mnth; WWAHSS; Chrch Yth Grp; Emplmnt; FBLA; Prom Com; Bskball (J); Vsy Clb (V); Secondary Education; Accounting; Clarion U; Lock Haven U

STINE, APRIL; BANGOR, PA; BANGOR AREA HS; (SO); Hnr Roll; MVP; Otst Ac Ach Awd; St of Mnth; DARE; Emplmnt; Vsity Clb; Spanish Clb; Chr; PP Ftbl (J); Rqtball (V); Tennis (VJCL); Wt Lftg (V); Most Improved Tennis Player; Most Wins Ever At First Singles - Tennis; Accounting; Marine Biology; Penn State; U of Pittsburgh

STINE, LINDSEY; WILLIAMSPORT, PA; LOYALSOCK TWP HS; (JR); Hnr Roll; Key Club; French Clb; Clr Grd; Mch Bnd; Veterinarian

STINSON, LAUREL T; DOYLESTOWN, PA; CTRL BUCKS HS EAST; (JR); F Lan Hn Soc; Hi Hnr Roll; WWAHSS; Hab For Humty Volntr; Peer Tut/Med; Emplmnt; Key Club; Mus Clb; P to P St Amb Prg; Prom Com; French Clb; Bnd; Chr; Mch Bnd; SP/M/VS; PP Ftbl; Track (V L); Cl Off (T); PMEA District II Band - 2004 / 2005; PMEA Region VI Band 2005; Music Education; Mathematics; Northwestern U; Rice U

STITZINGER, JENNIE; DOYLESTOWN, PA; CTRL BUCKS HS EAST; (SO); F Lan Hn Soc; Hi Hnr Roll; Otst Ac Ach Awd; WWAHSS; Comm Volntr; FCA; Key Club; Chr; Student Council Member; Principal's Award; Culinary Arts; Marine Biology; Johnson and Wales U; Culinary Institute of America

STOCK, ESTHER L.; FAIRVIEW, PA; MC DOWELL INT HS; (SO); Hi Hnr Roll; Hnr Roll; Comm Volntr; Chrch Yth Grp; FCA; Chr; Ch Chr; SP/M/VS; Stg Cre; Cr Ctry; Track (V); Church Volunteer; Poem Published in "Celebrate! Young Poets Speak Out"; Nurse Practitioner; Engineering; Gannon U; Waynesburg College

STODART, JAKE; OLANTA, PA; CLEARFIELD AREA HS; (JR); Hnr Roll; WWAHSS; Lib Aide; Prom Com

STOFFLET, GORDON; GOULDSBORO, PA; NORTH POCONO HS; (FR); Bnd; Mch Bnd; Marching Band/Concert Band; Rifle Club; Auto Mechanics; Technological College

STOKES, ALEXIS; BROWNSVILLE, PA; BROWNSVILLE AREA; (SO); Hi Hnr Roll; Nat Hon Sy; WWAHSS; Hosp Aide; ArtClub; DARE; FCCLA; Off Aide; Pep Squd; Photog; Prom Com; Vsity Clb; Chrldg (V); Stu Cncl (R); Yrbk (E, P); Youth Education Association; Forensics; Nursing; Penn State U; Waynesburg College

STOLEY, KARA; SHREWSBURY, PA; SUSQUEHANNOCK HS; (SO); Hi Hnr Roll; Otst Ac Ach Awd; Comm Volntr; Peer Tut/Med; Scouts; Svce Clb; SADD; Spanish Clb; Bnd; Jzz Bnd; Mch Bnd; Orch; Stu Cncl (R); Varsity Letter in Band; Spanish Award; Advertising; Journalism; Yale U; Columbia U

STOLTZFUS, ANGELICA; CAMP HILL, PA; CAMP HILL HS; (FR); Ctznshp Aw; Hnr Roll; MVP; Nat Hon Sy; Yth Ldrshp Prog; Peer Tut/Med; Chrch Yth Grp; Chr; Bskball (J); Track (V); Cl Off (P); Stu Cncl (R); CR (R); Volunteer Club; Soccer Travel Team Club; Lawyer; Broadcasting; Dickinson College; Messiah College

STOLTZFUS, SAMANTHA L; LITITZ, PA; MANHEIM TWP HS; (JR); Hnr Roll; WWAHSS; DARE; Key Club; Scouts; Acpl Chr; Bnd; Chr; Dnce; PP Ftbl (J); Sccr; Troubadours; PMEA District 7 Chorus; Performing Arts Major; Musical Theatre Major

STONER, MICHAEL R; GREENVILLE, PA; REYNOLDS JR/SR HS; (FR); Hnr Roll; Nat Hon Sy; Comm Volntr; Peer Tut/Med; Key Club; Off Aide; Tchrs Aide; Culinary Arts; Police Academy; Pittsburg State U; Penn State U

STOUDT, CHRIS; RICHBORO, PA; COUNCIL ROCK HS NORTH; (JR); F Lan Hn Soc; Hi Hnr Roll; Nat Hon Sy; Nat Mrt Fin; Perf Att; Sci/Math Olympn; Valdctrian; Comm Volntr; Peer Tut/Med; Red Cr Aide; Dbte Team; Emplmnt; Mth Clb/Tm; Quiz Bowl; Sci Clb; German Clb; Lcrsse (V); Model Congress, Political Science Club; Red Cross Jub Fundraising Chairman; Physics; Harvard College; Yale U

STOUFFER, MORGAN J; IRWIN, PA; HOMESCHOOL; (SR); WWAHSS; Comm Volntr; Chrch Yth Grp; Emplmnt; P to P St Amb Prg; Scouts; Ch Chr; SP/M/VS; Gold Medal of Achievement; Lead America; Music Therapy; Seton Hill U

STOVER, BRIANNA; MILLHEIM, PA; PENNS VALLEY JR/SR HS; (FR); 4H Awd; Hnr Roll; Perf Att; St of Mnth; Comm Volntr; Hab For Humty Volntr; Peer Tut/Med; 4-H; Chrch Yth Grp; DARE; Mus Clb; Chr; Stg Cre; Scr Kpr (L); Sftball (J); Elementary Phys. Ed. Teacher; Penn State U

STOVER, KIRK A; MILLHEIM, PA; CTRL PA INST OF SCI HS; (JR); 4H Awd; Hi Hnr Roll; Perf Att; St of Mnth; Comm Volntr; Hab For Humty Volntr; Red Cr Aide; 4-H; Chrch Yth Grp; Emplmnt; Lttrmn Clb; Ntl FFA; Vsity Clb; Fbball (VJ L); Yrbk (E); Crime Scene Investigator; Science; Central Penn College; Penn Tech

STRAUB, SARAH E; NEW KENSINGTON, PA; ST JOSEPH HS; (SO); Hi Hnr Roll; Sci Fairs; St of Mnth; Comm Volntr; Drma Clb; Mus Clb; Outdrs Clb; Chr; SP/M/VS; Stg Cre; Chrldg (J); Gmnstcs; Tennis (J); Cl Off (T); Level 7 Gymnast, Member ACA; PJAS State Finalist, PA History Day Com; Physical Therapy; Sports Therapy

STRAUSKULAGE, MATTHEW; LAKE ARIEL, PA; NORTH POCONO HS; (FR); Hi Hnr Roll; Hnr Roll; Otst Ac Ach Awd; Drma Clb; SP/M/VS; Sch Ppr (R); Johns Hopkins Cty Talent Search; Acting; Communications

STRAUSS, RACHEL A; NEW KENSINGTON, PA; BURRELL HS; (FR); Hi Hnr Roll; Hnr Roll; Pres Ac Ftns Aw; Comm Volntr; Red Cr Aide; ArtClub; Dbte Team; Drma Clb; Mus Clb; P to P St Amb Prg; Scouts; Svce Clb; French Clb; Chr; Dnce; Drl Tm; Swg Chr; Bskball (J); Tennis (V); Track (L); Stu Cncl (R); Sch Ppr (R); Distinguished Student Status - Based on SAT Scores from Johns Hopkins U; Law; Engineering; U of Pittsburgh; Georgetown U

STRAUSS, SANDRALEE; MARIANNA, PA; BETHLEHEM CTR SR HS; (FR); Hi Hnr Roll; Hnr Roll; AL Aux Girls; Chrch Yth Grp; American Legion Auxiliary Award (Twice); Bachelor's and Master's in Computer Programming; Culinary Arts

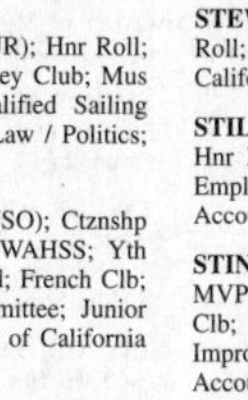

Stoley, Kara
Susquehannock HS
Shrewsbury, PA

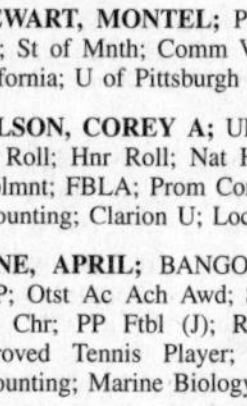

Stokes, Alexis
Brownsville Area
Brownsville, PA

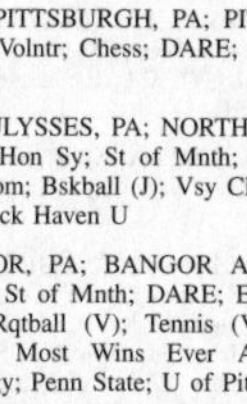

Sterngold, David
Muncy HS
Muncy, PA

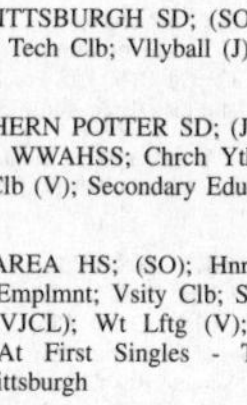

Stock, Esther L.
Mc Dowell Int HS
Fairview, PA

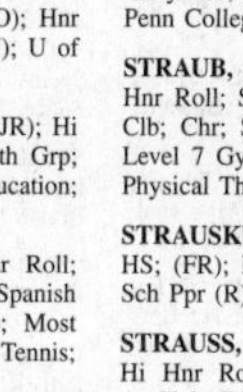

Stoltzfus, Samantha L
Manheim Twp HS
Lititz, PA

STRAYER, MEGAN; GREENSBURG, PA; GREATER LATROBE HS; (JR); F Lan Hn Soc; Nat Hon Sy; Pres Ac Ftns Aw; WWAHSS; Comm Volntr; Peer Tut/Med; Chrch Yth Grp; Emplmnt; Key Club; Lttrmn Clb; Off Aide; German Clb; Sccr (V L); Track (V L); Sch Ppr (E); Optometry Degree; Washington and Jefferson; Le Moyne

STRICKLER JR, GERALD E; TREMONT, PA; PINE GROVE AREA HS; (FR); Hnr Roll; ROTC; Clr Grd; Bsball (J); Ftball (J); Wrstlg (J); U.S. Naval Academy

STRIPLET, STEPHANIE; PHILADELPHIA, PA; OLNEY HS; (SR); Comm Volntr; Ch Chr; Vllyball (V); Community College of Philadelphia

STROSNIDER, MARLIE A; ELLWOOD CITY, PA; LINCOLN JR/SR HS; (SR); Hi Hnr Roll; Hnr Roll; Perf Att; CARE; Comm Volntr; Chrch Yth Grp; Dbte Team; Drma Clb; Emplmnt; Key Club; Photog; Scouts; French Clb; Chr; SP/M/VS; Bskball (J); Chrldg (V); Golf (VJ L); PP Ftbl (VJ); Skiing (VJ); Sftball (VJ); Swmg; Biology; Health; St Vincent U

STRUBY, CHRIS R; DOYLESTOWN, PA; CTRL BUCKS HS EAST; (SR); Duke TS; Hi Hnr Roll; MVP; Nat Hon Sy; Nat Mrt LOC; WWAHSS; Comm Volntr; Red Cr Aide; Chrch Yth Grp; Key Club; Scouts; Bnd; Chr; Dnce; Jzz Bnd; Ice Hky (V); Rlr Hky; Sccr (V); MVP- Varsity Ice Hockey; Coaches Award - Ice Hockey Princeton; Pre-Med / Medical School; Lehigh U

STUBBS, AMANDA; NEW KENSINGTON, PA; KISKI AREA HS; (JR); Hi Hnr Roll; Hnr Roll; Perf Att; Comm Volntr; Key Club; Spanish Clb; Bskball (J L); Scr Kpr (J); Skiing (J); Tennis (V L); Sch Ppr (R); Journalism; Communications; Robert Morris U; Westminster College

STUBERT, ADAM; GREENVILLE, PA; GREENVILLE HS; (SO); All Am Sch; Hi Hnr Roll; Hnr Roll; WWAHSS; Hosp Aide; Key Club; Lttrmn Clb; Sci Clb; Cr Ctry (V L); Track (V L); Stu Cncl (R); National Society of High School Scholars; Who's Who Among American High School Students; Chemistry; Medicine; U of Pittsburgh; Case Western Reserve

STUBERT, JAMES; GREENVILLE, PA; GREENVILLE HS; (SO); All Am Sch; Hi Hnr Roll; Hnr Roll; WWAHSS; Key Club; Lttrmn Clb; Sci Clb; Cr Ctry (V L); Track (J L); National Society of High School Scholars; Who's Who Among High School Students; History; Education; Westminster U; Indiana U of Pennsylvania

STUCKEY, REBECCA; CLEARVILLE, PA; EVERETT AREA HS; (SR); F Lan Hn Soc; Hi Hnr Roll; Jr Mshl; Nat Hon Sy; St of Mnth; Chrch Yth Grp; Emplmnt; FBLA; Prom Com; French Clb; Chr; GAA (V); Scr Kpr (J); Tennis (V L); Cl Off (S); Stu Cncl (R); Yrbk; Majorettes-Co-Captain; Major in Accounting; Saint Francis U; U of Pittsburgh

STUDENROTH, BETH; TYLERSPORT, PA; SOUDERTON AREA HS; (SR); Hi Hnr Roll; Hnr Roll; Perf Att; Comm Volntr; Spec Olymp Vol; Chrch Yth Grp; Bnd; Ch Chr; Clr Grd; Mch Bnd; Dvng (V); Nursing (RN); Mission; Montgomery County College

STUFFLE, DEAN; HANOVER, PA; SOUTH WESTERN HS; (JR); Hi Hnr Roll; Hnr Roll; Nat Hon Sy; Perf Att; Comm Volntr; Chrch Yth Grp; Cmptr Clb; DARE; Emplmnt; National Youth Leadership Forum Technology Nomination; The National Society of High School Scholars Member; Computer Networking; Computer Tech; Pennsylvania College of Technology, Williamsport

STULL, JESSICA; BRADFORD, PA; BRADFORD AREA HS; (FR); Hnr Roll; Chrch Yth Grp; DARE; Chrldg (J); Elementary Education; Youth Ministry; Mt Vernon U; Eastern Nazarene College

STUSH, ALAINA; MIFFLINBURG, PA; MIFFLINBURG AREA HS; (JR); Hi Hnr Roll; Hnr Roll; Nat Hon Sy; WWAHSS; Comm Volntr; Drma Clb; HO'Br Yth Ldrshp; Key Club; Prom Com; Spanish Clb; Chr; SP/M/VS; Sccr (J); CR; Sch Ppr (R); Certified SCUBA Diver; Building Leaders for the Susquehanna Valley; Biology; Dermatology; Villanova U

STUVEK, MEGAN; CARMICHAELS, PA; CARMICHAELS AREA JR/SR HS; (SO); Bskball (V L); Stu Cncl (R); Medial Field; Chiropractics; Bucknell U; West Virginia

SUBE, CLAIR; HERSHEY, PA; HERSHEY HS; (FR); Hnr Roll; Hab For Humty Volntr; Chrch Yth Grp; DARE; Emplmnt; Bnd; Jzz Bnd; Mch Bnd; Bskball (JC); Sftball (J); Psychology; Coaching; Villa Julie; Bloomsburg U

SUBE, DAVID; HERSHEY, PA; HERSHEY HS; (JR); Hi Hnr Roll; Hab For Humty Volntr; Chrch Yth Grp; DARE; Emplmnt; Quiz Bowl; Bnd; Jzz Bnd; Mch Bnd; Pep Bnd; Music Teacher; Math Teacher; Lebanon Valley College; Mansfield U

SULLIVAN, DUSTIE; SAYLORSBURG, PA; PLEASANT VALLEY HS; (JR); Hnr Roll; Comm Volntr; AL Aux Girls; Volunteer at Nursing Home HCR - MCHS; Business Management; Kutztown College; East Stroudsburg U

SUMMA, BRANDEN; DUNMORE, PA; DUNMORE SD; (MS); Hi Hnr Roll; Nat Hon Sy; Black Belt Karate; Medical Doctor

SUMMERS, ANDREA; LANCASTER, PA; MANHEIM TWP HS; (SO); Hi Hnr Roll; Hnr Roll; WWAHSS; Key Club; Medical Career; Franklin & Marshall College; Millersville U

SUMMERS, LYDIA; BLOOMSBURG, PA; WATSONTOWN CHRISTIAN AC; (FR); Chrch Yth Grp; Ch Chr; Sccr (V); Track (V); Cl Off (T); Yrbk (R); Psychology; Bible; Word of Life Bible Institute

SUMMERVILLE, CHARLISA; WHITEHALL, PA; WHITEHALL-COPLAY HS; (SO); Hi Hnr Roll; Hnr Roll; Pres Ac Ftns Aw; St of Mnth; Yth Ldrshp Prog; Peer Tut/Med; P to P St Amb Prg; Tchrs Aide; Sccr (V); Tennis (J); CR (R); Pharmacy; Temple U; Auburn U

SUN, FAN; DU BOIS, PA; DU BOIS AREA SD; (JR); Hnr Roll; Nat Hon Sy; BPA; Emplmnt; Mth Clb/Tm; Prom Com; Sci Clb; SP/M/VS; Sccr (V); Vllyball (V); Stu Cncl; Financial; International Business; Penn State U

SUNDRY, CHRISTINA; GREENSBURG, PA; GREENSBURG SALEM HS; (JR); Hi Hnr Roll; Hnr Roll; Perf Att; WWAHSS; Prom Com; Scouts; French Clb; Chr; PP Ftbl (V); Vllyball (VJ); Stu Cncl (R); CR (R); Business Management; Marketing; Penn State U; U of South Carolina

SURRY, PAUL; MECHANICSBURG, PA; TRINITY HS; (JR); Hnr Roll; Nat Hon Sy; Sci Fairs; Peer Tut/Med; Drma Clb; Emplmnt; Scouts; Latin Clb; Bnd; SP/M/VS; Ftball (J); CR (R); History; Saint Joseph's U; U of Scranton

SUYDAM, KRISTIE; LANCASTER, PA; MANHEIM TOWNSHIP HS; (SO); Hnr Roll; Comm Volntr; Spec Olymp Vol; Chrch Yth Grp; Key Club; Board Member of Key Club International; Secondary Education; Youth Ministry; Eastern U; Columbia International U

SWACKHAMMER, MATTHEW; PITTSBURGH, PA; PLUM SR HS; (SO); Hnr Roll; Bnd; Mch Bnd; SP/M/VS

SWANGO, JAMIE L; BENTLEYVILLE, PA; BENTWORTH HS; (JR); Hi Hnr Roll; Hnr Roll; Nat Hon Sy; Pres Sch; WWAHSS; Comm Volntr; Chrch Yth Grp; Drma Clb; FBLA; Prom Com; SADD; Chr; Ch Chr; Mch Bnd; SP/M/VS; Mar Art (V); PP Ftbl (V); Sftball (J); Track (J); Entworth Leo Club; Pre-Med; Psychology; Arcadia U; Washington and Jefferson U

SWANSON, GEORGE A; KERSEY, PA; SMA HS; (SO); Hnr Roll; German Clb; Diesel Mechanics; Metal Fabrication; Wyo Tech; Universal Technical Institute

SWART, JADA K; YOUNGSVILLE, PA; YOUNGSVILLE MIDDLE SR HS; (FR); Hi Hnr Roll; Hnr Roll; Otst Ac Ach Awd; DARE; Emplmnt; Off Aide; Photog; Svce Clb; SADD; Spanish Clb; Bskball (V); Chrldg (V); Track (J); Cl Off (T); CR (T); Yrbk (R, P); Ophelia Club, Yearbook Committee; Baseball-Stats; Psychologist; Pediatrician; Penn State; Pitt

SWARTZ, BROCK E; HANOVER, PA; SOUTH WESTERN HS; (SR); DAR; Hi Hnr Roll; Hnr Roll; Nat Hon Sy; WWAHSS; Yth Ldrshp Prog; Comm Volntr; Chrch Yth Grp; Dbte Team; Emplmnt; Key Club; Prom Com; Scouts; Tennis (J); Cl Off (P); Stu Cncl (R); Eagle Scout; Political Science; Pre-Law

SWARTZ, JESSICA; MIFFLINTOWN, PA; JUNIATA HS; (JR); Hnr Roll; Nat Hon Sy; WWAHSS; Comm Volntr; Spec Olymp Vol; Chrch Yth Grp; Key Club; Prom Com; Vsity Clb; Chr; Ch Chr; SP/M/VS; Stg Cre; Bskball (V); Sccr (V); Track (V); Vsy Clb (V); Dance-Private School; Messiah-Medical; Penn State-Medical; Messiah Medical; Penn State Medical

SWEELY, AMY; JERSEY SHORE, PA; JERSEY SHORE AREA SR HS; (JR); Hi Hnr Roll; Hnr Roll; Nat Hon Sy; WWAHSS; Chrch Yth Grp; FBLA; Key Club; Mod UN; Prom Com; Bskball (VJ L); Sftball (VJ L); Tennis (VJ L); Cl Off (R); Radiography; Pennsylvania College of Technology

SWEELY, EMILY; JERSEY SHORE, PA; JERSEY SHORE AREA SR HS; (FR); Ctznshp Aw; Hi Hnr Roll; WWAHSS; Chrch Yth Grp; FBLA; Key Club; Bskball (J); Tennis (J); Track (V L); CR (R)

SWEENEY, BRANDON; CRESCO, PA; POCONO MTN SR HS; (SO); Hnr Roll; Perf Att; St of Mnth; Comm Volntr; Spec Olymp Vol; DARE; Emplmnt; Scouts; Cr Ctry (V L); Track (V); CR (R); Eagle Scout; Criminal Justice; Police Administration; Temple U

SWEENEY JR, PAUL J; DARBY, PA; MONSIGNOR BONNER HS; (JR); Perf Att; WWAHSS; DARE; Psychology; Graphic Design; Widener U; Brown U

SWIDINSKY, JESSICA; STILLWATER, PA; BENTON AREA HS; (SR); Hi Hnr Roll; Hnr Roll; Nat Hon Sy; Pres Sch; WWAHSS; Peer Tut/Med; Red Cr Aide; ArtClub; Drma Clb; Emplmnt; Key Club; Mod UN; Mus Clb; Prom Com; Svce Clb; Bnd; Chr; Mch Bnd; SP/M/VS; Sch Ppr (R); Voted "Most Artistic Senior" By Class of 2005; President of 2004/2005 Art Club; Fashion Design; Accounting; Fashion Institute of Design and Merchandising; Drexel

SWISHER, COLTON L; LEWISTOWN, PA; LEWISTOWN AREA HS; (SO); Hnr Roll; Perf Att; Comm Volntr; Spec Olymp Vol; Chrch Yth Grp; Key Club; Bskball (J); Tobacco Busters; Key Club; Major in Education (Secondary); Shippensburg U; Penn State

SWITZER, SHEILA D; CAMP HILL, PA; CAMP HILL SD HS; (SO); Hi Hnr Roll; Hnr Roll; Peer Tut/Med; Lib Aide; Bnd; Drm Mjr; Jzz Bnd; Mch Bnd; Cr Ctry; Yrbk; Art; Medicine; U of Pittsburgh; York College

SZEWCZUK, BARBARA; SPARTANSBURG, PA; CORRY AREA HS; (JR); Hi Hnr Roll; Hnr Roll; Nat Hon Sy; Perf Att; WWAHSS; Peer Tut/Med; Acpl Chr; Chr; Scr Kpr (J); Biology; Pre-Med; Wittenburg U; Xavier U

SZRAMOWSKI, JESSICA L; GLENSHAW, PA; SHALER AREA HS; (JR); Hi Hnr Roll; Hnr Roll; MVP; Nat Hon Sy; Perf Att; Comm Volntr; ArtClub; Emplmnt; Bskball (J); Vllyball (V CL); CR (R); Advertising; Master's Degree / Business; U of Pittsburgh; Point Park U

TALARICO, ALYSSA; PHOENIXVILLE, PA; PHOENIXVILLE AREA HS; (JR); Ctznshp Aw; F Lan Hn Soc; Hi Hnr Roll; Yth Ldrshp Prog; Key Club; Prom Com; Spanish Clb; Lcrsse (V); Stu Cncl (R); CR (R); Fashion Merchandising; Business; Drexel U

TAMECKI, KAYLA; DILLSBURG, PA; NORTHERN YORK HS; (FR); Hnr Roll; Perf Att; Pres Ac Ftns Aw; Sci Fairs; Comm Volntr; Hosp Aide; Peer Tut/Med; DARE; Key Club; Lttrmn Clb; Pep Squd; SADD; French Clb; Dnce; Chrldg (J L); Gmnstcs (J)

TANNER, ASHLEY; PIPERSVILLE, PA; CTRL BUCKS EAST HS; (FR); 4H Awd; Hnr Roll; 4-H; Chrch Yth Grp; DARE; Chr; Sccr (J); CR (R); Science Degrees; Veterinarian; U of Pennsylvania; Oxford U

TAQE, SAYED; BETHLEHEM, PA; LIBERTY HS; (SR); Hnr Roll; Track (V); Cricket; Aviation Science; Lehigh Carbon Community College

TARTT-MINOR, CHANEL A; PHILADELPHIA, PA; PHILADELPHIA HS; (JR); Hnr Roll; WWAHSS; Comm Volntr; Vsity Clb; Cr Ctry (V C); Track (V C); Representative of Athletic Association; Communications; Spelman College; North Carolina A & T State U

TATE, BRYAN; PHILADELPHIA, PA; NORRIS S BARRATT MS; (MS); Perf Att; Sci/Math Olympn; SP/M/VS; Bsball (V); Computer Repair Technician; Temple U

TAWEH, JUMAH P; UPPER DARBY, PA; UPPER DARBY HS; (JR); Hi Hnr Roll; Hnr Roll; Nat Ldrshp Svc; Perf Att; St of Mnth; Yth Ldrshp Prog; CARE; Comm Volntr; Peer Tut/Med; DARE; Emplmnt; Svce Clb; Chr; Ch Chr; SP/M/VS; School President-Building W/Books; Tutor-ESL Adult Classes; Pre-Med (Pediatrician); Education (Elementary School Teacher); Penn State U Park; West Chester U

TAWNEY, MELISSA; STOYSTOWN, PA; SHANKSVILLE-STONYCREEK HS; (SO); Duke TS; Hnr Roll; Nat Hon Sy; Nat Sci Aw; Sci/Math Olympn; Comm Volntr; Peer Tut/Med; Chrch Yth Grp; Emplmnt; Quiz Bowl; Schol Bwl; Tchrs Aide; Dnce; Physical Therapist / Biology

TAWODA, TOMMY; PITTSBURGH, PA; UPPER ST CLAIR HS; (JR); Hnr Roll; USAA; Yth Ldrshp Prog; Comm Volntr; Red Cr Aide; Spec Olymp Vol; DARE; Emplmnt; FBLA; NYLC; Svce Clb; Spanish Clb; Bnd; Bskball; Ftball; Golf; Lcrsse; Skiing; Cl Off (V); Stu Cncl (V); CR (V); USC Community Day Plan Coordinator; Red Cross Volunteer; Engineering; Pre-Med; Penn State U; U of Pittsburgh

TAYLOR, ALITA; PHILADELPHIA, PA; (FR); Hnr Roll; Otst Ac Ach Awd; Perf Att; St of Mnth; Peer Tut/Med; Chrch Yth Grp; Emplmnt; French Clb; Ch Chr; Dnce; Yrbk (R); Masters; PhD; Howard U; Southern California U

TAYLOR, AMANDA C; FEASTERVILLE TREVOSE, PA; BENSALEM TOWNSHIP SD; (FR); Hi Hnr Roll; Hnr Roll; MVP; Otst Ac Ach Awd; Swmg (V); Interior Design; LaSalle U; U of Miami

TAYLOR, CHELSEA; BEAVER FALLS, PA; BIG BEAVER FALLS SR HS; (JR); Hi Hnr Roll; Nat Hon Sy; St of Mnth; WWAHSS; Comm Volntr; Chrch Yth Grp; Key Club; SADD; Vsity Clb; Spanish Clb; Bnd; Mch Bnd; Chrldg (V); Vsy Clb (V); Yrbk (P); Rachel Carson/9,000 Sch Award; Chosen Section Leader of My Band; Elementary Education; Communications; Slippery Rock U; Clarion U

TAYLOR, CHRIS; HERMITAGE, PA; HICKORY HS; (FR); Hi Hnr Roll; Pres Ac Ftns Aw; St of Mnth; WWAHSS; Bnd; Jzz Bnd; Mch Bnd; Bskball; Psychology

TAYLOR, CYNTHIA; SCHWENKSVILLE, PA; BOYERTOWN AREA SR HS; (JR); Hi Hnr Roll; Nat Hon Sy; Emplmnt; Key Club; Lcrsse (V); PP Ftbl; Scr Kpr; Sccr (V C); Track (V); PAC - 10 Honorable Mention; Top Soccer Buddy; Secondary Education; Shippensburg U; Gettysburg College

TAYLOR, JANITRA R; PHILADELPHIA, PA; CARVER ENG AND SCI; (SO); Hi Hnr Roll; Hnr Roll; Nat Hon Sy; Otst Ac Ach Awd; Red Cr Aide; Emplmnt; Ntl Beta Clb; Dnce; Chrldg (V); Mock Trial / Young Scholars Program; ACE Mentor Group / Women in Science and Engineering; Engineering; Business; U of Pennsylvania; Drexel U

TAYLOR, JEANITA; ERIE, PA; STRONG VINCENT HS; (JR); Hnr Roll; Perf Att; ROTC; Spanish Clb

TAYLOR, NICKESHA; READING, PA; READING HS; (SO); Hnr Roll; Otst Ac Ach Awd; Perf Att; Sci Fairs; St of Mnth; Peer Tut/Med; FBLA; Tchrs Aide; Dnce; Track; Law; Business; Cheney U; Kutztown U

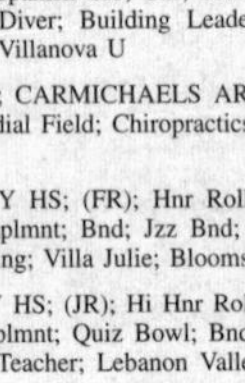

Taweh, Jumah P
Upper Darby HS
Upper Darby, PA

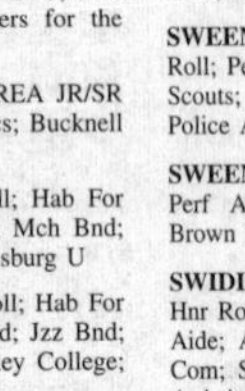

Sun, Fan
Du Bois Area SD
Du Bois, PA

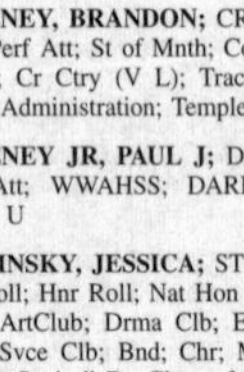

Summa, Branden
Dunmore SD
Dunmore, PA

National
Honor Roll
Spring 2005

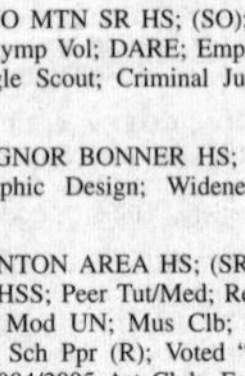

Struby, Chris R
Central Bucks HS East
Doylestown, PA

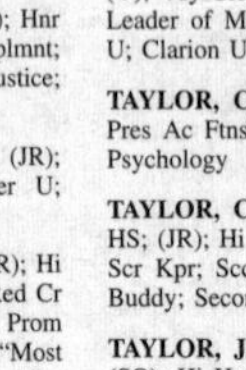

Tartt-Minor, Chanel A
Philadelphia HS
Philadelphia, PA

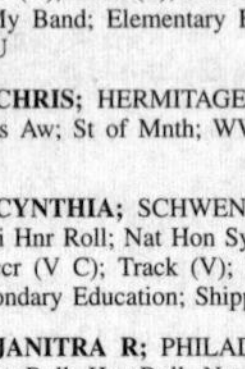

Taylor, Janitra R
Carver Eng And Sci
Philadelphia, PA

TAYLOR, SARA; LEWISTOWN, PA; LEWISTOWN AREA HS; (FR); Hi Hnr Roll; Nat Hon Sy; Hosp Aide; Spec Olymp Vol; Chrch Yth Grp; Key Club; Spanish Clb; Dnce; Sftball (J); Stu Cncl (P); CR (R); Yrbk (E, P); Radiology

TAYLOR, TRACEY N; PHILA, PA; (SO); Ctznshp Aw; Peer Tut/Med; DARE; Drma Clb; Quiz Bowl; SP/M/VS; Work with Electronics; Participated in Writing Contest; Biology; Chemistry; Temple U; Morgan State U

TE, KENNY; ROYERSFORD, PA; SPRING-FORD SR HS; (SO); Hnr Roll; Otst Ac Ach Awd; Perf Att; Pres Ac Ftns Aw; Ftball (J); Track (J); Have Won Many Karate Trophies; My Art Work Has Been Showcased In Middle & High School; Business; Marketing; U of Maryland U College; U of Delaware

TELL, LAYNIE A; MONROEVILLE, PA; GATEWAY SR HS; (JR); Hi Hnr Roll; Hnr Roll; Pres Ac Ftns Aw; WWAHSS; Comm Volntr; Drma Clb; Jr Cls League; Key Club; P to P St Amb Prg; Tmpl Yth Grp; Chr; SP/M/VS; Sccr; Stu Cncl (S); CR (R); Yrbk (R)

TELLO, MARCO A; ALLENTOWN, PA; WILLIAM ALLEN HS; (SO); Hnr Roll; Kutztown Upward Bound Program; 2nd Mile Leadership Programs; Lawyer; Chef; Penn State; Kutztown Upward Bound Program

TEME, JONA; PHILADELPHIA, PA; FRANKLIN LEARNING CTR; (SO); Hi Hnr Roll; Perf Att; St of Mnth; ALBAMIAN Clb; Aids Week Volunteer; Consistent Honor Roll; Pediatrician; Pharmacist; Temple U; Penn State U

TENGERES, JONATHAN P; ELLWOOD CITY, PA; LAWRENCE CTY VO-TECH; (SR); Emplmnt; Stage Crew for 3 Years; Enjoys Riding Dirt Bike; Triangle Tech-Carpentry; Triangle Tech

TESTA, CHRISSY; PHOENIXVILLE, PA; PHOENIXVILLE HS; (SO); Hi Hnr Roll; Hnr Roll; Nat Hon Sy; Dbte Team; Emplmnt; Schol Bwl; Scouts; Spanish Clb; Bnd; Stg Cre; Track; Girl Scout Silver Award; Finance; Business Management; Harvard U; U of Pennsylvania

TESTA, JOSEPH; AMITY, PA; TRINITY HS; (JR); Bskball (V L); Lcrsse (V L); Stu Cncl (R); Volunteer-Mayview State Hospital; Volunteer-American Respiratory Alliance

THERA, STEPHANIE S; PHILADELPHIA, PA; SAMUEL FELS HS; (SR); F Lan Hn Soc; Hnr Roll; Nat Mrt Semif; Perf Att; WWAHSS; Comm Volntr; Peer Tut/Med; Chrch Yth Grp; Prom Com; Tchrs Aide; French Clb; Ch Chr; Dnce; Bdmtn (J); Bskball; Chrldg (J); Gmnstcs; Tennis (VJ); Vllyball (V); Cl Off (V); White Williams Scholars; Honor Roll Each School Year; Nursing BSN / MSN; Pre-Med / Pediatrician; Penn State U Park; West Chester U of Pennsylvania

THISTLE, GINNY; WEXFORD, PA; NORTH ALLEGHENY INT HS; (FR); Hi Hnr Roll; MVP; Nat Hon Sy; Otst Ac Ach Awd; Sci/Math Olympn; St of Mnth; Valdctrian; Yth Ldrshp Prog; Comm Volntr; Chrch Yth Grp; Emplmnt; Key Club; Chr; Ch Chr; SP/M/VS; Bskball (J); Track (V L); Water Polo-Varsity/Letter Winner; All Freshman State Water Polo Team; Aviation/Aeronautics; Sports Medicine; Annapolis Naval Academy; Duke U

THOM, BRETT J; ROYERSFORD, PA; SPRING-FORD SR HS; (SO); Ctznshp Aw; Hi Hnr Roll; Hnr Roll; Pres Ac Ftns Aw; Sci/Math Olympn; St of Mnth; Emplmnt; Key Club; Mth Clb/Tm; Sci Clb; Stu Cncl (R); Computer Programming

THOMAS, ANGELA; SHAVERTOWN, PA; LAKE LEHMAN HS; (SO); Nat Hon Sy; Sci/Math Olympn; Key Club; Chrldg (V); Science Olympiad States 4th Place; Pharmacy; Physical Therapy

THOMAS, COURTLYN L; CHESTER, PA; CHESTER HS; (FR); Hnr Roll; Perf Att; Comm Volntr; Chrch Yth Grp; Key Club; ROTC; Spanish Clb; Ch Chr; Clr Grd; Dnce; Drl Tm; MCJROTC; Key Club; Law; Business; Clark Atlanta U

THOMAS, DAVID K; ALIQUIPPA, PA; CTR AREA SD; (SO); Hi Hnr Roll; WWAHSS; Yth Ldrshp Prog; Chrch Yth Grp; DARE; Lttrmn Clb; Scouts; Vsity Clb; Spanish Clb; Bnd; Drm Mjr; Jzz Bnd; Mch Bnd; Swmg (V L); Track (V)

THOMAS, EARL C; TUNKHANNOCK, PA; TUNKHANNOCK AREA HS; (SO); Hi Hnr Roll; Hnr Roll; MVP; WWAHSS; Comm Volntr; Spec Olymp Vol; Emplmnt; Key Club; Scouts; Bskball (JC); Ftball (V L); Track (V L); Wt Lftg (V); Adv Cncl (R); Stu Cncl (R); Eagle Scout Award; Aeronautics; United States Air Force Academy; Embry Riddle U

THOMAS, JAMAR N S; CHESTER, PA; CHESTER HS; (SO); Dnce; SP/M/VS; Art Institute of Philadelphia; Joe Hubert School of Cartoon and Graphic Art

THOMAS, JASON B; WINDSOR, PA; EASTERN YORK HS; (SR); Hi Hnr Roll; Hnr Roll; Chrch Yth Grp; Emplmnt; Ntl FFA; Bnd; Jzz Bnd; Mch Bnd; Pep Bnd; Electrician; Lawyer; Millersville; York College

THOMAS, JODI L; CENTRE HALL, PA; BELLEFONTE HS; (SO); Flg Crps; Chrldg (V); Yrbk; Real Estate Agent; Penn State

THOMAS, KELLY N; HOUTZDALE, PA; MOSHANNON VALLEY JR/SR HS; (FR); All Am Sch; Hi Hnr Roll; Hnr Roll; Nat Hon Sy; Otst Ac Ach Awd; Perf Att; St of Mnth; USAA; Comm Volntr; Peer Tut/Med; Chrch Yth Grp; DARE; Drma Clb; Mus Clb; French Clb; Bnd; Chr; Drm Mjr; Mch Bnd; Bskball (J); CR (R); Yrbk (R); United States Achievement Academy - All American Scholar Program; USAA National English Merit Award; History; Music Education; Duquesne U; Penn State U

THOMAS, KIARA M; PITTSBURGH, PA; WOODLAND HILLS HS; (SR); Hi Hnr Roll; Nat Hon Sy; Comm Volntr; Chrch Yth Grp; Emplmnt; Acpl Chr; Chr; Ch Chr; SP/M/VS; Chrldg; National Honors Society; High Honors; Psychology; Business Management; West Chester U

THOMAS, LEVI G; HOOVERSVILLE, PA; SHADE CTRL CITY SD; (FR); Hi Hnr Roll; WWAHSS; Comm Volntr; Peer Tut/Med; Chrch Yth Grp; Emplmnt; Outdrs Clb; Chr; Ch Chr; Ftball (J); Track (V L)

THOMAS, MEGAN K; CAMP HILL, PA; EAST PENNSBORO AREA HS; (FR); Hnr Roll; Sci Fairs; Key Club; Bnd; Chr; Key Club President; Registered Nurse; Psychiatrist; U of Pittsburgh; Penn State

THOMAS, MICHAEL; BENSALEM, PA; BENSALEM TOWNSHIP SD HS; (FR); Hnr Roll; St of Mnth; Comm Volntr; Peer Tut/Med; Emplmnt; ROTC; Scouts; Bnd; Drl Tm; Mch Bnd; Pep Bnd; Cl Off; Sea Scouts, Police Explorers; X-Site Service Program, Drama Work Shop; United States Coast Guard; Music Education; U of Delaware; Temple U

THOMAS, NICHOLAS M; STONEBORO, PA; LAKEVIEW HS; (SR); Hnr Roll; Computer Science; Business Management; DeVry; Full Sail

THOMAS, SHANNON M; PHILADELPHIA, PA; MULTI-CULTURAL AC; (FR); Otst Ac Ach Awd; Perf Att; Sci Fairs; St of Mnth; Comm Volntr; Peer Tut/Med; Chrch Yth Grp; DARE; Lib Aide; Mth Clb/Tm; Photog; Ch Chr; Cl Off (S); Yrbk (P); Ninth Grade Secretary; Law; West Chester U; Howard U

THOMAS, SUMMER; WASHINGTON, PA; WASHINGTON HS; (JR); Hnr Roll; WWAHSS; Pep Squd; Chr; Chrldg (V); Cl Off (P); Stu Cncl (P); I Want to Be a Lawyer; Be Successful in Everything.

THOMAS, TAEJA; PITTSBURGH, PA; PITTSBURGH SD; (SO); Hi Hnr Roll; Hnr Roll; Nat Hon Sy; WWAHSS; P to P St Amb Prg; Prom Com; Ice Hky (V); Heart Surgeon or Brain Surgeon; Judge; U of Pittsburgh; Harvard U

THOMAS, TEANA L; ERIE, PA; STRONG VINCENT HS; (JR); Nat Hon Sy; Comm Volntr; Dbte Team; Emplmnt; Spanish Clb; Benjamin Wiley Partnership Program; Peer Mentor/Educator; Pharmaceutical; Forensic Scientist; Drexel U; Iowa State-Lake Erie Cmty College

THOMPSON, CORY; WELLSVILLE, PA; DOVER AREA HS; (SR); 4H Awd; Hnr Roll; St of Mnth; WWAHSS; Hab For Humty Volntr; 4-H; Ntl FFA; Vllyball (V); FFA; Dairy Farmer/Animal Sciences; Agribusiness; Pennsylvania U

THOMPSON, DARREN; PHILADELPHIA, PA; SIMON GRATZ HS; (SR); Hi Hnr Roll; Hnr Roll; Physical Education

THOMPSON, FAITH; WEST NEWTON, PA; YOUGH SD HS; (SO); Hnr Roll; Chrch Yth Grp; FCA; Lib Aide; Clr Grd; Pre-Law

THOMPSON, JAMES; BUENA VISTA, PA; ELIZABETH FORWARD HS; (FR); Hi Hnr Roll; Otst Ac Ach Awd; WWAHSS; Comm Volntr; Chess; Wdwrkg Clb; Stu Cncl (R); Community Baseball 12 Presidential Outstanding Excellence Awards; Church Youth Group/Usher; Pitt-Pre-Med; Orthopedic Surgeon; U of Pittsburgh

THOMPSON, KRISTIN; SECANE, PA; RIDLEY SD; (JR); Hnr Roll; Pres Ac Ftns Aw; Sci Fairs; St of Mnth; Comm Volntr; Spec Olymp Vol; Emplmnt; Tchrs Aide; Foreign Clb; Fld Hky (V CL); Lcrsse (V); Elementary Education; Child Psychology; Elizabethtown College; Albright College

THOMPSON, STEVEN; UNIONTOWN, PA; LAUREL HIGHLANDS SD; (SO); Hi Hnr Roll; Hnr Roll; Scouts; Bnd; Jzz Bnd; Mch Bnd; Architecture; Music; Penn State

THOROGOOD, JAMIL; CHESTER, PA; (FR); Ctznshp Aw; Hnr Roll; Nat Hon Sy; Comm Volntr; Peer Tut/Med; Chrch Yth Grp; Ch Chr; Computer Tech; DeVry

THRESHER, COURTNEY D; LINCOLN UNIVERSITY, PA; ST MARK'S HS; (SO); Hnr Roll; Pres Sch; St of Mnth; Comm Volntr; Key Club; Track (V); Member of Z-Club International; Emergency Medicine; Nursing; Boston College; U of Scranton

THRESHER, KRISTINA F; LINCOLN UNIVERSITY, PA; ST MARK'S HS; (SO); Hnr Roll; Pres Sch; St of Mnth; Comm Volntr; Key Club; Track (V); Member of Z-Club International; Physical Medicine and Rehabilitation; Emergency Medicine; Boston College; U of Scranton

THURBER, RACHAEL; GIBSONIA, PA; PINE RICHLAND HS; (JR); Hi Hnr Roll; St Optmst of Yr; DARE; SADD; Vllyball (V)

THURSTON, JESSICA D; PITTSBURGH, PA; PENN HILLS HS; (SR); Hi Hnr Roll; Hnr Roll; Nat Hon Sy; Perf Att; WWAHSS; Peer Tut/Med; Chrch Yth Grp; Emplmnt; Key Club; Spanish Clb; Counseling Psychology; Chatham College

TIAN, KATHY S; MACUNGIE, PA; EMMAUS HS; (SO); F Lan Hn Soc; Nat Hon Sy; Otst Ac Ach Awd; Perf Att; Comm Volntr; Peer Tut/Med; Quill & Scroll; French Clb; Lit Mag (E); President, Anime Club; Royal Conservatory of Music 8th Grade (Piano); Psychology/Sociology; Archaeology; Princeton U; Lehigh U

TILBERRY, MIMI; TAYLOR, PA; RIVERSIDE JR/SR HS; (FR); Hi Hnr Roll; Nat Hon Sy; St of Mnth; Comm Volntr; Peer Tut/Med; Chrch Yth Grp; DARE; Photog; Ch Chr; Clr Grd; Dnce; Chrldg (J); PPSqd (J); Tennis (V); Presidential Education Award; Youth Representative-Skylake; Teacher / Education Major

TILEY, BRITTNEY; POTTSTOWN, PA; POTTSGROVE SR HS; (FR); Ctznshp Aw; Hi Hnr Roll; Nat Hon Sy; Otst Ac Ach Awd; Pres Sch; St of Mnth; Peer Tut/Med; ArtClub; Mth Clb/Tm; Sci Clb; French Clb; IPAA Basketball; Teaching Degrees; Temple U; Penn State

TILLER, BECCA; CAMP HILL, PA; CEDAR CLIFF HS; (SR); F Lan Hn Soc; Hi Hnr Roll; Nat Hon Sy; Otst Ac Ach Awd; Comm Volntr; Chrch Yth Grp; Emplmnt; Photog; Quill & Scroll; German Clb; Ch Chr; Dnce; Yrbk (R, P); Human Development; Messiah College

TIMCHECK, THERESA; PITTSBURGH, PA; NORTH ALLEGHENY INT HS; (SO); Hi Hnr Roll; Nat Hon Sy; Otst Ac Ach Awd; Pres Ac Ftns Aw; St of Mnth; WWAHSS; Comm Volntr; Peer Tut/Med; Chrch Yth Grp; FBLA; Key Club; Bnd; Ch Chr; CR (R)

TIMPSON, CARLI S; EAST STROUDSBURG, PA; EAST STROUDSBURG HS SOUTH; (SO); Gov Hnr Prg; Hi Hnr Roll; Sci/Math Olympn; WWAHSS; FTA; HO'Br Yth Ldrshp; Key Club; Mod UN; Schol Bwl; Sci Clb; Bnd; Jzz Bnd; Mch Bnd; Lit Mag (R); Second Mile Leadership Ambassador; Character, Leadership, Sportsmanship Awards; French; Advertising; Bryn Mawr; NYU

TINCH, BRITTANY; LAWRENCEVILLE, PA; NORTHERN TIOGA SD; (FR); Ctznshp Aw; Hi Hnr Roll; Hnr Roll; WWAHSS; Peer Tut/Med; DARE; Pep Squd; Chr; Skiing; Sccr; Sftball; Track; Vllyball; Yrbk (E, P); Sportsman Club; Teacher Grades 2-4; Science; Corning Community College; Mansfield U

TOCZYLOWSKA, ANETA; EAST STROUDSBURG, PA; EAST STROUDSBURG SR HS; (FR); Hi Hnr Roll; Hnr Roll; Sci Fairs; St of Mnth; Peer Tut/Med; Key Club; Foreign Clb; Chr; Dnce; Piano; Doctor; Arizona State U; Grand Canyon U

TOLLAND, AMANDA; READING, PA; READING HS; (FR); Hnr Roll; St of Mnth; Comm Volntr; DARE; Fr of Library; Lib Aide; Tchrs Aide; Nurse; Lawyer; Penn State U; Kutztown U

TOMKO, LESLIE C; HERMITAGE, PA; HICKORY HS; (SO); All Am Sch; Hi Hnr Roll; Comm Volntr; Chrch Yth Grp; Spanish Clb; Dnce; Drl Tm; Golf (V L); Sftball (V L)

TOMS, CHRIS; LANCASTER, PA; JP MC CASKEY HS; (JR); Hnr Roll; MVP; Ftball; Ice Hky; Wt Lftg; Criminal Justice; Sports Management; Florida State U; U of Pennsylvania

TONG, SOLOMON; WEXFORD, PA; NORTH ALLEGHENY HS; (SO); Otst Ac Ach Awd; Perf Att; WWAHSS; Yth Ldrshp Prog; Comm Volntr; Chrch Yth Grp; Key Club; Mth Clb/Tm; Tennis (VJ); ACT Math Competition Award; AIME Math; Medical School; Degree in Medicine; Johns Hopkins U

TOOMER, JAMES; PHILADELPHIA, PA; NORTHEAST CATHOLIC BOYS HS; (FR); Hnr Roll; Comm Volntr; DARE; Emplmnt; Off Aide; Ch Chr; SP/M/VS; Bskball (J); Ftball (V C); Stu Cncl (P); Sch Ppr (E); Law-Enforcement-SWAT; Drama-As a Minor; Virginia Tech College; Temple U

TORBIC, GREGORY; ERIE, PA; HARBORCREEK JR/SR HS; (SR); Hi Hnr Roll; Nat Hon Sy; Salutrn; WWAHSS; Yth Ldrshp Prog; Comm Volntr; Chrch Yth Grp; Bskball (J); Sccr (VJCL); Track (V L); WSEE 35/Arby's Scholar Athlete Nominee; 1st Team All-County-Soccer; Accounting; Law; U of Pittsburgh; Florida State U

TORRES, ANA; NORRISTOWN, PA; NORRISTOWN AREA HS; (FR); Ctznshp Aw; ArtClub; Emplmnt; ROTC; Orch; Lcrsse (J); Science Award; Reading-Communications Award; Fashion Designing; Lawyer; Penn State College; Harvard

TORRES, ERICA; PHILADELPHIA, PA; KENSINGTON HS; (JR); Hi Hnr Roll; Hnr Roll; Emplmnt; Mus Clb; Chr; SP/M/VS; School Choir (Ferris H.S., Jersey City, NJ); Forensic Science; Fashion Designer; Arcadia U; Alvernia College

TORRES, RICKY; SCRANTON, PA; ST MICHAEL'S SCH; (FR); Bskball

TORRES, VERONICA; ALLENTOWN, PA; WILLIAM ALLEN HS; (FR); Dnce; Drl Tm; To Become a Doctor; Pharmacist; Penn State U; Muhlenberg College

TORREY, DANEK; COUDERSPORT, PA; HEBRON CTR CHRISTIAN SCH; (SO); 4H Awd; All Am Sch; Hnr Roll; Nat Hon Sy; Otst Ac Ach Awd; St of Mnth; 4-H; Chrch Yth Grp; Quiz Bowl; Wdwrkg Clb; Bnd; SP/M/VS; Bskball (V); Skiing (V); Vllyball (V); Yrbk (P)

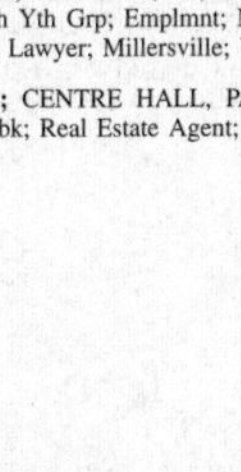
Thomas, Michael
Bensalem Township SD HS
Bensalem, PA

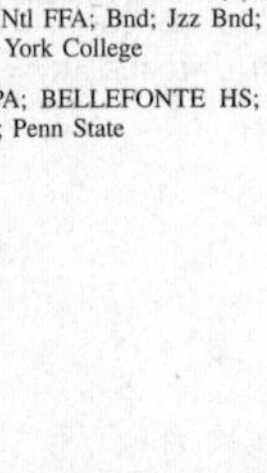
Thomas, Kelly N
Moshannon Valley JR/SR HS
Houtzdale, PA

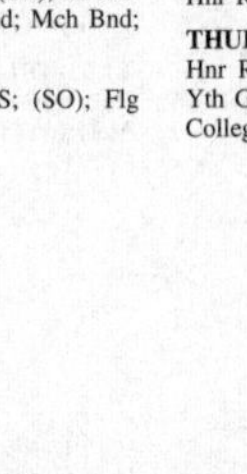
Thom, Brett J
Spring-Ford SR HS
Royersford, PA

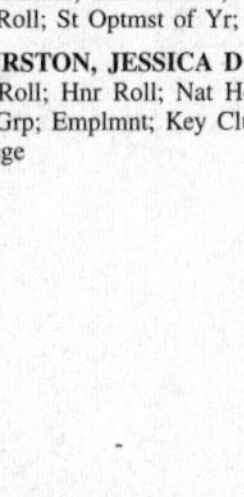
Thera, Stephanie S
Samuel Fels HS
Philadelphia, PA

National
Honor Roll
Spring 2005

Tello, Marco A
William Allen HS
Allentown, PA

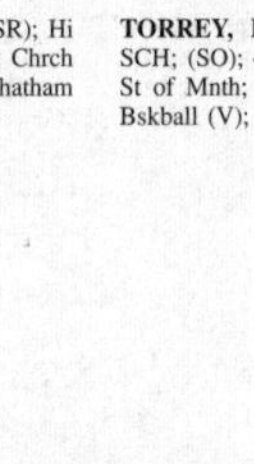
Thomas, Courtlyn L
Chester HS
Chester, PA

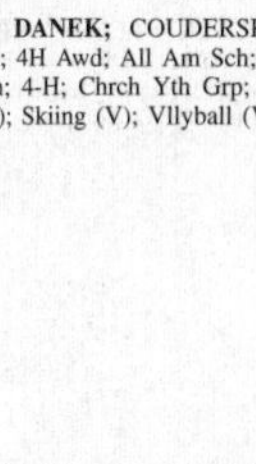
Thomas, Kiara M
Woodland Hills HS
Pittsburgh, PA

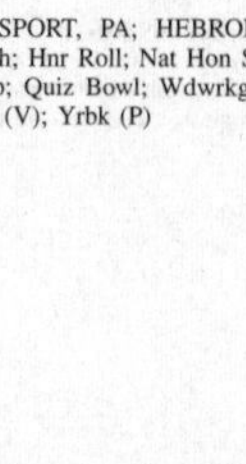
Thompson, Kristin
Ridley SD
Secane, PA

TOWNSEND, GEOFFREY; GLENOLDEN, PA; (SR); Bskball (V); Communications; Business; Immaculata; West Chester U

TRAN, LIEU; PHILADELPHIA, PA; EDISON-FAREIRA HS; (SO); Ctznshp Aw; Hi Hnr Roll; Hnr Roll; Nat Hon Sy; St of Mnth; Sccr (V); Track (V); Wrstlg (V); Engineering; Artist; Penn State College

TRAN, PHUC; MECHANICSBURG, PA; TRINITY HS; (JR); Hnr Roll; Nat Hon Sy; Key Club; Stu Cncl (R); CR (R); Yrbk; Yearbook Club; Astronomy Club; Pharmacology; Pharmaceutical Chemistry; Temple U; Pittsburgh U

TRAN, PHUOC; LANCASTER, PA; MANHEIM TOWNSHIP HS; (SO); Ctznshp Aw; Hnr Roll; WWAHSS; Hosp Aide; Peer Tut/Med; Spec Olymp Vol; Key Club; SADD; Track (V); Volunteer in LGH Culture Awareness; Operation Smile Club; Nursing; Pediatrician; Temple U; U of Phoenix

TREGO, JAMIE; POTTSTOWN, PA; POTTSTOWN SR HS; (FR); Ctznshp Aw; Hnr Roll; Comm Volntr; Chrch Yth Grp; DARE; Key Club; Scr Kpr (V); Secretary for Key Club; Psychology; Criminal Justice; Shippensburg U; Villanova U

TRIMBLE, JOHN C; MILL HALL, PA; CTRL MTN HS; (FR); Hi Hnr Roll; Hnr Roll; Perf Att; St of Mnth; Comm Volntr; Hab For Humty Volntr; Chrch Yth Grp; Emplmnt; Mus Clb; German Clb; Ch Chr; Mar Art; Blue Belt in Martial Arts; Will Earn Black Belt - May 2006; Dentist; Aviation; Penn State U

TRINH, ERIC; NEWTOWN, PA; COUNCIL ROCK HS NORTH; (JR); Hi Hnr Roll; Nat Hon Sy; Otst Ac Ach Awd; Perf Att; St of Mnth; Drma Clb; Mth Clb/Tm; German Clb; SP/M/VS; Stg Cre; Stu Cncl (R); International Thespian Society; Principal's Distinguished Honor Roll; Cardiology; Penn State U; Temple U

TRIVELPIECE, JULIA G; BERWICK, PA; BERWICK AREA SR HS; (SR); Hnr Roll; Peer Tut/Med; Bnd; Clr Grd; Track (J); Peer Tutor; Volunteer for the Extended Summer Program; Special Education Teacher; Luzerne County Community College

TROUT, TRAVIS M; NEW STANTON, PA; HEMPFIELD AREA HS; (JR); Hi Hnr Roll; Hnr Roll; Cr Ctry (J); Track (V); Electrical Engineer; Mechanical Engineer; U of Pittsburgh; Penn State U

TROUT, TYLER; HARRISBURG, PA; CTRL DAUPHIN HS; (JR); Hi Hnr Roll; Hnr Roll; Nat Hon Sy; WWAHSS; Comm Volntr; Emplmnt; Sccr (V); Pre-Med; Engineering; U of Pennsylvania; Bucknell U

TROYNACKI, DANIEL; PITTSTON, PA; PITTSTON AREA HS; (JR); Hi Hnr Roll; Nat Hon Sy; WWAHSS; Bskball (V); Golf (V); Biology

TRUAX, AMANDA; HOUTZDALE, PA; MOSHANNON VALLEY HS; (FR); Hi Hnr Roll; Hnr Roll; St of Mnth; Chrch Yth Grp; Emplmnt; Lttrmn Clb; Prom Com; Tchrs Aide; Vsity Clb; French Clb; Bnd; Chr; Ch Chr; Flg Crps; Bskball (J); Vsy Clb (VJ L); Vllyball (VJCL); Sch Ppr (R); Select Chorus; Music Aide

TRUNK, CARISSA; PLYMOUTH MEETING, PA; PLYMOUTH WHITEMARSH HS; (SO); Hi Hnr Roll; Hnr Roll; Nat Hon Sy; Otst Ac Ach Awd; Comm Volntr; Fld Hky (J L); Lcrsse (J); Track (L); Psychology; Sports Medicine; Muhlenberg U; Lafayette U

TRUONG, QUAN; BRACKENRIDGE, PA; HIGHLANDS SD; (MS); Hi Hnr Roll; Hnr Roll; Otst Ac Ach Awd; Perf Att; St of Mnth; Peer Tut/Med; DARE; Chr; SP/M/VS; Track; Medical Fields, Business; Teaching Career; Pittsburgh U; Pennsylvania State U

TRUPE, TRACI; LANCASTER, PA; MANHEIM TWP HS; (SR); Hnr Roll; ArtClub; Chrch Yth Grp; DARE; Emplmnt; Photog; Orch; SP/M/VS; Stg Cre; PP Ftbl (V); Graduated from Barbizon Modeling School; Photography; Cinematography; Millersville U

TU, SIYUAN; WEXFORD, PA; NORTH ALLEGHENY HS; (SO); Hi Hnr Roll; Nat Hon Sy; Perf Att; Pres Ac Ftns Aw; WWAHSS; Comm Volntr; Hosp Aide; Peer Tut/Med; Key Club; Mth Clb/Tm; Svce Clb; Chr; Cl Off; Stu Cncl; CR; Lit Mag (R); National French Exam (9th National)

TULLER, YASMINE; PHILADELPHIA, PA; (JR); Comm Volntr; Chrch Yth Grp; DARE; Chr; Ch Chr; Medicine; Science; U of Pennsylvania; Temple U

TUMBLESON, ABBIE A; WHITNEY, PA; GREATER LATROBE SR HS; (JR); Hi Hnr Roll; Hnr Roll; WWAHSS; Emplmnt; Key Club; NtlFrnscLg; Scouts; French Clb; Lit Mag (R); Yrbk (R); Westmoreland Interscholastic Reading Competition; Key Club; Journalism; Creative Writing; Point Park U; Franklin Pierce College

TURK, CARLY; HERMITAGE, PA; HICKORY HS; (FR); Hi Hnr Roll; MVP; Otst Ac Ach Awd; Pres Ac Ftns Aw; St of Mnth; Comm Volntr; Peer Tut/Med; Chrch Yth Grp; Quiz Bowl; SADD; Latin Clb; Bnd; Dnce; Drl Tm; Mch Bnd; Bskball (J); Sftball (J); Swmg (V L); Cl Off (T); Stu Cncl (R); Scholar-Athlete Award GPA & Varsity Letter; Students for Charities 3.75

TURNER, JAMIE L; ELVERSON, PA; OWEN J ROBERTS HS; (SR); Hi Hnr Roll; Hnr Roll; Emplmnt; PP Ftbl (V); Track (V CL); Most-Improved for Track; PAC 10 Champion, Ran 4x100 Relay in Districts; Health Related Field; Physical Therapy; Temple U-Accepted; Westchester U-Accepted

TURNER, MICHAEL; CLARION, PA; CLARION AREA JR/SR HS; (SO); Hi Hnr Roll; Hnr Roll; Chess; Chrch Yth Grp; Schol Bwl; Scouts; Student Leadership Seminar; Architecture; Computer Programming; Clarion U

TURNER, WHITNEE; HOMESTEAD, PA; STEEL VALLEY HS; (FR); Hnr Roll; WWAHSS; Comm Volntr; Chrch Yth Grp; DARE; Key Club; Spanish Clb; Chr; Vllyball (J); Stu Cncl (R); Fashion Designer; Model; ICM

TURNER, ZACKARY; PT ALLEGANY, PA; PT ALLEGANY HS; (JR); Hnr Roll; Comm Volntr; Quiz Bowl; Schol Bwl; Scouts; French Clb; Avid Piano Player for Six Years; Japanese; Teaching Degree; U of Toronto; U of Pittsburgh

TURR, LINDSEY; E STROUDSBURG, PA; EAST STROUDSBURG HS SOUTH; (SO); Hi Hnr Roll; Sci/Math Olympn; WWAHSS; Key Club; Mth Clb/Tm; Mod UN; Prom Com; Scouts; Foreign Clb; Bnd; Clr Grd; Mch Bnd; Orch; Psychology

TWEEDY, JOSHUA P; MC CONNELLSBURG, PA; MC CONNELLSBURG HS; (SO); Hi Hnr Roll; Comm Volntr; Chrch Yth Grp; Mus Clb; SADD; Bnd; Chr; Mch Bnd; Orch; Bsball (V); Stu Cncl (R); Campaign Volunteer Kerry / Edwards 2004; Public Opinion Writing Contest Winner; Music; Architecture; Pennsylvania State U; Shippensburg U

TWIFORD, IAN C; HARRISBURG, PA; CTRL DAUPHIN HS; (SO); Hi Hnr Roll; Hnr Roll; Comm Volntr; Emplmnt; Bsball (J); Bskball (J); Cl Off (S); Law; Enforcement; Coast Guard Academy

TYLER, JESSICA N; SPRING CITY, PA; OWEN J ROBERTS HS; (JR); DAR; Hi Hnr Roll; Hnr Roll; Kwnis Aw; Otst Ac Ach Awd; Pres Ac Ftns Aw; Peer Tut/Med; DECA; Emplmnt; Key Club; Spanish Clb; PP Ftbl (V); Sccr (V); Lit Mag (R); Sch Ppr (R); Yrbk (R); DECA State Champion; Pre-Med; Psychology; U of Delaware; Scranton U

TYLER, SARAH; JAMESTOWN, PA; JAMESTOWN AREA SD; (FR); Ctznshp Aw; F Lan Hn Soc; Hi Hnr Roll; Peer Tut/Med; Spanish Clb; Bnd; Pep Bnd; Track (VJ L); Vllyball (J); Stu Cncl (R); Forensic Science; U of Virginia, U of Tennessee; John Jay College of Criminal Justice

UDDIN, MOHAMMAD; TELFORD, PA; SOUDERTON AREA HS; (SR); Hnr Roll; Comm Volntr; Hab For Humty Volntr; Red Cr Aide; Chess; Chrch Yth Grp; Wdwrkg Clb; Walk Against Hunger; Chemical Engineering; Penn State U

ULMER, TIERNEY L; COGAN STATION, PA; JERSEY SHORE AREA SR HS; (FR); Hi Hnr Roll; Hnr Roll; Otst Ac Ach Awd; Pres Sch; WWAHSS; Chrch Yth Grp; Key Club; Chr; Tennis (J); Stu Cncl (R); Accountant, CPA; Penn State U; NYU

UMSTEAD, WESTON; POTTSTOWN, PA; POTTSGROVE HS; (FR); Ctznshp Aw; Hi Hnr Roll; Hnr Roll; Otst Ac Ach Awd; Pres Sch; St of Mnth; WWAHSS; Peer Tut/Med; Chrch Yth Grp; Latin Clb; Ch Chr; Ftball (J); President's Award; Forensics; Chemistry; Temple U; Elizabethtown College

UNDERWOOD, KAYLA; PITTSBURGH, PA; PENN HILLS SR HS; (JR); F Lan Hn Soc; Hi Hnr Roll; Nat Hon Sy; WWAHSS; Comm Volntr; Peer Tut/Med; Chrch Yth Grp; Key Club; French Clb; Dnce; Orch; SP/M/VS; Tennis (V CL); Track (V); Stu Cncl (V); Girl Scout Silver Award

UPSHUR-SPRATLEY, SHANICE; PHILADELPHIA, PA; PHILADELPHIA. GIRLS HS; (JR); Nat Hon Sy; WWAHSS; Comm Volntr; Emplmnt; P to P St Amb Prg; Scouts; Bnd; Cl Off (T); CR (R); Nursing; Business; Howard U; Delaware State U

URBIETA, SANTAMARIA; ERIE, PA; ERIE CITY SD HS; (SO); Hnr Roll; Nat Hon Sy; Accounting

URBON, GINA M; WILKES BARRE, PA; HANOVER AREA JR/SR HS; (JR); Hi Hnr Roll; Nat Hon Sy; WWAHSS; Comm Volntr; Peer Tut/Med; Chrch Yth Grp; DARE; Emplmnt; Key Club; Lttrmn Clb; Prom Com; Bskball (V); Fld Hky (V L); Sftball (V L); Stu Cncl (R); Athletic Training

VAKERAK, SARAH A; HOMESTEAD, PA; WILSON CHRISTIAN AC; (SO); Hi Hnr Roll; Nat Hon Sy; WWAHSS; Emplmnt; Lib Aide; Ch Chr; English Major; Library Science Degree; Grove City College; Carlow College

VALENTI, VALEREE; PITTSBURGH, PA; PENN HILLS SR HS; (SR); Hi Hnr Roll; Hnr Roll; Nat Hon Sy; WWAHSS; CARE; Comm Volntr; Chrch Yth Grp; Key Club; Scouts; Svce Clb; Spanish Clb; Dnce; Chrldg (J); Ice Sktg; Nursing; Medical Field; Robert Morris U

VALENTINO, JEN; POTTSTOWN, PA; POTTSGROVE HS; (SO); Hnr Roll; St of Mnth; WWAHSS; Comm Volntr; Hosp Aide; Emplmnt; FTA; Key Club; SP/M/VS; Elementary Education; Special Education Instructor; West Chester U

VALERIO, CHRIS; NEWTOWN, PA; COUNCIL ROCK HS NORTH; (SO); Comm Volntr; Temple U; West Chester U

VALJEE, SHRUTI; MC DONALD, PA; SOUTH FAYETTE TOWNSHIP HS; MS; All Am Sch; Hi Hnr Roll; Otst Ac Ach Awd; Sci/Math Olympn; St of Mnth; USAA; WWAHSS; Yth Ldrshp Prog; Comm Volntr; DARE; Emplmnt; Mth Clb/Tm; NYLC; P to P St Amb Prg; Schol Bwl; Tmpl Yth Grp; French Clb; Chr; Dnce; SP/M/VS; Stu Cncl (R); CR (R); Piano; Indian Classical Dance; Medicine; Business

VALLANA, RICKI; LATROBE, PA; GREATER LATROBE SR HS; (SO); F Lan Hn Soc; Sci/Math Olympn; WWAHSS; Emplmnt; Key Club; German Clb; Sccr (V); Elementary Education; Messiah College; Allegheny College

VAN, ALLEN; PHILADELPHIA, PA; EDISON-FAREIRA HS; (JR); Ctznshp Aw; Hi Hnr Roll; Hnr Roll; Yth Ldrshp Prog; Peer Tut/Med; Bskball (J); Ftball (J); Wt Lftg (V); Yrbk (E); Pharmacy; Psychology; Temple U; U of Pennsylvania

VAN BILLIARD, HEATHER; EASTON, PA; WILSON HS; (JR); Hnr Roll; AL Aux Girls; Emplmnt; Mathematics; UCLA

VANDENHENGEL, MEGAN; MECHANICSBURG, PA; CUMBERLAND VALLEY HS; (JR); Hnr Roll; Nat Hon Sy; Perf Att; Hab For Humty Volntr; Key Club; Chr; Orch; Cr Ctry (V L); Sccr (J); Track (V L); Elementary Education; Elizabethtown College; Millersville U

VAN DINNER, LAURA; LANCASTER, PA; PENN MANOR SD; (SR); Hi Hnr Roll; Hnr Roll; St of Mnth; WWAHSS; Dbte Team; Emplmnt; Foreign Clb; Poetry Merit Awards; Sociology-Criminal Psychology

VANESS II, ROBERT; MARCUS HOOK, PA; CHICHESTER SR HS; (FR); St of Mnth; Sccr (V L); Science Field; Harvard U

VAN NAME, BRITTANY E; PALMERTON, PA; PALMERTON AREA SD; (FR); Hnr Roll; Perf Att; St of Mnth; ArtClub; Registered Nurse; Lehigh-Carbon Community College

VANYO, IAN E; CORAOPOLIS, PA; CORNELL HS; (JR); Hi Hnr Roll; Hnr Roll; Model United Nations; Marine Biology; Forensics; Indiana U of Pennsylvania

VARGAS, JULIE B; BETHLEHEM, PA; LEHIGH VALLEY CH. HS. PERF ARTS HS; (JR); Hi Hnr Roll; Nat Hon Sy; Perf Att; Dnce; Dance; English; Fordham U; New York U

VARNER, CATHERINE; STATE COLLEGE, PA; STATE COLLEGE AREA HS; (JR); Hi Hnr Roll; Otst Ac Ach Awd; WWAHSS; Comm Volntr; Spec Olymp Vol; ArtClub; Chrch Yth Grp; Drma Clb; Emplmnt; Jr Ach; Key Club; Mus Clb; Bnd; Mch Bnd; SP/M/VS; Stg Cre; Tri-M Music Honor Society; Political Science; International Relations; Georgetown U; College of William and Mary

VARVAGLIONE, MARIA; PITTSTON, PA; PITTSTON AREA HS; (SO); Hnr Roll; St of Mnth; Comm Volntr; Pep Squd; Chrldg (J); Gmnstcs (J); Talent Show; Cheerleading Coach; Teaching; King's College; Wilkes U

VASILKO, JULIE A; JOHNSTOWN, PA; RICHLAND; (SR); Hnr Roll; Nat Hon Sy; WWAHSS; Comm Volntr; Peer Tut/Med; ArtClub; Key Club; Prom Com; Schol Bwl; SADD; French Clb; Sftball (V L); Cl Off (T); Stu Cncl (R); Sch Ppr (R); Physician Assistant; Saint Francis U

VEAZEY, MEGAN; EASTON, PA; WILSON AREA HS; (JR); Hi Hnr Roll; Hnr Roll; Nat Hon Sy; Sci/Math Olympn; WWAHSS; Peer Tut/Med; Emplmnt; HO'Br Yth Ldrshp; Key Club; Quill & Scroll; Cr Ctry (V L); Sccr (V L); Cl Off (P); Sch Ppr (R); Yrbk (R); Will to Win Gatorade Athlete for Last 2 Years in V Soccer; Lock Haven U; York College

VECCHIO, DANEEN M; MCKEESPORT, PA; MC KEESPORT AREA SD; (SO); Hnr Roll; Sci Fairs; Chrch Yth Grp; DARE; Emplmnt; Scouts; Tchrs Aide; Chrldg (V); Vllyball (J); Cultural Arts Awards; Art Fairs; Radiologic Tech; UPMC School of Radiologic Technology; Community College of Allegheny County

VEGESNA, SAGAR; SOUTHAMPTON, PA; CAMEL ROCK SOUTH; (SO); Hnr Roll; St of Mnth; Comm Volntr; DARE; Scouts; Spanish Clb; Chr; Sccr (J); Tennis (J)

VENERICK, MEGAN; CLEARFIELD, PA; CLEARFIELD AREA HS; (JR); F Lan Hn Soc; Hi Hnr Roll; Kwnis Aw; Nat Hon Sy; Nat Mrt Semif; Nat Sci Aw; Pres Sch; St of Mnth; USAA; WWAHSS; Amnsty Intl; JSA; Key Club; Mus Clb; Off Aide; German Clb; Bnd; Chr; Jzz Bnd; Mch Bnd; Principal's List (Top 10); District/Region Band; Pre-Law; Music; Cornell U; Georgetown U

VENSEL, JAMES R; PITTSBURGH, PA; PLUM SR HS; (SO); Hnr Roll; Emplmnt; Bskball (J); Track (V); Stu Cncl (V); Engineering; Business; U of Pittsburgh; Penn State

VERAS, DIANA D; WEST HAZLETON, PA; HAZLETON AREA HS; (JR); Hnr Roll; Nat Hon Sy; Emplmnt; Key Club; Off Aide; Step Club; Accounting; Finance; Penn State Hazleton; McCann School of Business

VERDETTO, NICOLE; MOSCOW, PA; NORTH POCONO HS; (FR); Hnr Roll; Emplmnt; FBLA; Dnce; Golf (J); Accounting; Law; U of Scranton; Marywood U

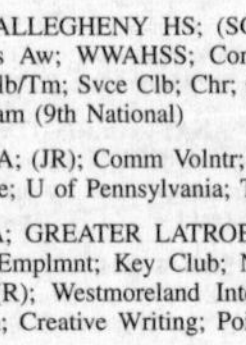
Turner, Zackary
Pt Allegany HS
Pt Allegany, PA

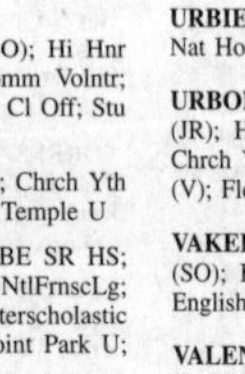
Truong, Quan
Highlands SD
Brackenridge, PA

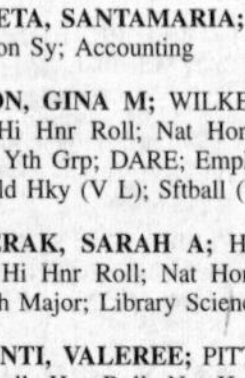
Trimble, John C
Central Mtn HS
Mill Hall, PA

National
Honor Roll
Spring 2005

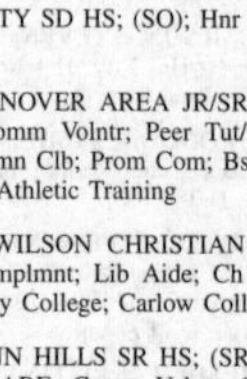
Townsend, Geoffrey
Glenolden, PA

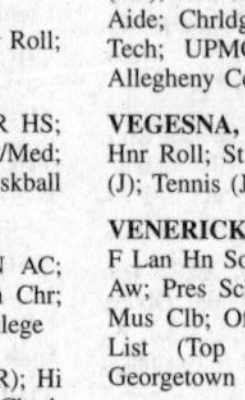
Turner, Jamie L
Owen J Roberts HS
Elverson, PA

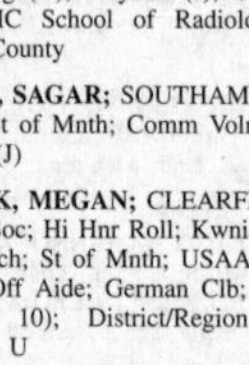
Upshur-Spratley, Shanice
Philadelphia. Girls HS
Philadelphia, PA

VERGARA, MYRA; UPPER DARBY, PA; UPPER DARBY HS; (JR); Nat Hon Sy; WWAHSS; Yth Ldrshp Prog; Comm Volntr; Peer Tut/Med; Spec Olymp Vol; ArtClub; Svce Clb; Yrbk (P); Major in Medicine; Minor in Business

VERNAT, JEANRORO; PHILADELPHIA, PA; OLNEY HS; (JR); Chrch Yth Grp; Bnd; Chr; Ch Chr; SP/M/VS; Bskball; Cyclg; Dvng; Ftball; Sccr; Tennis; Vllyball; Wrstlg; Mechanical Engineer; Temple U; Drexel U

VERNON, ASHLEY; WILLOW GROVE, PA; ABINGTON SR HS; (JR); Hi Hnr Roll; Hnr Roll; Nat Hon Sy; WWAHSS; Yth Ldrshp Prog; Comm Volntr; Key Club; Spanish Clb; Yrbk (E); Champions of Caring; Students Against Violence Everywhere

VETOVICH, KRISTALYN; PAXINOS, PA; SHAMOKIN AREA HS; (FR); Hi Hnr Roll; Hnr Roll; Nat Hon Sy; Sci Fairs; Comm Volntr; Peer Tut/Med; Chrch Yth Grp; Drma Clb; Key Club; Sci Clb; Chr; Dnce; SP/M/VS; Stu Cncl (R); Sch Ppr (R); Mission Trips; Community Theater; Drama; Music; NYU; Disney

VICKERS, JONATHAN; ELLWOOD CITY, PA; MC GUFFEY HS; (JR); Hi Hnr Roll; Nat Hon Sy; Comm Volntr; Chrch Yth Grp; Emplmnt; Mth Clb/Tm; Prom Com; Bnd; Mch Bnd; Ftball (V L); Skt Tgt Sh (V L); Club Lacrosse; Criminology; Psychology; West Virginia U; Millersville U PA

VIDMOSKO, GEORGE; TAYLOR, PA; RIVERSIDE JR/SR HS; (FR); Hnr Roll; Nat Hon Sy; WWAHSS; DARE; Wdwrkg Clb; CR (R); Yrbk (E); Design Games for Computers; Computer Engineering; U of Miami; Drexel U

VIDUMSKY, CHRISTINA; BETHLEHEM, PA; BETHLEHEM CATHOLIC HS; (JR); Hi Hnr Roll; Otst Ac Ach Awd; Pres Ac Ftns Aw; USAA; WWAHSS; Comm Volntr; Biology Clb; Chrch Yth Grp; Key Club; Pep Squd; Spanish Clb; Bskball (J); Elementary School Volleyball Coach; Elementary School Basketball Coach

VIJAYVARGIYA, NEHA; SINKING SPG, PA; WILSON SOUTHERN JR HS; (FR); Ctznshp Aw; Hi Hnr Roll; Otst Ac Ach Awd; Perf Att; Sci Fairs; Sci/Math Olympn; St of Mnth; Comm Volntr; Peer Tut/Med; Mth Clb/Tm; Mus Clb; NYLC; P to P St Amb Prg; Sci Clb; Wdwrkg Clb; Spanish Clb; Bnd; Chr; Clr Grd; Dnce; Mar Art; Stu Cncl (R); Sch Ppr (R); 1st Chair-Soprano 1 in County Chorus; State Award for SAT Scores; Doctor: Surgeon; Journalism; Johns Hopkins; Harvard

VINCENT, NYANDAI M; FREELAND, PA; HAZLETON AREA HS; (FR); Hnr Roll; Nat Hon Sy; Emplmnt; Bnd; Chr; Tennis (V L); Accounting & Business Manager; Arts, Performing Acting; New York U

VISHNESKY, JON A; MOOSIC, PA; RIVERSIDE JR/SR HS; (JR); Hnr Roll; MVP; Nat Hon Sy; WWAHSS; FBLA; Prom Com; SADD; Bsball (V); Bskball (V C); Golf (V L); Vllyball (V); Golf MVP; Political Science/History; Law; U of Pennsylvania; New York U

VODA, MICHAEL D; TUNKHANNOCK, PA; TUNKHANNOCK AREA HS; (SR); Hnr Roll; Hosp Aide; Emplmnt; Bnd; Jzz Bnd; Mch Bnd; Vice-President Robotics Club; Wilkes U

VODZAK, REBECCA; DALLAS, PA; DALLAS HS; (JR); Hi Hnr Roll; Nat Hon Sy; WWAHSS; Comm Volntr; Peer Tut/Med; Red Cr Aide; Key Club; Prom Com; Skiing; Track (V L); Cl Off (P); Stu Cncl (R); Yrbk (R); Sunday School Teacher; Big Brothers Big Sisters Volunteer; Physical Therapy

VOGAN, EMMA M; WATERFORD, PA; FT LEBOEUF HS; (SO); Hi Hnr Roll; Hnr Roll; Perf Att; FCA; Chr; SP/M/VS; Chrldg (J); Play the Piano; Music Therapy; Psychology; Slippery Rock U

VOJTAS, JESSICA; PITCAIRN, PA; GATEWAY HS; (SO); Hnr Roll; Perf Att; WWAHSS; Comm Volntr; Hab For Humty Volntr; Hosp Aide; FBLA; Key Club; Chr; Chrldg (JC); Athletic Training; California U of Pennsylvania; Slippery Rock U

VOLLMER, ADRIENNE; BRIDGEVILLE, PA; SOUTH FAYETTE TOWNSHIP HS; (SO); Hi Hnr Roll; Nat Hon Sy; Perf Att; St of Mnth; USAA; WWAHSS; Chrch Yth Grp; Drma Clb; Lttrmn Clb; Mth Clb/Tm; French Clb; Chr; SP/M/VS; Sccr (J); Swmg (V L); Political Science; Pre-Law; Harvard College; Washington and Jefferson U

VOLTZ, KELSEY; MECHANICSBURG, PA; MECHANICSBURG AREA SR HS; (SO); F Lan Hn Soc; Hi Hnr Roll; Perf Att; WWAHSS; Key Club; Photog; Bskball (J); Track (V L); Vllyball (V L); Stu Cncl (R); PalsatMash (Buddy to Special Needs Student); Fundraising for 4-Diamonds; Physical Therapy

WADE, CHRISTINA; PORT ROYAL, PA; JUNIATA CTY SD; (JR); Emplmnt; Prom Com; SP/M/VS; Stg Cre; Sftball (J); Pediatrician; Penn State U

WADE, WILLIAM; PHILADELPHIA, PA; GEORGE PEPPER MS; Ctznshp Aw; Hnr Roll; Otst Ac Ach Awd; Perf Att; Ch Chr; Bskball (V); Ftball; Tennis (V); Football Player

WAEGERLE, ROBERT K; WAYNE, PA; CONESTOGA HS; (JR); Comm Volntr; Hab For Humty Volntr; Off Aide; Photog; Tech Clb; Wdwrkg Clb; Arch; Started an Archery Club; Liberal Arts; Gettysburg College; U of Delaware

WAGNER, AMANDA K; MILLMONT, PA; MIFFLINBURG AREA SD; (SO); 4H Awd; Hi Hnr Roll; Pres Ac Ftns Aw; Comm Volntr; 4-H; Chrch Yth Grp; Scouts; Stg Cre; Sccr (V L)

WAGNER, ELISE; CRESCO, PA; POCONO MTN EAST HS; (SO); Hi Hnr Roll; Otst Ac Ach Awd; USAA; Comm Volntr; Peer Tut/Med; Chrch Yth Grp; Bnd; Mch Bnd; Sftball (V); Pocono Pride Fastpitch Softball Tournament Team; Sunday School Teacher - Mt Pocono UMC; Science; Psychology

WAGNER, EVAN; WAYNE, PA; UPPER MERION HS; (JR); Hi Hnr Roll; Hnr Roll; Otst Ac Ach Awd; Perf Att; St of Mnth; DARE; DECA; Emplmnt; Prom Com; SADD; Winning DECA State Competition and Going to Nationals; Winning Multiple Awards At the Center for Tech Studies; Construction; Architecture; Pennsylvania Institute for Technical Studies; Pennsylvania Institute of Technology

WAGNER, SARAH; MC CLURE, PA; MIDD-WEST SD HS; (JR); Hi Hnr Roll; Hnr Roll; Nat Hon Sy; Perf Att; WWAHSS; Comm Volntr; Chrch Yth Grp; Emplmnt; Prom Com; Vsity Clb; Bnd; Chr; Mch Bnd; SP/M/VS; Bskball (VJ L); Fld Hky (V L); Vsy Clb (V); Cl Off (S); Stu Cncl; Most Improved in Basketball; Homecoming Court-2003; Nursing (RN); Penn State U; Bloomsburg U

WAGNER, TYLER R; MIFFLINBURG, PA; MIFFLINBURG AREA SD; (SO); Ctznshp Aw; Hi Hnr Roll; Nat Hon Sy; Otst Ac Ach Awd; Pres Ac Ftns Aw; Comm Volntr; Chrch Yth Grp; Emplmnt; Key Club; French Clb; Bsball (V L); Ftball (V L); Youth Mission Work Camp in WV; Civil Engineering; Forestry; Bucknell U; Pennsylvania State U

WAITZ, DANIEL R; EAST STROUDSBURG, PA; EAST STROUDSBURG HS SOUTH; (SO); Hi Hnr Roll; Hnr Roll; Nat Ldrshp Svc; Comm Volntr; Scouts; Eagle Scout; Computer Hardware Engineer; Computer Networking

WALIZER, CHRIS; HERSHEY, PA; HERSHEY HS; (SO); Hi Hnr Roll; Hnr Roll; Comm Volntr; Chrch Yth Grp; Key Club; Ftball (J); Track (L); Veterinarian; Business; Pennsylvania State U

WALIZER, CHRISTY R; MILL HALL, PA; CTRL MTN HS; (SR); Hi Hnr Roll; Hnr Roll; Perf Att; Yth Ldrshp Prog; Chrch Yth Grp; Emplmnt; Mod UN; Vllyball (V L); Stu Cncl (R); Yrbk (R); Biology; Penn State U

WALKER, ALLISON; MERTZTOWN, PA; BRANDYWINE HEIGHTS HS; (SR); Hnr Roll; Nat Hon Sy; WWAHSS; Comm Volntr; Hosp Aide; Peer Tut/Med; ArtClub; Key Club; Photog; Spanish Clb; SP/M/VS; Chrldg (V CL); Telecom Club-Secretary; Cheerleading - UCA All-Star and All-American; Forensic Science Major; West Virginia U

WALKER, APRIL E; HARVEYS LAKE, PA; LAKE LEHMAN HS; (JR); Hi Hnr Roll; Nat Hon Sy; WWAHSS; Comm Volntr; Peer Tut/Med; Red Cr Aide; Chrch Yth Grp; Emplmnt; Key Club; Outdrs Clb; Scouts; French Clb; Chr; SP/M/VS; Sftball (V); Wt Lftg (V); Sch Ppr (R); Outstanding Math Student Award; Key Club Member of the Month Award; Business Management; U of Pittsburgh

WALKER, JESSE L; CAIRNBROOK, PA; SHADE-CENTRAL CITY SD; (SO); Hnr Roll; SADD; Spanish Clb; Student Council Member at Large

WALKER, JOHANNA; POTTSVILLE, PA; POTTSVILLE HS; (FR); F Lan Hn Soc; Hnr Roll; Perf Att; ArtClub; Key Club; SADD; Spanish Clb; Sccr (VJ); Track (V); Veterinarian Medical School

WALKER, MARK; WOODLAND, PA; (SR); All Am Sch; Hi Hnr Roll; Nat Hon Sy; St of Mnth; USAA; WWAHSS; Chrch Yth Grp; FCA; Bnd; Mch Bnd; National Honor Society; Mechanical Engineering; Penn State U

WALKER, RASHIDA; PHILADELPHIA, PA; BOK HS; (JR); Hnr Roll; Comm Volntr; DARE; Drl Tm; Business Management; Community College of Philadelphia; Cheyney U

WALKER JR, SHELLIE; HERMITAGE, PA; HICKORY HS; (SO); Drma Clb; Spanish Clb; Chr; SP/M/VS; Law; Pharmacy; Edinboro U; Slippery Rock U

WALLACE, KENDALL; MECHANICSBURG, PA; CUMBERLAND VALLEY HS; (JR); Hnr Roll; Key Club; Vllyball (J L); Graphic Arts; Penn State; Shippensburg U

WALLACE, STEPHEN; DOWNINGTOWN, PA; BISHOP SHANAHAN HS; (JR); Hi Hnr Roll; Yth Ldrshp Prog; Comm Volntr; Emplmnt; NYLC; Svce Clb; Golf (V L); Lcrsse (J); Placed in Several Jr PGA Golf Tournaments; Mock Trial Club; International Business; Law; George Washington U; U of Pittsburgh

WALLACE, TIMOTHY W; PHILADELPHIA, PA; NORTHEAST CATHOLIC BOYS HS; (FR); Hnr Roll; Doctor; Technician; Penn State U; Temple U

WALSH, CAMILLA; BETHEL PARK, PA; BETHEL PARK SD; (SO); Hi Hnr Roll; Nat Hon Sy; Sci/Math Olympn; WWAHSS; Chrch Yth Grp; Jr Ach; Mth Clb/Tm; Mus Clb; Vllyball (J); Cl Off (R); CR (R); Cake Decorator at Bethel Bakery; Go to Haiti in the Summers to Help Them; Medicine; Grove City; Messiah College

WALSH, COLLEEN E; GREENVILLE, PA; GREENVILLE HS; (SO); Ctznshp Aw; Hi Hnr Roll; Hnr Roll; Otst Ac Ach Awd; Pres Sch; St of Mnth; Comm Volntr; Key Club; Spanish Clb; Chr; SP/M/VS; Chrldg (VJ); Scr Kpr (VJ); Vllyball (VJ); Student Council; Relay for Life Captain; Dentistry; Physician; U of Pittsburgh; U of Miami

WALSH, ELORA; NEW KENSINGTON, PA; VALLEY HS; (FR); Hi Hnr Roll; Hnr Roll; Otst Ac Ach Awd; Perf Att; Drma Clb; Bnd; Jzz Bnd; Mch Bnd; SP/M/VS; Sccr (V); Track (V); Lawyer; Journalist; Penn State; Notre Dame U

WALSH, JACLYN M; FALLS CREEK, PA; DUBOIS AREA HS; (JR); F Lan Hn Soc; Hi Hnr Roll; Hnr Roll; WWAHSS; Key Club; Orch; SP/M/VS; Veterinary; Music Career (Violin)

WALTON, ZACHARY P; MECHANICSBURG, PA; CUMBERLAND VALLEY HS; (SR); Hnr Roll; WWAHSS; Key Club; Scouts; Tech Clb; Orch; Eagle Scout; Brotherhood in Order of the Arrow; Biomedical Engineer; U of Pittsburgh

WANG, JIZHON; UPPER DARBY, PA; UPPER DARBY HS; (SO); Ctznshp Aw; Hnr Roll; Comm Volntr; Peer Tut/Med; Spec Olymp Vol; FBLA; Mod UN; Sci Clb; Chr; Future Business Leaders of America, 3rd Place in Regional Comp.; Hero Club Member; Business; Law Degree; Princeton U; Harvard U

WANSON, JOSEPH D; DU BOIS, PA; DUBOIS AREA HS; (SR); Hnr Roll; MVP; Nat Hon Sy; Otst Ac Ach Awd; Perf Att; WWAHSS; Peer Tut/Med; Red Cr Aide; Spec Olymp Vol; Lttrmn Clb; Off Aide; Bsball (VJCL); Ftball (VJCL); Elementary Basketball Coach; Secondary Education (Social Studies); Edinboro U

WARD, KAREN; POTTSVILLE, PA; POTTSVILLE AREA HS; (SO); F Lan Hn Soc; Hi Hnr Roll; Hnr Roll; Comm Volntr; Peer Tut/Med; Biology Clb; Chrch Yth Grp; Key Club; French Clb; Chr; Ch Chr; Clr Grd; Honor Choirs; Veterinarian

WARD, ROSLYN B; PHILADELPHIA, PA; OVERBROOK HS; (SO); Hnr Roll; Perf Att; Emplmnt; Tchrs Aide; GAA (V); Help Keep Roll Book for Teacher; Help Grade Papers for Teacher; Nursing; Accountant; Cheyney U; Temple U

WARD, SHAWN M; MOOSIC, PA; RIVERSIDE JR/SR HS; (JR); Hi Hnr Roll; Hnr Roll; MVP; Nat Hon Sy; Otst Ac Ach Awd; St of Mnth; WWAHSS; Yth Ldrshp Prog; Comm Volntr; Chrch Yth Grp; DARE; Emplmnt; Jr Ach; Lttrmn Clb; Vsity Clb; Bsball (V L); Bskball (V CL); Golf (V CL)

WARD IV, BURFOOT S; WARREN, PA; WARREN CTY CAREER CTR; (SO); Hi Hnr Roll; Hnr Roll; Perf Att; Chrch Yth Grp; Scouts; Bnd; Jzz Bnd; Mch Bnd; Orch; Cl Off (V)

WARFIELD, ANGELA N; RED LION, PA; RED LION AREA SR HS; (SR); Hi Hnr Roll; Hnr Roll; St of Mnth; WWAHSS; Comm Volntr; Hab For Humty Volntr; Emplmnt; Mus Clb; Project Harmony Member; Big Brothers / Big Sisters Mentor; Psychology; English; Penn State York Campus; Harrisburg Area Community College

WARNER, ABBY; FACTORYVILLE, PA; MONTROSE AREA SD; (SO); Hi Hnr Roll; Amnsty Intl; Emplmnt; Vsity Clb; French Clb; Chrldg (V L); Fld Hky (V L); Track (V); Vsy Clb (V L); Stu Cncl (R); Church Youth Group; Nursing / CRNA; Pharmacy; Wake Forest U; Notre Dame U

WARNER, ASHLEIGH S; TITUSVILLE, PA; TITUSVILLE HS; (SR); 4H Awd; Hi Hnr Roll; Hnr Roll; St of Mnth; WWAHSS; Yth Ldrshp Prog; Comm Volntr; 4-H; ArtClub; Chrch Yth Grp; Scouts; SP/M/VS; Special Education/Elementary Education; Carlow U

WARNER, BRIAN C; GLENMOORE, PA; CTR FOR ART TECH-PICKERING; (JR)

WARNER, MICHELLE A; SCRANTON, PA; TRIBORO CHRISTIAN AC; (FR); Hi Hnr Roll; Hnr Roll; Chrch Yth Grp; Emplmnt; SP/M/VS; Chrldg (V); Occupational Therapy; Marywood U

WARNER, RACHEL E; MIFFLINTOWN, PA; JUNIATA CTY SD; (JR); Ctznshp Aw; Hi Hnr Roll; Nat Hon Sy; Pres Ac Ftns Aw; St of Mnth; WWAHSS; Comm Volntr; Peer Tut/Med; 4-H; Chrch Yth Grp; Drma Clb; Emplmnt; Prom Com; Scouts; Tchrs Aide; Spanish Clb; Bnd; Chr; Drm Mjr; SP/M/VS; Fld Hky (JC); Sftball (JC); Tennis (J); Cl Off (T); Migrant Education Student Aide; Pre-Med; Spanish Language Professor

Ward, Roslyn B
Overbrook HS
Philadelphia, PA

National
Honor Roll
Spring 2005

Vijayvargiya, Neha
Wilson Southern JR HS
Sinking Spg, PA

WARRENDER, ZACHARY S; TRANSFER, PA; REYNOLDS JR/SR HS; (JR); Hnr Roll; WWAHSS; Peer Tut/Med; Red Cr Aide; Chrch Yth Grp; Key Club; Scouts; Eagle Scout; Respiratory Therapy

WARRINGTON, CHRISTINA; CLIFTON HEIGHTS, PA; UPPER DARBY HS; Hi Hnr Roll; Spec Olymp Vol; Chrch Yth Grp; Ch Chr; Lcrsse (J); Adv Cncl (R); Cl Off (S); Stu Cncl (R); Runner -Up - Biology Student of the Year; Teaching

WARSHAW, BOBBY; MECHANICSBURG, PA; (SO); F Lan Hn Soc; Hi Hnr Roll; Otst Ac Ach Awd; Perf Att; St of Mnth; WWAHSS; Comm Volntr; Key Club; Sccr (V C); 17 National Soccer Team; All AmericanAthlete; Adidas Top 100 Soccer Players

WASKO, AMANDA; CARLISLE, PA; CUMBERLAND VALLEY HS; (FR); Hnr Roll; Sci Fairs; Comm Volntr; Peer Tut/Med; Chrch Yth Grp; Dbte Team; Drma Clb; Emplmnt; Key Club; Mod UN; Scouts; Spanish Clb; Track (J L); CR (R); Youth Tutor; Girl Scout Cadet-7 Yrs; Nutrition Science; Language; Princeton

WASSER, AMBER; GREENVILLE, PA; (JR); Hi Hnr Roll; Nat Hon Sy; St of Mnth; WWAHSS; Chrch Yth Grp; Emplmnt; Key Club; Pep Squd; Prom Com; Spanish Clb; Chrldg (V CL); Physician's Assistant

WASSER, JUSTIN; EBENSBURG, PA; CTRL CAMBRIA HS; (JR); Hi Hnr Roll; Nat Hon Sy; Pres Ac Ftns Aw; Yth Ldrshp Prog; Comm Volntr; Peer Tut/Med; AL Aux Boys; Dbte Team; Drma Clb; Emplmnt; Jr Ach; NtlFrnscLg; Spch Team; SADD; Chr; Dnce; SP/M/VS; Ice Hky (V); Rlr Hky (V); Sccr (V); Adv Cncl (R); Cl Off (P); Stu Cncl (R); CR (R); Executive Officer of Young Democrats of Cambria County; Political Science; Communications; Boston U; American U

WATERMAN, JOHN; MONROEVILLE, PA; FORBES ROAD CTC; (SO); Comm Volntr; Engineering; Wyotech

WATERS, CANDICE S; BROOKHAVEN, PA; CARDINAL O'HARA HS; (SR); Ctznshp Aw; Hnr Roll; Valdctrian; Chrch Yth Grp; Emplmnt; Chr; Ch Chr; SP/M/VS; Chrldg (V); Cl Off (R); Yrbk; Morgan State U

WATERS, MICHELLA; HARRISBURG, PA; HARRISBURG HS; (SR); Hi Hnr Roll; Hnr Roll; Otst Ac Ach Awd; Chrch Yth Grp; Drma Clb; Track (V); Cheerleading, Prayer Club; Modeling; Psychology; Business Management; Spelman College; Hampton U

WATKINS, BRITTANY R; PITTSBURGH, PA; PITTSBURGH SD; (SO); DAR; Hi Hnr Roll; Nat Hon Sy; Business Management; Nursing

WATKINS, DION; WEST MIFFLIN, PA; RIDGEVIEW AC CS; (SO); Hnr Roll; Perf Att; St of Mnth; DARE; Wdwrkg Clb; Ftball; Auto Body Repair; Business; Ohio State U; Akron U

WATKINS, JULIE M; SHIPPENSBURG, PA; SHIPPENSBURG AREA HS; (SR); Hi Hnr Roll; Hnr Roll; Otst Ac Ach Awd; Comm Volntr; FBLA; CR (R); Scholastic Certificate of Merit Award for Art; Member of Youth Assets in the Community - YAC; Accounting; Biology; Millersville U

WATSON, COLLEEN M; WHITEHALL, PA; WHITEHALL-COPLAY HS; (SO); Sftball (J); Tennis (VJ); Yrbk (E, P); SADD Club Vice President; Pep Club Officer; Pre-Med; Advertising; Temple U; West Chester U

WATSON, KYRA; PHILADELPHIA, PA; PHILADELPHIA HS FOR GIRLS; (JR); Nat Hon Sy; Yth Ldrshp Prog; Comm Volntr; NYLC; Tmpl Yth Grp; Sftball (V); Youth Adelphia, Youth Philanthropy Board; Mechanical Engineer; Chemistry; United States Air Force Academy; Temple U

WATTS, BRITTANY; PITTSBURGH, PA; PITTSBURGH SD; (SO); Hnr Roll; Sci Fairs; Comm Volntr; Peer Tut/Med; Chess; Chrch Yth Grp; Drma Clb; Mus Clb; Photog; Schol Bwl; Chr; Ch Chr; SP/M/VS; Chrldg (C); Dvng (J); Scr Kpr (J); CR (P); Yrbk (P); Manager of an Ensemble Singing Group; Master's Degree in Psychology; Associate's Degree Child Psychology; Georgia Tech; Clark U

WAYNE, SHARITA; PHILADELPHIA, PA; EDWARD BOK AVT SCH; (JR); Ctznshp Aw; Perf Att; St of Mnth; Red Cr Aide; DARE; Emplmnt; Photog; Tchrs Aide; Business Administration; Human Resources Management; Temple U; Widner U

WEATHERSPOON, BRITNEE L; CLAIRTON, PA; CLAIRTON CITY SD; (SO); Hi Hnr Roll; Nat Hon Sy; Otst Ac Ach Awd; Perf Att; WWAHSS; Bskball (VJ); Penn State Talent Search; Psychology; Sports Medicine; Akron U; U of Pittsburgh

WEAVER, CASSIE M; JERSEY SHORE, PA; JERSEY SHORE HS; (JR); Hi Hnr Roll; Nat Hon Sy; Pres Ac Ftns Aw; Sci Fairs; WWAHSS; Comm Volntr; Peer Tut/Med; Chrch Yth Grp; DARE; Emplmnt; FBLA; Prom Com; SADD; Bskball (V); Tennis (V L); Track (V L); Stu Cncl (R); Created Web Page for YMCA; Vice President of Tennis Club; Information Science and Technology; Penn State U Park

WEAVER, DANIELLE C M; KNOX, PA; KEYSTONE HS; (SR); Hi Hnr Roll; Nat Hon Sy; Otst Ac Ach Awd; St of Mnth; WWAHSS; Comm Volntr; Red Cr Aide; Chrch Yth Grp; FTA; Mus Clb; Off Aide; Prom Com; Bnd; Jzz Bnd; Mch Bnd; SP/M/VS; Bskball (L); Music Education; Grove City College

WEAVER, DANIELLE M; HARRISBURG, PA; CTRL DAUPHIN HS; (SR); Hnr Roll; MVP; Nat Hon Sy; Comm Volntr; Spec Olymp Vol; Emplmnt; Key Club; Bnd; Scr Kpr (VJ); Skiing; Vllyball (V CL); Stu Cncl (R); Athlete of the Month; Employee of the Month; Nurse Anesthetist; Registered Nurse; Harrisburg Area Community College; Penn State U

WEAVER, HANNAH; WILLIAMSBURG, PA; WILLIAMSBURG CMTY SD; (SO); Hi Hnr Roll; Pres Sch; St of Mnth; WWAHSS; ArtClub; Chrch Yth Grp; Drma Clb; Emplmnt; Mth Clb/Tm; Bnd; Ch Chr; Mch Bnd; Stg Cre; Cl Off (T); Church Drama Team; Lee U; Liberty U

WEAVER, NATALIE E; PALMYRA, PA; LEBANON CTY CAREER AND TECH HS; (SR); 4H Awd; Hi Hnr Roll; Hnr Roll; St of Mnth; Comm Volntr; 4-H; Chrch Yth Grp; Emplmnt; Ch Chr; Vllyball (V); Cl Off (S); Skills USA Food & Beverage State Winner; Management/Business; Hospitality Industry; Johnson and Wales

WEAVER, NICOLE; DENVER, PA; EPHRATA HS; (SR); F Lan Hn Soc; Hnr Roll; Comm Volntr; Chrch Yth Grp; DARE; Emplmnt; Lib Aide; Photog; Bnd; Chr; Mch Bnd; Nursing; Psychology; Hesston College; Goshen College

WEAVER, NIGERHA H; LANSDOWNE, PA; BEVERLY HILLS MS; (MS); Ctznshp Aw; Hi Hnr Roll; Hnr Roll; Nat Hon Sy; Perf Att; Comm Volntr; Chrch Yth Grp; DARE; CR (P); Howard U; North Carolina A & T State U

WEAVER, SAMANTHA; YORK, PA; WEST YORK AREA SCH; (FR); Hnr Roll; Nat Hon Sy; Pres Ac Ftns Aw; St of Mnth; National Junior Honor Society; 1st Place VFW Essay Winner; Interpreter; Elementary Education; York College of Pennsylvania; Harvard

WEBB, BECKY; LAURYS STATION, PA; PARKLAND HS; (JR); Cr Ctry (V L); Track (V L); Key Club; Elementary Education; Bloomsburg U; DeSales U

WEBB, RODNEY; CLAIRTON, PA; CLAIRTON CITY SD; (SO); Hi Hnr Roll; Bskball (J)

WEBER, JANEL; COUDERSPORT, PA; COUDERSPORT AREA SD; (FR); 4H Awd; Hi Hnr Roll; Hnr Roll; Sci Fairs; 4-H; Chrch Yth Grp; Drma Clb; Scouts; Bnd; Chr; Dnce; Mch Bnd

WEBER, JULIE; PITTSBURGH, PA; PLUM SR HS; (SO); Hnr Roll; Perf Att; WWAHSS; Emplmnt; Quiz Bowl; Chrldg (V L); The National Society of High School Scholars; Scholar Athlete Award; English Major; U of Pennsylvania; U of Miami

WEBER, KENT; WASHINGTON CROSSING, PA; COUNCIL ROCK HS NORTH; (JR); F Lan Hn Soc; Hi Hnr Roll; Hnr Roll; Nat Hon Sy; Pres Sch; Comm Volntr; Hosp Aide; Red Cr Aide; Emplmnt; German Clb; People to People Ambassador; History Degree; Professor

WEBSTER, SARA; PERKASIE, PA; PENNRIDGE HS; (JR); Hi Hnr Roll; Nat Hon Sy; Yth Ldrshp Prog; Comm Volntr; Peer Tut/Med; NYLC; Chr; Fld Hky (J); Sccr (VJ); Student Athletic Trainer; Stand Tall-Drug Awareness; Sports Med-Athletic Training; Marketing/Advertising; U of Maryland; U of North Carolina

WECKMAN, ANDREW; PITTSBURGH, PA; NORTH CATHOLIC HS; (JR); Ctznshp Aw; Hi Hnr Roll; MVP; Nat Hon Sy; Perf Att; Sci Fairs; Comm Volntr; Peer Tut/Med; Chess; Chrch Yth Grp; Dbte Team; Emplmnt; P to P St Amb Prg; Scouts; Bskball (J L); Ftball (V L); Vice Pres. Leadership Team; Certified CPR & First Aid Instructor; Technical Engineering; Business Management; Air Force Academy; Carnegie Mellon U

WEDNER, HILARY; PITTSBURGH, PA; TAYLOR ALLDERDICE HS; (JR); Hi Hnr Roll; Nat Hon Sy; Perf Att; WWAHSS; Comm Volntr; Key Club; Tennis (V); Track (V); Key Club Treasurer; Business; Penn State U Park

WEEAST, ASHLEY; FLEETWOOD, PA; BRANDYWINE HEIGHTS HS; (SR); Ctznshp Aw; DAR; Hi Hnr Roll; Hnr Roll; Nat Hon Sy; Yth Ldrshp Prog; Comm Volntr; ArtClub; Chrch Yth Grp; Drma Clb; FBLA; HO'Br Yth Ldrshp; Key Club; Mus Clb; Prom Com; Bnd; Chr; Mch Bnd; SP/M/VS; Cl Off (S); Business Communications; U of Pittsburgh

WEHAR, JACOB; BEAVER FALLS, PA; BLACKHAWK HS; (SO); Hi Hnr Roll; Hnr Roll; WWAHSS; Spec Olymp Vol; Key Club; Spanish Clb; Ftball (J); Sccr (VJ); Dentistry; Secondary Education; Tampa U; Slippery Rock U

WEIDEMOYER, SARAH; PERKIOMENVILLE, PA; ST PIUS X HS; (JR); Hnr Roll; Nat Hon Sy; St of Mnth; Comm Volntr; Hosp Aide; Chrch Yth Grp; Dbte Team; Drma Clb; Emplmnt; Scouts; Bnd; Chr; Ch Chr; SP/M/VS; Bskball (V); Sftball (V); Track (V); Yrbk (R); Lettered for Drama in May 05; Nursing; Art; Moravian College; Drexel U

WEIDNER, MARY; GILBERTSVILLE, PA; BOYERTOWN AREA SR HS; (SO); Hnr Roll; Peer Tut/Med; DARE; Chr; Ch Chr; HEARTS Program Award; History Teacher; Nurse; Clarion U of PA

WEIGEL, KEVIN; CHALFONT, PA; CB WEST HS; (SR); CARE; Comm Volntr; Hab For Humty Volntr; Hosp Aide; Peer Tut/Med; Red Cr Aide; Emplmnt; Voc Ind Clb Am; Stu Cncl (V); Criminal Justice; Lehigh Valley College

WEINHOFER, BETHANY; PAXINOS, PA; SUNBURY CHRISTIAN AC; (SR); Hi Hnr Roll; Hnr Roll; WWAHSS; Chrch Yth Grp; Emplmnt; Bskball (V CL); Sccr (V CL); Cl Off (P, V); Pennsylvania Governors' School of the Arts Alternate; Creative Writing; Eastern U

WEISMAN, ERIN L; LANCASTER, PA; MANHEIM TWP HS; (JR); Ctznshp Aw; Hi Hnr Roll; Hnr Roll; Nat Hon Sy; St of Mnth; WWAHSS; Comm Volntr; Spec Olymp Vol; Emplmnt; Key Club; Dnce; Vllyball (J); Students Against Starvation; Fashion Merchandising

WEISS, CODY; FEASTERVILLE TREVOSE, PA; NESHAMINY HS; (SO); Fut Prb Slvr; Hi Hnr Roll; Perf Att; Mth Clb/Tm; Golf (J); Tennis (J); Bowling (JV); World Affairs Club; Art History; Business; Stanford U; Princeton U

WEISS, OLIVIA; EFFORT, PA; PLEASANT VALLEY HS; (SO); Hi Hnr Roll; Hnr Roll; WWAHSS; Spec Olymp Vol; Key Club; Chr; SP/M/VS; Film Club; Elementary Education; Music / Performing Arts; Berklee School of Music; East Stroudsburg U

WELDON, NATILEE; DRUMS, PA; IMMANUEL CHRISTIAN SCH; (JR); Hi Hnr Roll; Pres Ac Ftns Aw; Comm Volntr; Red Cr Aide; Chrch Yth Grp; Emplmnt; Stu Cncl (T); Yrbk (E); Lifeguard @ YMCA; International Business; Grove City College; Penn State

WELLING, KRISTIN M; ROYERSFORD, PA; SPRING-FORD SR HS; (SO); Hnr Roll; Otst Ac Ach Awd; Peer Tut/Med; Lib Aide; Pep Squd; Photog; Scouts; SADD; Spanish Clb; Dnce; Sccr (V L); Track (V L); Stu Cncl (R); Outstanding Physical Education; Criminal Law; Business; Duke U; Elon U

WELLS, JESSICA; MONTROSE, PA; ELK LAKE; (SO); Hi Hnr Roll; Nat Hon Sy; St of Mnth; WWAHSS; Chrch Yth Grp; Emplmnt; Key Club; Prom Com; Bnd; Dnce; Mch Bnd; Cr Ctry (J); Fld Hky (J); Skiing (V); Sccr (J); Swmg (V); Stu Cncl (R); Yrbk (R, P); From Steering Committee Member; Certified Lifeguard; Veterinary Medicine; Elementary Education; Baptist Bible College; Cornell U

WELSH, ANNE; COLLEGEVILLE, PA; METHACTON HS; (SO); Hi Hnr Roll; Pres Ac Ftns Aw; WWAHSS; Yth Ldrshp Prog; Amnsty Intl; Comm Volntr; Hab For Humty Volntr; Chrch Yth Grp; Key Clb; Mod UN; P to P St Amb Prg; Vsity Clb; Swmg (V); Track (V); Stu Cncl (R); Peer Connection Club; Student Athletic Training Club; Neurological Surgeon; Mother; Penn State; Temple U

WELSH, JENNIFER; PHILADELPHIA, PA; KENNEDY KENRICK CHS; (SR); Ctznshp Aw; Hi Hnr Roll; Hnr Roll; WWAHSS; Yth Ldrshp Prog; Lib Aide; Off Aide; Lit Mag (E); Sch Ppr; Forensic Pathology-MD, PhD; LaSalle U; Drexel U

WENGER, ERICA L; SHARON, PA; SHARON HS; (JR); Ctznshp Aw; Hi Hnr Roll; St of Mnth; WWAHSS; Yth Ldrshp Prog; Comm Volntr; Peer Tut/Med; ArtClub; Sci Clb; Spanish Clb; Chr; SP/M/VS; Swmg (V CL); Tennis (V L); CR (R); Lit Mag (R); Education; Math / Chemistry / English; Duquesne U; Dennison College

WENNER, KEN; BLOOMSBURG, PA; COLUMBIA-MONTOUR AVTS; (SO); Hnr Roll; Nat Hon Sy; Comm Volntr; DARE; Voc Ind Clb Am; Ftball (VJCL); All-American Football Conference - All-Academic

WERGER, CLARK A; BIRD IN HAND, PA; LANCASTER MENNONITE; (SR); Hnr Roll; Nat Hon Sy; Pres Ac Ftns Aw; WWAHSS; Comm Volntr; Emplmnt; Ntl FFA; Golf (V CL); Physician (M.D.); Messiah College

WERKMEISTER, LORA I; MC DONALD, PA; SOUTH FAYETTE TOWNSHIP HS; (JR); Hi Hnr Roll; Nat Hon Sy; Otst Ac Ach Awd; Pres Sch; St of Mnth; WWAHSS; Yth Ldrshp Prog; Comm Volntr; Peer Tut/Med; Chrch Yth Grp; Emplmnt; Mth Clb/Tm; NtlFrnscLg; Off Aide; Prom Com; Svce Clb; Japanese Clb; Bnd; Ch Chr; Mch Bnd; SP/M/VS; PP Ftbl; Stu Cncl (P); CR (R); American Legion Award

WERT, MARY B; PORT ROYAL, PA; JUNIATA CTY SD; (JR); Hi Hnr Roll; Hnr Roll; Pres Sch; St of Mnth; WWAHSS; Chrch Yth Grp; Emplmnt; Prom Com; Clb; Bnd; Chr; Flg Crps; Mch Bnd; Cl Off; Veterinary Medical Technology; Continue to Grad School; Wilson College

WERTZ, CHELSEA; POTTSVILLE, PA; POTTSVILLE AREA HS; (FR); Hnr Roll; Peer Tut/Med; Red Cr Aide; ArtClub; Chrch Yth Grp; Key Club; Spanish Clb; Bnd; Mch Bnd; Cr Ctry (L); Track (V); Sch Ppr (R); Adolescent Psychology; Nursing

Webb, Becky
Parkland HS
Laurys Station, PA

Weatherspoon, Britnee L
Clairton City SD
Clairton, PA

Weaver, Samantha
West York Area Sch
York, PA

WERTZ JR, JOHN J; RED LION, PA; YORK CTY SCH OF TECH; (FR); Hi Hnr Roll; Hnr Roll; Comm Volntr; Lib Aide; Electronics/Computer Repair Technician; ITT Technical Institute; ECPI

WEST, ANGELICA; BRACKNEY, PA; MONTROSE AREA SD; (SO); F Lan Hn Soc; Hi Hnr Roll; Hnr Roll; WWAHSS; Comm Volntr; Emplmnt; Lttrmn Clb; Vsity Clb; French Clb; Dnce; PP Ftbl (V); Sftball (L); Tennis (V L); Stu Cncl (R); Biology; Temple U; U of Pittsburgh

WESTCOTT, MARTINA; PHILADELPHIA, PA; CENTRAL HS; Hi Hnr Roll; Nat Hon Sy; St of Mnth; WWAHSS; Comm Volntr; Chrch Yth Grp; Emplmnt; Off Aide; Dnce; Sch Ppr (E); Pediatrics; Harvard U; Stanford U

WETLING, DANIELLE; UPPER DARBY, PA; UPPER DARBY HS; (JR); Hi Hnr Roll; Hnr Roll; MVP; Perf Att; Peer Tut/Med; Red Cr Aide; Spec Olymp Vol; Chrch Yth Grp; Bskball (V L); Lcrsse (V); PP Ftbl; Track (V L); Vllyball (V L); Stu Cncl (R); CR (R); Yrbk (P); Summer Volleyball League (Not for School); Softball (Not for School); Forensics; Business; Penn State U; Villanova U

WETZEL, PHILIP; ZIONSVILLE, PA; SALEM CHRISTIAN SCH; (FR); Hi Hnr Roll; Perf Att; Comm Volntr; Chrch Yth Grp; Bnd; Bsball (V); Sch Ppr (R); Sports Media

WETZEL, RYAN; ASHVILLE, PA; PENN CAMBRIA HS; (SR); Hi Hnr Roll; Hnr Roll; Nat Hon Sy; WWAHSS; Comm Volntr; Bsball (V CL); Bskball (V CL); Ftball (V CL); National Honor Roll; National Honor Society; PhD Pharmacy; Temple U

WEXELBLATT, JESSE; ELKINS PARK, PA; ABINGTON HS; (JR); Ctznshp Aw; Hi Hnr Roll; Hnr Roll; Nat Hon Sy; Nat Ldrshp Svc; DARE; Key Club; Pep Squd; Tmpl Yth Grp; Spanish Clb; Skiing; Sccr (C); Tennis (J); CR (R); Play Piano / TADA (Teens Against Drug & Alcohol) - 9th Grade Captain; Law / Pre-Law; Business / Business Administration; Penn State U; American U

WEXELBLATT, REBECCA; ELKINS PARK, PA; ABINGTON SR HS; (JR); Hnr Roll; Spec Olymp Vol; DARE; Key Club; Prom Com; Tmpl Yth Grp; Track (V); CR (R); Competitive Gymnast for 14 Years / TADA Captain 9th; Level 9 & 8 States & Regionals; Elementary Education / Early Childhood; Working With Children; Towson State; Rider U

WHEATLEY, TANISHA; SALTSBURG, PA; KISKI AREA HS; (SO); Hi Hnr Roll; MVP; WWAHSS; Comm Volntr; Key Club; Vsity Clb; Bskball (V); Cr Ctry (V); Track (V); Yrbk (R); Education; Law; Clarion; Slippery Rock

WHITBRED, AMANDA; DOYLESTOWN, PA; CTRL BUCKS HS EAST; (SO); Hi Hnr Roll; Nat Hon Sy; Pres Sch; WWAHSS; Amnsty Intl; Comm Volntr; ArtClub; Emplmnt; Key Club; Mod UN; Scouts; SADD; Scr Kpr (J); Adv Cncl (R); CR (R); Lit Mag (E); Published Poet; Poet; Creative Writing Major; Cornell U; Sarah Lawrence College

WHITE, ANTHONY M; PHILADELPHIA, PA; MURRELL DOBBINS AVTS; (SR); Hnr Roll; Perf Att; St of Mnth; WWAHSS; Peer Tut/Med; Emplmnt; FBLA; Jr Ach; Prom Com; Bskball (J); Business Management; Journalism; Delaware Valley College; Cheyney U

WHITE, CARLA; SCRANTON, PA; SCRANTON HS; (SR); Hnr Roll; Early Childhood Education; Wilkes U; Lackawanna College

WHITE, KENDRIC J; HARRISBURG, PA; HARRISBURG HS; (FR); Ctznshp Aw; Hi Hnr Roll; Hnr Roll; Yth Ldrshp Prog; Peer Tut/Med; Key Club; Stu Cncl (R); CR (R); Paralegal; Business Marketing; Howard U; Florida State U

WHITE, TONI D; DRUMS, PA; HAZLETON HS; (SO); Hi Hnr Roll; WWAHSS; Chess; Chrch Yth Grp; Emplmnt; Key Club; Sci Clb; Cr Ctry (V); Sccr (V); CR (R); Counseling; Teaching; Oral Roberts U; Messiah

WHITE, WHITNEY; HARRISBURG, PA; HARRISBURG HS; (JR); Ctznshp Aw; DAR; Hi Hnr Roll; Hnr Roll; Nat Stu Ath Day Aw; Otst Ac Ach Awd; Perf Att; St Schl; St of Mnth; Yth Ldrshp Prog; Comm Volntr; Hosp Aide; Red Cr Aide; Drma Clb; Mth Clb/Tm; Mod UN; Mus Clb; Ntl Beta Clb; NYLC; Photog; SADD; Dnce; Drl Tm; Mch Bnd; SP/M/VS; Bskball (V); Chrldg (V); Dvng (V); GAA (V); Sftball (V); Swmg (V); Tennis (V); Vllyball (V); Nursing; Thompson Institute; Millersville U

WHITE, WILETTA; PHILADELPHIA, PA; SIMON GRATZ HS; (FR); Ctznshp Aw; Hi Hnr Roll; Hnr Roll; St of Mnth; Chrch Yth Grp; Ch Chr; Medical Degree; Heart Surgeon; Temple U; Drexel U

WHITENACK, KELLY; BRODHEADSVILLE, PA; PLEASANT VALLEY HS; (SR); Hi Hnr Roll; Sci Fairs; Sci/Math Olympn; WWAHSS; Spec Olymp Vol; Biology Clb; FBLA; Off Aide; Sci Clb; SADD; Cr Ctry (V CL); Skiing (V C); Swmg (V CL); Track (V CL); Science Olympiad; Biology; Pre-Med; Syracuse U; Kent State

WHITMAN, ARIN C; HERMITAGE, PA; HICKORY HS; (SO); Hi Hnr Roll; Pres Ac Ftns Aw; Chrch Yth Grp; Ch Chr; Orch; Bskball (VJ); Track (V L); Medical Field-Pharmacist; Westminster College, New Wilmington PA; U of Pittsburgh

WHITMOYER, EMILY; FREDERICKSBURG, PA; NORTHERN LEBANON JR/SR HS; (SR); 4H Awd; Gov Hnr Prg; Hi Hnr Roll; Hnr Roll; Nat Hon Sy; St of Mnth; WWAHSS; Comm Volntr; Spec Olymp Vol; 4-H; Chrch Yth Grp; Emplmnt; Ntl FFA; Outdrs Clb; Svce Clb; Spch Team; SADD; Bnd; Chr; Ch Chr; Mch Bnd; PP Ftbl (V); Tennis (J); Sch Ppr (R); Agricultural Journalism; Texas A & M U

WHITNEY, ASHTON L; BLOSSBURG, PA; NORTH PENN JR/SR HS; (SO); Hi Hnr Roll; Hnr Roll; Comm Volntr; Spec Olymp Vol; Chrch Yth Grp; Key Club; Prom Com; Tchrs Aide; Track (J); Cl Off (V); Peer Helpers; Key Club; Law Enforcement; Air Force (Military Police); U of North Texas; Remington College

WHITTINGTON, BROOKE; PHILADELPHIA, PA; UNIVERSITY CITY HS; (SR); Ctznshp Aw; Hnr Roll; Otst Ac Ach Awd; Perf Att; St of Mnth; WWAHSS; Chrch Yth Grp; Emplmnt; Tchrs Aide; Dnce; SP/M/VS; Stg Cre; School Bowling Team; Early Childhood Education; St. John's U; Neumann College

WIESE, ELIZABETH K; BADEN, PA; (SO); Hnr Roll; Nat Hon Sy; Otst Ac Ach Awd; Sci Fairs; St of Mnth; WWAHSS; Comm Volntr; Key Club; Acpl Chr; Chr; SP/M/VS; Lcrsse; Scr Kpr; Stu Cncl; James Madison; Notre Dame

WIESECKEL, ERIC; WEXFORD, PA; NORTH ALLEGHENY HS; (SO); Hnr Roll; Nat Hon Sy; WWAHSS; Comm Volntr; Chrch Yth Grp; Key Club; Key Club; Physician; Physical Therapy; Northwestern U; Carnegie Mellon U

WIGGINS, LAMONICA; KINGSTON, PA; WYOMING VALLEY WEST; (SR); Hnr Roll; Nat Hon Sy; Pres Sch; WWAHSS; Red Cr Aide; Lib Aide; Mus Clb; Bnd; Jzz Bnd; Mch Bnd; Orch; Fncg; Tennis (J); CR; Lit Mag (E); Sch Ppr; CIA; FBI; U of Pittsburgh

WIGGINTON, BRYAN; PITTSBURGH, PA; (JR); Hnr Roll; Otst Ac Ach Awd; Chess; Ftball (V); Track (V); Wt Lftg (V); Physical Education; Slippery Rock U

WILAMOWSKI, PAIGE L; CRANBERRY TWP, PA; SENECA VALLEY SHS; (SO); Hi Hnr Roll; WWAHSS; Comm Volntr; Chrch Yth Grp; Emplmnt; Key Club; SADD; Chr; Dnce; SP/M/VS; Swg Chr; Chrldg (V L); CR (R); Honors District Chorus; Competitive Dance Team; Music; Business; San Diego State; Juilliard

WILCOX, ASHLEY; PITTSFIELD, PA; YOUNGSVILLE MIDDLE SR HS; MS; Hi Hnr Roll; Hnr Roll; Psychology; Biology

WILDMAN, KAYTI; MECHANICSBURG, PA; CUMBERLAND VALLEY HS; (SO); Hnr Roll; Key Club; Spanish Clb; Forensic Science; U of Virginia; Villanova U

WILEMAN, DUSTIN; MC VEYTOWN, PA; LEWISTOWN HS; (JR); Hi Hnr Roll; Hnr Roll; Nat Hon Sy; St of Mnth; DARE; FCA; Im a Life Scout; Master Architecture Engineering; South Hills

WILKINS, TIA; PHILADELPHIA, PA; MERCY VOC HS; (FR); Hnr Roll; St of Mnth; Comm Volntr; Pediatric Nurse

WILKINSON, FAITH A; BELLEFONTE, PA; CTRL PA INST OF SCI HS; (SR); Hnr Roll; Comm Volntr; Red Cr Aide; Spec Olymp Vol; Scouts; Tchrs Aide; Stg Cre; Volunteer with Centre Life Link EMS

WILKOSZ, CINDY; CLIFTON HEIGHTS, PA; (JR); Hi Hnr Roll; Hnr Roll; Perf Att; Drma Clb; Emplmnt; Dnce; SP/M/VS; Pharmaceuticals; U of Sciences in Philadelphia

WILL, DANNILLE M; FRIEDENS, PA; SOMERSET AREA SD; (JR); Hnr Roll; MVP; Ntl FFA; Spanish Clb; Chr; Bskball (J); Skt Tgt Sh (V L); Sftball (V L); Player of the Game; Landscaping Design; Texas A & M; Texas Tech

WILLIAMS, AINSWAL; PHILADELPHIA, PA; BEN FRANKLIN HS; (MS); Ctznshp Aw; Otst Ac Ach Awd; Perf Att; St of Mnth; Chrch Yth Grp; Lib Aide; NYLC; Ch Chr; Cr Ctry (V); Track (V); Engineering / Mechanical; Computer Technology

WILLIAMS, ALEXIS; HARRISBURG, PA; SCI TECH HS; (SO); Hnr Roll; Sci Fairs; St of Mnth; Comm Volntr; Emplmnt; Key Club; Bnd; Mch Bnd; Pre-Med; Hampton U; North Carolina U

WILLIAMS, ALICIA; CARLISLE, PA; BOLING SPRINGS HS; (JR); Hnr Roll; WWAHSS; Comm Volntr; Hab For Humty Volntr; Chrch Yth Grp

WILLIAMS, ASHLEY; BERWICK, PA; BERWICK AREA HS; (JR); Hi Hnr Roll; Hnr Roll; Comm Volntr; Chrch Yth Grp; Key Club; Elementary Education; Bloomsburg U; Luzurn County Community College

WILLIAMS, ASHTON; LANCASTER, PA; MC KASKEY HS EAST; (FR); Hnr Roll; Chrch Yth Grp; Ch Chr; Dnce; Sccr (J); Outstanding Achievement in Social Studies, The DeJanee Award, Certificate of Merit Mathematics League; Meritorious Honors Award, Academic Excellence Communication Arts, Good Behavior Recognition Award; Surgeon; Oral Roberts U; Harvard U

WILLIAMS, CAITLIN; HONEY BROOK, PA; COATESVILLE; (JR); Hi Hnr Roll; Hnr Roll; Nat Hon Sy; WWAHSS; Comm Volntr; Emplmnt; P to P St Amb Prg; Svce Clb; Spanish Clb

WILLIAMS, COURTNEY A; CHICORA, PA; KARNS CITY HS; (SR); Hi Hnr Roll; Hnr Roll; Perf Att; St of Mnth; WWAHSS; Chrch Yth Grp; Emplmnt; SADD; Spanish Clb; Dnce; Bskball (J); PP Ftbl (V); Sftball (V); Track (V); 2005 Butler Leaders of Tomorrow Nominee; Communications / Public Relations; Slippery Rock U; Point Park U

WILLIAMS, EQUILLE V; LANSDOWNE, PA; MONSIGNOR BONNER HS; (FR); Hi Hnr Roll; Hnr Roll; Perf Att; Made Bowling Team; Meteorology Degree; Geology Degree; U of Miami; Duke U

WILLIAMS, ERIC S; PHILADELPHIA, PA; CENTRAL HS; (SR); Bskball; Math Award; PhD Programs; MD Programs; Howard U; Drexel U

WILLIAMS, EVAN L; PINE FORGE, PA; PINE FORGE SDA AC; (SR); Ctznshp Aw; Hnr Roll; Perf Att; Peer Tut/Med; Drma Clb; Emplmnt; Chr; SP/M/VS; Stg Cre; Bskball (V); Cr Ctry (V); Broadcast Communications; Auto Mechanics; Oakwood College; Columbia Union College

WILLIAMS, JUSTIN; LEVITTOWN, PA; (SR); Hnr Roll; Nat Hon Sy; Comm Volntr; Peer Tut/Med; Chrch Yth Grp; Spanish Clb; Bnd; Ch Chr; Clr Grd; Drm Mjr; Music Education; Indiana U; Millersville U

WILLIAMS, KELLY; TRUCKSVILLE, PA; DALLAS HS; (JR); Hnr Roll; Nat Hon Sy; St of Mnth; WWAHSS; Comm Volntr; Chrch Yth Grp; Emplmnt; Key Club; Scouts; Chr; Ch Chr; SP/M/VS; Graduate of Junior Leadership Wilkes-Barre; Recipient of Gold Award for Girl Scouts; Communications/ Journalism; Education; Ithaca College; Marywood U

WILLIAMS, KRYSTAL L; PHILADELPHIA, PA; RANDOLPH CAREER AC; (JR); Hnr Roll; Perf Att; Hosp Aide; Emplmnt; Bskball (VJ); Sccr (V); Tennis (V); Physical Therapy; U of Pittsburgh; Old Dominion U

WILLIAMS, LASHAELA; ERIE, PA; EAST HS; (MS); Hnr Roll; St of Mnth; Chrch Yth Grp; Mth Clb/Tm; Mus Clb; Ch Chr; Dnce; Drl Tm; CR (R); Pediatrician; Nurse

WILLIAMS, LAUREN; COLUMBIA, PA; HEMPFIELD HS; (JR); Hi Hnr Roll; Nat Hon Sy; WWAHSS; Comm Volntr; Chrch Yth Grp; Emplmnt; Key Club; Pep Squd; Svce Clb; Chr; Dnce; SP/M/VS; Chrldg (V); Early Childhood Education; Psychology; Temple U; Bloomsburg U

WILLIAMS, RYAN O; FREDONIA, PA; LAKEVIEW SD; (JR); St of Mnth; Peer Tut/Med; Hsbk Rdg (V)

WILLIAMS, SHELBY D; ELIZABETHTOWN, PA; ELIZABETHTOWN AREA HS; MS; Hi Hnr Roll; Otst Ac Ach Awd; St of Mnth; Comm Volntr; Sccr (J); Stu Cncl (R); Lit Mag (R); Sch Ppr (R); Teaching Degree; Penn State

WILLIAMS, STEPHEN; PHILADELPHIA, PA; MULTI-CULTURAL AC CHARTER SCH; (FR); Hi Hnr Roll; Hnr Roll; Perf Att; Sci Fairs; St of Mnth; Yth Ldrshp Prog; CARE; Comm Volntr; Cmptr Clb; Emplmnt; Fr of Library; Off Aide; Quiz Bowl; Schol Bwl; Tchrs Aide; Tech Clb; Bsball; Lit Mag (E)

WILLIAMS, WALTER; ERIE, PA; STRONG VINCENT HS; (JR); Hnr Roll; MVP; Otst Ac Ach Awd; St of Mnth; Yth Ldrshp Prog; French Clb; Ftball (V); Track (V); Stu Cncl (V); Yrbk (P); Sports Medicine; Criminal Justice; U of Miami; U of Southern California

WILLIAMSON, DEIRDRE; BETHLEHEM, PA; SAUCON VALLEY HS; (JR); Hi Hnr Roll; Hnr Roll; Perf Att; St of Mnth; Comm Volntr; Peer Tut/ Med; Chrch Yth Grp; Drma Clb; Emplmnt; SADD; Chr; Orch; SP/M/VS; Chrldg (J); PP Ftbl (J); Sccr (V L); Received Medals

Williams, Courtney A
Karns City HS
Chicora, PA

Wilkinson, Faith A
Central Pa Inst Of Sci HS
Bellefonte, PA

Whittington, Brooke
University City HS
Philadelphia, PA

White, Anthony M
Murrell Dobbins AVTS
Philadelphia, PA

White, Wiletta
Simon Gratz HS
Philadelphia, PA

Will, Dannille M
Somerset Area SD
Friedens, PA

Williams, Shelby D
Elizabethtown Area HS
Elizabethtown, PA

WILLIAMSON, MARLA; PHILADELPHIA, PA; SIMON GRATZ HS; (FR); Hnr Roll; Nat Hon Sy; Otst Ac Ach Awd; St of Mnth; Chrch Yth Grp; DARE; Emplmnt; ROTC; Dnce; Track (J); White Williams Scholar; Law; Kutztown U; Rosemount College

WILLIE, AARON K; PHILADELPHIA, PA; (SR); Ctznshp Aw; Hnr Roll; MVP; Perf Att; WWAHSS; Chrch Yth Grp; Dbte Team; Wdwrkg Clb; Clb; Sccr (J); CR (S); Business, Accounting; Drexel U; Lincoln U

WILLOW, RODNEY J; MIFFLINTOWN, PA; JUNIATA HS; (SR); Bsball (V); CADD; York Technical Institute

WILMARTH, VIRGINIA; SPRINGVILLE, PA; ELK LAKE SCH; (SO); Hi Hnr Roll; Hnr Roll; Nat Hon Sy; Pres Ac Ftns Aw; St of Mnth; WWAHSS; Hab For Humty Volntr; Peer Tut/Med; Chrch Yth Grp; Key Club; Schol Bwl; SADD; Spanish Clb; Acpl Chr; Bnd; Chr; Ch Chr; Tennis (V); Vice President-Spanish Club; Winner of School Talent Show; Communications-Public Relations; Business; Rensselaer Polytechnic Institute; U of Pennsylvania

WILSON, BRANDON; MESHOPPEN, PA; ELK LAKE HS; (SO); Hi Hnr Roll; Hnr Roll; Kwnis Aw; Nat Hon Sy; Perf Att; St of Mnth; Yth Ldrshp Prog; Comm Volntr; Emplmnt; HO'Br Yth Ldrshp; Key Club; Prom Com; Spanish Clb; Bnd; Mch Bnd; Sccr (V); Track (J); Vllyball (J); Stu Cncl (R); CR (R); Yrbk (R); MAAC-Mid Atlantic Alliance of Cooperatives; Elem Education; Gym Teacher; Lock Haven U; East Stroudsburg U

WILSON, JAMIE L; WASHINGTON, PA; TRINITY AREA SD; (JR); Hi Hnr Roll; Hnr Roll; Perf Att; Peer Tut/Med; Business; French; Shippensburg U; Temple U

WILSON, MOLLY; BRACKNEY, PA; MONTROSE AREA SD; (SO); 4H Awd; Comm Volntr; Peer Tut/Med; 4-H; SADD; Fld Hky (J); Nursing; Pediatrics; Broome Community College; SUNY Binghamton

WILSON, SAMUEL; LANSDALE, PA; NORTH PENN HS; (JR); Hi Hnr Roll; Hnr Roll; WWAHSS; Spec Olymp Vol; Cmptr Clb; Key Club; President of Book Club; Member of Key Club; Marine Biology; Political Science; U of Connecticut; Michigan State U

WILT, JOSH; SPRING MILLS, PA; CTRL PA INST OF SCI HS; (SO); DAR; Hi Hnr Roll; Hnr Roll; St of Mnth; Wdwrkg Clb; Chr; Ftball (J); Protective Services; Certified in First Responder / CPR / Firefighter; Conservation Officer; Police Officer; Penn State U

WILTROUT, ALEX M; MERTZTOWN, PA; BRANDYWINE HEIGHTS HS; (SO); Ctznshp Aw; Hi Hnr Roll; St of Mnth; WWAHSS; Comm Volntr; Chrch Yth Grp; Key Club; German Clb; Bskball (J); Tennis (V); Chemistry; History

WINDERMAN, DIANA; BENSALEM, PA; BENSALEM HS; (JR); Ctznshp Aw; Hi Hnr Roll; Comm Volntr; Peer Tut/Med; Emplmnt; Prom Com; Svce Clb; Student Government; Community Service; Psychology; Penn State U; U Central Florida

WINGATE, BROOKE; CONSHOHOCKEN, PA; PLYMOUTH WHITEMARSH HS; (SO); Ctznshp Aw; Hi Hnr Roll; Hnr Roll; Perf Att; Pres Ac Ftns Aw; St of Mnth; DARE; SP/M/VS; Mar Art; Track (V L); Class Steering Committee; Entertainment Law; Theatre; NYU; Howard U

WINGROVE, KRISTEN; WEXFORD, PA; NORTH ALLEGHENY INT HS; (FR); Hi Hnr Roll; Otst Ac Ach Awd; Perf Att; St of Mnth; WWAHSS; Comm Volntr; Peer Tut/Med; Chrch Yth Grp; Key Club; Ch Chr; Orch; Vllyball; Piano; Dance Committee; Secondary Education; Penn State U; Ohio U

WISDOM, ANDREW; PHILADELPHIA, PA; NORTHEAST HS; (SR); Hnr Roll; Off Aide; Prom Com; JAPAN Clb; Bnd; Chr; Dnce; Mch Bnd; Ftball (V); Mar Art; Track (V); Wt Lftg; Adv Cncl (R); Cl Off (P, V); Stu Cncl (R); CR (R); Anesthesiology; Penn State U

WISEHAUPT, HILLARY; PORT ROYAL, PA; JUNIATA CTY SD; (SR); Hnr Roll; Nat Hon Sy; Spec Olymp Vol; Jr Ach; Key Club; Lib Aide; Bnd; Mch Bnd; Dale Carnegie Award; VMT; Equestrian Studies; Wilson College

WISLER, BRIANA; COLLEGEVILLE, PA; METHACTON HS; (SR); WWAHSS; Yth Ldrshp Prog; Comm Volntr; Peer Tut/Med; Chrch Yth Grp; FCA; Key Club; Tchrs Aide; PP Ftbl (V); Track (VJ); Key Club - Treasurer; Student Ambassador; Physical Therapy / Biology Major; Messiah College

WISNICK, JUSTIN; PITTSBURGH, PA; (JR); Ctznshp Aw; Hnr Roll; MVP; Chrch Yth Grp; Emplmnt; Scouts; Vsity Clb; Bsball (V); Bskball (VJ L); Ftball (J); Physical Education; Sports Medicine; Point Park; Slippery Rock U-La Roche

WISOR, BETHANY; LEBANON, PA; CURWENSVILLE HS; (FR); 4H Awd; Hi Hnr Roll; Hnr Roll; St of Mnth; 4-H; FCA; Chr; Chrldg (J); Gmnstcs (J); Cl Off (S); Stu Cncl (R); Law; Criminal Justice; Penn State U; George Mason U

WISOWATY, JOSHUA; DANVILLE, PA; COLUMBIA-MONTOUR AVTS; (JR); Hnr Roll; Nat Hon Sy; Sci Fairs; Chrch Yth Grp; Emplmnt; Outdrs Clb; Wt Lftg; Nano Fabrication Manufacturing; Electrical Engineering; Penn State U

WISSINGER, CHASTITY A; EMLENTON, PA; MONITEAU JR/SR HS; (SR); Hnr Roll; Nat Hon Sy; Otst Ac Ach Awd; WWAHSS; Comm Volntr; Hosp Aide; Red Cr Aide; ArtClub; DARE; Emplmnt; Pep Squd; SADD; Tchrs Aide; Chr; Dnce; SP/M/VS; Chrldg (V CL); PP Ftbl (V); Track (V CL); Vllyball (V); Stu Cncl (R); Principal's Honor Award; BSN Degree; Pediatric Nurse Practitioner; Butler County Community College; U of Maryland

WITMER, MARANDIA K; NEWVILLE, PA; BIG SPRING SD; (JR); Hnr Roll; Comm Volntr; DARE; Drma Clb; Outdrs Clb; Chr; SP/M/VS; MLS; Kutztown U

WITTER, GRACE; MONROEVILLE, PA; GATEWAY SR HS; (SO); Hi Hnr Roll; St of Mnth; WWAHSS; Chrch Yth Grp; Drma Clb; Emplmnt; Jr Cls League; Key Club; Chr; Ch Chr; SP/M/VS; Magna Cum Laude in National Latin Exam (2003); Elementary Education; Pediatrics; U of Pennsylvania; U of Pittsburgh

WITTER, TYLER; SHIPPENSBURG, PA; BIG SPRING SD; (FR); Hnr Roll; Sci Fairs; Comm Volntr; Chrch Yth Grp; P to P St Amb Prg; Quiz Bowl

WLAZELEK, SARA; LENHARTSVILLE, PA; KUTZTOWN AREA HS; (SO); Hi Hnr Roll; MVP; Spec Olymp Vol; Emplmnt; Key Club; Scouts; Fld Hky (J); Track (V L); Stu Cncl (R); Cougar Award in Track & Field; Most Points Scored By Female Athlete (Track); Journalism; Education; Shippensburg U of PA; Elizabethtown College

WOCHNER, HALEY A; ERIE, PA; HARBOR CREEK HS; (FR); Hi Hnr Roll; Perf Att; WWAHSS; Comm Volntr; Peer Tut/Med; Quiz Bowl; Schol Bwl; Clr Grd; Dnce; SP/M/VS; Tennis (V); Cl Off (P); Yrbk (P); President of Busted! - Kids Against Tobacco; Coalition Pathways, Inc./ National Youth Anti-Drug; Law; Pharmacy; Harvard U; Yale U

WOLFE, JANEL L; HARRISBURG, PA; CTRL DAUPHIN HS; (SO); Hi Hnr Roll; Hnr Roll; Perf Att; St of Mnth; Yth Ldrshp Prog; Comm Volntr; Peer Tut/Med; Bskball (J); Track (J); Stu Cncl (R); Athletic Trainer; Volunteer at Hershey Medical Center; Nursing; Penn State U

WOLFE, JENN; LANCASTER, PA; MANHEIM TWP HS; (SR); Hnr Roll; Sci Fairs; Comm Volntr; Emplmnt; Key Club; Svce Clb; Radiology; Lancaster General College of Radiology

WOLGEMUTH, EMILY; LANCASTER, PA; MANHEIM TWP HS; (JR); Hi Hnr Roll; Hnr Roll; Nat Hon Sy; Nat Mrt LOC; WWAHSS; Comm Volntr; Spec Olymp Vol; Chrch Yth Grp; FCA; Key Club; Lcrsse (J L); PP Ftbl (V C); Scr Kpr (VJ); Sccr (J L); Track (J); Stu Cncl (R); CR (R); Yrbk (E); English; Taylor U; Gordon College

WONG, JONATHAN; BENSALEM, PA; BENSALEM HS; (JR); Hnr Roll; ROTC; Ftball (V); Engineering; Management; Pennsylvania State U; Lafayette College

WOOD, CHRISTIAN A; WARREN, PA; WARREN AREA HS; (SO); Hi Hnr Roll; MVP; Lttrmn Clb; Bskball (V L); Ftball (VJ L); Wt Lftg; All State Academic Team

WOOD, JOSH; MESHOPPEN, PA; ELK LAKE SCH; (SO); Hnr Roll; Nat Hon Sy; Perf Att; St of Mnth; WWAHSS; Comm Volntr; Drma Clb; Emplmnt; Key Club; Mus Clb; Spanish Clb; Bnd; Chr; Jzz Bnd; SP/M/VS; Yrbk (R); Elementary Education; Theatre; Lock Haven U; Mansfield

WOOD, KIMBERLY; MARCUS HOOK, PA; CHICHESTER SR HS; (SO); Hi Hnr Roll; WWAHSS; Emplmnt; Mod UN; Fld Hky (J); Lcrsse (J); JV Captain- Field Hockey / Lacrosse; Ski Club; Marine Biology; Journalism

WOOD, SADIE; LIBERTY, PA; LIBERTY JR/SR HS; (SO); Hi Hnr Roll; Hnr Roll; Otst Ac Ach Awd; Perf Att; Spec Olymp Vol; Key Club; Spanish Clb; Chr; Vllyball (VJ); Stu Cncl (S); Key Club Secretary; Psychology; Literature/English; Penn State U

WOODARD, TRACEY; NORRISTOWN, PA; NORRISTOWN AREA HS; (JR); Hnr Roll; WWAHSS; Spec Olymp Vol; Key Club; SP/M/VS; Stg Cre; Theater Major; English Major; Muhlenberg College; Penn U of Pennsylvania

WOODRING, COURTNEY E; HOLLIDAYSBURG, PA; HOLLIDAYSBURG AREA SR HS; (JR); Hnr Roll; Nat Hon Sy; Red Cr Aide; Chrch Yth Grp; Drma Clb; FBLA; Key Club; Prom Com; SADD; Vsity Clb; Stg Cre; Chrldg (V); Stu Cncl (V); Sports Marketing; Penn State U; Slippery Rock U

WOODRUFF, BRITTANY L; POTTSTOWN, PA; POTTSGROVE HS; (JR); Ctznshp Aw; Hi Hnr Roll; Hnr Roll; Pres Sch; Comm Volntr; Emplmnt; Key Club; Bnd; Chr; Secondary Education; Special Education; Kutztown U; Millersville U

WOODS, MEGHAN D; WEST CHESTER, PA; WEST CHESTER EAST HS; (SR); F Lan Hn Soc; Hnr Roll; Nat Hon Sy; St of Mnth; Comm Volntr; Peer Tut/Med; Prom Com; Sftball (V L); Stu Cncl (R); Service Above Self Award-From West Chester Rotary Club; Secretary of National Honor Society; Biochemistry; Biology; U of Delaware; U of Maryland

WOODWARD, KAITLYN R; YARDLEY, PA; NOTRE DAME HS; (JR); Hi Hnr Roll; Hnr Roll; Nat Hon Sy; Otst Ac Ach Awd; WWAHSS; Peer Tut/Med; Emplmnt; Chr; Dnce; PP Ftbl (J); Track (V L); 2005 Irish Way Scholarship Winner; English; Pennsylvania State U; Lehigh U

WOODWARD, KRISTIN; DILLSBURG, PA; NORTHERN HS; (JR); Hi Hnr Roll; Hnr Roll; Otst Ac Ach Awd; Pres Ac Ftns Aw; Sci Fairs; Comm Volntr; Peer Tut/Med; Spec Olymp Vol; DARE; Emplmnt; Key Club; Scouts; SADD; Tchrs Aide; Chr; Bskball (J); Hsbk Rdg; Ice Sktg; Skiing; Swmg; Red Cross Babysitters Course; Elementary Education; Shippensburg U

WOREK, MELANIE; APOLLO, PA; KISKI AREA HS; (SO); Hi Hnr Roll; Perf Att; Sci/Math Olympn; WWAHSS; Yth Ldrshp Prog; Hosp Aide; AL Aux Girls; ArtClub; Key Club; SADD; Bskball (J); Tennis (V); Track (J); Cl Off (V); Stu Cncl (R); Yrbk (R); President's Volunteer Service Award-Bronze; American Legion Award; Pre-Medicine; Chemical Engineering

WORLEY, ANNA; HARRISBURG, PA; CTRL DAUPHIN SD; (FR); Hnr Roll; Comm Volntr; Key Club; Chr; Dnce; Fld Hky; Sccr; Did Club Soccer Until Knee Surgery; Psychology; Journalism

WORONA, MYRON; HERMITAGE, PA; HICKORY HS; (SO); Hnr Roll; Pres Ac Ftns Aw; Comm Volntr; Chrch Yth Grp; Ftball (J)

WORST, CHRISTINA E; WEST CHESTER, PA; BISHOP SHANAHAN HS; (JR); Ctznshp Aw; Hnr Roll; Nat Hon Sy; Perf Att; Yth Ldrshp Prog; Comm Volntr; Peer Tut/Med; Emplmnt; NYLC; French Clb; Nursing; West Chester U; Drexel U

WRIGHT, BRITTNEA M; HARRISBURG, PA; JOHN HARRIS HS; (FR); Ctznshp Aw; Hnr Roll; Nat Hon Sy; Perf Att; Sci Fairs; DARE; Chr; Ch Chr; Dnce; Chrldg (J); Cr Ctry (V); Track (V); Stu Cncl (R); Pediatrician

WRIGHT, JEWEL; ERIE, PA; ERIE CITY SD HS; (SO); Nursing; Film

WRIGHT, SHAKIRA; PHILADELPHIA, PA; CITY CTR AC; (JR); F Lan Hn Soc; Hi Hnr Roll; Hnr Roll; Otst Ac Ach Awd; Perf Att; Salutrn; St of Mnth; WWAHSS; Peer Tut/Med; ArtClub; Chrch Yth Grp; Drma Clb; Emplmnt; Mth Clb/Tm; Prom Com; Scouts; Ch Chr; Dnce; Drl Tm; SP/M/VS; Cl Off (P); First Honors; Second Highest Average; PhD / Pediatric Medicine; Early Childhood Education; Howard U; U of Pennsylvania

WRUBEL, JOSHUA M; WILLIAMSTOWN, PA; WILLIAMS VALLEY JR/SR HS; (JR); Ctznshp Aw; Hi Hnr Roll; Nat Hon Sy; Perf Att; St of Mnth; WWAHSS; Yth Ldrshp Prog; Drma Clb; Emplmnt; HO'Br Yth Ldrshp; Mus Clb; Prom Com; Bnd; Chr; Jzz Bnd; Mch Bnd; Student Announcer; Chemistry; Pre-Med; Pennsylvania State U; Franklin and Marshall

WU, KATHLEEN; BRYN MAWR, PA; RADNOR HS; (SR); F Lan Hn Soc; Hnr Roll; Nat Hon Sy; Nat Mrt Semif; Pres Sch; Sci/Math Olympn; WWAHSS; Yth Ldrshp Prog; HO'Br Yth Ldrshp; Key Club; Mth Clb/Tm; Mus Clb; Spanish Clb; Orch; SP/M/VS; Track (V L); Cl Off (T); Stu Cncl (R); NCTE Writing Contest Achievement Award; Biochemical Engineering; Finance; U of Pennsylvania

WYNEGAR, RENEE E; MECHANICSBURG, PA; CUMBERLAND VALLEY HS; (JR); Hnr Roll; Comm Volntr; Emplmnt; Key Club; Photog; Track (V L); CR (P); Education; U of Pittsburgh At Johnstown; Indiana U of Pennsylvania

WYSHOCK, ANDREW; MONTOURSVILLE, PA; LOYALSOCK TWP HS; (SO); Ctznshp Aw; Hi Hnr Roll; WWAHSS; Chrch Yth Grp; Key Club; Tennis (VJ); Aerospace Engineer

WYTIAZ, NICHOLAS P; JEFFERSON HILLS, PA; THOMAS JEFFERSON HS; (JR); Ctznshp Aw; F Lan Hn Soc; Hi Hnr Roll; Nat Hon Sy; Perf Att; Pres Ac Ftns Aw; Sci Fairs; St of Mnth; Comm Volntr; Hosp Aide; Chrch Yth Grp; Cmptr Clb; Emplmnt; Jr Cls League; Sci Clb; Scouts; Vllyball (V CL); Sch Ppr (R); Eagle Scout; Pittsburgh Tribune-Review Outstanding Young Citizen; Medical Field; Pharmacy; U of Pittsburgh; U of Pennsylvania

XIAO, EILEEN; HUNTINGDON, PA; HUNTINGDON AREA HS; (SO); Hi Hnr Roll; Otst Ac Ach Awd; WWAHSS; Yth Ldrshp Prog; Comm Volntr; Peer Tut/Med; Spec Olymp Vol; Drma Clb; Key Club; Mus Clb; Quiz Bowl; Schol Bwl; Bnd; Chr; SP/M/VS; National History Day; Computer Crime Investigation; Computer Science; Massachusetts Institute of Technology; Yale U

XU, YIRAN; HERSHEY, PA; HERSHEY HS; (SO); Hi Hnr Roll; WWAHSS; Key Club; Mod UN; Tennis (J); Stu Cncl (R); Sch Ppr (R); Member of Cooking Club

YAM, KAREN; UPPER DARBY, PA; (JR); Hnr Roll; Perf Att; Comm Volntr; ArtClub; Tennis (J); Pharmacy; Graphic Designing; Temple U; Penn State U

YAMMUE, DARGAR; PHILADELPHIA, PA; BARTRAM HS; (JR); Hnr Roll; Perf Att; SP/M/VS; Member Neighborhood Bike Works; Science; Business; U of Miami; Lincoln U

YANCIK, SAMANTHA; PHOENIXVILLE, PA; PHOENIXVILLE AREA HS; (JR); Hi Hnr Roll; Nat Hon Sy; Peer Tut/Med; Emplmnt; Key Club; NYLC; French Clb; Fld Hky (J); Stu Cncl (R); Summer Mentoring for Elementary Students (Summer Activities For Enrichment Program); Mathematics; Lehigh U; Gettysburg College

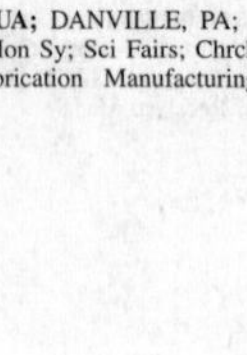
Yammue, Dargar
Bartram HS
Philadelphia, PA

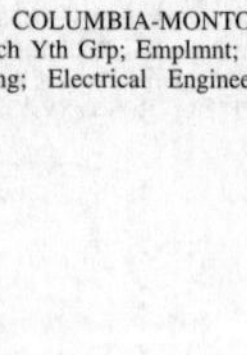
Wright, Shakira
City Ctr AC
Philadelphia, PA

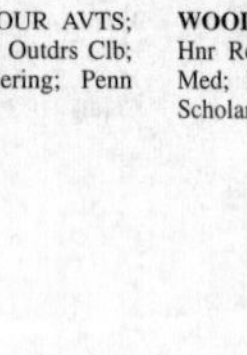
Wisowaty, Joshua
Columbia-Montour AVTS
Danville, PA

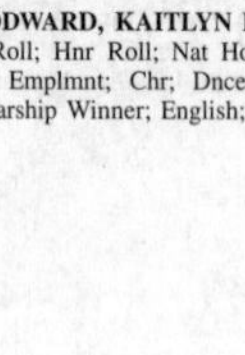
Wilson, Jamie L
Trinity Area SD
Washington, PA

National
Honor Roll
Spring 2005

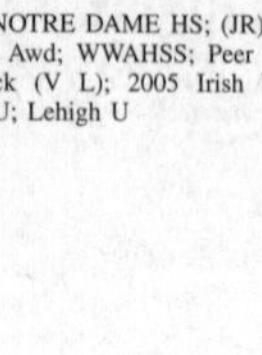
Willow, Rodney J
Juniata HS
Mifflintown, PA

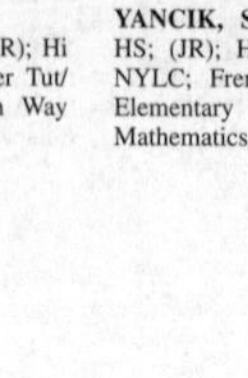
Woodward, Kaitlyn R
Notre Dame HS
Yardley, PA

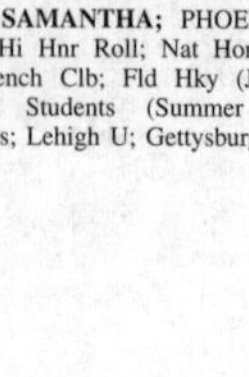
Wynegar, Renee E
Cumberland Valley HS
Mechanicsburg, PA

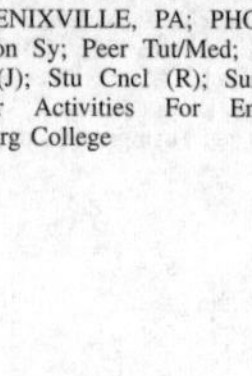
Yancik, Samantha
Phoenixville Area HS
Phoenixville, PA

YATZKANIC, AIMEE; BLAIRSVILLE, PA; BLAIRSVILLE HS; (SO); Hi Hnr Roll; Hnr Roll; Nat Hon Sy; Pres Ac Ftns Aw; WWAHSS; Comm Volntr; Red Cr Aide; FBLA; Key Club; Chrldg (V L); Sftball (V); Track (V); Vllyball (J); Secondary School Teacher; Physical Therapy; U of Pittsburgh; Duquesne U

YEAGER, KACIE; HARRISBURG, PA; CTRL DAUPHIN HS; (FR); Hnr Roll; Comm Volntr; Chrch Yth Grp; Key Club; Lib Aide; German Clb; Dnce; Psychology; BYU Utah; BYU Idaho

YEAGER JR, DANIEL M; SPRING GROVE, PA; YORK CTY SCH OF TECH; (JR); Hi Hnr Roll; St of Mnth; Computer Programming; Computer Sciences; Harrisburg U, PA; ITT Technical Institute, PA

YEZZI, ROBERT; GOULDSBORO, PA; NORTH POCONO HS; (FR); Ctznshp Aw; Hnr Roll; Comm Volntr; Ice Hky (V)

YODER, KAYLA M; LIBERTY, PA; LIBERTY JR SR HS; (SO); Hi Hnr Roll; Hnr Roll; Otst Ac Ach Awd; WWAHSS; Comm Volntr; Spec Olymp Vol; FBLA; Key Club; Spanish Clb; Flg Crps; Sccr (V L); Sftball (V L); Yrbk (E, R, P); Architecture; Arziona State U

YODER, PAUL R; BOSWELL, PA; NORTH STAR SD; (MS); Hnr Roll; Perf Att; Archery Champion-Benshoff Hill; ITT Technical Institute; U.S. Air Force

YOO, BENJAMIN; STATE COLLEGE, PA; STATE COLLEGE AREA HS; (SR); Hi Hnr Roll; Sci/Math Olympn; WWAHSS; Comm Volntr; Chess; FBLA; Key Club; Mth Clb/Tm; Mus Clb; Sci Clb; Tech Clb; French Clb; Orch; Bdmtn; Bskball; Ftball; Rqtball; Skiing; Sccr; Swmg; Tennis (V); 1st in State, 6th in Nation-Knowledge Masters 2002; 2nd in State-Technology Student Association 2003; Biomedical Engineering; Johns Hopkins U

YOON, JUNG; PLYMOUTH MTNG, PA; KENNEDY-KENDRICK CATHOLIC HS; (JR); Hnr Roll; Mth Clb/Tm; Off Aide; Svce Clb; Yrbk (E); Community Service Corps; Pre-Laws; Pennsylvania State U

YORK JR, JOSEPH O; BOILING SPRINGS, PA; BOILING SPRINGS HS; (SO); Hnr Roll; Spec Olymp Vol; Dbte Team; Drma Clb; Mod UN; Scouts; SADD; Acpl Chr; Chr; SP/M/VS; Ftball; Golf; Track; Cl Off (T); District & Regional & County Chorus; Model UN, SAAD Club, Drama Club; Music; Theatre

YORKO, TANYA; RURAL VALLEY, PA; LENAPE TECH; (JR); 4H Awd; Hnr Roll; Comm Volntr; Spec Olymp Vol; 4-H; ArtClub; Emplmnt; SADD; French Clb; Bnd; Pep Bnd; Vllyball (J); Hotel & Restaurant Management; IUP in PA, UNKY

YOST, KYRA L; BOYERTOWN, PA; BRANDYWINE HEIGHTS HS; (SO); Hnr Roll; Pres Ac Ftns Aw; WWAHSS; Comm Volntr; ArtClub; Emplmnt; FBLA; Key Club; Spanish Clb; Vllyball (V L); Yrbk (R, P); Biology; Sociology; Juniata College

YOUELLS, MEGAN L; DALLAS, PA; DALLAS SR HS; (SO); Hnr Roll; Kwnis Aw; Nat Hon Sy; WWAHSS; Comm Volntr; Hosp Aide; FBLA; Key Club; Scouts; SADD; Fld Hky (VJ); Sccr (V); Sch Ppr (P); FBLA-5th Place Regional Conference; Key Club-Head of Dinner Committee; Physical Therapy-Ithaca College; Ithaca College; U of the Sciences Philadelphia

YOUNG, ALYSSA; EASTON, PA; NAZARETH HS; (JR); Hi Hnr Roll; Hnr Roll; Perf Att; Comm Volntr; Spec Olymp Vol; ArtClub; Chrch Yth Grp; Drma Clb; Emplmnt; Key Club; Photog; Svce Clb; German Clb; Dnce; Fld Hky (J); Adv Cncl (R); Stu Cncl (R); Yrbk (P); The Morning Call Photo Contest 2nd Place; Graphic Design; Photography; Kutztown U; Cazenovia College

YOUNG, AMBER; BEAVER FALLS, PA; BLACKHAWK HS; (SO); Hi Hnr Roll; Hnr Roll; Nat Stu Ath Day Aw; Otst Ac Ach Awd; WWAHSS; Comm Volntr; Hab For Humty Volntr; Spec Olymp Vol; Drma Clb; Key Club; Spanish Clb; SP/M/VS; Stg Cre; Photographer; Architect; Art Institute of Pittsburgh

YOUNG, BETHANY; JERSEY SHORE, PA; JERSEY SHORE AREA SR HS; (SR); Ctznshp Aw; Hi Hnr Roll; MVP; Nat Hon Sy; Otst Ac Ach Awd; Pres Ac Ftns Aw; St of Mnth; Valdctrian; WWAHSS; Chrch Yth Grp; Emplmnt; FBLA; Key Club; Photog; Chr; SP/M/VS; Cr Ctry (V CL); Track (V CL); Stu Cncl (R); Yrbk (E, P); Nursing; Cedarville U

YOUNG, BRIAN T; PHILADELPHIA, PA; CENTRAL HS; (SR); Hnr Roll; Nat Mrt Semif; Pres Sch; Sci Fairs; Comm Volntr; Emplmnt; Photog; Tchrs Aide; Ch Chr; Bskball (V); Scr Kpr (V); Howard U

YOUNG, CYNTHIA; KUNKLETOWN, PA; PALMERTON AREA SD; (FR); Hi Hnr Roll; Hnr Roll; Pres Ac Ftns Aw; WWAHSS; ArtClub; Chrldg (J); Cl Off (T); Stu Cncl (T); UCA All-Star Cheerleader; Law; Fashion Design; U of North Carolina-Chapel Hill; Princeton U

YOUNG, JIMY; CRANBERRY TWP, PA; (JR); Hnr Roll; WWAHSS; Key Club; Who's Who Among High School Scholars; Computer Engineering; Computer Science

YOUNG, KIM; DREXEL HILL, PA; UPPER DARBY HS; (JR); Hi Hnr Roll; Hnr Roll; Nat Hon Sy; Otst Ac Ach Awd; Comm Volntr; Emplmnt; Acpl Chr; Bnd; Chr; Mch Bnd; Lcrsse (J); Algebra Award; Art Education; Art Major; Tyler School of Art; Temple U

YOUNG, KRISTINE R; SAYRE, PA; SAYRE AREA HS; (SR); Ctznshp Aw; Hi Hnr Roll; Hnr Roll; Jr Rot; MVP; Nat Hon Sy; Yth Ldrshp Prog; FBLA; Prom Com; Bnd; Chr; Sccr (V CL); Swmg (V CL); Track (V CL); PIAA Sportsmanship Award; 12 Letter Award; Communications; Penn State Altoona

YOUNG, KYLE; IVYLAND, PA; COUNCIL ROCK HS NORTH; (JR); Hi Hnr Roll; Hnr Roll; Perf Att; Mth Clb/Tm; Vsity Clb; German Clb; Ice Hky (V C); Rlr Hky (V); Vllyball (V); Architecture; Landscape Architecture; Syracuse U; Penn State U

YOUNG, LINDSAY; OAKMONT, PA; RIVERVIEW JR/SR HS; (JR); Hnr Roll; WWAHSS; Drma Clb; Emplmnt; Key Club; Lib Aide; Chr; Sftball (J); Sch Ppr (R); Journalism

YOUNG, SAIRIN K; WILLIAMSPORT, PA; WILLIAMSPORT AREA HS; (JR); Hi Hnr Roll; Hnr Roll; Key Club; Skiing; Culinary Arts

YOUNGDAHL, ALEX; BEAVER FALLS, PA; BLACKHAWK HS; (JR); Hi Hnr Roll; Nat Hon Sy; St of Mnth; WWAHSS; Drma Clb; Prom Com; Spanish Clb; SP/M/VS; Stg Cre; Track; Vllyball; Stu Cncl (R); Gifted Program Academic Games; Junior Historians Club; Film Studies; Pre-Med; Boston U; U of Pittsburgh

YU, SARAH M; CONNEAUTVILLE, PA; FRENCH CREEK VALLEY CHRN SCH; (SO); Ctznshp Aw; Hi Hnr Roll; Otst Ac Ach Awd; Sci Fairs; Comm Volntr; Peer Tut/Med; Chrch Yth Grp; P to P St Amb Prg; Sci Clb; Svce Clb; Orch; Sccr (V L); Cl Off (R); Stu Cncl (T); Sch Ppr (R); Yrbk (E); Outstanding Academic Achievement Award; Leo Club Charter Member; PhD in Immunology; U of California-Berkeley; Johns Hopkins U

YUAN YUAN, SUMMER; MONROEVILLE, PA; THE ELLIS SCH; (SO); F Lan Hn Soc; Hnr Roll; Otst Ac Ach Awd; Perf Att; Comm Volntr; Peer Tut/Med; Chrch Yth Grp; Cmptr Clb; Dbte Team; Drma Clb; Mth Clb/Tm; Svce Clb; French Clb; Dnce; Orch; Stg Cre; Tennis (J); CR (R); Sch Ppr (E); Co-President of School Spirit Club (Tiger Spirit); Law School; Medical School; Columbia U

YURICH, NICOLE; BEAVER FALLS, PA; BIG BEAVER FALLS HS; (SO); Hi Hnr Roll; Hnr Roll; Nat Hon Sy; Otst Ac Ach Awd; Comm Volntr; ArtClub; Drma Clb; FBLA; Key Club; Vsity Clb; Spanish Clb; Bnd; Mch Bnd; Orch; Sftball (J); Tennis (V); Vsy Clb (L); 1st Place in County Wide Art Contest; Parliamentarian For FBLA '05-'06 School Yr; Architecture; Business Administration; Kent State; Columbia U

YUROCHKO, JENNIFER A; HOMESTEAD, PA; PITTSBURGH SD; (SO); Ctznshp Aw; Hnr Roll; Nat Hon Sy; Sci Fairs; Hab For Humty Volntr; Chrch Yth Grp; Key Club; Scouts; Drl Tm; SP/M/VS; Sccr (J); Girl Scout Silver Award; Business; Fashion; IUP (Indiana U of PA); Slippery Rock U

ZABICKI, GREGORY W; PHOENIXVILLE, PA; PHOENIXVILLE AREA HS; (JR); Hi Hnr Roll; Emplmnt; Key Club; Scouts; Bnd; Jzz Bnd; Mch Bnd; Orch; The Young Authors of Onslow County & Camp Lejeune 1995-96; Engineering-Drexel; U of North Texas Drexel; Penn State U

ZABOROWSKI, TIM; ALLENTOWN, PA; SALISBURY HS; (JR); Hnr Roll; WWAHSS; Peer Tut/Med; Emplmnt; Key Club; Tennis (V CL); Key Club; Business; East Stroudsburg U; Penn State U

ZACHERL, HARRISON J; TITUSVILLE, PA; VENANGO CATHOLIC HS; (JR); Hi Hnr Roll; Hnr Roll; Nat Hon Sy; Otst Ac Ach Awd; Perf Att; Sci/Math Olympn; Comm Volntr; Hosp Aide; Chess; Lib Aide; Mth Clb/Tm; Scouts; German Clb; Chr; SP/M/VS; Bskball (V L); Cr Ctry (V CL); Wt Lftg; Cl Off (P); Stu Cncl (R); CR (R); Overall Excellence in French I & II; Super Scientist Award; Accounting; U of Notre Dame; Gannon U

ZAMAN, MOHAMMAD; BENSALEM, PA; BENSALEM TOWNSHIP SD; (FR); Hnr Roll; Schol Bwl; Pre-Med; Pharmacy; U of Pennsylvania; Temple U

ZAMBRANA, MANUEL; PHILADELPHIA, PA; EDISON-FAREIRA HS; (SO); Perf Att; St of Mnth; WWAHSS; Wrstlg (V L); Automotive-Technician; Baseball Player (Professional); Penn State; Drexel

ZAMBRANO, DANIELLE; PHILADELPHIA, PA; GIRARD AC MUSIC PROGRAM; (FR); Ctznshp Aw; Hi Hnr Roll; Hnr Roll; Otst Ac Ach Awd; Perf Att; Peer Tut/Med; Chrch Yth Grp; Mus Clb; Italian Clb; Acpl Chr; Clr Grd; Drl Tm; Stu Cncl (R); CR (R); Yrbk (E); Highest G.P.A. of Any C.C.D. Student; Pre-Med Studies; Pediatric Care; Harvard U; U of Pennsylvania

ZANAN, RACHEL B; HUNTINGDON VALLEY, PA; ABINGTON SR HS; (SO); Hnr Roll; Perf Att; Peer Tut/Med; Key Club; Tmpl Yth Grp; Spanish Clb; Journalism; Advertising; Penn State U; Temple U

ZANOTTI, ALEXANDRA N; LEECHBURG, PA; APOLLO-RIDGE SD; (SO); Hi Hnr Roll; Hnr Roll; Nat Hon Sy; DARE; Chr; Yrbk (P); High Honor Roll; Neonatal Nursing; Elementary School Teacher; Seton Hill U; Penn State College

ZARRIZSKI, JOHNATHON D; BETHLEHEM, PA; BETHLEHEM AREA VOC TECH SCH; (FR); Automotive Mechanics

ZATEZALO, LIZA; SALTSBURG, PA; KISKI AREA HS; (JR); Hi Hnr Roll; Nat Hon Sy; Comm Volntr; Peer Tut/Med; Key Club; Pep Squd; SADD; Stg Cre; Bskball (J); Sccr (J); YMCA Nerf Soccer Coach-5 years; Little League Baseball Coach-2 years; Medical Field; Engineering; Duquesne U; Seton Hill College

ZAVALA, MAGALY; OXFORD, PA;; Comm Volntr; Secretary; Business Management; Delaware Tech

ZAYZAY JR, MATTHEW; PHILADELPHIA, PA; GEORGE PEPPER MS; MS; Fut Prb Slvr; Hi Hnr Roll; Hnr Roll; Nat Hon Sy; Nat Sci Aw; Perf Att; Sci Fairs; St of Mnth; St Optmst of Yr; WWAHSS; ArtClub; Dbte Team; Fr of Library; Quiz Bowl; ROTC; Schol Bwl; Scouts; Wdwrkg Clb; Bnd; Dnce; Flg Crps; Stg Cre; Bskball; Dvng; Ftball; Mar Art; Scr Kpr; Sccr; Swmg; Vllyball; PhD in Science; Doctor; Penn State U; Harvard U

ZEAK, SARAH; ALTOONA, PA; BISHOP GUILFOYLE HS; (SO); Hi Hnr Roll; Comm Volntr; Chrch Yth Grp; Dnce; Chrldg (V)

ZEBLEY, AMY; UNIONTOWN, PA; LAUREL HIGHLANDS SD; (FR); Hi Hnr Roll; WWAHSS; Comm Volntr; Peer Tut/Med; Chrch Yth Grp; SADD; Spanish Clb; Vllyball (J); Cl Off (V); Stu Cncl (R); Interact Club; Qualifying for States in Bowling; Math Teacher; Medical Field; West Virginia U; Bucknell U

ZEBLEY, JUSTIN; MARCUS HOOK, PA; CHICHESTER SR HS; (FR); Hi Hnr Roll; Hnr Roll; Otst Ac Ach Awd; Pres Ac Ftns Aw; Sci Fairs; Sci/Math Olympn; St of Mnth; Mod UN; P to P St Amb Prg; Sci Clb; Chr; Stg Cre; Skiing; Cl Off (V); Stu Cncl (R); CR (V); Most Conscientious Award; Chichester Business Association Scholarship; Medicine; Government Intelligence; Harvard Medical School; Duke Medical School

ZECHMAN, BRADLEY C; MIDDLEBURG, PA; MIDD-WEST SD; (JR); Hi Hnr Roll; Hnr Roll; Nat Hon Sy; Perf Att; St of Mnth; Chess; Chrch Yth Grp; Emplmnt; Bnd; Chr; Jzz Bnd; Mch Bnd; Bsball (J); District Band; Regional Band; Mathematics; Physics; Elizabethtown College; Penn State U

ZEHNER, TIFFANY E; LARKSVILLE, PA; WYOMING VALLEY WEST; (JR); Ctznshp Aw; F Lan Hn Soc; Hi Hnr Roll; Nat Hon Sy; Otst Ac Ach Awd; Pres Sch; Sci Fairs; Sci/Math Olympn; WWAHSS; Yth Ldrshp Prog; Comm Volntr; Hosp Aide; Peer Tut/Med; Chrch Yth Grp; FBLA; Key Club; Mus Clb; NYLC; Pep Squd; Bnd; Chr; Drm Mjr; Jzz Bnd; Youth Salute Member; Pre-Medicine; Pediatrician; Bucknell; Franklin and Marshall

ZEHNGUT, NADIA; EASTON, PA; EASTON AREA HS; (JR); Hnr Roll; St of Mnth; Key Club; Business

ZEIGLER, DAVIS; CARLISLE, PA; BOILING SPRINGS HS; (FR); Hnr Roll; WWAHSS; Chrch Yth Grp; Chr; Golf (V); Business Management; Grove City; Messiah

ZEKLER, RACHELLE; TOWANDA, PA; TOWANDA JR/SR HS; (SO); Ctznshp Aw; DAR; Hi Hnr Roll; Hnr Roll; Nat Hon Sy; Salutrn; WWAHSS; Yth Ldrshp Prog; Comm Volntr; Chrch Yth Grp; HO'Br Yth Ldrshp; P to P St Amb Prg; Spanish Clb; Chr; Ch Chr; SP/M/VS; Bskball (J); Track (L); Marine Biologist; Biology Teacher; Florida Institute of Technology; Houghton College

ZENERT, DAVID; IRWIN, PA; NORWIN HS; (SR); Hnr Roll; Nat Hon Sy; Pres Sch; WWAHSS; Hab For Humty Volntr; ArtClub; Chrch Yth Grp; Scouts; Skiing; Lit Mag (E); Graphic Designer; Animator; Indiana U of Pennsylvania; California U of Pennsylvania

ZEOLI, LUCAS A; GREENSBURG, PA; GREENSBURG SALEM; (SO); Hi Hnr Roll; Hnr Roll; Comm Volntr; Emplmnt; Chr; Ftball (J); Wt Lftg (V)

ZHANG, YI R; DEVON, PA; CONESTOGA HS; (SO); Ctznshp Aw; Hnr Roll; Otst Ac Ach Awd; St of Mnth; Amnsty Intl; Comm Volntr; ArtClub; Chess; Drma Clb; Key Club; Mth Clb/Tm; Mod UN; SP/M/VS; Lit Mag (R); Service and Leadership Award; Certified Oral Presenter At Conestoga HS; Business; Pediatrics; U of Pennsylvania; New York U

ZHDANOV, IGOR; BOALSBURG, PA; STATE COLLEGE AREA HS; (JR); Hi Hnr Roll; WWAHSS; Ch Chr; International Boxing; Marketing; Business; Penn State U

ZHENG, HAO; MECHANICSBURG, PA; CUMBERLAND VALLEY HS; (SR); Ctznshp Aw; Hnr Roll; Nat Hon Sy; Perf Att; WWAHSS; Comm Volntr; Chess; Dbte Team; Key Club; Lib Aide; Mth Clb/Tm; Mod UN; Spch Team; Tchrs Aide; Track (V); Leaders of Tomorrow of 2004 Award; Merit Award for High School Math Modeling Contest; Biological Engineering; Northwestern U

Zatezalo, Liza
Kiski Area HS
Saltsburg, PA

Zambrano, Danielle
Girard AC Music Program
Philadelphia, PA

Zacherl, Harrison J
Venango Catholic HS
Titusville, PA

Zanotti, Alexandra N
Apollo-Ridge SD
Leechburg, PA

Zebley, Justin
Chichester SR HS
Marcus Hook, PA

Zabicki, Gregory W
Phoenixville Area HS
Phoenixville, PA

Young, Sairin K
Williamsport Area HS
Williamsport, PA

Young, Brian T
Central HS
Philadelphia, PA

Yoder, Paul R
North Star SD
Boswell, PA

Yoder, Kayla M
Liberty JR SR HS
Liberty, PA

National
Honor Roll
Spring 2005

Yatzkanic, Aimee
Blairsville HS
Blairsville, PA

Young, Alyssa
Nazareth HS
Easton, PA

Young, Kristine R
Sayre Area HS
Sayre, PA

Yu, Sarah M
French Creek Valley Chrn Sch
Conneautville, PA

Yuan Yuan, Summer
The Ellis Sch
Monroeville, PA

ZIGERELLI, JESSICA A; SCENERY HILL, PA; BENTWORTH; (JR); Hi Hnr Roll; Hnr Roll; Nat Ldrshp Svc; Pres Ac Ftns Aw; Pres Sch; WWAHSS; Comm Volntr; Hab For Humty Volntr; Spec Olymp Vol; Drma Clb; Emplmnt; FBLA; Prom Com; Svce Clb; Vsity Clb; Chr; SP/M/VS; Chrldg (V L); Vsy Clb (V)

ZIGO, ANTHONY; MERCER, PA; MERCER AREA HS; (SR); Hi Hnr Roll; Hnr Roll; Pres Ac Ftns Aw; Comm Volntr; Quill & Scroll; Chr; Bskball (V L); Sccr (V CL); Lit Mag (E); Sch Ppr; 4 Letter - Basketball; 3 Letter - Soccer; Thiel College

ZIMMER, AUDRA; WEXFORD, PA; PINE-RICHLAND HS; (SO); Pres Sch; WWAHSS; Comm Volntr; Drma Clb; Key Club; Scouts; SADD; Chr; Fld Hky (V C); Gmnstcs (V L); Key Communicator for My School; Highest Honor Award; Pre-Medicine

ZIMMERMAN, BLAINE; HARRISBURG, PA; STEELTON-HIGHSPIRE HS; (FR); Hi Hnr Roll; Hnr Roll; St of Mnth; Peer Tut/Med; Chrch Yth Grp; Chrldg (J); Stu Cncl (R); Attorney; Computer Technology; West Chester; Dickinson Law School

ZIMMERMAN, JOSHUA; DRIFTING, PA; WEST BRANCH HS; (SR); Nat Ldrshp Svc; St of Mnth; USAA; WWAHSS; Yth Ldrshp Prog; Comm Volntr; Peer Tut/Med; Emplmnt; NYLC; Scouts; SADD; Tchrs Aide; Ftball (J); Stu Cncl; Eagle Scout-BSA; Lead America Leadership Conference; Education-Secondary; Lock Haven U-PA

ZINBERG, LAURIE; JENKINTOWN, PA; ABINGTON SR HS; (JR); Hi Hnr Roll; Hnr Roll; Nat Hon Sy; Nat Ldrshp Svc; Comm Volntr; Key Club; Svce Clb; Orch; SP/M/VS; Stu Cncl (R); Yrbk (E); The Congressional Award Program: Bronze and Silver Medals; Astronomer; Neuroscientist; Boston U; Lehigh U

ZISA, STEPHANIE; JAMISON, PA; CTRL BUCKS HS EAST; (SO); Hi Hnr Roll; Otst Ac Ach Awd; Pres Ac Ftns Aw; WWAHSS; Comm Volntr; Hab For Humty Volntr; Chrch Yth Grp; DARE; Drma Clb; Emplmnt; Key Club; Tchrs Aide; Chr; Dnce; SP/M/VS; Stg Cre; PP Ftbl; National Junior Honor Society; Women's Ensemble; Education/History; Music; Harvard U; Oxford U

ZOEGAR JR, YANCY B; PHILADELPHIA, PA; BARTRAM HS; (SR); Hi Hnr Roll; Hnr Roll; St of Mnth; St Optmst of Yr; Comm Volntr; Red Cr Aide; ArtClub; Dbte Team; Drma Clb; Emplmnt; Chr; SP/M/VS; Sccr (V); Track (V); Vsy Clb (V); Vllyball (V); CR (R); Drama; Debate; Master's Degree Management; Temple U; Community College

ZOLTAK, MATTHEW; PHILADELPHIA, PA; PLYMOUTH WHITEMARSH HS; (JR); Hi Hnr Roll; Hnr Roll; Photog; Vsity Clb; Wdwrkg Clb; Bsball (V); AAU Championship - Baseball Tournaments; Sports Medicine; Professional Baseball; U of North Carolina Chapel Hill; Notre Dame U

ZURFLIEH, BEN; CAMP HILL, PA; CAMP HILL SD; (JR); Hnr Roll; Comm Volntr; Cr Ctry (V); Wrstlg (V L); CR (R)

ZYGMUNT, JOHN; PHOENIXVILLE, PA; PHOENIXVILLE AREA HS; (SO); Hi Hnr Roll; USAA; WWAHSS; Key Club

Rhode Island

ABATE, KATLYN S; NORTH SMITHFIELD, RI; BEACON CHARTER SCH; (JR); Hnr Roll; Nat Hon Sy; Sci/Math Olympn; St of Mnth; Comm Volntr; Drma Clb; Emplmnt; Sci Clb; Bnd; Dnce; Jzz Bnd; SP/M/VS; Yrbk (P)

ALAM, SAAD; CUMBERLAND, RI; CUMBERLAND HS; (SO); Hnr Roll; Sci/Math Olympn; WWAHSS; Comm Volntr; Hosp Aide; Dbte Team; Mth Clb/Tm; Quill & Scroll; Quiz Bowl; Lcrsse (V); Track (J); Sch Ppr (R)

ALLIENELLO, KAITLIN M; RUMFORD, RI; EAST PROVIDENCE HS; (JR); Hnr Roll; Peer Tut/Med; Spec Olymp Vol; Emplmnt; Scouts; Yrbk (E, R); Special Education; Education; Rhode Island College; U of Conn

AMAYA, ROSA; PROVIDENCE, RI; CLASSICAL HS; (SO); Hnr Roll; Comm Volntr; Peer Tut/Med; Photog; ROTC; Sftball (J); Track (J); Weightlifting Champ 6th Place; Knitting Club to Help the Homeless; Pharmaceuticals; Spanish Language; Johnson and Wales U; Rhode Island College

ANDRADE, EMILY; BRISTOL, RI; MT HOPE HS; (SR); WWAHSS; Yth Ldrshp Prog; Comm Volntr; DECA; DECA; NAFA; Fashion Designer; CCRI General Courses; Lasell College

ANGELL, ROBERT; WOONSOCKET, RI; BEACON CHARTER SCH; (FR); Hi Hnr Roll; Hnr Roll; Comm Volntr; DARE; ROTC; Scouts; SADD; Wdwrkg Clb; Drl Tm; Blackston Valley Young Marine; United States Marine Corps; West Point-Military Academy

AUBOURG, JEAN; PROVIDENCE, RI; MT PLEASANT HS; (SO); Hnr Roll; Perf Att; Hosp Aide; Medical Doctor; Degree in Business; Brown U

BAGLEY, CAITLYN J; JOHNSTON, RI; MT ST CHARLES AC; (SR); Hnr Roll; MVP; Perf Att; WWAHSS; Comm Volntr; Peer Tut/Med; Drma Clb; Emplmnt; Svce Clb; SP/M/VS; Bskball (J); Ice Hky (V); Sccr (J); Track (V); Christian Action Program; Special Education Teacher; Elementary Education Teacher; Assumption College

BAIRD, KATIE; SAUNDERSTOWN, RI; NORTH KINGSTOWN HS; (JR); F Lan Hn Soc; Hi Hnr Roll; Sci Fairs; Hosp Aide; ArtClub; Emplmnt; Photog; Sci Clb; History Club; (North-School Affiliated) Competitive Horseback Riding; Geology/Earth Sciences; Environmental Sciences; New York U; U of Hawaii

BELISLE, AMANDA M; HARRISVILLE, RI; BURRILLVILLE HS; (JR); Hi Hnr Roll; Hnr Roll; Comm Volntr; Peer Tut/Med; Works Part Time in Human Services; CPR & First Aid Certification; Social Work with Medical Background; U of Miami

BELTRE, JULIA; PROVIDENCE, RI; P.A.I.S. (PROVIDENCE AC OF INTERNATIONAL STUDIES); (SO); Hnr Roll; Peer Tut/Med; English Clb; Vllyball; Business Administration; Johnson and Wales; Bryan U

BELTRE, MARIA L; PROVIDENCE, RI; MT PLEASANT HS; (FR); Hnr Roll; Track; Participation Certificates; Chemical Engineer / Police Woman; Doctor / Administrator; Brown U

BERBERICK, JEFFREY D; PORTSMOUTH, RI; PORTSMOUTH ABBEY SCH; (SR); Hi Hnr Roll; WWAHSS; Yth Ldrshp Prog; Comm Volntr; Chrch Yth Grp; Dbte Team; NYLC; Scouts; Svce Clb; Russian Clb; Orch; Bsball (V); Ftball (V); Rqtball (J); Lit Mag (R); Eagle Scout; Co-Founder of the Russian Club; International Economics; Foreign Language; George Washington U; Lehigh U

BERLINSKY-SCHINE, LAURA; PROVIDENCE, RI; LINCOLN SCH; (JR); Hi Hnr Roll; Otst Ac Ach Awd; Amnsty Intl; Comm Volntr; Peer Tut/Med; Emplmnt; Lib Aide; Tchrs Aide; Lit Mag (R); Sch Ppr (R); Published in POHUCK Magazine; Published in Teen Ink; Journalism; Creative Writing; Johns Hopkins U; New York U

BISSONNETTE, JENNA M; FORESTDALE, RI; N SMITHFIELD JR/SR HS; (SR); Hnr Roll; Nat Hon Sy; WWAHSS; Emplmnt; Mus Clb; Outdrs Clb; Pep Squd; Prom Com; Chr; Dnce; Chrldg (V CL); Public Relations; Event Planning; U of New Hampshire; Quinnipiac U

BISSONNETTE, PATRICK; NORTH SMITHFIELD, RI; NORTH SMITHFIELD JR/SR HS; (SR); Hnr Roll; DECA; Networking; Johnson & Wales

BLACKMAR, JIMMY; RIVERSIDE, RI; EAST PROVIDENCE HS; (JR); Hnr Roll

BOGHOSSIAN, KIMBERLY; CRANSTON, RI; CRANSTON HS WEST; (JR); Ctznshp Aw; F Lan Hn Soc; Hnr Roll; Otst Ac Ach Awd; Perf Att; Comm Volntr; Chrch Yth Grp; DARE; Lib Aide; Mth Clb/Tm; Scouts; Tchrs Aide; Bnd; Mch Bnd; Pep Bnd; Tennis (V L); Spanish Language Honor Society; CUS Charity Classic Volunteer (Golf) 2 Years; Math Teacher; Research; U of Rhode Island; Rhode Island College

BROWN, KATHLEEN; WOONSOCKET, RI; BEACON CHARTER SCH; (SO); Hi Hnr Roll; Hnr Roll; WWAHSS

BURGESS, WILLIAM H; PORTSMOUTH, RI; PORTSMOUTH HS; (SO); Hnr Roll; Pres Ac Ftns Aw; Chrch Yth Grp; FCA; Bskball; Golf; Scr Kpr; Skiing; Run Own Lawn Service; Business

BURKE, MAEGAN; PROVIDENCE, RI; CLASSICAL HS; (SO); Hnr Roll; Nat Hon Sy; Comm Volntr; Emplmnt; Dnce; SP/M/VS; Tennis (J); Track (J); CR (R); Brotherhood; Helping Hand; Pre-Law; Architectural Engineering; Boston U; Northeastern U

CAMILO, ELIZABETH; PROVIDENCE, RI; (SR); Comm Volntr; Chrch Yth Grp; Drma Clb; Mus Clb; Spanish Clb; Chr; Dnce

CAREY, MARY K; SMITHFIELD, RI; SMITHFIELD HS; (JR); Hi Hnr Roll; MVP; Nat Hon Sy; Otst Ac Ach Awd; Yth Ldrshp Prog; Comm Volntr; Chr; Chrldg (V); Track (V); Stu Cncl (P, S); All-Class / All-Division - Track; National French Honor Society; International Business; French; Georgetown U; Bryant U

CARLINO, STEVEN; LINCOLN, RI; (FR); Hosp Aide; Cr Ctry; Tennis

CASTO, BRIAN J; EAST PROVIDENCE, RI; EAST PROVIDENCE HS; (SO); Hnr Roll; Sci Fairs; St of Mnth; Comm Volntr; Emplmnt; Track (J); Yrbk (E); Dirt Biking and 2 Years of Martial Arts; Computer Engineering-Repair or Design; U of Rhode Island; ITT Technical Institute

CHATEL, JAMIE; WARWICK, RI; LA SALLE AC; (JR); F Lan Hn Soc; Hi Hnr Roll; Hnr Roll; Nat Hon Sy; Otst Ac Ach Awd; St of Mnth; Hosp Aide; Peer Tut/Med; Spec Olymp Vol; ArtClub; Drma Clb; Mus Clb; P to P St Amb Prg; Acpl Chr; Chr; Dnce; SP/M/VS; CR (R); Arts Alive; History Day (Nationals); Communications; Journalism; Cornell; Emerson

CHRISTENSEN, JIMMY; ASHAWAY, RI; WESTERLY HS; (SR); WWAHSS; Eagle Scout; Architecture; Philadelphia U-Pennsylvania; Wentworth Institute of Technology-Boston

CIMORELLI, JOANNA; PROVIDENCE, RI; MT PLEASANT HS; Hnr Roll; St of Mnth; Nursing; Veterinarian; Rice

COSTA, ALEXANDRA N; RIVERSIDE, RI; OUR LADY OF FATIMA HS; (JR); Hi Hnr Roll; Hnr Roll; Nat Hon Sy; Nat Ldrshp Svc; St of Mnth; Peer Tut/Med; Drma Clb; SP/M/VS; Vllyball (V CL); Cl Off (V); Stu Cncl (S); Yrbk (E); Psychology; Pharmacy; Brown U; Boston U

COTE, DESIREE E; WOONSOCKET, RI; BEACON CHARTER SCH; (SO); Hi Hnr Roll; Hnr Roll; Perf Att; WWAHSS; Drma Clb; Mus Clb; Prom Com; SADD; Latin Clb; Bnd; Chr; Dnce; SP/M/VS; Stu Cncl (V); Lit Mag (E); Solo & Ensemble Awards for Band; Chef; Musician; Johnson & Wales U; Berklee School of Music

CURRAN, DANIEL P; GREENVILLE, RI; LASALLE AC; (JR); F Lan Hn Soc; Hi Hnr Roll; Hnr Roll; Nat Hon Sy; Otst Ac Ach Awd; Pres Sch; Sci Fairs; St of Mnth; WWAHSS; Yth Ldrshp Prog; Comm Volntr; Hab For Humty Volntr; Peer Tut/Med; Dbte Team; Drma Clb; Emplmnt; HO'Br Yth Ldrshp; Mth Clb/Tm; Mod UN; Prom Com; Scouts; SP/M/VS; Cl Off (V); Stu Cncl (V); Vice President of the RI State Student Council; Top 10% of Class; Law School / Lawyer; Would Like to Run for US Senate; Georgetown U; Boston College

DEIFIN, JAMIE; PROVIDENCE, RI; MT PLEASANT HS; (SR); Hnr Roll; Comm Volntr; Peer Tut/Med; DARE; Asian Clb; Dnce; Sftball (V); Vllyball (V); Pediatrician; Brown U; Rhode Island College

DELGADO, N'DEYE-KATIE G; PROVIDENCE, RI; CLASSICAL HS; (SO); Hnr Roll; St Schl; Comm Volntr; Peer Tut/Med; Ch Chr; Forensic Science; Psychiatry; New York U; Boston U

DIAS, BRITNEY M; EAST PROVIDENCE, RI; EAST PROVIDENCE HS; (FR); Hnr Roll; Otst Ac Ach Awd; St of Mnth; Comm Volntr; Chrch Yth Grp; DARE; Drma Clb; Mus Clb; Chr; SP/M/VS; (DICE) Drug Intervention Community Educators; Portuguese Academic Award; Foreign Language: Portuguese Teacher; Musical Theatre; Rhode Island College; U of Rhode Island

DOLAN, DEREK; HOPE VALLEY, RI; CHARIHO REG HS; (SR); Hnr Roll; Comm Volntr; FBLA; Vsity Clb; Bsball (V); FBLA - 2nd Place State Business Law Competition; Finance; MBA; Suffolk U; U of Rhode Island

DOMENICI, KAYLYN M; LINCOLN, RI; LINCOLN HS; (FR); Hnr Roll; MVP; Comm Volntr; Bnd; Mch Bnd; Pep Bnd; Sccr (V L); Varsity Soccer-"Rookie of the Year"-Freshman; EMS; Sports Medicine; RIC-Rhode Island College; U of Rhode Island

DUPONT, JENNA L; PAWTUCKET, RI; BISHOP FEEHAN HS; (SO); F Lan Hn Soc; Hi Hnr Roll; Comm Volntr; Scouts; SADD; Stg Cre; Education

DYER, MICHAEL C; RIVERSIDE, RI; EAST PROVIDENCE HS; (JR); Ctznshp Aw; Hnr Roll; DARE; Emplmnt; Computer Science; New England Technical Institute; Katherine Gibbs

EBELLING, ALESIA; PASCOAG, RI; BEACON CHARTER SCH; (JR); Hnr Roll; Nat Hon Sy; Chess; Fr of Library; Prom Com; Bnd; Chr; SP/M/VS; Hsbk Rdg (VJC)

EKSTROM, BRITTANY R; TIVERTON, RI; TIVERTON HS; (SR); F Lan Hn Soc; Hi Hnr Roll; Hnr Roll; Nat Hon Sy; Pres Ac Ftns Aw; USAA; WWAHSS; Comm Volntr; Emplmnt; Jr Ach; Lib Aide; Prom Com; Foreign Clb; Bnd; Mch Bnd; Bskball (V L); Sccr (V L); Tennis (V CL); Stu Cncl (R); CR (R); American History; Communications/Advertising; The George Washington U; Cornell U

ESPINAL, MERCY; PROVIDENCE, RI; MT PLEASANT HS; Hnr Roll; Perf Att; Comm Volntr; Chrch Yth Grp

EVORA, JESSICA L; PAWTUCKET, RI; CHARLES E SHEA SR HS; (JR); Hnr Roll; Comm Volntr; FBLA; Key Club; Mth Clb/Tm; SP/M/VS; Bskball; Tennis (J); Cl Off (V); Stu Cncl (R); CR (R); Yrbk; Volunteer at Boys & Girls Club and Woodlawn Community Center / Working Against Violence Group; FBLA / Mock Trial / Peer Helping Network / URI Guaranteed Admissions Program - 3 Summers; Public Communications; Business; Syracuse U; Pennsylvania State U

FARIA, AUGUSTO; BRISTOL, RI; MT. HOPE HS; (SO); Hnr Roll; Perf Att; Pres Sch; St Schl; WWAHSS; Bsball (VJ L); Ftball (VJ L)

FERRARO, DOMINIQUE M; WESTERLY, RI; WESTERLY HS; (SO); Hi Hnr Roll; Hnr Roll; Comm Volntr; Emplmnt; SADD; Cr Ctry (J); PP Ftbl; Track (J); Cl Off (R); Stu Cncl (R); CR (R); Forensic Sciences / Psychology; Biology Education; Boston U; U Mass Amherst

FINNEGAN, ERIK; CHARLESTOWN, RI; THE PROUT SCH; (SR); F Lan Hn Soc; Hi Hnr Roll; Hnr Roll; Nat Hon Sy; Nat Ldrshp Svc; Otst Ac Ach Awd; WWAHSS; Yth Ldrshp Prog; Comm Volntr; Peer Tut/Med; Emplmnt; Mod UN; Scouts; Spch Team; SP/M/VS; Stg Cre; Model United Nations Performance Awards; Lead Sound Technician-Theater; Mock Trial Performance Awards; Computer Science; Philosophy; Rensselaer Polytechnic Institute; U of Rochester

FONTES, JASON B; PAWTUCKET, RI; WILLIAM & TOLMAN HS; (FR); Hnr Roll; Engineering; Computers.; Rhode Island College; U of Rhode Island

FRECHETTE, RANDE E; WARWICK, RI; WARWICK VETERANS MEMORIAL HS; (JR); Hnr Roll; Perf Att; Emplmnt; Scouts; Swmg (V); Culinary Arts-Pastry Baking; Johnson & Wales U; U of Rhode Island

FRIAS, PAOLA P; PROVIDENCE, RI; CLASSICAL HS; (SO); Hi Hnr Roll; Hnr Roll; Otst Ac Ach Awd; Perf Att; Pres Sch; St of Mnth; WWAHSS; Peer Tut/Med; Cmptr Clb; Dbte Team; Photog; Tennis (J); Cl Off (T); Lit Mag (P); Yrbk (P); Business; Teaching / Education; New York U; Brown U

FRITZ, LISA M; WARWICK, RI; TOLL GATE HS; (JR); Hnr Roll; Perf Att; Pharmacy; Teacher; U of Rhode Island; Rhode Island College

GACIN, ERLANDE J; PROVIDENCE, RI; CLASSICAL HS; (SO); Hi Hnr Roll; Hnr Roll; Perf Att; Yth Ldrshp Prog; Comm Volntr; Chrch Yth Grp; Drma Clb; Sci Clb; Chr; Ch Chr; Stg Cre; Wt Lftg (V); Wrstlg (V); Pediatric Care / Nurse; U of Rhode Island; U of Mass Boston

Curran, Daniel P
Lasalle AC
Greenville, RI

Chatel, Jamie
La Salle AC
Warwick, RI

Belisle, Amanda M
Burrillville HS
Harrisville, RI

Carlino, Steven
Lincoln, RI

Domenici, Kaylyn M
Lincoln HS
Lincoln, RI

GARCIA, MIGUEL A; PROVIDENCE, RI; CLASSICAL HS; (FR); Hnr Roll; Ftball (J); Track (J); Computer Engineering; Law; Brown U

GERBER, CHARLENE; WOONSOCKET, RI; BEACON CHARTER SCH; (SO); Hnr Roll; Peer Tut/Med; Chr; SP/M/VS; Stg Cre; Stu Cncl (R); Helped in the Office - Organizing Attendance; Model for the Famous; Nursing; Brown U; Case U

GITTINGS, DANIEL; PORTSMOUTH, RI; PORTSMOUTH HS; (JR); Hi Hnr Roll; Hnr Roll; Otst Ac Ach Awd; Pres Ac Ftns Aw; Sci Fairs; Comm Volntr; Peer Tut/Med; Sci Clb; Scouts; Bnd; Mch Bnd; Cr Ctry (V CL); Tennis (V); Track (V C); Adv Cncl (V); Cl Off (V); Stu Cncl (R); CR (R); Science and Engineering Apprenticeship; Eagle Scout; Medical Doctor; Brown U; Dartmouth College

GLASHOW, ALEXANDRA; BARRINGTON, RI; BARRINGTON HS; (JR); Hosp Aide; Spec Olymp Vol; Emplmnt; SADD; Lcrsse (J); Swmg (V L); Hospital Volunteer / Ski Instructor; Lifeguard / Camp Counselor / SADD Girl Swimmer of the Year; Pediatric Physical Therapy; Endicott College; Lyndon State College

GOMES, DIANE M; RUMFORD, RI; EAST PROVIDENCE HS; (JR); Hnr Roll; Nat Hon Sy; DECA; Stu Cncl (R); Accounting; Business Major; Bryant College; Rhode Island College

GREEN, ROCKY; MAPLEVILLE, RI; BURRILLVILLE HS; (JR); Hnr Roll; Emplmnt; Automobile Repair & Replace; Power & Energy; Universal Technical Institute; New England Tech

HONGKHAM, NITHTAYA M; JOHNSTON, RI; JOHNSTON HS; (SO); Hi Hnr Roll; Hnr Roll; Perf Att; St of Mnth; WWAHSS; SADD; Bskball (JC); Vllyball (V L)

HOYLE, SARAH J; WOONSOCKET, RI; BEACON CHARTER SCH; (FR); Hi Hnr Roll; WWAHSS; Comm Volntr; Chrch Yth Grp

HUDSON, BARBARA; SMITHFIELD, RI; SMITHFIELD HS; (SO); Hi Hnr Roll; Hnr Roll; Otst Ac Ach Awd; Marine Biology; Psychology; Providence College; U of California, Los Angeles

HUYNH, JENNIFER Y; WOONSOCKET, RI; WOONSOCKET HS; (JR); Hi Hnr Roll; Jr Mshl; Nat Hon Sy; Otst Ac Ach Awd; Comm Volntr; Emplmnt; FBLA; HO'Br Yth Ldrshp; SADD; Cl Off (S, T); Sch Ppr (R); Yrbk (E); FBLA Chapter President, Vice Pres; FBLA State Reporter; Master's in International Business; PhD in Biochemistry; Quinnipiac U; Babson U

JOHNSON, DANIELLE H; MIDDLETOWN, RI; THE PROUT SCH; (SR); All Am Sch; Hnr Roll; Nat Hon Sy; Sci Fairs; St of Mnth; USAA; WWAHSS; Yth Ldrshp Prog; Comm Volntr; SADD; Yrbk (R, P); La Sallian Youth; Student Ambassador; Psychology; Law

JOYAL, DOROTHY M; JOHNSTON, RI; JOHNSTON SR HS; (SO); Hnr Roll; Otst Ac Ach Awd; Perf Att; Sci Fairs; St Schl; St of Mnth; WWAHSS; Comm Volntr; Prom Com; SADD; Chr; Dnce; Vllyball (J); Cl Off (R); Stu Cncl (R); CR (R); Received Foreign Language Award; Most Spirited Played Award (Volleyball); Majoring in Spanish Language (Masters); Minoring or Majoring in Italian; Providence College; Florida State U

JOYCE, DANIELLE; MAPLEVILLE, RI; BEACON CHARTER SCH; (FR); Hnr Roll; ArtClub; Bnd; Mch Bnd; Stg Cre; Scr Kpr; Sch Ppr (E); Architecture; Culinary Arts; U of Rhode Island; Johnson and Wales U

KARLINA, YULIYA A; EAST PROVIDENCE, RI; EAST PROVIDENCE HS; (JR); To Work for the ASPCA

KAZANTZIS, CHRYSTA D; BARRINGTON, RI; BARRINGTON HS; (JR); F Lan Hn Soc; Hnr Roll; Comm Volntr; Peer Tut/Med; FBLA; NYLC; P to P St Amb Prg; Photog; French Clb; Bnd; Mch Bnd; Bskball (J); Yrbk (E); Fluent in Greek; International Relations; American U; Eckerd College

LABBADIA, GIANA; CRANSTON, RI; CRANSTON CAREER AND TECH; (JR); Hi Hnr Roll; Hnr Roll; WWAHSS; Comm Volntr; Chrch Yth Grp; DECA; Prom Com; Tchrs Aide; Dnce; Drm Mjr; SP/M/VS; Ice Sktg (C); Dance Team Captain; Falconette / Majorette; Elementary Education; Curry College; Lynn U

LAURENCEAU, DEBBIE; PROVIDENCE, RI; MT PLEASANT HS; (FR); Chrch Yth Grp; NYLC; Tmpl Yth Grp; Ch Chr; Dnce; SP/M/VS; Bskball (V); Chrldg (V); Cr Ctry (V); Track (V); Doctor Taking Care of Infants; Business; Boston U; Gibbs College of Boston

LAURENT, RHODE; PROVIDENCE, RI; CLASSICAL HS; (SO); Hi Hnr Roll; Hnr Roll; Comm Volntr; Chrch Yth Grp; Ch Chr; Helping Hand; Business Management; Interior Decoration; Rhode Island College; Brown U

LE FEBVRE, AMANDA; PASCOAG, RI; BURRILLVILLE HS; (JR); Hi Hnr Roll; Hnr Roll; ArtClub; DARE; DECA; Prom Com; SP/M/VS; Chrldg (V L); Vllyball (VJC); Cl Off (R); DECA National List; Honor Roll 1-4; Business; Entrepreneurship; Bryant College; U of Rhode Island

LEVESQUE, DANIELLE; RIVERSIDE, RI; EAST PROVIDENCE HS; (SO); Hnr Roll; Prom Com; Scouts; Bnd; Chr; Bskball (J L); Track (VJ L); Cl Off (V); Political Science; Teaching; Boston College

LO BUONO, NADIA; HOPE, RI; SCITUATE HS; (SR); Hnr Roll; Nat Hon Sy; WWAHSS; Comm Volntr; Peer Tut/Med; FBLA; Chr; Chrldg (V); Sccr (V); United States Naval Sea Cadet Corps; Education; Rhode Island College

MACHADO, JOSEPH N; RIVERSIDE, RI; EAST PROVIDENCE HS; (JR); Hi Hnr Roll; Otst Ac Ach Awd; DARE; Bnd; Mch Bnd; Musicianship Award; RI Music Educators Assn Junior Division Honors; Rhode Island College; Providence College

MADRID, DEBORAH; PROVIDENCE, RI; MT PLEASANT HS; (SR); Hnr Roll; Dnce; Rhode Island College; Community College of Rhode Island

MASSIMINO, LAURA M; WESTERLY, RI; WESTERLY HS; (SR); Hi Hnr Roll; Nat Hon Sy; St of Mnth; Pep Squd; Bnd; Jzz Bnd; Mch Bnd; Orch; Chrldg (V L); Swmg (V); Stu Cncl

MC CARTHY, KRYSTAL; RIVERSIDE, RI; EAST PROVIDENCE HS; (FR); Chrch Yth Grp; Civil Air Pat; DARE; Chr; DICE; Community College of the Air Force

MC COLLUM, MATTHEW S; NORTH PROVIDENCE, RI; WILLIAM M DAVIES CAREER & TECH HS; (JR); Hnr Roll; Perf Att; Sci Fairs; WWAHSS; Chess; Cmptr Clb; DARE; Computer Club; Computer Programmer; U of Rhode Island; Rhode Island College

MEDEIROS, IVAN S; EAST PROVIDENCE, RI; EAST PROVIDENCE HS; (JR); Ctznshp Aw; F Lan Hn Soc; Fut Prb Slvr; Hnr Roll; MVP; Nat Hon Sy; St of Mnth; Comm Volntr; DARE; Emplmnt; Mus Clb; Photog; Tchrs Aide; Portuguese Clb; Bnd; Cr Ctry (J); Ice Hky (J); Sccr (J); Electrical; Gaming Software; New England Technical

MEEHAN, ERIKA; EAST PROVIDENCE, RI; EAST PROVIDENCE HS; (JR); Hnr Roll; Nat Hon Sy; Comm Volntr; Spec Olymp Vol; Chrch Yth Grp; Emplmnt; Chr; Sccr (V L); Swmg (V L); 2nd Team-All State (Swimming); Education; Sports Medicine; U of Connecticut; U of Rhode Island

MOORE, BRITTANY; WARWICK, RI; WARWICK VETERANS MEMORIAL HS; (JR); Hi Hnr Roll; Hnr Roll; Pres Ac Ftns Aw; Sci Fairs; USAA; Yth Ldrshp Prog; Comm Volntr; Peer Tut/Med; Chrch Yth Grp; Jr Ach; Mth Clb/Tm; Scouts; Tchrs Aide; Dnce; Bskball (J); Sccr (VJCL); Track (V L); Girl Scout Silver Award; Coach's Award 2004; Psychology; Physical Therapy; Georgetown U; Northeastern U

MORAN, MATTHEW D; WEST WARWICK, RI; BISHOP HENDRICKEN HS; (JR); Hi Hnr Roll; MVP; Nat Hon Sy; Spec Olymp Vol; Ftball (V C); Peer Ministry; National Honor Society; History Major, Psychology; BC (Boston College); Brown U

MORILLO, ELIANA; PROVIDENCE, RI; CLASSICAL HS; (SO); Hi Hnr Roll; Comm Volntr; Chrch Yth Grp; Dbte Team; Ch Chr; CR (T); Yrbk (P); Knitting Club; Debate Team; Pediatrician; Speech Pathologist; Boston U; Brown U

MORKEH, JOSHUA; PROVIDENCE, RI; MT PLEASANT HS; (JR); Hnr Roll; Comm Volntr; Outdrs Clb; Stg Cre; Sccr (V); East Tennessee State U; U of North Carolina

MOTTA, CHRISTINA; CRANSTON, RI; BEACON CHARTER SCH; (JR); Hnr Roll; Perf Att; Peer Tut/Med; Emplmnt; Sch Ppr (R)

MULLEN, ERIN C; RUMFORD, RI; EAST PROVIDENCE HS; (JR); Hnr Roll; Nat Hon Sy; Scouts; Chr; Flg Crps; SP/M/VS; 2005 French Academic Achievement Award; Girl Scout Silver Award; Creative Writing, English; History; Salve Regina U; U of Rhode Island

MURPHY, AMANDA; MAPLEVILLE, RI; BURRILLVILLE HS; (JR); Hi Hnr Roll; Hnr Roll; Perf Att; DARE; Emplmnt; Quiz Bowl; Chr; Physical Therapy; RIC; URI

NUNEZ, SAHONNY N; PROVIDENCE, RI; MT PLEASANT HS; (SO); F Lan Hn Soc; Hi Hnr Roll; Hnr Roll; Otst Ac Ach Awd; Sci Fairs; Peer Tut/Med; Pep Squd; Spanish Clb; Dnce; Vllyball (J); Excellence in Science 2003-04; Excellence in Math 2004-05; Law / Lawyer; Law Enforcement; Brown U; Rhode Island College

OAKLEY, KRISTA; HOPE, RI; SCITUATE HS; (JR); Hi Hnr Roll; Hnr Roll; Nat Hon Sy; Emplmnt; SADD; Bnd; Mch Bnd; Orch; Nursing; Northeastern U; U Mass Amherst

OK, CHANNA; PROVIDENCE, RI; CLASSICAL HS; (SO); Hnr Roll; Otst Ac Ach Awd; Perf Att; Clb; Cr Ctry (J); Ftball (J); Tennis (J); Track (J); CR (R); Manga Club; Go Club; Medical Field / Doctor; Astronomy

O'KEEFE, KYLE R; CUMBERLAND, RI; CUMBERLAND HS; (JR); Comm Volntr; Peer Tut/Med; Sccr (J); Track (VJ L); Yrbk (E); Save Our School

OLIVEIRA, STACY; EAST PROVIDENCE, RI; EAST PROVIDENCE HS; (FR); Comm Volntr; Chrch Yth Grp; Portuguese Clb; Chr; Dnce; Chrldg (V); Portuguese Club; Pediatrician; Brown U

OLIVO, JENNIFER L; NORTH PROVIDENCE, RI; NORTH PROVIDENCE HS; (SO); Hi Hnr Roll; Hnr Roll; Pres Ac Ftns Aw; Comm Volntr; DARE; Jr Ach; Tchrs Aide; Bskball (J); Cr Ctry (V L); Sftball (V L); Stu Cncl (R); National Junior Honor Society; Dentistry; Plastic Surgeon; Boston College; Boston U

ORELLANA, AURA A; PROVIDENCE, RI; MT PLEASANT HS; (FR); Hnr Roll; Comm Volntr; Lawyer; Writer; Bryant College; Rhode Island College

PACKER, RICHARD; KINGSTON, RI; SOUTH KINGSTOWN HS; (SR); Hi Hnr Roll; Nat Hon Sy; Otst Ac Ach Awd; Pres Sch; Comm Volntr; Peer Tut/Med; Chrch Yth Grp; Emplmnt; Mod UN; P to P St Amb Prg; Bskball (VJ L); Cr Ctry (V); Sccr (J); RI Interscholastic "All-Academic" Team; Captain-Renaissance Team; Accounting; General Business Admin; Boston College; U of Connecticut

PATTERSON, LANA; WARREN, RI; MT HOPE HS; (JR); Hi Hnr Roll; Hnr Roll; St of Mnth; WWAHSS; DARE; Emplmnt; Scouts; Math Teacher; Accountant; Rhode Island College; U of Rhode Island

PAYEN, MAGDALA; PROVIDENCE, RI; HOPE HS; (JR); Hi Hnr Roll; Hnr Roll; Nat Hon Sy; St of Mnth; Comm Volntr; ArtClub; Biology Clb; Chess; Chrch Yth Grp; Cmptr Clb; DARE; Dbte Team; Drma Clb; Ch Chr; Dnce; SP/M/VS; Bdmtn (V); Bsball (V); Bskball (V); Chrldg (V); Cyclg (V); Fld Hky (V); Gmnstcs (V); Hsbk Rdg (V); Sch Ppr (E, P); Yrbk (E, P); Cartoon Designs Into 3-D on the Computer; Teacher; Brown U; Johnson & Wales U

PEREZ, ALYSSA K; PROVIDENCE, RI; MT PLEASANT HS; (SO); Hi Hnr Roll; Hnr Roll; Drm Mjr; Medical; Business; Rhode Island College; Princeton U

PEREZ, JENNIFER; PROVIDENCE, RI; CLASSICAL HS; (SO); Hi Hnr Roll; Hnr Roll; SADD; Sftball (J); Tennis (J); Yrbk (R); Nursing; Culinary Arts; Brown U; Johnson & Wales U

PEREZ, YOLANDA I; PAWTUCKET, RI; CTRL FALLS SR HS; (JR); Hi Hnr Roll; Hnr Roll; Nat Ldrshp Svc; Otst Ac Ach Awd; Perf Att; Pres Sch; Sci Fairs; St of Mnth; US Army Sch Ath Aw; Yth Ldrshp Prog; Comm Volntr; Hab For Humty Volntr; Hosp Aide; ArtClub; Cmptr Clb; DARE; Emplmnt; Mth Clb/Tm; Mus Clb; NYLC; Scouts; Acpl Chr; Chr; Dnce; SP/M/VS; Bskball (V); Chrldg (V); Dvng (V); Ftball (V); Mar Art (J); Sccr (V); Sftball (V); Vllyball (V); Adv Cncl (P); Cl Off (V); Stu Cncl (S); CR (R); Lit Mag (R); Sch Ppr (R); U.S Army; Laws; Bryan College; U of Rhode Island

PICOT-VIERRA, JAMES; EAST PROVIDENCE, RI; EAST PROVIDENCE HS; (FR); Hi Hnr Roll; Otst Ac Ach Awd; Perf Att; Pres Sch; St of Mnth; Yth Ldrshp Prog; Comm Volntr; Chrch Yth Grp; DARE; NYLC; P to P St Amb Prg; Scouts; Bnd; Chr; Bskball (L); Sccr (L); Vllyball; Wrstlg

PRESTON, JESSICA; PAWTUCKET, RI; TOLMAN HS; (SO); Hnr Roll; Sci Fairs; Comm Volntr; DARE; Emplmnt; Dnce; Various Art Awards; Competing in Regional Cheerleading for Darlington Braves; Graphic Design/ Game Programmer; Computer Engineering; Rhode Island College; Rhode Island School of Design

RABIDEAU, MICHELLE; HARRISVILLE, RI; BURRILLVILLE HS; (JR); Hi Hnr Roll; Nat Hon Sy; Comm Volntr; Chr; Stu Cncl (R); Animal Shelter Volunteer; Animal Shelter Employee; Mathematics; Statistics; Mount Holyoke; U of Massachusetts Lowell

RAHEB, JENNA A; LINCOLN, RI; LINCOLN HS; (SO); Hnr Roll; Nat Hon Sy; FBLA; Yrbk (E); Figure Skating; Making Top 10 of Class; Business; Science; Boston U; Boston College

REDMAN, MARIBETH; EAST GREENWICH, RI; EAST GREENWICH HS; (JR); Hnr Roll; Comm Volntr; Peer Tut/Med; DARE; Bnd; Mch Bnd; Lcrsse (V); Sccr (V); Swmg (V); Track (V); I've Played a Sport Every Season in My HS Career; I've Been in Honors Classes Since Freshman Yr; Veterinary Medicine; Psychology; Michigan State U; Northeastern U

Morillo, Eliana
Classical HS
Providence, RI

Mc Collum, Matthew S
William M Davies Career & Tech HS
North Providence, RI

Machado, Joseph N
East Providence HS
Riverside, RI

Hudson, Barbara
Smithfield HS
Smithfield, RI

Joyce, Danielle
Beacon Charter Sch
Mapleville, RI

Medeiros, Ivan S
East Providence HS
East Providence, RI

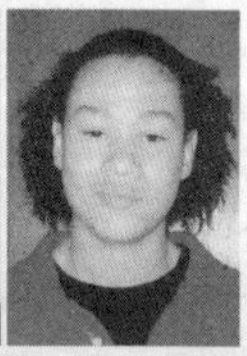
Picot-Vierra, James
East Providence HS
East Providence, RI

RINCON, FREDYS; PAWTUCKET, RI; CHARLES E SHEA SR HS; (SO); Hnr Roll; Perf Att; Comm Volntr; Chrch Yth Grp; Clr Grd; Drl Tm; Track (C)

ROLLAND, PITTER; PROVIDENCE, RI; MT PLEASANT HS; (JR); Hi Hnr Roll; Hnr Roll; MVP; Amnsty Intl; Red Cr Aide; Spec Olymp Vol; Chrch Yth Grp; Outdrs Clb; Spch Team; Bskball (J); Sccr (J); Track (V); Vllyball (V); Wrstlg (V); Business & Professional Sports; Economics; Any School Giving Scholarships

SHARIF, MAYSOON A; WOONSOCKET, RI; MT ST CHARLES AC; (JR); Hi Hnr Roll; Nat Hon Sy; Sci Fairs; Sci/Math Olympn; WWAHSS; Comm Volntr; Peer Tut/Med; Emplmnt; Svce Clb; Foreign Clb; Dnce; Sch Ppr; Writing Award; Art Award; Chemistry; Biochemistry; Cornell U; Tufts U

SILVA, APRYL; EAST PROVIDENCE, RI; EAST PROVIDENCE HS; (SR); Hnr Roll; Nat Hon Sy; St of Mnth; WWAHSS; Yth Ldrshp Prog; Comm Volntr; Peer Tut/Med; Emplmnt; Vsity Clb; Spanish Clb; Bnd; Chrldg (V CL); Track (V); Stu Cncl (R); CR (R); Townie Award; Management (Business); Communications; Bryant U

SOLAPHET, LAMMONE; PROVIDENCE, RI; MT PLEASANT HS; (SR); Ctznshp Aw; Hnr Roll; Otst Ac Ach Awd; Perf Att; Comm Volntr; Dnce; SP/M/VS; Elementary Education; Restaurant Management; U of Rhode Island; Johnson & Wales U

STENNING, MICHAEL; CRANSTON, RI; CRANSTON CAREER & TECH CTR; (SR); Hnr Roll; St of Mnth; Comm Volntr; Peer Tut/Med; DECA; Emplmnt; Mus Clb; Prom Com; Tech Clb; Bnd; Mch Bnd; Stu Cncl (R); 1st Place Marketing (10-12); Outstanding Marketing Student (10); Business Management; Newbury College; Fisher College

SULLIVAN, BRIAN; BRISTOL, RI; LASALLE AC; (SR); Hi Hnr Roll; Hnr Roll; Pres Sch; St of Mnth; Comm Volntr; Chess; Chrch Yth Grp; Drma Clb; Emplmnt; Scouts; Acpl Chr; Bnd; Chr; Pep Bnd; Eagle Scout; History; Sec Education; Marymount U

THOMAS, KIMBERLY; RIVERSIDE, RI; EAST PROVIDENCE HS; (SO); Hnr Roll; WWAHSS; Comm Volntr; Peer Tut/Med; Red Cr Aide; Lib Aide; Clr Grd; Flg Crps; SP/M/VS; Elementary Education; Law Associate; Rhode Island College; Johnson & Wales

TOWNE, SHAUN R; RIVERSIDE, RI; EAST PROVIDENCE HS; (JR); Hnr Roll; Perf Att; Chrch Yth Grp; Emplmnt; Mus Clb; Spanish Clb; Bnd; Ftball (VJ); Musicianship Award (3 Years); Black Belt in Kempo Karate; U of Rhode Island

TREMBLAY, JENNIFER; WARREN, RI; ST MARY AC-BAY VIEW HS; (JR); Nat Hon Sy; Sci Fairs; WWAHSS; DARE; P to P St Amb Prg; Prom Com; Scouts; French Clb; SP/M/VS; Stg Cre; Chrldg (V); Architecture; Mc Gill U; Drexel U

VANASSE, JESSE; WOONSOCKET, RI; BEACON CHARTER SCH; (JR); Hi Hnr Roll; Hnr Roll; WWAHSS; Peer Tut/Med; ArtClub; Drma Clb; Fr of Library; Lib Aide; Prom Com; Chr; Dnce; SP/M/VS; Stu Cncl (R); Sch Ppr (E, R); Actress; Writer; Salem State; U of Rhode Island

VEGA, SAMANTHA C; PAWTUCKET, RI; CHARLES E SHEA SR HS; (FR); Hnr Roll; Nat Hon Sy; Nat Mrt LOC; Otst Ac Ach Awd; Perf Att; Comm Volntr; Hosp Aide; Peer Tut/Med; DARE; Emplmnt; Scouts; Svce Clb; Ch Chr; Dnce; Nominated to the Teen Hall of Fame; Over 1000 Hrs in Volunteer Community Work; Business Management; Cosmetology; Arthur Angelo School; Johnson & Wales U

VEIGA, MARGARIDA; RUMFORD, RI; EAST PROVIDENCE HS; (FR); Hi Hnr Roll; Hnr Roll; Salutrn; Sci Fairs; St of Mnth; Peer Tut/Med; Chrch Yth Grp; DECA; Dnce; Sch Ppr (R); Kujenga Vongozi; Youth Christian Leadership Institute; Library Science; Sociology

VONGKAISONE, JONATHAN; PROVIDENCE, RI; MT PLEASANT HS; (FR); Hnr Roll; U of Rhode Island; Rhode Island College

VOTA, JOHN D; PASCOAG, RI; BURRILLVILLE HS; (JR); Cinema; Computer Graphics; School of the Museum of Fine Arts; U of Hartford

WHALEN, AMANDA; WOONSOCKET, RI; BEACON CHARTER SCH; (FR); Hi Hnr Roll; Hnr Roll; Perf Att; Sweet Shop; Interior Decorating; Architecture; RI School of Design (RISD)

WILLIAMS, LAKISHA R; WOONSOCKET, RI; BEACON CHARTER SCH; (JR); Hnr Roll; Chrch Yth Grp; Drma Clb; FBLA; Ch Chr; Dnce; Drl Tm; SP/M/VS; Started Own Drill Team; Degree in Business; To Become a Salon Owner; Arthur Angelo School; Community College of Rhode Island

Stenning, Michael
Cranston Career & Tech Ctr
Cranston, RI

Silva, Apryl
East Providence HS
East Providence, RI

National Honor Roll Spring 2005

Rincon, Fredys
Charles E Shea SR HS
Pawtucket, RI

Vega, Samantha C
Charles E Shea SR HS
Pawtucket, RI

Tennessee

ABERNATHY, ELIZABETH A; PULASKI, TN; GILES CTY HS; (JR); Hi Hnr Roll; Comm Volntr; Red Cr Aide; Chrch Yth Grp; Ntl Beta Clb; Prom Com; Tchrs Aide; International Clb; Bnd; Mch Bnd; Bausch & Lomb Honorary Science Award; American Chemical Society - Wilson Dam Section Chemistry Award; Chemistry Fields; Tennessee Technical U

ABSTON, WILLIAM J; CRAWFORD, TN; MONTEREY HS; (JR); 4H Awd; Ctznshp Aw; Hnr Roll; Sci Fairs; WWAHSS; Comm Volntr; 4-H; ArtClub; Ntl Beta Clb; Computer Technician; Computer Engineer; Tennessee Tech U

ADAM, SARAH M; MC MINNVILLE, TN; WARREN CTY HS; (FR); Hi Hnr Roll; Otst Ac Ach Awd; Pres Ac Ftns Aw; St of Mnth; Comm Volntr; ArtClub; Chrch Yth Grp; Key Club; Pep Squd; Bnd; Clr Grd; Flg Crps; Pep Bnd; Stu Cncl (S); National Junior Honor Society; Law; Communications; Harvard Law School; New York U

ADAMS, KARAH; MEMPHIS, TN; GERMANTOWN HS; (JR); Hnr Roll; Comm Volntr; Chrch Yth Grp; Key Club; SADD; Spanish Clb; Stg Cre; International Club; Writer's Guild; Pre-Medicine; U of Tennessee: Martin; U of Tennessee: Knoxville

ADAMSON, MALEA; LIBERTY, TN; DEKALB CTY HS; (JR); Hi Hnr Roll; Otst Ac Ach Awd; WWAHSS; AL Aux Girls; FBLA; FCCLA; Lib Aide; Ntl Beta Clb; French Clb; SP/M/VS; Psychology; Arts; U of Tennessee-Knoxville; Belmont U

ADDAI, EVETTE; BRENTWOOD, TN; DAVID LIPSCOMB HS; (JR); Nat Hon Sy; WWAHSS; Comm Volntr; Chrch Yth Grp; Drma Clb; Pep Squd; Svce Clb; Spanish Clb; Chr; Ch Chr; Cl Off (V); Pre-Med; Sociology; Duke U; Tulane U

ADDO-ATUAH, KWEKU; MEMPHIS, TN; CENTRAL HS; (SO); Hi Hnr Roll; Yth Ldrshp Prog; Comm Volntr; ArtClub; Chrch Yth Grp; French Clb; Tennis (J); Bridge Builders; French Club Secretary / International Club; Architecture; U of Pennsylvania; Yale U

ADEDOKUN, TOYIN; JACKSON, TN; JACKSON CTRL -MERRY HS; (SR); Hnr Roll; Nat Mrt LOC; Perf Att; Pres Ac Ftns Aw; Sci Fairs; Yth Ldrshp Prog; Comm Volntr; Peer Tut/Med; Chrch Yth Grp; DARE; Drma Clb; Emplmnt; FCCLA; Ch Chr; SP/M/VS; Track (V); FCCLA Secretary; Computer Science; Business; U of Memphis; Lambuth U

ADKISSON, DARCI; COLUMBIA, TN; SPRING HILL HS; (JR); Hnr Roll; Otst Ac Ach Awd; Perf Att; WWAHSS; Comm Volntr; Chrch Yth Grp; Emplmnt; FCA; FTA; Key Club; Ntl Beta Clb; Business; Physical Therapy; Freed-Hardeman U; Columbia State Community College

AGARWAL, SONIA S; MURFREESBORO, TN; SIEGEL HS; (JR); Gov Hnr Prg; Hi Hnr Roll; Nat Hon Sy; Comm Volntr; Hosp Aide; AL Aux Girls; Jr Cls League; Mth Clb/Tm; Mod UN; MuAlphaTh; Ntl Beta Clb; Prom Com; Sci Clb; Dnce; Tennis (V); Cl Off (P); CR (R); 1st Band for Mid-State Band 2002-2003; Summa Cum Laude on National Latin Exam; Pre-Med; George Washington U; Northwestern U

AGOLLI, FABJOLA F; NASHVILLE, TN; MC GAVOCK COMP HS; (SR); Hi Hnr Roll; Perf Att; WWAHSS; Comm Volntr; Emplmnt; German Clb; Chr; Nursing; Business; Belmont U

AGRESTA, JARED P; KNOXVILLE, TN; BEARDEN HS; (SR); Hnr Roll; Perf Att; Comm Volntr; DARE; Emplmnt; FBLA; Key Club; Base Place Award- Technology 2005; Technology Achievement Award - 2004; Computer Science; Pellissippi State College

AHMAD, WAQAS; NASHVILLE, TN; HILLSBORO COMP HS; (JR); Ctznshp Aw; Hnr Roll; Pres Sch; Comm Volntr; Hab For Humty Volntr; BPA; Sccr (V); Sch Ppr (R); More Than 60 Hours of Volunteering in 6 Days; Dentistry; Science; Vanderbilt U; U of Tennessee

AHMADIAN, ARMAN; COLLIERVILLE, TN; COLLIERVILLE HS; (SO); Hnr Roll; Perf Att; WWAHSS; Comm Volntr; German Clb; Rqtball (J); Bilingual; Medicine; Emory U

ALANIS CONTRERAS, JACQUELINNE L; KNOXVILLE, TN; CENTRAL HS; (SO); UC Berkeley; UCLA

ALDER, DANA R; JASPER, TN; SOUTH PITTSBURG HS; (FR); 4H Awd; Hnr Roll; St of Mnth; Comm Volntr; Hosp Aide; Peer Tut/Med; 4-H; Chrch Yth Grp; DARE; Emplmnt; Lib Aide; Off Aide; Pep Squd; Tchrs Aide; Chrldg (J); Gmnstcs (V); Sccr (V); Vllyball (J); Cl Off (S); Interact Club; Leo Club; Medical; Health; UTK; UTC

ALDREDGE, KRISTEN; JEFFERSON CITY, TN; JEFFERSON CTY HS; (JR); Hnr Roll; Nat Hon Sy; St of Mnth; WWAHSS; Comm Volntr; Chrch Yth Grp; DECA; Emplmnt; FCA; Ntl Beta Clb; Ch Chr; Chrldg (V); National Honor Society; National Technical Honor Society; Teaching; Carson Newman College; Mars Hill College

ALLEN, ABBY; HIXSON, TN; HIXSON HS; (JR); Comm Volntr; Hosp Aide; SADD; Mch Bnd; Majorette 4 Superior Ratings in Competitions; Bachelor in Science - RN; U of Tennessee at Chattanooga; Chattanooga State Technical College

ALLEN, BRITNEY; DUFF, TN; CAMPBELL CTY COMP HS; (FR); Hi Hnr Roll; Hnr Roll; Salutrn; Peer Tut/Med; 4-H; Chrch Yth Grp; DARE; Lib Aide; Scouts; Ch Chr; Nurse; Cosmetology; Lincoln Memorial U; Roane State

ALLEN, CHRISTINA N; LEBANON, TN; LEBANON HS; (JR); Duke TS; Hnr Roll; WWAHSS; Chrch Yth Grp; Emplmnt; Ntl Beta Clb; Chr; Ch Chr; Ob/Gyn; Nurse; Cumberland U

ALLEN, CODY; WALLING, TN; WHITE CTY HS; (SR); Hnr Roll; Pres Sch; Comm Volntr; Chrch Yth Grp; ROTC; Schol Bwl; Tech Clb; Spanish Clb; President of TSA; Industrial Engineering; Accounting; Mississippi State U

ALLEN, JUSTIN R; MILLINGTON, TN; MILLINGTON CTRL HS; (JR); Hnr Roll; Nat Hon Sy; WWAHSS; Comm Volntr; Emplmnt; FCA; Ntl Beta Clb; Off Aide; Football Manager; U of Memphis

ALLEN, TIMOTHY D; SEVIERVILLE, TN; SEVIER CTY HS; (FR); Hnr Roll; Perf Att; Emplmnt; Ntl Beta Clb; Beta Club 4 Bowling Team; Veterans Day Program; Software Developer; Computer Science; ITT Tech

ALLEN, TYESLIA; JACKSON, TN; LIBERTY TECH MAGNET HS; (JR); 4H Awd; Yth Ldrshp Prog; Peer Tut/Med; 4-H; DARE; Completion of WIA; Completion of DARE; Massage Therapist; Nurse Assistant; U of Phoenix; Jackson State

ALLEY, MICHELE; CORRYTON, TN; GIBBS HS; (FR); Comm Volntr; FCCLA; FCCLA Member; Veterinarian; Marine Biologist; Carson-Newman College; U of Tennessee

ALONZO, MARIA; CORDOVA, TN; CARDOVA HS; (SO); Ctznshp Aw; Hi Hnr Roll; Chrch Yth Grp; Emplmnt; Clb; Nursing; Memphis U; U of Tennessee

AL-SAAD, ROUA; HERMITAGE, TN; MC GAVOCK COMP HS; (JR); Hi Hnr Roll; Hnr Roll; Otst Ac Ach Awd; WWAHSS; Comm Volntr; Peer Tut/Med; Red Cr Aide; Fr of Library; Lib Aide; SADD; Stu Cncl (R); CR (R); I Was in GROTC and I Have National Honor Roll; Dentistry; Interior Design; Vanderbilt U; Austin Peay

ALUKO, ASHLEY; MEMPHIS, TN; WHITE STATION HS; (SO); Ctznshp Aw; Duke TS; Hi Hnr Roll; WWAHSS; Comm Volntr; Peer Tut/Med; Mod UN; Ntl Beta Clb; Bnd; Mch Bnd; Pep Bnd; Vllyball (V); Adv Cncl (R); Cl Off (S); Class Favorite (9th & 10th Grade); All West Tennessee Band (Red & Blue); Pre-Med

AMOS, CHRISTIN D; MEMPHIS, TN; WHITE HAVEN HS; (SO); Gov Hnr Prg; Hnr Roll; MVP; Nat Hon Sy; Sci Fairs; Sci/Math Olympn; WWAHSS; BPA; Orch; Chrldg (V); Track (V); Stu Cncl (S); CR (R); NCA All American Cheerleader; UCH All Star Cheerleader; Optometry; Criminology; U of Kentucky; U of Louisville

AMOS, TABITHA; SNEEDVILLE, TN; HANCOCK HS; (FR); 4H Awd; Hnr Roll; Perf Att; 4-H; Vllyball (J); Lab Technician; Nurse; East Tennessee State U; U of Tennessee

ANDERSON, CHRISTY; WHITWELL, TN; MARION CTY HS; (SR); Hnr Roll; Perf Att; 4-H; DARE; FCA; Ntl Beta Clb; Prom Com; SADD; Ch Chr; Chrldg (V); PP Ftbl (V); Cl Off (S); Child Development; Pediatrics; Middle Tennessee State U; U of Tennessee Chattanooga

ANDERSON, CLINT; MC KENZIE, TN; (SR); Hi Hnr Roll; Pres Ac Ftns Aw; USAA; WWAHSS; Yth Ldrshp Prog; Comm Volntr; AL Aux Boys; Chrch Yth Grp; DARE; FCA; Key Club; Lttrmn Clb; Lib Aide; Ntl Beta Clb; Bsball (V CL); Bskball (V CL); Ftball (V CL); Track (V L); Leo Club President; Math Education; Lambuth U

ANDERSON, DEBORAH; MURFREESBORO, TN; OAKLAND HS; (FR); Hi Hnr Roll; Hnr Roll; Chrch Yth Grp; Ch Chr; Journalism; Political Science; Belmont U; Middle Tennessee State U

ANDERSON, DEIDRA P; ARLINGTON, TN; ARLINGTON HS; (FR); Ctznshp Aw; Hnr Roll; Perf Att; Pres Ac Ftns Aw; Sci Fairs; Comm Volntr; ArtClub; Chrch Yth Grp; Cmptr Clb; Ntl Beta Clb; Bnd; Chr; Ch Chr; Dnce; Honor Club All through School; Policewoman; Animation Artist

ANDERSON, DWAYNE; HILHAM, TN; LIVINGSTON AC; (SO); Hnr Roll; Play Upright Bass in Bluegrass Band; Do Mechanic Work and Misc Work on Autos; Automotive Service Technician; Automotive Technical Engineer; Tennessee Technological U

ANDERSON, JENAE A; KNOXVILLE, TN; AUSTIN EAST HS; (SO); Hnr Roll; MVP; Otst Ac Ach Awd; WWAHSS; Comm Volntr; Peer Tut/Med; Chrch Yth Grp; FCA; FBLA; Ntl Beta Clb; Bnd; Dnce; Mch Bnd; SP/M/VS; Bskball (V L); Cr Ctry (J); Track (V CL); Cl Off (V); CR (V); State Runner Up As Freshman In 100 And 200 Meter Dash; Business; Law; Hampton U; North Carolina A & T

ANDERSON, JOSHUA; MEMPHIS, TN; CENTRAL HS; (SO); St of Mnth; Chess; Bskball (J); Student of the Month; Winning Spelling Bees; Actor; Wrestler; Memphis State U

ANDERSON, KATELYNN; BELLS, TN; CROCKETT CTY HS; (FR); Hnr Roll; Spec Olymp Vol; Chr; Registered Nurse BSN; Doctor (Endocrinologist); Jackson State Community College

ANDERSON, MONTIA; MEMPHIS, TN; CARVER HS; (SO); Hnr Roll; Perf Att; CARE; Comm Volntr; Peer Tut/Med; Chrch Yth Grp; DARE; Mod UN; Quiz Bowl; ROTC; Clr Grd; Dnce; Drl Tm; Bskball (V); Vllyball (V); CR (T); Yrbk (E); U of Memphis; U of Tennessee

ANDERSON, NATALIE R; SOUTH PITTSBURG, TN; RICHARD HARDY MEMORIAL SCH; (SR); 4H Awd; DAR; Hi Hnr Roll; Hnr Roll; Nat Hon Sy; Yth Ldrshp Prog; Comm Volntr; Peer Tut/Med; 4-H; Chrch Yth Grp; DARE; Lib Aide; Ntl Beta Clb; SADD; Tchrs Aide; Bnd; Chr; Ch Chr; Mch Bnd; Vllyball (J); TN/GA Delegate for the Cumberland Presbyteria; 3 Yrs Leo Club / 3 Honors; Master's Degree / Psychology; Chattanooga State Tech Community College; U of Memphis

ANDERSON, STEPHANIE; WARTBURG, TN; CENTRAL HS; (JR); Hi Hnr Roll; Hnr Roll; WWAHSS; Chrch Yth Grp; FCA; Criminal Justice; Accounting; Roane State Community College; ITT Technical Institute

ANDREWS, ASHLEY; HUMBOLDT, TN; HUMBOLDT HS; (JR); Nat Hon Sy; Perf Att; Sci Fairs; WWAHSS; Comm Volntr; Hosp Aide; Peer Tut/Med; Ntl Beta Clb; Off Aide; Prom Com; Bnd; Ch Chr; Drm Mjr; Jzz Bnd; Chrldg; Cl Off (T); Stu Cncl; Pre-Pharmacy; Xavier U

ANGLIN, SONYA; FRANKLIN, TN; CENTENNIAL HS; (JR); Ctznshp Aw; Hi Hnr Roll; Hnr Roll; Otst Ac Ach Awd; Comm Volntr; Chrch Yth Grp; Emplmnt; Off Aide; Prom Com; Tchrs Aide; Stu Cncl (R); CR (R); Forestry; Foreign Language; U of Tennessee Chattanooga; Middle Tennessee State U

ANITO, KELSEY; KNOXVILLE, TN; HALLS HS; (SO); Ctznshp Aw; Duke TS; Gov Hnr Prg; Hi Hnr Roll; Nat Hon Sy; Otst Ac Ach Awd; Pres Sch; WWAHSS; Comm Volntr; Chrch Yth Grp; DARE; FCA; Key Club; Mus Clb; Off Aide; Pep Squd; Prom Com; Acpl Chr; Chr; Ch Chr; Dnce; PPSqd (V); Adv Cncl (R); Cl Off (T); Stu Cncl (V); Sch Ppr; Alternate in All-East Women's Choir; Music; Law

ANJONRIN-OHU, AKIN; KINGSPORT, TN; SULLIVAN SOUTH HS; (JR); Hnr Roll; Kwnis Aw; Perf Att; WWAHSS; Hosp Aide; DARE; Emplmnt; Mth Clb/Tm; NYLC; French Clb; Track (V); Part Time Work; Volunteer Hours; Mechanical Engineering; Math; Iowa State U; Virginia Tech U

ANSARI, NADIA S; FRANKLIN, TN; CENTENNIAL HS; (JR); Hi Hnr Roll; Nat Hon Sy; Perf Att; Sci/Math Olympn; WWAHSS; Red Cr Aide; Emplmnt; Mth Clb/Tm; MuAlphaTh; Biomedical Engineering; Cardiology / MD; Vanderbilt U; Emory U

ANZALONE, ERIN N; FRANKLIN, TN; CENTENNIAL HS; (JR); Hi Hnr Roll; Hnr Roll; MVP; Nat Hon Sy; WWAHSS; Comm Volntr; Drma Clb; Emplmnt; Photog; Prom Com; SP/M/VS; Stg Cre; Sccr (VJ); Principal's List; Psychology; Creative Writing; U of Tennessee Knoxville; Middle Tennessee State U

ARCHER, JESSICA; MAURY CITY, TN; CROCKETT CTY HS; (FR); 4H Awd; Hnr Roll; 4-H; Chrch Yth Grp; DARE; Drma Clb; FCA; Ntl Beta Clb; Chr; Ch Chr; SP/M/VS; Stg Cre; X-Ray Tech; Jackson State; Memphis State

ARENDALE, BRITTANY; HARRISON, TN; CENTRAL HS; (FR); Hnr Roll; Chrch Yth Grp; FCA; FBLA; Bnd; Mch Bnd; Pep Bnd; Adv Cncl (R); Forensic Science; Criminal Justice; U of Tennessee Knoxville

ARMENTROUT, DANIEL; JONESBOROUGH, TN; DANIEL BOONE HS; (JR); Duke TS; Hi Hnr Roll; Nat Hon Sy; Perf Att; WWAHSS; Yth Ldrshp Prog; Chrch Yth Grp; FCA; Ntl Beta Clb; Spanish Clb; Chr; Bsball (V L); Cl Off (P); Pre-Medicine; Biochemistry; U of Tennessee; Duke U

ARMSTRONG, ANGELICA; NASHVILLE, TN; NASHVILLE SCH OF THE ARTS; (SO); Hnr Roll; Perf Att; Chrch Yth Grp; Bnd; Stg Cre; Belmont U

ARMSTRONG, DANIELLE; BLOUNTVILLE, TN; SULLIVAN CTRL HS; (SO); Hi Hnr Roll; Nat Sci Aw; WWAHSS; Key Club; Clr Grd; Flg Crps; Mch Bnd; Bachelor's Degree; Tennessee Tech; Memphis College of Art

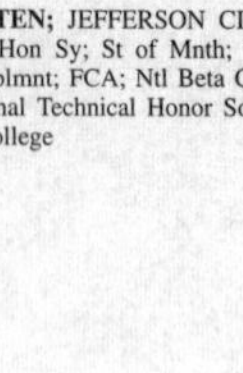

Armentrout, Daniel
Daniel Boone HS
Jonesborough, TN

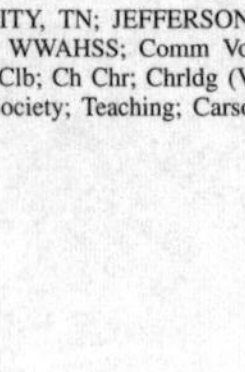

Allen, Christina N
Lebanon HS
Lebanon, TN

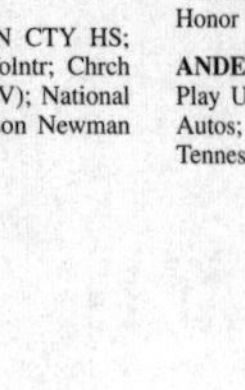

Agresta, Jared P
Bearden HS
Knoxville, TN

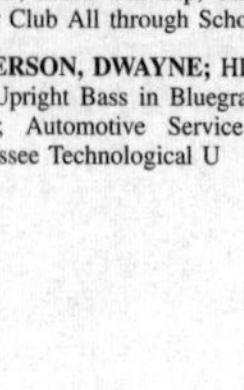

Addo-Atuah, Kweku
Central HS
Memphis, TN

National
Honor Roll
Spring 2005

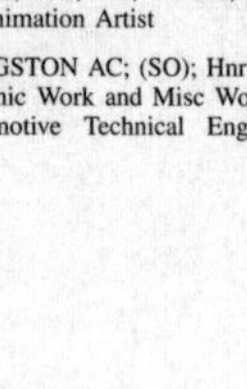

Adam, Sarah M
Warren Cty HS
Mc Minnville, TN

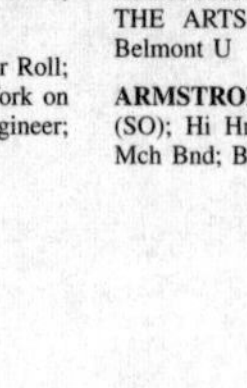

Alder, Dana R
South Pittsburg HS
Jasper, TN

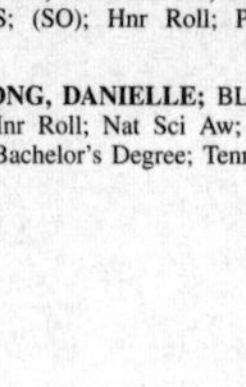

Anderson, Natalie R
Richard Hardy Memorial Sch
South Pittsburg, TN

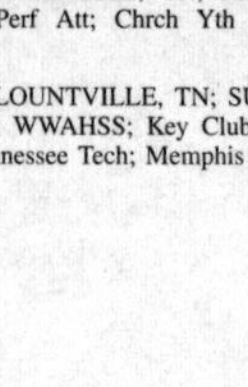

Armstrong, Angelica
Nashville Sch Of The Arts
Nashville, TN

ARNOLD, HOPE; LEBANON, TN; LEBANON HS; (JR); Duke TS; Hi Hnr Roll; Nat Hon Sy; St of Mnth; WWAHSS; Comm Volntr; Spec Olymp Vol; Chrch Yth Grp; DARE; Emplmnt; FCA; Jr Ach; Key Club; Ntl Beta Clb; Vsity Clb; Bskball (VJ); Sftball (VJ L); Yrbk (E); Student Athletic Trainer; Sports Medicine; Physical Therapy; U of Tennessee At Chattanooga; Tennessee Tech

ARNOLD, MIMI; MEMPHIS, TN; ST MARY'S EPISC SCH; (JR); Hi Hnr Roll; Sci Fairs; WWAHSS; Comm Volntr; Peer Tut/Med; Biology Clb; Fr of Library; Mod UN; Ntl Beta Clb; Quill & Scroll; Tmpl Yth Grp; Bnd; Dnce; Cr Ctry (VJ L); Track (V); Adv Cncl (V); CR (S); Lit Mag (R); 1st Place in Dance Competition; Awards at Model UN / Volunteer Counselor for Youth with Disability; Dartmouth College; Tulane U

ARWOOD, JESSICA M; JOHNSON CITY, TN; DANIEL BOONE HS; (SR); 4H Awd; Hnr Roll; Nat Hon Sy; WWAHSS; Comm Volntr; 4-H; Chrch Yth Grp; FCA; Ntl Beta Clb; Ntl FFA; Veterinary Medicine; East Tennessee State U

ASHABRANER, DESIREE; ADAMS, TN; JO BYRNS HS; (FR); Hi Hnr Roll; Otst Ac Ach Awd; Perf Att; Valdctrian; WWAHSS; FCCLA; Ntl Beta Clb; Dnce; Chrldg (V); PPSqd (V); Jr Beta; FCCLA; Medicine; Vanderbilt U

ASHWORTH, DENA E; MURFREESBORO, TN; BLACKMAN HS; (SR); Hnr Roll; Kwnis Aw; St of Mnth; Valdctrian; Peer Tut/Med; Key Club; Tchrs Aide; Spanish Clb; Sch Ppr (R); Renaissance; Beta Club; Chemistry Major; Pre-Professional Student in Medicine; U of Tampa

ASKEW, JUSTIN T; MEMPHIS, TN; CENTRAL HS; (SO); 4H Awd; Ctznshp Aw; Hi Hnr Roll; Hnr Roll; Nat Hon Sy; Otst Ac Ach Awd; Perf Att; WWAHSS; Comm Volntr; Peer Tut/Med; BPA; Chess; Chrch Yth Grp; Emplmnt; P to P St Amb Prg; Svce Clb; SADD; Bnd; Ch Chr; Mch Bnd; Ftball (V); Track (V); Wt Lftg (V); 2 Years of Band / Judge in Court Room / Shadow Attorney; Speaker at Churches; Pre-Law; Business; Howard U; Brown U

ASKEW, LATASHA; MEMPHIS, TN; GERMANTOWN HS; (JR); Hnr Roll; Perf Att; WWAHSS; Voc Ind Clb Am; French Clb; Secretary of VICA Skills USA; Business Owner; Cosmetology; Georgia State U; U of California At Los Angeles

ASKINS, LAUREN M; TULLAHOMA, TN; MOORE CTY HS; (JR); Duke TS; Hnr Roll; Nat Mrt LOC; USAA; Chrch Yth Grp; Degree in Education; U of Tennessee Chattanooga; Belmont U

ATKINS, KIARA M; BOLIVAR, TN; BOLIVAR CTRL HS; (SO); F Lan Hn Soc; Gov Hnr Prg; Hi Hnr Roll; Hnr Roll; Nat Hon Sy; Nat Mrt LOC; Otst Ac Ach Awd; USAA; WWAHSS; Yth Ldrshp Prog; Comm Volntr; Peer Tut/Med; BPA; Chrch Yth Grp; Emplmnt; Mth Clb/Tm; Ntl Beta Clb; NYLC; Sci Clb; SADD; Bnd; Ch Chr; Mch Bnd; Pep Bnd; Ice Hky (V); Sftball (J); Stu Cncl (V); Pre-Med; Psychiatry; Fisk U; Middle Tennessee State U

ATKINS, NATE; ESTILL SPRINGS, TN; FRANKLIN CTY HS; (SR); Hnr Roll; German Clb; Chr; SP/M/VS; Assistant Teacher at Clarke Memorial - Taught German to 5th Graders; Business and Leadership; Psychology; U of Illinois Springfield; Northern Illinois U

AUSTELL, JENNA; GERMANTOWN, TN; BRIARCREST CHRISTIAN HS; (JR); F Lan Hn Soc; Hi Hnr Roll; Nat Hon Sy; USAA; WWAHSS; Comm Volntr; Chrch Yth Grp; Emplmnt; FCA; Mth Clb/Tm; MuAlphaTh; Mus Clb; Svce Clb; Chr; SP/M/VS; Cr Ctry (V CL); Swmg (V L); Track (V L); Stu Cncl (S); Pediatric Oncology/Pediatric Medicine; Physical Therapy/ Sports Medicine; Princeton U; Clemson U

AUSTIN, ROBERT S; KINGSPORT, TN; SULLIVAN SOUTH HS; (JR); Hnr Roll; MVP; WWAHSS; Comm Volntr; Chrch Yth Grp; Spanish Clb; Cr Ctry (J); Sccr (V L); Either Sports Medicine or Sports Management; Clemson U; Spring Hill College

AUTARY, DANIELLE N; HEISKELL, TN; ANDERSON CTY HS; (SO); Hnr Roll; Comm Volntr; Chrch Yth Grp; Teens 4 Christ; Business; Child Care; Crown College; Bryan College

AVERHART, BRITTNEY; FRANKLIN, TN; CENTENNIAL HS; (JR); Hnr Roll; WWAHSS; 4-H; Chrch Yth Grp; FCA; Ntl Beta Clb; SADD; Chrldg; Student Aide; Pediatrician, Psychology (Child); Vanderbilt U; Michigan State

AVERY, JUSTIN; ROBBINS, TN; SUNBRIGHT SCH; (JR); Hi Hnr Roll; Hnr Roll; Nat Hon Sy; Otst Ac Ach Awd; Perf Att; WWAHSS; Chrch Yth Grp; Emplmnt; Lib Aide; Mth Clb/Tm; Mus Clb; Sci Clb; Tchrs Aide; Chr; Ch Chr; Technology; Music; Roane State in Crossville

AYLOR, AMY J; FRANKLIN, TN; RAVENWOOD HS; (JR); Hnr Roll; Yth Ldrshp Prog; Comm Volntr; Hab For Humty Volntr; Chrch Yth Grp; DARE; Drma Clb; Emplmnt; FCA; Prom Com; Tchrs Aide; SP/M/VS; Stg Cre; Chrldg (V C); Sccr (V); Yrbk (R); Nursing; Physical Therapist; Union U; Belmont U

AYTES, CHRISTOPHER; MURFREESBORO, TN; RIVERDALE HS; (FR); Hnr Roll; Perf Att; FCA; Ftball (J); Swmg (V); Track (J); Wt Lftg (J); State Qualifier for Swimming; Criminal Justice; U of Tennessee Knoxville; Middle Tennessee State U

BAE, SUNG H; FRANKLIN, TN; CENTENNIAL HS; (JR); Hi Hnr Roll; Nat Hon Sy; Perf Att; WWAHSS; Comm Volntr; Red Cr Aide; Mth Clb/Tm; MuAlphaTh; Vsity Clb; Ch Chr; Tennis (V); 6th Place in State in Advanced Calculus Topic; 6th Place in State in Pre-Calculus; Aerospace Engineer; Physics; Massachusetts Institute of Technology; Georgia Tech

BAGBY, NICHOLAS W; CLARKSVILLE, TN; KENWOOD HS; (JR); F Lan Hn Soc; Hnr Roll; Nat Hon Sy; WWAHSS; Comm Volntr; Chrch Yth Grp; Mth Clb/Tm; Tchrs Aide; Spanish Clb; Bsball (V); County Academic Award Recipient; Business Administration Bachelors; Health & Fitness Bachelors; Austin Peay State U; Murray State U

BAILEY, BEN; LAWRENCEBURG, TN; LAWRENCE CTY HS; (SR); Ctznshp Aw; DAR; Hnr Roll; Nat Hon Sy; St Schl; WWAHSS; Peer Tut/Med; Spec Olymp Vol; AL Aux Boys; Chrch Yth Grp; DECA; Ntl Beta Clb; Sccr (V); Sch Ppr (E); Biology Major; David Lipscomb U

BAILEY, JESSICA; GREENEVILLE, TN; GREENEVILLE HS; (JR); 4H Awd; MVP; Nat Hon Sy; Pres Ac Ftns Aw; Sci Fairs; WWAHSS; Comm Volntr; 4-H; Emplmnt; FCA; Lib Aide; Scouts; Bnd; Flg Crps; Sftball (J); High School Math Teacher; Early Childhood; U of Tennessee in Chattanooga; Tusculum College

BAILEY, JOSEPH; WHITWELL, TN; MARION CTY; (JR); Perf Att; Pres Ac Ftns Aw; St of Mnth; Spec Olymp Vol; 4-H; Chrch Yth Grp; Emplmnt; FCA; Lttrmn Clb; SADD; Vsity Clb; Spanish Clb; Bskball (V); Ftball (V); Vsy Clb (V); Wt Lftg (V); Cl Off (R)

BAILEY, KENDRA; PULASKI, TN; GILES CTY HS; (JR); Hi Hnr Roll; Salutrn; USAA; ArtClub; Chrch Yth Grp; Emplmnt; FCA; Ntl Beta Clb; Chemistry II Student of the Year; Vanderbilt U; Samford U

BAKER, CODY M; ARLINGTON, TN; ARLINGTON HS; (FR); Hnr Roll; Peer Tut/Med; Chess; Ntl Beta Clb; Degree in Architecture; City Planner; U of Memphis

BAKER, JONATHAN T; SEVIERVILLE, TN; SEVIER CTRY HS; (FR); Hnr Roll; Perf Att; Sci Fairs; St of Mnth; Emplmnt; Cr Ctry (L); Medical Field; Novelist; Tennessee U

BAKER, TIMOTHY D; NASHVILLE, TN; WHITES CREEK HS; (SO); Hnr Roll; Perf Att; St of Mnth; Chrch Yth Grp; DARE; Bskball (J); Accounting; Attorney; Memphis State U

BAKER, TITUS; CROSSVILLE, TN; CUMBERLAND CTY HS; (FR); Ctznshp Aw; Hnr Roll; Perf Att; St of Mnth; 4-H; Chess; Chrch Yth Grp; DARE; FCA; Ntl Beta Clb; ROTC; Scouts; Ch Chr; Sccr (J); Navy-Pilot

BALDO, SHANNON; HENDERSONVILLE, TN; BEECH HS; (SO); Duke TS; Hi Hnr Roll; St Schl; St of Mnth; WWAHSS; Peer Tut/Med; Ntl Beta Clb; Tchrs Aide; SP/M/VS; Stg Cre; Lit Mag (R); Yrbk (R, P); Published in - Short Stories By Young Americans

BARBEE, ANISHA B; MADISON, TN; MAPLEWOOD COMP HS; (FR); 4H Awd; Hnr Roll; Otst Ac Ach Awd; Perf Att; Sci Fairs; Peer Tut/Med; 4-H; DARE; FCA; Bskball; Track; Vllyball; Stu Cncl (R); Pediatrician; Nursing; U of Tennessee; Vanderbilt

BARBEE, JOSEPH A; SODDY DAISY, TN; SODDY-DAISY HS; (FR); Hnr Roll; Nat Hon Sy; Perf Att; WWAHSS; DARE; Dbte Team; Ntl Beta Clb; Computer Aided Design Technology; Electronic Engineering Technology; U of Tennessee At Chattanooga; U of Tennessee At Knoxville

BARBER, CREWS; HOHENWALD, TN; LEWIS CTY HS; (FR); Hi Hnr Roll; Hnr Roll; MVP; DARE; Lttrmn Clb; Quiz Bowl; Golf (V L); Freshman of the Year in Golf; Batting Champ 4 Years in Baseball; Law; U of Tennessee At Knoxville; U of Memphis (TN)

BARBER, LAUREN P; ROCKVALE, TN; BLACKMAN HS; (FR); Bnd; Ch Chr; Jzz Bnd; Mch Bnd; Sch Ppr (R); Blackman Renaissance Action Team; Student Youth Leader; Engineering; Architectural Studies; U of Tennessee; Tennessee Tech

BARBO, CHELSEE D; CLINTON, TN; CLINTON HS; (JR); Hnr Roll; Pres Ac Ftns Aw; St of Mnth; Yth Ldrshp Prog; Peer Tut/Med; 4-H; DARE; DECA; Drma Clb; FCA; Key Club; Tchrs Aide; Spanish Clb; Stg Cre; Bskball (V CL); Sch Ppr (R); DECA Member; Boy & Girls Club Youth of the Year; Business Management; Foreign Language; Brevard College; Northwestern State U

BARGERY, KYLE; MUNFORD, TN; MUNFORD HS; (FR); Hnr Roll; WWAHSS; FCA; Key Club; Bsball (J); Business; UT Knoxville

BARNETT, BRITTANY; COLLIERVILLE, TN; ROSSVILLE CHRISTIAN AC; (SR); Duke TS; Hi Hnr Roll; Nat Sci Aw; Pres Ac Ftns Aw; Sci Fairs; WWAHSS; Comm Volntr; Hosp Aide; Red Cr Aide; Chrch Yth Grp; Emplmnt; Sci Clb; Competitive Horseback Riding; Riding Instructor; Biology; Marketing; Middle Tennessee State U; U of Mississippi

BARNETT, COLLEEN; ALCOA, TN; ALCOA HS; (SO); Duke TS; Hi Hnr Roll; MVP; Otst Ac Ach Awd; Perf Att; WWAHSS; Comm Volntr; Peer Tut/ Med; ArtClub; Chrch Yth Grp; Emplmnt; FCA; FBLA; Key Club; MuAlphaTh; Schol Bwl; Ch Chr; PP Ftbl; Sccr (VLC); Manager Boy's Soccer - 2 Years; Academic Letter- 2 Years Science, 1 Year Math; Mathematics and Physics / Chemistry; Secondary Level Teacher; Yale; Michigan Institute of Technology

BARNETT JR, MICHAEL C; SEVIERVILLE, TN; SEVIER CTY HS; (FR); Perf Att; Chess; ROTC; Ftball (J); National Junior Honor Society; Presidential Award of Academic Achievement; Culinary Arts; Mississippi State U; U of Tennessee

BARNEY, DARRYL M; MURFREESBORO, TN; OAKLAND HS; (FR); Hnr Roll; Ftball (V); Wrstlg (V); Attorney At Law; U of Tennessee At Knoxville

BARRETT, APRIL M; KINGSPORT, TN; DOBYNS BENNETT HS; (FR); Hi Hnr Roll; Perf Att; WWAHSS; Comm Volntr; Chrch Yth Grp; FCA; Key Club; Svce Clb; Bnd; Chr; Ch Chr; Mch Bnd; Elementary School Teacher; East TN State U; U of TN

BARRETT, KENNETH A; MURFREESBORO, TN; SIEGEL HS; (SR); 4H Awd; F Lan Hn Soc; Hi Hnr Roll; Nat Hon Sy; Otst Ac Ach Awd; St Schl; USAA; Valdctrian; WWAHSS; Yth Ldrshp Prog; Comm Volntr; DARE; Drma Clb; Jr Cls League; Key Club; MuAlphaTh; Ntl Beta Clb; Pep Squd; Prom Com; SP/M/VS; Cl Off (P); Most Outstanding Senior; 2005 Senior Prom King; English; Law; Vanderbilt U

BARRINGER, CHELSEY; APISON, TN; (FR); Hnr Roll; Peer Tut/Med; Red Cr Aide; Drma Clb; Bnd; Ch Chr; Mch Bnd; Pep Bnd; Tutor in Geometry Every Wednesday Until 4:00; Piano During Marching Season; Photography; Writer; Bryan College; U of Tennessee At Knoxville

BARTON, HUGHES A; MURFREESBORO, TN; OAKLAND HS; (FR); Hnr Roll; MVP; Chrch Yth Grp; FCA; Golf (V); Young Life Membership; U of Kentucky; OSU (Oklahoma)

BASKIN, ASHLEY; OLD HICKORY, TN; MC GAVOCK COMP HS; (SO); Hnr Roll; Perf Att; Sci Fairs; Comm Volntr; Chrch Yth Grp; Emplmnt; Vllyball (J L); U of Tennessee; Tennessee Technological U

BASS, KAITLYN E; KINGSPORT, TN; SULLIVAN SOUTH HS; (SO); Nat Hon Sy; Nat Mrt Semif; WWAHSS; Scouts; French Clb; Ch Chr; Dnce; SP/ M/VS; Company Member of the Kingsport Ballet Company; Foreign Languages; Business; Georgetown U; Emory U

BASS, PAIGE; ALEXANDRIA, TN; DEKALB CTY HS; (JR); Comm Volntr; Chrch Yth Grp; FCA; Scouts; Spanish Clb; Chr; Bskball (V); Business Major; Middle Tennessee State U; U T Knoxville

BATES, JUSTIN; HUNTSVILLE, TN; SCOTT HS; (SO); Electrical Engineering; U of Tennessee; Tennessee Technology U

BATEY, LA BREESHA; MADISON, TN; NASHVILLE SCH OF THE ARTS; (SO); 4H Awd; Hi Hnr Roll; Hnr Roll; Otst Ac Ach Awd; Perf Att; Sci Fairs; Comm Volntr; Peer Tut/Med; 4-H; Chrch Yth Grp; DARE; Dbte Team; Drma Clb; Emplmnt; Ntl Beta Clb; P to P St Amb Prg; Ch Chr; SP/ M/VS; Stg Cre; Stu Cncl (V); Invited to the Young Leadership Council; Did on Stage Acting Outside of School; Goals: Actress or Top Executive Over Advertising Company; Major: Marketing/Advert; Spelman College; Xavier College

BATSON, MONIQUE J; ANTIOCH, TN; BRENTWOOD AC; (MS); Duke TS; Hi Hnr Roll; Otst Ac Ach Awd; Peer Tut/Med; Chrch Yth Grp; Dnce; Drl Tm; Chrldg; Vllyball; Sch Ppr (R); Pre-Med; Duke U; Stanford U

BATTLE, JANELL; KNOXVILLE, TN; CENTRAL HS; (SO); Hnr Roll; Chrch Yth Grp; Scouts; Tchrs Aide; Ch Chr; Bskball (J); Chrldg (J); PP Ftbl (J); Track (J); Law; Business; Middle TN State U

BATTLE JR, FRED; NASHVILLE, TN; MADISON SCH; Hnr Roll; Perf Att; WWAHSS; Key Club; Stu Cncl (S); To Become a Film Director

BATTS, IYSHA; MEMPHIS, TN; KIRBY HS; (FR); Hi Hnr Roll; Hnr Roll; Otst Ac Ach Awd; Perf Att; Comm Volntr; Chrch Yth Grp; Scouts; Dnce; Vllyball (J); Veterinary Medicine; Anatomy; Howard U; Georgetown U

BAYKO, HEATHER A; KINGSPORT, TN; DOBYNS BENNETT HS; (JR); Duke TS; Hnr Roll; Nat Hon Sy; Pres Ac Ftns Aw; WWAHSS; Comm Volntr; Peer Tut/Med; Chrch Yth Grp; FCA; Key Club; Mth Clb/Tm; MuAlphaTh; Ntl Beta Clb; Prom Com; French Clb; Chrldg (VJC); Track (V); Cl Off (V); Stu Cncl (R); CR (R); Yrbk (R, P); Mock Trial Team; Pre-Vet; Communications/Advertising; Vanderbilt; Ohio State

BEAN, MICAH L; SEYMOUR, TN; KINGS AC; (SO); All Am Sch; Ctznshp Aw; Hi Hnr Roll; Hnr Roll; MVP; Nat Hon Sy; Otst Ac Ach Awd; Perf Att; Pres Ac Ftns Aw; Pres Sch; CARE; Comm Volntr; ArtClub; Biology Clb; Chrch Yth Grp; DARE; FCA; Mth Clb/Tm; Mus Clb; Schol Bwl; Chr; Bskball (V L); Ftball (V L); Sccr (V L); Wt Lftg (V); Cl Off (R); Stu Cncl (R); Pharmaceuticals; Radiology; U of Tennessee; Walters State

Bates, Justin
Scott HS
Huntsville, TN

Barringer, Chelsey
Apison, TN

Barbo, Chelsee D
Clinton HS
Clinton, TN

Baker, Titus
Cumberland Cty HS
Crossville, TN

National
Honor Roll
Spring 2005

Askew, Justin T
Central HS
Memphis, TN

Barrett, April M
Dobyns Bennett HS
Kingsport, TN

Bass, Paige
Dekalb Cty HS
Alexandria, TN

Batson, Monique J
Brentwood AC
Antioch, TN

BEARD, AMANDA; KNOXVILLE, TN; SOUTH DOYLE HS; (SO); Hi Hnr Roll; Nat Hon Sy; Sci/Math Olympn; St of Mnth; WWAHSS; Comm Volntr; Key Club; Scouts; Vsity Clb; Latin Clb; Bnd; Chr; Jzz Bnd; Sftball (VJ); HOSA; Medicine; Education; Vanderbilt U; U of Georgia

BEARD, TIARA N; JACKSON, TN; NORTHSIDE HS; (JR); Hnr Roll; Nat Hon Sy; WWAHSS; Comm Volntr; Key Club; MuAlphaTh; Ntl Beta Clb; Spanish Clb; Bskball (V); Cl Off (T); Community Service Award (Sponsored By the Sorority of Alpha Kappa Alpha); Pre-Med; Biomedical Engineering; Clark Atlanta U; U of Knoxville

BEASLEY, ELIZABETH; CAMDEN, TN; CENTRAL HS; (FR); 4H Awd; Nat Hon Sy; 4-H; Ntl Beta Clb; Published in - Into the Mystical; Fashion Design and Merchandising; Writer; Middle Tennessee State U

BEATTY, ELISABETH; FRANKLIN, TN; FRANKLIN HS; (JR); Hnr Roll; Hab For Humty Volntr; Chrch Yth Grp; Habitat for Humanity; Tennessee Choral Academy; Child Psychology; Elementary Education; Duke U; U of South Carolina

BEATY, GRANT; COOKEVILLE, TN; COOKEVILLE HS; Drma Clb; Scouts; Spanish Clb; Ch Chr; Dnce; SP/M/VS; Sch Ppr (R); Seminary; Engineer; BYU Utah; BYU Idaho

BECK, JASMINE; NASHVILLE, TN; NASHVILLE SCH OF THE ARTS; (SO); Ctznshp Aw; Hnr Roll; Perf Att; Comm Volntr; Chrch Yth Grp; FCA; Bnd; Dnce; Flg Crps; Mch Bnd; Track (V); Forensics Science; Howard U; UT (Knoxville)

BECKMAN, CHELSEY A; LAWRENCEBURG, TN; LAWRENCE CTY HS; (JR); Duke TS; Hi Hnr Roll; Hnr Roll; Nat Hon Sy; WWAHSS; Peer Tut/Med; 4-H; Chrch Yth Grp; DARE; Emplmnt; FBLA; FCCLA; Key Club; Ntl Beta Clb; Sch Ppr (R); Secondary Education; UTC UNA; MTSU

BEDWELL, JEFFREY; WHITE HOUSE, TN; (FR); St of Mnth; WWAHSS; Comm Volntr; Key Club; Lib Aide; Ntl Beta Clb; Ntl FFA; Stu Cncl; Delta, FFA, Key Club; Fireman

BELL, LINDSAY; COLLIERVILLE, TN; HOUSTON HS; (JR); Duke TS; F Lan Hn Soc; Hi Hnr Roll; Nat Hon Sy; Perf Att; WWAHSS; Comm Volntr; Spec Olymp Vol; ArtClub; DECA; Emplmnt; Key Club; Ntl Beta Clb; P to P St Amb Prg; Vice President of DECA; Marketing; Advertising; Indiana U; Kansas U

BENCITO, JESSICA D; LA VERGNE, TN; LA VERGNE HS; (FR); Hnr Roll; Perf Att; Chrch Yth Grp; DARE; Drma Clb; FCA; SP/M/VS; Chrldg (J); Scientist (Chemistry); Photography; MTSU-Middle TN State U; Belmont

BENGE, JOHN J; SPEEDWELL, TN; CUMBERLAND GAP HS; (FR); Comm Volntr; Emplmnt; FCA; Ntl FFA; Heavy Equipment Operator; Agriculture Science/Wildlife Mgmt

BENGE, WILLIAM J; LA VERGNE, TN; LA VERGNE HS; (FR); Hnr Roll; Perf Att; St of Mnth; 4-H; DARE; Jr Cls League; Mth Clb/Tm; Ice Hky (V); National Geography Bee; Psychology; History; U of Kentucky

BENNETT, BRIAN; CARTHAGE, TN; SMITH CTY HS; (SR); Ctznshp Aw; Hnr Roll; Perf Att; WWAHSS; ArtClub; Chrch Yth Grp; FCA; FBLA; Ntl FFA; Sci Clb; Tchrs Aide; Spanish Clb; Ftball (V); Cl Off (R); Physical Therapy; Graphic Art; Tennessee Tech U

BENNETT, ERIKA K; JONESBOROUGH, TN; DAVID CROCKETT HS; (FR); 4H Awd; Duke TS; Hnr Roll; Pres Sch; 4-H; Chrch Yth Grp; DARE; Ch Chr; Vllyball (J); Sch Ppr (R); Pharmacy; U of Tennessee at Knoxville; Wake Forest

BENNETT, HEATHER B; ATOKA, TN; BRIGHTON HS; (FR); Ctznshp Aw; Hnr Roll; Otst Ac Ach Awd; ArtClub; Chrch Yth Grp; FCA; Ntl FFA; Tchrs Aide; Chr; Ch Chr

BENNETT, JAVONNE; RIPLEY, TN; RIPLEY HS; (JR); Hnr Roll; WWAHSS; 4-H; DECA; Ntl Beta Clb; Bnd; Mch Bnd; Pep Bnd; Who's Who Among HS Students; Most Improved & Outstanding Freshman in Band; Computer Science; Computer Systems Analyst; U of Tennessee At Martin; U of Memphis

BENNETT, MEGAN; ROCKVALE, TN; EAGLEVILLE SCH; (SO); Hnr Roll; MVP; Otst Ac Ach Awd; WWAHSS; Peer Tut/Med; Red Cr Aide; Chrch Yth Grp; FCA; Ntl FFA; SADD; Tchrs Aide; Spanish Clb; Ch Chr; Dnce; SP/M/VS; Bskball (L); Scr Kpr (V); Swmg (V); Vllyball (L); Wt Lftg (L); Become a Teacher; Become a Coach; U of Tennessee At Knoxville; U of Texas

BENSON, FLOYD; MEMPHIS, TN; NORTHSIDE HS; (SO); MVP; Nat Stu Ath Day Aw; Otst Ac Ach Awd; Perf Att; Comm Volntr; Chrch Yth Grp; DARE; Drma Clb; FCA; Outdrs Clb; Bsball (V); Bskball (J); Ftball (J); Stu Cncl (P); Baseball, Basketball, Football or Be a Policeman; T.S.U.

BENTON, MALEIGHA; LA VERGNE, TN; LA VERGNE HS; (FR); 4H Awd; Hnr Roll; St of Mnth; Comm Volntr; 4-H; DARE; Drma Clb; ROTC; SP/M/VS; Nurse; Massage Therapy; Middle Tennessee State U; U of Tennessee Knoxville

BENZ, CHRISTIAN C; MEMPHIS, TN; RIDGEWAY HS; (JR); Hi Hnr Roll; Hnr Roll; Nat Mrt LOC; Sci Fairs; WWAHSS; Peer Tut/Med; Chrch Yth Grp; Cmptr Clb; Mus Clb; Scouts; Arch; Bsball; Gmnstcs; Swmg; Guitarist; Medical Sciences

BERNAL, JOSE; NASHVILLE, TN; (FR); Hnr Roll; Sccr; Engineer; Tennessee State U

BERNARD, MORGAN A; BRENTWOOD, TN; BRENTWOOD HS; (JR); Ctznshp Aw; Duke TS; F Lan Hn Soc; Gov Hnr Prg; Hi Hnr Roll; Nat Hon Sy; Otst Ac Ach Awd; St Schl; Yth Ldrshp Prog; Comm Volntr; Peer Tut/Med; ArtClub; Chrch Yth Grp; DARE; Dbte Team; Emplmnt; Fr of Library; Jr Ach; Key Club; Stg Cre; Bskball (J); Golf (V); Teen Advisory Board At Library; President of Book Club; Pre-Law; Cinematography; Duke U; Vanderbilt U

BERNARD, NICOLE; GATES, TN; HALLS HS; (JR); Hnr Roll; Comm Volntr; Peer Tut/Med; Spanish Clb; Bnd; Ch Chr; Mch Bnd; Pep Bnd; Lit Mag (E); Made All-West, TN Honor Band 5 Times; Was Once Named Best Woodwind; Psychology; Music (Instruments); U of Martin; Middle Tennessee State U

BERRY, HEATHER; KINGSPORT, TN; SULLIVAN NORTH HS; (JR); Comm Volntr; Spec Olymp Vol; DARE; Emplmnt; FCA; Key Club; Chr; SP/M/VS; Stg Cre; Nursing-Surgical; Milligan College; East Tennessee State U

BERRY, JESSICA; CHRISTIANA, TN; (SO); Chrch Yth Grp; Key Club; Ntl Beta Clb; Bnd; Mch Bnd; Pep Bnd; Mid-State Honors Band, All-County Band; Tennessee Ambassador of Music; Nursing Program-RN; After Becoming RN, Study CRNA; Middle Tennessee State U

BERRY, TROY; MURFREESBORO, TN; OAKLAND HS; (FR); Hi Hnr Roll; Hnr Roll; Otst Ac Ach Awd; St of Mnth; Peer Tut/Med; Chrch Yth Grp; High Profile Student; Broadcasting; Coaching; Middle Tennessee State U; U of Tennessee

BERTRAND, DAVID Y; HOLLADAY, TN; CAMDEN CTRL HS; (SO); Hi Hnr Roll; Otst Ac Ach Awd; Sci/Math Olympn; Emplmnt; Mth Clb/Tm; Spanish Clb; Mar Art (L); 1st Degree Black Belt - Assistant Instructor; Medical Doctor; Intelligence Service / Law Enforcement; MIT; Vanderbilt U

BERVOETS, JEREMY; FRANKLIN, TN; FRANKLIN HS; (SO); Hi Hnr Roll; WWAHSS; Comm Volntr; Chrch Yth Grp; Emplmnt; French Clb; Ch Chr; Swmg (V L); Excel Award (Hard Work, Dedication); Maroon and Gray Award (Team Leader); Archaeology/Anthropology; Civil Engineering; Drury U; Georgia Institute of Technology

BEST, EMMA; MARYVILLE, TN; WILLIAM BLOUNT HS; (JR); All Am Sch; Hi Hnr Roll; Hnr Roll; MVP; WWAHSS; Comm Volntr; Peer Tut/Med; Spec Olymp Vol; Chrch Yth Grp; DECA; FCA; Mth Clb/Tm; MuAlphaTh; Ntl Beta Clb; Off Aide; Tchrs Aide; Vllyball (V CL); MVP of Volleyball Team, All-District Team; Accounting; Tennessee Tech U

BEURIS, LAUREN; KINGSPORT, TN; DOBYNS-BENNETT HS; (JR); All Am Sch; WWAHSS; Comm Volntr; ArtClub; Chrch Yth Grp; FCA; Key Club; Prom Com; Swmg (V); All American-100 Butterfly 2004; Interior Design; U of TN, Knoxville

BEVERING, AMBER; SEQUATCHIE, TN; MARION CTY HS; (SR); 4H Awd; Hnr Roll; Yth Ldrshp Prog; Comm Volntr; 4-H; FCA; FCCLA; Pep Squd; Prom Com; SADD; Chrldg (V); Gmnstcs (V); PP Ftbl (V); Crime Scene Investigator; Middle Tennessee State U

BIALK, EVAN N; CORDOVA, TN; FIRST ASSEMBLY CHRISTIAN SCH; (SO); Hi Hnr Roll; Hnr Roll; Nat Sci Aw; Otst Ac Ach Awd; Sci Fairs; Yth Ldrshp Prog; Comm Volntr; BPA; Chess; Chrch Yth Grp; FBLA; Scouts; Spch Team; Bnd; Ch Chr; Pep Bnd; SP/M/VS; Bskball (V); Ftball (V); Cl Off (P); Stu Cncl (R); CR (P); Eagle Scout; Mid-South Fair Winner; Air Force Academy Engineering; Air Force Academy

BICKFORD, MELISSA M; SODDY DAISY, TN; SODDY DAISY HS; (JR); WWAHSS; Comm Volntr; DECA; Key Club; Stu Cncl (R); Student of the Day 2 Yrs; Poet of Year of 2005 for National Poet Society; Child Psychology; UTC-U of Tennessee At Chattanooga

BILBO, JESSICA M; CLEVELAND, TN; CLEVELAND HS; (SO); Hnr Roll; Pres Sch; WWAHSS; Comm Volntr; Chrch Yth Grp; Drma Clb; Off Aide; Chr

BILBREY, AMBER L; CROSSVILLE, TN; MONTEREY HS; (SO); Hnr Roll; FCCLA; Lawyer; Social Worker; U of Tennessee; Roane State Community College

BILHARTZ, SARA M; NASHVILLE, TN; ST CECILIA AC; (SO); F Lan Hn Soc; Hnr Roll; WWAHSS; Peer Tut/Med; Mod UN; Spanish Clb; Chr; Cr Ctry (J); Track (V L); MTVA Mid-State Women's Choir; Pre-Law; Texas A & M U; Vanderbilt U

BILLINGS, KACI; ARLINGTON, TN; ST BENEDICT HS AT AUBURNDALE; (FR); Ctznshp Aw; Duke TS; Hnr Roll; Chrch Yth Grp; FCA; Ntl Beta Clb; Cr Ct Ski (V); Forensic Science Field; Medical Field; U of Tennessee

BIRSE, JOUNIVIE M; MEMPHIS, TN; OAKHAVEN MIDDLE HS; (SO); Hnr Roll; WWAHSS; Voc Ind Clb Am; Stu Cncl (T); CR (V); RN; Business Administration; UT Martin; Eastern-State

BISHOP, JENNIFER; KINGSTON SPGS, TN; HARPETH HS; (JR); Hnr Roll; Cosmetics

BIVENS, CHRISTOPHER; SWEETWATER, TN; SWEETWATER HS; (SR); Hnr Roll; MVP; St of Mnth; WWAHSS; Peer Tut/Med; Chrch Yth Grp; Dbte Team; DECA; Emplmnt; FCA; Bskball (V L); Sccr (V CL); All-State Soccer; MVP Soccer; Tennessee Wesleyan College

BIVENS, JARROD; OLDFORT, TN; POLK CTY HS; (FR); 4H Awd; Hi Hnr Roll; Perf Att; WWAHSS; Yth Ldrshp Prog; 4-H; Chrch Yth Grp; Ntl Beta Clb; P to P St Amb Prg; Scouts; Ch Chr; Student Ambassador to Australia-People to People

BJORKLAND, AMANDA; MEMPHIS, TN; LAUSANNE COLLEGIATE SCH; (FR); Hnr Roll; Sci Fairs; Comm Volntr; Key Club; Fncg (J); Hsbk Rdg; Vllyball (J); Art Honor Society; National Junior Honor Society; History; Art

BLACK, JANA; OAK RIDGE, TN; OAK RIDGE HS; (JR); Duke TS; F Lan Hn Soc; Gov Hnr Prg; Hi Hnr Roll; Nat Hon Sy; Sci/Math Olympn; WWAHSS; Comm Volntr; Chrch Yth Grp; Drma Clb; Key Club; Mth Clb/Tm; Tchrs Aide; Spanish Clb; Orch; SP/M/VS; Mar Art; Skiing; Track; Stu Cncl (R); Tennessee Honors Program; Biomedical Engineering; MD/PhD Program; GA Tech; Duke U

BLACKBURN, BOBBY; FRANKLIN, TN; CENTENNIAL HS; (JR); Hi Hnr Roll; WWAHSS; Red Cr Aide; AL Aux Boys; DARE; Mth Clb/Tm; MuAlphaTh; NYLC; Off Aide; Bsball (V L); Electrical Engineering; Biomedical Engineering; Vanderbilt U; Tennessee Tech

BLACKWELL, ELIZABETH J; HARRISON, TN; CHATTANOOGA CTRL HS; (JR); Duke TS; Gov Hnr Prg; Hi Hnr Roll; Nat Hon Sy; Otst Ac Ach Awd; Sci Fairs; Sci/Math Olympn; WWAHSS; Yth Ldrshp Prog; Comm Volntr; Chrch Yth Grp; Dbte Team; FBLA; Mod UN; MuAlphaTh; Ntl Beta Clb; Svce Clb; Bnd; Mch Bnd; Stu Cncl (V); School Letters / Academics and Band; Artist's Creativity Award; Registered Dietitian; East Tennessee State U; Tennessee Technological U

BLAIR, CRYSTAL M; SEYMOUR, TN; SEYMOUR HS; (SR); F Lan Hn Soc; Hnr Roll; Nat Hon Sy; Pres Ac Ftns Aw; WWAHSS; Peer Tut/Med; Red Cr Aide; Spec Olymp Vol; 4-H; Chrch Yth Grp; DARE; DECA; FCA; Key Club; Ntl Beta Clb; Tchrs Aide; Bskball (J); PP Ftbl (V); Student of Distinction; Pre-Law / Criminal Law; Vanderbilt U; U of Tennessee

BLAIR III, HARRY; MEMPHIS, TN; HAMILTON HS; (SR); Hi Hnr Roll; Hnr Roll; Nat Hon Sy; Perf Att; Chrch Yth Grp; Bnd; Ch Chr; Jzz Bnd; Mch Bnd; 1st Trumpet for the Memphis Honor Band; Music Education; Bachelor of Science in Music; Jackson State U Tennessee State U; Alabama A & M U

BLAKELY, CORRITA; NASHVILLE, TN; WHITE CREEK SCH; (FR); Perf Att; WWAHSS; Hosp Aide; Chrch Yth Grp; DARE; Pep Squd; Sci Clb; Scouts; Tmpl Yth Grp; Ch Chr; Chrldg (V); Medical Career; GA State U; U of San Diego

BLAKEMORE, RANDEE; NEWBERN, TN; DYERSBURG HS; (SO); Hnr Roll; Nat Hon Sy; Sci/Math Olympn; St Optmst of Yr; Yth Ldrshp Prog; Comm Volntr; Peer Tut/Med; ArtClub; Emplmnt; Key Club; Photog; Stu Cncl (R); Yrbk (R, P); Medical

BLAYLOCK, PAMELA R; CAMDEN, TN; CAMDEN CTRL HS; (JR); All Am Sch; WWAHSS; ArtClub; BPA; Spanish Clb; West TN Art Competition; Clean & Green Contest Winner; Journalism; Business Degree; Murray State U; Belmont U

BLEVINS, LANA B; COOKEVILLE, TN; COOKEVILLE HS; (SO); 4H Awd; Hnr Roll; Otst Ac Ach Awd; Perf Att; Sci Fairs; 4-H; DARE; Ntl Beta Clb; Chrldg (J); Cr Ctry (J); Cosmetology; Business; U of Tennessee-Knoxville

BOCK, ANDREW J; COOKEVILLE, TN; COOKEVILLE HS; (SR); Hnr Roll; MVP; WWAHSS; Chrch Yth Grp; FCA; Chr; Cr Ctry (V L); Track (V L); Cross Country MVP 2003; National Spanish Honor Society; Athletic Training; Health / Physical Education; Middle Tennessee State U; Tennessee Technological U

BOES, KEVIN A; CORDOVA, TN; CHRISTIAN BROTHERS HS; (SO); Hnr Roll; Perf Att; Comm Volntr; Hab For Humty Volntr; Peer Tut/Med; Chrch Yth Grp; Spanish Clb; CR (R); Varsity Bowling; Computer Sciences; Engineering; Vanderbilt U; Christian Brothers U

BOGGS, MICHAEL; JOHNSON CITY, TN; SCIENCE HILL; (SO); Hi Hnr Roll; WWAHSS; Chrch Yth Grp; Sccr (J)

BOHANON, CHIQUITA; MEMPHIS, TN; WOODDALE HS; (JR); Hi Hnr Roll; Hnr Roll; Otst Ac Ach Awd; WWAHSS; BPA; Chrch Yth Grp; DECA; Emplmnt; Pep Squd; Scouts; Tchrs Aide; William H. Sweet Honors Award; PTSA Honors Award; Criminal Lawyer- Prelaw; Business Administration; U of Memphis; Tennessee State U

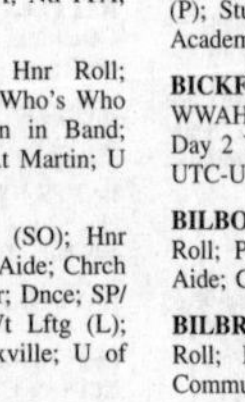

Blair, Crystal M
Seymour HS
Seymour, TN

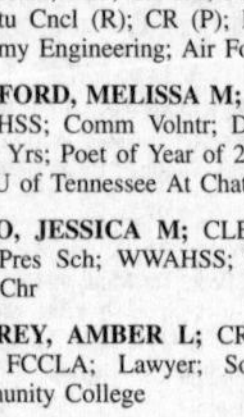

Bevering, Amber
Marion Cty HS
Sequatchie, TN

Beck, Jasmine
Nashville Sch Of The Arts
Nashville, TN

Bernard, Morgan A
Brentwood HS
Brentwood, TN

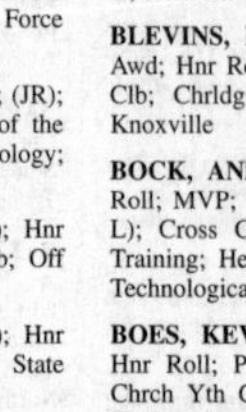

Bock, Andrew J
Cookeville HS
Cookeville, TN

BOMMER, MARK D; ESTILL SPRINGS, TN; FRANKLIN CTY HS; (SO); Hnr Roll; DARE; Web Design; Art-Animation

BONAGURA, ALYSSA; FRANKLIN, TN; FATHER RYAN HS; (JR); Yth Ldrshp Prog; Ch Chr; Dnce; SP/M/VS; Co Captain of Dance Team; Started the Dance Team; Music Production and Engineering; Berklee College of Music; New York U (Tish)

BOND, PROPHETESS P; NASHVILLE, TN; NASHVILLE SCH OF THE ARTS; (FR); Ctznshp Aw; Hnr Roll; Jr Eng Tech; Otst Ac Ach Awd; Perf Att; Yth Ldrshp Prog; Comm Volntr; Chrch Yth Grp; DARE; FCA; Lib Aide; Mus Clb; Ntl Beta Clb; Off Aide; Prom Com; Bnd; Chr; Ch Chr; Mch Bnd; Stu Cncl (P); Ministerial License-SOF; Ordination License-FVC; Architectural Engineer; Instrumental Musician

BONVILLE, MICHAEL; HOHENWALD, TN; GENERAL ASSEMBLY AC; (SO); Hnr Roll; MVP; Perf Att; Comm Volntr; Chrch Yth Grp; Emplmnt; Tchrs Aide; Wdwrkg Clb; Dnce; SP/M/VS; Stg Cre; Bskball (V C); Sccr (V); Tennis (V); Stu Cncl (T); College Dual Enrollment Program; Engineering; U of Tennessee; Middle Tennessee State U

BOOKER, ANITA; CLARKSVILLE, TN; NORTHWEST HS; (FR); Hnr Roll; Otst Ac Ach Awd; Perf Att; Pres Ac Ftns Aw; WWAHSS; Comm Volntr; DARE; P to P St Amb Prg; Chr; SP/M/VS

BORDEN, ROLONDA J; TEN MILE, TN; MIDWAY HS; (SO); Ctznshp Aw; Hnr Roll; Nat Hon Sy; Nat Ldrshp Svc; Nat Mrt LOC; Nat Mrt Sch Recip; Perf Att; St of Mnth; WWAHSS; Comm Volntr; Peer Tut/Med; Chrch Yth Grp; Emplmnt; FCA; Ntl Beta Clb; Ntl FFA; SADD; Chr; Ch Chr; Bskball (V); Hsbk Rdg (V); PP Ftbl (V); Veterinary Medicine; U of Tennessee Knoxville; Roane State Community College

BORUM, QUNETA; MEMPHIS, TN; FRAYSER MIDDLE HS; (JR); Hnr Roll; Comm Volntr; ROTC; Scouts; Drl Tm; Chrldg (V); Sftball (V); Medicine; Ob/Gyn; Arkansas State U

BOSHERS, AARON P; COLUMBIA, TN; COLUMBIA AC; (JR); Hnr Roll; USAA; Chrch Yth Grp; Emplmnt; Off Aide; Pep Squd; Bsball (V); Ftball (V)

BOTKIN, ALEX; PIGEON FORGE, TN; SEVIER CTY HS; (FR); 4H Awd; Hnr Roll; Perf Att; Sci Fairs; WWAHSS; 4-H; DARE; FCA; Key Club; Ntl Beta Clb; Quiz Bowl; SP/M/VS; Bskball (J); Chrldg (J); Cr Ctry (V); Sccr (J); Sftball (V); Track (V); Architectural Engineering; Pharmaceutical Sales; U of Tennessee; Florida State U

BOUNDS, EMILY E; KINGSPORT, TN; DOBYNS BENNETT HS; (JR); Duke TS; WWAHSS; Yth Ldrshp Prog; Comm Volntr; Chrch Yth Grp; Emplmnt; Key Club; Bnd; Ch Chr; Mch Bnd; Pep Bnd; SHOUT! Youth Leadership Graduate; AIMS Scholar; U of Tennessee At Knoxville; U of South Carolina

BOURG, ASHTON P; CLARKSVILLE, TN; NORTHEAST HS; (FR); Ctznshp Aw; Duke TS; Hnr Roll; Pres Ac Ftns Aw; Vllyball (J)

BOWEN, LANDON; MEMPHIS, TN; WHITEHAVEN HS; (FR); Hnr Roll; Nat Hon Sy; WWAHSS; Bskball (F); Architect / Engineer; UNC Chapel Hill; University of Tennessee Chattanooga

BOWERS, MISTY D; ATHENS, TN; MC MINN CTY HS; (SO); Ctznshp Aw; Hnr Roll; WWAHSS; Comm Volntr; Drma Clb; Emplmnt; Key Club; Tchrs Aide; Chr; SP/M/VS; Stg Cre; Vllyball (C); Physical Therapy; Teaching; Cleveland State; Technical

BOWES, MAXWELL A; CLARKSVILLE, TN; NORTHEAST HS; (SO); Hnr Roll

BOWMAN, ERIC; JONESBOROUGH, TN; DCHS; (SO); Hnr Roll; MVP; Otst Ac Ach Awd; WWAHSS; Chr; Wt Lftg (V)

BOYD, DANIEL; MC MINNVILLE, TN; WARREN CO HS; (FR); Hi Hnr Roll; St of Mnth; Comm Volntr; Chrch Yth Grp; Ntl Beta Clb; Ftball (J); Wt Lftg (J)

BOYD, DANIELLE A; NASHVILLE, TN; NASHVILLE SCH OF THE ARTS; (FR); Ctznshp Aw; Hnr Roll; Comm Volntr; Peer Tut/Med; Chrch Yth Grp; Ntl Beta Clb; Tchrs Aide; Bnd; Ch Chr; Mch Bnd; SP/M/VS; Stu Cncl (R); Mass Media; Business Degree (To Operate Own Business); Full Sail; Clark U

BOYTER, ANNA; WINCHESTER, TN; FRANKLIN CTY HS; (FR); Hnr Roll; WWAHSS; Comm Volntr; FBLA; Key Club; International Club; Accounting; Clemson U; U of Houston

BRADEN, KRISTEN M; PULASKI, TN; GILES CTY HS; (JR); Hi Hnr Roll; Hnr Roll; Perf Att; WWAHSS; Chrch Yth Grp; Pep Squd; Ch Chr; Excel Student; Pre-Med; Master's Degree; Tennessee State U; U of Tennessee Memphis

BRADFORD, HANNAH; DUNLAP, TN; SEQUATCHIE CTY HS; (SO); 4H Awd; Hi Hnr Roll; Hnr Roll; Otst Ac Ach Awd; WWAHSS; 4-H; DARE; Ntl Beta Clb; President's Award; Pediatrician; Pediatrician's Assistant; Sewanee; Middle Tennessee State U

BRADLEY, JOHN; CROSSVILLE, TN; CUMBERLAND CTY HS; (JR); Hi Hnr Roll; Hnr Roll; FCA; Mus Clb; Bsball (V CL); Fellowship of Christian Athletes; Play Baseball in College; Graduate to Be an Engineer; U of Tenn (Knox); Middle Tenn State U

BRADLEY, KELLEY A; MOUNT JULIET, TN; WILSON CTRL HS; (SO); Hnr Roll; Nat Hon Sy; WWAHSS; Chrch Yth Grp; FCA; Ntl Beta Clb; Ntl FFA; Quill & Scroll; Bnd; Chr; Clr Grd; Sccr (V); Track (L); Yrbk (E); Foreign Missions Volunteer; Humane Society Volunteer; Animal Science; Criminal Justice; Belmont; LSU

BRAGG, ASHLEY; KNOXVILLE, TN; FARRAGUT HS; (SO); Hnr Roll; Pres Ac Ftns Aw; WWAHSS; Comm Volntr; Chrch Yth Grp; Dnce; PPSqd (J); Y-Teens; Pre-Medicine; Auburn

BRAND, MAGGIE; CLARKSVILLE, TN; ROSSVIEW HS; (FR); Ctznshp Aw; Hnr Roll; Nat Hon Sy; Perf Att; Pres Sch; St of Mnth; Hosp Aide; SADD; Ftball (VJ); Sftball (J); Class Favorite; Interior Decorator; Austin Peay State U; International Academy of Arts

BRANDON, DUSTIN; LYNCHBURG, TN; MOORE CTY HS; (JR); 4H Awd; Hnr Roll; Nat Hon Sy; Perf Att; Comm Volntr; 4-H; AL Aux Boys; Emplmnt; Prom Com; Bsball (V); Ftball (V); Cl Off (V); CR (P); Real Estate; Lawyer; Middle Tennessee State U; Motlow State Community College

BRANNER, MICHELLE L; BRUSH CREEK, TN; GORDONSVILLE HS; (JR); Hnr Roll; Otst Ac Ach Awd; Perf Att; WWAHSS; Comm Volntr; Peer Tut/Med; Emplmnt; Ntl Beta Clb; Ntl FFA; Off Aide; Spch Team; Spanish Clb; Vice President of FFA Chapter; Accounting; International Business and Finance; Auburn U; MTSU

BRASEEL, SHELLY; SMITHVILLE, TN; DEKALB CTY HS; (JR); Gov Hnr Prg; Pres Ac Ftns Aw; WWAHSS; Mth Clb/Tm; Chr; Coroner; Archeology; Middle Tennessee State U; U of Tennessee

BRAXTON, KARYN; FRANKLIN, TN; FRANKLIN HS; (SO); Hnr Roll; WWAHSS; Spec Olymp Vol; 4-H; Chrch Yth Grp; DARE; Drma Clb; FCA; NYLC; ROTC; SADD; Bnd; Ch Chr; Dnce; Drm Mjr; Swmg (L); Adv Cncl (S); Honorary Bill At Youth Legislature 03 & 04; Neonatal-Nursing; Pediatric Nurse; Tennessee State U; U of Tennessee Memphis

BRAY, WILLIAM A; ELIZABETHTON, TN; SCIENCE HILL HS; (JR); Hi Hnr Roll; Hnr Roll; Nat Hon Sy; Perf Att; Pres Ac Ftns Aw; WWAHSS; Comm Volntr; Chrch Yth Grp; DARE; Emplmnt; FCA; Off Aide; Prom Com; Bsball (V); Ftball (V); Cl Off (V); Stu Cncl (V); Aeronautics; Air Force Academy

BREEDLOVE, MARY C; SOMERVILLE, TN; FAYETTE AC; (MS); Duke TS; Hnr Roll; Perf Att; Chrch Yth Grp; Bnd; Ch Chr; Mch Bnd; Pep Bnd; Cl Off (P); Law/Political Science; Film/Photography; Georgetown U; Mississippi State U

BREWER, ALEX; CORDOVA, TN; ARLINGTON HS; (MS); Duke TS; Hnr Roll; Nat Hon Sy; Comm Volntr; National Jr Honor Society; Presidential Honors; Fashion Design / Merchandising

BREWER, ALLISON J; CROSSVILLE, TN; CUMBERLAND CTY HS; MS; 4H Awd; Hnr Roll; Perf Att; Comm Volntr; 4-H; ArtClub; Chrch Yth Grp; Emplmnt; NYLC; Pep Squd; Wdwrkg Clb; Spanish Clb; Bnd; Jzz Bnd; Mch Bnd; Orch; Chrldg (J); Sftball (J); Vllyball (J); Went to State for 4-H for Fine Arts; Piano Performance; U of Tennessee; Juilliard School

BREWER, WHITNEY D; MEMPHIS, TN; FAIRLEY HS; (SO); Hi Hnr Roll; Otst Ac Ach Awd; Perf Att; WWAHSS; Comm Volntr; Chrch Yth Grp; Acpl Chr; Chr; SP/M/VS; Cl Off (V); CR (R); Classical Chorus; Club President; Medical Degree; Biology Major; Clark Atlanta U; Tennessee State U

BRIGGS, GRIFF R; CLARKSVILLE, TN; ROSSVIEW HS; (SR); Hnr Roll; Pres Sch; Sci Fairs; Peer Tut/Med; Cmptr Clb; FCA; Lttrmn Clb; SP/M/VS; Bsball (VJ L); Ftball (VJCL); Ice Hky (J); Lcrsse (J); Summer Mission - Russia; President's Scholarship - Austin Peay; English; Director/ Performing Arts; Austin Peay State U; Vanderbilt U

BRIGGS, JORDAN K; ERWIN, TN; U N 1001 CTY VOC SCH; (SR); Hnr Roll; 4-H; Chrch Yth Grp; Emplmnt; FCA; Ntl FFA; Pep Squd; Voc Ind Clb Am; German Clb; Ch Chr; SP/M/VS; Ftball (L); Track (L); CR (R); Turfgrass Management; U of Tennessee Knoxville; Middle Tennessee State U

BRIGHT, MARLON W; MARTIN, TN; MARTIN WESTVIEW HS; (SR); Hnr Roll; MVP; Nat Hon Sy; Otst Ac Ach Awd; Sci Fairs; WWAHSS; Comm Volntr; Spec Olymp Vol; BPA; Chrch Yth Grp; FCA; MuAlphaTh; Ntl Beta Clb; Sci Clb; Spanish Clb; Chr; Ch Chr; Bsball (V L); Bskball (V CL); Cl Off (P); Stu Cncl (R); National Achievement Corporation Scholar; Basketball - 004-2005 District 13AA MVP; Computer Engineering; Electrical Engineering; Florida International U; U of South Florida

BRITTON, MICHELLE; GREENBACK, TN; GREENBACK HS; (FR); 4H Awd; Hi Hnr Roll; Sci Fairs; 4-H; Ntl Beta Clb; Business

BROADHURST, DEL'ANDRE; GOODLETTSVILLE, TN; MADISON SCH; (FR); Hnr Roll; St of Mnth; Comm Volntr; DARE; Key Club; Vice President-Pokemon Club; President's Award for Educational Achievement; Military; SWAT Team / Police

BROADWAY, ANDREW C; COLUMBIA, TN; COLUMBIA CTRL HS; (FR); Duke TS; Hi Hnr Roll; USAA; Yth Ldrshp Prog; Comm Volntr; Hab For Humty Volntr; Chrch Yth Grp; DARE; Svce Clb; Bnd; Ch Chr; Jzz Bnd; Mch Bnd; Golf; Medicine; Law; Vanderbilt U

BROOKS, ALEX D; MEMPHIS, TN; CRAIGMONT HS; (JR); Hnr Roll; Sci Fairs; WWAHSS; DARE; DECA; Emplmnt; ROTC; Spanish Clb; Stu Cncl (R); CR (R); BA in Chemistry/Biology; BA in Criminology/Forensics; U of Tennessee At Chattanooga; U of Tennessee At Knoxville

BROOKS, ANGELICA; MEMPHIS, TN; HAMILTON HS; (JR); Perf Att; Sci Fairs; Peer Tut/Med; Mus Clb; NYLC; Chr; Ch Chr; CR (P); Criminal Justice; Music Education; TSU; Clark U

BROOKS, DELENA; MEMPHIS, TN; OAKHAVEN HS; (SR); Hnr Roll; Comm Volntr; Cmptr Clb; Emplmnt; Drm Mjr; Sftball (C); Cl Off (T); CR (V); Sch Ppr (P)

BROOKS, KENDALL; CORDOVA, TN; CORDOVA HS; (SR); Hnr Roll; Perf Att; Comm Volntr; Chrch Yth Grp; DECA; Bskball (V); Real Estate Management; Computer Repair; U of Tennessee Martin; Austin Peay State U

BROOKS, MARSHUN; MEMPHIS, TN; OVERTON HS; (SR); All Am Sch; Hi Hnr Roll; Hnr Roll; WWAHSS; Key Club; MuAlphaTh; Photog; Track (V)

BROOKS, VICTORIA L; THORN HILL, TN; WASHBURN HS; (SO); Hnr Roll; St of Mnth; FCCLA; Nursing; Walter State Community College; Lincoln Memorial U

BROWN, ALYSSA; MARTIN, TN; MARTIN WESTVIEW HS; (SR); Hnr Roll; WWAHSS; Comm Volntr; Chrch Yth Grp; Emplmnt; Off Aide; Clb; Bnd; Ch Chr; Jzz Bnd; Mch Bnd; Honor Band 4 Years; Quad State 2 Years; BS Education / History; Master's Degree / PhD; University of Tennessee Martin

BROWN, CAROLINE; PIKEVILLE, TN; BLEDSOE CTY HS; (FR); 4H Awd; Hnr Roll; USAA; WWAHSS; Comm Volntr; Peer Tut/Med; 4-H; Chrch Yth Grp; Svce Clb; Stu Cncl (R); United States Achievement Academy-Mathematics; RN / Medical Field; Chattanooga State; U of Chattanooga

BROWN, CHASTYNE; SAVANNAH, TN; HARDIN CTY HS; (SO); Comm Volntr; Hosp Aide; Chrch Yth Grp; Quill & Scroll; Tchrs Aide; Chrldg; Sch Ppr (E); U of Northern Alabama; U.T Knoxville

BROWN, INDIA; MEMPHIS, TN; RIDGEWAY HS; (SR); Hi Hnr Roll; WWAHSS; Comm Volntr; ArtClub; Key Club; MuAlphaTh; Ch Chr; Stu Cncl; William Sweet Award; US History BUILDERS Award; Pre-Dentistry; U of Tennessee Knoxville

BROWN, JAMES R; HUNTINGDON, TN; HUNTINGDON HS; (JR); Hnr Roll; Perf Att; St of Mnth; WWAHSS; Yth Ldrshp Prog; Comm Volntr; Hab For Humty Volntr; BPA; Chess; Chrch Yth Grp; Cmptr Clb; Emplmnt; FBLA; SP/M/VS; Sccr (V CL); English/Chemistry; Computer Science; Rhodes U; U of Virginia

BROWN, JESSICA; CHUCKEY, TN; DAVID D CROCKETT HS; (SO); Yth Ldrshp Prog; Comm Volntr; Ntl FFA; Track (V); Agricultural Science; King College; Milligan College

BROWN, JUSTIN; WARTRACE, TN; CASCADE HS; (SR); DARE; Drma Clb; Photog; Scouts; SP/M/VS; Stg Cre; Sch Ppr (P); United States Achievement Academy Recommendation; Architecture; Aerospace Engineering; Tennessee Technical U; Middle Tennessee State U

BROWN, JUSTIN L; MEMPHIS, TN; WHITEHAVEN HS; (SR); Hnr Roll; MVP; Nat Hon Sy; St of Mnth; WWAHSS; Chrch Yth Grp; DARE; Key Club; Bnd; Jzz Bnd; Mch Bnd; Pep Bnd; Bsball (V C); Physical Therapy; Engineering; U of Tennessee At Martin

BROWN, KATHERINE E; CAMDEN, TN; CENTRAL HS; (FR); 4H Awd; Hnr Roll; Nat Hon Sy; Nat Sci Aw; Otst Ac Ach Awd; Sci Fairs; USAA; WWAHSS; Comm Volntr; Spec Olymp Vol; 4-H; BPA; DARE; Emplmnt; Cl Off (T); Physical Therapy; Biology Sciences; U of Tennessee Knoxville; Middle Tennessee State U

BROWN, KAYLA; BAXTER, TN; UPPERMAN HS; (SO); Hi Hnr Roll; Hnr Roll; Comm Volntr; Chrch Yth Grp; DARE; FCA; Ntl Beta Clb; Bskball (V); Vllyball (V); Sch Ppr (R); Nurse Practitioner; Tennessee Tech; UT

BROWN, LAURA J; JOHNSON CITY, TN; SCIENCE HILL HS; (JR); Hnr Roll; Sci Fairs; Yth Ldrshp Prog; Comm Volntr; Peer Tut/Med; ArtClub; Chrch Yth Grp; DARE; Emplmnt; Marketing; Interior Design; Rochester Institute of Technology; Purdue U

BROWN, MEGAN A; MUNFORD, TN; MUNFORD HS; (SO); Hnr Roll; Comm Volntr; Chrch Yth Grp; Drma Clb; Ch Chr; SP/M/VS; Plays Piano for Church Choir; EMT; Theater Arts / Acting; Christian Brothers U

Brooks, Victoria L	Bradford, Hannah	Braden, Kristen M	Bond, Prophetess P	Borden, Rolonda J	Brewer, Allison J	Brown, Chastyne
Washburn HS	Sequatchie Cty HS	Giles Cty HS	Nashville Sch Of The Arts	Midway HS	Cumberland Cty HS	Hardin Cty HS
Thorn Hill, TN	Dunlap, TN	Pulaski, TN	Nashville, TN	Ten Mile, TN	Crossville, TN	Savannah, TN

BROWN, MIKEL D; COOKEVILLE, TN; LIVINGSTON AC; (SO); Perf Att; Comm Volntr; Peer Tut/Med; Chrch Yth Grp; Making Better Grades; Mechanics; Auto Body - Welding, Cutting (Torches)

BROWN, MYRON D; MEMPHIS, TN; CENTRAL HS; (SO); 4H Awd; Hi Hnr Roll; Hnr Roll; Red Cr Aide; Sci Fairs; WWAHSS; Comm Volntr; 4-H; Chess; DARE; Mus Clb; Sci Clb; SADD; Vsity Clb; Spanish Clb; Bnd; Mch Bnd; Bsball (V); Ftball (V); Wt Lftg (V); Business Management; Music; Howard U; Morehouse College

BROWN, SASHA M; MONTEREY, TN; MONTEREY HS; (SO); Hnr Roll; Perf Att; Hab For Humty Volntr; 4-H; BPA; Chrch Yth Grp; DARE; FCA; Ntl Beta Clb; Sftball (J); Vllyball (J); Cl Off (T); Student Congress on Policies in Education Delegate; 2004 / 2005 - Football Homecoming Attendant; Sports Medicine Degree; Physical Therapist; U of Tennessee; Tennessee Tech U

BROWN, STEVEN; DYERSBURG, TN; DYERSBURG HS; (JR); Duke TS; Hi Hnr Roll; Hnr Roll; MVP; Nat Hon Sy; Pres Ac Ftns Aw; Sci/Math Olympn; WWAHSS; Yth Ldrshp Prog; Comm Volntr; Peer Tut/Med; Spec Olymp Vol; Chrch Yth Grp; DARE; FCA; FTA; Key Club; Sci Clb; Svce Clb; Chr; Bsball (V CL); Bskball (V CL); Ftball (V L); Stu Cncl (R); CR (R); Basketball-ISAAA All-District and ISAAA All-Tournament; Baseball-ISAAA All-District and ISAAA All-Tournament; Pre-Medicine

BROWNER, SHANA; CHATTANOOGA, TN; BRAINERD HS; (SO); Nat Hon Sy; Perf Att; Red Cr Aide; Lib Aide; Bnd; Dnce; Sings Solo at Different Functions; Song at Local Radio Station; Acting & Singing Career; U of Georgia; U of Chattanooga Tennessee

BROYLES, MICHELLE L; ERWIN, TN; UNICOI CTY HS; Perf Att; Pres Sch; WWAHSS; ArtClub; FCA; FBLA; Key Club; Ntl Beta Clb; Scouts; Spanish Clb; Track (V); Sch Ppr; Girl Scout Gold & Silver Award; Girl Scout Cadet & Senior Leadership; Elem Ed Teacher; East Tennessee State U

BROYLES, STEVEN A; ERWIN, TN; UNICOI CTY HS; (FR); WWAHSS; Key Club; German Clb; Cr Ctry (V L); Track (V L); Top German I Award; Pharmacy; East Tennessee State U

BRUCE, ADAM G; LA FOLLETTE, TN; CAMPBELL CTY HS; (SR); Duke TS; Pres Sch; Sci Fairs; WWAHSS; Yth Ldrshp Prog; Comm Volntr; Chess; Chrch Yth Grp; DARE; Dbte Team; NYLC; Prom Com; Schol Bwl; Stg Cre; Pre-Law; U of Tennessee; Middle Tennessee State U

BRUMBALOUGH, KELLY; CROSSVILLE, TN; CUMBERLAND CTY HS; (FR); Chrch Yth Grp; Pep Squd; Pediatrician; Lawyer; Tennessee Technological U; Georgia State U

BRUNSON, NAKIA; MEMPHIS, TN; OAKHAVEN MIDDLE HS; (MS); Hi Hnr Roll; Hnr Roll; Nat Sci Aw; Perf Att; Peer Tut/Med; DARE; Scouts; Bskball (J); Track (V); College Track Trainer; Nurse; U of Memphis (MSU); Tennessee State U (TSU)

BRYANT, NIKKI; NEWPORT, TN; COCKE CTY HS; (SO); Perf Att; Sci Fairs; Hosp Aide; Chrch Yth Grp; FCA; FCCLA; Key Club; Bskball (V); Cr Ctry (V); PP Ftbl; Yrbk (R); Physical Therapy; Optometry; U of Southern California; UCLA

BRYANT, TABETHA; CLARKSVILLE, TN; ROSSVIEW HS; (JR); Hnr Roll; Chrch Yth Grp; Mus Clb; Tchrs Aide; Chr; Ch Chr; Chosen Christian Group; Massage Therapist; Music Teacher; U of Tennessee; Free Will Bible College

BRYCE, KELLYN E; LAWRENCEBURG, TN; LAWRENCE CTY VOC CTR; (SO); Hnr Roll; Perf Att; Vllyball (J); Interact Club, Educators Talent Search; Student Government & Association (SGA); A Degree in Interior Design; O'more College of Design; Middle Tennessee State U

BRYSON, TARAICA; MURFREESBORO, TN; OAKLAND HS; (FR); Hnr Roll; Perf Att; Hosp Aide; Chrch Yth Grp; DARE; Lib Aide; Cl Off (P); CR (R); DARE Essay 1st Place Winner; Health Care; Teacher; Middle Tennessee State U; Tennessee State U

BUCHANAN, ALISHA; MULBERRY, TN; MOORE CTY HS; (SO); 4H Awd; Perf Att; Spec Olymp Vol; 4-H; Pep Squd; Prom Com; PP Ftbl (V); Dental Hygienist; Elementary Teacher; Tennessee State U; Middle Tennessee State U

BUCKNER, SUSIE; MAYNARDVILLE, TN; UNION CTY HS; (SO); 4H Awd; Duke TS; Gov Hnr Prg; Hnr Roll; MVP; Nat Ldrshp Svc; Nat Mrt Fin; Perf Att; Pres Sch; Sci Fairs; Sci/Math Olympn; St of Mnth; USAA; Valdctrian; WWAHSS; Comm Volntr; Peer Tut/Med; Spec Olymp Vol; 4-H; Chrch Yth Grp; DARE; FCA; Fr of Library; Ntl FFA; Off Aide; Outdrs Clb; Voc Ind Clb Am; Wdwrkg Clb; Chr; Ch Chr; Clr Grd; Dnce; Cr Ctry; Dvng; Hsbk Rdg; Ice Sktg; PP Ftbl; Sccr; Sftball; Track; Vllyball; Wt Lftg; Sch Ppr (R); Doctor

BUGG, KIMBERLY; SPRINGFIELD, TN; SPRINGFIELD HS; (JR); Hnr Roll; Perf Att; WWAHSS; Comm Volntr; FCCLA; Education; Accounting; Austin Peay State U; Sullivan U

BUHL, JOANNA; POWELL, TN; HALLS HS; (SO); Ctznshp Aw; Hnr Roll; St of Mnth; Tchrs Aide; Elected Student Mentors; Psychology; Forensics Science; U of Tennessee

BULLARD, CHELSI; MEMPHIS, TN; MELROSE HS; (SO); Ctznshp Aw; Hi Hnr Roll; Hnr Roll; Nat Hon Sy; Sci Fairs; WWAHSS; Chrch Yth Grp; DARE; Ch Chr; Screen Writing; Psychology; Art Institute of California; Princeton U

BUMM, DANIEL; FRANKLIN, TN; FRANKLIN HS; (SO); Hi Hnr Roll; Hnr Roll; Comm Volntr; Chrch Yth Grp; Mod UN; Adv Cncl (R); Fishing Team; Architecture; Business; U of Kentucky; Harvard U

BURCH, AMBER; WOODLAWN, TN; NORTHWEST HS; (FR); Ctznshp Aw; Hnr Roll; Nat Hon Sy; Otst Ac Ach Awd; Perf Att; WWAHSS; Chrch Yth Grp; DARE; Chr; Ch Chr; Chrldg (V L); Highest Science Average; Lawyer; Harvard Law School; Princeton

BURDINE, TAURUS S; JACKSON, TN; SOUTH SIDE HS; (SO); Children's Doctor; Designer; Lane College

BURGESS, KATIE; PROSPECT, TN; GILES CTY HS; (JR); Hi Hnr Roll; Hnr Roll; Otst Ac Ach Awd; USAA; WWAHSS; Dbte Team; DECA; Emplmnt; FTA; Off Aide; Pep Squd; Prom Com; Chrldg (V CL); Stu Cncl (R); CR (R); Lit Mag (R); Sch Ppr (R); UCA All Star & Student-Athlete Merit Award; Distinguished Scholastic Achievement Award; Nutrition; Business & Communications; U of Tennessee (Knoxville); Belmont U

BURING, PAIGE; MEMPHIS, TN; RIDGEWAY HS; (JR); Hi Hnr Roll; Nat Hon Sy; Otst Ac Ach Awd; WWAHSS; Yth Ldrshp Prog; Comm Volntr; Key Club; Mod UN; MuAlphaTh; Off Aide; Tmpl Yth Grp; Stu Cncl (R); Student Rep at Board of Education; Criminal Justice; Foreign Language; U of Wisconsin; U of Kansas

BURKE, ANDREW; PINEY FLATS, TN; SULLIVAN EAST HS; (SO); WWAHSS; Key Club; Ntl Beta Clb

BURNS, CHRISTOPHER M; COTTONTOWN, TN; WHITE HOUSE HS; (SR); Ctznshp Aw; F Lan Hn Soc; Hnr Roll; Nat Hon Sy; Nat Mrt Fin; Nat Mrt LOC; Otst Ac Ach Awd; Pres Sch; WWAHSS; Comm Volntr; 4-H; Dbte Team; DECA; Jr Ach; Mod UN; Ntl Beta Clb; Cr Ctry (J); Ftball (J); Sccr (V L); Graduated in Top 10% W/Honors; Magna Cum Laude-Latin II Honors-2004; U of Tenn., Knoxville

BURNS, MOLLY R; DYERSBURG, TN; DYERSBURG HS; (JR); All Am Sch; Hi Hnr Roll; Hnr Roll; Nat Hon Sy; USAA; WWAHSS; Yth Ldrshp Prog; Comm Volntr; Peer Tut/Med; Spec Olymp Vol; Chrch Yth Grp; Drma Clb; Key Club; MuAlphaTh; Pep Squd; Prom Com; Spanish Clb; Chr; Ch Chr; Chrldg (V); Cl Off (P); Stu Cncl (R); CR (R); Yrbk (E); Pediatric Psychiatrist; U of Kentucky; Union U

BURNS, STEPHANIE; CLARKSVILLE, TN; MONTGOMERY CTRL HS; (MS); 4H Awd; Ctznshp Aw; Duke TS; Hnr Roll; Perf Att; Pres Sch; St of Mnth; Peer Tut/Med; 4-H; DARE; Drma Clb; Stg Cre; Bskball (J); Tennis (J); Vllyball (J); Yrbk (P); Bowling; Teaching; Nursing; Vanderbilt U; Austin Peay State U

BURNS, ZACHARY M; CARYVILLE, TN; CLINTON HS; (SR); Duke TS; Hnr Roll; WWAHSS; Emplmnt; Off Aide; Voc Ind Clb Am; Ftball; Wt Lftg; Lit Mag (R)

BUSH, ELISHIA A; MEMPHIS, TN; GERMANTOWN HS; (JR); Ctznshp Aw; Perf Att; WWAHSS; Yth Ldrshp Prog; Comm Volntr; Chrch Yth Grp; Emplmnt; SADD; Bnd; Ch Chr; Clr Grd; Mch Bnd; Chrldg (V); Health Care Administration; Business Management; Georgia State U; Xavier U

BUTLER, BOBBY; MT PLEASANT, TN; MOUNT PLEASANT HS; (JR); Hi Hnr Roll; Hnr Roll; Perf Att; Chrch Yth Grp; Emplmnt; FCA; Ntl Beta Clb; Ntl FFA; Pep Squd; Prom Com; Wdwrkg Clb; Ftball (V); Tennis (V); Adv Cncl (T)

BUTLER, JOSHUA; UNION CITY, TN; OBION CTY CTRL HS; (FR); MVP; Perf Att; Comm Volntr; Chrch Yth Grp; Mth Clb/Tm; Tchrs Aide; Graphic Art Degree

BYINGTON, AMY; SURGOINSVILLE, TN; VOLUNTEER HS; (SO); Hi Hnr Roll; Otst Ac Ach Awd; Comm Volntr; Peer Tut/Med; Chrch Yth Grp; Key Club; Svce Clb; Ch Chr; Pharmacist; Math Teacher; Carson Newman; Lincoln Memorial U

BYNUM, CYNTHIA R; SEVIERVILLE, TN; SEVIER CTY HS; (FR); 4H Awd; Ctznshp Aw; Duke TS; Hi Hnr Roll; Otst Ac Ach Awd; Sci Fairs; Sci/Math Olympn; St of Mnth; WWAHSS; Yth Ldrshp Prog; CARE; Comm Volntr; Chrch Yth Grp; Emplmnt; FCA; Mth Clb/Tm; P to P St Amb Prg; Quiz Bowl; Svce Clb; Bnd; Ch Chr; Jzz Bnd; Mch Bnd; CR (R); Junior Beta Club; Attorney At Law; Accountant; U of Tennessee; Harvard Law School

BYRD, LA TRICE; MILLINGTON, TN; MILLINGTON CTRL HS; (JR); Hnr Roll; Nat Hon Sy; Medical Assistant; Cosmetologist; Concord Career College; Southwest Community College

BYROM, PAUL E; JASPER, TN; RICHARD HARDY MEMORIAL SCH; (FR); Hnr Roll; Perf Att; Ntl Beta Clb; Bnd; Jzz Bnd

CABLE, MELANIE; RICEVILLE, TN; WALKER VALLEY HS; (SR); Hnr Roll; Nat Hon Sy; WWAHSS; Comm Volntr; Peer Tut/Med; FBLA; Ntl Beta Clb; National Society of High School Scholars; Treasurer of FBLA; Accounting; CPA; ETSU

CADWELL, CHRISSIE L; UNION CITY, TN; HOMESCHOOL; (SR); Hnr Roll; WWAHSS; Hab For Humty Volntr; ArtClub; Chrch Yth Grp; Drma Clb; Ntl Beta Clb; Spanish Clb; Bnd; Jzz Bnd; Mch Bnd; Track (L); Drama and Theatre; Music Education; Florida Southern College; U of South Florida

CAIN, MICHAEL C; MEDON, TN; SOUTH SIDE HS; (SO); Hi Hnr Roll; Nat Hon Sy; Perf Att; Pres Sch; Comm Volntr; Chrch Yth Grp; FCA; MuAlphaTh; Ntl Beta Clb; Ch Chr; Bsball (J); Ftball (V L); Aeronautical Engineering; Pharmacy; Middle Tennessee State U; Tennessee Technology U

CALDWELL, CAYLEE; LAWRENCEBURG, TN; LAWRENCE CTY HS; (SO); Hnr Roll; Nat Hon Sy; Chr; Vice-President of Anchor Club

CALDWELL, DAVID G; BRIGHTON, TN; BRIGHTON HS; (FR); Hnr Roll; USAA; Chrch Yth Grp; Scouts; Private Music Lessons-Trumpet & Guitar; NJHS - National Junior Honor Society

CALDWELL, JESSICA; COLUMBIA, TN; FRANKLIN HS; (SO); Duke TS; F Lan Hn Soc; Hi Hnr Roll; Hnr Roll; Pres Sch; St of Mnth; WWAHSS; Comm Volntr; 4-H; Chess; DARE; Key Club; Photog; Scouts; Presidential Service Award Nominee (for Volunteer Services at Saddle-Up Nashville); National Society of High School Scholars Member; Equine Management Major; Murray State U- Murray, KY; Midway U- Midway, KY

CALDWELL, ZACHARY L; RIPLEY, TN; RIPLEY HS; (JR); Hnr Roll; Nat Hon Sy; Chrch Yth Grp; DECA; Ntl Beta Clb; Ntl FFA; Electrician; Work for Power and Light

CALLISON, TRAVIS; ESTILL SPRINGS, TN; FRANKLIN CTY HS; (JR); Ntl FFA; Bachelor's of Science; UT Martin; UT Knoxville

CAMPBELL, ALLISON; RUTHERFORD, TN; GIBSON CTY HS; (SR); 4H Awd; Hnr Roll; St of Mnth; ArtClub; Chrch Yth Grp; Drma Clb; Emplmnt; Lib Aide; Pep Squd; Prom Com; Tchrs Aide; PP Ftbl (V); Vllyball (J); Sch Ppr (R); Yrbk (R); Health Occupations Students of America; Massage Therapy; West Tennessee Business College

CAMPBELL, HANNAH L; MEMPHIS, TN; EVANGELICAL CHRISTIAN SCH; (JR); Hi Hnr Roll; Hnr Roll; Nat Hon Sy; WWAHSS; Spec Olymp Vol; Chrch Yth Grp; Key Club; MuAlphaTh; Ntl Beta Clb; Photog; French Clb; Bnd; Ch Chr; Mch Bnd; Pep Bnd; PP Ftbl (J); Church Puppet Team-5 years

CAMPBELL, TALISHA; LA VERGNE, TN; LA VERGNE HS; (FR); Hnr Roll; WWAHSS; SP/M/VS; Chrldg (C); Pediatrician; U of Tennessee; Spelman

CAMPBELL, TIA L; ROAN MOUNTAIN, TN; CLOUDLAND HS; (JR); Hi Hnr Roll; St of Mnth; Yth Ldrshp Prog; Comm Volntr; Peer Tut/Med; ArtClub; Chrch Yth Grp; Drma Clb; Emplmnt; Fr of Library; Lib Aide; Ntl Beta Clb; Photog; Bnd; SP/M/VS; Cyclg; Wt Lftg; Cl Off (S); CR (R); Yrbk (P); Beta Club Library Tech / English, Science, Math, Music, Choir - Award / Principal's Pride Award; Major Science / Going to Become a Vet - Minor History / Music; Milligan College; King College

CAMPER, KASHIA; REAGAN, TN; SCOTTS HILL HS; (JR); SP/M/VS; Yrbk; Honors English / Biology

CAMPOS, JACOB; NASHVILLE, TN; MC GAVOCK COMP HS; (JR); Hi Hnr Roll; Yth Ldrshp Prog; Comm Volntr; DARE; Bnd; Jzz Bnd; Mch Bnd; Orch; Nashville Young Symphony; Mid State / All State; Music Performance; Composition & Theory; DePaul U; Eastman School of Music

CANNON, TESSILY N; LEBANON, TN; LEBANON HS; (SO); Hi Hnr Roll; Kwnis Aw; Otst Ac Ach Awd; Perf Att; Pres Ac Ftns Aw; Sci Fairs; WWAHSS; ArtClub; Chrch Yth Grp; Emplmnt; Key Club; Kwanza Clb; Spanish Clb; Spirit Award for English and Spanish; Genetics; Translator (Spanish); Duke U

CANTRELL, TIFFANY M; HARRISON, TN; CHATTANOOGA CTRL HS; (SO); Hi Hnr Roll; Hnr Roll; Pres Sch; WWAHSS; Comm Volntr; Emplmnt; FCA; Svce Clb; Tchrs Aide; Flg Crps; Chrldg (V); Stu Cncl (R); National Society of High School Scholars; English Award

CAO, THUYDUNG; MEMPHIS, TN; RIDGEWAY HS; (SO); Ctznshp Aw; Hi Hnr Roll; Hnr Roll; WWAHSS; Comm Volntr; ArtClub; Chrch Yth Grp; DARE; Key Club; Lib Aide; Outdrs Clb; SADD; Tchrs Aide; Ch Chr; Dnce; Scr Kpr (J); Tennis (V); Bridge Builder; Doctor; Fashion Designer; Christian Brothers U

CAO, THUYVAN; MEMPHIS, TN; RIDGEWAY HS; (JR); Ctznshp Aw; Hi Hnr Roll; Hnr Roll; Nat Hon Sy; Perf Att; WWAHSS; Comm Volntr; ArtClub; Chrch Yth Grp; DARE; Fr of Library; Key Club; Mth Clb/Tm; MuAlphaTh; Quill & Scroll; Ch Chr; Dnce; Scr Kpr (J); Cl Off (S); Stu Cncl (R); Bowling Team / Bridge Builder; Key Club Secretary / 1st & 2nd Places in Foreign Language Fair; Pediatrician; Pharmacist; Christian Brothers U; U of Tennessee

CAPPS, BRANDON; WAVERLY, TN; MC EWEN HS; (JR); All Am Sch; Hnr Roll; Sci Fairs; USAA; WWAHSS; Chrch Yth Grp; Emplmnt; Ntl Beta Clb; Sci Clb; Ch Chr; Cr Ctry (V); Tennis (V); Cl Off (V); Mechanical Engineering; Medical; Austin Peay-Clarksville; U.T-Martin

CARLTON, ANDREA B; ALAMO, TN; CROCKETT CTY HS; (FR); Hnr Roll; WWAHSS; Drma Clb; Chr; MD; Pharmacist; FL State; Miami State

Cao, Thuydung — Ridgeway HS — Memphis, TN

Caldwell, David G — Brighton HS — Brighton, TN

Bryce, Kellyn E — Lawrence Cty Voc Ctr — Lawrenceburg, TN

National Honor Roll Spring 2005

Brunson, Nakia — Oakhaven Middle HS — Memphis, TN

Campbell, Hannah L — Evangelical Christian Sch — Memphis, TN

Cao, Thuyvan — Ridgeway HS — Memphis, TN

CARMICHAEL, CHRISTOPHER; JACKSON, TN; NORTH SIDE HS; (SO); Hi Hnr Roll; Chrch Yth Grp; Latin Clb; Bsball (V); Ftball (V)

CARNEY, BRITTANY; CLARKSVILLE, TN; NORTHWEST HS; (FR); Hi Hnr Roll; Hnr Roll; MVP; Otst Ac Ach Awd; Perf Att; Hosp Aide; DARE; Vsity Clb; Bskball (V); Scr Kpr (J); Vllyball (V)

CARPENTER, KATIE M; MORRISTOWN, TN; MORRISTOWN-HAMBLEN HS EAST; (JR); Hnr Roll; Comm Volntr; Chrch Yth Grp; Registered Nurse; Walters State Community College

CARPENTER, KINSEY A; MEMPHIS, TN; EVANGELICAL CHRISTIAN SCH; (FR); Ctznshp Aw; Hnr Roll; WWAHSS; Comm Volntr; Chrch Yth Grp; Key Club; Lib Aide; Acpl Chr; Chr; Ch Chr; SP/M/VS; Key Club Grade Representative; Beta Club Secretary; Performing Arts; U of Alabama; Union U

CARRAWAY, LAWRENCE; MEMPHIS, TN; TREZEVANT MIDDLE HS; (SO); Hnr Roll; Bsball; Bskball; Mar Art (J); Marketing; Physical Therapy; Duke U; Baylor U

CARROLL, MICHAEL; MURFREESBORO, TN; RIVERDALE HS; (FR); 4H Awd; Hi Hnr Roll; Hnr Roll; MVP; Otst Ac Ach Awd; Perf Att; Sci Fairs; St of Mnth; 4-H; Chrch Yth Grp; DARE; FCA; Chr; Ch Chr; Bsball (J); Ftball (V); Skt Tgt Sh (V); Wt Lftg (V); Law / Lawyer; Architecture; Tennessee U; Florida State U

CARROUTH, WHITNEY; BELL BUCKLE, TN; CASCADE HS; (JR); Gov Hnr Prg; Hi Hnr Roll; Nat Hon Sy; Yth Ldrshp Prog; Chrch Yth Grp; Drma Clb; FCA; Key Club; Ch Chr; SP/M/VS; Cl Off (S); CR (R); Key Club - President; FCA Leader; Education / K-5; Physical Therapy; Middle Tennessee State U

CARSON, AARON; MARYVILLE, TN; WILLIAM BLOUNT HS; (SR); Hnr Roll; MVP; Nat Hon Sy; Peer Tut/Med; FCA; Bskball (V L); Ftball (V CL); Track (L); Business; Tennessee Tech U

CARSON, AMANDA L; ONEIDA, TN; SCOTT HS; (SR); Hnr Roll; Nat Hon Sy; USAA; WWAHSS; Hab For Humty Volntr; 4-H; Chrch Yth Grp; DARE; Drma Clb; Emplmnt; Mth Clb/Tm; Ntl Beta Clb; Pep Squd; Ch Chr; SP/M/VS; Chrldg (C); Gmnstcs (V); English Education; David Lipscomb U; Cumberland College

CARSON, DIANA; LA FOLLETTE, TN; CAMPBELL CTY HS; (JR); Hnr Roll; Nat Hon Sy; WWAHSS; ArtClub; BPA; Chrch Yth Grp; FCA; Key Club; Ntl Beta Clb; Golf (V C); Cl Off (V, S); Stu Cncl (P); Art; Architecture; Appalachian State U; Tennessee Tech U

CARTER, CHRISTA A; PORTLAND, TN; PORTLAND HS; (JR); Nat Hon Sy; WWAHSS; Comm Volntr; Chrch Yth Grp; DARE; Emplmnt; FCA; FBLA; Ntl Beta Clb; Scouts; Spch Team; Bnd; Ch Chr; Clr Grd; Jzz Bnd; Middle Tennessee State U; Western Kentucky U

CARTER, JAMES; MC KENZIE, TN; MC KENZIE HS; (SR); Ctznshp Aw; Hi Hnr Roll; Hnr Roll; Perf Att; Pres Sch; Sci Fairs; WWAHSS; Comm Volntr; Hab For Humty Volntr; Chrch Yth Grp; Emplmnt; Key Club; Lib Aide; Ntl Beta Clb; Ch Chr; Adv Cncl (T); Aeronautical Engineering; Visual Art; U of TN Knoxville

CARTER, PETER B; CLEVELAND, TN; BRADLEY HS; (SR); 4H Awd; Gov Hnr Prg; Hi Hnr Roll; Hnr Roll; Perf Att; 4-H; DARE; Wdwrkg Clb; Architect; U of Tennessee Chattanooga; U of Tennessee

CARTER, SHANTE N; SAVANNAH, TN; HARDIN CTY HS; (FR); Ctznshp Aw; Hnr Roll; Chrch Yth Grp; DARE; Emplmnt; Scouts; Bnd; Ch Chr; Mch Bnd; Hsbk Rdg (J)

CARTWRIGHT, ANNA; SMYRNA, TN; BLACKMAN HS; (JR); Hi Hnr Roll; Nat Hon Sy; Chrch Yth Grp; Key Club; Bnd; Mch Bnd; Over 20 Hours of Community Service; Clarinet Section Leader; Acute Care/Family Care Nurse Practitioner; Physician's Assistant; Trevecca Nazarene U; Middle Tennessee State U

CARUTHERS, ELISABETH; BIG SANDY, TN; CAMDEN CTRL HS; (SO); Hnr Roll; Nat Hon Sy; Chrch Yth Grp; Ch Chr; Chrldg (V); Stu Cncl (R); Yrbk (R); Middle Tennessee State U

CASON, LEE A; KNOXVILLE, TN; SOUTH DOYLE HS; (SO); Ctznshp Aw; Hnr Roll; Nat Hon Sy; St of Mnth; WWAHSS; Comm Volntr; Chrch Yth Grp; FBLA; FTA; Key Club; Chr; CR (R); Elementary Education; U of Tennessee At Knoxville; Furman U

CASTON, BRIAN; KINGSPORT, TN; DOBYNS BENNETT HS; (SO); Duke TS; Hi Hnr Roll; WWAHSS; Comm Volntr; Peer Tut/Med; Chrch Yth Grp; DARE; FCA; Jr Ach; Key Club; Ntl Beta Clb; Scouts; Spanish Clb; Bnd; Mch Bnd; Orch; Pep Bnd; Swmg (V L); Cl Off (P); Stu Cncl (R); CR; Veterinary Sciences; Engineering; U of Tennessee; Clemson U

CASTON, PAUL R; KINGSPORT, TN; DOBYNS BENNETT HS; (JR); Ctznshp Aw; Hi Hnr Roll; Nat Hon Sy; Nat Mrt LOC; Otst Ac Ach Awd; WWAHSS; Yth Ldrshp Prog; Comm Volntr; AL Aux Boys; Chrch Yth Grp; DARE; Emplmnt; Jr Cls League; Key Club; Mus Clb; Ntl Beta Clb; Bnd; Jzz Bnd; Mch Bnd; Orch; Swmg (J L); Track; Stu Cncl (R); Civil Engineering; Political Science; United States Military Academy; Clemson U

CASTOR, JONATHAN; LIMESTONE, TN; CHUCKEY-DOAK HS; (FR); Hi Hnr Roll; Hnr Roll; Bsball (VJ); Bskball (VJ); Cr Ctry (V); Engineering MSME degree; Natural Sciences, Physics, Biology & Chemistry; Georgia Institute of Technology

CATES, BRANDY N; CROSSVILLE, TN; CUMBERLAND CTY HS; MS; Hnr Roll; Perf Att; WWAHSS; Ntl Beta Clb; Orch; Chrldg (J); Solo Ensemble (Violin); CPA

CATES, ERIN M; BENTON, TN; POLK CO. HS; (FR); 4H Awd; Hi Hnr Roll; Hnr Roll; Otst Ac Ach Awd; Perf Att; Comm Volntr; 4-H; Chrch Yth Grp; DARE; FCA; Ntl Beta Clb; Pep Squd; Quiz Bowl; Sci Clb; Ch Chr; Vllyball (J); Stu Cncl (R); CR (R)

CATHEY, AMBER A; MEMPHIS, TN; MELROSE HS; (FR); Hnr Roll; Nat Hon Sy; 4-H; DARE; ROTC; Chr; Nursing; Music; U of Memphis

CESARINI, MARY C; PULASKI, TN; GILES CTY HS; (JR); 4H Awd; Ctznshp Aw; F Lan Hn Soc; Gov Hnr Prg; Hi Hnr Roll; Jr Rot; Pres Sch; St of Mnth; WWAHSS; Comm Volntr; Red Cr Aide; 4-H; AL Aux Girls; Chrch Yth Grp; DECA; Drma Clb; Emplmnt; FCA; FTA; Chr; Ch Chr; Dnce; SP/M/VS; Chrldg (V L); Hsbk Rdg; Stu Cncl (S, R); President of Rotary Sponsored Interest; Vice-President of DECA; Veterinary Medicine; Biochemistry; Vanderbilt U; Rhodes College

CHAFFIN, JENNIFER N; EAGLEVILLE, TN; EAGLEVILLE SCH; (SO); Hi Hnr Roll; Hnr Roll; Perf Att; WWAHSS; Chrch Yth Grp; P to P St Amb Prg; Spanish Clb; Sftball (C); Middle Tennessee State U; Tennessee State U

CHAMBERLIN, KEVIN; CROSSVILLE, TN; CUMBERLAND CTY HS; (SO); Hi Hnr Roll; Hnr Roll; Yth Ldrshp Prog; Emplmnt; Ntl Beta Clb; Outdrs Clb; German Clb; Bnd; Mch Bnd; Skt Tgt Sh (V CL); Student Tutor, Church Softball; Young Republicans, PTSA; Architecture; U of Cincinnati; Auburn U

CHAMBERS, MONICA; MEMPHIS, TN; CRAIGMONT HS; (JR); Hi Hnr Roll; Nat Hon Sy; WWAHSS; MuAlphaTh; Svce Clb; French Clb; Ch Chr; Vllyball (V); Cl Off (S); CR (R); Business Administration/Management/International; Pre-Law; Washington U in St Louis; DePaul U

CHAMBERS, TARA; LEBANON, TN; LEBANON HS; (JR); Nat Hon Sy; WWAHSS; Comm Volntr; Key Club; Spanish Clb; Dnce; Sccr (V L); Stu Cncl; Yrbk; Music; Fashion; Long Beach City College; Volunteer State Community College

CHANDLER, JEREMY; CLARKSVILLE, TN; CLARKSVILLE HS; (JR); Hnr Roll; Comm Volntr; Chrch Yth Grp; Drma Clb; FCA; Tchrs Aide; SP/M/VS; Sccr (VJ L); Wrstlg (VJ L); Stu Cncl (R); Academic Award Recipient; Letter Winner-Academics; Broadcast Communications; Western KY U; U of TN-Martin

CHANDLER, LEKIVA M; MEMPHIS, TN; MELROSE HS; (FR); Hnr Roll; Peer Tut/Med; 4-H; DARE; Drma Clb; Dnce; SP/M/VS; TSU; Miami U

CHANDLER, ROBERT C; CHATTANOOGA, TN; CENTRAL HS; (FR); Hi Hnr Roll; Hnr Roll; Perf Att; DARE; FBLA; Bnd; Mch Bnd; Pep Bnd; 4 Years- Chattanooga Boys Choir; Responsibility Character Trade Award; Robotics Engineering; Allied Health; U of Tennessee Chattanooga; Middle Tennessee State U

CHANGKACHITH, LOUANNE; CORDOVA, TN; HOUSTON HS; (SO); Ctznshp Aw; Hi Hnr Roll; Hnr Roll; Perf Att; Sci Fairs; Comm Volntr; Peer Tut/Med; DARE; Mus Clb; Pep Squd; Chr; Ch Chr; Dnce; Orch; Chrldg (J); PPSqd (J); Medical Field; Interior Designer; U of Memphis; U of Alabama

CHAPMAN, MICHELE; PINEY FLATS, TN; SULLIVAN EAST HS; Hnr Roll; Otst Ac Ach Awd; Perf Att; Chrch Yth Grp; FCA; Tchrs Aide; Dnce; SP/M/VS; Chrldg; Vllyball; Cl Off (V); Public Speaking 4-H Award

CHARLES, RALPH; NASHVILLE, TN; GLEN CLIFF HS; (MS); Sccr

CHASTAIN, ASHLEY E; HARRISON, TN; CHATTANOOGA CTRL HS; (JR); Hi Hnr Roll; Hnr Roll; WWAHSS; FBLA; Bnd; Dnce; Mch Bnd; PP Ftbl; 12 Years of Ballet; UT Chattanooga; UT Knoxville

CHATHAM, NATHAN; DYERSBURG, TN; DYERSBURG HS; (JR); Hi Hnr Roll; Kwnis Aw; Nat Hon Sy; WWAHSS; Comm Volntr; Peer Tut/Med; Spec Olymp Vol; Chrch Yth Grp; FCA; Key Club; Ch Chr; Bskball (V); Sccr (V); Stu Cncl (R)

CHEEKS, ERIC L; MEMPHIS, TN; CARVER HS; (SO); Ctznshp Aw; Hnr Roll; Nat Hon Sy; Nat Mrt LOC; Perf Att; WWAHSS; Comm Volntr; BPA; Chrch Yth Grp; Cmptr Clb; Drma Clb; FBLA; Chr; Ch Chr; SP/M/VS; Stg Cre; Sch Ppr (P); Yrbk (P); Stir Up the Gift Award; Lane College; U of Tennessee Martin

CHERRY, KAYLA D; RED BOILING SPRINGS, TN; HERMITAGE SPRINGS SCH; (JR); Hnr Roll; WWAHSS; 4-H; BPA; FCCLA; Ntl FFA; Prom Com; Who's Who; Cosmetology

CHINERY, SARA; JACKSON, TN; NORTH SIDE HS; (JR); Hnr Roll; WWAHSS; Comm Volntr; Chrch Yth Grp; Drma Clb; Latin Clb; Chr; Ch Chr; Dnce; SP/M/VS; Community Theatre; Communications; Theatre; Union U; Southern Methodist U

CHRISTIANER, DEVEN; SEVIERVILLE, TN; SEVIER CTY HS; (FR); Hnr Roll; Perf Att; Chrch Yth Grp; ITT Technical Institute

CHRISTIANSON, LAWREN; MURFREESBORO, TN; SIEGEL HS; (SO); Ctznshp Aw; Hnr Roll; WWAHSS; Comm Volntr; Hosp Aide; Chrch Yth Grp; Drma Clb; FCA; Jr Cls League; Key Club; Pep Squd; Latin Clb; Chr; Ch Chr; SP/M/VS; Bskball (V); Medicine; Business; U of Tennessee Knoxville; Middle Tennessee State U

CLABO, TIM; SEVIERVILLE, TN; SEVIER CTY HS; (FR); Hnr Roll; St of Mnth; DARE; Emplmnt; Algebra I Achievement Award; Regional Math Competition; Video Game Designs; Business Degree

CLARK, ALISON G; KINGSPORT, TN; SULLIVAN SOUTH HS; (JR); Duke TS; Nat Hon Sy; Chrch Yth Grp; Emplmnt; FCA; Cr Ctry (V); Sccr (V); Track (V); Vllyball (J); International Studies/Archeology; U of Tennessee; U of South Carolina

CLARK, CONSTANCE; SODDY DAISY, TN; SODDY DAISY HS; (SO); Hnr Roll; WWAHSS; Comm Volntr; Chrch Yth Grp; FCA; Key Club; Kwanza Clb; Ntl Beta Clb; Ch Chr; Chrldg (V CL); Yrbk (R, P); Marine Biology; Florida State; U of TN Knoxville

CLARK, GABRIELLE; MURFREESBORO, TN; OAKLAND HS; (SO); Perf Att; Sci Fairs; St of Mnth; Comm Volntr; Hab For Humty Volntr; Peer Tut/Med; Chrch Yth Grp; Emplmnt; FCA; Tchrs Aide; Spanish Clb; Chr; Dnce; SP/M/VS; Chrldg (V); Gmnstcs; PPSqd (V); Cl Off (S); Sch Ppr; Also Nominated for Who's Who; Journalism; Communications; Spelman College; Xavier U

CLARK, HANNAH E; MORRISTOWN, TN; MORRISTOWN EAST HS; (SR); WWAHSS; Peer Tut/Med; Spec Olymp Vol; Chrch Yth Grp; Emplmnt; Tchrs Aide; French Clb; Bskball (J L); Cr Ctry (V); PP Ftbl (V C); Track (V); Vllyball (VJCL); Stu Cncl (R); CR; Yrbk (P); TSSAA - Academic Achievement Award; Interact Club; BS / Master's Degree Nursing; Walters State Community College

CLARK, KATRINA; MONTEREY, TN; MONTEREY HS; (SO); Hnr Roll; Sci Fairs; St of Mnth; ArtClub; FCA; Ntl Beta Clb; Chrldg (VJC); PP Ftbl (V); Cl Off (S); CR (R); President's Award for Educational Achievement - 6th-8th; Occupational Therapy; Registered Nurse; U of Tennessee; Tennessee Technological U

CLARK, MARISSA; HENDERSONVILLE, TN; HENDERSONVILLE HS; (FR); Ctznshp Aw; DAR; Hi Hnr Roll; Nat Hon Sy; Pres Sch; St of Mnth; Comm Volntr; Peer Tut/Med; Chrch Yth Grp; Drma Clb; Emplmnt; FCA; FCCLA; P to P St Amb Prg; Photog; Scouts; Chr; Ch Chr; Dnce; SP/M/VS; PP Ftbl (J); Swmg (J); Track (J); Stu Cncl (R); CR (R); Sch Ppr (P); 2nd Place Winner Patriot's Pen Essay Contest; Theatre and the Arts; New York U; Western Kentucky U

CLARK, MARY E; COSBY, TN; COSBY HS; (SO); Hi Hnr Roll; Nat Hon Sy; Valdctrian; WWAHSS; Peer Tut/Med; Drma Clb; Emplmnt; Schol Bwl; Ch Chr; SP/M/VS; Vllyball (V); Cl Off (V); Stu Cncl; Sch Ppr (R); Yrbk (P); Drama Major; Liberal Arts & Sciences / Associate's Degree; Brandeis U; U of Nebraska Omaha

CLARK, NIKKI; CHURCH HILL, TN; VOLUNTEER HS; (SR); All Am Sch; Ctznshp Aw; Hi Hnr Roll; Hnr Roll; Nat Hon Sy; Otst Ac Ach Awd; Perf Att; WWAHSS; Comm Volntr; Hosp Aide; Peer Tut/Med; BPA; Chrch Yth Grp; Cmptr Clb; DARE; Emplmnt; Jr Ach; Key Club; Ntl Beta Clb; Chrldg (V CL); Track (V L); Wt Lftg (V); Yrbk (E, R, P); Pre-Med; Biology; East Tennessee State U

CLARY, AMANDA K; GALLATIN, TN; STATION CAMP HS; (JR); Chrch Yth Grp; Mus Clb; Prom Com; Spanish Clb; Chr; Ch Chr; Middle Tennessee State U; U of Tennessee-Knoxville

CLAY, RICHARD D; MADISON, TN; HUNTERS LANE HS; (SR); WWAHSS; Peer Tut/Med; Drma Clb; Key Club; MuAlphaTh; Photog; ROTC; Acpl Chr; Mch Bnd; SP/M/VS; Stg Cre; Cl Off (V); Yrbk (E, R, P); Recording Technology (Music); Middle Tennessee State U; U of Memphis

CLEGG, ANNA; SODDY DAISY, TN; SODDY-DAISY HS; (FR); Ctznshp Aw; DAR; Duke TS; Hi Hnr Roll; Kwnis Aw; Otst Ac Ach Awd; Sci Fairs; Comm Volntr; Chrch Yth Grp; DARE; Tchrs Aide; Church Basketball; Nursing; U of Tennessee At Knoxville; U of Tennessee At Chattanooga

CLELLAND, JOANIE; COSBY, TN; COSBY; (SO); Ctznshp Aw; Hnr Roll; Kwnis Aw; Nat Sci Aw; Yth Ldrshp Prog; Peer Tut/Med; Chrch Yth Grp; Drma Clb; Key Club; Ntl FFA; SP/M/VS; Scr Kpr (J); Sftball (J); Vllyball (J); Yrbk (R)

CLEMENS, CHRISTINA; KINGSPORT, TN; SULLIVAN SOUTH HS; (SO); Hi Hnr Roll; Hnr Roll; Otst Ac Ach Awd; Perf Att; Pres Sch; WWAHSS; Bnd; Pep Bnd; High Placing in Writing & Art Contest (NIE); Solo & Ensemble High Score (I); Psychology; Teaching

CLEMENT III, JOSEPH D A; MURFREESBORO, TN; FRANKLIN ROAD CHRISTIAN SCH; (SO); Hnr Roll; Nat Hon Sy; St of Mnth; USAA; WWAHSS; Chrch Yth Grp; Chr; Ch Chr; Bsball; Bskball; Cl Off (V); Coach Little League Basketball; Pensacola Christian College

Clark, Mary E
Cosby HS
Cosby, TN

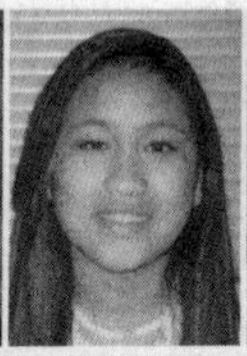
Changkachith, Louanne
Houston HS
Cordova, TN

Cates, Brandy N
Cumberland Cty HS
Crossville, TN

Chandler, Robert C
Central HS
Chattanooga, TN

Clegg, Anna
Soddy-Daisy HS
Soddy Daisy, TN

CLIMER, MEGAN; NASHVILLE, TN; FRANKLIN HS; (SO); Duke TS; Hi Hnr Roll; Nat Mrt LOC; WWAHSS; Comm Volntr; FCA; Jr Ach; Mth Clb/Tm; Mod UN; Scouts; Cl Off (P); Stu Cncl (P); Biology; Pre-Med; Duke U; Vanderbilt U

COBB, JUSTIN W; WHITE PINE, TN; JEFFERSON CTY HS; (JR); Hnr Roll; Perf Att; WWAHSS; 4-H; Chrch Yth Grp; Ntl FFA; Scouts; Bnd; Jzz Bnd; Mch Bnd; Arch; Skt Tgt Sh; Carson-Newman College; UT @ Knoxville

COBB, MYKILA; JACKSON, TN; NORTH SIDE HS; (SO); WWAHSS; Chrch Yth Grp; Key Club; Chrldg (V); Track (V); Stu Cncl (R); Clark Atlanta U

COBBS, KEVIN; MEMPHIS, TN; FRAYSER MIDDLE HS; (MS); Ctznshp Aw; Hnr Roll; Perf Att; Ftball (J); Art; Computer Animation; Duke U; Harvard U

COE, AMBER D; MURFREESBORO, TN; BLACKMAN HS; (SO); Ctznshp Aw; Duke TS; Hi Hnr Roll; Hnr Roll; Nat Hon Sy; Otst Ac Ach Awd; St of Mnth; WWAHSS; Comm Volntr; Peer Tut/Med; DARE; Key Club; Ntl Beta Clb; Off Aide; Svce Clb; Bnd; Mch Bnd; Sch Ppr (E, R); Volleyball Manager; Elementary Teacher; Middle Tennessee State U; UT Martin

COFFEY, SARAH A; SMYRNA, TN; BLACKMAN HS; (FR); 4H Awd; Ctznshp Aw; Hi Hnr Roll; Otst Ac Ach Awd; St of Mnth; WWAHSS; Comm Volntr; 4-H; Chrch Yth Grp; Key Club; Presidents Volunteer Service Award

COLE, ELIZABETH; MC MINNVILLE, TN; WARREN CTY HS; (SO); Hnr Roll; Sch Ppr (R, P); Bowling Team; New Age Beauty Academy; Motlow Community College

COLE, MARIO M; MEMPHIS, TN; KIRBY HS; (SR); Hnr Roll; Nat Hon Sy; Perf Att; Comm Volntr; Chrch Yth Grp; Emplmnt; FCA; Member of Christ Missionary Baptist Church Pastor Gina M. Steiner; I Want to Be a Chef; Physical Therapist; U of M College; Southwest Tennessee College

COLE, RAVEN S; ALAMO, TN; CROCKETT CTY HS; (FR); Hi Hnr Roll; Chrch Yth Grp; HOSA-Health Occupation Students of America; Major in Medical Field or Major in Law; Minor in Journalism; Lambuth U and Union U; Memphis State

COLE, STEVEN C; BLOUNTVILLE, TN; SULLIVAN CTRL HS; (SR); Hi Hnr Roll; Hnr Roll; Perf Att; WWAHSS; Yth Ldrshp Prog; Comm Volntr; Emplmnt; FBLA; Key Club; Ntl Beta Clb; Off Aide; Svce Clb; Tennis (VJ); Sch Ppr (R); AIM Scholar; Pre-Med; Biology; East Tennessee State U

COLEMAN, SIMONE R; CULLEOKA, TN; CULLEOKA HS; (JR); Sci Fairs; Yth Ldrshp Prog; Spec Olymp Vol; DECA; FCA; FBLA; FCCLA; Pep Squd; Prom Com; Pep Bnd; Bskball (V); Vllyball (V); Stu Cncl (S); Sch Ppr (R); National American Miss Pageant; Social Work; Journalism; U of Tennessee (Knoxville); U of Tennessee (Chattanooga)

COLLINS, KAYLA J; CELINA, TN; CLAY CTY HS; (FR); 4H Awd; Hnr Roll; 4-H; Chrch Yth Grp; DARE; FCA; FCCLA; Mth Clb/Tm; Ntl FFA; Chrldg (V); Fld Hky (V); Golf (V); Hsbk Rdg (V); Ice Hky (V); Tennis (V); U of Tennessee; Western Kentucky

COLQUITT, FAITH; KNOXVILLE, TN; WEST HS; (FR); Comm Volntr; Stu Cncl (R); Psychology; Law; U of Tennessee

COMBS, CHARLOTTE; KNOXVILLE, TN; BEREAN CHRISTIAN SCH; (SR); Nat Ldrshp Svc; USAA; Comm Volntr; ArtClub; Chrch Yth Grp; P to P St Amb Prg; Bskball (V); Yrbk (P); Egyptology; Photography; Boston U; U of Pennsylvania

COMBS, REIGAN; BRENTWOOD, TN; HUME-FOGG AC; (SR); Nat Hon Sy; Off Aide; Prom Com; Swg Chr; Cl Off (P); CR (R); National Achievement Scholar; Business Administration; Marketing/Advertising; U of Pennsylvania; Duke U

COMER, J C; HIXSON, TN; HIXSON HS; (JR); Duke TS; USAA; WWAHSS; Comm Volntr; Chrch Yth Grp; ROTC; Clr Grd; Drl Tm; National Youth Leadership Forum on Defense, Intelligence & Diplomacy; Drill Team & Flight Commander; International Relations; Military Science; U.S. Naval Academy; Norwich U

COMER, LAKEN; MC KENZIE, TN; MC KENZIE HS; (SO); Hi Hnr Roll; WWAHSS; Comm Volntr; Chrch Yth Grp; DARE; FCA; FBLA; FTA; Key Club; Lttrmn Clb; Ntl Beta Clb; Bskball (V); Sftball (V); Adv Cncl (S); Who's Who World Geography; Medical Degree; Psychology; Vanderbilt U; U of Alabama

CONLEY, BENJAMIN S; MEMPHIS, TN; GREY ROAD CHRISTIAN AC; (FR); Hi Hnr Roll; Hnr Roll; Sci Fairs; Peer Tut/Med; Chrch Yth Grp; Dbte Team; Drma Clb; Emplmnt; Mus Clb; Photog; Tchrs Aide; Chr; Ch Chr; SP/M/VS; Stg Cre; Stu Cncl (V); Youth Group; Audio Equipment At Church; Fed Ex Pilot; U of Memphis

CONNALLY, JORDAN; SODDY DAISY, TN; SODDY DAISY HS; (FR); Ctznshp Aw; Hnr Roll; Nat Hon Sy; Perf Att; Pres Ac Ftns Aw; WWAHSS; 4-H; DARE; FCA; Bsball (VJ); Ftball; Stu Cncl (R); Law; UTK; UGA

CONNER, ALICIA P; HUMBOLDT, TN; PEABODY HS; (SR); Hnr Roll; Perf Att; St of Mnth; 4-H; DARE; Lib Aide; Off Aide; Scouts; Tchrs Aide; Cosmetology; Nail Technician; West Tennessee Business College

CONNER, CHARLES L A; JONESBOROUGH, TN; DAVID CROCKETT HS; (FR); Ctznshp Aw; Duke TS; Hnr Roll; MVP; Sci Fairs; Chrch Yth Grp; DARE; Ntl Beta Clb; Off Aide; Photog; Ch Chr; Bsball (J); Ftball (J); Stu Cncl (R); Yrbk (E, P); Who's Who Babe Ruth Baseball 2004; Criminal Justice; Education; East Tennessee State U; U of Tennessee

COOK, SAMANTHA; SHELBYVILLE, TN; MOORE CTY HS; (JR); Hnr Roll; Sci Fairs; Comm Volntr; Red Cr Aide; Spec Olymp Vol; 4-H; ArtClub; Chrch Yth Grp; DARE; DECA; FCA; FBLA; FCCLA; Chr; Ch Chr; Clr Grd; Dnce; Bskball; PP Ftbl; Sftball; Nurse; Chef; MTSU or Motlow; Austin or Sullivan

COOLEY, CHRISTOPHER; MORRISTOWN, TN; JEFFERSON CTY HS; (JR); Yth Ldrshp Prog; Comm Volntr; ArtClub; Chess; Chrch Yth Grp; Emplmnt; Diocesan Youth Ministry Advisory (2yrs) Council; Youth Leadership Institute; Radiology; Teaching; U Tennessee Chattanooga; East Tennessee State U

COOPER, QUALEKQUA; MT PLEASANT, TN; MT PLEASANT HS; (JR); Hi Hnr Roll; Hnr Roll; MVP; Nat Hon Sy; WWAHSS; Peer Tut/Med; Chrch Yth Grp; Emplmnt; Pep Squd; Prom Com; Bskball (V C); PP Ftbl (J); Track (V); Adv Cncl (S); Clark Atlanta U; Albany State U

COPAS, ANDREA; CELINA, TN; CLAY CTY HS; (SO); 4H Awd; Hnr Roll; Comm Volntr; Peer Tut/Med; 4-H; Chrch Yth Grp; FCA; Mth Clb/Tm; Ntl Beta Clb; Ntl FFA; Bskball (V L); Sftball (V CL); Cl Off (V); Stu Cncl; National Land & Range Judging Winner; 4-H State Wildlife Winner; Veterinarian; U of Tennessee; Auburn U

COPAS, HAYLEY; CELINA, TN; CLAY CTY HS; (FR); 4H Awd; Hnr Roll; Comm Volntr; Peer Tut/Med; 4-H; Chrch Yth Grp; Mth Clb/Tm; Ntl Beta Clb; Ntl FFA; Sci Clb; Bskball (V L); Sftball (V L); Cl Off (P); Yrbk; Nursing; U of Tennessee; Tennessee Tech U

COPCIAC, MONICA; MURFREESBORO, TN; BLACKMAN HS; (FR); Chrch Yth Grp; Key Club; Bnd; Key Club Scrapbooking Chair; Second Grade Teacher; Michigan State U; Middle Tennessee State U

COPELAND, AMETHYST; HIXSON, TN; HIXSON HS; (SO); Ctznshp Aw; Duke TS; Hnr Roll; Perf Att; Pres Sch; WWAHSS; Comm Volntr; DARE; Emplmnt; ROTC; Specialize As Ob/Gyn; Medical Field; UTK; Stanford U

COPELAND, BLAKE; ADAMS, TN; J BYRNS SCH; (SO); 4H Awd; Hi Hnr Roll; Perf Att; WWAHSS; Comm Volntr; 4-H; Chrch Yth Grp; Key Club; Ntl Beta Clb; Sci Clb; Ftball (V); Wt Lftg (V); Cl Off (R); Stu Cncl (R)

COPELAND, JAMIYAN; MEMPHIS, TN; OVERTON HS; (SO); Hi Hnr Roll; Hnr Roll; Perf Att; WWAHSS; Chrch Yth Grp; Emplmnt; Dnce; Orch; SP/M/VS; Chrldg (V); Performance Arts; Orchestra

COPESKEY, CANDICE; WAVERLY, TN; WAVERLY CTRL HS; (JR); Hnr Roll; Nat Stu Ath Day Aw; Pres Sch; St of Mnth; WWAHSS; Yth Ldrshp Prog; Comm Volntr; FCA; FBLA; Ntl Beta Clb; Off Aide; Tchrs Aide; Chr; Chrldg (V); Tennis (V); Cl Off (S); Stu Cncl (R); Cheerleading Award; Performing Arts; Vet, Interior Design; U of Tennessee, Knoxville; Middle Tennessee State U

CORBITT, H CAITLIN; NASHVILLE, TN; NASHVILLE SCH OF THE ARTS; (SO); Ctznshp Aw; Duke TS; Hnr Roll; Otst Ac Ach Awd; WWAHSS; Yth Ldrshp Prog; Comm Volntr; Hab For Humty Volntr; Chrch Yth Grp; Dbte Team; Drma Clb; Emplmnt; Ntl Beta Clb; NtlFrnscLg; Photog; Spch Team; Ch Chr; Dnce; SP/M/VS; Stg Cre; Creative Dramatics Freshman of the Year; Journalism; Theatre; Belmont; Vanderbilt

CORDOVA, CASEY C; MONTEAGLE, TN; (JR); Duke TS; WWAHSS; AL Aux Boys; Chrch Yth Grp; FCA; Spanish Clb; Bnd; Mch Bnd; Pep Bnd; Who's Who Among American High School Students; Boy's State; Military; United States Military Academy At WestPoint; Virginia Military Institute

CORLEW, CHRIS; MURFREESBORO, TN; (JR); Gov Hnr Prg; Hnr Roll; Nat Hon Sy; WWAHSS; Chess; Chrch Yth Grp; Key Club; Mus Clb; Ntl Beta Clb; Bnd; Jzz Bnd; Mch Bnd; Pep Bnd; Lit Mag (R); Tennessee Governor's School for Humanities; All Mid-State Jazz Band; Philosophy; Jazz Studies; Middle Tennessee State U; Duke U

CORLEY, EMILY; FRANKLIN, TN; FRANKLIN HS; (JR); Comm Volntr; Chrch Yth Grp; Emplmnt; Sign Clb; Cr Ctry (V)

CORR, RACHEL; MEMPHIS, TN; WHITE STATION HS; (JR); F Lan Hn Soc; Gov Hnr Prg; Hi Hnr Roll; Nat Hon Sy; Yth Ldrshp Prog; Amnsty Intl; Comm Volntr; AL Aux Girls; Chrch Yth Grp; DECA; Drma Clb; HO'Br Yth Ldrshp; MuAlphaTh; Ntl Beta Clb; German Clb; Orch; Track (V); Stu Cncl (R)

CORUM, BRITTANY N; ATHENS, TN; MC MINN CTY HS; (SR); Ctznshp Aw; Hi Hnr Roll; Hnr Roll; Otst Ac Ach Awd; WWAHSS; Comm Volntr; Emplmnt; MuAlphaTh; Pep Squd; SADD; Tchrs Aide; Voc Ind Clb Am; Bowling Team; Business Administration; Law; U of Tennessee Knoxville

COSTA, ALEINA; MC EWEN, TN; MC EWEN HS; (JR); Ctznshp Aw; Hnr Roll; Perf Att; Sci Fairs; BPA; Drma Clb; FTA; Ntl Beta Clb; Ntl FFA; Prom Com; Sci Clb; Spanish Clb; Dnce; SP/M/VS; Bskball (J); Tennis (J L); Leo Club; Stars / Stars Executive Council; Fashion Merchandising; Graphic Design; Middle Tennessee State U; Murray State U

COTHREN, CALEB M; LAWRENCEBURG, TN; LAWRENCE CTY HS; (FR); Duke TS; Hnr Roll; USAA; Chrch Yth Grp; FBLA; Stu Cncl (R); Community Theatre Plays; Community Gymnastics; Drama; Psychology

COTTER, JEREMY W; ARLINGTON, TN; ARLINGTON HS; (FR); Duke TS; Hnr Roll; Ntl Beta Clb; Sccr (J); Architecture; Music Production

COUCH, CHRISTOPHER; JACKSON, TN; LIBERTY TECH MAGNET HS; (SO); Hnr Roll; WWAHSS; Comm Volntr; Hosp Aide; Red Cr Aide; Chrch Yth Grp; Emplmnt; Ntl Beta Clb; Ntl FFA; Spanish Clb; Scr Kpr; Student Achievement Award; Agriculture; U of Tennessee At Martin

COVINGTON, JAMES W; HIXSON, TN; HIXSON HS; (SO); Hi Hnr Roll; Hnr Roll; WWAHSS; Chrch Yth Grp; FCA; FBLA; Golf (V L); 2004/2005 Best All Around Superlative; 2003-2004 Church Mission Trips; Golf Course Architecture; Engineering; Tennessee Tech U

COWLES, SHARI; COUNCE, TN; HARDIN CTY HS; (FR); 4H Awd; Hnr Roll; Nat Hon Sy; Otst Ac Ach Awd; Sci Fairs; 4-H; DARE; Bnd; Dnce; Bskball (L); Cl Off (P); CR (P); Pediatrician; Psychologist; Argosy U, Nashville, Brentwood; Walden U

COX, ASHLEY; LAKE CITY, TN; ANDERSON CTY HS; (SO); 4H Awd; Duke TS; Hi Hnr Roll; Nat Hon Sy; Pres Sch; WWAHSS; Chrch Yth Grp; Ntl FFA; P to P St Amb Prg; Bnd; Ch Chr; Jzz Bnd; Mch Bnd; Stu Cncl (R); CR (R); Criminal Justice; Marine Biology

COX, BRANDON L; MEMPHIS, TN; FAIRLEY HS; (SR); Hnr Roll; Emplmnt; Ftball (V C); Most Dedicated Player; Best Defensive Lineman; Business Administration; General Business; Middle Tennessee State U; Tennessee State U

COX, COURTNEY D; SOUTH PITTSBURG, TN; RICHARD HARDY MEMORIAL SCH; (FR); 4H Awd; Duke TS; Hi Hnr Roll; Hnr Roll; Nat Hon Sy; Perf Att; Sci Fairs; USAA; WWAHSS; Comm Volntr; Hosp Aide; 4-H; Chrch Yth Grp; DARE; Emplmnt; FCA; Mth Clb/Tm; Ntl Beta Clb; P to P St Amb Prg; Chrldg (V); Vllyball (V L); Duke Talented Teen; Who's Who; Psychology; Rhodes; Union

COX, HANNAH E; OLIVER SPRINGS, TN; OLIVER SPRINGS HS; (SO); Duke TS; Otst Ac Ach Awd; Pres Sch; Sci Fairs; WWAHSS; Comm Volntr; Chrch Yth Grp; Drma Clb; Ntl Beta Clb; Spanish Clb; Ch Chr; Chrldg (V L); Cl Off (T); Yrbk; FCA Officer; Leader of My Youth Group Drama Group; Biology; Meteorology; Vanderbilt U; The U of Tennessee

COX, KIMMY; WILDERSVILLE, TN; CLARKSBURG HS; (SO); Nat Hon Sy; Perf Att; WWAHSS; 4-H; Chrch Yth Grp; FCA; FCCLA; FTA; Lttrmn Clb; Prom Com; Vsity Clb; Bskball (V); Scr Kpr (V); Sftball (V); Vsy Clb (V); Sch Ppr (E, R); Criminology; Union U

COX, TANYA; JONESBOROUGH, TN; SULLIVAN SOUTH HS; (JR); Hnr Roll; Kwnis Aw; Nat Hon Sy; Otst Ac Ach Awd; Perf Att; Pres Ac Ftns Aw; USAA; WWAHSS; Drma Clb; Key Club; SP/M/VS; Cr Ctry (V CL); Track (V L); Anchor Club; AIMS Scholar; Medical Field; Nursing; King College; East Tennessee State U

COX, TRAVIS C; KNOXVILLE, TN; BEREAN CHRISTIAN SCH; (FR); Duke TS; Peer Tut/Med; Chrch Yth Grp; Emplmnt; Bskball (V); Sccr (V); Business; Engineering; Duke U; U of Kentucky

CRAFTON, LEAH N; ATHENS, TN; MC MINN CTY HS; (JR); Duke TS; Hi Hnr Roll; Kwnis Aw; Nat Hon Sy; Otst Ac Ach Awd; Pres Ac Ftns Aw; Pres Sch; WWAHSS; Comm Volntr; Chrch Yth Grp; Emplmnt; FCA; FCCLA; MuAlphaTh; Outdrs Clb; Bnd; Sccr (V L); Stu Cncl (T); Marine Biology; U North Carolina Wilmington; Costal Carolina U

CRASS, RONNIE; CLINTON, TN; OLIVER SPRINGS HS; (SO); 4H Awd; Hnr Roll; Nat Hon Sy; Otst Ac Ach Awd; Perf Att; Comm Volntr; 4-H; Chrch Yth Grp; DARE; Ntl Beta Clb; Stg Cre; AMAF 8 2nd Place; Pharmacy; Engineering; U of Kentucky; U of Tennessee of Martin

CRAVEN, RACHEL K; HIXSON, TN; SODDY DAISY HS; (FR); Hi Hnr Roll; Hnr Roll; Perf Att; Sci Fairs; Bnd; Chr; Jzz Bnd; Yrbk; Science Fair - Honorable Mention Winner; Church Orchestra - Church Youth Handbells; Elementary Education; Veterinary Medicine; U of Tennessee Chattanooga

CRAWFORD, BRITTANY D; KINGSPORT, TN; SULLIVAN NORTH HS; (SR); Hnr Roll; Nat Hon Sy; Comm Volntr; DECA; Emplmnt; Key Club; Ntl Beta Clb; Business/Finance; Graphic Design; East Tennessee State U; U of Tennessee (In Chattanooga)

CRISP, CLINT A; DECATUR, TN; MC MINN CTY HS; (JR); 4H Awd; Hnr Roll; Nat Hon Sy; WWAHSS; Yth Ldrshp Prog; Comm Volntr; 4-H; Chrch Yth Grp; Emplmnt; FCA; Ntl FFA; NYLC; Ch Chr; Vice President - FFA / Chapter; Regional Vice President / FFA; Vet; U of Tennessee Knoxville

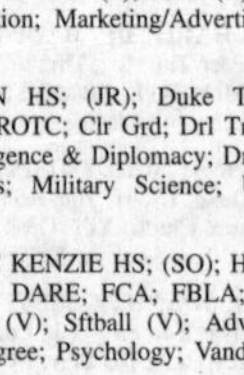
Cox, Kimmy
Clarksburg HS
Wildersville, TN

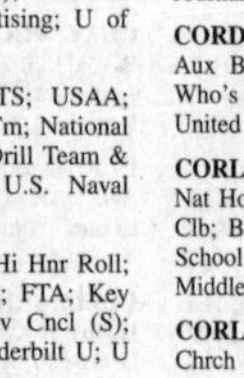
Conner, Charles L A
David Crockett HS
Jonesborough, TN

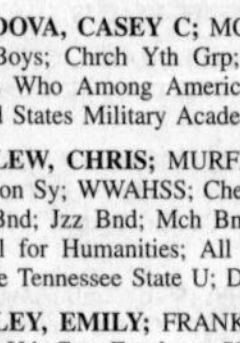
Conner, Alicia P
Peabody HS
Humboldt, TN

National
Honor Roll
Spring 2005

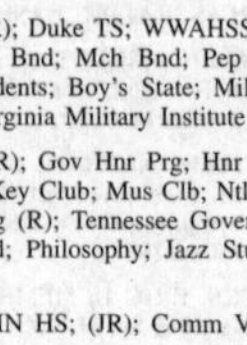
Cobb, Justin W
Jefferson Cty HS
White Pine, TN

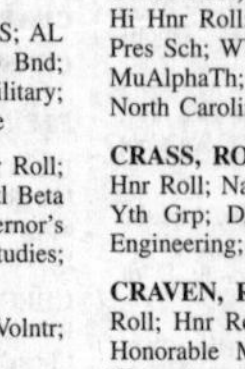
Corbitt, H Caitlin
Nashville Sch Of The Arts
Nashville, TN

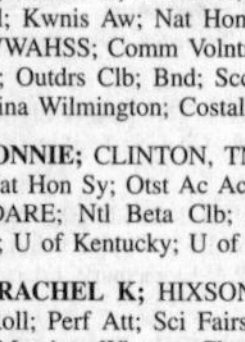
Cox, Travis C
Berean Christian Sch
Knoxville, TN

CRISS, DANNY; COTTONTOWN, TN; WHITE HOUSE HS; (SO); 4H Awd; Hi Hnr Roll; Hnr Roll; Jr Rot; Kwnis Aw; MVP; Nat Hon Sy; Otst Ac Ach Awd; St of Mnth; Yth Ldrshp Prog; 4-H; DARE; FCA; FBLA; Ntl Beta Clb; Ntl FFA; Ftball (V); Sccr (J); Wrstlg (V); Aeronautics; Aviation; United States Air Force Academy

CROCKETT JR, JAMES; HENDERSONVILLE, TN; HENDERSONVILLE CHRN AC; (FR); Hi Hnr Roll; Nat Hon Sy; Spch Team; Chr; SP/M/VS; Stg Cre; Bskball (V); Stu Cncl; Best of Show Humorous Interpretation/State; Evangelism; Bible; Trinity Baptist College

CROSBY, BRIAN; MORRISTOWN, TN; (FR); 4H Awd; Ctznshp Aw; Otst Ac Ach Awd; 4-H; Chrch Yth Grp; DARE; Scouts; Mar Art; Stu Cncl (R); Most Improvement; WSCC

CROSS, KAMI; BLOUNTVILLE, TN; SULLIVAN CTRL HS; (SO); Duke TS; Hi Hnr Roll; WWAHSS; Comm Volntr; Chrch Yth Grp; Drma Clb; Key Club; Chr; Ch Chr; SP/M/VS; Tennis; Vllyball; Cl Off (V); Middle Tennessee State U; U of Georgia

CROSSLIN, DANEE; WARTRACE, TN; CASCADE HS; (JR); Hnr Roll; WWAHSS; FCCLA; Prom Com; Sccr (V)

CROWDER, PAIGE; CELINA, TN; CLAY CTY HS; (SO); Hnr Roll; FCCLA; Ntl Beta Clb; Ntl FFA; Bskball (V); Veterinarian; Nursing; Tennessee Technological U; Vol State

CROWE, ASHLEY; DANDRIDGE, TN; JEFFERSON CTY HS; (SO); Hnr Roll; Pres Sch; WWAHSS; Chrch Yth Grp; DARE; FCA; Ntl Beta Clb; Pep Squd; Wt Lftg; Biology; Computer Art; East Tennessee State U; U of Tennessee (Knoxville)

CROWELL, SAMANTHA N; BIG SANDY, TN; CAMDEN CTRL HS; (SO); Hnr Roll; Comm Volntr; Peer Tut/Med; Biology Clb; Emplmnt; Sci Clb; Spanish Clb; Nursing; Law; Martin-U of Tennessee; Jackson State

CRUTCHER, CHARMISHA L; MEMPHIS, TN; WOODDALE HS; (JR); Ctznshp Aw; Hi Hnr Roll; Hnr Roll; Perf Att; WWAHSS; Comm Volntr; ArtClub; BPA; Chrch Yth Grp; Emplmnt; Mus Clb; Acpl Chr; Chr; Ch Chr; Dnce; CR (R); Most Talented of 2005 & Junior Class; Miss Public Relations at Wooddale HS; Medical Field - Anesthesiologist / Doctor; Performing Arts / Professional Singer; Tennessee State U; U of Tennessee

CRUZ, MARTIKA; CLARKSVILLE, TN; NORTHEAST HS; (FR); Ctznshp Aw; Hnr Roll; Otst Ac Ach Awd; Bsball; Sftball; Vllyball; Earned Savings Bond for Academic Excellence; Science; Forensics; Princeton U, Miami U, U of Tennessee; New York U, Florida State U

CULPEPPER, ETHAN; SOUTH PITTSBURG, TN; RICHARD HARDY MEMORIAL SCH; (FR); Hnr Roll; Comm Volntr; 4-H; Chrch Yth Grp; DARE; Scouts; Vsity Clb; Ch Chr; Bsball (VJ); Bskball (V)

CUMMINGS, TERRICA; MEMPHIS, TN; OAKHAVEN MIDDLE HS; (SO); Hi Hnr Roll; Chr; Cl Off (S); Medical Physician; Christian Brother; U of Tennessee

CUMMINS, KYLE; GERMANTOWN, TN; EVANGELICAL CHRISTIAN SCH; (SO); Ctznshp Aw; Duke TS; Hi Hnr Roll; Hnr Roll; Nat Hon Sy; WWAHSS; Chrch Yth Grp; FCA; Ntl Beta Clb; Pep Squd; Quill & Scroll; Bsball; Bskball (V); Cr Ctry (V); Tennis (V); Wt Lftg (V); Sch Ppr (R); Beta Club President; Principal's Honor Roll

CUNNINGHAM, COURTNEY; BLUFF CITY, TN; SULLIVAN EAST HS; (FR); Hnr Roll; Comm Volntr; Chrch Yth Grp; Quill & Scroll; Chr; Ch Chr; Vllyball (J); Sch Ppr (R); Health Science; RN; U of Tennessee; King College

CUNNINGHAM, DANIEL L; SEYMOUR, TN; SEYMOUR HS; (SO); Duke TS; Hi Hnr Roll; Hnr Roll; Nat Hon Sy; Otst Ac Ach Awd; Sci Fairs; USAA; Comm Volntr; Chrch Yth Grp; DARE; Drma Clb; Emplmnt; FCA; Ntl Beta Clb; NtlFrnscLg; Quiz Bowl; Bnd; Ftball (J); Track (V); Downhill Skier; In Christian Music Band; Liberal Arts; Vanderbilt U; Duke U

CUPPLES, JENNIE; COLUMBIA, TN; MT PLEASANT HS; (SR); Hi Hnr Roll; Hnr Roll; WWAHSS; Drma Clb; Mus Clb; Tchrs Aide; Bnd; Drm Mjr; Jzz Bnd; Mch Bnd; Cl Off (V); Interact Club; Music Education; Middle Tennessee State U

CURETON, AMBER; RUSSELLVILLE, TN; MORRISTOWN-HAMBLEN HS EAST HS; (JR); Peer Tut/Med; Spec Olymp Vol; Chrch Yth Grp; FCA; Off Aide; Tchrs Aide; French Clb; Chr; Sftball (J); Adv Cncl (R); Cl Off (R); Stu Cncl (R); CR (R); Fashion Degree (Major); Performing Arts (Minor); Savannah College of Art and Design

CURRY, NIKKITA J; MEMPHIS, TN; OVERTON HS; (JR); Hi Hnr Roll; WWAHSS; Chrch Yth Grp; Emplmnt; MuAlphaTh; Quill & Scroll; Spanish Clb; Ch Chr; Mu Alpha Theta; Who's Who Among American High School Students; Journalism; Creative Writing; Tennessee State U; U of Miami

CUTSHALL, JULIAN M; GREENEVILLE, TN; CHUCKEY DOAK HS; (JR); Hnr Roll; Nat Hon Sy; Peer Tut/Med; Ntl FFA; Tchrs Aide; Ftball (V); Wt Lftg (V); Doctor

CUTSHAW JR, RICHARD L; GREENEVILLE, TN; GREENEVILLE HS; (SO); Hnr Roll; Comm Volntr; Chrch Yth Grp; ALM Scholar of Greenville/ Greene County; Wildlife Management; Major in Biology; Tennessee Tech U; Walters State Community College

DAHLIN, CASSIE; BENTON, TN; POLK CTY HS; (SR); Hnr Roll; Perf Att; WWAHSS; Comm Volntr; ArtClub; Chrch Yth Grp; FCA; Prom Com; Sci Clb; Tchrs Aide; Bskball (V C); Cr Ctry (V); Vllyball (V); Class Officer - Sophomore-Senior; Family Career & Community Leaders of America; Radiology Technology; Cleveland State Community College; Chattanooga State Technical College

DAHLIN, DANIELLE A; KINGSPORT, TN; SULLIVAN CTRL HS; (JR); Hi Hnr Roll; Nat Hon Sy; WWAHSS; Comm Volntr; Emplmnt; Ntl Beta Clb; Psychology; Lawyer; U of Tennessee Knoxville; East Tennessee State U

DAILEY, LAKISHA; NASHVILLE, TN; STRATFORD HS; (JR); Perf Att; St of Mnth; Comm Volntr; Chrch Yth Grp; DARE; Scouts; Bskball (J); Vllyball (V); Football Manager; Medicine; Pediatrician; Tennessee State U; Middle Tennessee State U

DALSEM, CRYSTAL V; CLARKSVILLE, TN; CLARKSVILLE HS; (JR); Hnr Roll; WWAHSS; Drma Clb; Emplmnt; Stg Cre; International Thespian Society; Creative Writing; U of Tennessee; Memphis State U

DANIEL, LAUREN D; SODDY DAISY, TN; SODDY-DAISY HS; (FR); Ctznshp Aw; Hi Hnr Roll; Hnr Roll; Nat Hon Sy; Nat Stu Ath Day Aw; Otst Ac Ach Awd; Perf Att; Sci Fairs; WWAHSS; Yth Ldrshp Prog; Comm Volntr; Peer Tut/Med; Spec Olymp Vol; ArtClub; Chrch Yth Grp; DARE; Dbte Team; FCA; Key Club; Mus Clb; Photog; Ch Chr; SP/M/VS; Bskball (J); Cr Ctry (V); Track (V); Stu Cncl

DANIELL, SHAWN; MOUNT JULIET, TN; WILSON CTRL HS; (JR); Perf Att; Yth Ldrshp Prog; Chrch Yth Grp; Emplmnt; ROTC; Drl Tm; Skt Tgt Sh (V); Leadership ACD (ROTC); Drafting; Law Enforcement; Tennessee Tech; Western Kent

DANIELS, COLTON A; HIXSON, TN; SODDY-DAISY HS; (FR); Ctznshp Aw; Duke TS; Hi Hnr Roll; Kwnis Aw; WWAHSS; Chrch Yth Grp; FCA; Bskball (J); Golf (J); Ecology Award; U of TN At Chattanooga; Carson Newman

DANIELS, JAMISON W; HIXSON, TN; SODDY DAISY HS; (JR); Duke TS; Gov Hnr Prg; Hi Hnr Roll; Nat Hon Sy; Otst Ac Ach Awd; WWAHSS; Yth Ldrshp Prog; Comm Volntr; Peer Tut/Med; Chrch Yth Grp; Emplmnt; FCA; Ntl Beta Clb; Ch Chr; Skiing; Sccr; Algebra II Award / Spanish Award; Geometry Award; Teaching; Physician; U of TN Chattanooga; U Tenn

D'APICE, STACI; KNOXVILLE, TN; HALLS HS; (FR); WWAHSS; Comm Volntr; DARE; FCA; Chr; Bskball (J); Sftball (V L); Vllyball (J); Cl Off (R); CR (R); Physical Therapy; Accounting; U of Georgia; U of Florida

DAUGHERTY, AMANDA D; WARTBURG, TN; CENTRAL HS; (JR); Hi Hnr Roll; Hnr Roll; Perf Att; WWAHSS; Drma Clb; FCA; Ntl FFA; SP/ M/VS; Sftball (V); Cl Off (P); HOSA; Physical Therapist; Roane State Community College; UT College

DAUGHTDRILL, SABRINA; NASHVILLE, TN; PEARL COHN HS; (SR); Hnr Roll; WWAHSS; Yth Ldrshp Prog; Comm Volntr; Peer Tut/Med; Chrch Yth Grp; Ch Chr; Physical Therapy; Psychology; The U of Tennessee At Chattanooga; Xavier U of Louisiana

DAVENPORT, SARAH T; MURFREESBORO, TN; RIVERDALE HS; (FR); Ctznshp Aw; Hnr Roll; Nat Hon Sy; St of Mnth; Comm Volntr; Hosp Aide; Chrch Yth Grp; DARE; FCA; FBLA; Ntl Beta Clb; Pep Squd; Scouts; Bnd; Chr; SP/M/VS; Chrldg (VJ); Law; Duke U

DAVIDSON, EBONY J; NASHVILLE, TN; NASHVILLE SCH OF THE ARTS; (FR); Ctznshp Aw; Gov Hnr Prg; Hnr Roll; Nat Stu Ath Day Aw; Otst Ac Ach Awd; Sci Fairs; St of Mnth; Comm Volntr; Peer Tut/Med; Chrch Yth Grp; DARE; Drma Clb; FCA; Mus Clb; Bnd; Chr; Ch Chr; Drl Tm; Chrldg (C); Cl Off (P); Music; Management; Spelman College; U of South Florida

DAVIDSON, KEVIN; ARLINGTON, TN; ARLINGTON HS; (FR); Comm Volntr; FCA; Ntl Beta Clb; Ch Chr; Cr Ctry (V L); Track (V L); Political Science; Justice Studies; U of Memphis; U of Tennessee Martin

DAVIDSON, NICK; ENVILLE, TN; CHESTER CTY HS; (JR); All Am Sch; F Lan Hn Soc; Nat Hon Sy; USAA; WWAHSS; Comm Volntr; Peer Tut/Med; AL Aux Boys; Chrch Yth Grp; FCA; Lttrmn Clb; MuAlphaTh; Ntl Beta Clb; Quiz Bowl; Tchrs Aide; Bnd; Jzz Bnd; Mch Bnd; Pep Bnd; Tennis (V L); Cl Off (P, V); Sch Ppr (E, R); 2nd Place Beta English Competition-TN; Biology; Medicine; Vanderbilt U; Washington U St Louis

DAVIDSON, SARA; CROSS PLAINS, TN; EAST ROBERTSON HS; (JR); WWAHSS; FCA; Chiropractic; U of Sciences in Philly; Palmer Chiropractic

DAVIDSON, ZACHARY A; DOWELLTOWN, TN; DEKALB CTY HS; (SO); Hnr Roll; Sci/Math Olympn; Chrch Yth Grp; DARE; FCA; Mth Clb/Tm; Spanish Clb; Ch Chr; Orch; SP/M/VS; Bskball (J); Golf (V); Sccr (V); Engineering; Tennessee Tech U

DAVIS, ALYSSA C; RIPLEY, TN; RIPLEY HS; (JR); WWAHSS; Yth Ldrshp Prog; Comm Volntr; Chrch Yth Grp; Drma Clb; FCA; Ntl Beta Clb; SP/M/VS; English Literature; International Relations

DAVIS, BETHANY K; DOWELLTOWN, TN; DE KALB CTY HS; (JR); Hi Hnr Roll; WWAHSS; Chrch Yth Grp; FCA; FBLA; FCCLA; Ntl Beta Clb; Ntl FFA; Off Aide; Prom Com; Bskball (VJCL); Cl Off (V); Stu Cncl (V); CR (V); Murfreesboro Tenn State U

DAVIS, CODY A; WARTBURG, TN; CENTRAL HS; (JR); Hi Hnr Roll; Hnr Roll; Otst Ac Ach Awd; Ntl Beta Clb; Stu Cncl (R); Yrbk (R, P); National Beta Club; Academic Achievement Award Recipient; Technological Field; Computer Forensics; Vanderbilt U; Middle Tennessee State U

DAVIS, ERICA M; NASHVILLE, TN; NASHVILLE SCH OF THE ARTS; (SR); Hi Hnr Roll; Nat Hon Sy; WWAHSS; Comm Volntr; Peer Tut/Med; Chrch Yth Grp; Acpl Chr; Chr; Ch Chr; Dnce; Senior Committee Member; Graduation Committee Member; Pharmacist; Ob/Gyn Physician; Tennessee State U

DAVIS, HANNAH L; WASHBURN, TN; WASHBURN SCH; (JR); Ctznshp Aw; F Lan Hn Soc; Hnr Roll; Nat Hon Sy; Perf Att; St of Mnth; WWAHSS; Yth Ldrshp Prog; Chrch Yth Grp; FBLA; FCCLA; Ntl Beta Clb; SADD; Talent Search; FBLA State Conference (Compete); Radiology (Ultra Sound Technician); Optometry (Optometrist); South College; Roane State

DAVIS, HANNA J; BENTON, TN; POLK CTY HS; 4H Awd; Hi Hnr Roll; Hnr Roll; Chrch Yth Grp; DARE; FCA; Ntl Beta Clb; Tchrs Aide; Ch Chr; Bskball (V); Stu Cncl (P); Sch Ppr (R); Science Award; Vanderbilt; UTK

DAVIS, HOLLY R; LEBANON, TN; WILSON CTRL HS; (JR); Hi Hnr Roll; Nat Hon Sy; Otst Ac Ach Awd; Sci Fairs; Comm Volntr; Chrch Yth Grp; Drma Clb; Emplmnt; Mth Clb/Tm; MuAlphaTh; Mus Clb; Ntl Beta Clb; Photog; Acpl Chr; Chr; Dnce; SP/M/VS; CR (R); Yrbk (E); Editor-In-Chief of Yearbook; Photography and Journalism; Fine Arts and Literature; Northwestern; Boston U

DAVIS, JEFFERY R; EAGLEVILLE, TN; EAGLEVILLE SCH; (SR); Hnr Roll; USAA; WWAHSS; Hab For Humty Volntr; Chrch Yth Grp; FBLA; Ntl Beta Clb; Scouts; Bsball (V); Bskball (V); Ftball (V); Stu Cncl (V); Eagle Scout; Civil Engineer; Tennessee Tech U

DAVIS, JENNA L; MANCHESTER, TN; F C BOYD CHRISTIAN SCH; (FR); 4H Awd; All Am Sch; Hi Hnr Roll; Hnr Roll; 4-H; Ntl Beta Clb; Dnce; Bskball; Hsbk Rdg; Cl Off (V); Church Activities, Piano for 5 1/2 Yrs; Biology-Emphasis on Pre-Vet; Pre-Vet; David Lipscomb U; U of Tennessee At Knoxville

DAVIS, JENNIFER N; COOKEVILLE, TN; COOKEVILLE HS; (SO); Hnr Roll; Chrch Yth Grp; FCA; Key Club; Scouts; Tennessee Tech U

DAVIS, JESSICA; KODAK, TN; SEVIER CTY HS; (FR); Hi Hnr Roll; Hnr Roll; St of Mnth; WWAHSS; Ntl Beta Clb; Svce Clb; French Clb; Bnd; Golf (J); Bowling - V / L; Veterinarian; University of Tennessee Knoxville; North Carolina State U

DAVIS, JESSICA C; MEMPHIS, TN; OAKHAVEN MIDDLE HS; (SR); Voc Ind Clb Am; Ch Chr; Was a News Anchor on Cable 19; Mass Communications; Nursing; Southwest Tennessee Community College; U of Memphis

DAVIS, JUSTIN C; MEMPHIS, TN; OAK HAVEN HS; (JR); Ctznshp Aw; Hi Hnr Roll; Hnr Roll; Nat Hon Sy; Perf Att; St of Mnth; WWAHSS; Yth Ldrshp Prog; Comm Volntr; Peer Tut/Med; Chess; Chrch Yth Grp; Emplmnt; FBLA; Bsball (V); Accomplished Swimmer; Accomplished Chess Player; English Major-Business Major; Translator (Spanish); (UT) Martin-U Tennessee; (TN) State-Tennessee

DAVIS, KEVIN; MEMPHIS, TN; WHITE HAVEN HS; Ctznshp Aw; Hnr Roll; Nat Hon Sy; Perf Att; Comm Volntr; Hosp Aide; Chess; DARE; Emplmnt; ROTC; Spch Team; SADD

DAVIS, REBECCA J; NEWPORT, TN; SUNBRIGHT SCH; (SO); Hi Hnr Roll; Nat Hon Sy; WWAHSS; Chrch Yth Grp; Ntl Beta Clb; Ch Chr; Medical Doctor in the ER; U of Tennessee (Knoxville); U of Tennessee (Memphis)

DAVIS, RICKEYIA; MEMPHIS, TN; HILLCREST HS; (SO); Hi Hnr Roll; Hnr Roll; St of Mnth; BPA; DARE; Scouts; Yrbk (E); Medical; Nursing; Lane College; Med School

DAVIS, TRENT K; ALAMO, TN; CROCKETT CO HS; (JR); Duke TS; Hi Hnr Roll; MVP; Nat Hon Sy; WWAHSS; Comm Volntr; Chrch Yth Grp; DARE; Emplmnt; Ch Chr; Bsball (V CL)

DAVIS JOHNSON, ALISHA S; MEMPHIS, TN; WHITEHAVEN HS; (FR); Ctznshp Aw; Hi Hnr Roll; Hnr Roll; Otst Ac Ach Awd; Perf Att; Chrch Yth Grp; Spanish Clb; Chr; Ch Chr; Dnce; SP/M/VS; Gmnstcs; PPSqd; CR (R); Performance Art; Teacher; Georgia State U; Washington State U

DAWSON, ANTHONY P; PIKEVILLE, TN; BLEDSOE CTY HS; (SO); Hnr Roll; Nat Hon Sy; Perf Att; Comm Volntr; Emplmnt; Mod UN; Chr; SP/ M/VS; Software Programming; Video Game Producer; Tennessee Technical U; U of Michigan

Davis, Erica M
Nashville Sch Of The Arts
Nashville, TN

Cutshaw Jr, Richard L
Greeneville HS
Greeneville, TN

Cruz, Martika
Northeast HS
Clarksville, TN

National
Honor Roll
Spring 2005

Crosby, Brian
Morristown, TN

Davidson, Ebony J
Nashville Sch Of The Arts
Nashville, TN

Davis, Jenna L
F C Boyd Christian Sch
Manchester, TN

DEAL, IVY N; COPPERHILL, TN; COPPER BASIN HS; (JR); WWAHSS; Key Club; Lib Aide; Off Aide; Prom Com; Tchrs Aide; Chr; Chrldg (V); Cl Off (V); Boy's Basketball Manager; Nurse / RN; Epworth Community College; Tri-County Community College

DEAN, KASIE; MC EWEN, TN; WAVERLY CTRL HS; (FR); 4H Awd; Hnr Roll; Pres Ac Ftns Aw; Hab For Humty Volntr; BPA; Chrch Yth Grp; DARE; Off Aide; Pep Squd; Bskball; Vanderbilt, UTN Martin; Lipscomb

DEAN, SARAH; HARRIMAN, TN; OLIVER SPRINGS HS; (SO); Hnr Roll; WWAHSS; Comm Volntr; BPA; Chrch Yth Grp; FCA; Tchrs Aide; Spanish Clb; Ch Chr; Stu Cncl (R); Physical Science Award; Outstanding Academic Excellence; Elementary Education; Interior Design; Roane Community College; Union U

DEANS, ASHLEY L; GREENEVILLE, TN; GREENEVILLE HS; (SO); Duke TS; Hi Hnr Roll; Otst Ac Ach Awd; Perf Att; Pres Sch; Sci Fairs; Yth Ldrshp Prog; Comm Volntr; Hab For Humty Volntr; Peer Tut/Med; Chrch Yth Grp; FCA; Jr Ach; NYLC; Scouts; Svce Clb; Vsity Clb; Ch Chr; Bskball (V L); Sftball (V L); Track (V L); Vllyball (V L); Cl Off (R); Stu Cncl; Girl Scout Gold Award; Intro to Business Most Professional Award; Communications/Media; Business/Advertising

DEBLOIS, H R; MURFREESBORO, TN; RIVERDALE HS; (JR); Gov Hnr Prg; Hi Hnr Roll; Nat Hon Sy; Otst Ac Ach Awd; Comm Volntr; Peer Tut/Med; Chrch Yth Grp; Emplmnt; Key Club; MuAlphaTh; Mus Clb; Ntl Beta Clb; Quiz Bowl; Spanish Clb; Acpl Chr; Bnd; Orch; SP/M/VS; Cl Off (R); Stu Cncl (R); Music; Engineering; U of Virginia; U of Tennessee Knoxville

DEBORD, BEVERLY; PIKEVILLE, TN; BLEDSOE CTY HS; (FR); 4H Awd; Hi Hnr Roll; Otst Ac Ach Awd; Comm Volntr; 4-H; Chrch Yth Grp; Ntl Beta Clb; Bskball (V); Nursing; Physical Therapy; U of Tennessee Chattanooga

DEBORD, GARRETTE; PIKEVILLE, TN; BLEDSOE CTY HS; (FR); 4H Awd; Hi Hnr Roll; Hnr Roll; Perf Att; Sci Fairs; USAA; 4-H; Chrch Yth Grp; FTA; Ntl Beta Clb; 1st Degree Black Belt in Tae Kwon Do; Five Years of Piano Lessons; Bible; Missions; Freed-Hardeman U

DE GROFF, KYLE J; LAWRENCEBURG, TN; LAWRENCE CTY VOC CTR HS; (SO); Hi Hnr Roll; Hnr Roll; Nat Hon Sy; Nat Ldrshp Svc; Nat Sci Aw; Otst Ac Ach Awd; Perf Att; Pres Ac Ftns Aw; Yth Ldrshp Prog; Comm Volntr; Peer Tut/Med; Spec Olymp Vol; DARE; Emplmnt; Ntl Beta Clb; NYLC; P to P St Amb Prg; Quiz Bowl; Schol Bwl; Tchrs Aide; SP/M/VS; Sccr (J); Tennis (V); Track (J); Stu Cncl (R); National Young Leaders Conference; Teen Ambassador; Medical/Vet Med; Law; U of South Carolina; Duke or U of Arizona

DE HART, SAMANTHA J; FAYETTEVILLE, TN; LINCOLN CTY HS; (JR); All Am Sch; Hi Hnr Roll; Hnr Roll; Nat Hon Sy; Otst Ac Ach Awd; St of Mnth; WWAHSS; Comm Volntr; 4-H; ArtClub; Chrch Yth Grp; DARE; Emplmnt; FCA; Ntl Beta Clb; Ntl FFA; Cr Ctry (V); Sccr (V); Adv Cncl (R); Cl Off (T); Stu Cncl; CR (T); Yrbk (R); Winner of State Fire Marshall Contest; HOSA Member; Radiation Technician; Radiologist; Aquinas College; Tennessee Technical Institute Chatt. TN

DEITZ, ADAM; KINGSTON, TN; ROANE CTY HS; (SO); 4H Awd; Hi Hnr Roll; Perf Att; WWAHSS; Comm Volntr; 4-H; Chrch Yth Grp; DARE; DECA; Emplmnt; FCA; Photog; Sccr (V); Sch Ppr; Political Science

DELPLANE, AUTUMN P; SPRINGFIELD, TN; EAST ROBERTSON HS; (FR); 4H Awd; Otst Ac Ach Awd; 4-H; Chrch Yth Grp; DARE; Drma Clb; FCA; FTA; Mth Clb/Tm; Bnd; Sch Ppr (R); Writers Club; Literature/English Teacher; Drama/Actress

DEMMING, ASHLEY; KINGSPORT, TN; DOBYNS BENNETT HS; (JR); Nat Hon Sy; WWAHSS; Key Club; MuAlphaTh; Ntl Beta Clb; Prom Com; Spanish Clb; Track (V); Vllyball (J); Stu Cncl (V); Architecture; Georgia Tech

DEMOSS, KEETON M; SUMMERTOWN, TN; SUMMERTOWN HS; (FR); Comm Volntr; Peer Tut/Med; 4-H; Chrch Yth Grp; DARE; FCA; Scouts; SADD; Ch Chr; Cl Off (T); Attorney; Business Management; Louisiana State U

DENISON, CANDACE N; NEWBERN, TN; DYER CTY HS; (FR); 4H Awd; Duke TS; Hi Hnr Roll; Hnr Roll; Nat Hon Sy; Perf Att; Sci Fairs; St of Mnth; WWAHSS; Yth Ldrshp Prog; Comm Volntr; Hab For Humty Volntr; Red Cr Aide; ArtClub; Chess; Dbte Team; FCA; Mod UN; Ntl Beta Clb; ROTC; Spanish Clb; Bnd; Clr Grd; Drl Tm; Drm Mjr; Bskball (V); Chrldg (JC); Gmnstcs (V); Sftball (VJ); Tennis (VJCL); Track (VJ); Vllyball (VJ); Cl Off (S); Stu Cncl; CR (R); Yrbk (R, P); Expert Shooter Military Rifle Team; Most Decorated Freshman in AJROTC; Joining USMC; Legal Service Specialist; Yale U; U of Tennessee Martin

DENNENY, JACQUELLINE; KNOXVILLE, TN; WEST HS; (FR); Hnr Roll; Chrch Yth Grp; Mus Clb; Chr; SP/M/VS; Swmg (J); Received Black Belt in Martial Arts; Pediatrician; Massage Therapist; Northwestern; Central Methodist

DENNIS, JESSICA M; NASHVILLE, TN; PEARL COHN HS; (SO); Perf Att; WWAHSS; DARE; Jr Ach; Mod UN; Quiz Bowl; Bskball (J); Cr Ctry (V); Track (V); Stu Cncl (R); Nursing

DENNIS, RHEACHAL M; BELL BUCKLE, TN; CASCADE HS; (SO); Hi Hnr Roll; Nat Hon Sy; St of Mnth; WWAHSS; 4-H; ArtClub; Chrch Yth Grp; DARE; Drma Clb; FCA; Key Club; NYLC; Ch Chr; Stg Cre; Registered Nurse; Pediatric Doctor; Middle Tennessee State U; Vanderbilt U

DENTON, ANDREW H; SODDY DAISY, TN; SODDY-DAISY HS; (FR); Duke TS; Hi Hnr Roll; Perf Att; Comm Volntr; Chrch Yth Grp; Mod UN; Ntl Beta Clb; Bnd; Jzz Bnd; Mch Bnd; Pep Bnd; Character Education-Self Discipline; Optometry; Music; U of Kentucky; Middle Tennessee State U

DENTON, JASMINE; MEMPHIS, TN; WHITEHAVEN HS; (FR); Hi Hnr Roll; Otst Ac Ach Awd; St of Mnth; WWAHSS; Yth Ldrshp Prog; Comm Volntr; Peer Tut/Med; Chrch Yth Grp; Emplmnt; Mus Clb; Spanish Clb; Chr; Ch Chr; Bskball; Vice President of Youth Connection @ Church; Service Project Coordinator for the L.D.D.'s; Psychologist; Lawyer; Spelman College; Fisk U

DENWIDDIE, GWENDOLYN; JACKSON, TN; MADISON AC MAGNET HS; (SO); Perf Att; WWAHSS; Comm Volntr; Hosp Aide; Chrch Yth Grp; Ntl Beta Clb; Pep Squd; Acpl Chr; Bnd; Jzz Bnd; Bskball (V L); Cr Ctry (V L); Track (V L); Cl Off (P); CR (R); Sch Ppr (E, R, P); Yrbk (E); 5 Time Bible Bowl Winner at Church; Miss Tennessee State Congeniality; Journalism; Biology; Howard U; Abilene Christian U

DEROSSETT, JEFFREY D; ASHLAND CITY, TN; CHEATHAM CTY CTRL HS; (SO); Comm Volntr; 4-H; ArtClub; Chrch Yth Grp; DARE; Ntl FFA; Outdrs Clb; Scouts; Cr Ctry (V); Wt Lftg (V); Wrstlg (V); Hunter Safety Course - Education; Doctorial Degree; Law Degree; Middle Tennessee State U; Vanderbilt U

DERRICK, EDWARD; COLLIERVILLE, TN; COLLIERVILLE HS; (SR); Hnr Roll; Nat Hon Sy; Otst Ac Ach Awd; Perf Att; USAA; WWAHSS; Comm Volntr; Peer Tut/Med; Chrch Yth Grp; Emplmnt; Mth Clb/Tm; MuAlphaTh; Ntl Beta Clb; Quill & Scroll; Bnd; Mch Bnd; President's Award for Educational Excellence; National Society of High School Scholars; Mathematics; Business Administration; Middle Tennessee State U; Rhodes College

DESHAZIER, ASHLEY; SAVANNAH, TN; HARDIN CTY HS; (SO); Dental Hygienist; Cosmetologist; UT Martin

DE VRIES, LEIGH; NASHVILLE, TN; NASHVILLE SCH OF THE ARTS; (SO); Hnr Roll; Ntl Beta Clb; Tchrs Aide; Acpl Chr; Chr; Ch Chr; SP/M/VS; Beta Club; Art History; Creative Writing; NYU; Sewanee

DEW, KELLI; HEISKELL, TN; ANDERSON CTY HS; (SO); Hi Hnr Roll; Nat Hon Sy; Comm Volntr; Chrch Yth Grp; FCA; FBLA; Prom Com; Tchrs Aide; Chrldg (V L); CR (R); Teaching; Business / Master's Degree; Carson-Newman College; Lincoln Memorial U

DIGGS, JA'COLE; ANTIOCH, TN; MC GAVOCK COMP HS; (FR); Hnr Roll; Perf Att; Hosp Aide; Tennis; Pediatrician; RN; Spelman College; Georgia Tech College

DISHROON, KARA L; CHATTANOOGA, TN; CENTRAL HS; (FR); Hnr Roll; Otst Ac Ach Awd; Chrch Yth Grp; DARE; Tchrs Aide; Bnd; Chr; Ch Chr; Orch; Education; Photography; U of Tennessee Chattanooga; Lee U

DISIDORO, BRANDIE M; PIKEVILLE, TN; BLEDSOE CTY HS; (FR); Hnr Roll; Comm Volntr; Chrch Yth Grp; Beta Club 6th, 7th, 8th Grade; Child Psychology; Counselor; U of Tennessee; Chattanooga State

DISNEY, LOGAN J; HEISKELL, TN; ANDERSON CTY HS; (SO); Hnr Roll; WWAHSS; Comm Volntr; Chrch Yth Grp; Emplmnt; Ftball (V L); Track (V L); Young Life Member; Project Lead the Way; Aerospace Engineering; Teacher; Auburn; Air Force Academy

DISTERDICK, HANNAH D; HIXSON, TN; SODDY DAISY HS; (SO); Nat Hon Sy; Otst Ac Ach Awd; WWAHSS; Comm Volntr; Hosp Aide; Chrch Yth Grp; Emplmnt; FCA; Key Club; Mth Clb/Tm; Ntl Beta Clb; Bnd; Ch Chr; Dnce; Mch Bnd; Cr Ctry (V); Sccr (V); Stu Cncl (R); CR (R); Doctor; Model/Dance; Belmont; Vanderbilt

DISTERDICK, JOHNNA G; HIXSON, TN; SODDY DAISY HS; (JR); Hi Hnr Roll; Hnr Roll; Nat Hon Sy; Pres Sch; WWAHSS; Yth Ldrshp Prog; Comm Volntr; Hosp Aide; Chrch Yth Grp; DECA; Emplmnt; FCA; Key Club; Ntl Beta Clb; Prom Com; Tchrs Aide; SP/M/VS; Cr Ctry (V); Vllyball (J); Cl Off (S); Jr. Miss-1st Runner Up; Talent & Fitness & Prize Winner; Attorney At Law (Political Science Major); Business Major; U of Tennessee Chattanooga; Vanderbilt

DITTRICH, JULIA; KNOXVILLE, TN; (JR); Hi Hnr Roll; Hnr Roll; Kwnis Aw; Nat Hon Sy; Otst Ac Ach Awd; Perf Att; St of Mnth; WWAHSS; Comm Volntr; Chrch Yth Grp; Key Club; MuAlphaTh; P to P St Amb Prg; Prom Com; French Clb; Ch Chr; PP Ftbl; CR (R); Secondary Education; Austin-Peay State U

DODGEN, WHITNEY; SEVIERVILLE, TN; PIGEON FORGE HS; (SR); Ctznshp Aw; Hnr Roll; Perf Att; WWAHSS; Spec Olymp Vol; Emplmnt; Jr Cls League; Lttrmn Clb; Ntl Beta Clb; Prom Com; Vsity Clb; Latin Clb; Bskball (V CL); Cr Ctry (V L); Track (V); Vllyball (V CL); Girls Basketball-All District, All-District Tournament, All-Region Tournament; Psychology/Sociology Major; Lees-McRae College

DOHRMANN, MARY; NASHVILLE, TN; HILLSBORO COMP HS; (JR); F Lan Hn Soc; Hi Hnr Roll; Nat Hon Sy; WWAHSS; Comm Volntr; Jr Cls League; Off Aide; Quiz Bowl; Chr; Cl Off (R); Stu Cncl (R); Sch Ppr (E, R, P); Knitting Club

DOMINGUEZ CHAIDEZ, VALERIA; MEMPHIS, TN; ARLINGTON HS; (FR); Ctznshp Aw; Hnr Roll; Perf Att; Pres Ac Ftns Aw; St of Mnth; Sccr (J); Physician; Surgeon

DONATHAN, SAMANTHA L; CROSSVILLE, TN; CUMBERLAND CTY HS; (FR); Hnr Roll; MVP; Otst Ac Ach Awd; Chrch Yth Grp; FCA; Sftball (J); Tennessee Tech U; U of Tennessee

DONEY, JAMES A; DECHERD, TN; FRANKLIN CTY HS; (JR); Hnr Roll; MVP; Perf Att; Sci Fairs; Comm Volntr; 4-H; Chrch Yth Grp; DARE; Emplmnt; Voc Ind Clb Am; Ftball (V); Wt Lftg (V); Stu Cncl; Race Go-Karts; Machinist; Tennessee Technological Center

DONIHE, RACHEL L; KINGSPORT, TN; SULLIVAN NORTH; (JR); Ctznshp Aw; Hnr Roll; Perf Att; Comm Volntr; BPA; Jr Ach; Sftball (V)

DOSS, IAN; KNOXVILLE, TN; FARRAGUT HS; (SO); Duke TS; Hnr Roll; Perf Att; DARE; Bnd; Perfect Attendance Since 1st Grade; Engineering Computer Science; U of Tennessee; Stanford

DOTSON, STACEY; LEBANON, TN; LEBANON HS; (SO); Hnr Roll; Nat Hon Sy; WWAHSS; Key Club; Spanish Clb; Chr; Fashion Designing; Lawyer; U of Tennessee; Vol State

DOTY, SAMUEL B; UNICOI, TN; UNICOI CTY HS; (JR); Jr Mshl; Otst Ac Ach Awd; Pres Sch; USAA; WWAHSS; Yth Ldrshp Prog; Comm Volntr; Peer Tut/Med; Chrch Yth Grp; Emplmnt; Key Club; Lib Aide; Ntl Beta Clb; German Clb; Bskball (VJ); Cl Off

DOUGHERTY, ELEANOR E; MADISONVILLE, TN; MC MINN CTY HS; (SR); Duke TS; Hi Hnr Roll; Nat Hon Sy; WWAHSS; Yth Ldrshp Prog; Comm Volntr; Spec Olymp Vol; Chrch Yth Grp; FCCLA; HO'Br Yth Ldrshp; MuAlphaTh; Ntl FFA; Off Aide; Svce Clb; PP Ftbl; Tennis (J L); Stu Cncl (R); Yrbk (R, P); HOBY Representative; FCCLA Power of One; Interior Design; U of Tennessee Chattanooga

DOUGHMAN, GRANT; CLARKSVILLE, TN; CLARKSVILLE HS; (JR); Hi Hnr Roll; Hnr Roll; MVP; Sci Fairs; WWAHSS; Comm Volntr; Peer Tut/Med; Spec Olymp Vol; Chrch Yth Grp; DARE; FCA; Svce Clb; Tchrs Aide; Chr; Ch Chr; Swg Chr; Bsball (V CL); Ftball (V L); Stu Cncl (R); CR (R); Boys State; Dentistry; Austin Peay State U; U of Tennessee Knoxville

DOUGLASS, LUAREN; COLLIERVILLE, TN; COLLIERVILLE HS; (JR); Hnr Roll; Otst Ac Ach Awd; Perf Att; USAA; Yth Ldrshp Prog; Comm Volntr; Chrch Yth Grp; Drma Clb; Key Club; MuAlphaTh; Ntl Beta Clb; Spanish Clb; Chr; Ch Chr; SP/M/VS; Stg Cre; Bskball (J); Sftball (VJ); Sch Ppr (R, P); English; Public Relations; Christian Brothers U; Union U

DOVER, TANGELA; MEMPHIS, TN; CARVER HS; (SO); Hnr Roll; Nat Hon Sy; Ntl Beta Clb; ROTC; Drl Tm; PPSqd; Bachelor of Science; Doctor of Medicine; Christian Brothers U; U of Tennessee

DOYLE, TABITHA; JAMESTOWN, TN; ALVIN C YORK AGRI INS; (JR); 4H Awd; Hnr Roll; Otst Ac Ach Awd; Perf Att; St of Mnth; Peer Tut/Med; FCCLA; Pep Squd; Prom Com; Voc Ind Clb Am; Tennessee Technology University; Roane State Community College

DRAPER, SUSAN L; JONESBOROUGH, TN; DAVID CROCKETT HS; (JR); Duke TS; Hi Hnr Roll; Hnr Roll; Pres Sch; WWAHSS; Spanish Clb; Chr; English; Education; East Tennessee State U; Vanderbilt

DRISCOLL, CASEY A; GOODLETTSVILLE, TN; NASHVILLE SCH OF THE ARTS; (SO); Hi Hnr Roll; Nat Hon Sy; WWAHSS; Chrch Yth Grp; Ntl Beta Clb; Scouts; Bnd; Ch Chr; Orch; Swg Chr; Eagle Scout, Boy Scouts of America; Order of the Arrow, Boy Scouts of America; Doctorate of Music; Teach At a College or U; Belmont U in Nashville, TN

DRIVER, ARTAVEUS; MEMPHIS, TN; MITCHELL HS; (SR); Hnr Roll; Nat Hon Sy; Perf Att; WWAHSS; Comm Volntr; Drma Clb; Chr; Bsball; Bskball (V); Sch Ppr (P); Yrbk (E); Music Performance; Computer Technology; LeMoyne-Owen College; Clark Atlanta U

DUCK, EMILY D; JEFFERSON CITY, TN; JEFFERSON CTY HS; (JR); Hi Hnr Roll; Nat Hon Sy; WWAHSS; Yth Ldrshp Prog; Chrch Yth Grp; FCA; FCCLA; Ntl Beta Clb; Ch Chr; Swmg (V C); Yrbk (R); City League Swim Team-Most Improved; National Technical Honor Society; Family & Consumer Science Education

DUDAS, CHASETON; HALLS, TN; HALLS HS; (JR); Hnr Roll; MVP; Perf Att; WWAHSS; Comm Volntr; Peer Tut/Med; ArtClub; FCA; Ntl FFA; Bsball (V L); Ftball (V L); Golf; Wt Lftg (V); Stu Cncl (R); Forensic Science; History; U of Tennessee; U of Tennessee At Martin

DUDLEY, CHRIS; MURFREESBORO, TN; BLACKMAN HS; (SR); Hi Hnr Roll; Hnr Roll; WWAHSS; Comm Volntr; Peer Tut/Med; Chrch Yth Grp; Emplmnt; Key Club; Mth Clb/Tm; Tchrs Aide; Key Club Member, Committee Chair of Renaissance; Architect; Youth Pastor; Middle Tennessee State U

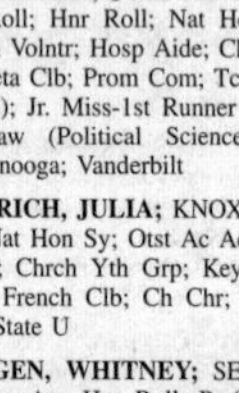

Disney, Logan J
Anderson Cty HS
Heiskell, TN

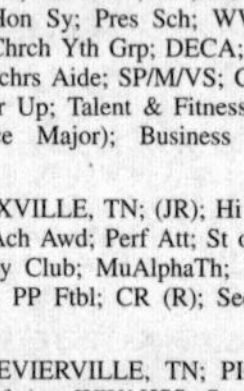

Denton, Andrew H
Soddy-Daisy HS
Soddy Daisy, TN

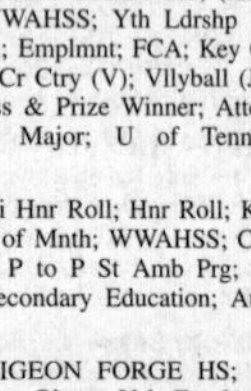

Derossett, Jeffrey D
Cheatham Cty Ctrl HS
Ashland City, TN

DUGGIN, RACHEL; BRADYVILLE, TN; CANNON CTY HS; (FR); Hi Hnr Roll; Hnr Roll; 4-H; Chrch Yth Grp; DARE; FCA; SADD; Sftball (J); Agriculture; Veterinary Medicine; U of Tennessee; Vanderbilt U

DUIGNAN, KAITLYN; STRAWBERRY PLAINS, TN; JEFFERSON CTY HS; (JR); Hi Hnr Roll; Nat Hon Sy; Perf Att; Valdctrian; WWAHSS; Yth Ldrshp Prog; Chrch Yth Grp; FCA; Ntl Beta Clb; Swg Chr; Sccr (V C); Yrbk (R); Pre-Medicine; Pre-Law; Vanderbilt; Baylor

DUKE, CHARLES; HENDERSONVLLE, TN; BEECH HS; (SO); Hnr Roll; Perf Att; 4-H; Chrch Yth Grp; Ntl FFA; Science

DUKE, HEATHER M; HENDERSONVILLE, TN; HENDERSONVILLE HS; (SR); Hnr Roll; Pres Sch; WWAHSS; Yth Ldrshp Prog; Comm Volntr; Chrch Yth Grp; DARE; Drma Clb; Emplmnt; FCA; FBLA; Ntl Beta Clb; Ntl FFA; Elementary Education; Maryville College; Samford U

DUKOVAC, THOMAS E; BRENTWOOD, TN; CENTENNIAL HS; (JR); Hi Hnr Roll; Hnr Roll; Nat Mrt LOC; Perf Att; Pres Ac Ftns Aw; St of Mnth; Comm Volntr; Chrch Yth Grp; Emplmnt; P to P St Amb Prg; Wdwrkg Clb; Latin Clb; Bnd; Pep Bnd; Ftball (J); 2-Time National Latin Exam Silver Medalist; 3 Yrs in Ski Club; BA in International Business with MBA; Belmont U; Vanderbilt U

DUMAS, JESSICA; KNOXVILLE, TN; HALLS HS; (SO); 4H Awd; Perf Att; WWAHSS; Peer Tut/Med; 4-H; Chrch Yth Grp; DARE; Dbte Team; Mus Clb; Chr; Mentor for Incoming Freshmen; Seeking RN Degree or Ob/Gyn

DUNCAN, CAITLYN; KINGSPORT, TN; DOBYNS-BENNETT HS; (SO); Ctznshp Aw; Hi Hnr Roll; Hnr Roll; Nat Hon Sy; WWAHSS; Comm Volntr; Key Club; Spanish Clb; Bnd; Dnce; Mch Bnd; Pep Bnd; Danced in the Nutcracker Ballet and Showtime; Pharmacy; U of Tennessee; East Tennessee State U

DUNCAN, LINDSAY; SMYRNA, TN; LA VERGNE HS; (FR); 4H Awd; Duke TS; Hi Hnr Roll; Hnr Roll; Comm Volntr; Peer Tut/Med; 4-H; Drma Clb; NtlFrnscLg; NYLC; Pep Squd; Tmpl Yth Grp; SP/M/VS; Stg Cre; Stu Cncl (R); CR (R); Debate Team; Poetic Dialect; Psychology; The Performing Arts; The U of Tennessee; Middle Tennessee State U

DUNN, BROOKE; FARRAGUT, TN; FARRAGUT HS; (JR); Perf Att; DARE; Bnd; Ch Chr; Mch Bnd; Track (J); Psychologist; Biologist; Pellissippi State; Louisiana State

DURFEE, VANESSA; CLINTON, TN; ANDERSON CTY HS; (JR); Hnr Roll; Comm Volntr; Hosp Aide; Chrch Yth Grp; NYLC; Voc Ind Clb Am; Cosmetology; Tennessee School of Beauty

DURHAM, LESLIE A; CLARKSVILLE, TN; CLARKSVILLE HS; (JR); Hi Hnr Roll; Otst Ac Ach Awd; Perf Att; WWAHSS; DARE; FCA; Jr Cls League; Mus Clb; Ntl Beta Clb; Svce Clb; Chr; SP/M/VS; Swg Chr; Mid-State Choir; Pre-Med; Austin Peay State U

DYKES, JODY; KNOXVILLE, TN; CENTRAL HS; (SR); Hnr Roll; Nat Hon Sy; WWAHSS; Comm Volntr; Key Club; MuAlphaTh; Bnd; Sccr (V L); U of Tennessee

DYSON, JASMINE; COVINGTON, TN; COVINGTON HS; (SO); Hnr Roll; Sci Clb; Ch Chr; UT Martin; Lain College

EARNHARDT, BRANDI; BRUSH CREEK, TN; GORDONSVILLE HS; (JR); Perf Att; St of Mnth; WWAHSS; ArtClub; Chess; Cmptr Clb; DARE; Scouts; Voc Ind Clb Am; Spanish Clb; Chr; Chrldg (V); Perfect Attendance; Jump Queen for Cheerleading; Middle Tennessee State U; Tennessee Tech

EASTHAM, LAUREN A; GALLATIN, TN; GALLATIN HS; (SO); Hnr Roll; WWAHSS; Hosp Aide; Spec Olymp Vol; Chrch Yth Grp; Emplmnt; Key Club; Stu Cncl (R); CR (R); Member of Tri-Hi-Y; Volunteer At Relay for Life; USDA Earth Team Volunteer; Volunteered At Special Olympics 2 Yrs.; Neo-Natal Nurse Practitioner; Pediatrician; Western Kentucky U; Volunteer State Community College

EAVES, TYLER; DRESDEN, TN; DRESDEN HS; (SR); Hnr Roll; Nat Hon Sy; Otst Ac Ach Awd; 4-H; AL Aux Boys; DARE; Mth Clb/Tm; MuAlphaTh; Ntl Beta Clb; Ntl FFA; Ftball (V); English; History; U of Tennessee At Knoxville; U of Tennessee At Martin

ECHOLS, PASSION; MURFREESBORO, TN; SIEGEL HS; (SO); Hi Hnr Roll; Hnr Roll; WWAHSS; Comm Volntr; Chess; Chrch Yth Grp; Civil Air Pat; Emplmnt; Key Club; Ch Chr; Bskball (V); Bowling Team, Key Club; Chess Club; Architecture; MTSU

EDEN, JENNIFER; ANTIOCH, TN; HOMESCHOOL; (SR); Comm Volntr; Chrch Yth Grp; Emplmnt; Prom Com; Ch Chr; Dnce; SP/M/VS; Cr Ctry (V); Yrbk (E, P); 2001 Harding Place YMCA Volunteer of the Year; Harding Place YMCA Board of Directors Member; Theatre/Drama; Graphic Design; Belmont U, Nashville, Tennessee

EDENS, MARK; HARROGATE, TN; CUMBERLAND GAP HS; (JR); Hnr Roll; Nat Hon Sy; Drma Clb; Key Club; Ntl Beta Clb; Ch Chr; PhD in Anesthesiology; U of Tennessee

EDWARDS, CASSIDY; HOHENWALD, TN; LEWIS CTY HS; (SR); Hi Hnr Roll; Hnr Roll; WWAHSS; BPA; Chrch Yth Grp; P to P St Amb Prg; Sci Clb; Tchrs Aide; Chr; Dnce; Mch Bnd; Chrldg (V); Majorette (Baton Twirler) Co-Captain; Dance Education; Mass Communications; U of Tennessee At Martin; Columbia State Community College

EDWARDS, RACHEL M; ERWIN, TN; U N 1001 CTY VOC SCH; (SR); Ctznshp Aw; Hnr Roll; MVP; Perf Att; WWAHSS; Peer Tut/Med; ArtClub; Chrch Yth Grp; Key Club; Pep Squd; Vsity Clb; German Clb; Sftball (V); King College; Virginia Intermont

EDWARDS, SARA; RIVES, TN; OBION CTY CTRL HS; (SO); All Am Sch; Hnr Roll; Nat Ldrshp Svc; Otst Ac Ach Awd; USAA; WWAHSS; Comm Volntr; ArtClub; Emplmnt; FBLA; Key Club; Ntl Beta Clb; Pep Squd; Svce Clb; Tchrs Aide; SP/M/VS; Tennis; Stu Cncl (R); CR (R); 1st Place Categories, Art Show OCCHS; Teen Advisory Board, Obion Cty Public Library; Visual Design, Computers; International Relations; Rhodes College; Memphis State U

EGGERS, MINDY D; JONESBOROUGH, TN; DAVID CROCKETT HS; (SO); 4H Awd; MVP; Nat Stu Ath Day Aw; Perf Att; Pres Ac Ftns Aw; Sci Fairs; Comm Volntr; Peer Tut/Med; 4-H; Chrch Yth Grp; DARE; FCA; Voc Ind Clb Am; Ch Chr; Bskball (J); Gmnstcs (J); Sftball (V); Doctor Degree; Duke U; U of Tennessee-Knoxville

EIDSON, DANIELLE R; ROGERSVILLE, TN; VOLUNTEER HS; (SR); Perf Att; WWAHSS; Peer Tut/Med; Chrch Yth Grp; Emplmnt; Tchrs Aide; Ch Chr; Physical Therapy; Massage Therapy; Lincoln Memorial U; Berea College

EIDSON, NIKKI; GALLATIN, TN; GALLATIN HS; (SO); Nat Hon Sy; WWAHSS; Key Club; Chrldg; Computer Information Systems; Business; Tennessee Technological U; Western Kentucky U

ELKINS, CHERI L; HEISKELL, TN; HALLS HS; (JR); Hi Hnr Roll; Hnr Roll; Nat Hon Sy; Perf Att; St of Mnth; WWAHSS; Chrch Yth Grp; Emplmnt; Mus Clb; French Clb; Acpl Chr; Chr; SP/M/VS; Church Organist; Pianist (II Years); Jazz Pianist; Choir Director; U of Tennessee, Knoxville; Carson-Newman College

ELLERSON, AISHA S; MEMPHIS, TN; (JR); Hnr Roll; Nat Hon Sy; Comm Volntr; Chrch Yth Grp; Emplmnt; Ch Chr; Drl Tm; Bskball (V); Cr Ctry (V); Mar Art; Track (V); Vllyball (V); Stu Cncl (R); ACT-SO; Mifa; Accounting; Business Management; U of Tennessee in Knoxville; Jackson State U

ELLERSON, CHANDRA R; MEMPHIS, TN; MIDDLE COLLEGE HS; (SO); Hnr Roll; Otst Ac Ach Awd; Perf Att; Sci Fairs; St of Mnth; WWAHSS; Comm Volntr; ArtClub; Chrch Yth Grp; Bskball (V); Cr Ctry (V); Mar Art; Sftball (V); Vllyball (V); Cl Off (R); CR; Psychology; Computer Technology; U of Tennessee Knoxville; Spelman College

ELLIS, COURTNEY; MURFREESBORO, TN; SIEGEL HS; (SO); Duke TS; Hi Hnr Roll; WWAHSS; ArtClub; Chrch Yth Grp; DARE; FCA; Key Club; Pep Squd; Spanish Clb; Sftball (V)

ELLIS, JANE; GERMANTOWN, TN; EVANGELICAL CHRISTIAN SCH; (FR); Cr Ctry (J L); Track (V); Medicine; Veterinary Medicine

ELLISON, ANDREA M F; ALAMO, TN; CROCKETT CTY HS; (FR); 4H Awd; Hnr Roll; Mas Aw; Nat Hon Sy; Yth Ldrshp Prog; Comm Volntr; Peer Tut/Med; 4-H; Chrch Yth Grp; FBLA; SADD; Bnd; Dnce; Jzz Bnd; Mch Bnd; Family Career Community Leaders of Am; Veterinarian; Biology; Tenn State U; Missouri Baptist College

ELLISON, BRITTANY; KNOXVILLE, TN; AUSTIN EAST MAGNET HS; (SO); Ctznshp Aw; Perf Att; Hosp Aide; ROTC; Jr Optimist; Most Improved; Nurse; Physical Therapy; Florida State; New York U

ELLISON, DANIEL M; ANTIOCH, TN; MC GAVOCK COMP HS; (JR); Hnr Roll; WWAHSS; Emplmnt; FCA; Scouts; Bnd; Chr; Mch Bnd; Bskball (VJ); Ftball (V); Political Science; Engineer; Alabama State U; Middle Tennessee State U

ELLISON, ERICA J; DECATUR, TN; MC MINN CTY HS; (FR); 4H Awd; Hnr Roll; Perf Att; Pres Ac Ftns Aw; 4-H; Chrch Yth Grp; Tchrs Aide; Ch Chr; Bskball (J); Vllyball (V); Cl Off (R); Reporter - FCCLA; Student Trainer / Physical Therapy; Medical Degree; Stanford U; U of Tennessee Knoxville

ELMORE, GRAYSON; CLEVELAND, TN; BRADLEY HS; (JR); Hnr Roll; MVP; Perf Att; WWAHSS; Spec Olymp Vol; Chrch Yth Grp; Emplmnt; FCA; Ntl Beta Clb; SP/M/VS; Ftball (V L); Track (V CL); Wt Lftg (V C); Stu Cncl (R); CR (R); Law Degree; Psychology; Coastal Carolina U; Middle Tennessee State

ELROD, ADAM; MURFREESBORO, TN; OAKLAND HS; (FR); Hnr Roll; Comm Volntr; Chrch Yth Grp; Ftball (V L); Wt Lftg (V); Architecture; Middle Tennessee State U; U of Tennessee Knoxville

ENGLE, CHRISTY N; ERWIN, TN; U N 1001 CTY VOC SCH; (SR); 4H Awd; Hi Hnr Roll; Hnr Roll; WWAHSS; Comm Volntr; 4-H; ArtClub; Chrch Yth Grp; DARE; Drma Clb; FCA; FCCLA; FTA; Yrbk (P); LMU; Northeast State

ENGLISH, NATASHA; MOUNTAIN CITY, TN; JOHNSON CTY HS; (FR); Hnr Roll; Perf Att; Comm Volntr; 4-H; Chrch Yth Grp; Bnd; Mch Bnd; Pep Bnd; Northeast State U; East Tennessee State U

ERICKSON, JESSICA A; NEWPORT, TN; COSBY HS; (SO); Hnr Roll; WWAHSS; Drma Clb; Key Club; Ntl Beta Clb; Bnd; SP/M/VS; Sftball (V); Business; Vanderbilt U; U of Tennessee

ESCUE, GERRI D; LAWRENCEBURG, TN; LAWRENCE CTY HS; (FR); Ctznshp Aw; Perf Att; Bnd; Mch Bnd; Pep Bnd; Interact Club; Mississippi State U; Columbia State Community College

EUBANKS, JESSICA E; GALLATIN, TN; GALLATIN HS; (SO); Hi Hnr Roll; Nat Hon Sy; Comm Volntr; Spec Olymp Vol; Chrch Yth Grp; Drma Clb; Key Club; Mus Clb; Svce Clb; Chr; Dnce; SP/M/VS; Cl Off (R); GHS National Honor Society; GHS Cotillion Club; Nursing; Medical Field

EULLS, ASHLEY R; MEMPHIS, TN; MIDDLE COLLEGE HS; (SR); Ctznshp Aw; Hnr Roll; Nat Hon Sy; Comm Volntr; DARE; DECA; Emplmnt; Prom Com; Chr; Ch Chr; Dnce; Cl Off (R); CR (R); Lawyer; Doctor; Clark Atlanta U; Jackson State U

EVANS, AMANDA R; NEW JOHNSONVILLE, TN; WAVERLY CTRL HS; (FR); 4H Awd; Hnr Roll; Perf Att; Peer Tut/Med; 4-H; DARE; Tchrs Aide; Tech Clb; Cl Off (T); Sch Ppr (E, R); Technology Award; Mentor Mates; Pharmacist Degree; U of Tennessee; Austin Peay U

EVANS, BRITTANY; CLEVELAND, TN; WALKER VALLEY HS; (SO); Hnr Roll; Nat Hon Sy; St of Mnth; WWAHSS; Chrch Yth Grp; FCA; FBLA; Key Club; Ntl Beta Clb; Dnce; Cr Ctry (V); Track (V); Agape Club; Anchor Club; Psychology; Law; East Tennessee State U; University of Tennessee Knoxville

EVANS, CECILIA A; MEMPHIS, TN; CRAIGMONT HS; (SR); Hi Hnr Roll; WWAHSS; Ch Chr

EVANS, CHRISTOPHER S; LEWISBURG, TN; MARSHALL CTY HS; (FR); Hnr Roll; FCA; Ftball (J); Computer Graphics; Engineering; Middle Tennessee State U; U of Tennessee

EVELY, THOMAS B; ERWIN, TN; U N 1001 CTY VOC SCH; (SR); Hnr Roll; Kwnis Aw; Nat Hon Sy; Pres Sch; WWAHSS; 4-H; AL Aux Boys; Chrch Yth Grp; Drma Clb; FCA; Ntl Beta Clb; German Clb; Ch Chr; Bsball (V L); Bskball (V CL); Ftball (V CL); Cl Off (P); Stu Cncl (P, V); Fellowship of Christian Athletes-President; Delegate to Boys' State; Physical Therapy; Teaching; East Tennessee State U

EWING, J R; LUTTRELL, TN; UNION CTY HS; (SR); All Am Sch; Hi Hnr Roll; Hnr Roll; Nat Hon Sy; Valdctrian; WWAHSS; Chrch Yth Grp; Emplmnt; Ntl Beta Clb; Ntl FFA; Tchrs Aide; Yrbk (E); United States Academic Decathlon; Star Greenhand Award (FFA); Pre-Med; U of Tennessee Knoxville; East Tennessee State U

EWING, MICHAEL L; POWELL, TN; TEMPLE BAPTIST AC; (FR); Hnr Roll; MVP; Otst Ac Ach Awd; Perf Att; Chrch Yth Grp; Mus Clb; Bnd; Orch; Pep Bnd; Bsball (V L); Bskball (VJCL); Sccr (V L); American History; U of Tennessee; Duke U

EZELL, DEREK; MARTIN, TN; MARTIN WESTVIEW HS; (SR); BPA; Chrch Yth Grp; FCA; Tchrs Aide; French Clb; Chr; Sccr (V); Pre-Med; Physical Therapy; Union U

EZELL, JESSICA B; SODDY DAISY, TN; RIVERDALE HS; (SR); Hi Hnr Roll; Hnr Roll; Nat Hon Sy; WWAHSS; Comm Volntr; Hosp Aide; Chrch Yth Grp; Ntl Beta Clb; Off Aide; Sci Clb; Svce Clb; Tchrs Aide; Swmg (V); Biology; Pre-Med; U of Tennessee Chattanooga

FAGAN II, JEFFERY G; MT JULIET, TN; MT JULIET HS; (JR); Hnr Roll; Nat Hon Sy; USMC Stu Ath Aw; WWAHSS; Yth Ldrshp Prog; Hosp Aide; Peer Tut/Med; ROTC; Vsity Clb; Bskball (J); Ftball (V); Mar Art (V); Track (V); Wt Lftg (V); Anesthetist / Pre-Med; U of Alabama; Tuskegee U

FAIRBEE, GABRIELLE A; MEMPHIS, TN; CENTRAL HS; (SO); Ctznshp Aw; Hi Hnr Roll; Nat Hon Sy; Otst Ac Ach Awd; Perf Att; Sci Fairs; St of Mnth; Comm Volntr; Chess; Chrch Yth Grp; DARE; Drma Clb; FBLA; NYLC; Ch Chr; SP/M/VS; Law; Business; Harvard Law School; U of Memphis Law School

FANIEL, RASHIEKA; MEMPHIS, TN; MELROSE HS; (FR); 4H Awd; Hnr Roll; MVP; Nat Hon Sy; Perf Att; WWAHSS; Comm Volntr; Peer Tut/Med; 4-H; Chrch Yth Grp; Cmptr Clb; DARE; Jr Ach; Ch Chr; Bskball (J); Chrldg (C); Cr Ctry (VJ); Sftball (JC); Track (VJ); Vllyball (C); Stu Cncl (S); Nurse Practitioner; Law and Order; Florida State U; Tennessee State U

FANN, GRANT; NASHVILLE, TN; MC GAVOCK COMP HS; (JR); Clr Grd; Drl Tm; Stu Cncl (R); CR (R); National Honor Society / National Forensics League; Donelson-Hermitage Youth Leadership / Youth Legislature; Architectural Engineering; Theology Degree; Vanderbilt U

Ewing, J R
Union Cty HS
Luttrell, TN

Ellison, Erica J
Mc Minn Cty HS
Decatur, TN

Eden, Jennifer
Homeschool
Antioch, TN

Echols, Passion
Siegel HS
Murfreesboro, TN

National
Honor Roll
Spring 2005

Duke, Heather M
Hendersonville HS
Hendersonville, TN

Eidson, Danielle R
Volunteer HS
Rogersville, TN

Evans, Amanda R
Waverly Ctrl HS
New Johnsonville, TN

Fairbee, Gabrielle A
Central HS
Memphis, TN

FANN, JAKOB P; MC MINNVILLE, TN; WARREN CTY HS; (JR); Ctznshp Aw; Hi Hnr Roll; Hnr Roll; Pres Sch; St of Mnth; WWAHSS; Comm Volntr; Chess; DARE; Emplmnt; Mth Clb/Tm; MuAlphaTh; Ntl Beta Clb; Stu Cncl; Aids in Structured Athletics for Challenged Children & the ARC of Warren County; Medical Technology/Nuclear Medicine; Radiography; U of Tennessee Knoxville; Austin Peay

FANNIN, JORJINA; LEBANON, TN; LEBANON HS; (SO); WWAHSS; Comm Volntr; Peer Tut/Med; 4-H; Key Club; Lttrmn Clb; Lib Aide; Voc Ind Clb Am; Bnd; Jzz Bnd; Mch Bnd; Forensics; Stanford U; Vanderbilt U

FARMER, DANIEL L; CAMDEN, TN; BENTON CO CAREER TECH CTR; (SR); All Am Sch; Hnr Roll; Pres Ac Ftns Aw; WWAHSS; Comm Volntr; Spec Olymp Vol; DECA; Drma Clb; FCA; Lttrmn Clb; Ntl Beta Clb; Off Aide; Prom Com; Vsity Clb; SP/M/VS; Bsball (V C); Bskball (V C); Adv Cncl; Cl Off (V); Stu Cncl (P); Yrbk; Deca President; All District-Baseball; Secondary Education; Business Administration; U of Tennessee Martin

FARMER, MEGAN D; WARTBURG, TN; CENTRAL HS; (JR); Hnr Roll; Otst Ac Ach Awd; St of Mnth; Comm Volntr; Drma Clb; FCA; Prom Com; SP/M/VS; Cl Off (P); Yrbk (R); Renaissance Awards; Poetry Awards; Psychology; Physical Therapy; Lee U; Austin Peay State U

FAULKNER, CRYSTAL; MEMPHIS, TN; FAIRLEY HS; (SR); Perf Att; Red Cr Aide; Chr; Cosmetology; Interior Doctoring; Southwest Community

FAULKNER, DUSTIN; LAWRENCEBURG, TN; LAWRENCE CTY HS; 4H Awd; Hnr Roll; MVP; Perf Att; Yth Ldrshp Prog; DARE; FCA; Lib Aide; Bskball; History Major; Coaching Basketball; Florida College

FEAR, DAVID; KNOXVILLE, TN; (SO); Hnr Roll; Perf Att; WWAHSS; Chrch Yth Grp; Key Club; Bsball (VJ); Perfect Attendance K Thru 11; Sports Management; U of TN

FEARS, LETIMICIA; SPRINGFIELD, TN; SPRINGFIELD HS; (SO); Hnr Roll; WWAHSS; Ntl Beta Clb; NtlFrnscLg; Track (V); Vllyball (V); Business Major; Medical Major; Columbia U of New York; U of Georgia

FEDON, LOURIENNE; SEVIERVILLE, TN; SEVIER CTY HS; (FR); Hnr Roll; Nat Hon Sy; WWAHSS; Ntl Beta Clb; Vllyball (V L); 2004-2005 Gatorade Rookie of the Year; Zoology; U of Tennessee; East Tennessee State U

FENAUGHTY, MAIRE A; MEMPHIS, TN; FOURNIER LEARNING STRATEGIES; (FR); Duke TS; Hi Hnr Roll; Nat Hon Sy; Sci Fairs; Comm Volntr; Spec Olymp Vol; Chrch Yth Grp; Emplmnt; Ntl Beta Clb; P to P St Amb Prg; Sign Clb; Bnd; Chr; Ch Chr; Orch; Skiing; Lit Mag (E); Harp / Guitar; Sign Language Memphis Girls Choir; Attorney; Harvard U; Yale U

FENG, XUE; NASHVILLE, TN; MARTIN LUTHER KING HS; (JR); Hnr Roll; Nat Hon Sy; Nat Mrt Semif; Sci Fairs; Sci/Math Olympn; Valdctrian; Comm Volntr; Hab For Humty Volntr; Emplmnt; Mth Clb/Tm; MuAlphaTh; Ntl Beta Clb; Prom Com; SP/M/VS; Adv Cncl (R); Publications of Research Project Done At Vanderbilt U; Tennessee Governor's School for the Sciences; Biomedical Engineering; Environmental Engineering; Massachusetts Institute of Technology; Stanford U

FENNELL, LAKEASHA S; MEMPHIS, TN; SHEFFIELD HS; (SO); Hnr Roll; WWAHSS; Chrldg (J); Sftball (V); Vllyball (V); Most Enthusiastic Cheerleader; MS Ninth Grade; Veterinary; Pediatrician; Tennessee State U

FERBY, TIFFANY; NASHVILLE, TN; MAPLEWOOD HS; (SO); Hi Hnr Roll; Hnr Roll; MVP; Perf Att; DARE; Bskball (V); Business / Management; Duke U; North Carolina U

FERDJALLAH, ASMAA; KNOXVILLE, TN; FARRAGUT HS; (SR); Gov Hnr Prg; Hi Hnr Roll; Hnr Roll; Nat Hon Sy; WWAHSS; Yth Ldrshp Prog; Comm Volntr; Hab For Humty Volntr; Peer Tut/Med; ArtClub; Dbte Team; Fr of Library; JSA; Key Club; MuAlphaTh; NtlFrnscLg; Svce Clb; Stu Cncl (R); CR (R); Sch Ppr (E, R); National Honor Society-Secretary; Mu Alpha Theta 3 Year Member; Pre-Medicine; Major in Chemistry; U of Tennessee, Knoxville

FERGUSON, A JADE; JACKSON, TN; MADISON AC; (JR); Gov Hnr Prg; Hnr Roll; Perf Att; Pres Sch; WWAHSS; Comm Volntr; Hosp Aide; Chrch Yth Grp; Emplmnt; FCA; Mus Clb; Ntl Beta Clb; Svce Clb; SADD; Spanish Clb; Chr; SP/M/VS; Chrldg (L); Track (V); Vllyball (V); Pre-Medical Studies; Vanderbilt U; Pepperdine U

FESMIRE, KELLEY; JACKSON, TN; NORTHSIDE HS; (SR); Hnr Roll; WWAHSS; Comm Volntr; ArtClub; Chrch Yth Grp; Lit Mag; Technical Illustration Composition; Journalism; Jackson State Community College; Lambuth U

FIELDS, ASHLEY L; CHESTNUT MOUND, TN; GORDONSVILLE HS; (JR); Perf Att; WWAHSS; Yth Ldrshp Prog; Hab For Humty Volntr; Biology Clb; Chrch Yth Grp; Emplmnt; FCA; Prom Com; SADD; Vsity Clb; Spanish Clb; Chr; Bskball (V C); Nursing-RN; School Teacher-K-4; Cumberland U; Tennessee Tech

FINLEY, REBEKAH; KNOXVILLE, TN; TEMPLE BAPTIST AC; (SO); Hnr Roll; Otst Ac Ach Awd; Comm Volntr; Peer Tut/Med; Chrch Yth Grp; Emplmnt; Ch Chr; Orch; Vllyball (V); National Fitness Award; Bible Quizzing Team; Nursing; Teaching; Pensacola Christian College; U of Tennessee

FISHER, MARY K; MC MINNVILLE, TN; WARREN CTY HS; (FR); Hnr Roll; Pres Sch; St of Mnth; WWAHSS; Comm Volntr; Chrch Yth Grp; Emplmnt; Lttrmn Clb; Ntl Beta Clb; Off Aide; Pep Squd; Ch Chr; Bskball (J); Sftball (J); Vllyball (V L); Stu Cncl (R); CR (R); All District Freshman for Volleyball; Law (Criminal)

FISHER, VIVIAN E; COLUMBIA, TN; COLUMBIA CTRL HS; (SR); Hi Hnr Roll; Hnr Roll; WWAHSS; Comm Volntr; Peer Tut/Med; Chrch Yth Grp; Drma Clb; Emplmnt; Mus Clb; Tchrs Aide; Acpl Chr; Chr; Ch Chr; SP/M/VS; Track (J); Lit Mag (E); Choral Departmental Award; Church Basketball Player / Coach; English Major; Theatre Arts Minor; Columbia State Community College; Middle Tennessee State U

FISKE, BROOKE; MANCHESTER, TN; COFFEE CTY CTRL HS; (SR); Hi Hnr Roll; Nat Hon Sy; ArtClub; PP Ftbl (V); U of Tennessee Martin

FISSEHA, TEEMAR Z; SHELBYVILLE, TN; TULLAHOMA HS; (SR); All Am Sch; Nat Hon Sy; Comm Volntr; Chrch Yth Grp; FCA; Key Club; MuAlphaTh; French Clb; 2005 Friendliest Superlative; 3rd Place Short Story Contest Winner for Tullahoma Women's Club Contest; Psychology; Linguistics; I Will Be Attending the U of Virginia in Fall 2005

FITHIAN, ZACKERY I; LEBANON, TN; LEBANON HS; (FR); Duke TS; Peer Tut/Med; Emplmnt; Bnd; Duke Talent Search; Completed Gateway in 8th Grade; Computer Field; Culinary Arts; U of Tennessee; Auburn

FITZHUGH, LEILANI; MEMPHIS, TN; MIDDLE COLLEGE HS; (SR); Nat Hon Sy; Comm Volntr; Chrch Yth Grp; Prom Com; Chr; Ch Chr; Jzz Bnd; Mch Bnd; Bskball (V); Cr Ctry (V); Sftball (V); Tennis (V); Stu Cncl (P); PhD Pharmacy; Fisk U; Xavier U

FLANARY, LAUREN; LIMESTONE, TN; DAVID CROCKETT HS; (SO); Duke TS; Hnr Roll; Nat Hon Sy; St of Mnth; WWAHSS; Chrch Yth Grp; FCA; Ntl FFA; Spanish Clb; Sccr (V L); Track (V); Cl Off (T); Yrbk (R); Civinettes; Clown Troupe, Hiking Club; Education-English Teacher; Tennessee Tech U

FLANIGAN, JADE; KNOXVILLE, TN; HALLS HS; (FR); Ctznshp Aw; Hnr Roll; Otst Ac Ach Awd; Sci/Math Olympn; St of Mnth; Comm Volntr; Chrch Yth Grp; Cmptr Clb; Drma Clb; Mus Clb; Pep Squd; Chr; Ch Chr; SP/M/VS; Stg Cre; Stu Cncl (R); Lit Mag (R); Degree in Acting, Drama/Stage; U of Tennessee; Art School in Atlanta

FLEET, CHELSEA L; ARLINGTON, TN; FAYETTE AC; (MS); Hi Hnr Roll; Sci Fairs; Comm Volntr; Chrch Yth Grp; Sign Clb; Ch Chr; SP/M/VS; Sccr (V); One of Ten 8th Grade Students Chosen Nationwide By the History Channel; To Participate In The "Just Ask Ben" Program; Theatre; Marine Biology

FLEISHOUR, AUSTIN; PEGRAM, TN; NASHVILLE CHRISTIAN SCH; (JR); 4H Awd; Ctznshp Aw; Hi Hnr Roll; Hnr Roll; MVP; Nat Hon Sy; Otst Ac Ach Awd; Perf Att; Pres Ac Ftns Aw; Chrch Yth Grp; Emplmnt; FCA; Bsball (V L); Bskball (J); Ftball (VJ L); Wt Lftg (VJ); All-State Team, Basketball, 8th Grade; All-Region, Honorable Mention, 11th Grade; Sports Medicine; Engineering; U of North Carolina of Chapel Hill; U of Tennessee At Knoxville

FLIPPIN, BILLIE; MEMPHIS, TN; KINGSBURY MIDDLE HS; (SR); Hnr Roll; Comm Volntr; Hosp Aide; Peer Tut/Med; ArtClub; FCCLA; ROTC; Spanish Clb; Registered Nurse; Southwest Tennessee Community College; U of Tennessee

FLOREZ, NIKKI; BIG ROCK, TN; STEWART CTY HS; (SO); 4H Awd; Hnr Roll; Perf Att; WWAHSS; Comm Volntr; 4-H; Spanish Clb; Bnd; Clr Grd; Mch Bnd; Forensic Scientist; Austin Peay State U

FLOWERS, JOSEPH; CHARLESTON, TN; WALKER VALLEY HS; (SR); Hi Hnr Roll; Jr Rot; Nat Hon Sy; Nat Mrt Sch Recip; Otst Ac Ach Awd; Perf Att; Comm Volntr; Chess; Chrch Yth Grp; FCA; Ntl Beta Clb; Bnd; Ch Chr; Jzz Bnd; Mch Bnd; 1st Chair-Concert Band, 4 Yrs on Drumline; Band "Best Player" 10 & 11th Grade, "Most Talented Senior Superlative"; Will Major in Music At Lee U School of Music; Lee U

FLOYD, ERIN; KINGSPORT, TN; DOBYNS BENNETT HS; (JR); Duke TS; Hi Hnr Roll; Jr Mshl; Nat Hon Sy; Valdctrian; WWAHSS; AL Aux Girls; Emplmnt; FCA; Jr Cls League; Key Club; MuAlphaTh; Ntl Beta Clb; Bnd; Cr Ctry (V); Track (J); Kamato's Waitress; Confirmation Mentor; Pre-Med; Swarthmore; Bates

FLOYD, MASON F; KNOXVILLE, TN; SOUTH DOYLE HS; (SO); Hnr Roll; Nat Hon Sy; Sci/Math Olympn; Peer Tut/Med; FBLA

FLOYD, TERRI L; WHITWELL, TN; WHITWELL HS; (JR); Hi Hnr Roll; Hnr Roll; Perf Att; St of Mnth; WWAHSS; Peer Tut/Med; FCA; Ntl Beta Clb; Prom Com; PP Ftbl (V); Cl Off (P); Stu Cncl (V); CR (R); Chattanooga State; U of Tennessee

FLUELLEN, CYNTHIA; MEMPHIS, TN; WHITEHAVEN HS; (JR); WWAHSS; Comm Volntr; Dnce; PPSqd (V); Cl Off (P); Stu Cncl (R); National English Merit Award; Who's Who Among America's High School; Majoring in Medicine/Obstetrician; Minor in Dance; U of Tennessee Martin; U of Texas Southern

FORBES, ALEX; COLLIERVILLE, TN; COLLIERVILLE HS; (JR); Hnr Roll; Comm Volntr; Drma Clb; Emplmnt; Ntl Beta Clb; SP/M/VS; Stg Cre; Yrbk (P); Mass Communications; Television Producer

FORD, ANISHA S; MEMPHIS, TN; MIDDLE COLLEGE HS; (JR); Hnr Roll; Nat Hon Sy; WWAHSS; Pep Squd; Photog; Prom Com; ROTC; Bskball (V); Cr Ctry (V); Track (V); Yrbk (P); Bowling Team-Top 10 in District; History; Biology; Tennessee State U; U of Memphis

FORD, MEGAN; FRANKLIN, TN; HOMESCHOOL; (JR); WWAHSS; Chrch Yth Grp; Emplmnt; Yrbk (P); Art Exhibits in School Talent Show, Library; 2nd Place Winner in Calendar Contest (WCMC); Production Design; New York U; Columbia U Chicago

FORD, SAMUEL A; UNICOI, TN; UNICOI CTY HS; (JR); Hnr Roll; Nat Hon Sy; Chrch Yth Grp; FCA; Ntl Beta Clb; Voc Ind Clb Am; Bsball (V); Reporter VICA Club; Engineer

FORNSHELL, RICHARD; SUMMERTOWN, TN; SUMMERTOWN HS; (FR); 4H Awd; Hnr Roll; WWAHSS; 4-H; Chrch Yth Grp; DARE; Schol Bwl; Scouts; Bnd; Pep Bnd; High School Bowling - Varsity Letter; Biochemistry; Medical Practitioner; Vanderbilt U

FORREST, SEAN C; HIXSON, TN; SODDY-DAISY HS; (FR); DAR; Duke TS; Hi Hnr Roll; Perf Att; Yth Ldrshp Prog; Chrch Yth Grp; Mod UN; Ntl Beta Clb; Bnd; Mch Bnd; Tennis (V L); Stu Cncl (R); YMCA Southeastern Middle School Model UN Vice-President; YMCA Youth Trust Leadership Conference; Medicine; Engineering; Duke U; Vanderbilt U

FORRESTER, JESSICA L; BUTLER, TN; HAMPTON HS; (SR); Hnr Roll; Nat Hon Sy; WWAHSS; Peer Tut/Med; BPA; Emplmnt; Pep Squd; Svce Clb; Tchrs Aide; Spanish Clb; Yrbk (R); Internet and Computer Core Certification; Diplomat Service Award; Cosmetology; Tennessee School of Beauty; Tri-City Beauty College

FORSYTH, CANDICE; BEERSHEBA SPRINGS, TN; GRUNDY CTY HS; (SO); Hi Hnr Roll; Hnr Roll; Nat Hon Sy; Nat Ldrshp Svc; Yth Ldrshp Prog; Comm Volntr; Peer Tut/Med; Chrch Yth Grp; Emplmnt; FBLA; Ntl FFA; Prom Com; Quill & Scroll; SADD; Spanish Clb; Chr; SP/M/VS; Sftball (V); Yrbk (E, R, P); Student Council - 2005-2006; Motlow State Community College; MTSU

FORTSON, KIRSTIN D; SODDY DAISY, TN; SODDY DAISY HS; (FR); Duke TS; Hnr Roll; Nat Hon Sy; Otst Ac Ach Awd; Pres Ac Ftns Aw; Sci Fairs; Comm Volntr; Chrch Yth Grp; DARE; FCA; SADD; Tchrs Aide; Bnd; Scr Kpr (VJ); Honor / Star Roll; Field of Medicine; U of Tennessee; Oklahoma U

FOSTER, BRITTANY L; MEMPHIS, TN; NORTHSIDE HS; (JR); Hnr Roll; Sci Fairs; Comm Volntr; Jr Ach; Bnd; Dnce; Drm Mjr; Mch Bnd; Nursing; Dancing; Jackson State U; Tennessee State U

FOSTER, DENTARIAS; MEMPHIS, TN; WHITE STATION HS; (FR); Hnr Roll; Chrch Yth Grp; DARE; Drma Clb; Ch Chr; Reading Awards, Honor Society Certificates; Citizenship Award, Science Fair Certificates; Business and Management, Drama/Theater; Computer Technician, and Engineering Jobs.; U of Tennessee, Louisiana State U; Texas, Kentucky, and Somewhere Close to the South

FOSTER, LAKESHIA; LA VERGNE, TN; LA VERGNE HS; (FR); Hnr Roll; Drma Clb; Scouts; Chr; SP/M/VS; Singer and Actress; Own A Restaurant; Le Cordon Bleu; New York U

FOSTER, WINDERFUL T; MEMPHIS, TN; OAKHAVEN MIDDLE HS; (FR); Hi Hnr Roll; Hnr Roll; MVP; Nat Hon Sy; Nat Mrt LOC; Sci Fairs; Sci/Math Olympn; St of Mnth; WWAHSS; Yth Ldrshp Prog; Comm Volntr; Hab For Humty Volntr; Hosp Aide; Chrch Yth Grp; Cmptr Clb; DARE; Dbte Team; Drma Clb; Fr of Library; Lttrmn Clb; Lib Aide; Ch Chr; Dnce; Flg Crps; Pep Bnd; Bskball (V); Chrldg (V); Fld Hky (V); Gmnstcs (V); Ice Hky (V); Ice Sktg (V); PPSqd (V); Rqtball (V); Adv Cncl (R); Yrbk (E); Award - Most Likely to Succeed; Award in Language Arts Certificate; Registered Nursing; Poet; The U of Memphis; The U of Tennessee

FOX, JORDAN; CLINTON, TN; CLINTON HS; (JR); Hnr Roll; DECA; FCA; Prom Com; Vsity Clb; Vllyball (VJCL); Cl Off (S); Stu Cncl (R); CR (R); Business; U of Tennessee Knoxville

FOX, RACHAEL; COLUMBIA, TN; COLUMBIA CTRL HS; (SR); 4H Awd; Gov Hnr Prg; Hnr Roll; MVP; Sci Fairs; St of Mnth; Valdctrian; Yth Ldrshp Prog; CARE; Comm Volntr; Red Cr Aide; 4-H; ArtClub; Chrch Yth Grp; DARE; Jr Ach; Key Club; Mod UN; Pep Squd; Chr; Ch Chr; SP/M/VS; Stg Cre; Chrldg (J); Fld Hky (J); Gmnstcs (J); PPSqd (J); Scr Kpr (J); Vsy Clb (J); Vllyball (J); CR (V); Yrbk (P); Guitar Club; Nursing; Lawyer; Columbia State Community College; MTSU

FOY, SERINA L; CLARKSVILLE, TN; NORTHWEST HS; (FR); Hnr Roll; Yth Ldrshp Prog; Peer Tut/Med; Spec Olymp Vol; Scouts; Dnce; Bskball (V); Scr Kpr (V); Sftball (V); AVID; Obstetrics; Basketball; U of California Los Angeles; U of Southern California

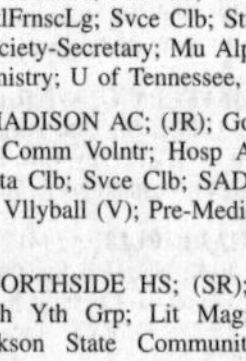

Flippin, Billie
Kingsbury Middle HS
Memphis, TN

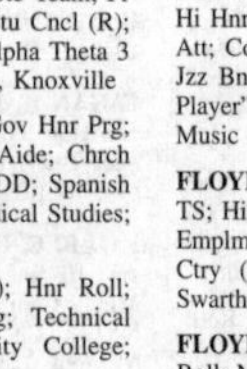

Fithian, Zackery I
Lebanon HS
Lebanon, TN

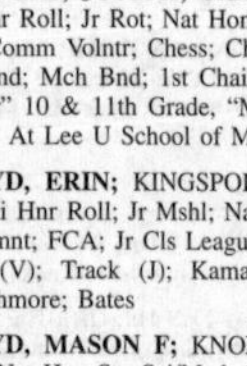

Fenaughty, Maire A
Fournier Learning Strategies
Memphis, TN

National
Honor Roll
Spring 2005

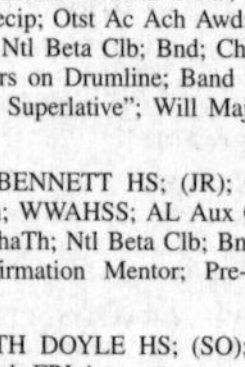

Fedon, Lourienne
Sevier Cty HS
Sevierville, TN

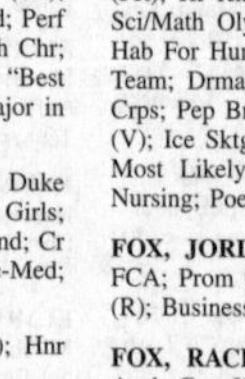

Fitzhugh, Leilani
Middle College HS
Memphis, TN

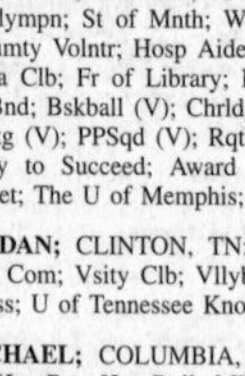

Foy, Serina L
Northwest HS
Clarksville, TN

FRADY, FELICIA L; NASHVILLE, TN; GLENCLIFF HS; (FR); 4H Awd; Hi Hnr Roll; Hnr Roll; Otst Ac Ach Awd; Perf Att; Comm Volntr; 4-H; DARE; Scouts; Former Girl Scout, Former Magnet School Attendee; Master's in Attorney At Law or Master's in Veterinary Medicine

FRANCIS, KRISTIN N; PLEASANT VIEW, TN; SYCAMORE HS; (JR); Hi Hnr Roll; Nat Hon Sy; Nat Mrt LOC; USAA; WWAHSS; Hab For Humty Volntr; Emplmnt; FCA; Ntl Beta Clb; Pep Squd; Prom Com; Dnce; Chrldg (V L); Cr Ctry (V); PPSqd (V); Cl Off (S, R); Stu Cncl (P); Yrbk (E); 2nd Runner - Up Fairest of the Fair; Mathematics; U of Tennessee; Vanderbilt U

FRANKLIN, ELEANOR R; KINGSPORT, TN; DOBYNS BENNETT HS; (JR); Duke TS; Hi Hnr Roll; WWAHSS; Comm Volntr; Chrch Yth Grp; Emplmnt; Key Club; Ntl Beta Clb; NYLC; Clr Grd; PP Ftbl (VJ); Captain-Color Guard; Global Youth Leader Conference; Business; Theatre/Dramatic Arts; New York U; George Washington U

FRANKLIN, RACHEL; LEBANON, TN; LEBANON HS; (JR); Ctznshp Aw; Duke TS; Hi Hnr Roll; Hnr Roll; Nat Hon Sy; St of Mnth; WWAHSS; Yth Ldrshp Prog; Hab For Humty Volntr; 4-H; ArtClub; FCA; Jr Ach; Key Club; Ntl Beta Clb; Off Aide; Scouts; Vllyball (V); Yrbk (E); Computer Engineer; Architect; UT Knoxville; TN Tech Cookeville

FRANKLIN JR, ROBERT A; LA VERGNE, TN; LA VERGNE HS; Hnr Roll; Ftball (J); Physical Therapy; North Caroline

FRAY, MATTHEW A; MEMPHIS, TN; GREY ROAD CHRISTIAN AC; (SR); Hnr Roll; Sci Fairs; Hosp Aide; ArtClub; Cmptr Clb; Dbte Team; Emplmnt; Scouts; Tchrs Aide; Bnd; Stg Cre; Stu Cncl (P); Part Time Worker (Manager); Literary Arts; Other Arts; U of M (U of Memphis)

FRAZER III, JOE; MEMPHIS, TN; OVERTON HS; (JR); Ctznshp Aw; Duke TS; Hi Hnr Roll; Perf Att; WWAHSS; Peer Tut/Med; Chrch Yth Grp; Jr Ach; MuAlphaTh; Ntl Beta Clb; Latin Clb; Adv Cncl (R); President of Sci-Fi Club; Physics; Mathematics; U of Alabama At Huntsville

FRAZIER, ASHLEY; CHATTANOOGA, TN; SEQUOYAH TECH CTR; (SR); Hnr Roll; WWAHSS; DARE; Emplmnt; FCCLA; Mus Clb; Clb; Early Childhood Education; Chattanooga State Tech Community College; Middle Tennessee State U

FREED, MELISSA; STRAWBERRY PLAINS, TN; BEREAN CHRISTIAN SCH; (SO); Duke TS; Hi Hnr Roll; Comm Volntr; Chrch Yth Grp; Ch Chr; Dnce; SP/M/VS; Vllyball (V); Stu Cncl (T); Art; Law Enforcement; Forensic Sciences

FREEMAN, MARVIN; MEMPHIS, TN; FRAYSER MIDDLE HS; (MS); Hnr Roll; MVP; Comm Volntr; SP/M/VS; Bskball (L); Track (C); Frayser Modeling Society; Law; Biology; Michigan State U; U of South Carolina

FREEMAN, ROGER; PIKEVILLE, TN; BLEDSOE CTY HS; (FR); Hnr Roll; Cars; Welding; U of Tennessee; U of Tennessee Chattanooga

FREYTAG, SHAUNA; WARTBURG, TN; CENTRAL HS; (JR); Hnr Roll; WWAHSS; Emplmnt; Voc Ind Clb Am; Veterinary Science; Biology; Lincoln Memorial U; U of Tennessee

FRIED, SARAH; MANCHESTER, TN; COFFEE CTY CTRL HS; (SO); Hi Hnr Roll; Otst Ac Ach Awd; Comm Volntr; Chrch Yth Grp; Quill & Scroll; Tchrs Aide; Latin Clb; Chr; Sch Ppr (E); Pre-Med; Foreign Languages and Cultures; Boston U; U of the South

FRIEDMAN, KATIE; MEMPHIS, TN; ST MARY'S EPISC SCH; (JR); F Lan Hn Soc; Nat Hon Sy; WWAHSS; Comm Volntr; Peer Tut/Med; Chrch Yth Grp; Mth Clb/Tm; MuAlphaTh; Ntl Beta Clb; Quill & Scroll; Sci Clb; Svce Clb; Clb; Bnd; Jzz Bnd; Cl Off (V); Stu Cncl (R); Director of School CD; Classical Piano; Chemical Engineering; Piano Performance; Yale U; Washington U

FUGATE III, JERRY C; JEFFERSON CTY, TN; JEFFERSON CTY HS; (SR); Comm Volntr; ROTC; Air Force

FULKERSON, NATHANIEL L; KINGSPORT, TN; SULLIVAN CTRL HS; (SO); Hi Hnr Roll; Perf Att; WWAHSS; Comm Volntr; Hosp Aide; DARE; FCA; FBLA; Key Club; Bnd; Mch Bnd; Orch; Sccr (V L); Stu Cncl (T, R); Honor Roll, Key Club, FBLA; Perfect Attendance; Engineering; Motor Sports Management/Business Admin; East Tennessee State U; U of Tennessee At Knoxville

FULLILOVE, PATRICIA; MEMPHIS, TN; CARVER HS; (SR); 4H Awd; Ctznshp Aw; Fut Prb Slvr; Hi Hnr Roll; Hnr Roll; Perf Att; Sci Fairs; St of Mnth; USAA; Yth Ldrshp Prog; CARE; Comm Volntr; Red Cr Aide; Chrch Yth Grp; Drma Clb; Emplmnt; Jr Ach; Ntl Beta Clb; ROTC; Scouts; SADD; Drl Tm; Mch Bnd; Chrldg (V); Vllyball (V); Nursing; U of Memphis; Rhodes U

FULTZ, STEVE; MURFREESBORO, TN; RIVERDALE HS; (SO); Hnr Roll; Perf Att; WWAHSS; DECA; Ntl Beta Clb; Voc Ind Clb Am; German Clb; Graphic Design; Film; Academy of Art College San Francisco; The Art Institute of California San Diego

FUQUA, KAYLA; JOELTON, TN; SYCAMORE HS; (FR); Ctznshp Aw; Nat Hon Sy; Nat Mrt Fin; Peer Tut/Med; Chrch Yth Grp; DARE; Key Club; Scouts; Bnd; Clr Grd; Mch Bnd; Marching Band Letter; Teacher; Doctor; Vanderbilt U; David Lipscomb U

GAINES, MAURICIA C; NASHVILLE, TN; EAST LITERATURE MAGNET SCH; (JR); Hnr Roll; Nat Hon Sy; Nat Ldrshp Svc; USAA; WWAHSS; Yth Ldrshp Prog; Hab For Humty Volntr; Peer Tut/Med; Chrch Yth Grp; DARE; FCA; Prom Com; Bnd; Chr; Ch Chr; Mch Bnd; Tennis (V); Track (V); Yrbk; Entrepreneurship, Prom Committee; Bowling, V; Pharmacy; Xavier U, New Orleans, LA; Howard U, Washington, DC

GALLAWAY, KATRINA; BRENTWOOD, TN; HILLSBORO HS; (JR); Hi Hnr Roll; Hnr Roll; French Clb; Drm Mjr; Flg Crps; Mch Bnd; Orch; Music Education Major; Music Performance Major; Western Kentucky U, KY; Shenandoah U, VA

GANNON, AMBER M; MURFREESBORO, TN; SIEGEL HS; (SR); Hi Hnr Roll; Hnr Roll; Nat Hon Sy; Comm Volntr; BPA; Chrch Yth Grp; Cmptr Clb; FCA; Ntl Beta Clb; Pep Squd; Scouts; Tchrs Aide; Bskball (L); Ftball (L); Scr Kpr (VJ); Business Administration; Tennessee Technological U

GANTT, DANA L; JACKSON, TN; LIBERTY TECH MAGNET HS; (SO); Comm Volntr; Chrch Yth Grp; Ntl FFA; Greenhand Award-FFA; Veterinarian; Murray State U; Sewanee U

GARCIA, EMILY; KINGSPORT, TN; DOBYNS BENNETT HS; (SR); WWAHSS; Spec Olymp Vol; Key Club; Off Aide; Scouts; Spanish Clb; Bnd; Mch Bnd; Sftball (J); Swmg (V L); Sch Ppr (R); Church Praise Team-Flutist; Athletic Training; Physical Therapy; Mars Hill College

GARD, NATHAN; SMITHVILLE, TN; DEKALB CTY HS; (JR); Hnr Roll; WWAHSS; Chrch Yth Grp; DARE; Emplmnt; Mth Clb/Tm; Spanish Clb; Ch Chr; Bsball (J); Aviation; Mechanics; Middle Tennessee State U; Tennessee Tech U

GARDNER, BRITTANY N; LOUDON, TN; LOUDON HS; (SR); 4H Awd; Hnr Roll; Nat Hon Sy; Nat Ldrshp Svc; Pres Ac Ftns Aw; WWAHSS; Yth Ldrshp Prog; Hab For Humty Volntr; Chrch Yth Grp; Emplmnt; Key Club; Prom Com; Acpl Chr; SP/M/VS; Chrldg (V CL); Gmnstcs; PP Ftbl; Track (V L); Dental / Orthodontist; Accounting; East Tennessee State U

GAREAU, BRITTANY; SEVIERVILLE, TN; SEVIER CTY HS; (FR); Ctznshp Aw; Hnr Roll; Otst Ac Ach Awd; St of Mnth; WWAHSS; Comm Volntr; Chrch Yth Grp; Emplmnt; JSA; Ch Chr; Chrldg (J); Vllyball (J); Freshman Homecoming Princess for Basketball; Lawyer; Cosmetologist or Performer (Dance & Sing); U of Tennessee; Liberty

GARNER, CHAS; DYERSBURG, TN; DYER CTY HS; (JR); Hnr Roll; Nat Hon Sy; WWAHSS; Yth Ldrshp Prog; Comm Volntr; Peer Tut/Med; Emplmnt; Chrldg; Sch Ppr (R); Yrbk (R); Ultrasound Technology; Surgical Nursing; MTSU; Jackson State Community College

GARNER, LAUREN; HUNTINGDON, TN; CLARKSBURG SCH; (SO); Ctznshp Aw; Hnr Roll; Otst Ac Ach Awd; Perf Att; Pres Ac Ftns Aw; St of Mnth; WWAHSS; Peer Tut/Med; Chrch Yth Grp; DARE; FCA; FCCLA; Ntl Beta Clb; Ntl FFA; Tchrs Aide; Chrldg (V); Cl Off (S); Stu Cncl (R); Sch Ppr (R); FCCLA Secretary; Class Representative; Dentistry; Psychology; Union U; U of TN At Martin

GARRETT, ANAWANISE M; MEMPHIS, TN; OAKHAVEN MIDDLE/HS; (JR); Ctznshp Aw; Hi Hnr Roll; Hnr Roll; Nat Hon Sy; Nat Sci Aw; Perf Att; WWAHSS; Comm Volntr; Chrch Yth Grp; DARE; Drma Clb; Emplmnt; Jr Ach; Chr; Vllyball (V); Cl Off (P); Stu Cncl (P); CR (V); Who's Who Awards; Choir Competitions; Psychology, Law; Medicine; TSU Tenn. State U; U of Memphis

GARRETT, ANDREA; MEMPHIS, TN; FRAYSER HS; (FR); Ctznshp Aw; Hnr Roll; Kwnis Aw; Perf Att; Comm Volntr; GAA (V); Girls Inc.; All Star Inc.; Business & Partnering; Fashion Majoring; Southwest Community College; Santa Monica College

GARRETT, CHARITY; LINDEN, TN; PERRY CTY HS; (JR); 4H Awd; Hi Hnr Roll; Hnr Roll; MVP; Nat Hon Sy; Otst Ac Ach Awd; Perf Att; Sci Fairs; US Army Sch Ath Aw; USMC Stu Ath Aw; Comm Volntr; Peer Tut/Med; Red Cr Aide; 4-H; ArtClub; DARE; Mth Clb/Tm; Ntl Beta Clb; Sci Clb; Tech Clb; Voc Ind Clb Am; Bnd; Chr; Ch Chr; SP/M/VS; Bskball (J); Gmnstcs (L); Hsbk Rdg (L); PP Ftbl (J); Scr Kpr (L); Sftball (J); Vllyball (J); Wt Lftg (L); Cl Off (P); Yrbk (P); 4-H Speech Winner; Medicine; Law; Columbia U; Jackson State U

GARRETT, JAMES; CELINA, TN; CLAY CTY HS; (FR); Sci Fairs; 4-H; DARE; FCA; Bnd; Mch Bnd; SP/M/VS; Master's Degree; Major in Engineering; U of Tennessee; Vanderbilt U

GARRETT, J ETHAN; WHITE HOUSE, TN; WHITE HOUSE HERITAGE HS; (FR); 4H Awd; Ctznshp Aw; Hi Hnr Roll; Hnr Roll; Nat Hon Sy; Perf Att; WWAHSS; Comm Volntr; 4-H; BPA; DARE; Emplmnt; FBLA; Key Club; Ntl Beta Clb; Scouts; Bnd; Jzz Bnd; Mch Bnd; Pep Bnd; Stu Cncl; Eagle Scout; Medicine; Vanderbilt U

GASKIN, EVAN L; EVA, TN; CENTRAL HS; (FR); Sci Fairs; 4-H; Lawyer; Wildlife Biology; Auburn U; U of Tennessee

GATES, WHITLEY E; ARDMORE, TN; ARDMORE HS; (FR); 4H Awd; Hi Hnr Roll; St of Mnth; Comm Volntr; Peer Tut/Med; Red Cr Aide; 4-H; Chrch Yth Grp; DARE; FCA; Ntl Beta Clb; SADD; Spanish Clb; Bnd; Ch Chr; Jzz Bnd; Mch Bnd; Pediatrician; Engineering Management; U of Alabama; U of Alabama Huntsville

GEABHART, SARA; CORDOVA, TN; EVANGELICAL CHRISTIAN SCH; (SO); Hnr Roll; Nat Hon Sy; WWAHSS; Yth Ldrshp Prog; Comm Volntr; Hab For Humty Volntr; Chrch Yth Grp; Emplmnt; Key Club; Bnd; Chr; Ch Chr; SP/M/VS; Who's Who Among American HS Students-05; National Society of HS Scholars-05; RN; Medical Field; U of TN Knoxville TN; Vanderbilt-Nashville TN

GEATER, MELVIN K; MEMPHIS, TN; WHITE STATION HS; (FR); Hi Hnr Roll; Hnr Roll; MVP; Otst Ac Ach Awd; Perf Att; ROTC; Chr; Drm Mjr; Stu Cncl (P); President of Middle School; Graduated with Honor; Law; Medical; Harvard; U of Tennessee

GENNETT, LYDIA M; HIXSON, TN; HIXSON HS; (FR); Chrldg (V); Sccr (V); Track (V)

GENTRY, CLAIRE; MEMPHIS, TN; RIDGEWAY HS; (SO); Hi Hnr Roll; MVP; Otst Ac Ach Awd; WWAHSS; Comm Volntr; Peer Tut/Med; Chrch Yth Grp; FCA; Key Club; P to P St Amb Prg; French Clb; Ch Chr; Bskball (V); Sccr (V); Freshman MVP Basketball; Coaches Award Basketball Sophomore; Computer Science; Production Engineering; Duke U; Stanford U

GEORGE, STEPHANIE M; EADS, TN; EVANGELICAL CHRISTIAN SCH; (JR); Hi Hnr Roll; WWAHSS; Comm Volntr; Peer Tut/Med; Chrch Yth Grp; Emplmnt; FCA; Key Club; Ntl Beta Clb; Latin Clb; Clr Grd; Baton Twirling; Pharmacy; U of Tennessee, Knoxville; U of Florida

GIBBS, MELANEICE; ANTIOCH, TN; NASHVILLE SCH OF THE ARTS; (SO); WWAHSS; Chrch Yth Grp; Ntl Beta Clb; Ch Chr; Dnce; Drm Mjr; Mch Bnd; Stu Cncl (R); CR (R); Who's Who; Business; Education; Alabama A & M U; Jackson State U

GIBSON, JOSHUA SHANE; PIONEER, TN; SCOTT HS; (JR); 4H Awd; Ctznshp Aw; Otst Ac Ach Awd; Comm Volntr; 4-H; Chrch Yth Grp; DARE; Ntl FFA; Ch Chr; Automotive Mechanic; Diesel Mechanic School

GIBSON, WM S; SEYMOUR, TN; SEYMOUR CMTY CHRISTIAN SCH; (JR); Hi Hnr Roll; Hnr Roll; Chrch Yth Grp; Emplmnt; Ch Chr; SP/M/VS; Bskball (V C); US History; Government; Tennessee Temple U; Ambassador Baptist College

GILBERT, PAUL; COOKEVILLE, TN; COOKEVILLE HS; (SO); Hnr Roll; WWAHSS; Chrch Yth Grp; Key Club; Bskball (L); Sccr (L); Communications; Broadcasting; Western Kentucky U; Belmont U

GILBERT, SARAH R; CLEVELAND, TN; WALKER VALLEY HS; (SR); Hi Hnr Roll; Nat Hon Sy; Nat Stu Ath Day Aw; St of Mnth; USAA; WWAHSS; Chrch Yth Grp; Civil Air Pat; Drma Clb; FCA; Mth Clb/Tm; MuAlphaTh; Ntl Beta Clb; Dnce; Sccr (V); Cl Off (T); CR (R); Aerospace Engineering; Georgia Institute of Technology

GILES, ETHAN T; LAWRENCEBURG, TN; SUMMERTOWN HS; (FR); Hnr Roll; WWAHSS; Chrch Yth Grp; Bnd; Ch Chr; Cr Ctry (J); Music Major; Youth Ministry; UT Knoxville

GILLIAM, JAPONICA; MASON, TN; FAYETTE-WARE HS; (SO); Hi Hnr Roll; Hnr Roll; Otst Ac Ach Awd; Perf Att; Comm Volntr; Chrch Yth Grp; FCCLA; Bnd; Ch Chr; Mch Bnd; Band 8-9th Grade; Basketball 9th Grade; Elementary-Teacher; Pharmacy; Lane College; U of Memphis

GILLIAM, STANTON; SOUTH PITTSBURG, TN; RICHARD HARDY; (SO); 4H Awd; Hnr Roll; Yth Ldrshp Prog; Comm Volntr; 4-H; DARE; Wdwrkg Clb; Stu Cncl (T)

GILLIAM, TIFFANY; MANCHESTER, TN; COFFEE CTY CTRL HS; (SO); Hi Hnr Roll; Hnr Roll; WWAHSS; Peer Tut/Med; Emplmnt; Key Club; ROTC; Spanish Clb; Drl Tm; Cl Off; Sch Ppr (R); Nominated for National Youth Leadership Forum - DID; Senate Page; Law; Psychiatry; U of Tennessee Knoxville; Middle Tennessee State U

GILMORE, LINDSAY; GRAY, TN; DANIEL BOONE HS; (JR); Duke TS; Hi Hnr Roll; WWAHSS; Chrch Yth Grp; Emplmnt; FCCLA; Key Club; Ntl Beta Clb; French Clb; Law; Accounting; U of Tennessee; Tennessee Tech

GIPSON, PRESTON; MEMPHIS, TN; FRAYSER MIDDLE HS; (JR); Hi Hnr Roll; Hnr Roll; Nat Hon Sy; Nat Ldrshp Svc; Perf Att; Comm Volntr; Peer Tut/Med; Chrch Yth Grp; DARE; Mus Clb; ROTC; Spanish Clb; Bnd; Mch Bnd; Pep Bnd; SP/M/VS; Principal's Honor Roll; Percussion Awards: Superior Leadership and Character; Music (Music Instructor); Mechanic Engineering; Prairie View A & M U; Bethune Cookman College

GIRDNER, SARAH; ATOKA, TN; BRIGHTON HS; (SO); Hnr Roll; Sci Fairs; Comm Volntr; Spec Olymp Vol; ArtClub; Chrch Yth Grp; Spanish Clb; (First Lady) Andrea Conte Walks for Tennessee's Children; National Junior Honor Society; Nursing; Business; U of Memphis; Tennessee State U

Gibson, Joshua Shane
Scott HS
Pioneer, TN

Gantt, Dana L
Liberty Tech Magnet HS
Jackson, TN

Fugate III, Jerry C
Jefferson Cty HS
Jefferson Cty, TN

National
Honor Roll
Spring 2005

Freytag, Shauna
Central HS
Wartburg, TN

Gates, Whitley E
Ardmore HS
Ardmore, TN

Gipson, Preston
Frayser Middle HS
Memphis, TN

GIRGIS, CHRISTINA; KNOXVILLE, TN; WEST HS; (JR); Hnr Roll; Perf Att; Comm Volntr; Peer Tut/Med; Chrch Yth Grp; Emplmnt; Lib Aide; Pep Squd; Stu Cncl (P); Yrbk; I'm in a Club Called Interfaith-Also As Peer Tutor; Pediatric MD; Author; East Tennessee State U; U of Tennessee

GIRTEN, JEFFREY T; GALLATIN, TN; (SR); Duke TS; Hi Hnr Roll; Nat Hon Sy; St of Mnth; Comm Volntr; Hab For Humty Volntr; Chrch Yth Grp; Emplmnt; FCA; Prom Com; Spanish Clb; Sccr (V); Adv Cncl (R); Stu Cncl (R); National Honor Society; Fellowship of Christian Athletes: Treasurer; Mechanical Engineering; U of TN At Martin

GIVENS, ZACHARY M; SMYRNA, TN; SMYRNA HS; (SR); Ctznshp Aw; Hnr Roll; Pres Ac Ftns Aw; Drma Clb; Emplmnt; Jr Cls League; Ntl Beta Clb; Latin Clb; Bnd; Jzz Bnd; Business; Meteorology; Middle Tennessee State U; David Lipscomb U

GLASS, PATTY; DYERSBURG, TN; DYERSBURG HS; (SO); Hnr Roll; Nat Hon Sy; Perf Att; USAA; WWAHSS; Yth Ldrshp Prog; Spec Olymp Vol; Chrch Yth Grp; FCA; Key Club; Lttrmn Clb; Pep Squd; Photog; Vsity Clb; Ch Chr; Chrldg (V L); Cr Ctry (V L); Swmg (V); Cl Off (V); Stu Cncl (R); CR (R); Sch Ppr (P); Student Athlete Award of Merit; Storm Assessor; Business; U of TN At Knoxville; U of Alabama

GLENN III, JOHN F; WAVERLY, TN; WAVERLY CTRL HS; (FR); 4H Awd; 4-H; Chrch Yth Grp; FCA; Ntl FFA; Scouts; Voc Ind Clb Am; Ftball (J); 4-H honor Club; Agri Science (Vet School); Welding; Middle Tennessee U

GLISSEN, COURTNEY N; MEMPHIS, TN; BOLTON HS; (SO); Hnr Roll; WWAHSS; Chrch Yth Grp; Key Club; Nurse; Baptist College; Memphis U

GLOVER, JAY; CORDOVA, TN; EVANGELICAL CHRISTIAN SCH; (JR); Duke TS; F Lan Hn Soc; Hnr Roll; Nat Hon Sy; WWAHSS; Yth Ldrshp Prog; Comm Volntr; Spec Olymp Vol; Chrch Yth Grp; Emplmnt; Key Club; Ntl Beta Clb; Quill & Scroll; Quiz Bowl; Latin Clb; Ch Chr; Stg Cre; Bsball (J); Ftball (V); Stu Cncl (R); Sch Ppr (E); Key Club President; Bausch & Lomb Science Award; Pre-Med; Marine Aviation (USMC); United States Naval Academy; Union U

GLOVER, STEPHANIE L; DELANO, TN; CENTRAL HS; (FR); Ctznshp Aw; Fut Prb Slvr; Hi Hnr Roll; Hnr Roll; Otst Ac Ach Awd; Perf Att; Pres Ac Ftns Aw; Sci Fairs; St of Mnth; Yth Ldrshp Prog; Comm Volntr; Peer Tut/Med; 4-H; ArtClub; Chrch Yth Grp; DARE; Emplmnt; FBLA; Mth Clb/Tm; Mus Clb; Chr; Ch Chr; Dnce; SP/M/VS; Chrldg (J); Hsbk Rdg (C); Sccr (L); Sftball (L); Swmg (V); Stu Cncl (R); CR (R); Waitress for a Year; Volunteer - Equine Assisted Therapeutic Riding Program; Doctor of Veterinary Medicine; MD; MTSU; Auburn U

GLUCK, EMILY K; UNICOI, TN; UNICOI CTY HS; (JR); Hnr Roll; Sci Fairs; Comm Volntr; Chrch Yth Grp; Key Club; Off Aide; Photog; Ch Chr; Bskball (V); PP Ftbl (V); Yrbk; Key Club; Secondary Education; Marketing; U of Tennessee; East Tennessee State U

GLYN-JONES, ASHLEY A; MONTEREY, TN; SMITHFIELD HS; (SO); Hnr Roll; Perf Att; 4-H; ArtClub; Fr of Library; Jr Cls League; Key Club; Ntl Beta Clb; Bnd; Jzz Bnd; Mch Bnd; Teacher; Vet; Tennessee Tech

GOAD, CRISTIE; MURFREESBORO, TN; BLACKMAN HS; (JR); Hi Hnr Roll; Hnr Roll; Kwnis Aw; Nat Hon Sy; WWAHSS; Comm Volntr; Peer Tut/Med; Red Cr Aide; BPA; Chrch Yth Grp; Drma Clb; FCA; Key Club; Ntl Beta Clb; Sci Clb; Scouts; Clr Grd; SP/M/VS; Hsbk Rdg; Accounting; Master's in Business Administration; Lipscomb U; Western Kentucky U

GODSEY, AMANDA; KINGSPORT, TN; DOBYNS BENNETT HS; (SO); Hi Hnr Roll; WWAHSS; Comm Volntr; Chrch Yth Grp; FCA; Key Club; MuAlphaTh; Ntl Beta Clb; Spanish Clb; Medical; Finance; Wake Forest; U of Tennessee

GOFORTH, LAUREN; BENTON, TN; POLK CTY HS; (FR); Hnr Roll; Perf Att; Chrch Yth Grp; Dnce; Dental Hygienist; Chef; Cleveland State

GOLDBERG, JENNIFER; ANTIOCH, TN; NASHVILLE SCH OF THE ARTS; (FR); Hnr Roll; Otst Ac Ach Awd; Sci Fairs; Chess; Photog; Chr; Dnce; SP/M/VS; Tennessean Newspaper Photography; Internship & Exhibition @ the First Museum; Fine Arts, Performing Arts; Filmmaking & Graphic Design; U of Michigan @ Ann Arbor

GOLDEN, ANTONIO; DENMARK, TN; SOUTHSIDE HS; (SO); Hnr Roll; Chrch Yth Grp; Ftball (V L); Business or Business Management; Accounting; Memphis State U, U of Tennessee; U of Michigan

GOLDSTON, PORTIA L; CHATTANOOGA, TN; CENTRAL HS; (FR); Hi Hnr Roll; Hnr Roll; Otst Ac Ach Awd; Perf Att; Sci Fairs; St of Mnth; DARE; Dbte Team; FCCLA; ROTC; Scouts; Tchrs Aide; Tech Clb; Scr Kpr (V); Track (V); Computer Engineering; Teaching; Middle Tennessee State U

GOMEZ, EVELYN; ATHENS, TN; ATHENS JHS; (MS); Hi Hnr Roll; Hnr Roll; MVP; Nat Hon Sy; Outdrs Clb; Bnd; Bskball (V); Sccr (V); Track (V); Dentistry; Duke U; U of Tennessee

GOOCH, ELIZABETH; NASHVILLE, TN; PEARL-COHN BUSINESS MAG; (JR); Hnr Roll; Perf Att; WWAHSS; Chrch Yth Grp; Tennis; Major in Child Care Development; Middle Tennessee State U; Howard U

GOOCH, NICOLE; WHITES CREEK, TN; MIDDLE COLLEGE HS; (JR); Hi Hnr Roll; Hnr Roll; Comm Volntr; Hab For Humty Volntr; Chrch Yth Grp; FCA; SADD; Chr; Ch Chr; Dnce; SP/M/VS; Housing Engineer; Doctor; Clark Atlanta U; Howard U

GOODMAN, ADAM W; MEMPHIS, TN; MELROSE HS; (FR); Hnr Roll; Nat Hon Sy; Perf Att; ROTC; JROTC Knowledge Bowl; Computer Graphics; Computer Repair; Massachusetts Institute of Technology; Christian Brothers U

GOODSON, WES; NASHVILLE, TN; MADISON SCH; (JR); Hnr Roll; St of Mnth; Comm Volntr; Emplmnt; Key Club; Lib Aide; Prom Com; Tchrs Aide; Cl Off (V); Stu Cncl (V); Writer of Poetry and Short Stories; Science; Literature

GORDON, JANEE; KNOXVILLE, TN; FULTON HS; (SO); DAR; Hnr Roll; Peer Tut/Med; Spec Olymp Vol; Chrch Yth Grp; DARE; DECA; Dnce; SP/M/VS; Cl Off (V); Stu Cncl (V); CR (V); SECHME; Path Mentor; Pediatrician; Neonatal Nurse; U of Tennessee; Carson Newman

GORDY, MICHELLE P; LAWRENCEBURG, TN; LAWRENCE CTY HS; (FR); Hnr Roll; Chrch Yth Grp; DARE; FCA; FBLA; Chr; Ch Chr; SP/M/VS; Stu Cncl (R); Safe and Smart Leaders of America; Bible Drill; Music; Drama; Mississippi State U

GOSNELL, ELAINE M; ROBBINS, TN; CENTRAL HS; (JR); Hi Hnr Roll; Otst Ac Ach Awd; St of Mnth; FCA; FCCLA; Ntl Beta Clb; Prom Com; Bskball (V); Cl Off (S); Stu Cncl (R); Received All-District Player 2005 / Player of the Week - Basketball - 2004 & 2005; Nurse; Pharmacist

GOSS, HEATHER A; TURTLETOWN, TN; COPPER BASIN HS; (SO); 4H Awd; Hi Hnr Roll; Hnr Roll; Kwnis Aw; Perf Att; Comm Volntr; 4-H; Emplmnt; FBLA; FCCLA; Key Club; Ntl Beta Clb; NYLC; Chr; Cl Off (S); 8th Grade History and Math Award; Beginning Tech Team and Heritage Club; Journalism Major; Law Major; Lee U; U of Tennessee Knoxville

GOSSETT, WILLIAM; DECHERD, TN; FRANKLIN CTY HS; (SO); Hnr Roll; WWAHSS; Ftball (V); Wt Lftg; Vet; Engineer; U of Tennessee; Middle Tennessee State U

GOTO, TAKUMI; MORRISTOWN, TN; MORRISTOWN-HAMBLEN HS WEST; (JR); Bsball (V L); Ftball (V L); Medical Field; Biological Field; U of Tennessee; Walter State Community College

GOUGE, BRIANNE A; JOHNSON CITY, TN; ELIZABETHTON HS; (SO); Hi Hnr Roll; WWAHSS; Yth Ldrshp Prog; Comm Volntr; FCA; HO'Br Yth Ldrshp; Scouts; Svce Clb; French Clb; Bskball (VJCL); Sccr (V L); Law; Vanderbilt; Georgetown

GRABNER, JOSH; GREENEVILLE, TN; GREENEVILLE HS; (SO); Svce Clb; Bnd; Mch Bnd; Sccr (J); Landscape Architecture; Education; U of Tennessee; Mississippi State U

GRAHAM, LEXIE; MORRISTOWN, TN; MORRISTOWN HAMBLEN HS WEST; (FR); Master's Degree; U of Arizona; U of Tennessee

GRANBERY, ANNE; NASHVILLE, TN; HARPETH HALL; (SR); F Lan Hn Soc; Hi Hnr Roll; Hnr Roll; Nat Hon Sy; Comm Volntr; Hosp Aide; Peer Tut/Med; Chrch Yth Grp; FCA; Outdrs Clb; Pep Squd; Prom Com; Quill & Scroll; Svce Clb; Spanish Clb; Lcrsse (V); Stu Cncl; Yrbk (E); Published in Tennessean as Nashville Eye; Cum Laude - Spanish Award; Nursing; Spanish; U of Virginia - Enrolled / Attending

GRANDBERRY, LESLIE; MEMPHIS, TN; MELROSE HS; (SO); 4H Awd; Ctznshp Aw; Hnr Roll; Nat Hon Sy; Nat Mrt LOC; Otst Ac Ach Awd; Comm Volntr; Peer Tut/Med; Chrch Yth Grp; Drma Clb; Emplmnt; Off Aide; Outdrs Clb; Prom Com; Svce Clb; French Clb; Ch Chr; SP/M/VS; Stg Cre; Sccr (V); Sftball (V); Track (V); Stu Cncl (R); Outstanding Award Poetry; Student Government Association - Service Award; Accounting / CPA; General Business; Tennessee State of U

GRANT, SHARON R; NASHVILLE, TN; HERMITAGE HALL; (JR); Hi Hnr Roll; Hnr Roll; Otst Ac Ach Awd; St of Mnth; Peer Tut/Med; Drl Tm; SP/M/VS; Bskball (V); Stu Cncl (R); CR (P); College Major-Science; U of Pennsylvania

GRANTHAM, ELIZABETH K; ESTILL SPRINGS, TN; TULLAHOMA HS; (JR); Gov Hnr Prg; Hnr Roll; Nat Hon Sy; Sci Fairs; Valdctrian; WWAHSS; Yth Ldrshp Prog; Comm Volntr; Chrch Yth Grp; Key Club; MuAlphaTh; Spanish Clb; Track (V L); Stu Cncl (R); Mayor's Youth Council-Mayor of Tullahoma 2005-2006; Barrett Browning Soc, Black Belt-Tae Kwon Do

GRANTHAM, THOMAS O; ESTILL SPRINGS, TN; TULLAHOMA HS; (FR); Hnr Roll; Pres Ac Ftns Aw; Sci Fairs; WWAHSS; Chess; Chrch Yth Grp; Key Club; Scouts; Spanish Clb; SP/M/VS

GRAPSKI, DOUGLAS; KNOXVILLE, TN; FARRAGUT HS; (SR); Duke TS; Hi Hnr Roll; MVP; Nat Hon Sy; Pres Ac Ftns Aw; WWAHSS; Yth Ldrshp Prog; Comm Volntr; Peer Tut/Med; Mth Clb/Tm; MuAlphaTh; Ice Hky (V L); Lcrsse (V CL); CR; All-State; MVP-Hockey; Biology; Chemistry; Vanderbilt; Lehigh

GRAVENOR, KIMBERLEY L; GERMANTOWN, TN; HUTCHISON HS; (JR); F Lan Hn Soc; Hi Hnr Roll; Hnr Roll; Nat Sci Aw; Comm Volntr; Hab For Humty Volntr; Mod UN; MuAlphaTh; Quill & Scroll; French Clb; Swmg (J); Sch Ppr (R); Yrbk (E); Placed 7th and 11th on National French Contest; Won 1st Place in a 90 Word Writing Competition; Dentistry; Medicine; Northwestern U; U of North Carolina At Chapel Hill

GRAY, CASEY R; JONESBOROUGH, TN; DANIEL BOONE HS; (SO); Hnr Roll; Chrch Yth Grp; DARE; FCCLA; Bskball (V); Summer Softball; Plastic Surgeon; Lawyer; East Tennessee State U; U of Tennessee

GREAVES, BRITTNEY; CLARKSVILLE, TN; CLARKSVILLE HS; (JR); Comm Volntr; Svce Clb; Tchrs Aide; Sccr (V); Surgical Nurse/Registered Nurse; Pre-Medical; King College; Bellarmine U

GREEN, BRITNEY C; LAVERGNE, TN; ANTIOCH HS; (SR); 4H Awd; Hnr Roll; Nat Hon Sy; Otst Ac Ach Awd; Sci Fairs; WWAHSS; Yth Ldrshp Prog; Comm Volntr; Peer Tut/Med; 4-H; ArtClub; BPA; Chrch Yth Grp; Drma Clb; Emplmnt; FCA; FBLA; Dnce; Tennis (V); English; Psychology; Oakwood College

GREEN, CHRISTINA; MEMPHIS, TN; GATEWAY CHRISTIAN SCH; (JR); Ctznshp Aw; Comm Volntr; Chrch Yth Grp; Mus Clb; Chr; Ch Chr; All Southwest Junior Honor Choir; All Southwest Senior Honor Choir; Major in Music; Psychology; U of Memphis; Lambuth U

GREEN, QUINDALYNN; MEMPHIS, TN; MITCHELL HS; (FR); Ctznshp Aw; F Lan Hn Soc; Hi Hnr Roll; Hnr Roll; Nat Hon Sy; Otst Ac Ach Awd; Perf Att; St of Mnth; WWAHSS; Yth Ldrshp Prog; CARE; Comm Volntr; Peer Tut/Med; Chrch Yth Grp; DARE; Emplmnt; Jr Ach; Prom Com; Scouts; SADD; French Clb; Chr; Ch Chr; Dnce; Stg Cre; Bsball (J); Bskball (J); GAA (J); Golf (J); Sftball (J); Tennis (J); Track (J); Vllyball (J); CR (R); Yrbk (R); Bowling-Captain; Coronation Runner-Up Queen; Law-Judge; Politics; Stanford U; Harvard U

GREEN, RYAN J; ALCOA, TN; ALCOA HS; (SR); Hi Hnr Roll; Hnr Roll; Nat Hon Sy; St of Mnth; Valdctrian; WWAHSS; Yth Ldrshp Prog; Chrch Yth Grp; Emplmnt; FCA; Key Club; Lib Aide; Schol Bwl; Tech Clb; Spanish Clb; Bsball (V L); Cr Ctry (V L); Golf (V L); Stu Cncl (P); Pre-Med / Orthopedics; U of Tennessee Knoxville

GREER, JASMON L; JACKSON, TN; SOUTH SIDE HS; (SO); 4H Awd; Hi Hnr Roll; Bnd; Jzz Bnd; Mch Bnd; Pep Bnd; CR (S); West Tennessee Honor Band; Band; Memphis State; Purdue

GREGG, HAYLEY; GREENEVILLE, TN; GREENEVILLE HS; (SO); Hnr Roll; Pres Ac Ftns Aw; Sci Fairs; WWAHSS; Comm Volntr; Peer Tut/Med; Spec Olymp Vol; Chrch Yth Grp; FCA; Sci Clb; Chr; Ch Chr; Dnce; SP/M/VS; Swg Chr; Chrldg (J, L); Golf (V); Sftball (JV); Yrbk (E, R, P); Who's Who Among American High School Students- Sports Edition; Pre-Med; Georgetown U- Washington, D.C.; U of Tennessee- Knoxville, Tennessee

GREGG, JOSH T; NEWPORT, TN; (SO); Wrstlg (V); USAF; Air Force Academy

GREGORY, RICHARD C; MOUNT JULIET, TN; WILSON CTRL HS; (JR); Chrch Yth Grp; Emplmnt; FCA; Sccr (V); Dental/Dentistry; Western Kentucky U; Middle Tennessee State U

GRESHAM, DANIELLE; FRANKLIN, TN; CENTENNIAL HS; (JR); Hi Hnr Roll; Hnr Roll; WWAHSS; Hab For Humty Volntr; Chrch Yth Grp; Emplmnt; Tchrs Aide; Cert; Pre-Med; U of Georgia; U of Tennessee

GRIFFIN, VALISA R; HERMITAGE, TN; NASHVILLE SCH OF THE ARTS; (SO); 4H Awd; Hi Hnr Roll; Hnr Roll; Otst Ac Ach Awd; Perf Att; Yth Ldrshp Prog; 4-H; Chrch Yth Grp; DARE; Dbte Team; Jr Ach; Ntl Beta Clb; Bnd; Chr; Ch Chr; Dnce; Sccr; Yrbk (R); Published First Book in August 2004; A Two-Time Mid-State Band Participant; Journalism; Sociology; U of Chicago; Belmont U

GRIFFITH, MICHAEL D; GOODLETTSVILLE, TN; HUNTERS LANE HS; (SR); Hi Hnr Roll; Hnr Roll; Nat Hon Sy; WWAHSS; Comm Volntr; Bnd; Jzz Bnd; Mch Bnd; Orch; Filmmaking (Screenwriting); Music Performance or Education; Watkins College of Art/Design; Austin Peay State U

GRIFFITH II, JAMES D; BELVIDERE, TN; FRANKLIN CTY HS; (SR); Hnr Roll; Voc Ind Clb Am; Going to NADC; Plan to Open My Own Shop One Day; Nashville Auto-Diesel College

GRIGSBY, RACHEL; HENNING, TN; RIPLEY HS; (SO); 4H Awd; Hi Hnr Roll; WWAHSS; 4-H; Drma Clb; Ntl Beta Clb; Voc Ind Clb Am; Bnd; Chr; Mch Bnd; Pep Bnd; U of Tennessee Martin

GRIMES, ALYSSA; MURFREESBORO, TN; BLACKMAN HS; (SO); Duke TS; Hi Hnr Roll; Kwnis Aw; St of Mnth; WWAHSS; Chrch Yth Grp; FCA; FBLA; JSA; Key Club; Ntl Beta Clb; Quiz Bowl; Latin Clb; Chr; Ch Chr; Clr Grd; Political Science

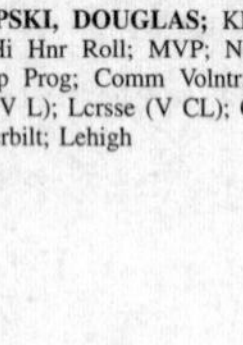
Gosnell, Elaine M
Central HS
Robbins, TN

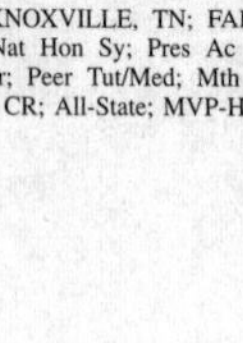
Givens, Zachary M
Smyrna HS
Smyrna, TN

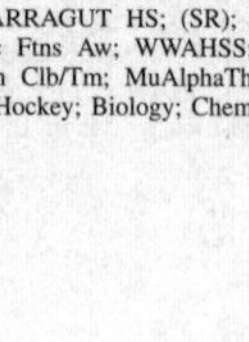
Goodson, Wes
Madison Sch
Nashville, TN

GRIMES, RYAN; CLARKSVILLE, TN; CLARKSVILLE HS; (JR); Hi Hnr Roll; Hnr Roll; Perf Att; WWAHSS; Spec Olymp Vol; Chrch Yth Grp; DARE; ROTC; Drl Tm; Drill Team Varsity / Letter Winner; Computer Science; Electronic Engineering; United States Military Academy - West Point; Austin Peay State U

GRISHAM, JONATHAN B; NASHVILLE, TN; NASHVILLE SCH OF THE ARTS; (SO); Hnr Roll; Otst Ac Ach Awd; Perf Att; DARE; Spanish Clb; SP/M/VS; Stg Cre; Performed in NSA Music Showcase; Performed with NSA Guitar Quartet; Major Music Engineering; Guitar; Austin Peay U; MTSU

GRISHAM, KASEY; CARTHAGE, TN; GORDONSVILLE HS; (JR); Hi Hnr Roll; Nat Hon Sy; Perf Att; WWAHSS; Yth Ldrshp Prog; Comm Volntr; FCA; Lttrmn Clb; Ntl Beta Clb; Prom Com; SADD; Vsity Clb; Spanish Clb; Chr; Dnce; Bskball (V); Vllyball (V); Cl Off (T); Girls State Representative; Miss Junior; Pharmacy; Nursing; Tennessee Tech U; Vanderbilt U

GROCOCK, ERIKA; ROCKVALE, TN; EAGLEVILLE SCH; (SO); Ctznshp Aw; Gov Hnr Prg; Hi Hnr Roll; Nat Hon Sy; Otst Ac Ach Awd; Perf Att; WWAHSS; Dbte Team; FBLA; Ntl Beta Clb; Ntl FFA; P to P St Amb Prg; Photog; Scouts; Spanish Clb; Bskball (V); Scr Kpr (VJ); Vllyball (V); State Winning Opening/Closing Team; Business; Computer Science; Tennessee Tech; ITT Tech

GROOMS, TESSA L; TRENTON, TN; GIBSON CTY HS; (SO); Hnr Roll; Perf Att; Comm Volntr; DARE; Emplmnt; FCCLA; Chr; SP/M/VS; PP Ftbl; CPA (Accounting & Business); Lawyer; Dyersburg State Community College; Union U

GROSS, ROBBEY; CHUCKEY, TN; CHUCKEY-DOAK HS; (JR); Ctznshp Aw; Hnr Roll; MVP; Nat Hon Sy; Otst Ac Ach Awd; Perf Att; WWAHSS; Yth Ldrshp Prog; Comm Volntr; Chrch Yth Grp; DARE; Lttrmn Clb; Lib Aide; Svce Clb; Vsity Clb; SP/M/VS; Stg Cre; Cr Ctry (V L); Scr Kpr (VJ); Sccr (V L); Vsy Clb (V L); Rotary Round Robin Team; Perfect Attendance Since Kindergarten; Computer Animation (Fine Arts); Game Art and Design (Fine Arts); Savannah of Art and Design

GROUP, JAMES; WINCHESTER, TN; FRANKLIN CTY HS; (SO); Hnr Roll; WWAHSS; Comm Volntr; Chrch Yth Grp; DARE; Emplmnt; Ntl Beta Clb; Tech Clb; Bnd; Mch Bnd; Pep Bnd; SP/M/VS; Tennis; Fish Christian Club; Middle Tennessee State U; U of Tennessee (Knoxville)

GROVES, ALICIA M; BRIGHTON, TN; BRIGHTON HS; (SO); Hi Hnr Roll; Nat Hon Sy; Perf Att; Pres Sch; St of Mnth; ArtClub; Chrch Yth Grp; Mus Clb; Sci Clb; French Clb; Chr; Orch; Visual Art; U of Tennessee Knoxville; Tennessee Tech Cookeville

GROWDEN, ANDREW; SMYRNA, TN; LA VERGNE HS; (FR); Hnr Roll; Chrch Yth Grp; Rlr Hky (V); Forensic Science/Ballistics

GRSENE, CHRISTOPHER S; ERWIN, TN; U N 1001 CTY VOC SCH; (SR); Hi Hnr Roll; Hnr Roll; Perf Att; Pres Sch; USAA; WWAHSS; Comm Volntr; Peer Tut/Med; Chrch Yth Grp; FCA; Key Club; Lttrmn Clb; Ntl Beta Clb; Ntl FFA; Pep Squd; Quiz Bowl; Ftball (V L); Scr Kpr; Track (L); Wt Lftg; Cl Off (T); Stu Cncl (T); CR (R); Psychology; U of Tennessee-Acc

GUTELIUS, KIMBERLY; MILLINGTON, TN; MILLINGTON CTRL HS; (JR); Hnr Roll; Nat Hon Sy; Bskball (V); National Honor Society; Accounting Major; Business Management; U of Tennessee-Knoxville; U of Tennessee-Martin

GUY, ANGEL; BLUFF CITY, TN; SULLIVAN EAST HS; (JR); WWAHSS; Comm Volntr; FTA; Key Club; ROTC; ETSU Upward Bound; Pres of FTA; Art, English; Teaching, Creative Writing; East Tennessee State U; Radford U

GUY, DENNIS C; MILLINGTON, TN; MILLINGTON CTRL HS; (JR); Ctznshp Aw; Hnr Roll; WWAHSS; Yth Ldrshp Prog; Spec Olymp Vol; Emplmnt; Key Club; ROTC; Drl Tm; ROTC Drill Team Leader, Distinguished Cadet; Education; The Citadel; U of Memphis

HAHN, MICHELLE; ATHENS, TN; ATHENS JHS; (MS); Duke TS; Nat Hon Sy; Pres Ac Ftns Aw; Comm Volntr; Chrch Yth Grp; Bnd; Accounting; Finance; Duke U; U of Tennessee Knoxville

HALE, JENNIFER; FAYETTEVILLE, TN; LINCOLN CTY HS; (SR); 4H Awd; Ctznshp Aw; DAR; Hi Hnr Roll; Nat Hon Sy; Sci Fairs; St of Mnth; Yth Ldrshp Prog; Comm Volntr; Peer Tut/Med; Red Cr Aide; 4-H; Chrch Yth Grp; Drma Clb; Emplmnt; FCCLA; Ntl FFA; Photog; Scouts; Dnce; Chrldg (J); Stu Cncl (R); Yrbk (E, P); Agriculture Communications; Education (Secondary); Tennessee Technological U

HALE, RACHAEL M; SEVIERVILLE, TN; SEVIER CTY HS; (FR); WWAHSS; Emplmnt; SP/M/VS; Principles of Business Award; Karate; Criminal Justice; Law; U of Tennessee; Carson Newman

HALL, BANDANA B; FRIENDSHIP, TN; CROCKETT CTY HS; (JR); Hi Hnr Roll; Hnr Roll; WWAHSS; Chrch Yth Grp; FCA; Ntl Beta Clb; Bnd; Ch Chr; Mch Bnd; Pep Bnd; Cr Ctry; PP Ftbl; Karate; Radiology; X-Ray Tech; Jackson State Community College; Union U

HALL, DE MICHAEL M; MEMPHIS, TN; FAIRLEY HS; (JR); Sci/Math Olympn; Chrch Yth Grp; Ch Chr; Upward Bound Math and Science Program; Neurosurgeon; Neurologist (Ped); Xavier; Clark Atlanta

HALL, JORDAN; TALBOTT, TN; JEFFERSON CTY HS; (JR); WWAHSS; Spec Olymp Vol; Ntl FFA; Voc Ind Clb Am; Hsbk Rdg; Masonry

HALL, LAUREN; GEORGETOWN, TN; WALKER VALLEY HS; (JR); Hnr Roll; Otst Ac Ach Awd; Comm Volntr; Chrch Yth Grp; FCA; FBLA; Key Club; Ntl Beta Clb; Tchrs Aide; Cr Ctry (V); Sccr (V); Medical Field; East Tennessee State U; U of Tennessee At Chattanooga

HAMBY, JAKE L; PULASKI, TN; GILES CTY HS; (JR); Hnr Roll; WWAHSS; AL Aux Boys; Chrch Yth Grp; Emplmnt; Ntl Beta Clb; Vsity Clb; Voc Ind Clb Am; Sccr (V); Engineering Degree; Tennessee Technological U

HAMPTON, ASHLEY; FRANKLIN, TN; FRANKLIN HS; (JR); Hnr Roll; Nat Hon Sy; Chrch Yth Grp; Mod UN; Prom Com; Scouts; Spanish Clb; Bnd; Clr Grd; Mch Bnd; Girl Scout Silver Award; International Studies; American U; Wheaton College

HAMPTON, JAREN J; NASHVILLE, TN; HUNTERS LANE HS; (SO); Hnr Roll; Drma Clb; SP/M/VS; Mar Art; Acting; Broadcast Journalism; U of Memphis; New York U

HANDY, MELISSA; OLIVER SPRINGS, TN; OLIVER SPRINGS HS; (JR); Hi Hnr Roll; Hnr Roll; Perf Att; Pres Sch; Sci Fairs; WWAHSS; FCA; Ntl Beta Clb; Prom Com; Spanish Clb; Award for Most Outstanding Exhibit in Materials Science; Awards for Achieving Excellence Algebra I / II and Pre-Calculus; Elementary Education; Math Teacher; Lipscomb U; Tusculum College

HANEY, WENDY C; WOODBURY, TN; CANNON CTY HS; (JR); HOSA President; Biochemistry; TN Wesleyan College; West Texas

HANGEY, CHRISTINE; MURFREESBORO, TN; RIVERDALE HS; (JR); Duke TS; Hnr Roll; WWAHSS; Chess; ROTC; Ice Hky; Rlr Hky; Political Science; Temple U; Boston College

HANLEY, LAUREN; LA FOLLETTE, TN; CAMPBELL CTY COMP HS; (SO); Hnr Roll; WWAHSS; Comm Volntr; Chrch Yth Grp; Drma Clb; ROTC; Bnd; Ch Chr; Nursing; Psychology; Evangel U; Azusa Pacific U

HANNS, CARL; CLARKSVILLE, TN; NORTHWEST HS; (SO); Hnr Roll; Ftball (VJ); Track (V)

HANSON, CURTIS W; OLIVER SPRINGS, TN; OLIVER SPRINGS HS; (SO); Hnr Roll; Drma Clb; Ntl Beta Clb; SP/M/VS; CR (R); Black Belt-Isshinryu Karate; President's Award for Educational Excellence (2004); History/Archaeology; Acting; U of Tennessee (Knoxville)

HARALSON, KAYLA; MOUNT JULIET, TN; WILSON CTRL HS; (FR); 4H Awd; Hi Hnr Roll; Hnr Roll; Sci Fairs; St of Mnth; Peer Tut/Med; 4-H; Biology Clb; Chrch Yth Grp; DARE; Emplmnt; Lib Aide; Sci Clb; Acpl Chr; Chr; Ch Chr; Ftball (V); Wrstlg (V); Marine Biology; Lawyer; U of Tennessee; Duke U

HARBISON, SUSAN; MC EWEN, TN; MC EWEN HS; (JR); Hi Hnr Roll; Hnr Roll; MVP; WWAHSS; Chrch Yth Grp; Ntl Beta Clb; Vsity Clb; Chr; Ch Chr; Bskball (V L); Vllyball (VJ); Volunteer Girls State; Beta Club; Small Business Management; Belmont U; Carson-Newman College

HARDY, ADERO K; ARLINGTON, TN; ARLINGTON HS; (FR); 4H Awd; Ctznshp Aw; Hi Hnr Roll; Otst Ac Ach Awd; Perf Att; Sci Fairs; Comm Volntr; Peer Tut/Med; 4-H; Chrch Yth Grp; Mth Clb/Tm; Ntl Beta Clb; Sci Clb; Bnd; Ch Chr; Dnce; Options Math and Science Club; Martial Arts; Pharmacy - Math and Science Degrees; Writer / Author; Fisk U; Spelman College

HARGIS, CODI; MONTEREY, TN; MONTEREY HS; (SO); Hnr Roll; St of Mnth; Comm Volntr; BPA; Chrch Yth Grp; DARE; FCA; Golf; Patient Spotlight from East TN Children's Hospital; Teaching; Architecture/Drafting; Tennessee Tech; U of Tennessee

HARGROVE, MORGAN R; FAYETTEVILLE, TN; LINCOLN CTY HS; (JR); Hi Hnr Roll; Hnr Roll; WWAHSS; DECA; Emplmnt; Pep Squd; Bnd; Psychology; Marketing/Public Relations; MISU, Murfreesoboro, TN; Matlow

HARMON, CRYSTAL R; MEMPHIS, TN; OAKHAVEN MIDDLE HS; (FR); Ctznshp Aw; Hnr Roll; Perf Att; DARE; Mus Clb; Prom Com; Scouts; Vsity Clb; Bnd; Dnce; Mch Bnd; Bskball; Chrldg; PPSqd; Medical; Education; U of Chattanooga; Harvard U

HARMS, TIMOTHY; FRANKLIN, TN; FRANKLIN HS; (JR); Duke TS; F Lan Hn Soc; Hi Hnr Roll; Otst Ac Ach Awd; Sci/Math Olympn; Yth Ldrshp Prog; Comm Volntr; AL Aux Boys; Chrch Yth Grp; Drma Clb; Emplmnt; FCA; Mod UN; MuAlphaTh; Clb; Bnd; Chr; SP/M/VS; Stu Cncl (P); First Priority Leader (4 Years); Appeared on a TV Reality Show; Business Administration; Engineer; Belmont U; Vanderbilt U

HARP, SEAVER; GALLATIN, TN; GALLATIN HS; (JR); Comm Volntr; ArtClub; Chrch Yth Grp; Emplmnt; Photog; Sch Ppr (R); Oceanography; Marine Biology; San Diego State U; U of San Diego California

HARPER, COREY J; MOUNT JULIET, TN; WILSON CTRL HS; (SO); Hnr Roll; WWAHSS; Emplmnt; Engineering; Auto/Aeronautical Design/Engineer; Georgia Tech; Vanderbilt U

HARRELL, TIFFANY L; MORRISON, TN; COFFEE CTY CTRL HS; (SR); Ctznshp Aw; Hi Hnr Roll; Nat Hon Sy; Otst Ac Ach Awd; WWAHSS; Spec Olymp Vol; ArtClub; BPA; Chrch Yth Grp; Emplmnt; Off Aide; Tchrs Aide; Spanish Clb; Cl Off (T); Peer Counselor; Registered Nurse; Criminal Law; Middle Tennessee State U; Motlow State Community College

HARRIS, ANGELA; INDIAN MOUND, TN; STEWART CTY HS; (JR); Hnr Roll; Perf Att; WWAHSS; Nurse Practitioner; Registered Nurse; Austin Peay State U; Murray State U

HARRIS, ANNA C; MANCHESTER, TN; COFFEE CTY CTRL HS; (JR); Hi Hnr Roll; Nat Hon Sy; Perf Att; Pres Sch; Comm Volntr; Chrch Yth Grp; Emplmnt; FCA; FCCLA; Quill & Scroll; Spanish Clb; Sch Ppr (E); English Major; Lee U

HARRIS, CHERRY D; MURFREESBORO, TN; SIEGEL HS; (JR); Hi Hnr Roll; WWAHSS; Comm Volntr; Peer Tut/Med; Chrch Yth Grp; Jr Cls League; Ntl Beta Clb; Pep Squd; Sign Clb; Sign Language Club President; Youth Drama / Dance Team; Forensic Science; Criminal Justice; Austin Peay State U; UT Martin

HARRIS, JENNIFER; ERWIN, TN; UNICOI CTY VOC SCH; (JR); Hnr Roll; 4-H; ArtClub; BPA; FCCLA; Ntl FFA; Pep Squd; Prom Com; CR (P); Work with Small Children; East Tennessee State U; North East State

HARRIS, JESSICA R; LENOIR CITY, TN; LENOIR CITY HS; (SR); Hi Hnr Roll; Nat Hon Sy; Pres Sch; Comm Volntr; 4-H; Jr Ach; MuAlphaTh; Ntl FFA; Prom Com; Cl Off (P); Stu Cncl (R); Girl's State Delegate; Animal Science; U of TN Knoxville

HARRIS, LAURA; DYERSBURG, TN; DYERSBURG HS; (SO); Hnr Roll; Comm Volntr; Peer Tut/Med; Chrch Yth Grp; Emplmnt; Key Club; Ntl Beta Clb; Chr; Ch Chr; SP/M/VS; Yrbk (E); Business; Pharmacy; Mississippi State U; Tulane U

HARRIS, NIALA E; ATHENS, TN; MC MINN CTY HS; (SO); 4H Awd; Ctznshp Aw; Hnr Roll; MVP; Comm Volntr; Chrch Yth Grp; DARE; Jr Ach; Bskball (V); All-District Basketball Team; Southeast Tournament Corp; Pharmacist; Physician; U of Tennessee; Duke U

HARRISON, KATHRYN; NASHVILLE, TN; NASHVILLE SCH OF THE ARTS; (SO); Ctznshp Aw; Duke TS; Hnr Roll; WWAHSS; Dbte Team; Drma Clb; Emplmnt; Mus Clb; NtlFrnscLg; Scouts; Acpl Chr; Orch; SP/M/VS; Writers Showcase & American Legion Writers Awards; Vanderbilt (Blair) Scholarship; Journalism, Music, Anthropology; Theatre, Peace Corps, Writer; Brown U, Oberlin U; New York U, Brandeis U

HART, FREDDY; LAWRENCEBURG, TN; LAWRENCE CTY HS; (FR); 4H Awd; Hi Hnr Roll; Hnr Roll; Nat Hon Sy; Nat Mrt Fin; Nat Mrt LOC; Nat Mrt Semif; Nat Sci Aw; Otst Ac Ach Awd; Perf Att; 4-H; DARE; Emplmnt; FCA; Ntl FFA; Outdrs Clb; Scouts; Ftball (V); Wt Lftg (V); FFA Award; Equine Science Major; Inter Collegiate Rodeo Association; Tennessee-Martin

HART, WHITNEY; MEDINA, TN; LIBERTY TECH MAGNET HS; (SO); Hnr Roll; 4-H; Ntl FFA; Medical Field; Law Enforcement Field (Lawyers); U of Tennessee; Murray State

HARTNESS, ROBIN; CLEVELAND, TN; BRADLEY HS; (JR); Hi Hnr Roll; Hnr Roll; Perf Att; Sci Fairs; St of Mnth; Tchrs Aide; Math Teacher; Lee U; Cleveland State

HARVEY, ALAINA M; MASCOT, TN; TEMPLE BAPTIST AC; (JR); Hnr Roll; Yth Ldrshp Prog; Comm Volntr; Peer Tut/Med; Chrch Yth Grp; DARE; Mth Clb/Tm; Ntl Beta Clb; NYLC; Chr; Ch Chr; Nurse; School Teacher; U of Tennessee; Pellissippi State

HARVEY, DOROTHY T; JACKSON, TN; JACKSON CHRISTIAN SCH; (SO); Duke TS; Hi Hnr Roll; MVP; USAA; Comm Volntr; Peer Tut/Med; Chrch Yth Grp; Drma Clb; FCA; Ntl Beta Clb; Vsity Clb; Ch Chr; SP/M/VS; GAA (V); Scr Kpr (V); Sccr (V L); Track (V L); Beta Club, Eagles for Christ, FCA; Varsity Basketball Manager, Homecoming Court; Nursing; Teaching; U of Mississippi

HARVEY, REBECCA; OLIVER SPRINGS, TN; OLIVER SPRINGS HS; (SO); Gov Hnr Prg; Hi Hnr Roll; Hnr Roll; MVP; Nat Hon Sy; Nat Ldrshp Svc; Nat Mrt Sch Recip; Otst Ac Ach Awd; Perf Att; Sci Fairs; Comm Volntr; Peer Tut/Med; Red Cr Aide; Chrch Yth Grp; Emplmnt; FCA; HO'Br Yth Ldrshp; Mus Clb; Ntl Beta Clb; NYLC; Spanish Clb; PP Ftbl (V); Tennis (V); Stu Cncl (R); CR (R); Yrbk (E); Basketball Certified Trainer; Youth Leadership Member; Industrial-Organizational Psychology; Forensics; U of Tennessee

HASKEW, CHRISTINA; CHATTANOOGA, TN; EAST RIDGE HS; (SR); Hnr Roll; MVP; Nat Hon Sy; Lttrmn Clb; Ntl Beta Clb; Off Aide; Vsity Clb; Sftball (V CL); Vllyball (V CL); All District Region, State in Volleyball & All District-Softball; Nursing; U of Tennessee At Knoxville

HASKIN, JILLIAN N; KODAK, TN; SEVIER CTY HS; (FR); 4H Awd; Hnr Roll; Perf Att; Sci Fairs; St of Mnth; 4-H; FCCLA; Chr; Ch Chr; Dnce; Vllyball (J); Ob/Gyn; Pediatrics; Walters State; UT

Harrell, Tiffany L
Coffee Cty Ctrl HS
Morrison, TN

Hanson, Curtis W
Oliver Springs HS
Oliver Springs, TN

Hall, Lauren
Walker Valley HS
Georgetown, TN

Grooms, Tessa L
Gibson Cty HS
Trenton, TN

Groves, Alicia M
Brighton HS
Brighton, TN

Harper, Corey J
Wilson Ctrl HS
Mount Juliet, TN

Harvey, Alaina M
Temple Baptist AC
Mascot, TN

HAUN, EMILY; LAWRENCEBURG, TN; LAWRENCE CTY HS; (FR); Hnr Roll; DARE; Bnd; Clr Grd; Pep Bnd

HAUSMAN, JOLIE; CLARKSVILLE, TN; CLARKSVILLE HS; (JR); Gov Hnr Prg; Hnr Roll; MVP; Sci Fairs; Drma Clb; SP/M/VS; Stg Cre; Tennis (V L); Chosen for TN Governor's School for the Arts; Member of the International Thespian Society; Theatre Arts / Performing Arts; Film and Video Production; Austin Peay State U; Middle Tennessee State U

HAUTH, AMY E; HARRIMAN, TN; OLIVER SPRINGS ELEM; (FR); Ctznshp Aw; Duke TS; Hnr Roll; Sci Fairs; Comm Volntr; Peer Tut/Med; Chrch Yth Grp; FCA; Ntl Beta Clb; Bskball (V)

HAWKES, CANDACE; JOHNSON CITY, TN; DANIEL BOONE HS; (SO); Hi Hnr Roll; Perf Att; Sci Fairs; WWAHSS; Peer Tut/Med; FCA; Key Club; Tchrs Aide; French Clb; Chr; Sftball (J)

HAWKINS, BRENDAN T; LIMESTONE, TN; DAVID CROCKETT HS; (FR); Hi Hnr Roll; Perf Att; Chrch Yth Grp; DARE; Emplmnt; Ch Chr; Cr Ctry (V); Track (V); Law School; U of Tennessee

HAWKINS, CYNTHIA; MEMPHIS, TN; HAMILTON HS; (FR); Hi Hnr Roll; Hnr Roll; Nat Hon Sy; DARE; Bnd; Ch Chr; Dnce; Drm Mjr; Bskball (V); Chrldg (V C); Sftball (V); Vllyball (V); CR; Health Science; PhD; Tennessee State U; Jackson State U

HAWN, BRANDI D L; WARTBURG, TN; CENTRAL HS; (JR); Hi Hnr Roll; Hnr Roll; Perf Att; St of Mnth; 4-H; Chrch Yth Grp; Emplmnt; FCA; Prom Com; Sftball (V); Cl Off (P); Stu Cncl (R); Yrbk (R, P); Nursing; Engineering; U of Tennessee; Tennessee Tech

HAYDEN, JESSICA; WAVERLY, TN; WAVERLY CTRL HS; (FR); 4H Awd; Ctznshp Aw; DAR; Fut Prb Slvr; Hnr Roll; MVP; Nat Hon Sy; Perf Att; Sci Fairs; St of Mnth; Comm Volntr; Hab For Humty Volntr; Peer Tut/Med; 4-H; ArtClub; Chrch Yth Grp; DARE; FCCLA; Lib Aide; Mus Clb; Voc Ind Clb Am; Chr; Ch Chr; Dnce; SP/M/VS; Chrldg (J); Gmnstcs (L); Mar Art (C); PPSqd; Sftball (J); Vsy Clb (J); Vllyball (J); Wt Lftg (J); Stu Cncl (T); Sch Ppr (E); Veterinarian; Doctor; Middle Tennessee State U; U of Tennessee

HAYGOOD, ERICA P; BRIGHTON, TN; BRIGHTON HS; (FR); Hnr Roll; Chrch Yth Grp; Dbte Team; Drma Clb; Mth Clb/Tm; Mus Clb; Bnd; Ch Chr; Mch Bnd; Pep Bnd; Surgeon; Veterinarian; U of Tennessee Martin

HAYNES, ADAM; WHITE PINE, TN; JEFFERSON CTY HS; (JR); Hnr Roll; WWAHSS; Spec Olymp Vol; BPA; DECA; Ntl Beta Clb; Political Science; Business Administrations; Austin Peay State U; Emory & Henry U

HAYNES, MEREDITH L; ALCOA, TN; ALCOA HS; (JR); Hi Hnr Roll; Nat Hon Sy; Perf Att; WWAHSS; Yth Ldrshp Prog; Peer Tut/Med; 4-H; Chrch Yth Grp; Drma Clb; Emplmnt; FBLA; Key Club; Tchrs Aide; Spanish Clb; Ch Chr; Stu Cncl (R); Academic Letter in Language Arts; Academic Letter in Social Studies

HEAD, SUSAN; CLARKSVILLE, TN; CLARKSVILLE HS; (JR); 4H Awd; Hi Hnr Roll; Hnr Roll; Otst Ac Ach Awd; Comm Volntr; Hab For Humty Volntr; 4-H; Chrch Yth Grp; FCCLA; Mth Clb/Tm; Ntl Beta Clb; Off Aide; Svce Clb; Tennis (V); Recipient of Academic Awards - 2 Yrs; Numerous Piano Excellence Awards; Pharmacy; Agriculture; U of Tennessee Knoxville; U of Tennessee Martin

HEARD, APRIL D; MEMPHIS, TN; WOODDALE HS; (JR); Fut Prb Slvr; Hnr Roll; Perf Att; WWAHSS; Yth Ldrshp Prog; Comm Volntr; DARE; Drma Clb; FBLA; Flg Crps; Adv Cncl (V); Sch Ppr (R); Bachelor's Degree; Master's Degree; New York U; U of Memphis

HEASTON, ANDREA E; MEMPHIS, TN; CENTRAL HS; (FR); 4H Awd; Hi Hnr Roll; Nat Hon Sy; Otst Ac Ach Awd; Perf Att; St of Mnth; Comm Volntr; Peer Tut/Med; 4-H; Chrch Yth Grp; Drma Clb; Mus Clb; Pep Squd; Chr; Ch Chr; Dnce; Mch Bnd; PPSqd (V); Cl Off (V); Business and Marketing; Performing Arts; Harvard U; U of Tennessee

HEATHMAN, BRITTANY N; KNOXVILLE, TN; BEARDEN HS; (JR); Hnr Roll; Nat Mrt LOC; WWAHSS; Comm Volntr; Key Club; Svce Clb; Latin Clb; Bnd; Chr; Mch Bnd; Skiing; Track (J); Vllyball (J); Lit Mag (R); Rock Climbing; Veterinary Medicine; Wildlife / Zoology; U of Tennessee Knoxville; Purdue U West Lafayette

HECK, AARON G; LOUISVILLE, TN; CENTRAL HS; (SO); Hi Hnr Roll; Hnr Roll; Perf Att; Bskball (J); Ftball (V L); U of Tennessee-Knoxville

HEFLIN, SHELBYE; COLLIERVILLE, TN; COLLIERVILLE HS; (SO); 4H Awd; Ctznshp Aw; Hi Hnr Roll; Hnr Roll; Sci Fairs; Yth Ldrshp Prog; Comm Volntr; Peer Tut/Med; DECA; Jr Cls League; Dnce; PPSqd (V CL); Rlr Hky (V); Biology; Pathology; U of Mississippi; St Louis U

HEFNER, DEREK L; NEWPORT, TN; COCKE CTY HS; (JR); Hi Hnr Roll; Hnr Roll; Psychology; Neurology; U of Tennessee; East Tennessee State U

HELM, MICHAEL; LANCASTER, TN; GORDONSVILLE HS; (JR); 4H Awd; Hnr Roll; Nat Hon Sy; WWAHSS; Comm Volntr; 4-H; Chrch Yth Grp; FCA; Mth Clb/Tm; Mus Clb; Outdrs Clb; Sci Clb; Spanish Clb; Chr; Ch Chr; Ftball (V); Wt Lftg (V); Black Belt in Karate; Tennessee Technical U

HELPER, BRITTANY; OBION, TN; OBION CTY CTRL HS; (SO); 4H Awd; Gov Hnr Prg; Hi Hnr Roll; Nat Hon Sy; Nat Ldrshp Svc; Perf Att; Pres Sch; St of Mnth; WWAHSS; Yth Ldrshp Prog; Comm Volntr; Hosp Aide; Peer Tut/Med; 4-H; Chrch Yth Grp; SADD; Tchrs Aide; Voc Ind Clb Am; Ch Chr; Clr Grd; Dnce; Drm Mjr; Chrldg (V); Gmnstcs (V); PPSqd (J); PP Ftbl (V); Cl Off (P); Yrbk (P); Nursing; Teaching; Columbia U; Urban College of Boston

HELTON, CHANCE F; HOHENWALD, TN; LEWIS CTY HS; (FR); Hnr Roll; Chrch Yth Grp; DARE; Ntl Beta Clb; Bskball (V L); Adv Cncl (R); Cl Off (P); CR (P); Education-College Major; NBA (National Basketball Association)-Profession; U of North Carolina; U of Tennessee

HENDERSON, BETHANY; ASHLAND CITY, TN; SYCAMORE HS; (FR); Ctznshp Aw; Hnr Roll; Perf Att; WWAHSS; Comm Volntr; Peer Tut/Med; 4-H; DARE; Ntl Beta Clb; Pep Squd; Chrldg (V); PPSqd (V); PP Ftbl (V); Best All-Around Student; Hall of Fame; Elementary Education; Centre College; Belmont U

HENDON, CANDACE N; OOLTEWAH, TN; OOLTEWAH HS; (FR); Hnr Roll; Otst Ac Ach Awd; Perf Att; Drma Clb; FCA; Mod UN; Off Aide; Ch Chr; Yrbk (P); Best Press Delegate (Model United Nations); Cosmetology; Graphic Design; Auburn U; Memphis College of Art & Design

HENRIS, NATHAN T; FRANKLIN, TN; FRANKLIN HS; (JR); Hnr Roll; ArtClub; Mod UN; Photog; Tchrs Aide; Bnd; Drm Mjr; Mch Bnd; Pep Bnd; Model UN; Logo Design Award; Graphic Design; Savannah College of Art & Design

HENRY, BRETT; FRANKLIN, TN; FRANKLIN HS; (SO); Duke TS; Hi Hnr Roll; Nat Hon Sy; Otst Ac Ach Awd; WWAHSS; Yth Ldrshp Prog; Hab For Humty Volntr; Chrch Yth Grp; FCA; Mth Clb/Tm; MuAlphaTh; P to P St Amb Prg; Tchrs Aide; Bskball (VJ); Cr Ctry (V L); Stu Cncl (R); Biology; Medical School; Wake Forrest; Lipscomb

HENRY, CHRISTOPHER W; WATERTOWN, TN; GORDONSVILLE HS; (SO); WWAHSS; Chr; Cl Off (V)

HERNANDEZ, JENNYFER; ANTIOCH, TN; GLENCLIFF COMP HS; (SR); Hi Hnr Roll; Hnr Roll; Otst Ac Ach Awd; Peer Tut/Med; Emplmnt; Off Aide; Sci Clb; Tchrs Aide; Sccr (V C); Vllyball (V CL); Learned English Language in Less Than a Year; Social Work; Education; Cumberland U (Lebanon, TN); Trevecca Nazarene U or Lipscomb U

HERRMANN, PAULINA; CELINA, TN; CLAY CTY HS; (SR); 4H Awd; Hi Hnr Roll; MVP; Otst Ac Ach Awd; Pres Ac Ftns Aw; US Army Sch Ath Aw; WWAHSS; Comm Volntr; Chrch Yth Grp; DARE; FCA; Lttrmn Clb; Mth Clb/Tm; Ntl Beta Clb; Prom Com; Vsity Clb; Bskball (V CL); Cl Off (P); Sch Ppr (R); Major in General Business; Tennessee Technological U

HERRON, KEOISHA N; MILAN, TN; MILAN HS; (JR); Hnr Roll; St of Mnth; Comm Volntr; Hosp Aide; 4-H; Chrch Yth Grp; DARE; DECA; Emplmnt; Prom Com; French Clb; Bnd; Ch Chr; Nursing; U of Tennessee Chattanooga; U of Memphis

HESS, ERIN; KINGSPORT, TN; DOBYNS-BENNETT HS; (JR); Hi Hnr Roll; Hnr Roll; Nat Hon Sy; Comm Volntr; Peer Tut/Med; Key Club; Prom Com; Scouts; Stu Cncl (R); Nursing; Social Services; East Tennessee State U; U of Tennessee Knoxville

HICKMAN, ADA; SPRING HILL, TN; (JR); Hi Hnr Roll; Hnr Roll; MVP; Nat Hon Sy; WWAHSS; Yth Ldrshp Prog; Comm Volntr; Hab For Humty Volntr; Spec Olymp Vol; AL Aux Girls; BPA; Chrch Yth Grp; FCA; Key Club; Ntl Beta Clb; SADD; Dnce; Cr Ctry (V L); Track (V L); Cl Off (V, S); Stu Cncl (V); Yrbk (P); MVP Distance Runner in Track '04; Most Improved Cross Country '02; Tennessee Tech; U of Tennessee At Knoxville

HICKS, CHRISTY M; KINGSPORT, TN; DOBYNS BENNETT HS; (FR); Hnr Roll; Nat Hon Sy; WWAHSS; Chrch Yth Grp; FCA; Jr Ach; Key Club; Scouts; Bnd; Mch Bnd; Major in Internal Medicine; Major in Music; U of Tennessee; Middle Tennessee State U

HICKS, MICHAEL A; MEMPHIS, TN; HAMILTON HS; (JR); Hnr Roll; Bsball (L); BA Fine Arts; BA Computer Engineering; U of Memphis; ITT Technical Institute

HIEMSTRA, SHANNON E; WOODLAWN, TN; NORTHWEST HS; (FR); Hnr Roll; Nat Hon Sy; WWAHSS; Chrch Yth Grp; DARE; FCA; Jr Ach; Mth Clb/Tm; Chr; Sccr (V L); Cl Off (P); Doctor; Forensic Scientist; Washington U; U of Tennessee in Knoxville

HIGGINBOTHAM, CASSIDY; SWEETWATER, TN; MC MINN CTY HS; (FR); FBLA; Chr; Tennis (J); National Junior Beta Club; Business; U of Florida; Emory U

HIGGINS, ARIEL; WOODBURY, TN; F C BOYD CHRISTIAN SCH; (JR); Hnr Roll; WWAHSS; Comm Volntr; Peer Tut/Med; AL Aux Girls; Drma Clb; Svce Clb; Tchrs Aide; SP/M/VS; Interact Club (Secretary); Bible School Teacher; Major In Culinary Arts; Business, Management; Le Cordon Bleu, Atlanta; Culinary Institute of America, New York

HIGGINS, JOHN; COLLIERVILLE, TN; COLLIERVILLE HS; (JR); Hnr Roll; WWAHSS; MuAlphaTh; Ntl Beta Clb; Vsity Clb; Ftball (V); Beta Club; National Society of High School Scholars; Engineering; U of Tennessee

HIGHTOWER, MEGHAN; JOELTON, TN; GREENBRIER HS; (JR); Duke TS; Fut Prb Slvr; Hnr Roll; Nat Hon Sy; WWAHSS; Comm Volntr; BPA; Ntl Beta Clb; Quiz Bowl; Svce Clb; Tchrs Aide; Spanish Clb; Clr Grd; Mch Bnd; SP/M/VS; Stu Cncl; NSHSS Member; Miss Tennessee Teen Pageant Finalist; Architecture; Interior Design; Savannah College of Art and Design; Pratt Institute

HILL, HASTINGS; MEMPHIS, TN; THE MASTERS SCH; (SO); Ctznshp Aw; DAR; Hnr Roll; Nat Hon Sy; Otst Ac Ach Awd; Yth Ldrshp Prog; Comm Volntr; Chrch Yth Grp; DECA; Drma Clb; Mod UN; Ntl Beta Clb; Pep Squd; Tchrs Aide; Dnce; SP/M/VS; Chrldg (V L); CR (R); Finalist for Rush Siler Outstanding Student Award; Phillips Academy Summer Session 1 - 2003 / 2004 Graduated with High Honors 2004 / 2005; Creative and Performing Arts; New York U; Columbia U

HILL, JAMIE R; CLEVELAND, TN; CLEVELAND HS; (SO); Ctznshp Aw; Hi Hnr Roll; Hnr Roll; MVP; Perf Att; USAA; Yth Ldrshp Prog; Comm Volntr; Peer Tut/Med; Chess; Chrch Yth Grp; DARE; Drma Clb; P to P St Amb Prg; Quiz Bowl; Scouts; Bnd; Ch Chr; Mch Bnd; Poetry Awards / Editor's Choice Award; Nursing; Pre-Med; Georgia State U; Belmont U

HILL, TINA M; SPARTA, TN; WHITE CTY HS; (SO); 4H Awd; Hi Hnr Roll; Hnr Roll; DARE; ROTC; Clr Grd; Bachelor Degree in Psychology; Ass. Degree in Electronics; Argosy U; Tennessee Tech

HILLIARD, STEVEN; WINCHESTER, TN; FRANKLIN CTY HS; (SO); Hnr Roll; Nat Hon Sy; FBLA; Voc Ind Clb Am; Engineer; Veterinarian; Auburn U; U of Alabama in Huntsville

HILL II, KELVIN L; MURFREESBORO, TN; SIEGEL HS; (JR); Hnr Roll; MVP; Nat Hon Sy; WWAHSS; Peer Tut/Med; Chrch Yth Grp; Drma Clb; FCA; Ntl Beta Clb; SP/M/VS; Cr Ctry (V L); Track (V CL); Best Actor in Supporting Role; Daily News Journal MVP Track 800 Run; Engineering

HINCKE, JACQUI; KINGSPORT, TN; DOBYNS BENNETT HS; (SO); Key Club; Ntl Beta Clb; Clr Grd; Flg Crps; Secondary Education-English; U of Tennessee; East Tennessee State U

HINDS, KAULA C; DEER LODGE, TN; CENTRAL HS; (JR); Hnr Roll; WWAHSS; Criminal Justice; Roane State Community College

HINEBORG, ANDREW; COLLIERVILLE, TN; COLLIERVILLE HS; (SO); Ctznshp Aw; Hnr Roll; Perf Att; WWAHSS; Chrch Yth Grp; FCA; Off Aide; Wrstlg (J); Nursing; Aerospace; Middle TN State U; U of Memphis

HISEY, MATTHEW; CHATTANOOGA, TN; CHATTANOOGA CHRISTIAN SCH; (SR); Hnr Roll; Chrch Yth Grp; Drma Clb; FCA; Prom Com; Tech Clb; Wdwrkg Clb; Ch Chr; SP/M/VS; Scr Kpr (V); Sccr (J); Web Site Designer / Editor / School Athletics; Education; Business; U of Kentucky; U of Alabama

HITCHCOCK, ANDRE; CHATTANOOGA, TN; TYNER AC; (SO); Ctznshp Aw; Hi Hnr Roll; Hnr Roll; Nat Hon Sy; Ntl Beta Clb; Track (V); Sports Medicine-Bachelor Degree; Criminal Justice-Bachelor Degree; Morehouse College; Tennessee State U

HITSON, MARISSA; BENTON, TN; POLK CTY HS; (SR); Duke TS; Hi Hnr Roll; Hnr Roll; Nat Hon Sy; Valdctrian; WWAHSS; Chrch Yth Grp; Emplmnt; FCA; HO'Br Yth Ldrshp; Off Aide; Pep Squd; Prom Com; Chr; Clr Grd; Mch Bnd; Yrbk (R, P); Biology Major; East Tennessee State U

HO, TRUC; MEMPHIS, TN; OVERTON HS; (JR); Hnr Roll; Comm Volntr; Lib Aide; MuAlphaTh; Optometrist; Business

HOAG, ELIZABETH; GERMANTOWN, TN; GERMANTOWN HS; (JR); Hnr Roll; Nat Hon Sy; Perf Att; WWAHSS; Comm Volntr; Chrch Yth Grp; Drma Clb; Ntl Beta Clb; NtlFrnscLg; Ch Chr; SP/M/VS; Stg Cre; Broadcast Journalism; U of Missouri-Columbia

HODGE, BRANDON; COOKEVILLE, TN; COOKEVILLE HS; (SR); Hi Hnr Roll; Hnr Roll; WWAHSS; Chrch Yth Grp; FCA; Spanish Clb; Bskball (V CL); Finance; Accounting; Tennessee Tech U

HOFF, ERIK; CLARKSVILLE, TN; ROSSVIEW HS; (JR); Chrch Yth Grp; Sccr (VJ L); Business Management; Accounting; Belmont U; Boston College

HOFFMAN, KURTIS; TROY, TN; OBION CTY CTRL HS; (JR); Hnr Roll; Perf Att; Comm Volntr; Hab For Humty Volntr; Wdwrkg Clb; Bskball (J); Community Service Award; Carpentry

HOLDEN, CARA L; SODDY DAISY, TN; SODDY DAISY HS; (JR); Ctznshp Aw; Duke TS; Hnr Roll; WWAHSS; Yth Ldrshp Prog; Comm Volntr; Chrch Yth Grp; Key Club; Ntl Beta Clb; Prom Com; Tchrs Aide; Dnce; Chrldg (V CL); Cl Off (S); Stu Cncl (R); Senior Leadership; English Award - 9th / 11th; Physical Therapy; Nursing; Carson Newman College; U of TN Knoxville

Hill, Jamie R
Cleveland HS
Cleveland, TN

Heard, April D
Wooddale HS
Memphis, TN

Hawn, Brandi D L
Central HS
Wartburg, TN

National
Honor Roll
Spring 2005

Hawkins, Brendan T
David Crockett HS
Limestone, TN

Hill, Hastings
The Masters Sch
Memphis, TN

Hill II, Kelvin L
Siegel HS
Murfreesboro, TN

HOLDEN, EMILY; SODDY DAISY, TN; SODDY DAISY HS; (FR); Hi Hnr Roll; Hnr Roll; WWAHSS; Comm Volntr; Chrch Yth Grp; FCA; Chrldg (V); Stu Cncl (R); Education; Medical / Pediatrician; U of Tennessee Knoxville; Tennessee Tech U

HOLDER, LAUREN M; NASHVILLE, TN; HILLWOOD HS; (JR); Hnr Roll; Perf Att; Comm Volntr; MuAlphaTh; Spanish Clb; Dnce; Perfect Attendance to Date; No Tardies to Date-Ranked #20 in My Class of 247; Nursing, RN; Belmont U-Nashville TN

HOLLAND, LINDSAY K; CHARLESTON, TN; WALKER VALLEY HS; (FR); Duke TS; Hi Hnr Roll; Perf Att; Sci Fairs; Sci/Math Olympn; St Schl; Peer Tut/Med; Chrch Yth Grp; Ntl Beta Clb; Ch Chr; Dnce; Chrldg (J); Track (J); Duke Tip Program-State Level Winner

HOLLIDAY, PAUL M; MEMPHIS, TN; WHITE STATION HS; (SO)

HOLLIFIELD, MEGAN G; ALCOA, TN; ALCOA HS; (SR); Hi Hnr Roll; Nat Hon Sy; St of Mnth; WWAHSS; Comm Volntr; ArtClub; Chrch Yth Grp; Emplmnt; FCA; Key Club; Off Aide; Photog; Prom Com; Ch Chr; Chrldg (V C); Tennis (V); Stu Cncl (V); Sch Ppr (R); Yrbk (R, P); U of Tennessee

HOLLOWAY, CANDACE L; PIKEVILLE, TN; BLEDSOE CTY HS; (FR); Hnr Roll; MVP; Chrch Yth Grp; Ntl Beta Clb; Bskball (V); Sftball (V); Stu Cncl (S); Top Ten of Class in 2004; Rookie of the Year 2004-2005; Accounting; Computer Sciences; U of Tennessee Knoxville; U of Tennessee Chattanooga

HOLLOWAY, JOSHUA A; MEMPHIS, TN; OAKHAVEN MS HS; (FR); Ctznshp Aw; Hnr Roll; Perf Att; St of Mnth; Chrch Yth Grp; DARE; Fr of Library; Tchrs Aide

HOLLOWAY, JUSTIN D; MEMPHIS, TN; MELROSE HS; (FR); Ctznshp Aw; Hnr Roll; MVP; Nat Hon Sy; Nat Stu Ath Day Aw; Otst Ac Ach Awd; Sci/Math Olympn; Yth Ldrshp Prog; Comm Volntr; ArtClub; Chrch Yth Grp; DARE; FCA; P to P St Amb Prg; Clb; Ch Chr; SP/M/VS; Bsball (V); Bskball (V); Ftball (V); Gmnstcs (C); Track (V); Stu Cncl (R); Mr Football; Mr Seventh Grade; Business; Social Worker; U of North Carolina; U of Tennessee

HOLMES, FELICIA; MEMPHIS, TN; KINGSBURY MIDDLE HS; (JR); F Lan Hn Soc; Hnr Roll; Comm Volntr; DARE; Prom Com; Cl Off (R); Stu Cncl (R); CR (R); Yrbk (P); Sisters of Legacy=Community Service Organization; I Have a Job.; Teaching; Nursing; U of Knoxville; Belmont U

HOLT, CARRIE; HARTFORD, TN; COSBY HS; (JR); DAR; Hi Hnr Roll; Hnr Roll; Nat Hon Sy; Perf Att; Valdctrian; WWAHSS; Chrch Yth Grp; FTA; Prom Com; Spanish Clb; Ch Chr; Chrldg (VJ); Teacher (Elementary or Spanish); Something in Medical Field

HOLT, JESSICA S; MOUNT PLEASANT, TN; MT PLEASANT HS; (SR); Ctznshp Aw; DAR; Hi Hnr Roll; MVP; Perf Att; WWAHSS; Comm Volntr; AL Aux Girls; Chrch Yth Grp; Drma Clb; Emplmnt; FCA; Lib Aide; Mth Clb/Tm; Ntl Beta Clb; Ch Chr; SP/M/VS; Bskball (V CL); Golf (V CL); Sftball (V L); Tennis (V L); Adv Cncl (P); Cl Off (P); Perfect Attendance 13 Yrs; Education English Major; Lambuth U; Martin Methodist

HOLT, MATTHEW W; MEMPHIS, TN; ARLINGTON HS; (FR); Hnr Roll; Pres Ac Ftns Aw; Comm Volntr; Chrch Yth Grp; DARE; Dbte Team; Emplmnt; Ntl Beta Clb; Spch Team; Business; Architect; U of Tennessee Knoxville

HOLT, SWEDEN; NASHVILLE, TN; MAPLEWOOD HS; (SO); Hnr Roll; Nat Hon Sy; Nat Sci Aw; Otst Ac Ach Awd; Perf Att; WWAHSS; DARE; Emplmnt; Scouts; Neonatal Nurse; Belmont U

HONG, BRYAN; COLLIERVILLE, TN; CHRISTIAN BROTHERS HS; (SO); Hnr Roll; Comm Volntr; Chrch Yth Grp; Track

HOOD, JAMES; BENTON, TN; POLK CTY HS; (FR); 4H Awd; Duke TS; Hnr Roll; Otst Ac Ach Awd; 4-H; Cmptr Clb; DARE; Veterinary Medicine; U of Tennessee

HOOPER, KRISTEN; MC EWEN, TN; MC EWEN HS; (JR); All Am Sch; Ctznshp Aw; Hnr Roll; MVP; Nat Hon Sy; Nat Ldrshp Svc; Sci Fairs; USAA; WWAHSS; Comm Volntr; Red Cr Aide; BPA; Chrch Yth Grp; FCA; FTA; Ntl Beta Clb; Ntl FFA; Off Aide; Prom Com; Bskball (V CL); Sftball (V CL); Stu Cncl (R); CR (R); Nursing; Education; Trevecca Nazarene U; Union U

HOOVER, KIMBERLY; JAMESTOWN, TN; CLARKRANGE HS; (SR); Hi Hnr Roll; Hnr Roll; St of Mnth; WWAHSS; 4-H; ArtClub; Chrch Yth Grp; Drma Clb; Emplmnt; FCA; Photog; Prom Com; SP/M/VS; Photographer for Art Club; Business; Roane State Community College; Tennessee Tech U

HOPPER, ALEX; OLIVER SPRINGS, TN; (FR); Duke TS; Hnr Roll; Perf Att; Comm Volntr; Peer Tut/Med; Chrch Yth Grp; Drma Clb; FCA; Mth Clb/Tm; International Clb; Dnce; SP/M/VS; Ftball (J); Junior Deacon; Engineering; Architecture; South Carolina State U; UT Knoxville

HOPSON, JOSHUA P; UNICOI, TN; U N 1001 CTY VOC SCH; (SR); Hi Hnr Roll; Jr Mshl; Nat Hon Sy; WWAHSS; Comm Volntr; Chrch Yth Grp; FCA; Key Club; Ntl Beta Clb; Ntl FFA; Pep Squd; Spanish Clb; Ftball (V); Stu Cncl (R); Biology I Award; US History Award; Political Science; Law; U of Tennessee

HORENKAMP, AMANDA; MURFREESBORO, TN; SIEGEL HS; (JR); Hi Hnr Roll; MVP; Nat Hon Sy; WWAHSS; FCA; Ntl Beta Clb; Pep Squd; Tchrs Aide; Vsity Clb; Spanish Clb; Stg Cre; Vllyball (V CL); Medical Field; Lincoln Memorial U

HORN, AUDREY L; PARIS, TN; HENRY CTY HS; (FR); Ctznshp Aw; Comm Volntr; Chrch Yth Grp; Mus Clb; Chr; SP/M/VS; Rating of 'Superior' in Choral Competition; Selected to "Honors Choir" for West TN; Interior Design; Freed Hardeman U--Henderson TN

HOSKINS, VALERIE; THORN HILL, TN; WASHBURN HS; (SO); 4H Awd; Ctznshp Aw; Fut Prb Slvr; Hnr Roll; Nat Hon Sy; Otst Ac Ach Awd; Perf Att; St of Mnth; Comm Volntr; 4-H; Chrch Yth Grp; DARE; FBLA; FCCLA; Mus Clb; Ntl FFA; SADD; Ch Chr; Pep Bnd; Chrldg (V); Physical Therapist; Pediatrician Doctor; Walter State; Lincoln Memorial U

HOUSE, CANDACE; CHATTANOOGA, TN; BRAINERD HS; (JR); Hnr Roll; WWAHSS; Emplmnt; Acpl Chr; Ch Chr; Dnce; International Society of Poets - Published Poet; Psychiatry; Psychology / Cosmetology; U of Georgia; U of Michigan

HOUSE, KANISHA R; MEMPHIS, TN; CENTRAL HS; (SO); Hnr Roll; Perf Att; Sci Fairs; St of Mnth; Yth Ldrshp Prog; Comm Volntr; Peer Tut/Med; Chrch Yth Grp; DARE; DECA; Emplmnt; FTA; Lib Aide; Mus Clb; Tchrs Aide; Bnd; Ch Chr; Mch Bnd; Orch; Rqtball (C); Vllyball (J); Educational Teacher; Child Social Worker; UAPB; TSU

HOUSER, HEATHER; KINGSPORT, TN; DOBYNS BENNETT HS; (SO); Ch Chr; Orch; Bskball; Golf; Beta Club; Fellowship of Christian Athletes; Physical Therapy; U of North Carolina; U of Tennessee

HOUSEWRIGHT, DUSTIN; CHURCH HILL, TN; VOLUNTEER HS; (SR); Hnr Roll; Perf Att; WWAHSS; Comm Volntr; Tchrs Aide; Voc Ind Clb Am; Bsball (V); Paramedic; Associate of Fire Science; Walters State Community College; East Tennessee State U

HOUSEWRIGHT, JAMISON; KINGSPORT, TN; SULLIVAN SOUTH HS; (SR); Hi Hnr Roll; Hnr Roll; Nat Hon Sy; Valdctrian; WWAHSS; Comm Volntr; Peer Tut/Med; Emplmnt; Jr Ach; Sci Clb; Latin Clb; SP/M/VS; Latin Club President; Young Business Minded American Award; Sociology; Psychology; U of TN; Baylor

HOUSLEY, CHEYENNE; LA FOLLETTE, TN; CAMPBELL CTY HS; (SO); 4H Awd; Hnr Roll; Perf Att; WWAHSS; Comm Volntr; 4-H; BPA; Chrch Yth Grp; Emplmnt; FCCLA; Key Club; Ntl FFA; SADD; Chr; Ch Chr; Pep Bnd; Cr Ctry (V); Track (V); Lincoln Memorial U; East Tennessee State U

HOWARD, CALEB; MOUNTAIN CITY, TN; JOHNSON CTY HS; (FR); Hnr Roll; Perf Att; Comm Volntr; Chrch Yth Grp; Bskball; Golf; Plays Piano; Medical Field; Pharmacist; U of North Carolina; U of Tennessee

HOWARD, JACOB B; SOUTH PITTSBURG, TN; RICHARD HARDY MEMORIAL SCH; (FR); 4H Awd; DAR; Hnr Roll; Pres Ac Ftns Aw; Sci Fairs; WWAHSS; Comm Volntr; 4-H; Chrch Yth Grp; DARE; Emplmnt; Lttrmn Clb; Lib Aide; Mth Clb/Tm; Ntl Beta Clb; Ch Chr; SP/M/VS; Bskball (VJ L); Golf (V); Cl Off (P); Life Scout with Boy Scouts of America; Law; Business; U of Tenn At Knoxville; U of Tenn At Chattanooga

HOWARD, SHEMEEKA; MEMPHIS, TN; KINGSBURY MIDDLE HS; (FR); Hnr Roll; Perf Att; Peer Tut/Med; DARE; ROTC; Ch Chr; Dnce; Doctor; Lawyer; Yale; Princeton

HOWELL, DANIELLE E; TIPTON, TN; MUNFORD HS; (SR); Hi Hnr Roll; Hnr Roll; WWAHSS; Comm Volntr; Red Cr Aide; Chrch Yth Grp; Key Club; Lib Aide; MuAlphaTh; French Clb; Bnd; Mch Bnd; Orch; Pep Bnd; Atoka Person of the Year; Pre-Med; Radiology; Christian Brothers U

HOWELL, SAM; LOUISVILLE, TN; ALCOA HS; (JR); Cr Ctry (L); Sccr (V); Cl Off (P); Stu Cncl (P, R); 3 Academic Letters - Sci, S.Sci, Eng; Multiple Academic Awards; Chemical Engineering; Nanotechnology; Maryville College; U of Tennessee

HOYT, CHRISTOPHER; NASHVILLE, TN; HERMITAGE HALL; (JR); Hi Hnr Roll; Pres Sch; St of Mnth; Comm Volntr; Hosp Aide; Peer Tut/Med; Scouts

HUBBARD, ASHLEY; PINEY FLATS, TN; SULLIVAN CTRL HS; (SR); All Am Sch; Hi Hnr Roll; Nat Hon Sy; Perf Att; Pres Sch; St of Mnth; USAA; US Army Sch Ath Aw; WWAHSS; Key Club; Mth Clb/Tm; Ntl Beta Clb; Sci Clb; Cr Ctry (V C); Track (V C); Pharmacy; Wingate U

HUDSON, BRANDON; GERMANTOWN, TN; GERMANTOWN HS; (JR); Hnr Roll; Perf Att; Sci Fairs; WWAHSS; Comm Volntr; Chrch Yth Grp; Emplmnt; Outdrs Clb; Spanish Clb; SP/M/VS; Stg Cre; Inaugural Movers Leadership School; Music Business; Middle Tennessee State U; Memphis U

HUDSON, DANIEL W; MURFREESBORO, TN; SIEGEL HS; (SO); 4H Awd; Ctznshp Aw; Duke TS; F Lan Hn Soc; Hi Hnr Roll; Nat Hon Sy; Perf Att; Sci/Math Olympn; Yth Ldrshp Prog; Comm Volntr; 4-H; Chess; Chrch Yth Grp; Jr Cls League; Key Club; Mth Clb/Tm; Mod UN; MuAlphaTh; Bnd; Chr; Jzz Bnd; Mch Bnd; Golf (J L); Sccr (J); Cl Off (T, R); Stu Cncl (R); CR (R); Sch Ppr (E); Eagle Scout; Church Honor-Torch Bearer; State 1st VP of Children of American Revolution; Finance; Marketing; U of North Carolina-Chapel Hill; U of Tennessee-Knoxville

HUDSON, GREGORY; GRAYSVILLE, TN; BLEDSOE CTY HS; (FR); 4H Awd; Ctznshp Aw; Hnr Roll; MVP; Nat Hon Sy; Sci Fairs; 4-H; Chrch Yth Grp; Ntl Beta Clb; Bskball (VJ); Member of the Beta Club; Lawyer; Sports Commentary; U of North Carolina; U of Tennessee Knoxville

HUDSON, JAMES; BIG SANDY, TN; CAMDEN CTRL HS; (JR); All Am Sch; Hi Hnr Roll; Otst Ac Ach Awd; Sci Fairs; WWAHSS; BPA; DARE; DECA; Emplmnt; Ntl Beta Clb; Quiz Bowl; Golf (V); Tennis (V); U Tennessee Martin; U of Tennessee Knoxville

HUGGINS, CHRIS; BRIGHTON, TN; BRIGHTON HS; (JR); Hnr Roll; Nat Hon Sy; Otst Ac Ach Awd; Chrch Yth Grp; DECA; SADD; Bsball (J); Cr Ctry (J); Architecture; Engineering; Freed Hardeman U; Arkansas State U

HUGHES, JESSICA A; DRUMMONDS, TN; MUNFORD HS; (SO); Ctznshp Aw; F Lan Hn Soc; Fut Prb Slvr; Hi Hnr Roll; Hnr Roll; Otst Ac Ach Awd; Perf Att; Comm Volntr; Mth Clb/Tm; MuAlphaTh; Ntl FFA; Spanish Clb; Clr Grd; Flg Crps; Mch Bnd; CR (R); Massage Therapy; Business Management; U of Miami; Hawaii Pacific U

HUGHES, MICHELLE L; ATHENS, TN; ATHENS JHS; (MS); Hnr Roll; Perf Att; Lawyer; Massage Therapist; Tennessee Wesleyan College; Cleveland State College

HUGHES, SOMMER; JONESBOROUGH, TN; DAVID CROCKETT HS; Chrch Yth Grp; Ntl FFA; I Want to Specialize in Orthopedic Surgery

HUNT, TROY W; ELIZABETHTON, TN; UNAKA HS; (JR); Hnr Roll; Chrch Yth Grp; Computer Technology; Northeast State; East Tennessee State U

HUNTER, HOPE D; RUGBY, TN; SUNBRIGHT SCH; (SR); Hi Hnr Roll; Nat Hon Sy; Valdctrian; WWAHSS; Peer Tut/Med; BPA; Emplmnt; Lib Aide; Ntl Beta Clb; Off Aide; Prom Com; Tchrs Aide; Bnd; Cl Off (P); Stu Cncl (S); Sch Ppr; Yrbk; Upward Bound; Major-Film & Business Management; Berea College

HURD JR, KENNETH W; STRAW PLAINS, TN; SEVIER CTY HS; (FR); Hnr Roll; U of Tennessee

HURST, ALEX; MEMPHIS, TN; ARLINGTON HS; (FR); Ctznshp Aw; Hnr Roll; FCA; Ntl Beta Clb; Bsball (J); Ftball (V L); Wt Lftg (V); Beta Club; Law Enforcement; Wildlife Management; U of Texas; U of Tennessee

HURST, APRIL; KNOXVILLE, TN; CENTRAL HS; (SO); 4H Awd; Hnr Roll; 4-H; DARE; ROTC; Bnd; Chr; Cosmetology; Tennessee School of Beauty

HUSKEY, AMY R; PIGEON FORGE, TN; PIGEON FORGE HS; (JR); Hnr Roll; Sci Fairs; St of Mnth; Emplmnt; Chr; SP/M/VS; Interact Club; Microbiology; Biochemistry; U of Tennessee; Carson-Newman College

HUTCHISON, HOLLY; CLARKSVILLE, TN; NORTHEAST HS; (SR); Hnr Roll; Nat Hon Sy; WWAHSS; Comm Volntr; Chrch Yth Grp; Ntl Beta Clb; Tchrs Aide; Chr; Ch Chr; Beta Club; Elementary Education; Bethel College

HYDE, ERIKA M; MURFREESBORO, TN; SIEGEL HS; (JR); Hi Hnr Roll; Nat Mrt LOC; Perf Att; WWAHSS; Comm Volntr; Key Club; Mth Clb/Tm; Mod UN; French Clb; Dnce; Most Outstanding Student French I; Most Outstanding Student Algebra II; Education / College Level; Vanderbilt U; Harvard U

IRONS, ASHLEY; WOODLAWN, TN; NORTHWEST HS; (FR); Ctznshp Aw; Hnr Roll; Nat Hon Sy; Biology Major; Business Major; Austin Peay State U; Vanderbilt

IRVIN, KRISTIE; SAVANNAH, TN; HARDIN CTY HS; (JR); Hi Hnr Roll; Hnr Roll; Nat Hon Sy; USAA; BPA; Chrch Yth Grp; Emplmnt; SP/M/VS; Stg Cre; Cl Off (T); Stu Cncl (R); CR (R); Pre-Med; Pharmacy; U of Tennessee At Knoxville; U of North Alabama

IRWIN, HANNAH L; MT PLEASANT, TN; MT PLEASANT HS; (SO); Hi Hnr Roll; Hnr Roll; Nat Hon Sy; 4-H; ArtClub; Chrch Yth Grp; DARE; Drma Clb; FCCLA; Prom Com; Bnd; SP/M/VS; Psychology; Art; Vanderbilt U; Middle Tennessee State U

ISAACS, STEPHANIE; HENDERSON, TN; CHESTER CTY HS; (FR); 4H Awd; Hi Hnr Roll; Hnr Roll; Otst Ac Ach Awd; Comm Volntr; Peer Tut/Med; 4-H; Chrch Yth Grp; Ntl Beta Clb; Tchrs Aide; Chr; Ch Chr; Scr Kpr (V); Sccr (V); Courtesy Club - Secretary; Beta Teacher Aide; PhD in Teaching; Freed-Hardeman U

Hunt, Troy W
Unaka HS
Elizabethton, TN

Hudson, Daniel W
Siegel HS
Murfreesboro, TN

Horn, Audrey L
Henry Cty HS
Paris, TN

Hopper, Alex
Oliver Springs, TN

National
Honor Roll
Spring 2005

Holder, Lauren M
Hillwood HS
Nashville, TN

Howard, Caleb
Johnson Cty HS
Mountain City, TN

Huggins, Chris
Brighton HS
Brighton, TN

Huskey, Amy R
Pigeon Forge HS
Pigeon Forge, TN

ISAACSON, SAMANTHA M; HARRIMAN, TN; OAKDALE HS; (SO); 4H Awd; Perf Att; Hosp Aide; 4-H; Chrch Yth Grp; DARE; Mus Clb; Bnd; Chr; Ch Chr; Lit Mag (P); Sch Ppr (R); Yrbk (P); Registered Nurse; Paramedic; Cumberland U; U of Tennessee

ISAACSON, WHITNEY; CROSSVILLE, TN; CUMBERLAND CTY HS; (JR); All Am Sch; Duke TS; Hi Hnr Roll; Nat Ldrshp Svc; Nat Sci Aw; Otst Ac Ach Awd; Perf Att; USAA; WWAHSS; Yth Ldrshp Prog; Spec Olymp Vol; Chrch Yth Grp; Ntl Beta Clb; Off Aide; Tchrs Aide; Chr; Stu Cncl; Architecture and Design; Medicine; U of Tennessee, Knoxville; Vanderbilt U

ISABELL, ASHLEY R; HUMBOLDT, TN; HUMBOLDT HS; (JR); Hnr Roll; Perf Att; WWAHSS; Comm Volntr; Peer Tut/Med; Chrch Yth Grp; Pep Squd; Prom Com; Spanish Clb; Bnd; Mch Bnd; Pep Bnd; Bskball (V C); Stu Cncl; Pre-Med / Biology; Clark Atlanta U; U of Tennessee Knoxville

ISBELL, KATIE; MEMPHIS, TN; CRAIGMONT HS; (SR); Ctznshp Aw; Hi Hnr Roll; MVP; Nat Hon Sy; Comm Volntr; Hab For Humty Volntr; Peer Tut/Med; Chess; Chrch Yth Grp; Mth Clb/Tm; MuAlphaTh; Ntl Beta Clb; Prom Com; French Clb; Sccr (V CL); Mock Trial Club; Library Sciences; Political Science; UT Knoxville

ISHAM, MONICA D; AFTON, TN; NORTH GREENE HS; (JR); Hnr Roll; Perf Att; Sci Fairs; DARE; Drma Clb; Emplmnt; Walter State; Milligan College

ISLEY, LINDSEY G; GREENEVILLE, TN; NORTH GREENE HS; (FR); Hnr Roll; Chrch Yth Grp; DARE; SADD; Cl Off (P); Stu Cncl; CR (P); Child Care; Cosmetology; U of TN; ETSU

ISMAIL, HEBA; MEMPHIS, TN; RIDGEWAY HS; (JR); Hi Hnr Roll; Nat Hon Sy; WWAHSS; Comm Volntr; Key Club; MuAlphaTh; French Clb; Stu Cncl (R); 1st Place Craft At U of Memphis Foreign Language Fair; 2nd Place Poetry At U of Memphis Foreign Language Fair; Business; Design; U of Memphis; Christian Brothers U

IVIE, SHARI; JACKSON, TN; NORTH SIDE HS; (JR); Hnr Roll; Kwnis Aw; Nat Hon Sy; Otst Ac Ach Awd; Perf Att; St Schl; St of Mnth; WWAHSS; Peer Tut/Med; Emplmnt; Key Club; MuAlphaTh; Ntl Beta Clb; Spanish Clb; Chr; Bskball (V); Cl Off (R); Stu Cncl (R); CR (R); Golden Basketball Award; Girls State (Alternate); Pharmacy; Physical Therapy; Clark-Atlanta U; Memphis U

JABER, LINDSEY; CLEVELAND, TN; WALKER VALLEY HS; (SR); Chrch Yth Grp; Key Club; Ntl Beta Clb; Off Aide; Ch Chr; Pres & Sec of Agape Club; Elementary Education; Lee U

JABLONSKI, ALICE; ROAN MOUNTAIN, TN; CLOUDLAND HS; (JR); Hi Hnr Roll; Hnr Roll; Jr Mshl; MVP; Pres Ac Ftns Aw; Sci Fairs; Comm Volntr; Peer Tut/Med; 4-H; Chrch Yth Grp; DARE; Drma Clb; Emplmnt; FCA; FCCLA; FTA; SP/M/VS; Chrldg (V CL); Cl Off (S); Sch Ppr (R); Yrbk (E, R, P); All-Star Cheerleading; Psychology; Business; U of Tennessee Knoxville; New York U

JACINTO, KAREN; DECHERD, TN; FRANKLIN CTY HS; (SR); Hnr Roll; Nat Mrt Sch Recip; Sci/Math Olympn; St Optmst of Yr; Yth Ldrshp Prog; Spec Olymp Vol; Chrch Yth Grp; Emplmnt; Off Aide; Tchrs Aide; Dnce; SP/M/VS; Sccr; I Like to Read; I Love the Movies.; I Want to Be a Doctor.; U of Alabama; Matlow College Tennessee

JACKSON, AARON; NEW TAZEWELL, TN; CLAIBORNE HS; (SR); Hnr Roll; Kwnis Aw; Nat Hon Sy; Nat Sci Aw; WWAHSS; Comm Volntr; Chrch Yth Grp; Emplmnt; Key Club; Sci Clb; Spanish Clb; Ftball (V CL); Track (V L); Outstanding Key Clubber; Pre-Med; Maryville College

JACKSON, BRIAN K; MEMPHIS, TN; WHITEHAVEN HS; (JR); Hi Hnr Roll; Hnr Roll; Perf Att; Ftball (V); Track (V); Business; Economic; U of Tennessee Knoxville; Auburn U

JACKSON, DENZEL M; NASHVILLE, TN; HILLSBORO HS; (FR); Perf Att; Comm Volntr; Chrch Yth Grp; Ch Chr; Track (J); Kindergarten Teacher or Pre-K; U of Florida; Tennessee State U

JACKSON, ELIZABETH S; MURFREESBORO, TN; OAKLAND HS; (FR); Off Aide; ROTC; Jr. ROTC; Nursing; Middle Tennessee State U

JACKSON, JENNIFER L; KNOXVILLE, TN; HALLS HS; (JR); Hnr Roll; Nat Hon Sy; Pres Sch; Peer Tut/Med; Chrch Yth Grp; DARE; Jr Ach; Key Club; Off Aide; French Clb; Chr; Ch Chr; Clr Grd; Education; Pellissippi State College; Union U

JACKSON, ZACHARY T; MIDDLETON, TN; MIDDLETON HS; (JR); All Am Sch; Hnr Roll; MVP; Nat Hon Sy; WWAHSS; Chrch Yth Grp; DECA; Emplmnt; Spanish Clb; Bsball (V); Golf (V); Tenn High School Rodeo; Agricultural; UT Martin; Jackson State

JAEGER, ASHLEY; CHATTANOOGA, TN; RED BANK HS; (FR); Hi Hnr Roll; Otst Ac Ach Awd; Perf Att; Pres Ac Ftns Aw; Sci/Math Olympn; Emplmnt; FCA; Ntl Beta Clb; Tchrs Aide; Bskball (VJCL); Chrldg (L); Cr Ctry (L); Golf (V L); Cl Off (T); Yrbk (E); Ranked 1 of 418 (9th Grade); Ph.D Architecture; Math; Massachusetts Institute of Technology; Georgia Institute of Technology

JAMES, HERSCHEL A; MEMPHIS, TN; WHITEHAVEN HS; (JR); Hnr Roll; WWAHSS; Peer Tut/Med; Chrch Yth Grp; Spanish Clb; USAA National English Merit Award; Computer Engineering; Middle Tennessee State U; Vanderbilt U

JAMES, JESSE; WAVERLY, TN; WAVERLY CTRL HS; (SR); 4H Awd; All Am Sch; Gov Hnr Prg; Hi Hnr Roll; Hnr Roll; Nat Hon Sy; Otst Ac Ach Awd; Perf Att; Pres Sch; Sci/Math Olympn; Comm Volntr; Peer Tut/Med; 4-H; Biology Clb; Chess; Chrch Yth Grp; Emplmnt; FCA; Mth Clb/Tm; Mus Clb; Chr; SP/M/VS; Ftball (V); Sccr (V); Adv Cncl (R); Stu Cncl (S); Youth of the Month Award; Region 5 AA Football Academic Award; Electrical Engineering; Computer Engineering; Tennessee Technology U; Nashville State Community College

JAMES, OLIVIA; FRANKLIN, TN; FRANKLIN HS; (SO); Hi Hnr Roll; Hnr Roll; Comm Volntr; Emplmnt; Dnce; Piano (10 Yrs); Elementary Education; Foreign Language (Spanish and French); College of Charleston; William & Mary

JAMES, TAYLOR; DYERSBURG, TN; DYERSBURG HS; (JR); Hi Hnr Roll; Hnr Roll; Nat Hon Sy; Perf Att; Pres Sch; Sci Fairs; WWAHSS; Comm Volntr; Peer Tut/Med; Red Cr Aide; AL Aux Girls; Chrch Yth Grp; Drma Clb; Emplmnt; Key Club; Mth Clb/Tm; MuAlphaTh; Spanish Clb; Bnd; Mch Bnd; Pep Bnd; SP/M/VS; National Honor Society; International Thespian Society; Pre Dentistry; U of Tennessee Knoxville

JANGA, SEEMA; CORDOVA, TN; CORDOVA HS; (JR); Hnr Roll; Nat Hon Sy; Otst Ac Ach Awd; Comm Volntr; Hosp Aide; Peer Tut/Med; ArtClub; Key Club; Lib Aide; MuAlphaTh; Tchrs Aide; President-Mu Alpha Theta (05-06); Secretary-Mu Alpha Theta (04-05); Pediatrician; Biology; U of Tennessee, Memphis; Southern Adventist U

JARRELL, AMBER; LASCASSAS, TN; BLACKMAN HS; (JR); Perf Att; WWAHSS; Comm Volntr; BPA; Chrch Yth Grp; Emplmnt; Key Club; Spanish Clb; Dnce; Most Dedicated Student -Chemistry; X-Ray Technician; Business; Middle Tennessee State U

JARRETT, SHARONDREA N; RIPLEY, TN; RIPLEY HS; (SO); 4H Awd; Hi Hnr Roll; Hnr Roll; Peer Tut/Med; 4-H; DARE; Bskball (C); Ob/Gyn; Pediatrician; Middle Tennessee State U; U of Tennessee Knoxville

JAYME, MARIE; ANTIOCH, TN; POPE JOHN PAUL II HS; (MS); Hnr Roll; MVP; Nat Hon Sy; Otst Ac Ach Awd; Perf Att; Salutrn; Chrch Yth Grp; Mus Clb; NtlFrnscLg; Pep Squd; Bnd; Ch Chr; Dnce; SP/M/VS; Chrldg (V); Sccr (V); Stu Cncl (R); Class Salutatorian/Middle School; St. Edward School Booster Club Academic Awardee; Medical Field; Arts; Vanderbilt U; Stanford U

JEFFERS, JONATHAN; MURFREESBORO, TN; SIEGEL HS; (SO); Duke TS; Hnr Roll; Chess; Chrch Yth Grp; Pep Squd; ROTC; Tchrs Aide; JROTC; Engineering; Middle Tennessee State U

JENKINS, CARESS; NASHVILLE, TN; NASHVILLE SCH OF THE ARTS; (FR); 4H Awd; Ctznshp Aw; Hnr Roll; Nat Sci Aw; Perf Att; Pres Sch; Sci Fairs; St Schl; St of Mnth; Comm Volntr; Chrch Yth Grp; Drma Clb; FCA; Tchrs Aide; Dnce; SP/M/VS; Bskball (V); Chrldg (V); Track (V); Vllyball (V); Cl Off (S); CR (S); Sch Ppr (R); Yrbk (E); Centennial of Flight Aviation Award; Church Plays; Psychology; Law (School); Yale U; Michigan State U

JENKINS, COURTNEY; CLEVELAND, TN; WAINER VALLEY HS; (SO); Hnr Roll; Ntl Beta Clb; Clr Grd; Anesthegiology; U of Tennessee At Knoxville

JENKINS, JIMIKA; MEMPHIS, TN; WHITE STATION HS; (FR); Hnr Roll; MVP; St of Mnth; Peer Tut/Med; ArtClub; DARE; Drma Clb; SP/M/VS; Bskball (J); PP Ftbl; Sftball; Track; Vllyball; Tennessee U; Vanderbilt U

JENNINGS, CODY; GREENEVILLE, TN; SOUTH GREENE HS; (SR); Hi Hnr Roll; Hnr Roll; Nat Hon Sy; Otst Ac Ach Awd; Perf Att; Pres Sch; Sci Fairs; St of Mnth; WWAHSS; Comm Volntr; Chrch Yth Grp; DECA; Emplmnt; Ntl FFA; SADD; Tchrs Aide; SP/M/VS; Freshman of the Year; Communications; Journalism; Tusculum College; East Tenn. State U

JENNINGS, HANNAH S; CLARKSVILLE, TN; CLARKSVILLE HS; (JR); Hnr Roll; Otst Ac Ach Awd; WWAHSS; Chrch Yth Grp; FCA; Chrldg (V); Cl Off (P); Stu Cncl (R); Nursing; U of Tennessee Chattanooga; Austin Peay State U

JERNIGAN, ADRIANNE; MEMPHIS, TN; RIDGEWAY HS; (FR); Hi Hnr Roll; Hnr Roll; WWAHSS; Comm Volntr; Chrch Yth Grp; Key Club; Cr Ctry (V); Track (V); Stu Cncl (R); CR (R); William Sweet Award; 1st Place in State History Fair - Sr Exhibits

JERNIGAN, ANDREA; MEMPHIS, TN; RIDGEWAY HS; (JR); Hi Hnr Roll; Hnr Roll; Nat Hon Sy; WWAHSS; Comm Volntr; Chrch Yth Grp; Emplmnt; Key Club; SADD; William Sweet Award - 2 Times; Health Related Field; Murray State; Abilene Christian

JERNIGAN, RACHAEL K; BRADYVILLE, TN; CANNON CTY HS; (JR); 4H Awd; All Am Sch; Hi Hnr Roll; Nat Hon Sy; Nat Ldrshp Svc; Nat Sci Aw; Otst Ac Ach Awd; WWAHSS; Comm Volntr; 4-H; BPA; Chrch Yth Grp; Drma Clb; Emplmnt; FCA; Ntl Beta Clb; French Clb; SP/M/VS; Yrbk (E); Various School Awards and National Awards; Photo Journalism; Western Kentucky; Middle Tenn State U

JETER, RACHEL M; LEWISBURG, TN; MARSHALL CTY HS; (FR); Hnr Roll; Otst Ac Ach Awd; WWAHSS; Comm Volntr; Chrch Yth Grp; Mus Clb; Acpl Chr; Chr; Ch Chr; Orch; MTVA Honors Choir - 10th Chair; Music Instruction / Elementary; Choral Performance; Belmont U; U of Tennessee

JOHANNIS II, ANDREW; CLARKSVILLE, TN; NORTHWEST HS; (FR); Hi Hnr Roll; Chrch Yth Grp; FCA; Ftball (J); AVID; Academic Award Recipient (A's); Architecture; Contractor; Auburn U

JOHNSEY, EVAN; JACKSON, TN; LIBERTY TECH MAGNET HS; (SO); 4H Awd; Hi Hnr Roll; Hnr Roll; MVP; Nat Hon Sy; Perf Att; St of Mnth; WWAHSS; Comm Volntr; 4-H; Chrch Yth Grp; Ntl Beta Clb; Tech Clb; Ftball (V CL); Sccr (V CL); Student Achievement Award; 2nd Team All Region-Football; Sports Medicine; U of Tennessee/Knoxville; Union U

JOHNSON, A B; ASHLAND CITY, TN; CHEATHAM CTY CTRL HS; (JR); Hnr Roll; Nat Hon Sy; Perf Att; WWAHSS; Comm Volntr; ArtClub; Chrch Yth Grp; FCA; Spanish Clb; Bible Club President; Elementary Education; American Literature; Austin Peay State U; Vanderbilt U

JOHNSON, ALLEE; GOODLETTSVILLE, TN; GREENBRIER HS; (SO); Hnr Roll; Comm Volntr; BPA; Chrch Yth Grp; FCA; Ntl Beta Clb; Spanish Clb; Ch Chr; Dnce; SP/M/VS; Bskball; Vllyball (V); Vice President of BPA (Class); Basketball Girls Manager; Medical Career

JOHNSON, ANTONY B; LENOIR CITY, TN; LENOIR CITY HS; (JR); Hnr Roll; Perf Att; 4-H; DARE; Honor Roll; Perfect Attendance; Game Warden; Carson Newman; Lincoln Memorial

JOHNSON, AUSTIN; AFTON, TN; CHUCKEY-DOAK HS; (JR); Ctznshp Aw; Hi Hnr Roll; Hnr Roll; Nat Hon Sy; Otst Ac Ach Awd; WWAHSS; Yth Ldrshp Prog; Comm Volntr; Peer Tut/Med; Dbte Team; Ntl FFA; Quiz Bowl; Svce Clb; Spch Team; Tchrs Aide; Ch Chr; Best of Show / Art Grotto at Provenance Gallery; Anthropology; Linguistics; Duke U; Yale U

JOHNSON, BENJAMIN; NASHVILLE, TN; HILLSBORO COMP HS; (JR); Duke TS; Hi Hnr Roll; Nat Hon Sy; Nat Sci Aw; Comm Volntr; Chrch Yth Grp; Drma Clb; Emplmnt; Mus Clb; Sci Clb; Latin Clb; Bnd; Chr; Orch; Swg Chr; National Thespian Society; International Business; NYU; Chicago

JOHNSON, CARLIN M; CAMDEN, TN; CENTRAL HS; (FR); Hosp Aide; Ntl FFA; Computer Technician; Jackson State Community College

JOHNSON, CARMEN L; MEMPHIS, TN; GREY ROAD CHRISTIAN AC; (FR); 4H Awd; Hi Hnr Roll; Sci Fairs; 4-H; ArtClub; Chrch Yth Grp; Cmptr Clb; Dbte Team; Drma Clb; Emplmnt; Mus Clb; Chr; Ch Chr; SP/M/VS; Stu Cncl (S); Praise Singer in Church Services; Literary Composition/Music; Medicine; U of Tennessee; Michigan State U

JOHNSON, DEVIN; OAKFIELD, TN; NORTH SIDE HS; (JR); Hi Hnr Roll; Hnr Roll; WWAHSS; Peer Tut/Med; Chrch Yth Grp; Emplmnt; Chr; SP/M/VS; All-West Honor Choir; Nursing; Nurse Practitioner; Austin Peay State U; Middle Tennessee State U

JOHNSON, JASMINE; MEMPHIS, TN; CITY UNIVERSITY OF LIBERAL ARTS; (FR); Hnr Roll; Scouts; Bskball (C); Yrbk (P); Been Voted for Ms Yearbook; Veterinary; Clark Atlanta U; Xavier U LA

JOHNSON, JENNIFER B; NEW TAZEWELL, TN; CLARBORNE HS; (SR); Hnr Roll; Nat Hon Sy; Sci Fairs; USAA; WWAHSS; Comm Volntr; Peer Tut/Med; Chrch Yth Grp; Emplmnt; Key Club; Ntl Beta Clb; Off Aide; Prom Com; Sci Clb; Ch Chr; SP/M/VS; Walters State Community College

JOHNSON, JEREMY; MURFREESBORO, TN; OAKLAND HS; (FR); Hnr Roll; Perf Att; St of Mnth; Chrch Yth Grp; DARE; Outdrs Clb; Mechanics; Middle Tennessee State U; U of Tennessee

JOHNSON, JERRICA; LEWISBURG, TN; MARSHALL CTY HS; (FR); Pres Ac Ftns Aw; Comm Volntr; Hab For Humty Volntr; FTA; Ch Chr; Dnce; Stu Cncl (R); Law; Psychology; Middle Tennessee State U; Tennessee State U

JOHNSON, KIARA R; MEMPHIS, TN; SHEFFIELD HS; (SO); Ctznshp Aw; Hi Hnr Roll; Hnr Roll; Perf Att; ArtClub; Spanish Clb; Spanish Club; Art Club; Graphic Art; Culinary Art; Lane College; Spelman College

JOHNSON, LAMARCUS T; NASHVILLE, TN; WHITE CREEK SCH; (FR); DARE; Emplmnt; Bskball; Engineering; Tennessee State U

JOHNSON, MICHAEL R; CHATTANOOGA, TN; TYNER AC; (SR); Hnr Roll; Otst Ac Ach Awd; Perf Att; St of Mnth; Comm Volntr; ArtClub; Chess; DARE; Emplmnt; Bskball (V); Track (V); Wt Lftg (V); Computer Architect; Business; Chattanooga State; Cleveland State

JOHNSON, NIKKI; MURFREESBORO, TN; BLACKMAN HS; (JR); Hi Hnr Roll; St of Mnth; Peer Tut/Med; Chrch Yth Grp; Key Club; Mth Clb/Tm; MuAlphaTh; Ntl Beta Clb; Quiz Bowl; Sci Clb; Spanish Clb; Chr; Stg Cre; Biomedical Engineer; U of Memphis; Tennessee Tech U

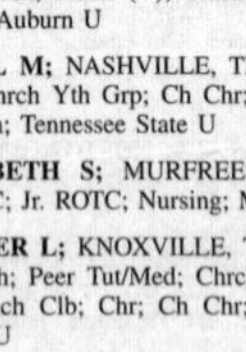

Johnson, Kiara R
Sheffield HS
Memphis, TN

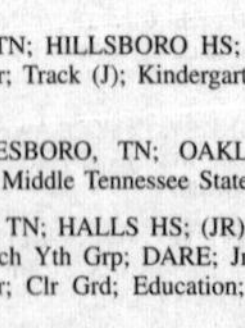

Johnson, Antony B
Lenoir City HS
Lenoir City, TN

Jennings, Cody
South Greene HS
Greeneville, TN

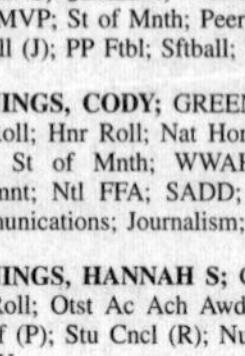

Jayme, Marie
Pope John Paul II HS
Antioch, TN

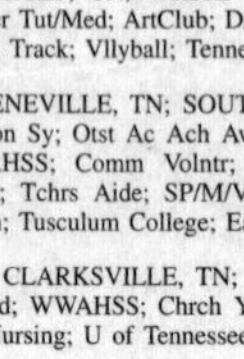

Ivie, Shari
North Side HS
Jackson, TN

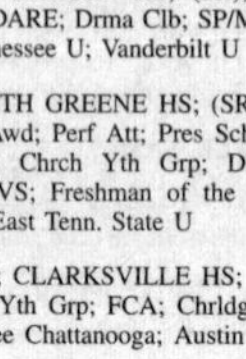

Jackson, Elizabeth S
Oakland HS
Murfreesboro, TN

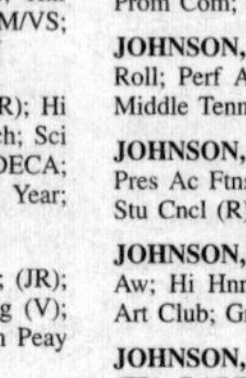

Johnsey, Evan
Liberty Tech Magnet HS
Jackson, TN

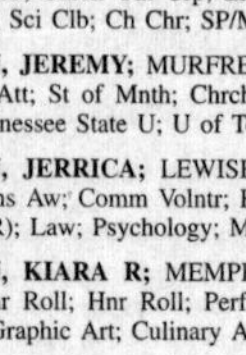

Johnson, Carlin M
Central HS
Camden, TN

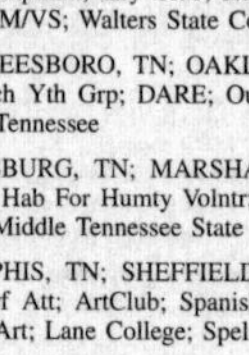

Johnson, Michael R
Tyner AC
Chattanooga, TN

JOHNSON, PHILLIP; ARLINGTON, TN; ARLINGTON HS; (FR); Hi Hnr Roll; Nat Hon Sy; Comm Volntr; Peer Tut/Med; BPA; Chrch Yth Grp; Ftball (VJ); Cl Off (P); Historian of BPA; Bachelor's; PhD; U of Miami; U of California Los Angeles

JOHNSON, RACKELLA; SAULSBURY, TN; MIDDLETON HS; (JR); Hnr Roll; Comm Volntr; Emplmnt; Lib Aide; Stg Cre; Scr Kpr (J); Major in Chemistry; U of Memphis

JOHNSON, RHONDA L; MEMPHIS, TN; FAIRLEY HS; (SO); Hnr Roll; Perf Att; DARE; Chr; Computer Programming

JOHNSON, TIFFANY; SWEETWATER, TN; SWEETWATER HS; (SR); 4H Awd; Hnr Roll; Nat Hon Sy; St of Mnth; WWAHSS; Yth Ldrshp Prog; Comm Volntr; Peer Tut/Med; ArtClub; Chrch Yth Grp; FCA; Ntl Beta Clb; NYLC; Photog; Svce Clb; Tchrs Aide; Ch Chr; PP Ftbl (V); Stu Cncl (P); CR (R); Yrbk (E); Pre-Pharmacy; Hiwassee College; Samford U

JOHNSON-EL, JAUHARA R; NASHVILLE, TN; PEARL-COHN MAGNET HS; (SO); Hnr Roll; WWAHSS; Drma Clb; Emplmnt; SP/M/VS; Sftball (J); Business Management; English Literature; Columbia U; Duke U

JOLLY, JESSICA; MURFREESBORO, TN; BLACKMAN HS; (JR); Hi Hnr Roll; Nat Hon Sy; St of Mnth; USAA; WWAHSS; Comm Volntr; 4-H; Chrch Yth Grp; Key Club; Lib Aide; Ntl Beta Clb; Tchrs Aide; Latin Clb; Bnd; Mch Bnd; SP/M/VS; Tennis ((V)); Stu Cncl (R); Renaissance Club; BHS Student of the Week; Pre-Med; Pediatrics; Middle Tennessee State U; University of Alabama

JOLLY, KAYLA; WOODLAWN, TN; STEWART CTY HS; (JR); Hnr Roll; Nat Hon Sy; Perf Att; Comm Volntr; Hab For Humty Volntr; Red Cr Aide; BPA; Chrch Yth Grp; Drma Clb; FCCLA; Ntl FFA; NYLC; Prom Com; SADD; SP/M/VS; Chrldg (J); Yrbk (R); Veterinary Medicine; Animal Science; Lipscomb State U

JONES, ALICIA; MEMPHIS, TN; TREZEVANT MIDDLE HS; (FR); Ctznshp Aw; Hi Hnr Roll; Hnr Roll; Nat Hon Sy; Valdctrian; Pediatrician; Nurse (RN); Tennessee State U; U of Memphis

JONES, ASHLEY N; KINGSPORT, TN; SULLIVAN NORTH HS; Duke TS; Hi Hnr Roll; Nat Hon Sy; FCA; Key Club; Ntl Beta Clb; Sftball (V); Stu Cncl (R); National Honor Society; Biology; Physician; East Tennessee State U

JONES, BRIAN S; MEMPHIS, TN; MANASSAS HS; (FR); Hnr Roll; MVP; Comm Volntr; ArtClub; Fr of Library; ROTC; Bnd; Pep Bnd; Swmg; Wt Lftg; Paralegal Degree / Bachelor's Degree; PhD; California State U

JONES, BRITTNEY; MEMPHIS, TN; EAST HS; (FR); Hi Hnr Roll; Hnr Roll; Comm Volntr; Chrch Yth Grp; Chr; Ch Chr; Drm Mjr; Stu Cncl (R); Journalism/Mass Communications; English; Tennessee State U; Middle Tennessee State U

JONES, CARA; LEOMA, TN; LAWRENCE CTY HS; (SO); Hnr Roll; Perf Att; Peer Tut/Med; FCCLA; Mus Clb; Sci Clb; Scouts; Chr; Clr Grd; FCCLA-Reporter; Earned Girl Scout Silver Award; Veterinarian; Interior Design; Middle Tennessee State U; U of Tennessee in Knoxville

JONES, CECILY; MEMPHIS, TN; NORTHSIDE HS; (FR); Ctznshp Aw; Hnr Roll; Perf Att; Comm Volntr; Peer Tut/Med; ROTC; Tchrs Aide; Clr Grd; Drl Tm; Master's Degree in Science; Dentistry Cosmetics; Atlanta U; New York City U

JONES, CHELSIE; SOMERVILLE, TN; FAYETTE AC; (MS); Hi Hnr Roll; FCA; Bnd; Sftball (J); Vllyball (C); 2nd Place in Pre-Algebra Math Meet

JONES, COURTNEY; MADISON, TN; HUNTERS LANE HS; (JR); Hnr Roll; Red Cr Aide; Chrch Yth Grp; Tchrs Aide; Chr; Ch Chr; Sch Ppr (R); Good Citizenship Award Twice; Psychology; Photography; Austin Peay U; Tennessee State U

JONES, JESSICA E; CROSSVILLE, TN; CUMBERLAND CTY HS; (SO); Perf Att; St of Mnth; WWAHSS; Chess; Chrch Yth Grp; DARE; FCA; Sci Clb; Spanish Clb; Ch Chr; Clr Grd; Cl Off (R); Attorney At Law; U of Tennessee

JONES, KE'ARRA D; MEMPHIS, TN; CENTRAL HS; (SO); Hnr Roll; Nat Hon Sy; Perf Att; St of Mnth; Comm Volntr; Hab For Humty Volntr; Biology Clb; Mar Art (V); All Girls Step Team; Ladies of Distinction - LOD; Veterinary Medicine; Artist; Tennessee State U; Memphis U

JONES, KELLYE D; CAMDEN, TN; CAMDEN CTRL HS; (JR); All Am Sch; Hi Hnr Roll; Hnr Roll; Nat Hon Sy; Otst Ac Ach Awd; Sci Fairs; WWAHSS; Yth Ldrshp Prog; Comm Volntr; Spec Olymp Vol; BPA; Chrch Yth Grp; DARE; DECA; Emplmnt; FCA; FBLA; Ntl Beta Clb; Golf (V L); Scr Kpr (V C); Cl Off (R); Stu Cncl (T); Medical; Optometry; U of Tennessee Knoxville; Middle Tennessee State U

JONES, MARTICE; MEMPHIS, TN; MELROSE HS; (SO); Ctznshp Aw; Perf Att; CARE; Comm Volntr; Chrch Yth Grp; Fr of Library; Mus Clb; Ch Chr; Doctor; Teacher; U of Memphis; Tennessee State U

JONES, MICHAEL E; WARTBURG, TN; CENTRAL HS; (JR); Hi Hnr Roll; Jr Eng Tech; Chrch Yth Grp; Auto Restoration / Auto Body; Mechanics; Automotive; Nashville Automotive Diesel College; Pellissippi Community College

JONES, MOLLY; GREENEVILLE, TN; GREENEVILLE HS; (SO); Hnr Roll; Otst Ac Ach Awd; Perf Att; St of Mnth; WWAHSS; Chrch Yth Grp; Mus Clb; NYLC; Svce Clb; Spanish Clb; Chr; Mch Bnd; SP/M/VS; Swg Chr; Tennis (V L); Cl Off (R); Government/Press Journalist; New York U; College of Charleston

JONES, STEPHEN; MURFREESBORO, TN; SIEGEL HS; (SO); Hnr Roll; MVP; Chrch Yth Grp; DARE; Mus Clb; Bnd; Mch Bnd; SP/M/VS; Swmg; Wrstlg; Tri-M Music Honor Society; Chamber Choir; Music; Norfolk State U; Middle Tennessee State U

JONES, TEATRA; MEMPHIS, TN; OAK HAVEN HS; (SO); Ctznshp Aw; Hnr Roll; Nat Hon Sy; St of Mnth; CARE; Comm Volntr; Hosp Aide; DARE; FCA; Jr Ach; Mth Clb/Tm; Outdrs Clb; Prom Com; Scouts; SADD; Clr Grd; Dnce; Adv Cncl (R); Cl Off (P); Stu Cncl (T); CR (R); Business Administrator; Xavier U New Orleans; TSU

JORDAN, ANDREW; PINEY FLATS, TN; ELIZABETHTON HS; (JR); Hi Hnr Roll; Hnr Roll; Pres Ac Ftns Aw; WWAHSS; Chrch Yth Grp; Emplmnt; FCA; Mus Clb; Track (V); School Guitar Club; Church Praise Team; Law; History; Northeast State Community College; East Tennessee State U

JORGE, CONSUELO; KNOXVILLE, TN; FARRAGUT HS; (SR); Drl Tm; PPSqd (J); FCCLA; Accounting; Pilot; The U of Tennessee-Knoxville

JOWERS, JESSICA L; BRIGHTON, TN; BRIGHTON HS; (FR); Ctznshp Aw; Comm Volntr; Scouts; Member of HOSA; Physical Therapist; Video Game Design; Dyersburg State Community College; U of Memphis

JUDKINS, COURTNEY D; MORRISON, TN; WARREN CTY HS; (SR); Hnr Roll; WWAHSS; Emplmnt; Pep Squd; Prom Com; Dnce; PPSqd (J); Who's Who Among High School Students; 2 Years of Dance Team (Fresh & Soph.); Education Degree; Motlow State Community College; Middle Tennessee State U

JUDKINS, DONALD; PULASKI, TN; GILES CTY HS; (JR); Hi Hnr Roll; WWAHSS; Comm Volntr; Ntl Beta Clb; HOSA; U of Tennessee

JULIAN, CHELSEA V; BUTLER, TN; CLOUDLAND HS; (JR); Ctznshp Aw; Hnr Roll; Nat Hon Sy; St of Mnth; Physical Therapist; Registered Nurse; Charleston South Carolina; Clemson U

JUNE, NICOLE; CLARKSVILLE, TN; NORTHWEST HS; (SO); Hnr Roll; Peer Tut/Med; Chrch Yth Grp; Ntl Beta Clb; Journalism; Creative Writing; U of Tennessee; Austin Peay State U

JUSTICE, JEREMIAH E; HARRIMAN, TN; OLIVER SPRINGS HS; (JR); Hnr Roll; Otst Ac Ach Awd; Perf Att; Comm Volntr; Chrch Yth Grp; Emplmnt; FCA; Lttrmn Clb; Ntl Beta Clb; Vsity Clb; Foreign Clb; Bsball (V L); Ftball (V L); Electrical Engineering; Tennessee Tech; Carson-Newman U

JUSTICE, JOSHUA B; HARRIMAN, TN; OLIVER SPRINGS HS; (JR); Hnr Roll; Otst Ac Ach Awd; Perf Att; Comm Volntr; Chrch Yth Grp; Emplmnt; FCA; Lttrmn Clb; Ntl Beta Clb; Vsity Clb; Foreign Clb; Bsball (V L); Ftball (V L); Cl Off (R); Electrical Engineering; Tennessee Tech; Carson-Newman U

JUSTICE, TONYA MARIE; LAKE CITY, TN; ANDERSON CTY HS; (JR); Hnr Roll; Nat Hon Sy; WWAHSS; Comm Volntr; Hab For Humty Volntr; 4-H; Emplmnt; FCA; Ntl FFA; Bskball (V CL); Cr Ctry (V L); Sftball (V CL); Oak Ridge Specific Site Advisory Board; Veterinarian Science; Lincoln Memorial U; Carson-Newman College

KALFAYAN, CAITLIN J; MEMPHIS, TN; RIDGEWAY HS; (FR); Duke TS; Hi Hnr Roll; Pres Sch; WWAHSS; Comm Volntr; Chrch Yth Grp; Key Club; Ch Chr; William Sweet Award; Optimist Essay Contest - 1st District / 3rd Region; Teacher; Psychologist; U of Mississippi; U of Virginia

KALFAYAN, JOHN A; MEMPHIS, TN; RIDGEWAY HS; (JR); Duke TS; Hi Hnr Roll; Nat Hon Sy; Sci Fairs; Sci/Math Olympn; WWAHSS; Comm Volntr; Chrch Yth Grp; Emplmnt; Key Club; Mod UN; MuAlphaTh; Ch Chr; Sccr (J); Bridge Builders Rep; William Sweet Award; Architecture; Engineering / Computer Science; Clemson U; U of Arkansas

KAPOOR, GITANJALI K; OAK RIDGE, TN; OAK RIDGE HS; (JR); F Lan Hn Soc; Nat Hon Sy; Comm Volntr; Peer Tut/Med; Key Club; Clb; Orch; Sftball (V); Key Club-Historian; Children's Museum Youth Advisory Board; MBA; Mathematics; U of California-Los Angeles; Northwestern U

KASPAR, KEVIN; ARLINGTON, TN; EVANGELICAL CHRISTIAN SCH; (JR); Hnr Roll; WWAHSS; Chess; Chrch Yth Grp; FCA; Key Club; MuAlphaTh; Bskball (J); Engineering; Business; Mississippi St; Tennessee Knoxville

KASPER, JASON; ARLINGTON, TN; (SO); Hnr Roll; Pres Sch; Chess; Chrch Yth Grp; FCA; Key Club; Tennis (V); Graduate; Duke U; Dartmouth U

KATZERMAN, BERNARD; CORDOVA, TN; RIDGEWAY HS; (JR); Hi Hnr Roll; Hnr Roll; Nat Hon Sy; Sci Fairs; WWAHSS; Comm Volntr; Peer Tut/Med; Biology Clb; Key Club; Mod UN; MuAlphaTh; Off Aide; SADD; Tmpl Yth Grp; Bnd; Cr Ctry (J); Most Improved Band - Trumpet; William B Sweet Honor; Mechanical Engineering; U of Tennessee; U of Texas

KEIFER, AMANDA; BAXTER, TN; COOKEVILLE HS; (JR); WWAHSS; Comm Volntr; Hab For Humty Volntr; 4-H; Fr of Library; Key Club; Outdrs Clb; French Clb; Sccr (V CL); Swmg (J); Track (V L); Joining the Peace Corps; Political Science; International Studies; Centre College; Rhodes College

KEIPER, RACHEL; MT JULIET, TN; WILSON CTRL HS; (SO); Hi Hnr Roll; Nat Hon Sy; Otst Ac Ach Awd; Quill & Scroll; Dnce; Yrbk (R, P); Grade IV Cecchetti Method of Ballet; Medicine; Vanderbilt U; U of Tennessee

KEISLING, MIA C; LAFAYETTE, TN; POPE JOHN PAUL II HS; (SR); Hnr Roll; Nat Hon Sy; WWAHSS; Comm Volntr; Hab For Humty Volntr; Hosp Aide; Chrch Yth Grp; FCA; Mth Clb/Tm; MuAlphaTh; Photog; Ch Chr; Chrldg (V); Yrbk (P); Pharmacy; U of Kentucky; U of Tennessee Knoxville

KEITH, KALEY; THOMPSONS STATION, TN; INDEPENDENCE HS; (SO); Hi Hnr Roll; MVP; St of Mnth; Hab For Humty Volntr; Peer Tut/Med; Red Cr Aide; Key Club; Off Aide; SADD; Tchrs Aide; Bskball (J); Track (V); Vllyball (V CL); Cl Off (R); Stu Cncl (V); CR (R); Yrbk (P); Doctor; Florida State U; Indiana U

KELLER, DANIELLE N; KELSO, TN; LINCOLN CTY HS; (JR); DAR; Hnr Roll; Perf Att; 4-H; Emplmnt; Pep Squd; Tchrs Aide; Stu Cncl (R); FCCLA; Pep Squad; Motlow College

KELLEY, GARRETT; RIPLEY, TN; RIPLEY HS; (FR); Hnr Roll; Chrch Yth Grp; DARE; FCA; Ntl FFA; Scouts; Ch Chr; Fld Hky (V); Ftball (V); Track (V); Wt Lftg (V); Law Degree; Criminal Justice; U of Mississippi; U of Tennessee

KELLY, JACOB; POWELL, TN; TEMPLE BAPTIST AC; (JR); Hi Hnr Roll; Hnr Roll; Otst Ac Ach Awd; Perf Att; Chrch Yth Grp; Mth Clb/Tm; Second Place in Algebra/Geometry in Tennessee Association of Christian Schools; Honor Roll in 8th-11th Grades; Mechanical Engineering; Pellissippi State Technical Community College; U of Tennessee Knoxville

KELLY, NAJIYAH; KNOXVILLE, TN; BEREAN CHRISTIAN SCH; (SO); Ctznshp Aw; Hnr Roll; Comm Volntr; Chrch Yth Grp; DARE; Chr; Dnce; Gmnstcs; Anthropology; Art; A & E

KESTERSON, KATRINA; MC KENZIE, TN; MC KENZIE HS; (SO); Hi Hnr Roll; Nat Hon Sy; Otst Ac Ach Awd; Sci Fairs; WWAHSS; Comm Volntr; Hab For Humty Volntr; FCA; Key Club; Ntl Beta Clb; Pep Squd; Sci Clb; Tech Clb; Spanish Clb; SP/M/VS; Skt Tgt Sh (V); Tennis (V); Track (V); Cl Off (V); Stu Cncl (S); Radiology; Vanderbilt U; U of TN Knoxville

KETCHUM, ANDREA; DYERSBURG, TN; DC HS; (FR); Fut Prb Slvr; Hnr Roll; Sci Fairs; St of Mnth; WWAHSS; Comm Volntr; Peer Tut/Med; Red Cr Aide; Chess; Emplmnt; Ntl FFA; Outdrs Clb; Photog; ROTC; Bnd; Ch Chr; Drl Tm; Mch Bnd; Cr Ctry (L); Mar Art (L); PP Ftbl (L); Sccr (L); Vllyball (L); Stu Cncl (R); Yrbk (P); Teacher Degree; Medical Degree

KEY, JESSICA; CELINA, TN; (JR); Hnr Roll; Comm Volntr; Hosp Aide; Ntl Beta Clb; Dnce; Fashion Designer; Physical Therapist; U of Indianapolis; Nashville State

KEY, JOSEPH; CELINA, TN; (SO); Doctor; Lawyer; U of Tennessee; Florida U

KEY, WILLIAM M; CELINA, TN; CLAY CTY HS; (JR); 4H Awd; Hnr Roll; Perf Att; Yth Ldrshp Prog; Hab For Humty Volntr; 4-H; Chrch Yth Grp; DARE; Emplmnt; FCA; Lttrmn Clb; Ntl FFA; Golf (V); Vice President of Local FFA Chapter; Outstanding Leader Award 9+ FFA Camp; Wildlife Conservation; Agriculture Engineering; U of Tennessee; Tennessee Technological U

KILGORE, LAUREN K; BLOUNTVILLE, TN; SULLIVAN CTRL HS; (JR); 4H Awd; Ctznshp Aw; Hi Hnr Roll; Hnr Roll; Nat Stu Ath Day Aw; Otst Ac Ach Awd; Pres Ac Ftns Aw; WWAHSS; Comm Volntr; Peer Tut/Med; 4-H; Chrch Yth Grp; DARE; Key Club; Mus Clb; SADD; Chr; Ch Chr; Dnce; Won Miss Congeniality, Won DARE Essay Contest 3 Years in a Row, Came in Top 20 4 Years; Homecoming Court 3 Times, Cougarette Dance Team 3 Years; Law; Child Care-Fashion

KILMON, ASHLEY; CELINA, TN; CLAY CTY HS; (JR); Hi Hnr Roll; Nat Hon Sy; Nat Mrt LOC; WWAHSS; Comm Volntr; Peer Tut/Med; DARE; Mth Clb/Tm; Ntl Beta Clb; Sci Clb; Tchrs Aide; SP/M/VS; Cl Off (V); Math Award; Beta Club Service Award; Nursing; Medicine; Tennessee Tech; U of Tennessee Knoxville

KIMBROUGH, KRISTOPHER D; KNOXVILLE, TN; AUSTIN-EAST MAGNET HS; (SO); WWAHSS; Comm Volntr; Chrch Yth Grp; FBLA; Ch Chr; Bskball (J); Ftball (V); Computer Science; Personal Trainer; U of North Carolina; U of Tennessee

Kilgore, Lauren K
Sullivan Ctrl HS
Blountville, TN

Keisling, Mia C
Pope John Paul II HS
Lafayette, TN

Jowers, Jessica L
Brighton HS
Brighton, TN

Jones, Michael E
Central HS
Wartburg, TN

Jones, Cara
Lawrence Cty HS
Leoma, TN

National
Honor Roll
Spring 2005

Jolly, Jessica
Blackman HS
Murfreesboro, TN

Jones, Stephen
Siegel HS
Murfreesboro, TN

Judkins, Courtney D
Warren Cty HS
Morrison, TN

Kelly, Najiyah
Berean Christian Sch
Knoxville, TN

Key, William M
Clay Cty HS
Celina, TN

KING, KATIE; LA FOLLETTE, TN; CAMPBELL CTY HS; (SO); Hnr Roll; WWAHSS; Emplmnt; Key Club; Tennis (V); Cl Off (S); Lifeguard & CPR Certification; Accounting; Physical Therapy; U of Tennessee; Tennessee Tech

KING, KENDRA; SEVIERVILLE, TN; SEVIER CTY HS; (SO); Hnr Roll; St of Mnth; Cosmetologist; Nurse; Tennessee School of Beauty

KING, KIMBERLY; LENOIR CITY, TN; GREENBACK PUBLIC SCH; (FR); 4H Awd; Hi Hnr Roll; Sci Fairs; Yth Ldrshp Prog; Comm Volntr; Peer Tut/Med; 4-H; Chrch Yth Grp; Emplmnt; FCA; FBLA; FCCLA; Ntl Beta Clb; Bnd; Ch Chr; Mch Bnd; Pep Bnd; Bskball (VJ); Hsbk Rdg; Cl Off (R); Yrbk; 4-H State Hippology Championship Team-2004; 4-H State Hippology High Individual 3rd-2004; Veterinary Medicine; Animal Science and Equine Studies; U of Tennessee; Middle Tennessee State U

KING, MEGAN R; RED BOILING SPRINGS, TN; HERMITAGE SPRINGS SCH; (JR); Hi Hnr Roll; MVP; Perf Att; WWAHSS; Comm Volntr; 4-H; Chrch Yth Grp; DARE; FCA; FCCLA; Ntl Beta Clb; Ntl FFA; Prom Com; Bskball (V C); Sftball (V C); Yrbk; Softball Most Valuable Player of District 2004; Softball Most Valuable Player of Team 2004; General Business; Athletic Trainer; Middle Tennessee State U; Western Kentucky U

KING, RACHEL; MURFREESBORO, TN; RIVERDALE HS; (JR); Hi Hnr Roll; Comm Volntr; Chess; Chrch Yth Grp; Key Club; Sci Clb; German Clb; Ch Chr; Secretary of German Club; Social Services; Middle Tennessee State U

KING, SARAH; JOHNSON CITY, TN; PROVIDENCE AC; (FR); Hnr Roll; Pres Ac Ftns Aw; Sci Fairs; Comm Volntr; ArtClub; Chrch Yth Grp; Mus Clb; Chr; Bskball (V L); Sccr (V); Service Award; Guest Chef; Culinary Arts; Business; Johnson and Wales U; Culinary Institute of America

KING, SARAH; LA FOLLETTE, TN; CAMPBELL CTY COMP HS; (SO); Hnr Roll; WWAHSS; Comm Volntr; Chrch Yth Grp; FCA; Key Club; Education; Writer; Brown U; Baylor U

KING JR, CHARLES A; RIPLEY, TN; RIPLEY HS; (SO); Hnr Roll; St of Mnth; Wt Lftg; Perfect Attendance; Student of the Year - Finger HS; Producer; Columbia U

KINNARD, LAWRENCE; MEMPHIS, TN; RALEIGH-EGYPT HS; (SR); Hnr Roll; Comm Volntr; Vsity Clb; SP/M/VS; Bskball (VJC); Cr Ctry (V C); Tennis (V); Outstanding Senior; NBA; UAB

KINNEY, TARA L; BRIGHTON, TN; BRIGHTON HS; (FR); All Am Sch; Ctznshp Aw; Hi Hnr Roll; Otst Ac Ach Awd; Comm Volntr; Chrch Yth Grp; Prom Com; Spanish Clb; Chrldg (V); PP Ftbl (V); Track (V); Stu Cncl (V); 2nd Runner-Up - Miss Atoka; 4th Runner-Up Miss Jr Tipton County; Orthopedics; Pediatrics; U of Tennessee Knoxville; U of Southern California

KINZER, JESSICA; KNOXVILLE, TN; BEARDEN HS; (SR); Hi Hnr Roll; MVP; Nat Hon Sy; WWAHSS; Comm Volntr; AL Aux Girls; Chrch Yth Grp; DECA; FCA; Key Club; MuAlphaTh; Prom Com; PP Ftbl; Sccr (V CL); Sch Ppr (R); Business Management; Education; Carson Newman College

KIRBY, CAITLIN; LAWRENCEBURG, TN; LAWRENCE CTY HS; (SO); All Am Sch; Duke TS; Hnr Roll; Nat Hon Sy; Otst Ac Ach Awd; WWAHSS; Comm Volntr; Drma Clb; Emplmnt; FBLA; SP/M/VS; Stg Cre; Theatre; Chemistry; Sewanee: U of the South; Duke U

KIRBY, CHRIS; CHATTANOOGA, TN; HOME SCH; (JR); Perf Att; Chrch Yth Grp; DARE; Chr; Bskball (V); Sccr (VJ)

KIRBY, GLIJUAN; GALLATIN, TN; GALLATIN HS; (SO); Hnr Roll; Chrch Yth Grp; Drma Clb; Mus Clb; Chr; Ch Chr; SP/M/VS; Journalism/ Communications; Performing Arts; U of Tennessee; Clark Atlanta U

KIRBY, TAMARA L; GORDONSVILLE, TN; GORDONSVILLE HS; (JR); Hnr Roll; Perf Att; WWAHSS; Yth Ldrshp Prog; Comm Volntr; FCA; Ntl Beta Clb; Photog; SADD; Tchrs Aide; Vsity Clb; Spanish Clb; Chr; Sftball (V); Yrbk (E, P); Secretary of SADD; Accounting; Mathematics; Tennessee Technological U; Cumberland U

KIRI, WANI G; CHATTANOOGA, TN; CENTRAL HS; (SO); Hnr Roll; MVP; St of Mnth; Hab For Humty Volntr; FCCLA; MuAlphaTh; Sccr (V); Honors Student; Academic Letter and Bar; Electrical Engineering; Nuclear Engineering; Tennessee Technological U; Florida Atlantic U

KIRKSEY, BRETT W; CLEVELAND, TN; WALKER VALLEY HS; (SO); Duke TS; Hi Hnr Roll; MVP; Nat Hon Sy; WWAHSS; Comm Volntr; Chrch Yth Grp; Key Club; Ntl Beta Clb; Chr; SP/M/VS; Cr Ctry (V); Ftball (V); Sccr (V); Track (V); CR (R); MVP Special Teams-Football; Iron Man Award-Soccer

KITZLER, KRISTEN; MURFREESBORO, TN; BLACKMAN HS; (SO); Hnr Roll; WWAHSS; Chrch Yth Grp; Key Club; Ntl Beta Clb; Scouts; Latin Clb; Bnd; Mch Bnd; Pep Bnd; Vllyball (V C); Pediatrician; Teacher; Vanderbilt U; Middle Tennessee State U

KIZER, KOURTNEY J A; HERMITAGE, TN; MC GAVOCK COMP HS; (JR); Ctznshp Aw; Hi Hnr Roll; Otst Ac Ach Awd; Comm Volntr; AL Aux Girls; Drma Clb; Bnd; Mch Bnd; Attendee of Various Honor Bands; Attendee of First Annual Writer's Workshop; Biology Major / Medical Field; Belmont U; Vanderbilt U

KLARHAN, JORDAN; DANDRIDGE, TN; JEFFERSON CTY HS; (SR); Hnr Roll; WWAHSS; Comm Volntr; DECA; Emplmnt; Key Club; Ntl Beta Clb; Pep Squd; Tchrs Aide; East Tennessee Vice President of DECA 04-05; National Marketing Education Honor Award, DECA Competitor and Board of Directors; Pacemaker Sales Representative; King College; Walter State Community College

KNIGHT, MADDIE; SMYRNA, TN; LA VERGNE HS; (FR); Hnr Roll; Drma Clb; Emplmnt; Vsity Clb; SP/M/VS; Stg Cre; Cr Ctry (V); Sccr (V); Track (V); Wt Lftg (V); Business Management; Photography; Florida State U; U of North Carolina

KNOX, SHANEQUA; CLARKSVILLE, TN; NORTHWEST HS; (FR); Hnr Roll; Perf Att; Chrch Yth Grp; DARE; Drma Clb; Scouts; Ch Chr; Sftball (V); Stu Cncl (V); Master's Degree; Bachelor's Degree; Duke U; U of Knoxville

KOKOREVA, NATALIJA; GERMANTOWN, TN; GERMANTOWN HS; (JR); F Lan Hn Soc; Hnr Roll; Nat Hon Sy; Otst Ac Ach Awd; Perf Att; WWAHSS; Comm Volntr; Ntl Beta Clb; Spanish Clb; Bnd; Pep Bnd; Chrldg (V); Cr Ctry (V); Swmg (V); Tennis; Track (V); Wrstlg; Yrbk (P); (Music) Superior Rating on Performance Test in Local Student Auditions; Certificardo De Merito en Espanol in 2003 & 2004; Arts; International Business

KOLP, ZACHARY; MURFREESBORO, TN; BLACKMAN HS; (JR); Hi Hnr Roll; Kwnis Aw; Otst Ac Ach Awd; St of Mnth; WWAHSS; Comm Volntr; Peer Tut/Med; Key Club; Lib Aide; Ntl Beta Clb; Tchrs Aide; President of Beta/Key Club/Environmental Society in National Society of High School Scholars; Piano Performance; History; Indiana U-Bloomington; Mobile Tennessee State U

KOOMEN, T J; NASHVILLE, TN; HILLSBORO COMP HS; (JR); Hi Hnr Roll; Comm Volntr; Lcrsse (C); Cl Off (P); Sch Ppr (R); Mock Trial Team

KOPLIN, SARAH; MEMPHIS, TN; LAUSANNE COLLEGIATE SCH; (SO); All Am Sch; Hnr Roll; MVP; Sci Fairs; Comm Volntr; Hab For Humty Volntr; Peer Tut/Med; Emplmnt; Key Club; Ntl Beta Clb; P to P St Amb Prg; Svce Clb; Ch Chr; Tennis (V C); Yrbk; Key Club; Beta Club; Public Relations; Marketing/Designs/Graphic Artist; U of Georgia; Sewanee College, Rhodes

KOZUB, CHRIS; MOUNT JULIET, TN; WILSON CTRL HS; (SO); 4H Awd; Hnr Roll; Otst Ac Ach Awd; Perf Att; Sci Fairs; Yth Ldrshp Prog; Chess; MuAlphaTh; ROTC; Spanish Clb; Drl Tm; NJROTC; Chess Club/ Team; Oceanography; Physics; United States Naval Academy; Tennessee Technological U

KRAMER, TYLER; ATOKA, TN; BRIGHTON HS; (SO); Hnr Roll; Nat Hon Sy; Perf Att; Chrch Yth Grp; Emplmnt; Bnd; Scr Kpr (J); Sccr (J); Tennis (J); Johns Hopkins U Center for Talented Youth; Engineering; US Naval Academy

KRANTZ, HEATHER; ASHLAND CITY, TN; CHEATHAM CTY CTRL HS; (SO); Hnr Roll; WWAHSS; Chrch Yth Grp; Scouts; Sftball (V L); Vllyball (V L); Bible Club; Sports Medicine

KRANTZ, HUGH S A; CHARLOTTE, TN; CREEKWOOD HS; (SO); Comm Volntr; Bsball (J L); Ftball (V L)

KRAVITZ, KAYLEY M; MURFREESBORO, TN; THE WEBB SCH; (JR); Duke TS; Hi Hnr Roll; Hnr Roll; Nat Hon Sy; Otst Ac Ach Awd; Comm Volntr; Mus Clb; Off Aide; Quill & Scroll; Bnd; SP/M/VS; Stg Cre; Sch Ppr (E, R); Book Awards / Spanish & Computer; Georgia Journalism Academy; Magazine Journalism; Music Theory; U of Georgia; Middle Tennessee State U

KRIZ, KYLE; MANCHESTER, TN; COFFEE CTY CTRL HS; (FR); 4H Awd; Ctznshp Aw; Hi Hnr Roll; Hnr Roll; Perf Att; Comm Volntr; Chrch Yth Grp; Bsball (J); Bskball (J); Ftball (V); Wt Lftg (V); Who's Who Babe Ruth Baseball; Bachelor's Degree; University of Georgia; University of Tennessee

KROCK, ALEX; COLLIERVILLE, TN; LAUSANNE COLLEGIATE SCH; (SO); Hnr Roll; Perf Att; Sci Fairs; WWAHSS; Comm Volntr; Key Club; Sccr (J); Received Coach's Award for 2004 Soccer Season; Elected Captain of 2005 Varsity Soccer Team; Medical Degree; Emory U; Drury U

KUCA, DIANE; OAK RIDGE, TN; OAK RIDGE HS; (JR); Otst Ac Ach Awd; Pres Ac Ftns Aw; St of Mnth; Comm Volntr; Emplmnt; FBLA; Pep Squd; Tchrs Aide; Dnce; Chrldg (V L); Track (V); State Finalist in Miss Tennessee Teen Pageant; Advanced Placement Classes; Radiology; Medical Doctor / MD; U of Tennessee Knoxville; Roane State Community College

KUMAH, YAA; COLLIERVILLE, TN; COLLIERVILLE HS; (FR); 4H Awd; Ctznshp Aw; Hi Hnr Roll; Hnr Roll; Otst Ac Ach Awd; WWAHSS; Comm Volntr; Peer Tut/Med; 4-H; ArtClub; Chrch Yth Grp; Drma Clb; Key Club; Scouts; French Clb; Chr; Ch Chr; SP/M/VS; #1 in Freshman Class; Mock Trial; Law; Architecture; Harvard U; Oxford U

KYLE, KEVIN; KNOXVILLE, TN; AUSTIN EAST HS; (FR); Hnr Roll; Comm Volntr; DARE; Voc Ind Clb Am; Bnd; Bsball (V); Bskball (J); Ftball (J); Engineering / Web Designer; U of Tennessee; Atlanta A & M

LAFEVER, OLIVIA L; GORDONSVILLE, TN; GORDONSVILLE HS; (JR); Perf Att; Hab For Humty Volntr; SADD; Voc Ind Clb Am; Spanish Clb; Chr; Yrbk; Nursing; Teaching; Tennessee Tech; Cumberland U

LAMB, KRISTEN P; TULLAHOMA, TN; TULLAHOMA HS; (JR); Hnr Roll; Nat Hon Sy; Sci Fairs; WWAHSS; Comm Volntr; Red Cr Aide; Key Club; Clr Grd; Flg Crps; Vllyball (VJ); Barrett Browning Society; Art Therapy; Art Education; Lipscomb U; Vanderbilt U

LAMBERT, ASHLEY; MURFREESBORO, TN; SIEGEL HS; (JR); Hnr Roll; Peer Tut/Med; Chrch Yth Grp; Drma Clb; Ntl Beta Clb; Clb; Chr; Drama Class; Work with Kids At My School's Pre-School for 3-5 years Old; Master's Degree in Social Work; Trevecca Nazarene U

LANCASTER, ARIEL; PULASKI, TN; GILES CTY HS; (JR); Hnr Roll; Nat Hon Sy; Otst Ac Ach Awd; Pres Sch; WWAHSS; Comm Volntr; Chrch Yth Grp; DARE; Drma Clb; Emplmnt; Ntl Beta Clb; Pep Squd; Prom Com; Ch Chr; Dnce; Chrldg (V L); Cl Off (V); CR; Yrbk (P); TSSAA Student-Athlete Award of Merit; TSSAA Distinguished Scholar Achievement Award; Pharmacy; Interior Design; U of Memphis; Spelman College

LANDRUM, ELIZABETH; WARTBURG, TN; CENTRAL HS; (JR); 4H Awd; Hnr Roll; Nat Hon Sy; St of Mnth; 4-H; Ntl Beta Clb; Prom Com; Sftball (V); Yrbk (P); Beta Club; Interior Design; Nursing; U of Tennessee; Roane State Community College

LANE, ELISABETH; FLINTVILLE, TN; LINCOLN CTY HS; (FR); 4H Awd; Ctznshp Aw; Hi Hnr Roll; Hnr Roll; Otst Ac Ach Awd; Perf Att; USAA; 4-H; Chrch Yth Grp; Ntl Beta Clb; Science and Technology; History; Tennessee Tech U; Middle Tennessee State U

LANE, SHEENA; GREENEVILLE, TN; SOUTH GREENE HS; (SR); 4H Awd; Perf Att; Sci Fairs; WWAHSS; 4-H; Chrch Yth Grp; DARE; Mus Clb; Tchrs Aide; Wdwrkg Clb; Stu Cncl (S); Teacher

LANE, THOMAS R A; MORRISTOWN, TN; MORRISTOWN-HAMBLEN HS EAST; (SR); Hi Hnr Roll; Hnr Roll; Nat Hon Sy; Otst Ac Ach Awd; Pep Squd; Photog; Stu Cncl (R); Sch Ppr (R); DVM; U of Tennessee Knoxville

LANE JR, TOMMIE F; CLARKSVILLE, TN; NORTHWEST HS; (FR); Hi Hnr Roll; Nat Ldrshp Svc; Nat Mrt Sch Recip; Nat Sci Aw; Chrch Yth Grp; DARE; ROTC; Scouts; Bnd; Ch Chr; Drl Tm; Bsball (J); CR (R); Excel Award, Debut Escort; Top Student on My Team in 8th Grade; Computer; Engineer; Morehouse College; Savannah State U

LANGFORD, ANNA M; HILHAM, TN; CLAY CTY HS; (JR); Hnr Roll; Comm Volntr; Chrch Yth Grp; Ntl Beta Clb; Prom Com; Ch Chr; Cl Off (V); Stu Cncl; Yrbk (P); Elementary School Teacher; Nurse; Vol State; Tennessee Tech

LANGFORD, CARRIE B; GORDONSVILLE, TN; GORDONSVILLE HS; (JR); Hnr Roll; Perf Att; WWAHSS; Yth Ldrshp Prog; Chrch Yth Grp; Ntl Beta Clb; Prom Com; SADD; Cl Off (P); Yrbk; Tennessee Honors Program; Tennessee Technological U; Middle Tennessee State U

LANKFORD, ARIELLE; HARRIMAN, TN; OLIVER SPRINGS HS; (JR); Duke TS; Hi Hnr Roll; MVP; WWAHSS; Yth Ldrshp Prog; Comm Volntr; Chrch Yth Grp; FCA; Ntl Beta Clb; Off Aide; Schol Bwl; Foreign Clb; Bskball (V CL); Cr Ctry (V L); Sccr (V CL); Cl Off (V, T); Stu Cncl (P, R); Beta Club - President; Physical Therapy; Nursing; U of Tennessee Chattanooga; Western Carolina U

LANKFORD, ASHLEY E; SMYRNA, TN; SMYRNA HS; (SO); Hnr Roll; Perf Att; Comm Volntr; 4-H; Chrch Yth Grp; DARE; Emplmnt; Sci Clb; SADD; Vsity Clb; Latin Clb; Bskball; Dvng; Swmg; Wt Lftg; Business Major; Law Major or Minor; Duke U; Middle Tennesse State U

LA PIER, KAYLA; CROSSVILLE, TN; CUMBERLAND CTY HS; (MS); 4H Awd; Hnr Roll; 4-H; ArtClub; DARE; FCA; Stu Cncl (R); Lawyer; Harvard; Yale

LARKINS, LAURA; KINGSPORT, TN; SULLIVAN NORTH HS; (FR); Duke TS; Hi Hnr Roll; Perf Att; WWAHSS; Spec Olymp Vol; Chrch Yth Grp; DARE; FCA; Ntl Beta Clb; Bnd; Ch Chr; Mch Bnd; Bskball (J); PP Ftbl (V); Stu Cncl (R); Physical Therapy; Duke U; Harvard

LASSITER, KAITLYN E; WHITE HOUSE, TN; WHITE HOUSE HS; (JR); Hi Hnr Roll; Hnr Roll; WWAHSS; Comm Volntr; Peer Tut/Med; Chrch Yth Grp; Emplmnt; FCA; FBLA; Ntl Beta Clb; Svce Clb; Acpl Chr; Chr; Swg Chr; Noah's Promise-Ambassador; Monday Morning Bible Club-Co-Founder; Music Education; Music Therapy

LAW, DANIEL; WHITE HOUSE, TN; WHITE HOUSE HS; (JR); Hnr Roll; Chrch Yth Grp; Emplmnt; FCA; FBLA; Ntl FFA; Ftball (V); Sccr (V); Wt Lftg (V); Technological Engineering; Aviation; U of Tennessee; Tennessee Tech

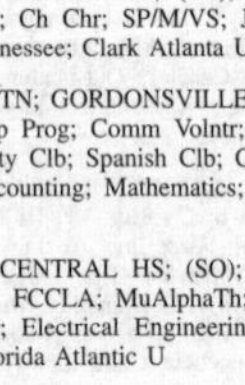
Lancaster, Ariel
Giles Cty HS
Pulaski, TN

Kumah, Yaa
Collierville HS
Collierville, TN

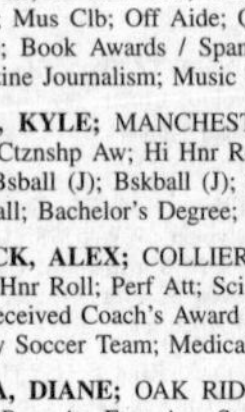
Krantz, Heather
Cheatham Cty Ctrl HS
Ashland City, TN

National
Honor Roll
Spring 2005

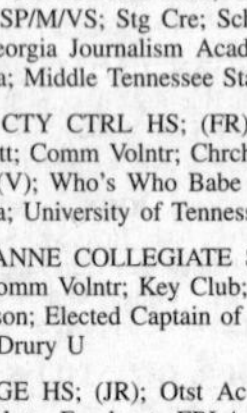
Kinnard, Lawrence
Raleigh-Egypt HS
Memphis, TN

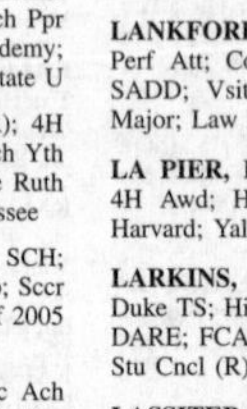
Lamb, Kristen P
Tullahoma HS
Tullahoma, TN

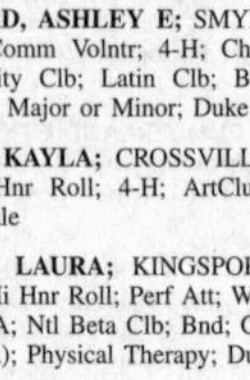
Lane Jr, Tommie F
Northwest HS
Clarksville, TN

LAWRENCE, RAYSHAWN M; NASHVILLE, TN; HERMITAGE HALL; (SO); Ctznshp Aw; Hnr Roll; Perf Att; St of Mnth; DARE; Pep Squd; SP/M/VS; Bskball (V); Cl Off (T); CR (T); Auto Mechanic (Certified); Computer Technician; Nashville Auto Diesel College; ITT Technical College

LAWSON, ADAM; CALHOUN, TN; WALKER VALLEY HS; (SR); Hnr Roll; WWAHSS; Comm Volntr; Peer Tut/Med; Ntl Beta Clb; SP/M/VS; Stg Cre; Geological Engineering; Geologist; Ole Miss; Tennessee Technical U

LAWSON, ASHLEE; ENGLEWOOD, TN; ATHENS JHS; (MS); Hi Hnr Roll; Hnr Roll; Comm Volntr; Chrch Yth Grp; Off Aide; Bskball (J); Swmg (J); CR (R)

LAWSON, AUDRA; GREENEVILLE, TN; GREENEVILLE HS; (JR); Nat Hon Sy; Perf Att; Peer Tut/Med; Chrch Yth Grp; FCA; Key Club; Svce Clb; Spanish Clb; Sccr (V L); Tennis (V); Psychology; Elementary Education; U of TN, Knoxville

LAWSON, SAMUEL A; CROSSVILLE, TN; CUMBERLAND CTY HS; (JR); Hnr Roll; Otst Ac Ach Awd; Perf Att; Comm Volntr; Chrch Yth Grp; Emplmnt; FCA; Off Aide; Stg Cre; Cr Ctry (V L); Perfect Attendance Throughout High School; Lettered in Cross Country At High School; Computer Programming; Car Audio & Video Specialist; Roane State Community College; U of Tennessee

LAY, JESSICA N; KNOXVILLE, TN; TEMPLE BAPTIST AC; (JR); Hnr Roll; Pres Ac Ftns Aw; Sci Fairs; Comm Volntr; Pep Squd; Photog; Spanish Clb; Chr; Ch Chr; Chrldg (V CL); Captain of Cheerleading Squad; Cosmetology & Design; Somatic Therapy; Roane State Community College; U of Tennessee

LAY, JONICA L; CARYVILLE, TN; CAMPBELL CTY HS; (FR); St of Mnth; USAA; Comm Volntr; Emplmnt; Lib Aide; Bnd; Chr; Sch Ppr (R); Education; Marine Mammal Trainer; Daytona Beach Community College; Clearwater Christian College

LAZAR, JENNIFER; MEMPHIS, TN; RIDGEWAY HS; (JR); Hi Hnr Roll; Otst Ac Ach Awd; WWAHSS; Comm Volntr; Key Club; Scouts; SADD; Tmpl Yth Grp; Gold President's Volunteer Service Award; Education; History; U of Arizona; New Mexico State

LEBOVITZ, LISA C; FRANKLIN, TN; FRANKLIN HS; (SR); Hnr Roll; Comm Volntr; Scouts; Tmpl Yth Grp; Bnd; Swmg (V L); Girl Scout Gold & Silver Awards; History Fair Regional Winner

LEE, JOSEPH; LA VERGNE, TN; LA VERGNE HS; (FR); Ctznshp Aw; Hnr Roll; Perf Att; St of Mnth; Chrch Yth Grp; Mus Clb; Bnd; Mch Bnd; Orch; Pep Bnd; Mar Art (J); Orthodontics; Musician; Sewanee U of the South; Vanderbilt U

LEE, KARA; LEXINGTON, TN; SCOTTS HILL HS; (SR); Hnr Roll; Nat Hon Sy; WWAHSS; FBLA; Acpl Chr; Chr; National Society of High School Scholars; Psychiatry / Psychology; Accounting; Jackson State Community College; Austin Peay

LEE, LINDSEY; NASHVILLE, TN; HILLSBORO COMP HS; (JR); Duke TS; Hi Hnr Roll; Nat Hon Sy; WWAHSS; Chrch Yth Grp; Prom Com; French Clb; Chrldg (V); Tennis (V); Sch Ppr (R); Journalism; Politics; U of Virginia; U of Georgia

LENOIR, BRANDON; MURFREESBORO, TN; RIVERDALE HS; (FR); Hnr Roll; Comm Volntr; Chess; FCA; ROTC; Swmg (V); Track (J); Math Major; Minor - Science and Robotics; Morehouse College; Tennessee State U

LENORE, TERRIKA J; MEMPHIS, TN; CRAIGMONT HS; (SO); Ctznshp Aw; Hi Hnr Roll; Hnr Roll; Otst Ac Ach Awd; Perf Att; St of Mnth; Comm Volntr; Peer Tut/Med; Chrch Yth Grp; DARE; Jr Ach; Lib Aide; Off Aide; ROTC; Scouts; Tchrs Aide; Clr Grd; Drl Tm; Flg Crps; Tennis; Two Published Poems; Basketball for Community Center; Elementary School Teacher; Master's in Teaching; Christian Brothers U; Rhodes College

LEONARD, LINDSEY; BLUFF CITY, TN; SULLIVAN EAST HS; (JR); WWAHSS; HOSA Club; Nursing; Northeast State U; East Tennessee State U

LESLIE, FRANCES E; MEMPHIS, TN; ST MARY'S EPISCOPAL SCH; (JR); Jr Cls League; Ntl Beta Clb; Quill & Scroll; Sccr (V L); Track (V L); Lit Mag (E, R); National Honor Society; 4 Gold Medals in National Latin Exam

LEWIS, ANNA; KNOXVILLE, TN; FARRAGUT HS; (SO); Hnr Roll; Nat Hon Sy; Perf Att; Comm Volntr; Chrch Yth Grp; Drma Clb; Emplmnt; FCA; Scouts; Svce Clb; Chr; Ch Chr; SP/M/VS; Destination Imagination Global Finalist; Junior Honor Society; Biology; Musical Theatre; U of Tennessee; New York U

LEWIS, CORY S B; NEWPORT, TN; COCKE CTY HS; (FR); Hnr Roll; Perf Att; Computers; Drafting

LEWIS, EBONI L; CLARKSVILLE, TN; NORTHWEST HS; (JR); 4H Awd; Ctznshp Aw; Hi Hnr Roll; Hnr Roll; Perf Att; Sci Fairs; St of Mnth; Comm Volntr; Peer Tut/Med; 4-H; Chrch Yth Grp; DARE; Emplmnt; Key Club; P to P St Amb Prg; Scouts; Tchrs Aide; Bnd; Chr; Ch Chr; Dnce; Chrldg (J); Sftball (J); County Spelling Bee; Student Ambassador; Nursing; Criminal Justice; Vanderbilt U; Austin Peay State U

LEWIS, HOLLY; NASHVILLE, TN; NASHVILLE CHRISTIAN SCH; (JR); 4H Awd; Ctznshp Aw; Hi Hnr Roll; Hnr Roll; Otst Ac Ach Awd; Perf Att; Pres Ac Ftns Aw; Pres Sch; Hab For Humty Volntr; Hosp Aide; 4-H; Chrch Yth Grp; Drma Clb; FCA; Pep Squd; Photog; Scouts; Bskball (V); Chrldg (V); Yrbk (R, P); All-District in Basketball Soph. & Jr. Year (Freshman Yr.); Medicine-Human & Animal; U of North Carolina At Chapel Hill; U of Tennessee At Knoxville

LEWIS, JEANNIE; MEMPHIS, TN; RALEIGH EGYPT HS; (FR); Ctznshp Aw; Hnr Roll; Perf Att; Sci Fairs; Comm Volntr; Fr of Library; SADD; GAA (L); Tennis (L); Bowling; Cosmetologist - Hair & Make-Up; Nail Technician - Manicure / Pedicure; Rhodes College; Christian Brothers U

LEWIS, LANCE; TAZEWELL, TN; CLABORNE HS; (SO); Nat Hon Sy; Pres Ac Ftns Aw; BPA; Key Club; Prom Com; Spanish Clb; Bsball (V); Golf (V); Business; East Tennessee State U; Appalachia College

LEWIS, MYRA S; CLARKSVILLE, TN; KENWOOD HS; (SR); Hi Hnr Roll; Hnr Roll; Otst Ac Ach Awd; WWAHSS; Comm Volntr; Peer Tut/Med; BPA; Emplmnt; Quiz Bowl; ROTC; Drl Tm; Attorney (Political Science); Tennessee State U

LEWIS, SELETA; GALLATIN, TN; GALLATIN HS; (SO); Nat Hon Sy; WWAHSS; Chrch Yth Grp; Ch Chr; Clr Grd; Mch Bnd; SP/M/VS; (RN)-Master's & Bachelor's Degree; Clark Atlanta U; Georgia State U

LEWIS, TATIJANA; MEMPHIS, TN; OAKHAVEN MIDDLE HS; (MS); Hnr Roll; ArtClub; Chess; DARE; Drma Clb; Scouts; Spanish Clb; Bnd; Chr; Drm Mjr; Mch Bnd; Bsball (V); Bskball (V); Sftball (V); Lawyer; Eastern Michigan U

LIDVALL, KRISTIN; ALCOA, TN; ALCOA HS; (SR); Hnr Roll; Nat Hon Sy; St of Mnth; WWAHSS; Comm Volntr; AL Aux Girls; Chrch Yth Grp; Emplmnt; FCA; Key Club; Scouts; Tchrs Aide; Bskball (J); Scr Kpr (V); Sccr (V CL); Cl Off (S); Stu Cncl (T); Yrbk (R); Chemistry; Carson-Newman College

LIGHTFOOT, ELIJAH; MEMPHIS, TN; MELROSE HS; (FR); 4H Awd; Ctznshp Aw; Hi Hnr Roll; Perf Att; 4-H; Chrch Yth Grp; DARE; Ch Chr; Mch Bnd; Bsball (V); Ftball (V); Rank #24 Out of 300 Graduates - 8th Grade; Professional Baseball Player; Vanderbilt U

LINDSAY, TREY; KNOXVILLE, TN; SOUTH DOYLE HS; (SO); Hnr Roll; St of Mnth; WWAHSS; Comm Volntr; Chrch Yth Grp; FCA; Key Club; Mus Clb; Scouts; Latin Clb; Bnd; Ch Chr; Jzz Bnd; Mch Bnd; Solo Piano in Federation, KMTA and National Guild; Honors Band; Engineering; Music; U of Tennessee; Middle Tennessee State U

LINK, RHONDA; DOVER, TN; STEWART CTY HS; (SR); Hi Hnr Roll; USAA; Spec Olymp Vol; Chrch Yth Grp; Drma Clb; FCA; Ntl Beta Clb; Prom Com; Sci Clb; Scouts; Foreign Clb; Dnce; SP/M/VS; PPSqd (V CL); Stu Cncl (R); Girl Scout Silver and Gold Awards; National Association of Parliamentarians Award; Spanish; French; U of Tennessee At Knoxville; Rhodes College

LINKOUS, MELANIE N; ROGERSVILLE, TN; VOLUNTEER HS; (SR); Comm Volntr; Peer Tut/Med; Chrch Yth Grp; Key Club; Tchrs Aide; Bnd; Mch Bnd; Pep Bnd; Cl Off (V); BSN Degree; Walter State; East Tennessee State U

LINN, NICOLE D; SMITHVILLE, TN; DEKALB CTY HS; (JR); Hi Hnr Roll; Nat Mrt LOC; Otst Ac Ach Awd; Sci Fairs; WWAHSS; Chrch Yth Grp; FBLA; Off Aide; Voc Ind Clb Am; Spanish Clb; Gmnstcs (V); Sccr (V); Tennis (J); Hospital Administrator; Tennessee Technical U

LINZ, LACIE; SODDY DAISY, TN; SODDY DAISY HS; (JR); Hnr Roll; Nat Hon Sy; WWAHSS; Comm Volntr; Chrch Yth Grp; FCA; Key Club; Ntl Beta Clb; Off Aide; Bskball (VJCL); Stu Cncl (R); CR (R); Nursing; Carson-Newman College

LITTRELL, TRENTON; LAWRENCEBURG, TN; LAWRENCE CTY HS; (FR); Hnr Roll; Comm Volntr; Chrch Yth Grp; Emplmnt; FCA; Svce Clb; Stu Cncl

LIVELY, AMY L; MERCER, TN; SOUTH SIDE HS; (JR); Gov Hnr Prg; Hnr Roll; WWAHSS; AL Aux Girls; Emplmnt; Jr Cls League; MuAlphaTh; Ntl Beta Clb; ROTC; Drl Tm; Exchange Student Iceland (03-04); Russian (Foreign Language); Pre-Med; Washington U (St Louis); Vanderbilt U

LIVESAY, HEATHER; JEFFERSON CITY, TN; JEFFERSON CTY HS; (JR); Hi Hnr Roll; Yth Ldrshp Prog; Spec Olymp Vol; Emplmnt; FCA; Ntl Beta Clb; Pep Squd; SP/M/VS; Pharmacy; Walters State Community College; East Tennessee State U

LLOYD III, RICHARD H; ERWIN, TN; UNICOI CTY HS; (SR); Hnr Roll; Otst Ac Ach Awd; Pres Ac Ftns Aw; WWAHSS; Comm Volntr; ArtClub; BPA; Chrch Yth Grp; Cmptr Clb; FCA; FCCLA; Key Club; Ntl Beta Clb; Ch Chr; Cr Ctry (V); Track (V); Stu Cncl (R); Secondary Education; East Tennessee State U

LOFTIS, LACY; SPARTA, TN; WHITE CTY HS; (SR); F Lan Hn Soc; Hi Hnr Roll; Kwnis Aw; MVP; Perf Att; Pres Ac Ftns Aw; WWAHSS; Emplmnt; FCA; Key Club; MuAlphaTh; Ntl Beta Clb; Outdrs Clb; Pep Squd; Tchrs Aide; Tennis (V L); Track (V L); Vllyball (V CL); Stu Cncl (R); Best All Around Player-Volleyball; Coaches Award-Tennis; Business; Pharmacy; Tennessee Technological U

LONG, JESSICA C; MEMPHIS, TN; TREZEVANT VOC TECH CTR; (SO); Ctznshp Aw; Hi Hnr Roll; Hnr Roll; Nat Hon Sy; Nat Stu Ath Day Aw; Otst Ac Ach Awd; Perf Att; St of Mnth; Yth Ldrshp Prog; CARE; Comm Volntr; Peer Tut/Med; ArtClub; BPA; Chrch Yth Grp; Cmptr Clb; DARE; DECA; Drma Clb; FBLA; Bnd; Ch Chr; Dnce; Drm Mjr; Bskball (V); Chrldg (C); Cr Ctry (J); PPSqd (J); PP Ftbl (V); Swmg (V); Track (V); Vllyball (J); CR (P); Won 2 National Hair Shows; To Be an Entrepreneur; To Be a Professional Cosmetologist; Tennessee State U; Jackson State U

LONG, VALENCIA; JACKSON, TN; SOUTHSIDE HS; (SO); Hnr Roll; Perf Att; WWAHSS; Comm Volntr; Peer Tut/Med; Drma Clb; Mth Clb/Tm; MuAlphaTh; Latin Clb; SP/M/VS; Stg Cre; Distinguished Student Award; Biology; Nursing; Tennessee State U; Clark Atlanta College

LOPP, TABETHA L; LAWRENCEBURG, TN; LAWRENCE CTY VOC CTR; (SO); Hnr Roll; Otst Ac Ach Awd; WWAHSS; FBLA; Vllyball (VJ)

LOVE, KENIYA S; HARRISON, TN; BROWN MIDDLE SCH; (MS); Perf Att; Comm Volntr; Chrch Yth Grp; DARE; Pep Squd; French Clb; Chr; Ch Chr; Dnce; Pep Bnd; Chrldg (VJ); Cr Ctry (J); Mar Art; PPSqd (J); Track (J L); Yrbk (P); Music / Voice; U of Louisville; UCLA

LOWE, BLAKE; HELENWOOD, TN; SCOTT HS; (SO); Hi Hnr Roll; MVP; Perf Att; Valdctrian; WWAHSS; Peer Tut/Med; Chrch Yth Grp; Ntl Beta Clb; P to P St Amb Prg; Ch Chr; Bskball (V); Cr Ctry (V); Sccr (V); Track (V); Cl Off (P); U of Tennessee Knoxville; Washington U

LOWERY, JAY; JACKSON, TN; NORTH SIDE HS; (SO); Duke TS; Hi Hnr Roll; MVP; WWAHSS; Yth Ldrshp Prog; Chrch Yth Grp; Mth Clb/Tm; Ntl Beta Clb; Sci Clb; Bsball (V); Ftball (V); Stu Cncl (R); CR (R)

LOWREY, ELIZABETH D; JASPER, TN; SOUTH PITTSBURG HS; (FR); 4H Awd; Hi Hnr Roll; 4-H; SADD; Spotted Saddle Horse & American Quarter; Horse & TN Walking Horse Youth Associations; Veterinarian; U of Tennessee Knoxville, TN

LOY, MATT; KNOXVILLE, TN; THE KINGS AC; Ctznshp Aw; Hnr Roll; Perf Att; Sci Fairs; Comm Volntr; Chrch Yth Grp; DARE; Emplmnt; Chr; Bskball (V); Ftball (V); Sccr (V); Sports Medicine; Broadcasting; U of North Carolina Chapel Hill; U of Tennessee

LUCAS, SARA N; MURFREESBORO, TN; SIEGEL HS; (JR); Nat Hon Sy; WWAHSS; Chrch Yth Grp; Emplmnt; MuAlphaTh; Ntl Beta Clb; Spanish Clb; SP/M/VS; Vllyball (V CL); Stu Cncl; Volunteer for Family Readiness Group Army Reserve; Nursing; U of Tennessee Knoxville; Middle Tennessee State U

LUCKEY, ZACHARY; FRIENDSVILLE, TN; WILLIAM BLOUNT HS; (JR); USAA; WWAHSS; Chrch Yth Grp; Emplmnt; Off Aide; Quiz Bowl; Tchrs Aide; Tennis (V); Nominated National Young Leaders Conference; Nominated National Society of High School Scholars; U of Tennessee

LUCO, STEPHEN; MC EWEN, TN; MC EWEN HS; (JR); Hnr Roll; Otst Ac Ach Awd; Sci Fairs; Comm Volntr; BPA; Chrch Yth Grp; Ntl Beta Clb; Prom Com; Sci Clb; Scouts; Cr Ctry (V L); Tennis (V L); 2nd Place Jr Academy of Science 2005; 2nd Place Jr Academy of Science 2004; Engineering; U. S. Naval Academy

LUMPKIN, SEAN D; OOLTEWAH, TN; OOLTEWAH HS; (FR); Chrch Yth Grp; DARE; Bsball (J); Certified Scuba Diver; Marine Biology; U of Miami; Florida State U

LUNA, HUNTER; GERMANTOWN, TN; EVANGELICAL CHRISTIAN SCH; (FR); Hnr Roll; WWAHSS; Spec Olymp Vol; Chrch Yth Grp; Key Club; Scouts; Chr; Stg Cre; Who's Who Among High School Students; Beta Club; Pre-Med (Medical School)

LUNA, TIMOTHY D; FLINTVILLE, TN; LINCOLN CTY HS; (SR); 4H Awd; Ctznshp Aw; Hi Hnr Roll; Nat Hon Sy; Otst Ac Ach Awd; Perf Att; Pres Sch; WWAHSS; Comm Volntr; 4-H; Chrch Yth Grp; Emplmnt; FCA; Ntl Beta Clb; Outdrs Clb; Pep Squd; Quiz Bowl; Ftball (V); Cl Off (P); Stu Cncl (P); SCOPE Delegate; Political Science; Ashland U; Sewanee

LUNCEFORD, TESSA N; ELIZABETHTON, TN; UNAKA HS; (SO); 4H Awd; Hi Hnr Roll; Nat Hon Sy; Otst Ac Ach Awd; Perf Att; Comm Volntr; 4-H; Chrch Yth Grp; FCA; Bskball (V); Sftball; Cl Off (V); Sch Ppr (R); Law; Physics; U of Tennessee-Knoxville; Duke U

LUNDIEN, BRADLEY; HIXSON, TN; SODDY DAISY HS; (SO); Ctznshp Aw; Hnr Roll; Perf Att; Pres Ac Ftns Aw; Chrch Yth Grp; FCA; Mth Clb/Tm; Ntl Beta Clb; Ftball (V L); Engineering Program Volunteer; Math Club / FCA / Humane Society; Veterinarian; Engineering; U of TN Chattanooga; U of TN Knoxville

Lucas, Sara N
Siegel HS
Murfreesboro, TN

Lightfoot, Elijah
Melrose HS
Memphis, TN

Lewis, Eboni L
Northwest HS
Clarksville, TN

Lenore, Terrika J
Craigmont HS
Memphis, TN

Lawson, Samuel A
Cumberland Cty HS
Crossville, TN

Lee, Joseph
La Vergne HS
La Vergne, TN

Lewis, Jeannie
Raleigh Egypt HS
Memphis, TN

Linn, Nicole D
Dekalb Cty HS
Smithville, TN

Luco, Stephen
Mc Ewen HS
Mc Ewen, TN

LUNSFORD, JENNIFER R; COSBY, TN; COSBY HS; Hi Hnr Roll; Hnr Roll; Nat Hon Sy; WWAHSS; Mth Clb/Tm; Ntl Beta Clb; Ntl FFA; Cl Off (V); Football Manager; Track Manager; Hotel Management; Walters State

LUSTER, ROBERT; HUMBOLDT, TN; HUMBOLDT HS; (SO); Hnr Roll; Perf Att; WWAHSS; Comm Volntr; Hab For Humty Volntr; ArtClub; Chrch Yth Grp; Emplmnt; Mus Clb; Wdwrkg Clb; Ch Chr; Bsball (V); Bskball (V); Ftball; Computer Program; Law; Duke; Temple

LY, ANHDAO; MEMPHIS, TN; CENTRAL HS; (SO); Ctznshp Aw; Hi Hnr Roll; Hnr Roll; St of Mnth; WWAHSS; Comm Volntr; Peer Tut/Med; ArtClub; Key Club; Tmpl Yth Grp; Chr; Stu Cncl; Winner of William Sweet Award; Member of Vietnamese Dance Group; Biology; Law; Rhodes College; Oxford U in Ohio

LYLE, MARY R; ERWIN, TN; UNICOI CTY HS; (SO); Sci Fairs; Chrch Yth Grp; Key Club; Bnd; Ch Chr; Mch Bnd; Orch; CR (R); Field Conductor-Marching Band; Drama Team/Bell Choir-Church; Veterinary Medicine; King College; U of Tennessee

LYNCH, NICOLE M; KNOXVILLE, TN; HALLS HS; (JR); Hnr Roll; Perf Att; Comm Volntr; Chrch Yth Grp; Emplmnt; FCA; French Clb; Chr; SP/M/VS; Went on Mission Trip to Venezuela; Mission Trip to Honduras (6-24-05); Veterinary Medicine; Psychology; U of Tennessee (Knoxville); U of Tennessee (Chattanooga)

LYNN, CATHERINE; OLIVER SPRINGS, TN; OLIVER SPRINGS; (JR); Duke TS; Hi Hnr Roll; Otst Ac Ach Awd; WWAHSS; BPA; Chrch Yth Grp; Drma Clb; Emplmnt; FCA; Ntl Beta Clb; Prom Com; International Clb; Bnd; Drm Mjr; Jzz Bnd; Mch Bnd; Cr Ctry (V); Cl Off (P); Stu Cncl (P); Law; David Lipscomb U

MABON, TAYLOR; NASHVILLE, TN; NASHVILLE SCH OF THE ARTS; (SO); Ctznshp Aw; Hnr Roll; WWAHSS; Comm Volntr; FCA; Ntl Beta Clb; Scouts; Bnd; Dnce; Mch Bnd; Criminal Justice; Middle Tennessee State U; Tennessee State U

MACKAY, JUSTIN; MURFREESBORO, TN; FRANKLIN ROAD CHRISTIAN SCH; (JR); Hnr Roll; MVP; Yth Ldrshp Prog; Chrch Yth Grp; DARE; Emplmnt; Ntl Beta Clb; Scouts; Chr; Bsball (V L); Bskball (V C); Sccr (V); Stu Cncl (R); Sports Medicine; Pre-Med; Olivet Nazarene U; Middle Tennessee State U

MACKAY, RYAN; TULLAHOMA, TN; TULLAHOMA HS; (JR); Hi Hnr Roll; Hnr Roll; Nat Hon Sy; Yth Ldrshp Prog; Comm Volntr; Peer Tut/Med; AL Aux Boys; Emplmnt; MuAlphaTh; NYLC; Photog; Svce Clb; Tmpl Yth Grp; Spanish Clb; Cr Ctry (V L); Ftball (V L); Scr Kpr (V L); Track (V L); Barrett-Browning English Honor Society

MACKLIN, CHANTISS; MEMPHIS, TN; OAKHAVEN MS; (SO); Ctznshp Aw; Gov Hnr Prg; Hi Hnr Roll; Hnr Roll; Perf Att; Pres Sch; Sci Fairs; St of Mnth; Valdctrian; Yth Ldrshp Prog; ArtClub; DARE; Scouts; Acpl Chr; Dnce; Drm Mjr; SP/M/VS; Chrldg (V); GAA (V); Gmnstcs (V); Mar Art (J); PPSqd (J); Sccr (V); Sftball (V); Vllyball (V); Stu Cncl (V); Ph.D; Bachelors Degree; Washington U; Emory U

MAEKAWA, AKIE; GERMANTOWN, TN; LAUSANNE COLLEGIATE SCH; (JR); F Lan Hn Soc; Hi Hnr Roll; Nat Hon Sy; Perf Att; Sci Fairs; USAA; WWAHSS; Peer Tut/Med; Key Club; Ntl Beta Clb; Bnd; Sftball; Cl Off (T); Word Smith; National French Exam; French; Mass Communication; Vanderbilt; Rhodes College

MAGGART, AMANDA; CARTHAGE, TN; GORDONSVILLE HS; (JR); Hnr Roll; Nat Hon Sy; WWAHSS; Chrch Yth Grp; FCA; Ntl Beta Clb; Prom Com; SADD; Vsity Clb; Bskball; Sccr; Vsy Clb; Cl Off (P, V); Stu Cncl (R); Perfect Attendance-Freshman To Present; Honor Roll-For 3 Years; Allied Sciences-Dental; Nursing RN; Tennessee Tech U; Cumberland U

MAHOLMES, LISA; JACKSON, TN; NORTH SIDE HS; (SR); Hnr Roll; Jr Mshl; Salutrn; WWAHSS; Comm Volntr; 4-H; Key Club; English/Spanish Clb; Stu Cncl (R); Ranked 6th in Honor Division for Tennessee's State Academic Decathlon; Graduated from Governor's School for the Humanities in 2004; English; Political Science; Lambuth U

MAIN, AMBER-SHEA; LA FOLLETTE, TN; CAMPBELL CTY HS; (FR); Duke TS; Hi Hnr Roll; Hnr Roll; Otst Ac Ach Awd; Pres Sch; USAA; WWAHSS; Comm Volntr; Peer Tut/Med; Chrch Yth Grp; Drma Clb; Key Club; Lib Aide; Prom Com; Tchrs Aide; SP/M/VS; Stg Cre; Criminology / FBI Agent; Psychology; Harvard U; Yale U

MAJMUDAR, BITTU R; NASHVILLE, TN; MARTIN LUTHER KING HS MAGNET; (SR); Hi Hnr Roll; Nat Hon Sy; Nat Mrt LOC; Perf Att; Sci Fairs; WWAHSS; Hosp Aide; Peer Tut/Med; Mth Clb/Tm; MuAlphaTh; Ntl Beta Clb; Orch; Tennis (J); CR (R); TN Governor's School For The Sciences; Outstanding Student of America; Biology; Psychology; Vanderbilt U; Belmont U

MAJORAS, IAN H; HIXSON, TN; SODDY-DAISY HS; (FR); Hnr Roll; Sci Fairs; St of Mnth; WWAHSS; Peer Tut/Med; DARE; FCA; Tchrs Aide; Bskball (J); Stu Cncl (R); Who's Who Among High School; Medical School; Duke U

MAJORS, DAVIDA; NASHVILLE, TN; HUNTERS LANE HS; (JR); Hnr Roll; Nat Hon Sy; Sci Fairs; WWAHSS; Comm Volntr; BPA; Chrch Yth Grp; Emplmnt; MuAlphaTh; French Clb; Ch Chr; Dnce; Cr Ctry (J); Cl Off (V); Sch Ppr (R); Journalism; New York U; Columbia U

MALONE, BRITTNY; MEMPHIS, TN; CENTRAL HS; (JR); Hnr Roll; WWAHSS; BPA; Chrch Yth Grp; DARE; Emplmnt; Lib Aide; Ch Chr; Clr Grd; Dnce; Stg Cre; PPSqd; Stu Cncl (R); Breast Cancer Marathon; Business Management; Lane College; University of Memphis

MALONE, JEREMY; MEMPHIS, TN; (JR); Nat Hon Sy; Perf Att; Peer Tut/Med; Emplmnt; Ntl Beta Clb; Computer Tech; Duke U; UT-Knoxville (U of Tennessee)

MALONE, J PAIGE; BRISTOL, TN; TENNESSEE HS; (JR); Yth Ldrshp Prog; Comm Volntr; Chrch Yth Grp; Emplmnt; FCA; SADD; Tchrs Aide; Chr; Ch Chr; Dnce; Chrldg (J); Gmnstcs (J); Sch Ppr (E, R); Dance Teacher & Student; Cheerleading Coach - Christian School; Nursing; Virginia Highlands Community College; Virginia Intermont College

MALOY, RACHEL; MIDDLETON, TN; MIDDLETON HS; (FR); 4H Awd; Hnr Roll; Comm Volntr; Lib Aide; Photog; Bnd; Mch Bnd; Tennis; Mentor; Forensic Science; U of Knoxville

MANGRUM, STACEY; LA VERGNE, TN; LA VERGNE HS; (FR); Ctznshp Aw; Hnr Roll; St of Mnth; I Helped Write A Play and Performed in it; Interior Design; Architect; Academy of Art U; Art Institute of Charlotte

MANI, SHARAD; MANCHESTER, TN; COFFEE CTY CTRL HS; (SR); Hi Hnr Roll; Nat Hon Sy; Otst Ac Ach Awd; Pres Sch; WWAHSS; Yth Ldrshp Prog; BPA; Emplmnt; Mth Clb/Tm; Off Aide; SP/M/VS; Reporter for BPA; Pre-Med; Tusculum College

MANNING, ANGELA M; CHATTANOOGA, TN; EAST RIDGE HS; (SR); Ctznshp Aw; DAR; Hnr Roll; Nat Ldrshp Svc; Nat Mrt LOC; Otst Ac Ach Awd; Perf Att; Pres Ac Ftns Aw; Sci Fairs; St of Mnth; Comm Volntr; Hosp Aide; Peer Tut/Med; Chrch Yth Grp; DARE; Jr Ach; Lttrmn Clb; Off Aide; Photog; Prom Com; ROTC; Ch Chr; Clr Grd; Drl Tm; Flg Crps; Tennis (J); Sch Ppr (R); Military Order of the Purple Heart; Cadet Challenge Medal; Neonatal Nursing; Graphic Communications; U of Tennessee At Chatham; U of Tennessee Knoxville

MARBURY, CHARLES L; SAVANNAH, TN; HARDIN CTY HS; Hnr Roll; Nat Ldrshp Svc; Yth Ldrshp Prog; Comm Volntr; 4-H; Chrch Yth Grp; Emplmnt; Outdrs Clb; Spanish Clb; Bnd; Hsbk Rdg (V); Rlr Hky (V); Tennis (VJ); Roller Hockey After-School Activities; Wakeboarding/Water Skiing; Aviation; Middle Tennessee State U

MARBUT, KAYLA L; PEGRAM, TN; HARPETH HS; (SO); 4H Awd; Ctznshp Aw; St of Mnth; Spec Olymp Vol; 4-H; AL Aux Girls; Chrch Yth Grp; Outdrs Clb; Photog; Chr; Bskball (J); Sftball (C); Yrbk (P); Teaching; Veterinarian; U of Tennessee; Vanderbilt U

MARION, ANTHONY L; MEMPHIS, TN; MITCHELL HS; (FR); Hnr Roll; Nat Hon Sy; Perf Att; Ftball; Team Placed 2nd in Track and Field; Tennessee State U

MARKL, KRISTOFER C; JOHNSON CITY, TN; SCIENCE HILL HS; (JR); Hnr Roll; Otst Ac Ach Awd; USAA; Chrch Yth Grp; NYLC; Ch Chr; Pre-Law; Law Degree; U of Tennessee; East Tennessee State U

MARKS, MYESHIA; MEMPHIS, TN; RIDGEWAY HS; (SO); Ctznshp Aw; Fut Prb Slvr; Hnr Roll; Perf Att; Sci Fairs; CARE; Comm Volntr; Spec Olymp Vol; Chrch Yth Grp; DARE; Drma Clb; Pep Squd; Spanish Clb; Ch Chr; Dnce; Drl Tm; Drm Mjr; Bsball (V); Bskball (V); Chrldg (V); PPSqd (V); Sftball (V); Tennis (V); Track (V); Vllyball (V); Lawyer; Cosmetologist; U of Memphis

MARSH, CHELSEA; PIKEVILLE, TN; BLEDSOE CTY HS; (FR); Hi Hnr Roll; Nat Hon Sy; WWAHSS; Bskball (V L); Sftball (V L); Computer Science; Tennessee Technological College; U of Chattanooga

MARSHALL, BETHANY M; KINGSPORT, TN; SULLIVAN NORTH HS; (SR); Duke TS; Hi Hnr Roll; Nat Hon Sy; Nat Stu Ath Day Aw; St of Mnth; WWAHSS; Comm Volntr; Spec Olymp Vol; Chrch Yth Grp; DARE; DECA; Emplmnt; FCA; Key Club; Ntl Beta Clb; Scouts; Chr; SP/M/VS; Tennis (V); Stu Cncl (R); Yrbk (R, P); Outstanding Senior; Anchor Club President; Communications; Psychology; East Tennessee State U; U of Tennessee Knoxville

MARSHALL, JOSHUA; ESTILL SPRINGS, TN; FRANKLIN CTY HS; (JR); 4H Awd; Sci Fairs; 4-H; DARE; Automotive; Tennessee Tech; Nashville Auto Tech

MARSHALL, RACHAEL; HERMITAGE, TN; MC GAVOCK COMP HS; (JR); Hi Hnr Roll; Nat Hon Sy; Sci Fairs; WWAHSS; Yth Ldrshp Prog; Comm Volntr; Peer Tut/Med; ArtClub; Drma Clb; Spanish Clb; Bnd; Mch Bnd; Lit Mag (E, R); Sch Ppr (E); Young Writers Festival; Science / Spanish & History Awards; Belmont U; LSU

MARTIN, ALEXANDER; NASHVILLE, TN; CMTY HS; (SR); Hnr Roll; Nat Hon Sy; ArtClub; DARE; German Clb; Bnd; Chr; Jzz Bnd; SP/M/VS; Cl Off (R); Stu Cncl (R); Music Production; Psychology; Emerson College; Austin Peay State U

MARTIN, ASHLEY B; MURFREESBORO, TN; BLACKMAN HS; (SO); Hnr Roll; Perf Att; St of Mnth; WWAHSS; Comm Volntr; Key Club; Ntl Beta Clb; Tchrs Aide; French Clb; Chr; Accounting; Middle Tennessee State U

MARTIN, KELLY L; COOKEVILLE, TN; COOKEVILLE HS; (JR); Hnr Roll; Kwnis Aw; Comm Volntr; Emplmnt; FCA; Key Club; Kwanza Clb; Pep Squd; Photog; SADD; Yrbk (E, R, P); Helped Design and Distribute '06 Football Shirts; Helped Organize School Pictures; Business Management; Psychology / Sociology; U of Tennessee Knoxville; Middle Tennessee State U

MARTIN, KELLY S; DECHERD, TN; FRANKLIN CTY HS; (JR); Hnr Roll; Nat Sci Aw; Perf Att; Sci Fairs; Chrch Yth Grp; DARE; Ntl Beta Clb; Prom Com; Chr; Ch Chr; Cl Off (S); Stu Cncl (S); CR (S); Lt of Explorers - Student Police Academy; Beta Club; Criminal Justice; Pre-Law; East Tennessee State U; Middle Tennessee State U

MARTIN, MC KENSIE; MEMPHIS, TN; EVANGELICAL CHRISTIAN SCH; (FR); Duke TS; Hi Hnr Roll; Nat Hon Sy; Chrch Yth Grp; Emplmnt; Key Club; Lib Aide; Ntl Beta Clb; Pep Squd; Clb; Chrldg (V); Cr Ctry (J); PPSqd (V); Sccr (J); Track (V L); Trampoline and Tumbling National Finalist

MARTIN, TIFFANY; ROGERSVILLE, TN; CHEROKEE HS; (SO); 4-H; DARE; Tchrs Aide; Cosmetology

MASON, DUSTIN D; PINEY FLATS, TN; SULLIVAN EAST HS; (JR); WWAHSS; Comm Volntr; Chrch Yth Grp; FCA; Bskball (VJC); Who's Who Among High School Students (Two Years); Medical; Engineering; East Tennessee State U; Northeast State

MASON, MELANIE M; NASHVILLE, TN; MAPLEWOOD HS; (SO); Ctznshp Aw; Hnr Roll; Otst Ac Ach Awd; Perf Att; St of Mnth; Cosmetology

MASON, RASHAD; NASHVILLE, TN; PEARL-COHN MAGNET HS; (SO); 4H Awd; Hnr Roll; MVP; Perf Att; Sci Fairs; Spec Olymp Vol; 4-H; Chrch Yth Grp; DARE; Emplmnt; Vsity Clb; Bskball (C); Ftball (V); Business Major; Engineer; U of Southern Cal; Orlando State

MASON, TIFFANY; KNOXVILLE, TN; AUSTIN EAST HS; (FR); Fut Prb Slvr; Hnr Roll; Comm Volntr; Peer Tut/Med; Chrch Yth Grp; DARE; FBLA; Dnce; Dance; Psychology; Morris Brown College

MASSA, JENNIFER; KINGSPORT, TN; DOBYNS-BENNETT HS; (JR); Ctznshp Aw; Hnr Roll; Key Club; Bnd; Drm Mjr; Mch Bnd; Swmg; Sch Ppr

MASSENGILL, JEREMY; HARROGATE, TN; CLAIBORNE CO HS & VOC CT; (JR); WWAHSS; Voc Ind Clb Am

MASSINGILLE, ALISON L; CELINA, TN; CLAY CTY HS; (SO); Hnr Roll; Chrch Yth Grp; DARE; Emplmnt; I Was in Band for Almost Seven Years; Business & Management; Tennessee Tech (After 18 Months Vocational School)

MATHES, NNEKA L; KNOXVILLE, TN; CENTRAL HS; (SO); MVP; Chrch Yth Grp; ROTC; Bskball (VJ); Track (VJ); 4 Year College; TCSU

MATHIS, HANNAH L; BRIGHTON, TN; BRIGHTON HS; (FR); Gov Hnr Prg; Hi Hnr Roll; Hnr Roll; Chrch Yth Grp; Chr; Ch Chr; Vllyball; Cl Off (S); Stu Cncl (R); Pediatric Medicine; Neonatology

MATTHEWS, CHAMESE; MEMPHIS, TN; OVERTON HS; (SO); Hi Hnr Roll; WWAHSS; Chrch Yth Grp; Key Club; Chr; Ch Chr; Cl Off (V); All West; Stax; Business Major; Vocal Performance; Howard U; UC Berkeley

MAXFIELD, TONI; ALLONS, TN; CLAY CTY HS; (SO); Hnr Roll; Comm Volntr; FCA; Mth Clb/Tm; Clr Grd; Football & Baseball Manager; Paramedic; Pharmacist

MAXWELL, ALEXI R; KINGSPORT, TN; SULLIVAN CTRL HS; (JR); DAR; Duke TS; Hi Hnr Roll; Hnr Roll; WWAHSS; Peer Tut/Med; FBLA; Statistics Award; Linguistics; Law; Dartmouth College, NH

MAXWELL, KYLE D; SODDY DAISY, TN; SODDY-DAISY HS; (FR); Hnr Roll; WWAHSS; Chrch Yth Grp; Emplmnt; Bnd

MAXWELL, MEREDITH G; BLOUNTVILLE, TN; SULLIVAN CTRL HS; (SR); All Am Sch; Ctznshp Aw; F Lan Hn Soc; Hi Hnr Roll; Nat Hon Sy; Pres Sch; WWAHSS; Comm Volntr; Chrch Yth Grp; Emplmnt; Key Club; Ntl Beta Clb; Off Aide; Svce Clb; Tchrs Aide; Foreign Clb; Ch Chr; Yrbk (R); Teacher Appreciation Award; Math Honor Society; Pharmacy; Northeast State Technical Community College

MAY, CASSANDRA L; KINGSPORT, TN; DOBYNS BENNETT HS; (SR); Hi Hnr Roll; Yth Ldrshp Prog; ArtClub; Chrch Yth Grp; Key Club; Ntl Beta Clb; Scouts; Bnd; Mch Bnd; Pep Bnd; PP Ftbl (J); Sftball (VJ L); Lit Mag (E); Silver Award-Girl Scouts; Interior Design; U of Tennessee in Knoxville

MAY, HALEY; SODDY DAISY, TN; SODDY DAISY HS; (FR); Hnr Roll; WWAHSS; Chrch Yth Grp; DARE; Clr Grd; Anesthesiology; Respiratory Therapy; University of Tennessee at Knoxville; University of Tennessee at Chattanooga

Mason, Tiffany
Austin East HS
Knoxville, TN

Mason, Dustin D
Sullivan East HS
Piney Flats, TN

Malone, J Paige
Tennessee HS
Bristol, TN

Martin, Kelly S
Franklin Cty HS
Decherd, TN

Massingille, Alison L
Clay Cty HS
Celina, TN

MAYFIELD, WILLIAM M; PULASKI, TN; GILES CTY HS; (JR); 4H Awd; Ctznshp Aw; Duke TS; Hnr Roll; Pres Ac Ftns Aw; Sci Fairs; WWAHSS; 4-H; AL Aux Boys; Chrch Yth Grp; Emplmnt; Ntl FFA; Prom Com; Quiz Bowl; Schol Bwl; Bsball (V); Ftball (V); Officer in 4-H; Officer in TN Jr. Angus Assn (President); Agricultural Engineering; U of Tennessee

MAYNARD, JONATHAN D; LIVINGSTON, TN; LIVINGSTON AC; (SR); 4H Awd; F Lan Hn Soc; Hnr Roll; Jr Rot; Perf Att; St of Mnth; WWAHSS; Yth Ldrshp Prog; 4-H; AL Aux Boys; Chrch Yth Grp; FCA; Ntl Beta Clb; Ntl FFA; NYLC; Sci Clb; Bsball (V L); Ftball (V CL); Cl Off (V); Stu Cncl; 4-H Vol State Award; Agriculture; U of Tennessee; Tennessee Technology U

MAYS, DANIEL; WOODLAWN, TN; NORTHWEST HS; (FR); 4H Awd; Hnr Roll; ROTC; Clr Grd; Drl Tm; Ftball (J); Golf (V)

MAZZIO, NICOLE; CLARKSVILLE, TN; CLARKSVILLE HS; (JR); Duke TS; Hnr Roll; WWAHSS; Yth Ldrshp Prog; Hosp Aide; Chrch Yth Grp; Drma Clb; Key Club; SP/M/VS; Stg Cre; Sccr (V); Track (V); CR (R); Yrbk (E, P); Youth Leadership of Clarksville; Vice President of Jr Civitan; Child Psychology; Theatre Arts

MC ADAMS, LA SHUNDA; MEMPHIS, TN; HAMILTON HS; (SO); Hnr Roll; Perf Att; WWAHSS; ROTC; Computer Technology; Clark Atlanta U; Jackson State U

MC AMIS, CARMEN; CLEVELAND, TN; WALKER VALLEY HS; (SO); WWAHSS; Chrch Yth Grp; Key Club; Ntl Beta Clb; Bnd; Mch Bnd; Pep Bnd; PP Ftbl; Music Major; Education; U of Tennessee in Knoxville; U of Tennessee in Chattanooga

MC AMIS, TRACI K; CLEVELAND, TN; WALKER VALLEY HS; (SR); Hi Hnr Roll; MVP; Nat Hon Sy; Nat Stu Ath Day Aw; St of Mnth; USAA; WWAHSS; Comm Volntr; Chrch Yth Grp; FCA; Key Club; Ntl Beta Clb; NYLC; Prom Com; Chr; Cr Ctry (V C); Sccr (V C); Track (V C); Adv Cncl (R); Cl Off (P); Stu Cncl (R); CR (R); Sports Medicine; ETSU

MC BEE, LINDSEY; PALMER, TN; GRUNDY CTY; (JR); Hi Hnr Roll; Jr Rot; Nat Hon Sy; WWAHSS; 4-H; DECA; FBLA; Ntl Beta Clb; Outdrs Clb; Pep Squd; Prom Com; Quill & Scroll; SP/M/VS; Cl Off (P); Stu Cncl (P); Yrbk (E); Radiology; Chattanooga State; Middle Tennessee State U

MC BRIDE, HAYLEY E; MEDON, TN; SOUTH SIDE HS; (SO); Hnr Roll; Chrch Yth Grp; Lib Aide; Pep Squd; Photog; Tchrs Aide; Chrldg (V); Scr Kpr (V); Yrbk (R); Nursing; Nurse Anesthetist

MC CARTER, MELODY D; KNOXVILLE, TN; SOUTH DOYLE HS; (SO); Hnr Roll; Otst Ac Ach Awd; Perf Att; St of Mnth; WWAHSS; Comm Volntr; Peer Tut/Med; DARE; Emplmnt; Key Club; Medical Career; Cosmetology

MC CAULEY, CRYSTEL; COVINGTON, TN; BRIGHTON HS; (SO); Perf Att; St of Mnth; Comm Volntr; Hab For Humty Volntr; Spec Olymp Vol; Chrch Yth Grp; FCA; Ntl FFA; Chr; Volunteer Work - Memphis Veterans Hospital; JC at Mid-South Youth Camp; Civil Engineer; Air Force Academy

MC CLAIN, EVIN T; MEMPHIS, TN; WOODDALE HS; (JR); Hi Hnr Roll; Hnr Roll; Perf Att; St of Mnth; Yth Ldrshp Prog; Comm Volntr; Svce Clb; SADD; Wdwrkg Clb; Bnd; Mch Bnd; Stg Cre; Bsball (V); Bskball (V); Ftball (V); Gmnstcs (V); Scr Kpr; Sccr (V); Swmg (V); Yrbk (P); Business; Accounting; U of Memphis; UCLA

MC CLAIN, JASMINE S; PARIS, TN; HENRY CTY HS; (JR); Ctznshp Aw; Perf Att; Peer Tut/Med; Key Club; Ntl Beta Clb; Svce Clb; Spanish Clb; Sftball (J); Leo's Club; Patriot Pals; Effort Scholar; Mass Communication; Journalism; Lambuth U; Memphis State U

MC CLAIN, LAVORSKER D; MEMPHIS, TN; WHITEHAVEN HS; (FR); Ctznshp Aw; Hi Hnr Roll; Hnr Roll; Perf Att; DARE; Mus Clb; Bnd; Jzz Bnd; Mch Bnd; Pep Bnd; Stu Cncl (V); CR (V); Music; Medicine; U of Arkansas at Pine Bluff; Tennessee State U

MC CLAIN, STEPHANIE; GUILD, TN; RICHARD HARDY MEMORIAL SCH; (JR); Hi Hnr Roll; Nat Hon Sy; Nat Mrt LOC; Perf Att; USAA; WWAHSS; Comm Volntr; Chrch Yth Grp; DARE; Emplmnt; Ntl Beta Clb; Bnd; Ch Chr; English Award, Spanish Award, Science Award; Christian Therapy; Carson Newman

MC CLURE, COTY; NASHVILLE, TN; MC GAVOCK COMP HS; (JR); Hi Hnr Roll; Hnr Roll; Nat Hon Sy; Otst Ac Ach Awd; Comm Volntr; Chrch Yth Grp; Dbte Team; Lttrmn Clb; Vsity Clb; Bskball (L); Sftball (L); Vllyball (L); Education; History; Vanderbilt U; Middle Tennessee State U

MC CLURE, JULIA; MURFREESBORO, TN; HOMESCHOOL; (SR); Chrch Yth Grp; Ch Chr; SP/M/VS; Stg Cre; Missions; Elementary Education; Baptist Bible College

MC CONNON, LAUREN B; KNOXVILLE, TN; TEMPLE BAPTIST AC; (FR); Hi Hnr Roll; Hnr Roll; MVP; Otst Ac Ach Awd; Comm Volntr; Chrch Yth Grp; Spch Team; Chr; Ch Chr; SP/M/VS; Bskball (VJCL); Vllyball (V L); Won Highest GPA Last Seven Years; BS-Secondary Degree

MC CORD, KANDICE M; LAWRENCEBURG, TN; LAWRENCE CTY VOC CTR; (JR); Hnr Roll; Comm Volntr; Chrch Yth Grp; FCA; Tchrs Aide; President of Anchor Club; Social Work; U of North Alabama; Middle Tennessee State U

MC CORMICK, CASEY J; MONTEREY, TN; MONTEREY HS; (SO); Ctznshp Aw; Hnr Roll; Otst Ac Ach Awd; Sci Fairs; St of Mnth; USAA; Comm Volntr; BPA; Ntl Beta Clb; Photog; SP/M/VS; Golf (VJ); Cl Off (V); Sch Ppr (E, R); Yrbk (E, R, P); Member of School Academic Team; Played "Pomp & Circumstance" on Piano for Sr Graduation; MD - Physician/Surgeon Pre-Med/Medicine; Pre-Law; U of Tennessee Knoxville; Vanderbilt U

MC COY, SABRINA; GREENBACK, TN; GREENBACK HS; (SO); Hnr Roll; WWAHSS; 4-H; ArtClub; DARE; Tchrs Aide; Spanish Clb; Mar Art (CL); Tae Kwon Do; Biochemical; Engineering; Maryville College; U of Tennessee

MC CRAVEN, DOMINIQUE; MEMPHIS, TN; EAST HS; (SR); All Am Sch; Ctznshp Aw; Hnr Roll; Nat Hon Sy; Nat Ldrshp Svc; Otst Ac Ach Awd; St of Mnth; WWAHSS; Yth Ldrshp Prog; Comm Volntr; Peer Tut/Med; ArtClub; Emplmnt; Key Club; NYLC; Off Aide; Prom Com; Dnce; Bskball (V C); Track (J); Vllyball (VJC); Cl Off (P); Stu Cncl (R); Paul Robeson Award; Scholastic Art and Writing Award; Major-Pharmacy; Minor-Business; Maryville College; Xavier U of Louisiana

MC CROSKY, KALA; ARLINGTON, TN; ARLINGTON HS; (FR); Hnr Roll; Comm Volntr; Peer Tut/Med; 4-H; Chrch Yth Grp; Lib Aide; Ntl Beta Clb; SADD; Chrldg (J); Special Education; Arkansas State U

MC CULLOUGH, SEAN M; DANDRIDGE, TN; JEFFERSON CTY HS; (SO); All Am Sch; Hi Hnr Roll; Nat Hon Sy; Perf Att; Comm Volntr; Chrch Yth Grp; DECA; FCA; NtlFrnscLg; Scouts; Sccr (V); Yrbk (R); Eagle Scout and Jr Assistant Scoutmaster; The Good Samaritan Award; Business / Marketing; Math; U of Tennessee Knoxville; U of Notre Dame

MC DANIEL, GENNIFER; GALLATIN, TN; STATION CAMP HS; (SO); 4H Awd; Ctznshp Aw; Hi Hnr Roll; Hnr Roll; Kwnis Aw; Otst Ac Ach Awd; St of Mnth; CARE; Peer Tut/Med; 4-H; Chrch Yth Grp; DARE; Emplmnt; FCA; Key Club; Scouts; Spanish Clb; Bnd; Jzz Bnd; Mch Bnd; Orch; Sccr; Education; Photographer; U of Tennessee; Middle Tennessee State U

MC DANIEL, KAITLIN; KINGSPORT, TN; SULLIVAN SOUTH HS; (SO); 4H Awd; Hnr Roll; Otst Ac Ach Awd; Perf Att; Comm Volntr; 4-H; Chrch Yth Grp; DARE; Photog; ROTC; French Clb; Chr; Ch Chr; Drl Tm; Orch; Digital Media; Photo Journalism; Appalachian State U; East Tennessee State U

MC DANIEL, LE ANNA; MEMPHIS, TN; KIRBY HS; (FR); Hi Hnr Roll; Hnr Roll; Otst Ac Ach Awd; Fashion Design; Business; Tennessee State U; The Fashion Institute of Design & Merchandising

MC DANIEL, THOMAS; KNOXVILLE, TN; AUSTIN-EAST MAGNET HS; (JR); Comm Volntr; Hab For Humty Volntr; Peer Tut/Med; Chrch Yth Grp; Svce Clb; Ch Chr; Adv Cncl (R); Sch Ppr (R); Certificates-100 Blackman of Knoxville; Certificate-Project Grad.; Attend College; Pellissippi State Community College; U of Tennessee-Knoxville

MC DAVID, JENNIFER; CHURCH HILL, TN; DOBYNS BENNETT HS; (SR); Hnr Roll; Nat Hon Sy; WWAHSS; JSA; Key Club; Ntl Beta Clb; Tchrs Aide; Orch; Yrbk (R); National Youth Leadership Forum; U of Tennessee

MCDONALD, HALEY; LA FOLLETTE, TN; CAMPBELL CTY COMP HS; (SO); Hi Hnr Roll; Hnr Roll; MVP; Comm Volntr; Chrch Yth Grp; Drma Clb; FCA; Key Club; SP/M/VS; Bskball (J); Scr Kpr (V); Sftball (V L); Vllyball (V CL); Carson Newman College

MC FADGON, DEEANDRIA; MEMPHIS, TN; WHITEHAVEN HS; (SR); Hi Hnr Roll; Nat Hon Sy; WWAHSS; Yth Ldrshp Prog; Comm Volntr; Chrch Yth Grp; DECA; Emplmnt; Ch Chr; Chrldg (V); Cl Off (P); CR (R); The National Society of High School Scholars; English Criminal Law, Pre Law; The U of TN, At Chattanooga; The U of TN, At Martin

MC GAHA, JOIA; MEMPHIS, TN; CRAIGMONT HS; (JR); Hi Hnr Roll; Hnr Roll; WWAHSS; ArtClub; Spanish Clb; Graphic Design; Digital Communications; U of Memphis

MC GEE, BLAIR A; LINDEN, TN; PERRY CTY HS; (SR); Hi Hnr Roll; Hnr Roll; Valdctrian; AL Aux Girls; Emplmnt; FBLA; Mth Clb/Tm; Ntl Beta Clb; Prom Com; Tchrs Aide; Spanish Clb; SP/M/VS; Scr Kpr (V); Adv Cncl; Cl Off (V); Yrbk (E); Writing Assessment (Score of 6); Belmont U; U of Tennessee At Martin

MC GEE, ERIC; LEBANON, TN; WILSON CTRL HS; (SO); Hnr Roll; Perf Att; Chrch Yth Grp; DARE; Emplmnt; Ftball (V L); Video Taped District & Regional Basketball Tournaments; Tennessee Tech U; Middle Tennessee State U

MC GEE, PAIGE; SODDY DAISY, TN; SODDY DAISY HS; Hnr Roll; Hosp Aide; Chrch Yth Grp; FCA; Chr; Chrldg (V); Cr Ctry (L); Dentistry; Psychology; U of Tennessee Chattanooga; U of Tennessee Knoxville

MC GEHEE, JEFFREY M; DYERSBURG, TN; DYERSBURG HS; (JR); Hi Hnr Roll; Nat Hon Sy; Yth Ldrshp Prog; Peer Tut/Med; Chrch Yth Grp; Key Club; Mth Clb/Tm; Spanish Clb; Chr; Ch Chr; Stu Cncl; Key Club, Honor Society; Spanish Club; Business; Dentistry; Belmont U-Nashville, TN; Union U-Jackson, TN

MC GINNIS, KATELYN; MEMPHIS, TN; RIDGEWAY HS; (JR); Hi Hnr Roll; Nat Hon Sy; WWAHSS; Peer Tut/Med; Chrch Yth Grp; Emplmnt; Key Club; MuAlphaTh; SADD; Cr Ctry (V); Sccr (V L); Track (V L); AP Biology Builder Award; William Sweet Award; Biology Major; Environmental / Geology Major; Appalachian State U; Coastal Carolina U

MC GRAIL, PATRICIA; DYERSBURG, TN; DYERSBURG HS; (JR); Hnr Roll; Nat Hon Sy; WWAHSS; Yth Ldrshp Prog; Chrch Yth Grp; Drma Clb; Key Club; SP/M/VS; Tennis (V L); Yrbk (E)

MC GRATH, GAVIN; MEMPHIS, TN; WHITE STATION HS; (FR); Ctznshp Aw; Duke TS; Hi Hnr Roll; Hnr Roll; Nat Hon Sy; St of Mnth; Bskball (J); U of Memphis

MC KINLEY, KATHLEEN; KNOXVILLE, TN; FARRAGUT HS; (FR); Hnr Roll; Bnd; Mch Bnd

MC KINNEY, WHITNEY; ANTIOCH, TN; MC GAVOCK COMP HS; (JR); Hnr Roll; Nat Hon Sy; WWAHSS; Yth Ldrshp Prog; Comm Volntr; FBLA; Jr Ach; NYLC; Chr; Clr Grd; Jzz Bnd; Mch Bnd; Swmg (V); Adv Cncl (R); Mayor's Youth Council Member; Marketing/Advertisement; Human Resources; UT Knoxville

MC KISSACK, RACHEL; LEOMA, TN; LORETTO HS; (MS); Hnr Roll; Yth Ldrshp Prog; Comm Volntr; Chrch Yth Grp; Drma Clb; FCA; Ntl Beta Clb; Off Aide; Photog; Ch Chr; Dnce; SP/M/VS; Stg Cre; Cl Off (T); Church Youth Group Leader; League Soccer; Business Degree; Education Degree; U of North Alabama; Belmont College Nashville, TN

MC LAUGHLIN, JENNIFFER; CELINA, TN; CLAY CTY HS; (SO); Hnr Roll; FCA; Mth Clb/Tm; Ntl Beta Clb; Ntl FFA; Sci Clb; Bskball (V); Golf (V); Vet; Pediatrician; U of Tennessee; Tennessee Tech U

MC LEARRAN, CHRISTOPHER L; JAMESTOWN, TN; YORK AGRICULTURAL INST; (SR); Hi Hnr Roll; Hnr Roll; Yth Ldrshp Prog; Peer Tut/Med; Chrch Yth Grp; Emplmnt; ROTC; Voc Ind Clb Am; Wdwrkg Clb; Spanish Clb; Welding & Maintenance; Spartan College; Crossville Technology Center

MC MULLINS, TYLER; BLOUNTVILLE, TN; SULLIVAN CTRL HS; (JR); Hnr Roll; WWAHSS; 4-H; Chrch Yth Grp; FCA; Key Club; Chr; Ch Chr; Northeast State Technical Community College

MC MURRY, KRISTA A; GERMANTOWN, TN; LCS; (FR); All Am Sch; Ctznshp Aw; Duke TS; F Lan Hn Soc; Hi Hnr Roll; MVP; Nat Hon Sy; Sci Fairs; Sci/Math Olympn; WWAHSS; ArtClub; DARE; Fr of Library; Vsity Clb; French Clb; Dnce; Cr Ctry (V); Swmg (V); Vllyball (V); National Art Society-Vice President; French National Honor Society

MC MURTRY, RACHAEL N; NASHVILLE, TN; DAVIDSON AC; (SR); All Am Sch; DAR; Hnr Roll; Kwnis Aw; Otst Ac Ach Awd; WWAHSS; Comm Volntr; Emplmnt; Key Club; Off Aide; Photog; Bnd; Mch Bnd; Pep Bnd; Sch Ppr (E); Nashville Humane Association Volunteer; Biology Major; Medical Field; David Lipscomb U

MC NEAL, LAUREN-MARGARET; MEMPHIS, TN; OVERTON HS; (SR); Hnr Roll; DARE; ROTC; Drl Tm; Child Development, Care, and Guidance; Small Business/Entrepreneurial Studies; U of Memphis; Southwest Tennessee Community College

MC NEIL, JENNIFER N; GALLATIN, TN; GALLATIN HS; (SO); 4H Awd; Ctznshp Aw; Hi Hnr Roll; Hnr Roll; MVP; Perf Att; 4-H; Chrch Yth Grp; FCA; Key Club; Scouts; Svce Clb; Dnce; Cr Ctry; Sccr (V); TIU Baton Award Best Female Police Explorer; Junior Cotillion; Major in Criminal Justice; Minor in Spanish; Middle Tennessee State U; U of Tennessee

MC NUTT, STEPHANIE; BRISTOL, TN; SULLIVAN CTRL HS; (JR); WWAHSS; Comm Volntr; Chrch Yth Grp; Key Club; Chr; Dnce; PPSqd (V); Nursing

MC VEIGH, SHANNON; SPRING HILL, TN; SPRING HILL HS; Hi Hnr Roll; Nat Hon Sy; USAA; WWAHSS; Hosp Aide; DARE; Drma Clb; Emplmnt; Key Club; Ntl Beta Clb; Prom Com; SADD; Bnd; Mch Bnd; SP/M/VS; Cr Ctry (J); Cl Off (P); Stu Cncl (P); CR (R); Who's Who Among American HS Students; Law; Advertising/Marketing; U of Tennessee; U of the South

MC VEY, KANNETHA M; NASHVILLE, TN; HUNTERS LANE HS; (SR); Chrch Yth Grp; Off Aide; Ch Chr; Bskball (VJ); Cr Ctry (J); Tennis (V); Physical Therapy; Middle Tennessee State U

MEDLEY, KRISTEN; GREENEVILLE, TN; GREENEVILLE HS; (SO); Hnr Roll; Otst Ac Ach Awd; Clr Grd; Tennis; Adv Cncl (R); Yrbk; I Am Involved in First Priority At School.; I Am Also Involved in Youth Action Group.; Get an MBA; Emory U; Carson-Newman College

Mc Gaha, Joia
Craigmont HS
Memphis, TN

Mc Fadgon, Deeandria
Whitehaven HS
Memphis, TN

Mc Clain, Jasmine S
Henry Cty HS
Paris, TN

Mcdonald, Haley
Campbell Cty Comp HS
La Follette, TN

Mc Kissack, Rachel
Loretto HS
Leoma, TN

MEEKS, DEANNA; GRUETLI LAAGER, TN; GRUNDY CTY HS; (JR); WWAHSS; FTA; Quill & Scroll; Yrbk (R, P); President of Future Teachers of America Society; President of Quill & Scroll; Pediatric Oncologist; Journalist; Harvard U; Yale U

MEIER, LINDA; CLARKSVILLE, TN; CLARKSVILLE HS; (JR); Hi Hnr Roll; Hnr Roll; Otst Ac Ach Awd; Comm Volntr; ArtClub; Emplmnt; FCA; Svce Clb; Spanish Clb; Tennis (J); Track (V); Vllyball (V); Wrstlg (L); Nursing; Middle Tennessee State U; U of Tennessee Knoxville

MELTON, JAMIE R; KNOXVILLE, TN; BEREAN CHRISTIAN SCH; (SR); Hnr Roll; Chrch Yth Grp; Emplmnt; Ch Chr; Dnce; Sccr (VJCL); Yrbk (E, R, P); Certified Soccer Referee; Samaritan's Purse Volunteer; Business Administration; Photography; U of Tennessee

MERRILL, WESLEY P; MURFREESBORO, TN; OAKLAND HS; (FR); Perf Att; Sci Fairs; Comm Volntr; Chrch Yth Grp; ROTC; Cr Ctry (J); Mar Art (J); Track (J); I Am Interested in Missionary Work.; Bible College

MERRIWEATHER, KAYLA J; MEDON, TN; SOUTH SIDE HS; (SO); Ctznshp Aw; Duke TS; Hi Hnr Roll; Hnr Roll; MVP; Nat Hon Sy; Perf Att; Comm Volntr; ArtClub; Chrch Yth Grp; FCA; Ntl Beta Clb; Pep Squd; Chr; Ch Chr; SP/M/VS; Bskball (V L); Vllyball (V C); Stu Cncl (R); CR (R); All West Tennessee Volleyball Team (1st Sophomore); 3rd Place GEMS Octathlon 02-03; Biology; Psychology; U of Tennessee, Knoxville; Ole Miss U

METCALF, KRYSTAL J; LENOIR CITY, TN; LENOIR CITY HS; (SO); Ctznshp Aw; Hnr Roll; Nat Hon Sy; Perf Att; Chrch Yth Grp; DARE; Scouts; Chr; Ch Chr; Roane State

MICHAEL, AARON; ARLINGTON, TN; BOCTON HS; (SO); Hnr Roll; Perf Att; Pres Ac Ftns Aw; Sci Fairs; Peer Tut/Med; FCA; Quiz Bowl; Ch Chr; SP/M/VS; Cr Ctry (V); Sccr (V); DDS; U of Tennessee; U of Memphis

MICHAEL, CASSIE; TULLAHOMA, TN; MOORE CTY HS; (SO); 4H Awd; Hnr Roll; Perf Att; St of Mnth; USAA; Comm Volntr; 4-H; Chrch Yth Grp; DARE; Emplmnt; Fr of Library; FBLA; Cl Off (P); Stu Cncl (R); Yrbk (R); Law; Freed Hardeman; David Lipscomb

MIKEL, NATASHIA S; CLEVELAND, TN; WALKER VALLEY HS; (SR); Hi Hnr Roll; Nat Hon Sy; USAA; WWAHSS; Yth Ldrshp Prog; Comm Volntr; AL Aux Girls; Chrch Yth Grp; Emplmnt; FCA; Key Club; Ntl Beta Clb; Tchrs Aide; Ch Chr; Clr Grd; SP/M/VS; PP Ftbl (L); Sch Ppr (R); Yrbk (P); Tennessee Valley Federal Credit Union Scholarship Essay; Marketing; Education; Austin Peay State U

MILLER, ASHLEY; CORDOVA, TN; WHITEHAVEN HS; (SR); Ctznshp Aw; F Lan Hn Soc; Hi Hnr Roll; Hnr Roll; WWAHSS; Comm Volntr; Key Club; Ntl Beta Clb; Off Aide; Spanish Clb; Dnce; Stu Cncl (R); Biology; Pre-Med; Christian Brothers U; Fisk U

MILLER, ASHLEY; JOELTON, TN; SYCAMORE HS; (FR); Ctznshp Aw; Hnr Roll; Otst Ac Ach Awd; Perf Att; Pres Sch; WWAHSS; 4-H; DARE; Bnd; Mch Bnd; Pep Bnd; Cr Ctry (J); PP Ftbl (J); Swmg (J); Doctor; Vanderbilt U; Yale U

MILLER, COURTNEY; SODDY DAISY, TN; SODDY DAISY HS; (SO); Hnr Roll; Perf Att; WWAHSS; Comm Volntr; Chrch Yth Grp; Key Club; Ntl Beta Clb; SP/M/VS; Chrldg (V L); Scr Kpr (V); Cl Off (S); Stu Cncl; Student Council Core; Opthamologist; U of Tennessee

MILLER, DYLAN; ERWIN, TN; UNICCI CTY HS; (JR); Hnr Roll; WWAHSS; 4-H; BPA; DARE; Drma Clb; Key Club; Pep Squd; German Clb; Who's Who Among American HS Students; Tusculum College; Law; East Tenn. State U; U of Tenn.

MILLER, JANE L; MURFREESBORO, TN; SIEGEL HS; (JR); All Am Sch; Duke TS; F Lan Hn Soc; Hi Hnr Roll; Nat Hon Sy; St of Mnth; WWAHSS; Yth Ldrshp Prog; BPA; Chrch Yth Grp; DARE; Emplmnt; FCA; MuAlphaTh; Ntl Beta Clb; NYLC; Dnce; Cl Off (R); Stu Cncl (R); CR (R)

MILLER, JESSICA K; MEMPHIS, TN; WOODDALE HS; (FR); Ctznshp Aw; Hnr Roll; Perf Att; Comm Volntr; Sftball (V); Stu Cncl (S); Psychiatrist; Teacher; Delta State U; U of Memphis

MILLER, KASEY; CROSSVILLE, TN; CUMBERLAND CTY HS; (JR); Hnr Roll; Spec Olymp Vol; Chrch Yth Grp; Emplmnt; Ntl Beta Clb; Bskball (V L); Sports Medicine; Basketball Coach; Middle Tennessee State; East Tennessee State

MILLER, KASEY A; KNOXVILLE, TN; HALLS HS; (JR); Ctznshp Aw; Hnr Roll; St of Mnth; Comm Volntr; Peer Tut/Med; Emplmnt; FCA; Off Aide; Prom Com; Chrldg (V); CR (R); Occupational Therapy; Elementary Education; U of Tennessee Knoxville; East TN State U

MILLER, MAX R; FRANKLIN, TN; CENTENNIAL HS; (JR); Hi Hnr Roll; Nat Hon Sy; Perf Att; USAA; WWAHSS; Peer Tut/Med; Emplmnt; Mth Clb/Tm; MuAlphaTh; Bnd; Mch Bnd; Tennis (V CL); YMCA Basketball-11 Years; History; Education; Auburn; U of Tennessee-Knoxville

MILLS, KYLE; CLARKSVILLE, TN; MONTGOMERY CTRL HS; (JR); Hi Hnr Roll; Hnr Roll; MVP; Nat Hon Sy; Perf Att; Sci Fairs; St of Mnth; WWAHSS; Comm Volntr; AL Aux Boys; Chrch Yth Grp; DARE; Drma Clb; FCA; Mth Clb/Tm; Prom Com; Bsball (VJ); Bskball (VJ); Cr Ctry (V); Golf (V); MVP All Area Baseball-2004; Architecture; Civil Engineering; U of Tennessee-Knoxville; Belmont U

MILLS, SARAH R; KINGSPORT, TN; (JR); Nat Hon Sy; WWAHSS; Yth Ldrshp Prog; Comm Volntr; Hab For Humty Volntr; Chrch Yth Grp; Drma Clb; Jr Cls League; Key Club; Ntl Beta Clb; Off Aide; Prom Com; Tchrs Aide; Cr Ctry (J); Dvng (V); Swmg (V); Sch Ppr (R); Beta Club; National Honor Society; Psychology; Clemson U, U of Tennessee; West Va. U

MINCEY, SHERITTA J; MEMPHIS, TN; HILLCREST HS; (SO); Ctznshp Aw; Hnr Roll; Chrch Yth Grp; Mus Clb; ROTC; Ch Chr; I Am a Musician, a Drummer; I Also Sing, Tenor; I Want to Be a Registered Nurse.; I Would Like a Degree in Music.; Tennessee State U-TSU; Dallas U

MINGLE, STEPHANIE; LIBERTY, TN; CANNON CTY HS; (SO); 4H Awd; Hnr Roll; CARE; 4-H; Chrch Yth Grp; DARE; Ntl Beta Clb; Ntl FFA; Ch Chr; Middle Tennessee State U

MISAIPHON, AMIE; LEBANON, TN; LEBANON HS; (SO); Dnce; Vllyball (V); Stu Cncl (S); CR (R); Key Club Vice President; Beta Club; Medicine; U of Tennessee Knoxville

MISCHKE, ELIZABETH; GERMANTOWN, TN; HOUSTON HS; (JR); Chrldg (VJ L); Cl Off (S); Yrbk; Rhodes College; Sewanee-U of the South

MITCHELL, ANA L; WOODBURY, TN; CANNON CTY HS; Hnr Roll; Otst Ac Ach Awd; Perf Att; Sci Fairs; Comm Volntr; Chrch Yth Grp; Dbte Team; Emplmnt; Ntl Beta Clb; Active in Beta; Honorary Writers Award; Psychologist; Psychiatrist; Boston U; Vanderbilt U

MITCHELL, ANGELA; LEBANON, TN; WILSON CTRL HS; (SO); Hnr Roll; Nat Hon Sy; USAA; Valdctrian; Key Club; Ntl Beta Clb; Bnd; Mch Bnd; Pep Bnd; Sch Ppr (R, P); Astronomy; Psychology

MITCHELL, CHARLES; OLIVER SPRINGS, TN; OLIVER SPRINGS HS; (JR); Hnr Roll; Chrch Yth Grp; Emplmnt; Fr of Library; Ntl Beta Clb; Bsball (V); Beta Club; Recommended for Who's Who HS Sports; Computer Science; Electrical Engineering; Tennessee Tech; Roane State

MITCHELL, JASMINE; MEMPHIS, TN; WHITE STATION HS; (JR); Ctznshp Aw; Hnr Roll; MVP; Nat Hon Sy; Perf Att; WWAHSS; Comm Volntr; Hab For Humty Volntr; Spec Olymp Vol; Jr Ach; Bowling Team; Pharmacy; Music; Florida A & M U; Arkansas State

MITCHELL, SAMARIA; MEMPHIS, TN; WOODDALE HS; (SO); Ctznshp Aw; Hi Hnr Roll; Hnr Roll; MVP; Otst Ac Ach Awd; Perf Att; St of Mnth; Comm Volntr; Chrch Yth Grp; DARE; Drma Clb; Key Club; Off Aide; Tech Clb; French Clb; Chr; Ch Chr; SP/M/VS; Stg Cre; Sccr; Track (L); Performing Arts/Acting; Psychology; Juilliard School; Harvard U

MITCHELL, SHANTARA T; MURFREESBORO, TN; RIVERDALE HS; (FR); 4H Awd; Ctznshp Aw; Hi Hnr Roll; Hnr Roll; Otst Ac Ach Awd; Perf Att; St of Mnth; Comm Volntr; Hab For Humty Volntr; Hosp Aide; 4-H; Chrch Yth Grp; DARE; Emplmnt; Pep Squd; Quiz Bowl; Scouts; Bnd; Ch Chr; Clr Grd; Dnce; Pharmacist; Medicine; Middle Tennessee State U; Tennessee State U

MOBLEY, GINNY; GERMANTOWN, TN; EVANGELICAL CHRISTIAN SCH; (JR); F Lan Hn Soc; Hnr Roll; Nat Hon Sy; WWAHSS; Spec Olymp Vol; Chrch Yth Grp; FTA; Key Club; MuAlphaTh; Ntl Beta Clb; SP/M/VS; Stg Cre; Placed 17th in National Spanish Exam; National Honor Society; Education; Spanish; U of Tennessee Chattanooga

MOFFITT, BOBBY D; UNION CITY, TN; OBION CTY CAREER/TECH CTR; (SO); Hnr Roll; Perf Att; St of Mnth; 4-H; Tech Clb; Voc Ind Clb Am; Ch Chr; OCCTC Most Respectful; Placed 4th in Art Show; Get Job Fabricating Metal; Mechanist; Newbern Technology Center; Nashville Automotive Diesel Technology College

MOLINA, GABRIELLE; HENDERSON, TN; CHESTER CTY HS; (FR); Hi Hnr Roll; Hnr Roll; Otst Ac Ach Awd; Comm Volntr; Ntl Beta Clb; Bnd; Mch Bnd; Pep Bnd; Cr Ctry (L); Sccr (L); PhD in Music; PhD in Art; Juilliard; Yale U

MONCEAUX, DARYL; SEYMOUR, TN; SEYMOUR HS; (SO); Duke TS; Hnr Roll; Emplmnt; Scouts; Digital Arts; Psychology; Duke U

MONGER, BRITTANY; LENOIR CITY, TN; LENOIR CITY HS; (SR); Hi Hnr Roll; WWAHSS; Comm Volntr; Peer Tut/Med; Chrch Yth Grp; Emplmnt; Jr Ach; Off Aide; Prom Com; Chr; PP Ftbl (V); Track (V); Health Occupation Students of America; Physical Therapy; Roane State Community College

MONTGOMERY, MATTHEW T; BLOUNTVILLE, TN; SULLIVAN CTRL HS; (SR); Hnr Roll; Perf Att; WWAHSS; Yth Ldrshp Prog; Comm Volntr; Chrch Yth Grp; Emplmnt; Key Club; Scouts; Bnd; Jzz Bnd; Mch Bnd; Pep Bnd; Eagle Scout; Who's Who Among American Students; Mechanical Engineering; Tennessee Tech U

MONTOYA, NATASHA; PINEY FLATS, TN; SULLIVAN EAST HS; (SO); Hnr Roll; WWAHSS; Comm Volntr; FCA; Key Club; Ntl Beta Clb; Quill & Scroll; ROTC; French Clb; Chr; Drl Tm; Mar Art; Tennis (J); Cl Off; CR; Sch Ppr (R); 2005 Queen of Hearts Candidate; Multi Channel Retail Buyer (Buyer); Fashion Merchandising/Marketing; Fashion Inst. of Design and Merchandising; American Intercontinental U. London

MOODY, TRAVIS; MURFREESBORO, TN; SIEGEL HS; (JR); Hnr Roll; WWAHSS; Chess; Cmptr Clb; Emplmnt; Ntl Beta Clb; Pep Squd; Tech Clb; German Clb; Tennis (V); Computer Science; Networking; Tennessee Tech; Middle Tennessee State U

MOON, BRIAN; MURFREESBORO, TN; SIEGEL HS; (SO); Hnr Roll; Hab For Humty Volntr; DARE; FCA; Pep Squd; Spanish Clb; Bsball (V); Gmnstcs (V); CR (T, R); Yrbk (P); Middle Tennessee State U; U of Tennessee Knoxville

MOONEYHAM, GEOFFREY K; NASHVILLE, TN; MC GAVOCK COMP HS; (SR); Bskball (V); Ftball (C); Wrstlg (V); Mechanical Engineering; Civil Engineering; Georgia Institute of Technology

MOORE, BILL; COLUMBIA, TN; COLUMBIA CTRL HS; (SO); Sci Fairs; St of Mnth; Hab For Humty Volntr; Chrch Yth Grp; Cyclg; Executive Producer - Student Produced Newscast; Winner - BPA- Region / Computer Contest-Data Base Application; Broadcast Journalism; Computer Consultant; Appalachian State U; Southwest Missouri State

MOORE, DONALD P; MEMPHIS, TN; WHITE STATION HS; (SR); WWAHSS; ArtClub; Chrch Yth Grp; ROTC; Lcrsse (V L); Architecture; Engineering; U of Memphis; Mississippi State U

MOORE, ELIZABETH; DYERSBURG, TN; DYERSBURG HS; (JR); Nat Hon Sy; Otst Ac Ach Awd; Yth Ldrshp Prog; Comm Volntr; Spec Olymp Vol; ArtClub; FCA; FTA; Lttrmn Clb; Bskball (V); Vllyball (V); 2 Keys to City of Dyersburg By Mayor; 2 Dyer County Mayoral Proclamations; Art; Marine Biology; Rhodes

MOORE, HEATHER; MEDINA, TN; GIBSON CTY HS; (FR); Hi Hnr Roll; Hnr Roll; Perf Att; 4-H; DARE; FCA; Lttrmn Clb; Ntl Beta Clb; Bnd; Dnce; Mch Bnd; Pep Bnd; Cr Ctry (V); PP Ftbl (V); Track (V); Honor Roll; Diagnostic Medical Sonographer; Health Professions and Related Clinical Sciences; Middle Tennessee State U; Austin Peay State U

MOORE, JUSTIN; MEMPHIS, TN; OVERTON HS; (FR); Hi Hnr Roll; Hnr Roll; Perf Att; Business Management; U of Memphis; U of Georgia

MOORE, LAUREN; COLLIERVILLE, TN; COLLIERVILLE HS; (SO); Hnr Roll; Nat Hon Sy; Otst Ac Ach Awd; FCA; Ntl Beta Clb; Ntl FFA; Spanish Clb; Dvng; PPSqd; Varsity Pom Squad 9th; Business / Management; U of Memphis

MOORE, SARAH; MURFREESBORO, TN; SIEGEL HS; (JR); Hi Hnr Roll; Hnr Roll; Yth Ldrshp Prog; Comm Volntr; Chrch Yth Grp; DARE; FCA; FCCLA; Jr Cls League; Key Club; Ntl Beta Clb; Svce Clb; Chr; Ch Chr; Dnce; Cl Off (R); Stu Cncl (V); CR (R); Varsity Dance Team; Elementary Education

MOORE, SHANAYE L; CLARKSVILLE, TN; NORTHEAST HS; (FR); Sci Fairs; Comm Volntr; Scouts; Bnd; Bskball (VJ); Vllyball (J); Played AAU-Basketball; Greeters Club-Middle School; Medical-Pediatrician; Austin Peay State U

MOORE, STEPHANIE S; UNICOI, TN; U N 1001 CTY VOC SCH; (SR); Hi Hnr Roll; Kwnis Aw; Nat Hon Sy; WWAHSS; BPA; Chrch Yth Grp; FCA; Key Club; Lib Aide; Ntl Beta Clb; Ntl FFA; Schol Bwl; Cl Off (T); CR; 7 United Mountain Horse World Championship Wins; 5 Rocky Mountain Horse International; Veterinary Medicine; U of Kentucky

MOORHOUSE, STACY; HIXSON, TN; SODDY DAISY HS; (FR); Hnr Roll; Otst Ac Ach Awd; Perf Att; WWAHSS; Chrch Yth Grp; Mod UN; Ntl Beta Clb; Chr; SP/M/VS; Interior Design; Acting; Bowling Green State U; Minnesota State U

MORELAND, BONNIE J; JONESBOROUGH, TN; DAVID CROCKETT HS; (SO); 4H Awd; Hnr Roll; Otst Ac Ach Awd; Perf Att; Sci Fairs; Peer Tut/Med; 4-H; DARE; Drma Clb; Mus Clb; Spanish Clb; Bnd; Chr; Sccr (J); Sch Ppr (R); HOSA; Secondary Education (7th & 8th Grade Math); Veterinary Assistant; U of Tennessee; East Tennessee State U

MORGAN, BRANDI S; NASHVILLE, TN; MC GAVOCK HS; (MS); Ctznshp Aw; Nat Hon Sy; Otst Ac Ach Awd; Comm Volntr; Peer Tut/Med; Chrch Yth Grp; DARE; FCA; Sci Clb; Chr; Ch Chr; Chrldg (C); Stu Cncl (R); Sch Ppr (R); Law; CSI; Harvard; Princeton

MORGAN, JEFFREY W; ROCKVALE, TN; EAGLEVILLE SCH; (SO); Hi Hnr Roll; Hnr Roll; Otst Ac Ach Awd; Red Cr Aide; Dbte Team; Emplmnt; Ntl FFA; Golf (V); Mar Art (V); Cl Off (T); Stu Cncl (T); Beta Club; Medical; Business; Vanderbilt; UT Health of Memphis

MORGAN, KYLE J; KINGSPORT, TN; SULLIVAN NORTH HS; (SR); Hi Hnr Roll; Nat Hon Sy; Perf Att; WWAHSS; Spec Olymp Vol; FCA; Key Club; Ntl Beta Clb; Bsball (J); Tennis (V); Stu Cncl (R); Pre-Med Major; East Tennessee State U

Mooneyham, Geoffrey K
Mc Gavock Comp HS
Nashville, TN

Mingle, Stephanie
Cannon Cty HS
Liberty, TN

Miller, Ashley
Whitehaven HS
Cordova, TN

National
Honor Roll
Spring 2005

Metcalf, Krystal J
Lenoir City HS
Lenoir City, TN

Montoya, Natasha
Sullivan East HS
Piney Flats, TN

Moore, Elizabeth
Dyersburg HS
Dyersburg, TN

MORGAN, LEANDRA; BARTLETT, TN; WHITE STATION HS; (SO); Ctznshp Aw; Duke TS; Hi Hnr Roll; Perf Att; Pres Ac Ftns Aw; St of Mnth; WWAHSS; Comm Volntr; Chrch Yth Grp; Jr Ach; MuAlphaTh; Ntl Beta Clb; ROTC; Svce Clb; 8th Grade Valedictorian

MORKOVIN, STEPHANY; CLARKSVILLE, TN; ROSSVIEW HS; (JR); Hi Hnr Roll; Hnr Roll; Nat Hon Sy; Comm Volntr; ArtClub; Chrch Yth Grp; Mus Clb; Off Aide; ROTC; Acpl Chr; Chr; Mar Art (L); Psychology / Business; Music; Washington U; Austin Peay U

MORRIELLO, MARY; CHRISTIANA, TN; BLACKMAN HS; (JR); Hnr Roll; Kwnis Aw; St of Mnth; WWAHSS; Comm Volntr; DECA; Key Club; Ntl Beta Clb; Tchrs Aide; Dnce; Middle Tennessee State U

MORRIS, KIMBERLY M; ATHENS, TN; MC MINN CTY HS; (SR); 4H Awd; Ctznshp Aw; Hnr Roll; Perf Att; Sci Fairs; St of Mnth; Comm Volntr; Spec Olymp Vol; 4-H; FBLA; Key Club; Off Aide; Outdrs Clb; Scouts; Tchrs Aide; Bnd; Chr; Ch Chr; Mch Bnd; Yrbk (E); Pharmacy; Sales Rep; Tennessee Wesleyan College; Long Island U

MORRIS, MALLORIE G; FRANKLIN, TN; FRANKLIN HS; (JR); Duke TS; Hi Hnr Roll; WWAHSS; Yth Ldrshp Prog; Comm Volntr; Hab For Humty Volntr; Red Cr Aide; Chrch Yth Grp; FCA; Mth Clb/Tm; Off Aide; Svce Clb; Top 25; Physician; Vanderbilt U; Lipscomb U

MORRIS, TERRA A; SAVANNAH, TN; HCHS; (SO); MVP; Nat Hon Sy; Otst Ac Ach Awd; WWAHSS; Comm Volntr; Chrch Yth Grp; DARE; FCA; SADD; Bskball (V); Cr Ctry (V); Vllyball (V); I Am a Member of Sub-Debs.; I Am a Member of Just Say No.; Dental Hygienist; Doctor; UT Knoxville; Memphis

MORROW, ANDREW D; MURFREESBORO, TN; OAKLAND HS; (FR); Hnr Roll; MVP; FCA; Vsity Clb; Bsball; Ftball; Wrstlg; Sports Management; Architecture; U of Tennessee; U of California At Los Angeles

MORROW, DOJE N; NASHVILLE, TN; NASHVILLE SCH OF THE ARTS; (SR); Hnr Roll; MVP; Comm Volntr; Emplmnt; FCA; Off Aide; Prom Com; Chr; President's Award; Business Administration; Human Resources; Western Kentucky U; Tennessee State U

MOTLEY, KATIE; SMYRNA, TN; BLACKMAN HS; (FR); Hnr Roll; WWAHSS; Comm Volntr; Key Club; Pep Squd; Tennis (V); Pep Club; Key Club; Elementary School Teacher; Middle Tennessee State U

MOTT, CURTIS; ORLINDA, TN; EAST ROBERTSON HS; (FR); Hnr Roll; Comm Volntr; Chrch Yth Grp; FCA; Ntl Beta Clb; Ntl FFA; Bskball (VJ); Ftball (V); Sr Beta Club; FFA; Dentist; Austin Peay State U

MOUNT, JEFFREY A; HENDERSONVLLE, TN; STATION CAMP HS; (SO); 4H Awd; Hnr Roll; Pres Sch; St of Mnth; Comm Volntr; DECA; Scouts; Bnd; Ftball (J); YMCA Teen Volunteer Award 2004; YMCA Teen Leader Vice President 03-05; Pilot-Aeronautics; United States Air Force Academy; Embry Riddle Aeronautical U

MUHAMMAD, JARRED R; MEMPHIS, TN; (JR); Ctznshp Aw; Hi Hnr Roll; Hnr Roll; Sci Fairs; Quiz Bowl; Sci Clb; Advanced State Testing Scores; Law; Graphic Design; U of Miami; Jackson State U

MUHAMMAD, KYAIRRA; MEMPHIS, TN; KINGSBURY VOC-TECH CTR; (SO); Ctznshp Aw; Hnr Roll; MVP; Sci Fairs; St of Mnth; Comm Volntr; BPA; Cmptr Clb; Off Aide; Pep Squd; SADD; Stg Cre; Vllyball (V); Cl Off (R); Archonette Club of Zeta Phi Beta; Computer Engineer; Chemist; Georgia State U; Clark Atlanta

MULLINS, BETHANY; MORRISTOWN, TN; MORRISTOWN HAMBLEN HS WEST; (FR); 4H Awd; Ctznshp Aw; St of Mnth; WWAHSS; Peer Tut/Med; Spec Olymp Vol; 4-H; Chrch Yth Grp; DARE; Ch Chr; Special Olympics; Law Enforcement; Human Services; Georgia Tech; North Carolina State

MULLINS, TANISHA; CLARKSVILLE, TN; NORTHWEST HS; (FR); Hnr Roll; Nat Hon Sy; Chrch Yth Grp; Drma Clb; Fr of Library; Lib Aide; Ch Chr; Studying Japanese and Sign Language, One of the Top Students in Algebra in 9th Grade; Computer Science/Web Design; Sign Language Interpreter

MURPHY, HEATHER C; LAWRENCEBURG, TN; LAWRENCE CTY HS; (FR); 4H Awd; Ctznshp Aw; Hi Hnr Roll; Hnr Roll; 4-H; Chrch Yth Grp; DARE; Bnd; Clr Grd; Mch Bnd; Pep Bnd; 2 Outstanding Characters Awards; 1st Place Winter Guard Championship 2004; Advertising; Pediatrics; U of Tennessee in Knoxville; David Lipscomb U

MYERS, RACHEL; COLLIERVILLE, TN; HOUSTON HS; (FR); Chr; SGA (Student Gov) Member; Student Impact Member; Psychology; History; Duke U

MYKYTKA, KATHERINE; KINGSPORT, TN; DOBYNS-BENNETT HS; (JR); Hnr Roll; Nat Hon Sy; WWAHSS; Comm Volntr; Chrch Yth Grp; JSA; Key Club; Ntl Beta Clb; Prom Com; Spanish Clb; Ch Chr; Chrldg (J); Sccr (V); Cl Off (R); Stu Cncl (T); Pharmacy

NAMER, ALEXANDRA V; CORDOVA, TN; RIDGEWAY HS; (JR); Hi Hnr Roll; Nat Hon Sy; Nat Ldrshp Svc; Otst Ac Ach Awd; WWAHSS; Comm Volntr; Peer Tut/Med; Chrch Yth Grp; Emplmnt; Key Club; Mth Clb/Tm; MuAlphaTh; SADD; Tchrs Aide; Tmpl Yth Grp; Chr; Ch Chr; SP/M/VS; Stg Cre; Cr Ctry (L); Tennis; All-West Orchestra-2nd Chair; Internship- U TN Molecular Science; Pre-Med; Communications / Journalism; Auburn U; Tulane U

NDAYISHIMIYE, CHRISTINA; MADISON, TN; HUNTERS LANE HS; (SR); Hnr Roll; Nat Hon Sy; Comm Volntr; Tennis; Nurse; Medical Assistant; Phoenix College; U of Phoenix

NEAL, KATELANDE; RIPLEY, TN; RIPLEY HS; (FR); Hnr Roll; Perf Att; 4-H; Chrch Yth Grp; DARE; Mus Clb; Ntl FFA; Acpl Chr; Chr; Radiologist; Registered Nurse; Lambuth U; U Tennessee Martin

NEAL, WILLIAM; MEMPHIS, TN; MITCHELL HS; (JR); Hnr Roll; Ftball (V); Physical Therapy; Athletic Trainer / Sports Administrator; U of Memphis; U of Texas Austin

NELSON, ASHLEY; MEMPHIS, TN; RALEIGH EGYPT HS; (MS); ROTC; Chr; Music and Dance Major

NELSON, JESSICA; OLD HICKORY, TN; MC GAVOCK COMP HS; (JR); Hnr Roll; Otst Ac Ach Awd; St of Mnth; Comm Volntr; DARE; Emplmnt; Photog; SADD; Dnce; SP/M/VS; PP Ftbl (C); Cl Off (R); Stu Cncl (R); CR (R); Yrbk (E, P); Future Community Career Leaders of America; Oasis Youth Council Member; Nursing; Medical Technology; Vanderbilt U; Tennessee State U

NELSON, PORSCHE D; MEMPHIS, TN; MEMPHIS CTRL HS; (FR); Ctznshp Aw; Hi Hnr Roll; Hnr Roll; Nat Hon Sy; Otst Ac Ach Awd; Perf Att; St of Mnth; Peer Tut/Med; DARE; Sci Clb; Scouts; French Clb; Bnd; Chr; SP/M/VS; GAA (L); Vllyball (C); Stu Cncl (R); Sch Ppr (R); Highest GPA in Several Subjects; Pediatrician / Doctor

NEPOMUCENO, TORIE; KNOX, TN; CENTRAL HS; (SO); Hnr Roll; Nat Hon Sy; WWAHSS; Comm Volntr; Peer Tut/Med; Emplmnt; Ntl Beta Clb; Bskball (J); PP Ftbl (V); Sftball (V); Part Time Job; Volunteer; Criminal Justice; Sports Broadcasting; Middle Tenn. State U; East Tenn State U

NETTERVILLE, LINDSEY; NEW JOHNSONVILLE, TN; WAVERLY CTRL HS; (JR); Hnr Roll; Nat Hon Sy; Pres Ac Ftns Aw; WWAHSS; Hab For Humty Volntr; Peer Tut/Med; Spec Olymp Vol; 4-H; Chrch Yth Grp; DARE; Drma Clb; FCA; Mus Clb; Off Aide; Tchrs Aide; Chr; Ch Chr; Dnce; SP/M/VS; Bskball (J); Chrldg (V); Gmnstcs (V); Scr Kpr (V); Stu Cncl (R); Aviation; Louisiana State U; Middle Tennessee State U

NEVILLE, CHRIS; LEBANON, TN; WILSON CTRL HS; (JR); Ctznshp Aw; Hnr Roll; MVP; Otst Ac Ach Awd; Perf Att; Sci Fairs; St of Mnth; Comm Volntr; Peer Tut/Med; 4-H; Chrch Yth Grp; DARE; Emplmnt; Scouts; Ftball (V L); Mar Art (C); Sccr (V L); Eagle Scout, Jr. Olympic Tae Kwon Do; Honor Roll Comp.; Archeology; Anthropology; Florida State U; Miami U

NEWBERN, KATHRYN; COTTONTOWN, TN; WHITE HOUSE HS; (SR); 4H Awd; Hnr Roll; MVP; Otst Ac Ach Awd; WWAHSS; Red Cr Aide; 4-H; FBLA; Key Club; Ntl Beta Clb; Ntl FFA; Off Aide; Scouts; Vsity Clb; Dnce; PP Ftbl (V); Sccr (V); Cl Off (S); Stu Cncl (S); Gold Award Recipient; Agriculture Business; U of Tennessee At Knoxville

NEWBERN, KIMBERLY M; MEMPHIS, TN; FAIRLEY HS; (SO); Ctznshp Aw; Hnr Roll; Nat Hon Sy; Perf Att; DARE; Jr Ach; Mch Bnd; Medical Business; Law Enforcement; Jackson State U; Florida Alabama

NEWBERRY, KALEIGH; READYVILLE, TN; OAKLAND HS; (SO); Hnr Roll; Sci Fairs; WWAHSS; 4-H; Ntl Beta Clb; Scouts; Pediatrician; Vet; Middle Tennessee State U; Tennessee State U

NEWBERRY, ZCHKULSHA T; MEMPHIS, TN; MELROSE HS; (FR); Ctznshp Aw; Hnr Roll; Pediatrician; Pharmacist; U of Memphis; Tennessee State U

NEWBY, KANESHA; MEMPHIS, TN; G W CARVER HS; (FR); Hi Hnr Roll; Perf Att; Ntl Beta Clb; Beta Club; Business Computers; Doctor; U of Memphis; Lemoyne Owen College

NEWTON, MEAGAN; PULASKI, TN; GILES CTY HS; (SO); 4H Awd; 4-H; AL Aux Girls; DARE; Bnd; Bskball; Veterinarian; Social Worker; U of Kentucky; U of North Alabama

NGUYEN, KELLY H; MEMPHIS, TN; WOODDALE HS; (JR); Hi Hnr Roll; Hnr Roll; Kwnis Aw; Nat Hon Sy; Perf Att; WWAHSS; Comm Volntr; Hab For Humty Volntr; Red Cr Aide; DECA; Key Club; Sci Clb; Orch; All Year Honor Roll; All Year Perfect Attendance; Accountant; Graphic Designer; Christian Brother U; Rhodes College

NGUYEN, TRANGDAI; MEMPHIS, TN; RIDGEWAY HS; (SO); All Am Sch; Hnr Roll; Nat Hon Sy; Nat Ldrshp Svc; WWAHSS; Comm Volntr; ArtClub; Key Club; French Clb; Vice President of Key Club; Rhodes; U of Memphis

NGUYEN, TUYEN; MEMPHIS, TN; SHEFFIELD HS; (SO); Hnr Roll; Perf Att; Clb; Ch Chr; Medical Physics; Biomedical Engineering; U of TN; U of Memphis

NHIEM, SOMPHAT; NASHVILLE, TN; EAST LITERATURE MAGNET SCH; (SO); Hnr Roll; Perf Att; Comm Volntr; Chrch Yth Grp; Business Management; Medical Diagnostics; Belmont U; Austin Peay

NICHOLS, BRITTANY; MURFREESBORO, TN; SIEGEL HS; (JR); Hnr Roll; Nat Hon Sy; WWAHSS; Comm Volntr; Chrch Yth Grp; DARE; FCA; Ntl Beta Clb; Tchrs Aide; Dnce; Stu Cncl (R); Dance Team-V; Nursing; Middle Tennessee State U

NICHOLS, JACQUELINE M; ENGLEWOOD, TN; TELLICO PLAINS HS; (SR); Hi Hnr Roll; Nat Hon Sy; Perf Att; WWAHSS; Yth Ldrshp Prog; Comm Volntr; Chrch Yth Grp; FCA; FCCLA; Ntl Beta Clb; Quill & Scroll; Schol Bwl; Scouts; Tchrs Aide; Chr; Ch Chr; Cl Off (V); Yrbk; Silver Award-Girl Scouts; Elementary Education; Tennessee Wesleyan College

NICHOLSON OWENS, BRITTNY E; SPRINGFIELD, TN; SPRINGFIELD HS; (FR); Ctznshp Aw; Hi Hnr Roll; Hnr Roll; MVP; Perf Att; Sci Fairs; St of Mnth; Comm Volntr; Quill & Scroll; ROTC; Sci Clb; SP/M/VS; Stg Cre; Skiing; Sccr; CR (T); Yrbk (P); South Carolina Senate Committee For the Care of the Ocean; Marine Biologist; Vanderbilt U

NIEGELBERG, DANIEL M; GERMANTOWN, TN; GERMANTOWN HS; (FR); Hnr Roll; Perf Att; St of Mnth; Comm Volntr; Spec Olymp Vol; Key Club; Tchrs Aide; Tmpl Yth Grp; Chr; Wild Life Research

NIPPER, JARED; HIXSON, TN; SODDY-DAISY HS; (FR); Fut Prb Slvr; Hnr Roll; WWAHSS; Chrch Yth Grp; Emplmnt; Mod UN; Ntl Beta Clb; Scouts; Ftball (V); Freshman Football Team; Freshman Basketball Team; Architecture; Graphic Design; Georgia Institute of Technology; U of Tennessee At Knoxville

NIXON, STEVEN; ALAMO, TN; CROCKETT CTY HS; (FR); 4H Awd; All Am Sch; Hi Hnr Roll; MVP; Nat Hon Sy; Sci/Math Olympn; St Schl; St of Mnth; Comm Volntr; Peer Tut/Med; 4-H; Chrch Yth Grp; DARE; Emplmnt; FCA; Mth Clb/Tm; Ntl Beta Clb; Ntl FFA; Ch Chr; Bsball (J); Bskball (J); Ftball (V); Golf (V); CR (V); Engineering; Law School; Middle Tennessee State U; Florida U

NOE, CHRISTIAN L; HARRIMAN, TN; OLIVER SPRINGS HS; (SO); Hnr Roll; Otst Ac Ach Awd; Perf Att; Chrch Yth Grp; Drma Clb; FCA; Ntl Beta Clb; International Clb; Bnd; Ch Chr; Jzz Bnd; Mch Bnd; Cr Ctry (V); Tennis (V); Psychology; Sociology; Baylor U; Middle Tennessee State U

NOE, LEEANNA M; OLIVER SPRINGS, TN; OLIVER SPRINGS HS; (FR); Duke TS; Hi Hnr Roll; Hnr Roll; Nat Hon Sy; Sci Fairs; Comm Volntr; Peer Tut/Med; Chrch Yth Grp; DARE; Drma Clb; FCA; Ntl Beta Clb; Schol Bwl; Sci Clb; Spanish Clb; Ch Chr; SP/M/VS; Stg Cre; Bskball (VJ L); PP Ftbl (VJ); Cl Off (V, S, T, R); CR (V); Forensic Science; Psychology; U of Tennessee Knoxville; Louisiana State U

NOLEN, SAMUEL R; KINGSPORT, TN; SULLIVAN SOUTH HS; (JR); Duke TS; Nat Hon Sy; WWAHSS; Yth Ldrshp Prog; Comm Volntr; Mth Clb/Tm; MuAlphaTh; ROTC; Acpl Chr; Cr Ctry (V); Sccr (J); Stu Cncl (R); Law

NORRIS, CHRISTINA; LANCING, TN; SUNBRIGHT SCH; (JR); Otst Ac Ach Awd; USAA; Comm Volntr; English Merit Award; Forensic Science (Medical Field); Lawyer; U of Tennessee; Tusculum

NORRIS, RACHEL L; COLLIERVILLE, TN; COLLIERVILLE HS; (SO); Hi Hnr Roll; Hnr Roll; WWAHSS; Sci Clb; Spanish Clb; Pharmacy; U of Tennessee; Samford U

NORTON, JONATHON C; PARROTTSVILLE, TN; COCKE CTY HS; (FR); Emplmnt; ROTC; Cr Ctry (J); Navy Pilot; NASA; Naval Academy; U of Tennessee

NUNLEY, ANDREW; LANCASTER, TN; DEKALB CTY HS; (JR); Hnr Roll; Spanish Clb; Sccr (V); Computer Science; Journalism; Middle TN State U

NUNLEY, MEAGAN; KNOXVILLE, TN; FARRAGUT HS; (SR); Hi Hnr Roll; Nat Hon Sy; Otst Ac Ach Awd; Pres Ac Ftns Aw; Pres Sch; Comm Volntr; Red Cr Aide; Chrch Yth Grp; DECA; Emplmnt; FBLA; Scouts; Voc Ind Clb Am; Gold Award Recipient, DECA Parliamentarian; Skills USA VICA President, Climbing Team Member; MBA; Business Management; U of Tennessee; Clemson U

OAKLEY, ANNA; PROSPECT, TN; GILES CTY HS; (SR); WWAHSS; Comm Volntr; FBLA; FCCLA; Pep Squd; Bnd; Clr Grd; Mch Bnd; SP/M/VS

OATSVALL, LESLI D; CAMDEN, TN; CENTRAL HS; (FR); 4H Awd; Hnr Roll; 4-H; Ntl Beta Clb; SP/M/VS; Chrldg (J); Cl Off (S); Stu Cncl (R); Sch Ppr (R); Beta Club; Nursing; UT Martin; U of Tennessee Knoxville

OCAMPO, FELICITAS; WHITLEYVILLE, TN; HERMITAGE SPRINGS SCH; (JR); Hnr Roll; Perf Att; WWAHSS; 4-H; FCCLA; Prom Com

O'CONNOR, GEORGE M; MEMPHIS, TN; WHITE STATION HS; (SO); Hi Hnr Roll; Hnr Roll; Ftball (VJ)

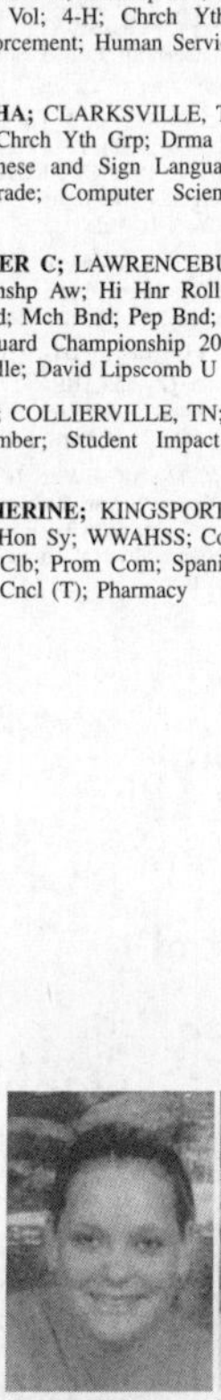
Norris, Christina
Sunbright Sch
Lancing, TN

Newberry, Zchkulsha T
Melrose HS
Memphis, TN

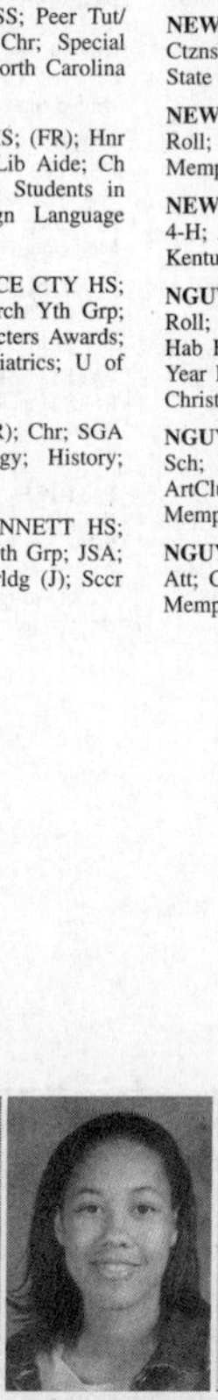
Nelson, Porsche D
Memphis Ctrl HS
Memphis, TN

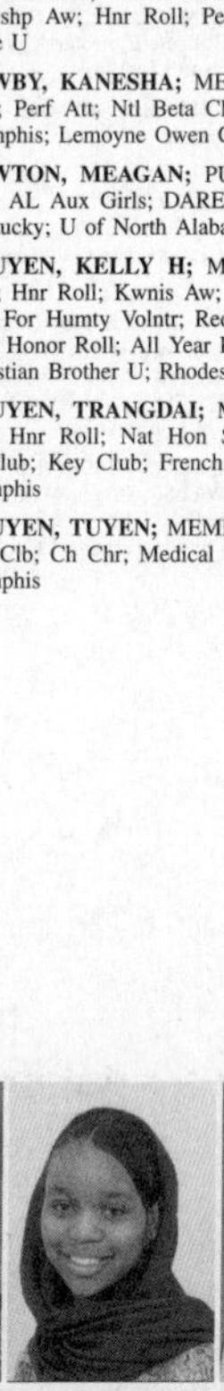
Muhammad, Kyairra
Kingsbury Voc-Tech Ctr
Memphis, TN

Morriello, Mary
Blackman HS
Christiana, TN

Morris, Mallorie G
Franklin HS
Franklin, TN

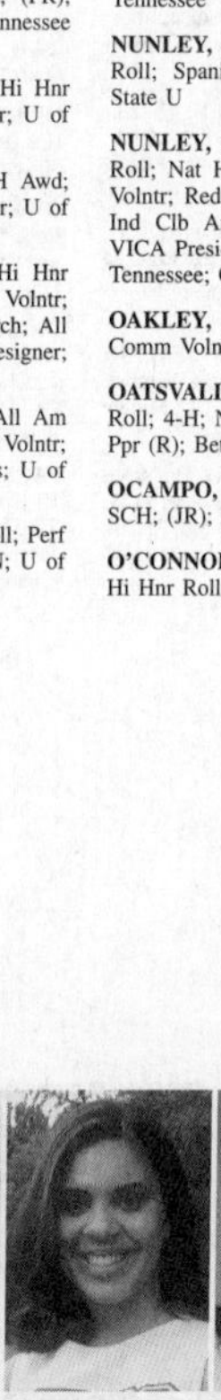
Netterville, Lindsey
Waverly Ctrl HS
New Johnsonville, TN

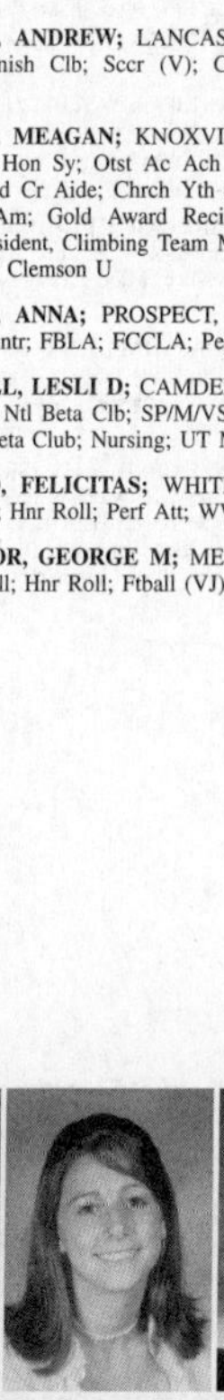
Noe, Leeanna M
Oliver Springs HS
Oliver Springs, TN

Oakley, Anna
Giles Cty HS
Prospect, TN

O'CONNOR, KATIE; COLLIERVILLE, TN; COLLIERVILLE HS; (JR); F Lan Hn Soc; Hnr Roll; MVP; Otst Ac Ach Awd; Sci Fairs; WWAHSS; Comm Volntr; Peer Tut/Med; Spec Olymp Vol; FCA; Key Club; Outdrs Clb; Pep Squd; Scouts; Clb; Track (V L); Pre-Med; UT Knoxville, M U of Alabama; UA Fayetteville, Ark U of Mississippi

O'CONNOR, KATLIN; MURFREESBORO, TN; BLACKMAN HS; (FR); Duke TS; St of Mnth; Comm Volntr; Key Club; Chr

O'CONNOR, RACHEL; MEMPHIS, TN; WHITE STATION HS; (FR); Ctznshp Aw; Duke TS; Hnr Roll; Perf Att; Comm Volntr; Peer Tut/Med; Chrch Yth Grp; FCA; Svce Clb; Latin Clb; Chr; Stu Cncl

ODHAM, JAMES T; SEYMOUR, TN; SEYMOUR HS; (SR); Hnr Roll; WWAHSS; Comm Volntr; Chrch Yth Grp; Drma Clb; Emplmnt; Ntl Beta Clb; Vsity Clb; Spanish Clb; SP/M/VS; Bskball (V L); Ftball (CL); Track (V CL); Education; Carson-Newman College

ODOM, MARRISSA; MURFREESBORO, TN; SIEGEL HS; (JR); 4H Awd; Ctznshp Aw; Hnr Roll; MVP; Sci Fairs; WWAHSS; Comm Volntr; Peer Tut/Med; ArtClub; Chrch Yth Grp; Emplmnt; Jr Cls League; Key Club; Ntl Beta Clb; Pep Squd; Photog; Bskball (VJ); National Art Honors Society; Teaching; Medical Assistant; Middle Tennessee State U; Shepard U

OGBONNAYA, KELECHI C; KINGSPORT, TN; DOBYNS BENNETT HS; (SR); MVP; Nat Hon Sy; WWAHSS; Emplmnt; FCA; Key Club; Ntl Beta Clb; Off Aide; Tchrs Aide; Spanish Clb; Bnd; Ch Chr; Mch Bnd; Bskball (J L); Track; Physical Therapy; U of Tennessee-Knoxville

OGLE, JOSH; SEYMOUR, TN; KINGS AC; (FR); Ctznshp Aw; Hi Hnr Roll; Hnr Roll; WWAHSS; Yth Ldrshp Prog; Chr; Ch Chr; Ftball (V); Pediatrician

OHM, ANDREA M; HARRISON, TN; CENTRAL HS; (SO); Hi Hnr Roll; Hnr Roll; Document Creation Award; Nominated-Nation Honor Who's Who; Business; UTC

OLIVER, KRISTEN L; FRANKLIN, TN; HAZARD HS; (SR); Hnr Roll; WWAHSS; 4-H; Off Aide; Prom Com; Tchrs Aide; Chrldg (V); Sch Ppr (R); Yrbk (R, P); Education (Childhood); Pharmacist; Morehead State U; Alice Lloyd College

OLIVER, MARIANA; MEMPHIS, TN; WHITE STATION HS; (FR); Ctznshp Aw; DAR; Duke TS; Hi Hnr Roll; Nat Hon Sy; Perf Att; Sci Fairs; Peer Tut/Med; JSA; Ntl Beta Clb; History; Design; Vanderbilt U; U of California, Berkeley

OLIVER, QUENTAVIOUS R; CHATTANOOGA, TN; EAST RIDGE HS; (SO); Hnr Roll; Otst Ac Ach Awd; St of Mnth; Yth Ldrshp Prog; FCA; Ntl Beta Clb; Scouts; Tech Clb; Voc Ind Clb Am; Bnd; SP/M/VS; Bskball (J); Stu Cncl (R); Boy Scouts; YMCA Leadership Conference; Major: Medicine, Science; Licensed Medical Practice; Austin Peay U; U of Tennessee-Knoxville

OLIVER, REBECCA; SODDY DAISY, TN; SODDY DAISY HS; (FR); Hnr Roll; Sci Fairs; Chrch Yth Grp; Key Club; Cl Off (T); Bowling Team - Varsity / Letter; Veterinarian; U of Alabama

OLIVER, WHITNEY E; KINGSPORT, TN; DOBYNS-BENNETT HS; (SO); Hnr Roll; French Clb; Bnd; Mch Bnd; Swmg (J); Chemical Engineering; Middle Tennessee State U

OLLIS, ANDY; ERWIN, TN; UNICOI CTY HS; (SO); Hnr Roll; WWAHSS; 4-H; Ntl FFA; German Clb; Bsball (V); Ftball (L); Landscape Management; Horticulture; U of Tennessee-Knoxville

OLSEN JR, JAMES G; HENDERSONVILLE, TN; HENDERSONVILLE CHRN AC; (FR); Hi Hnr Roll; MVP; Otst Ac Ach Awd; Pres Ac Ftns Aw; Sci Fairs; Comm Volntr; Chrch Yth Grp; Emplmnt; Spch Team; Chr; SP/M/VS; Bskball (VJCL); Golf (V); Sccr (V L); First Place in Art Competitions; Computers/Engineering; Pre-Law/Military Intelligence; Bob Jones U; West Point Military Academy

OLSWING, KIMBERLY; MEMPHIS, TN; RIDGEWAY HS; (JR); Hi Hnr Roll; Nat Hon Sy; WWAHSS; Comm Volntr; Emplmnt; Key Club; MuAlphaTh; SADD; Tmpl Yth Grp; William Sweet Award; Nursing; PR; U of North Carolina Chapel Hill; U of Georgia

O'NEAL, BRITTNEY A; M'BORO, TN; MONROE CTY CHRISTIAN AC; (FR); 4H Awd; Hnr Roll; Perf Att; Comm Volntr; 4-H; FCCLA; Hsbk Rdg; Cl Off (S); Carhart & Camo Club; Forensic Science; Middle Tennessee State U; Florida State

O'NEAL, YALISA; LEWISBURG, TN; MARSHALL CTY HS; (FR); 4H Awd; Hnr Roll; 4-H; Pep Squd; Ch Chr; Dnce; PP Ftbl (J); Was a Football Manager; X-Ray Technician; Pediatrician; Tennessee State U; Middle Tennessee State U

ORRAND, REBECCA M; FAIRVIEW, TN; FAIRVIEW HS; (SR); Hnr Roll; MVP; WWAHSS; Comm Volntr; Red Cr Aide; 4-H; ArtClub; Emplmnt; FCA; Key Club; Ntl FFA; Photog; Prom Com; Arch; Ftball; Hsbk Rdg; Skt Tgt Sh; Sftball (VJC); Vllyball (VJC); Wrstlg; Stu Cncl; Veterinary Technician; BS Minimum; U of Tennessee at Martin; Columbia State Community

ORTIZ, CRISTINA G; MEMPHIS, TN; WOODDALE HS; (JR); Hnr Roll; Sccr (V C); Kindergarten Teacher; Doctor; U of Memphis; Christian Brothers U

ORTIZ, KOSALBA P; COWAN, TN; FRANKLIN CTY HS; (JR); Hnr Roll; Nat Hon Sy; Perf Att; FBLA; Ntl Beta Clb; Sccr (V); Civil Engineer; Engineering (General); Middle Tennessee State U; The U of Alabama in Huntsville

ORTIZ, LEAH E; BRIGHTON, TN; BRIGHTON HS; (FR); Hi Hnr Roll; Otst Ac Ach Awd; Pres Sch; Sci Fairs; Sci/Math Olympn; Yth Ldrshp Prog; Chrch Yth Grp; Drma Clb; Lib Aide; Bnd; Mch Bnd; Pep Bnd; SP/M/VS; Community Theatre; Teen in Ministry; Forensic Scientist; Medical Doctor; Texas A & M U; U of Tennessee Knoxville

OSBORNE, CHRISTIE; CLARKSVILLE, TN; CLARKSVILLE HS; (JR); Hnr Roll; WWAHSS; Svce Clb; Bnd; Clr Grd; Mch Bnd; Pre-Law; Cumberland U; Tennessee Tech U

OSBORNE, JASMINE N; NASHVILLE, TN; MAPLEWOOD HS; Hnr Roll; Chr; Swg Chr; Bskball (V); Vllyball (V); Mass Communications; Journalism; Middle Tennessee State; Western Kentucky

OSBORNE, JONATHAN; ALAMO, TN; CROCKETT CO HS; (JR); Hnr Roll; Perf Att; WWAHSS; Ntl FFA

OSBORNE, SHARLEY N; MOUNTAIN CITY, TN; JOHNSON CTY HS; (SO); 4H Awd; Hnr Roll; 4-H; Scouts; SADD; Skiing (J); Clogging (High Country Christian); Daisy Assistant Leader for 5 Yr. Old Scouts; Law; Teaching; East Tennessee State U; Appalachian State U

OSMAN, RUWEIDA; NASHVILLE, TN; EAST LITERATURE MAGNET SCH; (JR); Ctznshp Aw; Peer Tut/Med; DARE; Pediatrician; Vanderbilt U; Tennessee State U

OSMENT, NICOLE; CAMDEN, TN; CAMDEN HS; (SO); Hnr Roll; WWAHSS; Spec Olymp Vol; 4-H; Chrch Yth Grp; DARE; DECA; FCA; Bskball (V); Ftball; Cl Off (S); Physical Therapy; Harding U; U of Alabama

OVERCAST, HALEY; MEMPHIS, TN; EVANGELICAL CHRISTIAN SCH; (SO); Duke TS; Hi Hnr Roll; Pres Sch; WWAHSS; Yth Ldrshp Prog; Comm Volntr; Chrch Yth Grp; Emplmnt; Key Club; Ntl Beta Clb; Tchrs Aide; Spanish Clb; SP/M/VS; Sftball (V L); Swmg (V CL); History; English; College of William & Mary; U of Virginia

OWEN, DANIELLE; COLLIERVILLE, TN; EVANGELICAL CHRISTIAN SCH; (SR); Duke TS; Hi Hnr Roll; Hnr Roll; Otst Ac Ach Awd; Perf Att; Pres Sch; WWAHSS; Yth Ldrshp Prog; Comm Volntr; Spec Olymp Vol; Chrch Yth Grp; Emplmnt; FCA; FTA; Key Club; Ntl Beta Clb; Off Aide; Pep Squd; Sftball (VJ L); Tennis (V L); Vllyball (VJCL); Cl Off (T); Yrbk (R); Education; Speech Pathology; Auburn U

OWENS, ASHLEY; MEMPHIS, TN; MELROSE HS; (FR); 4H Awd; Hi Hnr Roll; Otst Ac Ach Awd; Perf Att; St of Mnth; Comm Volntr; Mus Clb; Acpl Chr; Ch Chr; Sch Ppr (R); Honor Society for 3 Years; Graduated With Honors; Business Management / Sociology; Associate's / Bachelor's / Master's Degrees; Georgia State U; Princeton U

OWENS, JESSICA L; KNOXVILLE, TN; FARRAGUT HS; (FR); Duke TS; Yth Ldrshp Prog; Comm Volntr; Red Cr Aide; Chrch Yth Grp; Drma Clb; Emplmnt; Ch Chr; Nursing (Pediatrics); Architect/Home Designer; U of Tennessee; Vanderbilt

OWENS, JUSTON; KNOXVILLE, TN; BEREAN CHRISTIAN HS; (SO); Yth Ldrshp Prog; Comm Volntr; Golf; Tennis; Yrbk (P); Member of Student Panel; Medical; Tennessee; Vanderbilt

OWENS, KALON E; MEMPHIS, TN; NORTHSIDE HS; (JR); Hnr Roll; Otst Ac Ach Awd; Sci Fairs; WWAHSS; Comm Volntr; Peer Tut/Med; Jr Ach; Mus Clb; Quiz Bowl; Bnd; Mch Bnd; Pep Bnd; SP/M/VS; Sch Ppr (E); Yrbk (E, R, P); Mr. Sophomore 1st Alternate; Bridge Builder; Biotechnology; Pre-Med; U of Tennessee Knoxville; Coastal Carolina North Carolina

OWENS, KATIE; FRANKLIN, TN; FRANKLIN HS; (SO); 4H Awd; DAR; Hnr Roll; Comm Volntr; Chrch Yth Grp; Emplmnt; Ch Chr; Education (Teaching)

OWENS, PAMELA; GREENEVILLE, TN; SOUTH GREENE HS; (SR); Hnr Roll; Nat Hon Sy; Sci Fairs; St of Mnth; WWAHSS; FCCLA; FTA; Lib Aide; SADD; Tchrs Aide; Media Clb-President; FCCLA-Secretary; Master's in Education; Tusculum College

OXENDINE, SAVANNAH H; KNOXVILLE, TN; HALLS HS; (FR); 4H Awd; Ctznshp Aw; Duke TS; Hnr Roll; St of Mnth; WWAHSS; Hosp Aide; ArtClub; Chrch Yth Grp; DARE; Drma Clb; FCA; Pep Squd; Wdwrkg Clb; Ch Chr; SP/M/VS; Scr Kpr (J); Adv Cncl (R); Stu Cncl (R); CR (R); Photography; Custom Paint Jobs; U of Auburn; U of Louisiana

PACK, ROBERT C; ANDERSONVILLE, TN; ANDERSON CTY HS; (SO); Hi Hnr Roll; Nat Hon Sy; Otst Ac Ach Awd; WWAHSS; Comm Volntr; Peer Tut/Med; FCA; Lttrmn Clb; Spanish Clb; Bsball (V L); Ftball (V L); Mechanical Engineering / Aerospace Engineering; Sports Training / Coaching; Carson-Newman College; U of Tennessee

PAGE, BRITTNEY; CLARKSVILLE, TN; CLARKSVILLE HS; (JR); Duke TS; Hi Hnr Roll; WWAHSS; Comm Volntr; Chrch Yth Grp; Drma Clb; Emplmnt; FCA; Jr Cls League; Key Club; Svce Clb; Tchrs Aide; Sftball (J); Business Administration; Accounting; U of Tennessee Knoxville; Vanderbilt U

PAK, ETHELYN J; FRANKLIN, TN; CENTENNIAL HS; (JR); Gov Hnr Prg; Hi Hnr Roll; Pres Sch; WWAHSS; Peer Tut/Med; Red Cr Aide; Chrch Yth Grp; Mth Clb/Tm; MuAlphaTh; Ntl Beta Clb; Ch Chr; HOSA Secretary; Physician- Medical Field / Biochemistry; Biology; Vanderbilt U; Emory College / Main Campus

PALMER, TIFFANY; CLEVELAND, TN; CLEVELAND HS; (JR); Hnr Roll; Chrch Yth Grp; Prom Com; Cr Ctry (V); Track (V); Engineering; Education; Tennessee Tech; East Tennessee State U

PALMER, ZAVIER; MEMPHIS, TN; FRAYSER MIDDLE HS; (MS); Ctznshp Aw; Gov Hnr Prg; Hnr Roll; MVP; Nat Hon Sy; Otst Ac Ach Awd; Perf Att; St of Mnth; Yth Ldrshp Prog; Chess; Chrch Yth Grp; DARE; Mth Clb/Tm; Mus Clb; Quiz Bowl; Scouts; Ch Chr; Bsball (C); Bskball (C); Ftball (J); Wt Lftg (C); Stu Cncl (P); CR (P); I Want to Major in Math.

PANTCHER, ANDREY; MC EWEN, TN; MC EWEN HS; (JR); All Am Sch; 4-H; DARE; Ntl FFA; Sci Clb; Open Up My Own Shop; Nashville Auto Diesel College

PANTER, RANDY; WINCHESTER, TN; FRANKLIN CTY HS; (SR); Ctznshp Aw; Hnr Roll; Perf Att; St of Mnth; Spec Olymp Vol; Chrch Yth Grp; DARE; FCA; Scouts; SADD; Special Olympics-Track & Field, Swimming Bowling

PARIS, BRITTANY L.; JASPER, TN; MARION CTY HS; (JR); Duke TS; Hnr Roll; Otst Ac Ach Awd; WWAHSS; Chrch Yth Grp; FCA; Pep Squd; P to P St Amb Prg; Prom Com; Ch Chr; Bskball (V); PP Ftbl (V); Sftball (V); Vllyball (V); CR (V); All District and Best of Preps 1st Team; 2nd Team - Softball / Best Offensive Player Basketball; UTC Chattanooga; UT Knoxville

PARKER, ASHLEY L; BRADYVILLE, TN; F C BOYD CHRISTIAN SCH; (FR); 4H Awd; Hnr Roll; Hab For Humty Volntr; Peer Tut/Med; 4-H; Ntl Beta Clb; Hsbk Rdg (V); Vice President of Jr Beta Club, National; English Merit Award, National; Psychologist (Psychology); Middle Tennessee State U; Equine Science

PARKER, BRITANY; MEMPHIS, TN; WHITE STATION HS; (FR); Hnr Roll; Comm Volntr; Peer Tut/Med; Bnd; PhD; Memphis State

PARKER, GENNA; MURFREESBORO, TN; SIEGEL HS; (JR); All Am Sch; Duke TS; Hi Hnr Roll; Nat Hon Sy; Pres Sch; WWAHSS; Mth Clb/Tm; Sci Clb; German Clb; Dnce; SP/M/VS; Stg Cre; PPSqd (V); Cl Off (V); National Honor Society, Beta Club, Mu Alpha Theta, German Club; UT-Knoxville; Vanderbilt

PARKER II, GREGORY C; MEMPHIS, TN; WHITEHAVEN HS; (JR); Hnr Roll; WWAHSS; Chrch Yth Grp; DARE; Bnd; Jzz Bnd; Bachelor's of Arts and Music; U of Memphis; Berklee College of Music

PARKS, LAUREN E; TAZEWELL, TN; CLERBORNE HS; (JR); 4H Awd; Hnr Roll; Nat Hon Sy; Sci Fairs; WWAHSS; Comm Volntr; Hosp Aide; Spec Olymp Vol; 4-H; BPA; Key Club; Ntl Beta Clb; Off Aide; Prom Com; Sci Clb; Vsity Clb; Chrldg (V); Stu Cncl (S); Political Science; Investment Banking

PARNELL, LAUREN; WAVERLY, TN; WAVERLY CTRL HS; (JR); Hi Hnr Roll; Hnr Roll; WWAHSS; Comm Volntr; BPA; Emplmnt; FCCLA; Ntl Beta Clb; Tchrs Aide; Spanish Clb; Chr; I Was in the Eagle Squadron (Flying Club); The National Society of High School Scholars; Austin Peay State U; Belmont U

PARRISH, NATHAN B; MC EWEN, TN; MC EWEN HS; (JR); Ctznshp Aw; Hnr Roll; Jr Eng Tech; Otst Ac Ach Awd; Sci Fairs; Comm Volntr; ArtClub; Emplmnt; Ntl Beta Clb; Sci Clb; Bskball (J); Cr Ctry (V L); Golf (V CL); Cl Off (P, S); Nuclear Engineering; United States Naval Academy; United States Merchant Marine Academy

PARSONS, BRITTANY J; JONESBOROUGH, TN; DAVID CROCKETT HS; (FR); Fut Prb Slvr; Hnr Roll; St of Mnth; Peer Tut/Med; ArtClub; Chrch Yth Grp; DARE; FCA; Key Club; Ntl Beta Clb; ROTC; Scouts; Bnd; Mch Bnd; Pep Bnd; Cl Off (T); President's Award for Educational Excellence; Medicine; Forensic Scientist; New York U; Yale

PARTIN, KELLY; CHRISTIANA, TN; EAGLEVILLE SCH; (SO); Hnr Roll; Drma Clb; Emplmnt; Ntl Beta Clb; Prom Com; Spanish Clb; SP/M/VS; Sftball (V); Stu Cncl (R); CR (R); B.S.R.N; Middle Tennessee State U

PATEL, MITAL; WHITE PINE, TN; JEFFERSON CTY HS; (SO); Hi Hnr Roll; Hnr Roll; Perf Att; Sci/Math Olympn; USAA; Emplmnt; Key Club; Wrstlg; United States Achievement Academy; Key Club; Engineer; Mathematics; U of Tennessee-Knoxville; U of North Carolina-Asheville

PATRICK, JASON R; WAVERLY, TN; MC EWEN HS; (JR); 4H Awd; Hnr Roll; Otst Ac Ach Awd; Perf Att; Comm Volntr; Biology Clb; Chrch Yth Grp; FCA; Ntl Beta Clb; Ntl FFA; Sci Clb; Spanish Clb; Ftball (VJ L); Cl Off (T); All-American Christian Student Athlete; Physical Therapy; Automotive / Body Work; Austin Peay State U; Bethel U

Parker II, Gregory C
Whitehaven HS
Memphis, TN

Paris, Brittany L.
Marion Cty HS
Jasper, TN

Ogbonnaya, Kelechi C
Dobyns Bennett HS
Kingsport, TN

Panter, Randy
Franklin Cty HS
Winchester, TN

Parrish, Nathan B
Mc Ewen HS
Mc Ewen, TN

PATT, KELSEY; LAWRENCEBURG, TN; LAWRENCE CTY VOC CTR; (SO); Hi Hnr Roll; Nat Hon Sy; WWAHSS; Chrch Yth Grp; FBLA; Interior Design; U of Knoxville Tennessee; O'More

PATTERSON, CANDICE; ATOKA, TN; MUNFORD HS; (SO); Hnr Roll; Perf Att; WWAHSS; 4-H; Ntl FFA; Clr Grd; Archaeology; Astronomy

PATTERSON, DEXTER; MEMPHIS, TN; FAIRLEY HS; (SR); Ctznshp Aw; Hnr Roll; MVP; Nat Stu Ath Day Aw; Perf Att; Sci Fairs; WWAHSS; Comm Volntr; Chrch Yth Grp; DARE; FCA; Jr Ach; Vsity Clb; Ftball (V C); Track (V); CR (R); Volunteer for YMCA-Score Keeper; Tennessee State/ Alabama State/U of Memphis; Arkansas State

PATTERSON, LAKEISHA; MEMPHIS, TN; BOOKER T WASHINGTON HS; (FR); Ctznshp Aw; Hnr Roll; Perf Att; Chrch Yth Grp; DARE; Jr Ach; Ch Chr; Bskball (V); Cr Ctry (V); Sftball (V); Track (V); Most Defensive Player; Most Characteristic Award; Teaching; Day Care; Tennessee State U; Vanderbilt U

PATTERSON, RACHEL; MEMPHIS, TN; RIDGEWAY HS; (JR); Ctznshp Aw; Hi Hnr Roll; Hnr Roll; Nat Hon Sy; Otst Ac Ach Awd; Sci/Math Olympn; Yth Ldrshp Prog; Comm Volntr; Red Cr Aide; Drma Clb; Emplmnt; Key Club; Mod UN; MuAlphaTh; Quill & Scroll; SADD; Dnce; Co-President of Students Against Drunk Driving; Secretary of Key Club; Pre-Med / Medical School; Degree in History

PATTERSON, SARAH L; MEMPHIS, TN; GERMANTOWN HS; (JR); Comm Volntr; Chrch Yth Grp; Spanish Clb; Ch Chr; Essay Published in What Is Important to Me; Spring '05 Anthology; Pharmacy; Pre-Med; U of Tennessee At Knoxville; Washington U At St. Louis

PATTON, HANNAH; BIRCHWOOD, TN; MEJAS CTY HS; (SO); Ctznshp Aw; St of Mnth; WWAHSS; Comm Volntr; Dbte Team; Mus Clb; Chr; Girl Scouts of America; Registered Nurse; Crime Scene Investigator; U of Tennessee Knoxville; U of Tennessee Chattanooga

PATTON, JASMINE; MEMPHIS, TN; WHITE STATION HS; (FR); Ctznshp Aw; Hi Hnr Roll; Hnr Roll; Nat Hon Sy; Perf Att; Chrch Yth Grp; Chr; Ch Chr; Dnce; Outstanding Achievement Award; Pediatrician Doctor; U of Illinois; U of Los Angeles California

PATTON, KELLI L; MURFREESBORO, TN; BLACKMAN HS; (JR); Hi Hnr Roll; Hnr Roll; Nat Hon Sy; Perf Att; WWAHSS; Peer Tut/Med; Chrch Yth Grp; Key Club; Ntl Beta Clb; Sci Clb; Tchrs Aide; Spanish Clb; Cl Off; Stu Cncl (S); Renaissance Club; Bio-Genetics; Tennessee State U; Fisk U

PAYNE, CANDACE; SPRING CITY, TN; BLEDSOE CTY HS; (FR); 4H Awd; Hi Hnr Roll; Peer Tut/Med; 4-H; Emplmnt; FCCLA; Medical Doctor; Pediatrician; U of Tennessee Knoxville; Clemson U

PAYNE, JASMINE; NASHVILLE, TN; GOODPASTURE CHRISTIAN HS; (JR); Hi Hnr Roll; Hnr Roll; MVP; Nat Hon Sy; Perf Att; WWAHSS; Comm Volntr; Chrch Yth Grp; Emplmnt; FCA; Key Club; Pep Squd; Prom Com; Bskball (V); Scr Kpr (VJ); Track (V); Duke U; Vanderbilt U

PAZ, JOSHUA C; MC MINNVILLE, TN; WARREN CTY HS; (JR); Ctznshp Aw; Hi Hnr Roll; Hnr Roll; MVP; Otst Ac Ach Awd; Comm Volntr; Chrch Yth Grp; Emplmnt; FCA; Mth Clb/Tm; Ntl Beta Clb; Ftball (V); Track (V); Wt Lftg (V); U of TN At Knoxville; U of Louisville Kentucky

PEACE, LISA; ASHLAND CITY, TN; CHEATHAM CTY CTRL HS; (FR); Hnr Roll; Nat Sci Aw; Drma Clb; FCCLA; Scouts; President's Award; Pediatrician; Princeton U; Middle Tennessee U

PEDIGO, TINEKIA; RED BOILING SPRINGS, TN; HERMITAGE SPRINGS SCH; (JR); Hi Hnr Roll; Hnr Roll; WWAHSS; 4-H; FCCLA; Ntl Beta Clb; Prom Com; Cl Off (S); CR (S); Yrbk (E); Pre-Law; Pre-Physical Therapy; Vanderbilt; U of Tennessee At Knoxville

PENDERGRASS, CHRISTINA; ATHENS, TN; MC MINN CTY HS; (MS); Ctznshp Aw; Hnr Roll; Nat Hon Sy; St of Mnth; Hosp Aide; Chrch Yth Grp; Drma Clb; Emplmnt; Tchrs Aide; Yrbk (E); Foreign Affairs; History; Vanderbilt U; U of Tennessee

PENDERGRASS, WHITNEY N; BRISTOL, TN; THS; (FR); Ctznshp Aw; Hnr Roll; Otst Ac Ach Awd; Perf Att; Pres Ac Ftns Aw; DARE; FCA

PENNINGTON, TRAVIS C; CELINA, TN; CLAY CTY HS; (SO); Hnr Roll; Perf Att; Ftball (V); Wt Lftg (V); Business; Video Game Designer; Tennessee Technological U; U of Tennessee

PENNINGTON, WADE D; MEMPHIS, TN; ARLINGTON HS; (FR); Hnr Roll; Comm Volntr; Chrch Yth Grp; Emplmnt; FCA; Ntl Beta Clb; Bsball (J); Ftball (J); Broadcasting; Sports Management; U of Tennessee Knoxville; Freed-Hardeman U

PENNY, M SHANE; ESTILL SPRINGS, TN; FRANKLIN CTY HS; (JR); 4H Awd; Ctznshp Aw; Hnr Roll; MVP; 4-H; Chrch Yth Grp; DARE; FCA; Voc Ind Clb Am; Ftball (V CL); Wrstlg (V); Business Administration; U of Mississippi; U of Tennessee At Knoxville

PEPPARD, KIA H; CORDOVA, TN; OVERTON HS; (FR); Hnr Roll; DARE; Key Club; Mus Clb; Bnd; Clr Grd; Vllyball; Involvement in Inkwell Society (Writers Organization); Music; Psychology; Oberlin College

PERRITT, CAROL; MC KENZIE, TN; MC KENZIE HS; (SR); Hi Hnr Roll; Pres Sch; WWAHSS; Yth Ldrshp Prog; Hab For Humty Volntr; Peer Tut/Med; Chrch Yth Grp; FCA; Key Club; Lib Aide; Ntl Beta Clb; Sftball (V L); Cl Off (V); Sch Ppr (E); Yrbk (E); Mathematics Award; Danforth "I DARE You" Award; Biology; U of Tennessee Martin

PERRONE, KRISTEN; FRANKLIN, TN; CENTENNIAL HS; (JR); Hi Hnr Roll; Nat Hon Sy; Comm Volntr; Peer Tut/Med; Red Cr Aide; Emplmnt; Ntl Beta Clb; Off Aide; Prom Com; Chrldg (V); Stu Cncl (R); VP of Cert - Community Emergency Response Team; HOSA Parliamentarian; Nursing; Medical Field; Belmont U; UT Knoxville

PERRY, TINA J; WHITE HOUSE, TN; WHITE HOUSE HS; (JR); Hnr Roll; Chrch Yth Grp; Key Club; Ntl Beta Clb; Latin Clb; Chr; Ch Chr; Superior in Middle Tennessee Solo & Ensem; National Youth Leadership Forum of Nursing; Science; Nursing; Aquinas College (Nashville); Vol-State CC

PETERS, BRITNEE L; MEMPHIS, TN; WHITE STATION HS; (FR); Ctznshp Aw; Hi Hnr Roll; Hnr Roll; Otst Ac Ach Awd; Perf Att; Pres Sch; St of Mnth; Peer Tut/Med; Sci Clb; Scouts; Spanish Clb; National Junior Honor Society (Grade7-8); Medicine

PETERSEN, ROCIO; MEMPHIS, TN; RIDGEWAY HS; (SR); F Lan Hn Soc; Hi Hnr Roll; Hnr Roll; Nat Hon Sy; St of Mnth; WWAHSS; Yth Ldrshp Prog; Comm Volntr; Chrch Yth Grp; Fr of Library; Key Club; MuAlphaTh; Scouts; French Clb; Bell South Student Exchange to South Africa; City Language Fair - 1st Place French II Poetry; Biology; Spanish; Hendrix College; U of Oregon

PETERSON, BENJAMIN T; ERWIN, TN; UNICOI CTY HS; (SR); F Lan Hn Soc; Hnr Roll; MVP; Nat Hon Sy; Pres Ac Ftns Aw; WWAHSS; ArtClub; FCA; Ntl Beta Clb; Ntl FFA; Bsball (V CL); Ftball (V L); All Conference Baseball; All District Tournament & All Regional Teams; Physical Therapy; Business/Communications; East Tennessee State U; King College, Carson-Newman U

PETERSON, JOSHUA M; UNICOI, TN; U N 1001 CTY VOC SCH; (SR); 4H Awd; All Am Sch; Hnr Roll; Nat Hon Sy; Otst Ac Ach Awd; Perf Att; Pres Ac Ftns Aw; Sci Fairs; WWAHSS; Comm Volntr; 4-H; Emplmnt; Ntl FFA; Quiz Bowl; Voc Ind Clb Am; Spanish Clb; Landscape Architecture; Civil Engineering; U of Tennessee; Northeast State Technical Community College

PETTY, SAMUEL H; LEWISBURG, TN; MARSHALL CO HS; (FR); WWAHSS

PETTYS, ALI; FRANKLIN, TN; CENTENNIAL HS; (SO); Ctznshp Aw; Hi Hnr Roll; Otst Ac Ach Awd; Sci Fairs; Comm Volntr; Peer Tut/Med; Chrch Yth Grp; FCA; Ntl Beta Clb; Chr; Stg Cre; Sccr (V L); Track (V); Yrbk (P); Personal Fitness Trainer; Sports Medicine; U of Florida; U of Texas Austin

PHELPS, DOMINIQUE N; MEMPHIS, TN; RIDGEWAY HS; (SO); Hi Hnr Roll; Hnr Roll; WWAHSS; Comm Volntr; Chrch Yth Grp; Key Club; Bnd; Ch Chr; Pep Bnd; Stu Cncl; Bridge Builders; Heath Sciences & Allied Health Fields; Duke U; U of Miami

PHILLIPPI, SAMANTHA; BRISTOL, TN; SULLIVAN EAST HS; (SR); 4H Awd; Ctznshp Aw; Hnr Roll; WWAHSS; Comm Volntr; Hosp Aide; 4-H; Chrch Yth Grp; DARE; FCA; FCCLA; Spanish Clb; Ch Chr; Participant in Miss Pre-Teen TN Pageant; Physical Therapy; Northeast State; Walter State

PHILLIPS, LAYNE L; WAVERLY, TN; WAVERLY CTRL HS; (SO); Hi Hnr Roll; Hnr Roll; Nat Hon Sy; USAA; WWAHSS; Chrch Yth Grp; Lib Aide; Mod UN; Tchrs Aide; Sftball (V); Football Manager; Interior Design; Business Related; Middle Tennessee State U; U of Tennessee At Knoxville

PHILLIPS, MALLORY; WAVERLY, TN; WAVERLY CTRL HS; (JR); Hi Hnr Roll; Hnr Roll; USAA; WWAHSS; Yth Ldrshp Prog; Comm Volntr; 4-H; BPA; Chrch Yth Grp; Lib Aide; Mod UN; Ntl Beta Clb; Stu Cncl (R); Yrbk (R); American Legion Girls State Alternate; Model United Nations Best Delegate; International Relations; Mass Communications; Middle Tennessee State U; New York U

PHIPPS, CHRISTOPHER; STRAWBERRY PLAINS, TN; JEFFERSON CTY HS; (JR); Ctznshp Aw; Hnr Roll; Perf Att; USAA; Yth Ldrshp Prog; Comm Volntr; Peer Tut/Med; Spec Olymp Vol; Chrch Yth Grp; Drma Clb; FCA; Mus Clb; Ntl Beta Clb; Pep Squd; Chr; SP/M/VS; CR (R); Pre-Law; Business Administration; U of Vanderbilt; U of Texas-Austin

PIERCE, AINSLEY J; KNOXVILLE, TN; SOUTH DOYLE HS; (SO); Duke TS; Hi Hnr Roll; Nat Hon Sy; Chrch Yth Grp; DARE; Key Club; MuAlphaTh; Spanish Clb; Dvng (V); 2004 and 2005 Female TN State High School Diving Champion; Medical Doctor

PIERCEFIELD, BAILEY N; COTTONTOWN, TN; WHITE HOUSE HERITAGE HS; MS; Hnr Roll; MVP; Otst Ac Ach Awd; Comm Volntr; Hab For Humty Volntr; Chrch Yth Grp; Ntl Beta Clb; Bskball (J); Chrldg (J); Cr Ctry (V); Sftball (V); Stu Cncl (R); Hometown Insurance Player of the Week 4 Times, Social Studies Excellence Award; Principal's Award/Most Likely to Succeed

PIGG, ANNA M; PULASKI, TN; GILES CTY HS; (JR); Gov Hnr Prg; Hi Hnr Roll; Hnr Roll; Chrch Yth Grp; FCA; FTA; Ntl Beta Clb; Prom Com; Scouts; International Clb; Bnd; Jzz Bnd; Mch Bnd; Pep Bnd; Stu Cncl (R); Business; Music Education; Tennessee Technological U; U of Alabama-Huntsville

PIGG, MICHELE; IRON CITY, TN; COLLINWOOD; (SO); Hnr Roll; WWAHSS; Comm Volntr; Emplmnt; FTA; Ntl Beta Clb; Ntl FFA; Beautician; Registered Nurse; Columbia State Community College; U of North Alabama

PINKARD, ANDREA; MURFREESBORO, TN; BLACKMAN HS; (JR); Hi Hnr Roll; Hnr Roll; Pres Ac Ftns Aw; St of Mnth; WWAHSS; Comm Volntr; DARE; Emplmnt; Key Club; Ntl Beta Clb; Pep Squd; Photog; Tchrs Aide; Spanish Clb; Yrbk (P); Photography; Middle Tennessee State U; San Francisco Art Institute

PIPPENGER, RANDALL; ADAMSVILLE, TN; ADAMSVILLE HS; (SO); Duke TS; Hi Hnr Roll; Nat Hon Sy; Otst Ac Ach Awd; Pres Sch; WWAHSS; Comm Volntr; Peer Tut/Med; Chrch Yth Grp; Emplmnt; FCA; Mod UN; Ntl Beta Clb; NYLC; Ch Chr; Ftball (V); Vsy Clb (V); Wt Lftg (V); Law; History; Harvard; Yale

PITMAN, LAUREN N; HAMPTON, TN; HAMPTON HS; (JR); Hnr Roll; WWAHSS; Comm Volntr; Peer Tut/Med; Red Cr Aide; ArtClub; Chrch Yth Grp; Drma Clb; Emplmnt; FCA; Lib Aide; Pep Squd; Vsity Clb; Bskball (V); Sftball (V); Stu Cncl; Yrbk (P); Who's Who; Psychology; Business; Milligan College; East Tennessee State U

PITTS, KELLY; MEMPHIS, TN; WHITE STATION HS; (JR); Ctznshp Aw; F Lan Hn Soc; Hi Hnr Roll; Nat Hon Sy; Perf Att; Comm Volntr; Hab For Humty Volntr; Peer Tut/Med; Chrch Yth Grp; DECA; P to P St Amb Prg; Svce Clb; Spanish Clb; Dnce; Cl Off (R); Stu Cncl (R); CR (R); Yrbk (E); International Business; Spanish; U of Georgia; Auburn

PIVNICK, LILLA; MEMPHIS, TN; WHITE STATION HS; (FR); DAR; Hi Hnr Roll; Nat Hon Sy; Nat Sci Aw; USAA; WWAHSS; Comm Volntr; Drma Clb; Svce Clb; Acpl Chr; Chr; Orch; SP/M/VS; Cl Off (R); Stu Cncl; CR (R); Novus Canticus: Youth Chorale; Thespian Club; Archaeology, History; Evolutionary Biology/Genetics; North Western U; Yale U

PLOUCHA, BRET; JOHNSON CITY, TN; (SO); Hnr Roll; Comm Volntr; Chr; Bsball; Ftball; Psychology; Criminal Justice; U of North Carolina-Wilmington; Coastal Carolina U

POE, SARAH; DECATUR, TN; MEIGS CTY HS; (JR); F Lan Hn Soc; Hnr Roll; Perf Att; Pres Ac Ftns Aw; St of Mnth; WWAHSS; Comm Volntr; Peer Tut/Med; Chrch Yth Grp; Ntl FFA; ROTC; Sci Clb; Tchrs Aide; Spanish Clb; Drl Tm; Tennis (V); Nursing; Navy; U of North Carolina-Chapel Hill

POINTER JR, JAMES L; TALLASSEE, TN; WILLIAM BLOUNT HS; (SR); Hi Hnr Roll; Hnr Roll; MVP; USAA; WWAHSS; Comm Volntr; Business Degree; Culinary Degree; North Carolina U; U of Tennessee

POLAND, AMANDA; OLIVER SPRINGS, TN; OLIVER SPRINGS HS; (JR); Duke TS; Hnr Roll; WWAHSS; Comm Volntr; Peer Tut/Med; Chrch Yth Grp; Drma Clb; Emplmnt; FCA; Ntl Beta Clb; Prom Com; Vsity Clb; SP/M/VS; Stg Cre; Bskball (V); Cr Ctry (V); PP Ftbl (V); Sftball (V); Stu Cncl (R); Organized Own Volunteer Programs; Criminal Justice; Elementary Education; Belmont U; U of Tennessee Knoxville

POLKA, NEELEY; HENDERSONVILLE, TN; STATION CAMP HS; (JR); Duke TS; Nat Hon Sy; WWAHSS; Comm Volntr; AL Aux Girls; Chrch Yth Grp; DECA; FCA; FCCLA; Jr Cls League; Ntl Beta Clb; Prom Com; Ch Chr; Chrldg (V CL); Stu Cncl (S, T); Psychology; Marketing; U of Tennessee Knoxville; Emory U

POLLARD, CASSIE L; SODDY DAISY, TN; SODDY-DAISY HS; (FR); Hi Hnr Roll; Hnr Roll; Perf Att; Chrch Yth Grp; Ntl Beta Clb; Ch Chr; Participant in State Level Reader's Digest (National Word Power); Member of Church Basketball Team; Forensics (CSI); U of Tennessee Chattanooga; U of Tennessee Knoxville

POOLE, LANESHIA C; NASHVILLE, TN; STRATFORD HS; (FR); Hnr Roll; Otst Ac Ach Awd; Perf Att; St of Mnth; Comm Volntr; Chrch Yth Grp; DARE; Dbte Team; Emplmnt; Jr Ach; Ntl Beta Clb; Pep Squd; Scouts; Bnd; Ch; Ch Chr; Chrldg (V); PPSqd (V); Sftball (V); Stu Cncl (T); Yrbk (E); Medical; Vanderbilt U

POORE, ASHLEY N; TRENTON, TN; GIBSON CTY HS; (SO); Hi Hnr Roll; Hnr Roll; Perf Att; WWAHSS; Comm Volntr; Chrch Yth Grp; Emplmnt; FCA; Bskball (V L); Cr Ctry (V L); Sftball (V L); Math Major; Education; Union U; U of Tennessee @ Martin

POORE, DUSTIN; NEW TAZEWELL, TN; CLAIBORNE HS; (SR); Hnr Roll; Nat Hon Sy; Sci Fairs; Sci/Math Olympn; WWAHSS; Peer Tut/Med; Spec Olymp Vol; 4-H; Chrch Yth Grp; Key Club; Ch Chr; Bskball (V CL); Golf; Tennis (V C); Cl Off (V); Medical Field; Physical Therapist; U of Tennessee Knoxville

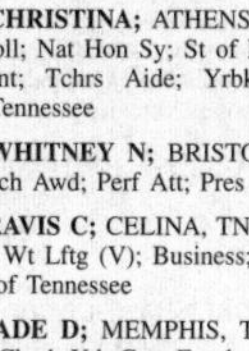
Pigg, Anna M
Giles Cty HS
Pulaski, TN

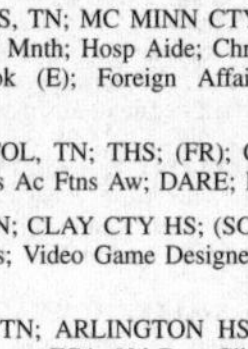
Petty, Samuel H
Marshall Co HS
Lewisburg, TN

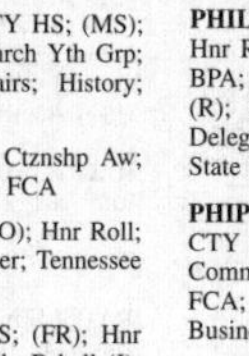
Perry, Tina J
White House HS
White House, TN

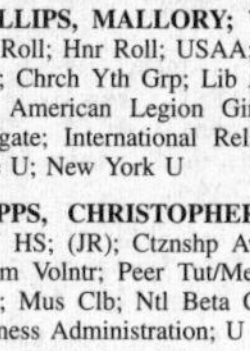
Pennington, Travis C
Clay Cty HS
Celina, TN

National
Honor Roll
Spring 2005

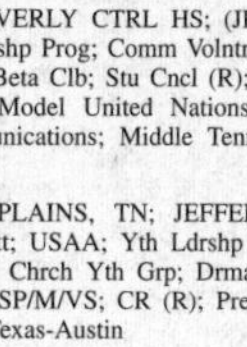
Patton, Hannah
Mejas Cty HS
Birchwood, TN

Peterson, Benjamin T
Unicoi Cty HS
Erwin, TN

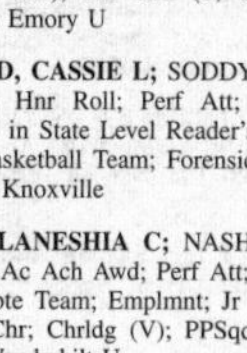
Piercefield, Bailey N
White House Heritage HS
Cottontown, TN

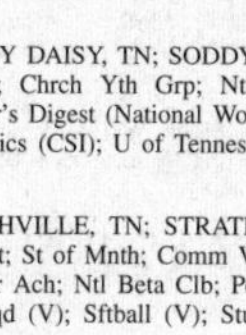
Pitman, Lauren N
Hampton HS
Hampton, TN

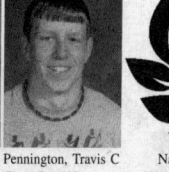

POPE, ASHLEY; CLEVELAND, TN; CLEVELAND HS; (SR); F Lan Hn Soc; Hi Hnr Roll; Nat Hon Sy; Otst Ac Ach Awd; Sci Fairs; Sci/Math Olympn; St of Mnth; WWAHSS; Comm Volntr; Peer Tut/Med; Cmptr Clb; DARE; Emplmnt; Mth Clb/Tm; Ntl Beta Clb; Svce Clb; Tchrs Aide; Tech Clb; PP Ftbl (J); Certified Web Master I; Certified Web Master II; Computer Tech; Lee U Cleveland TN

POPE, JOSHUA; LA VERGNE, TN; LA VERGNE HS; (JR); Hnr Roll; Perf Att; WWAHSS; ROTC; Scouts; Yrbk (R, P); Eagle Scout; Excalibur Science National Honor Society; Criminal Justice; Political Science; Austin Peay State U; United States Air Force Academy

POPE, RACHEL; CLARKSVILLE, TN; NORTHWEST HS; (FR); Sci Fairs; Veterinary Science; Tufts U

POPE JR, KEVIN B; WOODBURY, TN; CANNON CTY HS; (JR); 4H Awd; Hi Hnr Roll; Hnr Roll; MVP; Perf Att; Comm Volntr; 4-H; Biology Clb; Chrch Yth Grp; DARE; Emplmnt; FCA; Ntl Beta Clb; Ntl FFA; Bsball (V); Bskball (V); Ftball (V); Mechanical Engineering

PORTER, JAMIE C; THORN HILL, TN; WASHBURN SCH; (JR); Comm Volntr; FBLA; Spanish Clb; Sftball (V); Photography; Pharmacy Technician; Walter State Community College; Lincoln Memorial U

POSTER, ANGELA; KODAK, TN; SEVIER CTY HS; (FR); Ctznshp Aw; Hnr Roll; St of Mnth; Comm Volntr; Chrch Yth Grp; Ntl Beta Clb; Ch Chr; Veterinary Science; Marine Science; Walters State; U of Tennessee

POSTON, SAMANTHA J; LEBANON, TN; LEBANON HS; (SR); Hi Hnr Roll; Hnr Roll; WWAHSS; Comm Volntr; Spec Olymp Vol; Chrch Yth Grp; DARE; Emplmnt; Fr of Library; Key Club; Mus Clb; NtlFrnscLg; Scouts; Chr; Clr Grd; HOSA Secretary; Key Club Bulletin Editor; Nursing Bachelor of Science; Cumberland U; Middle Tennessee State U

POWELL, CHRISTOPHER G; HIXSON, TN; SODDY DAISY HS; (FR); Ctznshp Aw; Duke TS; Hnr Roll; WWAHSS; Comm Volntr; FCA; Bskball (J); History Award; Building Construction; History; U of Florida; US Naval Academy

POWERS, ADAM; ATHENS, TN; ATHENS JHS; (MS); Duke TS; Hi Hnr Roll; Nat Hon Sy; Otst Ac Ach Awd; Perf Att; Comm Volntr; Ntl Beta Clb; Bsball (V); Bskball (V); Ftball (V); Victor General; Radiology; Communications / Broadcast Journalism; U of Tennessee Knoxville; U of Oklahoma

POWERS, ZACKARY; ASHLAND CITY, TN; SYCAMORE HS; (JR); Hnr Roll; Nat Hon Sy; WWAHSS; Comm Volntr; 4-H; Chrch Yth Grp; DARE; Emplmnt; Pep Squd; Sccr (V); Wt Lftg (V); Business; Architecture; Vanderbilt U; Austin Peay State U

PRATER, CORY C; PIKEVILLE, TN; BLEDSOE CTY HS; (MS); 4H Awd; Hi Hnr Roll; Sci/Math Olympn; Comm Volntr; 4-H; Mth Clb/Tm; Ntl Beta Clb; Ftball (V); U of Tennessee Knoxville; U of Tennessee Chattanooga

PRATER, DUSTIN G; WOODBURY, TN; CANNON CTY HS; (JR); Hnr Roll; Nat Hon Sy; Nat Stu Ath Day Aw; Perf Att; Pres Ac Ftns Aw; WWAHSS; FCA; Ntl Beta Clb; Ntl FFA; SP/M/VS; Pharmacy; Computer Programming; Middle Tennessee State U

PRESLEY, BRITTNEY L; MURFREESBORO, TN; BLACKMAN HS; (JR); Hnr Roll; WWAHSS; Comm Volntr; Chrch Yth Grp; Emplmnt; Key Club; Ntl Beta Clb; Pep Squd; Spanish Clb; Pre-Med; Middle Tennessee State U

PRICE, JESSICA M M; JOHNSON CITY, TN; HAMPTON HS; (JR); All Am Sch; Hnr Roll; Jr Mshl; Nat Hon Sy; USAA; WWAHSS; Comm Volntr; ArtClub; Chrch Yth Grp; FCA; Lib Aide; NYLC; Spanish Clb; Bskball (V C); Cl Off (S, T); Yrbk (E, P); Algebra ll Award for Highest Average; New York City Mission Trip; East Tennessee State U; Milligan College

PRICE, MEIOSHA; MEMPHIS, TN; WHITEHAVEN HS; (JR); Hi Hnr Roll; Sci Fairs; St of Mnth; WWAHSS; Peer Tut/Med; DECA; Drma Clb; Emplmnt; Key Club; Prom Com; Spanish Clb; Chr; Nursing; Fashion Design; Middle Tennessee College

PRICE, PAIGE; BENTON, TN; POLK CTY HS; (FR); 4H Awd; Hnr Roll; 4-H; Chrch Yth Grp; FCA; Pep Squd; Dental Hygienist; Tennessee Wesleyan U

PRIJATEL, BENJAMIN; KNOXVILLE, TN; SOUTH DOYLE HS; (SR); Perf Att; St of Mnth; WWAHSS; Comm Volntr; Peer Tut/Med; Chrch Yth Grp; DECA; FBLA; Key Club; Prom Com; Schol Bwl; Tchrs Aide; Latin Clb; Bnd; Mch Bnd; Tennis (V); Cl Off (V); CR (R); Sch Ppr (E); Yrbk (P); Talent Show MC; Journalism and Electronic Media; Political Science; U of Tennessee

PRINCE, AMY; COPPERHILL, TN; COPPER BASIN HS; (SO); Hnr Roll; Comm Volntr; 4-H; Chrch Yth Grp; DARE; Emplmnt; FBLA; Key Club; Ntl Beta Clb; Prom Com; Bskball (V); Cl Off (V); Yrbk (R, P); Football Manager; Superlatives (Friendliest, Together Forever); Education (Teaching); Psychology; U of Tennessee At Knoxville; Lee U

PRINCE, NICHOLAS A; SWEETWATER, TN; SWEETWATER HS; (SR); All Am Sch; Hi Hnr Roll; Perf Att; Sci Fairs; Sci/Math Olympn; Valdctrian; WWAHSS; Peer Tut/Med; Emplmnt; Ntl Beta Clb; Sci Clb; Tchrs Aide; Valedictorian, Excellence Award Eng. I, II, III, IV; Monroe County Skeet Clay Target Shooting, 9th in State; Pharmacy; Tennessee Technical U; Maryville College

PROCTOR, AUNDREA; DRUMMONDS, TN; MUNFORD HS; (SR); Hnr Roll; Nat Hon Sy; Nat Mrt LOC; Otst Ac Ach Awd; WWAHSS; Chrch Yth Grp; FTA; Ntl FFA; Off Aide; Bnd; Mch Bnd; PP Ftbl (VJ); Track (J); High School Broadcasting; Agriculture; U of Tennessee Martin

PROFFITT, JESSICA D; LEBANON, TN; GORDONSVILLE HS; (JR); Perf Att; Chrch Yth Grp; Emplmnt; Off Aide; SADD; Voc Ind Clb Am; Spanish Clb; Chr; Bskball (V); Cl Off (S); Secretary of Skills USA; A Member Of SADD; Criminal Justice; Law; Vol State; Cumberland U

PROGAR, JORDAN A; EAGLEVILLE, TN; EAGLEVILLE SCH; (SO); Ctznshp Aw; Hnr Roll; Nat Hon Sy; Nat Mrt Sch Recip; Otst Ac Ach Awd; Comm Volntr; Chrch Yth Grp; FCA; ROTC; Spanish Clb; Clr Grd; Drl Tm; Lawyer; Political Science; West Point

PRUETT, HANK; CLARKSVILLE, TN; CLARKSVILLE HS; (JR); WWAHSS; Comm Volntr; Drma Clb; French Clb; Acpl Chr; Chr; SP/M/VS; Stg Cre; Ftball (J); Wt Lftg (V); Wrstlg (V); Lit Mag (E); International Thespian Society President; Video Production and Tech; Professional Theatre; Theatre Teacher

PRUETT, MICHELLE; BRADYVILLE, TN; CANNON CTY HS; (JR); Hnr Roll; WWAHSS; Comm Volntr; FCCLA; Off Aide; Ch Chr; Lioness Club; Teacher; Librarian; Motlow U; Middle Tennessee State U

PRYOR, JORDAN A; MEMPHIS, TN; CENTRAL HS; (SO); Hi Hnr Roll; Hnr Roll; Hab For Humty Volntr; Peer Tut/Med; Chrch Yth Grp; Fr of Library; MuAlphaTh; Ch Chr; Sch Ppr; Recreational Basketball - City of Memphis; Mentoring Program MIFA; PhD in Medicine; Business Master's Degree; U of Memphis; Moorehouse College

PUCKETT, JENNA; CLARKSVILLE, TN; CLARKSVILLE HS; (JR); Duke TS; Nat Hon Sy; WWAHSS; Drma Clb; Emplmnt; Svce Clb; Tchrs Aide; SP/M/VS; Stg Cre; Lit Mag (E); International Thespian Society; BFA; Film Major / Directing; Watkins Institute; Tulane U

PUCKETT, MALINDA; CLARKSVILLE, TN; NORTHEAST HS; (JR); Hnr Roll; Sci/Math Olympn; WWAHSS; Peer Tut/Med; Red Cr Aide; DECA; Drma Clb; FTA; Key Club; Mth Clb/Tm; Ntl Beta Clb; Photog; Sci Clb; Pharmacy; Special Education; U of Tennessee-Knoxville; Ohio State

PUGH, RACHEL; JACKSON, TN; JACKSON CHRISTIAN SCH; (SR); Duke TS; Hi Hnr Roll; Jr Rot; MVP; Nat Hon Sy; USAA; WWAHSS; Hab For Humty Volntr; Spec Olymp Vol; Chrch Yth Grp; FCA; MuAlphaTh; Vsity Clb; Chr; SP/M/VS; Bskball (V L); Sccr (V CL); Track (V CL); Harding U

PUGH, WHITNEY L; CROSSVILLE, TN; CUMBERLAND CO HS; (JR); Hi Hnr Roll; Hnr Roll; Peer Tut/Med; Chrch Yth Grp; Emplmnt; FCA; Ntl Beta Clb; Off Aide; Spanish Clb; Chr; Ch Chr; Mch Bnd; Majorette in Marching Band for 3 Years; Algebra 1 Award; Communications; Pre-Med; Belmont U; East Tennessee State U

PULLIAM, MEGAN W; ALAMO, TN; CROCKETT CTY HS; (FR); Hi Hnr Roll; Comm Volntr; Chrch Yth Grp; DARE; FCA; Ntl Beta Clb; Ntl FFA; Pep Squd; SADD; Ch Chr; Chrldg (V); Tennis (V); Cl Off (V); Class Favorite

PURDIE, ANGELA L; ATHENS, TN; MC MINN CTY HS; (JR); 4H Awd; Hi Hnr Roll; Hnr Roll; Nat Hon Sy; Perf Att; Pres Ac Ftns Aw; WWAHSS; 4-H; Chrch Yth Grp; FBLA; Ntl FFA; Tchrs Aide; Chr; Ch Chr; FFA Chapter Secretary; 4-H Chapter Secretary; Speech Therapy; Veterinary Medicine; U of Tennessee Knoxville; Middle Tennessee State U

PURSLEY, JESSICA D; MURFREESBORO, TN; SIEGAL HS; (JR); 4H Awd; Hnr Roll; Nat Mrt LOC; St of Mnth; WWAHSS; Comm Volntr; 4-H; Civil Air Pat; Jr Ach; Jr Cls League; ROTC; Scouts; Latin Clb; Ch Chr; Gmnstcs (V); Sftball (V); Sch Ppr (E, R, P); Yrbk (R, P); Marine Biology; Physician; U of West Florida; U of Charleston S Carolina

PUTMAN, ZACK; DYERSBURG, TN; NORTHSIDE CHRISTIAN AC; (JR); Hnr Roll; X-Ray Technician; EMT; Jackson State U; Dyersburg State Community College

PYLANT, JESSIE; PULASKI, TN; GILES CTY HS; (JR); Hnr Roll; Sci/Math Olympn; WWAHSS; Mus Clb; Sci Clb; Scouts; Bnd; Jzz Bnd; Mch Bnd; Pep Bnd; Most Improved Underclassman; Most Outstanding Sophomore; Aerospace Engineering; U of Alabama Huntsville; U of Tennessee Knoxville

QUARLES, ANNIE; CORDOVA, TN; EVANGELICAL CHRISTIAN SCH; (FR); Ctznshp Aw; Hi Hnr Roll; Nat Mrt LOC; Pres Ac Ftns Aw; WWAHSS; Key Club; Off Aide; Pep Squd; Dnce; Stg Cre; New York U; Baylor U

QUARLES, BRYANA K; NASHVILLE, TN; NASHVILLE SCH OF THE ARTS; (SR); Perf Att; Comm Volntr; Chrch Yth Grp; FCA; Off Aide; Tchrs Aide; Bnd; Ch Chr; Orch; Music Engineer/Producer; Massage Therapy; Middle Tennessee State U; Tennessee State U

QUARLES, JERRE; MEMPHIS, TN; KIRBY HS; (FR); Ctznshp Aw; Hi Hnr Roll; Hnr Roll; Perf Att; Business Management; Lawyer; U of Tennessee; U of Memphis

QUARLES, SHAQUITA; ANTIOCH, TN; ANTIOCH HS; (JR); Hnr Roll; Nat Hon Sy; Perf Att; Sci Fairs; Biology Clb; Chrch Yth Grp; DARE; Jr Ach; Pep Squd; Prom Com; Ch Chr; Clr Grd; Dnce; Mch Bnd; Stu Cncl (S); Vanderbilt Law School

QUIJANO, JENNIFER N; CLARKSVILLE, TN; THOMSON HS; (SR); Hnr Roll; Ch Chr; Ice Sktg (L); To Become a Biologist; Austin Peay State U; ITT Tech

QUILLEN, KIMBERLY F; ERWIN, TN; U N 1001 CTY VOC SCH; (SR); WWAHSS; Chrch Yth Grp; FTA; Key Club; Ntl Beta Clb; Ntl FFA; State FFA Degree; Floriculture Team; Kindergarten Teacher; East Tennessee State U; Northeast Community College

RAGAN, SARA; ERWIN, TN; UNICOI CTY HS; (SR); ArtClub; Chrch Yth Grp; Emplmnt; Key Club; Lib Aide; Pep Squd; Tchrs Aide; German Clb; Ch Chr; CR (R); Yrbk; Cutest Couple with My Boyfriend Steven Light (Voted in By Sr. Class); Early Childhood Education; East Tennessee State U

RAGSDALE, KATHERINE L; SPRING HILL, TN; CULLEOKA UNIT SCH; MS; 4H Awd; Hnr Roll; Comm Volntr; 4-H; DARE; Off Aide; Svce Clb; Vllyball (J); Seeds of Service Grant to Build; Press Box At Ball Field & Paint Buildings; Nursing At U of Tennessee; U of Tennessee

RAINEY, DORCAS E; MEMPHIS, TN; CENTRAL HS; (JR); Hnr Roll; Kwnis Aw; WWAHSS; Comm Volntr; Chrch Yth Grp; Emplmnt; Key Club; Mus Clb; Quill & Scroll; Chr; Ch Chr; Yrbk (R); 2005 - Miss Junior; Business Executive; Magazine Editor; Howard U; Tennessee State U

RAINEY, JEROMY; SAVANNAH, TN; HARDIN CTY HS; (SR); 4H Awd; Ctznshp Aw; WWAHSS; Yth Ldrshp Prog; 4-H; BPA; Chrch Yth Grp; Emplmnt; Outdrs Clb; Chr; SP/M/VS; UT Martin

RAINEY, SAMANTHA; FRANKLIN, TN; CENTENNIAL HS; (JR); Hi Hnr Roll; Otst Ac Ach Awd; Comm Volntr; Hab For Humty Volntr; Peer Tut/Med; Emplmnt; Mth Clb/Tm; MuAlphaTh; Tchrs Aide; Vllyball (J); Sch Ppr; Teens N Touch / Stars; U of Tennessee

RALLS, THOMAS; SMYRNA, TN; BLACKMAN HS; (SR); Hi Hnr Roll; Hnr Roll; Otst Ac Ach Awd; WWAHSS; Comm Volntr; BPA; Chrch Yth Grp; Emplmnt; Key Club; Ntl Beta Clb; Sci Clb; Tchrs Aide; Spanish Clb; Bnd; Jzz Bnd; Mch Bnd; Pep Bnd; Computer Emphasis Award; All-Rutherford County Honor Band; Music Education; Computer Generated Imagery; Middle Tennessee State U

RAMOS, MICHAEL; NASHVILLE, TN; MC GAVOCK COMP HS; (JR); Hnr Roll; Nat Hon Sy; St of Mnth; Comm Volntr; Orch; Community Volunteer

RAMSDALE, JACKIE; KINGSPORT, TN; DOBYNS BENNETT HS; (SR); Hi Hnr Roll; MVP; Nat Hon Sy; WWAHSS; Comm Volntr; Key Club; Ntl Beta Clb; Bskball (V L); Sftball (VJ L); Vllyball (V CL); Wendy's High School Heisman Award Nominee; Physician Assistant; Pharmacy; U of Tennessee, Knoxville

RANDOLPH, TURNER; CLEVELAND, TN; BRADLEY CTRL HS; (JR); Hnr Roll; Perf Att; Spec Olymp Vol; Emplmnt; Wrstlg (J)

RANSOM, MALLORY; MEMPHIS, TN; WHITE STATION HS; (FR); Ctznshp Aw; Duke TS; Hnr Roll; Nat Hon Sy; Perf Att; WWAHSS; Comm Volntr; Peer Tut/Med; Chrch Yth Grp; Svce Clb; Bnd; Ch Chr; Orch; Vllyball; CR (R); Who's Who Among American High School Students; National Jr, Honor Society; Education; Pharmacist; U of Memphis; Yale

RAPER, MALLORY E; DENMARK, TN; SOUTH SIDE HS; (SO); Hi Hnr Roll; Nat Hon Sy; Hosp Aide; Chrch Yth Grp; Emplmnt; MuAlphaTh; Ntl Beta Clb; Quiz Bowl; Latin Clb; Ch Chr; Pre-Med; Medical Technology; East Tennessee State U; Vanderbilt U

RATCLIFF, WALTER C; FRANKLIN, TN; CENTENNIAL HS; (SO); Hi Hnr Roll; Chrch Yth Grp; Drma Clb; Mth Clb/Tm; Mod UN; MuAlphaTh; Bnd; Chr; Ch Chr; Jzz Bnd; Swmg (L)

RATHER, JENNIFER M; OLIVER SPRINGS, TN; OLIVER SPRINGS HS; (JR); Hnr Roll; Otst Ac Ach Awd; Perf Att; WWAHSS; Comm Volntr; 4-H; BPA; DARE; FCA; Lttrmn Clb; SADD; Vsity Clb; Spanish Clb; PP Ftbl (V); Sftball (V CL); Secondary Education, History Major or Math Major; Bachelors; Kings College; Cumberland College in Kentucky

RATLEDGE, GEORGE; SODDY DAISY, TN; SODDY-DAISY HS; (JR); Hi Hnr Roll; WWAHSS; Yth Ldrshp Prog; Chrch Yth Grp; Key Club; Pharmacy School; East Tennessee State U; U of Tennessee At Chattanooga

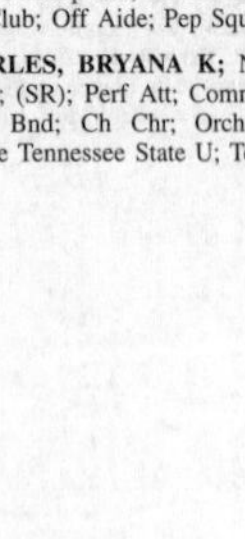

Pryor, Jordan A
Central HS
Memphis, TN

National
Honor Roll
Spring 2005

Presley, Brittney L
Blackman HS
Murfreesboro, TN

RATLIFF, SUEKEVA; MEMPHIS, TN; TREADWELL MIDDLE HS; Hi Hnr Roll; Hnr Roll; Nat Hon Sy; Nat Ldrshp Svc; Nat Stu Ath Day Aw; Otst Ac Ach Awd; Perf Att; Pres Sch; Sci Fairs; St Schl; CARE; Comm Volntr; Peer Tut/Med; ArtClub; BPA; Chrch Yth Grp; Cmptr Clb; Drma Clb; Emplmnt; FCA; Fr of Library; Chr; Ch Chr; Dnce; Mch Bnd; Bskball (J); GAA (V); Hsbk Rdg (V); Mar Art (V); PPSqd (V); Sccr (V); Sftball (V); Swmg (V); Adv Cncl (S); Cl Off (S); Stu Cncl (S); CR (S); Sch Ppr (P); Yrbk (P); Singer; Artist; Nursing Child Care; Computer; MPHS State; Shelby State

RAY, JACQUELINE; TULLAHOMA, TN; MOORE CTY HS; (JR); 4H Awd; Hnr Roll; Perf Att; 4-H; Pep Squd; Ch Chr; PP Ftbl (V); Sftball (V); Swmg (V); Cl Off (T); Teacher; Motlow State Community College; Middle Tennessee State U

RAYBURN, KATILYN; CAMDEN, TN; CAMDEN CTRL HS; (SO); Duke TS; Hnr Roll; Nat Hon Sy; Otst Ac Ach Awd; Perf Att; WWAHSS; Comm Volntr; Hosp Aide; BPA; FCA; Sci Clb; Ch Chr; Bskball; Ftball (V); Student Football Athletic Trainer; Student Basketball Athletic Trainer; Physical Therapy; Sports Athletic Training; U of Tennessee Martin

RAYNER, JAMES; JACKSON, TN; LIBERTY TECH MAGNET HS; (SO); Nat Hon Sy; Bsball; Real Estate; Business Management; Tennessee; North Carolina

REAMEY, BRITTNEY; MEMPHIS, TN; MIDDLE COLLEGE HS; (SR); Hnr Roll; Nat Hon Sy; Perf Att; WWAHSS; Chrch Yth Grp; DECA; Prom Com; Tchrs Aide; Ch Chr; Chrldg; STAX Music Academy - Vocalist; CFA Productions / Model; Psychology / Counseling; Physical Therapy; U of Tennessee Chattanooga

REBELLO, MEGAN L; WAVERLY, TN; WAVERLY CTRL HS; (JR); 4H Awd; Hnr Roll; WWAHSS; Comm Volntr; 4-H; FCA; FTA; Voc Ind Clb Am; Cl Off (V); Stars, Paws, HOSA, BPA, FCCLA; FBLA; Nursing; Teaching; APSU & Aquinas; MTSU

RECHENBACH, JAMES; KNOXVILLE, TN; BEREAN CHRISTIAN SCH; (FR); Duke TS; Hi Hnr Roll; MVP; Perf Att; Pres Ac Ftns Aw; Comm Volntr; Chrch Yth Grp; Chr; Bsball; Bskball (V); Scr Kpr (V); 6 out of 6 Years - Superior Rating in the National Federation Festival for Piano Solos; Tournament MVP Player of Middle School Tournament; Sports Analyst / Announcer; Financial Planner / Advisor; U of Tennessee; Duke U

REED, AMY; AUBURNTOWN, TN; CANNON CTY HS; (SO); Hi Hnr Roll; Hnr Roll; MVP; Perf Att; Pres Ac Ftns Aw; Sci Fairs; Valdctrian; Comm Volntr; 4-H; Chrch Yth Grp; DARE; Emplmnt; FCCLA; Ntl Beta Clb; Ch Chr; Sftball (V); Vllyball (JC); Head Start Volunteer; Theology; History; Belmont College; Middle Tennessee State U

REED, CHRIS B; MANCHESTER, TN; COFFEE CTY CTRL HS; (JR); Bnd; Mch Bnd; Eagle Scout; TSA - Technology Club; Computer Science; Computer Programming; TN Tech U; Middle TN State U

REED, LAUREN P; MURFREESBORO, TN; SIEGEL HS; (JR); Hi Hnr Roll; Hnr Roll; Comm Volntr; ArtClub; Chrch Yth Grp; DECA; FCA; Ntl Beta Clb; Photog; Chrldg (J); Sccr (V); Fashion; Bible; Lipscomb U; Omar U

REEVES, JASMINE C; MURFREESBORO, TN; SIEGEL HS; (JR); Hi Hnr Roll; Nat Hon Sy; WWAHSS; FCA; Beta Club; Forensic Science; Middle Tennessee State U; Motlow State Community College

REEVES, JOSHUA; LENOIR CITY, TN; LENOIR CITY HS; (SO); 4H Awd; Hnr Roll; Pres Ac Ftns Aw; Yth Ldrshp Prog; Peer Tut/Med; 4-H; Chrch Yth Grp; Emplmnt; FCA; Ntl FFA; Tchrs Aide; Bnd; Ch Chr; Golf (V); Carpenter; Mechanical Engineer; Tennessee Tech U

REID, DIANA; ELIZABETHTON, TN; UNAKA HS; (SO); Hnr Roll; Nat Hon Sy; Otst Ac Ach Awd; St of Mnth; 4-H; Chrch Yth Grp; Emplmnt; FCA; FCCLA; Chrldg (V); Sch Ppr (R); 4-H Congress; Elementary Education; Criminal Investigation; Tusculum College; King College

REPASS, ASHLEY J N; BLUFF CITY, TN; SULLIVAN EAST HS; (SO); 4-H; DARE; Drma Clb; FCA; ROTC; SADD; Ch Chr; Bskball (J); PP Ftbl (J); Award Club; Neonatal Doctor; Sports Medical Field; U of Tennessee; U of Cumberland

REYNOLDS, SAVANNA; SWEETWATER, TN; LOUDON HS; (FR); Hi Hnr Roll; Otst Ac Ach Awd; WWAHSS; Yth Ldrshp Prog; Comm Volntr; Peer Tut/Med; 4-H; Chrch Yth Grp; DARE; ROTC; Bnd; Ch Chr; Drl Tm; Mch Bnd; Sccr (VJ); Physical Therapy; Education; U of Tennessee; Georgetown U

REYNOLDS, TERRIKA; MEMPHIS, TN; GERMANTOWN HS; (JR); Hnr Roll; WWAHSS; Hosp Aide; Chrch Yth Grp; French Clb; Ch Chr; Orch; SP/M/VS; Veterinary Science; Tuskegee U; U of Tenn. Knoxville

REYNOLDS, TIFFANY N; CLARKSVILLE, TN; NORTHWEST HS; (FR); Hnr Roll; Nat Hon Sy; Comm Volntr; Hosp Aide; Chrch Yth Grp; Chr; Chrldg (V)

RICH, LAUREN M; CELINA, TN; HERMITAGE SPRINGS SCH; (JR); Hi Hnr Roll; Hnr Roll; WWAHSS; Comm Volntr; FCA; FCCLA; Ntl FFA; Prom Com; Chr; SP/M/VS; Bskball; Cl Off (R)

RICHARD, BENNEKIA; MEMPHIS, TN; MIDDLE COLLEGE HS; (SO); Hnr Roll; Nat Hon Sy; Peer Tut/Med; Pep Squd; Tchrs Aide; Dnce; Drm Mjr; Chrldg (V); Cl Off (S); Pediatrician; Fisk U

RICHARDS, EVAN; CELINA, TN; CLAY CTY HS; (FR); Hi Hnr Roll; Yth Ldrshp Prog; Comm Volntr; Chess; Chrch Yth Grp; DARE; FCA; Ch Chr; Bsball (V); Bskball (J); Ftball (V); Wrstlg (J); Master's Degree; Architect; UCLA; U of Notre Dame

RICHARDS, SHAWN M; ASHLAND CITY, TN; CHEATHAM CTY CTRL HS; (SO); Hi Hnr Roll; Hnr Roll; Perf Att; Comm Volntr; 4-H; Chrch Yth Grp; DARE; FCA; Outdrs Clb; Vsity Clb; Voc Ind Clb Am; Spanish Clb; Ftball (V); Sccr (V); FCA; Dentist; Ministry; Free Will Baptist Bible College; Vanderbilt U

RICHMOND JR, JOHN; KINGSPORT, TN; SULLIVAN SOUTH HS; (JR); Hnr Roll; Perf Att; Drma Clb; Emplmnt; Spanish Clb; SP/M/VS; Ftball (J); Run My Own Business; East Tennessee State U; Northeast State U

RIDDLE, MELLIE R; MURFREESBORO, TN; BLACKMAN HS; (JR); Hi Hnr Roll; Hnr Roll; St of Mnth; JSA; Key Club; Ntl Beta Clb; Scouts; Clr Grd; Dnce; SP/M/VS; 13th on National Spanish Exam; Complete High School in 3 Years; Theatre Major; Psychology / Human Behavior; Sarah Lawrence College; Oberlin College

RIDLEY, BROOKE A; MC KENZIE, TN; MC KENZIE HS; (JR); Hnr Roll; Sci Fairs; USAA; WWAHSS; Comm Volntr; BPA; Chrch Yth Grp; DECA; FCA; Key Club; Ntl Beta Clb; Prom Com; Sci Clb; Sftball (J); Track (V L); Yrbk (P); Pep Club; Community Service Projects; Nursing; Austin Peay State U; U of Tennessee Martin

RIEBEN, CONNIE; ARLINGTON, TN; BOLTON HS; (FR); Ctznshp Aw; F Lan Hn Soc; Hi Hnr Roll; Hnr Roll; Nat Hon Sy; Otst Ac Ach Awd; Pres Ac Ftns Aw; Pres Sch; St of Mnth; Comm Volntr; Hab For Humty Volntr; Peer Tut/Med; ArtClub; Chrch Yth Grp; DARE; Mus Clb; Spanish Clb; Ch Chr; Chrldg (J); Mar Art (J); Sccr (J); In Pageants; Honor Society at School; Nursing; Veterinary Assistant; Ole Miss; Southwest Community College

RILEY, DEANGELO; MEMPHIS, TN; KIRBY HS; (JR); French Clb; Bnd; Mch Bnd; Bskball (V); Ftball; Bachelor Degree; Business Degree; U of Tennessee; U of Tennessee Nashville, Tennessee

RILEY, SHADA L; MEMPHIS, TN; OAK HAVEN HS; (JR); Hi Hnr Roll; Hnr Roll; Perf Att; Mus Clb; Chr; Flg Crps; Swg Chr; Cl Off (T); Cosmetology; Business; UT Martin; Tennessee State U

RITCHEY, CHRISTOPHER M; MARYVILLE, TN; WILLIAM BLOUNT HS; (SR); Hnr Roll; Nat Hon Sy; WWAHSS; Chrch Yth Grp; Emplmnt; FCA; Ftball (V L); Swmg (V); CR (T); Mechanical Engineering; Tennessee Tech

RIVERA, COURTNEY; HENDERSONVILLE, TN; HENDERSONVILLE HS; (SR); F Lan Hn Soc; Nat Hon Sy; Comm Volntr; Chrch Yth Grp; Emplmnt; FCA; Ntl Beta Clb; Spanish Clb; Track (V); President of Beta Club; Recipient of Violet Richardson Award for Volunteer Service; Spanish; Wheaton College

ROBERSON, ALISHA L; SODDY DAISY, TN; SODDY DAISY HS; (SR); Hnr Roll; Perf Att; WWAHSS; Drma Clb; FCA; Key Club; Ntl Beta Clb; Lawyer; U of TN Knoxville

ROBERSON, CHASITY M; MEMPHIS, TN; WHITE STATION HS; (SO); Ctznshp Aw; Hnr Roll; Perf Att; Comm Volntr; Peer Tut/Med; Chrch Yth Grp; Drma Clb; Scouts; Spch Team; Tchrs Aide; Stg Cre; Sftball (J); Track (V); Sunday School Teachers Aid; History PhD; Forensic Science; The U of Memphis; Spelman U

ROBERSON, JOSHUA T; DUNLAP, TN; BLEDSOE CTY HS; (FR); Bskball (J); Football Statistician; Students of Service; Engineering / Computers; Tennessee Technological U; U of Tennessee

ROBERSON, TIFFANY S; CLARKSVILLE, TN; NORTHEAST HS; (SO); Hnr Roll; Chrch Yth Grp; Ntl Beta Clb; Pep Squd; Ch Chr; Drl Tm; Medical; Teacher; Austin Peay State U; U of Tennessee At Memphis

ROBERTS, EMILY; HIXSON, TN; GIRLS PREP SCH; (SO); Duke TS; Hnr Roll; Sci Fairs; Comm Volntr; Hab For Humty Volntr; Peer Tut/Med; Chrch Yth Grp; Emplmnt; Ntl Beta Clb; Off Aide; Svce Clb; Dnce; SP/M/VS; Bskball (J); Sccr (J); Vllyball (J); CR (R); National Junior Honor Society; State Level Piano Competitor (Top Ten); Government; Law; Georgetown; Vanderbilt

ROBERTS, KELLEY; LEBANON, TN; WILSON CTRL HS; (JR); 4H Awd; 4-H; Ntl Beta Clb; Sftball (L); Vllyball (L); Beta Club; Teacher; Vet; Cumberland U; Middle Tennessee State U

ROBERTSON, DUSTY; CULLEOKA, TN; MT PLEASANT HS; (FR); Hnr Roll; Stg Cre; Ftball (V); Wt Lftg (V); Game Designer; U of Tennessee

ROBINSON, ASHLEY; JACKSON, TN; NORTHSIDE HS; (FR); 4H Awd; Ctznshp Aw; Otst Ac Ach Awd; Sci Fairs; St of Mnth; WWAHSS; Comm Volntr; 4-H; Chrch Yth Grp; DARE; Key Club; Scouts; Chr; Stu Cncl (V); Member of Teen Court; Participate in Education Talent Search Prog.; Pediatrics; Industrial Engineering; Middle Tennessee State U; Clark Atlanta U

ROBINSON, ASHLEY; KNOXVILLE, TN; FARRAGUT HS; (SO); Bnd; Chr; Chrldg (J); Surgeon/Medical; Forensics; U of Tennessee; Carson Newman

ROBINSON, CHAMPAGNE; MADISON, TN; HUNTER'S LANE HS; (SO); Hi Hnr Roll; Perf Att; Chrldg (V); Co Captain Varsity; Ranking #1 GPA-383; Spelman Fisk U; Howard U

ROBINSON, COURTNEY; SPARTA, TN; WHITE CTY HS; (SO); Hnr Roll; Perf Att; Sci Fairs; 4-H; Vllyball (J); Business Management; Middle Tennessee State U

ROBINSON, JERICA; JACKSON, TN; SOUTH SIDE HS; (SO); Hi Hnr Roll; Hnr Roll; Perf Att; Chrch Yth Grp; Drma Clb; FCA; Ntl Beta Clb; Chr; Ch Chr; SP/M/VS; Vllyball (V); Stu Cncl (R); Leadership U Inductee; Nat'l Spanish Honor Society Vice Pres; Law; Criminal Justice; Spelman College; Duke U

ROBINSON, KRISTOPHER A D; SMITHVILLE, TN; DEKALB CTY HS; (JR); 4H Awd; Hi Hnr Roll; Hnr Roll; Pres Sch; WWAHSS; Comm Volntr; 4-H; Chrch Yth Grp; DARE; Emplmnt; FCA; FBLA; Ntl Beta Clb; Off Aide; Cl Off (P); Stu Cncl (P); Board Member of Local Car Club Team Agression-We Raise Money for Cancer Society; Major-Political Science; Minor-Business Administration & Psychology; Belmont U; Middle Tennessee State U

ROBINSON, REBECCA P; FRANKLIN, TN; FRANKLIN HS; (SO); Hi Hnr Roll; WWAHSS; Hab For Humty Volntr; Chrch Yth Grp; French Clb; Bnd; Clr Grd; Dnce; Flg Crps; Swmg (V); Pre-Emptors Fife and Drum Corps

ROBISON, MEGAN; GATES, TN; HALLS HS; (JR); Ctznshp Aw; Duke TS; Yth Ldrshp Prog; Comm Volntr; ArtClub; Chrch Yth Grp; DECA; Ntl FFA; Prom Com; Quiz Bowl; Adv Cncl (R); Stu Cncl (R); Yrbk (R, P); National Bible Bowl Finalist; Dyersburg State Community College; Jackson State Community College

ROCKEL, ELISHA; LEBANON, TN; WILSON CTRL HS; (JR); Prom Com; Medical School; MTSU-Middle Tennessee State U

RODGERS, HENRY; MEMPHIS, TN; WHITE STATION HS; (SO); Hnr Roll; Nat Hon Sy; Chrch Yth Grp; Bskball; Ftball; Sport Athlete; Sport Management; Michigan U; Louisville U

RODGERS, MICHAEL; MEMPHIS, TN; OAKHAVEN MIDDLE HS; (JR); MVP; Nat Ldrshp Svc; St of Mnth; WWAHSS; DARE; Ch Chr; Bsball (V C); Ftball (V); Cl Off (V); Engineering; Computer Repair; ITT Technical; U of Memphis

ROEHL, ABBY; POWELL, TN; TEMPLE AC; (FR); Hnr Roll; Chr; Bskball (J L); Vllyball (J); National Physical Fitness Award; X-Ray Technician; U of Tennessee

ROGERS, JONATHAN; MEMPHIS, TN; WHITE STATION HS; (FR); Hnr Roll; Nat Hon Sy; Bnd; Swmg; Art; Engineering; The U of Memphis; Rhodes College

ROLLINS, COURTNEY L; KNOXVILLE, TN; SOUTH DOYLE HS; (JR); Hi Hnr Roll; Hnr Roll; St of Mnth; WWAHSS; Yth Ldrshp Prog; Comm Volntr; Peer Tut/Med; Spec Olymp Vol; Chrch Yth Grp; FCA; Key Club; Lttrmn Clb; MuAlphaTh; Prom Com; French Clb; Sftball (V L); Stu Cncl (P, R); Knoxville's Promise Youth Action Council; Veterinary Medicine; Carson Newman; Maryville College

ROLLINS, MELANIE; CROSSVILLE, TN; CUMBERLAND CTY HS; (JR); Ctznshp Aw; Hi Hnr Roll; Nat Hon Sy; Otst Ac Ach Awd; Perf Att; St of Mnth; Hab For Humty Volntr; 4-H; Chrch Yth Grp; DARE; Emplmnt; Mth Clb/Tm; Off Aide; Pep Squd; French Clb; Chr; Interested in Psychology; Early Education; Roane State Community College; Berea College

RONCA, DAVID J; CLEVELAND, TN; WALKER VALLEY HS; (SR); Hnr Roll; Chess; Chrch Yth Grp; Drma Clb; Emplmnt; Jr Ach; SP/M/VS; 4th Place At Algebra II Competition Tennessee Western College; 1st Place in School Pre-Coloring Project; Business; Pre-Law (Political Science); Lee U; U of Miami (Florida)

ROOKS, JARON C; MARTIN, TN; (SO); Sccr (VJ)

ROSE, ROBERT; JOHNSON CITY, TN; DANIEL BOONE HS; (SO); Hnr Roll; Nat Hon Sy; WWAHSS; Peer Tut/Med; ArtClub; Spanish Clb; Optometrist

ROSE II, JOHNNIE M; MEMPHIS, TN; OVERTON HS; (FR); Hnr Roll; WWAHSS; Yth Ldrshp Prog; Comm Volntr; Chrch Yth Grp; Key Club; Ch Chr; Ftball; CR (R); Studying to Be a Minister; Being a Psychology Major (Child); Entrepreneur; U of Southern Mississippi; Jackson State U

ROSS, ABBY; KINGSTON, TN; ROANE CTY HS; (JR); 4H Awd; Yth Ldrshp Prog; Comm Volntr; 4-H; BPA; Chrch Yth Grp; DARE; FBLA; Mus Clb; Photog; Scouts; Bnd; Ch Chr; Mch Bnd; Pep Bnd; Music Education; Charleston Southern U; U of Tennessee, Knoxville

ROSS, BRITTANY A; BELL BUCKLE, TN; CASCADE HS; (SO); Hi Hnr Roll; Hnr Roll; WWAHSS; Chrch Yth Grp; FCA; Key Club; Bskball (V); Sftball (V); Pediatrician; U of Tennessee

Rollins, Melanie
Cumberland Cty HS
Crossville, TN

Rollins, Courtney L
South Doyle HS
Knoxville, TN

Roberson, Chasity M
White Station HS
Memphis, TN

Riddle, Mellie R
Blackman HS
Murfreesboro, TN

Richards, Evan
Clay Cty HS
Celina, TN

Reeves, Joshua
Lenoir City HS
Lenoir City, TN

Reed, Amy
Cannon Cty HS
Auburntown, TN

Reeves, Jasmine C
Siegel HS
Murfreesboro, TN

Richards, Shawn M
Cheatham Cty Ctrl HS
Ashland City, TN

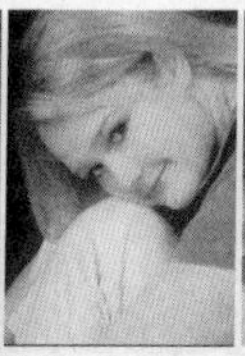
Rieben, Connie
Bolton HS
Arlington, TN

Robinson, Ashley
Northside HS
Jackson, TN

Robinson, Kristopher A D
Dekalb Cty HS
Smithville, TN

ROSS, IAN R; KINGSPORT, TN; DOBYNS BENNETT HS; (SR); Duke TS; Hi Hnr Roll; Nat Hon Sy; WWAHSS; Comm Volntr; Peer Tut/Med; AL Aux Boys; Chrch Yth Grp; Emplmnt; Jr Cls League; Key Club; Ntl Beta Clb; Tchrs Aide; Bnd; Jzz Bnd; Mch Bnd; Orch; Sch Ppr (R); Yrbk (E); Section Leader-Marching Band; Boys State, Teen BED-KPT Times News; Doctor of Medicine; East TN State U

ROSS, KELSEY; MC EWEN, TN; MC EWEN HS; (JR); 4H Awd; Hnr Roll; Perf Att; Comm Volntr; 4-H; BPA; Chrch Yth Grp; Drma Clb; FTA; Ntl Beta Clb; Ntl FFA; Sci Clb; SP/M/VS; Vllyball (V CL); Vol State Award Recipient; Tennessee FFA State Degree Recipient; Elementary Education; Agricultural Business; U of Tennessee At Knoxville; Middle Tennessee State U

ROSS, PHILLIP C; KINGSPORT, TN; DOBYNS BENNETT HS; (SR); Duke TS; Hi Hnr Roll; Nat Hon Sy; Nat Mrt LOC; WWAHSS; Comm Volntr; AL Aux Boys; Chrch Yth Grp; DARE; Emplmnt; Jr Cls League; JSA; Key Club; Ntl Beta Clb; Bsball (V L); Sch Ppr (R); Yrbk (R); Section Editor-Yearbook; Started New Club-"Athletes in Action"; Law School; East TN State U As a Roan Scholar

ROWLEY, BROOKE E; MURFREESBORO, TN; SIEGEL HS; (JR); Hi Hnr Roll; Nat Hon Sy; WWAHSS; Hosp Aide; Chrch Yth Grp; Emplmnt; Ntl Beta Clb; President of HOSA; Nursing / Pediatrics; Freed-Hardeman U; Middle Tennessee State U

RUCKER JR, WILLIE; CHATTANOOGA, TN; CHATTANOOGA SCH-ART & SCIENCE; (FR); 4H Awd; Hnr Roll; Perf Att; St of Mnth; Comm Volntr; 4-H; DARE; Mod UN; Scouts; SP/M/VS; Bskball (J); Cr Ctry (J); Track (J); CHOAT Panelist in CHOAT - Teen Abstinence Program; Received 3 High School Credits in the 8th Grade; Drama / Theatre; Engineer - Specifically Thrill Ride Engineer; Howard U; Florida A & M U

RUDOLPH, SARA; CLARKSVILLE, TN; CLARKSVILLE HS; (JR); Hnr Roll; Comm Volntr; ArtClub; Chrch Yth Grp; Drma Clb; Emplmnt; Svce Clb; French Clb; SP/M/VS; Track (J); Lead Role in School Play; Active Member of International Thespian Society; Law; Cosmetology; U of Memphis; Middle Tennessee State U

RUSHING, LAUREN E; RIPLEY, TN; RIPLEY HS; (FR); Hi Hnr Roll; Hnr Roll; Perf Att; Spec Olymp Vol; 4-H; Chrch Yth Grp; DARE; Ntl Beta Clb; Chr; Chrldg (J); Vllyball (J); Nurse Practitioner or Medical Doctor; Registered Nurse; U of Tennessee Knoxville

RUSSELL, LYNDSAY H; LA FOLLETTE, TN; CAMPBELL CTY HS; (JR); Hnr Roll; Nat Hon Sy; Perf Att; Yth Ldrshp Prog; Hab For Humty Volntr; Spec Olymp Vol; BPA; Chrch Yth Grp; DECA; Drma Clb; Emplmnt; FCA; FCCLA; Key Club; Golf (V L); PP Ftbl (V); Cl Off (S); Stu Cncl; CR (S); DECA Secretary / Class Officer - For 2 Years; Pharmacist or a Pharmaceutical Sales Rep; U of Tennessee (Knox); East Tennessee State U

RUTLEDGE, IVY; LYNCHBURG, TN; MOORE CTY HS; (SR); Hi Hnr Roll; Nat Hon Sy; Salutrn; Comm Volntr; Peer Tut/Med; AL Aux Girls; Chrch Yth Grp; DARE; Emplmnt; FBLA; FCCLA; Pep Squd; Prom Com; Chr; SP/M/VS; Cl Off (P); Stu Cncl (R); CR (R); Sch Ppr (P); Yrbk (E, P); Community Christmas Show; Chiropractic; Motlow State Community College; Middle Tennessee State U

RYANS, SHANE M; CHURCH HILL, TN; VOLUNTEER HS; (SR); Hnr Roll; Perf Att; WWAHSS; Comm Volntr; Peer Tut/Med; Emplmnt; MuAlphaTh; Off Aide; Bskball (V); Mar Art (V); Wt Lftg; Civil Engineering; Northeast State Technical Community College; Tennessee Technology

SADLER, TYLER; NASHVILLE, TN; NASHVILLE CHRISTIAN SCH; (JR); Ctznshp Aw; F Lan Hn Soc; Hi Hnr Roll; Otst Ac Ach Awd; Pres Sch; Yth Ldrshp Prog; Comm Volntr; Hab For Humty Volntr; Chess; Chrch Yth Grp; FCA; SP/M/VS; Bsball (V L); Cr Ctry (V L); Ftball (V L); Wrstlg (V L); Best Sophomore in Baseball; Marketing; Economics; Cumberland U; Washington St

SAILOR, NICOLE; WARTRACE, TN; CASCADE HS; (JR); Hnr Roll; Nat Hon Sy; Comm Volntr; Drma Clb; Emplmnt; FCA; Spanish Clb; SP/M/VS; Stg Cre; Sftball; Stu Cncl (R); Culinary Arts Major; Entrepreneurship Major; Middle Tennessee State U; Belmont U

SALAMEN, REMA; MC KENZIE, TN; MC KENZIE HS; (JR); Sftball (L); Tennis (V L); Cl Off (T); Stu Cncl (R); CR (T); Yrbk (E); Homecoming Royalty; Miss McKenzie; Pharmaceutical Sales; David Lipscomb U; U of Tennessee of Martin

SALAT, JUSTIN R; MEMPHIS, TN; WOODDALE HS; (JR); Ctznshp Aw; Hi Hnr Roll; Hnr Roll; MVP; Nat Hon Sy; Perf Att; Hosp Aide; ArtClub; Drma Clb; Voc Ind Clb Am; SP/M/VS; Stg Cre; Bskball (V); Scr Kpr (V); Sccr (L); Distinguished Honor Roll; Citizenship Award; Physical Therapy or Sports Medicine; U of Memphis; U of TN

SALSBURY, JORDAN; LEBANON, TN; LEBANON HS; (FR); Hi Hnr Roll; Hnr Roll; WWAHSS; Peer Tut/Med; Chrch Yth Grp; FCA; Key Club; Ftball (J); Engineer; Medical Doctor; Vanderbilt U; Tennessee Tech.

SAMPSEL, EMILY G; HARRIMAN, TN; OLIVER SPRINGS HS; (SO); Otst Ac Ach Awd; Pres Sch; WWAHSS; BPA; Chrch Yth Grp; FCA; Ch Chr; Stu Cncl (R); Psychology; Cosmetology; Tennessee School of Beauty

SAMPSON, ASHLEY; MURFREESBORO, TN; BLACKMAN HS; (FR); Ctznshp Aw; Hnr Roll; St of Mnth; WWAHSS; Comm Volntr; Chrch Yth Grp; Key Club; Ntl Beta Clb; Off Aide; Ch Chr; Dnce; SP/M/VS; Community Service Work With Key Club; Studies in Classical Dance; Law Enforcement / Criminal Justice; Middle Tennessee State U

SANDERS, APRIL; HORNSBY, TN; MC NAIRY CTRL HS; (JR); Duke TS; F Lan Hn Soc; Nat Hon Sy; USAA; WWAHSS; Yth Ldrshp Prog; Comm Volntr; Peer Tut/Med; Chrch Yth Grp; FTA; Svce Clb; Spanish Clb; Chr; Ch Chr; Secondary English Education; Union U; Bethel College

SANDERS, AUBREY L; MEMPHIS, TN; SHEFFEILD HS; (FR); All Am Sch; Ctznshp Aw; Fut Prb Slvr; Hnr Roll; Nat Hon Sy; Nat Mrt Fin; Nat Sci Aw; Nat Stu Ath Day Aw; Otst Ac Ach Awd; Sci Fairs; Comm Volntr; Hab For Humty Volntr; Cmptr Clb; Drma Clb; FBLA; Mus Clb; Photog; SADD; Tech Clb; Vsity Clb; Bskball (J); Adv Cncl (S); Technology; Doctor; Michigan State U; U of Memphis

SANDERS, BRYAN; LEWISBURG, TN; MARSHALL CTY HS; (FR); Hnr Roll; Perf Att; Scouts; Bnd; Mch Bnd; Pep Bnd; Robotics; Engineering; Middle Tennessee State U; Tennessee Technological U

SANDERS, LINDSAY; JACKSON, TN; SOUTH SIDE HS; (SO); Ctznshp Aw; Otst Ac Ach Awd; Perf Att; ROTC; Drl Tm

SANDERS, SIFFINI; MEMPHIS, TN; OAKHAVEN HS; (JR); Hnr Roll; Nat Hon Sy; Comm Volntr; ROTC; Drm Mjr; Lawyer; Masseuse; High Tech U; UT Martin

SANDERS IV, JOHN A; CARTHAGE, TN; SMITH CTY HS; (SR); Hnr Roll; Perf Att; WWAHSS; Yth Ldrshp Prog; Hab For Humty Volntr; Chrch Yth Grp; Drma Clb; Emplmnt; FCA; Chr; Ch Chr; SP/M/VS; Stg Cre; Bskball (V L); Golf (V L); Education, Coaching Basketball; Tennessee Technological U

SANDERSON, DANIELLE A; CROSSVILLE, TN; CUMBERLAND CTY HS; (SO); Hi Hnr Roll; Hnr Roll; Otst Ac Ach Awd; Sci Fairs; Peer Tut/Med; Chrch Yth Grp; Drma Clb; Ntl Beta Clb; Off Aide; Tchrs Aide; Spanish Clb; Bnd; Mch Bnd; Pep Bnd; Swmg (J); Wrstlg (L); Sch Ppr (R); Yrbk (R); Wrestling Manager; Lettered in Marching Band 8, 9, 10; Medical; Athletic Training

SANDS, BRITTANY D; MARYVILLE, TN; WILLIAM BLOUNT HS; (SO); Hnr Roll; Cr Ctry (V); Track (V); Criminal Investigation; Walter State; U of Tennessee-Chattanooga

SANNES, RACHEL W; MOUNTAIN CITY, TN; JOHNSON CTY HS; (FR); 4H Awd; Pres Sch; 4-H; DARE; Emplmnt; Scouts; Bnd; Mch Bnd; Bskball (J); Tennis (J); Marching Band 9th Grade Representative; Junior Clinic, Presidential Academic Awards 6th, 8th Grades; Social Science; Foreign Language; U of Tennessee

SAULSBERRY, PATRICK; MEMPHIS, TN; MELROSE HS; (FR); Hnr Roll; 4-H; Jr Ach; Ftball (VJ); Music Engineering; Computer Engineering

SAYLOR, AARON K; ERWIN, TN; U N 1001 CTY VOC SCH; (SR); Hnr Roll; WWAHSS; Comm Volntr; 4-H; ArtClub; BPA; Chrch Yth Grp; FCA; Ntl FFA; Voc Ind Clb Am; Spanish Clb; Ftball (V CL); Outstanding Running Back; Agriculture; Northeast State Technical Community College; U of Tennessee

SAYLOR, BRIAN A; NEWPORT, TN; COCKE CTY HS; (SO); Hi Hnr Roll; Hnr Roll; Perf Att; Sci Fairs; Mythology; College Professor; U of Tennessee; East Tennessee State U

SAYLOR, RACHEL; KNOXVILLE, TN; BEREAN CHRISTIAN SCH; (FR); Duke TS; Comm Volntr; Peer Tut/Med; Chrch Yth Grp; Prom Com; Chr; Bskball (V); Sccr (V); Swmg; Vllyball; CR (R); Yrbk (P); Piano (11 Years); Tutoring; Mathematics Teaching; Architecture; Bryan College; Liberty U

SCAIFE, REBECCA; MEMPHIS, TN; RIDGEWAY HS; (SO); Nat Hon Sy; WWAHSS; Amnsty Intl; BPA; Chrch Yth Grp; Key Club; MuAlphaTh; Psychology; Sociology; Spelman College

SCANTLAND, LEAH M; GAINESBORO, TN; JACKSON CTY HS; (SO); Hnr Roll; Nat Hon Sy; Emplmnt; FCA; FCCLA; Ntl Beta Clb; Vllyball (V); Orthodontics; Tennessee Tech; U of Kentucky

SCHAEFER, SARAH E; KINGSPORT, TN; DOBYNS BENNETT; (SO); Duke TS; Hi Hnr Roll; Comm Volntr; Chrch Yth Grp; Key Club; Ntl Beta Clb; Bnd; Mch Bnd; Orch; Pep Bnd

SCHEITERLEIN, ROBBY; EADS, TN; FAYETTE AC; (MS); Duke TS; Hi Hnr Roll; Nat Hon Sy; Otst Ac Ach Awd; Pres Sch; Sci/Math Olympn; Comm Volntr; Peer Tut/Med; ArtClub; Fr of Library; Mth Clb/Tm; Mus Clb; Scouts; Bnd; Jzz Bnd; Mch Bnd; Orch; Golf (J); National Geographic Bee State Finalist 2004 & 2005/Winner 1st Regional Math Meet; All West Band; Surgeon; Medical Research; Stanford; Duke

SCHIERMEYER, KATHERINE; TULLAHOMA, TN; TULLAHOMA HS; (JR); Hi Hnr Roll; Nat Hon Sy; WWAHSS; Comm Volntr; Peer Tut/Med; Key Club; Mth Clb/Tm; MuAlphaTh; Scouts; Tchrs Aide; Spanish Clb; Flg Crps; Jzz Bnd; Pre-Med

SCHOONMAKER, LAURA; KNOXVILLE, TN; FARRAGUT HS; (SR); Nat Hon Sy; Nat Mrt Fin; WWAHSS; Comm Volntr; Drma Clb; Mus Clb; Chr; Dnce; SP/M/VS; Swmg (V); Tennessee Ambassadors of Music Europe Tour; All-East Choir Participant-2 years; Vocal Performance; Musical Theater; Furman U

SCHORLE, ASHTON B; SODDY DAISY, TN; SODDY DAISY HS; (FR); Hnr Roll; USAA; WWAHSS; Chrch Yth Grp; Emplmnt; Dnce; Fashion Merchandising; U of Tennessee Chattanooga

SCHWENKE, ALI; ERWIN, TN; UNICOI CTY VOC SCH; (FR); Hi Hnr Roll; Otst Ac Ach Awd; Pres Sch; Comm Volntr; Chrch Yth Grp; DARE; FCA; Ntl FFA; Pep Squd; Spanish Clb; Ch Chr; Track (V); Vllyball (V L); Cl Off (P); CR; Volleyball All Conference & All Tournament; Winner District Creed Speaking FFA-2 & Regional; Tusculum College; U of Tennessee

SCOTT, ALANA; CELINA, TN; CLAY CTY HS; (SO); Hi Hnr Roll; Nat Hon Sy; WWAHSS; Biology Clb; Mth Clb/Tm; Ntl Beta Clb; Sci Clb; Yrbk (E, R, P)

SCOTT, ANGELLICA M; NASHVILLE, TN; MARTIN LUTHER KING HS; (SO); Hnr Roll; Sci Fairs; Photog; Ch Chr; Track (V); Cum Laude - National Latin Exam; Engineering - Top Math Student Tenn State U Summer; Psychiatry / Clinical Psychology; Pre-Law; Oxford College; Duke U

SCOTT, TIFFANY; WHITLEYVILLE, TN; HERMITAGE SPRINGS SCH; (JR); Hnr Roll; WWAHSS; BPA; Emplmnt; FCCLA; Ntl Beta Clb; Ntl FFA; Prom Com; Pediatrician; Teacher; Tennessee Tech

SCRUGGS, WHITNEY; MURFREESBORO, TN; BLACKMAN HS; (JR); Ctznshp Aw; Gov Hnr Prg; Hnr Roll; Nat Hon Sy; Otst Ac Ach Awd; St of Mnth; WWAHSS; Comm Volntr; Key Club; Ntl Beta Clb; Latin Clb; Bnd; Mch Bnd; Orch; Pep Bnd; All-State Orchestra / Mid-State Band; Tennessee Governor School for the Arts; Pre-Med; Music

SCURLOCK, MARKISS; MEMPHIS, TN; KINGSBURY VOC-TECH CTR; (JR); Ctznshp Aw; Hnr Roll; Perf Att; Comm Volntr; Chrch Yth Grp; Cmptr Clb; Mth Clb/Tm; Tchrs Aide

SEAL, TENIKA; MORRISTOWN, TN; (SO); Hi Hnr Roll; Nat Hon Sy; Comm Volntr; PP Ftbl (J); Sftball (V); Nursing; Cosmetology; U of Tennessee; Walter State

SEATON, KAYLA; WASHBURN, TN; WASHBURN SCH; (JR); Hi Hnr Roll; Perf Att; St of Mnth; WWAHSS; Ntl Beta Clb; Prom Com; Spanish Clb; Cl Off (T); Family, Career, and Community Leaders of America; Veterinary Medicine; Veterinary Technology; Lincoln Memorial U; Walters State Community College

SEIVENO, NATHAN; FRANKLIN, TN; RAVENWOOD HS; (FR); Hi Hnr Roll; Hnr Roll; DARE; Mus Clb; Chr; SP/M/VS; Meteorology; Fine Arts / Choir, Acting; Florida Institute of Technology; U of Tennessee

SELLERS, LEKESIA; MEMPHIS, TN; CENTRAL HS; (JR); Hnr Roll; Comm Volntr; Ntl Beta Clb; Spanish Clb; Cl Off; Stu Cncl (R); Teenage Improvement Club; Lovely Ladies of Elegance LLE; Psychology; Business Administration

SELPH, CHRYSTAL; STEWART, TN; STEWART CTY HS; (JR); All Am Sch; Hi Hnr Roll; Hnr Roll; MVP; WWAHSS; Spec Olymp Vol; 4-H; Chrch Yth Grp; DARE; FCA; Mth Clb/Tm; Ntl Beta Clb; Ntl FFA; Pep Squd; Ch Chr; Bskball (J); Sftball (V); Cl Off (P); Stu Cncl (T); CR (R); Miss Stewart County 2004; Miss Kentucky Bluegrass 2004; Special Education; Psychology (Applied and Mental Health); U of Tennessee At Martin; Union U

SEYMOUR, JACQUELINE M; BRISTOL, TN; SULLIVAN EAST; (MS); Duke TS; Hnr Roll; Chr; Chrldg (V C); Yrbk

SEYMOUR, TIERA; MEMPHIS, TN; MELROSE HS; (FR); Hi Hnr Roll; Hnr Roll; St of Mnth; Comm Volntr; Peer Tut/Med; DARE; Dnce; Stu Cncl (T); CR (V); Bachelor's Degree; Pediatrician; U of Memphis; Howard U

SHAFER, SARAH; LENOIR CITY, TN; LENOIR CITY HS; (JR); Nat Hon Sy; Yth Ldrshp Prog; Peer Tut/Med; Emplmnt; Prom Com; Scouts; Chr; SP/M/VS; Mar Art

SHAH, VARUN; MEMPHIS, TN; RIDGEWAY HS; (SO); Hi Hnr Roll; Key Club; Mth Clb/Tm; MuAlphaTh; EOL; Computer Science; Computer Engineering; Georgia Tech Atlanta; U of Washington Seattle

SHANNON, DJANINN M; WOODLAWN, TN; NORTHWEST HS; (SO); Hi Hnr Roll; Hnr Roll; Perf Att; Peer Tut/Med; Red Cr Aide; Mth Clb/Tm; Ntl Beta Clb; Spch Team; Chr; Sccr (V); Sftball (J); Track (V); Wt Lftg (J); CR (R); Mathematics; Geneticist

SHARP, ASHLEY P; JASPER, TN; MARION CTY HS; (JR); 4H Awd; Hnr Roll; Yth Ldrshp Prog; Comm Volntr; 4-H; Chrch Yth Grp; DARE; Emplmnt; Ntl Beta Clb; Pep Squd; SADD; Ch Chr; Chrldg (V); Big Brothers / Big Sisters

SHARP, JARED; SPRINGFIELD, TN; SPRINGFIELD HS; (SO); Hnr Roll; Chrch Yth Grp; Emplmnt; FCA; Ntl Beta Clb; Wrstlg (J); Engineer, Computer; Western Kentucky U; Austin Peay U

Selph, Chrystal
Stewart Cty HS
Stewart, TN

Scheiterlein, Robby
Fayette AC
Eads, TN

Sanders, April
Mc Nairy Ctrl HS
Hornsby, TN

Salat, Justin R
Wooddale HS
Memphis, TN

Rushing, Lauren E
Ripley HS
Ripley, TN

Russell, Lyndsay H
Campbell Cty HS
La Follette, TN

Sands, Brittany D
William Blount HS
Maryville, TN

Scott, Alana
Clay Cty HS
Celina, TN

Sharp, Ashley P
Marion Cty HS
Jasper, TN

SHARP, SARAH; NASHVILLE, TN; FRANKLIN HS; (JR); Duke TS; Nat Hon Sy; Chrch Yth Grp; FCA; Mth Clb/Tm; Mod UN; Prom Com; Spanish Clb; Bnd; Ch Chr; Flg Crps; Mch Bnd; National Honor Society; Top 10 of 450 Students; Pharmacy; Chemistry; Vanderbilt U; Wake-Forest U

SHARPE, LAUREN; JEFFERSON CITY, TN; JEFFERSON CTY HS; (SO); Duke TS; Hi Hnr Roll; Perf Att; Pres Ac Ftns Aw; USAA; WWAHSS; Chrch Yth Grp; DECA; FCA; FCCLA; Pep Squd; Ch Chr; SP/M/VS; Bskball (VJ); Sccr (V); Track (V); Stu Cncl (R); Communications; Magazine Editing

SHAW, TIMOTHY M; GREENBRIER, TN; GOODPASTURE CHRISTIAN SCH; (SR); Hi Hnr Roll; Hnr Roll; Pres Sch; WWAHSS; Comm Volntr; FCA; Bsball (V C); Cr Ctry (V); Class Rank-11th; Started My Own Lawn Care Business; Finance Major; U of Tennessee (Knoxville); Vanderbilt U

SHEETS, AARON; JOHNSON CITY, TN; HAPPY VALLEY HS; (JR); WWAHSS; Chrch Yth Grp; Emplmnt; Mus Clb; Bnd; Ftball (J); Track (V); Music; East Tennessee State U; Lee U

SHELBY, JOSEPH C; PULASKI, TN; GILES CTY HS; (JR); Duke TS; Hnr Roll; Pres Sch; Sci/Math Olympn; Yth Ldrshp Prog; Comm Volntr; FBLA; Quiz Bowl; Sci Clb; Scouts; Bnd; Mch Bnd; Eagle Scout; Computer Engineering; Business; Tennessee Technological U

SHELTON, HOLLY B; HARTFORD, TN; COSBY HS; (JR); Hi Hnr Roll; Hnr Roll; Nat Hon Sy; Perf Att; WWAHSS; Yth Ldrshp Prog; Peer Tut/Med; Chrch Yth Grp; FCA; Mth Clb/Tm; Mus Clb; Ntl Beta Clb; Pep Squd; Prom Com; Scouts; Chr; Ch Chr; SP/M/VS; Bskball (VJ); Vllyball (VJ); Cl Off (P, R); CR (P); Dentistry, Dental Hygiene; Business, Fashion; U of North Carolina UNC; East Tennessee State U

SHELTON, JESSI; KINGSPORT, TN; SULLIVAN NORTH HS; (SO); Hi Hnr Roll; Kwnis Aw; Comm Volntr; Spec Olymp Vol; Chrch Yth Grp; DARE; FCA; Key Club; Ntl Beta Clb; Ch Chr; Medical Field, Ob/Gyn; Forensic Science; U of Tennessee; East Tennessee State U

SHEPPARD, ROSE; MANCHESTER, TN; COFFEE CTY CTRL HS; (SR); 4H Awd; Hi Hnr Roll; Hnr Roll; MVP; Nat Mrt Fin; Nat Mrt LOC; Otst Ac Ach Awd; Perf Att; WWAHSS; Yth Ldrshp Prog; 4-H; ArtClub; Chrch Yth Grp; DARE; Emplmnt; Mth Clb/Tm; NYLC; Pep Squd; Veterinary Medicine; Middle Tennessee State U

SHERMAN, CASSANDRA; NIOTA, TN; MC MINN CTY HS; (FR); 4H Awd; Hi Hnr Roll; Hnr Roll; MVP; Nat Hon Sy; Otst Ac Ach Awd; Perf Att; 4-H; Chrch Yth Grp; DARE; Scouts; Ch Chr; SP/M/VS; Stg Cre; Bskball; Sftball (V); Vllyball (V); Student at Tennessee Tae Kwon Do Judo College; Marine Biologist / Science Major; Cleveland State TN; U of TN

SHERROD, NICK; MURFREESBORO, TN; SIEGEL HS; (SO); Yth Ldrshp Prog; Chrch Yth Grp; FCA; Key Club; Bsball (J); Engineering; Architect; U of Tennessee; U of Alabama

SHEUMAKER, BRITTNEY M; SPRING HILL, TN; SPRING HILL HS; (SO); Hi Hnr Roll; Hnr Roll; WWAHSS; DARE; Key Club; Ntl Beta Clb; ROTC; UT Knoxville; Vanderbilt U

SHIPLEY, AMBER; JASPER, TN; MARION CTY HS; (JR); Ctznshp Aw; Duke TS; Hnr Roll; WWAHSS; 4-H; DARE; FCA; FCCLA; Lib Aide; Sftball (V); Stu Cncl (R); Nursing; Radiology; Chattanooga State; U of Tennessee At Chattanooga

SHIPLEY, ERICA; KNOXVILLE, TN; HALLS HS; (SO); Hnr Roll; WWAHSS; Comm Volntr; Chrch Yth Grp; Emplmnt; Clb; Bnd; Mch Bnd; Mentor Program; Church Nursery & Welfare Ministry; Veterinary Medicine; U of Tennessee-Knoxville; Tennessee Tech-Pellissippi State

SHIPLEY, JESSI; MURFREESBORO, TN; BLACKMAN HS; (SR); Ctznshp Aw; DAR; Duke TS; Hi Hnr Roll; Hnr Roll; Nat Hon Sy; Otst Ac Ach Awd; St of Mnth; Yth Ldrshp Prog; Comm Volntr; Peer Tut/Med; Chrch Yth Grp; DARE; DECA; Emplmnt; Lib Aide; Ntl Beta Clb; Pep Squd; Tchrs Aide; Bnd; Chr; Ch Chr; SP/M/VS; Adv Cncl (R); Library Science; Interior Design; U of Tennessee At Martin

SHOLES, ASHELIE C; MEMPHIS, TN; WHITEHAVEN HS; (SR); Ctznshp Aw; F Lan Hn Soc; Hnr Roll; Nat Hon Sy; Otst Ac Ach Awd; St of Mnth; WWAHSS; Comm Volntr; Peer Tut/Med; DARE; Ntl Beta Clb; Off Aide; Sci Clb; Tchrs Aide; Dnce; CR; National Spanish Honor Society; Beta Club; Accounting; Performing Arts; Spelman College; Clark Atlanta U

SHORT, SAMUEL W; LAWRENCEBURG, TN; NEW PROSPECT SCH; (MS); Hi Hnr Roll; DARE; Ntl Beta Clb; Quiz Bowl; Tchrs Aide; Golf; Mar Art; Swmg; Beta Club-Entertainment Chairman 2004; Knowledge Bowl Team/ Church Youth Group; Pre-Med; U of Tennessee

SHORT, TAMEKA; NASHVILLE, TN; WHITE CREEK SCH; (FR); Hnr Roll; Perf Att; WWAHSS; Chrch Yth Grp; DARE; Jr Ach; French Clb; Ch Chr; Regular Degrees; PhD & Masters Degree; Tennessee State U; UT Knoxville

SHOUSE, EMMA; FRANKLIN, TN; FRANKLIN HS; (SO); Ctznshp Aw; Duke TS; Hnr Roll; Comm Volntr; Hab For Humty Volntr; Peer Tut/Med; Chrch Yth Grp; FCA; Key Club; Mus Clb; P to P St Amb Prg; Chr; SP/M/VS; Good Citizen for 2 Years At My School; Social Work; Special Education; Hendrix College; Earlham College

SIDDON, SARITA; NASHVILLE, TN; WHITES CREEK COMP HS; (FR); Hnr Roll; Perf Att; Peer Tut/Med; Prom Com; Dnce; Stu Cncl (R); Bachelor's Degree; TSU; Harvard

SIMMONS, BONNIE; EAGLEVILLE, TN; EAGLEVILLE SCH; (SO); Hnr Roll; Perf Att; WWAHSS; Ntl FFA; Vllyball (J); Respect and Responsibility Award; Psychology; Nutrition; Middle Tennessee State U

SIMMONS, BRITTNEY D; COOKEVILLE, TN; COOKEVILLE HS; (FR); 4H Awd; Hnr Roll; Yth Ldrshp Prog; Chrch Yth Grp; FCA; Clb; Bskball (J); PP Ftbl (V); Pharmacist Technician; Pharmacist; U of Tennessee; U of Kentucky

SIMMONS, MORGAN E; FRANKLIN, TN; CENTENNIAL HS; (SO); Ch Chr; Chrldg (J L); Best Overall for Cheerleading - 9th Grade; U of Tennessee

SIMMONS, TASHA J; HOHENWALD, TN; LEWIS CTY HS; (JR); WWAHSS; Peer Tut/Med; Spec Olymp Vol; Drma Clb; Fr of Library; Lib Aide; Sci Clb; Bnd; Dnce; Jzz Bnd; Mch Bnd; Teach CDC Students; Outstanding Soloist Award; Nursing; Teaching; Bethel College; U of Tennessee in Martin

SIMMONS JR, DARRYL T; MEMPHIS, TN; WHITE STATION HS; (FR); Hnr Roll; Perf Att; Comm Volntr; Hosp Aide; Chrch Yth Grp; Emplmnt; Jr Ach; Mus Clb; Off Aide; Chr; Ch Chr; Cl Off (V); CR (V); Lit Mag (R); Masters in Business; Masters in Music; U of North Carolina; Rhodes College

SIMPSON, DIAONDRA; KNOXVILLE, TN; (SO); Hnr Roll; WWAHSS; Chrch Yth Grp; Chr; Vet.; Doctor; U of Tennessee

SIMPSON, STEPHANIE; KNOXVILLE, TN; FARRAGUT HS; (JR); Ctznshp Aw; Hnr Roll; Pres Ac Ftns Aw; Comm Volntr; Hosp Aide; Peer Tut/ Med; Chrch Yth Grp; DARE; Emplmnt; Off Aide; Prom Com; Dnce; Yrbk; Major in Journalism/Broadcasting; U of Tennessee; East Tennessee State U

SIMS, ALICIA; HAMPSHIRE, TN; LEWIS CTY HS; (JR); Hi Hnr Roll; Hnr Roll; Nat Hon Sy; Sci Fairs; Comm Volntr; Peer Tut/Med; Red Cr Aide; 4-H; Biology Clb; DARE; Emplmnt; Mth Clb/Tm; Mus Clb; Outdrs Clb; P to P St Amb Prg; Bnd; Cl Off (S); CR (R); President of Anchor Club, Involved in 4-H, Math, Science and French Clubs; Nursing; Teaching; U of Memphis

SINDY, QIMAT; NASHVILLE, TN; GLENCLIFF COMP HS; (SR); Nat Hon Sy; Otst Ac Ach Awd; St of Mnth; Comm Volntr; 4-H; ArtClub; BPA; Lib Aide; Off Aide; Sci Clb; Yrbk (P); Tutor 3rd and 4th Graders After School; Write Poems; Registered Nurse; Doctorate Degree; Aquinas College; Tennessee State U

SISK, AARON; PHILADELPHIA, TN; LOUDON HS; (SO); 4H Awd; Duke TS; Hi Hnr Roll; Perf Att; Sci Fairs; WWAHSS; Peer Tut/Med; 4-H; Chrch Yth Grp; DARE; Ntl Beta Clb; Ch Chr; Stg Cre; Ftball (VJ L); Wt Lftg (VJ); PhD / Math Teaching; PhD / Science Teaching; U of South Carolina; Tennessee Wesleyan College

SISSOM, AMANDA R; BRADYVILLE, TN; CANNON CTY HS; (FR); Hnr Roll; Comm Volntr; Chrch Yth Grp; Ntl Beta Clb; Master's Degree; Bachelor's Degree; UNC Chapel Hill; Middle Tennessee State U

SIZEMORE, KAYLA; SNEEDVILLE, TN; HANCOCK HS; (SO); 4H Awd; Hnr Roll; MVP; Hab For Humty Volntr; Red Cr Aide; 4-H; Chrch Yth Grp; DARE; Ntl FFA; SADD; Voc Ind Clb Am; Ch Chr; Dnce; Chrldg (C); Gmnstcs (J); Mar Art (J); Swmg (J); Cl Off (V); Stu Cncl (S); CR (T); Sch Ppr (P); I Want to Be a Nurse in the Air Force.; East Tennessee U

SKINNER, LEAH K; ROCKFORD, TN; ALCOA HS; (JR); 4H Awd; Hnr Roll; Nat Hon Sy; WWAHSS; Comm Volntr; 4-H; ArtClub; Biology Clb; Chrch Yth Grp; Drma Clb; FCA; FBLA; Key Club; Ch Chr; SP/M/VS; Sccr (L); Sftball (V); Swmg (V L); Tennis (V L); Cl Off (T); Stu Cncl; Dentistry; Anthropology; U of Tennessee Chattanooga; U of Tennessee Knoxville

SLIGH, KEONTAE; CHATTANOOGA, TN; OOLTEWAH HS; (SO); Hnr Roll; WWAHSS; Fashion Design

SLONE, LATASHA; WOODLAWN, TN; NORTHWEST HS; (FR); 4H Awd; Hnr Roll; Nat Hon Sy; Comm Volntr; 4-H; Chrch Yth Grp; Clr Grd; Student to Student Ambassador; Medical; Law; Brown U; New York U

SMILEY, NIKKO; CHATTANOOGA, TN; (SO); Bskball; Dvng; Skt Tgt Sh; Wt Lftg; Law; UTC; Duke U

SMITH, AMANDA A; NEWPORT, TN; (FR); Hnr Roll; Nat Hon Sy; WWAHSS; Peer Tut/Med; P to P St Amb Prg; ROTC; Bnd; Mch Bnd; Orch; Pep Bnd; Bowling-High Average; Astronomer; Flutist in a Symphony Orchestra; King College; Carson Newman

SMITH, ANNA; TELFORD, TN; DAVID CROCKETT HS; (FR); Hnr Roll; Pres Sch; Yth Ldrshp Prog; Peer Tut/Med; 4-H; DARE; FCA; Hsbk Rdg; Sccr (V, L); Track (V, L); Stu Cncl (R); Tennessee State Duck Stamp Competition, 3rd place; Pre-Law; Vanderbilt U; U of Tennessee

SMITH, ANNA M; PIKEVILLE, TN; BLEDSOE CTY HS; (FR); 4H Awd; Hi Hnr Roll; USAA; WWAHSS; Comm Volntr; 4-H; Chrch Yth Grp; FTA; Ntl Beta Clb; Ntl FFA; Svce Clb; Vllyball (L); 4-H Honor Club-President; Cattle Kids-President; Attorney

SMITH, ANTHONY; KNOXVILLE, TN; WEST END AC; (FR); Hnr Roll; MVP; Nat Hon Sy; Perf Att; Chrch Yth Grp; Tchrs Aide; Bsball (V); Bskball (V C); Ftball (J); Golf (V C); Mechanical Engineering; Tennessee; Pellisippi Community College

SMITH, APRIL D; RED BOILING SPRINGS, TN; HERMITAGE SPRINGS SCH; (JR); 4H Awd; Hi Hnr Roll; Nat Sci Aw; Perf Att; WWAHSS; Yth Ldrshp Prog; Comm Volntr; 4-H; Chrch Yth Grp; DARE; FCA; FCCLA; Ntl Beta Clb; Ntl FFA; Prom Com; SP/M/VS; Chrldg (V C); Cl Off (V); Stu Cncl (V); CR (P); Yrbk (E); Pres. of FCA & FCCLA; Asst. Coach to Little Wildcat Cheerleaders; Business Management; Accounting; Tennessee Tech U

SMITH, CHARITY R; MOUNT JULIET, TN; WILSON CTRL HS; MS; Hnr Roll; Otst Ac Ach Awd; Chrch Yth Grp; DARE; Chr; Ch Chr; Music; U of Tennessee (Knoxville); U of Memphis

SMITH, GEORGANNA; COVINGTON, TN; COVINGTON HS; (FR); MVP; Hosp Aide; Red Cr Aide; FCA; Pep Squd; Voc Ind Clb Am; Sftball (V); Vllyball (V); Stu Cncl; CR (R); Yrbk (P); Sports Medicine; Lawyer; The U of Tennessee Knoxville; The U of West Florida

SMITH, GINA S; ATOKA, TN; MUNFORD HS; (SR); Hnr Roll; Comm Volntr; Chrch Yth Grp; DECA; Off Aide; Scouts; Tchrs Aide; Ch Chr; Student of the Week; Nursing / RN; Business Administration; U of Memphis; Tennessee State of U

SMITH, IMAN A; COLLIERVILLE, TN; (SO); Gov Hnr Prg; WWAHSS; Comm Volntr; DARE; Emplmnt; Swmg (V); Bridge Builders; Pharmacist; Physical Therapist; Howard U; Florida A & M U

SMITH, JAKE; KNOXVILLE, TN; FARRAGUT HS; (JR); Hnr Roll; U of Tennessee Knoxville; Middle Tennessee State U

SMITH, JENNIFER L; HARRIMAN, TN; OLIVER SPRINGS HS; (SO); Ctznshp Aw; Hnr Roll; MVP; Otst Ac Ach Awd; Pres Sch; Peer Tut/Med; ArtClub; Drma Clb; FCA; Bskball (V); Principal's Award; Certificate of Achievement in Computer Skills; Pharmaceutical Sales; Pediatric Care; Georgia U; Roane State

SMITH, JESSICA A; UNICOI, TN; UNICOI CTY HS; (FR); WWAHSS; BPA; Chrch Yth Grp; Key Club; Pep Squd; Vllyball (VJ); U of Tennessee; U of Florida

SMITH, JOSHUA G; HIXSON, TN; SODDY-DAISY HS; (FR); Hnr Roll; Perf Att; Chrch Yth Grp; DARE; FCA; ROTC; Cr Ctry (L); Track (L); Member of High School Bowling Team; Received 4 JROTC Awards-Spring 2005; Officer in US Navy; Marine Biology; U of Mississippi, Oxford; U of North Carolina Chapel Hill

SMITH, JULIE; SELMER, TN; MC NAIRY CTRL HS; (JR); Nat Hon Sy; WWAHSS; Comm Volntr; Chrch Yth Grp; Prom Com; Stu Cncl (V); Vice President Bobcat Community Service; HOSA; Pre-Med; Nursing; Jackson State Community College; Union U

SMITH, JUSTIN; SIGNAL MTN, TN; RED BANK HS; (SO); Duke TS; Chrch Yth Grp; Drma Clb; Stg Cre; Mechanical Engineering; Outdoor Guide; U of Tennessee Chattanooga; Chattanooga State College

SMITH, KATELYN; CROSSVILLE, TN; CUMBERLAND CTY HS; (JR); 4H Awd; Hnr Roll; MVP; Otst Ac Ach Awd; Perf Att; Sci Fairs; St of Mnth; WWAHSS; Yth Ldrshp Prog; Peer Tut/Med; 4-H; DECA; FCA; FBLA; Ntl Beta Clb; Ntl FFA; Scr Kpr (J); Vllyball (C); Business Management; Professional Sales; Tennessee Technological U; Maryville College

SMITH, LYNDSAY M; MURFREESBORO, TN; SIEGEL HS; (JR); Hi Hnr Roll; MVP; Nat Hon Sy; WWAHSS; Comm Volntr; Chrch Yth Grp; Emplmnt; FCA; Key Club; Ntl Beta Clb; Pep Squd; Scouts; Dnce; Stg Cre; PPSqd (V); Stu Cncl (R); Girl Scouts of America Gold Award; United Dance Association All-Star; Early Childhood Education; Psychology; U of Tennessee Knoxville; Middle Tennessee State U

SMITH, MEGAN J; ATHENS, TN; MC MINN CTY HS; (SO); Hnr Roll; Nat Hon Sy; Pres Ac Ftns Aw; WWAHSS; Comm Volntr; Peer Tut/Med; Chrch Yth Grp; FCA; Pep Squd; Prom Com; Svce Clb; Chr; Dnce; SP/M/VS; Bskball (J); Vllyball (J); Cl Off (S); Stu Cncl (R); Track Manager; Law / Paralegal; Public Relations / Communications; Duke U; U of North Carolina

SMITH, RACHEL; WHITE HOUSE, TN; WHITE HOUSE HS; (JR); Fut Prb Slvr; Hi Hnr Roll; Nat Hon Sy; Otst Ac Ach Awd; St of Mnth; WWAHSS; Comm Volntr; DECA; Mth Clb/Tm; Ntl Beta Clb; Scouts; Spanish Clb; Vice-President DECA; Secretary Beta; Elementary Education; Western Kentucky U; Middle Tennessee State U

SMITH, RACHELE E; KNOXVILLE, TN; SOUTH DOYLE HS; (SO); Duke TS; Hnr Roll; Nat Hon Sy; WWAHSS; Chrch Yth Grp; Emplmnt; Ch Chr; Bskball (V); U of Tennessee

Smith, Gina S
Munford HS
Atoka, TN

Smith, April D
Hermitage Springs Sch
Red Boiling Springs, TN

Slone, Latasha
Northwest HS
Woodlawn, TN

Sisk, Aaron
Loudon HS
Philadelphia, TN

Shelton, Holly B
Cosby HS
Hartford, TN

Simmons, Tasha J
Lewis Cty HS
Hohenwald, TN

Smith, Anna M
Bledsoe Cty HS
Pikeville, TN

Smith, Charity R
Wilson Ctrl HS
Mount Juliet, TN

Smith, Rachele E
South Doyle HS
Knoxville, TN

SMITH, SHANICE J; MADISON, TN; HUNTERS LANE HS; (JR); Hnr Roll; WWAHSS; DARE; Jr Ach; Voc Ind Clb Am; Dnce; Nursing; Middle Tennessee State U; Memphis State U

SMITH, SHARITA; NASHVILLE, TN; MC GAVOCK COMP HS; (JR); Hnr Roll; WWAHSS; Comm Volntr; Peer Tut/Med; Chrch Yth Grp; Drma Clb; Scouts; Ch Chr; Dnce; SP/M/VS; Girl Scouts Silver Award; Working Toward Gold Award; Psychology; Early Childhood Development; Alabama A & M U; U of Memphis

SMITH, SPENSER C; SODDY DAISY, TN; SODDY DAISY HS; (FR); All Am Sch; Duke TS; Hnr Roll; Sci Fairs; USAA; WWAHSS; Comm Volntr; Peer Tut/Med; Chrch Yth Grp; Emplmnt; Mod UN; Tchrs Aide; Ftball (V L); Stu Cncl (V); Anesthesiologist; Stock Investor

SMITH, TENESHA; MEMPHIS, TN; TREZEVANT VOC TECH CTR; (SO); Ctznshp Aw; Hnr Roll; Nat Sci Aw; Perf Att; Pres Ac Ftns Aw; St of Mnth; Comm Volntr; ArtClub; Chrch Yth Grp; FCCLA; Jr Ach; Scouts; Voc Ind Clb Am; Bnd; Drm Mjr; Flg Crps; Mch Bnd; Chrldg; Hsbk Rdg; Mar Art; Tennis; Fashion and Design; Cosmetology

SMITH, THOMAS L; HICKMAN, TN; GORDONSVILLE HS; (JR); Hnr Roll; Nat Hon Sy; WWAHSS; Chrch Yth Grp; FCA; Ntl Beta Clb; Prom Com; SADD; Chr; Ch Chr; Bskball (V); Cl Off (S); Psychology; Business; The U of Tennessee; U of California Los Angeles

SMITH, ZACH B; KNOXVILLE, TN; WEST HS; (FR); Hnr Roll; Nat Hon Sy; Perf Att; Chrch Yth Grp; U of Tennessee

SMOOT, TEELA; MEMPHIS, TN; CENTRAL HS; (JR); Hnr Roll; WWAHSS; DECA; Key Club; Ntl Beta Clb; Stu Cncl (R); Vanderbilt U; U of Tennessee Knoxville

SNEED, BRITTANY N; SODDY DAISY, TN; SODDY DAISY HS; (FR); Hnr Roll; WWAHSS; Chrch Yth Grp; Ntl Beta Clb; Chr; Ch Chr; Yrbk (P); Majorette; Meteorology; U of North Carolina Asheville

SNYDER, BENJAMIN R; MARYVILLE, TN; WILLIAM BLOUNT HS; (JR); All Am Sch; WWAHSS; Chrch Yth Grp; Emplmnt; Mathematics Secondary Education; History Secondary Education; Milligan College; Maryville College

SOHN, GEEHYUNG; CLARKSVILLE, TN; KENWOOD HS; (JR); Otst Ac Ach Awd; WWAHSS; ArtClub; Mth Clb/Tm; Orch; Accountant; Pharmacy; U of Texas; U of Tennessee

SOLOMAN, STEVEN; NEW MARKET, TN; JEFFERSON CTY HS; (JR); Hi Hnr Roll; Nat Hon Sy; Perf Att; WWAHSS; Yth Ldrshp Prog; Emplmnt; Ntl Beta Clb; Bsball (V); Bskball (V); Ftball (V); High Honors; Who's Who American High Schools; Walter State Community College; Maryville College

SONG, JUN; MEMPHIS, TN; WHITE STATION HS; (FR); Ctznshp Aw; Duke TS; Perf Att; Sci/Math Olympn; St of Mnth; Chess; Chrch Yth Grp; DARE; Mth Clb/Tm; Schol Bwl; Orch; Swmg (J); Math Counts; Science Olympiad; Medical; Law; Massachusetts Institute of Technology; Princeton

SORY, BRANDON; CHARLOTTE, TN; NASHVILLE CHRISTIAN SCH; (JR); Duke TS; Hi Hnr Roll; Nat Hon Sy; Comm Volntr; FCA; Bsball (J); Bskball (V); Ftball (VJ); Cl Off (V); Stu Cncl (V, T); Yrbk (R, P); Mock Trial Teen & Youth in Government; Athletic-Scholar Award; Structural/ Aerospace Engineering; Business; U of Tennessee

SOUTH, RACHEAL; JONESBOROUGH, TN; DAVID CROCKETT HS; (FR); 4H Awd; Duke TS; Hi Hnr Roll; Sci Fairs; 4-H; Chrch Yth Grp; ROTC; Bnd; Ch Chr; Mch Bnd; Pianist At Church; Pre-Med; Vanderbilt U; U of North Carolina

SPARE, DAVID; CULLEOKA, TN; CULLEOKA UNIT HS; (SO); Bsball (V L); Bskball (V L); CR (P); Middle Tennessee State U; U of Tennessee Chattanooga

SPAULDING, ADAM M; HIXSON, TN; SODDY-DAISY HS; (FR); Hnr Roll; Perf Att; Chess; DARE; ROTC; Corporate Lawyer; UTK; UTC

SPEARS, ZACK; SHELBYVILLE, TN; CASCADE HS; (JR); Hi Hnr Roll; Nat Hon Sy; AL Aux Boys; Chrch Yth Grp; Emplmnt; FCA; Key Club; Ntl FFA; Prom Com; Bskball (V L); Ftball (V L); Golf (V L); Sccr (V L); Stu Cncl (T, R); Architecture; Engineering; Princeton U; Duke U

SPITZER, ASHLEY; LAKE CITY, TN; ANDERSON CTY HS; (JR); Hnr Roll; Nat Hon Sy; Comm Volntr; Bnd; Flg Crps

SPRATTLIN JR, GERALD A; MEMPHIS, TN; WOODDALE HS; (JR); Ctznshp Aw; Hnr Roll; Nat Ldrshp Svc; Perf Att; WWAHSS; Comm Volntr; Chrch Yth Grp; DARE; NYLC; Stg Cre; Bsball (V); Bskball (V C); Ftball (V); Gmnstcs (V); Business Administrations/Financing; Communications/ Terminology; Tennessee State U/Texas Southern; Florida A & M U/Florida State

SSALI, MICHAEL; MEMPHIS, TN; WHITE STATION HS; (SO); F Lan Hn Soc; Hnr Roll; Comm Volntr; Chrch Yth Grp; P to P St Amb Prg; Spanish Clb; Participate in Pathfinder Club; Participate in Youth Congress; Engineer, Civil; Business Manager; U of Tennessee-Knoxville; Vanderbilt U

STAFFORD, ARIAL; LIMESTONE, TN; HOMESCHOOLED; (FR); Sci Fairs; Chrch Yth Grp; Drma Clb; Scouts; Sign Clb; Ch Chr; Dnce; SP/M/VS; Gmnstcs; Hsbk Rdg; National American Miss State Finalist; Sign Language Interp.; Dance

STALCUP, AMELIA F; CLEVELAND, TN; WALKER VALLEY HS; (SO); F Lan Hn Soc; Hi Hnr Roll; Hnr Roll; Jr Rot; Kwnis Aw; Otst Ac Ach Awd; USAA; WWAHSS; Comm Volntr; Peer Tut/Med; Drma Clb; Key Club; MuAlphaTh; Ntl Beta Clb; Prom Com; Svce Clb; SP/M/VS; Stg Cre; Track; Yrbk (R, P); Anchor Club, Drama Club; Junior Civitan Charter Member; Communications; Law; Duke U

STALCUP, LEAH D; PIGEON FORGE, TN; SEVIER CTY HS; (FR); Duke TS; Hi Hnr Roll; Hnr Roll; Nat Stu Ath Day Aw; Otst Ac Ach Awd; Perf Att; Sci Fairs; St of Mnth; Comm Volntr; Hosp Aide; Peer Tut/Med; Chrch Yth Grp; Mus Clb; Ntl Beta Clb; Scouts; Chr; Ch Chr; Dentist; Teacher; U of Tennessee, Knoxville TN; Duke U

STAMPS, RACHEL; PLEASANT VIEW, TN; SYCAMORE HS; (FR); Hnr Roll; WWAHSS; Key Club; Bnd; Mch Bnd; Veterinarian; Vet. Assistant; Austin Peay State U; Middle Tennessee U

STAPISH, BRITTANY; COLUMBIA, TN; MT PLEASANT HS; (SR); All Am Sch; Hi Hnr Roll; Hnr Roll; WWAHSS; Red Cr Aide; BPA; Emplmnt; FCCLA; Ntl Beta Clb; Pep Squd; Prom Com; Yrbk; Family Resource Center Mentor; Business; Entrepreneurship; Tennessee Technological U

STARK, KATHLEEN C; FRANKLIN, TN; RAVENWOOD-FRANKLIN ROAD AC MS; MS; Duke TS; Hi Hnr Roll; Nat Hon Sy; Otst Ac Ach Awd; Sci Fairs; Valdctrian; Chrch Yth Grp; Chr; Ch Chr; SP/M/VS; Chrldg (J); Track (J); Cl Off (P, V); Stu Cncl; National Junior Honor Society; Honors Choir; Belmont U; Furman U

STATEN, ANGELA; SPRINGFIELD, TN; SPRINGFIELD HS; (JR); Hnr Roll; WWAHSS; Peer Tut/Med; Red Cr Aide; Drma Clb; SP/M/VS; Member of HOSA; Acting; Nursing; Middle Tennessee State U; Volunteer State Community College

STATES, ERICA A; CLARKSVILLE, TN; ROSSVIEW HS; (JR); Perf Att; Comm Volntr; DARE; Key Club; Tchrs Aide; Vllyball (J); Blue Excel Card; Finance Exploring Program - Legends Bank; Business; CPA; Austin Peay State U

STEADING, DEBORAH; MURFREESBORO, TN; SIEGEL HS; (SR); 4H Awd; Hnr Roll; MVP; Otst Ac Ach Awd; Perf Att; St of Mnth; 4-H; Emplmnt; Jr Cls League; Lttrmn Clb; Ntl Beta Clb; Pep Squd; ROTC; Tchrs Aide; Bnd; Mch Bnd; Pep Bnd; Varsity Lettering in Marching Band; Aviation; Psychology; Middle Tennessee U; UT Martin

STEELE, JHERRICA R; KNOXVILLE, TN; WEST HS; (SO); 4H Awd; DAR; Duke TS; Hnr Roll; WWAHSS; 4-H; DARE; ROTC; Scouts; Squad Leader in ROTC; Chief Petty Officer in ROTC; Animal/Medicine; U of Texas

STEPHENS, JOSH R; ATHENS, TN; MC MINN CTY HS; (JR); Hnr Roll; WWAHSS; Comm Volntr; Chrch Yth Grp; Chr; Stu Cncl (R); CR (R); Young Southern Student Writers Winner - 2005; BS in Music Business; Marketing Minor; Lee U

STEVENS, ADAM; ROAN MOUNTAIN, TN; CLOUDLAND HS; (JR); Ctznshp Aw; Hi Hnr Roll; Hnr Roll; Nat Hon Sy; Perf Att; St of Mnth; Chrch Yth Grp; DARE; Drma Clb; Ntl Beta Clb; SP/M/VS; Stg Cre; Bskball (V C); Principal's Pride Award; 100% Award; Computer Programming; ETSU; Northeast State

STEVENS, REECE; JASPER, TN; SOUTH PITTSBURG HS; (FR); Hnr Roll; Perf Att; Comm Volntr; Ntl Beta Clb; Ftball; Wt Lftg; Pro Football Player; Forensic Scientist; U of Florida; U of Kentucky

STEVENSON, CHASITY D; MEMPHIS, TN; OAKHAVEN MIDDLE HS; MS; Hnr Roll; Nat Hon Sy; Perf Att; Chrch Yth Grp; DARE; Scouts; Bnd; Ch Chr; Mch Bnd; Bskball (J); U of Missouri; U of Memphis

STEVENSON, KIMBERLY; PULASKI, TN; GILES CTY HS; (JR); Hi Hnr Roll; Perf Att; WWAHSS; Comm Volntr; Ntl Beta Clb; Bnd; Mch Bnd; Member of HOSA; U of Tennessee

STEWART, AYOOLA W; MEMPHIS, TN; WHITE STATION HS; (JR); Ctznshp Aw; F Lan Hn Soc; Hi Hnr Roll; Hnr Roll; Nat Hon Sy; Perf Att; Comm Volntr; Peer Tut/Med; Dbte Team; DECA; Drma Clb; Ntl Beta Clb; Spch Team; Spanish Clb; Cl Off (R); CR (R); Pre-Law; Biomedical Engineering; Columbia U in New York City; Boston U

STEWART, CARA; MC EWEN, TN; MC EWEN HS; (JR); All Am Sch; Ctznshp Aw; Gov Hnr Prg; Hnr Roll; Nat Hon Sy; Nat Ldrshp Svc; Nat Sci Aw; Sci Fairs; USAA; Comm Volntr; Hab For Humty Volntr; FTA; Ntl Beta Clb; Ntl FFA; Off Aide; Prom Com; Sci Clb; Tchrs Aide; Spanish Clb; Bskball (V); Golf (V); Sftball (V L); Stu Cncl (R); Yrbk (R, P); Beta Club; Business Administration; Education; Cumberland U; Lamberth U

STEWART, CHRISTOPHER A; NASHVILLE, TN; (JR); Hi Hnr Roll; Hnr Roll; Perf Att; Sci Fairs; WWAHSS; Hab For Humty Volntr; Chess; Drma Clb; Mth Clb/Tm; French Clb; Cr Ctry (V L); Sccr (J); Tennis (V); Track (V); Yrbk (P); Ski Team-Private; Math-Teacher; Banking; Dickinson College; Rhodes College

STEWART, JAMIE; HENDERSONVLLE, TN; (FR); 4H Awd; Ctznshp Aw; Hi Hnr Roll; Hnr Roll; Yth Ldrshp Prog; Spec Olymp Vol; 4-H; Chrch Yth Grp; DARE; Drma Clb; FCA; Ntl FFA; Outdrs Clb; Photog; Chr; Cl Off (S); Stu Cncl (S); CR (S); Sch Ppr (P); Yrbk (P); Citizenship Awards; Photography; Psychology-Psychiatrist; Full Sail-Orlando, FL

STEWART, NICHOLAS M; ATHENS, TN; MC MINN CTY HS; (SO); Hi Hnr Roll; Hnr Roll; Nat Hon Sy; Perf Att; Pres Ac Ftns Aw; Pres Sch; WWAHSS; Comm Volntr; DECA; MuAlphaTh; Chr; SP/M/VS; Cr Ctry (V); Sccr; King and I - Community Play; State DECA Competitor; Medicine; Chemistry; New York U; Vanderbilt U

STEWART, TYLER B; SOUTH PITTSBURG, TN; RICHARD HARDY MEMORIAL SCH; (SO); All Am Sch; Hnr Roll; Otst Ac Ach Awd; Pres Sch; Sci Fairs; USAA; Yth Ldrshp Prog; Comm Volntr; 4-H; Chrch Yth Grp; FCA; Lttrmn Clb; Ntl Beta Clb; Quiz Bowl; Vsity Clb; Bsball (V L); Bskball (V L); Golf (V CL); Vsy Clb (L); History; Medical Field; U of Alabama; Vanderbilt

STEWART I, STEVEN; KNOXVILLE, TN; FARRAGUT HS; (JR); WWAHSS; Chess; MuAlphaTh; Bnd; Mch Bnd; 8th Place in Pre-Calculus State Test; Rugby All-Conference Team Player; Pharmacy; Astronomy; U of Tennessee; East Tennessee State U

STILLWELL, AMERETTE L; MC MINNVILLE, TN; WARREN CTY HS; (SO); Ctznshp Aw; Hnr Roll; Perf Att; St of Mnth; Peer Tut/Med; Ntl Beta Clb; Bnd; Orch; Published Twice At Poetry Com; Psychology; Child Education; Lincoln Memorial U

STOKES, RYONNA; MEMPHIS, TN; TREADWELL MIDDLE HS; (MS); Ctznshp Aw; Hnr Roll; Nat Hon Sy; Nat Sci Aw; Sci Fairs; USAA; Yth Ldrshp Prog; Comm Volntr; Peer Tut/Med; Spec Olymp Vol; BPA; Chrch Yth Grp; FCA; Outdrs Clb; Quill & Scroll; Sci Clb; SADD; Tmpl Yth Grp; Dnce; Drl Tm; SP/M/VS; Stg Cre; Bskball (V); Chrldg (V); Cr Ct Ski (V); Gmnstcs (V); Mar Art (V); Sftball (V); Track (J); CR (S); Lit Mag (E); Hair; Law Enforcing; TN State U; Delta State U

STOLWORTHY, RACHEL E; FRANKLIN, TN; FRANKLIN HS; (SO); Hi Hnr Roll; Comm Volntr; Hab For Humty Volntr; Chrch Yth Grp; DARE; Emplmnt; Key Club; Ntl Beta Clb; Off Aide; Scouts; Svce Clb; Ch Chr

STONE, RICHARD D; JACKSON, TN; SOUTHSIDE HS; (SO); Hnr Roll; Kwnis Aw; Nat Hon Sy; Nat Sci Aw; Otst Ac Ach Awd; Perf Att; St of Mnth; WWAHSS; Emplmnt; Lib Aide; Off Aide; Tchrs Aide; Vsity Clb; Ftball (V); Wt Lftg; Varsity Football

STRAHAN, TIARA N; MEMPHIS, TN; OVERTON HS; (MS); Ctznshp Aw; Hnr Roll; Chrch Yth Grp; Chr; Ch Chr; Flg Crps; All West Tennessee Honors Choir; Cordova Middle School Choir; Cosmetology; Business Administration; Alcorn State U; Jackson State U

STRATTON, AMY E; MADISON, TN; NASHVILLE SCH OF THE ARTS; (SO); 4H Awd; F Lan Hn Soc; Hnr Roll; Chrch Yth Grp; FCA; Ntl Beta Clb; P to P St Amb Prg; Acpl Chr; Ch Chr; Chrldg (V); Pediatric Nursing; Music; Vanderbilt U

STRATTON, TIMOTHY F; NASHVILLE, TN; NASHVILLE SCH OF THE ARTS; (SO); Hi Hnr Roll; Sci Fairs; Peer Tut/Med; Chrch Yth Grp; FCA; Ntl Beta Clb; Acpl Chr; Bnd; Chr; Ch Chr; Bowling-Varsity (Captain); Auto Mechanic Engineer; Mechanical Engineering; Wichita State U; Georgia Tech

STREET, DAVID; ARDMORE, TN; LINCOLN CTY HS; (SO); Hnr Roll; Nat Hon Sy; Comm Volntr; Chrch Yth Grp; Emplmnt; Lttrmn Clb; Voc Ind Clb Am; Ftball (VJ); Autobody Technician; Master Mechanic; Wyotech; Tennessee Tech

STREET, LAUREN; CLARKSVILLE, TN; CLARKSVILLE HS; (JR); Duke TS; Hi Hnr Roll; Hnr Roll; Perf Att; Pres Sch; St of Mnth; WWAHSS; Chrch Yth Grp; Drma Clb; SP/M/VS; Stg Cre; International Thespian Society; Cinematography; Television Production; Middle Tennessee State U; New York U

STREMIC, CAROLINE; BRENTWOOD, TN; FRANKLIN CLASSICAL SCH; Hnr Roll; Chrch Yth Grp; Drma Clb; SP/M/VS

STRINGER, MEGAN; SPRINGFIELD, TN; GREENBRIER HS; (SO); Hnr Roll; Perf Att; FBLA; Ntl Beta Clb; Spanish Clb; Bskball (J); Sccr (V); Austin Peay U; Vanderbilt U

STUARD, COLEY; SPRINGFIELD, TN; WHITE HOUSE HERITAGE HS; (SR); Hnr Roll; Valdctrian; Peer Tut/Med; Spec Olymp Vol; Emplmnt; FBLA; FCCLA; Key Club; Ntl Beta Clb; Off Aide; Yrbk (E, R, P); 2004 Homecoming Queen MS Heritage; Robertson Co. Senior of the Year Award; Pre-Medical; Middle Tennessee State U; Volunteer State Community College

Stevens, Reece
South Pittsburg HS
Jasper, TN

Stark, Kathleen C
Ravenwood-Franklin Road AC MS
Franklin, TN

Song, Jun
White Station HS
Memphis, TN

Stalcup, Leah D
Sevier Cty HS
Pigeon Forge, TN

Stone, Richard D
Southside HS
Jackson, TN

STUCKEY, EBONY; MEMPHIS, TN; CRAIGMONT HS; (JR); Hnr Roll; Nat Mrt LOC; WWAHSS; Yth Ldrshp Prog; Comm Volntr; Peer Tut/Med; DARE; ROTC; Tchrs Aide; Chr; Ch Chr; Dnce; Drl Tm; Bible Bowl Champion; Bible Reading Contest Winner; The U of Memphis; Christian Brothers U

STURGILL, SAMANTHA J; HARROGATE, TN; THOMAS WALKER HS; (SO); Hnr Roll; Peer Tut/Med; FBLA; Lib Aide; Pep Squd; Prom Com; Sci Clb; Spanish Clb; Bskball (J); Chrldg (V); Member of Enrichment Program; Magazine Journalist; Secondary Education/Librarian; U of Texas; U of North Carolina

STYKES, BART; JONESBOROUGH, TN; DANIEL BOONE HS; (SR); 4H Awd; All Am Sch; Hi Hnr Roll; Nat Hon Sy; Pres Sch; Valdctrian; WWAHSS; Comm Volntr; 4-H; Chrch Yth Grp; DECA; Emplmnt; FCA; Key Club; Ntl Beta Clb; Schol Bwl; Bnd; Chr; Ch Chr; Jzz Bnd; Sccr (J); Stu Cncl (V); Yrbk (R, P); Key Club-VP; Beta Club-VP; History Major-Goal College Profess; Austin Peay State U

SULLIVAN, CHERMONICA M; CLARKSVILLE, TN; NORTHWEST HS; (SO); Hnr Roll; Otst Ac Ach Awd; Chrch Yth Grp; Ntl Beta Clb; Off Aide; Chr; Ch Chr; Chrldg (V); Member of Elite All-American Team (Cheerleading); Attempting and Achieving Youth Banquet (Outstanding Academics); Pediatrician; Pharmacist

SULLIVAN, KELLY; CHRISTIANA, TN; RIVERDALE HS; (JR); Hnr Roll; Nat Hon Sy; Drma Clb; Scouts; Dnce; SP/M/VS; Stu Cncl (R); Humanities Governor's School 2005; TN Renaissance Fair '04/'05; 4 Community Plays; Lawyer/Politician; Theatre; Columbia College of Columbia U; Boston U

SUMMERS, KENDRA C; CAMDEN, TN; CENTRAL HS; (FR); 4H Awd; Hnr Roll; Otst Ac Ach Awd; Perf Att; Sci Fairs; Peer Tut/Med; 4-H; Chrch Yth Grp; Tourism; Athletic Training; U of Tennessee Knoxville

SUMMEY, JESSICA; BLOUNTVILLE, TN; SULLIVAN CTRL HS; (SO); Chrch Yth Grp; Key Club; Bnd; Mch Bnd

SUTTON, BETH; NEWPORT, TN; COSBY HS; (SO); DAR; Hnr Roll; Kwnis Aw; WWAHSS; Comm Volntr; Peer Tut/Med; Chrch Yth Grp; Emplmnt; FTA; Key Club; Lib Aide; Ntl Beta Clb; Svce Clb; Chr; Ch Chr; Yrbk (E); Key Club President - 3 Years; Special Education Teacher; Elementary Teacher; Walter's State Community College; U of Tennessee

SWAFFORD, ASHLEY R; EVENSVILLE, TN; BLEDSOE CTY HS; (SR); Gov Hnr Prg; Hi Hnr Roll; St of Mnth; WWAHSS; 4-H; Chrch Yth Grp; DECA; Drma Clb; FTA; Ntl Beta Clb; Ntl FFA; Off Aide; SP/M/VS; Stg Cre; Stu Cncl (P); Yrbk; 2004 Tennessee Governors School for Ag; Agribusiness; U of Tennessee Knoxville

SWAIN, HUNTER; GERMANTOWN, TN; MEMPHIS UNIVERSITY SCH; (SR); F Lan Hn Soc; Hnr Roll; Nat Hon Sy; Nat Mrt LOC; Hab For Humty Volntr; Mod UN; Quill & Scroll; SP/M/VS; Stg Cre; Lit Mag (E); Sch Ppr (E); Anthropology; Philosophy; Colorado College

SWALLOWS, KAYLA; MONTEREY, TN; MONTEREY HS; (SO); Hnr Roll; St of Mnth; WWAHSS; FCA; Ntl Beta Clb; Golf (V); Yrbk (R); Business Marketing; U of Tennessee; Tennessee Technological U

SWANSON, SIERRA M; MEMPHIS, TN; HAMILTON HS; (JR); Hnr Roll; MVP; Bskball (V); Cr Ctry (V); Track (V); Physical Therapist; Athletic Trainer; U of Memphis; U of Tennessee

SWEAT, KRISTEN E; RIPLEY, TN; DYERSBURG HS; (SR); Hi Hnr Roll; Hnr Roll; Nat Hon Sy; Pres Ac Ftns Aw; St of Mnth; WWAHSS; Comm Volntr; Peer Tut/Med; Red Cr Aide; AL Aux Girls; BPA; Chrch Yth Grp; DECA; Drma Clb; Emplmnt; FBLA; FCCLA; Ch Chr; SP/M/VS; Stg Cre; Tennis (J); Sch Ppr (E, P); Key Club President; FCCLA President; Communications-Major; Political Science-Minor; U of Tennessee At Knoxville

SWEENEY, GREGORY D; WHITE HOUSE, TN; WHITE HOUSE HS; (SO); Hnr Roll; Nat Hon Sy; St Schl; Comm Volntr; Peer Tut/Med; DECA; Ntl Beta Clb; Ntl FFA; SADD; Ch Chr; Tennis (V); Stu Cncl (R); Agricultural Majors-Any Degree; U of Tennessee At Knoxville

SWIFT, VALORIE; MEDON, TN; SOUTHSIDE HS; (SO); 4H Awd; Nat Hon Sy; Perf Att; St of Mnth; WWAHSS; Comm Volntr; Peer Tut/Med; 4-H; Chrch Yth Grp; FCA; Chr; Ch Chr; Track (V); Pre-Med; Education; Vanderbilt U; Meharry Medical College

TADE, AUTUMN J E; CELINA, TN; CLAY CTY HS; (FR); Hi Hnr Roll; Emplmnt; Cr Ctry (V); Sftball (V); Athletic Academic Award; PhD; X-Ray Technician; U of Kentucky; U of Tennessee

TAGGETT, STEVIE; LYNCHBURG, TN; MOORE CTY HS; (FR); Hnr Roll; Nat Hon Sy; WWAHSS; Spec Olymp Vol; Chrch Yth Grp; Pep Squd; Ch Chr; Dnce; Chrldg; CR (R); Yrbk (P); Crowned Miss Lynchburg; Homecoming Court; Veterinary Science; Bachelor's Degree; Middle Tennessee State U

TALLEY, DUSTIN L; ERWIN, TN; U N 1001 CTY VOC SCH; (SR); Hnr Roll; Nat Hon Sy; Pres Sch; WWAHSS; Comm Volntr; Drma Clb; FCA; Ntl FFA; Pep Squd; German Clb; SP/M/VS; Bsball (V C); Ftball (V); Stu Cncl (R); Chemistry I Award; Chemistry; Pharmacy; East Tennessee State U

TAMASHEVICH, KATE; CHATTANOOGA, TN; CMSCCA HS; (SR); Hnr Roll; Nat Hon Sy; Pres Sch; Yth Ldrshp Prog; Comm Volntr; Hosp Aide; Peer Tut/Med; ArtClub; Chess; Drma Clb; Mth Clb/Tm; Spch Team; Tchrs Aide; Russian Clb; Chr; SP/M/VS; Stg Cre; Vllyball (V); Cl Off (P); Stu Cncl (P); CR (P); Sch Ppr (E); Public Relations; Lee U

TARNER, CAITLIN R; CLINTON, TN; TEMPLE BAPTIST AC; (FR); Hnr Roll; Comm Volntr; Chrch Yth Grp; Mth Clb/Tm; Chr; Ch Chr; National Physical Fitness Award; Received Outstanding Achievement in Geography; Psychology; Forensics; George Mason U; Columbia U

TARR, LOREN A; COOKEVILLE, TN; COOKEVILLE HS; (JR); Ctznshp Aw; Pres Ac Ftns Aw; WWAHSS; Comm Volntr; Red Cr Aide; Emplmnt; FCA; FBLA; Clb; Bskball (J); PP Ftbl; Sccr (JC); Sftball (V); Who's Who - 2 Yrs; Best Sportsmanship Award - 2003-2004 / Soccer; Physical Therapy; Occupational Therapy; Vanderbilt U; Duke U

TATE, AUDREY S; COLLIERVILLE, TN; VANGUARD SCH; (JR); Hnr Roll; Kwnis Aw; WWAHSS; Yth Ldrshp Prog; Key Club; Ntl Beta Clb; NYLC; Prom Com; Svce Clb; Hsbk Rdg; Tennis; Track; Adv Cncl; Stu Cncl (S); CR; Key Club; Dorm Council

TAYLOR, AMBER M; TALBOTT, TN; MORRISTOWN HAMBLEN HS WEST; (SR); WWAHSS; Chrch Yth Grp; Chr; Ch Chr; Graduated with 1st Honors; Physical Therapy; Business; U of Tennessee

TAYLOR, ERIN M; CAMDEN, TN; CAMDEN CTRL HS; (FR); 4-H; Chrch Yth Grp; DARE; Fr of Library; Lib Aide; CR (R); Business; Teaching; U of Tennessee Knoxville; Vanderbilt U

TAYLOR, KATIE; TALBOTT, TN; JEFFERSON CTY HS; (JR); Duke TS; Hi Hnr Roll; Nat Hon Sy; Perf Att; USAA; WWAHSS; Yth Ldrshp Prog; Peer Tut/Med; Chrch Yth Grp; DECA; Golf (V)

TAYLOR, KIMBERLY D; CROSSVILLE, TN; CUMBERLAND CTY HS; (JR); Hi Hnr Roll; Hnr Roll; WWAHSS; Chrch Yth Grp; Emplmnt; FCA; Ntl Beta Clb; Off Aide; Pep Squd; Svce Clb; Vsity Clb; Ch Chr; Bskball (VJ L); Cr Ctry (VJ); Yrbk (P); Various Individual Subject Awards; Chemistry Major; Pre-Med / Physical Therapy; Belmont U; U of TN Chattanooga

TAYLOR, LAUREN; MURFREESBORO, TN; SIEGEL HS; (JR); Hi Hnr Roll; Hnr Roll; Nat Hon Sy; Otst Ac Ach Awd; WWAHSS; Comm Volntr; Chrch Yth Grp; FCA; MuAlphaTh; Ntl Beta Clb; Pep Squd; Sci Clb; Svce Clb; Spanish Clb; Chr; SP/M/VS; Stu Cncl; Nursing; Middle Tennessee State U; U of Tennessee, Knoxville

TAYLOR, MARTECIA; MEMPHIS, TN; MIDDLE COLLEGE HS; (JR); Ctznshp Aw; Hnr Roll; Nat Hon Sy; Perf Att; Comm Volntr; Chrch Yth Grp; DECA; Drma Clb; Pep Squd; Tchrs Aide; Dnce; SP/M/VS; Chrldg (V); PPSqd (V); Pre-Law; Public Broadcasting; U of Memphis; Christian Brothers U

TAYLOR, MICHELLE; NEWBERN, TN; DYER CTY HS; (SO); Nat Hon Sy; Comm Volntr; Chrch Yth Grp; Ch Chr; Dnce; Track

TAYLOR, SARA J; ARDMORE, TN; ARDMORE HS; (JR); Duke TS; Hi Hnr Roll; Nat Hon Sy; Otst Ac Ach Awd; WWAHSS; Yth Ldrshp Prog; Peer Tut/Med; Red Cr Aide; Spec Olymp Vol; Chrch Yth Grp; FCA; HO'Br Yth Ldrshp; MuAlphaTh; Ntl Beta Clb; Sci Clb; Spanish Clb; Bnd; Mch Bnd; Bskball (V); Sftball (V); Cl Off (V); Girls State Representative; Most Outstanding Bandsmen Award; Mathematics; Education; U of Alabama Huntsville; Martin Methodist College

TAYLOR, STEPHANIE L; MIDDLETON, TN; MIDDLETON HS; (JR); Hnr Roll; USAA; WWAHSS; Chrch Yth Grp; Ntl Beta Clb; ROTC; Spanish Clb; Clr Grd; Sftball (V); National Society of High School Scholars; Forensic Science and Technology; Criminal Justice; U of Central Florida

TAYLOR JR, JOHN; MEMPHIS, TN; MEMPHIS UNIVERSITY SCH; (SR); Duke TS; Hi Hnr Roll; Nat Hon Sy; Nat Mrt LOC; WWAHSS; Comm Volntr; Peer Tut/Med; MuAlphaTh; Quill & Scroll; Bsball (V); Bskball (V L); Stu Cncl (R); CR; Sch Ppr; National Honor Society; AP Scholar; Wake Forest U

TEAGUE, WHITNEY; CLAIRFIELD, TN; JELLICO HS; DAR; WWAHSS; Comm Volntr; Chrch Yth Grp; Emplmnt; Mth Clb/Tm; Ntl Beta Clb; German Clb; Ch Chr; Bskball (V); Sftball (V); Vllyball (V); Yrbk (P); Physical Therapy; German; Lambuth U

TENNANT, JALENE; COLUMBIA, TN; SPRING HILL HS; (JR); All Am Sch; Hnr Roll; Nat Hon Sy; WWAHSS; Prom Com; Tchrs Aide; Coach Jr Pee Wee Pop Warner Cheerleading; Creative Writing; Belmont U

TERRY, JESSICA E; CAMDEN, TN; CENTRAL HS; (FR); 4H Awd; Duke TS; Hnr Roll; Nat Hon Sy; Otst Ac Ach Awd; Sci Fairs; Peer Tut/Med; 4-H; Chrch Yth Grp; DARE; FCA; Ntl Beta Clb; Ch Chr; Lit Mag (R); Publication of Personal Poetry; Top Ten School Wide Geography Bee; Lawyer; Law Enforcement; Duke U; U of Tennessee Knoxville

TERRY, ROSALYN R; ROSSVILLE, TN; FAYETTE-WARE HS; (FR); Hnr Roll; Sci Fairs; WWAHSS; Comm Volntr; Red Cr Aide; Mus Clb; Chr; Ch Chr; Dnce; Drl Tm; Chrldg (V); Sch Ppr (E); Laboratory Technician; Radiology; Tennessee State U; U of Memphis

THARP, JOELLEN; MURFREESBORO, TN; BLACKMAN HS; (SO); Hi Hnr Roll; Chrch Yth Grp; FCA; FBLA; Key Club; Ntl Beta Clb; Chrldg (VJ); Business Administration; Psychology; Vanderbilt; U of Tennessee

THATCHER, CARRIE E; KNOXVILLE, TN; ALCOA HS; (SR); Duke TS; Hnr Roll; Nat Hon Sy; Comm Volntr; Emplmnt; FCA; Key Club; Prom Com; Sftball; Swmg; Nutrition / Communications; U of Tennessee

THIELECKE, ASHLEY; ATOKA, TN; BRIGHTON HS; (SO); Hi Hnr Roll; Hnr Roll; Otst Ac Ach Awd; 4-H; Chrch Yth Grp; Dbte Team; Scouts; Spanish Clb; Tennis (V); Fashion Designing; Lawyer; Florida U

THIGPEN, ALLISON; KNOXVILLE, TN; SOUTH DOYLE HS; (JR); Nat Hon Sy; St of Mnth; Comm Volntr; Chrch Yth Grp; FBLA; Key Club; MuAlphaTh; Prom Com; French Clb; Bnd; Jzz Bnd; Mch Bnd; Cl Off (P); Executive Women's International Regional Scholarship Winner

THOMAS, BEN; MURFREESBORO, TN; SIEGEL HS; (JR); Duke TS; Hnr Roll; Key Club; Mus Clb; Jzz Bnd; Mar Art; Second Degree Black Belt in Tae Kwon Do; Guitar Scholarship from Berklee School of Music; Music Performance; Berklee School of Music; The New School

THOMAS, DAQUANDRA S; MEMPHIS, TN; OVERTON HS; (FR); Ctznshp Aw; Hi Hnr Roll; Hnr Roll; Nat Hon Sy; Perf Att; Bnd; Jzz Bnd; Mch Bnd

THOMAS, JESSICA M; JASPER, TN; MARION CTY HS; WWAHSS; Emplmnt; Bnd; Mch Bnd; Pep Bnd; Culinary Arts in Pastry and Baking

THOMAS, MEGAN; BLOOMINGTON SPRINGS, TN; COOKEVILLE HS; (SO); Hi Hnr Roll; Hnr Roll; St of Mnth; WWAHSS; Key Club; Lib Aide; Bnd; Mch Bnd; Pep Bnd; Computer Science; Archaeologist; Tennessee Technological U; U of Tennessee

THOMAS, TAYLAR H; ATHENS, TN; ATHENS JHS; (MS); Yth Ldrshp Prog; Comm Volntr; Chrch Yth Grp; Drma Clb; Lib Aide; Outdrs Clb; Ch Chr; SP/M/VS; Mar Art (L); Community Theater; Business Major; Acting Minor; Tennessee Western College; Cleveland State

THOMAS, THESHIA; TRENTON, TN; DYERSBURG HS; (SO); Hi Hnr Roll; Hnr Roll; Perf Att; Peer Tut/Med; Chrch Yth Grp; DARE; FCCLA; Ntl Beta Clb; Bnd; Dnce; Mch Bnd; Track; To Go Into The Medical Field to Be a Plastic Surgeon; To Go Into the Law Field to Be an Attorney; U of Southern Alabama; Navy Academy

THOMPSON, CECILY; FRIENDSHIP, TN; CROCKETT CTY HS; (FR); 4H Awd; Hnr Roll; 4-H; Chrch Yth Grp; DARE; Ntl Beta Clb; Ntl FFA; Doctor of Veterinary Medicine; Veterinary Assistant; UT Knoxville; UT Martin

THOMPSON, CHRIS; KINGSTON SPRINGS, TN; YARPETH HS; (SO); Peer Tut/Med; Chrch Yth Grp; Emplmnt; Mth Clb/Tm; Golf (J); Honor Roll; Academic Awards for GPA; Mathematical Degree; Engineering; U of Tennessee

THOMPSON, JACKIE; STANTONVILLE, TN; ADAMSVILLE HS; (JR); 4H Awd; Gov Hnr Prg; 4-H; Emplmnt; Spanish Clb; Veterinary; Animal Science; U of Tennessee; U of Kentucky

THOMPSON, JOHN; LIMESTONE, TN; CHUCKEY-DOAK HS; (FR); Ctznshp Aw; Hi Hnr Roll; Hnr Roll; Perf Att; St of Mnth; DARE; ROTC; Round Robin; Military; U of Tennessee; Air Force Academy

THURMOND, AMBER; MEMPHIS, TN; GERMANTOWN HS; (JR); Ctznshp Aw; Hi Hnr Roll; Hnr Roll; Nat Hon Sy; Perf Att; Sci Fairs; WWAHSS; Comm Volntr; Cmptr Clb; Emplmnt; Key Club; Off Aide; SADD; Spanish Clb; Bnd; Mch Bnd; Ventures Scholars Program; Who's Who Among American High School Students; Pharmacy; Clark U; U of Memphis

TILLERY, RANDALL; LA VERGNE, TN; LA VERGNE HS; (FR); Hnr Roll; MVP; Ftball (VJ L); Track (V); Medical Field; U of Miami; U of Tennessee

TILLISON, SAMANTHA; NASHVILLE, TN; WHITES CREEK COMP HS; (JR); Hi Hnr Roll; Hnr Roll; Nat Hon Sy; Perf Att; WWAHSS; Comm Volntr; Peer Tut/Med; Mus Clb; Chr; Dnce; SP/M/VS; Certified Resistance Ed and Training; Doctor; TSU

TILLMAN, MELISSA; ADAMS, TN; JO BYRNS HS; (SO); Hnr Roll; WWAHSS; 4-H; Chrch Yth Grp; FCA; FCCLA; FTA; Key Club; Ntl Beta Clb; Bskball (V); Vllyball (J); Cl Off (T); Math Teacher

TILTON, MATTHEW C; MURFREESBORO, TN; RIVERDALE HS; (JR); Hi Hnr Roll; Hnr Roll; WWAHSS; Emplmnt; FCA; Tchrs Aide; Spanish Clb; Bskball (J); Tennis (V); Boys & Girls Basketball Statistician; Varsity Girls Basketball Scout Team; Nuclear Engineering; Chemical Engineering; United States Naval Academy; U of Tennessee

TIPTON, ALEXA N; KINGSPORT, TN; SULLIVAN NORTH HS; (SR); Duke TS; Nat Hon Sy; WWAHSS; Peer Tut/Med; Emplmnt; Key Club; Ntl Beta Clb; Respiratory Therapist; East Tennessee State U; Northeast State Community College

TIPTON, ASHLEY D; JASPER, TN; MARION CTY HS; (JR); Hnr Roll; 4-H; FCA; Track (J); Mathematics; Law; Tennessee State U; U Tennessee Knoxville

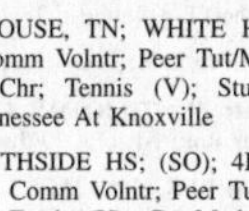
Thompson, John
Chuckey-Doak HS
Limestone, TN

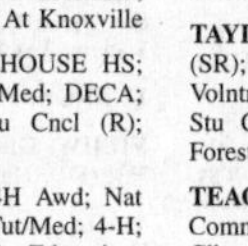
Taylor, Erin M
Camden Ctrl HS
Camden, TN

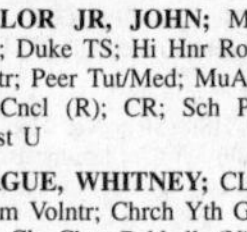
Swafford, Ashley R
Bledsoe Cty HS
Evensville, TN

National
Honor Roll
Spring 2005

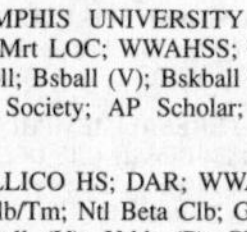
Sturgill, Samantha J
Thomas Walker HS
Harrogate, TN

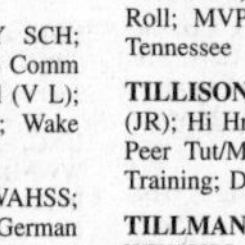
Taylor, Martecia
Middle College HS
Memphis, TN

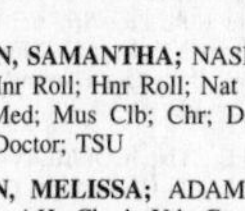
Thurmond, Amber
Germantown HS
Memphis, TN

TIPTON, DEANNA; TRACY CITY, TN; GRUNDY CTY HS; (SO); 4H Awd; Hi Hnr Roll; Hnr Roll; Nat Hon Sy; Otst Ac Ach Awd; Perf Att; St of Mnth; Yth Ldrshp Prog; 4-H; Chrch Yth Grp; DARE; Emplmnt; FCA; FBLA; Outdrs Clb; Photog; Sftball (V); Yrbk (E, R, P); Veterinarian

TODD, DONOVAN; HERMITAGE, TN; MC GAVOCK COMP HS; (SR); WWAHSS; Chrch Yth Grp; DARE; Emplmnt; FCA; Ftball (VJ); Cl Off (V); Stu Cncl (V); CR (V); Restaurant Management; Culinary Arts; Johnson & Wales U

TODD, SARAH; VONORE, TN; (MS); 4H Awd; Hnr Roll; Nat Hon Sy; St of Mnth; 4-H; DARE; Off Aide; Schol Bwl; Ch Chr; National Junior Honor Society; Talent Search; Fashion Design; Carpentry & Construction; Columbia; Long Island U

TORBETT, AMANDA L; CLEVELAND, TN; WALKER VALLEY HS; (SR); DAR; Duke TS; Hi Hnr Roll; Nat Hon Sy; Otst Ac Ach Awd; WWAHSS; Yth Ldrshp Prog; Spec Olymp Vol; Chrch Yth Grp; Emplmnt; FCA; Key Club; Ntl Beta Clb; Off Aide; Pep Squd; P to P St Amb Prg; Dnce; Chrldg (V C); PP Ftbl (V); Yrbk (R)

TORRES, BRITTANY; ONEIDA, TN; ONEIDA HS; (FR); 4H Awd; Hnr Roll; Nat Hon Sy; Otst Ac Ach Awd; 4-H; DARE; Ntl Beta Clb; Chr; Sftball; Medicine-Pediatrician; Photography; U of Tennessee; Florida State U

TORRES, MARIA D; MEMPHIS, TN; OAKHAVEN MIDDLE HS; (MS); Ctznshp Aw; Hnr Roll; Perf Att; Peer Tut/Med; DARE; Drma Clb; Emplmnt; Dnce; Sch Ppr (R); Poetry Club; Become a Famous Designer; Savannah College of Art and Design; Art Institute of America (In Dallas)

TREADWAY, LAKISHA N; RIPLEY, TN; RIPLEY HS; (JR); Hnr Roll; 4-H; DECA; Bnd; Mch Bnd; Pep Bnd; Veterinarian; Doctor; U of Tennessee Martin; Vanderbilt U

TREST, MATTHEW B; GOODLETTSVILLE, TN; DAVIDSON AC; (SR); Nat Mrt Fin; Nat Mrt Semif; WWAHSS; CARE; Comm Volntr; Chrch Yth Grp; Cmptr Clb; Emplmnt; Key Club; Outdrs Clb; Photog; Tech Clb; Ch Chr; Stg Cre; Track; Lit Mag (R); Architecture; Mechanical Engineering; U of TN, Knoxville; Belmont U

TRODGLEN, J.T.; ERIN, TN; HOUSTON CTY HS; (JR); Sch Ppr (E); Yrbk (E); Mechanics; Nashville Auto Diesel College

TROUPE, LEE; CLARKSVILLE, TN; CLARKSVILLE HS; (JR); Duke TS; Gov Hnr Prg; Hi Hnr Roll; Otst Ac Ach Awd; Pres Sch; WWAHSS; AL Aux Boys; Chrch Yth Grp; Jr Cls League; Mth Clb/Tm; Mus Clb; Bnd; Jzz Bnd; Mch Bnd; Lit Mag (E); Aerospace Engineering; Massachusetts Institute of Technology; Georgia Institute of Technology

TROUTT, CARTER; MURFREESBORO, TN; SIEGEL HS; (JR); Duke TS; Hi Hnr Roll; Hnr Roll; MVP; Nat Hon Sy; St of Mnth; WWAHSS; Yth Ldrshp Prog; Comm Volntr; Peer Tut/Med; BPA; Chess; Chrch Yth Grp; DARE; Dbte Team; Emplmnt; FCA; Key Club; Acpl Chr; Dnce; SP/M/VS; Golf (V); Track (V); Stu Cncl (R); Choreography At My Dance Studio; Half-Times/Studio Recitals/Dance Awards; Choreographer and Owner of Studies; U of North Carolina; Belmont U

TRUEHEART, PATRICK; ESTILL SPRINGS, TN; FRANKLIN CTY HS; (SO); Ctznshp Aw; St of Mnth; Chrch Yth Grp; FBLA; Ntl Beta Clb; Ch Chr; FBLA/Skills USA; Beta; Architect; U of Tenn

TRUESDALE, CARSHEBA; MEMPHIS, TN; WOODDALE HS; (JR); Hi Hnr Roll; Hnr Roll; Perf Att; WWAHSS; Comm Volntr; Hab For Humty Volntr; Peer Tut/Med; DARE; DECA; Jr Ach; Key Club; Mth Clb/Tm; Sci Clb; SADD; Biology; Aviation; Tennessee State U

TRUETT, TRAVIS D; KNOXVILLE, TN; FARRAGUT HS; (SR); Ctznshp Aw; Duke TS; Fut Prb Slvr; Hi Hnr Roll; Hnr Roll; Pres Sch; Sci Fairs; Sci/Math Olympn; WWAHSS; Comm Volntr; Chrch Yth Grp; DARE; Emplmnt; FBLA; Scouts; Sch Ppr (R); 1st Degree Black Belt; Eagle Scout; Aerospace Engineering; U of Tennessee; U of Colorado/Boulder

TRUJILLO, MICHELLE; COLLIERVILLE, TN; COLLIERVILLE HS; (SO); Chr; Dnce; Chrldg (V); Cr Ctry (J); Cr Ct Ski (J); Gmnstcs (V); PPSqd; Sccr; Track (J); Film and Video Editing; Mississippi State U; Jackson State U

TRUMPORE, SARAH; KNOXVILLE, TN; SOUTH DOYLE HS; (JR); Ctznshp Aw; Hi Hnr Roll; Hnr Roll; Nat Hon Sy; Perf Att; St of Mnth; WWAHSS; Yth Ldrshp Prog; Comm Volntr; Chrch Yth Grp; DARE; FCA; Key Club; Scouts; French Clb; Chr; Bridge Builders; National Honor Society; Psychology; Neonatology; Berea College; Vanderbilt U

TUCK, LAUREN E; KINGSPORT, TN; DOBYNS BENNETT HS; (SO); Duke TS; Hi Hnr Roll; Hnr Roll; Pres Ac Ftns Aw; Pres Sch; WWAHSS; Chrch Yth Grp; Key Club; Ntl Beta Clb; Bnd; Mch Bnd; Orch; Swmg (V); Swimming-State Qualifier; Band-Jr Clinic 9th Grade Senior Clinic 10th Grade; Medicine; U of Tennessee, Vanderbilt, Virginia Tech

TUCKER, DUSTIN; HENDERSONVILLE, TN; STATION CAMP HS; (JR); Ctznshp Aw; Perf Att; Comm Volntr; DECA; Ntl Beta Clb; Ntl FFA; Scouts; Tchrs Aide; Eagle Scout 2001; Auto-Diesel College

TUCKER, MARC R; KINGSPORT, TN; DOBYNS BENNETT HS; (JR); Ctznshp Aw; Duke TS; Hnr Roll; Nat Hon Sy; WWAHSS; Comm Volntr; Hab For Humty Volntr; Peer Tut/Med; Chrch Yth Grp; DARE; Key Club; Ntl Beta Clb; Scouts; Cr Ctry (J L); Track (J); AIM Scholar, Church Youth Rep-CE & Officer Nominating Committees; Shout Leadership Program, Rotary Youth Leadership Seminar; Accountant; Business Technology

TURNER, AMBER L; FAIRVIEW, TN; FAIRVIEW HS; (JR); Hnr Roll; WWAHSS; ArtClub; Emplmnt; FCA; Key Club; Ntl Beta Clb; Dnce; Mar Art (V); Sch Ppr (R); Dance Team Captain; National Art Honors Society; Graphic Design; Austin Peay State U; Middle Tennessee State U

TURNER, AMBER L; SPRINGFIELD, TN; SPRINGFIELD HS; (SR); Hnr Roll; Perf Att; Peer Tut/Med; 4-H; Chrch Yth Grp; DARE; DECA; FBLA; Off Aide; Scouts; Tchrs Aide; Ch Chr; Clr Grd; Flg Crps; Stg Cre; DECA (Pres.), Peer Mediator; Girl Talk; Marketing; Women's Health Studies; Western Kentucky U

TURNER, ASHLEY M; CELINA, TN; CLAY CTY HS; (SO); 4H Awd; Hi Hnr Roll; Hnr Roll; MVP; 4-H; Biology Clb; Chrch Yth Grp; Fr of Library; Mth Clb/Tm; Ntl Beta Clb; Sci Clb; Bdmtn (V); Bskball; Cl Off (T); Beta Club; Dentist; Vet; Western Kentucky U; Tennessee Tech

TURNER, BRITTANY; HARRIMAN, TN; HARRIMAN HS; (JR); Hnr Roll; Prom Com; Bskball (J); Sccr (V L); Sftball (V L); Vllyball (J); Radiologist; RN; U of Tennessee; Middle Tennessee State U

TURNER, BRITTNEY M; DUCKTOWN, TN; COPPER BASIN HS; (SR); Hnr Roll; WWAHSS; Comm Volntr; Chrch Yth Grp; DARE; FCA; FBLA; Key Club; Lttrmn Clb; Prom Com; Vsity Clb; Bskball (VJ L); Chrldg (V L); Business; Middle Tennessee State U; Lee U

TURNER, CACI; LASCASSAS, TN; OAKLAND HS; (FR); Ctznshp Aw; Hnr Roll; Nat Sci Aw; Perf Att; 4-H; ArtClub; Chrch Yth Grp; DARE; Scouts; Social Worker; Child Care; Middle Tennessee State U; David Lipscomb U

TURNER, CYERRA D; KINGSPORT, TN; SULLIVAN NORTH HS; (SR); Nat Hon Sy; WWAHSS; Key Club; Chrldg (V); Involved in HOSA; Nursing; Northeast State Technical Community College; East Tennessee State U

TURNER, ERICA; LEOMA, TN; LAWRENCE CTY HS; (FR); Hnr Roll; MVP; Perf Att; Comm Volntr; 4-H; ArtClub; Chess; Chrch Yth Grp; Cmptr Clb; DARE; Drma Clb; Emplmnt; Chr; Ch Chr; Dnce; SP/M/VS; Chrldg (V); Sccr (V); Yrbk (P)

TURNER, JOHN; OLD HICKORY, TN; MC GAVOCK COMP HS; (FR); Hnr Roll; Sci Fairs; Comm Volntr; Hab For Humty Volntr; Bsball (V); Ftball (J); Youth Council Member; United Methodist Youth Missions

TURNEY, KYLE; DYERSBURG, TN; DYERSBURG HS; (JR); Duke TS; Hi Hnr Roll; Nat Hon Sy; WWAHSS; Yth Ldrshp Prog; AL Aux Boys; Chrch Yth Grp; Key Club; NYLC; Ftball (V); Sccr (V); Electrical Engineering; Vanderbilt U; Rice U

TWILLEY, JENNIFER N; MEMPHIS, TN; FRAYSER MIDDLE HS; (MS); Hnr Roll; St of Mnth; Comm Volntr; Peer Tut/Med; Chess; Chrch Yth Grp; Cmptr Clb; DARE; FCA; Wdwrkg Clb; Ch Chr; Dnce; Mch Bnd; SP/M/VS; PPSqd; Majorette; Girls Inc.; Cosmetology; Nurse; Memphis State College; LeMoyne Owen College

UNCAPHER-COLLIER, KRISTIN D; SODDY DAISY, TN; SODDY-DAISY HS; (FR); Hi Hnr Roll; Hnr Roll; Otst Ac Ach Awd; Sci Fairs; St of Mnth; Comm Volntr; Chrch Yth Grp; FCA; Stu Cncl (R); National Jr. Beta Club; Book Club; Psychology BS; Bryan College; East Tennessee State U

UNDERWOOD, WILLIAM M G; CAMDEN, TN; CAMDEN CTRL HS; (FR); WWAHSS; Was in HOSA; Lawyer; FBI Agent; Vanderbilt U; U of Tennessee Martin

UNG, TERESA; MEMPHIS, TN; WOODDALE HS; (SR); Nat Hon Sy; WWAHSS; Biology Clb; DECA; Emplmnt; Key Club; Sci Clb; Scouts; Bridge Builders; Facing History and Ourselves; Business Owner/Management; Christian Brothers U

URESTI, FRANCISCO; SMYRNA, TN; LAVERGNE HS; (JR); Sccr (V); Swmg (V); Biology; Chemistry; Middle Tennessee State U; Belmont U

VALENTOUR, LAUREN; SODDY DAISY, TN; SODDY DAISY HS; (FR); Hi Hnr Roll; Otst Ac Ach Awd; Perf Att; WWAHSS; Chrch Yth Grp; DARE; Bnd; Mch Bnd; Orch; Medical School

VANCE, RACHAEL L; WOODBURY, TN; CANNON CTY HS; (SO); WWAHSS; Chrch Yth Grp; DARE; Ntl Beta Clb; French Clb; Ch Chr; Nursing; Fashion Design; Vanderbilt U; Sewanee College

VANDERGRIFF, LEE D; HIXSON, TN; HIXSON HS; (SR); Hi Hnr Roll; Hnr Roll; Nat Hon Sy; WWAHSS; Peer Tut/Med; FCA; Ntl Beta Clb; Golf (V CL); Wrstlg (V CL); Fellowship of Christian Athletes President; State Golf Championship Team; Psychology; Secondary Education; U of Tennessee At Chattanooga

VANDERHOFF, NICOLE; BRIGHTON, TN; BRIGHTON HS; (FR); Hnr Roll; Chrch Yth Grp; Chr; Pediatric Psychologist; Interior Designer; Ohio State U; Tennessee State U

VANDERLEE, AMBER; CLARKSVILLE, TN; NEW PROVIDENCE MS; (MS); Duke TS; Nat Hon Sy; Perf Att; Pres Ac Ftns Aw; Sci Fairs; Spec Olymp Vol; Off Aide; Scouts; Chrldg (J); Sftball (J); Stu Cncl (R); Girl Scout Bronze Award; Girl Scout God & Family; Religious; Forensic Science; Marine Biology; Nicholls State U; Austin Peay State U

VANE, JACOB; OAK RIDGE, TN; OAK RIDGE HS; (JR); Hnr Roll; WWAHSS; AL Aux Boys; Chrch Yth Grp; FCA; Prom Com; Bsball (V L); Ftball (V L); Adv Cncl (R); Stu Cncl (R); Business/Advertising; Clemson U; U of Tennessee

VAN ETTEN, EMILY; MURFREESBORO, TN; SIEGEL HS; (SO); Hnr Roll; Perf Att; Comm Volntr; Chrch Yth Grp; Pep Squd; Bnd; Ch Chr; Mch Bnd; Pep Bnd; Elementary Education; Business; Middle Tennessee State U; Belmont U

VAN WAGNER, ALISON; ENGLEWOOD, TN; MC MINN CTY HS; (SO); Duke TS; WWAHSS; Chrch Yth Grp; MuAlphaTh; Outdrs Clb; Sccr (V L); Stu Cncl (R); Pre-Law; Education; Auburn U; Vanderbilt U

VANWINKLE, KRISTA; SODDY DAISY, TN; SODDY DAISY HS; (JR); Ctznshp Aw; DAR; Hnr Roll; Nat Hon Sy; WWAHSS; Comm Volntr; DECA; Key Club; Ntl Beta Clb; Tchrs Aide; Chrldg (V); Tennis (V); Cl Off (V); Yrbk; Vice President of Key Club; Placed 2nd At National Cheerleading Competition; Psychologist; Writer; U of Louisville; Lee U

VARELA, LIA; GERMANTOWN, TN; EVANGELICAL CHRISTIAN SCH; (FR); Hi Hnr Roll; Perf Att; WWAHSS; Comm Volntr; Spec Olymp Vol; Key Club; Ntl Beta Clb; Bnd; Mch Bnd; Pep Bnd; Math (Major/PhD); Music (Minor); Christian College

VARGAS, ANDREINA; GALLATIN, TN; GALLATIN HS; (SR); Key Club; Spanish Clb; Chr; Dnce; Nursing; Vol State; TSU

VAUGHN, ANGELA; ELIZABETHTON, TN; UNAKA HS; (SO); Hnr Roll; Chrch Yth Grp; FCA; Bskball (J); Sch Ppr (R); Physical Therapist; Massage Therapist; U of Tennessee; East Tennessee State U

VAUGHN, TRAVIS; HIXSON, TN; SODDY DAISY HS; (FR); Hi Hnr Roll; Nat Sci Aw; Otst Ac Ach Awd; Perf Att; Sci Fairs; WWAHSS; Comm Volntr; Hab For Humty Volntr; Peer Tut/Med; 4-H; Chess; DARE; FBLA; Mod UN; Ntl Beta Clb; ROTC; Tchrs Aide; Cl Off (R); Stu Cncl (R); CR (R); Bowling Team - 2nd in State; PhD / Neurosurgeon or Plastic Surgery; Own A Business; Vanderbilt U; Stanford U

VAZQUEZ, JUAN C; MEMPHIS, TN; GERMANTOWN HS; (JR); F Lan Hn Soc; Hnr Roll; WWAHSS; Comm Volntr; Cmptr Clb; Spanish Clb; Radiology; Computer Engineering

VEACH, BRADLEY E; BRENTWOOD, TN; FRANKLIN HS; (JR); Hi Hnr Roll; Hab For Humty Volntr; Chrch Yth Grp; Scouts; Sccr (V L); Life Scout (Boy Scouts of America); Business; Wake Forest U; U of Richmond

VERGARA, ANDREA; THOMPSONS STATION, TN; FRANKLIN HS; (JR); Duke TS; Hi Hnr Roll; Hnr Roll; MVP; Otst Ac Ach Awd; Pres Sch; Comm Volntr; Peer Tut/Med; Chrch Yth Grp; Drma Clb; Emplmnt; FTA; Key Club; Tchrs Aide; Ch Chr; SP/M/VS; Stg Cre; Highest National Spanish Exam Grade in Class; Teaching (Elementary/Middle School)

VERISSIMO, JESSICA; CLARKSVILLE, TN; NORTHWEST HS; (JR); F Lan Hn Soc; Hnr Roll; Nat Hon Sy; St of Mnth; Comm Volntr; Chrch Yth Grp; DARE; Emplmnt; Mth Clb/Tm; Tchrs Aide; German Clb; Chr; Dnce; Sch Ppr (R); Yrbk (R); German National Honor Society; National Honor Society; Teacher; Egyptologist; Trevecca Nazarene U; Austin Peay State U

VERNON, KEVAN M; LAWRENCEBURG, TN; LCHS; (SO); SP/M/VS

VIEHWEGER JR, TIMOTHY L; CLEVELAND, TN; BRADLEY CTRL HS; (FR); Hnr Roll; Ntl FFA; Wdwrkg Clb

WADE, CHARLES C A; JACKS CREEK, TN; CHESTER CTY HS; (JR); Hi Hnr Roll; Hnr Roll; MVP; Perf Att; WWAHSS; Chrch Yth Grp; Lib Aide; Tchrs Aide; Bnd; Chr; Ch Chr; Drm Mjr; Bsball (C); Bskball (C); Sccr (C); Tennis; Vllyball (C); Yrbk (P); Dodge Ball; Commercial Airline Pilot; Business

WADE, MEGAN; BETHEL SPGS, TN; MC NAIRY CTRL HS; (JR); 4H Awd; Hi Hnr Roll; Hnr Roll; Nat Mrt LOC; Comm Volntr; Peer Tut/Med; 4-H; BPA; Chrch Yth Grp; Emplmnt; FCA; FTA; Off Aide; Prom Com; Chr; Ch Chr; Cl Off (R); Sch Ppr (R); Yrbk (E); Journalism; Medical; Journalism; Tennessee State U; U of Miami

WADE, TIMOTHY; MT PLEASANT, TN; MT PLEASANT HS; (SR); Hi Hnr Roll; MVP; WWAHSS; AL Aux Boys; FCA; Ntl Beta Clb; Ntl FFA; Tennis (V); Middle Tennessee State U

WADLEY, DOLLAVEESE; MURFREESBORO, TN; OAKLAND HS; (FR); PhD; Bachelor's Degree; Harvard U; Duke U

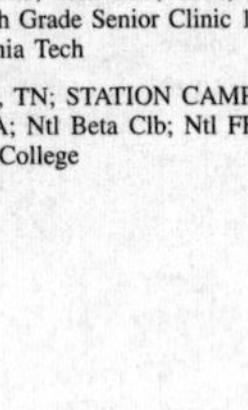
Turney, Kyle
Dyersburg HS
Dyersburg, TN

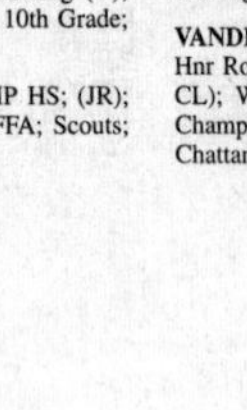
Tucker, Marc R
Dobyns Bennett HS
Kingsport, TN

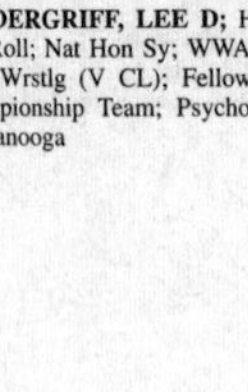
Truett, Travis D
Farragut HS
Knoxville, TN

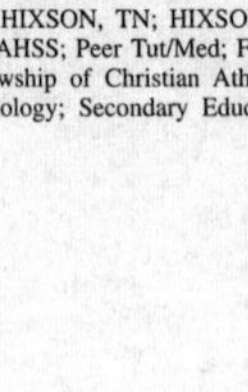
Torres, Brittany
Oneida HS
Oneida, TN

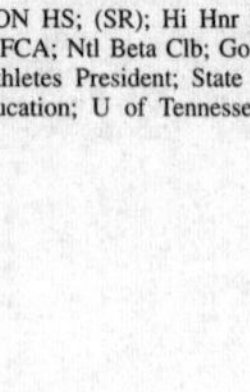
Trueheart, Patrick
Franklin Cty HS
Estill Springs, TN

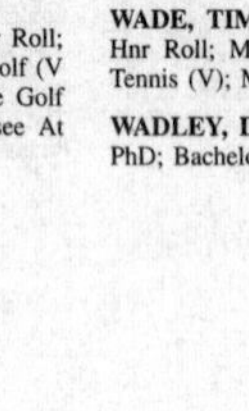
Turner, Erica
Lawrence Cty HS
Leoma, TN

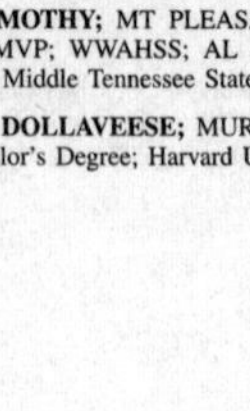
Uncapher-Collier, Kristin D
Soddy-Daisy HS
Soddy Daisy, TN

WALFORD, CONSUELA; JACKSON, TN; LIBERTY TECH MAGNET HS; (SO); Perf Att; WWAHSS; ArtClub; Chrch Yth Grp; Chr; Ch Chr; Yrbk (R); Choral Music Achievement Award; Superior Rating at Solo & Ensemble Festival; Cosmetology; RNA or Pediatrician; Baylor; Tennessee Tech

WALKER, AMANDA S H; CROSSVILLE, TN; CUMBERLAND CTY HS; (JR); 4H Awd; Hnr Roll; Otst Ac Ach Awd; Perf Att; St of Mnth; Peer Tut/Med; 4-H; ArtClub; Chrch Yth Grp; DARE; DECA; FCA; Pep Squd; German Clb; Ch Chr; Education; Law; Sullivan U; U of Virginia

WALKER, KIMBERLY; MEMPHIS, TN; WOODDALE HS; (JR); Ctznshp Aw; Hnr Roll; Perf Att; WWAHSS; Chrch Yth Grp; Emplmnt; Nursing; Psychology; Tennessee State U; Clark Atlanta U

WALKER, KRISTIN; BELLS, TN; CROCKETT CTY HS; (FR); 4H Awd; Hnr Roll; St of Mnth; Comm Volntr; Hab For Humty Volntr; 4-H; Chrch Yth Grp; DARE; Drma Clb; FCA; Ntl Beta Clb; Voc Ind Clb Am; Chr; SP/M/VS; 1st in My School to Make All-Northwest Honor Choir for a Freshman; Be a Pediatrician; Be a Singer

WALKER, MESHIA; LA VERGNE, TN; LA VERGNE HS; (FR); Hnr Roll; Perf Att; ArtClub; Chrch Yth Grp; Dnce; Chrldg (V); Sch Ppr (P); Dental Hygienist; Orthodontist; Middle Tennessee State U; U of Tennessee

WALLACE, AUBRIANNA; BURLISON, TN; BRIGHTON HS; (FR); Hnr Roll; Peer Tut/Med; Chrch Yth Grp; SADD; Hsbk Rdg; Lcrsse; PP Ftbl; Skiing; Sccr; Wt Lftg; CR (S); Rugby - Played for 1 Year; Biology; Medical Field; U of Memphis; U of Tennessee Martin

WALLEN, JESSICA M; KINGSPORT, TN; DOBYNS BENNETT HS; (JR); Ctznshp Aw; Hi Hnr Roll; Kwnis Aw; Nat Hon Sy; WWAHSS; Comm Volntr; Key Club; U of Virginia At Wise

WALLIS, AUDRA; CLEVELAND, TN; WALKER VALLEY HS; (FR); 4H Awd; Duke TS; Hnr Roll; WWAHSS; Hab For Humty Volntr; Civil Air Pat; Drma Clb; Key Club; Bnd; Jzz Bnd; Mch Bnd; Pep Bnd; Swmg; Winner of VFW Essay Contest; Teaching/Math; Library Science; Vanderbilt U; U of Tennessee At Knoxville

WALLS, LAURA; HENDERSON, TN; CHESTER CTY HS; (FR); Hosp Aide; Mus Clb; Bnd; Mch Bnd; Pep Bnd; Maternity Ward; Mid-Wife

WALTHER, KATIE; COLLIERVILLE, TN; COLLIERVILLE HS; (JR); F Lan Hn Soc; Fut Prb Slvr; Hi Hnr Roll; Hnr Roll; Nat Hon Sy; Otst Ac Ach Awd; WWAHSS; Yth Ldrshp Prog; Emplmnt; Ntl Beta Clb; Spanish Clb; Bnd; Mch Bnd; Pep Bnd; Swmg (J); Track (L); Attended National Youth Leadership Forum on Medicine; Lifeguard Certified; Medicine; U of Florida; U of Tennessee Knoxville

WALTHER, TROY R; COLLIERVILLE, TN; COLLIERVILLE HS; (FR); Hnr Roll; Ftball (J); U of Florida; Michigan State U

WALTON, AMIE L; CLARKSVILLE, TN; NORTHEAST HS; (SO); Ctznshp Aw; Otst Ac Ach Awd; Sci Fairs; DARE; Pep Squd; ROTC; Scouts; In JROTC; Elementary Teacher; Gonzaga U (Washington); Washington State U

WALTON, JAMES B; WAVERLY, TN; WAVERLY CTRL HS; (SR); Hnr Roll; St of Mnth; 4-H; BPA; DARE; Tchrs Aide; Cl Off (T); Automotive; Computer Science; Mechanic; Community College; NADC

WALTON, ROBERT C; TELLICO PLAINS, TN; MONROE CTY CHRISTIAN AC; (FR); 4H Awd; Hi Hnr Roll; Comm Volntr; Peer Tut/Med; 4-H; Chrch Yth Grp; Ch Chr; Has Completed 4 Years of Academics in 2 Years of Study; Equestrian Award; Mechanical Engineering; Electrical Computer Engineering; U of Tennessee Knoxville; Hiwassee College Madisonville

WAMBLES, ZACH; CAMDEN, TN; CAMDEN CTRL HS; (FR); Sci Fairs; WWAHSS; Yth Ldrshp Prog; Hab For Humty Volntr; 4-H; Chrch Yth Grp; Voc Ind Clb Am; Placed 3rd in Science Fair; U of Tennessee; Freed-Hardman College

WANG, YABIN; GREENEVILLE, TN; GREENVILLE HS; (SO); Hnr Roll; Perf Att; St of Mnth; USAA; ArtClub; Spanish Clb; Clr Grd; Flg Crps; Mch Bnd; Accounting; Engineering; Washington U in St. Louis; U of Tennessee

WARD, KIERRA R; JACKSON, TN; NORTHSIDE HS; (SO); Hnr Roll; Nat Hon Sy; Nat Stu Ath Day Aw; Perf Att; WWAHSS; Comm Volntr; Vsity Clb; Latin Clb; Chr; Dnce; Chrldg (V); Gmnstcs (V); Stu Cncl (R); Business Major; Vanderbilt U; Middle Tennessee State U

WARMSLEY, TITANIA; MEMPHIS, TN; HAMILTON HS; (JR); Hnr Roll; Nat Hon Sy; WWAHSS; Peer Tut/Med; Chrch Yth Grp; Vsity Clb; Ch Chr; Bskball (V); Cr Ctry (V); Track (V); UT Knoxville - Major: English or Education; Law School; U of Tennessee (Knoxville); Vanderbilt U

WARN, TYLER S; ETOWAH, TN; (MS); Hnr Roll; Chrch Yth Grp; Ch Chr; Chrldg; MC Minn. County Youth Leadership Award; Mountain View Energy War Competition; Equestrian Massage Therapy; Equestrian; U of Tennessee; U of Kentucky

WARREN, ELIZABETH; JASPER, TN; MARION CTY HS; (SO); Hi Hnr Roll; Hnr Roll; 4-H; Chrch Yth Grp; DARE; FCA; Lib Aide; Mus Clb; Ntl Beta Clb; Bnd; Jzz Bnd; Mch Bnd; Orch; Theology; Bible Study; Houghton College; Nyack College

WARREN, JOSLYN M; GALLATIN, TN; GALLATIN HS; (SR); Hnr Roll; Comm Volntr; Spec Olymp Vol; Spanish Clb; Ch Chr; Criminal Justice; Cosmetology; Volunteer State College; Vanderbilt U

WARRICK, STEPHANIE R; ROCKVALE, TN; RIVERDALE HS; (SO); Ctznshp Aw; F Lan Hn Soc; Hi Hnr Roll; Perf Att; Chrch Yth Grp; FCA; Jr Cls League; Photog; Bnd; SP/M/VS; Bskball (VJ); Swmg (J); Yrbk (R, P); Middle School Basketball - State Champions; Latin I & II JCL Silver Medal on NLE; Veterinary Medicine; Medical; Brigham Young U; Auburn U

WASHER, DUSTIN; GORDONSVILLE, TN; GORDONSVILLE HS; (JR); Hnr Roll; MVP; Perf Att; WWAHSS; Hab For Humty Volntr; Peer Tut/Med; Ntl Beta Clb; SADD; Spanish Clb; Chr; Bsball (V); Scr Kpr (V); Junior Beta Club; National Beta Club; Science; Technology; Cumberland U; Middle Tennessee State U

WASHINGTON, ALEISHA; MEMPHIS, TN; MIDDLE COLLEGE HS; (JR); Ctznshp Aw; Hnr Roll; Peer Tut/Med; Biology Clb; Chrch Yth Grp; Drma Clb; Prom Com; Sci Clb; Dnce; Drm Mjr; Chrldg (V); PPSqd (V); CR (R); Yrbk (E); Foreign Language; Spelman College; Xavier U

WASHINGTON, JASMINE D; MEMPHIS, TN; CENTRAL HS; (JR); Hi Hnr Roll; Nat Hon Sy; WWAHSS; Comm Volntr; Mus Clb; Ntl Beta Clb; Spanish Clb; Bnd; Mch Bnd; Pep Bnd; PP Ftbl (L); Stu Cncl (R); Computer Engineering; Accounting; Christian Brothers U; Tennessee State U

WASHINGTON, MICAELA M; CLARKSVILLE, TN; NORTHWEST HS; (SO); Hnr Roll; WWAHSS; Peer Tut/Med; Sftball (J); CR (R); 9th Grade-D. I.A. (Divas in Action) Step Team; Legal Studies; Temple U

WATKINS, KELSEY; HERMITAGE, TN; MC GAVOCK COMP HS; (JR); Hnr Roll; MVP; Peer Tut/Med; Spanish Clb; Bnd; Sftball (V); Cl Off (V); CR (R); Anesthesiologist; Physical Therapist; Tennessee State U; Western Kentucky U

WATKINS, REBEKAH; ALAMO, TN; CROCKETT CTY HS; (SO); Hi Hnr Roll; Hnr Roll; Perf Att; Sci Fairs; WWAHSS; Comm Volntr; Chrch Yth Grp; Ntl Beta Clb; Chr; Church Volunteer Work; UTM Honor Choir; Literature; Music; UT Knoxville; Union

WATKINS, RODSHEKA; MEMPHIS, TN; WESTWOOD HS; (JR); Ctznshp Aw; Hnr Roll; WWAHSS; Peer Tut/Med; FCA; Chrldg; Sftball; Tennis; Teens For Peace Club; Criminal Justice; English; Princeton U; New York U

WATSON, AMY L; WHITE BLUFF, TN; HARPETH HS; (SO); Hnr Roll; Otst Ac Ach Awd; P to P St Amb Prg; Vllyball (V); Junior Civitan; Athletic Trainer At High School

WATSON, HILLARY L; MANCHESTER, TN; COFFEE CTY CTRL HS; (SR); Hi Hnr Roll; Hnr Roll; Nat Hon Sy; Pres Ac Ftns Aw; St of Mnth; USAA; Peer Tut/Med; Red Cr Aide; ArtClub; BPA; Chrch Yth Grp; DARE; FCA; Ntl Beta Clb; Pep Squd; Vsity Clb; Chrldg (V L); PP Ftbl (V); Sftball (J L); President HOSA Club; Secretary FCLA Club; Nursing; Middle Tennessee U

WATSON, JACOB P; LOUDON, TN; LOUDON HS; (FR); Hi Hnr Roll; Otst Ac Ach Awd; WWAHSS; Chrch Yth Grp; Ntl FFA; Ch Chr; Ftball (J); Sftball (V); Vsy Clb (V); Vllyball (V); Wrstlg (V); Top Ten Freshman - Loudon High School; Wildlife Biology; Zoology

WEAVER, ELIZABETH H; UNICOI, TN; U N 1001 CTY VOC SCH; (SR); Hnr Roll; WWAHSS; 4-H; ArtClub; FCCLA; Lttrmn Clb; Pep Squd; German Clb; Bskball (V L); Sftball (VJ L); CR (P); Education; Game Warden/Park Ranger; Coastal Caroline

WEAVER, TEERINEY; MEMPHIS, TN; WHITE STATION HS; (SO); Hnr Roll; Nat Sci Aw; HOSA; Facing History and Ourselves; Pre Medicine; U of Tennessee At Knoxville

WEBB, ZAKIYA T; MEMPHIS, TN; KIRBY HS; (FR); Ctznshp Aw; Hnr Roll; Nat Hon Sy; Otst Ac Ach Awd; Perf Att; Comm Volntr; Drma Clb; CR (R); Principal's List; Appreciation Award; Dentistry (Orthodontist); Fashion Designer; U of Alabama

WEBBER, TERRICA; MEMPHIS, TN; NORTHSIDE HS; (FR); Hnr Roll; Peer Tut/Med; Fr of Library; Chr; Track; Yrbk (P); Ms. Snowden; Mathematics Degree; Music Degree; Tennessee State U; Memphis State U

WEBER, ELISSA; MURFREESBORO, TN; BLACKMAN HS; (SO); Hi Hnr Roll; Otst Ac Ach Awd; Perf Att; St of Mnth; WWAHSS; Comm Volntr; Chrch Yth Grp; FCA; Key Club; Scouts; Svce Clb; Chr; Ch Chr; Clr Grd; Mch Bnd; Skt Tgt Sh (J); Girl Scout Silver Award; National Beta Club; Teaching; Social Worker; Middle Tennessee State U; Vanderbilt

WEBSTER, CHRISTINE; MEMPHIS, TN; NORTHSIDE HS; (JR); Ctznshp Aw; Hi Hnr Roll; Hnr Roll; Nat Hon Sy; Otst Ac Ach Awd; WWAHSS; Hosp Aide; Peer Tut/Med; Emplmnt; Jr Ach; Pediatric Medicine; Veterinarian Medicine; East Tennessee State U

WEBSTER, SHATERRA T; MEMPHIS, TN; OVERTON HS; (SR); Ctznshp Aw; Perf Att; DECA; ROTC; Drl Tm

WEDDLE, ALISHA; NASHVILLE, TN; PEARL COHN HS; (FR); 4H Awd; Ctznshp Aw; Duke TS; Hi Hnr Roll; Hnr Roll; Nat Hon Sy; Otst Ac Ach Awd; Perf Att; Pres Sch; St Schl; Hab For Humty Volntr; Hosp Aide; Peer Tut/Med; DARE; Dbte Team; Lib Aide; Mth Clb/Tm; Off Aide; Photog; Prom Com; Tchrs Aide; Bnd; Clr Grd; SP/M/VS; Stg Cre; GAA; Rqtball; Rlr Hky; Scr Kpr; Sccr; Sftball; Tennis; Vllyball; Psychology; Accounting; Spelman College; Vanderbilt U

WEEDEN, LINDSEY B; BLUFF CITY, TN; SULLIVAN EAST HS; (SR); Duke TS; Hi Hnr Roll; Nat Hon Sy; Salutrn; WWAHSS; Comm Volntr; Spec Olymp Vol; FCA; Key Club; Ntl Beta Clb; Quill & Scroll; Chrldg (V); PP Ftbl (V); Sch Ppr (R); Beta Club President; National Honor Society Chaplain; Dental Hygiene; East Tennessee State U

WELCH, LINDSEY; MONTEREY, TN; MONTEREY HS; (SO); Hnr Roll; MVP; Pres Sch; St of Mnth; FCA; Lib Aide; Ntl Beta Clb; Off Aide; Chrldg (V); Sftball (J); Cl Off (S); Sch Ppr (E); MD; PhD; Tennessee Tech U; U of Tennessee Knoxville

WELLER, CAITLIN; MURFREESBORO, TN; SIEGEL HS; (JR); Duke TS; Hi Hnr Roll; Hnr Roll; Nat Hon Sy; Perf Att; Pres Ac Ftns Aw; St of Mnth; WWAHSS; Hosp Aide; Chrch Yth Grp; Drma Clb; FCA; Ntl Beta Clb; Pep Squd; Spanish Clb; Chr; SP/M/VS; Stg Cre; Vllyball (V CL); Alpha Delta Kappa Sorority Historian; Nursing; Physician's Assistant; MTSU; UT

WELLS, ASHLEY; TALBOTT, TN; JEFFERSON CTY HS; (SO); 4H Awd; Hi Hnr Roll; Hnr Roll; Sci Fairs; St Optmst of Yr; Peer Tut/Med; 4-H; Chrch Yth Grp; DARE; FCA; NtlFrnscLg; Chrldg (J); Gmnstcs (J); Vllyball (J); Law; Business; U of Tennessee

WEST, AUDRIANA; CLARKSVILLE, TN; NORTHWEST HS; (FR); Hnr Roll; Nat Hon Sy; Nat Sci Aw; Comm Volntr; Peer Tut/Med; DARE; Drma Clb; Mus Clb; Chr; Ch Chr; Cl Off (V); CR (V); Science Academic Award; Music Major; Pre-Law Major; Tennessee State U; Atlanta U

WEST, TARSHEIKA; MEMPHIS, TN; OAKHAVEN HS; (SO); Nat Hon Sy; Chrch Yth Grp; CR (T); Yrbk (E); Computer Science; Performing Arts; Jackson State U; Georgia Tech

WEST, WILLIAM; MURFREESBORO, TN; OAKLAND HS; (FR); All Am Sch; Duke TS; Hi Hnr Roll; Otst Ac Ach Awd; USAA; Yth Ldrshp Prog; Peer Tut/Med; Chrch Yth Grp; DARE; Jr Cls League; Mth Clb/Tm; Mission Trip with Church to New Orleans, LA; Scored a 25 on ACT As a Freshman; Medicine; Law; Duke U; Washington U

WESTBROOK, RAVEN; MEMPHIS, TN; MELROSE HS; (FR); 4H Awd; Ctznshp Aw; Hnr Roll; Nat Hon Sy; Otst Ac Ach Awd; 4-H; Chrch Yth Grp; DARE; Scouts; Ch Chr; Accounting; Law; U of Memphis; Tennessee State

WESTFALL, SARAH N; AFTON, TN; CHUCKEY-DOAK HS; (FR); Hi Hnr Roll; Perf Att; WWAHSS; Sch Ppr (R); Yrbk (E); Math Competition; Published in Sweet 16 Guide Posts; Forensic/Criminal Psychology; Art/Writing; U of Tennessee At Knoxville

WHATLEY, CHELSEA C; MEMPHIS, TN; CENTRAL HS; (SO); Ctznshp Aw; Hi Hnr Roll; Hnr Roll; Comm Volntr; Peer Tut/Med; ArtClub; Chrch Yth Grp; MuAlphaTh; Ch Chr; Dnce; Cr Ctry (V); Track (V); Piano; Youth Usher Board; Business Administration; Law; Spelman College; Clark Atlanta U

WHEATLEY, MELISSA; COLLIERVILLE, TN; COLLIERVILLE HS; (SR); F Lan Hn Soc; Hi Hnr Roll; Kwnis Aw; Nat Hon Sy; Nat Mrt LOC; WWAHSS; Comm Volntr; Chrch Yth Grp; Key Club; Chr; Ch Chr; SP/M/VS; Swg Chr; Chrldg (V L); Stu Cncl (R); United Methodist Church Leadership; Religion - Youth Ministry; Music Business - Production; Belmont U

WHEELER, ALISHA R; SODDY DAISY, TN; SODDY DAISY HS; (FR); Ch Chr; Drm Mjr; Stg Cre; Cr Ctry (L); Track (L); United Twirling; Math Degree

WHEELER, ANDREW J R; POWELL, TN; TEMPLE BAPTIST AC; (SO); Hi Hnr Roll; Hnr Roll; Pres Ac Ftns Aw; Bnd; Chr; Ch Chr; Orch; Sccr (V); Computer Engineering; Computer Science; Duke U; U of Tennessee

WHEELER, ERIC; FRANKLIN, TN; CENTENNIAL HS; (JR); Hi Hnr Roll; Nat Hon Sy; Otst Ac Ach Awd; Pres Sch; Sci/Math Olympn; Hab For Humty Volntr; Peer Tut/Med; Chrch Yth Grp; Drma Clb; Emplmnt; Mth Clb/Tm; MuAlphaTh; Scouts; Voc Ind Clb Am; SP/M/VS; Stg Cre; Eagle Scout; Engineering; Physics

WHEELER, PAIGE; GOODLETTSVLLE, TN; HUNTERS LANE HS; (SO); Hnr Roll; WWAHSS; Key Club; Ecology Club; Medicine (Pediatrician); Art; Vanderbilt U; Meharry U

WHITE, AMBER T; MEMPHIS, TN; WOODDALE HS; (FR); Ctznshp Aw; Hi Hnr Roll; Hnr Roll; Medicine; Law; Spelman U; Howard U

WHITE, CASSIE L; SAVANNAH, TN; HARDIN CTY HS; (JR); 4H Awd; Hi Hnr Roll; Hnr Roll; MVP; Otst Ac Ach Awd; Perf Att; St of Mnth; Comm Volntr; 4-H; Chrch Yth Grp; DARE; Emplmnt; Off Aide; Photog; Tchrs Aide; Ch Chr; Sftball (V L); Vllyball (V L); Stu Cncl (R); Teacher; Registered Nurse; U of Tennessee At Martin; Middle Tennessee State U

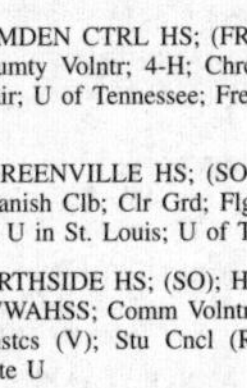
Weber, Elissa
Blackman HS
Murfreesboro, TN

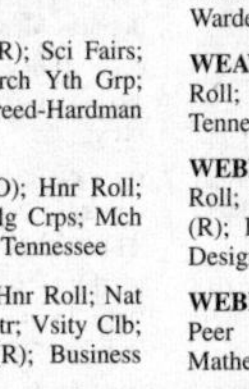
Washer, Dustin
Gordonsville HS
Gordonsville, TN

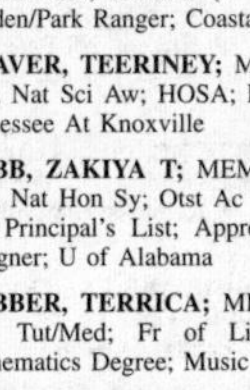
Walton, Robert C
Monroe Cty Christian AC
Tellico Plains, TN

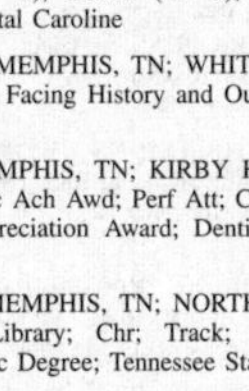
Wallen, Jessica M
Dobyns Bennett HS
Kingsport, TN

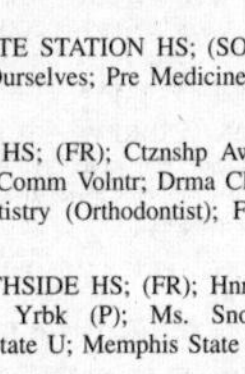
Walton, Amie L
Northeast HS
Clarksville, TN

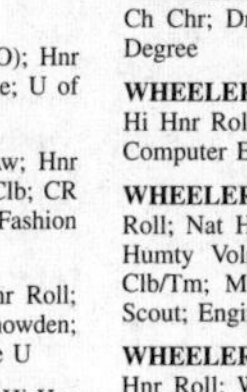
Washington, Micaela M
Northwest HS
Clarksville, TN

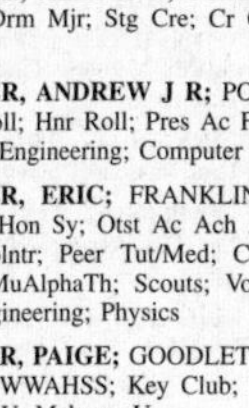
White, Cassie L
Hardin Cty HS
Savannah, TN

WHITE, KATHRYN; ASHLAND CITY, TN; SYCAMORE HS; (FR); Hi Hnr Roll; MVP; Comm Volntr; Spec Olymp Vol; Chrch Yth Grp; FCA; Pep Squd; Tchrs Aide; Bskball (J L); Sftball (V L); MVP-Softball; All District Player-Softball; Nursing; Medical Doctor; Vanderbilt U; Lipscomb U

WHITE, KEENAN C; ERWIN, TN; UNICOI CTY HS; (JR); Hnr Roll; WWAHSS; Chrch Yth Grp; Emplmnt; Key Club; Bnd; Jzz Bnd; Mch Bnd; Pep Bnd; Bass Guitar Player for the Band "Attica"

WHITE, LUCAS; LAWRENCEBURG, TN; LAWRENCE CTY HS; (SO); Hnr Roll; Emplmnt; Ftball (V); Student Government Assn

WHITE, MATTHEW C; ERWIN, TN; U N 1001 CTY VOC SCH; (SR); Ctznshp Aw; Hi Hnr Roll; Hnr Roll; Jr Mshl; MVP; Otst Ac Ach Awd; Pres Sch; Valdctrian; WWAHSS; Comm Volntr; ArtClub; Chrch Yth Grp; FCA; Lttrmn Clb; Mth Clb/Tm; Ntl Beta Clb; Ntl FFA; Schol Bwl; Ch Chr; Bsball (V L); Bskball (V CL); Cl Off (P); Business; U of Tennessee Knoxville

WHITE, RACHEL; MEMPHIS, TN; ST MARY'S SCH; (JR); F Lan Hn Soc; Nat Hon Sy; Nat Mrt Semif; WWAHSS; MuAlphaTh; Ntl Beta Clb; Quill & Scroll; French Clb; Dnce; Stu Cncl (R); CR (R); Yrbk (E); Piano Performances of Pieces By Chopin & Beethoven; Cum Laude Honor Society; Stanford U; Washington U in St Louis

WHITE, SHANIECE E; HERMITAGE, TN; MC GAVOCK COMP HS; (JR); Hnr Roll; Otst Ac Ach Awd; Comm Volntr; BPA; Chrch Yth Grp; DARE; Emplmnt; NtlFrnscLg; Ch Chr; Dnce; SP/M/VS; Stg Cre; PP Ftbl (J); Stu Cncl (R); CR (R); Family Career & Community Leaders of America; Oasis Youth Council Member; Nursing; Psychology; Tennessee State U; Meharry Medical College

WHITE, VALERIE D; MEMPHIS, TN; WOODDALE HS; Ctznshp Aw; Hi Hnr Roll; Hnr Roll; Emplmnt; ROTC; Bnd; Medical School; Law School; U of Memphis; Harvard Law School

WHITEAKER, JENNIFER; HERMITAGE, TN; DONELSON CHRISTIAN AC; MS; Duke TS; Hi Hnr Roll; Hnr Roll; Nat Hon Sy; Otst Ac Ach Awd; Comm Volntr; Chrch Yth Grp; Jr Ach; Scouts; Chr; Ch Chr; Cl Off (S); Top 10% of My Class; Chosen 4th Soprano in Mid-TN Honors Choir; BA / Education; BA Music / Fine Arts; Tennessee Technological U; Belmont U

WHITEFIELD, SHAE; OLIVER SPRINGS, TN; OLIVER SPRINGS HS; (FR); 4H Awd; Duke TS; Hnr Roll; Nat Hon Sy; Pres Sch; Sci Fairs; Comm Volntr; Hosp Aide; Peer Tut/Med; 4-H; Chrch Yth Grp; DARE; Drma Clb; FCA; Ntl Beta Clb; Tchrs Aide; Ch Chr; Dnce; SP/M/VS; Chrldg (J); Volunteering At Methodist Medical Center; Medical Field-Ob/Gyn; U of TN Knoxville; Vanderbilt or Duke U

WHITESIDE, ASHLEY E; CHATTANOOGA, TN; BRAINERD HS; (SR); Hnr Roll; Otst Ac Ach Awd; St of Mnth; Yth Ldrshp Prog; Comm Volntr; Chrch Yth Grp; Off Aide; SADD; Tchrs Aide; Ch Chr; Clr Grd; Dnce; Mch Bnd; Cr Ctry (V C); Track (V); Positive Role Model of the Year- 2001-2002; Physical Therapy; Master's Degree; Chattanooga State Community College; Meharry Medical School Nashville

WHITSON, CHASE E; ERWIN, TN; U N 1001 CTY VOC SCH; (SR); Hi Hnr Roll; Hnr Roll; MVP; Nat Hon Sy; WWAHSS; Comm Volntr; 4-H; ArtClub; FCCLA; Lttrmn Clb; Ntl FFA; Vsity Clb; German Clb; Bsball (V L); Master's Degree in Radiology; Minor Business; East Tennessee State U

WHITT, JACOB M; CHATTANOOGA, TN; EAST RIDGE HS; (SR); Hnr Roll; Comm Volntr; FBLA; Bnd; Jzz Bnd; Mch Bnd; U of Tennessee Chattanooga

WHITTENBARGER, SHEA A; CHATTANOOGA, TN; EAST RIDGE HS; (JR); Hnr Roll; Otst Ac Ach Awd; Perf Att; St of Mnth; Comm Volntr; Peer Tut/Med; DARE; Mus Clb; ROTC; Sign Clb; Bnd; Ch Chr; Mch Bnd; Orch; Martial Arts-Black Belt; Modeling for Sears; Anesthesiology Assistant; Nursing; Chattanooga State; U of TN At Chatt

WHITTINGTON, ASHLEY; TULLAHOMA, TN; (FR); Hnr Roll; Comm Volntr; BPA; Chrch Yth Grp; Key Club; French Clb; Member of International Society of Poets; Veterinarian; U of Alabama Huntsville

WIGGINS, HALLEY; FRANKLIN, TN; FRANKLIN HS; (FR); Hnr Roll; Scouts; Sftball (J); Vllyball (V L); Medicine; U of Missouri Columbia

WIKLE, SHAUNDA; DANDRIDGE, TN; JEFFERSON CTY HS; (JR); DECA; FCA; Ntl FFA; Voc Ind Clb Am; Sign Clb; Respiratory Therapist; Walter State; Roane State

WILBUR, TARA L; COLUMBIA, TN; SPRING HILL HS; (FR); Ctznshp Aw; Hnr Roll; WWAHSS; Chrch Yth Grp; Drma Clb; Key Club; Pep Squd; SP/M/VS; Stg Cre; Yrbk (R, P); Public Relations; Southern Adventist U

WILDER, AMANDA; KINGSPORT, TN; DOBYNS BENNETT HS; (SO); Hnr Roll; Sci Fairs; St of Mnth; Yth Ldrshp Prog; Chrch Yth Grp; Emplmnt; Key Club; Bnd; Chr; Ch Chr; Mch Bnd; Sccr (J); Swmg (V L); Dentistry; Sports Management; U of Tennessee; Carson Newman College

WILKEY, BLAKE A; SODDY DAISY, TN; SODDY-DAISY HS; (FR); Duke TS; WWAHSS; Comm Volntr; Peer Tut/Med; Chrch Yth Grp; DARE; Emplmnt; Photog; Bnd; Awards for Community Services; French Awards; Physicist; Physics Major; Duke U

WILKINS, ALISHA N; JACKSON, TN; JACKSON CTRL MERRY HS; (JR); DAR; Hnr Roll; Nat Hon Sy; Otst Ac Ach Awd; Yth Ldrshp Prog; Comm Volntr; Red Cr Aide; ArtClub; Chrch Yth Grp; DARE; FTA; ROTC; SADD; Tchrs Aide; Clr Grd; Drl Tm; Scottish Rite, Southern Jurisdiction; History; Military Intelligence; U of Tennessee Martin; Memphis State

WILKS, ANTWAN; MEMPHIS, TN; EAST HS; (JR); Hnr Roll; Perf Att; Comm Volntr; Peer Tut/Med; BPA; Chrch Yth Grp; Cmptr Clb; Emplmnt; Bnd; SP/M/VS; Ftball; Track; Accounting and Business Management; U of Memphis Rhodes College

WILLETT, EMILY; KINGSPORT, TN; DOBYNS BENNETT HS; (SO); Hnr Roll; Peer Tut/Med; Emplmnt; Key Club; Ntl Beta Clb; Spanish Clb; Scr Kpr; Stu Cncl (R); Pharmacy; Engineering; U of South Carolina; U of Tennessee

WILLIAMS, BRITTANY; CLEVELAND, TN; WALKER VALLEY HS; (JR); Hi Hnr Roll; Hnr Roll; Nat Hon Sy; WWAHSS; Yth Ldrshp Prog; Emplmnt; Key Club; Ntl Beta Clb; Pep Squd; Prom Com; Svce Clb; Tchrs Aide; Chrldg (V C); President of Anchor Club; Marine Biology; Law; U of Tennessee At Chattanooga; Jacksonville U

WILLIAMS, BRITTNEY D; MEMPHIS, TN; CENTRAL HS; (SO); Hnr Roll; Nat Hon Sy; Nat Stu Ath Day Aw; Perf Att; Peer Tut/Med; Chrch Yth Grp; Ntl Beta Clb; Sftball (V); Criminology; Nursing; Tenn State U; UT

WILLIAMS, BROOK A; ATOKA, TN; MUNFORD HS; (SR); Hi Hnr Roll; Hnr Roll; Kwnis Aw; MVP; WWAHSS; Yth Ldrshp Prog; Comm Volntr; Peer Tut/Med; Spec Olymp Vol; ArtClub; Chrch Yth Grp; Emplmnt; FTA; Key Club; Ntl FFA; Tchrs Aide; Acpl Chr; Chr; Ch Chr; Swg Chr; Allied Health Care; Paralegal; Concorde Career College

WILLIAMS, CHARITY K; GALLATIN, TN; GALLATIN HS; (SO); Chrch Yth Grp; Drma Clb; Ch Chr; Cr Ctry; I Work At McDonalds; Fisk U; Austin Pegy U

WILLIAMS, JEREE S; OAK RIDGE, TN; OAK RIDGE HS; (SR); Ctznshp Aw; Otst Ac Ach Awd; WWAHSS; Yth Ldrshp Prog; Comm Volntr; Hab For Humty Volntr; Chrch Yth Grp; Emplmnt; FBLA; Off Aide; Tchrs Aide; Chr; Ch Chr; Track (J); Stu Cncl (R); CR (R); SECME Member; SECME Scholar; Criminal Law; Social Work; U of Tennessee in Knoxville; Tennessee State U

WILLIAMS, MICHAEL; BELL BUCKLE, TN; CASCADE HS; (SO); Hi Hnr Roll; Nat Hon Sy; Comm Volntr; Chrch Yth Grp; Drma Clb; Key Club; Stg Cre; Yrbk; Psychology; Pharmaceutical Science

WILLIAMS, TYLER E; ELIZABETHTON, TN; UNAKA HS; (SO); Hnr Roll; Nat Hon Sy; Otst Ac Ach Awd; Perf Att; Chrch Yth Grp; Bnd; Mch Bnd; Chemist; Software Developer; East Tenn. State U; Northeast State Comm College

WILLIAMSON, DOMONIQUE; ATOKA, TN; MUNFORD HS; (SR); Hnr Roll; Perf Att; WWAHSS; Comm Volntr; BPA; Chrch Yth Grp; DARE; FCCLA; FTA; Lib Aide; SADD; Tchrs Aide; Ch Chr; Drl Tm; President's Circle of BPA; 2004 Poetry Contest; Banking / Finance; Accounting; U of Memphis; Southwest Tennessee Community College

WILLIAMSON, VICTORIA; MEMPHIS, TN; CENTRAL HS; (SO); Ctznshp Aw; Hnr Roll; Perf Att; Yth Ldrshp Prog; Comm Volntr; Hab For Humty Volntr; Emplmnt; French Clb; Member of French Club; Youth United Way; Physical Therapy; Dental Hygiene; Howard U; Dillard U

WILLIS, ANDREW; MURFREESBORO, TN; SIEGEL HS; (JR); WWAHSS; Comm Volntr; Chrch Yth Grp; FCA; Jr Cls League; Key Club; Mth Clb/Tm; Mod UN; MuAlphaTh; Ntl Beta Clb; Mechanical Engineering; Astronautical Engineering; Georgia Institute of Technology; Purdue U

WILSON, ALLISON L; KINGSPORT, TN; DOBYNS BENNETT HS; (SR); Hi Hnr Roll; Hnr Roll; Nat Hon Sy; Pres Ac Ftns Aw; WWAHSS; Comm Volntr; ArtClub; Chrch Yth Grp; FCA; Key Club; Mth Clb/Tm; Ntl Beta Clb; Svce Clb; Tchrs Aide; Ch Chr; Bskball (V); Cr Ctry (V CL); Track (V L); Physical Therapy; East Tennessee State U

WILSON, ANDREW; WHITEVILLE, TN; FAYETTE AC; (MS); Duke TS; Hi Hnr Roll; Hnr Roll; Perf Att; Emplmnt; Bnd; Jzz Bnd; Mch Bnd; Pep Bnd; Golf (J); Computer Specialist; Computer Repair; U of Tennessee Knoxville; U of Tennessee Martin

WILSON, APRIL; MEMPHIS, TN; KINGSBURY MIDDLE HS; (FR); Hnr Roll; Otst Ac Ach Awd; DARE; Bnd; SP/M/VS; Gmnstcs; Scr Kpr; Bachelor's Degree; Masters Degree; U of Memphis; Lemoyne-Owens

WILSON, ELIZABETH; SPRINGVILLE, TN; EASTWOOD CHRISTIAN AC; (JR); Hi Hnr Roll; Hnr Roll; Perf Att; St of Mnth; Chrch Yth Grp; Drma Clb; Emplmnt; P to P St Amb Prg; Spch Team; Chr; Chrldg (V); Stu Cncl (P); Yrbk (R); Piano; Soccer (Extra Curricular); Pre-Medicine

WILSON, ERICA A; MEMPHIS, TN; RIDGEWAY HS; (JR); F Lan Hn Soc; Hi Hnr Roll; Comm Volntr; Peer Tut/Med; Chrch Yth Grp; Cmptr Clb; Emplmnt; Mus Clb; Scouts; Spanish Clb; Bnd; Ch Chr; Pep Bnd; Youth United Way-Executive Board Member; Biology; Biomedical Research; U of Tennessee-Knoxville; Middle Tennessee State U

WILSON, JUSTIN K; GALLATIN, TN; GALLATIN HS; (SO); Nat Hon Sy; WWAHSS; Comm Volntr; Hosp Aide; Spec Olymp Vol; Chrch Yth Grp; DECA; Key Club; Voc Ind Clb Am; Chr; Mechanical Engineering; U of Alabama in Huntsville

WILSON, LAUREN E A; KINGSPORT, TN; DOBYNS-BENNETT; (SO); Duke TS; Nat Hon Sy; WWAHSS; Chrch Yth Grp; Dbte Team; Emplmnt; FCA; JSA; Key Club; Ntl Beta Clb; P to P St Amb Prg

WILSON, RACHEL A; PIGEON FORGE, TN; SEVIER CTY HS; (SO); Hnr Roll; Perf Att; Chrch Yth Grp; Mus Clb; SADD; Tchrs Aide; Chr; Ch Chr; SP/M/VS; Chrldg (J); Hair and Nails; Music; Tennessee School of Beauty; Maryville College

WILSON, SHARIEKA L; MEMPHIS, TN; TREADWELL MIDDLE HS; (FR); Ctznshp Aw; Hnr Roll; Perf Att; Sci Fairs; St of Mnth; Comm Volntr; Peer Tut/Med; DARE; Chr; Chrldg (V); Defensive Attorney; Business Administrator; U of California of Los Angeles; Rhodes College

WILSON, SHAWN D; COOKEVILLE, TN; COOKEVILLE HS; (SO); Ctznshp Aw; Hnr Roll; Sci Fairs; Chrch Yth Grp; Engineering; TN Tech

WINEGAR, MEGHAN; WARTBURG, TN; CENTRAL HS; (JR); Hnr Roll; St of Mnth; Comm Volntr; Chrch Yth Grp; Drma Clb; FCA; SP/M/VS; Bskball (V CL); CR (R); Dental Hygiene; Roane State Community College; Tennessee Tech

WINFREY, CHATUAN; MEMPHIS, TN; EAST HS; (SO); Hnr Roll; Nat Hon Sy; Perf Att; St of Mnth; Yth Ldrshp Prog; Comm Volntr; Hosp Aide; BPA; Chrch Yth Grp; Cmptr Clb; Emplmnt; Mus Clb; Ntl Beta Clb; NYLC; Outdrs Clb; Chr; Ch Chr; Dnce; SP/M/VS; Chrldg (J); PPSqd (L); Swmg (L); Tennis (L); Yrbk (E); General Surgeon / Surgery Major; Neuro Surgeon / Surgery Major; Georgia State U; UCLA

WINSETT, CHRISTIAN; LYNCHBURG, TN; (FR); Hnr Roll; St of Mnth; 4-H; Bnd; Mch Bnd; Pep Bnd; Lawyer; Master's Degree in Math; Yale U; Princeton U

WINTERS, PERRY R; ROAN MOUNTAIN, TN; CLOUDLAND HS; (JR); Drma Clb; Ntl Beta Clb; Spanish Clb; Ftball (J); Student Government Association / Member - ETSU Upward Bound; Pathology; Art; Belmont U; U of Tennessee Knoxville

WIRRICK, MEAGAN B; CLARKSVILLE, TN; CLARKSVILLE HS; (JR); Hnr Roll; St of Mnth; WWAHSS; BPA; Drma Clb; SP/M/VS; Stg Cre

WISECARVER, JORDAN C; ERWIN, TN; U N 1001 CTY VOC SCH; (SR); 4H Awd; Ctznshp Aw; Hnr Roll; MVP; 4-H; ArtClub; Ntl FFA; Acpl Chr; Ch Chr; SP/M/VS; Bsball (V); Won a District Baseball Championship; Won a Regional Baseball Championship; Agriculture; Engineering; Milligan College; Tusculum College

WITHERSPOON, JUSTIN; COLUMBIA, TN; CENTRAL HS; (SO); Hnr Roll; Yth Ldrshp Prog; Prom Com; Spanish Clb; Bskball (J); Ftball (V L); Track (V); Stu Cncl (V); Yrbk (R); Business; U South Carolina; U Tennessee

WITMER, JENNA; BUTLER, TN; JOHNSON CTY HS; (FR); Hnr Roll; Pres Sch; Comm Volntr; Chrch Yth Grp; Chrldg (J); Neurology; Medicine; East Tennessee State U; U of Pennsylvania

WITT, REBECCA; MOUNTAIN CITY, TN; JOHNSON CTY HS; (SR); Hnr Roll; Nat Hon Sy; Pres Ac Ftns Aw; WWAHSS; Drma Clb; Emplmnt; Bnd; Mch Bnd; Tennis (V); Band President 2004-2005; Communication Arts; Lees-Mc Rae College

WITTSCHECK, ALEX; IRON CITY, TN; WILSON HS; (JR); Duke TS; Hi Hnr Roll; Hnr Roll; Perf Att; Comm Volntr; Chess; Chrch Yth Grp; Drma Clb; Emplmnt; Key Club; Off Aide; Schol Bwl; Sci Clb; SP/M/VS; Stg Cre; Business Management; Commercial Music; Auburn U; U of North Alabama

WIX, HOLLYANNE; MANCHESTER, TN; (SR); WWAHSS; Who's Who Among American High School Students; Teacher; Medical; Motlow State; MTSU

WOLFE, COURTNEY; KINGSPORT, TN; DOBYNS BENNETT HS; (SO); Hnr Roll; Perf Att; WWAHSS; Key Club; Spanish Clb; Bnd; Mch Bnd; Pep Bnd; Yrbk (R); AIM Scholar; Pharmacy

WOLFE, RACHEL; KINGSPORT, TN; DOBYNS-BENNETT HS; (SO); Duke TS; Hi Hnr Roll; WWAHSS; Emplmnt; Jr Cls League; Key Club; Clr Grd; Pharmacy; East Tennessee State U; U of Tennessee

WOMBLE, AMBER; LAWRENCEBURG, TN; LAWRENCE CTY VOC CTR; (FR); Hnr Roll; Nat Hon Sy; Perf Att; Chrch Yth Grp; DARE; Stu Cncl (R); Educational Talent Search; Vet; Some Type of Child Care

WONG, TING; MEMPHIS, TN; RIDGEWAY HS; (JR); Hnr Roll; Nat Hon Sy; Otst Ac Ach Awd; WWAHSS; Comm Volntr; ArtClub; Emplmnt; Fr of Library; Key Club; Lib Aide; Mth Clb/Tm; MuAlphaTh; Quill & Scroll; Stu Cncl; Lit Mag; Sch Ppr (R); International Club; Designer of Vote Now Organization Logo; Pre-Pharmacy; International Business Administration; California State U Bakersfield; Christian Brothers U

Winfrey, Chatuan
East HS
Memphis, TN

Wilson, Erica A
Ridgeway HS
Memphis, TN

Whittenbarger, Shea A
East Ridge HS
Chattanooga, TN

Whitefield, Shae
Oliver Springs HS
Oliver Springs, TN

White, Shaniece E
Mc Gavock Comp HS
Hermitage, TN

Whiteaker, Jennifer
Donelson Christian AC
Hermitage, TN

Wilkey, Blake A
Soddy-Daisy HS
Soddy Daisy, TN

Winegar, Meghan
Central HS
Wartburg, TN

Witherspoon, Justin
Central HS
Columbia, TN

WONG, YING Y; MEMPHIS, TN; RIDGEWAY HS; (SR); Hnr Roll; Nat Hon Sy; WWAHSS; Comm Volntr; ArtClub; Emplmnt; Key Club; MuAlphaTh; Quill & Scroll; SP/M/VS; Art Club Vice President / Assistant Secretary; Quill and Scroll Honor Society; Biology / Pharmacy; Christian Brothers U

WOOD, JEFF; MURFREESBORO, TN; SIEGEL HS; (JR); Hnr Roll; USAA; WWAHSS; Comm Volntr; Peer Tut/Med; Chrch Yth Grp; Drma Clb; Emplmnt; Ntl Beta Clb; SP/M/VS; Ftball (V); Sccr (J); Middle Tennessee State U; U of Tennessee Knoxville

WOOD, JOSH; MONTEREY, TN; MONTEREY HS; (SO); Hnr Roll; St of Mnth; Comm Volntr; Chrch Yth Grp; FCA; Ntl Beta Clb; CR (R); Taking Honors Classes; Veterinarian; Law Enforcement; U of Tennessee; U of Kentucky

WOOD, LAUREN; BRENTWOOD, TN; RAVENWOOD HS; (SO); Hi Hnr Roll; Hnr Roll; Comm Volntr; Hab For Humty Volntr; Chrch Yth Grp; DARE; Dbte Team; FCA; Chr; Stg Cre; Lcrsse (J); Sftball; Track; Cl Off (S); First Priority Club; Lawyer; Doctor; Vanderbilt U; Baylor U

WOODARD, LAKEISHA; SPRINGFIELD, TN; SPRINGFIELD HS; (SO); Clr Grd; Mch Bnd; SP/M/VS; HOSA; Nursing Bachelor's Degree; Middle Tennessee State U; Tennessee State U

WOODS, ALYSE D; MEMPHIS, TN; CRAIGMONT HS; (MS); All Am Sch; Gov Hnr Prg; Hi Hnr Roll; Comm Volntr; Chrch Yth Grp; Bnd; Ch Chr; Stu Cncl (R); Yrbk

WOODS, AMANDA L; CORDOVA, TN; EVANGELICAL CHRISTIAN SCH; (SR); Comm Volntr; Peer Tut/Med; Spec Olymp Vol; FTA; Key Club; Quill & Scroll; Latin Clb; Cr Ctry (V); PP Ftbl (J); Track (J); Sch Ppr (E); Latin Club Secretary; Future Educator of America-President; Psychology; Journalism; U of Tennessee-Knoxville; U of Tennessee-Chattanooga

WOODS, KAYLA; BRISTOL, TN; SULLIVAN EAST HS; (FR); Hnr Roll; Nat Hon Sy; WWAHSS; Chrch Yth Grp; FCA; Key Club; Ntl Beta Clb; NtlFrnscLg; SP/M/VS; Bskball (J); Vllyball (J); Neonatal Nursing; Ob/Gyn; East Tennessee State U; U of Tennessee

WOODS, TIFFANEY M; CLINTON, TN; CLINTON HS; (MS); 4H Awd; Ctznshp Aw; Hi Hnr Roll; Hnr Roll; MVP; Nat Hon Sy; Otst Ac Ach Awd; Perf Att; Sci Fairs; St of Mnth; Comm Volntr; Peer Tut/Med; Chrch Yth Grp; Dbte Team; Drma Clb; Lib Aide; Pep Squd; Photgz; Scouts; Chr; Ch Chr; Dnce; SP/M/VS; Bskball (J); Chrldg (V); Golf (V); PPSqd (R); Sccr (J); Sftball (V); Track (J); Vllyball (J); Cl Off (S); Stu Cncl (S); CR (R); Yrbk (P); Homecoming Queen; Pediatrics; Master's Degree; Duke U; U of Tennessee

WOODSIDE, TIFFANY; SODDY DAISY, TN; SODDY-DAISY HS; (FR); Hi Hnr Roll; WWAHSS; Chrch Yth Grp; FCA; FBLA; Bnd; Ch Chr; Jzz Bnd; Mch Bnd; Stu Cncl (R); Church AWANA; Church Plays; Math Major; Music Major; Middle Tennessee State U; U of Tennessee Knoxville

WOODS JR, CHARLES; MEMPHIS, TN; MELROSE HS; (FR); Fut Prb Slvr; Perf Att; WWAHSS; Chrch Yth Grp; Wdwrkg Clb; Ch Chr; Ftball (J); Drives a Tracker Tractor Trailer; Truck Driver

WRIGHT, BRITTANY L; OLIVER SPRINGS, TN; OLIVER SPRINGS HS; (SO); Hnr Roll; WWAHSS; Peer Tut/Med; Spanish Clb; Bnd; Clr Grd; Mch Bnd; Nursing; Child Care; Vanderbilt U; Middle Tennessee State U

WRIGHT, JESSICA E; NUNNELLY, TN; HICKMAN CTY HS; (FR); Ctznshp Aw; Hnr Roll; Perf Att; Chrch Yth Grp; DARE; Drma Clb; FCA; Bnd; Clr Grd; Flg Crps; Mch Bnd; Bskball; Chrldg; Registered Nurse; Cosmetologist; U of Tennessee

WRIGHT, KAYCEE; WARTRACE, TN; CASCADE HS; (JR); 4H Awd; Hi Hnr Roll; Nat Hon Sy; Perf Att; WWAHSS; Comm Volntr; 4-H; AL Aux Girls; Chrch Yth Grp; Emplmnt; FCA; FBLA; Key Club; Pep Squd; Chrldg (V L); Cl Off (T); Nursing

WRIGHT, LAUREN; MEMPHIS, TN; WHITE STATION HS; (FR); Hnr Roll; Perf Att; Interior Design; Lambuth U

WRIGHT, NANCY; MURFREESBORO, TN; SIEGEL HS; (SR); Hi Hnr Roll; Nat Hon Sy; USAA; WWAHSS; BPA; Key Club; MuAlphaTh; Ntl Beta Clb; Sci Clb; Tchrs Aide; Clr Grd; Color Guard Captain; Accounting; U of Tennessee Knoxville

WRIGHT, SHERIKA; MEMPHIS, TN; MIDDLE COLLEGE HS; (JR); Nat Hon Sy; Peer Tut/Med; BPA; DECA; Mus Clb; Spanish Clb; Cl Off (T); Stu Cncl (R); Biochemistry; Biology; Washington U in St Louis; Howard U

WU, CUI X; MEMPHIS, TN; WOODDALE HS; (JR); Ctznshp Aw; Hnr Roll; Economics; U of Memphis

WUERFEL, KELLY; ARLINGTON, TN; (JR); Hnr Roll; FBLA; Key Club; Pharmacy; Business; Auburn U; Florida State U

WURTHMANN, TIFFANY L; JOELTON, TN; WHITES CREEK HS; (SR); All Am Sch; Hi Hnr Roll; Hnr Roll; Nat Hon Sy; Otst Ac Ach Awd; WWAHSS; Hosp Aide; Spec Olymp Vol; BPA; Chrch Yth Grp; FBLA; Off Aide; Pep Squd; Bnd; Mch Bnd; Yrbk (P); National Honor Society; Registered Nurse; U of Tennessee, Knoxville; Austin Peay State U

WYATT, JOEL; JACKSON, TN; LIBERTY TECH MAGNET HS; (SO); Hnr Roll; WWAHSS; Comm Volntr; Chrch Yth Grp; DECA; Emplmnt; Sch Ppr (V); Business Administration; U of North Carolina; U of Tennessee At Chattanooga

WYATT, TARA L; KNOXVILLE, TN; HALLS HS; (SO); Duke TS; Fut Prb Slvr; Hnr Roll; Nat Hon Sy; WWAHSS; Comm Volntr; Peer Tut/Med; Chrch Yth Grp; FCA; Mus Clb; P to P St Amb Prg; Acpl Chr; Bnd; Chr; Ch Chr; Sftball (VJ); Swmg (V); Elementary Education; Medical; U of Tennessee-Knoxville; Pellissippi State Community College-Knoxville

YANCEY, KAYLA; CHRISTIANA, TN; FRANKLIN ROAD CHRISTIAN SCH; (SO); Hnr Roll; Nat Hon Sy; Sci Fairs; St of Mnth; WWAHSS; Comm Volntr; Chrch Yth Grp; Emplmnt; Chr; Ch Chr; Chrldg (J); Mar Art (VJ); Teacher with Minor in Court; Pensacola Christian College

YANG, LI; NASHVILLE, TN; HILLSBORO COMP HS; (JR); WWAHSS; Peer Tut/Med; Dbte Team; Drma Clb; Emplmnt; Lib Aide; Mod Un UN; Photgz; Prom Com; Quiz Bowl; SP/M/VS; Cl Off (P); Sch Ppr (E); International Club; International Business; Biology; Vanderbilt U; Stanford U

YATES, NICHOLAS A; MARYVILLE, TN; WILLIAM BLOUNT HS; (JR); F Lan Hn Soc; Hi Hnr Roll; Hnr Roll; WWAHSS; Hab For Humty Volntr; Chrch Yth Grp; Emplmnt; FCA; Tchrs Aide; French Clb; Bskball (J); Ftball (J); Sccr (V L); Criminal Psychology; U of North Carolina; Carteret Community College

YENAMANDRA, TEJA; NASHVILLE, TN; HILLSBORO COMP HS; (JR); Hnr Roll; Nat Hon Sy; Perf Att; St of Mnth; WWAHSS; Yth Ldrshp Prog; Comm Volntr; Cmptr Clb; DARE; Emplmnt; Lib Aide; Mth Clb/Tm; Sci Clb; SP/M/VS; Swg Chr; Bsball; Ftball; Lcrsse; Tennis; Cl Off (S); Sch Ppr (E); Karate; Metlife Scholar Program Participant; Medical Field; Genetics; Vanderbilt U; Johns Hopkins U; Stanford U; NYU; Columbia U

YORK, AMANDA L; ERWIN, TN; UNICOI CTY HS; (SR); St of Mnth; Comm Volntr; Red Cr Aide; Key Club; Registered Nurse License; Flight Nurse License; Northeast State Community College

YORK, BRITTANY C; KNOXVILLE, TN; WEST HS; (SR); Hi Hnr Roll; Hnr Roll; Nat Hon Sy; Nat Mrt Fin; Nat Mrt LOC; WWAHSS; Comm Volntr; Peer Tut/Med; DARE; DECA; Prom Com; Sftball (VJ L); Miss Jr Tenn Teen 2004; Nutrition; Dietetics; U of Tennessee; Pellissippi State Technical Community College

YOUNG, ASHLEY; FRANKLIN, TN; FRED J PAGE HS; (SO); Hi Hnr Roll; Hnr Roll; Perf Att; 4-H; Chrch Yth Grp; DARE; Drma Clb; Emplmnt; Mth Clb/Tm; MuAlphaTh; Scouts; Spanish Clb; Vllyball (J); Pharmacy; Psychology; U of Memphis, TN; U of Tennessee, Knoxville

YOUNG, ASHLIE; CHATTANOOGA, TN; LOOKOUT VALLEY HS; (SO); 4H Awd; Ctznshp Aw; Perf Att; St of Mnth; Comm Volntr; Hosp Aide; Peer Tut/Med; 4-H; ArtClub; Chrch Yth Grp; DARE; Drma Clb; FCA; FBLA; Jr Ach; SP/M/VS; Sftball (J); Vllyball (J); Stu Cncl (R)

YOUNG, BRITTONIE L; MEMPHIS, TN; WHITEHAVEN HS; (JR); Ctznshp Aw; Hi Hnr Roll; Hnr Roll; Nat Hon Sy; WWAHSS; Comm Volntr; Chrch Yth Grp; DARE; Chr; Ch Chr; Cl Off (R); Stu Cncl; CR (R); Youth of the Year Award; Asst Sunday School Teacher; Cardiologist; Pediatrician; Baylor U; Tuskegee

YOUNG, MEAGAN; NASHVILLE, TN; ST CECILIA HS; (SO); Gov Hnr Prg; Hi Hnr Roll; Otst Ac Ach Awd; Pres Sch; Hab For Humty Volntr; Peer Tut/Med; ArtClub; Mth Clb/Tm; Outdrs Clb; Spanish Clb; Swmg (V L); Vllyball (J); Cl Off (P); Certified in CPR and Lifeguarding; Teach Private Lessons During the Summer; Wild Life; Marine Biology; U of Kentucky

YOUNG, MITCHELL A; ROCK ISLAND, TN; F C BOYD CHRISTIAN SCH; (FR); All Am Sch; Hi Hnr Roll; Hnr Roll; USAA; WWAHSS; Peer Tut/Med; Mth Clb/Tm; Ntl Beta Clb; Bsball (V); Bskball (VJ); Sftball (V); Stu Cncl; 8th Grade Class Valedictorian; Eastside Beta Club President; Education; Law; U of Tennessee-Knoxville; Tennessee Tech U

YOUNG, WINSTON; MEMPHIS, TN; LAUSANNE COLLEGIATE SCH; (JR); Sci Fairs; Comm Volntr; Peer Tut/Med; Key Club; Pep Squd; Svce Clb; Tmpl Yth Grp; Bnd; Jzz Bnd; Pep Bnd; Golf (V); School Publishing of Literary Works; Word Smith Winner in 03-04; Music; Sound Engineering; The New School U; Memphis State U

YUNGMEYER, LAURA L; KINGSPORT, TN; DOBYNS BENNETT HS; (SO); Sccr (V); Tennis (V); Cl Off (V); Yrbk (R)

ZACHARY, LISA D; KNOXVILLE, TN; HALLS HS; (SR); Hnr Roll; Nat Hon Sy; St of Mnth; Valdctrian; WWAHSS; Comm Volntr; Chrch Yth Grp; Emplmnt; FBLA; Key Club; Mth Clb/Tm; Bnd; Dnce; Mch Bnd; PPSqd (V CL); Voted "Most Likely to Succeed"; Who's Who Among American High School Students; Chemical Engineering; U of Tennessee-Knoxville

ZAGEL, EMMA; MEMPHIS, TN; WHITE STATION HS; (SO); Ctznshp Aw; Hnr Roll; Chess; Chrch Yth Grp; Tchrs Aide; Bnd; Ch Chr; Skiing; Publication in Poetry Anthology 1998; Bell Choir 2001, 2002, 2003; Meteorology; Interior/Fashion Design; U of Mississippi, U of Memphis; U of Tennessee

ZEIGLER, ANNIE; JACKSON, TN; SOUTH SIDE HS; (JR); 4H Awd; Ctznshp Aw; Hnr Roll; Otst Ac Ach Awd; Perf Att; Hosp Aide; Peer Tut/Med; 4-H; Chrch Yth Grp; Latin Clb; Presidential Education Award; Nominated 2 Years for Lead America; Pre-Medicine; Elementary Education; Jackson State Community College; Union U

ZEIGLER, ARIEL; JACKSON, TN; ROSE HILL MAGNET SCH; (MS); 4H Awd; Ctznshp Aw; Hnr Roll; MVP; Sci Fairs; Yth Ldrshp Prog; Comm Volntr; Hab For Humty Volntr; Spec Olymp Vol; 4-H; AL Aux Girls; Chrch Yth Grp; Drma Clb; Fr of Library; Jr Ach; Photgz; Scouts; Chr; Dnce; SP/M/VS; Swg Chr; Golf (J); Hsbk Rdg (J); Sftball (J); Cl Off (S); Yrbk (P); Modeling/Actress; Veter; Purdue U

ZHANG, ZI; CHATTANOOGA, TN; EAST RIDGE HS; (SO); Hnr Roll; Nat Hon Sy; Perf Att; Chess; ROTC; Extracurricular Award for Mathematics; Academic Honors; Computer-Engineer; Software Programmer; North Central Technical College; Princeton-U

ZHELTKOV, LYUDMILA; NASHVILLE, TN; HILLWOOD HS; (SO); Hnr Roll; WWAHSS; Red Cr Aide; Dbte Team; Drma Clb; Emplmnt; NtlFrnscLg; French Clb; SP/M/VS; Stg Cre; Teacher; Engineering; Vanderbilt U; Middle Tennessee State U

ZIBBLE, DANIELLE; HOHENWALD, TN; LEWIS CTY HS; (JR); All Am Sch; Hnr Roll; Otst Ac Ach Awd; USAA; WWAHSS; Chrch Yth Grp; DARE; Bnd; Jzz Bnd; Mch Bnd; Pep Bnd; Outstanding Discipline Award; Best Woodwind Award; Ob Nurse; U of Michigan; Bethel U

Yenamandra, Teja
Hillsboro Comp HS
Nashville, TN

Wurthmann, Tiffany L
Whites Creek HS
Joelton, TN

National Honor Roll Spring 2005

Woods, Tiffaney M
Clinton HS
Clinton, TN

Zagel, Emma
White Station HS
Memphis, TN

Vermont

ADAMS, CHRISTOPHER J; TROY, VT; NORTH CTRY UNION HS; (SR); Hnr Roll; Red Cr Aide; Emplmnt; Van Gogh Award; Computer Animator; PhotoShop Tech Work; Lyndon State College of Vermont; Art Institute of Massachusetts

AUREIMA, NICOLA; WOODSTOCK, VT; WOODSTOCK UNION HS; (JR); Hnr Roll; Emplmnt; Mod UN; Prom Com; Sccr (V); Tennis (J); Graphic Design; Writer (Fiction); Emerson; Barnard

BARRIERE, CHRISTOPHER; BENNINGTON, VT; MT ANTHONY UNION HS; (SO); Hi Hnr Roll; Hnr Roll; Otst Ac Ach Awd; Perf Att; Emplmnt; Mod UN; Bsball (J); Bskball (J); Fox Sports Net Funcaster Award; Journalism; Broadcasting; Syracuse U; Boston U

BERNSTEIN, REBECCA M; HUNTINGTON, VT; VT. COMMONS HS; (JR); Chr; CR (P); Communications; Psychology; Northeastern; Emerson

BUSHMAN, DANIELLE; DANBY, VT; MILL RIVER HS; (FR); Sci Fairs; Key Club; Bowling; Zoologist; Teacher

CASLIN, LIND E; BENNINGTON, VT; MT ANTHONY UNION HS; (JR); Hi Hnr Roll; Pres Ac Ftns Aw; Comm Volntr; Emplmnt; Scouts; Bnd; Mch Bnd; Cr Ct Ski (V L); Fld Hky (V CL); Lcrsse (L); 2 Year Position - Appointed to the VT State Board Education; Psychology / Social Work; Design; Middlebury College; Williams College

CHRISTIE, ANGELA M; WHITE RIV JCT, VT; HARTFORD HS; (JR); Hi Hnr Roll; Perf Att; St of Mnth; Yth Ldrshp Prog; Comm Volntr; Dbte Team; Drma Clb; Emplmnt; Mth Clb/Tm; NtlFrnscLg; Tchrs Aide; SP/M/VS; Stg Cre; Track; Yrbk (P); Physics; Mathematics; George Washington U; Cornell U

CONROY, EMILY C; S BURLINGTON, VT; RICE MEMORIAL HS; (JR); Hi Hnr Roll; Hnr Roll; Nat Hon Sy; Otst Ac Ach Awd; Pres Ac Ftns Aw; St of Mnth; WWAHSS; Comm Volntr; Chrch Yth Grp; Drma Clb; Mus Clb; Prom Com; Svce Clb; Acpl Chr; Chr; Ch Chr; SP/M/VS; Sccr (VJ L); Tennis (V L); Cl Off (R); Stu Cncl (R); CR (R); Yrbk (E); Yearbook Editor; Sunday School Teacher; Business / Fashion Industry; Boston College; Northeastern U

CORCORAN, MIKE; ESSEX JUNCTION, VT; ESSEX HS; (JR); Duke TS; Hnr Roll; WWAHSS; Comm Volntr; Emplmnt; Scouts; Ftball (J); Lcrsse (VJ); Wt Lftg; Governor's Institute of Vermont; Engineering; Science; U of Vermont, U of New Hampshire; Clarkson U, Montana State U

COWENS, KYLIE R; MONTPELIER, VT; U-32; (JR); Hi Hnr Roll; MVP; Perf Att; Pres Sch; WWAHSS; Comm Volntr; Peer Tut/Med; Chrch Yth Grp; Bnd; Ch Chr; Bskball (V L); Sccr (V CL); Sftball (V L); Track (V L); 7 Time Highest Honors / 2 Time High Honors; Physical Therapy; U of New England; Gordon College

DELONG, CHRISTOPHER M; WELLS, VT; POULTNEY HS; (FR); Hnr Roll; St of Mnth; Comm Volntr; DARE

DIDIO, SAMANTHA E; RUTLAND, VT; MILL RIVER UNION HS; (JR); Sci Fairs; St of Mnth; WWAHSS; Peer Tut/Med; Tchrs Aide; Veterinarian

DOANE, AARON; E FAIRFIELD, VT; ENOSBURG FALLS MIDDLE HS; (SO); Hi Hnr Roll; Sci Fairs; St of Mnth; Comm Volntr; Chess; Drma Clb; Mus Clb; Bnd; Chr; Jzz Bnd; SP/M/VS; Professional Musician; High School Band Director; U of Vermont; Johnson State College

DORAN, HEIDI A; BOMOSEEN, VT; FAIR HAVEN UNION HS; (SO); Hnr Roll; Otst Ac Ach Awd; Perf Att; Yth Ldrshp Prog; Drma Clb; HO'Br Yth Ldrshp; Bnd; Chr; Dnce; Mch Bnd; Sccr (V); Sftball (V); Track (V); Cl Off (S); Stu Cncl (V); Law Enforcement Explorer - Police Cadet; Master's Degree / Psychology; Law Enforcement Officer; U of North Carolina; Saint Michaels College of Vermont

DOSHI, VIRAL K; SOUTH BURLINGTON, VT; SOUTH BURLINGTON HS; (JR); Hi Hnr Roll; Nat Sci Aw; WWAHSS; Best Category Award By Intel Science Talent Discovery Fair in 2003; Tri-Lingual - Hindi / Gujareti / English; Biomedical Engineering; Genetic Engineering; U of Vermont; McGill U Canada

D'OTTAVIO, TONY; LUDLOW, VT; BLACK RIVER HS; (SO); Hnr Roll; MVP; Comm Volntr; Drma Clb; Emplmnt; NYLC; SP/M/VS; Bskball (JC); Golf (J); Cl Off (T); CR (T); Played Both Junior Varsity and Varsity During Basketball; Professional Basketball Player; U of Vermont; Boston College

DUPEE, BRENTON; BENNINGTON, VT; MT ANTHONY UNION HS; (JR); 4-H; Dbte Team; Mod UN; Off Aide; Scouts; Mar Art; Computer Graphics; Foreign Language; Graphic Art / Tech; Green Mountain College

DUTCHER, ALLYSON E; BENNINGTON, VT; MT ANTHONY UNION HS; (FR); Ctznshp Aw; Hi Hnr Roll; Hnr Roll; Nat Ldrshp Svc; Otst Ac Ach Awd; St of Mnth; Comm Volntr; AL Aux Girls; Chrch Yth Grp; DARE; Drma Clb; NYLC; Scouts; Chr; Dnce; SP/M/VS; Sch Ppr (R); Art History / Italian & US

GABORIAULT, HILAREE; GREENSBORO BEND, VT; HAZEN UNION HS; Hnr Roll; Pres Ac Ftns Aw; Comm Volntr; Emplmnt; Key Club; Prom Com; SP/M/VS; Bskball (JC); Sccr (JC); Cl Off (T); Key Club Secretary; Prom Committee; Social Work/Psychology; Nursing

GAGNE, ASHLEY R; SWANTON, VT; MISSISQUOI VALLEY UNION JSHS; (JR); Hi Hnr Roll; Nat Hon Sy; Perf Att; WWAHSS; Comm Volntr; Bskball (VJCL); Sccr (VJCL); Sftball (J); Stu Cncl (R); Physical Therapy; U of Vermont

GATES, KAREN A; FRANKLIN, VT; MISSISQUOI VALLEY UNION JSHS; (JR); Hi Hnr Roll; MVP; Nat Hon Sy; St of Mnth; Comm Volntr; Chrch Yth Grp; Drma Clb; Mth Clb/Tm; Mus Clb; Bnd; Drm Mjr; Jzz Bnd; Mch Bnd; Ice Hky (V L); Sccr (V L); Track (V L); CR (R); Local Grade Level Winner Twice - U of VT Writing Contest; Marine Biology; Medicine; Tufts U; U of Rhode Island

GORMLEY, ANN K; RUTLAND, VT; RUTLAND HS; (JR); Hi Hnr Roll; Pres Ac Ftns Aw; Comm Volntr; AL Aux Girls; ArtClub; Key Club; Mus Clb; Prom Com; Sci Clb; Acpl Chr; Chr; Cr Ctry; Fld Hky; Lcrsse; Skiing; Cl Off (V); CR; Senator Jeffords Art Award; Excellence in Art Award; Communications; Syracuse U

GRANT, KARA A; WATERBURY CTR, VT; RICE MEMORIAL HS; (JR); Hi Hnr Roll; Hnr Roll; St of Mnth; Comm Volntr; Peer Tut/Med; Spec Olymp Vol; Lib Aide; French Clb; Bnd; Sch Ppr (R); Student of the Month; Biomedical Engineering; Dartmouth College

GRENNON, WHITNEY J; FRANKLIN, VT; MISSISQUOI VALLEY UNION JSHS; (JR); Hi Hnr Roll; MVP; Nat Hon Sy; Otst Ac Ach Awd; St of Mnth; Comm Volntr; Red Cr Aide; AL Aux Girls; Chrch Yth Grp; Scouts; Svce Clb; Bnd; Mch Bnd; SP/M/VS; Bskball (VJC); Sccr (V C); Sftball (VJC); Stu Cncl (P); Vermont Athletic Leadership Conference; Executive Student Council President; Exercise Science / Sports Medicine; Physical Therapy; Sacred Heart U; U of North Carolina Chapel Hill

GROTE, GRETCHEN; SOUTH ROYALTON, VT; SOUTH ROYALTON SCH; (SR); Hnr Roll; Perf Att; Comm Volntr; Emplmnt; Prom Com; SADD; Tchrs Aide; Bskball (V CL); Golf (V); Sccr (V); Sports Management; Southern New Hampshire U

HAMMERL, MICHAEL R; WATERBURY, VT; HARWOOD UNION HS; (SR); Hnr Roll; Comm Volntr; Emplmnt; Bskball (VJC); Golf (V); Business Major; U of Vermont; U of Colorado @ Boulder

HARRIS, STEPHANIE; WILLISTON, VT; CHAMPLAIN VALLEY UNION HS; (JR); Hi Hnr Roll; Hnr Roll; Nat Hon Sy; Otst Ac Ach Awd; Comm Volntr; Emplmnt; Key Club; Fld Hky (J); Sftball (VJCL); International Club; Buddy Program; English; Film; Pomona College; Boston College

HART, MARIE; NEW HAVEN, VT; MT ABRAHAM HS; (SR); Hi Hnr Roll; Hnr Roll; Perf Att; WWAHSS; Comm Volntr; Peer Tut/Med; Chrch Yth Grp; Emplmnt; Tchrs Aide; Elementary Education; Castleton State College; Champlain College

HAWLEY, ANDREA L; RUTLAND, VT; RUTLAND HS; (JR); Hi Hnr Roll; Nat Hon Sy; Otst Ac Ach Awd; Sci Fairs; St of Mnth; Comm Volntr; ArtClub; Chrch Yth Grp; Emplmnt; Key Club; Sci Clb; Youth Group President; Science Club; PharmD; U of Sciences At Philadelphia; Campbell U

HEWITT, KAITLIN; DANBY, VT; MILL RIVER UNION HS; (FR); Ctznshp Aw; Hnr Roll; Comm Volntr; Key Club; Chr; TA Representative; Marine Biology; Zoology; U of New England; U of New Hampshire

HIGGINS, ASHLEY; WINOOSKI, VT; WINOOSKI HS; (JR); Gov Hnr Prg; Hi Hnr Roll; Hnr Roll; Nat Hon Sy; Pres Sch; Sci Fairs; St of Mnth; Comm Volntr; Drma Clb; Emplmnt; Schol Bwl; Tchrs Aide; Flg Crps; Orch; SP/M/VS; Chrldg (L); Track (V); Cl Off (P); Stu Cncl (S); CR (R); International Thespian Society; Governor's Institute on the Arts; Secondary Education; French; Vassar; U of North Carolina

HIGGINS, ZACH; BENNINGTON, VT; MT ANTHONY UNION HS; (JR); Hi Hnr Roll; Hnr Roll; Pres Ac Ftns Aw; Sci Fairs; Sci/Math Olympn; ArtClub; Bnd; Mch Bnd; Orch; Stg Cre; Sch Ppr (R); Graphic Design; Fine Art; Syracuse U; Digipen Technical Institute

HILL, DANIELLE; REXBURY, VT; NORTHFIELD MIDDLE HS; (JR); Hnr Roll; Perf Att; Hosp Aide; AL Aux Girls; DARE; Wdwrkg Clb; SP/M/VS; Stg Cre; Sftball (J); Journalism; Anthropology; Johnston State College; Boston U

HOUSTON, CHRISTINA M; E WALLINGFORD, VT; MILL RIVER UNION HS; (JR); Hnr Roll; Kwnis Aw; Sci Fairs; St of Mnth; WWAHSS; Peer Tut/Med; DARE; Emplmnt; Key Club; Lttrmn Clb; Prom Com; Scouts; Tchrs Aide; Bskball (J L); Chrldg (V L); Sftball (J); CR; Key Club; International Business; U of Maryland College Park; U of Maryland, Eastern Shore

LA FOUNTAIN, TAUSHA M; FAIRFAX, VT; BFA FAIRFAX; (SO); Hnr Roll; WWAHSS; Comm Volntr; Peer Tut/Med; ArtClub; Dbte Team; Emplmnt; Lib Aide; NYLC; Chr; Dnce; SP/M/VS; Stg Cre; Lions Club Award; Culinary Degree; New England Culinary Institute; Culinary Institute of America

LAQUERRE, ASHLEY; BARRE, VT; SPAULDING HS; (JR); Hi Hnr Roll; Hnr Roll; Prom Com; Vsity Clb; Golf (V); Ice Hky (V); Sccr (V); Cl Off (P, V); Leadership Award; Fitness Award; Physical Therapy; Sports Training; St Lawrence U; U of Vermont

LA ROSE, RENAE; ENOSBURG FALLS, VT; ENOSBURG FALLS HS; (JR); Hnr Roll; Perf Att; Prom Com; Tchrs Aide; Chr; Bskball (VJC); Scr Kpr (V); Sccr (JC); Sftball (VJC); Physical Therapy; Elementary Education; Castleton State College; Lyndon State College

LEADBEATER, SAMANTHA; HIGHGATE CTR, VT; MISSISQUOI VALLEY UNION JSHS; (JR); Hnr Roll; St of Mnth; WWAHSS; Comm Volntr; Tchrs Aide; Chr; Ch Chr; SP/M/VS; Fld Hky (J); Sftball (J); Secondary Teacher; Principal; Plymouth State; Rhode Island College

LEONARD, KAYLA J; CTR RUTLAND, VT; RUTLAND HS; (SO); Hi Hnr Roll; Pres Ac Ftns Aw; WWAHSS; ArtClub; Chrch Yth Grp; Emplmnt; Key Club; Bskball (V L); Fld Hky (J); Lcrsse (J); Pediatrician

LUBOLD, SARAH L; BRAINTREE, VT; RANDOLPH UNION HS; (JR); 4H Awd; Hi Hnr Roll; Nat Hon Sy; Comm Volntr; Peer Tut/Med; 4-H; AL Aux Girls; Drma Clb; Emplmnt; Bnd; Chr; Mch Bnd; SP/M/VS; Sch Ppr (E); Restorative Justice; Started Environmental Club; Anthropology / History; English / Foreign Languages

LUMSDEN, ELIZABETH M; HARDWICK, VT; HAZEN UNION HS; (SR); DAR; Hi Hnr Roll; Hnr Roll; Nat Hon Sy; Comm Volntr; Red Cr Aide; Chrch Yth Grp; Emplmnt; HO'Br Yth Ldrshp; Key Club; Lib Aide; Off Aide; Prom Com; Vsity Clb; Chr; Ch Chr; Bskball (V CL); Sccr (J); Sftball (V CL); Vsy Clb (V C); Cl Off (T); Sch Ppr (E, R); Yrbk; Girls State; NHS-President; Education; Business; Saint Michael's College

LUSSIER, LEAH M; JEFFERSONVILLE, VT; LAMOILLE UNION HS; (FR); Hi Hnr Roll; MVP; Nat Hon Sy; WWAHSS; Scouts; SADD; Vsity Clb; Dnce; Bskball (J L); Lcrsse (V L); Scr Kpr (V); Sccr (J L); Bachelors Degree in Science; RN; Boston College; North Carolina U

LYNDE, AUBREE; BRATTLEBORO, VT; BRATTLEBORO UNION HS; (SR); Hnr Roll; Chrch Yth Grp; DECA; Emplmnt; Photog; Prom Com; Vsity Clb; Fld Hky (V L); Lcrsse (V L); Yrbk (E, P); Early Childhood Education; Colby-Sawyer College

MACHIA, KAYSE A; HIGHGATE CTR, VT; NORTHWEST TECH CTR; (SR); Hi Hnr Roll; Hnr Roll; WWAHSS; Red Cr Aide; DECA; Emplmnt; Off Aide; P to P St Amb Prg; Tchrs Aide; Fld Hky (VJ L); Ice Hky (V L); Sftball (VJ L); Stu Cncl (R); Yrbk (E, P); Television Studies; Photography; Lyndon State College

MACK, LAURA; BRISTOL, VT; RICE MEMORIAL HS; (SR); Hnr Roll; Perf Att; Yth Ldrshp Prog; Amnsty Intl; Red Cr Aide; ArtClub; Chrch Yth Grp; Outdrs Clb; P to P St Amb Prg; Photog; Prom Com; Schol Bwl; French Clb; Ch Chr; Ice Hky (V); Vermont Teen Leadership Safety Program - President; Jamaica Missionary Trip; Liberal Arts; Hartwick College

MANNEY, MATTHEW; RUTLAND, VT; RUTLAND HS; (JR); Hi Hnr Roll; Hnr Roll; Nat Hon Sy; Otst Ac Ach Awd; Sci Fairs; St of Mnth; WWAHSS; Comm Volntr; Chrch Yth Grp; Emplmnt; Key Club; Bnd; Jzz Bnd; Orch; Golf (V L); Several Music Awards; Academic Awards; Forensic Science; U of Central Florida; Duquesne U

MARTIN, CALEY; SHAFTSBURG, VT; MT ANTHONY UNION HS; (SR); Hi Hnr Roll; Hnr Roll; Perf Att; Comm Volntr; 4-H; Cmptr Clb; Emplmnt; Mod UN; Scouts; Skiing (C); Sccr (J); Political Science; Foreign Trade Investing; SUNY Binghamton

MC CLEERY III, JAMES P; SOUTH ROYALTON, VT; SOUTH ROYALTON SR HS; (SR); Ctznshp Aw; Hnr Roll; Otst Ac Ach Awd; Pres Ac Ftns Aw; Sci Fairs; WWAHSS; Comm Volntr; Peer Tut/Med; Cmptr Clb; Emplmnt; Mth Clb/Tm; Prom Com; Sci Clb; Scouts; Tchrs Aide; Tech Clb; Bskball (J); Golf (V); Sccr (V); Sftball (JCL); Physics Awards/Computer Awards; Science Awards; Computer Game Design; Collins College of Art & Design

Harris, Stephanie
Champlain Valley Union HS
Williston, VT

Didio, Samantha E
Mill River Union HS
Rutland, VT

Conroy, Emily C
Rice Memorial HS
S Burlington, VT

National
Honor Roll
Spring 2005

Caslin, Lind E
Mt Anthony Union HS
Bennington, VT

Grennon, Whitney J
Missisquoi Valley Union Jshs
Franklin, VT

Higgins, Zach
Mt Anthony Union HS
Bennington, VT

NATIONAL HONOR ROLL SPRING 2005 — Vermont

MC DERMOTT, CAILEY; EAST CALAIS, VT; HAZEN UNION HS; (SR); Hnr Roll; Nat Hon Sy; Otst Ac Ach Awd; Perf Att; Sci Fairs; Comm Volntr; Peer Tut/Med; Drma Clb; Key Club; Outdrs Clb; Photog; Prom Com; Vsity Clb; French Clb; Chr; Mch Bnd; SP/M/VS; Bskball (JC); Skiing; Sccr (VJCL); Sftball (V L); Vsy Clb; Cl Off (V); Stu Cncl (R); CR (R); Sch Ppr (P); Yrbk (E, P); National Honor Society (Treasurer)/Mentor; Key Club (Vice Pres.)/Governor's Institute on the Arts; Visual Communications; Photojournalism; Saint Michael's College

MC DERMOTT, JESSICA L; ENOSBURG FLS, VT; ENOSBURG FALLS MIDDLE HS; (SO); Hi Hnr Roll; Hnr Roll; Nat Hon Sy; Otst Ac Ach Awd; FBLA; SP/M/VS; Bskball; Sccr (C); Cl Off (S); Business; Home Interior Design; U of Southern California

MILLAR, HEAVEN; BENNINGTON, VT; MT ANTHONY UNION HS; (SO); Hi Hnr Roll; Hnr Roll; Perf Att; Mod UN; Spch Team; SADD; Bnd; Chr; Fld Hky (J); Track (V L); Stu Cncl (R); Law; Forensics

MOLL, NATHAN; BENNINGTON, VT; GRACE CHRISTIAN SCH; (FR); Hi Hnr Roll; Perf Att; Sci/Math Olympn; Bsball; Bskball; Skiing; Sccr; Cl Off (T); Engineering; Liberty U

MOORE, NICOLE K; RUTLAND, VT; RUTLAND HS; (SR); Hnr Roll; Sci Fairs; Chrch Yth Grp; Emplmnt; Key Club; Bnd; Chr; Dnce; Mch Bnd; Bskball (J); Fld Hky (J); Yrbk (E, P); Dance Major; Dean College MA

MURPHY, SARAH; BARRE, VT; SPAULDING HS; (JR); Hnr Roll; Nat Mrt LOC; Peer Tut/Med; Chrch Yth Grp; Emplmnt; Tchrs Aide; Forensic Science; Business Management; U of Georgia; George Washington U

NAGAR, CAILEIGH G; POULTNEY, VT; POULTNEY HS; (FR); Hnr Roll; Comm Volntr; Scouts; Bskball (J); Chrldg (V L); Sccr (V L); Sftball (J); Cl Off (T); Veterinarian; Teacher

NEILL, JESSICA; WAITSFIELD, VT; HARWOOD UNION HS; (JR); Hi Hnr Roll; Nat Hon Sy; Yth Ldrshp Prog; Comm Volntr; Peer Tut/Med; Chrch Yth Grp; Emplmnt; Prom Com; Svce Clb; Tchrs Aide; French Clb; Bnd; Jzz Bnd; Mch Bnd; CR (R); National Honor Society President; Elementary Education; Saint Michael's College; Colgate U

NEWTON, LINDSEY; RUTLAND, VT; RUTLAND HS; (SO); Hi Hnr Roll; Hnr Roll; Otst Ac Ach Awd; Pres Sch; Sci Fairs; Comm Volntr; Bnd; Stu Cncl (R); Pediatrics; Child Psychology; Dartmouth Medical School; Harvard U

NORTHROP, WHITNEY P; RUTLAND, VT; RUTLAND HS; (JR); Hnr Roll; Comm Volntr; 4-H; Key Club; Prom Com; Bnd; Chr; Mch Bnd; Scr Kpr (VJ); Stu Cncl (R); Biology; Education; U of Vermont; U of North Carolina

OLSON, TOREY M; RUTLAND, VT; RUTLAND HS; (JR); Hi Hnr Roll; MVP; Nat Ldrshp Svc; Otst Ac Ach Awd; Pres Ac Ftns Aw; Pres Sch; Sci Fairs; St of Mnth; WWAHSS; Comm Volntr; Emplmnt; Key Club; Prom Com; SADD; Vsity Clb; Cr Ctry (V CL); Cr Ct Ski (V L); Track (V CL); Cl Off (T); Wildlife Biology; Wildlife Science; Cornell U; U of Vermont

PARK, JAMES; RUTLAND, VT; GRANVILLE HS; (FR); Hnr Roll; Emplmnt; Lawyer Pre-Law

PENAR, GEOFFREY; SHELBURNE, VT; ST JOHNSBURY AC; (SO); Hi Hnr Roll; Nat Hon Sy; Sci Fairs; Chrch Yth Grp; Drma Clb; Acpl Chr; Chr; Jzz Bnd; Orch; Tennis (V); All-State Vocal Scholarship Recipient; Classical Voice; U of Michigan; Oberlin College

POPE, MELISSA L; MONTPELIER, VT; WEBSTERVILLE BAPTIST CHRISTIAN SCH; (JR); Hnr Roll; Chrch Yth Grp; SP/M/VS; Bskball (V); Stu Cncl (T); Social Work; Psychology

POPOVAC, TAMARA; SOUTH BURLINGTON, VT; SOUTH BURLINGTON HS; (JR); Hi Hnr Roll; Comm Volntr; Red Cr Aide; Key Club; Prom Com; Chr; Half Semester Abroad in Germany; Speak Three Languages Fluently; High School Education; German; U of Vermont; Middlebury College

ROMEO, ANNA; RUTLAND, VT; RUTLAND HS; (SR); Hnr Roll; WWAHSS; Comm Volntr; AL Aux Girls; Chrch Yth Grp; Emplmnt; Key Club; Mus Clb; Chr; Ch Chr; Clr Grd; Dnce; Sftball; Hospitality; Johnson & Wales U

SANDOVAL, SHELLEY A; SHELBURNE, VT; CHAMPLAIN VALLEY UNION HS; (JR); Hnr Roll; Otst Ac Ach Awd; Perf Att; St Optmst of Yr; Amnsty Intl; Comm Volntr; Hab For Humty Volntr; ArtClub; Emplmnt; FBLA; Key Club; Mod UN; Prom Com; Bnd; Cr Ct Ski (J); Fld Hky (V); Track (J); Stu Cncl (R); Entrepreneurship; International Studies; Marquette U; Lawrence U

SARGOOD, CHRISTOPHER; BENNINGTON, VT; MT ANTHONY UNION HS; (SR); Hi Hnr Roll; Hnr Roll; MVP; Nat Hon Sy; Pres Sch; WWAHSS; Comm Volntr; Outdrs Clb; Skiing (V); Track (V CL); Automotive Technician; Universal Technical Institute

SCHIERMEYER, DANIEL; POWNAL, VT; MT ANTHONY UNION HS; (SO); Hi Hnr Roll; Otst Ac Ach Awd; Lcrsse (JC); Motocross Racing; Engineering; Photography; RPI Technical College; Hallmark Institute of Photography

SCHINDLER, ELIZABETH; RUTLAND, VT; RUTLAND HS; (JR); Hi Hnr Roll; Nat Mrt LOC; Sci Fairs; WWAHSS; Comm Volntr; Emplmnt; Key Club; Mod UN; Prom Com; Dnce; Skiing (V L); Sccr (VJCL); Cl Off (S); Stu Cncl; State Championship '03-'04 - Skiing; Marble Valley League Champion Soccer - Seasons '03 / '04; Doctor / Medical Field; Tufts U; Boston College

SOARES, NICHOLAS A; RANDOLPH CTR, VT; RANDOLPH UNION HS; (JR); Hi Hnr Roll; Hnr Roll; Nat Hon Sy; Pres Ac Ftns Aw; WWAHSS; Drma Clb; SP/M/VS; Stg Cre; History; Literature; Castleton State; Franklin Pierce College

STAPLES, JENNIFER M; MORRISVILLE, VT; PEOPLES AC; (SR); Ctznshp Aw; Hnr Roll; Nat Hon Sy; Otst Ac Ach Awd; Pres Sch; WWAHSS; Peer Tut/Med; Drma Clb; Emplmnt; Mus Clb; Prom Com; Spanish Clb; Chr; Dnce; SP/M/VS; Tennis (V); Governor's Institute of Vermont; Wellesley College Book Award; Communications; Psychology; Hofstra U

STEWART, SHEENA; DANVILLE, VT; DANVILLE HS; (SR); Hnr Roll; Otst Ac Ach Awd; Comm Volntr; Spec Olymp Vol; Chrch Yth Grp; Drma Clb; Emplmnt; Lib Aide; Scouts; Tchrs Aide; Bskball (L); Sccr (L); Merit Roll All Through High School; Special Olympics; Community College of VT St Johnsbury; Human Service & Day Care License; Community College of Vermont; Lyndon State College Lyndonville VT

STRINGER, KELLY; LUDLOW, VT; BLACK RIVER HS; (FR); Hnr Roll; Sci Fairs; Comm Volntr; DARE; Emplmnt; Vsity Clb; Chr; Skiing (V); Sccr (V); Catechism for 10 Years; Confirmation in 2005; Nursing; Interior Design

ST SAUVEUR, NATHAN T; WHITE RIV JCT, VT; HARTFORD HS; (JR); Comm Volntr; Chrch Yth Grp; Tchrs Aide; Fthall (V L); Ice Hky (V L); Lcrsse (V L); Junior Coach for Youth Football, Ice Hockey, Lacrosse; U of Arizona; Northern Arizona U

SWANN, KEVIN W; NORTHFIELD, VT; NORTHFIELD MIDDLE HS; (JR); Hnr Roll; Nat Hon Sy; Yth Ldrshp Prog; Chrch Yth Grp; DARE; Emplmnt; SP/M/VS; Golf (J); Skt Tgt Sh (V); Sccr (V); Church Praise Band; Mechanical Engineering; Forensic Science; Liberty U; Norwich U

TEMPLE, JUSTIN M; RUTLAND, VT; RUTLAND HS; (FR); Hi Hnr Roll; WWAHSS; Comm Volntr; Chrch Yth Grp; Key Club; Jzz Bnd; Ftball (J); Lcrsse (J); Orthopedic Medicine; Johns Hopkins U

THOMAS, MARGARET; WINOOSKI, VT; WINOOSKI HS; (JR); Ctznshp Aw; Hi Hnr Roll; Hnr Roll; Nat Hon Sy; St of Mnth; Emplmnt; Prom Com; Sccr (V L); Track (V L); Cl Off (V); Stu Cncl (R); Yrbk (R); Psychology; Marine Biology

THOMPSON, COLLIN; WINOOSKI, VT; WINOOSKI HS; (JR); Hnr Roll; Nat Hon Sy; Perf Att; Yth Ldrshp Prog; Comm Volntr; Peer Tut/Med; Chrch Yth Grp; Emplmnt; Prom Com; Quiz Bowl; Scouts; Bnd; Chr; Ch Chr; SP/M/VS; Bskball (J); Scr Kpr; Sccr; Stu Cncl (V, S); CR (R); Yrbk (R); Physical Therapy; Sports Medicine; U of North Carolina At Chapel Hill; Elon U

THOMPSON, LAURA; SOUTH HERO, VT; SOUTH BURLINGTON HS; (SR); Hi Hnr Roll; Hnr Roll; Comm Volntr; Spec Olymp Vol; 4-H; Chrch Yth Grp; Drma Clb; Emplmnt; Quiz Bowl; Scouts; Bnd; Chr; Ch Chr; SP/M/VS; Bskball (J); Fld Hky (JC); Lcrsse (J); Scr Kpr; Sccr; Stu Cncl (V, S); CR (R); Honor Roll - Since 6th Grade; Walk-A-Thons / Work to Benefit Homeless & Hungry; Fashion Design; Florida State U; U of Delaware

THORPE, JONATHON; STARKSBORO, VT; PATRICIA HANNAFORD CAREER CTR; (SR); Hnr Roll; Otst Ac Ach Awd; Perf Att; Comm Volntr; Chrch Yth Grp; Art Education (K-12); Green Mountain College

WELKER, REBECCA; FRANKLIN, VT; MISSISQUOI VALLEY UNION JSHS; (JR); Hi Hnr Roll; Otst Ac Ach Awd; St of Mnth; WWAHSS; Comm Volntr; Peer Tut/Med; Red Cr Aide; Emplmnt; Mod UN; Prom Com; Tchrs Aide; Stg Cre; Bskball (J); Scr Kpr (V); Sftball (J); Adv Cncl (S); Stu Cncl (S); CR (R); Yrbk (P); Clinical Psychology; U of San Diego; Duke U

WIGMORE, ALEXANDER; RUTLAND, VT; RUTLAND HS; Hi Hnr Roll; Key Club; Lcrsse (J); Skiing (V L); Sccr (J); Cl Off (T); Traveled to Japan on Exchange

Park, James — Granville HS — Rutland, VT

Nagar, Caileigh G — Poultney HS — Poultney, VT

National Honor Roll Spring 2005

Mc Dermott, Cailey — Hazen Union HS — East Calais, VT

Thompson, Collin — Winooski HS — Winooski, VT

Virginia

ABATE, ADEN; ALEXANDRIA, VA; T C WILLIAM HS; (JR); Hnr Roll; Otst Ac Ach Awd; WWAHSS; Comm Volntr; Peer Tut/Med; Red Cr Aide; SP/M/VS; Stg Cre; Member of Latin American Student Society; Ethio-Erietrean Club/Outstanding Community Service; Business Administration/Management

ABBAS, PAULINE; BLACKSBURG, VA; BLACKSBURG HS; (SR); WWAHSS; Chrch Yth Grp; Emplmnt; FCA; Key Club; Latin Clb; HOSA Secretary; Volunteered At 6 Blood Drives; Majoring in Chemistry; Pharmacy Degree; Virginia Tech

ABOAGYE, MAVIS; DUMFRIES, VA; NORTHWESTERN HS; (JR); Hnr Roll; Nat Hon Sy; WWAHSS; Yth Ldrshp Prog; Comm Volntr; Peer Tut/Med; ArtClub; Chrch Yth Grp; DARE; Lib Aide; Mth Clb/Tm; Svce Clb; Ch Chr; Dnce; Mentor Cares Program; (ISP) International Studies Program; Pre-Medicine; Art-Studio; Hampton U; Virginia Commonwealth U

ADEWODU, YOMI; VIRGINIA BEACH, VA; FLOYD KELLAM HS; (SO); Hnr Roll; Perf Att; St of Mnth; Bsball; Bskball (J); Pharmacy; Howard U; Hampton U

ADKINS, EMILY C; STAFFORD, VA; COLONIAL FORGE HS; (SR); Hnr Roll; Ch Chr; VICA; Art I / II / III; Primary Teacher; Cosmetologist; Mary Washington U; George Mason U

ADKINS, SANTINA K; RICHMOND, VA; VARINA HS; (FR); Hnr Roll; Perf Att; Bnd; Mch Bnd; All County Band (Henrico County Gr 8 & 9); Music (Composition); Design (Fashion, Architecture, Etc); North Carolina Agriculture & Technology

AFROILAN, EDWARD; MANASSAS, VA; OSBOURN HS; (JR); F Lan Hn Soc; WWAHSS; Key Club; SADD; Orch; Treasurer-Key Club; Physics; Marine Biology; U of Virginia; James Madison U

AFTAB, SHAZMA; CENTREVILLE, VA; CENTREVILLE HS; (FR); Duke TS; Hnr Roll; WWAHSS; Yth Ldrshp Prog; Amnsty Intl; Key Club; ISLAMIC Clb; Toastmasters; Amnesty International; Medical; Dentistry; Yale U; U of Virginia

AHMED, AZHAR; STERLING, VA; POTOMAC FALLS HS; (SO); Hnr Roll; WWAHSS; Comm Volntr; Key Club; Schol Bwl; Bskball (J); Track (V L); Cl Off (V); CR (R); National Spanish Honor Society; Duke U; Massachusetts Institute of Technology

AHMED, MOHAMMAD S; ARLINGTON, VA; WASHINGTON-LEE HS; (JR); Hi Hnr Roll; Hnr Roll; Nat Ldrshp Svc; Comm Volntr; DECA; FBLA; NYLC; Bnd; Business; Criminal Justice & Law; George Mason; U of Virginia

AHMED, SAMOAL I; FALLS CHURCH, VA; STUART HS; (SO); Hnr Roll; Otst Ac Ach Awd; Perf Att; Sci Fairs; St of Mnth; Peer Tut/Med; BPA; Dbte Team; Arabic Clb; Orch; Bsball (J); Ftball (J); Wt Lftg (J); PhD in Pharmaceutical Medicine; PhD in Physical Science; Harvard; U of Virginia

AKLILU, BETEL; SPRINGFIELD, VA; ROBERT E LEE HS; (SO); Ctznshp Aw; Hnr Roll; Sci Fairs; St of Mnth; WWAHSS; Comm Volntr; Peer Tut/Med; Track (V); Odyssey of the Mind / Book Club; Leaders to Promise / French Honor Society; Pre-Med; Master's Degree; Yale U; Johns Hopkins U

ALAM, RAYHAN; FALLS CHURCH, VA; STUART HS; (SO); Ctznshp Aw; Hnr Roll; Nat Hon Sy; Otst Ac Ach Awd; Comm Volntr; Peer Tut/Med; Sci Clb; Medical Science; Chemical Engineering; George Washington U; Johns Hopkins U

AL-BABA, SARA M; FALLS CHURCH, VA; J E B STUART HS; (JR); Hnr Roll; Otst Ac Ach Awd; Sci Fairs; Yth Ldrshp Prog; Amnsty Intl; Comm Volntr; ArtClub; FBLA; NYLC; Photog; Prom Com; Quill & Scroll; SP/M/VS; Track (V L); Vllyball (V); Adv Cncl (R); Stu Cncl (V); Lit Mag (R); Sch Ppr (E); Yrbk (R, P); National Young Leaders Conference; Most Responsible Student of the School; Science & Law - Double Major; Doctorate Degree; U of Virginia; Bryn Mawr College

AL-BAWARDY, REEMA; FALLS CHURCH, VA; ISLAMIC SAUDI AC; (SO); Hnr Roll; Sci Fairs; Comm Volntr; Bdmtn; Gmnstcs; Sccr (V); Photography; Business Management; George Washington U; Marymount U

ALDRIDGE, BREEANNA M; ARARAT, VA; PATRICK CTY HS; (SO); Gov Hnr Prg; Hnr Roll; Pres Ac Ftns Aw; Comm Volntr; Chrch Yth Grp; FCA; Ntl Beta Clb; P to P St Amb Prg; Scouts; Dnce; Junior Beta-Vice President 7th Grade; Marine Biologist; U of North Carolina of Wilmington, NC

ALFADLI, MUNEEF; GAINESVILLE, VA; STONEWALL JACKSON HS; (JR); Hnr Roll; Emplmnt; FBLA; Business Management Or Industrial Engineering & Management, Entrepreneurship; George Mason U; George Washington U

ALGARZAE, NORAH K M; SPRINGFIELD, VA; ISLAMIC SAUDI AC; (SO); Hi Hnr Roll; Hnr Roll; Nat Sci Aw; Sci Fairs; St of Mnth; Comm Volntr; Peer Tut/Med; ArtClub; Dbte Team; Svce Clb; Spanish Clb; Bdmtn (V); Organizer and Sponsor of Miss ISA; Cardiologist; Orthodontist; Harvard; Georgetown U

ALHUSSAIN, REEM; FAIRFAX, VA; ISLAMIC SAUDI AC; (SO); Ctznshp Aw; Hi Hnr Roll; Otst Ac Ach Awd; Sci Fairs; St of Mnth; Comm Volntr; Hosp Aide; Peer Tut/Med; Drma Clb; FBLA; Mod UN; French Clb; Bdmtn (L); Bskball (J); Sccr (J); Cl Off (P); CR (P); Won Silver in Academic Olympics; Participated in the Regional Science Fair; Dentistry; Pediatrics; Georgetown U; Johns Hopkins U

AL-KADHI, MAHA; VIENNA, VA; ISLAMIC SAUDI AC; (JR); Hnr Roll; Nat Mrt LOC; WWAHSS; Comm Volntr; Drma Clb; SP/M/VS; Stg Cre; CR (S); National Honor Society; Psychology; Graphic Arts; Georgetown U; George Washington U

ALLEN, DANIELLE; RICHMOND, VA; JOHN MARSHALL HS; (SR); Ctznshp Aw; Hnr Roll; Perf Att; WWAHSS; Yth Ldrshp Prog; Peer Tut/Med; 4-H; Chrch Yth Grp; DARE; Drma Clb; Emplmnt; FBLA; Off Aide; Prom Com; Chr; Mch Bnd; SP/M/VS; Stg Cre; Prom Committee; Forensics Team (Drama Club); Psychologists; Child Psychologists; Delaware State U; Elizabeth City State U

ALLEN, KENDRA D; SUFFOLK, VA; (JR); Ctznshp Aw; Red Cr Aide; Chrch Yth Grp; Off Aide; Member of FCCLA (2 Years); Hampton U; ODU U

ALLEN, RAVON; EASTVILLE, VA; NORTHAMPTON HS; (FR); Ctznshp Aw; Hi Hnr Roll; Hnr Roll; Nat Hon Sy; Otst Ac Ach Awd; Perf Att; St of Mnth; Peer Tut/Med; Chrch Yth Grp; Ntl Beta Clb; Bnd; Ch Chr; Mch Bnd; Pep Bnd; Stu Cncl (R); Architecture; Interior Design; Hampton U; Howard U

ALLEN, ROBINETTE; SANDSTON, VA; VARINA HS; (FR); Key Club; Pharmacist; Ophthalmologist; Virginia Commonwealth U; Hampton U

ALLEN, STEPHANIE R; CLAUDVILLE, VA; WHITE PLAINS CHRISTIAN SC; (FR); Hnr Roll; Otst Ac Ach Awd; Perf Att; St of Mnth; Comm Volntr; Red Cr Aide; Chrch Yth Grp; Mus Clb; Off Aide; Tchrs Aide; Ch Chr; SP/M/VS; Outstanding Academic Excellence; Degree of Excellence in Piano; Elementary Education; Sunny Community College

ALLERS, PANIDA; ASHBURN, VA; STONE BRIDGE HS; (FR); Hnr Roll; Comm Volntr; Key Club; Track (V); Thai Dancing

ALLERS, SIREE D; ASHBURN, VA; STONE BRIDGE HS; (SO); Hi Hnr Roll; Pres Ac Ftns Aw; Sci Fairs; Yth Ldrshp Prog; Amnsty Intl; Comm Volntr; Key Club; Tennis; Track (V); Middle Eastern and Asian Studies; Latin American Studies; James Madison U; U of Richmond

ALLISON, MAGGIE; TROUTVILLE, VA; ROANOKE CATHOLIC HS; (SO); Hnr Roll; WWAHSS; Comm Volntr; Chrch Yth Grp; Emplmnt; Jr Ach; Key Club; P to P St Amb Prg; SP/M/VS; Bskball (J); Hsbk Rdg; Sftball (V); Swmg (V); Vllyball (V); Serving Christ Through One Another Award; Major in Chemistry; Specialize in Forensic Science; Christopher Newport U

ALNESS, BRITTANY; ASHBURN, VA; STONE BRIDGE HS; (FR); All Am Sch; Hnr Roll; Pres Ac Ftns Aw; Chrch Yth Grp; Key Club; Chr; Dnce; Cl Off (P); Teaching; Dance/Arts; Montana U; George Mason U

ALSAADI, DANA; FAIRFAX, VA; ISLAMIC SAUDI AC; (FR); Hi Hnr Roll; Otst Ac Ach Awd; Pres Ac Ftns Aw; Sci Fairs; St of Mnth; Yth Ldrshp Prog; Peer Tut/Med; Emplmnt; Mod UN; Off Aide; Svce Clb; Bdmtn (J); Gmnstcs (J); Medicine and Health; Political Science; Georgetown U; U of Maryland College Park

ALSTON, WHITNEY N; SUFFOLK, VA; NANSEMOND RIVER HS; (JR); Hi Hnr Roll; Hnr Roll; Perf Att; Pres Ac Ftns Aw; Pres Sch; St of Mnth; WWAHSS; Chrch Yth Grp; FBLA; JSA; NYLC; Off Aide; Photog; Ch Chr; Drl Tm; Chrldg (J); Tennis (V L); Track (L); Vllyball (C); Yrbk (P); Church Sign Language Group; Business Administration; Law; Howard U; Morgan State U

AMANIN, ROSE; NEWPORT NEWS, VA; WARWICK HS; (JR); Ctznshp Aw; F Lan Hn Soc; Hi Hnr Roll; Hnr Roll; Nat Hon Sy; Otst Ac Ach Awd; Perf Att; Pres Ac Ftns Aw; Pres Sch; Valdctrian; Comm Volntr; Hosp Aide; Peer Tut/Med; Biology Clb; Chrch Yth Grp; DECA; Key Club; Sci Clb; French Clb; Dnce; SP/M/VS; Chrldg (V L); Gmnstcs (J L); Mar Art; Track (V); Adv Cncl (R); Stu Cncl (R); Pre-Medicine; Biology; Columbia U; Dartmouth

AMATO, JOSEPH; LAKE RIDGE, VA; WOODBRIDGE SR HS; (SR); Ctznshp Aw; Hnr Roll; MVP; Perf Att; St of Mnth; WWAHSS; Comm Volntr; Red Cr Aide; ROTC; Bsball (V L); Track; Congressional Student Leadership Conference

AMES, CIERRA C; CHERITON, VA; NORTHAMPTON HS; (SO); Ctznshp Aw; Hnr Roll; MVP; Nat Hon Sy; Nat Ldrshp Svc; Perf Att; Pres Sch; WWAHSS; Comm Volntr; Peer Tut/Med; Chrch Yth Grp; Emplmnt; Ntl Beta Clb; Prom Com; Svce Clb; Bnd; Ch Chr; Pep Bnd; Bskball (JC); Track (V); Stu Cncl (R); Sch Ppr (E, R, P); Yrbk (P); Presidential Award; Who's Who; Pediatrician; Johns Hopkins U; Old Dominion U

AMIRHADJI, NATASHA S; STERLING, VA; DOMINION HS; (JR); Ctznshp Aw; Hnr Roll; MVP; Nat Hon Sy; Otst Ac Ach Awd; Sci Fairs; St of Mnth; Peer Tut/Med; ArtClub; Drma Clb; FTA; Kwanza Clb; Photog; Scouts; Tchrs Aide; Ftball (L); Tennis (V CL); CR (T, R); Sch Ppr (E, P); Art Honor Society Council; Fine Arts

AMJED, MADIHA; HERNDON, VA; WESTFIELD HS; (JR); Hnr Roll; Comm Volntr; Peer Tut/Med; Emplmnt; Spanish Clb; Track (J); Cl Off (T); Stu Cncl (R); Cooking Club Treasurer; Student Government Historian; Biology; Comparative Religions; George Mason U; Virginia Commonwealth U

AMURRIO, MARICRUZ; FALLS CHURCH, VA; STUART HS; (JR); F Lan Hn Soc; Hnr Roll; Perf Att; St of Mnth; WWAHSS; Comm Volntr; Emplmnt; Fr of Library; SP/M/VS; Criminal Justice; Medicine; George Mason U; Averett U

ANACTA, SHIELA; VIRGINIA BEACH, VA; FRANK W COX HS; (JR); Hnr Roll; Key Club; Spanish Clb; Congressional Councils Medal Recognition (Student College 05); Neptune Festival Youth Art Show Merit Award; Fine Arts; Business Administration; Old Dominion U; U of Virginia

ANDERSON, JONATHAN P; NATHALIE, VA; HALIFAX CTY HS; (JR); All Am Sch; Hnr Roll; Nat Hon Sy; Chrch Yth Grp; Emplmnt; Bnd; Chr; Ch Chr; Jzz Bnd; Ftball (J); Wt Lftg (J); USAA All-American Winner; USAA Band Award Winner; Music Education; Music Therapy; U of Kentucky; Virginia Tech

ANDERSON, KATHERINE L; CLIFTON FORGE, VA; ALLEGHANY HS; (FR); Bnd; Chr; Mch Bnd; Track (V L); All-Area Band / All-District Band; All-District Chorus; Music; James Madison U; Virginia Tech

ANDERSON, MONIKA K; SALEM, VA; SALEM HS; (SO); F Lan Hn Soc; Hnr Roll; Nat Hon Sy; Comm Volntr; Spec Olymp Vol; National German Honor Society; Journalism; German; Virginia Commonwealth U; College of William & Mary

ANDERSON, SHANELLE; DRAKES BRANCH, VA; RANDOLPH HENRY HS; (SO); Hnr Roll; Nat Sci Aw; WWAHSS; Comm Volntr; Spanish Clb; SP/M/VS; Psychology; Virginia Military Institute; U of Virginia

ANDERSON JR, IAN; STERLING, VA; POTOMAC FALLS HS; (FR); Hnr Roll; WWAHSS; Comm Volntr; Key Club; Latin Clb; Aerospace Science; James Madison U; George Mason U

ANDREWS, BRITTANY; RICHMOND, VA; VARINA HS; (FR); Hnr Roll; Perf Att; DARE; Divorce Attorney; Criminal Attorney; Harvard; Yale

ANSELL, SARAH; LEESBURG, VA; HERITAGE HS; (SO); Hnr Roll; St of Mnth; Yth Ldrshp Prog; Comm Volntr; FTA; Key Club; Chr; Clr Grd; Sftball (J); Vice President of Key Club; Teaching; Psychology; Virginia Tech; Florida State U

ANTLE, ASHLEY; CLIFTON, VA; CENTREVILLE HS; (JR); Hi Hnr Roll; Nat Hon Sy; WWAHSS; Comm Volntr; FCA; Mus Clb; Sci Clb; Scouts; Acpl Chr; Chr; Swg Chr; Sftball (VJ L); Tae Kwon Do Black Belt; Member of Tri-M Music Honor Society; Crime Scene Investigation; Medical Invention; U of Virginia; UNC Chapel Hill (U of North Carolina)

ANTOZZI, BRITTNEY; FREDERICKSBURG, VA; JAMES MONROE HS; (JR); Hi Hnr Roll; Hnr Roll; Nat Hon Sy; Otst Ac Ach Awd; Pres Ac Ftns Aw; Comm Volntr; FCA; Key Club; Off Aide; French Clb; Bskball (VJCL); Sccr (V L); Psychology; Marine Biology; Virginia Tech; U of North Carolina (Chapel Hill)

APPLE, STEPHANIE; MANASSAS, VA; OSBOURN HS; (SO); Hi Hnr Roll; Hnr Roll; Nat Sci Aw; Sci Fairs; WWAHSS; Comm Volntr; Peer Tut/Med; FCCLA; Key Club; Photog; Cr Cty (V); Track (V L); Sch Ppr (R); Vice President FCCLA; Nat'l. Christopher Columbus Awards Finalist; Biology; Chemistry; Duke U; U of Southern CA

ARBAUGH, DERICK B; STUARTS DRAFT, VA; STUARTS DRAFT HS; (JR); Hi Hnr Roll; Hnr Roll; Nat Hon Sy; Otst Ac Ach Awd; WWAHSS; Yth Ldrshp Prog; Comm Volntr; AL Aux Boys; Chrch Yth Grp; Key Club; Svce Clb; Spanish Clb; National Honor Society Member; Attended Boys State of Virginia; International Relations; Language; Eastern Mennonite U; U of Virginia

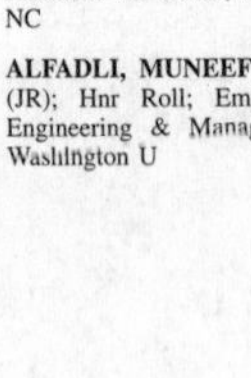
Anderson, Monika K
Salem HS
Salem, VA

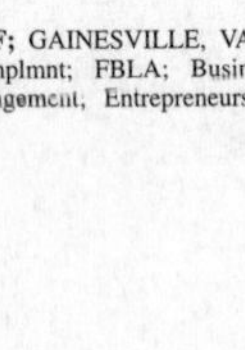
Alsaadi, Dana
Islamic Saudi AC
Fairfax, VA

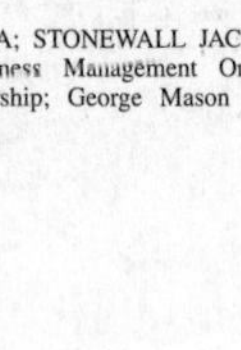
Alhussain, Reem
Islamic Saudi AC
Fairfax, VA

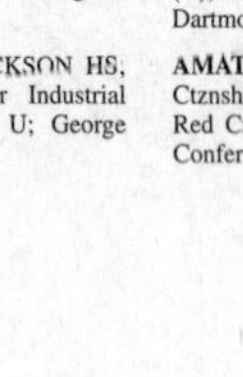
Al-Baba, Sara M
J E B Stuart HS
Falls Church, VA

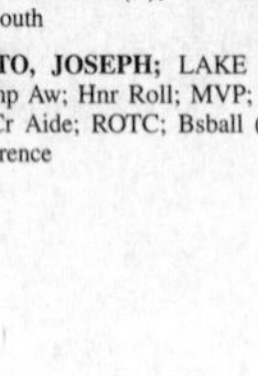
Ahmed, Samoal I
Stuart HS
Falls Church, VA

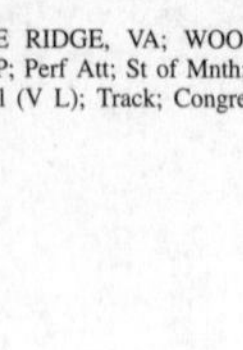
Abate, Aden
T C William HS
Alexandria, VA

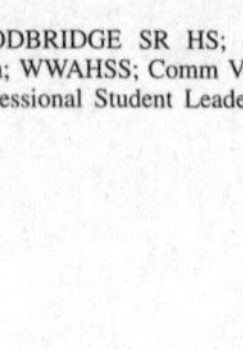
Afroilan, Edward
Osbourn HS
Manassas, VA

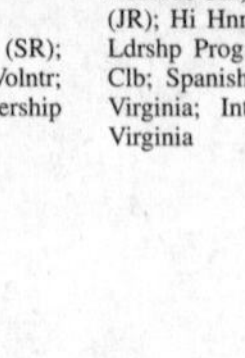
Algarzae, Norah K M
Islamic Saudi AC
Springfield, VA

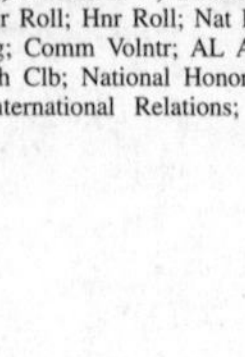
Allen, Stephanie R
White Plains Christian Sc
Claudville, VA

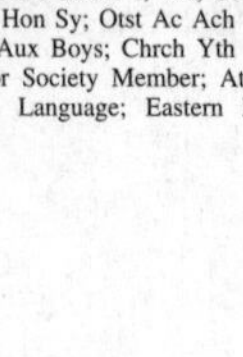
Ames, Cierra C
Northampton HS
Cheriton, VA

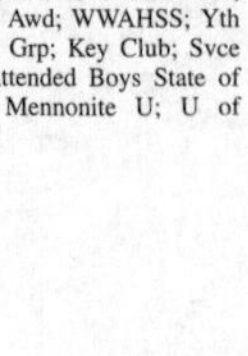
Anderson, Jonathan P
Halifax Cty HS
Nathalie, VA

ARBUCKLE, MICHAEL Y W; ALEXANDRIA, VA; T C WILLIAMS HS; (JR); Hnr Roll; Nat Hon Sy; Perf Att; Sci Fairs; WWAHSS; ArtClub; Key Club; Scouts; Latin Clb; Stg Cre; Cr Ctry (J); Lcrsse (J); Swmg (V); Sch Ppr (R); USAA National Mathematics Award; Scholar Athlete Award; Bachelor's of Architecture; Architecture and Design; Syracuse U; Cornell U

ARCHER JR, PHILLIP I; ASHBURN, VA; MONROE TECH CTR; (SR); Hnr Roll; Perf Att; St of Mnth; Tchrs Aide; Automotive Technician; U Technical Institute

ARENAS, ALEXANDRA; RESTON, VA; SOUTH LAKES HS; (JR); Hnr Roll; Pres Ac Ftns Aw; Comm Volntr; Emplmnt; Spanish Clb; Psychology; George Mason U; U of Miami

ARNOLD, KAYLA N; SALEM, VA; SALEM HS; (SO); Hnr Roll; French Clb; Lcrsse (V L); Junior Honor Association; Keyettes; Pre-Pharm; PharmD; Radford U; Averett U

ARRINGTON, CRYSTAL F; ROCKY MOUNT, VA; FRANKLIN CTY HS; (SR); Hnr Roll; Nat Hon Sy; Chrch Yth Grp; Emplmnt; Ch Chr; Loves Animals; Veterinarian; Veterinary Tech; Virginia Tech; Virginia Western CC

ARTIS, JAZMYN; PORTSMOUTH, VA; IC NORCOM; (SO); All Am Sch; Hnr Roll; Nat Hon Sy; WWAHSS; Yth Ldrshp Prog; Comm Volntr; Chrch Yth Grp; HO'Br Yth Ldrshp; Ch Chr; Dnce; Drm Mjr; Mch Bnd; Bskball (V); Highest GPA in Sophmore Class; Chemical Engineering

ARTRIP, RYAN; ABINGDON, VA; JOHN S BATTLE HS; (SR); Ctznshp Aw; Gov Hnr Prg; Hnr Roll; Nat Hon Sy; USAA; WWAHSS; Comm Volntr; Spec Olymp Vol; Dbte Team; Emplmnt; Scouts; Bnd; Jzz Bnd; Mch Bnd; SP/M/VS; Adv Cncl (R); Debate/Forensics Clubs, Destination Imagination; Governor's School; Political Science; Law; Virginia Tech; James Madison

ASHBY, CLAYTON L; MARSHALL, VA; FAUQUIER HS; (JR); Hnr Roll; Nat Hon Sy; Perf Att; Comm Volntr; Chrch Yth Grp; Emplmnt

ASHBY, ROBERT; AXTON, VA; MAGNA VISTA HS; (JR); Hnr Roll; Perf Att; Comm Volntr; Chrch Yth Grp; Emplmnt; Bnd; Jzz Bnd; Mch Bnd; Ftball (VJ L); Sccr (V); Wrstlg (V); Johnson Bible College

ASKEW, JAMES; NORFOLK, VA; BOOKER T WASHINGTON HS; (FR); Hnr Roll; Nat Hon Sy; Perf Att; Sci/Math Olympn; St of Mnth; WWAHSS; Comm Volntr; Peer Tut/Med; Spec Olymp Vol; DARE; DECA; FBLA; ROTC; Schol Bwl; Clr Grd; Dnce; Drl Tm; SP/M/VS; Chrldg (J); PPSqd (J); Stu Cncl (T); Prelaw; College of William and Mary; Norfolk State U

ASTBURY, JENNIFER L; CHESAPEAKE, VA; WESTERN BRANCH HS; (SO); Hnr Roll; Nat Hon Sy; Spec Olymp Vol; FBLA; Cr Ctry (V); Tennis (V); Track (V); Future Business Leader (FBLA); Special Olympics Fund Raiser; Forensic Science; Business; U of Virginia; Old Dominion U

ATOBRAH, AMA S; RESTON, VA; SOUTH LAKES HS; (JR); Ctznshp Aw; Fut Prb Slvr; Hi Hnr Roll; Hnr Roll; Nat Hon Sy; Nat Ldrshp Svc; Otst Ac Ach Awd; Perf Att; Pres Ac Ftns Aw; Sci Fairs; Comm Volntr; Hosp Aide; Peer Tut/Med; ArtClub; Chrch Yth Grp; Drma Clb; Jr Ach; Key Club; Lib Aide; Mus Clb; Pep Squd; Acpl Chr; Chr; Ch Chr; Dnce; Bskball (J); Chrldg (J L); Lcrsse (V); Adv Cncl (R); Cl Off (S); Stu Cncl (R); CR (R); President of the National Junior Society; Virginia District Chorus; Music Theatre; Music Law/Management/Advertising; Princeton U; New York U

AUGUSTINE, ELIZABETH; ASHBURN, VA; BROAD RUN HS; (SO); Hnr Roll; Otst Ac Ach Awd; WWAHSS; Comm Volntr; Emplmnt; Key Club; Bskball (J); Sftball (JC); Stu Cncl (R); Sch Ppr (R, P); MADD Volunteer; Journalism; International Relations; UNC Chapel Hill; U of Maryland

AUSTIN, CHANEY E; CROZIER, VA; GOOCHLAND HS; (JR); Gov Hnr Prg; Hnr Roll; MVP; Nat Hon Sy; Comm Volntr; Chrch Yth Grp; Emplmnt; Key Club; Prom Com; Ch Chr; Sftball (VJ); Vllyball (VJC); CR; Sch Ppr; Yrbk; Key Club President/Key Club Vice-President; National Honor Society Secretary; Communications; James Madison U; Longwood U

AWADALLAH, BAHA M; ANNANDALE, VA; ANNANDALE HS; (SO); Chrch Yth Grp; Arabic Clb; Ftball (J); Wrstlg (V L); 4 Time Student Of The Quarter; Business Management; Economics; George Mason U; Georgetown U

AWAN, SEEMAL; ALEXANDRIA, VA; ANNANDALE HS; (FR); Hi Hnr Roll; Sci Fairs; St of Mnth; Peer Tut/Med; FBLA; Mth Clb/Tm; Schol Bwl; Track (J); Cl Off (R); 3rd Place-Technology Project (Regional); Johns Hopkins Talent Search; Math Major; Science Major; George Mason U; Johns Hopkins U

AYALA, ASHLEY G; NORFOLK, VA; NORVIEW HS; (JR); Hnr Roll; WWAHSS; Peer Tut/Med; Bnd; Mch Bnd; Ftball (V L); Track (V CL); Sports Medicine; Cooking; U of Central Florida; U of Miami (Florida)

AYERS, KRISTEN; ROANOKE, VA; PATRICK HENRY HS; (SO); Hnr Roll; Otst Ac Ach Awd; Perf Att; Sci Fairs; St of Mnth; Peer Tut/Med; Chess; Chrch Yth Grp; DARE; Scouts; Medical; Business

AZIZ, FAISAL; SPRINGFIELD, VA; LEE HS; (JR); Drma Clb; Mth Clb/Tm; College Partnership Program; Math Honors in 7th Grade; American Ambassador to Pakistan; Serve in the UN; American U; Virginia Commonwealth U

BACON II, TROY P; VIRGINIA BEACH, VA; FLOYD KELLAM HS; (JR); Hnr Roll; Comm Volntr; Peer Tut/Med; Chrch Yth Grp; DARE; Emplmnt; Ch Chr; Dnce; SP/M/VS; Governor's School for the Performing Arts; Professional Entertainer; Choreographer; Carnegie Melon; Regent U

BAGBY, PATRINA O; RICHMOND, VA; HENRICO HS; (SR); Hi Hnr Roll; WWAHSS; Chrch Yth Grp; Emplmnt; FBLA; FCCLA; Ntl Beta Clb; Off Aide; Prom Com; Tchrs Aide; Ch Chr; Clr Grd; Mch Bnd; Cl Off (S); CR (S); Brotherhood to Sisterhood Award; Completed an Internship At Glenlea Elementary; Biology; Business Administration & Marketing (Retail); North Carolina Agricultural & Technical State U; Bethune Cookman College

BAIN, STEPHEN C; SALEM, VA; SALEM HS; (SO); F Lan Hn Soc; Hnr Roll; MVP; Nat Hon Sy; Pres Ac Ftns Aw; Pres Sch; Comm Volntr; Golf (V L); Junior Honor Society/National Honor Society; Spanish Honor Society

BAKER, M ELIZABETH; FREDERICKSBURG, VA; JAMES MONROE HS; (JR); Hi Hnr Roll; Nat Hon Sy; Pres Ac Ftns Aw; Sci Fairs; WWAHSS; Comm Volntr; Chrch Yth Grp; Emplmnt; Chrldg (V L); Cr Ctry (V L); Fld Hky (V CL); Track (V L); Sch Ppr (E); Yrbk (E); Monroe Scholar; National Latin Exam Silver Medalist; Biology

BAL, POONAM; BURKE, VA; ROBINSON SECONDARY SCH; (SR); Hi Hnr Roll; Hnr Roll; Nat Hon Sy; Perf Att; ArtClub; Chrch Yth Grp; Dbte Team; Drma Clb; FBLA; Key Club; Mod UN; Spch Team; Dnce; Stg Cre; Business Honor Society; Art Honor Society; Event Planner; VCU

BALABER, EVAN; VIENNA, VA; JAMES MADISON HS; (SO); Ctznshp Aw; Nat Hon Sy; Pres Ac Ftns Aw; Comm Volntr; Peer Tut/Med; Chrch Yth Grp; Emplmnt; Scouts; Tmpl Yth Grp; Bnd; Mch Bnd; Pep Bnd; Bskball; Track (V); Business; U of Virginia; Virginia Tech

BALACONIS, ZOE E; VIRGINIA BEACH, VA; PRINCESS ANNE HS; (SO); 4H Awd; F Lan Hn Soc; Gov Hnr Prg; Hi Hnr Roll; Hnr Roll; Kwnis Aw; Nat Hon Sy; Perf Att; Comm Volntr; Peer Tut/Med; 4-H; Emplmnt; Key Club; French Clb; Stu Cncl (R); CR (R); Crew Team 9

BALANCIO, HEATHER; CHESAPEAKE, VA; DEEP CREEK HS; (JR); Hnr Roll; Nat Mrt Sch Recip; Perf Att; WWAHSS; Comm Volntr; Key Club; Chr; Psychology; North Carolina State U; U of North Carolina

BALL, JAMIE; STRASBURG, VA; STRASBURG HS; (SO); Hnr Roll; Pres Ac Ftns Aw; Comm Volntr; 4-H; Drma Clb; Spanish Clb; Swmg (V L); Leo Club; Beta Club-Community Service; Business Management; Communications; James Madison U; Virginia Commonwealth U

BALLOU, PORTIA M; SOUTH BOSTON, VA; HALIFAX CTY HS; (FR); Ctznshp Aw; Hnr Roll; Perf Att; St of Mnth; WWAHSS; Comm Volntr; Hab For Humty Volntr; 4-H; Chrch Yth Grp; Emplmnt; FBLA; Chr; Ch Chr; Dnce; Member of Baccalaureate Committee; Physical Therapist; Advertising; VCU

BANKS, CIERRA; ROANOKE, VA; PATRICK HENRY HS; (SO); 4H Awd; Ctznshp Aw; F Lan Hn Soc; Hnr Roll; Perf Att; St of Mnth; WWAHSS; Comm Volntr; Peer Tut/Med; Red Cr Aide; 4-H; Chess; Chrch Yth Grp; DARE; Emplmnt; Jr Ach; Pep Squd; Scouts; Ch Chr; Dnce; Bskball (J); Track (J); Cl Off (P); Lawyer; Registered Nurse; Spelman College; Harvard U

BARACAT, TIFFANY A; STERLING, VA; POTOMAC FALLS HS; (JR); Hnr Roll; Nat Hon Sy; Sci Fairs; WWAHSS; Comm Volntr; Peer Tut/Med; Chrch Yth Grp; DARE; Drma Clb; Key Club; Off Aide; Scouts; SP/M/VS; Chrldg; Treasurer - Key Club; Psychology; Education; Virginia Tech

BARBER JR, WILLIAM M; FREDERICKSBURG, VA; COLONIAL FORGE HS; (SO); Hnr Roll; MVP; Otst Ac Ach Awd; WWAHSS; Comm Volntr; Peer Tut/Med; AL Aux Boys; Chrch Yth Grp; FBLA; Bsball (VJ); Bskball (J); Captain - City Tournament Bowling Team; Member - Virginia State Bowling Tournament; Pre-Med; Engineering; U of Miami; U of Virginia

BARE, HILLARY M; TROUTVILLE, VA; LORD BOTETOURT HS; (SR); 4H Awd; WWAHSS; Amnsty Intl; Comm Volntr; Red Cr Aide; 4-H; Chrch Yth Grp; Key Club; Ntl FFA; Off Aide; Photog; Prom Com; Scouts; Chrldg (JCL); Hsbk Rdg; Lit Mag (P); Yrbk (P); Large Animal Veterinarian; Emory & Henry College

BARKER, BETSY; COLONIAL HEIGHTS, VA; COLONIAL HEIGHTS HS; (JR); F Lan Hn Soc; Hi Hnr Roll; Hnr Roll; Nat Hon Sy; Otst Ac Ach Awd; Pres Ac Ftns Aw; Comm Volntr; Peer Tut/Med; Chrch Yth Grp; FCA; Jr Cls League; Key Club; Ntl Beta Clb; Quill & Scroll; Scouts; Latin Clb; Sccr (J); Tennis (V); Cl Off (R); Yrbk (E); Premed; Doctorate; U of Virginia; U of William and Mary

BARKER, NICOLE C; CULPEPER, VA; CORNERSTONE CHRISTIAN AC; (SR); 4H Awd; Hnr Roll; Nat Hon Sy; Otst Ac Ach Awd; Sci Fairs; St of Mnth; WWAHSS; Comm Volntr; 4-H; Chrch Yth Grp; Photog; Prom Com; SP/M/VS; Fld Hky (JCL); Scr Kpr (V); Sccr (V L); Cl Off (T); Physical Therapy; Christian Ministries; Campbell U; Eastern Minnesota U

BARNER, BETHANY; POWHATAN, VA; BANNER CHRISTIAN SCH; (JR); Chr; Ch Chr; Ice Sktg (J); Sccr (J); Vllyball (V); Sch Ppr (R); Elementary Education; Liberty U; John Tyler Community College

BARNES, KIMBERLY L; CHESTERFIELD, VA; MANCHESTER HS; (JR); F Lan Hn Soc; Gov Hnr Prg; Hi Hnr Roll; MVP; Nat Hon Sy; Nat Mrt Fin; Otst Ac Ach Awd; Perf Att; Pres Ac Ftns Aw; St of Mnth; Comm Volntr; Peer Tut/Med; Chrch Yth Grp; Dbte Team; Emplmnt; Jr Cls League; Key Club; Ntl Beta Clb; NtlFrnscLg; NYLC; Ch Chr; Adv Cncl (R); CR (R); Student Leader - 2002-03; Oral Interpreter of the Year - 2003-04; Public Relations; Business; Howard U; James Madison U

BARNETT, ERIN M; EAGLE ROCK, VA; ALLEGHENY HS,; (SO); Hnr Roll; MVP; Comm Volntr; Chrch Yth Grp; Key Club; SADD; Vsity Clb; Bnd; Mch Bnd; Bskball (V); Track (V); Vsy Clb (V); James Madison U

BARNWELL, JACQUELINE; MANASSAS, VA; STONEWALL JACKSON HS; (SO); Hnr Roll; WWAHSS; Comm Volntr; Key Club; American Clb; Orch; Vllyball (J); Key Club Editor; U of Mary Washington; Radford U

BARROS, BUSTAVO; STERLING, VA; DORAL AC HS; (JR); Hi Hnr Roll; Hnr Roll; Nat Hon Sy; Sch Ppr (E, R); Honor Roll; Best 9th Grader; Civil Engineering; Massachusetts Institute of Technology; Virginia Tech U

BARROW, JAMIE L; MARTINSVILLE, VA; MARTINSVILLE HS; (SR); Hi Hnr Roll; Nat Hon Sy; WWAHSS; Red Cr Aide; Chrch Yth Grp; Key Club; Swmg (V CL); Stu Cncl (R); CR (R); Woodmen of the World Award - 2004; Virginia High School League Academic Award; Roanoke College U of Virginia; College of William and Mary

BARTGIS, CAITLIN; HAMPTON, VA; BETHEL HS; (SO); Ctznshp Aw; Hi Hnr Roll; Hnr Roll; Nat Mrt LOC; Perf Att; St of Mnth; Comm Volntr; Jr Ach; Mus Clb; Vsity Clb; Bnd; Mch Bnd; Orch; Sccr (V)

BARTLEY, KEISHA; HAYSI, VA; HAYSI HS; (SO); Hnr Roll; Perf Att; Comm Volntr; Spec Olymp Vol; FBLA; Key Club; Ntl Beta Clb; Bskball (V); Sftball (V); Vllyball (V); Yrbk (P); Medical/Nursing; Pharmacy; Radford U; Tusculum

BASHIRUDDIN, SABAH T; WOODBRIDGE, VA; WOODBRIDGE SR HS; (SO); Hnr Roll; Pres Ac Ftns Aw; St of Mnth; Comm Volntr; DARE; Key Club; Off Aide; Mar Art; CR (P); Black Belt in Martial Arts; Law; Business Management; George Mason U; U of Virginia

BASS, KIMMIE; MANASSAS, VA; OSBOURN HS; (SO); 4H Awd; Hi Hnr Roll; Nat Ldrshp Svc; WWAHSS; Yth Ldrshp Prog; Comm Volntr; 4-H; Emplmnt; HO'Br Yth Ldrshp; Key Club; Tmpl Yth Grp; SP/M/VS; Chrldg (V L); Cl Off (P); Stu Cncl (R); CR (R); Yrbk (E); 4-H All-Star; Astronaut; Artist/Architect; College of William and Mary

BASSETT, ALETHIA; WILLIAMSBURG, VA; (SR); WWAHSS; FBLA; Social Work; Physical Therapy; Christopher Newport U; Old Dominion U

BASSETT, HAYDEN F; MARTINSVILLE, VA; MARTINSVILLE HS; (FR); Hnr Roll; Comm Volntr; Chrch Yth Grp; Key Club; Scouts; Bnd; Mch Bnd; Sccr (J); Swmg (V L); NC State U

BATES, NIYA M; CHARLOTTESVILLE, VA; MONTICELLO HS; (FR); Hnr Roll; Otst Ac Ach Awd; Perf Att; Peer Tut/Med; Key Club; Pep Squd; Scouts; Bnd; Mch Bnd; Pep Bnd; SHOUT Club; Pediatric Medicine; Veterinary Medicine; U of Virginia

BATTLE, DENISE N; PORTSMOUTH, VA; CHURCHLAND HS; (JR); Chr; SP/M/VS; Sccr (V); Track (V); All-State / All-District / All-City Chorus; Visual and Performing Arts Magnet Program; Vocal Performance / Opera; Music Theatre; Carnegie Mellon School of Music; Juilliard School of Performing Arts

BATWINAS, SHANNON; LYNCH STATION, VA; STAUNTON RIVER HS; (SR); Hi Hnr Roll; Hnr Roll; WWAHSS; DARE; Drma Clb; Emplmnt; Key Club; SP/M/VS; Stg Cre; Swmg (V); Key Club; Forensic Science; Asian Studies; Sweet Briar College; Cedar Crest College

BEACH, ANDREA; ASHBURN, VA; BROAD RUN HS; (JR); Hnr Roll; Kwnis Aw; Nat Hon Sy; Otst Ac Ach Awd; Peer Tut/Med; DECA; FCA; Key Club; Prom Com; Vsity Clb; Cr Ctry (V L); PP Ftbl; Sftball (V L); Adv Cncl (R); Cl Off (P); Stu Cncl (R); CR (R); Biology Student of the Year; Outstanding Cadd Award; Architecture; U of Virginia; Virginia Polytechnic Institute

BEALE, CHRISTOPHER; SOUTH BOSTON, VA; HALIFAX CTY HS; (JR); All Am Sch; Gov Hnr Prg; Hnr Roll; MVP; Nat Hon Sy; USAA; Yth Ldrshp Prog; Hosp Aide; Peer Tut/Med; 4-H; AL Aux Boys; Chrch Yth Grp; Jr Cls League; Schol Bwl; Sci Clb; Bnd; Jzz Bnd; Mch Bnd; Pep Bnd; Sccr (VJCL); Superior Piano Festival Performance Rating; Ecology/Envirothon Teams; International Studies; Musical Performance; Georgetown U; Hampton-Sydney College

BEALL, SYDNEY E; ASHBURN, VA; BROAD RUN HS; (SO); Hi Hnr Roll; Nat Hon Sy; Nat Stu Ath Day Aw; Peer Tut/Med; ArtClub; Dbte Team; Tennis (V); Art Award Grade 9 & 10; Malone Foundation Recipient; Fine Arts; Architecture

Barnes, Kimberly L
Manchester HS
Chesterfield, VA

Atobrah, Ama S
South Lakes HS
Reston, VA

Askew, James
Booker T Washington HS
Norfolk, VA

National
Honor Roll
Spring 2005

Arrington, Crystal F
Franklin Cty HS
Rocky Mount, VA

Bacon II, Troy P
Floyd Kellam HS
Virginia Beach, VA

Battle, Denise N
Churchland HS
Portsmouth, VA

BEASLEY, WORTH Z; STUART, VA; PATRICK CTY HS; (JR); 4H Awd; Hnr Roll; Otst Ac Ach Awd; Sci Fairs; Comm Volntr; 4-H; Chrch Yth Grp; Drma Clb; Emplmnt; NtlFrnscLg; Prom Com; Scouts; French Clb; SP/M/VS; Stg Cre; Cl Off (T); Yrbk (R); French Club Treasurer 3 Years; Challenge-Program for Talented & Gifted; Filmmaking; Theater/Acting; New York U; U of California

BEAUCHAMP, LESLIE; MONTROSS, VA; WASHINGTON & LEE HS; (MS); Ctznshp Aw; DAR; Hi Hnr Roll; Hnr Roll; Perf Att; 4-H; Art

BEAZELL, STEWART A; CHARLOTTESVILLE, VA; MONTICELLO HS; (FR); F Lan Hn Soc; Hnr Roll; Yth Ldrshp Prog; Comm Volntr; Key Club; Acpl Chr; Chr; SP/M/VS; Swg Chr; Fld Hky (J); Sccr (J); Pediatrician; U of Virginia

BEDI, SURMEEN; SPRINGFIELD, VA; ANNANDALE HS; (SR); Hi Hnr Roll; Hnr Roll; Nat Hon Sy; Otst Ac Ach Awd; Perf Att; Sci Fairs; St of Mnth; Comm Volntr; Lib Aide; Off Aide; Tchrs Aide; SP/M/VS; Tutor - Summer 2002-2003; Fundraising For Future Business Leaders of America; Health Science; George Mason U

BEDSWORTH, MEREDITH; RICHMOND, VA; GODWIN HS; (JR); Hnr Roll; Nat Hon Sy; Sci Fairs; Peer Tut/Med; Chrch Yth Grp; Emplmnt; Key Club; Ntl Beta Clb; Prom Com; Quill & Scroll; Svce Clb; SP/M/VS; Stg Cre; Track (V); Sch Ppr (E); Club Soccer; Journalism; U of Virginia

BEERS, TIFFANY L; LURAY, VA; LURAY HS; (SO); Hnr Roll; Hab For Humty Volntr; Emplmnt; Member of Interact Club; Botany; Marine Biology

BELCHER, BLAKE; ABINGDON, VA; ABINGDON HS; (SR); Ctznshp Aw; Hi Hnr Roll; Nat Hon Sy; Nat Mrt Fin; Otst Ac Ach Awd; Perf Att; St of Mnth; WWAHSS; Peer Tut/Med; DECA; Emplmnt; FCA; Mth Clb/Tm; Quiz Bowl; Scouts; Wrstlg (V); Two Time National Competition - DECA; School President & District President - DECA; Business; Marketing; Virginia Tech; Virginia Highlands Community College

BELCHER, LATISHA; MARTINSVILLE, VA; MAGNA VISTA HS; (JR); Ctznshp Aw; Hnr Roll; MVP; Perf Att; St of Mnth; Comm Volntr; ROTC; Drl Tm; Bskball (VJ L); Vllyball (VJCL); Player of Year / Regional Player of Year; AAU - Player for 5 Years; Army; Virginia Tech; U of Connecticut

BELCHER, MAGHAN; HAYSI, VA; ERVINTON HS; (JR); 4H Awd; Ctznshp Aw; Gov Hnr Prg; Hnr Roll; MVP; Nat Hon Sy; Otst Ac Ach Awd; Sci Fairs; Comm Volntr; Spec Olymp Vol; Biology Clb; Drma Clb; FBLA; Key Club; Prom Com; Sci Clb; Tchrs Aide; Bnd; SP/M/VS; Bskball (C); Chrldg (V CL); Scr Kpr (V); Track (V); Cl Off (V); Sch Ppr (R); Yrbk (E); Pharmacy; Occupational Therapy; Southwest Virginia Community College; U of VA College At Wise

BELL, AMANDA; PORTSMOUTH, VA; IC NORCOM; (SR); DAR; F Lan Hn Soc; Hi Hnr Roll; Nat Hon Sy; WWAHSS; Peer Tut/Med; Chrch Yth Grp; Emplmnt; Prom Com; Schol Bwl; Tchrs Aide; International Clb; Swmg (V CL); Sch Ppr (E); Yrbk (R); Access; Interact Club; Pharmacy; Hampton U; Virginia Commonwealth U

BELLAMY, SAMARIAM F; RICHMOND, VA; BINFORD MS; (MS); Fut Prb Slvr; Hnr Roll; Nat Hon Sy; Otst Ac Ach Awd; Perf Att; Sci Fairs; Comm Volntr; Physical Education; Child Lawyer; RN; A & T U; Virginia Union U

BENDER, JENNIFER; CHARLOTTESVILLE, VA; ALBERMARLE HS; (FR); Hnr Roll; St of Mnth; Comm Volntr; Hab For Humty Volntr; Chrch Yth Grp; Key Club; Fncg (J); Fld Hky (J); Lcrsse (J); CR (R); Engineering; Business Degree; James Madison U; College of William and Mary

BENEDICT, JOSEPH R; NEWPORT NEWS, VA; BETHEL HS; (SO); Hnr Roll; St of Mnth; Comm Volntr; Fr of Library; Lib Aide; Photog; ROTC; Tchrs Aide; Latin Clb; Cl Off (R); CR (R); Latin Club; ROTC; Culinary Arts; Computer Science; Culinary School of Pittsburgh; ITT Technical Institute

BENNETT, BROOKE; FREDERICKSBURG, VA; COURTLAND HS; (JR); Ctznshp Aw; F Lan Hn Soc; Hi Hnr Roll; Hnr Roll; Jr Eng Tech; Nat Hon Sy; Otst Ac Ach Awd; Pres Ac Ftns Aw; WWAHSS; Yth Ldrshp Prog; CARE; Comm Volntr; Peer Tut/Med; Emplmnt; P to P St Amb Prg; Prom Com; Tchrs Aide; Vsity Clb; Voc Ind Clb Am; Latin Clb; Dnce; Pep Bnd; SP/M/VS; Chrldg (V CL); Gmnstcs (V CL); PPSqd (V); PP Ftbl (J); Vsy Clb (V L); Adv Cncl (R); Cl Off (T); Stu Cncl (R); CR (T); Girls State Delegate; International DECA Rep; Pediatric Surgery; Fashion / Interior Design; U of Virginia; North Carolina State U

BENNETT, LAUREN; COVINGTON, VA; ALLEGHANY HS; (JR); Hi Hnr Roll; Hnr Roll; Nat Hon Sy; WWAHSS; Hosp Aide; Peer Tut/Med; HO'Br Yth Ldrshp; Key Club; NYLC; Prom Com; SADD; Cl Off (P); Stu Cncl (R); CR (R); Key Club Vice President; Students For Christ Club; Nursing; Radiologist; James Madison U; Edward Via School of Osteopathy

BENNETT, SHANE H; WAYNESBORO, VA; WAYNESBORO HS; (JR); Hnr Roll; Perf Att; Yth Ldrshp Prog; Comm Volntr; Peer Tut/Med; Chrch Yth Grp; DARE; Drma Clb; Jr Cls League; Key Club; Vsity Clb; Latin Clb; Chr; Ch Chr; SP/M/VS; Stg Cre; Sccr (VJCL); Sch Ppr (R); Reporter & Anchor for Broadcast News; Education; Social Studies

BENOMRAN, ARWA; FALLS CHURCH, VA; STUART HS; (SO); F Lan Hn Soc; Hi Hnr Roll; Hnr Roll; Nat Hon Sy; Otst Ac Ach Awd; Sci/Math Olympn; Amnsty Intl; Comm Volntr; Peer Tut/Med; Sftball (JC); Vllyball (J); Community Service & Volunteer; Join Clubs in School and Out; Mathematics/Bio Major; Education

BERNABE, DANIELLE; VIENNA, VA; BISHOP DENIS J O'CONNELL HS; (SO); Hnr Roll; Pres Ac Ftns Aw; Comm Volntr; Key Club; Mth Clb/Tm; Crew / Rowing Team; Nominated - Governor's School For French Immersion; Math Education; Virginia Polytechnic Institute; University of Virginia

BERRYMAN, RENATA; DILLWYN, VA; CUMBERLAND CTY HS; (MS); Ctznshp Aw; Hnr Roll; Otst Ac Ach Awd; Perf Att; St of Mnth; Comm Volntr; Chrch Yth Grp; DARE; Scouts; Clr Grd; Flg Crps; Chrldg (J); Leadership; Communications; California State U; Longwood U

BERTHA, MICHAEL L; SPRINGFIELD, VA; ROBERT E LEE HS; (JR); F Lan Hn Soc; Hnr Roll; Nat Hon Sy; Sci Fairs; St of Mnth; Yth Ldrshp Prog; Comm Volntr; Chrch Yth Grp; DARE; DECA; Emplmnt; MuAlphaTh; Mus Clb; ROTC; Scouts; Bnd; Clr Grd; Mch Bnd; Lcrsse (VJ L); Eagle Scout; History; Engineering; United States Military Academy; Pennsylvania State U

BEVERLEY, KASHAE C O; LOCUST HILL, VA; MIDDLESEX HS; (SR); Ctznshp Aw; Hi Hnr Roll; Hnr Roll; Pres Ac Ftns Aw; Comm Volntr; Chrch Yth Grp; DARE; DECA; FCA; FBLA; Prom Com; Ch Chr; Bskball (VJCL); PP Ftbl (V); Tennis (V); Wt Lftg (V); District Award for Apparel & Accessories ML; Coach's Award for Varsity Basketball; Accounting; Fashion Merchandise; Shaw U; Chowan College

BIBB, KATRINA; STAFFORD, VA; COLONIAL FORGE HS; (SO); Otst Ac Ach Awd; Sci Fairs; Peer Tut/Med; Chrch Yth Grp; George Mason U; Virginia Commonwealth U

BIDDLE JR, DARRYL C; BEAUMONT, VA; PAUL S BLANDFORD SCH; (SO); Hi Hnr Roll; Hnr Roll; Comm Volntr; Bnd; Drl Tm; Wrstlg (J); CR (R); Go to College; Own My Business; DeVry U; U of Virginia

BILLINGS, TERRA; VIRGINIA BEACH, VA; FLOYD KELLAM HS; (JR); Hi Hnr Roll; Hnr Roll; Perf Att; Comm Volntr; Chrch Yth Grp; Drma Clb; Emplmnt; Off Aide; Awards for Recreational Sports; Vacation Bible School Award; Degree in Elementary Education; Bachelor's Degree, Complete Education Program; Eastern Mennonite U; Virginia Commonwealth U

BILLUPS, CLAIRE E; RICHMOND, VA; GODWIN HS; (SR); Hnr Roll; Nat Hon Sy; Perf Att; WWAHSS; Comm Volntr; Chrch Yth Grp; Emplmnt; FCA; MuAlphaTh; Ntl Beta Clb; Prom Com; Quill & Scroll; Svce Clb; Dnce; Cr Ctry (VJCL); Track; Sch Ppr (E); Yrbk (E); Keyettes Vice President; Who's Who Among American HS Students; Communications; Education; James Madison U

BITTLER, CALEB A; FINCASTLE, VA; JAMES RIVER HS; (SR); Hnr Roll; Nat Hon Sy; Perf Att; WWAHSS; Comm Volntr; Chrch Yth Grp; Emplmnt; Quiz Bowl; Scouts; Ftball (J); Eagle Scout; Building Trades

BITTLER, ETHAN J; FINCASTLE, VA; JAMES RIVER HS; (SO); Hi Hnr Roll; Perf Att; Comm Volntr; Chess

BIZAL, TIMOTHY F; STERLING, VA; BROAD RUN HS; (SR); Hi Hnr Roll; Hnr Roll; Nat Hon Sy; Otst Ac Ach Awd; Perf Att; WWAHSS; Comm Volntr; Key Club; Schol Bwl; Cr Ctry (VJCL); Yrbk (R, P); Coaches' Award-Cross Country 2005; Loudoun Co. Volunteer SVSC of Year Award - 2001; Computer Science; Government; College of William & Mary

BLACK, KATELYN L; WAYNESBORO, VA; WILSON MEMORIAL HS; (FR); Fut Prb Slvr; Hnr Roll; Kwnis Aw; Otst Ac Ach Awd; St of Mnth; WWAHSS; Comm Volntr; Spec Olymp Vol; Chrch Yth Grp; FCA; Key Club; Sftball (J); Key Club Vice Pres.; Physical Therapy; Virginia Polytechnic Institute & State U; Duke U (Grad)

BLACK, LATASHA; WILLIAMSBURG, VA; BRUTON HS; (FR); Hnr Roll; Perf Att; Sci Fairs; St Optmst of Yr; Comm Volntr; FBLA; Photog; Dnce; Computer Sciences; Fashion; Drexel U; Jacksonville U

BLACKARD, KAITLIN R; FISHERSVILLE, VA; STUARTS DRAFT HS; (SO); Gov Hnr Prg; Hi Hnr Roll; Otst Ac Ach Awd; Comm Volntr; Chrch Yth Grp; Key Club; Schol Bwl; Spanish Clb; Ch Chr; Key Club Treasurer; Pharmacy; Medical; U of VA; William & Mary

BLACKWELL, JILLIAN; GRUNDY, VA; MOUNTAIN MISSION SCH; (FR); Ctznshp Aw; Duke TS; Hi Hnr Roll; Otst Ac Ach Awd; Pres Sch; WWAHSS; Comm Volntr; Peer Tut/Med; Drma Clb; P to P St Amb Prg; SP/M/VS; Fncg (J); Cl Off (V); Yrbk (E); Member of Lego Team; Member of Mock Trial; Art; Education; Duke U; Pratt U

BLAIR, KATIE; OAKTON, VA; OAKTON HS; (FR); Hnr Roll; Pres Ac Ftns Aw; WWAHSS; Key Club; Chr; Track (J); Volunteering At Sully Historic Plantation; Writing; History; College of William and Mary; Boston U

BLAKELY, CHELSEA; MARTINSVILLE, VA; MARTINSVILLE HS; (FR); 4H Awd; Hnr Roll; Otst Ac Ach Awd; Perf Att; Yth Ldrshp Prog; 4-H; Drma Clb; FBLA; Key Club; Ntl Beta Clb; Scouts; Bnd; Chr; Mch Bnd; SP/M/VS; Tennis (J); Piano / Voice Lessons; Criminal Justice / Forensic Science; Performing / Visual Arts; Appalachian State; U of North Carolina

BLANDON-MARTINEZ, JORMERY; ALEXANDRIA, VA; THOMAS A EDISON HS; (SR); Hnr Roll; WWAHSS; Comm Volntr; Hosp Aide; Peer Tut/Med; DECA; FBLA; Key Club; ROTC; Spanish Clb; Drl Tm; Lcrsse (J); Key Club, FCCLA, DECA; Spanish Honor Society, Spanish Club; Biology Major; Pre-Medicine; Virginia Commonwealth U; West Virginia Wesleyan College

BLANKENSHIP, SERENA; VANSANT, VA; GRUNDY HS; (JR); 4H Awd; Hnr Roll; Perf Att; Comm Volntr; 4-H; FBLA; Ntl Beta Clb; Off Aide; Scouts; Sccr (V); Biology Major; Nursing Degree; U of Virginia At Wise; Southwest Virginia Community College

BLAYLOCK, LANCE; ABINGDON, VA; JOHN S BATTLE HS; (SR); Hnr Roll; Perf Att; Pres Ac Ftns Aw; St of Mnth; WWAHSS; Comm Volntr; Biology Clb; DARE; Ntl Beta Clb; Prom Com; Bskball (J); Ftball (J); Cl Off (P); Stu Cncl (V); Sch Ppr (R); Yrbk (R); Prom Prince; Teacher/Coach (Math); King; VA Highlands

BLOWE, ASHLEY; HAMPTON, VA; BETHEL HS; (SO); Hnr Roll; Perf Att; Comm Volntr; Emplmnt; FBLA; Spanish Clb; Adv Cncl (R); Cl Off (P); Child Psychology; College of William and Mary; U of North Carolina

BOBEVA, GERGANA I; RICHMOND, VA; NORTH HURON HS; (SR); F Lan Hn Soc; Hi Hnr Roll; Hnr Roll; Nat Hon Sy; Sci/Math Olympn; Red Cr Aide; Emplmnt; SADD; Vsity Clb; Wdwrkg Clb; BULGARIAN Clb; Chrldg (V L); Sch Ppr (R, P); Yrbk (R, P); National Honor Society Member; FACTS Member; Advertising; Mass Communications; Virginia Commonwealth U

BOGGESS, JARED S; MECHANICSVILLE, VA; LEE DAVIS HS; (JR); Hnr Roll; Otst Ac Ach Awd; WWAHSS; Comm Volntr; ArtClub; Chrch Yth Grp; Emplmnt; Photog; Bnd; SP/M/VS; Lit Mag (E); Honor Certificate Award for Specific Artwork; Accepted in Gifted & Talented Program for Art; Art; Graphic Art; Virginia Commonwealth U

BOLEY, AMY; LYNCH STATION, VA; ALTAVISTA HS; (SR); Hnr Roll; St of Mnth; WWAHSS; Emplmnt; FBLA; ROTC; Drl Tm; Chrldg (VJ); Criminal Justice-Student of the 6 Weeks; Central Virginia Community College; Radford U

BOLT, CANDICE L; GALAX, VA; (MS); 4H Awd; Hi Hnr Roll; Hnr Roll; Nat Hon Sy; Otst Ac Ach Awd; Pres Ac Ftns Aw; St of Mnth; Comm Volntr; 4-H; DARE; FCA; Ntl FFA; Sign Clb; Chr; Ch Chr; Chrldg; Gmnstcs; Yrbk (E, P); President of FCA; Teacher of Deaf; Sign Language; U of Kentucky; NC State

BONNEY, MICHELLE; SMITHFIELD, VA; SMITHFIELD HS; (SO); Hi Hnr Roll; Hnr Roll; Nat Hon Sy; Pres Ac Ftns Aw; St of Mnth; Yth Ldrshp Prog; Peer Tut/Med; Fr of Library; FCCLA; Key Club; Ntl Beta Clb; Quiz Bowl; Schol Bwl; French Clb; SP/M/VS; Track (V); Law; Interior Design; William & Mary

BOONE, JONATHAN M; MADISON, VA; MADISON CTY HS; (SR); Hi Hnr Roll; Hnr Roll; Perf Att; DARE; Off Aide; Bnd; Mch Bnd; Second Degree Black Belt-Tae Kwon Do; Independent Studies-Writing a Novel; English Literature; Criminal Justice; Germanna Community College; U of Virginia

BOSCO, MELISSA J; OAKTON, VA; FLINT HILL SCH; (SR); Hnr Roll; Sci Fairs; Comm Volntr; Emplmnt; Mus Clb; Vsity Clb; Bskball (J); Sccr (V); Sftball (C); Stu Cncl (R); Paderewski Medal-National Piano Guild; 10-Year Gold Cup-National Federation Of Music; Business Marketing; Computer Engineering

BOSSARDT, MOLLY; CHARLOTTESVILLE, VA; ALBEMARLE HS; (JR); Hnr Roll; WWAHSS; Chrch Yth Grp; Emplmnt; Key Club; Fld Hky (V L); Sccr (J); Stu Cncl (R); All Academic Award; Antioch Team; Political Science; Virginia Tech; U of Mary Washington

BOSTIC, LAUREN; SUFFOLK, VA; LAKELAND HS; (JR); DAR; Hi Hnr Roll; Sci Fairs; Comm Volntr; Hab For Humty Volntr; Hosp Aide; FBLA; Key Club; Ntl Beta Clb; Schol Bwl; Bskball (J); Yrbk (R, P); Fleet Reserve Association 3rd Place Essay Winner; Virginia Tech; James Madison U

BOSTON, JESSICA A; SALEM, VA; SALEM HS; (SO); F Lan Hn Soc; Hi Hnr Roll; MVP; Nat Hon Sy; Comm Volntr; Chrch Yth Grp; DARE; Drma Clb; FCA; Jr Ach; Key Club; Spanish Clb; SP/M/VS; Stg Cre; Sftball (JC); Pre-Med; U of Virginia; James Madison U

BOSWORTH, MICHELLE; MANASSAS, VA; STONEWALL JACKSON HS; (SO); Emplmnt; Key Club; Tchrs Aide; Chr; Dnce; GMFL Cheerleading, MS Walk; Help W/Little League Football, Adopt a Child for Xmas; Computers; Coastal Carolina U

BOUCHTIA, YOSSERA; LORTON, VA; SOUTH CTY; (SO); Hi Hnr Roll; Hnr Roll; Mth Clb/Tm; French Clb; SP/M/VS; HAWC Club; Greensprings; Psychology; Drama; New York U

BOUKNIGHT, BRITTANY A; MANASSAS, VA; STONEWALL JACKSON HS; (SO); Hnr Roll; ArtClub; Bskball (J); International Club; Step Team; Psychology; Theater

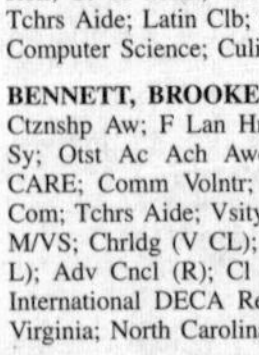
Bouknight, Brittany A
Stonewall Jackson HS
Manassas, VA

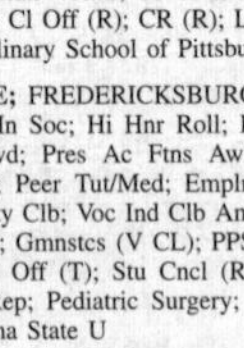
Bolt, Candice L
Galax, VA

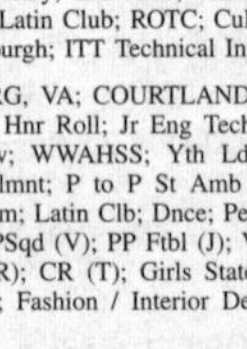
Blaylock, Lance
John S Battle HS
Abingdon, VA

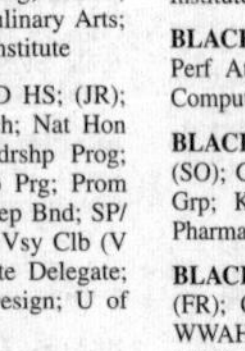
Benedict, Joseph R
Bethel HS
Newport News, VA

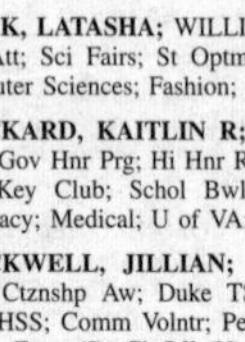
Belcher, Maghan
Ervinton HS
Haysi, VA

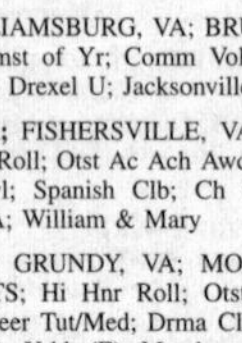
Beasley, Worth Z
Patrick Cty HS
Stuart, VA

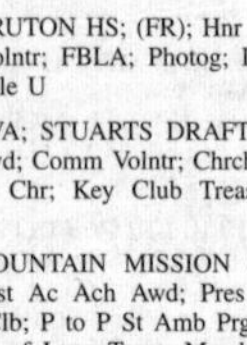
Belcher, Latisha
Magna Vista HS
Martinsville, VA

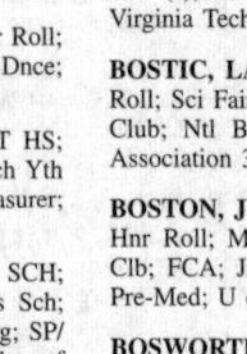
Blandon-Martinez, Jormery
Thomas A Edison HS
Alexandria, VA

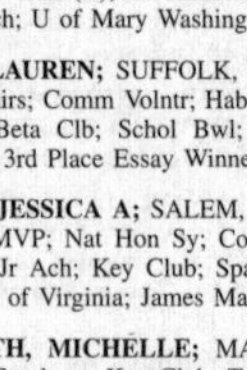
Blowe, Ashley
Bethel HS
Hampton, VA

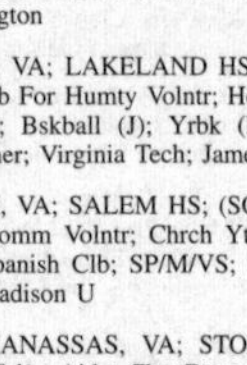
Boone, Jonathan M
Madison Cty HS
Madison, VA

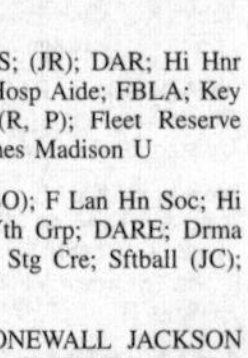
Bosco, Melissa J
Flint Hill Sch
Oakton, VA

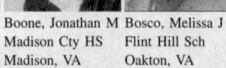

BOWERS, ADRIENNE; HAMPTON, VA; BETHEL HS; (SO); Hnr Roll; Otst Ac Ach Awd; Perf Att; Yth Ldrshp Prog; Hosp Aide; French Clb; Drm Mjr; Mch Bnd; Sch Ppr (R); 2005 Academic Award Recipient; Hampton U Media Production Employee; Mass Communications; Journalism; Virginia Commonwealth U; Christopher Newport U

BOWIE, MATORI; NEWPORT NEWS, VA; WOODSIDE HS; (JR); Hi Hnr Roll; Hnr Roll; Sci Fairs; Comm Volntr; Peer Tut/Med; DARE; FBLA; Pep Squd; Bnd; Clr Grd; Vllyball; honorary volunteer; meteorology; business; Georgia Tech; Ohio state

BOWMAN, MEGAN J; WILLIAMSBURG, VA; LAFAYETTE HS; (SR); Hnr Roll; WWAHSS; Comm Volntr; Red Cr Aide; Key Club; SADD; Tchrs Aide; French Clb; Cr Ctry (V); Track (V); Veterinary Technician; Marine Biology; Thomas Nelson Community College

BOWMAN, SAMANTHA M; CANA, VA; CARROLL CTY HS; (JR); 4-H; Ntl FFA; SADD; Bnd; Pep Bnd; Biology; Extension Education; Virginia Polytechnical Inst; U of Tennessee

BOYD, APRIL N; BEDFORD, VA; LIBERTY HS; (SO); Ctznshp Aw; Gov Hnr Prg; Hi Hnr Roll; Hnr Roll; Otst Ac Ach Awd; Perf Att; Sci Fairs; Comm Volntr; Red Cr Aide; 4-H; Chrch Yth Grp; DARE; Key Club; Scouts; SADD; SP/M/VS; Stg Cre; Cr Ctry (V L); Sccr (J); Track (V L); Key Club President; (Will Be Attending) Central Virginia Governors School for Science and Technology; Peace Corps; Science (Physical, Chemistry); William and Mary; Washington and Lee

BOYKIN, CARTER; VIRGINIA BEACH, VA; FRANK W COX HS; (SO); Hnr Roll; WWAHSS; Comm Volntr; Key Club; U of North Carolina Chapel Hill; College of Charleston

BOYSEN, JESSICA; ASHBURN, VA; STONE BRIDGE HS; (SR); F Lan Hn Soc; Hnr Roll; Nat Hon Sy; WWAHSS; Peer Tut/Med; Chrch Yth Grp; Emplmnt; Bnd; PP Ftbl (V); Scr Kpr (V); Sccr (L); Sch Ppr (E); English Major; College of William and Mary

BOZA, JUAN; STERLING, VA; DOMINION HS; (JR); Hnr Roll; Otst Ac Ach Awd; Sci Fairs; Comm Volntr; DECA; Sccr (J L); Computer Engineering; Architecture; Virginia Polytech Institute State U; James Madison U

BRACKEN, KATHLEEN; ASHBURN, VA; BROAD RUN HS; (JR); F Lan Hn Soc; Hi Hnr Roll; Nat Hon Sy; Sci Fairs; Sci/Math Olympn; Key Club; Bnd; PP Ftbl; Sccr (V L); Key Club Treasurer; William & Mary Leadership Award; Engineering; Accounting; U of Virginia; Purdue U

BRACKEN, KATHLEEN; STERLING, VA; BROAD RUN HS; (JR); F Lan Hn Soc; Hi Hnr Roll; Hnr Roll; Kwnis Aw; Nat Hon Sy; Otst Ac Ach Awd; Sci Fairs; Sci/Math Olympn; Spec Olymp Vol; Emplmnt; Key Club; Off Aide; Bnd; PP Ftbl (V); Sccr (V L); William & Mary Leadership Award; Loudoun County Community Service Award; Engineering; Accounting; U of Virginia; Purdue U

BRADSHAW, F KERSTIN; SANDY HOOK, VA; GOOCHLAND HS; (FR); Ctznshp Aw; Hi Hnr Roll; Sci Fairs; WWAHSS; Comm Volntr; Chrch Yth Grp; Key Club; Sftball (J); Vllyball (J); Virginia Junior Science Fair; Forensic Science; Photography Career; James Madison U; Virginia Tech

BRADSHAW JR, CALVIN; FINCASTLE, VA; JAMES RIVER HS; (SR); WWAHSS; Scouts; Voc Ind Clb Am; Ftball (V); Wrstlg (V); Aviation

BRANCH, KATHERYN; BUCKINGHAM, VA; BUCKINGHAM CTY HS; (SO); 4H Awd; Hnr Roll; Comm Volntr; 4-H; Fr of Library; Lib Aide; Scouts; Dnce; Pre-School Teacher; Veterinarian; Longwood College; Virginia Tech

BRANNAN, LINDSAY J; MIDLOTHIAN, VA; MIDLOTHIAN HS; (JR); F Lan Hn Soc; Hi Hnr Roll; Hnr Roll; Jr Mshl; Nat Hon Sy; Comm Volntr; Peer Tut/Med; Chrch Yth Grp; Dbte Team; Key Club; Mod UN; Quill & Scroll; French Clb; Lit Mag (E); U At Richmond Book Award; Volunteer Work for Adopt-A-Minefield; Anthropologic; Criminal Justice/Pre-Law; William & Mary

BRANTLEY, TEMPERANCE; MIDLOTHIAN, VA; MIDLOTHIAN HS; (SO); Hnr Roll; Yth Ldrshp Prog; Hab For Humty Volntr; Spanish Clb; SP/M/VS; Bskball (V); Spanish Club; AAU Basketball; Psychology / Communications; U of Miami; Various North Carolina Colleges

BRAVSTEIN, AARON; ASHBURN, VA; BROAD RUN HS; (JR); Hnr Roll; MVP; Comm Volntr; Chr; Bskball (J); Sccr (V L); Yrbk (E); Youth Chamber Orchestra; Business; Mechanical Engineering; Virginia Polytechnic Institute & State U; George Mason U

BRAYBOY, BRITTANY; NEWPORT NEWS, VA; DENBIGH HS; (JR); Hnr Roll; Comm Volntr; Peer Tut/Med; Emplmnt; Key Club; MuAlphaTh; Dnce; Cl Off (V); Marine Biology; Mythology

BREECE, LINDSAY; ASHBURN, VA; STONE BRIDGE HS; (JR); Hnr Roll; Comm Volntr; Key Club; Chr; Manager of JV softball; CPR and First-Aid Certified; Pediatric Nurse; Radford U; U of Virginia

BRENNER, MICHELLE; MANASSAS, VA; OSBOURN PARK SR HS; (JR); WWAHSS; Comm Volntr; 4-H; Chrch Yth Grp; Key Club; SP/M/VS; Tennis (J); Committee Head in Key Club; Next Year Editor of Key Club; Education; Longwood U; Lynchburg College

BRIGHTON, REBECCA D; SPOTSYLVANIA, VA; RIVERBEND HS; (JR); Nat Hon Sy; WWAHSS; Comm Volntr; Peer Tut/Med; HO'Br Yth Ldrshp; NYLC; French Clb; Chr; Dnce; Commonwealth Governor's School; National Art Honor Society; Foreign Affairs; Art History; American U; College of William and Mary

BRISCO, DARREN K; RICHMOND, VA; Cmty HS; (MS); Otst Ac Ach Awd; Perf Att; Comm Volntr; Chess; Scouts; Clb; SP/M/VS; Bskball (L); Track (J); CR (V); Yrbk (P); Participated in Garfield Memorial Fund- Danced for Hurricane; Participated in Collegent - 2 Summers; Veterinary Assistant; Veterinary; VCU; College of William and Mary

BRISENDINE, COURTNEY N; COVINGTON, VA; ALLEGHANY HS; (JR); Hnr Roll; WWAHSS; Yth Ldrshp Prog; Comm Volntr; Spec Olymp Vol; FBLA; Key Club; NYLC; Scouts; Vllyball (V); Girl Scout Gold Award; GS Presidential Award; Math Teacher; Radford VA; James Madison U

BRISENDINE, JONATHAN C; COVINGTON, VA; ALLEGHANY HS; (JR); Hnr Roll; WWAHSS; Comm Volntr; Chrch Yth Grp; FBLA; Key Club; Ntl Beta Clb; Scouts; Eagle Scout; Forensic Science; Radford, VA; Marshall-West VA

BRISSON, EVAN H; RICHMOND, VA; GODWIN HS; (FR); Hi Hnr Roll; MVP; Otst Ac Ach Awd; Pres Sch; Comm Volntr; ArtClub; Chrch Yth Grp; Key Club; Ch Chr; Swmg (J); Architecture; Engineering; NC State

BROCK, AMY N; SPRINGFIELD, VA; ROBERT E LEE HS; (JR); Hi Hnr Roll; Hnr Roll; Nat Stu Ath Day Aw; Otst Ac Ach Awd; Perf Att; Pres Ac Ftns Aw; Pres Sch; St Schl; St of Mnth; WWAHSS; Peer Tut/Med; DARE; DECA; FBLA; Sccr (V C); Biology; Drexel U; Howard U

BROCK, MAX; FREDERICKSBURG, VA; JAMES MONROE HS; (JR); Hi Hnr Roll; WWAHSS; Comm Volntr; Dbte Team; Key Club; Spanish Clb; Rlr Hky (V); Tennis (L); Cl Off (P); I Have Played Travel Ice Hockey for 8 Years, I Play the Guitar. I Have Traveled Throughout. Canada,; South America and Australia

BROCK, PIPER; FREDERICKSBURG, VA; JAMES MONROE HS; (SO); Hi Hnr Roll; Sci Fairs; WWAHSS; Comm Volntr; Dbte Team; Key Club; Spanish Clb; Dnce; Cl Off (V); Sch Ppr (R); I Have Been Trained in Classical Ballet for 13 Yrs; I Have Traveled Throughout the U.S., Canada, South America and Australia

BROOKBANK, LINDSEY; ASHBURN, VA; STONE BRIDGE HS; (SO); Hi Hnr Roll; Hnr Roll; Otst Ac Ach Awd; Sci Fairs; DARE; Key Club; Chrldg (J); Stu Cncl (R); William & Mary, James Madison; Virginia Tech

BROOKE, CRYSTAL; NORFOLK, VA; (SR); Chrch Yth Grp; Tchrs Aide; Dnce; Graduate of Charm Associates; Sr. Graduate of Evelyn Oh Dancing Sch; Tidewater Tech

BROOKS, AMANDA M; CLIFTON, VA; CENTREVILLE HS; (SR); Hi Hnr Roll; Nat Hon Sy; Pres Ac Ftns Aw; Comm Volntr; Red Cr Aide; Spec Olymp Vol; Key Club; Sign Clb; Bnd; Dnce; Vllyball (V C); Crew - Varsity; Elementary Education; U of North Carolina Greensboro

BROOKS, CYNTHIA Q; RICHMOND, VA; GEORGE WYTHE HS; (JR); Hi Hnr Roll; Hnr Roll; Nat Hon Sy; St of Mnth; WWAHSS; Peer Tut/Med; FBLA; Ch Chr; Chrldg (V); Stu Cncl (R); National Honor Society; National Society of HS Scholars; Pre-Med; Business

BROWN, ALICIA; SHENANDOAH, VA; PAGE CTY HS; (SO); Hnr Roll; Nat Hon Sy; St of Mnth; Comm Volntr; Chrch Yth Grp; Emplmnt; Mus Clb; Tech Clb; Chr; Ch Chr; National Leadership Bronze Award (FCCLA); Choir Medal-Most Improved; Agriculture Vet Technician; Blue Ridge Community College

BROWN, ANNE M; ROANOKE, VA; ROANOKE CATHOLIC HS; (JR); Hnr Roll; MVP; Perf Att; WWAHSS; Comm Volntr; Peer Tut/Med; Chrch Yth Grp; Cmptr Clb; Drma Clb; HO'Br Yth Ldrshp; Jr Ach; Key Club; Mth Clb/Tm; Prom Com; Orch; Cr Ctry (V); Swmg (V); Track (V); Cl Off (S); Stu Cncl (R); Lit Mag (E, R); Serving Christ in One Another - Award; Key Club - Lt Governor; Pre-Med; Chemistry; U of Virginia; College of William and Mary

BROWN, BRANDON D; PETERSBURG, VA; MATOCCA HS; (JR); Ctznshp Aw; Hnr Roll; Jr Mshl; Nat Hon Sy; Otst Ac Ach Awd; Pres Sch; St of Mnth; Yth Ldrshp Prog; Comm Volntr; Peer Tut/Med; AL Aux Boys; Chrch Yth Grp; DECA; Emplmnt; FBLA; Key Club; Mod UN; Prom Com; Ch Chr; Cl Off (P); CR (R); Lit Mag (E); National Student Leadership Conference; MHS Peer Ambassador; Marketing; Law; Longwood U; James Madison U

BROWN, DARIUS V; LORTON, VA; HAYFIELD SECONDARY SCH; (SR); Hi Hnr Roll; Hnr Roll; Kwnis Aw; Otst Ac Ach Awd; Perf Att; Comm Volntr; Emplmnt; FCA; Key Club; Bnd; Ch Chr; Jzz Bnd; Mch Bnd; Cr Ctry (J L); Track (V L); Academic Letter; Auto Cad 2000 (U.S) Brain Bench; Aerospace Engineering; Mechanical Engineering; The Pennsylvania State U

BROWN, GLENN; NEWPORT NEWS, VA; WOODSIDE HS; (JR); Hnr Roll; Photog; Vsity Clb; Bskball (J); Sccr (V); Yrbk (R, P); Business Management Degree; Old Dominion U; George Mason U

BROWN, KA-TARI B; CHARLOTTESVILLE, VA; MONTICELLO HS; (FR); Hnr Roll; Nat Hon Sy; Chrch Yth Grp; Cmptr Clb; DARE; Chr; AAU Basketball; City League Basketball; Music Production; Clothing Design; Georgia Tech; PVCC

BROWN, MICHAEL; CLIFTON, VA; ROBINSON HS; (JR); Hnr Roll; Nat Hon Sy; Otst Ac Ach Awd; Sci Fairs; Comm Volntr; Peer Tut/Med; DECA; Emplmnt; Photog; Golf (V L); DECA: 1 District-Runner Up State, National; Photography: Solo Exhibit; Engineering; Physics; U of Virginia; Bucknell

BROWN, PATRICK R; COLONIAL BEACH, VA; WASHINGTON & LEE HS; (SO); Ctznshp Aw; Hi Hnr Roll; Hnr Roll; St of Mnth; Comm Volntr; Peer Tut/Med; ArtClub; Chess; Lib Aide; Foreign Clb; SP/M/VS; Stu Cncl (P); Academic Club; Astro Physics; Computer Technology; Virginia Tech; Columbia U

BROWNLEE, AMBER M; CHARLOTTESVILLE, VA; ALBEMARLE HS; (SR); Hnr Roll; Comm Volntr; Peer Tut/Med; Red Cr Aide; Chrch Yth Grp; Key Club; Swmg (V); Babysitting; Salvation Army Volunteer; Nursing; Radford U

BRUNER, SARAH M; BURKE, VA; SOUTH RIVER HS; (JR); Hi Hnr Roll; Hnr Roll; Perf Att; Comm Volntr; Peer Tut/Med; Emplmnt; Tchrs Aide; Wdwrkg Clb; Chemical Engineering; Forensic Science; Carnegie Mellon U; Virginia Polytechnic U

BRYAN, BRITTANY L; VIRGINIA BEACH, VA; PRINCESS ANNE HS; (SO); F Lan Hn Soc; Hnr Roll; Nat Hon Sy; Pres Ac Ftns Aw; WWAHSS; Yth Ldrshp Prog; Comm Volntr; Peer Tut/Med; Chrch Yth Grp; Dbte Team; Drma Clb; Key Club; P to P St Amb Prg; Spch Team; Vsity Clb; French Clb; SP/M/VS; Sftball (V L); CR (R); Forensics; President of Global Outreach; International Affairs; Government & Politics; U of Virginia; College of William & Mary

BRYANT, CANDICE; NEWPORT NEWS, VA; DENBIGH BAPTIST CHRISTIAN SCH; (FR); Hnr Roll; Perf Att; Sci/Math Olympn; WWAHSS; Yth Ldrshp Prog; Comm Volntr; Peer Tut/Med; Chrch Yth Grp; Drma Clb; FCA; Lib Aide; Svce Clb; Chr; SP/M/VS; Stg Cre; Chrldg (VJ); Drama Club; TABB Library Volunteer and Teen Advisory Board Member; Premed; Dental Field; College of William and Mary; Virginia Commonwealth U

BUCHANAN, BETHANY; VIRGINIA BEACH, VA; PRINCESS ANNE HS; (SO); F Lan Hn Soc; Hnr Roll; Nat Hon Sy; Otst Ac Ach Awd; Pres Sch; Comm Volntr; Hosp Aide; Key Club; Quill & Scroll; Spch Team; French Clb; CR (R); Sch Ppr (E); President of Quill & Scroll Society; (News Paper) My Article Won 2nd Place in State-Wide Competition; Journalism; Psychology; Indiana U; College of William & Mary

BUDAGOV, ANASTAS; VIRGINIA BEACH, VA; NORFOLK COLLEGIATE SCH; (JR); Ctznshp Aw; Fut Prb Slvr; Hi Hnr Roll; Hnr Roll; MVP; Comm Volntr; Chrch Yth Grp; Greek Clb; Bnd; Dnce; Jzz Bnd; Pep Bnd; Bskball (J); Sccr (V); Tennis (V CL); Lit Mag (R); Engineering; Business; George Mason U; Virginia Tech U

BURGESS, ASHLEY; FREDERICKSBURG, VA; JAMES MONROE HS; (SO); Sccr (J); Yrbk (E, R); The Free Lance Star 2005 Star Search Contest Winner-Editorial Cartoon Category

BURKE, AEISHA; RICHMOND, VA; VARINA HS; (SR); Hnr Roll; Nat Stu Ath Day Aw; Perf Att; WWAHSS; Hab For Humty Volntr; DECA; Drma Clb; Emplmnt; SP/M/VS; Stg Cre; Bskball (V); Cr Ctry (V)

BURKE, CHRISTINE S; MANASSAS, VA; OSBOURN HS; (JR); F Lan Hn Soc; Hnr Roll; Nat Hon Sy; Pres Ac Ftns Aw; WWAHSS; Yth Ldrshp Prog; Peer Tut/Med; 4-H; Emplmnt; Key Club; NYLC; Scouts; Spanish Clb; Dnce; Drm Mjr; Bskball (JC); Cr Ctry (V L); Sccr (JC); Sch Ppr; Virginia Governor's School for Russian; Mid-Atlantic Regional Baton Champion; Business; Public Relations; Georgetown U; U of Miami

BURKE, ROBERT A; RICHMOND, VA; VARINA HS; (SR); MVP; USAA; WWAHSS; Yth Ldrshp Prog; Comm Volntr; Spec Olymp Vol; Emplmnt; Key Club; MuAlphaTh; Ntl Beta Clb; Quill & Scroll; French Clb; Cr Ctry (V); Ftball (VJ L); Sccr (VJCL); Adv Cncl (R); Stu Cncl (P); Pres. & Co-Founder-SAVIS (Students Against Violence in Schools); Communications-Broadcast Journalism; Secondary Education; George Mason U (Attending)

BURNETT, KATIE L; AUSTINVILLE, VA; FORT CHISWELL HS; (JR); Ctznshp Aw; F Lan Hn Soc; Hnr Roll; Nat Hon Sy; WWAHSS; Chrch Yth Grp; FCA; Scouts; Spanish Clb; Bnd; Chr; Jzz Bnd; Mch Bnd; Japanese Translation; Asian Studies

BURNHAM, SHARON; GAINESVILLE, VA; BATTLEFIELD HS; (SO); Hnr Roll; WWAHSS; Comm Volntr; Peer Tut/Med; Chess; Chrch Yth Grp; Photog; Sign Clb; Ch Chr; Stg Cre; VA State Finalist National American Miss; History / Education / Psychology

Bryant, Candice
Denbigh Baptist Christian Sch
Newport News, VA

Brighton, Rebecca D
Riverbend HS
Spotsylvania, VA

Bowers, Adrienne
Bethel HS
Hampton, VA

Brenner, Michelle
Osbourn Park SR HS
Manassas, VA

Burke, Robert A
Varina HS
Richmond, VA

BURRAGE, STACY; VIRGINIA BCH, VA; CALVARY CHRISTIAN SCH; (SO); Hi Hnr Roll; Hnr Roll; Perf Att; Sci Fairs; St of Mnth; Comm Volntr; ArtClub; Chrch Yth Grp; DARE; Photog; Svce Clb; Ch Chr; Stg Cre; Bskball (J); Scr Kpr (J); Basketball Manager JV / Poetry Contest / Poetry Published / State Finalist Miss VA Jr Teen Pageant; Beauty School Student / Junior Teen Miss America; Flight Attendant; Cosmetologist; Howard U; Southern State U Baton Rouge

BURRELL, ANTOINE J; KEYSVILLE, VA; RANDOLPH HENRY HS; (SO); Hi Hnr Roll; Hnr Roll; MVP; Otst Ac Ach Awd; Perf Att; Comm Volntr; Peer Tut/Med; 4-H; Chrch Yth Grp; DARE; Emplmnt; FBLA; Scouts; Wdwrkg Clb; Spanish Clb; Bnd; Ch Chr; Ftball (V L); Track (V L); Wt Lftg (V); CR (R); Plan to Go to College on a Football or Track Scholarship; What to Be One of the Best Athletes There Ever Was.

BURRITT, KRISTEN C; CHESAPEAKE, VA; DEEP CREEK HS; (SO); Hnr Roll; MVP; St of Mnth; WWAHSS; Comm Volntr; Chrch Yth Grp; Key Club; P to P St Amb Prg; Bnd; Jzz Bnd; Sftball (JC); Pre-Medical; Virginia Polytechnic Inst and State U

BURTON, CHYNNA M; RICHMOND, VA; JAMES RIVER HS; (SR); Hnr Roll; WWAHSS; Emplmnt; P to P St Amb Prg; Accountant/CPA; Old Dominion U

BUTERA, KRISTINA; VIRGINIA BEACH, VA; FLOYD E KELLAM HS; (SR); Hnr Roll; DECA; P to P St Amb Prg; Quiz Bowl; Elementary Education; Longwood U

BUTLER, REBECCA S; VIRGINIA BEACH, VA; PRINCESS ANNE HS; (SR); DAR; F Lan Hn Soc; Hnr Roll; Comm Volntr; Emplmnt; FBLA; Lib Aide; Quiz Bowl; Svce Clb; Japanese Clb; Optimist Club; Japanese; International Business; Old Dominion U; Georgetown U

BUTLER, SARAH V; ROANOKE, VA; WILLIAM FLEMING HS; (SR); Ctznshp Aw; Hnr Roll; Perf Att; Sci Fairs; Yth Ldrshp Prog; Comm Volntr; Peer Tut/Med; Chrch Yth Grp; Drma Clb; Key Club; Photog; Orch; Stg Cre; Chrldg (J); Tennis (J); Cl Off (R); CR (R); Lit Mag (E); Yrbk (E, P); English Major; History Major; Hollins College; Virginia Western Community College

BUTTAR, MANDEEP S; CENTREVILLE, VA; CENTREVILLE HS; (JR); Hnr Roll; Nat Mrt LOC; Perf Att; Pres Ac Ftns Aw; WWAHSS; Comm Volntr; FBLA; Clb; Ftball (V); Wt Lftg (V); Engineering; Virginia Tech; Virginia Commonwealth U

CALA, JOHN M; ALEXANDRIA, VA; T C WILLIAMS; (SO); Hi Hnr Roll; Emplmnt; Key Club; Bsball (J)

CALDERON, BIANCA K; BLOXOM, VA; ARCADIA HS; (SR); Hnr Roll; Otst Ac Ach Awd; St of Mnth; Hosp Aide; DARE; Emplmnt; Lib Aide; Prom Com; Clb; Chrldg (VJ L); Lit Mag (E, R); PASSS Club; Physical Therapy; Radiology; U of Maryland; Virginia Commonwealth U

CALHOUN, JASMINE N; CLINCHCO, VA; (SR); Hnr Roll; Nat Hon Sy; WWAHSS; Comm Volntr; Chrch Yth Grp; FBLA; FCCLA; Key Club; Sftball (V); Track (V); Criminal Justice; Law Enforcement; Mountain Empire Community College; Southwest Virginia Community College

CAMINOS, DESIREE; FREDERICKSBURG, VA; CHANCELLOR HS; MS; Hnr Roll; Perf Att; Sci Fairs; St of Mnth; Peer Tut/Med; Chrch Yth Grp; DARE; Drma Clb; FCA; Chr; SP/M/VS; Chrldg (JC); Sch Ppr (R); Wrote Proposals for Middle School; Tutored Students for School GPA; Associate's Degree; Majors in Law, Business, Economics; George Washington U; New York U

CAMP, TALAYA R; FREDERICKSBURG, VA; COURTLAND HS; (SO); Hnr Roll; WWAHSS; Emplmnt; FCCLA; SP/M/VS; Historian of FCCLA; 2005 Courtland Leader; Biochemistry; Medicine-Nursing; Hampton U; Old Dominion U

CAMPBELL, BRIAN W; BUENA VISTA, VA; PARRY MC CLUER HS; (SR); Ctznshp Aw; Hnr Roll; Otst Ac Ach Awd; DARE; Photog; Arch; Received Scholastic Patch-2004; HVAC-Completer; Mechanics

CAMPBELL, CARLIE; FREDERICKSBURG, VA; CHANCELLOR HS; (SR); Hnr Roll; Nat Hon Sy; Otst Ac Ach Awd; Comm Volntr; AL Aux Girls; Chrch Yth Grp; FCA; Quill & Scroll; SADD; Bnd; Lit Mag (E); Missionary (World Missions Major); Valley Forge Christian College

CAMPBELL, DANIEL G; GREENVILLE, VA; RIVERHEADS HS; (SR); Ctznshp Aw; Hnr Roll; Otst Ac Ach Awd; Perf Att; Yth Ldrshp Prog; Comm Volntr; Peer Tut/Med; Biology Clb; Emplmnt; Sci Clb; Tchrs Aide; Spanish Clb; Ftball (VJ); WVPT Channel 51 PBS Young Heroes Award; WNLR Radio 1150 AM Student Achievement Award; Biology / Pre-Professional Science; Chemistry / Forensic Science; Ferrum College VA

CAMPBELL, S GABRIELLE; PAMPLIN, VA; RANDOLPH HENRY HS; (SO); Hi Hnr Roll; Hnr Roll; Nat Hon Sy; Otst Ac Ach Awd; St of Mnth; Comm Volntr; Emplmnt; Mth Clb/Tm; Prom Com; Quill & Scroll; Bnd; Jzz Bnd; Mch Bnd; Hsbk Rdg; CR (R); Doctor of Veterinary Science; Virginia Tech

CAPITO, RACHEL; MIDLOTHIAN, VA; MIDLOTHIAN HS; (JR); Hi Hnr Roll; MVP; Chrch Yth Grp; Emplmnt; Quill & Scroll; Svce Clb; Vsity Clb; German Clb; Sccr (V CL); Track (V L); Cl Off (P); Yrbk (E); All-District Soccer Team; Meteorology; U of Virginia; North Carolina State U

CAPPS, ANDREA D; HAMPTON, VA; BETHEL HS; (SO); Ctznshp Aw; Hi Hnr Roll; Hnr Roll; Perf Att; Sci Fairs; St of Mnth; Comm Volntr; Tchrs Aide; Medical Field; Medical College of Virginia; Christopher Newport U

CARBAUGH, ALYSSA; VIRGINIA BEACH, VA; YOUNG MUSICIANS OF VIRGINIA HS; (JR); Hnr Roll; MVP; Comm Volntr; Chrch Yth Grp; Fr of Library; Lib Aide; Off Aide; Bnd; Chr; Ch Chr; Chrldg (V); Swmg; Most Improved Player; Early Childhood Development; Criminal Just; Old Dominion U; Tidewater Community College

CARBONE, THERESA; CHARLOTTESVILLE, VA; ALBEMARLE HS; (SR); Hnr Roll; WWAHSS; Comm Volntr; Chrch Yth Grp; Emplmnt; Jr Cls League; Key Club; Mus Clb; Ntl Beta Clb; Bnd; Chr; Mch Bnd; Pep Bnd; Vice President of Tri-M Music Honor Society; Nursing; Psychology; George Mason U

CARDEN, APRIL E; ALEXANDRIA, VA; T C WILLIAMS HS; (JR); Ctznshp Aw; Comm Volntr; Emplmnt; Training to Become a Child Educator; Won Many Art Awards; Cosmetology; Social Work; Northern Virginia Community College; Chowan College

CARL, JACLYN P; ROANOKE, VA; PATRICK HENRY HS; (JR); Gov Hnr Prg; Hi Hnr Roll; Perf Att; WWAHSS; Comm Volntr; Emplmnt; Key Club; Scouts; Sftball (J); Swmg (V); Vllyball (V); Key Club-PR and Board Member; Girl Scouts

CARLSON, KRISTEN N; CHESAPEAKE, VA; HICKORY HS; (SO); Hnr Roll; St of Mnth; DECA; Orch; DECA National Competition - Districts / States; Entrepreneurship; French; Old Dominion U; Virginia Wesleyan U

CARNES, KATIE; CHANTILLY, VA; BROAD RUN HS; (FR); Ctznshp Aw; Hi Hnr Roll; Otst Ac Ach Awd; Sci Fairs; Comm Volntr; Hab For Humty Volntr; Hosp Aide; Chrch Yth Grp; Dbte Team; Scouts; Tennis (V L); Stu Cncl (S); Doctor / Neonatologist; International Politician; Pennsylvania State U; Johns Hopkins U

CARON, MATTHEW G; CHESAPEAKE, VA; WESTERN BRANCH HS; (SO); Hi Hnr Roll; Hnr Roll; Otst Ac Ach Awd; Perf Att; St of Mnth; Yth Ldrshp Prog; Peer Tut/Med; Chrch Yth Grp; Drma Clb; Mus Clb; Photog; Orch; SP/M/VS; Stg Cre; All-City Orchestra; Regional Orchestra; Film Directing; Writing; Savannah College of Arts and Design; New York U

CARR, ASHLEY; LANEXA, VA; LAFAYETTE HS; (SR); Chrch Yth Grp; Ch Chr; Dnce; Design; Art Education; Pratt Community College; Thomas Nelson Community College

CARR, DASHANNA; NATHALIE, VA; HALIFAX CTY HS; (JR); Ctznshp Aw; Hi Hnr Roll; Otst Ac Ach Awd; Perf Att; Pres Ac Ftns Aw; Pres Sch; St of Mnth; Peer Tut/Med; FBLA; Mus Clb; NYLC; Pep Squd; Prom Com; Acpl Chr; Chr; Dnce; PPSqd (V); CR (R); Education; Music Arts; Longwood U; Virginia Commonwealth U

CARROLL, RACHEL; PORTSMOUTH, VA; STONEBRIDGE SCH; (JR); Hnr Roll; Nat Hon Sy; Hosp Aide; Emplmnt; Key Club; Sftball (V); Vllyball (V); CR (S); Nursing

CARROLL, THOMAS B; ALEXANDRIA, VA; T.C. WILLIAMS; (SO); Ctznshp Aw; Hi Hnr Roll; Hnr Roll; Pres Ac Ftns Aw; Sci Fairs; WWAHSS; Yth Ldrshp Prog; Key Club; Bsball (VJ L); Golf (V L)

CARROLL IV, F ANDREW; ALEXANDRIA, VA; T C WILLIAMS HS; (JR); Hi Hnr Roll; Hnr Roll; Nat Hon Sy; Pres Ac Ftns Aw; WWAHSS; Yth Ldrshp Prog; Key Club; Bsball (VJ L); Golf (V CL); Swmg (V L); Business; Engineering; William & Mary College; Emory U

CARTER, AMANDA; HAYMARKET, VA; OSBOURN PARK SR HS; (JR); Hnr Roll; Nat Hon Sy; WWAHSS; Peer Tut/Med; DECA; Emplmnt; FBLA; Key Club; Play Piano; Began Mentoring Program for Elementary-Aged Kids; Elementary Education

CARTER, JARVIS; MARTINSVILLE, VA; MARTINSVILLE HS; (SO); Ch Chr; Track (J); National Society of Black Engineers; Bowling Club / National Society of High School Scholars; Film / Dramatic Arts; A & T State; Virginia State

CARTER, JUSTIN R; MARTINSVILLE, VA; MAGNA VISTA HS; (JR); Ctznshp Aw; Hnr Roll; Nat Hon Sy; Perf Att; Comm Volntr; 4-H; Chrch Yth Grp; FBLA; Ntl Beta Clb; Ntl FFA; Scouts; French Clb; Cr Ctry (V); Computer Technology; Health Care; Radford U; James Madison U

CARTER, MICHAEL; HILTONS, VA; GATE CITY HS; (JR); Hnr Roll; Nat Hon Sy; WWAHSS; Comm Volntr; Peer Tut/Med; Key Club; Golf (V); Track (J); Cl Off (T); AIM Scholar; Dermatology; Virginia Tech

CARTER, RICKY D; DRYDEN, VA; LEE HS; (JR); 4H Awd; Hnr Roll; Jr Eng Tech; Sci Fairs; Yth Ldrshp Prog; CARE; Comm Volntr; Hab For Humty Volntr; 4-H; AL Aux Boys; Biology Clb; Civil Air Pat; DARE; DECA; Emplmnt; FBLA; Clr Grd; Drl Tm; Stg Cre; Ftball (J); Hsbk Rdg (J); Wt Lftg (J); Adv Cncl (R); Cl Off (V); Stu Cncl (R); CR (S); Yrbk (P); Awarded ROTC Medal; Join Military; Military Science; Virginia Military Institute

CARTY, COLLEEN; FAIRFAX, VA; (FR); Hnr Roll; MVP; Nat Sci Aw; Sci Fairs; St of Mnth; Photog; Scouts; Vllyball (J); CR (R); Select/Travel Softball; House League Basketball; Virginia Tech; U of Virginia

CARUSO, KATHERINE; GREAT FALLS, VA; TLC/CORTONA AC; (JR); Hnr Roll; Comm Volntr; Chrch Yth Grp; Emplmnt; Key Club; P to P St Amb Prg; Scouts; Chrldg (V); National Society of High School Scholars; American Heritage Award; Acting; Law; Stanford; Yale

CASE, ASHLEY E; LYNCHBURG, VA; E C GLASS HS; (SR); Nat Hon Sy; St of Mnth; WWAHSS; Key Club; Mth Clb/Tm; Prom Com; Spanish Clb; Dnce; Track (V); Medical Career; U of Virginia

CASERO, OLIVA; PALMYRA, VA; FLUVANNA CTY HS; (JR); Hi Hnr Roll; Hnr Roll; Otst Ac Ach Awd; Perf Att; Pres Ac Ftns Aw; Comm Volntr; Chrch Yth Grp; Key Club; Ntl Beta Clb; NYLC; P to P St Amb Prg; Prom Com; Quiz Bowl; Dnce; SP/M/VS; Chrldg (V C); Tennis (V C); Elementary Education; Political Science; Winthrop U; Virginia Wesleyan

CASILLAS, CARLOS; CULPEPER, VA; CULPEPER CTY HS; (JR); Hnr Roll; Perf Att; Pres Ac Ftns Aw; Chess; Drma Clb; Emplmnt; Jzz Bnd; SP/M/VS; CR (P); Telecommunications; Music; James Madison U; George Mason U

CASTELLOW, CHARLOTTE E; HAMPTON, VA; HAMPTON CHRISTIAN HS; (SR); Ctznshp Aw; Hi Hnr Roll; Otst Ac Ach Awd; Perf Att; Pres Ac Ftns Aw; Pres Sch; USAA; WWAHSS; Comm Volntr; Chrch Yth Grp; Drma Clb; Emplmnt; Ntl Beta Clb; Off Aide; SP/M/VS; Bible; Intercultural Studies; Columbia International U

CASTILLO, STEPHANIE; HAMPTON, VA; BETHEL HS; (SO); Hnr Roll; ROTC; Sccr (J); President's Academic Award; National Junior Honor Society; Journalism; Hampton U; U of Virginia

CATALDI, CHRISTOPHER; MIDLOTHIAN, VA; (SR); Hi Hnr Roll; Hnr Roll; WWAHSS; Latin Clb; Bnd; Lifeguard YMCA; Classical Guitar 12 Yrs.; Pre-Law; Psychology; Hampton-Sydney College; UVA

CATON, MICHAEL A; LEESBURG, VA; HOME SCH/HERITAGE HS; (SO); 4H Awd; Hi Hnr Roll; Otst Ac Ach Awd; Sci Fairs; St of Mnth; Valdctrian; Comm Volntr; Red Cr Aide; 4-H; ArtClub; Chrch Yth Grp; Drma Clb; FCA; P to P St Amb Prg; Scouts; German Clb; SP/M/VS; Stg Cre; Swmg (V L); Meritorious Action Medal for Saving a Life, Given from Boy Scouts; Programming; Government; Massachusetts Institute of Technology; Rochester Institute of Technology

CAUDILL, DESIREE; FREDERICKSBURG, VA; (SO); All Am Sch; Hnr Roll; WWAHSS; Comm Volntr; DARE; Key Club; French Clb; Key Club Member; James Monroe Scholar; Psychology; Anatomy; Virginia Tech, UV, Roanoke, Radford, JNW, Christopher Newport

CAVANO, MATTHEW C; CHESAPEAKE, VA; WESTERN BRANCH HS; (SO); Bnd; Drm Mjr; Jzz Bnd; Mch Bnd; Principal Horn for the Virginia Youth Symphony Orchestra; Principal Horn for the Hampton Roads Youth Wind Ensemble; Music; Architecture; Yale U; Michigan State U

CAYLOR, MEGHAN; LYNCHBURG, VA; EC GLASS HS; (SO); Hi Hnr Roll; Hnr Roll; WWAHSS; Hab For Humty Volntr; Spec Olymp Vol; Key Club; French Clb; Sccr (V); Cl Off (T); Yrbk (R); Medical Field-Nurse Practitioner; Business

CENTRA, MARCUS; CENTREVILLE, VA; WESTFIELD HS; (JR); Hnr Roll; Comm Volntr; SP/M/VS; Stg Cre; Honor Roll Every Quarter Except for One; Criminal Justice; Law Enforcement; Indiana U of PA; Penn State U of P.A.

CHACKO, LAUREN; SUFFOLK, VA; STONE BRIDGE SCH; (JR); Hi Hnr Roll; Hnr Roll; Nat Hon Sy; Sci Fairs; Comm Volntr; Hosp Aide; Peer Tut/Med; Chrch Yth Grp; Emplmnt; Key Club; Chr; Dnce; SP/M/VS; Tennis (J); CR; Multiple 1st / 2nd and 3rd Place Art Awards; Language Arts; Grove City College; Hillsdale College

CHANDLER, JUDAH D; FALLS CHURCH, VA; GEORGE MASON HS; (SO); WWAHSS; Comm Volntr; Peer Tut/Med; Chrch Yth Grp; Bskball (J); Ftball (V L); Mr. Sophomore Homecoming; AAU Basketball-Fairfax Stars; Veterinarian; Florida A & M U; Morehouse College

CHANG, SZE; ALEXANDRIA, VA; THOMAS A EDISON HS; (JR); F Lan Hn Soc; Hnr Roll; Nat Hon Sy; Perf Att; St of Mnth; FBLA; Key Club; Mth Clb/Tm; Mod UN; MuAlphaTh; Sci Clb; French Clb; Club Volleyball; Business (General); Finance; U of Virginia; New York U

CHANNA, BALTEJ S; CHESAPEAKE, VA; DEEP CREEK HS; (SO); Key Club; Computer Software Engineering; Web Designing; U of Virginia; Old Dominion U

Caylor, Meghan
Ec Glass HS
Lynchburg, VA

Caruso, Katherine
Tlc/Cortona AC
Great Falls, VA

Campbell, S Gabrielle
Randolph Henry HS
Pamplin, VA

Caminos, Desiree
Chancellor HS
Fredericksburg, VA

Burrage, Stacy
Calvary Christian Sch
Virginia Bch, VA

Burton, Chynna M
James River HS
Richmond, VA

Carter, Ricky D
Lee HS
Dryden, VA

Caton, Michael A
Home Sch/Heritage HS
Leesburg, VA

Chacko, Lauren
Stone Bridge Sch
Suffolk, VA

CHARALAMBOUS, ALEXANDRA; VIRGINIA BEACH, VA; FIRST COLONIAL HS; (FR); Kwnis Aw; St of Mnth; WWAHSS; Comm Volntr; Peer Tut/Med; Spec Olymp Vol; Chrch Yth Grp; Dbte Team; Key Club; Mth Clb/Tm; Gmnstcs (V L); Sccr (J L); U of Virginia

CHAWLA, NEETY; ASHBURN, VA; BROAD RUN HS; (SO); All Am Sch; Ctznshp Aw; Hi Hnr Roll; Hnr Roll; Otst Ac Ach Awd; Pres Ac Ftns Aw; Comm Volntr; Key Club; Prom Com; Dnce; Track (J); Cl Off (T); Stu Cncl (R); Certified in First Aid; Medical Degree; U of California Berkeley; U of Virginia

CHAWLA, RAVEEN; CENTREVILLE, VA; CENTREVILLE HS; (JR); F Lan Hn Soc; Hnr Roll; Nat Hon Sy; Otst Ac Ach Awd; WWAHSS; FBLA; Key Club; Mth Clb/Tm; Spanish Clb; Tennis (V); Biology; Cardiologist; Virginia Commonwealth U; U of Virginia

CHEBOLU, ADITYA; STERLING, VA; BROCO RUN HS; (SO); Comm Volntr; Peer Tut/Med; Dbte Team; Scouts; Bskball; Played in the House League; Engineering; Virginia Tech; U of VA

CHEESEBORO, LATESHA R; HAMPTON, VA; BETHEL HS; (SO); All Am Sch; Ctznshp Aw; Hnr Roll; USAA; Chrch Yth Grp; Acpl Chr; Chr; Ch Chr; Dnce; United States Academic Scholars; Old Dominion U

CHEN, XIA; STUART, VA; PATRICK CO HS; (JR); Emplmnt; Mth Clb/Tm; Spanish Clb

CHENG, KAI Y; ALEXANDRIA, VA; EPISCOPAL HS; (SR); Hnr Roll; Sci Fairs; Yth Ldrshp Prog; Comm Volntr; Spec Olymp Vol; Emplmnt; Tchrs Aide; Dnce; Bskball (L); Track (V); Vllyball; Yrbk (R, P); Psychology; Business; Syracuse U

CHENG, LANCE C; VIENNA, VA; MARSHALL HS; (FR); Ctznshp Aw; Hnr Roll; Nat Hon Sy; Nat Stu Ath Day Aw; Pres Ac Ftns Aw; Sci/Math Olympn; St of Mnth; WWAHSS; Yth Ldrshp Prog; Comm Volntr; NYLC; Cr Ctry (J); Track (V); Competed in Brain Bee Competition; Attorney; Medical Doctor; U of Virginia; Yale U

CHILDS, KARIS A; YORKTOWN, VA; HAMPTON CHRISTIAN HS; (SO); Ctznshp Aw; Hi Hnr Roll; Otst Ac Ach Awd; Perf Att; Pres Ac Ftns Aw; Comm Volntr; Ntl Beta Clb; Orch; Chrldg (V); Gmnstcs (V); Yrbk (E); Gymnastics-10 Years; Law; Medicine

CHO, JULIETTE; HAYMARKET, VA; BATTLEFIELD HS; (JR); F Lan Hn Soc; Hnr Roll; Nat Hon Sy; Nat Ldrshp Svc; Otst Ac Ach Awd; Perf Att; Pres Sch; Sci Fairs; Yth Ldrshp Prog; Comm Volntr; Peer Tut/Med; FCA; Key Club; Lttrmn Clb; Mod UN; NYLC; P to P St Amb Prg; Quill & Scroll; French Clb; Sch Ppr (E); Journalism Student of the Year - 2003-2004 / 2004-2005; History Student of the Year 2004-2005; Political Science / Political Law; Journalism; University of Virginia; University of Michigan

CHOI, NAK; CHARLOTTESVILLE, VA; ALBEMARLE HS; (JR); F Lan Hn Soc; Hi Hnr Roll; Hnr Roll; Nat Hon Sy; Perf Att; Sci Fairs; Comm Volntr; Hab For Humty Volntr; Peer Tut/Med; Chrch Yth Grp; Emplmnt; Jr Cls League; Key Club; Mth Clb/Tm; MuAlphaTh; Mus Clb; Ntl Beta Clb; Bnd; Ch Chr; Cr Ctry (J); Tennis (V L); Cl Off (T); Stu Cncl (T); National Latin Assessment-Gold Medal; Band-District Band (Qualified for State); Biomedical Engineering; Neuroscience; U of Virginia; Cornell U

CHOUDHURY, TASLIMA; LORTON, VA; HAYFIELD SECONDARY SCH; (JR); F Lan Hn Soc; Hnr Roll; Nat Hon Sy; Otst Ac Ach Awd; Sci Fairs; Yth Ldrshp Prog; Comm Volntr; Hab For Humty Volntr; Peer Tut/Med; Quill & Scroll; Sci Clb; Spanish Clb; Sch Ppr (E); 2nd Place at Regional Science Fair 2004-2005; Recognition from Chemical Society of Washington; MBA / 5-Year Program; Biology / 2nd Major; Georgetown U; U of Virginia

CHOWDHURY, AFSANA; LEESBURG, VA; HERITAGE HS; (SR); F Lan Hn Soc; Gov Hnr Prg; Hnr Roll; Nat Hon Sy; Otst Ac Ach Awd; St of Mnth; Comm Volntr; Peer Tut/Med; DECA; Emplmnt; FBLA; Key Club; Off Aide; Svce Clb; Spanish Clb; Dnce; Stu Cncl (T, R); 2004 Spanish Governor's Academy; 2004 Loudoun Co. Bar Association's Law Camp; Political Science; Business; Virginia Polytechnic Institute; College of William & Mary

CHRISTIANSEN, ALEXANDRA; MANASSAS, VA; OSBORN PARK HS; (SR); Nat Hon Sy; WWAHSS; Comm Volntr; Spec Olymp Vol; BPA; Chrch Yth Grp; FBLA; Key Club; Physical Therapist; Shenandoah U

CHUMBLE, ANUJA; MARTINSVILLE, VA; MARTINSVILLE HS; (FR); All Am Sch; Hnr Roll; Comm Volntr; FBLA; Key Club; Ntl Beta Clb; Bnd; Dnce; Mch Bnd; Stg Cre; Swmg (V L); Tennis (V L); CR (R); Political Science; Pre-Law; U of Virginia; Wake Forest U

CHUNG, PETER; VIRGINIA BEACH, VA; FRANK W COX HS; (SO); Hnr Roll; Perf Att; Comm Volntr; Peer Tut/Med; Chess; Cmptr Clb; Key Club; Photog; Golf; Tennis (V); Business; Medical; Virginia Tech; James Madison U

CHUNG, THERESA; POQUOSON, VA; POQUOSON HS; (JR); MVP; Nat Hon Sy; Pres Ac Ftns Aw; WWAHSS; Comm Volntr; Spec Olymp Vol; AL Aux Girls; Chrch Yth Grp; FBLA; Key Club; Quill & Scroll; SADD; Dnce; Swmg (V L); Cl Off (S); Yrbk (E); Most Valuable Swimmer; High Point Swimmer; Major in History; Major in Law; West Point; Bucknell

CLAPP, CHRISTEN E; CHESTERFIELD, VA; LLOYD C BIRD HS; (SR); F Lan Hn Soc; Hi Hnr Roll; Jr Mshl; Nat Hon Sy; Nat Mrt Fin; Otst Ac Ach Awd; Perf Att; Pres Sch; Sci Fairs; Valdctrian; Peer Tut/Med; Emplmnt; Key Club; MuAlphaTh; Svce Clb; Tchrs Aide; Stu Cncl (R); Presidential Scholarship; Nursing; U of Virginia; Virginia Commonwealth U

CLARK, ASHLEY; ROANOKE, VA; PATRICK HENRY HS; (SR); Hnr Roll; Otst Ac Ach Awd; Chrch Yth Grp; Off Aide; Photog; Ch Chr; Chrldg (J); Volunteered At Democratic Headquarters; Member At Church Mission Team (L.I.G.H.T.); Psychology; Radford U; Ferrum College

CLARK, CASSANDRA M; VIRGINIA BCH, VA; KEMPSVILLE HS; (SR); Hnr Roll; Peer Tut/Med; Emplmnt; FBLA; Photog; Business; Real Estate; Old Dominion U

CLARK, MADELEINE; GREAT FALLS, VA; LANGLEY HS; (JR); F Lan Hn Soc; Hi Hnr Roll; Hnr Roll; MVP; Nat Hon Sy; Pres Ac Ftns Aw; WWAHSS; Chrch Yth Grp; Emplmnt; Key Club; Cr Ctry (V L); Track (V L); U of North Carolina-Chapel Hill; U of Virginia

CLARK, MATTHEW E; NORFOLK, VA; LAKE TAYLOR HS; (JR); Hnr Roll; Nat Hon Sy; Perf Att; St of Mnth; WWAHSS; Yth Ldrshp Prog; Comm Volntr; Peer Tut/Med; Bsball (J); Bskball (J); Ftball (J); Sch Ppr (E); Youth Leader for YABA Bowling Program; Youth Coach for 5/6 yr Old T-Ball Team; Tidewater Community College - Norfolk Campus

CLAYTON, CHASITY C; ALEXANDRIA, VA; BISHOP DENIS J O'CONNELL HS; (FR); Hnr Roll; MVP; Nat Stu Ath Day Aw; Comm Volntr; Bskball (V); Yrbk (P); Freshman - Proud Leader Around School; Medical Field / Cardiologist; Medical Field / Obstetrician; Tennessee State; Duke U

CLEMENTS, BRITTENY; HURT, VA; GRETNA HS; (JR); Hnr Roll; MVP; Perf Att; Pres Ac Ftns Aw; Comm Volntr; Hab For Humty Volntr; FCCLA; Lttrmn Clb; Photog; Sci Clb; SADD; Vsity Clb; Spanish Clb; Bskball (V C); Cr Ctry (V C); Track (V CL); CR (P); Yrbk (P); Fastest girl on Track Team; Homecoming Court Rep; Clinical Laboratory Science; PhD; U of North Carolina; James Madison U

CLEMENTS II, ANDREW R; NORTH GARDEN, VA; MONTICELLO HS; (JR); Comm Volntr; Chrch Yth Grp; Bsball (J); Cr Ctry (J); Wrstlg (V L); Junior Fire Fighter; Police Science; Radford U; PU CC

CLINTON, KIMBERLY; FREDERICKSBURG, VA; STAFFORD HS; (JR); Hi Hnr Roll; Otst Ac Ach Awd; Perf Att; Yth Ldrshp Prog; Comm Volntr; Chrch Yth Grp; DARE; DECA; Emplmnt; FBLA; Scouts; Chr; Ch Chr; Drl Tm; Scr Kpr (V); Vllyball (V); Yrbk (P); Pre-Medicine; Business; Virginia State U; Virginia Commonwealth U

CLIPPARD, JAMES; ARARAT, VA; PATRICK CTY HS; (SO); Hi Hnr Roll; Hnr Roll; Perf Att; WWAHSS; Red Cr Aide; Mth Clb/Tm; Ntl Beta Clb; ROTC; Tennis (V); SAL Leadership Award; Automotive Engineering; Universal Technical Institute; U of North Carolina

CLOUSE, HANNAH R; ASHBURN, VA; STONE BRIDGE HS; (FR); Hi Hnr Roll; Otst Ac Ach Awd; Sci Fairs; Comm Volntr; Chrch Yth Grp; Key Club; Mus Clb; Foreign Clb; Chr; CR (R); 2nd Place Division Science Fair; Perfect Score SOL Math; Business Major; College of William and Mary-Virginia; James Madison U-Virginia

COATES, BRYNN L; VIRGINIA BEACH, VA; FRANK W COX HS; (SO); Ctznshp Aw; F Lan Hn Soc; Kwnis Aw; Nat Hon Sy; Perf Att; St of Mnth; Sftball (J L); Adv Cncl (R); Cl Off (R); Stu Cncl (R); CR (R); Sophomore Class Historian; Reflections Visual Arts 1st Place; Education; Studio Art; William and Mary College; U of North Carolina

COBB, MARCUS E; PATRICK SPRINGS, VA; PATRICK CTY HS; (SO); Ctznshp Aw; Gov Hnr Prg; Hi Hnr Roll; Hnr Roll; Perf Att; Pres Ac Ftns Aw; Pres Sch; WWAHSS; DARE; Ntl Beta Clb; Bskball (J); Bachelor's, Major, Doctorate; U of Virginia; U of Florida

COBLE, SHANNON; ASHBURN, VA; STONE BRIDGE HS; (JR); Hnr Roll; Pres Ac Ftns Aw; Comm Volntr; Hab For Humty Volntr; FBLA; Bskball (V L); Track (V L); Manager for Freshman Boys' Basketball; Business; Sports Management; Radford U; Old Dominion U

CODY, ERYN; MANASSAS, VA; OSBOURN PARK SR HS; (SO); Hnr Roll; Sci Fairs; WWAHSS; Chrch Yth Grp; Key Club; Pep Squd; Dnce; PPSqd; Gold & Platinum Competition Dance Winner; Dance Team Captain-8th Grade

CODY SEXTON, ADAM E; ROANOKE, VA; NORTHSIDE HS; (SO); Hi Hnr Roll; Nat Hon Sy; Sci Fairs; WWAHSS; Comm Volntr; Peer Tut/Med; Chrch Yth Grp; Key Club; Quiz Bowl; Spanish Clb; Stu Cncl (V); Lit Mag (R); U of Virginia

COLE, JESSICA; RICHMOND, VA; JOHN F KENNEDY HS; (SR); Hnr Roll; Perf Att; Comm Volntr; Emplmnt; FBLA; Off Aide; Chr; Computer Information Systems; Virginia Commonwealth U; Old Dominion U

COLE, KENZIE; LYNCHBURG, VA; E C GLASS HS; (FR); Hnr Roll; Comm Volntr; Peer Tut/Med; Chrch Yth Grp; Key Club; Lib Aide; Scouts; Svce Clb; Chr; SP/M/VS; Stg Cre; Girl Scout: Silver Award & Leadership Award; Special Education Teacher; School Psychologist; Liberty U

COLEMAN, ERICA D; JAMAICA, VA; MIDDLESEX HS; (FR); Ctznshp Aw; Hnr Roll; Perf Att; Comm Volntr; FBLA; Future Business Leaders of America - FBLA; Biologist; Social Worker; Virginia Commonwealth U; Sergeant Reynolds College

COLES, KIARRIA; RICHMOND, VA; HENRICO HS; (SO); MVP; Perf Att; Yth Ldrshp Prog; Comm Volntr; Chrch Yth Grp; DARE; FCA; Fr of Library; FBLA; P to P St Amb Prg; Bskball (V); Cr Ctry (J); GAA (J); Track (V); Virginia State U; St Augustine's College

COLGAN, MEREDITH; VIRGINIA BEACH, VA; FRANK W COX HS; (JR); Hi Hnr Roll; Hnr Roll; Perf Att; St of Mnth; Chrch Yth Grp; Key Club; Scouts; Dnce; SP/M/VS; Hsbk Rdg; Swmg; Nursing; Education; Virginia Wesleyan College; Tidewater Community College

COLLINS, BROOKE; NORTON, VA; APPALACHIA HS; (SO); Sftball (J); Active in Church Youth; Nurse Practitioner; Radford U; UVA Wise

COLLINS, KATIE; CHARLOTTESVILLE, VA; ALBEMARLE HS; (JR); Hnr Roll; Kwnis Aw; WWAHSS; Peer Tut/Med; Key Club; Fld Hky (J); Cl Off (R); YMCA Volunteer for Girls Basketball Team; Peer Counselor At Albemarle HS / National Art Honor Society; Architecture; Virginia Tech

COLLINS, KEITH D; EXMORE, VA; NORTHAMPTON HS; (SR); Ctznshp Aw; Hnr Roll; Perf Att; Emplmnt; Cooking School

CONNER, ASHANTA M; RICHMOND, VA; ARMSTRONG HS; (FR); Hi Hnr Roll; Hnr Roll; Perf Att; Yth Ldrshp Prog; Wildcats Leadership; Forensics Club; Theatre; Communications; Spelman College; U of Kentucky

CONNER, HOLLEY; ALTON, VA; HALIFAX CTY HS; (JR); Hnr Roll; Yth Ldrshp Prog; Chrch Yth Grp; Emplmnt; NYLC; Vllyball (V); Piano (10 Years); Automotive Mechanics; Auto Body Repair

CONNOLLY, TROY; WOODBRIDGE, VA; WOODBRIDGE HS; (JR); DARE; FBLA; Computer Science; Virginia Tech; Virginia

CONNORS, CHRISTINE; FAIRFAX, VA; ROBINSON SECONDARY SCH; (SR); F Lan Hn Soc; Hi Hnr Roll; Hnr Roll; Nat Hon Sy; Valdctrian; WWAHSS; Comm Volntr; Peer Tut/Med; DECA; FBLA; MuAlphaTh; Cr Ctry (V L); Track (V L); Student of the Quarter; Academic Letter Recipient; International Business; Economics; James Madison U

CONTEH, JALIKA; CHESAPEAKE, VA; DEEP CREEK HS; (JR); Hnr Roll; Kwnis Aw; Perf Att; Key Club; Sch Ppr (R); Young Author's Achievement Award; Journalism; Creative Writing

CONVY, ALLISON; VIENNA, VA; JAMES MADISON HS; St of Mnth; DECA; Emplmnt; FCA; SADD; Vsity Clb; Dnce; Drl Tm; Vsy Clb (V CL); 2005-2006 JMHS DECA President; 2005-2006 Varsity Crew Captain; Sports Marketing; Public Relations; U of Georgia; College of Charleston

COOGLE, LAUREN; ASHBURN, VA; STONE BRIDGE HS; (JR); F Lan Hn Soc; Hi Hnr Roll; Jr Rot; Nat Hon Sy; Perf Att; Pres Ac Ftns Aw; Sci Fairs; Yth Ldrshp Prog; Hosp Aide; Chrch Yth Grp; Jr Cls League; Key Club; NYLC; Tchrs Aide; Bnd; Chrldg (V L); Cl Off (S); Stu Cncl (R); Neuroscience; Pre-Med; Georgia Institute of Technology; U of Virginia

COOK, KRISTEN; CHESAPEAKE, VA; OSCAR FROMMEL SMITH HS; (JR); Hi Hnr Roll; Nat Hon Sy; Nat Mrt LOC; Pres Ac Ftns Aw; WWAHSS; Hosp Aide; Peer Tut/Med; Key Club; NYLC; Gmnstcs (V L); Sccr (V); Tennis (V L); Track (V L); Vllyball (J); Stu Cncl (V); Doctor; U of Florida

COOK PJ, PRESTON B; MONTROSS, VA; WASHINGTON & LEE SR HS; (FR); Hnr Roll; Peer Tut/Med; Chrch Yth Grp; Bnd; Ch Chr; Mch Bnd; Ftball (J); Track (J); Wt Lftg; James Farmer Scholars; Law, Criminal Justice; Medicine, Business; Virginia State U; James Madison U

COOPER, BRYATT; FORT EUSTIS, VA; WOODSIDE HS; (SR); Hnr Roll; MVP; Nat Hon Sy; Pres Ac Ftns Aw; Peer Tut/Med; DECA; Emplmnt; FBLA; Ntl Beta Clb; ROTC; Ftball (V); Track (V); Wt Lftg (V); Varsity Letter, Football and Track; Architecture; Hampton U, Hampton Virginia

COOPER, KAKILA S; DANVILLE, VA; GEORGE WASHINGTON HS; (SR); Hnr Roll; Nat Hon Sy; Comm Volntr; FBLA; Key Club; Prom Com; French Clb; Stu Cncl (R); CR (R); Bachelor's In Marketing; Bachelor's In Advertising; Old Dominion U; Virginia Commonwealth U

CORDLE, BRADLEY; RAVEN, VA; RICHLANDS HS; (SO); Hnr Roll; MVP; Nat Hon Sy; WWAHSS; Comm Volntr; 4-H; DARE; DECA; Ntl FFA; ROTC; Ch Chr; Pharmacy

CORDOVA, FATIMA; ROANOKE, VA; WILLIAM FLEMING HS; (SO); Hnr Roll; Sci Fairs; Comm Volntr; Hosp Aide; Peer Tut/Med; Mus Clb; Scouts; Adv Cncl (V); Stu Cncl (R); Youth Court, Vice President; Piano Player with Awards.; Criminal Justice; Sociology; Washington & Lee; U of California of San Barbara

Cole, Kenzie, E C Glass HS, Lynchburg, VA — Cody, Eryn, Osbourn Park SR HS, Manassas, VA — Chowdhury, Afsana, Heritage HS, Leesburg, VA — Cobb, Marcus E, Patrick Cty HS, Patrick Springs, VA — Collins, Keith D, Northampton HS, Exmore, VA

CORNELL, ALLISON E; CHARLOTTESVILLE, VA; ALBEMARLE HS; (FR); Hnr Roll; Otst Ac Ach Awd; Comm Volntr; Chrch Yth Grp; Key Club; Bnd; Veterinary Medicine; Virginia Tech

CORNELL, CRISTINA M; CHARLOTTESVILLE, VA; ALBEMARLE HS; (JR); F Lan Hn Soc; Hnr Roll; Otst Ac Ach Awd; Key Club; Bnd; PP Ftbl (V); Track (V); Math Honor Society; Environmental Science; Psychology; Virginia Tech; Mary Washington U

CORONA, ANNA; WOODBRIDGE, VA; C D HYLTON HS; (FR); Hi Hnr Roll; Hnr Roll; Bskball (C); CR (R); Medicine; U of Virginia; Virginia Tech

CORPREW, TIARA; NORFOLK, VA; GRANBY HS; (SR); Hnr Roll; Perf Att; St of Mnth; Business / Modeling; Performing Arts / Theater Dancing; Tidewater Community College; Out of State College

CORRELL, RAHEEN; NEWPORT NEWS, VA; WOODSIDE HS; (JR); Ctznshp Aw; Hnr Roll; CARE; Comm Volntr; Peer Tut/Med; DARE; Drma Clb; Lib Aide; Off Aide; Spanish Clb; SP/M/VS; Bskball (J); Ftball (J); Wt Lftg (J); Actor, Modeling, Filming; Medical, Actor, Drama, Modeling; Engineering Technology; Morehouse U; Bridgewater Point U

CORRIGAN, KEENAN; CHESAPEAKE, VA; WESTERN BRANCH HS; (SO); Hi Hnr Roll; Hnr Roll; Pres Ac Ftns Aw; Valdctrian; Yth Ldrshp Prog; Comm Volntr; Emplmnt; Off Aide; Scouts; Spanish Clb; Bskball (JC); Sftball (J); Tennis (V); Cl Off (P); Stu Cncl; CR (P); Girl Scout Silver Award; Girl Scout Community Service Bar; International Studies; Political Science; Duke U; Wake Forest

CORTES, RAYMOND P; ASBURN, VA; HAYFIELD SECONDARY SCH; (SR); Hnr Roll; Participated in High School Diplomat Program 2003-2004; Business; Psychology; George Mason U

COURTNEY, SHANNON; CHESAPEAKE, VA; WESTERN BRANCH HS; (FR); Ctznshp Aw; Hnr Roll; Nat Hon Sy; Otst Ac Ach Awd; Perf Att; Ch Chr; Optometry; Criminal Justice; U of Virginia; Hampton U

COYNE, SHANNON; STERLING, VA; POTOMAC FALLS HS; (SO); Hnr Roll; Otst Ac Ach Awd; ArtClub; Key Club; Chrldg (V L); Scer (J); CR (R); AP Courses; Freshmen All-Star; Advertising; Sports Medicine; Duke U; U of Virginia

COYNER, TOBY; CHURCHVILLE, VA; BUFFALO GAP HS; (SR); Hi Hnr Roll; Nat Hon Sy; Otst Ac Ach Awd; Perf Att; Comm Volntr; Hab For Humty Volntr; Chrch Yth Grp; Emplmnt; FCA; Lttrmn Clb; Ntl FFA; Sci Clb; Vsity Clb; Voc Ind Clb Am; Bskball (J); Ftball (VJ L); Track (V); Vsy Clb (VJ L); Wt Lftg (VJ); Wrstlg (J); Academic Excellence 2003-2004; Advanced Studies Diploma 2005; Wildlife Science; Forestry; Virginia Tech

COYNER, TRAVIS R; STAUNTON, VA; RIVERHEADS HS; (FR); Ctznshp Aw; Hi Hnr Roll; Otst Ac Ach Awd; Chrch Yth Grp; Mus Clb; Chr; Ch Chr; Tennis (V); Stu Cncl (P, R); CR (R); Yrbk (E, P); Member of District Youth; Member of Admin Council at Church; Business & Accounting; Computer Specialist; Virginia Polytechnic Institute; James Madison U

COZZENS, LAUREN N; GREAT FALLS, VA; (JR); Hnr Roll; MVP; Nat Hon Sy; Pres Ac Ftns Aw; Pres Sch; Sci Fairs; WWAHSS; Yth Ldrshp Prog; Comm Volntr; Peer Tut/Med; AL Aux Girls; Chrch Yth Grp; Key Club; Mth Clb/Tm; Mus Clb; Scouts; Svce Clb; Clb; Acpl Chr; Chr; Ch Chr; Dnce; Bskball (J); Cr Ctry (V CL); PP Ftbl (V); Swmg (V CL); Track (V L); Library Volunteer; Leadership in Sports Award; Orthodontist; Archaeologist; Stanford U; BYU

CRAIG, LAUREN; OAKTON, VA; FLINT HILL SCH; (SR); Hi Hnr Roll; Hnr Roll; Hab For Humty Volntr; Peer Tut/Med; Biology Clb; Mus Clb; Pep Squd; Prom Com; Scouts; Vsity Clb; Acpl Chr; Lcrsse (V L); Sccr (V L); Cl Off (R); CR (V); National Youth Leadership Forum on Medicine; Biology; Marketing; U of Virginia

CRAUN, STEFANIE E; RESTON, VA; SOUTH LAKES HS; (JR); Hnr Roll; Otst Ac Ach Awd; Pres Ac Ftns Aw; WWAHSS; Yth Ldrshp Prog; Comm Volntr; Peer Tut/Med; Vsity Clb; Tennis (V); Leadership; Sports Medicine

CRAVEN, ALEX; MIDLOTHIAN, VA; BENEDICTINE HS; (SO); Hi Hnr Roll; Hnr Roll; Otst Ac Ach Awd; US Army Sch Ath Aw; Key Club; Scouts; Foreign Clb; SP/M/VS; Cr Ctry (V L); Skt Tgt Sh (V CL); Wrstlg (V L); Military; Business; US Military Academy West Point; US Naval Academy Annapolis

CREASY, LAURA; ATKINS, VA; MARION SR HS; (JR); Hnr Roll; WWAHSS; Emplmnt; Quill & Scroll; Bnd; Mch Bnd; Pep Bnd; Cl Off (R); Lit Mag (E); Business Management; Emory; Henry College

CREGGER, DELAYNA A; THAXTON, VA; STAUNTON RIVER HS; (JR); Hi Hnr Roll; Otst Ac Ach Awd; Chrch Yth Grp; French Clb; Ch Chr; Sch Ppr (E); Radiology; Health Field; Virginia Polytechnic Institute; National Business College

CROCOLL, NICHOLAS J; ASHBURN, VA; STONE BRIDGE HS; (JR); Hnr Roll; Otst Ac Ach Awd; Pres Ac Ftns Aw; Sci Fairs; WWAHSS; Yth Ldrshp Prog; Comm Volntr; Peer Tut/Med; Cmptr Clb; Key Club; Sci Clb; Svce Clb; Tech Clb; Bsball (J L); Engineering; Business; Virginia Tech; James Madison

CROFT, KATIE; OAKTON, VA; FLINT HILL SCH; (JR); F Lan Hn Soc; Hi Hnr Roll; Hnr Roll; P to P St Amb Prg; Chr; Dnce; SP/M/VS; Swmg (V); Stu Cncl (R); Lit Mag

CRONIN, ERIN; CENTREVILLE, VA; WESTFIELD HS; (JR); F Lan Hn Soc; Hnr Roll; Pres Ac Ftns Aw; Sci Fairs; Comm Volntr; Hab For Humty Volntr; Peer Tut/Med; Chrch Yth Grp; Emplmnt; FCA; Prom Com; Quill & Scroll; Scouts; Chrldg (J); Fld Hky (VJCL); PP Ftbl (V); CR (R); Yrbk (E, R, P); Crew/Rowing-Varsity & Letter; U of North Carolina Wilmington; James Madison U

CROOK, LUCY; GWYNN, VA; MATHEWS HS; (SO); Ctznshp Aw; Gov Hnr Prg; Hi Hnr Roll; Nat Mrt LOC; Pres Sch; St of Mnth; Comm Volntr; Chrch Yth Grp; Key Club; Ntl Beta Clb; Bnd; Chr; Ch Chr; Mch Bnd; Cr Ctry (V L); Track (V L); Chesapeake Bay Governors School; Community Theatre; Environmental Science; Education; UVA At Wise (U of Virginia); Eastern Mennonite U

CROPPER, AMANDA S; HONAKER, VA; COUNCIL HS; (SO); Hnr Roll; Pres Ac Ftns Aw; Comm Volntr; French Clb; SP/M/VS; Pharmacist; Photographer; Southwest Virginia Community College; U At Wise

CROSS, NICHOLE; YORKTOWN, VA; YORK HS; F Lan Hn Soc; Hnr Roll; Sci Fairs; Comm Volntr; Chrch Yth Grp; Mod UN; Schol Bwl; French Clb; Most Outstanding Delegation Award; Horticulture; International Relations; U of Virginia; College of William and Mary

CROUCH, KRISTINA; HAMPTON, VA; KECOUGHTON HS; (SO); Hi Hnr Roll; Otst Ac Ach Awd; WWAHSS; Clubs: FCCLA; Arts: Guitar; Early Childhood Education; Psychology; Christopher Newport U; James Madison U

CROUCH, NINA F; PARTLOW, VA; FAITH BAPTIST SCH; (SR); Hi Hnr Roll; Nat Hon Sy; Yth Ldrshp Prog; Hosp Aide; Chrch Yth Grp; Emplmnt; Mus Clb; Pep Squd; Prom Com; Tchrs Aide; Vsity Clb; Acpl Chr; Bnd; Chr; Ch Chr; Chrldg (V CL); Sccr (V L); Vllyball (J); Cl Off (V); Stu Cncl (S); Volunteer EMS; USAA National Band Award; Bachelor of Science in Nursing Degree; Liberty U

CROWGEY, AARON A; WYTHEVILLE, VA; GEORGE WYTHE HS; (SR); 4H Awd; Hi Hnr Roll; MVP; Nat Hon Sy; Otst Ac Ach Awd; Pres Ac Ftns Aw; WWAHSS; Chrch Yth Grp; Emplmnt; FBLA; Ntl FFA; Vsity Clb; Stg Cre; Cr Ctry (V L); Ftball (V CL); Sccr (VJCL); Vsy Clb (V); FFA-President; FBLA; Agricultural Economics & Business; U of TN

CRUMPLER, JENNIFER L; POTOMAC FALLS, VA; DOMINION HS; (JR); Hnr Roll; Perf Att; WWAHSS; DECA; Key Club; Chrldg (V); Junior Golf Lowes Island Club Championship Winner; Dentistry; Virginia Tech; West Virginia U

CRUTE, MISHTWON; PORTSMOUTH, VA; IC NORCOM; (SO); Ctznshp Aw; Hi Hnr Roll; Hnr Roll; Nat Hon Sy; Otst Ac Ach Awd; Perf Att; WWAHSS; Comm Volntr; Peer Tut/Med; Dnce; Mar Art (V); Tennis (V); Alonzo Crim Student Award for Excellence in Math and Chrome Club Access Upward Bound; Science/Magnet Program; Pre-Med; Hampton U; Howard U

CRUZ, ALEJANDRO; EXMORE, VA; NORTHAMPTON HS; (JR); Hnr Roll; Nat Hon Sy; Comm Volntr; FBLA; Clb; Wrstlg (VJ); Architecture; Vocal

CRUZ, ERMI A; NEWPORT NEWS, VA; WOODSIDE HS; (JR); Hnr Roll; Perf Att; Comm Volntr; Peer Tut/Med; Chrch Yth Grp; Emplmnt; Photog; Prom Com; Spanish Clb; Started a Latin Dancing Club; Photography; Interior Decorator; New York U

CUBBAGE, NICHOLAS W; RILEYVILLE, VA; LURAY HS; (JR); 4H Awd; Hnr Roll; Comm Volntr; 4-H; DARE; Ntl FFA; Wdwrkg Clb; Ftball (VJ); Wt Lftg (V); 2 Years Automotive Technology; ITT Tech; National Diesel College

CUI, JING J; CHARLOTTESVILLE, VA; ALBEMARLE HS; (SO); DAR; Hnr Roll; CARE; Hab For Humty Volntr; Key Club; Bnd; Vllyball (J); Pre-Med; Biology; U of Virginia; Harvard U

CULLEN, JACQUELYN; ASHBURN, VA; STONE BRIDGE HS; (FR); Hi Hnr Roll; Hnr Roll; WWAHSS; Comm Volntr; Drma Clb; Key Club; Dnce; Stg Cre; Journalism; U of Virginia; Boston College

CULLEN, ROBERT E; ASHBURN, VA; STONE BRIDGE HS; (SR); Hnr Roll; Nat Hon Sy; Sci Fairs; Comm Volntr; Quiz Bowl; Tennis (V CL); Biology; Virginia Tech

CUMMINGS, COURTNEY; PORTSMOUTH, VA; L C NORCOM; (JR); Hnr Roll; Perf Att; Comm Volntr; Peer Tut/Med; Chrch Yth Grp; FBLA; ROTC; Bnd; Ch Chr; Clr Grd; Drl Tm; Sccr (V); Criminal Justice; Virginia Commonwealth U; Old Dominion U

CUNNINGHAM, AUSTIN W; SMITHFIELD, VA; JAMES RIVER CHRISTIAN AC; Hnr Roll; Nat Hon Sy; Sci Fairs; Comm Volntr; Chrch Yth Grp; Cmptr Clb; DARE; Emplmnt; Off Aide; Sci Clb; Tchrs Aide; Wdwrkg Clb; Adv Cncl (R); Varsity Bowling; Homecoming; Doctorate in Science; Doctorate in Law/Political Science; William & Mary; Christopher Newport U

CUNNINGHAM, PATRICK; STERLING, VA; POTOMAC FALLS HS; (JR); Hnr Roll; WWAHSS; Comm Volntr; Hab For Humty Volntr; Chrch Yth Grp; DECA; Emplmnt; Key Club; Bnd; Jzz Bnd; Mch Bnd; Pep Bnd; Sch Ppr (R); Most Outstanding - Earth Science 9th Grade; Most Improved- History / English 9th Grade

CURETON, KHIARA; FREDERICKSBURG, VA; STAFFORD SR HS; (SO); Perf Att; WWAHSS; Comm Volntr; Peer Tut/Med; Red Cr Aide; Chrch Yth Grp; Emplmnt; Key Club; Scouts; Svce Clb; Spanish Clb; Chrldg (J); Track (V); CR (R); Girl Scout Silver Award; Pediatrician; New York U; Harvard

CURTIS, REBECCA; PORTSMOUTH, VA; WOODROW WILSON HS; (JR); Hnr Roll; Nat Hon Sy; St of Mnth; WWAHSS; Emplmnt; COE Program

CUTITARU, MIHAIL; VIRGINIA BEACH, VA; FIRST COLONIAL HS; (JR); WWAHSS; Comm Volntr; Key Club; Future Leaders Exchange Program Scholarship; Close Up Foundation Workshop; Electrical Engineering; Old Dominion U

CYRUS, JENNIFER; MANASSAS, VA; STONEWALL JACKSON HS; (SO); Ctznshp Aw; Hnr Roll; Comm Volntr; Hab For Humty Volntr; Chrch Yth Grp; Key Club; Photog; Chr; Orch; Highest Community Service Hours; Graphic Designer; Computer Graphics; George Mason U

DANG, LONG B; HERNDON, VA; SOUTH LAKES HS; (JR); Hnr Roll; Nat Hon Sy; Comm Volntr; FBLA; Pediatrician; Pharmacist; Virginia Commonwealth U; College of William and Mary

DANIELS, DIONNE D; DANVILLE, VA; (FR); Hnr Roll; USAA; Comm Volntr; Hab For Humty Volntr; Peer Tut/Med; Roots and Shoots; Architect; Interior/Exterior Designer; Dickinson

DANTE, SNEHA K; FAIRFAX, VA; W.T. WOODSON HS; (JR); F Lan Hn Soc; Hnr Roll; MVP; Nat Hon Sy; Otst Ac Ach Awd; Perf Att; Sci Fairs; Sci/Math Olympn; St of Mnth; Comm Volntr; Peer Tut/Med; Red Cr Aide; Chrch Yth Grp; Dbte Team; Emplmnt; Key Club; Mth Clb/Tm; Mod UN; Quiz Bowl; Sci Clb; Bskball (V); Cl Off (R); Debate Team; Molecular Biology; Genetics; Yale U; Columbia U

DARBOUZE, REGGIE; ROANOKE, VA; FLEMING HS; (JR); Bskball (V); Business Management; Rutgers U in New Jersey; Maryland U

DAVENJAY, JEFF; CHARLOTTESVILLE, VA; ALBERMARLE HS; (JR); Hnr Roll; WWAHSS; Comm Volntr; Peer Tut/Med; Chrch Yth Grp; Jr Cls League; Key Club; Swmg (V L); Tennis (V L); Adv Cncl (R); Cl Off (V); CR (R); Patriot Athletic Leaders - PALS; Peer Counseling; Biology; Political Science and Government

DAVENPORT, ALEX; STERLING, VA; DOMINION HS; (SO); Hnr Roll; Yth Ldrshp Prog; Comm Volntr; Chrch Yth Grp; Dbte Team; Emplmnt; Key Club; Lib Aide; Mod UN; NtlFrnscLg; P to P St Amb Prg; Ch Chr; SP/M/VS; Stu Cncl (R); CR (R); Lit Mag; Sch Ppr (E, R); Co-Founder of the Students for Acceptance

DAVIDSON, SALINA; ROANOKE, VA; PATRICK HENRY HS; (SO); F Lan Hn Soc; Hi Hnr Roll; Hnr Roll; WWAHSS; Comm Volntr; Chrch Yth Grp; DARE; Jr Ach; Key Club; Scouts; French Clb; Ice Sktg; Lcrsse (V); Sccr (J); Architecture; U of Virginia; Virginia Tech

DAVIS, AMANDA S; VERNON HILL, VA; HALIFAX CTY HS; (JR); Hnr Roll; Nat Hon Sy; Peer Tut/Med; FBLA; Astronomy; Biology; U of North Carolina; Virginia Tech

DAVIS, CHAKA L; EMPORIA, VA; GREENSVILLE CTY HS; (FR); Ctznshp Aw; Hnr Roll; MVP; Otst Ac Ach Awd; St of Mnth; WWAHSS; Peer Tut/Med; Chrch Yth Grp; Emplmnt; Chr; Ch Chr; Drm Mjr; Stu Cncl (R); CR (R); Communications; Music; Norfolk State U-VA; Clark Atlanta U-GA

DAVIS, GREGORY N; VALENTINES, VA; HALIFAX AC CHRISTIAN SCH; (JR); Hnr Roll; Otst Ac Ach Awd; Valdctrian; Ntl Beta Clb; Prom Com; Quiz Bowl; Svce Clb; Bskball (VJ); Cl Off (P); Awards In: English, Algebra II, Environmental Science; Spanish I, World History, Algebra I, NC History; Business; The College of William and Mary; U of Virginia

DAVIS, TAMARA T; NORFOLK, VA; MAURY HS; (SO); All Am Sch; F Lan Hn Soc; Hi Hnr Roll; Hnr Roll; Nat Hon Sy; Nat Ldrshp Svc; USAA; Comm Volntr; Hosp Aide; Chrch Yth Grp; NtlFrnscLg; Ch Chr; Drl Tm; Venture Scholars Program; VA Pilot Scholastic Achievement; Clinical Laboratory Science MD-PhD; Howard U; Virginia Commonwealth U

DAWSON, DAVID; WOODBRIDGE, VA; C D HYLTON HS; (FR); Hnr Roll; Chrch Yth Grp; Emplmnt; Mission Trip to Bolivia; Computer Engineer; Virginia Tech; Penn State U

DAY, WILLIAM J; VIENNA, VA; (JR); F Lan Hn Soc; Hnr Roll; MVP; Nat Hon Sy; WWAHSS; DECA; Ice Hky (V C); 1st Team All-Star Northern Virginia Scholastic Hockey League; 2nd Team All-Star Washington Post; Business; Finance; U.S. Military Academy; U of Virginia

Davis, Tamara T
Maury HS
Norfolk, VA

Crumpler, Jennifer L
Dominion HS
Potomac Falls, VA

Cregger, Delayna A
Staunton River HS
Thaxton, VA

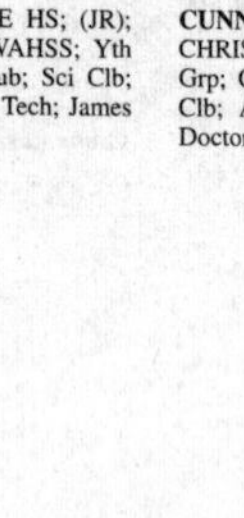
Craven, Alex
Benedictine HS
Midlothian, VA

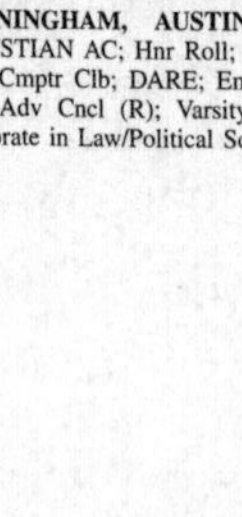
Coyner, Toby
Buffalo Gap HS
Churchville, VA

National
Honor Roll
Spring 2005

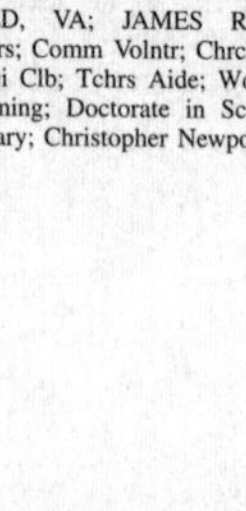
Corona, Anna
C D Hylton HS
Woodbridge, VA

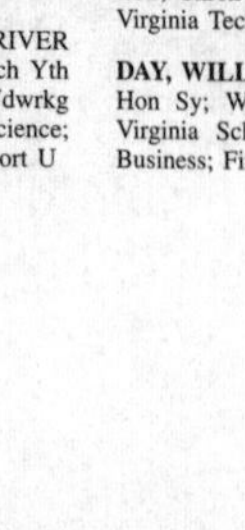
Creasy, Laura
Marion SR HS
Atkins, VA

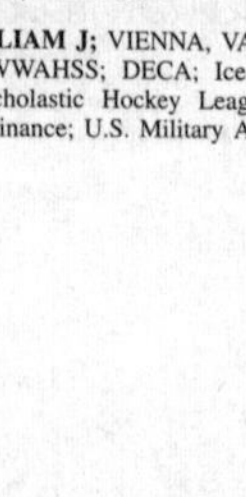
Crouch, Nina F
Faith Baptist Sch
Partlow, VA

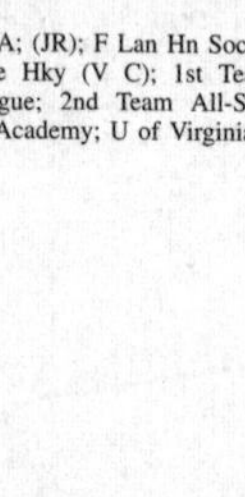
Cubbage, Nicholas W
Luray HS
Rileyville, VA

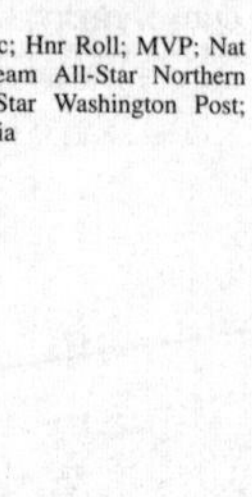
Cyrus, Jennifer
Stonewall Jackson HS
Manassas, VA

DEAK, DALIA M; MC LEAN, VA; ISLAMIC SAUDI AC; (FR); Hnr Roll; Sci Fairs; St of Mnth; Yth Ldrshp Prog; Comm Volntr; Peer Tut/Med; Emplmnt; Mod UN; SP/M/VS; Bskball (J); Interviewed for International Television; Chosen to Critique a U.S Government Agency Website for Youth Overseas; Medicine; Law; Princeton; Yale

DE BREW, LA TOYA; WILLIAMSBURG, VA; JAMES RIVER CHRISTIAN AC; (JR); Hnr Roll; Nat Hon Sy; Sci Fairs; USAA; WWAHSS; Emplmnt; Ntl Beta Clb; Prom Com; Scouts; SP/M/VS; Golf (V); Vllyball (V); Cl Off (R); Art Award; 11th Grade Homecoming Representative; Graphic Design; Music; Virginia Commonwealth U; Virginia State U

DECARMO, AMANDA; CHESAPEAKE, VA; OSCAR F SMITH HS; (JR); Hnr Roll; MVP; DARE; DECA; Emplmnt; Chrldg (V, L); Gmnstcs (V, L); Track; Get a Degree in Veterinary Medicine; U of Maryland: Eastern Shore; North Carolina State U

DEEL, TIFFANY L; VANSANT, VA; MTN MISSION SCH; (SO); Ctznshp Aw; Hnr Roll; Peer Tut/Med; Chrch Yth Grp; Scouts; Wdwrkg Clb; Chr; Bskball (V); Sccr (V); 98.8 Yr Avg High School Spanish / College Spanish I; Traveling Concert Choir / Soprano; Biology/Pre-Med 2nd Major Psychology; Medical Doctor, Pediatrics; Duke U; Johns Hopkins U

DEGEN, SARAH; FREDERICKSBURG, VA; FREDERICKSBURG CHRISTIAN SCH; (FR); Hi Hnr Roll; Hnr Roll; MVP; St of Mnth; Comm Volntr; Key Club; Scouts; Spch Team; Bnd; Gold Cups & Ribbons in Piano; 1st Place Soccer Team; Orthodontist; Music

DELANEY, ALEXANDER; BURKE, VA; JAMES W ROBINSON SECONDARY SCH; (JR); Hnr Roll; Nat Hon Sy; Sci Fairs; WWAHSS; Comm Volntr; Emplmnt; Key Club; Photog; Track (J); Crew; Virginia Polytechnic Institute; James Madison U

DELEON, SERGIO; ANNANDALE, VA; BISHOP DENIS J O'CONNELL HS; (SR); Hnr Roll; Sci Fairs; Yth Ldrshp Prog; Amnsty Intl; Cmptr Clb; Key Club; Sci Clb; Spanish Clb; Wt Lftg (V); Math and Science College Program; Virginia Junior Academy of Science; Engineering; Virginia Tech; Virginia Commonwealth U

DELPH, AMANDA; HAMPTON, VA; KECOUGHTON HS; (SO); Hnr Roll; Perf Att; WWAHSS; ArtClub; Emplmnt; Key Club; Tennis (V L); Yrbk (R, P); Academic Letter Award Recipient; Operation Smile, Aurora Society; Dentistry; U of Virginia; James Madison U

DE MARTINO, MEGHAN; ASHBURN, VA; STONE BRIDGE HS; (FR); Hi Hnr Roll; Hnr Roll; MVP; Pres Ac Ftns Aw; WWAHSS; Yth Ldrshp Prog; Comm Volntr; Peer Tut/Med; Chrch Yth Grp; DARE; Key Club; Scouts; Clb; Bnd; Lcrsse (V); Vllyball (J); Who's Who Among High School Students; (Nominated) International Foreign Language Award; Teacher; Business; College of William and Mary

DEMOSS, LAUREN; WAYNESBORO, VA; WAYNESBORO HS; (SO); Gov Hnr Prg; Hi Hnr Roll; Otst Ac Ach Awd; Perf Att; WWAHSS; Yth Ldrshp Prog; Comm Volntr; Chrch Yth Grp; Emplmnt; FCA; Key Club; Ntl Beta Clb; Photog; Tennis (V); Yrbk; Secretary of Beta Club; Attended Jr. Beta Club National Convention for Group Talent; Math; Architecture; James Madison U; U of Virginia

DESPOT, RENEE M; MARTINSVILLE, VA; MARTINSVILLE HS; (FR); Hi Hnr Roll; Hnr Roll; WWAHSS; Chrch Yth Grp; Key Club; Bnd; Mch Bnd; Sftball (V)

DEVENING, ERIN; LYNCHBURG, VA; EC GLASS HS; (JR); Hnr Roll; Nat Hon Sy; Comm Volntr; Hosp Aide; Peer Tut/Med; ArtClub; Emplmnt; Key Club; Mth Clb/Tm; Scouts; Svce Clb; SADD; French Clb; Clr Grd; Mch Bnd; SP/M/VS; Chrldg (V L); PP Ftbl (J); Sccr (J); Girl Scout Gold Award Recipient; NHS Member; Meteorology; Environmental Sciences; U of Virginia; College of William and Mary

DEVERS, CESAR; RESTON, VA; (SO); Hi Hnr Roll; Hnr Roll; Nat Hon Sy; Chrch Yth Grp; Bnd; Jzz Bnd; Mch Bnd; Pep Bnd; Bsball (J); Mar Art (V L); Engineering; Sales; Columbia U for the General Studies; Yale U

DHAMI, NAVJOT; MANASSAS, VA; STONEWALL JACKSON HS; (SO); Hnr Roll; Otst Ac Ach Awd; Perf Att; St of Mnth; Physician; Anesthesiology

DIAL, NATHAN E; COLONIAL HEIGHTS, VA; THOMAS DALE HS; (JR); Ctznshp Aw; F Lan Hn Soc; Hi Hnr Roll; MVP; Nat Hon Sy; Otst Ac Ach Awd; Perf Att; Pres Ac Ftns Aw; Sci Fairs; St of Mnth; Comm Volntr; Hab For Humty Volntr; Peer Tut/Med; Chrch Yth Grp; DARE; Dbte Team; Drma Clb; Emplmnt; FCA; Fr of Library; Mth Clb/Tm; Bnd; Orch; SP/M/VS; Bskball (V L); Golf (V L); Mar Art (V CL); Sccr (VJCL); Track; Adv Cncl (R); Cl Off (V); CR (R); Boys & Girls Club Youth of Year (Local) Pennsylvania; Presidential Physical/Fitness Award; Engineering; Pilot; Air Force Academy; Columbia

DIAMOND, TYLER; WARM SPRINGS, VA; (JR); Ctznshp Aw; Hi Hnr Roll; Hnr Roll; MVP; Nat Ldrshp Svc; St of Mnth; Yth Ldrshp Prog; Comm Volntr; Emplmnt; NYLC; P to P St Amb Prg; Bskball (J L); Cr Ctry (V L); Sccr (J); Tennis (V L); Cl Off (P, R); Stu Cncl (P); CR (R); ELA Member (Library); Ecology Club; History Major; Journalism; U of Virginia; Fordham U

DIKE, IKENNA; BRISTOW, VA; STONEWALL JACKSON; (JR); Ctznshp Aw; Hnr Roll; Nat Hon Sy; Sci Fairs; Comm Volntr; Hosp Aide; Peer Tut/Med; Biology Clb; BPA; FBLA; Kwanza Clb; NYLC; Vsity Clb; Bskball (VJ L); Ftball (VJ L); Lcrsse (VJ L); Stu Cncl (R)

DILCHER, CANDACE M; ROANOKE, VA; NORTHSIDE HS; (JR); Chrch Yth Grp; Key Club; SADD; French Clb; Tennis (L); Barbizon Modeling School Graduate; Accounting; Forensic Science; Randolph-Macon U; Greensboro College

DILLEY, URSULA S.; SALEM, VA; SALEM HS; (SO); Duke TS; F Lan Hn Soc; Hi Hnr Roll; Hnr Roll; Nat Hon Sy; Otst Ac Ach Awd; Pres Sch; Sci Fairs; Comm Volntr; ArtClub; Chrch Yth Grp; DARE; FCA; Jr Cls League; Latin Clb; Hsbk Rdg (V); Tennis (V); Scholastic Art Awards- Gold Key; Virginia General Assembly - Page; Visual Arts; Design; Cooper Union College; Rhode Island School of Design

DILWORTH, JENNIFER T; PETERSBURG, VA; PETERSBURG HS; (JR); Hnr Roll; Nat Hon Sy; WWAHSS; Chrch Yth Grp; Cmptr Clb; DECA; FBLA; Key Club; Ch Chr; Bdmtn (V); Bsball (V); Bskball (V); Mar Art (J); Rlr Hky (J); Scr Kpr (J); Skiing (J); West Point Leadership Award; NFTE 2005 Entrepreneur of the Year; Religious Studies; Marketing Management; Virginia Commonwealth U; Christopher Newport U

DIN, KIMBERLY W; NORFOLK, VA; GRANBY HS; (SR); Hnr Roll; Comm Volntr; Emplmnt; Mod UN; Orch; Fld Hky (VJCL); Participated in the National Field Hockey Festival; 3rd Place Winner in City Book Review Contest; Information Technology; Business Administration; George Mason U

DINH, MARGARET; ROANOKE, VA; WILLIAM FLEMING HS; (FR); Hnr Roll; Perf Att; Key Club; Dnce; Vllyball (J)

DISBROW, JULIA M; CULPEPER, VA; CULPEPER CTY HS; (SR); Hi Hnr Roll; Hnr Roll; Nat Sci Aw; Sci Fairs; Yth Ldrshp Prog; Hab For Humty Volntr; Red Cr Aide; 4-H; Hsbk Rdg (L); National Youth Leadership Forum on Medicine; Certified Lifeguard; Pre-Med; Want to Be a Pediatrician; Eastern Mennonite U; Bridgewater College

DIXON, MELISSA L; EVERGREEN, VA; APPOMATTOX HS; (JR); Hi Hnr Roll; Nat Hon Sy; Pres Sch; USAA; WWAHSS; Comm Volntr; Chrch Yth Grp; Drma Clb; FCA; NYLC; Ch Chr; SP/M/VS; Chrldg (V L); Cl Off (R); Sch Ppr (R); Speech Pathologist; U of Virginia

DIXON, TENESHA A; LONG ISLAND, VA; GRETNA HS; (JR); Hnr Roll; Perf Att; St of Mnth; WWAHSS; Comm Volntr; Chrch Yth Grp; DARE; Chr; Ch Chr; Pediatrician; Culinary Arts; Johnson & Wales U; A & T

DIXON-SMITH, BRITTNI; WOODBRIDGE, VA; (SO); Hi Hnr Roll; Hnr Roll; MVP; Nat Hon Sy; Otst Ac Ach Awd; Pres Ac Ftns Aw; Yth Ldrshp Prog; Comm Volntr; NYLC; Prom Com; Scouts; Vsity Clb; Bskball (V L); Track (V L); Vllyball (V L); Cl Off (R); Stu Cncl (P); CR (R); State Ambassador for VA (Jr Preteen); Outstanding French Student; Plastic Surgery (Pre-Med); Political Science; Duke U; Harvard U

DO, LIEN; ANNANDALE, VA; FALLS CHURCH HS; (JR); F Lan Hn Soc; Hnr Roll; Nat Hon Sy; St of Mnth; USAA; Comm Volntr; FBLA; Key Club; Mth Clb/Tm; Japanese Clb; Lcrsse (J); National Business Honor Society; Academic Letter Award; Chemistry Major; Doctor of Dentistry; U of Virginia; James Madison U

DO, MINHHA; ANNANDALE, VA; ANNANDALE HS; (JR); Hnr Roll; Nat Hon Sy; St of Mnth; Comm Volntr; Peer Tut/Med; Drma Clb; Emplmnt; FBLA; Lib Aide; Dnce; Employee of the Month; Finance; Master's Degree; George Mason U; U of Virginia

DODERO, BETHANY J; GAINESVILLE, VA; BATTLEFIELD HS; (SO); F Lan Hn Soc; Hi Hnr Roll; Otst Ac Ach Awd; Comm Volntr; Chrch Yth Grp; Emplmnt; Key Club; Quill & Scroll; Fld Hky (J); PP Ftbl (V); Sccr (V); Swmg (V); Cl Off (P); Stu Cncl (P); CR (R); News Channel 10 Internship; Key Club Vice President; Media; Business; UVA; NYU

DODSON, JENNIFER R; ALEXANDRIA, VA; THOMAS A EDISON HS; (JR); F Lan Hn Soc; Hnr Roll; ArtClub; Dbte Team; Key Club; French Clb; Orch; Bskball; Lcrsse (J); PP Ftbl (J); Track (J); Vllyball (V L); Lit Mag (E); Sch Ppr; American Vision Award/National Art Award; Governor's School Summer Program; Art Therapy; Art, Photography; The Cleveland Institute of Arts; Delaware College of Art & Design

DOHNALEK, ABIGAIL J; STERLING, VA; POTOMAC FALLS HS; (SO); Hnr Roll; Chrch Yth Grp; DARE; Key Club; Bnd; Bskball (J); Sccr (V L); Club Soccer; Recycling Club

DONG, XIN; FREDERICKSBURG, VA; JAMES MONROE; (FR); Hi Hnr Roll; Hnr Roll; Mary Washington U; Virginia Tech

DONOVAN, ASHLEY N; VIRGINIA BEACH, VA; FLOYD KELLAM HS; (JR); Hnr Roll; Chr; Orch

DONOVAN, CHRISTINE; VIRGINIA BEACH, VA; FLOYD KELLAM HS; (FR); CR (R)

DORTON, BRITTNEY D; RIDGEWAY, VA; MAGNA VISTA HS; (JR); Hnr Roll; WWAHSS; Comm Volntr; Peer Tut/Med; Emplmnt; FBLA; Prom Com; Chr; SP/M/VS; Cr Ctry (V L); Sftball (V L); Vllyball (JC); Most RBI's Award 2003 - Softball; Miss Utility Award 2003 - Softball; Sports Management & Administration; Liberty U; St John's U FL

DOSS, CHARLES; WINCHESTER, VA; MILLBROOK HS; (SR); Hi Hnr Roll; Nat Hon Sy; St of Mnth; WWAHSS; Comm Volntr; Peer Tut/Med; FBLA; Key Club; Mth Clb/Tm; Quiz Bowl; Academic Team, Coaches Award; Academic Team, Pioneer Award; College of William & Mary

DOTSON, BRIAN L; SUFFOLK, VA; NANSEMOND RIVER HS; (SR); F Lan Hn Soc; Nat Hon Sy; WWAHSS; Chrch Yth Grp; DECA; Emplmnt; Honor Graduate; Spanish Honor Society; Urban and Regional Planning; Civil Engineering; Frostburg State U; Virginia Tech

DOTSON, KATIE; CLIFTON FORGE, VA; ALLEGHANY HS; (SO); Hnr Roll; WWAHSS; Key Club; Pep Squd; Foreign Clb; Bnd; Mch Bnd; Tennis (V); Pharmacy

DOUGHERTY, KATHLEEN; CHARLOTTESVILLE, VA; ALBEMARLE HS; (JR); F Lan Hn Soc; Hnr Roll; Nat Hon Sy; Otst Ac Ach Awd; Perf Att; WWAHSS; Chrch Yth Grp; Emplmnt; Key Club; MuAlphaTh; Spanish Clb; Bnd; Jzz Bnd; Mch Bnd; Pep Bnd; Bskball (JC); PP Ftbl (V)

DOUGLAS, PATRICK; VIRGINIA BEACH, VA; (JR); Business; Management; Old Dominion U

DOUGLAS, TROY M; CLOVER, VA; HAILFAX HS; (SO); Fut Prb Slvr; Gov Hnr Prg; Hnr Roll; MVP; Otst Ac Ach Awd; Pres Ac Ftns Aw; St of Mnth; St Optmst of Yr; WWAHSS; Comm Volntr; Hab For Humty Volntr; ArtClub; Chrch Yth Grp; Cmptr Clb; FBLA; FTA; Outdrs Clb; P to P St Amb Prg; ROTC; Bsball; Ftball (V); Skiing; Track (J); Wt Lftg (V); Adv Cncl (P); Yrbk

DOWTIN, MACKENZIE; MIDLOTHIAN, VA; POWHATAN HS; (JR); Nat Hon Sy; WWAHSS; Comm Volntr; Drma Clb; HO'Br Yth Ldrshp; Mod UN; Off Aide; Photog; Prom Com; SP/M/VS; Chrldg (V L); PP Ftbl (J); Stu Cncl (R); Crew Leader - Richmond Animal League; Chemistry Major; Chemical Engineering / Doctor; Wake Forest U; U of Virginia

DRESSLER, CHELSEA E; COVINGTON, VA; ALLEGHENY HS,; (JR); Hi Hnr Roll; Kwnis Aw; Nat Hon Sy; WWAHSS; Comm Volntr; Peer Tut/Med; Chrch Yth Grp; DARE; Emplmnt; FBLA; Key Club; Ntl Beta Clb; Pep Squd; SADD; Hsbk Rdg (V); PP Ftbl (J); Scr Kpr (V L); Tennis (V L); Track (J L); Stu Cncl (R); Most Improved Tennis-Award; Equine Studies; Religion/Youth Ministries; Virginia Intermont College

DROGO, BRITTNEY; STAFFORD, VA; COLONIAL FORGE HS; (JR); Hnr Roll; Nat Hon Sy; WWAHSS; Comm Volntr; Peer Tut/Med; Spec Olymp Vol; Chrch Yth Grp; Key Club; Bskball; Sftball; Stu Cncl; CR; Physical Therapy; St. Francis U; Shenandoah

DRUMMOND, ANDREW; VIRGINIA BEACH, VA; FLOYD KELLAM HS; (JR); Black Belt-1st Degree Martial Arts; Soon to Be Certified to Teach; Martial Arts Instructor, Management; Virginia Polytechnic U; Old Dominion U

DRUMMOND, GREER; FALLS CHURCH, VA; BISHOP O'CONNELL HS; (FR); Sccr (V L); Johns Hopkins Center for Talented Youth; Distinction on Verbal SAT; Psychology; Journalism; U of Virginia; U of Southern California

DUFFY, ELLEN; STERLING, VA; POTOMAC FALLS HS; (SO); 4H Awd; Duke TS; Hnr Roll; MVP; Sci Fairs; Sci/Math Olympn; St of Mnth; Peer Tut/Med; 4-H; FTA; Key Club; Tchrs Aide; Acpl Chr; Bskball (J); Sftball (J); County Science Fair; Law; Biology; U of Kansas; Pepperdine U

DUKORE, LUCILE; BLACKSBURG, VA; BLACKSBURG HS; (JR); Hnr Roll; Emplmnt; Key Club; NtlFrnscLg; Spch Team; Acpl Chr; Flg Crps; Stg Cre; Swg Chr; Stu Cncl (R); U of Mary Washington

DUMERA, NAINA; ARLINGTON, VA; HAYFIELD SECONDARY SCH; (JR); Hnr Roll; Pres Sch; Peer Tut/Med; Quill & Scroll; Svce Clb; SP/M/VS; Yrbk (E, R, P); President of International Club 2-Yrs; Member of Odyssey of the Mind-7 yrs; Communications-Broadcasting; Finance; James Madison U; Georgetown U

DUNBAR, MICHELLE D; VIENNA, VA; JAMES MADISON HS; (SR); Hnr Roll; St of Mnth; Hosp Aide; Chrch Yth Grp; DECA; Drma Clb; Emplmnt; FCA; SADD; Chrldg (V L); Gmnstcs (V L); Track (V); Student of the Month; DECA Officer; Pre-Med the Medical Degrees; George Mason U

DUNCAN, SHERRY L; STUART, VA; PATRICK CTY HS; (SO); Hi Hnr Roll; Pres Ac Ftns Aw; Spec Olymp Vol; Ntl Beta Clb; Ntl FFA; Vsity Clb; French Clb; Bskball (V L); Sftball (V); Vllyball (V L); Law-Criminal Justice; Sports Medicine; Virginia Tech; Duke U

DUNGEE, MICHELLE S; TAPPAHANNOCK, VA; ESSEX HS; (JR); Hnr Roll; Perf Att; Comm Volntr; Spec Olymp Vol; Chrch Yth Grp; Dbte Team; Off Aide; Scouts; Bnd; Ch Chr; Mch Bnd; Pep Bnd; Sftball (J); Track (VJ); George Mason U Debate 3rd Place Reg Team; John Phillip Sousa Band Award 8th Grade; Music Education; Science Major; Virginia State U; Old Dominion U

Dunbar, Michelle D
James Madison HS
Vienna, VA

Disbrow, Julia M
Culpeper Cty HS
Culpeper, VA

Dhami, Navjot
Stonewall Jackson HS
Manassas, VA

Devers, Cesar
Reston, VA

National
Honor Roll
Spring 2005

Deel, Tiffany L
Mtn Mission Sch
Vansant, VA

Dial, Nathan E
Thomas Dale HS
Colonial Heights, VA

Dorton, Brittney D
Magna Vista HS
Ridgeway, VA

Dungee, Michelle S
Essex HS
Tappahannock, VA

DUNHAM, CHRISTOPHER D; CHESAPEAKE, VA; WESTERN BRANCH HS; (JR); Hnr Roll; Red Cr Aide; Chrch Yth Grp; Cr Ctry (V); Wrstlg (V); Red Cross Club; Cardiovascular Surgeon; Physical Therapist; Old Dominion U; Tidewater Community College

DURAN, KRISTEN; CHESAPEAKE, VA; INDIAN RIVER HS; (SR); Hnr Roll; Comm Volntr; DECA; Drma Clb; ROTC; Dnce; SP/M/VS; Stg Cre; Track (J); Alpha Member of the Month; Community Service Letter; Performing Arts; Culinary Arts; U of Nevada, Las Vegas; U of Arizona, Tucson

DURANT, HANNAH E; ALEXANDRIA, VA; T C WILLIAMS HS; (SO); Ctznshp Aw; Hi Hnr Roll; Hnr Roll; Perf Att; Comm Volntr; FBLA; Key Club; SADD; Vsity Clb; Wdwrkg Clb; Fld Hky (J); Golf; Sccr (V); Yrbk (E, R, P); City Art Winner (Reflections); City Writing Winner (Reflections); Business; James Madison U; U of Virginia

DURBIN, TRISHA; PHOENIX, VA; PRINCE EDWARD CTY HS; (SR); Gov Hnr Prg; Hi Hnr Roll; Nat Hon Sy; Otst Ac Ach Awd; Salutrn; St Schl; USAA; WWAHSS; Comm Volntr; Peer Tut/Med; Jr Cls League; Photog; Latin Clb; SP/M/VS; Tennis (V L); Stu Cncl (S); Lit Mag (P); Yrbk (E, P); Governor's Latin Academy; Kodak Young Leader's Award; College of William & Mary

DYE, CHASE; HONAKER, VA; HONAKER HS; (SO); Hnr Roll; Chrch Yth Grp; FBLA; Ntl Beta Clb; Ntl FFA; Bsball (V); Stu Cncl (R); CR (V, R); Chiropractor

DYSKO, JOHANNA; RICHMOND, VA; MILLS E GODWIN HS; (SO); Hnr Roll; Perf Att; Comm Volntr; Chrch Yth Grp; Emplmnt; Scouts; Tech Clb; Ch Chr; SP/M/VS; Gmnstcs; Track; Girl Scout Silver Award; Girl Scout Leadership Award; Hospital Social Worker; Physical Therapist; Virginia Commonwealth U; Roanoke College of Health & Sciences

EBERLE, VICTORIA; CLIFTON, VA; CENTREVILLE HS; (JR); Hnr Roll; Nat Hon Sy; WWAHSS; Yth Ldrshp Prog; Comm Volntr; Hab For Humty Volntr; Chrch Yth Grp; Key Club; Photog; PP Ftbl (V); Education; Psychology

EDMONDSON, MONIQUE; VIRGINIA BEACH, VA; LANDSTOWN HS; (JR); Ctznshp Aw; Hi Hnr Roll; Otst Ac Ach Awd; Perf Att; Pres Ac Ftns Aw; WWAHSS; Comm Volntr; DECA; Emplmnt; Spanish Clb; Dnce; Swmg (J); Track (J); Stu Cncl; Step Team; Interact Club; I Want to Major in Pediatrics; Howard U; U of Virginia

EDWARDS, HANNAH W; CHESAPEAKE, VA; STONE BRIDGE HS; (SR); Hi Hnr Roll; Nat Hon Sy; Key Club; Bskball (V CL); Yrbk; Graphic Design (Major); James Madison U (Attending)

EDWARDS, MITCHELL; KENTS STORE, VA; FLUVANNA CO HS; (JR); Hnr Roll; Nat Hon Sy; Perf Att; WWAHSS; Comm Volntr; Chrch Yth Grp; Emplmnt; Key Club; Ntl Beta Clb; Scouts; Bsball (VJ); Ftball (VJ)

EDWARDS, SHANNAN; MIDLOTHIAN, VA; MIDLOTHIAN HS; (SR); Hi Hnr Roll; Hnr Roll; WWAHSS; DECA; Emplmnt; Quill & Scroll; Spanish Clb; Yrbk (E, P); Inducted Into Quill & Scroll; Member of Spanish, Spirit, and Marketing Clubs; Nursing; George Mason U; Virginia Commonwealth U

EGGLESTON, JOSHUA W; CHESTER, VA; THOMAS DALE HS; (SR); F Lan Hn Soc; Hi Hnr Roll; Hnr Roll; Nat Hon Sy; Nat Mrt Sch Recip; Otst Ac Ach Awd; Perf Att; Pres Ac Ftns Aw; Sci Fairs; Sci/Math Olympn; Comm Volntr; Peer Tut/Med; Spec Olymp Vol; AL Aux Boys; Chrch Yth Grp; Mth Clb/Tm; Mus Clb; ROTC; Schol Bwl; Scouts; Svce Clb; Bnd; Chr; Ch Chr; Drm Mjr; Sccr (J); Air Force Academy Summer Seminar; Rifle Team; Aerospace Engineering; Astronautical Engineering; United States Air Force Academy; Virginia Polytechnic Institute and State U

EGGLESTON, ROBBIE; WILLIAMSBURG, VA; LAFAYETTE HS; (SO); Hnr Roll; Comm Volntr; Hosp Aide; Chrch Yth Grp; Emplmnt; FBLA; Key Club; French Clb; Ch Chr; Leader in church youth group; Help start a Christian Bible club at school with other people/ called LOGOS; History Major; Ministry at church; Virginia Polytechnic Institute; William & Mary College

EIDSON, ASHLEY M; RESTON, VA; SOUTH LAKES HS; (SO); Hnr Roll; Nat Hon Sy; WWAHSS; Comm Volntr; Peer Tut/Med; Scouts; French Clb; PP Ftbl; Sftball (V L); CR (R); Saturday Youth Bowling-Sr. Girls High Average; Captain of Travel Softball Team for 3 of 3 Years; Accounting; Computers

ELDER, HEATHER M; HURT, VA; GRETNA HS; (JR); 4H Awd; Ctznshp Aw; Hnr Roll; Nat Hon Sy; Nat Ldrshp Svc; Perf Att; St of Mnth; WWAHSS; Comm Volntr; Hab For Humty Volntr; Hosp Aide; 4-H; Biology Clb; Chrch Yth Grp; Cmptr Clb; DARE; Drma Clb; Emplmnt; FBLA; Bnd; Chr; Ch Chr; SP/M/VS; Cr Ctry (V CL); GAA (V L); Sftball (J L); Track (V CL); Vsy Clb (V L); Wt Lftg (V L); Adv Cncl (R); Stu Cncl (S); CR (P); President of National Honor Society; Secretary of HOSA; Nursing; Elementary Education; Radford U; George Mason U

ELDRIDGE, ELLEN C; SALEM, VA; ROANOKE CATHOLIC HS; (SR); Hi Hnr Roll; Hnr Roll; Jr Eng Tech; MVP; Nat Hon Sy; Nat Mrt Fin; WWAHSS; Comm Volntr; Peer Tut/Med; Chrch Yth Grp; Jr Ach; Key Club; Mth Clb/Tm; Spanish Clb; Ch Chr; PP Ftbl (VJ); Sftball (V CL); Vllyball (V L); Adv Cncl (T); Stu Cncl (T); Lit Mag (E, R); Toyota Scholar Nominee; 2003-2004 1st Team All-Conference Softball; Spanish; Psychology; Hillsdale College; Georgetown U

ELLIS, WHITNEY; CHURCH ROAD, VA; DINWIDDIE HS; (JR); Hnr Roll; Comm Volntr; Chrch Yth Grp; Ch Chr; Bskball (V); Track (V); Stu Cncl (R); Pre-Medicine; Anatomy; Hampton U; Virginia Commonwealth U

EL-SHERIF, YOUMNA; CENTREVILLE, VA; ISLAMIC SAUDI AC; (FR); Hi Hnr Roll; Sci Fairs; Sci/Math Olympn; St of Mnth; Yth Ldrshp Prog; Comm Volntr; Peer Tut/Med; Mod UN; Svce Clb; Cl Off (T); National Student Leadership Conference; 1st Place in Quran Contest; Astronomy & Rocket Science; Symbology; Harvard; Virginia Tech

EMERSON, KERRI A; LEESBURG, VA; HERITAGE HS; (SR); F Lan Hn Soc; Hnr Roll; Nat Hon Sy; WWAHSS; Comm Volntr; Chrch Yth Grp; Mus Clb; German Clb; Bskball (J); Guitar Student of the Year- 12th; National Honor Society of German; Liberty U

ENGH, CATHERINE; ALEXANDRIA, VA; T C WILLIAMS HS; (SO); Hi Hnr Roll; Hnr Roll; Comm Volntr; Key Club; Vsity Clb; Tennis (V); Artwork in Show; Field Hockey Manager; Engineering; Lawyer; U of Virginia; Dartmouth

ENGLISH, COURTNEY A; FREDERICKSBURG, VA; RIVERBEND HS; (JR); Ctznshp Aw; Gov Hnr Prg; Hi Hnr Roll; Hnr Roll; Nat Hon Sy; Otst Ac Ach Awd; Comm Volntr; Peer Tut/Med; Spec Olymp Vol; Chrch Yth Grp; FCA; French Clb; Dnce; Yrbk (R, P); National Junior Honor Society; National Honor Society; Dance; Business; Dickinson College; U of Richmond

ENGLISH, JESSICA; STAFFORD, VA; COLONIAL FORGE HS; (SR); Lit Mag; National Honor Society; Secretary of German Club; Business Major; U of Mary Washington

ENKHBOLD, NOMIN; ROANOKE, VA; (JR); F Lan Hn Soc; Hi Hnr Roll; Hnr Roll; Otst Ac Ach Awd; Perf Att; WWAHSS; FBLA; Dnce; Youth Court; PRIDE Team; Radford U; Art Institute of Arlington

EPPERSON, DERRALL R; HAYES, VA; GLOUCESTER HS; (SR); DARE; FBLA; Latin Clb; Computer Science; ITT Tech, Richmond VA; Rappahannock Community College

ERICKSON, SARAH S; RESTON, VA; SOUTH LAKES HS; (JR); Hi Hnr Roll; Hnr Roll; Nat Hon Sy; Otst Ac Ach Awd; Pres Ac Ftns Aw; Comm Volntr; ArtClub; Chrch Yth Grp; Emplmnt; Key Club; Mth Clb/Tm; Photog; Scouts; Tchrs Aide; Acpl Chr; SP/M/VS; Swg Chr; Ice Hky (J); Sccr (V); Relay for Life Team Leader; Pediatrician; Evergreen State College; U of California-Santa Cruz

ESPINAS, BRIAN A; ARLINGTON, VA; YORKTOWN HS; (FR); F Lan Hn Soc; Hnr Roll; Otst Ac Ach Awd; Perf Att; WWAHSS; Comm Volntr; Peer Tut/Med; Chess; Cmptr Clb; Emplmnt; Fr of Library; Outdrs Clb; ROTC; Scouts; SADD; Bdmtn (L); Bsball (L); Bskball (L); Cyclg (L); Ftball (L); Sccr (L); Track (L); Vllyball (L); Cl Off (R); CR (R); Computer Programming; Electronic Engineer; Georgetown U; Marymount U

ETHERINGTON, MEREDITH T; NORFOLK, VA; NORFOLK COLLEGIATE SCH; (JR); Comm Volntr; Photog; Tchrs Aide; Bskball (J); Sftball (V); Yrbk (R, P); U of Virginia; U of North Carolina Wilmington

EURE, KATELYN M; LYNCH STATION, VA; ALTAVISTA COMBINED SCH; (FR); Hnr Roll; Chrch Yth Grp; FCCLA; Spanish Clb; Neo-Natal Nurse; Teacher; U of Virginia; Roanoke Bible College

EVANS, ASHLAND; GALAX, VA; GALAX HS; (JR); Ctznshp Aw; Hnr Roll; Nat Hon Sy; Otst Ac Ach Awd; Perf Att; USAA; Chrch Yth Grp; Emplmnt; FCA; Mth Clb/Tm; Mus Clb; Prom Com; SADD; Spanish Clb; Scr Kpr (V); Cl Off (T); Interdenominational/Young People's Conference; All-District Band; Physical Therapy; Psychology; Virginia Polytechnic State U; James Madison U

EVANS, JENNIFER; MIDLOTHIAN, VA; MIDLOTHIAN HS; (JR); Hi Hnr Roll; Jr Mshl; Nat Hon Sy; Otst Ac Ach Awd; Comm Volntr; Peer Tut/Med; Chrch Yth Grp; Emplmnt; Jr Cls League; Pep Squd; Photog; Prom Com; Quill & Scroll; Svce Clb; Ch Chr; Dnce; Chrldg (V L); Sccr (J); Stu Cncl (R); Yrbk (E, R, P); Communication/Publications; Clemson U; U of South Carolina

EVANS, KATHERINE; YORKTOWN, VA; TABB HS; (SR); Hi Hnr Roll; Hnr Roll; Nat Hon Sy; Pres Sch; WWAHSS; Yth Ldrshp Prog; Comm Volntr; Peer Tut/Med; Chrch Yth Grp; Key Club; Mth Clb/Tm; Mod UN; MuAlphaTh; Quill & Scroll; Tchrs Aide; Chr; Ch Chr; Dnce; Sch Ppr (E, R, P); Irish Step Dancer; Horseback Riding; Elementary Education; Brigham Young U

EVANS, KAYLA; MARION, VA; MARION SR HS; (SR); Hi Hnr Roll; Hnr Roll; Key Club; GAA; Sftball (V); Vsy Clb; Yrbk (E); Virginia Highlands Community College; Emory & Henry

EVANS, TIMOTHY A; LYNCHBURG, VA; HERITAGE HS; (FR); Hnr Roll; MVP; Track (V); Health Care; Manager (Restaurant)

EZZELL, SHONTELL; FREDERICKSBURG, VA; RIVERBEND HS; (SR); Ctznshp Aw; Hnr Roll; Perf Att; Pres Sch; Comm Volntr; Chrch Yth Grp; DARE; DECA; Photog; Chr; Ch Chr; Track (J); Yrbk; FCCLA; Criminal Justice / Lawyer; Germanna Community College

FABIUS, ALEXANDRA; HAMPTON, VA; BETHEL HS; (SO); Ctznshp Aw; Hnr Roll; Nat Sci Aw; Nat Stu Ath Day Aw; Otst Ac Ach Awd; Perf Att; St of Mnth; Comm Volntr; Chrch Yth Grp; ROTC; Ch Chr; Pediatrician Nurse; Massage Therapist; Norfolk State U; Old Dominion U

FADELEY, EMILY S; STRASBURG, VA; STRASBURG HS; (SR); 4H Awd; Hi Hnr Roll; Hnr Roll; Nat Hon Sy; Perf Att; 4-H; Chrch Yth Grp; Emplmnt; Bnd; Mch Bnd; Pep Bnd; Outbound Japanese Exchange Club Delegate; 4-H All-Star; Nursing; Lord Fairfax Community College

FAISON, COURTNEY L; PETERSBURG, VA; DINWIDDIE HS; (FR); Hnr Roll; DECA; Track (J); Sch Ppr (R); Science Major (Meteorologist); English Major (Newspaper Reporter); Norfolk U; Duke U

FAMULARO, NICOLE; VIRGINIA BEACH, VA; FRANK W COX HS; (FR); F Lan Hn Soc; Hi Hnr Roll; Perf Att; Pres Ac Ftns Aw; Comm Volntr; Chrch Yth Grp; Key Club; Scouts; German Clb; Drl Tm; Sccr (J L); Randolph Macon Women's College; Mary Washington College

FARMAND, ELAHEH; FALLS CHURCH, VA; JEB STUART HS; (JR); F Lan Hn Soc; Hnr Roll; MVP; Otst Ac Ach Awd; Perf Att; St of Mnth; Comm Volntr; Emplmnt; Photog; Quill & Scroll; Orch; Vllyball (J); Lit Mag; Sch Ppr (R); Future Educators of America Club; Interact Club; Journalism; Writer/ Photographer; New York U; George Washington U

FARROW, LAFENNA L; NORFOLK, VA; LAKE TAYLOR HS; (JR); Hnr Roll; Otst Ac Ach Awd; St of Mnth; Comm Volntr; Chrch Yth Grp; FBLA; Chr; Ch Chr; Mch Bnd; SCA; Flag Girl; Surgical Technology; Physician's Assistant; Virginia Wesleyan; Old Dominion U

FAYYAD, DANA; SPRINGFIELD, VA; ISLAMIC SAUDI AC; (SO); Ctznshp Aw; Hi Hnr Roll; Nat Ldrshp Svc; Sci Fairs; Sci/Math Olympn; St of Mnth; Yth Ldrshp Prog; Comm Volntr; Peer Tut/Med; FBLA; Mod UN; NYLC; Bskball (V); Scr Kpr (V); Sccr (V); Cl Off (P); Sch Ppr; Prudential Spirit Award; President of Community Service Award; Medicine; Pediatrics; Princeton U; U of Virginia

FELDER, JASMINE; NEWPORT NEWS, VA; WARWICK HS; (JR); Hi Hnr Roll; Hnr Roll; Nat Hon Sy; WWAHSS; Chrch Yth Grp; Emplmnt; Key Club; Mth Clb/Tm; Chr; Ch Chr; Dnce; Chrldg (V); Track (V); National Achievement Scholarship Program; Pre-Med; Child Psychology; U of Virginia

FELLOWS, NICOLE M; STAFFORD, VA; COLONIAL FORGE HS; (JR); Hi Hnr Roll; Nat Hon Sy; Otst Ac Ach Awd; St of Mnth; Yth Ldrshp Prog; Peer Tut/Med; Chrch Yth Grp; DARE; Mod UN; Ch Chr; Bskball (V CL); Sccr (V CL); Tennis (V L); Stu Cncl (R); Accepted Into Showcase Dodds-Europe Creative Anthology; Accepted to Presidential Classroom; Physics Major; Brigham Young U; MIT

FENG, SUSAN; ASHBURN, VA; STONE BRIDGE HS; (JR); Hnr Roll; Nat Hon Sy; Perf Att; Comm Volntr; Peer Tut/Med; Key Club; Mth Clb/Tm; Vllyball (J); Computer Science; U of MD College Park

FERGUSON, GRACE A; RICHMOND, VA; VARINA HS; (FR); Peer Tut/ Med; Sch Ppr (R); Recreation Softball-4 years; Elementary Education; Secondary Education; Virginia Commonwealth U; U of Virginia

FERGUSON, KATHERINE; RICHMOND, VA; MILLS E GODWIN HS; (JR); F Lan Hn Soc; Hnr Roll; Nat Hon Sy; Perf Att; WWAHSS; Comm Volntr; Emplmnt; FCA; Key Club; Ntl Beta Clb; Pep Squd; Prom Com; Quill & Scroll; Spanish Clb; SP/M/VS; Cr Ctry (V); Track (V); Sch Ppr (E); Student Organization for Developing Attitudes - SODA; Nutrition / Dietician

FERGUSON, M DANE; HALIFAX, VA; HALIFAX CTY HS; (JR); 4H Awd; Hnr Roll; MVP; Comm Volntr; Hab For Humty Volntr; 4-H; Chrch Yth Grp; Svce Clb; SP/M/VS; Swmg (V L); Have 2nd Degree Black Belt in Karate; Accomplished Musician-Piano, Guitar, Drums; Something W/Music-Production; Christopher Newport U; Old Dominion U

FERGUSON, ZACHARY S; HAMPTON, VA; BETHEL HS; (SO); Hnr Roll; Perf Att; St of Mnth; Yth Ldrshp Prog; Comm Volntr; Chrch Yth Grp; Drma Clb; Emplmnt; Key Club; Stg Cre; Architecture / Engineering; Media Technology; Virginia Tech; Christopher Newport U

FEUCHT, ANNA M; MANASSAS, VA; OSBOURN HS; (JR); Hnr Roll; Nat Hon Sy; Sci Fairs; WWAHSS; Comm Volntr; Peer Tut/Med; Chrch Yth Grp; Emplmnt; Key Club; Mod UN; Quill & Scroll; SADD; French Clb; Chr; Ch Chr; SP/M/VS; Scr Kpr (L); Yrbk (E); District Choir; Tri-M Music Honors Society; English Language & Literature; Vocal Performance; The College of William and Mary; U of Virginia

FEUTZ, HILARY H; RESTON, VA; THE MADEIRA SCH; (SO); Hnr Roll; Nat Hon Sy; Sci Fairs; Comm Volntr; Hosp Aide; Chrch Yth Grp; Svce Clb; Tchrs Aide; Dnce; Sch Ppr (R); Dance Team Honors; Camp Counselor (3 Camps); Medicine (Cardiology); Stanford U; Emory U

Farrow, Lafenna L
Lake Taylor HS
Norfolk, VA

Espinas, Brian A
Yorktown HS
Arlington, VA

Enkhbold, Nomin
Roanoke, VA

National
Honor Roll
Spring 2005

El-Sherif, Youmna
Islamic Saudi AC
Centreville, VA

Evans, Ashland
Galax HS
Galax, VA

Fellows, Nicole M
Colonial Forge HS
Stafford, VA

FEYDO, ANDREW; CHESAPEAKE, VA; WESTERN BRANCH HS; (SO); Ctznshp Aw; Hi Hnr Roll; Hnr Roll; Nat Hon Sy; Otst Ac Ach Awd; Comm Volntr; Peer Tut/Med; Chrch Yth Grp; DARE; Lttrmn Clb; Spanish Clb; Acpl Chr; Chr; Ch Chr; Cr Ctry (V L); Track (V L); School Achievements Throughout School; All-District, Cross Country Southeastern District; Law Enforcement; Foreign Languages; Virginia Tech; U of North Carolina

FIGUEREDO, LUISA F; MARION, VA; (JR); Hi Hnr Roll; Hnr Roll; Nat Hon Sy; WWAHSS; Comm Volntr; Quill & Scroll; ROTC; Dnce; SP/M/VS; Stu Cncl (P); Lit Mag (E); 1st Place-Virginia Highlands Festival (Youth Art Exhibit); College Major-Biology; Become an Orthodontist; Virginia Commonwealth U; Harvard Dental School

FILLO, NORHAN; ASHBURN, VA; STONE BRIDGE HS; (JR); F Lan Hn Soc; Hnr Roll; Nat Hon Sy; Peer Tut/Med; Emplmnt; Key Club; Clb; National Society of High School Scholars; Governor School (Virginia) for French; Nursing; U of Virginia; James Madison U

FINKS, JOSHUA A; GREAT FALLS, VA; DOMINION HS; (JR); Hnr Roll; Pres Ac Ftns Aw; Comm Volntr; Chrch Yth Grp; Emplmnt; Ftball (VJC); Lcrsse (V); Track (V); Wt Lftg (V); Running for Senior Class President; Mission Trip to Honduras & Belize; Engineering; Architecture; VA Tech, Virginia Polytech; UVA, U of Virginia

FITZSIMMONS, JAMES V; OAKTON, VA; JAMES MADISON HS; (SO); Hnr Roll; Otst Ac Ach Awd; Pres Ac Ftns Aw; WWAHSS; ROTC; Drl Tm; Doctor; Lawyer; US Naval Academy; West Point

FLEEGER, CRYSTAL; VIRGINIA BEACH, VA; FIRST COLONIAL HS; (JR); F Lan Hn Soc; Hnr Roll; Nat Hon Sy; Pres Ac Ftns Aw; St of Mnth; WWAHSS; Yth Ldrshp Prog; Comm Volntr; Peer Tut/Med; Chrch Yth Grp; Key Club; MuAlphaTh; Sci Clb; French Clb; Math Analysis Student of the Year; Acceptance Into the Legal Studies Academy; Psychology; Education; College of William and Mary; U of Virginia

FLEMING, KAYLA M; CENTREVILLE, VA; WESTFIELD HS; (SO); Hi Hnr Roll; Comm Volntr; Peer Tut/Med; Quill & Scroll; Sch Ppr (E, R); Spanish Honor Society, College Partnership Program; Newspaper Center Spread Editor; Journalism; Education/Child Care Development; James Madison U; U of Virginia; New York U, VA Tech

FLETCHER, JADE; CLINTWOOD, VA; CLINTWOOD HS; (SO); 4H Awd; Hnr Roll; Pres Ac Ftns Aw; WWAHSS; 4-H; Drma Clb; Key Club; National Society of High School Scholars; Law; Education; Washington U St Louis; U of Virginia Wise

FLIPPO, DANIEL; RICHMOND, VA; VARINA HS; (SR); Hnr Roll; MVP; Perf Att; Pres Ac Ftns Aw; Comm Volntr; Hab For Humty Volntr; Peer Tut/Med; DARE; Emplmnt; Key Club; MuAlphaTh; Ntl Beta Clb; Sci Clb; Scouts; Tchrs Aide; Ftball (VJCL); Sccr (V L); Wrstlg (V CL); Eagle Scout; Criminal Justice/Science; Chemistry; Virginia Military Institute

FLOWERS, TIFFINY; MONTVALE, VA; LIBERTY HS; (SR); Hnr Roll; Kwnis Aw; Perf Att; Comm Volntr; Hosp Aide; 4-H; Chrch Yth Grp; FCA; Key Club; Spanish Clb; Ch Chr; Chrldg (VJCL); Sch Ppr (R, P); Yrbk (R, P); Nursing-Registered Nurse; Lynchburg College; Lynchburg General School of Nursing

FLOYD, MEGAN; WAYNESBORO, VA; STUARTS DRAFT HS; (JR); Hi Hnr Roll; Hnr Roll; WWAHSS; Chrch Yth Grp; Emplmnt; Key Club; Spanish Clb; Psychology; History; Virginia Commonwealth U; Guilford College

FLY, MICHAEL T; CHESAPEAKE, VA; WESTERN BRANCH HS; (SO); Hnr Roll; Nat Hon Sy; Otst Ac Ach Awd; Perf Att; St of Mnth; Comm Volntr; Chrch Yth Grp; DARE; Scouts; Bsball (V); Ftball (V L); Wt Lftg; Engineering; Architect; Old Dominion U

FLYNN, CASEY M; KEYSVILLE, VA; RANDOLPH-HENRY HS; (JR); Ch Chr; SP/M/VS; Cr Ctry (V L); Track (V L); Miss Southside Teen 2005; Professional Firefighter

FOCO, KATE; MIDLOTHIAN, VA; MIDLOTHIAN HS; (SO); Hi Hnr Roll; Comm Volntr; Red Cr Aide; Chrch Yth Grp; Drma Clb; Emplmnt; Jr Cls League; Latin Clb; Dnce; Stg Cre; Johns Hopkins Talent Search; President of Rock Climbing Club; PhD in Physics; Professor; U of Virginia; Cornell U

FORBES, BIANCA L; BURKE, VA; LAKE BRADDOCK SECONDARY SCH; MS; Hnr Roll; Otst Ac Ach Awd; St of Mnth; Comm Volntr; Chrch Yth Grp; Prom Com; Ch Chr; Dnce; Vllyball (J); 2005 National American Miss Finalist (Virginia); MPEE Academic Award 2004/2005; Registered Nurse; Talk Show Hostess (Communications Major); Virginia State U, Petersburg, VA; Hampton U, Hampton, VA

FORBES, ROBERT; NORFOLK, VA; GRANBY HS; (SO); Ctznshp Aw; Hnr Roll; Nat Ldrshp Svc; Otst Ac Ach Awd; Perf Att; Pres Ac Ftns Aw; Comm Volntr; Chrch Yth Grp; DARE; Chr; Ch Chr; Stg Cre; Cr Ctry (V); Black Belt in Karate; UNC-Charlotte

FOREMAN, AMBER; VIRGINIA BEACH, VA; FLOYD KELLAM HS; (JR); F Lan Hn Soc; Hi Hnr Roll; Hnr Roll; Nat Hon Sy; WWAHSS; Peer Tut/Med; Chess; Chrch Yth Grp; P to P St Amb Prg; French Clb; Dnce; Captain of the Knight Squad Step Team; Spanish; Hospitality Administration; James Madison U; Western Carolina U

FORREST, GREGORY E; CHESAPEAKE, VA; DEEP CREEK HS; (FR); Hnr Roll; Comm Volntr; Key Club; SADD; Bsball (J); Math; Science

FORTE, LUCY L; NEWPORT NEWS, VA; WOODSIDE HS; (JR); Ctznshp Aw; Hi Hnr Roll; Hnr Roll; Otst Ac Ach Awd; Perf Att; Pres Ac Ftns Aw; St of Mnth; Comm Volntr; Peer Tut/Med; DARE; Drma Clb; Emplmnt; Scouts; Spanish Clb; Ch Chr; CR (P); Sch Ppr (R); Peer Mediator; Girls Club; To Become a Lawyer and Chef; Write a Book; Howard U; Maryland U

FORTIER, ASHLEY; GLEN ALLEN, VA; DEEP RUN HS; (SO); Hnr Roll; Sci Fairs; Comm Volntr; 4-H; Dbte Team; Emplmnt; Fr of Library; Quill & Scroll; Scouts; Lit Mag (R); Sch Ppr (R); 3rd Place Winner VA Jr Academy of Science; DVM-Veterinary Medical Doctor; Writer; Tufts; Virginia Polytechnic Institute

FOSKETT, KEVIN A; MANASSAS, VA; OSBOURN PARK SR HS; (SO); Hnr Roll; Hab For Humty Volntr; Chrch Yth Grp; FBLA; Key Club; Sccr (V); Swmg (V); Microbiology; Science; United States Naval Academy; U of Virginia

FOSTER, E MEGAN; STAFFORD, VA; COLONIAL FORGE HS; (JR); Hnr Roll; Nat Hon Sy; Otst Ac Ach Awd; Comm Volntr; Chrch Yth Grp; Emplmnt; Orch; National Honor Society; Aquia Episcopal Youth Mission Trips; Bio-Technology; Biology; United States Air Force Academy; U of Virginia

FOSTER, LUKE; REVA, VA; MADISON HS; (SO); Hnr Roll; Nat Hon Sy; Otst Ac Ach Awd; Perf Att; FCA; Mus Clb; Ice Hky; Rlr Hky; Guitar; Snowboarding; Professional Musician; Professional Snowboarder; U of VA

FOSTER, VAQUEESA N; ROANOKE, VA; NORTHSIDE HS; (SR); WWAHSS; DECA; Bskball (V); Track (V); Who's Who Among Students; Political Science; Law Degree; Louisiana State U; U of Maryland

FOURNIER, CONNOR; MONROE, VA; HOMESCHOOLED/ALLIANCE CHRISTIAN AC; (JR); WWAHSS; Chrch Yth Grp; Civil Air Pat; Bnd; Adv Cncl (P); Stu Cncl (P); CR (P); Sch Ppr (E); 1st Degree Black in Tae Kwan Do, 2nd Degree in Shorin Ryu; Eaker Award (Lt. Colonel) in Civil Air Patrol; Law; Business/Economics; U of Virginia; College of William and Mary

FRAZIER, ERNEST D; DANVILLE, VA; GEORGE WASHINGTON HS; (SO); Hnr Roll; Nat Hon Sy; Perf Att; WWAHSS; Comm Volntr; Chrch Yth Grp; Key Club; Mus Clb; Ntl Beta Clb; Latin Clb; Ch Chr; Mch Bnd; Orch; Pep Bnd; Football; Volleyball; Practice Law; Musician; Howard U; Virginia Commonwealth U

FREED, STEPHANIE P; WAYNESBORO, VA; WAYNESBORO HS; (JR); Gov Hnr Prg; Hi Hnr Roll; Hnr Roll; Nat Hon Sy; WWAHSS; Comm Volntr; Chrch Yth Grp; Drma Clb; Emplmnt; Key Club; Acpl Chr; Chr; SP/M/VS; Sch Ppr (E); Community & Semi Professional Theatre; Shenandoah Valley Governor's School; Major-Musical Theatre; Minor-Business; East Carolina U; Christopher Newport U

FREEMAN, JESSICA N; PORTSMOUTH, VA; CHURCHLAND HS; (SR); Hnr Roll; DECA; ROTC; Received Nursing Certificate Jan - 2004; Graduated from School Jan 2005; Medical Administrative Management; Child Development; Tidewater Tech

FRIEDMAN, KARI; VIRGINIA BEACH, VA; KEMPSVILLE HS; (JR); Hnr Roll; Nat Hon Sy; Comm Volntr; Prom Com; Quill & Scroll; Scouts; Tmpl Yth Grp; Bnd; Mch Bnd; Cl Off (R); Yrbk (E); Vice President of Youth Group; Accounting; Psychology; James Madison U; Virginia Polytechnic Institute & State U

FRUCHTMAN, JESSICA; ASHBURN, VA; STONE BRIDGE HS; (FR); Hnr Roll; Comm Volntr; Peer Tut/Med; DECA; Key Club; Ntl FFA; Bnd; Jzz Bnd; Track (J); Manager-Freshman Basketball; Business; U of Virginia; James Madison U

FRUCHTMAN, REBECCA; ASHBURN, VA; STONE BRIDGE HS; (FR); Hnr Roll; Key Club; Bnd; Jzz Bnd; Track (J); Manager of Freshman Basketball; US Government; UVA; George Mason

FRY, MELISSA D; STERLING, VA; POTOMAC FALLS HS; (SO); Hnr Roll; Comm Volntr; ArtClub; Chrch Yth Grp; Key Club; Cr Ctry (J); Track (L); Architecture; Engineering

FU, ANN C; SPRINGFIELD, VA; ROBERT E LEE HS; Hnr Roll; Nat Hon Sy; Perf Att; Comm Volntr; FBLA; Clb; International Business; U of Virginia

FUEKANG, SOLANGE; FAIRFAX STATION, VA; HAYFIELD HS; (SR); Hnr Roll; Nat Hon Sy; Pres Sch; Comm Volntr; Peer Tut/Med; Chrch Yth Grp; Svce Clb; Tech Clb; Mechanical Engineering; Manufacturing Engineering; Virginia Commonwealth U

FULGHUM, JOHANNA M; VIENNA, VA; PAUL VI CATHOLIC HS; (JR); Hi Hnr Roll; Hnr Roll; Nat Hon Sy; Sci Fairs; Comm Volntr; Hab For Humty Volntr; Peer Tut/Med; FCA; Key Club; Spanish Clb; Cr Ctry (V L); Fld Hky; Lcrsse; Sccr; Track (V L); Yrbk (R, P); Virginia Polytechnic Institute; Mary Washington U

FULK, BYRON G; BRIDGEWATER, VA; TURNER ASHBY HS; (SR); F Lan Hn Soc; Hnr Roll; Nat Hon Sy; Yth Ldrshp Prog; Comm Volntr; Chrch Yth Grp; Emplmnt; FTA; Ntl FFA; Sci Clb; Tchrs Aide; Voc Ind Clb Am; Volunteer Firefighter/EMT; Chapter President-Turner Ashby FFA; Biology; Secondary Education; Bridgewater College

FULLER, BRITANY M; DANVILLE, VA; GEORGE WASHINGTON HS; (SR); Hi Hnr Roll; Hnr Roll; Pres Ac Ftns Aw; Sci Fairs; WWAHSS; Yth Ldrshp Prog; Comm Volntr; Peer Tut/Med; Red Cr Aide; Chrch Yth Grp; DECA; Emplmnt; Lib Aide; Prom Com; Scouts; Tchrs Aide; French Clb; Bnd; Chr; Ch Chr; SP/M/VS; PP Ftbl (V); CR (R); 5 Years of Project Discovery; Business Management; Associate's Degree; Danville Community College; Norfolk State U

FULLER, JUSTIN R; HONAKER, VA; COUNCIL HS; (SO); Ctznshp Aw; Hnr Roll; Pres Ac Ftns Aw; Comm Volntr; Spec Olymp Vol; Chrch Yth Grp; Scouts; Clr Grd; Bskball (VJC); Wt Lftg (J); Computers; Emory & Henry; Virginia Tech

FULWILER, KATHRYN; MANASSAS, VA; BATTLEFIELD HS; (JR); Hnr Roll; Sci Fairs; Comm Volntr; Chrch Yth Grp; DECA; Drma Clb; Emplmnt; FBLA; Prom Com; SADD; Cl Off (T); Future Business Leaders of America-Pres; Criminal Justice; Law Enforcement; Radford U; George Mason U

GABRO, CHRISTINA; ASHBURN, VA; BROAD RUN HS; (JR); Hnr Roll; MVP; Nat Hon Sy; Sci Fairs; WWAHSS; Chrch Yth Grp; Dbte Team; Emplmnt; NtlFrnscLg; Prom Com; Schol Bwl; Cl Off (R); Sch Ppr (R); VA State Forensics Tournament Participant; Policy Debate Captain; Political Science; Law; U of Virginia; Virginia Polytechnic Institute & State U

GAGEN, MATTHEW; STERLING, VA; POTOMAC FALLS HS; (JR); F Lan Hn Soc; Gov Hnr Prg; Hnr Roll; FBLA; Key Club; Vsity Clb; Spanish Clb; Bnd; Swmg (V L); Accepted - Academy of Science / Loudoun County; Engineering; Business Administration; Georgetown U; Johns Hopkins U

GALDAMEZ, GERALDINE E; MANASSAS, VA; STONEWALL JACKSON HS; (JR); F Lan Hn Soc; Hnr Roll; MVP; Nat Hon Sy; Pres Ac Ftns Aw; Sci Fairs; Comm Volntr; Peer Tut/Med; Chrch Yth Grp; FCA; Key Club; Photog; Vsity Clb; Bskball (V L); Fld Hky (V L); Lcrsse (V L); Stu Cncl (V); Pre-Medicine; Engineering; Brown U; U of Virginia

GALLAGHER, SHANNON D; CENTREVILLE, VA; CHANTILLY HS; (SR); F Lan Hn Soc; Hnr Roll; MVP; Nat Hon Sy; Otst Ac Ach Awd; Comm Volntr; Peer Tut/Med; Mth Clb/Tm; Vllyball (V CL); National Honor Society-President; Political Science Internship; U of Virginia

GALLIHER, WHITNEY; MARION, VA; MARION SR HS; (SR); WWAHSS; FBLA; SADD; Chrldg (V); Sftball (J); Vllyball (J); Stu Cncl; Old Dominion U

GANDHI, RONAK; NATURAL BRIDGE, VA; ROCKBRIDGE CTY HS; (JR); Mth Clb/Tm; Sci Clb; Tech Clb; Computer Science; University of Virginia Charlottesville; Virginia Tech

GARG, MITIKA; ASHBURN, VA; BROAD RUN HS; (JR); F Lan Hn Soc; Hi Hnr Roll; Hnr Roll; Nat Hon Sy; St of Mnth; Comm Volntr; Peer Tut/Med; Emplmnt; Key Club; Mth Clb/Tm; Business; Math; College of William and Mary; U of Virginia

GARLAND, AIXA M; HAMPTON, VA; TABB HS; (JR); Hnr Roll; WWAHSS; DARE; Prom Com; Scouts; Chrldg (J); Track (V); Cl Off (S); Gymnastics At World Class Level 8; Physical Therapist; Veterinarian; Clark Atlanta U; Spelman U

GATES, DIANA B; COLONIAL HEIGHTS, VA; COLONIAL HEIGHTS HS; (JR); F Lan Hn Soc; Hnr Roll; Nat Hon Sy; WWAHSS; Comm Volntr; Peer Tut/Med; AL Aux Girls; Chrch Yth Grp; DECA; HO'Br Yth Ldrshp; Ntl Beta Clb; Quill & Scroll; Schol Bwl; Scouts; Fld Hky (V); Sftball (V); Cl Off; Sch Ppr (E); National Honor Society President; French Club President; Journalism; International Affairs; New York U; U of Virginia

GAYLE, JAZMINE; ROANOKE, VA; PATRICK HENRY HS; (SO); Hnr Roll; Key Club; Sch Ppr; Participated in National "Stop Smoking" Ad Campaign; Political Science - BA/BS, MA/MS; Business Administration/Performing Arts - BA/BS, MBA/MS; Radford U; Roanoke, Virginia; U of Virginia at Charlottesville; Charlottesville, Virginia

GECKER, ALEXANDRA; RICHMOND, VA; MAGGIE L WALKER GOVERNOR'S SCH; (FR); Hi Hnr Roll; Mod UN; French Clb; Sccr (J); Stu Cncl (R); 2nd Level Lauriat National-Concour National De Francois; JD / Law; MBA; U of Virginia; Princeton U

GEORGE, JEFF; FALLS CHURCH, VA; J.E.B. STUART HS; (JR); Hnr Roll; Otst Ac Ach Awd; WWAHSS; Comm Volntr; Peer Tut/Med; ArtClub; Chrch Yth Grp; FBLA; SP/M/VS; Cr Ctry (V L); Track (V L); IB Diploma Candidate; Medal Winner in 5k Runner Run Conducted By DC Road Runners; Architecture; Aviation; Virginia Tech; George Mason U

Gabro, Christina
Broad Run HS
Ashburn, VA

Feydo, Andrew
Western Branch HS
Chesapeake, VA

Frazier, Ernest D
George Washington HS
Danville, VA

GEORGE, JEFF; FALLS CURCH, VA; J.E.B. STUART HS; (JR); Hnr Roll; Otst Ac Ach Awd; WWAHSS; Comm Volntr; Peer Tut/Med; ArtClub; Chrch Yth Grp; Emplmnt; FBLA; SP/M/VS; Cr Ctry (V L); Track (V L); Medal Winner in 5k Run (DC Road-Runners Club); (1st Place in Raider Run), Effort Award; Architecture (Civil Engineering); Design Engineer (Computers); Virginia Tech; George Mason U

GHAZANFARI, PARNIA; ASHBURN, VA; STONE BRIDGE HS; (FR); Hnr Roll; Sci Fairs; Comm Volntr; Key Club; Bnd; Law School; Dental School; U of Virginia; New York U

GIAMARINO, SARAH E; FREDERICKSBURG, VA; JAMES MONROE HS; (SO); Hi Hnr Roll; Key Club; Clr Grd; Veterinary Medicine

GIBBS, NATALIE; NEWPORT NEWS, VA; WARWICK HS; (JR); WWAHSS; Yth Ldrshp Prog; Comm Volntr; Peer Tut/Med; Chrch Yth Grp; Emplmnt; Jr Ach; Key Club; SADD; Ch Chr; CR (R); Religion; Virginia State U

GIBSON, DIONNE; VIRGINIA BEACH, VA; PRINCESS ANNE HS; (SR); Hnr Roll; MVP; Otst Ac Ach Awd; USMC Stu Ath Aw; DECA; Emplmnt; Spanish Clb; Cr Ctry; Track; Venture's Scholars; All-State Track and Field; Major in Nursing; Medical School / Pediatrician; Charleston Southern U

GILBERT, CHELSEA; CHESAPEAKE, VA; WESTERN BRANCH HS; (SO); Hnr Roll; Nat Hon Sy; Perf Att; Pres Ac Ftns Aw; Comm Volntr; Chrch Yth Grp; Lib Aide; Sftball (V L); Vllyball (JC); President of National Junior Honor Society; Special Education; Primary Education, Physical Therapy; Virginia Tech; Averett U

GILBERT, KRISTIN; ASHBURN, VA; STONE BRIDGE HS; (SR); F Lan Hn Soc; Hnr Roll; Nat Hon Sy; Pres Ac Ftns Aw; Comm Volntr; Key Club; Chr; Dnce; PP Ftbl; Music Education; Attending-James Madison U

GILBERT, ZACHARY I; CEDAR BLUFF, VA; RICHLANDS HS; (FR); Hnr Roll; Sci Fairs; Sci/Math Olympn; Ftball (V); Tennis (V); Wt Lftg (V); Virginia Tech; U North Carolina

GILEAU, RAVEN; WOODBRIDGE, VA; C D HYLTON HS; (FR); Hnr Roll; Nat Hon Sy; Otst Ac Ach Awd; Perf Att; Sci Fairs; Perfect Attendance; Dentistry; Architecture; Virginia Tech; Harvard U

GILES-OUTLAW, SORAENA V; NORFOLK, VA; B T WASHINGTON HS; (FR); Ctznshp Aw; Hnr Roll; Nat Hon Sy; St of Mnth; Comm Volntr; Peer Tut/Med; Chrch Yth Grp; FBLA; Fld Hky (V); Sftball (VJ); Track (J); Money Management / MBA; International Finances; Hampton U; Howard U

GILILLAND, SANDRA; ALEXANDRIA, VA; WEST POTOMAC HS; (SR); Hi Hnr Roll; Hnr Roll; Nat Hon Sy; Salutrn; Sci Fairs; St of Mnth; Hosp Aide; Peer Tut/Med; Emplmnt; Spanish Clb; Bnd; Clr Grd; Mch Bnd; Pep Bnd; Hsbk Rdg; Spanish Honor Society; Junior Volunteer of the Year (At Mt. Vernon Hospital); Biology; Pre-Medicine; The College of William and Mary

GILL, JEFFREY; RICHMOND, VA; BENEDICTINE HS; (SO); Hi Hnr Roll; Comm Volntr; Key Club; French Clb; Bskball (JC); Georgetown U; Virginia Tech

GILTNER, CATHRYN; ASHBURN, VA; BROAD RUN HS; (JR); Duke TS; Hi Hnr Roll; Hnr Roll; Kwnis Aw; Nat Hon Sy; Otst Ac Ach Awd; Pres Ac Ftns Aw; St of Mnth; WWAHSS; Yth Ldrshp Prog; Comm Volntr; Peer Tut/Med; Emplmnt; Key Club; Pep Squd; SADD; Vsity Clb; Tennis (V L); Vllyball (VJ L); Adv Cncl (R); Yrbk (E, R, P); Earth Science Student of the Year; Pre-Calculus Student of the Year; Pre-Med; Bioengineering; College of William and Mary; Duke U

GIVNER, DIONNE M; ASHBURN, VA; STONE BRIDGE HS; (SO); Hnr Roll; WWAHSS; Comm Volntr; Drma Clb; MULTI Clb; SP/M/VS; Stg Cre; Who's Who Among American HS Students; Doctor; Business; Emory U; New York U

GLADDEN, HEATHER; MILLBORO, VA; ALLEGHANY; (JR); Hnr Roll; St of Mnth; WWAHSS; Comm Volntr; Peer Tut/Med; ArtClub; Chrch Yth Grp; DARE; Key Club; Lib Aide; Photog; SADD; Bnd; Mch Bnd; Pep Bnd; SP/M/VS; Stu Cncl (V, S); CR (R); Lit Mag (E); Yrbk (P); Virginia Tech; Roanoke College

GLASBY, JANET M; LORTON, VA; MAYFIELD SECONDARY SCH; (SR); Hi Hnr Roll; Hnr Roll; Nat Hon Sy; WWAHSS; Comm Volntr; DECA; Dnce; Spelling Bee Competitor; Business Management; Music; Berklee College of Music; State U of New York

GLASCOCK, JEANA D; SCOTTSBURG, VA; CTRVILLE CHRISTIAN SC; (SO); Ctznshp Aw; Hnr Roll; MVP; Nat Hon Sy; Perf Att; Sci Fairs; Comm Volntr; Chrch Yth Grp; Mus Clb; Chr; Ch Chr; SP/M/VS; Bskball (V); Vllyball (V); Yrbk (P); Singing; Missionary/Missions; Crown College; Ambassador College

GLASS, RYAN A; ASHBURN, VA; STONE BRIDGE HS; (FR); Hnr Roll; Comm Volntr; Key Club; Meteorology; Music; James Madison U; VA Tech, UVA

GLASSMAN, ALYSSA; VIRGINIA BEACH, VA; FRANK W COX HS; (SO); F Lan Hn Soc; Nat Hon Sy; Pres Ac Ftns Aw; St of Mnth; Key Club; Tmpl Yth Grp; Cl Off (P, V); Stu Cncl (R); CR (R); Crew Club; Relay for Life; Business; U of Virginia; Virginia Tech

GLEISER, JOANNE; WILLIAMSBURG, VA; LAFAYETTE HS; (SR); F Lan Hn Soc; Nat Hon Sy; Otst Ac Ach Awd; WWAHSS; Comm Volntr; Peer Tut/Med; Drma Clb; Emplmnt; MuAlphaTh; NtlFrnscLg; Photog; Spanish Clb; Dnce; SP/M/VS; Child Psychology; Spanish; U of Virginia

GLENN, D JASEN; CHESAPEAKE, VA; WESTERN BRANCH HS; (JR); Gov Hnr Prg; Hnr Roll; Comm Volntr; Hosp Aide; Drma Clb; Chr; Dnce; SP/M/VS; Governor's School for the Arts; Musical Theatre; Physics; William and Mary; James Madison

GLORFIELD, MARY A; MIDLOTHIAN, VA; MAGGIE L WALKER GOVERNOR'S SCH; (JR); F Lan Hn Soc; Gov Hnr Prg; Nat Hon Sy; Comm Volntr; Key Club; P to P St Amb Prg; Prom Com; Cr Ctry (V L); Track (V L); Interior Design; Emory U

GLOVER, BRIAN; FALLS CHURCH, VA; GEORGE MASON HS; (SO); Nat Hon Sy; Comm Volntr; Peer Tut/Med; Cr Ctry (J); Lcrsse (V); Stu Cncl (R); CR (R); Stanford U; Princeton U

GOING, TIFFANY P; CHESAPEAKE, VA; STONE BRIDGE HS; (FR); Hnr Roll; WWAHSS; Comm Volntr; Chrch Yth Grp; Emplmnt; Key Club; Bskball (J); Sftball (VJ); Swmg (V L); CR (R); William & Mary; James Madison

GOLD, KEVIN T; VIENNA, VA; G C MARSHALL HS; (SR); DECA; Quill & Scroll; Tmpl Yth Grp; Sch Ppr (E); Indiana U

GOLIGHTLY, AMANDA; WINCHESTER, VA; JAMES WOOD HS; (JR); Hnr Roll; DARE; DECA; Emplmnt; Scouts; Flg Crps; Bsball; Chrldg (V L); Cr Ctry (J); Gmnstcs (J); Sftball (J); Nursing; Modeling; Shenandoah U

GOMEZ, NICOLE; VIRGINIA BEACH, VA; BRANDON MS; (MS); Hi Hnr Roll; Perf Att; Chr; Fld Hky (L); Sccr (CL); Played on Two Other Soccer Teams; Veterinarian & to Play Soccer

GOMEZ, TYLER B; RICHMOND, VA; VARINA HS; (FR); Ctznshp Aw; Hnr Roll; WWAHSS; Comm Volntr; Chrch Yth Grp; Key Club; Ch Chr; Dnce; Sch Ppr (R); Journalism/Broadcast; Virginia Commonwealth U; North Carolina State

GONZALEZ, JENNY; MANASSAS, VA; OSBOURN PARK HS; (JR); Hnr Roll; Nat Ldrshp Svc; Pres Ac Ftns Aw; WWAHSS; Comm Volntr; Hosp Aide; Peer Tut/Med; Chrch Yth Grp; FTA; Key Club; Quill & Scroll; Chr; Fld Hky (VJ L); Lcrsse (VJCL); Track (V); Cl Off (P); Stu Cncl (R); Sch Ppr (R, P); Yrbk (R, P); National Student Leadership Conference; William and Mary Leadership Award; Political Science/Law

GOOD, GILLIAN C; ALEXANDRIA, VA; ST. STEPHENS & ST. AGNES SCH; (JR); F Lan Hn Soc; Nat Mrt Semif; Comm Volntr; Emplmnt; Mth Clb/Tm; Mod UN; Quill & Scroll; Spanish Clb; Tennis (V); Cl Off (R); Yrbk (E); Varsity Crew Team Member, Cum Laude; Peer Helper (Counselor Program); Medical Degree; Orthodontics; U of Virginia; Princeton U

GOODE, CHENIQUA; PORTSMOUTH, VA; IC NORCOM; (SR); Hnr Roll; Nat Hon Sy; WWAHSS; Comm Volntr; Emplmnt; Off Aide; Prom Com; Fld Hky (V); Sftball (J); Sch Ppr (R); Yrbk (P); Academic Achievement Award, Access; Nomination for Youth Citizen Award; Mass Communications; Nursing; Virginia Commonwealth U; Virginia State U

GOODE, DEMETRIA L; PETERSBURG, VA; PETERSBURG HS; (JR); Hnr Roll; Nat Hon Sy; Key Club

GOODE, LATAVIA M; EMPORIA, VA; GREENSVILLE CTY HS; (SR); Hi Hnr Roll; Hnr Roll; Nat Hon Sy; WWAHSS; Forensic Science; Virginia Commonwealth, MN; Virginia State U

GOODIN, SARAH L; POWHATAN, VA; POWHATAN HS; (JR); Comm Volntr; Emplmnt; Prom Com; Tchrs Aide; SP/M/VS; Stu Cncl (R); Two Part-Time Jobs; Medical Engineering; Intelligence / Military History; College of William & Mary; Virginia Polytechnic

GOODMAN, ALEXANDER; SUFFOLK, VA; LAKELAND HS; (SR); Hnr Roll; Comm Volntr; DARE; Ftball (V); Wrstlg (V); Bachelors; Norfolk State U; Virginia Tech

GOODRICH, LAKEN R; NEWPORT NEWS, VA; WOODSIDE HS; (JR); Chrch Yth Grp; Emplmnt; German Clb; Elementary Education; Childcare Development; East Carolina U; U of North Carolina

GOODYEAR, ZACHARY L; STUARTS DRAFT, VA; STUARTS DRAFT HS; (FR); Ctznshp Aw; Hnr Roll; Pres Ac Ftns Aw; WWAHSS; Comm Volntr; FCA; Key Club; Lttrmn Clb; Ntl FFA; Bsball (VJ); Ftball (J); Stu Cncl (R); CR (T); Business; Engineering; Notre Dame

GOVANI, TIFFANY; VIRGINIA BEACH, VA; FRANK W COX HS; (JR); Hnr Roll; Perf Att; WWAHSS; Comm Volntr; Chrch Yth Grp; Emplmnt; Key Club; Spanish Clb; Tennis (V); Stu Cncl; Medical; U of Mary Washington

GOYAL, SAMITA S; ALEXANDRIA, VA; THOMAS JEFFERSON HS FOR SCI/TECH; (SR); Nat Hon Sy; Nat Mrt LOC; Pres Sch; Hosp Aide; Mth Clb/Tm; Mod UN; Fld Hky (J); Lcrsse (V L); Stu Cncl (R); National Honor Society Treasurer; Advanced Placement Scholar; Neuro-Cardiosurgeon; Research; Duke U; U of Virginia

GRAHAM, JENNIFER L; DANVILLE, VA; GALILEO MAGNET HS; (FR); Ctznshp Aw; Nat Hon Sy; Comm Volntr; Chrch Yth Grp; Excellence in Math; Recognition of Excellent Conduct; Degree in Psychology; Social Worker / Pediatrician; Liberty U; Nova Southeastern U

GRAMSKY, BABS R; FALLS CHURCH, VA; STUART HS; (SR); Hnr Roll; Nat Hon Sy; Comm Volntr; Peer Tut/Med; Emplmnt; Scouts; Chr; Stg Cre; Member of Virginia Academy of Fencing; ISI Ice Skating Institute Freestyle 6; Criminal Justice; Computer Graphics; George Mason U; LA Arts College, U of the Art

GRASSO, ZACK; MIDLOTHIAN, VA; MAGGIE L WALKER GOVERNOR'S SCH; (FR); Ctznshp Aw; DAR; Fut Prb Slvr; Hi Hnr Roll; Hnr Roll; Nat Hon Sy; Perf Att; Pres Ac Ftns Aw; Pres Sch; Sci Fairs; Comm Volntr; Chess; Key Club; Mth Clb/Tm; Spanish Clb; Bnd; Jzz Bnd; Sccr (J); Swmg

GRAVES, FELICIA; LONG ISLAND, VA; GRETNA HS; (JR); Ctznshp Aw; Hnr Roll; Comm Volntr; Peer Tut/Med; Lib Aide; Chr; SP/M/VS; Cl Off (R); Family Career and Community Leaders of America; Early Childhood Development; Child Care; Danville Community College; Hampton U

GRAVES, WHITNEY; HAMPTON, VA; BETHEL HS; (SO); Hnr Roll; FBLA; Spanish Clb; Cl Off (S); Elizabeth City State U; North Carolina A & T State U

GRAY, SHANICE D; CHARLOTTESVILLE, VA; CHARLOTTESVILLE HS; (JR); Hi Hnr Roll; Hnr Roll; WWAHSS; Biology Clb; Emplmnt; FBLA; Off Aide; Psychology; Business Technology; U of Virginia; Virginia Commonwealth U

GRAY, STEPHANIE; CHARLOTTESVILLE, VA; ALBEMARLE HS; (JR); Gov Hnr Prg; Hi Hnr Roll; Hnr Roll; Nat Hon Sy; Yth Ldrshp Prog; Comm Volntr; Hab For Humty Volntr; Chrch Yth Grp; Jr Cls League; Key Club; Bnd; Ch Chr; Orch; Cr Ctry (V CL); Lcrsse (VJ L); Track (V CL); CR (R); Attendance At The 2005 Governor's School For Fine Arts; Medical School-Pediatric Oncologist; Washington and Lee; William and Mary

GRAY III, THOMAS P; CHESTER, VA; THOMAS DALE HS; (SR); Hi Hnr Roll; Hnr Roll; Nat Hon Sy; Otst Ac Ach Awd; Comm Volntr; Peer Tut/Med; Chrch Yth Grp; Emplmnt; FCA; Vsity Clb; French Clb; Sccr (JC); Vllyball (V); Sch Ppr (R); Yrbk (E); Economics-MBA/JD; George Mason U; Virginia Tech

GREEN, ASHLEY A; WAYNESBORO, VA; STUARTS DRAFT HS; (JR); Hi Hnr Roll; ArtClub; Lawyer; Probation Officer; JMU College; Stanford College

GREEN, BRITTANY L; WHITE STONE, VA; LANCASTER HS; (SO); F Lan Hn Soc; Hnr Roll; Kwnis Aw; Otst Ac Ach Awd; Comm Volntr; Chrch Yth Grp; Emplmnt; HO'Br Yth Ldrshp; Key Club; Foreign Clb; Bnd; Ch Chr; Mch Bnd; Bskball (J); Scr Kpr (VJ); Adv Cncl (V); HOBY Certificate, Vice President of Leo Club Award; Bachelors in Psychology; Attending Modeling School; Old Dominion U; Howard U

GREEN, JESSICA H; GLEN ALLEN, VA; DEEP RUN HS; (JR); Hnr Roll; Comm Volntr; Hosp Aide; ArtClub; Key Club; Ntl Beta Clb; Pep Squd; Track (V); Best in Show - 2004 for the Arts; Numerous Piano Awards; Art History Professor; Archeologist; U of Virginia; James Madison U

GREEN, MARCO; SUFFOLK, VA; LAKELAND HS; (SR); Ctznshp Aw; Hnr Roll; Perf Att; ArtClub; Ch Chr; Art; Engineering; The Art Institute

GREEN, NIKITA; STERLING, VA; DOMINION HS; (JR); Hnr Roll; Perf Att; Pres Ac Ftns Aw; WWAHSS; Comm Volntr; Key Club; Vsity Clb; Track (V CL); Stu Cncl (R); CR (R); Athletic Trainer/Manager for Football; U of Miami; Florida Southern College

GREEN, SHANE M; RICHMOND, VA; VARINA HS; (JR); Hosp Aide; Chrch Yth Grp; Clr Grd; 2nd Place in Skills USA Spelling Competition; 3rd Place in Skills USA Cosmetology Technical Exam; Law / Lawyer; Science / Doctor; North Carolina Central U; Florida State U

GREENE, ABIGAIL; FREDERICKSBURG, VA; COLONIAL FORGE HS; (JR); Hi Hnr Roll; Hnr Roll; MVP; Nat Hon Sy; Otst Ac Ach Awd; WWAHSS; Comm Volntr; Hab For Humty Volntr; Peer Tut/Med; Chrch Yth Grp; DARE; Key Club; Mth Clb/Tm; Prom Com; SADD; Vsity Clb; Latin Clb; Sccr (V); Adv Cncl (V); Sch Ppr (E); Key Club - VP; Finance; Law; U of VA; Virginia Poly Technical U

GREGORY, GERALD A; PALMYRA, VA; FLUVANNA HS; (SO); Hnr Roll; Otst Ac Ach Awd; Perf Att; St of Mnth; Chrch Yth Grp; FCA; Key Club; Mus Clb; Chr; SP/M/VS; Bskball (J); Ftball (V L); Sound Eng.; Sport Medicine; Virginia Tech; Maryland

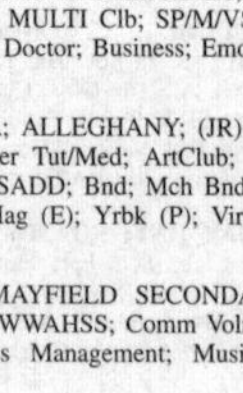
Greene, Abigail
Colonial Forge HS
Fredericksburg, VA

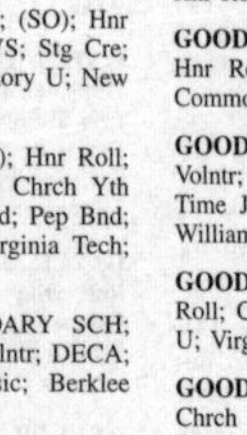
Green, Brittany L
Lancaster HS
White Stone, VA

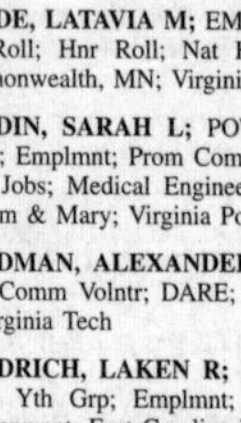
Green, Ashley A
Stuarts Draft HS
Waynesboro, VA

National
Honor Roll
Spring 2005

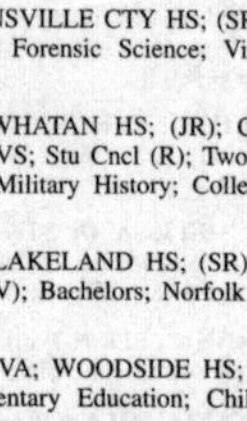
Goodrich, Laken R
Woodside HS
Newport News, VA

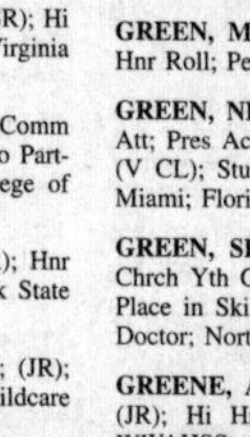
Green, Jessica H
Deep Run HS
Glen Allen, VA

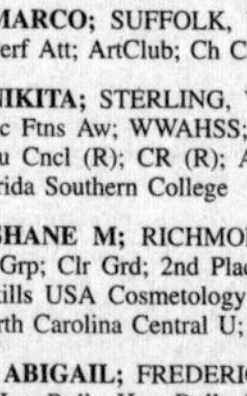
Gregory, Gerald A
Fluvanna HS
Palmyra, VA

GREGORY, JENNIFER J; NORFOLK, VA; GRANBY HS; (JR); F Lan Hn Soc; Gov Hnr Prg; Hnr Roll; Nat Hon Sy; Pres Sch; WWAHSS; Comm Volntr; Spec Olymp Vol; DARE; DECA; Emplmnt; FBLA; Chr; CR (R); Music Technology; Spanish; Georgia State U; Georgia Institute of Technology

GRIBLING, RACHEL L; SUFFOLK, VA; STONEBRIDGE SCH; (FR); Hi Hnr Roll; Hnr Roll; Salutrn; Sci Fairs; Chrch Yth Grp; Drma Clb; Key Club; Chr; Ch Chr; SP/M/VS; Bskball (VJ L); Sccr (V); Adv Cncl (R); Stu Cncl; CR (R); Participated in 30 Hour Famine March for Life, Washington DC; Political Science, Law; Veterinarian; Mary Washington College, William & Mary; U of Virginia, James Madison

GRIESER, JUSTIN; ALEXANDRIA, VA; THOMAS A EDISON HS; (SR); F Lan Hn Soc; Hi Hnr Roll; Nat Hon Sy; WWAHSS; Key Club; Spanish Clb; Bnd; International Relations; U of Virginia

GRIFFIN, DARCY; MANASSAS, VA; FOREST PARK; (FR); Ctznshp Aw; Hi Hnr Roll; Nat Hon Sy; Pres Ac Ftns Aw; St of Mnth; ArtClub; DARE; Scouts; Stg Cre; Sccr (J); Swmg (J); Track (J); Stu Cncl; CR; National Junior Honor Society; News Anchor-School Media Team; Television Journalism; Communications; U of Richmond; New York U

GRIFFIN, GABRIEL A; PETERSBURG, VA; PETERSBURG HS; (SR); Hnr Roll; Perf Att; Comm Volntr; Peer Tut/Med; DECA; FBLA; Mus Clb; Bnd; Ch Chr; Jzz Bnd; Mch Bnd; I Want to Go to College for Criminal Justice.; I Want to Be a Crime Scene Investigator.; Virginia State U; Norfolk State U

GRIMESEY, SARAH G; COVINGTON, VA; ALLEGHANY HS; (JR); Hi Hnr Roll; Hnr Roll; Nat Hon Sy; WWAHSS; Peer Tut/Med; Red Cr Aide; Chrch Yth Grp; FCA; FBLA; Key Club; Ntl Beta Clb; Prom Com; Chr; SP/M/VS; Sccr (V); Stu Cncl (R); Sch Ppr (R); Leadership Committee; Students for Christ; English; Education; George Mason U; U of Virginia

GRIMM, ZACHARY; ARRINGTON, VA; NELSON CTY HS; (SO); Hnr Roll; Sci Fairs; Yth Ldrshp Prog; Comm Volntr; Emplmnt; NYLC; Wt Lftg; Wrstlg; Yrbk; Congressional Student Leadership Conference; Independent Volunteer Work; Diplomacy and International Affairs; U of Virginia

GROSZ, ERIN; RICHMOND, VA; VARINA HS; (SO); Hnr Roll; Hosp Aide; HO'Br Yth Ldrshp; Orch; Vllyball (J L); Diversity Awareness Club; History Club; History; Librarian Science; U North Carolina Greensboro; Longwood U

GROVES, SHANNON C; ASHBURN, VA; BROAD RUN HS; (SO); Hi Hnr Roll; Hnr Roll; Perf Att; Pres Ac Ftns Aw; Sci Fairs; St of Mnth; Comm Volntr; ArtClub; Schol Bwl; Cr Ctry (V L); Sccr (J); 1st Place Science Award from FWQA; Soccer Player in Travel League for 5 Years; Marine Biology; Medicine; U of California Santa Barbara; U of Hawaii

GUARD, LUKE T; SALEM, VA; SALEM HS; (SO); Chrch Yth Grp; Emplmnt; SP/M/VS; Bskball (JC); Ftball (VJ L); Sch Ppr (R); Junior Honor Association; Teaching / Coaching; Psychology; Freed-Hardeman U

GUENDEL, NICK; SMITHFIELD, VA; SMITHFIELD HS; (SO); Hnr Roll; MVP; Comm Volntr; Chrch Yth Grp; Jr Cls League; Key Club; Ntl Beta Clb; Scouts; Cr Ctry (V); Swmg (V); Track (V); Most Valuable Runner - Cross Country; Most Dedicated Swimmer; College of William and Mary; Pennsylvania State U

GUERIN, CARRIE; MIDLOTHIAN, VA; MIDLOTHIAN HS; (SO); Hi Hnr Roll; Hnr Roll; Comm Volntr; Quill & Scroll; Latin Clb; Lit Mag (E); Academic Letter and 1 Bar; 2nd Place Write Now Contest; UN Ambassador; Best-Selling Novelist; College of William and Mary; U of Mary Washington

GUERRERO, ROBERT; ASHBURN, VA; STONE BRIDGE HS; (SO); Comm Volntr; Key Club; Architecture; Texas A&M; Virginia Tech

GULLE, ARAS; FALLS CHURCH, VA; STUART HS; (JR); Ftball (L); Swmg (V L); Crew: Rowing Varsity (Have Letter); Engineer's Civil or Aerospace; GMU; JMU

GUPTA, NATASHA; ALEXANDRIA, VA; THOMAS A EDISON HS; (SO); Hnr Roll; Sci/Math Olympn; WWAHSS; Comm Volntr; Dbte Team; Key Club; Sci Clb; Spanish Clb; Tennis (J); Lit Mag (R); Sch Ppr (R); Math Honor Society; It's Academic; U of Virginia

GUSTAVSON, ERICA K; WOODBRIDGE, VA; WOODBRIDGE SR HS; (JR); F Lan Hn Soc; Nat Hon Sy; Otst Ac Ach Awd; Chrch Yth Grp; Ntl Beta Clb; French Clb; Fld Hky (J); Lcrsse (VJ)

GUYNN, REBECCA E; SALEM, VA; SALEM HS; (SO); F Lan Hn Soc; Nat Hon Sy; Comm Volntr; Emplmnt; FCA; Prom Com; Scouts; Svce Clb; Spanish Clb; Bnd; Swmg (V L); Vllyball (VJ); Adv Cncl (R); Cl Off (T); Stu Cncl (R); Girl Scout Silver Award; Club Volleyball (Roanoke Juniors)

GWALTNEY, DANIELLE R; RANDOLPH, VA; RANDOLPH HENRY HS; (SO); 4H Awd; MVP; Nat Hon Sy; Nat Sci Aw; Otst Ac Ach Awd; Perf Att; 4-H; DARE; FBLA; SADD; Sftball (V L); Vllyball (JC); Basketball 2002; Architecture; Engineering; Lynchburg College; U of Virginia

GWYNN, KIYA M; STAFFORD, VA; NORTH STAFFORD HS; (SR); Hnr Roll; Otst Ac Ach Awd; Comm Volntr; DARE; Emplmnt; FBLA; Scouts; SADD; Member of Step Team; Psychology Minor in Cognitive Neuroscience; Marymount of Fordham U; Virginia Tech

HA, LORI; GLEN ALLEN, VA; MAGGIE L WALKER GOVERNOR'S SCH; (SR); Nat Hon Sy; Hab For Humty Volntr; Hosp Aide; Chrch Yth Grp; Key Club; Mod UN; Off Aide; Tennis (V); Stu Cncl (R); Club Asia Treasurer, Vice Pres; U of Richmond Book Award; Dentistry; Psychiatry; Virginia Commonwealth U

HA, THU; FALLS CHURCH, VA; STUART HS; (SO); Chr; Clr Grd; Mch Bnd; Chrldg (J); Pharmacy; U of Virginia; Virginia Commonwealth U

HADEED, KRISTINE L; FREDERICKSBURG, VA; HOME SCH; (JR); Comm Volntr; ArtClub; Chrch Yth Grp; Tchrs Aide; Cyclg (V); Mar Art (V); Wt Lftg (V); Sch Ppr (R); Active Member of Young Virginia Writer's Club; Journalism; Graphic Design; Fashion Institute of Technology; U of Mary Washington

HADJIKYRIAKOU, MARIA; CENTREVILLE, VA; CENTREVILLE HS; (FR); Ctznshp Aw; DAR; Hi Hnr Roll; Otst Ac Ach Awd; Perf Att; St of Mnth; Comm Volntr; Jr Ach; Key Club; Scouts; CR (R); Faculty Award (For Consistently Demonstrating Leadership, Character, and Academic Achievement); The AHEPA Medal of Scholastic Excellence; President's Award for Outstanding Academic Excellence; Biology- Genetic Engineering; Math; U of Virginia; Johns Hopkins U - Maryland

HAGA, KASIE; QUINTON, VA; NEW KENT HS; (JR); Hi Hnr Roll; MVP; Otst Ac Ach Awd; Pres Ac Ftns Aw; WWAHSS; Comm Volntr; Peer Tut/Med; FCA; Lttrmn Clb; Ntl Beta Clb; NtlFrnscLg; Prom Com; Vsity Clb; Foreign Clb; Chr; Bskball (J); Cr Ctry (J); Fld Hky (V L); PP Ftbl (J); Sccr (V L); Vsy Clb (V L); Cl Off (T, R); CR; CSLC; Math Teacher; College of William and Mary; Longwood U

HAGY, ELISHA M; CLIFTON FORGE, VA; ALLEGHANY HS; (JR); Hnr Roll; WWAHSS; Comm Volntr; FBLA; Key Club; Prom Com; FCCLA - President (JRTC) FBLA - Treasurer (JRTC); FCCLA - Secretary (AHS); Education / Teacher; DSLCC; ODU

HAIDER, SARA; CHARLOTTESVILLE, VA; ALBEMARLE HS; (JR); Hnr Roll; Otst Ac Ach Awd; WWAHSS; Comm Volntr; Drma Clb; MuAlphaTh; Scouts; Bnd; Math Honor Society; Kendo - Not with School; Orthodontist; Biology Major; U of Virginia; Virginia Commonwealth U

HAIRSTON, DASMOND; SUTHERLIN, VA; DAN RIVER HS; (SR); Ctznshp Aw; Hnr Roll; Perf Att; St of Mnth; USAA; WWAHSS; Comm Volntr; Chrch Yth Grp; DARE; FBLA; Ntl Beta Clb; Ch Chr; Mch Bnd; Ftball (V); Scr Kpr (V); Track (V); Electrical Engineering; Computer Engineering; Virginia State U; Virginia Commonwealth U

HAIRSTON, ELLEN-ROSE C; PETERSBURG, VA; PETERSBURG HS; (JR); 4H Awd; Ctznshp Aw; Hi Hnr Roll; Hnr Roll; Nat Hon Sy; Otst Ac Ach Awd; Sci Fairs; Comm Volntr; Peer Tut/Med; 4-H; Chrch Yth Grp; Jr Ach; Key Club; Prom Com; Scouts; Ch Chr; Dnce; Scr Kpr; Swmg; Adv Cncl; CR; Girl Scout 10 Year Membership; 4-H Member 7 Years, Counselor 4 Years; Business Administration & Organization; Fashion Merchandising; Morgan State U; U of Miami

HAIRSTON, JASMINE N; AXTON, VA; MAGNA VISTA HS; (SR); Hnr Roll; WWAHSS; Comm Volntr; FBLA; Prom Com; PP Ftbl (V); Vllyball (J); Adv Cncl; National Society of Black Engineers; Family Career and Community Leaders of America; Engineering; Computer Science; Norfolk State U; Virginia Union U

HAKANSON, LINDSAY L; VIRGINIA BEACH, VA; FRANK W COX HS; (JR); Hnr Roll; Perf Att; St of Mnth; Comm Volntr; Chrch Yth Grp; Key Club; Spanish Clb; Chr; Lcrsse (V); Education; Business; James Madison U; U of Virginia

HALES, BRYANT; CHESAPEAKE, VA; WESTERN BRANCH HS; (SO); Hnr Roll; Sccr (V); Virginia Tech

HALL, CRYSTAL L; HAYES, VA; MATHEWS HS; (SR); Hi Hnr Roll; Kwnis Aw; Nat Hon Sy; Pres Ac Ftns Aw; WWAHSS; Comm Volntr; Emplmnt; Key Club; Ntl Beta Clb; Tech Clb; Invited to Presidential Classroom; Invited to National Student Leadership Conference; Pre-Law; Political Science; Christopher Newport U

HALL, DOMINIQUE T; PORTSMOUTH, VA; CALVARY CHRISTIAN SCH; (FR); Hnr Roll; Chrch Yth Grp; Bnd; Ch Chr; Bskball (J); Cr Ctry (V); CIT / Children in Training - Volunteer Service for Christian Education; Law; Technology; Duke U; U of Maryland

HALL, ESSCENCE; NORFOLK, VA; NORVIEW HS; (SO); Hnr Roll; Nat Hon Sy; Otst Ac Ach Awd; Perf Att; St of Mnth; WWAHSS; Peer Tut/Med; Chrch Yth Grp; Pep Squd; Tchrs Aide; Bnd; Chr; Dnce; Mch Bnd; Chrldg (VJ); PPSqd (J); Track (VJ); Neighborhood Reader to Kids; Medical Degree; To Become a Doctor; Old Dominion U; Spelman College

HALL, JENNIFER D; PULASKI, VA; PULASKI CTY HS; (SR); Perf Att; Chrldg (J); Vllyball (J); Finished Health Assistant Class with B+; RN; Radiologist; New River Community College

HALL, RAVEN Y; CHESAPEAKE, VA; OSCAR SMITH HS; (SO); Hnr Roll; WWAHSS; Comm Volntr; DECA; Emplmnt; FBLA; Photog; Sccr (V); Sch Ppr (R); Veterinarian; Virginia Tech U; Clark Atlanta U

HALPIN, JONATHAN D; ASHBURN, VA; STONE BRIDGE HS; (SR); Hnr Roll; Nat Hon Sy; Otst Ac Ach Awd; Yth Ldrshp Prog; Comm Volntr; Peer Tut/Med; HO'Br Yth Ldrshp; Key Club; Mth Clb/Tm; Prom Com; Cr Ctry (J); Scr Kpr (VJCL); Vllyball; Governor's Youth Public Safety Advisory Commission; Architect; U of Virginia

HALPIN, KELLEY; LEESBURG, VA; FLINT HILL SCH; (SO); Hi Hnr Roll; Nat Hon Sy; WWAHSS; Yth Ldrshp Prog; Comm Volntr; Emplmnt; Bsball (V L); Bskball (J); Ftball (L); Spanish National Honor Society; Youth Basketball Coach; Pre Vet

HALPIN, PATRICK; LEESBURG, VA; FLINT HILL SCH; (JR); Hi Hnr Roll; MVP; Nat Hon Sy; WWAHSS; Yth Ldrshp Prog; Comm Volntr; Peer Tut/Med; Emplmnt; Bsball (V CL); Ftball (V CL); Adv Cncl; Spanish National Honor Society; Youth Basketball Coach; Pre Law; Tufts U; Boston College

HAMELOTII, MIKE D; CHESAPEAKE, VA; STONE BRIDGE HS; (SR); Hnr Roll; WWAHSS; Comm Volntr; Chess; Chrch Yth Grp; Drma Clb; Emplmnt; Key Club; Scouts; SP/M/VS; Stg Cre; Sccr; Swmg; Track; Wt Lftg; John Quincy Adams Servant Award; Who's Who American High Schools; Computer Science; Liberty U

HAMILTON, CHELSEA D; BUENA VISTA, VA; ROCKBRIDGE CTY HS; (SO); Hnr Roll; Nat Hon Sy; Otst Ac Ach Awd; WWAHSS; Comm Volntr; Chrch Yth Grp; FBLA; French Clb; Astronomy; Astrophysics; Australian National U; Sydney U

HAMRAZ, BRANDON; CHESAPEAKE, VA; WESTERN BRANCH HS; (FR); Hnr Roll; Peer Tut/Med; Spec Olymp Vol; Dbte Team; Schol Bwl; Latin Clb; Orch; SP/M/VS; Fncg (J); Swmg (V); Cl Off (V); Lawyer; Actor

HAN, JIHA; CENTREVILLE, VA; CENTREVILLE HS; (SO); Hnr Roll; Pres Ac Ftns Aw; Sci Fairs; Comm Volntr; Key Club; Korean Clb; Honorable Mention-Art Contest; School Science Fair- 2nd Place / Regional Science Fair- Honorable Mention; Jewelry Design; Product Design; Parsons School of Art and Design; Cooper Union

HANLEY, KELSEY; VIRGINIA BEACH, VA; 1ST COLONIAL HS; (FR); Hnr Roll; Comm Volntr; Key Club; Scouts; Beach EC, Travel Soccer Club; Operation Smile; Marketing; Advertising; U of Miami; New York U

HANNON, MICHELLE; POTOMAC FALLS, VA; DOMINION HS; (SO); Hi Hnr Roll; Hnr Roll; Otst Ac Ach Awd; Perf Att; Comm Volntr; ArtClub; Key Club; Prom Com; Bnd; Chrldg (J); Tennis (V L); CR (R); Virginia Tech; U of Virginia

HARBIN, JOHN M; WILLIAMSBURG, VA; LAFAYETTE HS; (SR); Hnr Roll; Nat Hon Sy; Perf Att; Pres Ac Ftns Aw; WWAHSS; Yth Ldrshp Prog; Comm Volntr; Hab For Humty Volntr; Peer Tut/Med; Chrch Yth Grp; Emplmnt; Key Club; Mod UN; MuAlphaTh; NYLC; SADD; Spanish Clb; SP/M/VS; Cr Ctry (VJ L); Tennis (V CL); Sch Ppr (E); Meteorology; Environmental Science; Virginia Tech

HARDIMAN, WYTHE; SANDSTON, VA; VARINA HS; (SO); F Lan Hn Soc; Hnr Roll; WWAHSS; Chrch Yth Grp; Emplmnt; Key Club; French Clb; Sch Ppr (R); Key Club; Teacher; U of Virginia; George Mason U

HARIHAN, CAMERON T; CHESAPEAKE, VA; WESTERN BRANCH HS; (SO); Hnr Roll; St of Mnth; Chrch Yth Grp; Scouts; Orch; Ftball (J); Eagle Scout in BSA; Engineering; Architecture; Virginia Tech; Old Dominion U

HARMS, JESSICA; WILLIAMSBURG, VA; LAFAYETTE HS; (SR); Hnr Roll; Nat Hon Sy; WWAHSS; Comm Volntr; Chrch Yth Grp; Cmptr Clb; Drma Clb; Emplmnt; Fr of Library; Mod UN; Mus Clb; NtlFrnscLg; Bnd; Chr; Ch Chr; Dnce; Sch Ppr (R); State Finals for Forensics; Played At National Flute Convention; BFA Musical Theatre; BFA AHS Administration; Christopher Newport U; Shenandoah U

HARPER, ALEXANDRA; HERNDON, VA; CHANTILLY HS; (SO); Hnr Roll; Nat Hon Sy; Otst Ac Ach Awd; Sci Fairs; St of Mnth; Comm Volntr; Peer Tut/Med; Spec Olymp Vol; Chrch Yth Grp; Emplmnt; Quill & Scroll; Bskball (V L); Sch Ppr (E); Interact Club Vice President, NHS; 3rd Team All-District (Basketball), Quill & Scroll Society

HARPER, ALEXIS; VIRGINIA BEACH, VA; NORFOLK COLLEGIATE MID-UPR SCH; (SR); Hnr Roll; Nat Hon Sy; Comm Volntr; Red Cr Aide; ROTC; Drl Tm; Bskball (J L); Chrldg (V L); Fld Hky (V L); PP Ftbl; Sftball (V L); NJROTC Boot Camp in Camping; Icelandic Amer. Azalea Princess; CIA Employed; Degree in Criminal Law; U of West Florida; Florida Gulf Coast U

HARPER, JASMINE R; STAFFORD, VA; NORTH STAFFORD HS; (SO); Hnr Roll; WWAHSS; FBLA; Track (J); National Society of High School Scholars; Computer Science; Computer Information Systems; Old Dominion U; Hampton U

Hall, Dominique T
Calvary Christian Sch
Portsmouth, VA

Hairston, Ellen-Rose C
Petersburg HS
Petersburg, VA

National
Honor Roll
Spring 2005

Gribling, Rachel L
Stonebridge Sch
Suffolk, VA

Harper, Alexandra
Chantilly HS
Herndon, VA

HARRIS, AQUISI; SALEM, VA; SALEM HS; (SO); F Lan Hn Soc; Hi Hnr Roll; Nat Hon Sy; Otst Ac Ach Awd; Perf Att; Pres Sch; Spanish Clb; Chr; Track (L); Keyette Club, District Choir, Young Poets Celebration; Spanish Department Award, Academic Distinction; Biology/Chemistry; Spanish; Virginia Tech; Roanoke College

HARRIS, AUSTIN N; HARTWOOD, VA; COLONIAL FORGE HS; (SR); Hi Hnr Roll; Hnr Roll; Nat Hon Sy; Peer Tut/Med; Dbte Team; Emplmnt; Off Aide; Ftball (J); Lcrsse (V L); Lit Mag; Attended Congressional Student Leadership Conference - July 2003; Winner - VHSL Creative Writing Contest - Sophomore Year; Science / Microbiology / Pharmacology; Virginia Tech

HARRIS, BRITTANY C; PALMYRA, VA; FLUVANNA CTY HS; (FR); Ctznshp Aw; Hnr Roll; Nat Mrt Fin; St of Mnth; Chrch Yth Grp; Mus Clb; Ntl Beta Clb; Scouts; Tchrs Aide; Bnd; Ch Chr; SP/M/VS; Stu Cncl (V); Yrbk (P); Writing Club

HARRIS, SHANIQUE; SOUTH BOSTON, VA; HALIFAX CTY HS; (JR); Hnr Roll; Nat Stu Ath Day Aw; Otst Ac Ach Awd; Perf Att; St of Mnth; ArtClub; Chrch Yth Grp; Emplmnt; FBLA; Ch Chr; Track (J L); CR (R); Bachelor's Degree; MD Degree; Virginia Commonwealth U

HARRIS, YVONNE; PETERSBURG, VA; PETERSBURG HS; (JR); Ctznshp Aw; Hnr Roll; Perf Att; St of Mnth; Hosp Aide; Chrch Yth Grp; Key Club; Ch Chr; Nursing; Secondary Teaching; John Tyler Community College; Virginia State U

HARRISON, CRYSTAL; PORTSMOUTH, VA; WOODROW WILSON HS; (SR); Hnr Roll; Peer Tut/Med; Chrch Yth Grp; DECA; Emplmnt; FBLA; Cl Off (R); Stu Cncl; Miss DECA; Fashion Design; Business Management; Norfolk State U; Old Dominion U

HARRISON, JESSICA; FLOYD, VA; FLOYD CTY HS; (SO); 4H Awd; Hi Hnr Roll; Hnr Roll; WWAHSS; Comm Volntr; 4-H; Chrch Yth Grp; FCA; FCCLA; Scouts; SADD; Bnd; Ch Chr; Mch Bnd; Cr Ctry (VJ L); Track (VJ L); 2003 State Champions-Cross Country (Team); MACC; Marine Biology; Elementary Science Teacher; King College; U of North Carolina

HARTRIDGE, C J; SOUTH BOSTON, VA; HALIFAX CTY HS; (JR); Hnr Roll; Perf Att; Yth Ldrshp Prog; Hab For Humty Volntr; 4-H; Drma Clb; Pep Squd; Dnce; Dixie Softball; Pre-Med; Architecture; Randolph-Macon College; U of Virginia

HARTZOG, HANNAH; ROANOKE, VA; ROANOKE CATHOLIC HS; (FR); Hi Hnr Roll; Otst Ac Ach Awd; WWAHSS; Comm Volntr; Chrch Yth Grp; Key Club; Sci Clb; Ch Chr; Roanoke City Soccer; Engineer; Architect; U of Virginia; Auburn U

HARVEY, CRYSTAL M; SUFFOLK, VA; KINGS FORK HS; (SO); Peer Tut/Med; Chrch Yth Grp; DARE; Scouts; SADD; Chr; Ch Chr; Dnce; Sccr (V); Cl Off (R); Law; Dance; Hampton U

HARVEY, MEGAN A; LYNCHBURG, VA; E C GLASS HS; (JR); Hnr Roll; Nat Hon Sy; Comm Volntr; Hab For Humty Volntr; Chrch Yth Grp; DARE; Emplmnt; Key Club; Scouts; French Clb; Tennis (JC); Pre-Med; St Andrews Presbyterian College; U of Virginia

HASAN, LUBABA; STERLING, VA; POTOMAC FALLS HS; (SO); Hnr Roll; Perf Att; Comm Volntr; Dbte Team; Key Club; Mod UN; Quiz Bowl; Schol Bwl; Vsity Clb; Bnd; Mch Bnd; Doctor; U of Virginia; Johns Hopkins U

HASH, CYNDLE A D; ROANOKE, VA; WILLIAM FLEMING HS; (JR); Hnr Roll; Kwnis Aw; Nat Hon Sy; WWAHSS; Comm Volntr; Peer Tut/Med; Chrch Yth Grp; Cmptr Clb; Key Club; Bnd; Ch Chr; Part of a Music Group Min. Bernard and Glory 2; Criminal Law; Harvard; JMU

HASKINS JR, MITCHELL K; BOYDTON, VA; BLUESTONE SR HS; (JR); Hnr Roll; Nat Hon Sy; Chrch Yth Grp

HASSAN, ABDURAHMAN A; FALLS CHURCH, VA; AMERICAN SCH; (SR); Hnr Roll; Otst Ac Ach Awd; Sci Fairs; St Optmst of Yr; Comm Volntr; Bsball (V); Bskball (V); Cyclg (J); Ftball (J); Sccr (J); Swmg (J); Track (J); Wt Lftg (J)

HASSANZADEH, FATIMA; GAINESVILLE, VA; BRENTSVILLE DISTRICT HS; (JR); F Lan Hn Soc; Otst Ac Ach Awd; St of Mnth; Comm Volntr; Hosp Aide; Peer Tut/Med; Drma Clb; FBLA; Lib Aide; Photog; SADD; Tchrs Aide; French Clb; Chr; SP/M/VS; Stu Cncl (R); President of French Club; Member of FCCLA and FBLA; Journalism; Communications; Georgetown U; George Mason U

HASSELL, LINDSEY; VIRGINIA BEACH, VA; KEMPSVILLE HS; (SR); Ctznshp Aw; F Lan Hn Soc; Hi Hnr Roll; Hnr Roll; Nat Hon Sy; WWAHSS; Comm Volntr; Peer Tut/Med; DECA; Emplmnt; Prom Com; Spanish Clb; Sccr (J); Stu Cncl (R); CR (R); Randolph Macon College Book Award; Marketing; Virginia Polytechnic Institute & State U

HATTER, ANNA; SMITHFIELD, VA; SMITHFIELD HS; (JR); Hi Hnr Roll; Jr Mshl; WWAHSS; Comm Volntr; Peer Tut/Med; 4-H; AL Aux Girls; Key Club; Ntl Beta Clb; Quiz Bowl; Schol Bwl; French Clb; PP Ftbl (V); Presidential Classroom; William and Mary Leadership Award; International Relations; History; College of William and Mary; U of Virginia

HAUN, INDIA B; CHARLOTTESVILLE, VA; MONTICELLO HS; (SO); F Lan Hn Soc; Hnr Roll; Perf Att; Peer Tut/Med; Chrch Yth Grp; Key Club; MuAlphaTh; Bskball (V L); PP Ftbl; Sftball (JC); Vllyball (VJ L); Stu Cncl (R); Sports Medicine; Engineering; Virginia Polytechnic Institute and State U; Randolph-Macon College

HAWES, SARAH; NATURAL BRG, VA; ROCKBRIDGE CTY HS; (JR); Hi Hnr Roll; Hnr Roll; Nat Hon Sy; Otst Ac Ach Awd; WWAHSS; Comm Volntr; Hosp Aide; Peer Tut/Med; ArtClub; Chrch Yth Grp; Emplmnt; FCCLA; Spanish Clb; Bnd; Dnce; Women's Club Poetry Contest; National Spanish Award; Biology; Psychology; U of Virginia; James Madison U

HAWKINS, STEPHANIE; YORKTOWN, VA; YORK HS; (SO); Hi Hnr Roll; Hnr Roll; Perf Att; Pres Sch; Comm Volntr; Peer Tut/Med; Chess; DARE; Dbte Team; Acpl Chr; Chr; Rec Soccer; Rec Basketball; Pre-Law; Law Enforcement; Harvard Law; William & Mary

HAYNES, AUSTIN; FREDERICKSBURG, VA; STAFFORD SR HS; (JR); WWAHSS; Stg Cre; Art; Music; Virginia Commonwealth U; Germana Community College

HAYNES, ERIN A; KING GEORGE, VA; JAMES MONROE HS; (SO); Hi Hnr Roll; Otst Ac Ach Awd; WWAHSS; Key Club; Latin Clb; Chrldg (J); Fld Hky (JC); Sccr (V); National Latin Exam-Gold Medal 2003, 2004 Silver Medal 2005; Medicine; U of Virginia; James Madison U

HAYNIE, JESSICA R; CALLAS, VA; NORTHUMBERLAND HS; (SR); Gov Hnr Prg; Hnr Roll; Otst Ac Ach Awd; St of Mnth; WWAHSS; Comm Volntr; Chrch Yth Grp; Emplmnt; Ntl Beta Clb; Bskball (J); Fld Hky (V); Sccr (V C); Sftball (V); Chesapeake Bay Governor's School; Virginia Tech; Clemson U

HAZELWOOD, BRIDGET; SUTHERLIN, VA; DAN RIVER HS; (SR); All Am Sch; Ctznshp Aw; Hi Hnr Roll; Jr Mshl; USAA; WWAHSS; Ntl Beta Clb; French Clb; Yrbk; SCAEL (Academic Team); Graduate of Merit; Biology (Physical Therapy); Occupational Therapy; Longwood U

HAZUR, CRISTEN; BURKE, VA; LAKE BRADDOCK SECONDARY HS; (SR); Dnce; Piano; Am Attending GMU 1 Year Early; Political Science; Aeronautical Engineering; George Mason U

HEADEN, TIMOTHY; EMPORIA, VA; GREENSVILLE CTY HS; (SO); Ctznshp Aw; Hnr Roll; Nat Hon Sy; Otst Ac Ach Awd; WWAHSS; FBLA; Ntl Beta Clb; Bsball (J); Bskball (J); Cl Off (P); Certificate of Merit for Superintendent's List; Invitation to Attend the National Leaders Conf.; Business Management; Computer Engineering; U of North Carolina; U of Richmond

HEALY, BRANDON; ANNANDALE, VA; ANNANDALE HS; (SO); Hnr Roll; MVP; Comm Volntr; Peer Tut/Med; Spec Olymp Vol; Dbte Team; DECA; Emplmnt; Fr of Library; Lib Aide; Bnd; Ice Hky (V); Lcrsse (J); Rlr Hky; DECA Vice President; Advertisement; Marketing; Christopher Newport U; U of Maine

HEARD, RONAE; FREDERICKSBURG, VA; MASSAPONAX HS; (SR); All Am Sch; Hnr Roll; Nat Hon Sy; Perf Att; Pres Sch; WWAHSS; Comm Volntr; Chrch Yth Grp; Dbte Team; Emplmnt; Key Club; Lib Aide; Prom Com; SADD; Tchrs Aide; Bnd; Clr Grd; CR; Key Club; Pre-Med; Psychology; Virginia Commonwealth U; Liberty U

HEATH, AMBER; SUFFOLK, VA; LAKELAND HS; (JR); Hnr Roll; Comm Volntr; FCCLA

HEAVENER, JESSICA; HAMPTON, VA; PHOEBUS HS; (FR); Ctznshp Aw; Hnr Roll; St of Mnth; Drma Clb; Bnd; Nursing; Spanish; ODV; Virginia Wesleyan

HEDRICK, HUNTER; MIDLOTHIAN, VA; MIDLOTHIAN HS; (JR); F Lan Hn Soc; Hi Hnr Roll; Hnr Roll; Jr Mshl; Nat Hon Sy; Otst Ac Ach Awd; Yth Ldrshp Prog; Peer Tut/Med; Chrch Yth Grp; Jr Cls League; Mod UN; MuAlphaTh; Mus Clb; Off Aide; Bnd; Chr; Ch Chr; Swg Chr; Club Officer (Latin Club President); 2002 Student of the Year; Music Minister; Pharmacy; Davidson College; Washington and Lee

HENDRICK, LINDSEY M; CHESAPEAKE, VA; COASTAL CHRISTIAN AC; (FR); All Am Sch; Hnr Roll; Nat Ldrshp Svc; USAA; Photog; Yrbk; High Red Belt in Tae Kwon Do; Pharmacy; Hampton U; Old Dominion U

HENDRICK, WILLY; STERLING, VA; NOTRE DAME AC; (JR); Hi Hnr Roll; Hnr Roll; Nat Ldrshp Svc; Perf Att; Yth Ldrshp Prog; Comm Volntr; Chrch Yth Grp; NYLC; Sci Clb; Vsity Clb; Bskball (J); Lcrsse (JCL); Cl Off (T); Stu Cncl (T); CR (R); Biological Studies Costa Rico; College Level Courses; Pre-Med

HENLEY, CAITLIN M; GOOCHLAND, VA; GOOCHLAND HS; (FR); Hnr Roll; St of Mnth; Chrch Yth Grp; DARE; Drma Clb; Emplmnt; Key Club; Photog; Church Softball; Junior Counselor for a Camp; Animal Vet; Math Teacher; Virginia Tech; Texas A & M International U

HENRY, DAMON; CHESAPEAKE, VA; WESTERN BRANCH HS; (JR); Fut Prb Slvr; Hi Hnr Roll; Hnr Roll; Nat Hon Sy; Pres Sch; Sci Fairs; WWAHSS; Comm Volntr; Peer Tut/Med; Chrch Yth Grp; Lib Aide; Ntl Beta Clb; Quiz Bowl; Schol Bwl; Tchrs Aide; Bnd; Ch Chr; Sccr (V); Cl Off (T); Attended "Linguafest" Program in Germany; Industries Award; Aeronautical Engineering; Architecture; Purdue U; Massachusetts Institute of Technology

HENSEL, MARCUS O; RICHMOND, VA; MILLS E GODWIN HS; (SR); Hnr Roll; Key Club; Bsball (VJ); Economics; Business Management; South Carolina U

HENSON, BRETT C; WOODBRIDGE, VA; C D HYLTON HS; (FR); Hi Hnr Roll; Hnr Roll; Nat Hon Sy; Pres Ac Ftns Aw; Sci Fairs; Comm Volntr; DARE; Dbte Team; Drma Clb; Mod UN; Tchrs Aide; Vsity Clb; Bnd; Chr; SP/M/VS; Stg Cre; Cr Ctry (V); Lcrsse (V); Track (V); Wt Lftg (V); Architecture; Theater Arts; UVA; UNC

HENSON, LAURA A; BRISTOL, VA; JOHN S BATTLE HS; (SR); 4H Awd; Gov Hnr Prg; Hi Hnr Roll; Hnr Roll; Nat Hon Sy; Otst Ac Ach Awd; Perf Att; Pres Ac Ftns Aw; WWAHSS; Yth Ldrshp Prog; Comm Volntr; Peer Tut/Med; Spec Olymp Vol; Chrch Yth Grp; Drma Clb; Emplmnt; FCA; Jr Ach; Mus Clb; Ntl Beta Clb; Pep Squd; Acpl Chr; Bnd; Chr; Ch Chr; Dvng (J); Cl Off (T); CR (T); Most Outstanding Band Student; Color Guard Captain; Medical; Music; Virginia Highlands Community College; East Tennessee State U

HEUNEMAN, BROOKE; VIRGINIA BEACH, VA; FLOYD KELLAM HS; (JR); Ctznshp Aw; Hnr Roll; Otst Ac Ach Awd; Comm Volntr; Hab For Humty Volntr; Chrch Yth Grp; Emplmnt; Dnce; Lettered in Academics in 02-04; Elementary Education; Old Dominion U; Virginia Wesleyan College

HEVIA, ALEXANDRA T; FAIRFAX, VA; JAMES W ROBINSON SECONDARY SCH; (JR); Comm Volntr; Chrch Yth Grp; DECA; Emplmnt; Key Club; Off Aide; Pep Squd; P to P St Amb Prg; SADD; Bskball (JC); Sccr (J); Track (V L); DECA Winner/Lettered; Black Belt/Karate; Marketing; Mass Communications; Tusculum College; Christopher Newport U

HICKEY, JUSTIN; WOODBRIDGE, VA; FREEDOM HS; (SO); Gov Hnr Prg; Hi Hnr Roll; Hnr Roll; MVP; Nat Hon Sy; Nat Mrt LOC; Nat Mrt Sch Recip; Nat Stu Ath Day Aw; Otst Ac Ach Awd; Pres Ac Ftns Aw; Comm Volntr; Peer Tut/Med; Chrch Yth Grp; ROTC; Ch Chr; Bsball (V L); Ftball (VJCL); Track; Wt Lftg (V); Wrstlg (V CL); Offensive Player of the Year (Football); 5th Place AAA State Tournament (Wrestling); Study Law At Michigan U; Law/Electronics; Michigan; Virginia Tech

HICKS, CORYNN; NEWPORT NEWS, VA; WARWICK HS; (JR); Gov Hnr Prg; Hnr Roll; Nat Hon Sy; Otst Ac Ach Awd; Perf Att; Sci Fairs; WWAHSS; Yth Ldrshp Prog; Comm Volntr; Hosp Aide; Peer Tut/Med; AL Aux Girls; Emplmnt; Key Club; Mod UN; MuAlphaTh; Bnd; Drm Mjr; Jzz Bnd; Mch Bnd; Sccr (V L); Swmg (J L); Tennis (J L); Best Delegate=Model United Nations Team; Youth Delegate At National League of Cities Conference 2004; Pre-Med; International Relations; U of Virginia

HICKS, DANIEL L; JARRATT, VA; GREENSVILLE CTY HS; (JR); Comm Volntr; Spec Olymp Vol; Chrch Yth Grp; Chr; Ch Chr; Yrbk (R); Member-The United Community Voices; Artist (Cartoonist); St. Paul's College; St. Augustine's College

HICKS, KEJUANA; CREWE, VA; NOTTAWAY HS; (MS); Hi Hnr Roll; Hnr Roll; Nat Hon Sy; Otst Ac Ach Awd; St of Mnth; Peer Tut/Med; DARE; Dbte Team; Bnd; Yrbk (E, P); Recognition as a Young Poet; Entry of Poetry Into National Contest; Veterinarian; Model / Actress; University of Virginia; Longwood University

HILL, NOAH; DALE CITY, VA; HOME STUDY INTERNATIONAL HS; (SR); Ctznshp Aw; Hnr Roll; WWAHSS; Yth Ldrshp Prog; Comm Volntr; Chrch Yth Grp; Outdrs Clb; Svce Clb; Bskball (V); Outstanding Achievement in Poetry Award; NASA Advanced Space Camp Graduate; Pastoral Evangelism; Hartland College

HILL, STEPHANY; ROANOKE, VA; WILLIAM FLEMING HS; (JR); 4H Awd; Hnr Roll; Perf Att; Sci Fairs; Comm Volntr; Hab For Humty Volntr; 4-H; Chrch Yth Grp; DARE; Emplmnt; FCA; Key Club; Off Aide; Prom Com; Vllyball (J); Cl Off (S); Stu Cncl (S); Law School; MBA; U of Virginia; Howard U

HINKLE JR, ROBERT W; COVINGTON, VA; JACKSON RIVER TECH CTR; (SR); Sci Fairs; St of Mnth; DARE; Emplmnt; Tchrs Aide; Voc Ind Clb Am; Bsball (VJ L); Ftball (V); Worked Part Time from 9th-12th Grade; Welder

HITE, MONICA H; RICHMOND, VA; MILLS E GODWIN HS; (JR); Hnr Roll; Nat Hon Sy; Pres Ac Ftns Aw; Pres Sch; WWAHSS; Comm Volntr; Peer Tut/Med; Chrch Yth Grp; FCA; Ntl Beta Clb; Prom Com; Quill & Scroll; Tchrs Aide; French Clb; Ch Chr; Cr Ctry (V); Gmnstcs (V C); Track (V); Cl Off (T); CR (R); Yrbk (E); Most Dedicated - Gymnastics & Cross Country; Junior Class Princess; Business; Engineering; U of Virginia; Wake Forest U

Hicks, Daniel L
Greensville Cty HS
Jarratt, VA

Hickey, Justin
Freedom HS
Woodbridge, VA

Henson, Laura A
John S Battle HS
Bristol, VA

Haynes, Austin
Stafford SR HS
Fredericksburg, VA

Hassanzadeh, Fatima
Brentsville District HS
Gainesville, VA

Hash, Cyndle A D
William Fleming HS
Roanoke, VA

Harris, Aquisi
Salem HS
Salem, VA

Harrison, Jessica
Floyd Cty HS
Floyd, VA

Haun, India B
Monticello HS
Charlottesville, VA

Hendrick, Lindsey M
Coastal Christian AC
Chesapeake, VA

Heuneman, Brooke
Floyd Kellam HS
Virginia Beach, VA

Hevia, Alexandra T
James W Robinson Secondary Sch
Fairfax, VA

HOANG, TERESA N; ALEXANDRIA, VA; STUART HS; (SR); Hnr Roll; Otst Ac Ach Awd; Perf Att; St of Mnth; Yth Ldrshp Prog; Comm Volntr; Peer Tut/Med; Emplmnt; FBLA; Key Club; Prom Com; Scouts; Tmpl Yth Grp; Chr; Ch Chr; Dnce; SP/M/VS; Chrldg (V); PP Ftbl (V); Stu Cncl (R); CR (R); Vietnamese Dance Choreographer and Instructor; Forensic Science; George Washington U; George Mason U

HOBBS, ROBERT J; BOYCE, VA; CLARKE CTY HS; (JR); 4H Awd; All Am Sch; Nat Hon Sy; WWAHSS; Comm Volntr; DECA; Emplmnt; Ntl FFA; Bskball (J); Sccr (VJ L); VA State President of DECA; Communications; Political Science; Elon U; U of Virginia

HOBSON, ASHLEY M; RICHMOND, VA; VARINA HS; (FR); Hi Hnr Roll; Hnr Roll; Otst Ac Ach Awd; Perf Att; Sci Fairs; St of Mnth; Comm Volntr; Peer Tut/Med; P to P St Amb Prg; Photog; Scouts; Sccr (V); U of Texas; William and Mary

HOEHNER, TIMOTHY J; CHARLOTTESVILLE, VA; MONTICELLO HS; (FR); Hnr Roll; Comm Volntr; Peer Tut/Med; Chrch Yth Grp; Emplmnt; Scouts; Skiing (V); Peer Counselor / Mediator; Honor Council; Private Business; Aviation; U of Virginia; Dartmouth College

HOFFMAN, BRADLEY J; GALAX, VA; GRAYSON CTY CAREERS-TECH CTR; (JR); 4H Awd; Hi Hnr Roll; Hnr Roll; Perf Att; St of Mnth; St Optmst of Yr; 4-H; Chrch Yth Grp; Spanish Clb; Army; Air Force

HOGAN, KATHERINE A; STERLING, VA; POTOMAC FALLS HS; (FR); Hnr Roll; St of Mnth; Comm Volntr; Key Club; Chr; Ch Chr; SP/M/VS; Selected to Sing National Anthem At Minor League Game 2 Years in a Row; All County Chorus 8th Grade; Music; Teaching; Christopher Newport U

HOLDER, DOMINIQUE; HAMPTON, VA; KECOUGHTON HS; (JR); DECA; Emplmnt; Mus Clb; Tchrs Aide; Tech Clb; Chr; All-District Chorus; Treasurer for DECA; Physical Therapy; Message Therapy; North Carolina A & T; Norfolk State U

HOLDER, WESLEY L; ARLINGTON, VA; NATIONAL CHRISTIAN AC; (SO); Sci Fairs; FCA; SP/M/VS; Bskball (J); CR (P); Marketing; Management; Georgetown U; Yale U

HOLLEY, KOURTNEY; VIRGINIA BEACH, VA; KELLAM HS; (SO); Ctznshp Aw; Hi Hnr Roll; Hnr Roll; Otst Ac Ach Awd; Perf Att; Pres Ac Ftns Aw; St of Mnth; Chrch Yth Grp; DARE; Drma Clb; P to P St Amb Prg; French Clb; Dnce; YST (Stop Smoking Organization); Law; William and Mary; Old Dominion U

HOLT, ALEXANDRIA; BASSETT, VA; BASSETT HS; (FR); Ctznshp Aw; Hnr Roll; Perf Att; Comm Volntr; Peer Tut/Med; Chrch Yth Grp; Emplmnt; Lib Aide; Ntl Beta Clb; Spanish Clb; Bnd; Chr; Ch Chr; Chrldg (J); Stu Cncl (R); Child Psychology; Medical / Pediatrician; Virginia State U; Virginia Commonwealth U

HON, TING; CENTREVILLE, VA; CENTREVILLE HS; (SO); Hnr Roll; Sci Fairs; USAA; WWAHSS; Comm Volntr; Peer Tut/Med; FBLA; Key Club; Orch; Stg Cre; Medical Field; Pediatrician; Virginia Tech; U of Virginia

HONBARRIER, WILLIAM; GOODE, VA; JEFFERSON FOREST HS; (SO); Duke TS; Hi Hnr Roll; Pres Ac Ftns Aw; Sci/Math Olympn; Peer Tut/Med; DECA; Emplmnt; Bskball (J); Ftball (V); Wt Lftg (V); Cl Off (V); Stu Cncl (T, R); College of William and Mary Leadership Award; Johns Hopkins Talent Identification Program; Dentistry; Medicine; UNC Chapel Hill; U of Virginia

HOOVER, ALYSON T; HAYES, VA; GLOUCESTER HS; (JR); Hnr Roll; Pres Ac Ftns Aw; WWAHSS; Comm Volntr; Peer Tut/Med; DARE; FCA; FBLA; Off Aide; Pep Squd; SADD; Tchrs Aide; Spanish Clb; Chr; Bskball (VJ L); Tennis (V CL); Academy of Finance (Inducted Sophomore Year); Business; Criminal Justice; Old Dominion U; East Carolina U

HOPKINS, FANTASIA F; VIRGINIA BEACH, VA; WESTERN BRANCH HS; (JR); Hnr Roll; Jr Mshl; Nat Hon Sy; WWAHSS; Yth Ldrshp Prog; Comm Volntr; Emplmnt; Jr Cls League; Prom Com; Latin Clb; Dnce; Drl Tm; Cl Off (R); Stu Cncl (R); Biology/Pre-Med; Ob/Gyn; Howard U; Duke U

HOPKINS, KATIE; MANASSAS, VA; OSBOURN PARK SR HS; (JR); Ctznshp Aw; Hnr Roll; St of Mnth; WWAHSS; Comm Volntr; Emplmnt; Key Club; Tchrs Aide; Lt. Governor-Key Club; Published Poems; Special Ed Teacher; Writer; Longwood U; Winthrop U

HOPKINS, MEGAN; FRANKLIN, VA; SOUTHAMPTON AC; (JR); Hnr Roll; Nat Hon Sy; USAA; WWAHSS; Chrch Yth Grp; Emplmnt; Ntl Beta Clb; Prom Com; SADD; Bskball (V CL); Chrldg (V C); Vllyball (V); Cl Off (T); All Conference-Varsity Basketball; Education; Psychology; James Madison U; Mary Washington

HORNER, DANIEL; SUFFOLK, VA; HOMESCHOOL; (SR); Hnr Roll; Perf Att; Yth Ldrshp Prog; Chrch Yth Grp; Emplmnt; Skt Tgt Sh (C); Sccr (V); Business Management; Virginia Military Institute

HORRICKS, BRIANNA; FREDERICKSBURG, VA; COLONIAL FORGE HS; (JR); Hi Hnr Roll; Nat Hon Sy; Nat Ldrshp Svc; Pres Ac Ftns Aw; Yth Ldrshp Prog; Comm Volntr; Red Cr Aide; FCA; Mth Clb/Tm; Off Aide; SADD; Bnd; Chr; Dnce; Cr Ctry (V); Sccr (J); Ballet Since Four; Veterinary Medicine; VA Tech; UVA

HORTON, AMANDA C; CUMBERLAND, VA; CUMBERLAND CTY HS; (SO); Ctznshp Aw; Hnr Roll; Nat Hon Sy; Otst Ac Ach Awd; Pres Ac Ftns Aw; St of Mnth; US Army Sch Ath Aw; DARE; ROTC; Sci Clb; Spanish Clb; Clr Grd; Drl Tm; Cr Ctry (V); Sftball (J); Track (V); JROTC; Public Speaking; Law; Communications; Longwood U; Virginia Commonwealth U

HORTON, NICOLE; LEESBURG, VA; HERITAGE HS; (SR); Hnr Roll; Perf Att; St of Mnth; Comm Volntr; Red Cr Aide; Spec Olymp Vol; Chrch Yth Grp; Emplmnt; Pep Squd; Svce Clb; Sign Clb; Dnce; Drl Tm; SP/M/VS; Captain/Founder of Heritage Step Team; Washington Wizards Student Achiever; Bachelor's Degree in Physical Therapy; Business Management (Health Spas); Florida A & M U; Shaw U

HOWARD, TOM; RADFORD, VA; RHS; (JR); Nat Mrt LOC; Pres Ac Ftns Aw; WWAHSS; Yth Ldrshp Prog; Red Cr Aide; AL Aux Boys; Chrch Yth Grp; DARE; Drma Clb; HO'Br Yth Ldrshp; Scouts; SADD; Spanish Clb; Acpl Chr; Chr; SP/M/VS; Cl Off (P); Eagle Scout; Boy's State; PhD; Virginia Polytechnic; U of Virginia

HOWE, LAUREN; EARLYSVILLE, VA; ALBEMARLE HS; (JR); Gov Hnr Prg; Hi Hnr Roll; Nat Hon Sy; WWAHSS; Comm Volntr; Peer Tut/Med; Key Club; MuAlphaTh; Mus Clb; German Clb; Chr; Fld Hky (J); Swmg (V L); Track (J); Stu Cncl (S); CR (R); Art Honors Society; Tri-M Musical Society; Psychology; Film Studies; U of Virginia; Washington U St. Louis

HOWERTON, LINDSAY; CLIFTON, VA; ROBINSON SECONDARY SCH; (SR); Sci Fairs; Comm Volntr; DECA; Emplmnt; Key Club; Photog; Bnd; Dnce; Cr Ctry (J); CR (R); Member of Ensemble of Fairfax; 1st Place National DECA Winner; Marketing; Public Relations; East Carolina U

HOWERTON, SIOBHAN; SOUTH BOSTON, VA; HALIFAX CTY HS; (SR); Hnr Roll; WWAHSS; Hab For Humty Volntr; Chrch Yth Grp; Ch Chr; Track (V L); Youth President of Church Group; Electrical Engineering; Graphic Communications; North Carolina A & T State U; Old Dominion U

HSU, JASMINE; STERLING, VA; POTOMAC FALLS HS; (FR); Hnr Roll; Perf Att; WWAHSS; Key Club; Stg Cre; Play the Piano, Guitar, and Drums; Computer and Information Sciences; Communications Technologies; University of Virginia

HU, MAGGY; FAIRFAX, VA; FAIRFAX HS; (JR); F Lan Hn Soc; Hi Hnr Roll; Nat Hon Sy; Perf Att; Sci Fairs; WWAHSS; Comm Volntr; Peer Tut/Med; Spec Olymp Vol; DECA; Key Club; Mth Clb/Tm; Sci Clb; Lcrsse (VJ L); PP Ftbl; Tennis (V L); Track (J); DECA - 1st Place at State Competition; DECA -Top 30 at International Competition; Pre-Med; Business; U of Virginia; U of Texas Austin

HUDSON, CARLY; MANASSAS, VA; OSBOURN HS; (SO); 4H Awd; Hnr Roll; Otst Ac Ach Awd; Pres Sch; 4-H; Chrch Yth Grp; Emplmnt; Key Club; Bnd; Chr; Ch Chr; Stg Cre; Yrbk (E); International Affairs; American U; U of Mary Washington

HUDSON, EMILY F; RICHLANDS, VA; RICHLANDS HS; (JR); Hnr Roll; Pres Ac Ftns Aw; Sci Fairs; Comm Volntr; Spec Olymp Vol; Chrch Yth Grp; FBLA; Key Club; Prom Com; Scouts; Ch Chr; Dnce; Pre-Med; Biology; College of William and Mary; Virginia Tech

HUDSON, LAURA; CHESAPEAKE, VA; WESTERN BRANCH HS; (SO); Hnr Roll; Comm Volntr; Hab For Humty Volntr; Hosp Aide; Chess; Chrch Yth Grp; Scouts; Spanish Clb; Orch; CR (R); Doctor (Pediatrician); Veterinarian; U of Maryland; Virginia Tech

HUFF, SARAH E; STAFFORD, VA; COLONIAL FORGE HS; (SO); Hnr Roll; Otst Ac Ach Awd; St of Mnth; Peer Tut/Med; DARE; Key Club; Scouts; Track; Finance; Foreign Language; Art Institute; Virginia Tech

HUGHES, ALLYN; ROANOKE, VA; PATRICK HENRY HS; (JR); Hi Hnr Roll; Nat Hon Sy; Sci Fairs; Comm Volntr; Drma Clb; Emplmnt; SP/M/VS, Lcrsse (V); PP Ftbl (J); Sccr (J); Stu Cncl (R); Sch Ppr (R, P); Environmental Science; Architecture; U of Virginia; Virginia Tech

HUGHES, ASHLEY D; NATHALIE, VA; HALIFAX CTY HS; (JR); Hnr Roll; Perf Att; Comm Volntr; Chrch Yth Grp; FCCLA; Ch Chr; FCCLA; HOSA; Health Care / Nursing; EMT / Firefighter; DCC; SVHEC

HUGHES, BRADLEY T; MARTINSVILLE, VA; MAGNA VISTA HS; (FR); Ctznshp Aw; Hnr Roll; 4-H; Chrch Yth Grp; DARE; Ntl FFA; Psychology; Teaching; Virginia Tech

HUGHES-PUKROP, CHEZ; VIRGINIA BEACH, VA; FRANK W COX HS; (SR); Ctznshp Aw; F Lan Hn Soc; Hnr Roll; Nat Hon Sy; WWAHSS; Comm Volntr; Peer Tut/Med; AL Aux Girls; Chrch Yth Grp; Emplmnt; Mod UN; MuAlphaTh; Prom Com; Quill & Scroll; Spanish Clb; PP Ftbl; Sftball (J L); Vsy Clb (V L); Adv Cncl; Cl Off (P, V, S); Stu Cncl; CR; Sch Ppr (E); Homecoming Queen; Falcon Medallion Recipient; Virginia Tech

HUH, DEBORAH; CHANTILLY, VA; BROAD RUN HS; (JR); Hnr Roll; Nat Hon Sy; Perf Att; Pres Ac Ftns Aw; WWAHSS; Comm Volntr; Chrch Yth Grp; Key Club; SADD; Track (V)

HUH, JEE S; HERNDON, VA; WESTFIELD HS; (SO); Hnr Roll; Nat Sci Aw; Sci Fairs; Comm Volntr; ArtClub; SADD; Spanish Clb; Orch; Architecture; Psychology

HUMMER, CANDACE M; WINCHESTER, VA; JAMES WOOD HS; (FR); Ctznshp Aw; Hnr Roll; Otst Ac Ach Awd; Perf Att; Pres Ac Ftns Aw; Pres Sch; St of Mnth; Comm Volntr; Peer Tut/Med; Scouts; French Clb; Bnd; Chrldg (J); Cr Ctry; Gmnstcs; Tennis (V); Track; Cl Off (T); CR (T); Art Show Awards; DARE Essay Winner; Genetics (Forensics); U of Virginia; Alabama U

HUNT, SAMANTHA; CENTREVILLE, VA; CENTREVILLE HS; (FR); DAR; Hnr Roll; Pres Ac Ftns Aw; Yth Ldrshp Prog; Comm Volntr; Chrch Yth Grp; Emplmnt; Key Club; Vllyball; Pharmacy; Physical Therapy; U of Virginia; Shenandoah U

HURWITCH, SARA; STERLING, VA; DOMINION HS; (JR); Ctznshp Aw; Hnr Roll; MVP; Otst Ac Ach Awd; Comm Volntr; DECA; Golf (V L); 2004-05 Washington Post All-District Golfer of the Year; 2004 Virginia High School Leagues Girls State Open Champion; Play Collegiate Golf-Turn Pro LPGA; Business/Psychology; Vanderbilt, UVA, Tennessee; Wake Forest, Tulane, Duke

HUSS, MAREN V; WAYNESBORO, VA; WAYNESBORO HS; (SO); Hnr Roll; Perf Att; WWAHSS; Comm Volntr; Drma Clb; Key Club; Ntl Beta Clb; Chr; Sccr (V); Track (V); Beta Club Vice President for 2005-2006

HUYNH, MARY; LORTON, VA; HAYFIELD SECONDARY SCH; (JR); Hnr Roll; Otst Ac Ach Awd; Perf Att; Pres Sch; WWAHSS; Svce Clb; Orch; Neuroscience; Biology; Johns Hopkins U; U of Virginia

HWANG, JUDITH; CENTREVILLE, VA; CENTREVILLE HS; (SO); F Lan Hn Soc; Hnr Roll; Comm Volntr; Peer Tut/Med; FBLA; Bnd; Mch Bnd; Pep Bnd; Piano for 11 Years; Chinese School Academic Awards; Business; U of Virginia; James Madison U

HWANG, SUN HAE; CENTREVILLE, VA; THOMAS JEFFERSON HS SCIENCE & TECH; (JR); F Lan Hn Soc; Comm Volntr; Hosp Aide; Biology Clb; Chrch Yth Grp; Sci Clb; Japanese Clb; Dnce; Vllyball (J); Medical Society, Vice President; Asian Awareness, Vice President; Medical Doctor (PhD); U of Virginia; Harvard U

HYATT, JAMES C; ROANOKE, VA; PATRICK HENRY HS; (SR); Hnr Roll; Perf Att; St of Mnth; WWAHSS; Chrch Yth Grp; Ntl Beta Clb; Bsball (V L); Ftball (V CL); Wendy's High School Heisman Nominee; Hamden-Sydney College

IBIA, YAKAYAMA; RESTON, VA; SOUTH LAKES HS; (SO); Ctznshp Aw; Hnr Roll; Comm Volntr; Chrch Yth Grp; FCA; FBLA; Bskball (J L); Ftball (V L); Track (V L); Wt Lftg (V); Lead America Congressional; Student Leadership (Summer Year); Computer Engineering/Programming; U of Virginia; Virginia Commonwealth U

IDOWU, OLALEKAN J; MANASSAS, VA; STONEWALL JACKSON HS; (SO); Tchrs Aide; Bskball (V L); Natural Sciences-Physics; Investigative Analyst for Government; Syracuse U; Virginia Polytechnic Institute and State U

ILIEV, ILIA A; MANASSAS, VA; OSBOURN HS; (SO); Gov Hnr Prg; Hi Hnr Roll; Nat Hon Sy; Otst Ac Ach Awd; Comm Volntr; Cmptr Clb; DARE; Key Club; Orch; Mar Art; First Place in NASKA "5A" Rated Tournaments; Physician/Medical Degree; U of Virginia/Harvard U; Georgetown U

ING, ANNA; SPRINGFIELD, VA; WEST SPRINGFIELD HS; (JR); Ctznshp Aw; DAR; F Lan Hn Soc; Nat Hon Sy; Pres Ac Ftns Aw; St of Mnth; Comm Volntr; DECA; Emplmnt; Key Club; Latin Clb; PP Ftbl (VJ); Sccr (J); Wrstlg (VJ L); (2005) VA State Champ-Deca: Financial Analysis; Marine Science/Biology; U of Virginia

INGRAM, KENDALL R; MANASSAS, VA; OSBOURN HS; (JR); Hnr Roll; Nat Hon Sy; Perf Att; Pres Ac Ftns Aw; Sci Fairs; WWAHSS; Yth Ldrshp Prog; Comm Volntr; Peer Tut/Med; DARE; Dbte Team; Emplmnt; FBLA; Key Club; SADD; Spanish Clb; SP/M/VS; Chrldg (V C); Cl Off (P); CR (R); Spanish Honor Society; Young Democrats Club; Accounting; Corporate Lawyer; U North Carolina Chapel Hill NC; Virginia Commonwealth U

IRBY, KATHLEEN; STAFFORD, VA; COLONIAL FORGE HS; (SO); 4H Awd; Hnr Roll; 4-H; Scouts; Acpl Chr; Chr; Dnce; SP/M/VS; Pre-Veterinary Medicine; Virginia Tech; Longwood

ISKRENOVA, NASTASSIA; BURKE, VA; LAKE BRADDOCK SECONDARY HS; (SO); Ctznshp Aw; Hnr Roll; Pres Ac Ftns Aw; Sci Fairs; Comm Volntr; Peer Tut/Med; Spec Olymp Vol; Dbte Team; Emplmnt; Stu Cncl (R); CR (R); Sch Ppr (E); Junior National Honor Society; Skiing Novice Ladies Figure Skater, Tennis Film School; Business; Fashion; New York U; George Mason U

Ingram, Kendall R
Osbourn HS
Manassas, VA

Horner, Daniel
Homeschool
Suffolk, VA

Holder, Wesley L
National Christian AC
Arlington, VA

Hoang, Teresa N
Stuart HS
Alexandria, VA

Hobson, Ashley M
Varina HS
Richmond, VA

Howe, Lauren
Albemarle HS
Earlysville, VA

Irby, Kathleen
Colonial Forge HS
Stafford, VA

ITTAH, ARIEL; CENTREVILLE, VA; WESTFIELD HS; (SO); F Lan Hn Soc; Hi Hnr Roll; Hnr Roll; Sci/Math Olympn; St of Mnth; Dbte Team; NtlFrnscLg; Quill & Scroll; Spch Team; German Clb; Sch Ppr (E); Lt. for Westfield Speech and Debate; Most Valuable Debater 2004-2005; Business and Economics; Political Science; College of William and Mary; Johns Hopkins U

IWUJI, FRANCIS; WOODBRIDGE, VA; OSBORN PARK HS; (FR); Ctznshp Aw; Perf Att; DARE; Off Aide; Bnd; Chr; Won 1st Place at USA World; Showcase / Most Photogenic; Computer Engineering / Medical Doctor; Programming; Virgnia Tech; U of VA

JACKSON, AMANDA N; AXTON, VA; MAGNA VISTA HS; (JR); Hnr Roll; Nat Hon Sy; Comm Volntr; 4-H; Chrch Yth Grp; FBLA; Ntl Beta Clb; Ntl FFA; Chrldg (J); State Winning FFA Team; National FFA Team; Agriculture Education; Virginia Tech; Patrick Henry Community College

JACKSON, CHEREESE; LOUISA, VA; LOUISA CTY HS; (SR); Hnr Roll; Otst Ac Ach Awd; Perf Att; Pres Ac Ftns Aw; WWAHSS; FCCLA; Veterinary Assistant; Veterinary Technology; Averett U; Bridgewater College

JACKSON, KESHIA; CONCORD, VA; RUSTBURG HS; (JR); Hnr Roll; Otst Ac Ach Awd; Chrch Yth Grp; Emplmnt; Bnd; Ch Chr; Dnce; Mch Bnd; Yrbk (P); Seminole District All-Academic / Athletic Team; Academic Achievement Award; Fashion Design; Hip Hop Dancer; Art Institute in Philadelphia; Radford U

JACKSON, STEPHANIE; ASHBURN, VA; STONE BRIDGE HS; (SO); Duke TS; Hi Hnr Roll; Hnr Roll; Otst Ac Ach Awd; Comm Volntr; Key Club; Pep Squd; P to P St Amb Prg; Foreign Clb; Dnce; All Star International and National Dance Titles; Business; Fashion; Florida State U; Stanford

JACOB, ELIZA A; BLACKSBURG, VA; BLACKSBURG HS; (SR); Nat Hon Sy; WWAHSS; Comm Volntr; Hosp Aide; Peer Tut/Med; Mth Clb/Tm; Sci Clb; Spanish Clb; Ch Chr; Biotechnology; Virginia Tech

JAIPRAKASH, ASHWIN; ASHBURN, VA; STONE BRIDGE HS; (SR); Gov Hnr Prg; Hnr Roll; Nat Hon Sy; Pres Ac Ftns Aw; WWAHSS; Comm Volntr; Chess; Key Club; Bnd; Sccr (V); Computer Engineering; Virginia Tech

JAMES, BIANCA; BRISTOL, VA; VIRGINIA HS; (FR); Comm Volntr; Chr; Dnce; Vice President of Keystone @ the Boys & Girls Club; Dance; Psychology; Norfolk State U; Howard U

JARAMILLO, PEDRO L; ASHBURN, VA; BROAD RUN HS; (SR); F Lan Hn Soc; Hnr Roll; Nat Hon Sy; Otst Ac Ach Awd; Perf Att; St of Mnth; WWAHSS; Comm Volntr; ArtClub; Chess; Emplmnt; Key Club; Computer Science; U of Virginia

JARAMILLO-UNDERWOOD, ALICIA; WOODBRIDGE, VA; OSBOURN PARK SR HS; (JR); Duke TS; F Lan Hn Soc; Hnr Roll; MVP; Nat Hon Sy; Chrch Yth Grp; Spanish Clb; Sccr (V L); Tennis (V L); Presidential Service Award; Academic Letter 2003-2004; Psychology; International Relations; U of Virginia; College of William and Mary

JARRELL, JESSICA; NEWPORT NEWS, VA; WOODSIDE HS; (SR); Hi Hnr Roll; Hnr Roll; Otst Ac Ach Awd; Peer Tut/Med; Bnd; I'm Known for Being a Great Drummer; I Have Done 25 Hr Community Service in ER; Business Management; Political Science; Christopher Newport U

JARVIS, CORY; BRISTOL, VA; JOHN S BATTLE HS; (SR); All Am Sch; Hnr Roll; MVP; Chrch Yth Grp; Emplmnt; FCA; Lttrmn Clb; Off Aide; Vsity Clb; Chr; Bsball (J); Bskball (VJCL); Ftball (VJCL); Tennis (V CL); Track (VJ L); Vsy Clb (V C); Sch Ppr (R, P); Yrbk (R, P); 2nd Team-All District Quarterback; Honorable Mention-Basketball; Biology Major-Doctorate; Open My Own Pediatric Clinic; U of Virginia WISE/Eastern VA Med School; Emory & Henry College

JAUDON, SHARLAY L; EVINGTON, VA; ALTAVISTA COMBINED SCH; (FR); Ctznshp Aw; Hnr Roll; Perf Att; Peer Tut/Med; 4-H; DARE; FCCLA; Scouts; Drl Tm; Step Team Ace; Pediatric Nurse; Registered Nurse; U of North Carolina; U of Virginia

JAYNE, BRAD; WAYNESBORO, VA; WAYNESBORO HS; (FR); Hnr Roll; Comm Volntr; Hab For Humty Volntr; Key Club; Ntl Beta Clb; Bnd; Mch Bnd; Swg Chr; Ftball (V); Key Club; Virginia Tech

JENNINGS, LATESHA; NATHALIE, VA; HALIFAX CTY HS; (SR); Hnr Roll; WWAHSS; Comm Volntr; Chrch Yth Grp; Business Accounting; National College of Business and Technology; North Carolina Agriculture & Technology

JENNINGS, LINDSAY E; ASHBURN, VA; FOXCROFT SCH; (JR); Ctznshp Aw; Hi Hnr Roll; MVP; Pres Ac Ftns Aw; WWAHSS; Hab For Humty Volntr; Aqrium Clb; DARE; Emplmnt; P to P St Amb Prg; Sccr (V CL); Sftball (V CL); Stu Cncl (V); Parents Association Award in 2005; Head of Blue Planet Society; Marine Biology; Brown U; Tufts U

JEONG, JENNY; LYNCHBURG, VA; HERITAGE HS; (JR); Ctznshp Aw; Hnr Roll; Nat Hon Sy; Comm Volntr; Chrch Yth Grp; Key Club; Mth Clb/Tm; Orch; Pre-Dentist; Biology; North Carolina State U; UNC

JETT, HEATHER A; BERRYVILLE, VA; CLARKE CTY HS; (SO); Yth Ldrshp Prog; Comm Volntr; DARE; Emplmnt; SADD; Lit Mag (P); Australian Shepherd Club of America High Score 13-17/ Overall '02-'03 & '03-'04 Sheep Region Six Junior 13-17; Blueridge Australian Shephard Club High in Trial Working - Junior; Physics; Art - Animation / Fire; Lord Fairfax Community College; U of the Arts

JHAVERI, DIMPI; ASHBURN, VA; STONE BRIDGE HS; (SO); Hnr Roll; Comm Volntr; Peer Tut/Med; Key Club; Dnce; Dental; Medical; George Mason U; U of Virginia

JHAVERI, SHIEL S; WINCHESTER, VA; JAMES WOOD HS; (SR); Hnr Roll; Nat Hon Sy; Valdctrian; WWAHSS; Comm Volntr; Red Cr Aide; Emplmnt; Key Club; Ntl FFA; Prom Com; Sci Clb; Tech Clb; Vsity Clb; Swmg (V); Track (J); Vsy Clb (V); Psychology; Pre-Med; Admitted to and Attending the U of Virginia

JIVIDEN, LILA D; MANASSAS, VA; OSBOURN HS; (SO); Gov Hnr Prg; Hi Hnr Roll; Pres Ac Ftns Aw; Sci Fairs; WWAHSS; Yth Ldrshp Prog; Comm Volntr; Chrch Yth Grp; FBLA; HO'Br Yth Ldrshp; Mod UN; French Clb; Cr Ctry (V); Swmg (V L); Track (V L); French Club President, Key Club Member; Future Business Leaders of America President, 1st Place Winner in Parliamentary Procedures in VA State; Medicine; Business; U of Virginia; William and Mary

JIVIDEN, MARIA; MANASSAS, VA; OSBOURN HS; (FR); SP/M/VS; Cr Ctry; Sccr (J); Swmg (V L); Future Business Leaders of America Parliamentarian; FBLA Regional Parliamentarian, French Club Member, 9th Place in Nation Parliamentarian Procedures; Medicine; Business; U of Virginia; William and Mary

JOHN, CAMERON A; FREDERICKSBURG, VA; JAMES MONROE HS; (JR); Hi Hnr Roll; Nat Hon Sy; Nat Mrt Fin; Nat Mrt LOC; WWAHSS; Comm Volntr; Chrch Yth Grp; Emplmnt; FCA; Key Club; Prom Com; Latin Clb; Cr Ctry (V L); Ftball (V L); Lcrsse (V L); Swmg (V L); Fredericksburg Rescue Squad-Junior Member

JOHNS, ANDREW W; FREDERICKSBURG, VA; JAMES MONROE; (FR); Hi Hnr Roll; Nat Hon Sy; Otst Ac Ach Awd; Pres Ac Ftns Aw; St of Mnth; WWAHSS; Comm Volntr; Biology Clb; FCA; Key Club; NtlFrnscLg; French Clb; Jzz Bnd; Golf (J); Lcrsse (J); Swmg (J); Tennis (V L); Stu Cncl (R); CR (R); Yrbk (P)

JOHNS, SIMONE; WILLIAMSBURG, VA; LAFAYETTE HS; (SO); F Lan Hn Soc; Hnr Roll; WWAHSS; Comm Volntr; Peer Tut/Med; Flg Crps; Track (J); U of Maryland; Morgan State U

JOHNS JR, MONTGOMERY; FREDERICKSBURG, VA; JAMES MONROE HS; (JR); Duke TS; Hi Hnr Roll; MVP; Nat Hon Sy; Otst Ac Ach Awd; Comm Volntr; Peer Tut/Med; Chrch Yth Grp; FCA; Key Club; NYLC; French Clb; Golf (V L); Swmg (V); Tennis (V L); CR (R); National Youth Leadership Forum in Technology; Technology Intern Fredericksburg City Schools; Computer Engineering; Patent Attorney; U of Virginia; Duke U

JOHNSON, ALEXANDER W; ALEXANDRIA, VA; T C WILLIAMS HS; (SO); Hi Hnr Roll; Hnr Roll; MVP; Nat Hon Sy; Otst Ac Ach Awd; WWAHSS; Comm Volntr; Peer Tut/Med; Key Club; Sccr (V L); Division 1 Soccer State Cup Winner; Principal's Honor Award; Engineering; Architecture; NYU, Yale; MIT, Berkeley

JOHNSON, ALICIA V; ASHBURN, VA; STONE BRIDGE HS; (SO); Hnr Roll; Comm Volntr; Key Club; Chr; Ch Chr; Key Club-(Community Service); Music; Business; George Mason; U of Virginia

JOHNSON, BATRICE; CHESAPEAKE, VA; DEEP CREEK HS; (JR); Hnr Roll; Perf Att; WWAHSS; Key Club; ROTC; Drl Tm; Pre-Medicine; Regis U; James Madison U

JOHNSON, CHRISTIANA E; ALEXANDRIA, VA; T C WILLIAMS HS; (JR); F Lan Hn Soc; Hi Hnr Roll; MVP; Nat Hon Sy; Otst Ac Ach Awd; Pres Ac Ftns Aw; USAA; WWAHSS; Key Club; German Clb; Bnd; Bskball (V); Fld Hky (V); Sccr (V); Lit Mag (R); Titan Pride Leadership Award

JOHNSON, DAVID; VIRGINIA BEACH, VA; FLOYD KELLAM HS; (FR); Hi Hnr Roll; Hnr Roll; Otst Ac Ach Awd; Perf Att; St of Mnth; Comm Volntr; Peer Tut/Med; Step Team; Pharmacist; U of Florida (FLU); U of Virginia (UVA)

JOHNSON, ELIZABETH; ASHBURN, VA; STONE BRIDGE HS; (SR); Nat Hon Sy; WWAHSS; Comm Volntr; Emplmnt; FBLA; Key Club; German Clb; Cr Ctry (V L); Sccr (V L); Track (V); Vllyball (J L); Yrbk (R, P); Cross Country Regional Champions 2004-05; Rookie of the Year Cross Country 2004; English; James Madison U

JOHNSON, KIRSTEN; VIRGINIA BCH, VA; COASTAL CHRISTIAN AC; (FR); Nat Hon Sy; Comm Volntr; Lib Aide; Yrbk (P); Piano; Doctor; Lawyer; Virginia State U; Old Dominion U

JOHNSON, LA NESHA N; WAVERLY, VA; SUSSEX CTRL HS; (SR); Hnr Roll; Sci Fairs; Yth Ldrshp Prog; Chrch Yth Grp; Cmptr Clb; DARE; Emplmnt; Fr of Library; ROTC; Track (V); Stu Cncl (R); Criminal Justice; Saint Paul U

JOHNSON, LAUREN; LOUISA, VA; LOUISA CTY HS; (SR); Hi Hnr Roll; Hnr Roll; WWAHSS; Chrch Yth Grp; DECA; FCA; FBLA; Prom Com; Quill & Scroll; Tchrs Aide; Vsity Clb; PP Ftbl (V); Track (V L); Vsy Clb (V L); Yrbk (E, R, P); Who's Who Among American Students; Management & Info Systems; George Mason U

JOHNSON, NATALIA K; CHANTILLY, VA; (FR); Hnr Roll; MVP; Sci Fairs; St of Mnth; Comm Volntr; Chrch Yth Grp; DARE; Scouts; SADD; Tchrs Aide; Sftball (J L); CYA Basketball Championship; Medicine; Doctorate Degree; Duke U; U of North Carolina

JOHNSON, NATASHA D; DANVILLE, VA; GEORGE WASHINGTON HS; (SR); Ctznshp Aw; Hnr Roll; Nat Hon Sy; WWAHSS; Comm Volntr; Chrch Yth Grp; Emplmnt; FBLA; Ch Chr; FBLA; Gear Up; Lawyer; Registered Nurse; Johnson C. Smith U; Morgan State U

JOHNSON, RYAN; HAMPTON, VA; HAMPTON HS; (SR); Ctznshp Aw; F Lan Hn Soc; Hnr Roll; Nat Hon Sy; Nat Ldrshp Svc; Nat Mrt Semif; St of Mnth; WWAHSS; Peer Tut/Med; Chrch Yth Grp; Emplmnt; Mod UN; Quiz Bowl; Schol Bwl; Svce Clb; Tchrs Aide; French Clb; Ch Chr; Lit Mag (R); Chair of Hampton VA/Neighborhood Youth; President-Model UN Club/ Advisory Board; Mechanical Engineering; Design Engineer; Virginia Commonwealth U; U of North Carolina-Charlotte

JONES, AMANDA; AXTON, VA; MAGNA VISTA HS; (FR); Hnr Roll; Comm Volntr; 4-H; Chrch Yth Grp; Ntl Beta Clb; Ntl FFA; Ch Chr; Sftball (J); Cl Off (R); Virginia Tech; Averett U

JONES, ASHLEY; NEWPORT NEWS, VA; WOODSIDE HS; (JR); Ctznshp Aw; Hnr Roll; WWAHSS; Comm Volntr; Spec Olymp Vol; Orch; Swmg (V L); CR (R); Coast Guard Blue Dolphins-Swimming; Communications; Swimming; James Madison U; West Virginia U

JONES, COURTNEY L; VIRGINIA BEACH, VA; FRANK W COX HS; (SO); Hnr Roll; Pres Ac Ftns Aw; St of Mnth; Comm Volntr; Emplmnt; Key Club; Mod UN; Photog; Japanese Clb; Chr; Lcrsse (VJC); Sccr (J); Lit Mag (P); Intern At Virginia Maritime Museum; Communications; International Relations; Averett U; James Madison U

JONES, CRISTINA; ROANOKE, VA; WILLIAM FLEMING HS; (FR); Hnr Roll; Sci Fairs; Comm Volntr; CR (S); Breckinridge Best Award; Computer Science; Georgia Tech; U of Georgia

JONES, CRYSTAL D; HURT, VA; GRETNA HS; (SR); Hi Hnr Roll; Jr Mshl; Nat Hon Sy; Nat Sci Aw; Perf Att; WWAHSS; Comm Volntr; Ntl Beta Clb; Spanish Clb; Clr Grd; Chrldg (V C); Health Occupations Students of America Secretary; Registered Nurse; Jefferson College of Health Sciences

JONES, DERRELL; PETERSBURG, VA; PETERSBURG HS; (JR); WWAHSS; Comm Volntr; Peer Tut/Med; Key Club; Photog; Chr; Bsball (V); Sch Ppr (R, P); Key Club/Treasurer; History Club FBLA; Pre-Law/Lawyer; Business Accounting/Accountant; Pepperdine U; Columbia U

JONES, HALLEE J; IVOR, VA; JAMES RIVER CHRISTIAN AC; (FR); Hnr Roll; Salutrn; USAA; Emplmnt; Chrldg (V); Vllyball; Architecture; Journalism; Longwood; UVA

JONES, KARI; MANASSAS, VA; OSBOURN HS; (JR); Hnr Roll; Comm Volntr; Peer Tut/Med; DARE; FBLA; Key Club; SADD; French Clb; Swmg (V); Elementary Education; Mathematics Education; U of North Carolina Greensboro; Christopher-Newport U

JONES, KELLEE G; VIRGINIA BEACH, VA; (JR); Hi Hnr Roll; Nat Hon Sy; Otst Ac Ach Awd; Pres Ac Ftns Aw; St of Mnth; Comm Volntr; Spec Olymp Vol; Chrch Yth Grp; Drma Clb; Emplmnt; Key Club; Quill & Scroll; Spanish Clb; SP/M/VS; Cr Ctry (V L); Fld Hky (JCL); Track (V L); Lit Mag; President-Key Club; Virginia Pilot Scholastic Team; Pediatric Oncologist; Teacher; James Madison U; College of Charleston

JONES, MARK T; VIRGINIA BEACH, VA; COX HS; (FR); Hi Hnr Roll; Pres Ac Ftns Aw; St of Mnth; Key Club; Sccr (J); Spanish Honor Society; Key Club; Opthamologist

JONES, RACHEL D; CARROLLTON, VA; SMITHFIELD HS; (JR); 4H Awd; Ctznshp Aw; Hi Hnr Roll; Hnr Roll; Nat Hon Sy; Otst Ac Ach Awd; Perf Att; Pres Sch; Sci Fairs; Sci/Math Olympn; Comm Volntr; Hab For Humty Volntr; Peer Tut/Med; Chrch Yth Grp; DARE; Emplmnt; Key Club; Ntl Beta Clb; Off Aide; Photog; Scouts; Ch Chr; Stg Cre; Vllyball (VJ L); Lit Mag (E, R)

JONES, SARAH E; ABINGDON, VA; JOHN S BATTLE HS; (JR); Hi Hnr Roll; Hnr Roll; Nat Hon Sy; USAA; WWAHSS; Comm Volntr; Chrch Yth Grp; Dbte Team; Bnd; Mch Bnd; Cr Ctry (V); Track (V); Lit Mag; District Concert Band / Superior Solo Rating; Author; Mental Health Activist; Cedarville U; Wellesley College

JONES, SHAROD M; NORFOLK, VA; LAKE TAYLOR HS; (SR); Hnr Roll; Nat Hon Sy; Pres Sch; St Optmst of Yr; WWAHSS; Prom Com; Bnd; Mch Bnd; Pep Bnd; Cl Off (R); CR (R); Yrbk (E); Hampton Roads Scholar - Old Dominion U; Principal's Award Recipient; Criminal Justice; Criminal Defense Attorney; Old Dominion U - Accepted

Johnson, Elizabeth
Stone Bridge HS
Ashburn, VA

Jarvis, Cory
John S Battle HS
Bristol, VA

James, Bianca
Virginia HS
Bristol, VA

National
Honor Roll
Spring 2005

Iwuji, Francis
Osborn Park HS
Woodbridge, VA

Jaudon, Sharlay L
Altavista Combined Sch
Evington, VA

Johnson, Natalia K
Chantilly, VA

JORDAN, DEANCA; FARMVILLE, VA; PRINCE EDWARD CTY HS; (FR); Hnr Roll; Nat Hon Sy; Perf Att; St of Mnth; Bskball (V); Track (J); English Academic Award; Being an Artist; Cosmetology; Hampton U; Norfolk State U

JORDAN, TIFFANY R; ROANOKE, VA; WILLIAM FLEMING HS; (FR); Hnr Roll; Perf Att; Pres Ac Ftns Aw; Chrch Yth Grp; Key Club; Bnd; Ch Chr; Chrldg (J); Stu Cncl (P); Yrbk (E); IB (Middle Years Program); Youth Council At Sweet Union Baptist Church; Bachelor's Degree; Master's Degree; U of North Carolina; Georgia Tech

JOYCE, JESSICA; LEXINGTON, VA; ROCKBRIDGE CTY HS; (JR); Hnr Roll; Pres Ac Ftns Aw; WWAHSS; Spanish Clb; Bnd; Dnce; Sccr (V L); Swmg (V); Scholar / Athlete Award; National Spanish Exam Award

JOYNER, AZALEA; SUFFOLK, VA; KING'S FORK HS; (SO); Comm Volntr; DARE; Key Club; P to P St Amb Prg; Foreign Clb; Fld Hky (J); Treasurer of Key Club; Member of the Academic Challenge Team; English Literature; Political Science; U of Hawaii At Manoa

JU, EUN-SON; ASHBURN, VA; STONE BRIDGE HS; (SO); Hi Hnr Roll; Hnr Roll; Nat Hon Sy; Perf Att; WWAHSS; Comm Volntr; HO'Br Yth Ldrshp; Key Club; Mth Clb/Tm; Bnd; Jzz Bnd; Track; Won A Lot of Art Awards (Geico Seat Belt Poster Contest, Etc.); Talking Art 3 Now; Skipped Art 1; Medical (Plastic Surgery); Medical Illustration; Johns Hopkins U; Duke U

JUDD, MISTY; LURAY, VA; LURAY HS; (FR); Hnr Roll; Hab For Humty Volntr; FBLA; Vsity Clb; Bskball; Sftball (VJ L); Vllyball (JC); Participated in Pride Club; Physical Therapy; Teacher/Coach; U of Texas; U of Virginia

JUSTUS, KAITLIN; GRUNDY, VA; GRUNDY HS; (SO); 4H Awd; Hnr Roll; Otst Ac Ach Awd; Perf Att; WWAHSS; Comm Volntr; Chrch Yth Grp; FBLA; Key Club; Chrldg (V L); Sftball (CL); Stu Cncl; Sch Ppr (E); Yrbk (P); Freshman Student of the Year; Young Republican's Club; Ophthalmology/ Optometry; Vanderbilt U; East Tennessee State U

KALASKAS, ANTHONY; DUMFRIES, VA; FOREST PARK SR HS; (JR); Ctznshp Aw; F Lan Hn Soc; Hi Hnr Roll; Hnr Roll; Nat Hon Sy; Otst Ac Ach Awd; Perf Att; St of Mnth; Comm Volntr; Chess; Cmptr Clb; Key Club; Quill & Scroll; Sci Clb; Spanish Clb; Sch Ppr (E, R); Piano-Have Played for 10 Years; Black History Month 2005 Essay Contest Winner; Political Science; Economics; U of Virginia; College of William and Mary

KAMARA, MARIE; SPOTSYLVANIA, VA; (MS); Hnr Roll; MVP; Otst Ac Ach Awd; Perf Att; Pres Sch; Comm Volntr; DARE; Drma Clb; Pep Squd; Chr; SP/M/VS; PPSqd (V); Stu Cncl (V); Pediatrician; Medicine Field / Doctorate; Harvard Medical School; Princeton U

KANAKIS, MARIA; FALLS CHURCH, VA; MC LEAN HS; (SR); F Lan Hn Soc; Nat Hon Sy; Pres Sch; Emplmnt; MuAlphaTh; Orch; SP/M/VS; Swmg (V); Participant in Three Performing Quartets; McLeader / Mentor to Underclassmen; Music Performance Degree - Violin; The Eastman School of Music at the U of Rochester

KANNEY, CHRIS; WAYNESBORO, VA; WAYNESBORO HS; (SR); Gov Hnr Prg; Hi Hnr Roll; Hnr Roll; Kwnis Aw; Nat Hon Sy; Nat Ldrshp Svc; Otst Ac Ach Awd; Perf Att; Pres Ac Ftns Aw; Sci Fairs; Chess; Chrch Yth Grp; DARE; Emplmnt; FCA; HO'Br Yth Ldrshp; Key Club; Mth Clb/Tm; Acpl Chr; Chr; Ch Chr; SP/M/VS; Cr Ctry (V CL); Sccr (VJCL); Track (VJ); Cl Off (P, V); Stu Cncl (V); CR (R)

KANNEY, MALOREE; WAYNESBORO, VA; WAYNESBORO HS; (FR); Hi Hnr Roll; Hnr Roll; Kwnis Aw; Otst Ac Ach Awd; Perf Att; Sci Fairs; WWAHSS; ArtClub; Chrch Yth Grp; DARE; DECA; Emplmnt; Key Club; Ntl Beta Clb; Scouts; Acpl Chr; Chr; Ch Chr; Dnce; Sccr (VJ); Tennis (V); Vllyball (J); CR (R)

KARDARAS, NICOLE A; MANASSAS, VA; BISHOP DENIS J O'CONNELL HS; (JR); Hnr Roll; Comm Volntr; Chrch Yth Grp; Drma Clb; Bnd; SP/M/VS; Track (V); U of Mary Washington

KARDASHIAN, BRIELLE N.; BERRYVILLE, VA; CLARKE CTY HS; (SO); Ctznshp Aw; Hnr Roll; Kwnis Aw; Otst Ac Ach Awd; Perf Att; St of Mnth; Comm Volntr; DARE; Chr; Dnce; SP/M/VS; Bskball (J); Chrldg (JC); Sccr (J); Tennis (V L); Yrbk (R, P); Select Travel Soccer - 5 Yrs / Multiple League & Tournament Champions; Undefeated JV Basketball Team-2004-05 (22-0-Dist-Champs); Exercise Sciences; Sports Law; U of Maryland College Park; Bowling Green State U

KARDASHIAN, JONATHAN; BERRYVILLE, VA; CLARKE CTY HS; (JR); Ctznshp Aw; Hnr Roll; Kwnis Aw; Otst Ac Ach Awd; Perf Att; Sci Fairs; St of Mnth; Comm Volntr; Peer Tut/Med; Chess; Emplmnt; P to P St Amb Prg; Bnd; Mar Art; Tae Kwon Do Black Belt; One Year of Kickboxing; Doctorate in Psychology; James Madison U

KARRAKCHOU, KHALIL; FALLS CHURCH, VA; GEORGE MASON HS; (FR); Ctznshp Aw; Hnr Roll; Chess; Mod UN; Wrstlg (J); CR (R); Medical School; World Politics; Georgetown U; UVA

KAZMAR, KIMBERLY; CHESAPEAKE, VA; WESTERN BRANCH HS; (SO); Hnr Roll; Nat Hon Sy; Comm Volntr; Hab For Humty Volntr; Hosp Aide; Chrch Yth Grp; FBLA; Mus Clb; Chr; Sftball (J); Vllyball (VJ L); Nursing

KEEL, STEPHEN W; CHESAPEAKE, VA; STONEBRIDGE CHRISTIAN SCH; (SO); Hi Hnr Roll; Hnr Roll; Nat Hon Sy; Perf Att; Sci Fairs; WWAHSS; Chrch Yth Grp; Drma Clb; Emplmnt; Key Club; SP/M/VS; Stg Cre; Bsball (V); Bskball (VJCL); CR (P); National Honor Society Member; Electrical Engineering; Mechanical Engineering; Virginia Polytechnic Institute; North Carolina State U

KEELER, AMANDA B; BERRYVILLE, VA; CLARKE CTY HS; (FR); Hnr Roll; Kwnis Aw; Comm Volntr; Chrch Yth Grp; Scouts; Vllyball (J); Pediatrician; U of South Carolina; U of North Carolina

KEITHLEY, KEVIN; RESTON, VA; BISHOP O'CONNELL HS; (JR); F Lan Hn Soc; Hi Hnr Roll; Nat Hon Sy; Pres Ac Ftns Aw; WWAHSS; Comm Volntr; Peer Tut/Med; Emplmnt; FCA; Key Club; Sci Clb; French Clb; Bsball (V L); Virginia Junior Academy Science-Honorable Mention Paper; 1st Place Math League, VA Baseball Club P/T work; Mathematics / Economics; Investment Banking; U of Virginia; George Washington U

KELLEY, ALICIA; PORTSMOUTH, VA; I.C. NORCOM HS; (SR); Perf Att; Chrch Yth Grp; DECA; Drma Clb; Prom Com; Vsity Clb; Fld Hky (V C); Cl Off (P); Sch Ppr (R); Miss Senior; English Teacher-7th Grade; Old Dominion U; Virginia Union U

KELLEY, CHRISTINA M; LEXINGTON, VA; ROCKBRIDGE CTY HS; (JR); Hnr Roll; Nat Hon Sy; WWAHSS; Ntl FFA; Scouts; French Clb; Lcrsse (V); Biochemistry; Biology

KELLY III, EUGENE W; ALEXANDRIA, VA; T C WILLIAMS HS; (SR); Hi Hnr Roll; Hnr Roll; Kwnis Aw; Nat Hon Sy; Otst Ac Ach Awd; Sci Fairs; WWAHSS; Comm Volntr; Peer Tut/Med; Chrch Yth Grp; Key Club; Latin Clb; TC Williams Titan Pride Award Next Step Superteen; Academic Letter Award and AP Scholar; History; Library Science; U of Virginia

KENNEDY, STEPHAN; BEDFORD, VA; LIBERTY HS; (JR); Hnr Roll; Kwnis Aw; WWAHSS; Key Club; Bnd; Jzz Bnd; Mch Bnd; Pep Bnd; Trauma Physician; Virginia Tech; Old Dominion U

KENT, WHITNEY G; CHESAPEAKE, VA; GREAT BRIDGE HS; (SR); Hnr Roll; Perf Att; WWAHSS; Peer Tut/Med; Emplmnt; Svce Clb; SADD; French Clb; Dnce; Orch; SP/M/VS; Varsity Dance Team; Chamber Orchestra; Education; Old Dominion U

KEOSOMBATH, JESSICA; ASHLAND, VA; PATRICK HENRY HS; (SO); Ctznshp Aw; Hnr Roll; Otst Ac Ach Awd; Perf Att; Sci Fairs; ArtClub; Chrch Yth Grp; Vsity Clb; Chr; Gmnstcs (V L); Show Choir; Medical Field; Virginia Commonwealth U

KERN, SARAH; VIRGINIA BEACH, VA; FIRST COLONIAL HS; (JR); Hnr Roll; MVP; Nat Hon Sy; WWAHSS; Key Club; Fld Hky (VJ); Sccr (VJ); Crew; James Madison U; George Mason U

KESSLER, COURTNEY B; NORFOLK, VA; MAURY HS; (SR); F Lan Hn Soc; Hi Hnr Roll; Hnr Roll; Nat Hon Sy; Comm Volntr; Emplmnt; FBLA; Jr Cls League; Photog; Latin Clb; Swmg (V); Tennis (V); Cl Off (S); Stu Cncl (V); Political Science; Communications; U of Virginia

KEY, SARAH; SCOTTSVILLE, VA; FLUVANNA HS; (SO); Hi Hnr Roll; Hnr Roll; Comm Volntr; Chrch Yth Grp; Scouts; Cr Ctry (L); Sccr (L); Track (L); Special Education Teacher; Design; U of Virginia; Longwood U

KHALID, UMAR; FALLS CHURCH, VA; STUART HS; (SO); Perf Att; SP/M/VS; Stg Cre; Medical; George Washington; Georgetown

KHALSA, RUE; HERNDON, VA; PAUL VI CHS; (SO); Hnr Roll; Amnsty Intl; Comm Volntr; Key Club; Bskball (J); Track (J); Sch Ppr (E); Critics & Awards Program (Cuppies) Critic; Young D.C. (Youth Newspaper) Reporter; Journalism; Political Science

KHAN, MYRA; ASHBURN, VA; STONE BRIDGE HS; (SR); Hnr Roll; Nat Hon Sy; WWAHSS; Comm Volntr; DECA; Emplmnt; Key Club; Off Aide; Tennis (V CL); Volunteer - Ashburn Fire & Rescue; Virginia Commonwealth U

KHAN, NADWA; FAIRFAX, VA; FAIRFAX HS; (SO); Hnr Roll; Peer Tut/Med; Sch Ppr (R); George Mason U

KHAN, SAADIA; STERLING, VA; DOMINION HS; (SO); Ctznshp Aw; Hnr Roll; Sci Fairs; Comm Volntr; ArtClub; Dbte Team; FTA; Key Club; NtlFrnscLg; Tennis (L); Sch Ppr (R); Letter in Training All Spring Sports; Letter in Debate; Pediatrics; Biology Major; James Madison U; George Mason U

KHASAWINAH, SARAH; ALEXANDRIA, VA; JEB STUART HS; (SR); Ctznshp Aw; Hi Hnr Roll; Nat Hon Sy; Pres Sch; Sci Fairs; Valdctrian; WWAHSS; Yth Ldrshp Prog; Amnsty Intl; Comm Volntr; Peer Tut/Med; AL Aux Girls; ArtClub; Chrch Yth Grp; Mth Clb/Tm; Photog; Schol Bwl; Svce Clb; Vsity Clb; Cr Ctry (J); Track (V); Adv Cncl (P); Stu Cncl (P); Princeton Prize in Race Relations; Raider Award; Political Science; Law; Bryn Mawr College

KHOSROWDAD, NADIA; CENTREVILLE, VA; CENTREVILLE HS; (SO); Nat Hon Sy; WWAHSS; Peer Tut/Med; Key Club; Education; English; U of Virginia; James Madison U

KIDNEY, RACHEL; CHARLOTTESVILLE, VA; ALBEMARLE HS; (FR); Hnr Roll; Comm Volntr; Emplmnt; Key Club; Bskball (J); Sccr (V L); Outstanding Achievement Award - Spring '05; Freshman Honorable Mention - Central Virginia Girls Soccer

KIECHLIN, JAMES; ASHBURN, VA; STONE BRIDGE HS; (SR); Hnr Roll; MVP; Otst Ac Ach Awd; Pres Ac Ftns Aw; Comm Volntr; DARE; DECA; Emplmnt; Key Club; Sccr (V C); Business Major; Christopher Newport U

KILLIAN, ERIC; GARRISONVILLE, VA; FREDERICKSBURG CHRISTIAN HS; (SO); Hnr Roll; Emplmnt; Ntl Beta Clb; Chemistry; College of William and Mary; U of Mary Washington

KIM, AMY; CENTREVILLE, VA; CENTREVILLE HS; (FR); WWAHSS; Peer Tut/Med; Chrch Yth Grp; Key Club; Scouts; Orch; Cl Off (R); Girl Scout Silver Award; Southwestern Youth Association Basketball Finalist; Pre-Med; Doctor; Johns Hopkins U; UC Berkeley

KIM, DAVID; FAIRFAX, VA; ROBINSON SECONDARY SCH; (JR); Hnr Roll; Pres Ac Ftns Aw; FBLA; Key Club; Bnd; Praise Band At Church; Economics; Political Science; James Madison U; New York U

KIM, ELISABETH; CENTREVILLE, VA; WESTFIELD HS; (SR); Hnr Roll; Nat Hon Sy; Comm Volntr; Chrch Yth Grp; Sci Clb; Orch; Science Honor Society; Soloist Award (Cello); Biology; Pre-Med; U of Virginia; Virginia Poly Technical Institute

KIM, EUNSOO; CENTREVILLE, VA; CENTREVILLE HS; (FR); Hnr Roll; Nat Hon Sy; WWAHSS; Key Club; Bnd; Tennis (V); Law; History

KIM, EVELYN; COLONIAL HEIGHTS, VA; COLONIAL HEIGHTS HS; (JR); F Lan Hn Soc; Hnr Roll; Nat Hon Sy; WWAHSS; Comm Volntr; Chrch Yth Grp; Emplmnt; FCA; Jr Cls League; Key Club; Ntl Beta Clb; Quill & Scroll; Latin Clb; Ch Chr; Sch Ppr (R); Optimist Essay Contest Winner; President Church Youth Group; New York U; Georgetown U

KIM, GINA E; FAIRFAX, VA; WOODSON HS; (MS); Ctznshp Aw; Hnr Roll; Comm Volntr; Peer Tut/Med; Chrch Yth Grp; Mth Clb/Tm; Chr; Orch; SP/M/VS; Stg Cre; Chrldg; Gmnstcs; Ice Sktg; Mar Art; Tennis; Stu Cncl (T); CR (R); Sch Ppr (R); National Junior Honor Society; Johns Hopkins Mathematics Talent Search; Medical; Journalism; Duke U; Yale U

KIM, HONG J; YORKTOWN, VA; YORK HS; (SO); Gov Hnr Prg; Hi Hnr Roll; USAA; WWAHSS; Comm Volntr; Red Cr Aide; Key Club; MuAlphaTh; Ftball (VJ); Regional Math Contest Team Champion; Bronze Medal in "Inquiry Announcement Meeting"; Johns Hopkins; Medical Engineer; Johns Hopkins U; U of Virginia

KIM, HWAPYEONG; CENTREVILLE, VA; CENTREVILLE HS; (JR); Perf Att; Peer Tut/Med; ArtClub; Chrch Yth Grp; FBLA; Key Club; Mth Clb/Tm; MuAlphaTh; Jzz Bnd; Accounting; Piano; U of Pennsylvania; George Mason U

KIM, JUNG-AH; CENTREVILLE, VA; CENTREVILLE HS; (SO); Ctznshp Aw; Hnr Roll; Nat Hon Sy; Perf Att; Pres Ac Ftns Aw; Pres Sch; Sci Fairs; Comm Volntr; Key Club; Mus Clb; Korean Clb; Bnd; Mch Bnd; Pep Bnd; Lcrsse (J); Honorable Mention at Regional Science Fair; Member of National Honor Society; Dental Careers; U of Virginia; Johns Hopkins U

KIM, KEVIN; ASHBURN, VA; BROAD RUN HS; (JR); Hnr Roll; St of Mnth; Comm Volntr; BPA; FBLA; Chr; Bskball (VJCL); Sccr (V L); Swmg (J); Cl Off (R); Yrbk (E); Advertising; Marketing; Virginia Polytechnic Institute & State U; U of Virginia

KIM, KO EUN; FAIRFAX, VA; OAKTON HS; (SO); Hi Hnr Roll; Hnr Roll; Comm Volntr; Peer Tut/Med; Chrch Yth Grp; Key Club; MuAlphaTh; Orch; Korean Society-Security; Oakton HS Orchestra David Chu Award-Most Improved; International Relationship; Political Science; U of Virginia; U of Pennsylvania

KIM, LUCY; ASHBURN, VA; STONE BRIDGE HS; (JR); F Lan Hn Soc; Hnr Roll; Nat Hon Sy; Sci Fairs; Hosp Aide; Dbte Team; FBLA; Key Club; CR (R); Debate JV; Political Science/Government; English Literature; U of Virginia

KIM, SHARON; YORKTOWN, VA; YORK HS; (SO); Hi Hnr Roll; WWAHSS; Comm Volntr; Chrch Yth Grp; Key Club; Mod UN; Asian Clb; Ch Chr; Cl Off (V); National Junior Honor Society President; Friends Club Representative; Medical; Cornell U; Harvard U

KIM, SOO; FAIRFAX, VA; CENTREVILLE HS; (JR); FBLA; Key Club; Photog; Interior Design; Parsons School of Design

KIM, SOYUB; BLACKSBURG, VA; BLACKSBURG HS; (SO); Hi Hnr Roll; Hnr Roll; Perf Att; Yth Ldrshp Prog; Hosp Aide; Emplmnt; Key Club; Svce Clb; Key Club Secretary; Mountain Academic Competition - Science; Psychiatrist; Art Therapist; Harvard U; U of Virginia

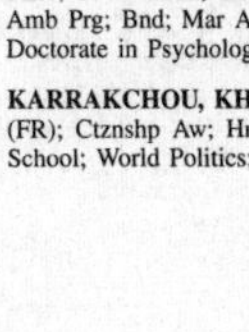
Kim, Soyub
Blacksburg HS
Blacksburg, VA

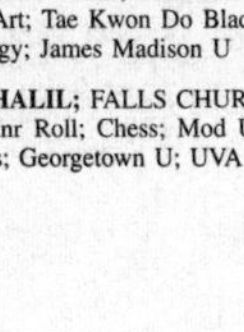
Key, Sarah
Fluvanna HS
Scottsville, VA

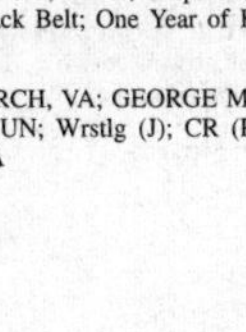
Keel, Stephen W
Stonebridge Christian Sch
Chesapeake, VA

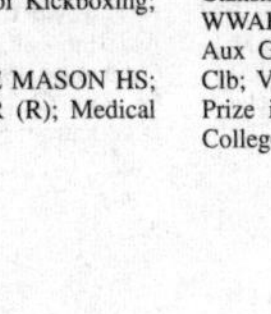
Kardashian, Jonathan
Clarke Cty HS
Berryville, VA

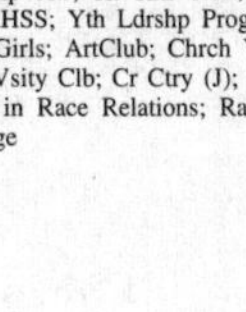
Kardashian, Brielle N.
Clarke Cty HS
Berryville, VA

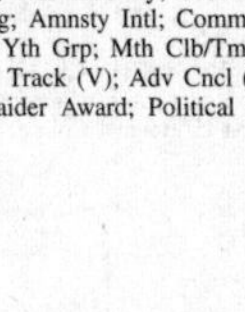
Joyce, Jessica
Rockbridge Cty HS
Lexington, VA

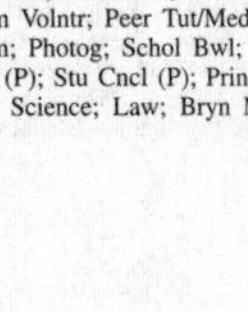
Ju, Eun-Son
Stone Bridge HS
Ashburn, VA

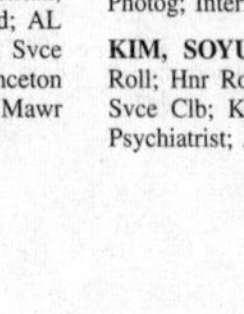
Karrakchou, Khalil
George Mason HS
Falls Church, VA

Kent, Whitney G
Great Bridge HS
Chesapeake, VA

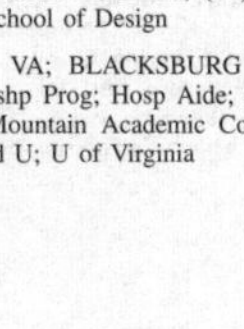
Kiechlin, James
Stone Bridge HS
Ashburn, VA

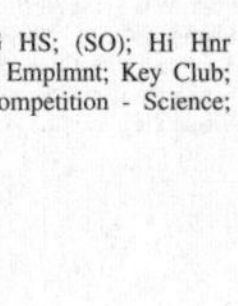
Kim, Gina E
Woodson HS
Fairfax, VA

KIME, KRISTEN E; MT CRAWFORD, VA; GRACE CHRISTIAN SCH; (JR); Hi Hnr Roll; Hnr Roll; Pres Ac Ftns Aw; Comm Volntr; Chrch Yth Grp; Sccr (V L); Vllyball (VJ L); Yrbk (E, R, P); 6 Years of Piano; Short-Term Mission Team Member; Sciences; English; Wheaton College; Messiah College

KINDER, BRIAN; RICHLANDS, VA; RICHLANDS HS; (FR); Ctznshp Aw; Hnr Roll; Otst Ac Ach Awd; Pres Ac Ftns Aw; Sci/Math Olympn; Peer Tut/Med; Chrch Yth Grp; FBLA; ROTC; Cr Ctry (V); CR (R); Upward Bound; Pre-Law; Forensic Science; U of Tennessee; Air Force Academy

KING, MOLLY L; SALEM, VA; SALEM HS; (SO); Ctznshp Aw; F Lan Hn Soc; Hnr Roll; Nat Hon Sy; Otst Ac Ach Awd; Yth Ldrshp Prog; Comm Volntr; Peer Tut/Med; Chrch Yth Grp; Emplmnt; Key Club; Svce Clb; SP/M/VS; Swmg (V); Stu Cncl (R); Young Heroes Award; Wolverine Award; Spanish; Concert Piano; College of William & Mary; U of Virginia

KING, SARAH; MILLBORO, VA; ALLEGHANY HS; (SR); Gov Hnr Prg; Hi Hnr Roll; Hnr Roll; Mas Aw; MVP; Nat Hon Sy; Nat Stu Ath Day Aw; Pres Ac Ftns Aw; WWAHSS; Comm Volntr; Hab For Humty Volntr; AL Aux Girls; ArtClub; Chrch Yth Grp; Key Club; Ntl Beta Clb; Quiz Bowl; Schol Bwl; SP/M/VS; Cr Ctry (V L); PP Ftbl (V); Tennis (V L); Lit Mag (E); VHSL Region III Female Athlete of the Year; Wendy's High School Heisman Award; Biology; Education; College of William and Mary

KINGSLEY, JASON M; ALEXANDRIA, VA; HAYFIELD SECONDARY SCH; (SR); Hnr Roll; Sci Fairs; WWAHSS; Comm Volntr; Peer Tut/Med; Emplmnt; Key Club; Mth Clb/Tm; Mod UN; Svce Clb; Bnd; Golf (J); Lcrsse (V L); Key Club Officer; Government/Political Science; International Affairs; Christopher Newport U

KISH, NICK; ASHBURN, VA; BROAD RUN HS; (JR); Hnr Roll; WWAHSS; Key Club; Bskball (VJ L); Ftball (VJ); Track (V CL); Model General Assembly Rep For Gov - History Club; Engineering; Politics; U of Virginia; Virginia Polytechnic Institute

KLANCHER, VICTORIA M; ASHBURN, VA; STONE BRIDGE HS; (JR); Hnr Roll; Comm Volntr; Hosp Aide; DARE; Key Club; Vllyball (J); CR (R); Key Club; Medicine; Dentistry; Virginia Tech; James Madison U

KLEIN, ASHLEY N; RESTON, VA; SOUTH LAKES HS; (SO); Hnr Roll; Comm Volntr; Emplmnt; Scouts; Sccr (J); Vllyball (J); Business Law; Marketing; James Madison U; Virginia Commonwealth U

KLYNSMA, HEIDI; SPRINGFIELD, VA; WEST SPRINGFIELD HS; (JR); Hnr Roll; Nat Hon Sy; Chrch Yth Grp; DECA; Key Club; French Clb; Chrldg (VJ L); Adv Cncl (V); Cl Off (V); State Champion Cheerleading; Marketing; James Madison U

KNOLL, HANGSIN; ASHBURN, VA; STONE BRIDGE HS; (FR); Hi Hnr Roll; Hnr Roll; Otst Ac Ach Awd; Perf Att; Sci Fairs; WWAHSS; Comm Volntr; Chrch Yth Grp; Key Club; Chr; Ch Chr; Cr Ctry (J); Finalist in the Loudoun County History Fair; Recipient of the Academic Excellence Award; Pre Medicine; Pediatrician; U of Virginia; The George Washington U

KO, JULIANA; CENTREVILLE, VA; CTRVILLE HS; (SO); F Lan Hn Soc; Hnr Roll; Kwnis Aw; Nat Hon Sy; Pres Ac Ftns Aw; Sci Fairs; WWAHSS; Comm Volntr; Hosp Aide; Peer Tut/Med; FBLA; Key Club; Mth Clb/Tm; Mus Clb; Latin Clb; Orch; Lcrsse (J); Officer of NHS; Teaching; U of Virginia; Virginia Tech

KOLLAR, JOHN; MANASSAS, VA; OSBOURN HS; (JR); F Lan Hn Soc; Hnr Roll; Comm Volntr; Emplmnt; Key Club; President of the Teenage Republicans; Virginia Teenage Republicans Treasurer; Mechanical Engineering; Computer Engineering; Virginia Polytechnic Institute and State U; U of Virginia

KORTZE, KATHERINE L; VIRGINIA BEACH, VA; TALLWOOD HS; (SR); F Lan Hn Soc; Hnr Roll; Pres Ac Ftns Aw; WWAHSS; Comm Volntr; Chrch Yth Grp; Key Club; Bnd; Ch Chr; Clr Grd; Dnce; Band Leadership Council President; Band Leadership Council Representative; Physical Therapist; Old Dominion U

KREMPASKY, BRANDIN; FREDERICKSBURG, VA; JAMES MONROE HS; (JR); Hi Hnr Roll; Nat Hon Sy; Pres Ac Ftns Aw; Comm Volntr; ArtClub; Chrch Yth Grp; Emplmnt; Key Club; Spanish Clb; Cr Ctry (V); Tennis (J); Vllyball (V); Figure Skating Regional Skater; Women Lee Hockey-Frostbites; Geology; Art-Photography; Mary Washing U

KUBISTEK, KATHERINE L; PALMYRA, VA; FLUVANNA CTY HS; (JR); Hnr Roll; 4-H; Emplmnt; Flg Crps; SP/M/VS; Lit Mag; Several Middle School Art Awards; Art, Graphic Design; Virginia Commonwealth U

KWINDJA, CEDRIC J D; ALEXANDRIA, VA; T C WILLIAMS HS; Hnr Roll; WWAHSS; Comm Volntr; Chrch Yth Grp; Key Club; French Clb; Ftball (V); Basketball; Computer Engineering; Virginia State U

LACEY, ERIN; WILLIAMSBURG, VA; LAFAYETTE HS; (SO); F Lan Hn Soc; WWAHSS; FBLA; Key Club; French Clb; Fld Hky (JC); Sccr (V L); Swmg (V L); 5th in State on Grand Concours (National French Test); Volunteer Coaching Summer Swim Team Kids Under 6 Yrs.; International Business; Architecture/Interior Design; Georgia Institute of Technology; Virginia Polytechnic Institute-Engineering School

LACKS JR, DAVID W; SCOTTSBURG, VA; HALIFAX CTY HS; (JR); Hnr Roll; Perf Att; WWAHSS; Bsball (V L); East Carolina U; Virginia Tech

LA CLAIR, EVAN; OILVILLE, VA; GOOCHLAND HS; (JR); Hnr Roll; Comm Volntr; Emplmnt; Fr of Library; Bsball (J); Bskball (J); Sccr (V); Swmg (V); National Leadership Forum on Law; CPR Certified/Musical Guitar Instrument; Finance; Psychology; VA Polytechnic Institute and State U; U of Virginia

LA FONTANT, SOPHIA; WOODBRIDGE, VA; GARFIELD HS; (JR); Hnr Roll; Nat Hon Sy; Otst Ac Ach Awd; WWAHSS; Comm Volntr; Chrch Yth Grp; Key Club; Prom Com; Tchrs Aide; Vsity Clb; Ch Chr; Dnce; Track (V); Cl Off (T); Stu Cncl (R); Thurgood Marshall Society; Political Science; Psychology; Spelman College; Hampton U, Clark Atlanta U

LAFRICAN, JENNIFER; CHANTILLY, VA; CHANTILLY HS; (JR); 4H Awd; Hnr Roll; Nat Hon Sy; Pres Ac Ftns Aw; Sci Fairs; Comm Volntr; Spec Olymp Vol; 4-H; Drma Clb; Emplmnt; Jr Cls League; Mus Clb; Ntl FFA; Outdrs Clb; Latin Clb; Dnce; Orch; SP/M/VS; 2003 4-H Virginia State Top Junior Dog Handler; Equine Veterinarian; Virginia Polytechnic Institution

LAI, KALOK; FALLS CHURCH, VA; GEORGE MASON HS; (FR); F Lan Hn Soc; Hnr Roll; Nat Mrt Fin; Perf Att; Pres Ac Ftns Aw; Pres Sch; Sci Fairs; Comm Volntr; Chrch Yth Grp; DARE; Mth Clb/Tm; Bnd; Tennis (V); Vllyball (J); Lit Mag (E); Medicine

LAITI, LAURA E; ASHBURN, VA; STONE BRIDGE HS; (SO); Hnr Roll; Otst Ac Ach Awd; Pres Ac Ftns Aw; Comm Volntr; DECA; Emplmnt; Key Club; Sftball (JC); Swmg (V); Coaches' Player of the Year Trophy-JV Softball; JV Softball Player and Manager; Education; Journalism; Virginia Polytechnic Institute and State U; U of Florida

LAKE, BRANTON E; KILMARNOCK, VA; NORTH CUMBERLAND HS; (JR); Fut Prb Slvr; Gov Hnr Prg; Hnr Roll; St of Mnth; WWAHSS; AL Aux Boys; Emplmnt; Ntl Beta Clb; Quiz Bowl; ROTC; Schol Bwl; Drl Tm; Ftball (V L); Wrstlg (V L); Army JROTC Battalion Commander; Quiz Band Captain; Psychology; Military Science; United States Military Academy; U of Virginia

LAM, KRISTEN L; SALEM, VA; WILLIAM FLEMING HS; (JR); Ctznshp Aw; Hnr Roll; Otst Ac Ach Awd; Sci Fairs; Comm Volntr; Chrch Yth Grp; Key Club; Ntl Beta Clb; Dnce; Youth Council High School Representative in Church; Psychology (Marriage & Family Counseling); Primary/Elementary Education; Liberty U; U of Virginia

LAMBERT, EVAN; VA BEACH, VA; OCEAN LAKES HS; (SO); Ctznshp Aw; F Lan Hn Soc; Hi Hnr Roll; Hnr Roll; Nat Hon Sy; Otst Ac Ach Awd; Pres Ac Ftns Aw; Pres Sch; Sci/Math Olympn; Yth Ldrshp Prog; Comm Volntr; Peer Tut/Med; Red Cr Aide; Chrch Yth Grp; Emplmnt; Jr Cls League; Mth Clb/Tm; MuAlphaTh; NYLC; Sci Clb; Scouts; Spanish Clb; Orch; SP/M/VS; Mar Art; Swmg; Cl Off (R); Yrbk (R); Excellence In Music Theory Award / National Winner Piano Guild / 1200+ SAT / PSAT Club / Dedicated Dolphin; National Junior Honor Society President / National Latin Honor Society / VA Pilot Scholastic Achievement; Pre-Med; Neurology / Brain Studies or Emergency; Johns Hopkins U; Duke U

LAMBERT, KATHRYN A; TAZEWELL, VA; TAZEWELL HS; (MS); Hnr Roll; Perf Att; Comm Volntr; DARE; Pep Squd; Spanish Clb; Dnce; Chrldg (V); Sccr (J); CR (R); Nursing-RN; Business; Radford; VA Tech

LAMBERT, MARCEL; HAMPTON, VA; HAMPTON HS; (FR); Ctznshp Aw; Hnr Roll; Perf Att; Pres Ac Ftns Aw; Bsball (V); Aerospace Engineering; Nuclear Engineering; U of Virginia; Virginia Polytechnic Institute

LAMB-MOODY, ALICIA K; MANASSAS, VA; STONEWALL JACKSON HS; (SO); Scouts; Bnd; Dnce; Step Team; Communications; Broadcasting; Georgia State U; Spelman U/Clark Atlanta U

LAMPROPOULOS, WILLIAM; CHESAPEAKE, VA; WESTERN BRANCH HS; (SO); Hi Hnr Roll; Hnr Roll; Nat Hon Sy; Pres Ac Ftns Aw; Jr Cls League; Latin Clb; Bnd; Ftball (J); Wt Lftg (V); Wrstlg (L); Virginia Tech; U of Virginia

LANCASTER, JACKIE N; DANVILLE, VA; TUNSTALL HS; (SR); Hnr Roll; WWAHSS; Chrch Yth Grp; Emplmnt; Bnd; Mch Bnd; Pep Bnd; Sccr (V); Track; Helmsmen-Winter Guard International Competition 2000-2004; Music Education; James Madison U

LANDERS, SHANNON; ASHBURN, VA; STONE BRIDGE HS; (FR); Chrch Yth Grp; Lcrsse (V); Swmg (V); 1st Chair Clarinet (Middle School); Presidential Fitness; U of North Carolina At Wilmington; Syracuse U

LANDES, BRIAN; HARRISONBURG, VA; TURNER ASHBY HS; (JR); Hnr Roll; Perf Att; Chrch Yth Grp; Emplmnt; Ntl FFA; Criminal Justice; Virginia Tech; U of Virginia

LANE, AMIRAH D; ALEXANDRIA, VA; WEST POTOMAC HS; (JR); Hi Hnr Roll; Hnr Roll; Nat Hon Sy; Otst Ac Ach Awd; Pres Sch; WWAHSS; Comm Volntr; Chrch Yth Grp; P to P St Amb Prg; ROTC; Chr; Clr Grd; Mch Bnd; PP Ftbl (J); Track (J); Vllyball (J); Cl Off (P); Cadet Corporal-JROTC Army; United States Presidents Award/Academic; Interior Architectural Design; Psychology; Hampton U; Bennett College

LANE, ANGEL; BLUEMONT, VA; LOUDOUN VALLEY HS; (SR); Hnr Roll; FBLA; FCCLA; ASL Clb; Vice President of American Sign Language Club; Business / Accounting; West Virginia U; James Madison U

LANE, VICTORIA; BURKE, VA; LAKE BRADDOCK SECONDARY; (SR); Hnr Roll; Comm Volntr; Chrch Yth Grp; Ch Chr; Dnce; Major in English; Theology; Christopher Newport U

LANG, CASSIE N; MARTINSVILLE, VA; MARTINSVILLE HS; (JR); Chrch Yth Grp; Ch Chr; Registered Nurse; Data Entry; Patrick Henry Community College; Danville Community

LANG, LUCY T; FREDERICKSBURG, VA; JAMES MONROE HS; (SO); 4H Awd; Hnr Roll; Pres Ac Ftns Aw; WWAHSS; Comm Volntr; 4-H; Drma Clb; Key Club; Latin Clb; SP/M/VS; Fld Hky (J); Sccr (V); Swmg (V); President of Junior National Honor Society; Past Ltg. for Division 10b of Key Club; Theatre; Interior Design; New York U; U of California Los Angeles (UCLA)

LANGLAIS, KRISTIN J; LURAY, VA; LURAY HS; (SO); F Lan Hn Soc; Hi Hnr Roll; Hnr Roll; Otst Ac Ach Awd; Perf Att; St of Mnth; Comm Volntr; Hab For Humty Volntr; Drma Clb; Mus Clb; Foreign Clb; Chr; SP/M/VS; Track (V); CR (R); Interact Club / Diversity Club / Pride Club; Mechanical Engineering; Marine Biology

LANTZ, RACHEL D; FREDERICKSBURG, VA; COURTLAND HS; (SO); Gov Hnr Prg; Hi Hnr Roll; Pres Sch; WWAHSS; Comm Volntr; Chrch Yth Grp; FCA; Clb; Ch Chr; Chrldg (V L); Film; Journalism

LA PRADE, D ANDREW; CHARLOTTESVILLE, VA; ALBEMARLE HS; (JR); Hnr Roll; WWAHSS; Comm Volntr; Key Club; Mus Clb; Bnd; Ch Chr; Jzz Bnd; Mch Bnd; All District Band-1st Chair; James Madison U Honors Youth Brass Band; Music Education; Jazz Performance Studies; James Madison U; Virginia Tech

LARSEN, DANE; WILLIAMSBURG, VA; BRUTON HS; (SO); Hi Hnr Roll; WWAHSS; Yth Ldrshp Prog; Chrch Yth Grp; Scouts; Chr; Ch Chr; SP/M/VS; District Chorus; Early Morning Bible Study Class - Seminary; Engineering; Computer Programming; Brigham Young U Idaho; Colorado School of Mines

LAW, REBECCA; CHANTILLY, VA; BROADRUN HS; (JR); Hi Hnr Roll; Hnr Roll; Nat Hon Sy; St of Mnth; WWAHSS; Hab For Humty Volntr; Peer Tut/Med; Chrch Yth Grp; Key Club; Yrbk (R, P); Mathematics; Virginia Polytechnic Institute and State U; North Carolina State U

LAWRENCE, BRITTNEY; CHESAPEAKE, VA; GREAT BRIDGE HS; (FR); Hnr Roll; Nat Hon Sy; Otst Ac Ach Awd; Pres Ac Ftns Aw; St of Mnth; Chrch Yth Grp; DARE; Pep Squd; P to P St Amb Prg; Bnd; Jzz Bnd; Mch Bnd; Pep Bnd; Chrldg (J); Old Dominion U; James Madison U

LAWSON, MEGAN; EXMORE, VA; NORTHAMPTON HS; (SO); Ctznshp Aw; Hnr Roll; MVP; Nat Hon Sy; Otst Ac Ach Awd; Pres Ac Ftns Aw; Sci Fairs; St of Mnth; WWAHSS; Comm Volntr; Peer Tut/Med; Chrch Yth Grp; Emplmnt; Mus Clb; Ntl Beta Clb; Outdrs Clb; Photog; Vsity Clb; Bnd; Mch Bnd; Pep Bnd; Sftball (V CL); Vllyball (V CL); Cl Off (V); Club Co-Ed Hi-Y, Club Tri-M; Law/Psychology; Music & the Arts; U of Virginia; James Madison U

LAZARIS, NICOLE; STERLING, VA; POTOMAC FALLS HS; (SR); Hnr Roll; MVP; Nat Hon Sy; Otst Ac Ach Awd; Perf Att; Pres Ac Ftns Aw; Sci Fairs; WWAHSS; Comm Volntr; Peer Tut/Med; Red Cr Aide; FBLA; Key Club; Vsity Clb; Clb; Cr Ctry (L); Sccr (J); Track (V); Youth and Government Club Secretary; Cross Country Coaches Award; International Affairs; International Business and Law; James Madison U

LE, MICHELLE; VIENNA, VA; GEORGE C MARSHALL HS; (JR); Hnr Roll; Nat Hon Sy; Pres Ac Ftns Aw; WWAHSS; Comm Volntr; Peer Tut/Med; Sci Clb; SADD; Latin Clb; Lcrsse (V); PP Ftbl (V); Academic Athletic Achievement; Interact Club; Medicine; PhD; U of Virginia; Georgetown U

LEAPHART, DESIRAE; PORTSMOUTH, VA; IC NORCOM; (SO); Hi Hnr Roll; Hnr Roll; Otst Ac Ach Awd; St of Mnth; Peer Tut/Med; FBLA; Lib Aide; Tennis (V); Youth Advisory Board; Access; Sociology; Psychology; Columbia U; New York U

LEE, ANDREA; LEESBURG, VA; STONE BRIDGE HS; (JR); Hnr Roll; Nat Hon Sy; WWAHSS; Comm Volntr; Dbte Team; Key Club; Mth Clb/Tm; Nursing; Medical Professional; U of Virginia; James Madison U

LEE, JISOO; FAIRFAX, VA; BISHOP O'CONNELL HS; (SO); F Lan Hn Soc; Comm Volntr; Chrch Yth Grp; Key Club; Chr; Ch Chr; Doctor; U of Virginia

LEE, LATRICE Y; CHESAPEAKE, VA; DEEP CREEK HS; (SR); Ctznshp Aw; Hnr Roll; Kwnis Aw; Nat Hon Sy; Perf Att; WWAHSS; Comm Volntr; Chrch Yth Grp; Key Club; NtlFrnscLg; ROTC; SADD; Spanish Clb; Ch Chr; Drl Tm; Cl Off (S); CR (P); PTA Reflections Contest 1st Place; Business Management; Marketing; Virginia State U; Virginia Commonwealth U

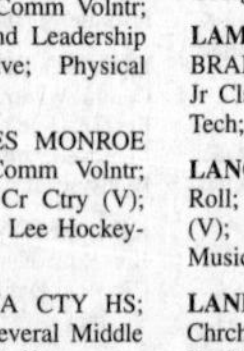

Lamb-Moody, Alicia K
Stonewall Jackson HS
Manassas, VA

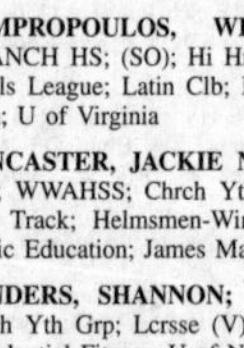

Laiti, Laura E
Stone Bridge HS
Ashburn, VA

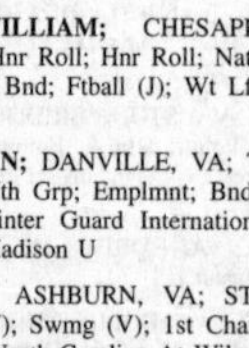

Kinder, Brian
Richlands HS
Richlands, VA

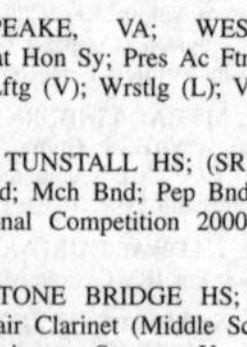

Kubistek, Katherine L
Fluvanna Cty HS
Palmyra, VA

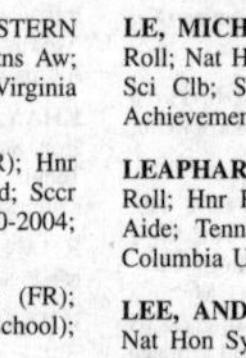

Lang, Cassie N
Martinsville HS
Martinsville, VA

LEE, LAUREN B; GLEN ALLEN, VA; DEEP RUN HS; (JR); Hnr Roll; Nat Hon Sy; WWAHSS; Yth Ldrshp Prog; Comm Volntr; Peer Tut/Med; DECA; Emplmnt; Key Club; Ntl Beta Clb; NYLC; P to P St Amb Prg; Tmpl Yth Grp; Sccr (J); Track (V); Vsy Clb (J); Vllyball; Stu Cncl (R); People to People Student Ambassador; Business; U of North Carolina Chapel Hill; Virginia Tech

LEE, MALLORY; CHESTER, VA; L C BIRD HS; (JR); 4H Awd; F Lan Hn Soc; Hi Hnr Roll; Jr Mshl; Nat Hon Sy; Perf Att; Sci Fairs; Sci/Math Olympn; WWAHSS; Comm Volntr; 4-H; ArtClub; Emplmnt; Jr Cls League; Key Club; MuAlphaTh; Photog; Latin Clb; Yrbk (P); Biology; Nursing; James Madison U; Virginia Tech

LEE, RICHARD; SPRINGFIELD, VA; EDISON HS; (SR); F Lan Hn Soc; Hi Hnr Roll; Hnr Roll; Otst Ac Ach Awd; Perf Att; St of Mnth; WWAHSS; Comm Volntr; Hosp Aide; ArtClub; DECA; Mth Clb/Tm; MuAlphaTh; Japanese Clb; Mar Art; Class President of Marketing Fundamentals DECA Officer; Nationally Certified Professional in Customer Service; Management; Counseling; George Mason U; James Madison U

LEE, SAE R; FAIRFAX, VA; JAMES W ROBINSON JR SECONDARY SCH; (SO); Chrch Yth Grp; Key Club; Korean Clb; Bnd; Mch Bnd; Skt Tgt Sh (J L); Psychology; U of Virginia; James Madison U

LEE, SEUNG Y; CENTREVILLE, VA; CENTREVILLE HS; (SO); Orch; Tennis (L); Psychology; Law; U of Virginia; New York U

LEE, SHAUNDA; NORFOLK, VA; AZALEA GARDEN CHRISTIAN SCH; (SO); Hi Hnr Roll; Mus Clb; RN; Georgia Tech / Georgia State

LEFEBVRE, VALENTINA; NORFOLK, VA; MAURY HS; (SR); F Lan Hn Soc; Hnr Roll; Otst Ac Ach Awd; Comm Volntr; Outdrs Clb; French Clb; Spanish & French Honor Societies; 2005 Most Outstanding Foreign Language Award; Political Science; International Relations; Flagler College

LEIZER, CELESTE E; MARTINSVILLE, VA; MARTINSVILLE HS; (JR); Hi Hnr Roll; Nat Hon Sy; WWAHSS; Comm Volntr; Peer Tut/Med; Red Cr Aide; Chrch Yth Grp; Drma Clb; Fr of Library; Key Club; Prom Com; SADD; Bnd; Jzz Bnd; Mch Bnd; Orch; Cr Ctry (V L); Gmnstcs; Hsbk Rdg; Mar Art; Sccr (VJ L); 2 Black Belts in Tae Kwon Do/ Piedmont Gov. Sch for Math, Sci, Tech / Attended Summer Gov. School -Russian Studies; Art; Music; Virginia Tech; James Madison U

LEMAN, ELIZABETH; ASHBURN, VA; BROAD RUN HS; (SO); F Lan Hn Soc; Hnr Roll; Sci Fairs; WWAHSS; Comm Volntr; Hab For Humty Volntr; Chrch Yth Grp; Dbte Team; Emplmnt; Key Club; German Clb; Chr; Ch Chr; Ice Sktg; Sftball; 2004 Science Student of the Year; History; Psychology; College of William & Mary; U of Virginia

LEMONS, CHRISTINA A; RIDGEWAY, VA; MAGNA VISTA HS; (SR); Hi Hnr Roll; Hnr Roll; Nat Hon Sy; Comm Volntr; Peer Tut/Med; Emplmnt; FBLA; Ntl Beta Clb; Prom Com; Chr; SP/M/VS; Lit Mag (E, R); Sch Ppr (E, R); English Major / Creative Writing Concentration; Patrick Henry Community College; Hollins College

LEON, MICHELLE; ASHBURN, VA; (FR); Hnr Roll; WWAHSS; FBLA; Key Club; Bskball; Track (L); Law; Business Administration; William and Mary; U of Virginia

LEONARD, TRACI; BRISTOL, VA; JOHN S BATTLE HS; (SR); Hnr Roll; Nat Hon Sy; USAA; WWAHSS; Comm Volntr; Ntl FFA; Off Aide; SADD; Bnd; Mch Bnd; Pep Bnd; Stg Cre; Scr Kpr (V); Honor Roll; Who's Who Among American High Schools; Architecture; Elementary Education; Virginia Tech; Radford U

LEONE, ROSELLA-ANNE; ROANOKE, VA; PATRICK HENRY HS; (JR); Hnr Roll; WWAHSS; Comm Volntr; Red Cr Aide; Emplmnt; Key Club; NYLC; Scouts; Orch; Vllyball (J); Virginia State Certification in American Sign Language; Recipient of Presidential Student Service Gold Award 2003 & 2004; Education; Educational Research; College of William & Mary; Roanoke College

LESE, KRISTINA; BERRYVILLE, VA; OSBOURN HS; (SO); Hnr Roll; Peer Tut/Med; FCCLA; Key Club; Scouts; SADD; Track (V L); Member of Sailing Team; President of FCCLA (FHA); Psychology; Anthropology; U of Virginia; Mary Washington College

LESTER, MOLLY; ROSEDALE, VA; RICHLANDS HS; (FR); Sci Fairs; Comm Volntr; ArtClub; DARE; FBLA; Mth Clb/Tm; Bnd; Mch Bnd; Teaching; Virginia Tech

LEWIS, ADRIAN N; COVINGTON, VA; ALLEGHANY HS; (JR); Hi Hnr Roll; Sci Fairs; WWAHSS; Yth Ldrshp Prog; Comm Volntr; Chrch Yth Grp; DARE; Drma Clb; Key Club; Mus Clb; Bnd; Chr; Ch Chr; Jzz Bnd; Tennis; Girl Scout Silver Award; District & Regional Acting Awards; Fashion Merchandising; Theatre; Kent State U; Philadelphia U

LEWIS, FRANKI L.; MEADOWS OF DAN, VA; PATRICK CTY HS; (JR); Hnr Roll; Yth Ldrshp Prog; Comm Volntr; Spec Olymp Vol; Chrch Yth Grp; DECA; Emplmnt; NYLC; Ch Chr; The National Youth Leadership Forum on Nursing, HOSA Club, Certified Nursing Assistant; Dual Enrollment; PARTY Club, Literature Team; Nursing; Medicine/Biology; The U of Virginia At Wise

LEWIS, WILLIAM B; SOUTH BOSTON, VA; HALIFAX CTY HS; (JR); Hi Hnr Roll; Nat Hon Sy; Perf Att; Chrch Yth Grp; FBLA; Bsball (J); Bskball (J); Cr Ctry; Golf (V); YABA Bowling-Sportsmanship-2 Yrs.; JV Baseball-Coach's Award; U of Virginia; Randolph Macon College

LEWIS-WHITSON, TESSA; SALEM, VA; SALEM HS; (SO); Hi Hnr Roll; Nat Hon Sy; Otst Ac Ach Awd; Perf Att; St of Mnth; Key Club; Spanish Clb; SP/M/VS; New York U; U of Virginia

LIGON, DIANA; NORFOLK, VA; LAKE TAYLOR SR HS; (SR); Hnr Roll; MVP; Nat Hon Sy; Perf Att; Comm Volntr; Peer Tut/Med; Red Cr Aide; Chrch Yth Grp; Cr Ctry (V L); Fld Hky (V CL); Sccr (V L); All-Eastern District First Team in Field Hockey; Earn an Aviation Degree; Phoenix East Aviation

LIN, TZYY-HAW (ERIC); ASHBURN, VA; STONE BRIDGE HS; (FR); Hi Hnr Roll; Hnr Roll; Nat Hon Sy; Perf Att; Comm Volntr; Chess; Key Club; Mth Clb/Tm; Swmg; Business; Medicine; U of Virginia; George Mason U

LIN, TZYY-YAW (PETER); ASHBURN, VA; STONE BRIDGE HS; (SO); Hnr Roll; WWAHSS; Chess; FTA; Key Club; Bskball; Swmg; Stu Cncl (R); Duke U; U of Virginia

LINDSAY, ALANA; CHESAPEAKE, VA; HICKORY HS; (SO); 4H Awd; Ctznshp Aw; WWAHSS; Comm Volntr; Peer Tut/Med; Spec Olymp Vol; 4-H; DARE; Dbte Team; Scouts; Spanish Clb; Chr; Dnce; SP/M/VS; Cl Off (S); CR (R); Aquilla Onxy; Dance; Nutrition; Virginia Commonwealth U; Sweet Briar College

LINDSAY, MELINDA; IRON GATE, VA; ALLEGHANY HS; (JR); DAR; Hi Hnr Roll; Hnr Roll; MVP; Nat Hon Sy; Pres Ac Ftns Aw; St of Mnth; WWAHSS; Yth Ldrshp Prog; Comm Volntr; Peer Tut/Med; Spec Olymp Vol; DARE; Emplmnt; FBLA; Key Club; Ntl Beta Clb; Ntl FFA; NYLC; P to P St Amb Prg; Bskball (JC); Cl Off (R); Stu Cncl (R); CR (R); Yrbk (R); Hospice Volunteer; Medicine; Business Administration; Virginia Tech

LIU, JIA; CHARLOTTESVILLE, VA; ALBEMARLE HS; (SO); DAR; F Lan Hn Soc; Hnr Roll; Key Club; MuAlphaTh; Orch; Sftball (J); Vllyball (J); Cl Off; U of Virginia

LIVESAY, RACHAEL R; COVINGTON, VA; ALLEGHANY HS; (SO); Hi Hnr Roll; Hnr Roll; Nat Hon Sy; WWAHSS; Comm Volntr; Peer Tut/Med; Spec Olymp Vol; Chrch Yth Grp; Emplmnt; Key Club; Pep Squd; Scouts; Bnd; Mch Bnd; Chrldg (V L); Tennis (V); Cl Off (P); Stu Cncl (R); Yrbk (P); Early Childhood Education; Elementary Education; Virginia Tech; Roanoke College

LIVINGSTON, JENNIFER I; AMHERST, VA; AMHERST CTY HS; (SO); F Lan Hn Soc; Hnr Roll; St of Mnth; Red Cr Aide; Tennis (V); Lit Mag (R); Member of Extend & VICA - Gifted Program / Vocational Program; Architecture; Theology or Philosophy; NYU; Ucla

LOGAN, KARA; LYNCHBURG, VA; HERITAGE HS; (JR); Hi Hnr Roll; Hnr Roll; Nat Hon Sy; Salutrn; Valdctrian; WWAHSS; Chrch Yth Grp; Key Club; NtlFrnscLg; Chr; Ch Chr; Yrbk (R, P); Forensics Award Winner; Forensic Biology; Master's Degree; Duke U; Virginia Commonwealth U

LOGAN, LEQUIA K; DANVILLE, VA; GEORGE WASHINGTON HS; (SR); Hnr Roll; Comm Volntr; Chrch Yth Grp; Chr; Ch Chr; Dnce; Chrldg (V L); Communications; Music Performance/Vocal; Old Dominion U; Averett U

LOHMANN, JACOB A; BERRYVILLE, VA; CLARKE CTY HS; (SR); Nat Hon Sy; Pres Ac Ftns Aw; Sci Fairs; St of Mnth; WWAHSS; Comm Volntr; Peer Tut/Med; Key Club; Prom Com; Sccr (V); Honorable Mention - Congressional Art Show; Nominated for Boys State; Architecture; Industrial Design; Pratt Institute; Rhode Island School of Design

LOMAKA, LAUREN; RICHMOND, VA; MILLS E GODWIN HS; (SO); Hnr Roll; Comm Volntr; Spec Olymp Vol; FCA; Pep Squd; Quill & Scroll; SADD; French Clb; Sch Ppr (E); Law; U of Virginia

LONG, JESSICA; VIRGINIA BEACH, VA; FRANK W COX HS; (JR); Hi Hnr Roll; Hnr Roll; Nat Hon Sy; Pres Ac Ftns Aw; Comm Volntr; Peer Tut/Med; Chrch Yth Grp; Emplmnt; Key Club; P to P St Amb Prg; Quiz Bowl; Spanish Clb; Bnd; Hsbk Rdg (V); CR (R); Varsity Crew Team, Lettered 3 Years; Law; Veterinary Medicine; U of Virginia; U of Southern California

LOPEZ, SHEILA M; NEWPORT NEWS, VA; WOODSIDE HS; (JR); Hi Hnr Roll; Sci Fairs; Sci/Math Olympn; Comm Volntr; Chrch Yth Grp; Tchrs Aide; Spanish Clb; Dnce; SP/M/VS; Chrldg (V); Vllyball (C); CR (S); Adopt a Grandparent Program (PR); Field Day Coordinator (PR.); Massage Therapy; Photography; Key Business College

LOPEZ, VICTOR; CHARLOTTESVILLE, VA; MONTICELLO; (FR); Nat Hon Sy; Sccr (J)

LOUHOFF, CHRISTY D; DANVILLE, VA; GEORGE WASHINGTON HS; (FR); Ctznshp Aw; Hi Hnr Roll; Nat Hon Sy; Sci Fairs; USAA; Chrch Yth Grp; Chr; World Changers & Florida Mission; NJHS (Historian); Honor Roll-3 Perfect Sol Scores in 8th Grade; Lawyer; Veterinarian; Averett College; U of Virginia

LOVETT, ZACHARY; MECHANICSVILLE, VA; LEE DAVIS HS; (SR); Ctznshp Aw; Hnr Roll; Otst Ac Ach Awd; Yth Ldrshp Prog; Comm Volntr; AL Aux Boys; Emplmnt; Key Club; Lttrmn Clb; ROTC; Svce Clb; Vsity Clb; Clr Grd; Drl Tm; Bsball (VJ L); Ftball (J L); PP Ftbl (VJ); Scr Kpr (J); Vsy Clb (V); Wrstlg (VJ L); NJROTC Lt. JG; Administration Officer; PTSA; Military Aptitude Award; NJROTC Leadership Academy; History; Military Science; U of North Carolina Pembroke; Virginia Commonwealth U

LOWE, REBEKAH; LEESBURG, VA; HERITAGE HS; (JR); F Lan Hn Soc; Hi Hnr Roll; Hnr Roll; Nat Hon Sy; Perf Att; St of Mnth; Peer Tut/Med; Chrch Yth Grp; FCA; Key Club; Chr; Dnce; Chrldg (J); Tennis (V CL); Vllyball (J); Sch Ppr (E, R); Graphic Design; Journalism/Media; James Madison U; George Mason U

LUND, SONJA; CHESAPEAKE, VA; WESTERN BRANCH HS; (SO); Gov Hnr Prg; WWAHSS; Comm Volntr; Chrch Yth Grp; Bnd; Mch Bnd; Orch; Professional Musician; General Surgeon

LUU, BINH; FALLS CHURCH, VA; STUART HS; (SO); Vietnamese Clb; George Mason U; U of Virginia

LYNCH, ASHLEE; PORTSMOUTH, VA; IC NORCOM; (SR); MVP; Nat Hon Sy; Salutrn; Peer Tut/Med; Schol Bwl; Dnce; Yrbk (E); Interact Club; Access; Architecture; Virginia Polytechnic and State U

LYON, JUSTIN D; STUART, VA; PATRICK CTY HS; (JR); Hi Hnr Roll; Hnr Roll; Perf Att; St of Mnth; Ntl Beta Clb; Vsity Clb; Golf; Trigonometry Award; Desktop Publishing Award; Mathematics/Teaching; Education; Radford U; Virginia Tech

LYON, MARY E; SMITHFIELD, VA; SMITHFIELD HS; (SR); DAR; Hi Hnr Roll; Hnr Roll; Jr Mshl; WWAHSS; Comm Volntr; Emplmnt; FCA; FBLA; Key Club; Lib Aide; Ntl Beta Clb; Spanish Clb; SP/M/VS; Chrldg (VJ); Cl Off (P); Sch Ppr (R); Most Likely to Succeed - Senior Superlative; Studio 92 News - School Broadcast; History; Accounting; George Mason U

LYONS, MEGAN M; STEPHENS CITY, VA; SHERANDO HS; (SR); Hnr Roll; Nat Hon Sy; Comm Volntr; Red Cr Aide; Emplmnt; FCCLA; FTA; Ntl FFA; Prom Com; Clr Grd; Flg Crps; Cl Off (T); Stu Cncl (T); CR (R); Sch Ppr (E); National Honor Society - President; Interact Club Board of Directors; Psychology; Virginia Tech

LYONS, SHEANARA; CHESAPEAKE, VA; DEEP CREEK HS; (SR); Hnr Roll; WWAHSS; Comm Volntr; Emplmnt; Key Club; Bskball (VJ L); Track (V); Most Improved Player (Varsity Basketball); Academic Award (Varsity Basketball); Nursing; Physical Therapy; Winston-Salem State U

MABERY, CASEY; MEADOWS OF DAN, VA; PATRICK CTY HS; (JR); Hi Hnr Roll; Comm Volntr; Spec Olymp Vol; 4-H; DARE; Emplmnt; Ntl Beta Clb; Vsity Clb; Spanish Clb; Sccr (V CL); Vllyball (VJ L); Emory & Henry College; Ferrum College

MABERY, KRYSTLE J; STAFFORD, VA; NORTH STAFFORD HS; (JR); Hi Hnr Roll; Hnr Roll; Nat Ldrshp Svc; Perf Att; Sci Fairs; WWAHSS; Yth Ldrshp Prog; Comm Volntr; Peer Tut/Med; Red Cr Aide; Chrch Yth Grp; Emplmnt; FBLA; NYLC; Scouts; Tchrs Aide; Ch Chr; Stu Cncl (R); CR (R); National Society of High School Scholars; Computer Programming; Virginia Tech

MACKEY, JEREMY; EARLYSVILLE, VA; ALBEMARLE HS; (JR); F Lan Hn Soc; Hnr Roll; WWAHSS; Hab For Humty Volntr; Spec Olymp Vol; Jr Cls League; Key Club; MuAlphaTh; Photog; Sccr (J); Track (V); Adv Cncl (R); Lit Mag (P); Photograph Published in "Floral Fusion Magazine"; Advanced to Second Round of National Math Exam Twice; PhD In Business; Mathematics Degree; U of Virginia; College of William and Mary

MAGGI, GINA; MIDLOTHIAN, VA; LLOYD C. BIRD HS; (SR); Hnr Roll; Jr Mshl; Nat Hon Sy; Nat Mrt LOC; Otst Ac Ach Awd; WWAHSS; Comm Volntr; Peer Tut/Med; Emplmnt; Key Club; MuAlphaTh; Schol Bwl; Svce Clb; SADD; Tchrs Aide; Tech Clb; Fld Hky (VJ L); Sccr (J); Adv Cncl (R); Cl Off (R); Stu Cncl (S, R)

MAGOE, ASHLEY K L; NEWPORT NEWS, VA; MENCHVILLE HS; MS; Hi Hnr Roll; Otst Ac Ach Awd; St of Mnth; Comm Volntr; Chrch Yth Grp; Drma Clb; Pep Squd; Chr; SP/M/VS; Chrldg (L); National Junior Honor Society (Treasure); Presidential Academic Award; Veterinarian; Business Administration; Princeton; Colorado State U

MAHESHWARI, DISHU; ASHBURN, VA; STONE BRIDGE HS; (FR); Ctznshp Aw; Gov Hnr Prg; Otst Ac Ach Awd; Perf Att; Pres Sch; St of Mnth; WWAHSS; Comm Volntr; Peer Tut/Med; Dbte Team; FBLA; Key Club; Adv Cncl (V); Part of International Club; Software Piracy Lawyer; Journalism; U of Virginia; Virginia Tech

MAHONE, WILLIAM; MARION, VA; MARION SR HS; (SR); Hi Hnr Roll; WWAHSS; Comm Volntr; Emplmnt; Key Club; Ntl Beta Clb; Prom Com; Spanish Clb; Cr Ctry (J); Golf (V); Sccr (V L); Sorensen Institute For Political Leadership; William & Mary Leadership Award; International Affairs; U of Virginia

Lyons, Megan M
Sherando HS
Stephens City, VA

Lopez, Sheila M
Woodside HS
Newport News, VA

Lewis, Franki L.
Patrick Cty HS
Meadows Of Dan, VA

Leizer, Celeste E
Martinsville HS
Martinsville, VA

National
Honor Roll
Spring 2005

Lee, Seung Y
Centreville HS
Centreville, VA

Lewis, William B
Halifax Cty HS
South Boston, VA

Lyon, Justin D
Patrick Cty HS
Stuart, VA

Magoe, Ashley K L
Menchville HS
Newport News, VA

MAHONEY, CHRISTOPHER; RICHMOND, VA; RICHMOND CMTY HS; (JR); F Lan Hn Soc; Hi Hnr Roll; Nat Hon Sy; Perf Att; WWAHSS; Hab For Humty Volntr; Peer Tut/Med; Key Club; MuAlphaTh; Scouts; Bskball (J); Ftball (V); Track (V); Mechanical Engineering; Electrical Engineering; Virginia Tech; James Madison U

MAI, TONY; CENTREVILLE, VA; CENTREVILLE HS; (JR); Hnr Roll; Sci Fairs; USAA; WWAHSS; Comm Volntr; Key Club; Sci Clb; Orch; Who's Who America; National Student Leadership Conference; Medicine (MD); Virginia Commonwealth U; U of Virginia

MAKARA, LINDSAY; ASHBURN, VA; STONE BRIDGE HS; (SR); F Lan Hn Soc; Hnr Roll; Nat Hon Sy; Otst Ac Ach Awd; WWAHSS; Emplmnt; Key Club; Cr Ctry (V CL); Sccr; Track (V L); Stu Cncl (R); U of Virginia (Attending in Fall)

MALONE, SENECA D; FREDERICKSBURG, VA; MASSAPONAX HS; (JR); Hnr Roll; Comm Volntr; Chrch Yth Grp; DARE; DECA; Emplmnt; FCA; FBLA; Ch Chr; Dnce; Stu Cncl; CR; Student Counsel Association; Black Belt - Tae Kwon Do; U of Virginia

MANGAN, ANNABELLE; CHARLOTTESVILLE, VA; ALBEMARLE HS; (JR); F Lan Hn Soc; Gov Hnr Prg; Hi Hnr Roll; Nat Hon Sy; Nat Mrt LOC; WWAHSS; Hab For Humty Volntr; Spec Olymp Vol; Jr Cls League; Key Club; MuAlphaTh; Fld Hky (L); Lcrsse (L); Stu Cncl (R); Spanish Honor Society; Art Honor Society; Biology; Medical Degree; Duke U; U of Virginia

MANGES, LAUREL A; MANASSAS, VA; OSBOURN HS; (FR); Hnr Roll; St of Mnth; WWAHSS; Comm Volntr; FBLA; Key Club; SADD; Dnce; Cl Off (T); Sch Ppr (R); Nominated & Submitted for Who's Who Among High School Students for Sophomore Year; Medical Field; Marine Biology; Penn State U; U of Virginia

MANGUERRA, SOPHIA A; CHANTILLY, VA; BROAD RUN HS; (SO); Hnr Roll; Otst Ac Ach Awd; Pres Ac Ftns Aw; Comm Volntr; Chrch Yth Grp; Emplmnt; Lib Aide; Scouts; Bnd; Dnce; SP/M/VS; Scr Kpr (J); Sccr (J); SIGNET - Academic Challenge; Pediatrician; UC San Francisco

MANLEY, ELIZABETH; CHANTILLY, VA; CHANTILLY HS; (JR); F Lan Hn Soc; Hnr Roll; Nat Hon Sy; Otst Ac Ach Awd; Sci Fairs; Comm Volntr; Peer Tut/Med; Chrch Yth Grp; Emplmnt; Quill & Scroll; Tchrs Aide; PP Ftbl (J); Swmg (V L); Sch Ppr (E, R); VHSL First Place Feature Story; Coach's Award for Swimming; Biomedical Engineering; Chemical Engineering; U of Virginia; North Carolina State U

MANNING, VANESSA C; HAMPTON, VA; BETHEL HS; (SO); Hnr Roll; Perf Att; St of Mnth; Drma Clb; FBLA; Stg Cre; GAA (V); Student Athletic Trainer; Drama Club Member; Physical Therapy; Dermatology; Georgia Tech; U of Georgia

MANNINO, ALEXANDRA; ASHBURN, VA; STONE BRIDGE HS; (JR); Hnr Roll; Nat Hon Sy; Pres Ac Ftns Aw; Comm Volntr; Key Club; Pep Squd; SADD; PP Ftbl; Swmg (V); Stu Cncl (R); Yrbk (R, P); Made It to States As a Sophomore and Freshman; Active in News Program; Communications-Journalism; Meteorology; James Madison U; U of North Carolina At Wilmington

MANNS, MARANDA; BASSETT, VA; BASSETT HS; (SO); Ctznshp Aw; Hnr Roll; WWAHSS; Yth Ldrshp Prog; Comm Volntr; Peer Tut/Med; Red Cr Aide; Chrch Yth Grp; FCA; HO'Br Yth Ldrshp; Lib Aide; Pep Squd; Tchrs Aide; Bnd; Chr; Ch Chr; Bskball (J); Chrldg (V L); Vllyball (J); Stu Cncl (R); CR (R); Radiology; Culinary Arts; James Madison U; Virginia Tech

MANSFIELD, JESSICA; VIRGINIA BEACH, VA; FIRST COLONIAL HS; (SR); Hnr Roll; Comm Volntr; Chrch Yth Grp; DARE; Emplmnt; Key Club; Sftball (V L); Nursing; Old Dominion U

MARAVETZ, ANNEMARIE; ASHBURN, VA; STONE BRIDGE HS; (JR); Hnr Roll; Pres Ac Ftns Aw; Yth Ldrshp Prog; Comm Volntr; Chrch Yth Grp; Key Club; Off Aide; Chrldg (VJCL); Track (V L); Advisory Commission of Youth Member; Walk for Water Teen Organizer; Psychology; Guidance Counselor; U North Carolina Wilmington; Virginia Tech

MARCHESE, HEATHER; NORFOLK, VA; MAURY HS; (SO); Hnr Roll; Perf Att; USAA; Comm Volntr; Hosp Aide; FBLA; ROTC; Scouts; Clr Grd; Drl Tm; Aviation; Old Dominion U; Embry-Riddle Aeronautical U

MARCUS, DAN; WILLIAMSBURG, VA; BRUTON HS; (JR); Hi Hnr Roll; WWAHSS; Hab For Humty Volntr; Dbte Team; Key Club; Mod UN; Schol Bwl; Sccr (V)

MARSH, AMY R; VIRGINIA BEACH, VA; FRANK W COX HS; (SR); Hnr Roll; Nat Hon Sy; Perf Att; Pres Ac Ftns Aw; Drma Clb; Emplmnt; Key Club; Varsity Letter Crew; Student Leadership Workshop Committee; Kinesiology; Psychology; James Madison U; Marietta College

MARSHALL, HEATHER; ARARAT, VA; PATRICK CTY HS; (SO); Gov Hnr Prg; Hi Hnr Roll; Spec Olymp Vol; Ntl Beta Clb; Vsity Clb; SP/M/VS; Tennis (V); Vsy Clb (V); Business Major; Law Degree; James Madison U; Averett College

MARTIN, DEANNA; CHESTER, VA; THOMAS DALE HS; (SR); Ctznshp Aw; Hnr Roll; Nat Hon Sy; Otst Ac Ach Awd; Perf Att; Pres Ac Ftns Aw; WWAHSS; Comm Volntr; Peer Tut/Med; Red Cr Aide; Chrch Yth Grp; Latin Clb; Chr; Swg Chr; Chrldg; Fld Hky (VJ L); Gmnstcs; Veterinary Medicine; Virginia Tech

MARTIN, RYAN; CHESAPEAKE, VA; STONE BRIDGE HS; (JR); Hnr Roll; Nat Hon Sy; WWAHSS; Dbte Team; Emplmnt; Key Club; Stg Cre; Bskball (V); Golf (V); Sccr (V); Business Administration; Marketing; Methodist College; Campbell U

MARTINEZ, CARLA R; STERLING, VA; POTOMAC FALLS HS; (SO); Hnr Roll; WWAHSS; Comm Volntr; Chrch Yth Grp; Emplmnt; FBLA; Key Club; Bnd; Dnce; Sftball (J); CR; Outstanding Achievement in Science Award Recipient; Outstanding Community Service Award, Neale Concert Series for Talented Teens; Education; Nutritionist

MARTINEZ, CHELSEA; ASHBURN, VA; BROAD RUN HS; (JR); F Lan Hn Soc; Hnr Roll; Nat Hon Sy; Otst Ac Ach Awd; WWAHSS; FTA; Key Club; Sci Clb; SADD; Vllyball (J L); Yrbk (R, P); English; Secondary Education

MASCARENHAS, NICOLE; SPRINGFIELD, VA; BISHOP DENIS J O'CONNELL HS; (JR); Perf Att; Pres Ac Ftns Aw; Sci Fairs; WWAHSS; Comm Volntr; Drma Clb; Emplmnt; Key Club; Svce Clb; Spanish Clb; SP/M/VS; Stg Cre; Track (J); Activities-Kickboxing; Tae Kwon Do; Civil Engineering; George Mason U; Virginia Polytechnic and State U

MASON, URANDA M; EMPORIA, VA; GREENSVILLE CTY HS; (JR); Ctznshp Aw; Hnr Roll; Otst Ac Ach Awd; Perf Att; USAA; Comm Volntr; Emplmnt; FBLA; Ntl Beta Clb; Bskball (VJ); Chrldg (J); Sftball (V); Vllyball (V); Stu Cncl (S); CR (R); Accounting; Child Care; Hampton U; Morgan State U

MASON-DEESE, WILL; MANASSAS, VA; OSBOURN PARK SR HS; (JR); Hnr Roll; Nat Hon Sy; Peer Tut/Med; Key Club; Tennis (V); Ping Pong Club

MATHERLY, BRITTANY R; MARTINSVILLE, VA; MARTINSVILLE HS; (FR); Hi Hnr Roll; WWAHSS; Comm Volntr; Chrch Yth Grp; FBLA; Key Club; Bnd; Dnce; Mch Bnd; SP/M/VS; Tennis (VJ); Key Club; FBLA; Design / Law; Cosmetology; UVA; Hampton U

MATHIAS, VALERIE; MANASSAS, VA; OSBOURN HS; (SO); Hi Hnr Roll; Comm Volntr; FBLA; Key Club; Photog; Track (V L); Golden Eagle Honor Award; Psychology; Marketing; U of Florida; College Of William and Mary

MATHIS, SALLY T; CHARLOTTESVILLE, VA; ALBEMARLE HS; (FR); Hnr Roll; Comm Volntr; Chrch Yth Grp; Key Club

MATHUR, AAGYA; YORKTOWN, VA; TABB HS; (SO); F Lan Hn Soc; Gov Hnr Prg; Hi Hnr Roll; Nat Sci Aw; Otst Ac Ach Awd; Sci Fairs; Comm Volntr; Peer Tut/Med; Spec Olymp Vol; Key Club; Mth Clb/Tm; Mod UN; MuAlphaTh; Quill & Scroll; Scouts; Tmpl Yth Grp; Chr; Dnce; SP/M/VS; Bskball (JC); Sccr (JC); Cl Off (V); Stu Cncl (R); CR (R); Sch Ppr (E); Sports Ambassadors Award; Secretary of York County Youth Commission; Law/Political Science; Medicine; U of Virginia; Harvard U

MATTAR JR, MICHAEL; LEESBURG, VA; HERITAGE HS; (JR); Hnr Roll; Ch Chr; Ftball (V); Track (L), Wt Lftg; Art Award; Psychology; Music Production; College of William and Mary; James Madison U

MAUME, DEREK; VIRGINIA BEACH, VA; FRANK W COX HS; (JR); Camp Counselor for 2 Years; Maintained Two Jobs for 1 Year; Business; Communications; U of Maryland College Park; West Virginia U

MAYO, CHRISTI; DANVILLE, VA; GEORGE WASHINGTON HS; (JR); Ctznshp Aw; Hnr Roll; Kwnis Aw; Nat Hon Sy; Otst Ac Ach Awd; Perf Att; Pres Ac Ftns Aw; Peer Tut/Med; Key Club; Orch; Cl Off (P); Health Careers Academy (President of Junior Class); Pre-Medicine; Norfolk State U Norfolk, Virginia; Danville Community College Danville, Virginia

MAZZEI, FRANCESCO; CROZET, VA; ALBEMARLE HS; (SR); Hnr Roll; WWAHSS; Emplmnt; Key Club; Ntl Beta Clb; Schol Bwl; Varsity Academic Team - 2 Years; Spanish Honor Society; Meteorology; Marine Science; North Carolina State U; Pennsylvania State U

MC ADOO, WILLIAM; ALEXANDRIA, VA; T C WILLIAMS HS; (JR); Hnr Roll; Chrch Yth Grp; Emplmnt; Key Club; Scouts; Golf (V); Ice Hky (V); Lcrsse (J); Tennis (V); Life Scout; Troop OA Representative; Physics; Biology; Emory U; U of Virginia

MC CARRON, COLLEEN A; CENTREVILLE, VA; WESTFIELD HS; (JR); F Lan Hn Soc; Hi Hnr Roll; Nat Hon Sy; WWAHSS; Comm Volntr; Emplmnt; MuAlphaTh; Quill & Scroll; Spanish Clb; Cl Off (R); CR (R); Yrbk (E); Graduation Choir; Media Arts and Design; Communications; James Madison U; U of Delaware

MC CAUGHAN, MEAGHAN A; LURAY, VA; LURAY HS; (FR); Hnr Roll; WWAHSS; Comm Volntr; Emplmnt; FCA; FBLA; Pep Squd; Svce Clb; SADD; Foreign Clb; Bskball (VJ L); Track (VJ); Vllyball (J); Cl Off (P, V); Stu Cncl (R); CR (R); AAU Basketball; Nursing; Orthodontist; James Madison U; U of Virginia

MC CENEY, SARAH A; RUTHER GLEN, VA; CAROLINE HS; (SR); Nat Hon Sy; Nat Ldrshp Svc; Peer Tut/Med; Cr Ctry (V C); Track (V); National Honor Society - Reporter; Computer Science; Virginia Tech; Christopher Newport U

MC CLANAHAN, JESSICA R; GRUNDY, VA; GRUNDY HS; (JR); Hnr Roll; Perf Att; WWAHSS; Comm Volntr; FBLA; Key Club; Chrldg (VJC); Cr Ctry; Track (VJ); Vllyball (J); President of Key Club; President of Health Occupations Students of America; Dentistry; U of Kentucky

MC CONNELL, KATLYN; CHESAPEAKE, VA; HICKORY HS; (JR); F Lan Hn Soc; Hi Hnr Roll; Nat Hon Sy; Otst Ac Ach Awd; Perf Att; Pres Sch; St of Mnth; Comm Volntr; Hosp Aide; Chrch Yth Grp; Emplmnt; Svce Clb; Spanish Clb; Bnd; Mch Bnd; James Madison U; Virginia Tech U

MC COTTER, AMBER L; NEWPORT NEWS, VA; DENBIGH HS; (FR); Hnr Roll; Perf Att; Comm Volntr; Chrch Yth Grp; Chr; Dnce; Lettered in Chorus; Lettered in Academics; Education; Criminal Justice; The George Washington U

MC COWAN, BRYAN; NORA, VA; ERVINTON HS; (SR); Hi Hnr Roll; Hnr Roll; Nat Hon Sy; Otst Ac Ach Awd; Perf Att; WWAHSS; Comm Volntr; Peer Tut/Med; 4-H; FBLA; Key Club; Tchrs Aide; Tech Clb; SP/M/VS; Ftball (J); Cl Off (P, V); Sch Ppr (R); ECMC Scholars; Engineering; Southwest Virginia Community College

MC COY, KRISTEN; YORKTOWN, VA; GRAFTON HS; (JR); F Lan Hn Soc; Hi Hnr Roll; Nat Hon Sy; Otst Ac Ach Awd; Hosp Aide; Chrch Yth Grp; Emplmnt; Quill & Scroll; Fld Hky (VJCL); Sccr (VJ L); Sch Ppr (R); Yrbk (E); Futures Field Hockey Olympic Development Program; Second Team All District Field Hockey 2004-2005; Biology; Health Sciences; U of Virginia; Virginia Tech

MC CULLOUGH, JONATHAN C; GATE CITY, VA; GATE CITY HS; (SO); Hnr Roll; Nat Hon Sy; WWAHSS; Comm Volntr; Chrch Yth Grp; FCA; Key Club; Bnd; Mch Bnd; Pep Bnd; AIM Scholar; Bachelor of Science in Music Education; Band Director; U of Tennessee

MC CULLOUGH, MERCEDES S; RICHMOND, VA; PRINCE EDWARD CTY HS; (FR); Ctznshp Aw; Hnr Roll; Perf Att; Pep Squd; Step Team; Medical Assistance; Cosmetology; Virginia State U; New York U

MC DOUGALD, PILANDA; HAMPTON, VA; BETHEL HS; (SO); Hnr Roll; Otst Ac Ach Awd; Comm Volntr; Peer Tut/Med; Chrch Yth Grp; FBLA; Spanish Clb; Acpl Chr; Ch Chr; Cl Off (T); 3rd Place in Business Calculations / FBLA Spring Regional 2003; Pre-Med; Biology; Howard U; Spelman College

MC ENHIMER, SHAUN C; CHESTERFIELD, VA; LLOYD C BIRD HS; (SR); F Lan Hn Soc; Hi Hnr Roll; Jr Mshl; Nat Hon Sy; Perf Att; Pres Ac Ftns Aw; WWAHSS; Comm Volntr; AL Aux Boys; Emplmnt; Jr Cls League; Key Club; MuAlphaTh; Latin Clb; Bnd; Mch Bnd; Bsball (V CL); Ftball (V); Track (V L); 2005 Leadership For The 21st Century Award; 2002 Sportsmanship Award; Computer Science; Information Systems; U of Virginia; Virginia Commonwealth U

MC GEE, GRACE B; VIRGINIA BEACH, VA; FLOYD KELLAM HS; (JR); F Lan Hn Soc; Hi Hnr Roll; Hnr Roll; Nat Hon Sy; WWAHSS; Yth Ldrshp Prog; Comm Volntr; Red Cr Aide; ArtClub; Biology Clb; Chess; DECA; Vsity Clb; French Clb; Chr; Ch Chr; Fld Hky (V CL); Swmg (V L); Stu Cncl (V); Virginia Beach Citywide SCA Vice-Chairman; 2005 Virginian Pilot Scholastic Achievement Team; Art History

MC GLOTHLIN, HOPE; BLACKSBURG, VA; BLACKSBURG HS; (SR); Hnr Roll; MVP; Nat Stu Ath Day Aw; Comm Volntr; FBLA; Bskball (VJ L); Yrbk (R, P)

MC HENRY, KELLY A; WILLIAMSBURG, VA; LAFAYETTE HS; (SO); WWAHSS; Comm Volntr; FBLA; Key Club; Mod UN; Spanish Clb; Fld Hky (V L); Sccr (V L); Genetics; Biology; U of Virginia; U of North Carolina

MC KEE, PATRICIA A; MONETA, VA; STAUNTON RIVER HS; (JR); Hnr Roll; WWAHSS; Tchrs Aide; Chr; Cl Off (S); National Society of High School Scholars; Marine Biologist; U of Miami; Christopher Newport U

MC LAUGHLIN, CAZUM C; VIRGINIA BEACH, VA; FLOYD KELLAM HS; (FR); Hnr Roll; Comm Volntr; DARE; Orch; Electrical Engineering; Biomedical; Virginia Tech; U of Virginia

MC LELLAN, KRISTINNA; AMHERST, VA; AMHERST CTY HS; (SR); Ctznshp Aw; Hnr Roll; Nat Hon Sy; Sci Fairs; St of Mnth; Emplmnt; Photog; Vllyball (J L); Clinical Psychologist; Lynchburg College

MC LEOD, TERNISHA; RICHMOND, VA; GEORGE WYTHE HS; (JR); Hnr Roll; Nat Sci Aw; Cmptr Clb; Nursing; Virginia State U; Hampton U

Mc Enhimer, Shaun C
Lloyd C Bird HS
Chesterfield, VA

Mansfield, Jessica
First Colonial HS
Virginia Beach, VA

Manns, Maranda
Bassett HS
Bassett, VA

National
Honor Roll
Spring 2005

Makara, Lindsay
Stone Bridge HS
Ashburn, VA

Mason, Uranda M
Greensville Cty HS
Emporia, VA

Mc Laughlin, Cazum C
Floyd Kellam HS
Virginia Beach, VA

MC MANUS, MOLLY; CHESAPEAKE, VA; WESTERN BRANCH HS; (SO); Hnr Roll; Comm Volntr; Chrch Yth Grp; Emplmnt; Gmnstcs (V L); National Junior Honor Society; Magnet Program; Psychology; Art; The College of William and Mary; George Macon U

MC MANUS, SARAH; WILLIAMSBURG, VA; LAFAYETTE HS; (SR); Peer Tut/Med; DARE; Emplmnt; French Clb; Agriculture; West Virginia U; Roanoke Bible College

MC NEILL, KATIE; BRISTOW, VA; STONEWALL JACKSON HS; (JR); F Lan Hn Soc; Hnr Roll; Nat Hon Sy; Comm Volntr; Red Cr Aide; Chrch Yth Grp; Key Club; Mod UN; Lcrsse (J); Swim Team Manager; History; Secondary Education; Brown; Ithaca

MC PHERSON, BRITTANY J; SUFFOLK, VA; NORFOLK COLLEGIATE SCH; (JR); Hnr Roll; Nat Hon Sy; Otst Ac Ach Awd; Perf Att; Pres Sch; Comm Volntr; Red Cr Aide; ArtClub; Chrch Yth Grp; Mod UN; Prom Com; Bnd; Chr; Drl Tm; SP/M/VS; Bskball (J); Chrldg (V L); Lcrsse (V L); Cl Off (T); Journalism (Photo); (Cosmetic) Dentistry; Brown U; Pepperdine U

MC PHERSON, KAYLA; MANASSAS, VA; OSBOURN HS; (JR); Hi Hnr Roll; Nat Hon Sy; Sci Fairs; WWAHSS; Comm Volntr; Hab For Humty Volntr; Hosp Aide; Key Club; Mod UN; Latin Clb; Bnd; Ch Chr; Vllyball (JC); Bowling-Captain; Biology; Doctorate in Medicine; Duke U; Johns Hopkins U

MEADE, RANDA; CLINTWOOD, VA; CLINTWOOD HS; (FR); Hnr Roll; USAA; WWAHSS; 4-H; Chrch Yth Grp; Drma Clb; Key Club; Ch Chr; Pace Team; Lawyer; Senator / Representative; Harvard U; Columbia U

MEHTA, SWATI; FALLS CHURCH, VA; JEB STUART HS; (JR); F Lan Hn Soc; Hnr Roll; Perf Att; St of Mnth; Comm Volntr; Hosp Aide; Chr; Stg Cre; Lit Mag; Sch Ppr (R); I Have Been in Raider Readers Club; Architect; Lawyer; George Washington; George Mason

MELTON, MEGAN; SUFFOLK, VA; LAKELAND HS; (SR); F Lan Hn Soc; Hnr Roll; WWAHSS; Yth Ldrshp Prog; Comm Volntr; AL Aux Girls; Chrch Yth Grp; Emplmnt; FBLA; Spanish Clb; Ch Chr; Vllyball (JV); Hampton Roads Young Achievers; Congressional Student Leadership Conference; Juris Doctorate; Pre-Law and Trust Management; Campbell U, Buies Creek, North Carolina

MENDEZ, JOSE A; FALLS CHURCH, VA; STUART HS; (JR); Hnr Roll; Programming/Networking; George Mason U

MEROLA, CHRISTINE; STERLING, VA; POTOMAC FALLS HS; (SO); F Lan Hn Soc; Hi Hnr Roll; Hnr Roll; Comm Volntr; ArtClub; Chrch Yth Grp; Key Club; National Art Honors Society; 1st Place Literary Arts Winner - County Wide Program; Creative Writing; Art

MERRICK, JOHN; CHARLOTTESVILLE, VA; ALGEMARLE HS; (JR); F Lan Hn Soc; Hi Hnr Roll; Hnr Roll; Nat Hon Sy; Otst Ac Ach Awd; Pres Ac Ftns Aw; St of Mnth; Comm Volntr; Jr Cls League; Key Club; MuAlphaTh; Outdrs Clb; Spanish Clb; Ftball (J); Lcrsse (V L); CR (R); Achievement Award for Having Above A 3.5 GPA In Sports; Vice Pres. of Los Caballeros Club; Medicine; Engineering; U of Virginia; Duke U

MERRITT, MONTRICE; RADFORD, VA; RADFORD HS; (SO); F Lan Hn Soc; Gov Hnr Prg; Hi Hnr Roll; Hnr Roll; Comm Volntr; Chess; Cmptr Clb; DARE; FCA; Lib Aide; Scouts; Spanish Clb; Bnd; Jzz Bnd; Mch Bnd; Pep Bnd; Tennis (V); Yrbk (P); Foreign Relations; Computer Graphic Design; Alliant International U; Washington U St Louis

MEYER, JENNIFER L; STAFFORD, VA; COLONIAL FORGE HS; (SR); Hnr Roll; MVP; Nat Hon Sy; Nat Ldrshp Svc; Otst Ac Ach Awd; USAA; WWAHSS; AL Aux Girls; ArtClub; Key Club; Jzz Bnd; Bskball (J); Fld Hky (V CL); Sccr (J); Co-President Key Club; Sophomore Student of the Year; Physics; Molecular Biology; Appalachian State - Attending 2005

MICKUNAS, ALLISON; VIRGINIA BEACH, VA; COX HS; (FR); Hnr Roll; WWAHSS; Key Club; Scouts; Chr; Swmg (V L); Most Valuable Newcomer Girl Swimming; Who's Who Among HS Students Nominee; Athletic Therapy; Gastroenterology; Florida State U; U of Florida

MIKUS, LAUREN; VIRGINIA BEACH, VA; FRANK W COX HS; (JR); Hnr Roll; Comm Volntr; Chrch Yth Grp; Emplmnt; Key Club; Prom Com; Svce Clb; Cr Ctry (VJ L); Cl Off (R); Stu Cncl (R); CR (R); Interior Design; Appalachian State U; James Madison U

MILES, RHEA E; ASHBURN, VA; STONE BRIDGE HS; (SR); Ctznshp Aw; F Lan Hn Soc; Hnr Roll; Nat Hon Sy; Otst Ac Ach Awd; St of Mnth; WWAHSS; Comm Volntr; Peer Tut/Med; Chrch Yth Grp; Emplmnt; FBLA; Key Club; Pep Squd; Bskball (J); Tennis (VJ L); Adv Cncl (R); Cl Off (R); CR (R); Football Manager-Varsity; Pre-Med; Randolph-Macon Woman's College

MILLER, AMANDA; YORKTOWN, VA; YORK HS; (SR); Hnr Roll; Nat Hon Sy; Peer Tut/Med; Emplmnt; Key Club; Mus Clb; Prom Com; SADD; Vsity Clb; Bnd; Dnce; Drm Mjr; Jzz Bnd; Vllyball (V L); CR (R); Virginia Student Council Association, Rep. Region II; Social Work; Earth and Space Science; Brigham Young U

MILLER, CRYSTAL A; ALEXANDRIA, VA; THOMAS A EDISON HS; (JR); Hi Hnr Roll; Hnr Roll; Otst Ac Ach Awd; Perf Att; Pres Sch; St of Mnth; Yth Ldrshp Prog; Comm Volntr; Emplmnt; Lttrmn Clb; Mth Clb/Tm; Tchrs Aide; Vsity Clb; Sftball (V L); Sch Ppr (R, P); Yrbk (P); Competitive Bowling (Outside of School); Played for a Select Travel Softball Team for 4 Yrs.; Business Management Degree; Animal Care; Northern VA Community College; George Mason U

MILLER, JACLYN V; WAYNESBORO, VA; WAYNESBORO HS; (FR); Hnr Roll; MVP; WWAHSS; Comm Volntr; Key Club; Ntl Beta Clb; Acpl Chr; Chr; Cr Ctry (V L); Track (V L); Accompanist; Soloist At Church and Jr District Chorus; Music Teacher

MILLER, STUART; ASHBURN, VA; BROAD RUN HS; (JR); Hi Hnr Roll; Perf Att; Pres Ac Ftns Aw; Yth Ldrshp Prog; Comm Volntr; DECA; Emplmnt; NYLC; Tmpl Yth Grp; German Clb; Bskball (VJ L); Cr Ctry (V L); Germany Club; DECA; Sports Marketing; Commercial Art; Old Dominion U; James Madison U

MILLER, TRACY M; PALMYRA, VA; FLUVANNA CTY HS; (JR); Hnr Roll; Otst Ac Ach Awd; Emplmnt; Photog; Prom Com; Tchrs Aide; Vsity Clb; Sftball (VJ L); Vllyball (VJCL); 1st Team All Central VA (Pitcher); Business Management; Commercial Advertisement; California U At Pennsylvania

MIMMS, LESLIE; CHARLOTTESVILLE, VA; ALBEMARLE HS; WWAHSS; Comm Volntr; Hab For Humty Volntr; Chrch Yth Grp; Key Club; MuAlphaTh; Ntl Beta Clb; Photog; German Clb; Pharmacy; Virginia Tech

MIMNA, TRISHA; VIRGINIA BEACH, VA; FRANK W COX HS; (JR); Hnr Roll; Otst Ac Ach Awd; Chrch Yth Grp; Key Club; Latin Clb; Chr; Latin Honor Society; Tri-M (Music Honor Society); Nurse Practitioner; Old Dominion U

MIN, JIHYUN; BURKE, VA; ROBINSON HS; (FR); Hi Hnr Roll; Hnr Roll; WWAHSS; Comm Volntr; Chrch Yth Grp; Key Club; Ch Chr; Korean Club - Officer; Guitar Ensemble; Accounting

MINES, CHANEL R; RICHMOND, VA; HENRICO HS; (SO); Hnr Roll; Perf Att; WWAHSS; FCCLA; P to P St Amb Prg; Ch Chr; Chrldg (V); Fashion Design; Hampton U; Howard U

MINNICK, MEGHAN; CHESAPEAKE, VA; WESTERN BRANCH HS; (SO); Hnr Roll; Comm Volntr; Peer Tut/Med; Chrch Yth Grp; Dnce; Doctor of Medicine; Pediatrician; U of Virginia; Eastern Virginia Medical School

MITCHELL, ASHLEY; NEWPORT NEWS, VA; JUDSON SR HS; (SR); Ctznshp Aw; Hi Hnr Roll; Hnr Roll; Otst Ac Ach Awd; Perf Att; Pres Ac Ftns Aw; St of Mnth; WWAHSS; Comm Volntr; Chrch Yth Grp; Drma Clb; Emplmnt; Mus Clb; Tchrs Aide; Ch Chr; SP/M/VS; Bskball (V); Chrldg (V L); Track (V); Nursing; Medical Careers Institute; Hampton U

MITCHELL, MEREDITH; ALEXANDRIA, VA; T C WILLIAMS HS; (FR); Hi Hnr Roll; Nat Hon Sy; Nat Stu Ath Day Aw; Otst Ac Ach Awd; Perf Att; Sci Fairs; WWAHSS; Comm Volntr; Peer Tut/Med; Chrch Yth Grp; Key Club; Orch; Girls Rowing Team-Varsity; National Junior Honor Society-Vice President; Major in Chemistry; Medical Degree; Duke U; U of Virginia

MITCHELL, TIMOTHY D; FRONT ROYAL, VA; WARREN CTY HS; (SO); Ctznshp Aw; Hi Hnr Roll; Hnr Roll; Otst Ac Ach Awd; Perf Att; Sci Fairs; St of Mnth; WWAHSS; Comm Volntr; Chrch Yth Grp; Key Club; P to P St Amb Prg; Scouts; Bsball (JC); Ftball (V L); Wt Lftg; Wrstlg; U West Virginia; Virginia Tech

MITCHELL, TIMOTHY J; MARTINSVILLE, VA; MAGNA VISTA HS; (FR); PhD; Science Associate's Degree; Virginia Tech; National College of Business & Tech

MITCHELL II, MICHAEL D; ASHBURN, VA; STONE BRIDGE HS; (JR); Hnr Roll; Nat Hon Sy; Pres Ac Ftns Aw; Sci Fairs; Comm Volntr; Key Club; Bskball (V); CR (R); Pre Law; Biomedical Engineering; New York U; U of Connecticut

MITCHEM, MADALYN; MATHEWS, VA; MATHEWS HS; (FR); Hi Hnr Roll; WWAHSS; Chrch Yth Grp; Key Club; Ntl Beta Clb; Bnd; Ch Chr; Dnce; Mch Bnd; Cl Off (V)

MITCHENER, SHANI H; ROANOKE, VA; NORTHSIDE HS; (SR); Yth Ldrshp Prog; Comm Volntr; Peer Tut/Med; Red Cr Aide; Chrch Yth Grp; DECA; Emplmnt; FBLA; Key Club; Photog; Spanish Clb; Bnd; Chr; Ch Chr; Dnce; Sccr (J); Alumni of the National Youth Leadership Forum on Law; English; Communications; Bridgewater College; Roanoke College

MOLINA, BRIAN; RESTON, VA; SOUTH LAKES HS; (JR); Hnr Roll; Nat Hon Sy; Peer Tut/Med; Emplmnt; ROTC; Orch; Air Force Pilot; Virginia Tech; UVA

MONEYMAKER, COLIN; CHARLOTTESVILLE, VA; ALBERMARLE HS; (FR); Hnr Roll; Comm Volntr; Key Club; Swmg (V); Multiple Medals-Virginia Gator Swimming; Key Club; Aviation; Averette U; U VA

MONTGOMERY, BRITTNEY A; AUSTINVILLE, VA; FORT CHISWELL HS; (SO); 4H Awd; Ctznshp Aw; Hnr Roll; Perf Att; Pres Ac Ftns Aw; Sci Fairs; Comm Volntr; 4-H; ArtClub; Chrch Yth Grp; DARE; FCA; FBLA; Pep Squd; SADD; Dnce; Bskball (V); PP Ftbl (J); Sftball (J); Vllyball (J); Stu Cncl; Jr. Miss FCHS Pageant Winner 04-05; Marine Mammal Biology; Texas A & M U; West Florida State Pensacola

MOODY, ERIKA G; PORTSMOUTH, VA; CHURCHLAND HS; (JR); Hnr Roll; Otst Ac Ach Awd; Perf Att; WWAHSS; Comm Volntr; ArtClub; Mth Clb/Tm; P to P St Amb Prg; Photog; Bskball (J); Forensic Science; Architecture; James Madison U; George Mason U

MOODY, LE MESHIA; HAMPTON, VA; PHOEBUS HS; (FR); Hi Hnr Roll; Perf Att; St of Mnth; WWAHSS; Yth Ldrshp Prog; Scouts; Dnce; Flg Crps; Stu Cncl (P); Accountant; Any Financial Career; U of Virginia; Old Dominion U

MOONEY, LISA; PORTSMOUTH, VA; WOODROW WILSON HS; (SR); Hnr Roll; Nat Hon Sy; WWAHSS; Comm Volntr; AL Aux Girls; Off Aide; Bnd; Mch Bnd; Sftball (J); Superintendent Awards; Old Dominion U

MOONEY, NICHOLAS; COVINGTON, VA; ALLEGHANY HS; (SO); Hi Hnr Roll; Key Club; Lit Mag

MOORE, DAVID W; AXTON, VA; MAGNA VISTA HS; (SR); Hnr Roll; Ntl FFA; Scouts; Software Design; Patrick Henry Community College

MOOSRI, SHAMAMA; CHANTILLY, VA; BROAD RUN HS; (SO); Hnr Roll; WWAHSS; Peer Tut/Med; Dbte Team; HO'Br Yth Ldrshp; Key Club; Track (J); Cl Off (R); Sch Ppr (E, R); Debate Metro Final Qualifier; Key Club Editor; Lawyer; Master's Degree; U of Virginia; George Mason U

MORELOCK, CANDACE; ST PAUL, VA; COEBURN HS; (SO); 4H Awd; F Lan Hn Soc; Hnr Roll; Otst Ac Ach Awd; Sci Fairs; Comm Volntr; Biology Clb; Chrch Yth Grp; DARE; Ntl Beta Clb; SADD; French Clb; Ch Chr; Dnce; Chrldg (J); Tennis (J); CR (R); Criminal Investigation; Crime Scene Investigation; SUNY Canton; John Jay College of Criminal Justice

MORENO, KRISTEN J; HAMPTON, VA; BETHEL HS; (SO); Ctznshp Aw; Hi Hnr Roll; Hnr Roll; Otst Ac Ach Awd; Perf Att; Comm Volntr; Chrch Yth Grp; Emplmnt; Bnd; Mch Bnd; Cr Ctry; Sccr (V); Marching Band Drumline Captain; Awarded Outstanding Technical Drawing Student 2003-2004; Engineering; Pre-Med; College of William and Mary; U of Virginia

MORGAN, ASHLEY M; DUMFRIES, VA; GAR-FIELD SR HS; (SR); Hnr Roll; Yth Ldrshp Prog; Chrch Yth Grp; Tchrs Aide; Vsity Clb; Bnd; Ch Chr; Clr Grd; Track (V C); Stu Cncl (R); CR (R); National Ventures Scholar; Pan-Hellenic Council Black Scholar; Pre-Med (Biology); BS; U of Arkansas, Fayetteville; Old Dominion U

MORGAN, KRISTA; SELMA, VA; JACKSON RIVER TECH CTR; (JR); Hnr Roll; Nat Hon Sy; Chrch Yth Grp; DARE; Ch Chr; Welding; Architecture; Dabney S Lancaster Community College

MORRELL, MARIE; VIRGINIA BEACH, VA; COX HS; (SO); Hi Hnr Roll; Hnr Roll; Peer Tut/Med; Chrch Yth Grp; Key Club; Sccr (VJ); Stu Cncl (R); Fantastic Falcon Eng 9th; Team Captain JV Soccer; Pepperdine U

MORRIS, ASHLEY D; PHENIX, VA; RANDOLPH HENRY HS; (SO); Hnr Roll; Nat Sci Aw; Comm Volntr; Drma Clb; Latin Clb; SP/M/VS; Scr Kpr (J); Forensics - Lettered; Junior National Honor Society; Teaching; Medicine; U of Virginia; James Madison U

MORRIS, WILLIAM; CHARLOTTESVILLE, VA; ALBEMARLE HS; (JR); F Lan Hn Soc; Hnr Roll; Pres Ac Ftns Aw; WWAHSS; Chrch Yth Grp; Emplmnt; Key Club; Mus Clb; Spanish Clb; Bnd; Ch Chr; Jzz Bnd; Mch Bnd; Hymn Leader At the Charlottesville Church of the Brethren / On the District Youth Cabinet For Church; Eastern Mennonite U; Manchester College

MORRISON, DANIELLE C; RICHLANDS, VA; RICHLANDS HS; (JR); 4H Awd; Ctznshp Aw; Hnr Roll; Otst Ac Ach Awd; St of Mnth; Hab For Humty Volntr; 4-H; Chrch Yth Grp; DARE; Fr of Library; CR (R); 3rd in Accelerated Reader Points; FCCLA; Novelist; Graphic Designers; Southwest Virginia Community; Christopher Newport U

MORRISON, KERRY; WILLIAMSBURG, VA; LAFAYETTE HS; (SR); F Lan Hn Soc; Hi Hnr Roll; Nat Hon Sy; Nat Sci Aw; Valdctrian; WWAHSS; Peer Tut/Med; Red Cr Aide; Jr Cls League; Key Club; Mod UN; MuAlphaTh; Latin Clb; Bnd; Mch Bnd; Fld Hky (V CL); Sftball (V L); Tennis (V); All-State Band; Field Hockey State Champion; Genetics; Virology; U of Virginia; College of William and Mary

MORSE, GLORIA; STAUNTON, VA; ROBERT E LEE HS; (JR); Hnr Roll; Otst Ac Ach Awd; WWAHSS; Yth Ldrshp Prog; Emplmnt; Quiz Bowl; Schol Bwl; French Clb; Bnd; Mch Bnd; Pep Bnd; SP/M/VS; Stu Cncl (R); National Spelling Bee; Electrical / Computer Engineering; Nuclear Physics; California Institute of Technology; U of Chicago

Moreno, Kristen J
Bethel HS
Hampton, VA

Miller, Crystal A
Thomas A Edison HS
Alexandria, VA

Mitchell, Meredith
T C Williams HS
Alexandria, VA

MORUZA, THOMAS; CHARLOTTESVILLE, VA; CHARLOTTESVILLE HS; (JR); Hnr Roll; MVP; Nat Hon Sy; Otst Ac Ach Awd; Comm Volntr; Chrch Yth Grp; Drma Clb; Scouts; SP/M/VS; Stg Cre; Cr Ctry (V); Sccr (V); Swmg (V); Lit Mag (R); 8 Time Swimming State Qualifier; 2004 Soccer VA State Champions / Selected for Leadership Seminar at West Point; West Point Military Academy; Degree in Engineering; West Point Military Academy; College of William and Mary

MOSES, DESIRE; VINTON, VA; ROANOKE CATHOLIC HS; (JR); Hi Hnr Roll; Nat Hon Sy; WWAHSS; Comm Volntr; Peer Tut/Med; Key Club; Spanish Clb; Bskball (VJ); Sccr (J); Stu Cncl (S); Sch Ppr (R); Yrbk (P); Destination Imagination (5 Yrs); Key Club Vice President; English; New York U; Virginia Tech

MOSLEY, SHRONDA; APPOMATTOX, VA; APPOMATTOX CTY HS; (FR); Ctznshp Aw; Hnr Roll; Otst Ac Ach Awd; Perf Att; Pres Ac Ftns Aw; Sci Fairs; Hab For Humty Volntr; 4-H; Chrch Yth Grp; DARE; Pep Squd; Chr; Ch Chr; Pep Bnd; Chrldg (J); PP Ftbl (J); Track (V L); Stu Cncl (S); Accounting; Dance/Singing Education; Georgia Tech; Florida State U

MOSS, KAYLEE N; YORKTOWN, VA; YORK HS; (FR); Ctznshp Aw; Hnr Roll; Nat Hon Sy; Key Club; Dnce; 10 Yrs of Private Dance; Ballet, Tap, Jazz & Pointe; Medical Field; Nursing; Medical College of VA; U of Virginia

MOTLEY, MARK E; RICHMOND, VA; LLOYD C BIRD HS; (JR); Hi Hnr Roll; Hnr Roll; Jr Mshl; Nat Hon Sy; Otst Ac Ach Awd; Perf Att; Sci Fairs; Yth Ldrshp Prog; Peer Tut/Med; Chrch Yth Grp; Emplmnt; FCA; Key Club; Quill & Scroll; Vsity Clb; Latin Clb; Bnd; Ftball (VJ L); Wt Lftg; Stu Cncl (R); CR (R); Sch Ppr (E, R, P); Senior Guide; Journalism; Business; James Madison U; George Mason U

MOUNCE, AMANDA; CHESTERFIELD, VA; MANCHESTER HS; (JR); F Lan Hn Soc; Hi Hnr Roll; Jr Mshl; Nat Hon Sy; Otst Ac Ach Awd; Perf Att; St of Mnth; Valdctrian; Comm Volntr; Chrch Yth Grp; Emplmnt; Mod UN; Ntl Beta Clb; Prom Com; Bnd; Dnce; Mch Bnd; Stu Cncl (R); School Liaison for Annual French Congress; Teaching; Journalism; College of William & Mary; U of Virginia

MOUNCE, CARLIE; VIRGINIA BEACH, VA; FLOYD KELLAM HS; (JR); Hi Hnr Roll; Nat Hon Sy; Perf Att; Pres Ac Ftns Aw; Comm Volntr; French Clb; Bskball (VJ L); Sftball (J L); Vllyball (V L); P.E. Teacher; Sports Trainer; James Madison U; Radford U

MOWERY, RENEE M; ALEXANDRIA, VA; THOMAS A EDISON HS; (SR); Hnr Roll; Comm Volntr; Key Club; ROTC; Tchrs Aide; Drl Tm; George Mason U; Northern Virginia Community College

MOXLEY, DAVID R; MANASSAS, VA; OSBOURN PARK SR HS; (SO); Gov Hnr Prg; Hnr Roll; WWAHSS; Key Club; Scouts; Bnd; Orch; SP/M/VS; Lcrsse (J); Boy Scouts: Life Scout Rank; Order of the Arrow Member; Football: Freshman Team; Business; Chemical Engineering; Shenandoah U; VA Tech

MOYNIHAN, LAURA C; CLIFTON, VA; PAUL VI CATHOLIC HS; (SO); Hi Hnr Roll; Sci Fairs; Yth Ldrshp Prog; Comm Volntr; Spec Olymp Vol; Chess; Chrch Yth Grp; Jr Cls League; Key Club; Mth Clb/Tm; Orch; SP/M/VS; Magna Cum Laude on National Latin Exam; Student Leadership Youth Corps; Law; Pilot; U of Virginia; College Of William and Mary

MUELLER, CARL; MIDLOTHIAN, VA; CLOVER HILL HS; (JR); Hi Hnr Roll; Hnr Roll; MVP; Pres Ac Ftns Aw; Yth Ldrshp Prog; Comm Volntr; Peer Tut/Med; Spec Olymp Vol; DECA; Drma Clb; FCA; Jr Ach; Prom Com; SADD; Spanish Clb; SP/M/VS; Chrldg (V CL); PPSqd (V); Track (J); Stu Cncl (R); CR (R); DECA District Winner; International DECA Finalist; Broadcast Journalism; Public Relations; U of South Carolina; U of Texas

MUIR, MELISSA W; ASHBURN, VA; STONE BRIDGE HS; (JR); DAR; F Lan Hn Soc; Hnr Roll; Nat Hon Sy; Pres Ac Ftns Aw; St of Mnth; Yth Ldrshp Prog; Comm Volntr; Peer Tut/Med; Chrch Yth Grp; Emplmnt; Key Club; Quiz Bowl; Spanish Clb; Chr; Chrldg (J); PP Ftbl (J); Sccr (V L); Adv Cncl (R); CR (R); Distinguished Key Club Vice President; Key Club President; Spanish; Business/Advertising/Marketing; U of Virginia; Pennsylvania State U

MULLEN, JENNIFER; HAMPTON, VA; BETHEL HS; (SR); Hnr Roll; Otst Ac Ach Awd; WWAHSS; Emplmnt; Jr Ach; Key Club; MuAlphaTh; Top GPA Junior 2003-2004; Academic Achievement 2003; Interior Design; Fashion Design; Old Dominion U; Christopher Newport U

MULLINS, MICHAEL B; CLIFTON, VA; CENTREVILLE HS; (SO); Hnr Roll; Kwnis Aw; Perf Att; WWAHSS; Comm Volntr; Peer Tut/Med; Key Club; Lcrsse (J); Stu Cncl (R); PTSA Student Representative; Student Government; Business; Public Relations; Chapman U; U of Southern California

MURPHY, LEE; SOUTH BOSTON, VA; HALIFAX CTY HS; (JR); Ctznshp Aw; Hnr Roll; Nat Hon Sy; Perf Att; WWAHSS; Chrch Yth Grp; Emplmnt; Prom Com; Ch Chr; Cl Off (V); Technology Student Association (TSA) - (State Officer); Transportation Safety Commission; Information Technology; U of Virginia; Virginia Commonwealth U

MURPHY, MEGAN; FREDERICKSBURG, VA; FREDERICKSBURG CHRISTIAN SCH; (FR); Hi Hnr Roll; Hnr Roll; Kwnis Aw; Perf Att; St of Mnth; WWAHSS; Comm Volntr; Chrch Yth Grp; Key Club; Ch Chr; Scr Kpr (V); Vllyball (J); Key Club Social Chairman; Varsity Boy's Volleyball Statistician

MURRAY, NATALIE S; MANASSAS, VA; OSBOURN HS; (FR); Hnr Roll; Otst Ac Ach Awd; Pres Sch; WWAHSS; Yth Ldrshp Prog; FBLA; Key Club; Sch Ppr (R); Youth Advisory Council of Prince William County; Founder and President of Female Institution of Revolutionizing Education; International, Business, and Domestic Law; Masters of Business Administration (MBA); Yale U, Duke U; Harvard U, U of North Carolina, Charlotte

MUSICK, LINDSEY L; WEBER CITY, VA; GATE CITY HS; (SR); DAR; Hnr Roll; MVP; Nat Hon Sy; Perf Att; WWAHSS; Comm Volntr; Peer Tut/Med; Chrch Yth Grp; FCA; FCCLA; Key Club; Mth Clb/Tm; MuAlphaTh; Ch Chr; Bskball (V CL); Track (VJ L); Vllyball (V CL); King College

NANCE, SANTIA; HAMPTON, VA; KECOUGHTAN HS; (JR); Gov Hnr Prg; Hi Hnr Roll; Hnr Roll; Perf Att; Comm Volntr; Biology Clb; Emplmnt; MuAlphaTh; ROTC; Sci Clb; Bnd; Mch Bnd; Vice President of Ecology Club; JROTC Drill Teams; Mathematics; Communications; U of Virginia; Virginia Tech

NAQVI, IMRAN H; RESTON, VA; SOUTH LAKES HS; (JR); Ctznshp Aw; F Lan Hn Soc; Fut Prb Slvr; Hi Hnr Roll; Hnr Roll; Nat Hon Sy; Nat Ldrshp Svc; Otst Ac Ach Awd; Perf Att; St of Mnth; CARE; Comm Volntr; Hab For Humty Volntr; Emplmnt; Fr of Library; Jr Ach; Jr Cls League; JSA; Lib Aide; Outdrs Clb; Svce Clb; Drl Tm; Flg Crps; SP/M/VS; Stg Cre; Arch (V); Bdmtn (V); Bsball (V); Bskball (V); Fncg; Scr Kpr (V); Skt Tgt Sh (V C); Sccr; Cl Off (P, T); CR (T, R); Mentoring Program (Tutor); SLICE Intramural Club & NHS; Major in Dentistry; Ambassador; Virginia Tech College; Harvard U

NARET, MATTHEW H; RICHMOND, VA; THE MATH & SCIENCE HS AT CLOVER HILL; (SR); Hi Hnr Roll; Nat Hon Sy; Pres Sch; WWAHSS; Lttrmn Clb; Lib Aide; MuAlphaTh; Quill & Scroll; Quiz Bowl; Bnd; Jzz Bnd; Mch Bnd; Eagle Scout; Forensic Science; Virginia Commonwealth U

NASH, CARI; STERLING, VA; THOMAS JEFFERSON HS FOR SCI/TECH; (SR); Nat Hon Sy; Nat Mrt LOC; WWAHSS; Comm Volntr; Peer Tut/Med; Chrch Yth Grp; Emplmnt; Prom Com; Svce Clb; Chrldg (V L); Piano-10 Yrs; Biology; Political Science; U of Virginia

NAVARRO-OROZCO, DANIEL; LEESBURG, VA; HERITAGE HS; (JR); F Lan Hn Soc; Hnr Roll; Otst Ac Ach Awd; Pres Ac Ftns Aw; St of Mnth; Comm Volntr; Peer Tut/Med; DECA; Key Club; Scouts; French Clb; Bskball; Cr Ctry; Ftball; Mar Art; Sccr (VJC); Wage Radio Academy Award; Vice President of French and Friends Without Borders Clubs; Dentistry; Marketing; George Washington U; U of Virginia

NAZERI, AHMAD S; RICHMOND, VA; HENRICO HS; (SO); Hi Hnr Roll; Perf Att; WWAHSS; Comm Volntr; Chess; Clb; Sccr (V); Track (V); Stu Cncl (R); International Baccalaureate; Academic Club; Architecture; Mathematics; Washington U in St Louis; Columbia U (NY)

NEAL, WILLIAM C; RICHMOND, VA; BENEDICTINE HS; (JR); Hi Hnr Roll; Nat Hon Sy; Perf Att; ArtClub; Chrch Yth Grp; Emplmnt; Key Club; ROTC; Skt Tgt Sh (V); Real Estate Development; James Madison U; Virginia Commonwealth U

NEALE, AMY E; VIRGINIA BEACH, VA; COX HS; Hnr Roll; Key Club; Fld Hky (J); Psych, Law; Business; VA Tech, JMU, CNU

NEALE, KEVIN T; VIRGINIA BEACH, VA; COX HS; (JR); Hnr Roll; Key Club; Ftball (VJ); Track (VJ); Business; Radford, Longwood; CNU

NEARY III, RICHARD J; VIRGINIA BEACH, VA; (FR); Hnr Roll; Comm Volntr; ArtClub; Chrch Yth Grp; DARE; Key Club; Scouts; French Clb; Sccr (J); Track (J); Architect; Computer Design; VA Tech; UVA

NEDELCOUYAH, MICHAEL; RESTON, VA; SOUTH LAKES HS; (SR); F Lan Hn Soc; Hi Hnr Roll; Hnr Roll; Nat Hon Sy; Nat Mrt LOC; Sci Fairs; WWAHSS; Comm Volntr; Chrch Yth Grp; FCA; Key Club; Mth Clb/Tm; SADD; Vsity Clb; Sccr (V C); Biochemistry Research; College of William & Mary

NEGRON-BOYLE, BRICE W; COLONIAL HGTS, VA; (JR); Hnr Roll; DECA; Tech Clb; Spanish Clb; Ftball (V L); Track (V L); Wrstlg (V L); Swimming (Yacht/Club) League Champions; All Academic First Team Football District; Business/Marketing; Sports Medicine; Virginia Tech/Virginia; William/Mary

NEUBERGER, MIRANDA; WARRENTON, VA; PA HS; (JR); Hnr Roll; WWAHSS; Comm Volntr; ArtClub; P to P St Amb Prg; French Clb; Bskball (V); Sccr (V); Swmg (V); Top 100 in Virginia for 2 Swimming Strokes (Breast/Free) Honorable Mention, National HSLDA Art Contest: Several Best of Show and 1st Place Art Awards; Awanas Regional Speed Record Holder (Girls Marathon); Fine Arts-Art

NEWSOME, ISAAC; GATE CITY, VA; GATE CITY HS; (JR); Hi Hnr Roll; Nat Hon Sy; WWAHSS; Comm Volntr; Chrch Yth Grp; Key Club; Bnd; Mathematics

NG, ABIGAIL; CHESAPEAKE, VA; DEEP CREEK HS; (FR); Hi Hnr Roll; WWAHSS; Peer Tut/Med; Key Club; Dnce; Orch; Chrldg (J); Young Life; Medicine; U of Michigan

NGO, AMANDA; MANASSAS, VA; OSBOURN HS; (SR); F Lan Hn Soc; Hnr Roll; Otst Ac Ach Awd; USAA; WWAHSS; Peer Tut/Med; FBLA; Key Club; P to P St Amb Prg; Spanish Clb; Vice President of Osbourn High School; Future Business Leaders of America; Business Management; U of Virginia; James Madison U

NGUYEN, ALEXANDER; STERLING, VA; (JR); Hnr Roll; Nat Hon Sy; Perf Att; St of Mnth; WWAHSS; Comm Volntr; Hosp Aide; Chess; Jr Cls League; Key Club; Bnd; Cr Ctry (J); Track; Latin Club Vice President; Interact Club; Medical; U of Virginia; College of William and Mary

NGUYEN, ANNA A; CLIFTON, VA; ROBINSON SECONDARY SCH; (FR); F Lan Hn Soc; Hi Hnr Roll; Nat Hon Sy; Otst Ac Ach Awd; Comm Volntr; Peer Tut/Med; Mus Clb; French Clb; SP/M/VS; Mar Art; Tennis; Member of National Piano Playing Auditions; Pediatrics / MD; Johns Hopkins U

NGUYEN, CHRISTINA-MAI; FAIRFAX, VA; FAIRFAX HS; (JR); Perf Att; Pres Ac Ftns Aw; DECA; Mth Clb/Tm; Prom Com; SADD; Tchrs Aide; Vsity Clb; Latin Clb; Chr; Chrldg (VJC); Dvng (V L); Fncg (V); Lcrsse (V L); PP Ftbl (VJ); Scr Kpr (V L); Vsy Clb (V); Cl Off (T); CR (R); Student Gov't Association; School Treasurer; Business Management; Journalist/News Reporter; George Mason U

NGUYEN, MINH; STERLING, VA; DOMINION HS; (JR); Perf Att; Comm Volntr; DECA; Key Club; Tmpl Yth Grp; Vsity Clb; Bnd; Ftball (V L); Track (V); Black Belt Karate/Tae Kwon Do; Played Piano for Nine Years; Biology; Dentist/Oral Surgeon; Virginia Polytech Institute and State U; James Madison U

NGUYEN, VI; MANASSAS, VA; OSBOURN HS; (SO); Hi Hnr Roll; Hnr Roll; Nat Hon Sy; Nat Stu Ath Day Aw; Otst Ac Ach Awd; Perf Att; Pres Ac Ftns Aw; St of Mnth; WWAHSS; Comm Volntr; FCCLA; Key Club; Photog; Spanish Clb; SP/M/VS; Dentistry; Engineering; Virginia Tech; U of Virginia

NICASTRI, PATRICIA; CLIFTON, VA; ROBINSON SECONDARY SCH; (FR); Hnr Roll; Comm Volntr; Drma Clb; Mus Clb; P to P St Amb Prg; Bnd; Mch Bnd; SP/M/VS; U of Virginia; College of William and Mary

NICHOLAS, RYAN A; CLIFTON, VA; THOMAS JEFFERSON HS FOR SCI/TECH; (JR); Duke TS; Gov Hnr Prg; Hi Hnr Roll; Nat Hon Sy; Nat Mrt LOC; Comm Volntr; BPA; FCA; Lttrmn Clb; Svce Clb; Vsity Clb; Bskball (VJCL); Ftball (VJCL); Developed & Sold Power Point Real Estate Marketing Program; Natl. Honor Society; Business and Management; Economics; Yale U; U of Virginia

NICHOLS, JODIE L; SAXE, VA; HALIFAX CTY HS; (SR); 4H Awd; Ctznshp Aw; Hnr Roll; Hab For Humty Volntr; Chrch Yth Grp; Emplmnt; SADD; Sftball (J); Sch Ppr (R); Certified in Microsoft Excel, Was in All-District Choir in 8th Grade; Certified in Microsoft Word; Teacher; Writer; Southside Virginia Community College; Old Dominion U

NIMMAGADDA, SAILEY; MC LEAN, VA; THE BULLIS SCH; (SO); Comm Volntr; Drma Clb; Emplmnt; JSA; Lib Aide; Chr; Dnce; SP/M/VS; Sccr (J); Computer Scientist; U of Virginia; U of Maryland

NISSEN, ANNIE E; GLEN ALLEN, VA; PATRICK HENRY HS; (FR); Ctznshp Aw; Hnr Roll; MVP; Otst Ac Ach Awd; Sci Fairs; Chrch Yth Grp; DARE; Dbte Team; Photog; Latin Clb; Acpl Chr; Chr; GAA (J); Sftball (J); Yrbk (P); Starting Pitcher JV Softball Umpire; Rec. Fast Pitch Player-Pitcher; Interior Design; (VCU) Virginia Commonwealth U; Randolph Macon College

NIXON, JUSTIN; SALEM, VA; SALEM HS; (SO); Hnr Roll; Nat Hon Sy; WWAHSS; Emplmnt; FCA; Cr Ctry (J); Track (J); Computers; Virginia Tech

NIZAM, AMANDA E; VIRGINIA BEACH, VA; FIRST COLONIAL HS; (JR); Hnr Roll; Nat Hon Sy; Perf Att; Comm Volntr; Hosp Aide; Peer Tut/Med; Chrch Yth Grp; Key Club; Mod UN; MuAlphaTh; German Clb; Track (J); Adv Cncl; Stu Cncl; Lit Mag; Mu Alpha Theta; National Honor Society; Biology; Medicine (MD); U of Virginia; Boston College

NIZAM, CHANTAL; VIRGINIA BEACH, VA; FIRST COLONIAL HS; (FR); Hnr Roll; Perf Att; WWAHSS; Comm Volntr; Chrch Yth Grp; Key Club; German Clb; Adv Cncl; Speak German and Lebanese; Studying Piano 8 Years+; Psychology; Nutrition

NOFFSINGER, ANNE-MERRIN; YORKTOWN, VA; GRAFTON HS; (SR); DAR; F Lan Hn Soc; Hi Hnr Roll; Nat Hon Sy; Nat Mrt Semif; Comm Volntr; Chrch Yth Grp; Drma Clb; Emplmnt; Quill & Scroll; Lit Mag (E); Sch Ppr (E, R); Lettered Twice in Forensics (Local League); Girls State Representative; English; Education; Already Enrolled At James Madison

NORMENT, COURTNEY E; MECHANICSVILLE, VA; ATLEE HS; (SR); F Lan Hn Soc; Hi Hnr Roll; Hnr Roll; Nat Hon Sy; Otst Ac Ach Awd; Pres Ac Ftns Aw; Comm Volntr; Peer Tut/Med; ArtClub; Chess; Chrch Yth Grp; Emplmnt; Ntl Beta Clb; Photog; Prom Com; Spanish Clb; PP Ftbl (VJ); Track (VJ L); Cl Off (P); Stu Cncl (R); Yrbk (R); Homecoming Queen; Virginia Tech; UVA

Nimmagadda, Sailey
The Bullis Sch
Mc Lean, VA

Nguyen, Christina-Mai
Fairfax HS
Fairfax, VA

Nazeri, Ahmad S
Henrico HS
Richmond, VA

Mullins, Michael B
Centreville HS
Clifton, VA

Naqvi, Imran H
South Lakes HS
Reston, VA

Nichols, Jodie L
Halifax Cty HS
Saxe, VA

Nissen, Annie E
Patrick Henry HS
Glen Allen, VA

NOYES, MAX A; VIRGINIA BEACH, VA; FRANK W COX HS; (SO); Hnr Roll; Perf Att; Comm Volntr; Emplmnt; Key Club; Orch; Swmg (V L); CR (R); Bowling-State (2004) Double Champ; Tidewater Team Bowling-(2004) Winning Team; Oceanography, Meteorology, Mechanical Engineer

NUNN, TESSA A; WILLIAMSBURG, VA; LAFAYETTE HS; (JR); F Lan Hn Soc; WWAHSS; Comm Volntr; Hosp Aide; Peer Tut/Med; Emplmnt; FBLA; Jr Cls League; Key Club; Lib Aide; Mod UN; MuAlphaTh; NtlFrnscLg; Bnd; Dnce; Mch Bnd; Lit Mag; Education; French; U of Virginia

NUNNALLY, MIAISHA; ROANOKE, VA; WILLIAM FLEMING HS; (JR); F Lan Hn Soc; Hnr Roll; Perf Att; Sci Fairs; Emplmnt; Ntl Beta Clb; Vllyball (V); Cl Off (V); 4.1 GPA (IB Program in School); Ranked #6 in My Class; I Would Like to Be a Pediatrician or Child Psychologist; Duke U; Emory College (In Georgia)

NUTLER, LAUREN; VIRGINIA BEACH, VA; FRANK W COX HS; (JR); Hi Hnr Roll; Hnr Roll; Otst Ac Ach Awd; Pres Ac Ftns Aw; WWAHSS; Comm Volntr; Chrch Yth Grp; Key Club; Photog; Quiz Bowl; Spanish Clb; Cr Ctry (VJ L); Outstanding Falcon for AP Psychology; Reflections Contest Winner (Photography); Psychology; Photography; U of California, Irvine; Pepperdine U

OCAMPO, EVANGELINE; ASHBURN, VA; BISHOP DENIS J O'CONNELL HS; (SO); Hi Hnr Roll; WWAHSS; Comm Volntr; 4-H; Key Club; Bnd; Dnce; Finance; Real Estate; U of Virginia; George Washington U

OCK, SUNGJIN; FAIRFAX, VA; ROBINSON SECONDARY SCH; (JR); WWAHSS; Comm Volntr; Chrch Yth Grp; FCA; Key Club; Mth Clb/Tm; Ch Chr; Orch; Mar Art (V); Vllyball (V); Youth Group President of Church; Dentistry; Virginia Commonwealth U; George Mason U

OCKERT, CLAUDIA; VIRGINIA BEACH, VA; FRANK W COX HS; (SO); F Lan Hn Soc; Hnr Roll; Chrch Yth Grp; FBLA; Key Club; German Clb; Swmg (V L); German Honor Society Secretary; U of Virginia

OCKERT, LYDIA S; VIRGINIA BEACH, VA; FRANK W COX HS; (JR); Hnr Roll; Chrch Yth Grp; FBLA; Key Club; German Clb; Swmg (V L); Occupational Therapy; James Madison U; U of Wisconsin-Madison

O'CONNELL, KATHRYN; VIRGINIA BEACH, VA; COX HS; Ctznshp Aw; F Lan Hn Soc; Hi Hnr Roll; Pres Ac Ftns Aw; St of Mnth; Comm Volntr; Jr Cls League; Key Club; Scouts; Latin Clb; Orch; Cr Ctry (V L); Cox Crew-JV-Letter; Engineering; Architecture; U of Virginia; U of North Carolina

O'DONNELL, KALEIGH; VIRGINIA BEACH, VA; CHURCHLAND HS; (JR); Hi Hnr Roll; Nat Hon Sy; Otst Ac Ach Awd; Comm Volntr; Prom Com; Dnce; Fld Hky (V L); Sftball (J); Adv Cncl; Nominated for Governors School Summer Program; Nominated for Girls State; Broadcasting; Communications; U of Virginia; James Madison U

OH, JEONG; STERLING, VA; POTOMAC FALLS HS; (JR); Hnr Roll; Nat Hon Sy; Otst Ac Ach Awd; WWAHSS; Comm Volntr; FBLA; Key Club; Bnd; Track (J); History Fair - 2nd Place; Outstanding History Student Award; Business; International Relations; George Mason U; College of William and Mary

OH, REBECCA S; WILLIAMSBURG, VA; LAFAYETTE HS; (JR); F Lan Hn Soc; Nat Hon Sy; Nat Mrt LOC; WWAHSS; Yth Ldrshp Prog; Peer Tut/Med; Chrch Yth Grp; Emplmnt; Key Club; Mod UN; MuAlphaTh; Quiz Bowl; Schol Bwl; Spanish Clb; Tennis (J); Adv Cncl; Lit Mag (E); Biology-Medicine; English; Brown U; U of Washington in St. Louis

OH, YEKYOO; ALDIE, VA; BROAD RUN HS; (SO); Hnr Roll; Red Cr Aide; Bnd; Mch Bnd; Bio Tech; Chemistry; U of Virginia; Yale U

O'LEARY, AMY; DUMFRIES, VA; FOREST PARK HS; (SR); F Lan Hn Soc; Hnr Roll; Nat Hon Sy; Red Cr Aide; Key Club; Mod UN; Quill & Scroll; Tchrs Aide; French Clb; Fld Hky (J L); Yrbk (E); Summa Cum Laude Graduate; Academic Letter-3 years; U of Virginia

OLSON, JOSHUA L; MANASSAS, VA; OSBOURN PARK HS; (JR); Gov Hnr Prg; Hnr Roll; Sci Fairs; Comm Volntr; Chrch Yth Grp; Key Club; Scouts; Eagle Scout; Governers School; Mathematics; U of Virginia; Brigham Young U

O'MALLEY, AMANDA; VIRGINIA BEACH, VA; COX HS; (FR); Ctznshp Aw; DAR; Hi Hnr Roll; Kwnis Aw; Otst Ac Ach Awd; St of Mnth; WWAHSS; Comm Volntr; JSA; Key Club; Spanish Clb; Stu Cncl (R); Yrbk (P); Received Above and Beyond Award At Key Club Convention; Designed Ornament for Kiwanis Club; Law; English; Mary Washington U; Georgetown U

ONAWOLE, OLADOYIN; VIRGINIA BEACH, VA; BRANDON MS; MS; Hnr Roll; Comm Volntr; Chrch Yth Grp; Drma Clb; FCA; Lib Aide; Chr; Ch Chr; Clr Grd; SP/M/VS; Yrbk (P); National Junior Honor Society Vice President; Obstetrics / Gynecology; Oakwood College

ONWUKA, OBINNA J; STERLING, VA; DOMINION HS; (JR); Hnr Roll; Pres Ac Ftns Aw; St of Mnth; Schol Bwl; Lit Mag (E); Academic Letter; Creative Writing; Music; U of Virginia; Oberlin U

O'QUINN, JARED W; HAYSI, VA; HAYSI HS; (SO); Ctznshp Aw; Hi Hnr Roll; 4-H; Emplmnt; Ntl Beta Clb; Ntl FFA; Engineering; UVA-U of Virginia (Wise); Virginia Tech

ORNELAS, STEFANNY; WINCHESTER, VA; OOLOGAH-TALALA HS; (FR); Hnr Roll

ORSINI, DAVID R; MANASSAS, VA; OSBOURN PARK SR HS; (JR); Hnr Roll; Perf Att; WWAHSS; Emplmnt; FBLA; Key Club; ROTC; Bskball (V L); Volunteer Prince William Public Library System; James Madison U; Virginia Tech

ORZELL, MATTHEW; VIRGINIA BEACH, VA; FIRST COLONIAL HS; (JR); F Lan Hn Soc; Hi Hnr Roll; Nat Hon Sy; Perf Att; WWAHSS; Comm Volntr; Chrch Yth Grp; FBLA; Key Club; MuAlphaTh; Bsball (J L); Track (V L); National Honor Society; Math Honor Society (Mu Alpha Theta); Dentistry; Business

OSINOVSKY, LEV; RESTON, VA; SOUTH LAKES HS; (JR); F Lan Hn Soc; Hnr Roll; Sci Fairs; Yth Ldrshp Prog; Peer Tut/Med; Key Club; Tmpl Yth Grp; Swmg (V L); Track (V L); Science Fair 1st Place in Physics; 9 Medals from Maccabi Games; Dentistry; Computer Field; U of Virginia; James Madison U

OSMAN, RAZAN A; HERNDON, VA; WESTFIELD HS; (SO); Hi Hnr Roll; Hnr Roll; Otst Ac Ach Awd; Perf Att; Pres Ac Ftns Aw; St of Mnth; Quill & Scroll; French Clb; Sch Ppr (E); Member of College Partnership Program; Criminal Psychology; Law; Virginia Tech; U of Virginia

OTT, REBECCA G; FREDERICKSBURG, VA; JAMES MONROE HS; (FR); Comm Volntr; ArtClub; Key Club; Latin Clb; Orch; Performed in Eugene Onegin; Violinist; Writer; Catholic U of America; Pratt Institute

OWEN, MEGAN L; STONY CREEK, VA; BRUNSWICK HS; (SR); All Am Sch; Hi Hnr Roll; Hnr Roll; Jr Mshl; Nat Hon Sy; WWAHSS; Comm Volntr; Hab For Humty Volntr; Chrch Yth Grp; Emplmnt; Tchrs Aide; Ch Chr; Dnce; Bskball (V C); Sftball (V); Cl Off (T); Business; Education; U of Richmond

OZA, DIPAN H; CHESAPEAKE, VA; WESTERN BRANCH HS; (SO); Hnr Roll; Nat Hon Sy; Perf Att; Yth Ldrshp Prog; Hosp Aide; Lib Aide; Mod UN; NYLC; Quiz Bowl; Tech Clb; Bnd; Cl Off (V); Volunteer Worker At Mary View Medical Center Since 3 Years.; Medicine; U of Virginia, William & Mary; Duke

PACQUE, DEREK J; MC LEAN, VA; MC LEAN HS; (SO); Hnr Roll; WWAHSS; DECA; Emplmnt; Mth Clb/Tm; NYLC; French Clb; Bskball (J); Tennis (V); Toshiba Explora Vision Honorable Mention; DECA Officer; Business / Marketing; Computer Science / Information Tech

PADGET, LAUREN; VIRGINIA BEACH, VA; FIRST COLONIAL HS; (JR); Hnr Roll; Perf Att; Comm Volntr; Key Club; Orch; Swmg (V L); Dentistry; Pharmacy

PALMA, JESSE; WILLIAMSBURG, VA; AMERICAN SCH; (SR); WWAHSS; DECA; Drma Clb; Emplmnt; Chr; Dnce; VICA-Skills USA; Project Reach Out-Community Service; Merchandise Marketing-Associate; Visual Communications-Associate; Fashion Institute of Design & Marketing

PALMER, ALISON; YORKTOWN, VA; GRAFTON HS; (JR); Hi Hnr Roll; Hnr Roll; Nat Hon Sy; Perf Att; Sci Fairs; Yth Ldrshp Prog; Comm Volntr; Spec Olymp Vol; Mod UN; Quill & Scroll; Spanish Clb; Track (V L); Sch Ppr (E); Competed History Course At College of William and Mary; Received College Credit; History (Historic Preservation); Archaeology; The College of William and Mary; U of Mary Washington

PALMER, KESHAWN R; LAWRENCEVILLE, VA; BRUNSWICK SR HS; (SO); Hi Hnr Roll; Hnr Roll; Nat Stu Ath Day Aw; Otst Ac Ach Awd; Sci Fairs; ArtClub; DARE; Ftball (V L); Track (V); CR (R); DARE Award Winner; Principal's Award - Honor Roll; Architecture; Business Management; Norfolk State U; Hampton U

PALOMO, MARK; RESTON, VA; SOUTH LAKES HS; (SO); Hnr Roll; FBLA; Computer Engineering; George Mason U

PARBADIA, KUNAL P; WARRENTON, VA; FAUQUIER HS; (JR); Ctznshp Aw; Hi Hnr Roll; Hnr Roll; Otst Ac Ach Awd; Perf Att; Pres Ac Ftns Aw; Sci Fairs; St of Mnth; WWAHSS; Comm Volntr; Hosp Aide; Cmptr Clb; FBLA; Mth Clb/Tm; Sci Clb; Tech Clb; Latin Clb; I Have Taken Art and Net & Computer Courses; Participated in Regional Competition of FBLA and TSA; Computer Engineering; Computer Science; Virginia Polytechnic Institute of Technology; U of Virginia

PARK, JANE; CLIFTON, VA; CTRVILLE HS; (FR); Hnr Roll; Chrch Yth Grp; Key Club; Bnd; Mch Bnd; Went to Missions to Vancouver Canada; Business Marketing; Psychology; Virginia Tech; U of Virginia

PARKER, C PAUL; SUFFOLK, VA; STONE BRIDGE HS; (SO); Sci Fairs; Comm Volntr; Key Club; Scouts; Bnd; Cr Ctry (V CL); Track (V CL); 1st Place Science Fair; North Carolina State U

PARKER, HALEY; MARTINSVILLE, VA; MARTINSVILLE HS; (SO); All Am Sch; Hi Hnr Roll; Nat Hon Sy; Perf Att; WWAHSS; Chrch Yth Grp; Key Club; Spanish Clb; Bnd; Dnce; Mch Bnd; SP/M/VS; Tennis (V); CR (R); Pharmacy; Accounting

PARKER, TIFFANY M; RICHMOND, VA; VARINA HS; (JR); Perf Att; WWAHSS; DECA; FBLA; Teaching; Nursing; North Carolina State U; Virginia State U

PATEL, MAYA; MIDLOTHIAN, VA; ST CATHERINE'S SCH; (SO); Hi Hnr Roll; Hnr Roll; Comm Volntr; Hosp Aide; Peer Tut/Med; Emplmnt; Mod UN; Svce Clb; Tmpl Yth Grp; Dnce; Adv Cncl (R); Lit Mag (E, R); Sch Ppr (E, R); Recipient of the Randolph Macon Women's College Book Award for Excellency; Medicine; Law; Duke; Georgetown

PATEL, PAYAL; MANASSAS, VA; OSBOURN HS; (SO); Hnr Roll; Perf Att; Comm Volntr; Hosp Aide; FBLA; Key Club; FCCLA; Medical (Major); U of Virginia (UVA); James Madison U (JMU)

PATILLO, SHERAY C; VIRGINIA BEACH, VA; PRINCESS ANNE HS; (SR); Hnr Roll; Perf Att; Pres Ac Ftns Aw; St of Mnth; WWAHSS; Comm Volntr; Hab For Humty Volntr; Peer Tut/Med; Chrch Yth Grp; DARE; Dbte Team; Emplmnt; Key Club; NtlFrnscLg; Photog; Prom Com; Ch Chr; Track (V L); Cl Off (R); Stu Cncl (R); Psychology; Criminology; Southern U; Howard U

PATRICIO, COURTNEY K; STAFFORD, VA; COLONIAL FORGE HS; (JR); Hi Hnr Roll; Hnr Roll; Nat Hon Sy; Pres Ac Ftns Aw; Comm Volntr; Peer Tut/Med; Chrch Yth Grp; FBLA; Key Club; Spanish Clb; Dnce; Lit Mag; Business; Public Relations; U of Virginia; Brown U

PAUL, SHARON; ASHBURN, VA; STONE BRIDGE HS; (JR); F Lan Hn Soc; Hi Hnr Roll; Hnr Roll; MVP; Nat Hon Sy; Perf Att; Pres Ac Ftns Aw; St of Mnth; WWAHSS; Comm Volntr; Peer Tut/Med; Biology Clb; Chrch Yth Grp; FCA; Key Club; Spanish Clb; SP/M/VS; Sccr (JC); Track (V L); Stu Cncl (R); CR (R); Pre-Medicine

PAULMINO, MARK; VIRGINIA BEACH, VA; FLOYD KELLAM HS; (FR); Hnr Roll; Perf Att; Peer Tut/Med; Chrch Yth Grp; German Clb; Fld Hky (J); Ftball (J); Recreation Basketball League; FCCLA; Physical Therapy; Business Administration; Virginia Tech; Virginia

PAXTON, ASHLEE N; COVINGTON, VA; ALLEGHANY HS; (SO); Hnr Roll; Nat Hon Sy; Sci Fairs; WWAHSS; Comm Volntr; Peer Tut/Med; 4-H; Chrch Yth Grp; DARE; Key Club; Mth Clb/Tm; Scouts; SADD; Bnd; Ch Chr; Clr Grd; Mch Bnd; Chrldg (J); PPSqd (V); CR (R); Talent Search; Medical Field / Pediatrics; Middle School Education; James Madison U; Bridgewater College

PAYNE, ALLYSON M.; GREAT FALLS, VA; DOMINION HS; (JR); F Lan Hn Soc; Hi Hnr Roll; Hnr Roll; Nat Hon Sy; Otst Ac Ach Awd; Perf Att; St Schl; Yth Ldrshp Prog; Comm Volntr; Peer Tut/Med; Chrch Yth Grp; Dbte Team; Emplmnt; Mus Clb; Prom Com; German Clb; Bnd; Jzz Bnd; Mch Bnd; Stu Cncl (R); VHSL Regional 5th Place for Congress Debate / State 4th Place; Music Education; English Education; College of William and Mary; James Madison U

PEAKE, RACHEL; SCOTTSVILLE, VA; FLUVANNA CTY HS; (SO); Hnr Roll; Chrch Yth Grp; Church Singing Group; Piano; History; Literature; Liberty U; Pensacola Christian College

PEARCE, WESLEY C; VIRGINIA BEACH, VA; FIRST COLONIAL HS; (JR); F Lan Hn Soc; Hnr Roll; Nat Hon Sy; Peer Tut/Med; Key Club; MuAlphaTh; Spanish Clb; Tennis (V L); Treasurer of National Honor Society; Biology, Psychiatry, Medical; The College of William and Mary; U of North Carolina

PEARSON, ALEX; VIRGINIA BEACH, VA; NORFOLK COLLEGIATE MID-UPR SCH; (JR); Ctznshp Aw; Hi Hnr Roll; Hnr Roll; Nat Hon Sy; Perf Att; St Optmst of Yr; Comm Volntr; ArtClub; Photog; Prom Com; French Clb; Bskball (V L); Lcrsse (V CL); PP Ftbl (V); Cl Off (R); Stu Cncl (T, R); CR (R); Yrbk (E, R, P); Social Science; Veterinary Medicine; Virginia Commonwealth U; Randolph Macon College

PECK, ANNE C; ASHBURN, VA; STONE BRIDGE HS; (FR); Hi Hnr Roll; WWAHSS; Comm Volntr; Key Club; Mus Clb; Bnd; Sftball (J); Law; Medicine; Virginia Tech; Stanford

PEGRAM, QUENTIN L; WOODBRIDGE, VA; GARFIELD HS; (SR); Hnr Roll; Chrch Yth Grp; Emplmnt; Ch Chr; Track (V); Auto CAD 2000 Certification; Architecture; Virginia Polytechnic Institute and State U; U of Maryland At College Park

PENDLETON, MALLORY L; SANDSTON, VA; VARINA HS; (FR); Hnr Roll; Comm Volntr; Chrch Yth Grp; Drma Clb; Key Club; Tchrs Aide; French Clb; Sch Ppr (R); Swim Team; Ballet, Jazz & Tap; Interior Decorator; Fashion Designer; U of Virginia

PERDOMO, JORGE; ANNANDALE, VA; ANNANDALE HS; (JR); Hnr Roll; Peer Tut/Med; Chess; Mathematics; Teaching; George Mason U; Northern Virginia Community College

PEREZ, CHLIRISSA; VIRGINIA BEACH, VA; FRANK W COX HS; (JR); Hi Hnr Roll; Hnr Roll; WWAHSS; Peer Tut/Med; AL Aux Girls; Emplmnt; Key Club; Quiz Bowl; Svce Clb; Russian Clb; Lit Mag (E); Yrbk (R); Operation Smile Club; Sociology; Psychology

Onawole, Oladoyin
Brandon MS
Virginia Beach, VA

Ocampo, Evangeline
Bishop Denis J O'Connell HS
Ashburn, VA

National
Honor Roll
Spring 2005

Nutler, Lauren
Frank W Cox HS
Virginia Beach, VA

Pegram, Quentin L
Garfield HS
Woodbridge, VA

PEREZ, JULIA; OAKTON, VA; (SO); WWAHSS; Yth Ldrshp Prog; Scouts; Orch; Girl Scouts; Pre-Law; Duke U; Brown U

PERIASAMY, MONICA; CROZET, VA; WESTERN ALBEMARLE HS; (JR); F Lan Hn Soc; Hi Hnr Roll; Hnr Roll; Otst Ac Ach Awd; Perf Att; Yth Ldrshp Prog; CARE; ArtClub; Chrch Yth Grp; Key Club; P to P St Amb Prg; Latin Clb; Dnce; Bskball (J); Cr Ctry (J); Sftball (J); Track (J); Gold Medal in National Junior Classical League for Latin Exam; B.S. in Biology; U of Virginia

PERKINS, TRINITY S; WOODBRIDGE, VA; HYLTON HS; (SR); Hnr Roll; St Schl; WWAHSS; Yth Ldrshp Prog; Comm Volntr; Chrch Yth Grp; Emplmnt; FCA; Quiz Bowl; Tchrs Aide; Ch Chr; Vllyball (J); Adv Cncl (R); Advisory Council-Parliamentarian; Elementary Education; Spanish; Old Dominion U; Christopher Newport U

PERO, AMBER; ROANOKE, VA; WILLIAM FLEMING HS; (JR); F Lan Hn Soc; Hnr Roll; Kwnis Aw; Sci Fairs; WWAHSS; Comm Volntr; Dbte Team; Drma Clb; Emplmnt; Key Club; NtlFrnscLg; Tchrs Aide; Clb; SP/M/VS; Stg Cre; Key Club Secretary-3 yrs/Theater Board of Dir.; French Honor Society; Science; Roanoke College; U of Virginia

PERRELLA, ELIZABETH M; VIRGINIA BEACH, VA; FIRST COLONIAL HS; (FR); Ctznshp Aw; Hnr Roll; Otst Ac Ach Awd; St of Mnth; Key Club; Track (L); Veterinarian; Criminal Science; Pennsylvania State U; Virginia Tech

PERSONIUS, LAURA L; FREDERICKSBURG, VA; COURTLAND HS; (SR); Hnr Roll; Nat Hon Sy; WWAHSS; Comm Volntr; Dbte Team; Drma Clb; Off Aide; Bnd; Fld Hky (VJC); PP Ftbl (V); Novice Debate Team 2002-03; Novice Debate 2003-04; Marine Science; Music; Coastal Carolina U

PETERS, SARAH A; HARRISONBURG, VA; SPOTSWOOD HS; (SR); F Lan Hn Soc; Hnr Roll; Nat Hon Sy; Perf Att; Valdctrian; Peer Tut/Med; Chrch Yth Grp; Emplmnt; FBLA; Mus Clb; NtlFrnscLg; Tchrs Aide; Spanish Clb; Bnd; Ch Chr; Drm Mjr; Mch Bnd; Medallion Awards; Wellesley College Book Award; Economics; Political Science; Lynchburg College

PETERSEN, DANIEL B; SALEM, VA; SALEM HS; (SO); F Lan Hn Soc; Hi Hnr Roll; MVP; Nat Hon Sy; Otst Ac Ach Awd; Pres Ac Ftns Aw; St of Mnth; Comm Volntr; Svce Clb; Spanish Clb; Chr; Ch Chr; Cr Ctry (V L); Sccr (V L); Eagle Scout; Construction Management; Pilot; Brigham Young U; U of Virginia

PETERSON, BRITTANY; FAIRFAX STATION, VA; ROBINSON SECONDARY SCH; (JR); F Lan Hn Soc; Hnr Roll; Nat Hon Sy; St of Mnth; Comm Volntr; DECA; Pep Squd; Spanish Clb; Dnce; Drl Tm; International Baccalaureate Diploma Candidate; Film Production; Marketing; U of Miami Florida; Virginia Tech

PETERSON, KATHERINE M; ASHBURN, VA; BROAD RUN HS; (JR); Hi Hnr Roll; Nat Hon Sy; Otst Ac Ach Awd; WWAHSS; Yth Ldrshp Prog; Comm Volntr; Peer Tut/Med; Chrch Yth Grp; Emplmnt; HO'Br Yth Ldrshp; Key Club; Lib Aide; Mod UN; Off Aide; Schol Bwl; Bnd; PP Ftbl (J); Track (J); Board of Directors, Girl Scout Council of the Nation's Capital; Executive Officer, Government and History Club; Cultural Anthropology; Randolph-Macon Woman's College; College of William & Mary

PETERSON, SHANICE R; WARFIELD, VA; BRUNSWICK SR HS; (JR); Hnr Roll; Business Administration; Cosmetologist; Virginia State U; Virginia Commonwealth U

PETTY, JOVAN K; CUMBERLAND, VA; CUMBERLAND HS; (SO); 4H Awd; Hnr Roll; Perf Att; St of Mnth; 4-H; Chrch Yth Grp; Dbte Team; FBLA; HO'Br Yth Ldrshp; Schol Bwl; Dnce; SP/M/VS; Track (V); Vllyball (J); Sch Ppr (R); Yrbk (P); Most Outstanding Student (3 Times); Track-Sprinter of the Year (2004); Journalism; Communications; American U; Howard U

PETWAY, SHARON; CHESTERFIELD, VA; LLOYD C BIRD HS; (JR); Hnr Roll; Jr Mshl; Nat Hon Sy; Otst Ac Ach Awd; Perf Att; WWAHSS; Peer Tut/Med; Drma Clb; Jr Cls League; Key Club; P to P St Amb Prg; French Clb; Bnd; Jzz Bnd; Mch Bnd; Pep Bnd; Sccr (J); Student Exchange Program to France; Music-History/Theory & Performance-Literature; French; U of Richmond; U of Virginia

PHAM, LINDA; ROANOKE, VA; WILLIAM FLEMING HS; (JR); F Lan Hn Soc; Hnr Roll; Nat Ldrshp Svc; Perf Att; Sci Fairs; Comm Volntr; Peer Tut/Med; Key Club; Ntl Beta Clb; Off Aide; Tchrs Aide; French Clb; Lit Mag (E); Presidential Classroom Alumni; Best All Around Female in 11th Grade; Business; Pharmaceuticals; Virginia Commonwealth U; U of North Carolina in Greensboro

PHAM-NGUYEN, TRANG T; SPRINGFIELD, VA; ANNANDALE HS; (FR); Hnr Roll; Perf Att; Sci Fairs; WWAHSS; Chrch Yth Grp; Drma Clb; Emplmnt; FCA; Mth Clb/Tm; SP/M/VS; Track (J); Vllyball (J); Video Production Club; Movie Club; Arts; Medicine; Virginia Commonwealth U; Christopher Newport U

PHELPS, JOSCELLYN; PETERSBURG, VA; EVANGEL CHRISTIAN; (JR); Hnr Roll; MVP; Otst Ac Ach Awd; Perf Att; Pres Ac Ftns Aw; WWAHSS; Comm Volntr; Spec Olymp Vol; 4-H; Chrch Yth Grp; DECA; Emplmnt; FBLA; SADD; Mch Bnd; Bskball (V C); Vllyball (V); Computer Science; Business Administration; Christopher Newport U; Elon U

PHILLIPS, ALYSA D; VIRGINIA BEACH, VA; FLOYD E KELLAM HS; (JR); Ctznshp Aw; Hnr Roll; Otst Ac Ach Awd; St of Mnth; Comm Volntr; Chrch Yth Grp; DECA; Chr; Cash Award for Leadership; Co-Op Achievement Award; Bachelor's Degree in Teaching; Degree in Performing Arts; Berklee School of Music; Indiana U

PHILYAW, TRAVIS J; PORTSMOUTH, VA; STONEBRIDGE HS; (JR); Hi Hnr Roll; Hnr Roll; Nat Hon Sy; Comm Volntr; AL Aux Boys; Drma Clb; Emplmnt; Key Club; Bnd; SP/M/VS; CR (P); Yrbk; Standard of Excellence Award in English; Business; Old Dominion U; William and Mary

PHO, NHIEN; SPRINGFIELD, VA; ROBERT E LEE HS; (SR); F Lan Hn Soc; Hi Hnr Roll; Hnr Roll; Nat Hon Sy; Perf Att; Pres Ac Ftns Aw; Sci Fairs; Sci/Math Olympn; St of Mnth; WWAHSS; Comm Volntr; Peer Tut/Med; BPA; Chrch Yth Grp; Emplmnt; FBLA; Key Club; Mth Clb/Tm; MuAlphaTh; Prom Com; Ch Chr; Dnce; SP/M/VS; Lcrsse (JC); CR; Varsity Letter - Academics; Anesthesiology; Biology; George Mason U

PICKENS, TYNEISHA; FARMVILLE, VA; CUMBERLAND HS; (SO); Hnr Roll; Perf Att; Comm Volntr; 4-H; Chrch Yth Grp; DARE; Drma Clb; FBLA; Tchrs Aide; Chr; Ch Chr; Poetry Contest; Virginia State; Longwood U

PICKETT, COLLEEN; MANASSAS, VA; OSBOURN PARK SR HS; (JR); Hnr Roll; Nat Hon Sy; WWAHSS; Comm Volntr; DECA; FBLA; Key Club; Prom Com; Chr; Cl Off (S, R); Academic Letter Recipient; Homecoming Committee; Marketing; Old Dominion U; George Mason U

PIPPIN, LYNDSEY A; LYNCHBURG, VA; E C GLASS HS; (SR); Hi Hnr Roll; Hnr Roll; Nat Hon Sy; WWAHSS; Yth Ldrshp Prog; Comm Volntr; Chrch Yth Grp; Emplmnt; FCA; Mth Clb/Tm; Prom Com; Bnd; Clr Grd; Dnce; Mch Bnd; Sccr (V); Sftball (V); Vllyball (V); Adv Cncl (S); Cl Off (S); Stu Cncl (T, R); CR (R); National Latin Exam-Highest Award; Most Improved Color Guard; Nursing; Liberty U

POLLY, MICHELLE; MONTROSS, VA; WASHINGTON & LEE HS; (SO); Ctznshp Aw; Hnr Roll; Perf Att; St of Mnth; 4-H; Bnd; FCCLA (L); Journalism/Photography

PONCE, VICTOR M; WOODBRIDGE, VA; OSBOURN PARK HS; (JR); Fut Prb Slvr; Nat Hon Sy; Comm Volntr; Peer Tut/Med; Emplmnt; Key Club; Tchrs Aide; National Honor Society; Electrical Engineering; Mechanical Engineering; Virginia Tech; Duke

POOLE, CAITLIN; ASHBURN, VA; STONE BRIDGE HS; (SR); Hi Hnr Roll; Hnr Roll; Nat Hon Sy; Otst Ac Ach Awd; Pres Ac Ftns Aw; Comm Volntr; Peer Tut/Med; FTA; Key Club; Prom Com; Chrldg (JC); Lcrsse (V L); Vllyball (V L); Stu Cncl (R); CR (R); Lacrosse and Volleyball Manager Positions; Education; Psychology; James Madison U

POON, NGA-LAI; CENTREVILLE, VA; CENTREVILLE HS; (JR); Hi Hnr Roll; Hnr Roll; Nat Hon Sy; Perf Att; Sci Fairs; WWAHSS; Comm Volntr; Peer Tut/Med; Chess; Emplmnt; FBLA; Key Club; Mus Clb; French Clb; Orch; Clinical Psychology; Sociology; U of Virginia; College of William and Mary

POPE, MOLLY M; STAFFORD, VA; COLONIAL FORGE HS; (JR); Hi Hnr Roll; Hnr Roll; Otst Ac Ach Awd; Perf Att; St of Mnth; Comm Volntr; Spec Olymp Vol; Chrch Yth Grp; DARE; FBLA; Off Aide; Bnd; Ch Chr; Jzz Bnd; Mch Bnd; Bskball (J); Vllyball (VJ L); Physical Therapy; Shenandoah U; Old Dominion U

PORTER III, HARVEY L; RICHMOND, VA; VARINA HS; (JR); Gov Hnr Prg; Hnr Roll; WWAHSS; DECA; CR (R); Japanese I and II; French I and II; Computer Engineer; Video Game Designer; Virginia Polytechnic Institute; Virginia Commonwealth U

POTOSKY, LEAH; CHANTILLY, VA; CHANTILLY HS; (JR); WWAHSS; Comm Volntr; DECA; Swmg (V L); DECA President (2006); Business; Marketing; Virginia Tech; Christopher Newport U

POWELL, DOMINIQUE J J; STAFFORD, VA; NORTH STAFFORD HS; MS; Hnr Roll; Otst Ac Ach Awd; St of Mnth; Comm Volntr; DARE; SP/M/VS; Bskball (V); Vllyball (V); Seeds Awards for Church; Doctor; An Actress; U of California, Los Angeles; Xavier U, LA

POWELL, RASHID; RICHMOND, VA; VARINA HS; (FR); Ctznshp Aw; Hnr Roll; Perf Att; Comm Volntr; Chess; Stu Cncl (T); Advanced SOL Scores in Advanced Classes; Electronics; Science; Duke U; Princeton U

POWERS, JACOB D; CHESAPEAKE, VA; DEEP CREEK HS; (SO); Ctznshp Aw; Hnr Roll; MVP; Perf Att; St of Mnth; Comm Volntr; Drma Clb; Emplmnt; Key Club; Lib Aide; Mus Clb; Prom Com; SADD; Acpl Chr; Chr; Adv Cncl (R); CR (R); District Chorus 2005; Superior Achievement Award in Chorus; Public Relations and Organizational Management; Business Management; State U of New York At Buffalo; San Diego State U

PRESNELL, WILLIAM; RICHLANDS, VA; RICHLANDS HS; (FR); Ctznshp Aw; Hnr Roll; Pres Ac Ftns Aw; Pres Sch; Sci Fairs; Sci/Math Olympn; NtlFrnscLg; Ftball (V); Tennis (V); Sports Medicine; Physical Therapy; U of Virginia; U of North Carolina

PRICE, DAN; CHANTILLY, VA; WESTFIELD HS; (JR); Hnr Roll; Perf Att; WWAHSS; Comm Volntr; Chrch Yth Grp; Civil Air Pat; Emplmnt; Mth Clb/Tm; Mus Clb; Sci Clb; Bnd; Jzz Bnd; Mch Bnd; Orch; Junior Math Team Top Scorer; Engineering; Music Industry; Virginia Poly Technical and State U; James Madison U

PRICE, KIMBERLY; RICHMOND, VA; VARINA HS; (FR); Hnr Roll; Nat Hon Sy; St of Mnth; WWAHSS; Peer Tut/Med; Key Club; Chrldg (J L); Sftball (J); Sch Ppr (R); Competition Cheers for an Organization Outside of School; William & Mary

PRIMUS, JASON; FORT EUSTIS, VA; WOODSIDE HS; (JR); Hnr Roll; Perf Att; Pres Ac Ftns Aw; Yth Ldrshp Prog; Comm Volntr; Peer Tut/Med; DARE; FCA; Jr Ach; Lib Aide; Mus Clb; Quiz Bowl; Spch Team; Ch Chr; Ftball (J); National Public Speaker; Johns Hopkins U PhD; Medical Doctor MD; Johns Hopkins U; Oakwood College

PRITCHARD, LINDSEY P; WILLIAMSBURG, VA; (JR); Hnr Roll; Perf Att; Peer Tut/Med; ArtClub; Chrch Yth Grp; Emplmnt; Photog; Bnd; Mch Bnd; Art Education; Psychology; Mary Washington

PRITCHETT, TEMPEST; RICHMOND, VA; HUGUENOT HS; (JR); Ctznshp Aw; F Lan Hn Soc; Hi Hnr Roll; Perf Att; WWAHSS; Comm Volntr; Spec Olymp Vol; Dbte Team; FBLA; Ntl Beta Clb; ROTC; Sci Clb; Scouts; Clb; Clr Grd; Drl Tm; criminal justice as a college major; to attend law school after college and become a lawyer; Brown U, Rhode Island; U of Virginia, Virginia

PROCTOR, EMILY A; ASHBURN, VA; STONE BRIDGE HS; (JR); Hnr Roll; Pres Ac Ftns Aw; Comm Volntr; Chrch Yth Grp; Emplmnt; FCA; Key Club; Chr; Ch Chr; PP Ftbl (J); Track (J); Vllyball (J); CR (R); Manager for Freshman Basketball; All County & All District Chorus; Education; Psychology; Christopher Newport U; James Madison U

PUGH, SARAH; CHARLOTTE C H, VA; RANDOLPH HENRY HS; (SO); Ctznshp Aw; Hnr Roll; Nat Hon Sy; WWAHSS; DARE; FBLA; Jr Ach; Ch Chr; Bskball (J); Sftball (JC); Swmg (J); Public Accounting; CPA; Longwood U; Radford U

QUADE, BEN; CHARLOTTESVILLE, VA; MONTICELLO HS; (JR); Hnr Roll; Nat Hon Sy; WWAHSS; Yth Ldrshp Prog; Comm Volntr; Emplmnt; Latin Clb; Cr Ctry (V); Track (V); Stu Cncl (S); Multiple Honor Societies / National, Math, Leadership - 2 Yrs; Engineering; Medicine; U of VA

QUERRY, SAMANTHA; MANASSAS, VA; (JR); Hnr Roll; WWAHSS; Key Club; Lcrsse (J); Veterinarian; Medicine; Virginia Tech

QUESENBERRY, JOSEPH; STUART, VA; PATRICK CTY HS; (SO); Hnr Roll; Nat Stu Ath Day Aw; Perf Att; Peer Tut/Med; Chrch Yth Grp; Emplmnt; FCA; Bnd; Ch Chr; Jzz Bnd; Mch Bnd; Cl Off (T); Stu Cncl (S, T); CR (R); Marching Band-Letter; Medical Field; Music Field; Virginia Tech; Radford U

QUESNEL, SUZANNE C E; CARROLLTON, VA; SMITHFIELD HS; (JR); Hi Hnr Roll; Hnr Roll; Perf Att; WWAHSS; Comm Volntr; Chrch Yth Grp; Emplmnt; Key Club; Mth Clb/Tm; Ntl Beta Clb; Scouts; French Clb; Orch; PP Ftbl; Stu Cncl (R); Forensic Science; Human Medicine; Eastern Virginia Medical School; Old Dominion U

QUICK, ERICKA; CHESAPEAKE, VA; GREAT BRIDGE HS; (FR); Ctznshp Aw; Hnr Roll; Pres Ac Ftns Aw; Sci Fairs; St of Mnth; WWAHSS; Comm Volntr; Chrch Yth Grp; Key Club; French Clb; Bnd; Chr; Ch Chr; Got Award for Most Outstanding in World History; Pre-Law; Art History; Oklahoma U; New York U

QUINN, KALA; VIRGINIA BEACH, VA; BRANDON MS; (MS); Hnr Roll; Nat Hon Sy; ArtClub; Chrch Yth Grp; DARE; Mus Clb; Scouts; Bnd; Jzz Bnd; National Junior Honor Society; Animator / Cartoonist; Voice Actor; U of Virginia

QUINTERO, CLAUDIA; FALLS CHURCH, VA; BISHOP O CONNELL HS; (SO); F Lan Hn Soc; Hnr Roll; Sci Fairs; Key Club; Spanish Clb; Dnce; Spanish Honor Society; President of Latin RHC/THMS Dance; Architecture; International Relations, Psychology; U of Virginia; William & Mary

RAFFO, TATIANNA; ASHBURN, VA; BROAD RUN HS; (JR); Hnr Roll; Nat Hon Sy; St of Mnth; WWAHSS; Comm Volntr; Emplmnt; Key Club; Prom Com; Sccr (V); Vllyball (V); Forensic Science; Marymount U; U of Virginia

RAFUS, SAMANTHA N; VIRGINIA BEACH, VA; KELLAM HS; (JR); Hnr Roll; WWAHSS; Chrch Yth Grp; Emplmnt; Wdwrkg Clb; Bnd; Mch Bnd; Pep Bnd; Band Manager; Pastry Chef; Johnson and Wales U

RAGSDALE, SCARLETT E; SOUTH BOSTON, VA; HALIFAX CTY HS; (SO); Hnr Roll; Scouts; Dental Hygienist; Old Dominion U; NC State U

RAINES, JESSIE; WAYNESBORO, VA; WAYNESBORO HS; (JR); Hi Hnr Roll; Hnr Roll; Key Club; Ntl Beta Clb; Chr; Sccr (J); Tennis (V); Vllyball (J); CR (R); James Madison U

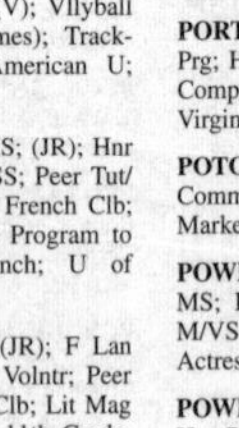
Powell, Dominique J J
North Stafford HS
Stafford, VA

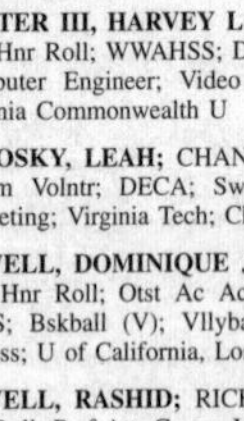
Polly, Michelle
Washington & Lee HS
Montross, VA

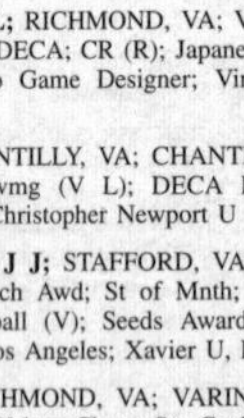
Perrella, Elizabeth M
First Colonial HS
Virginia Beach, VA

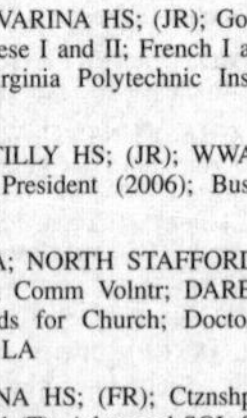
Phillips, Alysa D
Floyd E Kellam HS
Virginia Beach, VA

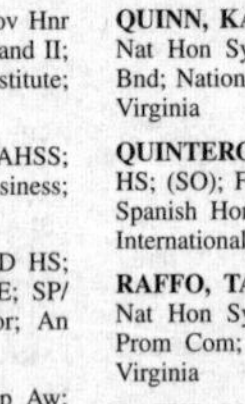
Quinn, Kala
Brandon MS
Virginia Beach, VA

RALSTON, ANNE; EARLYSVILLE, VA; ALBERMARLE HS; (SR); F Lan Hn Soc; Hi Hnr Roll; Hnr Roll; Otst Ac Ach Awd; Perf Att; WWAHSS; ArtClub; Emplmnt; Jr Cls League; Key Club; MuAlphaTh; Ntl Beta Clb; Prom Com; Cr Ctry (VJ); Lcrsse (VJCL); PP Ftbl (VJ); Track (J); Cl Off (S); CR (R); Blue Ridge Lacrosse Club Team; Athletic Training; Kinesiology; James Madison U

RAMEY, DEIDRA A; CLINTWOOD, VA; CLINTWOOD HS; (JR); Hnr Roll; Nat Hon Sy; Otst Ac Ach Awd; WWAHSS; 4-H; DECA; Drma Clb; FCA; Key Club; Prom Com; Sci Clb; SP/M/VS; Chrldg (VJ); Yrbk (R); Mathematics; Foreign Language; U of Virginia College Wise; U of Tennessee

RAMEY, SAMANTHA; BRISTOL, VA; GATE CITY HS; (SO); Hnr Roll; Perf Att; Comm Volntr; Hosp Aide; Peer Tut/Med; Key Club; Ch Chr; Nursing Degree; UVA Wise; Mountain Empire Community College

RAMOS, VERONICA; FREDERICKSBURG, VA; MASSAPONAX HS; (JR); F Lan Hn Soc; Gov Hnr Prg; Hnr Roll; Nat Hon Sy; Otst Ac Ach Awd; Pres Ac Ftns Aw; Pres Sch; Sci Fairs; Comm Volntr; Peer Tut/Med; Aqrium Clb; Chrch Yth Grp; Emplmnt; Off Aide; P to P St Amb Prg; French Clb; Chr; Ch Chr; SP/M/VS; Bskball (J); PP Ftbl; Swmg (V L); Track (V); Young Woman of the Year- Knights of Columbus - 2005; Youth Group President - St Jude's Church; Political Science; Travel; United States Naval Academy; U of VA

RAMUS-JONES, JANELLE A; NORFOLK, VA; NORFOLK COLLEGIATE SCH; (JR); Hnr Roll; Nat Hon Sy; Comm Volntr; Chrch Yth Grp; Emplmnt; Lcrsse (V); Lit Mag; Won National French Exam-3rd and 7th in State; Had an Essay Published on the Online Local Newspaper; International Business; Journalism; New York U; The College of William and Mary

RANDOF, TIFFANY; SKIPPERS, VA; GREENSVILLE CTY HS; (SO); Hnr Roll; Chrch Yth Grp; FBLA; Ntl Beta Clb; Quiz Bowl; SADD; Bnd; Sftball (V); Vllyball (J); Sch Ppr (R); Law; Journalism; Louisiana State U; Texas Madison U

RANGI, MANPREET; CENTREVILLE, VA; CENTREVILLE HS; (SO); Hnr Roll; Nat Hon Sy; Otst Ac Ach Awd; WWAHSS; Key Club; Key Club Member; Arts & Entertainment; Computer Graphics; U of Virginia; Virginia Tech

RANLIFF, CHANELL; RICHMOND, VA; BINFORD MS; (SR); Hnr Roll; Peer Tut/Med; Cmptr Clb; Dbte Team; FBLA; Computer Engineer; Music; Hampton U; Georgia State U

RAO, ANEESHA N; CENTREVILLE, VA; ROBINSON SECONDARY SCH; (FR); Bnd; Dnce; Won the "Honorable Delegation Award" at the Ivy League Model United Nations Conference; Won the Presidential Award for Excellence; Law; Political Science; New York U; Princeton U

RASHEED, MARIAM; ASHBURN, VA; BROAD RUN HS; (JR); Hnr Roll; Kwnis Aw; Nat Hon Sy; Otst Ac Ach Awd; Perf Att; Comm Volntr; Key Club; Muslim Student Association; BRACS; Lawyer; Interior Design; George Mason U

RASNAKE, KIMBERLY L; SWORDS CREEK, VA; HONAKER HS; (JR); Chrch Yth Grp; FCA; Ntl Beta Clb; SADD; Spanish Clb; Bnd; Clr Grd; Mch Bnd; Mountain Youth Drama; Biology; Chemistry; Southwest Virginia Community College

RATCLIFFE, TASHA E; DUBLIN, VA; PULASKI CTY HS; (SR); 4H Awd; Hnr Roll; Perf Att; Comm Volntr; 4-H; DECA; Ntl FFA; Chr; Sch Ppr; 4-H Since 3rd Grade; Head Teen Volunteer Service & Service Learning; Elementary Teacher; Horticulture & Landscape; New River Community College; Longwood U

RATLIFF, KAREN; GRUNDY, VA; BUCHANAN TECH & CAREER CTR & GHS; (SO); Ctznshp Aw; Hi Hnr Roll; Hnr Roll; Perf Att; Comm Volntr; Chrch Yth Grp; ROTC; Electrical Engineer; Neonatal RN; Wake Forest U; Morehead State U

RATLIFF, MONICA J; VANSANT, VA; HAYSI HS; (JR); FBLA; Key Club; Ntl Beta Clb; Chrldg (V); Vllyball (V); U of Virginia College At Wise

RAWLES, JESSICA; HAMPTON, VA; BETHEL HS; (SO); Ctznshp Aw; Hnr Roll; St of Mnth; Peer Tut/Med; Chrch Yth Grp; DARE; Mth Clb/Tm; ROTC; Spanish Clb; Ch Chr; Dnce; Drl Tm; Cl Off (V); Military Air Force; Medical Field; ODU; Florida State

RAYO, JORDAN; ANNANDALE, VA; ANNANDALE HS; (SO); Perf Att; DC Metro Poster Design Award 2001 - 2nd Place; Computer Graphics; Business/ Marketing Finance; U of Virginia; U of Mary Washington

RECUPERO, RYAN; RICHMOND, VA; LLOYD C BIRD HS; (SR); WWAHSS; Chrch Yth Grp; Emplmnt; FCA; Key Club; Off Aide; Photog; Prom Com; Chr; Dnce; GAA; Sccr (V CL); Sftball (J); Adv Cncl; Cl Off (V); Sportsmanship Award - Soccer; Most Improved - Soccer; Meteorology; Earth Science; Richard Bland College; Old Dominion U

REED, CAROLINE; WILLIAMSBURG, VA; LAFAYETTE HS; (JR); F Lan Hn Soc; Hi Hnr Roll; Hnr Roll; Nat Hon Sy; Perf Att; WWAHSS; Chrch Yth Grp; Key Club; Mod UN; MuAlphaTh; French Clb; Bnd; Mch Bnd; Pep Bnd; Bskball (V L); Cr Ctry (V L); Sccr (V L); Track (V L); Leo Club; Biology; Pre-Med

REEVES, ASHLEY; STAFFORD, VA; COLONIAL FORGE HS; (JR); Hnr Roll; Nat Hon Sy; Chrch Yth Grp; Emplmnt; NYLC; French Clb; Dnce; Jzz Bnd; French Club Secretary; Fashion Advisory Board; Political Science; French; Georgetown U; Brown U

REGINALDI, HEATHER M; ASHBURN, VA; STONE BRIDGE HS; (JR); Hnr Roll; DECA; Historian for DECA; Letter Winner for Academics; Marketing; Advertising; Virginia Polytechnic Institute and State U; George Mason U

REID, CIARA; MILLWOOD, VA; CLARKE CTY HS; (FR); Hnr Roll; Art; Taking Care of Mother; Art Major

REID, SUAVE; NASSAWADOX, VA; NORTHAMPTON HS; (FR); Ctznshp Aw; Hnr Roll; Perf Att; St of Mnth; Chrch Yth Grp; DARE; Drma Clb; Spch Team; Tchrs Aide; Vsity Clb; Wdwrkg Clb; Chr; Ch Chr; SP/M/VS; Stg Cre; Wrstlg (J); Management Classes; Study for Law

REILLY, COLIN; CHESAPEAKE, VA; STONE BRIDGE HS; (SO); Hi Hnr Roll; Hnr Roll; Nat Hon Sy; Comm Volntr; Chrch Yth Grp; Drma Clb; Key Club; Stg Cre; Bsball (V L); Bskball (VJ L); Computer Engineering; Virginia Polytechnic Institute

REILLY, MELISSA; CHARLOTTESVILLE, VA; ALBEMARLE HS; (SR); F Lan Hn Soc; Hnr Roll; Nat Hon Sy; WWAHSS; Emplmnt; Key Club; Quill & Scroll; Vsity Clb; Sccr (V L); Yrbk (E); Business; Virginia Polytechnic Institute

REITZ, DANIEL L; ROCKVILLE, VA; PATRICK HENRY HS; (JR); Hnr Roll; MVP; Perf Att; Quill & Scroll; MVP Defense Ashland Roller Hockey Senior JV; Defense Patrick Henry Roller Hockey JV Champion Team 2005; Music Video Production; James Madison U

REMENNIKOVA, RUSLANA; COLONIAL HEIGHTS, VA; COLONIAL HEIGHTS HS; (JR); F Lan Hn Soc; Hnr Roll; Nat Hon Sy; WWAHSS; Comm Volntr; Peer Tut/Med; Chess; Cmptr Clb; DECA; Drma Clb; Emplmnt; Key Club; Ntl Beta Clb; Pep Squd; Dnce; PP Ftbl (J); Tennis (VJ L); Adv Cncl (P); Sch Ppr (E); Player of the Year - 2003; Chemical Engineering; Virginia Commonwealth U

REMINGTON, CODY; ROANOKE, VA; PATRICK HENRY HS; (JR); Hi Hnr Roll; Hnr Roll; Nat Hon Sy; Sci Fairs; WWAHSS; Comm Volntr; Chrch Yth Grp; Emplmnt; FCA; Key Club; Off Aide; Tchrs Aide; Vsity Clb; Spanish Clb; Ch Chr; Cr Ctry (V L); Sccr (V); Track (VJ L); Adv Cncl (R); Law; Business; U of Virginia; Virginia Polytechnic Institute

RETTER, LEONARD; VIRGINIA BEACH, VA; LANDSTOWN HS; (SO); Hnr Roll; Perf Att; St of Mnth; Comm Volntr; Chrch Yth Grp; DECA; Emplmnt; FBLA; Jr Ach; French Clb; Swmg (V); Tennis (V); Stu Cncl; DECA Chapter Secretary; DECA State Competition Runner-Up; MBA; International Relations; U of Virginia; Columbia U

REVERE, NATHANIEL B; LOVETTSVILLE, VA; HOMESCHOOL; (JR); Hnr Roll; Nat Hon Sy; Comm Volntr; Drma Clb; Quiz Bowl; Japanese Clb; SP/M/VS; Stg Cre; Cr Ctry; Vllyball; National History Day Competition; Year Abroad in Japan; Japanese; Literature/Writing

REYNOLDS, AMANDA; MIDLOTHIAN, VA; MIDLOTHIAN HS; (SO); Hnr Roll; Chrch Yth Grp; Vllyball (J L); Honor Star in Missionetts; Journalism; Political Science; College of William and Mary; Marymount Manhattan

REYNOLDS, CHRISTINA J S; RICHLANDS, VA; RICHLANDS HS; (SO); Gov Hnr Prg; Hi Hnr Roll; Hnr Roll; WWAHSS; DARE; FBLA; Bnd; Mch Bnd; Pep Bnd; Track (V); Southwest Community College; East Tennessee State U

REYNOLDS, MELVIN L; NATHALIE, VA; HALIFAX CTY HS; (JR); Hnr Roll; MVP; Nat Hon Sy; Perf Att; Pres Ac Ftns Aw; WWAHSS; Yth Ldrshp Prog; AL Aux Boys; Chrch Yth Grp; Emplmnt; FBLA; Ntl FFA; P to P St Amb Prg; Prom Com; Schol Bwl; Ch Chr; Ftball (J L); Track (VJC); Cl Off (V); Stu Cncl (V, R); CR (R); Robotics Team; Ventures Scholar; Bio Medical Engineering; Computer Engineering; Norfolk State U; Virginia Commonwealth U

REYNOLDS, QUANEISHA; ROANOKE, VA; WILLIAM FLEMING HS; (FR); Hi Hnr Roll; MVP; Nat Hon Sy; Otst Ac Ach Awd; Perf Att; WWAHSS; Comm Volntr; Peer Tut/Med; Chrch Yth Grp; Key Club; Bnd; Ch Chr; Sftball (J); Track (J); Vllyball (JC); Neurosurgeon; Medical Chemist; Stanford U; Duke U

RICHARDS, AMBER; ROANOKE, VA; HIDDEN VALLEY HS; (JR); Pres Ac Ftns Aw; Emplmnt; Ntl Beta Clb; Pep Squd; Prom Com; Spanish Clb; Ch Chr; Dnce; Drl Tm; Sch Ppr (E); Lettered in Marching Band; Nomination for Governor's School of Dance; Dermatologist; U of Virginia; Vanderbilt U

RICHARDS, AMBER L; ROANOKE, VA; HIDDEN VALLEY HS; (JR); Hi Hnr Roll; Hnr Roll; Perf Att; WWAHSS; Chrch Yth Grp; Emplmnt; Ntl Beta Clb; Spanish Clb; Ch Chr; Dnce; Drl Tm; PP Ftbl (J); Stu Cncl (R); Sch Ppr (E); Beta President; Business Administration; Journalism; U of Virginia; James Madison U

RICHARDS, ERIC J; RESTON, VA; SOUTH LAKES HS; (SO); Hi Hnr Roll; Nat Hon Sy; St of Mnth; Comm Volntr; Tchrs Aide; Dnce; Computer Science; Engineer; U of Virginia; VA Tech-School of Engineering

RICHARDS, HEATHER E; MANASSAS, VA; PAUL IV CATHOLIC HS; (SR); Hnr Roll; Sci Fairs; WWAHSS; Comm Volntr; Peer Tut/Med; Key Club; Lib Aide; Scouts; Chr; Ch Chr; Stu Cncl (T); Paul VI Student Ambassador; Master's in Elementary Education; Lynchburg College

RICHARDS, JOHN H; LURAY, VA; LURAY HS; (SO); 4H Awd; F Lan Hn Soc; Hi Hnr Roll; MVP; Nat Hon Sy; Nat Stu Ath Day Aw; Pres Ac Ftns Aw; Sci Fairs; WWAHSS; Yth Ldrshp Prog; Comm Volntr; 4-H; Chrch Yth Grp; DARE; Emplmnt; FCA; Mth Clb/Tm; SADD; Vsity Clb; Ftball (V CL); Track (V CL); Wt Lftg (V CL); CR

RICHARDS, LINDSEY; LURAY, VA; LURAY HS; (FR); Hnr Roll; Emplmnt; Chrldg (V); Fashion Designing; Nursing

RICHARDSON, ANGEL; GRETNA, VA; GRETNA HS; (SR); Ctznshp Aw; Hnr Roll; Nat Hon Sy; Nat Sci Aw; USAA; WWAHSS; Comm Volntr; Biology Clb; Emplmnt; FBLA; Ntl Beta Clb; Sci Clb; Chr; Adv Cncl (T); Stu Cncl (T); Certified Nursing License; U.S. Student Council Award; Registered Nursing; Danville Community College; Danville Regional Medical Center School of Nursing

RICHARDSON, AUTUMN A; NEWPORT NEWS, VA; WOODSIDE HS; (JR); Hi Hnr Roll; Hnr Roll; WWAHSS; Comm Volntr; Emplmnt; Mod UN; Japanese Clb; Lit Mag (E); Medical Science; Criminal Law; The College of William and Mary; Old Dominion U

RICHTER, NATASHA; FAIRFAX, VA; PAUL VI CATHOLIC HS; (SO); Ctznshp Aw; Hi Hnr Roll; Otst Ac Ach Awd; Sci Fairs; St Optmst of Yr; Peer Tut/Med; Key Club; Mth Clb/Tm; Svce Clb; Spanish Clb; SP/M/VS; Tennis (J); Sch Ppr (E, R); Student Leadership Youth Corps; It's Academic; Medicine; Neurosurgical Degree; U of Virginia; Virginia Polytechnic Institute and State U

RICKARD, JESSICA N; ORANGE, VA; ORANGE CTY HS; (FR); Hnr Roll; Comm Volntr; ROTC; Dnce; FCCLA; Degree in Criminal Justice; Liberty U; Harvard

RICKERD, SHELLY; ROANOKE, VA; PATRICK HENRY HS; (SO); Ctznshp Aw; Hnr Roll; Perf Att; St of Mnth; WWAHSS; Comm Volntr; Photog; Clr Grd; Flg Crps; Mch Bnd; Longwood U; U of South Carolina

RIDDLE, JUSTON R; CHATHAM, VA; CHATHAM HS; (FR); Ctznshp Aw; Hnr Roll; Perf Att; WWAHSS; Ntl Beta Clb; Ntl FFA; ROTC; Help Parents on 105 Acre Farm with Livestock / Garden / Greenhouse; Help Parents Run Greenhouse Business / Helps Father Run Construction Business; Marine Biologist; Biologist; College of William and Mary; U of Georgia

RIDGEWAY, KATIE; MANASSAS, VA; OSBOURN HS; (SO); Hnr Roll; Peer Tut/Med; DARE; Key Club; Dnce; SP/M/VS; Virginia Commonwealth Governors School; Environmental Science; U of Virginia

RIGGS, DAVID; COLONIAL BEACH, VA; WASHINGTON & LEE HS; (FR); Ctznshp Aw; Hnr Roll; Perf Att; Sci/Math Olympn; ArtClub; Chess; Cmptr Clb; Photog; Tech Clb; Ftball (J); Sccr (J); Art/Anime; Computer or Video Game Design

RILEY II, ANTHONY; WINCHESTER, VA; JAMES WOOD HS; (SO); Hnr Roll; Otst Ac Ach Awd; Perf Att; St of Mnth; Always Been on Honor Roll; Plan to Take 5 Years of Spanish in High School; Accounting; Federal Law Enforcement; James Madison U; Virginia Tech

RINEHART, LAURI; ASHBURN, VA; BROAD RUN HS; (JR); Ctznshp Aw; Hnr Roll; Nat Hon Sy; Otst Ac Ach Awd; Pres Ac Ftns Aw; WWAHSS; Comm Volntr; Peer Tut/Med; Spec Olymp Vol; Emplmnt; Key Club; Prom Com; SADD; Dnce; Bskball (VJ L); Sccr (J); Adv Cncl (R); Stu Cncl (R); CR (R); Virginia Tech; James Madison U

RISTOW, ANNA K; NEWPORT NEWS, VA; MENCHVILLE HS; (SR); Hi Hnr Roll; Nat Hon Sy; Otst Ac Ach Awd; Perf Att; Spec Olymp Vol; Chrch Yth Grp; Vsity Clb; Bnd; Mch Bnd; Bskball (J); Sftball (V CL); Track (V L); Vsy Clb (V L); Human Biology / Sports Training; Pediatrics; Bethany Lutheran College

RIVERA, TATIANA; HAMPTON, VA; BETHEL HS; (SO); Ctznshp Aw; Hnr Roll; Perf Att; Comm Volntr; Chrch Yth Grp; Mus Clb; ROTC; Acpl Chr; Chr; Ch Chr; Sccr (J); Lit Mag (R); YCOPE - Youth Corp on Public Envolvement; Jag Officer in Navy; Music Major; Christopher Newport U; Virginia Commonwealth U

RIZZIO, MELISSA A; CHESAPEAKE, VA; HICKORY HS; (SR); Hnr Roll; Nat Hon Sy; Otst Ac Ach Awd; DARE; Emplmnt; Lit Mag (E); Art I Student of the Year; Arts and Crafts Student of the Year; Journalism; Massage Therapy; Virginia Commonwealth U; Christopher Newport U

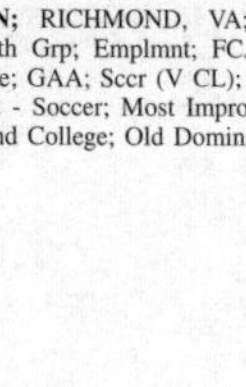
Riggs, David
Washington & Lee HS
Colonial Beach, VA

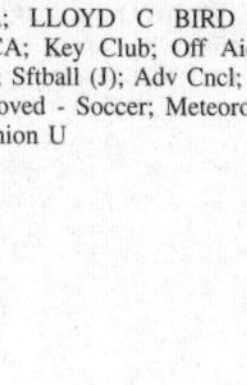
Retter, Leonard
Landstown HS
Virginia Beach, VA

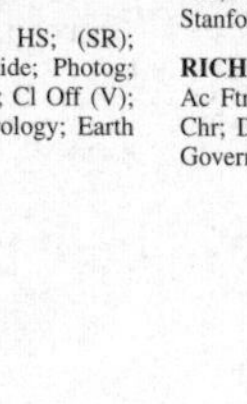
Ratliff, Monica J
Haysi HS
Vansant, VA

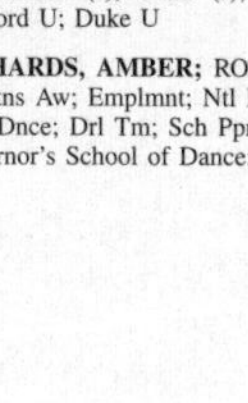
Ratcliffe, Tasha E
Pulaski Cty HS
Dublin, VA

National
Honor Roll
Spring 2005

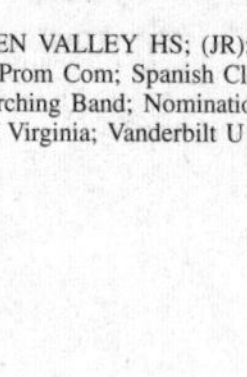
Ramos, Veronica
Massaponax HS
Fredericksburg, VA

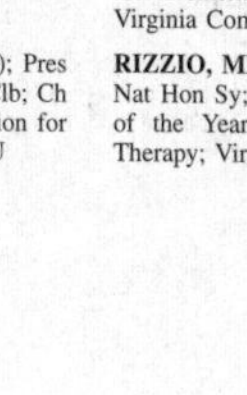
Reid, Ciara
Clarke Cty HS
Millwood, VA

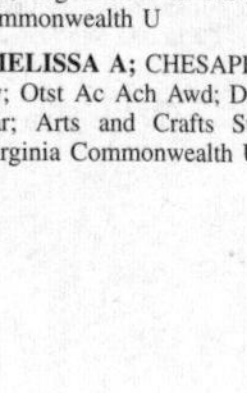
Rickard, Jessica N
Orange Cty HS
Orange, VA

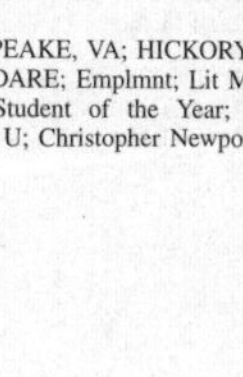
Riley II, Anthony
James Wood HS
Winchester, VA

ROACH, ANDY; VIENNA, VA; FLINT HILL SCH; (SR); Hi Hnr Roll; MVP; Golf (V); Swmg (V); Adv Cncl (P); Husky Award-Golf; Capt Golf Team 2002, 2003, 2004; William-Mary Leadership Award

ROACH, KASEY M; DANVILLE, VA; WESTOVER CHRISTIAN AC; (MS); Hi Hnr Roll; Perf Att; Pres Ac Ftns Aw; Chrch Yth Grp; Mus Clb; Chr; Dnce; Chrldg (JC); Forensic Science; Law; Liberty U; Virginia Tech

ROAN, COREY; VIRGINIA BEACH, VA; FLOYD KELLAM HS; (JR); Hnr Roll; Nat Hon Sy; Emplmnt; NtlFrnscLg; Vsity Clb; Bskball (J L); Sccr (V L); Law; Journalism; U of North Carolina At Wilmington; Elon U

ROANE DAVIS, ALEXANDRA T; NEWPORT NEWS, VA; WOODSIDE HS; (FR); Hi Hnr Roll; Hnr Roll; Nat Hon Sy; Perf Att; Pres Ac Ftns Aw; Sci Fairs; Red Cr Aide; Chrch Yth Grp; DARE; Drma Clb; Outdrs Clb; Scouts; Spanish Clb; Chr; SP/M/VS; Stg Cre; Chrldg (J); Fld Hky (J); Cl Off (P); Virginia General Assembly House of Delegates Page; Medicine; Psychiatry; Theater Arts; William and Mary College; Virginia Commonwealth U

ROBAIR, KALIA A; CAPE CHARLES, VA; NORTHAMPTON HS; (SO); Hnr Roll; Comm Volntr; ArtClub; Photog; Poetry-Published; Culinary Arts, Sculpture; Business Class; Johnson & Wales U

ROBBINS, AARON; NORFOLK, VA; NORFOLK COLLEGIATE MID-UPR SCH; (SR); All Am Sch; F Lan Hn Soc; Hi Hnr Roll; Hnr Roll; Nat Hon Sy; Perf Att; USAA; WWAHSS; Comm Volntr; French Clb; Yrbk (E, R); The Virginian Pilot Scholastic Team; Norfolk Collegiate Honor Council; Old Dominion U

ROBERSON, ASHLEIGH; FREDERICKSBURG, VA; MASSAPONAX HS; (SO); Hnr Roll; WWAHSS; Chrch Yth Grp; DECA; Emplmnt; FCA; FBLA; FTA; Scouts; Ch Chr; Fld Hky (J); Girl Scout-Gold Award; DECA Officer; Special Ed Sign Language; Seclusion/ 1D Classes; Christopher Newport; Old Dominion

ROBERTS, REBECCA L; CLINTWOOD, VA; CLINTWOOD HS; (SO); Hnr Roll; WWAHSS; DECA; Key Club; Bskball (JC); Sftball (J); Tennis (V L); Vllyball (V L); Geology; Crime Scene Investigation

ROBERTSON, BLAIR J; WAYNESBORO, VA; WAYNESBORO HS; (SO); Ctznshp Aw; F Lan Hn Soc; Hi Hnr Roll; Perf Att; Pres Ac Ftns Aw; Sci Fairs; WWAHSS; Comm Volntr; Hab For Humty Volntr; Chrch Yth Grp; Key Club; Lib Aide; Latin Clb; Chr; Swmg (V); Tennis (V); Vllyball (V); CR (P); VP Latin Club; VP Key Club; Pre-Med; UVA; College of William & Mary

ROBERTSON, JAZMINE; SMITHFIELD, VA; SMITHFIELD HS; (FR); Fut Prb Slvr; Hi Hnr Roll; WWAHSS; Peer Tut/Med; Chrch Yth Grp; FBLA; Jr Cls League; Key Club; Ntl Beta Clb; Ch Chr; Chrldg (J); A Career in Pathology; U of Virginia

ROBERTSON JR, JOHN B; ROANOKE, VA; PATRICK HENRY HS; DAR; Hnr Roll; Sci Fairs; Comm Volntr; Chrch Yth Grp; Emplmnt; Scouts; Sccr (J); U of North Carolina-Chapel Hill

ROBINSON, ALYSHIG R; RICHMOND, VA; VARINA HS; (SR); All Am Sch; Hnr Roll; Nat Hon Sy; WWAHSS; Comm Volntr; FTA; Key Club; Ntl Beta Clb; Quill & Scroll; Tchrs Aide; Spanish Clb; Clr Grd; Sch Ppr (E, R, P); Barbizon Modeling Academy Graduate; Business Management; Fashion Design; Hampton U; Virginia Commonwealth U

ROBINSON, JEREL; RICHMOND, VA; VARINA HS; Chrch Yth Grp; Emplmnt; Ftball (VJC); Track (V)

ROBINSON, RACHEL; CHESAPEAKE, VA; DEEP CREEK HS; (JR); Hnr Roll; Comm Volntr; FTA; ROTC; Scouts; Drl Tm; JROTC; Master's Degree in Elementary Education; Bachelor's Degree in Secondary Education; Old Dominion U; Washington State

ROBISON, NICHOLE A; MANASSAS, VA; BRENTSVILLE DISTRICT HS; MS; Ctznshp Aw; St of Mnth; Yth Ldrshp Prog; Comm Volntr; Chrch Yth Grp; Drma Clb; Fr of Library; Mus Clb; Scouts; Tchrs Aide; Chr; Ch Chr; SP/M/VS; Cr Ctry (J); Belong to IMTA / L & M Modeling Agency; Girl Scout Silver Award; Communication Degrees; Teaching Degree

ROCKWOOD, ASHLEY; COLONIAL BEACH, VA; COLONIAL BEACH HS; (FR); 4H Awd; Hnr Roll; Perf Att; St of Mnth; Comm Volntr; Hosp Aide; Drma Clb; Spanish Clb; Dnce; Scr Kpr (J); Sccr (J); CR; Defense Lawyer; Bowie U

RODEBAUGH, STASE L; FREDERICKSBURG, VA; COLONIAL FORGE HS; (JR); Hi Hnr Roll; Nat Hon Sy; Otst Ac Ach Awd; WWAHSS; Comm Volntr; Chrch Yth Grp; Key Club; Spanish Clb; Swmg (V L); Tennis (J); Lit Mag (R); Spanish Club Secretary; Babysitter - Red Cross Certified; Education / Teacher; English; Central Michigan U; U of California San Diego

RODGERS, JESSICA; SALEM, VA; SALEM HS; (SO); F Lan Hn Soc; Hnr Roll; Nat Hon Sy; Perf Att; Comm Volntr; Chrch Yth Grp; Latin Clb; Chr; Ch Chr; Dnce; Scr Kpr (J); Track (J); English Major; U of Virginia; Radford U

ROGERS, AMANDA; ASHBURN, VA; BROAD RUN HS; (SO); Hnr Roll; Nat Hon Sy; Perf Att; Pres Ac Ftns Aw; Comm Volntr; Peer Tut/Med; Emplmnt; Key Club; Tchrs Aide; Chrldg (VJ L); Wt Lftg; Freshman Homecoming Princess / Varsity Competitive Cheerleader; Semifinalist for International Poetry Contest; Communications; Education; Virginia Tech U; Radford U

ROGERSON, DAVID M; WINCHESTER, VA; MILLBROOK HS; (FR); Hnr Roll; Golf (J)

ROJAS, GABY F; RESTON, VA; SOUTH LAKES HS; (JR); Hi Hnr Roll; Hnr Roll; Nat Hon Sy; St of Mnth; Comm Volntr; Peer Tut/Med; ArtClub; Latin Clb; Taking Flight Ignite Mentor; Archaeology; History; William and Mary; U of Virginia

ROMERO, PAOLA; GAINESVILLE, VA; BATTLEFIELD HS; (JR); DAR; Hnr Roll; St of Mnth; DECA; Emplmnt; Photog; Forensic Science; Criminal Justice (Law); George Mason U; Marymount U

RONAYNE, MICHAEL; FAIRFAX, VA; (FR); MVP; Sci Fairs; St of Mnth; Yth Ldrshp Prog; Amnsty Intl; Comm Volntr; Chess; Chrch Yth Grp; Drma Clb; Scouts; Svce Clb; SP/M/VS; Mar Art; Adv Cncl (P); Toil Foundation for Africa (Fund Raising); Cystic Fibrosis Volunteer Fund Raiser; Science

RONQUEST, SAMANTHA; MONTPELIER, VA; PATRICK HENRY HS; (JR); Ctznshp Aw; F Lan Hn Soc; Hi Hnr Roll; Nat Hon Sy; Nat Mrt Semif; Otst Ac Ach Awd; Perf Att; USAA; WWAHSS; Yth Ldrshp Prog; Comm Volntr; Hab For Humty Volntr; Peer Tut/Med; Mth Clb/Tm; Ntl Beta Clb; Prom Com; Quill & Scroll; Tchrs Aide; Vsity Clb; French Clb; Dnce; PP Ftbl (V); Sftball (JC); CR (R); Sch Ppr (E, R); Yrbk (R); History & Education; Performing Arts; U of Richmond; Randolph Macon College

ROOT, LAUREN E; WINCHESTER, VA; MILLBROOK HS; (JR); Hnr Roll; Otst Ac Ach Awd; Perf Att; Pres Sch; Comm Volntr; Chrch Yth Grp; FCA; Scouts; Sccr (JCL); Track; Girl Scouting-Silver Award; Graphic Design; Virginia Tech; Longwood U

ROSALES, INGRID; MANASSAS, VA; OSBOURN HS; (JR); F Lan Hn Soc; Hnr Roll; Nat Hon Sy; Perf Att; WWAHSS; Comm Volntr; Emplmnt; FBLA; Key Club; Mus Clb; Clb; Chr; Lit Mag; I Want to Become a Lawyer.; Help my Community and Make My Culture Be Known To Everyone; George Madison, VA; College Of William and Mary, VA

ROSALES, KRISTINA; ALEXANDRIA, VA; EDISON HS; (JR); F Lan Hn Soc; Hi Hnr Roll; Hnr Roll; MVP; Nat Hon Sy; Otst Ac Ach Awd; WWAHSS; Comm Volntr; Red Cr Aide; DECA; Mod UN; Vllyball (V L); Adv Cncl (P); Stu Cncl (R); DECA (District President & Chapter VP); Model UN President; National Honor Society; International Relations; Georgetown U; George Washington U

ROSALES, PAOLA; FALLS CHURCH, VA; BISHOP IRETON HS; (JR); Hi Hnr Roll; Nat Hon Sy; Otst Ac Ach Awd; Comm Volntr; Spanish Clb; Biology; Veterinary Medicine; Loyola College in Maryland; St Josephs College in PA

ROSCHER, ERICH S; STAUNTON, VA; GRACE CHRISTIAN SCH; (JR); Hnr Roll; Comm Volntr; Chrch Yth Grp; Emplmnt; Scouts; Bsball (J); Sccr (VJ L); Tennis (J); Track (V); Aeronautical Engineering; Culinary; Virginia Tech; Liberty U

ROSE, ASHLEY; CLINTWOOD, VA; CLINTWOOD HS; (JR); Ctznshp Aw; Hnr Roll; Pres Ac Ftns Aw; WWAHSS; Spec Olymp Vol; 4-H; DECA; Drma Clb; FCA; FBLA; Key Club; Lttrmn Clb; Vsity Clb; Bskball (V C); Cr Ctry (V); Sftball (V); Track (V); Vllyball (V); CR (S); All LPD in Volleyball - First Team; Honorable Mention in Basketball; Physical Education; Business; East Tennessee State U; Radford U

ROTHMAN, DANIEL; STERLING, VA; POTOMAC FALLS HS; (SO); F Lan Hn Soc; Hi Hnr Roll; WWAHSS; Comm Volntr; Key Club; Bnd; Most Outstanding Math Student; Chemistry; Psychology; U of Virginia; James Madison U

ROTHRAUFF, CASSANDRA; STERLING, VA; POTOMAC FALLS HS; (SO); Hnr Roll; Perf Att; WWAHSS; Comm Volntr; Chrch Yth Grp; Drma Clb; Key Club; Dnce; SP/M/VS; Stg Cre; Won Many Dance Awards Competitive; Award for Composing Piano Piece; Famous Actress; Movie Producer; George Mason U; Virginia Tech

ROTHRAUFF, CATHERINE; STERLING, VA; POTOMAC FALLS HS; (FR); Hnr Roll; Comm Volntr; Peer Tut/Med; Spec Olymp Vol; Chrch Yth Grp; Drma Clb; Key Club; Chrldg (V); Gmnstcs (V); Won Many Cheerleading Awards / Trophies; Registered Nurse / Doctor; Virginia Tech U; U of Kentucky

ROTKAEN, THITRENDY; SOUTH RIDING, VA; BROAD RUN HS; (JR); Hnr Roll; Comm Volntr; ArtClub; National Art Honors Society; Business Marketing; George Mason U

ROWAN, CHRISTOPHER; FARMVILLE, VA; RANDOLPH HENRY HS; (MS); Hnr Roll; 4-H; Chrch Yth Grp; SP/M/VS; Ftball (J); Wrstlg (J); Cl Off (S); College Major in Law; College Major in Performance Arts; Longwood U; U of North Carolina

ROWELL, SADE; WAVERLY, VA; SURRY CTY HS; (FR); Hnr Roll; Perf Att; Pres Ac Ftns Aw; St of Mnth; Yth Ldrshp Prog; Comm Volntr; Peer Tut/Med; Chrch Yth Grp; DARE; ROTC; SADD; Chr; Ch Chr; Clr Grd; Drl Tm; Pre/Postnatal Nursing; Massage Therapy; Florida State U; Atlanta state U

RUCKER, JESSICA S; STERLING, VA; DOMINION HS; (SR); Hnr Roll; Perf Att; St of Mnth; WWAHSS; Hab For Humty Volntr; 4-H; Emplmnt; Key Club; French Clb; Chr; Ch Chr; SP/M/VS; Chrldg (J); Cl Off (R); CR (R); Biology; Psychology; Virginia Union U; Norfolk State U

RUDEBUSCH, RACHEL; SPRINGFIELD, VA; LAKE BRADDOCK SECONDARY SCH; (SO); Hnr Roll; Nat Hon Sy; Otst Ac Ach Awd; Sci Fairs; Comm Volntr; Chrch Yth Grp; Quill & Scroll; Chrldg (J); Sch Ppr (E); 2nd Place - '03 NASA Student Involvement Project; National Honor Society / Academic Letter; Journalism; New York U; U of Virginia

RUSSELL, DESIREE Y; PETERSBURG, VA; MATOACA HS; (MS); Hnr Roll; Nat Hon Sy; St of Mnth; Red Cr Aide; Drma Clb; FCA; Photog; ROTC; Chr; Drl Tm; SP/M/VS; Track; Stu Cncl (V); Yrbk (R, P); Track MVP; Teacher; Model/Fashion Designer; Harvard; Spelman

RUTHERFORD, MARQUITA; HAMPTON, VA; BETHEL HS; (SO); Hnr Roll; St of Mnth; Comm Volntr; Chrch Yth Grp; FBLA; Spanish Clb; Ch Chr; Drl Tm; Citizen of the Month; Business Management; Music; U of North Carolina

RYAN, EMILY; STERLING, VA; POTOMAC FALLS HS; (SO); F Lan Hn Soc; Hi Hnr Roll; WWAHSS; Key Club; Vsity Clb; Bnd; Vllyball (V L); Biology; College of William & Mary

RYAN, MATTHEW T; RICHMOND, VA; BENEDICTINE HS; (SO); Hnr Roll; Key Club; Lcrsse (V L); Sccr (VJ L); Tennis (V L); Business Major; Real Estate Investment; Kenyon College; U of Virginia

RYDER, ASHLEY; RICHMOND, VA; VARINA HS; (JR); Hnr Roll; St of Mnth; WWAHSS; Comm Volntr; Chrch Yth Grp; Emplmnt; FCA; FTA; Key Club; Scouts; Chr; Ch Chr; Dnce; SP/M/VS; Cr Ctry (V); Captain in 2 Show Choirs; Member of Volunteer Rescue Squad; Nursing; Teaching

RYDER, DANIEL; MANASSAS, VA; OSBOURN PARK SR HS; (SR); Hnr Roll; Kwnis Aw; Perf Att; Pres Ac Ftns Aw; WWAHSS; Yth Ldrshp Prog; Comm Volntr; Red Cr Aide; Spec Olymp Vol; ArtClub; DARE; Key Club; Mus Clb; ROTC; Bnd; Ftball (L); CR (T); Guitar for 8 Years; Graphic Designer; Small Business; Lynchburg U; Longwood U

SABAS, CATHERINE A; STERLING, VA; POTOMAC FALLS HS; (SO); F Lan Hn Soc; Hi Hnr Roll; Hnr Roll; Perf Att; Comm Volntr; Chrch Yth Grp; Key Club; Vsity Clb; Chr; Bskball (V L); Vllyball (V); Church & Community Volunteer; National Spanish Honor Society; Business Administration; Education; Penn State U; College of William & Mary

SABOOR, ZOHAL; CHANTILLY, VA; STONEWALL JACKSON HS; (JR); F Lan Hn Soc; Hnr Roll; Nat Hon Sy; WWAHSS; FBLA; Key Club; Mod UN; P to P St Amb Prg; SP/M/VS; Stg Cre; National Honor Society Member; French Honor Society Member; Anthropologist; Peace Corps; Georgetown U; New York U

SACHS, MATTHEW D; CHARLOTTESVILLE, VA; ALBEMARLE HS; (SO); Hnr Roll; Perf Att; WWAHSS; Comm Volntr; Chrch Yth Grp; Key Club; Sccr (J); Key Club Member; History; Foreign Languages

SACKMAN, CHELSEA N; VIRGINIA BEACH, VA; COX HS; (JR); Hnr Roll; Yth Ldrshp Prog; Comm Volntr; Peer Tut/Med; Red Cr Aide; Chrch Yth Grp; Key Club; Pep Squd; Quiz Bowl; Vsity Clb; Ch Chr; Chrldg; Treasurer of Cox Medical Association; Interior Design; Fashion; George Mason U; James Madison U

SADIQ-ALI, SARA G; RESTON, VA; SOUTH LAKES HS; (JR); Hnr Roll; Nat Hon Sy; Sci Fairs; WWAHSS; Comm Volntr; National Society of High School Scholar; Pre-Med; Biology; Harvard U; Johns Hopkins U

SAGER, STEPHANIE R; WOODSTOCK, VA; CENTRAL HS; (SR); Hnr Roll; Otst Ac Ach Awd; Comm Volntr; 4-H; Chrch Yth Grp; DARE; Emplmnt; FCCLA; Ntl FFA; Prom Com; SADD; Chrldg (VJ L); Sftball (J); Sports Medicine / Physical Therapy; Radford U

SALEETID, LALANA; FAIRFAX STATION, VA; (JR); Hnr Roll; Quill & Scroll; Sch Ppr (E); Pre-Med; Biology; George Mason; Virginia State

SALUJA, DEEPIKA; LEESBURG, VA; HERITAGE HS; (JR); F Lan Hn Soc; Fut Prb Slvr; Gov Hnr Prg; Hi Hnr Roll; Hnr Roll; Nat Hon Sy; Nat Ldrshp Svc; Otst Ac Ach Awd; St of Mnth; Comm Volntr; Peer Tut/Med; DARE; DECA; Emplmnt; FBLA; FTA; Key Club; Spanish Clb; Peer Mediation (8th Grade); Optometry; Education; Georgetown U; George Washington U

SAMFORD, MORGAN M; VIRGINIA BEACH, VA; FRANK W COX HS; (SR); Hnr Roll; Comm Volntr; DARE; DECA; Emplmnt; P to P St Amb Prg; DECA District Leadership Conference-First Place-Communication & Interpersonal Skills; English Major; Elementary Education; James Madison U; Radford U

Rutherford, Marquita
Bethel HS
Hampton, VA

Rothrauff, Cassandra
Potomac Falls HS
Sterling, VA

Rojas, Gaby F
South Lakes HS
Reston, VA

Robinson, Rachel
Deep Creek HS
Chesapeake, VA

Robbins, Aaron
Norfolk Collegiate Mid-Upr Sch
Norfolk, VA

National
Honor Roll
Spring 2005

Roach, Andy
Flint Hill Sch
Vienna, VA

Robison, Nichole A
Brentsville District HS
Manassas, VA

Rothman, Daniel
Potomac Falls HS
Sterling, VA

Rothrauff, Catherine
Potomac Falls HS
Sterling, VA

Rotkaen, Thitrendy
Broad Run HS
South Riding, VA

SAMMAN, KENNAN; VIENNA, VA; GEORGE C MARSHALL HS; (SR); MVP; Otst Ac Ach Awd; Pres Ac Ftns Aw; Sci Fairs; Comm Volntr; Spec Olymp Vol; DECA; Emplmnt; FBLA; Off Aide; SADD; Tchrs Aide; Vsity Clb; Bskball (V); Sccr (V); 1st Team All-State, Region and District: Soccer; Captain of Both Soccer and Basketball; Sports Advertising; West Virginia U; Rider U

SAMPSON, LANCE; LURAY, VA; LURAY HS; (FR); Hnr Roll; Nat Hon Sy; Perf Att; SP/M/VS; Wt Lftg (J); Archaeology; Doctor; Notre Dame U; James Madison U

SAMUELS, JODIANN N; HAMPTON, VA; PHOEBUS HS; (FR); Hnr Roll; USMC Stu Ath Aw; Hosp Aide; ArtClub; Drma Clb; ROTC; French Clb; Psychology

SANDERS, JADE; RICHMOND, VA; OPEN HS; (SO); Ctznshp Aw; Nat Hon Sy; Otst Ac Ach Awd; St Schl; Comm Volntr; Peer Tut/Med; Emplmnt; Lib Aide; Scouts; Orch; Stu Cncl (R); American Youth Harp Ensemble; Partnership for the Future; Psychology; Music; Syracuse U; Howard U

SANDERS, JAREL; SUFFOLK, VA; NANSEMOND RIVER HS; (SO); Ctznshp Aw; Hnr Roll; Perf Att; Ntl Beta Clb; Video Game Designer / Programmer

SANDERS, NATALIA L; NEWPORT NEWS, VA; WARWICK HS; (JR); Ctznshp Aw; Hi Hnr Roll; Hnr Roll; Nat Hon Sy; Otst Ac Ach Awd; Perf Att; Pres Ac Ftns Aw; Sci Fairs; WWAHSS; Hosp Aide; Chrch Yth Grp; DECA; Emplmnt; Key Club; Ch Chr; Dnce; Orch; SP/M/VS; Gmnstcs; CR (R); National Honor Society

SANDERSEN, DANIELLE; ASHBURN, VA; BROAD RUN HS; (JR); Hi Hnr Roll; MVP; Nat Hon Sy; Perf Att; Pres Ac Ftns Aw; St of Mnth; WWAHSS; Comm Volntr; Chrch Yth Grp; DECA; Emplmnt; Key Club; Dnce; Sccr; Track (V); Vllyball (V); Occupational Therapy; Physical Therapy

SANDRIDGE, CARMEN; CHARLOTTESVILLE, VA; ALBEMARLE HS; (JR); Hnr Roll; Nat Hon Sy; WWAHSS; Chrch Yth Grp; Key Club; MuAlphaTh; Bnd; Dnce; Mch Bnd; President of Church Youth Group; Nursing / Nurse Practitioner; Medicine

SANTOS, MURAE; MANASSAS, VA; OSBOURN HS; (JR); Hnr Roll; Otst Ac Ach Awd; WWAHSS; Comm Volntr; Emplmnt; Key Club; P to P St Amb Prg; Photog; Forensic Psychology; Architecture; Florida Institute of Technology; Christopher Newport

SARTAIN, DEAN P C; MC LEAN, VA; BISHOP DENIS J O'CONNELL HS; (JR); Hnr Roll; Pres Ac Ftns Aw; Comm Volntr; Hosp Aide; Chrch Yth Grp; Key Club; Ftball; Skiing; Wt Lftg; German AP Test- Top Score 5; Guitar; Architecture; Catholic U; Virginia Tech

SARVAY, STEFFANY; RICHMOND, VA; VARINA HS; (SR); All Am Sch; Hnr Roll; Nat Hon Sy; WWAHSS; Comm Volntr; Emplmnt; MuAlphaTh; Quill & Scroll; Svce Clb; Sch Ppr (E, R, P); Center for Communications; Pediatric Physical Therapy; Psychology; Virginia Commonwealth

SAUNDERS, LAUREN; BEAVERDAM, VA; HANOVER HS; (JR); Hnr Roll; Otst Ac Ach Awd; Chrch Yth Grp; DARE; Bnd; Ch Chr; Clr Grd; Mch Bnd; Medicine; Drama; Virginia Commonwealth U; James Madison U

SAUNDERS, MARY CATHERINE; FREDERICKSBURG, VA; JAMES MONROE HS; (SO); Hi Hnr Roll; Otst Ac Ach Awd; Valdctrian; WWAHSS; Yth Ldrshp Prog; Amnsty Intl; Comm Volntr; Chrch Yth Grp; Dbte Team; Emplmnt; FCA; HO'Br Yth Ldrshp; Key Club; Latin Clb; Dnce; Vllyball (J); Engineering; Linguistics; New York U; Yale

SAUNDERS, VICTORIA S; SURRY, VA; SURRY CTY HS; (FR); FBLA; Ch Chr; Scr Kpr (J); Track (V); CR (R); Ethics for Life Committee; Culinary Arts; Law; U of Richmond; U of Virginia

SAVAGE, DEWAN; CHERITON, VA; NORTHAMPTON HS; (FR); Ctznshp Aw; DAR; Hi Hnr Roll; Hnr Roll; Perf Att; St of Mnth; Mus Clb; Clb; Bnd; Pep Bnd; Track (V); 2-Time Junior All-Shore Band (2003, 2004); Senior All-Shore Band Alternate (2005); Journalism; Communications; U of North Carolina; U of Virginia

SAWYERS, CHELSEA L; ROCKY MOUNT, VA; FRANKLIN CTY HS; (SR); Hnr Roll; Nat Hon Sy; Pres Sch; WWAHSS; Comm Volntr; Chrch Yth Grp; Tchrs Aide; Voc Ind Clb Am; Ch Chr; Stu Cncl (R); Nursing (RN); Jefferson College of Health Sciences; Liberty U

SAXBY, LINDSEY E; RICHMOND, VA; GODWIN HS; (FR); Hnr Roll; Comm Volntr; Chrch Yth Grp; Drma Clb; Spanish Clb; Chr; Stg Cre; Sccr; CR (R); Sch Ppr (E); Acting; Writing; U of Virginia; Boston U

SAYGBE, JOHNETTA N; FALLS CHURCH, VA; STUART HS; (FR); Hnr Roll; MVP; Otst Ac Ach Awd; Perf Att; Comm Volntr; Orch; Bskball; Track; Vllyball; Scholar Athlete (Volleyball Basketball); Medical; Business; Johns Hopkins U; U of Virginia

SCALES, KENNETTA; CHESAPEAKE, VA; DEEP CREEK HS; (SO); Hnr Roll; Otst Ac Ach Awd; Comm Volntr; Chrch Yth Grp; Key Club; SADD; Spanish Clb; Clr Grd; Psychology; Hampton U; Virginia State

SCHNITTKA, ANDREA; CHARLOTTESVILLE, VA; ALBEMARLE HS; (JR); Hnr Roll; Nat Hon Sy; Otst Ac Ach Awd; WWAHSS; Comm Volntr; Chrch Yth Grp; Key Club; MuAlphaTh; Photog; Bnd; Mch Bnd; Pep Bnd; National Math Honor Society; U of Virginia; U of Mary Washington

SCHOLZ, CANDACE; ALEXANDRIA, VA; WEST POTOMAC HS; (SO); Hi Hnr Roll; Hnr Roll; Sci Fairs; WWAHSS; Drma Clb; Scouts; French Clb; Chr; Dnce; SP/M/VS; Stg Cre; Best Actress-Award 2004; American Model and Talent Convention-4 first Places; Psychology-Major; Acting Industry; Stanford; U of Virginia

SCHULTE, DENISE J; CLIFTON, VA; JAMES W ROBINSON SECONDARY SCH; (SR); Otst Ac Ach Awd; DECA; Emplmnt; FBLA; Clr Grd; Sports Management; Human Resources; St. Johns U

SCHUMACHER, BECKY; CHESAPEAKE, VA; WESTERN BRANCH HS; (SO); Hnr Roll; MVP; Perf Att; St of Mnth; Comm Volntr; Chrch Yth Grp; Drma Clb; NtlFrnscLg; Orch; SP/M/VS; Stg Cre; Sftball (JC); CR (R); Church Praise and Worship Dance Team Member; Bowling Duckpin; Science Major; Criminal Justice Major; Texas Agricultural and Manufacturing; Virginia Commonwealth U

SCHWAB, JOHN; VIRGINIA BEACH, VA;; F Lan Hn Soc; Hi Hnr Roll; Hab For Humty Volntr; Mod UN; Chr; SP/M/VS; Lit Mag (E); Drama Award; National Latin Exam-Gold Medal; History Teacher; Actor

SCHWARTZ, KIMBERLY; STERLING, VA; DOMINION HS; (JR); Ctznshp Aw; Hnr Roll; Comm Volntr; Vsity Clb; Chr; Stg Cre; Chrldg (V L); Gmnstcs (V L); CR (R); District Chorus; Coaching Gymnastics; Business Finance; U of Virginia; Virginia Tech

SCHWARZ, KRISTEN; DUMFRIES, VA; FOREST PARK HS; (JR); Comm Volntr; Chrch Yth Grp; Jr Cls League; Latin Clb; Ch Chr; Clr Grd; Digital Media; Graphic Design; Waynesburg College, Waynesburg, Pennsylvania; Liberty U, Lynchburg, Virginia

SCOFIELD, LAUREN E; LEESBURG, VA; STONE BRIDGE HS; (FR); Hnr Roll; Sci Fairs; WWAHSS; Key Club; Bskball; Track

SCOTT, TERRA G; NORFOLK, VA; LAKE TAYLOR HS; (FR); Ctznshp Aw; Comm Volntr; Chrch Yth Grp; ROTC; Drl Tm; SP/M/VS; Tennis (V); Marines (Communications); Spokes Person; (UAB) U Alabama Birmingham; Norfolk State U

SCRANTON, MELISSA R; VIRGINIA BEACH, VA; OCEAN LAKES HS; MS; Hnr Roll; Otst Ac Ach Awd; Perf Att; Pres Ac Ftns Aw; Pres Sch; St of Mnth; DARE; Tchrs Aide; Gymnastics Out of School; U of California, Los Angeles

SEABORN JR, SHELTON L; EMPORIA, VA; GREENSVILLE CTY HS; (SO); 4H Awd; Ctznshp Aw; F Lan Hn Soc; Hi Hnr Roll; Hnr Roll; Nat Mrt LOC; Otst Ac Ach Awd; Pres Ac Ftns Aw; Sci Fairs; WWAHSS; Peer Tut/Med; Spec Olymp Vol; 4-H; Chrch Yth Grp; HO'Br Yth Ldrshp; Ntl Beta Clb; Quiz Bowl; ROTC; Vsity Clb; Spanish Clb; Ch Chr; Clr Grd; Drl Tm; Cr Ctry (V); Skt Tgt Sh (J); Track (V); Attendee of 2005 Presidential Youth Leadership Conference; Selected for 05/06 Southside Regional Governor's School; Architecture; Engineering; West Point; Norwich U

SEAL, PATRICK D; CUMBERLAND, VA; CUMBERLAND HS; (SO); Hnr Roll; Perf Att; USAA; Chrch Yth Grp; Bsball (J); Yrbk

SEALAND, J B; ORANGE, VA; MADISON HS; (SR); F Lan Hn Soc; Hnr Roll; Pres Ac Ftns Aw; 4-H; AL Aux Boys; Chrch Yth Grp; Ntl Beta Clb; Cr Ctry (V L); Sccr (V CL); Cl Off (S); Sch Ppr (R); Yrbk (R, P); Church Council; Boy's State; Medicine; Biology; U of the South Sewanee

SEARCY, DELTRESS M; NORFOLK, VA; LAKE TAYLOR HS; (SR); Hnr Roll; MVP; Otst Ac Ach Awd; Comm Volntr; Peer Tut/Med; Red Cr Aide; Chrch Yth Grp; DARE; Pep Squd; Tchrs Aide; Bnd; Drm Mjr; Mch Bnd; Pep Bnd; Bskball (V C); Track (V CL); CR (R); Computer Tech.; Computer Engineering; Virginia State U; Shaw U

SEGAL, DANIELLE A; FREDERICKSBURG, VA; CHANCELLOR HS; MS; Hi Hnr Roll; Otst Ac Ach Awd; Perf Att; Comm Volntr; Peer Tut/Med; Chrch Yth Grp; Scouts; Dnce; Orch; Chrldg (J); Rqtball (J); Tennis (J); Law; Politics; Harvard U; Princeton U

SELKOW, JOSEPH L; WOODBRIDGE, VA; WOODBRIDGE SR HS; (SR); Ctznshp Aw; Perf Att; ROTC; International Club Member.; West Point; The Art Institute in Arlington VA

SESE, ANDREW R; WOODBRIDGE, VA; BISHOP IRETON CATHOLIC HS; (SO); Hnr Roll; Sci Fairs; WWAHSS; Yth Ldrshp Prog; Comm Volntr; Key Club; Mod UN; Bnd; Dnce; SP/M/VS; Step Team; Tap Dance Classes; Medical Lawyer; Nurse / Doctor; U of Virginia

SEWAH, CHRISTIANA; ALEXANDRIA, VA; T C WILLIAMS HS; (SO); Nat Ldrshp Svc; Yth Ldrshp Prog; Dnce; SP/M/VS; Tennis (J); I Would Like to Be an Actress

SHAFER, LESLIE J; VIRGINIA BEACH, VA; FRANK W COX HS; (JR); Hnr Roll; Nat Mrt Fin; WWAHSS; Peer Tut/Med; Key Club; Varsity Letter in Crew-3 Years; Founding Member Ruritan/French Honor Society; Virginia Commonwealth U; U of Virginia

SHAH, KARAN S; NEWPORT NEWS, VA; WARWICK HS; (JR); Hi Hnr Roll; Kwnis Aw; Nat Hon Sy; Otst Ac Ach Awd; Perf Att; Pres Sch; St of Mnth; WWAHSS; Comm Volntr; Hosp Aide; Dbte Team; Emplmnt; FCA; FBLA; Jr Ach; JSA; Key Club; Mth Clb/Tm; Drl Tm; SP/M/VS; Bsball (J); Bskball (J); Sccr (J); Vsy Clb (V); Vllyball (V); Adv Cncl; Yrbk; District Forensics Champion; District Quiz Bowl Champion; Physician; Brown U; Harvard U

SHAH, SONAM; VIRGINIA BEACH, VA; FIRST COLONIAL HS; (JR); F Lan Hn Soc; Hi Hnr Roll; Nat Hon Sy; Comm Volntr; Emplmnt; FBLA; Key Club; MuAlphaTh; Cl Off (T); Microsoft Office Certified; Business Student for 9 Wks; Business; Hotel Management; U of California; U of Virginia

SHAHEEN, SASHA; ANNANDALE, VA; ANNANDALE HS; (FR); Comm Volntr; Spec Olymp Vol; FCA; Mth Clb/Tm; Scouts; Social Work; Criminal Justice; Virginia Commonwealth U; Howard U

SHANK, TAYLOR; MARTINSVILLE, VA; MARTINSVILLE HS; (FR); Hi Hnr Roll; Otst Ac Ach Awd; Perf Att; WWAHSS; Chrch Yth Grp; Key Club; Mus Clb; Ntl Beta Clb; Scouts; Bnd; Mch Bnd; Stg Cre; Sccr (JC); Swmg (V); Ralph Shank Hustle Award / Best Freshman in Marching Band; Biology / Veterinary Medicine; Economics / History; U of Virginia; North Carolina State U

SHAPIRO, PHILIP L; CENTREVILLE, VA; CENTREVILLE HS; (SO); Hnr Roll; Nat Hon Sy; Otst Ac Ach Awd; Pres Sch; Sci Fairs; WWAHSS; Comm Volntr; Key Club; Outdrs Clb; Scouts; Mar Art; Skiing; Stu Cncl (R); Eagle Scout-Bronze / Gold Palm Awards; Martial Arts-2nd Degree Black Belt; Computer Engineering; Business; Virginia Tech; James Madison U

SHARMA, KRITIKA; STERLING, VA; DOMINION HS; (SO); Hnr Roll; WWAHSS; Comm Volntr; Key Club; Sch Ppr (R); U of Virginia

SHARROFNA, JENAN A; LORTON, VA; ISLAMIC SAUDI AC; (SO); Hnr Roll; Sci Fairs; Comm Volntr; Dbte Team; Mod UN; Svce Clb; French Clb; Bdmtn (V); Bskball (V); Scr Kpr (V); Architecture; Business Management; George Mason U; Marymount U

SHAVER, ELIZABETH; BLACKSBURG, VA; BLACKSBURG HS; (SR); Ctznshp Aw; Hnr Roll; Comm Volntr; Emplmnt; Ntl FFA; Scouts; Tchrs Aide; Bnd; Chr; Gmnstcs (L); Hsbk Rdg (V); Skt Tgt Sh (L); Swmg (L); Animal and Poultry Sciences; Biology; Virginia Tech; Radford U

SHEEHAN, PATRICK M; ASHBURN, VA; BROAD RUN HS; (JR); Ctznshp Aw; F Lan Hn Soc; Hi Hnr Roll; Hnr Roll; Nat Hon Sy; Pres Sch; Comm Volntr; Scouts; Bskball (VJ L); Tennis (V CL); Vllyball (V L); Cl Off (P); Sch Ppr (R, P); Lions Club Award for Academic Excellence; National Junior Honor Society; International Relations; Pre-Law; College of William and Mary; U of Notre Dame

SHEETS, TARA N; WEBER CITY, VA; GATE CITY HS; (SO); 4H Awd; All Am Sch; Hnr Roll; Otst Ac Ach Awd; Perf Att; WWAHSS; Yth Ldrshp Prog; Comm Volntr; Chrch Yth Grp; Emplmnt; FCA; FBLA; Tennis (V); State Champion-Tennis; Shout-Youth Leadership Program; Wofford U; Virginia Tech

SHELTON, HANNAH; DANVILLE, VA; WESTOVER CHRISTIAN AC; (MS); Hi Hnr Roll; Hnr Roll; Comm Volntr; Chrch Yth Grp; Tchrs Aide; Chr; Chrldg (J); Liberty U (VA); Life Pacific Bible College (CA)

SHENK, LATASHA; LURAY, VA; LURAY HS; (FR); FCCLA; James Madison U; Blue Ridge Community College

SHEPHERD, ASHLEY; NEWPORT NEWS, VA; WARWICK HS; (JR); Hnr Roll; Nat Hon Sy; WWAHSS; Yth Ldrshp Prog; Peer Tut/Med; Key Club; Bnd; Mch Bnd; Gmnstcs; National Honor Society; Who's Who; Lawyer; Duke; William & Mary

SHERIDAN, SARA G; BLACKSBURG, VA; BLACKSBURG HS; (SR); Hnr Roll; WWAHSS; Key Club; Acpl Chr; Chr; Clr Grd; Yrbk (R, P); New River Valley Lacrosse Team; Psychology; Virginia Tech

SHERMAN, CHRISTINE M; MANASSAS, VA; OSBOURN HS; (JR); Hnr Roll; WWAHSS; Emplmnt; FBLA; Key Club; Off Aide; Sftball (VJC); Business Admin; Human Resources; Florida State U; George Mason

SHIELDS, PATRICIA; LORTON, VA; HAYFIELD SECONDARY SCH; (JR); F Lan Hn Soc; Hi Hnr Roll; Hnr Roll; Nat Hon Sy; WWAHSS; Comm Volntr; Emplmnt; FCCLA; Mth Clb/Tm; Pep Squd; Quill & Scroll; CR (R); Yrbk (E); All "A" Honor Roll - All-Year; Psychology; English; Virginia Tech; U of Virginia

SHIM, YOOSUN; CENTREVILLE, VA; CENTREVILLE HS; (FR); Hnr Roll; WWAHSS; Comm Volntr; Key Club; Orch; Tennis (J); U of Virginia

SHIN, CHRISTINA; CENTREVILLE, VA; CENTREVILLE HS; (SO); Hnr Roll; Nat Hon Sy; Comm Volntr; Peer Tut/Med; FBLA; Key Club; Orch; Mathematics; Chemistry; Brown U; Cornell U

SHIN, HYUN H; CENTREVILLE, VA; CENTREVILLE HS; (SO); Hnr Roll; Nat Hon Sy; Sci Fairs; WWAHSS; Comm Volntr; FBLA; Key Club; Mth Clb/Tm; MuAlphaTh; Orch; Track (J); Fairfax County Regional Science Fair Winner - Honorable Medalist; International Business; Economics; U of Pennsylvania; Cornell U

Shaheen, Sasha Annandale HS Annandale, VA	Segal, Danielle A Chancellor HS Fredericksburg, VA	Saygbe, Johnetta N Stuart HS Falls Church, VA	Schumacher, Becky Western Branch HS Chesapeake, VA	Sheehan, Patrick M Broad Run HS Ashburn, VA

SHIPE, MAGGIE K; CHARLOTTESVILLE, VA; ALBERMARLE HS; (JR); Comm Volntr; Key Club; Photog; Svce Clb; James Madison U; Old Dominion U

SHIRLEY, AIMIE M; STUARTS DRAFT, VA; STUARTS DRAFT HS; (JR); Hnr Roll; WWAHSS; DARE; Emplmnt; FCCLA; Key Club; Chr; Invited to Gov. School for Visual Arts; Art; Chorus

SHOFNER, MOLLY J; CHESAPEAKE, VA; WESTERN BRANCH HS; (SR); Hnr Roll; Nat Hon Sy; Comm Volntr; Acpl Chr; Chr; Upward Bound Program; Old Dominion U

SHOUP, NICOLE; VIRGINIA BEACH, VA; FLOYD KELLAM HS; (SO); Hnr Roll; Pres Ac Ftns Aw; St of Mnth; Comm Volntr; FBLA; Vllyball (V L); CR (P); Academic Letter; Honorable Mention All-Beach District Team; Criminology; Sociology; U of Virginia; Christopher Newport U

SHOWALTER, BAILEY; AXTON, VA; MARTINSVILLE HS; (JR); DAR; Hi Hnr Roll; Hnr Roll; Nat Hon Sy; WWAHSS; Yth Ldrshp Prog; Comm Volntr; Drma Clb; Key Club; NtlFrnscLg; Sci Clb; Bnd; Jzz Bnd; Mch Bnd; Stg Cre; Hsbk Rdg; PP Ftbl; Business Manager for Robotics Team; Engineering; Business; Princeton U; U of Virginia

SHRIEVES, CHRIS; STAFFORD, VA; COLONIAL FORGE HS; (JR); Hnr Roll; MVP; Pres Ac Ftns Aw; Peer Tut/Med; Bnd; Ice Hky (V, C); Rlr Hky (V); Sportsmanship Awards; Leadership Awards; Architectural Design; Engineering; Boston College; University of Maryland Baltimore

SHULTZ, JASON; MANASSAS, VA; STONEWALL JACKSON HS; (SO); Hnr Roll; Otst Ac Ach Awd; WKA Go-Kart Racing 2004 Junior Animal Champion-National; WKA Go-Kart Racing 2004 VA State Champion-Jr. Light & Heavy; Engineering

SHULTZ, KELSEY F; ASHBURN, VA; STONE BRIDGE HS; (FR); Hi Hnr Roll; Nat Hon Sy; Otst Ac Ach Awd; Key Club; German Clb; Swmg (V); Sch Ppr (R); Piano; Archery; U of Virginia

SHUM, YI YAN V; ROANOKE, VA; ROANOKE CATHOLIC SCH; (JR); Hi Hnr Roll; Hnr Roll; Nat Hon Sy; Perf Att; WWAHSS; Peer Tut/Med; Jr Ach; Key Club; Spanish Clb; Orch; Swmg; Sch Ppr (R); Kathryn Ann Rattenbury Student Scholarship; VCEE Economics Challenge State Runner-Up; International Business

SHUMAKER, KRISTIN; HIGHLAND SPRINGS, VA; VARINA HS; (SR); Hnr Roll; Otst Ac Ach Awd; Pres Sch; Comm Volntr; Chrch Yth Grp; FTA; Key Club; Photog; Quill & Scroll; Scouts; Sftball (VJCL); Sch Ppr (R, P); Quill and Scroll Society; Elementary Education; Sports Management; Virginia Commonwealth U

SHUMAN, KELLY K; FORK UNION, VA; FLUVANNA CTY HS; (JR); Hnr Roll; MVP; Perf Att; St of Mnth; WWAHSS; Peer Tut/Med; 4-H; Chrch Yth Grp; DARE; Emplmnt; FBLA; Mus Clb; Ntl Beta Clb; Off Aide; Chr; SP/M/VS; Bskball (J); Track (V L); Vllyball (VJCL); 2nd Team All-District Volleyball; Domino's Pizza Athlete of the Week; Nursing; Teaching; Radford U; Roanoke College

SIDDIQI, AYESHA; LEESBURG, VA; BROAD RUN HS; (SR); F Lan Hn Soc; Hnr Roll; Nat Hon Sy; Perf Att; Pres Ac Ftns Aw; St of Mnth; WWAHSS; Comm Volntr; Hosp Aide; Spec Olymp Vol; DECA; Emplmnt; Key Club; Mod UN; French Clb; Bskball (J L); PP Ftbl (V); Track (J L); Broadcast Journalism; Marketing / Business; Pennsylvania State U

SIEDOW, ERIK; GLEN ALLEN, VA; HENRICO HS; (JR); Hnr Roll; Nat Hon Sy; WWAHSS; Hosp Aide; Emplmnt; Prom Com; Bsball (V L); Wrstlg (J); Registered/Licensed Pharmacy Technician; IBMYP Diploma; Pharmacy; Medicine; James Madison U; George Mason U

SIELATY, STEPHANIE; SPRINGFIELD, VA; ANNANDALE HS; (JR); Hnr Roll; MVP; Nat Stu Ath Day Aw; Otst Ac Ach Awd; WWAHSS; DECA; Bskball (J); Vllyball (VJ L); 4 Year DECA Enrollment & DECA President; A-B Honor Roll & Student of Quarter; Sports & Entertainment Management; Marketing/Advertising; U of South Carolina; U of Georgia

SIGMON, HANNAH C; ABINGDON, VA; ABINGDON HS; (SR); Hi Hnr Roll; Hnr Roll; Nat Hon Sy; Otst Ac Ach Awd; Perf Att; WWAHSS; Comm Volntr; Peer Tut/Med; ArtClub; Chrch Yth Grp; Drma Clb; SADD; Spanish Clb; Chr; Swmg (V L); Governor's School Nominee and Alternate; Accepted Into National Art Honor Society; Spanish; Social Work; David Lipscomb U

SILIEZAR, JUSTIN B; OAKTON, VA; BISHOP O'CONNELL HS; (JR); Hnr Roll; Nat Ldrshp Svc; WWAHSS; Yth Ldrshp Prog; Comm Volntr; Peer Tut/Med; Key Club; NYLC; Schol Bwl; Fncg; Wrstlg (V); Johns Hopkins Center for Talented Youth; Cambridge (England) College Programmer; Medicine; Bio-Medical Engineering; UC Berkeley; UC Davis

SIMPSON, CARMEN J; WOODBRIDGE, VA; POTOMAC SR HS; (SO); Ctznshp Aw; Hnr Roll; Pres Ac Ftns Aw; Comm Volntr; Prom Com; Chr; Dnce; Bskball (J); Chrldg (V); Track (V); CR (V); Tri-M Music Honor Society; Dentistry, Medicine, Business; Management; Spelman College; U of Maryland

SINGH, GURJAS; MANASSAS, VA; STONEWALL JACKSON HS; (JR); Gov Hnr Prg; Hi Hnr Roll; Hnr Roll; Otst Ac Ach Awd; Perf Att; St of Mnth; Yth Ldrshp Prog; Comm Volntr; Hosp Aide; Red Cr Aide; ArtClub; Chess; Cmptr Clb; Dbte Team; FBLA; Key Club; Lib Aide; Mod UN; Sci Clb; Chr; Ch Chr; Dnce; Mch Bnd; Bdmtn (J); Bskball (J); Golf (J); Sccr (L); Vllyball (J); Adv Cncl (S); Cl Off (R); Stu Cncl (R); 2005 Legislative Youth Tour Delegate (Novel), Officer in the United Nations; DeVry U Summer Scholar, GPA=A+, ID Advisers Council, Also Newspaper; MBA in Management; MBA in Marketing; George Washington U; George Mason U

SINGH, KARAN; STERLING, VA; DOMINION HS; (JR); Hnr Roll; Nat Mrt LOC; Comm Volntr; Peer Tut/Med; Emplmnt; Dnce; Bskball (V); Biochemistry; Dentistry; George Mason U; George Washington U

SINGH, TANDEEP; MANASSAS, VA; OSBOURN HS; (SO); Ctznshp Aw; DAR; Hnr Roll; Nat Hon Sy; Otst Ac Ach Awd; Perf Att; Pres Ac Ftns Aw; St of Mnth; WWAHSS; Comm Volntr; Hosp Aide; Chrch Yth Grp; Dbte Team; Key Club; Lib Aide; Mus Clb; Off Aide; Scouts; Tchrs Aide; Ch Chr; Dnce; Orch; SP/M/VS; Fncg; Gmnstcs; Ice Sktg; Skiing; Sccr; Swmg; Tennis; Honorable Mention from MetLife; Psychiatrist; Child Custody Lawyer; Johns Hopkins U; Penn State U

SINGHAL, PRIYANKA; GLEN ALLEN, VA; DEEP RUN HS; (SO); Ctznshp Aw; Hnr Roll; Pres Ac Ftns Aw; Pres Sch; Yth Ldrshp Prog; Comm Volntr; Hosp Aide; Red Cr Aide; ArtClub; DARE; Dbte Team; Drma Clb; Jr Ach; Photog; Spanish Clb; Chr; Clr Grd; Dnce; Mch Bnd; Stu Cncl (R); CR (R); Lit Mag (E); Reflections; Leadership Conferences; Medicine / Ob-Gyn; Residency Fellowship; U of Virginia; Stanford U

SINGLETARY-CLAFFEE, ASHLEY; VIRGINIA BEACH, VA; FRANK W COX HS; (JR); Hnr Roll; Nat Hon Sy; WWAHSS; Hosp Aide; Peer Tut/Med; AL Aux Girls; Chrch Yth Grp; Emplmnt; Jr Cls League; Key Club; Latin Clb; Ch Chr; SP/M/VS; Sccr; Cl Off (V); Stu Cncl (R); Student Athletic Trainer; Architecture; Engineering; U of Virginia; Virginia Tech

SIODMOK, SARAH; MIDLOTHIAN, VA; CLOVER HILL HS; (SR); F Lan Hn Soc; Gov Hnr Prg; Jr Mshl; Nat Hon Sy; Otst Ac Ach Awd; Valdctrian; Comm Volntr; Peer Tut/Med; Emplmnt; MuAlphaTh; Tchrs Aide; French Clb; Bnd; Drm Mjr; Mch Bnd; Biology; Pre-Med; U of Virginia; Duke U

SIST, JOSEPH W; WYTHEVILLE, VA; WYTHE CTY TECH SCH; (JR); Hnr Roll; Lttrmn Clb; Quiz Bowl; Schol Bwl; Sci Clb; Vsity Clb; Ftball (V L); Track (V L); Cl Off (V); Automotive Engineering; Law; Virginia Tech

SKELTON, MATTHEW; MONTPELIER, VA; PATRICK HENRY HS; (SO); Hnr Roll; Yth Ldrshp Prog; Comm Volntr; Chrch Yth Grp; FCA; NYLC; Lcrsse (V); SLU 101 (Student Leadership); SLU 102 (Student Leadership); Liberty U

SLAGLE, MATTHEW D; STAFFORD, VA; COLONIAL FORGE HS; (JR); Perf Att; Pres Ac Ftns Aw; Comm Volntr; Peer Tut/Med; Tech Clb; Bskball (VJCL); Cr Ctry (V L); Vllyball (V L); Martial Arts / Individual; Basketball Camps Advisor / Assistant; Sports Health; Sports Marketing; Randolph Macon U; Eastern Mennonite U

SLAGLE III, GEORGE D; SKIPPERS, VA; GREENSVILLE CTY HS; (SO); Hi Hnr Roll; Hnr Roll; Otst Ac Ach Awd; Wt Lftg; Art (Drawing); Virginia Commonwealth U; Old Dominion U

SLATE, JAMES M; STUART, VA; PATRICK CTY HS; (JR); Hi Hnr Roll; Jr Mshl; Perf Att; Comm Volntr; Spec Olymp Vol; Chrch Yth Grp; Ntl Beta Clb; Vsity Clb; Bsball (V); Bskball (V); Ftball (V); Criminology; Criminal Justice; Virginia Tech; Ferrum College

SLONE, MATTHEW; HURLEY, VA; HURLEY HS; (SR); Hnr Roll; Perf Att; WWAHSS; Ntl Beta Clb; SADD; Bskball (V); Track (V); Yrbk (E); U of Virginia-Wisc

SMALES, WHITNEY M; ROANOKE, VA; WILLIAM FLEMING HS; (SR); Ctznshp Aw; Hi Hnr Roll; Nat Hon Sy; Nat Mrt LOC; Otst Ac Ach Awd; Pres Sch; WWAHSS; Comm Volntr; Chrch Yth Grp; Dbte Team; Key Club; Ntl Beta Clb; Mar Art; Tennis (V); CR; Lit Mag; Yrbk; Kung-Fu Demonstration Team; Education; Missions/Bible; Azusa Pacific U

SMALL, NAOMI; CHARLOTTESVILLE, VA; ALBERMARLE HS; (FR); Hnr Roll; Nat Hon Sy; WWAHSS; Comm Volntr; 4-H; Chrch Yth Grp; Jr Cls League; Key Club; Mth Clb/Tm; Pep Squd; Scouts; Spch Team; Bnd; Chr; Cl Off (R); CR (R); Lit Mag (E, R); Sch Ppr (E, R); Junior Classical League; Law; Psychology; U of Virginia; Virginia Tech

SMALLEY III, R W; BERRYVILLE, VA; CLARKE CTY HS; (SR); All Am Sch; Nat Hon Sy; WWAHSS; Outdrs Clb; Cr Ctry (V L); Track (V L); Lead America Alumnus; U of Virginia

SMALLS, JASMINE; CHESAPEAKE, VA; DEEP CREEK HS; (SO); Hnr Roll; Perf Att; Key Club; SADD; Bnd; Clr Grd; Chrldg (V); Fld Hky (V); Psychology Major; Duke U; Old Dominion U

SMART, CHELSEA; FREDERICKSBURG, VA; STANFORD SR HS; (SO); 4H Awd; Hi Hnr Roll; Hnr Roll; Nat Hon Sy; Otst Ac Ach Awd; 4-H; Chrch Yth Grp; Emplmnt; Lib Aide; Photog; Hsbk Rdg; 3 Years of 4-H - 2 Years Secretary, Recreational Horseback Riding - 5 Years; Veterinary Science; Psychology; Tufts U

SMITH, AMY L; BASSETT, VA; MARTINSVILLE HS; (FR); Hnr Roll; WWAHSS; Comm Volntr; Red Cr Aide; Spec Olymp Vol; Key Club; Bnd; Cr Ctry (V L); Track (V L); CR (R); VA. High School League Leaders Conference & Sportsmanship Summit; Sports & Fitness Administration; U of Virginia; James Madison U

SMITH, CHASITY; RIDGEWAY, VA; MAGNA VISTA HS; (JR); Ctznshp Aw; Hnr Roll; St of Mnth; Comm Volntr; Chrch Yth Grp; ROTC; Chr; Ch Chr; Drl Tm; Cl Off (V); Lit Mag (R); EMT / Martinville Rescue Square; Cardiologist; UNC Chapel Hill; Patrick Henry Community

SMITH, DEIDRE M; CHARLOTTESVILLE, VA; ALBERMARLE HS; (SO); Hi Hnr Roll; Hnr Roll; MVP; Otst Ac Ach Awd; St of Mnth; Comm Volntr; Hab For Humty Volntr; Chrch Yth Grp; NYLC; P to P St Amb Prg; Photog; German Clb; Chr; Ch Chr; Swmg (V L); CR (R); Yrbk (E, R, P); People to People Sports Ambassador; Orthodontics; Sports Medicine; U of Florida; U of Virginia

SMITH, JILL; COVINGTON, VA; ALLEGHANY HS; (SO); Hnr Roll; Nat Hon Sy; WWAHSS; Yth Ldrshp Prog; Comm Volntr; Peer Tut/Med; Chrch Yth Grp; HO'Br Yth Ldrshp; Key Club; Scouts; SADD; Foreign Clb; Bnd; Chr; Mch Bnd; Pep Bnd; Bskball (JC); Track (V L); Vllyball (VJ L); Stu Cncl (R); Girl Scout Silver Award; Advertising; Acting; Virginia Tech

SMITH, LAUREN R; MANASSAS, VA; OSBOURN HS; (SR); Nat Hon Sy; Pres Ac Ftns Aw; Sci Fairs; WWAHSS; Comm Volntr; Chrch Yth Grp; Key Club; SADD; Clr Grd; Orch; Bskball (J); Track (J); Edge Club Leader; Tri-M Music Society Member; Biology; Pre-Med; Southeastern College

SMITH, LINDSAY; VIRGINIA BEACH, VA; FLOYD KELLAM HS; (JR); Hnr Roll; MVP; Nat Hon Sy; Pres Ac Ftns Aw; Comm Volntr; Prom Com; Vsity Clb; Fld Hky (J L); Swmg (V L); Vllyball (V); Stu Cncl (R); MVP Swimming; 1st in Reflections (Lit) in School, 3rd in City; Education; Guidance; College of William and Mary; U of Virginia

SMITH, MARY E; LOUISA, VA; LOUISA CTY HS; (JR); Hi Hnr Roll; Otst Ac Ach Awd; WWAHSS; Peer Tut/Med; Chrch Yth Grp; Emplmnt; Ntl FFA; Bskball (V); PP Ftbl (V); Perfect Score on Algebra II SOL; SODA - Student Organization for Developing Attitudes; Horse Vet; Virginia Poly Technic Institute

SMITH, SALLY; CLINTWOOD, VA; CLINTWOOD HS; (JR); Nat Hon Sy; Perf Att; WWAHSS; Drma Clb; FCA; Key Club; Sftball (V L); Teaching Degree; U of Virginia College Wise

SNAPP, JENNIFER; WINCHESTER, VA; JAMES WOOD HS; (SO); Hnr Roll; St of Mnth; FBLA; FCCLA; FTA; Tchrs Aide; Blue and Gold Award, 2004; Major in Secondary Education; Become Middle School Science Teacher; U of Virginia; James Madison U

SNEAD, CHELSIE D; HAMPTON, VA; BETHEL HS; (SO); Hnr Roll; Perf Att; Pres Ac Ftns Aw; St of Mnth; Interior Designer; Old Dominion U

SNEDDEN, ADELAIDE E; FREDERICKSBURG, VA; JAMES MONROE HS; (JR); Tennis (V); Sch Ppr (R); Top Science Student; Top Math Student

SNYDER, CRYSTAL R; RICHMOND, VA; LLOYD C BIRD HS; (FR); Hnr Roll; Comm Volntr; Peer Tut/Med; Key Club; Orch; SP/M/VS; Stg Cre; Stu Cncl (R); Part of Award Winning Orchestra; Registered Nurse / Master's Degree; Family Practitioner; Virginia Commonwealth U

SOLANKI, JIGNA; RICHMOND, VA; VARINA HS; (FR); Hi Hnr Roll; Hnr Roll; St of Mnth; Comm Volntr; ArtClub; Emplmnt; Spanish Clb; Dnce; Sftball (J); Track (J); Sch Ppr; A chance to graduate one year earlier; Ruriteens Volunteer Club; Pre-medical/Medical; Journalism; Princeton U, Princeton, New Jersey; Harvard U, Cambridge, Massachusetts

SOLEMAN, BURHAN; ANNANDALE, VA; FALLS CHURCH HS; (JR); F Lan Hn Soc; Fut Prb Slvr; Hi Hnr Roll; Hnr Roll; Jr Eng Tech; Nat Hon Sy; Otst Ac Ach Awd; St of Mnth; WWAHSS; Comm Volntr; Peer Tut/Med; Chess; FBLA; Mth Clb/Tm; French Clb; Bskball (J); Business Major; U of Pennsylvania; Duke U

SOLLIDAY, KELLY; VIRGINIA BEACH, VA; FLOYD KELLAM HS; (SO); Hnr Roll; Perf Att; St of Mnth; Comm Volntr; Emplmnt; Fld Hky; Virginia Tech; James Madison U

SONG, JIN A; CENTREVILLE, VA; CENTREVILLE HS; (JR); F Lan Hn Soc; Gov Hnr Prg; Hnr Roll; Nat Hon Sy; Nat Ldrshp Svc; Otst Ac Ach Awd; Sci Fairs; WWAHSS; Yth Ldrshp Prog; Comm Volntr; Hosp Aide; Peer Tut/Med; Key Club; Mth Clb/Tm; MuAlphaTh; Mus Clb; Sci Clb; Spanish Clb; Acpl Chr; Chr; Sftball (J); Published a Book of Poetry - Pacific Bridge; Selected to Attend Governor's School for Humanities; English Literature / Creative Writing; Choir; Princeton U

SONNEK, SYLVIA; JEFFERSONTON, VA; CULPEPER CTY HS; (JR); Hnr Roll; Nat Hon Sy; WWAHSS; Comm Volntr; Outdrs Clb; Scouts; Bnd; Mch Bnd; Vllyball (V L); Medicine; U of Virginia

Smith, Chasity
Magna Vista HS
Ridgeway, VA

Slate, James M
Patrick Cty HS
Stuart, VA

Slagle, Matthew D
Colonial Forge HS
Stafford, VA

Simpson, Carmen J
Potomac SR HS
Woodbridge, VA

Singhal, Priyanka
Deep Run HS
Glen Allen, VA

Slone, Matthew
Hurley HS
Hurley, VA

Smith, Deidre M
Albermarle HS
Charlottesville, VA

SORENSON, KATHRYN; CLIFTON, VA; CENTREVILLE HS; (JR); F Lan Hn Soc; Hnr Roll; Nat Hon Sy; Pres Sch; WWAHSS; Comm Volntr; Peer Tut/Med; Emplmnt; FCA; Key Club; Tchrs Aide; Spanish Clb; Sch Ppr (E); Attended National Student Leadership Conference and Penn State Institute for Journalist; Political Science; Pre-Law; U of Rhode Island; Boston U

SOUTH, LOURDES E; OAKTON, VA; PAUL VI CATHOLIC HS; (SO); Hi Hnr Roll; Hnr Roll; Yth Ldrshp Prog; Amnsty Intl; Comm Volntr; Hab For Humty Volntr; Chrch Yth Grp; Key Club; NYLC; Spanish Clb; SP/M/VS; CR (P); Fencing Not in School & Surfing; Play Guitar, Model Judiciary, Painter, President of SLATE Recycling Club & NSLC; Medical Profession; Doctor; Politics, Like Senator; William & Mary, Georgetown; James Madison U

SPARROW, LESLIE ANN; PORTSMOUTH, VA; I C NORCOM; (SR); Hnr Roll; Nat Hon Sy; Otst Ac Ach Awd; WWAHSS; Comm Volntr; Dnce; Mch Bnd; Sccr (V L); Cl Off (T); Sch Ppr; Yrbk; Pillar of Character Award; Political Science; Hampton U; Old Dominion U

SPINNER, BRITTNEY A; LYNCHBURG, VA; HERITAGE HS; (JR); Hnr Roll; Nat Hon Sy; Otst Ac Ach Awd; WWAHSS; Comm Volntr; DARE; Mus Clb; Scouts; Acpl Chr; Chr; Orch; SP/M/VS; Chrldg (V CL); Miller Lewis International; Demo Production; Bachelor's Business & Marketing; Virginia Commonwealth U; Old Dominion U

SPURLOCK, BRANDON J; GLEN ALLEN, VA; HENRICO HS; (SO); Hnr Roll; Perf Att; Ftball (V C); Track; Wt Lftg

STALEY, COREY; CHESAPEAKE, VA; ATLANTIC SHORES CHRISTIAN SCH; (SR); Hi Hnr Roll; Hnr Roll; Nat Hon Sy; Perf Att; Pres Ac Ftns Aw; WWAHSS; Comm Volntr; Chrch Yth Grp; Prom Com; Spch Team; SP/M/VS; Chrldg (VJ); Sccr (V); Vllyball (J); Stu Cncl (S); Yrbk (P); Communication Degree / Social Influence; Old Dominion U

STANKOVIC, ALEKSANDAR; MIDDLEBURG, VA; HIGHLAND SCH; (SO); F Lan Hn Soc; Fut Prb Slvr; Hi Hnr Roll; Hnr Roll; Sci/Math Olympn; St of Mnth; WWAHSS; Comm Volntr; Hosp Aide; Peer Tut/Med; Biology Clb; Chess; DARE; Dbte Team; Fr of Library; Lib Aide; Mth Clb/Tm; Sci Clb; Bnd; SP/M/VS; Bskball (J); Lcrsse (J); Mar Art (V); Virginia School for Gifted Students; Advanced Classes (Mathematics, Science); Business Major, Economic; U of Virginia, Syracuse U, Duke U; Harvard U, UC Berkeley, Stanford U, Princeton U

STANLEY, SARAH; SALEM, VA; SALEM HS; (SO); F Lan Hn Soc; Hi Hnr Roll; Nat Hon Sy; Comm Volntr; ArtClub; Chrch Yth Grp; Emplmnt; Lib Aide; Prom Com; Svce Clb; French Clb; Tennis (V); Cl Off (S); Treasurer-Interact Club; Art; Graphic Design

STARR, BROOKE; VIRGINIA BEACH, VA; FRANK W COX HS; (JR); F Lan Hn Soc; Hi Hnr Roll; Hnr Roll; Nat Hon Sy; Perf Att; WWAHSS; Yth Ldrshp Prog; Comm Volntr; Peer Tut/Med; Red Cr Aide; Chrch Yth Grp; Drma Clb; Emplmnt; Jr Cls League; MuAlphaTh; Prom Com; Latin Clb; Dnce; SP/M/VS; Lcrsse (VJ); Adv Cncl (R); Cl Off (R); Stu Cncl (R); CR (R); Key Club; 3 Honor Societies (National, Math, Latin); Public Relations; Film; Virginia Polytechnic Institute; James Madison U

ST CLAIR, KONTESSA; SALEM, VA; SALEM HS; (SO); Hi Hnr Roll; Hnr Roll; French Clb; Chr; Ch Chr; SP/M/VS; Lit Mag (E); Keyettes Club; Veterinary Medicine; Virginia

STECH, JESSICA C; MIDLOTHIAN, VA; MANCHESTER HS; (SR); Hnr Roll; Nat Hon Sy; Otst Ac Ach Awd; St of Mnth; Comm Volntr; Chrch Yth Grp; Emplmnt; Pep Squd; Photog; Prom Com; Tchrs Aide; Chr; Ch Chr; Cl Off (R); Stu Cncl (R); CR (R); Jobs for VA Graduates-Officer; Pep Club-Rep; Education; Marketing / Fashion; Virginia Commonwealth U

STEPALOVITCH, BONNIE C; ROANOKE, VA; WILLIAM FLEMING HS; (FR); Hi Hnr Roll; Pres Ac Ftns Aw; Sci Fairs; Emplmnt; Dnce; Virginia Western Community College; Radford U

STERN, AARON M; OAKTON, VA; JAMES MADISON HS; (SO); Sci Fairs; WWAHSS; Comm Volntr; Chrch Yth Grp; Emplmnt; SADD; Bnd; Mch Bnd; Pep Bnd; Lcrsse (J)

STEWART, LEAVETRICE M; DANVILLE, VA; GEORGE WASHINGTON HS; (FR); Ctznshp Aw; Hnr Roll; Nat Hon Sy; Otst Ac Ach Awd; Perf Att; Pres Ac Ftns Aw; Pres Sch; Sci Fairs; Chrch Yth Grp; Spanish Clb; Orch; Youth of the Year for 2000 (Courage By Boys & Girls Club); Editor's Choir Award (2004); Accountant; Cosmetology; U of Virginia; Rutgers U

STODOLA, KATHERINE; MANASSAS, VA; OSBOURN HS; (JR); F Lan Hn Soc; Hi Hnr Roll; Nat Hon Sy; Key Club; Quill & Scroll; Bnd; Bskball (JC); Sccr (JC); Lit Mag (R)

STOKES, LAUREN Y N; HOPEWELL, VA; TRINITY EPISCOPAL SCH; (JR); Hi Hnr Roll; Hnr Roll; Nat Hon Sy; Yth Ldrshp Prog; Comm Volntr; Emplmnt; Mod UN; NYLC; Bnd; Chr; Ch Chr; SP/M/VS; Fld Hky (VJ); Sccr (V L); Cl Off (V); Co-Founder of Trinity's Diversity Club & Band, National Youth Leadership Forum on Medicine; St Christopher's School's Summer Institute on Leadership & Public Service; Culinary Arts School of Performing Arts; U of Virginia Medical or Business College; Spelman College

STOLTZ, NERECE; SALEM, VA; SALEM HS; (SO); Nat Hon Sy; St of Mnth; Peer Tut/Med; Tennis (V L); English Second Language Student; Aviation; Language; College of William & Mary; U of Virginia

STONE, SARAH D; STANLEYTOWN, VA; BASSETT HS; (SO); Ctznshp Aw; Hi Hnr Roll; MVP; WWAHSS; Yth Ldrshp Prog; Comm Volntr; Chrch Yth Grp; FCA; ROTC; Foreign Clb; Ch Chr; Clr Grd; Drl Tm; Sccr (J); Track (V L); Vllyball (J); Stu Cncl (R); J-ROTC Officer, Exhibition Drill Team; Psychology; Social Work

STRASSER, AMANDA; STERLING, VA; (SO); Hnr Roll; St of Mnth; ArtClub; Key Club; Clr Grd; SYSA Soccer Participation

STRATTON, ERIKA; BURKE, VA; LAKE BRADDOCK SECONDARY HS; (SO); Nat Hon Sy; Sci Fairs; Comm Volntr; Chrch Yth Grp; Emplmnt; FCA; Mth Clb/Tm; Quill & Scroll; Bnd; Swmg (V L); Sch Ppr (E); Medicine; Missions; U of Virginia; William and Mary College

STRICKLER, MATTHEW D; FRONT ROYAL, VA; WARREN CTY HS; (SO); Hi Hnr Roll; Sci Fairs; WWAHSS; Emplmnt; Key Club; Ftball (VJ L); Maintained Honor Roll Since Elem. School; Advanced Proficiency on Science Sol's; Software/Graphic Engineer; Networking Engineer; Virginia Tech-Virginia Poly Technical Institute; James Madison U

STROOP, DEREK; PENN LAIRD, VA; SPOTSWOOD HS; (JR); F Lan Hn Soc; Hnr Roll; Sci Fairs; Chrch Yth Grp; Quiz Bowl; Schol Bwl; Spanish Clb; Bnd; Mch Bnd; Orch; Pep Bnd; 4th Place in Science Fair; Psychology; Biology; The Citadel; U of Michigan

STUART, JEB; FALLS CHURCH, VA; STUART HS; (JR); Hi Hnr Roll; Hnr Roll; Nat Hon Sy; St of Mnth; WWAHSS; Hosp Aide; Outdrs Clb; Vsity Clb; Spanish Clb; Sccr (V); College Partnership Program; Spanish Honor Society; Medicine

STUCKE, MARIA; ASHBURN, VA; BISHOP DENIS J O'CONNELL HS; (JR); Hnr Roll; MVP; Nat Hon Sy; Yth Ldrshp Prog; Comm Volntr; Peer Tut/Med; Emplmnt; Lib Aide; Scr Kpr (V); Sftball (V); Vllyball (J); Lifeguard Assistant Manager / Swim Lesson Instructor; Volunteer - Pediatrics Office; Nursing; Psychology; U of Virginia; Virginia

STYER, AMBER; CHESAPEAKE, VA; WESTERN BRANCH HS; (SO); Ctznshp Aw; Hnr Roll; Comm Volntr; P to P St Amb Prg; Scouts; Orch; 2000 Top Girl Scout At Blackston, Virginia; Math Teacher; Carson-Newman College; Christopher Newport U

SULLIVAN, EMILY J; RICHMOND, VA; (JR); Hi Hnr Roll; Otst Ac Ach Awd; WWAHSS; Comm Volntr; Emplmnt; Mod UN; Ntl Beta Clb; Photog; Prom Com; Quill & Scroll; Bskball (J L); Cl Off (R); Lit Mag (R, P); Model UN Delegate; Film Production

SULLIVAN, SALENA; ROANOKE, VA; WILLIAM FLEMING HS; (FR); Hnr Roll; Emplmnt; Fr of Library; Dnce; SP/M/VS; Lit Mag (E); Member of Free Dance Company; History (Major); Business Management; Brown U; Howard U

SULSER, KRISTA; WINCHESTER, VA; JOHN HANDLEY HS; (JR); Nat Ldrshp Svc; Chrch Yth Grp; DECA; Emplmnt; Spanish Clb; Bnd; Ch Chr; Mch Bnd; Pep Bnd; State Finalist/International Competition in DECA; Music; Christian Education; Christian Life College; Gateway College of Evangelism

SUMRELL, TATIANA; YORKTOWN, VA; TABB HS; (SO); Gov Hnr Prg; Hi Hnr Roll; Comm Volntr; Chrch Yth Grp; Key Club; Pep Squd; Quill & Scroll; Chrldg (V L); Cl Off (V); Sch Ppr (E); Key Club, Operation Smile, Spirit Club.; Honor Program; Medical Research; Forensics; U of Virginia; James Madison U

SUNIGA, SARA; SOUTH BOSTON, VA; HALIFAX CTY HS; (JR); Duke TS; Hi Hnr Roll; Hnr Roll; Jr Mshl; Nat Hon Sy; Yth Ldrshp Prog; Comm Volntr; HO'Br Yth Ldrshp; Mod UN; P to P St Amb Prg; Voc Ind Clb Am; French Clb; Orch; Chrldg (V); Track (V); Lettered in Cross-Country and Track; Foreign Language/Study Abroad; Aeronautics/Engineering; United States Air Force Academy

SUPINGER, CHRISTOPHER L; LYNCHBURG, VA; FISHBURNE MILITARY SCH; (SR); Hnr Roll; Peer Tut/Med; Chrch Yth Grp; DARE; FCA; ROTC; Clr Grd; Bsball (V L); Ftball (VJCL); Wrstlg (V); CR (V); Junior High School Basketball-Team Capt; Cadet of the Month-Fishburne Military School; Military; Criminal Justice; Georgia Military College; The Citadel

SURAT, ERIC M; ROANOKE, VA; ROANOKE CATHOLIC HS; (JR); Ctznshp Aw; Duke TS; Hi Hnr Roll; Nat Hon Sy; Nat Mrt Fin; Nat Mrt LOC; WWAHSS; Yth Ldrshp Prog; Comm Volntr; Peer Tut/Med; Chess; Chrch Yth Grp; Emplmnt; Key Club; Ch Chr; Swmg (V L); Lit Mag (R); High Honor Roll; English/Theology; U of Notre Dame; Duke U

SURAT, MARIA; ROANOKE, VA; ROANOKE CATHOLIC HS; (FR); Hi Hnr Roll; WWAHSS; Comm Volntr; Peer Tut/Med; Chrch Yth Grp; Key Club; Sci Clb; Bnd; Ch Chr; Mch Bnd; Pep Bnd; Swmg (V); Leading Prayer Services At Nursing Homes; Theology Major; Biology Major; Catholic U of America; U of Notre Dame

SUTTON, NATALIE M; STERLING, VA; POTOMOC FALLS HS; (FR); Hnr Roll; Key Club; Scouts; Bnd; Manager-Varsity Swim Team; Manager - Girl's Lacrosse; Sociology; College of William & Mary; UVA

SUTTON, TIPHANIE G; HAMPTON, VA; KECAUGHTAN HS; (JR); F Lan Hn Soc; Hnr Roll; Pres Ac Ftns Aw; Sci Fairs; St of Mnth; WWAHSS; Comm Volntr; Hosp Aide; Peer Tut/Med; FBLA; MuAlphaTh; Dnce; Cr Ctry (L); Track (V); Cl Off (V); Biomedical Engineering; Chemistry; U of Virginia; Georgetown U

SWAN, PIERRETTE A; VIRGINIA BEACH, VA; KEMPSVILLE HS; (SR); Ctznshp Aw; Hi Hnr Roll; Hnr Roll; Nat Hon Sy; Otst Ac Ach Awd; Pres Sch; Yth Ldrshp Prog; Comm Volntr; DECA; Emplmnt; Key Club; Photog; Prom Com; Tchrs Aide; French Clb; SP/M/VS; Sftball (J); Swmg (V L); Stu Cncl (R); Lit Mag (R); Theatre / Fine Arts; Virginia Wesleyan College

SZOKE, HOLLY M; STERLING, VA; POTOMAC FALLS HS; (FR); Hi Hnr Roll; WWAHSS; Comm Volntr; Key Club; Cr Ctry (J); Track (J); Art; Foreign Language; U of Virginia; College of William and Mary

TA, HIEU; STERLING, VA; BISHOP O'CONNELL HS; (JR); F Lan Hn Soc; Hi Hnr Roll; Hnr Roll; Nat Hon Sy; Otst Ac Ach Awd; Perf Att; WWAHSS; Peer Tut/Med; Emplmnt; Key Club; NYLC; Cr Ctry (J); Mar Art (V C); Track (J); Spanish National Honor Society; History; Neurosurgery; College of William and Mary; Washington & Lee U

TABILAS, AILEEN; CHARLOTTESVILLE, VA; ALBEMARLE HS; (JR); Hnr Roll; Kwnis Aw; WWAHSS; Key Club; Photog; Mar Art; PP Ftbl (V); Track (V); James Madison U; George Mason U

TABOR, MATTHEW W B; NORFOLK, VA; GRANBY HS; (SR); Hnr Roll; Nat Ldrshp Svc; Yth Ldrshp Prog; Comm Volntr; Hab For Humty Volntr; Red Cr Aide; ArtClub; Chrch Yth Grp; DARE; Drma Clb; Emplmnt; Lttrmn Clb; NYLC; Photog; Stg Cre; Ftball (V L); Lit Mag (P); Chrome; Selected for Nat'l Leadership Scholar; Art Award; Criminal Justice; Architectural Engineering; Accepted/Attending Va. Wesleyan College; Accepted-Old Dominion U

TAGGART, JESSICA; GLEN ALLEN, VA; HERMITAGE SD; (JR); Hnr Roll; Sci Fairs; DARE; Ntl Beta Clb; Vsity Clb; Chr; Sftball (V); Vllyball (J); Yrbk (E); Sportsmanship Award-Softball; Elementary Education; Social Work; Virginia Tech; Longwood U

TAGHAVIE-MOGHADAM, PARESA; VIRGINIA BEACH, VA; FLOYD KELLAM HS; (JR); Ctznshp Aw; Hnr Roll; Nat Hon Sy; Perf Att; Pres Ac Ftns Aw; Sci Fairs; St of Mnth; Comm Volntr; Peer Tut/Med; Drma Clb; Outdrs Clb; Schol Bwl; Svce Clb; Spanish Clb; Chr; SP/M/VS; Stg Cre; CR (R); Yrbk (R, P); Courthouse Recreation Volleyball; International Thespian; Medical Scientist; Chemical Engineer; College of William and Mary; Virginia Commonwealth U

TAMM, NICOLAS; CHARLOTTESVILLE, VA; CHARLOTTESVILLE HS; (JR); Hnr Roll; MVP; Perf Att; Pres Ac Ftns Aw; WWAHSS; Emplmnt; German Clb; Bnd; Jzz Bnd; Mch Bnd; Cr Ctry (V CL); Lcrsse (V L); Sccr (J); Track (V L); Stu Cncl (R); 3rd Place in Poetry Contest; Won State Championship in Track; Business; Physician; U of Virginia; James Madison U

TAN, STEPHANIE; MANASSAS, VA; OSBOURN HS; (JR); Hnr Roll; Nat Hon Sy; Sci Fairs; WWAHSS; Yth Ldrshp Prog; Peer Tut/Med; 4-H; Emplmnt; Key Club; NYLC; Prom Com; SADD; French Clb; Acpl Chr; Chr; Swg Chr; Chrldg (VJ L); Cl Off (S); Tri-M Music Honor Society; Government & Politics; Pre-Law; College of William & Mary; U of North Carolina-Chapel Hill

TANNER, LINDSAY; ASHBURN, VA; BROAD RUN HS; (JR); Hnr Roll; Nat Hon Sy; Pres Ac Ftns Aw; Comm Volntr; Hosp Aide; Peer Tut/Med; Chrch Yth Grp; DECA; Chrldg (V CL); Track (J); CR (R); Academic Biology Student of the Year; PE Student of the Year; Marketing; James Madison U; Virginia Tech

TATEM, AMBER N; CHESAPEAKE, VA; INDIAN RIVER HS; (SR); Hnr Roll; WWAHSS; Comm Volntr; Peer Tut/Med; Spec Olymp Vol; ArtClub; Chess; Chrch Yth Grp; Drma Clb; FCA; Mus Clb; Svce Clb; Foreign Clb; Chr; Ch Chr; Orch; SP/M/VS; Lit Mag; Miss Congeniality (In Miss Indian River Pageant); People's Choice (In Miss Indian River Pageant); Pre-Law; Liberty U

TATIYA, IRIN; ALEXANDRIA, VA; THOMAS A EDISON; (JR); Hnr Roll; Comm Volntr; Peer Tut/Med; DECA; Emplmnt; FBLA; Mod UN; Prom Com; ROTC; Scouts; Vsity Clb; Drl Tm; PP Ftbl (V); Vllyball (V); Cl Off (P); Sch Ppr (R); Purple Heart Leadership Award; Marketing; Entrepreneurship; Bentley College; U of Michigan

TATO, MICHAEL R; ANNANDALE, VA; BISHOP DENIS J O'CONNELL HS; (JR); Hnr Roll; Nat Hon Sy; Comm Volntr; Peer Tut/Med; Emplmnt; P to P St Amb Prg; Scouts; Bsball (VJ L); Mar Art; Wrstlg (V CL); Life Scout; Engineering; Environmental Studies; U of Southern California; U of California Santa Barbara

TAVENNER, SARAH; PARIS, VA; CLARKE CTY HS; (SR); Hnr Roll; Nat Hon Sy; Emplmnt; Outdrs Clb; Bnd; Dnce; Mch Bnd; Orch; Lit Mag (E); Art; Virginia Commonwealth U

Tabilas, Aileen
Albemarle HS
Charlottesville, VA

Sumrell, Tatiana
Tabb HS
Yorktown, VA

Stankovic, Aleksandar
Highland Sch
Middleburg, VA

Spinner, Brittney A
Heritage HS
Lynchburg, VA

National
Honor Roll
Spring 2005

South, Lourdes E
Paul VI Catholic HS
Oakton, VA

Styer, Amber
Western Branch HS
Chesapeake, VA

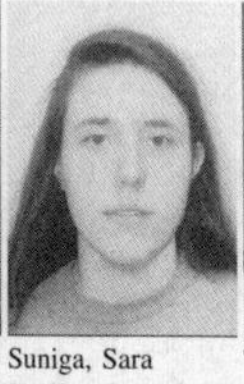
Suniga, Sara
Halifax Cty HS
South Boston, VA

Tatiya, Irin
Thomas A Edison
Alexandria, VA

TAYLOR, COURTNEY A; HAMPTON, VA; BETHEL HS; (SO); Hnr Roll; Otst Ac Ach Awd; Perf Att; Comm Volntr; Chrch Yth Grp; DECA; Scouts; Ch Chr; Dnce; Flg Crps; Track (V); Mass Communications; Business Management; Virginia State U; North Carolina A & T State U

TAYLOR, EMMA; CHARLOTTESVILLE, VA; ALBEMARLE HS; (FR); 4H Awd; Hnr Roll; Comm Volntr; 4-H; Key Club; SP/M/VS; Stg Cre; Lcrsse (J); Animal Science - Equine; Veterinarian Science; New York U; U of Virginia

TAYLOR, MEGAN; NORFOLK, VA; MAURY HS; (JR); Hnr Roll; Mas Aw; Comm Volntr; Spec Olymp Vol; Emplmnt; Chr; SP/M/VS; Past Honored Queen of International Order of Jobs Daughters; Award for Top 30% National Spanish Exam; Criminal Justice; Forensic Science; Virginia Common Wealth U; James Madison U

TEHEYFIO, LIZ; ASHBURN, VA; STONE BRIDGE HS; (SR); Hnr Roll; WWAHSS; DECA; Emplmnt; Key Club; Prom Com; SP/M/VS; PP Ftbl (V); Track (V); Multicultural Club Vice President; Top Ten State Finalist At DECA Competition; Medical Degree; Virginia Commonwealth U; U of Pittsburgh

TELLAWI, HEBA; ALEXANDRIA, VA; ISLAMIC SAUDI AC; (SO); Hi Hnr Roll; Hnr Roll; Sci Fairs; St of Mnth; Yth Ldrshp Prog; Comm Volntr; Hosp Aide; Peer Tut/Med; Drma Clb; FBLA; Mod UN; NYLC; Quiz Bowl; Bskball (J, V); Sccr (V); Cl Off (V); Sch Ppr (R); I have received a Best Delegation,3 Outstanding Delegations, and 1 Honorable Mention Award at MUN; I have completed Honors Algebra I, and Honors Geometry with the Center for Talented Youth at JHU.; Journalism; Pre-law; Harvard; U of Virginia

TELLER, JEANETTE; MANASSAS, VA; OSBOURN HS; (SO); 4H Awd; Hi Hnr Roll; MVP; Sci Fairs; St of Mnth; Comm Volntr; 4-H; Chrch Yth Grp; Key Club; Mus Clb; Bnd; Jzz Bnd; Mch Bnd; Pep Bnd; Bskball (J); Vllyball (J); Group Workcamps; U of Mary Washington; U of Virginia

TESTERMAN, IVORY; ARODA, VA; MADISON HS; (FR); Hnr Roll; Hosp Aide; DARE; Spanish Clb; Dnce; Stepp Team; English Teacher; Dancer; Princeton U; Atlanta U

THEMIDES, JAMES; VIRGINIA BEACH, VA; KEMPSVILLE HS; (JR); Hnr Roll; Perf Att; St of Mnth; Business; Longwood U

THOMAS, AJA J; SPRINGFIELD, VA; ROBERT E LEE HS; (MS); Perf Att; Peer Tut/Med; Chrch Yth Grp; Orch; Member of Chamber Orchestra; Fine Arts, Journalism; Private Investigators

THOMAS, BRELYNN; SMITHFIELD, VA; SMITHFIELD HS; (SO); Hnr Roll; WWAHSS; Red Cr Aide; Key Club; Ntl Beta Clb; ROTC; Chr; Ch Chr; Bskball (J); Adv Cncl (R)

THOMAS, DEREK; PORTSMOUTH, VA; I C NORCOM; (SR); All Am Sch; Hi Hnr Roll; Hnr Roll; MVP; Nat Hon Sy; Otst Ac Ach Awd; Perf Att; WWAHSS; Comm Volntr; Peer Tut/Med; Emplmnt; Prom Com; Quiz Bowl; Schol Bwl; Svce Clb; Scr Kpr (V); Vllyball (V L); Interact Club; Chrome Club; Physician-Biology Major; U of Virginia

THOMAS, KATHRYN S; RICHMOND, VA; DEEP RUN HS; (SO); Hnr Roll; WWAHSS; Emplmnt; Key Club; Sci Clb; SADD; Cr Ctry (V); Track (J); Key Club

THOMAS, LLOYD; ROANOKE, VA; PATRICK HENRY HS; (SO); Ctznshp Aw; Hnr Roll; Perf Att; WWAHSS; Peer Tut/Med; Chrch Yth Grp; DECA; Emplmnt; FBLA; Jr Ach; Chr; Ch Chr; Dnce; Ftball (J); Track (J); Wt Lftg (J); DECA; Forensic Science; Computer Technology; Virginia Common-Wealth U; Virginia Tech

THOMAS, SHANNON A; HIGHLAND SPRINGS, VA; PATRICK HENRY HS; (JR); Ctznshp Aw; Hnr Roll; Otst Ac Ach Awd; St of Mnth; Hab For Humty Volntr; Peer Tut/Med; Spec Olymp Vol; AL Aux Girls; Ntl Beta Clb; P to P St Amb Prg; Quill & Scroll; Dnce; SP/M/VS; CR (R); Lit Mag (R); Sch Ppr (R); President of Leo Club, Ashland, VA; High Academic Achievement; News/Radio Personality; Journalist; George Mason U; Virginia Commonwealth U

THOMAS, TIFFANY N; CAPE CHARLES, VA; NORTHAMPTON HS; (SR); Ctznshp Aw; Hnr Roll; Nat Mrt LOC; Nat Mrt Semif; WWAHSS; Comm Volntr; Emplmnt; FBLA; Ntl Beta Clb; Off Aide; Svce Clb; SP/M/VS; Manager of Girls Basketball Team; Held Part-Time Job Since Sophomore Year; Physical Therapy; Counseling; Old Dominion U-Accepted; Hampton U-Accepted

THOMBS, CAROLYN; DUMFRIES, VA; FOREST PARK HS; (SO); F Lan Hn Soc; Hi Hnr Roll; Hnr Roll; Otst Ac Ach Awd; Pres Ac Ftns Aw; Comm Volntr; Peer Tut/Med; Chrch Yth Grp; Jr Cls League; Mod UN; NYLC; Spanish Clb; Ch Chr; Sccr (J); Tennis (J); State Finalist in National American Miss; Spanish Major; Business Major; Christopher Newport U; Manhattanville College

THOMPSON, CHRISTINE E; STAFFORD, VA; COLONIAL FORGE HS; (JR); Hi Hnr Roll; Nat Hon Sy; Otst Ac Ach Awd; Peer Tut/Med; FBLA; French Clb; Dnce; French Club Vice President; History Major; Law; College of William & Mary; U of Virginia

THOMPSON, KATHARINE A; WINCHESTER, VA; JAMES WOOD HS; (SR); Hnr Roll; Pres Ac Ftns Aw; St of Mnth; Yth Ldrshp Prog; Chrch Yth Grp; DARE; Chr; Ch Chr; Swmg (L); Choral Librarian; Virginia All State Chorus; Elementary Education; Christian Education; Westminster College; Presbyterian College

THOMPSON, KELLY N; CLOVERDALE, VA; LORD BOTETOURT HS; (JR); Hnr Roll; Nat Hon Sy; Perf Att; WWAHSS; Peer Tut/Med; Chrch Yth Grp; Voc Ind Clb Am; Spanish Clb; Ch Chr; Presidential Physical Fitness Award; Nutrition; Dietetics; Carson-Newman College; Lenoir-Rhyne College

THOMPSON, MICHELLE; COLONIAL BEACH, VA; WASHINGTON & LEE HS; (JR); Ctznshp Aw; Perf Att; Emplmnt; Foreign Clb; Bnd; Drm Mjr; Mch Bnd; Anea Band; Pre-Medicine; Howard U; Johns Hopkins

THOMPSON, USAVADEE; CHESAPEAKE, VA; DEEP CREEK HS; (JR); Hnr Roll; Yth Ldrshp Prog; Dbte Team; Key Club; Mod UN; NtlFrnscLg; SADD; Bnd; Mch Bnd; Stu Cncl (T); Key Club Sophomore Director; JMU International Relations; James Madison; Virginia Tech

THORNHILL, KRISTEN A; MADISON HEIGHTS, VA; AMHERST CTY HS; (SR); Hi Hnr Roll; Nat Hon Sy; Pres Sch; WWAHSS; Emplmnt; Photog; Prom Com; Scouts; Bnd; Mch Bnd; Bskball (J); Sccr (V L); Vllyball (V CL); Cl Off (S); Honor Graduate - 7th in Class of 319; History Education; U of Virginia - Attending

TIEU, ROBIN; STERLING, VA; DOMINION HS; (JR); Perf Att; St of Mnth; DECA; FCA; Key Club; Vsity Clb; Lcrsse (V); PP Ftbl; Vllyball (V L); Student Athletic Trainer-Letter; Sports Medicine; Athletic Trainer; Emory & Henry; Virginia Commonwealth U

TIMPONE, GENEVIEVE; FREDERICKSBURG, VA; JAMES MONROE HS; (JR); Hi Hnr Roll; Sci Fairs; Amnsty Intl; Comm Volntr; ArtClub; Drma Clb; Emplmnt; Key Club; Spanish Clb; SP/M/VS; Stg Cre; Amnesty International Communications Officer; Key Club Poster Contest 2nd Place; Linguistics; Theatre; U of Virginia; Mary Washington U

TIPTON, MEGAN; ASHBURN, VA; STONE BRIDGE HS; (JR); Hnr Roll; Comm Volntr; Peer Tut/Med; Key Club; SADD; Bnd; Dnce; Vice President of SADD; Biology; Psychology; James Madison U; College of William & Mary

TIWANA, SHAHEEN; CENTREVILLE, VA; CENTREVILLE HS; (JR); Ctznshp Aw; F Lan Hn Soc; Hnr Roll; Nat Hon Sy; Otst Ac Ach Awd; Perf Att; WWAHSS; Amnsty Intl; Comm Volntr; Emplmnt; Key Club; Photog; Wdwrkg Clb; French Clb; Guitar Ensemble; Selected Into the National Student Leadership Conference; Pre-Med; Liberal Arts and Sciences; U of Virginia; George Mason U

TOMICK, BRITTANY D; STERLING, VA; POTOMAC FALLS; (SR); DAR; F Lan Hn Soc; Hi Hnr Roll; Nat Hon Sy; Otst Ac Ach Awd; St of Mnth; WWAHSS; Comm Volntr; Peer Tut/Med; ArtClub; Chrch Yth Grp; Emplmnt; SADD; Dnce; Animation; Savannah College of Art and Design

TORABINEJAD, MOHAMMAD; BLACKSBURG, VA; BLACKSBURG HS; (JR); F Lan Hn Soc; Gov Hnr Prg; Hi Hnr Roll; Hnr Roll; Nat Hon Sy; Nat Mrt LOC; Otst Ac Ach Awd; Sci/Math Olympn; WWAHSS; Comm Volntr; Peer Tut/Med; Cmptr Clb; Dbte Team; Key Club; Mth Clb/Tm; Mod UN; Ntl Beta Clb; NtlFrnscLg; Off Aide; Cr Ctry (V L); Track (J); Varsity Scholastic Bowl Captain; Debate Team (Varsity) Vice-Captain; Biochemistry; MD/PhD; Stanford U; Harvard College

TORGERSON, JESSICA R; DUMFRIES, VA; FOREST PARK HS; (JR); Hnr Roll; WWAHSS; Comm Volntr; Hosp Aide; Peer Tut/Med; Tchrs Aide; Chr; Chrldg; Swmg; Sch Ppr (R); Nursing; George Mason U; U of Nevada Reno

TORRES, EDWIN; STERLING, VA; MONROE TECH CTR; (JR); Hnr Roll; Perf Att; St of Mnth; Business Administration; Marketing; Universal Technical Institute; George Mason U

TOSO, CHRISTOPHER L; STAFFORD, VA; NORTH STAFFORD HS; (SR); Perf Att; Comm Volntr; Chrch Yth Grp; Emplmnt; FCA; FBLA; Scouts; Chr; Master's Degree; Computer Security; German Community College

TOUSLEY, CHRIS; ASHBURN, VA; BROAD RUN HS; (JR); Hnr Roll; Nat Hon Sy; Dbte Team; DECA; FBLA; Key Club; Boy Scouts: Eagle Scout; Pre-Law; Business

TRACY, ELIZABETH A; VIRGINIA BEACH, VA; FIRST COLONIAL HS; (FR); Ctznshp Aw; Hnr Roll; Otst Ac Ach Awd; Perf Att; St of Mnth; WWAHSS; Comm Volntr; Key Club; Scouts; Chr; Sccr (J L); Cl Off (S); Citizenship Awards; Captain of 8th Grade Soccer Team; Pediatrics; Psychology; U of Virginia; U of Mary Washington

TRAINOR, JESSICA; CHESTER, VA; LLOYD C BIRD HS; (SR); Hi Hnr Roll; Hnr Roll; Jr Mshl; Nat Hon Sy; Otst Ac Ach Awd; Sci Fairs; St of Mnth; WWAHSS; Comm Volntr; Peer Tut/Med; Key Club; Spanish Clb; Engineering Governor's Program; Biomedical Engineering; Medicine; U of Virginia; Virginia Commonwealth U

TRAVIS, OLIVIA R; ASHLAND, VA; PATRICK HENRY HS; (JR); F Lan Hn Soc; Hnr Roll; Jr Mshl; Nat Hon Sy; Otst Ac Ach Awd; WWAHSS; Comm Volntr; Chrch Yth Grp; Drma Clb; FCA; Jr Cls League; Ntl Beta Clb; Photog; Quill & Scroll; Latin Clb; Chr; Ch Chr; Stg Cre; Lit Mag (P)

TREFZGER, ANNA; STERLING, VA; DOMINION HS; (JR); F Lan Hn Soc; Hnr Roll; Otst Ac Ach Awd; Comm Volntr; ArtClub; Chrch Yth Grp; Emplmnt; Key Club; Photog; Chrldg (J L); Yrbk (R); Interior Design; Psychology; U of Virginia; Geneva College

TRELAWNY, DILLON T; WOODSTOCK, VA; CENTRAL HS; (JR); Ctznshp Aw; Hi Hnr Roll; Hnr Roll; Nat Hon Sy; Otst Ac Ach Awd; Perf Att; Pres Ac Ftns Aw; Chess; Chrch Yth Grp; Lttrmn Clb; SADD; Bnd; Jzz Bnd; Mch Bnd; SP/M/VS; Bskball (J); Cr Ctry (L); Track (V L); Aerospace Engineering; Architecture; U of Virginia; James Madison U

TRENT, RONINA L; RICHMOND, VA; VARINA HS; (JR); Hnr Roll; Hosp Aide; Chrch Yth Grp; Church Choir; Volunteer Work At McGuire Hospital; Biology; Veterinarian; Virginia Commonwealth U; Virginia Union U

TREXLER, AMANDA; VIRGINIA BEACH, VA; FIRST COLONIAL HS; (SO); Hnr Roll; Otst Ac Ach Awd; Perf Att; Comm Volntr; Peer Tut/Med; Key Club; Clr Grd; Mch Bnd; The Get Involved Award; Landscape Painting; Mathematics; Child and Elderly Care; Virginia State U; Old Dominion U

TRIMMER, KELLEY; BUMPASS, VA; THE STEWARD SCH; (FR); Hnr Roll; Pres Ac Ftns Aw; Comm Volntr; Bskball (J); Lcrsse (V); Mar Art (V); Wt Lftg (J)

TROTMAN, OWEN; CHESAPEAKE, VA; GREAT BRIDGE HS; (JR); Hnr Roll; WWAHSS; Comm Volntr; Civil Air Pat; Emplmnt; ROTC; Ftball (J); Cl Off (S); JROTC; Civil Engineering; Biology; Virginia Military Institute; Old Dominion U

TROTTA, CHRISTINE; EARLYSVILLE, VA; ALBEMARLE HS; (JR); F Lan Hn Soc; Hnr Roll; Nat Hon Sy; Otst Ac Ach Awd; Perf Att; WWAHSS; Hab For Humty Volntr; Chrch Yth Grp; Key Club; MuAlphaTh; Photog; Bnd; Sccr (V L); Second Team All-Central Virginia Girls' Soccer; Biology; College of William and Mary; U of Virginia

TRUSLOW, BRANDON; VERONA, VA; FT DEFIANCE HS; (JR); Hi Hnr Roll; Perf Att; Chrch Yth Grp; Tech Clb; Latin Clb; Track (V); Engineer; Virginia Military Institute; Virginia Tech

TUASON, KATRINA T; CHESTER, VA; THOMAS DALE HS; (SR); Hnr Roll; Nat Hon Sy; Otst Ac Ach Awd; Perf Att; Hab For Humty Volntr; Peer Tut/Med; Drma Clb; P to P St Amb Prg; Photog; Prom Com; Tchrs Aide; Chr; Dnce; SP/M/VS; Stg Cre; CR (R); Mixed Show Choir-Knight Scene; Publisher's Choice for Outstanding Poetry; Psychology; Psychiatry; Virginia Commonwealth U; The College of William and Mary

TUERFF, DAVID T; MC LEAN, VA; ST. STEPHEN'S AND ST. AGNES SCH; (SO); Hi Hnr Roll; Hnr Roll; Peer Tut/Med; Chrch Yth Grp; Jzz Bnd; Chrldg (C); Golf (V); Sch Ppr (R)

TUNSTALL, KIERRA C M; RICHMOND, VA; VARINA HS; (JR); Hnr Roll; Nat Ldrshp Svc; Sci Fairs; USAA; WWAHSS; Yth Ldrshp Prog; Hab For Humty Volntr; Chrch Yth Grp; DARE; DECA; Emplmnt; Off Aide; Prom Com; Bnd; Ch Chr; Dnce; Mch Bnd; Leaders of Tomorrow; History Club; Neuroscience (Medicine); Law; UVA; Clark Atlanta U

TURNER, LINDSEY; RICHMOND, VA; BANNER CHRISTIAN SCH; (JR); Hnr Roll; Comm Volntr; Red Cr Aide; Chrch Yth Grp; Mus Clb; Chr; Vllyball (V); Sch Ppr (R); Yrbk (R); Business

TUTOR, JAMES H; PORTSMOUTH, VA; CHURCHLAND HS; (FR); F Lan Hn Soc; Hnr Roll; Hosp Aide; Mth Clb/Tm; Stu Cncl (T); Ping-Pong; Medical Sciences; French

TWIMASI, LUCY; LORTON, VA; HAYFIELD SECONDARY SCH; (JR); Hnr Roll; Nat Hon Sy; Nat Mrt LOC; WWAHSS; DECA; FBLA; French Clb; Orch; Hayfield DECA Leader/Officer; Finalist in Virginia DECA Competition/ ICDC; Business; Public Relations; Virginia Polytechnic Institute & State U; U of MD; College Park

TWINE, CHANTE'L; HAMPTON, VA; PHOEBUS HS; (SR); Hnr Roll; WWAHSS; Emplmnt; Key Club; Sci Clb; Tchrs Aide; Bnd; Ch Chr; Mch Bnd; Miss Band 04-05; Accounting; CPA; Hampton U

ULSH, J RYAN; STERLING, VA; POTOMAC FALLS HS; (FR); Hi Hnr Roll; Hnr Roll; Comm Volntr; DARE; Key Club; Scouts; Cr Ctry (J); Track (J); Cl Off (V); Penn State; Virginia Tech

UNGERMAN, ANNABELLE J; NORFOLK, VA; NORFOLK COLLEGIATE MID-UPR SCH; (JR); Hnr Roll; MVP; Comm Volntr; ArtClub; Chrch Yth Grp; Emplmnt; Mus Clb; Off Aide; Prom Com; Bnd; Lcrsse (VJ L); Swmg (V L); Vllyball (VJCL); U of South Carolina; College of Charleston

UPSHAW, CHARLIE; BOWLING GREEN, VA; LEE DAVIS HS; (SR); Track (V C); Agricultural Economics; VA Tech; Virginia Polytechnic Institute & State U

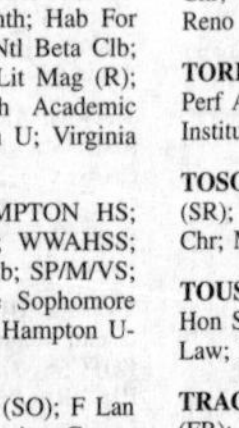
Tuason, Katrina T
Thomas Dale HS
Chester, VA

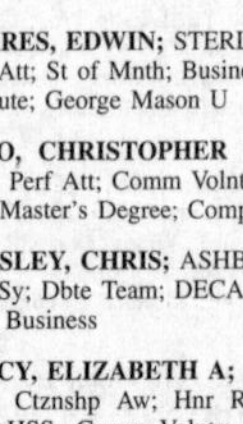
Toso, Christopher L
North Stafford HS
Stafford, VA

National
Honor Roll
Spring 2005

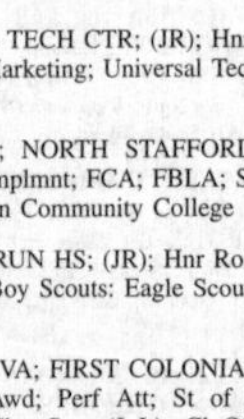
Tiwana, Shaheen
Centreville HS
Centreville, VA

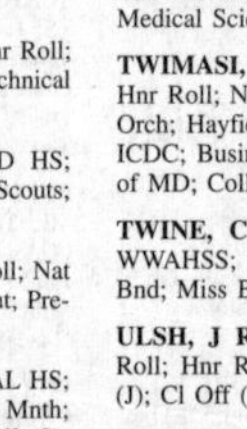
Ungerman, Annabelle J
Norfolk Collegiate Mid-Upr Sch
Norfolk, VA

UPSHAW, TIANNA L; RICHMOND, VA; SBCS; (SO); All Am Sch; Hnr Roll; Nat Hon Sy; Perf Att; Sci Fairs; St of Mnth; WWAHSS; Comm Volntr; Peer Tut/Med; Chess; Chrch Yth Grp; Mod UN; Off Aide; Spanish Clb; Acpl Chr; Chr; Ch Chr; Chrldg (V); Vllyball (V); Stu Cncl (T); CR (R); Sch Ppr (R); Yrbk (R); Science Fair - 2nd Place; Delegate to Model UN; Physical Education; Business Management; Virginia Commonwealth U; U of Richmond

UPSHUR, ROCHELLE; MANASSAS, VA; FOREST PARK HS; (JR); Hnr Roll; MVP; Yth Ldrshp Prog; Peer Tut/Med; AL Aux Girls; Chrch Yth Grp; Emplmnt; FBLA; Prom Com; Quill & Scroll; SADD; Vsity Clb; Sftball (V CL); Cl Off (S); CR (S); Yrbk (E); Assistant Editor of Yearbook; World of Difference Trainer; Neurosurgeon; Doctorate; U of Virginia

USMANI, AARZOO; ANNANDALE, VA; ANNANDALE HS; (SO); Hnr Roll; St of Mnth; Comm Volntr; FBLA; Excellence Award From President George W. Bush; Excellence Award From Mustafa Center; Medical Field; Law; George Mason U; U of Virginia

UYGUR, SHAFKAT; RESTON, VA; SOUTH LAKES HS; (JR); Peer Tut/Med; Fr of Library; FBLA; Bskball (J); Ftball (J); Mar Art (C); Sccr (J); Track (J); Wrote a Book on My Family History; Dentist; George Mason U; James Madison U

VAN DER LINDE, MELISSA; EARLYSVILLE, VA; ALBEMARLE HS; (SR); Hnr Roll; WWAHSS; 4-H; Emplmnt; Key Club; German Clb; Chr; PP Ftbl; Architecture; Clemson U

VANI, NINA; MC LEAN, VA; MC LEAN HS; (SO); Comm Volntr; Peer Tut/Med; Sci Clb; Svce Clb; Spanish Clb; Dnce; Health; Clinical Sciences; U of Virginia; Johns Hopkins U

VARGAS, JAIMIE L; VIRGINIA BEACH, VA; BRANDON MS; (MS); Hi Hnr Roll; Hnr Roll; MVP; Nat Hon Sy; Perf Att; Pres Ac Ftns Aw; St of Mnth; Yth Ldrshp Prog; Comm Volntr; Chrch Yth Grp; DARE; Drma Clb; Prom Com; Scouts; Bnd; Dnce; SP/M/VS; Bsball; Chrldg (C); Gmnstcs; PPSqd; Sftball; Swmg; Track (L); Vllyball (L); Stu Cncl; CR (R); 9 Year Jr. Graduate Evelyn Ott School of Dance - Gymnastics; 9 Year Jr. Graduate Evelyn Ott School of Dance (Jazz); Marine Biology; Performing Arts; Old Dominion U; James Madison U

VASQUEZ, ROBERTO A; FALLS CHURCH, VA; GEORGE C MARSHALL HS; (JR); Hnr Roll; Perf Att; Chrch Yth Grp; Scouts; Ch Chr; Hospitality Management; Business Management; Michigan State U; Brigham Young U

VAUGHAN, JOHANNA; RESTON, VA; SOUTH LAKES HS; (SO); Hnr Roll; MVP; Nat Hon Sy; Otst Ac Ach Awd; Sci Fairs; St of Mnth; Comm Volntr; Peer Tut/Med; Spec Olymp Vol; Chrch Yth Grp; Chr; Bskball (J); Mar Art (V); Sftball (J); Yrbk (P); First Degree Black Belt; Medicine; Family Physician; U of Toronto; Yale

VAUGHAN, RACHEL; CLIFTON FORGE, VA; ALLEGHANY HS; (JR); Hnr Roll; Nat Hon Sy; WWAHSS; Comm Volntr; Hosp Aide; AL Aux Girls; Chrch Yth Grp; Emplmnt; Key Club; Ntl Beta Clb; Prom Com; SADD; Foreign Clb; Bnd; Mch Bnd; Pep Bnd; Stg Cre; Cr Ctry (V L); Lit Mag; AHYD Swim Team; Creative Writing / Journalism; British Literature; Christopher Newport U; High Point U

VAUGHN, DANIELLE; CLOVER, VA; HALIFAX CTY HS; (JR); Hnr Roll; Perf Att; Yth Ldrshp Prog; Chrch Yth Grp; FBLA; Pep Squd; Scouts; Ch Chr; Dnce; Pep Bnd; PPSqd; Future Career Community Leaders of America; Young Democrats; Communications; Dancing; North Carolina Central U; Virginia Commonwealth

VEASEY, MEGAN; EARLYSVILLE, VA; ALBEMARLE HS CHARLOTTESVILLE VA; (FR); Hi Hnr Roll; Comm Volntr; Chrch Yth Grp; Key Club; Chr; Swmg (V L)

VENEY, LORENZO; TAPPAHANNOCK, VA; ESSEX HS; (FR); Bnd; Ch Chr; Mch Bnd; Bskball (J); Track (V); I Was MVP of Band; I Received a Perfect Score on the Algebra; Law; Computer Technician; Harvard U; Penn State U

VENNE, TORI; ASHBURN, VA; BROAD RUN HS; (SO); Hi Hnr Roll; Hnr Roll; Otst Ac Ach Awd; Perf Att; St of Mnth; Chrch Yth Grp; DARE; Emplmnt; Scouts; Animal Biology; Zoology; Ohio Wesleyan U; North Carolina State U

VENSKOSKE, JEREMY E; WINCHESTER, VA; JAMES WOOD HS; (SO); 4H Awd; Hnr Roll; Comm Volntr; 4-H; Chrch Yth Grp; Ntl FFA; Bnd; Mch Bnd; Orch; Pep Bnd; Star Greenhand; Outstanding Agriculture Student; Band Teacher; Farmer; Lord Fairfax Community College; Virginia Tech

VICK, CAROLINE E; MEHERRIN, VA; FUQUA SCH; (FR); All Am Sch; Hnr Roll; Sci Fairs; USAA; Chrch Yth Grp; Fr of Library; SADD; Wdwrkg Clb; Spanish Clb; Chrldg (J); Swmg (VJ); US President's Award for Academic Excellence; Academic Advancement for Youth @ Johns Hopkins U; Elementary Education; Business; Elon College; Longwood College

VILLA, ELIZABETH A; ASHBURN, VA; BRIARWOODS HS; (FR); Duke TS; Hnr Roll; Otst Ac Ach Awd; St of Mnth; WWAHSS; Comm Volntr; Peer Tut/Med; Key Club; Ntl Beta Clb; Beta Club Member 2001-2003; Key Club International; Veterinary Science; Business Law; Virginia Tech; U VA

VILLANUEVA, ROSE; ARLINGTON, VA; YORKTOWN HS; (JR); Ctznshp Aw; Comm Volntr; Peer Tut/Med; Emplmnt; NYLC; SADD; Dnce; Vllyball (V); 1st Place - National Peruvian Dance called - Marinera Nortena / NJ; Executive Board for the 2006 School Year at Yorktown HS; Dentist; Biomedical Engineer; University of North Carolina; Christopher Newport University

VINT, ERIK S; RIDGEWAY, VA; MAGNA VISTA HS; (JR); Hi Hnr Roll; Nat Hon Sy; Perf Att; WWAHSS; Hosp Aide; Chrch Yth Grp; FBLA; Ntl Beta Clb; Sci Clb; Bnd; Ch Chr; Mch Bnd; SP/M/VS; Bskball (J); Ftball (VJ L); Wrstlg (V L); Chemistry Major; Astronomy Major; Virginia Tech; U of Notre Dame

VOLODIN, DMITRY; FAIRFAX, VA; THOMAS JEFFERSON HS SCIENCE & TECH; (SR); Nat Mrt Fin; Cmptr Clb; Emplmnt; Mth Clb/Tm; Sci Clb; Chrldg (V L); German National Exam-99th Percentile 9th/11th Grades; Virginia Polytechnic Institute; U of Virginia

WADE, DANIELLE J; FREDERICKSBURG, VA; STAFFORD SR HS; (SR); Hi Hnr Roll; WWAHSS; Voc Ind Clb Am; Bskball (J); Vice President of Skills-USA; Business Administration; Virginia State U

WADE, JUSTIN J; MARTINSVILLE, VA; MARTINSVILLE HS; (SR); Ctznshp Aw; F Lan Hn Soc; Hi Hnr Roll; Hnr Roll; MVP; Nat Stu Ath Day Aw; Otst Ac Ach Awd; Pres Sch; WWAHSS; Yth Ldrshp Prog; Comm Volntr; Spec Olymp Vol; 4-H; Chrch Yth Grp; Cmptr Clb; DARE; Drma Clb; Emplmnt; FBLA; Off Aide; Ch Chr; SP/M/VS; Stg Cre; Bsball; Ftball; PP Ftbl (C); Scr Kpr; Track (V CL); Wt Lftg; Cl Off (T); Stu Cncl (R); CR (P); National Society Black Engineers; Medicine / Obstetrician; Old Dominion U; Christopher Newport U

WADE, SARAH; LYNCHBURG, VA; E C GLASS HS; (JR); Gov Hnr Prg; Hi Hnr Roll; Hnr Roll; Nat Hon Sy; Nat Mrt Fin; Otst Ac Ach Awd; Comm Volntr; Chrch Yth Grp; Key Club; Mth Clb/Tm; Mus Clb; Latin Clb; Ch Chr; Orch; SP/M/VS; Sccr (JC); Track (J); Adv Cncl (R); National History Day Participant; State Winner-Virginia History Day; English; Political Science/ Foreign Policy; U of Virginia; Princeton U

WAKEFIELD, MEGAN R; STERLING, VA; POTOMAC FALLS HS; (SO); Ctznshp Aw; Hi Hnr Roll; Hnr Roll; Otst Ac Ach Awd; Pres Sch; St of Mnth; Comm Volntr; ArtClub; Key Club; NtlFrnscLg; Quiz Bowl; Schol Bwl; Spch Team; Tmpl Yth Grp; Dnce; Varsity Baseball Manager; Dance Team; Journalism; English Literature; U of Virginia

WALDEN, TYREME R; HAMPTON, VA; PHOEBUS HS; (JR); Emplmnt; Computer Engineer; Architect; Hampton U; Christopher Newport U

WALKER, CANDACE N; ROANOKE, VA; PATRICK HENRY HS; (SO); Ctznshp Aw; Perf Att; Yth Ldrshp Prog; Comm Volntr; Chrch Yth Grp; DARE; Drma Clb; NYLC; Pep Squd; ROTC; Scouts; Ch Chr; Dnce; SP/M/VS; Chrldg (J); Scr Kpr (VJ); Tennis (J); Captain of Dance Team; Social Work; Education/Or Buss.; Bennett College; Clark Atlanta U

WALKER, DESARAY E.; STAFFORD, VA; COLONIAL FORGE HS; (SO); Ctznshp Aw; Hnr Roll; Otst Ac Ach Awd; Pres Ac Ftns Aw; Sci Fairs; St of Mnth; Chrch Yth Grp; DARE; Chr; Stg Cre; Virginia Society of Certified Public Accountants; Homecoming Committee; Teacher's Degree; Business; U of Virginia; Mary Washington U

WALKER, MASON R; ROANOKE, VA; WILLIAM FLEMING HS; (JR); Peer Tut/Med; Drma Clb; Ntl Beta Clb; NtlFrnscLg; Spch Team; Tchrs Aide; SP/M/VS; Stg Cre; Computer Engineering; Physics; James Madison U; Rochester Institute of Technology

WALKER, TY'RICA; CHERITON, VA; NORTHAMPTON HS; (FR); Ctznshp Aw; Hnr Roll; Nat Hon Sy; Otst Ac Ach Awd; Perf Att; St of Mnth; Comm Volntr; Mus Clb; Ntl Beta Clb; Bnd; Ch Chr; Mch Bnd; Fld Hky (V); Tennis (J); Work for FBI; Harvard U; Virginia Tech

WALLACE, ASHLEY; MANASSAS, VA; WOODBRIDGE SR HS; (JR); Otst Ac Ach Awd; Perf Att; Pres Ac Ftns Aw; WWAHSS; Comm Volntr; Emplmnt; Lttrmn Clb; Pep Squd; Vsity Clb; Dnce; SP/M/VS; PPSqd (V L); Vsy Clb (V); CR (R); Varsity Dance Team-Letter Received; Journalism; Dance; James Madison U; George Mason U

WALLER, BLAKE E; NATHALIE, VA; HALIFAX CTY HS; (SR); 4H Awd; Hi Hnr Roll; Nat Hon Sy; WWAHSS; Comm Volntr; 4-H; Chrch Yth Grp; FBLA; Lttrmn Clb; Ntl FFA; Ch Chr; Bsball (VJ L); Cr Ctry (VJ L); Ftball (VJ L); Swmg (VJ L); North Halifax Fire Dept.; Environmental Science; Virginia Tech

WALSTON, STEVEN T; CHARLOTTESVILLE, VA; ALBEMARLE HS; (JR); F Lan Hn Soc; Hnr Roll; Nat Hon Sy; Key Club; MuAlphaTh; Bnd; Bskball (J); Sccr (VJ L); Track (V L); Engineering; Ophthalmology

WALTERS, JACQUIE; VIRGINIA BEACH, VA; FRANK W COX HS; (SO); F Lan Hn Soc; Hi Hnr Roll; Nat Hon Sy; Otst Ac Ach Awd; WWAHSS; Comm Volntr; Key Club; Mus Clb; Spch Team; French Clb; Chr; SP/M/VS; Stu Cncl (R); Virginian Pilot 2005 Scholastic Achievement Team; PTSA Class Representative; Actor; U of Virginia; Yale U

WALTHER, BRANDON D; CHARLOTTESVILLE, VA; ALBEMARLE HS; (SO); Hnr Roll; WWAHSS; Peer Tut/Med; Key Club; Bsball (J); CR (R); Peer Counseling; Young Life; Business; Virginia Tech; U of Virginia

WALTON, CHRIS; PORTSMOUTH, VA; STONEBRIDGE SCH; (SR); Hnr Roll; Nat Hon Sy; WWAHSS; Comm Volntr; Peer Tut/Med; Chess; Chrch Yth Grp; Emplmnt; FCA; Key Club; Tchrs Aide; Bnd; SP/M/VS; Cr Ctry (V); Tennis (V CL)

WALTON, RHETT; VIRGINIA BEACH, VA; FRANK W COX HS; (FR); Hnr Roll; Comm Volntr; Key Club; Rush Advanced Soccer

WANG, DINGQIU; HAYMARKET, VA; STONEWALL JACKSON HS; (JR); F Lan Hn Soc; Hnr Roll; St of Mnth; Comm Volntr; Art Award in Montgomery County; Mathematics; Business; Columbia U; Yale U

WARD, JONATHAN; DANVILLE, VA; CHATHAM HS; (JR); Ctznshp Aw; Hnr Roll; Jr Mshl; WWAHSS; Emplmnt; FBLA; Ntl Beta Clb; Scouts; Drl Tm; Ftball (J); Golf (V); Track (V); Cl Off (P); Eagle Scout Candidate - Member of Boy Scouts; Selected to Represent School at Boys State; Law; Surgeon; Virginia Military Academy; James Madison U

WARD, M SUTTON; CHESTER, VA; LLOYD C BIRD HS; (JR); Perf Att; Comm Volntr; Peer Tut/Med; FBLA; Jr Cls League; Key Club; Dnce; Key Club, Future Business Leaders, Latin Club, Academic Award; Business Management; Radford U; Longwood U

WARF, SHELLY R; HILLSVILLE, VA; CARROLL CTY HS; (SR); Hi Hnr Roll; Hnr Roll; St of Mnth; Comm Volntr; Mus Clb; Acpl Chr; Chr; Ch Chr; Vllyball (JC); Law School; New River College

WARREN, ASHLEE R; EAGLE ROCK, VA; ALLEGHANY HS; (SO); Hi Hnr Roll; Nat Hon Sy; WWAHSS; Comm Volntr; Peer Tut/Med; Chrch Yth Grp; Emplmnt; Key Club; Scouts; SADD; Vsity Clb; Bnd; Dnce; Mch Bnd; Bskball (J); Track (V L); Vsy Clb; Girls AAU Basketball, Symphonic Band; Girl Scouts, Hand Bell Choir; Athletic Training; Duke U

WASHINGTON, APRIL; COLONIAL HEIGHTS, VA; (SR); The National Dean's List; Criminal Justice Technology; ECPI College / Technical

WASHINGTON, DONNIE; TROY, VA; FLUVANNA CTY HS; (JR); Ctznshp Aw; Hnr Roll; Otst Ac Ach Awd; St of Mnth; WWAHSS; Chrch Yth Grp; Ntl Beta Clb; Chr; Ch Chr; Track (V); Yrbk; Medical; Law; Harvard Law; U of Virginia

WASHINGTON, GENOVA D; WOODBRIDGE, VA; GAR-FIELD HS; (JR); Hnr Roll; MVP; Otst Ac Ach Awd; Comm Volntr; Quill & Scroll; Cr Ctry (V CL); Track (V L); Yrbk (R, P); International Baccalaureate Student; Leo Club (Volunteer Service), Homecoming Committee; Pharmacy; Chemistry; Florida A & M U, (La); Xavier U

WASHINGTON, KEONNA; PORTSMOUTH, VA; I C NORCOM; (SO); Hi Hnr Roll; Hnr Roll; Salutrn; WWAHSS; Comm Volntr; Ch Chr; Chrome Club and Access Program; Magnet Student; Forensic Scientist; Business Owner; Hampton U; Old Dominion U

WASHINGTON, ZACHARY A; TAPPAHANNOCK, VA; ESSEX HS; (FR); Perf Att; Comm Volntr; 4-H; Chrch Yth Grp; DARE; Bnd; Mch Bnd; Pep Bnd; Computer Science; Medical Sciences; Pennsylvania State U; James Madison U

WATKINS, DANA; HAMPTON, VA; BETHEL HS; (SO); Hi Hnr Roll; Perf Att; Comm Volntr; FBLA; Latin Clb; Jzz Bnd; Chrldg (V); Cr Ctry (J); Track (J); Outstanding World History Student; Honor Roll; Business; Finance; U of Virginia; James Madison U

WATSON, SEKIA M; SOUTH BOSTON, VA; HALIFAX CTY HS; (JR); Ctznshp Aw; Hi Hnr Roll; Jr Mshl; Nat Hon Sy; Pres Ac Ftns Aw; Yth Ldrshp Prog; Comm Volntr; Peer Tut/Med; 4-H; ArtClub; Chrch Yth Grp; Mth Clb/Tm; Pep Squd; Prom Com; Scouts; Latin Clb; Ch Chr; Cl Off (P, R); Mortuary Science; Business Degree; Norfolk State U; Old Dominion U

WATTIE, SALONE D D; RICHMOND, VA; HENRICO HS; (SO); Hnr Roll; Perf Att; Comm Volntr; Peer Tut/Med; Drma Clb; Scouts; Dnce; Chrldg (C); Golf (J); PP Ftbl (J); Sftball (J); Track (J); Vllyball (J); Cl Off (V); Sch Ppr (E); Peer Mediator; Doctor/Nurse; Mary Washington College; Old Dominion U

WATTS, MANDY; SOUTH BOSTON, VA; HALIFAX CTY HS; (JR); Hnr Roll; Nat Hon Sy; Otst Ac Ach Awd; Perf Att; WWAHSS; Peer Tut/Med; Bskball (JC); Sftball (VJ); Vllyball (VJ L); Sch Ppr (R); Dixie Softball & Jr. Leadership; Travel Softball; Physical Therapy; Athletic Training; Greensboro College; Lynchburg College

WEANING, SARAH M; BERRYVILLE, VA; CLARKE CTY HS; (SR); All Am Sch; Hnr Roll; Nat Hon Sy; Pres Ac Ftns Aw; WWAHSS; Comm Volntr; Peer Tut/Med; Red Cr Aide; AL Aux Girls; Emplmnt; Prom Com; Bskball (JC); Vllyball (J); Classical Studies; Latin; Virginia Polytechnic and State U; U of Virginia

WEARLY, JAMIE; NEWPORT NEWS, VA; WARWICK HS; (SO); Hnr Roll; Key Club; Acpl Chr; Chr; Interior Designing

Vargas, Jaimie L
Brandon MS
Virginia Beach, VA

Usmani, Aarzoo
Annandale HS
Annandale, VA

Van Der Linde, Melissa
Albemarle HS
Earlysville, VA

WEATHERSTINE, SARAH V; PORTSMOUTH, VA; WOODROW WILSON HS; (SR); Hnr Roll; Nat Hon Sy; Otst Ac Ach Awd; WWAHSS; Comm Volntr; Emplmnt; FBLA; FBLA-Parliamentarian; Criminal Law; Virginia Wesleyan College

WEBB, CLINTON R; HILLSVILLE, VA; CARROLL CTY HS; (SO); 4H Awd; Ctznshp Aw; Hnr Roll; Perf Att; Sci Fairs; Scouts; Bnd; Engineering; Virginia Tech; U of North Carolina

WEDDELL, EMMA S.; VIRGINIA BEACH, VA; FRANK W COX HS; (SO); Hnr Roll; Sci Fairs; St of Mnth; WWAHSS; Comm Volntr; Chrch Yth Grp; Emplmnt; Key Club; Ch Chr; SP/M/VS; Chrldg (CL); Swmg (V L); Wt Lftg (V); CR (R); Computer Technology Outstanding Student of the Year; FCCLA; James Madison U; Virginia Polytechnic Institute and State U

WEDEL, ELISE; MANASSAS, VA; OSBOURN PARK SR HS; (JR); Hi Hnr Roll; Nat Hon Sy; Nat Ldrshp Svc; Yth Ldrshp Prog; Comm Volntr; Hosp Aide; Peer Tut/Med; Emplmnt; FTA; Key Club; Svce Clb; SADD; Adv Cncl (R); Girls State; Youth Salute; Education; Psychology; U of Virginia; U of North Carolina Chapel Hill

WEIDERHOLD, LIZ; SPRINGFIELD, VA; WEST SPRINGFIELD HS; (JR); Ctznshp Aw; F Lan Hn Soc; Hi Hnr Roll; Nat Hon Sy; Pres Ac Ftns Aw; WWAHSS; Comm Volntr; Peer Tut/Med; Emplmnt; Mth Clb/Tm; Quill & Scroll; Sci Clb; Scouts; Latin Clb; Sch Ppr (E, R); Yrbk (R); AAUW Diversity Award; Journalism; English; Columbia; Northwestern

WEIGLE, MEGHAN E; FALLS CHURCH, VA; STUART HS; (SR); Hnr Roll; Emplmnt; NYLC; Photog; Prom Com; International Studies; International Relations; Elon U; Wesley College

WELKER, SARA; WOODBRIDGE, VA; C D HYLTON HS; (FR); Ctznshp Aw; Hnr Roll; Otst Ac Ach Awd; Perf Att; Pres Ac Ftns Aw; Sci Fairs; Comm Volntr; Peer Tut/Med; Chrch Yth Grp; DARE; FCA; Tchrs Aide; Chr; Ch Chr; SP/M/VS; Stg Cre; Cl Off (R); CR (P); Advanced Gymnastics; Select Choir Ensemble; Marine Biology; Culinary Arts

WELLS, CHRISTINA M; CHESAPEAKE, VA; DEEP CREEK HS; (SR); F Lan Hn Soc; Hi Hnr Roll; Nat Hon Sy; WWAHSS; Comm Volntr; Red Cr Aide; Chrch Yth Grp; Emplmnt; Key Club; Chrldg (V C); Stu Cncl (V); Homecoming Queen; National Honor Society; Accounting; James Madison U

WELLS, JESSICA; RICHMOND, VA; RICHMOND CMTY HS; (SO); Ctznshp Aw; Hi Hnr Roll; Hnr Roll; Perf Att; Sci Fairs; WWAHSS; Yth Ldrshp Prog; Comm Volntr; Peer Tut/Med; Chrch Yth Grp; FBLA; Key Club; Mod UN; Quiz Bowl; Scouts; Adv Cncl (R); Cl Off (R); Stu Cncl (R); CR (R); Business & Information Technology Student of the Year - 2002-2003; Poetry.Com - Semi-Finalist; Pre-Law; Forensics

WELLS, ZACHARY A; BOYCE, VA; CLARKE CTY HS; (FR); Ctznshp Aw; Kwnis Aw; Comm Volntr; Civil Air Pat; Emplmnt; Scouts; Bnd; Eagle Scout Boy Scout Troop 10; Air Force Pilot; Professional Fire Fighter; US Air Force Academy; Air Force ROTC- U of Maryland

WENTWORTH, JACKIE; DULLES, VA; (JR); Hi Hnr Roll; Hnr Roll; St of Mnth; Yth Ldrshp Prog; Comm Volntr; Mod UN; Bskball (J); Global Youth Leadership Conference; Private Voice/Piano Lessons; Veterinary Medicine; Law; Brown; Tufts

WERNER, KELSEY; ASHBURN, VA; STONE BRIDGE HS; (JR); Hi Hnr Roll; Hnr Roll; Nat Hon Sy; St of Mnth; WWAHSS; Comm Volntr; Emplmnt; Jr Cls League; Key Club; SADD; Latin Clb; Chr; SP/M/VS; Cr Ctry (V L); Track (V L); Lit Mag (E); Forensics; Reed College; U of California At Berkeley

WEST, ASHLEY E; ASHBURN, VA; STONE BRIDGE HS; (SO); Hnr Roll; Comm Volntr; Emplmnt; Key Club; Sftball (JC); Hours of Community Service/Key Club; Teach Swimming to Small Children; Lawyer; Genetics; Duke U; U of Virginia

WEST, JENNIFER; WILLIAMSBURG, VA; JAMESTOWN HS; (JR); Ctznshp Aw; Hnr Roll; Special Education Teacher; Milligan Christian College; Carson-Newman Christian College

WHARTON, EDGAR D; DANVILLE, VA; GALILEO; (FR); Ctznshp Aw; Hnr Roll; Perf Att; Sci Fairs; St Optmst of Yr; Amnsty Intl; Comm Volntr; Peer Tut/Med; Dbte Team; Lib Aide; Sci Clb; Scouts; GERMANY Clb; Bnd; Chr; SP/M/VS; Stg Cre; Lit Mag (P); Roots & Shoots; PhD in International Affairs; Master's Degree in Theology; Columbia U; Duke U

WHEELER, JESSICA; ASHBURN, VA; STONE BRIDGE HS; (JR); Hnr Roll; MVP; Nat Hon Sy; WWAHSS; Comm Volntr; FBLA; Key Club; Chrldg (V CL); PP Ftbl; CR (R); Sch Ppr; Psychology; Virginia Tech; Ohio State U

WHELAN, CARLY A; COLONIAL HEIGHTS, VA; COLONIAL HEIGHTS HS; (JR); Sftball (VJ L); 600 Club; Photography; Pre-Law; Virginia Commonwealth U; College of William and Mary

WHITAKER, JENNIFER; AMELIA COURT HOUSE, VA; AMELIA CTY HS; (SO); SP/M/VS; Chrldg (V); Track (V); Stu Cncl (V); CR (R); Yrbk (P); Who's Who; Dentistry; UVA; James Madison U

WHITE, CAMERON A; WILLIAMSBURG, VA; JAMESTOWN HS; (SO); Ctznshp Aw; Hi Hnr Roll; Hnr Roll; Nat Sci Aw; Nat Stu Ath Day Aw; Perf Att; Sci Fairs; Yth Ldrshp Prog; Comm Volntr; Hab For Humty Volntr; Peer Tut/Med; ArtClub; Chrch Yth Grp; Drma Clb; Emplmnt; Outdrs Clb; Tchrs Aide; German Clb; Chr; Ch Chr; Drl Tm; Qualified for E AP1; Captain of Step Team in Toano Middle School; Music Major; Entertainment Business-Singer & Actor; Hampton U; Florida State

WHITE, CAMERON E; PALMYRA, VA; ALBEMARLE HS; (JR); Hnr Roll; WWAHSS; Chrch Yth Grp; Key Club; Bnd; Ch Chr; Jzz Bnd; Mch Bnd; Bskball (J); Track (VJ); Wt Lftg (VJ); Stu Cncl (R); All Star Percussionist-State of VA; Computer Engineering; Duke U; Georgia Tech

WHITE, JARED; VERONA, VA; FT DEFIANCE HS; (JR); Hnr Roll; Otst Ac Ach Awd; WWAHSS; Ntl FFA; Poultry Judging-2nd in State; Dairy Judging-10th in State; Diesel Mechanic; Forestry

WHITE, JESSICA R; ROANOKE, VA; WILLIAM FLEMING HS; (JR); F Lan Hn Soc; Hnr Roll; Perf Att; Sci Fairs; WWAHSS; Comm Volntr; Peer Tut/Med; Chrch Yth Grp; DARE; Emplmnt; Key Club; Ntl Beta Clb; Chr; Flg Crps; Lit Mag (E); Premedicine; Teaching; Roanoke College; U of Virginia

WHITE, JESSIE A; EARLYSVILLE, VA; ALBEMARLE HS; (SR); F Lan Hn Soc; Hi Hnr Roll; Hnr Roll; Kwnis Aw; MVP; Nat Hon Sy; Otst Ac Ach Awd; Pres Ac Ftns Aw; WWAHSS; Comm Volntr; Peer Tut/Med; ArtClub; Emplmnt; Key Club; Photog; Spanish Clb; Swmg (V L); Track (V); Semi Finalist for Ayn Rand's Novel "Anthem", Essay Contest; Photography Exhibit Drexel U / First Place 2d Art in Exhibit; Environmental Science/Law; International Studies; The U of Virginia

WHITE, MAC; BANDY, VA; RICHLANDS HS; (SO); Hnr Roll; Nat Hon Sy; Otst Ac Ach Awd; Perf Att; Sci Fairs; Sci/Math Olympn; St Optmst of Yr; WWAHSS; Yth Ldrshp Prog; Comm Volntr; Hab For Humty Volntr; Emplmnt; Ntl FFA; Off Aide; ROTC; Scouts; Vsity Clb; Clr Grd; Drl Tm; Sccr (J); Cl Off (P); Stu Cncl (P); Tournament Paintball Captain; Criminal Justice; Virginia Tech; Southwest Virginia Community

WHITE, MARGARET; MANASSAS, VA; OSBOURN HS; (SR); F Lan Hn Soc; Nat Hon Sy; Sci Fairs; WWAHSS; Yth Ldrshp Prog; Comm Volntr; Red Cr Aide; Chrch Yth Grp; Drma Clb; Emplmnt; Mus Clb; SADD; Tchrs Aide; Spanish Clb; Chr; Ch Chr; SP/M/VS; Stg Cre; Lcrsse (V L); Tri-M Music Honor Society; Thespian Honor Society; Psychology; Marine Biology; Coastal Carolina U

WHITE, QUIANA C; RICHMOND, VA; HERMITAGE CTR FOR THE ARTS; (FR); Hnr Roll; Perf Att; Yth Ldrshp Prog; Comm Volntr; Chrch Yth Grp; Emplmnt; NYLC; Dnce; Drl Tm; SP/M/VS; Track (J); Student Leadership Workshop of VA; Teen Metro of Richmond; Business Mgmt./ Accounting; Dance; Virginia Tech & U of Penn

WHITE, VICTORIA A; CULPEPER, VA; CULPEPER CTY HS; (JR); Hi Hnr Roll; Nat Hon Sy; Otst Ac Ach Awd; Pres Ac Ftns Aw; USAA; WWAHSS; Comm Volntr; 4-H; AL Aux Girls; Emplmnt; Jr Cls League; Outdrs Clb; Latin Clb; Bnd; Jzz Bnd; Wind Ensemble/Honor Band; Academic Spotlight (Twice); Business; Mathematics; U of Virginia

WHITE JR, DEREK W; RICHLANDS, VA; RICHLANDS HS; (FR); Hnr Roll; Perf Att; Sci Fairs; USAA; Comm Volntr; Chrch Yth Grp; Mus Clb; Schol Bwl; Bnd; Mch Bnd; CR (R)

WHITING, BRITTANY; CHARLOTTESVILLE, VA; ALBEMARLE HS; (JR); Hnr Roll; Kwnis Aw; Perf Att; Comm Volntr; Chrch Yth Grp; Emplmnt; Jr Cls League; Key Club; Tmpl Yth Grp; Clb; Fld Hky (J); Track (J); Chemistry; Medical; James Madison U; U of Virginia

WHITLEY, ERIKA; ROANOKE, VA; WILLIAM FLEMING HS; (FR); Ctznshp Aw; Hnr Roll; Sci Fairs; Comm Volntr; DARE; Lib Aide; Dnce; Forensic Science; Forensic Engineer; Georgetown U; New York U

WHITNEY, COLLEEN; ALEXANDRIA, VA; THOMAS A EDISON HS; (JR); Hnr Roll; Otst Ac Ach Awd; Perf Att; Comm Volntr; Chrch Yth Grp; FCA; Key Club; Vsity Clb; PP Ftbl; Swmg (V L); Vsy Clb; Adv Cncl (V, R); Lit Mag (R); Essay Published in "Teen Ink" Magazine; Journalism; Advertising; Longwood U; Christopher Newport U

WHITTINGTON, JASMIN R; HAMPTON, VA; BETHEL HS; (SO); Hnr Roll; Acpl Chr; Chr; Ch Chr; Chrldg (J); Stu Cncl (R); Children's Church; Praise Dance; Major -Education; Minor - Child Development; Spelman College; Norfolk State U

WILLGRUBER, HOLLY L; PALMYRA, VA; FLUVANNA CTY HS; (JR); Hi Hnr Roll; Hnr Roll; Otst Ac Ach Awd; Perf Att; Pres Ac Ftns Aw; Comm Volntr; Hab For Humty Volntr; Chrch Yth Grp; Key Club; Ntl Beta Clb; Prom Com; Tchrs Aide; PP Ftbl (V); Sccr (V L); Track (V L); Sch Ppr (R); Domino's Athlete of the Week; Marine Biology; Physical Therapy; Christopher Newport U; Duke U

WILLIAMS, BROOKS; RICHMOND, VA; BENEDICTINE HS; (SO); Hi Hnr Roll; Otst Ac Ach Awd; St of Mnth; Comm Volntr; Chess; Key Club; French Clb; Clr Grd; Drl Tm; Cr Ctry (V L); Track (V L); Top Academic Honors for All Course Subjects; American Legion Post 125 Award for Military Excellence; Pre-Med / Medical Degree in Surgery; PhD Anatomy / Physiology; United States Naval Academy; U of Notre Dame

WILLIAMS, CAPRI M; RICHMOND, VA; BINFORD MS; (MS); Hi Hnr Roll; Perf Att; Comm Volntr; Jr Ach; Photog; Scouts; Spanish Clb; Track (L); Yrbk (E); National Junior Honor Society; Medical Field; Neurology; Duke U; Columbia U

WILLIAMS, DEBRIELLE K; DANVILLE, VA; GEORGE WASHINGTON HS; (FR); Ctznshp Aw; Hi Hnr Roll; Hnr Roll; Nat Hon Sy; Otst Ac Ach Awd; Chrch Yth Grp; French Clb; Ch Chr; Orch; Business-Public Relations; Fashion Designing; North Carolina A & T State U; U of Virginia

WILLIAMS, DELVON; RICHMOND, VA; JOHN F KENNEDY HS; (JR); Ctznshp Aw; Hnr Roll; MVP; Perf Att; Yth Ldrshp Prog; Chrch Yth Grp; Emplmnt; FCA; Chr; CR (P); Business; Computer Technology; Virginia State U; Virginia Union U

WILLIAMS, DEREK W; LURAY, VA; LURAY HS; (SO); Hnr Roll; Perf Att; Scouts; Bsball (J); Bskball (J); Chrldg (V L); Ftball (VJ L); Track (J); Wt Lftg (VJ)

WILLIAMS, EBONEE; WILLIAMSBURG, VA; BRUTON HS; (SO); Hnr Roll; Nat Hon Sy; Perf Att; Sci Fairs; WWAHSS; Peer Tut/Med; Chrch Yth Grp; DECA; Tennis (J); Nursing; Engineering; Old Dominion U; Virginia Tech

WILLIAMS, JOSH; PEMBROKE, VA; (SR); Hnr Roll; WWAHSS; Lttrmn Clb; Scouts; Ftball (VJ L); Track (VJ L); Engineering; Virginia Tech

WILLIAMS, KANISHIA K; DANVILLE, VA; GALILEO MAGNET HS; (FR); Ctznshp Aw; Hnr Roll; Perf Att; Sci Fairs; St of Mnth; Comm Volntr; Peer Tut/Med; Chrch Yth Grp; DARE; Science Fair Award; Veterinary Medicine; Forensic Science; North Carolina State U; Virginia Polytechnic Institute and State U

WILLIAMS, KAYLYN R; ROANOKE, VA; WILLIAM BYRD HS; (SO); Ctznshp Aw; F Lan Hn Soc; Gov Hnr Prg; Hnr Roll; Perf Att; Pres Ac Ftns Aw; Sci Fairs; Yth Ldrshp Prog; Comm Volntr; Chrch Yth Grp; Drma Clb; Scouts; French Clb; Chr; Stg Cre; Cr Ctry (V L); Tennis (V); Track (V L); Attend Roanoke Valley Governor's School for Science & Technology; President's Award Academic Excellence; Medical; Engineering; U of Virginia; College of William & Mary

WILLIAMS, KIANA A; ASHBURN, VA; STONE BRIDGE HS; (FR); Hnr Roll; WWAHSS; Yth Ldrshp Prog; Comm Volntr; BPA; DARE; Dbte Team; DECA; Emplmnt; FBLA; Jr Ach; Key Club; Stu Cncl (P); CR (P); Business Owner; Howard U, Virginia Tech; Penn State, UVA

WILLIAMS, KIARA I; MANASSAS, VA; OSBOURN HS; (SO); Hnr Roll; Nat Sci Aw; WWAHSS; Chrch Yth Grp; DARE; Key Club; Mus Clb; Chr; Ch Chr; Dnce; Bskball (JC); Track (V L); Cl Off (V); National Winner of Internet & Science Technology Fair; First Place Reflections Contest (Poetry); U of Virginia

WILLIAMS, LAUREN; BEDFORD, VA; LIBERTY HS; (SO); Key Club; Chr; Clr Grd; SP/M/VS; Track (L); Random Volunteer Work; Music Major; Film Major; Christopher Newport U; Berklee College of Music

WILLIAMS, MALLORY; CHESAPEAKE, VA; GREAT BRIDGE HS; (SR); Hnr Roll; Yth Ldrshp Prog; Comm Volntr; French Clb; Bnd; Mch Bnd; Pep Bnd; Stg Cre; Lettered in Band; Major in Political Science; Become a Teacher/Psychologist; Attending Old Dominion U in the Fall

WILLIAMS, MORENIKE C; NEWPORT NEWS, VA; WARWICK HS; (SR); F Lan Hn Soc; Hnr Roll; Perf Att; Red Cr Aide; Key Club; Yrbk; Psychology; Spanish; Old Dominion U; Hampton U

WILLIAMS, NATASCHA F; CHESTER, VA; THOMAS DALE HS; (SR); F Lan Hn Soc; Hnr Roll; Perf Att; ArtClub; Chess; DECA; Drma Clb; Mod UN; German Clb; Orch; Cr Ctry (V CL); Track (V CL); Psychology; Sociology; Virginia Commonwealth U; Old Dominion U

WILLIAMS, SARAH V; CHESAPEAKE, VA; (SO); Chrch Yth Grp; Bnd; Ch Chr; Drl Tm; SP/M/VS; Track; Yrbk (P); Eighth Grade Step Team Recognition from City Council of Chesapeake, VA; Media-Telecommunication; Theater-Drama; Norfolk State U; U of Virginia

WILLIAMS, SHANNON C; BOYDTON, VA; BLUESTONE SR HS; (SO); WWAHSS; FBLA; Ntl Beta Clb; Prom Com; Spanish Clb; Bnd; Mar Art; Lit Mag (E); Computer Science; History; Christopher Newport U; Virginia Military Institute

WILLIAMS, SHAUNTE; CHARLES CITY, VA; (FR); Hnr Roll; Nat Hon Sy; Sci Fairs; St of Mnth; Hosp Aide; Peer Tut/Med; Lib Aide; Chr; SP/M/VS; Bskball (V); Pediatrician; Virginia Commonwealth U; Duke U

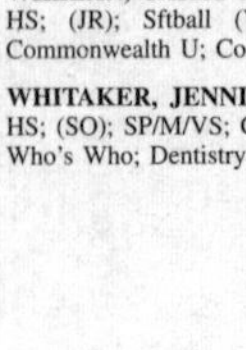
Williams, Sarah V
Chesapeake, VA

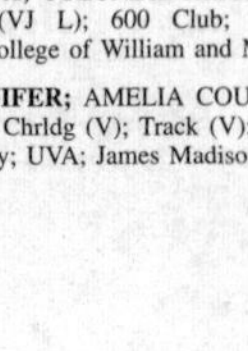
Whitney, Colleen
Thomas A Edison HS
Alexandria, VA

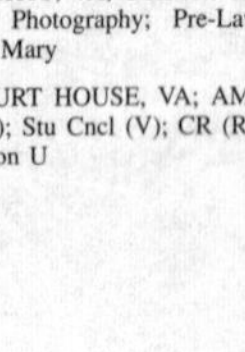
White, Cameron A
Jamestown HS
Williamsburg, VA

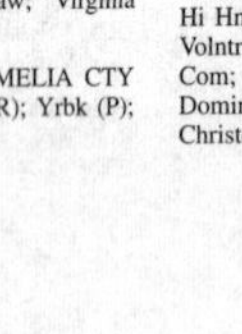
Werner, Kelsey
Stone Bridge HS
Ashburn, VA

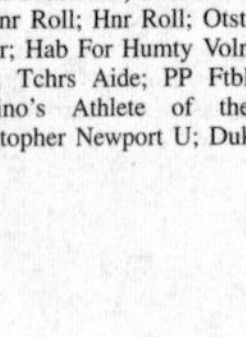
Wells, Zachary A
Clarke Cty HS
Boyce, VA

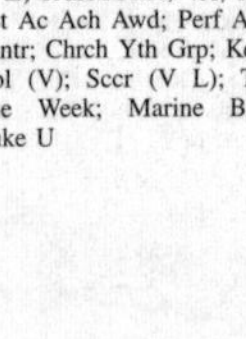
Webb, Clinton R
Carroll Cty HS
Hillsville, VA

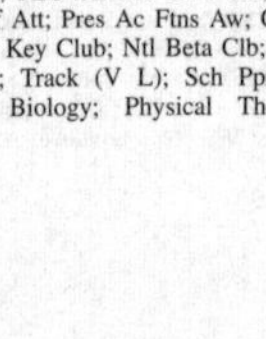
Welker, Sara
C D Hylton HS
Woodbridge, VA

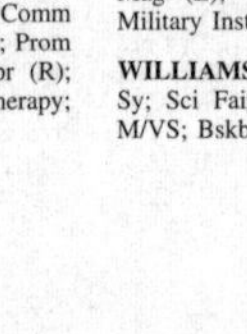
Wharton, Edgar D
Galileo
Danville, VA

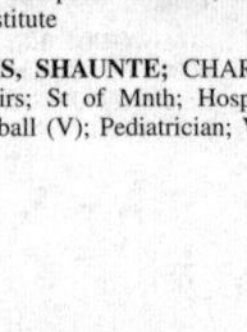
White, Margaret
Osbourn HS
Manassas, VA

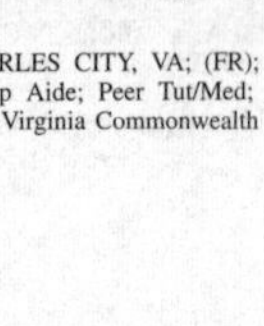
Williams, Mallory
Great Bridge HS
Chesapeake, VA

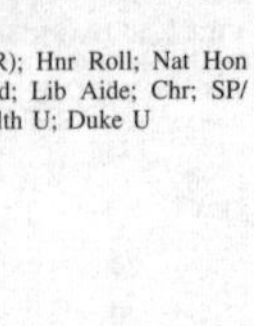
Williams, Natascha F
Thomas Dale HS
Chester, VA

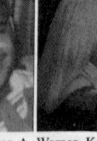

WILLIAMS II, JOHN; CHESAPEAKE, VA; DEEP CREEK HS; (JR); Ctznshp Aw; Hi Hnr Roll; Nat Hon Sy; Nat Ldrshp Svc; Perf Att; Pres Sch; WWAHSS; Comm Volntr; Peer Tut/Med; Chrch Yth Grp; Emplmnt; Key Club; Mod UN; NYLC; Ch Chr; Ftball (V L); Track (V L); CR (R); Architecture; Engineering; Yale U; Penn State

WILLIAMSON, EMILY A; MANASSAS, VA; OSBOURN PARK SR HS; (JR); Hi Hnr Roll; Hnr Roll; Nat Hon Sy; Pres Ac Ftns Aw; Sci Fairs; WWAHSS; Comm Volntr; Hosp Aide; Emplmnt; FCA; FBLA; Key Club; SADD; Latin Clb; Chr; Swg Chr; Sftball (J); FBLA Chapter Vice President; Choir Section Leader; Psychology; Business; Christopher Newport U; James Madison U

WILLIS, OLIVIA; DANVILLE, VA; WESTOVER CHRISTIAN AC; (MS); Hi Hnr Roll; Comm Volntr; Chrch Yth Grp; Drma Clb; Clr Grd; Teacher; Small Business Owner; Trevecca Nazarene U; Olivet Nazarene U

WILSON, CHYNITA; CULPEPER, VA; CULPEPER CTY HS; (SR); Ctznshp Aw; Hnr Roll; DARE; Mus Clb; Acpl Chr; Chr; SP/M/VS; All District Choir; Computer System Technology; Computer Networking; Strayer U; Germana Community College

WILSON, LINDSEY; AXTON, VA; MAGNA VISTA HS; (JR); All Am Sch; Jr Mshl; WWAHSS; Comm Volntr; Red Cr Aide; Chrch Yth Grp; Ntl FFA; Sftball (V); Vllyball (V); FFA State CDE Contest - 1st Place Individual & Team; Iriswood District Student Award; Educational Administration; Horticultural Science; Virginia Polytech Institute; Radford U

WILSON, MATTHEW S; EMPORIA, VA; GREENSVILLE CTY HS; (SO); Hnr Roll; Otst Ac Ach Awd; Yth Ldrshp Prog; FBLA; Ntl FFA; ROTC; SADD; Bskball (J); Ftball (J); Track (V); Engineering; Computer Technology

WILSON, NOAH A; PINEY RIVER, VA; NELSON CTY HS; (SO); Hnr Roll; WWAHSS; Chrch Yth Grp; Emplmnt; Scouts; Sccr (J); Photography; Pyrotechnics; New York Institute of Photography

WILSON, TERESA E; CHESAPEAKE, VA; DEEP CREEK HS; (JR); Hi Hnr Roll; Hnr Roll; Key Club; I've Been Published; Social Work; Sociology; U of Virginia At Wise; William & Mary

WILSON, ZACHARY V; STAFFORD, VA; NORTH STAFFORD HS; (SR); Bskball (V L); Ftball (V L); Track (V); 1st Degree Black Belt Kempo Karate; 1st Degree Black Belt Ju Jitsu; Computer Engineering; Christopher Newport U

WINCHELL, ROSA-ANNA; HAMPTON, VA; BETHEL HS; (SO); Chrch Yth Grp; FCA; Bnd; Fld Hky (V); Sccr (V); Physical Therapist; Johns Hopkins U

WINKELJOHN, STEPHANIE; RESTON, VA; SOUTH LAKES HS; (JR); Hi Hnr Roll; Nat Hon Sy; Pres Sch; Sci Fairs; Amnsty Intl; Comm Volntr; Peer Tut/Med; Bnd; Mch Bnd; Pep Bnd; Honor Band of America 2005; George Mason U Honor Band; History-General; Religion/Theology; U of Virginia; James Madison U

WINLAND, EMILY; ASHBURN, VA; STONE BRIDGE HS; (FR); Hi Hnr Roll; Otst Ac Ach Awd; WWAHSS; Comm Volntr; Peer Tut/Med; Chrch Yth Grp; Key Club; Quiz Bowl; SADD; Chr; Cr Ctry (J); Swmg (V); History Fair; Pre-Med; Biology; U of Virginia; Pennsylvania State U

WINSLOW, KAYLA L; CHESAPEAKE, VA; DEEP CREEK HS; (FR); Hi Hnr Roll; WWAHSS; Comm Volntr; Key Club; Chr; Ch Chr; Dnce; Chrldg (J); CR (R); All District Chorus

WISE, PATRICK M; PETERSBURG, VA; PETERSBURG HS; (JR); Ctznshp Aw; Hnr Roll; MVP; Sci Fairs; WWAHSS; Yth Ldrshp Prog; Comm Volntr; Peer Tut/Med; Chess; DARE; Emplmnt; Key Club; ROTC; Clr Grd; Drl Tm; Golf (V); Stu Cncl (V); CR (R); Sch Ppr (R); Rifle Team; Raider Team; Psychology; Law Enforcement; West Point Military Academy; Virginia Military Institute

WISE, TALIA; NEWPORT NEWS, VA; WARWICK HS; (SR); Hnr Roll; MVP; Nat Hon Sy; WWAHSS; Yth Ldrshp Prog; Comm Volntr; Key Club; Vsity Clb; Spanish Clb; Acpl Chr; Chr; Bskball (V CL); Track (V CL); CR (R); Marketing; Communications; U of Virginia; U of Maryland At Eastern Shore

WISER, WESLEY; CHANTILLY, VA; BROAD RUN HS; (SO); Hnr Roll; Ftball; Football at Freshman Level; Medicine

WITTE, CHELSEA; WINCHESTER, VA; MILLBROOK HS; (SO); Hnr Roll; Comm Volntr; Peer Tut/Med; DECA; Key Club; Skiing (J); Sccr (J); CR (S); Fashion Marketing; Business; Virginia Tech; Ohio State

WOOD, ERIKA N; KING GEORGE, VA; KING GEORGE HS; (SO); Hnr Roll; Sci Fairs; St of Mnth; Comm Volntr; Chrch Yth Grp; DECA; FCA; P to P St Amb Prg; Scouts; Fld Hky (J); Sftball (VJ); Coach's Award; 1st Place Regional Science Fair; Math; English; College of William and Mary; Virginia Polytechnic Institute and State U

WOOD, JUSTIN D; PALMYRA, VA; FLUVANNA CTY HS; (FR); Ctznshp Aw; Hi Hnr Roll; Otst Ac Ach Awd; Pres Ac Ftns Aw; Traditional Shotokan "Black Belt"; Doc. Veterinary Medicine; Virginia Tech; U of Virginia

WOOD JR, PAUL T; MARTINSVILLE, VA; MAGNA VISTA HS; (SO); FBLA; Ch Chr; Biology; Virginia Tech; Radford U

WOODS, MADELINE M; MANASSAS, VA; OSBOURN PARK SR HS; (JR); Hnr Roll; WWAHSS; Drma Clb; Emplmnt; Key Club; Prom Com; Wdwrkg Clb; Acpl Chr; Chr; Ch Chr; SP/M/VS; Cl Off (R); Piano; Baseball Manager; Scenic and Lighting Design; Stage Management; Shenandoah U

WOODS JR, RANDALL A; FALLS CHURCH, VA; J E B STUART HS; (SR); Hnr Roll; Otst Ac Ach Awd; Chrch Yth Grp; 3rd Place in Drama Rock Challenge Competition; Best Movie Award in Drama; Film; Multimedia; Abilene Christian U

WOOLSEY, JACOB T; FARNHAM, VA; RAPPAHANNOCK HS; (SR); Hnr Roll; WWAHSS; Emplmnt; Scouts; Ftball (V L); Volunteer Fire Fighter; Computer Networking and Security

WRAY, MEAGAN; FAIRFAX, VA; FAIRFAX HS; (JR); F Lan Hn Soc; Hnr Roll; MVP; Nat Hon Sy; Otst Ac Ach Awd; Sci Fairs; St of Mnth; WWAHSS; Comm Volntr; Peer Tut/Med; Emplmnt; Lib Aide; Photog; Tchrs Aide; Spanish Clb; Bnd; Fld Hky (V L); Lcrsse (V L); PP Ftbl; Swmg (V L); Yrbk (P); Piano Festival Honors X 11 Years; NVSL X 11 Years/Spanish Honor Society; Nursing; Old Dominion U; James Madison U

WRIGHT, JEFFERY D; HAMPTON, VA; BETHEL HS; (JR); Ctznshp Aw; Hi Hnr Roll; Hnr Roll; Perf Att; Pres Ac Ftns Aw; St of Mnth; Yth Ldrshp Prog; ArtClub; Chrch Yth Grp; DARE; Drma Clb; Mus Clb; Off Aide; P to P St Amb Prg; Photog; Bnd; Ch Chr; Mch Bnd; SP/M/VS; Track (V); Adv Cncl (R); CR (P); Soccer Referee; Computer Engineering; Music Engineering; North Carolina A & T; Miami U

WRIGHT, LEAH; WOODBRIDGE, VA; WOODBRIDGE SR HS; (SR); Otst Ac Ach Awd; Pres Ac Ftns Aw; Drma Clb; Photog; Quill & Scroll; SP/M/VS; Stg Cre; Adv Cncl (R); Stu Cncl (R); CR (R); Yrbk (E); International Studies; Japanese; College of William and Mary; Christopher Newport U

WRIGHT, MEGHAN B; HOT SPRINGS, VA; ALLEGHANY HS; (SO); Hnr Roll; Nat Hon Sy; WWAHSS; Comm Volntr; Chrch Yth Grp; DARE; Key Club; SADD; Chr; Ch Chr; SP/M/VS; Sccr (V); Lit Mag (R); Babysitter; Older Sister; Psychology, Communications / Broadcasting; Teaching / Journalism; James Madison U VA; College of William and Mary

WRIGHT, MIKELA; PORTSMAHN, VA; I C NORCOM; (JR); Hnr Roll; Nat Hon Sy; Nat Mrt LOC; Otst Ac Ach Awd; WWAHSS; Peer Tut/Med; Chess; FBLA; Prom Com; Tech Clb; Flg Crps; Mch Bnd; Bskball (J); Cl Off (T); Sch Ppr (E, R); Yrbk (R); Mechanical Engineering; Business Administration; Virginia Tech; North Carolina A & T

WRIGHT, NICHOLAS; WAYNESBORO, VA; STUART HALL SCH; (SO); Hi Hnr Roll; WWAHSS; Comm Volntr; Spec Olymp Vol; DARE; Sccr (J); Tennis (VJ); Cl Off (T); Engineering; Computer Tech

WRIGHT, RICKY; WILLIAMSBURG, VA; BRUTON HS; (FR); Comm Volntr; Key Club; NFL Youth Flag Football; Mentorship Program; Computer Engineer

WUYEK, THOMAS; FREDERICKSBURG, VA; SPOTSYLVANIA CAREER TECH CTR; (JR); Hnr Roll; Comm Volntr; Emplmnt; Off Aide; Quiz Bowl; Voc Ind Clb Am; Bskball (V L); Stu Cncl; CR (R); To Become a Chef; Johnson and Wales U; Culinary Institute of America

WYATT, LAUREN E; MARTINSVILLE, VA; MARTINSVILLE HS; (JR); Hi Hnr Roll; Nat Hon Sy; WWAHSS; Comm Volntr; Chrch Yth Grp; Key Club; International Clb; Bnd; Ch Chr; Mch Bnd; Sccr (VJ); Vllyball (J); Yrbk (R, P); Big M; National Technical Honor Society; Pharmacy

WYCHE, JASMINE L; EMPORIA, VA; GREENSVILLE CTY HS; (SO); Hnr Roll; Chrch Yth Grp; Ntl Beta Clb; Computer Engineer; Lawyer; Drexel U; Georgetown U

WYETT-FINNEY, JAMES S; CULPEPER, VA; CULPEPER CTY HS; (JR); Hnr Roll; DECA; Emplmnt; Stg Cre; Went to State DECA in First Year; Went to Nationals DECA - 2nd Year / Made Competency; Marketing; Business Management; Texas A & M U; Texas Tech

WYNN, NAKIA D; CHESAPEAKE, VA; WESTERN BRANCH HS; (SO); Hnr Roll; Nat Hon Sy; St of Mnth; Comm Volntr; Chrch Yth Grp; Ch Chr; Mch Bnd; Jr. National Honor Society; Architectural Engineer; Finance; Duke U; Old Dominion U

YASSIN, SARAH; ARLINGTON, VA; ISLAMIC SAUDI AC; (SO); Hnr Roll; Sci Fairs; St of Mnth; Comm Volntr; Peer Tut/Med; Svce Clb; I Was in the School Academic Olympics; I Join a Community Service Club; Medicine; Computer Technology; Duke U; New York U

YATES, KATHLEEN E; HALIFAX, VA; HALIFAX CTY HS; (JR); Hnr Roll; Nat Hon Sy; Comm Volntr; Chrch Yth Grp; Svce Clb; Pharmacy

YEH, BESS; HERNDON, VA; OAKTON HS; (SR); F Lan Hn Soc; Hnr Roll; Nat Hon Sy; Otst Ac Ach Awd; Perf Att; Sci Fairs; WWAHSS; Comm Volntr; Peer Tut/Med; AL Aux Girls; ArtClub; Chrch Yth Grp; Mth Clb/Tm; MuAlphaTh; Mus Clb; Sci Clb; French Clb; Orch; SP/M/VS; VA Summer Residential Governor's School for Humanities; Rocketry Club & National TARC Finalist; Biochemistry; U of Virginia

YELLAND, ERICA S; WARRENTON, VA; LIBERTY HS; (JR); Hnr Roll; WWAHSS; Hab For Humty Volntr; DARE; Emplmnt; French Clb; Bnd; Jzz Bnd; Mch Bnd; Pep Bnd; Church Young Group; Graphic Arts; Forensic Science; James Madison U; Virginia Polytechnic Institute

YEZZI, KRISTEN; MANASSAS, VA; OSBOURN PARK; (JR); Hnr Roll; Pres Ac Ftns Aw; Comm Volntr; Hosp Aide; Peer Tut/Med; Emplmnt; FTA; Key Club; Quill & Scroll; Chrldg (V L); Sch Ppr (R); Yrbk (R)

YI, CRYSTAL H; NEWPORT NEWS, VA; WARWICK HS; (JR); F Lan Hn Soc; Hi Hnr Roll; Nat Hon Sy; Otst Ac Ach Awd; Perf Att; Sci Fairs; Sci/Math Olympn; WWAHSS; Comm Volntr; Peer Tut/Med; Chrch Yth Grp; FCA; FBLA; Key Club; MuAlphaTh; Sci Clb; Svce Clb; Spanish Clb; Ch Chr; Tennis (J); CR (R); National Student Leadership Conference; Japanese Governor's School At VCU; Political Sciences; International Business; Georgetown U; Duke U

YOO, JOY J; ALEXANDRIA, VA; WEST POTOMAC; (SR); F Lan Hn Soc; Nat Hon Sy; Pres Ac Ftns Aw; Sci Fairs; WWAHSS; Yth Ldrshp Prog; Comm Volntr; Peer Tut/Med; AL Aux Girls; Emplmnt; FCA; Key Club; Quill & Scroll; Svce Clb; Vsity Clb; Spanish Clb; Orch; Mar Art (C); PP Ftbl (V C); Swmg (V L); Vllyball (V CL); Stu Cncl (R); Sch Ppr (E); 2002-2005 Tae Kwon Do National Champion; Public Relations; Business/Finance; Syracuse U; Boston College

YOPP, SHANNON J; ROANOKE, VA; PATRICK HENRY HS; (SO); Ctznshp Aw; Hnr Roll; Sci Fairs; Mus Clb; Pep Squd; Orch; Chrldg (JC); CR (R); Keyboarding Awards; Law; Music; U of South Carolina; Virginia Commonwealth U

YORI, COLETTE E; ALEXANDRIA, VA; THOMAS A EDISON HS; (SR); Hi Hnr Roll; Hnr Roll; Nat Hon Sy; WWAHSS; ArtClub; Drma Clb; Emplmnt; Key Club; MuAlphaTh; Prom Com; Latin Clb; Dnce; SP/M/VS; PP Ftbl (V); Cl Off (P); VA Governor's School for the Performing Arts for Dance; Cappie Award for Female Dancer in DC Metro Area; Biochemistry; Medicine; U of Miami

YOU, DEBORAH; FAIRFAX, VA; OAKTON HS; (SO); Ctznshp Aw; Hi Hnr Roll; Hnr Roll; Otst Ac Ach Awd; Perf Att; Comm Volntr; Peer Tut/Med; 4-H; Chrch Yth Grp; Emplmnt; Key Club; Mth Clb/Tm; Orch; Adv Cncl (R); Law Degree; Georgetown U; Cornell U

YOU, SYLVIA; CENTREVILLE, VA; CENTREVILLE HS; (JR); Hnr Roll; Sci Fairs; Hosp Aide; FCA; Key Club; Orch; Yrbk (P); Nursing; U of Virginia; Virginia Technology

YOUNG, ASHLIE; MARTINSVILLE, VA; MAGNA VISTA HS; (SO); WWAHSS; Sci Clb; Bnd; Flg Crps; Mch Bnd; Pep Bnd; Chrldg (J); Band Council-Secretary; Flag Corps-Squad Leader; Chemistry; Secondary Education; East Tennessee State U; Virginia Tech

YOUNG, BRITTANY N; COVINGTON, VA; ALLEGHANY HS; (SO); 4H Awd; Hi Hnr Roll; Perf Att; Comm Volntr; Hosp Aide; Peer Tut/Med; 4-H; Chrch Yth Grp; Key Club; Pep Squd; Scouts; Bnd; Mch Bnd; Chrldg (J L); Sftball (J); Stu Cncl (R); CR (R); U of Virginia; James Madison U

YOUNG, CAROLINE; HUSTLE, VA; ESSEX HS; (FR); 4H Awd; Hnr Roll; MVP; Otst Ac Ach Awd; Perf Att; St of Mnth; Peer Tut/Med; 4-H; DARE; Bnd; Ch Chr; Mch Bnd; Bskball (J); Science; Education; U of North Carolina; Liberty U

YOUNG, CHELSEA; MANASSAS, VA; OSBOURN HS; (SO); Hi Hnr Roll; WWAHSS; Comm Volntr; Chrch Yth Grp; Key Club; P to P St Amb Prg; Chr; Ch Chr; Dnce; Stg Cre; Yrbk (E); Tri-M Music Honor Society; Historian of Key Club; American Studies; Medicine; U of Virginia; Harvard U

YU, CATHERINE C; BURKE, VA; LAKE BRADDOCK SECONDARY HS; (JR); F Lan Hn Soc; Hnr Roll; Nat Hon Sy; Perf Att; WWAHSS; Yth Ldrshp Prog; Comm Volntr; ArtClub; Chrch Yth Grp; FCA; Key Club; Mus Clb; Quiz Bowl; JAPANSESE Clb; Orch; Mar Art (V); Track (J); Participant of TEH 04 High School Diplomats Program; Selected for the Prudential Youth Institute 04; International Relations; International Business; Georgetown U; American U

Young, Caroline
Essex HS
Hustle, VA

You, Deborah
Oakton HS
Fairfax, VA

Wright, Meghan B
Alleghany HS
Hot Springs, VA

Wood Jr, Paul T
Magna Vista HS
Martinsville, VA

Wise, Patrick M
Petersburg HS
Petersburg, VA

Wilson, Zachary V
North Stafford HS
Stafford, VA

Wilson, Lindsey
Magna Vista HS
Axton, VA

Wilson, Matthew S
Greensville Cty HS
Emporia, VA

Wood, Justin D
Fluvanna Cty HS
Palmyra, VA

Woods Jr, Randall A
J E B Stuart HS
Falls Church, VA

Wynn, Nakia D
Western Branch HS
Chesapeake, VA

Yoo, Joy J
West Potomac
Alexandria, VA

YUILLE, SHAKENA; LYNCHBURG, VA; HERITAGE HS; (JR); Hnr Roll; Nat Hon Sy; Perf Att; Sci/Math Olympn; WWAHSS; Comm Volntr; Chrch Yth Grp; Key Club; Chr; Bskball (J); Nursing; U of Virginia; James Madison U

ZAKARIAN, KATHLEEN M; CLIFTON, VA; CENTREVILLE HS; (SR); F Lan Hn Soc; Otst Ac Ach Awd; WWAHSS; Comm Volntr; Hosp Aide; Peer Tut/Med; Emplmnt; FBLA; Key Club; History; Education; George Mason U

ZEIGLER, ANNAMARIE; SUFFOLK, VA; STONE BRIDGE HS; (FR); Hnr Roll; Chrch Yth Grp; Key Club; Sccr (V); Cl Off (S); School Art Awards; ACSI Art Awards, Metro Art Awards; Psychiatry; English; Boston U

ZEITZ, JESSICA A; FREDERICKSBURG, VA; JAMES MONROE HS; (JR); F Lan Hn Soc; Hi Hnr Roll; Nat Hon Sy; Otst Ac Ach Awd; Perf Att; Sci Fairs; WWAHSS; Comm Volntr; ArtClub; Key Club; Prom Com; Vsity Clb; Latin Clb; Bnd; Chrldg (J); Fld Hky (J); PP Ftbl; Sccr (J); Cl Off (S, T); Stu Cncl (R); Soccer Manager-(l) Varsity; Monroe Scholar

ZEITZ, KIMBERLY A; FREDERICKSBURG, VA; JAMES MONROE HS; (FR); F Lan Hn Soc; Hi Hnr Roll; Sci Fairs; Comm Volntr; ArtClub; Key Club; Latin Clb; Orch; Fld Hky (J); Sccr (J); National Junior Honor Society; Monroe Scholar

ZEITZ, REBECCA A; FREDERICKSBURG, VA; JAMES MONROE HS; (FR); F Lan Hn Soc; Hi Hnr Roll; Sci Fairs; Comm Volntr; ArtClub; Key Club; Latin Clb; Orch; Chrldg (J); Sccr (J); National Junior Honor Society; Monroe Scholar

ZHENG, JIA; ROANOKE, VA; CAVE SPRING HS; (MS); Hnr Roll; Otst Ac Ach Awd; Perf Att; Mus Clb; Bnd; Dnce; Drl Tm; Orch; Gifted Art Program; 1st Runner Up National American Miss Talent Competition VA; Optometry; International Business; Duke U; U of Virginia

Zheng, Jia
Cave Spring HS
Roanoke, VA

West Virginia

ABRAHAM, WILLIAM; OMAR, WV; LOGAN SR HS; (JR); Hi Hnr Roll; Hnr Roll; Otst Ac Ach Awd; Pres Ac Ftns Aw; WWAHSS; Comm Volntr; Emplmnt; Prom Com; Vsity Clb; Bskball (J); Ftball (V C); Wt Lftg (V); Cl Off (P); Stu Cncl (R); Pharmacy; Tennessee; West Virginia

ABRAHAMSON, MEGAN A; WILLIAMSTOWN, WV; WILLIAMSTOWN; (FR); F Lan Hn Soc; Hi Hnr Roll; Hnr Roll; Kwnis Aw; Nat Hon Sy; Pres Ac Ftns Aw; Sci Fairs; Comm Volntr; Peer Tut/Med; Red Cr Aide; Chrch Yth Grp; DARE; Key Club; Photog; Prom Com; Quiz Bowl; Bnd; Jzz Bnd; Mch Bnd; Pep Bnd; Tennis (V L); Cl Off (P); Stu Cncl (S); CR (R); Lit Mag (R); Sch Ppr (R, P); Honor Society; Johns Hopkins Center for Talented Youth; Law; International Studies; Yale

ACORD, KRISTAN; BECKLEY, WV; WOODROW WILSON HS; (SO); Hnr Roll; Perf Att; 4-H; ArtClub; DARE; Drma Clb; Elementary Education; Medical School; Concord U; West Virginia U

ADAMS, EMMA; WEIRTON, WV; WEIR HS; (FR); Hnr Roll; WWAHSS; Comm Volntr; Chrch Yth Grp; Drma Clb; Key Club; Sci Clb; Swmg (V L); Forensic Science; Criminal Justice

ADAMS, MICHAEL C; CHARLESTON, WV; NITRO HS; (JR); Hi Hnr Roll; Hnr Roll; Nat Hon Sy; Perf Att; WWAHSS; Chrch Yth Grp; Emplmnt; FCA; Key Club; MuAlphaTh; Spanish Clb; Bnd; Jzz Bnd; Mch Bnd; National Honor Society; Inducted in Mu Alpha Theta; Plan to Major in Chemistry; Plan to Go to Pharmacy School; West Virginia U; Ohio State U

ADKINS, AMANDA; HUNTINGTON, WV; HUNTINGTON HS; (JR); Hnr Roll; Nat Hon Sy; Comm Volntr; Peer Tut/Med; Spec Olymp Vol; ArtClub; Chrch Yth Grp; Drma Clb; Emplmnt; Key Club; Mus Clb; Ntl Beta Clb; Photog; Acpl Chr; Chr; SP/M/VS; Stg Cre; WV Key Club District Lt. Gov. Div. 10A; Soul/Raze/Community Theater; Fine Arts (Visual or Theater); Teaching; Ohio State U; Fine Arts

ADKINS, WHITNEY; HUNTINGTON, WV; HUNTINGTON HS; (SO); Hi Hnr Roll; Nat Hon Sy; WWAHSS; Comm Volntr; Chrch Yth Grp; Key Club; Ntl Beta Clb; Latin Clb; Sch Ppr (E); Yrbk (P); English; Psychology; New York U

ALBERS, COREY W; WHEELING, WV; WHEELING PARK HS; (FR); Hi Hnr Roll; Otst Ac Ach Awd; Perf Att; Key Club; Sci Clb; Svce Clb; Ftball (V); Swmg (V); Architecture; West Virginia U

ALIFF, CURTIS; HEDGESVILLE, WV; HEDGESVILLE HS; (FR); Hnr Roll; Nat Hon Sy; Bsball (J); Ftball (J); Tennis (J); Track (J); Marine Biology; West Virginia U

ALLEN, L DAVID; CRUM, WV; TUG VALLEY HS; (FR); SP/M/VS; National Beta English Award Winner; UCLA-U of Southern California; West Virginia U

ALLEY JR, GARY W; INWOOD, WV; MUSSELMAN HS; (SO); Hnr Roll; Off Aide; SADD; Tchrs Aide; Ftball (J); Wt Lftg (J); U of South Carolina; Maryland U College Park

AL-QAWASMI, HALIMA; HUNTINGTON, WV; HUNTINGTON HS; (JR); Hi Hnr Roll; Nat Hon Sy; WWAHSS; Key Club; MuAlphaTh; Ntl Beta Clb; Sci Clb; Latin Clb; Gold Medal Winner on the National Latin Exam; Biology; Chemistry; Marshall U; Washington U in St. Louis

ANDERSON, ALEXANDRA; BARBOURSVILLE, WV; CADELL MIDLAND HS; (SO); WWAHSS; Hosp Aide; Fashion Merchandising; WVU

ANDERSON, JOSHUA; HEDGESVILLE, WV; MUSSELMAN HS; (SO); Hnr Roll; Chrch Yth Grp; SADD; Sccr (J); Wrstlg (V CL); State Qualifier in Wrestling; WVU

ANDERSON, KAYLA D; RIPLEY, WV; RIPLEY HS; (JR); 4H Awd; Hnr Roll; Perf Att; Pres Ac Ftns Aw; Hab For Humty Volntr; 4-H; DARE; Chr; Sftball (J); Marine Mammal Training; Biology; Washington State Community College; Salem

ANDERSON, KIRBY; BUNKER HILL, WV; MUSSELMAN HS; (JR); Hnr Roll; Otst Ac Ach Awd; Wdwrkg Clb; Bsball (V L); Wt Lftg; People 2 People Ambassador; Join the Navy and Become a Navy Seal

ANDERSON, WILLIAM E; WEIRTON, WV; WEIR HS; (SO); Hnr Roll; Key Club; Bsball (V L); Ftball (J); Physical Therapy

ANDREWS, TABITHA; WAR, WV; BIG CREEK HS; (SR); All Am Sch; Hi Hnr Roll; Nat Hon Sy; USAA; Valdctrian; WWAHSS; Peer Tut/Med; Red Cr Aide; Spec Olymp Vol; ArtClub; Key Club; Off Aide; Prom Com; Yrbk (E, P); National Society of High School Scholars; International Foreign Language Award; Concord U

ANTHONY, TONI L; PHILIPPI, WV; PHILIP BARBOUR HS COMPLEX; (SO); Hnr Roll; Emplmnt; Chr; SP/M/VS; Stg Cre; I Have Overcome Some Physical Disabilities to Get Where I Am.; Fairmont State-Psychology and Construction; Fairmont State College

ARMENDARIZ, LUIS; TALCOTT, WV; SUMMERS CTY HS; (SO); Hnr Roll; 4-H; Dbte Team; Quiz Bowl; Spanish Clb; Bnd; Mch Bnd; Track (C); Business/Marketing

ARNESON, EMMA; HUNTINGTON, WV; HUNTINGTON HS; (FR); Hnr Roll; Nat Hon Sy; Otst Ac Ach Awd; Chrch Yth Grp; Scouts; Bnd; Ch Chr; Dnce; Mch Bnd; Track (V); Silver Award Girl Scouts; Marine Biology; Food Science; Hood College; Wittenberg U

ARNOLD, LUCKY; KEYSER, WV; KEYSER HS; (FR); Hnr Roll; MVP; Pres Ac Ftns Aw; Sci Fairs; St of Mnth; Comm Volntr; Chrch Yth Grp; DARE; Drma Clb; FCA; Dnce; Bsball (J); Bskball (J); Ftball (J); Adv Cncl (T); Cl Off (T); Stu Cncl (T); CR (T); Potomac State; West Virginia U

ARNWINE, CANDICE J; CHARLES TOWN, WV; JEFFERSON HS; (FR); Hi Hnr Roll; Hnr Roll; Sci Fairs; Chrch Yth Grp; Key Club; Chr; Ch Chr; Won County Social Studies Fair Two Years in a Row; Participated in Tri-County Spelling Bee; Medicine; Law; West Virginia U; Johns Hopkins U

ASH, GABRIELLE; SALEM, WV; DODDRIDGE CTY HS; (SO); 4H Awd; Hnr Roll; Nat Hon Sy; Pres Ac Ftns Aw; Pres Sch; Sci Fairs; WWAHSS; Comm Volntr; Peer Tut/Med; 4-H; Chrch Yth Grp; FCA; Svce Clb; SP/M/VS; Chrldg (V); Track (V); Stu Cncl (S); Duke U; Concord U

BAILES, SAMANTHA; MOUNT NEBO, WV; NICHOLAS CTY HS; (FR); Hnr Roll; Nat Hon Sy; Perf Att; Pres Ac Ftns Aw; DARE; Lib Aide; Scouts; Chrldg (V); Sftball; Stu Cncl; Yrbk; #1 Club; Honors Society; Teacher; Lawyer; West Virginia U; Marshall U

BAILEY, CHRISTOPHER R; PAX, WV; MT HOPE HS; (SO); Masonry; Basketball

BAILEY, JACOB B; PRINCETON, WV; (SO); Hnr Roll; Otst Ac Ach Awd; Perf Att; St of Mnth; Comm Volntr; Hab For Humty Volntr; Peer Tut/Med; Chrch Yth Grp; Church Youth - Helping Repair Run Down Homes for the Homeless; Sports Announcing; Sports Medicine

BAILEY, LAURA; SUTTON, WV; BRAXTON CTY HS; (SO); Hnr Roll; Photog; Quill & Scroll; Bnd; Jzz Bnd; Mch Bnd; Orch; Track (J L); Yrbk (R, P); Student Council Member; Competed in State Track Meet - 2004; Education; Sciences; West Virginia U; Muskingham College

BAILEY, MEGAN J; MT CLARE, WV; BRIDGEPORT HS; (JR); 4H Awd; Ctznshp Aw; Hnr Roll; Perf Att; WWAHSS; 4-H; Chrch Yth Grp; Emplmnt; Pep Squd; Dnce; Pep Bnd; Chrldg (J); Radiology; United Hospital Center School of Radiology; West Virginia U

BAISDEN, ANDREA; MONAVILLE, WV; LOGAN HS; (SR); Hnr Roll; Nat Hon Sy; WWAHSS; Comm Volntr; Hosp Aide; ArtClub; FCA; Sftball (VJ); Architecture; Carpenter; Southern West Virginia Community & Technical College

BAKER, BRANDY J; RODERFIELD, WV; MT VIEW HS; (SR); WWAHSS; Peer Tut/Med; Key Club; Prom Com; Vllyball (V); Accounting; Bluefield State College; West Virginia U

BAKER, WHITNEY B; HUNTINGTON, WV; HUNTINGTON HS; (SO); 4H Awd; Hnr Roll; Hosp Aide; 4-H; Chr; Swg Chr; Nursing; Education; Glenville State College; Marshall U

BALES, CHARLES C; BALLARD, WV; SUMMERS CTY HS; (SR); Hnr Roll; Perf Att; WWAHSS; Ntl FFA; Bskball (VJ); Golf (VJ); Mechanical Engineering; Virginia Tech

BALL, ASHLEY N; IAEGER, WV; IAEGER HS; (FR); Ctznshp Aw; Hi Hnr Roll; Hnr Roll; Nat Stu Ath Day Aw; Otst Ac Ach Awd; Perf Att; Pres Ac Ftns Aw; St of Mnth; DARE; Bnd; Clr Grd; Dnce; Flg Crps; Bdmtn (V); Bskball (V); Skiing (V); Sftball (V); Swmg (V); Vllyball (V); Golden Horseshoe; Spelling Bee; RN Classes; Nursing; Concord College; Bluefield State

BALL, CHELSEA N; HUNTINGTON, WV; HUNTINGTON HS; (SO); Hnr Roll; Comm Volntr; Red Cr Aide; Spec Olymp Vol; ArtClub; Chrch Yth Grp; Key Club; Ntl Beta Clb; Off Aide; Scouts; Vllyball (J); S.O.U.L.; Medical Career-Pediatrician; Culinary Arts; U of Tennessee; Marshall U

BALL, CRYSTAL L.; BRADSHAW, WV; IAEGER HS; (FR); 4H Awd; Hnr Roll; Perf Att; Sci Fairs; Comm Volntr; Peer Tut/Med; 4-H; DARE; Quiz Bowl; Scouts; Chr; Bsball; Bskball; Chrldg; Gmnstcs; PPSqd; Sftball; Horse Riding-On My Own Time.; Virginia Tech-Veterinary Medicine; Concord College/U-Pre Vet.; Virginia Tech; Concord U

BALLARD, TARA; BRADLEY, WV; WOODROW WILSON HS; (JR); Gov Hnr Prg; Hi Hnr Roll; Kwnis Aw; WWAHSS; CARE; Drma Clb; Key Club; Spanish Clb; Stu Cncl (R); Accounting; Banking/Finance; North Carolina U; U of North Carolina-Charlotte

BALLATO, DANA M; WEIRTON, WV; MADONNA HS; (SO); All Am Sch; Hnr Roll; Drma Clb; Pep Squd; SADD; SP/M/VS; Chrldg; Skiing; Track

BANKS, ASHLEY R; SHEPHERDSTOWN, WV; JEFFERSON HS; (SR); 4H Awd; Hnr Roll; Nat Hon Sy; 4-H; Chrch Yth Grp; Emplmnt; FBLA; FCCLA; Prom Com; Tchrs Aide; Chr; Chrldg (VJ L); The President's Volunteer Service Award; 1st Place on Community Service Project for FBLA; Baking and Pastry Arts; Catering; York Technical Institute

BARBERY, ENNIS; ATHENS, WV; PIKEVIEW HS; (SO); Gov Hnr Prg; Hi Hnr Roll; 4-H; Mod UN; Quiz Bowl; Cr Ctry (V); Track (V); Environmental Club President; Member of Model UN Team; Psychology; Journalism

BARKER, ALEX; HURRICANE, WV; POCA HS; (SR); Hi Hnr Roll; USAA; WWAHSS; Comm Volntr; DECA; Emplmnt; Wdwrkg Clb; Cr Ctry (L); Most Valuable Dot - Nominee; Campus Christian Fellowship; Occupational Therapy; Business Administration; Dalton State College; Marshall U

BARKER, KORY; HEDGESVILLE, WV; MUSSELMAN HS; (SO); Perf Att; Photog; Achieving Appleman; Perfect Attendance

BARKER, NATHAN W; PHILIPPI, WV; PHILIP BARBOUR HS COMPLEX; (SO); Hi Hnr Roll; Hnr Roll; Perf Att; Comm Volntr; Chess; Ntl FFA; Off Aide; Stu Cncl (R); Yrbk (R); Dedicated to the FFA-Barbour Chapter; Participated in FFA Competitions; Graduate from Diesel College; Graduate from Trucking School; Universal Technical Institute

BARTOE, KAITLIN; NITRO, WV; NITRO HS; (JR); Nat Hon Sy; Comm Volntr; Hosp Aide; Chrch Yth Grp; Emplmnt; Key Club; Mth Clb/Tm; Prom Com; Cr Ctry (V); Sccr (V); Track (V); Cl Off (P); CR (P); Nursing; Marshall U; Ohio State U

BARTON JR, MICHAEL C; PRINCETON, WV; (SO); Hnr Roll; Comm Volntr; Chrch Yth Grp; FCA; Golf (V); AWANA / Sparks Team Leader; Law Enforcement; FBI Academy; Concord U; West Virginia U

BAUER, STEPHANIE; PETERSBURG, WV; PETERSBURG; (FR); Hnr Roll; Comm Volntr; Chess; Chrch Yth Grp; DARE; Bnd

BAXA, DANIELLE; BUCKHANNON, WV; BUCKHANNON-UPSHUR HS; (SR); 4H Awd; Hnr Roll; WWAHSS; Comm Volntr; 4-H; Chrch Yth Grp; DARE; DECA; Prom Com; Chr; Ch Chr; CR (V); Family and Consumer Sciences; Accounting; West Virginia Wesleyan College; Fairmont State U

BAXA, DERRICK; BUCKHANNON, WV; BUCKHANNON UPSHUR HS; (FR); Hnr Roll; Perf Att; Chess; Ftball (VJ); Wt Lftg (VJ); West Virginia U; West Virginia Wesleyan College

BECHETT, AMANDA R; WHEELING, WV; MT DE CHANTAL VISTATION AC; (FR); Ctznshp Aw; Hnr Roll; Kwnis Aw; Sci Fairs; WWAHSS; DARE; Drma Clb; Emplmnt; Key Club; Mth Clb/Tm; Spanish Clb; Chr; SP/M/VS; Stg Cre; Cl Off (P, R); CR (R); Wheeling Associates of Anime and Comics Treasurer; Voice Actress; English Teacher in Japan

BECKETT, SEAN M; BARBOURSVILLE, WV; CABELL MIDLAND HS; (SO); Ctznshp Aw; Hi Hnr Roll; Hnr Roll; Comm Volntr; Chrch Yth Grp; DARE; Scouts; Bnd; Mch Bnd; SP/M/VS; Eagle Scout; Fire Science; Eastern Kentucky; U of Cincinnati

BEECH, GABRIELLE; BRIDGEPORT, WV; BRIDGEPORT HS; (SO); Hi Hnr Roll; WWAHSS; Comm Volntr; Chrch Yth Grp; Key Club; Lttrmn Clb; Ftball (V); TATU - Teens Against Tobacco Use; Key Club; Elementary Education

BEEGLE, AMANDA D; LEON, WV; BUFFALO HS; 4H Awd; Hnr Roll; St of Mnth; Comm Volntr; Red Cr Aide; Spec Olymp Vol; Chrch Yth Grp; Chr; Community Service; 1995 Ruller Clean Up; LPNS; Labor and Delivery Nurse; WVU Medical School

BELCHER, AMANDA N; OCEANA, WV; WESTSIDE HS; (FR); Hi Hnr Roll; Hnr Roll; Perf Att; St of Mnth; Yth Ldrshp Prog; Comm Volntr; Peer Tut/Med; Chrch Yth Grp; Drma Clb; Mus Clb; SADD; Bnd; Ch Chr; Mch Bnd; SP/M/VS; Yrbk (P); National Junior Honor Society Historian; Nursing; Child Protective Services; West Virginia U; World Harvest College

BELLAMY, DONALD; ROCK, WV; PIKEVIEW HS; (SR); Hnr Roll; Nat Hon Sy; Perf Att; Pres Ac Ftns Aw; WWAHSS; AL Aux Boys; Lib Aide; Scouts; Tchrs Aide; Pharmacology; Concord U; West Virginia U

BENDER, JESSICA; MONTCALM, WV; MONTCALM HS; (SO); Hnr Roll; Chrch Yth Grp; Yrbk (R)

Barker, Nathan W
Philip Barbour HS Complex
Philippi, WV

Ball, Ashley N
Iaeger HS
Iaeger, WV

Bailey, Christopher R
Mt Hope HS
Pax, WV

Anthony, Toni L
Philip Barbour HS Complex
Philippi, WV

National
Honor Roll
Spring 2005

Andrews, Tabitha
Big Creek HS
War, WV

Baisden, Andrea
Logan HS
Monaville, WV

Banks, Ashley R
Jefferson HS
Shepherdstown, WV

Bender, Jessica
Montcalm HS
Montcalm, WV

BENDER, NICHOLE K; HACKER VALLEY, WV; WEBSTER CTY HS; (FR); Hi Hnr Roll; Comm Volntr; Scouts; French Clb; Dnce; Register Nurse; Accountant; Davis and Elkins; West Virginia U

BENNETT, AMY M; FRENCH CREEK, WV; BUCKHANNON-UPSHUR HS; (JR); Hnr Roll; Perf Att; Pres Ac Ftns Aw; Comm Volntr; 4-H; Chrch Yth Grp; DARE; Mus Clb; Scouts; Bnd; Mch Bnd; Pep Bnd; Juniorettes; Teen Institute / RAZE; Zoology; Park Activities Coordinator; Fairmont State U; West Virginia U

BERARDI, ASHLEY; FOLLANSBEE, WV; BROOKE HS; (SR); F Lan Hn Soc; Gov Hnr Prg; Nat Hon Sy; Perf Att; Valdctrian; WWAHSS; Comm Volntr; Emplmnt; Key Club; Off Aide; Photog; SADD; Spanish Clb; Ch Chr; Lit Mag (E); 2nd Degree Black Belt in Karate; Bronze, Silver & Gold Academic Awards; Veterinary Medicine; Bethany College

BERG, BRYCE T; MAYSVILLE, WV; PETERSBURG HS; (FR); Hnr Roll; Comm Volntr; Chrch Yth Grp; Emplmnt; Bnd; Forester; Potomac State College

BERRY, JESSI; WILLIAMSTOWN, WV; WILLIAMSTOWN HS; Hi Hnr Roll; Hnr Roll; Otst Ac Ach Awd; Comm Volntr; Peer Tut/Med; Chrch Yth Grp; Emplmnt; FCA; Key Club; Lttrmn Clb; NYLC; Tchrs Aide; Vsity Clb; Cr Ctry (JCL); Track (V L); Sch Ppr (R); All Star Cheerleading National Champion; Sports Medicine; Medical Field; Marietta College; U of Kentucky

BERRY, REBEKAH F; PARKERSBURG, WV; PARKERSBURG CHRISTIAN SCH; (FR); Hi Hnr Roll; Hnr Roll; Nat Hon Sy; WWAHSS; Vllyball (V); Teaching; Nursing; West Virginia U Parkersburg

BIAS, BETHANY N; BARBOURSVILLE, WV; CABELL MIDLAND HS; (FR); Ctznshp Aw; Hnr Roll; Comm Volntr; Chrch Yth Grp; Mus Clb; Scouts; Bnd; Clr Grd; Dnce; Mch Bnd; CR (R); Child Care and Teaching Academy; Pre-School Teacher / Aide; Child Care Director

BLANKENSHIP, DUSTIN; WELCH, WV; WELCH NAZARENE CHRN AC; (SO); 4H Awd; Hnr Roll; Perf Att; 4-H; Chrch Yth Grp; DARE; Mus Clb; Outdrs Clb; Photog; Prom Com; Wdwrkg Clb; Ch Chr; SP/M/VS; Stu Cncl (R); Air Force/Aviation Mechanic; Engineering; West Virginia U; Marshall U

BLANKENSHIP, DUSTIN S; BAISDEN, WV; GILBERT HS; (SO); All Am Sch; Hi Hnr Roll; Hnr Roll; St of Mnth; Comm Volntr; Peer Tut/Med; Chrch Yth Grp; FCA; HO'Br Yth Ldrshp; Mth Clb/Tm; Bnd; Chr; Ch Chr; Mch Bnd; Golden Horseshoe Award Winner; Gifted Education's Best Public Speaker (Mingo County, WV); Law (Pre-Law); Psychology; Oral Roberts U; Yale U

BLANKENSHIP, EMILY A; GILBERT, WV; GILBERT HS; (SO); Hnr Roll; Perf Att; Vllyball (V); Forensics; Mountain State U; Marshall U

BLANKENSHIP, JASON R; BAISDEN, WV; GILBERT HS; (MS); Hi Hnr Roll; Hnr Roll; Perf Att; St of Mnth; WWAHSS; Law; Education; Marshall U

BLANKENSHIP, SARA; WEIRTON, WV; BROOKE HS; (SR); F Lan Hn Soc; Hi Hnr Roll; Hnr Roll; Nat Hon Sy; Nat Ldrshp Svc; Otst Ac Ach Awd; Perf Att; WWAHSS; Hosp Aide; Chrch Yth Grp; DECA; FBLA; Key Club; SADD; Tchrs Aide; French Clb; Presidents Community Service Award; Gold / Silver & Bronze Academic Achievement Awards; Master's Degree in Nursing; Bachelor's Degree in Political Science; West Virginia U

BLEVINS, AMBER J; BERWIND, WV; BIG CREEK HS; (FR); Hnr Roll; Perf Att; Comm Volntr; Key Club; Veterinarian; Bluefield State College; Concord College

BLEVINS, NICHOLAS K; BECKLEY, WV; WOODROW WILSON HS; (SO); Hnr Roll; Pres Ac Ftns Aw; WWAHSS; Yth Ldrshp Prog; FCA; Off Aide; National Society of High School Scholars; National Honor Roll & Presidential Classroom; Civil Engineering; Marshall U/Virginia Tech U; West Virginia U

BOBO JR, RICKY L; FISHER, WV; MOOREFIELD HS; (SR); Ftball (VJ L); Track (VJ L); Wt Lftg (VJ); Science and Natural Resources; Criminal Justice; Fairmont State U

BOLDVC, BRANDON; WEIRTON, WV; WEIR HS; (FR); Hi Hnr Roll; Hnr Roll; WWAHSS; Bnd; Mch Bnd; Ftball (J); Pharmacy; West Virginia U

BOLIN, RIDGE T; PENNSBORO, WV; RITCHIE CTY HS; (SO); Hi Hnr Roll; Hnr Roll; Pres Ac Ftns Aw; Comm Volntr; Chrch Yth Grp; Vsity Clb; Bsball (V L); Bskball (J); Golf (V L); Junior National Honor Society; Pharmacy; Computer Engineering; West Virginia U; Marshall U

BOLLINGER, CYNTHIA G; JUMPING BR, WV; SUMMERS CTY HS; (SO); Hnr Roll; Perf Att; Pres Ac Ftns Aw; Comm Volntr; Peer Tut/Med; Chrch Yth Grp; FCA; Spanish Clb; Dnce; Chemistry; Sciences; Appalachian State U; Concord U

BOOTH, JESSICA L; DANVILLE, WV; SCOTT HS; (SR); Hnr Roll; WWAHSS; Chr; Sch Ppr; Yrbk (R, P); Potomac State College; West Virginia U

BOUBERHAN, HANNA; SHEPHERDSTOWN, WV; JEFFERSON HS; (FR); Hi Hnr Roll; St of Mnth; Key Club; Bnd; Mch Bnd; Key Club; Youth Theatre 2002-2004; Nursing; Law; Yale (Yale) U; Notre Dame

BOWEN, HEATHER M; HUNTINGTON, WV; HUNTINGTON HS; (SO); Hnr Roll; Comm Volntr; Chrch Yth Grp; Dnce; Mch Bnd; Pediatric Nurse; Child Care; Marshall U; West Virginia U

BOWEN, LAURA; DINGESS, WV; TUG VALLEY HS; (FR); Hnr Roll; Pres Ac Ftns Aw; Ntl Beta Clb; Chrldg (V); Sftball (J); Teacher; Lawyer; West Virginia State; Marshall U

BOWEN, PHILLIP A; BRADSHAW, WV; IAEGER HS; (FR); Ctznshp Aw; Hnr Roll; Pres Ac Ftns Aw; St of Mnth; DARE; Prom Com; Bskball (V)

BOWMAN, MEGHAN; RIDGELEY, WV; FRANKFORT HS; (SO); Ctznshp Aw; Hnr Roll; Perf Att; St of Mnth; DARE; Emplmnt; Quiz Bowl; Chr; Bskball (J); Sccr (J); Stu Cncl (R); Social Work / Child Services; Law; West Virginia; Potomac State

BOYD, JOHN B; GERRARDSTOWN, WV; MUSSELMAN HS; (FR); 4H Awd; Hnr Roll; 4-H; Ntl FFA; Bskball; Sccr (VJC); Tennis (V); CR (R); Agri-Business; WVU; Virginia Tech

BRADLEY, STEPHANIE S; WELLSBURG, WV; BROOKE HS; (SR); Hi Hnr Roll; Nat Hon Sy; Otst Ac Ach Awd; Perf Att; WWAHSS; Comm Volntr; Peer Tut/Med; AL Aux Girls; Chrch Yth Grp; Drma Clb; FBLA; Key Club; Off Aide; SADD; French Clb; Acpl Chr; Chr; Ch Chr; SP/M/VS; Bskball (J); Cr Ctry (V L); Usher's Club; Teens for Life; Speech Pathology / Audiology; West Liberty State College

BRANHAM, NATALIE R; DINGESS, WV; TUG VALLEY HS; (FR); Hi Hnr Roll; Hnr Roll; Nat Hon Sy; Perf Att; Drma Clb; Ntl Beta Clb; SP/M/VS; Chrldg (V); Gmnstcs (V); To Be a Vet; WV U

BRIGHT, MORGAN D; CHARLESTON, WV; NITRO HS; (SO); 4H Awd; Hnr Roll; Comm Volntr; 4-H; SP/M/VS; Ftball (J); Junior Leader- West Virginia 4-H Program; Charting Pin- West Virginia 4-H Program; Law; Journalism; West Virginia U; Marshall U

BRITCHER II, JOHN M; BRIDGEPORT, WV; BRIDGEPORT HS; (FR); Hnr Roll; Pres Ac Ftns Aw; Sci Fairs; Comm Volntr; Spec Olymp Vol; Chrch Yth Grp; DARE; Scouts; Ftball (J); Stu Cncl (R); Forensic Science; West Virginia U; Pennsylvania State U

BROOKS, CHANTAL; KEYSER, WV; KEYSER HS; (FR); Hnr Roll; Otst Ac Ach Awd; Perf Att; Sci Fairs; St of Mnth; Comm Volntr; DARE; Drma Clb; SP/M/VS; Bskball (J); Modeling/Basketball Trophy; Hall Patrol Award; Private Detective; Counselor; Shepherdstown College; West Virginia U

BROWN, C EDWARD; CHARLESTON, WV; RIVERSIDE HS; (JR); Hnr Roll; Otst Ac Ach Awd; WWAHSS; Comm Volntr; Chrch Yth Grp; DECA; Emplmnt; FCA; Mus Clb; Prom Com; Bnd; Chr; Ch Chr; Drm Mjr; WV Symphony Young Conductor; 2 Time National DECA Winner; Doctor of Music / Band Director; Business Owner; Marshall U; James Madison U

BROWN, EMILY; KINCAID, WV; OAK HILL HS; (JR); Hi Hnr Roll; Hnr Roll; Nat Hon Sy; WWAHSS; Spec Olymp Vol; Key Club; Mth Clb/Tm; Prom Com; Chr; Sccr (V CL); Junior Class Representative for Miss Red Devil; All Coalfield Conference 1st Team; Veterinary Medicine; Animal Science; West Virginia U; Concord U

BROWN, JOSHUA; BRIDGEPORT, WV; BRIDGEPORT HS; (SO); F Lan Hn Soc; Hi Hnr Roll; Hnr Roll; MVP; Nat Hon Sy; Pres Ac Ftns Aw; WWAHSS; Emplmnt; Key Club; Lttrmn Clb; NYLC; SADD; Vsity Clb; French Clb; Bskball (J); Ftball (J); Sccr (V CL); Track (J); Young Life; Doctor of Pharmacology; Ohio Northern U; Ohio State U

BROWN, JOSHUA R; LINN, WV; GILMER CTY HS; (SR); Ctznshp Aw; Hi Hnr Roll; Nat Hon Sy; Otst Ac Ach Awd; Perf Att; St of Mnth; USAA; WWAHSS; Comm Volntr; Hosp Aide; Chrch Yth Grp; Emplmnt; NYLC; Wdwrkg Clb; Bsball (V CL); Ftball (V CL); Bachelor's Degree in Nursing; Glenville State College

BROWN, SHAY; VALLEY GROVE, WV; WHEELING PARK; (SO); Hi Hnr Roll; MVP; Otst Ac Ach Awd; Sci Fairs; St of Mnth; WWAHSS; Comm Volntr; Peer Tut/Med; Spec Olymp Vol; Chrch Yth Grp; DARE; Drma Clb; Key Club; Tchrs Aide; Vsity Clb; SP/M/VS; Chrldg (V); Gmnstcs; Ice Sktg; Skiing; Sftball (J)

BROWN, TIFFANY N; BLUEFIELD, WV; BLUEFIELD HS; (SO); Sci Fairs; Scouts; Sftball (VJ); Medical; RN; Bluefield State College; Southern Connecticut State U

BROWN, VERONICA L; SURVEYOR, WV; LIBERTY HS; (FR); Hnr Roll; Kwnis Aw; Chrch Yth Grp; Key Club; Ch Chr; Track (J); Jr. National Honor Society; M.D. General; Forensics; Loyola in M.D.; Harvard, U

BROWNING, HANNAH; ROCK CAVE, WV; BUCKHANNON-UPSHUR HS; (FR); Hi Hnr Roll; Hnr Roll; St of Mnth; Track (V); Physical Therapy; Counseling; West Virginia U; West Virginia Wesleyan College

BROWNING, SEAN A; WHARNCLIFFE, WV; GILBERT HS; (SO); Hi Hnr Roll; Hnr Roll; Otst Ac Ach Awd; WWAHSS; Comm Volntr; Chrch Yth Grp; Emplmnt; Bnd; Mch Bnd; Honors Band At Va. Tech; All County Band-1st Choir; Law Degree; Criminal Justice; West Virginia U; Marshall U

BROWN-STOBBE, BROOKE; MORGANTOWN, WV; UNIVERSITY HS; (JR); Ctznshp Aw; F Lan Hn Soc; Hi Hnr Roll; Hnr Roll; Nat Hon Sy; WWAHSS; Yth Ldrshp Prog; Comm Volntr; Hab For Humty Volntr; Hosp Aide; Chrch Yth Grp; HO'Br Yth Ldrshp; Key Club; Off Aide; Svce Clb; French Clb; Stu Cncl (R); CR (R); Started Key Club At UHS; Started Student Service Award (200+ Hours); Pharmacy; Physical Therapy; West Virginia U; Boston U

BRUMFIELD, MELISSA; HUNTINGTON, WV; HUNTINGTON HS; (SO); Hnr Roll; Nat Hon Sy; Pres Ac Ftns Aw; St of Mnth; WWAHSS; Spec Olymp Vol; Acpl Chr; Chr; Bskball (J); Spanish Honorary; Health; Ohio State U

BRYANT, JOSHUA; BLUEFIELD, WV; BEAVER HS; (FR); Hnr Roll; Pres Ac Ftns Aw; Bsball; Bskball; Radio Broadcasting; Engineering; Bluefield State College; Concord U

BRYANT, STACI L; MORGANTOWN, WV; MORGANTOWN HS; (FR); Hi Hnr Roll; Hnr Roll; Comm Volntr; Peer Tut/Med; Key Club; Pep Squd; Scouts; Wdwrkg Clb; Lcrsse (J); Track (J); Sch Ppr (R); "4" on Writing Assessment; Medical; U of Kentucky

BUDDEN, KATY; KENOVA, WV; SPRING VALLEY HS; (SO); Hnr Roll; Nat Hon Sy; Sci/Math Olympn; Chrch Yth Grp; P to P St Amb Prg; Quiz Bowl; Bnd; Mch Bnd; Optimist Club Essay-3rd Place; SCORES Competition At Marshall U; Orthodontist; Singer; Columbia U; Marshall U

BURKS, ASHLEY N; KIMBALL, WV; MT VIEW HS; Hnr Roll; Sci Fairs; WWAHSS; Comm Volntr; Peer Tut/Med; Drma Clb; Key Club; Mth Clb/Tm; Mus Clb; Ntl Beta Clb; Prom Com; French Clb; Bnd; Flg Crps; Mch Bnd; Pep Bnd; Swmg; Tennis (V); Yrbk; Volunteer; Flag Corps Captain; Psychologist; School Counselor; Mountain State U; Bluefield State College

BURNETT, ANDREA; SHINNSTON, WV; LINCOLN HS; (JR); Ctznshp Aw; Hi Hnr Roll; Nat Hon Sy; Otst Ac Ach Awd; Perf Att; St of Mnth; WWAHSS; Peer Tut/Med; Spec Olymp Vol; Chrch Yth Grp; Prom Com; Tchrs Aide; Bnd; Ch Chr; Drm Mjr; Mch Bnd; Bskball (C); Chrldg (V CL); Gmnstcs; Track (V CL); Cl Off (P); Stu Cncl (R); CR (R); Yrbk (R); State Cheerleading Champion; Kodak Young Leaders Award; Physical Therapy; Biology Major; Fairmont State U; West Virginia Wesleyan College

BURNS, AMY N; VIENNA, WV; PARKERSBURG HS; (SO); Hi Hnr Roll; Hnr Roll; Nat Hon Sy; Key Club; Scouts; Tchrs Aide; Acpl Chr; Chr; Chrldg (V L); 4th Year All Star Cheerleader; Volunteer Jr Pee Wee All Star Cheerleader Coach; Education; Sports Therapist; West Virginia U; West Virginia U of Parkersburg

BURTT, ZACK C; HEDGESVILLE, WV; HEDGESVILLE HS; (JR); Hnr Roll; Engineering; Architecture; Massachusetts Institute of Technology; West Virginia U

BUSICK, STEPHEN W; WHEELING, WV; WHEELING PARK HS; (JR); Gov Hnr Prg; Hi Hnr Roll; Nat Hon Sy; Sci/Math Olympn; Yth Ldrshp Prog; Comm Volntr; Spec Olymp Vol; AL Aux Boys; Key Club; Mth Clb/Tm; Tchrs Aide; Bnd; Mch Bnd; Orch

BUTCHER, HEATHER G; ALUM BRIDGE, WV; LEWIS CTY HS; (FR); Comm Volntr; Hosp Aide; ROTC; Ch Chr; Had Poem Published; Nursing; Fairmont State; West Virginia U

BUTTS, PAUL; MARTINSBURG, WV; MARTINSBURG HS; (SO); Hnr Roll; Perf Att; Pres Ac Ftns Aw; St of Mnth; Comm Volntr; Red Cr Aide; FCA; Tech Clb; Chr; Cr Ctry (V); Ftball (V); Wt Lftg (V); Cl Off (R); Masonry; Welding; West Virginia State U

BUTTS, SECILY M; GERRARDSTOWN, WV; MUSSELMAN HS; (SO); Ctznshp Aw; Hnr Roll; Perf Att; Pres Ac Ftns Aw; Chr; Dnce; Swg Chr; Skiing; Vllyball; Stu Cncl (R); CR (R); Yrbk (P); Freshman Volleyball; Elementary School Teacher; Dental Hygenist; Shepherd U; West Virginia U

CANNON, MEG; HUNTINGTON, WV; HUNTINGTON HS; (SO); Hi Hnr Roll; Hnr Roll; Comm Volntr; Hosp Aide; Spec Olymp Vol; ArtClub; Chrch Yth Grp; Ntl Beta Clb; Stu Cncl (R)

CAPITO, STEPHANIE M; WEIRTON, WV; MADONNA HS; (JR); All Am Sch; F Lan Hn Soc; Hnr Roll; Nat Hon Sy; WWAHSS; Yth Ldrshp Prog; Comm Volntr; ArtClub; Dbte Team; Emplmnt; Prom Com; Sci Clb; Svce Clb; SADD; Stg Cre; Sccr (V); CR (R); Lit Mag (R); Chamber of Commerce Business Symposium; JETS Academic Team

CARDER, COLE; BRIDGEPORT, WV; BRIDGEPORT HS; (SO); Hi Hnr Roll; Hnr Roll; WWAHSS; Chrch Yth Grp; DARE; Emplmnt; Orch; Ftball (V); Swmg (V); Track (V); Wt Lftg (V); Criminal Defense / Law; Northwestern U; Brown U

CAREY, ANDREA; HUNTINGTON, WV; SPRING VALLEY HS; (SR); Ctznshp Aw; Hnr Roll; DARE; Bnd; Mch Bnd; Elementary Education; Marshall U

Budden, Katy
Spring Valley HS
Kenova, WV

Bowman, Meghan
Frankfort HS
Ridgeley, WV

Boldvc, Brandon
Weir HS
Weirton, WV

Bobo Jr, Ricky L
Moorefield HS
Fisher, WV

Blankenship, Dustin S
Gilbert HS
Baisden, WV

Blevins, Nicholas K
Woodrow Wilson HS
Beckley, WV

Bowen, Phillip A
Iaeger HS
Bradshaw, WV

Bryant, Staci L
Morgantown HS
Morgantown, WV

Burtt, Zack C
Hedgesville HS
Hedgesville, WV

CARNAL, JENNIFER; EGLON, WV; TUCKER CTY HS; (FR); Hi Hnr Roll; Hnr Roll; Otst Ac Ach Awd; Prom Com; SADD; Stu Cncl (V); Young Writers; Social Studies Fair; Creative and Performing Arts; Applied Arts; West Virginia U; Fairmont State

CARTER, ADAM M; WHEELING, WV; WHEELING PARK HS; (SO); Hi Hnr Roll; Perf Att; WWAHSS; Hosp Aide; Key Club; Sccr (JC); Track (V); Physical Therapy; Ohio U/Slippery Rock; Pittsburgh U

CARTER, MEGAN; RAVENSWOOD, WV; RAVENSWOOD HS; (JR); Hnr Roll; MVP; Perf Att; Pres Ac Ftns Aw; WWAHSS; Comm Volntr; Hosp Aide; Pep Squd; Photog; Prom Com; Wdwrkg Clb; Chr; Chrldg (V); PP Ftbl (V); Sch Ppr (R); Radiology; U of Charleston; West Virginia U

CASDORPH, AMY; MORGANTOWN, WV; UNIVERSITY HS; (JR); F Lan Hn Soc; Hi Hnr Roll; Nat Hon Sy; St of Mnth; WWAHSS; Yth Ldrshp Prog; Comm Volntr; Hosp Aide; Spec Olymp Vol; HO'Br Yth Ldrshp; Key Club; Mod UN; MuAlphaTh; Mus Clb; SADD; Tchrs Aide; French Clb; Bnd; Dnce; SP/M/VS; Scr Kpr (V); Cl Off (S); Stu Cncl (R); CR (R); Presidential Student Service Award; Psychology (Under Grad); Law School; Clemson U; U of Kentucky

CASSELLS, MELANIE M; MORGANTOWN, WV; UNIVERSITY HS; (SO); Hnr Roll; St of Mnth; Comm Volntr; Mus Clb; Tchrs Aide; Bnd; Scr Kpr (J); Vllyball (J); Yrbk (E); A and B Honor Roll; Veterinarian (Veterinary Medicine); Duke U, NC; Wake Forest U, NC

CASTLE, MICHAEL A; HUNTINGTON, WV; SPRING VALLEY HS; (SO); Hi Hnr Roll; Nat Hon Sy; Otst Ac Ach Awd; Perf Att; St of Mnth; Peer Tut/Med; Spec Olymp Vol; Chrch Yth Grp; Quiz Bowl; Chr; Bskball (VJ L); Ftball (J); Sccr (VJ L); Sch Ppr (R); WV Governor's School for Mathematics and Science; Marshall U Booth Scholar; Architecture; Civil Engineering; Massachusetts Institute of Technology; Duke U

CASTO, BOBBI J; FAIRMONT, WV; FAIRMONT SR HS; (SR); Hi Hnr Roll; WWAHSS; Comm Volntr; Chrch Yth Grp; Drma Clb; Prom Com; Sci Clb; Svce Clb; Spch Team; SP/M/VS; Stu Cncl; Radiography; Physical Therapist; West Virginia U; Fairmont State U

CAUDILL, KAYLIN A; HUNTINGTON, WV; HUNTINGTON HS; (SO); Ctznshp Aw; Hnr Roll; Nat Hon Sy; WWAHSS; Chrch Yth Grp; Chr; Dnce; Bskball (J); Track (J); Ebony Club; Church Dance Group; Sports Medicine; Nurse & Choreographer; U of North Carolina; Howard U

CERAN, MATTHEW P; WEIRTON, WV; MADONNA HS; (JR); Hnr Roll; Otst Ac Ach Awd; Pres Ac Ftns Aw; USAA; Yth Ldrshp Prog; Peer Tut/Med; ArtClub; DARE; Prom Com; SADD; Bsball (V L); Bskball (V L); Ftball (V L); Cl Off (P); Stu Cncl (P); National Honor Society; JETS Academic Team; Physical Therapist; Surgeon; West Virginia U; U of Charleston

CERNUTO, BRITTANY L; BECKLEY, WV; WOODROW WILSON HS; (SO); Ctznshp Aw; Hnr Roll; Nat Hon Sy; Perf Att; Pres Ac Ftns Aw; Sci Fairs; St of Mnth; WWAHSS; Hosp Aide; 4-H; Chrch Yth Grp; DARE; Off Aide; Pep Squd; Prom Com; Scouts; Spanish Clb; Chrldg (V); Swmg (V); 1st & 3rd Place on Civic Oration Essay Contest; 1st Place-DARE. Essay; Major-Atmospheric Sciences/Meteorology; Minor-Adv. Communications/Broadcasting; Ohio State U; U of Louisville

CHAFFIN, OLIVIA; WAYNE, WV; WAYNE HS; (SO); Hnr Roll; Nat Hon Sy; St of Mnth; Comm Volntr; Spec Olymp Vol; Chrch Yth Grp; Chr; Ch Chr; Bskball (V); Vllyball (J); Rookie of the Year Basketball; HOSA Club; Nursing; Doctoring; Marshall U; Davis and Elkins

CHAFIN, KRISTAIN R; DELBARTON, WV; BURCH HS; (MS); Hnr Roll; Nat Hon Sy; Perf Att; Pres Ac Ftns Aw; Sci Fairs; St of Mnth; Drma Clb; Mth Clb/Tm; Off Aide; Scouts; Ch Chr; Dnce; SP/M/VS; Stg Cre; Drama; Registered Nurse / RN; LPN; Princeton U; North Carolina U

CHALLA, SUPRIYA R; CHARLESTON, WV; GEORGE WASHINGTON HS; (JR); Gov Hnr Prg; Hi Hnr Roll; Nat Mrt Semif; Perf Att; Sci Fairs; WWAHSS; Comm Volntr; Hab For Humty Volntr; Hosp Aide; Key Club; Mth Clb/Tm; Ntl Beta Clb; Prom Com; Dnce; Tennis (V L); Cl Off (T); Stu Cncl; CR (R); Vocal Lessons (Carnatic Music); (Indian Classical Dance)-Bharatha Natyam; Medicine; Economics; Duke U; U of Pennsylvania

CHANDLER, AMBER; FAIRMONT, WV; EAST FAIRMONT HS; (SO); Hnr Roll; Otst Ac Ach Awd; St of Mnth; Comm Volntr; Photog; Chr; Ch Chr; Gmnstcs (V); Veterinarian; Pediatrician Nurse; Florida State U; Arizona State U

CHANDLER, JOEL T; HUNTINGTON, WV; ST JOSEPH CTRL CATHOLIC HS; (JR); All Am Sch; Hi Hnr Roll; Hnr Roll; Kwnis Aw; Nat Hon Sy; Otst Ac Ach Awd; Pres Ac Ftns Aw; Sci Fairs; St of Mnth; WWAHSS; Comm Volntr; Hab For Humty Volntr; AL Aux Boys; Chrch Yth Grp; DARE; Dbte Team; Emplmnt; HO'Br Yth Ldrshp; Jr Ach; Key Club; Acpl Chr; Bnd; Chr; Ch Chr; Golf; Editor State Key Club Officer/Boys State; HOBY International Rep; Missiology; Marshall U; Berea College

CHAPMAN, JUSTIN S; SHADY SPRING, WV; SHADY SPRING HS; (SR); All Am Sch; Hi Hnr Roll; MVP; Otst Ac Ach Awd; Pres Ac Ftns Aw; Sci Fairs; WWAHSS; Comm Volntr; Peer Tut/Med; Chrch Yth Grp; DARE; Dbte Team; DECA; FCA; Prom Com; SADD; Vsity Clb; Cr Ctry (V); Wrstlg (V); Architecture; Engineering; U of Kentucky; Virginia Polytechnic Institute

CHARNEY, JESSICA; WILCOE, WV; MT VIEW HS; (SO); Hi Hnr Roll; Hnr Roll; Otst Ac Ach Awd; Pres Ac Ftns Aw; Sci Fairs; St of Mnth; WWAHSS; Comm Volntr; DARE; Dbte Team; Key Club; Mod UN; Quiz Bowl; Scouts; Tchrs Aide; Chrldg (J); Gmnstcs (V); CR (V); Yrbk (E, R, P); Physical Therapy; Nursing; Virginia Tech; West Virginia U

CHENOWETH, MAGGIE; BARBOURSVILLE, WV; CABELL MIDLAND HS; (JR); DAR; Hi Hnr Roll; Nat Hon Sy; Otst Ac Ach Awd; Perf Att; WWAHSS; Comm Volntr; Peer Tut/Med; Chrch Yth Grp; Key Club; Mth Clb/Tm; MuAlphaTh; Mus Clb; Prom Com; French Clb; Bnd; Mch Bnd; SP/M/VS; Tennis (V); All-Area Band; USAA National Mathematics Award

CHURCH, FRANKLIN; VERDUNVILLE, WV; LOGAN SR HS; (JR); Hnr Roll; DARE; SADD; Taking Classes to Get Ready for College; Engineering Computers

CHURCH, MEGAN; PRINCETON, WV; PRINCETON HS; (JR); Hnr Roll; Nat Hon Sy; WWAHSS; Comm Volntr; Hosp Aide; Key Club; Chr; Awards in English / History; Nuclear Medicine Technologist; Marshall U; Concord U

CIONNI, CAMILLA; FOLLANSBEE, WV; BROOKE HS; (SO); Hnr Roll; Perf Att; FBLA; Key Club; Psychiatrist; West Virginia U

CIPOLETTI, ALLISON N; WELLSBURG, WV; MT DE CHANTAL VISITATION AC; (FR); Hi Hnr Roll; WWAHSS; Drma Clb; Key Club; Lib Aide; Spanish Clb; Stg Cre; Cl Off (V); 2nd in the State in 8th Grade SAT Verbal Scores; Psychology

CITRO, MICHAEL A; HARPERS FERRY, WV; JEFFERSON HS; (FR); Gov Hnr Prg; Hi Hnr Roll; Otst Ac Ach Awd; Pres Ac Ftns Aw; Sci Fairs; Sci/Math Olympn; St of Mnth; Comm Volntr; Chrch Yth Grp; Key Club; Bnd; Jzz Bnd; Bsball (J); Destination Imagination State Champs; Governor's School for Math & Science; Science; Chemistry; West Virginia U; Shepherd College

CLAGETT, BRICE; FAIRMONT, WV; LINCOLN HS; (FR); Hi Hnr Roll; Sci Fairs; Peer Tut/Med; Chess; DARE; Lttrmn Clb; Quiz Bowl; ROTC; Bnd; Mch Bnd; Pep Bnd; Swg Chr; Track (V L); Science Bowl Team; Biology/Animal; Psychology

CLAGG, AMANDA; MILTON, WV; CABELL MIDLAND HS; (SR); 4H Awd; Hnr Roll; WWAHSS; Comm Volntr; 4-H; Emplmnt; Ntl FFA; 4 Years of Academic Awards; Vet Tech; Morehead State U

CLAPROOD, KELSEY A; BRIDGEPORT, WV; BRIDGEPORT HS; (FR); Hi Hnr Roll; WWAHSS; Young Life Member; West Virginia U; Ohio State U

CLARK, BRITTANY; BEAVER, WV; SHADY SPRING HS; (SO); 4H Awd; Hnr Roll; Otst Ac Ach Awd; Sci Fairs; 4-H; Chrch Yth Grp; DARE; FCA; Off Aide; Dnce; Drl Tm; Chrldg (V); Gmnstcs; Wt Lftg; Yrbk (R); Pharmacy; West Virginia U; U of North Carolina

CLARK, BRITTANY A; HUNTINGTON, WV; CABELL MIDLAND HS; (SO); Hi Hnr Roll; Pres Ac Ftns Aw; WWAHSS; Hosp Aide; Chrch Yth Grp; DARE; P to P St Amb Prg; Bskball (V); Sccr (V); People to People Ambassador - Australia-New Zealand 2004; Participate in AAU Ball / ODP Soccer; Wildlife Biology; U of North Carolina; U of Tennessee

CLARK, MEGAN; INWOOD, WV; MUSSELMAN HS; (FR); Ctznshp Aw; Hi Hnr Roll; Hnr Roll; Otst Ac Ach Awd; Perf Att; Pres Sch; Sci Fairs; Sci/Math Olympn; Comm Volntr; Chrch Yth Grp; Drma Clb; Jr Ach; P to P St Amb Prg; Sci Clb; Spanish Clb; SP/M/VS; Bskball (J); Sccr; Sftball (J); Tennis; Vllyball (J); Cl Off (V); Stu Cncl (R); 3rd Runner Up in Berkeley County Scholarship Pageant; Pre-Med / Cardiologist; West Virginia U; U of Maryland

CLAUDIO, CHRISTOPHER; MOOREFIELD, WV; WATKINS GLEN CTRL HS; (SO); 4H Awd; Hi Hnr Roll; Hnr Roll; Nat Hon Sy; Comm Volntr; 4-H; Chrch Yth Grp; DARE; Emplmnt; FCA; Ntl FFA; Mch Bnd; Bskball (VJ); Ftball (J); Track (V L); Wt Lftg (J); CR (V); 4-H State Camp - Leadership Camp-County Camp; Church Youth Group; Psychiatry; Forensics; James Madison U; West Virginia U

CLAYTON, COREY; MANNINGTON, WV; NORTH MARION HS; (FR); Hnr Roll; SP/M/VS; Theatre; Med School

CLINE, A J; BAISDEN, WV; GILBERT HS; (FR); Hnr Roll; Perf Att; St of Mnth; Comm Volntr; Peer Tut/Med; Chrch Yth Grp; Emplmnt; Ftball (J); Wt Lftg (J); Science Award, Writing Award; Math Award; Medical; Architecture; Southern Community College of W. VA; West Virginia U

CLINE, HILARY E; PANTHER, WV; IAEGER HS; (FR); Hnr Roll; Perf Att; Sci Fairs; Yth Ldrshp Prog; 4-H; Chrch Yth Grp; DARE; SADD; Sftball (V); Vllyball (V); National on President's Test; Major in the Medical Field; Marshall U; West Virginia U

CLINE, RACHELLE; PRINCETON, WV; PSHS; (JR); Ctznshp Aw; Hi Hnr Roll; Hnr Roll; Kwnis Aw; Nat Hon Sy; Comm Volntr; Peer Tut/Med; Spec Olymp Vol; Chrch Yth Grp; Key Club; Bnd; Clr Grd; Flg Crps; Mch Bnd; Stu Cncl (R); CR (R); Yrbk (R); National Honors Society- Representative; Physician's Assistant; Registered Nurse; BSC; MSU

COBB, ERIK; HEDGESVILLE, WV; MUSSELMAN HS; (FR); Scouts

COEBURN, MEGAN C; MC COMAS, WV; MONTCALM HS; (FR); Hnr Roll; Peer Tut/Med; DARE; Chr; Ch Chr; Bskball (V L); Sftball (J); Criminal Law; Family Law; U of North Carolina; Harvard U

COFFMAN, JORDAN; NEW MILTON, WV; DODDRIDGE CTY HS; (SO); Hi Hnr Roll; Hnr Roll; Nat Hon Sy; Pres Ac Ftns Aw; Comm Volntr; Peer Tut/Med; Chrch Yth Grp; Drma Clb; FCA; Prom Com; Dnce; Bskball (V); Chrldg (V); Cr Ctry (V); Track (V); Cl Off (V); Stu Cncl (R); CR (R); MD / Pediatrics; West Virginia U

COLEMAN, GORDON; SCARBRO, WV; MOUNTAIN VIEW CHRISTIAN; (SO); Hnr Roll; Nat Hon Sy; Otst Ac Ach Awd; WWAHSS; Yth Ldrshp Prog; Chrch Yth Grp; Golf (V); Stu Cncl (R); Degree in Music; Lee U

COLLINS, DUSTIN; PRINCETON, WV; PRINCETON SR HS; (SO); Hnr Roll; Kwnis Aw; Comm Volntr; Chess; Chrch Yth Grp; Key Club; Bnd; Ch Chr; Mch Bnd; Fine Arts; Music; Marshall U

COMBS, AMANDA N; BUNKER HILL, WV; MUSSELMAN HS; (SO); 4H Awd; Ctznshp Aw; Hnr Roll; Otst Ac Ach Awd; Perf Att; 4-H; Emplmnt; Ntl FFA; President of Musselman FFA Chapter 2005-2006; President of Blue Ridge Pioneers 4-H Club; General Agriculture & Animal Sciences; Pre-Veterinary; West Virginia U; Ohio State U

CONLIN, GENEVIEVE; WHEELING, WV; WHEELING PARK HS; (SO); Hi Hnr Roll; Perf Att; Sci Fairs; St of Mnth; WWAHSS; Comm Volntr; Chrch Yth Grp; DARE; Drma Clb; Jr Ach; Key Club; NtlFrnscLg; Spch Team; Spanish Clb; Chr; Orch; SP/M/VS; Cr Ctry (V); Track (J); State Champion in Declamation for Speech Team; Member of the Thespians; Architecture; Interior Design; New York School of Design; Art Institute of Pittsburgh

COOPER, AMANDA; WEIRTON, WV; WEIR HS; (JR); Kwnis Aw; Nat Hon Sy; WWAHSS; Comm Volntr; Emplmnt; Chrldg (V L); Sftball (V L); Vllyball (J); Cl Off (S); Yrbk (E); National Society of High School Scholars; Chemistry Club; Business and Marketing; Communications; West Virginia U; Marshall

COOPER, TERESA A; CULLODEN, WV; CABELL MIDLAND HS; (SO); Hnr Roll; Comm Volntr; Child Care and Teaching Academy; Child Psychiatrist; Social Work; Marshall U

CORDONE, BEVERLY; INWOOD, WV; MUSSELMAN HS; (SO); Hnr Roll; Sci Fairs; USAA; WWAHSS; Library Club; Art Education

CORNELL, ALISHA D; APPLE GROVE, WV; HANNAN HS; (SO); Hnr Roll; Perf Att; Sci Fairs; Comm Volntr; Drma Clb; Ntl FFA; Stg Cre; Bskball (V); Vllyball (V C); Police Officer; Correctional Officer; WV State Police Academy

COX, AARON; LESTER, WV; LIBERTY HS; (FR); Hnr Roll; Chess; DARE; FCA; SADD; Stg Cre; CR (R); Creative Arts; Computer Engineering; Mountain State U

COX, SAMANTHA; LOST CREEK, WV; SOUTH HARRISON HS; (JR); Hnr Roll; WWAHSS; 4-H; Swg Chr; Sccr (V); Stu Cncl; Yrbk (R, P); Teaching; Marshall U; Fairmont State U

CRONK, SAMANTHA; MARTINSBURG, WV; HEDGESVILLE HS; (JR); Gov Hnr Prg; Hi Hnr Roll; Yth Ldrshp Prog; Comm Volntr; Hab For Humty Volntr; Chrch Yth Grp; Emplmnt; Mus Clb; Bnd; Ch Chr; Mch Bnd; Orch; Sch Ppr (R); 4.0 on Writing Assessment Test; First Place in WV Promising Young Writers; English; Creative Writing; Boston U; Syracuse U

CROSS, JERICA; VOLGA, WV; BUCKHANNON-UPSHUR HS; (JR); 4H Awd; Hnr Roll; Comm Volntr; Hosp Aide; 4-H; Chrch Yth Grp; History Major; Political Science Minor; Wesleyans; Fairmont State

CUMBERLEDGE, STEPHANIE; PHILIPPI, WV; (SR); Hnr Roll; Perf Att; CARE; Comm Volntr; Spec Olymp Vol; Chr; Dnce; SP/M/VS; Stg Cre; CR (R); Getting the NHR Award; Fairmont State; West Virginia U

CURRENCE, JOHN T; MILL CREEK, WV; TYGARTS VALLEY HS; (SR); Hnr Roll; Comm Volntr; Red Cr Aide; DARE; Emplmnt; FCA; Bsball (V L); Ftball (V L); Track (J); Wt Lftg (V); Volunteer Fire Department; Diesel Mechanic; Northwestern

CUSICK, DONIELLE R; INWOOD, WV; MUSSELMAN HS; (SR); Hnr Roll; Comm Volntr; Peer Tut/Med; Red Cr Aide; Dbte Team; DECA; Key Club; Ntl FFA; Tchrs Aide; Aerospace Engineering; Law School; WVU - Accepted

D'ANGELO, RYAN C; HARPERS FERRY, WV; JEFFERSON HS; (FR); Fut Prb Slvr; Hnr Roll; Nat Hon Sy; Perf Att; Pres Ac Ftns Aw; Sci Fairs; St of Mnth; WWAHSS; Key Club; P to P St Amb Prg; ROTC; Track (J); Aerospace Engineer; Psychologist; West Virginia U

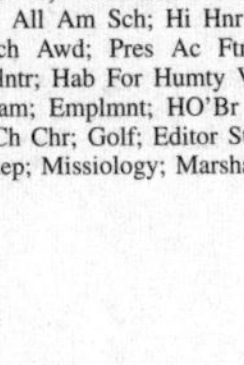
Combs, Amanda N
Musselman HS
Bunker Hill, WV

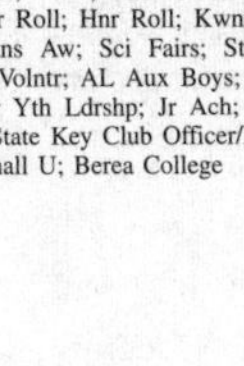
Clark, Megan
Musselman HS
Inwood, WV

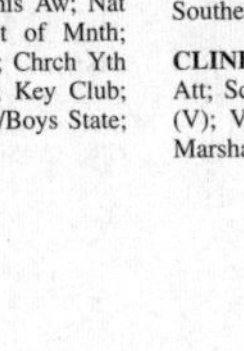
Clagg, Amanda
Cabell Midland HS
Milton, WV

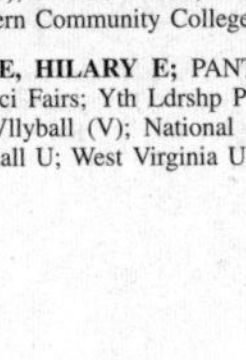
Clagett, Brice
Lincoln HS
Fairmont, WV

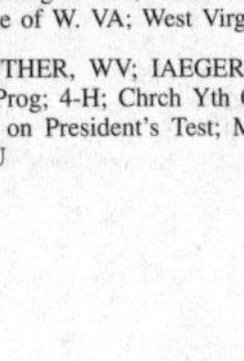
Chafin, Kristain R
Burch HS
Delbarton, WV

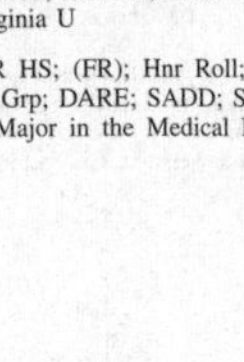
Challa, Supriya R
George Washington HS
Charleston, WV

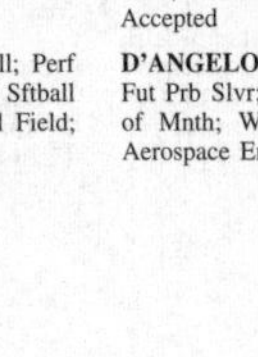
Clark, Brittany A
Cabell Midland HS
Huntington, WV

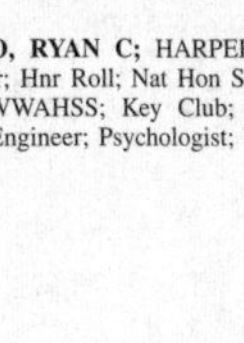
Cobb, Erik
Musselman HS
Hedgesville, WV

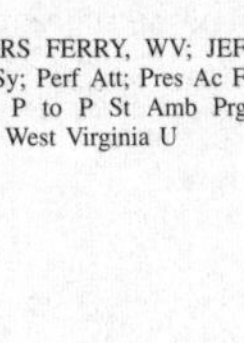
Cronk, Samantha
Hedgesville HS
Martinsburg, WV

DANKOVCHIK, LEAH; WEIRTON, WV; WEIR HS; (FR); Hi Hnr Roll; USAA; WWAHSS; Comm Volntr; Chrch Yth Grp; Drma Clb; Key Club; Sci Clb; Bskball (V L); GAA; Sccr (V L); Track (V)

DARBY, JESSE; NORMANTOWN, WV; GILMER CTY HS; (JR); Gov Hnr Prg; Hnr Roll; Nat Hon Sy; WWAHSS; Peer Tut/Med; Lib Aide; Prom Com; Bsball (L); Golf (L); Cl Off (P); Rotary Youth Leadership Award; Business / Marketing; Pre-Med; Rollins College; Miami U

DAVIDSON, BILLY; WARRIORMINE, WV; BIG CREEK HS; (SO); Ctznshp Aw; Hnr Roll; Nat Hon Sy; Sci Fairs; Sci/Math Olympn; St of Mnth; Comm Volntr; Peer Tut/Med; ArtClub; Fr of Library; Key Club; Prom Com; Quiz Bowl; Bnd; Chr; Mch Bnd; Culinary Arts; Business; Virginia Tech; Concord College

DAVIDSON, DOUG; FOLLANSBEE, WV; BROOKE HS; (JR); Hnr Roll; Nat Hon Sy; Perf Att; WWAHSS; Comm Volntr; Chess; Chrch Yth Grp; DECA; FBLA; Key Club; Mth Clb/Tm; Photog; Cultural Arts Literature Winner - County & State; Business and Accounting; Bethany College

DAVIDSON, JESSE; KANAWHA HEAD, WV; BUCKHANNON UPSHUR HS; (FR); Hnr Roll; Perf Att; WWAHSS; CR (T); Yrbk (P)

DAVIS, AMANDA B; DRENNEN, WV; NICHOLAS CTY; (JR); WWAHSS; FBLA; FCCLA; Lib Aide; Prom Com

DAVIS, JESSICA; CHARLESTON, WV; RIVERSIDE HS; (JR); Hi Hnr Roll; Comm Volntr; Chrch Yth Grp; Emplmnt; FCA; MuAlphaTh; Track (V); Plays the Piano; Pre-Law; Law; Concord U; West Virginia U

DAWSON, MICHAEL; LOST CREEK, WV; SOUTH HARRISON HS; (SR); 4H Awd; Hi Hnr Roll; Hnr Roll; Nat Hon Sy; Comm Volntr; Peer Tut/Med; 4-H; Chess; Cmptr Clb; DARE; Emplmnt; HO'Br Yth Ldrshp; Key Club; Mth Clb/Tm; Track (V C); Computer Engineering; Electrical Engineering; West Virginia U Institute of Technology

DAY, KAYLA D; RAYSAL, WV; IAEGER HS; (FR); Hi Hnr Roll; Hnr Roll; Perf Att; USAA; Comm Volntr; Peer Tut/Med; 4-H; DARE; Mth Clb/Tm; Sftball (V); Golden Horseshoe; Youth and Government; Pharmacist; Optometrist; Concord U; Mountain State U

DAY, TIMOTHY; CUCUMBER, WV; BIG CREEK HS; (FR); Ctznshp Aw; Hnr Roll; Perf Att; Comm Volntr; Peer Tut/Med; Diesel Mechanic

DEAN, NICHOLAS; GILBERT, WV; GILBERT HS; (SO); Hnr Roll; Perf Att; Pres Ac Ftns Aw; St of Mnth; USAA; WWAHSS; Comm Volntr; Chrch Yth Grp; Ftball (V); Wt Lftg (V); CR (R); 8th Grade Reading Award; 9th Grade English & Spanish II Awards; Carpentry; Mechanics; Southern West Virginia Community; National Institute of Technology

DEBERRY, FREDERICA S; BECKLEY, WV; WOODROW WILSON HS; (SO); Hnr Roll; Pres Ac Ftns Aw; French Clb; Dnce; Track; CR (R); Major-Therapeutic Services; Physical Therapist

DEFRUSCIO, ANNE E; WHEELING, WV; WHEELING PARK HS; (FR); Ctznshp Aw; Hi Hnr Roll; WWAHSS; Peer Tut/Med; Drma Clb; Key Club; Vsity Clb; SP/M/VS; Bskball (V L); Vsy Clb (V); Vllyball (V L); Member of National Junior Honor Society; Principal's Citizenship Award

DELAUDER, KASSIE; BELINGTON, WV; PHILIP BARBOUR HS COMPLEX; (SO); DAR; Hnr Roll; Perf Att; Sci Fairs; St of Mnth; Comm Volntr; Ntl FFA

DELGADO, ARYELLE; TRIADELPHIA, WV; WHEELING PARK HS; (SO); 4H Awd; Gov Hnr Prg; Hi Hnr Roll; Perf Att; St of Mnth; WWAHSS; Comm Volntr; 4-H; Chess; Chrch Yth Grp; Mth Clb/Tm; Svce Clb; Chr; Orch; Music Education; Baylor U; Wheaton College

DE LONG, MISTY; PHILIPPI, WV; PHILIP HARBOUR HS COMPLEX; (JR); Hnr Roll; Photog; Dnce; Accepted to the CSLC Business Conference 2005; In the Barbour County Art Show 2004; Pre-Law; Business and Management; Capital U; John Carroll U

DELP, LOUISE E; SHADY SPRING, WV; SHADY SPRING HS; (JR); Hi Hnr Roll; Hnr Roll; WWAHSS; Chrch Yth Grp; Emplmnt; FCA; Mus Clb; Bnd; Mch Bnd; Medical Assisting / Nursing; Music; Bluefield College; Mountain State U

DEMARCO, LAUREN A; LOST CREEK, WV; ROBERT C BYRD HS; (SO); Hnr Roll; Otst Ac Ach Awd; Peer Tut/Med; DARE; Key Club; SADD; Orch; Cr Ctry (V L); Sccr (V L); Track (V L); Social Study Fair Winner / Economic - State Winner; Medical Field; College of William & Mary; U of California

DE MARCO, ZACHARY M; SHINNSTON, WV; LINCOLN HS; (JR); Hi Hnr Roll; Jr Eng Tech; Nat Hon Sy; Comm Volntr; AL Aux Boys; Chrch Yth Grp; Emplmnt; Mth Clb/Tm; Bsball (V L); Bskball (J L); Ftball (V L); Golf (V L); Wt Lftg; Stu Cncl; CR; National Honor Society; JETS; Engineering; West Virginia U

DENNIS, DESIREE; WEIRTON, WV; WEIR HS; (FR); Hi Hnr Roll; Hnr Roll; Perf Att; Pres Ac Ftns Aw; Comm Volntr; Chrch Yth Grp; Key Club; Lib Aide; Chr; Ch Chr; SP/M/VS; Bskball (J); GAA (V); Track (V); Cl Off (R); Stu Cncl (R); Lit Mag (E); Sec & Treas of Church Youth Group; Egyptology; Marine Biology; Brown U; Harvard U

DEREMER, MICHELLE; RIDGELEY, WV; FRANKFORT HS; (JR); 4H Awd; Hi Hnr Roll; Hnr Roll; Nat Hon Sy; Sci Fairs; 4-H; DARE; Ntl FFA; Bnd; Mch Bnd; Chrldg (V L); Tennis (V L); Track (J); Adv Cncl (R); Forensic Science; Biologist; West Virginia U; Marshall U

DIGGS, SHALANDA C; BECKLEY, WV; WOODROW WILSON HS; (SO); Hi Hnr Roll; Hnr Roll; Nat Hon Sy; Otst Ac Ach Awd; St of Mnth; Chrch Yth Grp; Ch Chr; Dnce; Bskball (V); Cr Ctry (V); Track (V); Basketball (Best All Around Player); Medical (Nurse Practitioner); Georgetown U; U of North Carolina

DILLON, REBECCA L; FANROCK, WV; WESTSIDE HS; (SO); Ctznshp Aw; Hi Hnr Roll; Hnr Roll; Nat Hon Sy; Otst Ac Ach Awd; St of Mnth; WWAHSS; Comm Volntr; Chrch Yth Grp; DARE; FCA; Quiz Bowl; Ch Chr; The National Society of High School Scholars; Pharmacy; Medical; West Virginia U; Liberty U

DILORENZO, PHILLIP A; WELLSBURG, WV; BROOKE HS; (SR); Hi Hnr Roll; Hnr Roll; Nat Hon Sy; Nat Stu Ath Day Aw; Otst Ac Ach Awd; Perf Att; WWAHSS; Yth Ldrshp Prog; Peer Tut/Med; DECA; Emplmnt; FBLA; HO'Br Yth Ldrshp; Key Club; Off Aide; Golf (V L); Stu Cncl (R); HOBY / Bruins Best / Business Symposium Rep; Business Management / Golf Course Management; Marshall U Huntington

DINGESS, BRITTANY N; ELEANOR, WV; BUFFALO HS; (FR); Hnr Roll; Nat Hon Sy; Spec Olymp Vol; Scouts; Chr; Bskball (VJ); Sftball (VJ); Nurse; Veterinarian; West Virginia U; Marshall U

DINGESS, MYKEL R; HARTS, WV; HARTS HS; (SO); 4H Awd; All Am Sch; Ctznshp Aw; Hi Hnr Roll; Hnr Roll; MVP; Otst Ac Ach Awd; Sci/Math Olympn; USAA; Comm Volntr; Spec Olymp Vol; 4-H; Lttrmn Clb; Mth Clb/Tm; Mus Clb; Vsity Clb; Bnd; Bskball (V); Ftball (V); Vsy Clb (V); Wt Lftg (V); Cl Off (P); Stu Cncl (R); Math Field Day; Pre-Med; Marshall U; Concord College

DINGESS, PATRICIA; WHARNCLIFFE, WV; GILBERT HS; (SO); Hnr Roll; Perf Att; Pres Ac Ftns Aw; St of Mnth; Chrch Yth Grp; Mus Clb; Pep Squd; Scouts; SADD; Bnd; Mch Bnd; Chrldg (V); Gmnstcs (V); Honors Band; Honors All State Chorus; Mountain State U

DISHMAN, AMANDA; GARY, WV; MOUNT VIEW HS; (SO); Gov Hnr Prg; Hnr Roll; Kwnis Aw; Nat Hon Sy; Sci Fairs; St Schl; WWAHSS; Peer Tut/Med; Key Club; Ntl Beta Clb; Spanish Clb; Drm Mjr; Mch Bnd; Tennis (V); Runner-Up Spelling Bee @ State Beta Convention; Psychology; West Virginia U; Washington U in St. Louis

DITTO, ELIZABETH; HEDGESVILLE, WV; HEDGESVILLE HS; (SR); F Lan Hn Soc; Hi Hnr Roll; Hnr Roll; Nat Hon Sy; WWAHSS; Yth Ldrshp Prog; Peer Tut/Med; Chrch Yth Grp; Spanish Clb; Ch Chr; Sccr (VJ); Swmg (V L); National Honors Society (Co-Treasurer); National Spanish Society (Treasurer); Dentistry; West Virginia Wesleyan

DODRILL, BRETT M; CHARLESTON, WV; POCA HS; (JR); Hi Hnr Roll; Hnr Roll; USAA; WWAHSS; Comm Volntr; Spec Olymp Vol; Chrch Yth Grp; DECA; Emplmnt; Photog; Bnd; Chr; Ch Chr; Dnce; Journalism; Communications; Concord U

DOVE, VIRGIL A; BRANDYWINE, WV; PENDLETON HS; (SO); Hnr Roll; Chrch Yth Grp; Ntl FFA; Track (L); Wt Lftg; Astronomer; WVU; JMU

D'SOUZA, KELLIE; MORGANTOWN, WV; UNIVERSITY HS; (JR); Hi Hnr Roll; Nat Hon Sy; WWAHSS; Comm Volntr; Key Club; MuAlphaTh; Tchrs Aide; Bnd; Mch Bnd; Bskball (J); Forensics; West Virginia U

DUKE, PATRICK M; WEIRTON, WV; WEIR SR HS; (FR); Hnr Roll; WWAHSS; Key Club; Bsball (VJ L); Bskball; Sccr (V L); Dentistry; West Virginia U

DUNBAR, JORDAN M; CLEAR CREEK, WV; LIBERTY HS; (FR); Hi Hnr Roll; Hnr Roll; Nat Hon Sy; Perf Att; Sci Fairs; Comm Volntr; Chrch Yth Grp; DARE; FCA; Tchrs Aide; Chr; Ch Chr; FCA; Anesthesiologist; Mountain State U

DUNSMORE, JEREMY J; MAYSVILLE, WV; PETERSBURG HS; Chrch Yth Grp; Ch Chr

DURAN, ALEX D; NITRO, WV; POCA HS; (JR); Hnr Roll; Nat Hon Sy; St of Mnth; WWAHSS; Spec Olymp Vol; AL Aux Boys; FCA; FBLA; Bskball (V L); Cr Ctry (V L); Golf (V); Tennis (V L); Cl Off (S); Stu Cncl (R); Forensic Science; Georgetown U; Eastern Kentucky U

EARLEY, SHANE; MOUNDSVILLE, WV; LINSLY SCH; (JR); F Lan Hn Soc; Gov Hnr Prg; Hi Hnr Roll; Hnr Roll; Jr Eng Tech; MVP; WWAHSS; Comm Volntr; Hosp Aide; Peer Tut/Med; Drma Clb; FCA; Jr Cls League; Key Club; Mod UN; Prom Com; SADD; German Clb; Chr; SP/M/VS; Cr Ctry (V CL); Tennis (V L); Yrbk (P); Governor's School For The Arts; National Student Leadership Conference / Medicine; International Relations; Medicine; Yale U; Stanford U

EFFLAND, DENVER R; HEDGESVILLE, WV; HEDGESVILLE HS; (FR); Hnr Roll; Nat Stu Ath Day Aw; Pres Ac Ftns Aw; Chrch Yth Grp; Bskball (V L); Ftball (JC); Track (J); Wt Lftg (V); Physical Therapy; Zoology/ Archaeology; Virginia Tech; West Virginia U

EISENTROUT, BEKI; BRUCETON MILLS, WV; PRESTON HS; (FR); Hi Hnr Roll; Hnr Roll; Perf Att; Sci/Math Olympn; St of Mnth; St Optmst of Yr; Yth Ldrshp Prog; Peer Tut/Med; Chess; Chrch Yth Grp; DARE; Sign Clb; Chr; Ch Chr; Skiing (J); Sftball (V); CR (R); Law School; Journalism; U of Wisconsin; West Virginia U

ELLINGTON, DANA L; PRINCETON, WV; PRINCETON SR HS; (SO); Ctznshp Aw; Hi Hnr Roll; Kwnis Aw; Otst Ac Ach Awd; Perf Att; Pres Ac Ftns Aw; USAA; WWAHSS; Comm Volntr; Chrch Yth Grp; Key Club; Svce Clb; Bnd; Chr; Dnce; Flg Crps; Stu Cncl (R); Biology or Equine Science; DVM (Veterinarian); Virginia Tech; Marshall U

ELLIOTT, DEBBIE L; ROCK CAVE, WV; BUCKHANNON-UPSHUR HS; (SO); Hnr Roll; Comm Volntr; 4-H; Chrch Yth Grp; DARE; Tchrs Aide; Chr; Medical Assistant; Associate's Degree; The Hi-Tech College

ELLIOTT, KATIE; FAIRMONT, WV; EAST FAIRMONT HS; (FR); Hnr Roll; Perf Att; Pres Ac Ftns Aw; St of Mnth; Chrch Yth Grp; Scouts; Chr; Ch Chr; Track (J); Doctor or Nurse; WVU; Fairmont State

ELLISON, CASEY; MOUNT HOPE, WV; (FR); Ctznshp Aw; F Lan Hn Soc; Gov Hnr Prg; Hnr Roll; Nat Hon Sy; Nat Mrt Fin; Nat Stu Ath Day Aw; Pres Ac Ftns Aw; Sci/Math Olympn; St of Mnth; Comm Volntr; Hosp Aide; Peer Tut/Med; Chrch Yth Grp; Cmptr Clb; Dbte Team; Drma Clb; FCA; Mth Clb/Tm; Off Aide; Tech Clb; Chr; Ch Chr; SP/M/VS; Stg Cre; Bsball (J); Bskball (J); Ftball (J); Sccr (J); Track (J); Adv Cncl (R); Pharmacist; Culinary Arts; Mountain State U

ERDIE, RYAN C; FAIRMONT, WV; FAIRMONT SR HS; (SR); Hnr Roll; MVP; St of Mnth; WWAHSS; Comm Volntr; Spec Olymp Vol; Chrch Yth Grp; Emplmnt; Lttrmn Clb; Off Aide; Prom Com; SADD; Vsity Clb; French Clb; Ftball (V CL); Track (V L); Vsy Clb (V); Wt Lftg (V); TV Productions, Anchor/Crew; Student Representative East-West Stadium Committee; Business; West Virginia U; West Virginia Wesleyan College

ERWIN, STEPHEN T; BARBOURSVILLE, WV; HUNTINGTON HS; (JR); All Am Sch; Ctznshp Aw; Hnr Roll; WWAHSS; Comm Volntr; Chrch Yth Grp; Bnd; Ftball (V); Stu Cncl (R); Computer Engineering; West Virginia Tech; Virginia Tech

ESPOSITO, KENNETH; WEIRTON, WV; WEIR HS; (FR); Hi Hnr Roll; Sci Fairs; St of Mnth; WWAHSS; Astrophysics; Nuclear Physics

EXLINE, MICHELLE; ELLAMORE, WV; (JR); Hnr Roll; Perf Att; St of Mnth; Comm Volntr; Tchrs Aide; Chr; Adv Cncl (S); Yrbk (R); Did Community Service; Nursing; Davis Elkins; Mountain State

FARKASOVSKY, CHELSEA P; BRIDGEPORT, WV; BRIDGEPORT HS; (FR); Hnr Roll; Perf Att; Pres Ac Ftns Aw; Sci Fairs; Comm Volntr; Chrch Yth Grp; DARE; Key Club; Kwanza Clb; Photog; Bnd; Flg Crps; Mch Bnd; Sftball (VJ); Vllyball (J); Yrbk (P); Gatorade Rookie of the Year in Softball; Nurse

FERRARA, NOEL M; GERRARDSTOWN, WV; MARTINSBURG HS; (JR); Hnr Roll; Chrch Yth Grp; Emplmnt; ROTC; Psychology; Concord College; Shepherd U

FILE, AUDREY; BECKLEY, WV; WOODROW WILSON HS; (JR); Dnce; Chrldg (V L); Tennis (J); Track (V); Cl Off (P); Stu Cncl (P)

FILIUS, COURTNEY; FAIRMONT, WV; EAST FAIRMONT HS; (SO); Hi Hnr Roll; St of Mnth; WWAHSS; Chrldg (V)

FILTER, JULIET N; WHEELING, WV; WHEELING PARK HS; (SO); Hi Hnr Roll; Perf Att; WWAHSS; Comm Volntr; Drma Clb; Key Club; SADD; Orch; SP/M/VS; Chrldg (J); Stu Cncl (R); High Honors; Perfect Attendance; Pharmacy; Physicians Assistant; Ohio Northern; Wheeling College

FINKEL, SHERRY; MORGANTOWN, WV; UNIVERSITY HS; (JR); F Lan Hn Soc; Fut Prb Slvr; Hi Hnr Roll; Jr Eng Tech; Nat Hon Sy; Nat Mrt LOC; Pres Ac Ftns Aw; St of Mnth; WWAHSS; Spec Olymp Vol; Key Club; Mth Clb/Tm; Mod UN; MuAlphaTh; SADD; Bskball (J); Sftball (L); Vllyball (L); Yrbk (E); U of Delaware; Bucknell U

FISHER, BRITTANY; JANE LEW, WV; LEWIS CTY HS; (SO); Hnr Roll; WWAHSS; Yth Ldrshp Prog; Peer Tut/Med; Bnd; Flg Crps; Mch Bnd; Secondary English Education; Education / Kindergarten; Marshall University; Glenville State College

Earley, Shane
Linsly Sch
Moundsville, WV

Dove, Virgil A
Pendleton HS
Brandywine, WV

Deremer, Michelle
Frankfort HS
Ridgeley, WV

National
Honor Roll
Spring 2005

Demarco, Lauren A
Robert C Byrd HS
Lost Creek, WV

Dunbar, Jordan M
Liberty HS
Clear Creek, WV

Erdie, Ryan C
Fairmont SR HS
Fairmont, WV

FOOTE, AMANDA; BUNKER HILL, WV; MUSSELMAN HS; (JR); Hi Hnr Roll; Hnr Roll; Comm Volntr; Ntl FFA; Quill & Scroll; Chr; SP/M/VS; CR (R); Chapter FFA Degree; 2nd Place - Berkeley County Social Studies Fair; Equine Studies; BA; Delaware Valley College; Salem International U

FORTNEY, KATHERYN N; PARKERSBURG, WV; PARKERSBURG CHRISTIAN SCH; MS; Hi Hnr Roll; Hnr Roll; Perf Att; Sci Fairs; Peer Tut/Med; Chrch Yth Grp; Scouts; Acpl Chr; Chr; Ch Chr; SP/M/VS; Arch; Bskball (V); Vllyball (VJ); Sports Medicine; BS; Marshall U; Duke U

FOUTS, BENJAMIN K; BRIDGEPORT, WV; BRIDGEPORT HS; (FR); All Am Sch; Hi Hnr Roll; Pres Ac Ftns Aw; Sci Fairs; USAA; WWAHSS; Quiz Bowl; Scouts; Sccr (J); Cl Off (S); Academic Challenge Team, Eagle Scout; County, Regional, State - Math Field Days; Engineering; Mathematics; Carnegie Mellon; West Virginia U

FOX, JUSTIN M; GLENVILLE, WV; GILMER CTY HS; (SR); Hnr Roll; Ntl FFA

FRANCIS, MEGHAN B; RAVENSWOOD, WV; RAVENSWOOD HS; (FR); Hi Hnr Roll; St of Mnth; Comm Volntr; Chrch Yth Grp; Quiz Bowl; Chr; Ch Chr; Stg Cre; Track (V); Honor Bowl / Honor Choir / Concert Choir Select / Student of the Month; Pathology; Medical; Duke U; West Virginia U

FRANKLIN, BETHANY; HUNTINGTON, WV; HUNTINGTON HS; (SO); Comm Volntr; Peer Tut/Med; Chrch Yth Grp; Scouts; Ch Chr; Secretary at Church; Marshall U

GAINES, AMBER; LOST CREEK, WV; SOUTH HARRISON HS; (JR); 4H Awd; Hi Hnr Roll; Hnr Roll; Nat Hon Sy; WWAHSS; Comm Volntr; 4-H; AL Aux Girls; Key Club; Lib Aide; Prom Com; Bnd; Mch Bnd; PP Ftbl (V); Sccr (V L); Track (V L); Stu Cncl (T); Yrbk (E); Elementary Education; Pharmacist; Glenville State College; Fairmont State U

GAJTKA, MARK A; WEIRTON, WV; MADONNA HS; (JR); All Am Sch; Hi Hnr Roll; MVP; Nat Hon Sy; St of Mnth; USAA; WWAHSS; Yth Ldrshp Prog; Comm Volntr; Hab For Humty Volntr; ArtClub; Chrch Yth Grp; DARE; Key Club; Pep Squd; Prom Com; Svce Clb; SADD; Stg Cre; Bskball (VJ L); Ftball (V L); Golf (V L); Sccr (V CL); Tennis (V CL); Cl Off (V); Stu Cncl (V); Youth Leadership Program; All-Star 4 Club Soccer Teams; Architecture; Architectural Engineering; U of Cincinnati; Miami U

GAMES, DAVID; WEIRTON, WV; WEIR HS; (JR); Hnr Roll; Sci Fairs; St of Mnth; Emplmnt; Key Club; Mth Clb/Tm; Sci Clb; Yrbk; Engineer; CEO; West Virginia U; West Liberty State College

GAMPOLO, CANDICE; WEIRTON, WV; WEIR HS; (FR); Hnr Roll; Sci Fairs; St of Mnth; Hosp Aide; Key Club; Dnce; SP/M/VS; Chrldg (J); GAA (V); Gmnstcs (V); Mar Art (V); Piano-9 yrs.; Lawyer; Nurse; West Liberty; Bethany

GARRETT, ZACHARY D; VIENNA, WV; PARKERSBURG HS; (JR); Hnr Roll; MVP; Perf Att; Pres Ac Ftns Aw; Sci Fairs; Comm Volntr; Chrch Yth Grp; Dbte Team; Emplmnt; FCA; Scouts; Ftball (V CL); Eagle Scout BSA; Medicine; Sciences; WVU-West Virginia U; Pittsburgh

GARTEN, CHUCKY; BLOUNT, WV; RIVERSIDE HS; (JR); Sci Fairs; Chess; Emplmnt; Outdrs Clb; Ftball (V); National Technical Honor Society; 1st Place Kanauta County Special Studies Fair; Welding

GIBBONS, KAITLIN; WHEELING, WV; WHEELING CTRL CATHOLIC HS; (SO); F Lan Hn Soc; Hi Hnr Roll; Hnr Roll; Comm Volntr; ArtClub; Drma Clb; Key Club; Stg Cre; Vllyball (J); Can Food Drives, Worked Lebanese Festival, Greeter At Church, RAZE, Helped Salvation Army; Lawyer; Government; Bethany College

GIBSON, TABITHA A; HUNTINGTON, WV; SPRING VALLEY HS; (SO); Hnr Roll; Red Cr Aide; Spec Olymp Vol; Chrch Yth Grp; Key Club; ROTC; Chr; Ch Chr; SP/M/VS; Stg Cre; Published Art Work on www.Artsonia.com; Marshall U

GIFFEN, LAUREN A; BRIDGEPORT, WV; BRIDGEPORT HS; (SO); Hi Hnr Roll; Hnr Roll; Perf Att; Sci Fairs; USAA; Comm Volntr; Chrch Yth Grp; DARE; Key Club; Bnd; Clr Grd; Dnce; Flg Crps; Psychology; West Virginia U

GIFFORD, CHAD A; VOLGA, WV; BUCKHANNON-UPSHUR HS; (SR); All Am Sch; Hi Hnr Roll; Nat Hon Sy; St of Mnth; WWAHSS; AL Aux Boys; Chrch Yth Grp; DARE; FCA; SADD; Tchrs Aide; Bnd; Drm Mjr; Mch Bnd; SP/M/VS; Cr Ctry (V); Track (V); 1st Place Talent Shows - Playing Piano / Singing; Radiology/Radiologist; Alderson Broaddus College

GILKESON IV, SAMUEL T; HARPERS FERRY, WV; JEFFERSON HS; (FR); Hnr Roll; Sci Fairs; St of Mnth; WWAHSS; Comm Volntr; Key Club; Mth Clb/Tm; Bnd; Jzz Bnd; Track (J); 8th Grade Student of Year; Sergeant At Arms-Key Club; Medical Field-Surgery; West Virginia U

GILLENWATER, BROOKE A; PRINCETON, WV; PIKE VIEW; (JR); Hosp Aide; Emplmnt; Bnd; Chr

GOFF, ABRAM J L; ELIZABETH, WV; WIRT CTY HS; (JR); All Am Sch; Hi Hnr Roll; Nat Hon Sy; Sci/Math Olympn; WWAHSS; Comm Volntr; Chrch Yth Grp; Emplmnt; FBLA; HO'Br Yth Ldrshp; Mth Clb/Tm; Photog; Quill & Scroll; SADD; Bnd; Mch Bnd; Bskball (V); Ftball (V); Golf (V); Track (V); Wt Lftg (V); Cl Off (T); Sch Ppr (P); Yrbk (E, P); Future Business Leaders of America-WV State Treasurer; Graphic Design; Multimedia; Concord U; Pittsburgh Technical Institute

GOLDEN, BENJAMIN G; BRADLEY, WV; WOODROW WILSON HS; (JR); Hi Hnr Roll; Hnr Roll; Perf Att; WWAHSS; Chrch Yth Grp; Ch Chr; Bskball (JC); Ftball (V); Received Christian Character Award; Music; Business / Marketing; Appalachian Bible College

GOLDEN, SAMANTHA R; PHILIPPI, WV; PHILIP BARBOUR HS COMPLEX; (SO); Hnr Roll; Perf Att; Chrch Yth Grp; Mch Bnd; Teaching Degree; Alderson Broaddus College; Fairmont State College

GOLDIZEN, CECILY D; NEW CREEK, WV; PETERSBURG HS; (FR); Hnr Roll; Comm Volntr; Chrch Yth Grp; FCA; Bnd; Mch Bnd; Tennis (J); Vllyball (J); Cl Off (P); Stu Cncl (R); Pharmacy; West Virginia U; Potomac State College

GONDOLIA, RAHUL; VIENNA, WV; PARKERSBURG HS; (JR); Nat Hon Sy; Nat Ldrshp Svc; Otst Ac Ach Awd; Sci Fairs; WWAHSS; Comm Volntr; Hosp Aide; Key Club; Mod UN; Quiz Bowl; Sci Clb; Chr; Skiing; Tennis (V CL); Bio Major; U of Richmond; U of North Carolina-Chapel Hill

GOODFELLOW, SHANDRA C; FRIENDLY, WV; TYLER CONSOLIDATED HS; (JR); Hnr Roll; Nat Hon Sy; WWAHSS; Comm Volntr; Chrch Yth Grp; Mus Clb; Bnd; Chr; Ch Chr; Jzz Bnd; PP Ftbl; WV All-State Chamber Choir; First Runner-Up in Miss Knight Pageant; Music Education; Marshall U; West Liberty State College

GORDON II, DANIEL; BELINGTON, WV; PHILIP BARBOUR HS COMPLEX; (SO); Hnr Roll; WWAHSS; Comm Volntr; Spec Olymp Vol; Chrch Yth Grp; Ntl FFA

GORE, CASSANDRA; LOGAN, WV; LOGAN SR HS; Hi Hnr Roll; Hnr Roll; Nat Hon Sy; Otst Ac Ach Awd; WWAHSS; Comm Volntr; Spec Olymp Vol; Chrch Yth Grp; Key Club; Prom Com; Spanish Clb; Stu Cncl (R); CR (P); Team Leader for Relay 4 Life; American History; Law; West Virginia U

GOUNDEN, KRIYAN; BRIDGEPORT, WV; BRIDGEPORT HS; (SO); Hnr Roll; Otst Ac Ach Awd; Perf Att; Sci Fairs; Sci/Math Olympn; Peer Tut/Med; Chess; Cmptr Clb; Quiz Bowl; Ch Chr; SP/M/VS; Mar Art; Sccr; Swmg; Tennis; Chess - Excelled at Tournament Level; Achieved English / Math / Science Olympians; Physiology; Microbiology and Immunology; West Virginia U; Virginia Commonwealth U School of Medicine

GRASSER, TERRENCE; MULLENS, WV; WYOMING CTY EAST HS; (FR); Hi Hnr Roll; Hnr Roll; Perf Att; St of Mnth; WWAHSS; Chrch Yth Grp; FCA; Ftball (V); Wt Lftg (V); Athletic Coaching Education; West Virginia U; Georgia U

GRAY, NICOLE; HUNTINGTON, WV; HUNTINGTON HS; (SR); Hnr Roll; Nat Hon Sy; WWAHSS; Comm Volntr; Drma Clb; Key Club; Spch Team; Chr; SP/M/VS; Communications; Capital U

GREEN, JANNA R; RODERFIELD, WV; IAEGER HS; (SR); Hi Hnr Roll; Nat Hon Sy; Perf Att; Pres Ac Ftns Aw; Pres Sch; Sci Fairs; Valdctrian; WWAHSS; Comm Volntr; Peer Tut/Med; Chrch Yth Grp; DARE; Off Aide; Tchrs Aide; Bnd; Ch Chr; Business/Marketing; Culinary Arts

GREEN, MATTHEW T; SHINNSTON, WV; LINCOLN HS; (FR); Hnr Roll; WWAHSS; Chrch Yth Grp; Key Club; ROTC; Scouts; Bnd; Mch Bnd; Pep Bnd; Cr Ctry (V); Track (J); Stu Cncl (R); CR (R); Engineering; Aero-Space; West Virginia U; Miami U

GREEN, MICHAEL L; DAVY, WV; MOUNT VIEW HS; (FR); Hnr Roll; Perf Att; St of Mnth; Peer Tut/Med; ArtClub; Chrch Yth Grp; Mth Clb/Tm; Quiz Bowl

GRIFFITH, SAMANTHA; HANSFORD, WV; RIVERSIDE HS; (SO); Hi Hnr Roll; Nat Hon Sy; Perf Att; WWAHSS; Comm Volntr; Peer Tut/Med; FCA; NYLC; Spanish Clb; Upward Band Program; Pharmacy; West Virginia U; West Virginia Technical Institute

GRINDSTAFF, AMY; LANARK, WV; WOODROW WILSON HS; (SO); Hnr Roll; Drma Clb; Fine Arts; Marshall U; Mountain State U

HACKNEY, ADAM; BLOUNT, WV; RIVERSIDE HS; (SR); Hnr Roll; Nat Hon Sy; Perf Att; Yth Ldrshp Prog; Comm Volntr; Peer Tut/Med; Chrch Yth Grp; Mth Clb/Tm; MuAlphaTh; Ntl Beta Clb; Quiz Bowl; Tmpl Yth Grp; Bsball (V); Individual Weightlifting; Community Service; Pre-Med / Biology; Medical School / Tutoring Math; U of Charleston

HACKNEY, MICHELLE K; RAVENSWOOD, WV; RAVENSWOOD HS; (JR); Hnr Roll; Nat Stu Ath Day Aw; Otst Ac Ach Awd; Perf Att; Pres Ac Ftns Aw; Yth Ldrshp Prog; Comm Volntr; Peer Tut/Med; Chrch Yth Grp; Emplmnt; Bnd; Clr Grd; Dnce; Mch Bnd; Sch Ppr (E, R, P); Physician's Assistant; Law Enforcement; WV U; Fairmont State

HAGGERTY, BRITTANY; MOOREFIELD, WV; MOOREFIELD HS; (SR); Hi Hnr Roll; Hnr Roll; Sci Fairs; St of Mnth; WWAHSS; Comm Volntr; Chrch Yth Grp; Emplmnt; FCA; Mth Clb/Tm; Tchrs Aide; Sch Ppr; Yrbk; Forensics; Marshall U

HALL, CASEY L; BUCKHANNON, WV; BUCKHANNON-UPSHUR HS; (MS); 4H Awd; Hnr Roll; Perf Att; St of Mnth; Bnd; Cl Off (P, V, T); 4-H - Horseback Riding; American Youth Soccer Organization - AYSO; Science and Natural Resources

HALL, KRYSTAL; CHARLESTON, WV; SISSONVILLE HS; (JR); Hnr Roll; Otst Ac Ach Awd; Perf Att; Comm Volntr; Chrch Yth Grp; Jr Ach; Chrldg (V L); Interior Designing; UCLA; West Virginia U

HALL, RYAN; BUCKHANNON, WV; BUCKHANNON UPSHUR HS; (SO); WWAHSS; 4-H; Drma Clb; SP/M/VS; Stg Cre; Ftball (J); Wt Lftg (J)

HALSTEAD, MEGHAN; ST ALBANS, WV; SOUTH CHARLESTON HS; (JR); Hnr Roll; WWAHSS; Comm Volntr; Chrch Yth Grp; Chr; Ch Chr; Dnce; I Have a Job; Education; West Virginia State U; West Virginia U

HAMILTON, TONYA; BRADSHAW, WV; BIG CREEK HS; (JR); Ctznshp Aw; Hnr Roll; MVP; Otst Ac Ach Awd; Perf Att; St of Mnth; Peer Tut/Med; DARE; Off Aide; Pep Squd; Prom Com; Chrldg (V); American Legion Award; Pediatrics; Forensic Lab Scientist; Concord U; West Virginia U

HAMMACK, SEAN; HUNTINGTON, WV; ST JOSEPH CTRL CATHOLIC HS; (JR); Hi Hnr Roll; Nat Hon Sy; St of Mnth; WWAHSS; Peer Tut/Med; AL Aux Boys; Chrch Yth Grp; Drma Clb; Key Club; Mth Clb/Tm; MuAlphaTh; Prom Com; Quiz Bowl; Ch Chr; SP/M/VS; Bskball (J); Sccr (V); Tennis (V); Stu Cncl (R); $750 Scholarship from Catholic Daughters; 1st Place Carter Gr Woodson Scholarship; Business; Theatre; U of Notre Dame; Yale U

HAMMONDS, KAYLA N; BUFFALO, WV; BUFFALO HS; (SO); Chrch Yth Grp; DARE; Special Olympics Volunteer; Hurricane WV Civil War Reenactment; Dental Assistant; Dental Hygiene; Tennessee U; Marshall U

HAMRICK, TIFFANY; BUCKHANNON, WV; BUCKHANNON-UPSHUR HS; (JR); Hi Hnr Roll; Hnr Roll; Education; Veterinary Medicine

HARDIN, ASHLEY; PRINCETON, WV; PRINCETON SR HS; (JR); Hi Hnr Roll; Nat Hon Sy; Perf Att; Pres Ac Ftns Aw; Prom Com; Tchrs Aide; Bskball (V); Sccr (V); Sftball (V); Stu Cncl (R); CR (R); Help to Start Culture Club at School; Physical Therapy / Sports Medicine; Highest Degree; Marshall U; West Virginia U

HARDY, BRITTANY; SMITHERS, WV; VALLEY HS; (SR); Hnr Roll; Nat Hon Sy; St of Mnth; WWAHSS; Red Cr Aide; Drma Clb; Off Aide; Prom Com; Chr; SP/M/VS; Bskball (C); Cl Off (S); Stu Cncl (R); Sch Ppr (R); Yrbk (R, P); Outstanding Black HS Student; Homecoming Queen; Business Management; Marshall U; West Virginia U Institute of Technology

HARDY, HEATHER A; BELINGTON, WV; PHILIP BARBOUR HS COMPLEX; (SO); Hi Hnr Roll; Hnr Roll; Comm Volntr; Chrch Yth Grp; Emplmnt; Ntl FFA; FFA Greenhand Award (2004); Air Force Academy-Licensed Pilot; Ohio Wesleyan College

HARPER, AMY B; CAIRO, WV; RITCHIE CTY HS; (SO); 4H Awd; Hi Hnr Roll; Perf Att; Pres Ac Ftns Aw; Comm Volntr; 4-H; FCCLA

HARPER, LAUREN M; FAYETTEVILLE, WV; FAYETTEVILLE HS; (FR); Hnr Roll; Chrch Yth Grp; DARE; ROTC; Chr; Clr Grd; Drl Tm; Law; Cardiologist; West Virginia U; Marshall U

HARRIS, JOANNA; WEBSTER SPRINGS, WV; WEBSTER CTY HS; (FR); Hi Hnr Roll; Hnr Roll; St of Mnth; Comm Volntr; Chrch Yth Grp; DARE; FCA; Scouts; Bnd; Jzz Bnd; Mch Bnd; Pep Bnd; Bskball (J); Sftball (J); Track (L); Stu Cncl (V, R); Sch Ppr (E, R, P); Yrbk (P); Educational Talent Search Program; Health, Science, Technology Academy (HSTA); Law; Psychology; Harvard U; Stanford U

HARVEY, ANDREW G; SHADY SPRING, WV; GREATER BECKLEY CHRN SCH; (SR); Hnr Roll; Pres Sch; WWAHSS; Chrch Yth Grp; Emplmnt; FCA; Bnd; Ch Chr; SP/M/VS; Bskball (V L); Ftball (V L); Cl Off (R); Stu Cncl (R); CR (R); Theatre; Music; Concord U; Liberty U

HATFIELD, BRANDON; GILBERT, WV; GILBERT HS; (FR); Hnr Roll; Pres Ac Ftns Aw; St of Mnth; DARE; Scouts; Ftball (J); Wt Lftg (J); CR (P); PhD-Surgeon; Lawyer; Marshall U; West Virginia U

HAWKINS, ASHLEY M; HARPERS FERRY, WV; JEFFERSON HS; (SO); Hi Hnr Roll; Hnr Roll; Kwnis Aw; Pres Ac Ftns Aw; Sci Fairs; St of Mnth; Comm Volntr; Drma Clb; Emplmnt; HO'Br Yth Ldrshp; Key Club; Chr; SP/M/VS; Stg Cre; Chrldg (JC); Cl Off; Stu Cncl (T, R); Golden Horseshoe; Communications-Broadcast Journalism; Concord U; West Liberty State

HAYES, SARAH; COTTAGEVILLE, WV; RAVENSWOOD HS; (SO); Hnr Roll; Nat Hon Sy; Perf Att; WWAHSS; Hab For Humty Volntr; Spec Olymp Vol; 4-H; Chrch Yth Grp; Drma Clb; Chr; Ch Chr; SP/M/VS; Stg Cre; 4H Secretary; 2nd Place AR Student; Foreign Relations; Linguistics

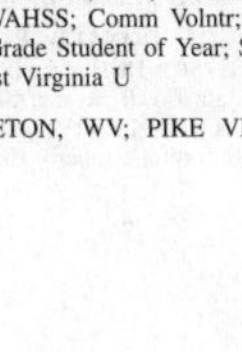
Harper, Amy B
Ritchie Cty HS
Cairo, WV

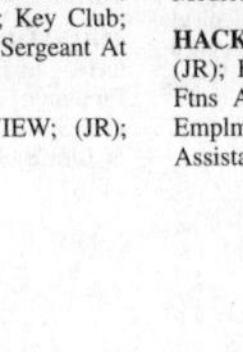
Golden, Samantha R
Philip Barbour HS Complex
Philippi, WV

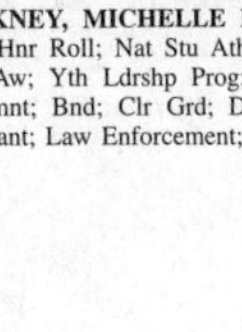
Gifford, Chad A
Buckhannon-Upshur HS
Volga, WV

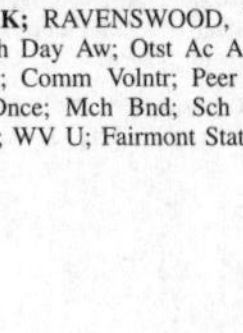
Francis, Meghan B
Ravenswood HS
Ravenswood, WV

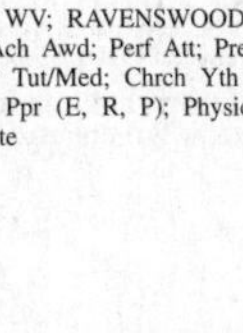
Gibbons, Kaitlin
Wheeling Ctrl Catholic HS
Wheeling, WV

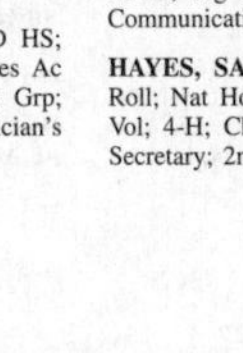
Gounden, Kriyan
Bridgeport HS
Bridgeport, WV

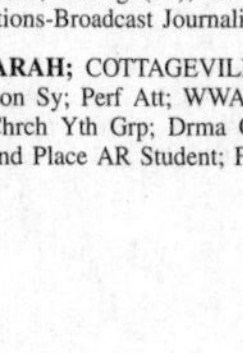
Harris, Joanna
Webster Cty HS
Webster Springs, WV

HAYES, TAMARA D; PINE GROVE, WV; VALLEY HS; (JR); Hnr Roll; Pres Ac Ftns Aw; Comm Volntr; 4-H; Chrch Yth Grp; Drma Clb; Emplmnt; Pep Squd; Prom Com; Bnd; Ch Chr; Mch Bnd; Pep Bnd; Chrldg (VJ L); WV Sheriffs Academy; Business; Accounting; West Virginia U; West Virginia Northern Community College

HAYNIE, CALEB; MAYSEL, WV; CLAY CHRISTIAN AC; (SR); Hnr Roll; Sci Fairs; Emplmnt; SP/M/VS; Arch (V); Bskball (V C); Tennis (V C); 3rd Place in National Land & Range Judging Contest; 5th Place in Engineering Science Project at ACE Convention; Joined the Navy as a Corpsman; BSN; Ohio State U; Virginia Tech U

HEDAYATNIA, MICHAEL R; MARTINSBURG, WV; HEDGESVILLE HS; (FR); Hnr Roll; Emplmnt; Scouts; Ftball (J); Architect; Chef; U of Texas

HELMICK, BILLY; SISSONVILLE, WV; SISSONVILLE HS; (SO); Ctznshp Aw; ROTC; 1st Place Colored Pencil Award in Loor County; 1st Place Drawings; Animation; Joining the Marines

HELPER, MARIDITH; ELKVIEW, WV; HERBERT HOOVER HS; (FR); Hi Hnr Roll; Hnr Roll; Perf Att; Comm Volntr; Mus Clb; Drl Tm; Drm Mjr; Flg Crps; Mch Bnd; Dancer; Majorette for High School; Business & Marketing; Engineering & Technical; Marshall U; West Virginia U

HENRY, JORDAN R; PRINCETON, WV; PRINCETON SR HS; (FR); Ctznshp Aw; Hi Hnr Roll; Perf Att; Sci Fairs; WWAHSS; Comm Volntr; Chrch Yth Grp; Key Club; Mch Bnd; Pep Bnd; Mar Art

HENRY, MELISSA; WEIRTON, WV; WEIR HS; Nat Hon Sy; Comm Volntr; AL Aux Girls; Emplmnt; Key Club; Bskball (V); GAA (V); Sccr (V); Stu Cncl (R); National Merit Scholar; Physical Therapy; West Virginia U

HERSHBERGER, BETHANY; FALLING WTRS, WV; HEDGESVILLE HS; (JR); Hnr Roll; Yth Ldrshp Prog; Dnce; Physical Therapy; Shenandoah U; Shepherd U

HESS, CHELSEA; WEIRTON, WV; (SO); Hnr Roll; WWAHSS; Hosp Aide; Drma Clb; Key Club; Sci Clb; SADD; Foreign Clb; Stg Cre; Who's Who; Pharmacy; X-Ray Technician; Duquesne U; West Liberty State College

HESS, KYLE M; MORGANTOWN, WV; UNIVERSITY HS; (FR); Ftball (J); Lcrsse (J); CR (R); Business; Law; Harvard; Yale

HICKEY, GREGORY A; HURRICANE, WV; HURRICANE HS; (SO); Hnr Roll; Perf Att; Comm Volntr; Hosp Aide; DARE; Jr Ach; Bnd; Automotive Engineering Science; Math/Science; NIT (National Institute of Technology); Marshall

HILL, ASHLEY; MOUNDSVILLE, WV; BISHOP DONAHUE HS; (FR); Hi Hnr Roll; Spec Olymp Vol; Biology Clb; Spanish Clb; Bskball (V); Sftball (V); Cl Off (S); GPA Average 4.2; Teacher; Physical Therapy; West Virginia U; Wheeling Jesuit

HILL, JEN; MOUNDSVILLE, WV; BISHOP DONAHUE HS; Bskball; Sftball; Vllyball; Teacher; WVU; West Liberty State

HILL, SANDI; CLENDENIN, WV; HERBERT HOOVER HS; (FR); Hnr Roll; Perf Att; Sci Fairs; Sccr (V CL); Lawyer; Doctor; West Virginia Mountaineers; Marshall U

HILLYARD, ERIC; LUMBERPORT, WV; LINCOLN HS; (JR); Ctznshp Aw; Hi Hnr Roll; Nat Hon Sy; Otst Ac Ach Awd; St of Mnth; WWAHSS; Yth Ldrshp Prog; Comm Volntr; Peer Tut/Med; 4-H; BPA; Chrch Yth Grp; Cmptr Clb; Emplmnt; Key Club; Prom Com; Tech Clb; Bnd; Chr; Ch Chr; Pep Bnd; Golf (V); United Methodist Person of the Year; Pharmacy; Automotive Engineer; West Virginia Wesleyan College

HITE, MEGAN; INWOOD, WV; MUSSELMAN HS; (FR); DAR; Hi Hnr Roll; Hnr Roll; Otst Ac Ach Awd; Comm Volntr; Chrch Yth Grp; Emplmnt; Fr of Library; Lttrmn Clb; Mus Clb; Spanish Clb; Chr; Ch Chr; SP/M/VS; Bskball; Scr Kpr; Sftball; Track (J); Avid Reader; Most Dedicated in Show Choir - Voted by Peers; Shenandoah U; New York U

HODGES, HILLARY V; LAVALETTE, WV; WAYNE HS; (SO); 4H Awd; Hnr Roll; Perf Att; Pres Ac Ftns Aw; Yth Ldrshp Prog; 4-H; Sch Ppr (R); Marshall U

HODGES, JAMIE; BUCKHANNON, WV; BUCKHANNON-UPSHUR HS; (JR); Hi Hnr Roll; Hnr Roll; St of Mnth; Comm Volntr; Prom Com; Spanish Clb; CR (R); Spirit Education Award; Attend College; Medical Field with a Business Degree; West Virginia U; Concord U

HODGES, SABRINA; BUCKHANNON, WV; BUCKHANNON-UPSHUR HS; (FR); Hi Hnr Roll; Hnr Roll; Perf Att; WWAHSS; Comm Volntr; Chrch Yth Grp; FCA; Bskball (J); Member of National Society of High School Scholars; National Youth Leadership Forum on Medicine; Medicine/MD; Medical; WVU Medical School; West Virginia School of Osteopathic Medicine

HODGES, SAMANTHA; BUCKHANNON, WV; BUCKHANNON-UPSHUR HS; (FR); Hnr Roll; Perf Att; WWAHSS; Comm Volntr; Chrch Yth Grp; FCA; Bskball (J); School Spirit Award; Perfect Attendance; Law Enforcement; Human Services; Fairmont State College; West Virginia U

HOGGARTH, TINA E Y; PETERSBURG, WV; PETERSBURG HS; (FR); 4H Awd; Hi Hnr Roll; Comm Volntr; FCA; Spanish Clb; Bnd; Mch Bnd; Sftball (J); Track (J); Vllyball (J); Interior Design; Oceanographer; U of Notre Dame; UCLA

HOHN, LEANDRA L; NEW MARTINSVILLE, WV; MAGNOLIA HS; (SR); F Lan Hn Soc; Hnr Roll; Perf Att; Sci Fairs; St of Mnth; WWAHSS; Yth Ldrshp Prog; Emplmnt; Mth Clb/Tm; MuAlphaTh; Prom Com; Sci Clb; Vllyball (JC); Congressional Student Leadership Conf; Homeroom Officer, USAA National Honors Student; Forensic & Investigative Science; Forensic Pathologist; West Virginia U

HOLBERT, DANNY J; BELINGTON, WV; PHILIP BARBOUR HS COMPLEX; (SO); Ctznshp Aw; DAR; Hi Hnr Roll; Hnr Roll; Kwnis Aw; Nat Sci Aw; Otst Ac Ach Awd; Sci Fairs; St of Mnth; Peer Tut/Med; Key Club; Ntl FFA; Tchrs Aide; Clb; SP/M/VS; Bsball; Bskball; Ftball (VJ); Wt Lftg; Cl Off (T); Stu Cncl (R); CR (R); Scholastic Honors Award; Medical Professions; Law and Legal Professions; West Virginia U; Ohio State U

HOLBROOK, ECIL M; RED HOUSE, WV; CALVARY BAPTIST AC; (FR); Hi Hnr Roll; Hnr Roll; Aqrium Clb; ArtClub; Biology Clb; Chess; Chrch Yth Grp; DARE; FCA; Lttrmn Clb; Chr; Ch Chr; SP/M/VS; Bskball (VJ L); Chrldg (J L); GAA (VJ); Sccr (J); Track (V); 1st Place- Watercolors / ACE - Regional Convention; 1st Place Long Jump; Medicine; Language; Duke U; Florida State U

HOLISKEY, ZACK; BUNKER HILL, WV; MUSSELMAN HS; (JR); Hnr Roll; Comm Volntr; Peer Tut/Med; P to P St Amb Prg; Golf (V L); Mechanical Engineering; West Virginia U; West Virginia Technical Institute

HOLSTINE, MICHELLE; DUNMORE, WV; POCAHONTAS CTY HS; (SO); Bnd; Jzz Bnd; Mch Bnd; Orch; Bskball (V L); Sccr (V L); Track (V L); All Conference Athlete - Soccer

HOOD III, DENNY L; PRINCETON, WV; PRINCETON SR HS; (JR); DAR; Hi Hnr Roll; Nat Hon Sy; WWAHSS; Chrch Yth Grp; Key Club; Mod UN; Scouts; Bsball (J); Sccr (V); Pharmacist; West Virginia U; Concord U

HOOVER, ANDREW; BRIDGEPORT, WV; BRIDGEPORT HS; (FR); WWAHSS; Key Club; Lttrmn Clb; Ftball (J); Track (V L); Wrstlg (J); U of Southern California; Marshall U

HOOVER, SARAH; BRIDGEPORT, WV; BRIDGEPORT HS; (JR); Hi Hnr Roll; Hnr Roll; Perf Att; Pres Ac Ftns Aw; Chrch Yth Grp; Emplmnt; Pep Squd; Prom Com; Chrldg (J); Gmnstcs; Yrbk (E); Participate on a National Champion Cheerleading Squad; Psychology; Journalism; West Virginia U; Marshall U

HORAN, CODY; BELLE, WV; CARVER CAREER & TECH ED CTR; (JR); 4H Awd; Comm Volntr; Chrch Yth Grp; Bsball (V); Ftball (V); WV State U

HORN, SARAH N; KERMIT, WV; TUG VALLEY HS; (SO); Gov Hnr Prg; Hnr Roll; MVP; Nat Hon Sy; St of Mnth; Comm Volntr; Chrch Yth Grp; Mth Clb/Tm; Ntl Beta Clb; Chr; Flg Crps; SP/M/VS; Bskball (V); Sftball (V); Physical Therapy 6 Yrs College; Pikeville Community College; West Virginia U

HORNICK, W JONATHAN; GARY, WV; MOUNT VIEW HS; (SO); Gov Hnr Prg; Hi Hnr Roll; Hnr Roll; Key Club; Ntl Beta Clb; Tennis; Yrbk; Computer Technology; Concord College; WV U

HOUGH, BRANDON; WHEELING, WV; WHEELING PARK HS; (JR); Hi Hnr Roll; Nat Hon Sy; Perf Att; Sci Clb; Clb; Sch Ppr (R); Yrbk (E); West Virginia U

HUBBARD, KELLIE N; BLUEFIELD, WV; MONTCALM HS; (FR); Hnr Roll; Master's Degree in Nursing; Marshall U

HUFF, ELIZABETH M; CHARLES TOWN, WV; JEFFERSON HS; (FR); Hnr Roll; Comm Volntr; Chrch Yth Grp; Key Club; Mus Clb; Chr; Ch Chr; Dnce; CR (R); National Honor Choir; Regional Honor Choir; Music; Drama; Brigham Young U; Shepard U

HUFFMAN, BENTON R; COXS MILLS, WV; GILMER CTY HS; (SR); Hnr Roll; Pres Ac Ftns Aw; WWAHSS; Peer Tut/Med; Prom Com; Bsball (V L); Bskball (V L); Ftball (V L); Adv Cncl (R); Young Democrats; 9th Junior Trooper Academy; Criminal Justice; Concord College

HUFFMAN, JASON; BUCKHANNON, WV; BUCKHANNON-UPSHUR HS; (FR); Hi Hnr Roll; Hnr Roll; Perf Att; St of Mnth; Ftball; Wt Lftg; Music; West Virginia U

HUFFMAN, SAMANTHA K; GILBERT, WV; GILBERT HS; (SO); All Am Sch; Hi Hnr Roll; Perf Att; St of Mnth; Comm Volntr; FCA; Scouts; SADD; Vllyball (J L); CR (R); Housing Award; Math Field Day Team; Medical Secretary; Physician's Assistant (P.A.C.); Southern West Virginia Community and Technical College; Mountain State U

HUGHES, TYLER; BRADSHAW, WV; IAEGER HS; (FR); Hnr Roll; Otst Ac Ach Awd; DARE; Bskball (J); Wt Lftg (J); Arts; Designs; West Virginia

HUGHES JR, LONNIE A.; BECKLEY, WV; WOODROW WILSON HS; (SO); Hnr Roll; Perf Att; WWAHSS; Comm Volntr; FCA; Mch Bnd; Bskball (V); Ftball (J); West Virginia U, Marshall U; Ohio State, Florida State, Tennessee U

HURLEY, LAUREN; HUNTINGTON, WV; HUNTINGTON HS; (SO); Hi Hnr Roll; Nat Hon Sy; Otst Ac Ach Awd; WWAHSS; Comm Volntr; Chrch Yth Grp; Dbte Team; Drma Clb; Key Club; Ntl Beta Clb; Sch Ppr (E); Yrbk (R); 3rd Place in Scores for Journalism; Alternate for the Hugh O'Brian Youth Leadership; Psychiatrist; Creative Writer; Tulane U; Sarah Lawrence College

HURLEY, SCOTT; BLUEFIELD, WV; MONTCALM HS; (FR); Ctznshp Aw; Hnr Roll; Comm Volntr; Peer Tut/Med; Chrch Yth Grp; Criminal Justice; Health / Human Services; Bluefield State College; Concord U

HYATT, BRITTANY N; IAEGER, WV; IAEGER HS; (FR); Hnr Roll; Perf Att; Sci Fairs; Peer Tut/Med; DARE; Quiz Bowl; Ch Chr; CR (T); Sch Ppr (E); Yrbk (E); Health; Bluefield State

JACKSON, DAVID E; BARBOURSVILLE, WV; CABELL MIDLAND HS; (JR); Hnr Roll; Emplmnt; Bowling Scholarship; Engineering / Technical; Car Designing; Marshall U; Virginia Tech

JACKSON, NIYA; MOUNT HOPE, WV; WOODROW WILSON HS; (FR); Hnr Roll; Nat Sci Aw; Perf Att; Sci Fairs; Chrch Yth Grp; Cmptr Clb; DARE; Drma Clb; Bnd; Chr; Dnce; Bskball; Medical Field; Computer Software; New York U; North Carolina A & T State U

JACOBS, SHAWN; PHILIPPI, WV; PHILIP BARBOUR HS COMPLEX; (FR); Hnr Roll; Ntl FFA; Ftball (VJ L); Engineering; Environmental Science; Texas A & M U; Virginia Tech

JAFRI, SARAH; BRIDGEPORT, WV; BRIDGEPORT HS; (JR); Hnr Roll; AL Aux Girls; Chrch Yth Grp; Emplmnt; Swmg (V L); Interior Design; Law; U of North Carolina; West Virginia U

JAMES, BRIAN D; MARTINSBURG, WV; MUSSELMAN HS; (SO); Ctznshp Aw; DAR; Hi Hnr Roll; Hnr Roll; MVP; Nat Hon Sy; Otst Ac Ach Awd; Perf Att; Pres Sch; Sci Fairs; CARE; Comm Volntr; Peer Tut/Med; Chrch Yth Grp; DARE; Drma Clb; Emplmnt; Mus Clb; SADD; Spanish Clb; Chr; Ch Chr; SP/M/VS; Stg Cre; Stu Cncl (R); CR (R); Achieving Applemen; Acting / Stage or Television; Theatre Teacher; New York U / Acting School in New York; UCLA

JAMISON, RADIANCE; MT HOPE, WV; MT HOPE HS; (SO); Hi Hnr Roll; Nat Hon Sy; Otst Ac Ach Awd; Perf Att; St of Mnth; Comm Volntr; Peer Tut/Med; Chrch Yth Grp; DARE; Drma Clb; FCA; Bnd; Dnce; Flg Crps; Mch Bnd; Medicine; West Virginia State College; West Virginia U

JEFFERSON, LESLIE J; BARBOURSVILLE, WV; CABELL MIDLAND HS; (JR); Hnr Roll; MVP; Peer Tut/Med; Chrch Yth Grp; FCA; Lib Aide; MuAlphaTh; Tchrs Aide; Vsity Clb; Sftball (V); Elementary Education; Marshall U; U of Kentucky

JEWELL, LINDSEY C; PRINCETON, WV; PRINCETON HS; (JR); Hnr Roll; Nat Hon Sy; Key Club; Sch Ppr (R); National Tech Honor Society; Pharmacy; Campbell U

JEWELL, MEGAN; WHEELING, WV; SR; (SR); F Lan Hn Soc; Hi Hnr Roll; Nat Hon Sy; Sci Fairs; WWAHSS; Chrch Yth Grp; Drma Clb; Emplmnt; SADD; Tech Clb; Chr; Speech Pathology; American Sign Language; Kent State U

JIN, MIN H; WHEELING, WV; BISHOP DONAHUE HS; (SR); Hnr Roll; Nat Hon Sy; WWAHSS; Spec Olymp Vol; Chrch Yth Grp; Key Club; Mth Clb/Tm; Mus Clb; P to P St Amb Prg; Prom Com; Scouts; Chr; SP/M/VS; Bskball (J); Cl Off (P); Stu Cncl (P); CR (P); Economics & Business; Penn State U

JIN, SUNG HO; HUNTINGTON, WV; HUNTINGTON HS; (FR); Bnd; Mch Bnd; Medicine School; Engineering; Ohio State U; West Virginia State U

JOHNSON, COLBY; FRANKLIN, WV; PENDLETON HS; (FR); Ntl FFA; Agriculture Technology; Fairmont State U; Potomac State College

JOHNSON, MYSTIN; FOLLANSBEE, WV; BROOKE HS; (JR); Hi Hnr Roll; Nat Hon Sy; Otst Ac Ach Awd; Pres Sch; Valdctrian; WWAHSS; Yth Ldrshp Prog; Comm Volntr; Chess; Chrch Yth Grp; DARE; Mth Clb/Tm; SADD; Clb; Bskball (VJ); Vllyball (VJCL); Dental Hygiene; Teaching; Bethany; West Liberty State College

JOHNSON, TIFFANY L; POCA, WV; POCA HS; (SO); Hi Hnr Roll; Hnr Roll; Pres Ac Ftns Aw; Sci Fairs; St of Mnth; WWAHSS; Comm Volntr; Spec Olymp Vol; Chrch Yth Grp; DARE; DECA; FCA; FBLA; Pep Squd; SADD; Dnce; Chrldg (V); Gmnstcs (V); Sftball (V); Stu Cncl (S); 2003 Sept / 2005 Feb - Student of Month; 2005 Sophomore - Homecoming Attendant; Physical Therapy; Nursing; Marshall U; WVU

JOHNSON III, DONALD E; BRADLEY, WV; GREATER BECKLEY CHRN SCH; (SR); Hi Hnr Roll; Hnr Roll; Pres Sch; Chrch Yth Grp; DARE; Emplmnt; Quiz Bowl; Scouts; Bnd; Jzz Bnd; Mch Bnd; Bskball (V); Ftball (V); Sftball (L); Wt Lftg (V); Handbell Choir; Computer Programming; Word of Life Bible Institute; Liberty U

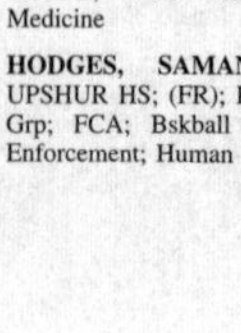
Jin, Sung Ho
Huntington HS
Huntington, WV

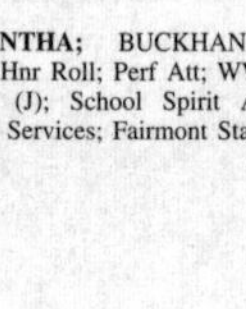
Holiskey, Zack
Musselman HS
Bunker Hill, WV

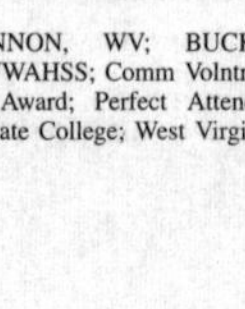
Hodges, Samantha
Buckhannon-Upshur HS
Buckhannon, WV

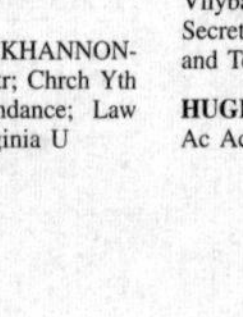
Hodges, Jamie
Buckhannon-Upshur HS
Buckhannon, WV

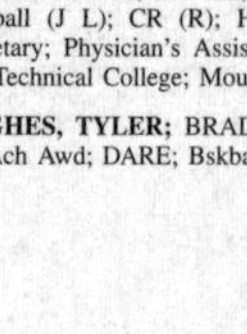
Hodges, Hillary V
Wayne HS
Lavalette, WV

National
Honor Roll
Spring 2005

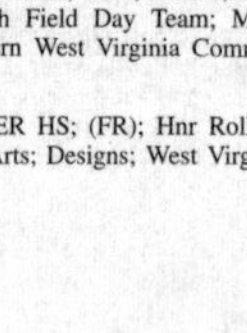
Hayes, Tamara D
Valley HS
Pine Grove, WV

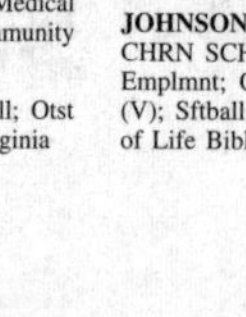
Hodges, Sabrina
Buckhannon-Upshur HS
Buckhannon, WV

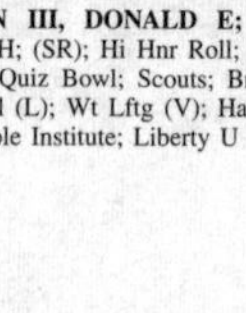
Holbert, Danny J
Philip Barbour HS Complex
Belington, WV

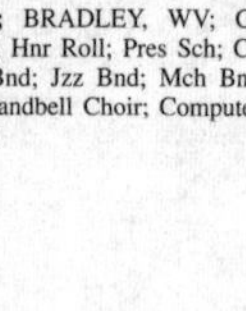
Hood III, Denny L
Princeton SR HS
Princeton, WV

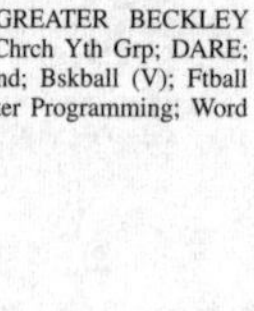
Huffman, Benton R
Gilmer Cty HS
Coxs Mills, WV

JOHNSTON, CHRISTOPHER S; WHEELING, WV; WHEELING PARK HS; (SR); Hi Hnr Roll; Kwnis Aw; Nat Hon Sy; Nat Ldrshp Svc; Otst Ac Ach Awd; Yth Ldrshp Prog; Comm Volntr; Hosp Aide; Emplmnt; Key Club; NYLC; Scouts; Svce Clb; Vsity Clb; Cr Ctry (J L); Golf (J L); Track (V L); Wt Lftg (V); Stu Cncl (R); CR (R); Eagle Scout-Boy Scouts of America; National Spanish Honor Society; Biology; Virginia Military Institute; West Virginia Wesleyan College

JONES, RYAN; OAK HILL, WV; OAK HILL HS; (JR); Gov Hnr Prg; Hi Hnr Roll; Nat Hon Sy; Perf Att; Sci/Math Olympn; WWAHSS; Peer Tut/Med; Key Club; Mth Clb/Tm; Prom Com; Spanish Clb; Bnd; Jzz Bnd; Mch Bnd; Junior Prom Court 2005

JONES, SAMANTHA K; CHARLESTON, WV; NITRO HS; (JR); Hnr Roll; Nat Hon Sy; Sci Fairs; Comm Volntr; Chrch Yth Grp; French Clb; Ch Chr; Day Care Worker; Active in Church Youth; Neonatal Nurse; Small Business Owner; West Virginia State; Mountain State U

JOSEPH, KASEY; CHARLESTON, WV; CAPITAL HS; (SR); Hi Hnr Roll; Nat Hon Sy; WWAHSS; Comm Volntr; Chrch Yth Grp; Emplmnt; FTA; Key Club; Vllyball (V L); Sch Ppr (R, P); Business, Human Resources; Elon U

JUSTICE, AMANDA; GILBERT, WV; GILBERT HS; (FR); Hi Hnr Roll; Hnr Roll; Nat Sci Aw; Otst Ac Ach Awd; St of Mnth; FCA; Mth Clb/Tm; Mch Bnd; Majorette; Nursing; West Virginia U; Marshall U

KANOSKY, KAYLA M; MORGANTOWN, WV; UNIVERSITY HS; (JR); Hnr Roll; Nat Hon Sy; WWAHSS; Yth Ldrshp Prog; Comm Volntr; Chrch Yth Grp; Emplmnt; Key Club; MuAlphaTh; Scouts; Spanish Clb; Bnd; Mch Bnd; Stg Cre; Bskball (J); Stu Cncl (R); National Youth Leadership Forum for Medicine; National Honor Society; Medicine; WVU (West Virginia U)

KEEN, NATHAN L; PETERSBURG, WV; PETERSBURG HS; (JR); Hnr Roll; Perf Att; DARE; FCA; FBLA; Lttrmn Clb; Ntl FFA; SADD; Voc Ind Clb Am; Ftball (VJ L); 1 Semester - Perfect Attendance; Masonry; Marshall U

KEETON, JOSEPH D; HUNTINGTON, WV; HUNTINGTON HS; (MS); Hnr Roll; Chrch Yth Grp; Ch Chr; Bskball; Ftball; Plays AAU Basketball; Accounting; OSU; UNC

KELLEY, GLENN E; RAVENSWOOD, WV; RAVENSWOOD HS; (SR); Hnr Roll; WWAHSS; AL Aux Boys; Photog; Wdwrkg Clb; Cr Ctry (J L); Track (V L); Volunteens President 2004-05 / Hospital Volunteer; RAZE Member; Bible Study; Theology; Berea College; Ohio Valley College

KENNEDY, CYNTHIA; CARETTA, WV; BIG CREEK HS; (SO); Hi Hnr Roll; Hnr Roll; Nat Hon Sy; Nat Sci Aw; Otst Ac Ach Awd; Perf Att; Pres Ac Ftns Aw; Sci Fairs; St of Mnth; WWAHSS; ArtClub; Chrch Yth Grp; DARE; Drma Clb; Emplmnt; Quiz Bowl; SADD; Bnd; Chr; Ch Chr; Dnce; Bskball (V); Sftball (J); Stu Cncl (P); CR (T); Heart Specialist; RN; WVU; Concord

KENNEDY, PAUL A; BUCKHANNON, WV; BUHS; (JR); Hnr Roll; Chrch Yth Grp; Scouts; Almost Eagle Scout; History; Spanish

KEPLINGER, JONATHAN; PETERSBURG, WV; SOUTH BRANCH CAREER & TECH CTR; (SR); Hnr Roll; Chrch Yth Grp; DARE; Ntl FFA; SADD; Wdwrkg Clb

KEYS, PATRICK; NORTHFORK, WV; MT VIEW HS; (SO); Hnr Roll; WWAHSS; Comm Volntr; Ntl Beta Clb; Bsball (V); Law; West Virginia U

KHADER, WASEEM; HUNTINGTON, WV; HUNTINGTON HS; (SR); Hi Hnr Roll; Hnr Roll; Kwnis Aw; Nat Hon Sy; Nat Ldrshp Svc; WWAHSS; Key Club; Mth Clb/Tm; MuAlphaTh; Ntl Beta Clb; Sci Clb; Pre-Med; Biology; Marshall U; West Virginia U

KIEFER, KYLIE; BRIDGEPORT, WV; BRIDGEPORT HS; (SO); Chrldg (V); Swmg (V); Track (V); Stu Cncl (R); Yrbk (R); Dance; Nursing; West Virginia U

KIMBLE, PAYDEN A; PETERSBURG, WV; PETERSBURG HS; (FR); 4H Awd; Hi Hnr Roll; Otst Ac Ach Awd; Sci Fairs; 4-H; Chrch Yth Grp; Bnd; Mch Bnd; Pep Bnd; Outstanding Male Band Member - 3 Yrs; Wright Brothers Writing Award Essay About Flight

KINCAID, MARY; FAYETTEVILLE, WV; FAYETTEVILLE HS; (SO); Hi Hnr Roll; Otst Ac Ach Awd; Sci Fairs; 4-H; Chrch Yth Grp; DARE; Emplmnt; ROTC; Scouts; SADD; Tchrs Aide; Chr; Bskball; Sftball (V); Paramedic; Registered Nurse; Marshall U; Concorde College

KINCAID JR, MICHAEL W; BUNKER HILL, WV; MUSSELMAN HS; (FR); Ctznshp Aw; Hnr Roll; MVP; Perf Att; Sci Fairs; St of Mnth; Comm Volntr; Chess; Chrch Yth Grp; P to P St Amb Prg; Bnd; Jzz Bnd; Mch Bnd; Orch; 2003-05 Superior Rating Shepherd U / Solo and Ensemble Festival; 2003-05 Musselman High Band Tournament of Bands & Chapter III Group 2 Champions; Music Education / Management; Marshall U; West Virginia U

KINDER, JENNIFER M; NELLIS, WV; SHERMAN HS; (JR); Comm Volntr; DARE; Registered Nurse; Marshall U; West Virginia U

KING, JESSICA B; MILLWOOD, WV; RAVENSWOOD HS; (FR); 4H Awd; Hnr Roll; Perf Att; Pres Ac Ftns Aw; Pres Sch; Sci Fairs; 4-H; Acpl Chr; Chr; SP/M/VS; Swg Chr; Honor Student; Published Poetry Writer; Journalism; Voice / Music; Concord U; U of Missouri Columbia

KING, REBECCA; PRINCETON, WV; PRINCETON SR HS; (FR); 4H Awd; Gov Hnr Prg; Hi Hnr Roll; Pres Ac Ftns Aw; Sci/Math Olympn; St of Mnth; WWAHSS; Peer Tut/Med; 4-H; Chrch Yth Grp; Dbte Team; FCA; Key Club; Mth Clb/Tm; Mod UN; Chr; Ch Chr; Dnce; Jzz Bnd; Golf (V); PPSqd (V); Tennis (V); Cl Off (R); Stu Cncl (R); Marine Biologist; Aeronautical Engineer; Tampa U; West Virginia U

KIRSCH, MORGAN; WHEELING, WV; MOUNT DE CHANTAL HS; (JR); Hnr Roll; Nat Hon Sy; WWAHSS; Hab For Humty Volntr; Key Club; German Clb; Chr; Bskball (VJ); Sccr (V); Track (V); Cl Off (R); Stu Cncl (T); CR (T); Yrbk (P); Health Care Management; Human Resources; Chatham College; Duquesne U

KISAMORE, LINDSEY; SENECA ROCKS, WV; PENDLETON HS; (FR); County Social Studies Winner; Musician; Writer; Potomac State College; Glenville State College

KLEIN, BEVERLY A; HUNTINGTON, WV; CABELL MIDLAND HS; (FR); Hnr Roll; CR (S, T, R); Yrbk (P); Bat-Mitzvah; Photography; Journalism; West Virginia U

KNAPP, MAXWELL L; RAVENSWOOD, WV; RAVENSWOOD HS; (FR); Hnr Roll; Pres Ac Ftns Aw; St of Mnth; Chess; Bsball (VJ); Golf (V L); Scr Kpr (VJ); Sccr (J); Natural Helpers; Physical Therapy; Physician's Assistant; Marshall U; Wake Forest U

KNIGHTEN, REBECCA A; MARTINSBURG, WV; HEDGESVILLE HS; (SO); 4H Awd; DAR; Hnr Roll; Otst Ac Ach Awd; Perf Att; Sci Fairs; 4-H; Chrch Yth Grp; Emplmnt; Bnd; Ch Chr; Mch Bnd; Church Awards; Elementary Teacher; Middle School Teacher; Shepherd U; West Virginia U

KNOX, ELIZABETH L; BRUCETON MILLS, WV; PRESTON HS; (SO); Hnr Roll; Chr; Pharmacist; Teacher; West Virginia U; Fairmont State

KNOX, JERICHA; LOGAN, WV; RALPH R WILLIS CAREER TECH SCH; (JR); Hnr Roll; St of Mnth; Comm Volntr; Spec Olymp Vol; Chrch Yth Grp; SADD; Chr; Dnce; Drl Tm; Drm Mjr; Bsball (V); Cr Ctry (C); Sftball (V); Cl Off (P); Stu Cncl (P); CR (P); Leo Club; BAPS; Go to College

KOCH, DEREK; GAULEY BRIDGE, WV; MIDLAND TRAIL HS; (FR); Hi Hnr Roll; Hnr Roll; Pres Ac Ftns Aw; Bnd; Ftball (VJ L); Track (VJCL); Wt Lftg; Mechanical Engineering; Underwater Welding; West Virginia U; Virginia Tech

KOCHER, CAITLIN; WELLSBURG, WV; BROOKE HS; (FR); Hi Hnr Roll; Perf Att; St Schl; Comm Volntr; Hosp Aide; Chrch Yth Grp; DARE; DECA; Key Club; French Clb; Sccr (V L); Sftball (V L); Forensic Pathologist

KRESSIN, ASHLEY N; CHARLES TOWN, WV; JEFFERSON HS 9TH GRADE COMPLEX; (FR); Hnr Roll; WWAHSS; Key Club; Key Club Treasurer; Arts & Humanities; Communications; West Virginia U; U of Virginia

KRYANINKO, CHRIS; WEIRTON, WV; WEIR HS; (JR); Nat Hon Sy; WWAHSS; Peer Tut/Med; AL Aux Boys; Chrch Yth Grp; HO'Br Yth Ldrshp; Key Club; Sci Clb; Chr; Ch Chr; SP/M/VS; Lit Mag; WLC HOBY Attendant; Key Club State Board; Zoology; Veterinary; George Washington U; Ohio State U

LAMBERT, BRITTANY E; MARTINSBURG, WV; MARTINSBURG HS; (SO); Hnr Roll; Peer Tut/Med; Chrch Yth Grp; Chr; Ch Chr; Dnce; Criminal Justice; Paralegal / Lawyer; West Virginia State U; U of Maryland

LAMOTHE, KYLE A; PRINCETON, WV; PRINCETON SR HS; (SO); WWAHSS; Comm Volntr; Chess; Chrch Yth Grp; Key Club; Scouts; Chr; Ch Chr; Sunday School Teacher; Altar Server

LAMP, ANGELA; WEIRTON, WV; WEIR HS; (FR); Pres Ac Ftns Aw; St of Mnth; WWAHSS; Comm Volntr; Chrch Yth Grp; Key Club; Scouts; GAA; Sccr (V L); Sftball (L); Swmg (L); Track; Softball Coach; Student Teacher-CCD

LANE, MEGAN; HINTON, WV; SUMMERS CTY HS; (SR); Hnr Roll; Nat Hon Sy; WWAHSS; Comm Volntr; Ntl FFA; Hsbk Rdg; New River Community and Technical College; Salem International U

LARCH, JASON; WEIRTON, WV; WEIR HS; (JR); All Am Sch; Hi Hnr Roll; Nat Hon Sy; Nat Sci Aw; USAA; WWAHSS; Emplmnt; HO'Br Yth Ldrshp; Key Club; Mth Clb/Tm; Sci Clb; Svce Clb; Bskball (J); Ftball (V L); Tennis (V L); Cl Off (V); Stu Cncl; Martial Arts-Chun Kuk Do; Key Club Presidents; Engineering; Ohio State U; The U of Notre Dame

LARCH, JULIE; WEIRTON, WV; WEIR HS; (FR); Hi Hnr Roll; USAA; WWAHSS; Drma Clb; Key Club; Sci Clb; Foreign Clb; Sccr (V); Tennis (V L); Cl Off (T); Key Club Treasurer; Math Major; Chemist; Notre Dame; Ohio State

LARCH, JULIE R; WEIRTON, WV; WEIR HS; (FR); Hi Hnr Roll; USAA; WWAHSS; Drma Clb; Key Club; Sci Clb; Foreign Clb; Sccr (V); Tennis (V L); Cl Off (T); US Ach Academy-Nat'l English Merit Award; Math Major; Science Minor; Notre Dame; Ohio State

LAYNE, ERICA; BRIDGEPORT, WV; BRIDGEPORT HS; (JR); F Lan Hn Soc; Hnr Roll; Nat Hon Sy; Otst Ac Ach Awd; WWAHSS; Comm Volntr; Peer Tut/Med; Red Cr Aide; FCA; Key Club; Lttrmn Clb; Tchrs Aide; Bnd; Clr Grd; Mch Bnd; Track (J); Young Author's Award; Band Letterman; Nutritionist; Psychology; West Virginia U; Marietta College

LEACOCK, KRYSTYNNE A; BECKLEY, WV; WOODROW WILSON HS; (SO); Ctznshp Aw; F Lan Hn Soc; Gov Hnr Prg; Hi Hnr Roll; Nat Hon Sy; Perf Att; Pres Ac Ftns Aw; Pres Sch; Salutrn; WWAHSS; Comm Volntr; Hosp Aide; Peer Tut/Med; ArtClub; Chrch Yth Grp; DARE; Drma Clb; FCA; Fr of Library; Key Club; Off Aide; Tennis (VJ); Track (V); Cl Off (P); Stu Cncl (V); Best of Show: Raleigh County Art Show 2005; Highest Score WV Writing; Biochemistry; Medical Degree; Georgetown U; Howard U

LEATHERMAN, CHIP; FALLING WATERS, WV; HEDGESVILLE HS; (SO); Hnr Roll; WWAHSS; Chrch Yth Grp; Off Aide; Scouts; Tchrs Aide; Ch Chr; Tennis (V); Stu Cncl (R); Yrbk (R); Page in WV Legislature-House of Delegates; Mechanical Engineering; Shepherd U; West Virginia U

LEDSOME, JAMIE; REEDY, WV; ROANE CTY HS; (FR); Ctznshp Aw; Hi Hnr Roll; Hnr Roll; MVP; Otst Ac Ach Awd; Pres Ac Ftns Aw; Sci Fairs; St of Mnth; USAA; Comm Volntr; 4-H; Ntl FFA; Sftball (VJ); Veterinarian; Lawyer; West Virginia U; Harvard U

LEIVA, CHRISTOPHER S; POCA, WV; POCA HS; (FR); 4H Awd; Ctznshp Aw; Hnr Roll; Perf Att; Comm Volntr; Hab For Humty Volntr; Red Cr Aide; 4-H; Chrch Yth Grp; Outdrs Clb; Ch Chr; SP/M/VS; Arch; Winner State Poster Contest-Promo; Winner State Poster Contest-Dairy; Science Teacher; NASA; Marshall U; Virginia Tech

LESTER, KURT; PAYNESVILLE, WV; IAEGER HS; (FR); Hnr Roll; Comm Volntr; Bsball (L); Ftball (J); Wt Lftg (V); Stage Crew "Rock Band"; Lawyer; Teacher; Florida State U; Marshall U

LEWIS, CASSIE; RICHWOOD, WV; RICHWOOD HS; (JR); Nat Hon Sy; ArtClub; Tchrs Aide; Art; Auto Mechanic

LIEBY, JOE; HEDGESVILLE, WV; HEDGESVILLE HS; (JR); St of Mnth; Chess; DARE; Drma Clb; Scouts; Chr; Ch Chr; Stg Cre; Member of Thespian International Society; Graphic Novelist

LINES, MICHAEL; BECKLEY, WV; WOODROW WILSON HS; (JR); Hnr Roll; Pres Ac Ftns Aw; DARE; Bskball (V); Ftball (V L); Wt Lftg (V); Engineering

LIPFORD, STEPHANIE; CHARLESTON, WV; HURRICANE HS; (SR); Ctznshp Aw; Hnr Roll; Nat Hon Sy; Otst Ac Ach Awd; St Schl; Comm Volntr; DARE; Emplmnt; Key Club; Kwanza Clb; Mus Clb; Off Aide; Tchrs Aide; Spanish Clb; Chr; Dnce; West Virginia Promise Scholar; Winner of the Mabel C Merical Grant-in-Aid Scholarship; West Virginia University; Elementary Education

LIPSCOMB, CRYSTAL L; BAYARD, WV; UNION HS; (SR); Red Cr Aide; Chr; Stu Cncl (R); Yrbk (P)

LITTLETON, BOBBY; WEIRTON, WV; WEIR HS; (SO); Hnr Roll; Perf Att; WWAHSS; Key Club; Scouts; Bskball (V); Sccr (V); Building Construction

LOCKE, JESIMAE J; SALEM, WV; LIBERTY HS; (FR); Hnr Roll; Pres Ac Ftns Aw; Comm Volntr; 4-H; Chrch Yth Grp; DARE; Emplmnt; Key Club; Pep Squd; Bnd; Chr; Ch Chr; Mch Bnd; Chrldg (V); Gmnstcs (V); Relay for Life Volunteer 4-H Volunteer; Energy Express Volunteer, Humane Society Volunteer; Cosmetology; Auto Mechanics; Virginia Tech; Fairmont State College

LOCKETT, CHERELLE; MARTINSBURG, WV; MARTINSBURG HS; (SO); Hi Hnr Roll; St of Mnth; Comm Volntr; Chrch Yth Grp; Bskball (VJ); Perfect Attendance; Teacher; Elementary School; Tennessee U Knoxville; Maryland U College Park

LONEGAN, JOSHUA; ELKINS, WV; ELKINS HS; (FR); Chrch Yth Grp; Voc Ind Clb Am; Fairmont States Dean 3 List for Honor Roll; Culinary; Fairmont Culinary; Pittsburgh Culinary

LONG, MARY BETH; FRANKFORD, WV; GREENBRIER EAST HS; (JR); Chr; Bskball (VJ L); Sftball (V L); Tennis (V); Vllyball (V L); Cl Off (V); Stu Cncl (R); National 4-H Conference Delegate; DECA Competition in LA; Teaching; Therapist; Elon U

LONO, JESSICA C; BRIDGEPORT, WV; BRIDGEPORT HS; (SR); F Lan Hn Soc; Gov Hnr Prg; Hi Hnr Roll; Jr Eng Tech; Nat Hon Sy; Perf Att; Comm Volntr; Hosp Aide; Chrch Yth Grp; DECA; Scouts; Orch; Sccr (V L); Track (V L); Urban Planner; Environmental Planning; Brigham Young U; Utah State U

LOPEZ, SAMANTHA J; BRIDGEPORT, WV; BRIDGEPORT HS; (JR); Hnr Roll; Perf Att; Comm Volntr; Spec Olymp Vol; Key Club; Bnd; Clr Grd; Mch Bnd; Medicine; Law; West Virginia U; Fairmont State

Lambert, Brittany E
Martinsburg HS
Martinsburg, WV

Kressin, Ashley N
Jefferson HS 9th Grade Complex
Charles Town, WV

Johnston, Christopher S
Wheeling Park HS
Wheeling, WV

Kincaid Jr, Michael W
Musselman HS
Bunker Hill, WV

Lockett, Cherelle
Martinsburg HS
Martinsburg, WV

LUPARDUS, DANIEL L; ELEANOR, WV; BUFFALO HS; (SO); 4H Awd; Hnr Roll; MVP; Otst Ac Ach Awd; Comm Volntr; 4-H; Chrch Yth Grp; DARE; Ftball (VJCL); Wt Lftg (VJCL); All-County Player; Mechanics; Collison Repair; West Virginia U

LUTYENS, LINDSEY; FAIRMONT, WV; BRIDGEPORT HS; (FR); 4H Awd; Hi Hnr Roll; Nat Hon Sy; Pres Ac Ftns Aw; WWAHSS; 4-H; Key Club; Cr Ctry (V); Hsbk Rdg; Track (J); Alternate Team Member for NWVQHA; Owning Own Business; Sales / Marketing; West Virginia U; Ohio State U

LYNCH, LARISSA H; HUNTINGTON, WV; HUNTINGTON HS; (JR); All Am Sch; Hi Hnr Roll; Nat Hon Sy; WWAHSS; Spec Olymp Vol; ArtClub; Emplmnt; Photog; French Clb; Golf (V L); 2004 WV Junior Female Golfer of the Year; 2004 Champion WV Junior Amateur-Female

LYONS, BETH A; KEYSER, WV; KEYSER HS; (JR); Hnr Roll; WWAHSS; Chrch Yth Grp; Scouts; Bnd; Ch Chr; Jzz Bnd; Mch Bnd; Scr Kpr (V); College Jazz Choir/Community Choir; College Musicals; Nursing

MALLOW, ANNE; UPPER TRACT, WV; PENDLETON HS; (JR); 4H Awd; Gov Hnr Prg; Hi Hnr Roll; Nat Hon Sy; Nat Sci Aw; Otst Ac Ach Awd; Pres Ac Ftns Aw; Sci Fairs; St of Mnth; Hab For Humty Volntr; Peer Tut/Med; 4-H; Chrch Yth Grp; FCA; Ntl Beta Clb; Off Aide; Prom Com; SADD; Tchrs Aide; Bnd; Ch Chr; Mch Bnd; Bskball (J); Track (V L); Cl Off (P); Engineering; Architecture; West Virginia U

MANLEY, LISA A; BUCKHANNON, WV; BUCKHANNON UPSHUR HS; (FR); Ctznshp Aw; Hi Hnr Roll; Nat Sci Aw; Comm Volntr; Chrch Yth Grp; FCA; Lttrmn Clb; Chrldg (V L); Sftball (VJ); Stu Cncl; Optometry; Physical Therapy; West Virginia U; Ohio State for Optometry

MANNS, BOBBY; BECKLEY, WV; WOODROW WILSON HS; (FR); Hnr Roll; WWAHSS; Bskball (J); Ftball (VJ); Wt Lftg (VJ); Art Picture (Honorable Mention); Engineering; Duke U; U of North Carolina

MANZO, CECILIA R; FAIRMONT, WV; NORTH MARION HS; (SR); Hi Hnr Roll; Nat Hon Sy; St of Mnth; WWAHSS; Comm Volntr; Spec Olymp Vol; FCA; MuAlphaTh; Off Aide; Tchrs Aide; SP/M/VS; Chrldg (V L); Track (V L); Accolades for Academics-2 Years; National Honor Society Secretary; Radiology; West Virginia U

MAPES, STEPHEN; RAVENSWOOD, WV; RAVENSWOOD HS; (SR); Hi Hnr Roll; Nat Hon Sy; Nat Mrt Fin; Salutrn; St of Mnth; USAA; WWAHSS; Comm Volntr; Red Cr Aide; Chrch Yth Grp; Cmptr Clb; Drma Clb; Mth Clb/Tm; Prom Com; Quiz Bowl; SP/M/VS; Cl Off (T); Sch Ppr (E); Perfect 1600 on SAT; Secondary Education; Psychology; Mount Vernon Nazarene U; Eastern Nazarene College

MARRS, KRISTA R; RED HOUSE, WV; BUFFALO HS; (JR); Ctznshp Aw; Pres Ac Ftns Aw; WWAHSS; Comm Volntr; Hab For Humty Volntr; Spec Olymp Vol; Emplmnt; FCCLA; Prom Com; SADD; PP Ftbl (V); Sftball (J); Vice President of FCLLA; President of Prom Committee; Early Education; Social Work; West Virginia U; Marshall U

MARSH, JASON E; BUCKHANNON, WV; BUCKHANNON-UPSHUR HS; (SR); Hnr Roll; St of Mnth; Comm Volntr; Spec Olymp Vol; Chrch Yth Grp; DARE; DECA; FCA; Tchrs Aide; Ch Chr; Bskball (L); Ftball (L); Track (L); Wt Lftg (V); DECA / Teens for Life / Teen in FCA; WV Raze; Photography; Fairmont State U

MARSHALL, MATTHEW I; CHARLESTON, WV; NITRO HS; (SO); Hnr Roll; Sccr (V L); Marshall U

MARTIN, ASHLEY; BECKLEY, WV; INDEPENDENCE HS; (JR); Hnr Roll; Chrch Yth Grp; FCA; Chrldg; Dvng; Gmnstcs; Swmg; Track; Treasurer of the Young Republicans; Dental Assistant; Lawyer; Bluefield State College

MARTIN, DANIELLE; CHARLESTON, WV; RIVERSIDE HS; (JR); All Am Sch; Gov Hnr Prg; Hi Hnr Roll; USAA; Comm Volntr; Hosp Aide; FCA; Prom Com; Skiing; Vllyball (J); Crime Scene Investigator; Radiologist; Marshall U; U of Charleston

MARTIN, JUSTIN; OAK HILL, WV; OAK HILL HS; (FR); Hnr Roll; Kwnis Aw; Comm Volntr; Chrch Yth Grp; Drma Clb; Key Club; Mus Clb; Bnd; Chr; Jzz Bnd; Mch Bnd; Business Admin.; Music; West Virginia U; Duke U

MARTIN, LEIGHA M; BECKLEY, WV; WOODROW WILSON HS; (FR); Hnr Roll; St of Mnth; WWAHSS; Dnce; Her Majesty's Players (Renefair Club); Tiger T (School News Program); Forensics Degree; Chemistry Degree; Mountain State U; Marshall

MARTIN, MATTHEW; CRAB ORCHARD, WV; GREATER BECKLEY CHRN SCH; (SR); Hnr Roll; Chrch Yth Grp; Emplmnt; History/Archaeology; Short-Term Missionary; Concord College; Bryan College

MARTIN, SUSAN; FRENCH CREEK, WV; BUCKHANNON UPSHUR HS; (SO); Hnr Roll; Comm Volntr; Scouts; Skiing (J); Tennis (J); Vllyball (J)

MARTIN IV, ROBERT E.; PRINCETON, WV; PRINCETON SR HS; (SO); Ctznshp Aw; Hi Hnr Roll; Hnr Roll; Perf Att; Pres Ac Ftns Aw; Sci/Math Olympn; St of Mnth; WWAHSS; Chrch Yth Grp; DARE; Key Club; Mth Clb/Tm; Bnd; Jzz Bnd; Mch Bnd; Orch; Pharmacist; Engineering; WVU; Lee U

MASON, CRAIG T; BUCKHANNON, WV; BUCKHANNON-UPSHUR HS; (FR); Pres Ac Ftns Aw; St of Mnth; WWAHSS; Sccr (VJ); Engineering

MASON, DANIEL; BUCKHANNON, WV; BUCKHANNON-UPSHUR HS; (JR); Hi Hnr Roll; Hnr Roll; Pres Ac Ftns Aw; St of Mnth; Comm Volntr; Emplmnt; Scouts; Bskball (J); Sccr (VJ L); Stu Cncl (R); Sch Ppr (R); Engineering; Medical Field

MATTHEY, BRITTNEY; CLARKSBURG, WV; LIBERTY HS; (FR); F Lan Hn Soc; Hi Hnr Roll; Hnr Roll; Pres Ac Ftns Aw; Sci Fairs; Comm Volntr; Hab For Humty Volntr; Chrch Yth Grp; DARE; Drma Clb; Key Club; Quiz Bowl; Bnd; Ch Chr; Clr Grd; Dnce; Stu Cncl (R); CR (R); Civic Oration Speech Contest Winner; Participated in Youth in Government; Law; Journalism; West Virginia U; U of Pittsburgh

MAXEY, JOYCE; BRIDGEPORT, WV; BRIDGEPORT HS; (FR); F Lan Hn Soc; Hnr Roll; Pres Ac Ftns Aw; Comm Volntr; Hosp Aide; 4-H; Key Club; PP Ftbl; Anesthesiology; Columbia U; New York U

MAYNOR, CALLYN B; BECKLEY, WV; WOODROW WILSON HS; (SR); Hnr Roll; Nat Hon Sy; WWAHSS; Off Aide; SP/M/VS

MC BEE, AMY; BUCKHANNON, WV; BUCKHANNON-UPSHUR HS; (JR); Hnr Roll; WWAHSS; Lib Aide; West Virginia U

MC CABE, SUNNIE J; WHEELING, WV; WHEELING PARK HS; (JR); Hi Hnr Roll; Perf Att; Peer Tut/Med; Chrch Yth Grp; Drma Clb; Emplmnt; Key Club; Tchrs Aide; Accounting; Pre Law.

MC CALLISTER, BRADLEY; HUNTINGTON, WV; CABELL MIDLAND HS; (JR); Gov Hnr Prg; Hi Hnr Roll; Nat Hon Sy; Pres Ac Ftns Aw; WWAHSS; Comm Volntr; Spec Olymp Vol; Chrch Yth Grp; Emplmnt; FCA; Prom Com; Tchrs Aide; Cr Ctry (V L); Track (V L); Cl Off (T); Computer / Electronics Engineer; Christian Ministry; Virginia Tech; Marshall U

MC CALLISTER, KYLE; ONA, WV; CABELL MIDLAND HS; (SO); Hnr Roll; Perf Att; Comm Volntr; Hosp Aide; Peer Tut/Med; Chrch Yth Grp; Emplmnt; FCA; Cr Ctry (J L); Track (J L); Wt Lftg (J); Journalism; Communications; Morehead State U; West Virginia State U

MC CANN, JACKIE; BUCKHANNON, WV; BUCKHANNON-UPSHUR HS; (SO); Hnr Roll; Track (V); Poem Published in Gardens of Youth; 3rd Place in County Essay Contest; Criminologist; Davis and Elkins College; Marshall U

MC CARTNEY, ERIC S; BUCKHANNON, WV; BUCKHANNON-UPSHUR HS; (JR); Hi Hnr Roll; Hnr Roll; Business; Accounting; Marshall U; West Virginia U

MC CAULEY, RYAN; MEADOWBROOK, WV; LINCOLN HS; (JR); Hnr Roll; WWAHSS; Who's Who; Honor Roll; Electrician

MC CLAUGHERTY, BRYANA; PRINCETON, WV; PRINCETON SR HS; (JR); Hnr Roll; Nat Hon Sy; Comm Volntr; Chrch Yth Grp; FCA; Key Club; Pep Squd; Chr; Sccr (J); Youth Group President; Concord U; Marshall U

MC CLAUGHERTY, MORGAN P; PRINCETON, WV; PRINCETON SR HS; (SO); Hnr Roll; Perf Att; WWAHSS; Chrch Yth Grp; Emplmnt; Key Club; Gmnstcs (V); Nursing / RN; Physical Therapy; Bluefield State College

MC CLELLAND, JEREMY; WHEELING, WV; (JR); Hi Hnr Roll; MVP; Nat Hon Sy; WWAHSS; Drma Clb; Key Club; Lttrmn Clb; Off Aide; Quill & Scroll; Tchrs Aide; Vsity Clb; Bskball (J); Cr Ctry (J); Tennis (V CL); Vsy Clb (V L); Sch Ppr (E, R); Yrbk (E, R); All State Tennis Team; USTA National Ranking; Florida Gulf Coast U; Colleges W/Division I or II Men's Tennis

MC COMAS, COURTNEY; HUNTINGTON, WV; HUNTINGTON HS; (JR); Ctznshp Aw; St of Mnth; WWAHSS; Peer Tut/Med; Spec Olymp Vol; ArtClub; DARE; Latin Clb; Bskball (V C); Track (V L); Yrbk (P); Art Award-1st Place, Pumpkin Festival

MC CORMICK, CODY; ALUM CREEK, WV; DUVAL HS; (FR); Ctznshp Aw; Hi Hnr Roll; Hnr Roll; Perf Att; Pres Ac Ftns Aw; St of Mnth; WWAHSS; Dbte Team; FCA; Mth Clb/Tm; NtlFrnscLg; Spch Team; Bsball (V L); Bskball (V L)

MC COY, BECKY; RAYSAL, WV; IAEGER HS; (FR); Hi Hnr Roll; Hnr Roll; USAA; Peer Tut/Med; 4-H; DARE; SADD; Cosmetology; Social Work; Concord U; Mountain State U

MC COY, CHANCE P; WEBSTER SPRINGS, WV; WEBSTER CTY HS; (FR); Hi Hnr Roll; Otst Ac Ach Awd; Perf Att; Pres Ac Ftns Aw; Sci Fairs; St of Mnth; Valdctrian; Emplmnt; Mth Clb/Tm; Bsball (C); Bskball (JCL); Ftball (JCL); Stu Cncl (P); Sch Ppr (E, R); Scholar Athlete Award; Red Cross Lifeguard; CWVAC All Tournament Basketball Award. CWVAC All Conference Football Award; Civil Engineering; Education in Math/Science; Computer Software Engineering; West Virginia U Institute of Technology; Virginia Tech, West Virginia Wesleyan

MC COY, TERRI; PANTHER, WV; IAEGER HS; (FR); F Lan Hn Soc; Hnr Roll; MVP; DARE; Dnce; Drm Mjr; Bsball; Bskball (V); Vllyball; Sch Ppr (R); Yrbk (P)

MC DANIEL, KERRI; CHARLESTON, WV; GEORGE WASHINGTON HS; (SR); DAR; Hnr Roll; Sci Fairs; WWAHSS; Hsbk Rdg; Sch Ppr (R); 2 World Championship Horse Show Wins; Business; Psychology; West Virginia U

MC DONALD, DERIC T; VIENNA, WV; PARKERSBURG HS; (JR); Hi Hnr Roll; Hnr Roll; MVP; Pres Ac Ftns Aw; Sci Fairs; Comm Volntr; Peer Tut/Med; Chrch Yth Grp; Sccr (V L); Camp Counselor for Soccer; Took National Spanish Exam; Medical Degree; Master's Degree; Marshall U; Ohio State U

MC ELFRESH, TYLER W; BRIDGEPORT, WV; BRIDGEPORT HS; (FR); Hnr Roll; Bsball (J); Bskball; Ftball (J)

MC GLONE, CHRISTOPHER W; HUNTINGTON, WV; ST JOSEPH CTRL CATHOLIC HS; (FR); Nat Hon Sy; Sci Fairs; WWAHSS; Comm Volntr; Key Club; Bsball (VJ L); Bskball (J L); U of Florida; U of Louisville

MC GLONE, JOSHUA R; HUNTINGTON, WV; ST JOSEPH CTRL CATHOLIC SCH; Hnr Roll; Pres Sch; WWAHSS; Comm Volntr; Key Club; Bsball (VJCL); Bskball (VJ L); Optimist Club Essay Winner; Garrison Scholarship Winner; History; Political Sciences; Bellarmine U

MC GORTY, BRIANA; RIDGELEY, WV; FRANKFORT HS; (FR); Hi Hnr Roll; Hnr Roll; Otst Ac Ach Awd; Pres Ac Ftns Aw; Sci Fairs; Yth Ldrshp Prog; Comm Volntr; Peer Tut/Med; Svce Clb; Dnce; PP Ftbl (J); Vllyball (J); CR (R); S.M.I.L.E. Service Project Group; Forensic Science; Criminal Law; West Virginia U; Marshall U

MC GRAW, MEGAN E; CHARLESTON, WV; RIVERSIDE HS; (JR); Hnr Roll; Nat Hon Sy; Sci Fairs; Emplmnt; FCA; Tennis (V); Stu Cncl (R); Yrbk (R, P); Upward Bound - 2002 / 2003; Interior Design; Arts / Various Areas; U of Charleston; Marshall U

MC INTOSH, OLIVIA; WHEELING, WV; WHEELING PARK HS; (FR); Hi Hnr Roll; Hnr Roll; Sci Fairs; Hosp Aide; Key Club; Bnd; Mch Bnd; Outstanding Woodwind (8th); Music (Performing Arts); Teaching; Wheeling Jesuit U

MC MILLAN, ERIC; BECKLEY, WV; WOODROW WILSON HS; (SO); St of Mnth; WWAHSS; Ftball (J L); Wt Lftg (J); History Professor; Medicine; West Virginia U

MC QUILLIAN, KILEY N; SAINT MARYS, WV; ST MARYS HS; (SR); 4H Awd; Hnr Roll; 4-H; Emplmnt; Art Picture Won 1st in Fairmont (Middle School); United States Achievement Academy; Going to Get RN; West Virginia Northern Community College

MEADOWS, BRITTANY; CRAB ORCHARD, WV; INDEPENDENCE HS; (SO); Hi Hnr Roll; Comm Volntr; Chrch Yth Grp; Bskball; Sftball; Sports Medicine; Pharmacy; Virginia Tech; West Virginia

MEDINA, KAYLA A; ENTERPRISE, WV; LINCOLN HS; (SO); Gov Hnr Prg; Hi Hnr Roll; Jr Eng Tech; USAA; WWAHSS; Hosp Aide; HO'Br Yth Ldrshp; Key Club; Bnd; Jzz Bnd; Mch Bnd; SP/M/VS; Adv Cncl (R); National Spelling Bee-2 times; Aerospace Engineer; West Virginia U

MEEKER, CATEY; MOUNDSVILLE, WV; BISHOP DONAHUE HS; (FR); Hnr Roll; WWAHSS; Comm Volntr; Key Club; Chr; Ch Chr; SP/M/VS; Journalism; Wheeling Jesuit College

MELKUS, BRITTANY; HEDGESVILLE, WV; HEDGESVILLE HS; (SR); Hi Hnr Roll; Nat Hon Sy; Perf Att; St of Mnth; WWAHSS; Chrch Yth Grp; SADD; Tchrs Aide; Bnd; Mch Bnd; Pep Bnd; Sch Ppr (R, P); Business; Music; Shepherd U

METHENY, STEPHANIE L; TERRA ALTA, WV; PRESTON HS; (FR); Hi Hnr Roll; Hnr Roll; Otst Ac Ach Awd; Pres Ac Ftns Aw; Sci Fairs; St of Mnth; Hosp Aide; DARE; Mus Clb; Pep Squd; Chr; Chrldg (V); Gmnstcs (V); Stu Cncl (R); CR (R); Buckwheat Festival Junior Princess; Nursing; Fairmont State U; Potomac State College

METZ, JASMINE M; PETROLEUM, WV; RITCHIE CTY HS; (SO); All Am Sch; Hi Hnr Roll; Hnr Roll; St of Mnth; USAA; Chrch Yth Grp; Ch Chr; Helping Hands; Criminal Justice / Forensics; Archaeology; Yale U; West Virginia U

MILLER, BROOKE; SPENCER, WV; ROANE CTY HS; (FR); Hnr Roll; Perf Att; Sci Fairs; Hosp Aide; Chrch Yth Grp; Ntl FFA; Scouts; Ch Chr; Bskball (J); Track (V L); Stu Cncl (R); Medical Degree; West Virginia U; Marshall U

MILLER, CASSONDRA; BUCKHANNON, WV; BUCKHANNON-UPSHUR HS; (JR); Hnr Roll; WWAHSS; Ntl FFA; Most Outstanding Junior Counselor of WVSY-LA; Veterinarian; West Virginia U; Ohio State U

MILLER, CHELSEA L; HEDGESVILLE, WV; HEDGESVILLE HS; (JR); F Lan Hn Soc; Hnr Roll; Photog; National French Honors Society; Aviation (Pilot); Interior Design; Fairmont State U (Fairmont, WV); Shepherd College (Shepherdstown, WV)

MILLER, EMILY; ANAWALT, WV; MT VIEW HS; (SO); Hi Hnr Roll; Pres Ac Ftns Aw; WWAHSS; Comm Volntr; Peer Tut/Med; Ntl Beta Clb; Quiz Bowl; Spanish Clb; Yrbk (R); Lawyer; Architect; WV U; Concord College

Metheny, Stephanie L
Preston HS
Terra Alta, WV

Mc Coy, Terri
Iaeger HS
Panther, WV

Mc Cormick, Cody
Duval HS
Alum Creek, WV

Mc Comas, Courtney
Huntington HS
Huntington, WV

Martin, Ashley
Independence HS
Beckley, WV

Martin IV, Robert E.
Princeton SR HS
Princeton, WV

Mc Coy, Chance P
Webster Cty HS
Webster Springs, WV

Mc Donald, Deric T
Parkersburg HS
Vienna, WV

Miller, Brooke
Roane Cty HS
Spencer, WV

MILLER, JUSTIN; WEST LIBERTY, WV; WHEELING PARK HS; (JR); 4H Awd; Hnr Roll; Kwnis Aw; Perf Att; WWAHSS; 4-H; Emplmnt; Key Club; Tchrs Aide; Acpl Chr; Chr; Hsbk Rdg (V); 4-H Outstanding Boy; Ohio County Country Fair Board Member; Equestrian Teacher/Trainer; Business; Otterbein College; U of Findley

MILLER, KARRI B; PRINCETON, WV; PIKEVIEW HS; (SR); 4H Awd; DAR; Hnr Roll; Nat Hon Sy; Perf Att; Pres Ac Ftns Aw; Salutrn; St of Mnth; WWAHSS; Comm Volntr; 4-H; AL Aux Girls; Chess; Key Club; Mod UN; Prom Com; Bnd; Mch Bnd; Pep Bnd; Scr Kpr (J); Sftball (VJCL); Vllyball (VJCL); Wt Lftg (V L); Stu Cncl (R); Lit Mag (P); Yrbk (E); Concord College Book Award; John Philip Sousa Award; Math Education Grades 5-Adult; Pre-Law; Concord U

MILLER, SETH A; BUCKHANNON, WV; BUCKHANNON-UPSHUR HS; (JR); Hnr Roll; Pres Ac Ftns Aw; WWAHSS; DARE; Emplmnt; FCA; Scouts; Ftball (V CL); Track (V); Wt Lftg (V); Wrstlg (V L); 2X Conference Tackle in Football; Criminal Justice; Law; Notre Dame U; Stanford U

MILLER, SHAWNEE; HARPERS FERRY, WV; JEFFERSON HS; (SR); Ctznshp Aw; Hnr Roll; MVP; Otst Ac Ach Awd; Perf Att; Pres Ac Ftns Aw; St of Mnth; WWAHSS; Spec Olymp Vol; Emplmnt; Key Club; Lib Aide; ROTC; Tchrs Aide; Bskball (J); Track (J); All Tournament Team for Basketball; Top 25 Student in 8th Grade; Public Services; Corrections; Community Technical College of Shepherd; Shepherd U

MILLER, SHAYLA; RIPLEY, WV; RIPLEY HS; (SO); Hnr Roll; Nat Hon Sy; Pres Ac Ftns Aw; Comm Volntr; Hosp Aide; Spec Olymp Vol; Drma Clb; Emplmnt; Lttrmn Clb; Pep Squd; Quill & Scroll; Vsity Clb; SP/M/VS; Sccr (V L); Sch Ppr (E, R); Miss Teen West Central 2005; Young Democrats Club Member/Debater; Journalism; Public Relations; U of Charleston; Ohio U

MILLER, TIMIKA; WEIRTON, WV; WEIR HS; (JR); Hi Hnr Roll; Hnr Roll; Nat Hon Sy; Perf Att; USAA; WWAHSS; Key Club; Bnd; Mch Bnd; SP/M/VS; Stg Cre; National Honor Society; Music Education; Business Management; Davis and Elkins; West Liberty State College

MILLER II, BRADLEY; MAYSVILLE, WV; PETERSBURG HS; (JR); Hnr Roll; Chess; DARE; ROTC; Drl Tm; Honor Guard; Army

MILLS, KURT; BRIDGEPORT, WV; BRIDGEPORT HS; (FR); Hi Hnr Roll; Hnr Roll; WWAHSS; Vsity Clb; Bnd; Mch Bnd; Swmg (V); BHS Swimming Regional Team; Architecture; Optometry; Cornell U; Virginia Polytechnic Institute

MITCHELL, KRISTIN; CHARLESTON, WV; CAPITAL HS; (JR); Hnr Roll; MVP; St of Mnth; Comm Volntr; Peer Tut/Med; Biology Clb; Chrch Yth Grp; FCA; Key Club; Tchrs Aide; Vllyball (V L); Sch Ppr (R, P); Yrbk (E, P); Won Young Writers Award; State Volleyball Tournament Runner-Up 2004 AAA; Biology; Physical Therapy; Wingate U; West Virginia U

MOLLOHAN, CHELSEA; PARKERSBURG, WV; PARKERSBURG HS; (SR); Hnr Roll; Nat Hon Sy; WWAHSS; Emplmnt; Key Club; Sccr (V); Track (V); Psychology; Criminal Justice; Marshall U

MONGENI, SARA; MULLENS, WV; WYOMING CTY EAST HS; (FR); 4H Awd; Hi Hnr Roll; WWAHSS; Comm Volntr; 4-H; Chrch Yth Grp; Juilliard; Harvard Law School

MONGOLD, ASHLEE B; PETERSBURG, WV; PETERSBURG HS; (FR); Hnr Roll; Comm Volntr; Peer Tut/Med; Chrch Yth Grp; Emplmnt; FCA; Bnd; Ch Chr; Mch Bnd; Bskball (J); PP Ftbl (J); Tennis (V); 1st Place Cty Social Studies Fair; Secretary-Church Youth Group; Physical Therapy, Occupational Therapy; Respiratory Therapy

MONGOLD, MARISSA T; PETERSBURG, WV; PETERSBURG HS; Hnr Roll; Perf Att; Chrch Yth Grp; Spanish Clb; Ch Chr; Dnce; Dance & Gymnastics- 9 Yrs; Baton & Drill Team-Baton- 4 Yrs / Drill Team - 1 Yr; Veterinarian; Cosmetologist; West Virginia U; Indiana U Pennsylvania

MOORE, DESIREE'; VAN, WV; VAN JR SR HS; (SR); Ctznshp Aw; Hnr Roll; Sci Fairs; WWAHSS; Red Cr Aide; Drma Clb; Prom Com; Tchrs Aide; Bnd; Mch Bnd; Sftball (VJ); Cl Off (V); Biology; Forensic Science; Auburn U; Marshall U

MOORE, JOSHUA T; WAYNE, WV; WAYNE HS; (SO); Ctznshp Aw; Hnr Roll; Pres Ac Ftns Aw; Spec Olymp Vol; 4-H; Chrch Yth Grp; SADD; Ch Chr; Ftball (V); Track (V); Wt Lftg (V); Electronics; Graphic Arts; Marshall U

MOORE, LYNN; HEDGESVILLE, WV; HEDGESVILLE HS; (SO); Hnr Roll; Sci Fairs; Pep Squd; Chrldg (V); Sftball (J); Academic Challenge; Education; Engineering; WVU

MORAN, ANGELA; COLLIERS, WV; BROOKE HS; (JR); Hi Hnr Roll; Hnr Roll; Otst Ac Ach Awd; WWAHSS; DECA; Emplmnt; FBLA; Key Club; Lib Aide; Outstanding Accounting Student; Record for Faithful Attendance - School; Business Administration in Finance; Franciscan U

MORAN, TRACEY D; PARKERSBURG, WV; PARKERSBURG HS; (SO); Ctznshp Aw; Hnr Roll; Kwnis Aw; Nat Hon Sy; Sci Fairs; Comm Volntr; Hosp Aide; Peer Tut/Med; Chrch Yth Grp; Key Club; Acpl Chr; Track (V); Stu Cncl (R); CR (R); Raze; American Cancer Society Teen Board; Physical Therapy; Occupational Therapy; West Virginia U; Marshall U

MORGAN, BRITTANY; TUNNELTON, WV; SOUTH PRESTON MS; MS; 4H Awd; Comm Volntr; Peer Tut/Med; 4-H; DARE; Pep Squd; Quiz Bowl; Bnd; Mch Bnd; Pep Bnd; Bskball (V); Hsbk Rdg; Attended Youth and Government Seminars; Attended County Math Field Day; Veterinary Medicine; Animal Sciences; West Virginia U; Ohio State U

MORRIS, TIFFANI; CHARLESTON, WV; NITRO HS; (JR); Hnr Roll; Comm Volntr; Emplmnt; Chr; 50 Hours Community Service; Many Awards in Chorus; Nursing; Photography; Mount Olive-North Carolina; Marshal U

MORTON, JAMIE; MOOREFIELD, WV; (FR); Hnr Roll; Perf Att; Sci Fairs; Chrch Yth Grp; Scouts; Massage Therapist

MOSSOR, AMANDA; PENNSBORO, WV; RITCHIE CTY HS; (SO); Hi Hnr Roll; Hnr Roll; Pres Ac Ftns Aw; St of Mnth; Comm Volntr; 4-H; Chess; Chrch Yth Grp; Quiz Bowl; Vsity Clb; Bskball (VJ); Cr Ctry (J); Accounting / Finance Management; Central Pennsylvania College; Oral Roberts U

MOTES, KIRSTIE L; CHARLES TOWN, WV; JEFFERSON HS; (JR); Hnr Roll; Perf Att; Advertising; Business; U of North Carolina At Charlotte; Appalachian State U

MOULD, RYAN A; BLUEFIELD, WV; PRINCETON SR HS; (JR); DAR; Hnr Roll; Nat Hon Sy; WWAHSS; Chrch Yth Grp; Key Club; Mod UN; Pep Squd; Prom Com; Bnd; Ch Chr; Drm Mjr; Jzz Bnd; Stu Cncl (R); CR (R); Key Club District Treasurer; Key Club Local Secretary; Music; Business Education; West Virginia U; Concord U

MULLINS, ELIZABETH; NAUGATUCK, WV; TUG VALLEY HS; (SO); Hi Hnr Roll; Hnr Roll; Perf Att; Comm Volntr; Key Club; Ntl Beta Clb; West Virginia U; U of Kentucky

MULLINS, MIRANDA L; HUNTINGTON, WV; HUNTINGTON HS; (JR); F Lan Hn Soc; Hi Hnr Roll; Nat Hon Sy; WWAHSS; Spec Olymp Vol; Key Club; Tchrs Aide; Spanish Clb; Advertising; Journalism; Coastal Carolina; Marshall U

MUNCY, ANNA N; SQUIRE, WV; BIG CREEK HS; (FR); Hi Hnr Roll; Hnr Roll; Sci Fairs; WWAHSS; Comm Volntr; Chrch Yth Grp; FCCLA; Key Club; Bnd; Chr; Dnce; Drm Mjr; Tennis (V); Received 2nd Runner-Up - School Beauty Pageant; Pharmacy; Medicine; West Virginia U; Bluefield State College

MUNCY, DANIEL C; WARRIORMINE, WV; BIG CREEK HS; (FR); Hi Hnr Roll; Kwnis Aw; St of Mnth; Comm Volntr; Peer Tut/Med; Spec Olymp Vol; Key Club; Mus Clb; Bnd; Chr; Drm Mjr; Mch Bnd; Bdmtn (V); CR (P); Sch Ppr (R); Band Awards; Solo Pindent; Medical Doctor; Surgery Doctor; Virginia Tech; Marshall U

MUNDELL, MATTHEW R; HUNTINGTON, WV; ST. JOSEPH CTRL CATHOLIC HS; (FR); Hi Hnr Roll; Nat Hon Sy; Otst Ac Ach Awd; Perf Att; Sci Fairs; Sci/Math Olympn; St of Mnth; WWAHSS; Hosp Aide; Peer Tut/Med; Drma Clb; Key Club; Mth Clb/Tm; Mus Clb; Quiz Bowl; Svce Clb; Latin Clb

MURPHY, BRANDI; KEYSER, WV; KEYSER HS; (FR); Hnr Roll; MVP; Nat Stu Ath Day Aw; Otst Ac Ach Awd; Sci Fairs; Comm Volntr; Spec Olymp Vol; Chrch Yth Grp; DARE; Drma Clb; Key Club; Scouts; SADD; Dnce; Gmnstcs (J); Dance Class (Out of School) for Almost 14 Years; Dancer; Dance Choreographer; Break the Floor; Florida State

MURPHY, BRIANNA; BRIDGEPORT, WV; BRIDGEPORT HS; (FR); Hnr Roll; Perf Att; Pres Ac Ftns Aw; St of Mnth; WWAHSS; Chrch Yth Grp; DARE; Scouts; Chr; Psychology; Pediatrician; Marshall U; West Virginia U

MURRAY, ALLISON; OAK HILL, WV; OAK HILL HS; (FR); Hi Hnr Roll; Hnr Roll; WWAHSS; Yth Ldrshp Prog; Comm Volntr; Peer Tut/Med; Chrch Yth Grp; FCA; Dnce; Drama Team At Church; Biology; Archaeology

MURRAY, SAMUEL C; BRIDGEPORT, WV; BRIDGEPORT HS; (JR); Hi Hnr Roll; Hnr Roll; St of Mnth; Comm Volntr; Chrch Yth Grp; Civil Air Pat; Emplmnt; Key Club; Scouts; Student of the Month; Bridgeport Co. 2 Firefighter; Firefighting; EMT; West Virginia U; Fairmont State U

MYERS, KAYLA; PADEN CITY, WV; PADEN CITY HS; (SR); Hnr Roll; Nat Hon Sy; WWAHSS; Comm Volntr; ArtClub; Prom Com; Quiz Bowl; Cl Off (S); Yrbk (E, R, P); Vet. Tech; Fairmont State U

MYERS, STACI; TERRA ALTA, WV; PRESTON HS; (FR); Hi Hnr Roll; Perf Att; Pres Ac Ftns Aw; Sci Fairs; Comm Volntr; Spanish Clb; Bnd; 4th Place in Young Writers; Physician; Ob /Gyn; West Virginia U; Alderson-Broadus College

NASH, MARGARET L; BLUEFIELD, WV; PRINCETON SR HS; (JR); Hnr Roll; Nat Hon Sy; WWAHSS; Comm Volntr; Chrch Yth Grp; Drma Clb; Key Club; Pep Squd; SP/M/VS; VP - Key Club; Business / Accounting; Business / Marketing; Mount Olive; U of North Carolina Charlotte

NAUGHTON, BRANDON; KEYSER, WV; KEYSER HS; (JR); Hnr Roll; Pres Ac Ftns Aw; Sci Fairs; Chrch Yth Grp; Drma Clb; Emplmnt; SP/M/VS; Stg Cre; Ftball (VJ); Physical Therapy; Potomac State College; West Virginia U

NEAL, LAUREN N; HUNTINGTON, WV; HUNTINGTON HS; (SR); F Lan Hn Soc; Hnr Roll; Nat Hon Sy; Comm Volntr; ArtClub; Emplmnt; FBLA; Key Club; Photog; Prom Com; Svce Clb; Tchrs Aide; Chr; Stg Cre; Sccr (J); Sftball (J); Swmg; Wt Lftg; CR (R); Key Club Secretary; Art Honorary; Public Relations; Education; Shepherd U

NELSON, ASHLEY; TRIADELPHIA, WV; WHEELING PARK HS; (JR); Hi Hnr Roll; Hnr Roll; Sci Fairs; St of Mnth; WWAHSS; Comm Volntr; 4-H; Chess; Chrch Yth Grp; Off Aide; Dnce; Biology; Chemistry

NIDA, KRISTA; PHILIPPI, WV; PHILIP BARBOUR HS COMPLEX; (JR); Hi Hnr Roll; Nat Hon Sy; WWAHSS; Key Club; Tennis (V L); Vllyball (V L); Stu Cncl (S); Key Club Treasurer; 1st Team Big Ten (Volleyball); Accounting; Elementary Education; WV Wesleyan College; West Virginia U

NILAND, SHAY; BUNKER HILL, WV; MUSSELMAN HS; (JR); Hi Hnr Roll; Hnr Roll; Otst Ac Ach Awd; Sci Fairs; St of Mnth; 4-H; ArtClub; Chrch Yth Grp; Prom Com; Sci Clb; Scouts; Spanish Clb; Dnce; Scr Kpr (V); Sccr (J); Cl Off (T); 2nd Place - Character Counts - Berkeley County; Political Science / History; Law School; Shepherd U; NYU

NOTTINGHAM, STACI; BARBOURSVILLE, WV; CABELL MIDLAND HS; (SR); Hnr Roll; Nat Hon Sy; WWAHSS; Comm Volntr; Peer Tut/Med; Chrch Yth Grp; FCA; Ch Chr; Lit Mag (R); Sch Ppr (R); National Honors Society; French Honorary; Journalism; Marshall U

O'DELL, ALISHA J; FARMINGTON, WV; NORTH MARION HS; (FR); Hnr Roll; Otst Ac Ach Awd; St of Mnth; Comm Volntr; Sch Ppr (E, R); I Was in the Bible Club.; Human Services; Cosmetology; Fairmont State U; Clarksburg Beauty Academy

OOTEN, SARAH C M; LENORE, WV; TUG VALLEY HS; (JR); 4H Awd; Hnr Roll; WWAHSS; 4-H; Chrch Yth Grp; Ntl Beta Clb; SP/M/VS; Bskball (V); Sftball (C); Vllyball (J); Athletic Trainer/Sports Medicine; Marshall U

OSBORNE, ELIZABETH A; LUMBERPORT, WV; LINCOLN HS; (SO); Jr Eng Tech; Perf Att; WWAHSS; Comm Volntr; 4-H; Chrch Yth Grp; FCCLA; Pep Squd; Bnd; Mch Bnd; Pep Bnd; Cr Ctry (L); Track (L); Cl Off (S); Stu Cncl (R); Dentistry; West Virginia U

OURS, BRITTANY; SHINNSTON, WV; BRIDGEPORT HS; (FR); Hnr Roll; Nat Hon Sy; WWAHSS; Comm Volntr; DARE; Dnce; Vllyball (J); Lit Mag (R); Chemistry Degree; Mathematics Degree; West Virginia U; Louisiana State U

OURS, KEVIN M; BUCKHANNON, WV; BUCKHANNON UPSHUR HS; (FR); Hi Hnr Roll; Hnr Roll; Perf Att; St of Mnth; WWAHSS; Spec Olymp Vol; Chess; Chrch Yth Grp; DARE; Jr Ach; Lib Aide; Spch Team; Tchrs Aide; Wdwrkg Clb; Chr; Bsball (V); Bskball (V); Ftball (V)

OWENS, ALLISON; FOLLANSBEE, WV; BROOKE HS; (FR); Hi Hnr Roll; Otst Ac Ach Awd; Chrch Yth Grp; DECA; Key Club; Lttrmn Clb; Mth Clb/Tm; SADD; Spanish Clb; Chr; Bskball (J); Track (V L); Vllyball (J); Stu Cncl (R); Business; Health Professions; Graceland U; West Virginia U

PARK, AARON M; ROMNEY, WV; HAMPSHIRE HS; (FR); Hnr Roll; Comm Volntr; Chess; Chess Club; Information Technology Support Systems; Visual Design; ITT Technical Institute

PARK, MOLLY; FORT ASHBY, WV; MINERAL CTY VOTECH CTR HS; (SO); Hi Hnr Roll; Hnr Roll; Sci Fairs; DARE; DECA; Vllyball (V); Business

PARNICZA, ELIZABETH; WEIRTON, WV; WEIR HS; (SO); Gov Hnr Prg; Hi Hnr Roll; Perf Att; Sci/Math Olympn; WWAHSS; Peer Tut/Med; Dbte Team; HO'Br Yth Ldrshp; Key Club; Off Aide

PARSONS, JON; WORTHINGTON, WV; LINCOLN HS; (JR); Hnr Roll; WWAHSS; Key Club; Photog; French Clb; Bskball (V); Stu Cncl (R); Fairmont State U; West Virginia U

PATE, CAITIE; OAK HILL, WV; FAYETTEVILLE HS; (MS); Hi Hnr Roll; Nat Hon Sy; Otst Ac Ach Awd; Sci Fairs; St of Mnth; Peer Tut/Med; Off Aide; Tchrs Aide; Chr; Delegate to Youth and Government Seminars; Plays Electric Guitar; Education (9-12 English); Lawyer; Concord U; Shepherd U

PATTERSON, BIONKA; CHARLESTON, WV; CAPITAL HS; (FR); Ctznshp Aw; Hnr Roll; Otst Ac Ach Awd; St of Mnth; Spec Olymp Vol; Key Club; Dnce; Accelerated Reader Award; Student of the Year; Biology; Pre-Med; Spelman College; West Virginia U

PAYNE, ADAM J; CHARLESTON, WV; NITRO HS; (SO); Hi Hnr Roll; Nat Hon Sy; Spec Olymp Vol; Emplmnt; FCA; ROTC; Ftball (VJ); Track (VJ); Wt Lftg (VJ); Engineering

PEAL, JOSHUA; CHARLESTON, WV; RIVERSIDE HS; (SR); SP/M/VS; Sccr (V); Computer Programming; WV U of Technology

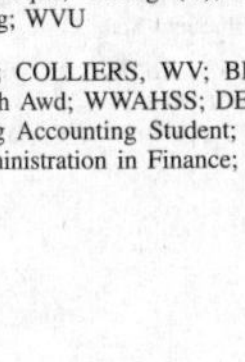
O'Dell, Alisha J
North Marion HS
Farmington, WV

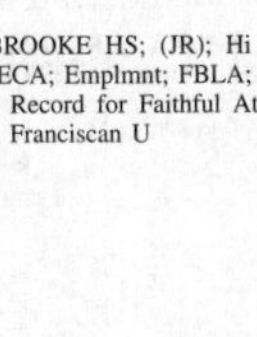
Morgan, Brittany
South Preston MS
Tunnelton, WV

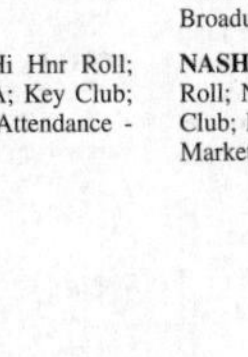
Mongold, Marissa T
Petersburg HS
Petersburg, WV

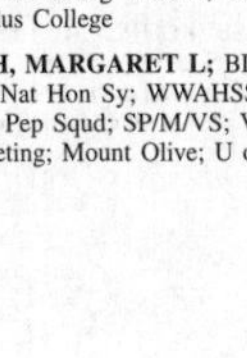
Mongeni, Sara
Wyoming Cty East HS
Mullens, WV

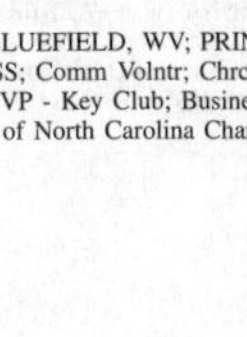
Miller, Shawnee
Jefferson HS
Harpers Ferry, WV

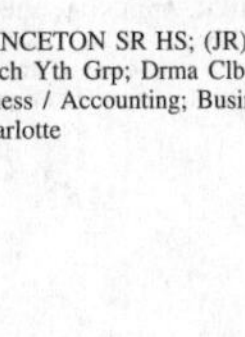
Miller, Shayla
Ripley HS
Ripley, WV

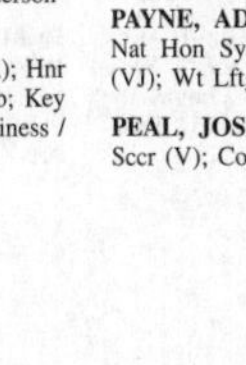
Moore, Desiree'
Van JR SR HS
Van, WV

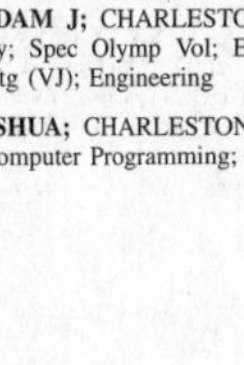
Neal, Lauren N
Huntington HS
Huntington, WV

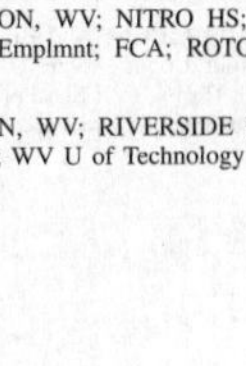
Payne, Adam J
Nitro HS
Charleston, WV

PELFREY, HANNAH E; KENOVA, WV; SPRING VALLEY HS; (SR); Ctznshp Aw; DAR; Hi Hnr Roll; Hnr Roll; Nat Hon Sy; Yth Ldrshp Prog; Comm Volntr; Hab For Humty Volntr; Hosp Aide; Chrch Yth Grp; Emplmnt; Key Club; Mus Clb; Off Aide; Prom Com; Tchrs Aide; Bnd; Chr; Clr Grd; Drm Mjr; PP Ftbl; Yrbk (R, P); Booth Scholars Program; Senior Salute Winner; Biology; Marshall U

PELIKAN, LANEY; SHINNSTON, WV; LINCOLN HS; (SR); Hi Hnr Roll; Hnr Roll; Kwnis Aw; St of Mnth; WWAHSS; Comm Volntr; Peer Tut/Med; Chrch Yth Grp; DARE; Drma Clb; FCCLA; Key Club; Lib Aide; Off Aide; SADD; Bnd; Chr; Ch Chr; Dnce; Top Scholar (English 9 and 11); Academic Achievement Award

PENTASUGLIA, ERICA J; PRINCETON, WV; PRINCETON SR HS; (FR); WWAHSS; Hosp Aide; Key Club; Finance; Accounting; Concord U; West Virginia U

PERINE, DANIELLE K; WELLSBURG, WV; BROOKE HS; (JR); Hi Hnr Roll; Hnr Roll; Nat Hon Sy; Perf Att; WWAHSS; Spec Olymp Vol; Chrch Yth Grp; Key Club; SADD; Acpl Chr; Bnd; Chr; Ch Chr; Interact Club - Associated with Rotary; HOSA; Registered Nurse; West Liberty State College

PERRI, VINCENT; NEW CUMBERLAND, WV; WEIR HS; (SO); Hi Hnr Roll; Pres Ac Ftns Aw; USAA; WWAHSS; Comm Volntr; Drma Clb; Emplmnt; Ftball (L); Wt Lftg (L); Stu Cncl (R); 2003-2004 English Merit Award; Hi-Y treasurer; Business Law Degree; PhD in Psychology; Harvard U; West Virginia U

PERRY, AARON; LENORE, WV; TUG VALLEY HS; (FR); Hi Hnr Roll; Hnr Roll; Ntl Beta Clb; Bskball (V); Ftball (V); Cl Off (P); Marshall U

PERRY, BRITTANY; DOROTHY, WV; LIBERTY HS; (FR); Hi Hnr Roll; Hnr Roll; Salutrn; St of Mnth; Law; Travel; Duke U; Virginia Tech

PETERS JR, EDWARD P; MOUNDSVILLE, WV; JOHN MARSHALL HS; (FR); Hi Hnr Roll; Hnr Roll; Perf Att; Sci Fairs; Comm Volntr; Peer Tut/Med; Chrch Yth Grp; Cmptr Clb; Dbte Team; P to P St Amb Prg; Spanish Clb; Golf (J); Scr Kpr (J); Salvation Army Volunteer; WV Nazarene Children Help Volunteer; Computer Science; Engineering; Carnegie Mellon U; Johns Hopkins U

PFEIFFER, SPENCER; DANIELS, WV; WOODROW WILSON HS; (SO); Hnr Roll; Otst Ac Ach Awd; Perf Att; Pres Ac Ftns Aw; Sci Fairs; Comm Volntr; Peer Tut/Med; Chrch Yth Grp; Key Club; Lib Aide; Spanish Clb; Sccr (J); Swmg (V L); Tennis (V); A Honor Roll; J3 Eastern Junior Olympics (Skiing); U of British Columbia; Colorado College

PHILLIPS, CATHERINE; SPRINGFIELD, WV; HAMPSHIRE HS; (JR); Hnr Roll; Sci Fairs; Comm Volntr; Spec Olymp Vol; DECA; Tchrs Aide; Vllyball (J); 1st Place State Competition-DECA; Chapter President-2005-2005-DECA; Nursing; Mortuary; Shepherd U; Marshall U

PHILLIPS, SAMANTHA B; CLARKSBURG, WV; LINCOLN HS; (SO); Hi Hnr Roll; Nat Hon Sy; Otst Ac Ach Awd; Pres Ac Ftns Aw; Pres Sch; Comm Volntr; Chrch Yth Grp; Bnd; Chr; Dnce; Mch Bnd; Stu Cncl (R); CR (R); WV Chanticleer Chamber Choir; Lincoln H.S. Gospel Choir; Public Relations; Business; David Lipscomb U, Nashville TN; Ohio Valley U, Vienna, WV

PHILLIPS, SANDRA N; CHARMCO, WV; GREENBRIER WEST HS; (JR); Hnr Roll; Perf Att; Pres Ac Ftns Aw; St of Mnth; Tennis (V); Spokesmodel; Veterinarian; Nurse; Davidson College; Greensboro College

PHILLIPS, VICTORIA L; INWOOD, WV; MUSSELMAN HS; (SO); Hi Hnr Roll; Pres Ac Ftns Aw; Sci Fairs; WWAHSS; Peer Tut/Med; Emplmnt; FCA; Sci Clb; Chr; Sccr (V L); Sftball (VJ); Cl Off (P); Stu Cncl (R); Math Field Day Winner; State Social Studies Fair Winner; Engineering; Finance; Virginia Tech

PIRLO, KARA; MORGANTOWN, WV; UNIVERSITY HS; (JR); 4H Awd; Hi Hnr Roll; Jr Mshl; Nat Hon Sy; WWAHSS; Comm Volntr; 4-H; Chrch Yth Grp; Key Club; MuAlphaTh; SADD; Tchrs Aide; Spanish Clb; Chrldg (JCL); Cl Off (T); Stu Cncl (R); Elementary Education; West Virginia U

PISKE, ALYS C; FRENCH CREEK, WV; BUCKHANNON-UPSHUR HS; (SR); Hnr Roll; WWAHSS; Tchrs Aide; Wrstlg (V L); Juniorettes Club; Pharmacy; West Virginia Wesleyan College

PLANTS, SAMANTHA; GALLIPOLIS FERRY, WV; HANNAN HS; (SR); Hi Hnr Roll; Nat Hon Sy; Perf Att; St of Mnth; WWAHSS; Comm Volntr; Peer Tut/Med; Chess; Chrch Yth Grp; Drma Clb; FCA; Lib Aide; Prom Com; Chr; Ch Chr; SP/M/VS; Vllyball (V); RAZE Crew Member; Math Education; Theatre Education; Berea College; Alice-Lloyd College

PLEASANT, JACQUELINE A; LESLIE, WV; WESTERN GREENBRIER HS; (FR); Hnr Roll; Perf Att; Comm Volntr; Cmptr Clb; FCA; Mus Clb; Bnd; Drm Mjr; Flg Crps; Mch Bnd; West Virginia Golden Horseshoe Participant; The Greenbrier Award Exemplary Performances; Health Care; West Virginia U

PLYMALE, MARY; ERBACON, WV; BRAXTON CTY HS; (SO); 4H Awd; Hi Hnr Roll; Hnr Roll; Comm Volntr; 4-H; DECA; Quill & Scroll; Spch Team; Bnd; Mch Bnd; Chrldg (V); Sch Ppr (R); Yrbk (R); Youth Community Theatre; Mass Communications; Broadcast Journalism; West Virginia U; Point Park U

POTTER, AMANDA; DAVY, WV; MOUNT VIEW HS; (SO); All Am Sch; F Lan Hn Soc; Hi Hnr Roll; Nat Hon Sy; Otst Ac Ach Awd; Perf Att; Pres Sch; Sci Fairs; St of Mnth; WWAHSS; 4-H; ArtClub; Cmptr Clb; Fr of Library; FTA; Ntl Beta Clb; Quiz Bowl; French Clb; Chr; Chrldg (V); CR; Yrbk (R); Young Writers Winner 2005; Teaching; Writing; Marshall U; Bluefield State

POTTS, KELLI; BLUEFIELD, WV; BLUEFIELD HS; (FR); Hnr Roll; Otst Ac Ach Awd; Perf Att; Chrch Yth Grp; DARE; Bnd; Chr; Ch Chr; Swg Chr; Bdmtn (J); Gmnstcs (J); Hsbk Rdg (J); Vllyball (J); CR (P); Editor's Choice Award - Poem; Medical / Surgeon; Performing Arts-Singer / Actor; Wake Forest U; Bluefield State College

POWERS, DATHA; BUCKHANNON, WV; BUCKHANNON-UPSHUR HS; (SO); Hnr Roll; WWAHSS; Chrch Yth Grp; Orch; Vllyball (J); Health Information Services; Education; Fairmont State U

PREECE, CASSIDY; HURRICANE, WV; HURRICANE HS; (SO); Hnr Roll; WWAHSS; Comm Volntr; Hab For Humty Volntr; Peer Tut/Med; Chrch Yth Grp; Emplmnt; Key Club; P to P St Amb Prg; Prom Com; Scouts; Ch Chr; Hospitality Management; International College of Hospitality City Management; Davis and Elkins

PRIDEMORE, DONNETTE; FAYETTEVILLE, WV; FAYETTEVILLE HS; (FR); Hnr Roll; Pres Ac Ftns Aw; St of Mnth; Chrch Yth Grp; FCA; ROTC; Scouts; Clr Grd; Drl Tm; Bskball (V); (MD) Pediatrician Endocrinologist; U of Kentucky; West Virginia U

PRINTZ, AMBER; KEARNEYSVILLE, WV; JEFFERSON HS; (FR); Hnr Roll; Perf Att; Comm Volntr; Chrch Yth Grp; Emplmnt; Key Club; Ntl FFA; United Day of Caring; Relay for Life-Lots of Community Service; Hydrologist (Water Resources); Environmental Sciences; West Virginia U

PROCTOR, CHRIS; CHARLESTON, WV; HERBERT HOOVER HS; (FR); Ctznshp Aw; Hnr Roll; St of Mnth; Comm Volntr; Spec Olymp Vol; Chrch Yth Grp; FCA; Mus Clb; Bnd; Ch Chr; Mch Bnd; Pep Bnd; Wildlife Management; Water Management / Oceanography; West Virginia U

QUINN, DAMON; CLEVELAND, WV; WEBSTER CTRY HS; (JR); Hi Hnr Roll; Hnr Roll; Nat Hon Sy; Otst Ac Ach Awd; Perf Att; Pres Sch; Sci Fairs; WWAHSS; Comm Volntr; Chrch Yth Grp; DARE; FCA; Prom Com; Bnd; Ch Chr; Mch Bnd; Pep Bnd; Scr Kpr (C); Yrbk (P); National Honor Society; PhD; Registered Nurse; West Virginia U; Marshall U

RACER, BRITTANY; NITRO, WV; NITRO HS; (SO); Hnr Roll; Nat Hon Sy; FCA; Key Club; MuAlphaTh; Bnd; Clr Grd; Flg Crps; Mch Bnd; Psychology; Pharmacy; Marshall U; West Virginia U

RAKES, JOHN M; BECKLEY, WV; WOODROW WILSON HS; (SO); Hnr Roll; Yth Ldrshp Prog; Hab For Humty Volntr; Chrch Yth Grp; DARE; Emplmnt; Ftball (J); Wrstlg (J); Physician

RAMBO, MEGAN; IKES FORK, WV; (FR); 4H Awd; Hi Hnr Roll; Hnr Roll; Otst Ac Ach Awd; Sci Fairs; St of Mnth; Yth Ldrshp Prog; Peer Tut/Med; 4-H; Chrch Yth Grp; Dnce; Vllyball (V); Psychology; Nursing; Concord U; Bluefield State

RAMSBY, RYAN; MILTON, WV; CABELL MIDLAND HS; (FR); Hnr Roll; Nat Hon Sy; Comm Volntr; Chrch Yth Grp; Ftball; Track; Own a Small Outdoor Business; Virginia Technical; U of Virginia

RAMSEY, JILLIAN M; OAK HILL, WV; OAK HILL HS; (FR); Hi Hnr Roll; Nat Hon Sy; St of Mnth; WWAHSS; Yth Ldrshp Prog; Comm Volntr; Peer Tut/Med; Chrch Yth Grp; DARE; FCA; Off Aide; Pep Squd; Tchrs Aide; Dnce; Adv Cncl (R); Stu Cncl (P); CR (P); Medical Doctor; West Virginia U (Morgantown WV)

RANDALL, ERIC R; BECKLEY, WV; WOODROW WILSON HS; (SO); Hnr Roll; Pres Ac Ftns Aw; St of Mnth; Yth Ldrshp Prog; Chrch Yth Grp; DARE; FCA; Bskball (J); Ftball (J); Sccr (V); Track (V); Received a Math Award in Jr. HS; Business Major; Marshall U; West Virginia U

RASICCI, DAVID; WEIRTON, WV; WEIR HS; (SO); Hi Hnr Roll; WWAHSS; Comm Volntr; Drma Clb; Sci Clb; Ftball (L); Wt Lftg (V); HI-Y club; Chem. Club; Medicine; Mathematics; U of Southern California; West Virginia U

RATLIFF, RACHEL L; MOOREFIELD, WV; MOOREFIELD HS; (SR); Hnr Roll; Sci Fairs; WWAHSS; Peer Tut/Med; DARE; Emplmnt; Ntl FFA; Prom Com; Dnce; Sch Ppr (R); Yrbk (P); Business

REED, JIMMY L; AVONDALE, WV; IAEGER HS; (FR); Ctznshp Aw; Hi Hnr Roll; Hnr Roll; Nat Hon Sy; Perf Att; St of Mnth; Chess; DARE; Chr; Yrbk; Science; Astronomy; West Virginia U; Virginia Tech

REED, SABRINA; JOLO, WV; IAEGER HS; (FR); Hi Hnr Roll; Perf Att; Peer Tut/Med; Chrch Yth Grp; Chr; Psychologist; Teacher; Concord U; Bluefield State College

REEDER, AMANDA; VIENNA, WV; PARKERSBURG HS; (JR); Hnr Roll; WWAHSS; ArtClub; Acpl Chr; The National Society of High School Scholars; Astronomy Club; Peta; Design (Industrial or Interior); Arts (Media, Fine, or Theater); Davis and Elkins College; North Carolina School of the Arts

REESE, NATHAN P; BRUCETON MLS, WV; PRESTON HS; (JR); Hi Hnr Roll; Hnr Roll; Nat Hon Sy; Perf Att; WWAHSS; Chrch Yth Grp; Emplmnt; FCA; Chr; Ch Chr; Religion; Christian Education; Mount Vernon Nazarene U

RICE, LEE E; HUNTINGTON, WV; SPRING VALLEY HS; (FR); Hi Hnr Roll; Hnr Roll; Yth Ldrshp Prog; Comm Volntr; Chrch Yth Grp; Key Club; Bnd; Dnce; Mch Bnd; Tennis (V); Stu Cncl (S); CR (S); Youth Leadership Corp; English Major; Law Degree; Wake Forest; Wheaton College (IL)

RIFFLE, MELISSA D; CLARKSBURG, WV; LIBERTY HS; (JR); Ctznshp Aw; Hnr Roll; Sci Fairs; Key Club; Clb; Bnd; Mch Bnd; Social Studies Fair; Associate/Interior Decorating; Bachelors/Fashion Design, Etc. Arts.; Fairmont State; West Virginia U

RIMMEY, BRITTANY; NEW HAVEN, WV; WAHAMA HS; (JR); All Am Sch; Hnr Roll; Nat Hon Sy; Otst Ac Ach Awd; Pres Ac Ftns Aw; USAA; WWAHSS; Red Cr Aide; FBLA; Sftball (J L); Cl Off (T); Law; Psychology; West Virginia U; Marshall U

RINE, JULIA; WEIRTON, WV; WEST HS; (SO); Hnr Roll; Sci Fairs; WWAHSS; Yth Ldrshp Prog; Comm Volntr; Hosp Aide; Chrch Yth Grp; Dbte Team; Drma Clb; Key Club; Spanish Clb; SP/M/VS; Stg Cre; Sccr (J); Track (L); Science; Medical; West Virginia U

RINER, SAMANTHA; HEDGESVILLE, WV; HEDGESVILLE HS; (FR); Hnr Roll; Crime Scene Investigator; SWAT Cop

RITTER, STACIE; WHITMAN, WV; LOGAN SR HS; (SO); All Am Sch; Hnr Roll; WWAHSS; Chrch Yth Grp; Mus Clb; Chr; Ch Chr; SP/M/VS; Stu Cncl (R); Nursing; Physical Therapy; Southern West Virginia Community and Technical College; West Virginia U

ROBERSON, CHANDRA; GILBERT, WV; GILBERT HS; (SO); All Am Sch; Hnr Roll; Perf Att; Art Reward; Pediatrician; X-Ray Technician; Southern Community and Technical College

ROBERTS, AARON; IAEGER, WV; IAEGER HS; (SR); Hi Hnr Roll; Hnr Roll; Nat Hon Sy; SP/M/VS; Ftball (V); Wt Lftg (V); Pharmacy; U of Charleston

ROBERTS, EMILY; HENDRICKS, WV; TUCKER CTY HS; (SO); Hi Hnr Roll; Otst Ac Ach Awd; Perf Att; Sci Fairs; Chrch Yth Grp; Drma Clb; Emplmnt; Photog; SADD; SP/M/VS; Stg Cre; Bskball (VJ); Cl Off (P); Degree in Culinary Arts; Nutritionist Degree; Mountain State U; Pennsylvania Culinary Institute

ROBERTS, JAMES D; CHARLESTON, WV; RIVERSIDE HS; (JR); Hnr Roll; WWAHSS; Chrch Yth Grp; Emplmnt; FCA; Track; Wt Lftg; Pre-Law; Concord U; U of Denver

ROBERTS, JESSICA D; LE ROY, WV; ROANE CTY HS; (FR); 4H Awd; Hnr Roll; Perf Att; Pres Ac Ftns Aw; WWAHSS; Comm Volntr; 4-H; Mth Clb/Tm; Ntl FFA; Bskball (J); Track (V L); Cl Off (V); Physical Therapy; Teaching

ROBINSON, MICHAEL; PRINCETON, WV; PRINCETON SR HS; (SR); Chr; Ch Chr; Bsball (V); All-State Chorus; BS / Management; Concord U

ROE, CHEYENNE; WEIRTON, WV; WEIR HS; (SO); Hi Hnr Roll; Hnr Roll; Nat Hon Sy; WWAHSS; Comm Volntr; Hosp Aide; Chess; Chrch Yth Grp; Dbte Team; Drma Clb; Key Club; Mth Clb/Tm; P to P St Amb Prg; SADD; SP/M/VS; Stg Cre; GAA; Scr Kpr (J); Envirothon; Chemistry Club; Surgical Doctor; Physical Therapy; West Virginia U; Shepard College

ROGERS, LINDSEY N; PRINCETON, WV; PRINCETON SR HS; (SO); Hnr Roll; Otst Ac Ach Awd; Perf Att; WWAHSS; Chrch Yth Grp; Mod UN; Off Aide; ROTC; Chr; Ch Chr; Clr Grd; Drl Tm; Criminal Law; WVU; Naval Academy

ROMAGE, NATASHA M; HUNTINGTON, WV; HUNTINGTON HS; (SO); Hnr Roll; Chrldg (V); HOSA; Nurse; Pediatric Nurse; Saint Mary's Nursing School; Marshall U

ROSE, CHRISTOPHER; JOLO, WV; IAEGER HS; (FR); All Am Sch; Hi Hnr Roll; Hnr Roll; MVP; Perf Att; Pres Ac Ftns Aw; Pres Sch; Sci Fairs; DARE; Mth Clb/Tm; Ftball (V); Wt Lftg (V); Yrbk (E, R, P); Lawyer; Virginia Tech; Louisville

ROSNICK, JOCELYN; WEIRTON, WV; WEIR HS; (SR); All Am Sch; Hnr Roll; Jr Eng Tech; Nat Hon Sy; Nat Sci Aw; Perf Att; Pres Sch; WWAHSS; Drma Clb; Emplmnt; Key Club; P to P St Amb Prg; Sci Clb; SADD; GAA; Skiing; Yrbk; Law Degree; Master's-Psychology; West Virginia U

ROSS, CHRISTY J; WHEELING, WV; WHEELING PARK HS; (SR); F Lan Hn Soc; Hnr Roll; Drma Clb; Emplmnt; Tchrs Aide; Spanish Clb; Stg Cre; Stu Cncl (R); CR (R); BS in Nursing; Wheeling Jesuit U

ROWE, EDEN; BEAVER, WV; SHADY SPRING HS; (SO); Hi Hnr Roll; Hnr Roll; MVP; Nat Hon Sy; Pres Ac Ftns Aw; Chrch Yth Grp; FCA; Vllyball (V); Mountain State U; Bluefield State College

ROWLEY, LAURA L; RIPLEY, WV; RIPLEY HS; (JR); 4H Awd; Hnr Roll; Sci Fairs; St of Mnth; 4-H; FCCLA; Ntl FFA; Quill & Scroll; Hsbk Rdg; Scr Kpr; 4-H Treasurer; Astronomy; Marine Biology; West Virginia U/ Parkersburg; U of Texas/Austin

Roberts, Emily
Tucker Cty HS
Hendricks, WV

Pridemore, Donnette
Fayetteville HS
Fayetteville, WV

Pleasant, Jacqueline A
Western Greenbrier HS
Leslie, WV

National
Honor Roll
Spring 2005

Piske, Alys C
Buckhannon-Upshur HS
French Creek, WV

Reed, Jimmy L
Iaeger HS
Avondale, WV

Rowe, Eden
Shady Spring HS
Beaver, WV

ROWSEY, KEVIN; HUNTINGTON, WV; HUNTINGTON HS; (SO); Hnr Roll; Nat Hon Sy; WWAHSS; Spec Olymp Vol; ArtClub; Emplmnt; Key Club; Stu Cncl (R); Medicine; Criminal Justice; U of Michigan; Yale U

ROY, SAKEIA M; CHARLES TOWN, WV; JEFFERSON HS; (JR); Hnr Roll; Otst Ac Ach Awd; St of Mnth; Comm Volntr; Peer Tut/Med; Chrch Yth Grp; DECA; Prom Com; Scouts; Ch Chr; Bskball (J); Track (V); Cl Off (R); CR (R); Business / Management; Interior Design; Hampton U; Marshall U

RUBLE, MASON R; BUNKER HILL, WV; MUSSELMAN HS; (FR); Hnr Roll; Nat Mrt LOC; Otst Ac Ach Awd; Perf Att; Sci Fairs; St of Mnth; Peer Tut/Med; Ntl FFA; Wdwrkg Clb; Bnd; Outstanding Penmanship Award 1998-99; Master Mechanic Degree; Master Welder Degree; Universal Technical Institute

RUCKER, TANIKA; NORTHFORK, WV; MT VIEW HS; (SO); Hnr Roll; Comm Volntr; Chrch Yth Grp; Yrbk; Member of Upward Bound; Member of HSTA; Cosmetologist; Pharmacy; West Virginia State; Concord U

RUCKER III, WILLIAM J; BECKLEY, WV; MTN STATE AC; (JR); Hi Hnr Roll; MVP; Nat Hon Sy; Perf Att; Pres Ac Ftns Aw; WWAHSS; Yth Ldrshp Prog; Hab For Humty Volntr; Peer Tut/Med; Red Cr Aide; Chess; Drma Clb; FCA; Mth Clb/Tm; Pep Squd; Sci Clb; SP/M/VS; Bskball (V CL); Sccr (V CL); Tennis (V L); Cl Off (S); Stu Cncl (P); CR (P); Community Volunteer; Biology / Radiology; Law; Duke U; Wake Forest U

RUSSELL, SAMANTHA D; LAVALETTE, WV; SPRING VALLEY HS; (SO); Hi Hnr Roll; Nat Hon Sy; Pres Ac Ftns Aw; Peer Tut/Med; Spec Olymp Vol; Ch Chr; Bskball (V); Vllyball (V); Cl Off (V); Booth Scholar; National Honor Society; Business; Law; College of William & Mary; U of Colorado At Boulder

SABBAGH, EBRAHIM; BRIDGEPORT, WV; BRIDGEPORT HS; (SR); Hnr Roll; St of Mnth; Comm Volntr; Hosp Aide; DARE; Bskball (J); Sccr (J); Sch Ppr (P); West Virginia U

SADOWSKI, ADAM M; BECKLEY, WV; WOODROW WILSON; (JR); Hi Hnr Roll; Nat Hon Sy; Nat Sci Aw; WWAHSS; Peer Tut/Med; Chrch Yth Grp; Emplmnt; Key Club; Skiing (V); Sccr (V); Tennis (V); Eagle Scout; Medical

SANDERS, SAMANTHA; ELKVIEW, WV; HERBERT HOOVER HS; (FR); Hnr Roll; Photog; Chorus Award; Psychology; Psychiatry; West Virginia U; Marshall U

SAPORITO, COURTNEY; WHEELING, WV; MT DE CHANTAL VISITATION AC; (FR); Ctznshp Aw; Hi Hnr Roll; St of Mnth; WWAHSS; Comm Volntr; DARE; Key Club; Mth Clb/Tm; French Clb; Bnd; Stg Cre; Cl Off (S); Play the Violin and the Clarinet; Pediatrician

SASEEN, JENA; WHEELING, WV; BISHOP DONAHUE HS; (JR); Hi Hnr Roll; WWAHSS; Yth Ldrshp Prog; Comm Volntr; Hosp Aide; Spec Olymp Vol; AL Aux Girls; Drma Clb; HO'Br Yth Ldrshp; Key Club; Prom Com; Chr; SP/M/VS; Chrldg (V L); Yrbk (E); Homecoming Committee Wheeling Symphony Volunteer, Church Lector & Sunday School Teacher; Elementary Education; Wheeling Jesuit U; California U of PA

SAUER, KAYLA R; SHOCK, WV; (JR); Hnr Roll; Comm Volntr; Chrch Yth Grp; DARE; Lttrmn Clb; Prom Com; Vsity Clb; Voc Ind Clb Am; Chr; Chrldg (V); Track (V); Health and Nursing Occupations; West Virginia State College; Glenville State College

SAUNDERS, ELIZABETH; WAR, WV; BIG CREEK HS; (SO); Hnr Roll; Perf Att; St of Mnth; Quiz Bowl; Spch Team; "B" Honor Roll; RN; Secretary

SAVILLE, KATLYN A; INWOOD, WV; MUSSELMAN HS; (FR); 4H Awd; Ctznshp Aw; Gov Hnr Prg; Hnr Roll; Pres Ac Ftns Aw; Sci Fairs; Yth Ldrshp Prog; Comm Volntr; Hosp Aide; 4-H; ArtClub; DARE; Ntl FFA; Photog; Scouts; Svce Clb; Chrldg (J); Gmnstcs (J); Scr Kpr (J); Governors School of Arts - PAVAN; President of FFA Aylor Chapter; Veterinary Science; Animal Husbandry; Wilson College; West Virginia U

SAYERS, JONATHAN E; PRINCETON, WV; PRINCETON SR HS; (SO); Hi Hnr Roll; WWAHSS; Comm Volntr; Chrch Yth Grp; FCA; Sccr (J); Orthodontics; Optometry; Concord U; Bluefield State College

SAYRE, ANTHONY; RIPLEY, WV; RAVENSWOOD HS; (JR); Hnr Roll; MVP; Nat Hon Sy; Pres Ac Ftns Aw; St of Mnth; Comm Volntr; Peer Tut/Med; Spec Olymp Vol; Chrch Yth Grp; Tchrs Aide; Bskball (V CL); Track (V L); Cl Off (R); Stu Cncl (R); Sch Ppr (R); National & World Champion Archer; All-State Basketball; Industrial Engineering; Mechanical Engineering; West Virginia U; West Virginia U of Technology

SAYRE, MANDI M; CHARLESTON, WV; NITRO HS; (SO); Hi Hnr Roll; Hnr Roll; WWAHSS; Hosp Aide; Chrch Yth Grp; FCA; MuAlphaTh; Spanish Clb; Nurse Anesthetist; Accounting; West Virginia U; Alderson-Broaddus College

SCONISH, SAMANTHA; FAIRMONT, WV; EAST FAIRMONT HS; (SO); F Lan Hn Soc; Hnr Roll; Emplmnt; Chr; Mch Bnd; Pep Bnd; West Virginia U

SEGANTINI, GIOVANNA T; LOST CREEK, WV; SOUTH HARRISON HS; (SR); All Am Sch; Hnr Roll; WWAHSS; Comm Volntr; Key Club; Spanish Clb; Bnd; Mch Bnd; Foreign Exchange Student; Accounting

SELLERS, VALERIE J; HEDGESVILLE, WV; HEDGESVILLE HS; (SR); Hnr Roll; Otst Ac Ach Awd; Perf Att; Comm Volntr; Photog; ROTC; Ch Chr; Drl Tm; Orch; Stu Cncl (R); Videography; International Beauty School, Martinsburg WV; Appalachia Bible College, West Virginia

SERRA, JACKIE; RAYSAL, WV; BIG CREEK HS; (SR); Hnr Roll; Kwnis Aw; MVP; Perf Att; Pres Ac Ftns Aw; Sci Fairs; St of Mnth; WWAHSS; Comm Volntr; Hosp Aide; Peer Tut/Med; ArtClub; DARE; Emplmnt; Key Club; Lttrmn Clb; Off Aide; Prom Com; Sci Clb; Chr; Ch Chr; Dnce; SP/M/VS; Chrldg (V CL); Mar Art (J L); Swmg (V L); Cl Off (T); Stu Cncl (T); CR (R); Radiology; RN; Southwest Virginia Community College

SHARP, KAYLA N; CABINS, WV; PETERSBURG HS; (FR); Hnr Roll; Otst Ac Ach Awd; Bnd; Mch Bnd; Sftball (J); Lady of the Golden Horseshoe; Doctor; Forensic Science; West Virginia U; Fairmont College

SHAW, CASEY; PETERSBURG, WV; PETERSBURG HS; (FR); Hnr Roll; Sci Fairs; 4-H; Chess; Drma Clb; Bnd; SP/M/VS; Sccr (J); Acting; Secret Agent; West Virginia U; Harvard U

SHAWYER, JILLIAN; HEDGESVILLE, WV; MUSSELMAN HS; (FR); Hnr Roll; MVP; Sci/Math Olympn; Comm Volntr; Chr; Sftball (V L); Most Valuable Player; Law Enforcement; North Carolina State; Florida State U

SHEILS, KATIE; HUNTINGTON, WV; HUNTINGTON HS; (JR); Hi Hnr Roll; Nat Hon Sy; WWAHSS; Hosp Aide; Spec Olymp Vol; Chrch Yth Grp; FCA; Key Club; Off Aide; Spanish Clb; Sccr (V); Honors Program

SHEPHERD, JESSICA; ELKINS, WV; ELKINS HS; (JR); Hnr Roll; WWAHSS; ArtClub; Voc Ind Clb Am; Bnd; Mch Bnd; Pep Bnd; Automotive Technician; Music; U of Northwestern Ohio; Ohio State U

SHERMAN, SAMANTHA D; MOOREFIELD, WV; MOOREFIELD HS; (FR); Hnr Roll; Otst Ac Ach Awd; Sci Fairs; St of Mnth; WWAHSS; Comm Volntr; Peer Tut/Med; DARE; Emplmnt; Fr of Library; FCCLA; Lib Aide; Ntl FFA; Off Aide; Scouts; SP/M/VS; Stu Cncl (R); CR (R); Pediatrician; Teacher; West Virginia U; North Carolina State

SHIFFLETTE, MATTHEW C; CORINNE, WV; WYOMING CTY EAST HS; (FR); Hi Hnr Roll; Nat Mrt LOC; WWAHSS; Comm Volntr; FCA; Scouts; Bsball (V); Ftball (J); West Virginia U; Concord U

SHORT, CYNTHIA; WEBSTER SPRINGS, WV; WEBSTER CTY HS; (SR); 4H Awd; Hnr Roll; Nat Hon Sy; USAA; WWAHSS; 4-H; Chrch Yth Grp; DARE; Drma Clb; Emplmnt; FCA; SADD; Tchrs Aide; SP/M/VS; Stg Cre; CR (R); Sch Ppr (E); Yrbk (E); Int'l Thespian Society; Journalism; West Virginia U

SHORT, DELLANNA; WELCH, WV; IAEGER HS; (FR); Hnr Roll; Nat Hon Sy; WWAHSS; Peer Tut/Med; DARE; Scouts; Dnce; Flg Crps; Bskball (V); Chrldg (V); Sftball (V); Vllyball (V); Swimming Welch Stingrays; Soccer-County League; ROTC-College; Marshall U

SHOUB, TYLER; HUNTINGTON, WV; HUNTINGTON HS; (SO); Hi Hnr Roll; Nat Ldrshp Svc; Otst Ac Ach Awd; Perf Att; Yth Ldrshp Prog; Spec Olymp Vol; Emplmnt; Tchrs Aide; Bsball (J); Golf (L); Spanish Honorary; Forensic Science; Marine Biology; U of North Carolina; Ohio State U

SHOWEN, AUSTIN; CHARLESTON, WV; NITRO HS; (SO); Hi Hnr Roll; Nat Hon Sy; Yth Ldrshp Prog; Comm Volntr; Chrch Yth Grp; FCA; MuAlphaTh; NYLC; Swg Chr; Stu Cncl (R); Yrbk (P); Law; Political Science; Marshall U; U of Maryland

SHOWEN, KRISTIN; CHARLESTON, WV; NITRO HS; (SO); Hi Hnr Roll; Hnr Roll; Nat Hon Sy; Comm Volntr; Chrch Yth Grp; Key Club; MuAlphaTh; Chr; Dnce; CR (S); Medicine; Marshall U; U of Cincinnati

SHREWSBURY, MACKENZIE; NITRO, WV; NITRO HS; (JR); Hi Hnr Roll; Hnr Roll; Nat Hon Sy; WWAHSS; Comm Volntr; Red Cr Aide; Chrch Yth Grp; Emplmnt; Key Club; MuAlphaTh; Prom Com; Sccr (V); Cl Off (V); Stu Cncl (V); CR (P, V); Rhododendron Girls' State; English As Second Lang. Volunteer; Pre-Dentistry; Nursing; Marshall U; Eastern Kentucky U

SHROYER, REBECCA; FAIRMONT, WV; EAST FAIRMONT HS; (SO); Hnr Roll; St of Mnth; WWAHSS; Emplmnt; Lib Aide; Medical; Psychology; West Virginia U; Fairmont State U

SIGLEY, AMANDA; WANA, WV; CLAY-BATTELLE HS; (SR); 4H Awd; Hnr Roll; WWAHSS; Hab For Humty Volntr; Red Cr Aide; 4-H; Emplmnt; Mus Clb; Ntl FFA; Off Aide; Sci Clb; Chr; Sch Ppr (R); Nursing; West Virginia U; Fairmont State College

SIGMON, SARAH A; CHARLESTON, WV; NITRO HS; (FR); Hi Hnr Roll; WWAHSS; Comm Volntr; Red Cr Aide; Chrch Yth Grp; DARE; Key Club; Bnd; Mch Bnd; Skiing (V); Swmg (V); Fundraiser for Women and Children's Abuse Fund and Breast Cancer; Medical School

SILVER, ROBERT L; BUNKER HILL, WV; MUSSELMAN HS; (FR); 4H Awd; DAR; Hnr Roll; Perf Att; Comm Volntr; 4-H; Zoology; Herpetology

SIMON JR, GERALD L; BECKLEY, WV; WOODROW WILSON HS; (JR); Hnr Roll; DECA; Cl Off (R); Business Degree; U of North Carolina; Marshall U

SIUDAK, BRITTANY; WEIRTON, WV; WEIR HS; (FR); Hi Hnr Roll; WWAHSS; Hosp Aide; Chrch Yth Grp; Drma Clb; Key Club; Teacher

SIUDAK, JAIME; WEIRTON, WV; WEIR HS; (FR); Hi Hnr Roll; WWAHSS; Hosp Aide; Chrch Yth Grp; Drma Clb; Key Club; Chr; Ch Chr; Teaching

SKILES, MISTY D; FRANKLIN, WV; PENDLETON CTY HS; (JR); Hnr Roll; Nat Hon Sy; WWAHSS; 4-H; Chrch Yth Grp; Drma Clb; FCA; Ntl Beta Clb; Tchrs Aide; Dnce; SP/M/VS; Stu Cncl (R); Criminal Justice; Glenville State College

SLATER, LEASA M; CHARLESTON, WV; NITRO HS; (SO); Hi Hnr Roll; Hnr Roll; Nat Hon Sy; Hosp Aide; Chrch Yth Grp; Emplmnt; FCA; Lib Aide; MuAlphaTh; Scouts; Spanish Clb; Chr; Ch Chr; Vllyball (VJ); Stu Cncl (R); Pediatric Oncology; Ohio State U; Marshall U

SLAVEY, TONI M; MABSCOTT, WV; WOODROW WILSON HS; (JR); Hnr Roll; Peer Tut/Med; DARE; FBLA; Pep Squd; ROTC; Child Psychologist; Florida State U; Mountaineer U

SMILEY, ESTHER; CHARLESTON, WV; (JR); F Lan Hn Soc; Hnr Roll; MVP; Sci Fairs; WWAHSS; Chrch Yth Grp; Drma Clb; Emplmnt; HO'Br Yth Ldrshp; Prom Com; Tchrs Aide; Spanish Clb; Chr; Dnce; Track (V); Stu Cncl (S); Yrbk (P); Occupational Therapy; Drama Voice

SMITH, ALEX; HURRICANE, WV; HURRICANE HS; (JR); Hnr Roll; Nat Hon Sy; WWAHSS; Chrch Yth Grp; FCA; MuAlphaTh; Scouts; Bnd; Chr; SP/M/VS; Architecture; Engineering; Ohio State U; U of Kentucky

SMITH, CASEY; FAYETTEVILLE, WV; FAYETTEVILLE HS; (FR); Hnr Roll; MVP; Nat Hon Sy; St of Mnth; Peer Tut/Med; Chrch Yth Grp; Off Aide; Tchrs Aide; Bskball (V); Sftball (V); Cl Off (P); Yrbk (E)

SMITH, EDDIE R; GILBERT, WV; GILBERT HS; (FR); Hnr Roll; Perf Att; Comm Volntr; FCA; Tchrs Aide; Chr; Ftball (J); Wt Lftg (J); Wrstlg (J); 2005-West Award-Achieved Mastery in All Tested Areas; 2003-All County Football Player for Mingo County-Gilbert Middle School; Dentist; Lawyer; West Virginia U; Ohio State U

SMITH, MICHAEL; CAMDEN ON GAULEY, WV; NEW LIFE CHRISTIAN AC; (FR); Hnr Roll; St Optmst of Yr; Drma Clb; Bskball; Social Studies Fair-2nd Place; Dentistry; UNC

SMITH, SCOTT; KEYSER, WV; KEYSER HS; (FR); Hnr Roll; MVP; Perf Att; Bsball (J L); Bskball (V C); Ftball (V); Freshman Football MVP; Freshman Basketball MVP; Architect; Military; U of Michigan; West Virginia U

SMITH, ZACHARY B; RIVERTON, WV; PENDLETON HS; (SO); 4H Awd; Hnr Roll; Perf Att; Sci Fairs; St of Mnth; 4-H; Chrch Yth Grp; Emplmnt; FCA; Ntl Beta Clb; Ntl FFA; Bsball (VJ); Bskball (VJ); Ftball (V); Sccr (J); FFA Star Farmer Award; Young Writers Award; Sports Medicine/ Professional Athlete; PE Teacher; Potomac State College; West Virginia U

SMITH, ZAN; WILLIAMSON, WV; TUG VALLEY HS; (JR); Hi Hnr Roll; Hnr Roll; Nat Hon Sy; WWAHSS; Comm Volntr; Peer Tut/Med; Spec Olymp Vol; Chrch Yth Grp; Key Club; Ntl Beta Clb; Prom Com; State Social Studies Fair; Computer Science; History; Marshall U; U of Kentucky

SMITH III, JAMES E; GILBERT, WV; GILBERT HS; (FR); Hnr Roll; Perf Att; Comm Volntr; FCA; Tchrs Aide; Chr; Ftball (J); Wt Lftg (J); Wrstlg (J); 2003-All County Football Player for Mingo County-Gilbert Middle School; 2005-Finished 2nd in Freshman Heavyweight Wrestling Tournament At Nitro, WV; Department of Natural Resources (DNR); Electrical Engineer; West Virginia U; Ohio State U

SOBOTKA, LINDSAY; WEIRTON, WV; WEIR HS; (SO); Hi Hnr Roll; Perf Att; WWAHSS; Comm Volntr; Emplmnt; Sci Clb; Swmg (V L); Vllyball (V L); Cl Off (S); Sch Ppr (R); Radiology; Journalism; U of Pittsburgh; Penn State

SPEARS, BRANDON C; SHADY SPRING, WV; SHADY SPRING HS; (FR); Hnr Roll; Ntl FFA

SPENCER, MATT; FRAMETOWN, WV; (FR); Hi Hnr Roll; Hnr Roll; Ntl FFA; Bnd; Jzz Bnd; Mch Bnd; Pep Bnd; PhD; Harvard U; Yale U

SPORMAN, HEATHER; BUNKER HILL, WV; MUSSELMAN HS; (JR); Ctznshp Aw; Hi Hnr Roll; Hnr Roll; Sci Fairs; USAA; WWAHSS; Peer Tut/ Med; Photog; Graduating Year Earlier Than Expected; Psychology; Shepherd U

SQUIRES, JOSHUA K; WESTON, WV; LEWIS CTY HS; (SR); WWAHSS; Computer Sciences; Business Administration; West Virginia U; Fairmont State College

STACKETT, EMILY M; HURRICANE, WV; CALVARY BAPTIST AC; (FR); Hi Hnr Roll; Hnr Roll; Chrch Yth Grp; Ch Chr; Bskball (V L); 3rd Place Job Winner - Females/ WV and VA Regional Convention; Liberty U; West Virginia State U

Smith III, James E
Gilbert HS
Gilbert, WV

Smith, Zachary B
Pendleton HS
Riverton, WV

Slater, Leasa M
Nitro HS
Charleston, WV

Shroyer, Rebecca
East Fairmont HS
Fairmont, WV

Sharp, Kayla N
Petersburg HS
Cabins, WV

Rucker III, William J
Mtn State AC
Beckley, WV

Roy, Sakeia M
Jefferson HS
Charles Town, WV

Ruble, Mason R
Musselman HS
Bunker Hill, WV

Shifflette, Matthew C
Wyoming Cty East HS
Corinne, WV

Silver, Robert L
Musselman HS
Bunker Hill, WV

Smith, Eddie R
Gilbert HS
Gilbert, WV

Smith, Scott
Keyser HS
Keyser, WV

STACY, AIMIE; JOLO, WV; IAEGER HS; (FR); Hnr Roll; Sci Fairs; USAA; Chrch Yth Grp; Dnce; Sftball; Gear Up / Upward Bound / State Government; Program / Summer Program - Youth & Government; Pharmacy; Medical Career; Concord U; Marshall U

STACY, DANIELLE; JOLO, WV; IAEGER HS; (FR); Nat Hon Sy; Perf Att; DARE; Sftball; Pre-Vet; Concord U

STADVEC, JORDAN E; PRINCETON, WV; (PSHS) PRINCETON SR HS; (SO); DAR; Hnr Roll; WWAHSS; ArtClub; Chrch Yth Grp; Key Club; Bnd; Ch Chr; Clr Grd; Mch Bnd

STAHL, PHILIP; WHEELING, WV; WHEELING PARK HS; (JR); Hi Hnr Roll; Nat Hon Sy; Nat Ldrshp Svc; Perf Att; WWAHSS; Yth Ldrshp Prog; Comm Volntr; Hosp Aide; ArtClub; Drma Clb; Emplmnt; Key Club; Off Aide; Tchrs Aide; Orch; Cl Off (S); Stu Cncl (R); Radio/TV Club; Student Ambassador; Business

STALEY, CHELSEA S; HURRICANE, WV; HURRICANE HS; (JR); Hi Hnr Roll; Hnr Roll; Nat Hon Sy; WWAHSS; Spec Olymp Vol; Chrch Yth Grp; FCA; Key Club; Sftball (V); Yrbk (E); Elementary Education; Marshall U

STARCHER, JACOB C; SPENCER, WV; ROANE CTY HS; (SR); Hnr Roll; Perf Att; St of Mnth; Emplmnt; Ftball (VJ L); Wt Lftg (VJ L)

STAUFFER, ERIN; WILLIAMSTOWN, WV; WILLIAMSTOWN; (JR); F Lan Hn Soc; Hi Hnr Roll; Nat Hon Sy; WWAHSS; Yth Ldrshp Prog; Comm Volntr; Peer Tut/Med; Red Cr Aide; Chrch Yth Grp; Emplmnt; FCA; Key Club; Lttrmn Clb; Prom Com; Svce Clb; Vsity Clb; Chrldg (V CL); PP Ftbl (V); Track (J); Vllyball (J); Cl Off (V); Stu Cncl (V); 6 Year Member of Student Council; Bachelor of Architecture; Masters of Architecture; U of Kentucky; West Virginia U

STEARNS, GORDON R; BRIDGEPORT, WV; BRIDGEPORT HS; (SR); F Lan Hn Soc; Gov Hnr Prg; Hnr Roll; WWAHSS; AL Aux Boys; Chrch Yth Grp; Emplmnt; Key Club; Swmg (V L); Member of Student Council; Virginia Polytechnic Inst State U; Virginia Military Institute

STEPHENS, DANIEL K; WAYNE, WV; WAYNE HS; (SR); Hnr Roll; Perf Att; Spec Olymp Vol; Chess; Chrch Yth Grp; Emplmnt; Lib Aide; Ch Chr; Bskball (L); Track (L); Vllyball (L); Get a Good Job

STEPHENS, TIFFANI; BARBOURSVILLE, WV; WAYNE HS; (FR); Hi Hnr Roll; Hnr Roll; Pres Ac Ftns Aw; Peer Tut/Med; Tchrs Aide; Bnd; Mch Bnd; Sftball (J); Invited to Go to Washington DC to See How Gov't Is Run; Forensic Science; English; Marshall U; West Virginia U

STEPHENSON, ANGELICA; SAINT ALBANS, WV; ST ALBANS HS; (SO); Ctznshp Aw; Hnr Roll; St of Mnth; Spec Olymp Vol; Chrch Yth Grp; Drma Clb; Scouts; Ch Chr; Dnce; Flg Crps; Mch Bnd; Physical Therapy; Ministry

STEVENS, AMBER; BARBOURSVILLE, WV; CABELL MIDLAND HS; (SO); Hnr Roll; Perf Att; WWAHSS; Hosp Aide; Photog; International Business; Marketing; University of Tampa; University of Adelaide

STEVENS, BRADEN G; CHARLESTON, WV; NITRO HS; (SO); Hnr Roll; Comm Volntr; Chrch Yth Grp; Bnd; Chr; Mch Bnd; SP/M/VS; CR (V); I Am a Participant in My Church Praise Band.; Engineering; West Virginia U; U of Kentucky

STICKLEY, ELIZABETH; KEYSER, WV; KEYSER HS; (SO); Hi Hnr Roll; Hnr Roll; St of Mnth; WWAHSS; Chrch Yth Grp; SADD; Chr; Medical Receptionist/Secretary; Potomac State College

STONE, BETHANY A; BECKLEY, WV; INDEPENDANCE HS; (SO); DAR; Hnr Roll; Comm Volntr; Chrch Yth Grp; DARE; FCA; Off Aide; Prom Com; Tchrs Aide; Ch Chr; CR (R); Hilltop Baptist Church Drama Team; Hilltop Baptist Church Puppet Team; Diabetic Educator; Concord U; Marshall U

STONE, TRAVIS; LEON, WV; BUFFALO HS; (FR); 4H Awd; Ctznshp Aw; Hnr Roll; St of Mnth; Comm Volntr; 4-H; Chrch Yth Grp; Fncg (V); Nursing; Teacher; Marshall U; West Virginia U of Technology

STONEKING, AMANDA R; FAIRMONT, WV; EAST FAIRMONT HS; (SO); Hnr Roll; St of Mnth; Comm Volntr; Chrch Yth Grp; Emplmnt; Bnd; Ch Chr; Senior Soldier (The Salvation Army); Psychiatrist; Lawyer; West Virginia U; A Christian College or U

STRADER, THEODORE J; FRENCH CREEK, WV; BUCKHANNON-UPSHUR HS; (FR); All Am Sch; Hi Hnr Roll; Hnr Roll; Perf Att; USAA; WWAHSS; Comm Volntr; Chrch Yth Grp; DARE; Scouts; Ftball (C); Wt Lftg (V); Wrstlg (V L); Stu Cncl (R); Order of the Arrow - Brotherhood-BSA; Sports Medicine; Business; West Virginia U; Fairmont State U

STREET, KAYLA M; JOLO, WV; IAEGER HS; (FR); Hnr Roll; Peer Tut/Med; DARE; SADD; Dnce; Bsball (L); Veterinary; Concord U; Virginia Tech

STRICKLAND, TABITHA; BUCKHANNON, WV; (JR); Hnr Roll; Ntl FFA; Sftball (VJ); FFA; Social Worker; Probation Officer; Davis & Elkins College; WV Wesleyan College

STRIDER, ADAM K; BUNKER HILL, WV; MUSSELMAN HS; (FR); Hnr Roll; Emplmnt; Scouts; Bnd; Jzz Bnd; Mch Bnd; Pep Bnd; Golf (J); Letterman in Academic Competition for Excellence; Academic Games League of America / Nationals Team Member; English / Political Science; Law; James Madison U; U of South Carolina

STROPE, ANDREA L; GLEN DALE, WV; BISHOP DONAHUE HS; (JR); Hi Hnr Roll; MVP; Nat Hon Sy; Sci Fairs; WWAHSS; Yth Ldrshp Prog; Comm Volntr; Peer Tut/Med; Spec Olymp Vol; Chrch Yth Grp; DARE; Key Club; Pep Squd; SP/M/VS; Chrldg (V); Psychology; Wheeling Jesuit U

STULL, AMBER D; CORE, WV; CLAY-BATTELLE HS; (SR); Ctznshp Aw; Hnr Roll; Perf Att; WWAHSS; Ntl FFA; Off Aide; Prom Com; Quiz Bowl; Sch Ppr (R); Nursing / Registered Nurse; West Virginia U

SUMMERS, SARAH R; WALKER, WV; WILLIAMSTOWN HS; (FR); Hnr Roll; Otst Ac Ach Awd; Perf Att; Comm Volntr; Chrch Yth Grp; Key Club; Bnd; Mch Bnd; Golden Horseshoe; Commendation List; Medicine; Law; WVU; Washington U in St. Louis

SURBAUGH, KAITLIN R; BECKLEY, WV; SHADY SPRING HS; (JR); Gov Hnr Prg; Hi Hnr Roll; MVP; Nat Hon Sy; Otst Ac Ach Awd; Pres Ac Ftns Aw; Pres Sch; Sci/Math Olympn; WWAHSS; Yth Ldrshp Prog; Comm Volntr; Hab For Humty Volntr; Spec Olymp Vol; Chrch Yth Grp; DARE; Emplmnt; FCA; Mth Clb/Tm; Off Aide; Outdrs Clb; SADD; Dnce; Cr Ctry (V); Ftball (J); Gmnstcs (V); Track (V); Wt Lftg (L); Wrstlg (J); CR (P); Sch Ppr (R); Health Sciences Technology Academy Secretary; Earned 360 Cmty-Service Hours Freshman Year; Detective in Drug/Sex Crimes; Resort Owner; West Virginia U; Marshall U

SURGEON, SANDRA; ALDERSON, WV; GREENBRIER EAST SR HS; (SR); Hi Hnr Roll; Nat Hon Sy; WWAHSS; FBLA; MuAlphaTh; Ntl FFA; Sftball (V L); Agricultural Education; West Virginia U; Virginia Tech

SUTPHIN, JOANNA D; MADISON, WV; STRATFORD CAREER INST; (SR); Hnr Roll; WWAHSS; ArtClub; Chr; Orch; SP/M/VS; Leo Club; All County Strings: 1st Violin; Nursing; Dental Assistant; Southern WV Community & Technical College

SWANNER V, JOSEPH T; PRINCETON, WV; PRINCETON SR HS; (FR); Ctznshp Aw; Hi Hnr Roll; Hnr Roll; Nat Hon Sy; Otst Ac Ach Awd; Pres Ac Ftns Aw; WWAHSS; Comm Volntr; Chess; Chrch Yth Grp; Dbte Team; Key Club; Mod UN; Bnd; Chr; Ch Chr; Mch Bnd; Physics; Music

SWAYNE, KATIE A; KEYSER, WV; KEYSER HS; (FR); 4H Awd; Hnr Roll; Perf Att; Sci Fairs; St of Mnth; 4-H; Chrch Yth Grp; Clr Grd; Dnce; SP/M/VS; Elementary Education; Dance/Fine Arts; West Virginia U Creative Arts Center; Wilson College in Pennsylvania

TALBOTT, RICHARD B L; GERRARDSTOWN, WV; MUSSELMAN HS; (FR); 4H Awd; Ctznshp Aw; Hi Hnr Roll; Hnr Roll; Otst Ac Ach Awd; Perf Att; Sci Fairs; Comm Volntr; Peer Tut/Med; 4-H; Chrch Yth Grp; Emplmnt; Ntl FFA; Ch Chr; Sccr (J); Track (V); Business Administration; West Virginia U; Shepherd U

TALKINGTON, KAYLA M; WEIRTON, WV; WEIR HS; (JR); Hi Hnr Roll; Nat Hon Sy; WWAHSS; Comm Volntr; Biology Clb; Emplmnt; Key Club; Prom Com; Dnce; The National Society of HS Scholars; Masters; Environmental Science; Warren Wilson College; Slippery Rock U

TALLMAN, SAMANTHA; ELKINS, WV; ELKINS HS; (FR); Otst Ac Ach Awd; Pres Ac Ftns Aw; Comm Volntr; Drma Clb; Bnd; Drl Tm; Drm Mjr; Mch Bnd; Chrldg (V); Track (V L); West Virginia U

TANNER, RACHEAL; SPENCER, WV; ROANE CTY HS; (JR); 4H Awd; Hnr Roll; WWAHSS; 4-H; Ntl FFA; West Virginia U Parkersburg

TAYLOR, CHRISTOPHER P; CLEAR CREEK, WV; LIBERTY HS; (FR); Hnr Roll; Perf Att; St of Mnth; Peer Tut/Med; DARE; Wt Lftg (J); Wrstlg (VJ); Business Ownership; Mathematics Major; Concord U; West Virginia U

TAYLOR, JAMAR L; KEYSER, WV; KEYSER HS; (FR); Hnr Roll; Comm Volntr; Chrch Yth Grp; Key Club; Ice Hky (V); School Choir; Fine Arts (Artist); Engineering (Engineer); West Virginia U; Marshall U

TENNEY, JUSTIN; BUCKHANNON, WV; BUCKHANNON-UPSHUR HS; (JR); Hnr Roll; MVP; Perf Att; Bskball (V); Ftball (J); Track (V); CR (R); Yrbk (E); Dentistry; Optometry; Marshall U; West Virginia U

TENNEY, STACEY; BUCKHANNON, WV; BUCKHANNON-UPSHUR HS; (SO); Hnr Roll; Quill & Scroll; Tennis (J); Yrbk; Registered Nurse; West Virginia U; Fairmont State

THOMAS, KRISTEN; PRINCETON, WV; PRINCETON SR HS; (FR); Hnr Roll; WWAHSS; Chrch Yth Grp; Key Club; Health Services

THOMAS, MACHELL; REEDSVILLE, WV; PRESTON HS; (FR); West Virginia U; Fairmont State U

THOMAS, MEGAN; BRAMWELL, WV; MONTCALM HS; (FR); DAR; Bnd; Mch Bnd; Doctor; Veterinarian; Concord U; Bluefield State

THOMAS, SHAWNA M; BARBOURSVILLE, WV; CABELL MIDLAND HS; (SO); Hnr Roll; St of Mnth; WWAHSS; Chrch Yth Grp; Prom Com; Ch Chr; Sccr (V); Virginia Tech

THOMASON, TABITHA A; BLUEFIELD, WV; BLUEFIELD HS; (SR); Hnr Roll; WWAHSS; Comm Volntr; ArtClub; Drma Clb; SP/M/VS; Psychology

THOMPSON, JENNIFER R; MURRAYSVILLE, WV; RAVENSWOOD HS; (SR); Ctznshp Aw; Hnr Roll; Otst Ac Ach Awd; Perf Att; WWAHSS; Comm Volntr; FBLA; Ntl FFA; Yrbk (R, P); Monsanto Award Winner; Computer Information Technology; West Virginia U Parkersburg

TOLEN, MEGAN A; MOUNT HOPE, WV; WOODROW WILSON HS; Hnr Roll; Peer Tut/Med; Chrch Yth Grp; Scouts; Chr; Sccr; Track (J); Theatre West Virginia Acting I & II; Medical Field; Professional Modeling; West Virginia U; Mountain State U

TOMASIK, SARAH K; BRIDGEPORT, WV; BRIDGEPORT HS; (SR); Hi Hnr Roll; Nat Hon Sy; Otst Ac Ach Awd; Perf Att; Pres Ac Ftns Aw; Yth Ldrshp Prog; Comm Volntr; Peer Tut/Med; Red Cr Aide; AL Aux Girls; Chrch Yth Grp; Emplmnt; Key Club; Prom Com; Tchrs Aide; French Clb; Bnd; Dnce; SP/M/VS; PP Ftbl (J); Track (J L); Cl Off (S); Stu Cncl (R); Secretary of Teens Against Tobacco Use; Nursing; West Virginia U

TOMBLIN, RANDY; HUNTINGTON, WV; SPRING VALLEY HS; (SO); Hnr Roll; Nat Hon Sy; WWAHSS; Comm Volntr; Peer Tut/Med; Spec Olymp Vol; HO'Br Yth Ldrshp; Key Club; Ftball (J); Cl Off (P); Stu Cncl (R); Sch Ppr (E); RAZE Crew Leader; Created School Newspaper; Health Care-Surgical; Marshall U; U of North Carolina

TORDIFF, JEFFREY; HARPERS FERRY, WV; JEFFERSON HS 9TH GRADE COMPLEX; (FR); Hnr Roll; Kwnis Aw; Otst Ac Ach Awd; Perf Att; Sci Fairs; Key Club; Tennis (J); Golden Horseshoe; Education-Major; Special Education-Minor; Radford U; Shepherd U

TRACY, BRIANNA M; WHEELING, WV; WHEELING PARK HS; (JR); Hi Hnr Roll; Nat Hon Sy; Perf Att; Sci Fairs; WWAHSS; Yth Ldrshp Prog; Comm Volntr; Peer Tut/Med; Red Cr Aide; 4-H; AL Aux Girls; ArtClub; Chrch Yth Grp; Emplmnt; Jr Ach; Key Club; P to P St Amb Prg; Ch Chr; Stg Cre; Chrldg (JC); Score of a 4 on Writing Assessment; Young Writers Contest Essay Winner; Marine Biology/Vet Med; Us History; Coastal Carolina; South Carolina U

TRICKETT, KRISTEN; BRIDGEPORT, WV; BRIDGEPORT HS; (SO); Ctznshp Aw; Hi Hnr Roll; Perf Att; Pres Ac Ftns Aw; WWAHSS; Yth Ldrshp Prog; Hosp Aide; Peer Tut/Med; Chrch Yth Grp; DARE; Key Club; Scouts; Bnd; Dnce; Drm Mjr; Flg Crps; Stu Cncl (R); Medicine; West Virginia U; Ohio State U

TUCKWILLER, KELLY; LEWISBURG, WV; GREENBRIER EAST HS; (SR); 4H Awd; Ctznshp Aw; Hnr Roll; MVP; WWAHSS; Comm Volntr; 4-H; AL Aux Girls; DARE; DECA; Emplmnt; FBLA; Bskball (VJ L); Sccr (V CL); Sftball (V L); Stu Cncl (V); I DARE You Award; Broadcast Journalism; West Virginia U

TULLY, MEGHAN R; CAMERON, WV; CAMERON HS; (SO); Hi Hnr Roll; Hnr Roll; Sci Fairs; Hab For Humty Volntr; Red Cr Aide; Bnd; Chr; Ch Chr; Chrldg (V L); Track (V); Region I Honor Band; Medical Science; Ohio State U; West Virginia U

TURNER, CHARLES D; BECKLEY, WV; WOODROW WILSON HS; (SO); Ctznshp Aw; Hnr Roll; MVP; Perf Att; Pres Ac Ftns Aw; Sci Fairs; St of Mnth; WWAHSS; Comm Volntr; Peer Tut/Med; Chrch Yth Grp; Emplmnt; FCA; Key Club; Scouts; Sccr (V); Swmg (V L); Tennis (V); Raze; Physical Therapy; Sports Medicine; West Virginia U

TURNER, KAYLA; HUNTINGTON, WV; HUNTINGTON HS; (JR); Hnr Roll; WWAHSS; Chrch Yth Grp; Key Club; Lib Aide; Mus Clb; Japanese Clb; Acpl Chr; Chr; SP/M/VS; All-State Chorus; Show Choir; Music; History; Marshall U

TUTTLE, KATHY; WHEELING, WV; WHEELING PARK HS; (JR); Hi Hnr Roll; Hnr Roll; Nat Hon Sy; Yth Ldrshp Prog; Comm Volntr; Hab For Humty Volntr; Hosp Aide; Chrch Yth Grp; Drma Clb; Emplmnt; Key Club; Svce Clb; Tchrs Aide; Superior Ratings in Piano Competitions; Volunteer of the Year; Med School; Marshall U

UNDERWOOD, MICHAEL; OAK HILL, WV; OAK HILL HS; (SO); Hi Hnr Roll; WWAHSS; Peer Tut/Med; Governor's School for Math and Science; Golden Horseshoe Winner; West Virginia U

URVAL, NIKITA; WHEELING, WV; LINSLY SCH; (SO); F Lan Hn Soc; Hi Hnr Roll; Nat Hon Sy; Perf Att; Yth Ldrshp Prog; Comm Volntr; Dbte Team; Key Club; Mus Clb; Outdrs Clb; P to P St Amb Prg; SADD; Spanish Clb; Chr; Dnce; SP/M/VS; Scr Kpr (V); Tennis (L); Vllyball (J); Medicine; Neuroscience; Johns Hopkins U; Emory U

VANCE, GABRIELLE; INWOOD, WV; MUSSELMAN HS; (SO); Hnr Roll; Chr; Accounting; Nursing; Shepherd U

VANCE, MICHAEL; RANGER, WV; HARTS HS; (SO); Bsball; Hunting; Fishing; Logan Community College

VANCE, SHANNON; MOUNT GAY, WV; LOGAN SR HS; (FR); St of Mnth; Key Club; Spanish Clb; Geography Bee Winner of School; Something to Do with Guitars; Acting; Marshall U; West Virginia U

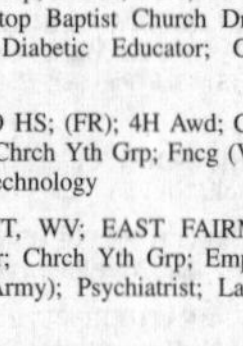
Tuttle, Kathy
Wheeling Park HS
Wheeling, WV

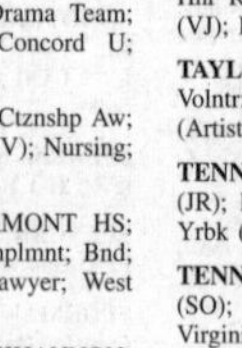
Taylor, Christopher P
Liberty HS
Clear Creek, WV

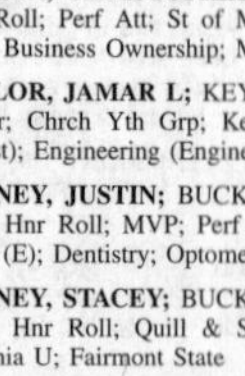
Tallman, Samantha
Elkins HS
Elkins, WV

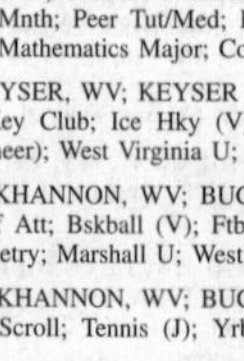
Starcher, Jacob C
Roane Cty HS
Spencer, WV

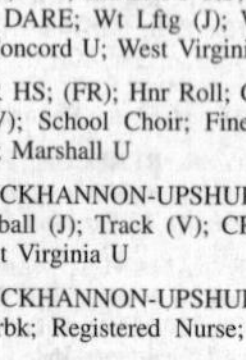
Stephens, Tiffani
Wayne HS
Barboursville, WV

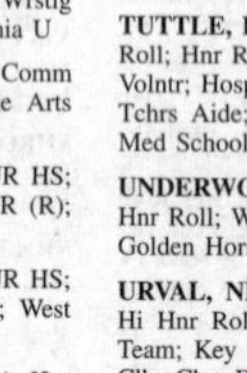
Turner, Charles D
Woodrow Wilson HS
Beckley, WV

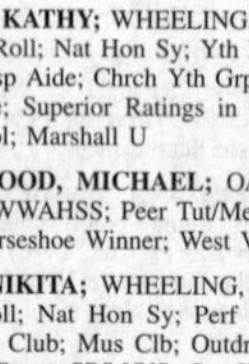
Urval, Nikita
Linsly Sch
Wheeling, WV

VAUGHN, JOSH; ELBERT, WV; MT VIEW HS; (SO); Hnr Roll; Nat Hon Sy; WWAHSS; Key Club; Sccr (V); Interact, Gear Up; Psychiatrist; Psychologist

VAUGHN, JUSTIN A; MILTON, WV; CABELL MIDLAND HS; (JR); Hnr Roll; Perf Att; WWAHSS; Chrch Yth Grp; Chr; Taking French as a Foreign Language; Member of Upward Bound Program; Airline Pilot; Marshall U

VEIT, BEN; BRIDGEPORT, WV; BRIDGEPORT HS; (SO); Hnr Roll; WWAHSS; Chrch Yth Grp; DECA; Key Club; Scouts; Welding Technology; Culinary Arts; West Virginia U Parkersburg; Marshall U

VIGH, RANDI L; GERRARDSTOWN, WV; MUSSELMAN HS; Hnr Roll; Sci Fairs; Emplmnt; Scouts; Chr; Sccr (VJ); Wt Lftg; Strawberry Festival Princess Nominee; Second Place-County Social Studies Fair; Teaching-Special Education; Fairmont State College; Glenville State College

VIGLIANCO, EMILY R; WEIRTON, WV; BROOKE HS; (FR); Hi Hnr Roll; Perf Att; Pres Ac Ftns Aw; Hosp Aide; Key Club; Mth Clb/Tm; Spanish Clb; Sccr (J); Swmg (V); Tennis (V); Cl Off (S); Cultural Arts Winner / Photography Literary; Medical Field; WV U

VIGLIANCO, RACHEL L; SAINT ALBANS, WV; ST ALBANS HS; (SO); Fut Prb Slvr; Pres Ac Ftns Aw; Sci Fairs; Comm Volntr; Chrch Yth Grp; Drma Clb; FCA; Jr Ach; Mus Clb; NtlFrnscLg; Quiz Bowl; Scouts; Acpl Chr; Chr; Ch Chr; SP/M/VS; Bskball (V CL); PP Ftbl (V); Sccr (V CL); Tennis (V L); Vllyball (V CL); Stu Cncl (P); CR; Yrbk (E, P); All-Conference in Soccer and Basketball; All-State Chorus; Physical Therapy; Performing Arts; West Virginia U; New York U

VIRDEN, CHELSEA D; WEIRTON, WV; WEIR HS; (FR); Hnr Roll; Nat Mrt Fin; Perf Att; WWAHSS; Chrch Yth Grp; Key Club; Lib Aide; Ch Chr; Scr Kpr; Lit Mag; National English Merit Award; Church Pianist

VLASIC, KRISTINA; PHILIPPI, WV; PHILIP BARBOUR HS; (SO); Hi Hnr Roll; Perf Att; WWAHSS; Comm Volntr; Chrch Yth Grp; Emplmnt; Outdrs Clb; SADD; Bnd; Ch Chr; Mch Bnd; Stg Cre; Ice Sktg; Friends & Fellowship Vice President 2004; Friends & Fellowship President 2005; Psychology History; Travel & Tourism; DeVry U, Marshall U; Argosy U, North Carolina

WAGGY, JULIE; FRANKLIN, WV; PENDLETON HS; (FR); Hnr Roll; Sci Fairs; St of Mnth; 4-H; Ntl FFA; Dnce; Chemistry; Business/Marketing; James Madison U; Eastern Mennonite U

WAGNER, ANDREW; EDMOND, WV; THE AC OF MOUNTAIN STATE U; (JR); Hi Hnr Roll; Otst Ac Ach Awd; USAA; WWAHSS; Comm Volntr; Peer Tut/Med; Spec Olymp Vol; ArtClub; Chrch Yth Grp; Drma Clb; Emplmnt; Mth Clb/Tm; Scouts; Mch Bnd; SP/M/VS; Sccr (V); Tennis (V); Cl Off (P); Chemical Engineering; Nuclear Engineering; Furman U; Purdue U

WAGONER, APRIL; RIDGELEY, WV; FRANKFORT HS; (JR); Gov Hnr Prg; Hi Hnr Roll; Hnr Roll; MVP; Nat Hon Sy; St of Mnth; WWAHSS; Emplmnt; Prom Com; Bnd; Mch Bnd; Sftball (VJ); Track (V); S.M.I.L.E. Team; Lawyer; Shepherd College; West Virginia U

WALLACE, SCOTT J; PARKERSBURG, WV; PARKERSBURG HS; (SO); Hi Hnr Roll; Hnr Roll; Pres Ac Ftns Aw; St of Mnth; Comm Volntr; Peer Tut/Med; Red Cr Aide; Emplmnt; Off Aide; Acpl Chr; Chr; Swmg (V L); Stu Cncl (R); CR (R); Swim Coach for Recreation League; American Red Cross Swim Lesson Instructor; Medicine; Culinary Arts; Ohio U; Wheeling Jesuit U

WALLS, AMBER; MARTINSBURG, WV; MARTINSBURG HS; (JR); Hnr Roll; St of Mnth; Ntl FFA; Drm Mjr; Nursing Assistant; Veterinary Assistant; James Rumsey Tech; Shepherd U

WALLS, ANTHONY C; VERNER, WV; GILBERT HS; (SR); Hnr Roll; Yrbk (R); Highest Grade in Class (Geography) (Applied Math II); O.D.; Chemistry; Marshall U

WALTER, STACY; BUNKER HILL, WV; MUSSELMAN HS; (SO); Hi Hnr Roll; Hnr Roll; Otst Ac Ach Awd; Sci Fairs; Sci/Math Olympn; Yth Ldrshp Prog; Comm Volntr; Spec Olymp Vol; DARE; ROTC; SADD; Tchrs Aide; Vsity Clb; Ftball (V); National Student Leadership Conference; Youth and Government Seminar / West VA; Biology & Life Sciences; Teaching; Shepherd U; Virginia Tech

WARD, DOUGLAS; HURRICANE, WV; HURRICANE HS; (JR); Hi Hnr Roll; Otst Ac Ach Awd; WWAHSS; Chief Engineer at Pontiac; President of General Motors; West Virginia U; Virginia Tech

WARD, LAUREN; HURRICANE, WV; HURRICANE HS; (JR); Hi Hnr Roll; Otst Ac Ach Awd; WWAHSS; Spec Olymp Vol; Key Club; MuAlphaTh; NYLC; Education; Biological Engineer; Marshall U; U of North Carolina

WARDER, DAVID J; GRAFTON, WV; FELLOWSHIP CHRISTIAN AC; (MS); Hnr Roll; Comm Volntr; Chrch Yth Grp; Emplmnt; Photog; Ch Chr; Stg Cre; Arch; Bsball; Skiing; Forestry; Fairmont State College

WARE, CHARLES; MARTINSBURG, WV; MARTINSBURG HS; (SR); 4H Awd; Hnr Roll; Nat Hon Sy; Sci Fairs; Comm Volntr; Red Cr Aide; 4-H; Chrch Yth Grp; Emplmnt; Ntl FFA; Ch Chr; Ftball (VJ); Wt Lftg (VJ); FFA-4 years Reporter; President 2 Yrs; Degree in Agriculture; Veterinarian Science Degree-Veterinarian; West Virginia U

WARNER, CIARA D; FRANKLIN, WV; PENDLETON HS; (FR); 4H Awd; Hnr Roll; MVP; Otst Ac Ach Awd; Pres Ac Ftns Aw; Pres Sch; Sci Fairs; 4-H; Chrch Yth Grp; DARE; FCA; Ntl FFA; Chrldg (V); Stu Cncl (S); Medical; Business; WVU; JMU

WASHINGTON, SHANEQUA; FAIRMONT, WV; FAIRMONT SR HS; (SO); Hnr Roll; Nat Hon Sy; Pres Ac Ftns Aw; WWAHSS; Peer Tut/Med; Sccr (J); Track (L); Vllyball (J); Fairmont State

WATSON, BRITTANY; MONTCALM, WV; MONTCALM HS; (SO); Hnr Roll; Perf Att; DARE; Chr; WV Golden Horseshoe Award; Zoology; Doctor; Duke U; Wake Forest U

WAYBRIGHT, ANDREW; NEWBURG, WV; PRESTON HS; (JR); Hnr Roll; Nat Hon Sy; Otst Ac Ach Awd; Perf Att; Comm Volntr; Peer Tut/Med; ROTC; Navy Seal; Tech Eng; West Virginia U; Harvard U

WEAVER, SARAH A; MT CLARE, WV; BRIDGEPORT HS; (JR); 4H Awd; Hi Hnr Roll; Hnr Roll; Pres Ac Ftns Aw; Comm Volntr; 4-H; Chrch Yth Grp; DARE; Emplmnt; Pep Squd; Dnce; Orch; Psychology; Dentistry; West Virginia U; U of Maine

WEIGLE, JASON; HEDGESVILLE, WV; HEDGESVILLE HS; (SO); Outdrs Clb

WEIKEE, LACEY J; UNION, WV; JAMES MONROE HS; (SR); 4H Awd; Hi Hnr Roll; Hnr Roll; Perf Att; Pres Ac Ftns Aw; St of Mnth; WWAHSS; Comm Volntr; Hosp Aide; Red Cr Aide; 4-H; Chrch Yth Grp; Emplmnt; Prom Com; Scouts; Voc Ind Clb Am; CR (R); 4-H Secretary of the Year (3 Years in a Row); Nursing; RN; Northern Virginia Community College

WEIKLE, BRIAN; UNION, WV; JAMES MONROE HS; (SR); Hnr Roll; Perf Att; Pres Sch; WWAHSS; Peer Tut/Med; Chrch Yth Grp; DARE; Emplmnt; FCA; FBLA; Mth Clb/Tm; Bnd; Bsball (J); Bskball (J); Track (J); Wt Lftg (V)

WEIKLE, STEPHANIE; UNION, WV; JAMES MONROE HS; (SR); Hnr Roll; Nat Hon Sy; FBLA; Lib Aide; Prom Com; Dnce; Sftball (V); Secretary of FBLA; Accounting; Business Management; Mercer County Technical School (College); Valley College of Technology

WELCH, KAYLEIGH M; SPRINGFIELD, WV; FRANKFORT HS; (JR); 4H Awd; Hi Hnr Roll; Hnr Roll; Nat Hon Sy; WWAHSS; Comm Volntr; 4-H; Chrch Yth Grp; Veterinary; CPA; Potomac State College; West Virginia U

WELSH, STEPHANIE N; WHEELING, WV; WHEELING PARK HS; (FR); Hi Hnr Roll; Perf Att; WWAHSS; Comm Volntr; Drma Clb; Key Club; Mth Clb/Tm; Chr; Stg Cre; United States Achievement Academy Award; Leo Club; Lawyer; Performing Arts; Harvard; Yale

WEST, SARA; BLUEFIELD, WV; MONTCALM HS; (SO); Perf Att; Chr; Social Studies - US History Award; Astronomical Science / NASA; Archaeology; Bluefield State

WESTMORELAND, JAYTESE; HUNTINGTON, WV; HUNTINGTON HS; (SO); Hnr Roll; Comm Volntr; Peer Tut/Med; Chrch Yth Grp; Emplmnt; Ch Chr; Fashion Buyers; Pediatrician; Marshall U; U of Charleston

WHIPP, KYLEN P; GLEN DALE, WV; JOHN MARSHALL HS; (FR); Gov Hnr Prg; Hi Hnr Roll; Kwnis Aw; Perf Att; Pres Ac Ftns Aw; Sci Fairs; St of Mnth; WWAHSS; Chrch Yth Grp; Dbte Team; Emplmnt; FCA; Quiz Bowl; Bsball (J); Bskball (J); Ftball (J); Stu Cncl (R); CR (R); Received 4.0 on State Writing Assessment; Selected to Attend Governor's School for Math & Science; Orthopedic Surgeon; Medicine; UNC Chapel Hill; West Virginia U

WHITE, BERNICE; BLUEFIELD, WV; MONTCALM HS; (FR); Ctznshp Aw; Hnr Roll; Perf Att; Sci Fairs; St of Mnth; Comm Volntr; Ch Chr; Stu Cncl (R); Elementary School Teacher; Bachelor's Degree; Concord U; West Virginia U

WHITE, BLAKE; ATHENS, WV; PINEVIEW HS; (JR); FCA; Track (V); Wt Lftg (V); State Champion in Powerlifting; Farming; Ag; Concord U; West Virginia U

WHITE, SARAH C; FAYETTEVILLE, WV; OAK HILL HS; (SR); Hnr Roll; Nat Hon Sy; Perf Att; St of Mnth; Valdctrian; WWAHSS; Comm Volntr; Chrch Yth Grp; Prom Com; Quiz Bowl; Clb; Bnd; Chr; Ch Chr; Mch Bnd; Sccr (V CL); Sch Ppr (R); Historic Fayette Theatre Actress; National Honor Society Secretary; Biology; Veterinarian; Wake Forest U

WHITMORE, AMBER N; OAK HILL, WV; OAK HILL HS; (JR); Hnr Roll; Nat Hon Sy; USAA; WWAHSS; Chrch Yth Grp; DARE; Key Club; Prom Com; SADD; Tchrs Aide; Chrldg (V L); Tennis (V); Stu Cncl; CR (S); Sch Ppr (R); Yrbk (R); Pharmacy; West Virginia U; Concord U

WHITMORE, TYLER D; OAK HILL, WV; OAK HILL HS; (FR); Hnr Roll; Chrch Yth Grp; DARE; FCA; Key Club; SADD; Sccr (V L)

WILDE JR, WILLIAM; MAIDSVILLE, WV; (FR); Hnr Roll; Perf Att; Sports Broadcaster; West Virginia U; U North Carolina

WILFONG, GARRETT E; SENECA ROCKS, WV; PENDLETON HS; (FR); 4H Awd; Hnr Roll; 4-H; Chrch Yth Grp; FCA; Ntl FFA; Bsball (J); West Virginia U; Fairmont State U

WILHELM, ASHLEY; BRIDGEPORT, WV; BRIDGEPORT HS; (JR); Hi Hnr Roll; Nat Hon Sy; WWAHSS; AL Aux Girls; Chrch Yth Grp; Key Club; Bnd; Clr Grd; Dnce; Secretary-Band-2005-2006; Chemistry; West Virginia U; Ohio State U

WILLIAMS, ASHLEY; KERMIT, WV; TUG VALLEY HS; (FR); Ctznshp Aw; Hnr Roll; St of Mnth; Comm Volntr; Drma Clb; Ntl Beta Clb; SP/M/VS; Sftball (J); Vllyball (J); Lawyer; X-Ray Tech; Marshall; Southern

WILLIAMS, LOGAN; MILTON, WV; CABELL MIDLAND HS; (JR); WWAHSS; Comm Volntr; Emplmnt; Chr; Cr Ctry (J); Ftball (J); Track (V); Business; Medical; Marshall U; Alice Lloyd College

WILLIAMS, VANESSA; CLARKSBURG, WV; ROBERT C BYRD HS; (FR); Duke TS; F Lan Hn Soc; Hi Hnr Roll; Yth Ldrshp Prog; Peer Tut/Med; Jr Cls League; SADD; SP/M/VS; WV Golden Horseshoe Winner; National Latin Exam - Summa Cum Laude Winner; Optometrist; Pediatrician; Seton Hill U; West Liberty State College

WILLIAMSON, JEFFREY S; DANVILLE, WV; LOGAN HS; (SR); Hnr Roll; Comm Volntr; Spec Olymp Vol; Chrch Yth Grp; Lib Aide; Bskball (V CL); Physical Education; Coaching; Fairmont State U

WILSON, SARAH; WHEELING, WV; WHEELING PARK HS; (JR); Nat Hon Sy; WWAHSS; Drma Clb; Key Club; Mus Clb; NtlFrnscLg; Spch Team; Chr; SP/M/VS; Stg Cre; Treasurer of Drama Club; Elementary Education; Business; Marshall U; Marietta State

WIND, EMILY; HUNTINGTON, WV; HUNTINGTON HS; (SR); Hi Hnr Roll; Nat Hon Sy; St of Mnth; WWAHSS; Red Cr Aide; Spec Olymp Vol; Chrch Yth Grp; Drma Clb; Key Club; Ntl Beta Clb; Sci Clb; Ch Chr; Stg Cre; Spanish Honorary; International Thespian Society; Accounting; Education; Marshall U, Huntington, West Virginia

WINTERS, JESSICA L; VALLEY GROVE, WV; WHEELING PARK HS; (SO); 4H Awd; Hi Hnr Roll; Hnr Roll; Perf Att; Hosp Aide; 4-H; Key Club; SADD; Orch; Member Key Club, Cheerleader-Freshman Squad; 8 Yr Member 4-H; Accounting; Business; West Virginia U; West Liberty State College

WINTZ, JESSICA B; CYCLONE, WV; WESTSIDE HS; (SR); Ctznshp Aw; DAR; F Lan Hn Soc; Hi Hnr Roll; Nat Hon Sy; Perf Att; St of Mnth; WWAHSS; Yth Ldrshp Prog; Comm Volntr; AL Aux Girls; Drma Clb; FCA; Off Aide; Pep Squd; Sci Clb; Svce Clb; Spanish Clb; SP/M/VS; Adv Cncl (R); Sch Ppr (R); Yrbk (E); 2005 DAR Good Citizen; Most School Spirit; Journalism; Marshall U

WOMACK, LAUREN K; HUNTINGTON, WV; CABELL MIDLAND HS; (JR); Hi Hnr Roll; Nat Hon Sy; WWAHSS; Comm Volntr; Chrch Yth Grp; Emplmnt; FCA; Mus Clb; Off Aide; Prom Com; Bnd; Ch Chr; Mch Bnd; SP/M/VS; GAA (V); Section Leader-Marching Band; Music Education; Elementary Education; Marshall U; Belmont U Nashville

WOODS, LUCAS T; PRINCETON, WV; PRINCETON SR HS; (FR); All Am Sch; Hi Hnr Roll; Otst Ac Ach Awd; Perf Att; St of Mnth; WWAHSS; Comm Volntr; Chrch Yth Grp; Dbte Team; Key Club; Mth Clb/Tm; Mod UN; Svce Clb; Bnd; Jzz Bnd; Mch Bnd; Orch; Mar Art (V); Swmg (J); CR (R); Yrbk (E, P); District Junior Civitan Chaplain; Director's Award - Band; Doctor of Music; West Virginia U; Marshall U

WRIGHT, AMANDA R.; MARTINSBURG, WV; HEDGESVILLE HS; (SO); Hnr Roll; Chrch Yth Grp; Emplmnt; SADD; Dnce; Sccr (J); Dance; Criminal Justice; Shepherd U; West Virginia U

WRIGHT, STEVEN A; OAK HILL, WV; OAK HILL HS; (JR); Hi Hnr Roll; Nat Hon Sy; St of Mnth; USAA; WWAHSS; Yth Ldrshp Prog; Comm Volntr; Peer Tut/Med; AL Aux Boys; Emplmnt; Tech Clb; Sccr (J L); Web Page Team; Natural Helper; Engineering; Business; Marshall U; West Virginia U

WRISTON, AMANDA S; OAK HILL, WV; OAK HILL HS; (JR); Hnr Roll; Comm Volntr; Chrch Yth Grp; FCA; Tchrs Aide; Bnd; Mch Bnd; Bskball (V); Sccr (V); Tennis (V); CR; Sch Ppr; To Be a Vet

YAQUINTA, GINA M; BRIDGEPORT, WV; BRIDGEPORT HS; (FR); F Lan Hn Soc; Hi Hnr Roll; Hnr Roll; Perf Att; Pres Ac Ftns Aw; WWAHSS; Comm Volntr; Chrch Yth Grp; Key Club; Bnd; Ch Chr; Dnce; Mch Bnd; Cl Off; Majorette; Optometrist; Pediatric Optometrist; Ohio State U; Marshall U

Williams, Ashley
Tug Valley HS
Kermit, WV

Weikle, Brian
James Monroe HS
Union, WV

White, Bernice
Montcalm HS
Bluefield, WV

YOST, JESSICA L; GLENWOOD, WV; ST. JOSEPH CTRL CATHOLIC HS; (FR); Hnr Roll; Nat Hon Sy; WWAHSS; Chrch Yth Grp; Key Club; Sccr (V); Sftball (V)

YOUNG, BRANDON; PRINCETON, WV; PIKEVIEW HS; (SR); Hi Hnr Roll; Hnr Roll; Nat Hon Sy; WWAHSS; Chess; Dbte Team; Tchrs Aide; Bnd; Mch Bnd; Pep Bnd; Bsball (J); Sccr (V C); Radiologic Technician; Bluefield State College

YOUNG, MEGAN L; SAINT ALBANS, WV; ST ALBANS HS; (FR); Ctznshp Aw; Hnr Roll; Comm Volntr; Hab For Humty Volntr; Spec Olymp Vol; Chrch Yth Grp; Key Club; Ch Chr; Track (V); Adv Cncl (P); Mission Team Work; President Church Youth Group; Journalism; English; West Virginia Wesleyan; West Virginia U

YOUNG JR, MARK A; RIPLEY, WV; RIPLEY HS; (JR); Hnr Roll; Ntl FFA; Engineering; West Virginia U; Marshall U

ZATEZALO, JENNIFER; WEIRTON, WV; WEIR HS; (SO); Ctznshp Aw; Hi Hnr Roll; Otst Ac Ach Awd; Perf Att; St of Mnth; WWAHSS; Comm Volntr; Hosp Aide; Chrch Yth Grp; Drma Clb; Emplmnt; Sci Clb; SADD; Cl Off (T); Stu Cncl (T); Tri-Hi-Vice President; National English Merit Award; Radiology; Pediatrics; West Virginia U; Duke U

ZUCOSKY, HEATHER C; WEIRTON, WV; WEIR SR HS; (SO); Hnr Roll; Otst Ac Ach Awd; WWAHSS; Comm Volntr; Chrch Yth Grp; Dbte Team; Drma Clb; Key Club; Dnce; SP/M/VS; Stg Cre; West Virginia U

ZUMPETTA, JOHN A; WELLSBURG, WV; BROOKE HS; (SO); Hi Hnr Roll; Jr Eng Tech; Perf Att; WWAHSS; Yth Ldrshp Prog; Key Club; Mth Clb/Tm; SADD; Vsity Clb; Spanish Clb; Acpl Chr; Chr; SP/M/VS; Sccr (V); Swmg (V); Tennis (V); Cl Off (P); Stu Cncl (R); Engineering; Law; Duke U; West Virginia U

ZUROS, PAUL J; WEIRTON, WV; WEIR SR HS; (JR); All Am Sch; Hnr Roll; USAA; WWAHSS; Yth Ldrshp Prog; Comm Volntr; AL Aux Boys; Emplmnt; Key Club; Prom Com; Sci Clb; Scouts; Eagle Scout; West Virginia U; West Liberty State College

Zuros, Paul J
Weir SR HS
Weirton, WV